W9-BGX-671

VOLUME 2

Mandell, Douglas, and Bennett's

PRINCIPLES AND PRACTICE OF Infectious Diseases

Fifth Edition

Edited by

Gerald L. Mandell, M.D.
Professor of Medicine
Owen R. Cheatham Professor of the Sciences
Chief, Division of Infectious Diseases
University of Virginia Health Sciences Center
Charlottesville, Virginia

John E. Bennett, M.D.
Head, Clinical Mycology Section
Laboratory of Clinical Investigation
National Institute of Allergy and Infectious Diseases
National Institutes of Health
Bethesda, Maryland

Raphael Dolin, M.D.
Dean for Clinical Programs
Maxwell Finland Professor of Medicine
Harvard Medical School
Boston, Massachusetts

CHURCHILL LIVINGSTONE
A Harcourt Health Sciences Company
New York Edinburgh London Philadelphia

CHURCHILL LIVINGSTONE
A Harcourt Health Sciences Company

The Curtis Center
Independence Square West
Philadelphia, Pennsylvania 19106

Library of Congress Cataloging-in-Publication Data

Mandell, Douglas, and Bennett's principles and practice of infectious diseases / edited by Gerald L. Mandell, John E. Bennett, Raphael Dolin.—5th ed.

p. cm.

Includes bibliographical references and index.

ISBN 0–443–07593–X

1. Communicable diseases. I. Mandell, Gerald L. II. Douglas, R. Gordon (Robert Gordon). III. Bennett, John E. (John Eugene). IV. Dolin, Raphael. V. Title: Principles and practice of infectious diseases. [DNLM: 1. Communicable Diseases. WC 100 M2713 2000]

RC111.P78 2000 616.9—dc21

DNLM/DLC 99-16736

MANDELL, DOUGLAS, AND BENNETT'S PRINCIPLES AND PRACTICE OF INFECTIOUS DISEASES

ISBN 0–443–07593–X (set)
ISBN 0–443–07983–8 (Vol. 1)
ISBN 0–443–07524–7 (Vol. 2)

Copyright © 2000, 1995, 1990, 1985, 1979 by Churchill Livingstone

All rights reserved. No part of this publication may be reproduced or transmitted in any form or by any means, electronic or mechanical, including photocopy, recording, or any information storage and retrieval system, without permission in writing from the publisher.

Churchill Livingstone® is a registered trademark of Harcourt, Inc.

™ is a trademark of Harcourt, Inc.

Printed in the United States of America.

Last digit is the print number: 9 8 7 6 5 4 3 2

Contributors

N. Franklin Adkinson, Jr., M.D.
Professor of Medicine, Johns Hopkins University School of Medicine; Co-Director, Division of Allergy and Clinical Immunology, Johns Hopkins Asthma and Allergy Center, Baltimore, Maryland
β-Lactam Allergy

David M. Allen, M.D., FAMS
Adjunct Assistant Professor of Medicine, Weill Medical College of Cornell University, New York, New York; Partner and Attending Physician, ID Associates, Dallas, Texas
Acinetobacter *Species*

Harvey J. Alter, M.D.
Clinical Professor of Medicine, Georgetown University School of Medicine, Washington, DC; Chief, Infectious Diseases Section, and Associate Director, Research Department of Transfusion Medicine, Warren G. Magnuson Clinical Center, National Institutes of Health, Bethesda, Maryland
Hepatitis G Virus and TT Virus

Guy W. Amsden, Pharm.D.
Adjunct Assistant Professor, Department of Pharmacology, Columbia University College of Physicians and Surgeons, New York; Adjunct Assistant Professor, Department of Pharmacy Practice, Albany College of Pharmacy, Union University, Albany; Clinical Pharmacy Specialist and Research Scientist, Clinical Pharmacology Research Center, Bassett Healthcare, Cooperstown, New York
Pharmacokinetics and Pharmacodynamics of Anti-infective Agents; Tables of Antimicrobial Agent Pharmacology

Elias Anaissie, M.D.
Professor of Medicine and Director of Clinical Affairs, Myeloma and Transplantation Research Center, University of Arkansas Medical Sciences, Little Rock, Arkansas
Stenotrophomonas maltophilia *and* Burkholderia cepacia

Suresh J. Antony, M.D., FACP, FRCP
Assistant Professor, Texas Tech University Health Sciences Center School of Medicine; Infectious Disease Consultant, Texas Oncology Physician Associates, El Paso, Texas
Streptococcus intermedius *Group*

Michael A. Apicella, M.D.
Professor and Head, Department of Microbiology, University of Iowa College of Medicine, Iowa City, Iowa
Neisseria meningitidis

Gordon L. Archer, M.D.
Professor of Medicine and Microbiology/Immunology; Chairman, Division of Infectious Diseases, Department of Medicine, Virginia Commonwealth University School of Medicine, Richmond, Virginia
Staphylococcus epidermidis *and Other Coagulase-Negative Staphylococci*

David A. Ashford, D.V.M., M.P.H., D.Sc.
Medical Epidemiologist, Meningitis and Special Pathogens Branch, Division of Bacterial and Mycotic Diseases, Center for Infectious Diseases, Centers for Disease Control and Prevention, Atlanta, Georgia
Leptospira *Species (Leptospirosis)*

Carol J. Baker, M.D.
Professor and Head, Section of Infectious Diseases, Department of Pediatrics, and Professor, Department of Microbiology and Immunology, Baylor College of Medicine; Attending Physician, Texas Children's Hospital, Houston, Texas
Streptococcus agalactiae *(Group B Streptococcus)*

Ronald C. Ballard, Ph.D., M.I.Biol.
Associate Professor, Department of Clinical Microbiology and Infectious Diseases, School of Pathology, University of the Witwatersrand and South African Institute for Medical Research, Johannesburg, South Africa
Calymmatobacterium granulomatis *(Donovanosis, Granuloma Inguinale)*

Charles H. Ballow, M.S., Pharm.D.
Clinical Associate Professor, School of Pharmacy, State University of New York at Buffalo; Director, Antiinfectives Research, The Clinical Pharmacokinetics Laboratory, Kaleida Health/Millard Fillmore Hospital, Buffalo, New York
Pharmacokinetics and Pharmacodynamics of Anti-infective Agents

Kenneth J. Bart, M.D.
Dean, San Diego State University School of Public Health, San Diego, California
Immunization

Byron E. Batteiger, M.D.
Professor of Medicine and Microbiology and Immunology, Indiana University School of Medicine, Indianapolis, Indiana
Chlamydia trachomatis *(Trachoma, Perinatal Infections, Lymphogranuloma Venereum, and Other Genital Infections); Introduction to Chlamydial Diseases*

Stephen G. Baum, M.D.
Professor of Medicine and Microbiology and Immunology, Albert Einstein College of Medicine of Yeshiva University, Bronx; Chairman, Department of Medicine, Beth Israel Medical Center, New York, New York
Adenovirus; Introduction to Mycoplasma *Diseases; Mumps Virus;* Mycoplasma pneumoniae *and Atypical Pneumonia*

Arnold S. Bayer, M.D.
Professor of Medicine, University of California, Los Angeles, UCLA School of Medicine, Los Angeles; Associate Chief, Adult Infectious Diseases, Harbor–UCLA Medical Center, Torrance, California
Endocarditis and Intravascular Infections

John E. Bennett, M.D.
Head, Clinical Mycology Section, Laboratory of Clinical Investigation, National Institute of Allergy and Infectious Diseases, National Institutes of Health, Bethesda, Maryland
Antifungal Agents; Introduction to Mycoses; Miscellaneous Fungi and Prototheca

Joseph S. Bertino, Jr., Pharm.D.
Associate Professor of Clinical Pharmacology (in Medicine), Columbia University College of Physicians and Surgeons, New York; Co-Director, Clinical Pharmacology Research Center, Bassett Healthcare, Cooperstown, New York
Pharmacokinetics and Pharmacodynamics of Anti-infective Agents

Alan L. Bisno, M.D.
Professor and Vice-Chairman, Department of Medicine, University of Miami School of Medicine; Chief, Medical Service, Veterans Affairs Medical Center, Miami, Florida
Classification of Streptococci; Nonsuppurative Poststreptococcal Sequelae: Rheumatic Fever and Glomerulonephritis; Pharyngitis; Streptococcus pyogenes *(Including Streptococcal Toxic Shock Syndrome and Necrotizing Fasciitis)*

Martin J. Blaser, M.D.
Addison B. Scoville Professor of Medicine and Professor of Microbiology and Immunology, and Director, Division of Infectious Diseases, Vanderbilt University School of Medicine; Staff Physician, Veterans Affairs Medical Center, Nashville, Tennessee
Campylobacter jejuni *and Related Species;* Helicobacter pylori *and Related Organisms*

Thomas P. Bleck, M.D.
Louise Nerancy Professor of Neurology and Professor of Neurological Surgery and Internal Medicine, University of Virginia School of Medicine; Director, Neuroscience Intensive Care Unit, University of Virginia Hospital, Charlottesville, Virginia
Approach to the Patient with Central Nervous System Infection; Clostridium botulinum *(Botulism);* Clostridium tetani *(Tetanus); Epidural Abscess; Rabies Virus; Subdural Empyema; Suppurative Intracranial Phlebitis*

David A. Bobak, M.D.
Associate Professor of Medicine and Microbiology, University of Virginia School of Medicine; Director, Traveler's Clinic, and Attending Physician, University of Virginia Health Sciences Center, Charlottesville, Virginia
Nausea, Vomiting, and Noninflammatory Diarrhea

William Bonnez, M.D.
Associate Professor of Medicine, University of Rochester School of Medicine and Dentistry; Attending Physician, Department of Medicine, Strong Memorial Hospital, Rochester, New York
Papillomaviruses

R.C. Boucher, M.D.
Professor of Medicine, University of North Carolina at Chapel Hill School of Medicine; Director, Division of Pulmonary/Critical Care Medicine, and Director, Cystic Fibrosis/Pulmonary Research and Treatment Center, UNC Hospitals, Chapel Hill, North Carolina
Cystic Fibrosis

Barry D. Brause, M.D.
Clinical Professor of Medicine, Weill Medical College of Cornell University; Attending Physician, New York Presbyterian Hospital–Cornell Campus, and Hospital for Special Surgery, New York, New York
Infections with Prostheses in Bones and Joints

Arthur E. Brown, M.D.
Professor of Clinical Medicine and Pediatrics, Weill Medical College of Cornell University; Attending Physician, Infectious Disease Service, Memorial Sloan-Kettering Cancer Center; Attending Physician, New York Presbyterian Hospital–Cornell Campus; and Visiting Associate Physician, The Rockefeller University Hospital, New York, New York
Other Corynebacteria and Rhodococcus

Barbara A. Brown, M.S., MT, ASCP, SM
Senior Research Scientist and Supervisor, Mycobacteria/Nocardia Laboratory; Study Coordinator, Mycobacterial Clinical Trials, University of Texas Health Center, Tyler, Texas
Infections Due to Nontuberculous Mycobacteria

Eric J. Brown, M.D.
Professor, Program in Microbial Pathogenesis and Host Defense, University of California, San Francisco, School of Medicine, San Francisco, California
Cell-Mediated Immunity in Host Defense against Infectious Diseases

Kevin E. Brown, M.D.
Visiting Scientist, Hematology Branch, National Heart, Lung and Blood Institute, National Institutes of Health, Bethesda, Maryland
Parvovirus B19

Patricia D. Brown, M.D.
Assistant Professor of Medicine, Department of Internal Medicine, Division of Infectious Diseases, Wayne State University School of Medicine, Detroit, Michigan
Infections in Injection Drug Users

Ralph T. Bryan, M.D.
Clinical Associate Professor of Medicine, University of New Mexico School of Medicine, Albuquerque, New Mexico; Medical Epidemiologist, National Center for Infectious Diseases, Centers for Disease Control and Prevention, Atlanta, Georgia
Microsporidia

Richard E. Bryant, M.D.
Professor of Medicine (Emeritus), Department of Medicine, Infectious Diseases Division, Oregon Health Sciences University School of Medicine, Portland, Oregon
Pleural Effusion and Empyema

James E. Burns, M.D., M.B.A.
Attending Physician, University of Virginia Health System, Department of Pediatrics, Division of Infectious Diseases, Charlottesville, Virginia
Epiglottitis

Larry M. Bush, M.D., FACP
Chief of Staff and Chairman, Infectious Diseases, JFK Medical Center, West Palm Beach, Florida; formerly Assistant Clinical Professor of Medicine, Medical College of Pennsylvania (now MCP–Hahnemann School of Medicine), Philadelphia, Pennsylvania
Peritonitis and Other Intra-abdominal Infections

Thomas Butler, M.D.
Professor of Internal Medicine, Texas Tech University Health Sciences Center School of Medicine; Chief of Infectious Diseases, Department of Internal Medicine, University Medical Center, Lubbock, Texas
Yersinia *Species, Including Plague*

Jason Calhoun, M.D., FACS
Professor and Chair, Department of Orthopedics and Rehabilitation, University of Texas Medical Branch, University of Texas Medical School at Galveston, Galveston, Texas
Osteomyelitis

Ellis S. Caplan, M.D.
Associate Professor of Medicine, Program in Traumatology, University of Maryland School of Medicine; Chief, Section of Infectious Diseases, R. A. Cowley Shock Trauma Center, Baltimore, Maryland
Hyperbaric Oxygen; Multiple Trauma

Charles C. J. Carpenter, M.D.
Professor of Medicine, Brown University School of Medicine, Providence, Rhode Island
Other Pathogenic Vibrios

Mary T. Caserta, M.D.
Assistant Professor of Pediatrics, University of Rochester School of Medicine and Dentistry; Attending Physician, Department of Pediatrics, Strong Memorial Hospital, Rochester, New York
Acute Laryngitis

Richard E. Chaisson, M.D.
Professor of Medicine, Epidemiology, and International Health, Johns Hopkins University School of Medicine, Baltimore, Maryland
Gastrointestinal and Hepatobiliary Manifestations of Human Immunodeficiency Virus Infection; General Clinical Manifestations of Human Immunodeficiency Virus Infection (Including Oral, Cutaneous, Renal, Ocular, and Cardiac Diseases)

Henry F. Chambers, M.D.
Professor of Medicine, University of California, San Francisco, School of Medicine; Chief, Infectious Diseases, San Francisco General Hospital, San Francisco, California
Other β-Lactam Antibiotics; Penicillins

Stanley W. Chapman, M.D.
Professor of Medicine and Associate Professor of Microbiology, University of Mississippi School of Medicine; Director, Division of Infectious Diseases, University of Mississippi Medical Center, Jackson, Mississippi
Blastomyces dermatitidis

Linda A. Chiarello, R.N., M.S.
Hospital Infections Program, National Center for Infectious Diseases, Centers for Disease Control and Prevention, Atlanta, Georgia
Human Immunodeficiency Virus in Health Care Settings

Anthony W. Chow, M.D., FRCPC, FACP
Professor of Medicine and Director, MD/PhD Program, Faculty of Medicine and Graduate Studies, University of British Columbia; Consultant, Division of Infectious Diseases, Department of Medicine, Vancouver Hospital and Health Sciences Centre, Vancouver, British Columbia, Canada
Infections of the Oral Cavity, Neck, and Head

Jeffrey D. Chulay, M.D., DTM&H
Principal Clinical Program Head, HIV and Opportunistic Infections Clinical Development, Glaxo Wellcome Inc., Research Triangle Park, North Carolina
Treponema *Species (Yaws, Pinta, Bejel)*

Claudia Cicala, Ph.D.
Staff Scientist, National Institute of Allergy and Infectious Diseases, National Institutes of Health, Bethesda, Maryland
The Immunology of Human Immunodeficiency Virus Infection

H. Fred Clark, D.V.M., Ph.D.
Research Professor of Pediatrics, University of Pennsylvania School of Medicine, Philadelphia, Pennsylvania
Rotavirus

Rebecca A. Clark, M.D., Ph.D.
Associate Professor of Medicine, Tulane University School of Medicine; HIV Division Director, HIV Outpatient Program, Tulane University Hospital, New Orleans, Louisiana
Human Immunodeficiency Virus Infection in Women

Robert A. Clark, M.D.
Professor and Chairman, Department of Medicine, and Dan F. Parman Distinguished Chair in Medicine, University of Texas Medical School at San Antonio; Attending Physician, South Texas Veterans Health System and University Hospital, San Antonio, Texas
Granulocytic Phagocytes

Myron S. Cohen, M.D.
Professor of Medicine and Microbiology and Epidemiology, University of North Carolina at Chapel Hill School of Medicine; Chief, Division of Infectious Diseases, and Director, UNC Center for Infectious Diseases, Chapel Hill, North Carolina
The Acutely Ill Patient with Fever and Rash

Oren Cohen, M.D.
Assistant Director for Medical Affairs, National Institute of Allergy and Infectious Diseases, National Institutes of Health, Bethesda, Maryland
The Immunology of Human Immunodeficiency Virus Infection

Susan E. Cohn, M.D., M.P.H.
Associate Professor of Medicine, University of Rochester School of Medicine and Dentistry, Rochester, New York
Human Immunodeficiency Virus Infection in Women

Lawrence Corey, M.D.
Professor of Laboratory Medicine and Medicine, University of Washington School of Medicine; Head, Virology Division, University of Washington Medical Center, and Head, Program in Infectious Diseases, Fred Hutchinson Cancer Research Center, Seattle, Washington
Herpes Simplex Virus

J. Thomas Cross, Jr., M.D., M.P.H.
Associate Professor, Department of Internal Medicine, Division of Infectious Diseases, and Department of Pediatrics, Louisiana State University School of Medicine in Shreveport, Shreveport, Louisiana
Francisella tularensis *(Tularemia)*

Kent B. Crossley, M.D.
Professor of Medicine, University of Minnesota Medical School–Minneapolis; Chief, Education Service, Minneapolis Veterans Affairs Medical Center, Minneapolis, Minnesota
Infections in the Elderly

Clyde S. Crumpacker, M.D.
Professor of Medicine, Harvard Medical School; Attending Physician, Infectious Diseases Division, Beth Israel Deaconess Medical Center, Boston, Massachusetts
Cytomegalovirus

James W. Curran, M.D., M.P.H.
Professor of Epidemiology and Dean, Rollins School of Public Health of Emory University, Atlanta, Georgia
Epidemiology and Prevention of Acquired Immunodeficiency Syndrome and Human Immunodeficiency Virus Infection

Rabih O. Darouiche, M.D.
Associate Professor, Departments of Physical Medicine and Rehabilitation and Medicine, and Director, Center for Prostheses Infection, Baylor College of Medicine; Staff Physician, Spinal Cord Injury and Medical Services, Infectious Disease Section, Veterans Affairs Medical Center, Houston, Texas
Infections in Patients with Spinal Cord Injuries

George S. Deepe, Jr., M.D.
Morgan Professor of Medicine, University of Cincinnati College of Medicine; Chief, Division of Infectious Diseases, University Hospital, Cincinnati, Ohio
Histoplasma capsulatum

Carlos Del Rio, M.D.
Associate Professor of Medicine (Infectious Diseases), Emory University School of Medicine, and Adjunct Associate Professor of International Health, Rollins School of Public Health of Emory University; Associate Director of Clinical Activities, Grady Memorial Hospital and the Ponce de Leon Center, Atlanta, Georgia
Epidemiology and Prevention of Acquired Immunodeficiency Syndrome and Human Immunodeficiency Virus Infection; Other Gram–Negative Bacilli

Lisa M. Demeter, M.D.
Assistant Professor of Medicine and Microbiology and Immunology, University of Rochester School of Medicine and Dentistry, Rochester, New York
Detection of Human Immunodeficiency Virus Infection; JC, BK, and Other Polyomaviruses; Progressive Multifocal Leukoencephalopathy

David W. Denning, M.B.B.S., FRCP, FRCPath
Senior Lecturer in Medicine (Infectious Diseases), University of Manchester; Consultant in Infectious Diseases, North Manchester General and Hope Hospitals, Manchester, England
Aspergillus *species*

Peter Densen, M.D.
Professor of Internal Medicine and Associate Dean, University of Iowa College of Medicine, Iowa City, Iowa
Complement

Ben E. De Pauw, M.D., Ph.D.
Professor of Medicine for Supportive Care, Catholic University; Head, Blood Transfusion Service and Clinical Department of Hematology, University Hospital St. Radboud, Nijmegen, The Netherlands
Infections in the Immunocompromised Host: General Principles; Infections in Patients with Acute Leukemia and Lymphoma

Terence S. Dermody, M.D.
Associate Professor of Pediatrics and Microbiology and Immunology and Director, Elizabeth B. Lamb Center for Pediatric Research, Vanderbilt University School of Medicine, Nashville, Tennessee
Introduction to Viruses and Viral Diseases

Richard D. Diamond, M.D.
Professor of Medicine and Research and Professor of Biochemistry, Boston University School of Medicine; Attending Physician, Section of Infectious Diseases, Boston Medical Center, Boston, Massachusetts
Cryptococcus neoformans

William E. Dismukes, M.D.
Professor and Vice-Chairman, Department of Medicine, and Director, Division of Infectious Diseases, University of Alabama School of Medicine; Director, Internal Medicine Residency Training Program, University of Alabama at Birmingham Medical Center, Birmingham, Alabama
Chronic Pneumonia

Raphael Dolin, M.D.
Professor of Medicine and Dean for Clinical Programs, Harvard Medical School, Boston, Massachusetts
Astroviruses, Toroviruses, and Picobirnaviruses; Norwalk Virus and Other Caliciviruses; Vaccines for Human Immunodeficiency Virus Infection

J. Peter Donnelly, B.Sc., Ph.D.
Microbiologist, Division of Hematology, University Hospital, Nijmegen, The Netherlands
Infections in the Immunocompromised Host: General Principles

Gerald R. Donowitz, M.D.
Professor of Medicine, University of Virginia School of Medicine; Attending Physician, Department of Internal Medicine, Division of Infectious Diseases, University of Virginia Health Sciences Center, Charlottesville, Virginia
Acute Pneumonia; Oxazolidinones

J. Stephen Dumler, M.D.
Associate Professor, Departments of Pathology and Molecular Microbiology and Immunology, and Cellular and Molecular Medicine, Johns Hopkins University School of Medicine and School of Hygiene and Public Health; Director, Division of Medical Microbiology, Department of Pathology, Johns Hopkins Hospital, Baltimore, Maryland
Ehrlichia chaffeensis *(Human Monocytotropic Ehrlichiosis),* Ehrlichia phagocytophila *(Human Granulocytotropic Ehrlichiosis), and Other Ehrlichiae;* Rickettsia typhi *(Murine Typhus)*

J. Stephen Dummer, M.D.
Professor of Medicine, Vanderbilt University School of Medicine; Director, Transplant Infectious Diseases, The Transplant Center, Vanderbilt University Hospital, Nashville, Tennessee
Infections in Solid Organ Transplant Recipients; Risk Factors and Approaches to Infections in Transplant Recipients

Herbert L. DuPont, M.D.
H. Irving Schweppe, Jr., M.D. Chair in Internal Medicine, Baylor College of Medicine, and Mary W. Kelsey Professor, University of Texas Medical School at Houston; Chief, Internal Medicine Service, St. Luke's Episcopal Hospital, Houston, Texas
Shigella *Species (Bacillary Dysentery)*

David T. Durack, M.B., D.Phil., FRCP, FRACP, FACP
Consulting Professor of Medicine, Duke University School of Medicine, Durham, North Carolina; Worldwide Medical Director, Becton Dickinson Microbiology Systems, Sparks, Maryland
Fever of Unknown Origin; Prophylaxis of Infective Endocarditis

Michael B. Edmond, M.D., M.P.H.
Associate Professor and Associate Chair for Education, Department of Internal Medicine, Virginia Commonwealth University School of Medicine; Hospital Epidemiologist, Medical College of Virginia Hospitals, Richmond, Virginia
Isolation; Organization for Infection Control

John E. Edwards, Jr., M.D.
Professor of Medicine, University of California, Los Angeles, UCLA School of Medicine, Los Angeles; Chief, Division of Infectious Diseases, Harbor/UCLA Medical Center, Torrance, California
Candida *Species*

Morven S. Edwards, M.D.
Professor of Pediatrics, Baylor College of Medicine; Attending Physician, Texas Children's Hospital, Houston, Texas
Streptococcus agalactiae *(Group B Streptococcus)*

Barry I. Eisenstein, M.D.
Professor of Medicine, Harvard Medical School; Vice President, Office of Science and Technology, Beth Israel Deaconess Medical Center, Boston, Massachusetts
Enterobacteriaceae; Introduction to Bacterial Diseases

Jerrold J. Ellner, M.D.
Professor of Medicine, Case Western Reserve University School of Medicine; Executive Vice Chair, Department of Medicine, University Hospitals of Cleveland, Cleveland, Ohio
Chronic Meningitis; Mycobacterium avium *Complex*

Suzanne U. Emerson, Ph.D.
Head, Molecular Hepatitis Section, Laboratory of Infectious Diseases, National Institute of Allergy and Infectious Diseases, National Institutes of Health, Bethesda, Maryland
Hepatitis E Virus

N. Cary Engleberg, M.D.
Professor and Chief, Division of Infectious Diseases, Department of Internal Medicine, University of Michigan Medical School, Ann Arbor, Michigan
Chronic Fatigue Syndrome

Lawrence M. Fagan, M.D., Ph.D.
Co-Director, Medical Informatics Training Program, and Associate Director for External Affairs, Stanford Medical Informatics, Stanford University School of Medicine, Stanford, California
The Infectious Diseases Physician and the Internet

Stanley Falkow, Ph.D.
Professor of Microbiology and Immunology, Stanford University School of Medicine, Stanford, California
A Molecular Perspective of Microbial Pathogenicity

Judith Falloon, M.D.
Senior Investigator, National Institute of Allergy and Infectious Diseases, National Institutes of Health, Bethesda, Maryland
Pulmonary Manifestations of Human Immunodeficiency Virus Infection

Barry M. Farr, M.D., M.Sc.
Professor of Medicine, Division of Epidemiology, University of Virginia School of Medicine, Charlottesville, Virginia
Rifamycins

W. Edmund Farrar, M.D.
Professor Emeritus of Medicine, Medical University of South Carolina College of Medicine, Charleston, South Carolina
Erysipelothrix rhusiopathiae

Anthony S. Fauci, M.D.
Director, National Institute of Allergy and Infectious Diseases, National Institutes of Health, Bethesda, Maryland
The Immunology of Human Immunodeficiency Virus Infection

Daniel P. Fedorko, Ph.D.
Senior Staff Microbiologist, Department of Clinical Pathology, Warren G. Magnuson Clinical Center, National Institutes of Health, Bethesda, Maryland
The Clinician and the Microbiology Laboratory

Stephen M. Feinstone, M.D.
Chief, Laboratory of Hepatitis Viruses, Center for Biologic Evaluation and Research, Food and Drug Administration, Bethesda, Maryland
Acute Viral Hepatitis; Hepatitis A Virus

Robert Fekety, M.D.
Professor Emeritus of Internal Medicine, University of Michigan Medical School; Attending Physician, Division of Infectious Diseases, Department of Internal Medicine, University of Michigan Health System, Ann Arbor, Michigan
Vancomycin, Teicoplanin, and the Streptogramins: Quinupristin and Dalfopristin

Jo-David Fine, M.D.
Professor of Dermatology and Clinical Professor of Epidemiology, University of North Carolina at Chapel Hill School of Medicine; Attending Physician, UNC Hospitals; Principal Investigator and Head, National Epidermolysis Bullosa Registry, Chapel Hill, North Carolina
The Acutely Ill Patient with Fever and Rash

Steven M. Fine, M.D., Ph.D.
Senior Instructor in Medicine, Infectious Diseases Unit, University of Rochester School of Medicine and Dentistry; Attending Physician, Strong Memorial Hospital, Rochester, New York
Vesicular Stomatitis and Related Viruses

Sydney M. Finegold, M.D.
Professor of Medicine and Microbiology and Immunology, University of California, Los Angeles, UCLA School of Medicine; Staff Physician, Infectious Diseases Section, Veterans Affairs Medical Center West Los Angeles, Los Angeles, California
Anaerobic Bacteria: General Concepts; Lung Abscess; Metronidazole

Anthony E. Fiore, M.D.
Medical Epidemiologist, Division of Viral and Rickettsial Diseases, National Center for Infectious Diseases, Centers for Disease Control and Prevention, Atlanta, Georgia
Multiple Trauma

Neil O. Fishman, M.D.
Assistant Professor of Medicine, University of Pennsylvania School of Medicine; Director, Antimicrobial Management Program, University of Pennsylvania Health System, Philadelphia, Pennsylvania
Antimicrobial Management and Cost Containment

Michael O. Frank, M.D.
Associate Professor of Medicine, Division of Infectious Diseases, Medical College of Wisconsin, Milwaukee, Wisconsin
Immunomodulators

John Galgiani, M.D.
Professor of Medicine and Director, Valley Fever Center for Excellence, University of Arizona; Program Director, Infectious Diseases, Veterans Affairs Medical Center, Tucson, Arizona
Coccidioides immitis

Joel E. Gallant, M.D., M.P.H.
Associate Professor of Medicine, Division of Infectious Diseases, Johns Hopkins University School of Medicine; Director, Moore HIV Clinic, Johns Hopkins Hospital, Baltimore, Maryland
Global Perspectives on Human Immunodeficiency Virus Infection and Acquired Immunodeficiency Syndrome

John I. Gallin, M.D.
Director, Warren G. Magnuson Clinical Center, and Chief, Laboratory of Host Defenses, National Institute of Allergy and Infectious Diseases, National Institutes of Health, Bethesda, Maryland
Evaluation of the Patient with Suspected Immunodeficiency

Robert C. Gallo, M.D.
Institute of Human Virology, University of Maryland School of Medicine, Baltimore, Maryland
Human Immunodeficiency Viruses

Robert H. Gelber, M.D.
Clinical Professor of Medicine and Dermatology, University of California, San Francisco, School of Medicine; Attending Physician, San Francisco General Hospital, San Francisco, California
Mycobacterium leprae *(Leprosy, Hansen's Disease)*

Jeffrey A. Gelfand, M.D.
Professor of Medicine and Dean for Research, Tufts University School of Medicine; Senior Vice President, Research and Technology, New England Medical Center, Boston, Massachusetts
Babesia

Julie Louise Gerberding, M.D., M.P.H.
Hospital Infections Program, National Center for Infectious Diseases, Centers for Disease Control and Prevention, Atlanta, Georgia
Human Immunodeficiency Virus in Health Care Settings

Anne A. Gershon, M.D.
Professor of Pediatrics and Director, Pediatric Infectious Diseases, Columbia University College of Physicians and Surgeons, New York, New York
Measles Virus (Rubeola); Rubella Virus (German Measles)

David N. Gilbert, M.D.
Professor of Medicine, Oregon Health Sciences University School of Medicine; Director, Medical Education and Earle A. Chiles Research Institute, Providence Portland Medical Center, Portland, Oregon
Aminoglycosides

Vee J. Gill, Ph.D.
Special Expert, Microbiology, Microbiology Service, Department of Clinical Pathology, Warren G. Magnuson Clinical Center, National Institutes of Health, Bethesda, Maryland
Capnocytophaga; *The Clinician and the Microbiology Laboratory*

P. H. Gilligan, Ph.D.
Professor, Departments of Microbiology and Immunology and Pathology and Laboratory Medicine, University of North Carolina at Chapel Hill School of Medicine; Director, Clinical Microbiology/Immunology Laboratory, UNC Hospitals, Chapel Hill, North Carolina
Cystic Fibrosis

Howard S. Gold, M.D.
Instructor, Harvard Medical School; Attending Physician, Division of Infectious Diseases, Department of Medicine, Beth Israel Deaconess Medical Center, Boston, Massachusetts
Introduction to Bacterial Diseases

Ellie J. C. Goldstein, M.D.
Clinical Professor of Medicine, University of California, Los Angeles, UCLA School of Medicine, Los Angeles; Director, R. M. Alden Research Laboratory, Santa Monica–UCLA Medical Center; Private Practice, Santa Monica, California
Bites

Linnie M. Golightly, M.D.
Assistant Professor of Medicine, Division of International Medicine and Infectious Diseases, Weill Medical College of Cornell University; Assistant Attending Physician, New York Presbyterian Hospital–Cornell Campus, New York, New York
Borrelia *Species (Relapsing Fever)*

Eduardo Gotuzzo, M.D.
Professor, Universidad Peruana Cayetano Heredia; Head, Infectious Disease Department, Hospital Nacional Cayetano Heredia, Lima, Peru
Vibrio cholerae

Paul S. Graman, M.D.
Associate Professor of Medicine, University of Rochester School of Medicine and Dentistry; Attending Physician, and Clinical Director, Infectious Diseases Unit, Strong Memorial Hospital, Rochester, New York
Esophagitis

J. Thomas Grayston, M.D.
Professor, Department of Epidemiology, School of Public Health and Community Medicine, University of Washington, Seattle, Washington
Chlamydia pneumoniae

John E. Greenlee, M.D.
Professor and Vice-Chair, Department of Neurology, University of Utah School of Medicine; Chief, Neurology Service, Veterans Affairs Medical Center, Salt Lake City, Utah
Approach to the Patient with Central Nervous System Infection; Epidural Abscess; Subdural Empyema; Suppurative Intracranial Phlebitis

Diane E. Griffin, M.D., Ph.D.
Professor and Chair, Department of Molecular Microbiology and Immunology, Johns Hopkins University School of Hygiene and Public Health, and Professor of Medicine and Neurology, Johns Hopkins University School of Medicine, Baltimore, Maryland
Encephalitis, Myelitis, and Neuritis

Barbara M. Gripshover, M.D.
Assistant Professor of Medicine, Case Western Reserve University School of Medicine; Medical Director, John T. Carey Special Immunology Unit, University Hospitals of Cleveland, Cleveland, Ohio
Chronic Meningitis

David I. Grove, M.D.
Clinical Professor, Departments of Medicine and Microbiology, University of Adelaide; Director, Departments of Clinical Microbiology and Infectious Diseases, The Queen Elizabeth Hospital, Adelaide, South Australia, Australia
Tissue Nematodes (Trichinosis, Dracunculiasis, Filariasis)

Richard L. Guerrant, M.D.
Thomas H. Hunter Professor of International Medicine, Department of Medicine, University of Virginia School of Medicine; Chief, Division of Geographic and International Medicine, and Director, Office of International Health, University of Virginia Hospital, Charlottesville, Virginia
Enteric Fever and Other Causes of Abdominal Symptoms with Fever; Inflammatory Enteritides; Nausea, Vomiting, and Noninflammatory Diarrhea; Principles and Syndromes of Enteric Infection; Tropical Sprue/Enteropathy

Ian D. Gust, M.D.
Professor, Monash University Faculty of Medicine, Chadstone; Professional Associate, University of Melbourne Faculty of Medicine, Dentistry and Health Sciences, Parkville; Director, Research and Development, CSL Limited, Parkville, Victoria, Australia
Hepatitis A Virus

Jack M. Gwaltney, Jr., M.D.
Wade Hampton Frost Professor of Internal Medicine, Department of Medicine, University of Virginia School of Medicine; Head, Division of Epidemiology and Virology, and Director, Center for the Prevention of Disease and Injury, University of Virginia Health Sciences Center, Charlottesville, Virginia
Acute Bronchitis; The Common Cold; Pharyngitis; Rhinovirus; Sinusitis

David W. Haas, M.D.
Associate Professor of Medicine, Vanderbilt University School of Medicine; Director, Clinical Infectious Diseases Services, Vanderbilt University Medical Center, Nashville, Tennessee
Mycobacterium tuberculosis

Caroline Breese Hall, M.D.
Professor of Pediatrics and Medicine in Infectious Diseases, University of Rochester School of Medicine and Dentistry, Rochester, New York
Acute Laryngotracheobronchitis (Croup); Bronchiolitis; Respiratory Syncytial Virus

W. Lee Hand, M.D.
Professor and Assistant Dean for Research, Department of Internal Medicine, Texas Tech University Health Sciences Center School of Medicine, El Paso, Texas
Haemophilus *Species (Including Chancroid)*

H. Hunter Handsfield, M.D.
Professor of Medicine, University of Washington School of Medicine; Director, STD Control Program, Public Health–Seattle and King County, Seattle, Washington
Neisseria gonorrhoeae

George J. Hanna, M.D.
Research Fellow in Medicine, Harvard Medical School; Clinical and Research Fellow in Medicine, Massachusetts General Hospital, Boston, Massachusetts
Antiretroviral Therapy of Human Immunodeficiency Virus Infection

Barry J. Hartman, M.D.
Clinical Professor of Medicine, Weill Medical College of Cornell University; Attending Physician, New York Presbyterian Hospital–Cornell Campus, New York, New York
Acinetobacter *Species*

M. Shahbaz Hasan, M.B.B.S.
Assistant Professor, Department of Internal Medicine, University of Texas Southwestern Medical Center at Dallas Southwestern Medical School; Staff Physician, Dallas Veterans Affairs Medical Center, Dallas, Texas
Infectious Arthritis

Diane V. Havlir, M.D.
Associate Professor, Division of Infectious Disease, Department of Medicine, University of California, San Diego, School of Medicine, La Jolla, California
Mycobacterium avium *Complex*

Roderick J. Hay, D.M., FRCP, FRCPath
Mary Dunhill Professor of Cutaneous Medicine, St. John's Institute of Dermatology, Guys, King's and St. Thomas School of Medicine (KCL), London, England
Dermatophytosis and Other Superficial Mycoses

Frederick G. Hayden, M.D.
Stuart S. Richardson Professor of Clinical Virology and Professor of Internal Medicine and Pathology, University of Virginia School of Medicine; Associate Director, Clinical Microbiology Laboratory, University of Virginia Health Sciences Center, Charlottesville, Virginia
Antiviral Drugs (Other Than Antiretrovirals)

Craig W. Hedberg, Ph.D.
Acute Disease Epidemiology Section, Minnesota Department of Health, Minneapolis, Minnesota
Epidemiologic Principles

Frederick P. Heinzel, M.D.
Associate Professor, Department of Medicine, Division of Geographic Medicine, Case Western Reserve University School of Medicine; Staff Physician, Veterans Affairs Medical Center, Cleveland, Ohio
Antibodies

David K. Henderson, M.D.
Deputy Director, Warren G. Magnuson Clinical Center, National Institutes of Health, Bethesda, Maryland
Infections Due to Percutaneous Intravascular Devices; Nosocomial Herpesvirus Infections

J. Owen Hendley, M.D.
Professor of Pediatrics, University of Virginia School of Medicine; Attending Physician, Department of Pediatrics, Division of Pediatric Infectious Diseases, University of Virginia Health System, Charlottesville, Virginia
Epiglottitis

Erik L. Hewlett, M.D.
Professor of Medicine and Pharmacology and Associate Dean for Research, University of Virginia School of Medicine, Charlottesville, Virginia
Bordetella *Species; Toxins*

Adrian V. S. Hill, D.Phil., D.M.
Professor of Human Genetics, University of Oxford; Noffield Department of Medicine, John Radcliffe Hospital, Oxford, England
Human Genetics and Infection

David R. Hill, M.D.
Associate Professor, Department of Medicine, Division of Infectious Diseases, University of Connecticut School of Medicine; Director, International Travelers' Medical Service, University of Connecticut Health Center, Farmington, Connecticut
Giardia lamblia

Alan R. Hinman, M.D., M.P.H.
Senior Consultant for Public Health Programs, Task Force for Child Survival and Development, Decatur, Georgia
Immunization

Martin S. Hirsch, M.D.
Professor of Medicine, Harvard Medical School; Director, AIDS Clinical Research, Massachusetts General Hospital, Boston, Massachusetts
Antiretroviral Therapy of Human Immunodeficiency Virus Infection

Monto Ho, M.D.
Professor of Medicine and Microbiology and Pathology, Emeritus, Graduate School of Public Health and School of Medicine, University of Pittsburgh, Pittsburgh, Pennsylvania
Infections in Solid Organ Transplant Recipients; Risk Factors and Approaches to Infections in Transplant Recipients

Steven M. Holland, M.D.
Investigator and Head, Immunopathogenesis Unit, Clinical Pathophysiology Section, Laboratory of Host Defenses, National Institute of Allergy and Infectious Diseases, National Institutes of Health, Bethesda, Maryland
Evaluation of the Patient with Suspected Immunodeficiency

Robert G. Holloway, Jr., M.D., M.P.H.
Assistant Professor of Neurology and Community and Preventive Medicine, University of Rochester School of Medicine and Dentistry, Rochester, New York
Neurologic Manifestations of Human Immunodeficiency Virus Infection

David C. Hooper, M.D.
Associate Professor of Medicine, Harvard Medical School; Fellowship Program Director, Infectious Disease Division, and Associate Chief, Infection Control Unit, Massachusetts General Hospital, Boston, Massachusetts
Quinolones; Urinary Tract Agents: Nitrofurantoin and Methenamine

David L. Hoover, M.D.
Associate Professor, Department of Medicine, Uniformed Services University of the Health Sciences, F. Edward Hébert School of Medicine, Bethesda, Maryland; Department of Bacterial Diseases, Walter Reed Army Institute of Research, Washington, D.C.
Innate (General or Nonspecific) Host Defense Mechanisms

Duane R. Hospenthal, M.D., Ph.D.
Assistant Chief, Infectious Disease Service (MCHK-DMI), Tripler Army Medical Center, Honolulu, Hawaii
Miscellaneous Fungi and Prototheca

James M. Hughes, M.D.
Clinical Associate Professor of Medicine, Division of Infectious Diseases, Department of Medicine, Emory University School of Medicine, and Adjunct Professor, Department of Epidemiology, Rollins School of Public Health of Emory University; Director, National Center for Infectious Diseases, Centers for Disease Control and Prevention, Atlanta, Georgia
Foodborne Disease; New and Emerging Infectious Diseases

Jainulabdeen J. Ifthikharuddin, M.D., MRCP(UK), MRCPath
Senior Instructor, University of Rochester School of Medicine and Dentistry; Attending Physician, Strong Memorial Hospital, Rochester, New York
Human T-Cell Lymphotropic Virus Types I and II

Jonathan R. Iredell, M.B.B.S., Ph.D., FRACP, FRCPA
Senior Lecturer, Faculty of Medicine, University of Sydney; Staff Specialist, Centre for Infectious Diseases and Microbiology, Westmead Hospital, Westmead, New South Wales, Australia
Nocardia *Species*

Lisa A. Jackson, M.D., M.P.H.
Assistant Professor, Department of Epidemiology, School of Public Health and Community Medicine, University of Washington; Assistant Investigator, Center for Health Studies, Group Health Cooperative, Seattle, Washington
Chlamydia pneumoniae

Selma M. B. Jeronimo, M.D., Ph.D.
Professor of Biochemistry, Universidade Federal do Rio Grande do Norte, Natal, Rio Grande do Norte, Brazil
Leishmania *Species: Visceral (Kala-Azar), Cutaneous, and Mucosal Leishmaniasis*

Caroline C. Johnson, M.D.
Associate Professor of Medicine, MCP–Hahnemann School of Medicine; Medical Director, Acute Communicable Disease Control Program, Philadelphia Department of Public Health, Philadelphia, Pennsylvania
Viridans Streptococci and Groups C and G Streptococci

Raymond M. Johnson, M.D., Ph.D.
Howard Hughes Postdoctoral Fellow, Department of Infectious Diseases, Washington University School of Medicine, St. Louis, Missouri
Cell-Mediated Immunity in Host Defense against Infectious Diseases

Warren D. Johnson, Jr., M.D.
B. H. Kean Professor of Tropical Medicine and Professor of Medicine, Weill Medical College of Cornell University; Attending Physician and Medical Director, International Health Care Service, and Chief, Division of International Medicine and Infectious Diseases, New York Presbyterian Hospital–Cornell Campus, New York, New York
Borrelia *Species (Relapsing Fever)*

Robert B. Jones, M.D., Ph.D.
Professor of Medicine and Microbiology and Immunology, Indiana University School of Medicine, Indianapolis, Indiana
Chlamydia trachomatis *(Trachoma, Perinatal Infections, Lymphogranuloma Venereum, and Other Genital Infections); Introduction to Chlamydial Diseases*

Manjari Joshi, M.D.
R. A. Cowley Shock Trauma Center, University of Maryland Medical System, Baltimore, Maryland
Multiple Trauma

Allen B. Kaiser, M.D.
Professor and Vice-Chairman, Department of Medicine, Vanderbilt University School of Medicine, Nashville, Tennessee
Postoperative Infections and Antimicrobial Prophylaxis

Adolf W. Karchmer, M.D.
Professor of Medicine, Harvard Medical School; Chief, Division of Infectious Diseases, Beth Israel Deaconess Medical Center, Boston, Massachusetts
Cephalosporins; Infections of Prosthetic Valves and Intravascular Devices

Hiroshi Kawai, M.D.
Department of Internal Medicine, University of Kanazawa School of Medicine, Kanazawa, Japan
Acute Viral Hepatitis

Donald Kaye, M.D.
Professor of Medicine, MCP–Hahnemann School of Medicine, Philadelphia, Pennsylvania
Urinary Tract Infections

Michael C. Keefer, M.D.
Associate Professor of Medicine, University of Rochester School of Medicine and Dentistry, Rochester, New York
Vaccines for Human Immunodeficiency Virus-1 Infection

Douglas S. Kernodle, M.D.
Associate Professor, Department of Medicine, Vanderbilt University School of Medicine; Chief, Infectious Diseases Section, Veterans Affairs Medical Center, Nashville, Tennessee
Postoperative Infections and Antimicrobial Prophylaxis

Jay S. Keystone, M.D., M.Sc.(CTM), FRCPC
Professor of Medicine, University of Toronto Faculty of Medicine; Staff Physician, Centre for Travel and Tropical Medicine, Toronto General Hospital, Toronto, Ontario, Canada
Isospora belli, Sarcocystis *Species,* Blastocystis hominis, *and* Cyclospora

Karl D. Kieburtz, M.D., M.P.H.
Associate Professor of Neurology and Community and Preventive Medicine, University of Rochester School of Medicine and Dentistry, Rochester, New York
Neurologic Manifestations of Human Immunodeficiency Virus Infection

Charles H. King, M.D.
Associate Professor of Medicine and International Health, Case Western Reserve University School of Medicine; Attending Physician, University Hospitals, Cleveland, Ohio
Cestodes (Tapeworms)

Louis V. Kirchhoff, M.D., M.P.H.
Professor, Department of Internal Medicine, University of Iowa College of Medicine; Staff Physician, Medical Service, Department of Veterans Affairs Medical Center, Iowa City, Iowa
Agents of African Trypanosomiasis (Sleeping Sickness); Trypanosoma *Species (American Trypanosomiasis, Chagas' Disease): Biology of Trypanosomes*

Jerome O. Klein, M.D.
Professor of Pediatrics, Boston University School of Medicine; Vice-Chairman for Academic Affairs, Boston Medical Center, Boston, Massachusetts
Otitis Externa, Otitis Media, and Mastoiditis

M. R. Knowles, M.D.
Professor of Medicine, University of North Carolina at Chapel Hill School of Medicine; Associate Director, Division of Pulmonary Critical Care Medicine, and Director, Adult Cystic Fibrosis Center, UNC Hospitals, Chapel Hill, North Carolina
Cystic Fibrosis

Phyllis Kozarsky, M.D.
Associate Professor of Medicine, Emory University School of Medicine; Chief of Infectious Diseases, Emory Crawford Long Hospital, Atlanta, Georgia
Isospora belli, Sarcocystis *Species,* Blastocystis hominis, *and* Cyclospora

John N. Krieger, M.D.
Professor of Urology, University of Washington School of Medicine; Chief of Urology, Veterans Affairs Puget Sound Health Care System, and Attending Surgeon, University of Washington Medical Center and Harborview Medical Center, Seattle, Washington
Prostatitis, Epididymitis, and Orchitis

Donald J. Krogstad, M.D.
Henderson Professor and Chair, Department of Tropical Medicine, Tulane University School of Public Health and Tropical Medicine, New Orleans, Louisiana
Plasmodium *Species (Malaria)*

Joshua Lederberg, Ph.D., M.D.(Hic.)
Professor, The Rockefeller University, New York, New York
Biological Warfare and Bioterrorism

James W. Leduc, Ph.D.
Associate Director for Global Health, National Center for Infectious Diseases, Centers for Disease Control and Prevention, Atlanta, Georgia
Global Epidemiology of Infectious Diseases

Stanley M. Lemon, M.D.
Professor and Chairman, Department of Microbiology and Immunology, University of Texas Medical Branch University of Texas Medical School of Galveston, Galveston, Texas
Hepatitis C

Donald P. Levine, M.D.
Professor of Medicine, Department of Medicine, Division of Infectious Diseases, Wayne State University School of Medicine; Vice-Chief of Medicine and Section Head, Infectious Diseases, Detroit Receiving Hospital, Detroit, Michigan
Infections in Injection Drug Users

Matthew E. Levison, M.D.
Professor of Medicine and Public Health, MCP–Hahnemann School of Medicine; Chief, Division of Infectious Diseases, Hahnemann University Hospital, Philadelphia, Pennsylvania
Peritonitis and Other Intra-abdominal Infections

Daniel P. Lew, M.D.
Professor of Medicine, Geneva University Medical School; Chief, Infectious Diseases Division, Geneva University Hospital, Geneva, Switzerland
Bacillus anthracis *(Anthrax)*

Aldo A. M. Lima, M.D., Ph.D.
Professor of Medicine, Federal University of Ceará, Fortaleza, Brazil
Inflammatory Enteritides

Nathan Litman, M.D.
Professor of Pediatrics, Albert Einstein College of Medicine of Yeshiva University; Chief, Pediatric Service, Montefiore Medical Center, Bronx, New York
Mumps Virus

Bennett Lorber, M.D., D.Sc. (Hon.)
Thomas M. Durant Professor of Medicine and Professor of Microbiology and Immunology, Temple University School of Medicine; Chief, Section of Infectious Diseases, Temple University Hospital, Philadelphia, Pennsylvania
Bacteroides, Prevotella, Porphyromonas, *and* Fusobacterium *Species (and Other Medically Important Anaerobic Gram-Negative Bacilli); Gas Gangrene and Other* Clostridium-*Associated Diseases;* Listeria monocytogenes

Larry I. Lutwick, M.D.
Professor of Medicine, State University of New York Health Science Center at Brooklyn College of Medicine; Director, Infectious Diseases, Veterans Affairs New York Harbor Health Care System, Brooklyn Campus, Brooklyn, New York
Infections in Asplenic Patients

Rob Roy MacGregor, M.D.
Professor of Medicine, Department of Medicine, Division of Infectious Diseases, University of Pennsylvania School of Medicine; Attending Physician, Hospital of the University of Pennsylvania, and Acting Chief, Infectious Disease Division, Philadelphia Veterans Affairs Medical Center, Philadelphia, Pennsylvania
Corynebacterium diphtheriae

Philip A. Mackowiak, M.D.
Professor and Vice Chairman, Department of Medicine, University of Maryland School of Medicine; Chief, Medical Care Clinical Center, Veterans Affairs Maryland Health Care System, Baltimore, Maryland
Fever of Unknown Origin; Temperature Regulation and Pathogenesis of Fever

Antone A. Madeiros, M.D.
Professor of Medicine, Brown University School of Medicine; Director, Division of Infectious Diseases, Miriam Hospital, and Medical Director, Clinical Microbiology Laboratory, Lifespan Academic Medical Center, Providence, Rhode Island
Mechanisms of Bacterial Antibiotic Resistance

Jon T. Mader, M.D.
Professor, Department of Internal Medicine, Division of Infectious Diseases, University of Texas Medical Branch University of Texas Medical School at Galveston, Galveston, Texas
Osteomyelitis

El Sheikh Mahgoub, M.D., Ph.D., FRCPath
Professor of Medical Microbiology, Faculty of Medicine, University of Science and Technology, Jordan; Formerly Regional Adviser, Research Promotion and Strategy Coordination, World Health Organization, Eastern Mediterranean Region, Alexandria, Egypt
Agents of Mycetoma

Adel A. F. Mahmoud, M.D., Ph.D.
Formerly Professor and Chairman of Medicine, Case Western Reserve University School of Medicine, and Physician-in-Chief, University Hospitals, Cleveland, Ohio; President, Merck Vaccines, Merck & Co., Inc., Whitehouse Station, New Jersey
Intestinal Nematodes (Roundworms); Introduction to Helminth Infections; Trematodes (Schistosomiasis) and Other Flukes

Gerald L. Mandell, M.D.
Professor of Medicine and Owen R. Cheatham Professor of the Sciences, University of Virginia School of Medicine; Chief, Division of Infectious Diseases, University of Virginia Health Sciences Center, Charlottesville, Virginia
Acute Pneumonia; Immunomodulators

Lionel A. Mandell, M.D.
Professor of Medicine and Chief, Division of Infectious Diseases, McMaster University School of Medicine, Hamilton, Ontario, Canada
Fusidic Acid

Barbara J. Mann, Ph.D.
Assistant Professor of Research, Department of Internal Medicine, Division of Infectious Diseases, University of Virginia School of Medicine, Charlottesville, Virginia
Microbial Adherence

Lewis Markoff, M.D.
Chief, Laboratory of Vector-Borne Virus Diseases, Division of Viral Products, Center for Biologic Evaluation and Research, Food and Drug Administration, Bethesda, Maryland
Alphaviruses

Thomas J. Marrie, M.D., FRCPC
Professor and Chair, Department of Medicine, University of Alberta Faculty of Medicine; Site Chief, Medicine, University of Alberta Hospital, Edmonton, Alberta, Canada
Coxiella burnetii *(Q Fever)*

Thomas Marth, M.D.
Professor of Internal Medicine II, Saarland University, Homburg, Germany
Whipple's Disease

Ellen M. Mascini, M.D., Ph.D.
Senior Fellow in Medical Microbiology, Eijkman-Winkler Institute for Microbiology, Infectious Diseases, and Inflammation, University Medical Centre, Utrecht, The Netherlands
Anaerobic Cocci; Anaerobic Gram-Positive Nonsporulating Bacilli

Henry Masur, M.D.
Chief, Critical Care Medicine Department, Clinical Center, National Institutes of Health, Bethesda, Maryland
Management of Opportunistic Infections Associated with Human Immunodeficiency Virus Infection

Michael Eric Mathieu, M.D.
Clinical Instructor in Dermatology, Dermatology Department, University of Virginia School of Medicine; Associate, Dermatology PLC of Charlottesville, Charlottesville, Virginia
Introduction to Ectoparasitic Diseases; Lice (Pediculosis); Mites (Including Chiggers); Myiasis; Scabies; Ticks (Including Tick Paralysis)

Kenneth H. Mayer, M.D.
Professor of Medicine and Community Health, Brown University School of Medicine, Providence, Rhode Island; Chief, Infectious Disease Service, Memorial Hospital of Rhode Island, Pawtucket, Rhode Island, and Medical Research Director, Fenway Community Health Center, Boston, Massachusetts
Mechanisms of Bacterial Antibiotic Resistance; Sulfonamides and Trimethoprim

John T. McBride, M.D.
Professor of Pediatrics, Northeast Ohio Universities College of Medicine, Rootstown; Vice-Chair, Department of Pediatrics, Children's Hospital Medical Center of Akron, Akron, Ohio
Acute Laryngotracheitis (Croup); Bronchiolitis

Carol A. McCarthy, M.D.
Associate Professor of Pediatrics, University of Vermont College of Medicine, Burlington, Vermont; Director, Pediatric Infectious Disease, Maine Medical Center, Portland, Maine
Respiratory Syncytial Virus

William M. McCormack, M.D.
Professor of Medicine and Obstetrics and Gynecology, State University of New York Health Science Center at Brooklyn College of Medicine, Brooklyn, New York
Urethritis

Joseph E. McDade, Ph.D.
Deputy Director, National Center for Infectious Diseases, Centers for Disease Control and Prevention, Atlanta, Georgia
New and Emerging Infectious Diseases

Kenneth McIntosh, M.D.
Professor of Pediatrics, Harvard Medical School; Chief, Division of Infectious Diseases, Children's Hospital, Boston, Massachusetts
Coronaviruses

Philip B. Mead, M.D.
Professor and Chair, Department of Obstetrics and Gynecology, University of Vermont College of Medicine; Obstetrician and Gynecologist-in-Chief, Fletcher Allen Health Care, Burlington, Vermont
Infections of the Female Pelvis

Michael H. Merson, M.D.
Professor and Dean of Public Health, and Chairman, Department of Epidemiology and Public Health, Yale University School of Medicine, New Haven, Connecticut
Global Perspectives on Human Immunodeficiency Virus Infection and Acquired Immunodeficiency Syndrome

Françoise Meunier, M.D., Ph.D.
Director, Central Office—Data Center, and Chairman, Invasive Fungal Infections Cooperative Group, European Organization for Research and Treatment of Cancer, Brussels, Belgium
Infections in Patients with Acute Leukemia and Lymphoma

Samuel I. Miller, M.D.
Professor of Medicine and Microbiology, Department of Medicine, Division of Allergy and Infectious Diseases, University of Washington School of Medicine, Seattle, Washington
Salmonella *Species, Including* Salmonella typhi

David H. Mitchell, M.B.B.S., M.Med.Sci.(Epi.)
Clinical Lecturer, Department of Infectious Disease, University of Sydney, Sydney; Staff Specialist, Centre for Infectious Diseases and Microbiology, Institute of Clinical Pathology and Medical Research, Westmead Hospital, Westmead, New South Wales, Australia
Nocardia *Species*

John F. Modlin, M.D.
Professor of Pediatrics and Medicine and Acting Chair, Department of Pediatrics, Dartmouth Medical School, Hanover; Attending Physician, Infectious Disease Section, Dartmouth–Hitchcock Medical Center, Lebanon, New Hampshire
Coxsackieviruses, Echoviruses, and Newer Enteroviruses; Introduction to Picornaviridae; Poliovirus

Robert C. Moellering, Jr., M.S., M.D., D.Sc.(hon)
Herrman L. Blumgart Professor of Medicine, Harvard Medical School; Physician-in-Chief and Chairman, Department of Medicine, and Chief Executive Officer, Harvard Medical Faculty Physicians, Beth Israel Deaconess Medical Center, Boston, Massachusetts
Enterococcus *Species,* Streptococcus bovis, *and* Leuconostoc *Species; Principles of Anti-infective Therapy*

Jose G. Montoya, M.D.
Assistant Professor of Medicine, Division of Infectious Diseases and Geographic Medicine, Stanford University School of Medicine, Stanford, California
Toxoplasma gondii

Kristine A. Moore, M.D., M.P.H.
Medical Director, Infection Control Advisory Network, Inc., Eden Prairie, Minnesota
Epidemiologic Principles

J. Glenn Morris, Jr., M.D., M.P.H.T.M.
Professor of Medicine, Epidemiology and Preventive Medicine, and Microbiology and Immunology, University of Maryland School of Medicine, Baltimore, Maryland
Human Illness Associated with Harmful Algal Blooms

E. Richard Moxon M.A., M.B., B.Chir.
Professor and Head, Department of Paediatrics, University of Oxford, and Head, Molecular Infectious Diseases Group, University of Oxford Institute of Molecular Medicine, John Radcliffe Hospital, Oxford, England
Haemophilus influenzae

Robert R. Muder, M.D.
Associate Professor of Medicine, University of Pittsburgh School of Medicine; Hospital Epidemiologist, Veterans Affairs Pittsburgh Healthcare System, Pittsburgh, Pennsylvania
Other Legionella *Species*

Jean Marie Mulinde, M.D.
Assistant Professor of Medicine, Program in Traumatology, University of Maryland School of Medicine; Attending Physician, Section of Infectious Diseases, R. A. Cowley Shock Trauma Center, Baltimore, Maryland
Hyperbaric Oxygen

Timothy F. Murphy, M.D.
Professor of Medicine and Microbiology, State University of New York at Buffalo School of Medicine and Biomedical Sciences; Chief, Division of Infectious Diseases, Veterans Affairs Medical Center, Buffalo, New York
Haemophilus influenzae; Moraxella (Branhamella) catarrhalis *and Other Gram-Negative Cocci*

Daniel M. Musher, M.D.
Professor of Medicine and Microbiology and Immunology, Baylor College of Medicine; Chief, Infectious Diseases Section, Veterans Affairs Medical Center, Houston, Texas
Streptococcus pneumoniae

Theodore E. Nash, M.D.
Senior Scientist, Laboratory of Parasitic Diseases, National Institute of Allergy and Infectious Diseases, National Institutes of Health, Bethesda, Maryland
Visceral Larva Migrans and Other Unusual Helminth Infections

William M. Nauseef, M.D.
Professor, Department of Internal Medicine, Inflammation Program, University of Iowa College of Medicine; Attending Physician, Veterans Affairs Medical Center, Iowa City, Iowa
Granulocytic Phagocytes

John M. Neff, M.D.
Professor of Pediatrics, University of Washington School of Medicine; Director, Center for Children with Special Needs and Chronic Health Conditions, Children's Hospital and Regional Medical Center, Seattle, Washington
Introduction to Poxviridae; Parapoxviruses, Molluscum Contagiosum, and Tanapox Viruses; Vaccinia *Virus (Cowpox); Variola (Smallpox) and Monkeypox Viruses*

Marguerite A. Neill, M.D.
Associate Professor, Department of Medicine, Division of Infectious Diseases, Brown University School of Medicine, Providence; Attending Physician, Division of Infectious Diseases, Memorial Hospital of Rhode Island, Pawtucket, Rhode Island
Other Pathogenic Vibrios

Terrence P. O'Brien, M.D.
Assistant Professor, Wilmer Eye Institute, Johns Hopkins Hospital, Baltimore, Maryland
Conjunctivitis; Endophthalmitis; Keratitis; Periocular Infections

Paul A. Offit, M.D.
Henle Professor of Immunologic and Infectious Diseases, University of Pennsylvania School of Medicine; Chief, Section of Infectious Diseases, Children's Hospital of Philadelphia, Philadelphia, Pennsylvania
Rotavirus

Pablo C. Okhuysen, M.D.
Associate Professor of Medicine, Division of Infectious Diseases, University of Texas Medical School at Houston; Assistant Professor of Biological Sciences, University of Texas–Houston School of Public Health, Houston, Texas
Sporothrix schenckii

Steven M. Opal, M.D.
Professor of Medicine, Brown University School of Medicine, Providence; Director, Infection Control Service, Memorial Hospital of Rhode Island, Pawtucket, Rhode Island
Mechanisms of Bacterial Antibiotic Resistance

Walter A. Orenstein, M.D.
Director, National Immunization Program, Centers for Disease Control and Prevention, and Assistant Surgeon General, U.S. Public Health Service, Atlanta, Georgia
Immunization

Michael T. Osterholm, Ph.D., M.P.H.
Chairman and Chief Executive Officer, Infection Control Advisory Network, Inc., Eden Prairie, Minnesota
Epidemiologic Principles

Stephen M. Ostroff, M.D.
Associate Director for Epidemiologic Science, National Center for Infectious Diseases, Centers for Disease Control and Prevention, Atlanta, Georgia
Global Epidemiology of Infectious Diseases

Michael N. Oxman, M.D.
Professor of Medicine and Pathology, University of California, San Diego, School of Medicine, La Jolla; Staff Physician, Infectious Diseases Section, Veterans Affairs San Diego Healthcare System, San Diego, California
Myocarditis and Pericarditis

Richard D. Pearson, M.D.
Professor, Department of Medicine, Division of Geographic and International Medicine, and Department of Pathology, University of Virginia School of Medicine, Charlottesville, Virginia
Agents Active Against Parasites and Pneumocystis carinii; *Enteric Fever and Other Causes of Abdominal Symptoms with Fever;* Leishmania *Species: Visceral (Kala-Azar), Cutaneous, and Mucosal Leishmaniasis*

David A. Pegues, M.D.
Assistant Clinical Professor, Department of Medicine, University of California, Los Angeles, UCLA School of Medicine; Hospital Epidemiologist and Attending Physician, Division of Infectious Diseases, UCLA Center for Health Sciences, Los Angeles, California
Salmonella *Species, Including* Salmonelli typhi

Robert L. Penn, M.D.
Professor, Department of Medicine, Louisiana State University School of Medicine in Shreveport; Chief, Infectious Diseases Section, Louisiana State University Hospital–Shreveport, Shreveport, Louisiana
Francisella tularensis *(Tularemia)*

Bradley A. Perkins, M.D.
Centers for Disease Control and Prevention, Atlanta, Georgia
Leptospira *Species (Leptospirosis)*

C. J. Peters, M.D.
Adjunct Professor, Department of Microbiology and Immunology, Emory University School of Medicine; Chief, Special Pathogens Branch, Centers for Disease Control and Prevention, Atlanta, Georgia
California Encephalitis, Hantavirus Pulmonary Syndrome, and Bunyaviridae Hemorrhagic Fevers; Lymphocytic Choriomeningitis Virus, Lassa Virus, and the South American Hemorrhagic Fevers; Marburg and Ebola Virus Hemorrhagic Fevers

Phillip K. Peterson, M.D.
Professor of Medicine, University of Minnesota Medical School; Director, Infectious Diseases Division, Department of Medicine, Hennepin County Medical Center, Minneapolis, Minnesota
Infections in the Elderly

William A. Petri, Jr., M.D., Ph.D.
Professor, Department of Internal Medicine, Division of Infectious Diseases, and Departments of Microbiology and Pathology, University of Virginia School of Medicine; Attending Physician and Associate Director of Clinical Microbiology, University of Virginia Hospital, Charlottesville, Virginia
Free-Living Amebas; Microbial Adherence

Peter Piot, M.D., Ph.D.
Executive Director, Joint United Nations Programme on HIV/AIDS, Geneva, Switzerland
Global Perspectives on Human Immunodeficiency Virus Infection and Acquired Immunodeficiency Syndrome

Philip A. Pizzo, M.D.
Thomas Morgan Rotch Professor and Chair, Department of Pediatrics, Harvard Medical School; Physician-in-Chief and Chair, Department of Medicine, Children's Hospital, Boston, Massachusetts
Empirical Therapy and Prevention of Infection in the Immunocompromised Host

Matthew Pollack, M.D.
Professor of Medicine, F. Edward Hébert School of Medicine, Uniformed Services University of the Health Sciences; Attending Staff Physician Internal Medicine, Infectious Diseases, National Naval Medical Center, Bethesda, Maryland
Pseudomonas aeruginosa

Debra Poutsiaka, M.D., Ph.D.
Assistant Professor of Medicine, Tufts University School of Medicine; Assistant Physician, Division of Geographic Medicine and Infectious Diseases, Department of Medicine, New England Medical Center, Boston, Massachusetts
Babesia

Robert H. Purcell, M.D.
Head, Hepatitis Viruses Section, Laboratory of Infectious Diseases, National Institute of Allergy and Infectious Diseases, National Institutes of Health, Bethesda, Maryland
Hepatitis E Virus

Anastacio de Queiroz Sousa, M.D.
Professor of Medicine, Department of Tropical Medicine, Universidade Federal do Ceará, Fortaleza; Secretary of Health, Ceará, Brazil
Leishmania *Species: Visceral (Kala-Azar), Cutaneous, and Mucosal Leishmaniasis*

Ronald P. Rabinowitz, M.D.
Assistant Professor, Department of Medicine, Division of Infectious Diseases, University of Maryland School of Medicine, Baltimore, Maryland
Multiple Trauma

Didier Raoult
Rickettsia Unit, Bacteriology-Serology-Virology Laboratory, Groupe Hospitalier de la Timone; Director, National Rickettsia Reference Center, Marseilles, France
Rickettsia rickettsii *and Other Spotted Fever Group Rickettsiae (Rocky Mountain Spotted Fever and Other Spotted Fevers)*

Jonathan I. Ravdin, M.D.
Nesbitt Professor and Chairman, Department of Medicine, University of Minnesota Medical School–Minneapolis; Chief of Medicine, Fairview–University Medical Center, Minneapolis, Minnesota
Entamoeba histolytica *(Amebiasis); Introduction to Protozoal Diseases*

Thomas H. Rea, M.D.
Emeritus Professor of Medicine (Dermatology), University of Southern California, Attending Physician, Los Angeles County/USC Medical Center, Los Angeles, California
Mycobacterium leprae *(Leprosy, Hansen's Disease)*

Annette C. Reboli, M.D.
Associate Professor of Medicine, University of Medicine and Dentistry of New Jersey Robert Wood Johnson Medical School at Camden; Hospital Epidemiologist, Cooper Hospital/University Medical Center, Camden, New Jersey
Erysipelothrix rhusiopathiae

Richard C. Reichman, M.D.
Professor of Medicine and Microbiology and Immunology, University of Rochester School of Medicine and Dentistry; Head, Infectious Diseases Unit, Strong Memorial Hospital, Rochester, New York
Detection of Human Immunodeficiency Virus Infection; Papillomaviruses

Michael F. Rein, M.D.
Professor, Department of Medicine, Division of Infectious Diseases, University of Virginia School of Medicine; Medical Director, Sexually Transmitted Disease Clinic, Thomas Jefferson District Health Department, Charlottesville, Virginia
Genital Skin and Mucous Membrane Lesions; Trichomonas vaginalis; *Urethritis; Vulvovaginitis and Cervicitis*

Marvin S. Reitz, Jr., Ph.D.
University of Maryland School of Medicine; Institute of Human Virology, Baltimore, Maryland
Human Immunodeficiency Viruses

David A. Relman, M.D.
Assistant Professor of Medicine and Microbiology and Immunology, Stanford University School of Medicine, Stanford; Staff Physician, Veterans Affairs Palo Alto Health Care System, Palo Alto, California
A Molecular Perspective of Microbial Pathogenicity

Jack S. Remington, M.D.
Professor, Department of Medicine, Division of Infectious Diseases and Geographic Medicine, Stanford University School of Medicine, Stanford; Marcus A. Krupp Research Chair and Chairman, Department of Immunology and Infectious Diseases, Research Institute, Palo Alto Medical Foundation, Palo Alto, California
Toxoplasma gondii

Angela Restrepo, Ph.D.
Senior Researcher and Scientific Director, Corporación para Investigaciones Biologicas (CIB), Medellin, Colombia
Paracoccidioides brasiliensis

John H. Rex, M.D.
Associate Professor of Medicine, University of Texas Medical School at Houston; Medical Director for Epidemiology, Hermann Hospital, Houston, Texas
Sporothrix schenckii

Herbert Y. Reynolds, M.D.
Professor and Chairman, Department of Medicine, Pennsylvania State University College of Medicine; Chief, Medical Clinical Operations, South Central Region, and Associate Director, Division of Medicine, Penn State Geisinger Health System, Hershey, Pennsylvania
Chronic Bronchitis and Acute Infectious Exacerbations

William S. Robinson, M.D.
Division of Infectious Diseases, Stanford University School of Medicine, Palo Alto, California
Hepatitis B Virus and Hepatitis D Virus

Joseph D. Rosenblatt, M.D.
Professor of Medicine and Microbiology and Immunology, University of Rochester School of Medicine and Dentistry; University of Rochester Cancer Center, Rochester, New York
Human T-Cell Lymphotropic Virus Types I and II

Mark E. Rupp, M.D.
Associate Professor, Department of Internal Medicine, University of Nebraska College of Medicine; Medical Director, Department of Healthcare Epidemiology, Nebraska Health System, Omaha, Nebraska
Meidastinitis

Charles E. Rupprecht, V.M.D., Ph.D.
Division of Viral and Rickettsial Diseases, Centers for Disease Control and Prevention, Atlanta, Georgia
Rabies Virus

Thomas A. Russo, M.D.
Assistant Professor, Department of Medicine, Division of Infectious Diseases, State University of New York at Buffalo School of Medicine and Biomedical Sciences; Staff Physician, Veterans Affairs Medical Center and Erie County Medical Center, Buffalo, New York
Agents of Actinomycosis

Alfred J. Saah, M.D., M.P.H.
Associate Director, Clinical Research, Infectious Diseases, Merck Research Laboratories, West Point, Pennsylvania
Introduction to Rickettsioses and Ehrlichioses; Orientia tsutsugamushi *(Scrub Typhus);* Rickettsia akari *(Rickettsialpox);* Rickettsia prowazekii *(Epidemic or Louse-Borne Typhus)*

Christopher J. Salmon, M.D.
Chest Radiologist, Scottsdale Medical Imaging, Ltd., Scottsdale, Arizona
Pleural Effusion and Empyema

Frank T. Saulsbury, M.D.
Professor of Pediatrics and Head, Division of Immunology and Rheumatology, Department of Pediatrics, University of Virginia School of Medicine, Charlottesville, Virginia
Kawasaki Syndrome

Maria C. Savoia, M.D.
Professor of Clinical Medicine and Associate Dean for Curriculum and Student Affairs, University of California, San Diego, School of Medicine, San Diego, California
Myocarditis and Pericarditis

W. Michael Scheld, M.D.
Professor of Medicine (Infectious Disease) and Neurosurgery, University of Virginia School of Medicine, Charlottesville, Virginia
Acute Meningitis; Brain Abscess; Endocarditis and Intravascular Infections

David Schlossberg, M.D.
Professor of Medicine, Jefferson Medical College of Thomas Jefferson University; Director, Department of Medicine, and Head, Infectious Disease Section, Episcopal Hospital, Philadelphia, Pennsylvania
Chlamydia psittaci *(Psittacosis)*

Robert T. Schooley, M.D.
Tim Gill Professor of Medicine, University of Colorado School of Medicine; Head, Division of Infectious Diseases, University of Colorado Health Sciences Center, Denver, Colorado
Epstein-Barr Virus (Infectious Mononucleosis)

David A. Schwartz, M.D.
Associate Professor of Pathology and Medicine, Emory University School of Medicine; Department of Pathology, Grady Memorial Hospital, Atlanta, Georgia
Microsporidia

Carlos Seas, M.D.
Assistant Professor of Medicine, Universidad Peruana Cayetano Heredia; Attending Physician, Hospital Nacional Cayetano Heredia, Lima, Peru
Vibrio cholerae

Kent A. Sepkowitz, M.D.
Associate Professor of Medicine, Weill Medical College of Cornell University; Associate Chairman, Clinical Affairs, Memorial Sloan-Kettering Cancer Center, New York, New York
Nosocomial Hepatitis and Other Infections Transmitted by Blood and Blood Products

Thomas A. Shaw-Stiffel, M.D.C.M., M.M.M.
Associate Professor of Medicine, University of Rochester School of Medicine and Dentistry; Director of Hepatology, Konar Center for Digestive and Liver Diseases, University of Rochester Medical Center, Rochester, New York
Chronic Hepatitis

Edward H. Shortliffe, M.D., Ph.D.
Professor, Departments of Medicine and Computer Science; Director, Medical Informatics Training Program; and Associate Dean for Information Resources and Technology, Stanford University School of Medicine; Attending Physician, UCSF Stanford Health Care System, Stanford, California
The Infectious Diseases Physician and the Internet

Upinder Singh, M.D.
Fellow, Department of Microbiology, Stanford University School of Medicine, Stanford, California
Free-Living Amebas

Leonard N. Slater, M.D.
Professor, Department of Medicine, University of Oklahoma College of Medicine; Vice-Chief, Infectious Diseases Section, Department of Medicine, University of Oklahoma Health Sciences Center; Attending Physician, University Hospital, Veterans Affairs Medical Center, and Presbyterian Hospital, Oklahoma City, Oklahoma
Bartonella *Species, Including Cat-Scratch Disease*

James W. Smith, M.D.
Professor, Department of Internal Medicine, University of Texas Southwestern Medical Center at Dallas Southwestern Medical School; Staff Physician, Infectious Diseases Section, Dallas Veterans Affairs Medical Center, Dallas, Texas
Infectious Arthritis

Jack D. Sobel, M.D.
Professor of Medicine, Wayne State University School of Medicine; Chief, Division of Infectious Diseases, Detroit Medical Center, Detroit, Michigan
Urinary Tract Infections

Tania C. Sorrell, M.D., FRACP
Professor of Clinical Infectious Diseases, Faculty of Medicine, University of Sydney, Sydney; Director, Centre for Infectious Diseases and Microbiology, Westmead Hospital, Westmead, New South Wales, Australia
Nocardia *Species*

P. Frederick Sparling, M.D.
J. Herbert Bate Professor of Medicine and Professor of Microbiology and Immunology, University of North Carolina at Chapel Hill School of Medicine, Chapel Hill, North Carolina
Neisseria gonorrhoeae

Carol A. Spiegel, Ph.D.
Associate Professor, Department of Pathology and Laboratory Medicine, University of Wisconsin Medical School; Director, Clinical Microbiology, University of Wisconsin Hospital and Clinics, Madison, Wisconsin
Gardnerella vaginalis *and* Mobiluncus *Species*

Harold C. Standiford, M.D.
Professor of Medicine, University of Maryland School of Medicine; Deputy Director, Medical Care Center, Veterans Affairs Maryland Health Care System, Baltimore, Maryland
Tetracyclines and Chloramphenicol

Allen C. Steere, M.D.
Zucker Professor of Medicine, Tufts University School of Medicine; Chief, Rheumatology/Immunology, New England Medical Center, Boston, Massachusetts
Borrelia burgdorferi *(Lyme Disease, Lyme Borreliosis)*

Neal H. Steigbigel, M.D.
Professor of Medicine, Albert Einstein College of Medicine of Yeshiva University; Head, Division of Infectious Diseases, Montefiore Medical Center, Bronx, New York
Macrolides and Clindamycin

James P. Steinberg, M.D.
Associate Professor, Department of Medicine, Division of Infectious Diseases, Emory University School of Medicine; Associate Chief of Medicine and Hospital Epidemiologist, Crawford W. Long Memorial Hospital, Atlanta, Georgia
Other Gram-Negative Bacilli

Theodore S. Steiner, M.D.
Assistant Professor, Department of Medicine, Division of Geographic and International Medicine, University of Virginia School of Medicine, Charlottesville, Virginia
Principles and Syndromes of Enteric Infection

Timothy R. Sterling, M.D.
Assistant Professor of Medicine and Epidemiology, Johns Hopkins University School of Medicine; Medical Director, Baltimore City Health Department TB Clinic, Baltimore, Maryland
General Clinical Manifestations of Human Immunodeficiency Virus Infection (Including Oral, Cutaneous, Renal, Ocular, and Cardiac Diseases)

David A. Stevens, M.D.
Professor, Department of Medicine, Stanford University School of Medicine, Stanford; Chief, Division of Infectious Diseases, Department of Medicine, Santa Clara Valley Medical Center; Principal Investigator, Infectious Diseases Research Laboratory, California Institute for Medical Research, San Jose, California
Antifungal Agents

Dennis L. Stevens, Ph.D., M.D.
Professor, Department of Medicine, University of Washington School of Medicine, Seattle, Washington; Chief, Infectious Disease Section, Veterans Affairs Medical Center, Boise, Idaho
Streptococcus pyogenes *(Including Streptococcal Toxic Shock Syndrome and Necrotizing Fasciitis)*

Charles W. Stratton, M.D.
Vanderbilt University School of Medicine, Nashville, Tennessee
Streptococcus intermedius *Group*

Stephen E. Straus, M.D.
Chief, Laboratory of Clinical Investigation, National Institute of Allergy and Infectious Diseases, National Institutes of Health, Bethesda, Maryland
Herpes B Virus; Human Herpesvirus Type 8 (Kaposi's Sarcoma–Associated Herpesvirus); Human Herpesvirus Types 6 and 7; Introduction to Herpesviridae

Larry J. Strausbaugh, M.D.
Professor of Medicine, Oregon Health Sciences University School of Medicine; Hospital Epidemiologist and Staff Physician, Veterans Affairs Medical Center, Portland, Oregon
Nosocomial Respiratory Infections

Howard Z. Streicher, M.D.
National Institutes of Health; Warren G. Magnuson Clinical Center, Bethesda, Maryland
Human Immunodeficiency Viruses

Alan M. Sugar, M.D.
Professor of Medicine, Boston University School of Medicine, Boston; Director HIV/AIDS Program, Cape Cod Hospital, Hyannis, Massachusetts
Agents of Mucormycosis and Related Species

Mark S. Sulkowski, M.D.
Assistant Professor, Department of Medicine, Division of Infectious Diseases, Johns Hopkins University School of Medicine, Baltimore, Maryland
Gastrointestinal and Hepatobiliary Manifestations of Human Immunodeficiency Virus Infection

Morton N. Swartz, M.D.
Professor of Medicine, Harvard Medical School; Chief, Jackson Firm Medical Service and Infectious Disease Unit, Massachusetts General Hospital, Boston, Massachusetts
Cellulitis and Subcutaneous Tissue Infections; Lymphadenitis and Lymphangitis; Myositis

David L. Swerdlow, M.D.
Medical Epidemiologist, Foodborne and Diarrheal Diseases Branch, National Center for Infectious Diseases, Centers for Disease Control and Prevention, Atlanta, Georgia
Foodborne Disease

Jordan W. Tappero, M.D., M.P.H.
Chief, Epidemiology Section, Division of Bacterial and Mycotic Diseases, National Center for Infectious Diseases, Centers for Disease Control and Prevention, Atlanta, Georgia
Leptospira *Species (Leptospirosis)*

Robert V. Tauxe, M.D., M.P.H.
Chief, Foodborne and Diarrheal Diseases Branch, Division of Bacterial and Mycotic Diseases, National Center for Infectious Diseases, Centers for Disease Control and Prevention, Atlanta, Georgia
Foodborne Disease

David Taylor-Robinson, M.D., MRCP, FRCPath
Emeritus Professor of Genitourinary Microbiology and Medicine, Department of Genitourinary Medicine and Communicable Diseases, Imperial College School of Medicine; St. Mary's Hospital, London, England
Ureaplasma urealyticum, Mycoplasma hominis, *and* Mycoplasma genitalium

Nathan M. Thielman, M.D., M.P.H.
Assistant Professor, Department of Medicine, Division of Infectious Diseases, Medical University of South Carolina, Charleston, South Carolina
Antibiotic-Associated Colitis

David L. Thomas, M.D., M.P.H.
Associate Professor of Medicine and Epidemiology, Johns Hopkins University School of Medicine, Baltimore, Maryland
Hepatitis C

Alan D. Tice, M.D.
Clinical Associate Professor, University of Washington School of Medicine, Seattle; Partner, Infections Limited, Tacoma, Washington
Outpatient Intravenous Antibiotic Therapy

Edmund C. Tramont, M.D.
Professor of Medicine (Infectious Diseases), University of Maryland School of Medicine; Associate Director, Institute of Human Virology, University of Maryland Biotechnology Institute, Baltimore, Maryland
Innate (General or Nonspecific) Host Defense Mechanisms; Treponema pallidum *(Syphilis)*

John J. Treanor, M.D.
Associate Professor, Department of Medicine, Division of Infectious Diseases, University of Rochester School of Medicine and Dentistry, Rochester, New York
Astroviruses, Toroviruses, and Picobirnaviruses; Influenza Virus; Norwalk Virus and Other Caliciviruses

Phoebe R. Trubowitz, M.D.
Clinical Fellow, Department of Medicine, Division of Hematology/Oncology, University of California, San Francisco, School of Medicine, San Francisco, California
Malignancies in Human Immunodeficiency Virus Infection

Theodore F. Tsai, M.D., M.P.H.
Director, Clinical Research, Wyeth Lederle Vaccines, Pearl River, New York
Coltiviruses (Colorado Tick Fever); Flaviviruses (Yellow Fever, Dengue, Dengue Hemorrhagic Fever, Japanese Encephalitis, St. Louis Encephalitis, Tick-Borne Encephalitis); Orthoreoviruses and Orbiviruses

Carmelita U. Tuazon, M.D., M.P.H.
Professor of Medicine, George Washington University School of Medicine and Health Sciences; Attending Physician, George Washington University Hospital, Washington, D.C.
Other Bacillus *Species*

Allan R. Tunkel, M.D., Ph.D.
Professor of Medicine and Associate Chair for Education, Department of Medicine, MCP–Hahnemann University; Director, Internal Medicine Residency Program, Hahnemann University Hospital, Philadelphia, Pennsylvania
Acute Meningitis; Brain Abscess; Topical Antibacterials; Viridans Streptococci and Groups C and G Streptococci

Kenneth L. Tyler, M.D.
Professor and Vice-Chairman, Department of Neurology, and Professor, Departments of Medicine and Microbiology and Immunology, University of Colorado School of Medicine; Chief, Neurology Service, Denver Veterans Affairs Medical Center, Denver, Colorado
Introduction to Viruses and Viral Diseases; Prions and Prion Diseases of the Central Nervous System (Transmissible Neurodegenerative Diseases)

Beth L. P. Ungar, M.D.
Clinical Associate Professor of Medicine, Georgetown University School of Medicine, Washington, D.C.
Cryptosporidium

Mauro Vaccarezza, M.D.
Visiting Fellow, National Institute of Allergy and Infectious Diseases, National Institutes of Health, Bethesda, Maryland
The Immunology of Human Immunodeficiency Virus Infection

Jo-Anne Van Burik, M.D.
Assistant Professor, Department of Medicine, Division of Infectious Diseases, University of Minnesota Medical School–Minneapolis, Minneapolis, Minnesota
Infections in Recipients of Blood and Marrow Transplantation

Ivo van de Rijn, Ph.D.
Professor, Department of Microbiology and Immunology, and Associate Professor, Department of Internal Medicine, Bowman Gray School of Medicine of Wake Forest University, Winston-Salem, North Carolina
Classification of Streptococci

Shahe Vartivarian, M.D.
Private Practice, Metropolitan Infectious Disease Associates, Houston, Texas
Stenotrophomonas maltophilia *and* Burkholderia cepacia

Jan Verhoef, M.D., Ph.D.
Professor of Medical Microbiology, University of Utrecht; Director, Eijkman-Winkler Institute for Microbiology, Infectious Diseases, and Inflammation, University Medical Centre, Utrecht, The Netherlands
Anaerobic Cocci; Anaerobic Gram-Negative Nonsporulating Bacilli

Paul A. Volberding, M.D.
Professor of Medicine, University of California, San Francisco, School of Medicine; Director, AIDS Program, San Francisco General Hospital, San Francisco, California
Malignancies in Human Immunodeficiency Virus Infection

Kenneth F. Wagner, D.O.
Associate Professor, Department of Medicine, Uniformed Services University of the Health Sciences, F. Edward Hébert School of Medicine; Attending Physician and Infectious Diseases Consultant, Department of Internal Medicine, National Naval Medical Center, Bethesda, Maryland
Agents of Chromomycosis

Francis A. Waldvogel, M.D.
Professor of Medicine, University of Geneva Medical School; Chairman, Department of Internal Medicine, University Hospital, Geneva, Switzerland
Staphylococcus aureus

David H. Walker, M.D.
Chair, Department of Pathology, University of Texas Medical Branch, Galveston, Texas
Ehrlichia chaffeensis *(Human Monocytotropic Ehrlichiosis),* Ehrlichia phagocytophila *(Human Granulocytotropic Ehrlichiosis) and Other Ehrlichiae;* Rickettsia rickettsii *and Other Spotted Fever Group Rickettsiae (Rocky Mountain Spotted Fever and Other Spotted Fevers);* Rickettsia typhi *(Murine Typhus)*

Richard J. Wallace, Jr., M.D.
Professor, Department of Medicine and Professor and Chairman, Department of Microbiology; Chief, Infectious Diseases, University of Texas Health Center, Tyler, Texas
Antimycobacterial Agents; Infections Due to Nontuberculous Mycobacteria

Peter D. Walzer, M.D.
Professor of Medicine, University of Cincinnati College of Medicine; Associate Chief of Staff for Research, Veterans Affairs Medical Center, Cincinnati, Ohio
Pneumocystis carinii

Christine A. Wanke, M.D.
Associate Professor of Community Health and Medicine, Tufts University School of Medicine; Staff Physician, Division of Infectious Diseases, New England Medical Center, Boston, Massachusetts
Tropical Sprue/Enteropathy

John W. Warren, M.D.
Professor and Head, Division of Infectious Diseases, Department of Medicine, University of Maryland School of Medicine, Baltimore, Maryland
Nosocomial Urinary Tract Infections

Ronald G. Washburn, M.D.
Associate Professor of Medicine, University of Nevada School of Medicine; Chief, Infectious Diseases, Veterans Affairs Medical Center, Reno, Nevada
Spirillum minus *(Rat-Bite Fever);* Streptobacillus moniliformis *(Rat-Bite Fever)*

David J. Weber, M.D.
Associate Professor of Medicine, Pediatrics, and Epidemiology and Assistant Dean, University of North Carolina at Chapel Hill School of Medicine; Associate Chief of Staff, UNC Hospitals, Chapel Hill, North Carolina
The Acutely Ill Patient with Fever and Rash

Rainer Weber, M.D.
Assistant Professor (Infectious Diseases), University of Zurich; Acting Head, Division of Infectious Diseases and Hospital Epidemiology, Department of Internal Medicine, University Hospital, Zurich, Switzerland
Microsporidia

Arnold N. Weinberg, M.D.
Professor of Medicine, Harvard Medical School, Boston; Attending Physician, Massachusetts General Hospital, Boston, and Medical Director, Massachusetts Institute of Technology, Cambridge, Massachusetts
Zoonoses

Geoffrey A. Weinberg, M.D.
Associate Professor, Department of Pediatrics, Division of Infectious Diseases, University of Rochester School of Medicine and Dentistry; Director, Pediatric HIV Program, Children's Hospital at Strong, Strong Memorial Hospital, Rochester, New York
Pediatric Human Immunodeficiency Virus Infection

Daniel Weisdorf, M.D.
Professor of Medicine, Department of Medicine, Division of Hematology, Oncology, and Transplantation, University of Minnesota Medical School–Minneapolis; Director, Adult Blood and Marrow Transplant Program, University of Minnesota Hospital and Clinic, Minneapolis, Minnesota
Infections in Recipients of Blood and Marrow Transplantation

Michael E. Weiss, M.D.
Clinical Associate Professor, Department of Medicine, Division of Allergy, University of Washington School of Medicine, Seattle, Washington
β-Lactam Allergy

David F. Welch, Ph.D.
Clinical Associate Professor of Pathology, University of Texas Southwestern Medical Center at Dallas Southwestern Medical School; Director, Clinical Microbiology Laboratories, Laboratory Corporation of America, Dallas, Texas
Bartonella *Species, Including Cat-Scratch Disease*

Richard P. Wenzel, M.D., M.Sc.
William Branch Porter Professor and Chair, Department of Internal Medicine, Virginia Commonwealth University School of Medicine, Richmond, Virginia
Health Care Reform and the Specialist in Infectious Diseases; Isolation; Organization for Infection Control; Disinfection, Sterilization, and Control of Hospital Waste

Melinda Wharton, M.D.
National Immunization Program, Centers for Disease Control and Prevention, Atlanta, Georgia
Immunization

Richard J. Whitley, M.D.
Professor of Pediatrics, Microbiology, and Medicine, University of Alabama School of Medicine, Birmingham, Alabama
Varicella-Zoster Virus

Barbara Braunstein Wilson, M.D.
Associate Professor, Department of Dermatology, University of Virginia School of Medicine; Attending Physician, University of Virginia Hospitals, Charlottesville, Virginia
Introduction to Ectoparasitic Diseases; Lice (Pediculosis); Mites (Including Chiggers); Myiasis; Scabies; Ticks (Including Tick Paralysis)

Brian Wispelwey, M.D.
Associate Professor, Department of Medicine, University of Virginia School of Medicine, Charlottesville, Virginia
Brain Abscess

Frank G. Witebsky, M.D.
Acting Chief, Microbiology Service, Clinical Pathology Department, Warren G. Magnuson Clinical Center, National Institutes of Health, Bethesda, Maryland
The Clinician and the Microbiology Laboratory

Martin S. Wolfe, M.D., D.C.M.T., FACP
Clinical Professor of Medicine, Georgetown University School of Medicine, and George Washington University School of Medicine and Health Sciences; Director, Traveler's Medical Service of Washington, D.C., Washington, D.C.
Protection of Travelers

Peter F. Wright, M.D.
Professor of Pediatrics, Microbiology and Immunology, and Pathology, and Director, Division of Infectious Disease, Vanderbilt University School of Medicine; Staff Physician, Department of Pediatrics, and Director, Clinical Diagnostic Virology Laboratory, Vanderbilt University Hospital, Nashville, Tennessee
Parainfluenza Viruses

Edward J. Young, M.D., M.S.
Professor of Medicine and Microbiology and Immunology, Baylor College of Medicine; Staff Physician, Veterans Affairs Medical Center, Houston, Texas
Brucella *Species*

Lowell S. Young, M.D.
Clinical Professor of Medicine, University of California, San Francisco, School of Medicine; Director, Kuzell Institute for Arthritis and Infectious Diseases, California Pacific Medical Center, San Francisco, California
Sepsis Syndrome

Victor L. Yu, M.D.
Professor of Medicine, University of Pittsburgh School of Medicine; Chief, Infectious Disease Section, Veterans Affairs Medical Center, Pittsburgh, Pennsylvania
The Infectious Diseases Physician and the Internet; Legionella pneumophila *(Legionnaires' Disease)*

Roger W. Yurt, M.D.
Johnson and Johnson Distinguished Professor and Vice-Chairman, Department of Surgery, Weill Medical College of Cornell University; Director, The Burn Center, New York Presbyterian Hospital–Cornell Campus, New York, New York
Burns

Mussaret Zaidi, M.D.
Associate Researcher, Department of Investigation, Hospital General O'Horán, Merida, Yucatan, Mexico
Disinfection, Sterilization, and Control of Hospital Waste

Dori F. Zaleznik, M.D.
Assistant Professor of Medicine, Harvard Medical School; Staff Physician, Beth Israel Deaconess Medical Center, Boston, Massachusetts
Enterobacteriaceae

Stephen H. Zinner, M.D.
Charles S. Davidson Professor of Medicine, Harvard Medical School, Boston; Chair, Department of Medicine, Mount Auburn Hospital, Cambridge, Massachusetts
Sulfonamides and Trimethoprim

John J. Zurlo, M.D.
Associate Professor, Department of Medicine, Section of Infectious Diseases and Epidemiology, Pennsylvania State University College of Medicine, Hershey, Pennsylvania
Pasteurella *Species*

Preface to the Fifth Edition

Infectious diseases remain the number one killer of human beings in the world as we approach the new millennium. Our knowledge of the role of infectious agents in malignancies, heart disease, rheumatic disease, gastrointestinal disease, and other "idiopathic" diseases continues to grow and expand. Preventive options and therapeutic strategies are changing rapidly, with the development of new vaccines, new antimicrobial agents, and innovative immunotherapies.

Our goal was to make this the most complete, authoritative, and up-to-date reference book in the world, and we believe that we and the contributing authors have succeeded.

In this, the fifth edition, we have added new chapters (e.g., Human genetics and infection; Global Epidemiology; New and Emerging Infectious Diseases; Hyperbaric oxygen; Oxazolidinones; Antimicrobial agent utilization and cost control; Home intravenous therapy; Human herpesvirus 8; Microbial warfare and terrorism; Health care reform and the ID specialist; The ID physician and the internet). The AIDS/HIV section has been completely rewritten and expanded. All chapters have been revised or rewritten, and new authors have been selected for many chapters. We are grateful to our authors and are in awe of their dedication and expertise.

Marc Strauss at Churchill Livingstone has been our advocate for excellence, and we thank him for that. Once again, Judith, Shirley, and Kelly get our thanks for putting up with distracted, overworked, and sometimes cranky husbands during the 2 years that it took to complete this latest and best edition.

Gerald L. Mandell, M.D.
John E. Bennett, M.D.
Raphael Dolin, M.D.

Preface to the First Edition

Infectious diseases traverse the usual boundaries established by medical specialists. All organ systems may be involved, and all physicians caring for patients may have to deal with infected patients. The format of this book was chosen with the intent that it would contain the necessary information to aid the practitioner in the understanding, diagnosis, and treatment of infectious diseases. Thus, internists, family or general practitioners, pediatricians, surgeons, obstetrician-gynecologists, urologists, residents and fellows in training, medical students, hospital infection control personnel, and clinical microbiologists should find the book a valuable reference.

In planning this book the editors considered several different patterns of organization. The system adopted allows the reader to approach an infected patient three different ways: (a) by major clinical syndrome, (b) by specific etiologic organisms, and (c) by host characteristics for patients who are compromised.

Principles and Practice of Infectious Diseases consists of four major parts. The book may be perused as whole, or individual chapters may be examined when the reader is concerned with a specific problem. Part I covers the basic principles necessary for a clear understanding of the concepts of diagnosis and management of infectious disease. Chapters dealing with microbial virulence factors, host defense mechanisms, the epidemiology of infectious diseases, and the clinician and microbiology laboratory are included. In addition, there is a comprehensive discussion of anti-infective chemotherapy.

Part II considers major clinical syndromes. The syndromes are described, followed by a discussion of the potential etiologic agents, evaluation of differential diagnostic possibilities, and an outline of presumptive therapy. All major infectious diseases are discussed in this part of the book.

Part III describes all important pathogenic microbes for man and the diseases they cause. The pathogen is classified and described, the epidemiology is discussed, clinical manifestations are listed, and specific information on therapy and prevention is presented. The most comprehensive discussion of a disease entity can be found by reading about both the etiologic agent and the clinical syndrome. Thus, a comprehensive treatment of pneumococcal pneumonia could be found in reading the appropriate sections of the chapters on acute pneumonia and *Streptococcus pneumoniae*. We attempted to make the chapters dealing with etiologic agents and those dealing with syndromes complete. Therefore some repetition was unavoidable.

The final section, Part IV, covers special problems in infectious diseases including nosocomial infections, infections in impaired hosts, immunizations, and protection of travelers.

The editors are grateful to our expert contributors. These physicians are the world's leaders in their fields, and they diligently prepared carefully written, well-referenced "state of the art" chapters. Our secretaries were skillful and meticulous in their attention to the complexities of assembling *Principles and Practice of Infectious Diseases.* John de Carville, executive editor of John Wiley & Sons, encouraged, cajoled, and advised us from the formative steps all the way through to completion. Lastly, and perhaps most important, we are grateful to our wives and children for putting up with interminable editorial work and meetings.

Gerald L. Mandell, M.D.

R. Gordon Douglas, Jr., M.D.

John E. Bennett, M.D.

NOTICE

Medicine is an ever-changing field. Standard safety precautions must be followed, but as new research and clinical experience broaden our knowledge, changes in treatment and drug therapy become necessary or appropriate. Readers are advised to check the product information currently provided by the manufacturer of each drug to be administered to verify the recommended dose, the method and duration of administration, and the contraindications. It is the responsibility of the treating physician, relying on experience and knowledge of the patient, to determine dosages and the best treatment for the patient. Neither the Publisher nor the editor assumes any responsibility for any injury and/or damage to persons or property.

THE PUBLISHER

Contents

PART III

Infectious Diseases and Their Etiologic Agents

SECTION A

VIRAL DISEASES

Chapter 119

Introduction to Viruses and Viral Diseases

TERENCE S. DERMODY
KENNETH L. TYLER

HISTORY

Accounts of viral diseases in humans date from antiquity, and new viral diseases continue to emerge in the contemporary era.[1] Scientific approaches to the study of viruses and viral diseases began in the 19th century and led to the characterization of specific disease entities of viral etiology. Careful clinical observations enabled the identification of many viral illnesses and allowed several viral diseases to be differentiated (e.g., smallpox versus chickenpox, and measles versus rubella). Enhancements in pathologic techniques, exemplified by the work of Virchow, allowed the pathology of many viral diseases to be defined. Finally, the work of Pasteur ushered in the systematic use of laboratory animals for studies of the pathogenesis of infectious diseases, including those caused by viruses.

As the 19th century ended, the first viruses were identified. Ivanovsky and Beijerinck identified tobacco mosaic virus, and Loeffler and Frosch discovered foot and mouth disease virus. These observations were quickly followed by the discovery of yellow fever virus and the seminal work on the pathogenesis of yellow fever by Walter Reed and the U.S. Army Yellow Fever Commission.[2] By the end of the 1930s, tumor viruses, bacteriophages, influenza viruses, mumps virus, and many arboviruses had been identified. This process of discovery has continued unabated to the present, with the human retroviruses and several new hepatitis viruses and herpesviruses being the most recent additions to the catalog of human disease–causing viruses.

In the 1940s, Delbrück, Luria, and others used bacteriophages as models to establish many basic principles of microbial genetics and molecular biology and identified key steps in viral replication.[3, 4] The pioneering experiments of Avery and associates on the transformation of pneumococci established that DNA is the genetic material[5] and set the stage for the experiments by Hershey and Chase[6] showing that the genetic material of bacteriophage T2 is also DNA. In the late 1940s, Enders and colleagues cultivated poliovirus in tissue culture.[7] This accomplishment led to the development of both formalin-inactivated (Salk) and live-attenuated (Sabin) vaccines for polio[8, 9] and ushered in the modern era of virology.

In the 1980s and 1990s, the use of x-ray crystallography allowed the structural definition of viruses and their components at an atomic level of resolution. Nucleotide sequences of entire genomes of many human viruses became known, and functional domains of many viral structural and enzymatic proteins were defined. This information is being applied to the development of new strategies to diagnose viral illnesses and the design of effective antiviral therapies. The polymerase chain reaction is an example of a technique that allows viral nucleotide sequences to be detected with a high degree of sensitivity and specificity. Methods like the polymerase chain reaction to detect viral genomes have proved superior to conventional serologic assays and culture techniques for the diagnosis of many viral diseases. For example, the polymerase chain reaction is now used routinely in the diagnosis of infections caused by enteroviruses, hepatitis C virus (HCV), herpesviruses, and human immunodeficiency virus (HIV).

Perhaps an even more exciting development is the means to introduce new genetic material into viral genomes. Strategies now exist in which specific mutations or even entire genes can be inserted into the genomes of many viruses. Such approaches can be exploited in the rational design of vaccines and in the development of viral vectors for use in gene therapy. Among the challenges for the future are the application of these powerful new techniques to expand our understanding of how viruses interact with target cells to alter their physiology, how the interactions of viruses and cells within a living host produce disease, and how events in the infected host result in the transmission of disease and the maintenance of infectious viruses in the environment. Improved understanding of these aspects of viral infection should facilitate new approaches to the diagnosis, prevention, and treatment of viral diseases.

VIRAL STRUCTURE AND CLASSIFICATION

The first classification of viruses as a group distinct from other microorganisms was based on their capacity to pass through filters of a small pore size ("filterable agents"). Initial subdivisions were based primarily on pathologic properties such as specific organ tropisms (e.g., enteroviruses) or common epidemiologic features such as transmission by arthropod vectors (e.g., arboviruses). Since the 1950s, classification has depended predominantly on morphologic and physicochemical criteria.[10] More recently, the availability of nucleotide sequences of many viral genomes has led to the development of classification schemes based on genetic relatedness. The key components of current classification systems are (1) the type and structure of the viral nucleic acid and the strategy used in its replication, (2) the type of symmetry of the virus capsid (helical versus icosahedral), and (3) the presence or absence of a lipid envelope (Table 119–1).

Virus particles or *virions* can be schematically represented as a delivery system that surrounds a payload (Fig. 119–1).[11] The delivery system consists of structural components used by the virus to survive in the environment and to bind host cells. The payload contains the viral genome and often includes enzymes required for the initial steps in viral replication. In virtually all cases, the delivery system must be removed from the virion to allow viral replication to commence.

In addition to facilitating attachment to target cells, the delivery system also plays a crucial role in determining the mode of transmission between hosts. Viruses containing lipid envelopes are sensitive to desiccation in the environment and are often transmitted by the respiratory, parenteral, and sexual routes. Nonenveloped viruses are stable to harsh environmental conditions and often are transmitted by the fecal-oral route.

Over the years, techniques to study viral structure have steadily improved, yielding a definition of structural details of many viruses at an atomic level of resolution (Fig. 119–2). General features of viral structure can be gained from examination of electron micrographs of negatively stained virions and thin-section electron micrographs of virus-infected tissues and cultured cells. These techniques allow the rapid identification of viral size, shape, symmetry, and surface features; the presence or absence of an envelope; and the intracellular

TABLE 119–1 Classification of Viruses

Family	Example	Type of Nucleic Acid	Genome Size (Kilobases or Kilobase Pairs)	Envelope	Capsid Symmetry
RNA-containing viruses					
Picornaviridae	Poliovirus	SS (+)RNA	7.2–8.4	No	I
Caliciviridae	Norwalk virus	SS (+)RNA	7.4–7.7	No	I
Astroviridae	Astrovirus	SS (+)RNA	7.2–7.9	No	I
Togaviridae	Rubella virus	SS (+)RNA	10–12	Yes	I
Flaviviridae	Yellow fever virus	SS (+)RNA	9.5–13	Yes	Unk
Coronaviridae	Coronavirus	SS (+)RNA	20–30	Yes	H
Rhabdoviridae	Rabies virus	SS (−)RNA	13–16	Yes	H
Filoviridae	Ebola virus	SS (−)RNA	19	Yes	H
Paramyxoviridae	Measles virus	SS (−)RNA	16–20	Yes	H
Orthomyxoviridae	Influenza virus	8 SS (−)RNA segments*	10–14	Yes	H
Bunyaviridae	California encephalitis virus	3 circular SS (ambisense) RNA segments	11–21	Yes	H
Arenaviridae	Lymphocytic choriomeningitis virus	2 circular SS (ambisense) RNA segments	10–14	Yes	H
Reoviridae	Rotavirus	10–12 DS RNA segments†	16–27	No	I
Retroviridae	Human immunodeficiency virus type 1	2 identical SS (+)RNA segments	7–11	Yes	I-capsid H-nucleocapsid
DNA-containing viruses					
Hepadnaviridae	Hepatitis B virus	Circular DS DNA with SS portions	3.2	Yes	I
Parvoviridae	Human parvovirus B-19	SS (+) or (−)DNA	5	No	I
Papoviridae	Human papillomavirus	Circular DS DNA	5–8	No	I
Adenoviridae	Adenovirus	Linear DS DNA	36–38	No	I
Herpesviridae	Herpes simplex virus	Linear DS DNA	120–240	Yes	I
Poxviridae	Vaccinia virus	Linear DS DNA with covalently closed ends	130–380	Yes	Complex

*Influenza C virus: seven segments.
†Reovirus, mammalian reovirus and orbivirus: 10 segments; rotavirus: 11 segments; Colorado tick fever virus: 12 segments.
Abbreviations: DS, Double stranded; H, helical; I, icosahedral; SS, single stranded; Unk, unknown; (+), message sense; (−), complement of message sense.
Data from Murphy and Kingsbury.[10]

site of viral assembly. More recently, electron cryomicroscopy and computer image-processing techniques have been used as powerful tools to determine the three-dimensional structures of spheric viruses at a level of resolution superior to that of negatively stained electron micrographs. A major advantage of electron cryomicroscopy is that it allows structural studies of viruses to be performed using conditions that do not alter the native virion structure. High-resolution x-ray crystallographic techniques provide views of viral structure at an atomic level of resolution. In addition to providing information about viral structure, both image reconstructions of electron cryomicrographs and x-ray crystallography can be used to investigate structural aspects of various viral functions, including binding to receptors[12, 13] and interaction with antibodies.[14, 15] The identification of key structural motifs, such as receptor-binding sites or immunodominant domains, provides the framework for understanding the structural basis for virus-cell interactions.

Viral genomes exist in a variety of forms and sizes and are

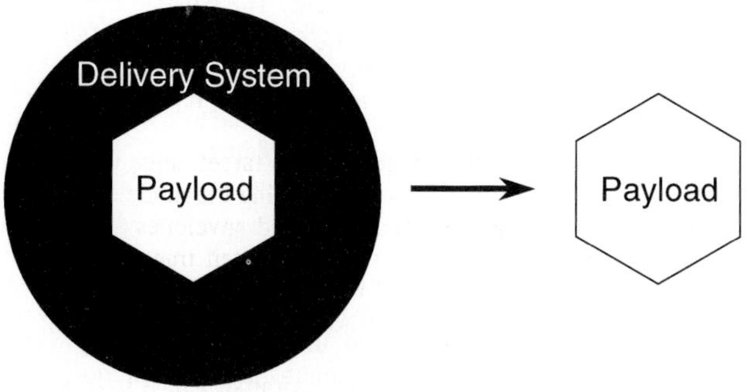

FIGURE 119–1. Schematic diagram of a virus particle. Viruses are simple structures consisting of a delivery system and a payload. The delivery system of a virus protects it against degradation in the environment and contains structures used to bind target cells in the host. The payload of a virus contains the genome and enzymes necessary to initiate the first steps in viral replication. (Figure prepared by Mehmet Goral, Vanderbilt University, Nashville, Tenn.)

composed of either RNA or DNA (Fig. 119–3; see also Table 119–1). Viral genomes range in size from 3 kilobases in small viruses such as the Hepadnaviridae to more than 300 kilobases in large viruses such as the Poxviridae. The genomes of the smallest viruses encode only three or four proteins, whereas those of the largest viruses can encode several hundred. Viral genomes are either single- or double-stranded and are either circular or linear. RNA genomes comprise either a single molecule of nucleic acid or multiple discrete segments. The number of RNA segments can vary from as few as two in the Arenaviridae to as many as 12 in some members of the Reoviridae. Viral nucleic acid is packaged in a protein coat, or *capsid*, that consists of multiple protein subunits termed *capsomeres*. The combination of the viral nucleic acid and the surrounding protein capsid is referred to as the *nucleocapsid* (Fig. 119–4).

A number of general principles have emerged from studies of viral structure.[16] In almost all cases, the capsid is composed of a repeating series of structurally similar subunits, each of which is in turn composed of only a few different proteins. The parsimonious use of structural proteins in a repetitive motif minimizes the amount of genetic information that must be committed to encode the capsid components. The repetition of subunits also leads to structural arrangements of viral capsids with symmetric features. All but the most complex viruses exhibit either helical or icosahedral symmetry (see Table 119–1). Viruses with helical symmetry contain repeating protein subunits that are bound at regular intervals along a helical spiral formed by the viral nucleic acid. Interestingly, all animal viruses that show this type of symmetry have RNA genomes. Viruses with icosahedral symmetry usually have a spheric shape, with two-fold, threefold, and fivefold axes of rotational symmetry. The nucleic acid is packed inside the spheric core and is intimately associated with specific viral capsid proteins.

The use of repeating subunits with symmetric protein-protein interactions undoubtedly facilitates the assembly of the viral capsid. In most cases, viral assembly appears to be a spontaneous process that occurs under the appropriate physiologic conditions and often can be reproduced when recombinant viral proteins are expressed in the absence of viral replication.[17] For many viruses, assembly of the capsid proceeds through a series of intermediates or subassemblies,

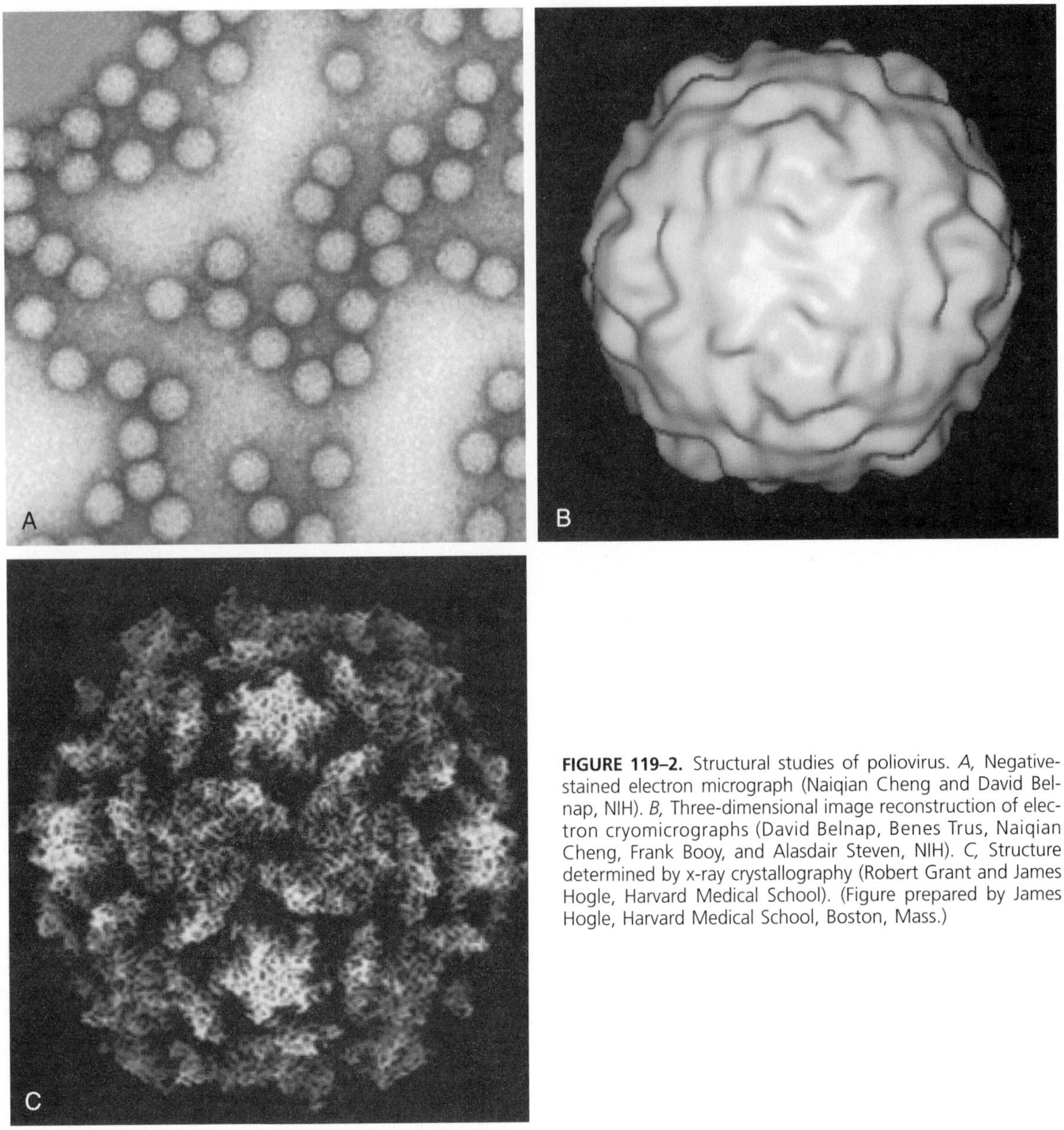

FIGURE 119–2. Structural studies of poliovirus. *A,* Negative-stained electron micrograph (Naiqian Cheng and David Belnap, NIH). *B,* Three-dimensional image reconstruction of electron cryomicrographs (David Belnap, Benes Trus, Naiqian Cheng, Frank Booy, and Alasdair Steven, NIH). *C,* Structure determined by x-ray crystallography (Robert Grant and James Hogle, Harvard Medical School). (Figure prepared by James Hogle, Harvard Medical School, Boston, Mass.)

each of which nucleates the addition of subsequent components in the assembly sequence.

One of the most poorly understood aspects of viral assembly is the process that ensures that the viral nucleic acid is correctly packaged into the capsid. In the case of viruses with helical symmetry, there may be an initiation site on the nucleic acid to which the initial capsid protein subunit binds, triggering the addition of subsequent subunits. In preparations of many icosahedral viruses, empty capsids (i.e., capsids lacking nucleic acid) are frequently observed, which indicates that assembly may proceed to completion without a requirement for the presence of the viral genome.

In some viruses the nucleocapsid is surrounded by a lipid envelope acquired as the viral particle buds from the host cell cytoplasmic, nuclear, or endoplasmic reticular membrane (see Fig. 119–4). Inserted into this lipid bilayer are virus-encoded proteins (e.g., the hemagglutinin and neuraminidase proteins of influenza virus), which are exposed on the surface of the viral particle. These viral proteins typically contain a glycosylated hydrophilic external portion and internal hydrophobic domains that span the lipid membrane and anchor the protein into the viral envelope. In some cases another viral protein may associate with the internal (cytoplasmic) surface of the lipid envelope, where it can interact with the cytoplasmic domains of the envelope glycoproteins. These matrix proteins may play roles in stabilizing the interaction between viral glycoproteins and the lipid envelope, in directing the viral genome to intracellular sites of viral assembly, or in facilitating viral budding.

VIRUS-CELL INTERACTIONS

Viruses are fundamentally different from all other pathogenic microorganisms in that they require an intact cell to replicate and can direct the synthesis of hundreds to thousands of progeny viruses during a single cycle of infection. In contrast to other microorganisms that replicate by fission, viruses must disassemble the infecting particle in order to direct synthesis of viral progeny.

Attachment

Viral replication occurs through an ordered series of steps (Table 119–2). The interaction between a virus and its target cell begins

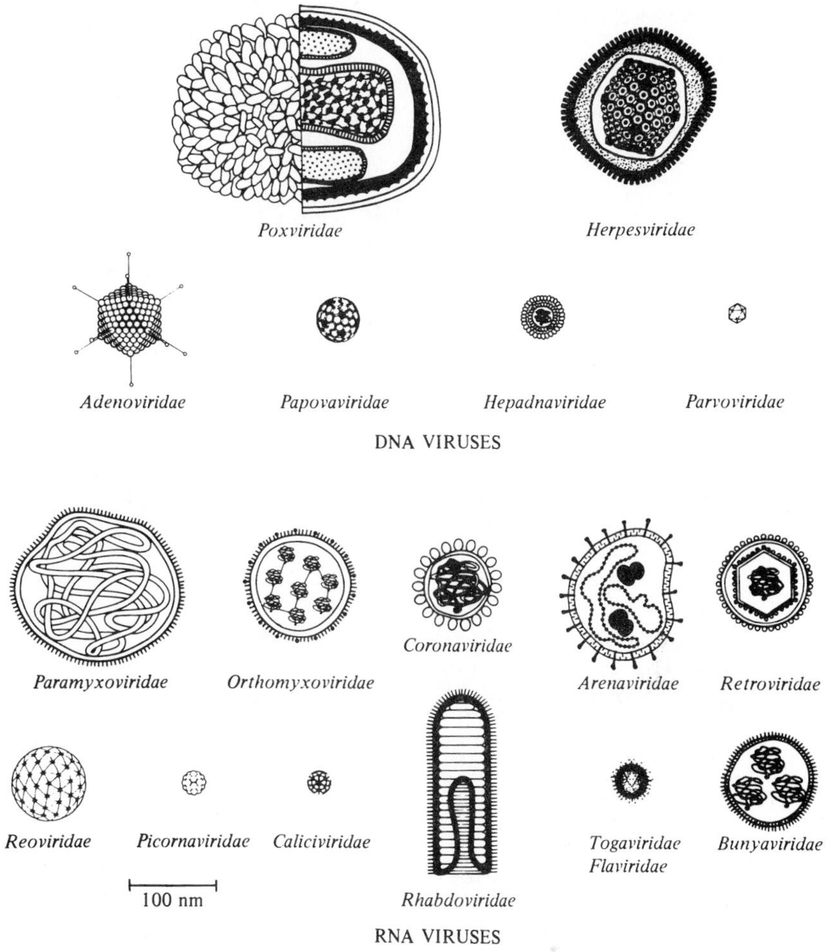

FIGURE 119–3. Sizes and shapes of animal viruses belonging to families known to be pathogenic in humans. (From White DO, Fenner FJ. Medical Virology. 3rd ed. Orlando, Fla: Academic Press; 1986.)

with attachment of the virus particle to specific receptors on the cell surface. Viral proteins that mediate the attachment (viral attachment proteins) include single capsid components that extend from the virion surface, such as the attachment proteins of adenovirus,[18, 19] reovirus,[20] and rotavirus[21]; surface glycoproteins of enveloped viruses, such as influenza virus (Fig. 119–5)[12, 22] and HIV[23, 24]; viral capsid proteins that form binding pockets that engage cellular receptors, such as the canyon formed by the capsid proteins of poliovirus[25] and rhinovirus[26]; or viral capsid proteins that contain extended loops capable of binding receptors, such as foot and mouth disease virus.[27] A rather simple mechanism of viral attachment was originally envisaged in which the virus makes stable contact with the cell via a monophasic binding event involving one type of cellular receptor and a single structure on the virus. However, studies of the attachment of several diverse virus groups, including adenoviruses, coronaviruses, herpesviruses, lentiviruses, and reoviruses, are rapidly establishing a unifying mechanistic theme in which multiple interactions between the virus and the cell occur during the attachment step. These observations are reshaping thoughts on virus-receptor interactions so that the process is increasingly regarded as a multidimensional interface between the virus and the cell that optimizes specificity of viral attachment and contributes significant stability to the association.[28]

TABLE 119–2 Stages in Virus-Cell Interaction

Attachment	Translation
Penetration	Replication
Disassembly	Assembly
Transcription	Release

One of the most dynamic areas of current research in virology concerns the identification of viral receptors on host cells. This interest stems in part from the critical importance of the attachment step as a determinant of target cell selection by many viruses. Several viral receptors have been identified (Table 119–3), and a number of important principles have emerged from studies of these receptors. First, viruses have adapted to utilize host cell surface molecules designed to facilitate a variety of normal cellular functions. Virus receptors may be either highly specialized proteins with limited tissue distribution such as complement receptors, growth factor receptors, or neurotransmitter receptors, or more ubiquitous components of cellular membranes such as integrins, phospholipids, or sialic acid–containing oligosaccharides. Second, many viruses use more than a single receptor to mediate multistep attachment and initiate the process of viral entry. For example, adenovirus binds the integrins $\alpha_V\beta_3$ or $\alpha_V\beta_5$[29] and the coxsackievirus and adenovirus receptor CAR[30]; herpes simplex virus (HSV) binds heparan sulfate[31–33] and herpesvirus entry mediator[34]; and HIV binds CD4[35, 36] and chemokine receptors CXCR4[37, 38] or CCR5.[39–41] Finally, in many cases, receptor expression is not the sole determinant of viral tropism for particular cells and tissues in the host. Therefore, although receptor binding is the first step in the interaction between the virus and the cell, subsequent events in the viral replication cycle also must be supported for productive viral infection to occur.

A detailed description of physical interactions between viruses and their receptors is limited to a few higher-resolution analyses performed with complexes of the receptor and the attachment protein, as illustrated by the association of sialic acid with the influenza hemagglutinin (see Fig. 119–5)[12] and polyomavirus VP1[42, 43]; intercellular adhesion molecule 1 bound to VP1 of rhinovirus[13]; and a

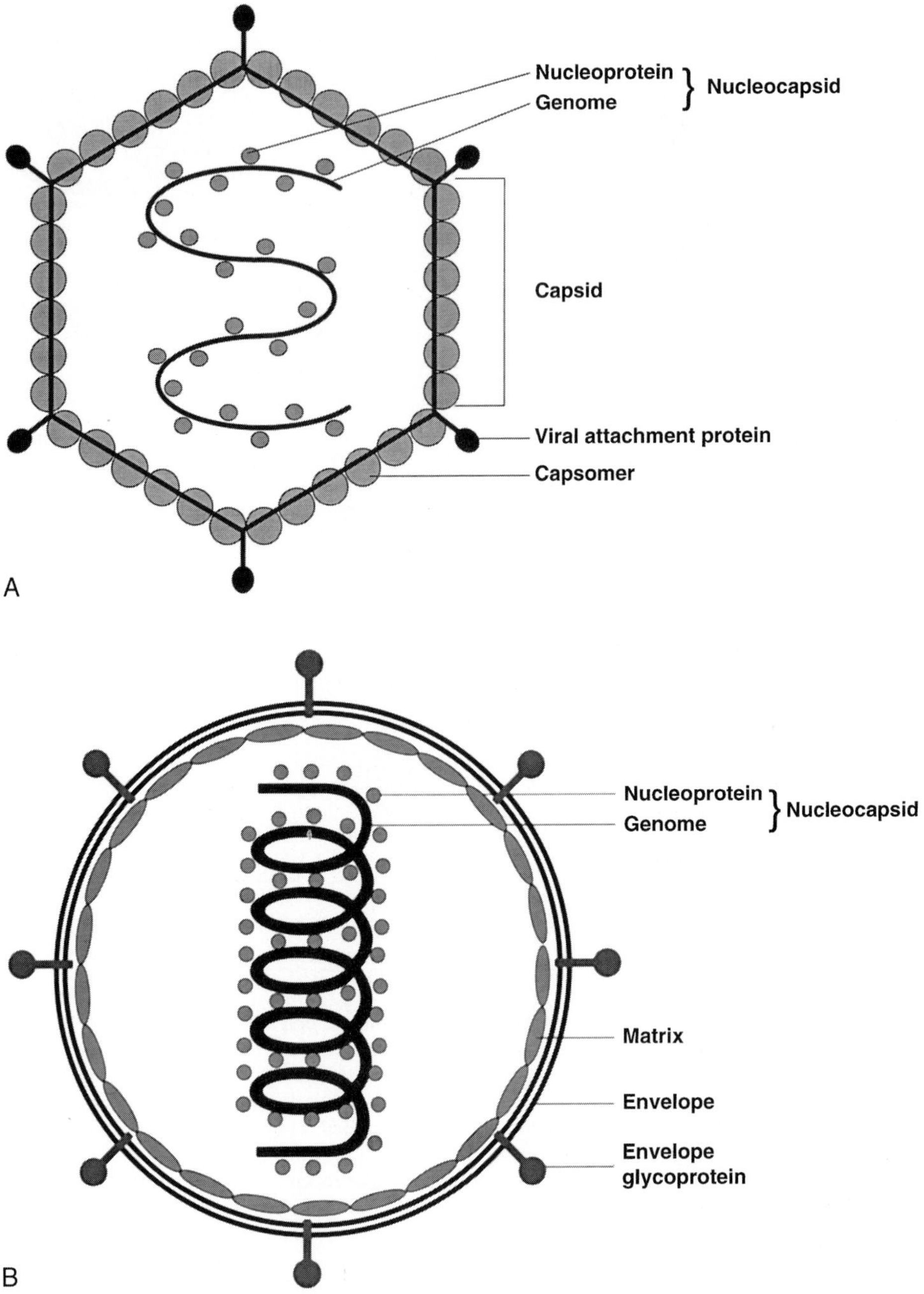

FIGURE 119–4. Schematic diagrams of the structure of a nonenveloped icosahedral virus *(A)* and an enveloped helical virus *(B)*. (Figure prepared by Mehmet Goral, Vanderbilt University, Nashville, Tenn.)

fragment of CD4 bound in solution to glycoprotein 120 (gp120) of HIV.[44] Although these studies have, in some cases, permitted examination of virus-receptor interactions at atomic resolution, they do not address the potential for more complex receptor engagement mechanisms that may represent the "functional" events leading to viral entry.

Penetration and Disassembly

Once attachment has occurred, the virus must penetrate the cell membrane and the capsid must undergo a series of disassembly steps (uncoating) that prepare the virus for the next steps in viral replication. Enveloped viruses such as the paramyxoviruses and retroviruses enter cells by fusion of the viral envelope with the cell membrane.[45] The attachment of these viruses to the cell surface induces changes in viral envelope proteins required for membrane fusion. For example, the binding of CD4 and certain chemokine receptors by HIV envelope glycoprotein gp120 induces a series of conformational changes in gp120 that lead to the exposure of sequences in the gp120-associated envelope transmembrane protein gp41.[46, 47] The fusion of viral and cellular membranes is believed to proceed through a subsequent interaction of the hydrophobic gp41 fusion peptide with the cell membrane.[48–50] Paramyxoviruses enter cells by a mechanism analogous to that used by HIV. After receptor binding by the paramyxovirus G protein, a hydrophobic domain within the viral F protein mediates fusion of viral and cellular membranes.[45]

Other viruses enter cells by receptor-mediated endocytosis (Fig. 119–6).[51] After receptor binding, virus-receptor complexes induce the formation of clathrin-coated pits that invaginate from the cell membrane to form coated vesicles. These vesicles are rapidly uncoated and fuse with early endosomes, which sort internalized proteins for recycling to the cell surface or other cellular compartments,

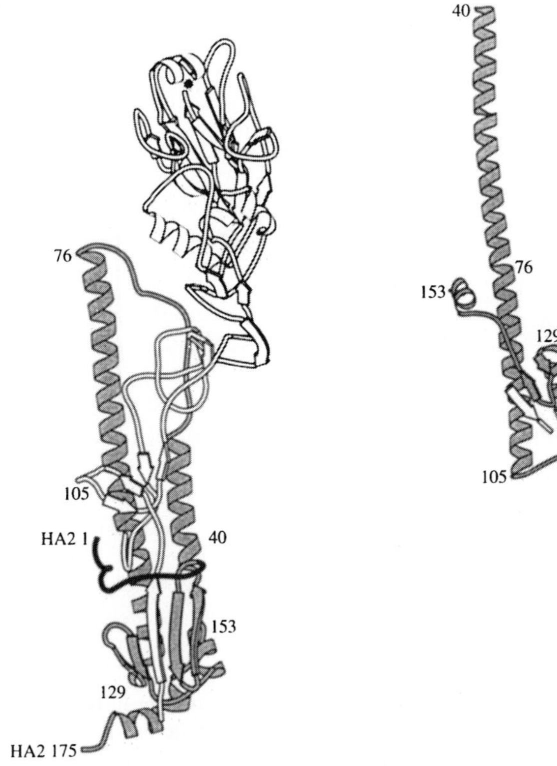

FIGURE 119–5. The folded structure of the influenza virus hemagglutinin (HA) and its rearrangement when exposed to low pH. *(Left)* The HA monomer. HA1 is light, HA2 is dark, and the fusion peptide at the N-terminus of HA2 is black. The receptor-binding pocket in the virion-distal domain of HA is indicated with a star. The viral membrane would be at the bottom of this figure. *(Right)* Conformational change in HA2 induced by exposure to low pH. Note the dramatic structural rearrangement in which amino acid residues 40–105 become a continuous alpha-helix. (From Harrison S, Wiley DC, Skehel JJ. Virus structure. *In:* Fields BN, ed. Fields Virology. 3rd ed. Philadelphia: Lippincott–Williams & Wilkins, 1995:59–99. Figure prepared by Donald Wiley and Frederick Hughson, Harvard University, Boston, Mass.)

such as late endosomes or lysosomes.[52] Acidification of endosomes and lysosomes is mediated by vacuolar proton–adenosine triphosphates (ATPases), and the pH in the endocytic compartment varies from approximately 5.5 to 6.5 (early endosomes) to 5.0 to 5.5 (late endosomes and lysosomes).[53] For enveloped viruses like influenza virus,[54, 55] Semliki Forest virus,[56, 57] and tick-borne encephalitis virus,[58] acid-dependent conformational changes involving envelope glycoproteins are required for fusion of the viral envelope with the endocytic membrane. Viewed at high resolution at acidic pH, structures of the influenza virus hemagglutinin demonstrate the dramatic alterations in the conformation of viral attachment proteins required for membrane fusion (see Fig. 119–5).[55]

Far less is known about the internalization and disassembly of nonenveloped viruses, which must traverse cell membranes without a fusion mechanism involving a viral envelope. Endocytic uptake and acidification are clearly required for the entry of some nonenveloped viruses, such as adenovirus,[59, 60] astrovirus,[61] parvovirus,[62] and reovirus.[63, 64] Moreover, proteolysis of certain capsid components by endosomal proteases also appears to be required for the entry of some of these viruses.[65] However, other nonenveloped viruses, such as poliovirus[66–68] and rotavirus,[69–72] do not require endocytic uptake for cell entry and are postulated to enter host cells by direct penetration.

Genome Replication

Once a virus has entered a target cell, it must replicate its genome and proteins. Replication strategies used by single-stranded–RNA–containing viruses depend on whether the genome can be used as messenger RNA (mRNA).[73] Translation-competent genomes, which include those of the alphaviruses, flaviviruses, and picornaviruses, are termed *plus sense,* or (+)sense, and are translated by cellular ribosomes immediately after the entry of the genome into the cytoplasm. For most viruses containing (+)sense-RNA genomes, translation results in the synthesis of a large polyprotein that is cleaved into several smaller proteins through the action of viral proteases. One of these proteins is an RNA-dependent RNA polymerase, which serves to replicate the viral RNA. Genome replication of (+)sense-RNA–containing viruses requires the synthesis of a *minus sense,* or

TABLE 119–3 Receptors for Selected Viruses

Virus	Receptor	Reference
Adenovirus	Coxsackievirus and adenovirus receptor CAR	30
	Integrins $\alpha_v\beta_3$, $\alpha_v\beta_5$	29
Coronavirus	Carcinoembryonic antigen glycoprotein family	206–208
	Aminopeptidase N	209, 210
	9-*O*-Acetylated sialic acid–containing oligosaccharides	211
Coxsackievirus	Decay-accelerating factor (CD55)	212, 213
	Integrin $\alpha_v\beta_3$	214
	Coxsackievirus and adenovirus receptor CAR	30
Echovirus	Integrin VLA-2	215
	Decay-accelerating factor (CD55)	216, 217
Epstein-Barr virus	Complement receptor 2 (CD21)	218, 219
Herpes simplex virus	Heparan sulfate	31–33
	Herpesvirus entry mediator HVEM	34
Human immunodeficiency virus type 1	CD4	35, 36
	Chemokine receptor CXCR4	37, 38
	Chemokine receptor CCR5	39–41
Influenza virus	Sialic acid–containing oligosaccharides	12, 220
Measles virus	CD46	221, 222
Parvovirus	Erythrocyte P antigen (globoside)	223
Poliovirus	Poliovirus receptor PVR	132
Rabies virus	Acetylcholine receptor	119, 120
	Gangliosides	224
Reovirus type 3	Sialic acid–containing oligosaccharides	225–227
Rhinovirus	Intercellular adhesion molecule 1	228–230
Rotavirus	Sialic acid–containing oligosaccharides	231–234
Vaccinia virus	Epidermal growth factor receptor	235
Vesicular stomatitis virus	Phosphatidylserine	236

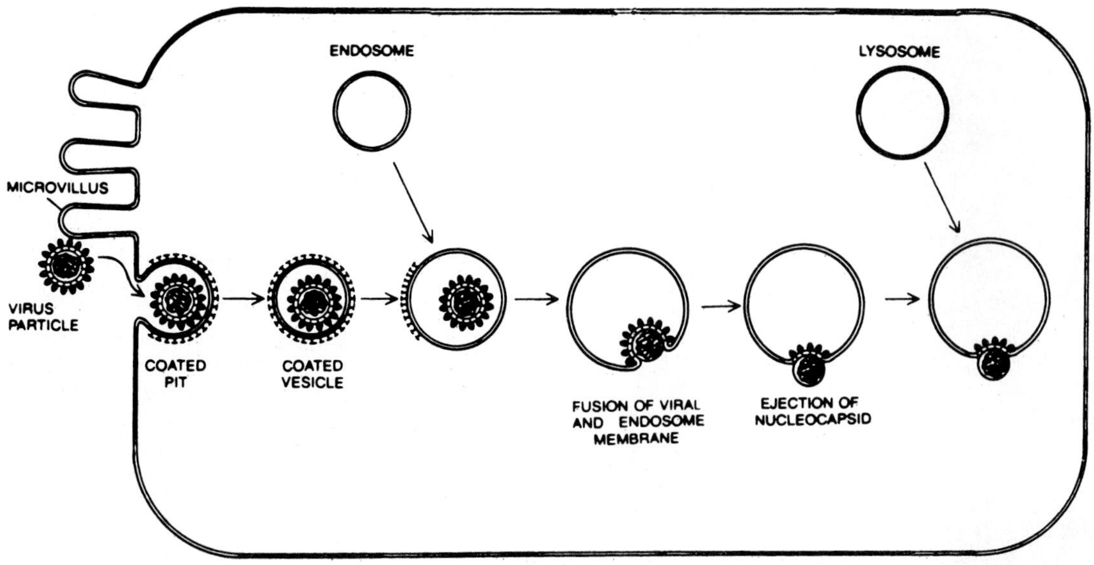

FIGURE 119–6. Viral entry into cells by receptor-mediated endocytosis. (Modified from Simons K, Garoff H, Helenius A. How an animal virus gets into and out of its host cell. Sci Am. 1982;246:58–66.)

(−)sense, RNA intermediate, which acts as a template for the production of (+)sense genomic RNA.

A different strategy is used by viruses containing (−)sense-RNA genomes. The genomes of these viruses, which include the orthomyxoviruses, paramyxoviruses, and rhabdoviruses, cannot serve directly as mRNA. The virions of these viruses must contain a preformed RNA-dependent RNA polymerase to transcribe (+)sense mRNAs using the (−)sense genomic RNA as the template. Genome replication of (−)sense-RNA–containing viruses requires the synthesis of a (+)sense-RNA intermediate, which serves as the template for the production of (−)sense genomic RNA. Mechanisms that regulate whether the (+)sense RNAs transcribed from (−)sense genomic RNA are used as templates for translation or genome replication are not well understood.

RNA-containing viruses belonging to the family Reoviridae have a segmented double-stranded RNA genome.[74] The innermost protein shell of these viruses (termed a *single-shelled particle* or *core*) contains an RNA-dependent RNA polymerase that catalyzes the synthesis of (+)sense mRNA using as template the (−)sense strand of each double-stranded RNA segment. The reovirus mRNAs are capped at their 5′-termini by virus-encoded enzymes and then extruded into the cytoplasm through channels in the single-shelled particle.[75] These (+)sense mRNAs also serve as the template for the replication of double-stranded RNA gene segments.

The retroviruses are RNA-containing viruses that replicate using a DNA intermediate.[76] The viral genomic RNA is (+)sense and single-stranded; however, it does not serve as mRNA. The retrovirus RNA genome is the template for the synthesis of a double-stranded DNA copy, termed the *provirus*. The synthesis of the provirus is mediated by a virus-encoded RNA-dependent DNA polymerase, or *reverse transcriptase*, so named because of the reversal of genetic information from RNA to DNA. The provirus is translocated to the nucleus and is integrated into host chromosomal DNA. Transcription of this integrated DNA is regulated for the most part by cellular transcriptional machinery. However, the human retroviruses HIV[77] and human T-cell lymphotropic virus (HTLV)[78] encode proteins that augment the transcription of viral genes. It is also apparent that intracellular signaling pathways are capable of activating retroviral gene expression and are postulated to play important roles in inducing high levels of viral replication in response to certain stimuli.[79] Transcription of the provirus yields mRNAs that encode viral proteins and genome-length RNAs that are packaged into progeny virions. Such a replication strategy results in persistent infection in the host, since the viral genome is maintained in the host cell and replicated with each cell division.

With the exception of the poxviruses, viruses containing DNA genomes replicate in the nucleus and for the most part use cellular enzymes for transcription and replication of their genomes.[73] Transcription of most DNA-containing viruses is tightly regulated and results in the synthesis of early and late mRNA transcripts. The early transcripts encode regulatory proteins and proteins required for DNA replication, whereas the late transcripts encode structural proteins. Several DNA-containing viruses, such as adenovirus and human papillomavirus (HPV), use strategies to induce cells to become permissive for viral DNA replication by stimulating cell-cycle progression. For example, the adenovirus E1A gene products bind the retinoblastoma gene product pRB and liberate transcription factor E2F, which induces progression of the cell cycle.[80] To prevent programmed cell death in response to E1A-mediated unscheduled cell-cycle progression, the adenovirus E1B 55-kDa protein inactivates tumor suppressor protein p53.[81, 82] An additional degree of complexity is added by the fact that some DNA-containing viruses, such as the herpesviruses, can establish latent infections in the host.[83] Unlike the retroviruses, genomes of the herpesviruses do not integrate into host chromosomes but instead exist as episomes. Factors that govern reactivation from latency are not well understood.

Cell Killing

Viral infection can compromise numerous cellular processes, such as nucleic acid and protein synthesis, the maintenance of cytoskeletal architecture, and the preservation of membrane integrity.[84] Many viruses are capable of inducing the genetically programmed mechanism of cell death that results in apoptosis of host cells.[85, 86] Apoptotic cell death is characterized by cell shrinkage, membrane blebbing, condensation of nuclear chromatin, and activation of an endogenous endonuclease, which results in cleavage of cellular DNA into oligonucleosome-length DNA fragments (Fig. 119–7).[87] These changes occur according to predetermined developmental programs or in response to certain environmental stimuli. In some cases, apoptosis may serve as an antiviral defense mechanism to limit viral replication by either destruction of virus-infected cells[88, 89] or reduction of potentially harmful inflammatory responses elicited by viral infection.[90] In other cases, apoptosis may result from the viral induction of cellular

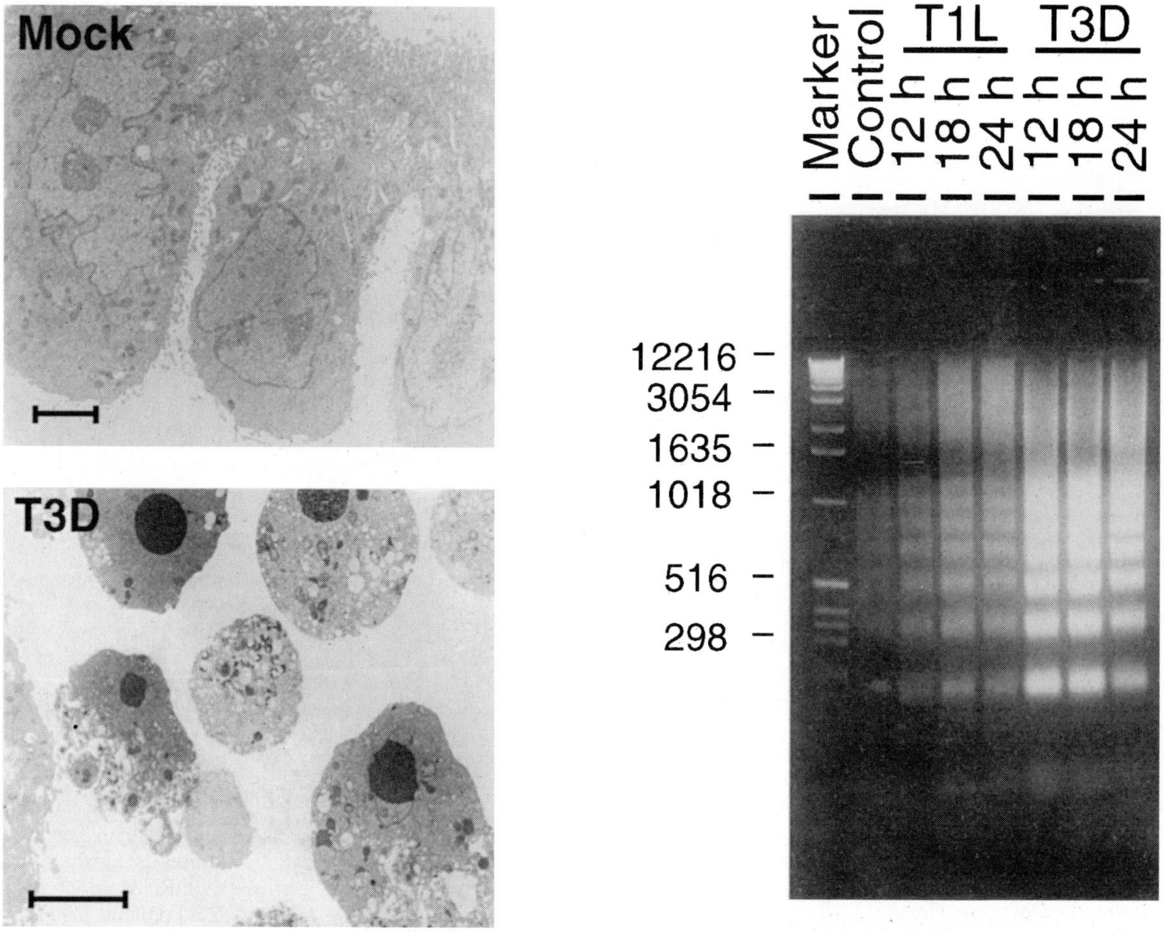

FIGURE 119–7. Induction of apoptosis by reovirus. *(Left)* Electron micrographs of MDCK epithelial cells infected with reovirus strain type 3 Dearing (T3D). Note cytoplasmic and nuclear membrane blebbing, cytoplasmic vacuolization, and condensation of nuclear chromatin. Bars, 5 μm. *(Right)* Agarose gel electrophoresis of low molecular weight cellular DNA extracted at various intervals from MDCK cells infected with reovirus strains type 1 Lang (T1L) and T3D. Size markers (in base-pairs) are indicated on the left. Note the presence of 200 base-pair concatemers of DNA. (From Rodgers SE, Barton ES, Oberhaus SM, et al. Reovirus-induced apoptosis of MDCK cells is not linked to viral yield and is blocked by Bcl-2. J Virol. 1997;71:2540–2546.)

factors required for efficient viral replication.[85, 86] In a general sense, RNA-containing viruses, including HIV, influenza virus, measles virus, poliovirus, reovirus, and Sindbis virus, induce apoptosis of their host cells, whereas DNA-containing viruses, including adenovirus, cytomegalovirus (CMV), Epstein-Barr virus (EBV), HPV, and the poxviruses, encode proteins that block apoptosis. For some viruses, the duration of the viral infectious cycle may determine whether apoptosis is induced or inhibited. Viruses capable of completing an infectious cycle before the induction of apoptosis would not require a means to inhibit this cellular response to viral infection. For other viruses, induction versus inhibition of apoptosis may determine the balance between lytic and persistent infections in the host.[91]

Antiviral Drugs

Knowledge of viral replication strategies has provided insights into critical steps in the viral life cycle that can serve as potential targets for antiviral therapy.[92] For example, drugs can be designed to interfere with viral binding to target cells or prevent penetration and disassembly once receptor engagement has occurred. Steps involved in the replication of the viral genome are also obvious targets for antiviral therapy. A number of currently available antiviral agents inhibit viral polymerases, including those active against herpesviruses (e.g., acyclovir) and HIV (e.g, zidovudine). The most recent additions to the antiviral formulary are drugs that inhibit viral proteases. Drugs that inhibit HIV protease block the processing of the Gag and Gag-Pol polyproteins and serve as potent inhibitors of HIV replication.[93] The use of these drugs in combination with agents that inhibit HIV reverse transcriptase has resulted in dramatic improvements in the survival of persons with HIV infection.[94]

In the future, a better understanding of viral replication strategies and mechanisms of virus-induced cell killing will undoubtedly pave the way for the rational design of novel antiviral agents. One of the most exciting approaches to the development of antiviral agents is the use of high-resolution x-ray crystallography to optimize studies of interactions between viral proteins and antiviral drugs.[95–98] Structures determined at high resolution combined with techniques in combinatorial chemistry may allow the design of antiviral agents with improved specificity for their targets.

VIRUS-HOST INTERACTION

One of the most fundamental challenges in virology is to apply knowledge gained from studies of virus-cell interactions in tissue culture systems to an understanding of how viruses interact with living hosts to produce disease. Virus-host interactions are often described in terms of pathogenesis and virulence. Viral *pathogenesis* is the process by which a virus interacts with its host in a discrete series of stages to produce disease (Table 119–4). Viral *virulence* is the capacity of a virus to produce disease in a susceptible host.

TABLE 119–4 Stages in Virus-Host Interaction

Entry into the host	Secondary replication
Primary replication	Cell injury or persistence
Spread	Host immune response
Cell and tissue tropism	

Virulence is often measured in terms of the quantity of virus required to produce illness or death in 50% of a cohort of animals infected with the virus. Virulence is dependent on both viral and host factors and must be measured using carefully defined conditions (e.g., viral strain, dose, and route of inoculation; and host species, age, and immune status). In many cases, it has been possible to identify roles played by individual viral proteins at specific stages in viral pathogenesis and to define the importance of these proteins in viral virulence.

Entry

The first step in the process of virus-host interaction is exposure of a susceptible host to viable virus under conditions that promote infection (Fig. 119–8).[99] Infectious virus may be present in respiratory droplets or aerosols, in fecally contaminated food or water, or in a body fluid or tissue (e.g., blood, saliva, urine, semen, or a transplanted organ) to which the susceptible host is exposed. In some cases, the virus is inoculated directly into the host through the bite of an insect or animal vector or through the use of a contaminated needle.

Infection also can be transmitted from mother to infant through virus carried in the germ line, virus that has infected the placenta or birth canal, or virus in breast milk. In some cases, acute viral infections result from the reactivation of endogenous latent virus (e.g., reactivation of HSV giving rise to herpes labialis) rather than de novo exposure to exogenous virus.

Exposure of respiratory mucosa to virus by direct inoculation or inhalation is an important means of viral entry into the host. A simple cough can generate up to 10,000 small, potentially infectious aerosol particles, and a sneeze can produce nearly 2 million! The distribution of these particles depends on a variety of environmental factors, the most important of which are temperature, humidity, and air currents. In addition to these factors, particle size is an important determinant of particle distribution. In general, smaller particles remain airborne longer than larger ones. Particle size also contributes to the fate of the particle after inhalation. Larger particles (>6 μm) are generally trapped in the nasal turbinates, whereas smaller particles may ultimately travel to the alveolar spaces of the lower respiratory tract.

Fecal-oral spread represents an additional important route of viral entry into the host. Food, water, or hands contaminated by infected fecal material can facilitate the entry of a virus by way of the mouth into the gastrointestinal (GI) tract. Once a virus has reached the GI tract, it faces a formidable physicochemical environment. Gastric contents are extremely acidic, at times approaching pH 2.0. Bile and proteolytic enzymes secreted from the gallbladder and pancreas enter the duodenum. Intestinal epithelial cells are covered by a carpet of mucus secreted by adjacent goblet cells. Secretory immunoglobulin A (IgA) as well as nonimmunoglobulin inhibitory substances are also present.

The environment of the GI tract requires viruses that infect by this route to have certain physical properties. Viruses capable of enteric transmission must be acid stable and resistant to bile salts. Since conditions in the GI tract are destructive to lipids contained in viral envelopes, most viruses spread by the fecal-oral route are nonenveloped. Interestingly, many viruses that enter the host via the GI tract require proteolysis of certain capsid components to productively infect intestinal cells. Treatment of mice with inhibitors of intestinal proteases blocks infection by reovirus[100] and rotavirus,[101] which demonstrates the critical importance of proteolysis in the initiation of infection by these viruses.

To produce systemic disease, a virus must cross the mucosal barrier that separates the luminal compartments of the respiratory, GI, and genitourinary tracts from the host's parenchymal tissues. Studies with reovirus illustrate one strategy used by viruses to cross mucosal surfaces to invade the host after entry into the GI tract.[102, 103] After oral inoculation of mice, reovirus adheres to the surface of intestinal microfold cells (M cells) that overlie collections of intestinal lymphoid tissue (Peyer's patches). In electron micrographs, reovirus virions can be followed sequentially as they are transported within vesicles from the luminal to the subluminal surface of M cells. Virions subsequently appear within Peyer's patches and then spread to regional lymph nodes and extraintestinal lymphoid organs such as the spleen. A similar pathway of spread also has been described for poliovirus[104] and HIV,[105] which suggests that M cells represent an important pathway for viral invasion of the host after entry into the GI tract.

Spread

Once a virus has entered the host, it can replicate locally or spread from the site of entry to distant organs to produce systemic disease (see Fig. 119–8). Examples of localized infections in which viral entry and replication occur at the same anatomic site include the respiratory infections caused by influenza virus, respiratory syncytial virus, and rhinovirus; the enteric infections produced by astrovirus, calicivirus, and rotavirus; and the dermatologic infections caused by HPV (warts) and paravaccinia virus (milker's nodules). Other viruses spread to distant sites in the host after primary replication at the sites of entry. For example, poliovirus spreads from the GI tract to the central nervous system (CNS) to produce meningitis, encephalitis, or poliomyelitis. Measles virus and varicella-zoster virus enter the host through the respiratory tract and then spread to lymph nodes, skin, and viscera.

The release of some viruses occurs preferentially from either the apical or the basolateral surface of polarized cells, such as epithelial cells.[106] In the case of enveloped viruses, polarized release is frequently determined by preferential sorting of envelope glycoproteins to sites of viral budding. Specific amino acid sequences in these viral proteins direct their transport to a particular cell surface.[107, 108] Mechanisms responsible for the polarized release of most nonenveloped viruses are not understood. The polarized release of virus at apical surfaces may facilitate the local spread of infection, whereas release at basolateral surfaces may facilitate systematic invasion by providing the virus access to subepithelial lymphoid, neural, or vascular tissues.

In the host, many viruses use the blood stream to spread from sites of primary replication to distant target tissues (see Fig. 119–8).[99, 109] In some cases, viruses may enter the blood stream directly, such as during a blood transfusion or an insect bite. More commonly, viruses enter the blood stream after replication at some primary site. Important sites of primary replication preceding hematogenous spread of viruses include Peyer's patches and mesenteric lymph nodes for enteric viruses; epithelial and alveolar cells for respiratory viruses; and skeletal muscle and subcutaneous tissue for togaviruses and some enteroviruses.

Fenner's classic studies with mousepox virus suggest that an initial low-titer viremia (*primary viremia*) serves to seed virus to a variety of organs where a period of further replication leads to a high-titer viremia (*secondary viremia*) that disseminates virus to target organs (Fig. 119–9).[110] It is often extremely difficult to identify primary and secondary viremias in naturally occurring viral infections; however, the replication of many viruses in reticuloendothelial organs (liver, spleen, lymph nodes, and bone marrow), muscle, fat, and even vascular endothelial cells can play an important role in maintaining viremia.

Viruses that reach the blood stream may travel either free in

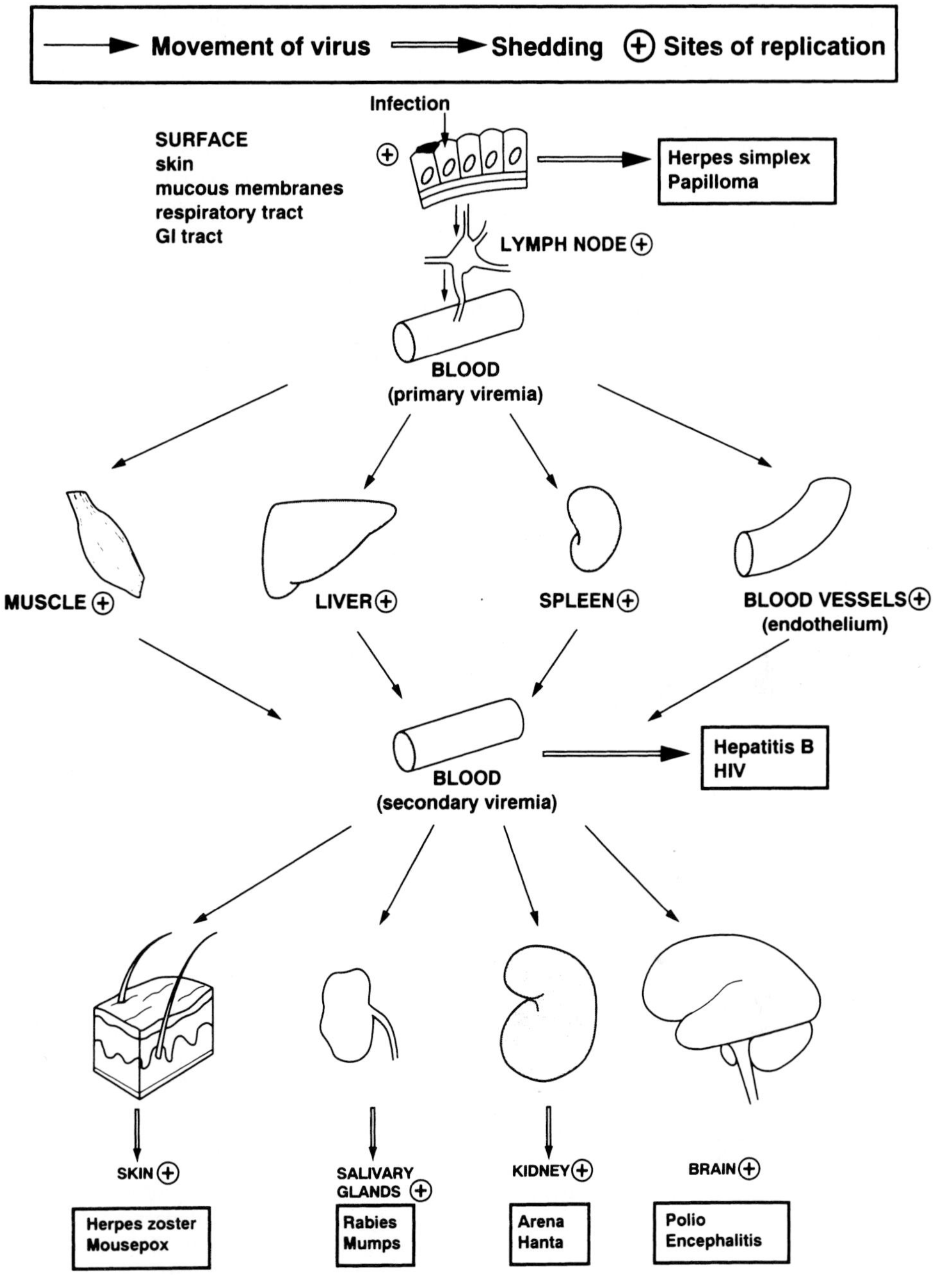

FIGURE 119–8. Entry and spread of viruses in human hosts. This scheme illustrates entry, primary replication, primary viremia, secondary replication, secondary viremia, and invasion of target organs. A few illustrative examples are shown. This scheme does not illustrate neural spread. (From Nathanson N, Tyler KL. Entry, dissemination, shedding, and transmission of viruses. In: Nathanson N, ed. Viral Pathogenesis. Philadelphia: Lippincott-Raven; 1997:13–33.)

plasma (e.g., picornaviruses and togaviruses) or in association with specific blood cells.[99, 109] A number of viruses are spread hematogenously by macrophages (e.g., CMV, HIV, and measles virus) or lymphocytes (e.g., CMV, EBV, HIV, HTLV, and measles virus). Although many viruses have the capacity to agglutinate erythrocytes in vitro (a process called *hemagglutination*), only in exceptional cases (e.g., Colorado tick fever virus) have erythrocytes been shown to transport virus in the blood stream.

The maintenance of viremia depends on the interplay between factors that promote viral production and those that favor viral clearance.[99, 109] A number of variables have been identified that can affect the efficiency of virus removal from plasma. In general, the larger the viral particle, the more efficiently it is cleared. Viruses that induce high titers of neutralizing antibodies are more efficiently cleared than those that do not induce humoral immune responses. Finally, phagocytosis of virus by cells in the host reticuloendothelial system can contribute to viral clearance.

A major pathway used by viruses to spread from sites of primary replication to the nervous system is through nerves. A large number of diverse viruses, including bornavirus,[111] coronavirus,[112] HSV,[113] poliovirus,[114] rabies virus,[115, 116] reovirus,[117] and Venezuelan equine encephalitis virus,[118] are capable of neural spread. Several of these viruses have been shown to accumulate at the neuromuscular junction after inoculation and replication in skeletal muscle. It has been suggested that the acetylcholine receptor serves as the rabies virus receptor that leads to viral entry into distal axon terminals of motor neurons.[119, 120] Interestingly, the major envelope glycoprotein of rabies virus has an amino acid sequence similarity with certain snake neurotoxins that also are known to bind the acetylcholine receptor.[121] HSV also appears to enter nerve cells via receptors that are located primarily at synaptic endings rather than on the nerve cell body.[122] Spread to the CNS of both rabies virus[115, 116] and HSV[123] can be inhibited by interruption of the appropriate nerves or by chemical agents that inhibit axonal transport. Studies of the kinetics of neural spread of these viruses suggest that they travel in nerves by the microtubule-based system of fast axonal transport.

Viruses are not limited to a single route of spread. Varicella-zoster virus, for example, enters the host by the respiratory route and then spreads from respiratory epithelium to the reticuloendothelial system and skin via the blood stream. Infection of the skin produces the characteristic exanthem of chickenpox. The virus subsequently enters distal terminals of sensory neurons and travels to dorsal root ganglia, where it establishes latent infection. Reactivation of varicella-zoster virus from latency results in the transport of virus in the sensory nerve axon to skin, where it gives rise to vesicular lesions in a dermatomal distribution characteristic of zoster or shingles.[124]

Poliovirus is also capable of spreading by both hematogenous and neural routes. Poliovirus is generally postulated to spread from the GI tract to the CNS via the blood stream, although it has been suggested that the virus may spread via autonomic nerves in the intestine to the brain stem and spinal cord.[125, 126] This hypothesis is supported by experiments using transgenic mice expressing the human poliovirus receptor.[127] When these mice are inoculated with poliovirus intramuscularly in the hind limb, virus does not reach the CNS if the sciatic nerve ipsilateral to the site of inoculation is sectioned.[114] Once poliovirus has reached the CNS, axonal transport is the major route of viral dissemination.

Little is known about mechanisms that determine pathways used by viruses to spread from sites of inoculation to target tissues. Experiments with reovirus have provided insights into the viral determinants of the capacity of viruses to use either hematogenous or neural routes of spread.[117] After intramuscular inoculation, reovirus strain type 1 Lang spreads via the blood stream to reach the spinal cord, whereas reovirus strain type 3 Dearing spreads via nerves. By using viruses containing different combinations of genes derived from the type 1 Lang and type 3 Dearing strains (reassortant viruses), it was found that the viral gene encoding the viral attachment protein determines the pathway of reovirus spread in the host. Studies using intertypic recombinants of HSV types 1 and 2 have identified specific regions in the HSV genome that influence the efficiency of neural spread of this virus.[128] In these experiments, the enhanced capacity of HSV type 2 to spread from the cornea to the CNS was found to segregate with a region of the HSV genome that encodes the viral DNA–dependent DNA polymerase. Similarly, studies comparing the neuroinvasiveness of two strains of HSV type 1 identified a region of the genome containing the gene encoding DNA polymerase as critical for neuroinvasiveness.[129] These studies indicate that the genomic region encoding the viral DNA polymerase plays a critical role in determining HSV interactions with neural tissues. Thus, as illustrated by both reovirus and HSV, specific viral factors can determine the pathways used by viruses to spread in the host.

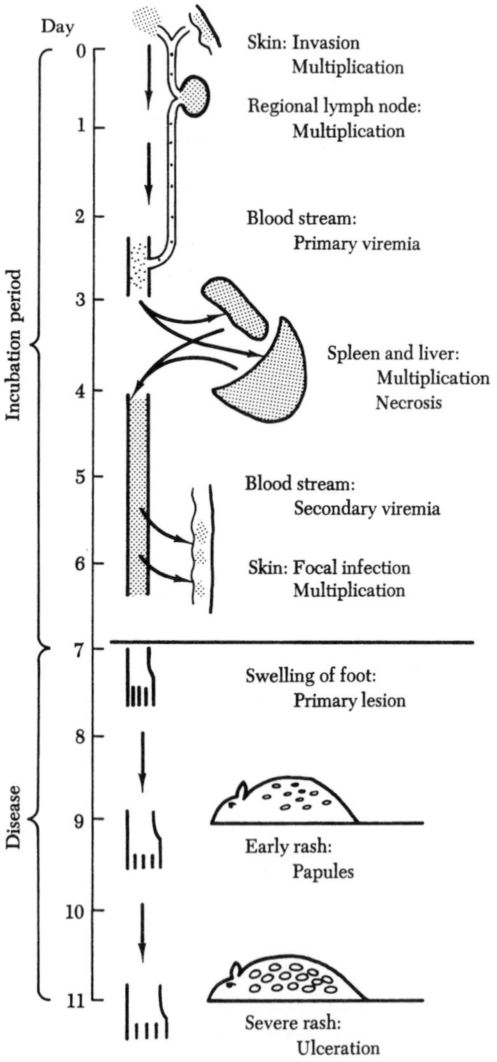

FIGURE 119–9. The pathogenesis of mousepox virus infection (ectromelia). Successive waves of viremia are shown to seed the spleen and liver and then skin. (From Fenner F. Mousepox [infectious ectromelia of mice]: A review. J Immunol. 1949;63:341–373. Copyright 1949. The American Association of Immunologists.)

Tropism

The capacity of a virus to infect a distinct group of cells in the host is referred to as *tropism*. For many viruses, tropism is determined by the availability of virus receptors on the surface of a given cell. This concept was first appreciated in studies of poliovirus when it was recognized that the capacity of the virus to infect specific tissues paralleled its capacity to bind homogenates of the susceptible tissues in vitro.[130] The importance of receptor expression as a determinant of poliovirus tropism was conclusively demonstrated by showing that cells not permissive for poliovirus replication could be made permissive by transfection of poliovirus genomic RNA[131] (thus abrogating the need for virus binding) or by recombinant expression of the poliovirus receptor.[132] In addition to poliovirus, the availability of virus receptors is a critical determinant of the tropism of many other viruses, including HIV,[36] rabies virus,[119, 120] and reovirus.[133]

However, it is important to note that the attachment of a virus to its receptor is only the first in series of events that lead to productive virus infection. In addition to the availability of virus receptors, tropism also can be determined by postattachment steps in viral replication, such as the regulation of viral gene expression. For example, some viruses contain genetic elements, termed *enhancers*, that stimulate the transcription of viral genes.[134, 135] Some enhancers are active in virtually all types of cells, whereas others show exquisite tissue specificity. The promoter-enhancer region of the JC polyomavirus is active in cultured human glial cells but not in HeLa cervical epithelial cells.[136] This tissue-specific expression of the JC viral genome correlates well with the capacity of this virus in immunocompromised persons to produce progressive multifocal leukoencephalopathy, a disease in which JC viral infection is limited to oligodendroglia in the CNS.

Specific steps in virus-host interaction, such as the route of entry and the pathway of spread, also can strongly influence viral tropism.[109] For example, encephalitis viruses such as Venezuelan equine encephalitis virus are transmitted to humans by insect bites. These viruses undergo primary replication and then spread to the CNS by both hematogenous and neural routes.[118] After oral inoculation, Venezuelan equine encephalitis virus is incapable of primary replication and spread to the CNS, which illustrates that tropism can be determined by the site of entry into the host. Influenza virus buds exclusively from the apical surface of respiratory epithelial cells,[106] which may limit its capacity to spread within the host and infect cells at distant sites.

In addition to the route of entry and pathway of spread, a wide variety of host factors can influence viral tropism. These include the host's age, nutritional status, and immune state as well as certain genetic polymorphisms that affect susceptibility to viral infection. Age-related patterns of infection are observed for many viruses, including respiratory syncytial virus[137–139] and rotavirus.[140, 141] The high rate of infections with these viruses in young children reflects the immunologic naiveté of such children but may also be related to intrinsic age-specific host or environmental factors that increase rates of viral infection.[109] The host's nutritional status is a critical determinant of the tropism and virulence of many viruses. For example, persons with vitamin A deficiency have enhanced susceptibility to measles virus infection.[142, 143] Similarly, the outcome of most viral infections is strongly linked to the immune competence of the host.

The basis for genetic determinants of host susceptibility to viral infections is complex. Studies with inbred strains of mice indicate that genetic variations can alter susceptibility to viral disease by a variety of mechanisms.[144] These can involve differences in immune responses, variability in the capacity to induce antiviral mediators such as interferon, and the differential expression of functional virus receptors. Polymorphisms in the expression of chemokine receptor CCR5, which serves as a coreceptor for HIV,[39–41] are associated with alterations in susceptibility to HIV infection in humans.[145, 146]

Persistent Infections

Many viruses are capable of establishing persistent infections in the host. Two types of persistent infections are recognized: chronic and latent.[147] *Chronic* viral infections are characterized by continuous shedding of virus for prolonged periods of time. Congenital infections with rubella virus[148] and CMV[149] and chronic infections with hepatitis B virus (HBV)[150] and HCV[151] are examples of chronic viral infections. Disease associated with chronic viral infections may be caused by progressive injury to host tissues as a consequence of viral infection or by immune-mediated destruction of virus-infected cells. *Latent* viral infections are characterized by maintenance of the viral genome in host cells in the absence of viral replication. Herpesviruses[83] and retroviruses[76] can establish latent infections. Disease produced by latent viral infections is usually associated with reactivation of productive viral infection with subsequent cytopathicity[152] or alteration of cell-cycle control mechanisms leading to neoplasia.[153] The distinction between chronic and latent infections is not readily apparent for some viruses, such as HIV, which can establish both chronic and latent infections in the host.[154–156]

Viruses capable of establishing persistent infections must have a means to evade the host immune response and a mechanism to attenuate their virulence.[147] Viruses use several strategies to evade immune-mediated clearance. Lentiviruses, such as equine infectious anemia virus[157] and HIV,[158–160] are capable of extensive antigenic variation resulting in escape from neutralizing-antibody responses of the host. Several viruses encode proteins that directly attenuate the host immune response. The adenovirus E3/19K protein blocks the cell surface expression of major histocompatibility class I proteins, resulting in diminished presentation of viral antigens to cytotoxic T lymphocytes.[161] Similarly, the CMV US11 gene product downregulates major histocompatibility class I protein expression by targeting these molecules to proteosomes for degradation.[162] The poxviruses encode a variety of immunomodulatory molecules including CrmA, which is capable of blocking T-cell–mediated apoptosis of virus-infected cells.[163] Viruses capable of establishing latent infections can evade both humoral and cell-mediated immune responses by decreasing the expression of viral proteins.

Many viruses that cause persistent infections can regulate their lytic potential. Some viruses, such as lymphocytic choriomeningitis virus, which establishes persistent infections in rodent species,[164] replicate without producing cell lysis or alterations in cell growth.[165] Cells infected with lymphocytic choriomeningitis virus survive, and persistent infections are established. Other viruses must restrict viral gene expression to establish persistent infections. For example, latent HSV infections of neurons are not associated with the synthesis of viral proteins.[166]

A number of tissues within the host are preferred sites for the establishment of persistent viral infections.[147] Several viruses, including HSV, measles virus, poliovirus, JC virus, and varicella-zoster virus, establish persistent infections in the nervous system. HBV and HCV establish persistent infections in the liver, and CMV, EBV, HIV, and HTLV establish persistent infections in either lymphocytes or monocytes. In some cases (e.g., the CNS), preferential sites for persistent viral infections are not readily accessible by the immune system,[167] which may favor the establishment of persistent infection.

Viruses and Cancer

Some viruses produce disease by promoting the malignant transformation of host cells.[168] Work by Peyton Rous with an avian retrovirus was the first to demonstrate that viral infections can cause cancer.[169] Rous sarcoma virus encodes an oncogene, v-*src*, which is a homologue of a cellular protooncogene, c-*src*.[170, 171] Cells infected with Rous sarcoma virus become transformed[172, 173] and give rise to tumors as a consequence of perturbations of cell-cycle control mediated by the v-*src* gene product.[174–176] Several viruses are associated with malignancies in humans. EBV is associated with many neoplasms,[177] including Burkitt's lymphoma, Hodgkin's disease, leiomyosarcoma, nasopharyngeal carcinoma, and CNS lymphomas in persons with HIV infection. HBV[150] and HCV[178, 179] are associated with hepatocellular carcinoma. HPV is associated with cervical cancer and a variety of anogenital neoplasms.[180] Human herpesvirus 8 is associated with Kaposi's sarcoma.[181, 182]

In many cases, the linkage of a virus to a particular neoplasm can be attributed to transforming properties of the virus itself. For example, EBV encodes several latency-associated proteins that are responsible for immortalization of B cells;[153] these proteins likely play crucial roles in the pathogenesis of EBV-associated malignancies.[183] Similarly, HPV encodes proteins that induce cell-cycle progression[184, 185] and block apoptosis.[186–188] It is hypothesized that the unregulated expression of these proteins induced by the aberrant integration of the HPV genome into the host genome is responsible for malignant transformation.[189] In other cases, mechanisms of malignancy triggered by viral infection are less clear. HCV is not known to encode transforming proteins but is strongly associated with hepatocellular cancer.[179] It is possible that increased cell turnover and the presence of inflammatory mediators in response to chronic HCV infection increase the risk of genetic damage, which results in malignant transformation.

Viral Virulence Determinants

One of the most important areas of recent research in viral pathogenesis has been the identification of determinants of viral virulence. It has now been possible to identify specific *virulence determinants* for many viruses. Although the nature of these virulence determinants varies for each viral group, a common theme is that virulence determinants are often viral surface proteins involved in attachment and entry. For example, polymorphisms in the attachment proteins of influenza virus,[190, 191] reovirus,[192] rotavirus,[193] and Venezuelan equine encephalitis virus[194] are strongly linked to the virulence of these viruses. Polymorphisms in viral attachment proteins can influence virulence by altering the affinity of virus-receptor interactions or modulating the kinetics of viral disassembly. Importantly, sequences in viral genomes that do not encode protein also can influence viral virulence. Mutations that contribute to the attenuated virulence of the Sabin strains of poliovirus are located in the 5′ nontranslated region of the viral genome.[195] These mutations attenuate poliovirus virulence by altering the efficiency of viral protein synthesis.

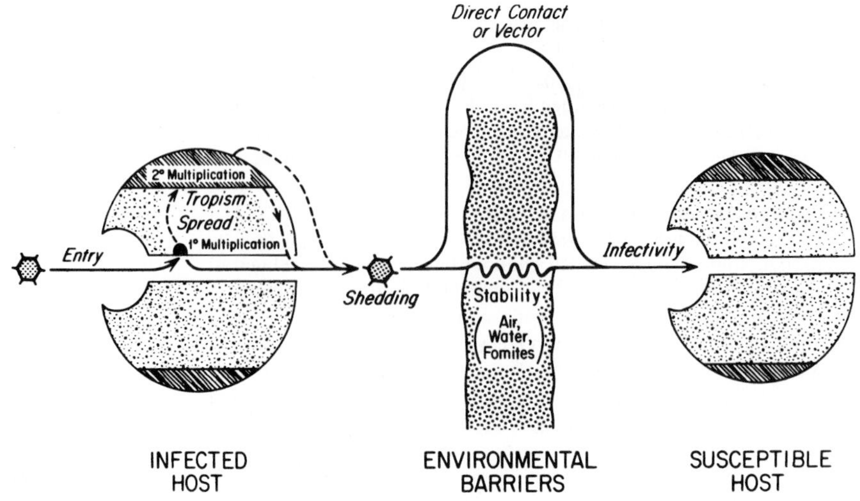

FIGURE 119–10. The life cycle of an enteric virus in the host and the environment. (From Keroack M, Fields BN. Viral shedding and transmission between hosts determined by reovirus L2 gene. Science. 1986;232:1635–1638.)

Ongoing studies to define roles played by viral genes and the proteins they encode at specific stages in viral pathogenesis will complement studies to identify cellular targets, such as receptors, that are involved in virus-host interactions. Knowledge of the precise mechanisms by which a virus engages its host to produce disease will likely lead to the development of new strategies for the prevention and treatment of viral diseases.

VIRUS-ENVIRONMENT INTERACTIONS

For a virus to survive in nature, the outcome of virus-host interaction must be the shedding of infectious virus into the environment in a manner that results in its spread to susceptible hosts (Fig. 119–10). Viruses can be shed from infected hosts by a variety of mechanisms. Virus in respiratory secretions can be expelled in aerosols generated by coughing or sneezing. Virus in saliva can be transmitted through biting or intimate personal contact. Virus in feces can contaminate food or water. Virus in semen or genital secretions can be transmitted during sexual intercourse. Each of these modes of transmission requires that the virus be stable (i.e., remain infectious) under defined environmental conditions. Because of the public health implications of viral stability in the environment, the effects of temperature, pH, and a variety of chemical and physical agents on the infectivity of a number of viruses have been defined. For example, poliovirus is resistant to inactivation by ether, chloroform, bile, detergents, and acidic pH but is quite sensitive to heat, ultraviolet irradiation, formalin, and chlorine.[196]

In some cases, it is possible to correlate the susceptibility of viruses to specific inactivating agents with particular aspects of viral structure. In the case of poliovirus, many conditions that result in viral inactivation (e.g., basic pH, heat, and ultraviolet irradiation) are associated with loss or alteration of structural protein VP4.[197] The absence of functional VP4 promotes the escape of viral RNA from the poliovirus capsid, which renders the virus noninfectious. Extensive studies of the effects of chemical and physical inactivating agents on the infectivity of reovirus indicate that viral surface proteins play critical roles in determining viral susceptibility to inactivation.[198, 199]

The effects of physical and chemical treatments on viral infectivity can be used to predict the survival of viruses in the environment and facilitate the development of rational inactivation strategies. Future directions for research on the transmission of viruses between hosts will focus in part on defining how specific viral structural components determine the stability of viral particles in defined physicochemical settings. In addition to improving an understanding of factors that affect the survival of viruses in the environment, this work is applicable to the development of viral vaccines with enhanced stability.

REFERENCES

1. Waterson AP, Wilkinson L. An Introduction to the History of Virology. London: Cambridge University Press; 1978.
2. Reed W. Recent researches concerning the etiology, propagation and prevention of yellow fever by the United States Army Commission. J Hyg. 1902;2:101–109.
3. Delbruck M. The growth of bacteriophage and lysis of the host. J Gen Physiol. 1940;23:643.
4. Luria SE. Bacteriophage: An essay on virus reproduction. Science. 1950;111: 507–511.
5. Avery OT, MacLeod CM, McCarty M. Studies on the chemical nature of the substance inducing transformation of pneumococcal types. Induction of transformation by a desoxyribonucleic acid fraction isolated from pneumococcus type III. J Exp Med. 1944;79:137–158.
6. Hershey AD, Chase M. Independent functions of viral protein and nucleic acid in the growth of bacteriophage. J Gen Physiol. 1952;36:39–56.
7. Enders JF, Weller TH, Robbins FC. Cultivation of the Lansing strain of poliomyelitis virus in cultures of various human embryonic tissues. Science. 1949;109:85–87.
8. Salk JE, Bennett BL, Lewis LJ, et al. Studies in human subjects on active immunization against poliomyelitis. I. A preliminary report of experiments in progress. JAMA. 1953;151:1081–1098.
9. Sabin AB, Boulger LR. History of Sabin attenuated poliovirus oral live vaccine strains. J Biol Stand. 1973;1:115–118.
10. Murphy FA, Kingsbury DW. Virus taxonomy. In: Fields BN, Knipe DM, Howley PM, eds. Fields Virology. 3rd ed. Philadelphia: Lippincott-Raven; 1996:15–57.
11. Nibert ML, Furlong DB, Fields BN. Mechanisms of viral pathogenesis: Distinct forms of reoviruses and their roles during replication in cells and host. J Clin Invest. 1991;88:727–734.
12. Weis W, Brown JH, Cusack S, et al. Structure of the influenza virus haemagglutinin complexed with its receptor, sialic acid. Nature. 1988;333:426–431.
13. Olson NH, Kolatkar PR, Oliveira MA, et al. Structure of a human rhinovirus complexed with its receptor molecule. Proc Natl Acad Sci U S A. 1993;90: 507–511.
14. Prasad BVV, Burns JW, Marietta E, et al. Localization of VP4 neutralization sites in rotavirus by three-dimensional electron microscopy. Nature. 1990;343:476–479.
15. Wang GJ, Porta C, Chen ZG, et al. Identification of a Fab interaction footprint site on an icosahedral virus by cryoelectron microscopy and x-ray crystallography. Nature. 1992;355:275–278.
16. Harrison S, Wiley DC, Skehel JJ. Virus structure. In: Fields BN, Knipe DM, Howley PM, eds. Fields Virology. 3rd ed. Philadelphia: Lippincott-Raven; 1996:59–99.
17. Crawford SE, Labbe M, Cohen J, et al. Characterization of virus-like particles produced by the expression of rotavirus capsid proteins in insect cells. J Virol. 1994;68:5942–5952.
18. Green NM, Wrigley NG, Russel WC, et al. Evidence for a repeating β-sheet structure in the adenovirus fibre. EMBO J. 1983;8:1357–1365.
19. Stewart PL, Burnett RM, Cyrklaff M, Fuller SD. Image reconstruction reveals the complex molecular organization of adenovirus. Cell. 1991;67:145–154.
20. Furlong DB, Nibert ML, Fields BN. Sigma 1 protein of mammalian reoviruses extends from the surfaces of viral particles. J Virol. 1988;62:246–256.
21. Shaw AL, Rothnagel R, Chen D, et al. Three-dimensional visualization of the rotavirus hemagglutinin structure. Cell. 1993;74:693–701.

22. Wilson IA, Skehel JJ, Wiley DC. Structure of the hemagglutinin membrane glycoprotein of influenza virus at 3 angstrom resolution. Nature. 1981;289:366–373.
23. Lasky LA, Nakamura G, Smith DH, et al. Delineation of a region of the human immunodeficiency virus type 1 gp120 glycoprotein critical for interaction with the CD4 receptor. Cell. 1987;50:975–985.
24. Moore JP, McKeating JM, Norton WA, Sattentau QJ. Direct measurement of soluble CD4 binding to human immunodeficiency virus type 1: gp120 dissociation and its implications for virus-cell binding and fusion reactions and their neutralization by soluble CD4. J Virol. 1991;65:1133–1140.
25. Hogle JM, Chow M, Filman DJ. Three dimensional structure of poliovirus at 2.9 angstrom resolution. Science. 1985;229:1358–1365.
26. Rossmann MG, Arnold E, Erickson JW, et al. Structure of a human common cold virus and functional relationship to other picornaviruses. Nature. 1985;317: 145–153.
27. Acharya R, Fry E, Stuart D, et al. The three dimensional structure of foot-and-mouth disease virus at 2.9 angstrom resolution. Nature. 1989;327:709–716.
28. Haywood AM. Virus receptors: Binding, adhesion strengthening, and changes in viral structure. J Virol. 1994;68:1–5.
29. Wickham TJ, Mathias P, Cheresh DA, Nemerow GR. Integrins alpha v beta 3 and alpha v beta 5 promote adenovirus internalization but not virus attachment. Cell. 1993;73:309–319.
30. Bergelson JM, Cunningham JA, Droguett G, et al. Isolation of a common receptor for Coxsackie B viruses and adenoviruses 2 and 5. Science. 1997;275:1320–1323.
31. WuDunn D, Spear PG. Initial interaction of herpes simplex virus with cells is binding to heparan sulfate. J Virol. 1989;63:52–58.
32. Lycke E, Johansson M, Svennerholm B, Lindahl U. Binding of herpes simplex virus to cellular heparan sulphate; an initial step in the adsorption process. J Gen Virol. 1991;72:1131–1137.
33. Shieh MT, WuDunn D, Montgomery RI, et al. Cell surface receptors for herpes simplex virus are heparan sulfate proteoglycans. J Cell Biol. 1992;116:1273–1281.
34. Montgomery RI, Warner MS, Lum BJ, Spear PG. Herpes simplex virus-1 entry into cells mediated by a novel member of the TNF/NGF receptor family. Cell. 1996;87:427–436.
35. Dalgleish AG, Beverley PCL, Clapham PR, et al. The CD4 (T4) antigen is an essential component of the receptor for the AIDS retrovirus. Nature. 1984;312: 763–767.
36. Maddon PJ, Dalgleish AG, McDougal JS, et al. The T4 gene encodes the AIDS virus receptor and is expressed in the immune system and the brain. Cell. 1986;47:333–348.
37. Feng Y, Broder CC, Kennedy PE, Berger EA. HIV-1 entry cofactor: Functional cDNA cloning of a seven-transmembrane, G protein–coupled receptor. Science. 1996;272:872–877.
38. Oberlin E, Amara A, Bachelerie F, et al. The CXC chemokine SDF-1 is the ligand for LESTR/fusin and prevents infection by T-cell-line-adapted HIV-1. Nature. 1996;382:833–835.
39. Deng H, Liu R, Ellmeier W, et al. Identification of a major co-receptor for primary isolates of HIV-1. Nature. 1996;381:661–666.
40. Dragic T, Litwin V, Allaway GP, et al. HIV-1 entry into CD4+ cells is mediated by the chemokine receptor CC-CKR-5. Nature. 1996;381:667–673.
41. Alkhatib G, Combadiere C, Broder CC, et al. CC CKR5: A RANTES, MIP-1alpha, MIP-1beta receptor as a fusion cofactor for macrophage-tropic HIV-1. Science. 1996;272:1955–1958.
42. Stehle T, Yan Y, Benjamin TL, Harrison SC. Structure of murine polyomavirus complexed with an oligosaccharide receptor fragment. Nature. 1994;369:160–163.
43. Stehle T, Harrison SC. High-resolution structure of a polyomavirus VP1-oligosaccharide complex: Implications for assembly and receptor binding. EMBO J. 1997;16:5139–5148.
44. Moebius U, Clayton LK, Abraham S, et al. The human immunodeficiency virus gp120 binding site on CD4: Delineation by quantitative equilibrium and kinetic binding studies of mutants in conjunction with a high-resolution CD4 atomic structure. J Exp Med. 1992;176:507–517.
45. Hernandez LD, Hoffman LR, Wolfsberg TG, White JM. Virus-cell and cell-cell fusion. Annu Rev Cell Dev Biol. 1996;12:627–661.
46. Doranz BJ, Berson JF, Rucker J, Doms RW. Chemokine receptors as fusion cofactors for human immunodeficiency virus type 1 (HIV-1). Immunol Res. 1997;16:15–28.
47. Moore JP, Trkola A, Dragic T. Co-receptors for HIV-1 entry. Curr Opin Immunol. 1997;9:551–562.
48. Kowalski M, Potz J, Basiripour L, et al. Functional regions of the envelope glycoprotein of human immunodeficiency virus type 1. Science. 1988;237:1351–1355.
49. Sattentau QJ. CD4 activation of HIV fusion. Int J Cell Clon. 1992;10:323–332.
50. Weissenhorn W, Dessen A, Harrison SC, et al. Atomic structure of the ectodomain from HIV-1 gp41. Nature. 1997;387:426–430.
51. Marsh M, Pelchen-Matthews A. The endocytic pathway and virus entry. In: Wimmer E, ed. Cellular Receptors for Animal Viruses. Cold Spring Harbor, NY: Cold Spring Harbor; 1994:215–240.
52. Trowbridge IS, Collawn JE, Hopkins CR. Signal-dependent membrane protein trafficking in the endocytic pathway. Annu Rev Cell Biol. 1993;9:129–161.
53. Mellman I, Fuchs R, Helenius A. Acidification of the endocytic and exocytic pathways. Annu Rev Biochem. 1985;55:663–700.
54. Stegmann T, White JM, Helenius A. Intermediates in influenza induced membrane fusion. EMBO J. 1990;9:4231–4241.
55. Bullough PA, Hughson FM, Skehel JJ, Wiley DC. Structure of influenza haemagglutinin at the pH of membrane fusion. Nature. 1994;371:37–43.
56. Kielian MC, Helenius A. pH-induced alterations in the fusogenic spike protein of Semliki Forest virus. J Cell Biol. 1985;101:2284–2291.
57. Wahlberg JM, Bron R, Wischut J, Garoff H. Membrane fusion of Semliki Forest virus involves homotrimers of the fusion protein. J Virol. 1992;66:7309–7318.
58. Allison SL, Schalich J, Stiansy K, et al. Oligomeric rearrangement of tick-borne encephalitis virus envelope proteins induced by an acidic pH. J Virol. 1995;69: 695–700.
59. Varga MJ, Weibull C, Everitt E. Infectious entry pathway of adenovirus type 2. J Virol. 1991;65:6061–6070.
60. Greber UF, Willetts M, Webster P, Helenius A. Stepwise dismantling of adenovirus 2 during entry into cells. Cell. 1993;75:477–486.
61. Donelli G, Superti F, Tinari A, Marziano ML. Mechanism of astrovirus entry into Graham 293 cells. J Med Virol. 1992;38:271–277.
62. Basak S, Turner H. Infectious entry pathway for canine parvovirus. Virology. 1992;186:368–376.
63. Maratos-Flier E, Goodman MJ, Murray AH, Kahn CR. Ammonium inhibits processing and cytotoxicity of reovirus, a nonenveloped virus. J Clin Invest. 1986;78:617–625.
64. Sturzenbecker LJ, Nibert M, Furlong D, Fields BN. Intracellular digestion of reovirus particles requires a low pH and is an essential step in the viral infectious cycle. J Virol. 1987;61:2351–2361.
65. Baer GS, Dermody TS. Mutations in reovirus outer-capsid protein $\sigma3$ selected during persistent infections of L cells confer resistance to protease inhibitor E64. J Virol. 1997;71:4921–4928.
66. Kaplan G, Freistadt MS, Racaniello VR. Neutralization of poliovirus by cell receptors expressed in insect cells. J Virol. 1990;64:4697–4702.
67. Curry S, Chow M, Hogle JM. The poliovirus 135S particle is infectious. J Virol. 1996;70:7125–7131.
68. Tosteson MT, Chow M. Characterization of the ion channels formed by poliovirus in planar lipid membranes. J Virol. 1997;71:507–511.
69. Kaijot J-KT, Shaw RD, Rubin DH, Greenberg HB. Infectious rotavirus enters cells by direct cell membrane penetration, not by endocytosis. J Virol. 1988;62:1136–1144.
70. Nandi P, Charpilienne A, Cohen J. Interaction of rotavirus particles with liposomes. J Virol. 1992;66:3363–3367.
71. Ruiz MC, Alonso-Torre SR, Charpilienne A, et al. Rotavirus interaction with isolated membrane vesicles. J Virol. 1994;68:4009–4016.
72. Falconer MM, Gilbert JM, Roper AM, et al. Rotavirus-induced fusion from without in tissue culture cells. J Virol. 1995;69:5582–5591.
73. Roizman B, Palese P. Multiplication of viruses: An overview. In: Fields BN, Knipe DM, Howley PM, eds. Fields Virology. 3rd ed. Philadelphia: Lippincott-Raven; 1996:101–111.
74. Fields BN. Reoviridae. In: Fields BN, Knipe DM, Howley PM, eds. Fields Virology. 3rd ed. Philadelphia: Lippincott-Raven; 1996:1553–1556.
75. Lawton JA, Estes MK, Prasad BVV. Three-dimensional visualization of mRNA release from actively transcribing rotavirus particles. Nat Struct Biol. 1997;4: 118–121.
76. Coffin JM. Retroviridae: The viruses and their replication. In: Fields BN, Knipe DM, Howley PM, eds. Fields Virology. 3rd ed. Philadelphia: Lippincott-Raven; 1996:1767–1847.
77. Luciw P. Human immunodeficiency viruses and their replication. In: Fields BN, Knipe DM, Howley PM, eds. Fields Virology. 3rd ed. Philadelphia: Lippincott-Raven; 1996:1881–1952.
78. Cann AJ, Chen ISY. Human T-cell leukemia virus types I and II. In: Fields BN, Knipe DM, Howley PM, eds. Fields Virology. 3rd ed. Philadelphia: Lippincott-Raven; 1996:1849–1880.
79. Nabel GJ. The role of cellular transcription factors in the regulation of human immunodeficiency virus gene expression. In: Cullen BR, ed. Human Retroviruses. Oxford: IRL; 1993:49–73.
80. Whyte P, Buchkovich KJ, Horowitz JM, et al. Association between an oncogene and an anti-oncogene: The adenovirus E1A proteins bind to the retinoblastoma gene product. Nature. 1988;334:124–129.
81. Rao L, Debbas M, Sabbatini P, et al. The adenovirus E1A proteins induce apoptosis which is inhibited by the E1B 19K and Bcl-2 proteins. Proc Natl Acad Sci U S A. 1992;89:7742–7746.
82. Yew PR, Berk AJ. Inhibition of p53 activation required for transformation by adenovirus early 1B protein. Nature. 1992;357:82–85.
83. Roizman B. Herpesviridae. In: Fields BN, Knipe DM, Howley PM, eds. Fields Virology. 3rd ed. Philadelphia: Lippincott-Raven; 1996:2221–2230.
84. Wagner RR. Cytopathic effects of viruses: A general survey. In: Fraenkel-Conrat H, Wagner RR, eds. Comprehensive Virology. New York: Plenum; 1984:1–63.
85. Razvi ES, Welsh RM. Apoptosis in viral infections. Adv Virus Res. 1995;45:1–60.
86. Shen Y, Shenk TE. Viruses and apoptosis. Curr Opin Gen Dev. 1995;5:105–111.
87. Wyllie AH, Kerr JFR, Currie AR. Cell death: The significance of apoptosis. Int Rev Cytol. 1980;68:251–306.
88. Martz E, Howell DM. CTL: Virus control cells first and cytolytic cells second? DNA fragmentation, apoptosis and the prelytic halt hypothesis. Immunol Today. 1989;10:79–86.
89. Clouston WM, Kerr JF. Apoptosis, lymphocytotoxicity and the containment of viral infections. Med Hypotheses. 1985;18:399–404.
90. Cohen JJ. Programmed cell death in the immune system. Adv Immunol. 1991;50:55–85.
91. Levine B, Huang Q, Isaacs JT, et al. Conversion of lytic to persistent alphavirus infection by the *bcl*-2 cellular oncogene. Nature. 1993;361:739–742.

92. Galasso GJ, Merigan TC, Buchanan RA, eds. Antiviral Agents and Viral Diseases of Man. 3rd ed. New York: Raven; 1990.
93. McQuade TJ, Tomasselli AG, Liu L, et al. A synthetic HIV-1 protease inhibitor with antiviral activity arrests HIV-like particle maturation. Science. 1990;247: 454–456.
94. Palella FJ Jr, Delaney KM, Moorman AC, et al. Declining morbidity and mortality among patients with advanced human immunodeficiency virus infection. N Engl J Med. 1998;338:853–860.
95. Smith TJ, Kremer MJ, Luo M, et al. The site of attachment in human rhinovirus 14 for antiviral agents that inhibit uncoating. Science. 1986;233:1286–1293.
96. Badger J, Minor I, Kremer MJ, et al. Structural analysis of a series of antiviral agents complexed with human rhinovirus 14. Proc Natl Acad Sci U S A. 1988;85:3304–3308.
97. Kohlstaedt LA, Wang J, Friedman JM, et al. Crystal structure at 3.5 angstrom resolution of HIV-1 reverse transcriptase complexed with an inhibitor. Science. 1992;256:1783–1790.
98. Wlodawer A, Erickson JW. Structure-based inhibitors of HIV-1 protease. Ann Rev Biochem. 1993;62:543–585.
99. Mims CA, White DO. Viral Pathogenesis and Immunology. Oxford: Blackwell Scientific; 1984.
100. Bass DM, Bodkin D, Dambrauskas R, et al. Intraluminal proteolytic activation plays an important role in replication of type 1 reovirus in the intestines of neonatal mice. J Virol. 1990;64:1830–1833.
101. Vonderfecht SL, Miskuff RL, Wee S, et al. Protease inhibitors suppress the in vitro and in vivo replication of rotaviruses. J Clin Invest. 1988;82:2011–2016.
102. Wolf JL, Rubin DH, Finberg R, et al. Intestinal M cells: A pathway of entry of reovirus into the host. Science. 1981;212:471–472.
103. Wolf JL, Kauffman RS, Finberg R, et al. Determinants of reovirus interaction with the intestinal M cells and absorptive cells of murine intestine. Gastroenterology. 1983;85:291–300.
104. Sicinski P, Rowinski J, Warchol JB, et al. Poliovirus type 1 enters the human host through intestinal M cells. Gastroenterology. 1990;98:56–58.
105. Amerongen HM, Weltzin R, Farnet CM, et al. Transepithelial transport of HIV-1 by intestinal M cells: A mechanism for transmission of AIDS. J AIDS. 1991;4: 760–765.
106. Tucker SP, Compans RW. Virus infection of polarized epithelial cells. Adv Virus Res. 1993;42:187–247.
107. Ball JM, Mulligan MJ, Compans RW. Basolateral sorting of the HIV type 2 and SIV envelope glycoproteins in polarized epithelial cells: Role of the cytoplasmic domain. AIDS Res Hum Retroviruses. 1997;13:665–675.
108. Huang XF, Compans RW, Chen S, et al. Polarized apical targeting directed by the signal/anchor region of simian virus 5 hemagglutinin-neuraminidase. J Biol Chem. 1997;272:27,598–27,604.
109. Tyler KL, Fields BN. Pathogenesis of viral infections. In: Fields BN, Knipe DM, Howley PM, eds. Fields Virology. 3rd ed. Philadelphia: Lippincott-Raven; 1996:173–218.
110. Fenner F. The pathogenesis of acute exanthems. Lancet. 1948;2:915.
111. Carbone KM, Duchala CS, Griffin JW, et al. Pathogenesis of Borna disease in rats: Evidence that intra-axonal spread is the major route for virus dissemination and the determination for disease incubation. J Virol. 1987;61:3431–3440.
112. Barnett E, Perlman S. The olfactory nerve and not the trigeminal nerve is the major site of CNS entry for mouse hepatitis virus, strain JHM. Virology. 1993;194:185–191.
113. Card JP, Whealy ME, Robbins AK, et al. Two alpha-herpesviruses are transported differentially in the rodent visual system. Neuron. 1991;6:957–969.
114. Ren R, Racaniello VR. Poliovirus spreads from muscle to central nervous system by neural pathways. J Infect Dis. 1992;166:747–752.
115. Tsiang H. Evidence for intraaxonal transport of fixed and street rabies virus. J Neuropathol Exp Neurol. 1979;38:286–297.
116. Lycke E, Tsiang H. Rabies virus infection of cultured rat sensory neurons. J Virol. 1987;61:2733–2741.
117. Tyler KL, McPhee DA, Fields BN. Distinct pathways of viral spread in the host determined by reovirus S1 gene segment. Science. 1986;233:770–774.
118. Davis NL, Grieder FB, Smith JF, et al. A molecular genetic approach to the study of Venezuelan equine encephalitis virus pathogenesis. Arch Virol Suppl. 1994;9:99–109.
119. Lentz TL, Burrage TG, Smith AL, et al. Is the acetylcholine receptor a rabies virus receptor? Science. 1982;215:182–184.
120. Hanham CA, Zhao F, Tignor GH. Evidence from the anti-idiotypic network that the acetylcholine receptor is a rabies virus receptor. J Virol. 1993;67:530–542.
121. Lentz TL, Wilson PT, Hawrot E, Speicher DW. Amino acid sequence similarity between rabies virus glycoprotein and snake venom curaremimetic neurotoxins. Science. 1984;226:847–848.
122. Ziegler RJ, Herman RE. Peripheral infection in culture of rat sensory neurons by herpes simplex virus. Infect Immun. 1980;28:620–623.
123. Kristensson K, Lycke E, Sjostrand J. Spread of herpes simplex virus in peripheral nerves. Acta Neuropathol (Berl). 1971;17:44–53.
124. Arvin AM. Varicella-Zoster virus. In: Fields BN, Knipe DM, Howley PM, eds. Fields Virology. 3rd ed. Philadelphia: Lippincott-Raven; 1996:2547–2585.
125. Bodian D. Poliomyelitis: Pathogenesis and histopathology. In: Rivers TM, Horsfall FL, eds. Viral and Rickettsial Infections of Man. 3rd ed. Philadelphia: Lippincott; 1959:479–518.
126. Sabin AB. Paralytic poliomyelitis: Old dogmas and new perspectives. Rev Infect Dis. 1981;3:543–564.
127. Ren R, Costantini FC, Gorgacz EJ, et al. Transgenic mice expressing a human poliovirus receptor: A new model for poliomyelitis. Cell. 1990;63:353–362.
128. Day SP, Lausch RN, Oakes JE. Evidence that the gene for herpes virus type 1 DNA polymerase accounts for the capacity of an intertypic recombinant to spread from eye to central nervous system. Virology. 1988;163:166–173.
129. Thompson RL, Cook ML, Devi-Rao GB, et al. Functional and molecular analysis of the avirulent wild-type herpes simplex virus type 1 strain KOS. J Virol. 1986;58:203–211.
130. Holland JJ. Receptor affinities as major determinants of enterovirus tissue tropisms in humans. Virology. 1961;15:312–326.
131. Holland JJ, McLauren SC, Syverton JT. The mammalian cell virus relationship. IV. Infection of naturally insusceptible cells with enterovirus ribonucleic acid. J Exp Med. 1959;110:65–80.
132. Mendelsohn CL, Wimmer E, Racaniello VR. Cellular receptor for poliovirus: Molecular cloning, nucleotide sequence, and expression of a new member of the immunoglobulin superfamily. Cell. 1989;56:855–865.
133. Weiner HL, Powers ML, Fields BN. Absolute linkage of virulence and central nervous system tropism of reoviruses to viral hemagglutinin. J Infect Dis. 1980;141:609–616.
134. McKnight S, Tijan R. Transcriptional selectivity of viral genes in mammalian cells. Cell. 1986;46:795–805.
135. Maniatis T, Goodbourn S, Fischer JA. Regulation of inducible and tissue-specific gene expression. Science. 1987;236:1237–1245.
136. Kenney S, Natarajan V, Strike D, et al. JC virus enhancer-promoter active in human brain cells. Science. 1984;226:1337–1339.
137. Hall CB, Hall WJ, Speers DM. Clinical and physiologic manifestations of bronchiolitis and pneumonia: Outcome of respiratory syncytial virus. Am J Dis Child. 1979;133:798–802.
138. Henderson FW, Collier AM, Clyde J, et al. Respiratory syncytial virus infections: Reinfections and immunity: A prospective, longitudinal study in young children. N Engl J Med. 1979;300:530–534.
139. Glezen WP, Taber LH, Frank AL, Kasel JA. Risk of primary infection and reinfection with respiratory syncytial virus. Am J Dis Child. 1986;140:543–546.
140. Rodriguez WJ, Kim HW, Brandt CD, et al. Rotavirus gastroenteritis in the Washington, DC area. Incidence of cases resulting in admission to the hospital. Am J Dis Child. 1980;134:777–779.
141. Bishop RF. Natural history of human rotavirus infections. In: Kapikian AZ, ed. Viral Infections of the Gastrointestinal Tract. New York: Marcel Dekker; 1994: 131–168.
142. Barclay AJG, Foster A, Sommer A. Vitamin A supplements and mortality related to measles: A randomised clinical trial. BMJ. 1987;294:294–296.
143. Hussey GD, Klein M. Routine high-dose vitamin A therapy for children hospitalized with measles. J Trop Pediatr. 1993;39:342–345.
144. Rosenstreich DL, Weinblatt AC, O'Brien AD. Genetic control of resistance to infection in mice. Crit Rev Immunol. 1982;3:263–300.
145. Dean M, Carrington M, Winkler C, et al. Genetic restriction of HIV-1 infection and progression to AIDS by a deletion allele of the *CKR5* structural gene. Hemophilia Growth and Development Study, Multicenter AIDS Cohort Study, Multicenter Hemophilia Cohort Study, San Francisco City Cohort, ALIVE Study. Science. 1996;273:1856–1862.
146. Hoffman TL, MacGregor RR, Burger H, at al. CCR5 genotypes in sexually active couples discordant for human immunodeficiency virus type 1 infection status. J Infect Dis. 1997;176:1093–1096.
147. Ahmed R, Morrison LA, Knipe DM. Persistence of viruses. In: Fields BN, Knipe DM, Howley PM, eds. Fields Virology. 3rd ed. Philadelphia: Lippincott-Raven; 1996:219–249.
148. Rawls WE. Viral persistence in congenital rubella. Prog Med Virol. 1974;17: 273–288.
149. Britt WJ, Alford CA. Cytomegalovirus. In: Fields BN, Knipe DM, Howley PM, eds. Fields Virology. 3rd ed. Philadelphia: Lippincott-Raven; 1996:2493–2523.
150. Hollinger FB. Hepatitis B virus. In: Fields BN, Knipe DM, Howley PM, eds. Fields Virology. 3rd ed. Philadelphia: Lippincott-Raven; 1996:2738–2807.
151. Houghton M. Hepatitis C viruses. In: Fields BN, Knipe DM, Howley PM, eds. Fields Virology. 3rd ed. Philadelphia: Lippincott-Raven; 1996:1035–1058.
152. Roizman B, Sears AE. Herpes simplex viruses and their replication. In: Fields BN, Knipe DM, Howley PM, eds. Fields Virology. 3rd ed. Philadelphia: Lippincott-Raven; 1996:2231–2295.
153. Kieff E. Epstein-Barr virus and its replication. In: Fields BN, Knipe DM, Howley PM, eds. Fields Virology. 3rd ed. Philadelphia: Lippincott-Raven; 1996:2343–2396.
154. Ho DD, Neumann AU, Perelson AS, et al. Rapid turnover of plasma virions and CD4 lymphocytes in HIV-1 infection. Nature. 1995;373:123–126.
155. Wong JK, Hezareh M, Gunthard HF, et al. Recovery of replication-competent HIV despite prolonged suppression of plasma viremia. Science. 1997;278:1291–1295.
156. Finzi D, Hermankova M, Pierson T, et al. Identification of a reservoir for HIV-1 in patients on highly active antiretroviral therapy. Science. 1997;278:1295–1300.
157. Montelaro RC, Parekh B, Orrego A, Issel CJ. Antigenic variation during persistent infection by equine infectious anemia virus, a retrovirus. J Biol Chem. 1984;259:10,539–10,544.
158. Robert-Guroff M, Brown M, Gallo RC. HTLV-III-neutralizing antibodies in patients with AIDS and AIDS-related complex. Nature. 1985;316:72–74.
159. Weiss RA, Clapham PR, Cheingsong-Popou R, et al. Neutralization of human T lymphotropic virus type III by sera of AIDS and AIDS-risk patients. Nature. 1985;316:69–72.
160. Fauci A. Immunopathogenesis of HIV infection. AIDS. 1993;6:655–662.
161. Burgert H, Maryanski J, Kvist S. "E3/19K" protein of adenovirus type 2 inhibits

lysis of cytolytic T lymphocytes by blocking cell-surface expression of histocompatibility class I antigens. Proc Natl Acad Sci U S A. 1987;84:1356–1360.
162. Wiertz E, Jones T, Sun L, et al. The human cytomegalovirus US11 gene product dislocates MHC class I heavy chains from the endoplasmic reticulum to the cytosol. Cell. 1996;84:769–779.
163. Tewari M, Telford WG, Miller RA, Dixit VM. CrmA, a poxvirus-encoded serpin, inhibits cytotoxic T-lymphocyte-mediated apoptosis. J Biol Chem. 1995;270:22,705–22,708.
164. Lehmann-Grube F. Portraits of viruses: Arenaviruses. Intervirology. 1984;22: 121–145.
165. Buchmeier MJ, Welsh RM, Dutko FJ, Oldstone MBA. The virology and immunobiology of lymphocytic choriomeningitis virus infection. Adv Immunol. 1980;30:275–331.
166. Fraser NW, Block TB, Spivack JG. The latency-associated transcripts of herpes simplex virus: RNA in search of function. Virology. 1992;191:1–8.
167. Barker CF, Billingham RE. Immunologically privileged sites. Adv Immunol. 1977;25:1–54.
168. Nevins JR, Vogt PK. Cell transformation by viruses. In: Fields BN, Knipe DM, Howley PM, eds. Fields Virology. 3rd ed. Philadelphia: Lippincott-Raven; 1996:301–343.
169. Rous P. A transmissible avian neoplasm: Sarcoma of the common fowl. J Exp Med. 1910;12:696–705.
170. Stehelin D, Varmus HE, Bishop JM, Vogt PK. DNA related to the transforming gene(s) of avian sarcoma viruses is present in normal avian DNA. Nature. 1976;260:170–173.
171. Takeya T, Hanafusa H. Nucleotide sequences of *c-src*. Cell. 1983;32:881–890.
172. Manaker RA, Groupe V. Discrete foci of altered chicken embryo cells associated with Rous sarcoma virus in tissue culture. Virology. 1956;2:838–840.
173. Temin HM, Rubin H. Characteristics of an assay for Rous sarcoma virus and Rous sarcoma cells in tissue culture. Virology. 1958;6:669–688.
174. Toyoshima K, Vogt PK. Temperature sensitive mutants of an avian sarcoma virus. Virology. 1969;39:930–931.
175. Martin GS. Rous sarcoma virus: A function required for the maintenance of the transformed state. Nature. 1970;227:1021–1023.
176. Cooper JA, Howell B. The when and how of Src regulation. Cell. 1993;73:1051–1054.
177. Rickinson AB, Kieff E. Epstein-Barr virus. In: Fields BN, Knipe DM, Howley PM, eds. Fields Virology. 3rd ed. Philadelphia: Lippincott-Raven; 1996:2397–2446.
178. Kiyosawa K, Sodeyama T, Tanaka E, et al. Interrelationship of blood transfusion non-A, non-B hepatitis and hepatocellular carcinoma: Analysis by detection of antibody to hepatitis C virus. Hepatology. 1990;12:671–675.
179. Tsukuma H, Hiyana T, Tanka S, et al. Risk factors for hepatocellular carcinoma among patients with chronic liver disease. N Engl J Med. 1993;328:1797–1801.
180. Shah KV, Howley PM. Papillomaviruses. In: Fields BN, Knipe DM, Howley PM, eds. Fields Virology. 3rd ed. Philadelphia: Lippincott-Raven; 1996:2077–2109.
181. Chang Y, Cesarman E, Pessin MS, et al. Identification of herpesvirus-like DNA sequences in AIDS-associated Kaposi's sarcoma. Science. 1994;266:1865–1869.
182. Martin JN, Ganem DE, Osmond DH, et al. Sexual transmission and the nature history of human herpesvirus 8 infection. N Engl J Med. 1998;338:948–954.
183. Leibowitz D. Epstein-Barr virus and a cellular signaling pathway in lymphomas from immunosuppressed patients. N Engl J Med. 1998;338:1413–1421.
184. Dyson N, Howley PM, Munger K, Harlow E. The human papilloma virus-16 E7 oncoprotein is able to bind to the retinoblastoma gene product. Science. 1989;243:934–937.
185. Dyson N, Guida P, Munger K, Harlow E. Homologous sequences in adenovirus E1A and human papillomavirus E7 proteins mediate interaction with the same set of cellular proteins. J Virol. 1992;66:6893–6902.
186. Scheffner M, Werness BA, Huibregtse JM, et al. The E6 oncoprotein encoded by human papillomavirus types 16 and 18 promotes the degradation of p53. Cell. 1990;63:1129–1136.
187. Werness BA, Levine AJ, Howley PM. Association of human papillomavirus types 16 and 18 E6 proteins with p53. Science. 1990;248:76–79.
188. Scheffner M, Huibregtse JM, Vierstra RD, Howley PM. The HPV-16 E6 and E6-AP complex functions as a ubiquitin-protein ligase in the ubiquitination of p53. Cell. 1993;75:495–505.
189. Schwarz E, Freese UK, Gissmann L, et al. Structure and transcription of human papillomavirus sequences in cervical carcinoma cells. Nature. 1985;314:111–114.
190. Nestorowicz A, Kawaoka Y, Bean WJ, Webster RG. Molecular analysis of the hemagglutinin genes of Australian H7N7 influenza viruses: Role of passerine birds in maintenance or transmission? Virology. 1987;11:400–418.
191. Horimoto T, Kawaoka Y. Reverse genetics provides direct evidence for a correlation of hemagglutinin cleavability and virulence of an avian influenza A virus. J Virol. 1994;68:3120–3128.
192. Bassel-Duby R, Spriggs DR, Tyler KL, Fields BN. Identification of attenuating mutations on the reovirus type 3 S1 double-stranded RNA segment with a rapid sequencing technique. J Virol. 1986;60:64–67.
193. Offit PA, Blavat G, Greenberg HB, Clark HF. Molecular basis of rotavirus virulence: Role of gene segment 4. J Virol. 1986;57:46–49.
194. Grieder FB, Davis NL, Aronson JF, et al. Specific restrictions in the progression of Venezuelan equine encephalitis virus–induced disease resulting from single amino acid changes in the glycoproteins. Virology. 1995;206:994–1006.
195. Brown F, Lewis BP. Poliovirus attenuation: Molecular mechanisms and practical aspects. Dev Biol Stand. 1993;78:1–187.
196. Melnick JL. Enteroviruses: Polioviruses, coxsackieviruses, echoviruses, and newer enteroviruses. In: Fields BN, Knipe DM, Howley PM, eds. Fields Virology. 3rd ed. Philadelphia: Lippincott-Raven; 1996:655–712.
197. Rueckert R. Picornaviridae: The viruses and their replication. In: Fields BN, Knipe DM, Howley PM, eds. Fields Virology. 3rd ed. Philadelphia: Lippincott-Raven; 1996:609–654.
198. Drayna D, Fields BN. Genetic studies on the mechanism of chemical and physical inactivation of reovirus. J Gen Virol. 1982;63:149–160.
199. Wessner DR, Fields BN. Isolation and genetic characterization of ethanol-resistant reovirus mutants. J Virol. 1993;67:2442–2447.
200. White DO, Fenner FJ. Medical Virology. 3rd ed. Orlando, Fla: Academic Press; 1986.
201. Simons K, Garoff H, Helenius A. How an animal virus gets into and out of its host cell. Sci Am. 1982;246:58–66.
202. Rodgers SE, Barton ES, Oberhaus SM, et al. Reovirus-induced apoptosis of MDCK cells is not linked to viral yield and is blocked by Bcl-2. J Virol. 1997;71:2540–2546.
203. Nathanson N, Tyler KL. Entry, dissemination, shedding, and transmission of viruses. In: Nathanson N, ed. Viral Pathogenesis. Philadelphia: Lippincott-Raven; 1997:13–33.
204. Fenner F. Mousepox (infectious ectromelia of mice): A review. J Immunol. 1949;63:341–373.
205. Keroack M, Fields BN. Viral shedding and transmission between hosts determined by reovirus L2 gene. Science. 1986;232:1635–1638.
206. Williams RK, Jiang GS, Holmes KV. Receptor for mouse hepatitis virus is a member of the carcinoembryonic antigen family of glycoproteins. Proc Natl Acad Sci U S A. 1991;88:5533–5536.
207. Yokomori K, Lai MM. Mouse hepatitis virus utilizes two carcinoembryonic antigens as alternative receptors. J Virol. 1992;66:6194–6199.
208. Dveksler GS, Diffenbach CW, Cardellichio CB, et al. Several members of the mouse carcinoembryonic antigen-related glycoprotein family are functional receptors for the coronavirus mouse hepatitis virus-A59. J Virol. 1993;67:1–8.
209. Delmas B, Gelfi J, L'Haridon R, et al. Aminopeptidase N is a major receptor for the entero-pathogenic coronavirus TGEV. Nature. 1992;357:417–420.
210. Yeager CL, Ashmun RA, Williams RK, et al. Human aminopeptidase N is a receptor for human coronavirus 229E. Nature. 1992;357:420–422.
211. Vlasak R, Luytjes W, Spaan W, Palese P. Human and bovine coronaviruses recognize sialic acid–containing receptors similar to those of influenza C viruses. Proc Natl Acad Sci U S A. 1988;85:4526–4529.
212. Bergelson JM, Mohoanty JG, Crowell RL, et al. Coxsackievirus B3 adapted to growth in RD cells binds to decay-accelerating factor (CD55). J Virol. 1995;69:1903–1906.
213. Shafren DR, Bates RC, Agrez MV, et al. Coxsackieviruses B1, B3, and B5 use decay accelerating factor as a receptor for cell attachment. J Virol. 1995;69:3873–3877.
214. Roivainen M, Piirainen L, Hovi T, et al. Entry of coxsackievirus A9 into host cells: Specifiic interactions with alpha v beta 3 integrin, the vitronectin receptor. Virology. 1994;203:357–365.
215. Bergelson JM, Shepley MP, Chan BM, et al. Identification of the integrin receptor VLA-2 as a receptor for echovirus 1. Science. 1992;225:1718–1720.
216. Bergelson JM, Chan M, Solomon KR, et al. Decay-accelerating factor (CD55), a glycosylphosphatidylinositol-anchored complement regulatory protein, is a receptor for several echoviruses. Proc Natl Acad Sci U S A. 1994;91:6245–6249.
217. Ward T, Pipkin PA, Clarkson NA, et al. Decay-accelerating factor CD55 is identified as the receptor for echovirus 7 using CELICS, a rapid immuno-focal cloning method. EMBO J. 1994;13:5070–5074.
218. Fingeroth JD, Weis JJ, Tedder TF, et al. Epstein-Barr virus receptor of human B lymphocytes is the C3d receptor CR2. Proc Natl Acad Sci U S A. 1984;81:4510–4514.
219. Frade R, Barel M, Ehlin-Henriksson B, Klein G. gp140, the C3d receptor of human B lymphocytes, is also the Epstein-Barr virus receptor. Proc Natl Acad Sci U S A. 1985;82:1490–1493.
220. Higa HH, Rogers GN, Paulson JC. Influenza virus hemagglutinins differentiate between receptor determinants bearing *N*-acetyl-, *N*-glycollyl-, and *N,O*-diacetyl-neuraminic acid groups. Virology. 1985;144:279–282.
221. Dorig RE, Marcil A, Chopra A, Richardson CD. The human CD46 molecule is a receptor for measles virus (Edmonston strain). Cell. 1993;75:295–305.
222. Naniche D, Varior-Krishnan G, Cervoni F, et al. Human membrane cofactor protein (CD46) acts as a cellular receptor for measles virus. J Virol. 1993;67:6025–6032.
223. Brown KE, Anderson SM, Young NS. Erythrocyte P antigen: Cellular receptor for B19 parvovirus. Science. 1993;262:114–117.
224. Superti F, Hauttecoeur B, Morelec MJ, et al. Involvement of gangliosides in rabies virus infection. J Gen Virol. 1986;67:47–56.
225. Gentsch JR, Pacitti AF. Effect of neuraminidase treatment of cells and effect of soluble glycoproteins on type 3 reovirus attachment to murine L cells. J Virol. 1985;56:356–364.
226. Paul RW, Choi AH, Lee PWK. The α-anomeric form of sialic acid is the minimal receptor determinant recognized by reovirus. Virology. 1989;172:382–385.
227. Chappell JD, Gunn VL, Wetzel JD, et al. Mutations in type 3 reovirus that determine binding to sialic acid are contained in the fibrous tail domain of viral attachment protein 1. J Virol. 1997;71:1834–1841.
228. Greve JM, Davis G, Meyer AM, et al. The major human rhinovirus receptor is ICAM-1. Cell. 1989;56:839–847.
229. Staunton DE, Merluzzi VJ, Rothlein R, et al. A cell adhesion molecule, ICAM-1, is the major surface receptor for rhinoviruses. Cell. 1989;56:849–853.
230. Tomassini JE, Graham D, DeWitt CM, et al. cDNA cloning reveals that the major

group rhinovirus receptor on HeLa cells is intercellular adhesion molecule 1. Proc Natl Acad Sci U S A. 1989;86:4907–4911.
231. Fukudome K, Yoshie O, Konno T. Comparison of human, simian, and bovine rotaviruses for requirement of sialic acid in hemagglutination and cell adsorption. Virology. 1989;172:196–205.
232. Willoughby RE, Yolken RH, Schnaar RL. Rotaviruses specifically bind to the neutral glycosphingolipid asialo-GM1. J Virol. 1990;64:4830–4835.
233. Superti F, Donelli G. Gangliosides as binding sites in SA-11 rotavirus infection of LLCC-MK2 cells. J Gen Virol. 1991;72:2467–2474.
234. Rolsma MD, Gelberg HB, Kuhlenschmidt MS. Assay for evaluation of rotavirus-cell interactions: Identification of an enterocyte ganglioside fraction that mediates group A porcine rotavirus recognition. J Virol. 1994;68:258–268.
235. Eppstein DA, Marsh YV, Schreiber AB, et al. Epidermal growth factor receptor occupancy inhibits vaccinia virus infection. Nature. 1985;318:663–665.
236. Schlegel R, Tralka S, Willingham MC, Pastan I. Inhibition of VSV binding and infectivity by phosphatidylserine. Is phosphatidylserine a VSV binding site? Cell. 1983;32:639–646.

DNA VIRUSES

Poxviridae

Chapter 120

Introduction to Poxviridae

JOHN M. NEFF

The poxviruses are a complex group of viruses whose classification is based primarily on the morphology of the virion and the viral nucleic acid.[1] This group represents the largest of all virus groups. These viruses replicate in cytoplasm rather than in the nucleus of cells, and by this characteristic they differ from most other DNA viruses. The virus particles are asymmetric and brick-shaped, with round corners, and are very resistant to chemical and physical inactivation. They contain double-stranded DNA and have specific enzymes not found in other DNA viruses that allow them to replicate in the cytoplasm. Within the cytoplasm, they produce eosinophilic inclusions called *Guanieri's bodies*. Originally, the poxviruses were classified according to their capability to produce vesicular skin lesions or cytoplasmic inclusion bodies. Since 1966, with the establishment of the International Committee on the Nomenclature of Viruses, their classification has depended on the large shape of the virion and the presence of a large single linear molecule of double-stranded DNA.[2] The accepted classification of poxviruses of vertebrates is as follows:

Family	Poxviridae
Subfamily	Chordopoxvirinae
Genera	*Orthopoxvirus*
	Avipoxvirus (fowlpox)
	Capripoxvirus (sheep-pox)
	Leporipoxvirus (myxoma)
	Parapoxvirus (milker's nodule)
	Suipoxvirus (swinepox)
	Molluscipoxvirus (molluscum contagiosum)
	Yatapoxvirus (tanapox)

The genus *Orthopoxvirus* includes at least nine different species that are generally very homogeneous. They are the causative agents for vaccinia, variola, cowpox, monkeypox, ectromelia, camelpox, taterapox, raccoonpox, and Uasin Gishu disease (probable member).[2]

The two major viruses of the *Orthopoxvirus* genus, vaccinia and variola, are closely related and have similar chemical and physical characteristics. Morphologically, they cannot be distinguished. The viral surface is composed of tubular structures surrounding a central nucleoid with a dense, dumbbell-shaped core. They can be separately identified by molecular genetic analysis.[3, 4] Restriction endonuclease and DNA-DNA hybridization techniques have shown that these viruses have extensive homology between the central regions of their genomes but less relatedness within the genome termini. These techniques are effective in describing the genetic variations of these viruses and differentiating among them.[3, 4]

The virions are generally resistant to drying agents and to many disinfectants. They can maintain infectivity for months at room temperature and for years at temperatures lower than $-20°C$. They can be inactivated by autoclaving, by heating at 60°C for 10 minutes, and by the chlorine preparations, formaldehyde, iodophores, and quaternary ammonium compounds.

The vaccinia and variola viruses share common antigens. Infection produces hemagglutination-inhibition and neutralizing antibodies. Routine serologic testing is not useful in distinguishing variola from vaccinia infection. They can, however, be differentiated by the following techniques: enzyme-linked immunosorbent assay, radioimmunoassay, monoclonal antibodies, polymerase chain reaction, and atomic force microscopy, by which structured details may be resolved at a scale of a few nanometers.[5–8] Polymerase chain reaction is the most rapid means of identification and differentiation available.[9]

Because of the interest in recombinant poxviruses as vehicles for new vaccines, much has been learned about the molecular biology of these viruses.[10]

REFERENCES

1. Fenner F, Henderson DA, Arita L, et al. Smallpox and Its Eradication. Geneva: World Health Organization; 1988:69–103.
2. Esposito JJ. Classification and nomenclature of viruses: Poxvirus group. Arch Virol Suppl. 1991;2:91–102.
3. Mercer A, Fleming S, Robinson A, et al. Molecular genetic analyses of parapoxviruses pathogenic for humans. Arch Virol Suppl. 1997;13:25–34.
4. Shchelkunov SN, Safronov PF, Totmenin AV, et al. The genomic sequence analysis of the left and right species-specific terminal region of a cowpox virus strain reveals unique sequences and a cluster of intact ORFs for immunomodulatory and host range proteins. Virology. 1998;243:432–460.
5. Marennikova SS, Malceva NN, Habahpaseva NA. ELISA: A simple test for detecting and differentiating antibodies to closely related orthopoxviruses. Bull World Health Organ. 1981;59:365.
6. Walls HH, Ziegler DW, Nakano JH. Characterization of antibodies to orthopoxviruses in human sera by radioimmunoassay. Bull World Health Organ. 1981;59:253.
7. Czerny CP, Waldmann R, Scheubeck T. Identification of three distinct antigenic sites in parapoxviruses. Arch Virol. 1997;142:807–821.
8. Ohnesorge FM, Horber JK, Haberle W, et al. AFM review study on pox viruses and living cells. Biophys J. 1997;73:2183–2194.
9. Ropp SL, Jin Q, Knight JC, et al. PCR strategy for identification and differentiation of small pox and other orthopoxviruses. J Clin Microbiol. 1995;33:2069–2076.
10. Moss B. Poxviridae: The viruses and their replication. In: Fields BN, Knipe DM, Howley PM, eds. Field's Virology, 3rd ed. Philadelphia: Lippincott–Raven; 1995.

Chapter 121

Vaccinia Virus (Cowpox)

JOHN M. NEFF

Little is known about the origins of vaccinia virus.[1] The virus was used for vaccination before there was any ability to characterize it or standardize its use. Vaccinia itself now has no natural host. One plausible theory of origin, currently backed by data from comparative analyses of genetic sequences, is that vaccinia is derived from the cowpox virus.[2] In the early 19th century it was gradually transformed into the current virus as a result of person-to-person vaccination.

Edward Jenner, in his "Inquiry into the Causes and Effects of the Variolae Vaccinae" in 1798, was the first to observe that pustular material from the lesions of cowpox, when inoculated into humans, protected them from infection with smallpox. Woodville and Pearson of the Smallpox Hospital in London experimented extensively with this technique and distributed vaccination material to many physicians throughout England. The practice of vaccination then spread throughout the world and has been directly responsible for the eradication of smallpox.[3]

VACCINES AND VACCINATION TECHNIQUES

Before vaccine standardization many vaccine strains were in use. Under the leadership of the World Health Organization (WHO), the use of strains was reduced to derivatives of one of three strains: Elstree strain (Lister Institute), the EM63 strain (Moscow Research Institute of Virus Preparation), and the New York Board of Health strain.[4] WHO also established standards for production and use.[5] In general, smallpox vaccines are produced from a seed virus propagated on the skin of calves and then processed to eliminate bacterial contamination. The final vaccine is stored in liquid form or as a freeze-dried preparation. The latter preparations can maintain their titer even after incubation at 37°C for 4 weeks.[4] With the development of freeze-dried vaccines, it has been possible to distribute standard vaccines to remote and temperate countries throughout the world without loss of titer.

To pass WHO standards, a vaccine should be able to produce major reactions in 95% of the primary vaccinees and in 90% of those who were vaccinated more than 10 years previously. To obtain such results, most vaccines should have a titer of at least 10^8 pock-forming units per milliliter.

Vaccinations should be made over the deltoid region of the upper arm. The preferred method of vaccination is to use a bifurcated needle that has been dipped into the vaccine. The needle is held perpendicular to the skin and pressed in and out, 5 times for primary vaccinees and 15 times for revaccinees, producing a trace of blood on the skin. Successful vaccination produces a major response in both primary vaccinees and revaccinees. A *major* response is defined by WHO as a "pustular lesion or an area of definite induration or congestion surrounding a central lesion (scab or ulcer) 6 to 8 days after vaccination." Any other response is called *equivocal*.[4]

Primary vaccinees in general demonstrate a vesicle within 3 to 5 days after vaccination. This becomes pustular and reaches its maximum size approximately 9 days after vaccination. The lesion forms a scab and ultimately leaves a small circular scar approximately 1 cm in diameter. Revaccinations yield variable results, ranging from an accelerated reaction, which becomes vesicular within 1 to 2 days, to lesions that are similar to primary reactions. Usually revaccinations do not result in scar formation, even in remote revaccinees.

IMMUNITY RESULTING FROM VACCINATION

After vaccination there is local replication of virus. There also may be some replication of virus in the regional lymph nodes. Viremia, however, has not been demonstrated in uncomplicated vaccinations using modern, standardized vaccines.[6] The protection against smallpox that results from vaccination is probably a result of both T- and B-cell–mediated antibodies. The dermal reaction that results from revaccination is a rough measurement of T-cell function and the circulating antibodies of B-cell function. The dermal evidence of immunity and circulating antibodies can be demonstrated within 4 to 5 days and increases for up to 4 weeks after vaccination.[7, 8] Circulating antibodies may persist for years after vaccination, and the dermal response after vaccination may demonstrate evidence of modification for up to 20 years. Although a primary vaccinee may rarely demonstrate seroconversion without a dermal response, the absence of a primary take and its accompanying scar is considered to be an inadequate response to immunization.

Successful vaccination is highly protective against smallpox. Protection is almost 100% for the first 1 to 3 years after vaccination. Persons who have not been vaccinated within 3 years may acquire smallpox on exposure, but this is a modified, nonfatal form of the disease, and protection may last for up to 20 years after vaccination. After 20 years, there is very little remaining protection.[4] Although the exact factors responsible for this protection are not clear, studies on the poxvirus proteins that are expressed but nonessential for replication may increase understanding of the pathogenesis of these viruses and the response of the immune system.[9]

PASSIVE IMMUNITY

Hyperimmune vaccinial globulin obtained from recent revaccinees is probably effective in reducing the incidence and severity of smallpox in intimate family contacts of an index case. If immune globulin is administered shortly after exposure and simultaneously with vaccination, there is limited evidence indicating that the resulting morbidity and mortality from smallpox is less than would be expected in those who receive only a vaccination.[10]

COMPLICATIONS RESULTING FROM VACCINATION

In most situations, primary vaccination results in modified swelling and tenderness at the site of vaccination, some regional lymphadenopathy, and occasionally a low-grade fever at the peak of the dermal response. At times, the pustular lesion may be as large as 4 cm, but usually it does not exceed 2 cm in diameter. Occasionally, abnormal reactions occur that may be mild or could be severe enough to result in death. Complications that result from vaccination have been broadly classified into central nervous system, dermal, and other complications.[11]

Central Nervous System Complications

The principal central nervous system complication that results from vaccination is a postinfectious encephalitis[12–21] that is similar to the encephalitis that occurs after measles and a few other acute viral illnesses. The vaccinia virus cannot be isolated from the central nervous system lesions. Most cases occur 1 to 2 weeks after vaccination, and the signs and symptoms are those of a generalized encephalitis. There also may be spinal cord signs (when there is transverse myelitis) or, rarely, focal neurologic signs. Routine diagnostic tests are of little help except to rule out other possible causes of the illness. Treatment is supportive and symptomatic. The extent and degree of residual neurologic problems depend on the severity and location of the original lesions. Mortality is in the range of 10 to 30% There is no known predilection for this disorder.[15]

The reported incidence of this disease has varied considerably from country to country, and the explanation for this variance is not clear.[16] The incidence in the United States, where the New York Board of Health strain was used, was a little more than 1 per 100,000 primary vaccinees. The incidence was slightly higher when vaccination occurred before the first birthday. Similar rates were observed in Great Britain, where the Elstree strain was used.[12] Although some countries have reported a higher incidence of this complication in adult primary vaccinees, compared with children, this has not been observed either in the United States or in Great Britain.

Dermal Complications

The most frequent complications reported after smallpox vaccination are dermal. These may or may not be associated with an underlying illness.[11, 22] The former group includes vaccinia necrosum, or progressive vaccinia, and eczema vaccinatum; the latter includes accidental infection, generalized vaccinia, and erythematous urticarial eruptions.

Vaccinia Necrosum. Vaccinia necrosum is the most severe complication occurring after smallpox vaccination.[23–25] It invariably results when a person with an immunologic deficiency is inadvertently vaccinated. The disease is insidious. The lesion begins as a normal vaccination but continues to progress, and in fatal cases shows no evidence of resolution. The patient initially may have no systemic signs, no regional lymphadenopathy or erythema, but only progressive necrosis at the site of vaccination. As the disease continues, the patient develops metastatic lesions throughout the body. Vaccinia virus can easily be isolated from any of the lesions.

Eczema Vaccinatum. Patients with eczema are unusually susceptible to two viral infections—herpes simplex and vaccinia. In both infections the clinical picture, Kaposi's varicelliform eruption, is similar, and the syndrome can be distinguished only by the history and viral isolation. Eczema vaccinatum is the clinical result of local spread or dissemination of vaccinia virus infection in such persons.[26–28] The complication may be a result of inadvertent vaccination or of intimate contact with a recently vaccinated person.

The treatment of eczema vaccinatum is administration of vaccinia immunoglobulin (VIG) in the therapeutic dose of 0.6 ml/kg per 24 hours, repeated daily until no new lesions appear.

Accidental Infection. Not uncommonly, a healthy person acquires vaccinial lesions accidentally as a result of autoinoculation at the time of vaccination or intimate body contact with a person recently vaccinated.[13] These lesions almost always occur in primary vaccinees. They are identical to a primary vaccination and are self-limited. When autoinoculation occurs, it is generally a coprimary reaction on a mucous membrane, the palpebral margins of the eyelid (ocular vaccinia), the nose, the mouth, or the anus.[29, 30]

Generalized Vaccinia. *Generalized vaccinia* is a nonspecific term that is used to describe a vesicular rash that develops after vaccination. If cases of eczema vaccinatum and vaccinia necrosum (illnesses that truly represent a generalized vaccinia) are excluded, it is extremely rare to document a generalized, systemic viral dissemination resulting from vaccination. On the other hand, it is not uncommon to see, at about 7 to 12 days after vaccination, a rash characterized by multiple small vesicular lesions, each with an erythematous base.[13, 22, 26, 31] The patient is nontoxic and often afebrile. Vaccinia virus cannot be isolated from the blood or from the peripheral lesions. These cases have often been reported as generalized vaccinia. They occur in primary vaccinees and are seen most frequently in children vaccinated before their first birthday. The cause is not known, and there is no specific treatment.

Erythematous Urticarial Eruptions. Several erythematous rashes similar to enterovirus-like or roseola-like rashes are frequently observed 7 to 12 days after vaccination.[31] These are self-limited reactions lasting no more than a few days. The patients are not acutely ill and require no specific treatment. The pathogenesis is unknown.

Other Complications

Many other complications of vaccination have been reported, including myocarditis, thrombocytopenia, arthritis, and pericarditis. There also have been cases of malignant melanoma occurring in vaccination scars and reports of acute erythema nodosum leprosum or lepra reactions after vaccination of patients with lepromatous leprosy.[11, 32]

Three more frequent but still rare reactions should be noted: bullous erythema multiforma, overwhelming viremia resulting in sudden death in infancy, and fetal vaccinia.

FURTHER ATTENUATED VACCINES

The two strains that have been tested most widely were derived from the CV-1 and CV-2 strains of Rivers. In the United States the CV-1 strain has been studied most thoroughly.[33] It was found to be safe when administered to more than 1000 eczematous children as a preimmunizing agent.[34] In healthy children, it has been demonstrated to be more attenuated than standard calf lymph vaccine, and it may not provide full protection against smallpox.

Laboratory attenuation has been accomplished by insertional inactivation of a virus gene by a foreign gene. Through this technique, virulence genes can be identified and replaced while vaccine immunogenicity is maintained.[35]

Since the routine discontinuation of vaccination, complications have been rare. There may, however, be new situations that could result in more frequent use of vaccinia and in a reappearance of complications. The first is vaccination of military personnel because of the concern of biologic warfare.[36] This potential risk was demonstrated in a report of disseminated vaccinia occurring in a military recruit who was immunologically impaired because of a concurrent infection with human immunodeficiency virus (HIV).[37]

The second potential risk is from the use of experimental recombinant live virus vaccines. In these vaccines, vaccinia is used as the biologic carrier for immunizing genes. Extensive work has been done in this field, recombining vaccinia with genes for use in both animal vectors and humans to administer many immunizing agents, including rabies virus, hepatitis B virus, Japanese encephalitis virus, HIV, *Mycobacterium tuberculosis*, and Newcastle virus.[38, 39] Vaccinia is an ideal agent for such recombinant research because of the large size of its genome and its extraordinary stability. This may be an important advance allowing the simultaneous delivery of several immunizing antigens through one vehicle. This agent, because of its stability, ease of storage, and mode of delivery, can be used in areas of the world where the use of other vaccines may not be practical.

The third risk is the use of vaccinia for immunotherapy. This vaccine approach in cancer therapy is still in early experimental stages. The approach is to destroy tumors that contain virus-specific tumor antigens by the administration of a vaccinia virus tumor antigen recombinant.[40] This ongoing experimental use of vaccinia virus will require knowledge and evaluation of its immunogenic characteristics and its complications as an immunizing agent and as a recombinant.[41]

REFERENCES

1. Baxby D. The origins of vaccinia virus. J Infect Dis. 1977;136:453.
2. Shchelkunov SN, Safronov PF, Totmenin AV, et al. The genomic sequence analysis of the left and right species-specific terminal region of a cowpox virus strain reveals unique sequences and a cluster of intact ORFs for immunomodulatory and host range proteins. Virology. 1998;243:432–460.
3. Dixon CW. Smallpox. London: Churchill Livingstone; 1962:249.
4. WHO Technical Report, Series No 493, WHO Expert Committee on Smallpox Eradication, Second Report. Geneva: World Health Organization; 1972.
5. WHO Technical Report, Series No 323, WHO Expert Group on Requirements for Biological Substances. Geneva: World Health Organization; 1965.
6. Glattner RJ, Norman JO, Hays FM, et al. Antibody response to cutaneous inoculation with vaccinia virus: Viremia and viruria in vacc children. J Pediatr. 1964;64:839.
7. Pincus WB, Flick JA. The role of hypersensitivity in the pathogenesis of vaccinia virus infection in humans. J Pediatr. 1963;62:57.

8. Wulff H, Chin TDY, Wenner HA. Serological responses of children after primary vaccination and revaccination against smallpox. Am J Epidemiol. 1969;90:312.
9. Smith GL, Symons JA, Khanna A, et al. Vaccinia virus immune evasion. Immunol Rev. 1997;159:137–154.
10. Kempe CH, Bowles C, Meiklejohn G, et al. The use of vaccinia hyperimmune gamma globulin in the prophylaxis of smallpox. Bull World Health Organ. 1961;25:41.
11. Lane JM, Millar JD, Neff JM. Smallpox and smallpox vaccination policy. Annu Rev Med. 1971;22:251.
12. Conybeare ET. Illness attributed to smallpox vaccination during 1951–60: Part II. Illness reported as affecting the central nervous system. Monthly Bull Ministry Health Public Health Lab Serv. 1964;23:150.
13. Lane JM, Ruben FL, Neff JM, et al. Complications of smallpox vaccination 1968: National Surveillance in the United States. N Engl J Med. 1969;281:1201.
14. Scott TFM. Postinfectious and vaccinial encephalitis. Med Clin North Am. 1967;51:701.
15. Keuter EJW. Predisposition of Post Vaccinial Encephalitis. Amsterdam: Elsevier; 1969.
16. Stuart G. Memorandum on post-vaccinial encephalitis. Bull World Health Organ. 1947;1:36.
17. Nanning W. Prophylactic effect of antivaccinia gamma-globulin against post-vaccinial encephalitis. Bull World Health Organ. 1962;27:317.
18. Noordaan J van der, Dekking F, Posthuma J, et al. Primary vaccination with an attenuated strain of vaccinia virus. Arch Gesamte Virusforsch. 1967;22:210.
19. Ehrengut W, Ehrengut-Lang J. Non-infectious smallpox vaccine in the prophylaxis of postvaccinial encephalitis. Int Symp Smallpox Vaccine, Bilthoven; 1972;19:319.
20. Polak MF. Complication of smallpox vaccination in the Netherlands 1959–1970. Int Symp Smallpox Vaccine, Bilthoven; 1972;19:235.
21. Berger K, Heinrich W. Decrease of postvaccinial deaths in Austria and introduction of less pathogenic virus strain. Int Symp Smallpox Vaccine, Bilthoven; 1972;19:119.
22. Conybeare ET. Illness attributed to smallpox vaccination during 1951–60: Part I. Illnesses reported as "generalized vaccinia." Monthly Bull Ministry Health Public Health Lab Serv. 1964;23:126.
23. O'Connell CJ, Karzon DT, Barron AL. Progressive vaccinia with normal antibodies. Ann Intern Med. 1964;60:282.
24. Lane JM, Ruben FL, Abrutyn E, et al. Deaths attributed to smallpox vaccination 1959 to 1966 and 1968. JAMA. 1970;212:441.
25. Neff JM, Lane JM. Vaccinia necrosum following smallpox vaccination for chronic herpetic ulcers. JAMA. 1970;213:123.
26. Lane JM, Ruben FL, Neff JM, et al. Complications of smallpox vaccination, 1968: II. Results of ten statewide surveys. J Infect Dis. 1970;122:303.
27. Copeman PWM, Wallace HJ. Eczema vaccinatum. Br Med J. 1964;2:5415, 906.
28. Rachelefsky GS, Opelz G, Mickey R. Defective T cell function in atopic dermatitis. J Allergy Clin Immunol. 1976;57:569.
29. Ruben FL, Lane JM. Ocular vaccinia, an epidemiologic analysis of 348 cases. Arch Ophthalmol. 1970;84:45.
30. Fulginiti VA, Winograd LA, Jackson M, et al. Therapy of experimental vaccinial keratitis: Effect of idoxuridine and VIG. Arch Ophthalmol. 1965;74:539.
31. Neff JM, Drachman RH. Complications of smallpox vaccination, 1968: Surveillance in a comprehensive care clinic. Pediatrics. 1972;50:481.
32. Conybeare ET. Illness attributed to smallpox vaccination during 1951–60: Part III. Fatal illnesses reported as associated with vaccination (but not as generalized vaccinia or as post-vaccinial encephalomyelitis). Monthly Bull Ministry Health Public Health Lab Serv. 1964;23:182.
33. Galasso GJ, Karzon DT, Katz SL, et al, eds. Clinical and serological study of four smallpox vaccines comparing variations of dose and routes of administration. J Infect Dis. 1977;135:131.
34. Kempe CH, Fulginiti V, Minamitani M, et al. Smallpox vaccination of eczematous patients with a strain of attenuated live vaccinia (CVI-78). Pediatrics. 1968;42:980.
35. Binns MM, Smith GL. Recombinant poxviruses. Boca Raton, Florida: CRC Press; 1992:235–267.
36. Halsey NA, Henderson DA. HIV infection and immunization against other agents. N Engl J Med. 1987;316:683–685.
37. Redfield RR, Wright DC, James WD, et al. Disseminated vaccinia in a military recruit with human immunodeficiency virus disease. N Engl J Med. 1987;316:673–676.
38. Paoletti E. Applications of pox virus vectors to vaccination: An update. Proc Natl Acad Sci U S A. 1996;93:11349–11353.
39. The Jordan Report 98: Accelerated Development of Vaccines. Division of Microbiology and Infectious Diseases, National Institutes of Allergy and Infectious Disease, National Institutes of Health. 1998;68–69.
40. Hodge JW. Carcinoembryonic antigen as a target for cancer vaccines. Cancer Immunol Immunother. 1996;43:127–134.
41. Centers for Disease Control and Prevention. Vaccinia (smallpox) vaccine: Recommendations of the Immunization Practices Advisory Committee (ACIP). MMWR Morb Mortal Wkly Rep. 1991;40(RR-14).

Chapter 122

Variola (Smallpox) and Monkeypox Viruses

JOHN M. NEFF

Although a great deal is known about the chemical and biologic properties of vaccinia virus, the study of variola virus has been limited because of the laboratory hazards involved. When comparative studies have been possible, very similar characteristics between the two viruses have been found. The differences between variola and vaccinia lie in their predilection for certain hosts and their different growth characteristics in the laboratory.[1] Whereas vaccinia virus infects a wide range of hosts, variola infection is limited to humans and, under certain circumstances, to monkeys. In the laboratory, the two viruses can be distinguished by the appearance of the pock lesions formed on the chorioallantoic membrane of the chick embryo.[2] The pocks caused by variola are small and gray-white, whereas those caused by vaccinia are large and sometimes hemorrhagic. The two viruses can also be distinguished by their different growth characteristics in tissue culture.

There are at least two strains of variola virus. The most virulent strain causes variola major, with a mortality of 20 to 50%. Variola minor, or alastrim, has a mortality of less than 1%. These two strains can easily be distinguished by their temperature-sensitive growth characteristics on the chorioallantoic membrane.

LABORATORY DIAGNOSIS OF SMALLPOX

One of the most important factors in the control of smallpox is the availability of rapid diagnostic techniques that differentiate smallpox from other vesicular illnesses.[2] The two techniques that are most commonly used are electron microscopy and gel diffusion. In both tests, vesicular scrapings are used. Under the electron microscope the poxvirus particles can be distinguished from herpes simplex or varicella-zoster virus. If this technique is not available, variola viral particles, Guarnieri's bodies, may be seen under light microscopy after staining by the Giemsa method. Gel diffusion tests the vesicular fluid antigen against known hyperimmune vaccinia antiserum. It is not as sensitive as the electron microscope or as direct virus isolation on the chorioallantoic membrane. It is, however, a good, rapid diagnostic tool in a laboratory in which an electron microscope is not available.[3, 4] Polymerase chain reaction techniques now allow rapid identification and differentiation of variola major from variola minor, monkeypox, vaccinia, and other orthopoxvirus infections (see Chapter 120).[5]

CLINICAL ILLNESS

Variola no longer exists in an indigenous state in nature. The last reported case was in Somalia in October 1977. In 1980 the World Health Organization (WHO) Global Commission for the Certification of Smallpox Eradication officially declared that smallpox eradication had been achieved.[6] Since 1977, there have been no indigenous cases of variola despite extensive surveillance.

The history, epidemiology, and clinical manifestations of smallpox have been well documented and are summarized in the 1988 WHO publication, *Smallpox and Its Eradication*.[7] Clinically, smallpox is a homogeneous illness that begins after an incubation period of 12 days, with a prodromal period of 2 to 4 days during which the virus can easily be isolated from the blood. The ensuing rash progresses in a uniform pattern, from maculopapules to vesicles to pustules and scabs, over 1 to 2 weeks. The rash follows a centrifugal pattern. The progress of the disease varies: death may occur before the appearance of any rash in the most fulminant form; on the other hand, a discrete form follows a full course to recovery. Except when the disease appears in its toxic or vaccinia-modified form, it is easily diagnosed.

Smallpox is a relatively noncontagious disease requiring close contact for spread. It can be contained by careful identification and vaccination of contacts.

MONKEYPOX

Monkeypox is the only other member of the *Orthopoxvirus* group that has any significant clinical application to humans. This virus creates a vesicular illness in monkeys that is very similar to variola. Monkeypox virus infection is enzootic among squirrels and monkeys in the rainforests of western and central Africa. Infection occurs sporadically in humans in these areas. When the illness occurs in humans, it produces a vesicular rash very much like variola, and secondary infection does occur. There is one report of its spread through four generations.[8] WHO carefully investigates all sporadic cases of monkeypox and has an active surveillance program in the geographic area where monkeypox is likely to occur. The most recent and largest reported epidemic in humans occurred in Kasai Oriental, Democratic Republic of Congo, from February 1996 to October 1997. A total of 511 cases were identified; 85% occurred in persons younger than 16 years of age. The case fatality ratio was 1.5%. Twenty-two percent of the cases were primary and the rest were secondary, with a secondary attack rate of 8.0%. Human to human transmission occurred for 2 years. One possible explanation for this large outbreak was the cessation of smallpox vaccinations. Vaccinations targeted to this population may be an effective way of preventing human infections.[9]

It is unlikely that any of the other orthopoxviruses cause significant pathologic disease in humans. There is no natural reservoir of variola, and it is extremely unlikely that the genomes of any of the other orthopoxviruses can alter in nature to a form that infects and persists in humans.[10] The only credible source of variola is from infection in a laboratory where the virus is stored.[11] At present, only two laboratories in the world contain the virus. If for any reason this virus were once again introduced to humans, the resulting disease could easily be contained by vaccination of identified contacts. Control depends on early recognition of cases and knowledge of the clinical and epidemiologic characteristics of the disease. Another possibility is that the laboratory variola virus stocks will eventually be destroyed and the causative agent of this disease will no longer exist.[12]

REFERENCES

1. Bedson HS, Dumbell KR. Smallpox and vaccinia. Br Med Bull. 1967;23:119.
2. World Health Organization: Guide to the Laboratory Diagnosis of Smallpox for Smallpox Eradication Programs. Geneva: World Health Organization; 1969.
3. Mitra AC, Sarkar SK, Mukherjee MK, et al. Evaluation of the precipitation-in-gel reaction in the diagnosis of smallpox. Bull World Health Organ. 1973;49:555.
4. Nakano JH. Evaluation of virological laboratory methods in smallpox diagnosis. Bull World Health Organ. 1973;48:529.
5. Ropp SL, Jin Q, Knight JC, et al. PCR strategy for identification and differentiation of smallpox and other orthopoxviruses. J Clin Microbiol. 1995;33:2069–2076.
6. WHO Declaration of global eradication of smallpox. Wkly Epidemiol Rec. 1980;55:145–152.
7. Fenner F, Henderson DA, Arita I, et al. Smallpox and Its Eradication. Geneva: World Health Organization; 1988.
8. Jezek Z, Arita I, Mutombo M, et al. Four generations of probably person to person transmission of human monkeypox. Am J Epidemiol 1986;123:1004–1012.
9. Human Monkeypox—Kasai Oriental, Democratic Republic of Congo, February 1996–October 1997. MMWR Morb Mortal Wkly Rep. 1997;46:1168–1171.
10. Douglas N, Dumbell K. Independent evolution of monkeypox and variola viruses. J Virol. 1992;66:7565–7567.
11. Dumbell K. What should be done about smallpox virus? Lancet. 1987;2:957–958.
12. WHO sets date to destroy smallpox stocks. Public Health Rep. 1996;111:388.

Chapter 123

Parapoxviruses, Molluscum Contagiosum, and Tanapox Viruses

JOHN M. NEFF

Within the Poxviridae family there are a few other viruses, other than the *Orthopoxvirus* genus, that produce diseases in humans. They are certain members of the parapoxviruses; the molluscum contagiosum virus, the only member of the genus *Molluscipoxvirus*; and the tanapox virus, a species of the *Yatapoxvirus* genus.

PARAPOXVIRUSES

The parapoxviruses are morphologically distinct from other poxviruses but share some common antigens. Cross-protection exists between certain, but not all, members of the group. These viruses are indigenous to a wide variety of nonhuman species. Several prototypes have demonstrated cross-infectivity to humans. The members of this genus are bovine papular stomatitis virus, pseudocowpox virus (milker's nodule or paravaccinia), and parapoxvirus of red deer in New Zealand. Orf is primarily a disease of sheep and goats; bovine papular stomatitis and pseudocowpox occur primarily in cattle, with

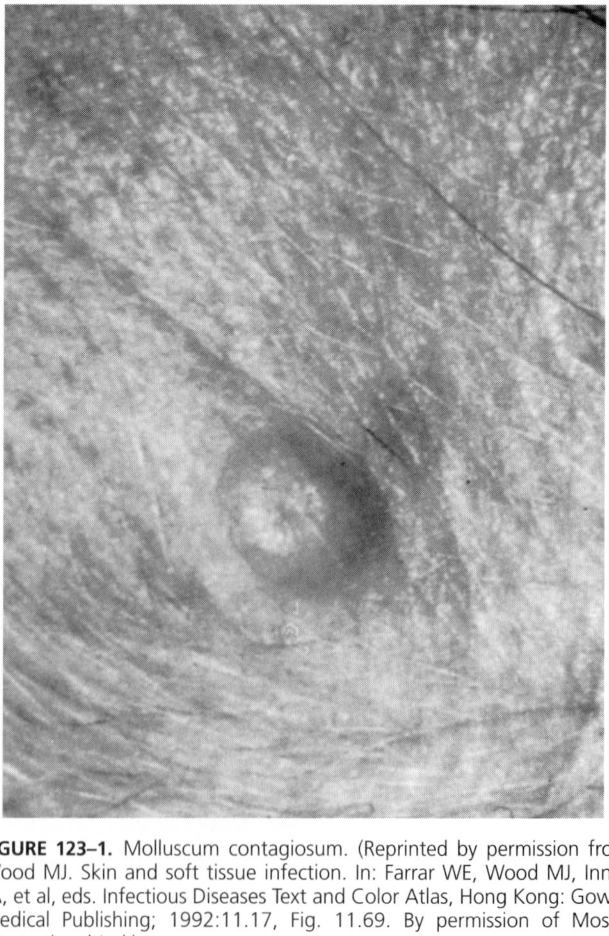

FIGURE 123–1. Molluscum contagiosum. (Reprinted by permission from Wood MJ. Skin and soft tissue infection. In: Farrar WE, Wood MJ, Innes JA, et al, eds. Infectious Diseases Text and Color Atlas, Hong Kong: Gower Medical Publishing; 1992:11.17, Fig. 11.69. By permission of Mosby International Ltd.)

cross-infectivity to other species. Tentative members of the genus are camel contagious ecthyma virus, chamois contagious ecthyma virus, and sealpox virus; sealpox can be transmitted to humans. The viruses have a worldwide distribution. They can persist in a herd for a long time because of chronic infection and the great stability of the viruses in the environment. All but the recently reported parapoxvirus of red deer have infected humans.[1]

The pathologic lesions in sheep and cattle occur in the oral mucosa and skin. The incubation period is several days, and infection results in vesicles that progress slowly to pustular formation, coalescent with adjacent lesions and extensive scabbing. Resolution occurs in 4 to 6 weeks. When these viruses infect humans, there is generally a history of direct contact with the originally infected species or contact with contaminated objects such as fences or feeding troughs. The lesions in humans are similar to, but milder than, those in the infected animal. The incubation period may be longer, up to several weeks. Lesions may persist for weeks and can be painful and pruritic. They occur on the sites of contact, mostly the hands and arms. These lesions are sometimes described as markedly granulomatous and may take months to heal. In patients with immune deficiency, the lesions may be larger and may not resolve.

The virus can be isolated in tissue culture and identified by electron microscopy.[2]

MOLLUSCUM CONTAGIOSUM

Now that smallpox has been eradicated, the molluscum contagiosum virus is the only poxvirus that is specific for humans.[3] This disease is worldwide and is spread by close human contact, including sexual intercourse. The disease is characterized by small, firm, umbilicated papules that are present on exposed epithelial surface areas of children or genital areas of adults (Fig. 123–1). The lesions may resolve spontaneously without significant associated systemic symptoms; however, they may persist for months or years in patients with significant immunosupression, and they may be generalized in patients with atopy. The virus has been cultivated but not propagated in human foreskin grafted on athymic mice.[4] Electron microscopic studies have revealed a virus indistinguishable from other poxviruses.[3] Restrictive endonuclease mapping of viral DNA has classified molluscum contagiosum into three major subtypes and minor variants. Epidemiologic studies indicate some geographic specificity but no clinical differentiation.[3]

Molluscum contagiosum occurs frequently as an opportunistic infection in patients with the acquired immunodeficiency syndrome.[5, 6] Infection can be generalized, frequently appearing on the face and upper body rather than in the genital area only. Ophthalmic involvement is usually of the eyelid and rarely of the conjunctiva and cornea.[3] The lesions may become large and atypical. The disease may be unremitting. In some cases, giant hyperkeratotic mollusca develop. The lesions may look like basal cell carcinoma or keratoacanthoma. The disease often represents a manifestation of advanced human immunodeficiency virus infection, and there seems to be a correlation between the extent and severity of molluscum contagiosum and a low count of CD4-positive T lymphocytes. Diagnosis is confirmed by histologic examination, by the demonstration of Henderson-Paterson inclusion cells, and by electron microscopy. Local therapy with carbon dioxide laser, cryotherapy with liquid nitrogen, electrodesiccation, or incision and curettage is beneficial in some patients. In an uncontrolled study, three patients with extensive molluscum contagiosum lesions responded to treatment with cidofovir, a nucleotide analogue of deoxycytidine monophosphate (see Chapter 36). Further controlled studies are warranted.[7] The most effective treatments to date are those that are directed toward improvement of immunologic functions.

TANAPOX VIRUS

The tanapox virus is a species of the new genus *Yatapoxvirus*. This virus causes vesicular lesions in monkeys and secondarily in humans. Clinically it is like monkeypox. It occurs along the Tana River in Kenya and in Zaire.[8, 9]

REFERENCES

1. Mercer A, Fleming S, Robinson A, et al. Molecular genetic analysis of parapoxviruses pathogenic for humans. Arch Virol. 1997(Suppl);13:25–34.
2. Lard SL, Roehrig JT, Pearson LD. Differentiation of parapoxviruses by application of orf virus-specific monoclonal antibodies against cell surface proteins. Vet Immunol Immunopathol. 1991;28:247–258.
3. Birthistle K, Carrington D. Molluscum contagiosum virus. J Infect. 1997;34:21–28.
4. Fife KH, Whitfeld M, Faust H, et al. Growth of Molluscum contagiosum virus in a human foreskin xenograft model. Virology. 1996;226:95–101.
5. Husak R, Garbe C, Orfanos CE. Molluscum contagiosa in HIV infection: Clinical manifestation, relation to immune status and prognostic value in 39 patients. Hautarzt. 1997;48:103–109.
6. Cotell SL, Roholt NS. Molluscum contagiosum in a patient with the acquired immunodeficiency syndrome. N Engl J Med. 1998;338:888.
7. Meadows KP, Tyring SK, Paviz AT, et al. Resolution of recalcitrant molluscum contagiosum virus lesions in human immunodeficiency virus-infected patients treated with cidofovir. Arch Dermatol. 1997;133:987–990.
8. Jezek Z, Arita I, Szczeniowski M, et al. Human tanapox in Zaire: Clinical and epidemiological observations on cases confirmed by laboratory studies. Bull World Health Organ. 1985;63:1027–1035.
9. Knight JC, Novembre FJ, Brown DR, et al. Studies on Tanapox virus. Virology. 1989;172:116–124.

Herpesviridae

Chapter 124

Introduction to Herpesviridae

STEPHEN E. STRAUS

The members of the Herpesviridae family are large, DNA-containing, enveloped viruses. Nearly 100 known herpesviruses infect a broad spectrum of the animal kingdom. Eight human viruses are recognized (Table 124–1). Several other herpesviruses infect new- or old-world monkeys, one of which, the herpes B virus (see Chapter 131), is a rare cause of disease in humans. Among other herpesviruses that do not infect humans are several economically important viruses of horses, pigs, and cattle.[1]

CLASSIFICATION

The herpesviruses are classified into three subfamilies according to their genome organization and homology, viral host range, and other biologic properties (see Table 124–1).[2]

STRUCTURE

All herpesviruses are large particles (150 to 250 nm) that are composed of four fundamental structural elements (Fig. 124–1) that, from the outside in, include an outer envelope, the tegument (an amorphous aggregate of viral structural proteins), the nucleocapsid, and an internal core consisting of proteins and the viral genome.

The envelope derives from portions of the host cellular membranes that are pinched off by the developing particle as it traverses the nucleus into the cytoplasm and eventually exits the cell. In the process, viral glycoproteins that had been inserted into the cellular

TABLE 124–1 Classification and Structure of Herpesviridae That Infect Humans

Common Name	Other Designation	Subfamily	Genome Size (kbp × 10⁶)	No. of Genome Isomers	Genome Type	Guanine-plus-Cytosine Content (%)
Human virus						
Herpes simplex virus type 1	Human herpesvirus 1	α	152	4	E	67
Herpes simplex virus type 2	Human herpesvirus 2	α	152	4	E	69
Varicella-zoster virus	Human herpesvirus 3	α	125	D	D	46
Epstein-Barr virus	Human herpesvirus 4	γ	172	1	C	59
Cytomegalovirus	Human herpesvirus 5	β	229	1	E	57
Human herpesvirus 6	—	β	165	1	A	43
Human herpesvirus 7	—	β	145	1	A	42
Human herpesvirus 8	Kaposi's sarcoma herpesvirus	γ	165	1	B	55
Simian virus						
Herpes B virus	Herpesvirus simiae; cercopithicine herpesvirus 1	α	150	4	E	74

Abbreviation: kbp, Kilobase pairs.

membranes are captured, with the end result that they project outward from the virion envelope.

The envelope glycoproteins of herpesviruses exhibit a number of biologic properties, some obvious and some still obscure. Certain of the glycoproteins, such as glycoproteins B and D of herpes simplex viruses 1 and 2, are responsible for the binding and penetration of virions into cells.[3, 4]

The cell surface receptors to which herpesvirus glycoproteins must bind to initiate infection are generally not known except for Epstein-Barr virus, which binds to the cellular C3d complement receptor.[5] Binding to a newly recognized member of the tumor necrosis factor receptor family of proteins has been shown to be one mechanism by which herpes simplex viruses enter cells.[6] Herpes simplex virus glycoprotein E is an Fc receptor, glycoprotein C has C3b-binding activity,[7, 8] and glycoprotein H is required for spread from infected to contiguous uninfected cells. Antibodies to many of the herpesvirus envelope glycoproteins neutralize viral infectivity.[4]

The virion tegument consists of a seemingly amorphous assemblage of virus-encoded proteins that, for some of the herpesviruses, help initiate the replicative cycle within susceptible cells.

Herpesvirus nucleocapsids are approximately 100 nm in diameter and consist of 162 discrete protein capsomeres in an icosapentahedral array. The nucleocapsids contain linear double-stranded DNA molecules. Herpesvirus DNAs are structurally organized into sets of patterns depending on the relative number, size, and position of repeated sequences. For example, herpes simplex viruses 1 and 2 possess two major, virtually uninterrupted expanses of unique DNA sequences, each of which is flanked by repeated sequences (Fig. 124–2).[9] For some herpesviruses, the unique sequences can be inverted, one relative to the other, during the course of replication. Each virion contains one of the possible isomeric forms of the genome. All isomers of herpesvirus DNAs are infectious. Although many herpesvirus DNAs are similarly organized, most individual virus types show little nucleic acid sequence homology. For herpes simplex viruses 1 and 2, more than 50% of their DNA sequences are identical, with sufficient differences to consider them discrete virus types. The individual subtypes A and B of Epstein-Barr virus are nearly identical except for sequences in a few genes. The same is true for subtypes of herpesvirus type 6. Across the virus types, there are only scattered regions of DNA homology such that there is a weak (<5%) overall sequence identity. The relatedness among herpesviruses is best appreciated by comparing the amino acid sequences of domains of selected viral proteins and the clustering of their coding elements in the genome.

As herpesviruses spread serially through the community, minor mutations that do not appreciably influence virulence gradually accrue in their DNA sequences. Ultimately, these minor changes can be detected by sensitive molecular techniques such as restriction endonuclease cleavage analysis and sequencing. The viral strain recovered from one person is indistinguishable from that of the person from whom the virus was acquired. Viruses from individuals who have not been in contact with one another usually differ. This powerful molecular epidemiologic tool has aided in our understanding of herpesvirus spread and reactivation.[10]

Herpesvirus DNA sequences are used very efficiently, expressing sufficient numbers of RNAs to encode from 70 to over 150 distinct proteins. The viral RNAs are transcribed from both strands of the genome in a generally nonoverlapping manner, with very few noncoding regions. Few herpesvirus transcripts are spliced, except for those of gammaherpesviruses such as Epstein-Barr virus.

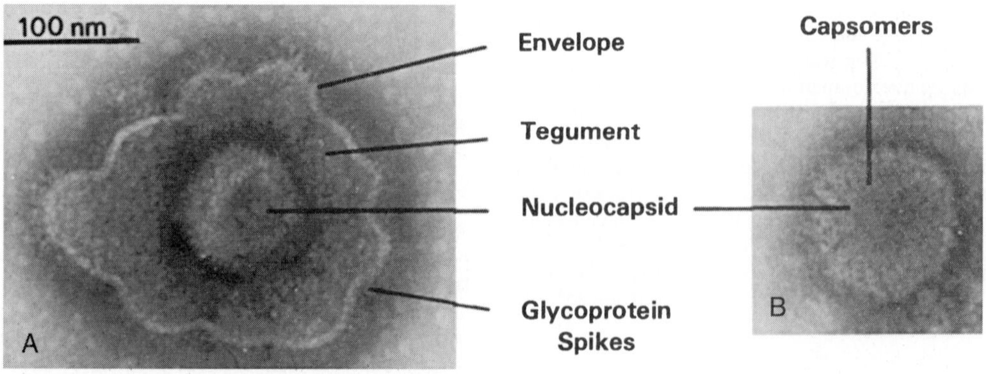

FIGURE 124–1. Electron micrographs of varicella-zoster virus negatively stained with phosphotungstic acid (×40,000). *A,* The complete enveloped virion. *B,* A purified viral nucleocapsid. (From Straus SE, Ostrove JM, Inchauspe G, et al. Varicella-zoster virus infections: Biology, natural history, treatment, and prevention. Ann Intern Med. 1988;108:221–237.)

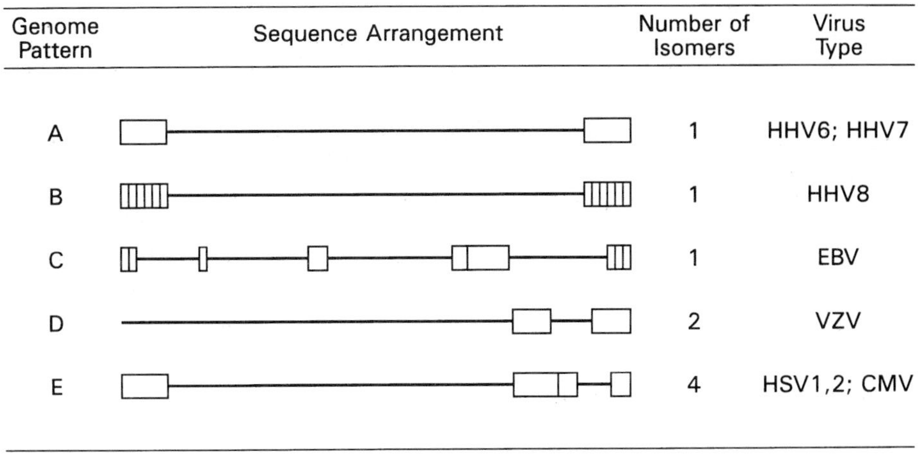

Genome Pattern
Sequence Arrangement
Number of Isomers
Virus Type
A
1
HHV6; HHV7
B
1
HHV8
C
1
EBV
D
2
VZV
E
4
HSV1,2; CMV

FIGURE 124–2. Organization of five genome types of human herpesviruses. The large boxes denote major repeat elements, between or adjacent to which are unique sequences. Some major repeats contain multiple copies of the same sequences, as indicated by vertically divided boxes. (Based on Roizman B. Herpesviridae. In: Fields BN, Knipe DM, Rowley RM, eds. Fields Virology. 3rd ed. Philadelphia: Lippincott-Raven; 1996:2221–2230.)

VIRUS REPLICATION

Herpesvirus replication is a carefully regulated, multistep process.[11] Shortly after infection, one or few *immediate-early* genes are transcribed. These encode proteins that regulate their own synthesis and stimulate the synthesis of a second, larger wave of proteins from the *early* set of viral genes. In some herpesviruses, synthesis of the immediate-early transcripts is first induced by tegument proteins. Herpesvirus early proteins support genome replication. The best characterized of these include the thymidine kinases and DNA polymerases.

All herpesvirus DNAs contain terminal repeat sequences that permit their circularization as a prelude to genome replication. Progeny DNA molecules appear to be generated continuously from the circular parental molecules by a rolling circle mechanism.[12] Newly synthesized multimers of the genome are then cleaved at specific terminal region sequences and then packaged into newly assembled nucleocapsids.

Most herpesvirus genes are expressed after DNA replication. These *late* gene products are incorporated into or aid in the assembly of progeny virions. New particles bud from their host cells and promptly infect contiguous susceptible cells. The predominant means by which herpesviruses spread through the body is from cell to cell. Cell-free virus does not accumulate.

TROPISM

Herpesviruses vary widely in their abilities to infect different types of cells, a feature that is considered in classifying the virus into subfamilies (see Table 124–1). For example, herpes simplex viruses grow readily in epithelial cells and fibroblasts of humans, monkeys, rabbits, mice, and many other animals. Varicella-zoster virus grows best in human epithelial cells and fibroblasts in vitro. In cell culture, cytomegalovirus grows well only in human fibroblasts. Epstein-Barr virus can be cultivated only in B lymphocytes. Herpesvirus types 6 and 7 replicate in vitro in $CD4^+$ T lymphocytes.[13] Herpesvirus type 8 has yet to be grown efficiently in the laboratory.

The relative breadth of a herpesvirus's host range, however, has more than taxonomic importance; it is highly predictive of the tissues that are clinically infected by the virus. Thus, the diseases associated with the lymphotropic herpesviruses are predominantly lymphoproliferative ones. In contrast, the herpesviruses that replicate readily in tissues of epithelial origin are primarily associated with mucocutaneous infections.

LATENCY

All herpesviruses induce lifelong latent infection in their natural hosts. The process of viral latency is still incompletely understood, but key questions regarding its nature have been resolved in the past few years. It is clear that for any herpesvirus, latency occurs within small numbers of specific types of cells (Table 124–2). Latent herpes simplex viruses, varicella-zoster virus, and Epstein-Barr virus genomes are carried extrachromosomally.[14, 15] Integrated copies of the genome also exist for Epstein-Barr virus.[16]

There had been a long-standing debate as to whether latent herpesvirus genomes are totally quiescent or whether viral genes are expressed. Compelling data now show that latency is characterized by the expression of a very limited repertoire of viral genes. Up to nine Epstein-Barr virus latency genes are expressed as proteins displayed on the cell surface or within the nucleus of virus-immortalized cell lines.[17] Only two of these genes are expressed in latently infected lymphocytes in vivo. Viral transcripts of only a single family of herpes simplex accumulate in latently infected neurons.[18] Analyses of herpesvirus latency genes suggest that they are predominantly regulatory in nature and may be serving to maintain the virus in its latent state or to keep it poised for reactivation.

PATHOGENESIS

Herpesviruses induce disease in three ways: by the direct destruction of tissues, by provoking immunopathologic responses, and by facilitating neoplastic transformation.

Mucocutaneous herpes simplex virus, varicella-zoster virus, and herpesvirus simiae lesions represent the direct consequences of tissue destruction by replicating virus. Visceral infections with these viruses or with cytomegalovirus, such as encephalitis, pneumonitis, and hepatitis, also reflect virus-induced cytopathogenicity.

Certain complications of herpesvirus infections, however, such as erythema multiforme, hemolytic anemia, and thrombocytopenia, are primarily immune mediated.[19, 20] Whether the neurologic complications of varicella and zoster are also immune mediated has been widely debated. Because encephalitis, transverse myelitis, and cranial nerve palsies typically develop in association with varicella-zoster infection as the cutaneous lesions are resolving, they are often considered to be immune mediated.[21] Isolated instances in which the virus or its DNA have been detected in the involved central nervous system tissues, however, suggest that the virus itself can directly contribute to neurologic disease in some settings.[22]

Most manifestations of Epstein-Barr virus infection, including the hematologic and neurologic complications, are immunopathologically mediated. Except with cellular immunodeficiency disorders, only a minute fraction of cells that infiltrate the lymph nodes, liver, and spleen during primary Epstein-Barr virus infection are actually virus-infected B lymphocytes.[23] Most are reactive T cells. For this reason, corticosteroids have a role in the management of some complications of Epstein-Barr virus infection, and, conversely,

TABLE 124–2 Features of Productive, Latent, and Transforming Herpesvirus Infections of Humans

Virus	Typical Primary Infections	Typical Recurrent Infections	Infection in the Compromised Host	State of Latency	Association with Human Cancers
Herpes simplex virus 1	Gingivostomatitis Keratoconjunctivitis Cutaneous herpes Genital herpes Encephalitis	Herpes labialis Keratoconjunctivitis Cutaneous herpes Encephalitis	Gingivostomatitis Keratoconjunctivitis Cutaneous herpes Esophagitis Pneumonitis Hepatitis, etc.	Sensory neurons	None
Herpes simplex virus 2	Genital herpes Cutaneous herpes Gingivostomatitis Meningoencephalitis Neonatal herpes	Genital herpes Cutaneous herpes Aseptic meningitis	Genital herpes Cutaneous herpes Disseminated infection	Sensory neurons	Cervical cancer?
Varicella-zoster virus	Varicella	Dermatomal zoster	Disseminated infection	Sensory nerve ganglia	None
Cytomegalovirus	Mononucleosis Hepatitis Congenital cytomegalic inclusion disease	?	Hepatitis Retinitis Pneumonitis Encephalitis Colitis, etc.	Monocytes? Neutrophils?	None
Epstein-Barr virus	Mononucleosis Hepatitis Encephalitis	?	Polyclonal and monoclonal lymphoproliferative syndromes Oral hairy leukoplakia	B lymphocytes	African-type Burkitt's lymphoma, CNS lymphoma, and other lymphomas; nasopharyngeal carcinoma; leiomyosarcoma
Human herpesvirus 6	Roseola infantum Fever and otitis media Encephalitis	?	Pneumonitis? Encephalitis?	CD4 lymphocytes?	Rare B-cell lymphomas?
Human herpesvirus 7	Roseola infantum	?	?	CD4 lymphocytes?	None
Human herpesvirus 8	?	?	Kaposi's sarcoma	?	Kaposi's sarcoma; multicentric Castleman's disease; primary effusion lymphoma
Simian herpes B virus	Mucocutaneous lesions Encephalitis	?	?	Sensory neurons	None

Abbreviation: CNS, Central nervous system.

acyclovir is not useful in the treatment of acute infectious mononucleosis.[24, 25]

Herpesviruses persist in humans and can induce recurrent disease because they have captured and altered cellular genes that prevent their clearance by permitting latency, inhibiting apoptosis, and avoiding immune detection. Latency is sustained by virus sequestration in immunologically privileged sites, such as the neuron, in the case of herpes simplex viruses,[18] and by a lack of expression of proteins that could be detected by the immune system, as in some B cells infected with Epstein-Barr virus.[26] Several gammaherpesviruses, including Epstein-Barr virus, express proteins that directly block tumor necrosis factor receptor-1 or Fas-mediated apoptosis of lymphocytes.[27]

Many herpesviruses can transform cells in vitro. Some of the viruses transform only cells of animals different from their natural hosts, whereas others transform their hosts' cells as well. There is probably no clinical relevance to transformation that occurs only in laboratory-derived model systems, as is seen with herpes simplex virus type 1 or 2, herpesvirus type 6, cytomegalovirus, or parts of their genomes.[28]

To date, only lymphotropic herpesviruses have been proved to be tumorigenic; most lead to lymphoproliferative malignancies. Epstein-Barr virus, however, is associated not only with various B- and T-cell lymphomas but also with nasopharyngeal carcinoma and leiomyosarcomas in acquired immunodeficiency syndrome patients. Human herpesvirus type 8 has been implicated in Kaposi's sarcoma, multicentric Castleman's disease, and primary effusion lymphomas.[29, 30]

Several herpesvirus gene products "cloak" infected cells from immune surveillance and destruction. In binding the Fc portion of immunoglobulin molecules or C3b, herpes simplex virus envelope glycoproteins E and C, respectively, inhibit neutralization by antibody and complement.[8] Herpes simplex virus–infected cell protein 47 blocks peptide transport into the Golgi apparatus so that it will not be presented in the context of major histocompatibility complex (MHC) class I.[31] Epstein-Barr virus nuclear-associated antigen 1 is the only protein expressed in some forms of B-cell latency. It contains glycine-arginine repeats that prevent peptide presentation by MHC class I.[26] Cytomegalovirus encodes four gene products that downregulate class I presentation.[32] This leaves infected cells vulnerable, though, to natural killer cells, which destroy only targets that display no MHC proteins. To solve this problem, cytomegalovirus encodes an MHC homologue.[33] If these strategies were not sufficient, some herpesviruses encode proteins that mimic cytokines, chemokines, or their receptors. An example of this is the Epstein-Barr virus interleukin-10 analogue that, like its human counterpart, induces B-cell growth and suppresses T-cell responses.[34]

EPIDEMIOLOGY AND TRANSMISSION

Herpesviruses are fragile and do not survive for prolonged periods in the environment. Transmission generally requires the inoculation of a fresh virus-containing body fluid of an infected person directly onto the susceptible tissues of a previously uninfected person. Susceptible sites include oral, ocular, genital, or anal mucosa; the respiratory tract; and the blood stream. Herpesviruses do not penetrate keratinized skin efficiently.

The six herpesviruses whose modes of transmission to humans are understood to some degree are acquired predominantly by intimate contact (Table 124–3). Direct contact with infected lesions and body fluids transfers herpes simplex, varicella-zoster, and herpesvirus simiae (B virus). Sexual intercourse and oral-genital contact transmit herpes simplex viruses and cytomegalovirus. The major vehicle for Epstein-Barr virus is probably infected saliva, although the virus has been detected in exfoliated cervical cells.[35] Herpesvirus types 6 and 7 are very common early in childhood; their presence in the saliva of healthy adults suggests a simple and efficient means of transmission.[36, 37] Herpesvirus type 8 has been detected in the saliva and semen of patients with Kaposi's sarcoma.[38, 39]

Given the prolonged intimate contact between mother and baby during pregnancy and delivery, it is not surprising that human herpesviruses cause congenital and neonatal infections; those associated with cytomegalovirus are the most prevalent.[40] At least one herpesvirus is transmitted without person-to-person contact: varicella is spread by infectious aerosols.[41] Cytomegalovirus and Epstein-Barr virus can also be transmitted by blood transfusion and transplantation.[42, 43]

Herpesviruses are transmitted by individuals in whom active viral replication is occurring either during the course of their own primary infections or during reactivation infections. Most people who transmit herpesviruses, however, are asymptomatic. Over the course of a lifetime, episodes of asymptomatic shedding of herpesviruses exceed those of symptomatic shedding, and thus there are more opportunities to transmit these viruses asymptomatically than symptomatically. With herpes simplex viruses, asymptomatic reactivation and shedding of infectious virus occurs on about 1 to 3% of days; viral DNA can be detected on genital swabs even more frequently.[44, 45] Epstein-Barr virus and herpesvirus type 7 shedding rates are much higher, exceeding 15% and 80% of the days in normal seropositive individuals, respectively.[37, 46]

The likelihood of transmission depends on the quantity of virus shed. The titer of virus recoverable during symptomatic infections greatly exceeds that of asymptomatic infections.[45] The net result of these factors is that both symptomatic and asymptomatic infections contribute substantially to rates of herpesvirus transmission. The best data are available for genital herpes infections. Between one half and three fourths of infections are acquired from asymptomatic sexual partners.[47]

DIAGNOSIS

Many herpesvirus infections can be diagnosed clinically, but there are situations in which specific tests are needed. Laboratory confir-

TABLE 124–3 Transmission and Seroepidemiology of Herpesviruses That Infect Humans

Virus	Modes of Transmission: *Perinatal*	*Blood Products*	*Intimate Contact*	*Aerosol*	Seroprevalence (%) in United States: *Healthy Children*	*Healthy Adults*	Groups or Activities with Higher Risk of Infection
Herpes simplex virus 1	+	–	+	–	20–40	50–70	Frequent intimate contact
Herpes simplex virus 2	+	–	+	–	0–5	20–50	Frequent intimate contact
Varicella-zoster virus	+	–	+	+	50–75	85–95	Children in day care
Cytomegalovirus	+	+	+	–	10–30	40–70	Children in day care Promiscuous gay men Transplant or blood recipients
Epstein-Barr virus	+	+	+	–	10–30	80–95	Frequent intimate contact
Human herpesvirus 6	?	?	?	?	80–100	60–100	Cellular immune deficiency states
Human herpesvirus 7	?	?	?	?	40–80	60–100	?
Human herpesvirus 8	?	?	?	?	<3%?	<3%?	Cellular immune deficiency states
Simian herpes B virus	–	–	+	–	0	<<1	Monkey handlers

Abbreviations: +, well-recognized association; –, rare or no association; ?, inadequate data.

TABLE 124–4 Clinical Syndromes Associated with Herpesviruses

Syndrome	Herpes Simplex Virus 1	Herpes Simplex Virus 2	Varicella-Zoster Virus	Cytomegalovirus	Epstein-Barr Virus	Human Herpesvirus 6	Human Herpesvirus 7	Human Herpesvirus 8	Herpesvirus Simiae
Gingivostomatitis	+	+	−						
Genital lesions	+	+	+						
Cutaneous lesions	+	+	+					+	+
Neonatal infection	+	+	+	+					
Keratoconjunctivitis	+	+	+						+
Retinitis	+	+	+	+					
Esophagitis	+	+	+	+					
Pneumonitis	+	+	+	+	+	+			
Hepatitis	+	+	+	+	+				
Myopericarditis	−	−	+	+	+				
Meningitis	−	+	+						
Encephalitis	+	+	+	+	+	+			+
Myelitis	+	+	+	+	+				+
Erythema multiforme	+	+	+						
Other rash				+	+	+	+		
Arthritis			+		+				
Hemolytic anemia			+	+	+				
Leukopenia			+	+	+	+			
Thrombocytopenia			+	+	+	+			
Mononucleosis				+	+	+	+		
Lymphoma					+			+	
Kaposi's sarcoma								+	

mation of a herpesvirus infection excludes other similar illnesses, may allay anxiety, guides counseling and treatment, and can detect drug-resistant viruses.

A practical example of the value of confirmatory testing is genital herpes, the diagnosis of which often implies recurrent discomfort and chronic psychological and social distress. It would be unfair to casually render this diagnosis, recommend behavioral modification, and prescribe treatment. Another example of the value of testing is recurrent zosteriform eruptions, which are frequently misdiagnosed as repeated zoster outbreaks rather than as recurrent cutaneous herpes simplex virus infections.[48] Timely proof of the diagnosis of herpes simplex encephalitis, neonatal herpes, cytomegalovirus pneumonia, and other life-threatening infections permits the most efficient use of clinical resources and avoids the hazards and expense of ceaseless empiricism.

Serologic tests are used for diagnosing recent infections or confirming past infections. Serial serologic tests are of little value in considering chronic or recurrent infections. Most herpesvirus infections are best diagnosed by virus culture or detection of viral antigens or DNA.[49] Unfortunately, herpesviruses are ubiquitous, and their detection in some clinical settings does not prove that they cause the symptoms in question.

CLINICAL SYNDROMES

Herpesviruses are associated with a wide spectrum of clinical disease (Table 124–4). These can be grouped into mucocutaneous, visceral,

TABLE 124–5 Available Means to Prevent or Treat Herpesvirus Infections

Virus	Host	Indication	Prevention	Treatment
Herpes simplex virus 1	Any	Primary mucocutaneous infection	Avoid contact	PO ACV, FAM, VAL
	Normal	Recurrent mucocutaneous infection	Sunscreen	None or PO ACV, VAL, FAM
	Immune compromised	Any syndrome	None	IV ACV or PO ACV, FAM, VAL
	Any	Visceral infection	None	IV ACV
Herpes simplex virus 2	Any	Primary mucocutaneous infection	Avoid contact	PO VAL, FAM, ACV or IV ACV
	Normal	Recurrent mucocutaneous infection	None	PO ACV, VAL, FAM
	Neonate	Visceral infection	Cesarean section	IV ACV
	Immune compromised	Any syndrome	None	IV ACV
Varicella-zoster virus	Normal	Varicella	Vaccine	None, or PO ACV
	Immune compromised		Varicella-zoster immunoglobulin, vaccine	IV ACV, or PO VAL
	Normal	Zoster	None	None, or PO FAM, VAL, ACV
	Immune compromised		None	PO VAL, FAM, ACV or IV ACV
Cytomegalovirus	Normal	Any syndrome	None	None
	Immune compromised	Visceral or retinal infection	Seronegative donor tissues and blood; specific immunoglobulin, ACV, VAL, GCV	GCV, FOS, CDV
Epstein-Barr virus	Normal	Infectious mononucleosis	None	None, steroids in selected cases
	Immune compromised	Any infection	None	None, or ACV?, GCV?
Human herpesvirus 6	Normal	Any infection	?	None
	Immune compromised	Any infection	?	GCV?
Human herpesvirus 7	Any	Any infection	?	?
Human herpesvirus 8	Immune compromised	Kaposi's sarcoma	None	Radiation, cytotoxic drugs, IFN-α
Herpesvirus simiae	Any	Any infection	Avoid infected monkeys	IV ACV, GCV

Abbreviations: ACV, Acyclovir; CDV, cidofovir; FAM, famciclovir; FOS, foscarnet; GCV, ganciclovir; IFN-α, interferon alfa; IV, intravenous; PO, oral; VAL, valacyclovir.

central nervous system, malignant, and reactive syndromes. The specific infections are covered in detail in Chapters 125 through 130.

PREVENTION AND TREATMENT

Formidable progress has been made in the prevention and treatment of some herpesvirus infections (Table 124–5). A live varicella vaccine has been approved for universal use in children and is recommended for susceptible adults and selected immunocompromised patients.[50, 51] Varicella-zoster immunoglobulin modifies acute disease if administered within 4 days of exposure.[52] Cytomegalovirus-specific immunoglobulin may prevent serious infection in selected transplant recipients, and candidate vaccines may do so as well.[53, 54] Infusions of Epstein-Barr virus–specific and cytomegalovirus-specific cytotoxic T cells, respectively, have shown encouraging activity in clearing post-transplantation lymphoproliferative disorders[55] and might be effective treatment for cytomegalovirus infections in transplant recipients.[56]

Acyclovir and its related congener, valacyclovir, and famciclovir, are indicated for the treatment of several forms of herpes simplex infections, varicella, and zoster.[57–59] Ganciclovir, a more toxic nucleoside analogue, treats and suppresses sight- and life-threatening cytomegalovirus infections in immunocompromised patients.[60] Cidofovir is an effective alternative for the long-term management of cytomegalovirus retinitis.[61] Foscarnet is also useful for severe cytomegalovirus infections as well as for acyclovir-resistant infections with herpes simplex viruses and varicella-zoster virus.[62, 63]

REFERENCES

1. Roizman B. Herpesviridae. In: Fields BN, Knipe DM, Howley RM, eds. Fields Virology. 3rd ed. Philadelphia: Lippincott-Raven; 1996:2221–2230.
2. Roizman B, desRosiers RC, Fleckenstein B, et al. The family Herpesviridae: An update. Arch Virol. 1992;123:425–449.
3. Cai WH, Gu B, Person S. Role of glycoprotein B of herpes simplex virus type 1 in viral entry and cell fusion. J Virol. 1988;62:2596–2604.
4. Highlander SL, Sutherland SL, Gage PJ, et al. Neutralizing monoclonal antibodies specific for herpes simplex virus glycoprotein D inhibit virus penetration. J Virol. 1987;61:3356–3364.
5. Frade R, Barel M, Ehlin-Henriksson B, et al. gp140, the C3d receptor of human B lymphocytes, is also the Epstein-Barr virus receptor. Proc Natl Acad Sci U S A. 1985;82:1490–1493.
6. Montgomery RI, Warner MS, Lum BJ, Spear PG. Herpes simplex virus-1 entry into cells mediated by a novel member of the TNF/NGF receptor family. Cell. 1996;87:427–436.
7. Baucke RB, Spear PG. Membrane proteins specified by herpes simplex virus. V. Identification of an Fc-binding glycoprotein. J Virol. 1979;32:779-789.
8. Friedman HM, Cohen GH, Eisenberg RJ, et al. Glycoprotein C of HSV-1 functions as a C3b receptor on infected endothelial cells. Nature. 1984;309:633–635.
9. Roizman B. The structure and isomerization of herpes simplex virus genomes. Cell. 1979;16:481–494.
10. Roizman B, Tognon M. Restriction endonuclease patterns of herpes simplex virus DNA: Applications to diagnosis and molecular epidemiology. Curr Top Microbiol Immunol. 1983;104;273–286.
11. Jones PC, Roizman B. Regulation of herpesvirus macromolecular synthesis. VII. The transcription program consists of three phases during which transcription and accumulation of RNA in the cytoplasm are regulated. J Virol. 1979;31:299–314.
12. Ben-Porat T, Tokazewski S. Replication of herpesvirus DNA. II. Sedimentation characteristics of newly synthesized DNA. Virology. 1977;79:292–301.
13. Frenkel N, Schirmer EC, Wyatt LS, et al. Isolation of a new herpesvirus from CD4$^+$ T cells. Proc Natl Acad Sci U S A. 1990;87:748–752.
14. Mellerick DM, Fraser NW. Physical state of the latent herpes simplex virus genome in a mouse model system: Evidence suggesting an episomal state. Virology. 1987;158:265–275.
15. Adams A, Lindahl T. Epstein-Barr virus genomes with properties of circular DNA molecules in carrier cells. Proc Natl Acad Sci U S A. 1975;72:1477–1481.
16. Adams A, Lindahl T, Klein G. Linear associations between cellular DNA and EBV DNA in a human lymphoblastoid cell line. Proc Natl Acad Sci U S A. 1973;70:2888–2892.
17. Kieff E. Epstein-Barr virus and its replication. In: Fields BN, Knipe DM, Howley PM, eds. Fields Virology. 3rd ed. Philadelphia: Lippincott-Raven; 1996:2343–2396.
18. Stevens JG, Wagner EK, Devi-Rao GB, et al. RNA complementary to a herpes virus α gene mRNA is prominent in latently infected neurons. Science. 1987;235:1056–1059.
19. Orton PW, Huff JC, Tonnesen MG, Weston WL. Detection of a herpes simplex viral antigen in skin lesions of erythema multiforme. Ann Intern Med. 1984;101;48–50.
20. Harris AI, Meyer RJ, Brody EA. Cytomegalovirus-induced thrombocytopenia and hemolysis in an adult (Letter). Ann Intern Med. 1975;83:670–671.
21. Jemsek J, Greenberg SB, Taber L, et al. Herpes zoster–associated encephalitis: Clinicopathologic report of 12 cases and review of the literature. Medicine. 1983;62:81–97.
22. Puchhammer-Stockl E, Popow-Kraupp T, Heinz FX, et al. Detection of varicella-zoster virus DNA by polymerase chain reaction in the cerebrospinal fluid of patients suffering from neurological complications associated with chicken pox or herpes zoster. J Clin Microbiol. 1991;29:1513–1516.
23. Rocchi G, Felici A, Ragona G, et al. Quantitative evaluation of Epstein-Barr virus-infected mononuclear peripheral blood leukocytes in infectious mononucleosis. N Engl J Med. 1977;296:132–134.
24. Bender CE. The value of corticosteroids in the treatment of infectious mononucleosis. JAMA. 1967;199:529–531.
25. Andersson J, Britton S, Ernberg I, et al. Effect of acyclovir on infectious mononucleosis: A double-blind placebo-controlled study. J Infect Dis. 1986;153:283–290.
26. Levitskaya J, Coram M, Levitsky V, et al. Inhibition of antigen processing by the internal repeat region of the Epstein-Barr virus nuclear antigen-1. Nature. 1995;375:685–688.
27. Kawanishi M. Epstein-Barr virus BHRF1 protein protects intestine 407 epithelial cells from apoptosis induced by tumor necrosis factor α and anti-Fas antibody. J Virol. 1997;71:3319–3322.
28. Tevethia MJ. Transforming potential of herpes simplex viruses and human cytomegalovirus. In: Roizman B, ed. The Herpesviruses. v. 3. New York: Plenum; 1982: 257–314.
29. Chang Y, Cesarman E, Pessin MS, et al. Identification of herpesvirus-like DNA sequences in AIDS-associated Kaposi's sarcoma. Science. 1994;266:1865–1869.
30. Cesarman E, Knowles DM. Kaposi's sarcoma–associated herpesvirus: A lymphotropic human herpesvirus associated with Kaposi's sarcoma, primary effusion lymphoma, and multicenter Castleman's disease. Semin Diagn Pathol. 1997;14:54–66.
31. Hill A, Jugovic P, York I, et al. Herpes simplex virus turns off the TAP to evade host immunity. Nature. 1995;375:411–415.
32. Wiertz E, Hill A, Tortorello D, Ploegh H. Cytomegaloviruses use multiple mechanisms to elude the host immune response. Immunol Lett. 1997;57:213–216.
33. Farrell HE, Vally H, Lynch DM, et al. Inhibition of natural killer cells by a cytomegalovirus MHC class I homologue in vivo. Nature. 1997;386:510–514.
34. Vieira P, deWaal-Malefyt T, Dang MN, et al. Isolation and expression of human cytokine synthesis inhibitory factor cDNA clones: Homology to Epstein-Barr virus open reading frame BCRFI. Proc Natl Acad Sci U S A. 1991;88:1172–1176.
35. Sixbey JW, Lemon SM, Pagano JS. A second site for Epstein-Barr virus shedding: The uterine cervix. Lancet. 1986;2:1122–1124.
36. Levy JA, Ferro F, Greenspan D, Lennette ET. Frequent isolation of HHV-6 from saliva and high seroprevalence of the virus in the population. Lancet. 1990;335:1047–1050.
37. Wyatt LS, Frenkel N. Human herpesvirus 7 is a constitutive inhabitant of adult human saliva. J Virol. 1992;66:3206–3209.
38. Viera J, Huang ML, Koelle DM, Corey L. Transmissible Kaposi's sarcoma–associated herpesvirus (human herpesvirus 8) in saliva of men with a history of Kaposi's sarcoma. J Virol. 1997;71:7083–7087.
39. Huang YQ, Li JJ, Poiesz BJ, et al. Detection of the herpesvirus-like DNA sequences in matched specimens of semen and blood from patients with AIDS-related Kaposi's sarcoma by polymerase chain reaction in situ hybridization. Am J Pathol. 1997;150:147–153.
40. Nelson CT, Demmler GJ. Cytomegalovirus infection in the pregnant mother, fetus, and newborn infant. Clin Perinatol. 1997;42:151–160.
41. Leclair JM, Zaia JA, Levin MJ, et al. Airborne transmission of chickenpox in a hospital. N Engl J Med. 1980;302:450–453.
42. Prince AM, Szmuness W, Millian SJ, David DS. A serologic study of cytomegalovirus infections associated with blood transfusions. N Engl J Med. 1971;284:1125–1131.
43. Gerber P, Walsh JH, Rosenblum EN, Purcell RH. Association of EB-virus infection with the post-perfusion syndrome. Lancet. 1969;2:593--595.
44. Wald A, Zeh J, Barnum G, et al. Suppression of subclinical shedding of herpes simplex virus type 2 with acyclovir. Ann Intern Med. 1996;124:8–15.
45. Cone RW, Hobson AC, Brown Z, et al. Frequent detection of genital herpes simplex virus DNA by polymerase chain reaction among pregnant women. JAMA. 1994;272:792–796.
46. Chang RS, Lewis JP, Abildgaard CF. Prevalence of oropharyngeal excreters of leukocyte-transforming agents among a human population. N Engl J Med. 1973;289:1325–1329.
47. Mertz GJ, Schmidt O, Jourden JL, et al. Frequency of acquisition of first-episode genital infection with herpes simplex virus from symptomatic and asymptomatic source contacts. Sex Transm Dis. 1985;12:33–39.
48. Kalman CM, Laskin OL. Herpes zoster and zosteriform herpes simplex virus infections in immunocompetent adults. Am J Med. 1986;81:775–788.
49. Cohen PR. Tests for detecting herpes simplex virus and varicella-zoster virus infections. Dermatol Clin. 1994;12:51–68.
50. Weibel RE, Neff BJ, Kuter BJ, et al. Live attenuated varicella virus vaccine: Efficacy trial in healthy children. N Engl J Med. 1984;310:1409–1415.
51. Gershon AA, Steinberg SP, Gelb L. Live attenuated varicella vaccine use in immunocompromised children and adults. Pediatrics. 1986;78:757–762.
52. Centers for Disease Control and Prevention. Varicella-zoster immune globulin for the prevention of chickenpox: Recommendations of the Immunization Practices Advisory Committee. Ann Intern Med. 1984;100:859–865.
53. Condie RM, O'Reilly RJ. Prevention of cytomegalovirus infection by prophylaxis

with an intravenous, hyperimmune, native, unmodified cytomegalovirus globulin. Randomized trial in bone marrow transplant recipients. Am J Med. 1984;76(Suppl 3A):134–141.
54. Plotkin SA, Starr SE, Friedman HM, et al. Effects of Towne live virus vaccine on cytomegalovirus disease after renal transplant: A controlled trial. Ann Intern Med. 1991;114:525–531.
55. Rooney CM, Smith CA, Ng CY, et al. Use of gene-modified virus-specific T lymphocytes to control Epstein-Barr virus–related lymphoproliferation. Lancet. 1995;345:9–13.
56. Walter EA, Greenberg PD, Gilbert MJ, et al. Reconstitution of cellular immunity against cytomegalovirus in recipients of allogeneic bone marrow by transfer of T-cell clones from the donor. N Engl J Med. 1995;333:1038–1044.
57. Whitley RJ, Gnann JW Jr. Acyclovir: A decade later. N Engl J Med. 1992;327: 782–789.
58. Beutner KR, Friedman DJ, Forszpaniak C, et al. Valacyclovir HCL compared with acyclovir for improved therapy for herpes zoster in immunocompetent adults. Antimicrob Agents Chemother. 1995:39:1546–1553.
59. Sacks SL, Aoki FY, Diaz-Mitoma F, et al. Patient-initiated, twice-daily oral famciclovir for early recurrent genital herpes. A randomized, double-blind, multicenter trial. JAMA. 1996;276:44–49.
60. Crumpacker CS. Ganciclovir. N Engl J Med. 1996;335:721–729.
61. Parenteral cidofovir for cytomegalovirus retinitis in patients with AIDS: The HPMPC peripheral cytomegalovirus retinitis trial. A randomized, controlled trial. Studies of Ocular complications of AIDS Research Group in Collaboration with the AIDS Clinical Trials Group. Ann Intern Med. 1997;126:264–274.
62. Safrin S, Crumpacker C, Chatis P, et al. A controlled trial comparing foscarnet with vidarabine for acyclovir-resistant mucocutaneous herpes simplex in the acquired immunodeficiency syndrome. N Engl J Med. 1991;325:551–555.
63. Safrin S, Berger TG, Gilson I, et al. Foscarnet therapy in five patients with AIDS and acyclovir-resistant varicella-zoster virus infection. Ann Intern Med. 1991;115:19–21.

Chapter 125

Herpes Simplex Virus

LAWRENCE COREY

Herpes simplex virus (HSV-1 and HSV-2) produce a wide variety of illnesses, including mucocutaneous infections, infections of the central nervous system, and an occasional infection of visceral organs; many of these conditions may be life-threatening. The advent of effective chemotherapy for HSV infection has made their prompt recognition of clinical importance.

The word herpes (from the Greek, "to creep") has been used in medicine since antiquity. Cold sores (herpes febrilis) were described by the Roman physician Herodotus in 100 AD.[1] Genital herpes was first described by John Astruc, physician to the king of France in 1736, and the first English translation appeared in his treatise on venereal disease in 1754.[2, 3] Infection in oral labial lesions was transmitted to other humans in the late 19th century. The disease was successfully transferred to rabbits in the early 20th century, and HSV was grown in vitro in 1925.[4, 5]

DESCRIPTION OF THE AGENT

The eight known human herpesviruses (HHVs) are divided by genomic and biologic behavior into three groups: the α-herpesviruses (HSV-1, HSV-2, and varicella-zoster), the β-herpesviruses (cytomegalovirus, HHV-6, HHV-7) and the γ-herpesviruses (Epstein-Barr virus, Kaposi's sarcoma–associated herpes virus [KSHV], or HHV-8)[6] (see Chapter 124). All herpesviruses are morphologically similar, possessing an internal core containing double-stranded DNA, an icosahedral capsid with 162 capsomers, and a lipid envelope. Their overall diameter is about 160 nm. Despite this common morphologic feature, the biologic and epidemiologic features of each of the herpesviruses are distinct. Although HSV-1 and HSV-2 are the two most closely related herpesvirus, these two agents are serologically and genetically distinct.[7]

The genome of HSV is a linear, double-stranded DNA molecule (molecular weight about 100×10^6) that encodes about 80 gene products. The genomic structures of the two HSV subtypes are similar, and the overall sequence homology between HSV-1 and HSV-2 is about 50%. The homologous sequences are distributed over the entire genome map, and most of the polypeptides specified by one viral type are antigenically related to polypeptides of the other viral type.[6] Many type-specific regions unique to HSV-1 and HSV-2 proteins do exist, however, and many of these regions appear to be important in host immunity. Restriction endonuclease analysis of viral DNA can be used to distinguish between the two subtypes and among strains of each subtype.[8, 9] The variability of nucleotide sequences from clinical strains of HSV-1 and HSV-2 is such that HSV isolates obtained from two individuals can be differentiated by restriction enzyme patterns unless the isolates are from epidemiologically related sources, such as sexual partners, mother-infant pairs, or victims of a common-source outbreak.[10–13]

The viral genome is packaged in a regular icosahedral protein shell (capsid) composed of 162 capsomers. The outer covering of the virus is a lipid-containing membrane (envelope) derived from a modified cell membrane and acquired as the DNA-containing capsid buds through the inner nuclear membrane of the host cell. Between the capsid and lipid bilayer of the envelope is the tegument. Viral replication has both nuclear and cytoplasmic phases. The initial steps of replication include attachment, fusion between the viral envelope and the cell membrane to liberate the nucleocapsid into the cytoplasm of the cell, and disassembly of the nucleocapsid to release the viral DNA. Recent work has identified several of the receptors for viral attachment. One is the heparin sulfate receptor and another is a member of the tumor necrosis factor family of proteins.[15–17] The wide ubiquity of these receptors underscores the wide host range of both HSV-1 and HSV-2.

Replication of HSV is highly regulated. After fusion of the virion envelope with the host cell membrane, several viral proteins are released from the HSV virion and are expressed immediately. These immediate early gene products shut off host protein synthesis (by increasing cellular RNA degradation), whereas others "turn on" transcription of early genes of HSV replication. These early gene products designated in α-genes, are required for synthesis of the subsequent polypeptide group, the β-polypeptides, many of which are regulatory proteins and enzymes required for DNA replication. Most current antiviral drugs interfere with β-proteins, such as the viral DNA polymerase enzyme. The third (γ) class of HSV genes requires viral DNA replication for expression and constitutes most of the structural proteins specified by the virus. DNA replication takes place in a "rolling circle" pattern much like a roll of toilet paper. Specific viral genes "clip" the end of the viral DNA into the procapsid.[18]

Nucleocapsids are assembled in the nucleus of the cell. Envelopment occurs as the nucleocapsids bud through the inner nuclear membrane into the perinuclear space. In some cells, viral replication in the nucleus forms two types of inclusion bodies: type A basophilic Feulgen-positive bodies that contain viral DNA and an eosinophilic inclusion body that is devoid of viral nucleic acid or protein and represents a "scar" of viral infection. Virions are then transported via the endoplasmic reticulum and the Golgi apparatus to the cell surface. The entire replication cycle takes from 4 to 12 hours, depending on the cell type. HSV is cytopathic to cells that harbor the full cycle of HSV replication.

HSV infection of some neuronal cells does not, however, result in cell death. Instead, viral genomes are maintained by the cell in a repressed state compatible with survival and normal activities of the cell, a condition called *latency*.[19, 20] Latency is associated with transcription of only a limited number of virus-encoded proteins.[21–23] Subsequently, activation of the viral genome may occur, resulting in the normal pattern of regulated viral gene expression, replication, and release of HSV.[24] The release of virus from the neuron and its subsequent entry into epithelial cells result in viral replication.[25, 26] This process is termed *reactivation*.[27, 28] Although infectious virus rarely can be recovered from sensory or autonomic nervous system ganglia dissected from cadavers, maintenance and growth of the neural cells in tissue culture result in production of infectious virions *(explantation)* and in subsequent permissive infection of susceptible cells *(cocultivation)*.[29, 30] The fact that HSV replication was first detected in neurons during reactivation in vitro suggested that the neuron harbors the latent virus in vivo. Viral DNA and RNA have since been found in neural tissue at times when infectious virus cannot be isolated.[31] Three RNA "latency-associated" transcripts that overlap the immediate early (α) gene products, called *ICP-O,* are in abundance in the nuclei of latently infected neurons. These latency-associated transcripts code proteins in an antisense direction.[32–34] Deletion mutants of this region that can become latent have been made; however, the efficiency of their later reactivation is reduced[35, 36]; thus, the antisense transcripts may play a role in maintaining, rather than in establishing, latency.[37, 38] At present, the molecular mechanisms of the latency of HSV-1 and HSV-2 are not well understood, and strategies to interrupt latency or to maintain molecular latency in neurons are not available.

EPIDEMIOLOGY

Herpes simplex viruses have a worldwide distribution and are found even in the most remote human populations. There are no known animal vectors for HSV, and although experimental animals can easily be infected, humans appear to be the only natural reservoir.[39]

Infection with HSV-1 is acquired more frequently and earlier than is infection with HSV-2.[40] More than 90% of adults have antibodies to HSV-1 by the fifth decade of life.[41, 43] Prevalence of antibody to HSV increases with age and correlates with socioeconomic status. In western populations in the post–World War II era, 80 to 100% of middle-aged adults of lower socioeconomic status possessed antibodies to HSV, as compared with 30 to 50% of adults of higher socioeconomic groups.[44, 45] In the United States in the 1970s, HSV-1 antibodies were detected in about 50% of high and 80% of lower socioeconomic class persons by age 30 years. The prevalence of HSV-1 infection in young adults appears to be 10 to 20% higher in western Europe than in the United States.[43, 46]

Antibodies to HSV-2 appear routinely in puberty and correlate with past sexual activity of either the individuals or their partners.[45–49] In the United States, two nationwide surveys indicated that the HSV-2 seroprevalence has increased from 16.4 to 21.7% of adults.[46, 48] The cumulative lifetime incidence of HSV-2 reaches 25% in white women, 20% in white men, 80% in African American women, and 60% in African American men. Other serologic studies conducted in more select populations support the high prevalence of HSV-2 infection worldwide.[49–51] The HSV-2 seroprevalence appears somewhat lower in Europe, including Great Britain and Australia, but in all situations, rates of HSV-2 are at least 10% and often approach 60 or 80%. The frequency of HSV-2 antibody is higher among persons recruited from sexually transmitted disease (STD) clinics and among homosexual men.[52–55] It has been seen consistently among studies that HSV-2 antibody is closely related to the lifetime number of sexual partners, age of sexual debut and a history of other STDs.[55–58]

Evaluation of the seroprevalence to HSV-1 and HSV-2 has been markedly enhanced by the development of type-specific serologic assays. These assays allow the detection of HSV-2 in the presence of HSV-1 antibodies and vice versa. Most of these assays use purified type-specific proteins such as glycoprotein gG1, and glycoprotein gG2, which are antigenically distinct between the two subtypes.[59, 60] The gG1 and gG2 assays are quite accurate for defining persons with long-standing HSV infections. Another assay using an immunoblot format that identifies several type-specific antibodies, for example, gG2 and ICP-35 complex, has also been developed.[60–63] It is the most sensitive assay for detecting recent HSV seroconversion.[60, 61] The Western blot assay has a sensitivity of greater than 98% and a specificity of greater than 98% for distinguishing HSV-1–specific and HSV-2–specific antibodies. Assays that use prototype viral antigens are inaccurate and should not be used for clinical diagnosis or seroepidemiologic studies.[62]

Incidence rates of HSV infection are difficult to estimate. In prospective studies of sexually active populations such as pregnant women and persons attending STD clinics, rates of HSV-1 seroconversion were between 1 and 4% per 100 person years; for HSV-2 they were 2 to 6% yearly.[64, 65] Among HSV-seronegative women, 50% of the seroconversions were clinically symptomatic.[66] For men these figures were 30% and 70%, respectively. Persons with prior HSV-1 are three times as likely to acquire HSV-2 subclinically.[66] Retrospective surveys indicate that only 20 to 25% of persons who possess HSV-1 antibodies and 10 to 20% of persons with HSV-2 antibodies report oral-labial or genital lesions.[48, 55, 67] The differences in the prospective and retrospective studies suggest that many acquisitions are only mildly symptomatic and do not bring persons to regular medical attention. Many persons who acquire genital infection subclinically manifest symptomatic reactivation on follow-up.[68]

TRANSMISSION OF HERPES SIMPLEX VIRUS INFECTION

In 1921, Lipshultz inoculated material from genital herpetic lesions into the skin of humans, eliciting clinical infection within 48 to 72 hours in six persons and within 24 days in one case.[2] Transmission of HSV infections most frequently occurs through close contact with a person who is shedding (excreting) virus at a peripheral site, mucosal surface, or in genital or oral secretions.[69] Since HSV is readily inactivated at room temperature and by drying, aerosol and fomitic spread are unusual means of transmission.[70–73] Infection occurs via inoculation of virus onto susceptible mucosal surfaces (e.g., the oropharynx, cervix, conjunctivae) or through small cracks in the skin.[69, 76] As discussed in detail further on, subclinical or asymptomatic shedding of HSV in oral and genital secretions is common even in immunocompetent persons.[75] Transmission to any mucosal site via direct contact can occur. Transmission of HSV-1 from oral-genital contact is being increasingly recognized, perhaps because of the reduction in age-specific prevalence of HSV-1 at the time of sexual debut.[76] In a recent study, the acquisition rates of genital HSV-1 and oral-labial HSV-1 were similar among sexually active adults.[66]

Spread of HSV-1 infection from oral secretions to other skin areas is a hazard of certain occupations, for example, dentists, respiratory care unit personnel, and wrestlers.[77, 78] Laboratory-acquired and nosocomial outbreaks in hospital personnel or in neonatal nurseries have been reported.[77, 78] Transmission of HSV can occur in infants born to mothers excreting HSV at delivery.[80] Anal and perianal infections with HSV-2 are common among sexually active male homosexual populations.[81–83] Autoinoculation from genital areas to other sites, including hands, thighs, and buttocks, is not uncommon.[83]

PATHOGENESIS

Exposure to HSV at mucosal surfaces or abraded skin sites permits entry of the virus and initiation of its replication in cells of the epidermis and dermis.[84] Initial HSV infection is often subclinical—that is, without clinically apparent lesions.[64–66] Both clinical acquisition and subclinical acquisition are associated with sufficient viral replication to permit infection of either sensory or autonomic nerve endings.[84] On entry into the neuronal cell, the virus, or, more likely, the nucleocapsid, is transported intra-axonally to the nerve cell bodies in ganglia.[25] For HSV-1 infection, trigeminal ganglia are most commonly infected, albeit extension to other areas, for example, inferior and superior cervical ganglia, also occurs.[19, 20, 30] With genital infection, sacral nerve root ganglia (S2–S5) are most commonly affected.[29] In humans, the interval from inoculation of virus in peripheral tissue to spread to the ganglia is unknown. During the initial phase of infection, viral replication occurs in ganglia and contiguous neural tissue.[84–86] Virus then spreads to other mucosal skin surfaces through centrifugal migration of infectious virions via peripheral sensory nerves. This mode of spread helps explain the large surface area involved, the high frequency of new lesions distant from the initial crop of vesicles that is characteristic in patients with primary genital or oral-labial HSV infection, and the recovery of virus from neural tissue distant from neurons innervating the inoculation site.[69, 83] Contiguous spread of locally inoculated virus also may take place and allow further mucosal extension of disease. Historically, herpetic lesions involve a thin-walled vesicle or ulceration in the basal region, multinucleated cells that may include intranuclear inclusion, necrosis, and an acute inflammatory infection.

After the resolution of primary disease, infectious HSV can no longer be recovered in the ganglia. However, viral DNA can be found in 10 to 50% of ganglion cells in the anatomic region of the initial infection.[22, 23, 86] Only about 1% of such cells express latency-associated transcripts of RNA detectable by current techniques.[22, 23] The mechanisms by which various stimuli cause the reactivation of HSV infection are unknown. Ultraviolet light, immunosuppression, and trauma to the skin or ganglia are associated with reactivation.[26, 27]

One of the intriguing differences in reactivation relates to the interaction between viral subtype and anatomic site of infection. Among immunocompetent persons who acquire HSV-1 both orally and genitally, HSV-1 will reactivate more frequently in the oral than in the genital region. Similarly for HSV-2, reactivation in the genital region is 8 to 10 times more frequent than is oral-labial reactivation of HSV-2.[87] In experimental animal systems, both sacral and trigeminal ganglia contain latent virus, but reactivation differs according to the anatomic site of injection.[34, 35, 88, 89] When the region containing the latency-associated transcripts of HSV-2 is inserted into an HSV-1 virus, increasing reactivation in sacral nerve root ganglia has occurred, indicating that viral factors influence reactivation.[35, 38]

Host factors clearly influence rates of reactivation. Immunocompromised patients have both more frequent and more severe reactivation.[90–96] Alterations in T-cell immunity are critical to viral containment. Although agammaglobulinemic patients appear to handle HSV infection well, widespread local extension and dissemination are common in infants and immunocompromised patients such as organ transplant recipients and human immunodeficiency virus (HIV)-infected persons.[91–96] Viremic spread of virus to visceral organs can lead to life-threatening disease.[95–97] Experimental ablation of lymphocytes indicates that T cells play a major role in preventing lethal disseminated disease, although antibodies help reduce viral titer in neural tissue.[98, 99] The surface viral glycoproteins have been shown to be antigens recognized by antibodies mediating neutralization and immune-medicated cytolysis (antibody-dependent cell-mediated cytotoxicity).[100, 101] Monoclonal antibodies specific for each of the known viral glycoproteins have, in experimental infections, conferred protection against subsequent neurologic disease or ganglionic latency.[102, 103] Multiple cell populations, including natural killer cells, macrophages, a variety of T lymphocytes, and lymphokines generated by these cells, play a role in host defenses against HSV infections.[104] In animals, passive transfer of primed lymphocytes confers protection from subsequent challenge.[105, 106] Maximal protection usually requires the activation of multiple T-cell subpopulations, including cytotoxic T cells and T cells responsible for delayed hypersensitivity. The latter cells may confer protection by the antigen-stimulated release of lymphokines (e.g., interferons), which may have a direct antiviral effect or may activate other nonspecific effector cells. Both HSV-1 and HSV-2 encode for proteins that are directed at subverting host T-cell responses.[107] One protein in particular, ICP-47 (infected cell protein No. 47), interacts with the transporter activity protein to prevent the interaction between HSV-specific peptides and HLA class I molecules.[108] This downregulates certain HSV peptides with HLA class I antigen on the cell surface and subverts the host $CD8^+$ cytotoxic T cell response to HSV.[109, 110]

Biopsies of herpetic lesions have shown that initially the predominant infiltrating cell is the $CD4^+$ lymphocyte.[111, 112] Staining of such lesions shows the presence of activation markers on these CD4-bearing cells. These include interleukin-2 receptor, DR^+, ICAM-1^+ and large amounts of γ-interferons within 2 to 4 days, and later the lesions are infiltrated with $CD8^+$ T cells.[113, 114] Clearance of HSV-2 from genital lesions is associated with the ability to detect cytolytic killing to HSV-2 in lesional T cells.[114] Most of this cytotoxic T-cell activity appears to be in the $CD8^+$ fraction of T lymphocytes. In addition, among HIV-positive persons there is an inverse correlation between quantity of circulating $CD8^+$ T cells to HSV and severity of infection.[115]

Some aspects of HSV disease may be related to immunopathologic events. In experimental animals, strand keratitis associated with HSV-1 infection is precipitated by HSV-specific T cells.[116–118] Molecular cross-reactivity between the HSV proteins and cellular proteins appear to play a role in this phenomenon.[119]

SPECTRUM OF DISEASES CAUSED BY HERPES SIMPLEX VIRUS

HSV has been isolated from nearly all visceral or mucocutaneous sites. The clinical manifestations and course of HSV infection depend on the anatomic site involved, the age and immune status of the host, and the antigenic type of the virus. First episodes of HSV disease, especially primary infections (i.e., first infections with either HSV-1 or HSV-2 in which the host lacks HSV antibodies in acute-phase serum), are frequently accompanied by systemic signs and symptoms, involve both mucosal and extramucosal sites, and have a longer duration of symptoms, a longer duration of virus isolation from lesions, and a higher rate of complications than do recurrent episodes of disease.[65, 69, 120] Both viral subtypes can cause genital and oral-facial infections, and the infections caused by the two subtypes are clinically indistinguishable. However, the frequency of reactivation of infection is influenced by anatomic site and virus type.[121, 122] Genital HSV-2 infection is twice as likely to reactivate and recurs 8 to 10 times more frequently than genital HSV-1 infection.[87, 121, 122] Conversely, oral-labial HSV-1 infection recurs more frequently than oral-labial HSV-2 infection.[87]

ORAL-FACIAL HERPES SIMPLEX VIRUS INFECTION

Gingivostomatitis and pharyngitis are the most frequent clinical manifestations of first-episode HSV-1 infection, whereas recurrent herpes labialis is the most frequent clinical manifestation of reactivation HSV infection.[123–127] HSV pharyngitis and gingivostomatitis usually result from primary infection and are most commonly seen in children and young adults.[123, 124] Clinical symptoms and signs, which include fever, malaise, myalgias, inability to eat, irritability, and cervical adenopathy, may last from 3 to 14 days. Lesions may involve the hard and soft palate, gingiva, tongue, lip, and facial areas (Fig. 125–1). HSV-1 and HSV-2 infection of the pharynx usually results in exudative or ulcerative lesions of the posterior pharynx or tonsillar pillars, or both. Lesions of the tongue, buccal mucosa, or gingiva may occur later in the course in one third of cases. Fever lasting from 2 to 7 days and cervical adenopathy are common. It can be difficult to differentiate HSV pharyngitis clinically from bacterial pharyngitis, *Mycoplasma pneumoniae* infections, and pharyngeal ulcerations of noninfectious causes (e.g., Stevens-Johnson syndrome). No substantial evidence suggests that reactivation of oral-labial HSV infection is associated with symptomatic recurrent pharyngitis.[128]

Reactivation of HSV from the trigeminal ganglia may be associated with asymptomatic virus excretion in the saliva, development of intraoral mucosal ulcerations, or herpetic ulcerations on the vermilion border of the lip or external facial skin.[126–128] About 50 to 70% of seropositive patients undergoing trigeminal nerve root decompression and 10 to 15% of those undergoing dental extraction acquire oral-labial HSV infection a median of 3 days after these procedures.[129, 130]

In immunosuppressed patients, infection may extend into mucosal

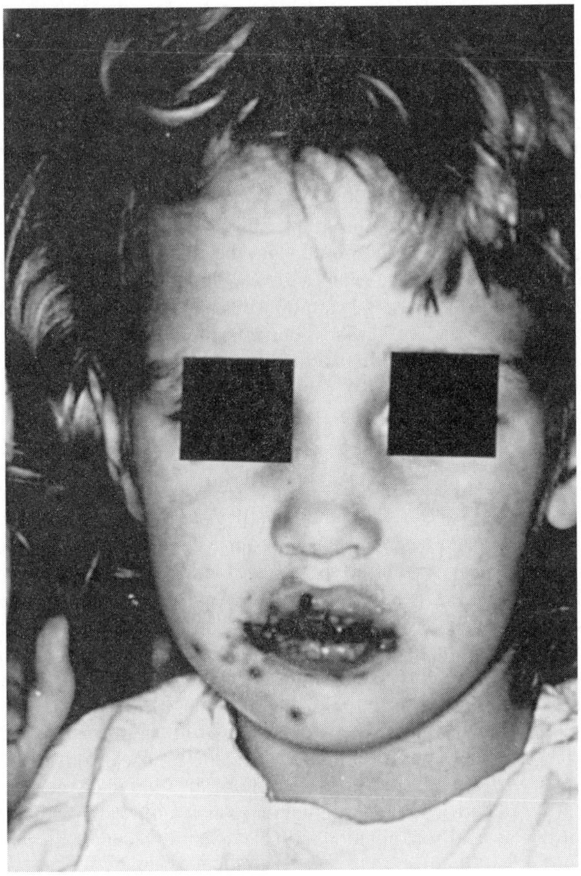

FIGURE 125–1. Primary herpes simplex virus gingivostomatitis in a child, extending to involve the cheek, chin and periocular skin.

and deep cutaneous layers. Friability, necrosis, bleeding, severe pain, and inability to eat or drink may result.[131–133] The lesions of HSV mucositis are clinically similar to mucosal lesions caused by cytotoxic drug therapy, trauma, or fungal or bacterial infection. Persistent ulcerative HSV infections are among the most common infections in patients with acquired immunodeficiency syndrome.[133] HSV and *Candida* infections often occur concurrently. Systemic acyclovir therapy speeds the rate of healing and relieves the pain of mucosal HSV infections in immunosuppressed patients.[91, 131, 132] Patients with atopic eczema or burns may also acquire severe oral-facial HSV infections (eczema herpeticum), which may rapidly come to involve extensive areas of skin and occasionally disseminate to visceral organs.[134, 135] Extensive eczema herpeticum has resolved promptly with the administration of intravenous acyclovir.[136] Erythema multiforme also may be associated with HSV infections, and evidence suggests that HSV infection is the precipitating event in about 75% of cases of cutaneous erythema multiforme.[137–139] HSV antigen has been demonstrated both in circulatory immune complexes and in skin lesion biopsy samples from these patients.[140] Patients with severe HSV-associated erythema multiforme are candidates for chronic suppressive oral antiviral therapy.[141]

HSV-1 and varicella-zoster virus have, for several years, been implicated in the cause of Bell's palsy (facial paralysis of the mandibular portion of the facial nerve).[142] Recently, typical DNA has been found in endometrial fluid in a high percentage of persons undergoing decompressive surgery for this entity, suggesting recent viral reactivation as the cause of the disease.[143, 144] This has led to more frequent use of antiviral chemotherapy for this infection. However, whether such therapy alters the course of this disease is unclear.

GENITAL INFECTION

First-episode primary genital herpes is characterized by fever, headache, malaise, and myalgias. Pain, itching, dysuria, vaginal and urethral discharge, and tender inguinal lymphadenopathy are the predominant local symptoms. Widely spaced bilateral lesions of the external genitalia are characteristic (Fig. 125–2). Lesions may be present in varying stages, including vesicles, pustules, or painful erythematous ulcers (Fig. 125–3).[146–150] The cervix and urethra are involved in more than 80% of women with first-episode infections (Fig. 125–4). First episodes of genital herpes in patients who have had prior HSV-1 infection are associated with less frequent systemic symptoms and faster healing than primary genital herpes.[83] The clinical course of acute first-episode genital herpes among patients with HSV-1 and HSV-2 infections are similar; however, the recurrence rates of genital disease differ with the viral subtype: the 12-month recurrence rates among patients with first-episode HSV-2 and HSV-1 infections are 90% and 55%, respectively.[122, 123] HSV has been isolated from the urethra and urine of men and women without external genital lesions.[151, 152] A clear mucoid discharge and dysuria are characteristics of symptomatic HSV urethritis. HSV has been isolated from the urethra of 5% of women with the dysuria-frequency syndrome.[152] Occasionally, HSV genital tract disease is manifested by endometritis and salpingitis in women and by prostatitis in men.[153–155]

Both HSV-1 and HSV-2 can cause symptomatic or asymptomatic rectal and perianal infections.[156–159] HSV proctitis is usually associated with rectal intercourse. However, subclinical perianal shedding of HSV is detected both in heterosexual men and in women who report no rectal intercourse.[160, 161] This phenomenon is due to the

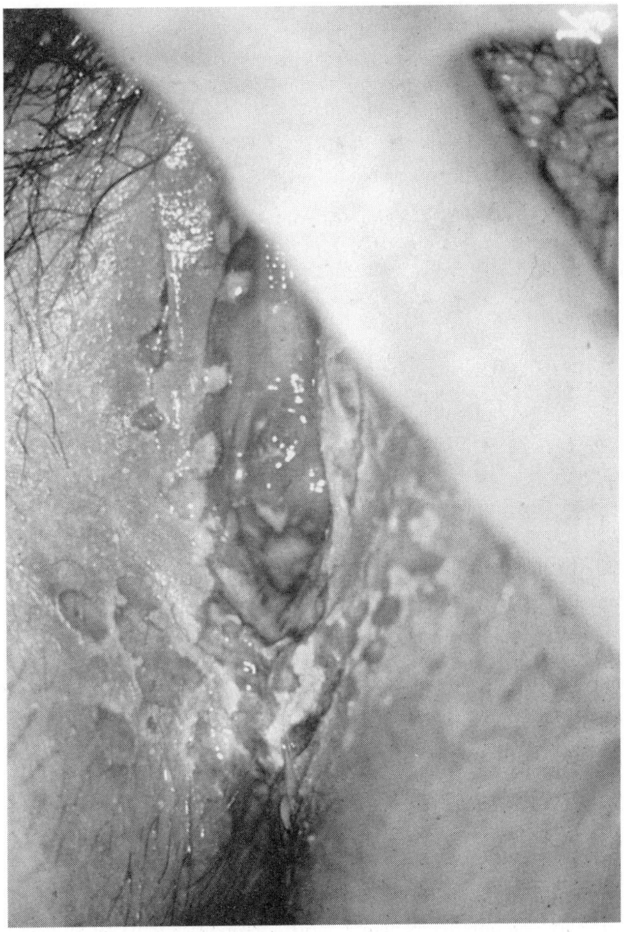

FIGURE 125–2. Primary genital herpes simplex virus-2 infection of the vulva.

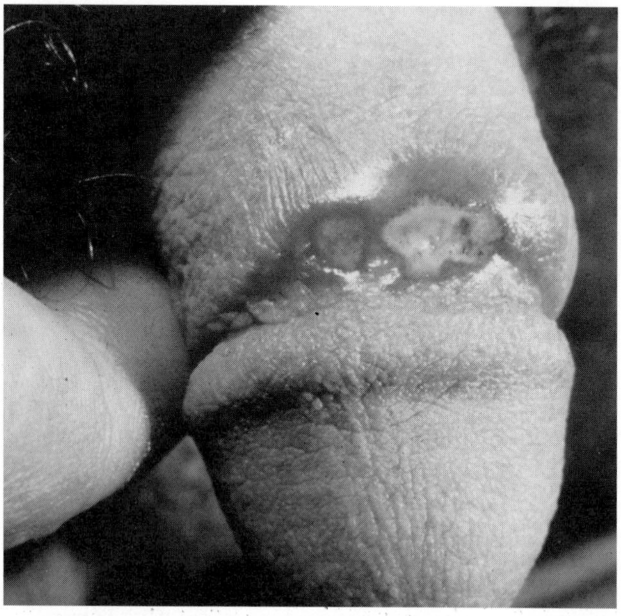

FIGURE 125–3. Chancroidal herpes simplex virus lesion on penis. (From Corey L. Herpes simplex virus infections. In: Mandell GL, series ed. Atlas of Infectious Diseases. Vol. V, Sexually Transmitted Diseases. Rein M, ed. Philadelphia: Churchill Livingstone/Current Medicine; 1996, Fig. 15–35.)

establishment of latency in the sacral dermatome from prior genital tract infection, with subsequent reactivation in epithelial cells in the perianal region. Such reactivations are often subclinical. Symptoms of HSV proctitis include anorectal pain, anorectal discharge, tenesmus, and constipation. Sigmoidoscopy reveals ulcerative lesions of the distal 10 cm of the rectal mucosa. Rectal biopsies show mucosal ulceration, necrosis, polymorphonuclear and lymphocytic infiltration of the lamina propria, and (in occasional cases) multinucleated intranuclear inclusion-bearing cells.[156] Antiviral therapy will speed healing.[159] Perianal herpetic lesions are also found in immunosuppressed patients receiving cytotoxic therapy. Extensive perianal herpetic lesions or HSV proctitis, or both, are common among patients with HIV infection.

COMPLICATIONS OF GENITAL HERPES

The complications of genital herpes are related both to local extension and to spread of virus to extragenital sites.[83, 162–164] Complications of primary genital herpes occur more frequently in women than in men.[83]

Aseptic Meningitis

Central nervous system involvement may be manifested as aseptic meningitis, transverse myelitis, or sacral radiculopathy.[163–168] In one series 36% of women and 13% of men with primary genital HSV-2 infection had stiff neck, headache, and photophobia on two consecutive examinations. Hospitalization was necessary in 6.4% of women and 1.6% of men for aseptic meningitis in association with primary HSV-2 infections.[83] A high frequency of cerebrospinal fluid (CSF) pleocytosis in patients without overt clinical evidence of meningeal irritation, was reported in a study of primary genital herpes in the early 1900s, suggesting that meningeal involvement may be a frequent occurrence with primary genital herpes.[169]

Both HSV-1 and HSV-2 have been isolated from CSF, although overt viral meningitis is much more common with HSV-2. Fever, headache, vomiting, photophobia, and nuchal rigidity are the predominant symptoms of HSV aseptic meningitis. Meningeal symptoms usually start 3 to 12 days after the onset of genital lesions. Symptoms generally reach a maximum 2 to 4 days into the illness and gradually recede over 2 to 3 days. The CSF in HSV aseptic meningitis is usually clear, and the opening pressures may be somewhat elevated. White blood cell counts in the CSF may range from 10 to more than 1000 cells/mm^3. The pleocytosis is predominantly lymphocytic in adults, although early in the course of disease and in neonates, a predominantly polymorphonuclear response may be seen. The CSF glucose level is usually more than 50% of the blood glucose, although hypoglycorrhachia has been reported on occasion. The CSF protein is usually slightly elevated.[170] In cases of aseptic meningitis HSV may be isolated from the CSF, although HSV DNA polymerase chain reaction (PCR) assay is a more sensitive diagnostic test.[160] The differential diagnosis of HSV aseptic meningitis includes diseases that result in neurologic involvement and genital ulcerations: sacral herpes zoster, Behcet's syndrome, collagen vascular disease, inflammatory bowel disease, and porphyria.[166]

Aseptic meningitis associated with genital herpes is usually a benign, albeit uncomfortable, disease in immunocompetent persons. Signs and symptoms of encephalitis are unusual, and neurologic sequelae are rare. Use of systemic antiviral chemotherapy of primary genital herpes decreases the subsequent development of aseptic meningitis. Controlled trials of intravenous acyclovir for established HSV meningitis have not been conducted. However, we recommend that intravenous acyclovir 5 mg/kg every 8 hours be given for hospitalized symptomatic patients (Table 125–1).

Autonomic nervous system dysfunction as well as transverse myelitis can occur in association with genital HSV infection.[171–177] Autonomic nervous system dysfunction can be associated with hyperesthesia or anesthesia of the perineal, lower back, or sacral regions, as well as urinary retention and constipation. This complication occurs more frequently among women and men with HSV proctitis. Physical examination reveals a large bladder, decreased

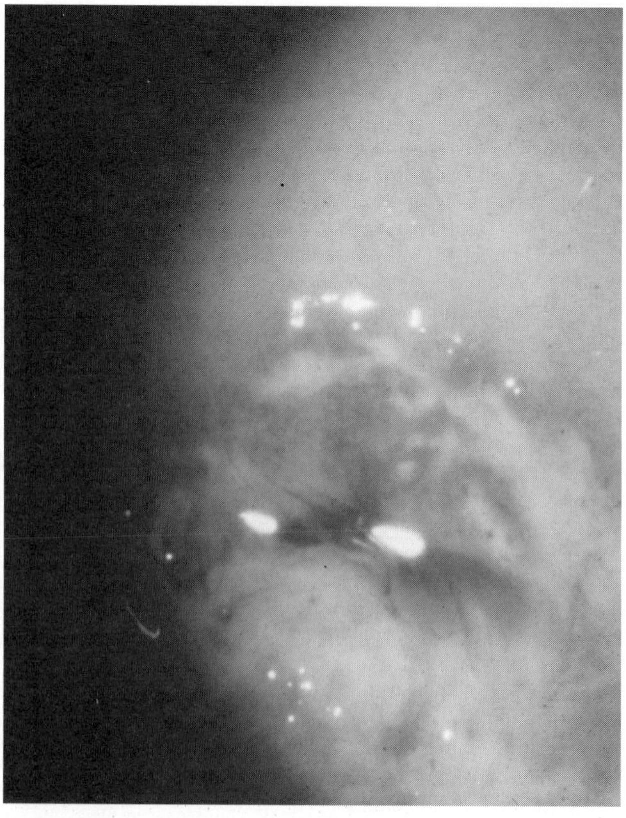

FIGURE 125–4. Herpes simplex virus cervicitis. (From Corey L. Herpes simplex virus infection. In: Mandell GL, series ed. Atlas of Infectious Diseases. Vol. V, Sexually Transmitted Diseases. Rein M, ed. Philadelphia: Churchill Livingstone/Current Medicine; 1996, Fig. 15–21.)

TABLE 125-1 Recommended Regimens of Antiviral Chemotherapy for Herpes Simplex Virus Infections

Indication	Drug	Dose	Duration	Comments
Mucocutaneous HSV Infections				
First episode genital or oral labial herpes	Acyclovir	200 mg PO 5×/day	10–14 days	Therapy has substantial benefit for all clinical and virologic aspects of the infection. Patients who have not healed after 2 weeks of therapy should be treated for an additional 7 days.
	Acyclovir	400 mg PO 3×/day		
	Valacyclovir	500 mg–1000 mg PO 2×/day		
	Famciclovir	250 mg PO 3×/day		
First episode of herpes proctitis	Acyclovir	400 mg PO 5×/day	10–14 days	
Recurrent genital herpes	Acyclovir	400 mg PO 3×/day	5 days	Therapy shortens episode by 1–2 days. May be useful in patients with prolonged recurrences or significant distress during recurrences.
	Acyclovir	200 mg PO 5×/day		
	Valacyclovir	500 mg PO 2×/day		
	Famciclovir	125 mg PO 2×/day		
Suppressive therapy	Acyclovir	400 mg PO 2×/day		Benefit of suppressive therapy is usually evident after 3–6 months of daily antiviral treatment. However, unless contraindications develop, it is preferable to continue therapy for at least 1 year.
	Valacyclovir*	500 mg PO 1×/day		
	Famciclovir	250 mg PO 2×/day		
Recurrent oral labial HSV	Penciclovir cream	Apply	5 days	Topical therapy shortens lesion time and pain.
	Oral acyclovir	400 mg PO 3×/day	5 days	For selected patients, especially if therapy initiated with prodrome.
Herpetic Whitlow	Oral acyclovir	400 mg PO 3×/day	7 days	
Infections in immunosuppressed patients	Famciclovir	250 mg PO tid	7–10 days	Relieves pain and speeds healing.
	or Valacyclovir	500 mg PO bid	7–10 days	
CNS HSV Infections				
HSV encephalitis	Intravenous acyclovir	10 mg/kg q 8 h, 30 mg/kg per day	10–14 days	
Aseptic meningitis	Acyclovir, intravenous	5 mg/kg q8h		After clinical improvement, oral administration of valacyclovir (500 mg to 1 g bid) is recommended for a total of 10–14 days of treatment.
Autonomic radiculopathy				No studies available. I recommend intravenous acyclovir for 5 days, followed by valacyclovir 500 mg PO bid for 10 additional days
Neonatal HSV	Intravenous acyclovir	60 mg/kg/day	21 days	Neonates appear to tolerate this high dose
Visceral HSV Infections				
HSV esophagitis	Systemic acyclovir	15 mg/kg/day		In milder forms of immunosuppression, oral therapy with valacyclovir or famciclovir is effective
HSV pneumonitis				No controlled studies exist. Systemic acyclovir (15 mg/kg/day) should be considered
Disseminated HSV infections				No controlled studies exist. Intravenous acyclovir (10 mg/kg q8h) nevertheless should be tried. No definite evidence indicates that therapy will decrease the risk of death.
Erythema multiforme associated with HSV	Oral acyclovir	400 mg bid or tid		Anecdotal observations suggest the oral acyclovir (400 mg bid or tid) will suppress erythema multiforme.
Infections due to acyclovir resistant HSV	Foscarnet	40 mg/kg IV q8h	Until lesions heal	The optimal duration of therapy and the usefulness of its continuation to suppress lesions are unclear. Some patients may benefit from cutaneous application of trifluorothymidine, 5% cidofovir gel, or systemic cidofovir

*Patient with very frequent recurrences (≥10/year) may benefit from valacyclovir 250 mg PO bid or 1000 mg qd.
Abbreviations: CNS, Central nervous system; HSV, herpes simplex virus.

sacral sensation, and poor rectal and perineal sphincter tone. Impotence and absent bulbocavernous reflexes have been noted in men. CSF pleocytosis may be present in some patients. Electromyography usually reveals slowed nerve conduction velocities and fibrillation potentials in the affected area, and urinary cystometric examination shows a large atonic bladder. Resolution occurs in most cases over 4 to 8 weeks.

Transverse myelitis has also been reported in association with primary genital HSV infection.[176, 177] Decreased deep tendon reflexes and muscle strength in the lower extremities, as well as the previously described autonomic nervous system signs and symptoms, are present. Residual neurologic dysfunction may occur. Whether autonomic nervous system dysfunction results from viral invasion of the central nervous system or an unusual immunologic response to infection is unknown.

Extragenital Lesions

Extragenital lesions commonly develop during the course of a first episode of primary genital herpes and are seen more commonly in women than in men.[178, 179] Extragenital lesions are most frequently located in the buttock, groin, or thigh area, although the finger and eye can also be involved. Among patients with primary HSV-2, 9% acquire extragenital lesions, most commonly on the buttocks.[179] Among patients with primary HSV-1, 25% acquire extragenital lesions, most commonly in or around the mouth.[179] Typically, the extragenital lesions develop after the onset of genital lesions, usually during the second week of disease. The distribution of lesions on the extremities or areas near the genital lesions, or both, and their occurrence later in the course of disease suggest that the majority of extragenital lesions develop by autoinoculation of virus or by viral reactivation in another part of the affected dermatome rather than viremic spread.[83, 178, 179] However, I have recently seen several patients with primary HSV in whom HSV DNA is present in plasma, suggesting that viremic spread may also be a factor in these lesions. As noted earlier, both HSV-1 and HSV-2 have been shown to be rare causes of pelvic inflammatory disease. Although this may represent dual infection with other sexually transmitted pathogens such as *Neisseria gonorrhoeae* and *Chlamydia trachomatis,* extension of HSV infection into the uterine cavity and laparoscopic evidence of vesicular lesions on the fallopian tube from which HSV has been isolated have been reported.[153, 154]

Disseminated Infection

Blood-borne dissemination as manifested by multiple vesicles over widespread areas of the thorax and extremities occurs rarely in persons with primary mucocutaneous herpes.[180–182] Cutaneous dissemination usually occurs early in the disease and is often associated with aseptic meningitis, hepatitis, pneumonitis, or arthritis. Other complications of primary genital HSV-2 infection include monoarticular arthritis,[183, 184] hepatitis,[185, 186] thrombocytopenia,[187] and myoglobinuria.[188] Pregnancy may predispose to severe visceral dissemination of primary genital HSV disease.[189–192] Reactivation of genital HSV in immunosuppressed patients, especially those with impaired cellular immune responses, can be associated with interstitial pneumonia, hepatitis, and pneumonitis, similar to the manifestations of disseminated infection of the neonate.[97, 193–195] Disseminated visceral infections in the immunosuppressed and pregnant patients have high mortality and should be treated with systemic antiviral chemotherapy.

Superinfection

Bacterial superinfection of genital herpes in immunocompetent patients is not a common complication. Rarely, pelvic cellulitis presenting as an advancing erythema and swelling of the perineal area can be seen, and systemic antimicrobial therapy should be administered to such patients. Fungal vaginitis is, however, frequently encountered during the course of initial genital herpes, and concurrent yeast infection was reported to occur more frequently in women with genital herpes.[120]

RECURRENT MUCOCUTANEOUS HERPES SIMPLEX VIRUS INFECTIONS

In contrast to first episodes of genital infection, the symptoms, signs, and anatomic sites of infection of recurrent genital or oral-labial herpes are usually localized to a defined mucocutaneous site.[125–127, 196, 197] Local symptoms such as pain and itching are mild to moderate compared with first episodes of infection, and the duration of the episode is shorter. Lesions are usually confined to one side, and the area of involvement is usually one-tenth that of primary infection.[65, 83] Recurrent oral-labial HSV tends to be of shorter duration than genital HSV. Oral-labial lesions tend to pass through clinical stages of infection more rapidly and the median time from onset of tingling to healing averages 5 days. Both oral and genital HSV reactivations are frequently associated with "prodromal signs and symptoms."[198] Prodromal symptoms vary from a mild tingling sensation, occurring 0.5 to 48 hours before eruption, to shooting pains in the buttocks, legs, or hips 1 to 5 days before the episode. In many patients, the prodromal symptoms are the most bothersome part of the episode. HSV is present on mucosal surfaces more frequently during these prodrome-only episodes, suggesting that viral reactivation is associated with these symptoms.

Increasingly, the diverse clinical spectrum of recurrent HSV ulcerations is being recognized. As described further on, subclinical reactivation of virus on mucosal surfaces is common. Some evidence suggests that such reactivation is associated with "microscopic" perineal lesions.[81] In addition, studies of both oral-labial and genital ulcerative lesions have found a surprisingly high frequency of HSV isolated from "atypical" clinical syndromes; lesions that are described as linear fissures, serpiginous ulcers without an erythematous base (see Fig. 125–3). Suffice it to say that all ulcerative lesions on oral and genital mucosa should be sampled for HSV. A definitive etiologic diagnosis can be established only with isolation of virus from lesions or demonstration of viral nucleic acid or isolation from the affected area.[199, 200]

FREQUENCY OF REACTIVATION

The major morbidity of HSV reactivations, especially genital herpes, is a result of the frequency of reactivation rates.[122, 123, 201, 202] Recent studies using both frequent viral isolation and the PCR methods have indicated that HSV shedding from mucosal surfaces is much more frequent than previously appreciated.[203–206] Because of its lifelong latency, HSV infection is a chronic life-long disease. Studies of clinical reactivation of HSV-2 infection show a steady but gradual decrease in recurrence rates over time.[207] In one study, clinical reactivations of genital herpes decreased from an average of five to an average of two recurrences per year over a 5- to 8-year period. This decrease is gradual and appears to occur most frequently 3–5 years after acquisition. However, great variability is seen and up to 20% of patients report increasing reactivations over time.[207]

Subclinical or asymptomatic viral shedding is an important aspect of the clinical and epidemiologic features of genital herpes because most episodes of sexual and vertical transmission appear to occur during such shedding.[209–213] HSV has been cultured from the lower genitourinary tract of women and men in the absence of genital ulcerations or other lesions.[203–205, 214–216] In women, the anatomic sites of asymptomatic shedding include the cervix, vulva, anus, and urethra.[203–205] In men, asymptomatic shedding occurs from the penile skin, urethra, anus, and occasionally semen.[215–217] Transmission of genital herpes can occur by sexual contact with a person who is shedding HSV without symptoms or lesions.[210, 212]

The rate of detection of subclinical shedding of HSV correlates with the frequency of swabbing of the genital mucosa, the anatomic sites sampled, and the technique used to detect HSV. HSV DNA PCR assays detect HSV on mucosal surfaces two to three times more frequently than does viral isolation.[204, 205] Studies of antiviral therapy have shown chronic daily therapy reduces viral excretion by 60 to 95% (from 30 to 5% of days), indicating that HSV DNA as detected by PCR on mucosal surfaces represents potentially infectious virus.[204, 206] Subclinical episodes of HSV reactivation share several characteristics with clinical episodes: (1) 25% of episodes last more than 1 day, (2) 17% of subclinical versus 22% of clinical episodes involve more than one anatomic site, (3) subclinical shedding is most likely to occur in temporal proximity to recurrences, and (4) women with frequent recurrences have frequent subclinical shedding.[203] Subclinical HSV reactivation is highest in the 6 months after the acquisition of infection. During this period, HSV can be isolated from genital sites a mean of 6% of days by viral isolation and 20 to 45% of days by HSV PCR.[204] Over the course of infection, the frequency of HSV shedding decreases, and persons who have had genital herpes for 5 to 10 years appear to have about half the subclinical shedding as women with disease of less than 2 years' duration. Counseling of patients with genital herpes needs to emphasize the potential for infectivity during episodes of subclinical shedding and provide appropriate strategies to decrease the risk to patients' sexual partners.

HERPES SIMPLEX VIRUS INFECTION IN PERSONS WITH HUMAN IMMUNODEFICIENCY VIRUS INFECTION

Case-control and cohort studies have both shown that prior HSV-2 infection is associated with an increased risk of acquisition of

HIV.[218–224] Estimates of the relative risk for HIV seroconversion among persons with genital herpes has varied from 1.2 to 8.5 but most studies found an increased relative risk of 2 to 3.[224, 225] The elevated risk has been found in male-to-male, male-to-female, and female-to-male transmission. These epidemiologic data support the role of genital herpes and other ulcerative STDs in fueling the HIV epidemic in developed and developing countries. In the United States, the attributable risk of HIV transmission to genital ulcers may be especially great among heterosexuals, who are currently the fastest growing segment of the HIV-infected population.[226, 227]

Laboratory studies have provided supportive evidence that HSV may be an important cofactor for HIV expression. The HSV regulatory proteins ICPO and ICP4 can upregulate the rate of HIV replication in vitro.[228, 229] Herpetic lesions are associated with an influx of activated CD4-bearing lymphocytes,[230] which may result in increased expression of HIV on mucosal surfaces. In vivo, HSV-1 and HIV coinfection of epithelial cells results in a higher copy number of HSV virions.[231, 232] A recent report detected HIV virions in nearly all genital herpes lesions in HSV- and HIV-infected persons, providing virologic confirmation of epidemiologic observations that HSV facilitates HIV transmission.[232]

HSV infections are one of the most common clinical presentations and manifestations of HIV infection. Almost all homosexual men with HIV infection possess antibodies to HSV; 80 to 90% with HSV-1 and 80 to 95% with HSV-2.[53, 218, 219] Moreover, HSV reactivation, especially perianal shedding in men and subclinical vulvar shedding in women, is more frequent in HIV-positive persons when compared with HIV-negative controls.[233] CD4 counts less than 200/mm^3 are associated with an increased risk of subclinical shedding.[215] Acyclovir suppression has been advocated as a means of reducing frequent HSV shedding in HIV-infected persons.[234, 235]

HERPETIC WHITLOW

Herpetic whitlow or HSV infection of the finger, may occur as a complication of primary oral or genital herpes by inoculation of virus via a break in the epidermal surface or by direct introduction of virus into the hand through occupational or some other type of exposure.[72, 77, 178] Before the universal use of gloves in health care settings, HSV-1 was most commonly isolated from herpetic infections of the hand.[72] However, one recent survey of herpetic infection of the hand found HSV-2 as the predominant causative agent.[236] Clinical signs and symptoms of herpetic whitlow include the abrupt onset of edema, erythema, and localized tenderness of the infected finger. Vesicular or pustular lesions of the fingertip that are difficult to distinguish from lesions of pyogenic bacterial infection are seen (Fig. 125–5). Fever, lymphadenititis, and epitrochlear and axillary lymphadenopathy are common. The infection may recur. Prompt diagnosis (to avoid unnecessary and potentially exacerbating surgical therapy or transmission, or both) is essential. Antiviral chemotherapy to speed the healing of the process is usually recommended (see further on).

HERPES GLADIATORUM

HSV may infect almost any area of skin. Mucocutaneous HSV infections of the thorax, ears, face, and hands have been described among wrestlers.[79, 237] Transmission of these infections is facilitated by trauma to the skin sustained during wrestling. Prompt diagnosis and therapy are required to contain the spread of this infection.

EYE INFECTIONS

HSV infection of the eye is the most frequent cause of corneal blindness in the United States.[238–240] HSV keratitis presents with an acute onset of pain, blurring of vision, chemosis, conjunctivitis, and characteristic dendritic lesions of the cornea (Fig. 125–6). Use of topical glucocorticoids may exacerbate symptoms and lead to involvement of deep structures of the eye. Débridement, topical antiviral treatment, interferon therapy, or a combination of these methods, hastens healing. However, recurrences are common, and the deeper structures of the eye may sustain immunopathologic injury. Chorioretinitis, usually a manifestation of disseminated HSV infection, may occur in neonates or in patients with HIV infection. HSV and varicella-zoster virus can cause acute necrotizing retinitis.[241–243] This entity can be seen both in immunocompetent persons and in persons with HIV-1 infection. Retinal necrosis is rapid, and prompt systemic antiviral chemotherapy is required. Residual blindness is common.[243]

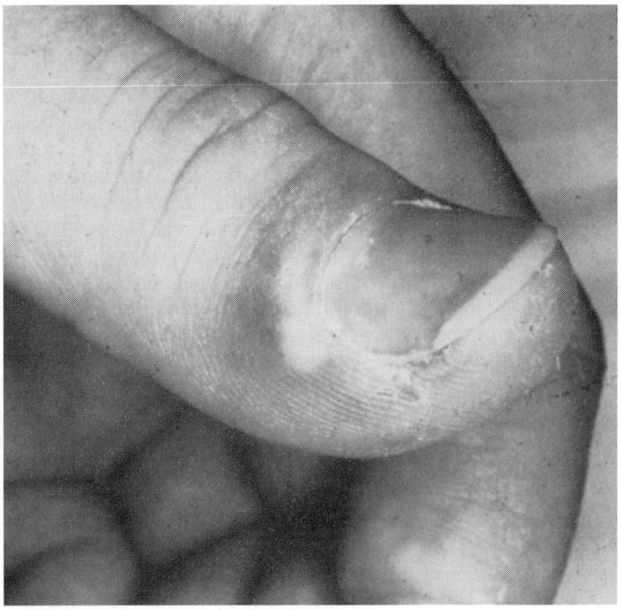

FIGURE 125–5. Herpetic whitlow (herpes simplex virus infection of the thumb). (From Corey L. Herpes simplex virus infection. In: Mandell GL, series ed. Atlas of Infectious Diseases. Vol. V, Sexually Transmitted Diseases. Rein M, ed. Philadelphia: Churchill Livingstone/Current Medicine; 1996.)

HERPES SIMPLEX VIRUS ENCEPHALITIS

HSV is the most commonly identified cause of acute, sporadic viral encephalitis in the United States, accounting for 10 to 20% of all cases.[244] The estimated incidence is about 2.3 cases/million persons/year. Cases are distributed throughout the year, and the age distribu-

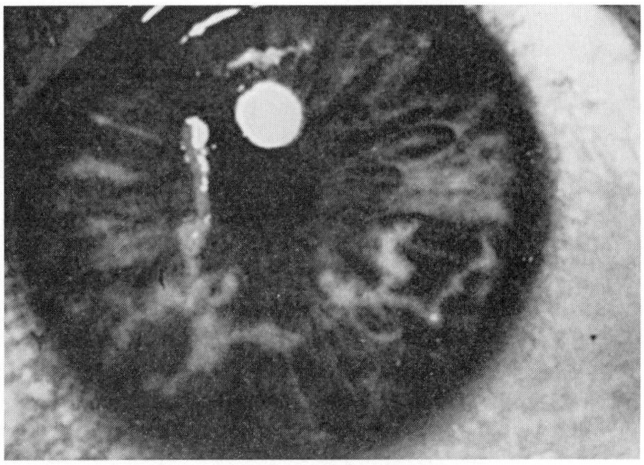

FIGURE 125–6. Herpes simplex virus-1 dendritic keratitis. (From Pavan-Langston D, ed. Ocular Viral Disease, v. 15. Boston: Little, Brown; 1975:19–36.)

tion appears to be biphasic, with peaks at 5 to 30 and greater than 50 years of age. Subtype 1 virus causes more than 95% of cases of HSV encephalitis.[245–247]

The pathogenesis of HSV encephalitis varies. In children and young adults, primary HSV infection may result in encephalitis; presumably, exogenously acquired virus enters the central nervous system (CNS) by neurotropic spread from the periphery via the olfactory bulb. However, most adults with HSV encephalitis have clinical or serologic evidence of mucocutaneous HSV-1 infection before the onset of the CNS symptoms.[247, 248] In about 25% of the patients examined, the HSV-1 strains from the oropharynx and brain tissue of the same patient differ; thus some cases may result from reinfection with another strain of HSV-1 that reaches the CNS.[247] The mechanisms behind the development of actively replicating HSV in localized areas of the CNS in persons whose ganglionic and CNS isolates are similar is unclear. Reactivation of latent HSV-1 infection in trigeminal or autonomic nerve roots may be associated with extension of virus into the CNS via nerves innervating the middle cranial fossa. HSV DNA has been demonstrated by DNA hybridization in brain tissue obtained at autopsy, even from healthy adults.[249] Thus, reactivation of long-standing latent CNS infection may be another mechanism of the development of HSV encephalitis.

The clinical hallmark of HSV encephalitis has been the acute onset of fever and focal neurologic (especially temporal lobe) symptoms.[250] Differentiation of HSV encephalitis from other viral encephalitides, as well as from other focal infections and noninfectious processes, is difficult.[251] The most sensitive noninvasive method for early diagnosis of HSV encephalitis is the demonstration of HSV DNA in CSF by PCR. Although titers of CSF and serum antibodies to HSV increase in most cases of HSV encephalitis, they rarely do so earlier than 10 days into the illness and therefore, although useful retrospectively, are generally not helpful in establishing an early clinical diagnosis. Magnetic resonance imaging is the neuroimaging technique of choice for detection of abnormalities associated with HSV encephalitis.[252–257] Demonstration of HSV antigen, HSV DNA, or HSV replication in brain tissue obtained by biopsy is highly sensitive and has a low complication rate. Brain biopsy is infrequently used now, but it provides the best opportunity to identify alternative, potentially treatable causes of encephalitis and may be considered when the clinical presentation is atypical or the diagnosis remains unclear. Intravenous acyclovir is more effective than vidarabine.[258] Even with therapy, however, neurologic sequelae are frequent, especially in persons older than 35 years of age. Most authorities recommend the administration of intravenous acyclovir to patients with presumed HSV encephalitis until the diagnosis is confirmed or an alternative diagnosis is made.

VISCERAL INFECTIONS

HSV infection of visceral organs usually results from viremia, and multiple-organ involvement is common. Occasionally, however, the clinical manifestations of HSV infection involve only the esophagus, lung, or liver. HSV esophagitis may result from direct extension of oral-pharyngeal HSV infection into the esophagus or may occur de novo by reactivation and spread of HSV to the esophageal mucosa via the vagus nerve.[259–261] The predominant symptoms of HSV esophagitis are odynophagia, dysphagia, substernal pain, and weight loss. There are multiple oval ulcerations on an erythematous base with or without a patchy white pseudomembrane. The distal esophagus is most commonly involved. With extensive disease, diffuse friability may spread to the entire esophagus. Neither endoscopic nor barium examination can differentiate HSV esophagitis from *Candida* esophatitis or from esophageal ulcerations due to thermal injury, radiation, or corrosives. Endoscopically obtained secretions for cytologic examination and culture provide the most useful material for diagnosis. Systemic antiviral chemotherapy usually reduces symptoms and heals esophageal ulcerations.

HSV pneumonitis is uncommon except in severely immunosuppressed patients and may result from extension of herpetic tracheobronchitis into lung parenchyma.[297] Focal necrotizing pneumonitis usually ensues. Hematogenous dissemination of virus from sites of oral or genital mucocutaneous disease also may occur and produce bilateral interstitial pneumonitis. Bacterial, fungal, and parasitic pathogens are commonly present in HSV pneumonitis. The mortality rate from untreated HSV pneumonia in immunosuppressed patients is high (>80%). HSV also has been isolated from the lower respiratory tract in persons with adult respiratory distress syndrome. However, the relationship between the isolation of HSV and the pathogenesis of adult respiratory distress syndrome is unclear.[262, 263]

HSV is an uncommon cause of hepatitis in immunocompetent patients. HSV infection of the liver is associated with fever, abrupt elevations of bilirubin and serum aminotransferase levels, and leukopenia (<4000 white blood cells/μl). Disseminated intravascular coagulation also may develop.[185, 186]

HERPES SIMPLEX VIRUS INFECTIONS IN IMMUNOCOMPROMISED HOSTS OTHER THAN HUMAN IMMUNODEFICIENCY VIRUS–INFECTED PATIENTS

Organ transplant patients, patients undergoing cancer chemotherapy, or those compromised by malnutrition or disorders of skin integrity such as burns or eczema are at greater risk for the development of severe HSV infections[263–266] (Fig. 125–7). Besides extensive mucocutaneous infections, HSV may disseminate to visceral organs such as adrenal glands, liver, bone marrow, and the gastrointestinal tract in such persons. Most kidney, liver, and bone marrow transplant recipients excrete HSV-1 in saliva during the first 2 to 3 weeks after grafting.[267, 268] Although often these reactivations are asymptomatic, extensive mucocutaneous ulcerations may occur, which if they persist may extend to the esophagus or lung. Because of the difficulty in distinguishing HSV from chemotherapy-related mucositis, most oncology centers use routine "prophylaxis" against HSV reactivation during the initial period after transplantation or initiation of chemotherapy.[269, 270]

HERPES SIMPLEX VIRUS IN PREGNANCY

A major concern of patients with genital herpes is the effect the disease might have on pregnancy and the risk of transmission to

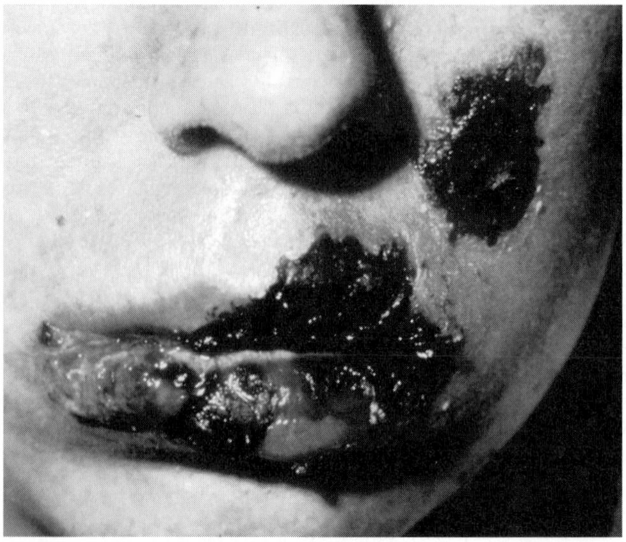

FIGURE 125–7. Severe mucocutaneous herpes simplex virus-1 infection in a bone-marrow transplant patient. (From Corey L. Herpes simplex virus infection. In: Mandell GL, series ed. Atlas of Infectious Diseases. Vol. V, Sexually Transmitted Diseases. Rein M, ed. Philadelphia: Churchill Livingstone/Current Medicine; 1996, Fig. 15–47.)

the newborn, which has high mortality and morbidity.[80, 271, 272] The prevalence of genital HSV infection during pregnancy as well as the relative incidence of neonatal HSV infection is influenced by the socioeconomic status, age, and past sexual activity of the patient population being examined.[272–274] In the United States, serologic evidence of past HSV-2 infection is present in about 30% of middle class women attending prenatal clinics; the percentage is 50 to 70% in nonwhite lower socioeconomic class women who receive obstetric care.[275]

Recent studies have shown that the highest risk for transmitting HSV in the perinatal period occurs during the acquisition of HSV at or near the time of labor.[64, 273–275] As such, populations with a high risk of acquiring HSV in pregnancy have the highest neonatal HSV infection rates. Scandinavia and the western coastal areas of the United States appear to have the highest neonatal HSV rates (about 1/3000 live births).[277]

CLINICAL COURSE OF GENITAL HERPES IN PREGNANCY

In general, the clinical manifestations of recurrent genital herpes, including the frequency of subclinical versus clinical infection and the duration of lesions, pain, and constitutional symptoms are similar in pregnant and nonpregnant women.[179, 280] Recurrences appear to increase in frequency over the course of pregnancy. Among women who are HSV-2 seropositive entering pregnancy, several clinical series and a recent study indicates that there is no effect of recurrent clinical infection on neonatal outcome, including birth weight and gestational age.[280, 281] First-episode infections in pregnancy have more severe consequences to mother and infant.[282–284] Visceral dissemination during the third trimester occasionally occurs and prematurity or intrauterine growth retardation, or both, may be seen.[288, 289] The acquisition of primary disease in pregnancy carries the risk of potential transplacental transmission of virus to the neonate.[64, 290, 291] Primary HSV infection in pregnancy can result in spontaneous abortion, albeit this appears to be relatively uncommon.[292]

Criteria for laboratory screening and surveillance, as well as delivery procedures for women with recurrent genital HSV infections, are the most frequently encountered questions of physicians caring for pregnant women with genital herpes.[276] The high prevalence rate of HSV-2 infection in pregnancy (antibody prevalence 30 to 60% and the low incidence of neonatal disease (1/6000 to 1/20,000 live births) indicates that only a few infants are at risk of acquiring disease. Cesarean section is therefore not routinely warranted for all women with recurrent genital disease.[293, 294] Because intrapartum transmission of infection accounts for the vast majority of cases, only those women who shed HSV at the time of delivery need be considered for abdominal delivery.[295] Several studies have shown no correlation between recurrences or viral shedding before delivery and the presence of viral shedding at term.[295] Therefore, weekly cytologic and virologic monitoring is no longer recommended.

Patients with recurrent genital herpes should be encouraged to come to the delivery room early at the time of delivery. At this time, careful examination of the external genitalia and cervix should be performed. In addition, a swab of the cervix or vulvar area, or both, for viral isolation should be performed. Women who have no clinical evidence of lesions should have a vaginal delivery. The presence of active lesions of the cervix or external genitalia, that is, clinical evidence of HSV infection of the lower genital tract, is an indication for abdominal delivery.[264] This policy will result in the exposure of some infants to episodes of cervical or vulvar shedding, or both. Only a few infants exposed to maternal excretions containing HSV acquire neonatal herpes.[262] Identification of such infants to communicate the HSV exposure to the attending pediatrician is necessary. Currently, most experts advise obtaining viral cultures from the throat, nasopharynx, eyes, and rectum of these infants immediately and then at 5- to 10-day intervals.[296] Any clinical evidence of lethargy, skin lesions, or other symptoms of neonatal HSV should be evaluated promptly.[297] All infants from whom HSV is isolated 24 hours after delivery should be treated with systemic antiviral chemotherapy.

The relationship between the duration of ruptured membranes in the woman with clinically apparent lesions and transmission of HSV to the infant is not well defined. Delivery of infants by cesarean section, even in women with intact membranes, will occasionally result in neonatal herpes.[298] Prolonged contact with infected secretions may increase the relative risk of acquisition of disease. Many authorities recommend that if membranes have been ruptured for more than 4 to 6 hours, cesarean section should no longer be considered for protection against HSV transmission. However, studies of neonatal HSV infection in Seattle have shown that transmission can occur from exposure to external genital lesions alone, that is, from women who are culture-positive only on vulvar and not cervicovaginal swabs.[273] Thus, in women with recurrent genital herpes who have active external genital lesions at the time of labor, I still recommend abdominal delivery.

PREVENTION OF HERPES SIMPLEX VIRUS ACQUISITION IN PREGNANCY BY USE OF ANTIVIRALS IN PREGNANCY

Controversy exists regarding the use of antiviral therapy during pregnancy.[299] As discussed further on, because the incidence of neonatal HSV-2 is low among women with recurrent genital herpes, the use of oral antiviral agents in late pregnancy to prevent neonatal HSV would not be cost-effective; one would treat 99 to 100 women to prevent one case of neonatal HSV-2. However, the incidence of cesarean delivery is much higher, and studies are under way to evaluate if routine antiviral suppression is effective in reducing subclinical shedding of HSV and reduce the frequency of abdominal delivery without increasing the risk to the infant via vaginal delivery. Until these studies are completed, no recommendations can be given.

NEONATAL HERPES

Ninety percent of neonatal herpes is perinatally acquired, 5 to 8% is congenital, and a few cases are acquired postnatally[300]; the infant acquires infection at the time of delivery through contact with HSV-infected secretions. More than 70% of infants with neonatal HSV infection are born to mothers who lack symptoms or signs of HSV lesions at delivery. The risk of transmission of neonatal herpes to the infant from a woman with primary HSV infection is about 50%. HSV-2 infection from a woman with past HSV-1 and recurrent HSV-2 is 20%, and the risk of neonatal transmission through vaginal delivery is less than 1%.[273]

Neonates (infants <6 weeks of age) have the highest frequency of visceral or CNS infection, or both, of any HSV-infected patient population. If not treated, neonatal herpes undergoes dissemination or develops into CNS infection in more than 70% of cases. Without therapy, the overall rate of death from neonatal herpes is 65%; less than 20% of neonates with CNS infection develop normally.[80] Although skin lesions are the most commonly recognized features of disease, many infants do not acquire lesions until well into the course of disease. Of the 70% of neonatal HSV infections caused by HSV-2, almost all result from contact with infected genital secretions at the time of delivery. However, congenitally infected infants have been reported.[288, 289] Usually these infants are born to mothers who have acquired primary HSV infection during pregnancy.[283] In most series, 30% of neonatal HSV infections are due to HSV-1.[304] Most of these cases are associated with the maternal acquisition of primary genital HSV-1 late in pregnancy and the consequent contact of the infant with infectious genital secretions at birth.[273] Neonatal HSV-1 infections may also be acquired through postnatal contact with immediate family members who have symptomatic or asymptomatic oral-labial HSV-1 infection through nosocomial transmission within the hospital.[13, 73, 307] CNS morbidity is less severe with HSV-1 than with HSV-2 infection.[304] Antiviral chemotherapy has reduced the rate of death from neonatal herpes to 25%.[305, 306] However, the rate of morbidity, especially in infants with HSV-2 infection involving the CNS, is still very high.[304]

The key to prevention of neonatal HSV is the prevention of acquisition of genital HSV-1 or HSV-2 infection late in pregnancy. Several approaches are possible. In high-incidence areas, such as the West Coast of the United States and Scandinavia, a case can be made for serologic screening in the third trimester to identify women at risk. Risk exists in HSV-seronegative women with an HSV-1– or HSV-2–seropositive partner or HSV-1–seropositive women with a HSV-2–seropositive partner. This requires the availability of accurate serologic assays in both the pregnant woman and her HSV-2–seropositive partner. Counseling to avoid sexual contact, including oral-genital contact, in late pregnancy is recommended. Greater appreciation of the potential to acquire HSV-1 via oral-genital sex in late pregnancy is needed, as nearly 30% of neonatal HSV is due to HSV-1.

Another approach is to serologically screen only women and to counsel regarding the risk of acquisition in the late third trimester. The disadvantage of this approach is that only about 20% of couples have discordant HSV serologic pictures and are "at risk." In low-prevalence settings, where neonatal HSV is uncommon, the cost of serologic screening may outweigh the benefits.

Infants born by cesarean section to women before the rupture of membranes or by vaginal delivery to women with no evidence of recent HSV infection are at minimal risk for the development of HSV infection, and most hospitals do not recommend segregating the infant from the rest of the newborn nursery. If a more cautious approach is desired, the infant can be put into an Isolette to make hospital personnel aware of the necessity to use wound and skin precautions and proper hand-washing techniques.

Infants born to women at risk of transmitting disease to the neonate (i.e., women with active lesions) should be placed in isolation. Viral cultures, liver function studies, and CSF examinations should be obtained, and the infant should be observed closely for the first month of life. Any symptoms of neonatal disease (e.g., poor feeding, fever, hypothermia, skin lesions, or CNS such as seizures) should be investigated expeditiously for evidence of neonatal HSV infection. Management of contact between infant and mother should also be handled on an individual basis. In women who acquire primary genital herpes late in pregnancy, the high incidence of extragenital lesions developing and the potential of viremia suggest that separation between mother and infant is warranted until therapy has produced a clinical and virologic response. Because recurrent genital herpes is rarely associated with frequent dissemination of disease or the development of extragenital lesions in exposed extremities, protection of the infant from exposure to infected genital secretion is adequate. When handling the infant in the hospital, the mother should wear a gown and observe proper hand-washing techniques. Oral-labial herpes presents a greater risk of postnatal acquisition of HSV infections to the newborn than genital herpes.[17] Thus, nursery personnel and other adults with external labial lesions caused by HSV should also be excluded for intimate contact with the newborn infant.

DIAGNOSIS

Both clinical and laboratory criteria are useful for establishing the diagnosis of HSV infections. A clinical diagnosis can be made accurately when characteristic multiple vesicular lesions on an erythematous base are present. However, it is increasingly being recognized that herpetic ulcerations may clinically resemble skin ulcerations of other causes. Mucosal HSV infection may also present as urethritis or pharyngitis without cutaneous lesions. Thus, laboratory studies to confirm the diagnosis and to guide therapy are recommended. Staining of scrapings from the base of the lesions with Wright, Giemsa (Tzanck preparation), or Papanicolaou stain demonstrates characteristic giant cells or intranuclear inclusions of HSV infection. These cytologic techniques are often useful as quick office procedures to confirm the diagnosis. Limitations of the cytologic method are that it does not differentiate between HSV and varicella-zoster virus infections, that it is relatively insensitive, and that the correct identification of giant cells requires experience.

HSV infection is best confirmed in the laboratory by isolation of virus in tissue culture or by demonstration of HSV antigens or DNA in scrapings from lesions. HSV causes a discernible cytopathic effect in a variety of cell culture systems, and most specimens can be identified within 48 to 96 hours after inoculation. Spin-amplified culture with subsequent staining for HSV antigen has shortened the time needed to identify HSV to less than 24 hours. The sensitivity of viral isolation depends on the stage of lesions (with higher sensitivity in vesicular than in ulcerative lesions), on whether the patient has a first or a recurrent episode of the disease (with higher sensitivity in first than in recurrent episodes), and on whether the sample is from an immunosuppressed or an immunocompetent patient (with more antigen in immunosuppressed patients). Antigen detection procedures have approached viral isolation in terms of sensitivity in detecting HSV in genital or oral-labial lesions; however, antigen detection appears to be only about 50% as sensitive as viral isolation for the identification of HSV in cervical or salivary secretions of asymptomatic patients. PCR techniques appear to be more sensitive for HSV than viral isolation, especially for the diagnosis of CNS infections and the detection of HSV as a cause of late-stage ulcerative lesions. Laboratory confirmation permits subtyping of the virus; information on subtype may be useful epidemiologically and may help to predict the frequency of reactivation after first-episode oral-labial or genital HSV infection.

Acute- and convalescent-phase serum can be useful in demonstrating seroconversion during primary HSV-1 or HSV-2 infection. However, only 5% of patients with recurrent mucocutaneous HSV infections have a fourfold or greater rise in titer of antibody to HSV in the interval between the collection of first and second samples. Serologic assays, especially type-specific assays, should be used to identify asymptomatic carriers of HSV-1 or HSV-2 infection.[61, 62]

Several studies have shown that persons seropositive for HSV-2 to whom the clinical manifestations of HSV have been explained are able to identify symptomatic reactivations. Individuals seropositive for HSV-2 should be told about the high frequency of subclinical reactivation in mucosal surfaces not visible to the eye (e.g., cervix, urethra, perianal skin) or in microscopic ulcerations that may not be clinically symptomatic. Transmission of infection during such episodes is well established.

TREATMENT

The advent of antiviral drugs for HSV-1 and HSV-2 infections has made clinical management of these infections a part of standard clinical practice (see Chapter 36).[307] For mucocutaneous and visceral HSV infections, acyclovir and its related compounds famciclovir and valacyclovir, have been the mainstay of therapy. Several antiviral agents are available for topical use in HSV eye infections: idoxuridine, trifluorothymidine, topical vidarabine, and cidofovir. For HSV encephalitis and neonatal herpes, intravenous acyclovir is the treatment of choice. Acyclovir-resistant virus can be encountered in immunocompromised hosts (see further on).

Acyclovir was the first antiviral clearly demonstrated to be effective against HSV infections. It is an acyclic nucleoside analogue that is a substrate for HSV-specified thymidine kinase.[308–310] Acyclovir is selectively phosphorylated by HSV-infected cells to acyclovir-monophosphate. Cellular enzymes then phosphorylate acyclovir-monophosphate to acyclovir-triphosphate, a competitive inhibitor of viral DNA polymerase.[311] Acyclovir-triphosphate is incorporated into the growing DNA chain of the virus and causes chain termination. Acyclovir has potent in vitro activity against both HSV-1 and HSV-2.[312] Numerous trials of acyclovir in mucocutaneous HSV infections of the immunocompetent and immunosuppressed host have been conducted.[313–321] General recommendations are outlined in Table 125–1.

Famciclovir, the oral formulation of penciclovir, is also clinically effective in the treatment of a variety of HSV-1 and HSV-2 infections.[322–326] Valacyclovir is a valyl ester of acyclovir that has greater bioavailability than acyclovir.[327–329] Ganciclovir has activity against both HSV-1 and HSV-2; however, because it is more toxic than acyclovir, valacyclovir, and famciclovir, it is generally not recommended for treatment of HSV infections.

Acyclovir has been shown to be effective in shortening the duration of symptoms and lesions of mucocutaneous HSV infections in immunocompromised patients (see Table 125–1). Intravenous and oral acyclovir as well as intravenous penciclovir and famciclovir also prevent reactivation of HSV in seropositive immunocompromised patients during induction chemotherapy for acute leukemia or in the period immediately after bone marrow transplantation.

Oral acyclovir, famciclovir, and valacyclovir have been shown to speed the healing and resolution of symptoms in first and recurrent episodes of genital HSV-1 and HSV-2 infections. Chronic daily suppressive therapy reduces the frequency of reactivation disease among patients with frequent genital herpes.

Intravenous acyclovir (30 mg/kg/day, given as a 10 mg/kg infusion over 1 hour at 8-hour intervals) is effective in reducing the rates of death and morbidity from HSV encephalitis.[258] Early initiation of therapy is a critical factor in outcome. The major side effect associated with intravenous acyclovir is transient renal insufficiency, usually caused by crystallization of the compound in the renal parenchyma. This adverse reaction can be avoided if the medication is given slowly over 1 hour and the patient is well hydrated. Because CSF levels of acyclovir average only 30 to 50% of plasma levels, the dosage of acyclovir used for treatments of CNS infection (30 mg/kg/day) is double that used for the treatment of mucocutaneous or visceral disease (15 mg/kg/day). For neonatal HSV, high-dose intravenous therapy is recommended (60 mg/kg/day in three divided doses). Intravenous therapy for neonatal herpes should be given for 21 days.[330]

Acyclovir-resistant strains of HSV are being identified with increasing frequency, especially in HIV-infected persons.[331–335] Almost all clinically significant acyclovir resistance has been seen in immunocompromised patients. Most acyclovir-resistant strains of HSV have a deficiency in thymidine kinase, the enzyme that phosphorylates acyclovir.[311] Thus, cross-resistance to famciclovir is usually found (see Chapter 36). Occasionally, an isolate with altered thymidine kinase specificity will arise and will be sensitive to famciclovir but not to acyclovir. In some patients infected with thymidine kinase–deficient virus, higher doses of acyclovir are associated with clearing of lesions. In others, clinical disease progresses despite high-dose therapy.[335–339] Isolation of HSV from persisting lesions despite adequate dosages and blood levels of acyclovir should raise the suspicion of acyclovir resistance. Therapy with the antiviral drug foscarnet is useful.[340, 341] Because of its toxicity and cost, this drug is usually reserved for patients with extensive mucocutaneous infections. Cidofovir is a nucleotide analogue and exists as a phosphonate or monophosphate form. Most thymidine kinase–deficient strains of HSV are sensitive to cidofovir. Cidofovir ointment has been shown to speed healing of acyclovir-resistant lesions.[342, 343] Similarly, trifluorothymidine ointment has also been reported to be of utility.[344]

REFERENCES

1. Wildy P. Herpes history and classification. In: As K, ed. The Herpes Viruses. New York: Academic Press; 1973:1.
2. Astruc J. De morbis venereis libri sex Paris. 1736.
3. Hutfield D. History of herpes genitalis. Br J Vener Dis. 1996;42:263.
4. Parker F, Nye R. Studies on filterable viruses: II. Cultivation of herpes virus. Am J Pathol. 1925;1:337.
5. Lipschutz B. Untersuchungen uber die aetiologie der Krankheiten der herpes gruppe (herpes zoster, herpes genitalis, herpes febrillis). Arch Dermatol Symp (Berlin). 1921;136:428.
6. Roizman B, Sears AE. Herpes simplex viruses and their replication. In: Fields BN, Knipe DM, Howley PM, eds. Field's Virology, v. 2, 3rd ed. Philadelphia: Lippincott-Raven; 1996:2231.
7. Nahmias A, Dowdle W. Antigenic and biologic differences in herpesvirus hominis. Prog Med Virol. 1968;10:110.
8. Buchman TG, Roizman B, Adams G, et al. Restriction endonuclease fingerprinting of herpes simplex virus DNA: A novel epidemiological tool applied to a nosocomial outbreak. J Infect Dis. 1978;138:488.
9. Schmidt OW, Fife KH, Corey L. Reinfection is an uncommon occurrence in patients with symptomatic recurrent genital herpes. J Infect Dis. 1984;149:645.
10. Hammer SM, Buchman TG, D'Angelo LJ, et al. Temporal cluster of herpes simplex encephalitis: Investigation by restriction endonuclease cleavage of viral DNA. J Infect Dis. 1980;141:436.
11. Lakeman AD, Nahmias AJ, Whitley RJ. Analysis of DNA from recurrent genital herpes simplex virus isolates by restriction endonuclease digestion. J Sex Trans Dis. 1986;13:61.
12. Buchman TG, Roizman B, Nahmias AJ. Demonstration of exogenous genital reinfection with herpes simplex virus type 2 by restriction endonuclease fingerprinting of viral DNA. J Infect Dis. 1979;140:259.
13. Douglas JM, Schmidt O, Corey L. Acquisition of neonatal HSV-1 infection from a paternal source contact. Pediatrics. 1983;103:908–910.
14. Lonsdale DM, Brown SM, Subak-Sharpe JH, et al. The polypeptide and the DNA restriction enzyme profiles of spontaneous isolates of herpes simplex virus type 1 from explants of human trigeminal, superior cervical and vagus ganglia. J Gen Virol. 1979;43:151.
15. Montgomery RI, Warner MS, Lum BJ, Spear PG. Herpes simplex virus-1 entry into cells mediated by a novel member of the TNF/NGF receptor family. Cell. 1996;87:427.
16. Krummenacher C, Nicola AV, Whitbeck JC, et al. Herpes simplex virus glycoprotein D can bind to poliovirus receptor-related protein 1 of herpesvirus entry mediator, two structurally unrelated mediators of virus entry. J Virol. 1998;72:6064.
17. Mauri DN, Ebner R, Montgomery RI, et al. LIGHT, a new member of the TNF superfamily, and lymphotoxin α are ligands for herpesvirus entry mediator. Immunity. 1998;8:21.
18. Ward PL, Roizman B. Herpes simplex genes: The blueprint of a successful human pathogen. Trends Gener. 1994;10:267.
19. Stevens JG, Cook ML. Latent herpes simplex virus in spinal ganglia. Science. 1971;173:843.
20. Baringer JR, Pisani P. Herpes simplex virus genomes in human nervous system tissue analyzed by polymerase chain reaction. Ann Neurol. 1994;36:823.
21. Galloway DA, Fenoglio C, Shevchuck M, et al. Detection of herpes simplex RNA in human sensory ganglia. Virology. 1979;95:265.
22. Stevens JG, Haarr L, Porter DD, et al. Prominence of the herpes simplex virus latency-associated transcript in trigeminal ganglia from seropositive humans. J Infect Dis. 1988;158:117.
23. Stevens JG, Wagner EK, Devi-Rao GB, et al. RNA complementary to a herpesvirus alpha gene mRNA is prominent in latently infected neurons. Science. 1987;235:1056.
24. Swartz J, Roizman B. Concerning the egress of HSV from infected cells electron and light microscopic observations. Virology. 1969;38:42.
25. Hill TJ, Field HJ, Roome APC. Intra-axonal location of herpes simplex virus particles. J Gen Virol. 1972;15:253.
26. Blyth WA, Hill TJ, Field HJ. Reactivation of HSV infection by ultraviolet light a possible role of prostaglandins. J Gen Virol. 1976;33:547.
27. Carlton CA, Kilbourne ED. Activation of latent herpes simplex by trigeminal sensory-root section. N Engl J Med. 1952;246:172.
28. Sawtell NM, Thompson RL. Rapid in vivo reactivation of HSV in latently infected murine ganglionic nerves after transient hypothermia. J Virol. 1992;66:2150.
29. Barringer J. Recovery of herpes simplex virus from human sacral ganglions. N Engl J Med. 1974;291:828.
30. Warren K, Brown SM, Wroblewska Z, et al. Isolation of latent herpes simplex virus from the superior cervical and vagus ganglions of human being. N Engl J Med. 1978;298:1068.
31. Rock DL, Fraser NW. Latent HSV type 1 DNA contains two copies of the DNA joint region. J Virol. 1985;55:849.
32. Javier RT, Stevens JG, Dissette VB, Wagner EK. A herpes simplex virus transcript abundant in latently infected neurons is dispensable for establishment of the latent state. Virology. 1988;166:254.
33. Rodahl E, Steven JG. Differential accumulation of HSV-1 type 1 latency associated transcripts in sensory and autonomous ganglia. Virology. 1992;189:385.
34. Burke R, Hartog K, Croen KD, Ostrove JMI. Detection and characterization of latent HSV RNA by in situ and northern blot hybridization in guinea pigs. Virology. 1991;181:793.
35. Block TM, Spivack JG, Steiner I, et al. A HSV type 1 latency associated transcript mutant reactivates with normal kinetics from latent infection. J Virol. 1990;64:3417.
36. Perng GC, Thompson RL, Sawtell NM, et al. An avirulent ICP34.5 deletion mutant of herpes simplex virus type 1 is capable of in vivo spontaneous reactivation. J Virol. 1995;69:3033.
37. Yoshikawa T, Hill JM, Stanberry LR, et al. The characteristic site-specific reactivation phenotypes of HSV-1 and HSV-2 depend upon the latency-associated transcript region. J Exp Med. 1996;184:659.
38. Sawtell NL, Thompson RL. HSV type 1 latency associated transcription promotes anatomal site dependent establishment and reactivation from latency. J Virol. 1992;66:2157.
39. Gentry GA, Lowe M, Alford G, Nevins R. Sequence analyses of herpesviral

enzymes suggest an ancient origin for human sexual behavior. Proc Natl Acad Sci U S A. 1988;85:2658.

40. Nahmias A, Josey WE, Naib ZM, et al. Antibodies to herpesvirus hominis types 1 and 2 in humans: Patients with genital infections. Am J Epidemiol. 1970;92:539.
41. Wentworth B, Alexander E. Seroepidemiology of infections due to members of the herpesvirus group. Am J Epidemiol. 1971;94:496.
42. Porter D, Wimberly I, Benyesh-Melnick M. Prevalence of antibodies to EB virus and other herpesviruses. JAMA. 1979;208:1675.
43. Cowan FM, Johnson AM, Ashley R, et al. Relationship between antibodies to herpes simplex virus (HSV) and symptoms of HSV infection. J Infect Dis. 1996;174:470.
44. Smith FW. Incidence of herpesvirus hominis antibody in the population. J Hyg. 1967;65:395.
45. Rawls WE, Iwamoto K, Adam E, Melnick JL. Measurement of antibodies to herpesvirus type 1 and 2 in human sera. J Immunol. 1970;104:599.
46. Johnson R, Nahmias AJ, Magder LS, et al. A seroepidemiologic survey of the prevalence of herpes simplex virus type 2 infection in the United States. N Engl J Med. 1990;321:7.
47. Rawls W, Gardner HL, Flunders RW, et al. Genital herpes in 2 social groups. Am J Obstet Gynecol. 1971;110:682.
48. Fleming DT, McQuillan GM, Johnson RE, et al. Herpes simplex virus type 2 in the United States, 1976 to 1994. N Engl J Med. 1997;337:1105–1111.
49. Oberle M, Rosero-Bixby L, Lee FK, et al. Herpes simplex virus type 2 antibodies: High prevalence in monogamous women in Costa Rica. Am J Trop Med Hyg. 1989;41:224.
50. Cowan F, Johnson AM, Ashley R, et al. Antibody to herpes simplex virus type 2 as serological marker of sexual lifestyle in populations. BMJ. 1994;9:1325.
51. Cunningham A, Lee FK, Ho DW, et al. Herpes simplex virus type 2 antibody in patients attending antenatal or STD clinics. Med J Aust. 1993;158:525.
52. Pasquini P, Mele LA, Franco E, et al. Prevalence of herpes virus type 2 antibodies in selected population groups in Italy. Eur J Clin Microbiol Infect Dis. 1988;7:54.
53. Siegel D, Golden E, Washington AG, et al. Prevalence and correlates of herpes simplex infections: The population-based AIDS in multiethnic neighborhoods study. JAMA. 1992;268:1700.
54. Oliver L, Wald A, Kim M, et al. Seroprevalence of herpes simplex virus infections in a family medicine clinic. Arch Fam Med. 1995;4:228.
55. Koutsky LA, Ashley RL, Holmes KK, et al. The frequency of unrecognized type 2 herpes simplex virus infection among women: Implications for the control of genital herpes. Sex Trans Dis. 1990;17:90–94.
56. Duenas A, Adam E, Melnick JL, Rawls WE. Herpes virus type 2 in a prostitute population. Am J Epidemiol. 1972;98:483.
57. Daling J, Weiss NS, Hislop G, et al. Sexual practices, sexually transmitted diseases, and the incidence of anal cancer. N Engl J Med. 1987;317:973.
58. Josey W, Nahmias A, Naib Z. The epidemiology of type 2 (genital) herpes simplex virus infection. Obstet Gynecol Surv. 1972;17:295.
59. Lee F, Coleman RM, Pereira L, et al. Detection of herpes simplex virus type 2 specific antibody with glycoprotein G. J Clin Microbiol. 1985;22:642.
60. Ashley RL, Wu L, Pickering JW, et al. Premarket evaluation of a commercial glycoprotein-G based enzyme immunoassay for herpes simplex virus type-specific antibodies. J Clin Microbiol. 1998;36:294.
61. Ashley RL, Militoni J, Lee F, et al. Comparison of Western blot (Immunoblot) and glycoprotein G-specific immunodot enzyme assay for detecting antibodies to herpes simplex virus types 1 and 2 in human sera. J Clin Microbiol. 1988;26:662.
62. Ashley R, Cent A, Maggs V, et al. Inability of enzyme immunoassays to discriminate between infections with herpes simplex virus types 1 and 2. Ann Intern Med. 1991;115:520.
63. Ashley RL, Dalessio J, Dragavon J, et al. Underestimation of HSV-2 seroprevalence in a high risk population by microneutralization assay. Sex Trans Dis. 1993;20:230.
64. Brown Z, Selke S, Zeh J, et al. Acquisition of herpes simplex virus during pregnancy. N Engl J Med. 1997;337:509.
65. Corey L, Wald A. Genital Herpes. In: Holmes KK, Sparling PF, Mardh PA, et al, eds. Sexually Transmitted Diseases, 3rd ed. New York: McGraw-Hill; 1999:285–312.
66. Langenberg AGM, Corey L, Ashley RL, et al. Acquisition of symptomatic and asymptomatic HSV-1 and HSV-2 infections: A prospective study of their incidence and clinical spectrum. N Engl J Med. In press.
67. Breinig MK, Kingsley LA, Armstrong JA, et al. Epidemiology of genital herpes in Pittsburgh: Serologic, sexual, and racial correlates of apparent and inapparent herpes simplex infections. J Infect Dis. 1990;162:299.
68. Diamond C, Selke S, Ashley R, et al. Clinical course of patients with serologic evidence of recurrent genital herpes presenting with signs and symptoms of first episode disease. Sex Trans Dis. 1999;26:221.
69. Corey L, Spear PG. Infections with herpes simplex viruses. N Engl J Med. Part 1: 1986;314:686–691; Part 2: 1986;314:749–757.
70. Stern H, et al. Herpetic whitlow, a form of cross infection in hospitals. Lancet. 1959;2:871.
71. Blank H, Haines HG. Experimental human reinfection with herpes simplex virus. J Invest Dermatol. 1973;61:223.
72. Perl T, Haugen TH, Pfaller MA, et al. Transmission of herpes simplex virus type 1 infection in an intensive care unit. Ann Intern Med. 1992;117:584.
73. Francis DP, Herrmann KL, MacMahon JR, et al. Nosocomial and maternally acquired herpesvirus hominis infections. Am J Dis Child. 1975;129:889.
74. Selling B, Kibrick S. An outbreak of herpes simplex among wrestlers (herpes gladiatorum). N Engl J Med. 1964;170:979.
75. Cesario T, Poland JD, Wulff H, et al. Six years' experience with herpes simplex virus in a children's home. Am J Epidemiol. 1969;90:416.
76. Wsooley P, Kudesia G. Incidence of herpes simplex virus type-1 and type-2 from patients with primary (first attack) genital herpes in Sheffield. Int J STD AIDS. 1990;1:184.
77. Rosato FE, Rosato EF, Plotkin SA. Herpetic-paronychia—an occupational hazard of medical personnel. N Engl J Med. 1970;283:804.
78. Light IJ. Postnatal acquisition of herpes simplex virus by the newborn infant: A review of the literature. Pediatrics. 1979;63:480.
79. Belongia EA, Goodman JL, Holland EJ, et al. An outbreak of herpes gladiatorum at a high-school wrestling camp. N Engl J Med. 1991;325:906.
80. Nahmias A, Dowdle WR, Josey WE, et al. Newborn infection with herpesvirus hominis types 1 and 2. J Pediatr. 1969;75:1194.
81. Quinn T, Corey L, Chaffee RG, et al. The etiology of anorectal infection in homosexual men. Am J Med. 1981;71:395.
82. Goldmeier D. Herpetic proctitis and sacral radiculomyelopathy in homosexual men. BMJ. 1979;2:549.
83. Corey L, Adams HG, Brown ZA, Holmes KK. Genital herpes simplex virus infection: Clinical manifestations, course and complications. Ann Intern Med. 1983;98:958.
84. Stanbury LR, Kern ER, Richards JT, et al. Genital herpes in guinea pigs: Pathogenesis of primary infection and description of recurrent disease. J Infect Dis. 1983;146:397.
85. Stanberry LR, Kit S, Myers MG. Thymidine kinase-deficient herpes simplex virus type 2 genital infection in guinea pigs. J Virol. 1985;55:322.
86. Rock DL, Fraser NW. Detection of HSV-1 genome in central nervous system of latently infected mice. Nature. 1983;302:523.
87. Lafferty WE, Coombs RW, Benedetti J, et al. Recurrences after oral and genital herpes simplex virus infection: Influence of anatomic site and viral type. N Engl J Med. 1987;316:1444–1449.
88. Landry ML, Zibello TA. Ability of herpes simplex virus (HSV) types 1 and 2 to induce clinical disease and establish latency following previous genital infection with the heterologous HSV type. J Infect Dis. 1988;158:1220.
89. Thomas E, Lycke E, Vahlne A. Retrieval of latent HSV type 1 genital infection by murine trigeminal ganglia by superinfection with heterotypic virus in vivo. J Gen Virol. 1985;66:1763.
90. Montgomerie JZ, Croxson MC, Becroft DMO, et al. Herpes simplex virus infection after renal transplantation. Lancet. 1969;2:867.
91. Meyers JD, Wade JC, Mitchell CD, et al. Multicenter collaborative trial of intravenous acyclovir for treatment of mucocutaneous herpes simplex virus infection in immunocompromised host. Am J Med. 1982;73:229.
92. Pass RF, Whitley RJ, Whelchel JD, et al. Identification of patients with increased risk of infection with herpes simplex virus after renal transplantation. J Infect Dis. 1979;140:487.
93. Kusne S, Schwartz M, Breinig MK, et al. Herpes simplex virus hepatitis after solid organ transplantation in adults. J Infect Dis. 1991;163:1001.
94. St. Geme J, et al. Impaired cellular resistance to herpes simplex virus in Wiskott-Aldrich syndrome. N Engl J Med. 1965;173:229.
95. Johnson JR, Egaas S, Gleaves CA, et al. Hepatitis due to herpes simplex virus in marrow-transplant recipients. Clin Infect Dis. 1992;14:38.
96. Muller SA, Herrmann EC Jr, Winkelmann RD. Herpes simplex infections in hematologic malignancies. Am J Med. 1972;52:102.
97. Ramsey PG, Fife KH, Hackman RC, et al. Herpes simplex virus pneumonia: Clinical, virological, and pathologic features in 20 patients. Ann Intern Med. 1982;97:813.
98. Kapor AK, Nash AA, Wildy P, et al. Pathogenesis of herpes simplex virus in congenitally athymic mice: The relative roles of cell-mediated and humoral immunity. J Gen Virol. 1982;60:225.
99. Simmons A, Tschmuke D, Speck P. The role of immune mechanisms in the control of HSV infection of the peripheral reservoir system. Curr Top Microbiol Immunol. 1992;179:31.
100. Dubin G, Fishman NO, Eisenberg RJ, et al. The role of herpes simplex virus glycoproteins in immune evasion. Curr Top Microbiol Immunol. 1992;179:111.
101. Norrild B, Shore SL, Cromeans TL, Nahmias AJ. Participation of three major glycoprotein antigens of herpes simplex virus type 1 early in the infectious cycle as determined by antibody-dependent cell-mediated cytotoxicity. Infect Immun. 1980;28:38.
102. Balachandran N, Bacchetti S, Rawls WE. Protection against lethal challenge of BALB/c mice by passive transfer of monoclonal antibodies to five glycoproteins of herpes simplex virus type-2. Infect Immun. 1982;37:1132.
103. Eisenberg R, Cerini CP, Heilman CJ, et al. Synthetic glycoprotein D–related peptides protect mice against herpes simplex virus challenge. J Virol. 1985;55:1014.
104. Notkins A. Immune mechanisms by which the spread of viral infections is stopped. Cell Immunol. 1974;11:478.
105. Manickan E, Rouse BT. Role of different T cell subsets in control of herpes simplex virus infection determined by using T-cell-deficient mouse-models. J Virol. 1995;69:8178.
106. Niemialtowski MG, Rouse BT. Cytotoxic T lymphocyte response to herpes simplex virus type 1 is composed of both $CD8^+$ and $CD4^+$ T cell phenotypes in acute and memory states. Arch Immunol Ther Exp Warsz. 1994;42:319.
107. Banks TA, Rouse BT. Herpesviruses: Immune escape artists? Clin Infect Dis. 1992;14:933.
108. York IA, Roop C, Andrews DW, et al. A cytosolic herpes simplex virus protein inhibits antigen presentation to $CD8^+$ T lymphocytes. Cell. 1994;77:525.
109. Posavad CM, Koelle DM, Corey L. Tipping the scales of herpes simplex virus reactivation: The important responses are local. Nature Med. 1998;4:381–382.
110. Tigges M, Levy S, Johnson DC, et al. Human herpes simplex virus (HSV)-specific

CD8+ CTL clones recognize HSV-2 infected fibroblasts after treatment with IFN-gamma or when virion host shutoff functions are disabled. J Immunol. 1996;156:3901.
111. Cunningham A, Turner RR, Miller AC, et al. Evolution of recurrent herpes simplex lesions. An immunohistologic study. J Clin Invest. 1985;75:226.
112. Koelle DM, Abbo H, Ziegwied K, et al. Direct recovery of HSV-specific T cell clones from human recurrent HSV-2 lesions. J Infect Dis. 1994;169:956.
113. Cunningham AL, Merican TC. γ Interferon production appears to predict time of recurrence of herpes labialis. J Immunol. 1983;130:2397.
114. Koelle D, Posavad C, Barnum GR, et al. Clearance of HSV-2 from recurrent genital lesions correlates with infiltration of HSV-specific cytotoxic T lymphocytes. J Clin Invest. 1998;101:1500.
115. Posavad CM, Koelle DM, Shaughnessy MF, Corey L. Severe genital herpes infections in HIV-infected individuals with impaired HSV-specific CD8+ CTL responses. Proc Nat Acad Sci USA. 1997;94:10289–10294.
116. Doymaz MZ, Rouse BT. Herpetic stromal keratitis: An immunopathologic disease mediated by CD4+ T lymphocytes. Invest Ophthalmol Vis Sci. 1992;33:2165.
117. Meyers-Elliott RH, Pettit TH, Maxwell WA. Viral antigens in the immune ring of herpes simplex stromal keratitis. Arch Ophthalmol. 1980;90:897.
118. Thomas J, Rouse BT. Immunopathogenesis of herpetic ocular disease. Immunol Res. 1997;16:375.
119. Zhao Z, Granucci F, Yeh L, et al. Molecular mimicry by herpes simplex virus-type 1: Autoimmune disease after viral infection. Science. 1998;279:1344–1347.
120. Corey L, Holmes KK. Genital herpes simplex virus infection: Current concepts in diagnosis, therapy and prevention. Ann Intern Med. 1983;98:973–983.
121. Reeves W, Corey L, Adams HG, et al. Risk of recurrence after first episodes of genital herpes: relation to HSV type and antibody response. N Engl J Med. 1981;305:315.
122. Benedetti J, Corey L, Ashley R. Recurrence rates of genital herpes after acquisition of symptomatic first episode infection. Ann Intern Med. 1994;121:847.
123. Glezen WP, Fernald GW, Lohr JA. Acute respiratory disease of university students with special reference to the etiologic role of herpesvirus hominis. Am J Epidemiol. 1975;101:111.
124. Schmitt DL, Johnson DW, Henderson FW. Herpes simplex type 1 infections in a group day care. Pediatr Infect Dis J. 1991;10:729.
125. Spruance ST, Overall JC Jr, Kern ER. The natural history of recurrent herpes simplex labialis—implications for antiviral therapy. N Engl J Med. 1977;297:69.
126. Bader C, Crumpacker CS, Schnipper LE, et al. The natural history of recurrent facial-oral infection with herpes simplex virus. J Infect Dis. 1978;138:897.
127. Young SK, Rowe NH, Buchanan RA. A clinical study for the control of facial mucocutaneous herpes virus infections. I. Characterization of natural history in a professional school population. Oral Surg Oral Med Oral Pathol. 1976;41:498.
128. Kriesel JD, Pisani PL, McKeough MB, et al. Correlation between detection of herpes simplex virus in oral secretions by PCR and susceptibility to experimental UV radiation-induced herpes labialis. J Clin Microbiol. 1994;32:3088.
129. Openshaw H, Bennett HE. Recurrence of herpes simplex virus after dental extraction. J Infect Dis. 1982;146:707.
130. Pazin GJ, Armstrong JA, Lam MT, et al. Prevention of reactivated herpes simplex infection by human leukocyte interferon after operation on the trigeminal root. N Engl J Med. 1978;301:225.
131. Shepp DH, Newton BA, Dandliker PA, et al. Oral acyclovir therapy for mucocutaneous herpes simplex virus infections in immunocompromised marrow transplant recipients. Ann Intern Med. 1985;102:783.
132. Straus SE, Smith HA, Brickman C, et al. Acyclovir for chronic mucocutaneous herpes simplex virus infection in immunosuppressed patients. Ann Intern Med. 1982;96:270.
133. Seigal FP, Lopez C, Hammer GS, et al. Severe acquired immunodeficiency in male homosexuals manifested by chronic perianal ulcerative herpes simplex lesions. N Engl J Med. 1981;305:1439.
134. Foley FD, Greenwald KA, Nash G, Pruitt BA Jr. Herpes virus infection in burned patients. N Engl J Med. 1970;282:652.
135. Hazen PG, Bennett-Eppes R. Eczema herpeticum caused by herpesvirus type 2. A case in a patient with Darier disease. Arch Dermatol. 1977;113:1085.
136. Garland SM, Hill PJ. Eczema herpeticum in pregnancy successfully treated with acyclovir. Aust NZ J Obstet Gynaecol. 1994;34:214.
137. Shelley WB. Herpes simplex virus as a cause of erythema multiforme. JAMA. 1967;201:153.
138. Bean SF, Quezada RK. Recurrent oral erythema multiforme: Clinical experience with 11 patients. JAMA. 1967;201:153.
139. Britz M, Sibulkin D. Recurrent erythema multiforme and herpes genitalis (type 2). JAMA. 1975;233:812.
140. Orton PW, Huff JC, Tonnesen MG, et al. Detection of a herpes viral antigen in skin lesions of erythema multiforme. Ann Intern Med. 1984;101:48.
141. Green JA, Spruance SL, Wenerstrom G, Piepkorn MW. Post-herpetic erythema multiforme prevented with prophylactic oral acyclovir. Ann Intern Med. 1985;102:632.
142. Valne A, Edstrom S, Arstila P, et al. Bell's palsy and herpes simplex virus. Arch Otolaryngol. 1981;107:72.
143. Furuta Y, Fukuda S, Chida E, et al. Reactivation of herpes simplex virus type 1 in patients with Bell's palsy. J Med Virol. 1998;54:162.
144. Burgess RC, Michaels L, Bale JR Jr, Smith RJ. Polymerase chain reaction amplification of herpes simplex viral DNA from the geniculate ganglion of a patient with Bell's palsy. Ann Otol Rhinol Laryngol. 1994;103:775.
145. Spruance SL. Bell palsy and herpes simplex virus. Ann Intern Med. 1994;120:1045.
146. Adams H. Genital herpetic infection in men and women: Clinical course and effect of topical application of adenine arabinoside. J Infect Dis. 1976;133:A151.
147. Vontver A, Reeves WC, Rattray M, et al. Clinical course and diagnosis of genital herpes simplex virus infection and evaluation of topical surfactant therapy. Am J Obstet Gynecol. 1979;133:548.
148. Mertz GJ, Critchlow C, Benedetti J, et al. Double-blind placebo-controlled trial of oral acyclovir in first-episode genital herpes simplex virus infection. JAMA. 1984;252:1147.
149. Bryson YJ, Dillon M, Lovett M, et al. Treatment of first episodes of genital herpes simplex virus infection with oral acyclovir. N Engl J Med. 1983;308:916.
150. Corey L, Fife KH, Benedetti JK, et al. Intravenous acyclovir for the treatment of primary genital herpes. Ann Intern Med. 1983;98:914.
151. Koutsky LA, Stevens CE, Holmes KK, et al. Underdiagnosis of genital herpes by current clinical and viral isolation procedures. N Engl J Med. 1992;326:1533–1539.
152. Stamm WE, Wagner KF, Amsel R, et al. Causes of the acute urethral syndrome in women. N Engl J Med. 1980;303:409.
153. Lehtinen M, Rantala I, Teisala J, et al. Detection of herpes simplex virus in women with acute pelvic inflammatory disease. J Infect Dis. 1985;152:78.
154. Schneider V, Behm FG, Mumaw VR. Ascending herpetic endometritis. Obstet Gynecol. 1982;59:259.
155. Morrisseau PM, Phillips CA, Leadbetter GW. Viral prostatitis. J Urol. 1970; 103:767.
156. Goodell S, Quinn TC, Mkrtichian E, et al. Herpes simplex virus proctitis in homosexual men: clinical, sigmoidoscopic, and histopathological features. N Engl J Med. 1983;308:868.
157. Goldmeier D. Proctitis and herpes simplex virus in homosexual men. Br J Vener Dis. 1980;56:111.
158. Schacker T, Hu HL, Koelle DM, et al. Famciclovir for the suppression of symptomatic and asymptomatic herpes simplex virus reactivation in HIV-infected persons. Ann Intern Med. 1998;128:21–28.
159. Rompalo A, Meitz GJ, Davis LG, et al. Oral acyclovir for treatment of first-episode herpes simplex virus proctitis. JAMA. 1988;259:2879–2881.
160. Wald A, Zeh J, Selke S, et al. Virologic characteristics of subclinical and symptomatic genital herpes infections. N Engl J Med. 1995;333:770–775.
161. Whitley R. Mucocutaneous herpes simplex virus infections in immunocompromised patients. Am J Med. 1982;73:236.
162. Tustin A, Kaiser A. Life threatening pharyngitis caused by herpes simplex virus type 2. Sex Trans Dis. 1979;6:23.
163. Skoldenberg B, et al. Herpes simplex virus 2 and acute aseptic meningitis. Scand J Infect Dis. 1975;7:227.
164. Ross C, Stevenson J. Herpes simplex meningoencephalitis. Lancet. 1961;2:682.
165. Klastensky J, Cappel R, Snoeck JM, et al. Ascending myelitis in association with herpes simplex virus. N Engl J Med. 1972;187:182.
166. Schlesinger Y, Tebas P, Gaudreault-Keener M, et al. Herpes simplex virus type 2 meningitis in the absence of genital lesions: Improved recognition with use of the polymerase chain reaction. Clin Infect Dis. 1995;20:842.
167. Tedder D, Ashley R, Tyler KL, et al. Herpes simplex virus infection as a cause of benign recurrent lymphocytic meningitis. Ann Intern Med. 1994;121:334–338.
168. Caplan L, Kleman FJ, Berg S. Urinary retention probably secondary to herpes genitalis. N Engl J Med. 1977;197:920.
169. Ravaut P, Darre M. Les reactions nerveuses au cours de herpes genitaux. Ann Derm Syph (Paris). 1904;5:481.
170. Brenton D. Hypoglycorrhachia in herpes simplex type 2 meningitis. Arch Neurol. 1980;37:317.
171. Goldmeier D, Bateman JR, Rodin P, et al. Urinary retention and intestinal obstruction associated with anorectal herpes simplex virus infection. Br Med J. 1975;1:425.
172. Oates J, Greenhouse P. Retention of urine in anogenital herpetic infection. Lancet. 1978;1:691.
173. Jacobs S, Jacobs SC, Herbert LA, et al. Acute motor paralytic bladder in renal transplant patients with anogenital herpes infection. J Urol. 1980;123:426.
174. Riehle R, Williams J. Transient neuropathic bladder following herpes simplex genitalis. J Urol. 1979;122:263.
175. Jacome D, Yanez G. Herpes genitalis and neurogenic bladder and bowel. J Urol. 1980;124:752.
176. Samarasinghe P, Oates JK, MacLennan IP, et al. Herpetic proctitis and sacral radiomyelopathy: A hazard for homosexual men. Br Med J. 1979;2:365.
177. Shturman-Ellstein R, Borkowsky W, Fish I, et al. Myelitis associated with genital herpes in a child. J Ped. 1976;88:523.
178. Crane L, Lerner A. Herpetic whitlow: A manifestation of primary infection with herpes simplex virus type 1 and 2. J Infect Dis. 1978;137:855.
179. Benedetti J, Zeh J, Selke S, et al. Frequency and reactivation of nongenital lesions among patients with genital herpes simplex virus. Am J Med. 1995;98:237.
180. Moedy JL, Lerman SJ, White RJ, et al. Fatal disseminated herpes simplex virus infection in a healthy child. Am J Dis Child. 1981;135:45.
181. Nahmias A. Dissiminated herpes simplex virus infections. N Engl J Med. 1979;282:684.
182. Ruchman I, Dodd K. Recovery of herpes simplex virus from the blood of a patient with herpetic rhinitis. J Lab Clin Med. 1950;35:434.
183. Friedman HM, Pincus T, Gibilisco P, et al. Acute monarticular arthritis caused by herpes simplex virus and cytomegalovirus. Am J Med. 1980;69:241.
184. Shelley W. Herpetic arthritis associated with disseminated herpes simplex virus and cytomegalovirus. Am J Med. 1980;69:241.
185. Flewett T, Parker RG, Philip WM, et al. Acute hepatitis due to herpes simplex in an adult. J Clin Pathol. 1969;22:60.
186. Joseph T, Bogt P. Disseminated herpes with hepatoadrenal necrosis in an adult. Am J Med. 1974;56:735.
187. Whittaker J, Hardson M. Severe thrombocytopenia after generalized HSV-2 infection. South Med J. 1978;72:864.

188. Schlesinger J, et al. Myoglobinuria associated with herpes group viral infections. Arch Intern Med. 1978;138:422.
189. Goyette R, et al. Fulminant hepatitis during pregnancy. Obstet Gynecol. 1974;43:191.
190. Young E, et al. Disseminated herpesvirus infection associated with primary genital herpes in pregnancy. JAMA. 1976;235:2731.
191. Koberman T, et al. Maternal death secondary to disseminated herpesvirus hominis. Am J Obstet Gynecol. 1980;137:742.
192. Hillard P, Seeds J, Cefalo R. Disseminated herpes simplex in pregnancy: Two cases and a review. Obstet Gynecol Surv. 1982;37:449.
193. Sutton A, et al. Fatal disseminated herpesvirus hominis type 2 infection in an adult with associated thymic dysplasia. Am J Med. 1974;56:545.
194. Keane J, et al. Herpesvirus hominis hepatitis and disseminated intravascular coagulation: Occurrence in an adult with pemphigus vulgaris. Arch Dermatol. 1976;93:1312.
195. Linnemann C, et al. *Herpesvirus hominis* type 2 meningo-encephalitis following renal transplantation. Am J Med. 1976;61:703.
196. Corey L, Nahmias AJ, Guinan ME, et al. A trial of topical acyclovir in genital herpes simplex virus infections. N Engl J Med. 1982;306:1313.
197. Frenkel LM, Garratty EM, Shen JP, et al. Clinical reactivation of herpes simplex virus type 2 infection in seropositive pregnant women with no history of genital herpes. Ann Intern Med. 1993;118:414.
198. Sacks S. Frequency and duration of patient-observed recurrent genital herpes simplex virus infection: Characterization of the nonlesional prodrome. J Infect Dis. 1984;150:873.
199. Morse S, et al. Comparison of clinical diagnosis and standard laboratory and molecular methods for the diagnosis of genital ulcer disease in Lesotho: Association with human immunodeficiency virus infection. J Infect Dis. 1997;175:01.
200. Chapel T, et al. Simultaneous infection with *Treponema pallidum* and herpes simplex virus. Cutis. 1979;24:191.
201. Catotti D, et al. Herpes revisited: Still a cause of concern. Sex Trans Dis. 1993;20:77.
202. Rand K, et al. Daily stress and recurrence of genital herpes simplex. Arch Intern Med. 1990;150:1889.
203. Wald A, Zeh J, Selke S, et al. Virologic characteristics of subclinical and symptomatic genital herpes infections. N Engl J Med. 1995;333:770–775.
204. Wald A, Corey L, Cone R, et al. Frequent genital herpes simplex virus 2 shedding in immunocompetent women: effect of acyclovir treatment. J Clin Invest. 1997;99:1092–1097.
205. Cone RW, Hobson AC, Brown Z, et al. Frequent reactivation of genital herpes simplex viruses among pregnant women. JAMA. 1994;272:792.
206. Wald A, Zeh J, Barnum G, et al. Suppression of subclinical shedding of herpes simplex virus type 2 with acyclovir. Ann Intern Med. 1996;124:8–15.
207. Benedetti JK, Zeh J, Corey L. Clinical reactivation of HSV-2 decreases in frequency over time. Ann Intern Med. 1999;131:14–20.
208. Rattray MC, Corey L, Reeves WC, et al. Recurrent genital herpes among women: Symptomatic versus asymptomatic viral shedding. Br J Vener Dis. 1978;54:262.
209. Mertz G, et al. Risk factors for the sexual transmission of genital herpes. Ann Intern Med. 1992;116:197.
210. Rooney J, et al. Acquisition of genital herpes from an asymptomatic sexual partner. N Engl J Med. 1986;314:1561.
211. Bryson Y, et al. Risk of acquisition of genital herpes simplex virus type 2 in sex partners of persons with genital herpes: a prospective couple study. J Infect Dis. 1993;167:942.
212. Mertz G, et al. Transmission of genital herpes in couples with one symptomatic and one asymptomatic partner: A prospective study. J Infect Dis. 1988;157:1169–1177.
213. Mertz G, et al. Frequency of acquisition of first-episode genital infection with herpes simplex virus from symptomatic and asymptomatic source contacts. Sex Trans Dis. 1985;12:33.
214. Douglas J, et al. A double-blind, placebo-controlled trial of the effect of chronic oral acyclovir on sperm production in men with frequently recurrent genital herpes. J Infect Dis. 1988;157:588.
215. Schacker T, Zeh J, Hu HL, et al. Frequency of symptomatic and asymptomatic HSV type 2 reactivation among HIV infected men. J Infect Dis. 1998;178:1616.
216. Krone MR, Tabet SR, Paradise M, et al. Herpes simplex virus shedding among HIV-negative men who have sex with men (MSM): Site and frequency of herpes shedding. J Infect Dis. 1998;178:978.
217. Moore D, et al. Transmission of genital herpes by donor insemination. JAMA. 1989;261:3441.
218. Greenblatt R, et al. Genital ulceration as a risk factor for human immunodeficiency virus infection. AIDS. 1988;2:47.
219. Stamm W, et al. Association between genital ulcer disease and acquisition of HIV infection in homosexual men. JAMA. 1988;260:1429.
220. Boulos R, et al. Herpes simplex virus type 2 infection, syphilis, and hepatitis B virus infection in Haitian women with human immunodeficiency virus type 1 and human T lymphotropic virus type 1 infections. J Infect Dis. 1992;166:418.
221. Hook E, et al. Herpes simplex virus infection as a risk factor for human immunodeficiency virus infection in heterosexuals. J Infect Dis. 1992;165:251.
222. Holmberg S, et al. Prior HSV type 2 infection as a risk factor for HIV infection. JAMA. 1988;259:1048.
223. Keet I, et al. Herpes simplex virus type 2 and other genital ulcerative infections as a risk factor for HIV-1 acquisition. Genitourin Med. 1990;66:330.
224. Telzak E, et al. HIV-1 seroconversion in patients with and without genital ulcer disease. Ann Intern Med. 1993;119:1181–1186.
225. Dickerson M, et al. The causal role for genital ulcer disease as a risk factor for transmission of human immunodeficiency virus: An application of the Bradford Hill criteria. Sex Trans Dis. 1996;23:429–440.
226. de Vincenzi I. A longitudinal study of human immunodeficiency virus transmission by heterosexual partners. N Engl J Med. 1994;331:341.
227. O'Farrell N, Torer ST. High cumulative incidence of genital herpes among HIV-1 seropositive heterosexuals in South London. Int J STD AIDS. 1994;5:415.
228. Albrecht M, et al. The herpes simplex virus immediate-early protein, ICP4 is required to potentiate replication of human immunodeficiency virus in $CD4^+$ lymphocytes. J Virol. 1989;63:1861.
229. Margolis DM, Rabson AB, Straus SE, Ostrove JM. Transactivation of the HIV-1 LTR by HSV-1 immediate early genes. Virology. 1992;186:788.
230. Koelle D, et al. Direct recovery of herpes simplex virus (HSV)-specific T lymphocyte clones from recurrent genital HSV-2 lesions. J Infect Dis. 1994;169:956.
231. Kucera L, et al. Human immunodeficiency virus type 1 (HIV-1) and herpes simplex virus type 2 (HSV-2) can coinfect and simultaneously replicate in the same human $CD4^+$ cell: Effect of coinfection on infectious HSV-2 and HIV-1 replication. AIDS Res Hum Retro. 1990;6:641.
232. Schacker T, Ryncarz AJ, Goddard J, et al. Frequent recovery of HIV-1 from genital herpes simplex virus lesions in HIV-1 infected men. JAMA. 1998;280:61.
233. Augenbraun M, et al. Increased genital shedding of herpes simplex virus type 2 in HIV-seropositive women. Ann Intern Med. 1995;123:845.
234. Conant MA. Prophylactic and suppressive treatment with acyclovir and the management of herpes in patients with acquired immunodeficiency syndrome. J Am Acad Dermatol. 1988;18:186.
235. Ioannidis JPA, Collier AC, Cooper DA, et al. Clinical efficacy of high dose acyclovir in human immunodeficiency virus infection: A meta-analysis of randomized individual patient data. J Infect Dis. 1998;178:349.
236. Gill J, et al. Herpes simplex virus infections of the hand. A profile of 79 cases. Am J Med. 1988;84:89.
237. Selling B, Kibrick S. An outbreak of herpes simplex among wrestlers (herpes gladiatorium). N Engl J Med. 1964;270:979.
238. Liesengang TJ, Melton III J, Daly PJ, Ilstrup DM. Epidemiology of ocular herpes simplex. Incidence in Rochester, Minn, 1950 through 1982. Arch Ophthalmol. 1989;107:1155.
239. Dawson CR, Togni B. Herpes simplex eye infections: Clinical manifestations, pathogenesis and management. Surv Ophthalmol. 1976;21:121.
240. Pepose JS, Leib DA, Stuart PM, Easty DL. Herpes simplex virus diseases: Anterior segment of the eye. In: Pepose JS, Holland GN, Wilhelmus KR, eds. Ocular Infection and Immunity. St. Louis: CV Mosby; 1996:905.
241. Culbertson WW, Blumenkrantz MS, Haines H, et al. The acute retinal necrosis syndrome. Ophthalmology. 1982;89:1317.
242. Forster DJ, Dugel PU, Frangieh GT, et al. Rapidly progressive outer retinal necrosis in the acquired immunodeficiency syndrome. Am J Ophthalmol. 1990;110:341.
243. Holland GN. Acquired immunodeficiency syndrome and ophthalmology. The first decade. Am J Ophthalmol. 1992;114:86.
244. Olson L, et al. Herpesvirus infections of the human central nervous system. N Engl J Med. 1967;172:1271.
245. Whitley R, et al. Adenine arabinoside therapy of biopsy-proved herpes simplex encephalitis. National Institute of Allergy and Infectious Diseases Collaborative Antiviral Study. N Engl J Med. 1977;197:389.
246. Whitley RH, Soong S-J, Hirsch MS, et al. Herpes simplex encephalitis. Vidarabine therapy and diagnostic problems. N Engl J Med. 1981;304:313.
247. Whitley R, Lakeman AD, Nahmias A, et al. DNA restriction-enzyme analysis of a herpes simplex virus isolate obtained from patients with encephalitis. N Engl J Med. 1982;307:1060.
248. Nahmias AJ, Whitley RJ, Visintine AM, et al. Herpes simplex virus encephalitis: laboratory evaluations and their diagnostic significance. J Infect Dis. 1982;145:829.
249. Fraser NW, Lawrence WC, Wroblewska A, et al. Herpes simplex type 1 DNA in human brain tissue. Proc Natl Acad Sci USA. 1981;78:6461.
250. Whitley RJ, Soong S-J, Linneman C Jr, et al. Herpes simplex encephalitis. Clinical assessment. JAMA. 1982;247:217.
251. Whitley RJ, Cobbs CG, Alford CA Jr, et al. Diseases that mimic herpes simplex encephalitis. Diagnosis, presentation, and outcome. JAMA. 1989;262:234.
252. Aurelius E, Johansson B, Skoldenberg B, et al. Rapid diagnosis of herpes simplex encephalitis by nested polymerase chain reaction assay of cerebrospinal fluid. Lancet. 1991;337:189.
253. Aurelius E, Johansson B, Skoldenberg B, Forsgren M. Encephalitis in immunocompetent patients due to herpes simplex virus type 1 or 2 as determined by type-specific polymerase chain reaction and antibody assays of cerebrospinal fluid. J Med Virol. 1993;39:179.
254. Rowley A, Lakeman F, Whitley R, Wolinsky S. Rapid detection of herpes simplex virus DNA in cerebrospinal fluid of patients with herpes simplex encephalitis. Lancet. 1990;335:440.
255. Lakeman FD, Whitley RJ. National Institute of Allergy and Infectious Disease CASG. Diagnosis of herpes simplex encephalitis: Application of polymerase chain reaction to cerebrospinal fluid from brain biopsied patients and correlation with disease. J Infect Dis. 1995;171:857.
256. Yamamoto LJ, Tedder DG, Ashley R, et al. Herpes simplex virus type 1 DNA in cerebrospinal fluid of a patient with Mollaret's meningitis. N Engl J Med. 1991;325:1082.
257. Kimura H, Futamura M, Kito H, et al. Detection of viral DNA in neonatal herpes simplex virus infections: Frequent and prolonged presence in serum and cerebrospinal fluid. J Infect Dis. 1991;164:289.
258. Whitley RJ, Alford CA, Hirsch MS, et al. Vidarabine versus acyclovir therapy in herpes simplex encephalitis. N Engl J Med. 1986;314:144.

259. McDonald GB, Sharma P, Hackman RC, et al. Esophageal infections in immunosuppressed patients after marrow transplantation. Gastroenterology. 1985;88:1111.
260. McBane RD, Gross JB. Herpes esophagitis: Clinical syndrome, endoscopic appearance, and diagnosis in 23 patients. Gastrointest Endosc. 1991;37:600.
261. Buss DH, Scharyj M. Herpes virus infection of the esophagus and other visceral organs in adults: incidence and clinical significance. Am J Med. 1979;66:457.
262. Graham BS, Snell JD. Herpes simplex virus infection of the adult lower respiratory tract. Medicine. 1983;62:384.
263. Tuxen DV, Cade JF, McDonald MI, et al. Herpes simplex virus from the lower respiratory tract in adult respiratory distress syndrome. Am Rev Respir Dis. 1982;126:416.
264. Montgomerie J, et al. Herpes simplex virus infection after renal transplantation. Lancet. 1969;2:867–871.
265. Wade J, et al. Intravenous acyclovir to treat mucocutaneous herpes simplex virus infection after marrow transplantation: A double-blind trial. Ann Intern Med. 1982;96:265.
266. Whitley R, et al. Infections caused by the herpes simplex virus in the immunocompromised host: Natural history and topical acyclovir therapy. J Infect Dis. 1984;150:323–329.
267. Meyers J, et al. Infection with herpes simplex virus and cell-mediated immunity after marrow transplant. J Infect Dis. 1980;142:338.
268. Saral R, et al. Acyclovir prophylaxis of herpes-simplex-virus infections: A randomized double-blind controlled trial in bone-marrow-transplant recipients. N Engl J Med. 1981;305:63.
269. Straus S, et al. Oral acyclovir to suppress recurring herpes simplex virus infection in immunodeficient patients. Ann Intern Med. 1984;100:522.
270. Shepp DH, Newton BA, Dandliker PS, et al. Oral acyclovir therapy for mucocutaneous herpes simplex virus infections in immunocompromised marrow transplant recipients. Ann Intern Med. 1985;102:783.
271. Nahmias A, et al. Perinatal risk associated with maternal genital herpes simplex virus infection. Am J Obstet Gynecol. 1971;110:825.
272. Forsgren M. Prevalence of antibodies to herpes simplex virus in pregnant women in Stockholm in 1969, 1983 and 1989: Implications for STD epidemiology. Int J STD AIDS. 1994;5:113.
273. Brown Z, et al. Neonatal herpes simplex virus infection in relation to asymptomatic maternal infection at the time of labor. N Engl J Med. 1991;324:1247.
274. Prober C, et al. Low risk of herpes simplex virus infections in neonates exposed to the virus at the time of vaginal delivery to mothers with recurrent genital HSV infections. N Engl J Med. 1987;316:240.
275. Nahmias AJ, Lee FK, Beckman-Nahmias S. Sero-epidemiological and -sociological patterns of herpes simplex virus infection in the world. Scand J Infect Dis Suppl. 1990;69:19–36.
276. Prober C, et al. The management of pregnancies complicated by genital infections with herpes simplex virus. Clin Infect Dis. 1992;15:1031.
277. Sullivan-Bolyai J, Hull HF, Wilson C, Corey L. Neonatal herpes simplex virus infections in King County, Washington. JAMA. 1983;250:3059–3062.
278. Malm G, Berg U, Forsgren M. Neonatal herpes simplex: Clinical findings and outcome in relation to type of maternal infection. Acta Paediatr. 1995;84:256.
279. Vontver L, et al. Recurrent genital herpes simplex virus infection in pregnancy: Infant outcome and frequency as asymptomatic recurrences. Am J Obstet Gynecol. 1982;143:75.
280. Brown Z, et al. Genital herpes in pregnancy: Risk factors associated with recurrences and asymptomatic shedding. Am J Obstet Gynecol. 1985;153:24.
281. Brown ZA, Benedetti JK, Selke S. Asymptomatic maternal shedding of herpes simplex virus at the onset of labor: relationship to preterm labor. Obstet Gynecol. 1996;87:483.
282. Yeager A, et al. Relationship of antibody to outcome in neonatal herpes simplex virus infections. Infect Immun. 1980;19:532.
283. Hain J, et al. Ascending transcervical herpes simplex infection with intact fetal membranes. Obstet Gynecol. 1980;56:106.
284. Florman A. Intrauterine infection with herpes simplex virus: Resultant congenital malformations. JAMA. 1973;225:129.
288. Hutto C, Arvin A, Jacobs R, et al. Intrauterine herpes simplex virus infections. J Pediatr. 1987;110:97.
289. Abrams CA. Isolation of herpes simplex from a mother and aborted fetus. Ghana Med J. 1966;5:41.
290. Kulhanjian J, et al. Identification of women at unsuspected risk of primary infection with herpes simplex virus type 2 during pregnancy. N Engl J Med. 1992;326:916.
291. Chalub E, et al. Congenital herpes simplex type II infection with extensive hepatic calcification, bone lesions and cataracts: Complete postmortem examination. Dev Med Child Neurol. 1977;19:527.
292. Naib Z, et al. Association of maternal genital herpetic infection with spontaneous abortion. Obstet Gynecol. 1970;35:260.
293. Libman MD, Dascal A, Kramer MS, et al. Strategies for the prevention of neonatal infection with herpes simplex virus: A decision analysis. Rev Infect Dis. 1991;13:1093.
294. Gibbs RS, Mead PB. Preventing neonatal herpes—current strategies. N Engl J Med. 1991;326:946.
295. Arvin A, et al. Failure of antepartum maternal cultures to predict the infant's risk of exposure to herpes simplex virus at delivery. N Engl J Med. 1986;315:796.
296. Sullivan-Bolyai J, et al. Presentation of neonatal HSV infections: Implications for a change in therapeutic strategy. Pediatr Infect Dis. 1986;5:309.
297. Whitley R, et al. Changing presentation of herpes simplex virus infection in neonates. J Infect Dis. 1988;158:109.
298. Light I, Linnemann C. Neonatal herpes simplex infection following delivery by cesarean section. Obstet Gynecol. 1974;44:496.
299. Frenkel L, et al. Pharmacokinetics of acyclovir in the term human pregnancy and neonate. Am J Obstet Gynecol. 1991;164:569.
300. Whitley R, et al. The natural history of genital herpes simplex virus infection of mother and newborn. Pediatrics. 1980;66:489.
301. Arvin AM, Yeager AS, Bruhn FW, Grossman M. Neonatal herpes simplex infection in the absence of mucocutaneous lesions. J Pediatr. 1982;100:715.
302. Whitley RJ, Arvin A, Prober C, et al. Predictors of morbidity and mortality in neonates with herpes simplex virus infections. N Engl J Med. 1991;324:450.
303. Parvey LS, Chien LT. Neonatal herpes simplex infection introduced by fetal monitor scalp electrodes. Pediatrics. 1980;65:1140.
304. Corey L, Whitley RJ, Stone EF, Mohan K. Difference in neurologic outcome after antiviral therapy of neonatal central nervous system herpes simplex virus type I versus herpes simplex virus type 2 infection. Lancet. 1988;2:1.
305. Whitley R, Arvin A, Prober C, et al. A controlled trial comparing vidarabine with acyclovir in neonatal herpes simplex virus infection. N Engl J Med. 1991;324:444.
306. Whitley RJ, Nahmias AJ, Soong S, et al. Vidarabine therapy of neonatal herpes simplex virus infection. Pediatrics. 1980;66:495.
307. Dorsky D, Crumpacker C. Acyclovir: Drugs 5 years later. Ann Intern Med. 1987;207:859.
308. Elion G, et al. Selectivity of action of an antiherpetic agent, 9-(2-hydroxyethoxymethyl)guanine. Proc Natl Acad Sci USA. 1977;79:5716–5720.
309. Schaeffer H, et al. 9-(2-Hydroxyethoxymethyl) guanine activity against viruses of herpes group. Nature. 1978;272:583.
310. Brigden D, Whitman P. The clinical pharmacology of acyclovir and its prodrug. Scand J Infect Dis. 1985;47(Suppl):33.
311. Coen D, Schaffer P. Two distinct loci confer resistance to acycloguanosine in herpes simplex virus type 1. Proc Natl Acad Sci USA. 1980;77:2265.
312. Crumpacker C, et al. Growth inhibition by acycloguanosine of herpes virus isolated from human infections. Antimicrob Agents Chemother. 1979;15:642.
313. Raborn GW, McGaw WT, Grace M, et al. Oral acyclovir and herpes labialis: A randomized, double-blind, placebo controlled study. J Am Dent Assoc. 1987;115:38.
314. Spruance SL, Stewart JCB, Rowe NM, et al. Treatment of recurrent herpes simplex labialis with oral acyclovir. J Infect Dis. 1990;161:185.
315. Rooney JF, Straus SE, Mannix ML, et al. Oral acyclovir to suppress frequently recurrent herpes labialis. A double-blind placebo-controlled trial. Ann Intern Med. 1993;118:268.
316. Reichman R, et al. Treatment of recurrent genital herpes simplex infections with oral acyclovir: A controlled trial. JAMA. 1984;251:2103.
317. Douglas J, et al. A double blind study of oral acyclovir for suppression of recurrences of genital herpes simplex virus infection. N Engl J Med. 1984;310:1551.
318. Straus S, et al. Suppressing of frequently recurring genital herpes: A placebo-controlled double blind trial of oral acyclovir. N Engl J Med. 1984;310:1545.
319. Mindel A, et al. Dosage and safety of long term suppressive therapy for recurrent genital herpes. Lancet. 1988;1:926.
320. Kaplowitz L, et al. Prolonged continuous acyclovir treatment of normal adults with frequently recurring genital herpes simplex virus infection. The Acyclovir Study Group. JAMA. 1991;265:747–751.
321. Goldberg L, et al. Long-term suppression of recurrent genital herpes with acyclovir. Arch Dermatol. 1993;129:582–587.
322. Hodge R, Cheng Y. The mode of action of penciclovir. Antiviral Chem Chemo. 1993;4S1:13.
323. Weinberg A, et al. In vitro activities of penciclovir and acyclovir against herpes simplex virus types 1 and 2. Antimicrob Agents Chemo. 1992;36:2037.
324. Pue M, Benet L. Pharmacokinetics of famciclovir in man. Antiviral Chem Chemo. 1993;4(s):47.
325. Sacks S, et al. Patient-initiated, twice-daily oral famciclovir for early recurrent genital herpes. A randomized, double-blind multicenter trial. JAMA. 1996;276:44.
326. Mertz G, et al. Oral famciclovir for suppression of recurrent genital herpes simplex virus infection in women: A multicenter, double-blind, placebo-controlled trial. Arch Intern Med. 1997;157:343.
327. Burnette T, et al. Purification and characterization of a rat liver enzyme that hydrolyzes valaciclovir, the L-valyl ester prodrug of acyclovir. J Biol Chem. 1995;270:15827.
328. Soul-Lawton J, et al. Absolute bioavailability and metabolic disposition of valaciclovir, the L-Val ester of acyclovir, following oral administration to humans. Antimicrob Agents Chemother. 1995;36:2759.
329. Reitano M, Tyring S, Levy W, et al. Valaciclovir for the suppression of recurrent genital HSV infection, a large scale dose range finding study. J Infect Dis. 1998;176:603.
330. Kimberlin DW, et al. Neonatal herpes simplex virus therapy. In press.
331. Erlich K, et al. Acyclovir-resistant herpes simplex virus infections in patients with the acquired immunodeficiency syndrome. N Engl J Med. 1989;320:293.
332. Englund JA, Zimmerman ME, Swierkoz EM, et al. Herpes simplex resistant to acyclovir. A study in a tertiary care center. Ann Intern Med. 1990;112:416.
333. Birch CJ, Tachedjian G, Doherty RR, et al. Altered sensitivity to antiviral drugs of herpes simplex isolates from a patient with acquired immunodeficiency syndrome. J Infect Dis. 1990;162:731.
334. Sacks S, et al. Progressive esophagitis from acyclovir-resistant herpes simplex. Clinical roles for DNA polymerase mutants and viral heterogeneity. Ann Intern Med. 1989;111:893–899.

335. Kost R, et al. Brief report: Recurrent acyclovir-resistant genital herpes in an immunocompetent patient. N Engl J Med. 1993;329:1777.
336. McLaren C, et al. In vitro sensitivity to acyclovir in genital herpes simplex viruses from acyclovir treated patients. J Infect Dis. 1983;148:868.
337. Nusinoff-Lehrman S, et al. Recurrent genital herpes and suppressive oral acyclovir therapy: Relationship between clinical outcome and in vitro drug sensitivity. Ann Intern Med. 1986;204:686.
338. Safrin S, et al. Correlation between response to acyclovir and foscarnet therapy and in vitro susceptibility result for isolates of herpes simplex virus from human immunodeficiency virus-infected patients. Antimicrob Agents Chemother. 1994;38:1246.
339. Engel J, et al. Treatment of resistant herpes simplex virus with continuous-infusion acyclovir. JAMA. 1990;263:1662–1664.
340. Safrin S, et al. Foscarnet therapy for acyclovir-resistant mucocutaneous herpes simplex virus infection in 26 AIDS patients: Preliminary data. J Infect Dis. 1990;161:1078.
341. Safrin S, et al. A controlled trial comparing foscarnet with vidarabine for acyclovir-resistant mucocutaneous herpes simplex in the acquired immunodeficiency syndrome. N Engl J Med. 1991;325:551.
342. Mendel D, et al. Biochemical basis for increased susceptibility to cidofovir of herpes simplex viruses with altered or deficient thymidine kinase activity. Antimicrob Agents Chemother. 1995;39:2120.
343. Lalezari J, et al. Treatment with intravenous (S)-1[3-Hydroxy-2(Phosphonylmethoxy) propyl]-cytosine of acyclovir resistant mucocutaneous infection with herpes simplex virus in a patient with AIDS. J Infect Dis. 1994;170:570.
344. Kessler H, et al. Pilot study of topical trifluridine for the treatment of acyclovir-resistant mucocutaneous herpes simplex disease in patients with AIDS (ACTG 172). J Acquir Immune Defic Syndr Hum Retrovirol. 1996;12:147.

Chapter 126

Varicella-Zoster Virus

RICHARD J. WHITLEY

Varicella-zoster virus (VZV) causes two distinct clinical diseases. *Varicella*, more commonly called chickenpox, is the primary infection and results from exposure of a person susceptible to the virus. Chickenpox is ubiquitous and extremely contagious, but for the most part, it is a benign illness characterized by a generalized exanthematous rash. It occurs seasonally and in epidemics. Recurrence of infection results in the more localized phenomenon known as *herpes zoster*, often referred to as shingles, a common infection among the elderly. A live, attenuated vaccine for the prevention of chickenpox is available in the United States and is recommended for use in normal children and in susceptible adults (see Chapter 312). The incidence of chickenpox has approached the annual birth rate: 3 to 4×10^6 cases yearly, although this is likely to be reduced as use of the vaccine becomes more widespread. Annually, from 300,000 to 500,000 persons seek medical care for chickenpox, and nearly half of these patients require a second office appointment. It is estimated that there are approximately 500,000 cases of herpes zoster yearly in the United States, which result in over 1.5 million physician visits per year. Many of these individuals require long-term follow-up medical care for postherpetic neuralgia.

HISTORICAL OVERVIEW

Shingles has been recognized since ancient times as a unique clinical entity because of the dermatomal vesicular rash; however, chickenpox was often confused with smallpox.[1] In 1875, Steiner successfully transmitted VZV by inoculation of the vesicular fluid from a person suffering from chickenpox to "volunteers."[2] The infectious nature of VZV was further defined by von Bokay, who observed chickenpox in persons who had close contact with others suffering from herpes zoster.[3, 4] He correctly described the mean incubation period for the development of chickenpox in susceptible patients as well as the average range in days. Kundratitz in 1925 showed that the inoculation of vesicular fluid from patients with herpes zoster into susceptible persons resulted in chickenpox.[5] Similar observations were reported by Brunsgaard[6] and others,[7] and in 1943 Garland suggested that herpes zoster was the consequence of the reactivation of latent VZV.[8]

Since early in the 20th century, similarities in the histopathologic features of skin lesions and in epidemiologic and immunologic studies indicated that varicella and herpes zoster were caused by the same agent.[9, 10] Tyzzer described the histopathologic features of skin lesions resulting from VZV infections and noted the development of intranuclear inclusions and multinucleated giant cells.[11] These descriptions came from histologic studies performed on serial skin biopsy specimens that were obtained during the first week of illness. The histopathologic descriptions were amplified by Lipschutz in 1921 for herpes zoster.[12]

Isolation of VZV in 1958 permitted a definition of the biology of this virus.[10] Viral isolates from patients with chickenpox and from patients with herpes zoster demonstrated similar changes in tissue culture, specifically the appearance of eosinophilic intranuclear inclusions and multinucleated giant cells. These findings are virtually identical to those encountered with clinically available biopsy material. Taken together, these data provided a universal acceptance that both diseases were caused by VZV. By 1958, Weller and colleagues had been able to establish that there were no differences between the viral agents isolated from patients with these two clinical entities from either a biologic or immunologic standpoint.[10, 13–15]

Later studies provided their identity by rigorous biochemical methods.[16] Viral DNA from a patient with chickenpox who subsequently developed herpes zoster was examined by restriction endonuclease analysis, and the molecular identity of these two viruses was verified.[17, 18]

THE PATHOGEN AND ITS REPLICATION

Varicella-zoster virus is a member of the Herpesviridae family and shares structural characteristics with other members of the family. The virus has icosapentahedral symmetry and contains centrally located double-stranded DNA with a surrounding envelope. The size of the virus is approximately 150 to 200 nm, and it has a lipid-containing envelope with glycoprotein spikes.[17] The naked capsid has a diameter of approximately 90 to 95 nm.[19–21] The DNA contains 125,000 base pairs, or approximately 80 megadaltons, and encodes approximately 75 proteins. The organization of the viral genome is similar to that of other herpesviruses. There are unique long (105 kilobases) and unique short (5.2 kilobases) regions of the viral genome. Each unique sequence contains terminal repeat sequences. With replication, the unique short (U_s) region can invert upon itself and result in two isomeric forms.[22–24]

Five families of VZV glycoproteins (gp) have been identified: gp I, gp II, gp III, gp IV, and gp V. The herpes simplex virus homologues are gE, gB, gH, U_s7, and gC, respectively. Viral infectivity can be neutralized by monoclonal antibodies directed against gp I, gp II, and gp III. These glycoproteins have been the subject of intense investigative interest because they represent the primary markers for both humoral and cell-mediated immunity.

Only enveloped virions are infectious; this may account for the lability of VZV. Furthermore, the envelope is sensitive to detergent, ether, and air drying.

Varicella-zoster virus is highly cell-associated and spreads from cell to cell by direct contact. Virus can be isolated in a variety of continuous and discontinuous cell culture systems of human and simian origin. Approximately 8 to 10 hours after infection, virus-specific immunofluorescence can be detected in the cells immediately adjacent to the initial focus of infection. This parallels the microscopic observation of the radial spread of the cytopathologic process.[25, 26] Electron microscopic studies demonstrate the appearance of immature viral particles within 12 hours of the onset of infection. As with herpes simplex virus, the naked capsids acquire their envelope at the nuclear membrane, being released into the perinuclear space where large vacuoles are formed.[19, 27] Infectious virus is then spread to adjacent cells after fusion of plasma membranes.

EPIDEMIOLOGY OF VARICELLA-ZOSTER VIRUS INFECTIONS

Chickenpox

Humans are the only known reservoir for VZV. Chickenpox follows exposure of the susceptible or seronegative person to VZV and represents the primary form of infection. Although it is assumed that the virus is spread by the respiratory route and replicates in the nasopharynx or upper respiratory tract, retrieval of virus from persons incubating VZV has been uncommon. However, the application of polymerase chain reaction (PCR) techniques to nasopharyngeal secretions of exposed and susceptible persons has detected VZV DNA, supporting this hypothesis. Chickenpox is a common infection of childhood and affects both genders equally and people of all races. To a certain extent, the virus is endemic in the population at large; however, it becomes epidemic among susceptible persons during seasonal periods, namely, late winter and early spring.[28] Intimate contact appears to be the key determinant for transmission.

Overall, chickenpox is a disease of childhood, because 90% of cases occur in children younger than 13 years of age. Typically, the virus is introduced into the susceptible school-aged or preschool child. In a study by Wells and Holla, 61 of 67 susceptible children in kindergarten through the fourth grade contracted chickenpox.[29] Approximately 10% of persons older than 15 years of age are considered susceptible to VZV infection. The incubation period of chickenpox, namely, the time interval between exposure of a susceptible person to an infected one, representing the index case, and the development of a vesicular rash is generally regarded as being 14 to 15 days, but disease can appear within a range of 10 to 20 days.[30, 31] Secondary attack rates in susceptible siblings within a household are between 70 and 90%.[32] Patients are infectious for a period of approximately 48 hours before the period of vesicle formation and generally 4 to 5 days thereafter until all vesicles are crusted.

Although chickenpox exists worldwide among children, it occurs more frequently in adults who reside in tropical regions than in those who reside in other geographic areas. Stokes noted a higher incidence of chickenpox among soldiers serving abroad during World War II, in whom the incidence was 1.41 to 2.27 per 1000 persons annually. These rates contrast with those in the United States, which were approximately half those reported among the soldiers.[33]

Herpes Zoster

The epidemiology of herpes zoster is somewhat different. VZV characteristically becomes latent after primary infection. The virus establishes latency within the dorsal root ganglia. Reactivation leads to herpes zoster, a sporadic disease. Histopathologic examination of the nerve root after infection with VZV demonstrates characteristics indicative of VZV infection. In persons who die after recent herpes zoster infection, an examination of the dorsal root ganglia reveals satellitosis, lymphocytic infiltration in the nerve root, and degeneration of the ganglia cells.[34, 35] Intranuclear inclusions can be found within the ganglia cells. Although it is possible to demonstrate the presence of VZV by electron microscopy, it has not been possible to isolate this virus in cultures, usually from explants of dorsal root ganglia, as has been done after herpes simplex virus infection. The biologic mechanism by which VZV establishes latency remains unknown.

Herpes zoster is a disease that occurs at all ages, but it will afflict about 20% or more of the population overall, mainly the elderly.[36, 37] Herpes zoster, known also as shingles, occurs in persons who are seropositive for VZV or, more specifically, in those who have had chickenpox. Reactivation appears to be dependent on a balance between virus and host factors. Most patients who develop herpes zoster have no history of exposure to other persons with VZV infection at the time of the appearance of lesions. The highest incidence of disease varies between 5 and 10 cases per 1000 for persons older than 60 years of age.[13] It has been suggested that approximately 4% of patients will suffer a second episode of herpes zoster; however, recurrences of dermatomal lesions are usually caused by herpes simplex virus. In a 7-year study performed by McGregor the annualized rate of herpes zoster was 4.8 cases per 1000 patients, three fourths of those patients being older than 45 years of age.[38] Persons who are immunocompromised have a higher incidence of both chickenpox and shingles.[39–42]

Herpes zoster has occurred within the first 2 years of life in children born to women who have had chickenpox during pregnancy. These particular cases probably reflect in utero chickenpox with reactivation early in life.

PATHOGENESIS

The pathogenesis of VZV infection that results in chickenpox reflects the natural history of the disease. Chickenpox occurs in susceptible persons who are exposed to virus after intimate contact. The appearance of a diffuse vesicular rash has been well studied from a pathologic standpoint. Histopathologic findings in human VZV infections, whether chickenpox or herpes zoster, are virtually identical. The vesicles involve the corium and dermis. As viral replication progresses, the epithelial cells undergo degenerative changes characterized by ballooning, with the subsequent appearance of multinucleated giant cells and prominent eosinophilic intranuclear inclusions. Under unusual circumstances, necrosis and hemorrhage may appear in the upper portion of the dermis. As the vesicle evolves, the collected fluid becomes cloudy as a consequence of the appearance of polymorphonuclear leukocytes, degenerated cells, and fibrin. Ultimately, either the vesicles rupture and release infectious fluid, or the fluid gradually becomes reabsorbed.

Transmission is likely by the respiratory route, followed by localized replication at an undefined site, which leads to seeding of the reticuloendothelial system and, ultimately, viremia. The occurrence of viremia in patients with chickenpox is supported by the diffuse and scattered nature of the skin lesions and can be verified in selected cases by the recovery of virus from the blood.[43] As noted, the mechanism of the reactivation of VZV that results in herpes zoster is unknown.

CLINICAL MANIFESTATIONS

Chickenpox

The medical importance of chickenpox should be stressed. There are approximately 250 deaths per year in the United States from this infection. For the normal child, chickenpox-associated mortality is less than 2 per 100,000 cases. This risk increases by more than 15-fold for adults. The presenting manifestations of chickenpox are a rash, low-grade fever, and malaise. A prodrome of symptoms may occur 1 to 2 days before the onset of the exanthem in a few patients. For the most part, chickenpox in the immunocompetent child is a benign illness associated with lassitude and a temperature of 100 to 103°F of only 3 to 5 days' duration. Constitutional symptoms that develop after the onset of rash include malaise, pruritus, anorexia, and listlessness. These symptoms gradually resolve as the illness abates. The skin manifestations, the hallmark of infection, consist of maculopapules, vesicles, and scabs in varying stages of evolution. The lesions initially contain clear vesicular fluid, but over a very short period of time they pustulate and scab. Most lesions are small, having an erythematous base with a diameter of 5 mm to as large as 12 to 13 mm. The lesions can be round or oval, with the occurrence of central umbilication as healing progresses. The lesions themselves have often been referred to as "dew-drop–like" during the early stages of formation. If they do not rupture within a few hours, the contents will rapidly become purulent in appearance. The lesions appear on the trunk and face and rapidly spread centripetally to involve other areas of the body. Successive crops of lesions generally appear over a period of 2 to 4 days. Thus, early in the disease, the hallmark of the infection is the appearance of lesions at all stages, as noted previously. The lesions can also be found on the mucosa of the oropharynx and even the vagina; however, these sites are less commonly involved. The crusts completely fall off within 1 to 2 weeks after the onset of infection and leave a slightly depressed area of skin.

Immunocompromised children, particularly those with leukemia, have more numerous lesions, often with a hemorrhagic base. Healing takes nearly three times longer in this population.[39] These children are at greater risk for visceral complications, which occur in 30 to 50% of cases and can be fatal in as many as 15% of cases. A notable complication of cutaneous lesions is secondary bacterial infection—often in association with gram-positive organisms. Streptococcal toxic shock is a rare but potentially lethal complication of varicella. Infection in the neutropenic host can be systemic.

The most frequent noncutaneous site of involvement after chickenpox is the central nervous system; the neurologic abnormalities are manifested as acute cerebellar ataxia or encephalitis.[28, 44–46] Cerebellar ataxia has been estimated to occur in 1 in 4000 cases among children younger than 15 years of age. Cerebellar ataxia can appear as late as 21 days after the onset of rash. It is more common, however, for acute cerebellar ataxia to present within a week of the onset of the exanthem. An extensive review by Underwood of 120 cases demonstrated that ataxia, vomiting, altered speech, fever, vertigo, and tremor all were common on physical examination.[46] Cerebrospinal fluid from these patients often demonstrates lymphocytosis and elevated levels of cerebrospinal fluid protein. This is usually a benign complication in children, and resolution occurs within 2 to 4 weeks. PCR techniques can be used to detect VZV DNA in the cerebrospinal fluid.[47]

A more serious central nervous system complication is encephalitis, which can be life-threatening in adults. Encephalitis is reported to occur in 0.1 to 0.2% of persons suffering from the disease.[48] Underwood's review reveals this illness to be characterized by depression in the level of consciousness with progressive headaches, vomiting, altered thought patterns, fever, and frequent seizures.[46] The duration of disease in these patients is at least 2 weeks. Some patients suffer from progressive neurologic deterioration leading to death. Mortality in patients who develop encephalitis has been estimated to range between 5 and 20%, and neurologic sequelae have been detected in as many as 15% of survivors.

A neurologic complication of note is the late appearance of cerebral angiitis after herpes zoster ophthalmicus. This problem has been noted in several patients and defined as being progressive, with a high mortality. Other nervous system manifestations of chickenpox include meningitis, transverse myelitis, and Reye's syndrome.

A serious and life-threatening complication is the appearance of varicella pneumonitis, a complication that occurs more commonly in adults and in immunocompromised persons.[28, 44, 49] Among adults, it is estimated to occur in 1 in 400 cases of infection and, not infrequently, in the absence of clinical symptoms. It generally appears 3 to 5 days into the course of illness and is associated with tachypnea, cough, dyspnea, and fever. Chest radiographs usually reveal nodular or interstitial pneumonitis. Varicella pneumonitis can be life-threatening when it occurs in pregnant women during the second or third trimester.

In a prospective study of male military personnel, radiographic abnormalities were detected in nearly 16% of enlisted men who developed varicella, yet only one quarter of these persons had evidence of cough.[50] Only 10% of those with radiographic abnormalities developed evidence of tachypnea, thus indicating that asymptomatic pneumonitis may exist more commonly than was initially predicted. Other manifestations of noncutaneous and non-neurologic involvement include the appearance of myocarditis, nephritis, bleeding diatheses, and hepatitis.

Perinatal varicella is associated with a high death rate when maternal disease develops 5 days before delivery or up to 48 hours post partum.[51, 52] In large part, this is the consequence of the fact that the newborn does not receive protective transplacental antibodies and of the immaturity of the neonatal immune system. It has been reported that under such circumstances, the mortality is as high as 30%. Affected children have progressive disease involving visceral organs, especially the lung. The outcome in these children has been summarized by Brunell.[53] Congenital varicella with clinical manifestations at birth is uncommon, but it has been characterized by skin scarring, hypoplastic extremities, eye abnormalities, and evidence of central nervous system impairment.[54]

Varicella has been associated epidemiologically with the development of Reye's syndrome.[55] The syndrome begins in the later stages of varicella with vomiting, followed by restlessness, irritability, and a progressive decrease in the level of consciousness, associated with progressive cerebral edema. The encephalopathy is associated with elevated levels of ammonia, a bleeding diathesis, hyperglycemia, and elevated serum transaminase levels.[56] The administration of aspirin as an antipyretic has been statistically associated with the development of Reye's syndrome. Therefore, administration of aspirin is contraindicated in persons with varicella.

Chickenpox in the Immunocompromised Patient

Chickenpox in the immunocompromised child or adult is a cause of significant morbidity and mortality. As noted previously, the duration of healing of cutaneous lesions can be extended by a minimum of threefold. However, a more important problem is the progressive involvement of visceral organs. Data from a variety of immunocompromised patient populations indicate a broad spectrum of disease in persons with lymphoproliferative malignancies and solid tumors versus bone marrow transplant recipients. In studies at St. Jude's Hospital by Feldman and colleagues, approximately one third of children developed progressive disease with involvement of multiple organs, including the lungs, liver, and central nervous system.[39] Most of these children developed pneumonitis within the first week after the onset of infection, as do 20% of all of those who acquire chickenpox. Mortality in this patient population has approximated 15 to 18%.[39, 57, 58] Patients with lymphoproliferative malignancies who require continuous chemotherapy appear to be at the greatest risk for visceral involvement.

In persons undergoing bone marrow transplantation, the incidence of VZV infections over the first year has been estimated to be 30% by 1 year after transplant. Eighty percent of these infections occurred within the first 9 months after transplantation, and 45% of these patients had cutaneous or visceral dissemination. Overall, 23 deaths occurred in one prospective series.[59] Risk factors identified for the acquisition of VZV infection included an age between 10 and 29 years, a diagnosis other than chronic myelogenous leukemia, the post-transplant use of anti-thymocyte globulin, allogenic transplant, and acute or chronic graft-versus-host disease. Notably, graft-versus-host disease increases the probability of visceral dissemination significantly.

Herpes Zoster

Herpes zoster, or shingles, is characterized by a unilateral vesicular eruption with a dermatomal distribution. Thoracic and lumbar dermatomes are most commonly involved. Herpes zoster may involve the eyelids when the first or second branch of the fifth cranial nerve is affected, but keratitis heralds a sight-threatening condition, herpes zoster ophthalmicus. Although lesions on the tip of the nose are said to presage corneal lesions, absence of such skin lesions does not guarantee corneal sparing. Keratitis may be followed by severe iridocyclitis, secondary glaucoma, or neuroparalytic keratitis. Ophthalmologic consultation should be requested for any patient with suspected herpes zoster ophthalmicus. Generally, the onset of disease is heralded by pain within the dermatome that precedes the lesions by 48 to 72 hours. Early in the disease course, erythematous, macropapular lesions appear that rapidly evolve into a vesicular rash. Vesicles may coalesce to form bullous lesions. In the normal host, these lesions continue to form over a period of 3 to 5 days, with the total duration of disease being 10 to 15 days. However, it may take as long as 1 month before the skin returns to normal.

Unusual cutaneous manifestations of herpes zoster, in addition to herpes zoster ophthalmicus, include the involvement of the maxillary or mandibular branch of the trigeminal nerve, which results in intraoral involvement with lesions on the palate, tonsillar fossa, floor of the mouth, and tongue. When the geniculate ganglion is involved, the Ramsay Hunt syndrome may occur, with pain and vesicles in the external auditory meatus, loss of taste on the anterior two thirds of the tongue, and ipsilateral facial palsy.

No known factors are responsible for the precipitation of the episodes of herpes zoster. If herpes zoster occurs in children, the course is generally benign and not associated with progressive pain or discomfort. In adults, systemic manifestations are mainly those associated with pain, as noted in the following paragraphs.

The most significant clinical manifestations of herpes zoster are the associated acute neuritis and, later, postherpetic neuralgia. Postherpetic neuralgia, although uncommon in young people, may occur in as many as 25 to 50% of patients older than 50 years of age.[60–62] As many as 50% of persons older than 50 years of age will have debilitating pain that persists for more than 1 month. Postherpetic neuralgia may cause constant pain in the involved dermatome or consist of intermittent stabbing pain. Pain may be worse at night or on exposure to temperature changes. At its worst, the neuralgia can be incapacitating, as recently reviewed.[63]

Extracutaneous sites of involvement include the central nervous system, as manifested by meningoencephalitis or encephalitis. The clinical manifestations are similar to those of other viral infections of the central nervous system. However, a rare manifestation of central nervous system involvement by herpes zoster is granulomatous cerebral angiitis, which usually follows zoster ophthalmicus. It should be noted that involvement of the central nervous system in cutaneous herpes zoster probably is more common than is recognized clinically. Frequently, patients who undergo cerebrospinal fluid examination for other reasons during episodes of shingles are found to have evidence of pleocytosis without elevated cerebrospinal fluid protein levels. These patients are without signs of meningeal irritation and infrequently complain of headaches.

Classically, VZV infection involves dorsal root ganglia. Motor paralysis can occur as a consequence of the involvement of the anterior horn cells, in a manner similar to that encountered with polio. Patients with involvement of the anterior horn cells are particularly likely to have excruciating pain. Other neuromuscular disorders associated with herpes zoster include Guillain-Barré syndrome, transverse myelitis[64] and myositis.[65, 66]

Herpes zoster in the immunocompromised patient is more severe than in the normal person. Lesion formation continues for up to 2 weeks, and scabbing may not take place until 3 to 4 weeks into the disease course.[42] Patients with lymphoproliferative malignancies are at risk for cutaneous dissemination and visceral involvement, including varicella pneumonitis, hepatitis, and meningoencephalitis. However, even in the immunocompromised patient, disseminated herpes zoster is rarely fatal.

In recent years, herpes zoster has been recognized as a frequent infection in persons with human immunodeficiency virus (HIV) infection, occurring in 8 to 11% of patients. Although the occurrence of cutaneous dissemination is infrequent, complications such as VZV retinitis, acute retinal necrosis, and chronic progressive encephalitis have been reported.[67]

Chronic herpes zoster may also occur in immunocompromised patients, particularly those persons with a diagnosis of HIV infection. Patients have experienced new lesion formation with an absence of healing of the existing lesions. These syndromes can be particularly debilitating and, of interest, have been associated with the isolation of VZV isolates resistant to acyclovir.

DIAGNOSIS

The diagnosis of both chickenpox and shingles is usually made by history and physical examination. In the latter part of the 20th century, the differential diagnosis of varicella and herpes zoster is less confusing than it was 20 to 30 years ago. Smallpox or disseminated vaccinia was confused with varicella because of the similar appearance of the cutaneous lesions. With the worldwide eradication of smallpox and the discontinuation of vaccination, these disease entities no longer confound the clinical diagnosis. For the most part, the characteristic skin rash with lesions in all stages of development provides the basis for the clinical diagnosis of infection. The presence of pruritus, pain, and low-grade fever also helps to establish a diagnosis of chickenpox. The localization and distribution of a vesicular rash make the diagnosis of herpes zoster highly likely; however, other viral exanthems can occasionally be confused with this disease.

Impetigo and varicella can also be confused clinically. Impetigo is usually caused by group A β-hemolytic streptococci, often follows an abrasion of the skin or inoculation of bacteria at the site of the skin break, and can be associated with the formation of small vesicles in the surrounding area. Systemic signs of disease may be present if progressive cellulitis or secondary bacteremia develops. Unroofing these lesions and careful Gram staining of the scraping of the base of the lesion should reveal gram-positive cocci in chains, which is suggestive of streptococci, or gram-positive cocci in clusters, which is suggestive of staphylococci, another cause of vesicular skin lesions. Treatment for these latter infections is distinctly different from that for chickenpox and requires administration of an appropriate antibacterial antibiotic.

In a smaller number of cases, disseminated vesicular lesions can be caused by herpes simplex virus. In these cases, disseminated herpes simplex virus infection is usually a consequence of an underlying skin disease such as atopic dermatitis or eczema. An unequivocal diagnosis can be made only by isolation of the virus in tissue culture.

More recently, it has been recognized that disseminated enteroviral infections, particularly those caused by group A coxsackieviruses, can cause widespread distal vesicular lesions. These rashes are more commonly morbilliform in nature, with a hemorrhagic component rather than vesicular or vesiculopustular appearance. Generally, these infections occur during the enterovirus season in late summer and early fall and are associated with lesions of the oropharynx, palms, and soles. This latter finding is helpful in distinguishing enteroviral disease from chickenpox.

Unilateral vesicular lesions in the dermatomal pattern should immediately lead the clinician to suspect a diagnosis of shingles. Herpes simplex virus infections and coxsackievirus infections can also cause dermatomal vesicular lesions. In such situations, diagnostic viral cultures remain the best method of establishing the cause of infection. Confirmation of the diagnosis is possible through the isolation of VZV in susceptible tissue culture cell lines or by the demonstration of either seroconversion or serologic rises using standard antibody assays of acute and convalescent serum specimens. A Tzanck smear, performed by scraping the base of the lesion, can demonstrate multinucleated giant cells; however, the sensitivity of this test is no better than 60%. Commercially available reagents are useful for direct fluorescent antibody staining of smears obtained from scraping vesicular lesions. With atypical skin lesions, such smears have adequate sensitivity and specificity to guide early management decisions. In research laboratories, PCR is being evaluated as a diagnostic tool. Useful antibody assays include immune adherence hemagglutination assay, fluorescence antibody to membrane antigen (FAMA) assay, or enzyme-linked immunosorbent assay (ELISA).[68]

The application of PCR to the cerebrospinal fluid can be used to detect VZV DNA and, therefore, infections of the central nervous system.

THERAPY

The medical management of chickenpox and shingles in the normal host is directed toward reduction of the risk of complications. For chickenpox, hygiene is important, including bathing, astringent soaks, and closely cropped fingernails to avoid a source for secondary bacterial infection associated with scratching of the pruritic skin lesions. Pruritus can be decreased with topical dressing or the administration of antipruritic drugs. Aluminum acetate or soaks with Burow's solution in the management of herpes zoster can be both soothing and cleansing.[69] Acetaminophen should be used to reduce fever in the child suffering from chickenpox because of the association between aspirin and Reye's syndrome.

Acyclovir is approved in the United States for the treatment of both chickenpox and herpes zoster in the normal host. Oral acyclovir therapy in normal children, adolescents, and adults shortens the duration of lesion formation by about 1 day, reduces the total number of new lesions by approximately 25%, and diminishes constitutional symptoms in one third of patients.[69–72] The American Academy of Pediatrics recommends therapy for adolescents and adults as well as for high-risk groups of patients (e.g., premature infants, children with bronchopulmonary dysplasia) within 24 hours of onset of disease. In children 2 to 16 years of age, the oral dosage is 20 mg/kg four times daily for 5 days (maximum of 800 mg qid). Adolescents and adults can receive up to 800 mg 5 times a day. Oral therapy of herpes zoster in the normal host accelerates cutaneous healing and reduces acute neuritis.

Acyclovir has been evaluated in controlled studies for all herpesvirus infections. Acyclovir is a guanine derivative that has a high degree of selectivity for the inhibition of VZV replication because of its selected phosphorylation and activation by the virus-coded thymidine kinase and its subsequent selective inhibition of the viral DNA polymerase. It is estimated that the concentration of acyclovir required to inhibit VZV replication in vitro is between 2.1 and 6.3 μM, which is a concentration easily achieved after intravenous administration of acyclovir.[73] It should be noted, however, that such concentrations are not easily achieved even after administration of high-dose oral acyclovir. These data have been summarized.[74]

The recommended dosage for acyclovir is from 5 to 10 mg/kg administered intravenously every 8 hours or, as suggested by some, 500 mg/m^2 intravenously every 8 hours, especially for children.

Recently, the prodrugs of acyclovir and penciclovir, namely, valaciclovir and famciclovir, respectively, have been licensed for therapy of herpes zoster.[75, 76] The use of valaciclovir results in enhanced oral bioavailability—approximately 60%, as compared with acyclovir. Famciclovir's oral bioavailability is approximately 80%. Both drugs appear superior to acyclovir for acceleration of cutaneous healing and are at least equally, if not more, efficacious for resolution of pain. Valaciclovir is administered at 1 g three times daily for 7 to 10 days.[75] Famciclovir is given at 500 mg three times daily for 7 to 10 days.[75] Both medications are well tolerated.

The concomitant administration of corticosteroids and an antiviral remains controversial. In one study, such regimens failed to affect postherpetic neuralgia, although resolution of acute neuritis was accelerated.[77] This study was not placebo-controlled. A more recent placebo-controlled trial, using a 2 × 2 factorial design, demonstrated significant improvement in quality of life.[78] Patients older than 50 years of age who received acyclovir (800 mg five times daily for 3 weeks) and tapering doses of prednisone (60 mg daily for 7 days, 30 mg daily for 7 days, and 15 mg daily for 7 days) experienced resolution of acute neuritis, were able to sleep uninterrupted, and returned to their usual activity levels more promptly than controls and also had lower analgesic requirements. Complications were not encountered; however, patients at risk for complications of high-dose steroid therapy were excluded.

Management of varicella pneumonitis and other complications requires excellent supportive nursing care in addition to evaluation, on an individual basis, of the potential need for antiviral therapy. The management of acute neuritis and postherpetic neuralgia can be particularly problematic. It requires the judicious use of analgesics ranging from non-narcotic to narcotic derivatives and may include the deployment of such drugs as amitriptyline hydrochloride and fluphenazine hydrochloride.

PREVENTION

In the normal host, prophylaxis of chickenpox is achieved by vaccination, as noted later on. The potential for transmission of VZV within the hospital to immunosuppressed patients, particularly children, is a serious problem, which is discussed in detail in Chapter 297. It is important to recognize that patients who require hospitalization because of varicella are a source of nosocomial infection within the hospital environment. Because approximately 10% of adults are seronegative, the risks in the medical care environment can be extremely high. Those most likely to become infected are nurses and medical personnel providing care to infected persons. Airflow can be documented as a means of transmission of infection from one area to another in the hospital environment.

In the immunocompromised person who has not been previously exposed to chickenpox, the administration of varicella-zoster immune globulin (VZIG) and varicella-zoster immune plasma (ZIP) has been shown to be useful for both prevention and amelioration of symptomatic chickenpox in high-risk persons.[79–82] VZIG should be administered to the immunodeficient patient younger than 15 years of age who has a negative or unknown history of chickenpox, who has not been vaccinated against VZV, and who has had contact in the household with a playmate or in a shared hospital room for more than 1 hour. Recent guidelines also recommend administration of VZIG to a pregnant woman who is known to be seronegative and who has had a significant exposure. VZIG should also be administered to a newborn infant whose mother had onset of chickenpox less than 5 days before delivery or up to 48 hours post partum. The use of VZIG for susceptible immunocompetent persons older than 15 years of age must be evaluated on an individual basis.

A vaccine is licensed for the prevention of chickenpox in immunocompetent persons.[83–89] Studies performed to date indicate a high probability of protection after vaccination.

The Oka strain of VZV has been developed by Takahashi and colleagues in Japan and studied as a vaccine extensively in both healthy and leukemic children. In immunocompromised children, serologic evidence of host response after vaccination has been achieved in between 89 and 100% of vaccinated individuals. These studies now have encompassed well over 1000 patients. Vaccine-induced rash, however, is not uncommon and occurs in variable percentages of patients from approximately 6% to as high as 47%. The factor most predictive of the appearance of rash is the degree of immunosuppression. Specifically, for children with acute lymphoblastic leukemia, the likelihood of rash can be as high as 40 to 50%. The subsequent occurrence of natural varicella after community exposure is decreased in the larger control studies and averages 8 to 16%. Vaccination did not appear to increase the likelihood of subsequent herpes zoster during the period of follow-up.

Similar studies have been performed in healthy children, with total numbers of subjects well in excess of 2000, as noted.[22] In these studies the development of antibody responses was higher than in the immunocompromised host and varied between 94% and 100%. Vaccine-induced rash was far less common in these individuals and occurred at a frequency of 0.5% to approximately 19% overall, with the rate for subsequent appearance of varicella after community exposure averaging between 1 and 5%. Theoretically, this vaccine might be useful for boosting immunity in older persons as a mechanism to prevent herpes zoster infection; however, this hypothesis remains to be tested. It should be noted that the risk of subsequent development of herpes zoster does not appear to be increased in vaccine recipients.[90]

REFERENCES

1. Gordon JE, Meader FM. The period of infectivity and serum prevention of chickenpox. JAMA. 1929;93:2013.
2. Steiner P. Zur Inokulation der Varicellen. Wein Med Wochenschr. 1875;25:306.
3. von Bokay J. Das Auftreten der Schafblattern uter besonderen Umstanden. Unger Arch Med. 1892;1:159.
4. von Bokay J. Uberden atiologischen zusammenhang der varizellen mit gewissen fallen von herpes zoster. Wein Klin Wochenschr. 1909;22:1323.
5. Kundratitz K. Experimentelle ubertragungen von herpes zoster auf menschen und die beziehungen von herpes zoster zu varicellen. Z Kinderheilkd. 1925;39:379.
6. Brunsgaard E. The mutual relation between zoster and varicella. Br J Dermatol Syph. 1932;44:1.
7. School Epidemics Committee of Great Britain. Epidemics in Schools. Medical Research Council. Special Report Series, No. 227. London: His Majesty's Stationary Office; 1938.
8. Garland J. Varicella following exposure to herpes zoster. N Engl J Med. 1943;228:336.
9. Seiler HE. A study of herpes zoster particularly in its relationship to chickenpox. J Hyg. 1949;47:253–262.
10. Weller TH, Witton HM. The etiologic agents of varicella and herpes zoster: Serologic studies with the viruses as propagated in vitro. J Exp Med. 1958;228:336–337.
11. Tyzzer EE. The histology of the skin lesions in varicella. Philippine J Sci. 1906;1:349.
12. Lipschutz B. Untersuchengen uber die Atiologies der Krankheiten der Herpesgruppe (Herpes Zoster, Herpes Genitalis, Herpes Febrilis). Arch Dermatol Syph. 1921;136:428.
13. Weller TH. Serial propagation in vitro of agents producing inclusion bodies derived from varicella and herpes zoster. Proc Soc Exp Biol Med. 1953;83:340–346.
14. Weller TH, Coons AH. Fluorescent antibody studies with agents of varicella and herpes zoster propagated in vitro. Proc Soc Exp Biol Med. 1954;86:789.
15. Weller TH, Stoddard MB. Intranuclear inclusion bodies in cultures of human tissue inoculated with varicella vesicle fluid. J Immunol. 1952;68:311.
16. Davison AJ, Scott JE. The complete DNA sequence of varicella-zoster virus. J Gen Virol. 1986;67:1759–1816.
17. Sawyer MH, Ostrove JM, Felser JM, et al. Mapping of the varicella-zoster virus deoxypyrimidine kinase gene and preliminary identification of its transcript. Virology. 1986;149:1–9.
18. Dumas AM, Geelen JL, Mares W, et al. Infectivity and molecular weight of varicella-zoster virus DNA. J Gen Virol. 1980;47:233–235.
19. Achong BC, Meurisse EV. Observations on the fine structure and replication of varicella virus in cultivated human amnion cells. J Gen Virol. 1968;3:305.
20. Almeida JD, Howatson AF, Williams MG. Morphology of varicella (chickenpox) virus. Virology. 1962;16:353.
21. Tournier P, Cathala F, Bernhard W. Ultrastructure et developpement intracellulaire du virus de la varicelle. Observe ou microscope electronique. Presse Med. 1957;65:1229.
22. Straus SE, Ostrove JM, Inchauspe G. Varicella-zoster virus infections: Biology, natural history, treatment and prevention. Ann Intern Med. 1988;108:221–237.
23. Gelb L. Varicella-zoster virus. In: Fields B, Knipe DM eds. Virology. New York: Raven Press; 1990:2011–2054.
24. Arvin AM. Varicella-zoster virus. In: Fields BN, Knipe DM, Howley PM, et al, eds. Fields Virology. 3rd ed. New York: Lippincott-Raven; 1996:2547.
25. Rapp F, Vanderslice D. Spread of zoster virus in human embryonic lung cells and the inhibitory effect of idoxyuridine. Virology. 1964;22:321.
26. Vaczi L, Geder L, Koller M, et al. Influence of temperature on the multiplication of varicella virus. Acta Microbiol Acad Sci Hung. 1963;10:109.
27. Grose C, Perrotta DM, Brunell PA, et al. Cell-free varicella-zoster virus in cultured human melanoma cells. J Gen Virol. 1979;43:15.
28. Preblud SR. Varicella: Complications and costs. Pediatrics. 1986;78:728–735.
29. Wells MW, Holla WA. Ventilation in the flow of measles and chickenpox through a community. JAMA. 1950;142:1337.
30. Preblud SR, Orenstein WA, Bart KJ. Varicella: Clinical manifestations, epidemiology, and health impact in children. Pediatr Infect Dis. 1984;3:505–509.
31. Hope-Simpson RE. Infectiousness of communicable diseases in the household (measles, chickenpox, and mumps). Lancet. 1952;2:549.
32. Ross AH. Modification of chickenpox in family contacts by administration of gamma globulin. N Engl J Med. 1962;267:369–376.
33. Stokes J Jr. Chickenpox. Communicable diseases transmitted chiefly through respiratory and alimentary tracts. In: Preventive Medicine in World War II. v. 4. Washington, DC: Department of the Army; 1958:55.
34. Bastian FO, Rabson AS, Yee CL, et al. Herpesvirus varicellae: Isolated from human dorsal root ganglia. Arch Pathol. 1974;97:331.
35. Esiri MM, Tomlinson AH. Herpes zoster: Demonstration of virus in trigeminal nerve and ganglion by immunofluorescence and electron microscopy. J Neurol Sci. 1972;15:35.
36. Ragozzino MW, Melton LJ III, Kurland LT, et al. Population-based study of herpes zoster and its sequelae. Medicine (Baltimore). 1982;51:310–316.
37. Hope-Simpson RE. The nature of herpes zoster: A long-term study and a new hypothesis. Proc R Soc Med. 1965;58:9.
38. McGregor RM. Herpes zoster, chickenpox, and cancer in general practice. Br Med J. 1957;1:84.
39. Feldman S, Hughes WT, Daniel CB. Varicella in children with cancer; Seventy-seven cases. Pediatrics. 1975;56:388–397.
40. Arvin AM, Pollard RB, Rasmussen LE, et al. Cellular and humoral immunity in the pathogenesis of recurrent herpes viral infections in patients with lymphoma. J Clin Invest. 1980;68:869–878.
41. Locksley RM, Flournoy N, Sullivan KM, et al. Infection with varicella-zoster virus after marrow transplantation. J Infect Dis. 1985;152:1172–1181.
42. Whitley RJ. Varicella-zoster infections. In: Galasso G, Merigan T, Buchanan R, eds. Antiviral Agents and Viral Infections of Man. New York: Raven Press; 1984:517–541.
43. Asano Y, Itakura N, Hiroishi Y, et al. Viremia is present in incubation period in nonimmunocompromised children with varicella. J Pediatr. 1985;106:69–71.
44. Fleisher G, Henry W, McSorley M, et al. Life-threatening complications of varicella. Am J Dis Child. 1981;135:896–899.
45. Johnson R, Milbourne PE. Central nervous system manifestations of chickenpox. Can Med Assoc J. 1970;102:831–834.
46. Underwood EA. The neurological complications of varicella: A clinical and epidemiological study. Br J Child Dis. 1935;32:83,177,241.
47. Burke DG, Kalayjian RC, Vann VR, et al. Polymerase chain reaction detection and clinical significance of varicella-zoster virus in cerebrospinal fluid from human immunodeficiency virus–infected patients. J Infect Dis. 1996;176:1080.
48. Johnson R, Milbourn PE. Central nervous system manifestations of chickenpox. Can Med J. 1970;102:831.
49. Triebwasser JH, Harrie RE, Bryant RE, et al. Varicella pneumonia in adults: Report of seven cases and a review of literature. Medicine (Baltimore). 1967;46:409–423.
50. Weber DM, Pellechia JA. Varicella pneumonia. JAMA. 1965;192:572.
51. Brunell PA. Fetal and neonatal varicella zoster infections. Semin Perinatol. 1983;7:47–56.
52. Preblud SR, Bregman DJ, Vernon LL. Deaths from varicella in infants. Pediatr Infect Dis. 1985;4:503–507.
53. Brunell PA. Placental transfer of varicella-zoster antibody. Pediatrics. 1966;38:1034.
54. Paryani SG, Arvin AM. Intrauterine infection with varicella zoster virus after maternal varicella. N Engl J Med. 1986;314:1542–1546.
55. Linnemann CC, Shea L, Partin JC, et al. Reye's syndrome: Epidemiologic and viral studies. Am J Epidemiol. 1975;101:517.
56. Hilty MD, Romshe CA, Delamater PV. Reye's syndrome and hyperaminoacidemia. J Pediatr. 1974;84:362.
57. Arvin AM, Kushner JH, Feldman S, et al. Human leukocyte interferon for treatment of varicella in children with cancer. N Engl J Med. 1982;306:761.
58. Whitley RJ, Soong SJ, Dolin R, et al. Early vidarabine therapy to control the complications of herpes in immunosuppressed patients. N Engl J Med. 1982;307:971.
59. Loxley RM, Flournoy N, Sullivan KM, et al. Infection with varicella-zoster virus after marrow transplantation. J Infect Dis. 1985;6:1172–1181.
60. deMoragas JM, Kierland RR. The outcome of patients with herpes zoster. Arch Dermatol. 1957;73:193–196.
61. Watson PN, Evans RJ. Postherpetic neuralgia; A review. Arch Neurol. 1986;43:836–840.
62. Esmann V, Kroon S, Petersblund NA, et al. Prednisolone does not prevent post-herpetic neuralgia. Lancet. 1987;2:126–129.
63. Kost RG, Straus SE. Drug therapy: Postherpetic neuralgia—pathogenesis, treatment, and prevention. N Engl J Med. 1996;335:32.
64. Hogan EL, Krigman MR. Herpes zoster myelitis. Arch Neurol. 1973;29:309.
65. Norris FH, Dramov B, Calder CD, et al. Virus-like particles in myositis accompanying herpes zoster. Arch Neurol. 1969;21:25.
66. Rubin D, Fusfeld RD. Muscle paralysis in herpes zoster. Calif Med. 1965;103:261.
67. Gnann JW, Whitley RJ. Natural history and treatment of varicella-zoster in high risk populations. J Hosp Infect. 1991;18:317–329.
68. Forghani B, Schmidt NJ, Dennis J. Antibody assays for varicella-zoster virus; comparison of enzyme immunoassay with neutralization, immune adherence hemagglutination and complement fixation. J Clin Microbiol. 1978;8:545–552.
69. Balfour HH, Kelly JM, Suarez, CS, et al. Acyclovir treatment of varicella in otherwise healthy children. J Pediatr. 1990;116:633–639.
70. Dunkle LM, Arvin LM, Whitley RW, et al. A controlled trial of acyclovir for chickenpox in the normal host. N Engl J Med. 1991;325:1539–1544.
71. Balfour HH, Dunkle LM, Feder HM, et al. Acyclovir treatment in otherwise healthy adolescents. J Pediatr. 1992;120:627–633.
72. Wallace MR, Bowler WA, Murray NB, et al. Treatment of adult varicella with oral acyclovir. A randomized, placebo-controlled trial. Ann Intern Med. 1992;117:358–363.
73. Huff JC, Bean B, Balfour HH, et al. Therapy of herpes zoster with oral acyclovir. Am J Med. 1988;85(2A):84–89.
74. Whitley RJ, Gnann JW. Acyclovir: A decade later. N Engl J Med. 1992;327:782–789.
75. Beutner KR, Friedman DJ, Forszpaniak C, et al. Valaciclovir compared with acyclovir for improved therapy for herpes zoster in immunocompetent adults. Antimicrob Agents Chemother. 1995;39:1546.
76. Tyring S, Barbarash, RA, Nahlik JE, et al. Famciclovir for the treatment of acute herpes zoster: Effects on acute disease and postherpetic neuralgia. A randomized,

double-blind, placebo-controlled trial. Collaborative Famciclovir Herpes Zoster Study Group. Ann Intern Med. 1995;123:89.
77. Wood MJ, Johnson RW, McKendrick MW, et al. A randomized trial of acyclovir for 7 days or 21 days with and without prednisolone for treatment of acute herpes zoster. N Engl J Med. 1994;330:896.
78. Whitley RJ, Weiss H, Gnann JW Jr, et al. Acyclovir with and without prednisone for the treatment of herpes zoster. A randomized placebo-controlled trial. The National Institute of Allergy and Infectious Diseases Collaborative Antiviral Study Group. Ann Intern Med. 1996;125:831.
79. Brunell PA, Ross A, Miller LH, et al. Prevention of varicella by zoster immune globulin. N Engl J Med. 1969;280:1191–1194.
80. Gershon AA, Steinberg S, Brunell PA. Zoster immune globulin: A further assessment. N Engl J Med. 1974;290:243–245.
81. Zaia J, Levin MJ, Preblud SR, et al. Evaluation of varicella zoster immune globulin: Protection of immunosuppressed children after household exposure to varicella. J Infect Dis. 1983;147:737–743.
82. Centers for Disease Control and Prevention. Varicella zoster immune globulin for the prevention of chickenpox: Recommendations of the immunization practices advisory committee. Ann Intern Med. 1984;100:859–865.
83. Takahashi M, Otsuka T, Okuno Y, et al. Live vaccine used to prevent the spread of varicella in children in hospital. Lancet. 1974;2:1288–1290.
84. Gershon AA, Steinberg SP, Gelb L. Live attenuated varicella vaccine use in immunocompromised children and adults. Pediatrics. 1986;78:757–762.
85. Takahashi M. Clinical overview of varicella vaccine: Development and early studies. Pediatrics. 1986;78:736–741.
86. Yabuuchi H, Baba K, Tsuda N, et al. A live varicella vaccine in a pediatric community. Biken J. 1984;27:43–49.
87. Horiuchi K. Chickenpox vaccination of healthy children: Immunological and clinical responses and protective effect in 1978–1982. Biken J. 1984;27:37–38.
88. Weibel RE, Neff BJ, Kutter BJ, et al. Live attenuated varicella virus vaccine: Efficacy trial in healthy children. N Engl J Med. 1984;310:1409–1415.
89. Asano Y, Nagai T, Miyata T, et al. Long-term protective immunity of recipients of the OKA strain of live varicella vaccine. Pediatrics. 1985;75:667–671.
90. Lawrence R, Gershon AA, Holzman R, et al. The risk of zoster after vaccination in children with leukemia. N Engl J Med. 1988;318:543–548.

Chapter 127

Cytomegalovirus

CLYDE S. CRUMPACKER

Human cytomegalovirus (HCMV) is a β herpes virus (see Chapter 124) and is the largest virus to infect human beings. Its genome is sufficient to encode 230 proteins, many of which play a significant role in downregulation of the immune response. Infection is common in all human populations, reaching 60 to 70% in urban U.S. cities[1] and nearly 100% in some parts of Africa. Disease is varied in humans infected with CMV, ranging from no disease in normal hosts; congenital CMV syndrome in neonates, which is frequently fatal; to the infectious mononucleosis syndrome in young adults. In the immunocompromised patient, CMV produces its most significant and severe disease syndromes in lung, liver, kidney, and heart transplant recipients. CMV is the most common opportunistic pathogen detected and causes significant mortality and morbidity.[2] In bone marrow transplant recipients, CMV pneumonia is the most common life-threatening infectious complication after transplantation.[3] In patients with the acquired immunodeficiency syndrome, CMV is the most common viral pathogen, and CMV retinitis is the most frequent sight-threatening infection even in the era of highly active antiretroviral therapy.[4] Fortunately, effective therapies for treatment and prevention of serious CMV disease in the immunocompromised patients are being established, and principles for the use of these therapies are becoming more clear.[5]

As with all the herpesviruses, CMV has the ability to establish latent infection in the host after recovery from acute infection. The exact mechanisms controlling latency are unclear, but polymorphonuclear cells, T lymphocytes, endothelial vascular tissue, renal epithelial cells, and salivary glands may all harbor the virus in a nonreplicating or slowly replicating form. Activation from this latent state can occur after immunosuppression, other illness, or the use of chemotherapeutic agents.[6]

Both primary and secondary infection with CMV can occur. Primary infection occurs in seronegative patients who have never been infected with CMV. Secondary infection represents activation of a latent infection or reinfection in a seropositive immune person. Infants and adults can be infected with multiple strains. Patients with AIDS have been shown to have several different strains of CMV present in the urine at the same time.[7] Clinical CMV disease can result from either primary or secondary infection, although in primary infection, virus usually replicates to a higher level and disease is more severe. Congenital infection of the neonate while in the mother's womb is almost always the result of primary infection of the mother during pregnancy.[8]

The emphasis in this chapter is on the clinical manifestations of CMV disease and the mechanisms of pathogenesis. Treatment and prevention of CMV disease with antiviral drugs has greatly changed the way CMV disease is managed in the immunocompromised patient and is highlighted. The limitations of antiviral therapy such as resistance to antiviral drugs are discussed.

DESCRIPTION OF THE PATHOGEN

The era of modern virology of CMV began with the isolation of murine CMV.[9] Shortly after the isolation of human CMV was reported by three independent groups led by Smith, Weller, Rowe, and their colleagues.[10–12] Human CMV was isolated from the human salivary gland and the term *cytomegalovirus* was first used to replace the term *salivary gland virus* or *cytomegalic inclusion disease virus*.[13] The first description of recognizable CMV disease in a normal healthy adult was in 1965.[14] A syndrome of CMV mononucleosis was found to occur sporadically and after transfusion with blood[15] or leukocyte products.[16]

Human CMV is the largest member of the human herpesvirus group and in fact is the largest known virus to infect humans. The CMV genome is a linear double-stranded DNA molecule of 230 million Da. The genome has been completely sequenced[17] and shown to contain nonoverlapping open reading frames for 230 proteins. Not all the proteins have been identified, and the functions of many of the proteins are not known. The laboratory strain AD169 has been the best studied and was the first strain to have its nucleotide sequence determined. The genome of AD169 has been shown to have a shorter genome than many clinical isolates and the Toledo strain of HCMV contains an additional 15 kb of DNA that is not present in strain AD169.[18] This large block of duplex DNA contains 19 genes encoding viral glycoproteins. The structure of the HCMV genome make it a member of the β group of human herpesviruses because it contains terminal repeat sequences that are complementary to each other. The HCMV genome contains a single origin of replication, and like all the human herpesviruses it encodes a DNA polymerase gene and a complete package of genes needed for its own DNA replication. The viral DNA polymerase is an important target for antiviral drugs, and all the current therapies for CMV disease inhibit the viral DNA polymerase as the final target.[5] The CMV DNA polymerase is encoded by a CMV open reading frame designated UL 54, and it has an important asssessory protein UL 44 that enhances the processivity of the DNA polymerase.[19] The UL 54 and UL 44 proteins form the functional complex of the complete DNA polymerase in infected cells.

The CMV genome also encodes a protein phosphotransferase enzyme, the product of UL97, whose role in CMV DNA replication is not well understood.[20] This UL97 protein is able to phosphorylate ganciclovir to form ganciclovir monophosphate, and this activation step is needed for ganciclovir to become an effective inhibitor of CMV DNA replication.[5, 21, 22] The role of UL 97 in CMV replication is still being defined, but recent work has shown that it is able to phosphorylate serine residues.[23] The UL97 protein may phosphorylate other proteins involved in DNA replication.

CMV also contains many genes that encode proteins directly involved in downregulating the host immune system as a way of evading immune control of the virus. One of the most important of these CMV proteins prevents cellular HLA-1 molecules from reaching the cell surface.[24] Thus, HLA-1 and CMV glycoproteins cannot form complexes on the cell surface to trigger recognition and destruction by $CD8^+$ T lymphocytes. This enables the CMV genome to remain in infected cells and avoid immune destruction.

In the infectious virion, CMV double-stranded DNA is wrapped in a nucleoprotein core, and this is surrounded by matrix proteins, the pp65 antigen of CMV, which is important for diagnosis of CMV, as it can be readily detected in the infected cells of patients by immunofluorescence, immunoperoxidase, and other antigen detection methods.[25] A lipid envelope surrounds the matrix and inner core, and this envelope contains many viral glycoproteins, which are involved in viral entry.

The cellular protein that serves as the specific receptor for CMV entry has not been identified, but CMV infects cells by a process of endocytosis. The CMV genome is uncoated within the cell, and the DNA protein core is transported to the nucleus of the cell. Following synthesis of viral DNA polymerase, CMV replication occurs in the nucleus of infected cells, and the large nuclear inclusions that are the hallmark of CMV infection in tissue culture and in infected cells from patients represent aggregates of replicating CMV nucleoprotein cores. Recognition of these CMV nuclear inclusions is valuable in establishing a diagnosis of CMV infection in patients.[26]

The ability of CMV to remain latent after infection contributes a great deal to serious CMV disease. Evidence for persistent CMV genomes and antigens exists in many tissues after initial infection, and CMV has been found in circulating mononuclear cells and in polymorphonuclear neutrophils.[27] CMV antigens have been detected in vascular endothelial cells, and this site has been suggested as a cause of vascular inflammation and development of atherosclerosis. Detection of cells containing CMV intranuclear inclusions in renal epithelial tissue and in pulmonary secretions provides evidence that CMV may persist in these tissues as well. The mechanisms controlling latency are not known, but CMV's ability to evade immune destruction of infected cells by downregulating cell surface markers such as HLA-1, may contribute to the capacity of the virus to remain undetected.[24] When immune suppression occurs in patients by HIV infection or by immunosuppressive therapy such as OKT3 antibody infusion,[28] CMV can reactivate and grow to high titers, producing end-organ disease.

Previous claims that CMV had oncogenic properties are now regarded with great skepticism. CMV is not associated with immortalization of cells in culture or enhanced proliferation of cell DNA; rather, CMV infection may be associated with cellular arrest or decreased growth. CMV is not closely linked to any tumor in immunocompromised patients and as distinguished from the oncogenic associations of viruses such as Epstein-Barr virus (see Chapter 128).

LABORATORY DIAGNOSIS

The laboratory diagnosis of CMV infection depends on the growth of the virus from urine or other body fluids or on the demonstration of virion components such as viral antigens or viral DNA. Diagnosis almost always depends on laboratory confirmation and cannot be made on clinical grounds alone. The first useful laboratory test relied on the detection of large nuclear inclusion–bearing cells in the urine sediment.[26] This was particularly useful in the newborn period, and the associated disease was called cytomegalic inclusion disease of infancy. Growth of virus in human fibroblast cultures (MRC-5 cells) was laborious and required several weeks for cell cultures to grow the virus. The culture technique could be greatly speeded up with the use of "shell vials" of cultured cells in which immediate early antigens were detected by the use of monoclonal antibodies.[25, 29]

The direct detection of antigens in neutrophils by the use of a monoclonal antibody against the CMV matrix protein pp65 has proved particularly useful.[30] This test provides a direct measure for the presence of CMV and can detect CMV antigen in the spinal fluid of patients with CMV polyradiculopathy syndrome as well as in the peripheral blood of immunocompromised patients. Other methods to detect CMV DNA or RNA have employed labeled viral nucleic acid probes and nucleic acid hybridization in body fluids or tissue specimens.[1, 31, 32]

The polymerase chain reaction (PCR), employing primers in the gene encoding CMV immediate early antigen[33] or the CMV DNA polymerase,[34] has provided a very sensitive technique with which to detect CMV. The PCR can detect small amounts of CMV DNA in many body fluids. It has been useful in the detection of CMV DNA in the cerebrospinal fluid of patients with CMV encephalitis or the CMV polyradiculopathy syndrome.[35, 36]

In 1997, three important papers described the use of PCR to detect CMV DNA in the blood of AIDS patients and showed that the presence of CMV DNA could predict the development of CMV retinitis several months later.[37–39] Although all three studies employed different PCR techniques, these papers showed remarkable agreement with positive predictive value of approximately 60% in correlating the presence of CMV DNA with the subsequent development of clinical disease. Quantitative PCR has also been employed to show that a high quantitative number of CMV DNA copies/ml of plasma was correlated with CMV disease activity in patients with AIDS.[40] The PCR assay for CMV DNA is also revolutionizing the approach to the management of CMV disease in liver, kidney, and bone marrow transplant recipients[41] (see further on). With the availability of effective antiviral therapy, a goal of management is to prevent CMV disease by using the PCR assay to detect CMV DNA in plasma before end-organ disease has developed. Antiviral therapy can then be used to lower CMV DNA levels and prevent development of CMV end-organ disease. This approach has been labeled "preemptive therapy."[42] CMV antigen detection in cerebrospinal fluid cells and cerebrospinal fluid DNA levels by PCR has provided comparable information on the course of antiviral therapy for CMV infection of the central nervous system (CNS).[43] Another study has suggested that prophylactic treatment with ganciclovir may be better than CMV antigen–guided preemptive therapy in preventing CMV pneumonia in the first 100 days after transplantation.[44] Further comparative studies on the use of the assays in plasma and neutrophils are needed to assess their relative merits in different clinical conditions. As further studies become available, rapid laboratory diagnosis and its correlation with clinical conditions and outcomes will likely significantly change the clinical management of multiple aspects of CMV disease.

CULTIVATION OF CYTOMEGALOVIRUS

HCMV has been cultured in human cells only, and previous claims that CMV could be grown in other animal cells have not been substantiated.[45] Although CMV can be readily cultured in human fibroblast cells, growth is characteristically slow. It may require 1 to 4 weeks of growth to develop the typical cytopathic changes in tissue culture. CMV produces characteristic infected cells, which are large, rounded, and contain "ground glass"–appearing inclusions in the cytoplasm. These infected cells are the hallmark of CMV and indicate the presence of CMV in the sample.[26]

CMV can be readily isolated from urine, mouth swabs, buffy coat, cervical tissue, and tissues obtained by biopsy or at post mortem examination. Virus is demonstrable even in the presence of neutralizing antibody.

CMV is not usually cultured from normal adults and may be difficult to culture from blood even in immunocompromised patients. Virus may be cultured from the cervix in healthy women[46] and from semen in healthy homosexual men.[47]

The growth of CMV from throat, urine, or blood is an abnormal finding, but only culture from blood is highly suggestive of a pathogenic CMV infection because CMV in throat or urine is frequently associated with asymptomatic infection. Patients recovering from acute CMV mononucleosis may shed CMV in the urine and throat for several weeks. Immunosuppressed patients may also shed CMV in throat washings or bronchoalveolar lavage. In the latter cases, the presence of histologic changes, such as intranuclear inclusions, is needed to establish a diagnosis of CMV pneumonitis.[26]

CYTOMEGALOVIRUS MONONUCLEOSIS

A primary infection with CMV in a young adult can produce an infectious mononucleosis syndrome with fever, lymphadenopathy, and relative lymphocytosis. It is estimated that 79% of infectious mononucleosis is caused by the Epstein-Barr virus (EBV) (see Chapter 128), and the other 21% is caused by acute CMV infection.[48] The heterophile agglutinin test is negative in CMV mononucleosis and usually positive in EBV mononucleosis. Another distinguishing feature between disease caused by these two viruses is that of a sore throat with enlarged, exudate covered tonsils which is more common with EBV infection. The CMV-induced infectious mononucleosis syndrome has been termed *typhoidal* because the symptoms may be more systemic in nature, with fever predominating and fewer signs of enlarged lymph nodes or splenomegaly.[48]

The hematologic hallmark of the infectious mononucleosis syndrome is a relative lymphocytosis, in which greater than 50% of the peripheral white blood cell differential is composed of lymphocytes. Of these, 10% or greater should be atypical lymphocytes that possess abnormal nuclei and exhibit rosetting around red blood cells.

The landmark study defining the clinical features of infectious mononucleosis was an 8-year prospective study on 494 cases by investigators from Finland.[48] In that study, 79% had a positive heterophile-agglutinin and had acute EBV infection. There were 73 patients older than 15 years of age who had a negative heterophil response, and 33 of these patients (45%) had CMV infection. The first serum taken 3 to 20 days after the onset of disease showed that 11 of 19 patients were seronegative (titer $\leq$1:4) and experienced a rise in complement-fixing antibodies. The peak titer was reached 4 to 7 weeks after the onset of disease. The presence of CMV in the urine was documented in 10 of 12 patients tested. This analysis led to the conclusion that CMV mononucleosis represents a primary infection in previously seronegative persons. The age range of infected patients was 18 to 66 years with a median of age 29 years; which was higher than in the group with EBV-induced mononucleosis. Fever was common in all patients and persisted from 9 to 35 days, with a mean of 19 days. The lymphocytosis in these patients varied from 55 to 86%, with 12 to 55% of total leukocytes being atypical lymphocytes. In the CMV-infected patients, pharyngitis and tonsillitis were rare. The enlargement of lymph nodes and the spleen was not a prominent feature of CMV mononucleosis, although this can occur. Low-level liver function abnormalities are regular features of CMV mononucleosis and can be an important clue to diagnosis. The occurrence of severe hepatitis or jaundice is rare.

CMV mononucleosis may occur without a clear source, but "kissing" and direct transfer of infected lymphocytes and polymorphonuclear cells is sometimes identified as a source. Other forms of intimate sexual contact are also important in the transmission of CMV.

The most clearly identified source for transmission of CMV and EBV is blood transfusion. CMV is also readily transmitted by transfusion of leukocytes alone.[49] The more units of transfused blood a patient receives, the greater the risk of being infected from this source. When large amounts of blood have been transfused. CMV should be considered as a source of postoperative fever. The risk of transmission of CMV from blood has been greatly reduced by screening blood for the presence of antibodies and eliminating units from seropositive donors.[46, 50]

In both CMV- and EBV-induced mononucleosis, laboratory abnormalities of transient immunologic aberrations can occur. These abnormalities include the appearance of cold agglutinins, rheumatoid factor, mixed cryoglobulinemia, antinuclear antibodies and anticomplementary activity.[48]

ASSOCIATED COMPLICATIONS

A series of associated findings can occur with CMV infection and these may be the initial manifestation of disease even in the normal host. The following sections describe these complications.

Interstitial Pneumonia

Interstitial pneumonia is the most severe complication of CMV disease in the bone marrow transplant patient, and it may also occur uncommonly in CMV-induced mononucleosis in the normal host. In the large series from Finland,[48] CMV pneumonitis occurred in 2 of 33 patients. The main findings are seen as interstitial infiltrates on chest radiographs, which eventually clear (Fig. 127–1). This is in sharp distinction to the finding of CMV pneumonitis in bone marrow transplant recipients, in whom CMV pneumonitis has a high mortality rate even with aggressive antiviral therapy. CMV pneumonitis in the setting of CMV mononucleosis is usually mild, and no treatment is required.

Hepatitis

Hepatitis is commonly associated with CMV mononucleosis, but it is usually mild and rarely symptomatic in the immunocompetent patient. A 21-year-old immunocompetent patient has been described in whom infectious hepatitis was suspected and who had a large and tender liver but did not have atypical lymphocytes. CMV was isolated from the urine and the patient had a significant rise in complement-fixing antibodies, which confirmed a diagnosis of acute CMV infection.[51] Granulomatous hepatitis may also be an initial manifestation of CMV infection accompanying mononucleosis.[52] In these patients, fever, vomiting, and a profound atypical lymphocytosis of

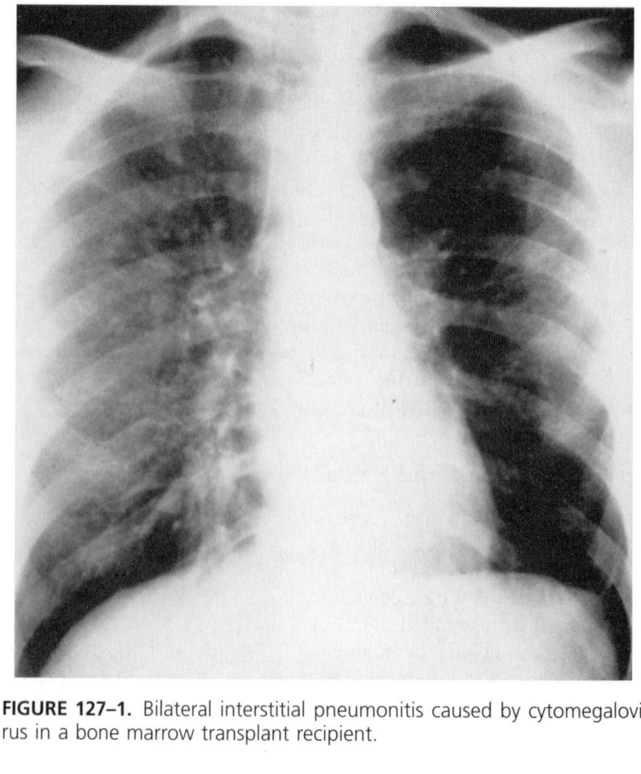

FIGURE 127–1. Bilateral interstitial pneumonitis caused by cytomegalovirus in a bone marrow transplant recipient.

nearly 50% has been noted. CMV was isolated from the throat and a diagnostic rise in complement-fixing antibodies was found. Liver biopsy in these patients revealed a resolving hepatitis with mononuclear cells infiltrating portal areas along with microscopic granulomas with giant cells. In the setting of acute CMV infection, hepatitis usually resolves fully. When scattered microscopic granulomas are found on liver biopsy, CMV infection should be considered.

Guillain-Barré Syndrome

The association of the Guillain-Barré syndrome and CMV mononucleosis was initially described in 1971 with nine patients having acute CMV mononucleosis who presented with polyneuritis characterized by sensory and motor weakness in the extremities. Cranial nerve involvement was also common, and four patients were treated in the respiratory unit.[53] Return of sensation was followed by motor improvement, and complete recovery required about 3 months for most patients.

In a large series of 94 cases of Guillian-Barré syndrome, acute CMV infection was documented in 10 cases.[54] In 9 of 10 of these patients, there was a high IgM immunofluorescent antibody titer on the initial specimen, and this showed a decline that was diagnostic for acute CMV infection by the time of discharge. The complement fixation antibody titer was already elevated in these patients, and no further rises were observed. All these patients had atypical lymphocytes in a blood smear, and all recovered.

The strongest evidence that CMV may be a direct cause of polyradiculopathy and myopathy is found in AIDS, in which CMV inclusions have been demonstrated in the nuclei of Schwann cells in association with a syndrome of motor weakness leading to a loss of bowel and bladder control (see further on).[55]

Meningoencephalitis

In association with CMV-induced infectious mononucleosis, meningoencephalitis has been infrequently reported in immunocompetent patients.[56] These patients may also have motor and sensory weakness, which is very similar to polyradiculopathy. The presence of severe headache, photophobia, lethargy, and pyramidal tract findings are features more indicative of meningocephalitis. The spinal fluid usually shows a moderate number of lymphocytes. In both CMV meningoencephalitis and CMV polyradiculopathy, the presence of CMV DNA detected by PCR can be helpful in establishing a diagnosis.[35, 36]

Myocarditis

A complication of CMV-induced mononucleosis can be myocardial involvement. In three of eight cases, inversion of T waves was noted.[57] One of the patients was a 14-year-old boy who died with serologic evidence of acute CMV infection, hepatitis, myocarditis, and consumptive coagulopathy. Another report described a 43-year-old immunocompetent woman who acquired myocarditis, heart failure, encephalitis, hepatitis, and adrenal insufficiency.[58] At autopsy, CMV was cultured from the adrenals. In children with congenital CMV infection, myocardial involvement is rarely reported.

Thrombocytopenia and Hemolytic Anemia

Thrombocytopenia and hemolytic anemia occur regularly in children with congenital CMV disease and also occasionally occur as a complication of CMV mononucleosis in healthy adults. A 33-year-old man with serologic evidence of acute CMV infection and viruria experienced a profound decrease in platelet count to 500/mm^3, a hemolytic anemia and hemoglobin of 3.6 g/dl, and a reticulocyte count of 12%.[59] The patient had a generalized purpura and bleeding gums and recovered completely with prednisone treatment. In a 26-year-old man with acute CMV infection, who presented with thrombocytopenia and purpura, a decreased red cell survival and elevated reticulocyte count were demonstrated.[60]

Skin Eruptions

Maculopapular and rubelliform rashes may also occur in the setting of CMV mononucleosis. These rashes may also develop after administration of ampicillin[61] and are thought to result from immunologic reactions to cellular antigens that are uncovered or expressed in association with the acute CMV infection. In an unusual report, a 40-year-old man with acute CMV viremia and viruria acquired epidermolysis 8 weeks after the onset of hepatitis.[62] Thus, the skin manifestation of acute CMV infection are usually mild, but can occasionally be severe.

CYTOMEGALOVIRUS INFECTION IN PATIENTS WITH ACQUIRED IMMUNODEFICIENCY SYNDROME

The profound immunodeficiency caused by infection with the human immunodeficiency virus-1 (HIV-1) results in defects in cellular immunity to many common infectious agents, including CMV. Coinfection with CMV has been noted in greater than 90% of homosexual men with HIV-1 infection by serologic status.[63] A high percentage of homosexual men also have CMV detected in the urine, even in the absence of HIV-1 infection.[64] Patients who are infected with HIV-1 and have a decrease in CD4 cells to less than 100 cells/mm^3 have a significantly increased risk for the development of serious CMV disease.

CMV is the most common viral opportunistic infection in patients with AIDS, and it has been estimated that 21 to 44% of patients with AIDS acquired CMV disease in the era before the availability of highly active antiretroviral therapy (HAART).[4] CMV retinitis is by far the most common form of CMV disease and usually occurs when the CD4 cell count falls to less than 50 cell/mm^3.[65] Autopsy studies have shown that up to 81% of HIV-infected patients had clinical or pathologic evidence of CMV disease by the time they died, and 32% had CMV retinitis.[66] Retinal disease due to CMV occurs only rarely in patients with bone marrow or solid organ transplants. CMV retinitis causes a complete-thickness infection through the retinal cells and results in progressive retinal destruction leading to blindness in 4 to 6 months. Now that HAART is able to suppress HIV, the incidence of CMV end-organ disease has decreased by more than 80%.[67] This has greatly changed the management of CMV retinitis, which is discussed in detail in Chapter 116.[4] The most likely reason for the reduction in CMV disease is an improvement in CMV-specific immune responses occurring with HAART.[68]

CMV retinitis is diagnosed predominantly on the basis of its clinical appearance. The characteristic appearance is a white fluffy retinal infiltrate occurring with several areas of hemorrhage (Fig. 127–2). It can also occur as a granular white area without hemorrhage. This form must be distinguished from cotton wool spots, which occur on the retinal tissue of patients with AIDS and are unrelated to CMV.

Initially, treatment of CMV retinitis was intravenous ganciclovir for 3 weeks at a dose of 7.5 to 15 mg/kg/day in three divided doses for 14 to 21 days, followed by a maintenance regimen of 5 to 6 mg/kg/day for 5 to 7 days per week[69] to prevent a relapse. Oral ganciclovir, despite its low oral bioavailability of 8%,[70] administered at a dose of 1000 mg taken three times a day, was found to be nearly equivalent to intravenous ganciclovir in preventing progression and preserving vision, particularly if the initial CMV retinitis was not sight-threatening.[71] Oral ganciclovir is not approved for initial treatment of CMV retinitis.

The use of a sustained-release ganciclovir implant device plus oral ganciclovir (4.5 g/day) to prevent infection in the other eye has significant advantages in the therapy for CMV retinitis. The device

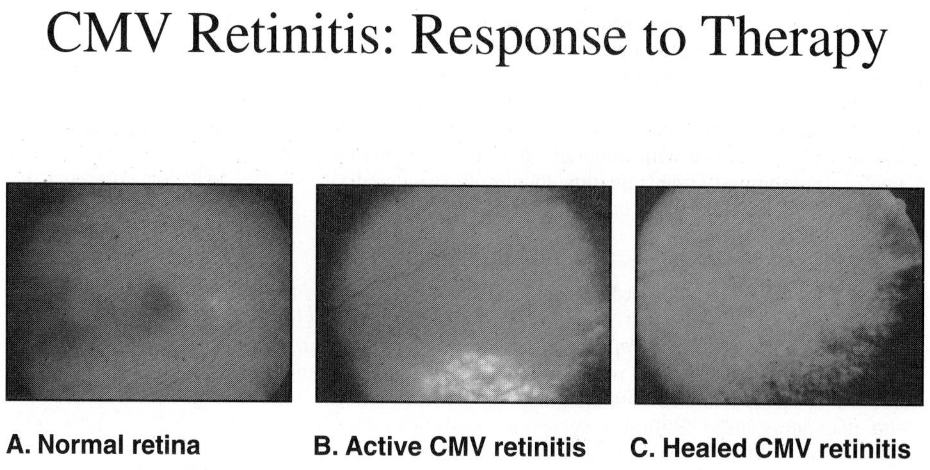

FIGURE 127–2. Cytomegalovirus (CMV) retinitis: response to therapy. *A*, Normal retina; *B*, active CMV retinitis; *C*, healed CMV retinitis. (Courtesy of Baruch D. Kuppermann, M.D., Ph.D.)

is implanted surgically in the eye and does not interfere with vision. The implant releases a high intravitreal concentration of ganciclovir that maintains adequate levels of drug for 8 to 10 months.[71] New implants that can release ganciclovir for up to 2 years are now in use. The ganciclovir implant plus oral ganciclovir was able to prevent relapse of CMV retinitis for about 270 days in 25% of patients. This was far superior to patients on intravenous ganciclovir alone and compared favorably with patients receiving implant and intravenous ganciclovir. The incidence of severe complications of ganciclovir toxicity, namely, marrow suppression leading to neutropenia and thrombocytopenia, was also decreased by approximately 40% in patients receiving oral ganciclovir.[71] However, in patients who recived oral ganciclovir at a dose of 4.5 g/day there was a higher rate of neutropenia than in those who received either intravenous ganciclovir or placebo, limiting this effective dose for some patients.[73] Another important benefit in patients who received oral ganciclovir at a dose of 4.5 g/day with the ganciclovir implant was a statistically significant decrease in the occurrences of Kaposi's sarcoma associated with AIDS.[73] Kaposi's sarcoma is closely linked with human herpesvirus 8 (see Chapter 130), and this virus is sensitive to ganciclovir in vitro.

Central Nervous System

In patients with AIDS, the most common CNS infection caused by CMV is polyradiculopathy.[55] This syndrome has a characteristic onset of ascending weakness in the lower extremities associated with a loss of deep tendon reflexes and ultimately loss of bowel and bladder control. The syndrome frequently begins as low back pain with a radicular or perianal radiation, followed in 1 to 6 weeks by a progressive flaccid paralysis. Marked pathologic changes are found in the cauda equina and lumbosacral nerve roots with a distinct mononuclear cell infiltrate destruction of axons, and CMV inclusion in Schwann cells and epithelial cells.[55] Lumber puncture reveals a characteristic picture of polymorphonuclear cells, mildly elevated protein, and a modest lowering of cerebrospinal fluid sugar. The findings are frequently mistaken for those of a bacterial meningitis, but bacterial cultures are negative. The diagnosis is usually made by detection of CMV DNA by PCR in the spinal fluid,[35, 36] or culture of CMV from the spinal fluid.

Treatment with ganciclovir has improved the weakness and polyradiculopathy in a few patients who were treated with ganciclovir alone or with ganciclovir and foscarnet early in the disease,[74, 75] but treatment with ganciclovir alone has generally been disappointing.[76] Some of the disappointing results of treatment may be due to the fact that only about one third of the plasma concentration of intravenous ganciclovir is found in the cerebrospinal fluid, and the CNS may represent a privileged site where only low concentrations of ganciclovir penetrate.[77]

The current favored treatment for CMV polyradiculopathy is early therapy with ganciclovir and foscarnet, even though no vigorous clinical trials to document benefit have been published. Anecdotal observations have been reported that suggest that CMV meningoencephalitis in patients with AIDS will respond to ganciclovir and foscarnet.[78]

Other CNS findings in patients with AIDS include mononeuritis multiplex and painful peripheral neuropathy, which have been attributed to CMV.[79] The benefits of antiviral therapy for those conditions are uncertain.

CYTOMEGALOVIRUS DISEASE OF THE GASTROINTESTINAL TRACT

Infection of the gastrointestinal tract with CMV had been frequent in patients with AIDS before the era of HAART. CMV can cause ulcers in the esophagus, and patients present with pain and difficulty swallowing. By endoscopic examination, shallow ulcers are seen. The diagnosis of CMV esophagitis is made by demonstration of intranuclear inclusions on biopsy specimens of the ulcers or by culture of CMV from biopsy tissue.

Patients with AIDS may also present with explosive watery diarrhea as a result of CMV colitis. Fever is common with CMV colitis, and occasionally bloody diarrhea may be present. The diagnosis is made by sigmoidoscopy which reveals plaquelike pseudomembranes, numerous erosions, and serpiginous ulcers.[80]

CMV colitis may also present as a mass lesion producing partial obstruction or with lesions that resemble Kaposi's sarcoma.[81] CMV may be present in the colon with other pathogens such as *Mycobacterium avium* complex and *Cryptosporidium*. With severe CMV colitis, perforation and gangrene have been described, although CMV infection alone may not be the only organisms found in association with those findings. The diagnosis of CMV colitis is made by biopsy, which demonstrates typical CMV inclusion bodies, or culture of CMV from biopsy material. The CMV inclusion bodies are usually seen in the mucosal epithelium[80] or mucosal crypts.[81] The first report of successful treatment of CMV colitis was with ganciclovir in 1986[82] followed by a placebo-controlled study with intravenous ganciclovir at a dose of 5 mg/kg for 14 days, in which there was a reduction in the frequency of CMV-infected colonic and urinary cultures in the ganciclovir treatment group, compared with the placebo group ($p = .03$ and $p < .001$, respectively). Colonoscopy scores improved more frequently in those who received ganciclovir (23% of patients) compared with 9% in the placebo group ($p = .03$).[83] However, diarrhea persisted at the end of treatment in both groups. These results suggest that treatment for 14 days may be inadequate for the colon to heal and diarrhea to resolve. In another study in bone marrow transplant patients with CMV colitis who were treated with ganciclovir, the cultures became negative with ganciclovir treatment, but gastrointestinal symptoms improved in both the ganciclovir- and placebo-treated groups, and ganciclovir had no apparent clinical benefit.[84] There is no evidence that maintenance therapy with ganciclovir is useful in preventing a relapse of CMV colitis.

Other parts of the digestive system can be infected with CMV. Patients with AIDS may acquire acute CMV pancreatitis.[85] Cholecystitis has been associated with the presence of CMV in the bile duct, gallbladder, and biliary tree,[85] including acalculous cholecystitis, papillary stenosis, and sclerosing cholingitis.[86]

ANTIVIRAL THERAPY

Three antiviral drugs that act to inhibit the viral DNA polymerase have been shown to be effective in treating CMV end-organ disease and have been approved for use in the United States. They are ganciclovir, foscarnet, and cidofovir (see Chapters 36 and 116). Another drug, valacyclovir, appears to delay the time to retinitis progression in patients with CMV retinitis.[86] An antisense inhibitor of CMV, Fomivirsen, can be used for direct injection into intravitreal fluid for treatment of CMV retinitis and has also been recently approved.[88] These drugs have been used to treat many forms of CMV disease in patients with AIDS and other immunocompromised patients, for example, recipients of bone marrow transplants or solid organ transplants. Individual drugs that have been useful in treatment of CMV-associated disease are discussed in the following sections.

Ganciclovir

Ganciclovir is a nucleoside analogue of guanosine and a homologue of acyclovir. Ganciclovir was the first antiviral drug to be demonstrated to be effective in the treatment of CMV disease in humans.[5, 89–91] It inhibits all the herpesviruses and blocks transformation of normal cord blood lymphocytes by EBV.[92, 93]

For antiviral activity, ganciclovir required phosphorylation by a viral-specific enzyme, but CMV does not have a thymidine kinase enzyme homologue to the herpes simplex virus thymidine kinase. The phosphotransferase product of the UL 97 gene of CMV converts ganciclovir to ganciclovir monophosphate. The monophosphate is then phosphorylated by cellular enzymes to the triphosphate. Ganciclovir triphosphate is a potent inhibitor of the CMV DNA polymerase enzyme. Ganciclovir triphosphate is a competitive inhibitor of the incorporation of deoxyguanosine triphosphate into elongating viral DNA. After cleavage of the pyrophosphate, ganciclovir monophosphate is incorporated into the end of the growing chain of viral DNA, greatly slowing replication.[94] Ganciclovir is not an absolute chain terminator, and short fragments of CMV DNA continue to be synthesized.[95, 96] All the drug's antiviral effects are due to the ability to inhibit the synthesis of CMV DNA and CMV replication by slowing elongation of viral DNA.[5]

The half-life of ganciclovir triphosphate in CMV-infected cells is 16.5 hours, compared with only 2.5 hours for acyclovir triphosphate.[97] Although ganciclovir triphosphate is not as effective an inhibitor of CMV DNA polymerase as is acyclovir triphosphate, this concentration of ganciclovir triphosphate in CMV-infected cells is 10 times the concentration of acyclovir triphosphate.[97] The high level of ganciclovir triphosphate and the prolonged intracellular half-life make ganciclovir a more effective inhibitor of CMV replication in vivo than acyclovir.

Resistance to Ganciclovir

The major mechanism of CMV resistance to ganciclovir is by the selection of mutants that are unable to phosphorylate ganciclovir. These viruses have mutations in two main regions of the UL97 protein. These are point mutations at codon 460 and point mutations or deletions around codons 590 to 596.[98, 99] A mutation at codon 520 also confers an inability to phosphorylate ganciclovir.[100] Ganciclovir-resistant viruses that have mutations or deletions in regions of the UL97 protein that affect nucleotide binding and phosphate transfer have also been described.

CMV clinical isolates that were resistant to ganciclovir were first reported in 1989.[101] These isolates were from three immunocompromised patients with CMV disease who had disease progression and died despite therapy, and in whom all viral cultures remained positive. In a subsequent study of 72 patients with CMV retinitis who were receiving maintenance ganciclovir therapy, 80% became culture-negative after 3 months of treatment.[102] In those who remained culture-positive, resistant CMV was isolated in 38%, with an overall incidence of 8%, and resistance was clearly associated with disease progression. Nine resistant strains of CMV were obtained from these 72 patients, and all failed to phosphorylate ganciclovir (Fig. 127–3).[103] All the strains remained sensitive to foscarnet, a drug that acts directly on the viral DNA polymerase (see farther on).

Another mechanism of resistance to ganciclovir is by mutations that occur in the CMV DNA polymerase gene.[104] These have been identified in clinical isolates and are less common than mutations in the UL97 gene.[105] CMV strains with mutations in both the UL97 and CMV DNA polymerase gene have also been reported.[166] These exhibit a very high degree of resistance with an ID_{50} (50% inhibiting concentration) greater than 30 μM. The inhibitory concentration for CMV clinical isolates that are sensitive to ganciclovir is 6.0 μM or less.[106] Some clinical isolates reveal an intermediate sensitivity between 6 and 12 μM. In a study to correlate mutations in either the UL97 gene or the DNA polymerase with resistance, the presence of a mutation in either gene was associated with an ID_{50} greater than 7 μM.[105] In an analysis of variability in the DNA polymerase gene of CMV, among 40 clinical isolates that were all sensitive to ganciclovir and foscarnet, less than 4% variability was found among all the isolates. No mutations were found in highly conserved regions of the viral DNA polymerase in wild type isolates, indicating that mutations that occur in these highly conserved regions are more likely to be a result of selection by antiviral drugs.[107]

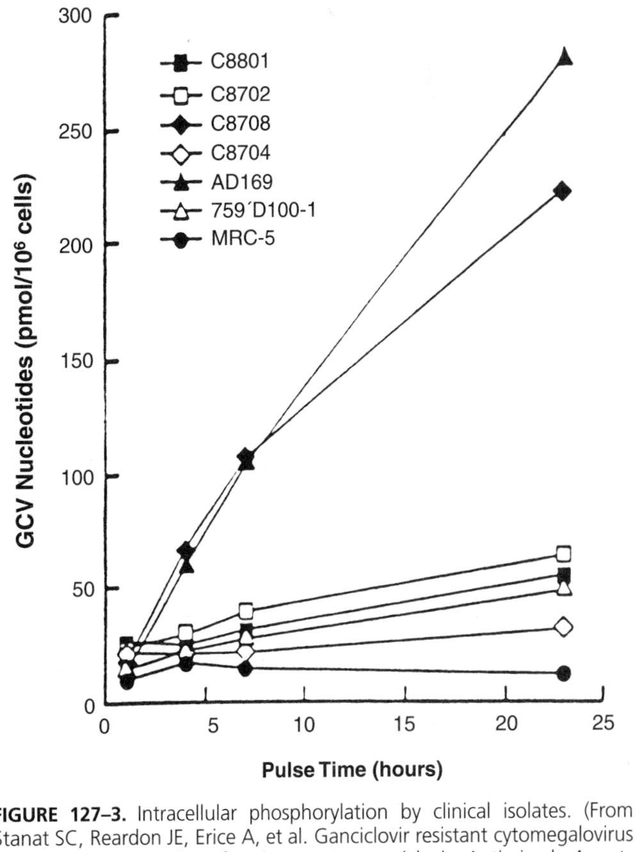

FIGURE 127–3. Intracellular phosphorylation by clinical isolates. (From Stanat SC, Reardon JE, Erice A, et al. Ganciclovir resistant cytomegalovirus clinical isolates: Modes of resistance to ganciclovir. Antimicrob Agents Chemother. 1991;35:2191–2197.

Foscarnet

Foscarnet is a pyrophosphate analogue that binds directly to the DNA polymerase of CMV and other herpesviruses (see Chapter 36). Foscarnet is a reversible competitive inhibitor that does not become incorporated into elongating viral DNA. Foscarnet must be present in high concentrations inside the cell to remain in contact with the DNA polymerase enzyme and inhibit DNA polymerase activity. When the intracellular concentration of foscarnet decreases, foscarnet no longer binds to the DNA polymerase, and viral DNA synthesis resumes.[108] Ganciclovir-resistant strains of CMV that have a mutation or a deletion in the UL97 protein kinase gene and are not able to phosphorylate ganciclovir remain sensitive to foscarnet.

Foscarnet has been used to treat patients with AIDS and CMV retinitis who have ganciclovir-resistant virus or are intolerant of ganciclovir,[109] and has resulted in stabilization of the retinitis and healing. Patients also need to be on long-term maintenance regimens with intravenous foscarnet to prevent the relapse or progression of CMV retinitis.

CMV strains exhibiting resistance to foscarnet have been reported, with mutations within the CMV DNA polymerase gene at codons 711 and 714[110] in the highly conserved region II of the polymerase. To date, the resistance mutations in the CMV DNA polymerase that confer resistance to foscarnet do not occur in regions of the polymerase conferring resistance to ganciclovir.

Foscarnet at a dose of 90 mg/kg/day intravenously in two divided doses had been shown to be equivalent to ganciclovir for the initial treatment of CMV retinitis,[111] but the mortality in patients with AIDS was improved in those who received foscarnet. In a subsequent study of CMV retinitis in patients with AIDS, the survival benefit was not confirmed,[112] but the combination of ganciclovir and foscarnet was superior for treatment of retinitis.

Foscarnet is associated with significant nephrotoxicity and metabolic toxicity.[109] Renal failure, hypocalcemia, hypomagnesemia, and hypophosphatemia are serious consequences of foscarnet therapy. They can be effectively managed by closely following serum creatinine levels and replacing magnesium, calcium, and phosphate losses with oral supplements.

Cidofovir

Cidofovir ((S)-1[3-hydroxy-2(phosphorylmethoxy) propyl] cytokine) is a nucleotide analogue of cytosine that has significant antiviral activity against CMV in vitro (see Chapter 36). The ID_{50} for cidofovir against CMV clinical isolates is 2.0 μM.[113] Cidofovir contains a phosphonate group, and does not need to be phosphorylated by a viral enzyme. It is therefore active against thymidine kinase–deficient herpes simplex virus[114] and cytomegalovirus with mutations in the UL97 gene conferring resistance to ganciclovir. Cidofovir is converted by cellular enzymes to cidofovir triphosphate, which is the active inhibitor of the viral DNA polymerase. Cidofovir triphosphate has a long intracellular half-life and needs to be given only once weekly. The maximal tolerated dose is 5 mg/kg weekly given intravenously.[115] The dose is given weekly for 2 weeks for induction and then is given once every 2 weeks. The drug has been approved for treatment only for CMV retinitis in patients with AIDS. Cidofovir must be administered with oral probenecid (2 g) before each intravenous dose. The major toxicity of cidofovir results from its uptake by the proximal convoluted renal tubular cells, producing a degeneration and necrosis of these cells, which may be irreversible.[116] Patients have experienced irreversible nephrotoxicity when cidofovir is given without probenecid and have required dialysis. Probenecid prevents the uptake of cidofovir and spares the renal tubular cells from degenerative damage.

Cross-Resistance to Antiviral Drugs in Cytomegalovirus Clinical Isolates

All the clinically approved systemic antiviral drugs act to inhibit the viral DNA polymerase as a final target. The possibility for cross-resistance among all the drugs acting on the viral DNA polymerase exists, but at present distinct patterns appear to be emerging. An early study showed that resistance to ganciclovir in the viral DNA polymerase of herpes simplex virus could be overcome by an analogue of foscarnet, phosphonoactive acid, suggesting that drugs that act on the viral polymerase could act synergistically[117] to overcome resistance to drugs that act on the DNA polymerase. Synergistic activity of ganciclovir and foscarnet against CMV has been shown in vitro.[118] If a clinical isolate of CMV is highly resistant to ganciclovir ($ID_{50} \geq 30$ μM) and contains mutations in both the UL97 and DNA polymerase genes, cross-resistance to cidofovir may also be observed.[119, 120] These isolates still remain sensitive to foscarnet. Cross-resistance between ganciclovir and foscarnet has not been observed, and this may reflect the fact that ganciclovir and foscarnet bind to different regions of the viral DNA polymerase. The resistance mutations to antiviral drugs against CMV appear to cluster in three distinct regions on the DNA polymerase, and significant overlap has not been observed (Fig. 127–4).[120]

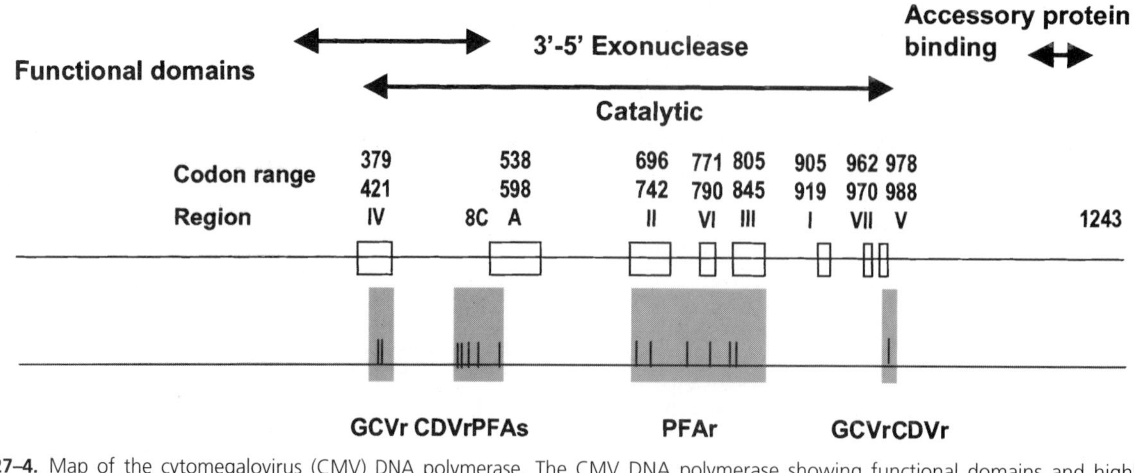

FIGURE 127–4. Map of the cytomegalovirus (CMV) DNA polymerase. The CMV DNA polymerase showing functional domains and highly conserved regions of DNA nucleotide sequences (I–VII). The shaded areas are regions associated with drug-resistance phenotypes. Codons mapped to drug resistance in clinical isolates are shown as bars. *Abbreviations:* CDV, Cidofovir; GCV, ganciclovir; PFA, foscarnet. (Adapted from Chou S, Lurain NS, Weinberg, et al. Interstrain variation in the human cytomegalovirus DNA polymerase sequence and its effect on genotype diagnosis of antiviral drug resistance. Antimicrob Agents Chemother. 1999;43:1500–1502.)

PREVENTION OF CYTOMEGALOVIRUS DISEASE

One of the most significant advances in the field was the demonstration that serious CMV disease could be prevented after bone marrow and solid organ transplantation with antiviral therapy. Prevention of life-threatening CMV pneumonia or other CMV-associated disease in recipients of bone marrow, heart, and liver transplants by administration of ganciclovir was clearly demonstrated in four independent studies in 1991 to 1995. In bone marrow transplant patients in particular, the development of interstitial pneumonia up to 120 days after the transplant is most frequently caused by CMV and has a very high mortality. In one of the studies from 1991, the use of a positive CMV culture from any site at any time after bone marrow transplantation was used as an indication to start intravenous ganciclovir.[121] This was found to be more effective in prevention of CMV pneumonia or death (97% efficacy) than screening for CMV by means of bronchoalveolar lavage at day 35 (75% efficacy)[122] as the indication to start ganciclovir. In a study in which CMV was detected by bronchoalveolar lavage in 20 patients who then received a full course of ganciclovir treatment, CMV pneumonia did not develop in any patient.[122] The strategy of preventing CMV pneumonia was quickly confirmed in heart transplant recipients who were seropositive for CMV and received ganciclovir or placebo for 28 days after transplantation.[123] In the patients who received ganciclovir, the incidence of CMV disease at 120 days after transplantation was reduced from 46 to 9%. The incidence of CMV infection at day 60 was 56% in the placebo group and only 19% in the ganciclovir group.[123] Among 250 patients who received ganciclovir or acyclovir intravenously after liver transplantation, ganciclovir almost completely prevented CMV disease during a follow-up period of 120 days, whereas CMV infection occurred in 38% of the acyclovir recipients.[124]

Oral ganciclovir was first shown to be effective in preventing CMV disease in patients with AIDS who had fewer than 100 CD4 cells/mm^3 of blood. In a study comparing oral ganciclovir at a dose of 1000 mg every 8 hours with placebo in 725 patients, only 14% of patients in the ganciclovir group acquired CMV disease compared with 26% of the patients in the placebo group.[125] There was a trend toward longer survival in the ganciclovir group. The patients receiving ganciclovir also had significantly fewer positive urine cultures for CMV than did those receiving placebo, thus providing a virologic correlation with clinical benefits. Analysis of plasma CMV DNA in the patients who acquired CMV disease showed that oral ganciclovir was primarily benefitting those with very low plasma CMV DNA at baseline, and was effective in preventing CMV retinitis in those with a low copy number of CMV DNA at baseline.[40] If a high copy number of CMV DNA was present at baseline, there was little evidence that oral ganciclovir would prevent CMV disease.[126] Since oral ganciclovir has a low oral bioavailability of 6 to 8%, the maximal serum concentration is 1.2 μg/ml.[70] This is probably too low a concentration to be active against high copy numbers of actively replicating CMV.

Oral ganciclovir has also been shown to be effective in prevention of CMV disease in liver transplant recipients and in reduction of mortality due to CMV infection.[70, 127] In kidney transplant patients, oral ganciclovir has also been effective in the prevention of CMV disease and in reducing CMV DNA levels in plasma. In patients who have received oral ganciclovir, the level of CMV DNA in plasma may be reduced to undetectable levels, but rejection of transplanted kidneys still occurred. This suggests that CMV disease may not be the only cause of kidney transplant rejection because rigorous control of CMV replication does not eliminate renal graft rejection.[128]

CYTOMEGALOVIRUS INFECTION IN TRANSPLANT PATIENTS

After bone marrow and solid organ transplantation, the severe immunosuppressive regimens that are employed to prevent rejection of the transplant make the recipient prone to severe CMV disease. In each form of transplantation the occurrence of CMV disease is different. The severity of the end-organ disease caused by CMV is related to the degree of immune suppression. The more severe the immune suppression, such as that required after bone marrow transplantation, the more severe the disease that occurs. Therefore, CMV pneumonia in the period of 120 days after bone marrow transplantation is much more severe and life-threatening than in a patient after renal transplantation. All major transplantations are associated with an increased risk of CMV infection. This includes kidney, liver, heart, heart–lung, and bone marrow transplants. In a summary of 16 studies of 1276 patients, it was found that the rate of infection after renal transplantation as measured by a serologic rise in antibody to CMV or isolation of virus from blood, urine, or throat had a range of 59 to 70%, with a median of 70%.[46] The infection rate was significantly higher in recipients who were seropositive before organ transplantation (84%) and lower in seronegative recipients (52%). Primary infections can occur in which a patient is infected from exposure to blood in a dialysis center or intensive care unit. The most important source for many patients is the transplanted organ or transfused blood. Secondary infection after activation of latent virus is also an important source of infection in any seropositive patient.[46]

CYTOMEGALOVIRUS INFECTION ACQUIRED FROM DONATED ORGANS

Even though attempts to isolate infectious CMV from organs of normal hosts are usually unsuccessful, the presence of CMV antigen in major visceral organs has been reported. This makes it likely that CMV will be activated after transplantation. In the case of kidney transplant recipients, two studies have reported the development of primary infection in 83% of seronegative recipients who received kidneys from seropositive donors.[129, 130] The development of CMV infection in those who received kidneys from seronegative donors was rare. CMV infection is also common in seronegative recipients who receive liver transplants from seropositive donors, in which as many as 50 to 70% of recipients will acquire CMV disease. In a trial comparing oral ganciclovir at 3 g/day with placebo for the prevention of CMV disease, 44% of seronegative recipients who received a liver transplant from a seropositive donor acquired CMV disease.[127] Evidence that the donor organ is a source of CMV is provided by the demonstration that identical CMV strains were found in two organ recipients who acquired CMV disease and shared a common organ donor.[46]

IMMUNOSUPPRESSIVE THERAPY

Immunosuppressive drugs play a major role in reactivation of CMV.[131] The cytologic drugs such as cyclophosphamide and azathioprine are sufficient in themselves to reactivate CMV.[132] Corticosteroids alone are not able to enhance CMV infection but act synergistically with other agents. The use of very high doses of corticosteroids plus azathioprine was associated with a very high incidence of CMV reactivation.[133]

Cyclosporine has been widely used as a primary immunosuppressive agent, and its potency has contributed to the success of transplants. The use of cyclosporine by itself does not increase CMV disease. A controlled trial in kidney transplant patients comparing azathioprine and prednisone with cyclosporine and prednisone showed that infection and severity of CMV disease was comparable in both groups of patients.[134] The other mainstay of immunosuppression, tacrolimus, does not enhance CMV infection, although CMV-associated disease is not eliminated.[135] Some novel immunosuppressive regimens, however, increase the frequency of severe CMV disease, and the most notable of these is the OKT3 antiserum infusion, which is used to treat rejection in liver transplant patients.[28] The use of OKT3 is associated with an increase in CMV hepatitis and dissemination of CMV in such patients. The type of transplant is also an important determinant of the morbidity of CMV disease as discussed in the following sections.

Bone Marrow Transplantation

The most common life-threatening infectious complication of allogenic bone marrow transplant is interstitial pneumonia due to CMV, which usually occurs in the first 120 days after transplantation. The pneumonitis usually shows an interstitial pattern rather than alveolar disease, but nodules may also be present on chest x-ray films. CMV pneumonia is usually rapid in onset with respiratory complaints being less than 2 weeks in duration. Fever, nonproductive cough, dyspnea progressing to hypoxia are common in severe cases. Hypoxia frequently requires assisted ventilation. In bone marrow transplant patients, CMV pneumonia has a very high mortality, which in one large series was 84%.[3] It has been suggested that part of the severity of CMV pneumonia in bone marrow transplant patients may be due to a graft-versus-host reaction in the lung. Graft-versus-host disease has been reported more commonly in those with CMV pneumonia (82%) than in those without CMV pneumonia (27%).[3]

In kidney transplant recipients, pneumonia due to CMV is less severe, and ganciclovir treatment has been lifesaving, but in bone marrow transplant recipients, the severe interstitial pneumonia has been difficult to treat with any single therapy. Attempts to treat with ganciclovir, acyclovir, vidarabine, human leukocyte interferon, lymphoblastoid interferon plus acyclovir have had only limited success.[82, 136, 137] In 10 bone marrow transplant recipients treated with ganciclovir for CMV pneumonia, only one patient survived, even though CMV was promptly cleared from the urine and pulmonary secretions of all 10.[136] In 20 bone marrow transplant recipients with CMV pneumonia, only 38% survived after treatment with ganciclovir. Four of these survivors also received high-titer CMV immune globulin.[137] In three uncontrolled trials, survival rates among bone marrow transplant patients treated with intravenous ganciclovir and high-dose intravenous CMV immune globulin ranged from 52 to 69%.[138–140] Although these trials were uncontrolled, the combination of ganciclovir and high-titer CMV immune globulin is the currently recommended therapy for CMV pneumonia in bone marrow transplant patients.

Results from European studies have not supported the favorable results observed in these three studies.[141] A retrospective study of 49 allogeneic bone marrow transplant recipients treated with ganciclovir and intravenous immune globulin showed that only 35% responded to treatment. At 1 month after diagnosis, the mortality of the combined treatment was 69%. It has been suggested that the American patients may not be comparable to European patients who received this treatment.

Liver Transplantation

CMV remains the most common pathogen isolated after solid organ transplantation, including liver transplantation.[142, 143] The problem of CMV hepatitis is an important problem after transplantation in both adults and infants and is more common after primary CMV infection. CMV disease is a leading cause of morbidity during the first 14 weeks after transplantation and increases costs and length of hospital stay.[144] The incidence of CMV hepatitis is greatest after transplantation from a CMV-seropositive donor. All cases of CMV hepatitis are characterized by prolonged fever, elevated bilirubinemia, and elevated liver enzyme concentrations. CMV hepatitis can also lead to liver failure requiring repeat transplantation. Management may be difficult because the signs of severe CMV hepatitis can be difficult to distinguish from graft rejection. Liver biopsy is the only reliable way to distinguish rejection from CMV hepatitis.[145] It is important to distinguish between these two possibilities because rejection is treated by increasing immunosuppression, whereas CMV infection is treated by decreasing immunosuppression and starting antiviral therapy. CMV predisposes to other opportunistic infection[146] and increases the risk for allograft rejection.[147] Attempts to prevent CMV disease in liver transplant recipients by adminstration of CMV immune globulin[148] or oral acyclovir[149, 150] or a combination of both[151] have had little effect on the incidence of CMV disease in seronegative recipients. The best results of prophylaxis of CMV disease in liver transplant recipients have been achieved with prolonged course of intravenous ganciclovir.[123] Among 250 patients randomly assigned to receive ganciclovir or acyclovir intravenously after liver transplantation, ganciclovir recipients had an incidence of CMV disease of 0.8% during a follow-up period of 120 days, whereas CMV disease occurred in 38% of acyclovir recipients. Intravenous ganciclovir reduced the incidence of CMV infection in patients who were positive for CMV antigen and in those who were CMV antigen–negative. The striking decrease in CMV disease included decreases in pneumonia, gastrointestinal disease, hepatitis, retinitis, encephalitis, and "CMV syndrome."

A long course of oral ganciclovir was compared with placebo in liver transplant recipients who received either oral ganciclovir at 1000 mg three times/day or a matching placebo.[127] The drug was administered no later than 10 days after transplantation and was continued until the 98th day after transplantation. Oral ganciclovir reduced the incidence of CMV disease in all subgroups when compared with placebo. The 6-month incidence of CMV disease was 18.9% in the placebo group and 4.8% (7 of 150) in the ganciclovir group ($p<0.001$). In the high-risk group of seronegative recipients of seropositive livers, the incidence of CMV disease was 44% in the placebo group and 14.8% in the ganciclovir group. There was also a benefit in those who received antilymphocyte globulin in whom the frequency of CMV disease was 32.9% in the placebo group and 4.6% in the ganciclovir group. The study showed that oral ganciclovir prophylaxis was still effective despite the intense immunosuppression of antilymphocyte antibodies. The use of oral ganciclovir for prophylaxis was still not as effective as intravenous ganciclovir, which was associated with an incidence of 0.8% of CMV disease compared with 4.8% in the oral ganciclovir recipients.[127]

The usual dose-limiting toxicity of ganciclovir is myelosuppression, which is less common in solid organ transplant recipients[123] than in bone marrow transplant patients[121] or in patients with AIDS.[125] In the study of oral ganciclovir for liver transplant recipients, there was no associated significant myelotoxicity. A trend toward a higher serum creatinine concentration was noted in ganciclovir recipients, which reflects the mild nephrotoxic effects of ganciclovir.[123]

Kidney Transplantation

The morbidity due to CMV is lowest in kidney transplant recipients, but primary infections from a seropositive donor to a seronegative recipient can occur and are significantly more symptomatic than secondary infections. Two studies[129, 130] reported the clinical and laboratory findings on a total of 154 renal transplant patients with CMV infection. In one of the series, 13 of 18 primary infections were associated with at least two of the following symptoms: fever, leukopenia, atypical lymphocytes, lymphocytosis, hepatosplenomegaly, myalgia, and arthralgia. This constellation of findings has been called the *CMV syndrome* and is now defined as CMV infection accompanied by an otherwise unexplained fever over 48 hours, malaise, and a fall in neutrophil count over 3 consecutive days.[127] This is the most common manifestation of CMV-associated illness in kidney transplant recipients. This is in contrast to secondary CMV infections, of which only 19% were associated with fever.

Clinically significant CMV hepatitis is a rare occurrence in patients after renal transplantation,[152] but elevated hepatic enzymes (aspartate aminotransferase) were seen in 10 of 16 (63%) cases of primary CMV infection in kidney transplant recipients.[130] There were also five cases of CMV interstitial pneumonia in this group.

Rejection of the transplanted kidney was also found in 4 of 16 patients with primary infection. In this study, 24 seronegative patients who received kidneys from seronegative donors and remained seronegative did not undergo rejection. This is one of the very few studies that reached the conclusion that CMV infection may increase rejection of the transplanted organ.[130] In a large series of 126 kidney transplant patients, hepatic dysfunction was observed in 22%.[153] Severe hepatitis was observed in seven, and CMV was isolated from bodily fluids of all seven. At autopsy, five of these patients had evidence of CMV in the liver.

In a small series of kidney transplant patients in whom CMV pneumonia developed, there was a mortality of 48%.[154] This is much less than that observed in bone marrow transplant patients in whom a mortality as high as 84% has been reported.[3] In kidney transplant recipients who acquire CMV pneumonia, ganciclovir alone has been effective therapy for severe interstitial pneumonia as noted earlier.[155]

Kidney transplant recipients have also been extensively studied in attempts to prevent CMV disease. In a study of CMV, hyperimmune globulin administered to 24 seronegative kidney transplant recipients within 72 hours of transplantation and continued for 16 weeks, the rate of CMV infection was 71% compared with 77% in 35 controls, but the rate of symptomatic disease decreased from 60 to 21%.[156] This study reported one death due to CMV in the treated group and five deaths in the control group, and the higher rate of CMV disease and death may have been related to the widespread use of antithymocyte globulin. Prophylaxis with immunoglobulin was not shown to be effective in primary CMV disease in other solid organ transplants, such as liver transplants.[157] CMV antigen detection has been employed to start ganciclovir as preemptive therapy in CMV antibody–positive kidney transplant patients and has met with success in prevention of CMV disease.[158] Oral ganciclovir therapy has also been successful in lowering CMV DNA levels and preventing CMV disease in renal transplantation.[128]

CONGENITAL CYTOMEGALOVIRUS INFECTION

Intrauterine CMV infections occur in 0.5 to 22% of all live births.[159] This is a less frequent mode of infection than perinatal infection but is associated with the most serious CMV disease in the neonatal period. The diagnosis of congenital infection is best demonstrated by viruria within the first week of life. The presence of IgM antibodies against CMV in cord serum is suggestive but not completely specific for congenital infection. The most important source of clinically significant congenital infections are in infants born to primiparous mothers with a primary infection during pregnancy.[46] These infections are diagnosed in the mothers by a change in antibody titer from negative to positive or by detection of IgM antibody.

In a large group of 3712 pregnant women in upper and lower socioeconomic groups from Alabama, 21 primary infections were found in 1382 seronegative mothers.[160] In this group of 21 mothers, 11 congenital infections occurred and three were symptomatic. This indicates that intrauterine infection of infants after primary CMV infection is high (55%). The rate of primary infection (0.52%) did not vary with socioeconomic status or immune status of the population. The rate of intrauterine CMV infection (24 in 8416 pregnancies) resulting from primary infection was 0.3%, 25% of which were symptomatic. These data indicate that primary infection at any stage of pregnancy presents a risk for intrauterine infection and that the risk is highest during the first half of pregnancy.[161]

Congenital infection was also observed in 20 babies from 2330 mothers (0.5%) who were seropositive.[160] This type of congenital infection occurs more frequently in mothers of lower socioeconomic group with a high prevalence of past infection. None of the 20 babies had symptoms of congenital infection.[160] Other reports have claimed that symptomatic infection may rarely result from infection in an immune mother.[162] These results indicate that the neonate who acquires CMV disease generally acquires infection from a mother who is not immune. In immune mothers, most of the infections in the babies are asymptomatic. A small number of infections develop from transplacental infection. Perinatal infection occurs from CMV carried in the cervix during late stages of pregnancy and from CMV in breast milk.

The symptoms that occur in children who are infected congenitally from nonimmune mothers include the fulminant cytomegalic inclusion disease, which consists of jaundice, hepatosplenomegaly, petechial rash, and multiple organ involvement. CNS findings of microcephaly, motor disability chorioretinitis, and cerebral calcifications are present.[163] At birth or shortly thereafter, there is onset of lethargy, respiratory distress, and seizures. The child may die in days or a few weeks. The jaundice and hepatosplenomegaly may subside, but neurologic sequelae, microcephaly, and mental retardation persists. Many extraneural defects, including hearing disorders, have been associated with congenital infection, and most of the disease manifestations are a result of inflammation secondary to virus invasion.[163] Interference with organ development such as occurs with rubella is not seen with CMV infection.

Infections that occur in babies postnatally are very different, and diffuse visceral and CNS disease does not develop. The picture may resemble some of the aspects of CMV mononucleosis, although the full mononucleosis syndrome is usually absent. CMV mononucleosis may occur rarely in young children,[14] and much more severe CMV-associated disease can occur as a result of exchange transfusions.[164]

Although perinatal infections are completely asymptomatic and without obvious long-term abnormalities, subtle effects on hearing and intelligence have been reported. In a study of 8644 neonates from middle-class socioeconomic families, 53 were identified with IgM antibodies against CMV in cord blood (0.6%).[165] Forty-four of these children were evaluated at 3.5 to 7.0 years of age. The mean IQ for the group was 103 and was lower than a matched control group. The school failure rate for this group was 2.7 times that of matched controls of the same socioeconomic status. Thirteen percent of these children (5 of 40) had severe bilateral hearing loss, and 3 had profound deafness. Inapparent CMV infection in the perinatal period is being invoked as a cause of the 1 in 1000 incidence of profound deafness in American children. Another report described the incidence of sensorineural hearing loss in neonatal CMV infection. In this study, 59 patients had congenital intrauterine infection and 8 had symptoms at birth.[166] Twenty-one children had perinatal CMV infection and none experienced hearing loss. Late-onset hearing loss developed in 17% of symptomatic congenital infections and 14% of asymptomatic congenital CMV infections. In this study, pathology demonstrated virus in the cells of the organ of Corti and in neurons of the spira ganglia.[166] Rare typical nuclear inclusions were seen in cells of the cochlea. The problem of hearing loss associated with CMV cannot be predicted by severity of infection or the IgM level at birth. This problem of hearing loss due to CMV has been cited as a major stimulus for the development of an effective vaccine for CMV and for development of other preventive measures.

CYTOMEGALOVIRUS INFECTION IN PREGNANT WOMEN

Two possible sources of sexual transmission of CMV are virus in the uterine cervix and in semen. About 1 to 2% of women in the United States who undergo a routine medical examination in a private practice setting are found to carry the virus in the cervix.[46] In Taiwan, it was observed that 18% of a group with infrequent sexual relations had CMV isolated from the cervix.[167] A study of 134 women attending a sexually transmitted diseases clinic in Seattle revealed that 34% of women older than 21 years of age shed CMV in the cervix, and many of these women had evidence of shedding multiple strains of CMV from the same patient.[168] The frequency of colonization correlated with the number of sexual partners and a younger age of sexual intercourse, although there is not direct evidence that CMV in the cervix comes from sexual intercourse or that it is transmitted by sexual intercourse. CMV is also found in high titers in the semen of both homosexual and heterosexual men.[47]

TABLE 127–1 Cervical Cytomegalovirus Infection during Pregnancy

Source	Infection in Trimester			Overall Infection
	First	*Second*	*Third*	
Numazaki et al.[169]	0/30 (0%)*	6/62 (9.7%)	17/61 (27.9%)	23/153 (15.0%)
Montgomery et al.[171]	1/43 (2%)	6/83 (7.2%)	6/49 (12.2%)	13/175 (7.4%)
Stagno et al.[170]	3/183 (1.6%)†	22/359 (6.1%)	42/371 (11.3%)	63/659 (9.6%)
Total infected/tested	4/256	34/504	65/481	99/987
Percentage infected	1.6	6.7	13.5	10.0

*Represents number of positive patients per number of patients tested.
†Number infected per number of specimens tested.
From Ho M. Cytomegalovirus. In: Mandell GL, Bennett JE, Dolin R, eds. Principles and Practice of Infectious Diseases, 4th ed. New York: Churchill Livingstone; 1995:1351.

An increased rate of cervical infection occurs in the late stages of pregnancy. CMV in the uterine cervix is a source of infection to the neonate during passage through the birth canal. Three studies of 987 pregnant women showed an increasing prevalence of infection progressing from first (0 to 2%), second (6 to 10%) and third trimesters (11 to 28%) (Table 127–1).[169–171] These three studies examined distinct populations. The study from Japan[169] included a nonpromiscuous middle-class population that was 85% CMV-seropositive. The study from Alabama in the United States included a young, sexually promiscuous group with a 10% rate of gonorrhea and a CMV seropositive status of 89%.[170] The third study included 71 native American Navajo and 125 middle-class white and African American pregnant women.[171]

The high cervical CMV excretion during the third trimester of pregnancy presents a risk of infection for the neonate during the birth process, but this risk may not be as important as transmission from infected milk as a cause of perinatal infection. In a study of 50 babies born to mothers who were nonsecretors, only 2 (4%) became infected, but 12.5% of babies born to mothers who secreted CMV from the cervix in the first or second trimester became infected and 37% of babies born to mothers who secreted in the third trimester became infected. The infection rate of babies whose mothers shed virus post partum and who were presumably shedding at birth rose to 57%.[172] During pregnancy, a primary infection in the mother may present with a mild mononucleosis syndrome but is usually asymptomatic and is associated with CMV viruria for 4 to 7 days. Recurrent infections in pregnant women are completely asymptomatic.

REFERENCES

1. Zhang LJ, Hanpf P, Rutherford C, et al. Detection of cytomegalovirus, DNA, RNA, and antibody in normal donor blood. J Infect Dis. 1995;171:1002–1006.
2. Patel R, Surydman DR, Rubin RH, et al. Cytomegalovirus prophylaxis in solid organ transplant recipients. Transplantation. 1996;61:1279–1289.
3. Myers JD, Flournoy N, Thomas ED. Risk factors for cytomegalovirus infection after human marrow transplantation. J Infect Dis. 1986;153:478–488.
4. Masur H, Whitcup SM, Cartwright C, et al. Advances in the management of AIDS-related CMV retinitis. Ann Intern Med. 1996;125:126–136.
5. Crumpacker CS. Ganciclovir. N Engl J Med. 1996;335:721–729.
6. Ho M. Cytomegalovirus. In Mandell GM, Bennett JE, Dolin R, eds. Principles and Practice of Infectious Diseases. 4th ed. New York: Churchill Livingstone; 1995.
7. Spector SA, Hirata KK, Neumann TR. Identification of multiple cytomegalovirus strains in homosexual men with acquired immunodeficiency syndrome. J Infect Dis. 1984;6:953–956.
8. Griffiths PD, Stagno S, Pass RF, et al. Infection with cytomegalovirus during pregnancy: Specific IgM antibodies as a marker of recent primary infection. J Infect Dis. 1982;145:647–653.
9. Smith MG. Propagation of salivary gland virus of the mouse in tissue cultures. Proc Soc Exp Biol Med. 1954;86:435–440.
10. Smith MG. Propagation in tissue cultures of a cytopathogenic virus from human salivary gland virus (SGV) disease. Proc Soc Exp Biol Med. 1956;92:424–430.
11. Weller TH, Macauley JC, Craig JM, et al. Isolation of intranuclear inclusion producing agents from infants with illnesses resembling cytomegalic inclusion disease. Proc Soc Exp Biol Med. 1957;94:4–12.
12. Rowe WP, Hartley JW, Waterman S, et al. Cytopathogenic agent resembling human salivary gland virus recovered from tissue cultures of human adenoids. Proc Soc Exp Biol Med. 1956;92:418–424.
13. Weller TH, Hanshaw JB, Scott DE. Serologic differentiation of viruses responsible for cytomegalic inclusion disease. Virology. 1960;12:130–132.
14. Klemola E, Kaariainen L. Cytomegalovirus as a possible cause of a disease resembling infectious mononucleosis. Br Med J. 1965;1099:102.
15. Kaarianen L, Klemola E, Paloheimo J. Rise of cytomegalovirus antibodies in an infectious-mononucleosis-like syndrome after transfusion. Br Med J. 1966;2:1270–1272.
16. Winston DJ, Ho WG, Howell CL, et al. Cytomegalovirus infections associated with leukocyte transfusions. Ann Intern Med. 1980;93:671–675.
17. Chee MS, Bankier AT, Becks S, et al. Analysis of the protein-coding content of the sequence of human cytomegalovirus strain. AD 169 Curr Top Microbiol Immunol. 1990;154:125–169.
18. Cha T, Tom S, Kemble GW, et al. Human cytomegalovirus clinical isolates carry at least 19 genes not found in laboratory strains. J Virol. 1996;70:78–83.
19. Rul PF, Powell KL. Physical and functional interaction of human cytomegalovirus DNA polymerase and its accessory protein (ZCP36) expressed in insect cells. J Virol. 1992;66:4126–4133.
20. Chee MS, Lawrence GL, Barell BG. Alpha-, beta- and gamma-herpesviruses encode a putative phosphotransferase. J Gen Virol. 1989;70:1151–1160.
21. Sullivan V, Talarico CL, Stanat SC, et al. A protein kinase homologue controls phosphorylation of ganciclovir in human cytomegalovirus infected cells. Nature. 1992;358:162–164. [Errata, Nature. 1992;359:85, 1993;366:756.]
22. Littler E, Stuart AD, Chee MS. Human cytomegalovirus UL 97 open reading frame encodes a protein that phosphorylates the antiviral nucleoside analogue ganciclovir. Nature. 1992;358:160–162.
23. He Z, He YS, Kim Y, et al. The human cytomegalovirus UL97 protein is a protein kinase that autophosphorylates on serines and threonines. J Virol. 1997;71:405–411.
24. Beersma MF, Bizlemaker MJ, Ploegh HL. Human cytomegalovirus down regulates HLA class I expression by reducing the stability of class I H chains. J Immunol. 1993;151:4455–4464.
25. Schuster EA, Bencke JS, Tegtmeier GE, et al. Monoclonal antibody for rapid laboratory detection of cytomegalovirus infections: Characterization and diagnostic application. Mayo Clin Proc. 1985;60:577–585.
26. Fetterman GH. A new laboratory aid in the clinical diagnosis of inclusion disease of infancy. Am J Clin Pathol. 1952;22:424–425.
27. Rinaldo CR, Black PH, Hirsch MS. Interactions of cytomegalovirus with leukocytes from patients with mononucleosis due to cytomegalovirus. J Infect Dis. 1977;136:667–678.
28. Singh N, Dummer JS, Ho M, et al. Infections with cytomegalovirus and other herpesviruses in 121 liver transplant recipients: Transmission by donated organ and the effect of OKT3 antibodies. J Infect Dis. 1988;158:124–131.
29. Martin WJ, Smith TJ. Rapid detection of cytomegalovirus in bronchoalveolar lavage specimens by a monoclonal antibody method. J Clin Microbiol. 1986;23:1006–1008.
30. van der Bij W, Schirm J, Torensma R, et al. Comparison between viremia and antigenemia for detection of cytomegalovirus in blood. J Clin Microbiol. 1988;26:2531–2535.
31. Chou S, Merigan TC. Rapid detection and quantitation of human cytomegalovirus in urine through DNA hybridization. N Engl J Med. 1983;308:921–925.
32. Churchill MA, Zaia JA, Forman SJ, et al. Quantitation of human cytomegalovirus DNA in lungs from bone marrow transplant recipients with interstitial pneumonia. J Infect Dis. 1987;155:501–509.
33. Stanier P, Kitchen AD, Taylor DL, et al. Detection of human cytomegalovirus in peripheral mononuclear cells and urine samples using PCR. Mol Cell Probes. 1992;6:51–58.
34. Gerna G, Zipeto D. Parea M, et al. Monitoring of human cytomegalovirus infections and ganciclovir treatment in heart transplant recipients by determination of viremia, antigenemia, and DNAemia. J Infect Dis. 1991;164:488–498.
35. Wolf DG, Spector SA. Diagnosis of human cytomegalovirus central nervous system disease in AIDS patients by DNA amplification from cerebrospinal fluid. J Infect Dis. 1992;166:1412–1415.
36. Fox JD, Brink NS, Zuckerman MA, et al. Detection of herpesvirus DNA by nested polymerase chain reaction in cerebrospinal fluid of human immunodeficiency virus-infected persons with neurologic disease: A prospective evaluation. J Infect Dis. 1995;172:1087–1090.
37. Bowen F, Sabiwca, Wilson P, et al. Cytomegalovirus (CMV) viraemia detected by polymerase chain reaction identifiers. A group at high risk of CMV disease. Aids 1997;11:889–893.

38. Shinkai M, Boizette SA, Powderly W, et al. Utility of urine and leukocyte cultures and plasma DNA PCR for identification of AIDS patients at risk for developing human cytomegalovirus disease. J Infect Dis. 1997;175:302–332.
39. Dodt KK, Jacobsen PH, Hofman B, et al. Development of cytomegalovirus (CMV) disease can be predicted in HIV infected patients by CMV polymerase chain reaction and antigenemia test. Aids. 1997;11F:21–28.
40. Spector SA, Wong R, Hiza K, et al. Plasma cytomegalovirus (CMV) DNA load predicts CMV disease and survival in AIDS patients. J Clin Invest. 1998;101:497–502.
41. Imbert-Marcille BM, Cantarovich D, Ferre-Aubineau V, et al. Usefulness of DNA viral load quantification for cytomegalovirus diseases monitoring in renal and pancreas/renal transplant recipients. Transplantation. 1997;63:1476–1481.
42. Singh N, Yu VL, Mieles L, et al. High-dose acyclovir compared with short-course preemptive ganciclovir therapy to prevent cytomegalovirus disease in liver transplant recipients: A randomized trial. Ann Intern Med. 1994;120:375–381.
43. Flood J, Drew WL, Miner R, et al. Diagnosis of cytomegalovirus (CMV) polyradiculopathy and documentation of in vivo anti-CMV activity in cerebrospinal fluid by using branched DNA signal amplification and antigen assays. J Infect Dis. 1997;176:348–352.
44. Boeckl M, Gooley TA, Myerson D, et al. Cytomegalovirus pp65 antigenemia guided early treatment with ganciclovir marrow transplantation: A randomized double blind study. Blood. 1997;88:4063–4071.
45. Dunkel EC, Scheer DI, Zhu Q, et al. A rabbit model for human cytomegalovirus-induced chorioretinal disease (retraction). J Infect Dis. 1998;177:1778.
46. Ho M. Cytomegalovirus: Biology and Infection. 2nd ed. New York: Plenum; 1991:440.
47. Lang DJ, Kummer JF. Demonstration of cytomegalovirus in semen. N Engl J Med. 1972;287:756–758.
48. Klemola E, von Essen R, Henle G, et al. lnfectious-mononucleosis-like disease with negative heterophil agglutination test. Clinical features in relation to Epstein-Barr virus and cytomegalovirus and antibodies. J Infect Dis. 1970;121:608–614.
49. Chou S, Kim DY, Norman DJ. Transmission of cytomegalovirus by pretransplant leukocyte transfusions in renal transplant candidates. J Infect Dis. 1987;155:565–567.
50. Bowden RA, Sayers M, Flourney N, et al. Cytomegalovirus immune globulin and seronegative blood products to prevent primary cytomegalovirus infection after marrow transplantation. N Engl J Med. 1986;314:1006–1010.
51. Carter AR. Cytomegalovirus disease presenting as hepatitis. Br Med J. 1968;3:786.
52. Bonkowsky HL, Lee RV, Klatskin G. Acute granulomatous hepatitis: Occurrence in cytomegalovirus mononucleosis. JAMA. 1984;37:1284–1288.
53. Leonard JC, Tobin JOH. Polyneuritis associated with cytomegalovirus infections. Q J Med. 1971;40:435–442.
54. Schmitz H, Enders G. Cytomegalovirus as a frequent cause of Guillain-Barre syndrome. J Med Virol. 1977;1:21–27.
55. Eidelberg D, Sotrel A, Vogel H, et al. Progressive polyradiculopathy in acquired immune deficiency syndrome. Neurology. 1986;36:912–916.
56. Klemola E, Kaariainen L, von Essen R, et al. Further studies on cytomegalovirus mononucleosis in previously healthy individuals. Acta Med Scand. 1967;182:311–322.
57. Tiula E, Leinikki P. Fatal cytomegalovirus infection in a previously healthy boy with myocarditis and consumption coagulopathy as presenting signs. Scand J Infect Dis. 1972;4:57–60.
58. Waris E, Rasanen P, Kreus KE, et al. Fatal cytomegalovirus disease in a previously healthy adult. Scand J Infect Dis. 1972;4:61–67.
59. Chanarin I, Walford DM. Thrombocytopenic purpura in cytomegalovirus mononucleosis. Lancet. 1973;1:238–239.
60. Harris AI, Meyer RJ, Brody EA. Cytomegalovirus-induced thrombocytopenia and hemolysis in an adult. Ann Intern Med. 1975;83:670–671.
61. Klemola E. Hypersenistivity reactions to ampicillin in cytomegalovirus mononucleosis. Scand J Infect Dis. 1970;2:29–31.
62. Muller-Stamou A, Senn HJ, Emody G. Epidermolysis in a case of severe cytomegalovirus infection. Br Med J. 1974;3:609–610.
63. Collier AC, Meyers JD, Corey L, et al. Cytomegalovirus infection in homosexual men. Am J Med. 1987;82:493–600.
64. Drew WL, Mills J, Levy J, et al. Cytomegalovirus infection and abnormal T-leukocyte subset ratios in homosexual men. Ann Intern Med. 1985;103:61–63.
65. Gallant JE, Moore RD, Richman DP, et al. Incidence and natural history of cytomegalovirus disease in patients with advanced human immunodeficiency virus disease treated with zidovudine. J Infect Dis. 1992;166:1223–1227.
66. McKenzie R, Travis WD, Dolan SA, et al. The causes of death in patients with human immunodeficiency virus infection: A clinical and pathologic study with emphasis on the role of pulmonary diseases. Medicine (Baltimore) 1991;70:326–343.
67. Hammer SM, Squires KE, Hughes MD, et al. A controlled trial of two nucleosides analogues plus indinavir in persons with immunodeficiency virus infection and CD4 cell counts of 200 per cubic millimeter or less. N Engl J Med. 1997;337:725–732.
68. Autran B, Carcelain G, Li TS, et al. Positive effects of combined antiretroviral therapy on CD4 T-cell homeostasis and function in advanced HIV disease. Science. 1997;277:112–116.
69. Mills J, Jacobsen MA, O'Donnell JJ, et al. Treatment of cytomegalovirus retinitis in patients with AIDS. Rev Infect Dis. 1988;3:5522–5531.
70. Anderson RD, Griffy KG, Jung D, et al. Ganiciclovir absolute bioavailability and steady state pharmacokinetics after oral administration of two 3000-mg/d dosing regimens in human immunodeficiency virus- and cytomegalovirus-seropositive patients. Clin Ther. 1995;17:425–432.
71. Drew WI, Ives D, Lalezari JP, et al. Oral ganciclovir as maintenance treatment for cytomegalovirus retinitis in patients with AIDS. N Engl J Med. 1995;333:615–620.
72. Martin, DF, Parks DJ, Mellow SD, et al. Treatment of cytomegalovirus retinitis with an intraocular sustained release ganciclovir implant: A randomized controlled clinical trial. Arch Ophthamol. 1994;112:1531–1539.
73. Martin DF, Kuppermann BD, Wolitz RA, et al. Oral ganciclovir for patients with cytomegalovirus retinitis treated with a ganciclovir implant. Roche Ganciclovir Study Group. N Engl J Med. 1999;340:1063–1070.
74. Miller RG, Storcy JR, Greco CM. Ganciclovir in the treatment of progressive AIDS-related polyradiculopathy. Neurology. 1990;40:569–574.
75. Fuller GN, Gill SK, Guiloff RJ, et al. Ganciclovir for lumbosacral polyradiculopathy in AIDS. Lancet. 1990;335:48–49.
76. Jacobson MA, Mills J, Rush J, et al. Failure of antiviral therapy for acquired immunodeficiency syndrome-related cytomegalovirus myelitis. Arch Neurol. 1988;45:1090–1092.
77. Fletcher CV, Balfour HH. Evaluation of ganciclovir for cytomegalovirus disease. DICP. 1989;23:5–12.
78. Enting R, de Gans J, Reiss P, et al. Ganciclovir/foscarnet for cytomegalovirus meningoencephalitis in AIDS. Lancet. 1992;340:559–560.
79. Fuller GN. Cytomegalovirus and the peripheral nervous system in AIDS. J Acquir Immune Defic Syndr. 1992;5(Suppl 1):S33–S36.
80. Knapp, AB, Horst DA, Eliopoulos G, et al. Widespread cytomegalovirus gastroenterocolitis in a patient with acquired immunodeficiency syndrome. Gastroenterology. 1983;85:1399–1402.
81. Meiselman MS, Cello JP, Margaretten W. Cytomegalovirus colitis. Report of the clinical, endoscopic, and pathologic findings in two patients with acquired immune deficiency syndrome. Gastroenterology. 1985;88:171–175.
82. Collaborative DHPG Treatment Study Group. Treatment of serious cytomegalovirus infections with 9-(1,3-dihydroxy-2-propoxymethyl)guanine in patients with AIDS and other immunodeficiencies. N Engl J Med. 1986;314:801–805.
83. Dieterich DT, Kotler DP, Busch DF, et al. Ganciclovir treatment of cytomegalovirus colitis in AIDS: A randomized, double-blind, placebo-controlled multicenter study. J Infect Dis. 1992;167:278–282.
84. Reed EC, Bowden RA, Dandliker PS, et al. Treatment of cytomegalovirus pneumonia with ganciclovir and intravenous cytomegalovirus immunoglobulin in patients with bone marrow transplants. Ann Intern Med. 1988;109:783–788.
85. Texidor HS, Honig CL, Norsoph E, et al. Cytomegalovirus infection of the alimentary canal: Radiologic findings with pathologic correlation. Radiology. 1987;163:317–323.
86. Blumberg RS, Kelsey P, Perrone T, et al. Cytomegalovirus- and cryptosporidium-associated acalculous gangrenous cholecystitis. Am J Med. 1984;76:1118–1123.
87. Feinberg JE, Hurwitz S, Cooper D, Satler FR. A randomized double-blend trial of valaciclovir prophylates for cytomegalovirus disease in patients with advanced human immunodeficiency virus infection. J Infect Dis. 1998;177:48–56.
88. Goudrield J, Khardori N. Cytomegalovirus: The taming of the beast? Lancet. 1997;350:1718–1719.
89. Martin JC, Dvorak CA, Smee DF, et al. 9-[(1,3-Dihydroxy-2-propoxy)methyl] guanine: A new potent and selective antiherpes agent. J Med Chem. 1983;26:759–761.
90. Ashton WT, Karkas JD, Field AK, Tolman RI. Activation by thymidine kinase and potent antiherpetic activity of 2′-nor-2′-deoxyguanosine (2′NDG). Biochem Biophys Res Commun. 1982;108:1716–1721.
91. Ogilvie UK, Cheriyan UD, Radatus OX, et al. Biologically active acyclonucleoside analogues. II. The synthesis of 9-(2-hydroxy-1-[hydroxymethyl, ethoxymethyl]guanine) BIOLF-62. Can J Chem. 1982;60:3005–3010.
92. Cheng YC, Huang ES, Lin JC, et al. Unique spectrum of activity of 9-[(1,3-dihydroxy-2-propoxy)methyl]-guanine against herpesviruses in vitro and its mode of action against herpes simplex virus type 1. Proc Natl Acad Sci USA. 1983;80:2767–2770.
93. Field AK, Davies ME, DeWitt C, et al. 9[{2-Hydroxy-1-(hydroxymethyl)ethoxy}-methyl]guanine: A selective inhibitor of herpes group virus replication. Proc Natl Acad Sci USA. 1983;80:4139–4143.
94. Cheng YC, Grill SP, Dutschman GE, et al. Metabolism of 9-(1,3-dihydroxy-2-propoxymethyl)guanine, a new anti-herpes virus compound, in herpes simplex virus-infected cells. J Biol Chem. 1983;258:12460–12464.
95. Hamzeh FM, Lietman PS. Intranuclear accumulation of subgenomic noninfectious human cytomegalovirus DNA in infected cells in the presence of ganciclovir. Antimicrob Agents Chemother. 1991;35:1818–1823.
96. Hamzeh FM, Lietman PS, Gibson W, Hayward GS. Identification of the lytic origin of DNA replication in human cytomegalovirus by a novel approach utilizing ganciclovir-induced chain termination. J Virol. 1990;64:6184–6195.
97. Biron KK, Stanat SC, Sorrell JB, et al. Metabolic activation of the nucleoside analog 9-[{hydroxy-1-(hydroxymethyl)ethoxy}methyl]guanine in human diploid fibrolasts infected with human cytomegalovirus. Proc Natl Acad Sci USA. 1985;82:2473–2477.
98. Chou S, Erice A, Jordan MC, et al. Analysis of the UL 97 phosphotransferase coding sequence in clinical cytomegalovirus isolates and identification of mutations conferring ganciclovir resistance. J Infect Dis. 1995;171:576–583.
99. Lurain NS, Spatford LE, Thompson KD. Mutation in the UL 97 open reading frame of human cytomegalovirus strains resistant to ganciclovir. J Virol 1994;68:4427–4431.
100. Erice A, Gil-Roda C, Perez JL, et al. Antiviral susceptibilities and analysis of UL97 and DNA polymerase sequences of clinical cytomegalovirus isolates from immunocompromised patients. J Infect Dis. 1997;175:1087–1092.
101. Erice A, Chou S, Biron KK, et al. Progressive disease due to ganciclovir-resistant cytomegalovirus in immunocompromised patients. N Engl J Med. 1989;320:289–293.

102. Drew WL, Miner RC, Busch DF, et al. Prevalence of resistance in patients receiving ganciclovir for serious cytomegalovirus infection. J Infect Dis. 1991;163:716–719.
103. Stanat SC, Reardon JE, Erice A, et al. Ganciclovir resistant cytomegalovirus clinical isolates: Mode of resistance to ganciclovir. Antimicrob Agents Chemother. 1991;35:2191–2197.
104. Lurain NS, Thompson KD, Holmes EW, Read GS. Point mutations in the DNA polymerase gene of human cytomegalovirus that result in resistance to antiviral agents. J Virol. 1992;66:7146–7152.
105. Chou S, Guentzel S, Michels KR, et al. Frequency of UL 97 phosphotransferase mutations related to ganciclovir resistance in clinical cytomegalovirus isolates. J Infect Dis. 1995;172:239–242.
106. Sullivan V, Biron KK, Talarico C, et al. A point mutation in the human cytomegalovirus DNA polymerase gene confers resistance to ganciclovir and phosphonylmethoxyalkyl dirvatives. Antimicrob Agents Chemother. 1993;37:19–25.
107. Chou S, Lurain NS, Weinberg A, et al. Interstrain variation in the human cytomegalovirus DNA polymerase sequence and its effect on genotype diagnosis of antiviral drug resistance. Antimicrob Agents Chemother. 1999;43:1500–1502.
108. Crumpacker CS. Mechanism of action of foscarnet against viral polymerases. Am J Med. 1992;92(Suppl 2A):2A3S–2A7S.
109. Jacobson MA, Wulfsohn M, Feinberg JE, et al. Phase II dose-ranging trial of foscarnet salvage therapy for cytomegalovirus retinitis in AIDS patients intolerant of or resistant to ganciclovir (ACTG protocol 093). AIDS. 1994;8:451–459.
110. Baldanti F, Underwood MR, Stant SC, et al. Single amino acid changes in the DNA polymerase confer foscarnet resistance and slow growth phenotype, while mutation in the UL 97 encoded phosphotransferase confers ganciclovir resistance in the double-resistant human cytomegalovirus strains removed from patients with AIDS. J Virol. 1996;70:1390–1395.
111. Studies of Ocular Complications of AIDS Research Group, AIDS Clinical Trials Group. Mortality in patients with the acquired immunodeficiency syndrome treated with either foscarnet or ganciclovir for cytomegalovirus retinitis. N Engl J Med. 1992;326:213–220. [Erratum, N Engl J Med. 1992;326:1172.]
112. The studies of Ocular Complications of AIDS Research Group, AIDS Clinical Trials Group. Combination foscarnet and ganciclovir therapy vs. monotherapy for the treatment of relapsed cytomegalovirus retinitis in patients with AIDS: The Cytomegalovirus Retreatment Trial. Arch Ophthalmol. 1996;114:23–33.
113. Ho HT, Woods KL, Bronson JJ, et al. Intercellular metabolism of the antiherpes agent (S)-1-{3-hydroxy-2-(phosphonylmethoxy)propyl}cytosine. Mol Pharmacol. 1992;41:197–202.
114. Lalezari JP, Jaffe HS, Stagg RG, et al. Randomized controlled study of the safety and efficacy of intravenous cidofovir for the treatments of relapsing cytomegalovirus retinitis in patients with AIDS. J AIDS. 1998;17:339–344.
115. Polis MA, Spooner KM, Baird BF, et al. Anticytomegaloviral activity and safety of ganciclovir in patients with human immunodeficiency virus infection and cytomegaloviruses. Antimicrob Agents Chemother. 1995;39:882–886.
116. Lalezari JP, Stagg RJ, Kupperman BD, et al. Intravenous ganciclovir for peripheral cytomegalovirus retinitis in patients with AIDS. Ann Intern Med. 1997;126:257–263.
117. Crumpacker CS, Kowalsky PN, Oliver SA, et al. Resistance of herpes simplex virus to 9-{[2-hydroxy-1-(hydroxymethyl)ethoxy]methyl}guanine: Physical mapping of drug synergism within the viral DNA polymerase locus. Proc Natl Acad Sci USA. 1984;81:1556–1560.
118. Manischevitz JF, Quinnan GV, Lane HC, Witter AE. Synergistic effect of ganciclovir and foscarnet on cytomegalovirus replication in vitro. Antimicrob Agents Chemother 1990;34:373–375.
119. Cherrington JM, Fuller MD, Lamy PD, et al. In vitro antiviral susceptibilities of isolates from CMV retinitis patients receiving first or second line cidofovir therapy, relationship to clinical outcome. J Infect Dis. 1998;178:1821–1825.
120. Chilar T, Fuller MD, Cherrington JM. Characterization of drug resistance associated mutations in the human cytomegalovirus DNA polymerase gene by using recombinant mutant viruses generated from overlapping DNA fragments. J Virol. 1998;72;5927–5936.
121. Goodrich JM, Mori M, Gleaves CA, et al. Early treatment with ganciclovir to prevent cytomegalovirus disease after allogeneic bone marrow transplantation. N Engl J Med 1991;325:1601–1607.
122. Schmidt GM, Horack DA, Niland JC, et al. A randomized, controlled trial of prophylactic ganciclovir for cytomegalovirus pulmonary infection in recipients of allogeneic bone marrow transplants. N Engl J Med 1991;324:1005–1011.
123. Merigan TC, Renlund DG, Keay S, et al. A controlled trial of ganciclovir to prevent cytomegalovirus disease after heart transplantation. N Engl J Med. 1992;326:1182–1186.
124. Winston DJ, Wirin D, Shaked A, Busuttil RW. Randomized comparison of ganciclovir and high-dose acyclovir for long-term cytomegalovirus prophylaxis in liver-transplant recipients. Lancet. 1995;346:69–74.
125. Spector SA, McKinley GF, Lalezari JP, et al. Oral ganciclovir for the prevention of cytomegalovirus disease in persons wth AIDS. N Engl J Med. 1996;334:1491–1497.
126. Spector SA, Wong R, Hiza K, et al. Plasma cytomegalovirus (CMV) DNA load predicts CMV disease and survival in AIDS patients. J Clin Invest. 1998;101:497–502.
127. Gane E, Salida F, Valdecasas GJC, et al. Randomized trial of efficacy and safety of oral ganciclovir in the prevention of cytomegalovirus disease in live transplant recipients. Lancet. 1997;350:1729–1733.
128. Brennan D, Garlick K, Singer G, et al. Prophylactic oral ganciclovir compared to deferred therapy for control of cytomegalovirus disease in renal transplant patients. Transplantation. 1997;64:1843–1846.
129. Ho M, Suwansirikul S, Dowling JN, et al. The transplanted kidney as a source of cytomegalovirus infection. N Engl J Med. 1975;293:1109–1112.
130. Betts RF, Freeman RB, Douglas RG Jr, et al. Transmission of cytomegalovirus infection with renal allograft. Kidney Int. 1975;8:387–394.
131. Ho M. Virus infections after transplantation in man. Arch Virol. 1977;55:1–24.
132. Dowling JN, Saslow AR, Ho M, et al. Cytomegalovirus infection in patients receiving immunosuppressive therapy for rheumatologic disorders. J Infect Dis. 1976;133:399–408.
133. Rubin RH. Infection in the renal transplant patient. In: Rubin RH, Young LS, eds. Clinical Approach to Infection in the Compromised Host. New York: Plenum; 1981:553–605.
134. Dummer JS, Hardy A, Poorsatter A, et al. Early infections in kidney, heart and liver transplant recipients on cyclosporine. Transplantation. 1983;36:259–267.
135. Thomason AW. FK-506—How much potential? Immunol Today. 1990;11:6–9.
136. Shepp DH, Dandliker PS, de Miranda P, et al. Activity of 9-[2-hydroxy-1-(hydroxymethyl)ethoxymethyl]guanine in the treatment of cytomegalovirus pneumonia. Ann Intern Med. 1985;103:368–373.
137. Crumpacker CS, Marlowe S, Zhang JL, Abrams S, Watkins P. Ganciclovir Bone Marrow Transplant Treatment Group. Treatment of cytomegalovirus pneumonia. Rev Infect Dis. 1988;10(Suppl 3):S538–S546.
138. Emmanuel D, Cunningham I, Jules-Elysee K, et al. Cytomegalovirus pneumonia after bone marrow transplantation successfully treated with the combination of ganciclovir and high-dose intravenous immune globulin. Ann Intern Med. 1988;109:783–788.
139. Reed EC, Bowden RA, Dandliker PS, et al. Treatment of cytomegalovirus pneumonia with ganciclovir and intravenous cytomegalovirus immunoglobulin in patients with bone marrow transplants. Ann Intern Med. 1988;109:783–788.
140. Schmidt GM, Kovacs A, Zaia JA, et al. Ganciclovir/immunoglobulin combination therapy for the treatment of human cytomegalovirus-associated interstitial pneumonia in bone marrow allograft recipients. Transplantation. 1988;46:905–907.
141. Ljungman P, Engelhard D, Link H. Treatment of interstitial pneumonitis due to cytomegalovirus with ganciclovir and intravenous immune globulin: Experience of European bone marrow transplantation. Clin Infect Dis. 1992;14:831–835.
142. Patel R, Snydman DR, Rubin RH, et al. Cytomegalovirus prophylaxis in solid organ transplant recipients. Transplantation. 1996;61:1279–1289.
143. Stratta RJ, Shaeffer MS, Markin RS, et al. Clinical patterns of cytomegalovirus disease after liver transplantation. Arch Surg. 1989;124:1433–1450.
144. McCarthy JM, Karim MA, Keown PA. The cost impact of cytomegalovirus disease in renal transplant recipients. Transplantation. 1993;55:1277–1282.
145. Demetris AJ, Lasky S, Van Thiel DH, et al. Pathology of hepatic transplantation. Am J Pathol. 1985;116:151–161.
146. Paya CV, Weisner RH, Hermans PE, et al. Risk factors for cytomegalovirus and severe bacterial infections following liver transplantation: A prospective multivariate time-dependent analysis. J Hepatol. 1993;18:185–195.
147. O'Grady JG, Alexander GJ, Sutherland S, Williams R. CMV infection and donor/recipients HLA antigens: Interdependent co-factors in the pathogenesis of vanishing bile duct syndrome after liver transplantation. Lancet. 1988;2:302–305.
148. Snydman DR, Werner BG, Dougherty NN, et al. Cytomegalovirus immune globulin prophylaxis in liver transplantation. A randomized, double-blind, placebo-controlled trial. The Boston Center for Liver Transplantation CMVIG Study Group. Ann Intern Med. 1993;119:984–991.
149. Singh N, Yu VL, Mieles L, et al. High-dose acyclovir compared with short-course preemptive ganciclovir therapy to prevent ctyomegalovirus disease in liver transplant recipients. Ann Intern Med. 1994;120:375–381.
150. Martin M, Manez R, Linden P, et al. A prospective randomized trial comparing sequential ganciclovir-high dose acyclovir to high dose acyclovir for prevention of cytomegalovirus disease in adult liver transplant recipients. Transplantation. 1994;58:779–785.
151. Stratta RJ, Shaefer MS, Cushing KA, et al. A randomized prospective trial of acyclovir and immune globulin prophylaxis in liver transplant recipients receiving OKT3 therapy. Arch Surg. 1992;127:55–64.
152. Ho M. Cytomegalovirus. In: Mandell J, Bennett J, Dolin R, eds. Principles of Infectious Disease. Philadelphia: WB Saunders; 1996.
153. Aldrete JS, Sterling WA, Hathaway BM, et al. Gastrointestinal and hepatic complications affecting patients with renal allografts. Am J Surg. 1975;129:115–124.
154. Petersen PK, Balfour HH Jr, Marker SC, et al. Cytomegalovirus disease in renal allograft recipients: A prospective study of the clinical features, risk factors and impact on renal transplantation. Medicine (Baltimore). 1980;59:283–300.
155. Hecht DW, Snydman DR, Crumpacker CS, et al. Boston Renal Transplant CMV Study Group. Ganciclovir for treatment of renal transplant-associated primary cytomegalovirus pneumonia. J Infect Dis. 1988;157:187–190.
156. Snydman DR, Werner BG, Heinze-Lacey B, et al. Use of cytomegalovirus immune globulin to prevent cytomegalovirus disease in renal-transplant recipients. N Engl J Med. 1987;317:1049–1054.
157. Snydman DR, Werner BG, Dougherty NN, et al. Cytomegalovirus prophylaxis in liver transplantation. Ann Intern Med. 1993;119:984–991.
158. Hibberd PL, Tolkoff-Rubin NE, Conti D, et al. Preemptive ganciclovir therapy to prevent cytomegalovirus disease in cytomegalovirus antibody-positive renal transplant recipients: A randomized controlled trial. Ann Intern Med. 1995;123:18–26.
159. Stagno S, Pass RF, Dworsky ME, et al. Congenital and perinatal cytomegalovirus infections. Semin Perinatol. 1983;7:31–42.
160. Stagno S, Pass RF, Dworsky ME, et al. Congenital cytomegalovirus infection: The relative importance of primary and recurrent maternal infection. N Engl J Med. 1982;306:945–949.
161. Stagno S, Whitley RJ. Herpesvirus infections of pregnancy. Part I: Cytomegalovirus and Epstein-Barr virus infection. N Engl J Med. 1985;313:1270–1274.

162. Ahlfors K, Harris S, Ivarsson S, et al. Secondary maternal cytomegalovirus infection causing symptomatic congenital infection. N Engl J Med. 1981;305:284.
163. Hanshaw JB. Developmental abnormalities associated with congenital cytomegalovirus infection. In: Wollam DHM, ed. Advances in Teratology. v. 4. New York: Academic Press; 1970:64.
164. Yeager AS, Grumet FC, Hafleigh EB, et al. Prevention of transfusion-acquired cytomegalovirus infection in newborn infants. J Pediatr. 1981;98:281–287.
165. Hanshaw JB, Scheiner AP, Moxley AW, et al. School failure and deafness after "silent" congenital cytomegalovirus infection. N Engl J Med. 1976;295:468–470.
166. Stagno S, Reynolds DW, Amos CS, et al. Auditory and visual defects resulting from symptomatic and subclinical congenital cytomegaloviral and toxoplasma infections. Pediatrics. 1977;59:669–678.
167. Alexander ER. Maternal and neonatal infection with cytomegalovirus in Taiwan (Abstract). Pediatr Res. 1967;1:210.
168. Chandler SH, Handsfield HH, McDougall JK. Isolation of multiple strains of cytomegalovirus from women attending a clinic for sexually transmitted diseases. J Infect Dis. 1987;155:655–660.
169. Numazaki Y, Yano N, Morizuka T, et al. Primary infection with human cytomegalovirus: Virus isolation from healthy infants and pregnant women. Am J Epidemiol. 1970;91:410–417.
170. Stagno S, Reynolds D, Tsiantos A, et al. Cervical cytomegalovirus excretion in pregnant and non-pregnant women: Suppressions in early gestation. J Infect Dis. 1975;131:522–527.
171. Montgomery RL, Youngblood LA, Medearis DN Jr. Recovery of cytomegalovirus from the cervix in pregnancy. Pediatrics. 1972;49:524–531.
172. Reynolds DW, Stagno S, Hosty TS, et al. Maternal cytomegalovirus excretion and perinatal infection. N Engl J Med. 1973;289:1–5.

Chapter 128

Epstein-Barr Virus (Infectious Mononucleosis)

ROBERT T. SCHOOLEY

Epstein-Barr virus (EBV) is a ubiquitous human herpesvirus. Infection with EBV is common, worldwide in distribution, and largely subclinical in early childhood. EBV has been established as the causative agent of heterophile-positive infectious mononucleosis, which occurs most frequently in late adolescence or early adulthood. In addition, an association between EBV and African Burkitt's lymphoma, as well as between EBV and nasopharyngeal carcinoma, has been suggested by seroepidemiologic data and by the detection of the EBV genome in cells from both tumors. However, the potential causative relationship between EBV and these tumors remains to be established.

HISTORY

Historical accounts of infectious mononucleosis often ascribe the initial description of the disease to Filatov or Pfeiffer who nearly simultaneously at the end of the 19th century described an illness characterized by malaise, fever, hepatosplenomegaly, lymphadenopathy, and abdominal discomfort.[1, 2] This illness came to be known as Drusenfieber (glandular fever) and occurred in family outbreaks. However, without specific techniques with which to establish the diagnosis, the concept of Drusenfieber as a clinical entity fell into disrepute. Between 1910 and 1920 a number of observers reported cases of apparent spontaneous remission of leukemia, with a clinical course that is consistent with the spontaneous resolution of infectious mononucleosis.[3, 4] The establishment of infectious mononucleosis as a clinical entity is credited to Sprunt and Evans, who in 1921 described six cases of fever, lymphadenopathy, and prostration occurring in previously healthy young adults.[5] The authors pointed out the mononuclear lymphocytosis that developed in each of the patients and contrasted the "pathologic" appearance of these lymphocytes to the uniform lymphocyte morphologic characteristics observed in children with other infections. Two years later, Downey and McKinlay described additional cases of infectious mononucleosis and provided a more detailed morphologic description of the atypical lymphocyte.[6] The recognition of atypical lymphocytosis as a hematologic marker for the disease led to more accurate descriptions of the clinical manifestations of illness.

A major advance occurred in 1932 when Paul and Bunnell, investigating immunologic mechanisms in serum sickness, unexpectedly encountered high titers of spontaneously occurring sheep red blood cell agglutinins in the sera of patients with infectious mononucleosis.[7] Davidsohn later enhanced the specificity of detection of this heterophile antibody by differential absorption of serum with guinea pig kidney and beef erythrocytes.[8]

During the 1940s and 1950s, substantial efforts were made to detect a causative agent for infectious mononucleosis. Attempts to culture etiologically related bacteria and viruses from patients with infectious mononucleosis proved unsuccessful. The disease could not be transmitted to animals. Interpretation of experimental attempts to transmit the disease to humans was hindered by the failure to appreciate the widespread occurrence of asymptomatic infection in preadolescents as well as the absence of a serologic marker of immunity.[9–11]

The identification of EBV followed the description by Burkitt in 1958 of an unusual lymphoma with a predilection for the head and neck.[12] The geographic distribution of this tumor paralleled that of certain mosquito-borne diseases in Africa, and a search for an etiologically related arbovirus was undertaken. Epstein and associates in 1964 described the presence of particles that resembled herpesviruses in tissue cultures of biopsy specimens from patients with Burkitt's lymphoma.[13] However, attempts to propagate the virus in conventional tissue cultures were unsuccessful. An indirect immunofluorescent antibody technique to this virus, now called *Epstein-Barr virus,* was developed by Werner and Gertrude Henle,[14] and high titers of this antibody were detected in patients with Burkitt's lymphoma. Additional studies revealed that 90% of American adults had demonstrable EBV antibodies as well.[14] The development of infectious mononucleosis in a technician in the Henles' laboratory on whom sequentially obtained sera were analyzed for EBV antibody suggested that acute EBV infection may be associated with this illness.[15] Large-scale epidemiologic studies[16–19] demonstrated that heterophile-positive infectious mononucleosis occurred in patients without preexisting EBV antibody and, conversely, heterophile-positive infectious mononucleosis was always accompanied by acquisition of EBV antibodies. These epidemiologic studies indicated that subclinical EBV infection also occurred. With specific antibody tests for EBV, it became apparent that 10 to 20% of the cases of mononucleosis, of which most are heterophile-negative, were caused by other agents, of which the most frequent was cytomegalovirus. This chapter deals primarily with EBV-induced infectious mononucleosis.

DESCRIPTION OF EPSTEIN-BARR VIRUS

Physical Properties

Epstein-Barr virus has the characteristic morphologic features of the Herpesviridae family of viruses of which it is a member. By electron microscopy, individual virions are 180 to 200 nm in diameter and appear as hexagonal nucleocapsids surrounded by a complex envelope. The nucleocapsids are 100 nm in diameter and consist of an orderly array of capsomeres with the 5:3:2 symmetry seen in herpesviruses.[20] EBV DNA is double-stranded with a molecular weight of $101 \pm 3 \times 10^6$ and a buoyant density of 1.718 g/cm^3 in CsCl.[21] The EBV genome encodes about 80 proteins.[22]

Biologic Properties

The host range of the virus is limited. In vitro cultivation of the virus has been described primarily in B lymphocytes and nasopharyngeal epithelial cells of humans and certain nonhuman primates.[28] The virus generally does not produce cytopathic effects in infected cells. After infection by the virus, B lymphocytes that contain the EBV genome are capable of continuous in vitro cultivation, and are termed *transformed* or *immortalized.* EBV has been confirmed as the transforming agent through the detection of viral antigens by indirect immunofluorescence within the nuclei of transformed cells or by hybridization of cellular DNA with purified EBV DNA.

Epstein-Barr virus receptors are demonstrable on B lymphocytes and nasopharyngeal epithelial cells of humans and certain nonhuman primates.[29, 30] EBV receptors are also present on a smaller proportion of complement receptor–bearing, non-B, non-T lymphocytes.[31–33] The EBV receptor is also the receptor for the d region of the third component of complement.[34, 35] The C3d receptor (also known as CR2 or CD21), a 145-kD glycoprotein, is encoded by a member of a multiple gene family that specifies a number of cell membrane molecules.

After attachment to the receptor, the virus gains entry to susceptible B lymphocytes. Before the detection of virus-directed protein synthesis, Epstein-Barr nuclear antigens (EBNA) are demonstrable in nuclei of infected cells.[36] At high multiplicities of infection, up to 25% of EBV-exposed B lymphocytes express EBNA.[37] Viral DNA synthesis is initiated with the production of multiple copies of the EBV genome. In transformed cells from patients with infectious mononucleosis or Burkitt's lymphoma, some viral DNA may be incorporated into the DNA of the host cell, although most of the DNA remains in a circular nonintegrated form as an episome. Linear integration of EBV DNA into host cell DNA may be enhanced by stimulation of the host cells by B-cell mitogens such as bacterial lipopolysaccharide at the time of transformation.[38] The host cell gains the property of immortality whether the virus is present in integrated or episomal forms, or a combination of the two forms.[38] Immortalization of B lymphocytes is a complex process that involves a coordinated interplay among a number of viral and host cell gene products.[22, 39–47] Latent infection of B cells by EBV is determined by binding of the EBNA-1 protein to a viral promoter termed *oriP.* EBNA-1 also transactivates the EBNA-2 protein, which, in turn, activates production of three EBV-encoded latent membrane proteins (LMP-1, 2A, and 2B), as well as several B-cell gene products (CD21, CD23 and *c-fgr*). LMP-1 activates production of several intercellular adhesion cell proteins (ICAM-1, LFA-1, and LFA-3), as well as an autocrine growth factor for B cells (CD23). LMP-1 may play an important role in EBV-associated oncogenesis in that it morphologically transforms epithelial and B cells[48] and prevents apoptosis (programmed cell death).[49]

Under most culture conditions, 10% or less of EBV-exposed B lymphocytes form continuous cell lines.[37] After transformation, the host cell replicates, and the progeny cells contain several EBV genocopies in latent form. In addition to viral antigens, EBV-transformed B lymphocytes produce or secrete immunoglobulin, or do both.[50–53] Although most polyclonally transformed lines produce immunoglobulin of the IgM class, studies of clonally transformed B lymphocytes indicate that EBV is capable of induction of the synthesis of immunoglobulin of the IgG, IgA, or IgM class.[54]

Cell lines that contain EBV genomes are characterized as producer or nonproducer lines. Most of the time, EBV remains in latent form both in vitro in established cell lines and in vivo in circulating lymphocytes. Three general patterns of expression of EBV-encoded proteins have been observed in association with latency (Table 128–1).[23] In Burkitt's lymphoma (latency I) only EBV-encoded RNAs (EBERs) and EBNA1 are expressed.[24] In latency II exemplified by nasopharyngeal carcinoma, three latent membrane proteins (LMP1, LMP2A, and LMP2B) are expressed in addition to EBERs and EBNA1.[25, 26] In lymphoid cell lines (latency III), six nuclear antigens (EBNA1, EBNA2, EBNA3A, EBNA3B, EBNA3C, and LP) are expressed in addition to factors expressed in latency I. Latent virus can be activated by stimulation of host B cells by certain chemicals or by antibodies to surface immunoglobulin.[22] After such stimulation, in the case of B-cells an immediate early gene of EBV (the EBV BZLF1 gene product or ZEBRA protein) is activated. In the case of epithelial cells, expression of another viral protein (BRLF1) triggers the transition from latency to lytic infection.[27] Expression of these proteins leads to a cascade of events culminating in the production of early EBV gene (EA) products responsible for viral replication (thymidine kinase and DNA polymerase), and late (structural) genes of the virus including viral capsid antigens (VCAs). On induction of early and viral capsid antigens, the virus enters a lytic cycle of infection that results in both the production of progeny virions and destruction of the host cell.

EPIDEMIOLOGY

Serum Antibody Prevalence

Antibodies to EBV have been found in all population groups studied, and most studies have shown no predilection for either sex. Antibodies are acquired earlier in life in tropical than in industrialized countries, but by adulthood 90 to 95% of most populations have demonstrable EBV antibodies.[55, 56]

Two strains of EBV have been defined on the basis of viral gene sequences expressed during latency and on their ability to transform B lymphocytes.[22] The strains (Type 1 [A] or 2 [B]) are not distinguishable serologically, but they do express unique epitopes that are identified by cytotoxic T cells. Although it was initially thought that there were specific geographic distributions for these two strains of EBV, it is now clear that both strains are widely distributed and that individuals can be coinfected with both strains. In the United States and in Great Britain, EBV seroconversion occurs before the age of 5 years in about 50% of the population.[56–58] A second wave of seroconversion occurs midway through the second decade of life. EBV seroconversion may occur at a younger average age in the southern United States than in other areas of that country.[59] Lower socioeconomic groups have a higher EBV antibody prevalence than do more affluent age-matched controls. The reported increased prevalence of EBV antibodies among blacks probably reflects this socioeconomic distribution.

Incidence of Infection

Clinically apparent infectious mononucleosis occurs most frequently in populations in which primary EBV exposure is delayed until the second decade of life. The disease is diagnosed most frequently among adolescents of higher socioeconomic groups in industrialized countries.[60] The incidence of infectious mononucleosis in a large epidemiologic study in the United States was 45.2 cases/100,000/year.[61] The incidence was highest in the 15- to 24-year-old age group. The incidence was the same for women as for men, but the

TABLE 128–1 Forms of Epstein-Barr Virus Latency

	Epstein-Barr Virus Expression	Clinical Condition
Latency I	EBNA1, EBV-encoded RNAs	African Burkitt's lymphoma, infectious mononucleosis
Latency II	EBNA1, EBV-encoded RNAs, LMP1, LMP2A, and LMP2B	Nasopharyngeal carcinoma, infectious mononucleosis
Latency III	EBNA1, 2, 3A, 3B, 3C, and LP LMP1, LMP2A, and LMP2B, EBV-encoded RNAs	Lymphoid cell lines, infectious mononucleosis

TABLE 128–2 Frequency of Epstein-Barr Virus Shedding

Population Description	Oropharyngeal Shedding Rate (%) (Range)	Reference
EBV-seronegatives	0	66
Seropositive healthy adults	12–25	66, 69–71
Solid tumor patients	27	70, 71
HIV-1–infected individuals	50	72
Renal transplant recipients	56–70	69, 71
Infectious mononucleosis patients	50–100	65–68
Critically ill leukemia or lymphoma patients	74–92	70, 71

Abbreviations: EBV, Epstein-Barr virus; HIV, human immunodeficiency virus.

peak age-specific incidence occurred 2 years earlier in women. The incidence of infectious mononucleosis was 30 times higher for whites than for blacks. The infrequency of infectious mononucleosis among blacks, noted as early as 1940, is probably a reflection of earlier primary EBV infection and the higher frequency of subclinical infections in children.[62–64] No clear seasonal incidence has been noted.

Methods of Spread

Low titers of EBV are present in throat washings of those with infectious mononucleosis.[65–67] Susceptible roommates of students with infectious mononucleosis or with inapparent EBV infection experience EBV seroconversion no more frequently than the general susceptible college population does.[18, 59] Only 6% of those with infectious mononucleosis cite previous contact with another case of infectious mononucleosis.[61] The virus persists in the oropharynx of patients with infectious mononucleosis for up to 18 months after clinical recovery.[68] It can be cultured from throat washings from 10 to 20% of normal healthy adults, from 50% of kidney transplant recipients, and from greater proportions of those critically ill with leukemia or lymphoma (Table 128–2).[69–71] Approximately 50% of human immunodeficiency virus (HIV)-1–infected homosexual men shed EBV in oropharyngeal secretions.[72] EBV sequences or antigens, or both, have also been identified in parotid duct and uterine cervical epithelia, although the implications of this distribution are unclear with respect to viral transmission.[73, 74]

EBV, like other herpesviruses, is relatively labile in the laboratory, and the virus has not been recovered from environmental sources, including fomites. These data suggest that EBV is a widespread agent of low contagiousness and that most cases of infectious mononucleosis are probably contracted by intimate contact between susceptible individuals and asymptomatic shedders of EBV. Among young adults, spread of the virus may be facilitated by the transfer of saliva with kissing.[75, 76] Serologic evidence suggests that the virus may also be spread among susceptible individuals within families.[77, 78] Infectious mononucleosis has also been spread by blood transfusion and after open heart surgery as the "postpump perfusion" syndrome.[79] Most postpump perfusion infectious mononucleosis is, however, attributable to cytomegalovirus.

Although several apparent epidemics of infectious mononucleosis have been described, these reports have not been substantiated with EBV serologic data and have lacked rigorous epidemiologic, clinical, or laboratory support. Some of these have resulted from errors in the performance of Monospot tests.[80] On the basis of the previously discussed information, it is unlikely that true epidemics of infectious mononucleosis occur.

Public Health Impact

College and military populations experience the highest morbidity from infectious mononucleosis, although cases occur in other groups as well. Infectious mononucleosis accounted for 5% of all hospitalizations of University of Wisconsin students, with an incidence of 450 admissions/100,000 students/year. Other American universities have reported similar incidences.[81, 82] Approximately 12% of susceptible college students undergo EBV seroconversion yearly.[18, 19] Many of these infections are subclinical (see further on).[18, 59] Although primary EBV infection may be clinically apparent in only about 10% of military cases, infectious mononucleosis ranked fourth as the cause of days lost due to illness in army personnel.[83, 84] Detailed information on the impact of infectious mononucleosis on the general population is not available because infectious mononucleosis is not a reportable disease in most states. However, it is likely that morbidity from infectious mononucleosis is generally underestimated because a specific diagnosis may not be made and the nonspecific illness can be attributed to a variety of other causes.

PATHOGENESIS

Histopathologic Findings

The usually benign course of infectious mononucleosis has limited pathologic examination to tissues obtained from fatal cases or from cases with atypical features from which biopsy specimens were obtained for diagnostic evaluation. During the acute phase of the illness, lymph nodes throughout the body are moderately enlarged. Individual nodes reveal increased numbers of enlarged, moderately active lymphoid follicles. Germinal centers are also enlarged, with cores containing blast cells, histiocytes, and lymphocytes. Although the reticulin framework remains intact, invasion by the hyperplastic pulp makes its borders less distinct.[85] In studies of spleens obtained at autopsy or at surgery after rupture, the organ is usually two to three times its normal weight.[86] The splenic capsule and trabeculae are edematous, thinned, and invaded by lymphoid cells. Most of the increased splenic size is the result of hyperplasia of the red pulp. Throughout the red pulp, pleomorphic blast cells are evident. The spleen is often congested with focal, particularly subcapsular, hemorrhages. The white pulp is relatively normal. Tonsillar biopsy specimens obtained during the course of mononucleosis reveal intense proliferation with numerous mitoses.[87] Bone marrow aspirate and biopsy specimens are often strikingly normal when compared with the florid changes noted in peripheral blood. Biopsy specimens are usually normocellular to mildly hypercellular. Small granulomas may be present, but these are not specific for mononucleosis and have no prognostic significance.[88, 89]

Changes in hepatic histologic features are usually mild. Hepatocytes demonstrate minimal swelling and vacuolization. Pleomorphic lymphocytic and monocytic portal infiltration is usually evident. Bile ducts may be minimally swollen, but frank biliary stasis is rare.[90, 91] A number of histopathologic changes have been reported in the nervous system of fatal cases of infectious mononucleosis.[87, 92, 93] These changes include neuronal degeneration, perivascular cuffing, perivascular hemorrhage, and astrocytic hyperplasia. Little mononuclear infiltration may be present despite demonstrable degenerative changes in the neurons of the cortex, basal ganglia, cerebellum, or spinal cord.

Humoral and Cell-Mediated Immune Responses

On the basis of the available evidence, the likely route of initial EBV infection is via the oropharynx. Cytohybridization studies have demonstrated EBV DNA within oropharyngeal epithelial cells. The virus presumably infects susceptible B lymphocytes within lymphoid tissue of the pharynx either simultaneously or subsequently.[94] Although a prior epidemiologically based study suggested that the incubation period of acute infectious mononucleosis is 30 to 50 days, this observation has not yet been confirmed using molecular epidemiologic techniques.[59] Thus, the incubation period of the illness is somewhat speculative. The immune response to EBV-infected transformed lymphocytes is complex and involves both humoral and cell-mediated immune mechanisms.[95]

EBV-induced infectious mononucleosis results in the synthesis of circulating antibodies directed against viral antigens as well as against unrelated antigens found on sheep, horse, and beef red cells. These latter are the so-called heterophile antibodies, which are detected as sheep and horse red cell agglutinins and beef cell hemolysins. The role of these antibodies in the pathogenesis or recovery from the illness is unclear. Heterophile antibodies are a heterogeneous group of predominantly IgM antibodies that may be separated by affinity chromatography into antibody populations with either Paul-Bunnell or Forssman specificity.[96] Heterophile antibodies do not cross-react with antibodies specific for EBV.[97] Immunization with sheep erythrocytes elicits sheep red cell agglutinins but has no effect on preexisting antibodies to EBV.[98, 99] There is no good correlation between the heterophile titer and the severity of the illness. Specific antibodies directed against EBV capsid antigen and often against other EBV antigens are demonstrable in most patients with infectious mononucleosis. These EBV-specific antibodies are discussed in detail under "Laboratory Diagnosis." In addition, a number of antibodies with other specificities have been detected during primary EBV infection. Among these are antibodies that bind platelets, neutrophils, lymphocytes, nuclear antigens, and ampicillin.[100–108] The potential role of these antibodies in some of the complications of infectious mononucleosis is not yet clear.

Non-EBV-specific cell-mediated immune functions are depressed early in the course of the illness, as measured by cutaneous anergy and decreased proliferative responses to mitogens and antigens.[109] During the first few weeks of clinical illness, a mononuclear lymphocytosis is present. Although earlier studies have suggested that an increase in B lymphocytes may occur as well, most of the increased numbers of lymphocytes have T-cell markers.[110–112] Studies using monoclonal antibodies have demonstrated an increase in both the relative and absolute number of T lymphocytes expressing surface antigens that have been associated with suppressor-cytotoxic function in vitro.[113–115] At the height of the illness, 0.005 to 0.5% of circulating mononuclear cells are capable of forming continuous cell lines in vitro.[116] Up to 20% of peripheral blood non-T lymphocytes may express EBNA during the first week of illness.[117] In acute infectious mononucleosis, the pattern of expression of EBV-associated products in peripheral blood B cells is heterogeneous with individual cells exhibiting expression patterns characteristic of latency I, II, or III.[118] In cell expressing the EBV-associated latent membrane protein-1 (LMP-1), a 30–base pair deletion variant often associated with EBV-associated malignancy is frequently observed in acute infection.[119, 120] In addition, lower levels of transcripts associated with lytic infection can be demonstrated in acute infectious mononucleosis.[121] Presumably, as a result of the vigorous cellular and humoral EBV-specific immune response that arises during acute infectious mononucleosis, lytic transcripts are rarely observed in EBV-seropositive individuals after convalescence.

The cellular immune response to EBV is complex, well integrated and includes both T lymphocytes and natural killer cells.[122–125] T lymphocytes from adults with immunity to EBV or from patients who are recovering from infectious mononucleosis have the capacity to suppress the outgrowth of autologous EBV-infected B lymphocytes.[125] Epitope mapping studies have demonstrated that EBV-specific cytotoxic T lymphocytes are directed against a broad array of latent and lytic proteins, including LMP-1, several of the Epstein-Barr virus nuclear antigens and several immediate early and early lytic cycle proteins.[95, 126–136]

During the acute phase of infectious mononucleosis, T lymphocytes capable of suppression of immunoglobulin synthesis are demonstrable in the peripheral blood.[137, 138] Elevations in serum cytokine levels including interleukin-2, interleukin-6, and interleukin-10 tumor necrosis factor–α have also been reported.[139–141] However, these elevations have not been observed in all studies and their role in disease pathogenesis is uncertain.

With recovery from illness, the atypical lymphocytosis gradually resolves. Functional and surface phenotypic abnormalities of circulating T lymphocytes also subside. Despite clinical recovery and the presence of both humoral and cell-mediated immune functions specific for EBV, the virus is not eliminated from the host. EBV DNA which is detectable by polymerase chain reaction in plasma during acute infectious mononucleosis, decreases in concentration during convalescence and is not detectable in healthy EBV-seropositive persons after convalescence.[142] Thus, EBV shares the property of latency or persistence with other members of the herpesvirus group. The virus can be cultivated from oropharyngeal washings for up to 12 to 18 months after recovery from infectious mononucleosis and can be recovered from the oropharynx and blood intermittently from both healthy and immunosuppressed persons.[68, 71] In addition, EBV DNA can be detected by polymerase chain reaction in peripheral blood mononuclear cells in approximately 50% of EBV-seropositive healthy children.[142] Although asymptomatic shedding of EBV by healthy persons does not appear to be associated with demonstrable immunologic abnormalities, reactivation of EBV by immunosuppressive drugs may be associated with a return of the abnormal distribution of T-lymphocyte surface phenotypes.[143]

CLINICAL MANIFESTATIONS

Spectrum of Illness

EBV induces a broad spectrum of illness in humans. Classic or typical infectious mononucleosis is an acute illness characterized clinically by sore throat, fever, and lymphadenopathy; serologically by the transient appearance of heterophile antibodies; and hematologically by a mononuclear leukocytosis that consists, in part, of atypical lymphocytes (Table 128–3). An individual case may have most but not necessarily all the aforementioned characteristics. Specific serologic tests for EBV infection indicate that infection results in a spectrum of clinical manifestations. Attempts to exclude cases that fail to meet the classic criteria for infectious mononucleosis result in artificial and often misleading distinctions.

The age of the patient has a profound influence on the clinical expression of EBV infection. In children, primary EBV infection is often asymptomatic. Young children may be more likely to exhibit rashes, neutropenia, or pneumonia than might individuals undergoing primary EBV infection at an older age.[144] Clinically apparent infections in very young children are heterophile-negative in about one-half of the cases.[145] The ratios of clinically apparent to inapparent disease and of EBV-induced heterophile-positive to heterophile-negative cases increase with age. By 4 years of age, 80% of children undergoing primary EBV infection are heterophile antibody–positive.[146]

In patients of college age, the ratio of clinically apparent to inapparent EBV infection ranges from 1:3 to 3:1.[18, 59] In military recruits, this ratio has been as low as 1:10.[84] Because of previously existing immunity, the disease is less common in older patients. When it does occur, however, clinical and serologic manifestations are similar to those found in adolescents.[147] During the course of the illness, 90% of the adolescents with clinically apparent infectious

TABLE 128–3 Manifestations of Epstein-Barr Virus–Induced Infectious Mononucleosis

Clinical
Fever
Sore throat
Lymphadenopathy
Hematologic
More than 50% mononuclear cells
More than 10% atypical lymphocytes
Serologic
Transient appearance of heterophile antibodies
Permanent emergence of antibodies to EBV

Abbreviation: EBV, Epstein-Barr virus.

TABLE 128–4 Symptoms of Infectious Mononucleosis

Symptom	Rate	Percentage	Range (%)
Sore throat	409/502	82	70–88
Malaise	243/426	57	43–76
Headache	216/426	51	37–55
Anorexia	117/546	21	10–27
Myalgias	66/326	20	12–22
Chills	54/326	16	9–18
Nausea	18/156	12	2–17
Abdominal discomfort	37/426	9	2–14
Cough	3/56	5	5
Vomiting	3/56	5	5
Arthralgias	1/56	2	2

Data from refs. 81 and 149–151.

mononucleosis should be heterophile-positive. Therefore, EBV infection is generally inapparent or is a self-limited illness lasting 2 or 3 weeks. In rare cases the disease can be devastating and can be accompanied by severe prostration, major complications, and even death,[148] as is discussed further on.

Symptoms

In most cases, the clinical manifestation of infectious mononucleosis is that of the clinical triad of sore throat, fever, and lymphadenopathy (Table 128–4). The onset may be abrupt, but often several days of prodromal symptoms can be elicited, including chills, sweats, feverish sensations, anorexia, and malaise. Loss of taste for cigarettes is common early in the illness but is not specific for infectious mononucleosis. Retro-orbital headaches, myalgias, and feelings of abdominal fullness are other common prodromal symptoms. The most frequent complaint is sore throat, which may be the most severe the patient has experienced.[149, 150] Other patients seek medical attention because of prolonged fever or malaise and less frequently because of incidentally encountered lymphadenopathy. Rarely, the first manifestation of illness is one of the complications of infectious mononucleosis described further on.

Signs

The signs of infectious mononucleosis are summarized in Table 128–5. Fever is present in more than 90% of the patients with infectious mononucleosis. The fever usually peaks in the afternoon with temperatures of 38°C to 39°C, although a temperature as high as 40°C is not uncommon. In most cases, fever resolves over a 10- to 14-day period. A rash, which may be macular, petechial, scarlatinaform, urticarial, or erythema multiforme–like, is present in about 5% of patients. The administration of ampicillin produces a pruritic, maculopapular eruption in 90 to 100% of the patients, and this rash may appear after cessation of treatment with the drug.[154, 155] Periorbital edema has been reported in up to one third of cases in some series,[150] but it has been observed less frequently in others.[151] Tonsillar enlargement is usually present, occasionally with tonsils meeting at the midline. The pharynx is erythematous with an exudate in about one third of cases. Palatal petechiae may be seen in 25 to 60% of cases but are not diagnostic of infectious mononucleosis. The petechiae are usually multiple, 1 to 2 mm in diameter, occur in crops lasting 3 to 4 days, and are usually seen at the junction of the hard and soft palate.[152] Cervical adenopathy, usually symmetric, is present in 80 to 90% of patients. Posterior adenopathy is most common, but submandibular and anterior adenopathy are quite frequent as well, and axillary and inguinal adenopathy also occur. Individual nodes are freely movable, are not spontaneously painful, and are only mildly tender to palpation. The results of examination of the lungs and heart are usually normal. Abdominal examination may detect hepatomegaly in 10 to 15% of cases, although mild tenderness to fist percussion over the liver is present somewhat more frequently.[149, 151] Jaundice is present in approximately 5% of cases.[150] Splenomegaly is present in about one half of cases if sought carefully over the course of the illness. The splenomegaly is usually maximal at the beginning of the second week of illness and regresses over the next 7 to 10 days. The results of neurologic examination are generally normal, although occasional complications may occur (see further on).

Complications

Most patients with infectious mononucleosis recover uneventfully. Complications that occasionally occur have been extensively reported in the literature, but even these complications have generally resolved fully, although there have been rare fatalities.

Hematologic. Autoimmune hemolytic anemia occurs in 0.5 to 3% of the patients with infectious mononucleosis.[156, 157] Cold agglutinins, almost always of the IgM class, are present in 70 to 80% of cases.[158] Anti-i specificity has been reported in 20 to 70% of cases.[105, 159] Most but not all cases of autoimmune hemolytic anemia in infectious mononucleosis are mediated by antibodies of this specificity.[160–163] The hemolysis usually becomes clinically apparent during the second or third week of illness and subsides over a 1- to 2-month period.[164] Corticosteroids may hasten recovery in some cases. Hematophagocytic syndrome has also been reported with both acute and chronic EBV infection.[165, 166]

Mild thrombocytopenia is common in infectious mononucleosis. Platelet counts less than 140,000/mm^3 were noted in 50% of patients with uncomplicated infectious mononucleosis in one series.[167] Profound thrombocytopenia with bleeding occurs rarely,[168] but platelet counts less than 1000/mm^3 and deaths from intracerebral bleeding have been reported.[169, 170] The mechanism for the thrombocytopenia is not known. The presence of normal or increased numbers of megakaryocytes in the marrow coupled with reports of antiplatelet antibodies suggest that peripheral destruction of platelets may be occurring, possibly on an autoimmune basis.[105, 106, 162] Corticosteroids have been reported to be beneficial for the thrombocytopenia in some but not all cases.[168–171] For refractory cases splenectomy may be indicated.[106] Mild neutropenia is seen rather frequently in uncomplicated infectious mononucleosis. The neutropenia is usually mild and self-limiting, although deaths associated with bacterial sepsis or pneumonia, or both, have been reported.[108, 172–178] Anaerobic sepsis without associated granulocytopenia, presumably of pharyngeal origin, has also been reported.[179]

Splenic Rupture. Splenic rupture is a rare but dramatic complication of infectious mononucleosis. Lymphocytic infiltration of the capsule, trabeculae, and vascular walls coupled with rapid splenic enlargement predisposes the organ to rupture. The incidence of rupture is highest in the second or third week of illness but may be the first sign of infectious mononucleosis. Abdominal pain is uncommon in infectious mononucleosis,[180] and splenic rupture must be strongly considered whenever abdominal pain occurs. The onset of this pain

TABLE 128–5 Signs of Infectious Mononucleosis

Sign	Rate	Percentage	Range (%)
Lymphadenopathy	495/526	94	93–100
Pharyngitis	444/526	84	69–91
Fever	399/526	76	63–100
Splenomegaly	244/470	52	50–63
Hepatomegaly	34/370	12	6–14
Palatal enanthem	18/156	11	5–13
Jaundice	37/426	9	4–10
Rash	49/470	10	0–15

Data from refs. 149–151 and 153.

may be insidious or abrupt. Pathologic examination of some of the ruptured spleens has revealed subcapsular hematomas that suggest that rupture may be preceded by intermittent subcapsular bleeding. The pain, usually in the left upper quadrant, may radiate to the left scapular area. Left upper quadrant tenderness to palpation, with or without rebound tenderness, is usually present along with peritoneal signs or shifting dullness. In rare cases, splenic rupture is unaccompanied by pain and is manifested as shock. Laboratory findings include a falling hematocrit and, in some cases, an elevated left hemidiaphragm. The abdominal catastrophe may reverse the usual differential count of infectious mononucleosis and evoke a neutrophilia. Confirmatory findings should not be awaited if splenic rupture is suspected. Prompt splenectomy is the treatment of choice, although nonoperative observation and splenorrhaphy have a role in the management of selected patients with subcapsular splenic hematoma.[181, 182] Because a history of trauma may be elicited in about one half the cases of splenic rupture,[183] elimination of contact sports, attention to constipation, and caution in splenic palpation are prudent measures in the first few weeks after diagnosis.

Neurologic. Neurologic complications, which occur in less than 1% of the cases, can dominate the clinical presentation[184–199] (Table 128–6). On occasion, these neurologic signs can be the first or only manifestation of infectious mononucleosis. In many cases, the heterophile antibody determination is negative, atypical lymphocytes may be low in number or delayed in appearance, and the diagnosis must be made by changes in EBV-specific antibodies.[184, 185, 190] The encephalitis seen with infectious mononucleosis may be acute in onset and rapidly progressive and severe but is usually associated with a complete recovery. The encephalitis is commonly manifested as a cerebellitis but may also be global.[186–188] The clinical presentation may also resemble aseptic meningitis. In both encephalitis and meningitis, changes in the spinal fluid are mild. The opening pressure is normal or slightly elevated. A predominantly mononuclear pleocytosis may be present, with most cell counts much less than 200/mm^3. Atypical lymphocytes have been seen in the cerebrospinal fluid in a number of cases. The protein level is usually normal to mildly elevated, and the glucose concentration is usually normal. Low titers of EBV VCA can be found in the cerebrospinal fluid.[189] Cases of Guillain-Barré syndrome, Bell's palsy, and transverse myelitis have been reported in primary EBV infection.[190] Although neurologic complications are the most frequent cause of death in infectious mononucleosis, the benign outcome of most of these episodes should be emphasized.[200] Eighty-five percent of the patients with neurologic complications recover completely.[184]

Hepatic. Hepatic manifestations consist largely of self-limited elevations of hepatocellular enzyme levels, which are present in 80 to 90% of the cases of infectious mononucleosis.[201] Reported cases of infectious mononucleosis leading to cirrhosis or other chronic sequelae are poorly documented.

Renal. Abnormal urinary sediment is not uncommon in acute infectious mononucleosis.[202, 203] Microscopic hematuria and proteinuria are the most frequently noted abnormalities.[204] Overt renal dysfunction is, however, extremely rare, although sporadic cases of acute renal failure in association with acute infectious mononucleosis have been reported.[205] It has been hypothesized that the renal manifestations of infectious mononucleosis are usually attributable to interstitial nephritis, which occurs as a manifestation of renal infiltration by activated T lymphocytes.[205] Renal dysfunction in association with EBV-associated rhabdomyolysis has also been reported, although not all cases of rhabdomyolysis are accompanied by renal dysfunction.[206]

Cardiac. Clinically significant cardiac disease is very uncommon. Electrocardiographic abnormalities, usually confined to ST-T wave abnormalities, were reported in 6% of the cases in one series.[207] Pericarditis and fatal myocarditis have also been observed.[208, 209]

Pulmonary. Pulmonary manifestations of infectious mononucleosis are rare.[210–213] Early studies reported the presence of interstitial infiltrates in 3 to 5% of the cases. However, systematic examination for other causes of nonbacterial pneumonias, for example, *Mycoplasma,* were not carried out in these studies, and it is not clear that these infiltrates were related to EBV infection. Pneumonia has, however, been reported, and in at least one instance, EBV-encoded RNA (EBERs) have been demonstrated in pulmonary tissue.[214, 215] The attribution of pulmonary lesions to EBV infection should be made only after other pathogens have been carefully excluded.

Death. Death from infectious mononucleosis is rare.[200, 216] Death may occur either as a result of overwhelming EBV infection or from complications of the disease. Overwhelming infection with demonstrable virus in lymph nodes, spleen, thymus, and other organs may occur in apparently healthy persons, but a familial syndrome of immunodeficiency and EBV infection has also been described.[217] This immunodeficiency syndrome is passed in an X-linked recessive pattern and has acquired the name of the originally described affected kindred (Duncan).[218, 219] Within families with this syndrome, individual cases may end in overwhelming infection and death during the acute phase of the illness, or agammaglobulinemia or lymphoma may develop over a several-year period after infectious mononucleosis.[220–225] The immunologic defect in this syndrome is not yet defined, but disordered immunoregulation after the induction of anomalous killer cells has been postulated.[225]

Neurologic complications of the illness, splenic rupture, or upper airway obstruction are the most frequent causes of death from infectious mononucleosis in otherwise apparently healthy persons. Deaths from complications associated with granulocytopenia, thrombocytopenia, hepatic failure, and myocarditis have also been reported.[163, 176, 200, 209, 226, 227]

TABLE 128–6 Neurologic Complications of Infectious Mononucleosis

Neurologic Complication	Reference
Encephalitis	185–189
Meningitis	185
Myelitis	189
Guillain-Barré syndrome	189
Optic neuritis	191
Retrobulbar neuritis	192
Cranial nerve palsies	189
Mononeuritis multiplex	193
Brachial plexus neuropathy	194
Seizures	185, 189
? Subacute sclerosing panencephalitis	195
Transverse myelitis	196
Psychosis	197
Demyelination	198
Hemiplegia	199

Clinical Course

Most cases of infectious mononucleosis resolve spontaneously over a 2- to 3-week period. The sore throat is usually maximal for 3 to 5 days and then gradually resolves over the course of a week to 10 days. Patients remain febrile for 10 to 14 days, but in the last 5 to 7 days, the fever is usually low grade and associated with little morbidity. The prostration associated with infectious mononucleosis is generally more gradual in its resolution. As the illness resolves, patients often have days of relative well-being that alternate with recrudescence of the symptoms.

Chronic or Persistent Epstein-Barr Virus Infection

It has been suggested that persistent EBV infection is a frequent cause of fatigue and malaise in young and middle-aged adults.[228–231]

This speculation has arisen from reports of a syndrome characterized by fatigue, sore throat, mild cognitive dysfunction, and myalgias initially noted in association with an apparent increase in antibody titers to the EBV early antigen complex.[228, 229] (See "Laboratory Diagnosis," further on). These reports have included primarily young adults, usually with a female preponderance, who acquire a nonspecific symptom complex more reminiscent of the prodrome of infectious mononucleosis than of the syndrome itself (often known as "chronic mononucleosis syndrome" or "chronic fatigue syndrome"). These patients have been noted either sporadically[228, 229, 232] or in epidemic clusters.[231] The initial suggestion that the syndrome is attributable to EBV has become untenable on the basis of serologic and epidemiologic observations.[232, 233] Investigation of the syndrome has been hampered by the vagueness of the symptoms and the absence of objective laboratory diagnostic criteria. A consensus case definition has emerged that focuses on fatigue rather than on EBV as the central feature of the syndrome.[234, 235] The chronic fatigue syndrome is discussed in more detail in Chapter 118.

In contrast to patients with the nonspecific syndrome just noted, rare patients have been identified in which EBV appears to be playing a direct role in ongoing objective organ system dysfunction.[236–240] These patients may present with fever, pulmonary parenchymal involvement, pancytopenia, or ophthalmologic or neurologic abnormalities. Such patients may be distinguished from those with the chronic fatigue syndrome by the presence of objective symptoms and signs and by extremely abnormal EBV-specific serologic findings. Temporary partial or complete responses to acyclovir have been reported in occasional patients.

Association with Burkitt's Lymphoma, Other Lymphomas, and Nasopharyngeal Carcinoma

Virtually all African patients with Burkitt's lymphoma and most patients with nasopharyngeal carcinoma possess high antibody titers to EBV. Viral capsid antibody titers are 10- to 15-fold higher in patients with these tumors than in matched controls.[55, 241] DNA hybridization studies have demonstrated the presence of the EBV genome in biopsy specimens from both Burkitt's lymphoma and nasopharyngeal carcinoma.[242] EBNA-1 but not EBNA-2, EBNA-3, or the LMP are expressed in Burkitt's lymphoma biopsy specimens, and the virus can be recovered from tissue cultures established from these biopsies.[243] EBNA-2, EBNA-3, and the LMP, but not EBNA-1, have been demonstrated to be targets for cytotoxic T lymphocytes[126–131]; thus, expression of these antigens in immunocompetent individuals would render such tumors susceptible to immunologically mediated attack. In addition to EBNA-1, EBERs are also expressed in Burkitt's lymphoma.[24] This pattern of latency, termed *latency I*, is the most restricted pattern of EBV expression in EBV-associated malignant diseases. In the case of nasopharyngeal carcinoma, EBV expression is less restricted and three latent membrane proteins (LMP1, LMP2A, and LMP2B) are expressed in addition to EBERs and EBNA1.[25, 26, 244] This pattern of EBV expression is termed *latency II*. In contrast, evidence for the association of EBV with histologically identical Burkitt's lymphoma tumors in the American population has been lacking.[245] The geographic restriction of Burkitt's lymphoma in Africa and the apparent predilection of nasopharyngeal carcinoma for certain ethnic groups suggests that genetic or environmental factors (including other viruses), or both, may also play a role in tumor development.

Increasing evidence suggests that EBV may also be related to neoplasia in several other settings. The recent demonstration of EBV nucleic acids and EBNA-1 in neoplastic tissue obtained from 20 to 40% cases of Hodgkin's lymphoma has raised the possibility that EBV might also contribute to the pathogenesis of Hodgkin's disease.[118, 246–251] EBV DNA appears to reside primarily within the Reed-Sternberg cell and is found relatively more frequently in pediatric Hodgkin's disease and in tumors of the mixed cellularity type.[249, 252, 253] Within any given histologic type, the presence of EBV does not appear to have a significant effect on prognosis.[254]

Uncontrolled EBV-induced lymphoproliferation may occur in patients with the X-linked lymphoproliferative syndrome (see earlier).[217–224] Occasional sporadic cases of primary EBV infection evolve into uncontrolled lymphoproliferative syndromes.[255, 257] In the setting of immunodeficiency, EBV plays a more important role in the induction of B-cell lymphomas than was previously appreciated.[258] Fatal T-cell lymphomas have been reported in three patients with chronic EBV infection.[259]

EBV-related lymphoproliferative syndromes have been observed after renal and bone marrow transplantation and in association with the acquired immunodeficiency syndrome.[260–269] EBV-related lymphoproliferative syndromes associated with immunosuppression may be a particular problem for patients treated with cyclosporine A.[263] EBV genomes are present in approximately one third of B-cell lymphomas arising in patients with acquired immunodeficiency syndrome[268] and is detected in virtually all central nervous system lymphomas arising in this patient population.[269] EBV is also associated with an unusual form of body cavity lymphomas in HIV-1–infected individuals.[270, 271] Human herpesvirus-8, the etiologic agent for Kaposi's sarcoma, is also implicated in the pathogenesis of these rapidly progressive tumors that initially present with involvement of the pleural, pericardial, or peritoneal cavity. In the setting of immunosuppression, EBV-associated tumors are less likely to display the restricted EBV gene product expression observed in EBV-related tumors that arise outside the setting of immunosuppression.[272, 273] The EBV genome has been detected in a tumor from a patient with a primary central nervous system B-cell lymphoma without the presence of overt immunosuppression, which suggests a possible association between EBV and lymphoma in that setting.[274]

LABORATORY DIAGNOSIS

Hematologic Findings

The central hematologic manifestation of the illness is the circulating lymphocytosis. At presentation, a relative and absolute mononuclear lymphocytosis is found in about 70% of the cases. The lymphocytosis peaks during the second or third week of illness, and monocytes and lymphocytes account for 60 to 70% of the total white cell counts of 12,000 to 18,000/mm³. However, higher white cell counts are not uncommon, and occasional patients manifest 30,000 to 50,000 leukocytes/mm³. Atypical lymphocytes are the hematologic hallmark of infectious mononucleosis and account for about 3% of the differential count at the height of the atypical lymphocytosis.[150, 151] The wide range in the atypical lymphocytosis is well recognized, and some cases show none or only a few atypical lymphocytes, whereas 90% or more of the circulating lymphocytes may be atypical in other cases. However, atypical lymphocytes are not pathognomonic for infectious mononucleosis (Table 128–7). They are also noted in other syndromes, including cytomegalovirus infection, viral hepatitis, toxoplasmosis, rubella, mumps, and roseola as well as in drug reactions.[275, 276] The atypical lymphocyte is generally larger than is the mature lymphocyte encountered in peripheral blood. The cytoplasm is often vacuolated and basophilic, and its edges have a rolled-up appearance. Nuclei are often lobulated and are eccentrically placed.

TABLE 128–7 Syndromes in Which Atypical Lymphocytosis May Be Found

Epstein-Barr virus–induced infectious mononucleosis
Cytomegalovirus infections
Toxoplasmosis
Acute viral hepatitis
Rubella
Roseola
Mumps
Drug reactions

Although the cells may appear quite immature, the heterogeneity of morphologic and tinctoral characteristics of such cells helps to distinguish atypical lymphocytes from the more uniform lymphoblasts of acute lymphocytic leukemia.[6, 275]

A relative and absolute neutropenia is evident in 60 to 90% of the cases, and neutrophils that remain in circulation exhibit a mild left shift.[172, 173] In most cases, the neutropenia is mild, with total granulocyte counts of 2000 to 3000/mm^3, although profound granulocytopenia has also been reported.[108, 174–178, 221, 277] The neutropenia is usually self-limited, and counts rise gradually toward normal by a month after presentation.[172]

Thrombocytopenia is also common, and 50% of the patients in one series manifested platelet counts of less than 140,000/mm^3.[167] Although cases of profound thrombocytopenia with bleeding have been reported,[168–171] these are rare and contrast markedly with the generally benign course of the common, mild thrombocytopenia.

Heterophile Antibodies

Heterophile antibodies, originally described by Paul and Bunnell[7] as sheep erythrocyte agglutinins, are present in about 90% of the cases at some point during the illness. Beef erythrocyte hemolysins and agglutinating antibodies to horse, goat, and camel erythrocytes are also demonstrable in infectious mononucleosis. The classic heterophile antibody titer is reported as the highest serum dilution at which sheep erythrocytes are agglutinated after absorption of the test serum by guinea pig kidney (Table 128–8). The differential absorption permits a distinction between naturally occurring Forssman antibodies, the antibodies of serum sickness, and heterophile antibodies of infectious mononucleosis. Beef red cell hemolysins do not require differential absorption for interpretation. Although titers may vary depending on laboratory techniques, a titer of 40 or greater after guinea pig absorption along with a compatible clinical presentation is strong evidence for infectious mononucleosis.

Heterophile antibodies may be demonstrable at the onset of illness or may appear later in the course of the illness. A delayed appearance of heterophile antibodies may be associated with a more prolonged convalescence.[278] Horse red cell agglutination is more sensitive than are tests for sheep red cell agglutination or beef red cell hemolysis. Horse red cell agglutinins persist for a year after diagnosis in 75% of the cases,[279] whereas sheep cell agglutinins fall to titers of less than 40 by a year in 70% of cases. False-positive titers greater than 40 of sheep and horse erythrocyte agglutinins have been found in 12 and 6.7% of sera, respectively[274] Commercial, generally specific and sensitive spot kits for the demonstration of heterophile antibodies have become available. The correlation between the results obtained by the use of these kits and by the classic tube heterophile method is quite good, although the sensitivity of the spot and slide tests is slightly greater than that of the classic tube heterophile test. Occasional false-positive Monospot test responses have been reported in patients with lymphoma or hepatitis, but the rarity of this event makes confirmation of a positive Monospot test result by classic sheep cell agglutination unnecessary.[280–282]

Epstein-Barr Virus–Specific Antibodies

In addition to the transient heterophile antibodies, infection with EBV results in the development of virus-specific antibodies. A determination of EBV-specific antibodies is rarely necessary for the diagnosis of infectious mononucleosis because 90% of the cases are heterophile-positive and few false-positive results are obtained if the test is properly performed (see earlier). For heterophile-negative cases and for diagnosis in atypical cases, a determination of EBV antibodies may help to establish a cause (Table 128–9).[283]

Antibodies to VCA as measured by immunofluorescence arise early in the course of the illness and are demonstrable at presentation in most cases. IgG antibodies to VCA are usually present at titers of 80 or greater on the first visit to a physician. Because these initially detected levels are close to peak VCA titers, a fourfold rise in titer is demonstrable in only 10 to 20% of the cases. After recovery, detectable titers of VCA IgG antibody are maintained for life. Thus, IgG VCA antibody titers may be of little help in the establishment of the diagnosis of infectious mononucleosis. Conversely, IgM antibodies to VCA are sensitive and specific for infectious mononucleosis. IgM antibody titers of greater than 5 as measured by indirect immunofluorescence are demonstrable in 90% of the cases early in illness. Titers fall rapidly thereafter, and in only 10% of the cases are titers of greater than 5 retained by 4 months after diagnosis.[279, 285] IgM VCA antibodies are not demonstrable in the general population, and thus their presence is virtually diagnostic of acute EBV infection.

Serum antibodies to early antigens are also demonstrable by indirect immunofluorescence and two distinct patterns of fluorescence emerge.[283, 285] Certain sera stain both nuclei and cytoplasm diffusely (anti-D), whereas others stain cytoplasmic aggregates (anti-R). Anti-D antibody is found in about 70% of patients with acute infectious mononucleosis (see Table 128–9). Anti-D titers arise later in the course of illness than do those to VCA and disappear after recovery. Anti-D antibodies may be found in the sera of patients with advanced nasopharyngeal carcinoma but are absent from the general population. The appearance of anti-D antibodies in a patient with IgG VCA antibodies suggests recent EBV infection. Unfortunately, only 70% of EBV-induced cases manifest anti-D antibodies. The presence and titer of anti-D antibodies correlate with the duration and severity of clinical illness.[285] Anti-R antibodies are only occasionally seen in infectious mononucleosis (see Table 128–9). They are present more often in protracted or atypical cases, arise after the anti-D antibodies peak, and remain detectable for up to 2 years.[286] Anti-R antibodies are also present in higher titers in patients with African Burkitt's lymphoma and occasionally in healthy persons who also possess high VCA titers.[287]

Antibodies to EBNA appear late in the course of all cases of infectious mononucleosis and persist for life.[288] The appearance of EBNA antibodies in a patient who was previously VCA-positive and EBNA-negative is strong evidence of recent EBV infection. The recent resolution of a number of distinct EBNAs has provided an additional serologic tool that might provide useful insights into EBV pathogenesis.[240] Neutralizing antibodies to EBV also appear late in the course of infectious mononucleosis and reach maximal levels 6 to 7 weeks after the onset of illness.[289] Neutralizing antibodies persist at stable titers (mean of 40) for life. The appearance or a rise in titer of neutralizing antibodies to EBV also indicates recent EBV infection. Neutralizing antibodies are, however, difficult to measure, and tests for them are not routinely available. Complement-fixing antibodies to soluble antigens (anti-S) appear in infectious mononucleosis in a time course similar to the appearance of EBNA antibodies.[290] A fourfold rise in titer of anti-S antibody suggests recent EBV infection. Anti-S antibody persists for life.

TABLE 128–8 Heterophile Antibodies: Effect of Absorption

		After Absorption with:	
Source of Serum	***Unabsorbed***	***Guinea Pig Kidney***	***Beef Red Cells***
Infectious mononucleosis	+ + + +	+ + +	0
Serum sickness	+ + +	0	0
Normal serum (Forssman antibody)	+	0	+

Detection of Epstein-Barr Virus

Epstein-Barr virus may be cultured from oropharyngeal washings or from circulating lymphocytes of 80 to 90% of patients with infectious mononucleosis.[65–68, 75, 116] Cultivation of the virus is, however, not routinely available in most diagnostic virology laboratories. This, coupled with the ubiquity of virus shedding in both healthy persons and in those with unrelated illnesses, renders cultivation of the virus

TABLE 128–9 Antibodies to Epstein-Barr Virus

Antibody Specificity	Time of Appearance in Infectious Mononucleosis	Percentage of Epstein-Barr Virus–Induced Mononucleosis Cases with Antibody	Persistence	Comments
Viral capsid antigens				
IgM VCA	At clinical presentation	100	4–8 wk	Highly sensitive and specific, major diagnostic utility
IgG VCA	At clinical presentation	100	Lifelong	High titer at presentation and lifelong persistence make IgG VCA more useful as epidemiologic tool than in diagnosis of individual cases
Early antigens				
Anti-D	Peaks at 3–4 wk after onset	70	3–6 mo	Correlated with severe disease; also seen in nasopharyngeal carcinoma
Anti-R	2 wk to several months after onset	Low	2 mo to >3 yr	Occasionally seen with unusually severe or protracted illness; also seen in African Burkitt's lymphoma
Epstein-Barr nuclear antigen	3–4 wk after onset	100	Lifelong	Late appearance helpful in diagnosis of heterophile-negative cases
Soluble complement-fixing antigens (anti-S)	3–4 wk after onset	100	Lifelong	Late appearance helpful in diagnosis of heterophile-negative cases

Abbreviation: VCA, Viral capsid antigen.

of little clinical use (see Table 128–2). Rapid diagnostic techniques based on DNA hybridization or monoclonal antibody techniques have also been developed.[142, 259, 292]

Other Laboratory Abnormalities

Liver function test results are abnormal in almost all cases of infectious mononucleosis[201, 293, 294] The hepatocellular enzyme (aspartate aminotransferase), alanine aminotransferase, and lactic dehydrogenase levels are the most commonly elevated, and one of the three is abnormal in about 90% of the cases. Elevations are usually mild, with individual values in the range of two to three times the upper limit of normal. Elevation to more than 10 times the upper limit of normal requires a search for another diagnosis.[201] The alkaline phosphatase level is elevated in about 60% of the cases.[293, 294] Mild elevation of the bilirubin level is noted in approximately 45% of cases, although frank jaundice occurs in only about 5%. Elevations are maximal in the second week of illness and decline gradually over a 3- to 4-week period.

Cryoproteins are present in modest amounts in 90 to 95% of patients.[159, 295] The cryoproteins are generally mixed cryoglobulins of IgG and IgM classes. When the cryoglobulins are dissociated, antibody of anti-i or anti-I, or both specificities, is usually demonstrable.[295, 296]

Differential Diagnosis

In most cases, the diagnosis of infectious mononucleosis is straightforward. The clinical manifestations of sore throat, fever, lymphadenopathy, and malaise coupled with atypical lymphocytosis and a positive heterophile test result establish the diagnosis of EBV-induced infectious mononucleosis. Difficulties arise, however, when the clinical manifestations are less striking, particularly when the heterophile test response is negative.

Heterophile-negative infectious mononucleosis may be caused by several different agents. Attention to the clinical manifestations of the illness and proper use of the laboratory will provide an etiologic diagnosis in 85 to 90% of all cases of infectious mononucleosis. The frequency with which heterophile-negative infectious mononucleosis is seen depends largely on three factors: (1) age of the patient population—EBV-induced infectious mononucleosis tends to be a milder illness and is more often heterophile-negative in pediatric populations than in young adults; (2) sensitivity of the heterophile test—heterophile antibodies are more often demonstrable by horse red cell agglutination than by beef red cell hemolysis or by sheep red cell agglutination; and (3) diligence with which heterophile antibodies are sought—typical cases of infectious mononucleosis may be heterophile-negative on presentation but, if retested later in the course of the illness, may become heterophile-positive.

The most frequent cause of heterophile-negative infectious mononucleosis in most populations is CMV.[297] Although differentiation of individual cases of EBV- versus CMV-induced infectious mononucleosis may be difficult, certain features are more common in CMV infections. CMV more frequently follows transfusion and is more frequently manifested as a typhoid-like syndrome without sore throat and lymphadenopathy. Splenomegaly may be slightly more prominent with CMV-induced disease, whereas the atypical lymphocytosis is usually less intense in CMV-induced infectious mononucleosis. In age-matched controls, the results of liver function tests are less elevated when the agent is CMV. Cryoglobulins are demonstrable in both EBV- and CMV-induced disease, but anti-i specificity is not seen in CMV-induced mononucleosis.[296] The illness may be attributed to CMV if there is serologic evidence of acute CMV infection and no evidence of acute EBV infection.

Heterophile-negative infectious mononucleosis may also be caused by EBV. As previously noted, this is not uncommon in the pediatric age group.[145, 146] The diagnosis rests on the demonstration of appropriate changes in specific EBV serologic tests (see Table 128–9).

Viral hepatitis may result in fever, lymphadenopathy, malaise, and an atypical lymphocytosis. Generally, the atypical lymphocytosis is of lesser magnitude, and atypical lymphocytes account for less than 10% of the leukocytes. In viral hepatitis, hepatocellular enzyme levels are usually markedly elevated at the initial visit, in contrast to infectious mononucleosis in which the results of liver function tests are only mildly elevated initially and rise gradually over a 1- to 2-week period. In addition, specific serologic tests are currently available for the detection of infection with hepatitis A, B, and C viruses.

Acute toxoplasmosis may also give rise to an infectious mononucleosis–like illness. Usually the degree of the lymphocytosis is mild, and a diagnosis can be made by serologic tests for *Toxoplasma.* Rubella may also occasionally be manifested by fever, lymphadenopathy, and a mild atypical lymphocytosis, but the appearance of the exanthem and the clinical course of the illness are generally not confused with those of infectious mononucleosis. A serologic diagnosis of recent rubella infection can be obtained if the diagnosis remains in doubt. Infectious lymphocytosis of childhood is a disease of uncertain cause that is characterized by fever, lymphadenopathy, occasionally diarrhea, and a lymphocytosis that consists almost exclusively of small mature lymphocytes. The disease is most common in the pediatric age group, may occur in epidemics, and is not associated with EBV infection.[298]

A streptococcal sore throat may also mimic infectious mononucleosis clinically. Adenopathy is generally submandibular and anterior cervical, and splenomegaly is absent in streptococcal sore throat. Culture of group A β-hemolytic streptococci from the throat is supportive but not conclusive evidence for this diagnosis because colonization with the organism is common in this patient population. Serologic tests for recent infection with group A streptococci may help to establish the cause.

Primary HIV-1 infection may also present with fever, lymphadenopathy, and pharyngitis.[299–301] Such patients may also exhibit a maculopapular rash and signs of aseptic meningitis. Patients with primary HIV-1 infection are not heterophile-positive and are diagnosed by the detection of HIV-1 p24 antigen in serum or plasma, or by seroconversion to HIV-1, or HIV-1 RNA or both (see Chapter 106).

TREATMENT

Treatment of infectious mononucleosis is largely supportive because more than 95% of the patients recover uneventfully without specific therapy. The level of activity is generally tailored to what the individual patient can comfortably tolerate. Contact sports or heavy lifting should be avoided during the first 2 to 3 weeks of illness, especially if splenomegaly is present. Aspirin or acetaminophen is helpful in relieving the sore throat and in suppressing the fever. Sore throat may be further alleviated by gargling with warm salt water. If constipation is present, it should be treated with a gentle laxative.

Corticosteroids are often advocated, but their use in uncomplicated illness is still controversial. Corticosteroids generally decrease the period of febrility and hasten the resolution of constitutional symptoms.[302–305] However, most infectious disease consultants prefer not to administer corticosteroids in this self-limited disease in the absence of certain specific indications. Corticosteroids are generally used in the following situations: (1) impending airway obstruction, (2) severe thrombocytopenia, or (3) hemolytic anemia. Some also advocate the use of corticosteroids for central nervous system involvement, myocarditis, or pericarditis. If corticosteroids are administered in these situations, treatment should be initiated in doses equivalent to 60 to 80 mg of prednisone per day given in a split daily regimen. The response is usually rapid, and the dosage can be tapered over a 1- to 2-week period. In selected cases of severe or prolonged prostration, a short tapering course of lower doses of prednisone may be of benefit. In these situations, an initial dose equivalent to 40 mg of prednisone is usually sufficient to produce the desired effect.

Phosphonoacetic acid, adenine arabinoside, acyclovir, desciclovir, ganciclovir and interferon-alfa and interferon-γ inhibit EBV replication in vitro.[306–318] Controlled trials of parenteral or oral acyclovir in infectious mononucleosis have demonstrated inhibition of viral shedding from the oropharynx but have not demonstrated sufficient clinical benefit to recommend the use of acyclovir in the setting of uncomplicated infectious mononucleosis.[319–322] Antiviral therapy has been insufficiently studied to make recommendations regarding its use in the setting of complicated infectious mononucleosis. Interferon-alfa decreased the incidence of shedding of EBV by renal allograft recipients in a prophylactic placebo-controlled study, but it has not been widely used for ongoing infection.[323] Acyclovir and desciclovir have each been shown to temporarily reverse EBV-associated oral hairy leukoplakia in individuals with HIV-1 infection.[318, 324] Acyclovir did not appear to benefit two patients with X-linked lymphoproliferative syndrome but did appear to induce a temporary remission of a polyclonal B-cell lymphoproliferative disorder observed in a patient after renal transplantation and in two patients with EBV-associated fever and interstitial pneumonitis.[236, 259, 325, 326]

More innovative approaches to the treatment of EBV-associated malignancies including the use of tumor-directed monoclonal antibodies and EBV-specific cytotoxic T cells may be on the horizon.[327, 328] however, although several agents have been shown to have in vitro antiviral activity against EBV, at this point the indications for the clinical use of antiviral agents in the treatment of EBV infection remain relatively limited.

PREVENTION

Public Health Measures

Because the spread of virus requires intimate contact, isolation of patients with infectious mononucleosis is not necessary. Because virocytemia is demonstrable for several months after recovery, consideration should be given to postponement of blood donation by patients with infectious mononucleosis for at least 6 months after the onset of illness.

Immunization against EBV, particularly of high-risk groups such as susceptible students or military populations, has been considered in the past. Immunization with sheep red cells gives rise to heterophile antibodies, but these are neither persistent nor protective.[98] Cell lines that produce large quantities of virus are available, and the possibility exists that an inactivated vaccine could be produced. However, additional data on the risk of administration of inactivated EBV need to be gathered before trials in humans can be contemplated. The potential oncogenicity of EBV requires that this hazard be carefully evaluated in any potential vaccine.

Antibodies to a surface glycoprotein of the virus, gp350, which binds to the cellular receptor for the virus have been shown to possess neutralizing activity against the virus. A study in cotton-top marmosets has demonstrated that vaccination with the EBV gp350 glycoprotein protects the animals from lymphoma after subsequent challenge with EBV, and other novel vaccine approaches using recombinant DNA technologies are under investigation.[309]

REFERENCES

1. Filatov NF. Lektuse ob ostrikh infektsion Nikh Lolieznyak (Lectures on Acute Infectious Disease of children). Moscow: U. Deitel; 1885.
2. Pfeiffer E. Drusenfieber. Jahrb f Kinderheilk. 1889;29:257.
3. Türk W. Septische Erkrankungen bei Verkümmerung des Granulozytensystems. Wein Klin Wochenschr. 1907;20:157.
4. Hall AJ. A case resembling acute lymphatic leukaemia, ending in complete recovery. Proc R Soc Med. 1915;8:15–19.
5. Sprunt TP, Evans FA. Mononuclear leukocytosis in reaction to acute infections ("infectious mononucleosis"). Johns Hopkins Hosp Bull. 1920;31:410.
6. Downey H, McKinlay CA. Acute lymphadenosis compared with acute lymphatic leukemia. Arch Intern Med. 1923;32:82–112.
7. Paul JR, Bunnell W. The presence of heterophile antibodies in infectious mononucleosis. Am J Med Sci. 1932;183:90–104.
8. Davidsohn I. Serologic diagnosis of infectious mononucleosis. JAMA. 1937;108:289–95.
9. Evans AS. Experimental attempts to transmit infectious mononucleosis to man. Yale J Biol Med. 1947;20:19–26.
10. Evans AS. Further experimental attempts to transmit infectious mononucleosis to man. J Clin Invest. 1950;29:508–512.
11. Niederman JC, Scott RB. Studies on infectious mononucleosis: Attempts to transmit the disease to human volunteers. Yale J Biol Med. 1965;38:1–10.
12. Burkitt D. A sarcoma involving the jaws in African children. Br J Surg. 1958;46:218–223.
13. Epstein MA, Achong BA, Barr YM. Virus particles in cultured lymphoblasts from Burkitt's lymphoma. Lancet. 1964;1:702–703.
14. Henle G, Henle W. Immunofluorescence in cells derived from Burkitt lymphoma. J Bacteriol. 1966;91:1248–1256.
15. Henle G, Henle W, Diehl V. Relation of Burkitt's tumor associated herpestype virus to infectious mononucleosis. Proc Natl Acad Sci U S A. 1968;59:94–101.
16. Niederman JC, McCollum RW, Henle G, et al. Infectious mononucleosis: Clinical manifestations in relation to EB virus antibodies. JAMA. 1968;203:205–209.
17. Evans AS, Niederman JC, McCollum Rw. Seroepidemiologic studies of infectious mononucleosis with EB virus. N Engl J Med. 1968;279:1121–1127.
18. Sawyer RN, Evans AS, Niederman JC, et al. Prospective studies of a group of Yale University freshmen. I. Occurrence of infectious mononucleosis. J Infect Dis. 1971;123:263–270.
19. University Health Physicians and PHLS Laboratories. A joint investigation of infectious mononucleosis and its relationship to EB virus antibody. Br Med J. 1971;4:643.
20. Miller S, Lipman M. Release of infectious Epstein-Barr virus by transformed marmoset leukocytes. Proc Natl Acad Sci U S A. 1973;70:190–194.

21. Pritchett RF, Hayward SD, Kieff E. DNA of Epstein Barr virus. Comparative studies of the DNA of Epstein-Barr virus from HRI and B95-8 cells: I. Size, structure, and relatedness. J Virol. 1975;15:556–559.
22. Straus SE, Cohen JI, Tosato G, et al. Epstein-Barr virus infections: Biology, pathogenesis and management. Ann Intern Med. 1992;118:45–58.
23. Rowe M, Lear A, Croom-Carter D, et al. Three pathways of Epstein Barr virus (EBV) gene activation from EBNA1 positive latency in B lymphocytes. J Virol. 1992;66:122–131.
24. Niedobitek G, Agathanggelou A, Rowe M, et al. Heterogeneous expression of Epstein-Barr latent proteins in endemic Burkitt's lymphoma. Blood, 1995;86:659–665.
25. Busson P, McCoy R, Sadler R, et al. Consistent transcription of the Epstein Barr virus LMP2 gene in nasopharyngeal carcinoma. J Virol. 1992;66:3257–3262.
26. Brooks L, Yao QY, Rickinson AB, Young LS. Epstein-Barr virus latent gene transcription in nasopharyngeal carcinoma cells: Coexpression of EBNA1, LMP1, and LMP2 transcripts. J Virol. 1992;66:2689–2697.
27. Zalani S, Holley-Guthrie E, Kenney S. Epstein-Barr viral latency is disrupted by the immediate-early BRLF1 protein through a cell-specific mechanism. Proc Natl Acad Sci U S A 1996;93:9194–9199.
28. Sixbey JW, Vesterinen EH, Nedrud JG, et al. Replication of Epstein-Barr virus in human epithelial cells infected in vitro. Nature. 1983;306:480–483.
29. Young LS, Sixbey JW, Clark D, et al. Epstein-Barr virus receptor on human pharyngeal epithelia. Lancet. 1986;1:240–242.
30. Sixbey JW, Davis DS, Young LS, et al. Human epithelial cell expression of an Epstein-Barr virus receptor. J Gen Virol. 1987;68:805–811.
31. Jondal M, Klein G. Surface markers on human B and T lymphocytes. II.Presence of Epstein-Barr virus receptors on B lymphocytes. J Exp Med. 1973;138:1365–1378.
32. Yefenof E, Bakacs T, Einhorn L, et al. Epstein-Barr virus receptors, complement receptors and EBV infectibility of different lymphocyte fractions of human peripheral blood. I. Complement receptor distribution and complement binding by separated lymphocyte subpopulations. Cell Immunol. 1978;35:34–42.
33. Einhorn L, Steinitz M, Yefenof E, et al. Epstein-Barr virus receptors, complement receptors and EBV infectibility of different lymphocyte fractions of human peripheral blood. II. Epstein-Barr virus studies. Cell Immunol. 1978;35:43–58.
34. Fingeroth JD, Weiss JJ, Tedder TF, et al. Epstein-Barr virus receptor of human B lymphocytes is the C3d receptor CR2. Proc Natl Acad Sci U S A. 1984;81:4510–4514.
35. Frade R, Barel M, Ehlin-Eriksson B, et al. gp140, the C3d receptor of human B lymphocytes, is also the Epstein-Barr virus receptor. Proc Natl Acad Sci U S A. 1985;82:1490–1493.
36. Robinson J, Smith D. Infection of human B lymphocytes with high multiplicities of Epstein-Barr virus: Kinetics of EBNA expression, cellular DNA synthesis, and mitosis. Virology. 1981;109:336–343.
37. Henderson E, Miller G, Robinson J, et al. Efficiency of transformation of lymphocytes by Epstein-Barr virus. Virology. 1977;76:152–163.
38. Andersson-Anvret M, Falk L, Lindahl T. Integration of EBV DNA. In: Proceedings of the Third International Symposium on Oncogenesis and Herpesviruses. Boston, July 25–29. Lyons, France: IARC Press; 1977:46.
39. Hennessy K, Kieff E. A second nuclear protein is encoded by Epstein-Barr virus in latent infection. Science. 1984;227:1238–1240.
40. Mueller-Lantzsch N, Lenoir GM, Sauter M, et al. Identification of the coding region for a second Epstein-Barr virus nuclear antigen (EBNA 2) by transfection of cloned DNA fragments. EMBO J. 1985;4:1805–1811.
41. Hennessy K, Fennewald S, Kieff E. A third viral nuclear protein in lymphoblasts immortalized by Epstein-Barr virus. Proc Natl Acad Sci U S A. 1985;82:5944–5948.
42. Hennessy K, Wang F, Bushman EW, et al. Definitive identification of a member of the Epstein-Barr virus nuclear protein 3 family. Proc Natl Acad Sci U S A. 1986;83:5693–5697.
43. Killner J, Kallin B, Alexander H, et al. An Epstein-Barr virus (EBV)-determined nuclear antigen (EBNA5) partly encoded by the transformation-associated *Bam* WYH region of EBV DNA: Preferential expression in lymphoblastoid cell lines. Proc Natl Acad Sci U S A. 1986;83:6641–6645.
44. Petti L, Sample J, Wang F, et al. A fifth Epstein-Barr virus nuclear protein (EBNA3C) is expressed in latently infected growth-transformed lymphocytes. J Virol. 1988;62:1330–1338.
45. Swendenman S, Thorley-Lawson DA. The activation antigen BLAST-2, when shed, is an autocrine BCGF for normal and transformed B cells. EMBO J. 1987;6:1637–1642.
46. Calender A, Billaud M, Aubry JP, et al. Epstein-Barr virus (EBV) induces expression of B-cell activation markers on in vitro infection of EBV-negative B-lymphoma cells. Proc Natl Acad Sci U S A. 1987;84:8060–8064.
47. Wang F, Gregory CD, Rowe M, et al. Epstein-Barr virus nuclear antigen 2 specifically induces expression of the B-cell activation antigen CD23. Proc Natl Acad Sci U S A. 1987;84:3452–3456.
48. Fahraeus R, Rymo R, Rhim JS, et al. Morphological transformation of human keratinocytes expressing the LMP gene of Epstein-Barr virus. Nature. 1990;345:447–449.
49. Henderson S, Rowe M, Gregory C, et al. Induction of bcl-2 expression by Epstein-Barr virus latent membrane protein 1 protects infected B-cells from programmed cell death. Cell. 1991;65:1107–1115.
50. Rosen A, Gergely P, Jondal M, et al. Polyclonal Ig production after Epstein-Barr virus infection of human lymphocytes in vitro. Nature. 1977;267:52–54.
51. Luzzatti AL, Hengartner H, Schrier MH. Induction of plaque-forming cells by combined action of antigen and Epstein-Barr virus. Nature. 1977;269:419–420.
52. Kirchner H, Tosato G, Blaese M, et al. Polyclonal immunoglobulin in secretion by human B-lymphocytes exposed to Epstein-Barr virus in vitro. J Immunol. 1979;122:1310–1313.
53. Schooley RT, Haynes BF, Payling-Wright CR, et al. Mechanisms of Epstein-Barr virus induced human B-lymphocyte activation. Cell Immunol. 1980;56:518–525.
54. Brown NA, Miller G. Immunoglobulin expression by human B lymphocytes clonally transformed by Epstein Barr virus. J Immunol. 1982;28:24–29.
55. Henle G, Henle W, Clifford P, et al. Antibodies to Epstein-Barr virus in Burkitt's lymphoma and control groups. J Natl Cancer Inst. 1969;43:1147–1154.
56. Pereira MS, Blake JM, Macrae AD. EB virus antibody at different ages. Br Med J. 1969;4:526–527.
57. Porter DD, Wimberly I, Benyesh-Melnick M. Prevalence of antibodies to EB virus and other herpesviruses. JAMA. 1969;208:1675–1679.
58. Gerber P, Birch SM, Rosenblum EN. The incidence of complement fixing antibodies in sera of human and non-human primates to viral antigens derived from Burkitt's lymphocyte cells. Proc Natl Acad Sci U S A. 1967;58:478–484.
59. Hallee TJ, Evans AS, Niederman JC, et al. Infectious mononucleosis at the United States Military Academy. A prospective study of a single class over 4 years. Yale J Biol Med. 1974;47:182–195.
60. Nye FJ. Social class and infectious mononucleosis. J Hyg (Lond). 1973;71:145–149.
61. Heath CW Jr, Brodsky AL, Potolsky AI. Infectious mononucleosis in a general population. Am J Epidemiol. 1972;95:46–52.
62. Bernstein A. Infectious mononucleosis. Medicine (Baltimore). 1940;19:85–159.
63. Henle G, Henle W. Observations on childhood infections with the Epstein-Barr virus. J Infect Dis. 1970;121:303–310.
64. Tamir D, Benderly A, Levy J, et al. Infectious mononucleosis and Epstein-Barr virus in childhood. Pediatrics. 1974;53:330–335.
65. Chang RS, Golden HD. Transformation of human leukocytes from throat washings from infectious mononucleosis patients. Nature. 1971;234:359–360.
66. Gerber P, Nonoyama M, Lucas S, et al. Oral excretion of Epstein Barr virus by healthy subjects and patients with infectious mononucleosis. Lancet. 1972;2:988–989.
67. Niederman JC, Miller G, Pearson HA, et al. Infectious mononucleosis: Epstein Barr virus shedding in saliva and the oropharynx. N Engl J Med. 1976; 294:1355–1359.
68. Miller G, Niederman JC, Andrews LL. Prolonged oropharyngeal excretion of Epstein Barr virus after infectious mononucleosis. N Engl J Med. 1973;288:229–232.
69. Strauch B, Siegel N, Andrews LL, et al. Oropharyngeal excretion of Epstein Barr virus by renal transplant recipients and other patients treated with immunosuppressive drugs. Lancet. 1974;1:234–237.
70. Chang RS, Lewis JP, Abildgaard CF. Prevalence of oropharyngeal excreters of leukocyte transforming agents among a human population. N Engl J Med. 1973;289:1325–1329.
71. Chang RS, Lewis JS, Reynolds RD, et al. Oropharyngeal excretion of Epstein Barr virus by patients with lymphoproliferative disorders and by recipients of renal homografts. Ann Intern Med. 1978;88:34–40.
72. Ferbas J, Rahman MA, Kingsley LA, et al. Frequent oropharyngeal shedding of Epstein-Barr virus in homosexual men during early HIV infection. AIDS. 1992;6:1273–1278.
73. Wolf H, Haus M, Wilmer E. Persistence of Epstein Barr virus in the parotid gland. J Virol. 1984;51:795–798.
74. Sixbey JW, Lemon SM, Pagano JS. A second site for Epstein-Barr virus shedding: The uterine cervix. Lancet 1986;2:122–124.
75. Lipman M, Andrews L, Niederman J, et al. Direct visualization of enveloped Epstein-Barr herpesvirus in throat washing with leukocyte transforming activity. J Infect Dis. 1975;132:520–523.
76. Hoagland RS. The transmission of infectious mononucleosis. Am J Med Sci. 1955;229:262–272.
77. Fleisher GR, Pasquariello PS, Warren WS, et al. Intrafamilial transmission of Epstein-Barr virus infections. J Pediatr. 1981;98:16–19.
78. Larsson BO, Linde A. Intrafamilial transmission of Epstein-Barr virus infection among six adult members of one adult family. Scand J Infect Dis. 1990;22:363–366.
79. Gerber P, Walsh JH, Rosenblum EN, et al. Association of EB virus infection with the post perfusion syndrome. Lancet. 1969;1:593–595.
80. Herbert JT, Feorino P, Caldwell GG. False-positive epidemic infectious mononucleosis. Am Fam Physician. 1977;115:119–121.
81. Evans AS. Infectious mononucleosis in University of Wisconsin students. Report of a 5 year investigation. Am J Hyg. 1960;71:342–362.
82. Evans AS. Epidemiology and pathogenesis of infectious mononucleosis. In: Proceedings of the International Infectious Mononucleosis Symposium. Evanston, IL: American College Health Association; 1967:40.
83. Evans AS. Infectious mononucleosis in the Armed Forces. Milit Med. 1970;135:300–304.
84. Lehane DE. A seroepidemiologic study of infectious mononucleosis. The development of EB virus antibody in a military population. JAMA. 1970;212:2240–2242.
85. Downey H, Stasney J. The pathology of the lymph nodes in infectious mononucleosis. Folia Haematol (Leipz). 1936;54:417–438.
86. Smith EB, Custer RP. Rupture of spleen in infectious mononucleosis: Clinicopathologic report of 7 cases. Blood. 1946;1:317–333.
87. Custer RP, Smith EB. The pathology of infectious mononucleosis. Blood. 1948; 3:830–857.
88. Hovde RF, Sundberg RD. Granulomatous lesions in the bone marrow in infectious mononucleosis. Blood. 1950;5:209–232.

89. Pease GL. Granulomatous lesions in bone marrow. Blood. 1956;11:720–734.
90. Nelson RS, Darragh JH. Infectious mononucleosis hepatitis. A clinicopathologic study. Am J Med. 1956;21:26–33.
91. Sullivan BH, Irey NS, Pieggi VJ, et al. The liver in infectious mononucleosis. Am J Dig Dis. 1957;2:210–223.
92. Bergin JD. Fatal encephalopathy in glandular fever. J Neurol Neurosurg Psychiatry. 1960;23:69–73.
93. Ambler M, Stoll J, Tzamaloukas A, et al. Focal encephalomyelitis in infectious mononucleosis. A report with pathologic description. Ann Intern Med. 1971;75: 579–583.
94. Lemon SM, Hutt LM, Li J-LH, et al. Replication of Epstein Barr virus occurs in epithelial cells during infectious mononucleosis. In: Proceedings of the Third International Symposium on Oncogenesis and Herpesviruses. Boston, July 25–29. Lyons, France: IARC Press; 1977:98.
95. Thorley-Lawson DA, Israelsohn ES. Generation of specific cytotoxic T cells with a fragment of the Epstein-Barr virus-encoded p63/latent membrane protein. Proc Natl Acad Sci U S A. 1987;84:5384–5388.
96. Langhorne J, Feizi T. Studies on the heterophile antibodies of infectious mononucleosis. I. Separation of four antibody populations, one of which contains lymphocytotoxic activity. Clin Exp Immunol. 1977;30:354–363.
97. Henle W, Henle G, Hewetson J, et al. Failure to detect heterophile antigens in Epstein Barr virus infected cells and to demonstrate interaction of heterophile antibodies with Epstein Barr virus. Clin Exp Immunol. 1974;17:281–286.
98. Leikola J, Aho K. Experimentally induced mononucleosis-like heterophile antibodies in man. Clin Exp Immunol. 1969;5:67–73.
99. Mangi RJ, Niederman JC, Kelleher JE, et al. Depression of cell mediated immunity during acute infectious mononucleosis. N Engl J Med. 1974;291:1149–1153.
100. Stevens DL, Everett ED, Boxer LA, et al. Infectious mononucleosis with severe neutropenia and opsonic antineutrophil activity. South Med J. 1979;72:519–521.
101. Carter RL. Antibody formation in infectious mononucleosis. II. Other 19S antibodies and false positive serology. Br J Haematol. 1966;12:268–275.
102. Kaplan ME, Tan EM. Antinuclear antibodies in infectious mononucleosis. Lancet. 1968;1:561–563.
103. McKenzie, Pavat D, White RG. IgM and IgG antibody levels to ampicillin in patients with infectious mononucleosis. Clin Exp Immunol. 1976;26:214–221.
104. Chartlesworth JA, Quin JW, MacDonald GJ, et al. Complement, lymphocytotoxins, and immune complexes in infectious mononucleosis: Serial studies in uncomplicated cases. Clin Exp Immunol. 1978;34:241–247.
105. Jenkins WJ, Koster HG, Marsh WL, et al. Infectious mononucleosis: An unsuspected source of anti-i. Br J Haematol. 1965;11:480–483.
106. Ellman L, Carvalho A, Jacobson BM, et al. Platelet autoantibody in a case of infectious mononucleosis presenting as thrombocytopenic purpura. Am J Med. 1973;55:723–726.
107. Kernoff LM. Demonstration of increased platelet bound IgG in infectious mononucleosis complicated by severe thrombocytopenia. Scand J Infect Dis. 1980;12: 67–69.
108. Schooley RT, Densen P, Harmon D, et al. Antineutrophil antibodies in infectious mononucleosis. Am J Med. 1984;76:85–90.
109. Haider S, Coutinho M de L, Emond RTD, et al. Tuberculin anergy and infectious mononucleosis. Lancet. 1973;2:74.
110. Papamichail M, Sheldon PJ, Holborow EJ. T- and B-cell subpopulations infectious mononucleosis. Clin Exp Immunol. 1974;18:1–11.
111. Engberg RN, Eberle BJ, Williams RC. T- and B-cells in peripheral blood during infectious mononucleosis. J Infect Dis. 1974;130:104–111.
112. Pattengale PK, Smith RW, Perlin E. Atypical lymphocytes in acute infectious mononucleosis. Identification by multiple T and B markers. N Engl J Med. 1974;291:1145–1148.
113. DeWaele M, Thielemans C, Van Camp BKG. Characterization of immunoregulatory T-cells in EBV induced infectious mononucleosis by monoclonal antibodies. N Engl J Med. 1981;304:460–462.
114. Reinherz EL, O'Brien C, Rosenthal P, et al. The cellular basis for viral-induced immunodeficiency: Analysis by monoclonal antibodies. J Immunol. 1980;125:1269–1274.
115. Reinherz EL, Schlossman SF. The differentiation and function of human T-lymphocytes. Cell. 1980;19:821–827.
116. Rocchi G, DeFelici A, Ragona G, et al. Quantitative evaluation of Epstein-Barr virus infected mononuclear peripheral blood leukocytes in infectious mononucleosis. N Engl J Med. 1977;296:132–134.
117. Robinson JE, Smith D, Niederman J. Plasmacytic differentiation of circulating Epstein-Barr virus infected B-lymphocytes during acute infectious mononucleosis. J Exp Med. 1981;153:235–244.
118. Niedobitek G, Kremmer E, Herbst H, et al. Immunohistochemical detection of the Epstein-Barr virus–encoded latent membrane protein 2A in Hodgkin's disease and infectious mononucleosis. Blood 1997;90:1664–1672.
119. Kingma DW, Weiss WB, Jaffe ES, et al. Epstein-Barr virus latent membrane protein-1 oncogene deletions: Correlations with malignancy in Epstein-Barr virus–associated lymphoproliferative disorders and malignant lymphomas. Blood 1996;88:242–251.
120. Berger C, McQuain C, Sullivan JL, et al. The 30-bp deletion variant of Epstein-Barr virus-encoded latent membrane protein-1 prevails in acute infectious mononucleosis. J Infect Dis 1997;176:1370–1373.
121. Prang NS, Hornef MW, Jager M, et al. Lytic replication of Epstein-Barr virus in the peripheral blood: analysis of viral gene expression in B lymphocytes during infectious mononucleosis, and in the normal carrier state. Blood. 1997;89:1665–1677.
122. Blazar B, Patarroyo M, Klein E, et al. Increased sensitivity of human lymphoid lines to natural killer cells after induction of the Epstein-Barr viral cycle by superinfection or sodium butyrate. J Exp Med. 1980;151:614–627.
123. Rickinson AB, Crawford D, Epstein MA. Inhibition of the in vitro outgrowth of Epstein-Barr virus transformed lymphocytes by thymus dependent lymphocytes from infectious mononucleosis patients. Clin Exp Immunol. 1977;28:72–79.
124. Thorley-Lawson DA, Chess L, Strominger JA. Suppression of in vitro Epstein Barr virus infection: A new role for the adult human T lymphocyte. J Exp Med. 1977;146:495–508.
125. Schooley RT, Haynes BF, Payling-Wright CR, et al. Development of suppressor T-lymphocytes for Epstein-Barr virus induced B-lymphocyte outgrowth: Assessment by two quantitative systems. Blood. 1981;57:510–517.
126. Burroughs S, Sculley TB, Misko IS, et al. An Epstein-Barr virus-specific cytotoxic T cell epitope in EBV nuclear antigen 3 (EBNA 3). J Exp Med. 1990;171:345–349.
127. Murray RJ, Kurilla MG, Griffin HM, et al. Human cytotoxic T-cell responses against Epstein-Barr virus nuclear antigens demonstrated by using recombinant vaccinia viruses. Proc Natl Acad Sci U S A. 1990;87:2906–2910.
128. Misko IS, Schmidt C, Moss DJ, et al. Cytotoxic T-lymphocyte discrimination between type A Epstein-Barr virus transformants is mapped to an immuno-dominant epitope in EBNA 3. J Gen Virol. 1991;72:405–409.
129. Murray RJ, Kurilla MG, Brooks JM, et al. Identification of target antigens for the human cytotoxic T cell response to Epstein-Barr (EBV): Implications for the immune control of EBV-positive malignancies. J Exp Med. 1992;176:157–168.
130. Gavioli R, de Campos-Lima PO, Kurilla MG, et al. Recognition of the Epstein-Barr virus–encoded nuclear antigens EBNA-4 and EBNA-6 by HLA-All-restricted cytotoxic T lymphocytes: Implications for down-regulation of HLA-A11 in Burkitt lymphoma. Proc Natl Acad Sci U S A. 1992;89:5862–5826.
131. Gavioli R, Kurilla MG, de Campos-Lima PO, et al. Multiple HLA-A11 restricted cytotoxic T-lymphocyte epitopes of different immunogenicities in the Epstein-Barr virus-encoded nuclear antigen 4. J Virol. 1993;67:1572–1578.
132. Callan MF, Steven N, Krausa P, et al. Large clonal expansions of CD8+ T cells in acute infectious mononucleosis. Nature Med 1996;2:906–911.
133. Silins SL, Cross SM, Elliott SL, et al. Development of Epstein-Barr virus-specific memory T cell receptor clonotypes in acute infectious mononucleosis. J Exp Med. 1996;184:1815–1824.
134. Steven NM, Leese AM, Annels NE, et al. Epitope focusing in the primary cytotoxic T cell response to Epstein-Barr virus and its relationship to T cell memory. J Exp Med 1996;184:1801–1813.
135. White CA, Cross SM, Kurilla MG, et al. Recruitment during infectious mononucleosis of CD3+CD4+CD8+ virus-specific cytotoxic T cells which recognise Epstein-Barr virus lytic antigen BHRF1. Virology 1996;219:489–492.
136. Steven NM, Annels NE, Kumar A, et al. Immediate early and early lytic cycle proteins are frequent targets of the Epstein-Barr virus–induced cytotoxic T cell response. J Exp Med 1997;185:1605–1617.
137. Haynes BF, Schooley RT, Payling-Wright CR, et al. Emergence of suppressor cells of immunoglobulin synthesis during acute Epstein-Barr virus-induced infectious mononucleosis. J Immunol. 1979;123:2095–2101.
138. Tosato G, Magrath I, Koski I, et al. Activation of suppressor T cells during Epstein-Barr virus–induced infectious mononucleosis. N Engl J Med. 1979;301:1133–1137.
139. Biglino A, Sinicco A, Forno B, et al. Serum cytokine profiles in acute primary HIV-1 infection and in infectious mononucleosis. Clin Immunol Immunopathol 1996;78:61–69.
140. Wright-Browne V, Schnee AM, Jenkins MA, et al. Serum cytokine levels in infectious mononucleosis at diagnosis and convalescence. Leukemia Lymphoma 1998;30:583–589.
141. Taga H, Taga K, Wang F, et al. Human and viral interleukin-10 in acute Epstein-Barr virus–induced infectious mononucleosis. J Infect Dis 1995;171:1347–1350.
142. Yamamoto M, Kimura H, Hironaka T, et al. Detection and quantification of virus DNA in plasma of patients with Epstein-Barr virus-associated diseases. J Clin Microbiol 1995;33:1765–1768.
143. Schooley RT, Hirsch MS, Colvin RB, et al. Association of herpesvirus infections with T-lymphocyte subset alterations, glomerulopathy, and opportunistic infections after renal transplantation. N Engl J Med. 1983;308:307–313.
144. Sumaya CV, Ench Y. Epstein-Barr virus infectious mononucleosis in children. I. Clinical and general laboratory findings. Pediatrics. 1985;75:1003–1010.
145. Schmitz H, Volz D, Krainick-Riechert CH, et al. Acute Epstein-Barr virus infections in children. Med Microbiol Immunol. 1972;158:58–63.
146. Sumaya CV, Ench Y. Epstein-Barr virus infectious mononucleosis in children. II. Heterophil antibody and viral-specific responses. Pediatrics. 1985;75:1011–1019.
147. Horwitz CA, Henle W, Henle G, et al. Clinical and laboratory evaluation of elderly patients with heterophile antibody positive infectious mononucleosis. Report of seven patients ages 40 to 78. Am J Med. 1976;61:333–339.
148. Britton S, Andersson-Anvret M, Gergely P, et al. Epstein Barr virus immunity and tissue distribution in a fatal case of infectious mononucleosis. N Engl J Med. 1978;298:89–92.
149. Cameron D, MacBear LM. A Clinical Study of Infectious Mononucleosis and Toxoplasmosis. Baltimore: Williams & Wilkins; 1973:8.
150. Hoagland RJ. Infectious mononucleosis. Am J Med. 1952;13:158–171.
151. Mason WR Jr, Adams EK. Infectious mononucleosis. An analysis of 100 cases with particular attention to diagnosis, liver function tests, and treatment of selected cases with prednisone. Am J Med Sci. 1958;236:447–459.
152. Caird FI, Holt PR. The enanthem of glandular fever. BMJ. 1958;1:85–87.
153. Joncas J, Chaisson JP, Turcotte J, et al. Studies on infectious mononucleosis. III. Clinical data, serologic and epidemiologic findings. Can Med Assoc J. 1968;98:848–854.

154. Pullen H, Wright N, Murdock J McC. Hypersensitivity reactions to antibacterial drugs in infectious mononucleosis. Lancet. 1967;2:1176–1178.
155. Patel BM. Skin rash with infectious mononucleosis and ampicillin. Pediatrics. 1967; 40:910–911.
156. Karzon DT. Infectious mononucleosis. Adv Pediatr. 1976;22:231–265.
157. Hoagland RJ. Infectious Mononucleosis. New York: Grune & Stratton; 1967:64.
158. Horwitz CA, Moulds J, Henle W, et al. Cold agglutinins in infectious mononucleosis and heterophile antibody negative mononucleosis like syndromes. Blood. 1977;50:195–202.
159. Capra JD, Dowling P, Cook S, et al. An incomplete cold reactive γ G antibody with i specificity in infectious mononucleosis. Vox Sang. 1969;16:10–17.
160. Bowman HS, Marsh WL, Schumacher HR, et al. Auto anti-N immunohemolytic anemia in infectious mononucleosis. Am J Clin Pathol. 1974;61:465–472.
161. Troxel DB, Innella F, Cohen RJ. Infectious mononucleosis complicated by hemolytic anemia due to anti-i. Am J Clin Pathol. 1966;46:625–631.
162. Wilkinson LS, Petz LD, Garraty G. Reappraisal of the role of anti-i in haemolytic anemia in infectious mononucleosis. Br J Haematol. 1973;25:715–722.
163. Rosenfield RE, Schmidt PJ, Calvo RC, et al. Anti-i, a frequent cold agglutin in infectious mononucleosis. Vox Sang. 1965;10:631–634.
164. Worlledge SM, Dacie JV. Hemolytic and other anemias in infectious mononucleosis. In: Carter RL, Penman HG, eds. Infectious Mononucleosis. Oxford: Blackwell Scientific 1969:82–120.
165. Ohshima K, Kikuchi M, Eguchi F, et al. Virus-associated haemophagocytic syndrome with Epstein-Barr virus syndrome. Virchows Arch Pathol Anat Histopathol. 1991;419;519–522.
166. Ross CW, Schnitzer B, Weston BW, et al. Chronic active Epstein-Barr virus infection and virus-associated hemophagocytic syndrome. Arch Pathol Lab Med. 1991;115:470–474.
167. Carter RL. Platelet levels in infectious mononucleosis. Blood. 1965;25:817–821.
168. Clark BF, Davies SH. Severe thrombocytopenia in infectious mononucleosis. Am J Med Sci. 1964;248:703–708.
169. Radel EG, Schorr JB. Thrombocytopenic purpura with infectious mononucleosis. J Pediatr. 1963;63:46–60.
170. Goldstein E, Porter DY. Fatal thrombocytopenia with cerebral hemorrhage in mononucleosis. Arch Neurol. 1969;20:533–535.
171. Grossman LA, Wolff SM. Acute thrombocytopenic purpura in infectious mononucleosis. JAMA. 1959;171:2208–2210.
172. Carter RL. Granulocyte changes in infectious mononucleosis. J Clin Pathol. 1966;19:279–283.
173. Cantow EK, Kostinas JE. Studies on infectious mononucleosis. iv. Changes in the granulocytic series. Am J Clin Pathol. 1966;46:43–47.
174. Wulff HR. Acute agranulocytosis following infectious mononucleosis. Report of a case. Scand J Haematol. 1965;2:180–182.
175. Habib MA, Babka JC, Burningham RA. Case Report. Profound granulocytopenia associated with infectious mononucleosis. Am J Med Sci. 1973;265:339–346.
176. Neel EU. Infectious mononucleosis. Death due to agranulocytosis and pneumonia. JAMA. 1976;236:1493–1494.
177. Eriksson KF, Holmberg L, Gustafbergstrand C. Infectious mononucleosis and agranulocytosis. Scand J Infect Dis. 1979; 11:307–309.
178. Hammond WP, Harlan JM, Steinberg SE. Severe neutropenia in infectious mononucleosis. West J Med. 1979;131:92–97.
179. Dagan R, Powell KR. Postanginal sepsis following infectious mononucleosis. Arch Intern Med. 1987;147:1581–1583.
180. Hoagland RJ, Henson HM. Splenic rupture in infectious mononucleosis. Ann Intern Med. 1957;46:1184–1191.
181. Peters RM, Gordon LA, Nonsurgical treatment or splenic hemorrhage in an adult with infectious mononucleosis. Am J Med. 1986;80:123–125.
182. McLean ER, Diehl W, Edoga JK, et al. Failure of conservative management of splenic rupture in a patient with mononucleosis. J Pediatr Surg. 1987;22:1034–1035.
183. Smith EB. The anatomic pathology of infectious mononucleosis and its complications. In: Proceedings of the International Infectious Mononucleosis Symposium. Washington, DC: American College Health Association; 1967:109.
184. Bernstein TC, Wolff HG. Involvement of the nervous system in infectious mononucleosis. Ann Intern Med. 1950;33:1120–1138.
185. Silverstein A, Steinberg S, Nathanson M. Nervous system involvement in infectious mononucleosis. The heralding and/or major manifestation. Arch Neurol. 1972;26:353–358.
186. Bennett DR, Peters HA. Acute cerebellar syndrome secondary to infectious mononucleosis in a 52 year old man. Ann Intern Med. 1961;55:147–149.
187. Gilbert JW, Culebras A. Cerebellitis in infectious mononucleosis. JAMA. 1972;220:727.
188. Bejada S. Cerebellitis in glandular fever. Med J Aust. 1976;1:153–156.
189. Joncas JH, Chicoine L, Thivierge R, et al. Epstein-Barr virus antibodies in the cerebrospinal fluid. Am J Dis Child. 1974;127:282–285.
190. Grose C, Henle W, Henle G, et al. Primary Epstein Barr virus infections in acute neurologic diseases. N Engl J Med. 1975;292:392–395.
191. Tanner OR. Ocular manifestations of infectious mononucleosis. Arch Ophthalmol. 1954;51:229–241.
192. Shechter FR, Lipsius EI, Rasansky HN. Retrobulbar neuritis. Am J Dis Child. 1955;89:58–61.
193. Gautier-Smith PC. Neurological complications of glandular fever (infectious mononucleosis). Brain. 1965;88:323–324.
194. Watson P, Ashby P. Brachial plexus neuropathy associated with infectious mononucleosis. Can Med Assoc J. 1976;114:758–767.
195. Forino PM, Humphrey D, Hochberg F, et al. Mononucleosis associated subacute sclerosing panencephalitis. Lancet. 1975;2:530–532.
196. Cotton PB, Webb-Peploe MM. Acute transverse myelitis as a complication of glandular fever. BMJ. 1966;654–655.
197. Raymond RW, Williams RL. Infectious mononucleosis with psychosis. Report of a case. N Engl J Med. 1948;239:542–544.
198. Bray PF, Culp KW, McFarlin DE, et al. Demyelinating disease after neurologically complicated primary Epstein-Barr virus infection. Neurology. 1992;42:278–282.
199. Adamson DJ, Gordon PM. Hemiplegia—a rare complication of acute Epstein-Barr virus (EBV) infection. Scand J Infect Dis. 1992;24:379–380.
200. Penman HG. Fatal infectious mononucleosis: A critical review. J Clin Pathol. 1970;23:765–771.
201. Finkel M, Parker GW, Fanselau HA. The hepatitis of infectious mononucleosis: Experience with 235 cases. Milit Med. 1964;129:533–538.
202. Hoagland RJ. The clinical manifestations of infectious mononucleosis: A report of two hundred cases. Am J Med Sci 1960;240:21–29.
203. Stevens JE. Infectious mononucleosis: A clinical analysis of 210 sporadic cases. Va Med Mon 1952;79:74–80.
204. Lee S, Kjellstrand CM. Renal disease in infectious mononucleosis. Clin Nephrol 1978;9:236–240.
205. Mayer HB, Wanke CA, Williams M, et al. Epstein-Barr virus–induced infectious mononucleosis complicated by acute renal failure: Case report and review. Clin Infect Dis 1996;22:1009–1018.
206. Osmah H, Finkelstein R, Brook JG. Rhabdomyolysis complicating, acute Epstein-Barr virus infection. Infection. 1995;23:119–120.
207. Hoagland RJ. Mononucleosis and heart disease. Am J Med Sci. 1964;248:1–6.
208. Shapiro SC, Dimich I, Steier M. Pericarditis as the only manifestation of infectious mononucleosis. Am J Dis Child. 1973;126:662–663.
209. Frishman W, Kraus ME, Zabkar J, et al. Infectious mononucleosis and fatal myocarditis. Chest. 1977;72:535–538.
210. Mundy GR. Infectious mononucleosis with pulmonary parenchymal involvement. BMJ. 1972;1:219–220.
211. Offit PA, Fleisher GR, Koven NI, et al. Severe Epstein-Barr virus pulmonary involvement. J Adolesc Health Care. 1981;2:121–125.
212. Andiman WA, McCarthy P, Markowitz RI, et al. Clinical, virologic, and serologic evidence of Epstein-Barr virus infection in association with childhood pneumonia. J Pediatr. 1981;99:880–886.
213. Barbera JA, Hayashi S, Hegele RG, et al. Detection of Epstein-Barr virus in lymphocytic interstitial pneumonia by in situ hybridization. Am Rev Respir Dis. 1992;145:940–946.
214. Sriskandan S, Labrecque LG, Schofield J. Diffuse pneumonia associated with infectious mononucleosis: Detection of Epstein-Barr virus in lung tissue by in situ hybridization. Clin Infect Dis 1996;22:578–579.
215. Haller A, von Segesser L, Baumann PC, Krause M. Severe respiratory insufficiency complicating Epstein-Barr virus infection: Case report and review. Clin Infect Dis 1995;21:206–209.
216. Lukes RJ, Cox FH. Clinical and morphologic findings in 30 fatal cases of infectious mononucleosis. Am J Pathol. 1958;34:586.
217. Bar RS, Delor CJ, Clausen KP, et al. Fatal infectious mononucleosis in a family. N Engl J Med. 1974;290:363–367.
218. Purtilo DT, Cassel CK, Yang JPS, et al. X-linked recessive progressive combined variable immunodeficiency (Duncan's disease). Lancet. 1975;1:935–940.
219. Purtilo DT, Cassel CK, Yang JPS. Fatal infectious mononucleosis in familial lymphohistiocytosis. N Engl J Med. 1974;291:736.
220. Purtilo DT, Bhawan J, Hutt LM, et al. Epstein-Barr virus infections in the X-linked recessive lymphoproliferative syndrome. Lancet. 1978;1:798–801.
221. Provisor AJ, Iacuone JJ, Chilcote RR, et al. Acquired agammaglobulinemia after a life-threatening illness with clinical and laboratory features of infectious mononucleosis in three related male children. N Engl J Med. 1975;293:62–65.
222. Purtilo DT, Yang JP, Cassel CK, et al. X-linked recessive progressive combined variable immunodeficiency. Lancet. 1975;1:935–940.
223. Hamilton JK, Paquin L, Sullivan J, et al. X-linked lymphoproliferative syndrome registry report. J Pediatr. 1980;96:669–673.
224. Purtilo DT, DeFloria D Jr, Hutt L, et al. Variable phenotypic expression of an X-linked expressive lymphoproliferative syndrome. N Engl J Med. 1977;297:1077–1080.
225. Sullivan JL, Byron KS, Brewster FE, et al. X-linked lymphoproliferative syndromes: Natural history of the immunodeficiency. J Clin Invest. 1983; 71:1765–1778.
226. Allen UR, Bass BH. Fatal hepatic necrosis in glandular fever. J Clin Pathol. 1963;16:337–341.
227. Dorman JM, Glick TH, Shannon DC, et al. Complications of infectious mononucleosis: A fatal case in a 2-year-old child. Am J Dis Child. 1974;128:239–243.
228. Jones JF, Ray CG, Minnich LL, et al. Evidence for active Epstein Barr virus infection in patients with persistent, unexplained illnesses: Elevated anti-early antigen antibodies. Ann Intern Med. 1985;102:1–7.
229. Straus SE, Tosato G, Armstrong G, et al. Persisting illness and fatigue in adults with evidence of Epstein-Barr virus infection. Ann Intern Med. 1985;102:7–16.
230. Straus SE. The chronic mononucleosis syndrome. J Infect Dis. 1988;157:405–412.
231. Holmes GP, Kaplan JE, Stewart JA, et al. A cluster of patients with a chronic mononucleosis-like syndrome. JAMA. 1987;257:2297–3302.
232. Buchwald D, Sullivan JL, Komaroff AL. Frequency of "chronic active Epstein-Barr virus infection" in a general medical practice. JAMA. 1987;257:2303–2307.
233. Horwitz CA, Henle W, Henle G, et al. Long-term serological follow-up of patients

for Epstein-Barr virus after recovery from infectious mononucleosis. J Infect Dis. 1985;151:1150–1153.
234. Holmes GP, Kaplan JE, Gantz NM, et al. Chronic fatigue syndrome: A working case definition. Ann Intern Med. 1988;108:387–389.
235. Holmes GP. Defining the chronic fatigue syndrome. Rev Infect Dis. 1991;13:S54–55.
236. Schooley RT, Carey RW, Miller G, et al. Chronic Epstein-Barr virus infection associated with fever and interstitial pneumonitis. Ann Intern Med. 1986;104:636–643.
237. Snydman DR, Rudders RA, Daquest P, et al. Infectious mononucleosis in an adult progressing to fatal immunoblastic lymphoma. Ann Intern Med. 1982;96:737–742.
238. Virelizier J-L, Lenoir G, Griscelli C. Persistent Epstein-Barr virus infection in a child with hypergammaglobulinaemia and immunoblastic proliferation associated with a selective defect in immune interferon secretion. Lancet. 1978;2:231–234.
239. Kuis W, Roord JJ, Zegers BJM, et al. Heterogeneity of immune defects in three children with a chronic active Epstein-Barr virus infection. J Clin Immunol. 1985;5:377–385.
240. Miller G, Grogan E, Rowe D, et al. Selective lack of antibody to a component of EB nuclear antigen in patients with chronic active Epstein-Barr virus infection. J Infect Dis. 1987;156:26–35.
241. Henle W, Henle G, Ho HC, et al. Antibodies to Epstein-Barr virus in nasopharyngeal carcinoma, other head and neck neoplasms, and control groups. J Natl Cancer Inst. 1970;44:225–231.
242. Zur Hausen H, Schulte-Holthausen H, Klein G, et al. EBV DNA in biopsies of Burkitt's tumors and anaplastic carcinomas of the nasopharynx. Nature. 1970;228:1056–1058.
243. Pagano JS, Huang CH, Levine P. Absence of Epstein Barr viral DNA in American Burkitt's lymphoma. N Engl J Med. 1973;289:1395–1399.
244. Sample J, Brooks L, Sample C, et al. Restricted Epstein-Barr virus protein expression in Burkitt's lymphoma is due to a different Epstein-Barr virus nuclear antigen-1 transcriptional initiation site. Proc Natl Acad Sci U S A. 1991;88:6343–6347.
245. Young LS, Dawson CW, Clark D, et al. Epstein-Barr virus gene expression in nasopharyngeal carcinoma. J Gen Virol. 1988;69:1051–1065.
246. Weiss LM, Movahed LA Warnke RA, et al. Detection of Epstein-Barr virus genomes in Reed-Sternberg cells of Hodgkin's disease. N Engl J Med. 1989;320:502–506.
247. Pallesen G, Hamilton-Dutoit SJ, Rowe M, et al. Expression of Epstein-Barr virus latent gene products in tumour cells of Hodgkin's disease. Lancet. 1991;337:320–322.
248. Herbert H, Steinbecher E, Neidobitek G, et al. Distribution and phenotype of Epstein-Barr virus-harboring cells in Hodgkin's disease. Blood. 1992;80:484–491.
249. Khan G, Norton AJ, Slavin G. Epstein-Barr virus in Hodgkin's disease. Relation to age and subtype. Cancer. 1993;71:3124–3129.
250. Kanaveros P, Jiwa M, van der Valk P, et al. Expression of Epstein-Barr virus latent genome products and related cellular activation and adhesion molecules in Hodgkin's disease and non-Hodgkin's lymphoma arising in patients without overt preexisting immunosuppression. Hum Pathol. 1993;24:725–729.
251. Oudejans JJ, Dukers DF, Jiwa NM, et al. Expression of Epstein-Barr virus encoded nuclear antigen 1 in benign and malignant tissues harbouring EBV. J Clin Pathol 1996;49:897–902.
252. Armstrong AA, Alexander FE, Paes RP, et al. Association of Epstein-Barr virus with pediatric Hodgkin's disease. Am J Pathol. 1993;142:1683–1688.
253. Delsol G, Brousset P, Chittal S, et al. Correlation of the expression of Epstein-Barr virus latent membrane protein and *in situ* hybridization with biotinylated BamHI-W probes in Hodgkin's disease. Am J Pathol. 1992;140:247–253.
254. Fellbaum C, Hansmann ML, Niedermeyer H, et al. Influence of Epstein-Barr virus genomes on patient survival in Hodgkin's disease. Am J Clin Pathol. 1992;98:319–323.
255. Robinson J, Brown N, Andiman W, et al. Diffuse polyclonal B-cell lymphoma during primary infection with Epstein-Barr virus. N Engl J Med. 1980;302:1293–1297.
256. Snydman DR, Rudders RA, Daoust P, et al. Infectious mononucleosis in an adult progressing to fatal immunoblastic lymphoma. Ann Intern Med. 1982;96:737–742.
257. Gaillard F, Mechinaud-Lacroix F, Papin S, et al. Primary Epstein-Barr virus infection with clonal T-cell lymphoproliferation. Am J Clin Pathol. 1992;98:324–333.
258. Andiman W, Gradonville L, Heston L, et al. Use of cloned probes to detect Epstein-Barr viral DNA in tissues of patients with neoplastic and lymphoproliferative disease. J Infect Dis. 1983;148:967–977.
259. Jones JF, Shurin S, Abramowsky C, et al. T cell lymphomas containing Epstein-Barr viral DNA in patients with chronic Epstein-Barr virus infections. N Engl J Med. 1988;318:733–741.
260. Hanto DW, Frizzera G, Gajl-Peczalska KJ, et al. Epstein-Barr virus induced B-cell lymphoma after renal transplantation. Acyclovir therapy and transition from polyclonal to monoclonal B-cell proliferation. N Engl J Med. 1982;306:913–918.
261. Frizzera G, Hanto DW, Gajl-Peczalska J, et al. Polymorphic diffuse B-cell hyperplasias and lymphomas in renal transplant recipients. Cancer Res. 1981;41:4262–4279.
262. Hanto DW, Frizzera G, Gajl-Peczalska J, et al. The Epstein-Barr virus in the pathogenesis of post-transplant lymphoma. Transplant Proc. 1981;13:756–760.
263. Crawford DH, Thomas JA, Janossy G, et al. Epstein-Barr virus nuclear antigen positive lymphoma after cyclosporins: A treatment in a patient with a renal allograft. Lancet. 1980;1:1355–1356.
264. Zeigler JL, Miner RC, Rosenbaum E, et al. Outbreak of Burkitt's-like lymphoma in homosexual men. Lancet. 1982;2:631–633.
265. Ho M, Jaffe R, Miller G, et al. The frequency of Epstein-Barr virus infection and associated lymphoproliferative syndrome after transplantation and its manifestations in children. Transplantation. 1988;45:719–727.
266. Borisch B, Gatter KC, Tobler A, et al. Epstein-Barr virus-associated anaplastic large cell lymphoma in renal transplant recipients. Am J Clin Pathol. 1992;98:312–318.
267. Carbone A, Gloghini A, Zanette I, et al. Demonstration of Epstein-Barr viral genomes by in situ hybridization in acquired immunodeficiency syndrome–related high grade and anaplastic large cell CD30+ lymphomas. Am J Clin Pathol. 1993;99:289–297.
268. Cohen JI. Epstein-Barr virus lymphoproliferative disease associated with acquired immunodeficiency. Medicine. 1991;70:137–160.
269. Ballerini P, Gaidano G, Gong J, et al. Molecular pathogenesis of HIV-associated lymphoma. AIDS Res Hum Retroviruses. 1992;8:731–735.
270. Cesarman E, Chang Y, Moore PS, et al. Kaposi's sarcoma–associated herpesvirus-like DNA sequences in AIDS-related body-cavity-based lymphomas. N Engl J Med 1995;332:1186–1191.
271. Cesarman E, Nador RG, Aozasa K, et al. Kaposi's sarcoma–associated herpesvirus in non-AIDS related lymphomas occurring in body cavities. Am J Pathol 1996;149:53–57.
272. Young L, Alfieri C, Hennessey K, et al. Expression of Epstein-Barr virus transformation associated antigens in B-cell disorders from immunocompromised individuals. N Engl J Med. 1989;321:1080–1085.
273. Thomas JA, Hothcin NA, Allday MJ, et al. Immunohistology of Epstein-Barr virus transformation-associated antigens in B-cell disorders from immunocompromised individuals. Transplantation. 1990;49:944–953.
274. Hochberg FG, Miller G, Schooley RT, et al. Central nervous system lymphoma related to Epstein-Barr virus. N Engl J Med. 1983;309:745–748.
275. Wood TA, Frenkel EP. The atypical lymphocyte. Am J Med. 1967;42:923–936.
276. Chin TDY. Diagnosis of infectious mononucleosis. South Med J. 1976;69:654–658.
277. Penman HG. Extreme neutropenia in glandular fever. J Clin Pathol. 1968;21:48–49.
278. Chretien JH, Esswein JG, Holland WG, et al. Predictors of the duration of infectious mononucleosis. South Med J. 1977;70:437–439.
279. Evans AS, Niederman JC, Cenabre LC, et al. A prospective evaluation of heterophile and Epstein Barr virus specific IgM antibody tests in clinical and subclinical infectious mononucleosis. Specificity and sensitivity of the tests and persistence of antibody. J Infect Dis. 1975;132:546–554.
280. Basson V, Sharp AA. Monospot: A differential slide test for infectious mononucleosis. J Clin Pathol. 1969;22:324–325.
281. Seitanidis B. A comparison of the Monospot with the Paul-Bunnell test in infectious mononucleosis and other diseases. J Clin Pathol. 1969;22:321–323.
282. Wolf P, Dorfman R, McClenahan J, et al. False-positive infectious mononucleosis spot test in lymphoma. Cancer. 1970;25:626–628.
283. Henle W, Henle G, Horwitz CA. Epstein-Barr virus specific diagnostic tests in infectious mononucleosis. Hum Pathol. 1974;5:551–565.
284. Schimitz H, Scherer M. IgM antibodies to Epstein Barr virus in infectious mononucleosis. Arch Gesamte Virusforsch. 1972;37:332–339.
285. Henle W, Henle G, Niederman JC, et al. Antibodies to early antigens induced by Epstein Barr virus in infectious mononucleosis. J Infect Dis. 1971;124:58–67.
286. Horwitz CA, Henle W, Henel G, et al. Clinical evaluation of patients with infectious mononucleosis and development of antibodies to the R component of the Epstein-Barr virus induced early antigen complex. Am J Med. 1975;58:330–338.
287. Reedman BM, Klein G. Cellular localization of an Epstein Barr virus associated complement fixing antigen in producer and nonproducer lymphoblastoid cell lines. Int J Cancer. 1973;11:499–520.
288. Henle G, Henle W, Horwitz CA. Antibodies to Epstein Barr virus associated nuclear antigen in infectious mononucleosis. J Infect Dis. 1974;130:231–239.
289. Hewetson JF, Rocchi S, Henle W, et al. Neutralizing antibodies to Epstein Barr virus in healthy populations and patients with infectious mononucleosis. J Infect Dis. 1973;128:283–289.
290. Benyesh-Melnick M, Lewis RT, Wimberly I. Some properties of the soluble (S) antigen of cultured lymphoblastoid cell lines. Arch Gesamte Virusforsch. 1970;31:113–124.
291. Thorley-Lawson DA, Schooley RT, Bhan AK, et al. Epstein-Barr virus superinduces a new human B cell differentiation antigen (B-LAST 1) expressed on transformed lymphoblasts. Cell. 1982;30:415–425.
292. Diaz-Mitoma F, Preiksaitis JK, Leung WC, et al. DNA-DNA dot hybridization to detect Epstein-Barr virus in throat washings. J Infect Dis. 1987;155:297–303.
293. Baron DN, Bell JL, Demmett WN. Biochemical studies on hepatic involvement in infectious mononucleosis. J Clin Pathol. 1965;18:209–211.
294. Rosalki SB, Jones TG, Verney AF. Transaminase and liver function studies in infectious mononucleosis. BMJ. 1960;1:929–932.
295. Kaplan ME. Cryoglobulinemia in infectious mononucleosis: Quantitation and characterization of the cryoproteins. J Lab Clin Med. 1968;71:754–765.
296. Horwitz CA, Moulds J, Henle W, et al. Cold agglutinins in infectious mononucleosis and heterophil-antibody-negative mononucleosis-like syndromes. Blood. 1977;50:195–202.
297. Horwitz CA, Henle W, Henle G, et al. Heterophile negative infectious mononucleosis and mononucleosis-like illness. Laboratory confirmation of 43 cases. Am J Med. 1977;63:947–957.
298. Blacklow NR, Kapikian AZ. Serological studies with EB virus in infectious lymphocytosis. Nature. 1970;226:647.
299. Ho DD, Sarngadharan MG, Resnick L, et al. Primary human T-lymphotropic virus type III infection. Ann Intern Med. 1985;103:880–883.

300. Cooper DA, Gold J, MacLean P, et al. Acute AIDS retrovirus infection: Definition of a clinical illness associated with seroconversion. Lancet. 1985;1:537–540.
301. Goudsmit J, de Wolf F, Paul DA, et al. Expression of human immunodeficiency virus antigen (HIV-Ag) in serum and cerebrospinal fluid during acute and chronic infection. Lancet. 1986;2:177–180.
302. Schumacher HR, Jacobson WA, Bemiller CR. Treatment of infectious mononucleosis. Ann Intern Med. 1963;58:217–228.
303. Bender CE. The value of corticosteroids in the treatment of infectious mononucleosis. JAMA. 1967;15:529–531.
304. Klein EM, Cochran JF, Buck RL. The effects of short-term corticosteroid therapy on the symptoms of infectious mononucleosis pharyngotonsilitis: A double blind study. J Am Coll Health Assoc 1969;17:446–452.
305. Collins M, Fleischer G, Kreisberg J, Fager S. Role of steroids in the treatment of infectious mononucleosis in the ambulatory college student. J Am Coll Health Assoc 1984;33:101–105.
306. Thorley-Lawson D, Strominger JL. Transformation of human lymphocytes by Epstein-Barr virus is inhibited by phosphonoacetic acid. Nature. 1976;263:332–334.
307. Nyormoi O, Thorley-Lawson DA, Elkington J, et al. Differential effect of phosphonoacetic acid on the expression of Epstein-Barr viral antigens and virus production. Proc Natl Acad Sci U S A. 1976;73:1745–1748.
308. Summers WC, Klein G. Inhibition of Epstein-Barr virus DNA synthesis and late gene expression by phosphonoacetic acid. J Virol. 1976;18:151–155.
309. Rickinson AB, Epstein MA. Sensitivity of the transforming and replicative functions of Epstein-Barr virus to inhibition by phosphonoacetate. J Gen Virol. 1978;40:409–420.
310. Thorley-Lawson DA, Strominger JL. Reversible inhibition by phosphonoacetic acid of human B-lymphocyte transformation by Epstein-Barr virus. Virology. 1978;86:423–431.
311. Coker-Vann M, Dolin R. Effect of adenine arabinoside on Epstein Barr virus in vitro. J Infect Dis. 1977;135:447–453.
312. Colby BM, Shaw JE, Elion GB, et al. Effect of acyclovir [9-(2-hydroxyethoxymethyl)guanine] on Epstein-Barr virus DNA replication. J Virol. 1980;34:560–568.
313. Colby BM, Shaw JE, Datta AK, et al. Replication of Epstein-Barr virus DNA in lymphoblastoid cells treated for extended periods with acyclovir. Am J Med. 1982;73:77–81.
314. Pagano JS, Datta AK. Perspectives on interactions of acyclovir with Epstein-Barr and other herpes viruses. Am J Med. 1982;73:18–26.
315. Adams A, Strander H, Cantell K. Sensitivity of the Epstein-Barr virus transformed human lymphoid cell lines to interferon. J Gen Virol. 1975;28:207–217.
316. Thorley-Lawson DA. The transformation of adult but not newborn lymphocytes by Epstein-Barr virus and phytohemagglutinin is inhibited by interferon: The early suppression by T-cells of Epstein-Barr infection is mediated by interferon. J Immunol. 1981;126:829–833.
317. Garner JG, Hirsch MS, Schooley RT. Prevention of Epstein-Barr virus-induced β-cell outgrowth by interferon-alpha. Infect Immun. 1984;43:920–924.
318. Greenspan D, DeSouza YG, Conant MA, et al. Efficacy of desciclovir in the treatment of Epstein-Barr virus infection in oral hairy leukoplakia. J AIDS. 1990;3:571–578.
319. Andersson J, Skoldenberg B, Henle W, et al. Acyclovir treatment in infectious mononucleosis: A clinical and virological study. Infection. 1987;15:14–20.
320. Andersson J, Britton S, Ernberg I, et al. Effect of acyclovir on infectious mononucleosis: A double-blind, placebo-controlled study. J Infect Dis. 1986;153:283–290.
321. van der Horst C, Joncas J, Aronheim G, et al. Lack of effect of peroral acyclovir for the treatment of infectious mononucleosis. J Infect Dis. 1991;164:788–792.
322. Tynell E, Aurelius E, Brandell A, et al. Acyclovir and prednisolone treatment of acute infectious mononucleosis: A multicenter, double-blind, placebo-controlled study. J Infect Dis 1996;174:324–331.
323. Cheeseman SH, Henle W, Rubin RH, et al. Epstein-Barr virus infection in renal transplant recipients: Effects of anti-thymocyte globulin and interferon. Ann Intern Med. 1980;93:39–42.
324. Resnick L, Herbst JS, Ablashi DV, et al. Regression of oral hairy leukoplakia after orally administered acyclovir therapy. JAMA. 1988;259:384–388.
325. Sullivan JL, Byron KS, Brewster FE, et al. Treatment of life-threatening Epstein-Barr virus infections with acyclovir. Am J Med. 1982;73:262–266.
326. Sullivan JL, Baker JN, Byron KS, et al. Failure of acyclovir to inhibit polyclonal Epstein-Barr virus induced lymphoproliferation. Fed Proc. 1983;42:458.
327. Fischer A, Blanche S, LeBidois J, et al. Anti-B-cell monoclonal antibodies in the treatment of severe B-cell lymphomoproliferative syndrome following bone marrow and organ transplantation. N Engl J Med. 1991;324:1451–1456.
328. Boyle TJ, Berend KR, DiMaio JM, et al. Adoptive transfer of cytotoxic T-lymphocytes for the treatment of transplant-associated lymphoma. Surgery. 1993;114:218–225.
329. Morgan AJ, Allison AC, Finerty S, et al. Validation of a first generation Epstein-Barr virus vaccine preparation suitable for human use. J Med Virol. 1989;29:74–78.

Chapter 129

Human Herpesvirus Types 6 and 7

STEPHEN E. STRAUS

Human herpesvirus (HHV) types 6 and 7 are ubiquitous lymphotropic agents whose biologic features and clinical relevance are still being defined. In the last few years, rapid progress has been made in developing tests for these viruses, and rational approaches to therapy of selected cases are now conceivable.

HISTORY

The fact that no new HHVs had been discovered in more than 2 decades, since Epstein and Barr reported their eponymous virus, suggested that no additional ones remained to be discovered. However, by the mid-1980s methods for cultivating human lymphocytes in the presence of trophic factors like interleukin-2 fortuitously amplified and permitted the recognition not only of the human T-lymphotropic retroviruses, but also of novel HHVs such as HHV-6 and HHV-7.

HUMAN HERPESVIRUS TYPE 6

Biology

HHV-6 was originally called human B-lymphotropic virus when Salahuddin, Gallo, and coworkers described it in 1986.[1] Subsequent in vitro studies showed that it grows in cells of diverse origin including T cells, monocytes, macrophages, megakaryocytes, and human embryonic glial cells as well as in Epstein-Barr–transformed B cells.[2] In vivo, most HHV-6–infected cells bear T-cell markers. The range of cells in which HHV-6 can replicate in vivo, however, is quite broad.

As summarized in Chapter 124, Introduction to Herpesviridae, HHV-6 is a typical herpesvirus—in view of its structure, genome organization, and expression.[3] As more strains of HHV-6 were isolated, it became apparent that they can be segregated into subtypes A and B, which differ with respect to epidemiology, growth, and antigenic composition.[4] HHV-6A and HHV-6B genes share 75 to 97% nucleotide identity.

Epidemiology

Initial studies using relatively insensitive assays suggested that the HHV-6 seroprevalence is high only in immunocompromised patient populations.[5] Methodologic improvements led to the recognition that HHV-6 infects nearly all humans by the age of 2 years. Several studies estimated HHV-6 seroprevalence at 64 to 83% by the age of 13 months, and upward of 95% in older children—with no clear differences according to gender, race, socioeconomic status, or country.[6–9] One study of blood from 2427 U.S. children found 10 and 66% of these to be polymerase chain reaction (PCR)-positive for HHV-6 DNA at 1 month and 1 year, respectively—verifying high rates of infection during the first year and persistence of virus in peripheral blood (Fig. 129–1).[10]

Serologic tests do not readily distinguish between the HHV-6A and HHV-6B variants, but molecular studies can do so. With these techniques, their distribution in various populations was determined. Although both HHV-6A and HHV-6B have been recovered with some frequency from the peripheral blood of immunocompromised

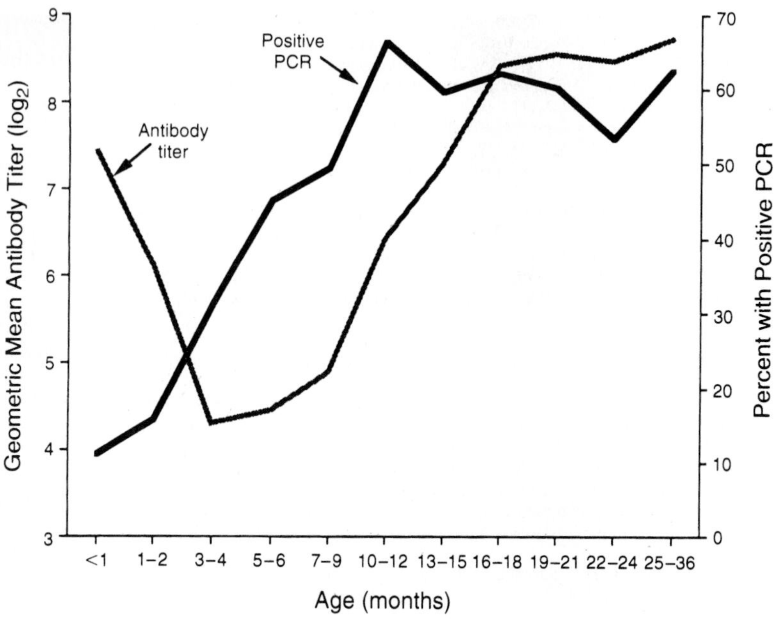

FIGURE 129–1. Antibody titers to HHV-6 and detection of HHV-6 DNA in peripheral blood by polymerase chain reaction in 2427 children, by age. (From Hall CB, Long CE, Schnabel KC, et al. Human herpesvirus-6 infection in children: A prospective study of complications and reactivation. N Engl J Med. 1994;331:432–438. Copyright © 1994 Massachusetts Medical Society. All rights reserved.)

or otherwise chronically ill patients,[1, 11] nearly all isolates from otherwise healthy adults and children represent variant B.[12] Although HHV-6B has been definitively associated with certain clinical syndromes, HHV-6A has yet to be causally linked to any illness.

Several studies suggest that intrauterine or perinatal transmission of HHV-6 may occur,[13] but most infections probably arise from the exchange of maternal (or other) saliva during the first years of life. HHV-6 is commonly detected in saliva, although rates have varied widely in different studies, in part owing to initial misidentification of HHV-7 isolates as HHV-6.[14, 15] Viruses recovered from the blood of several acutely infected children were shown by molecular analysis to be identical to those in their mothers' saliva.[16]

Pathogenesis

General

The existing data that implicate saliva as a potential vehicle for HHV-6, the known tropism of the virus for T cells, and analogies drawn to other herpesviruses suggest that the primary infection may proceed from the oropharynx, through the regional lymphoid tissue, and then to mononuclear cell populations distributed throughout the body. Productive replication, persistence, and eventual virus activation in the setting of immune suppression could incite the known spectrum of HHV-6–associated clinical syndromes.

Although HHV-6 is found in circulating lymphocytes during primary infection, during convalescence, and in healthy adults, it can be detected most readily in monocyte-macrophages.[17] The state of HHV-6 gene expression in persistently infected macrophages is not known, but chemical and cytokine activation of macrophages, or superinfection with HHV-7, induces lytic growth of HHV-6.[18]

Human immunodeficiency virus type 1 (HIV-1) and HHV-6 enjoy a curious, and potentially important, synergy. Both viruses infect and replicate in $CD4^+$ lymphocytes in vitro.[19] HHV-6 infection induces CD4 expression in otherwise $CD4^-$ subpopulations of lymphocytes and natural killer cells, rendering them available for HIV-1 entry.[20] Moreover, HHV-6 accelerates HIV-1 transcription and replication.[19] In turn, HIV-1 has been shown to upregulate HHV-6 gene expression and replication, whereas immune deficiency associated with progressive HIV disease permits the growth and spread of HHV-6.[21, 22]

Immune Avoidance

The capacity of HHV-6 to persist and to be transmitted efficiently reflects its successful adaptation to its host by capturing human genes that deter immune surveillance. HHV-6 open reading frames U12 and U51 encode G-protein receptor homologues that bind the β-chemokines macrophage inflammatory protein-1α (MIP-1α), MIP-1β, and RANTES (regulated upon activation, normal T-expressed, and secreted). The expression of these receptors on infected cells may enhance viral persistence in the face of otherwise formidable immune defenses.[3, 23]

Clinical Manifestations

Exanthem Subitum (Roseola Infantum; Sixth Disease)

Exanthem subitum is an illness of infants and young children that is heralded by 3 to 5 days of high, but otherwise unremarkable, fever, mild upper respiratory symptoms, and occasional cervical adenopathy.[24] As the fever abates, a classic diffuse macular or maculopapular exanthem emerges (Fig. 129–2; Table 129–1). Blood studies at this time often reveal a modest, atypical lymphocytosis and relative neutropenia. The course is generally a benign one, but febrile seizures, meningitis, and encephalitis are well-recognized complications.

In 1950, exanthem subitum was successfully transmitted by inoculation of serum from ill infants to susceptible ones[25]; however, the identity of the pathogen was not determined until 1988, when Yamanishi and colleagues reported acute infection and seroconversion to the recently described HHV-6.[26] Extensive subsequent studies verified that HHV-6 is the major cause of exanthem subitum, the

TABLE 129–1 Signs and Symptoms in 34 Febrile Children with Acute HHV-6 Infection

	No. (%) of Children
Malaise, irritability	28 (82)
Temperature ≥40°C	22 (65)
Inflamed tympanic membranes	21 (62)
Nasal congestion	19 (56)
Diarrhea	10 (29)
Cough	9 (27)
Rhonchi, wheezing, crackles	8 (24)
Vomiting	7 (21)
Rash	6 (18)
Seizure	1 (3)

Abbreviation: HHV, Human herpesvirus.

Modified from Pruksananonda P, Hall CB, Insel RA, et al. Primary human herpesvirus 6 infection in young children. N Engl J Med. 1992;326:1445–1450. Copyright © 1992 Massachusetts Medical Society. All rights reserved.

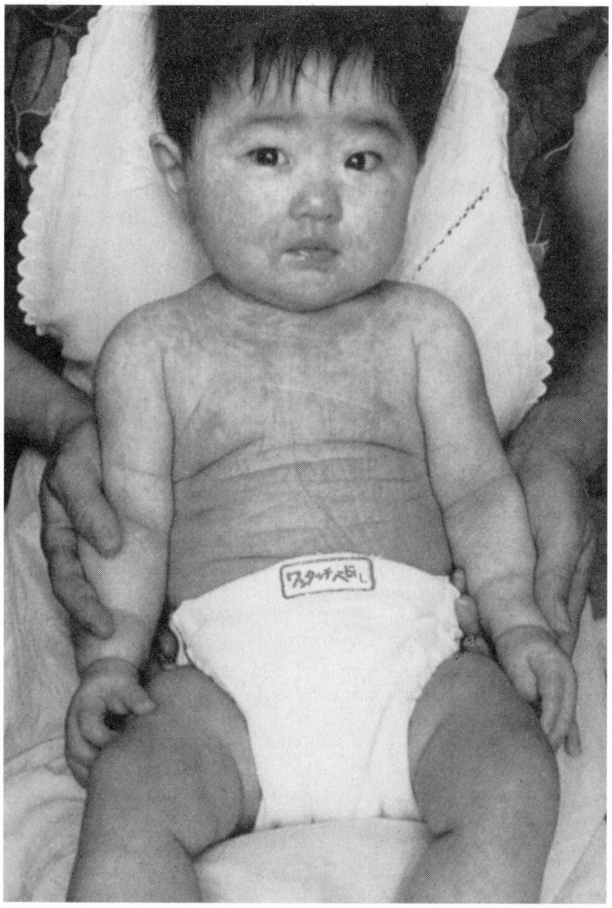

FIGURE 129–2. A child with roseola. (Courtesy of Professor K. Yamanishi.)

other cause being HHV-7.[10, 27, 28] Most infants are infected subclinically; only 9% of subjects in one study,[29] and 17% in another,[10] developed exanthem subitum.

Infantile Fever

In infants, a more common manifestation of primary HHV-6 infection than exanthem subitum is fever without rash.[30] In fact, HHV-6 is a prominent cause of fevers in infants and young children. In one hospital, of 1653 infants and young children who were evaluated prospectively for acute febrile illnesses, nearly 10% were experiencing primary HHV-6 infection (Fig. 129–3).[10] These infections were commonly associated with irritability, otitis, respiratory symptoms, or diarrhea, or all of these. Seizures accompanied 3 to 13% of febrile episodes.

Febrile Seizures

HHV-6 is a major precipitant of seizures in infants, not merely because of the high fever that the infection provokes, but also because HHV-6 replicates in the central nervous system.[10, 31] Using PCR, HHV-6 DNA is commonly detected in the spinal fluid, not only during acute primary infection but for years afterward.[31, 32]

Encephalitis and Other Neurologic Disorders

Reports of encephalitis as a complication of exanthem subitum and the appreciation that HHV-6 is highly neurotropic predicted that the virus might be associated with encephalitis in other settings as well. The detection of HHV-6 DNA in cerebrospinal fluids from patients with otherwise undiagnosed focal encephalitis supported this prediction—as did the direct demonstration, in one case, of the virus in brain parenchyma.[33, 34] The frequent presence of HHV-6 in the central nervous system, however, complicates its definitive attribution in individual cases of encephalitis, as well as in other acute or chronic neurologic syndromes. This problem underlies the current controversy regarding reports of HHV-6 in the brain of patients with multiple sclerosis.[35, 36] It has been postulated, but far from proved, that active HHV-6 infection in the central nervous system promotes inflammatory injury and demyelination.

Infectious Mononucleosis

Although Epstein-Barr virus is the most common cause of classic infectious mononucleosis and similar syndromes, other organisms can do so as well (see Chapter 128, Epstein-Barr Virus). It is not surprising, then, that the description of HHV-6, another human lymphotropic virus, would be followed by reports linking it to mononucleosis-like syndromes. These cases have been highly variable in the age of presentation and in severity, but most of them have been mild, with a modest number of atypical lymphocytes, and heterophil antibody responses are not often seen.[37–39]

Hepatitis

Elevations in aminotransferase levels were not appreciated as a common feature of roseola in large case series,[10] but in neonates and young children there are several reports of hepatitis associated with primary HHV-6 infection—some of which cases have been fulminant.[40, 41]

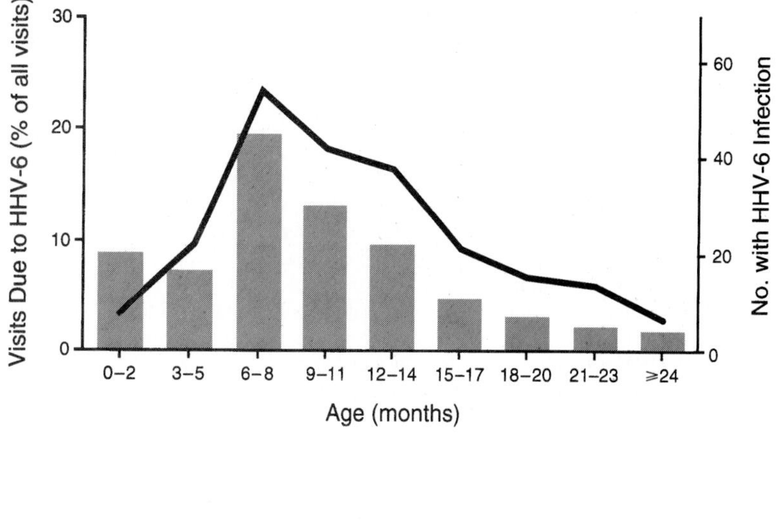

FIGURE 129–3. Percent of all emergency department visits for acute febrile illnesses that were associated with primary HHV-6 infections *(curve)* and the number of such cases by age. (From Hall CB, Long CE, Schnabel KC, et al. Human herpesvirus-6 infection in children: A prospective study of complications and reactivation. N Engl J Med. 1994;331:432–438. Copyright © 1994 Massachusetts Medical Society. All rights reserved.)

Infection in the Immunocompromised Host

As with other herpesviruses, cellular immune deficits permit HHV-6 to replicate, providing it opportunities to provoke potentially severe clinical illness. Such associations have been sought in multiple patient populations, with mixed and conflicting results.

Several studies demonstrated acute increases in HHV-6–specific antibody titers, and higher rates of viral DNA detection in the peripheral blood by PCR, or viral antigen detection in kidney biopsies in renal transplant recipients experiencing acute rejection.[42] None of these associations are understood.

Studies in bone marrow transplants have associated HHV-6 with particular clinical syndromes: graft-versus-host disease, delayed bone marrow engraftment, and pneumonitis. For each of these, there have been provocative reports describing increased HHV-6–specific antibodies, or viral DNA or antigen in peripheral blood mononuclear cells or tissues.[43–45] Bone marrow transplant recipients with pneumonitis were shown to have high levels of HHV-6 DNA in the lung, but these patients with complex conditions often had other opportunistic pathogens as well.[46, 47] It is likely that the more important cause of pneumonitis in transplant recipients is cytomegalovirus, which is usually found together with HHV-6 in affected lungs.[47]

Because of the synergy that HHV-6 and HIV manifest in vitro, many studies sought evidence that HHV-6 promotes the progression of acquired immunodeficiency syndrome (AIDS). In summary, it is clear that HHV-6 disseminates widely in advanced AIDS,[48, 49] but there is no compelling evidence for any prominent HHV-6–associated opportunistic illnesses in AIDS patients, and there are no consistent data to suggest that HHV-6 directly speeds the course of AIDS.[50–52]

HHV-6 has also been detected in and associated with various leukemias and lymphomas. Most interesting are instances of the nodular sclerosis type of Hodgkin's disease, in which high levels of HHV-6 DNA were detected in the absence of Epstein-Barr virus DNA, and even these data could not be confirmed.[53–55]

Chronic Fatigue Syndrome

Early studies identified a higher HHV-6 seroprevalence or rate of virus recovery from saliva or peripheral blood in patients with chronic fatigue syndrome than in controls, adding this virus to the many postulated causes of the syndrome. For each positive study, however, there are ones of equal or greater size and quality showing no association between HHV-6 and chronic fatigue syndrome.[56–58]

Diagnosis

Serodiagnosis

Commercial assays now reliably detect HHV-6–specific immunoglobulin G (IgG) antibody responses, but they do not distinguish infection with variants A and B, and there is cross-reactivity with HHV-7.[59, 60] Because nearly everyone older than 2 years is positive, a single HHV-6 serologic test result is generally meaningless; however, seroconversion from negative to positive in paired sera is good evidence of recent primary infection. IgM assays for HHV-6 are not reliable indicators of acute infection.[61]

Virus Detection

HHV-6 can be cultured from peripheral blood mononuclear cells. In the setting of an acute exanthem subitum–like illness, virus recovery may be truly diagnostic.[62] In healthy older children and adults, the isolation of HHV-6 is very uncommon. Higher rates of viral replication and recovery in immunocompromised patients, unrelated to the clinical presentation, negate culture as a useful tool in that setting. Antigen-specific monoclonal antibodies permit the definitive identification of HHV-6 in tissues, as does in situ hybridization, but it is always difficult to assign an etiologic role to the virus. Qualitative and quantitative PCR techniques for HHV-6 DNA in serum, plasma, or spinal fluid may eventually prove useful in identifying pathologically elevated levels of virus, but their current value is undefined.[63, 64]

Treatment

Multiple HHV-6 isolates have been tested for their sensitivity to antiviral drugs. The in vitro virus sensitivity roughly parallels that of cytomegalovirus: acyclovir is inactive; ganciclovir responsiveness is variable, and foscarnet is inhibitory in pharmacologically meaningful concentrations.[65, 66] There are anecdotes supporting the effectiveness of each of these drugs in selected patient settings, but there are no controlled trials.[67] Good prospective studies in patients with encephalitis, post-transplant pneumonia, and multiple sclerosis are needed.

HUMAN HERPESVIRUS TYPE 7

Biology and Pathogenesis

Frenkel and colleagues demonstrated in 1990 a novel herpesvirus in peripheral blood mononuclear cells of a healthy individual.[68] Since that time, the viral epidemiology and DNA sequence have been defined. All that is lacking is an understanding of what role HHV-7 plays in human disease, and whether there is ever a need for treatment.

HHV-7 infects activated cord blood or peripheral blood $CD4^+$ lymphocytes.[68] In fact, CD4 is a component of the cellular receptor for HHV-7, allowing infection with it to interfere with HIV-1 infection.[69] HHV-7 persists in circulating $CD4^+$ cells and can be induced from latency by T-cell activation.[18] HHV-7 possesses limited nucleic acid homology to HHV-6, but there is sufficient antigenic relatedness to have complicated earlier serologic tests of these viruses.[70, 71] As with HHV-6, HHV-7 encodes genes that could potentially interfere with host immune responses to it.[72] One such interesting effect relates to the profound downregulation by HHV-7 of CD4 expression on T cells.[73] Two HHV-7 genes (situated in a location identical to that of homologues in HHV-6) encode putative G-coupled protein receptors of chemokines. Although still not proved, these could enhance the survival of virally infected cells.[72]

Epidemiology

HHV-7 infects nearly all humans by the age of 5 years, the infections peaking at a later age than HHV-6 infections (Fig. 129–4). Among those infected, HHV-7 is virtually a commensal inhabitant of saliva.[15, 74] This easy spread probably depends on these high rates of salivary excretion.

Diagnosis

HHV-7–specific serologic tests, antigen detection, and PCR assays now exist but remain the province of research laboratories that are investigating the biology and significance of the virus.[75, 76]

Clinical Syndromes

The clear biologic and epidemiologic relatedness of HHV-6 and HHV-7 suggest that they should share similar clinical manifestations. The demonstration of acute HHV-7 seroconversion and viral shedding in association with second cases of exanthem subitum in HHV-6–positive Japanese infants suggests that it may be another cause of the syndrome.[77] Isolated reports of HHV-7 in encephalitis or hepatitis suggest that there may be a broader, still-undefined spectrum of illness provoked by this virus.[78, 79] Its cellular tropism—more restricted than that of HHV-6 in vitro—may limit the extent of its

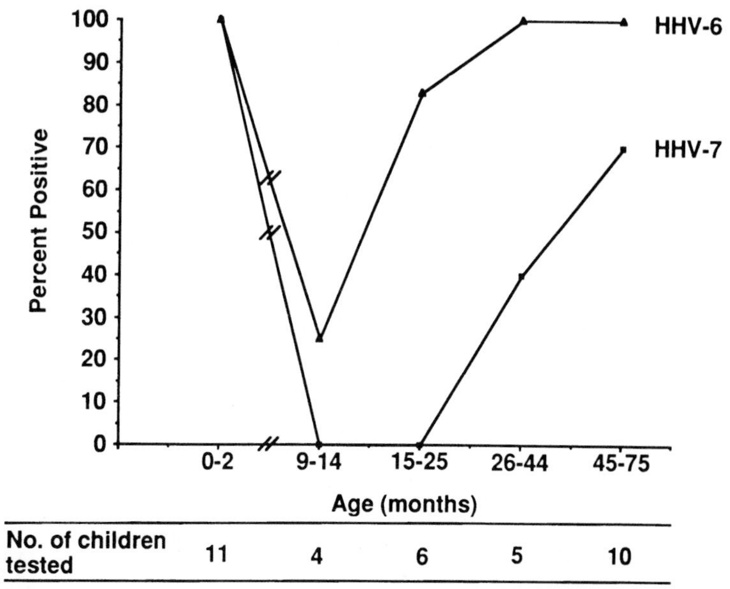

FIGURE 129–4. The percentage of children seropositive for HHV-6 and HHV-7, by age. (From Wyatt LS, Frenkel J. Human herpesvirus 7 is a constitutive inhabitant of adult human saliva. J Virol. 1992;66:3206–3209.)

clinical expression as well, whereas its ubiquitousness in patients will confound efforts to establish causation.

Treatment

HHV-7 replication in vitro is inhibited by achievable concentrations of foscarnet, but there are as yet no settings in which treatment seems warranted.[80]

REFERENCES

1. Salahuddin SZ, Ablashi DV, Markham PD, et al. Isolation of a new virus, HBLV, in patients with lymphoproliferative disorders. Science. 1986;234:596–601.
2. Ablashi DV, Salahuddin SZ, Josephs SF, et al. HBLV (or HHV-6) in human cell lines. Nature. 1987;329:207.
3. Gompels UA, Nicholas J, Lawrence G, et al. The DNA sequence of human herpesvirus-6: Structure, coding content, and genome evolution. Virology. 1995;209:29–51.
4. Schirmer EC, Wyatt LS, Yamanishi K, et al. Differentiation between two distinct classes of viruses now classified as human herpesvirus 6. Proc Natl Acad Sci U S A. 1991;88:5922–5926.
5. Saxinger C, Polesky H, Eby N, et al. Antibody reactivity with HBLV (HHV-6) in U.S. populations. J Virol Methods. 1988;21:199–208.
6. Briggs M, Fox J, Tedder RS. Age prevalence of antibody to human herpesvirus 6. Lancet. 1988;1:1058–1059.
7. Huang LM, Lee CY, Chen JY, et al. Primary human herpesvirus 6 infections in children: A prospective serologic study. J Infect Dis. 1992;165:1163–1164.
8. Okuno T, Takahashi K, Balachandra K, et al. Seroepidemiology of human herpesvirus 6 infection in normal children and adults. J Clin Microbiol. 1989;27:651–653.
9. Yoshikawa T, Suga S, Asano Y, et al. Distribution of antibodies to a causative agent of exanthem subitum (human herpesvirus-6) in healthy individuals. Pediatrics. 1989;84:675–677.
10. Hall CB, Long CE, Schnabel KC, et al. Human herpesvirus-6 infection in children: A prospective study of complications and reactivation. N Engl J Med. 1994;331:432–438.
11. Ablashi DV, Balachandran N, Josephs, SF, et al. Genomic polymorphism, growth properties, and immunologic variations in human herpesvirus-6 isolates. Virology. 1991;184:545–552.
12. Dewhurst S, McIntyre K, Schnabel K, et al. Human herpesvirus 6 (HHV-6) variant B accounts for the majority of symptomatic primary HHV-6 infections in a population of U.S. infants. J Clin Microbiol. 1993;31:416–418.
13. Aubin JT, Poirel L, Agut H, et al. Intrauterine transmission of human herpesvirus 6. Lancet. 1992;340:482–483.
14. Levy JA, Ferro F, Greenspan D, et al. Frequent isolation of HHV-6 from saliva and high seroprevalence of the virus in the population. Lancet. 1990;335:1047–1050.
15. Wyatt LS, Frenkel J. Human herpesvirus 7 is a constitutive inhabitant of adult human saliva. J Virol. 1992;66:3206–3209.
16. Mukai T, Yamamoto T, Kondo T, et al. Molecular epidemiologic studies of human herpesvirus 6 in families. J Med Virol. 1994;42:224–227.
17. Kondo KT, Kondo T. Okuno T, et al. Latent human herpesvirus 6 infection of human monocytes/macrophages. J Gen Virol. 1993;72:1401–1408.
18. Katsafanas GC, Schirmer EC, Wyatt LS, et al. In vitro activation of human herpesviruses 6 and 7 from latency. Proc Natl Acad Sci U S A. 1996;93:9788–9792.
19. Lusso P, Ensoli B, Markham PD, et al. Productive dual infection of human CD4+ T lymphocytes by HIV-1 and HHV-6. Nature. 1989;337:370–373.
20. Lusso P, Malnati MS, Garzino-Demo A, et al. Infection of natural killer cells by human herpesvirus 6. Nature. 1993;362:458–462.
21. Carrigan DR, Knox KK, Tapper MA. Suppression of human immunodeficiency virus type 1 replication by human herpesvirus-6. J Infect Dis. 1990;162:844–851.
22. Knox, KK, Carrigan DR. Disseminated active HHV-6 infections in patients with AIDS. Lancet. 1994;343:577–578.
23. Isegawa Y, Ping Z, Nakano K, et al. Human herpesvirus 6 open reading frame U12 encodes a functional β-chemokine receptor. J Virol. 1998;72:6104–6112.
24. Asano Y, Yoshikawa T, Suga S, et al. Clinical features of infants with primary human herpesvirus-6 infection (exanthem subitum, roseola infantum). Pediatrics. 1994;93:104–108.
25. Kempe CH, Shaw EB, Jackson JR, et al. Studies on the etiology of exanthem subitum (roseola infantum). J Pediatr. 1950;37:561–568.
26. Yamanishi K, Okuno T, Shiraki K, et al. Identification of human herpesvirus-6 as a causal agent for exanthem subitum. Lancet. 1988;1:1065–1067.
27. Okada K, Ueda K, Kusuhara K, et al. Exanthem subitum and human herpesvirus-6 infection: Clinical observations in fifty-seven cases. Pediatr Infect Dis J. 1993;12:204–208.
28. Tanaka K, Kondo T, Torigoe S, et al. Human herpesvirus 7: Another causal agent for roseola (exanthem subitum). J Pediatr. 1994;125:1–5.
29. Pruksananonda P, Hall CB, Insel RA, et al. Primary human herpesvirus 6 infection in young children. N Engl J Med. 1992;326:1445–1450.
30. Suga S, Yoshikawa T, Asano Y, et al. Human herpesvirus-6 infection (exanthem subitum) without rash. Pediatrics. 1989;83:1003–1006.
31. Kondo K, Nagafuji H, Hata A, et al. Association of human herpesvirus 6 infection of the central nervous system with recurrence of febrile convulsions. J Infect Dis. 1993;167:1197–1200.
32. Caserta MT, Hall CB, Schnabel K, et al. Neuroinvasion and persistence of human herpesvirus 6 in children. J Infect Dis. 1994;170:1586–1589.
33. McCullers JA, Lakeman FD, Whitley RJ. Human herpesvirus 6 is associated with focal encephalitis. Clin Infect Dis. 1995;21:571–576.
34. Drobyski WR, Knox KK, Majewski D, et al. Fatal encephalitis due to variant B human herpesvirus-6 infection in a bone marrow-transplant recipient. N Engl J Med. 1994;330:1356–1360.
35. Challoner PB, Smith KT, Parker JD, et al. Plaque-associated expression of human herpesvirus 6 in multiple sclerosis. Proc Natl Acad Sci U S A. 1995;92:7440–7444.
36. Sanders VJ, Felisan S, Waddell A, et al. Detection of Herpesviridae in postmortem multiple sclerosis brain tissue and controls by polymerase chain reaction. J Neurovirol. 1996;2:249–258.
37. Niederman JC, Liu C-R, Kaplan MH, et al. Clinical and serological features of human herpesvirus-6 infection in three adults. Lancet. 1988;10:817–819.
38. Steeper TA, Horwitz CA, Ablashi DV, et al. The spectrum of clinical and laboratory findings resulting from human herpesvirus-6 (HHV-6) in patients with mononucleosis-like illnesses not resulting from Epstein-Barr virus or cytomegalovirus. Am J Clin Pathol. 1990;93:776–783.
39. Akashi K, Eizuru Y, Sumiyoshi Y, et al. Brief report: Severe infectious mononucleosis-like syndrome and primary human herpesvirus 6 infection in an adult. N Engl J Med. 1993;328:168–171.
40. Asano Y, Yoshikawa T, Suga S, et al. Fatal fulminant hepatitis in an infant with human herpesvirus-6 infection. Lancet. 1990;335:862–863.

41. Mendel I, de Matteis M, Bertin C, et al. Fulminant hepatitis in neonates with human herpesvirus-6 infection. Pediatr Infect Dis J. 1995;14:993–997.
42. Okuno T, Higashi K, Shiraki K, et al. Human herpesvirus 6 infection in renal transplantation. Transplantation. 1990;49:519–522.
43. Carrigan DR, Drobyski WR, Russler SK, et al. Interstitial pneumonitis associated with human herpesvirus-6 infection after marrow transplantation. Lancet. 1991;338:147–149.
44. Carrigan DR, Knox KK. Human herpesvirus 6 (HHV-6) isolation from bone marrow: HHV-6–associated bone marrow suppression in bone marrow transplant patients. Blood. 1994;84:3307–3310.
45. Carrigan DR. Human herpesvirus-6 and bone marrow transplantation. In: Ablashi DV, Krueger GRF, Salabuddin SZ, eds. Human Herpesvirus-6: Epidemiology, Molecular Biology, and Clinical Pathology, v. 4. Amsterdam: Elsevier Biomedical; 1992:281–302.
46. Cone RW, Hackman RC, Huang ML, et al. Human herpesvirus-6 in lung tissue from patients with pneumonitis after bone marrow transplantation. N Engl J Med. 1993;329:156–161.
47. Knox KK, Carrigan DR. HHV-6 and CMV pneumonitis in immunocompromised patients. Lancet. 1994;343:1647.
48. Clark DA, Ait-Khaled M, Wheeler AC. Quantification of human herpesvirus 6 in immunocompetent persons and post-mortem tissues from AIDS patients by PCR. J Gen Virol. 1996;77:2271–2275.
49. Corbellino, M, Lusso P, Gallo RC, et al. Disseminated human herpesvirus 6 infection in AIDS. Lancet. 1993;342:1242.
50. Fox J, Briggs M, Tedder RS. Antibody to human herpesvirus 6 in HIV-1 positive and negative homosexual men. Lancet. 1988;2:396–397.
51. Spira TJ, Bozeman LH, Sanderlin KC, et al. Lack of correlation between human herpesvirus-6 infection and the course of human immunodeficiency virus infection. J Infect Dis. 1990;161:567–570.
52. Fairfax MR, Schacker T, Cone RW, et al. Human herpesvirus 6 DNA in blood cells of human immunodeficiency virus-infected men: Correlation of high levels with high CD4 cell counts. J Infect Dis. 1994;169:1342–1345.
53. Di Luca D, Dolcetti R, Mirandola P, et al. Human herpesvirus 6: A survey of presence and variant distribution in normal peripheral lymphocytes and lymphoproliferative disorders. J Infect Dis. 1994;170:211–215.
54. Torelli G, Marasca R, Luppi M, et al. Human herpesvirus-6 in human lymphomas: Identification of specific sequences in Hodgkin's lymphomas by polymerase chain reaction. Blood. 1991;77:2251–2258.
55. Valente G, Secchiero P, Lusso P, et al. Human herpesvirus 6 and Epstein-Barr virus in Hodgkin's disease: A controlled study by polymerase chain reaction and in situ hybridization. Am J Pathol. 1996;149:1501–1510.
56. Buchwald D, Cheney PR, Peterson DL, et al. A chronic illness characterized by fatigue, neurologic and immunologic disorders, and active human herpesvirus type 6 infection. Ann Intern Med. 1992;116:103–113.
57. Yalcin S, Kuratsune H, Yamaguchi K, et al. Prevalence of human herpesvirus 6 variants A and B in patients with chronic fatigue syndrome. Microbiol Immunol. 1994;38:587–590.
58. Buchwald D, Ashley RL, Pearlman T, et al. Viral serologies in patients with chronic fatigue and chronic fatigue syndrome. J Med Virol. 1996;50:25–30.
59. Coyle PV, Briggs M, Tedder RS, et al. Comparison of three immunoassays for the detection of anti-HHV6. J Virol Methods. 1992;38:283–295.
60. Black JB, Schwarz TF, Patton JL, et al. Evaluation of immunoassays for detection of antibodies to human herpesvirus 7. Clin Diagn Lab Immunol. 1996;3:79–83.
61. Suga S, Yoshikawa T, Asano Y, et al. IgM neutralizing antibody responses to human herpesvirus-6 in patients with exanthem subitum or organ transplantation. Microbiol Immunol. 1992;36:495–506.
62. Asano Y, Yoshikawa T, Suga S, et al. Viremia and neutralizing antibody response in infants with exanthem subitum. J Pediatr. 1989;114:535–539.
63. Cone RW, Huang ML, Ashley R. Human herpesvirus 6 DNA in peripheral blood cells and saliva from immunocompetent individuals. J Clin Microbiol. 1993;31:1262–1267.
64. Kondo K, Hayakawa Y, Mori H, et al. Detection by polymerase chain reaction amplification of human herpesvirus 6 DNA in peripheral blood of patients with exanthem subitum. J Clin Microbiol. 1990;28:970–974.
65. Williams MV. HHV-6: Response to antiviral agents. In: Ablashi DV, Krueger GRF, Salahuddin SZ, eds. Human Herpesvirus-6: Epidemiology, Molecular Biology, and Clinical Pathology, v. 4. Amsterdam: Elsevier Biomedical, 1992:317–335.
66. Reyman D, Naesens L, Balzarini J, et al. Antiviral activity of selected acyclic nucleoside analogues against human herpesvirus 6. Antiviral Res. 1995;28:343–357.
67. Drobyski, WR, Dunne WM, Burd EM, et al. Human herpesvirus-6 (HHV-6) infection in allogeneic bone marrow transplant recipients: Evidence of a marrow-suppressive role for HHV-6 in vivo. J Infect Dis. 1993;167:735–739.
68. Frenkel N, Schirmer EC, Wyatt LS, et al. Isolation of a new herpesvirus from human CD4+ T cells. Proc Natl Acad Sci U S A. 1990;87:748–752.
69. Lusso P, Secchiero P, Crowley RW, et al. CD4 is a critical component of the receptor for human herpesvirus 7: Interference with human immunodeficiency virus. Proc Natl Acad Sci U S A. 1994;91:3872–3876.
70. Berneman ZN, Ablashi DV, Li G, et al. Human herpesvirus 7 is a T-lymphotropic virus and is related to, but significantly different from, human herpesvirus 6 and human cytomegalovirus. Proc Natl Acad Sci U S A. 1992;89:10,552–10,556.
71. Foà-Tomasi L, Avitabile E, Ke L, et al. Polyvalent and monoclonal antibodies identify major immunogenic proteins specific for human herpesvirus 7–infected cells and have weak cross-reactivity with human herpesvirus 6. J Gen Virol. 1994;75:2719–2727.
72. Nicholas J. Determination and analysis of the complete nucleotide sequence of human herpesvirus 7. J Virol. 1996;70:5975–5989.
73. Secchiero P, Gibellini D, Flamand L, et al. Human herpesvirus 7 induces the downregulation of CD4 antigen in lymphoid T cells without affecting p56lck levels. J Immunol. 1997;159:3412–3423.
74. Yoshikawa T, Asano Y, Kobayashi I. Seroepidemiology of human herpesvirus 7 in healthy children and adults in Japan. J Med Virol. 1993;41:319–323.
75. Tanaka-Taya K, Kondo T, Mukai T, et al. Seroepidemiological study of human herpesvirus-6 and -7 in children of different ages and detection of these two viruses in throat swabs by polymerase chain reaction. J Med Virol. 1996;48:88–94.
76. Kidd IM, Clark DA, Ait-Khaled M, et al. Measurement of human herpesvirus 7 load in peripheral blood and saliva of healthy subjects by quantitative polymerase chain reaction. J Infect Dis. 1996;174:396–401.
77. Tanaka K, Kondo T, Torigoe S, et al. Human herpesvirus 7: Another causal agent for roseola (exanthem subitum). J Pediatr. 1994;125:1–5.
78. Torigoe S, Koide W, Yamada M, et al. Human herpesvirus 7 infection associated with central nervous system manifestations. J Pediatr. 1996;129:301–305.
79. Hashida T, Komura E, Yoshida M, et al. Hepatitis in association with human herpesvirus-7 infection. Pediatrics. 1995;96:783–785.
80. Black JB, Burns D, Goldsmith CS, et al. Biologic properties of human herpesvirus 7 strain SB. Virus Res. 1997;52:25–41.

Chapter 130

Human Herpesvirus Type 8 (Kaposi's Sarcoma–Associated Herpesvirus)

STEPHEN E. STRAUS

Powerful molecular techniques recently identified human herpesvirus type 8 (HHV-8; Kaposi's sarcoma–associated herpesvirus) in several important human neoplasms. Vast gaps exist in our understanding of how it contributes to these tumors, its overall clinical and epidemiologic significance, and whether the virus will prove amenable to practical therapeutic and preventive strategies.

HISTORY

In 1872, Moritz Kaposi described a pigmented multicentric reddish-brown sarcoma involving the skin, mucous membranes, and multiple viscera.[1] It was most prevalent in older men of eastern European and Mediterranean descent. As a relatively uncommon and often indolent process, Kaposi's sarcoma evoked limited interest until it was found to be endemic and more aggressive, frequently affecting children, in indigenous black populations across eastern Africa.[2] In 1981, the existence of a new relentlessly fatal immune deficiency disorder was, in part, recognized owing to the sudden and inexplicable clustering in New York and California of Kaposi's sarcoma cases among promiscuous homosexual men.[3] After numerous efforts to discern its cause, Chang, Moore, and associates applied an exquisitely sensitive molecular tool known as representational difference analysis to DNA isolated from Kaposi's sarcoma tissue, leading to their seminal 1994 report of novel herpesvirus-like sequences in the tumor.[4] Basically, the technique enriches for amplification, by polymerase chain reaction, rare and unique sequences that distinguish the neoplastic cell from its normal counterpart. Numerous studies confirmed and extended these observations, making rapid inroads into our understanding of the viral biology, pathogenesis, and epidemiology.

CLASSIFICATION AND BIOLOGY

Analysis of the entire HHV-8 DNA sequence revealed that it is a typical gammaherpesvirus similar to Epstein-Barr virus but even more similar to herpesvirus saimiri, which causes lymphomas in owl monkeys, placing HHV-8 in the genus Rhadinovirus.[5, 6] Another HHV-8–like virus was found to cause retroperitoneal fibromatosis in monkeys.[7]

The HHV-8 genome consists of a long unique segment of approximately 141,000 base pairs (bp) flanked by multiple GC-rich 801-bp direct repeats.[5] There is a large reduplication of part of the genome in a chronically infected body cavity lymphoma cell line frequently used to study HHV-8, leading to an early overestimate of the normal genome size.[8] Sixty-six of the HHV-8 genes encode conserved herpesvirus replication and structural proteins. There are also a number of genes that are homologous to eukaryotic cell-cycle regulatory, complement-binding, cytokine, and chemokine genes, indicating the exploitation of host sequences during the evolution of HHV-8.[6, 9, 10]

A variety of cell culture systems have been explored for their ability to support productive HHV-8 replication and to release infectious progeny.[11, 12] The most successful ones are continuous, chronically infected acquired immunodeficiency syndrome (AIDS)-associated body cavity lymphoma cell lines. By treating these cells with phorbol esters or butyrate, the viral lytic cycle can be induced, and small amounts of cell-free virus are released.[13, 14]

PATHOGENESIS

The sites of HHV-8 replication and persistence in the body are not known, but viral DNA has been detected variably in saliva and semen and reproducibly in peripheral blood mononuclear cells, suggesting that the infection disseminates and involves leukocytes.[4, 15–20] The mechanisms by which HHV-8 could promote the development of Kaposi's sarcoma or other malignant disorders with which it is associated remain speculative but would likely involve the cell-cycle regulatory proteins and cytokine homologues that they encode.[9, 10]

EPIDEMIOLOGY

Several epidemiologic investigations suggested that an infectious agent is involved in the pathogenesis of Kaposi's sarcoma and that this putative agent is likely to be transmitted sexually.[21, 22] Kaposi's sarcoma is over 20,000 times more common in persons with AIDS than in the general population. Over 95% of human immunodeficiency virus (HIV)-associated Kaposi's sarcoma cases occur in homosexual men. It is sevenfold to 15-fold more common in them than in others who acquire HIV by nonsexual routes, such as hemophiliac patients. Moreover, among women with AIDS, Kaposi's sarcoma is three to four times more common in those who report having sex with bisexual men than in those who report having sex with infected strictly heterosexual intravenous drug users.

Virtually all Kaposi's sarcoma lesions are HHV-8–positive by polymerase chain reaction.[4, 23–25] This is true of HIV-associated Kaposi's sarcoma and Kaposi's sarcoma that arises in immunosuppressed transplant recipients as well as endemic Kaposi's sarcoma in Africa, eastern Europe, and the Mediterranean basin.

The seroprevalence of HHV-8 infection is less clear-cut (Table 130–1). There are two conflicting bodies of data, depending entirely on the assay methodology. Several serologic studies involving the detection of antibodies to latency-associated nuclear antigens in body cavity lymphoma cell lines report antibodies to HHV-8 in 70 to 80% of patients with Kaposi's sarcoma, 25 to 30% of HIV-positive gay men without Kaposi's sarcoma, 2 to 4% of HIV-positive female hemophiliac patients, and only 1 to 2% of healthy HIV-negative U.S. blood donors.[13, 14, 26] Using these assays, HIV-positive patients were retrospectively found to seroconvert to HHV-8 positivity for a median of 33 months before they developed Kaposi's sarcoma.[14]

In contrast have been the findings of studies involving HHV-8 lytic-cycle antigens, in which virtually all Kaposi's sarcoma patients are seropositive, as are 90% of HIV-infected gay men without Kaposi's sarcoma and 20 to 25% of HIV-positive intravenous drug users and women. Among healthy adults and children, 25 and 8% were HHV-8 positive, respectively.[27, 28]

The prevalence of HHV-8 in semen is equally controversial. Given the hypothesis that HHV-8 is transmitted sexually, this is an important issue. Nested polymerase chain reaction assays yielded evidence of HHV-8 DNA sequences in the semen of the vast majority of HIV-infected gay men and healthy heterosexual men in Italy.[17] With a non-nested assay, which is less likely to be contaminated (and less prone to contamination), semen from 64% of gay men and 0% of heterosexual men was positive in one study, whereas semen specimens from zero of 99 HIV-infected men were positive in another study.[18, 19]

Saliva from HIV-infected patients with Kaposi's sarcoma usually contains HHV-8; saliva from HIV-infected patients without Kaposi's sarcoma commonly does; and saliva from healthy controls does not.[15, 16]

TABLE 130–1 Detection of Antibodies to Human Herpesvirus 8 and Human Herpesvirus 8 DNA in Diverse Populations

	Proportion (%) Positive by	
Group	*IFA**	*PCR†*
AIDS-KS: UK/US	84/103 (82)	48/52 (59)
Classic KS: Greece	17/18 (94)	9/15 (60)
HIV-infected, no KS		
Homosexual men	10/33 (30)	4/28 (14)
Women in STD clinics	3/15 (20)	2/15 (13)
HIV-positive		
Hemophiliac patients	0/26 (0)	0 26 (0)
IV drug users	0/38 (0)	—‡
HIV-negative		
IV drug users	0/25 (0)	—
Homosexual men	8/65 (12)	—
Heterosexual men in STD clinics	4/25 (5)	—
Heterosexual women in STD clinics	2/26 (8)	—
Children with rash and fever	0/24 (0)	—
Blood donors		
UK	4/150 (3)	—
US	0/117 (0)	—
Controls		
Greece	3/26 (12)	0/15 (0)
Ugandans, HIV-positive	18/34 (53)	—
Ugandans, HIV-negative	9/17 (53)	—

*Immunofluorescence assay for human herpesvirus 8 latent antigen.
†DNA detected by non-nested PCR.
‡Not tested.
Abbreviations: AIDS, Acquired immunodeficiency syndrome; HIV, human immunodeficiency virus; IFA, immunofluorescence assay, IV, intravenous; KS, Kaposi's sarcoma; PCR, polymerase chain reaction; STD, sexually transmitted disease; UK, United Kingdom; US, United States.
Modified from Simpson GR, Schulz TF, Whitby D, et al. Prevalence of Kaposi's sarcoma associated herpesvirus infection measured by antibodies to recombinant capsid protein and latent immunofluorescence antigen. Lancet. 1996;349:1133–1138. © by The Lancet Ltd, 1996.

CLINICAL MANIFESTATIONS

Kaposi's Sarcoma

Kaposi's sarcoma is characterized by the appearance of one or more vascular nodules in the skin (Fig. 130–1), mucous membranes, or the viscera, particularly the lung and biliary systems (reviewed by Knowles and Cesarman[29]). In its endemic form, Kaposi's sarcoma can be extremely indolent and of little prognostic significance. Even in advanced AIDS, Kaposi's sarcoma is less important as a cause of morbidity and mortality than are opportunistic infections.

The National Institute of Allergy and Infectious Diseases AIDS Clinical Trials Group staging system is useful in evaluating patients and designing approaches to their management (Table 130–2).

Isolated cutaneous lesions of no cosmetic impact can be observed. Individual lesions can be x-irradiated or treated with intralesional

TABLE 130–2 National Institute of Allergy and Infectious Diseases AIDS Clinical Trials Group TIS Staging System for Kaposi's Sarcoma

Parameter	Good Risk (Stage 0): All These Characteristics	Poor Risk (Stage 1): Any of These Characteristics
Tumor (T)	Confined to skin and/or lymph nodes and/or minimal oral disease	Tumor-associated edema or ulceration; extensive oral lesions; gastrointestinal lesions; non-nodal visceral lesions
Immune system (I)	CD4+ T-cell count ≥ 200/μl	CD4+ T-cell count < 200/μl
Systemic illness (S)	No B symptoms*; Karnofsky performance status > 70; no history of opportunistic infection, neurologic disease, lymphoma, or thrush	B symptoms* present; Karnofsky performance status < 70; history of opportunistic infection, neurologic disease, lymphoma, or thrush

*Defined as unexplained fever, night sweats, >10% involuntary weight loss, or diarrhea persisting for more than 2 wk.

vinblastine. Extensive non–life-threatening disease is treated with recombinant interferon-alfa or single-agent cytotoxic chemotherapy. Life-threatening disease may justify combination chemotherapy.

Histologically, the tumor consists of spindle cells and endothelial cells, extravasation of red blood cells, and a variable inflammatory component.[30] HHV-8 DNA and RNA are present in the vast majority of Kaposi's sarcoma lesion spindle cells; 1 to 5% of these cells are lytically infected with HHV-8.[31]

Primary Effusion (Body Cavity–Based) Lymphoma

This uncommon and distinct form of aggressive B-cell lymphoma arises in AIDS patients exclusively or mainly in their pleural, pericardial, and peritoneal cavities as lymphomatous effusions (reviewed by Knowles and Cesarman[29]). In one series in which lymphoma tissues from 42 AIDS patients and 151 patients without AIDS were studied by polymerase chain reaction, the only ones containing HHV-8 DNA were the eight primary effusion lymphomas from the AIDS patients.[32] Cell lines prepared from these tissues are latently infected with HHV-8 and can be chemically induced to release infectious virus particles.[11]

Castleman's Disease

When localized, angiofollicular lymph node hyperplasia, or Castleman's disease, is a benign disorder amenable to surgical excision and cure. Multicentric Castleman's disease, however, is an aggressive and usually fatal disorder that conveys a risk of infectious complications, malignant lymphoma, and Kaposi's sarcoma (reviewed by Herrada and associates[33]). Multicentric Castleman's disease is associated with HIV infection. Nearly all cases in HIV patients, and in many without HIV, are positive for HHV-8 DNA by polymerase chain reaction.[34]

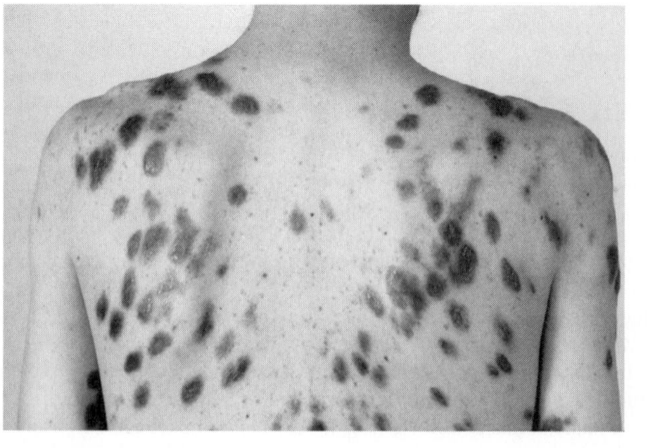

FIGURE 130–1. Kaposi's sarcoma lesions on the back of a man with acquired immunodeficiency syndrome. (Courtesy of Dr. Robert Yarchoan.)

Other Syndromes

Several skin cancers as well as multiple myeloma have been reported to contain HHV-8 DNA sequences.[35, 36] These claims have not been substantiated. No other acute or chronic illnesses have been convincingly ascribed to primary or reactivated infections with HHV-8.

TREATMENT AND PREVENTION

Assays of viral DNA synthesis or particles released by infected body cavity lymphoma cell lines revealed that HHV-8 is sensitive to cidofovir, moderately sensitive to foscarnet and ganciclovir, and insensitive to acyclovir.[37, 38] Nonetheless, antiviral drugs have no established role in treating HHV-8–associated malignancies. Small retrospective surveys suggest that incidental treatment of AIDS patients with foscarnet or ganciclovir may reduce the subsequent risk of developing Kaposi's sarcoma, and larger prospective studies are needed to resolve this issue.

REFERENCES

1. Kaposi M. Idiopathisches multiples Pigmentsarkom der Haut. Arch Derm Syph. 1872;4:265–273.
2. Lothe F. Kaposi's sarcoma in Ugandan Africans. Acta Pathol Microbiol Scand Suppl. 1963;161:5–71.
3. Centers for Disease Control. Kaposi's sarcoma and *Pneumocystis* pneumonia among homosexual men in New York City and California. MMWR Morb Mortal Wkly Rep. 1981;30:305–308.
4. Chang Y, Cesarman E, Pessin MS, et al. Identification of herpesvirus-like DNA sequences in AIDS-associated Kaposi's sarcoma. Science. 1994;266:1865–1869.
5. Russo JR, Bohenzky RA, Chien M-C, et al. Nucleotide sequence of the Kaposi's sarcoma–associated herpesvirus (HHV 8). Proc Natl Acad Sci U S A. 1996;93:14,862–14,867.
6. Neipel F, Albrecht J-C, Fleckenstein B. Cell-homologous genes in the Kaposi's sarcoma–associated Rhadinovirus human herpesvirus 8: Determinants of its pathogenicity? J Virol. 1997;71:4187–4192.
7. Rose TM, Strand KB, Schultz ER, et al. Identification of two homologs of the Kaposi's sarcoma–associated herpesvirus (human herpesvirus 8) in retroperitoneal fibromatosis of different macaque species. J Virol. 1997;71:4138–4144.
8. Moore PS, Gao S-J, Dominguez G, et al. Primary characterization of a herpesvirus agent associated with Kaposi's sarcoma. J Virol. 1996;70:549–558.
9. Goodden-Kent D, Talbot SJ, Boshoff C, et al. The cyclin encoded by Kaposi's sarcoma–associated herpesvirus stimulates cdk6 to phosphorylate the retinoblastoma protein and histone H1. J Virol. 1997;71:4193–4198.
10. Boshoff C, Endo Y, Collins PD, et al. Angiogenic and HIV-inhibitory functions of KSHV-encoded chemokines. Science. 1997;278:290–294.
11. Renne R, Zhong W, Herndier B, et al. Lytic growth of Kaposi's sarcoma–associated herpesvirus (human herpesvirus 8) in culture. Nature Med. 1996;2:342–346.
12. Foreman KE, Friborg J, Kong W-P, et al. Propagation of a human herpesvirus from AIDS-associated Kaposi's sarcoma. N Engl J Med. 1997;336:163–171.
13. Miller G, Rigsby MO, Heston L, et al. Antibodies to butyrate-inducible antigens of Kaposi's sarcoma–associated herpesvirus in patients with HIV-1 infections. N Engl J Med. 1996;334:1292–1297.
14. Gao S-J, Kingsley L, Hoover DR, et al. Seroconversion to antibodies against Kaposi's sarcoma–associated herpesvirus-related latent nuclear antigens before the development of Kaposi's sarcoma. N Engl J Med. 1996;335:233–241.
15. Vieira J, Huang M-L, Koelle DM, Corey L. Transmissible Kaposi's sarcoma–associated herpesvirus (human herpesvirus 8) in saliva of men with a history of Kaposi's sarcoma. J Virol. 1997;71:7083–7087.
16. Koelle DM, Huang M-L, Chandran B, et al. Frequent detection of Kaposi's sarcoma–associated herpesvirus (human herpesvirus 8) DNA in saliva of human immunodeficiency virus–infected men: Clinical and immunologic correlates. J Infect Dis. 1997;176:94–102.

17. Monini P, deLellis L, Fabris M, et al. Kaposi's sarcoma–associated herpesvirus DNA sequences in prostate tissue and human serum. N Engl J Med. 1996;334:1168–1172.
18. Lin J-C, Lin S-C, Mar E-C, et al. Is Kaposi's sarcoma–associated herpesvirus detectable in semen of HIV-infected homosexual men? Lancet. 1995;346:1601–1602.
19. Diamond C, Huang M-L, Kedes DH, et al. Absence of detectable human herpesvirus 8 in the semen of human immunodeficiency virus–infected men without Kaposi's sarcoma. J Infect Dis. 1997;176:775–777.
20. Blasig C, Zietz C, Haar B, et al. Monocytes in Kaposi's sarcoma lesions are productively infected by human herpesvirus 8. J Virol. 1997;71:7963–7968.
21. Beral V, Peterman TA, Berkelman RL, Jaffe HW. Kaposi's sarcoma among persons with AIDS: A sexually transmitted infection? Lancet. 1990;335:123–128.
22. Albrecht H, Helm EB, Plettenberg A, et al. Kaposi's sarcoma in HIV infected women in Germany: More evidence for sexual transmission. A report of 10 cases and review of the literature. Genitourin Med. 1994;70:394–398.
23. Moore PS, Chang Y. Detection of herpesvirus-like DNA sequences in Kaposi's sarcoma in patients with and those without HIV infection. N Engl J Med. 1995;332:1181–1185.
24. Huang YQ, Li JJ, Kaplan MH, et al. Human herpesvirus–like nucleic acid in various forms of Kaposi's sarcoma. Lancet. 1995;345:759–761.
25. Dupin N, Grandadam M, Calvez V, et al. Herpesvirus-like DNA sequences in patients with Mediterranean Kaposi's sarcoma. Lancet. 1995;345:761–762.
26. Simpson GR, Schulz TF, Whitby D, et al. Prevalence of Kaposi's sarcoma associated herpesvirus infection measured by antibodies to recombinant capsid protein and latent immunofluorescence antigen. Lancet. 1996;349:1133–1138.
27. Lennette ET, Blackbourn DJ, Levy JA. Antibodies to human herpesvirus type 8 in the general population and in Kaposi's sarcoma patients. Lancet. 1996;348:858–861.
28. Davis DA, Humphrey RW, Newcomb FM, et al. Detection of serum antibodies to a Kaposi's sarcoma–associated herpesvirus-specific peptide. J Infect Dis. 1997;175:1071–1079.
29. Knowles DM, Cesarman E. The Kaposi's sarcoma-associated herpesvirus (human herpesvirus 8) in Kaposi's sarcoma, malignant lymphoma, and other diseases. Ann Oncol. 1997;8:S123–S129.
30. Cockerell CJ. Histopathological features of Kaposi's sarcoma in HIV-infected individuals. Cancer Surv. 1991;10:73–89.
31. Staskus KA, Zhong W, Gebhard K, et al. Kaposi's sarcoma–associated herpesvirus gene expression in endothelial (spindle) tumor cells. J Virol. 1997;71:715–719.
32. Cesarman E, Chang Y, Moore PS, et al. Kaposi's sarcoma–associated herpesvirus-like DNA sequences in AIDS-related body-cavity-based lymphomas. N Engl J Med. 1995;332:1186–1191.
33. Herrada J, Cabanillas F, Rice L, et al. The clinical behavior of localized and multicentric Castleman disease. Ann Intern Med. 1998;128:657–662.
34. Soulier J, Grollet L, Oksenhenler E, et al. Kaposi's sarcoma–associated herpesvirus-like DNA sequences in multicentric Castleman's disease. Blood. 1995;86:1276–1280.
35. Nishimoto S, Inagi R, Yamanishi K, et al. Prevalence of herpesvirus-8 in skin lesions. Br J Dermatol. 1997;137:179–184.
36. Rettig MB, Ma HJ, Vescio RA, et al. Kaposi's sarcoma–associated herpesvirus infection of bone marrow dendritic cells from multiple myeloma patients. Science. 1997;276:1851–1854.
37. Medveczky MM, Horvath E, Lund T, Medveczky PG. In vitro antiviral drug sensitivity of the Kaposi's sarcoma–associated herpesvirus. AIDS. 1997;11:1327–1332.
38. Kedes DH, Ganem D. Sensitivity of Kaposi's sarcoma–associated herpesvirus replication to antiviral drugs. J Clin Invest. 1997;99:2082–2086.

Chapter 131

Herpes B Virus

STEPHEN E. STRAUS

Herpes B virus is relatively benign and enzootic in some monkey species but can initiate dramatic illness on experimental inoculation into small nonprimate animals or after inadvertent infection of humans. The occupational exposure of many thousands of individuals to captive monkeys and their tissues has, over the past 65 years, resulted in about 45 instances of herpes B virus infection. Most of these have been fatal and preventable.[1–3]

HISTORY

Herpes B virus was so named by Sabin and Wright after the individual from whom it was recovered.[4] In 1932, Dr. W. B. was bitten on his left hand by a rhesus monkey during experimental studies of poliomyelitis. Lesions emerged at the wound site in 3 days and progressed to form a cluster of small vesicles. On day 10 after the bite, generalized abdominal cramps were experienced and then followed by a progressive and ultimately fatal ascending myelitis.

Gay and Holden recovered a transmissible virus from autopsy tissues of W. B. but considered it a variant of herpes simplex virus (HSV).[5] Sabin and Wright undertook an extensive parallel series of experiments, which established definitively several of the key facts with regard to this virus.[6] They identified herpes B virus as distinct from, yet antigenically related to, HSV and proved that herpes B virus naturally infects monkeys and can do so asymptomatically.

In the ensuing years, only a few dozen additional cases were recognized. Human herpes B virus infections have been most common during periods of intense use of monkeys for medical research: in the mid-1950s for poliovirus vaccine development, and in the late 1980s for retrovirus studies.[1–3] The first instance of case clustering and person-to-person transmission of herpes B virus was documented among four individuals infected in Pensacola, Florida, in 1987.[7, 8] Two monkey handlers succumbed to progressive encephalitis, and a supervisor at the same facility experienced cutaneous infection. The wife of one of the patients who later died inadvertently inoculated herpes B virus onto a patch of eczematous skin of her finger while attending to her husband's lesions; her lesions resolved on acyclovir therapy. In the last several years, additional cases were identified, leading to other new observations regarding herpes B virus biology, transmission, and treatment.[9–11]

CLASSIFICATION AND BIOLOGY

Herpes B virus is an alphaherpesvirus related to HSV. At times it has been called herpesvirus simiae, which is a misleading term because there are numerous distinct herpesviruses of monkeys.[12] Now the virus is formally called cercopithecine herpesvirus 1.[3, 13] It possesses the typical structural elements of all herpesviruses: a double-stranded viral genome in an icosahedral nucleocapsid, tegument proteins, and an envelope bearing virally encoded glycoproteins.[14]

Herpes B virus exhibits a broad host range in vitro, causing a productive cytocidal infection in the cells of virtually all types of human and nonhuman primates, small mammals, and many birds. Herpes B virus infection progresses rapidly in vitro, leading to infectious progeny in 12 to 16 hours. The limited knowledge of its replicative cycle suggests that it closely resembles HSV in terms of a coordinately regulated process involving the successive synthesis of immediate-early (regulatory), early (replicative), and then late (structural) genes.[15]

The natural hosts of herpes B virus are diverse members of the *Macaca* genus of Asian monkeys, most notable of which are the rhesus (*Macaca mulatta*) and cynomolgus (*Macaca fascicularis*) species, frequently used for medical research, but all species of macaques may be susceptible. Many African and New World monkeys and humans suffer serious infections with herpes B virus, although its natural host species experiences relatively mild infection largely analogous to that caused by HSV in humans.[16–21]

It appears that herpes B virus is transmitted from monkey to monkey primarily by direct contact of mucous membranes or injured skin with virus-containing oral or genital secretions.[18, 19] The prevalence of infection increases with age and the conditions of crowding. Captive monkey colonies average 30 to 100% seroprevalence rates.[21–23]

Most herpes B virus infections of *Macaca* monkeys are asymptomatic. The virus persists latently in trigeminal and sacral sensory nerve root ganglia, from which it may reactivate periodically.[16, 17, 21, 24] Conditions of stress, such as shipping and crowding, and immunosuppression stimulate virus reactivation.[25] One large series of virologic studies of stable monkey colonies showed that 2.3% of all *Macaca* genus monkeys were culture-positive from conjunctival, oral, or genital secretions.[16] Symptomatic primary or recurrent mucocutaneous lesions are seen occasionally, with features strikingly similar to those associated with HSV-1 or HSV-2 infections in humans (Fig. 131–1).[20] Disseminated infections involving encephalitis, pneumonitis, hepatitis, and a diffuse exanthem have been reported in severely compromised monkeys.

HUMAN EPIDEMIOLOGY

Herpes B virus infection in humans is largely acquired from bites and scratches inflicted while handling monkeys, or in the course of working directly with monkey tissues or primary cell cultures.[1, 2] There have been isolated instances in which the mode of transmission was unknown; two cases that involved needlestick injuries; one case that is presumed to have arisen when a monkey handler was scratched with a jagged edge of the cage housing rhesus monkeys; two cases in which aerosol transmission was suspected; one case that followed an eye splash; and, as reported from the Pensacola, Florida, outbreak, a single instance of person-to-person transmission.[7, 8] Symptomatic herpes B virus infections have shown an incubation period of 2 to 14 days.[8, 26] Asymptomatic human infection is unrecognized. A controlled seroprevalence study has identified no asymptomatic infections among 321 monkey handlers, many of whom had suffered numerous episodes of being scratched and injured by rhesus monkeys.[27]

CLINICAL MANIFESTATIONS

Most herpes B virus infections of humans have been progressive and fatal, involving myelitis and hemorrhagic encephalitis with concomitant multiorgan involvement (Fig. 131–2). These progressive illnesses are variable in character but begin, typically, with symptoms of fever, malaise, diffuse pain, and headache. Regional lymphadenitis or frank lymphadenopathy is reported proximal to the site of inoculation. Abdominal pain and nausea may occur. These nonspecific symptoms gradually merge into a crescendo neurologic syndrome with dysesthesia, ataxia, diplopia, seizures, and ascending flaccid paralysis, leading to death in days. Cerebrospinal fluid studies reveal a moderate lymphocytic pleocytosis and elevated protein levels, increased red cells, and rising titers of specific antibodies to herpes B virus. In short, the clinical findings indicate a multifocal, hemorrhagic myelitis or encephalomyelitis. This is in contrast to herpes simplex encephalitis, in which focal involvement of the temporal lobe is typical.

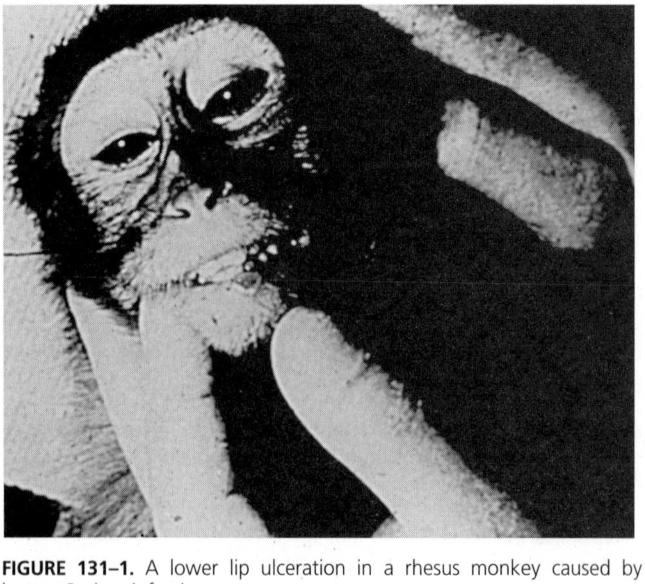

FIGURE 131–1. A lower lip ulceration in a rhesus monkey caused by herpes B virus infection.

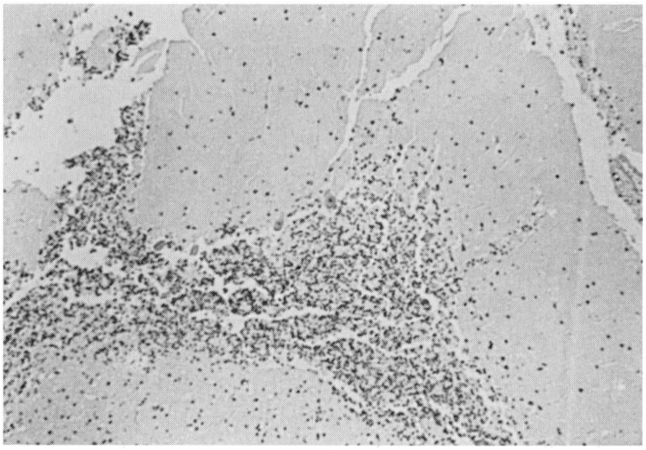

FIGURE 131–2. Herpes B virus encephalitis. Intense lymphocytic infiltration and isolated cells displaying eosinophilic intranuclear inclusions are seen in the cortical gray matter from a fatal human infection. (Courtesy of J. Hilliard, Southwest Foundation for Biomedical Research, San Antonio, Tex.)

Other clinical syndromes occur as well. Infections limited to the skin have been recognized, particularly in cases treated with acyclovir. Herpetic lesions were not common features of most earlier cases. One report involved an apparently self-limited aseptic meningitis.[9, 11]

It is uncertain whether herpes B virus establishes latency and can reactivate in humans. An instance in which conjunctival and buccal cultures became positive again after acute antiviral treatment was discontinued is compatible with viral reactivation, but even in experimentally infected animals, the resolution of primary infection is very slow with available drugs.[9, 28, 29] One controversial case report, however, suggests a zosteriform recurrence and subsequent encephalitis in a virologist several years after he discontinued active work with monkeys and their tissues.[30] Putative herpes B virus cases have been maintained on chronic acyclovir therapy and have thus not afforded an opportunity to learn whether asymptomatic or symptomatic reactivation and virus shedding can occur.

DIAGNOSIS

The potential severity of this viral infection and the possible need for prolonged or even lifelong suppressive treatment make it imperative that efforts be undertaken to define the exposure and to confirm a diagnosis promptly.[31] If the monkey can be identified and safely evaluated, samples should be cultured extensively and the monkey bled for antibody determinations.

All potential inoculation sites of the patient should be vigorously swabbed or biopsied, as appropriate, for culture. Serum should be held for later antibody determinations. Additional samples for culture should be taken from suspicious lesions and from the spinal fluid of symptomatic patients.

There are few facilities in the world suitable to undertake the isolation and identification of herpes B virus. As a class 4 pathogen, herpes B virus handling requires special training and protective equipment. In the United States, the current reference laboratory is that of Dr. Julia Hilliard at the Southwest Foundation for Biomedical Research in San Antonio, Texas (telephone: 210-674-1410).

Because herpes B virus cross-reacts antigenically with HSV-1 and HSV-2, serologic determination of recent or past infection of humans is very difficult.[12, 27, 32, 33] Current methods require extensive adsorption of serum to remove cross-reacting antibodies and parallel testing by immunoblot or competition enzyme-linked immunosorbent assay. Some patients with documented infection have shown slow or

TABLE 131-1 Arguments for and against Prophylactic Administration of Acyclovir to Persons Who May Have Been Exposed to Herpes B Virus

Pro

1. The initiation of acyclovir therapy within minutes of exposure may prevent herpes B virus infection.
2. The initiation of acyclovir therapy within 24 h of infection may prevent symptomatic herpes B virus disease.

Con

1. Infection with herpes B virus is quite rare relative to the number of possible exposures; thus, acyclovir therapy is unnecessary in most instances.
2. The ability of immediate empirical therapy to prevent infection or symptomatic illness in humans is undocumented.
3. The administration of intravenous therapy removes the employee from the workplace for several days, is costly, and is usually unnecessary.
4. Acyclovir therapy can suppress viral shedding and seroconversion, making accurate diagnosis difficult.

Modified from Holmes GP, Chapman LE, Stewart JA, et al. Guideline for the prevention and treatment of B-virus infections in exposed persons. Clin Infect Dis. 1995;20:421–439.

minimal virus-specific antibody rises, which confounds the problem of assessment and management of suspected cases.[8]

The development of polymerase chain reaction technology has facilitated the study of herpes B virus biology and may permit faster and more accurate assessment of individuals who are actively shedding virus.[34]

TREATMENT

Prompt, vigorous, and exhaustive cleaning with strong soap, iodine, or bleach solutions is recommended to decontaminate monkey-inflicted wounds. A sample from the wound should be immediately cultured and serum saved for antibody determination. Suspected lesions are best cultured by shave or punch biopsies. Depending on the circumstances and the severity of the wound, authorities differ as to the advisability of immediate or delayed institution of antiviral therapy (Table 131–1).[31] Immediate therapy should be instituted in cases of deep wounds or ones inflicted during contact with symptomatic monkeys. In other cases, many authorities recommend the initiation of treatment only if initial surveillance cultures of samples from the monkey or wound site are positive for herpes B virus. A case of fatal infection after an eye splash has substantially lowered the threshold for empirical therapy at many centers.

Acyclovir blocks herpes B virus replication in vitro with an inhibitory $dose_{50}$ concentration of about 1 μg/ml, readily achieved with intravenous or high-dose oral administration.[28] Ganciclovir is about three times more potent in vitro.[29] Early treatment with acyclovir or ganciclovir has successfully arrested infection in some animal studies. In humans, the results of antiviral treatments have been mixed. Intravenous acyclovir and ganciclovir have not halted disease progression in all encephalitic patients. Prompt treatment, though, has been associated with limited disease in a number of cases.[8–11] Valacyclovir is now preferable to oral acyclovir and could even substitute for intravenous acyclovir while laboratory confirmation of infection is awaited in asymptomatic persons who sustained high-risk exposures to herpes B virus. Because viral shedding has been documented to resume after early discontinuation of treatment and because of the theoretical possibility of serious symptomatic recurrence and viral transmission, there has been a reluctance to discontinue antiviral drugs once treatment has been initiated[10, 11]; however, it would seem appropriate to discontinue them eventually and to observe the patient carefully, with repeated cultures and serologic examinations, in instances in which infection has not been proved.

PREVENTION

Expert primate veterinarians working with the Centers for Disease Control and Prevention have recommended a series of practical guidelines to avoid herpes B virus infection.[31, 35] When feasible, animal studies should exclude *Macaca* species. All monkeys of the *Macaca* genus should be considered infected and never handled directly while they are awake or without extensive full arm and facial protection. Efforts to create herpes B virus–free colonies of rhesus and cynomolgus monkeys have begun.[36]

An inactivated herpes B virus candidate developed years ago is no longer available, and its efficacy was never adequately assessed.[37]

REFERENCES

1. Palmer AE. B virus, herpesvirus simiae: Historical perspective. J Med Primatol. 1987;16:99–130.
2. Weigler BJ. Biology of B virus in macaque and human hosts: A review. Clin Infect Dis. 1992;14:555–567.
3. Whitley RJ. Cercopithecine herpes virus 1 (B virus). In: Fields BN, Knipe DM, Howley PM, eds. Fields Virology. 3rd ed. Philadelphia: Lippincott-Raven; 1996:2623–2635.
4. Sabin AB, Wright AM. Acute ascending myelitis following a monkey bite, with the isolation of a virus capable of reproducing the disease. J Exp Med. 1934;59:115–136.
5. Gay FP, Holden M. The herpes encephalitis problem. II. J Infect Dis. 1933;53:287–303.
6. Sabin AB. Studies on the B virus. III. The experimental disease in *Macacus rhesus* monkeys. Br J Exp Pathol. 1934;15:321–334.
7. Centers for Disease Control and Prevention. B-virus infection in humans—Pensacola, Florida. MMWR Morb Mortal Wkly Rep. 1987;36:289–296.
8. Holmes GP, Hilliard JK, Klontz KC, et al. B virus (herpesvirus simiae) infection in humans: Epidemiologic investigation of a cluster. Ann Intern Med. 1990;112:833–839.
9. Centers for Disease Control and Prevention. B virus infection in humans—Michigan. MMWR Morb Mortal Wkly Rep. 1989;38:453–454.
10. Artenstein AW, Hicks CB, Goodwin BS, et al. Human infection with B virus following a needlestick injury. Rev Infect Dis. 1991;13:288–291.
11. Davenport DS, Johnson DR, Holmes GP, et al. Diagnosis and management of human B virus (herpesvirus simiae) infections in Michigan. Clin Infect Dis. 1994;19:33–41.
12. Eberle R, Hilliard J. The simian herpesviruses. Infect Agents Dis. 1995;4:55–70.
13. Roizman B, Carmichael LE, Deinhardt F, et al. Herpesviridae: Definition, provisional nomenclature and taxonomy. Intervirology. 1981;16:201–217.
14. Ludwig H, Pauli G, Gelderblom H, et al. B virus (herpesvirus simiae). In: Roizman B, ed. The Herpesvirus, v. 2. New York: Plenum; 1983;385–428.
15. Roizman B, Sears A. Herpes simplex viruses and their replication. In: Fields BN, Knipe DM, Howley PM, eds. Fields Virology, 3rd ed. Philadelphia: Lippincott-Raven; 1996:2231–2295.
16. Keeble SA. B virus infection in monkeys. Ann N Y Acad Sci. 1960;85:960–969.
17. Vizoso AD. Recovery of herpes simiae (B virus) from both primary and latent infections in rhesus monkeys. Br J Exp Pathol. 1975;56:485–488.
18. Zwartouw HT, Boulter EA. Excretion of B virus in monkeys and evidence of genital infection. Lab Anim. 1984;18:65–70.
19. Zwartouw HT, MacArthur JA, Boulter EA, et al. Transmission of B virus infection between monkeys especially in relation to breeding colonies. Lab Anim. 1984;18:125–130.
20. Anderson DC, Swenson RB, Orkin JL, et al. Primary Herpesvirus simiae (B-virus) infection in infant macaques. Lab Anim Sci. 1994;44:526–530.
21. Weigler BJ, Scinicariello F, Hilliard JK. Risk of venereal B virus (cercopithecine herpesvirus 1) transmission in rhesus monkeys using molecular epidemiology. J Infect Dis. 1995;171:1139–1143.
22. Pryor WH Jr, Chiang H-S, Raulston GL, et al. Incidence of neutralizing antibodies to herpes B virus in the Taiwan monkey (Macaca cyclopis). Primates. 1970;11:297–301.
23. Weigler B, Roberts JA, Hird DW, et al. A cross-sectional survey for B virus antibody in a colony of group housed rhesus macaques. Lab Animal Care. 1990;40:257–261.
24. Boulter EA. The isolation of monkey B virus (herpesvirus simiae) from the trigeminal ganglia of a healthy seropositive rhesus monkey. J Biol Stand. 1975;3:279–80.
25. Chellman GJ, Lukas VS, Eugui EM, et al. Activation of B virus (herpesvirus simiae) in chronically immunosuppressed cynomolgus monkeys. Lab Anim Care. 1992;42:146–151.
26. Davidson WL, Hummelev K. B virus infection in man. Ann N Y Acad Sci. 1960;85:970–979.
27. Freifeld AG, Hilliard J, Southers J, et al. A controlled seroprevalence survey of primate handlers for evidence of asymptomatic herpes B virus infection. J Infect Dis. 1995;171:1031–1034.
28. Boulter EA, Thornton B, Bauer DJ, et al. Successful treatment of experimental B virus (herpesvirus simiae) infection with acyclovir. BMJ. 1980;280:681–683.
29. Zwartouw HT, Humphreys CR, Collins P. Oral chemotherapy of fatal B virus (herpesvirus simiae) infection. Antiviral Res. 1989;11:275–284.
30. Fierer J, Bazeley P, Braude AI. Herpes B virus encephalomyelitis presenting as ophthalmic zoster. A possible latent infection reactivated. Ann Intern Med. 1973;79:225–228.
31. Holmes GP, Chapman LE, Stewart JA, et al. Guideline for the prevention and treatment of B-virus infections in exposed persons. Clin Infect Dis. 1995:20:421–439.

32. Eberle R, Black D, Hilliard JK. Relatedness of glycoproteins expressed on the surface of simian herpesvirus virions and infected cells to specific HSV glycoproteins. Arch Virol. 1989;109:233–252.
33. Blewett EL, Black D, Eberle R. Characterization of virus-specific and cross-reactive monoclonal antibodies to herpesvirus simiae (B virus). J Gen Virol. 1996;77:2787–2793.
34. Scinicariello F, English WJ, Hilliard J. Identification by PCR of meningitis caused by herpes B virus. Lancet. 1993;341:1660–1661.
35. Wells DL, Lipper SL, Hilliard JK, et al. Herpesvirus simiae contamination of primary rhesus monkey kidney cell cultures. CDC recommendations to minimize risks to laboratory personnel. Diagn Microbiol Infect Dis. 1989;12:333–336.
36. Ward JA, Hilliard JK. B virus-specific pathogen-free (SPF) breeding colonies of macaques: Issues, surveillance, and results in 1992. Lab Anim Sci. 1994;44:222–228.
37. Hull RN, Nash JC. Immunization against B virus infection. I. Preparation of an experimental vaccine. Am J Hyg. 1960;71:15–28.

Adenoviridae

Chapter 132

Adenovirus

STEPHEN G. BAUM

Adenoviruses are most important clinically because of their capacity to cause acute infections of the respiratory system and conjunctivae. The current intense biologic interest in these viruses derives from their ability to cause tumors in animals and to oncogenically transform cells in tissue culture, their propensity for latent infection in several types of host cells, their ability to induce or inhibit apoptosis through suppression or expression of early viral proteins, and their utility as vectors for introducing foreign genes into mammalian cells of diverse types. These varied capacities are exhibited by a virus with a relatively simple genetic composition, a fact that offers the promise of resolving the mechanisms of a number of important biologic phenomena.

The adenoviruses were discovered in 1953 by Rowe and colleagues, who noted that adenoidal tissues removed at the time of surgery spontaneously underwent a characteristic degeneration when maintained in culture for several weeks.[1] An agent was isolated from these degenerating tissues, and this agent, called *adenovirus* to denote its origin, could be serially passed in epithelial cells, leading to the typical cytopathic changes that have come to be attributed to the adenovirus group (Fig. 132–1). Over the next few years, several adenovirus serotypes were isolated from adenoidal tissues in which the virus appeared to cause a latent infection.[2] Other serotypes were isolated from pulmonary secretions of young adults with acute respiratory tract disease, and still other types were isolated from the eyes of patients with conjunctivitis. In the dozen years after the initial adenovirus isolation, 31 human serotypes were isolated and characterized; several new serotypes have since been described, bringing the total to at least 47. Although many serotypes have been shown to cause specific syndromes, a role in human disease remains obscure for more than half of the known types.

Adenovirus types 2, 5, 7, and 12 have been the subject of intensive physical and biochemical analysis. The genetic maps of these viruses have been constructed, and functions have been assigned to most of the regions of the DNA viral genome.[3]

Viruses similar to human adenoviruses are found in many animal classes, including monkeys, bovine species, birds, and lower mammals. With the exception of avian adenoviruses, these agents share a cross-reacting group-specific antigen. All adenoviruses have similar morphology and nucleic acid composition and produce characteristic cytopathic changes in susceptible cells. The adenoviruses of lower animals play no known role in human disease.

DESCRIPTION OF THE PATHOGEN

Human adenoviruses have DNA as their genetic material. The outer covering of the virus is a protein coat, or capsid, containing 252 subunits called *capsomeres*. These capsomeres are arranged in an icosahedral structure that has 20 sides and 12 vertices (Fig. 132–2). The capsid subunits are of three morphologic types. *Hexons*, which account for 240 of the capsomeres, have six nearest neighbors. The 12 vertices are occupied by *pentons*, which, as the name implies, have five nearest neighbors. Rodlike structures with knobs at the ends project from the penton base capsomeres; these rods are called *fibers*. The hexons, pentons, and fibers differ from one another immunologically as well as morphologically. The hexon appears to have some antigenic sites that are common to all human adenoviruses and other sites that show type specificity. Fiber antigen seems to be primarily type specific with some group specificity, whereas the penton base antigen is common to the adenovirus family.[4] Neutralizing antibody is directed at the hexon type-specific antigen.

In addition to these surface structural proteins, there are at least 10 other proteins surrounding the DNA in the adenovirion. These proteins have been identified electrophoretically, and some play a role in maintaining the integrity of the DNA genome. Others have enzymatic activity.[4] Adenovirus DNA is double-stranded and linear and has a molecular weight of about 23×10^6. The DNA represents 10 to 15% of the mass of the virus, and the intact virion has a diameter of about 70 nm, which places it in the middle range of animal viruses.[5]

In the decades since their discovery, the adenoviruses have been classified variously depending on the viewpoint of the taxonomist and the state of knowledge in virology at the time. Some of these classifications and their interrelationships are given in Table 132–1. Of particular note is the association of a high oncogenic potential with a low guanine plus cytosine content in the virus DNA. The adenovirus family has now been divided into two genera: adenoviruses of mammals (mastadenoviruses) and those of birds (aviadenoviruses). Mastadenoviruses of humans have been further subdivided (see Table 132–1) on the basis of antigenicity into subgenera and serotypes designated by the letter h (for human) and a type number (i.e., mastadenovirus h 7).[6]

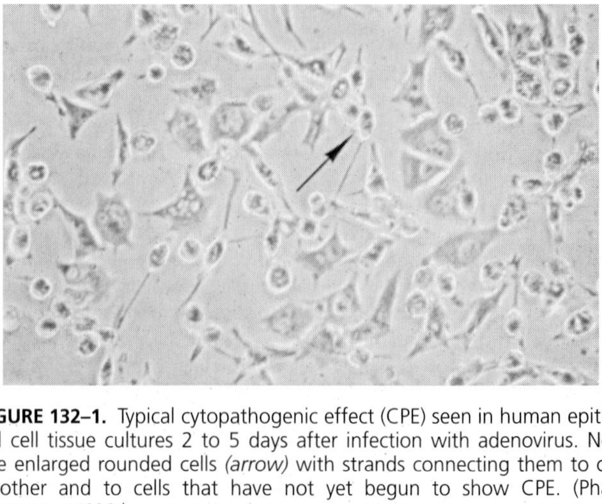

FIGURE 132–1. Typical cytopathogenic effect (CPE) seen in human epithelial cell tissue cultures 2 to 5 days after infection with adenovirus. Note the enlarged rounded cells *(arrow)* with strands connecting them to one another and to cells that have not yet begun to show CPE. (Phase contrast, ×400.)

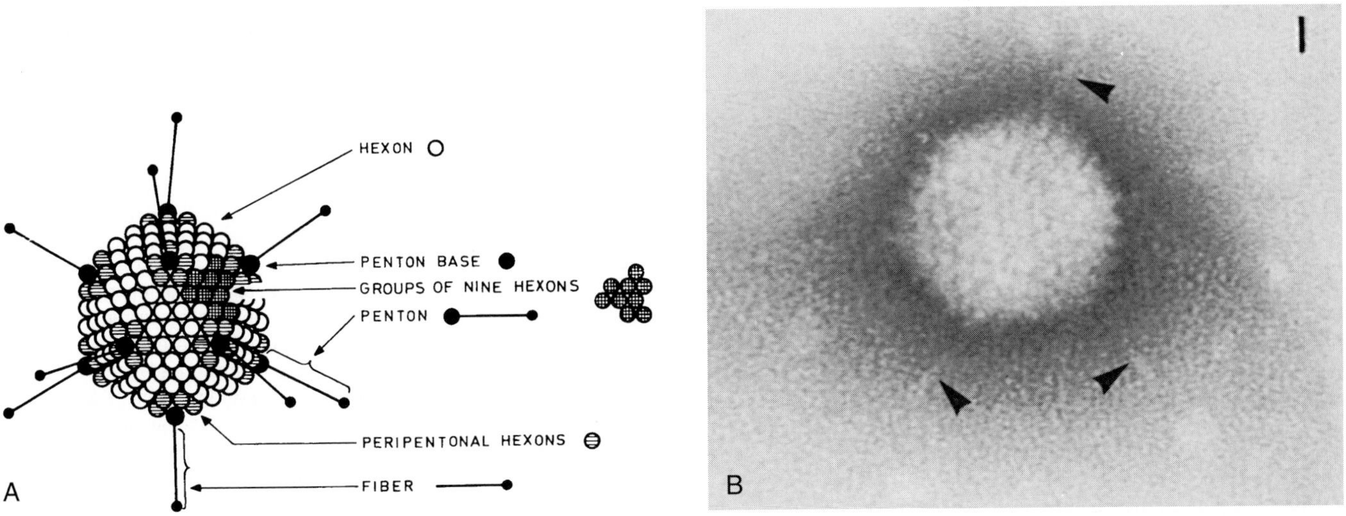

FIGURE 132–2. *A*, Adenovirion and its components. (From Philipson L, Pettersson U, Lindberg U. Molecular Biology of Adenoviruses. Virology Monographs 14. New York: Springer Publishing; 1975.) *B*, Electron micrograph of type 5 adenovirus negatively stained. (Arrows indicate fibers; bar represents 10 nm.)

As stated, the DNA of adenoviruses is currently being mapped, and functions are being assigned to different regions of the genome. The regions coding for the three capsid proteins have been identified, and the oncogenic potential of these viruses appears to reside in a small area comprising less than 10% of the genome near one end. The genomes of several adenovirus types have been elucidated in their entirety, and these viruses are being used extensively to analyze regulation of mammalian gene expression.

The most intense area of research involves the use of modified adenoviruses as vectors for the insertion of genetic material into many different types of mammalian cells. Attempts at gene therapy using adenovirus vectors have been directed at regeneration of the central nervous system[19] and treatment of inherited cardiomyopathies,[20] hematopoeitic malignancies,[21] cystic fibrosis,[22] and colon cancer,[23] among other entities. A complete discussion of adenovirus molecular biology is outside the scope of this chapter. Adenoviruses

TABLE 132–1 Classification Schemes for Adenoviruses of Humans (Mastadenovirus h)

Subgenus*	Hemagglutination Groups†	Serotypes	Oncogenic Potential‡: *Tumors in Animals*	Oncogenic Potential‡: *Transformation in Tissue Culture*	Percentage of Guanine and Cytosine in DNA	Syndromes in Humans Associated with Some Members
A	IV (little or no agglutination)	12, 18, 31	High	Moderate	48–49	Meningoencephalitis (T12)
B	I (complete agglutination of monkey erythrocytes)	3, 7	Moderate	Moderate	50–52	Pharyngitis, tracheobronchitis, pneumonia, pharyngoconjunctival fever, meningoencephalitis
		11, 21				Hemorrhagic cystitis in children
		14, 16				Pneumonia and urinary tract infection in immunocompromised patients
		34, 35§				
C	III (partial agglutination of rat erythrocytes)	1, 2, 5, 6	Low or none	Low	57–59	Respiratory infection in children, intussusception
D	II (complete agglutination of rat erythrocytes)	8, 9, 37‖	Low or none	Moderate	57–61	Epidemic keratoconjunctivitis
		9, 10, 13, 15, 17, 42¶				
		19, 20, 22–30				
		32, 33, 36,** 38,†† 39‡‡				
		42,¶ 43–47,§§ (48, 49)‖‖				Opportunistic infection in patients with AIDS
E	III	4	Low or none	Low	57–59	Respiratory tract infection in children and closed populations
F		40, 41¶¶	Unknown			Enteritis and pneumonia in children

*According to Matthews.[6]
†According to Rosen.[7]
‡Derived from Freeman et al[8] and Ginsburg.[9]
§Stalder et al.[10]
‖Keenlyside et al.[11]
¶Wigand et al.[12]
**Wigand et al.[13]
††de Jong et al.[14]
‡‡Hierholzer et al.[15]
§§Hierholzer et al.[16]
‖‖Schnurr and Dondera[17] (candidate serotypes).
¶¶de Jong et al.[18]

as vectors are the subject of several reviews,[24–26] and the molecular biology of adenoviruses is described in detail by Shenk,[3] Philipson,[27] and Horowitz.[28]

PATHOGENESIS

Adenoviruses appear to be capable of at least three types of interaction with cells. The first is a lytic infection in which the virus goes through an entire replicative cycle.[3] Lytic infection occurs in human epithelial cells and results in cell death and in the production of 10,000 to 1 million progeny viruses per cell, of which 1 to 5% are infectious.

The second interaction is a latent or chronic infection. This usually involves lymphoid cells, as in the tonsillar infection from which the virus was first isolated.[1, 2] Studies have shown that monkey epithelial cells can also undergo latent infection with human adenoviruses.[29] During latent infection only small numbers of viruses may be released, and cell death may be outstripped by cell multiplication, thereby resulting in inapparent infection. The mechanisms of latency are not clearly established.

The third significant virus-cell interaction occurring with adenoviruses is that of oncogenic transformation.[30, 31] In this situation, only the early steps in virus replication occur. The viral DNA is apparently integrated into and replicated with the cell's DNA, but no infectious virions are produced.

In all three types of infection, virus-specific proteins (T antigens) are synthesized.[29, 32] These antigens give evidence of adenoviral presence even in the absence of infectious virus. The T antigens are detected either by complement fixation or by immunofluorescence assays using serum from hamsters bearing tumors induced by adenovirus. The tumor cells contain large amounts of virus-specific T antigen to which the hamster makes antibody. Figure 132–3 shows the typical pattern of adenovirus T antigen as shown by immunofluorescence of human cells infected with adenovirus.

EPIDEMIOLOGY

Human adenovirus infections are ubiquitous, although there are slight variations in the association of specific serotypes with various syndromes in different parts of the world. Primary infection with an adenovirus usually takes place in the first few years of life, and most of the population has experienced infection with one or more adenovirus serotypes by the end of the first decade.[33] The serotype of adenovirus that causes infection and the type of disease induced are closely related to the age of the patient.

Types 1, 2, 5, and 6 are frequently isolated from the in situ tonsils and adenoids of young children. The children may be asymptomatic or may have upper respiratory tract infection at the time of isolation, and it is clear from the work of Rowe and associates,[1] Schlesinger,[34] and others that the virus can remain latent in lymphoepithelial tissue in the nasopharynx and elsewhere. Types 3, 4, and 7 are most frequently isolated from young adults with acute upper and lower respiratory tract disease.[33] Military recruits seem particularly likely to be infected with these agents, as well as mycoplasmal and meningococcal organisms. The reasons for these increased infection rates are probably related to crowding of a susceptible population. Infection in these cases seems to be spread by aerosols. Adenovirus types 8 and 19 have frequently been isolated from eye infections in adults,[35, 36] and types 11 and 21 have been linked to infections of the lower urinary tract in children.[37–40]

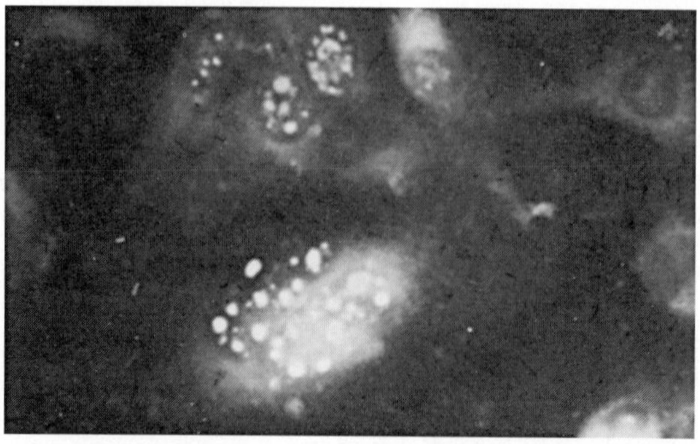

FIGURE 132–3. Adenovirus T antigen detected by immunofluorescence assay of human epithelial cells infected 24 hours earlier with adenovirus type 7. (×500.)

Two major viral epidemiologic studies have been carried out in the United States in the last 30 years.[41, 42] Both studies sought to establish the prevalence of various viruses in clinical and subclinical infections over an extended period in a large population. In each study, adenoviruses comprised the largest number of isolates in children. Types 1, 2, 3, and 5 were most commonly isolated, and the stool rather than respiratory secretions was the most common source. It was estimated that 5% of all infectious illnesses in infants and 3% in children aged 2 to 4 years were caused by adenoviruses. When seroconversion rather than virus isolation was the criterion of infection, the proportion of illness caused by adenovirus was even higher. A study using modern molecular and serologic diagnostic methods would be welcome.

CLINICAL SYNDROMES

Table 132–2 lists the syndromes caused by adenovirus serotypes.

Respiratory Infection

In nonepidemic circumstances in the general population, at least half of the infections caused by adenovirus do not lead to clinically apparent illness.[33] On the other hand, serologic surveys have shown that about 10% of all respiratory diseases in children are caused by adenoviruses.[43]

When respiratory disease in children results from infection with adenovirus, the illness usually takes the form of mild pharyngitis or tracheitis. In infants, adenovirus type 7 can cause fulminant bronchiolitis and pneumonia.[44] Some investigators have implicated adenovirus as the cause of whooping cough syndrome when *Bordetella pertussis* cannot be incriminated, and the virus has also been isolated in cases in which the bacterium was cultured.[45] Adenoviruses have been isolated more commonly than any other nonbacterial pathogen from patients with the whooping cough syndrome, although a causal relation has not been clearly established.

The first isolation of adenoviruses from patients with acute illness was in a study of military recruits in 1954.[46] The patients had a variety of influenza-like syndromes grouped under the term *acute respiratory disease*, and up to one fifth of these patients required hospitalization. Most of the recruits had tracheobronchitis. It was recognized that the isolates from these patients were similar to those first described by Rowe in 1953 and further characterized by Huebner and colleagues as adenoidal-pharyngeal-conjunctival viruses.[2] Serum specimens saved from patients having similar syndromes in World War II were later shown to contain antibodies against these viruses. Volunteer studies showed the incubation period to be 4 to 5 days.

Cough, fever, sore throat, and rhinorrhea are the most common signs and symptoms and usually last 3 to 5 days. Physical examination reveals pharyngitis, rales, and rhonchi commonly. Radiography of the chest in patients with pneumonia shows patchy ground-glass infiltrates primarily in the lower lung fields. The correlation between physical and radiographic findings in adenoviral pneumonia seems to be better than it is in *Mycoplasma*-induced pneumonia. In the latter condition, the extent of infiltrates on the roentgenogram is surprising because physical findings on chest examination are minimal.

TABLE 132-2 Diseases Caused by Adenoviruses

Group Affected	Syndromes	Common Causal Adenovirus Serotypes
Neonates	Fatal disseminated infection	3, 7, 21, 30
Infants	Coryza, pharyngitis (most asymptomatic)	1, 2, 5
Children	Upper respiratory disease	1, 2, 4–6
	Pharyngoconjunctival fever	3, 7
	Hemorrhagic cystitis	7, 11, 21
	Diarrhea	2, 3, 5, 40, 41
	Intussusception	1, 2, 4, 5
	Meningoencephalitis	2, 6, 7, 12
Young adults	Acute respiratory disease and pneumonia	3, 4, 7
Adults	Epidemic keratoconjunctivitis	8, 19, 37
Immunocompromised patients	Pneumonia with dissemination, urinary tract infection	5, 31, 34, 35, 39
	Intestinal infection	42–47 (48, 49)*
	CNS disease including encephalitis	7, 12, 32

*Schnurr and Dondera[17] (candidate serotypes).

Other infectious agents that cause a similar syndrome of "atypical" pneumonia in this population are influenza and parainfluenza viruses and *Mycoplasma pneumoniae*. From cases of atypical pneumonia caused by adenoviruses, types 4 and 7 are the ones most often isolated. The disease usually is self-limited, and superinfection and death are rare.[33]

Pharyngoconjunctival Fever

In children, the best described syndrome attributed to adenoviruses is the so-called pharyngoconjunctival fever. This disease occurs in small outbreaks and is one of the most common illnesses seen by physicians at children's summer camps. It is characterized by conjunctivitis, pharyngitis, rhinitis, cervical adenitis, and temperatures to 38°C. The onset is acute, and the fever and other symptoms last 3 to 5 days. Bulbar and palpebral conjunctivitis may be the only finding, and the palpebral conjunctivae usually have a granular appearance. Although the onset is frequently monocular, the other eye usually becomes involved. There is little bacterial superinfection and no permanent damage to the eye.

Early reports of this syndrome in the 1950s mentioned meningismus as a prominent symptom in one sixth of the cases. At that time, this finding led to some diagnostic confusion with poliomyelitis. Today, other enteroviral infections and infectious mononucleosis should be considered in young patients with conjunctivitis and pharyngitis.

Respiratory involvement in this syndrome usually does not progress to the bronchi or lungs, and bacterial superinfection is rare. Contaminated swimming pools and ponds have been implicated as sources of spread in this disease, and several of the most complete studies of this syndrome have shown type 3 adenovirus to be the causative agent.[47]

Epidemic Keratoconjunctivitis

Keratoconjunctivitis occurring in epidemic form in adult populations was first ascribed to adenovirus infection by Jawetz and coworkers in 1955.[35] They showed that eyes of shipyard workers that had sustained minor trauma from paint and rust chips were frequently infected with adenovirus type 8. Other serotypes have caused sporadic cases, but the only other serotypes that have been involved in major epidemics are types 19 and 37.[11] An epidemic involving both types simultaneously has also been reported.[36] Infection in one epidemic was through the use of a roller towel for drying hands and faces.[48] Contaminated ophthalmic solutions have also provided a vector.[11]

The incubation period is 4 to 24 days, and the conjunctivitis may last 1 to 4 weeks. The onset of conjunctivitis is insidious and frequently bilateral, and preauricular adenopathy is common. Keratitis begins as the conjunctivitis wanes, and the cornea may remain involved for several months and produce visual disturbance. There is secondary spread to household contacts in about 10% of the cases, with a higher incidence of secondary cases occurring with increased duration of the index case.[36] Virus can be isolated readily for at least 9 days after the onset of symptoms.[49]

Hemorrhagic Cystitis

A review of cases of hemorrhagic cystitis in Japanese and American children showed that 23 to 51% of these children had adenoviruria. Adenovirus types 11 and 21 were isolated more frequently than any other single bacterial or viral agent. Boys were affected two to three times more often than girls, whereas in bacterial hemorrhagic cystitis girls predominated. The average duration of gross hematuria was 3 days. Microscopic hematuria, dysuria, and urinary frequency persisted for several days longer.[37] Adenovirus type 7 has been also reported to cause this syndrome in children.[38]

The duration and severity of the disease were increased in the Japanese compared with the American children. There was no seasonal preponderance. Serologic studies indicated a large proportion of subclinical infections with adenovirus type 11 in children.

No structural abnormalities were discovered in the sick children, and this fact plus the predominance in boys made it likely that the cystitis was not caused by retrograde spread from the urethra. However, no viremia was demonstrated. There have been increasing reports of hemorrhagic cystitis and tubulointerstitial nephritis in adults and children receiving bone marrow transplants (BMT). Allogeneic BMT recipients are twice as likely as autologous BMT recipients to develop hemorrhagic cystitis, and adenoviruria is the principal predictive risk factor.[39,40]

Infantile Diarrhea

There has been much investigation of the viral cause of infantile diarrhea. Studies have shown that rotaviruses (see Chapter 139) and adenoviruses are the predominant pathogens in this disease.[50, 51] Adenoviruses are readily seen in large numbers but are not culturable on standard human tissue culture cells. They are defective and for in vitro culture require the use of tissue culture cells transformed by adenovirus[51] or Chang conjunctival cells.[50] These have also been called "enteric" or "uncultivatable" adenoviruses, but they have now been serotyped and are known as types 40 and 41 (see Table 132–1). In a 1993 study, adenovirus type 41 was the predominant serotype.[52]

Diarrhea is watery, is associated with fever, and may last for 1 to 2 weeks.

Intussusception

Another intestinal syndrome in which adenoviruses have been etiologically implicated is intussusception in children. In one study, adenoviruses were the most commonly isolated agent, representing 41% of all cases and 80% of all isolates. Serotypes 1, 2, 3, and 5 predominated, and many of the patients had a preceding or concurrent respiratory tract infection.[53] Viral isolations were, however, rarely accompanied by type-specific rises in antibody.

Central Nervous System Infection

Encephalitis and meningoencephalitis cases occurring sporadically have been caused by adenoviruses. In addition, epidemics of central nervous system infection have occurred as complications of respiratory epidemics. Serotype 7 is most commonly found,[54] but serotypes 1, 6, and 12 is also found regularly. Pneumonia is a frequent finding in cases of adenovirus central nervous system disease. Spinal fluid findings are variable, and the values for cell count and protein and glucose levels are not helpful in establishing a diagnosis. Chronic meningoencephalitis with serotypes 7, 12, and 32 is well documented in patients with hypogammaglobulinemia.

Infections in Immunosuppressed Patients

Adenovirus infections have emerged as important pathogens in immunosuppressed patients, particularly those undergoing bone marrow or solid organ transplantation.[55] Infection frequently involves the organ system transplanted (e.g., hepatitis in liver transplants, hemorrhagic cystitis in renal transplants), but disseminated disease involving the lung, colon, and central nervous system can also occur.[56–58] Disseminated disease occurs more frequently in children but is also seen in adults and is associated with a high mortality rate.[59]

Adenoviruses are frequently detected in patients with the acquired immunodeficiency syndrome (AIDS), most commonly in the urine or in the gastrointestinal tract. Serotypes from all subgenera have been isolated in AIDS patients, but particularly notable are types 34 and 35 (in urine) and types 42 through 49, which are highly unusual in immunocompetent patients.[17, 60, 61] The significance and spectrum of diseases associated with adenoviruses in these patients are unclear, because many patients are asymptomatic with respect to these adenoviral infections and others harbor multiple opportunistic pathogens. Diseases that have been attributed to adenovirus infections in AIDs patients include colitis,[62] parotitis,[63] and encephalitis.[64]

Other Diseases Infrequently Attributed to Adenoviruses

Fatal disseminated neonatal infections with adenovirus types 3, 7, 21, and 30 have been reported.[65]

Adenoviruses have at one time or another been implicated as a cause of pericarditis,[66] chronic interstitial fibrosis,[67] rubelliform illness,[68] and congenital anomalies.[69] Although adenovirus may be involved in these syndromes, it is unproved and unlikely that these viruses commonly play an etiologic role in any of these illnesses.

DIAGNOSIS

A diagnosis of adenoviral infection is frequently made in the proper setting on clinical criteria alone. A definitive diagnosis rests on visualization of the virus by electron microscopy,[70] isolation of the virus in tissue culture, or demonstration of adenovirus antigens in infected cells, adenoviral DNA in tissue samples,[71] or a fourfold rise in serum antibodies to adenovirus during the course of the illness. Adenoviruses may be cultured from pharynx, sputum, stool, and conjunctival scrapings and from fresh urine in the appropriate syndromes. Vital culture is performed in monolayers of human epithelial cells, and typical cytopathogenic changes occur in 2 to 7 days, depending on the amount of virus in the inoculum. Isolated adenovirus can be grouped by hemagglutination (see Table 132–1) and then specifically serotyped. Virus can be isolated in 50 to 70% of serologically confirmed cases of respiratory disease or conjunctivitis.

Adenovirus antigens have been demonstrated in exfoliated cells in cases of epidemic keratoconjunctivitis, pharyngoconjunctival fever, and hemorrhagic cystitis. The indirect immunofluorescence technique has been used and has correlated very well with virus isolation. This technique is much quicker and cheaper than virus culture, and it can be used to demonstrate both T antigens and capsid antigens in infected cells.[37, 72]

Serologic diagnosis of adenovirus infection involves the demonstration of a fourfold rise in antibodies that fix complement, neutralize the virus, or prevent adenoviral hemagglutination or that can be detected in an enzyme-linked immunosorbent assay or radioimmunoassay. Complement-fixing antibodies are group specific, whereas neutralizing and hemagglutination-inhibiting antibodies are type specific.

The rise in antibodies begins about 1 week after infection. As in other viral infections, complement-fixing antibodies are the earliest to fall and disappear by 1 year after infection. Neutralizing antibodies may persist for a decade or longer in relatively undiminished titer. Heterotypic reinfection may be responsible for repeated boosts of these long-lived antibodies.

Mufson and Belshe reported that a single determination of neutralizing antibodies to adenovirus types 11 or 21 at a titer of greater than 1:32 in a patient with hemorrhagic cystitis may be taken as a confirmatory evidence of adenovirus disease.[37]

TREATMENT

Most adenoviral infections are self-limited and require no or minimally supportive therapy. For severe cases, especially in immunosuppressed patients, specific antiviral therapy would be of interest but none has been demonstrated to be efficacious. Anecdotal case reports have suggested possible benefits after administration of ribavirin,[73] vidarabine,[74] or ganciclovir.[75] Cidofovir showed promise in an animal model of ocular adenovirus disease.[76] The use of human immune globulin as treatment for adenovirus infection in an immunosuppressed patient has been described[77] but has not otherwise been studied.

PREVENTION

Because of the ubiquity and severity of adenovirus respiratory disease in certain populations, vaccines were developed to prevent the disease. Although these live and inactivated virus vaccines were reasonably effective, the findings that adenoviruses were oncogenic and that they could combine with simian virus 40 to produce an even more oncogenic hybrid virus curtailed the use of parenteral vaccines. Vaccines have also been produced by the use of capsid components free of DNA. These vaccines were effective in volunteer studies but are not currently available for general administration.[33]

Oral vaccines have been developed for use in military recruits. These vaccines contain live adenovirus types 4 and 7 in an enteric-coated capsule. These viruses are not attenuated but take advantage of the fact that infection of the gastrointestinal tract by these adenoviruses does not result in illness, in contrast to infection of the respiratory tract. Their efficacy and safety have been well established, and the problem of acute respiratory tract disease in recruits has been markedly diminished.[78]

ADENO-ASSOCIATED VIRUSES

Adenovirus preparations are often contaminated with a 22-nm icosahedral virus that has been called *adeno-associated virus* (AAV). These contaminants have been classified as parvoviruses, and they are defective in that they require adenovirus coinfection of cells to replicate.[79] Herpesviruses and vaccinia can also provide a helper function for these viruses.[80] AAV contain single-stranded DNA that is not homologous to adenovirus DNA and has a molecular weight of 1.4×10^6. AAV are unique among DNA animal viruses in that complementary strands of viral DNA are made within the cell and either strand may enter the virus particle to give rise to some virions with DNA of one polarity and some with the complementary strand. The presence of AAV in an adenovirus preparation diminishes the infectivity of the adenovirus by an unknown mechanism.[81]

There are four serotypes of AAV, and although they have not been implicated in any human disease, the viruses have been isolated from human pharyngeal secretions and stool, and most people have antibodies to one or another AAV serotype by 10 years of age.[82] Another parvovirus (B19) has been proved to cause erythema infectiosum (fifth disease) and hydrops fetalis and causes aplastic crises in patients with hemoglobinopathies[83, 84] (see Chapter 136). AAV have also proved extremely useful as gene insertion vectors.[85, 86]

REFERENCES

1. Rowe WP, Huebner RJ, Gillmore LK, et al. Isolation of a cytopathogenic agent from human adenoids undergoing spontaneous degeneration in tissue culture. Proc Soc Exp Biol Med. 1953;84:570.
2. Huebner RJ, Rowe WP, Ward TG, et al. Adenoidal-pharyngeal-conjunctival agents: A newly recognized group of common viruses of the respiratory system. N Engl J Med. 1954;251:1077.
3. Shenk T. Adenoviridae: The viruses and their replication. In: Fields BN, Knipe DM, Howley PM, eds. Virology, 3rd ed. Philadelphia: Lippincott-Raven; 1996:2111–2148.
4. Russel WC, Kemp GD. Role of adenovirus structural components in the regulation of adenovirus infection. Curr Top Microbiol Immunol. 1995;19:81–98.
5. Green M, Pina M, Kimes R, et al. Adenovirus DNA: I. Molecular weight and conformation. Proc Natl Acad Sci U S A. 1967;57:1302.
6. Matthews REF. The classification and nomenclature of viruses: Summary of results of meetings of the international committee on taxonomy of viruses in Strasbourg, August 1981. Intervirology. 1981;16:53.
7. Rosen L. Hemagglutination by adenoviruses. Virology. 1958;5:574.
8. Freeman AE, Black PH, Vanderpool EA, et al. Transformation of primary rat embryo cells by adenovirus type 2. Proc Natl Acad Sci U S A. 1967;58:1205.
9. Ginsberg HS. Adenoviruses. In: Davis BD, Dulbecco R, Eisen HN, et al., eds. Microbiology. Hagerstown, Md: Harper & Row; 1980:1047.
10. Stalder H, Hierholzer JC, Oxman MN. New human adenovirus (candidate adenovirus type 35) causing fatal disseminated infection in a renal transplant recipient. J Clin Microbiol. 1977;6:257.
11. Keenlyside RA, Hierholzer JC, D'Angelo LJ. Keratoconjunctivitis associated with adenovirus type 37: An extended outbreak in an ophthalmologist's office. J Infect Dis. 1983;147:191.
12. Wigand R, Adrian T, Bricout F. A new human adenovirus of subgenus D: Candidate adenovirus type 42. Arch Virol. 1987;94:283–286.
13. Wigand R, Gelderblom H, Wadell G. New human adenovirus (candidate adenovirus 36): A novel member of subgroup D. Arch Virol. 1980;64:225.
14. de Jong JC, Wigand R, Adrian T, et al. Adenovirus 38: A new human adenovirus species of subgenus D. Intervirology. 1984;22:164–169.
15. Hierholzer JC, Kemp MC, Gary W Jr, et al. New human adenovirus associated with respiratory illness: Candidate adenovirus type 39. J Clin Microbiol. 1982;16:15–21.
16. Hierholzer JC, Wigand R, Anderson LJ, et al. Adenoviruses from patients with AIDS: A plethora of serotypes and a description of five new serotypes of subgenus D (types 43–47). J Infect Dis. 1988;158:804–813.
17. Schnurr D, Dondera ME. Two new candidate adenovirus serotypes. Intervirology. 1993;36:79–83.
18. de Jong JC, Wigand R, Kidd AH, et al. Candidate adenoviruses from human infant stool. J Med Virol. 1983;11:215.
19. Verhaagen J, Hermens WT, Dijkhuizen PA, et al. Use of viral vectors to promote neuroregeneration. Clin Neurosci. 1996;3:275–283.
20. Bowles NE, Wang Q, Towbin JA. Prospects for adenovirus-mediated gene therapy of inherited diseases of the myocardium. Cardiovasc Res. 1997;35:422–430.
21. Huang MR, Olsson M, Kallin A, et al. Efficient adenovirus-mediated gene transduction of normal and leukemic hematopoietic cells. Gene Ther. 1997;4:1093–1099.
22. Bellon G. Cystic fibrosis (CF) gene therapy. Pediatr Pulmonol. 1997;16:278–279.
23. Ogawa N, Fujiwara T, Kagawa S, et el. Novel combination therapy for human colon cancer with adenovirus-mediated wild-type p53 gene transfer and DNA-damaging chemotherapeutic agent. Int J Cancer. 1997;73:367–370.
24. Brody SL, Crystal RG. Adenovirus-mediated in vivo gene transfer. Ann N Y Acad Sci. 1994;716:90–101.
25. Miller N, Vile R. Targeted vectors for gene therapy. FASEB J. 1995;9:190–199.
26. Ilan Y, Droguett G, Chowdhury NR, et al. Insertion of the adenoviral E3 region into a recombinant viral vector prevents antiviral humoral and cellular immune responses and permits long-term gene expression. Proc Natl Acad Sci U S A. 1997;94:2587–2592.
27. Philipson L. Adenovirus: An eternal archetype. Curr Top Microbial Immunol. 1995;99:1–24.
28. Horowitz MS. Adenoviruses. In: Fields BN, Knipe DM, Howley PM, eds. Virology, 3rd ed. Philadelphia: Lippincott-Raven; 1996;2149–2171.
29. Baum SG. Persistent adenovirus infections of nonpermissive monkey cells. J Virol. 1977;23:412.
30. Huebner RJ, Rowe WP, Lane WT. Oncogenic effects in hamsters of human adenoviruses types 12 and 18. Proc Natl Acad U S A. 1962;48:2051.
31. Trentin JJ, Yabe Y, Taylor G. The quest for human cancer viruses. Science. 1962;137:835.
32. Pope JH, Rowe WP. Immunofluorescent studies of adenovirus 12 tumors and of cells transformed or infected by adenovirus. J Exp Med. 1964;120:577.
33. Knight V, Kasel JA. Adenoviruses. In: Knight V, ed. Viral and Mycoplasmal Infections of the Respiratory Tract. Philadelphia: Lea & Febiger; 1973:65.
34. Schlesinger RW. Adenoviruses: The nature of the virion and controlling factors in productive or abortive infection and tumorigenesis. Adv Virus Res. 1969;14:1.
35. Jawetz E, Kimura S, Nicholas AN, et al. New type of APC virus from epidemic keratoconjunctivitis. Science. 1955;122:1190.
36. Guyer B, O'Day DM, Hierholzer JC, et al. Epidemic keratoconjunctivitis: A community outbreak of mixed adenovirus type 8 and type 19 infection. J Infect Dis. 1975;132:142.
37. Mufson MA, Belshe RB. A review of adenoviruses in the etiology of acute hemorrhagic cystitis. J Urol. 1976;115:191.
38. Lee H-J, Pyo J-W, Choi E-H, et al. Isolation of adenovirus type 7 from the urine of children with acute hemorrhagic cystitis. Pediatr Infect Dis J. 1996;7:633–634.
39. Ito M, Hirabayashi N, Uno Y, et al. Necrotizing tubulointerstitial nephritis associated with adenovirus infection. Human Pathol 1991;22:1225–31.
40. Sencer SF, Haake RJ, Weisdorf DJ. Hemorrhagic cystitis after bone marrow transplantation. Transplantation. 1993;4:875–879.
41. Fox JP, Brandt CD, Wasserman FE, et al. The virus watch program: A continuing surveillance of viral infections in metropolitan New York families. Am J Epidemiol. 1969;89:25.
42. Fox JP, Hall CE, Cooney M. The Seattle virus watch: VII. Observations of adenovirus infections. Am J Epidemiol. 1977;105:362.
43. Brandt CD, Hyun WK, Vargosko AJ, et al. Infections in 18,000 infants and children in a controlled study of respiratory tract disease: I. Adenovirus pathogenicity in relation to serologic type and illness syndrome. Am J Epidemiol. 1969;90:484.
44. Angella JJ, Connor JD. Neonatal infection caused by adenovirus type 7. J Pediatr. 968;72:474.
45. Olson LC. Pertussis. Medicine (Baltimore). 1975;54:427.
46. Hilleman MR, Werner JH. Recovery of a new agent from patients with acute respiratory illness. Proc Exp Biol Med. 1954;85:183.
47. Sobel G, Aronson B, Aronson S, et al. Pharyngoconjunctival fever. AM J Dis Child. 1956;92:596.
48. Sprague JB, Hierholzer JC, Currier RW II, et al. Epidemic keratoconjunctivitis: A severe industrial outbreak due to adenovirus type 8. N Engl J Med. 1973;289:1341.
49. Koc J, Wigand R, Weil M. The efficacy of various laboratory methods for the diagnosis of adenovirus conjunctivitis. Zentralbl Bakteriol Mikrobiol Hyg [A]. 1987;263:607–615.
50. Kidd M., Cosgrove BP, Brown RA, et al. Faecal adenoviruses from Glasgow babies. J Hyg (Camb). 1982;88:463.
51. Yolken RH, Lawrence F, Leister F, et al. Gastroenteritis associated with enteric type adenovirus in hospitalized infants. J Pediatr. 1982;101:21.
52. deJong JC, Bijlsma K, Wermenbol AG, et al. Detection, typing and subtyping of enteric adenoviruses 40 and 41 from fecal samples and observation of changing incidences of infections with these types and subtypes. J Clin Microbiol. 1993;31:1562–1569.
53. Montgomery EA, Popek EJ. Intussusception, adenovirus and children: A brief reaffirmation. Hum Pathol. 1994;25:169–174.
54. Simila S, Jouppila R, Salmi A, et al. Encephalomeningitis in children associated with an adenovirus type 7 epidemic. Acta Pediatr Scand. 1970;59:310.
55. Carrigan DR. Adenovirus infections in immunosuppressed patients. Am J Med. 1997;102:71–74.
56. Whimbey E, Champlin KE, Couch RB. Community respiratory virus infections among hospitalized adult bone marrow transplant recipients. Clin Infect Dis. 1996:22:778–782.
57. Flomenberg P, Babbitt J, Drobyski WR. Increasing incidence of adenovirus disease in bone marrow transplant recipients. J Infect Dis. 1994;169:775–781.
58. Michael MG, Green M, Wald ER, et al. Adenovirus infection in pediatric liver transplant recipients. J Infect Dis. 1992;165:170–174.
59. Flomenberg P, Babbit J, Drobyski WR, et al. Increasing incidence of adenoviral disease in bone marrow transplant recipients. J Infect Dis. 1994;169:475–481.
60. Flomenberg PR, Chen M, Munk G, et al. Molecular epidemiology of adenovirus type 35 infections in immunocompromised hosts. J Infect Dis. 1987;155:1127–1134.
61. Khoo SH, Bailey AS, deJong JC. Adenovirus infections in human immunodeficiency virus-positive patients: Clinical features and molecular epidemiology. J Infect Dis. 1995;172:629–637.
62. Janoff EN, Orenstein JM, Manischewitz JF, et al. Adenovirus colitis in the acquired immunodeficiency syndrome. Gastroenterology. 1991;100:976–979.
63. Gelfand MS, Cleveland KO, Lancaster D, et al. Adenovirus parotitis in patients with AIDS. Clin Infect Dis. 1994;19:1045–1048.
64. Schnurr D, Bollen A, Crawford-Miksza L, et al. Adenovirus mixture isolated from the brain of an AIDS patients with encephalitis J Med Virol. 1995;47:168–171.
65. Abzug MJ, Levine MJ. Neonatal adenovirus infection: Four patients and review of the literature. Pediatrics. 1991;87:890–896.
66. Rahal JJ, Millian SJ, Noriega ER. Coxsackie and adenovirus infection. Association with acute febrile and juvenile rheumatoid arthritis. JAMA. 1976;235:2496.
67. Kawai T, Fujiwara T, Aoyama Y, et al. Diffuse interstitial fibrosing pneumonitis and adenovirus infection. Chest. 1976;69:692.
68. Gutekunst RR, Heggie AD. Viremia and viruria in adenovirus infection: Detection in patients with rubella and rubelliform illness. N Engl J Med. 1961;264:374.
69. Evans TN, Brown GC. Congenital anomalies and virus infection. Am J Obstet Gynecol. 1963;87:749.
70. Madely CR, Cosgrove BP, Bell EJ, et al. Stool viruses in babies in Glasgow. J Hyg (Lond). 1977;78:261.
71. Kidd AH, Jonsson M, Garwicz D. Rapid subgenus identification of human adenovirus isolates by a general PCR. J Clin Microbiol. 1996;34:622–627.
72. Schwartz HS, Vastine DW, Yamashiroya H, et al. Immunofluorescent detection of adenovirus antigen in epidemic keratoconjunctivitis. Invest Ophthalmol. 1976;15:199.
73. Aebi C, Headrick CL, McCracken GH Jr, et al. Intravenous ribavirin therapy in a neonate with disseminated adenovirus infection undergoing extracorporeal membrane oxygenation: Pharmacokinetics and clearance by hemofiltration. J Pediatr. 1997;130:612–615.
74. Kitabayashi A, Hirokawa M, Kuroki J, et al. Successful vidarabine therapy for

adenovirus type ll-associated acute hemorrhagic cystitis after allogeneic bone marrow transplantation. Bone Marrow Transplant. 1994;14:853–854.
75. Duggan JM, Farrehi J, Duderstadt S, et al. Treatment with ganciclovir of adenovirus pneumonia in a cardiac transplant patient. Am J Med. 1997;103:439–440.
76. Gordon YJ, Romanowski E, Araullo-Cruz T, et al. Pretreatment with topical 0.2% (*S*)-1-(3-hydroxy-2-phosphonylmethoxypropyl) cytosine inhibits adenovirus type 5 replication in the New Zealand rabbit ocular model. Cornea. 1992;11:529–533.
77. Dagan R, Schwartz RH, Insel RA, et al. Severe diffuse adenovirus 7a pneumonia in a child with combined immunodeficiency: Possible therapeutic effect of human immune serum globulin containing specific neutralizing antibody. Pediatr Infect Dis J. 1984;3:246.
78. Dudding BA, Top FH Jr, Winter PE, et al. Acute respiratory disease in military trainees: The adenovirus surveillance program 1966–1971. Am J Epidemiol. 1973;97:187.
79. Ward P, Dean FB, O'Donnell ME. Role of the adenovirus DNA-binding protein in in vitro adeno-associated virus DNA replication. J Virol. 1998;72:420–427.
80. Schlehofer JR, Ehbar M, zur-Hausen H. Vaccinia virus, herpes simplex virus and carcinogens induce DNA amplification in a human cell line and support replication of helper virus dependent parvovirus. Virology. 1986;152:110–117.
81. Hoggan MD, Blacklow NR, Rowe WP. Studies of small DNA viruses found in various adenovirus preparations: Physical, biological and immunological characteristics. Proc Natl Acad Sci U S A. 1966;55:1467.
82. Parks WP, Boucher DW, Melnick JL, et al. Seroepidemiological and ecological studies of the adenovirus associated satellite viruses. Infect Immun. 1970;2:716–722.
83. Anderson MJ. Human parvovirus infections. J Virol Methods. 1987;17:175–181.
84. Conrad JR, Studdard H, Anderson LJ. Aplastic crisis in sickle cell disorders: Bone marrow necrosis and human parvovirus infection. Am J Med Sci. 1988;295:212–215.
85. Dunbar CE. Gene transfer to hematopoietic stem cells: Implications for gene therapy of human disease. Annu Rev Med. 1996;47:11–20.
86. Xiao X, Li J, Samulski RJ. Production of high-titer recombinant adeno-associated virus vectors in the absence of helper adenovirus. J Virol. 1998;72:2224–2232.

Papovaviridae

Chapter 133

Papillomaviruses

WILLIAM BONNEZ
RICHARD C. REICHMAN

Human papillomaviruses (HPVs) are widespread throughout the population, produce epithelial tumors of the skin and mucous membranes, and have been closely associated with genital tract malignancies. Papillomaviruses have been detected in a variety of vertebrates. HPVs are highly species specific, and cross-species infections do not occur even under experimental conditions. The infectious nature of human warts was initially demonstrated in the late 19th century when human wart extracts were shown to produce warts when injected into humans. Ciuffo suggested that the infectious agent of warts was a virus after he was able to transmit the infection, via cell-free filtrates, in 1907.[1] Despite these early observations, HPVs have not been studied by standard virologic techniques because they have not been propagated successfully in tissue culture or in standard laboratory animals. For this reason, much of our knowledge of the biology of HPVs and the diseases with which they are associated has depended on the use of molecular biologic techniques. These techniques have led to an understanding of the genomic organization of these viruses, the functions of different viral genes, and the multiplicity of HPV types. Detailed reviews of these subjects are available.[2–8]

VIROLOGY

Papillomaviruses constitute the *Papillomavirus* genus of the Papovaviridae family.[9] They are nonenveloped viruses that are 55 nm in diameter and have an icosahedral capsid composed of 72 capsomeres enclosing a double-stranded, circular DNA genome. Virion particles contain at least two capsid proteins. The major capsid protein constitutes 80% of the virion by weight and has a molecular weight of about 56,000 Da. The minor capsid protein has a molecular weight of approximately 76,000 Da.

The HPV genome consists of approximately 7900 base pairs. All putative coding sequences (open reading frames [ORFs]) are arranged on one DNA strand, and all papillomaviruses share the same genomic organization.[6] Specific protein products are derived from these ORFs. However, analyses of viral messenger RNA (mRNA) transcripts suggest that most viral proteins derive from splicing of more than one ORF-specific mRNA. The genome is divided functionally into three regions. A noncoding, upstream regulatory region contributes to the control of DNA replication and transcription of eight to nine ORFs that are divided into "early" (E1–E7) and "late" (L1 and L2) regions.[6] E1 is involved in viral plasmid replication. E2 is an important modulator of viral transcription and also plays a role in viral replication. E4 proteins form filamentous cytoplasmic networks and share the same cellular distribution as cytokeratin intermediate filaments, with which they may interact.[10] They appear to play a role in viral replication.[11] The E5 protein is located in the cellular membrane, prevents the acidification of endosomes, and can stimulate the transforming activity of the epidermal growth factor receptor and contribute to the oncogenicity of HPV.[12, 13] E6 and E7 are two other proteins that have important transforming properties. The E6 protein of oncogenic HPVs binds to the p53 tumor suppressor gene product and abrogates its activity by accelerating its degradation.[4] The E7 protein of oncogenic HPVs also binds to a tumor suppressor gene product, the retinoblastoma protein, and to related proteins, thus inhibiting their functions.[4] The L1 and L2 0RFs encode the major and minor capsid proteins, respectively.

Although the genomes of several papillomaviruses can transform certain cell lines in tissue culture, the complete replicative cycle of HPV has not yet been duplicated in vitro. However, HPV virions can be recovered in vitro from naturally infected or experimentally transfected keratinocytes by induction of terminal differentiation of the cells.[14, 15] In addition, HPV types 6, 11, 16, and 40 have been propagated successfully in human skin grafted in the athymic (nude) mouse or the severe combined immunodeficiency mouse.[16, 17] HPV-infected grafts recovered from these animals can maintain viral particle production in vitro.[18]

Virions of most HPV types cannot be purified from naturally occurring lesions in significant quantities, and well-characterized, type-specific antigens are not yet widely available. Therefore, types are determined according to the degree of nucleic acid sequence homology rather than by serologic techniques. Distinct HPV types share less than 90% of their DNA sequences in the L1 ORF. Seventy-five HPV types have now been characterized, and many others have been recognized. HPVs are host specific, and each type is, to a large extent, associated with a distinct histopathologic process (Table 133–1).

Broadly cross-reactive, genus-specific antigenic determinants, located in the middle of the major capsid protein,[19] can be prepared by denaturation of viral particles, typically from bovine papillomavirus, with detergents and reducing agents. Antisera prepared against this papillomavirus *common antigen* have been used in the immunocytochemical diagnosis of HPV infections[20] (see "Diagnosis"). The antigenic characteristics of native viral particles also can be studied by the use of virus-like particles (VLPs). These are obtained by the expression in eukaryotic systems of the L1 or L1 and L2 ORFs (see "Prevention"). There appears to be a close correlation between genotype and serotype.[21, 22]

TABLE 133–1 Human Papillomavirus Types and Their Disease Association

Disease	Human Papillomavirus (HPV) Types*	
	Frequent Association	*Less Frequent Association*
Plantar warts	1, 2	4, 63
Common warts	2, 1	4, 26,† 27, 29, 41, 57, 65, 77
Common warts of meat, poultry, and fish handlers	7, 2	1, 3, 4, 10, 28
Flat and intermediate warts	3, 10	26, 27,† 28, 38, 41,‡ 49,† 75, 76
Epidermodysplasia verruciformis	2, 3, 10, 5,‡ 8,‡ 9, 12, 14,‡ 15, 17‡	19, 20,‡§ 21, 22, 23, 24, 25, 36, 37, 38,‡ 47, 50
Condylomata acuminata	6, 11	30, 42, 43, 44, 45,‡ 51,‡ 54, 55, 70‡
Intraepithelial neoplasia, unspecified		30,‡ 34, 39,‡ 40, 53, 57, 59,‡ 61, 62, 64, 66,‡ 67, 68,‡ 69, 71
Low-grade	6, 11	16,‡ 18,‡ 31,‡ 33,‡ 35,‡ 42, 43, 44, 45,‡ 51,‡ 52,‡ 74†
High-grade	16,‡ 18‡	6, 11, 31,‡ 34, 33,‡ 35,‡ 39,‡ 42, 44, 45,‡ 51,‡ 52,‡ 56,‡ 58,‡ 66‡
Cervical carcinoma	16,‡ 18‡	31,‡ 33,‡ 35,‡ 39,‡ 45,‡ 51,‡ 52,‡ 56,‡ 58,‡ 66,‡ 68,‡ 70‡
Recurrent respiratory papillomatosis	6, 11	
Focal epithelial hyperplasia of Heck	13, 32	
Conjunctival papillomas and carcinomas	6, 11, 16‡	
Other cutaneous lesions‖		6, 11, 16,‡¶, 30,‡ 33,‡ 36, 37, 38,‡ 41,‡ 48,†‡ 60, 72,† 73†

*The distinction between frequent and less frequent association is arbitrary in many instances. Large descriptive statistics of HPV type distribution by disease are not available for the majority of HPV types. Moreover, many HPV types have been looked for or identified only once.
†Types first recovered from immunosuppressed patients.
‡Types with high malignant potential or isolated in only one or a few lesions that were malignant.
§HPV-46 was found to be HPV-20, and there is no HPV-71.
‖Includes epidermoid cysts, keratoacanthoma, laryngeal carcinoma, and malignant melanoma.
¶Kaposi's sarcoma and normal and neoplastic prostatic tissues.
The authors are grateful to Drs. Ethel-Michele de Villiers and Gérard Orth for sharing information. Further information on HPV DNA sequences and novel isolates is available on the World Wide Web at http://hpv-web.lanl.gov.

EPIDEMIOLOGY

Incidence and Prevalence

The epidemiology of HPV infections is incompletely understood. With the exception of some investigations of genital tract diseases, few systematically conducted studies have been carried out. In addition, techniques for seroepidemiologic investigation remain inadequate, and diagnoses of nongenital infections have been based primarily on physical examination alone. However, several generalizations regarding the epidemiology of some HPV infections can be made.

Three types of cutaneous HPV infections are widespread throughout the general population.[23] Common warts, which represent up to 71% of all cutaneous warts, occur frequently among school-aged children, with prevalence rates of 4 to 20%.[24, 25] Although less common (34% of cutaneous warts), plantar warts are observed frequently among adolescents and young adults. Juvenile or flat warts are the least common of the three types (4%) and occur predominantly in children. Other groups at high risk for the development of cutaneous warts include butchers, meat packers, and fish handlers.[26–29] Epidermodysplasia verruciformis is a rare, probably autosomal recessive condition characterized by the appearance early in life of disseminated cutaneous warts and frequent malignant transformation.[30]

Condyloma acuminatum (pl., condylomata acuminata), or anogenital warts, is the most common viral sexually transmitted disease (STD) in the United States, and appears to be increasing rapidly in incidence. Using data collected by the National Disease and Therapeutic Index, the Centers for Disease Control and Prevention (CDC) estimated that the number of patient-physician interactions in the private sector related to this disease increased from 169,000 in 1966 to 1,150,000 in 1984 in the United States.[31] In an STD clinic setting in the United Kingdom, the rate of attendance for genital warts grew by 390% for men and 594% for women from 1971 to 1994.[32] Smaller studies in better-defined patient populations have also shown dramatic increases in the prevalence of this disease.[33, 34] It is estimated that approximately 500,000 persons each year acquire symptomatic genital warts.[35] HPV infection of the cervix gives rise to the most common cause of squamous cell abnormalities on Papanicolaou (Pap) smears.[36–38]

Prevalence data on recurrent respiratory papillomatosis, primarily a disease of the larynx, are not available, but the rate is estimated to be 11 per 100,000 for the juvenile-onset form of the disease and 4.5 per 100,000 for the adult-onset form.[39]

Transmission

Close personal contact is assumed to be important for the transmission of most cutaneous warts, although strong epidemiologic evidence for this assumption is lacking.[40] Minor trauma at the site of inoculation may also be important, as suggested by the high frequency of disease among meat handlers.[26–29]

Evidence that anogenital warts are sexually transmitted includes the observations that the age of onset is similar to that in other STDs and that the disease develops in approximately two thirds of sexual contacts of patients with anogenital warts.[41, 42] In addition, patients with anogenital warts often have other concomitant STDs or a history of such infections. Also, as outlined in Table 133–1, particular HPV types are associated with these lesions. These types are rarely found at other sites. Finally, having a large number of sexual partners is associated with greater risk of condylomata acuminata or HPV infection of the cervix.[43–45] Despite these observations in adults, it appears that young children may acquire genital warts from hand contact with nongenital lesions.[46] Approximately one fifth of prepubertal children with condyloma acuminatum have HPV type 1 or 2 in their lesions.[47–49] Conversely, HPV-6 DNA has been identified in cutaneous warts of family contacts of children with anogenital warts.[48]

Recurrent respiratory papillomatosis in young children is thought to be acquired by passage through an infected birth canal. This hypothesis is based on the observations that similar HPV types are associated with both respiratory papillomatosis and anogenital warts and that a large percentage of the mothers of these children have a history of genital tract HPV disease. In addition, neonates are more likely to harbor HPV DNA in their oral cavity if the cervix of the mother contains HPV DNA.[50] Many children with recurrent respiratory papillomatosis are first-born babies who were delivered vaginally to young (often teenaged) mothers.[39, 51] Although the median age of onset of recurrent respiratory papillomatosis is 3 years, cases have been documented at birth, even after cesarean section.[52, 53] This observation suggests that the disease may be acquired in utero, probably by ascending infection from the mother's genital tract. The role of cesarean section, if any, in prevention of transmission is unknown, and the procedure is not recommended for that purpose.[53] Family members and others having close personal contact with these patients are not at risk for development of the disease. In the adult-onset form, recurrent respiratory papillomatosis is associated with a higher than expected number of lifetime sexual partners and with oral-genital contact.[39]

The role of fomites in the transmission of HPV infection is uncertain. However, nosocomial transmission appears possible because infectious virus can be recovered from the fumes released from lesions during treatment with carbon dioxide laser or electrocoagulation.[54] In addition, HPVs are resistant to heat, and use of an autoclave is probably necessary for sterilization of contaminated instruments.[55, 56]

Association between Human Papillomavirus and Malignancies

Early work clearly documented the oncogenic potential of animal papillomaviruses.[57] Observations of patients with epidermodysplasia verruciformis provided the initial evidence suggesting that HPVs might also be carcinogenic. In these patients, characteristic skin lesions induced by specific HPV types frequently undergo malignant transformation, particularly when they occur in sun-exposed areas.[30] Most research investigating the oncogenic potential of HPVs has focused on genital tract malignancies.

A variety of clinical and epidemiologic observations suggest that a sexually transmissible agent is important in the pathogenesis of cancer of the uterine cervix. These observations include the low prevalence of cervical cancer among Catholic nuns,[58] the direct association of risk with number of sexual partners, and the increased risk of malignancy that is associated with having a male sexual partner whose previous consort had developed cervical cancer.[2, 59, 60] A history of condyloma acuminatum has also been linked prospectively with the development of cervical and other anogenital cancers.[61]

Evidence suggesting that HPVs represent the putative agent includes the finding that more than 93% of cervical cancers contain HPV DNA, usually of types 16, 18, 31, or 45; the observation that these same HPV types are also found in the precursor lesions, or cervical intraepithelial neoplasias (CIN); the detection of HPV mRNA in cervical cancer tissues, indicating that the HPV genome is expressed in these lesions; and the higher prevalence of antibodies to HPV-16, -18, or -33 VLPs in the sera of patients with cervical cancer compared with controls.[2, 3, 59, 60, 62–64] Furthermore, infection by specific HPV types, the "high-risk" types, is not simply associated with progression of CIN but precedes it. For example, longitudinal studies demonstrated that CIN lesions associated with HPV type 16 or 18 are more likely to progress than are lesions containing HPV type 6 or 11, which are generally associated with benign condyloma acuminatum.[65] Two years after enrollment in a prospective cohort study of women with normal cervical cytology, the cumulative incidence of CIN was 28% among women with cervical HPV DNA detected by dot blot hybridization, compared with 3% among those without detectable HPV DNA.[66] Moreover, the risk of developing CIN was 11-fold greater among women with HPV type 16 or 18 than among women without HPV DNA.

As expected in a causal relationship, the more sensitive methods of HPV detection, such as polymerase chain reaction assays, demonstrate the strongest association of HPV with CIN. In a case-control study of CIN patients diagnosed cytologically, the percentage of cases attributable to HPV infection was 76% or as high as 92% after adjustment for errors in cytologic diagnosis.[67] Cofactors were not necessary to explain the risk of CIN. As in other studies, the highest relative risk (RR = 51) was associated with the presence of HPV types 16 and 18; HPV types 31, 33, 35, 39, 45, 51, and 52 were associated with an intermediate risk (RR = 33); and infections with HPV types 6, 11, 42, and others were associated with a lower but still increased risk (RR = 8.7). Persistence of the HPV cervical infection is a correlate of high viral load, and when associated with high-risk types it increases the chance of CIN development.[68–70]

Cofactors such as cigarette smoking, use of oral contraceptives, and serologic evidence of current or past infection with *Chlamydia trachomatis* have been inconsistently linked with the development of CIN or invasive cervical carcinoma.[2, 60] As stated by a consensus panel gathered by the World Health Organization in 1995, a large body of epidemiologic and biologic data (discussed later) has now established that at least HPV-16 and -18 infections cause cervical cancers.[2]

Similar lines of evidence, although not necessarily as strong, also implicate HPV as a major factor in the development of at least some vaginal, vulvar, anal, and penile squamous cell cancers.[2, 60, 71, 72] HPVs may also have a role in the pathogenesis of oral,[73] laryngeal,[74] and esophageal[74] squamous carcinomas, as well as of nonmelanoma skin cancers.[74a, b]

PATHOGENESIS

The pathogenesis of HPV disease has been reviewed by several authors.[3, 64, 75, 76] The incubation period was established experimentally by inoculation of human subjects with extracts of cutaneous warts.[1, 77] Most often, warts developed within 3 to 4 months, although lesions occasionally grew as early as 6 weeks or as long as 2 years after inoculation. A similar incubation period was observed for genital warts among wives of American soldiers returning from the Korean War.[78] All types of squamous epithelium may be infected by HPV, but other tissues appear to be relatively resistant. Gross histologic appearances of individual lesions vary with the site of infection and the virus type. Figure 133–1 is a schematic diagram of a typical exophytic, cutaneous wart.

Although little is known about the first stage of HPV infection, it is assumed that the virus replicative cycle begins with the entry of particles into the stratum germinativum, because viral DNA has been detected in the nuclei of the basal cells.[79] As the basal cells differentiate and progress to the surface of the epithelium, HPV DNA replicates and is transcribed and viral particles are assembled in the nucleus. Ultimately, complete virions are released when dead keratinocytes are shed. In a wart or condyloma, viral replication is associated with excessive proliferation of all of the epidermal layers except the basal layer. This process produces acanthosis, parakeratosis, and hyperkeratosis. There is also, where normally present, a deepening of the rete ridges, which produces the typical papillomatous cytoarchitecture. Some infected cells undergo the characteristic transformation of koilocytosis. By histology, koilocytes (from the Greek *koilos*, meaning "cavity") are large, usually polygonal, squamous cells with a shrunken nucleus lodged inside a large cytoplasmic vacuole. Cytoplasmic keratohyalin inclusion bodies may also be observed. Excessive proliferation of the basal cells (basaloid proliferation) accompanied by a high number of mitoses, some abnormal (dyskaryosis), is a feature of premalignant and malignant HPV disease.

Normal-appearing epithelium may contain HPV DNA,[80, 81] and the presence of residual DNA after the treatment of warts may lead to recurrent disease.

In benign lesions caused by HPV, viral DNA is located extrachromosomally in the nuclei of infected cells. However, when HPV DNA is detected in high-grade intraepithelial neoplasias and cancers, it is generally integrated.[3] Integration of HPV DNA may occur at preferential sites in host cell chromosomes,[82] and it specifically disrupts the E2 ORF. Interruption of E2 probably plays a role in the pathogenesis of malignancy, because expression of this ORF normally leads to downregulation of E6 and E7, whose products interfere with the p53 and retinoblastoma tumor suppressor proteins (see "Virology").[3, 75] Additional potential mechanisms of HPV oncogenicity[76] include induction of chromosomal instability,[83] cooperation with activated oncogenes,[82] methylation of viral and cellular DNA sites,[3, 84] telomerase activation,[85] and hormonal[86] and immunogenetic factors.[87, 88]

Host defense responses to HPV infection are poorly understood. Nevertheless, several clinical observations suggest that an effective immune system is important in the resolution of HPV infection.

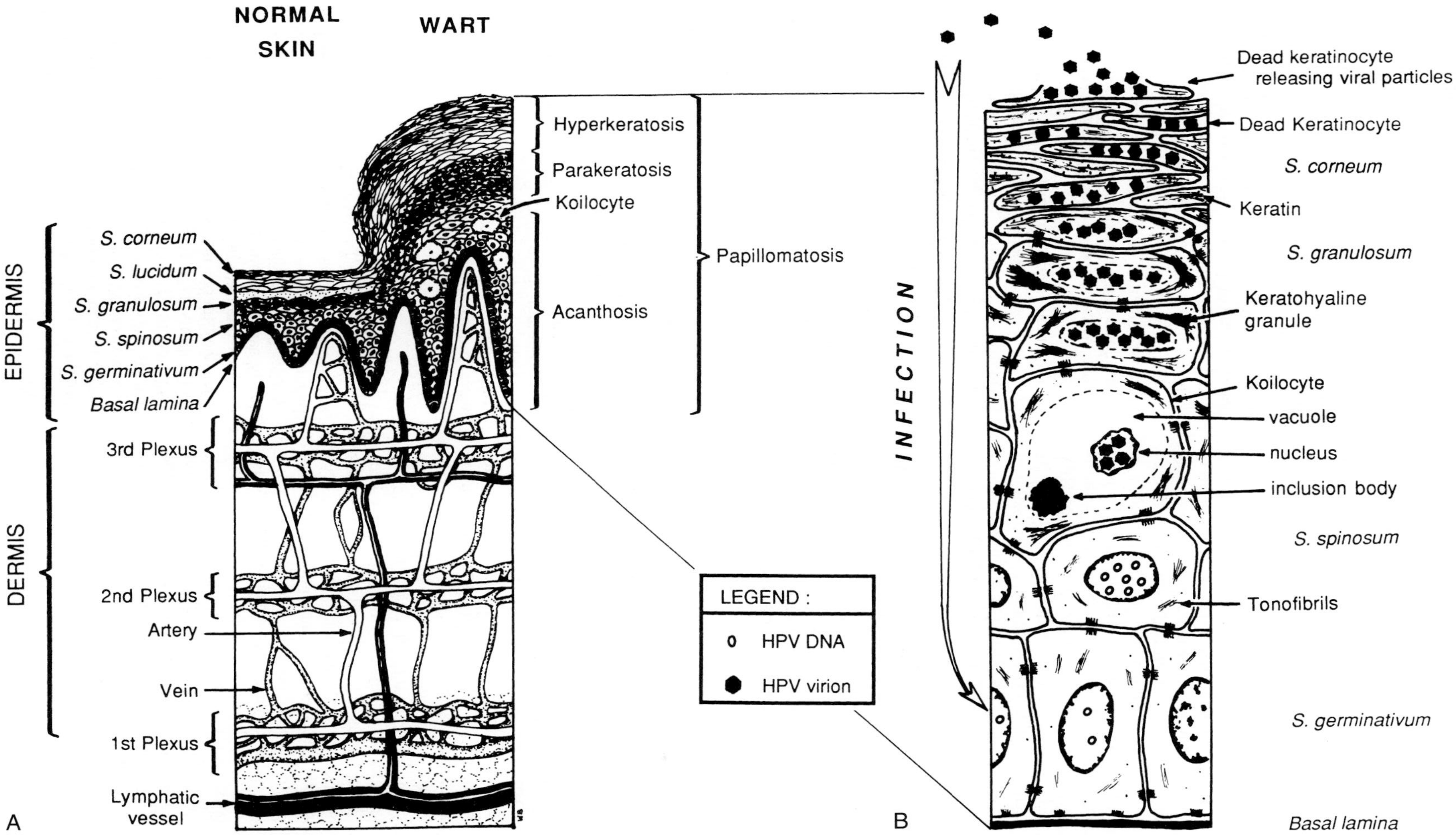

FIGURE 133–1. Exophytic cutaneous wart: Human papillomavirus pathogenesis. *A*, Histologic features. *B*, Cytologic features (see text for details).

HPV diseases occur frequently and are often severe in patients with both primary and secondary immunodeficiencies (e.g., Wiskott-Aldrich syndrome, common variable immunodeficiency.[89]) Severe, frequent HPV disease is also seen in patients with lymphoproliferative disorders and in those with human immunodeficiency virus (HIV) infections.[7, 89–94] The range of HPV-related diseases in HIV infection includes anogenital warts, CIN in women, and anal intraepithelial neoplasia and cancer in homosexual men.[71, 90–94] The prevalence of these conditions is greater with low counts of CD4-positive T lymphocytes and high HIV-1 RNA levels.[95–98] Although the presence of invasive cervical cancer is part of the 1993 CDC case-definition of AIDS,[99] there is more conclusive evidence documenting a rise in the incidence of anal rather than cervical cancers in HIV-infected patients.[72, 100, 101] This may reflect better appreciation among health care providers for disease in women and earlier detection of more easily treated lesions. Immunosuppressive therapy, notably in renal allograft recipients, has also been associated with high rates of extensive HPV infection.[102–106] Another clinical observation indicating the importance of the immune system in the resolution of HPV disease is that regression of one wart is frequently followed by regression of others.[107] Although the relative immunosuppression of pregnancy appears to be associated with an increased incidence and severity of HPV disease,[42] it is not clear that rates of HPV infection are substantially higher in this population than in nonpregnant women.[108, 109]

Various nonspecific alterations of the immune system have been described among patients with HPV diseases.[89] However, except for the decreased, local cell-mediated immunity observed in patients with epidermodysplasia verruciformis, most of these are of uncertain importance.[110]

Few studies have investigated HPV-specific cell-mediated immunity in humans. Delayed hypersensitivity reactions and lymphoproliferative and cytotoxic responses to HPV antigens do occur in infected patients but have been observed inconsistently.[111–115]

Histologic studies of HPV lesions have demonstrated alterations in the degree of immunologic activation of keratinocytes and natural killer cells and in the numbers of Langerhans and T-helper cells.[116–118] In most patients, T cells infiltrating genital warts develop a proliferative response when exposed to E7 or L1 proteins of HPV-6.[119] The presence of an epidermal lymphomonocytic infiltrate in resolving warts is consistent with a significant role of these T cells in curbing HPV infection.[120] These observations and others, along with the well-localized nature of HPV disease, suggest that lymphoid tissue associated with skin (or mucous membrane) may be more relevant to the pathogenesis and resolution of HPV infections than circulating peripheral blood mononuclear leukocytes.[110, 119]

HPV infection may elicit a serologic response. In patients with cutaneous warts, condyloma acuminatum, or recurrent respiratory papillomatosis, antibodies directed against the viral capsid have been detected.[111, 121, 122] VLPs based on the L1 or L1 and L2 proteins offer the same antigenic properties as viral capsids.[123] They have been used extensively to show by enzyme-linked immunosorbent assay that about one half to two thirds of patients with HPV infection have capsid antibodies.[124–127] In diseases associated with HPV-16, including cervical carcinoma, antibodies develop to various antigens derived from the early ORFs, most notably E7.[128] Anti-HPV antibodies tend to disappear with disease resolution but can persist for several years in asymptomatic patients.[129–131] The significance of the serologic response to HPV remains unknown, but antibodies may contribute to virus neutralization.[132]

CLINICAL MANIFESTATIONS

Cutaneous Warts

Cutaneous warts include deep plantar warts, common warts, and plane or flat warts.[133, 134]

Deep plantar warts, also called *myrmecia* (from the Greek, meaning "ant hill"), affect mostly adolescents and young adults. The lesions characteristically look like raised bundles of soft keratotic fibers 2 mm to 1 cm in diameter, and shaving reveals punctate, bleeding blood vessels. These lesions are often painful and may also be located on the palms of the hands.

Common warts appear as well-demarcated, exophytic, hyperkeratotic papules with a rough surface. They may occur on the dorsum of the hand, between the fingers, around the nails (periungual warts), on the palms or soles, or, rarely, on mucous membranes. Warts may coalesce and reach a diameter of 1 cm. Morphologic variants of common warts include mosaic warts, which appear as cobblestone-like patches measuring several square centimeters in diameter and barely rising above an indurated base. Filiform warts on the head and vegetating, hyperproliferative warts on the hands of butchers, fish handlers, and meat packers also occur.[26–29]

Plane warts are commonly found on children and appear as multiple, slightly elevated papules with an irregular contour and distribution and a smooth surface. They occur on the face, neck, and hands. When more protuberant, these lesions are called *intermediate warts*.

Cutaneous warts are usually asymptomatic, although they may bleed and can be painful when located over weight-bearing surfaces or points of friction. Very rarely, cutaneous warts may degenerate into verrucous carcinomas.[135] The natural history of cutaneous warts is poorly characterized. Spontaneous resolution appears to occur in 50 and 90% of children within 1 and 5 years, respectively.[23]

Epidermodysplasia Verruciformis

In this disease that is governed by genetic factors, lesions are associated with a large array of HPV types (see Table 133–1) most of which are specific for epidermodysplasia verruciformis.[30, 133, 136] These warts have several morphologic variants. They may resemble flat warts but more commonly resemble lesions of pityriasis versicolor, covering the torso and upper extremities. Over extensor surfaces these warts may become hypertrophic and coalescent. In most patients, warts appear in the first decade of life. Beginning in young adulthood, in about one third of patients, the lesions undergo malignant transformation into invasive squamous cell carcinomas, particularly in sun-exposed areas. Although these patients may have depressed cellular immunity,[110] they appear to have normal resistance to other pathogens. Epidermodysplasia verruciformis does not appear to be contagious to healthy contacts. It is of interest that lesions resembling epidermodysplasia verruciformis have been observed in solid organ allograft recipients.[74a, b] Furthermore, epidermodysplasia verruciformis–associated HPV types have been identified in many psoriatic lesions.[136a]

Anogenital Warts

Anogenital warts are flesh- to gray-colored, hyperkeratotic, exophytic papules, either sessile on the skin or, more frequently, attached by a short, broad peduncle (Fig. 133–2). Lesions range from smooth, pearly papules to more jagged, acuminate growths. They vary in size from less than a millimeter in diameter to several square centimeters when they merge into plaques. In uncircumcised men, the preputial cavity is involved in 85 to 90% of cases.[42, 137] In the United States, where about 85% of the male population is circumcised, the penile shaft is the most common site of lesions.[33] The urethral meatus is also involved in 1 to 25% of patients.[138, 139] Urethral warts are clearly visible by eversion of the meatus or with the use of a pediatric nasal speculum. They are mostly confined to the fossa navicularis or, less frequently, to the distal 3 cm of the urethra. Involvement of the bladder or proximal urethra is exceptional.[138, 139] Involvement of the perianal area varies according to sexual practice, from very high among homosexual men to low among heterosexual men.[140, 141] Lesions are only occasionally observed on the scrotum, perineum, groin, or pubic area.

In women, most lesions are distributed over the posterior introitus

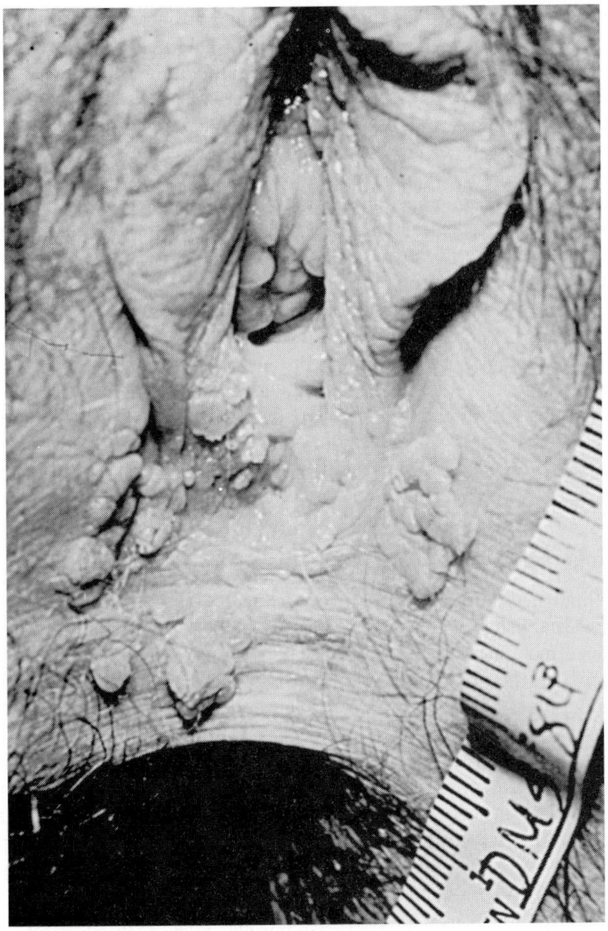

FIGURE 133–2. Vulvar condylomata acuminata.

and, to a lesser degree, over the labia majora and minora and the clitoris (see Fig. 133–2). In order of decreasing frequency, the perineum, vagina, anus, cervix, and urethra each represent less than one quarter of the sites of involvement.[33, 42]

The use of the colposcope and prior soaking of examined tissues with 3% to 5% acetic acid has expanded the clinical spectrum of anogenital warts, particularly those caused by HPV types 16 and 18. This technique was initially used to demonstrate the existence of flat condylomas on the uterine cervix. Typically, these lesions are shiny, white patches with poorly defined borders and an irregular surface containing characteristic capillary loops.[142] The presence of external genital warts may indicate the existence of cervical HPV squamous epithelial lesions, including CIN.[143, 144] Morphologic differentiation among the grades of squamous epithelial lesions is not reliable, and biopsy is strongly recommended for diagnosis.[145]

In the vagina, in addition to flat condylomas, small white nodosities centered on a capillary loop, called *spiked condylomas*, have been described.[146] The vulvar introitus may display prominent, sometimes painful, papillae whose relation to HPV infection is unlikely but controversial.[147, 148] HPV infection of the vulva may also appear as white patches revealed or accentuated by the application of acetic acid, but acetowhitening lacks specificity.[149–151] A link that remains questioned has been proposed between HPV infection and vulvar vestibulitis.[152–154] This syndrome, which may be recognized in up to 15% of women,[155] is characterized by severe pain on touching of the vestibule, tenderness limited to the vestibule, and vestibular erythema, either focal or diffuse, of various extent or intensity.[156, 157]

In men, acetic acid soaking or examination with a colposcope has shown HPV-infected papules and macules to be up to two times more common than exophytic condylomas, particularly on the prepuce and scrotum.[158, 159] Ranging in size from minuscule to 1 cm in diameter, round, sessile papules with brown to slate blue pigmentation are encountered on both male and female external genitalia (Fig. 133–3). These lesions, as well as similarly colored macules, are important to recognize because they may represent either HPV-6- or HPV-11–infected benign condylomas,[160, 161] seborrheic keratoses,[149] or intraepithelial neoplasias associated with HPV type 16 or 18 infection.[149, 161, 162]

About three quarters of patients with anogenital warts are asymptomatic.[33] However, itching and burning, pain, and tenderness are encountered frequently.[33] In addition, the disease can have serious psychological effects.[163] The natural history of genital warts, particularly of subclinical HPV disease, is poorly understood, but spontaneous remission may occur, as demonstrated by the results of randomized, placebo-controlled therapeutic trials that indicate a 10 to 20% spontaneous remission rate in untreated lesions over a 3- to 4-month period.[164–167]

Exophytic genital warts may rarely transform into invasive squamous cell carcinomas, including verrucous carcinoma.[135] They may also reach considerable size, particularly during pregnancy or immunosuppression. When large condylomas reveal histologic features of local destructive invasion without metastases, they may be called *Buschke-Löwenstein tumors*, condylomatous carcinomas, or giant condylomas.[168, 169] Genital HPV infections may also belong to the spectrum of penile, vulvar, vaginal, and cervical intraepithelial neoplasias.[170, 171] Pigmented papules of the external genitalia may histologically demonstrate condylomatous cytoarchitecture with evidence of intraepithelial neoplasia.[161] This clinicopathologic entity is called *bowenoid papulosis* (see Fig. 133–3).[172] Bowenoid papulosis can evolve to *Bowen's disease*, which manifests as a flat, red to brown plaque with well-demarcated borders and a scaly, irregular surface.[173] On the glans penis the lesion is known as *erythroplasia of Queyrat*. Histologically, carcinoma in situ is present. HPV-16 and HPV-18 have been recovered from both bowenoid papulosis and Bowen's disease.[174] The natural history of intraepithelial neoplasias is best understood in cervical lesions.[175] It is clear that the outcome (regression, no change, or progression) is highly variable and depends on the histologic grade of the tumor, the HPV type, and the method of diagnosis (conization, punch biopsy, or scraping). CIN grade 1 lesions have an approximate probability of 60% to regress, 30% to remain unchanged, 10% to progress to CIN 3, and 1% to progress to invasive cancer.[175] For CIN 2, the figures are 40%, 40%, 20%, and 5%, respectively. The risk of progression to cancer is the highest with CIN 3, 12%; only a third of these lesions spontaneously disappear.

Perianal warts are common among homosexual men, and up to

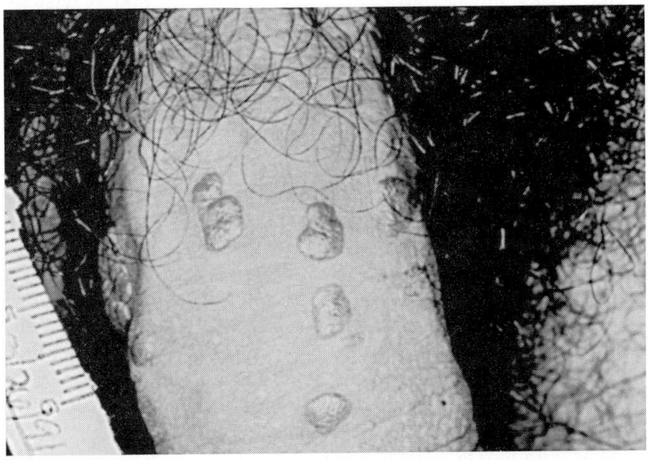

FIGURE 133–3. Pigmented penile warts mimicking bowenoid papulosis.

two thirds of patients with external anal warts also have internal lesions.[176] Although malignant transformation of anal condyloma has been described,[177] the association between anorectal dysplasia or cancer and HPV infection was only recently recognized in homosexual men.[178, 179] Passive anal intercourse carries a risk of anal cancer in homosexual men, and heterosexual men and women with a history of anogenital warts have a 30-fold increased risk of disease compared with control populations.[180] In the general population, a history of anal warts increases by about 10 times the risk of anal cancer.[72] During pregnancy, condylomas may become so large as to impair normal delivery mechanically.[181] Anogenital warts in children should always raise the possibility of sexual abuse, but in very young children nongenital or possibly perinatal transmission may be the predominant mode of acquisition.[182–184]

Recurrent Respiratory Papillomatosis

Recurrent respiratory papillomatosis has been described by several authors.[39, 52, 185–187] Patients present with hoarseness or, in infants, with an altered cry. Sometimes these symptoms are accompanied by respiratory distress or stridor. The disease may spread to the trachea and lungs, leading to obstruction, infection, and respiratory failure. In young children, rapid growth of lesions often threatens the upper respiratory tract and frequently necessitates surgical excision to avoid asphyxiation. In adults, the course of the disease is usually less aggressive. Lesions may, however, undergo malignant transformation, particularly in patients who have received radiation therapy.[188]

Other Human Papillomavirus Infections

Focal epithelial hyperplasia of the oral cavity (Heck's disease) is caused predominantly by HPV-13 and tends to regress spontaneously.[189] Other HPV infections may also occur in the oral cavity.[190] In particular, HPV may coinfect Epstein-Barr virus–induced oral hairy leukoplakia lesions in HIV-infected patients.[191] Conjunctival HPV-related papillomas and carcinomas have been described,[192, 193] and HPV DNA has been identified in epidermoid cysts.[194]

TREATMENT

Highly effective and safe treatments for HPV diseases are not yet available, and the current therapies are not designed to eradicate HPV infection. Rather, their purpose is to decrease or, if possible, eliminate clinical manifestations. Historically, the development of treatments for HPV diseases has been largely empirical. However, in the past 15 years evaluation of new therapies has become more rigorous through the use of randomized controlled clinical trials and in vitro and in vivo models. Whereas traditional approaches have relied mostly on the physical or chemical destruction of lesions, current approaches are directed at molecular viral targets and immunomodulation.[195, 196]

Cutaneous Warts

Because of the benign, usually self-limited nature of cutaneous warts, treatment should be individualized. On the basis of several randomized, non–placebo-controlled comparative trials, Bunney and colleagues[197] proposed several treatment approaches, usually involving paring of the wart. For hand warts, self-application of salicylic and lactic acid paint (salicylic acid, lactic acid, collodion, 1:1:4; SAL; DuoFilm, Occlusal, Paplex) daily for up to 12 weeks has produced a 69% cure rate. About the same cure rate (67%) was obtained with cryotherapy given every 3 weeks. For deep plantar warts, SAL paint cured 84% of patients, which is a response comparable to the 81% cure rate in patients treated with podophyllin resin. About half of patients with mosaic plantar warts were cured with SAL paint, 10% glutaraldehyde, or 5-fluorouracil. Another study of SAL found cure rates at 3 months of 54% for hand warts and 60% for plantar warts.[198] Twenty-five percent of patients with both hand and foot warts were cured. Those in whom this treatment failed were randomly assigned to cryotherapy or treatment with inosine pranobex (an immunomodulator), or both. Overall, 41% of the patients were cured, with no significant benefit of cryotherapy or inosine pranobex over placebo. This observation emphasizes the fact that most cutaneous warts undergo rapid, spontaneous resolution (see "Epidemiology"). Controlled localized heat therapy with a radiofrequency generator has also been used with success to treat cutaneous warts.[199] Flat warts usually do not require treatment. Cryotherapy is preferred for the management of eyelid, nasal, and periungual warts.[200, 201]

Several alternative treatments for cutaneous warts are available.[40, 201] Curettage may be appropriate for partial removal of deep plantar warts. Wedge resection should be avoided because of the resulting painful scarring. Electrosurgery includes electrocautery, electrocoagulation, and electrodesiccation. The last may be useful for removal of flat or filiform warts of the face or other well-localized warts. Scarring is a potential complication.

Anogenital Warts

Optimal methods of treatment of condyloma acuminatum have not been established,[202–207a] and currently available therapies may have little effect on eradication of HPV or transmission of infection.[80] Moreover, there is no evidence that treatment affects the uncommon development of neoplasms.[208, 209] Consequently, the principal indications for treatment of condyloma acuminatum are cosmesis, relief of local symptoms, alleviation of the adverse psychological impact caused by the presence of anogenital warts,[163] and restoration of normal physiologic function (e.g., debulking of lesions obstructing the birth canal). Before treatment is initiated, the goals of therapy, alternatives, costs, and potential side effects should be discussed with patients. It should also be remembered that within 3 to 4 months 10 to 20% of patients have spontaneous resolution of their disease.[164–166]

Cryotherapy is administered with liquid nitrogen or cryoprobe. Lesions are frozen every 1 or 2 weeks. Cryotherapy is regarded as an effective treatment, with cure rates in the 50 to 100% range, and it is safe even during pregnancy.[203, 210] One comparative study suggested that cryotherapy is more effective than podophyllin but probably less effective than electrosurgery.[211–213] Side effects are tolerable. They include burning, which resolves within a few hours, and ulceration, which heals in 7 to 10 days with little or no scarring.

Podophyllin, a resin extract from the rhizome of *Podophyllum peltatum* (podophyllum resin, USP) or *Podophyllum emodi*, has been the principal mode of therapy for many years.[214] The active molecules are lignans, particularly podophyllotoxin. Although podophyllin is a mitotic poison, its mode of action in warts is unknown. The compound is usually applied as a 10% solution in benzoin, directly on the wart, once weekly. Washing of lesions within 12 hours is recommended to minimize local reactions. Lack of regression after four applications suggests the need for alternative therapy. Although initial reports of podophyllin therapy suggested almost complete efficacy, more recent observations demonstrated cure rates ranging from 20 to 40%[137, 214, 215] Side effects are both local and systemic.[214, 216] Chemical burns are seen in one third to one half of the patients. Transient pseudoneoplastic histopathologic changes have also been reported. Neurologic, hematologic, and febrile complications, sometimes leading to death, as well as allergic sensitization, have been associated with administration of topical podophyllin. The drug is contraindicated in pregnancy.

Podophyllotoxin is available in the United States under the generic name podofilox. Podofilox offers distinct advantages over podophyllin. It is chemically uniform and of standardized potency. Podofilox is also more efficacious and less toxic than podophyllin.[137, 216, 217] Finally, it does not need to be washed off. Randomized, controlled studies have shown that 0.5% podofilox applied twice daily for three consecutive days every week for up to 4 weeks results in rates of complete response ranging from 45 to 58%.[218–220] Side effects are mostly mild and similar in nature to those of podophyllin. As with podophyllin, relapses are common, occurring in 33 to 91% of patients.[218–220] Application of podofilox to prevent recurrences is effective and well tolerated, but the long-term outcome after cessation of treatment is unknown.[221] A podofilox gel is being developed.[222]

Many other compounds, with an uncertain mode of action, have been employed in the treatment of external anogenital warts. 5-Fluorouracil, used topically as a 5% cream applied daily, has been reported to have cure rates of 30 to 95%; the best results have been obtained with intraurethral warts.[137, 223, 224] In a comparative trial in men, 5-fluorouracil appeared to be equivalent in efficacy to podophyllin.[225] In addition, prophylactic activity of 5-fluorouracil has been reported for vulvar warts.[226] This drug is not widely used because it often produces substantial pain, ulceration, and, if applied in the urethra, dysuria.[137] A novel formulation of 5-fluorouracil is in development. It incorporates the compound along with epinephrine in a collagen gel that is injected into the wart. This preparation (AccuSite) was evaluated for the treatment of condyloma acuminatum.[227] Patients were treated by intralesional injection, once a week for up to 6 weeks. At the end of treatment, 61% (96/158) of the patients randomly assigned to receive AccuSite had a complete response. The complete response was 43% (69/160) in the group receiving 5-fluorouracil alone in the collagen gel and 5% (2/41) in the placebo group. However, about half of the complete responders relapsed by the third month. The treatment caused local pain, inflammation, and erosions but was nonetheless well tolerated. Like other antimetabolites, 5-fluorouracil is contraindicated during pregnancy.

Trichloracetic acid and, to a lesser extent, bichloracetic acid have been used for the treatment of genital warts.[228] Trichloracetic acid in a 10% to 90% solution is used topically at weekly intervals. The application is painful and can cause ulcers. The unreacted acid should be removed with talcum powder or bicarbonate of soda. In one comparative trial, trichloracetic acid therapy appeared to be equivalent to cryotherapy, with complete response and relapse rates of 81 and 36%, respectively.[210] In another study, it was inferior to cryotherapy, with complete response rates of 70 and 86%, respectively.[229] It has been shown that 50% trichloracetic acid does not add to the effects of podophyllin alone and is ineffective in the treatment of vaginal and cervical warts.[230, 231]

Various surgical techniques for the treatment of anogenital warts have also been used. Conventional surgery offers the advantage of providing immediate eradication of visible lesions. This technique has been reserved mainly for the treatment of perianal warts, but it can be advantageously applied to other genital warts if they are limited in number. Up to one third of patients have recurrences, and scarring, typically limited to some skin discoloration, is the most common complication.[232–235] Electrosurgical techniques have often been applied for the treatment of external genital warts, with results probably superior to those of cryotherapy, but scarring may occur.[212, 213] Complete response rates of 80 to 90% have been reported with carbon dioxide laser therapy.[236–238] In a comparative assessment, however, laser therapy was not deemed to be superior to conventional surgery,[233] and more recent, better-designed studies indicate a long-term complete response rate of 19 to 39%.[239, 240] Laser therapy is expensive, may require general anesthesia, and is frequently accompanied by pain and scarring. Surgical methods have also been found to be variably effective in HIV-infected patients.[241, 242] Healing usually is not a problem in these patients, unless they are profoundly immunosuppressed.[243]

Immunotherapy has been directed predominantly at the treatment of recalcitrant warts. Autogenous vaccination with an extract of the patient's own warts appeared promising in initial studies but was not effective in a subsequent controlled trial.[244–246] Dinitrochlorobenzene skin sensitization is a tedious, protracted, and painful approach that has been claimed to be effective.[247, 248] Proper comparative studies have not been conducted.

Interferons have antiviral, immunomodulatory, and antiproliferative properties.[249] Encouraging in vitro and preliminary clinical studies were confirmed by four randomized, double-blind trials that demonstrated the efficacy of intralesionally administered interferon-α and interferon-β, compared with placebo.[107, 250–252] In these studies, 1 million units of interferon was administered per wart, three times per week for 3 to 4 weeks; 35 to 60% of interferon-injected warts resolved, compared with 20% of placebo-injected lesions. HIV-infected patients have not responded to this treatment.[253, 254] Parenterally administered interferons have also been evaluated for treatment of condyloma acuminatum. Although in one trial interferon-β gave results far superior to those of placebo,[164] more recent studies of various parenterally administered interferon-α preparations revealed clinically nonsignificant effects compared with placebo[165, 166] and complete response rates less than those of podophyllin.[255] Interferon, in the doses used, has been generally well tolerated. Side effects (influenza-like symptoms, neutropenia, and thrombocytopenia) are usually mild and are seen more frequently with higher doses.

Addition of interferon-α may or may not augment the effects of podophyllin treatment or electrosurgery,[254, 256, 257] but it does not add significantly to the effects of cryotherapy.[258, 259] Interferon reduces relapse rates after laser surgery,[239] but this advantage disappears with longer follow-up.[240, 260] Although interferon has a limited role in the treatment of condyloma acuminatum, imiquimod, an inducer of interferon-α and other cytokines, is an important addition to the therapeutic armamentarium.

Imiquimod is an imidazoquinolineamine that was introduced on the American market in June 1997 as a 5% cream (Aldara) for the self-treatment of condyloma acuminatum.[261] This preparation was compared with vehicle alone in a randomized, double-blind trial and was given three times a week, on alternate days, for up to 8 weeks.[262] At the end of the treatment period 108 patients were evaluable and the complete response rate was 37% in the imiquimod group, compared with nil in the control group ($p < .001$). Nineteen percent of the patients had a recurrence during the 10 weeks of follow-up. In a similar study, the treatment duration was extended for up to 16 weeks, and imiquimod 5% cream was compared with a 1% cream and with vehicle.[263] At the end of treatment the complete response rates were 50, 21, and 14% in the three respective groups. Imiquimod 5% cream was significantly superior to either of the two other preparations ($p < .001$). In the 5% imiquimod group, 72% of women had a complete response, compared with 33% of the men. During the 12 weeks of follow-up, recurrences were noted in 13, 0, and 10% of the subjects in the three groups, respectively. The adverse reactions were local and included itching and burning sensations, erythema, erosions, and swelling; they were well tolerated. The daily administration of imiquimod 5% cream offers some enhancement of efficacy, mostly in men, but a substantially higher incidence of side effects.[264] Therefore, Aldara is approved for thrice-weekly use only.

Two cost-benefit analyses have given markedly divergent results on the best approach to the treatment of condyloma acuminatum.[202, 265] Intralesional interferon and laser surgery are probably among the least cost-effective approaches. Availability, convenience, adverse reactions, location of lesions, and patient characteristics are other important considerations in the choice of treatment. Warts of the urinary meatus can be treated by careful application of podophyllin, podofilox,[137] or 5-fluorouracil.[137, 266] Cryotherapy may also be used.[267] Laser therapy[158] and interferon-α instillations[268] are alternative forms of treatment that are also applicable to intraurethral warts. Anal and rectal warts may be treated with scalpel removal, cryotherapy,[269] or laser treatment.[270] For vaginal warts, cryotherapy (sprays), trichloracetic acid, and podophyllin are simple options[207]; laser therapy[271, 272] and cryotherapy[273] have the advantage of being relatively safe during pregnancy, and they may be used for treatment of cervical warts as well. Except possibly for interferon, these treatments can be administered to HIV-infected patients, although it is unclear whether these patients respond to therapy as well as immunocompetent persons do.[274, 275] Although intralesional interferon may be indicated for the treatment of single, very large warts, laser therapy seems to be better suited for large, extensive lesions. Because internal genital warts are often associated with genital dysplasias and malignancies, and because of the special skills and technical resources required for proper diagnosis and management, patients with internal lesions should be referred to a qualified specialist.

Other Warts

The lesions of epidermodysplasia verruciformis should be carefully observed, and any malignant changes should be treated by surgical techniques (cold blade or laser), cryotherapy, or 5-fluorouracil ointments.[133] Oral retinoids and intralesional interferon improve but do not cure the lesions of epidermodysplasia verruciformis.[30, 276]

Recurrent respiratory papillomatosis is managed by endoscopic cryotherapy or, more often, by laser surgery,[39, 52, 185–187] which can be augmented by photodynamic therapy.[277] Tracheostomy should be avoided because of the possible risk of spreading disease to the distal respiratory tree. Similarly, radiotherapy is contraindicated in view of the risk of malignant transformation.[188] Although a large study indicated that the benefit of interferon alfa-n3 as an adjunctive treatment is probably limited to the first 6 months of treatment,[278] more encouraging results were reported subsequently by different investigators, who found that interferon alfa-n1 induced a long-lasting, complete response in one fourth of treated patients.[279] Interferon-α does not eradicate HPV DNA from involved tissues.[81] In a small, uncontrolled study, intralesional cidofovir (Vistide), an acyclic nucleotide analogue available for the treatment of cytomegalovirus retinitis, was found to be effective in the treatment of laryngeal papillomas.[280]

In the oral cavity, verruca vulgaris can be treated by 20% podophyllin in ethanol solution or by cryotherapy, and condyloma acuminatum can be treated by cryotherapy, electrosurgery, or surgical excision.[190] Because of its benign natural history, focal epithelial hyperplasia should not be treated.

DIAGNOSIS

The diagnosis of warts is usually made clinically by physical examination. Exophytic warts have a characteristic appearance. Deep plantar warts may be confused with calluses, but paring usually reveals typical punctated, thrombosed capillaries. Nevi, seborrheic keratoses, acrochordons, acanthomas, molluscum contagiosum, lichen planus, syringomas, and dermofibromas may be confused with cutaneous warts. Lesions of epidermodysplasia verruciformis may be similar to those of flat warts or pityriasis versicolor, but the patient's history should clarify the diagnosis.

Condyloma acuminatum of the external anogenital tract should rarely be confused with other STDs such as condyloma latum of syphilis, nodular scabies, genital herpes, lymphogranuloma venereum, chancroid, or granuloma inguinale. Nevertheless, molluscum contagiosum, particularly in its more atypical presentations, may be difficult to distinguish from anogenital warts. In contrast to condyloma acuminatum, the lesions of molluscum contagiosum tend to predominate over the pubis and are rarely pedunculated but rather appear as very smooth, sessile domes with a depressed center, from which cheesy material can be expressed. In men, a normal anatomic variant of the corona, hirsutoid papillomatosis (pearly coronal papules, papillae corona glandis), can be difficult to differentiate from small warts. A similar anatomic presentation exists in the vulvar introitus, where lesions may appear identical to those of HPV-related vulvar papillomatosis. On the keratinized vulva, hidradenoma papilliferum may be confused with a large wart. On the scrotum, epidermoid cysts and angiokeratomas should be easy to identify. Small and flat HPV lesions may sometimes be difficult to distinguish from lichen planus, lichen sclerosus et atrophicus, lichen nitidus, or syringomas, even with the help of the colposcope and acetic acid application. Finally, pigmented HPV lesions may be confused with nevi or seborrheic keratoses (Fig. 133–3).

Although initially designed for the evaluation of the female internal genital tract, the colposcope, with prior application for 3 to 5 minutes of a 3% to 5% acetic acid solution, has become an important diagnostic tool for other HPV infections as well.[281] In studies of male partners of women with either cervical condylomas or dysplasias, biopsy-proven genital condylomas were detected in 65 to 88% of the patients. More significantly, 43 to 73% of the lesions were seen only with a colposcope, whereas aceto-whitening alone made the diagnosis in 22% of patients.[159, 282, 283] The same technique applied to the vulva revealed subclinical papillomavirus infection in 96% of women with vulvar warts and 80% of women who were partners of men with penile warts.[284] In the oral cavity, 83% of HPV lesions are seen only with the colposcope.[285] The clinical significance of lesions that are detectable by aceto-whitening only is unknown, and aceto-whitening lacks specificity for the diagnosis of HPV infection, particularly for external anogenital warts.[149–151]

Lesions of the external genitalia that are pigmented (see Fig. 133–3), appear as plaques, bleed, or are large should be biopsied to establish the diagnosis.[161] Biopsy is also indicated to confirm the diagnosis of epidermodysplasia verruciformis and to determine the cause of lesions of the oral cavity and upper airways.

Anoscopic examination should be considered in patients with perianal warts or a history of receptive anal intercourse. Most intra-anal lesions are below the pectinate line, and sigmoidoscopy is not routinely indicated.[286, 287] The oral cavity should be examined in all patients with anogenital warts, because they may have concomitant oral warts.[285]

Appropriate evaluation of the vagina and cervix should include colposcopy and acetic acid application and should seek to rule out invasive cancer.[281] Women with a history of anogenital HPV disease, or whose sexual partners have had anogenital HPV disease, should have a cytologic examination of a cervical smear (Pap smear). Koilocytes on a cytologic smear are the hallmark of HPV infection.[288] More importantly, diagnoses of dysplasia and cancer can also be made from the smear.[289, 290] Depending on the patient's age and the location and nature of the HPV infection, the sensitivity of the Pap smear in detecting HPV infection ranges from 30 to 90%.[289–291] Cytology has also been applied with success to the diagnosis of intra-anal HPV infection.[292] Improvements in cervical cytology are becoming available. They include better smear preparation with liquid suspensions (Thin Prep, Cyto Rich) and automated systems for rescreening of negative smears (Pap Net, Auto Pap).[292a, b]

The general histopathologic features of HPV infection are usually characteristic (see "Pathogenesis"). Therefore, biopsy can be used to confirm most diagnoses. In addition, histologic examination can identify the presence of intraepithelial neoplasia or invasive cancer.

To enhance the sensitivity and specificity of cytohistopathology, several techniques are available, mostly in research settings.[293] They rely on demonstration of either papillomavirus antigens or nucleic acids in biopsy specimens. The papillomavirus common antigen is usually detected by peroxidase-antiperoxidase immunocytochemical staining. It is present in about half of HPV lesions, although less frequently with HPV-16 or-18 infections.[20] Various techniques exist for the detection and typing of HPV DNA.[293] They are all based on demonstration, under controlled conditions, of the ability of the nucleic acid being tested to reassociate with a probe (i.e., a known HPV DNA or RNA labeled with either radioisotopes or chemically reactive ligands). If hybridization occurs, the hybrid can be detected by an autoradiogram or a color reaction. The sensitivity of nucleic acid detection techniques can be enhanced by DNA amplification with the polymerase chain reaction.[294, 295] There is at present only one detection kit approved by the U.S. Food and Drug Administration: the Hybrid Capture assay. The reaction between target DNA and RNA probe occurs in a tube in liquid phase. The complex is immobilized by an antibody and recognized by a second antibody

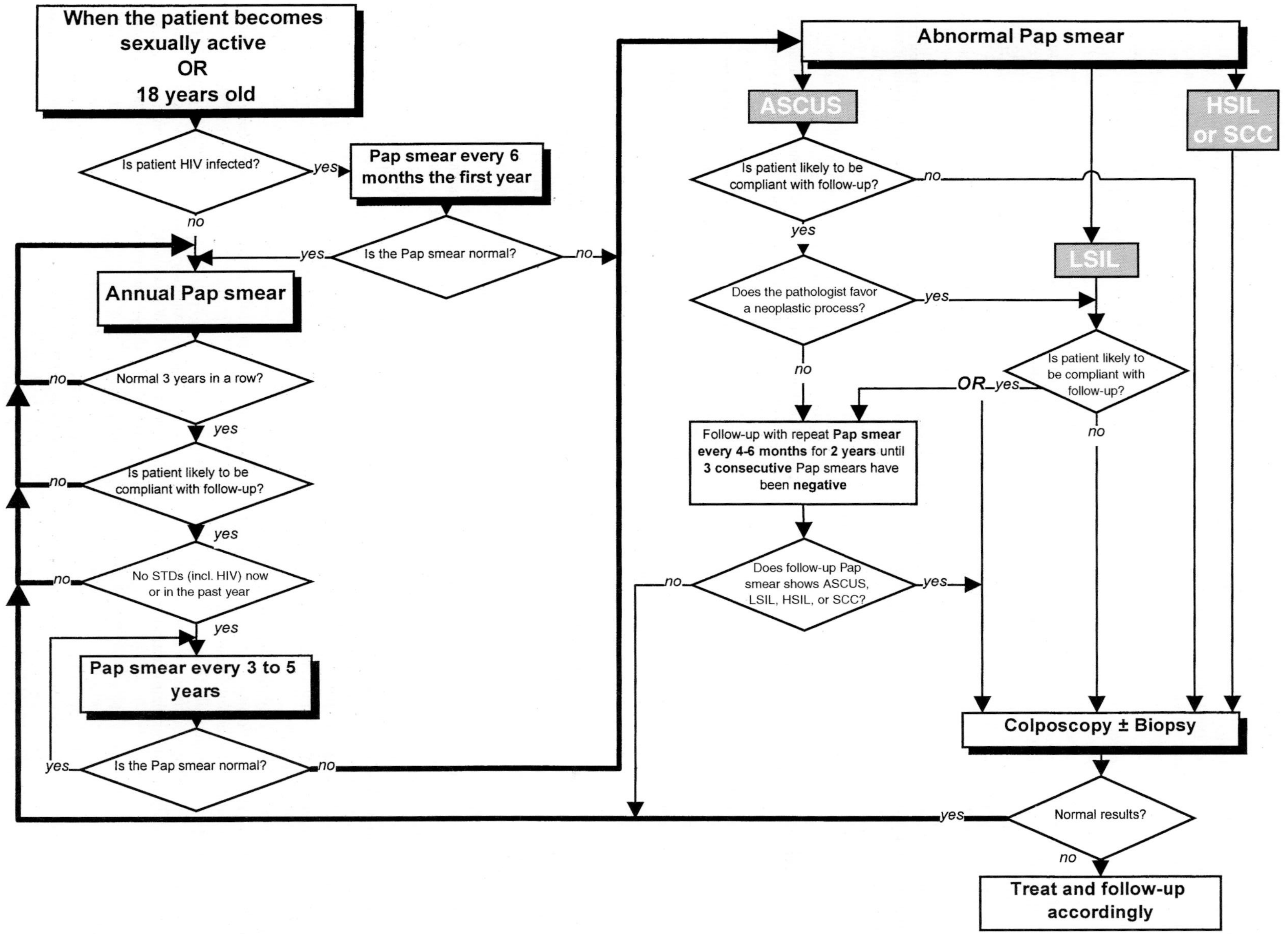

FIGURE 133–4. Cervical human papillomavirus disease: Screening and management of the abnormal Pap smear. *Abbreviations*: ASCUS, Atypical squamous cell of unknown significance; HSIL, high-grade squamous intraepithelial lesion; LSIL, low-grade squamous intraepithelial lesion; SCC, squamous cell carcinoma (see text for further comments).

conjugated to alkaline phosphatase. The assay is quantitative. Two pools of probes are used. Pool A is directed at the detection of low-risk HPVs (types 6, 11, 42, 43, and 44), and pool B targets high-risk HPVs (types 16, 18, 31, 33, 35, 45, 51, 52, and 56). PCR is more sensitive than the Hybrid Capture assay (0.89 versus 0.43) but less specific for the detection of cytologic cervical abnormalities (0.48 versus 0.93).[296, 297] A new version of the Hybrid Capture assay is in development. It uses a plate format, offers greater sensitivity, and incorporates more high-risk HPV types in probe pool B (types 39, 58, 59, and 68).[298]

Although there is now ample evidence that the development of genital cancer, particularly cervical cancer, is greatly increased in the presence of high-risk HPVs (see "Epidemiology"), the cost-effectiveness of HPV DNA detection and typing remains to be defined and validated by the results of large, multicenter, randomized studies that are now being completed. Therefore, the standard management of diseases related to HPV infection does not rely on HPV typing.[207] In the future, HPV typing may prove to be helpful, with quality control in the cytology laboratory, in resolving cases with inconclusive cytology or nondiagnostic histology, in the triage of patients referred for colposcopy, and in the screening of postmenopausal women.[299]

Virus cultivation and accurate serologic techniques are not available for diagnosis of HPV infections.

PREVENTION

At present, no effective methods of prevention are available for warts other than avoiding contact with infectious lesions.[300] It is unclear whether barrier methods of contraception are helpful in preventing the transmission of HPV infection of the genital tract.[301, 302] Whether reactivation of latent infection rather than reinfection is responsible for wart recurrence is unknown, but limited evidence suggests that examination and treatment of sexual partners does not affect the course of a patient's anogenital warts.[207]

The Pap smear is an essential tool for the screening and prevention of cervical cancer. Figure 133–4 summarizes a set of general guidelines offered by the American Cancer Society, the CDC, and the National Institutes of Health's Bethesda classification system regarding when to obtain Pap smears and what to do with the results.[207, 303–305] Some authorities advocate a more frequent and intensive screening in HIV-infected women.[306] In addition to providing an assessment of Pap smear quality, the Bethesda system establishes a four-category classification of the squamous cell abnormalities that are pertinent for the diagnosis and management of cervical HPV disease: (1) atypical squamous cell of unknown significance; (2) low-grade squamous intraepithelial lesion; (3) high-grade intraepithelial lesion; and (4) squamous cell carcinoma.[304, 305]

Cesarian section has probably only a limited role in the prevention of recurrent respiratory papillomatosis.[305a]

Although vaccines are not currently available against HPV disease, vaccines based on VLPs (see "Virology") have shown excellent protection against animal papillomavirus diseases. VLP vaccines are actively being developed for anogenital HPVs.[307, 308] An HPV-11 VLP vaccine administered to healthy volunteers was shown to generate very high titers of binding and neutralizing antibodies.[309]

REFERENCES

1. Ciuffo G. Imnesto positivo con filtrato di verruca volgare. Giorn Ital Mal Veneree. 1907;48:12–17.
2. Anon. Human papillomaviruses. IARC Monogr Eval Carcinog Risks Hum. 1995;94:1–379.
3. zur Hausen H. Papillomavirus infections: A major cause of human cancers. Biochim Biophys Acta. 1996;1288:F55–F78.
4. Kubbutat MHG, Vousden KH. Role of E6 and E7 oncoproteins in HPV-induced anogenital malignancies. Semin Virol. 1996;7:295–304.
5. Myers G, Lu H, Calef C, Leitner T. Heterogeneity of papillomaviruses. Semin Cancer Biol. 1996;7:349–358.
6. Howley PM. *Papillomavirinae*: The viruses and their replication. In: Fields BN, Knipe DM, Howley PM, et al., eds. Fields Virology, 3rd ed. Philadelphia: Lippincott-Raven; 1996:2045–2076.
7. Shah KV, Howley PM. Papillomaviruses. In: Fields BN, Knipe DM, Howley PM, et al., eds. Fields Virology. Philadelphia: Lippincott-Raven; 1996:2077–2109.
8. Bonnez W. Papillomavirus. In: Richman DD, Whitley RJ, Hayden FG, eds. Clinical Virology, 1st ed. New York: Churchill Livingstone; 1997:569–611.
9. Murphy FA, Fauquet CM, Bishop DHL, et al., eds. Virus Taxonomy: Classification and Nomenclature of Viruses. Sixth Report of the International Committee on Taxonomy of Viruses ed. Vienna: Springer-Verlag, 1995.
10. Ashmole I, Gallimore PH, Roberts S. Identification of conserved hydrophobic C-terminal residues of the human papillomavirus type 1 E1E4 protein necessary for E4 oligomerisation in vivo. Virology. 1998;240:221–231.
11. Doorbar J, Foo C, Coleman N, et al. Characterization of events during the late stages of HPV16 infection in vivo using high-affinity synthetic Fabs to E4. Virology. 1997;238:40–52.
12. Stoppler MC, Straight SW, Tsao G, et al. The E5 gene of HPV-16 enhances keratinocyte immortalization by full-length DNA. Virology. 1996;223:251–254.
13. Crusius K, Auvinen E, Alonso A. Enhancement of EGF- and PMA-mediated MAP kinase activation in cells expressing the human papillomavirus type 16 E5 protein. Oncogene. 1997;15:1437–1444.
14. Frattini MG, Lim HB, Doorbar J, et al. Induction of human papillomavirus type 18 late gene expression and genomic amplification in organotypic cultures from transfected DNA templates. J Virol. 1997;71:7068–7072.
15. Meyers C, Mayer TJ, Ozbun MA. Synthesis of infectious human papillomavirus type 18 in differentiating epithelium transfected with viral DNA. J Virol. 1997;71:7381–7386.
16. Howett MK, Christensen ND, Kreider JW. Tissue xenografts as a model system for study of the pathogenesis of papillomaviruses. Clin Dermatol. 1997;15:229–236.
17. Bonnez W. Murine models of human papillomavirus-infected human xenografts. Papillomavirus Rep. 1998;9:27–38.
18. Dollard SC, Wilson JL, Demeter LM, et al. Production of human papillomavirus and modulation of the infectious program in epithelial raft cultures. Genes Dev. 1992;6:1131–1142.
19. Strike DG, Bonnez W, Rose RC, et al. Expression in *Escherichia coli* of seven DNA segments comprising the complete L1 and L2 open reading frames of human papillomavirus type 6b and the location of the "common antigen." J Gen Virol. 1989;70:543–555.
20. Jenson AB, Kurman RJ, Lancaster WD. Detection of papillomavirus common antigens in lesions of skin and mucosa. Clin Dermatol. 1985;3:56–63.
21. Rose RC, Bonnez W, Da Rin C, et al. Serologic differentiation of human papillomavirus (HPV) types 11, 16, and 18, using recombinant virus-like particles (VLPs). J Gen Virol. 1994;75:2445–2449.
22. White WI, Wilson SD, Bonnez W, et al. *In vitro* infection and type-restricted antibody-mediated neutralization of authentic human papillomavirus type 16. J Virol. 1998;72:959–964.
23. Massing AM, Epstein WL. Natural history of warts: A two-year study. Arch Dermatol. 1963;87:306–310.
24. Williams HC, Pottier A, Strachan D. The descriptive epidemiology of warts in British schoolchildren. Br J Dermatol. 1993;128:504–511.
25. Larsson P-Å, Lidén S. Prevalence of skin diseases among adolescents 12–16 years of age. Acta Derm Venereol (Stockh). 1980;60:415–423.
26. Rüdlinger R, Bunney MH, Grob R, et al. Warts in fish handlers. Br J Dermatol. 1989;120:375–381.
27. Stehr-Green PA, Hewer P, Meekin GE, et al. The aetiology and risk factors for warts among poultry processing workers. Int J Epidemiol. 1993;22:294–298.
28. Keefe M, Al-Ghamdi A, Coggon D, et al. Cutaneous warts in butchers. Br J Dermatol. 1994;130:9–14.
29. Aziz MA, Bahamdan K, Moneim MA. Prevalence and risk factors for warts among slaughterhouse workers. East Afr Med J. 1996;73:194–197.
30. Majewski S, Jablonska S. Epidermodysplasia verruciformis as a model of human papillomavirus-induced genetic cancer of the skin. Arch Dermatol. 1995;131:1312–1318.
31. Becker TM, Blount JF, Guinan ME. Trends in genital herpes infections among private practitioners in the United States, 1966–1981. J Am Med Assoc. 1985;253:1601–1603.
32. Simms I, Fairley CK. Epidemiology of genital warts in England and Wales: 1971 to 1994. Genitourin Med. 1997;73:365–367.
33. Chuang T-Y, Perry HO, Kurland LT, et al. Condyloma acuminatum in Rochester, Minn., 1950–1978: I. Epidemiology and clinical features. Arch Dermatol. 1984;120:469–475.
34. Becker TM. Genital human papillomavirus infection: An epidemiological perspective. In: Norrby SR, ed. New Antiviral Strategies. Edinburgh: Churchill Livingstone; 1988;44–49.
35. Stone KM. Epidemiologic aspects of genital HPV infection. Clin Obstet Gynecol. 1989;32(1):112–116.
36. de Villiers E-M, Schneider A, Miklaw H, et al. Human papillomavirus infections in women with and without abnormal cytology. Lancet. 1987;2:703–706.
37. Garrido JL. Pathological incidence study of human papilloma virus (HPV) carried out on 1,439 patients between 1982–1985 in Panama. Eur J Gynaecol Oncol. 1988;9:144–148.
38. Rosenfeld WD, Vermund SH, Wentz SJ, et al. High prevalence rate of human papillomavirus infection and association with abnormal Papanicolaou smears in sexually active adolescents. Am J Dis Child. 1989;143:1443–1447.

39. Derkay CS. Task force on recurrent respiratory papillomatosis: A preliminary report. Arch Otolaryngol Head Neck Surg. 1995;121:1386–1391.
40. Bunney MH, Benton C, Cubie HA. Viral Warts: Biology and Treatment, 2nd ed. Oxford: Oxford University Press; 1992.
41. Campion MJ, Singer A, Carkson PK, et al. Increased risk of cervical neoplasia in consorts of men with penile condylomata acuminata. Lancet. 1985;1:943–946.
42. Oriel JD. Natural history of genital warts. Br J Vener Dis. 1971;47:1–13.
43. Koutsky LA, Galloway DA, Holmes KK. Epidemiology of genital human papillomavirus infection. Epidemiol Rev. 1988;10:122–163.
44. van den Eeden SK, Habel LA, Sherman KJ, et al. Risk factors for incident and recurrent condylomata acuminata among men: A population-based study. Sex Transm Dis. 1998;25:278–284.
45. Habel LA, van den Eeden SK, Sherman KJ, et al. Risk factors for incident and recurrent condylomata acuminata among women: A population-based study. Sex Transm Dis. 1998;25:285–292.
46. Fairley CK, Gay NJ, Forbes A, et al. Hand-genital transmission of genital warts? An analysis of prevalence data. Epidemiol Infect. 1995;115:169–176.
47. Obalek S, Jablonska S, Favre M, et al. Condylomata acuminata in children: Frequent association with human papillomaviruses responsible for cutaneous warts. J Am Acad Dermatol. 1990;23:205–213.
48. Cohen BA, Honig P, Androphy E. Anogenital warts in children: Clinical and virologic evaluation for sexual abuse. Arch Dermatol. 1990;126:1575–1580.
49. Gutman LT, Herman-Giddens ME, Phelps WC. Transmission of human genital papillomavirus disease: Comparison of data from adults and children. Pediatrics. 1993;91:31–38.
50. Fredericks BD, Balkin A, Daniel HW, et al. Transmission of human papillomaviruses from mother to child. Aust N Z J Obstet Gynaecol. 1993;33:30–32.
51. Kashima HK, Shah F, Lyles A, et al. A comparison of risk factors in juvenile-onset and adult-onset recurrent respiratory papillomatosis. Laryngoscope. 1992;102:9–13.
52. Kashima HK, Shah K. Recurrent respiratory papillomatosis: Clinical overview and management principles. Obstet Gynecol Clin North Am. 1987;14:581–588.
53. Kosko JR, Derkay CS. Role of cesarean section in prevention of recurrent respiratory papillomatosis: Is there one? Int J Pediatr Otorhinolaryngol 1996;35:31–38.
54. Sawchuk WS, Weber PJ, Lowy DR, et al. Infectious papillomavirus in the vapor of warts treated with carbon dioxide laser or electrocoagulation: Detection and protection. J Am Acad Dermatol. 1989;21:41–49.
55. Bonnez W, Rose RC, Borkhuis C, et al. Evaluation of the temperature sensitivity of human papillomavirus (HPV) type 11 using the human xenograft severe combined immunodeficiency (SCID) mouse model. J Clin Microbiol. 1994;32:1575–1577.
56. Roden RB, Lowy DR, Schiller JT. Papillomavirus is resistant to desiccation. J Infect Dis. 1997;176:1076–1079.
57. Lancaster WD, Olson C. Animal papillomaviruses. Microbiol Rev. 1982;46:191–207.
58. Fraumeni JF, Lloyd JM, Smith EM, et al. Cancer mortality among nuns: Role of the marital status in etiology of neoplastic disease in women. J Natl Cancer Inst. 1969;42:455–468.
59. Morris M, Tortolero-Luna G, Malpica A, et al. Cervical intraepithelial neoplasia and cervical cancer. Obstet Gynecol Clin North Am. 1996;23:347–410.
60. Franco EL. Epidemiology of anogenital warts and cancer. Obstet Gynecol Clin North Am. 1996;23:597–623.
61. Friis S, Kjaer SK, Frisch M, et al. Cervical intraepithelial neoplasia, anogenital cancer, and other cancer types in women after hospitalization for condylomata acuminata. J Infect Dis. 1997;175:743–748.
62. Wang Z, Konya J, Avall-Lundkvist E, et al. Human papillomavirus antibody responses among patients with incident cervical carcinoma. J Med Virol. 1997;52:436–440.
63. Chaouki N, Bosch FX, Muñoz N, et al. The viral origin of cervical cancer in Rabat, Morocco. Int J Cancer. 1998;75:546–554.
64. Arends MJ, Buckley CH, Wells M. Aetiology, pathogenesis, and pathology of cervical neoplasia. J Clin Pathol. 1998;51:96–103.
65. Campion MJ, Cuzick J, McCance DJ, et al. Progressive potential of mild cervical atypia: Prospective cytological, colposcopic, and virological study. Lancet. 1986;2:237–240.
66. Koutsky LA, Holmes KK, Critchlow CW, et al. A cohort study of the risk of cervical intraepithelial neoplasia grade 2 or 3 in relation to papillomavirus infection. N Engl J Med. 1992;327:1272–1278.
67. Schiffman MH, Bauer HM, Hoover RN, et al. Epidemiologic evidence showing that human papillomavirus infection causes most cervical intraepithelial neoplasia. J Natl Cancer Inst. 1993;85:958–964.
68. Brown DR, Rawlings K, Handy V, et al. Human papillomavirus detection by Hybrid Capture in paired cervicovaginal lavage and cervical biopsy specimens. J Med Virol. 1996;48:210–214.
69. Londesborough P, Ho L, Terry G, et al. Human papillomavirus genotype as a predictor of persistence and development of high-grade lesions in women with minor cervical abnormalities. Int J Cancer. 1996;69:364–368.
70. Ho GY, Bierman R, Beardsley L, et al. Natural history of cervicovaginal papillomavirus infection in young women. N Engl J Med. 1998;338:423–428.
71. Northfelt DW, Swift PS, Palefsky JM. Anal neoplasia: Pathogenesis, diagnosis, and management. Hematol Oncol Clin North Am. 1996;10:1177–1187.
72. Frisch M, Glimelius B, van den Brule AJC, et al. Sexually transmitted infection as a cause of anal cancer. N Engl J Med. 1997;337:1350–1358.
73. Sugerman PB, Shillitoe EJ. The high risk human papillomaviruses and oral cancer: Evidence for and against a causal relationship. Oral Diseases 1997;3:130–147.
74. Snijders PJF, van den Brule AJC, Meijer CJLM, et al. Papillomaviruses and cancer of the upper digestive and respiratory tracts. Curr Top Microbiol Immunol. 1994;186:177–198.
74a. Majewski S, Jablonska S. Human papillomavirus-associated tumors of the skin and mucosa. J Am Acad Dermatol. 1997;36:659–685.
74b. de Villiers EM. Human papillomavirus infections in skin cancers. Biomed Pharmacother. 1998;52:26–33.
75. Alani RM, Munger K. Human papillomaviruses and associated malignancies. J Clin Oncol. 1998;16:330–337.
76. Southern SA, Herrington CS. Molecular events in uterine cervical cancer. Sex Transm Infect 1998;74:101–109.
77. Goldschmidt H, Klingman AM. Experimental inoculation of humans with ectodermotropic viruses. J Invest Dermatol. 1958;31:175–182.
78. Barrett TJ, Silbar JD, McGinley JP. Genital warts: A venereal disease. JAMA. 1954;154:333–334.
79. Stoler MH, Broker TR. *In situ* hybridization detection of human papillomavirus DNAs and messenger RNAs in genital condylomas and cervical carcinoma. Hum Pathol. 1986;17:1250–1258.
80. Ferenczy A, Mitao M, Nagai N, et al. Latent papillomavirus and recurring warts. N Engl J Med. 1985;313:784–788.
81. Steinberg BM, Gallagher T, Stoler M, et al. Persistence and expression of human papillomavirus during interferon therapy. Arch Otolaryngol Head Neck Surg. 1988;114:27–32.
82. Lazo PA, Gallego MI, Ballester S, et al. Genetic alterations by human papillomaviruses in oncogenesis. FEBS Lett. 1992;300:109–113.
83. Mullokandov MR, Kholodilov NG, Atkin NB, et al. Genomic alterations in cervical carcinoma: Losses of chromosome heterozygosity and human papilloma virus tumor status. Cancer Res. 1996;56:197–205.
84. Rössl F, Arab A, Klevenz B, et al. The effect of DNA methylation on gene regulation of human papillomaviruses. J Gen Virol. 1993;74:791–801.
85. Anderson S, Shera K, Ihle J, et al. Telomerase activation in cervical cancer. Am J Pathol. 1997;151:25–31.
86. Khan MA, Canhoto AJ, Housley PR, et al. Glucocorticoids stimulate growth of human papillomavirus type 16 (HPV16)-immortalized human keratinocytes and support HPV16-mediated immortalization without affecting the levels of HPV16 E6/E7 mRNA. Exp Cell Res. 1997;236:304–310.
87. Breitburd F, Ramoz N, Salmon J, et al. HLA control in the progression of human papillomavirus infections. Semin Cancer Biol. 1996;7:359–371.
88. Helland A, Olsen AO, Gjoen K, et al. An increased risk of cervical intra-epithelial neoplasia grade II-III among human papillomavirus positive patients with the HLA-DQA1*0102-DQB1*0602 haplotype: A population-based case-control study of Norwegian women. Int J Cancer. 1998;76:19–24.
89. Kirchner H. Immunobiology of human papillomavirus infection. Prog Med Virol. 1986;33:1–41.
90. Biggar RJ, Rabkin CS. The epidemiology of AIDS-related neoplasms. Hematol Oncol Clin North Am. 1996;10:997–1010.
91. Robinson WR, Morris CB. Cervical neoplasia: Pathogenesis, diagnosis, and management. Hematol Oncol Clin North Am. 1996;10:1163–1176.
92. Wright TC Jr, Sun XW. Anogenital papillomavirus infection and neoplasia in immunodeficient women. Obstet Gynecol Clin North Am. 1996;23:861–893.
93. Palefsky JM. Cutaneous and genital HPV-associated lesions in HIV-infected patients Clin Dermatol. 1997;15:439–447.
94. Chopra KF, Tyring SK. The impact of the human immunodeficiency virus on the human papillomavirus epidemic. Arch Dermatol. 1997;133:629–633.
95. Klein RS, Ho GYF, Vermund SH, et al. Risk factors for squamous intraepithelial lesions on Pap smear in women at risk for human immunodeficiency virus infection. J Infect Dis. 1994;170:1404–1409.
96. Ho GY, Burk RD, Fleming I, et al. Risk of genital human papillomavirus infection in women with human immunodeficiency virus-induced immunosuppression. Int J Cancer. 1994;56:788–792.
97. Chirgwin KD, Feldman J, Augenbraun M, et al. Incidence of venereal warts in human immunodeficiency virus-infected and uninfected women. J Infect Dis. 1995;172:235–238.
98. Luque A, Demeter LM, Reichman RC. Prediction of cervical human papillomavirus infection and disease by magnitude of HIV-1 plasma RNA level. J Infect Dis. 1999;179. In press.
99. 1993 Revised classification system for HIV infection and expanded surveillance case definition for AIDS among adolescents and adults. MMWR Morb Mortal Wkly Rep. 1992;41(RR-17):1–19.
100. Maiman M, Fruchter RG, Clark M, et al. Cervical cancer as an AIDS-defining illness. Obstet Gynecol. 1997;89:76–80.
101. Tilston P. Anal human papillomavirus and anal cancer. J Clin Pathol. 1997;50:625–634.
102. Boyle J, Briggs JD, Mackie RM, et al. Cancer, warts and sunshine in renal transplant patients: A case-control study. Lancet. 1984;1:702–705.
103. Barr BBB, Benton EC, McLaren K, et al. Human papillomavirus infection and skin cancer in renal allografts recipients. Lancet. 1989;1:124–128.
104. Alloub MI, Barr BBB, McLaren KM, et al. Human papillomavirus infection and cervical intraepithelial neoplasia in women with renal allografts. BMJ 1989;298:153–156.
105. McGregor JM, Proby CM, Leigh IM. Virus infection and cancer risk in transplant recipients. Trends Microbiol 1996;4:2–3.
106. Euvrard S, Kanitakis J, Chardonner Y, et al. External anogenital lesions in organ transplant recipients: A clinicopathologic and virologic assessment. Arch Dermatol. 1997;133:175–178.
107. Reichman RC, Oakes D, Bonnez W, et al. Treatment of condyloma acuminatum

with three different interferons administered intralesionally: A double-blind, placebo-controlled trial. Ann Intern Med. 1988;108:675–679.
108. Kemp EA, Hakenewerth AM, Laurent SL, et al. Human papillomavirus prevalence in pregnancy. Obstet Gynecol. 1992;79:649–656.
109. Morrison EA, Gammon MD, Goldberg GL, et al. Pregnancy and cervical infection with human papillomaviruses. Int J Gynaecol Obstet. 1996;54:125–130.
110. Majewski S, Jablonska S, Orth G. Epidermodysplasia verruciformis: Immunological and nonimmunological surveillance mechanisms. Role in tumor progression. Clin Dermatol. 1997;15:321–334.
111. Kienzler JL, Lemoine MT, Orth G, et al. Humoral and cell-mediated immunity to human papillomavirus type 1 (HPV-1) in human warts. Br J Dermatol. 1983;108:665–672.
112. Höpfl R, Sandblicher M, Sepp N, et al. Skin test for HPV-16 proteins in cervical intraepithelial neoplasia. Lancet. 1991;337:373–374.
113. Viscidi RP, Shah KV. Immune response to genital tract infections with human papillomaviruses. In: Quinn TC, ed. Sexually Transmitted Diseases. New York: Raven Press, 1992:239–260. (Gallin JI, Fauci AS, eds. Advances in Host Defense Mechanisms; 8).
114. Nimako M, Fiander AN, Wilkinson GW, et al. Human papillomavirus-specific cytotoxic T lymphocytes in patients with cervical intraepithelial neoplasia grade III. Cancer Res. 1997;57:4855–4861.
115. Nakagawa M, Stites DP, Farhat S, et al. Cytotoxic T lymphocyte responses to E6 and E7 proteins of human papillomavirus type 16: Relationship to cervical intraepithelial neoplasia. J Infect Dis. 1997;175:927–931.
116. Charleson FC, Norval M, Benton EC, et al. Lymphoproliferative responses to human papillomaviruses in patients with cutaneous warts. Br J Dermatol. 1992;127:551–559.
117. Malejczyk J, Malejczyk M, Majewski S, et al. NK-cell activity in patients with HPV 16-associated anogenital tumors: Defective recognition of HPV 16-harboring keratinocytes and restricted unresponsiveness to immunostimulatory cytokines. Int J Cancer. 1993;54:917–921.
118. Schneider A. Pathogenesis of genital HPV infection. Genitourin Med. 1993;69:165–173.
119. Hong K, Greer CE, Ketter N, et al. Isolation and characterization of human papillomavirus type 6-specific T cells infiltrating genital warts. J Virol. 1997;71:6427–6432.
120. Oguchi M, Komura J, Tagami H, et al. Ultrastructural studies of spontaneously regressing plane warts: Macrophages attack verruca-epidermal cells. Arch Dermatol Res. 1981;270:403–411.
121. Bonnez W, DaRin C, Rose RC, et al. Use of human papillomavirus type 11 virions in an ELISA to detect specific antibodies in humans with condylomata acuminata. J Gen Virol. 1991;72:1343–1347.
122. Bonnez W, Kashima HK, Leventhal B, et al. Antibody response to human papillomavirus (HPV) type 11 in children with juvenile-onset recurrent respiratory papillomatosis. Virology. 1992;188:384–387.
123. Rose RC, Reichman RC, Bonnez W. Human papillomavirus type 11 (HPV-11) recombinant virus-like particles (VLPs) induce the formation of neutralizing antibodies and detect HPV-specific antibodies in human sera. J Gen Virol. 1994;75:2075–2079.
124. Wideroff L, Schiffman MH, Nonnenmacher B, et al. Evaluation of seroreactivity to human papillomavirus type 16 virus-like particles in an incident case-control study of cervical neoplasia. J Infect Dis. 1995;172:1425–1430.
125. Carter JJ, Wipf GC, Hagensee ME, et al. Use of human papillomavirus type 6 capsids to detect antibodies in people with genital warts. J Infect Dis. 1995;172:11–18.
126. De Sanjose S, Hamsikova E, Muñoz N, et al. Serological response to HPV16 in CIN-III and cervical cancer patients: Case-control studies in Spain and Colombia. Int J Cancer. 1996;66:70–74.
127. Olsen AO, Dillner J, Gjoen K, et al. Seropositivity against HPV 16 capsids: A better marker of past sexual behaviour than presence of HPV DNA. Genitourin Med. 1997;73:131–135.
128. Gissmann L. Immunologic responses to human papillomavirus infection. Obstet Gynecol Clin North Am. 1996;23:625–639.
129. Bonnez W, DaRin C, Rose RC, et al. Evolution of the antibody response to human papillomavirus type 11 (HPV-11) in patients with condyloma acuminatum according to treatment response. J Med Virol. 1993;39:340–344.
130. Lehtinen M, Leminen A, Kuoppala T, et al. Pre- and posttreatment serum antibody responses to HPV 16 E2 and HSV 2 ICP8 proteins in women with cervical carcinoma. J Med Virol. 1992;37:180–186.
131. af Geijersstam V, Kibur M, Wang Z, et al. Stability over time of serum antibody levels to human papillomavirus type 16. J Infect Dis. 1998;177:1710–1714.
132. Leiserowitz GS, Hall KS, Foster CA, et al. Detection of serologic neutralizing antibodies against HPV-11 in patients with condyloma acuminata and cervical dysplasia using an in vitro assay. Gynecol Oncol. 1997;66:295–299.
133. Grussendorf-Conen E-I. Papillomavirus-induced tumors of the skin: Cutaneous warts and epidermodysplasia verruciformis. In: Syrjänen K, Gissmann L, Koss LG, eds. Papillomaviruses and Human Disease. Berlin: Springer Verlag; 1987;158–181.
134. Jablonska S, Orth G, Obalek S, et al. Cutaneous warts: Clinical, histologic, and virologic correlations. Clin Dermatol. 1985;3:71–82.
135. Schwartz RA. Verrucous carcinoma of the skin and mucosa. J Am Acad Dermatol. 1995;32:1–21.
136. Lutzner MA, Blanchet-Bardon C. Epidermodysplasia verruciformis. Curr Probl Dermatol. 1985;13:164–185.
136a. Favre M, Orth G, Majewski S, et al. Psoriasis: A possible reservoir for human papillomavirus type 5, the virus associated with skin carcinomas of epidermodysplasia verruciformis. J Invest Dermatol. 1998;110:311–317.
137. von Krogh G. Podophyllotoxin for condylomata acuminata eradication: Clinical and experimental comparative studies on *Podophyllum lignans*, colchicine and 5-fluorouracil. Acta Derm Venereol (Stockh). 1981(suppl 98):1–48.
138. Davey DD, Naryshkin S, Nielsen ML, et al. Atypical squamous cells of undetermined significance: Interlaboratory comparison and quality assurance monitors. Diagn Cytopathol. 1994;11:390–396.
139. Kaplinsky RS, Pranikoff K, Chasan S, et al. Indications for urethroscopy in male patients with penile condylomata. J Urol. 1995;153:1120–1121.
140. Goorney BP, Waugh MA, Clarke J. Anal warts in heterosexual men. Genitourin Med. 1987;63:216.
141. Oriel JD. Anal warts and anal coitus. Br J Vener Dis. 1971;47:373–376.
142. Reid R, Laverty CR, Coppleson M, et al. Noncondylomatous cervical wart virus infection. Obstet Gynecol. 1980;55:476–483.
143. Walker PG, Colley NV, Grubb C, et al. Abnormalities of the uterine cervix in women with vulvar warts. Br J Venereol Dis. 1983;59:120–123.
144. Schwebke JR, Zajackowski ME. Effect of concurrent lower genital tract infections on cervical cancer screening. Genitourin Med. 1997;73:383–386.
145. Väyrynen M, Syrjänen H, Castrén O, et al. Colposcopy in women with papillomavirus lesions of the uterine cervix. Obstet Gynecol. 1985;65:409–415.
146. Roy M, Meisels A, Fortier M, et al. Vaginal condylomata: A human papillomavirus infection. Clin Obstet Gynecol. 1981;24:461–483.
147. Strand A, Wilander E, Zehbe I, et al. Vulvar papillomatosis, aceto-white lesions, and normal-looking vulvar mucosa evaluated by microscopy and human papillomavirus analysis. Gynecol Obstet Invest. 1995;40:265–270.
148. Gentile G, Formelli G, Pelusi G, et al. Is vestibular micropapillomatosis associated with human papillomavirus infection? Eur J Gynaecol Oncol. 1997;18:523–525.
149. Gross G, Ikenberg H, Gissmann L, et al. Papillomavirus infection of the anogenital region: Correlation between histology, clinical picture, and virus type. Proposal of a new nomenclature. J Invest Dermatol. 1985;85:147–152.
150. Reid R, Greenberg M, Jenson AB, et al. Sexually transmitted papillomaviral infections: I. The anatomic distribution and pathologic grade of neoplastic lesions associated with different viral types. Am J Obstet Gynecol. 1987;156:212–222.
151. Jonsson M, Karlsson R, Evander M, et al. Acetowhitening of the cervix and vulva as a predictor of subclinical human papillomavirus infection: Sensitivity and specificity in a population-based study. Obstet Gynecol. 1997;90:744–747.
152. Prayson RA, Stoler MH, Hart WR. Vulvar vestibulitis: A histopathologic study of 36 cases, including human papillomavirus in situ hybridization analysis. Am J Surg Pathol. 1995;19:154–160.
153. Bornstein J, Shapiro S, Rahat M, et al. Polymerase chain reaction search for viral etiology of vulvar vestibulitis syndrome. Am J Obstet Gynecol. 1996;175:139–144.
154. Lundqvist EN, Hofer PA, Olofsson JI, et al. Is vulvar vestibulitis an inflammatory condition? A comparison of histological findings in affected and healthy women. Acta Derm Venereol. 1997;77:319–322.
155. Friedrich EG. The vulvar vestibule. J Reprod Med. 1983;28:773–777.
156. McKay M, Frankman O, Horowitz BJ, et al. Vulvar vestibulitis and vestibular papillomatosis: Report of the ISSVD Committee on vulvodynia. J Reprod Med. 1991;36:413–415.
157. White G, Jantos M, Glazer H. Establishing the diagnosis of vulvar vestibulitis. J Reprod Med. 1997;42:157–160.
158. Rosemberg SK, Jacobs H, Fuller T. Some guidelines in the treatment of urethral condylomata with carbon dioxide laser. J Urol. 1982;127:906–908.
159. Barrasso R, De Brux J, Croissant O, et al. High prevalence of papillomavirus-associated penile intraepithelial neoplasia in sexual partners of women with cervical intraepithelial neoplasia. N Engl J Med. 1987;317:916–923.
160. Campion MJ. Clinical manifestations and natural history of genital human papillomavirus infection. Obstet Gynecol Clin North Am. 1987;14:363–388.
161. Demeter LM, Stoler MH, Bonnez W, et al. Penile intraepithelial neoplasia: Clinical presentation and an analysis of the physical state of human papillomavirus DNA. J Infect Dis. 1993;168:38–46.
162. Löwhagen G-B, Bolmstedt A, Ryd W, et al. The prevalence of "high-risk" HPV types in penile condyloma-like lesions: Correlation between HPV type and morphology. Genitourin Med. 1993;69:87–90.
163. Reitano M. Counseling patients with genital warts. Am J Med. 1997;102 (suppl 4S):38–43.
164. Schonfeld A, Nitke S, Schattner A, et al. Intramuscular human interferon-β injections in treatment of condylomata acuminata. Lancet. 1984;1:1038–1042.
165. Reichman RC, Oakes D, Bonnez W, et al. Treatment of condyloma acuminatum with three different alpha interferon preparations administered parenterally: A double-blind, placebo-controlled trial. J Infect Dis. 1990;162:1270–1276.
166. Condylomata International Collaborative Study Group. Recurrent condylomata acuminata treated with recombinant interferon alfa-2a: A multicenter double-blind placebo-controlled clinical trial. J Am Med Assoc. 1991;265:2684–2687.
167. Schiffman MH. Latest HPV findings: Some clinical implications. Contemp OB/GYN 1993;38:27–40.
168. Becker FT, Walder HJ, Larson DM. Giant condylomata acuminata: Buschke-Lowenstein tumor. Arch Dermatol. 1969;100:184–186.
169. Kibrite A, Zeitouni NC, Cloutier R. Aggressive giant condyloma acuminatum associated with oncogenic human papilloma virus: A case report. Can J Surg. 1997;40:143–145.
170. Anderson MC, Brown CL, Buckley CH, et al. Current views on cervical intraepithelial neoplasia. J Clin Pathol. 1991;44:969–978.
171. Okagaki T. Impact of human papillomavirus research on the histopathologic concepts of genital neoplasms. Curr Top Pathol. 1992;85:273–307.

172. Wade TR, Kopf AW, Ackerman AB. Bowenoid papulosis of the penis. Cancer. 1978;42:1890–1903.
173. De Villez RL, Stevens CS. Bowenoid papules of the genitalia: A case progressing to Bowen's disease. J Am Acad Dermatol. 1980;3:149–152.
174. Ikenberg H, Gissmann L, Gross G, et al. Human papillomavirus type 16-related DNA in genital Bowen's disease and in bowenoid papulosis. Int J Cancer. 1983;32:563–565.
175. Östör AG. Natural history of cervical intraepithelial neoplasia: A critical review. Int J Gynecol Pathol. 1993;12:186–192.
176. Schlappner OLA, Schaffer EA. Anorectal condylomata acuminata: A missed part of the condyloma spectrum. Can Med Assoc J. 1978;118:172–173.
177. Prassad ML, Abcarian H. Malignant potential of perianal condyloma acuminatum. Dis Colon Rectum. 1980;23:191–197.
178. Metcalf AM, Dean T. Risk of dysplasia in anal condyloma. Surgery. 1995;118:724–726.
179. Koblin BA, Hessol NA, Zauber AG, et al. Increased incidence of cancer among homosexual men, New York City and San Francisco, 1978–1990. Am J Epidemiol. 1996;144:916–923.
180. Daling JR, Weiss NS, Hislop TG, et al. Sexual practices, sexually transmitted diseases, and the incidence of anal cancer. N Engl J Med. 1987;317:973–977.
181. Osborne NG, Adelson MD. Herpes simplex and human papillomavirus genital infections: Controversies around obstetric management. Clin Obstet Gynecol. 1990;33:801–811.
182. Watts DH, Koutsky LA, Holmes KK, et al. Low risk of perinatal transmission of human papillomavirus: Results from a prospective cohort study. Am J Obstet Gynecol. 1998;178:365–373.
183. Armstrong DK, Handley JM. Anogenital warts in prepubertal children: Pathogenesis, HPV typing and management. Int J STD AIDS. 1997;8:78–81.
184. Hammerschlag MR. Sexually transmitted diseases in sexually abused children: Medical and legal implications. Sex Transm Dis. 1998;74:167–174.
185. Bauman NM, Smith RJ. Recurrent respiratory papillomatosis. Pediatr Clin North Am. 1996;43:1385–1401.
186. Gabbott M, Cossart YE, Kan A, et al. Human papillomavirus and host variables as predictors of clinical course in patients with juvenile-onset recurrent respiratory papillomatosis. J Clin Microbiol. 1997;35:3098–3103.
187. Somers GR, Tabrizi SN, Borg AJ, et al. Juvenile laryngeal papillomatosis in a pediatric population: A clinicopathologic study. Pediatr Pathol Lab Med. 1997;17:53–64.
188. Lindeberg H, Elbrond O. Malignant tumours in patients with a history of multiple laryngeal papillomas: The significance of irradiation. Clin Otolaryngol. 1991;16:149–151.
189. Cohen PR, Hebert AA, Adler-Storthz K. Focal epithelial hyperplasia: Heck disease. Pediatr Dermatol. 1993;10:245–251.
190. Praetorius F. HPV-associated diseases of oral mucosa. Clin Dermatol. 1997;15:399–413.
191. Adler-Storthz K, Ficarra G, Woods KV, et al. Prevalence of Epstein-Barr virus and human papillomavirus in oral mucosa of HIV-infected patients. J Oral Pathol Med. 1992;21:164–170.
192. Tabrizi SN, McCurrach FE, Drewe RH, et al. Human papillomavirus in corneal and conjunctival carcinoma. Aust N Z J Ophthalmol. 1997;25:211–215.
193. Karcioglu ZA, Issa TM. Human papilloma virus in neoplastic and non-neoplastic conditions of the external eye. Br J Ophthalmol. 1997;81:595–598.
194. Elston DM, Parker LU, Tuthill RJ. Epidermoid cyst of the scalp containing human papillomavirus. J Cutan Pathol. 1993;20:184–186.
195. Phelps WC, Alexander KA. Antiviral therapy for human papillomaviruses: Rationale and prospects. Ann Intern Med. 1995;123:368–382.
196. Tyring SK, Arany I, Stanley MA, et al. A randomized controlled, molecular study of condylomata acuminata clearance during treatment with imiquimod. J Infect Dis. 1998;178:551–555.
197. Bunney MH, Nolan MW, William DA. An assessment of methods of treating viral warts by comparative treatment trials based on a standard design. Br J Dermatol. 1976;94:667–669.
198. Berth-Jones J, Hutchinson PE. Modern treatment of warts: Cure rates at 3 and 6 months. Br J Dermatol. 1992;127:262–265.
199. Stern P, Levine N. Controlled localized heat therapy in cutaneous warts. Arch Dermatol. 1992;128:945–948.
200. Bunney MH. Viral Warts: Their Biology and Treatment, 1st ed. Oxford: Oxford University Press; 1982.
201. Rees RB. The treatment of warts. Clin Dermatol. 1985;3:179–184.
202. Ling MR. Therapy of genital human papillomavirus infection: Part II. Methods of treatment. Int J Dermatol. 1992;31:769–776.
203. Stone KM. Human papillomavirus infection and genital warts: Update on epidemiology and treatment. Clin Infect Dis. 1995;20(suppl 1):S91–S97.
204. Mayeaux EJ Jr, Harper MB, Barksdale W, Pope JB. Noncervical human papillomavirus genital infections. Am Fam Physician. 1995;53:19.
205. Reid R. The management of genital condylomas, intraepithelial neoplasia, and vulvodynia. Obstet Gynecol Clin North Am. 1996;23:917–991.
206. Baker GE, Tyring SK. Therapeutic approaches to papillomavirus infections. Dermatol Clin. 1997;15:331–340.
207. 1998 Guidelines for the treatment of sexually transmitted diseases. MMWR Morb Mortal Wkly Rep. 1998;47(RR-1):1–116.
207a. Beutner KR, Reitano MV, Richwald GA, Wiley DJ. External genital warts—Report of the American Medical Association Consensus Conference. Clin Inf Dis. 1998;27:796–806.
208. Krebs H-B, Helmkamp BF. Does the treatment of genital condylomata in men decrease the treatment failure rate of cervical dysplasia in the female sexual partner? Obstet Gynecol. 1990;76:660–666.
209. Sigurgeirsson B, Lindelöf B, Eklund G. Condylomata acuminata and risk of cancer: An epidemiological study. BMJ. 1991;303:341–344.
210. Godley MJ, Bradbeer CS, Gellan M, Thin RNT. Cryotherapy compared with trichloracetic acid in treating genital warts. Genitourin Med. 1987;63:390–392.
211. Bashi SA. Cryotherapy versus podophyllin in the treatment of genital warts. Int J Dermatol. 1985;24:535–536.
212. Stone KM, Becker TM, Hadgu A, et al. Treatment of external genital warts: A randomised clinical trial comparing podophyllin, cryotherapy, and electrodessication. Genitourin Med. 1990;66:16–19.
213. Simmons PD, Langlet F, Thin RNT. Cryotherapy versus electrocautery in the treatment of genital warts. Br J Vener Dis. 1981;57:273–274.
214. Miller RA. Podophyllin. Int J Dermatol. 1985;24:491–498.
215. Simmons PD. Podophyllin 10% and 25% in the treatment of anogenital warts: A comparative double-blind study. Br J Vener Dis. 1981;57:208–209.
216. Beutner KR. Podophyllotoxin in the treatment of genital human papillomavirus infection: A review. Semin Dermatol. 1987;6:10–18.
217. Edwards A, Atma-Ram A, Thin RN. Podophyllotoxin 0.5% v podophyllin 20% to treat penile warts. Genitourin Med. 1988;64:263–265.
218. Beutner KR, Friedman-Kien AE, Artman NN, et al. Patient-applied podofilox for treatment of genital warts. Lancet. 1989;1:831–834.
219. Kirby P, Dunne A, King DH, et al. Double-blind randomized clinical trial of self-administered podofilox solution versus vehicle in the treatment of genital warts. Am J Med. 1990;88:465–469.
220. Greenberg MD, Rutledge LH, Reid R, et al. A double-blind, randomized trial of 0.5% podofilox and placebo for the treatment of genital warts in women. Obstet Gynecol. 1991;77:735–739.
221. Bonnez W, Elswick RK Jr, Bailey-Farchione A, et al. Efficacy and safety of 0.5% podofilox solution in the treatment and suppression of anogenital warts. Am J Med. 1994;96:420–425.
222. Tyring S, Edwards L, Cherry LK, et al. Safety and efficacy of 0.5-percent podofilox gel in the treatment of anogenital warts. Arch Dermatol. 1998;134:33–38.
223. de Benedictis JT, Marmar JL, Praiss DE. Intraurethral condylomata acuminata: Management and a review of the literature. J Urol. 1977;118:767–769.
224. Dretler SP, Klein LA. The eradication of intraurethral condyloma acuminata with 5 per cent 5-fluorouracil cream. J Urol. 1975;113:195–198.
225. Wallin J. 5-Fluorouracil in the treatment of penile and urethral condylomata acuminata. Br J Vener Dis. 1977;53:240–243.
226. Krebs H-B. Prophylactic topical 5-fluorouracil following treatment of human papillomavirus-associated lesions of the vulva and vagina. Obstet Gynecol. 1986;68:837–841.
227. Swinehart JM, Sperling M, Phillips S, et al. Intralesional fluorouracil/epinephrine injectable gel for treatment of condylomata acuminata: A phase 3 clinical study. Arch Dermatol. 1997;133:67–73.
228. Richart RM, Kaufman RM, Woodruff JD. Advances in managing condylomas. Contemp OB/GYN 1982;20:164–171, 175, 177, 180, 182, 187, 188, 190–192, 194.
229. Abdullah AN, Walzman M, Wade A. Treatment of external genital warts comparing cryotherapy (liquid nitrogen) and trichloracetic acid. Sex Transm Dis. 1993;20:344–345.
230. Gabriel G, Thin RNT. Treatment of anogenital warts: Comparison to trichloracetic acid and podophyllin versus podophyllin alone. Br J Vener Dis. 1983;59:124–126.
231. Boothby RA, Carlson JA, Rubin M, et al. Single application treatment of human papillomavirus infection of the cervix and vagina with trichloracetic acid: A randomized trial. Obstet Gynecol. 1990;76:278–280.
232. Jensen SL. Comparison of podophyllin application with simple surgical excision in clearance and recurrence of perianal condylomata acuminata. Lancet. 1985;2:1146–1148.
233. Duus BR, Philipsen T, Christensen JD, et al. Refractory condylomata acuminata: A controlled clinical trial of carbon dioxide laser versus conventional surgical treatment. Genitourin Med. 1985;61:59–61.
234. McMillan A, Scott GR. Outpatient treatment of perianal warts by scissor excision. Genitourin Med. 1987;63:114–115.
235. Bonnez W, Oakes D, Choi A, et al. Therapeutic efficacy and complications of excisional biopsy of condyloma acuminatum. Sex Transm Dis. 1996;23:273–276.
236. Baggish MS. Improved laser techniques for the elimination of genital and extragenital warts. Am J Obstet Gynecol. 1985;153:545–550.
237. Reid R. Physical and surgical principles governing expertise with the carbon dioxide laser. Obstet Gynecol Clin North Am. 1987;14:513–535.
238. Bar-Am A, Shilon M, Peyser MR, et al. Treatment of male genital condylomatous lesions by carbon dioxide laser after failure of previous nonlaser methods. J Am Acad Dermatol. 1991;24:87–89.
239. Petersen CS, Bjerring P, Larsen J, et al. Systemic interferon alpha-2b increases the cure rate in laser treated patients with multiple persistent genital warts: A placebo-controlled study. Genitourin Med. 1991;67:99–102.
240. Condylomata International Collaborative Study Group. Randomized placebo-controlled double-blind combined therapy with laser surgery and systemic interferon-alpha 2a in the treatment of anogenital condylomata acuminatum. J Infect Dis. 1993;167:824–829.
241. Beck DE, Jaso RG, Zajac RA. Surgical management of anal condylomata in the HIV-positive patient. Dis Colon Rectum. 1990;33:180–183.
242. Miles AJG, Mellor CH, Gazzard B, et al. Surgical management of anorectal disease in HIV-positive homosexuals. Br J Surg. 1990;77:869–871.
243. Lord RVN. Anorectal surgery in patients infected with human immunodeficiency virus: Factors associated with delayed wound healing. Ann Surg. 1997;226:92–99.

244. Abcarian H, Sharon N. Long-term effectiveness of the immunotherapy of anal condyloma acuminatum. Dis Colon Rectum. 1982;25:648–651.
245. Malison MD, Morris R, Jones LW. Autogenous vaccine therapy for condyloma acuminatum: A double-blind controlled study. Br J Vener Dis. 1982;58:62–65.
246. Powell LC Jr. Condyloma acuminatum: Recent advances in development, carcinogenesis, and treatment. Clin Obstet Gynecol. 1978;21:1061–1079.
247. Dunagin WG, Millikan LE. Dinitrochlorobenzene immunotherapy for verrucae resistant to standard treatment modalities. J Am Acad Dermatol. 1982;6:40–45.
248. Sanders BB, Smith KW. Dinitrochlorobenzene immunotherapy of human warts. Cutis. 1981;27:389–392.
249. Rockley PF, Tyring SK. Interferons alpha, beta and gamma therapy of anogenital human papillomavirus infections. Pharmacol Ther. 1995;65:265–287.
250. Eron LJ, Judson F, Tucker S, et al. Interferon therapy for condylomata acuminata. N Engl J Med. 1986;315:1059–1064.
251. Friedman-Kien A, Eron LJ, Conant M, et al. Natural interferon alfa for treatment of condylomata acuminata. J Am Med Assoc. 1988;259:533–538.
252. Vance JC, Bart BJ, Hansen RC, et al. Intralesional recombinant alpha-2 interferon for the treatment of patients with condyloma acuminatum or verruca plantaris. Arch Dermatol. 1986;122:272–277.
253. Douglas JM, Rogers M, Judson FN. The effect of asymptomatic infection with HTLV-III on the response of anogenital warts in intralesional treatment with recombinant α_2 interferon. J Infect Dis. 1986;154:331–334.
254. Douglas JM Jr, Eron LJ, Judson FN, et al. A randomized trial of combination therapy with intralesional interferon α_{2b} and podophyllin versus podophyllin alone for the therapy of anogenital warts. J Infect Dis. 1990;162:52–59.
255. Condylomata International Collaborative Study Group. A comparison of interferon alfa-2a and podophyllin in the treatment of primary condylomata acuminata. Genitourin Med. 1991;67:394–399.
256. Potkul RK, Lancaster WD, Kurman RJ, et al. Vulvar condylomas and squamous vestibular micropapilloma: Differences in appearance and response to treatment. J Reprod Med. 1990;35:1019–1022.
257. Fleshner PR, Freilich MI. Adjuvant interferon for anal condyloma: A prospective, randomized trial. Dis Colon Rectum. 1994;37:1255–1299.
258. Handley JM, Maw RD, Horner T, et al. A placebo controlled observer blind immunocytochemical and histologic study of epithelium adjacent to anogenital warts in patients treated with systemic interferon alpha in combination with cryotherapy or cryotherapy alone. Genitourin Med. 1992;68:100–105.
259. Bonnez W, Oakes D, Bailey-Farchione A, et al. A randomized, double-blind trial of parenteral low dose versus high dose interferon-β in combination with cryotherapy for treatment of condyloma acuminatum. Antiviral Res. 1997;35:41–52.
260. Nieminen P, Aho M, Lehtinen M, et al. Treatment of genital HPV infection with carbon dioxide laser and systemic interferon alpha-2b. Sex Transm Dis. 1994;21:65–69.
261. Slade HB, Owens ML, Tomai MA, et al. Imiquimod 5% cream (Aldara™). Exp Opin Invest Drugs. 1998;7:437–449.
262. Beutner KR, Spruance SL, Hougham AJ, et al. Treatment of genital warts with an immune-response modifier (imiquimod). J Am Acad Dermatol. 1998;38:230–239.
263. Edwards L, Ferenczy A, Eron L, et al. Self-administered topical 5-percent imiquimod cream for external anogenital warts. Arch Dermatol. 1998;134:25–30.
264. Beutner KR, Tyring SK, Trofatter KF Jr, et al. Imiquimod, a patient-applied immune-response modifier for treatment of external genital warts. Antimicrob Agents Chemother. 1998;42:789–794.
265. Strauss MJ, Khanna V, Koenig JD, et al. The cost of treating genital warts. Int J Dermatol. 1996;35:340–348.
266. Ng N, Vuignier BI, Hart LL. Fluorouracil in condyloma acuminatum. Drug Intell Clin Pharm. 1987;21:175–176.
267. Sand PK, Shen W, Bowen LW, et al. Cryotherapy for the treatment of proximal urethral condyloma acuminatum. J Urol. 1987;137:874–876.
268. Levine LA, Elterman L, Rukstalis DB. Treatment of subclinical intraurethral human papilloma virus infection with interferon alfa-2b. Urology. 1996;47:553–557.
269. Dodi G, Infantino A, Moretti R, et al. Cryotherapy of anorectal warts and condylomata. Cryosurgery. 1982;19:287–288.
270. Bullingham RP, Lewis RG. Laser versus electrical cautery in the treatment of condylomata acuminata of the anus. Surg Gynecol Obstet. 1982;155:865–867.
271. Ferenczy A. Treating genital condyloma during pregnancy with the carbon dioxide laser. Am J Obstet Gynecol. 1984;148:9–12.
272. Wertheimer A. Indirect colposcopy and laser vaporization in the management of vaginal condylomata. J Reprod Med. 1986;31:39–42.
273. Matsunaga J, Bergman A, Bhatia NN. Genital condylomata acuminata in pregnancy: Effectiveness, safety and pregnancy outcome following cryotherapy. Br J Obstet Gynaecol. 1987;94:168–172.
274. McMillan A, Bishop PE. Clinical course of anogenital warts in men infected with human immunodeficiency virus. Genitourin Med. 1989;65:225–228.
275. von Krogh G, Wikström A, Syrjänen K, et al. Anal and penile condylomas in HIV-negative and HIV-positive men: Clinical, histological and virological characteristics correlated to therapeutic outcome. Acta Derm Venereol (Stockh). 1995;75:470–474.
276. Majewski S, Skopinska M, Bollag W, et al. Combination of isotretinoin and calcitriol for precancerous and cancerous skin lesions. Lancet. 1994;344:1510–1511.
277. Abramson AL, Shikowitz MJ, Mullooly VM, et al. Clinical effects of photodynamic therapy on recurrent laryngeal papillomas. Arch Otolaryngol Head Neck Surg. 1992;118:25–29.
278. Healy GB, Gelber RD, Trowbridge AL, et al. Treatment of recurrent respiratory papillomatosis with human leukocyte interferon. N Engl J Med. 1988;319:401–407.
279. Leventhal BG, Kashima HK, Mounts P, et al. Long-term response of recurrent respiratory papillomatosis to treatment with lymphoblastoid interferon alfa-n1. N Engl J Med. 1991;325:613–617.
280. Snoeck R, van Ranst M, Andrei G, et al. Treatment of anogenital papillomavirus infections with an acyclic nucleoside phosphonate analogue. N Engl J Med. 1995;333:943–944.
281. Wright VC, ed. Contemporary Colposcopy. Obstetrics and Gynecology Clinics, v. 20. Philadelphia: WB Saunders; 1993.
282. Sedlacek TV, Cunnane M, Carpiniello V. Colposcopy in the diagnosis of penile condyloma. Am J Obstet Gynecol. 1986;154:494–496.
283. Krebs H-B, Schneider V. Human papillomavirus-associated lesions of the penis: Colposcopy, cytology, and histology. Obstet Gynecol. 1987;70:299–304.
284. Singer A, Campion MJ, Clarkson PK, et al. Recognition of subclinical human papillomavirus infection of the vulva. J Reprod Med. 1986;31:985–986.
285. Panici PB, Scambia G, Perrone L, et al. Oral condyloma lesions in patients with extensive genital human papillomavirus infection. Am J Obstet Gynecol. 1992;167:451–458.
286. McMillan A. Sigmoidoscopy: A necessary procedure in the routine investigation of homosexual men? Genitourin Med. 1987;63:44–46.
287. Parker BJ, Cossart YE, Thompson CH, et al. The clinical management and laboratory assessment of anal warts. Med J Aust. 1987;147:59–63.
288. Sidawy MK. Cytology in gynecological disorders. Curr Top Pathol. 1992;85:233–272.
289. Eddy DM. Screening for cervical cancer. Ann Intern Med. 1990;113:214–226.
290. Koss LG. Cervical (Pap) smear. Cancer. 1993;71:1406–1412.
291. Purola E, Savia E. Cytology of gynecologic condyloma acuminatum. Acta Cytol. 1977;21:26–31.
292. Palefsky JM, Holly EA, Hogeboom CJ, et al. Anal cytology as a screening tool for anal squamous intraepithelial lesions. J Acquir Immun Defic Syndr Hum Retrovir. 1997;14:415–422.
292a. Walsh JM. Cervical cancer: Developments in screening and evaluation of the abnormal Pap smear. West J Med. 1998;169:304–310.
292b. Spitzer M. Cervical screening adjuncts: Recent advances. Am J Obstet Gynecol. 1998;179:544–556.
293. Lörincz AT. Molecular methods for the detection of human papillomavirus infection. Obstet Gynecol Clin North Am. 1996;23:707–730.
294. Gravitt PE, Manos MM. Polymerase chain reaction-based methods for the detection of human papillomavirus DNA. In: Muñoz N, Bosch FX, Shah KV, et al. eds. The Epidemiology of Cervical Cancer and Human Papillomavirus. IARC Scientific Publications No. 119. Lyon, France: International Agency for Research on Cancer, 1992:121–133.
295. van den Brule AJC, Snijders PJF, Meijer CJLM, et al. PCR-based detection of genital HPV genotypes: An update and future perspectives. Papillomavirus Rep. 1993;4:95–99.
296. Shah KV, Solomon L, Daniel R, et al. Comparison of PCR and Hybrid Capture methods for detection of human papillomavirus in injection drug-using women at high risk of human immunodeficiency virus infection. J Clin Microbiol. 1997;35:517–519.
297. Cope JU, Hildesheim A, Schiffman MH, et al. Comparison of the Hybrid Capture tube test and PCR for detection of human papillomavirus DNA in cervical specimens. J Clin Microbiol. 1997;35:2262–2265.
298. Ferris DG, Wright TCJ, Litaker MS, et al. Triage of women with ASCUS and LSIL on Pap smear reports: Management by repeat Pap smear, HPV DNA testing, or colposcopy? J Fam Pract 1998;46:125–134.
299. Cox JT. Clinical role of HPV testing. Obstet Gynecol Clin North Am. 1996;23:811–851.
300. Bunney MH. Prevention of plantar warts by the use of protective footwear in swimming pool. Community Med. 1972;127:127–129.
301. Evans BA, Kell PD, Bond RA, et al. Heterosexual relationships and condom-use in the spread of sexually transmitted diseases to women. Genitourin Med. 1995;71:291–294.
302. Schiffman MH, Brinton LA. The epidemiology of cervical carcinogenesis. Cancer. 1995;76:1888–1901.
303. Update January 1992: The American Cancer Society guidelines for cancer-related check-up. CA, Cancer J Clin 1992;42:44–45.
304. The Bethesda system for reporting cervical/vaginal cytologic diagnoses. Acta Cytol. 1993;37:115–124.
305. Kurman RJ, Henson DE, Herbst AL, et al., for the National Cancer Institute Workshop. Interim guidelines for management of abnormal cervical cytology. J Am Med Assoc. 1994;271:1866–1869.
305a. Kosko JR, Derkay CS. Role of cesarean section in prevention of recurrent respiratory papillomatosis—is there one? Int J Pediatr Otorhinolaryngol. 1996;35:31–38.
306. Maiman M. Management of cervical neoplasia in human immunodeficiency virus-infected women. Monogr Natl Cancer Inst. 1998;23:43–49.
307. Hines JF, Ghim S-J, Schlegel R, et al. Prospects for a vaccine against human papillomavirus. Obstet Gynecol. 1995;86:860–866.
308. Frazer IH. The role of vaccines in the control of STDs: HPV vaccines. Genitourin Med. 1996;72:398–403.
309. Reichman RC, Bonnez W, O'Brien D, et al. A phase I study of recombinant virus like particle vaccine against human papillomavirus type 11 in healthy adult volunteers. 38th Interscience Conference on Antimicrobial Agents and Chemotherapy, San Diego. Washington, DC: American Society for Microbiology; 1998.

Chapter 134

JC, BK, and Other Polyomaviruses; Progressive Multifocal Leukoencephalopathy

LISA M. DEMETER

JC virus (JCV) and BK virus (BKV) are human polyomaviruses. Infections with these viruses appear to be widespread but asymptomatic in the majority of patients. JCV or BKV infection is acquired during childhood and persists in the kidney. JCV is the cause of progressive multifocal leukoencephalopathy (PML), a rare demyelinating disease of immunosuppressed patients. Asymptomatic shedding of JCV and BKV can be detected in the urine of pregnant women and of immunocompromised patients such as organ transplant recipients. Polyomavirus viruria has been associated with ureteral stenosis in renal transplant patients and with hemorrhagic cystitis in bone marrow transplant patients. This chapter summarizes characteristics of JCV and BKV infections and the associated clinical manifestations, including PML.

DESCRIPTION OF THE PATHOGENS

Polyomaviruses are members of the Papovaviridae family, which are small, nonenveloped viruses with a covalently closed, circular, doubled-stranded DNA genome. The Papovaviridae capsid has icosahedral symmetry and consists of 72 capsomeres.[1] The Papovaviridae family is divided into the polyomavirus and papillomavirus genera. Polyomaviruses are distinguished from papillomaviruses by a smaller virion size (45 versus 55 nm diameter) and a different genome size and organization.[1] Polyomaviruses are ubiquitous in nature and can be isolated from a number of different species, including humans (JCV, BKV), monkeys (simian virus 40 [SV40]), and mice (mouse polyomavirus, K virus).[1] Infection with polyomaviruses is relatively species-specific, and natural infection with a given polyomavirus occurs in only one or a few related species.

JCV and BKV were first isolated in 1971. (J.C. and B.K. are the initials of the patients from whom the initial virus isolates were obtained.) JCV was first isolated from brain tissue obtained from a patient with PML.[2] BKV was initially isolated from urine specimens obtained from a renal transplant patient who developed ureteral stenosis postoperatively.[3] BKV and JCV share 75% homology at the level of nucleotide sequence, and each is 70% homologous with SV40.[4, 5] JCV and BKV virions contain both species-specific and cross-reacting epitopes.[1, 6] Polyomaviruses contain a genus-specific epitope that appears after denaturation of the virus capsid.[1, 6] Intact JCV and BKV virions are not cross-reactive serologically,[7] and serologic tests for JCV and BKV antibodies in human sera are able to distinguish the two.[1] Viruses that are antigenically almost indistinguishable from SV40 (SV40-PML viruses) have been isolated from small numbers of patients with PML and may represent a third serologic type of human polyomavirus.[7–11]

The genomes of JCV and BKV are approximately 5000 base pairs long and can be divided into three regions: (1) the early region, which encodes the large and small T antigens that function in transformation, viral replication, and regulation of gene expression; (2) the late region, which codes for the three viral capsid proteins VP1, VP2, and VP3; and (3) a noncoding regulatory region that contains the replication origin, T antigen-binding sites, and transcriptional regulatory elements.[4, 5, 12] Transcription of the early region and that of the late region occur from different strands of the DNA genome.[4, 5, 12] Sequence variants of human polyomaviruses have been described that exhibit significant heterogeneity in their regulatory regions. For example, variants of JCV or BKV may contain insertions, deletions, or duplications, or all three, in the regulatory region.[13–16] The functional significance of this marked variation is unknown, but it may play a role in the pathogenicity or tissue tropism of human polyomaviruses.

EPIDEMIOLOGY

Approximately 60 to 80% of adults in the United States and Europe have antibodies to JCV or BKV or both.[17–23] Antibodies are prevalent even in remote populations that have had no exposure to influenza or measles.[24] Comparison of the population distributions of JCV and BKV antibodies suggests that the two viruses circulate independently.[24] The seroprevalence of both JCV and BKV antibodies increases sharply during childhood.[17–21, 23, 25] Although the time of acquisition of antibodies to JCV and to BKV has not been examined comparatively in a single study, it appears that BKV infection is acquired in the majority of children at an earlier age (3 to 4 years) than is JCV infection (10 to 14 years).[17–20, 25] There is no evidence that an animal reservoir exists for JCV or BKV.[26]

Asymptomatic viruria with JCV or BKV occurs primarily in immunosuppressed patients and in pregnant women (see later on). The rising incidence of human immunodeficiency virus (HIV) infection has significantly altered the epidemiology of PML. In the pre-HIV era, PML was seen primarily in older patients with underlying hematologic malignancies.[27, 28] PML was also sometimes seen in patients with other causes for depression of cell-mediated immunity, such as steroid use.[29] Rarely, patients have been described who developed PML in the absence of any identifiable immunodeficiency.[30–32] Reported deaths due to PML significantly increased with the rise in cases of acquired immunodeficiency syndrome (AIDS), from 1.5/10 million persons in 1974 to 6.1/10 million persons in 1987.[33] It is estimated that over half of the deaths due to PML are associated with HIV infection and that approximately 1 to 4% of patients with HIV infection will develop PML.[33–35] PML, which is extremely rare in children with other immunodeficiencies, has been reported in some children with HIV infection.[36–38] PML has also been described as the initial manifestation of idiopathic $CD4^+$ lymphopenia.[39]

PATHOGENESIS

Little is known about transmission of BKV and JCV or about events during primary infection. It is thought that transmission of JCV requires sustained close contact. Transmission of JCV to children can occur frequently from either parent, although approximately half of infections occur outside the family.[40, 41] The possibility of perinatal transmission of BKV in humans has been raised by studies that identified BKV immunoglobulin M (IgM) in newborns.[23, 42] However, other studies have shown no evidence for viruria or acquisition of IgM in infants born to mothers with reactivation of BKV or JCV infection.[43–45] Perinatal transmission of polyomavirus infection can occur in mice if the mother develops a primary infection during pregnancy.[46, 47] At present there is no definitive evidence that perinatal transmission of polyomavirus infection occurs in the setting of maternal JCV or BKV viruria. The question of whether polyomavirus transmission to the fetus can occur during primary maternal infection is still unresolved.

It is hypothesized that viremia during primary infection results in seeding of the kidney,[48] where a clinically latent infection is established. JCV and BKV sequences can be detected in peripheral blood mononuclear cells obtained from patients with leukemia, HIV infection, or PML.[49] In addition, JCV DNA and capsid antigen can be demonstrated in mononuclear cells in bone marrow, central nervous system, and peripheral blood.[50] In one study, JCV DNA was detected more frequently in peripheral blood mononuclear cells from HIV-infected patients without PML than in those from healthy blood donors.[51] It is postulated that JCV infection of mononuclear cells may be important in the transport of virus to the central nervous system, although it does not appear that production of infectious JCV occurs in peripheral blood.[51]

The neuropathologic findings of PML are probably a result of direct infection of the oligodendrocytes with JCV, leading to decreased myelin production and demyelination. Electron microscopy and in situ hybridization techniques have been used to demonstrate the presence of polyomavirus in oligodendrocyte nuclei.[52–54] This hypothesis is further supported by the observation that transgenic mice with genomes containing the JCV early region develop a demyelinating disease related to the expression of JCV T antigens in oligodendrocytes.[55, 56] In addition, macaques that spontaneously develop a PML-like illness have evidence of SV40 infection in the white matter lesions.[57, 58] Tropism of JCV for oligodendrocytes may be explained by an effect of cell-specific transcription factors on viral gene expression.[59] It is not known whether PML results from reactivation of latent JCV infection in the central nervous system established during primary infection, reactivation of latent infection in the kidney with subsequent viremia and seeding of the central nervous system, or primary infection in an immunocompromised host. JCV DNA can be detected by polymerase chain reaction (PCR) assay in brain tissue of patients with and without PML, suggesting that latent JCV infection does exist in the central nervous system.[60] The factors that determine whether PML develops in neural tissue infected with JCV are unknown.

Support for the hypothesis that a clinically latent viral infection exists in renal tissue is provided by the observation that approximately 30 to 50% of normal persons have detectable BKV or JCV sequences in renal tissue obtained at surgery or autopsy.[61–63] JCV DNA can also be detected in the kidneys of patients with PML,[64] although the frequency with which JCV exists in renal tissue in patients with PML is unknown. During periods of immunosuppression, such as after organ transplantation, it is postulated that viral infection is reactivated in the kidney, leading to viruria. Patients excrete the same JCV genotype in the urine for prolonged periods of time, suggesting that renal shedding of JCV reflects persistent infection rather than repeated reinfections.[65] In the majority of patients, reactivation of JCV or BKV infection appears to be subclinical. Clinical manifestations reported to be associated with polyomavirus excretion, such as ureteral stenosis and hemorrhagic cystitis (see later on), are thought to result from the direct effects of viral replication. Cofactors that are important in the genesis of these clinical syndromes presumably exist, because specific syndromes occur only in a subset of patients at risk for reactivation of polyomavirus infections.

CLINICAL MANIFESTATIONS

Primary Infection

The majority of primary infections with BKV appear to be asymptomatic or minimally symptomatic.[21, 66] A study of children in whom BKV seroconversion was demonstrated identified associated mild upper respiratory tract symptoms in approximately one third.[21] Another study of children with upper respiratory tract illnesses demonstrated BKV seroconversion in 8%, and BKV viruria and seroconversion were reported in one child with tonsillitis.[66, 67] In addition, case reports have implicated polyomavirus infection as a cause of acute cystitis in three children.[68–71]

Progressive Multifocal Leukoencephalopathy

PML was first identified as a separate clinical entity by Åström and coworkers[27] in 1958. Patients with PML characteristically present with rapidly progressive focal neurologic deficits without signs of increased intracranial pressure.[27, 28, 72] Neurologic abnormalities most commonly seen at the time of presentation include hemiparesis, visual field deficits, and cognitive impairment (Table 134–1).[27–34, 72–76] Aphasia, ataxia, or cranial nerve deficits may also be noted. Late in the course of PML, patients can develop severe neurologic deficits, including cortical blindness, quadriparesis, profound dementia, and coma. The neurologic abnormalities are usually localized to cerebral white matter, although cerebellar and brain stem involvement can occur also. Spinal cord involvement is rare in PML. Patients most commonly undergo rapid deterioration, and death usually occurs within 6 months of the diagnosis.[27, 28, 34] However, there is a subset of patients who experience spontaneous fluctuations in the clinical course over a period of 2 to 3 years after the onset of symptoms and signs.[34, 75–78] The clinical presentation of PML in patients with HIV infection is similar to that in patients with other underlying immunodeficiencies.[34, 73, 74, 79] PML is an AIDS-defining disease according to the Centers for Disease Control and Prevention (CDC) surveillance case definition[80] and may be the initial presentation of HIV infection.[34, 73, 74, 79]

TABLE 134–1 Neurologic Presentation of Progressive Multifocal Leukoencephalopathy

Neurologic Manifestation	Frequency (% of Patients)
Aphasia	17
Ataxia	21
Cognitive disturbance	36
Cranial nerve deficits	13
Hemiparesis	42
Sensory deficits	9
Visual field deficits	32

Data from references 28, 34, and 72–76.

BK Virus and JC Virus Viruria

BKV and JCV viruria, detected by cytologic examination, culture, or electron microscopy, is rare in humans with intact immune function. However, PCR assay can detect viral sequences in the urine of patients without any evidence of immunocompromise. Shedding of JCV DNA appears to increase with age, with a significant increase in prevalence occurring during young adulthood.[40]

Pregnant Women

Asymptomatic JCV or BKV viruria can be detected by cytologic examination in approximately 3% of pregnant women.[81] Virus shedding occurs primarily during the third trimester of pregnancy[81, 82] and usually ceases in the immediate postpartum period.[81] The high seroprevalence of JCV and of BKV antibodies and the absence of seroconversion in the women studied suggest that polyomavirus excretion in pregnant women usually represents reactivation of previously acquired infection.[81] Both JCV and BKV shedding can occur, although JCV viruria is more common.[81]

Pregnant women appear to have more severe manifestations of infections in which cell-mediated immunity is important, although there is no consensus on the nature of the immune defects associated with pregnancy.[83] One study reported that monocytosis and lymphopenia were associated with reactivation of polyomavirus infection in pregnant women, which is consistent with the hypothesis that alterations in the immune system predispose these patients to polyomavirus reactivation.[82] An alternative hypothesis, based on studies of polyomavirus reactivation in mice, suggests that hormonal changes during pregnancy may lead to JCV and BKV reactivation.[46]

Renal Transplant Recipients

Urinary excretion of human polyomaviruses can be demonstrated by cytologic examination, culture, or electron microscopy in approximately 10 to 45% of patients after renal transplantation.[84–87] Serologic studies suggest that the majority of JCV and BKV infections in renal transplant recipients represent reactivation, although primary infection has also been documented.[84, 88] Both primary and reactivation infections are more common in patients who receive a kidney from a seropositive donor, suggesting that reactivation of latent virus in the donated tissue plays a role in viruria.[89] The majority of JCV and BKV infections occur within the first 3 months after transplantation, although infections occurring later than 2 years after transplantation have been reported.[88]

The majority of renal transplant recipients with JCV or BKV viruria have no symptoms attributable to polyomavirus infection. BKV viruria has been associated with localized ureteral ulceration and subsequent ureteral stenosis in a small number of renal transplant patients.[3, 84–88, 90] Nuclear inclusions and viral particles can be detected in epithelial cells lining the involved ureters.[3, 90] On the basis of these observations, ureteral stenosis associated with human polyomavirus infection is postulated to result from direct cytopathic effects of reactivated virus present in the epithelium of the donor ureter during periods of immunosuppression.[3, 90] The frequency with which postoperative ureteral stenosis in renal transplant recipients is associated with polyomavirus excretion is not known. Different studies have found conflicting results as to whether polyomavirus excretion after transplantation influences other clinical outcomes such as graft survival or risk of rejection.[84, 89]

Bone Marrow Transplant Recipients

BKV viruria occurs in approximately 50% of patients after bone marrow transplantation,[91–93] usually within the first 2 months after the procedure.[93] Published reports have described virus shedding only in patients who were seropositive before transplantation, suggesting that viruria is secondary to reactivation of latent infection.[92, 93] Late-onset prolonged hemorrhagic cystitis, which is thought to be unrelated to cyclophosphamide therapy, was present in 64% of patients with BKV viruria and was significantly more common in patients with BKV viruria than in those without detectable virus shedding.[92] BKV viruria frequently preceded the onset of clinical symptoms, suggesting that viral shedding was not a result of the cystitis.[91, 92] Excretion of JCV has been detected in small numbers of bone marrow transplant patients.[91–93] There has been no consistent association of JCV viruria with clinical manifestations in bone marrow transplant patients.

Other Patients

BKV viruria has been associated with tubulointerstitial nephritis in a child with hyper-IgM immunodeficiency[94] and with renal failure in a child with Hodgkin's disease and cartilage-hair hypoplasia.[95] A causal effect of BKV infection in both cases was supported by the presence of intranuclear inclusions and BKV DNA in renal tubular epithelium.[94, 95] BKV has also been isolated from the urine of patients with Wiskott-Aldrich syndrome.[96] No characteristic clinical manifestations of BKV reactivation have been described in these patients. Polyomavirus excretion can also be detected in the urine of approximately 10% of patients with malignancies, particularly in those patients with lymphoma.[97] Viruria detected using cytologic techniques appears to be rare in nonimmunosuppressed patients, occurring in less than 1% of samples tested.[98]

In summary, BKV and JCV viruria can be seen in patients with a variety of immunodeficiencies but appears to be most frequent among renal and bone marrow transplant recipients. In addition, pregnant women may excrete JCV or BKV in the third trimester, perhaps as a result of defects in cell-mediated immunity observed during pregnancy.[83] The majority of immunosuppressed patients who excrete BKV and JCV are asymptomatic. However, polyomavirus viruria has been associated in renal transplant patients with ureteral stenosis and in bone marrow transplant patients with late-onset hemorrhagic cystitis. The prevalence and associated clinical manifestations of JCV and BKV viruria are summarized in Table 134–2.

Association of BK Virus and JC Virus Infections with Malignancy

BKV and JCV can induce tumors in mice and hamsters after intracerebral, intraperitoneal, subcutaneous, or intravenous injection.[99–102] The early region of the BKV genome can transform cells in culture, either alone or in cooperation with an activated *ras* oncogene.[103–106] There are a number of reports of human polyomavirus isolation or detection of polyomavirus sequences in human tumors,[16, 107–109] particularly brain tumors.[16, 96, 107, 110, 111] Despite these suggestive reports, a causal relationship between polyomavirus infection and the development of tumors in humans has not been established.

DIAGNOSIS

Routine use of virus isolation for detection of JCV and BKV infection is hampered by the relatively slow growth of these viruses in tissue culture and the lack of readily available susceptible cells. Initial isolation of JCV or BKV from clinical specimens often requires weeks to months.[48] BKV-susceptible cells include human embryonic kidney, human diploid lung fibroblasts, infant urothelial cells, and human fetal brain cells.[1] JCV is more limited in its host range in cell culture and grows best in primary human fetal glial cells or in transformed cell lines derived from them.[1, 112]

Cytologic examination of urinary epithelial cells is the most widely used method to detect JCV or BKV viruria. The most characteristic abnormality of infected cells is an enlarged nucleus with a single large basophilic intranuclear inclusion.[85, 98] Cytoplasmic inclusions are not seen in association with JCV or BKV infections, in contrast to cytomegalovirus infections.[85, 98] Advantages of this technique include its accuracy and its utility in analyzing large numbers of clinical specimens. However, cytologic examination of the urine does have limitations in the diagnosis of polyomavirus infections. Although strongly suggestive of polyomavirus infection, the cytopathologic changes induced by polyomaviruses can be confused with those due to malignancy or to other virus infections, such as those caused by cytomegalovirus and adenovirus.[113] In addition, JCV and BKV infections cannot be distinguished from each other on the basis

TABLE 134–2 Prevalence and Associated Clinical Manifestations of JC Virus and BK Virus Viruria*

Risk Group	Frequency (%)	Usual Time of Onset	Associated Clinical Manifestations	Type of Infection	Reference(s)
Pregnant women	3	Third trimester	None	Reactivation	81
Renal transplant recipients	10–45	First 3 mo after transplant	Ureteral stenosis	Reactivation or primary infection	84–87
Bone marrow transplant recipients	50	First 2 mo after transplant	Late-onset hemorrhagic cystitis	Reactivation	91–93
Oncology patients	10	No correlation with chemotherapy	None	Reactivation	97
Nonimmunosuppressed patients	0.3	Not known	None	Not known	98

*Cases of polyomavirus excretion detected by cytopathologic study, electron microscopy, or culture are included.

of cytologic findings.[48, 85] Finally, JCV or BKV viruria can occur in the absence of detectable cytologic abnormalities.[48, 86] JCV or BKV viruria can also be discerned using electron microscopic examination of urinary sediment for viral particles,[3, 87] detection of viral nucleic acids by hybridization methods or PCR assay,[114, 115] and detection of viral antigens by immunofluorescence assay[116] or enzyme-linked immunosorbent assay (ELISA).[115]

PCR testing can detect JCV and BKV sequences in the urine of a significant proportion of HIV-infected patients,[114, 117] apparently normal control populations,[114] and elderly patients without evidence of overt immunosuppression.[118] Whether PCR positivity can be correlated with a positive result on urine culture or cytologic studies is not known, and the clinical significance of excretion of polyomavirus nucleic acids has not been established.

A definitive diagnosis of PML requires identification of the characteristic pathologic changes on brain biopsy, which are illustrated in Figure 134–1. Multiple asymmetric foci of demyelination at various stages of evolution can be seen in the cerebral white matter.[27, 28, 119] The oligodendrocytes, which are the myelin-producing cells of the central nervous system, demonstrate characteristic cytopathic effects that include nuclear enlargement, loss of normal chromatin pattern, and intranuclear accumulation of deeply basophilic homogenous staining material (see Fig. 134–1A).[28, 119] A significant proportion of lesions contain astrocytes that have undergone marked enlargement and that often have intensely hyperchromatic and irregularly shaped nuclei (see Fig. 134–1*B*).[27, 28, 119] Although PML lesions typically demonstrate minimal inflammatory changes, a subset of patients may have lesions with a marked inflammatory response.[27, 75] Electron microscopy can be used to demonstrate polyomavirus particles in enlarged oligodendrocyte nuclei.[52, 54] The techniques of fluorescent antibody staining, electron microscopic agglutination techniques, immunocytochemistry, and in situ hybridization have demonstrated JCV infection in almost all PML lesions studied,[53, 75, 120–124] although a small number of cases have been linked with the SV40 PML group of viruses.[9–11, 120] BKV infection has not been detected in PML. Although PML lesions in patients with AIDS may demonstrate increased numbers of JCV-infected cells and more extensive necrosis, there are no pathologic characteristics that can reliably distinguish PML in patients with AIDS from PML in patients with other immunodeficiencies.[125, 126]

Computed tomography (CT) scans in patients with PML characteristically reveal hypodense, nonenhancing lesions of the cerebral white matter.[34, 76, 127] The severity of the clinical findings is often greater than suggested by the extent of involvement on CT scan. This dissociation of clinical and CT findings in a patient with a compatible clinical picture should raise the possibility of PML.[76, 128] Magnetic resonance imaging (MRI) appears to be more sensitive than CT in detecting PML lesions.[34, 128, 129] PML lesions typically appear as areas of increased signal intensity on proton density– and T2-weighted MRI scans (Fig. 134–2).[128, 130] Stereotactic brain biopsy using computer-assisted imaging techniques such as CT and MRI has been used successfully to diagnose PML in HIV-infected patients.[131–133]

PCR testing has been used to amplify JCV DNA in cerebrospinal fluid (CSF) samples from patients with PML.[134–143] Methods used in these studies differ with regard to specimen preparation, region of the genome amplified, amplification conditions, and methods for detection. Reported sensitivities range from 60% to 100%, reflecting differences in the case definition of PML, the patient population studied, and the PCR methodology used. JCV DNA can be detected in the CSF of some immunosuppressed patients without clinical evidence for PML, although the frequency of JCV DNA in CSF in these patients is significantly lower than in those with biopsy- or autopsy-proven PML. PCR testing for JCV DNA in the CSF should not be used to diagnose PML in the absence of compatible clinical and radiographic findings. The detection of JCV DNA in the CSF of a patient with a compatible clinical picture supports the diagnosis of PML, but the absence of detectable JCV DNA cannot be used to rule out the diagnosis.

Other diagnostic tests may increase the clinician's index of suspicion for PML but are not helpful in establishing the diagnosis. Serum antibodies to JCV are common in the general population and are not helpful in predicting which patients are at risk for PML.[73] CSF cell count and chemistries are usually normal. Electroencephalography may reveal focal slowing or may be normal early in the course of PML.[144]

PREVENTION AND TREATMENT

The majority of patients with BKV and JCV infections are asymptomatic and do not require treatment. Case reports of patients with PML who have received cytosine arabinoside (cytarabine, or Ara-C) have provided conflicting data on the efficacy of this drug. The AIDS Clinical Trials Group (ACTG) of the National Institute of Allergy and Infectious Diseases conducted a randomized multicenter study comparing the efficacy of adding intravenous or intrathecal cytarabine to dual nucleoside antiretroviral therapy with that of antiretroviral therapy alone in HIV-infected patients with biopsy-

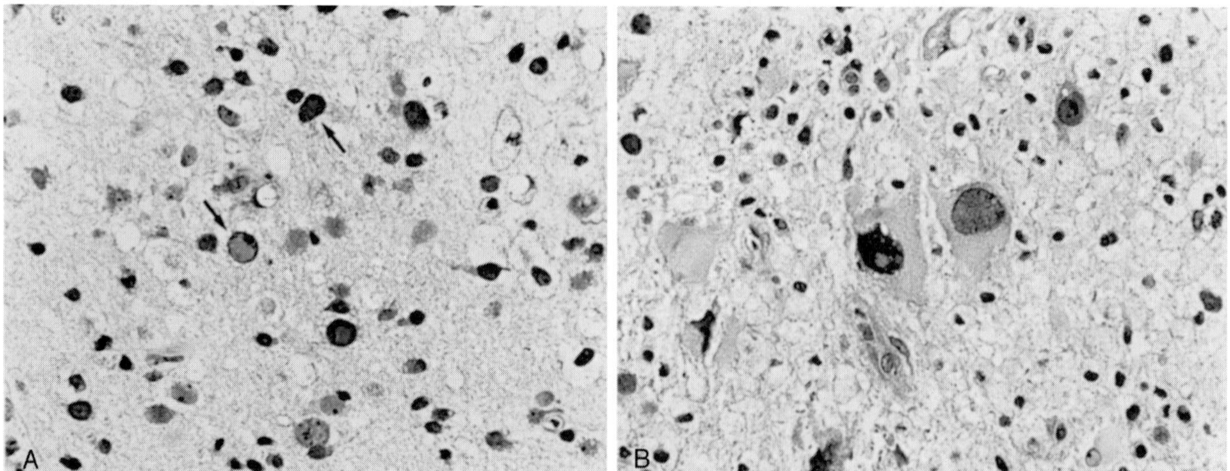

FIGURE 134–1. Progressive multifocal leukoencephalopathy. *A, Arrows* point to oligodendrocytes, each of which contains a homogeneous basophilic nuclear inclusion. *B*, Markedly enlarged astrocytes with hyperchromatic, irregularly shaped nuclei are apparent. (H&E, ×500). (Courtesy of Dr. Joshua Sickel, University of Rochester Department of Pathology.)

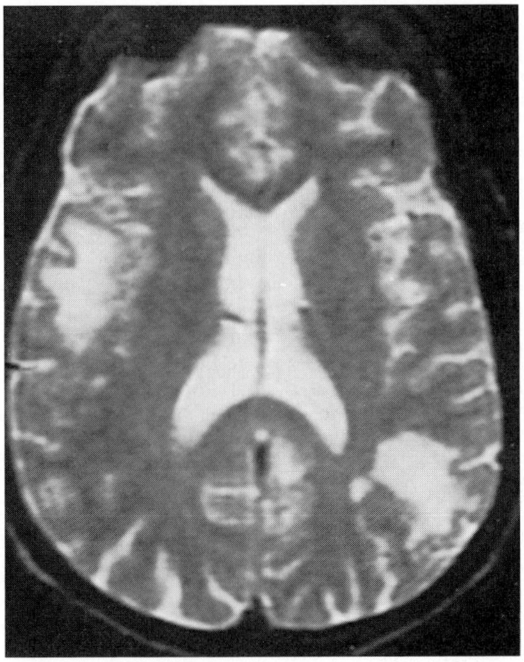

FIGURE 134–2. Axial T2-weighted magnetic resonance imaging scan of biopsy-proven progressive multifocal leukoencephalopathy. High signal lesions are seen in the right parietal and left parieto-occipital white matter. (From Keetonen L, Tuite MJ. Brain imaging in the human immunodeficiency virus infection. Semin Neurol. 1992;12:57–69.)

proven PML (ACTG 243).[145] No clinical benefit of either mode of administration of cytosine arabinoside was seen in this trial, and anemia and thrombocytopenia were more frequent in those patients who received intravenous cytarabine.[145] Thus, there is no evidence to support the use of this drug in HIV-infected patients with PML.

Other drugs reported to improve the clinical course of PML include interferon,[146, 147] IUDR,[148] and interleukin-2.[149] The reported studies all were uncontrolled, and no firm recommendations can be made regarding the use of these agents in the treatment of JCV infection in PML.

Cidofovir, a nucleoside analogue that is active against mouse and primate polyomaviruses,[150] has been reported to provide benefit in PML[151] and is being studied in an open label trial (ACTG 363). Topoisomerase I inhibitors, such as camptothecin and its analogue, inhibit JCV in vitro[152] and are being considered for clinical trials.

There are reports describing marked clinical and radiographic improvement in HIV-infected patients with PML after initiation of potent combination antiretroviral regimens that include a protease inhibitor.[153–155] If tolerated, aggressive antiretroviral treatment of underlying HIV infection appears to be the most reasonable therapeutic approach to the management of PML in HIV-infected patients.

Interferon has some activity against BKV in vitro but had no effect on BKV viruria in renal transplant patients.[156] Treatment of immunosuppressed patients with polyomavirus viruria is largely supportive and directed toward control of symptoms.

REFERENCES

1. Shah KV. Polyomaviruses. In: Fields BN, Knipe DM, Howley PM, et al, eds. Fields Virology. 3rd ed. Philadelphia: Lipincott-Raven Publishers; 1996:2027–2043.
2. Padgett BL, Walker DL, ZuRhein GM, et al. Cultivation of papova-like virus from human brain with progressive multifocal leukoencephalopathy. Lancet. 1971;1: 1257–1260.
3. Gardner SD, Field AM, Coleman DV, et al. New human papovavirus (B.K.) isolated from urine after renal transplantation. Lancet. 1971;1:1253–1257.
4. Yang RCA, Wu R. BK virus DNA: Complete nucleotide sequence of a human tumor virus. Science. 1979;206:456–462.
5. Frisque RJ, Bream GL, Cannella MT. Human polyomavirus JC virus genome. J Virol. 1984;51:458–469.
6. Shah KV, Ozer HL, Ghazey HN, et al. Common structural antigen of papovaviruses of the simian virus 40-polyoma subgroup. J Virol. 1977;21:179–186.
7. Penney JB Jr, Narayan O. Studies of the antigenic relationships of the new human papovaviruses by electron microscopy agglutination. Infect Immun. 1973;8:299–300.
8. Weiner LP, Herndon RM, Narayan O, et al. Isolation of virus related to SV40 from patients with progressive multifocal leukoencephalopathy. N Engl J Med. 1972;286:385–390.
9. Scherneck S, Geissler E, Jänisch W, et al. Isolation of a SV40-like virus from a patient with progressive multifocal leukoencephalopathy. Acta Virol. 1981;25:191–198.
10. Weiner LP, Herndon RM, Narayan O, et al. Further studies of a simian virus 40–like virus isolated from human brain. J Virol. 1972;10:147–149.
11. Weiner LP, Narayan O. Virologic studies of progressive multifocal leukoencephalopathy. Prog Med Virol. 1974;18:229–240.
12. Seif I, Khoury G, Dhar R. The genome of human papovavirus BKV. Cell. 1979;18:963–977.
13. Grinnell BW, Padgett BL, Walker DL. Comparison of infectious JC virus DNAs cloned from human brain. J Virol. 1983;45:299–308.
14. Martin JD, Foster GC. Multiple JC virus genomes from one patient. J Gen Virol. 1984;65:1405–1411.
15. Martin JD, King DM, Slauch JM, et al. Differences in regulatory sequences of naturally occurring JC virus variants. J Virol. 1985;53:306–311.
16. Negrini M, Rimessi P, Mantovani C, et al. Characterization of BK virus variants rescued from human tumors and tumor cell lines. J Gen Virol. 1990;71:2731–2736.
17. Flaegstad T, Rönne K, Filipe AR, et al. Prevalence of anti BK virus antibody in Portugal and Norway. Scand J Infect Dis. 1989;21:145–147.
18. Padgett BL, Walker DL. Prevalence of antibodies in human sera against JC virus, an isolate from a case of progressive multifocal leukoencephalopathy. J Infect Dis. 1973;127:467–470.
19. Shah KV, Daniel RW, Warszawski RM. High prevalence of antibodies to BK virus, an SV 40–related papovavirus, in residents of Maryland. J Infect Dis. 1973;128:784–787.
20. Gardner SD. Prevalence in England of antibody to human polyomavirus (B.K.). Br Med J. 1973;1:77–78.
21. Mäntyjärvi RA, Meurman OH, Vihma L, et al. A human papovavirus (B.K.), biological properties and seroepidemiology. Ann Clin Res. 1973;5:283–287.
22. Portolani M, Marzocchi A, Barbanti-Brodano G, et al. Prevalence in Italy of antibodies to a new human papovavirus (BK virus). J Med Microbiol. 1974;7:543–546.
23. Rziha HJ, Bornkamm GW, zur Hausen H. BK virus: Seroepidemiologic studies and serologic response to viral infection. Med Microbiol Immunol. 1978;165:73–81.
24. Brown P, Tsai T, Gajdusek DC. Seroepidemiology of human papovaviruses: Discovery of virgin populations and some unusual patterns of antibody prevalence among remote peoples of the world. Am J Epidemiol. 1975;102:331–340.
25. Dei R, Marmo F, Corte D, et al. Age-related changes in the prevalence of precipitating antibodies to BK virus in infants and children. J Med Microbiol. 1982;15:285–291.
26. Hogan TF, Padgett BL, Wallker DL. Human polyomaviruses. In: Belshse RB, ed. Textbook of Human Virology. 2nd ed. St. Louis: Mosby–Year Book; 1991:970–1000.
27. Åström K-E, Mancall EL, Richardson EP Jr. Progressive multifocal leukoencephalopathy: A hitherto unrecognized complication of chronic lymphatic leukemia and Hodgkin's disease. Brain. 1958;81:93–110.
28. Richardson EP Jr. Progressive multifocal leukoencephalopathy. N Engl J Med. 1961;265:815–823.
29. Newton P, Aldridge RD, Lessells AM, et al. Progressive multifocal leukoencephalopathy complicating systemic lupus erythematosus. Arthritis Rheum. 1986;29:337–343.
30. Rockwell D, Ruben FL, Winkelstein A, et al. Absence of immune deficiencies in a case of progressive multifocal leukoencephalopathy. Am J Med. 1976;61:433–436.
31. Bolton CF, Rozdilsky B. Primary progressive multifocal leukoencephalopathy: A case report. Neurology. 1971;21:72–77.
32. Fermaglich J, Hardman JM, Earle KM. Spontaneous progressive multifocal leukoencephalopathy. Neurology. 1970;20:479–484.
33. Holman RC, Janssen RS, Buehler JW, et al. Epidemiology of progressive multifocal leukoencephalopathy in the United States: Analysis of national mortality and AIDS surveillance data. Neurology. 1991;41:1733–1736.
34. Berger JR, Kaszovitz B, Post JD, et al. Progressive multifocal leukoencephalopathy associated with human immunodeficiency virus infection: A review of the literature with a report of sixteen cases. Ann Intern Med. 1987;107:78–87.
35. Levy RM, Bredesen DE, Rosenblum ML. Neurological manifestations of the acquired immunodeficiency syndrome (AIDS): Experience at UCSF and review of the literature. J Neurosurg. 1985;62:475–495.
36. Berger JR, Scott G, Albrecht J, et al. Progressive multifocal leukoencephalopathy in HIV-1–infected children. AIDS. 1992;6:837–841.
37. Vandersteenhoven JJ, Dbaibo G, Boyko OB, et al. Progressive multifocal leukoencephalopathy in pediatric acquired immunodeficiency syndrome. Pediatr Infect Dis J. 1992;11:232–237.
38. Morriss MC, Rutstein RM, Rudy B, et al. Progressive multifocal leukoencephalopathy in an HIV-infected child. Neuroradiology. 1997;39:142–144.

39. Chikezie PU, Greenberg AL. Idiopathic CD4+ T lymphopenia presenting as progressive multifocal leukoencephalopathy: Case report. Clinical Infect Dis. 1997;24:526–527.
40. Kitamura T, Kunitake T, Guo J, et al. Transmission of human polyomavirus JC virus occurs both within the family and outside the family. J Clin Microbiol. 1994;32:2359–2363.
41. Kunitake T, Kitamura T, Guo J, et al. Parent-to-child transmission is relatively common in the spread of human polyomavirus JC virus. J Clin Microbiol. 1995;33: 1448–1451.
42. Taguchi F, Nagaki D, Saito M. Transplacental transmission of BK virus in humans. Jpn J Microbiol. 1975;19:395–398.
43. Gibson PE, Field AM, Gardner SD, et al. Occurrence of IgM antibodies against BK and JC polyomaviruses during pregnancy. J Clin Pathol. 1981;34:674–679.
44. Daniel R, Shah K, Madden D, Stagno S. Serological investigation of the possibility of congenital transmission of papovavirus JC. Infect Immun. 1981;33:319–321.
45. Shah K, Daniel R, Madden D, et al. Serological investigation of BK papovavirus infection in pregnant women and their offspring. Infect Immun. 1980;30:29–35.
46. McCance DJ, Mims CA. Reactivation of polyoma virus in kidneys of persistently infected mice during pregnancy. Infect Immun. 1979;25:998–1002.
47. McCance DJ, Mims CA. Transplacental transmission of polyoma virus in mice. Infect Immun. 1977;18:196–202.
48. Arthur RR, Shah KV. Occurrence and significance of papovaviruses BK and JC in the urine. Prog Med Virol. 1989;36:42–61.
49. Schneider EM, Dörries K. High frequency of polyomavirus infection in lymphoid cell preparations after allogeneic bone marrow transplantation. Transplant Proc. 1993;25:1271–1273.
50. Gallia GL, Houff SA, Major EO, Khalili K. Review: JC virus infection of lymphocytes—revisited. J Infect Dis. 1997;176:1603–1609.
51. DuBois V, Dutronc H, Lafon M-E, et al. Latency and reactivation of JC virus in peripheral blood of human immunodeficiency virus type 1–infected patients. J Clin Microbiol. 1997;35:2288–2292.
52. Silverman L, Rubinstein LJ. Electron microscopic observations on a case of progressive multifocal leukoencephalopathy. Acta Neuropathol. 1965;5:215–224.
53. Dörries K, Johnson RT, ter Meulen V. Detection of polyoma virus DNA in PML-brain tissue by in situ hybridization. J Gen Virol. 1979;42:49–57.
54. ZuRhein GM, Chou S-M. Particles resembling papova viruses in human cerebral demyelinating disease. Science. 1965;148:1477–1479.
55. Trapp BD, Small JA, Pulley M, et al. Dysmyelination in transgenic mice containing JC virus early region. Ann Neurol. 1988;23:38–48.
56. Small JA, Scangos GA, Cork L, et al. The early region of human papovavirus JC induces dysmyelination in transgenic mice. Cell. 1986;46:13–18.
57. Holmberg CA, Gribble DH, Takemoto KK, et al. Isolation of simian virus 40 from rhesus monkeys *(Macaca mulatta)* with spontaneous progressive multifocal leukoencephalopathy. J Infect Dis. 1977;136:593–596.
58. Gribble DH, Haden CC, Schwartz LW, et al. Spontaneous progressive multifocal leukoencephalopathy in macaques. Nature. 1975;254:602–604.
59. Wegner M, Drolet DW, Rosenfeld MG. Regulation of JC virus by the POU-domain transcription factor Tst-1: Implications for progressive multifocal leukoencephalopathy. Proc Natl Acad Sci U S A. 1993;90:4743–4747.
60. White FA III, Ishaq M, Stoner GL, et al. JC virus DNA is present in many human brain samples from patients without progressive multifocal leukoencephalopathy. J Virol. 1992;66:5726–5734.
61. Chesters PM, Heritage J, McCance DJ. Persistence of DNA sequences of BK virus and JC virus in normal human tissues and in diseased tissues. J Infect Dis. 1983;147:676–684.
62. Tominaga T, Yogo Y, Kitamura T, et al. Persistence of archetypal JC virus DNA in normal renal tissue derived from tumor-bearing patients. Virology. 1992;186:736–741.
63. Heritage J, Chesters PM, McCance DJ. The persistence of papovavirus BK DNA sequences in normal renal tissue. J Med Virol. 1981;8:143–150.
64. Dörries K, ter Meulen V. Progressive multifocal leukoencephalopathy: Detection of papovavirus JC in kidney tissue. J Med Virol. 1983;11:307–317.
65. Kitamura T, Sugimoto C, Kato A, et al. Persistent JC virus (JCV) infection is demonstrated by continuous shedding of the same JCV strains. J Clin Microbiol. 1997;35:1255–1257.
66. Goudsmit J, Wertheim-van Dillen P, van Strien A, et al. The role of BK virus in acute respiratory tract disease and the presence of BKV DNA in tonsils. J Med Virol. 1982;10:91–99.
67. Goudsmit J, Baak ML, Slaterus KW, et al. Human papovavirus isolated from urine of a child with acute tonsillitis. Br Med J. 1981;283:1363–1364.
68. Padgett BL, Walker DL, Desquitado MM, et al. BK virus and non-hemorrhagic cystitis in a child. Lancet. 1983;1:770.
69. Hashida Y, Gaffney PC, Yunis EJ. Acute hemorrhagic cystitis of childhood and papovavirus-like particles. J Pediatr. 1976;89:85–87.
70. Mininberg DT, Watson C, Desquitado M. Viral cystitis with transient secondary vesicoureteral reflux. J Urol. 1982;127:983–985.
71. Saitoh K, Sugae N, Koike N, et al. Diagnosis of childhood BK virus cystitis by electron microscopy and PCR. J Clin Pathol. 1993;46:773–775.
72. Brooks BR, Walker DL. Progressive multifocal leukoencephalopathy. Neurol Clin North Am. 1984;2:299–313.
73. Gillespie SM, Chang Y, Lemp G, et al. Progressive multifocal leukoencephalopathy in persons infected with human immunodeficiency virus, San Francisco, 1981–1989. Ann Neurol. 1991;30:597–604.
74. von Einsiedel RW, Fife TD, Aksamit AJ, et al. Progressive multifocal leukoencephalopathy in AIDS: A clinicopathologic study and review of the literature. J Neurol. 1993;240:391–406.
75. Hair LS, Nuovo G, Powers JM, et al. Progressive multifocal leukoencephalopathy in patients with human immunodeficiency virus. Hum Pathol. 1992;23:663–667.
76. Krupp LB, Lipton RB, Swerdlow ML, et al. Progressive multifocal leukoencephalopathy: Clinical and radiographic features. Ann Neurol. 1985;17:344–349.
77. Price RW, Neilsen S, Horten B, et al. Progressive multifocal leukoencephalopathy: A burnt-out case. Ann Neurol. 1983;13:485–490.
78. Berger JR, Mucke L. Prolonged survival and partial recovery in AIDS-associated progressive multifocal leukoencephalopathy. Neurology. 1988;38:1060–1065.
79. Fong IW, Toma E, Canadian PML Study Group. The natural history of progressive multifocal leukoencephalopathy in patients with AIDS. Clin Infect Dis. 1995;20: 1305–1310.
80. Centers for Disease Control and Prevention. 1993 Revised classification system for HIV infection and expanded surveillance case definition for AIDS among adolescents and adults. MMWR Morb Mortal Wkly Rep. 1992;41:1–20.
81. Coleman DV, Wolfendale MR, Daniel RA, et al. A prospective study of human polyomavirus infection in pregnancy. J Infect Dis. 1980;142:1–8.
82. Coleman DV, Gardner SD, Mulholland C, et al. Human polyomavirus in pregnancy: A model for the study of defence mechanisms to virus reactivation. Clin Exp Immunol. 1983;53:289–296.
83. Weinberg ED. Pregnancy-associated depression of cell-mediated immunity. Rev Infect Dis. 1984;6:814–831.
84. Hogan TF, Borden EC, McBain JA, et al. Human polyomavirus infections with JC virus and BK virus in renal transplant patients. Ann Intern Med. 1980;92:373–378.
85. Traystman MD, Gupta PK, Shah KV, et al. Identification of viruses in the urine of renal transplant recipients by cytomorphology. Acta Cytol. 1980;24:501–510.
86. Coleman DV, Gardner SD, Field AM. Human polyomavirus infection in renal allograft recipients. Br Med J. 1973;3:371–375.
87. Lecatsas G, Prozesky OW, Van Wyk J, et al. Papova virus in urine after renal transplantation. Nature. 1973;241:343–344.
88. Gardner SD, MacKenzie EFD, Smith C, et al. Prospective study of the human polyomaviruses BK and JC and cytomegalovirus in renal transplant recipients. J Clin Pathol. 1984;37:578–586.
89. Andrews CA, Shah KV, Daniel RW, et al. A serological investigation of BK virus and JC virus infections in recipients of renal allografts. J Infect Dis. 1988;158:176–181.
90. Coleman DV, MacKenzie EFD, Gardner SD, et al. Human polyomavirus (BK) infection and ureteric stenosis in renal allograft recipients. J Clin Pathol. 1978; 31:338–347.
91. Apperley JF, Rice SJ, Bishop JA, et al. Late onset hemorrhagic cystitis associated with urinary excretion of polyomaviruses after bone marrow transplantation. Transplantation. 1987;43:108–112.
92. Arthur RR, Shah KV, Baust SJ, et al. Association of BK viruria with hemorrhagic cystitis in recipients of bone marrow transplants. N Engl J Med. 1986;315:230–234.
93. Arthur RR, Shah KV, Charache P, et al. BK and JC virus infections in recipients of bone marrow transplants. J Infect Dis. 1988;158:563–569.
94. Rosen S, Harmon W, Krensky AM, et al. Tubulo-interstitial nephritis associated with polyomavirus (BK type) infection. N Engl J Med. 1983;308:1192–1196.
95. de Silva LM, Bale P, de Courcy J, et al. Renal failure due to BK virus infection in an immunodeficient child. J Med Virol. 1995;45:192–196.
96. Takemoto KK, Rabson AS, Mullarkey MF, et al. Isolation of papovavirus from brain tumor and urine of a patient with Wiskott-Aldrich syndrome. J Natl Cancer Inst. 1974;53:1205–1207.
97. Hogan TF, Padgett BL, Walker DL, et al. Survey of human polyomavirus (JCV, BKV) infections in 139 patients with lung cancer, breast cancer, melanoma, or lymphoma. Prog Clin Biol Res. 1983;105:311–324.
98. Kahan AV, Coleman DV, Koss LG. Activation of human polyomavirus infection—detection by cytologic techniques. Am J Clin Pathol. 1980;74:326–332.
99. Greenlee JE, Narayan O, Johnson RT, et al. Induction of brain tumors in hamsters with BK virus, a human papovavirus. Lab Invest. 1977;36:636–641.
100. Corallini A, Barbanti-Brodano G, Bortoloni W, et al. High incidence of ependymomas induced by BK virus, a human papovavirus: Brief communications. J Natl Cancer Inst. 1977;59:1561–1563.
101. Varakis J, ZuRhein GM, Padgett BL, et al. Induction of peripheral neuroblastomas in Syrian hamsters after injection as neonates with JC virus, a human polyomavirus. Cancer Res. 1978;38:1718–1722.
102. Walker DL, Padgett BL, ZuRhein GM, et al. Human papovavirus (JC): Induction of brain tumors in hamsters. Science. 1973;181:674–676.
103. Corallini A, Pagnani M, Viadana P, et al. Induction of malignant subcutaneous sarcomas in hamsters by a recombinant DNA containing BK virus early region and the activated human c-Harvey-*ras* oncogene. Cancer Res. 1987;47:6671–6677.
104. Corallini A, Pagnani M, Caputo A, et al. Cooperation in oncogenesis between BK virus early region gene and the activated human c-Harvey-*ras* oncogene. J Gen Virol. 1988;69:2671–2679.
105. Pagnani M, Corallini A, Caputo A, et al. Cooperation in cell transformation between BK virus and the human c-Harvey *ras* oncogene. Int J Cancer. 1988;42: 405–413.
106. Grossi MP, Caputo A, Meneguzzi G, et al. Transformation of human embryonic fibroblasts by BK virus, BK virus DNA and a subgenomic BK virus DNA fragment. J Gen Virol. 1982;63:393–403.
107. Corallini A, Pagnani M, Viadana P, et al. Association of BK virus with human brain tumors and tumors of pancreatic islets. Int J Cancer. 1987;39:60–67.
108. Caputo A, Corallini A, Grossi MP, et al. Episomal DNA of a BK virus variant in a human insulinoma. J Med Virol. 1983;12:37–49.

109. Fiori M, Di Mayorca G. Occurrence of BK virus DNA in DNA obtained from certain human tumors. Proc Natl Acad Sci U S A. 1976;73:4662–4666.
110. Bergsagel DJ, Finegold MJ, Butel JS, et al. DNA sequences similar to those of simian virus 40 in ependymomas and choroid plexus tumors of childhood. N Engl J Med. 1992;326:988–993.
111. Dörries K, Loeber G, Meixensberger J. Association of polyomaviruses JC, SV40, and BK with human brain tumors. Virology. 1987;160:268–270.
112. Beckmann AM, Shah KV, Padgett BL. Propagation and primary isolation of papovavirus JC in epithelial cells derived from human urine. Infect Immun. 1982;38:774–777.
113. Coleman DV. The cytodiagnosis of human polyomavirus infection. Acta Cytol. 1975;19:93–96.
114. Markowitz RB, Thompson HC, Mueller JF, et al. Incidence of BK virus and JC virus viruria in human immunodeficiency virus–infected and –uninfected subjects. J Infect Dis. 1993;167:13–20.
115. Arthur RR, Beckmann AM, Li CC, et al. Direct detection of the human papovavirus BK in urine of bone marrow transplant recipients: Comparison of DNA hybridization with ELISA. J Med Virol. 1985;16:29–36.
116. Hogan TF, Padgett BL, Walker DL, et al. Rapid detection and identification of JC virus and BK virus in human urine by using immunofluorescence microscopy. J Clin Microbiol. 1980;11:178–183.
117. Shah KV, Daniel RW, Strickler HD, Goedert JJ. Investigation of human urine for genomic sequences of the primate polyomaviruses simian virus 40, BK virus and JC virus. J Infect Dis. 1997;176:1618–1621.
118. Kitamura T, Aso Y, Kuniyoshi N, et al. High incidence of urinary JC virus excretion in nonimmunosuppressed older patients. J Infect Dis. 1990;161:1128–1133.
119. Richardson EP Jr, Webster HDF. Progressive multifocal leukoencephalopathy: Its pathological features. Prog Clin Biol Res. 1983;105:191–203.
120. Narayan O, Penney JB Jr, Johnson RT, et al. Etiology of progressive multifocal leukoencephalopathy: Identification of papovavirus. N Engl J Med. 1973;289:1278–1282.
121. Aksamit AJ, Sever JL, Major EO. Progressive multifocal leukoencephalopathy: JC virus detection by in situ hybridization compared with immunohistochemistry. Neurology. 1986;36:499–504.
122. Hulette CM, Downey BT, Burger PC. Progressive multifocal leukoencephalopathy: Diagnosis by in situ hybridization with a biotinylated JC virus DNA probe using an automated histomatic code-on slide stainer. Am J Surg Pathol. 1991;15:791–797.
123. Knowles WA, Sharp IR, Efstratiou L, et al. Preparation of monoclonal antibodies to JC virus and their use in the diagnosis of progressive multifocal leukoencephalopathy. J Med Virol. 1991;34:127–131.
124. Itoyama Y, Webster HDF, Sternberger NH, et al. Distribution of papovavirus, myelin-associated glycoprotein, and myelin basic protein in progressive multifocal leukoencephalopathy lesions. Ann Neurol. 1982;11:396–407.
125. Aksamit AJ, Gendelman HE, Orenstein JM, Pezeshkpour GH. AIDS-associated progressive multifocal leukoencephalopathy (PML): Comparison to non-AIDS PML with in situ hybridization and immunohistochemistry. Neurology. 1990;40:1073–1078.
126. Kuchelmeister K, Gullotta F, Bergmann M, et al. Progressive multifocal leukoencephalopathy (PML) in the acquired immunodeficiency syndrome (AIDS): A neuropathological autopsy study of 21 cases. Pathol Res Pract. 1993;189:163–173.
127. Heinz ER, Drayer BP, Haenggeli CA, et al. Computed tomography in white-matter disease. Radiology. 1979;130:371–378.
128. Whiteman MLH, Post MJD, Berger JR, et al. Progressive multifocal leukoencephalopathy in 47 HIV-seropositive patients: Neuroimaging with clinical and pathologic correlation. Radiology. 1993;187:233–240.
129. Ciricillo SF, Rosenblum ML. Use of CT and MR imaging to distinguish intracranial lesions and to define the need for biopsy in AIDS patients. J Neurosurg. 1990;73:720–724.
130. Mark AS, Atlas SW. Progressive multifocal leukoencephalopathy in patients with AIDS: Appearance on MR images. Radiology. 1989;173:517–520.
131. Zimmer C, Märzheuser S, Patt S, et al. Stereotactic brain biopsy in AIDS. J Neurol. 1992;239:394–400.
132. Chappell ET, Guthrie BL, Orenstein J. The role of stereotactic biopsy in the management of HIV-related focal brain lesions. Neurosurgery. 1992;30:825–829.
133. Levy RM, Russell E, Yungbluth M, et al. The efficacy of image-guided stereotactic brain biopsy in neurologically symptomatic acquired immunodeficiency syndrome patients. Neurosurgery. 1992;30:186–190.
134. Gibson PE, Knowles WA, Hand JF, et al. Detection of JC virus DNA in the cerebrospinal fluid of patients with progressive multifocal leukoencephalopathy. J Med Virol. 1993;39:278–281.
135. Henson J, Rosenblum M, Armstrong D, et al. Amplification of JC virus DNA from brain and cerebrospinal fluid of patients with progressive multifocal leukoencephalopathy. Neurology. 1991;41:1967–1971.
136. Ferrante P, Caldarelli-Stefano R, Omodeo-Zorini E, et al. Comprehensive investigation of the presence of JC virus in AIDS patients with and without progressive multifocal leukoencephalopathy. J Med Virol. 1997;52:235–242.
137. Vago L, Cinque P, Sala E, et al. JCV-DNA and BKV-DNA in the CNS tissue and CSF of AIDS patients and normal subjects. Study of 41 cases and review of the literature. J Acquir Immune Defic Syndr Hum Retrovirol. 1996;12:139–146.
138. McGuire D, Barhite S, Hollander H, Miles M. JC virus DNA in cerebrospinal fluid of human immunodeficiency virus–infected patients: Predictive value for progressive multifocal leukoencephalopathy. Ann Neurol. 1995;37:395–399.
139. Weber T, Turner RW, Frye S, et al. Specific diagnosis of progressive multifocal leukoencephalopathy by polymerase chain reaction. J Infect Dis. 1994;169:1138–1141.
140. Hammarin A-L, Bogdanovic G, Svedhem V, et al. Analysis of PCR as a tool for detection of JC virus DNA in cerebrospinal fluid for diagnosis of progressive multifocal leukoencephalopathy. J Clin Microbiol. 1996;34:2929–2932.
141. Fong IW, Britton CB, Luinstra KE, et al. Diagnostic value of detecting JC virus DNA in cerebrospinal fluid of patients with progressive multifocal leukoencephalopathy. J Clin Microbiol. 1995;33:484–486.
142. De Luca, Cingolani A, Linzalone A, et al. Improved detection of JC virus DNA in cerebrospinal fluid for diagnosis of AIDS-related progressive multifocal leukoencephalopathy. J Clin Microbiol. 1996;34:1343–1346.
143. Antinori A, Ammassari A, De Luca A, et al. Diagnosis of AIDS-related focal brain lesions: A decision-making analysis based on clinical and neuroradiologic characteristics combined with polymerase chain reaction assays in CSF. Neurology. 1997;48:687–694.
144. Farrell DF. The EEG in progressive multifocal leukoencephalopathy. Electroencephalogr Clin Neurophys. 1969;26:200–205.
145. Hall CD, Dafni U, Simpson D, et al. Failure of cytarabine in progressive multifocal leukoencephalopathy associated with human immunodeficiency virus infection. N Engl J Med. 1998;338:1345–1351.
146. Steiger MJ, Tarnesby G, Gabe S, et al. Successful outcome of progressive multifocal leukoencephalopathy with cytarabine and interferon. Ann Neurol. 1993;33:407–411.
147. Tashiro K, Doi S, Moriwaka F, et al. Progressive multifocal leucoencephalopathy with magnetic resonance imaging verification in therapeutic trials of infection. J Neurol. 1987;234:427–429.
148. Tarsy D, Holden EM, Segarra JM, et al. 5-Iodo-2′-deoxyuridine (IUDR; NSC-39661) given intraventricularly in the treatment of progressive multifocal leukoencephalopathy. Cancer Chemother Rep. 1973;57:73–78.
149. Przepiorka D, Jaecle KA, Birdwell RR, et al. Successful treatment of progressive multifocal leukoencephalopathy with low-dose interleukin-2. Bone Marrow Transpl. 1997;20:983–987.
150. Andrei G, Snoeck R, Vandeputte M, et al. Activity of various compounds against murine and human polyomaviruses. Antimicrob Agents Chemother. 1997;41:587.
151. Snoeck R, DeWit, Ross C, et al. Treatment of progressive multifocal leukoencephalopathy (PML) with cidofovir in an AIDS patient. Abstract 113. Presented at the Ninth International Conference on Antiviral Research, Urabandai, Fukushima, Japan, May 1996.
152. Kerr DA, Chang CF, Gordon J, et al. Inhibition of human neurotropic virus (JCV) DNA replication in glial cells by camptothecin. Virology. 1993;196:612.
153. Elliot B, Aromin I, Gold R, et al. 2.5 year remission of AIDS-associated progressive multifocal leukoencephalopathy with combined antiretroviral therapy. Lancet. 1997;349:850.
154. Domingo P, Guardiola JM, Iranzo A, Margall N. Remission of progressive multifocal leucoencephalopathy after antiretroviral therapy. Lancet. 1997;349:1554–1555.
155. Baqi M, Kucharczyk W, Walmsley SL. Regression of progressive multifocal encephalopathy with highly active antiretroviral therapy. AIDS. 1997;11:1526–1527.
156. Cheeseman SH, Black PH, Rubin RH, et al. Interferon and BK papovavirus—clinical and laboratory studies. J Infect Dis. 1980;141:157–161.
157. Keetonen L, Tuite MJ. Brain imaging in human immunodeficiency virus infection. Semin Neurol. 1992;12:57–69.

Hepadnaviridae

Chapter 135

Hepatitis B Virus and Hepatitis D Virus

WILLIAM S. ROBINSON

Hepatitis B virus (HBV) is a small, hepatotropic, DNA virus that in nature infects only humans, and infected humans are the only known reservoir of virus for new human infections. Other similar viruses have been found in woodchucks in the eastern United States,[1] ground squirrels in California,[2] Peking ducks in China and the United States,[3] and other avian and rodent hosts. These viruses have unique ultrastructural, molecular, antigenic, and biologic features that distinguish them from members of all other recognized virus families,[4, 5] and they constitute a virus family called Hepadnaviridae.[4, 6]

Primary HBV infections (or infection with any hepadnavirus) can be self-limited and resolve or become persistent and continue for many years, often for the remaining lifetime of the infected individual. Acute and chronic infections are almost always accompanied by detectable viral antigen and often by infectious virus continuously in the blood. New HBV infections are often asymptomatic but may be associated with mild to severe symptomatic acute hepatitis (hepatitis B). Persistent infection can be accompanied by little or no liver disease, but chronic persistent or chronic active hepatitis is common. The life expectancy of patients with chronic hepatitis B is shortened by the significant risk of the development of cirrhosis or hepatocellular carcinoma (HCC), or both. Although HBV does not appear to infect and cause disease in organs other than liver, extrahepatic disease in the form of immune complex–mediated syndromes such as "serum sickness," glomerulonephritis, and polyarteritis involving viral antigen-antibody complexes are not rare manifestations of HBV infection.

The protean and serious disease manifestations that may accompany HBV infections and the significant prevalence of these infections in the United States make HBV an important human pathogen in this country. Its importance is far greater in many other regions of the world such as in populations of eastern Asia and sub-Saharan Africa, where infections commonly occur at a very young age. In those regions, chronic HBV infection may exceed 10%, and HBV-associated liver disease can represent the most important health problems in those populations. HBV infection is one of the most common causes of acute viral hepatitis in the United States and in other parts of the world. HBV is a major (if not the most common) cause of chronic liver disease and hepatocellular carcinoma in the world today, and it is a major cause of necrotizing vasculitis (polyarteritis).

HISTORY

The first recorded cases of "serum hepatitis" (acute hepatitis with a long incubation period after the percutaneous transfer of material containing human serum) appear to be those that followed the administration of smallpox vaccine containing human lymph to shipyard workers in Bremen in 1833.[7] In the early and middle parts of the 20th century, serum hepatitis was repeatedly observed after the use of contaminated needles and syringes; for example, at diabetic[8] and venereal disease clinics,[9–11] after plasma administration for immunoprophylaxis in measles[12] and mumps,[13] after the administration of vaccines containing human serum such as yellow fever vaccine,[14, 15] and after the transfusion of blood.[16, 17] Although some of these cases may have been due to agents such as hepatitis C virus (HCV), most were undoubtedly due to the virus now known as HBV.

Serum hepatitis was not clearly distinguished from "infectious hepatitis" until the 1940s and 1950s, when apparent antigenic[18–22] and other biologic[18, 19, 23–28] differences were demonstrated in experimental transmission studies in human volunteers. One of the most important discoveries leading to the rapid advancement of knowledge of the viral etiology of serum hepatitis, and its epidemiology and disease spectrum, occurred in 1965 when Blumberg and colleagues[29] fortuitously found an antigen in human serum while investigating human serum protein polymorphism. The antigen was first found in the serum of an Australian Aboriginal when a precipitin line formed in agar gel diffusion between that serum and the serum of a patient with hemophilia who had received multiple blood transfusions. Thus, the antigen was first named Australia antigen[30] and was first thought to be a host antigen. Several years of investigation led to its eventual association with acute hepatitis,[31–33] and it was then named hepatitis-associated antigen and later given the current name, hepatitis B surface antigen (HBsAg).

The discovery of HBsAg and the recognition that it was a viral antigen led to the appreciation that HBV has a worldwide distribution and that infection rates in some parts of the world, such as parts of Asia, Africa, and Oceania, are extremely high.[34] It became clear that most HBsAg particles in serum were not virions. Virions or Dane particles were eventually identified as larger and more complex HBsAg particles[35, 36] than the much more numerous and smaller HBsAg particles originally detected.[37]

Serologic testing provided direct evidence that many serum hepatitis cases were associated with HBV infection, that HBV infection could persist for many years, and that HBV was distinct from the virus associated with most infectious hepatitis cases (hepatitis A virus [HAV]).[38] Later, it became clear that not all post-transfusion hepatitis was associated with HBV infection, but additional agents designated post-transfusion non-A, non-B hepatitis viruses were responsible for many cases.[38–40] The most important of these, HCV, was isolated by cDNA cloning in 1987[41] and shown to be a flavivirus, an RNA virus that is unrelated to HBV.

The name *serum hepatitis,* used for many years, indicated that the first recognized common route of HBV transmission was by percutaneous transfer of serum or blood by virus-contaminated needles or by injected blood products. It is now clear that HBV is transmitted from infected to uninfected individuals most commonly by routes that may not involve such direct or overt percutaneous transfer, that is, by sexual contact and by mother-to-newborn infant transmission. These are now recognized as typical routes of transmission for blood-borne viruses of humans.

THE VIRUS

Viral Genome Structure

HBV contains among the smallest genomes of all known animal viruses. It consists of an approximately 3200-base pair circular DNA molecule that contains a single-stranded region of different length in different molecules[42, 43] (Fig. 135–1), reflecting the fact that DNA molecules are packaged into virions before viral DNA replication (i.e., synthesis of the DNA plus strand) is complete. The HBV genome has four long open reading frames in the complete or long (minus) virion DNA strand.[44] The C (core or nucleocapsid) gene encodes the major viral core or nucleocapsid polypeptide of approximately 21,000 Da, and when assembled into core particles it manifests hepatitis B core antigen (HB_cAg) specificity. A truncated form of this protein (truncated at the carboxy terminus) with a mass of approximately 17,500 Da possesses hepatitis B e antigen (HB_eAg)

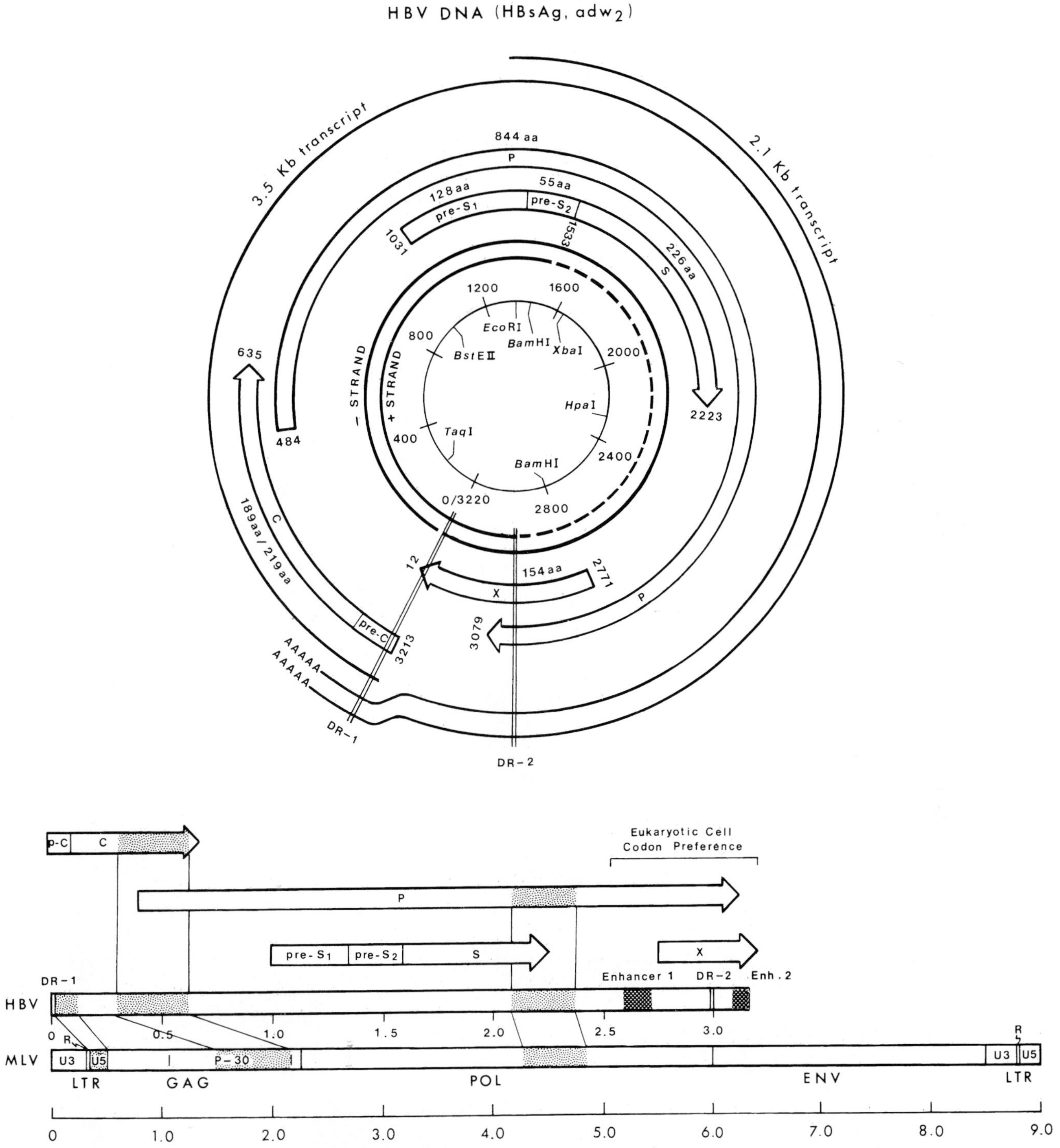

FIGURE 135–1. Physical and genetic map of hepatitis B virus (HBV) DNA and comparison with a murine leukemia virus (MLV) genome. The broken line in the + strand of circular HBV DNA represents the region within which the 3′ end of this strand may occur in different molecules, and the corresponding region of the − strand is that which may be single-stranded in different molecules. Regions of sequence homology of HBV and MLV are indicated by the shaded regions. The large arrows represent open reading frames, and DR1 and DR2 are 11 bp direct repeat sequences.

specificity.[45] This open reading frame includes a short pre-C (precore) sequence delineated by an in frame initiation codon. In cells, when translation is initiated at the first or pre-C initiation codon, the truncated polypeptide with HB_eAg specificity is secreted by the cells, suggesting that the pre-C sequence acts as a signal sequence. The extracellular HB_eAg polypeptide is found in a soluble form. When translation is initiated at the second or C initiation codon, the full-length C polypeptide is synthesized and assembled into core particles in the cell. Naturally occurring as well as experimentally constructed HBV mutants, which result in a stop codon in there-C sequence, infect cells and replicate but do not express HB_eAg[46, 47] because the HB_eAg precursor protein initiated at the first (pre-C) initiation codon cannot be made, although HB_cAg is expressed.

The S (surface or envelope) gene (see Fig. 135–1) including pre-

S1, pre-S2, and S regions delineated by 3 in frame initiation codons, encodes the viral surface antigen (HBsAg) reactive polypeptides in the virion envelope and in incomplete viral forms (surface antigen particles) found in the serum and liver of infected individuals. These consist of the glycosylated and nonglycosylated forms of three polypeptides of 24,000, 33,000, and 39,000 Da (termed *small, medium,* and *large HBsAg proteins,* respectively) coded, respectively, by the S sequence alone, by pre-S2 plus S sequence, and pre-S1, pre-S2 plus S regions of the S open reading frame.[48, 49]

The P (pol or polymerase) gene, which encompasses three fourths of the viral genome and overlaps a carboxyl-terminal portion of the C-gene, the entire S-gene, and an amino-terminal portion of the X-gene, encodes a basic polypeptide of approximately 90,000 Da (see Fig. 135–1) with DNA polymerase (or reverse transcriptase) activity and ribonuclease H activity. It also serves as a protein primer for DNA minus strand synthesis.[50–52]

The small X-gene encodes a polypeptide of 154 amino acids (see Fig. 135–1), which can transactivate transcription regulated by HBV,[53, 54] as well as by several heterologous viral (including human immunodeficiency virus)[54–58] and cellular[59–62] enhancers and promoters.

The hepadnavirus genome is unusually compact and efficiently organized in that much of the genome is used for multiple functions. This includes overlapping genes in different reading frames so that the same nucleotide sequence encodes more than one protein, and all *cis*-acting regulatory sequences (e.g., transcriptional enhancer and promoter elements) are contained in genomic sequences also encoding protein (see Fig. 135–1). Cleavage of the circular genome at any site interrupts some essential sequence and renders the DNA noninfectious. Hepadnaviruses share nucleotide sequence homology and genome organization with retroviruses and cauliflower mosaic virus,[50, 51] suggesting that these viruses are evolutionarily related.

Virion Structure

The hepatitis B virion has a diameter of approximately 42 nm. It has an outer layer or envelope approximately 7 nm in width that contains HBsAg proteins and glycoproteins and cellular lipid. Enclosed by the envelope is an electron-dense 28-nm–diameter spherical internal core or nucleocapsid (Fig. 135–2*A*).[35] The virion surface manifests HBsAg specificity, which is contained in the small, middle, and large HBsAg proteins that are the principal protein components of the viral envelope.[48, 49] HBsAg proteins not only are components of the virion envelope but also are released from infected cells as components of small spherical particles. These are heterogeneous in size and appearance (diameters from approximately 16 to 25 nm and called 22-nm particles) and are filamentous or rod-shaped particles (approximately 22 nm wide and up to several hundred nanometers in length) (Fig. 135–3). They consist of HBsAg proteins and glycoproteins and cellular lipid. They share antigenic determinants (HBsAg) with the surface of virions.[35] No nucleic acid has been found in them, and they are considered to be incomplete viral envelope particles. The small (22 nm) spherical particles contain mostly small HBsAg protein and little or no large HBsAg protein.[48, 49]

HBsAg is a complex antigen, and the antibody response to the antigen reflects this. At least five antigenic specificities are regularly found on HBsAg particles that appear to be contained in sequences of the S region of HBsAg proteins. A group-specific determinant *(a)*

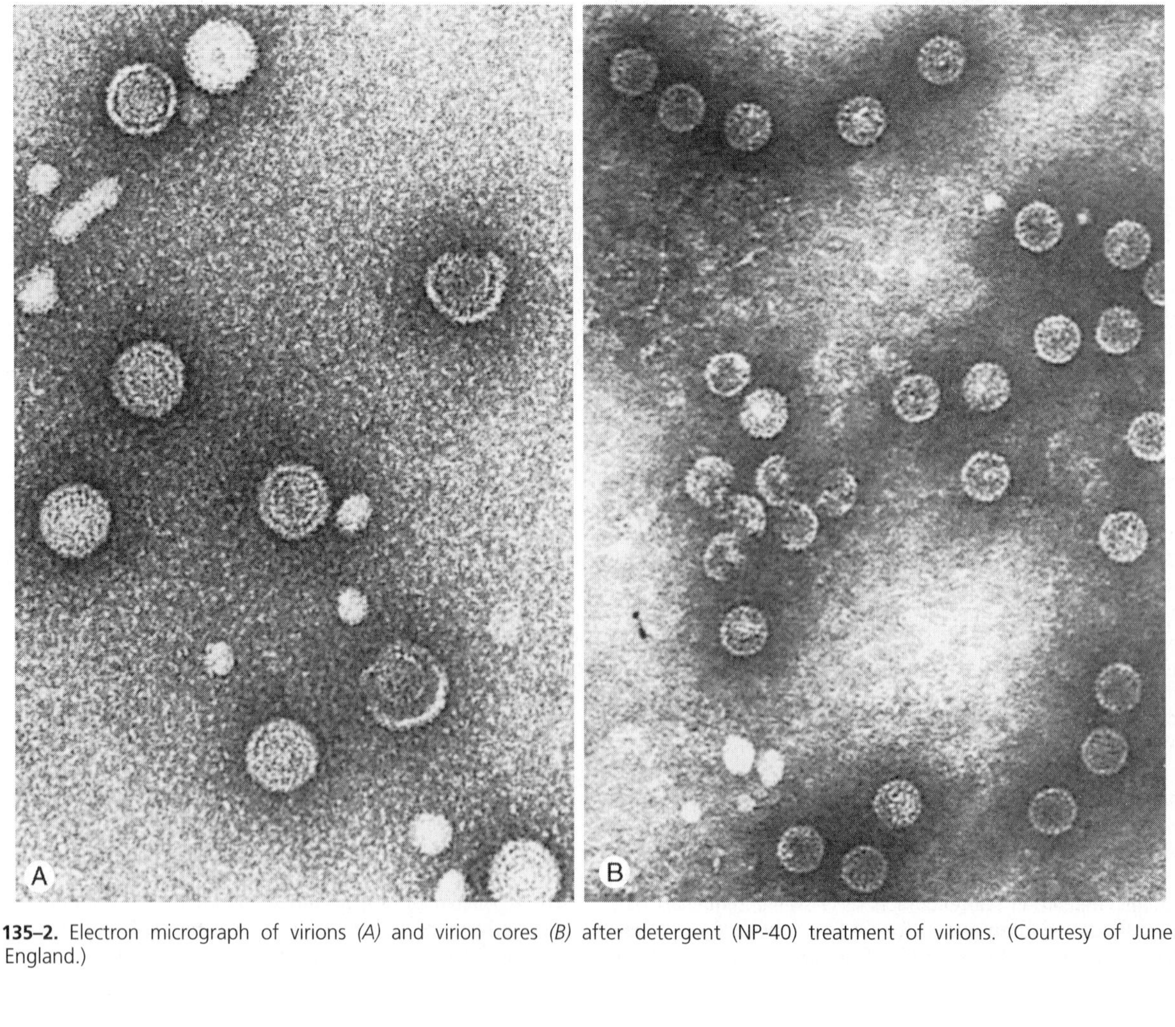

FIGURE 135–2. Electron micrograph of virions *(A)* and virion cores *(B)* after detergent (NP-40) treatment of virions. (Courtesy of June Almedia, London, England.)

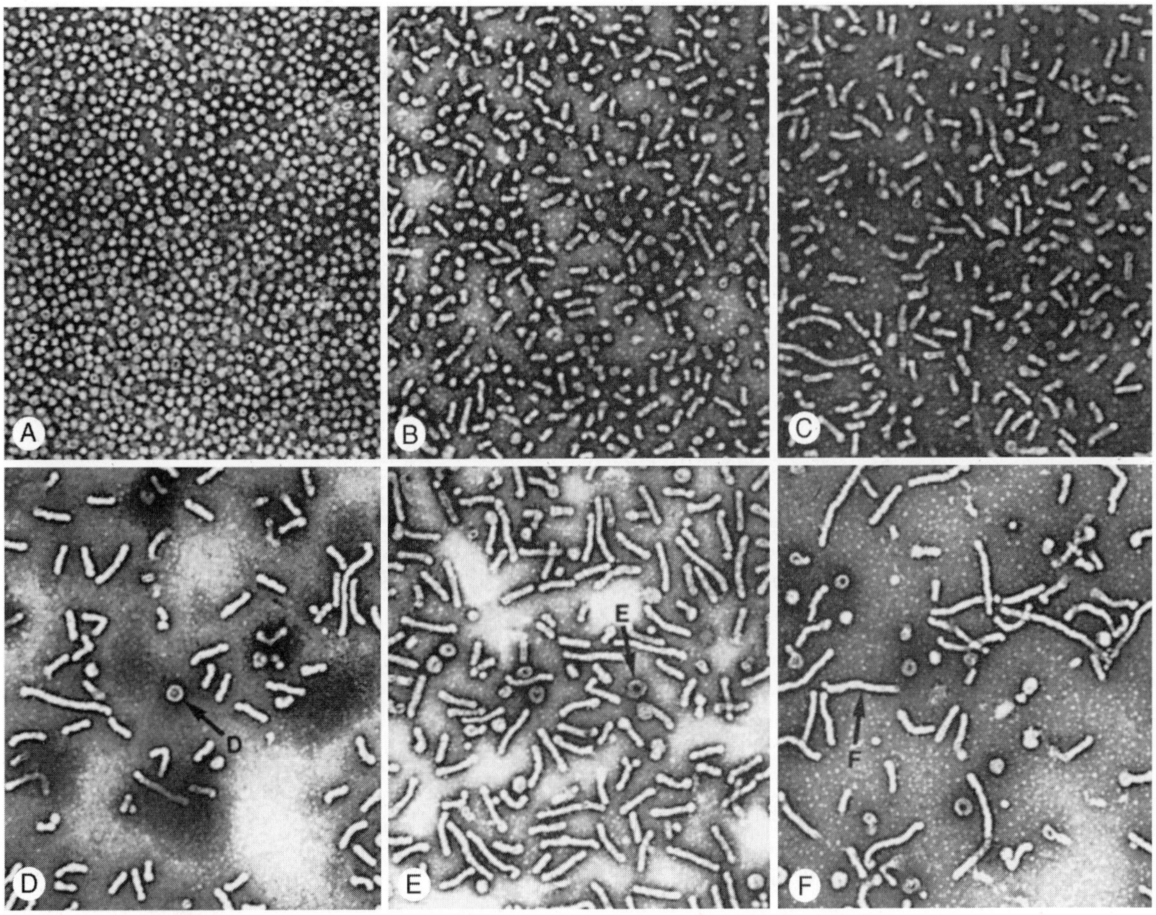

FIGURE 135–3. *A–F,* Electron micrographs of hepatitis B viral forms in the blood of an infected patient showing sucrose density gradient fractions after rate-zonal sedimentation of particles. *D,* virion with an electron-dense core; *E,* empty virion; *F,* filamentous form. (Courtesy of John L. Gerin, Rockville, Md.)

is shared by all HBsAg preparations; more than one antigenic site appears to share this broad specificity, and thus each would be defined as part of the *a* determinant. Two pairs of subtype determinants have been found (*d,y* and *w,r*). The determinants of each pair are mutually exclusive for the most part and thus usually behave as alleles.[63, 64] The four major subtypes of HBsAg have been designated *adw, ayw, adr,* and *ayr.* Antigenic heterogeneity of the w determinant and additional determinants such as j, k, q, and x or g have also been described.[62–65] Several serotypes including *ayw1, ayw2, ayw3, ayw4, ayr, adw2* (both q+ and q−), *adw4,* and *adr* (both q+ and q−) have been identified in sera of different patients.[65] Isolated and usually single cases from the Far East with unusual combinations of HBsAg subtype determinants, such as *awr, adwr, adyw, adyr,* and *adywr,* have been reported.[65] The subtype determinants in these cases are found on the same particles, suggesting that phenotypic mixing or unusual genetic recombinants have formed during mixed infections. Subtype determinants have been used as viral markers to follow spread of virus among individuals and in populations.

The *a* determinant can elicit protective immunity against virus of any subtype, and subtype determinants appear to elicit protection that is subtype-specific.[66] Specific B-cell and T-cell epitopes have been identified in pre-S1 and pre-S2 peptide sequences on the surfaces of virions and filamentous particles. Certain epitopes in both the pre-S1[67] and pre-S2[68] regions appear able to elicit protective immune responses, as do those of the S region noted earlier. Some evidence suggests that an amino acid sequence of the pre-S1 region (pre-S1 21–47) has binding affinity for hepatocytes and may represent a receptor on the virus for attachment to liver cells.[69]

The outer envelope of the virion with HBsAg can be removed by treatment with nonionic detergents, leaving free core particles (see Fig. 135–2*B*) bearing HB_cAg specificity that is antigenically distinct from HBsAg.[63] The viral core contains the viral DNA[70] with a covalently attached primer protein[71] (derived from the pol protein), DNA polymerase (reverse transcriptase) activity,[36, 72] and protein kinase activity.[73] Thus, a principal enzyme (reverse transcriptase) involved in viral DNA replication is contained in virions and is carried into cells as the virus enters cells.

The third antigen associated with HBV infection, HB_eAg, is a truncated form of the major core polypeptide that contains 10 contiguous additional amino acids encoded by the precore sequence at its amino terminus and lacks 34–36 amino acid of the core polypeptide sequence at its carboxy terminus.[74] It is released from infected liver cells in which HBV is replicating and is found as a soluble antigen in the serum of many HBV-infected patients. HB_eAg is also released when virion cores are disrupted with detergents,[45, 75, 76] and the isolated major polypeptide of core particles (21,000 Dad) appears to react with anti-HBe.[45] Thus, the major polypeptide of virion cores manifests different antigenic specificities when assembled in core particles (HB_cAg) and as free polypeptide after disruption of core particles (HB_eAg). Although there are distinct B-cell epitopes for HB_cAg and HB_eAg, these different antigenic forms of the same peptide appear to share major T-cell epitopes.[77]

Viral Forms in the Blood

A characteristic of HBV infections is the production of large amounts of viral antigen forms in the liver, which are detected in the blood,

FIGURE 135–4. Schematic representation of hepatitis B viral forms found in the blood of infected patients.

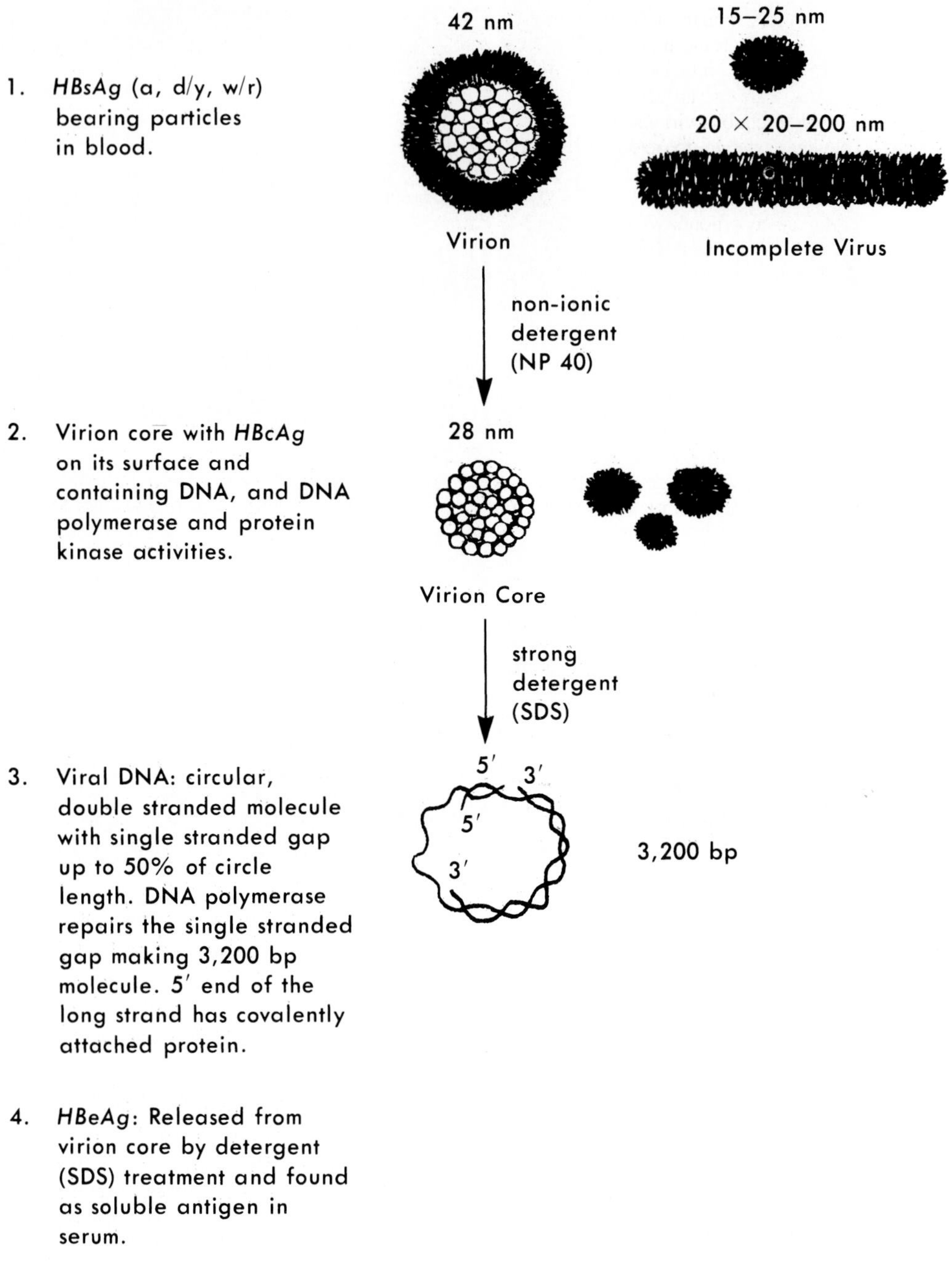
1. HBsAg (a, d/y, w/r) bearing particles in blood.
42 nm
15–25 nm
20 × 20–200 nm
Virion
Incomplete Virus
non-ionic detergent (NP 40)
2. Virion core with HBcAg on its surface and containing DNA, and DNA polymerase and protein kinase activities.
28 nm
Virion Core
strong detergent (SDS)
3. Viral DNA: circular, double stranded molecule with single stranded gap up to 50% of circle length. DNA polymerase repairs the single stranded gap making 3,200 bp molecule. 5′ end of the long strand has covalently attached protein.
5′
3′
5′
3′
3,200 bp
4. HBeAg: Released from virion core by detergent (SDS) treatment and found as soluble antigen in serum.

often in very high concentrations during acute infections and for the duration of most chronic infections. HBsAg in the blood remains the most useful marker of active HBV infection. It appears in the blood exclusively as a component of virions and incomplete particulate viral forms, and no soluble or low-molecular-weight form has been detected.[37, 78] Figure 135–4 summarizes the viral structures found in the blood. The serum of infected patients has been a principal source of viral material for physical characterization of HBV and was used for production of the original plasma vaccine because this virus grows poorly if at all in cell culture.

The concentrations of incomplete viral forms in serum usually greatly exceed the concentrations of complete virions or Dane particles. Concentrations of 22-nm HBsAg particles in serum can exceed 100 μg/ml (up to 500 μg/ml or approximately 10^{13} particles/ml or higher in some sera). Filamentous HBsAg particle concentrations are commonly 100-fold lower (e.g., 1 μg/ml), and virions or Dane particles when present are found in even lower concentrations. Dane particle concentrations may reach levels as high as 0.1 μg/ml (10^8 particles ml, which is usually 10^4 to 10^5-fold lower than the concentration of 22-nm particles in the same serum). Concentrations of HB$_e$Ag in serum may reach 10 μg/ml. HB$_c$Ag and core particles are not present in blood in a free form but are found only as internal components of Dane particles. The very high concentrations of viral antigens found during HBV infection may be present continuously for many years when infection is chronic and are not matched by any other known virus infection.

Some HBsAg-reactive sera, which have detectable virions or Dane particles and HB$_e$Ag, have infected humans or chimpanzees when 1 ml of dilutions up to 10^{-7} or 10^{-8} are inoculated,[79–81] indicating that such patients circulate high concentrations of infectious virus. Such infectivity titers correlate well with measured Dane particle concentrations, suggesting that very few virions are required to infect a susceptible human or chimpanzee. Other HBsAg-reactive sera without detectable Dane particles or HB_eAg and with antibody to HB_eAg have failed to infect chimpanzees when undiluted,[80] suggesting that some HBsAg carriers circulate only incomplete HBsAg particles and not infectious virions.

HBV has been shown to retain infectivity for humans for 6 months when stored in serum at 30°C to 32°C[82] and for 15 years when frozen at −20°C. All infectivity for human volunteers is not lost at 60°C for up to 4 hours when HBV is in serum, but it is lost at 60°C after 10 hours when HBV is in albumin.[83–86] Infectivity in serum was destroyed at 90°C after 1[87] or 20 minutes.[88] Infectivity has also been destroyed by dry heat at 160°C after 1 hour.[89]

Virus in Cells and in Liver

When hepadnaviruses infect and enter cells, the relaxed circular virion DNA is converted to closed circular DNA, which serves as a template for viral transcription. The resulting transcripts (see Fig. 135–1) include a longer than genome length RNA with a terminal redundancy (the long transcript), and smaller transcripts that serve as mRNA from which viral proteins are translated. The long transcript and pol gene product (reverse transcriptase) are encapsidated in core particles in which new viral DNA synthesis takes place by reverse transcription of the long transcript[90] (Fig. 135–5). Viral DNA replication by reverse transcription is a unique mechanism for a DNA virus and is shared only by hepadnaviruses and the plant virus cauliflower mosaic virus. This replication mechanism and nucleotide sequence homology among HBV, cauliflower mosaic virus, and retroviruses[50, 51] indicates a phylogenetic relationship between these virus families. Details of hepadnavirus DNA replication have been reviewed.[91, 92] Core particles in which viral DNA synthesis takes place have been found in cytoplasmic fractions isolated from duck hepatitis B virus, ground squirrel hepatitis virus, and HBV-infected livers. In contrast, HBcAg detected by immunofluorescent staining[93–95] and core particles detected by electron microscopy[96–98] have been found almost exclusively in hepatocyte nuclei of HBV-infected livers. HBsAg is detected by immunofluorescence staining as a cytoplasmic antigen and on cell surfaces.[93–95]

HBV DNA is found in infected liver not only in the episomal forms described earlier that are involved in virus replication but also

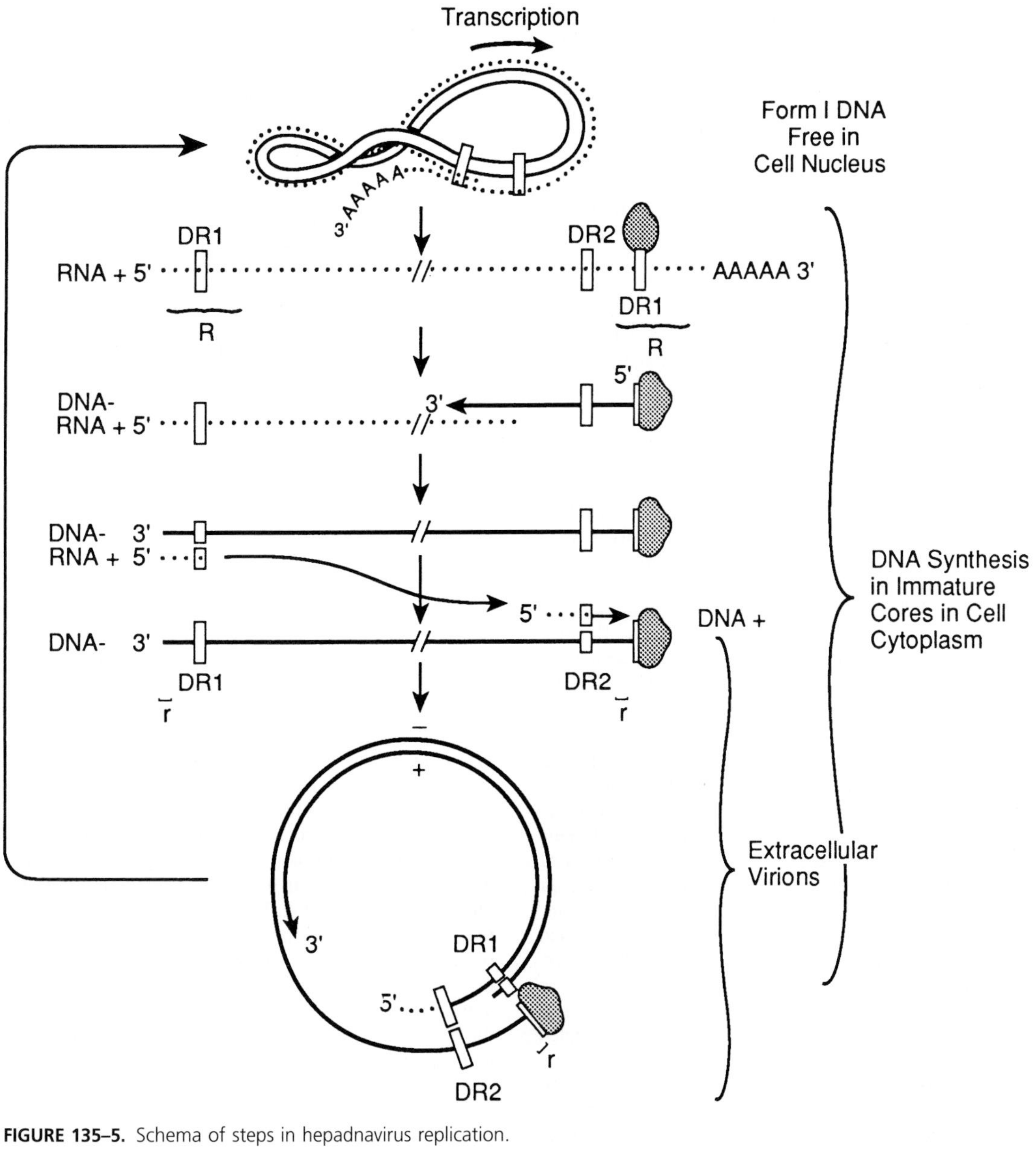

FIGURE 135–5. Schema of steps in hepadnavirus replication.

integrated in cellular DNA.[99, 100] It is not known whether such viral integration occurs in all or only some virus-infected cells, and integrated viral DNA is found at many (perhaps random) cellular DNA sites. Hepadnaviruses do not encode an integrase protein that catalyzes orderly integration of the viral genome as do retroviruses. Integrated hepadnavirus sequences are never completely preserved, and at least small deletions and often gross rearrangements of viral sequences are present in all integrants studied,[101] suggesting that integration occurs by a mechanism such as illegitimate recombination. Hepadnavirus integration interrupts the viral genome in a way that precludes synthesis of the long viral transcript so that virus replication is not possible from integrated sequences in naturally infected liver cells. Thus integration is not an integral step in virus replication, as it is for retroviruses. However, viral genes can be expressed from at least some HBV integrants. Because there are preferred sites in HBV DNA for interruption of the circular genome and for joining cell DNA in viral integrations,[101] the surface antigen gene is the one most often not interrupted, and HBsAg can be expressed by some cells only with integrated virus.

During persistent HBV infection, a variable number of liver cells contain viral antigens detected by immunofluorescent staining (from <1% to virtually all hepatocytes in different patients).[93–95] The pattern of viral antigen expression appears to be different in different cells of the same chronically infected liver. Commonly, most positive cells stain only for HBsAg, fewer have only detectable HB_cAg, and even fewer cells contain both HBsAg and HB_cAg. At least some cells expressing only HBsAg may contain only integrated viral DNA. In the liver of some chronic carriers, HBsAg is the only detectable viral antigen. In such carriers with no detectable virions or HB_eAg in serum, liver cells with replicating virus (and expressing HB_cAg) may have been eliminated by a cytopathic effect of replicating virus or by an immune response directed at HB_cAg; HBsAg may be expressed in remaining infected cells with only integrated virus. In all chronic carriers producing relatively high concentrations of virions and HB_eAg, significant numbers of HB_cAg-positive cells can be found in the liver. The different patterns of viral antigen synthesis in individual cells of the same chronically infected liver indicate that individual viral genes are expressed differently in different cells.

TISSUE TROPISM

Liver cells are clearly the most readily infected and permissive cells for HBV in vivo,[102–104] and permanent eradication of HBV infection after liver transplantation[105] suggests that liver is the only site of HBV replication in at least some cases. However, several studies have suggested that most chronically infected patients have low levels of nonreplicating HBV DNA and sometimes viral antigens in peripheral blood mononuclear cells including monocytes, B cells, $CD4^+$ and $CD8^+$ T cells, and polymorphonuclear leukocytes.[106–108] Interestingly, the presence of high-molecular-weight forms of HBV DNA found to be concatemers of viral DNA suggests aberrant viral DNA replication in such cells. Mitogen stimulation of peripheral blood lymphocytes (PBL) of woodchucks infected with woodchuck hepatitis virus resulted in activation of virus replication,[109] indicating that this closely related virus can replicate in lymphocytes under some conditions. HBV has also been reported in cultures of bone marrow cells of chronic HBV carriers.[106–110] High concentrations of HBsAg have been found in pancreatic juice of some HBV carrier patients,[111] and HBsAg and HB_cAg have been detected by immunofluorescent staining in occasional pancreatic cells in HBV-infected humans.[112] This suggests that limited infection of the pancreas occurs in some patients. High concentrations of duck hepatitis B virus DNA have been detected in the pancreas of infected Peking ducks,[3] suggesting that the pancreas of that species may be regularly infected by another hepadnavirus closely related to HBV. HBV antigens have also been reported in rare cells of skin and kidney of some infected patients.[113] Thus, cells of some tissues other than liver appear to be infected on occasion, but such cells support limited HBV replication, and no disease related to infection of extrahepatic tissues has been shown. Liver cells are most regularly and extensively infected and are the most permissive cell for HBV replication. Tissue tropism appears to be controlled at least in part at the level of viral transcription, because the viral transcriptional enhancers and certain viral promoters are active in liver cells but are not at all or poorly active in other cell types.[114] HBV does not regularly infect tissue culture cells, including primary hepatocyte cultures or cell lines with properties of liver cells, even though HBV can replicate in such cells when introduced as viral DNA. This suggests that the block in virus infection of cultured cells is an early step such as virus attachment to cells, penetration of cells, or uncoating of viral DNA.

VIRUS HOST RANGE

Hepatitis B virus has a narrow host range that is probably restricted to humans and some other primates. Tests for HBsAg in the sera of captive nonhuman primates have revealed infection in chimpanzees,[115–118] gibbons,[116, 117] orangutans,[118] African green monkeys,[115, 118] and squirrel monkeys.[115, 118] Testing for anti-HBs has revealed evidence of past infection in the same species,[118, 119] as well as in baboons, *Celebes*, apes, macaques, and some other Old World and some New World monkeys.[118] Only negative tests results have been found in numerous other primate species. It is not clear in these studies whether HBV infection occurred in any of the nonhuman primates in their natural habitat, or whether the virus was acquired in captivity by exposure to humans. It seems likely that natural infection with HBV or a cross-reactive virus analogous to woodchuck hepatitis virus and ground squirrel hepatitis virus may occur at least in some of these species.

HBV has also been experimentally transmitted to chimpanzees,[93, 120, 121] which are highly susceptible and demonstrate patterns of infection similar to those in humans (see section on the course of HBV infection), except for less severe liver disease. Experimental infection has also been reported in gibbons,[122] African green monkeys,[123] rhesus monkeys,[124] and wooly monkeys.[125] The latter three species appear to be much more resistant to infection than are chimpanzees and humans, because much higher virus doses are required, infection is irregular and very transient when it occurs, and little or no liver disease is seen. Because of this, these monkeys are unsuitable as animal models for HBV infection and infectivity titrations. No successful infections of subprimate species have been reported.

COURSE OF THE VIRUS INFECTION

Studies of natural HBV infections in humans and experimental infections in humans and chimpanzees have defined several patterns of infection with this virus. Most primary infections in adults are self-limited and completely resolve within 6 months of onset. Most infections also appear to be subclinical and are detected only by serologic testing and other methods. A fraction of infections fail to resolve, become persistent, and may continue for many years. A unique feature of infections with HBV is the presence of viral forms continuously in the blood during active infection in almost all patients. These forms are most commonly detected by their antigenicity (e.g., HBsAg). Tests for HBsAg essentially detect the incomplete viral forms described earlier (22-nm particles and filaments), which greatly outnumber complete virions in most patients. Although most persistently infected patients appear to have complete infectious virus in the blood as well as incomplete viral forms, some of these patients appear to have no infectious virus. The presence of viral forms in the blood that can be detected by serologic testing and other methods, and the immune responses to the viral antigens, offer markers that can be used to follow the course of HBV infections. Several patterns of infection that define the spectrum of responses to this virus are described here in detail.

Self-Limited HBsAg-Positive Primary Infection

When HBsAg can be detected transiently in the blood it is called *self-limited* HBsAg-positive primary infection is the most common pattern of primary HBV infection in adults. HBsAg is usually the first viral marker to appear in the blood after HBV infection (Fig. 135–6). The presence of this antigen is considered to be synonymous with active infection. HBsAg can be detected as early as 1[126] or 2[127] weeks and as late as 11 or 12 weeks[127] after exposure to HBV when very sensitive assays are used. Evidence of hepatitis was found to follow the appearance of HBsAg by an average of 4 weeks (usual range, 1 to 7 weeks)[128] and after at least 3 to 6 weeks[127] in different studies. In self-limited infections, HBsAg was found to remain detectable by complement fixation in the blood for 1 to 6 weeks in most patients,[128] although it may persist for up to 20 weeks.[127] Patients who remain HBsAg-positive for less than 7 weeks rarely appear to acquire symptomatic hepatitis.[127] The severity of hepatitis as measured by bilirubin elevations has been roughly correlated with the duration of HBsAg positivity in patients with self-limited experimental infections.[127] As symptoms and jaundice clear, the HBsAg titer usually falls and HBsAg becomes undetectable in most symptomatic patients several weeks after resolution of hepatitis. However, in experimental transmission studies, 9% of patients had become HBsAg-negative even before the onset of symptoms, and 28% were negative by the time symptoms had resolved.[127]

HB_eAg is another regular and early marker of HBV infection, as depicted in Figure 135–6. Highly sensitive assays such as passive hemagglutination[129, 130] and radioimmunoassay[131–134] have demonstrated that HB_eAg appears simultaneously or within a few days of the appearance of HBsAg in all or almost all primary infections, and its titer peaks and then declines in parallel with HBsAg. The prevalence of HB_eAg declines constantly over the first 10 weeks after the onset of symptoms.[134] HB_eAg usually disappears just before the disappearance of HBsAg in self-limited infections. Patients who remain HB_eAg-positive for 10 weeks or longer appear likely to become persistently infected.[133] Anti-HBe appears in most patients at the time HB_eAg becomes undetectable or shortly thereafter. Anti-HB_e persists for 1 to 2 years after resolution of HBV infection.[126]

The third viral marker in order of appearance is DNA and DNA polymerase–containing virions. These particles, detected by their DNA polymerase activity or by hybridization for viral DNA, appear in the blood of most patients soon after the appearance of HBsAg. They rise to high concentrations during the late incubation period of hepatitis B and fall with the onset of hepatic disease,[135, 136] as shown in Figure 135–6.

A fourth marker of infection that appears in virtually all patients and before the onset of hepatic injury in most, is anti-HB_c, the antibody directed against the internal antigen of virions. Anti-HB_c can usually be detected 3 to 5 weeks after the appearance of HBsAg in the blood and before the onset of clinically apparent hepatitis,[126, 127, 136] as shown in Figure 135–6. Anti-HB_c titers usually rise during the period of HBsAg positivity, level off, and eventually fall after HBsAg becomes undetectable. The highest titers of anti-HBc appear in the patients with the longest period of HBsAg positivity.[136] Anti-HB_c titers fall three- to fourfold in the first year after acute infection, and then drop more slowly.[137] Anti-HB_c can still be detected by immunoelectroosmophoresis 5 to 6 years after acute infection in most patients.[126, 137] The high correlation between the prevalence of anti-HB_c detected by immunoelectroosmophoresis[138] or radioimmunoassay (RIA)[127] and anti-HBs detected by RIA, indicates that these two antibodies persist for a similar time after acute self-limited infections.

Although most of the anti-HB_c activity is in the IgG class, IgM anti-HB_c has been found in almost all patients with acute hepatitis

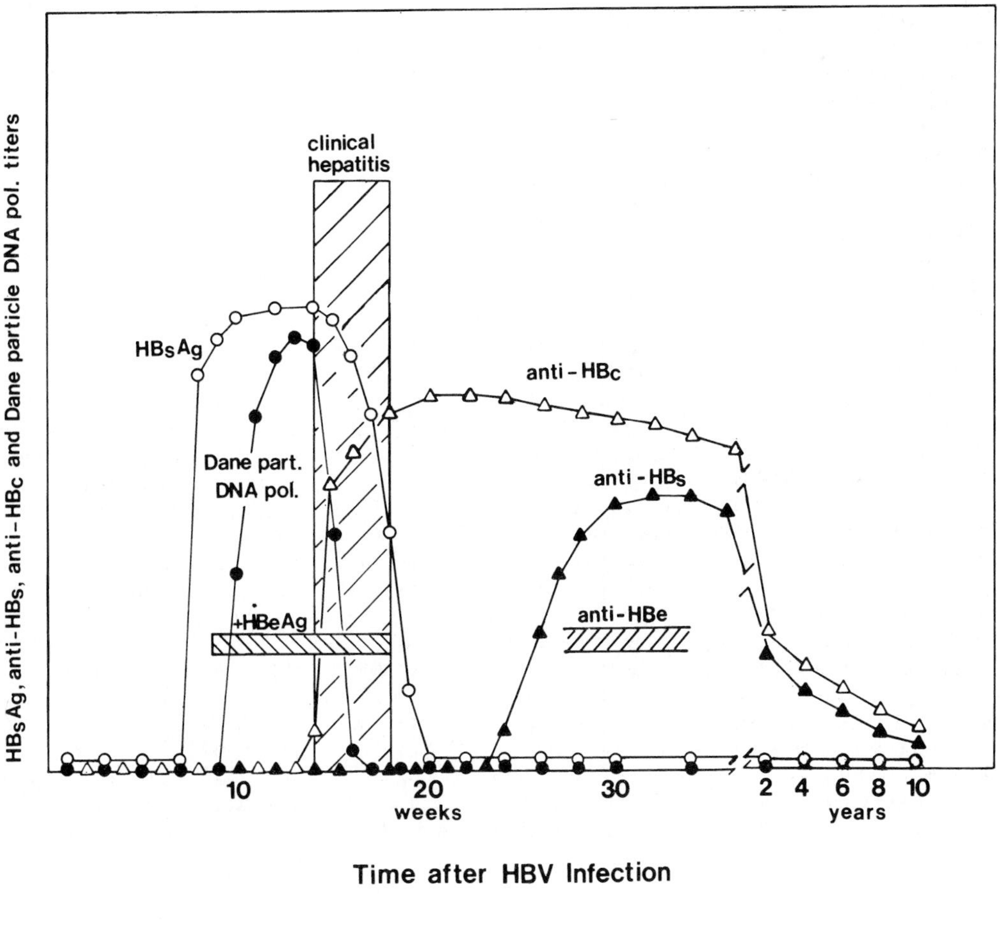

FIGURE 135–6. Schematic representation of viral markers in the blood through a typical course of self-limited HBsAg-positive primary hepatitis B virus infection.

B.[139–142] Using a sensitive enzyme-linked immunosorbent assay, anti-HB_c IgM was found to decline rapidly in titer after disappearance of HBsAg in only 40% of patients with self-limited acute hepatitis B; in the remainder, the decline was slow, with 20% still showing anti-HB_c IgM after 2 years.[142]

Antibody to HBsAg (anti-HBs) has been shown to appear during antigenemia and before the onset of clinically apparent hepatitis in the 10 to 20% of patients who acquire arthritis and rash associated with immune complex formation.[143] HBsAg–anti-HBs complexes have also been detected in a significant fraction of acute hepatitis B cases without well-recognized immune complex disease.[144–146] In most patients with self-limited HBV infection, however, anti-HBs can be detected only after HBsAg disappears from the blood,[23, 126–128, 136–147] as illustrated in Figure 135–6. Anti-HBs cannot be detected even by the most sensitive tests in many patients immediately after HBsAg disappears. There is a time interval of up to several months between the disappearance of detectable HBsAg and the appearance of anti-HBs in approximately one half of patients with self-limited infections.[127, 136] In approximately 10% of patients with transient antigenemia, anti-HBs never appears even when the most sensitive assays are used.[127] In patients with measurable anti-HBs responses, the antibody titer rises slowly during recovery and may still be rising 6 to 12 months after the disappearance of HBsAg.[127, 128] In contrast to the anti-HBc response, the highest titers of anti-HBs appear in those patients with the shortest period of antigenemia.[127] This antibody may persist for years after HBV infection and is associated with protection against reinfection.[23, 148–150]

In contrast to the extensive studies of viral markers in the blood early in the course of primary HBV infection, only a few investigators have examined the state of virus in cells in liver at this early time. During the late incubation period and early during the acute disease, almost all hepatocytes have been reported to be positive by immunofluorescent staining for HBsAg and HB_cAg.[93–95] The state of viral DNA in liver has not been adequately studied during acute hepatitis B, although evidence for integrated viral DNA has been reported for two patients.[151] However, the forms of virus in blood and antigen expression in liver suggest that almost all hepatocytes are replicating complete virions during early stages of primary infection.

Self-Limited Primary Infections without Detectable Serum HBsAg

A significant fraction of patients with evidence of acute self-limited primary HBV infection apparently never have detectable HBsAg in the blood. Anti-HBs usually appears 4 to 12 weeks after exposure to HBV (at about the time HBsAg appears in patients with detectable antigen), and the titer typically rises rapidly to high levels and is sustained,[127] as depicted in Figure 135–7. Anti-HB_c response is also detected, but the antibody usually appears only in low titer and may not persist for as long as in patients who manifest antigenemia.[127] IgM anti-HB_c is probably regularly found in these patients because it was detected in each of 31 patients with apparent acute hepatitis B who were HBsAg-negative from the time of their admission to the hospital.[142] Although some of the patients in this study may have been HBsAg-positive before testing began, undoubtedly some represented HBsAg-negative primary infections. Infections associated with a primary antibody response without detectable HBsAg in the blood are usually accompanied by asymptomatic disease with only minor elevations in serum transaminase activity.[136, 148, 152] Although the pattern of anti-HBs and anti-HB_c response differs in order and relative magnitude compared with the responses of patients with detectable antigenemia, the fact that both antibodies (including IgM anti-HB_c) and liver function abnormalities appear after a length of time consistent with the incubation period of HBV infection indicates

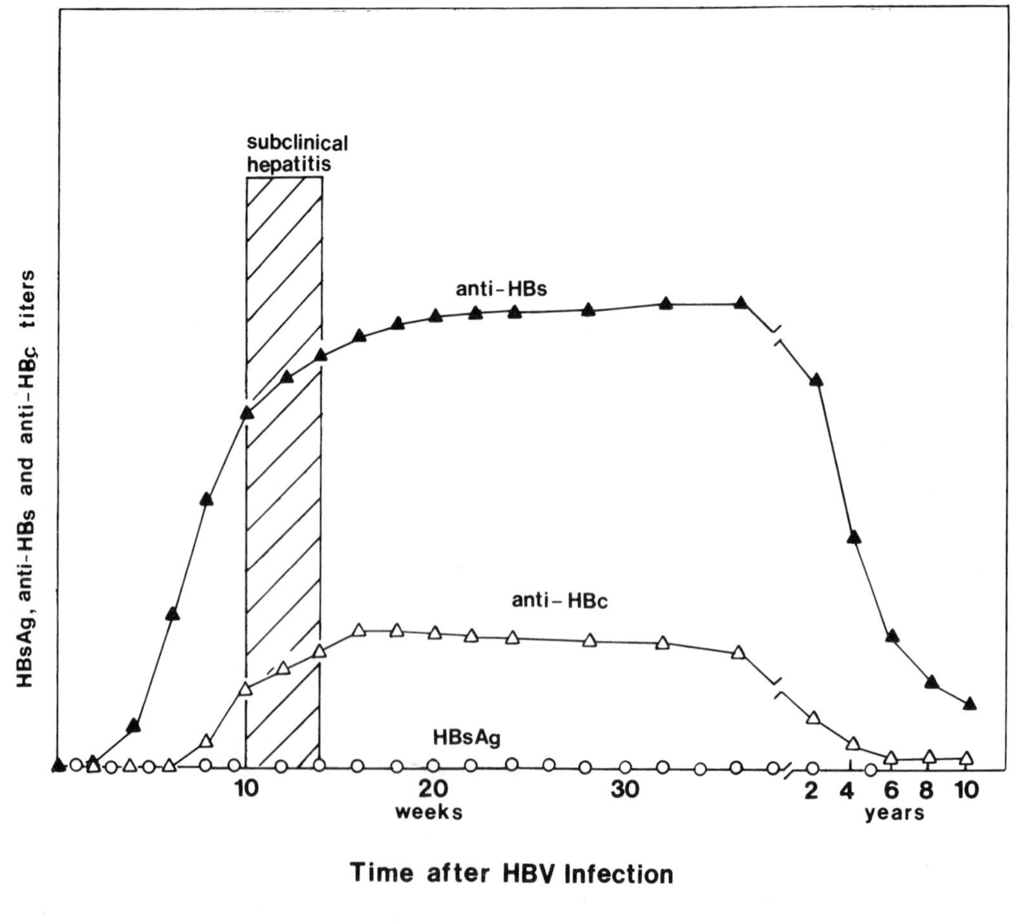

FIGURE 135–7. Schematic representation of the serologic response through a typical course of HBsAg-negative primary hepatitis B virus infection.

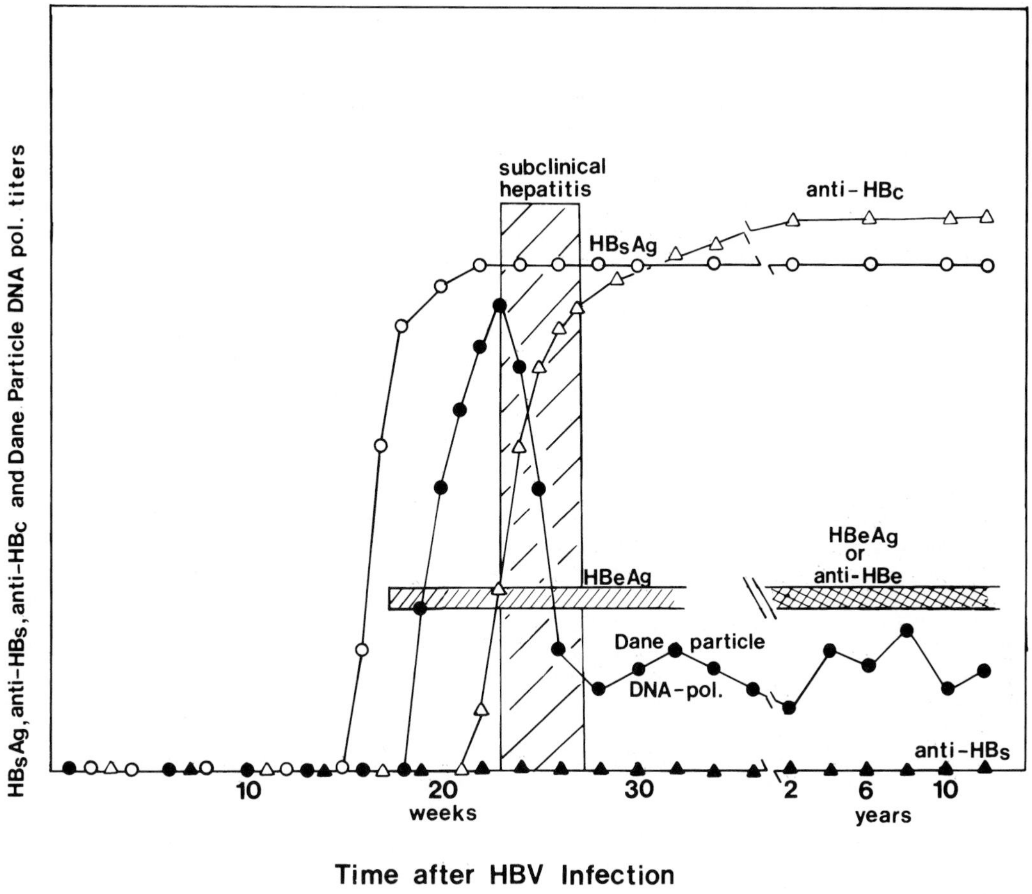

FIGURE 135–8. Schematic representation of viral markers in the blood through a typical course of hepatitis B virus infection that becomes persistent.

that actual infection with HBV has taken place. DNA polymerase–containing virions and HB_cAg have not been studied in such cases. No studies have been performed to assess the state of virus in liver cells during infection of this kind.

In a large series of adult patients experimentally infected with HBV, 70% had self-limited infection with transient HBsAg positivity, and 23% had no detectable antigenemia but a primary anti-HBs and anti-HB_c response.[127] The frequency of each response after natural infections would probably depend on the infecting dose of virus and other factors that might differ for different populations.

HBsAg-Positive Persistent Hepatitis B Virus Infection

Patients who remain HBsAg-positive for 20 weeks or longer after primary infection are likely to remain positive indefinitely and be designated chronic HBsAg carriers (Fig. 135–8). Virions (Dane particles),[153] DNA polymerase activity,[154, 155] HB_eAg,[156] or virion DNA[153] can be detected in the blood of a significant fraction of persistently infected patients who are positive for HBsAg. By a sensitive assay for virion DNA polymerase, approximately 50% of persistently infected patients tested positive and 5 to 10% had very high levels.[154] All patients with detectable virion DNA polymerase in the blood have HB_cAg detected by immunofluorescence in liver biopsies,[155] and when a highly sensitive assay for virions is used, all patients with HB_cAg in liver have detectable virions in serum.[157]

Almost all persistently infected patients have high titers of anti-HB_c in the blood,[127] as shown in Figure 135–8. The titers of this antibody are significantly higher during persistent infection than during most self-limited infections or in convalescence.[127] Although most of the anti-HB_c is undoubtedly in the IgG fraction, interestingly, IgM anti-HBc continues to be made and can be detected indefinitely in the serum of most persistently infected patients.[142, 158] Very rarely, HBV carriers fail to produce antibody to HB_cAg, which is thought to be on the basis of a selective defect in the immune response.[159]

As described earlier, HB_eAg can be detected in the serum of almost all patients early in primary HBV infection, and anti-HB_e appears in almost all during resolution of the infection. Conversely, in persistent infection, sensitive assays such as RIA or passive hemagglutination have detected HB_eAg in one fourth to one half of patients, and anti-HB_e in almost all of the remainder.[129, 160] When less sensitive assays are used, neither marker may be detected in 50% or more of persistently infected patients.[161–164] The observation that the high-molecular-weight form of HB_eAg in serum represents a complex between HB_eAg and immunoglobulin[165, 166] suggests that anti-HB_e may be produced by many or all HB_eAg-positive patients, but is present exclusively as a complex with HB_eAg so that no free antibody can be detected. There is a very high correlation between the presence of serum HB_eAg and virions detected by electron microscopy[167] or by their DNA polymerase activity.[167–171]

There is a wide range of HBsAg titers in persistently infected patients. In general, those with the highest titers of infectious virus[148, 152] and detectable virion DNA polymerase activity[172] or HB_eAg, or both,[172–174] have the highest HBsAg titers.

The most sensitive assay for complete virions is undoubtedly infectivity titrations by inoculation into susceptible hosts such as humans or chimpanzees because, as described earlier, infectious HBV can be demonstrated in some sera after dilution by as much as 10^{-8} [80, 81] Although most HBsAg carriers have high titers of infectious HBV in serum, some carriers appear to have no detectable infectious virus. The highest titers are found in patients with detectable HB_eAg[80, 81] or virion DNA polymerase activity[80], or both, in serum, and those without these markers[81] or with anti-HB_e have much lower titers. In one study, undiluted sera from six HBsAg carriers without detectable virion DNA polymerase or HB_eAg failed to infect chimpanzees.[80] This was a direct demonstration that some persistently infected patients who continue to produce HBsAg do not produce detectable amounts of infectious HBV, and these would appear to be HBsAg carriers without detectable virion DNA polymerase or HB_eAg. The fraction of HBsAg carriers who have no detectable infectious virus is not known. Patients with detectable virion DNA polymerase and HB_eAg in their serum, but not those without them, appear to be highly contagious,[168, 173, 175] which is in agreement with the data on titers of infectious HBV in the blood. A few HBsAg carriers with HB_eAg, and DNA and DNA polymerase–containing virions in the blood have been shown to have free replicating forms of viral DNA (closed and relaxed circular, and linear double-stranded, single-stranded, and DNA-RNA hybrids) and probably integrated viral DNA in the liver,[96, 97, 151, 176] providing biochemical evidence that complete virus replication is proceeding at least in some cells. A variable number of liver cells in such patients appear to contain HBsAg or HB_cAg, or both, by immunofluorescent staining. Such patients frequently, but not always, have chronic persistent or chronic active hepatitis.[171, 177, 178]

Investigation of a few HBsAg carriers with no detectable DNA and DNA polymerase–containing virions or HB_eAg in the blood has revealed evidence of integrated viral DNA sequences but no detectable free viral DNA forms or HB_cAg in liver cells.[96, 97, 151, 176] As described earlier, not all cells (and frequently only a small fraction of cells) are HBsAg-positive by immunofluorescent staining. These findings and the infectivity studies cited previously indicate that these patients are replicating complete virus at a very low level or not at all, and that the only viral gene expressed appears to be the HBsAg gene in an integrated state. Many but not all of these patients appear to have little or no liver disease[94, 171, 177] and are considered to be "healthy carriers."

Anti-HBs has been regularly detected as a complex with HBsAg in the serum of patients with certain extrahepatic disease syndromes such as HBV-associated polyarteritis nodosa and membranous glomerulonephritis.[143] In addition, there is evidence for HBsAg–anti-HBs complexes in the serum of a significant fraction of persistently infected patients with chronic liver disease and in some so-called healthy carriers.[144–146, 179] This indicates that anti-HBs is made in some patients in the face of ongoing persistent infection and without significant associated disease. Standard assays for anti-HBs rarely detect this antibody in serum of persistently infected subjects because of the great antigen excess. It is not known whether the anti-HBs response in these cases is quantitatively diminished; however, the frequent presence of this antibody, anti-HB_c, and anti-HB_e during persistent HBV infection would suggest that complete immunologic tolerance to these respective viral antigens does not account for the persistence of the infection.

Although the long-term natural history of persistent HBV infection is not completely defined, prolonged infection (e.g., for many years) appears to be the rule for most chronic carriers, and HBsAg positivity lasting as long as 20 years has been documented.[178] The titers of HBsAg and virion DNA polymerase levels have been shown to be relatively stable over a period of weeks or a few months.[155] However, evidence suggests that persistent HBV infections tend to spontaneously "wind down" over a period of many months to years, with HBsAg titers slowly falling and virion DNA polymerase and HB_eAg titers falling to less than detectable levels. In one prospective study of persistently infected patients with significant levels of virion DNA polymerase activity in their sera, virion DNA polymerase levels spontaneously fell to less than detectable levels in approximately 10% of patients per year, and a similar rate of disappearance of serum HB_eAg was observed.[155] In a different group of patients with HB_eAg, this antigen disappeared from serum in 45% of patients over a 2- to 7-year period.[180] Similar spontaneous disappearance of HB_eAg or virion DNA polymerase activity, or both, has been shown in many other cases.[170, 177, 180–183]

Anti-HB_e can eventually be detected in most patients after they become HB_eAg-negative. In HBsAg carriers without virion DNA polymerase activity or HB_eAg in serum, these markers have infrequently been observed to reappear spontaneously.[184, 185] Although the time after onset of infection when HB_eAg and virion levels fall to less than detectable levels appears to vary greatly and these markers may remain detectable in persistently infected patients for years, the duration of infection is clearly an important factor that is strongly correlated with the presence of detectable HB_eAg and virions. Spontaneous clearance of all viral markers of active HBV infection, although unusual, can occur at any time. HBsAg became undetectable at a rate of approximately 2% per year, using data combined from three different studies, including a total of 800 HBsAg-positive blood donors, most of whom were undoubtedly chronic carriers, and with individual follow-ups of 2 to 44 months.[186–188] In another study of persistently infected patients, most of whom had chronic hepatitis, HBsAg became undetectable in 1.5% of cases over a 10-month period.[172] Spontaneous disappearance of HBsAg in persistently infected patients has been observed in numerous other cases.[170, 177, 189] A number of factors that appear to influence the prevalence of persistent infection—such as age, sex, immunologic status, and possibly race—may also influence rates of spontaneous remission. Some evidence suggests that persistent infections resolve at a faster rate in females than in males.[190] Evidence is not available concerning the influence of other factors.

HBsAg-Negative Persistent Hepatitis B Virus Infection

There is good evidence that some patients with persistent HBV infection do not have detectable HBsAg in their serum. Hoofnagle and colleagues[127] described a patient with persistent HBV infection with a high anti-HB_c titer and HBsAg titer that fluctuated to just greater than and just less than the level of detection by RIA so that at certain times the patient's serum was HBsAg-negative by the most sensitive tests, although active infection apparently continued. A small but significant fraction of blood donors whose sera are HBsAg-negative by the most sensitive tests transmit HBV infection to recipients of their blood.[191–193] Although some of these donors could be in the incubation period of hepatitis B before the appearance of detectable HBsAg, they most probably are persistently infected, with HBsAg at less than detectable levels, because they have high titers of anti-HB_c. Finally, cases of chronic hepatitis without detectable HBsAg have been ascribed to active HBV infection because of persistent high titers of anti-HB_c.[194]

Exogenous Factors That May Alter the Course of Persistent Hepatitis B Virus Infection

Corticosteroid therapy appears to regularly alter the course of persistent HBV infection. Initiation of approximately 20 to 30 mg of prednisone per day has been shown to be rapidly and regularly followed by a rise in virion DNA polymerase activity and HBsAg titer in blood.[195] Occasional HBsAg-negative patients with anti-HB_c[196] or anti-HBs[197] have been shown to become positive during immunosuppressive therapy. This suggests the possibility that HBV may be present in a latent state in some patients and that virus replication can be activated in such patients by immunosuppression. Withdrawal of corticosteroid is usually associated with a fall in HBsAg titers and virion DNA polymerase levels, the latter sometimes to less than the level of detection.[195] The mechanism of the effects observed with corticosteroids is not proved, but either suppression of the immune response or direct stimulation of HBV replication and HBsAg expression through the action of corticosteroids on a steroid-responsive transcriptional enhancer element in the viral genome[198] may be involved.

Certain antiviral agents such as interferons and adenine arabinoside have been shown to inhibit HBV replication in all persistently infected patients.[155,156–199,200] Experimental treatment with either antiviral agent or with the two together has been accompanied by a rapid reduction in the level of virions in the serum of all patients and a much more gradual reduction of HBsAg titers in only some patients, which suggests that these antiviral agents act primarily on a step involved in virion production and not on incomplete HBsAg particle production. In some patients, permanent disappearance of only virions and HB$_e$Ag has been observed, and in a few patients disappearance of those markers as well as HBsAg has been noted (see "Management of Hepatitis B"). Although these responses to antiviral treatment have been well documented, the frequency with which each response occurs can only be determined in carefully designed trials including placebo-treated controls.

Finally, several cases have been observed in which HB$_e$Ag and virion DNA polymerase levels have fallen to undetectable levels and HBsAg titers have fallen significantly in persistently infected patients during intercurrent infections with other agents such as hepatitis A virus (W. S. Robinson, unpublished results). Although these anecdotal cases are suggestive, more evidence is needed to establish a causal effect and to elucidate a mechanism for these observations.

PROTECTIVE IMMUNITY AGAINST HEPATITIS B VIRUS INFECTION

The presence of anti-HBs in the serum of convalescent patients appears to confer almost complete resistance to reinfection. The anti-HBs produced after primary HBV infection is primarily of anti-a specificity, although anti-d, anti-y, or other type-specific antibody appropriate to the subtype of the infecting virus may also appear.[201] Protection against reinfection with HBV of either the same or a different subtype has been shown,[148] suggesting that immunity is probably conferred mostly by anti-a. In exceptional cases, however, second infections with HBV in patients with anti-HBs have been reported,[202–204] and in some cases, HBV of a different subtype infected an individual with antibody of restricted (e.g., only subtype) specificity.[202] It has also been shown that chimpanzees can be reinfected when challenge doses are sufficiently large, even when the identical strain of HBV is used for the initial and the challenge exposure.[148,205] Second infection with HBV overcoming immunity by either mechanism must be unusual because individuals having multiple episodes of acute viral hepatitis have not been found to acquire hepatitis B more than once.[206–208]

Evidence from primary immunization with purified HBsAg (after which anti-HBs but no anti-HB$_c$ appears)[149] and passive immunization with high-titer anti-HBs[150] indicates that anti-HBs protects against reinfection; however, patients with anti-HB$_c$ and no detectable anti-HBs have also been shown to resist reinfection.[127] Immunization of chimpanzees with HB$_c$Ag purified from infected liver[209] and HB$_c$Ag produced in bacterial cells transformed with a plasmid expression vector containing the HB$_c$Ag gene[210] has protected the animals against challenge with HBV. Anti-HB$_e$ also appears to be protective.[211] These results suggest a role of the immune response to HB$_c$Ag and HB$_e$Ag in protection against HBV infection and raise the question of whether HB$_c$Ag as well as HBsAg could be used as a vaccine.

Cellular immune responses directed against HBsAg and HB$_c$Ag are described under "Pathogenesis of Disease." The role of cellular immunity in resolution of HBV infection and protection against reinfection is undoubtedly important.

PATHOGENESIS OF DISEASES ASSOCIATED WITH HEPATITIS B VIRUS INFECTION

Acute and Chronic Hepatitis B

Acute and chronic hepatitis B represent syndromes of hepatocellular necrosis and inflammatory and regenerative responses associated with HBV infection of hepatocytes. Primary HBV infection may be associated with little or no liver disease or with acute hepatitis of severity ranging from mild to fulminant.[212] Persistent HBV infection is sometimes associated with a histologically normal or nearly normal liver and normal liver function and sometimes with syndromes designated as chronic persistent hepatitis (CPH) or chronic active hepatitis (CAH).[212] All possible mechanisms contributing to liver cell injury in hepatitis B are not established, but there has long been evidence implicating the immune response.[213,214]

Several factors have been identified that appear to correlate with the severity of acute or chronic hepatitis B and that may provide clues about pathogenesis. Among these is the infecting dose of virus, with high doses of HBV usually resulting in shorter incubation periods and more severe acute hepatitis than low infecting doses.[79] A second factor appears to be age. HBV infection at a very young age is usually associated with very mild initial hepatitis.[215,216] Anecdotal cases suggest that HBV infections are associated with milder initial disease in immunologically impaired hosts than in immunologically normal individuals.[217,218] These observations are consistent with a role of the immune response in influencing the severity of acute hepatitis B.

The mechanism or mechanisms involved in liver cell injury during acute and chronic hepatitis B have been difficult to define, and at least three mechanisms that could play a role have been identified. The first (and considered by many to be the most important) is an HLA class I restricted cytotoxic T-cell (CTL) response directed at HB$_c$Ag/HB$_e$Ag on HBV-infected hepatocytes. This possibility was suggested by cytotoxicity of peripheral blood cells of patients with chronic active hepatitis B for autologous hepatocyte target cells, and the cytotoxic effect was blocked by anti-HBc.[219,220] More recently, HLA class I restricted CTLs were demonstrated in patients with acute hepatitis B in studies in which target cells were autologous PBLs immortalized by Epstein-Barr virus infection and which expressed HBcAg after transfection with an Epstein-Barr virus–based expression vector carrying the HB$_c$Ag gene.[221] HB$_c$Ag-specific CTLs were not detected directly in freshly isolated PBLs of acute hepatitis B patients but only after sequential stimulation of PBLs with HB$_c$Ag synthetic peptides followed by HB$_c$Ag expressing HLA-matched cells.[221] This suggests that CTLs were present in very low concentrations in the blood of these patients and that a higher density of HB$_c$Ag on target cell surfaces was needed for CTL activation and detection than that provided by HB$_c$Ag expression via the transfected recombinant plasmid. Demonstration of a CTL response directed at HB$_c$Ag/HB$_e$Ag has required several years of difficult work and has been achieved in very few patients so that more studies are needed to define the role of this CTL response in acute and chronic hepatitis B.

A second possible mechanism for hepatocyte injury in hepatitis B is a direct cytopathic effect of HB$_c$Ag expression in infected hepatocytes. This possibility is suggested by the observation that cells in culture expressing HB$_c$Ag (and not those expressing HBsAg alone) experience cytopathic changes and die.[222] This indicates that HB$_c$Ag expression can be toxic to cells and suggests that such a mechanism might operate in infected cells in vivo when HB$_c$Ag is expressed.

Certain viral markers in the serum and liver of persistently infected patients appear to be present more often in patients who have chronic hepatitis than in those who do not. HB$_e$Ag[161–166,171–223,224] and virion DNA polymerase activity[171] in serum, and HB$_c$Ag as well as HBsAg in the liver detected by immunofluorescent staining,[171] are often found in patients with CAH or CPH. There is little difference between the prevalence of these markers, however, in CAH and CPH.[163–165,171] In contrast, "healthy" carriers,[223–225] including those with little or no abnormality documented by liver biopsy,[171,226] appear most often to be HB$_e$Ag-negative, virion DNA polymerase–negative,[71] and frequently anti-HB$_e$-positive.[165,171,224–226] In such patients, liver biopsies reveal HBsAg but no HB$_c$Ag by immunofluorescent staining.[94,95,171] These findings suggest that complete virus replication proceeds more often in liver cells of patients with chronic hepatitis B compared with liver cells of carriers with little or no hepatitis, which most often express only HBsAg. These findings are consistent with the hypothesis that the mechanism of liver cell injury in hepatitis B is either via a CTL response directed at HB$_c$Ag or HB$_e$Ag in infected liver cells (and not a response to HBsAg) or by a direct cytopathic effect of HB$_c$Ag expression in infected hepatocytes with replicating virus.

A third possible mechanism for liver cell injury in hepatitis B is high-level expression and inefficient secretion of HBsAg. This mechanism is suggested by observations in HBsAg transgenic mice expressing the large HBsAg protein alone.[227] This protein is inefficiently secreted (secretion of the large HBsAg protein is facilitated by coexpression of the small HBsAg protein), accumulates in cells of the mouse liver, and results in liver cell injury. Such cells in the mouse have the appearance of the "ground glass" cells observed in human liver of some hepatitis B patients, which are cells containing large amounts of accumulated HBsAg.[228] Whether HBsAg secretion is sufficiently blocked in any infected liver cells in vivo to cause liver cell injury by this mechanism in humans is not clear, but it is a mechanism that must be considered.

A final mechanism for liver cell injury in some cases during HBV infection appears to be coinfection with a second cytopathic virus, the hepatitis delta virus (HDV). Delta antigen was discovered by immunofluorescent staining as a nuclear antigen distinct from HBsAg, HB$_c$Ag, and HB$_e$Ag in hepatocytes of some HBsAg carriers in Italy, which is the area with the highest prevalence of delta antigen.[229] Most patients with delta antigen in liver have antibody to delta antigen (anti-delta) in their sera. Surveys show a high prevalence of anti-delta in Italians residing in southern Italy[230] and in other Mediterranean populations,[231] and it is particularly high in those in North Africa.[232] Epidemics have been reported in parts of South America.[233] In the United States, the prevalence is low in the general population but high in some groups such as certain intravenous drug users and polytransfused HBsAg carriers.[230] Although delta antigen has not been found in HBsAg-negative patients, anti-delta is found in low prevalence in polytransfused HBsAg-negative patients, but only in those with anti-HBs.

Delta antigen is contained in a 68,000-Da protein encoded by the HDV genome, which is a small single-stranded circular RNA with features of viroids. Virions of HDV consist of a core of delta antigen and RNA enclosed in an HBsAg-containing envelope.[234] Inoculation of HDV-containing sera into chimpanzees who are HBsAg carriers but who do not have delta antigen in the liver, resulted in the appearance of delta antigen in the hepatocyte nuclei of these animals, along with the disappearance of HB$_c$Ag detected by immunofluorescent staining in the liver, and a rise in serum alanine aminotransferase.[235] Thus, HDV appears to be a defective virus, and its replication requires coinfection with HBV. Phenotypic mixing results in delta antigen–containing particles with HBsAg-containing envelopes, and infection with the agent results in hepatic injury and suppression of HBV replication.

There is a higher incidence of HDV infection in HBsAg-positive patients with acute and chronic hepatitis compared with asymptomatic carriers.[230] Simultaneous infection with HBV and HDV may lead to severe or fulminant hepatitis more often than do infections with HBV alone, and cases of fulminant hepatitis B positive for delta antigen in populations with a high prevalence of delta agent have been observed.[233, 236, 237] In countries with a low prevalence of HDV infection such as the United States[237] and Ireland,[238] delta antigen appears to be present in only a small fraction of fulminant hepatitis B cases, and thus delta agent probably plays no role in most cases. HDV may play a more prominent role in chronic liver disease, especially in geographic areas where it is common, such as in Italy where 32% of HBsAg carriers with CAH and 52% with cirrhosis were found to be delta antigen–positive compared with HBsAg carriers with no liver disease, none of whom had detectable delta antigen.[239, 240] Exacerbations of hepatitis may occur in HBsAg carriers when they subsequently acquire HDV infection,[238, 239] but how often this mechanism accounts for exacerbations and the precise impact of HDV on the severity of acute and chronic hepatitis B in the United States remain to be determined. HDV may be present in blood in higher concentrations than HBV markers and rarely is present in blood that is HBsAg-negative. Such individuals represent a particular risk as blood donors for HBsAg carriers. Because new infection of HBsAg carriers with HDV can result in severe or fulminant hepatitis, great care is needed in selecting blood donors for patients who are HBsAg carriers. Donor blood should be negative for anti-delta, HBsAg, and anti-HB$_c$. The mechanism of liver cell injury associated with HDV infection has not been studied. Figure 135–9 illustrates the recognized patterns of HDV infection.

Hepatocellular Carcinoma

A second form of disease associated with chronic HBV infection is HCC. It has a worldwide distribution and, numerically, is one of the major cancers in the world today.[34, 241] Although HCC is rare in most parts of the world, it occurs commonly in sub-Saharan Africa, Southeast Asia, Japan, Oceania, Greece, and Italy. In certain areas of Asia and Africa, it is the most common cancer. Geographic areas with the highest incidence of HCC are also areas where HBV infection is common and where persistent HBV infections occur at the highest known frequencies. Within the limits of the data available, there appears to be a good correlation between the worldwide geographic distribution of HCC and active HBV infection, with the highest frequency of both occurring in sub-Saharan Africa and Southeast Asia.[34, 241] In addition, active HBV infection occurs significantly more frequently in patients with HCC than in controls in geographic areas with either a high or low incidence of HCC.[34, 241] A recent prospective study of HBsAg-positive and HBsAg-negative middle-aged men in Taiwan revealed an incidence of HCC more than 200 times higher in the HBsAg-positive group than in the HBsAg-negative group.[242] Similar results have been obtained in Japan.[243] Such prospective studies provide compelling evidence for a role of chronic HBV infection in the development of HCC.

The high incidence of persistent HBV infection in mothers of HCC patients, in contrast to that in fathers,[244] suggests that transmission from mothers to newborn or infant children may be a frequent mode and time of HBV infection in HCC patients. The findings of low serum HBsAg titers and the absence of HB$_e$Ag, together with the rare occurrence of hepatic HB$_c$Ag in most HCC patients,[34, 245] also suggest that the persistent infections in HCC patients are of long duration. If HBV infection does occur frequently at a very early age in HCC patients in areas of high HCC incidence, the age distribution of patients with clinically recognized tumors would suggest that these tumors appear after a mean duration of approximately 35 years of HBV infection.[246] Very few cases of HCC occur in children.[246] Between 60 and 90% of HCC patients have coexisting cirrhosis,[242, 246–249] suggesting that this lesion in association with persistent HBV infection increases the risk for the development of HCC.

HBV infection in humans is not the only hepadnavirus infection associated with HCC. A much higher incidence of HCC formation occurs in woodchuck hepatitis virus–infected woodchucks,[1, 250] and ground squirrel hepatitis virus–infected ground squirrels[251] than is observed in humans with HBV.

Although the association of HBV infection with HCC is very strong, a viral hepatocarcinogenic mechanism has not been identified. HCC in HBV-infected individuals often contains integrated viral DNA,[252] but such viral integrations are at different cellular DNA sites in every tumor, and they have not been implicated in an oncogenic mechanism in HCC in humans. Genetic changes that could contribute an oncogenic effect have been identified in some human HCCs (e.g., point mutations in the p53 tumor suppressor gene).[253, 254] These have been found in HCC not associated with HBV infection as well as in HCC or HBV-infected patients. The lack of exclusive association with HBV infection and the absence of an

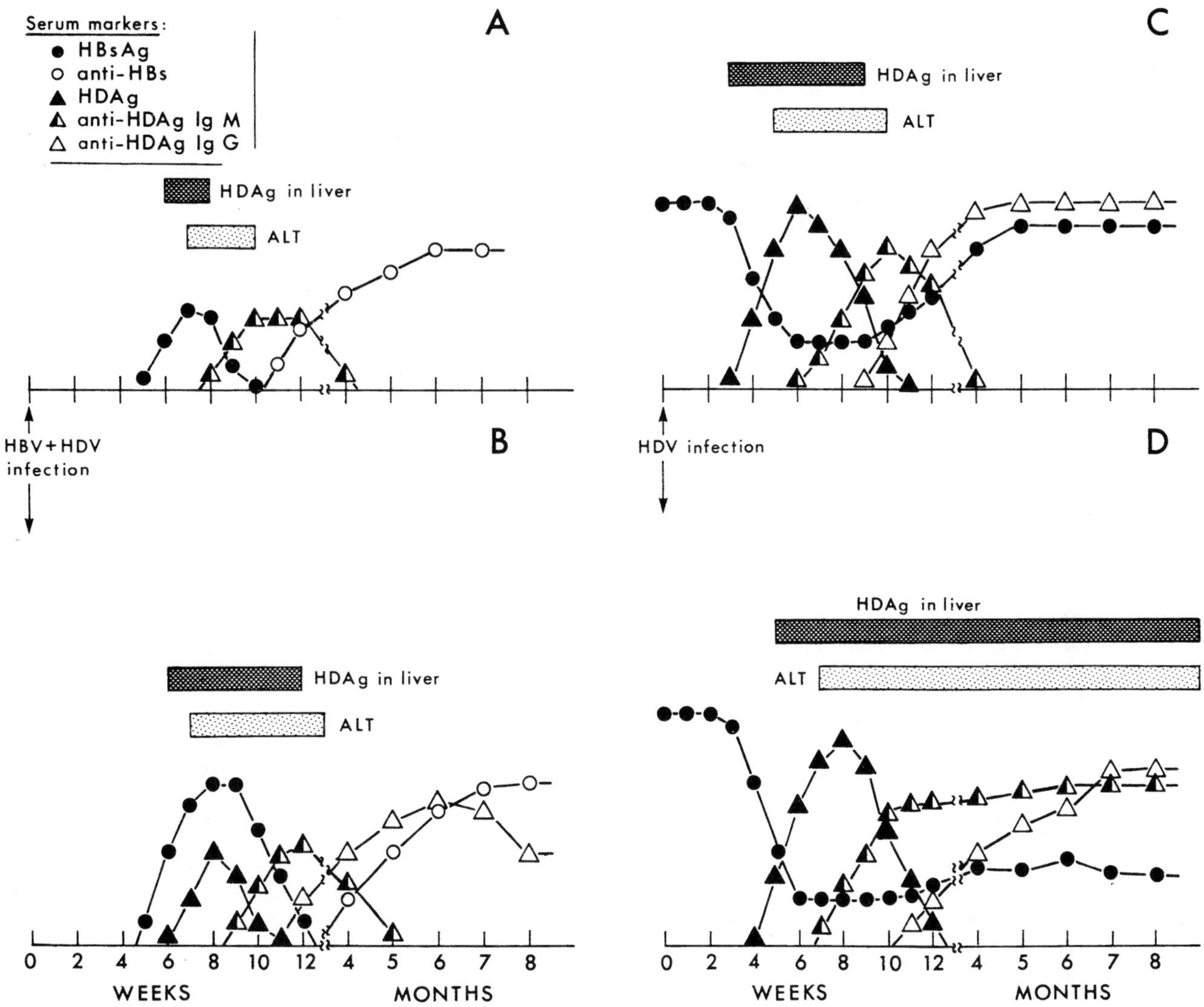

FIGURE 135–9. *A–D,* Typical patterns of serologic markers during hepatitis D virus (HDV) infection. Simultaneous primary infection with HDV and hepatitis B virus is usually self-limited and resolves (i.e., does not become chronic), and HDAg may (*B*) or may not (*A*) be detected in serum. Following such HDV infections without detectable HD-antigenemia, an anti-HDag IgG response may not be detected (*A*). HDV superinfection of HBsAg carriers may be self-limited and resolve (*C*) or become chronic (*D*) with persisting HDAg in liver and anti-HDAg IgM in serum. (Modified from Rizzetto M, Verme G. Delta hepatitis: Present status. J Hepatal. 1985;1:187. © 1985 EASL, the European Association for the Study of the Liver.)

obvious mechanism by which the virus might cause such point mutations make a direct role for HBV in causing this kind of change unlikely. Although it has been estimated that 80% of HCCs in the world are associated with HBV infection,[255] there are other recognized risk factors for the remaining HCC cases. These include chronic HCV infection, chronic alcoholic liver disease, hemochromatosis, and other causes of cirrhosis. Chronic hepatitis B and other risk factors for HCC appear to share the common feature of causing chronic necroinflammatory liver disease (liver cell necrosis, regeneration, inflammation, sometimes leading to cirrhosis), and when this pathologic process continues for many years, it may lead to carcinogenesis. Thus, the role of HBV in HCC may not be through a specific viral oncogenic mechanism but as an agent that causes chronic necroinflammatory liver disease, which is a process that may be carcinogenic, irrespective of the agent that causes the liver cell injury.

Extrahepatic Disease

Several additional syndromes with extrahepatic manifestations have been associated with HBV infection, and for some of these, there is evidence that HBsAg–anti-HBs complexes play a role in pathogenesis.[143, 256] The serum sickness–like syndrome consisting of fever, rash, urticaria, arthralgias, and sometimes acute arthritis, which occurs in 10 to 20% of patients during the incubation period of acute hepatitis B, is accompanied by HBsAg-antibody complexes and low levels of complement components in serum, synovial fluid, and synovial membranes in involved joints.[257, 258]

In several series, one third to one half of patients with biopsy-proven polyarteritis nodosa have had persistent HBV infection.[143, 256] Among all HBsAg carriers, however, this syndrome occurs infrequently (1 of 43 in one series).[259] Such patients have low serum complement levels and circulating HBsAg-anti-HBs complexes. Immune complexes and complement components have also been regularly detected in diseased vessels by immunofluorescent staining.[260, 261]

A significant number of cases of membranous glomerulonephritis have been associated with CAH and persistent HBV infection.[143, 256] Immune complex deposits can be found along the subepithelial surfaces of glomerular basement membranes by electron microscopy, and nodular deposits of HBsAg, immunoglobulin, and C3 in glomeruli have been observed by immunofluorescent staining in these cases.[262–266]

Several additional syndromes with unknown pathogenesis have also been associated with HBV infection. Infantile papular acrodermatitis appears to be frequently associated with persistent HBV infection in Mediterranean countries[267] and Japan.[268] In a series of 19 patients with essential mixed cryoglobulinemia, cryoprecipitates were shown to contain HBsAg in 6 cases and anti-HBs in 11,[269] suggesting that some cases of cryoglobulinemia may be related to HBV infection. This association, however, could not be confirmed in a subsequent study.[270] A significant number of cases of aplastic anemia have been observed after acute viral hepatitis.[271] Although in most cases the specific hepatitis virus has not been identified, in a few cases acute hepatitis B has been documented.[272, 273] The basis of this apparent association is not yet clear. Further work is needed to clarify the pathogenesis of these syndromes and to determine whether HBsAg-antibody complexes or HBV infection play an important role.

Clearly, infections with HBV and other hepadnaviruses have protean manifestations, and different pathogenetic mechanisms appear to be responsible for a number of different syndromes.

EPIDEMIOLOGY

Incidence of Primary Hepatitis B Virus Infection

It has been estimated by the Centers for Disease Control and Prevention[274, 275] that there are approximately 300,000 primary HBV infections per year in the United States. Most are in young adults, and approximately one fourth are associated with acute icteric disease. More than 10,000 patients are hospitalized with hepatitis B each year, and 300 die with fulminant hepatitis B. Between 6 and 10% of patients (18,000 to 30,000 cases) fail to resolve primary infection and become persistently infected (i.e., become chronic HBsAg carriers). There are approximately 750,000 to 1 million HBV carriers in the United States. Approximately 4000 to 5000 die each year in the United States from chronic HBV infection (3000 to 4000 with cirrhosis and 600 to 1000 with liver cancer). The lifetime risk of HBV infection is estimated to be 5% for the whole U.S. population, but for certain high-risk groups it may reach nearly 100%.

Most acute hepatitis B cases in the United States are in young adults, unlike the younger age distribution of hepatitis A.[190] The age distribution is related to the circumstances leading to transmission (see farther on). More cases occur in males than in females,[190] unlike hepatitis A for which there is no apparent sex predilection. The incidence of acute hepatitis B differs in different populations within the United States.[274, 275] Individuals at greatest risk are percutaneous drug users, patients receiving blood transfusions or certain other blood products, patients requiring hemodialysis, laboratory personnel who work with human blood or blood products, homosexuals and others with frequent and different sexual contacts, and medical and dental personnel with frequent contact with blood. Blood donor screening for HBsAg by the most sensitive tests, and a shift away from paid blood donors to the use of volunteer donors, greatly reduced but did not completely eliminate post-transfusion hepatitis B during the 1970s.[39, 191–193, 276] Recent studies of post-transfusion hepatitis indicate that less than 5% of cases are still caused by hepatitis B. Most of these occur after transfusion of blood that is negative for HBsAg by the most sensitive tests available, indicating that such tests do not detect all individuals with infectious HBV in the blood.

The prevalence of serum antibody to HBsAg (anti-HBs) indicating past HBV infection (or in recent years, vaccination) as determined by the most sensitive techniques, increases with age in the general U.S. population up to around ages 30 to 45, to rates of 5 to 20% in most studies.[190, 277] The prevalence of serum anti-HBs and other HBV serologic markers also differs significantly in different population groups within the United States, and the groups described previously with the highest risk of acute hepatitis B also have the highest prevalence of serum anti-HBs (Table 135–1). Different

TABLE 135–1 Prevalence of Hepatitis B Virus Serologic Markers in Different U.S. Populations

	Serum HBsAg Prevalence (%)	Any Markers* (%)
Visitors or immigrants from high HBV endemic geographic areas	10–20	70–85
Alaskan natives	5–15	40–70
Patients of institutions for mentally disabled	10–20	35–80
Parenteral drug users who share needles	5–10	60–80
Homosexual men	4–8	35–80
Household contacts of HBsAg-positive individuals	3–6	30–60
Hemodialysis patients	3–10	20–80
Medical, dental, and laboratory workers with exposure to blood	1–2	15–30
Prison inmates	1–8	10–80
Heterosexuals with multiple sex partners	0.5	5–20
Health care workers without frequent blood contact	0.3	3–10
General U.S. population		
Blacks	0.9	14
Whites	0.2	3

*HBsAg, anti-HBs, or anti-HBc.
Abbreviation: HBV, Hepatitis B virus.
Modified from Advisory Committee for Immunization Practices. Recommendations for protection against viral hepatitis. MMWR Morb Mortal Wkly Rep. 1990;39:725–729.

socioeconomic groups also have different risks for infection. Cherubin and colleagues[278] found the frequency of anti-HBs to be 44%, 18%, and 10% for persons older than 30 years of age in New York City in sections of Harlem, Staten Island, and Park Avenue, respectively.

Primary HBV infections occur at much higher frequencies and at much earlier ages in high-prevalence geographic areas of the world such as parts of Asia and Africa.[190] This is undoubtedly because the important routes of transmission (see "Routes of Transmission") are different from those in the United States and most often involve transmission from infected mothers to their children. In countries such as China, Senegal, Thailand, and Taiwan, infection rates are very high in infants, and continue through early childhood when the prevalence of HBsAg in serum may exceed 25%.[190] In Panama, Papua New Guinea, the Solomon Islands, Greenland, and in Alaskan Native Americans, infection rates in infants are relatively low and increase rapidly during early childhood.[190] In all these populations, the prevalence of serum anti-HBs reaches a plateau, usually much greater than 50% between the ages of 10 and 20 years.[190]

Clinically apparent acute viral hepatitis, often severe, was the first manifestation of primary HBV infection to be recognized. However, it is now clear that this is probably not the most common response to infection, except possibly when infection involves iatrogenic routes of transmission to susceptible adults, such as by blood transfusion or other direct percutaneous transfer of serum that contains virus. In geographic areas of the world with very high infection rates at early ages, routes of transmission that do not involve overt percutaneous transfer are the rule. Primary infections in those settings most often appear to be clinically silent or mild, as is the persistent infection that appears to be a common outcome of primary infection in those areas. Similarly, the natural infections of woodchucks, ground squirrels, and ducks by their respective hepadnaviruses that are related to HBV appear to be silent until late forms of disease (e.g., HCC) appear in some animals. Thus, much of the severe acute viral hepatitis that was first associated with primary HBV infection appears to be a manifestation of medical procedures and other practices (e.g., blood transfusions and parenteral drug abuse) found in technologically advanced cultures.

Persistent Hepatitis B Virus Infections

Persistent or chronic HBV infection (usually designated the HBsAg carrier state) is one of the most common persistent viral infections in humans. It has been estimated that more than 200 million persons in the world today are persistently infected with HBV.[34] A large fraction of these are in eastern Asia and sub-Saharan Africa, where the prevalence of chronic infection is very high and where the associated chronic liver disease and liver cancer are among the most important health problems. It is estimated that there are between 750,000 and 1 million chronic carriers in the United States and that as many as 25% of them may have chronic active hepatitis.[274, 275] As many as 5000 persons per year die of hepatitis B–related cirrhosis and 800 or more die of liver cancer. Although a small number of long-established chronic carriers apparently terminate their active infection and become HBsAg-negative (approximately 2% per year),[155, 186–188] most chronic carriers remain infected for many years,[178] and infection for life appears to be common.

The HBsAg carrier rate varies from 0.1 to 20% in different populations around the world.[34] The incidence of the HBsAg carrier state in populations is related most importantly to the incidence and age at primary infection, but there are also other host and viral factors that appear to increase the risk for the development of persistent infection, which may be important in establishing carrier rates for some epidemiologic groups. A genetic predisposition for persistent infection has been suggested by family studies in which the chronic carrier state appears to cluster in families with a distribution consistent with segregation as an autosomal recessive trait.[279, 280] An association between persistent infection and certain HLA types has also been reported.[281] Other studies, however, have failed to confirm either of these findings.[282, 283] Some evidence suggests that after primary HBV infection, New York City residents of Chinese origin are more likely to become carriers than are whites.[284] Whether this represents a genetic predisposition for persistent HBV infection remains to be determined.

Very young age appears to be one of the most important factors predisposing to persistent HBV infection. Although only a small fraction of adults (10%,[259] 5%,[127] and less than 1%[285] in different studies) with acute hepatitis B in the United States have been shown to become chronically infected,[127, 259] persistent infection almost invariably follows acute neonatal hepatitis B, which is most commonly anicteric.[215, 216] The HBsAg carrier state appears to be most common in the young adult age group in the United States, and the frequency in males is several times that in females in this age group.[190] The higher proportion of male carriers observed in many populations[190, 286–288] is at least in part due to the greater probability that males become persistently infected after primary infection, as well as to the apparently more rapid rate at which females terminate the carrier state.[190]

Anecdotal cases suggest that immunosuppression may be associated with milder initial disease and more frequent persistent infection. For example, HBV infection in renal dialysis patients frequently becomes persistent.[289] Finally, the HBsAg carrier state appears to be more common in patients with certain diseases such as Down syndrome, lepromatous leprosy, and chronic lymphocytic leukemia than in the general population.[287, 288] The mechanism by which each of these conditions leads to persistent infection is not clear. A possible common mechanism could be a modified or inadequate immune response, which results in failure to eliminate virus in such patients, in contrast to the situation in immunologically normal older children and adults, who usually clear the virus after an acute infection.

The infecting virus dose and severity of initial disease also appear to correlate with the likelihood of persistent infection developing. Persistent infection occurs more frequently after initial anicteric hepatitis than after initial icteric disease.[79, 290] Survivors of fulminant hepatitis rarely become persistently infected, and HBsAg carriers frequently give no history of recognized acute hepatitis.[259] Experimental infections with different dilutions of infectious serum suggest that smaller doses of virus result more often in long incubation periods, mild initial disease, and subsequent chronic infection compared with larger doses of virus.[79] This relationship has been so consistent that the infecting dose can usually be estimated from the incubation period in experimental transmission studies.[79, 81, 148] There is no evidence that hepatitis B virus strains (e.g., HBsAg subtypes) have different virulence properties or different propensities for persistent infection.

Striking differences occur in HBsAg carrier rates in different populations in the United States (see Table 135–1) and different geographic areas of the world. In most areas of the United States, less than 0.1% of volunteer blood and plasma donors are HBsAg-positive.[34] Almost all these are chronic HBsAg carriers, whereas the carrier rate in paid donors is usually closer to 1%. Among certain populations, such as percutaneous drug abusers, patients in some hemodialysis centers, and certain homosexual populations, the carrier rate may be 1 to 10%[291] (see Table 135–1). These high rates appear to reflect the frequent exposure to virus by members of these groups. The carrier rates in most Western European countries are similar to those in the United States,[34] but in other highly endemic areas of the world, such as in many countries in Africa, Asia, and Oceania, the rate may be as high as 20% of the population, and almost all HBsAg-negative adults are positive for anti-HBs or anti-HB_c, or both.[34, 190, 287] The increased carrier rates in some developing countries may be related not only to poor sanitary conditions and increased exposure at very early ages but also to differences in predisposition for chronic infection on a genetic, nutritional, or other basis. Transmission of virus from persistently infected mothers to newborn or young infants in whom persistent infection then usually develop has been estimated to account for 40% of carriers in Taiwan.[292, 293]

Among HBsAg carriers in the world, there is an uneven geographic distribution of HBsAg subtypes. As described previously, almost all antigens contain either determinants *d* or *y* and either *w* or *r*. The *d* determinant is common in the United States, northern Europe, Asia, and Oceania, although the *y* determinant is found at a lower frequency in these regions.[294, 295] The *d* determinant to the near exclusion of *y* is found in Japan. The *y* determinant, and rarely *d*, are found in Africa and in Australian Aboriginals. The *y* determinant also is found frequently in India and around the Mediterranean. The *w* determinant predominates in Europe, the United States, Africa, India, Australia, and Oceania. The *r* determinant predominates in Japan, China, and Southeast Asia. Subtypes *adw*, *ady*, and *adr* are each found in extensive geographic regions of the world. Subtype *ayr* is rare in the world, although it is commonly found in small populations in Oceania. The geographic distributions of subtypes probably reflect the locations of their origins (i.e., diversion from a common HBsAg ancestor), and the migrations of infected human populations.

Routes of Hepatis B Virus Transmission

It appears that the only important source or reservoir of virus for human infections are humans themselves. No important animal reservoir is known. Although some higher primates other than humans may be infected in nature (see "Virus Host Range"), there is no evidence that they are important sources for human infections. If nonhuman primates are infected in nature, it is unlikely they would infect humans because transmission from infected individuals requires specific patterns of intimate contact such as those described farther on. Although some environmental surfaces such as toothbrushes, razors, needles, toys, and so on may mediate person-to-person transmission in some cases, there are no important environmental reservoirs such as water or food, which are sometimes involved in the transmission of HAV. HBV does not appear to be present very often in feces, and there is no evidence for fecal-oral transmission, as there is for HAV. These features of HBV and the particular kinds of close contact required for transmission probably account for the infrequent epidemic pattern of spread, in contrast to many agents that are spread by enteric (e.g., HAV) or respiratory routes. Persistent infections in which infectious HBV may be present continuously in the blood and certain other body fluids for many years or for a lifetime, represent a stable human reservoir of virus so that HBV can be maintained indefinitely, even in small isolated populations (e.g., some island populations).

Although blood and blood products are the best-documented sources of infectious virus, HBsAg has also been found in feces, urine, bile, sweat, tears, saliva, semen, breast milk, vaginal secretions, cerebrospinal fluid, synovial fluid, and cord blood. Only serum,[79] saliva,[122, 296] and semen[296] have actually been shown to contain infectious HBV in experimental transmission studies. The report of transmission by the bite of an infected patient[297] is consistent with the presence of HBV in saliva. During the 1940s, more than 50 attempts to transmit "serum hepatitis" to human volunteers using feces from persons after experimental infections were unsuccessful.[19, 24] This suggests that infectious HBV probably enters feces infrequently in the absence of gastrointestinal bleeding, and thus feces must not be a common source of virus for HBV infections acquired in the community. Other body fluids have not been tested for infectious virus. Often the concentration of HBsAg in fluids other than the serum of infected patients are lower or not detectable at all. When present, antigen can sometimes be demonstrated only after concentration. When infectious virus is also present in such fluids, its concentration is undoubtedly lower than that in serum. Infectious HBV can also be present in blood without detectable HBsAg[39, 191–193, 297] so that the failure to detect antigen does not exclude the presence of infectious virus.

Several specific routes of transmission are well established. The most important routes of transmission in the United States are undoubtedly by percutaneous transfer and probably mucous membrane contact of blood and possibly other body fluids (e.g., saliva) and by heterosexual and homosexual contacts. Direct percutaneous inoculation of virus by needles can occur with contaminated blood or blood products, hemodialysis, tattooing, ear piercing, acupuncture, sharing needles during illicit drug use, or accidental needlesticks by hospital personnel. Clearly HBV is commonly transmitted by routes other than these overt parenteral ones.[298] Infectious material contacting open skin breaks or mucous membranes such as the eye can also be expected to result in infection. Because HBV is quite stable, transmission can be expected by means of environmental surfaces that may contact mucous membranes or open skin breaks, such as toothbrushes, baby bottles, toys, eating utensils, razors,[299, 300] hospital equipment such as respirators or endoscopes,[301, 302] or laboratory glassware and instruments.[303] In households, transmission is more common from HBV-infected patients to sexual partners than to other kinds of household contacts.[175, 304–306] HBV infection rates are unusually high among female prostitutes[307] and male homosexuals,[308, 309] who are commonly exposed to many different sexual partners. Cases of apparent direct transmission from HBV-infected persons to susceptible individuals after sexual intercourse have been reported.[310] The exact route of transmission in these cases is not yet proved, but it seems likely that sexual contact would be among the most common circumstances leading to HBV transmission in populations with high carrier rates. The demonstration of infectious virus in semen and saliva of infected patients[296] supports the possibility of sexual transmission.

Health care personnel have been shown to be at greater risk for HBV infection than is the general public,[311–313] and this is undoubtedly because of their more frequent exposure to infected patients. The specific routes of transmission from patients to medical and dental workers are not known, although it appears that the greater the direct exposure to blood and serum (e.g., as for surgeons[313, 314] and workers in renal dialysis units[313]), the greater the frequency of HBV infection.

A few persistently infected physicians,[315] dentists,[316] and oral surgeons,[317, 318] as well as acutely infected health care personnel,[319, 320] have been implicated in the transmission of HBV infection to multiple patient contacts; however, most health care personnel who are carriers,[321] as well as those with acute infection,[321, 322] appear to represent little risk to their patients. Transmission of infection only from certain chronic HBsAg carrier women and not from others to their newborn infants has also been observed.[173, 292] Transmission of virus from chronic carriers via administration of their blood products or via accidental needle puncture in a medical setting has also been frequently observed. Although these are the best-documented instances of the spread of HBV infection from chronic carriers, transmission also appears to occur commonly from chronic carriers to sexual contacts,[306, 308, 310] to those taking illicit drugs by self-injection when needles are "shared," and to individuals by other routes described earlier. However, proof of transmission from patients during the persistent phase of infection rather than during the acute phase has not been as clearly demonstrated for the latter routes of transmission.

Infection after oral intake of infectious material has been clearly demonstrated, although the dose of virus needed for successful infection by the oral route appears to be higher than that needed for parenteral infection.[23] That oral infection does not occur via the intestinal tract, but may occur through small breaks in the oral mucosa, was suggested by experiments in which two susceptible chimpanzees were not infected by infectious material placed directly into their stomachs but were infected by an oral spray of infectious material after their gums were lightly brushed with a toothbrush.[323] The detection of anti-HBs of the IgA class in feces is consistent with an intestinal or biliary tract phase of HBV infection.[324] However, HBsAg has not been detected by immunofluorescence in the cells of any tissue except liver, and occasionally in pancreases and in leukocytes of infected humans and chimpanzees. Although food and water appear to almost never be sources of virus for HBV infections, HBsAg has been detected in clams from coastal waters into which untreated sewage has been drained.[325] Despite this finding, published outbreaks of shellfish-associated hepatitis have not been of type B. Although HBV can infect by the oral route, it is not clear how important this portal of entry is in community-acquired infections. There is no evidence that the fecal-oral route plays a significant role in HBV transmission.

Persistent viremia appears to be a favorable condition for transmission by blood-feeding insects such as mosquitoes. Although some populations of wild mosquitoes and bedbugs caught in Africa[326–329] and in the United States[329] have been shown to contain HBsAg, there has been no direct demonstration of transmission to humans by insect vectors. Unlike arboviruses, HBV will probably not infect cells of insects so that passive transfer would be required.

In areas of the world where HBV infection rates are much higher than in the United States, inapparent parenteral routes of transmission appear to be important. In this setting, transmission from infected mothers to newborn infants or young children appears to account for a large fraction of HBV infections. Neonatal transmission from chronic carrier mothers and mothers with acute hepatitis B in the third trimester or the first 2 months postpartum have been clearly documented in the United States[215, 216] as well as in highly endemic populations[173, 292] and such infected infants commonly acquire persistent infection. In Taiwan it has been estimated that 40 to 50% of HBsAg carriers acquired their infection in the perinatal period.[173] Only 5 to 10% of these appear to be infected in utero, and the others appear to be infected at the time of delivery by exposure to maternal blood.[330] Many infants of mothers who are chronic carriers but escape perinatal infection are infected in the first few months or years of life, probably by contact with their infected mothers or siblings, although the exact routes of transmission are not known. Clustering of carriers in families in which mothers are infected[331] is consistent with this pattern of spread. It is thought that failure to sterilize acupuncture needles and other similar exposures, including the use of the same needle and syringe for vaccination of many different children, may account for many HBV infections and contribute to maintaining high carrier rates for many decades in China and certain other countries. The presence of HBsAg in maternal milk would suggest that breast-feeding might be an important route, although one study[332] indicated that this may not be the case. Mastication of food by mothers before feeding to infants is common in some cultures, and this might be expected to lead to infection of infants in those populations, although this has not been shown directly. Other kinds of intimate contact between mothers and children, as well as between siblings, are undoubtedly important. Bedbugs, mosquitoes, or other blood-feeding insects would appear to offer an opportunity for transmission between individuals sharing the same household or bed, but there is little direct evidence supporting this possibility.

The presence of significant Dane particle concentrations or HB_eAg in the blood, or both, has been shown to be correlated with the transmission of infection from carrier mothers to neonates,[173, 174, 216] from carriers to normal health care personnel accidentally inoculated with contaminated needles,[333] from health care personnel who are carriers to patient contacts (W.S. Robinson, unpublished results), and among sexual partners in households.[175] The regular appearance of Dane particles in high concentrations and of HB_eAg in the serum of patients during the late incubation period of acute hepatitis B,[135, 136] suggests that this is a time when patients are probably highly contagious. This also appears to be the case in the few chronic HBsAg carriers with high Dane particle concentration, or HB_eAg in their blood, or both. The very frequent transmission of infection from mothers with acute hepatitis B during the third trimester of pregnancy or the first 2 months postpartum[215, 216] also occurs at a time when high Dane particle or HB_eAg concentration, or both, are present in the blood.

CLINICAL MANIFESTATIONS AND PROGNOSIS

Acute Hepatitis B

The incubation period of acute serum hepatitis (most of which was undoubtedly hepatitis B) was long ago established to be 4 to 28 weeks, but in most cases the interval is between 60 and 110 days.[18, 19, 334–337] Among patients with acute icteric hepatitis B, between 10 and 20% have a serum sickness–like illness with an erythematous maculopapular rash, urticaria, arthralgias, occasional arthritis, and sometimes fever several days to weeks before the onset of clinically apparent liver disease.[143, 256] Symmetric involvement of distal joints or large joints is the rule. The symptoms usually last 2 to 10 days and clear without residual changes, although findings can persist for weeks or even months in unusual cases.

The clinical course of acute hepatitis B in individual cases is indistinguishable from that of acute hepatitis A. The severity varies widely, and many infections appear to be clinically inapparent.[79, 126, 127, 338–340] Although inapparent hepatitis is not associated with symptoms or abnormal physical findings, most cases are accompanied by abnormal serum transaminase activity. Less commonly, HBV infection occurs without associated liver function abnormalities and is detected only by specific serologic tests for the virus.

Symptomatic acute hepatitis B can be mild and anicteric or more severe and associated with icterus. Typically, symptoms of headache, malaise, loss of appetite, nausea and occasionally vomiting, moderate fever (temperatures of 37.5°C to 39°C), and chilliness are present initially and appear 2 to 7 days before the onset of jaundice in icteric cases. Loss of appetite is common and is often characterized by actual distaste or aversion for food and tobacco. The smell of food or tobacco may induce nausea in these patients. Abdominal discomfort or pain localized in the right upper quadrant is common. Urine becomes dark and stools light or clay colored.

In icteric cases, symptoms may progress, persist unchanged, decrease in severity, or rapidly clear with the onset of jaundice. Scleral icterus can be observed when the serum bilirubin level exceeds 2.5 or 3.0 mg/dl. Mild pruritus lasting only a few days occurs in one half of patients, but patients may occasionally have protracted or severe itching. Arthralgias may occur in 10 to 20% of patients.

Common physical findings include right upper quadrant tenderness, enlargement of the liver (up to 15 cm increase in vertical breadth), usually with a rounded tender edge; and scleral, mucous membrane, and cutaneous icterus. Massive hepatic enlargement is rare. The spleen can be palpated in 10 to 15% of patients. Mild enlargement of lymph nodes, particularly in the posterior cervical region, may be noted. Spider angiomats may develop and disappear after recovery. Transient gynecomastia occurs but is unusual. Children usually recover in 2 weeks and adults in 4 to 6 weeks.

Laboratory tests may reveal normal or moderately reduced hematocrit and hemoglobin concentrations. Mild hemolysis is often observed. Total white blood cell count is usually normal and rarely exceeds 12,000 cells/mm^3. There may, however, be granulocytopenia and a relative lymphocytosis. Large, atypical lymphocytes are commonly present but rarely exceed 10%.[341] Mild proteinuria may occur. Urobilinogen and bilirubin are common in the urine before the onset of jaundice and decrease in amount as jaundice progresses. Transient steatorrhea may occur early in the illness.

Liver function abnormalities may include an increase in direct-reacting serum bilirubin early when total bilirubin is normal. Total serum bilirubin usually increases for 10 to 14 days and does not exceed 10 mg/dl in most patients.[342] Occasional patients have higher values. The bilirubin concentration usually falls gradually over 2 to 4 weeks. The hallmark of acute viral hepatitis is the striking elevation in serum transaminase (aminotransferase) activity.[343, 344] Elevations may precede the onset of symptoms and usually peak in the first week of symptoms. Peak levels greater than 1000 units/ml are common, and serum alanine aminotransferase levels usually exceed serum aspartate aminotransferase levels. The peak level may correlate roughly with the extent of liver injury but is not a prognostic factor. The serum transminase activity usually returns to normal as the illness subsides. Serum alkaline phosphatase activity may be normal or mildly elevated. Concentrations of serum albumin and globulins are usually normal, although in severe or protracted viral hepatitis albumin levels may be decreased and gamma globulin increased up to two times the normal level. Glucose tolerance may be decreased during acute viral hepatitis, yet fasting blood glucose may be low. Most patients with icteric acute hepatitis B eliminate the virus and have no residual disease.

Acute hepatitis B may be accompanied or followed by severe depression (infrequently); neurologic syndromes such as meningitis, Guillain-Barré syndrome, myelitis, or encephalitis; hematologic disorders such as agranulocytosis, thrombocytopenia, or aplastic anemia; and electrocardiographic abnormalities, including arrhythmias. The role of the viral infection in these problems is unclear.

Acute hepatitis B may be clinically indistinguishable from acute hepatitis A and hepatitis C, infections with Epstein-Barr virus, cytomegalovirus, yellow fever virus, leptospirosis, and less commonly other infectious agents. Toxic hepatitis caused by ethanol, numerous drugs (e.g., halothane), and numerous industrial chemicals (e.g., benzene) may also produce similar syndromes.

A number of variants of hepatitis B may occur. Fulminant hepatitis is a severe form accompanied by hepatic failure with encephalopathy. The mortality in such cases is exceedingly high.[345] Occasionally, death occurs before the onset of jaundice; one half of deaths occur within 10 days of the onset of symptoms and three fourths within 3 weeks. Encephalopathy with hepatic failure is associated with hyperexcitability, impaired mentation, asterixis, confusion, obtundation, and eventually coma. Vomiting and seizures may also occur. Extensive hepatic necrosis may be associated with rapid reduction in the size of an enlarged liver, a fall in previously elevated serum transaminase activity and HBsAg, and progressive prolongation of prothrombin time. Oliguria and azotemia as well as edema and ascites may develop. Primary infection with HBV accompanied by delta agent may carry a special risk for fulminant hepatitis.[233, 236, 237]

Other variant forms of hepatitis B include prolonged acute hepatitis in which abnormal laboratory findings, mild symptoms, and abnormal physical findings may persist beyond 3 or 4 months and up to 12 months or more. Probably only 3 to 5% of cases of acute icteric viral hepatitis extend beyond 3 or 4 months.[346] The ultimate prognosis for patients with prolonged acute hepatitis B is probably no different from that of patients with a more typical shorter course, but prolonged acute hepatitis B may be difficult to distinguish from chronic forms of hepatitis (described further on) until they become HBsAg-negative and hepatitis resolves.

Relapsing hepatitis B follows a course of recovery followed by one or more episodes similar to, although usually milder than, the initial acute illness. Relapses occur in a small proportion of cases and have been attributed to premature ambulation, consumption of alcohol, and treatment with corticosteroids during the acute illness in anecdotal cases. A relapse must be distinguished from a second episode of acute hepatitis with a different infectious agent.

Although most infections with HBV appear to result in anicteric initial disease, and acute icteric hepatitis is usually a benign self-limited disease, relatively high fatality rates among icteric cases occur under certain circumstances. Several factors are known to influence the severity of acute hepatitis B. One is age. In general, infants and young children have milder initial disease than do older age groups,[215, 347] and the older the patient the longer the icteric phase.[259] The mortality in post-transfusion hepatitis appears to be related to age.[348] In patients with hepatic failure during acute hepatitis, the mortality can also be correlated with age. Survival is rare in such patients older than 40 years of age, compared with a significant number of younger patients who survive.[259] Severe or fulminant hepatitis appears to be uncommon in infants and young children, although it does occur.[349] It has been stated that the better prognosis of younger patients with severe hepatitis is due to their capacity for hepatocyte regeneration after hepatic necrosis.[259]

A second factor influencing severity of disease is virus dose. Experimental transmission studies have shown that the higher the virus dose, the shorter the incubation period and the more likely that icteric hepatitis will result.[79] The highest virus doses received by patients may occur in transfusions of infectious blood. The mortality of transfusion-associated icteric hepatitis was 10% more in many series before blood banks began testing for HBsAg,[350] and most of the cases in these studies were undoubtedly hepatitis B. The poor prognosis in such patients may be related to the large virus dose resulting from blood transfusion or to the severity of associated underlying diseases, or both. Since the advent of HBsAg testing, the mortality of post-transfusion hepatitis appears to be lower.[348] This may in part reflect the elimination of the blood units with very high concentrations of HBV. The mortality of acute hepatitis B appears to be unusually high in patients with malignant disease or preexisting cirrhosis.[259]

A third factor that may sometimes influence the severity of neonatal hepatitis B is the HB$_e$Ag status of the mother. Although newborns of HB$_e$Ag-positive mothers are frequently infected with HBV, the infections are usually subclinical with little acute hepatitis, and persistence of the infection is the usual outcome. This is thought to be related to the induction of immunologic tolerance to HB$_e$Ag and HB$_c$Ag in utero resulting from exposure of the fetus to transplacentally passed HB$_e$Ag.[351] In contrast, neonatal infection with an HB$_e$Ag-negative variant of HBV (a stop codon mutant in the precore sequence) from HB$_e$Ag-negative, anti-HBe–positive mothers resulted in fulminant hepatitis B in two infants,[352] which is consistent with absence of HB$_c$Ag/HB$_e$Ag-specific tolerance in these infants. Most neonatal infections from HB$_e$Ag-negative, anti-HBe-positive mothers, however, are not associated with severe liver disease, and the role of the viral mutants in severe disease in the two infants was not established.

Viral mutants have also been isolated from older children and adults with severe hepatitis B. Both precore and core gene mutant viruses have been recovered.[46, 47, 353–355] The finding of such mutants in patients with severe disease has raised the question as to whether mutant virus causes severe hepatitis B. Precore stop codon mutants have been detected in most chronic carriers at the time of HB$_e$Ag to anti-HB$_e$ seroconversion, and thus they are very common in some patient groups with mild disease.[46, 47, 356] Such mutants created experimentally in Woodchuck hepatitis virus–[357] and deck hepatitis B virus were shown not to have increased virulence, and to replicate less well than wild-type virus. Thus, current evidence suggests that precore mutants do not cause severe hepatitis B, although they are recovered from some patients. Mutations in the core protein coding sequence have not been analyzed as completely, and the question of altered virulence for such mutants remains undetermined.

A final factor associated with severe acute hepatitis B in some cases is coinfection with HDV[224, 227, 228] as noted earlier.

Persistent Hepatitis B Virus Infection

In a 1- to 5-year follow-up of 429 patients hospitalized with acute icteric hepatitis B, 90% became HBsAg-negative and 10% became persistent HBsAg carriers.[259] Seventy percent of the latter group had CPH and 30% had CAH. One of these patients acquired polyarteritis nodosa and one acquired membranous glomerulonephritis. No persisting liver disease was found in any of the patients who became HBsAg-negative after acute hepatitis. A more recent study of a large number of young men infected with HBV via contaminated yellow fever vaccine revealed that less than 1% acquired chronic infection.[285] The reason for the apparent difference in the number of persistent infections arising from primary HBV infection in adults in the two studies is not certain, but different patient populations were studied and different criteria were used to select patients for each study. Persistent infection with HBV is most often asymptomatic, but a significant number of patients chronically infected with HBV eventually experience cirrhosis.[358] When HBV infection is associated with CPH, patients are generally in good health and have persistent or recurrent elevations of AST and ALT without jaundice.[259] Persistent mild hepatomegaly is common and splenomegaly is occasionally present. Long-term follow-up of such patients shows no evidence of progression, and complete resolution occurs in some cases. Late disappearance of HBsAg occurs rarely.[259]

CAH associated with persistent HBV infection is sometimes difficult to distinguish from prolonged acute viral hepatitis or CPH in the first 6 or 12 months on either clinical or histologic grounds; however, in time the distinction can be made.[259] Patients with CAH may have chronic jaundice, intermittent episodes of jaundice, or no jaundice throughout their course. Episodes of jaundice are usually associated with significant transaminase elevations. The prognosis of patients in whom CAH develops is variable. Progression to cirrhosis occurs in many patients, and in some the progression to cirrhosis, hepatic failure, and death can occur within 1 year. Superinfections of HBsAg carriers with delta agent can lead to exacerbations of active hepatitis[238, 239] and persistent delta agent infection in HBsAg carriers may be commonly associated with chronic hepatitis[238, 239] as described earlier.

MAKING A VIRAL DIAGNOSIS

A diagnosis of acute viral hepatitis can usually be made from clinical findings, and the responsible viral agent can often be suspected from the epidemiologic setting and features such as the incubation period; however, only virus-specific tests can conclusively identify the infecting virus. Highly sensitive and specific tests are commercially available for HBsAg, anti-HBs, anti-HB$_c$, anti-HB$_c$ IgM, HB$_e$Ag, anti-HB$_e$, and anti-HDAg, and are of great diagnostic use. Tests specific for Dane particles or DNA and DNA polymerase–containing virions, and for HDAg and HDV RNA in liver and serum are available only in research laboratories. Table 135–2 shows typical serologic test findings at different stages of HBV infection and in convalescence. This table does not include all variations and does not convey the dynamic nature of infection during which individual markers appear or disappear, or both (not always in the same order

TABLE 135–2 Hepatitis B Virus (HBV) Serologic Markers in Different Stages of Infection and Convalescence

Stage of Infection	HBsAg	Anti-HBs	Anti-HBc *IgG*	Anti-HBc *IgM*	HB_eAg	Anti-HB_e
Late incubation period of hepatitis B	+	−	−	−	+ or −	−
Acute hepatitis B	+	−	+	+	+	−
HBsAg-negative acute hepatitis B	−	−	+	−	−	−
Healthy HBsAg carrier	+	−	+ + +	+ or −	−	+
Chronic hepatitis B	+	−	+ + +	+ or −	+	−
HBV infection in recent past	−	+ +	+ +	+ or −	−	+
HBV infection in distant past	−	+ or −	+ or −	−	−	−
Recent HBV vaccination	−	+ +	−	−	−	−

in different patients), during the evolution of infection as indicated in Figures 135–6 to 135–9 and discussed under "Course of Infection."

Tests for serum HBsAg, anti-HBs, anti-HB_c, and anti-HB_c IgM are important for clinical evaluation of patients for active and past HBV infection.[359, 360] HBsAg is the most important and commonly used marker for active infection because its presence in serum indicates active infection with HBV in almost all cases, with the rare exception being the passive transfer of HBsAg (e.g., by blood transfusion). HBsAg can be detected in most, although not all, patients with infectious HBV in the blood as described previously.[127, 191–193] Sera or other body fluids or secretions should be considered infectious when HBsAg is present.

When serum HBsAg is positive in patients with apparent acute hepatitis, acute hepatitis B is suggested, although superimposed hepatitis caused by another agent or acute exacerbations of CAH may give similar findings in a patient persistently infected with HBV. Falling titers of HBsAg or rising anti-HB_c titers, or both, and positive anti-HB_c IgM in such patients suggest acute hepatitis B (see Fig. 135–6). As described under "Course of Infection," in a fraction of patients with acute HBV infection, HBsAg can never be detected (see Fig. 135–7); in some, HBsAg becomes undetectable before the end of clinical disease; and in a few, it becomes negative even before the onset of disease. In such patients with acute hepatitis, HBV infection may be established only by the presence of anti-HB_c IgM, a rising titer of anti-HB_c, or the subsequent appearance of anti-HBs, or a combination.

HBsAg in the absence of detectable anti-HBc suggests early infection, that is, during the first few weeks after becoming HBsAg-positive and before the appearance of anti-HB_c (see Fig. 135–6). HBsAg can also occur alone in any infected patient unable to mount an antibody response (e.g., as in agammaglobulinemia). HBsAg in the presence of anti-HB_c IgM suggests primary infection sometime after the preceding early period (see Fig. 135–6), and a high titer of anti-HB_c (IgG) without anti-HB_c IgM suggests persistent infection (see Fig. 135–8). Anti-HB_c titers are usually significantly higher during persistent infection than during or after self-limited infection.[127, 359, 360]

The presence of anti-HBs and anti-HB_c in the absence of HBsAg anti-HB_c IgM indicates past infection with HBV and immunity.[127, 359, 360] In general, the more recent the infection, the higher the titers of these antibodies. The presence of either anti-HBs or anti-HB_c alone in low titers most commonly occurs after infection in the distant past in individuals who have since lost the second antibody. Anti-HB_c alone may be present in relatively high titer after the disappearance of HBsAg and before the appearance of anti-HBs (see Fig. 135–6), thus indicating recent infection. Anti-HB_c is the only antibody detected after self-limited infection in 10% of patients who never acquire detectable anti-HBs.

Infrequently, blood containing high titers of anti-HB_c but not detectable HBsAg has been shown to transmit HBV infection to recipients.[127] Such blood probably comes from persistently infected patients or those with self-limited infection who have HBsAg titers too low for detection by even the most sensitive assays. Thus, blood containing anti-HBc alone, particularly when in high titer, should be considered potentially infectious.

The presence of anti-HBs in the absence of anti-HB_c and HBsAg indicates past HBV infection or past vaccination for HBV.[127, 359, 360] Low anti-HBs titers in patients without past HBV vaccination suggests infection in the distant past in patients in whom anti-HB_c had fallen to less than the level of detection. High anti-HBs titers alone may occur after a secondary anti-HBs response after exposure to HBV and HBsAg (e.g., by receiving HBsAg-containing blood products or immunization with HBV vaccine) without a reinfection that would result in a rise in anti-HB_c as well as anti-HBs. Blood containing detectable anti-HBs appears to rarely if ever transmit HBV infection.[361, 362]

Passive transfer of HBsAg, anti-HBs, or anti-HB_c, or a combination, can produce any of the patterns described earlier after transfusion with blood containing the appropriate serologic activity.

Although analysis of a single blood sample may provide an accurate diagnosis in some cases, a second sample 1 month or more after the first, or serial samples may be required to establish HBV infection fully and the stage of infection or convalescence in some patients. For example, falling HBsAg titers in serial blood samples suggest resolving acute infection (see Fig. 135–6). A fourfold or greater rise in anti-HB_c titer and anti-HB_c IgM suggests ongoing infection (see Figs. 135–6 and 135–7). Such a rise in anti-HBs suggests recent infection (see Figs. 135–6 and 135–7), a secondary response after exposure to HBsAg without infection, or recent vaccination. Persistent infection (i.e., the chronic carrier state) usually cannot be established until HBsAg has been shown to be present for at least 6 months.

Assays for Dane particles, HBV DNA, HB_eAg, and anti-HB_e in serum are also clinically useful for assessing patients with HBV infection. Dane particles detected by their DNA polymerase activity[154] or their viral DNA content by nucleic acid hybridization,[157] and HB_eAg, are not found in serum without detectable HBsAg. High levels of Dane particle DNA polymerase activity, and HB_eAg appear regularly in the late incubation period of hepatitis B, and their presence with HBsAg in sera of patients without anti-HB_c suggests the early stage of infection (see Fig. 135–6). The presence of Dane particles and HB_eAg during acute or persistent infection may be used to identify patients who are more likely to transmit infection than are infected patients without these markers. As described under "Epidemiology," the presence of these markers correlates well with transmission of HBV infection from carriers via percutaneous routes,[168, 333] from carrier pregnant women to their newborn infants,[173, 174, 216, 292] from medical care personnel such as dentists to their patients (W. S. Robinson, unpublished results), and from persistently infected patients to their sexual contacts.[175] HBsAg carriers with anti-HB_e in their serum appear to transmit infection by these routes much less frequently. These correlations are not absolute,[363] and some blood samples containing HBsAg and anti-HB_e have been clearly shown to contain infectious HBV,[79, 364] although in much lower titer than in blood containing HB_eAg.[79] Thus, these viral markers clearly distinguish infected patients who readily transmit infection from those unlikely to infect others, at least by certain routes of transmission. However, these correlations are not absolute, and the outcome of contacts with infected patients in individual cases cannot be predicted with certainty from knowledge of these viral markers. HBV DNA can be detected in serum by polymerase chain reaction (PCR) in much lower concentrations than by DNA hybridization, and sera that are negative for HBV DNA by dot blot hybridization have been found to be positive by PCR. Such sera should be presumed to contain infectious virus, although no evidence for infectivity of any such sera has been published, and the clinical significance of PCR positivity with a negative hybridization test for viral DNA has not been established. PCR is a test with extremely high sensitivity, and it cannot be reliably performed without great care in avoiding contamination of reagents or equipment with HBV DNA. False-positive reactions can be expected from many laboratories that do not use the strict conditions required to eliminate contamination.

MANAGEMENT OF HEPATITIS B

Acute Hepatitis B

No therapeutic measure has proved to have beneficial effect on the disease process in the liver during acute viral hepatitis. The benefit of bed rest and the harm of exercise have been much debated, and many of the opinions about physical activity have been based on uncontrolled observations.[365] It has been claimed that relapses and deaths may be increased by severe exercise or even early ambulation. Conversely, several controlled studies have failed to confirm a deleterious effect of exercise.[366, 367] However, most of these studies have involved young, otherwise healthy adult patients with relatively mild disease. Under such circumstances, early ambulation or even light exercise is probably not harmful. For older patients and those with more severe disease, ambulation should be more gradual and determined by the severity of the disease, and by the patient's strength and sense of well-being. If evidence suggests that improvement in liver disease may have been halted or reversed by increasing physical activity, the level of activity can be reduced to determine whether this has a beneficial effect. Because prolonged bed rest may be deleterious to a patient's overall condition, it should be avoided unless needed for sound medical reasons.

No specific dietary alterations appear to affect the outcome of acute viral hepatitis, with the exception of hepatic failure for which protein or salt restriction, or both, may be indicated. The choice of foods should be dictated by taste and tolerance of individual patients and should be directed toward maintenance of the best possible nutritional state. High carbohydrate, high protein, or other special additions to the diet have not been shown to be of benefit.

Corticosteroids have been used by some for severe acute viral hepatitis, but controlled trials in severe[368] and fulminant[369] hepatitis have shown no difference, or even a less favorable outcome, for patients treated with corticosteroids compared with controls. Exchange transfusions, hemodialysis, cross-perfusion, and gamma-globulin containing high titers of anti-HBs[370] have not been shown to affect the course of fulminant hepatitis favorably.

Chronic Hepatitis B

Goals of therapy of chronic hepatitis B include the suppression or complete resolution of active hepatitis (or associated nonhepatic disease such as glomerulonephritis or polyarteritis), halting progression of liver disease, and rendering patients noninfectious. With the belief that elimination of the virus infection will lead to resolution of the disease, development of antiviral therapy for hepatitis B virus infection has been pursued in the past 2 decades with partial success. This success has led to the licensing of recombinant interferon-α (INF-α) and more recently the nucleoside lamivudine (3TC) in the United States for therapy of chronic hepatitis B. HBV replication in vivo was first shown to be suppressed in all patients treated with leukocyte interferon in 1975[156] and with nucleoside drugs in 1978,[199] and numerous studies since that time have confirmed these effects. Three kinds of responses to interferon therapy are well recognized.[155, 156] In a small fraction of patients, all markers of infection in serum (HBsAg, HB_eAg, virion DNA polymerase, virion DNA, and infectious HBV) and liver (HB_cAg and HBsAg) fall to less than the level of detection during treatment and remain so indefinitely after treatment is stopped (type I response). In other patients, HB_eAg, virion DNA polymerase, virion DNA, infectious HBV,[80] and HB_cAg disappear from serum and liver, respectively, and anti-HB_e appears in serum during treatment; these changes remain permanently after treatment is stopped, although serum and hepatic HBsAg persists (type II response). In most patients, virion DNA polymerase, virion DNA levels, and HB_eAg are partially suppressed during treatment and return to pretreatment levels when treatment is stopped (type III response). Type I and type II, but not type III, responses are associated with improvements in liver function and histologic characteristics[200, 377–379] and elimination of infectious virus from the serum of all or most patients,[80] making these clinically significant responses. The elimination of detectable serum HBsAg very infrequently results from the antiviral therapies used to date, and this remains an important goal because the risk of liver cancer developing appears to remain increased in such patients.

Recombinant interferon-α 2b (INF-α) given subcutaneously in doses of 5×10^6 units per day or 10×10^6 units 3 times per week for 4 to 6 months have been recommended for therapy of chronic HBV infection.[380] Analysis of the responses to such therapy for 4 to 6 months in 15 clinical trials of a subgroup of patients with chronic HBV infection, namely, those with hepatitis B virions and HB_eAg in their serum, revealed that serum HB_eAg became undetectable and remained so in 33% of INF-α–treated patients (a type II response) and in 12% of untreated controls, and very few patients became serum HBsAg-negative (a type I response).[381] It is the serum HB_eAg-positive subgroup of patients (a minority of adult patients who are chronically serum HBsAg-positive) for which antiviral therapy is recommended. Recommended indications for therapy include persistently elevated levels of serum aminotransferases in patients with HBsAg, HB_eAg, and HBV DNA in serum, and chronic hepatitis established by liver biopsy. Type I and type II responses occur more frequently in patients with (1) low virion DNA polymerase or virion DNA levels, or both, than in those with high levels[55, 377, 378]; (2) CAH (rather than CPH)[155]; (3) high serum aminotransferase levels; (4) a short duration of infection before therapy; and (5) absence of immunosuppressive underlying conditions. Therapy is not recommended for patients with: (1) serum HBsAg without HB_eAg or HBV DNA, or both; (2) normal serum aminotransferase levels; (3) advanced liver disease with hepatic failure; or (4) impaired immunity such as with renal failure, hemodialysis, organ transplantation, or HIV infection with reduced CD4 cell concentrations because such patients infrequently have type I or type II responses to INF-α therapy. Patients with cirrhosis and hepatic failure may have worsening of liver failure and other serious complications when treated with high doses of interferon.

The response of children with chronic hepatitis B to INF-α therapy appears to be similar to that of adults[382] and a dose of 6×10^6 units per square meter of body surface three times per week for 4 to 6 months is recommended for therapy of such patients.[383] Remission of HBV-associated glomerulonephritis has been reported in small numbers of patients[384] and INF-α therapy indicated for such patients. Polyarteritis nodosa patients with hepatitis B often have high serum levels of HBV DNA and respond poorly to INF-α, and those with severe vasculitis require immunosuppressive drug therapy.[382]

Interferon in high doses causes acute side effects of fever, myalgia, headache, fatigue, and malaise lasting for several hours after each dose but often decreasing in severity after several days of therapy.[156] To reduce such effects, therapy with interferon can be started at a low dose such as 1×10^6 units per day and increased to full doses over several days as the acute side effects decrease. Chronic side effects include persistent and sometimes severe fatigue and depression, hair loss (rarely), and suppression of white blood cell and platelet counts; these effects are usually dose-related and reversible when therapy is stopped.[155, 156, 377, 378]

The mechanism by which interferon therapy inhibits HBV replication in vivo is not established. In addition to suppression of steps in virus replication, interferon may increase HLA class I gene expression in liver cells[383] and affect the immune response[384, 385] in ways that contribute to its antiviral effect in vivo. Consistent with this is the regular finding of evidence for liver cell injury (serum alanine amino transferase rises) in patients who respond favorably to interferon therapy.[155, 156] This suggests that interferon may have activated a mechanism (e.g., a CTL response) for destruction of infected liver cells. Experimental studies with other interferons (e.g., β and γ) have also demonstrated suppression of HBV replication in vivo.[385–387]

A class of antiviral drugs that suppresses HBV replication is nucleoside analogues that act by inhibiting viral DNA synthesis. The first antiviral nucleoside used, ara-A (adenine arabinoside) in doses up to 10 mg/kg, strongly inhibited HBV replication in all infected patients, but the toxic effects of prolonged administration of the doses required preclude its regular use.[155, 199, 391, 392] Some other nucleoside analogues approved for use in humans for other viral infections such as acyclovir (10 mg/kg/day) produced only modest suppression of levels of HBV DNA and DNA polymerase in serum compared with ara-A.[395] Zidovudine (ZDV) has an even smaller effect on HBV. More recently nucleoside analogues such as lamivudine (2′,3′-dideoxy-3′-thiacytidine or 3TC)[393–395] approved for therapy of HIV, and famciclovir[396] approved for therapy of herpesvirus, have been shown to strongly suppress HBV replication at oral doses with less toxicity than nucleosides such as ara A (see Chapter 103). Clinical trials have shown type II responses in 12%[393] and 16%[394] of patients treated with 100 to 300 mg. orally per day for 12 weeks or more, and a larger percentage of patients experienced a reduction in levels of serum aminotransferase levels. There were no type I responses. Based on such studies, lamuvidine was recently approved by the U.S. Food and Drug Administration for therapy of chronic hepatitis B, providing an oral agent with acceptable side effects. The indications for lamivudine therapy of chronic HBV infection are those described previously for INF-α. Oral lamivudine doses of 100 mg one to three times per day for 4 to 6 months may be used.

A second clinical use for lamivudine is in suppression of HBV replication in HBV-infected liver transplant recipients before and after transplantation. Liver transplantation in patients with chronic HBV infection, particularly when they are serum HB_eAg- and HBV DNA–positive, is likely to result in HBV infection of the transplanted liver and subsequent rapidly progressive, and often fatal, liver disease.[397] High doses of hepatitis B hyperimmune globulin (HBIG) have had some efficacy in blocking HBV infection of transplanted liver in patients undergoing transplantation for fulminant hepatitis B and in those with chronic hepatitis B with undetectable or low levels of serum HBV DNA or HB_eAg, or both, but not in patients with high levels of such markers of HBV replication. Interferon therapy in this setting has not proved very useful. Preliminary studies suggest that treatment of such patients with lamivudine before transplantation and for prolonged periods or indefinitely after transplantation is successful in suppressing HBV replication and disease in transplanted livers infected with HBV, and this results in increased patient survival.[398–403] HBV is not eliminated from the infected transplant so that lifelong therapy may be required.

A third clinical setting in which lamivudine may be useful is in HBV-infected patients who are immunosuppressed by organ transplantation or cancer chemotherapy. Such patients may have activation of HBV replication and associated severe progressive fatal liver disease. There have been recent reports of the use of lamivudine therapy to suppress HBV replication and ameliorate liver disease in such patients.[404–408] Again, HBV is not eliminated by such therapy, so continuous therapy may be needed as long as patients remain immunosuppressed.

An increasingly apparent problem with prolonged therapy with lamivudine (and with famciclovir) has been selection of drug-resistant variants (usually mutations in the viral reverse transcriptase gene)[409–412] that make infections resistant to drug therapy. There have been numerous reports[399, 409–418] of development of such resistance during prolonged therapy, and this problem may prove to significantly affect the previously described uses of lamivudine (as well as prolonged therapy with famciclovir) (see Chapter 103).

Other antiviral compounds such as phosphonoformic and phosphonoacetic acid are also potent in suppressing hepadnavirus replication and are under study.

Thus, the approved therapies (interferon or lamivudine) for chronic hepatitis B are only partially successful, and improved therapy is needed. Trials of interferon combined with one or more other antiviral drugs is one approach that deserves more investigation because some evidence suggests that interferon plus ara-A is more virus-suppressive than either used alone.[155] A clinical trial combining IFN-α with lamivudine in patients in whom IFN-α monotherapy had failed, however, resulted in a sustained type II response in only 1 of 20 patients,[420] suggesting that better approaches are needed. The strategy of combination antiviral therapy deserves more investigation, with goals of both improving therapeutic efficacy and reducing the development of drug-resistant mutants to agents such as lamivudine. In addition, strategies to activate appropriate immune responses during chronic virus infections may offer the best approach for terminating such infections. Studies of the effects of newer antiviral agents in acute hepatitis B have been too limited to draw conclusions, but efficacy has not yet been demonstrated.

In the management of HBsAg carriers, it may be useful to inform patients of the course of certain serologic markers. As described under "Routes of Transmission," the presence of serum HB_eAg indicates a high level of contagiousness for contacts, and the absence of HB_eAg and presence of anti-HB_e indicate low contagiousness. In HB_eAg-positive carriers this test might be performed at yearly intervals to make the patient aware of a seroconversion that occurs in approximately 15% of HB_eAg-positive carriers per year, and the accompanying change in contagiousness. Similarly, periodic testing (every 1 or 2 years) for HBsAg would detect complete resolution of the infection (which occurs in 1 to 2% of carriers per year) with loss of contagiousness and risk of HBV-associated liver disease.

The high risk of HCC formation in certain HBsAg carriers (as high as 3% per year in Chinese male carriers older than 50 years of age and more than 12% per year for those with cirrhosis[242]) is a serious problem for these individuals. Several studies have shown that when serum α-fetoprotein (AFP) followed serially in HBsAg carriers rises to significantly more than the patient's own baseline (e.g., $> 100\ \mu g/ml$), HCC can often be detected by liver scanning or ultrasonography at a stage when the tumor can be cured by surgical resection.[421, 422] This suggests that many HBsAg carriers should have regular serial serum AFP determinations, although larger prospective studies are needed to better define the sensitivity, specificity, and predictive value of AFP screening and to better establish its indications. The interval between infection and development of HCC is usually many years, and the risk goes up in proportion to duration of infection.[242] Thus, in individuals infected in infancy or childhood, AFP testing and ultrasonographic examination at 6-month intervals might be carried out for those older than 35 or 40 years of age. It is recommended that all HBsAg carriers with cirrhosis have regular serum AFP testing and ultrasonographic examinations.

The progression of autoimmune chronic active hepatitis has been favorably altered by administration of corticosteroids and sometimes azothioprine in controlled trials.[371–373] In contrast, HBsAg-positive patients with CAH respond significantly less often to corticosteroids than do HBsAg-negative patients,[374] and HBsAg-positive patients with HB_eAg may be particularly unresponsive.[375] In addition, corticosteroid therapy regularly appears to enhance HBV replication with rises in titers of HBsAg, HB_eAg, and Dane particles, or induces the appearance of the latter markers in carriers without them.[195–197] This effect reverses the gradual winding down of the infection over months and years that is observed in many carriers. It has been recommended that corticosteroid therapy be used only for CAH patients who are symptomatic, who are HBsAg-negative, and who have severe histologic lesions in liver biopsy specimens, and not be used for HBsAg-positive patients.[376]

PREVENTION OF HEPATITIS B VIRUS INFECTION

Several measures have been used successfully to prevent spread of HBV. These include application of environmental control measures to contain virus and prevent exposure and the use of passive and active immunization to render individuals or groups resistant to infection. The development of successful control measures has depended to a large extent on the growing understanding of the epidemiologic and biologic features of this virus and the availability of serologic assays to identify infected and immune individuals.

Immunization

Preexposure Passive Immunization. Passive immunization with either hyperimmune serum globulin (HBIG) or standard immune serum globulin (ISG) has afforded protection against HBV infection /or disease, or both, under certain circumstances. HBIG preparations that are protective have titers of anti-HBs that approach or exceed 1:100,000 by sensitive tests such as passive hemagglutination assay or RIA; preparations of ISG that are protective have titers of 1:16 to 1:1000 by these tests.[423, 424] Preparations of ISG have regularly had anti-HBs titers of that magnitude since 1970.

Preexposure prophylaxis with HBIG was shown to provide protection for hemodialysis patients[425, 426] and staff,[427, 428] and for institutionalized children in the 1970s. Several studies failed to show a difference in incidence of hepatitis or HBsAg positivity in patients who received ISG that contained measurable anti-HBs titers, compared with patients who received HBIG in these settings,[425, 427, 429] suggesting that HBIG was not superior to ISG for preexposure prophylaxis. In some studies[428–430] there appeared to be a greater frequency of primary antibody response in the ISG-treated group than in those given HBIG. These results suggest that ISG might be superior to HBIG in producing passive-active immunity. If so, ISG could be more effective in providing long-term protection for persons at high risk for infection.

With the availability of an effective vaccine, there appears to be little or no indication for preexposure passive immunization except in individuals failing to respond to vaccine, or in patients with disorders that preclude a response (e.g., agammaglobulinemia), in settings in which the risk of exposure remains high despite environmental control measures designed to prevent infection.

Preexposure Immunization with Hepatitis B Vaccine. Plasma-derived hepatitis B vaccine was licensed in the United States in 1981. It consisted of HBsAg particles highly purified from plasma of HBsAg carriers and processed to inactivate the infectivity of HBV and other viruses.[431–433] This vaccine proved safe and effective. It was used in the United States until recombinant vaccines were licensed in 1986, after which production of plasma vaccine was discontinued in the United States. Plasma-derived hepatitis vaccines are still used in China and in many other parts of the world. Recombinant vaccines that consist of highly purified HBsAg particles expressed in yeast (*Saccharomyces cerevisiae*) cells were shown to be safe and equivalent to the plasma vaccines in immunogenicity and protective efficacy. Table 135–3 lists the hepatitis B vaccines currently manufactured in the United States and recommended dosage schedules.[274] Anti-HBs responses with these dosage schedules in experimental vaccine trials are excellent; greater than 90% of patients younger than 40 or 50 years of age, including infants, have high antibody titers after the third dose of vaccine[434–439] (Table 135–4). In children and young adults, titers may exceed 10,000 MIU/ml. Age is an important factor influencing the response to vaccine, and younger vaccinees (including newborn infants) have the highest rates of seroconversion in experimental trials. Older age, obesity, heavy smoking, and immunologic impairment have been associated with lower anti-HBs responses.[440, 441]

Although anti-HBs titers fall with time after vaccination, 85% of homosexual men who responded to three doses of vaccine retained detectable anti-HBs 5 years after vaccination,[434, 440] and more than 50% had antibody after 8 years.[442–448] The higher the anti-HBs titer after vaccination, the longer anti-HBs persists.[440] When the anti-HBs titer falls to less than 10 MIU/ml, HBV infections may occur but are always subclinical and usually without detectable serum HBsAg (such infections are detected only by development of anti-HBc or by a rise in the titer of anti-HBs).[443, 444] Thus, even when anti-HBs is no longer detectable after vaccination, protection against disease remained if HBV infection occurs. Whether vaccines will require regular booster doses and at what time intervals remains to be determined. Immunologically impaired individuals, such as those undergoing hemodialysis or those with organ transplants, respond less well (see Table 135–4), and a higher vaccine dose is recommended (see Table 135–3). Such patients may also be given a four-dose regimen with doses at 0, 1, 2, and 6 or 12 months.

Simultaneous administration of ISG with high anti-HBs titers does not impair the anti-HBs response to vaccine.[449, 450] Administration of vaccine to HBsAg carriers resulted in no recognizable ill effects and no alteration in the course of the infection.[451] Administration of vaccine to individuals who have anti-HBs in serum results in a rise in titer of this antibody and no recognizable ill effects. Although no special ill effects have been associated with vaccination of individuals with serum HBsAg or anti-HBs, vaccination of such individuals is of no value and is not indicated.

The safety of hepatitis B vaccines has been established by pro-

TABLE 135–3 U.S. Licensed Hepatitis B Vaccines

	Vaccine and Dose*					
	Hepatavax-B† Dose		*Recombivax HB Dose*		*Engenix-B Dose*	
Vaccination Group	*μg*	*ml*	*μg*	*ml*	*μg*	*ml*
Infants of HBsAg-positive mothers	10	0.5	5	0.5	10	0.5
Others less than age 10 yr	10	0.5	2.5	0.25	10	0.5
Ages 10–19 yr	20	1.0	5	0.5	20	1.0
Ages >19 yr	20	1.0	10	1.0	20	1.0
Immunologically impaired, including dialysis patients	40	2.0	40	1.0‡	40	2.0§

*Three doses given at 0, 1, and 6 months.
†Plasma vaccine no longer manufactured in United States, but similar vaccines are produced and used in China and some other countries.
‡Concentrated.
§Four doses recommended at 0, 1, 2, and 6 months.
Modified from Advisory Committee for Immunization Practices. Recommendations for protection against viral hepatitis. MMWR Morb Mortal Wkly Rep. 1990;39:725–729.

TABLE 135-4 Anti-HBs Seroconversion Rates after Hepatitis B Vaccination (%)

Neonates	>95
Age (years)	
2–19	≈99
20–29	~95
30–39	~90
40–49	~85
50–59	~70
>59	~50
Renal failure, HIV infection, other immunosuppression	50–70
Liver disease	60–70

Abbreviation: HIV, Human immunodeficiency virus.

spective clinical trials involving many thousands of individuals and by the subsequent administration of millions of doses worldwide. Side effects of hepatitis B vaccine have been moderate soreness at the injection site in approximately 12% of vaccinees, mild fever in less than 2%, and other mild constitutional symptoms. In placebo-controlled trials, no difference in side effects between recipients of vaccine or placebo was found.[435–437]

At this time there is no evidence that more serious side effects are associated with current HBV vaccines. Although a few cases of Guillain-Barré syndrome[452, 453] or other neurologic disorders[454] have been observed after vaccination, there is no evidence that the incidence of Guillain-Barré is higher among recipients of HBV vaccine than that in the general population. In controlled trials in homosexual men, the incidence of acquired immunodeficiency syndrome has been the same in groups receiving plasma-derived vaccine and placebo.[455] No cases of non-A, non-B hepatitis have been reported after plasma-derived vaccine. Hypersensitivity reactions can be expected in some individuals who are allergic to yeast antigens, and the yeast-derived vaccine is not recommended for such individuals. Very rare anaphylactic reactions have been reported. Cases of erythema nodosum and polyarthralgia after repeated doses of vaccine have been reported[456], if such a rare event were to occur, among additional vaccine doses should not be given.

Four prospective, double-blind, placebo-controlled trials of plasma vaccine have been carried out in homosexual males,[455, 457–459] hemodialysis unit staff,[460] and hospital personnel[450] and demonstrated more than 90% protection. Almost all the vaccinated individuals who were subsequently infected with HBV were among the small fraction of vaccine recipients who failed to seroconvert. Yeast-derived vaccine has been shown to reduce the rate of perinatal infection significantly in babies of HBsAg-positive mothers.[461–465] In summary, both plasma-derived and yeast-derived hepatitis B vaccines appear to be effective and safe in prevention of HBV infection. Susceptible individuals with a significant risk of infection with HBV should be vaccinated.

Indications for hepatitis B vaccination in the United States include individuals with a high risk of exposure to HBV and who have not been infected (Table 135–5). Because the policy of vaccination of high-risk groups in the first decade of hepatitis B vaccine use had little impact on the incidence of new HBV infections,[275, 466] and because of the overwhelming evidence of safety of hepatitis B vaccines, universal vaccination of all infants born in the United States was recommended and instituted in 1991.[467] Avoidance of administration of an additional parenteral vaccine would result from development of multicomponent vaccines, such as a combination of hepatitis B vaccine to diphtheria-pertussis-tetanus when trials of such combined vaccines demonstrate efficacy and safety. In 1996, the U.S. Food and Drug Administration licensed a combined *Haemophelus influenzae* conjugate and hepatitis B (recombinant) vaccine (Comvax) for infants. Vaccine-preventable diseases such as hepatitis B continue to occur among adolescents (i.e., persons aged 11 to 21 years). In 1996, the Advisory Committee on Immunization Practices (ACIP), the American Academy of Pediatrics, the American Academy of Family Physicians, and the American Medical Association published joint recommendations for hepatitis B vaccination of adolescents aged 11 to 12 years who have not been previously vaccinated because of continuing high rates of injecting-drug use, teenage pregnancy, sexually transmitted diseases, or a combination of these factors, in adolescents and young adults in many communities. School entry requirements are an effective mechanism for ensuring high vaccination coverage among children, and some states now require all persons entering seventh grade to be vaccinated with three doses of hepatitis B vaccine. In high-prevalence regions of the world, such as eastern Asia, vaccination of all newborn infants is the preferred strategy for control of HBV. Whether individuals vaccinated at early ages will require vaccine boosters at later times remains to be determined.

Before vaccination, individuals in high-risk groups may be tested for either anti-HBs or anti-HBc (the markers most likely to detect past infection)[457] to avoid unnecessary vaccination of individuals who are already immune. Serum anti-HBc would also be positive in HBsAg carriers, for whom vaccination is not beneficial. Some have recommended testing for anti-HB_c in preference to anti-HBs because anti-HB_c may be a more specific indication of past HBV infection and appears to correlate with high anti-HBs titers.[457] Also, rare patients with low anti-HBs titers that may or may not be nonspecific appear to remain susceptible to HBV infection.[202–204] Such prevaccination testing is not cost-effective in populations with low HBV prevalence, and vaccination of such populations without prior testing is recommended. After vaccination of seronegative health care workers, testing for anti-HBs should be performed to determine whether seroconversion has resulted. It is important for individuals to know when they have failed to seroconvert after vaccination because they remain susceptible to HBV infection and should receive ISG for significant future exposures to HBV. Such passive immunization is unnecessary for HBV exposure of those who successfully seroconvert after vaccination. Revaccination (by the same three-dose schedule) of individuals who have no detectable anti-HBs response after the third vaccine dose of a primary immunization series has resulted in an anti-HBs response in more than 50% of persons. However, the titers tend to be low and are not as persistent as in those in subjects who respond to the first vaccination series.[440] Several studies have shown that doses of 2 to 5 μg administered intradermally give seroconversion rates similar to 20- to 40-μg doses of the same HBV vaccine given intramuscularly.[458, 459] The possibility of intradermal vaccination is attractive for countries for which vaccine cost is critical because the intradermal route of administration requires smaller amounts of vaccine than does intramuscular administration.

A potential problem for hepatitis B vaccines may be naturally occurring HBV mutants[468–473] that alter HBsAg specificity and permit mutant virus to "escape" the immune response to vaccination. A case has been reported of an infant who was infected with HBV and became an HBsAg carrier despite vaccination accompanied by

TABLE 135-5 Groups with Increased Risk of Hepatitis B Virus Infection for Whom Hepatitis B Vaccine Is Recommended

Medical, dental, and laboratory workers and others with exposure to human blood
Homosexual men
Heterosexuals with multiple sex partners or with sexually transmitted diseases
Highly HBV endemic populations, e.g., Alaskan natives
Household contacts of HBsAg-positive individuals
Parenteral drug users who share needles
Hemophilia patients
Hemodialysis patients
Patients for whom multiple blood or blood product infusions are anticipated
Prison inmates and staff
Staff and patients of institutions for mentally disabled
Travelers to high HBV endemic areas with anticipated exposure to human blood, sexual contacts with locals or prolonged living in households with locals
Newborn infants of serum HBsAg-positive mothers

Abbreviation: HBV, Hepatitis B virus.

seroconversion.[468] A single point mutation was found within the region of the viral S-gene, which encodes the *a* epitope of HBsAg and that resulted in altered HBsAg specificity. This was considered to be an "escape mutant." Such mutants appear to be rare at present, but if they were to arise more frequently, they would present an important problem that may require changes in HBV vaccines and in diagnostic testing procedures.

Postexposure Immunization of Children and Adults. Krugman and Giles in 1973 conducted placebo-controlled trials that showed that serum immunoglobulin preparations with high titers of anti-HBs, given 4 hours after experimental inoculation of children with relatively high doses of infectious HBV, reduced but did not eliminate the incidence of infection.[474] ISG with a low anti-HBs titer appeared to give a significant but lower level of protection.

Most prospective controlled trials of postexposure prophylaxis of adults since that time have compared HBIG with ISG rather than with placebo. HBIG conferred significant protection compared with ISG in large trials in hospital personnel with needlestick or mucous membrane exposure to blood containing HBsAg[150] and for spouses of patients with acute hepatitis B.[475] A significant difference in protection between HBIG and ISG was not shown in a second similarly designed "needlestick" trial.[476, 477] The rate of HBV infection in both ISG- and HBIG-treated groups, however, was lower than anticipated for untreated patients in this study. The difference in the results of the different studies appears to be due to a difference in the ISG employed. The ISG used in the first two trials contained no detectable anti-HBs, whereas that in the latter trial contained a significant anti-HBs titer. These studies indicate that HBIG provides protection when given after exposure to HBV. It also appears that ISG containing significant amounts of anti-HBs may provide similar protection, unlike ISG without anti-HBs, which is clearly inferior to HBIG.

The timing of HBIG doses resulting in the most effective postexposure prophylaxis has not been well defined. In most clinical trials, two doses at a 1-month interval were used, and because of this, the Public Health Service Advisory Committee on Immunization Practices currently has recommended this two-dose schedule.[478] It is not clear, however, that two doses offer more protection than a single dose. In some studies that clearly demonstrated protection,[474, 475] a single dose was employed, and in some trials that employed two doses,[477] no increased protection by HBIG in comparison to ISG was shown. In one study,[479] a single dose of HBIG was compared directly with one half of the same dose given at the time of exposure and repeated after 1 month, and there was no statistically significant difference in the subsequent infection rates. Thus, a single dose at the time of exposure appears to provide significant protection, and the addition of a second dose has not been clearly shown to increase the beneficial effect.

There is also little information about the effect of time of administration of HBIG after exposure on the protective effect that is conferred. Because HBIG was given within 7 days of exposure in some studies that showed protection,[150, 476, 477] administration of the first HBIG dose within 7 days has been recommended by the Public Health Service Advisory Committee on Immunization Practices.[478] An unexpected finding of one study,[475] however, was apparent protection even when HBIG was not given until several weeks after the postulated time of exposures. Conversely, there is evidence that when HBIG or ISG is given within 48 hours of "needlestick" exposure, it is more effective than when given between 3 and 7 days after such exposure.[429] Thus, administration of HBIG soon after exposure to HBV appears to be important for maximal protection.

The dose of HBIG required for effective postexposure treatment is not precisely known, but a dose shown to protect adults successfully in two different controlled trials was 0.07 ml/kg.[150, 475–477]

There is no evidence in the studies to date that suggests that ISG or HBIG can transmit HBV infection or can increase the rate at which subsequent primary infections become persistent.

A major indication for HBIG is for prophylaxis after a single acute direct exposure to HBV, such as might occur with an accidental needlestick, with mucous membrane or broken skin exposure to blood or other body fluids known to contain HBsAg, or after sexual intercourse or oral exchange of saliva such as by kissing or sharing a toothbrush with a partner who is HBsAg-positive. If HBIG is not available, ISG containing detectable anti-HBs should be used after such exposures. Patients who are known to have anti-HBs or anti-HB_c in serum are resistant to infection and need not be given prophylaxis after exposure. Similarly, individuals who are HBsAg-positive do not benefit. Because of the apparent benefit of administration of immunoglobulin as soon as possible after exposure, a delay to test an exposed individual for anti-HBs is not recommended, and HBIG (or ISG) should be promptly administered after a significant exposure to HBV. Delaying passive immunization after a significant exposure to a patient with evidence of acute or chronic hepatitis of unknown type in order to identify a viral agent by serologic testing is not recommended. Again, HBIG (or ISG) should be rapidly given to the exposed individual, and such treatment should provide protection against HBV as well as HAV. All individuals receiving HBIG (or ISG) for exposure to HBV should also receive hepatitis B vaccine. The first dose of vaccine should be given within 7 days of the exposure.

Postexposure Immunization of Newborns. An important indication for postexposure immunization is for neonates born of HBsAg-positive mothers. Such infants are commonly infected, especially when mothers are HB_eAg-positive, and 90% or more of infected infants appear to become chronic carriers.[173, 174, 480–482] Several studies have shown that prompt administration of high doses of HBIG to infants born of HB_eAg-positive mothers reduces the infection rate by 70 to 80%.[481–483] When low doses were administered and when the administration of the first dose was delayed beyond 48 hours, little or no protection was observed.[484] A significant fraction of infants protected by HBIG in the neonatal period are infected later when passive antibodies have disappeared.[481, 485] Use of vaccine alone shortly after birth has been shown to give a similar level of protection.[486] Almost 100% of newborn infants have anti-HBs responses to the vaccine.[330, 481]

When HBIG and vaccine were used together in the neonatal period, 94% protection was achieved.[330] One half of the few infants who became chronic carriers in that study had moderate HBsAg titers in cord blood, which suggests that intrauterine infection had occurred, which is not likely to be reversed by immunization after birth. It is currently recommended that 0.5 ml of HBIG be administered intramuscularly in the delivery room to infants born of an HBsAg-positive mother, and 0.5 ml of vaccine be given intramuscularly at the same time or within the first week after delivery[274] (see Table 135–3). Second and third vaccine doses should be given at 1 and 6 months, respectively. Although the risk of infection is greatest when mothers are HB_eAg-positive, a small risk for infants remains when HBsAg-positive mothers also have anti-HB_e, and these infants should be managed in the same way. All pregnant women should be routinely tested for HBsAg before delivery so that newborns of positive mothers can be appropriately immunized after birth.

Environmental and Other Control Measures

Among the most important and effective approaches for control of spread of HBV are the use of environmental barriers and personal hygiene, which effectively prevent virus transmission. As described under "Epidemiology", the principal modes of transmission that must be interrupted in the United States appear to be (1) direct percutaneous inoculation of infective blood or serum (e.g., by administration of contaminated blood or blood products, tattooing, ear piercing, acupuncture, drug abuse, accidental needlesticks by hospital personnel, and so on), (2) contamination of mucosal surfaces by infective blood or serum (e.g., by mouth, pipetting, slashes in eyes or transfer from hands to eye or mouth, and so on) or by other infective secretions (e.g., by sexual or other activity involving semen or saliva, and so on), and (3) transfer of such infective material on environmental surfaces into skin breaks or mucous membranes (e.g., by contaminated objects such as toothbrushes, toys, baby bottles, cups or glasses, rubber gloves, razors, towels, or hospital equipment, and so on). Feces and urine are not important sources of HBV in the absence of gastrointestinal bleeding. The ability to identify infected patients and susceptible individuals through serologic testing permits application of containment measures in situations in which a risk of transmission is recognized. Education of HBsAg-positive individuals and their contacts, and particularly of high-risk populations such as health care personnel, about common sources of HBV, routes of transmission, and methods of prevention of transmission is essential for the most effective application of control measures. When contact with HBV is anticipated, an individual should be vaccinated before the anticipated exposure. Disease surveillance and consistent case reporting are also important for recognition of changes in epidemiologic trends so that community-wide control measures can be rationally applied.

Several methods have been recommended for disinfection or sterilization of contaminated material.[487, 488] Heat is the treatment of choice for materials that tolerate the required conditions. Boiling in water (100°C for 10 minutes), autoclaving at 121°C and 15 lb. per square inch for 15 minutes, or dry heat (160°C) for 2 hours exceed to conditions known to inactivate HBV. Alternative methods presumed to be effective because they have been shown to destroy HBsAg antigenicity or are bacteriocidal for bacterial endospores (although not demonstrated to render HBV noninfective) are solutions of sodium hypochlorite of 0.5 to 1.0% (5000 to 10,000 ppm chlorine) for 30 minutes, 40% aqueous formalin (16% aqueous formaldehyde) for 12 hours, or gas sterilization with ethylene oxide. Very active detergents such as sodium dodecyl sulfate (1%), which completely disrupt Dane particles and are virucidal for most viruses, are also undoubtedly virucidal for HBV. Thorough mechanical cleaning of surfaces to remove adherent material that might interfere with chemical disinfection is also important.

The Committee on Viral Hepatitis of the Division of Medical Sciences of the National Academy of Sciences, the National Research Council, and the Public Health Service Advisory Committee on Immunization Practices have made recommendations for minimizing transmission in specific settings.[488]

Households. Although spouses and other intimate contacts of HBsAg-positive patients with acute or persistent infection appear to be at greatest risk for infection in households, all household members who are not HBsAg- or anti-HBs-positive should be vaccinated.

General Patient Care in Hospital Areas. HBsAg-positive patients, whether acutely or persistently infected with HBV, need not be isolated or confined to hospital rooms. However, blood and other body fluids likely to be infective, and instruments, bed clothes, and other objects contaminated with potentially infective material must be handled in a manner that prevents transmission and appropriately decontaminated. Gloves should be worn by personnel drawing blood from HBsAg-positive patients or when handling potentially contaminated objects. Additional protective clothing such as gowns, masks, and glasses should be worn for procedures that could result in splashing of potentially infective material. Whether or not gloves are worn, careful hand washing should be practiced after any contact with HBsAg-positive patients or contaminated objects before contact with other patients. HBsAg-positive and HBsAg-negative patients should not share personal objects. Items such as tourniquets, blood pressure cuffs, marking pens used on the skin, antiseptics, skin care lotion, and so on should not be used for HBsAg-negative patients after use on HBsAg-positive patients unless first decontaminated. Potentially infective specimens such as blood of HBsAg-positive patients should be appropriately labeled to alert all who handle them of their infective nature. Bed linen, towels, and environmental surfaces in patient rooms, such as tops of eating tables, should be decontaminated before using for HBsAg-negative patients. Any spill of blood or other potentially infective material should be cleaned up immediately in a manner that contains and inactivates the virus. Susceptible (e.g., anti-HBs negative) hospital personnel or others should be given HBIG only after a recognized episode of direct percutaneous or mucous membrane exposure as described earlier. These preventive measures should be discontinued only after patients become HBsAg-negative at which time they can be considered to be noninfective. The same general approaches can be used for HBsAg-positive patients in nursing homes and institutions for the mentally retarded.

Hospital Patient Care Areas with Special High Risks. Special hospital patient care areas where the risk of HBV infection is high for patients and staff, such as hemodialysis units, may require procedures in addition to those outlined for general patient care areas to control the spread of infection. Patient care personnel assigned to these hospital areas, as well as those assigned to care for HBsAg-positive patients in any hospital area, should be vaccinated, be anti-HBs positive by virtue of past infection, or be HBsAg-positive and not at risk for HBV infection. Education of patients and staff about sources of HBV, routes of transmission, and methods of prevention of spread is particularly important in high-risk hospital units. Geographic separation of HBsAg-positive and HBsAg-negative patients has been quite successful in preventing spread of HBV to staff and susceptible patients in many hemodialysis units. Other important measures include use of separate wards and dialysis rooms, separate dialysis machines and all other pieces of equipment, proper decontamination of nondisposable items of equipment; use of disposable equipment or materials when possible, use of separate nursing personnel for HBsAg-positive and -negative patient groups, and administration of HBV vaccine to susceptible patients who have a high risk of infection.

Laboratory Processing of Infective Material. Clinical serology, chemistry, hematology, and pathology laboratories, as well as research laboratories, that handle infective material should employ procedures that reduce the risk of HBV infection of personnel. Mouth pipetting, smoking, and eating should be forbidden in laboratories that handle HBsAg-positive material. Gloves should be used to handle potentially infective material. In addition, gowns and masks should be used for any procedures during which splashing might occur (e.g., performing autopsies, and so on). HBsAg-positive specimens should be appropriately packaged and labeled, confined to specified areas of the laboratory (e.g., benches, refrigerators, freezers, and so on) designated for infective material, and these areas should be thoroughly cleaned and disinfected regularly. However, none of these procedures to contain HBV in the laboratory can substitute for careful laboratory techniques and appropriate personal habits (e.g., hand washing) to avoid spread of virus. Personnel working with potentially infective material in a laboratory should be vaccinated against HBV.

Management of Persistently Infected Persons with Special Risk for Transmission to Others

HBsAg-positive persons in certain occupations (e.g., health care personnel) and other circumstances may represent a special risk for transmission of HBV to contacts. During acute hepatitis B infection, it is prudent to restrict activity and contact of the individual with others until HBsAg negativity can be shown. Persistent HBV infection, in contrast, is not necessarily a reason to restrict an individual's activities, although clearly personal precautions should be taken.

Health Care Personnel. Persistently infected health care personnel with direct patient contact, such as dentists, nurses, physicians, and some technicians, should not be restricted from patient contact unless transmission to patients is documented. As discussed under "Epidemiology," most health care workers appear to represent little risk to patient contacts, although transmission has occurred in some cases. The presence of high blood concentrations of Dane particles and HBeAg appears to correlate with the risk of transmission. The potential for transmission by any carrier must be recognized, however. It is important that such persons have an understanding of the sources of HBV, the routes of transmission, and the personal procedures and practices that should be used to reduce the chances of transmission. Scrupulous aseptic technique, avoidance of personal hand injuries, and use of gloves for minor surgery, blood drawing, dental procedures, and wound dressing, should be practiced. Such persistently infected individuals should be tested for HBsAg at 6-month intervals because they may become HBsAg-negative and thus would no longer be infective to others. Some surveillance of patient contacts to determine whether virus transmission occurs is desirable. If implicated in transmission, certain restrictive measures (e.g., limiting or eliminating some types of procedures or patient contact) may be required.

Food Handlers. Although no cases of virus transmission from HBV-infected food handlers have been documented, it is reasonable to educate persistently infected food handlers about sources of HBV and routes of transmission and the need to practice good personal hygiene, frequent hand washing, and avoidance of hand injuries. Food handlers with acute hepatitis B should be restricted from work until they become HBsAg-negative.

Elimination of Infective Blood Products

Among the most important ways to prevent hepatitis B cases in the population is to eliminate infective blood used for transfusions and blood products. Since 1972, the U.S. Food and Drug Administration has required that blood banks test all blood donors for HBsAg. Although such testing eliminates much of the infective blood, evidence shows that even the most sensitive tests for HBsAg, such as RIA, do not identify a small number of blood donors whose blood transmits HBV to recipients.[191–193] The exclusive use of blood from volunteer donors also significantly reduces the incidence of post-transfusion hepatitis compared with the use of blood from paid donors.[489] The shift from paid to volunteer donors and HBsAg testing reduced post-transfusion HBV infection by 80% or more in the 1970s, and almost all cases of post-transfusion hepatitis were then due to HCV and possibly other undefined agents.[490–495] Methods for eliminating the remaining blood units infective for HBV and not eliminated by the preceding measures must be developed.

REFERENCES

1. Summers J, Smolec JM, Snyder R. A virus similar to human hepatitis B virus associated with hepatitis and hepatoma in woodchucks. Proc Natl Acad Sci U S A. 1978;75:4533–4537.
2. Marion PL, Oshiro L, Regnery DC, et al. A virus in Beechey ground squirrels that is related to hepatitis B virus of man. Proc Natl Acad Sci U S A. 1980;77:2941–2945.
3. Mason WS, Seal G, Summers J. Virus of Peking ducks with structural and biological relatedness to human hepatitis B virus. J Virol. 1980;36:829–836.
4. Robinson, WS. Genetic variation among hepatitis B and related viruses. Ann N Y Acad Sci. 1980;354:371–378.
5. Robinson WS, Marion PL, Feitelson M, et al. The hepadnavirus group: Hepatitis B and related viruses. In: Szmuness W, Alter HJ, Maynard JE, eds. Viral Hepatitis. Philadelphia: Franklin Institute Press; 1982:57–68.
6. Gust ID, Coulepis AG, Robinson WS, et al. Taxonomic classification of hepatitis B virus. Intervirology. 1986;25:14–29.
7. Lurman A. Eine icterus epidemic. Berl Klin Wochenschr. 1855;22:20.
8. Flaum A, Malmros H, Persson E. Eine nosocomiale icterus epidemic. Acta Med Scand Suppl. 1926;16:544.
9. Bigger JW, Dubi SD. Jaundice in syphilitics under treatment. Lancet. 1943;1:457.
10. MacCallum FO. Transmission of arsenotherapy jaundice by blood: Failure with feces and nasopharyngeal washings. Lancet. 1945;1:342.
11. McNatty AS. Great Britain Ministry Health Report of Chief Medical Officer, Annual Report. London; 1937.
12. Propert SA. Hepatitis after prophylactic serum. BMJ. 1938;2:677.
13. Beeson PB, Chesney G, McFarlan AM. Hepatitis following injection of mumps convalescent plasma. Lancet. 1944;1:814.
14. Findlay GM, MacCallum FO. Note on acute hepatitis and yellow fever immunization. Trans Soc Trop Med Hyg. 1937;31:297.
15. Anonymous. Jaundice following yellow fever vaccine. JAMA. 1942;119:1110.
16. Beeson PB. Jaundice occurring one to four months after transfusion of blood or plasma. JAMA. 1943;121:1332.
17. Morgan HW, Williamson DAJ. Jaundice following administration of human blood products. BMJ. 1943;1:750.
18. Paul RJ, Havens WP, Sabin AB, et al. Transmission experiments in serum jaundice and infectious hepatitis. JAMA. 1945;128:911.
19. Neefe JR, Gellis SS, Stokes J Jr. Homologous serum hepatitis and infectious (epidemic) hepatitis: Studies in volunteers bearing on immunological and other characteristics of the etiological agents. Am J Med. 1946;1:3.
20. Krugman S, Giles JP, Hammon J. Infectious hepatitis: Evidence for two distinctive clinical, epidemiological and immunological types of infection. JAMA. 1967;200:365.
21. Havens WP. Experiment in cross immunity between infectious and homologous serum jaundice. Proc Soc Exp Biol Med. 1945;59:148.
22. Neefe JR, Stokes J, Gellis SS. Homologous serum hepatitis and infectious (epidemic) hepatitis: Experimental study of immunity and cross immunity in volunteers. Am J Med Sci. 1945;210:561.
23. Krugman S, Giles JP. Viral hepatitis: New light on an old disease. JAMA. 1970;212:1019.
24. Neefe JR, Stokes J Jr, Reinhold JG. Oral administration to volunteers of feces from patients with homologous serum hepatitis and infectious (epidemic) hepatitis. Am J Med Sci. 1945;210:29.
25. Havens WP. Period of infectivity of patients with homologous serum jaundice and routes of infection in this disease. J Exp Med. 1946;83:441.
26. Stokes J, Berk JE, Malamut LL. The carrier state of viral hepatitis. JAMA. 1954;154:1059.
27. Voegt H. Zur Aetiologie der Hepatitis Epidemica. Muchen Med Wochenschr. 1942;89:76.
28. Neefe RJ, Norris RF, Reinhold JG, et al. Carriers of hepatitis virus in blood and viral hepatitis in whole blood recipients: 1. Studies on donors suspected as carriers of hepatitis virus and as sources of post-transfusion viral hepatitis. JAMA. 1954;154:1066.
29. Blumberg BS, Alter HJ, Visnich S. A "new" antigen in leukemia sera. JAMA. 1965;191:541.
30. Alter HJ, Blumberg BS. Further studies on a "new" human isoprecipitin system (Australia antigen). Blood. 1966;27:297.
31. Blumberg BS, Gerstley JS, Hungerford DA, et al. A serum antigen (Australia antigen) in Down's syndrome leukemia and hepatitis. Ann Intern Med. 1967;66:924.
32. Okachi K, Murakami S. Observations on Australia antigen in Japanese. Vox Sang. 1968;15:374.
33. Prince AM. An antigen detected in the blood during the incubation period of serum hepatitis. Proc Natl Acad Sci U S A. 1968;60:814.
34. Szmuness W. Hepatocellular carcinoma and the hepatitis B virus: Evidence for a causal association. Prog Med Virol. 1978;24:40.
35. Dane DS, Cameron CH, Briggs M. Virus-like particles in serum of patients with Australia antigen associated hepatitis. Lancet. 1970;2:695–698.
36. Kaplan PM, Greenman RL, Gerin JL, et al. DNA polymerase associated with human hepatitis B antigen. J Virol. 1973;12:995–1005.
37. Bayer ME, Blumberg BS, Werner B. Particles associated with Australia antigen in the sera of patients with leukemia, Down's syndrome and hepatitis. Nature (London). 1968;218:1057–1059.
38. Feinstone SM, Kapikian AZ, Purcell RH, et al. Transfusion associated hepatitis not due to viral hepatitis type A or B. N Engl J Med. 1975;282:767.
39. Knodell RG, Conrad ME, Dienstag JL, et al. Etiological spectrum of post-transfusion hepatitis. Gastroenterology. 1975;69:1278.
40. Alter HL, Purcell RH, Feinstone SM, et al. NonA/nonB hepatitis: A review and interim report of an ongoing prospective study. In: Vyas GN, Cohen SN, Schmid R, eds. Viral Hepatitis: A Contemporary Assessment of Etiology, Epidemiology, Pathogenesis and Prevention. Philadelphia: Franklin Institute Press; 1978:359.
41. Choo QL, Kuo G, Weiner AJ, et al. Isolation of a cDNA clone derived from a blood-borne non-A, non-B viral hepatitis genome. Science. 1989;244:359–362.
42. Landers TA, Greenberg HB, Robinson WS. Structure of hepatitis B Dane particle DNA and nature of the endogenous DNA polymerase reaction. J Virol. 1977;23:368–376.
43. Hruska JF, Clayton DA, Rubenstein JLR, et al. Structure of hepatitis B Dane particle DNA before and after the Dane particle DNA polymerase reaction. J Virol. 1977;21:666–672.
44. Tiollais P, Pourcel C, Dejean A. The hepatitis B virus. Nature. 1985;317:489–495.
45. Takahashi K, Akahane Y, Gotanda T, et al. Demonstration of hepatitis e antigen in the core of Dane particles. J Immunol. 1979;122:275–279.
46. Ralmondo G, Stemler M, Schneider R, et al. Latency and reactivation of a precore mutant hepatitis B virus in a chronically infected patient. J Hepatol. 1990; 11:374–380.
47. Wakita T, Kakumu S, Shibata M, et al. Detection of pre-C and core region mutants of hepatitis B virus in chronic hepatitis B virus carriers. J Clin Invest. 1991;88:1793–1801.
48. Heermann KH, Goldmann U, Schwartz W, et al. Large surface proteins of hepatitis B virus containing the pre-s sequence. J Virol. 1984;52:396–402.

49. Stibbe W, Gerlich WH. Structural relationships between minor and major proteins of hepatitis B surface antigen. J Virol. 1983;46:626–628.
50. Toh H, Hayashida H, Miyata T. Sequence homology between retroviral reverse transcriptase and putative polymerases of hepatitis B virus and cauliflower mosaic virus. Nature. 1983;305:827–829.
51. Miller RH, Robinson WS. Common evolutionary origin of hepatitis B virus and retroviruses. Proc Natl Acad Sci U S A. 1986;83:2531–2535.
52. Bosh V, Bartenschlager R, Radziwill G, et al. The duck hepatitis B virus P-gene codes for protein strongly associated with the 5′ end of the viral DNA minus strand. Virology. 1988;166:475–485.
53. Colgrove R, Simon G, Ganem D. Transcriptional activation of homologous and heterologous genes by the hepatitis B virus X gene product in cells permissive for viral replication. J Virol. 1989;63:4019–4026.
54. Spandau DF, Lee CH. Trans-activation of viral enhancers by the hepatitis B virus X protein. J Virol. 1988;62:427–434.
55. Zahm P, Hofschneider P, Koshy R. The HBV X-ORF encodes a transactivator: A potential factor in viral hepatocarcinogenesis. Oncogene. 1988;3:169–177.
56. Seto ET, Yen TSB, Peterlin BM, et al. Transactivation human immunodeficiency virus long terminal repeat by the hepatitis B virus x-protein. Proc Natl Acad Sci U S A. 1988;85:8286–8290.
57. Twu S Jr, Robinson WS. Hepatitis B virus X gene can transactivate heterologous viral sequences. Proc Natl Acad Sci U S A. 1989;86:2046–2050.
58. Siddiqui A, Gaynor R, Srinivasan A, et al. Trans-activation of viral enhancers including long terminal repeat of the human immunodeficiency virus by the hepatitis B virus X protein. Virology. 1989;169:479–484.
59. Twu JS, Schloemer RH. Transcriptional transactivating functions of hepatitis B virus. J Virol. 1987;61:3448–3453.
60. Koike K, Kobayashi M, Yaginama K, et al. Structure and function of integrated HBV DNA. In: Robinson WS, Koike K, Will H, eds. Hepadnaviruses. New York: Alan Liss; 1987:267–286.
61. Koike K, Shirakata Y, Yaginuma K, et al. Oncogenic potential of hepatitis B virus. Mol Biol Med. 1989;6:151–160.
62. Zhou D-X, Taraboulos A, Ou J-H, et al. Activation of class I major histocompatibility complex gene expression by hepatitis B virus. J Virol. 1990;64:4025–4028.
63. Almeida JD, Rubenstein D, Stott EJ. New antigen antibody system in Australia antigen positive hepatitis. Lancet. 1971;2:1225–1227.
64. LeBouvier GL. The heterogenicity of Australia antigen. J Infect Dis. 1971;123:671–675.
65. Bancroft WH, Mundo FK, Russel PK. Detection of additional determinants of hepatitis B antigen. J Immunol. 1972;109:842–848.
66. Gerin JL, Alexander H, Shih J W-K, et al. Proc Natl Acad Sci U S A. 1983;80:2365
67. Thornton GB, Moriarty AM, Milich D, et al. Protection of chimpanzees from hepatitis B virus infection after immunization with synthetic peptides. Presented at the Cold Spring Harbor Vaccine Meeting, New York, 1988.
68. Itoh Y, Taka E, Ohnuma H, et al. A synthetic peptide vaccine involving the product of the pre-S(2) region of hepatitis B virus DNA: Protective efficacy in chimpanzees. Proc Natl Acad Sci U S A. 1986;83:9174–9178
69. Neurath AR, Kent SBH, Strick N, et al. Identification and chemical synthesis of a host cell receptor binding site on hepatitis B virus. Cell. 1986;46:429–436.
70. Robinson WS, Clayton DA, Greenman RL. DNA of a human hepatitis B virus candidate. J Virol. 1974;14:384–391.
71. Gerlich W, Robinson WS. Hepatitis B virus contains protein attached to the 5′ terminus of its complete DNA strand. Cell. 1980;21:801.
72. Robinson WS, Greenman RL. DNA polymerase in the core of the human hepatitis B virus candidate. J Virol. 1974;13:1231–1236.
73. Albin C, Robinson WS. Protein kinase activity in hepatitis B virus. J Virol. 1980;34:297–302.
74. Schlicht HJ, Waseneur G. The quarternary structure and aggregational behavior of the secretory core protein of human hepatitis B virus are determined by its signal sequence. J Virol. 1991;65:6817–6825.
75. Neurath AR, Strick N. Association of hepatitis B e-antigen (HBeAg) determinants with the core of Dane particles. J Gen Virol. 1979;42:645–649.
76. Ohori H, Onodera S, Ishida N. Demonstration of hepatitis B e antigen (HBeAg) in association with intact Dane particles. J Gen Virol. 1979;43:423–427.
77. Bertoletti A, Chisari FV, Penna A, et al. Definition of a minimal optimal cytotoxic T-cell epitope within the hepatitis B virus nucleocapsid protein. J Virol. 1993;67:2376–2380.
78. LeBouvier GL, McCollum RW. Australia (hepatitis associated) antigen: Physicochemical and immunological characteristics. Adv Virus Res. 1970;16:357.
79. Barker LF, Murray R. Relationship of virus dose of incubation time of clinical hepatitis and time of appearance of hepatitis-associated antigen. Am J Med Sci. 1972;263:27.
80. Scullard G, Greenberg HB, Smith JL, et al. Antiviral treatment of chronic hepatitis B virus infection: Infectious virus cannot be detected in patient serum after permanent responses to treatment. Hepatology. 1982;2:39.
81. Shikata T, Karasawa T, Abe K, et al. Hepatitis B e antigens and infectivity of hepatitis B virus. J Infect Dis. 1977;136:571.
82. Redeker AG, Hopkins CE, Jackson B, et al. A controlled study of the safety of pooled plasma stored in the liquid state at 30–32°C for 6 months. Transfusion. 1968;8:60.
83. Murray R, DieFenbach WC. Effect of heat on the agent of homologous serum hepatitis. Proc Soc Exp Biol Med. 1953;84:230.
84. Gellis SS, Neefe JR, Stokes J Jr, et al. Chemical, clinical and immunological studies on the products of human plasma fractionation. XXXVI. Inactivation of the virus of homologous serum hepatitis in solution of normal serum albumin by means of heat. J Clin Invest. 1948;27:239.
85. Soulier JP, Blatix C, Courouce AM, et al. Prevention of virus B hepatitis (SH virus). Am J Dis Child. 1972;123:429–433.
86. Shikata T, Karasawa T, Abe K, et al. Incomplete inactivation of hepatitis B virus after heat treatment at 60°C for 10 hours. J Infect Dis. 1978;138:242–244.
87. Krugman S, Giles JP, Hammond J. Hepatitis virus: Effect of heat infectivity and antigenicity of MS-1 and MS-2 strains. J Infect Dis. 1970;122:432–436.
88. Wewalka F. Zur epidemiologie des ikterus bei der antisyphlitischen behandlung. Schweiz Z Allg Pathol. 1953;16:307–312.
89. Salaman MH, Williams DI, King AJ, et al. Prevention of jaundice resulting from antisyphilitic treatment. Lancet. 1944;2:7–8.
90. Summers J, Mason WS. Replication of the genome of a hepatitis B-like virus by reverse transcription of an RNA intermediate. Cell 1982;29:403–415.
91. Seeger C, Ganem D, Varmus HE. Biochemical and genetic evidence for the hepatitis B virus replication strategy. Science. 1986;232:477.
92. Will H, Reiser W, Weimer T, et al. Replication strategy of human hepatitis B virus. J Virol. 1987;61:904–911.
93. Barker LF, Chisari F, McGrath PP, et al. Transmission of type B viral hepatitis to chimpanzees. J Infect Dis. 1973;127:648.
94. Gudat F, Bianchi O, Sonnabend W. Pattern of core and surface expression in liver tissue reflects state of specific immune response in hepatitis B. Lab Invest. 1975;32:1.
95. Ray MB, Desmet VI, Bradburne AF. Distribution patterns of hepatitis B surface antigen (HBsAg in liver of hepatitis patients). Gastroenterology. 1976;71:462.
96. Almedia JD, Watterson AP, Trowel JM, et al. The finding of virus-like particles in two Australia-antigen-positive human livers. Microbios. 1970;2:145–153.
97. Huang SA. Hepatitis associated antigen hepatitis: An electronmicroscopic study of virus-like particles in liver cells. Am J Pathol. 1971;64:783.
98. Camamia F, DeBac C, Ricci G. Virus-like particles within hepatocytes of Australia antigen carriers. Am J Dis Child. 1972;123:309.
99. Miller RH, Robinson WS. Hepatitis B viral DNA forms in infected liver. Virology. 1984;137:390–399.
100. Kam W, Rall L, Smuckler E, et al. Hepatitis B viral DNA in liver and serum of asymptomatic carriers. Proc Natl Acad Sci U S A. 1982;79:7522–7526.
101. Matsubara K, Tokina T. Integration of hepatitis B virus DNA and its implications for hepatocarcinogenesis. Mol Biol Med. 1990;7:243–260.
102. Nowoslawski A, Krawczyuski K, Brzosko WJ. Tissue localization of Australia antigen immune complexes in acute and chronic hepatitis and liver cirrhosis. Am J Pathol. 1972;68:31–48.
103. Shikata T. Australia antigen in liver tissue. Jpn J Exp Med. 1973;43:231–245.
104. Murphy BL, Peterson JM, Ebert JW. Immunofluorescent localization of hepatitis B antigens in chimpanzee tissues. Intervirology. 1975;6:207–211.
105. Johnson PJ, Wansbrough-Jones MH, Portmann B. Familial HBsAg positive hepatoma: Treatment with orthotopic liver transplantation and specific immunoglobulin. BMJ. 1978;1:216.
106. Romet-Lemonne JL, McLane MF, Elfassi E, et al. Hepatitis B virus infection in cultured human lymphoblastoid cells. Science. 1983;221:667–669.
107. Lie-Injo LE, Balasegaram M, Lopez CG, et al. Hepatitis B virus DNA in liver and white blood cells of patients with hepatoma. DNA. 1983;2:301–308.
108. Bouffard P, Lamelin JP, Zoulim F, et al. Different forms of hepatitis B virus DNA and expression of HBV antigens in peripheral blood mononuclear cells in chronic hepatitis B. J Med Virol. 1990;31:312–317.
109. Korba BE, Cote PJ, Gerin JL. Mitogen-induced replication of woodchuck hepatitis virus in cultured peripheral blood lymphocytes. Science. 1988;241:1212–1216.
110. Elfassi E, Romet-Lemonne JL, Essex M, et al. Evidence of extrachromosomal forms of hepatitis B viral DNA in a bone marrow culture obtained from a patient recently infected with hepatitis B virus. Proc Natl Acad Sci U S A. 1984;81:3526–3528.
111. Hoefs JC, Renner IG, Ashcavai M, et al. Hepatitis B surface antigen in pancreatic and biliary secretion. Gastroenterology. 1980;79:191–194.
112. Karasawa T, Tsukagoshi S, Yoshimura M, et al. Light microscopic localization of hepatitis B virus antigens in the human pancreas: Possibility of multiplication of hepatitis B virus in the human pancreas. Gastroenterology. 1981;81:998–1005.
113. Dejean A, Lugassy C, Zafrani S, et al. Detection of hepatitis B virus DNA in pancreas, kidney and skin of two human carriers of the virus. J Gen Virol. 1984;65:651–655.
114. Antonucci TK, Rutter WJ. Hepatitis B virus (HBV) promoters are regulated by the HBV enhancer in a tissue-specific manner. J Virol. 1989;63:579–583.
115. Blumberg BS, Sutnick AI, London WT. Hepatitis and leukemia: Their relation to Australia antigen. Bull N Y Acad Med. 1968;44:1566.
116. Hirschman RJ, Shulman NR, Barker LF. Virus-like particles in sera of patients with infectious and serum hepatitis. JAMA. 1969;208:1667.
117. Maynard JE, Hartwell WV, Berquist KR. Hepatitis associated antigen in chimpanzees. J Infect Dis. 1971;126:660.
118. World Health Organization. Viral hepatitis: Report of a scientific group. WHO Tech Rep Ser. 1973;512.
119. Lichter EA. Chimpanzee antibodies to Australia antigen. Nature. 1969;224:810.
120. Prince AM. Infection of chimpanzees with hepatitis B virus. In: Vyas GN, Perkins HA, Schmid R, eds. Hepatitis and Blood Transfusions. New York: Grune & Stratton; 1972:403.
121. Markenson JH, Gerety RJ, Hoofnagle JH. Effects of cyclophosphamide on hepatitis B virus infection and challenge in chimpanzees. J Infect Dis. 1975;131:79.
122. Bancroft WH, Snitbhan R, Scott RM, et al. Transmission of hepatitis B virus to

gibbons by exposure to human saliva containing hepatitis B surface antigen. J Infect Dis. 1977;135:79.
123. London TW, Milman I, Sutnick AI. Transmission, replication and passage of Australia antigen in African green monkeys (vervets). Clin Res. 1970;18:636.
124. London WT, Alter HJ, Lander J. Serial transmission in rhesus monkeys of an agent related to hepatitis-associated antigen. J Infect Dis. 1972;125:382.
125. Barker LF, Maynard JE, Purcell RH, et al. Viral hepatitis, type B, in experimental animals. Am J Med Sci. 1975;270:189.
126. Krugman S, Overby LR, Mushahwar IK, et al. Viral hepatitis, type B: Studies on natural history and prevention reexamined. N Engl J Med. 1979;300:101–106.
127. Hoofnagle JH, Seeff LB, Bales ZB, et al. Serologic responses in hepatitis B. In: Vyas GN, Cohen SN, Schmid R, eds. Viral Hepatitis: A Contemporary Assessment of Etiology, Epidemiology, Pathogenesis and Prevention. Philadelphia: Franklin Institute Press; 1978:219–242.
128. Shulman RN. Hepatitis-associated antigen. Am J Med. 1971;49:669–692.
129. Takahashi K, Fukuda M, Baba K, et al. Determination of e antigen and antibody to e by means of passive hemagglutination method. J Immunol. 1977;119:1556–1559.
130. Aikawa T, Sairenji H, Furuta S, et al. Seroconversion from hepatitis B e antigen to anti-HBe in acute hepatitis B virus infection. N Engl J Med. 1978;298:439–441.
131. Fields HA, Bradley DW, Davis C, et al. Radioimmunoassay for the detection of hepatitis B e antigen (HBeAg) and its antibody (anti-HBe). J Immunol. 1978;121:273.
132. Myakawa Y, Akahane Y, Gotand T. Application of microtiter solid phase radioimmunoassay to the determination of hepatitis B "e" antigen. J Immunol. 1979;122:273.
133. Ling C, Mushahwar IK, Overby LR, et al. Hepatitis B e-antigen and its correlation with other serologic markers in chimpanzees. Infect Immun. 1979;24:352–356.
134. Aldershvile J, Frosner GG, Nielsen JO, et al. Hepatitis B e antigen and antibody radioimmunoassay in acute hepatitis B surface antigen–positive hepatitis. J Infect Dis. 1980;141:293.
135. Kaplan PM, Gerin JL, Alter HJ. Hepatitis B–specific DNA polymerase activity during post-transfusion hepatitis. Nature. 1974;249:762.
136. Krugman S, Hoofnagle JH, Gerety RJ, et al. Viral hepatitis type B: DNA polymerase activity and antibody to hepatitis B core antigen. N Engl J Med. 1974;290:1331–1335.
137. Hansson BG. Age and sex-related distribution of antibodies to hepatitis B surface and core antigens in Swedish population. Acta Pathol Microbiol Scand, Sect. B. 1976;84:342.
138. Hansson BG. Persistence of antibody to hepatitis B core antigen. J Clin Microbiol. 1977;6:209.
139. Brzosko WJ, Mikulska B, Cianciara J, et al. Immunoglobulin classes of antibody to hepatitis B core antigen. J Infect Dis. 1975;132:1–5.
140. Cohen BJ. The IgM antibody responses to the core antigen of hepatitis B virus. J Med Virol. 1978;3:141–150.
141. Neimeijer P, Gips CH. Antibodies and the infectivity of serum in hepatitis B. N Engl J Med. 1978;299:958.
142. Gerlich WH, Luer W, Thomssen R. Diagnosis of acute and inapparent hepatitis B virus infections by measurement of IgM antibody to hepatitis B core antigen. J Infect Dis. 1980;142:95–101.
143. Gocke DJ. Extrahepatic manifestations of viral hepatitis. Am J Med Sci. 1975;270:49–52.
144. Almeida JD, Waterson AP. Immune complexes in hepatitis. Lancet. 1969;2:983–986.
145. Madalinski L, Bragiel I. HBsAg immune complexes in the course of infection with hepatitis B virus. Clin Exp Immunol. 1979;36:371–378.
146. Lambert PH, Tribollet E, Celada A, et al. Quantitation of immunoglobulin associated HBs antigen in patients with acute and chronic hepatitis, in healthy carriers, and in polyarteritis nodosa. J Clin Lab Immunol. 1980;3:1–8.
147. Lander JJ, Giles JP, Purcell RH, Viral hepatitis type B (MS-2 strain): Detection of antibody after primary infection. N Engl J Med. 1970;283:303.
148. Barker LF, Maynard JE, Purcell RH, et al. Hepatitis B virus infection in chimpanzees: Titration of subtypes. J Infect Dis. 1975;132:451.
149. Purcell RH, Gerin JL. Hepatitis B subunit vaccine: A preliminary report of safety and efficacy tests in chimpanzees. Am J Med Sci. 1975;270:395–399.
150. Seef LB, Wright EC, Zimmerman HJ, et al. Type B hepatitis after needle-stick exposure: Prevention with hepatitis B immune globulin. A final report of the Veterans Administration Cooperative Study. Ann Intern Med. 1978;88:285.
151. Brechot C, Hadchouel M, Scotto J, et al. State of hepatitis B virus DNA in hepatocytes of patients with hepatitis B surface antigen-positive and -negative liver disease. Proc Natl Acad Sci U S A. 1981;78:3906–3910.
152. Hoofnagle JH. Hepatitis B surface antigen (HBsAg) and antibody (anti-HBs). In: Bianchi L, Gerok W, Sickinger K, et al., eds. Virus and the Liver. Lancaster: MTP Press; 1980:27.
153. Nielsen JO, Nielsen MH, Elling P. Differential distribution of Australia-antigen-associated particles in patients with liver disease and normal carriers. N Engl J Med. 1973;288:484.
154. Robinson WS. DNA and DNA polymerase in the core of Dane particles. Am J Med Sci. 1975;270:151.
155. Scullard GH, Pollard RB, Smith JL, et al. Antiviral treatment of chronic hepatitis B virus infection. I. Changes in viral markers with interferon combined with adenine arabinoside. J Infect Dis. 1981;143:772.
156. Greenberg HB, Pollard RB, Lutwixk LI, et al. Effect of human leukocyte interferon on hepatitis B virus infection in patients with chronic active hepatitis. N Engl J Med. 1976;295:517.
157. Bonino F, Hoyer B, Moriarty A, et al. Hepatitis B virus DNA in the sera of HBsAg carriers: A marker of active HBV replication in the liver. Gastroenterology. 1980;79:1009.
158. Kryger P, Mathiesen LR, Aldershvile J, et al. Presence and meaning of anti-HBc IgM as determined by ELISA in patients with acute type B hepatitis and healthy HBsAg carriers. Hepatology. 1981;1:233–237.
159. Lee JH, Paglieroni TG, Holland PV, et al. Chronic hepatitis B virus infection in an anti-HBc-nonreactive blood donor: Variant virus or defective immune response? Hepatology. 1992;16:24–30.
160. Aldershvile J, Skinhoj P, Frosner GG, et al. The expression pattern of hepatitis B e antigen and antibody in different ethnic and clinical groups of hepatitis B surface antigen carriers. J Infect Dis. 1980;142:18–22.
161. Eleftheriou N, Heathcoate J, Thomas HC, et al. Incidence and clinical significance of e antigen and antibody in acute and chronic liver diseases. Lancet. 1975;2:1171.
162. Smith JL, Murphy BL, Auslander MO, et al. Studies of the "e" antigen in acute and chronic hepatitis. Gastroenterology. 1976;71:208.
163. Nielsen JO, Dietrichson O, Juhl E. Incidence and meaning of the "e" determinant among hepatitis-B-antigen positive patients with acute and chronic liver diseases. Lancet. 1974;2:913–915.
164. Fay O, Tanno H, Ronocoroni M, et al. Prognostic implications of the e antigen of hepatitis B virus. JAMA. 1977;238:2501.
165. Takahashi K, Imai M, Miyakawa Y, et al. Duality of hepatitis B e antigen in serum of persons infected with hepatitis B virus: Evidence for non-identity of e antigen and immunoglobulin. Proc Natl Acad Sci U S A. 1978;75:1952.
166. Takahashi K, Miyakawa Y, Gotanda T, et al. Shift from free "small" hepatitis B e antigen to IgG-bound "large" form in the circulation of human beings and a chimpanzee acutely infected with hepatitis B virus. Gastroenterology. 1979;77:1193.
167. Hindman SH, Gravelle CR, Murphy BL, et al. "e" antigen, Dane particles, and serum DNA polymerase activity in HBsAg carriers. Ann Intern Med. 1976;85:458–460.
168. Alter HJ, Seeff LB, Kaplan PM, et al. Type B hepatitis: The infectivity of blood positive for e antigen and DNA polymerase after accidental needlestick exposure. N Engl J Med. 1976;295:909–913.
169. Takahashi K, Imai M, Tsuda F, et al. Association of Dane particles with e antigen in the serum of asymptomatic carriers of hepatitis B surface antigen. J Immunol. 1976;117:102–105.
170. Nordenfeldt E, Andren-Sandberg M. Dane particle associated DNA polymerase and e antigen: Relation to chronic hepatitis among carriers of hepatitis B surface antigen. J Infect Dis. 1976;134:85–89.
171. Hess G, Arnold W, Shih JWK, et al. Expression of hepatitis B virus–specific markers in asymptomatic hepatitis B surface antigen carriers. Infect Immun. 1977;17:550–554.
172. Andres LL, Sawhney VK, Scullard GH, et al. Dane particle DNA polymerase and HBeAg: Impact on clinical, laboratory, and histologic findings in hepatitis B-associated chronic liver disease. Hepatology. 1981;1:583–585.
173. Okada K, Kainiyama I, Inometa M, et al. e Antigen and anti-e in the serum of asymptomatic carrier mothers as indicators of positive and negative transmission of hepatitis B virus in their infants. N Engl J Med. 1976;294:746.
174. Beasley RP, Trepo C, Stevens CE, et al. The e antigen and vertical transmission of hepatitis B surface antigen. Am J Epidemiol. 1977;105:94–98.
175. Perrillo RP, Gelb L, Campbell C, et al. Hepatitis B e antigen, DNA polymerase activity, and infection of household contacts with hepatitis B virus. Gastroenterology. 1979;76:1319–1325.
176. Koshy R, Maupas P, Muller R, et al. Detection of hepatitis B virus-specific DNA in the genomes of human hepatocellular carcinoma and liver cirrhosis tissue. J Gen Virol. 1981;57:95.
177. Norkrans G, Nordenfeldt E, Hermodsson ES, et al. Long-term follow-up of chronic hepatitis patients with HBsAg, HBeAg and Dane particle associated DNA polymerase. Scand J Infect Dis. 1980;12:159.
178. Zuckerman AJ, Taylor PE. Persistence of the serum hepatitis (SH-Australia) antigen for many years. Nature. 1969;223:81.
179. Maruyama T, Thornton GB, Iino S, et al. Use of anti-peptide antibodies for the design of antigen-specific immune complex assays. J Immunol Methods. 1992;155:65–75.
180. Realdi G, Alberti A, Rugge M, et al. Seroconversion from hepatitis B e antigen to anti-HBe in chronic hepatitis B virus infection. Gastroenterology. 1980;79:195.
181. Aikawa T, Seirenji S, Furuta S, et al. Seroconversion from hepatitis B e antigen to anti-HBe in acute hepatitis B virus infection. N Engl J Med. 1978;298:439.
182. Alberti A, Diana S, Scullard GM, et al. Full and empty Dane particles in chronic hepatitis virus infection: Relationship to hepatitis B e antigen and presence of liver damage. Gastroenterology. 1978;75:869.
183. Hoofnagle JH, Seef LB, Dusheiko GM, et al. Seroconversion from hepatitis B e antigen to antibody during chronic type B hepatitis. Gastroenterology. 1980;79:1026.
184. Perrillo RP, Campbell CR, Saunders GE, et al. Spontaneous clearance and reactivation of HBV infection among male homosexuals with chronic type B hepatitis. Ann Intern Med. 1984;100:43.
185. Davis GL, Hoofnagle JH, Waggoner JG. Spontaneous reactivation of chronic hepatitis B virus infection. Gastroenterology. 1984;86:230.
186. Szmuness W, Prince AM, Brotman B. Hepatitis B antigen and antibody in blood donors: An epidemiologic study. J Infect Dis. 1973;127:17.
187. Helske T. Carriers of hepatitis B antigen and transfusion hepatitis in Finland. Scand J Haematol Suppl. 1974;22:1.
188. Sampliner RE, Hamilton FA, Iseri OA. The liver histology and frequency of

clearance of the hepatitis B surface antigen in chronic carriers. Am J Med Sci. 1979;277:17.
189. Feinman SV, Cooter N, Sinclair JC, et al. Clinical and epidemiological significance of the HBsAg (Australia antigen): Carrier state. Gastroenterology. 1975;68:113.
190. Szmuness W, Harley EJ, Ikran H, et al. Sociodemographic aspects of the epidemiology of hepatitis B. In: Vyas GN, Cohen SN, Schmid R, eds. Viral Hepatitis. Philadelphia: Franklin Institute Press; 1978:297.
191. Hollinger FB, Werch J, Melnick JL. A prospective study indicating that double-antibody radioimmunoassay reduces the incidence of post-transfusion hepatitis B. N Engl J Med. 1974;290:1104–1109.
192. Alter HJ, Holland PV, Purcell RH. The emerging pattern of post-transfusion hepatitis. Am J Med Sci. 1975;270:329.
193. Hoofnagle JH, Seeff LB, Bales ZB, et al. The Veterans Administration Hepatitis Cooperative Study Group. Type B hepatitis after transfusion with blood containing antibody to hepatitis B core antigen. N Engl J Med. 1978;298:1379–1383.
194. Bories P, Coursaget P, Degott C, et al. Antibody to hepatitis B core antigen in chronic active hepatitis. BMJ. 1978;1:396–397.
195. Scullard GH, Smith CI, Merigan TC, et al. Effect of immunosuppressive therapy on viral markers in chronic active hepatitis B. Gastroenterology. 1981;81:978.
196. Nagington J, Cossart YE, Cohen BJ. Reactivation of hepatitis B after transplantation operations. Lancet. 1977;1:558.
197. Wands JR, Chura CM, Roll FJ, et al. Serial studies of hepatitis associated antigen and antibody in patients receiving anti-tumor chemotherapy for myeloproliferative and lymphoproliferative disorders. Gastroenterology. 1975;68:105.
198. Tur-Kaspa R, Burk R, Shaul Y, et al. Hepatitis B virus DNA contains a glucocorticoid-responsive element. Proc Natl Acad Sci U S A. 1986;83:1627–1631.
199. Pollard RB, Smith JL, Beal A, et al. Effect of vidarabine on chronic hepatitis B virus infection. JAMA. 1978;239:1648.
200. Scullard GH, Andres LL, Greenberg HB, et al. Antiviral treatment of chronic hepatitis B virus infection: Improvement in liver disease with interferon and adenine arabinoside. Hepatology. 1981;1:228.
201. Gold JWM, Alter HJ, Holland PV. Passive hemagglutination assay for antibody to subtypes of hepatitis B antigen. J Immunol. 1976;117:2260.
202. Koziol DE, Alter HJ, Dirchner JP. Development of HBsAg positive hepatitis despite previous existence of antibody to HBsAg. J Immunol. 1976;117:2260–2262.
203. Sheretz RJ, Spindel E, Hoofnagle JH. Antibody to hepatitis B surface antigen may not always indicate immunity to hepatitis B virus infection. N Engl J Med. 1983;309:1519.
204. Linnemann CC, Askey PA. Susceptibility to hepatitis B despite high titer anti-HBs antibody. Lancet. 1984;1:346.
205. Trepo CG, Prince AM. Absence of complete homologous immunity to hepatitis B infection after massive exposure. Ann Intern Med. 1976;85:427.
206. Karvountzis GG, Mosley JW, Redecker AG. Serologic characterization of patients with two episodes of acute viral hepatitis. Am J Med. 1975;58:815.
207. Mosley JW. Hepatitis types B and non-B: Epidemiologic background. JAMA. 1975;233:967.
208. Mosley JW, Redecker AG, Feinstone SM. Multiple hepatitis viruses in multiple attacks of acute viral hepatitis. N Engl J Med. 1977;296:75.
209. Tabor E, Gerety RJ. Possible role of immune response to hepatitis B core antigen in protection against hepatitis B infection. Lancet. 1984;1:172.
210. Murray K, Bruce SA, Hinnen A, et al. Hepatitis B virus antigens made in microbial cells immunise against viral infection. EMBO J. 1984;3:645–650.
211. Prince AM. Mechanism of protection against hepatitis B infection by immunization with hepatitis B virus cores. Lancet. 1984;1:512.
212. Peters RL. Viral hepatitis: A pathologic spectrum. Am J Med Sci. 1975;270:17.
213. Edgington TS, Chisari FV. Immunological aspects of hepatitis B infection. Am J Med Sci. 1975;270:213–227.
214. Dienstag JL, Khan AK, Klingenstein RJ, et al. Immunopathogenesis of liver disease associated with hepatitis B. In: Szmuness W, Alter HJ, Maynards JE, eds. Viral Hepatitis. Philadelphia: Franklin Institute Press; 1982:221–236.
215. Schweitzer IL, Dunn AEF, Peters RL, et al. Viral hepatitis in neonates and infants. Am J Med. 1973;55:762.
216. Tong MJ, Thursby M, Rakela J, et al. Studies of the maternal-infant transmission of the viruses which cause acute hepatitis. Gastroenterology. 1981;80:999.
217. London WT, DiFiglia M, Sutnick AI, et al. An epidemic of hepatitis in a chronic hemodialysis unit. N Engl J Med. 1969;281:571–578.
218. Nordenfeldt E, Lindholm T, Dailquist E. A hepatitis epidemic in a dialysis unit: Occurrence of persistence of Australia-antigen among patients and staff. Acta Pathol Microbiol Scand Sect B. 1970;78:692.
219. Eddleston ALWF, Mondelle M, Mieli-Vergani G, et al. Lymphocyte cytotoxicity to autologous hepatocytes in chronic hepatitis B virus infection. Hepatology. 1982;2:122s.
220. Naumov NW, Mondelli M, Alexander GJM, et al. Relationship between expression of hepatitis B virus antigens in isolated hepatocytes and autologous lymphocyte cytotoxicity in patients with chronic hepatitis B virus infection. Hepatology. 1984;4:13.
221. Bertoletti A, Ferrari C, Fiaccardori F, et al. HLA class I–restricted human cytotoxic T cells recognize endogenously synthesized hepatitis B virus nucleocapsid antigen. Proc Natl Acad Sci U S A. 1991;88:10445–10449.
222. Yoakum GH, Korba BE, Lechner JR, et al. High-frequency transfection and cytopathology of hepatitis B virus core antigen gene in human cells. Science. 1983;222:385–389.
223. Trepo CG, Magnius LO, Schaefer RA, et al. Detection of e antigen and antibody: Correlations with hepatitis B surface and hepatitis B core antigen, liver disease, and outcome in hepatitis B infections. Gastroenterology. 1976;71:804.
224. Aldershvile J, Nielsen JO, Dietrichson O, et al. Long-term followup of e antigen (HBeAg) positive acute viral hepatitis. Scand J Gastroenterol. 1979;14:845.
225. Magnius LO, Lindholm A, Lundin P, et al. A new antigen-antibody system. Clinical significance in long term carriers of hepatitis B surface antigen. JAMA. 1975;231:356.
226. Reinicke V, Dybkjaer E, Poulsen H, et al. A study of Australia-antigen-positive blood donors and their recipients, with special reference to liver histology. N Engl J Med. 1972;286:867.
227. Chisari FV. Analysis of hepadnavirus gene expression, biology, and pathogenesis in the transgenic mouse. Curr Top Microbiol Immunol. 1991;168:85–101.
228. Chisari FV, Filippi P, Buras J, et al. Structural and pathological effects of synthesis of hepatitis B virus large envelope polypeptide in transgenic mice. Proc Natl Acad Sci U S A. 1987;84:6909–6913.
229. Rizzetto M, Canese MG, Arico S. Immunofluorescence detection of a new antigen system (delta/anti-delta) associated to the hepatitis B virus in the liver and the serum of HBsAg carriers. Gut. 1977;18:997.
230. Rizzetto M, Purcell RH, Gerin JL. Epidemiology of HBV-associated data agent: Geographical distribution of anti-delta and prevalence of polytransfused HBsAg carriers. Lancet. 1980;1:1215.
231. Hadziyannis S, Hatzakis A, Karamanos B. Clinical features of chronic delta infection. In: Vyas GN, Dieustag JL, Hoofnagle JH, eds. Viral Hepatitis and Liver Disease. New York: Grune & Stratton; 1984:701.
232. Ponzetta A, Forzani E, Shafi MS. Delta agent infection in Saudi Arabia: A general population study. In: Vyas GN, Dienstage JL, Hoofnagle JH, eds. Viral Hepatitis and Liver Disease. New York: Grune & Stratton; 1984:643.
233. Hadler S, Monzon M, Ponzetto A, et al. Delta virus infection and serum hepatitis: An epidemic in the Yucpa Indians of Venezuela. Ann Intern Med. 1984;100:339.
234. Rizzetto M, Hoyer B, Canese MG, et al. Delta agent: The association of delta antigen with hepatitis B surface antigen and ribonucleic acid in the serum of delta-infected chimpanzees. Proc Natl Acad Sci U S A. 1980;77:6124.
235. Rizzetto M, Canese MG, Gerin JL, et al. Transmission of the hepatitis B virus-associated delta antigen to chimpanzees. J Infect Dis. 1980;141:590.
236. Smedile A, Farci P, Verme G. Influence of delta infection on severity of hepatitis B. Lancet. 1982;2:945.
237. Tabor E, Ponzetto A, Gerin JL, et al. Does delta agent contribute to fulminant hepatitis? Lancet. 1983;1:765.
238. Shattock A, Morgan B, Peutherer J, et al. High incidence of delta antigen in serum. Lancet. 1983;2:104–105.
239. Columbo M, Cambieri R, Rumi M, et al. Long-term delta superinfection in hepatitis B surface antigen carriers and its relationship to the course of chronic hepatitis. Gastroenterology. 1983;85:235–239.
240. Rizzetto M, Verme G, Recchia S. Chronic hepatitis in carriers of hepatitis B surface antigen, with intrahepatic expression of delta antigen: An active and progressing disease unresponsive to immunosuppressive treatment. Ann Intern Med. 1983;98:437.
241. Kew MC. The development of hepatocellular cancer in humans. Cancer Surv 1986;5:719–739.
242. Beasley RP, Lin CC, Hwang LY, et al. Hepatocellular carcinoma and hepatitis B virus: A prospective study of 22,707 men in Taiwan. Lancet. 1981;2:1129–1133.
243. Obata H, Hayashi N, Motoike Y. A prospective study of development of hepatocellular carcinoma from liver cirrhosis with persistent hepatitis b virus infection. Int J Cancer. 1980;25:741.
244. Larouze B, London WT, Saimot G, et al. Host responses to hepatitis-B infection in patients with primary hepatic carcinoma and their families: A case-control study in Senegal, West Africa. Lancet. 1976;2:534.
245. Nishioka K, Hirayama T, Sekine T, et al. Australia antigen and hepatocellular carcinoma. Gann Monogr Cancer Res. 1973;14:167.
246. Steiner PE. Cancer of the liver and cirrhosis in trans-Saharan Africa and the United States of America. Cancer. 1960;13:1085.
247. Trichopoulos D, Violaki M, Sparros L, et al. Epidemiology of hepatitis B and primary hepatic carcinoma. Lancet. 1975;2:1038.
248. Peters RL. Pathology of hepatocellular carcinoma. In: Okuda K, Peters RL, eds. Hepatocellular Carcinoma. New York: John Wiley & Sons; 1976:107.
249. Kew MD. Hepatoma and HBV. In: Vyas GM, Cohen SN, Schmid R, eds. Viral Hepatitis: A Contemporary Assessment of Etiology, Epidemiology, Pathogenesis and Prevention. Philadelphia: Franklin Institute Press; 1978:439.
250. Popper H, Shih JWK, Gerin JL, et al. Woodchuck hepatitis and hepatocellular carcinoma: Correlation of histologic with virologic observations. Hepatology. 1981;1:91.
251. Marion PL, Van Davelaar MJ, Knight SS, et al. Hepatocellular carcinoma in ground squirrels persistently infected with ground squirrel hepatitis virus. Proc Natl Acad Sci U S A. 1983;83:4543–4546.
252. Miller RH, Lee SC, Liaw YF, et al. Hepatitis B viral DNA in infected liver and hepatocellular carcinoma. J Infect Dis. 1985;151:1081–1092.
253. Hsu IC, Metcalf RA, Sun T, et al. Mutational hotspot in the p53 gene in human hepatocellular carcinomas. Nature. 1991;350:427–428.
254. Bressac B, Kew M, Wands J, et al. Selective G to T mutations of p53 gene in hepatocellular carcinoma from southern Africa. Nature. 1991;350:429–431.
255. World Health Organization. Prevention of liver cancer. WHO Technical Rep Ser. 1988;691:8–9.
256. Gocke JD. Immune complex phenomena associated with hepatitis. In: Vyas GN, Cohen SN, Schmidt R, eds. Viral Hepatitis: A Contemporary Assessment. Philadelphia: Franklin Institute Press; 1978:27.
257. Schumacher HR, Gall EP. Arthritis in acute hepatitis and chronic active hepatitis:

Pathology of the synovial membrane with evidence for the presence of Australia antigen in synovial membranes. Am J Med. 1974;57:655.
258. Wands JR, Mann EA, Isselbacher KJ. The pathogenesis of arthritis associated with acute hepatitis B surface antigen positive hepatitis. Complement activation and characterization of circulating immune complexes. J Clin Invest. 1975;55:930.
259. Redeker AG. Viral hepatitis: Clinical aspects. Am J Med Sci. 1975;270:9.
260. Gocke DJ, Hsu K, Morgan C, et al. Vasculitis in association with Australia antigen. J Exp Med. 1971;134:330s.
261. Fye KH, Becker MJ, Theofilopoulos AN, et al. Immune complexes in hepatitis B antigen associated polyarteritis nodosa: Detection by antibody dependent cell mediated cytotoxicity in Raji cell assay. Am J Med. 1977;62:783.
262. Combes B, Stastny P, Shorey J, et al. Glomerulonephritis with deposition of Australia antigen-antibody complexes in glomerular basement membrane. Lancet. 1971;2:234.
263. Kohler PF, Croniln RE, Hammond WS. Chronic membranous glomerulonephritis caused by hepatitis B antigen-antibody immune complexes. Ann Intern Med. 1974;81:488.
264. Knieser WR, Jens EH, Howenthal DT, et al. Pathogenesis of renal disease associated with viral hepatitis. Arch Pathol. 1974;97:193.
265. Ozawa T, Levisohn P, Orsini E, et al. Acute immune complex disease associated with hepatitis. Arch Pathol Lab Med. 1976;100:484.
266. McIntosh RH, Koss MN, Gocke DJ. The nature and incidence of cryoproteins in hepatitis B antigen (HBsAg) positive patients. J Med. 1976;45:23.
267. Gianotti F. Papular acrodermatitis of childhood: An Australia antigen disease. Arch Dis Child. 1973;48:794.
268. Ishimaru Y, Ishimaru H, Toda G, et al. An epidemic infantile papular acrodermatitis in Japan associated with hepatitis B surface antigen subtype *ayw*. Lancet. 1976;1:707.
269. Levo Y, Gorevic PD, Kassab HJ, et al. Association between hepatitis B virus and essential mixed cryoglobulinemia. N Engl J Med. 1977;296:1501.
270. Popp JW, Dienstag JL, Wands JR, et al. Essential mixed cryoglobulinemia without evidence for hepatitis B virus infection. Ann Intern Med. 1980;92:383.
271. Hagler L, Pastore RN, Bergin JJ. Aplastic anemia following viral hepatitis. Medicine. 1975;54:139.
272. Nakamura S, Sato T, Maeda T, et al. Viral hepatitis B and aplastic anemia. Tohoku J Exp Med. 1975;116:101.
273. Casciato DA, Klein CA, Kaplowitz N, et al. Aplastic anemia associated with type B viral hepatitis. Arch Intern Med. 1978;138:1557.
274. Advisory Committee for Immunization Practices. Recommendations for protection against viral hepatitis. MMWR Morb Mortal Wkly Rep. 1990;39:725–729.
275. Centers for Disease Control and Prevention. Hepatitis Surveillance Report No. 52. Atlanta: U.S. Department of Health and Human Services, Public Health and Human Services, Health Service; 1989.
276. Holland PV. Available methods to further reduce post-transfusion hepatitis. In: Szmuness W, Alter HJ, Maynard JE, eds. Viral Hepatitis. Philadelphia: Franklin Institute Press; 1982:563.
277. Lander JJ, Holland PV, Alter HJ, et al. Antibody to hepatitis-associated antigen. Frequency and pattern of response as detected by radioimmunoprecipitation. JAMA. 1972;220:1079–1081.
278. Cherubin CE, Purcell RH, Landers JJ, et al. Acquisition of antibody to hepatitis B antigen in three socioeconomically different medical populations. Lancet. 1972;2:149.
279. Blumberg BS, Friedlander JS, Woodside A, et al. Hepatitis and Australia antigen: Autosomal recessive inheritance of susceptibility to infection in humans. Proc Natl Acad Sci U S A. 1969;62:1108.
280. Grossman RA, Benenson MW, Scott RM, et al. An epidemiologic study of hepatitis B virus in Bangkok, Thailand. Am J Epidemiol. 1975;101:144.
281. Hillis WD, Hillis A, Bias WB, et al. Association of hepatitis B surface antigenemia with HLA locus B specificities. N Engl J Med. 1977;296:1310–1314.
282. Stevens EC, Beasley RP. Lack of an autosomal recessive genetic influence in the vertical transmission of hepatitis B antigen. Nature. 1976;260:715.
283. Patterson MJ, Hourani MR, Mayor GH, et al. HLA antigens and hepatitis B virus. N Engl J Med. 1977;297:1124.
284. Szmuness W, Stevens CE, Ikram H, et al. Prevalence of hepatitis B virus infection and hepatocellular carcinoma in Chinese-Americans. J Infect Dis. 1978;137:822.
285. Norman JE, Beebe GW, Hoofnagle J, et al. Mortality follow-up of the 1942 epidemic of hepatitis B in the U.S. army. Hepatology. 1993;18:790–797.
286. Mosley JW. Epidemiologic implications of changing trends in type A and type B hepatitis. In: Vyas GN, Perkins HA, Schmid R, eds. Hepatitis and Blood Transfusion. New York: Grune & Stratton; 1972:349.
287. Blumberg BS. Australia antigen: The history of its discovery with comments on genetic and family aspects. In: Vyas GN, Perkins HA, Schmid R, eds. Hepatitis and Blood Transfusion. New York: Grune & Stratton; 1972:63.
288. Blumberg BS, Sutnick AI, London WT, et al. Sex distribution of Australia antigen. Arch Intern Med. 1972;130:231.
289. London WT, Drew JS, Lustbader DE, et al. Host response to hepatitis B infection in patients in a chronic hemodialysis unit. Kidney Int. 1977;12:51.
290. Krugman S. Hepatitis B immune globulin. In: Vyas GN, Perkins HA, Schmid R, eds. Hepatitis and Blood Transfusion. New York: Grune & Stratton; 1972:349.
291. Szmuness W, Much WM, Prince AM, et al. On the role of sexual behavior in the spread of hepatitis B infection. Ann Intern Med. 1975;83:489.
292. Stevens CE, Beasley RP, Tsui V, et al. Vertical transmission of hepatitis B antigen in Taiwan. N Engl J Med. 1975;292:771.
293. Beasley RP, Hwang LY, Lin CC, et al. Incidence of hepatitis B virus infections in preschool children in Taiwan. J Infect Dis. 1982;147:185.
294. Mazzur S, Burget S, Blumberg BS. Geographical distribution of Australia antigen determinants *d*, *y* and *w*. Nature. 1974;247:38.
295. Bancroft WH, Holland PV, Mazzur S, et al. The geographical distribution of HBsAg subtypes. Bibliotheca Haematol. 1976;42:42.
296. Alter JH, Purcell RH, Gerin JL. Transmission of hepatitis B to chimpanzees by hepatitis B surface antigen-positive saliva and semen. Infect Immun. 1977;16:928.
297. Center for Disease Control and Prevention. Hepatitis transmitted by a human bite. MMWR Morb Mortal Wkly Rep. 1974;23:24.
298. Prince AM, Hargrove RI, Szmuness W. Immunologic distinction between infectious and serum hepatitis. N Engl J Med. 1970;282:987.
299. Gocke DJ. Type B hepatitis—good news and bad news. N Engl J Med. 1974;291:1409.
300. Pattison CP, Boyer KM, Maynard JE. Epidemic hepatitis in a clinical laboratory: Possible association with computer card handling. JAMA. 1974;230:854.
301. Morris IM, Cattle DS, Smits BJ. Endoscopy and transmission of hepatitis B. Lancet. 1975;2:1152.
302. McDonald GB, Silverstein FE. Can gastrointestinal endoscopy transmit hepatitis B to patients? Gastrointest Endosc. 1975;22:168.
303. Lauer JL, Van Drunen NA, Washburn JW, et al. Transmission of hepatitis B virus in clinical laboratory areas. J Infect Dis. 1979;140:513.
304. Mirick GS, Shank RE. An epidemic of serum hepatitis studied under controlled conditions. Trans Am Climatol Assoc. 1959;71:176.
305. Hersh T, Melnick JL, Goyal RK, et al. Nonparenteral transmission of viral hepatitis type B (Australia antigen-associated serum hepatitis). N Engl J Med. 1971;285:1363.
306. Heathcote J, Gateau P, Sherlock S. Role of hepatitis B antigen carriers in non-parenteral transmission of hepatitis B virus. Lancet. 1974;2:370.
307. Papaevangllon D, Trichopoulos D, Kemagtinon T, et al. Prevalence of hepatitis B antigen and antibody in prostitutes. BMJ. 1974;2:256.
308. Szmuness W, Much WM, Prince AM. On the role of sexual behavior in the spread of hepatitis B infection. Ann Intern Med. 1975;83:489.
309. Dietzman DE, Harmisch JP, Ray CG, et al. Hepatitis B surface antigen (HBsAg) and antibody to HBsAg: Prevalence in homosexual and heterosexual men. JAMA. 1977;238:2625.
310. Wright RA. Hepatitis B and the HBsAg carrier: An outbreak related to sexual contact. JAMA. 1975;232:717.
311. Lewis TL, Alter HJ, Chalmers TC. A comparison of the frequency of hepatitis B antigen and antibody in hospital and non-hospital personnel. N Engl J Med. 1973;289:647.
312. Mosley JW, Edwards VM, Casey BS. Hepatitis virus infection in dentists. N Engl J Med. 1975;293:730.
313. Maynard JE. Viral hepatitis as an occupational hazard in the health care professional. In: Vyas GN, Cohen SN, Schmid R, eds. Viral Hepatitis. A Contemporary Assessment of Etiology, Epidemiology, Pathogenesis and Prevention. Philadelphia: Franklin Institute Press; 1978:321.
314. Rosenberg JL, Jones DP, Lipitz LR. Viral hepatitis: An occupational hazard to surgeons. JAMA. 1973;223:395.
315. Graf JP, Moeschlin P. Risk to contacts of a medical practitioner carrying HBsAg. N Engl J Med. 1975;293:197.
316. Levin ML, Maddrey CW, Wands JR. Hepatitis B transmission by dentists. JAMA. 1974;228:1139.
317. Goodwin D, Fannin SL, McCracker BB. An oral surgeon related hepatitis B outbreak. In: California Morbidity (California State Department of Health); April 16, 1976.
318. Rimland D, Parkin WE, Miller GB. Hepatitis B outbreak traced to an oral surgeon. N Engl J Med. 1977;296:153.
319. Syndmen DR, Hindman SH, Wineland MD. Nosocomial viral hepatitis B: A cluster among staff with subsequent transmission to patients. Ann Intern Med. 1976;85:573.
320. Garibaldi RA, Rasmussen CM, Holmes AW. Hospital acquired serum hepatitis: Report of an outbreak. JAMA. 1972;219:1577.
321. Alter HJ, Chalmer TC, Freeman BM. Health-care workers positive for hepatitis B surface antigen: Are their contacts at risk? N Engl J Med. 1975;292:454.
322. Williams SV, Pattison CP, Berquist KR. Dental infection with hepatitis B. JAMA. 1975;232:1231.
323. Centers for Disease Control and Prevention. Hepatitis Surveillance Report, No. 41, September, 1977.
324. Ogra PL. Immunologic aspects of hepatitis associated antigen and antibody in body fluids. J Immunol. 1974;110:1197.
325. Mohoney P, Gleischner G, Millman I. Australia antigen: Detection and transmission in shellfish. Science. 1974;183:80.
326. Prince AM, Metselaar D, Kapuko GW. Hepatitis B antigen in wild caught mosquitoes in Africa. Lancet. 1972;2:247.
327. Brotman B, Prince AM, Godfrey HK. Role of arthropods in transmission of hepatitis B virus in the tropics. Lancet. 1973;1:1305.
328. Wills W, Laroiuze B, London WT. Hepatitis B in bedbugs from Senegal. Lancet. 1977;2:217.
329. Dick SJ, Tamborro CH, Leevy CM. Hepatitis B antigen in urban caught mosquitoes. JAMA. 1974;229:1627.
330. Beasley RP, Hwang LY, Lee GC, et al. Prevention of perinatally transmitted hepatitis B virus infections with hepatitis B immunoglobulin and hepatitis B vaccine. Lancet. 1983;2:1099.
331. Ohbayashi A, Okochi K, Mayumi M, et al. Familial clustering of asymptomatic carriers of Australia antigen and patients with primary liver disease and primary liver cancer. Gastroenterology. 1972;62:618.

332. Beasley RP, Stevens CE, Shiao IS, et al. Evidence against breast feeding as a mechanism for vertical transmission of hepatitis B. Lancet. 1975;2:740.
333. Grady GF, Gitnick FL, Prince AM. Relation of e antigen to infectivity of HBsAg-positive inoculation among medical personnel. Lancet. 1976;2:492.
334. Oliphant JW. Jaundice following administration of human serum. Public Health Rep. 1943;58:1233.
335. MacCallum FO, Bauer DJ. Homologous serum jaundice: Transmission experiments with human volunteers. Lancet. 1944;1:622.
336. Oliphant JW. Jaundice following administration of human serum. Bull N Y Acad Med. 1944;20:429.
337. Havens WP. Properties of the etiologic agent of infectious hepatitis. Proc Soc Exp Biol Med. 1945;58:203.
338. DeRitis F, Mallucci L, Coltorti M, et al. Anicteric virus hepatitis in a closed environment as shown by serum transaminase activity. Bull World Health Organ. 1959;20:589.
339. Shimizu Y, Kitamoto O. The incidence of viral hepatitis after blood transfusion. Gastroenterology. 1963;44:740.
340. Hampers CL, Prager D, Senior JR. Past transfusion anicteric hepatitis. N Engl J Med. 1964;271:747.
341. Litwins J, Leibowitz S. Abnormal lymphocytes in virus diseases other than infectious mononucleosis. Acta Haematol. 1951;5:223.
342. Swift WE, Gardner HT, Moore DJ, et al. Clinical course of viral hepatitis and the effect of exercise during convalescence. Am J Med. 1950;8:614.
343. Madsen S, Bang NU, Iverson K. Serum glutamic oxalacetic transaminase in disease of the liver and biliary tract. BMJ. 1958;1:543.
344. Schneider AJ, Mosley JW. Studies of variations of glutamic-oxalacetic transaminase in serum and infectious hepatitis. Pediatrics. 1959;24:367.
345. Lucke B, Mallory T. The fulminant form of epidemic hepatitis. Am J Pathol. 1946;22:867.
346. Galambos JT. Chronic persisting hepatitis. Am J Pathol. 1946;22:867.
347. Merril DN, Dubois RS, Kohler PF. Neonatal onset of the hepatitis associated antigen carrier state. N Engl J Med. 1972;287:1280.
348. Goldfield M, Bill J, Colosimo F. The control of transfusion-associated hepatitis. In: Vyas GN, Cohen SN, Schmidt R, eds. Viral hepatitis: A contemporary assessment. Philadelphia: Franklin Institute Press; 1978;405.
349. Dupuy JM, Frommel D, Alagille D. Severe viral hepatitis type B in infancy. Lancet. 1975;1:191.
350. Allen JG, Sayman WA. Serum hepatitis from transfusions of blood. JAMA. 1962;180:1079.
351. Milich DR, Jones JE, Hughes JL, et al. Is a function of the secreted hepatitis B e antigen to induce immunologic tolerance in utero? Proc Natl Acad Sci U S A. 1990;87:6599–6603.
352. Terazawa S, Kojima M, Yamanaka T, et al. Hepatitis B virus mutants with precore region defects in two babies with fulminant hepatitis and their mothers positive for antibody to hepatitis B e antigen. Pediatr Res. 1991;29:5–9.
353. Carman WF, Hadziyannis S, Karayiannis P, et al. Association of the precore variant of HBV with acute and fulminant hepatitis B infection. In: Hollinger FB, Lemon SM, Margolis HS eds. Viral Hepatitis and Liver Disease. Baltimore: Williams & Wilkins; 1991:216–219.
354. Kosaka Y, Takase K, Kojima M, et al. Fulminant hepatitis B: Induction by hepatitis B virus mutants defective in the precore region and incapable of encoding e antigen. Gastroenterology. 1991;324:1087–1094.
355. Liang TJ, Hasegawa K, Rimon N, et al. A hepatitis B virus mutant associated with an epidemic of fulminant hepatitis. N Engl J Med. 1991;324:1705–1709.
356. Okamoto H, Yotsumoto S, Akahane Y, et al. Hepatitis B viruses with pre-core region defects prevail in persistently infected hosts along with seroconversion to the antibody against an antigen. J Virol. 1990;64:1298–1303.
357. Chen HS, Kew MC, Hornbuckle WE, et al. The precore gene of the woodchuck hepatitis virus genome is not essential for viral replication in the natural host. J Virol. 1992;66:5682–5684.
358. Liaw YF, Lai DI, Chu CM, et al. The development of cirrhosis in patients with chronic type B hepatitis: A prospective study. Hepatology. 1988;8:493–496.
359. Hoofnagle JH. Type B viral hepatitis: Virology, serology and clinical course. Semin Liver Dis. 1981;1:7.
360. Overby LR, Ling CM, Decker RH, et al. Serodiagnostic profiles of viral hepatitis. In: Szmuness W, Alter HJ, Maynard JE, eds. Viral Hepatitis: 1981 International Symposium. Philadelphia: Franklin Institute Press; 1982:169.
361. Aach RD, Alter HJ, Hollinger FB, et al. Risk of transfusing blood containing antibody to hepatitis B surface antigen. Lancet. 1974;2:190.
362. Renton PH, Wadsworth LD. Infectivity of blood containing hepatitis B antibody. Lancet. 1975;1:736.
363. Schweitzer IL, Edwards VM, Brezina M. E antigen in HBsAg-carrier mothers. N Engl J Med. 1975;293:940.
364. Berquist KR, Maynard JE, Murphy BL. Infectivity of serum containing HBsAg and antibody to e antigen. Lancet. 1976;1:1026.
365. Kirkler DM, Zilberg B. Activity and hepatitis. Lancet. 1966;2:1046.
366. Chalmers TC, Eckhardt RD, Reynolds WD, et al. The treatment of infectious hepatitis: Controlled studies of the effects of diet, rest and physical reconditioning on the acute course of disease and the incidence of relapses and residual abnormalities. J Clin Invest. 1955;34:1163.
367. Repsher LH, Freebern RK. Effects of early and vigorous exercise on recovery from infectious hepatitis. N Engl J Med. 1969;281:1393.
368. Gregory PB, Knauer M, Hempson RL, et al. Steroid therapy in severe viral hepatitis: A double blind randomized trial of methy-prednisolone versus placebo. N Engl J Med. 1976;294:728.
369. Redeker AG, Schweitzer IL, Yamahiro HS, et al. Randomization of corticosteroid therapy in fulminant hepatitis. N Engl J Med. 1976;294:728.
370. Acute Hepatic Failure Study Group. Failure of specific immunotherapy in fulminant type hepatitis. Ann Intern Med. 1977;86:272.
371. Cook CG, Mulligan R, Sherlock S. Controlled prospective trial of corticosteroid therapy in active chronic hepatitis. Q J Med. 1971;40:159.
372. Soloway RD, Summerskill WHJ, Baggenstoss AH, et al. Clinical, biochemical and histological remission of severe chronic active liver disease: A controlled study of treatments and early prognosis. Gastroenterology. 1972;63:820.
373. Murray-Lyon IM, Stern RB, Williams R. Controlled trial of prednisone and azothioprine in active chronic hepatitis. Lancet, 1973;1:735.
374. Schalm SW, Summerskill WHJ, Gitnick GL, et al. Contrasting features and responses to treatment of severe chronic active liver disease with and without hepatitis B s antigen. Gut. 1976;17:781.
375. Vogten AJM, Summerskill WHJ, Gilnick GL, et al. Behavior of e antigen and antibody during chronic liver disease. Relation to HB antigen-antibody system and prognosis. Lancet. 1976;2:126.
376. Wright EC, Seef LB, Berk PD, et al. Treatment of chronic active hepatitis. Gastroenterology. 1977;73:1422.
377. Hoofnagle JH, Peters M, Mullen KD, et al. Randomized controlled trial of recombinant human α-interferon in patients with chronic hepatitis B. Gastroenterology. 1988;95:1318.
378. Perrilo RP, Schiff ER, Davis GL, et al. A randomized, controlled trial of interferon alfa-2b alone and after prednisone withdrawal for the treatment of chronic hepatitis B. N Engl J Med. 1990;323:295.
379. Korenman J, Baker B, Waggoner J, et al. Long-term remission of chronic hepatitis B after alpha-interferon therapy. Ann Intern Med. 1991;114:629.
380. Hoofnagle JH, di Bisceglie AM. The treatment of chronic viral hepatitis. N Engl J Med. 1997;336:347–356.
381. Wong DK, Cheung AM, O'Rourke K, Naylor CD, et al. Effect of alpha-interferon treatment in patients with hepatitis B e antigen-positive chronic hepatitis B. A meta-analysis. Ann Intern Med. 1993;119:312–323.
382. Ruiz-Moreno M, Rua MJ, Molina J, et al. Prospective, randomized controlled trial of interferon-alpha in children with chronic hepatitis B. Hepatology. 1991;13:1035–1039.
383. Hoofnagle JH. Therapy of acute and chronic viral hepatitis. Adv Intern Med. 1994;39:241–275.
384. Conjeevaram HS, Hoofnagle JH, Austin HA, et al. Long-term outcome of hepatitis B virus–related glomerulonephritis after therapy with interferon alfa. Gastroenterology. 1995;109:540–546.
385. Eisenberg M, Rosno S, Garcia G, et al. Preliminary trial of recombinant *Fibroblast Interferon* in chronic hepatitis B virus infection. Antimicrob Agents Chemother. 1986;29:122–126.
386. Bissett JD, Eisenbert M, Gregory P, et al. A phase I/II study of the tolerance and effect of viral markers of recombinant fibroblast and immune interferons in chronic hepatitis B infection. J Infect Dis. 1988; 163:308–318.
387. Bissett JD, Eisenberg M, Gregory P, et al. Recombinant fibroblast interferon and immune interferon for treating chronic hepatitis B virus infection patients' tolerance and the effect on viral markers. J Infect Dis. 1988;157:1076–1080.
388. Pignatelli M, Waters J, Brown D, et al. HLA class I antigens on the hepatocyte membrane during recovery from acute hepatitis B virus infection and during interferon therapy in chronic hepatitis B virus infection. Hepatology. 1986;6:349.
389. Kirschner H. Interferons, a group of multiple lymphokines. Springer Semin Immunopathol. 1984;7:347.
390. Chen L, Mathieu-Mahul D, Bach FH, et al. Recombinant interferon alpha can induce rearrangement of T cell antigen receptor alpha genes and maturation to cytotoxicity in T lymphocyte clones in vitro. Proc Natl Acad Sci U S A. 1986;83:4887.
391. Scullard GH, Andres LL, Greenberg HB, et al. Antiviral treatment of chronic hepatitis B virus infection: Improvement in liver disease with interferon and adenine arabinoside. Hepatology. 1981;1:228.
392. Perrillo RP, Regenstein FG, Bodicky CJ, et al. Comparative efficacy of adenine arabinoside 5′ monophosphate and prednisone withdrawal followed by adenine arabinoside 5′ monophosphate in the treatment of chronic active hepatitis type B. Gastroenterology. 1985;88:780.
393. Dienstag JL, Perrillo RP, Schiff ER, et al. A preliminary trial of lamivudine for chronic hepatitis B infection. N Engl J Med. 1995;333:1657–1661.
394. Lai CL, Chien RN, Leung NW, et al. A one-year trial of lamivudine for chronic hepatitis B. Asia Hepatitis Lamivudine Study Group. N Engl J Med. 1998;339:61–68.
395. Nevens F, Main J, Honkoop P, et al. Lamivudine therapy for chronic hepatitis B: A six-month randomized dose-ranging study. Gastroenterology. 1997;113:1258–1263.
396. Main J, Brown JL, Howells C, et al. A double blind, placebo-controlled study to assess the effect of famciclovir on virus replication in patients with chronic hepatitis B virus infection. J. Viral Hepatitis. 1996;3:211–215.
397. Angus PW. Review: Hepatitis B and liver transplantation. J Gastroenterol Hepatol. 1997;12:217–223.
398. Markowitz JS, Martin P, Conrad AJ, et al. Prophylaxis against hepatitis B recurrence following live transplantation using combination lamivudine and hepatitis B immune globulin. Hepatology. 1998;28:585–589.
399. Marzano A, Debernardi-Venon W, Condreay L, Rizzetto M. Efficacy of lamivudine retreatment in a patient with hepatitis B virus (HBV) recurrence after liver transplantation and HBV-DNA breakthrough during the first treatment. Transplantation. 1998;65:1499–1500.
400. Van Thiel DH, Friedlander L, Kania RJ, et al. Lamivudine treatment of advanced

and decompensated liver disease due to hepatitis B. Hepatogastroenterology. 1997;44:808–812.
401. Ben-Ari Z, Shmueli D, Mor E, et al. Beneficial effect of lamivudine in recurrent hepatitis B after liver transplantation. Transplantation. 1997;63:393–396.
402. Grellier L, Mutimer D, Ahmed M, et al. Lamivudine prophylaxis against reinfection in liver transplantation for hepatitis B cirrhosis. Lancet. 1996;348:1212–1215.
403. Nery JR, Weppler D, Rodriguez M, et al. Efficacy of lamivudine in controlling hepatitis B virus recurrence after liver transplantation. Transplantation. 1998;65:1615–1621.
404. Picardi M, Selleri C, De Rosa G, et al. Lamivudine treatment for chronic replicative hepatitis B virus infection after allogeneic bone marrow transplantation. Bone Marrow Transplant. 1998;21:1267–1269.
405. Clark FL, Drummond MW, Chambers S, et al. Successful treatment with lamivudine for fulminant reactivated hepatitis B infection following intensive therapy for high-grade non-Hodgkin's lymphoma. Ann Oncol. 1998;9:385–387.
406. Chan TM, Wu PC, Li FK, et al. Treatment of fibrosing cholestatic hepatitis with lamivudine. Gastroenterology. 1998;115:177–181.
407. Rostaing L, Henry S, Cisterne JM, et al. Efficacy and safety of lamivudine on replication of recurrent hepatitis B after cadaveric renal transplantation. Transplantation. 1997;64:1624–1627.
408. Al Faraidy K, Yoshida EM, Davis JE, et al. Alteration of the dismal natural history of fibrosing cholestatic hepatitis secondary to hepatitis B virus with the use of lamivudine. Transplantation. 1997;64:926–928.
409. Tipples GA, Ma MM, Fischer KP, et al. Mutation in HBV RNA–dependent DNA polymerase confers resistance to lamivudine in vivo. Hepatology. 1996;24:714–717.
410. Melegari M, Scaglioni PP, Wands JR. Hepatitis B virus mutants associated with 3TC and famciclovir administration are replication defective. Hepatology. 1998;27:628–633.
411. Fu L, Cheng YC. Role of additional mutations outside the YMDD motif of hepatitis B virus polymerase in L(-)SddC (3TC) resistance. Biochem Pharmacol. 1998;55:1567–1567.
412. Allen MI, Deslauriers M, Andrews CW, et al. Identification and characterization of mutations in hepatitis B virus resistant to lamivudine. Lamivudine Clinical Investigation Group. Hepatology. 1998;27:1670–1677.
413. Niesters HG, Honkoop P, Haagsma EB, et al. Identification of more than one mutation in the hepatitis B virus polymerase gene arising during prolonged lamivudine treatment. J. Infect Dis. 1998;177:1382–1385.
414. Yoshida EM, Ma MM, Davis JE, et al. Postliver transplant allograft reinfection with a lamivudine-resistant strain of hepatitis B virus: Long-term follow-up. Can J Gastroenterol. 1998;12:125–129.
415. Buti M, Jardi R, Cotrina M, Rodriguez-Frias F, et al. Transient emergence of hepatitis B variants in a patient with chronic hepatitis B resistant to lamivudine. J. Hepatol. 1998;28:510–513.
416. Chayama K, Suzuki Y, Kobayashi M, et al. Emergence and takeover of YMDD motif mutant hepatitis B virus during long-term lamivudine therapy and re-takeover by wild type after cessation of therapy. Hepatology. 1998;27:1711–1716.
417. Ladner SK, Miller TJ, King RW. The M539V polymerase variant of human hepatitis B virus demonstrates resistance to 2′-deoxy-3′-thiacytidine and a reduced ability to synthesize viral DNA. Antimicrob Agents Chemother. 1998;42:2128–2131.
418. Jaeckel E, Manns MP. Experience with lamivudine against hepatitis B virus. Intervirology. 1997,40:322–336.
419. Smith CI, Scullard GH, Gregory PB, et al. Preliminary studies of acyclovir in chronic hepatitis B. In: King D Galasso G, eds. Proceedings of the Symposium of Acyclovir. Am J Med. 1982;73:267–270.
420. Mutimer D, Naoumov N, Honkoop P, et al. Combination alpha-interferon and lamivudine therapy for alpha-interferon-resistant chronic hepatitis B infection: Results of a pilot study. J Hepatol. 1998;28:923–929.
421. Heyward WL, Lanier AP, Bender TR. Early detection of primary hepatocellular carcinoma by screening for alpha fetoprotein in high risk families. Lancet. 1983;2:1161.
422. Centers for Disease Control and Prevention. Early detection of primary hepatocellular carcinoma—Alaska. MMWR Morb Mortal Wkly Rep. 1984;33:53.
423. Hoofnagle JH, Gerety RI, Barker LF. Antibody to the hepatitis B surface antigen in immune serum globulin. Transfusion. 1975;15:408.
424. Grady GF, Rodman M, Larsen L. Hepatitis B antibody in conventional globulin. J Infect Dis. 1975;132:474.
425. Courouce-Pauty AM, Delons S, Soulier JP. Attempt to prevent hepatitis B by using specific anti-HBs immunoglobulin. Am J Med Sci. 1975;270:375.
426. Desmyter J, Bradbourne AF, Vermylen C, et al. Hepatitis B immunoglobulin in prevention of HBs antigenaemia in haemodialysis patients. Lancet. 1975;2:377.
427. Iwarson S, Ahlmen J, Erickson E, et al. Hepatitis B immune serum globulin and standard gamma globulin in prevention of hepatitis B infection among hospital staff: A preliminary report. Am J Med Sci. 1975;270:385.
428. Iwarson S, Ahlmen J, Erickson E, et al. Hepatitis B immune globulin in prevention of hepatitis B among hospital staff members. J Infect Dis. 1977;135:473.
429. Grady GF. Viral hepatitis passive prophylaxis with globulins: State of the art in 1978. In: Vyas GN, Cohen SN, Schmidt R, eds. Viral Hepatitis: A Contemporary Assessment. Philadelphia: Franklin Institute Press; 1978.
430. Szmuness W, Prince AM, Goodman N, et al. Hepatitis B immune serum globulin in prevention of non-parenteral transmitted hepatitis B. N Engl J Med. 1974;290:701.
431. Tabor E, Gerety RJ. Inactivation of an agent of human non-A, non-B hepatitis with formalin. J Infect Dis. 1980;142:767.
432. Yoshizawa H, Itoh Y, Iwakiri S. Non A, non B (type 1) hepatitis agent capable of inducing tubular ultrastructures in the hepatocyte cytoplasm of chimpanzees: Inactivation by formalin and heat. Gastroenterology. 1982;82:502.
433. Gerety RJ, Tabor E. Newly licensed hepatitis B vaccine: Known safety and unknown risks. JAMA. 1983;249:745.
434. Hilleman MR, Buynak EB, McAleer WJ, et al. Hepatitis A and hepatitis B vaccines. Viral Hepatitis 1981 International Symposium 1981;34:385–397.
435. Szmuness W, Stevens CE, Harley EJ. Hepatitis B vaccine: Demonstration of efficacy in a controlled clinical trial in a high-risk population in the United States. N Engl J Med. 1980;303:833–841.
436. Szmuness W, Stevens CE, Zang FA. A controlled trial on the efficacy of the hepatitis B vaccine (Heptavax B): A final report. Hepatology. 1982;1:377.
437. Dienstag JL, Werner BG, Polk BF. Hepatitis B vaccine in health care personnel: A randomized, double-blind, placebo-controlled trial. Hepatology. 1982;2:696.
438. Francis DP, Hadler SC, Thompson SE. The prevention of hepatitis B with vaccine. Report of the Centers for Disease Control Multi-Center Trial Among Homosexual Men. Ann Intern Med. 1982;97:362.
439. Szmuness W, Stevens CE, Harley E, et al. Hepatitis B vaccine in medical staff of hemodialysis units. Efficacy and subtype cross-protection. N Engl J Med. 1982;307:385.
440. Hadler SC, Francis DP, Maynard JE, et al. Long term immunogenicity and efficacy of hepatitis B vaccine in homosexual men. N Engl J Med. 1986;315:209–214.
441. Horowitz MM, Ershler WB, Balliola RJ. Duration of immunity after hepatitis B vaccination: Efficacy of low dose booster vaccine. Ann Intern Med. 1988;108:185–189.
442. Jilg W, Schmidt M, Deinhardt F. Persistence of specific antibodies after hepatitis B vaccination. J Hepatol. 1988;6:201–207.
443. Wainwright RB, McMahon BJ, Bulkow LR, et al. Duration of immunogenicity and efficacy of hepatitis B vaccine in a Yupik Eskimo population. JAMA. 1989;261:2362–2366.
444. Hadler SC, Judson FN, O'Malley PM, et al. Studies of hepatitis B vaccine in homosexual men. In: Coursaget P, Tong MJ, eds. Progress in Hepatitis B Immunization. Paris: John Libby Eurotext; 1990:165–174.
445. Gibas A, Watkins E, Hindle C, et al. Long-term persistence of protective antibody after hepatitis B vaccine. In: Zuckermann AJ, ed. Viral Hepatitis and Liver Disease. New York: Alan R. Liss; 1988:998–1001.
446. Hwang LY, Lee CY, Beasley RP. Five-year follow-up of HBV vaccination with plasma derived vaccine in neonates: Evaluation of immunogenicity and efficacy against perinatal transmission. In: Hollinger FB, Lemon SM, Margolis HS, eds. Viral Hepatitis and Liver Disease. Baltimore: Williams & Wilkins; 1991:759–761.
447. Ko KJ, Lee SD, Tsai YT, et al. Long-term immunogenicity and efficacy of hepatitis B vaccine in infants born to HBeAg-positive HBsAg-carrier mothers. Hepatology. 1988;8:1647–1650.
448. Taylor PE, Stevens CE. Persistence of antibody to hepatitis B surface antigen after vaccination with hepatitis B vaccine. In: Zuckermann AJ, ed. Viral Hepatitis and Liver Disease. New York: Alan R. Liss; 1988:995–997.
449. Deinhardt F. Aspects of vaccination against hepatitis B: Passive-active immunization schedules and immune responses in different age groups. Scand J Infect Dis. 1983;(Suppl 38):17.
450. Szmuness W, Stevens CE, Oleszko WR. Passive-active immunization against hepatitis B: Immunogenicity studies in adult Americans. Lancet. 1981;1:575.
451. Deinstag JL, Stevens CE, Bhan AK, et al. Hepatitis B vaccine administered to chronic carriers of hepatitis B surface antigen. Ann Intern Med. 1982;96:575.
452. Kreider SD, Lange WR. Hepatitis B vaccine. N Engl J Med. 1984;310:466.
453. Centers for Disease Control and Prevention. The safety of hepatitis B vaccine. MMWR Morb Mortal Wkly Rep. 1983;32:134.
454. Herroelen L, De Keyser J, Ebinger G. Central-nervous-system demyelination after immunisation with recombinant hepatitis B vaccine. Lancet. 1991;338:1174–1175.
455. Stevens CE. No increased incidence of AIDS in recipients of hepatitis B vaccine. N Engl J Med. 1983;308:1163.
456. Goolsby PL. Erythema, nodosum after recombivax HB hepatitis B vaccine. N Engl J Med. 1989;321:1198–1199.
457. Grady GF. Hepatitis B immunity in hospital staff targeted for vaccination: Role of screening tests in immunization programs. JAMA. 1982;248:2266.
458. Miller KD, Gibbs RD, Mulligan MM, et al. Intradermal hepatitis B virus vaccine: Immunogenicity and side effects in adults. Lancet. 1983;2:1454.
459. Zoulek G, Lorbeer B, Jilg W, et al. Antibody responses and skin reactivity after intradermal hepatitis B vaccine. Lancet. 1984;1:568.
460. Miyanohara A, Toh-E A, Nozaki C, et al. Expression of hepatitis B surface antigen gene in years. Proc Natl Acad Sci U S A. 1983;80:1.
461. Stevens CE, Taylor PE, Tong MJ, et al. Yeast-recombinant hepatitis B vaccine: Efficacy with hepatitis B immune globulin in prevention of perinatal hepatitis B virus transmission. JAMA. 1987;257:2612–2616.
462. Stevens CE, Taylor PE, Tong MJ, et al. Prevention of perinatal hepatitis B virus infection with hepatitis B immune globulin and hepatitis B vaccine. In: Zuckermann AJ, ed. Viral Hepatitis and Liver Disease. New York: Alan R. Liss; 1988:982–988.
463. Poovorawan Y, Sanpaviat S, Pongpunlert W, et al. Comparison of a recombinant DNA hepatitis B vaccine alone or in combination with hepatitis B immune globulin for the prevention or perinatal acquisition of hepatitis B carriage. Vaccine. 1990;8S:S56–S62.
464. Xu Z-Y, Liu C-B, Francis D, et al. Prevention of perinatal acquisition of hepatitis B virus carriage using vaccine: Preliminary report of a randomized, double-blind placebo controlled and comparative trial. Pediatrics. 1985;76:713–718.
465. Tin KM. Studies of efficacy of hepatitis B vaccine in preventing perinatal HBV transmission in Burma. Presented at the symposium on Control of Hepatitis B

Infection in Infants and Children in High-Risk Areas of the World. Whakatane, New Zealand; November 12–14, 1987.
466. Centers for Disease Control and Prevention. Hepatitis Surveilance Report No. 51. Atlanta: U.S. Department of Health and Human Services, Public Health Service. 9–22, 1987.
467. Advisory Committee for Immunization Practices. Hepatitis B virus: A comprehensive strategy for eliminating transmission in the United States through universal childhood vaccination. MMWR Morb Mortal Wkly Rep. 1991;40:PR-13.
468. Carman WF, Zanetti AR, Karayiannis P, et al. Vaccine-induced escape mutant of hepatitis B virus. Lancet. 1990;336:325–329.
469. Harrison TJ, Hopes EA, Oon CJ, et al. Independent emergence of a vaccine induced escape mutant of hepatitis B virus. J Hepatol. 1991;13:S105–S107.
470. Fujii H, Moriyama K, Sakamoto N, et al. Gly 145 to Arg substitution in HBs antigen of immune escape mutant of hepatitis B virus. Biochem Biophys Res Commun. 1992;184:1152–1157.
471. Okamoto H, Yano K, Nozaki Y, et al. Mutations within the s gene of hepatitis-B virus transmitted from mothers to babies immunized with hepatitis-B immune globulin and vaccine. Pediatr Res. 1992;32:264–268.
472. McMahon G, Ehrlich PH, Moustafa ZA, et al. Genetic alternations in the gene encoding the major HBsAg: DNA and immunological analysis of recurrent HBsAg derived from monoclonal antibody-treated liver transplant patients. Hepatology. 1992;15:757–766.
473. Waters JA, Kennedy M, Voect P, et al. Loss of the common "a" determinant of hepatitis B surface antigen by a vaccine-induced escape mutant. J Clin Invest. 1992;90:254–257.
474. Krugman S, Giles JP. Viral hepatitis, type B (MS-2 strain). Further observations on natural history and prevention. N Engl J Med. 1973;288:755.
475. Redeker AJ, Mosely JW, Gocke DJ, et al. Hepatitis B immune globulin as a prophylactic measure for spouses exposed to acute type B hepatitis. N Engl J Med. 1975;293:1055.
476. Grady GF, Gitnick GL, Prince AM, et al. Hepatitis B immune globulin: Prevention of hepatitis from accidental exposure among medical personnel. N Engl J Med. 1975;293:1067.
477. Grady GF, Lee VA, Prince AM, et al. Hepatitis B immune globulin for accidental exposures among medical personnel. Final report of a multicenter controlled trial. J Infect Dis. 1978;137:131.
478. Centers for Disease Control and Prevention. Immune globulins for protection against viral hepatitis. MMWR Morb Mortal Wkly Rep. 1977;26:425.
479. Klein HG, Alter HA. Comparison of hepatitis B immune globulin given in single or divided doses for protection against hepatitis B virus infection. In: Vyas GN, Cohen SN, Schmidt R, eds. Viral Hepatitis: A Contemporary Assessment. Philadelphia: Franklin Institute Press; 1978:483.
480. Stevens CE, Neurath RA, Beasley RP, et al. HBeAg and anti-HBe detection by radioimmunoassay: Correlation with vertical transmission of hepatitis B virus in Taiwan. J Med Virol. 1979;3:237.
481. Beasley RP, Hwang LY, Lin CC, et al. Hepatitis B immunoglobulin (HBIG) efficacy in the interruption of perinatal transmission of hepatitis B virus carrier state. Lancet. 1981;2:388–393.
482. Beasley RP, Hwang YL, Stevens CE, et al. Efficacy of hepatitis B immune globulin (HBIG) for prevention of perinatal transmission of the HBV carrier state: Final report of a randomized double-blind placebo-controlled trial. Hepatology. 1983;3:135–141.
483. Reesink HW, Reesink-Brongers EE, Lafeber-Schut BJT, et al. Prevention of chronic HBsAg carrier state in infants of HBsAg-positive mothers by hepatitis B immunoglobulin. Lancet. 1979;2:436.
484. Beasley RP, Stevens CE. Vertical transmission of HBV and interruption with globulin. In: Vyas GN, Cohen SN, Sched R, eds. Viral Hepatitis. Philadelphia: Franklin Institute Press; 1978:333.
485. Beasley RP, Hwant LY. Postnatal infectivity of HBeAg carrier mothers. J Infect Dis. 1983;147:185.
486. Beasley RP, Hwang LY, Lee GC, et al. Prevention of perinatally transmitted hepatitis B virus infections with hepatitis B virus infections with hepatitis B immune globulin and hepatitis B vaccine. Lancet. 1983;2:1099–1102.
487. Centers for Disease Control and Prevention. Perspectives on control of viral hepatitis, type B. MMWR Morb Mortal Wkly Rep. 1976;25(Suppl):3.
488. Bond WW, Peterson NJ, Fauero MS. Viral hepatitis B: Aspects of environmental control. Health Lab Sci. 1977;14:235.
489. Aach RD, Lander JJ, Sherman LA, et al. Transfusion-transmitted virus: Interim analysis of hepatitis among transfused and non-transfused patients. In: Vyas GN, Cohen SN, Schmid R, eds. Viral Hepatitis. Philadelphia: Franklin Institute Press; 1978:383.
490. Porchon C, Kremsdorf D, Pol S, et al. Serum hepatitis C virus RNA and hepatitis B virus DNA in non-A, non-B post-transfusional and sporadic chronic hepatitis. J Hepatol. 1992;16:184–189.
491. Alter MJ, Margolis HS, Krawczynski K, et al. The natural history of community-acquired hepatitis C in the United States. The sentinel counties chronic non-A, non-B hepatitis study team. N Engl J Med. 1992;327:1899–1905.
492. Donahue JG, Munoz A, Ness PM, et al. The declining risk of post-transfusion hepatitis C virus infection. N Engl J Med. 1992;327:369–373.
493. Barbara JA, Contreras M. Post-transfusion NANBH in the light of a test for anti-HCV. Blood Rev. 1991;5:234–239.
494. Aach RD, Stevens CE, Hollinger FB, et al. Hepatitis C virus infection in post-transfusion hepatitis. An analysis with first- and second-generation assays. N Engl J Med. 1991;325:1325–1329.
495. Ebeling F, Leikola J. Post-transfusion hepatitis. Ann Intern Med. 1991;23:361–366.

Parvoviridae

Chapter 136

Parvovirus B19

KEVIN E. BROWN

Parvovirus B19, the only known human pathogenic parvovirus, was first discovered in 1974 during evaluations of assays for hepatitis B surface antigen using panels of serum samples.[1] Sample number 19 in panel B (hence B19) gave an anomalous, "false-positive" result in the relatively insensitive counter immune-electrophoresis assay. When the precipitin line was excised, electron microscopy showed the presence of 23-nm particles resembling parvoviruses. Although it was originally labeled "serum parvovirus-like particle" or "human parvovirus," in 1985 the virus was officially recognized as a member of the Parvoviridae, and the International Committee on Taxonomy of Viruses recommended the name B19 to prevent confusion with other viruses.

An association of B19 with significant clinical disease was not made until 1981, but it is now known that B19 infection has a wide variety of disease manifestations, depending on the immunologic and hematologic status of the host (Table 136–1). In normal, immunocompetent children B19 is the cause of erythema infectiosum (EI), also called fifth disease or slapped-cheek disease, an innocuous rash illness. Occasionally, especially in adults, fifth disease leads to an acute symmetric polyarthropathy that can mimic rheumatoid arthritis. In persons with underlying hemolytic disorders or increased erythropoiesis, or both, infections lead to a temporary failure of red blood cell production and transient aplastic crisis (TAC). In the immunocompromised host persistent B19 viremia manifests as pure red cell aplasia (PRCA) and chronic anemia, and in the fetus, where the immune response is immature, infection can lead to fetal death in utero, hydrops fetalis, or congenital anemia.

THE VIRUS

Parvum is the Latin word for "small," and Parvoviridae are among the smallest known DNA-containing viruses that infect mammalian cells. The virions are nonenveloped particles of approximately 22 nm diameter with icosahedral symmetry. The Parvoviridae are divided into two subfamilies, Parvovirinae and Densovirinae, on the basis of their ability to infect vertebrate or invertebrate cells, respectively. The Parvovirinae are further subdivided into three genera on the basis of their transcription maps and the ability to replicate either autonomously (genus *Parvovirus*), with a helper virus (genus *Dependovirus*), or only in erythroid cells (genus *Erythrovirus*). Par-

TABLE 136–1 Disease Manifestations and Persistence of Parvovirus B19 Infection in Various Host Populations

Disease	Persistence	Host
Fifth disease	Acute	Normal children
Polyarthropathy syndrome	Acute/chronic	Normal adults
Transient aplastic crisis	Acute	Patients with increased erythropoiesis
Hydrops fetalis/congenital anemia	Acute/chronic	Fetus (<20 weeks)
Persistent anemia	Chronic	Immunodeficient/immunocompromised patients

vovirus B19 replication occurs only in human erythrocyte precursors, and B19 is therefore classified as a member of the *Erythrovirus* genus, of which it is the type species.[2]

By electron microscopy, B19 particles have the typical parvovirus morphology (Fig. 136–1). Mature infectious particles have a molecular weight of 5.6×10^6 and a buoyant density in cesium chloride gradients of 1.41 g/ml. As a consequence of the lack of envelope and the limited DNA content, B19 is extremely resistant to physical inactivation. The virus resists inactivation at 56°C for much longer than 60 minutes and, at high viral concentration, 80°C for 72 hours,[3] and it is stable in lipid solvents such as ether and chloroform. It can be inactivated by formalin, β-propiolactone, oxidizing agents, and γ-irradiation.

The B19 genome size is limited, consisting of a single strand of DNA of approximately 5500 nucleotides, with identical inverted, 365-nucleotide-long terminal repeat sequences at each end. The transcription map of B19 distinguishes it from other Parvovirinae. There is a single strong promoter at the far left side of the genome and unusual polyadenylation signals in the middle of the genome.[4] The three major viral proteins, one nonstructural protein, and two capsid proteins are produced by alternative splicing from the promoter and its accompanying leader sequence. The relative quantities of the major and minor capsid proteins are in part regulated by the presence of multiple upstream AUG codons situated before the authentic transcription initiation codon.[5] In addition, there are transcripts for several smaller peptides of 7.5 and 11 kd and of unknown function.

The only unspliced transcript encodes the nonstructural protein, a 78-kd phosphoprotein.[6] Consistent with its role in viral propagation, the protein has DNA-binding properties, adenosine and guanosine triphosphatase activity, and nuclear localization signals (M Momeda, NS Young, and S Kajigaya, unpublished observations). Expression of the nonstructural protein causes host cell death through induction of apoptosis.[7]

The B19 virion is an icosahedron consisting of 60 copies of the capsid proteins. Most of the capsid is VP2, a 58-kd protein, with 5% or less of the larger, 84-kd, VP1 protein. VP1 protein differs from VP2 by an additional 227 amino acids at the amino terminus. Using genetic engineering techniques, the capsid proteins can be expressed in a variety of both mammalian[8, 9] and insect[10, 11] cell lines. Capsid proteins self-assemble in the absence of B19 DNA, and in these systems protein expression leads to formation of recombinant empty capsids; VP1 is not required for capsid formation.

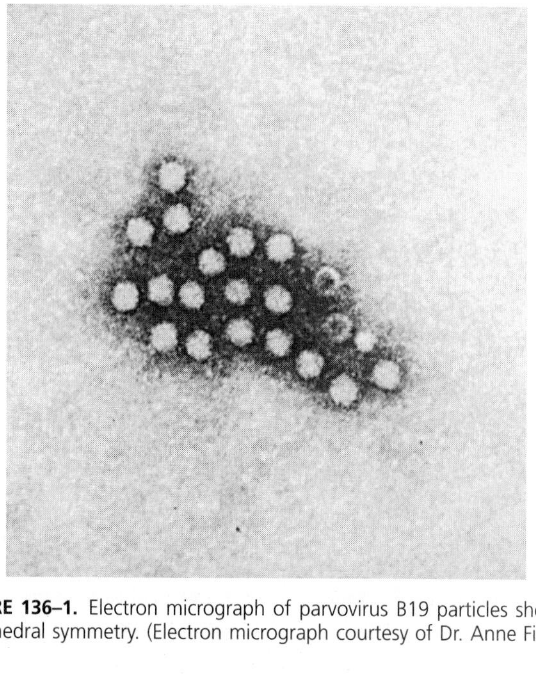

FIGURE 136–1. Electron micrograph of parvovirus B19 particles showing icosahedral symmetry. (Electron micrograph courtesy of Dr. Anne Field.)

The atomic structure of B19 VP2 empty capsids has now been resolved to 0.8 nm,[12] and the virus has also been visualized by cryoelectron microscopy.[13] The virion surface has a major depression encompassing the five-fold axis, similar to the canyon structure found in RNA-containing icosahedral viruses. In B19 capsids there is also a hollow cylindrical structure about the five-fold axes that appears to penetrate to the inside of the virion. The distribution of VP1 in the B19 capsid structure cannot be inferred from crystallographic analysis, but, based on antibody-binding studies, the VP1 unique region may extend through the five-fold axis cylinder of native capsids to the outside of the virion.[14]

No antigenic variation in B19 has been demonstrated. Small changes of nucleotide sequence have been detected by several investigators using restriction enzyme analysis or direct sequence analysis. Although isolates could be divided into groups (genome types) with particular enzyme digestion patterns, there is no correlation to specific disease presentation. Sequence divergence is generally less than 1%, with evidence for less variation in regions where antigenic epitopes are coded.[15] However, two isolates from China have shown significant difference (4.8%) from the prototype isolates, suggesting that geographically determined genotypes may exist.[16]

PATHOGENESIS

Parvovirus B19, like the other autonomous parvoviruses, is dependent on mitotically active cells for replication. However, B19 has a very narrow target cell range and apparently can be propagated only in human (or primate) erythroid cells. The virus cannot easily be cultivated in the laboratory. Humans are the only known host of parvovirus B19; all primates tested are resistant to B19 infection, although primates appear to have their own related erythroviruses.[17]

In human erythroid cells derived from bone marrow, susceptibility to parvovirus B19 increases with differentiation; the pluripotent stem cell appears to be spared, and the main target cells are erythroid progenitors (cells capable of giving rise to erythroid colonies in vitro) and erythroblasts.[18] The virus is cytotoxic, producing a cytopathic effect with characteristic light and electron microscopic[19] changes. Infected cultures are characterized by the presence of giant pronormoblasts, 25 to 32 μm in diameter, with cytoplasmic vacuolization, immature chromatin, and large eosinophilic nuclear inclusion bodies. By electron microscopy, virus particles are seen in the nucleus and lining cytoplasmic membranes, and infected cells show marginated chromatin, pseudopod formation, and cytoplasmic vacuolation, all typical of cells undergoing apoptosis.[20]

Erythroid specificity of parvovirus B19 results from the tissue distribution of the virus' cellular receptor, *globoside*, also known as *blood group P antigen*.[21] P antigen is found on erythroid progenitors, erythroblasts, and megakaryocytes. It is also present on endothelial cells, which may be targets of viral infection involved in the pathogenesis of transplacental transmission, possibly vasculitis, and the rash of fifth disease, and on fetal myocardial cells.[22] Rare individuals who genetically lack P antigen on erythrocytes are resistant to B19 infection, and their bone marrow cannot be infected with B19 in vitro.[23] However, erythroid specificity may also be modulated by specific erythroid cell transcription factors.[24]

Studies in normal volunteers showed that B19 infection leads to an acute but self-limited (4 to 8 days) cessation of red blood cell production and a corresponding decline in hemoglobin level.[25] In patients with normal erythroid turnover, this short interruption of red cell production does not lead to anemia, but in patients with high red cell turnover due to hemolysis, blood loss, or other causes, the temporary failure of erythropoiesis can precipitate an aplastic crisis. The anemia improves as the immune response develops. In patients who are immunocompromised, infection may persist and produce chronic PRCA.

The infected fetus may suffer severe effects because red blood cell turnover is high and the immune response is deficient. During the second trimester there is a great increase in red cell mass.

Parvovirus particles can be detected by electron microscopy within the hematopoietic tissues of liver and thymus.[26] B19 DNA and capsid antigen have been detected in the myocardium of infected fetuses,[27] and the fetus may develop myocarditis,[28] compounding the severe anemia and secondary cardiac failure. By the third trimester, a more effective fetal immune response to the virus probably accounts for the decrease in fetal loss at this stage of pregnancy.

The pathogenesis of the rash in EI and polyarthropathy is almost certainly immune complex mediated. In volunteer studies, the rash appeared when viremia was no longer detectable and coincident with a detectable immune response.[25] Similar findings have been reported in chronically infected persons who received immunoglobulin therapy.[29] However, in vitro studies have shown that the B19 nonstructural protein, in addition to inducing apoptosis in host cells, also induces activation of interleukin-6,[30] which could contribute in vivo to the B19-induced arthropathy and/or autoimmune antibody production.

EPIDEMIOLOGY

Prevalence and Incidence

Parvovirus B19 infection is common in childhood, and by the age of 15 years approximately 50% of children have detectable immunoglobulin G (IgG). Infection also occurs in adult life, so that more than 90% of elderly persons have detectable antibody.[31] Women of child-bearing age in the United States show an annual seroconversion rate of 1.5%.[32] Studies in different countries (United States, France, Germany, Japan) show similar patterns, with a slightly higher prevalence in children from countries such as Africa and Brazil. Some isolated tribal populations have a much lower prevalence: 2% on Rodriguez Island, Africa,[33] and 4 to 10% among the tribesmen around Belem, Brazil.[34]

Although antibody is prevalent in the general population, viremia is rare. Among blood donors, approximately 1 in 20,000 to 40,000 units of blood during epidemic seasons contains high titers of B19.[35] Screening of pooled samples from blood donors showed that 1 in 3000 units contained detectable B19 DNA by the more sensitive polymerase chain reaction (PCR) technique.[36]

Mechanism and Routes of Transmission

Parvovirus B19 infections in temperate climates are more common in the late winter, spring, and early summer months.[37] Rates of infection may also increase every 3 to 4 years, as reflected by corresponding increases in the major clinical manifestations of B19 infection, TAC, and EI.[38]

B19 DNA has been found in the respiratory secretions of patients at the time of viremia,[39] suggesting that infection is generally spread by a respiratory route of transmission. The virus can be transmitted readily by close contact, and the secondary attack rate has been calculated in various settings; in one study the secondary attack rate from symptomatic TAC or EI patients to susceptible (IgG-negative) household contacts was approximately 50%.[39] In school outbreaks, serologic studies are generally not available, but 10 to 60% of students may develop a rash disease consistent with B19 infection.[40–42] The highest secondary attack rates and annual seroconversion rates, even in the absence of known community outbreaks, are for workers in close contact with affected children, such as daycare providers and school personnel.[43] Nosocomial transmission in hospital situations has been described[44, 45] but is probably infrequent,[44] especially from patients with chronic infection. Nevertheless, patients with TAC or persistent disease should be considered infectious, and appropriate precautions should be taken to limit interaction with other patients and susceptible staff (see section on prevention).

The virus can be found in serum, and infection also can be transmitted by blood and blood products. As described previously, parvoviruses, including B19, are very resistant to heat and can withstand the usual thermal treatment aimed at infectious agents in blood products. In addition, solvent-detergent methods, which inactivate only lipid-enveloped viruses, are ineffective. B19 infection has been transmitted by steam- or dry-heated factor VIII or IX[3, 46] and by solvent-detergent–treated factor VIII.[47] Hemophiliacs who received heat-treated factor VIII alone had lower prevalence of B19 antibody and lower rates of seroconversion than those receiving non–heat-treated factor.[48]

CLINICAL MANIFESTATIONS

Erythema Infectiosum

Manifestations of parvovirus B19 infection vary even in the normal host, from asymptomatic or subclinical infection (most people with B19 specific antibody have no recollection of any specific symptoms) to a biphasic illness with symptoms during the viremic and immune complex–mediated stages of the disease. However, EI is the major clinical manifestation. EI was well characterized clinically before the discovery of B19.[49] This exanthematous rash illness of childhood was probably first described by Robert Willan in 1799 and illustrated in his 1808 textbook. The disease was rediscovered in Germany, where in 1899 Sticker gave it the name *erythema infectiosum*, and 6 years later Cheinisse classified it as the "fifth rash disease" of the six classic exanthema of childhood.[50] Often the epidemiologic data showed "a low rate of infection among extrafamilial contacts and a high infection rate within families,"[49] and an atypical rubella virus or echovirus was thought to be responsible. However, neither virus could be reproducibly isolated from patients with fifth disease. In 1983, after an outbreak of EI in London, 31 of 31 affected children and adolescents were found to have anti-B19–specific IgM.[51] Similar results were obtained in other epidemics of fifth disease, and parvovirus B19 is now recognized as the etiologic agent.

Clinical symptoms begin with a nonspecific prodromal illness, which often goes unrecognized; there may be symptoms of fever, coryza, headache, and mild gastrointestinal distress, including nausea and diarrhea. Two to 5 days later, the classic slapped-cheek rash appears, a fiery red eruption on the cheek accompanied by relative pallor circumorally. A second-stage rash, an erythematous maculopapular exanthemum on the trunk and limbs, may erupt within a few days; as this eruption fades it produces a typical lacey appearance. There is great variation in the dermatologic symptoms; the classic slapped-cheek appearance is much more common in children than in adults, and the second-stage eruption can vary from a faint, barely perceptible erythema to a florid exanthema. The rash may be transient, or recurrent for weeks. Rarely, other dermatologic presentations are seen: vesicopustular rash,[52] glove-and-stocking syndrome,[53–55] other purpuric rashes with or without Koplik's spots,[56, 57] and erythema multiforme.[58–60] Pruritus, especially on the soles of the feet, can be the dominant symptom.[53, 61, 62]

Arthropathy

Although B19 infection in children is usually mild and of short duration, a large proportion of adults, especially women, experience arthralgia or frank arthritis with painful joints, often with accompanying swelling and stiffness.[42] The arthralgia is usually symmetric, involving mainly the small joints of the hands and feet, and generally lasts for 1 to 3 weeks, although it may persist or recur for months and even years. In the absence of a history of rash, the symptoms may be mistaken for those of acute rheumatoid arthritis, especially because prolonged symptoms do not correlate with serologic studies, such as the duration of B19 IgM response, or persistent viremia. In addition, B19 infection can be associated with transient production of rheumatoid factor.[63] In one large study of patients attending an "early synovitis" clinic in England, 12% had evidence of recent infection with B19.[64] Three patients would have fulfilled the American Rheumatism Association's diagnostic criteria for definite rheumatoid arthritis. B19 infection should be considered as part of the differential diagnosis in any patient presenting with an acute polyarthritis. In contrast to rheumatoid arthritis, B19 infection is not associated with joint destruction. However, differentiation between early rheumatoid arthritis and B19 arthropathy is important, because the immunosuppressive therapy prescribed for rheumatoid arthritis is not indicated in parvovirus B19 infection.

The role of parvovirus B19 in chronic arthritis is unclear. Parvovirus B19 DNA has been found in the synovial fluid of a woman with serologically proven B19 infection[65] and in synovial fluid cells of a patient with "reactive arthritis."[66] However, PCR amplification studies should be interpreted with care: in one carefully performed controlled study, B19 DNA was indeed detected in synovial tissue of 28% of children with chronic arthritis but also was found in 48% of nonarthropathy controls,[67] indicating that PCR-detectable DNA can persist in synovial tissues for months or years.

Transient Aplastic Crisis

TAC, the abrupt cessation of erythropoiesis characterized by reticulocytopenia, absent erythroid precursors in the bone marrow, and precipitous worsening of anemia, was the first clinical illness associated with B19 infection. When stored sera from children admitted to a London hospital were examined for B19 virus, samples from six—all Jamaican immigrants with sickle cell disease presenting with TAC—showed evidence of recent infection with B19 (either antigenemia or seroconversion).[68] Retrospective studies of sera from Jamaican sickle cell patients showed that 86% of TAC episodes were associated with recent parvovirus infection.[69]

TAC due to B19 has now been described in a wide range of patients with underlying hemolytic disorders, including hereditary spherocytosis, thalassemia, red cell enzymopathies such as pyruvate kinase deficiency, and autoimmune hemolytic anemia.[70] TAC can also occur under conditions of erythroid "stress," such as hemorrhage or iron deficiency anemia and after kidney or bone marrow transplantation. Acute anemia has been described in hematologically normal persons,[71] and a drop in the red blood cell count (within the normal range) and also in the reticulocyte count was seen in healthy volunteers.[25]

Although they have an ultimately self-limited disease, patients with TAC can be severely ill. Symptoms may include dyspnea, lassitude, and even confusion resulting from the worsening anemia. Congestive heart failure and severe bone marrow necrosis may develop,[72] and the illness has been fatal.[38] TAC can be the first presentation of an underlying hemolytic disease in a well compensated patient.

Community-acquired red cell aplastic crisis is almost always caused by parvovirus B19,[73] and B19 infection should be the presumptive diagnosis in any patient with anemia due to abrupt cessation of erythropoiesis as documented by reduced reticulocytes and a bone marrow appearance of scattered, giant pronormoblasts. In contrast to patients with EI, those with TAC are often viremic at the time of presentation, with concentrations of virus as high as 10^{14} genome copies per milliliter; therefore, the diagnosis is readily made by detection of B19 DNA in the serum. As B19 DNA levels fall in serum, B19-specific IgM becomes detectable. TAC is easily treated by blood transfusion. After acute infection, immunity is lifelong.

TAC and B19 infection in hematologically normal patients are often associated with changes in other blood lineages, varying degrees of neutropenia,[74] and thrombocytopenia.[75] Some cases of idiopathic thrombocytopenia purpura[76] and Henoch-Schöenlein purpura[77] have been reported to occur after parvovirus B19 infection. Transient pancytopenia after parvovirus infection is rare.[78] Some cases of chronic neutropenia of childhood have also been ascribed to parvovirus B19 infection,[79] but in a study of serum from children and adults with chronic neutropenia we were unable to confirm an association.[80] A more convincing case of recurrent agranulocytosis ascribed to persistent parvovirus B19 has also been published.[81]

Parvovirus B19 does not appear to be the cause of true (permanent) aplastic anemia[78] or transient erythroblastopenia of childhood,[82] the temporary failure of red cell production in normal children: sporadic cases of transient erythroblastopenia with thrombocytopenia have been described with evidence of recent B19 infection, whereas the classic syndrome is associated with high platelet counts.

Pure Red Blood Cell Aplasia

Persistent B19 infection resulting in PRCA has been reported in a wide variety of immunosuppressed patients, ranging from patients with congenital immunodeficiency, acquired immunodeficiency syndrome (AIDS), or lymphoproliferative disorders to patients undergoing transplantation.[83] The stereotypic presentation is with persistent anemia rather than immune-mediated symptoms of rash or arthropathy. Patients have absent or low levels of B19-specific antibody and persistent or recurrent parvoviremia as detected by B19 DNA in the serum. Bone marrow examination generally reveals the presence of scattered giant pronormoblasts. Administration of immunoglobulin can be beneficial and ameliorative, if not curative.[84]

The prevalence of B19-induced anemia in patients who are seropositive for the human immunodeficiency virus (HIV) is probably higher than is recognized at present. In one early study of 50 patients with AIDS, no patients with B19 viremia were identified. In a larger cohort study, B19 DNA was found in only 1 (0.5%) of 191 HIV-seropositive homosexuals. However, B19 DNA was found in 5 (17%) of 30 transfusion-dependent HIV-seropositive homosexuals, and when a hematocrit of less than 20 was used as a criterion, 4 (31%) of 13 were positive.[85] In contrast to the earlier studies, the marrow morphology need not be suggestive of PRCA and giant pronormoblasts may not be present.

In less severely immunosuppressed patients (e.g., patients with systemic lupus erythematosus receiving steroid therapy), prolonged anemia after B19 infection has also been described.[86] However, in these patients there was a spontaneous, albeit delayed, development of antibodies, and viremia resolved without therapy. Presumably such patients represent one end of the spectrum of disease manifestations of B19 in patients with a compromised immune system.

Virus-Associated Hemophagocytic Syndrome

Virus-associated hemophagocytic syndrome is characterized by histiocytic hyperplasia, marked hemophagocytosis, and cytopenia in association with a systemic viral illness.[87] In contrast to malignant histiocytosis, this is usually a benign, self-limited illness, in which histiocytic proliferation is reversible. Hemophagocytosis is not uncommon, and it occurs in the setting of a wide range of infections, not only viral but also bacterial, rickettsial, fungal, and parasitic.[88] However, in many patients there is underlying immunosuppression, usually iatrogenic, so that the role of the incriminated pathogen as etiologic agent or coincidental opportunistic infection remains unclear. In two reported cases of virus-associated hemophagocytic syndrome, PRCA was concurrent.[88, 89]

Parvovirus B19 infection has been detected in 15 children and adults with hemophagocytosis syndrome.[90] The majority of patients were previously healthy, but four were immunosuppressed by drug therapies. In all but one case there was a favorable outcome (one immunosuppressed patient died of fulminant aspergillosis). Further studies are required to determine whether parvovirus B19 is a major cause of virus-associated hemophagocytic syndrome and the rate of this syndrome in otherwise uncomplicated cases of parvovirus B19 infection.

Fetal Infection (Hydrops Fetalis and Miscarriage)

Parvovirus B19 probably causes 10 to 15% of all cases of nonimmune hydrops. Nonimmune hydrops fetalis is rare (1 in 3000 births), and in approximately 50% of cases the cause is unknown.[91] In a study of 50 cases, the majority were caused by cardiovascular or chromosomal abnormalities, but parvovirus B19 DNA was detected by in situ hybridization in the lungs of 4 fetuses.[92] When pathologic studies have been undertaken, B19-infected fetuses showed evidence of leukoerythroblastic reaction in the liver and large pale cells with eosinophilic inclusion bodies and peripheral condensation or margination of the nuclear chromatin. Parvovirus B19 DNA could be detected by DNA dot-blot or in situ hybridization, and viral particles by electron microscopy.

Nevertheless, an adverse fetal outcome is not typical after maternal B19 infection. In a prospective British study of more than 400 women with serologically confirmed B19 during pregnancy, the excess rate of fetal loss was confined to the first 20 weeks of pregnancy and averaged only 9%.[93] No abnormalities were found at birth in the surviving infants, even when there was evidence of intrauterine infection by the presence of B19 IgM in the umbilical cord blood, and no long-term sequelae were found in the 129 children who were monitored for longer than 7 years.

No systematic studies have shown evidence for congenital abnormalities after maternal B19 infection,[93, 94] although there are case reports of congenital ocular[95] and/or neurologic abnormalities.[96] In addition, three infants born with chronic anemia after a history of maternal B19 exposure and intrauterine hydrops have been described.[97] In these cases, the virus load was low and localized: B19 DNA could be detected in bone marrow samples by PCR but not in concurrent serum samples. All three infants were treated with immunoglobulin therapy; one patient died, but in the other two cases B19 DNA became undetectable in bone marrow (by PCR), although the children remained severely anemic. The role of in utero B19 infection in inducing constitutional bone marrow failure such as Diamond-Blackfan anemia is still under investigation.

Other Disease Manifestations

B19 infection has been associated with a range of other disease manifestations, including neurologic disease, myocarditis, hepatitis, and vasculitis. However, most of these are case reports or limited PCR-based studies with poorly documented controls.

Encephalitis and, more often, aseptic meningitis have been described in serologically confirmed cases of B19 infection,[98–102] with detection of B19 DNA in cerebrospinal fluid. No long-term neurologic sequelae have been reported. Brachial plexus neuropathy with weakness and sensory loss has also been described in patients with B19 infection.[103, 104] In one study, 50% of patients with classic fifth disease (confirmed serologically) experienced neurologic symptoms (tingling and numbness in the fingers or toes).[105]

Case reports of myocarditis associated with B19 infection have been reported in both children[106–109] and adults.[110–112] The role of B19 in the pathogenesis of myocarditis warrants further investigation, particularly because P antigen is found on fetal myocardial cells and B19 appears to cause myocarditis in the fetus.[28, 113]

In addition, the role of parvovirus B19 in both hepatitis and vasculitis remains unclear. Although transient elevation of liver transaminases is not uncommon in B19 infection, frank hepatitis associated with B19 infection has rarely been reported.[114] Parvovirus B19 has been suggested as a possible causative agent of fulminant liver failure and associated aplastic anemia based on PCR studies.[115] However, the numbers were small (4 of 6 patients), and more studies in this area are required. In our own studies of livers of patients with both fulminant hepatitis and hepatitis-associated aplastic anemia, we have been unable to confirm this putative relationship.

Several case reports have described positive B19 serology in patients with vasculitis and/or polyarteritis nodosum,[116–119] systemic necrotizing vasculitis,[120] or Kawasaki disease, a multisystem vasculitis of early childhood. However, other studies have not shown a relationship between Kawasaki disease and parvoviral infection.[121, 122]

IMMUNE RESPONSE

Both virus-specific IgM and IgG antibodies are made after experimental[25] and natural B19 parvovirus infection (Fig. 136–2). After intranasal inoculation of volunteers, virus can first be detected at days 5 to 6, and levels peak at days 8 to 9. IgM antibody to virus appears about 10 to 12 days after experimental inoculation, and IgG antibody at about 2 weeks. The time course is similar in natural infections. In patients with TAC, 10^8 to 10^{14} genome copies of virus DNA per milliliter may circulate. IgM antibody may be present in patients with TAC at the time of reticulocyte nadir and during the next 10 days; IgG usually appears during the period of hematopoietic recovery. Viremia is not detectable in patients with clinical fifth disease (the manifestations are secondary to immune complex formation).

IgM antibody may be found in serum samples for several months after exposure.[123] IgG presumably persists for life, and levels rise with reexposure.[25] Measurable IgA antibodies specific to B19 parvovirus may play a role in protection against infection by the nasopharyngeal route.[124]

In immunocompetent persons, the early antibody response is to the major capsid protein VP2, but as the immune response matures reactivity to the minor capsid protein VP1 dominates. Sera from patients with persistent B19 infection typically contain antibody to VP2 but not to VP1.[125] That an immune response to VP1 might be necessary for protective immunity has been confirmed in animal experiments using recombinant capsids. Rabbits immunized with capsids containing only VP2 produced a strong antibody response as measured by enzyme-linked immunosorbent assay (ELISA), but the sera had low neutralization titers. In contrast, rabbits immunized with capsids containing VP1 produced antibody with neutralizing titers comparable to those produced in humans after acute B19 infection.[126] The role of the cellular immune response in limiting parvovirus B19 infection is uncertain: a lymphocyte proliferative response to B19 capsid proteins has been described in seropositive individual patients with the use of recombinant capsids, but not native virions.[127] The importance of the humoral arm of the immune response is shown by recovery from infection with the appearance of circulating specific antiviral antibody; in addition, administration of commercial immunoglobulins can cure or ameliorate persistent parvovirus infection in immunodeficient patients (see later discussion).

Persistent B19 parvovirus infection results from failure of the immunocompromised host to produce effective neutralizing antibodies. Perhaps because of the limited numbers of epitopes presented to the immune system by B19 parvovirus, the congenital immunodeficiency states associated with persistent infection may be clinically subtle, with susceptibility largely restricted to parvovirus, although multiple immune system defects are apparent once directed testing of T- and B-cell function is performed.

DIAGNOSIS

There is no suitable method for virus isolation from clinical specimens, and the detection of virus relies on DNA hybridization techniques. B19 DNA can be detected in serum at the time of TAC by dot-blot hybridization, and in situ hybridization has been used to identify B19 DNA within bone marrow and other cells.

In immunocompetent persons B19 DNA is detectable only for 2 to 4 days by dot-blot hybridization (see Fig. 136–2), and the diagnosis of acute B19 infection is therefore based on IgM assays, ideally performed by the capture technique.[128] In a radioimmunoassay or ELISA format, antibody can be detected in more than 90% of cases by the third day of TAC or at the time of rash in EI. IgM antibody remains detectable for 2 to 3 months after infection.

B19 IgG can be detected by capture assay or indirect assay. IgG usually is present by the seventh day of illness and probably for life thereafter. Because more than 50% of the population have IgG

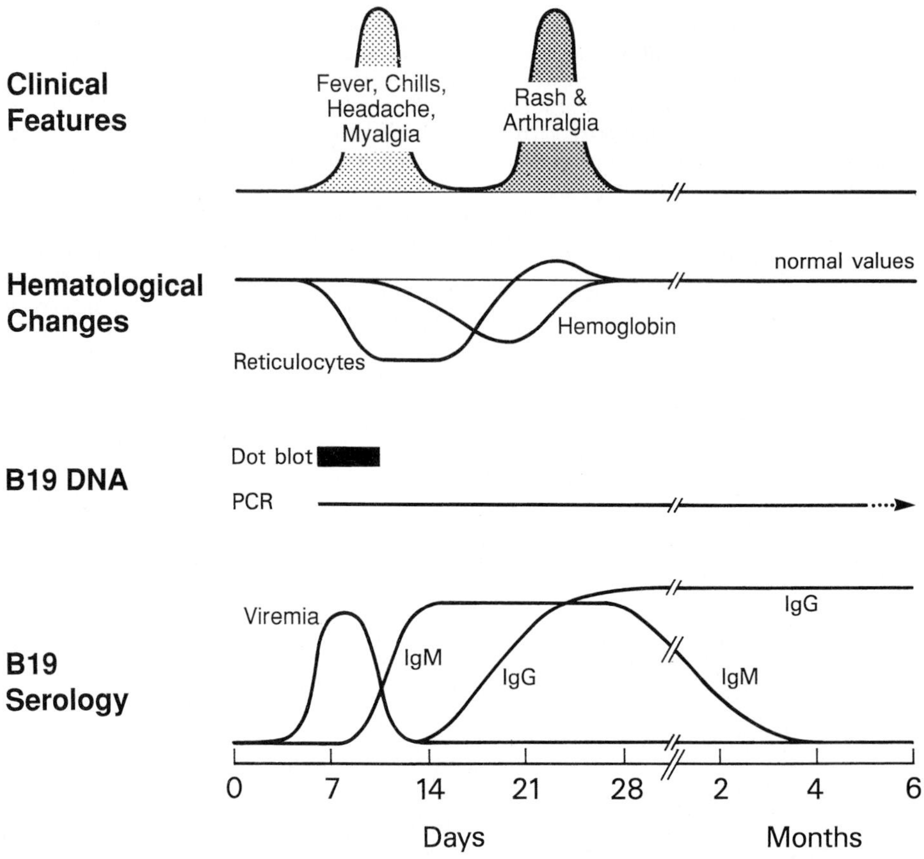

FIGURE 136–2. Virologic, immunologic, and clinical course after acute B19 infection in a normal individual. (From Brown KE, Young NS. Parvovirus B19 infection and hematopoiesis. Blood Rev. 1995;9:176–182.)

antibody to B19 infection, this test is not helpful for the diagnosis of acute infection. Immunocompromised and immunodeficient patients with chronic infection typically do not mount an immune response to the virus, and testing for B19 antigens or, more usually, for viral DNA is necessary to document recent infection.

The sensitivity level of detection of B19 has greatly increased with the use of PCR techniques, but at the risk of possible contamination and false-positive results that confuse interpretation. Even in immunocompetent persons, B19 DNA may be detectable by PCR for more than 4 months in serum after acute infection[129, 130] and for years in bone marrow,[131] synovial tissue,[67] and liver (K Brown and NS Young, unpublished data). In general, the diagnosis of acute or chronic infection can be made on the basis of standard DNA hybridization in combination with serologic assays for B19-specific IgG or IgM, or both.

Investigation of B19 fetal or congenital infection should be accompanied by serologic studies of the maternal serum. At the time of fetal infection, the mother should have evidence of recent B19 infection with detectable IgG and possibly IgM. If the IgM titer is low or absent, recent infection can be documented by IgG avidity studies. Fetal infection can be confirmed by amniotic fluid sampling, by fetal blood sampling, or from postmortem tissue.

Diagnosis of chronic arthropathy due to parvovirus B19 is problematic. Because of the presence of PCR-detectable B19 DNA in a significant number of healthy persons, detection of B19 in serum, bone marrow, or synovial fluid does not confirm the diagnosis, although parvovirus B19–specific IgM or IgG avidity may suggest recent B19 infection.

TREATMENT

In most children and adults, B19 infection is a benign and self-limited infection that results in lifelong immunity and requires no treatment other than symptomatic relief. Patients with arthralgia and arthritis usually respond to nonsteroidal anti-inflammatory drugs, although in some patients symptoms can persist for months and even years.[64] In patients with hematologic disease or persistent infection, specific treatment may be necessary.

Immunocompetent patients with TAC have a self-limited illness, and typical TAC is readily treated by blood transfusion and supportive therapy alone. In one study of sickle cell patients with TAC, 87% required blood transfusions and 61% required hospitalization for their symptoms; one patient died before transfusion could be given,[132] underscoring the importance of prompt medical intervention.

In immunosuppressed patients with documented persistent B19 infection, temporary cessation of immunosuppression may be sufficient to allow the host to mount an immune response and resolve the B19 infection, with no additional treatment being required.[133] In cases where cessation of immunosuppression is not feasible or is ineffective, administration of immunoglobulin can be beneficial,[29, 84] the usual regimen being intravenous IgG (IVIG) at a dose of 0.4 g/kg for 5 days. Patients often respond with a marked reduction in the level of B19 viremia, reticulocytosis, and resolution of the anemia within 1 to 2 weeks of treatment. However, monitoring for relapse is important, by observation of the reticulocyte count and assays for B19 viremia when indicated. If relapse occurs less than 6 months after the initial treatment, especially in HIV-positive patients, an empirical maintenance treatment with a single-day infusion of 0.4 g/kg IgG every 4 weeks may control the B19 viremia.

The role of intrauterine blood transfusions in the treatment of hydrops fetalis caused by maternal parvovirus B19 infection remains controversial. Intrauterine blood transfusions have risks, and B19-associated hydrops is known to resolve spontaneously, with the fetus being normal at delivery. However, several case reports have suggested that treatment with intrauterine blood transfusions leads to increased survival of B19-infected fetuses. In the best of these studies, 12 of 38 hydropic fetuses were treated with intrauterine blood transfusions, and 26 were treated conservatively.[134] Nine of the 12 treated fetuses survived, compared with 13 of the 26 treated conservatively, a difference in survival that was significant after adjustment for the severity of the ultrasound findings and the gestational age. Therefore, intrauterine blood transfusions may be beneficial in some cases of hydrops, but there remains a risk that treatment may be confounded by an increased incidence of antibody-enhanced infection and damage especially to myocardial cells and the immune system.[97]

PREVENTION AND VACCINATION

The only measures currently available to prevent B19 infection are those designed to interrupt virus transmission. However, because patients are viremic and infectious before the symptoms of EI appear, isolation of patients with fifth disease is not rational. Patients with TAC or PRCA are both viremic and infectious and should be appropriately separated from high-risk contacts. The Centers of Disease Control and Prevention recommends that patients with TAC be placed on droplet isolation precautions (door closed, mask used at all times, gown and gloves for all direct contacts) for 7 days or the duration of illness, whichever is longer, and for patients with chronic infection, for the duration of their hospitalization.[135] Pregnant health care workers should not care for patients with TAC or with chronic B19 infection.

The humoral immune response plays the major role in the normal immune response to parvovirus. Although antibodies appear to be protective in both passive and active immunizations, insufficient data are available to assess the efficacy of immunoprophylaxis.[136, 137]

Prospects for vaccination are good, and a B19 empty capsid vaccine is under development. The presence of VP1 protein in the capsid immunogen appears to be critical for the production of antibodies that neutralize virus activity in vitro, and capsids with supranormal VP1 content are even more efficient in inducing neutralizing activity in immunized animals.[138] Phase I trials of one B19 vaccine formulation commenced in early 1995, and further phase I trials are scheduled to begin in late 1999. However, the targets for such a vaccine remain to be determined. Should only those at high risk of severe or life-threatening disease, such as patients with sickle cell disease, be protected? Or, in view of the wide variety of disease manifestations affecting all strata of the population, should a universal vaccine policy be pursued?

REFERENCES

1. Cossart YE, Field AM, Cant B, et al. Parvovirus-like particles in human sera. Lancet. 1975;1:72–73.
2. Anonymous. Virus Taxonomy. Sixth Report of the International Committee on Taxonomy of Viruses. New York: Springer-Verlag; 1995.
3. Bartolomei Corsi O, Azzi A, Morfini M, et al. Human parvovirus infection in haemophiliacs first infused with treated clotting factor concentrates. J Med Virol. 1988;25:165–170.
4. Ozawa K, Ayub J, Hao YS, et al. Novel transcription map for the B19 (human) pathogenic parvovirus. J Virol. 1987;61:2395–2406.
5. Ozawa K, Ayub J, Young N. Translational regulation of B19 parvovirus capsid protein production by multiple upstream AUG triplets. J Biol Chem. 1988;263:10922–10926.
6. Ozawa K, Young N. Characterization of capsid and noncapsid proteins of B19 parvovirus propagated in human erythroid bone marrow cell cultures. J Virol. 1987;61:2627–2630.
7. Parravicini C, Lauri E, Baldini L, et al. Kaposi's sarcoma-associated herpesvirus infection and multiple myeloma (Technical comment). Science. 1997;278:1969–1970.
8. Kajigaya S, Shimada T, Fujita S, et al. A genetically engineered cell line that produces empty capsids of B19 (human) parvovirus. Proc Natl Acad Sci U S A. 1989;86:7601–7605.
9. Beard C, St Amand J, Astell CR. Transient expression of B19 parvovirus gene products in COS-7 cells transfected with B19-SV40 hybrid vectors. Virology. 1989;172:659–664.
10. Kajigaya S, Fujii H, Field A, et al. Self-assembled B19 parvovirus capsids, produced in a baculovirus system, are antigenically and immunogenically similar to native virions. Proc Natl Acad Sci U S A. 1991;88:4646–4650.
11. Brown CS, Van Lent JW, Vlak JM, et al. Assembly of empty capsids by using baculovirus recombinants expressing human parvovirus B19 structural proteins. J Virol. 1991;65:2702–2706.
12. Agbandje M, Kajigaya S, McKenna R, et al. The structure of human parvovirus B19 at 8 Å resolution. Virology. 1994;203:106–115.
13. Chipman PR, Agbandje-McKenna M, Kajigaya S, et al. Cryo-electron microscopy studies of empty capsids of human parvovirus B19 complexed with its cellular receptor. Proc Natl Acad Sci U S A. 1996;93:7502–7506.
14. Rosenfeld SJ, Yoshimoto K, Kajigaya S, et al. Unique region of the minor capsid protein of human parvovirus B19 is exposed on the virion surface. J Clin Invest. 1992;89:2023–2029.
15. Umene K, Nunoue T. Genetic diversity of human parvovirus B19 determined using a set of restriction endonucleases recognizing four or five base pairs and partial nucleotide sequencing: Use of sequence variability in virus classification. J Gen Virol. 1991;72:1997–2001.
16. Erdman DD, Durigon EL, Wang Q, et al. Genetic diversity of human parvovirus B19: Sequence analysis of the VP1/VP2 gene from multiple isolates. J Gen Virol. 1996;77:2767–2774.
17. Brown KE, Young NS. The simian parvoviruses. Rev Med Virol. 1997;7:211–218.
18. Takahashi T, Ozawa K, Takahashi K, et al. Susceptibility of human erythropoietic cells to B19 parvovirus in vitro increases with differentiation. Blood. 1990;75:603–610.
19. Young N, Harrison M, Moore J, et al. Direct demonstration of the human parvovirus in erythroid progenitor cells infected in vitro. J Clin Invest. 1984;74:2024–2032.
20. Morey AL, Ferguson DJ, Fleming KA. Ultrastructural features of fetal erythroid precursors infected with parvovirus B19 in vitro: Evidence of cell death by apoptosis. J Pathol. 1993;169:213–220.
21. Brown KE, Anderson SM, Young NS. Erythrocyte P antigen: Cellular receptor for B19 parvovirus. Science. 1993;262:114–117.
22. Rouger P, Gane P, Salmon C. Tissue distribution of H, Lewis and P antigens as shown by a panel of 18 monoclonal antibodies. Rev Fr Transfus Immunohematol. 1987;30:699–708.
23. Brown KE, Hibbs JR, Gallinella G, et al. Resistance to parvovirus B19 infection due to lack of virus receptor (erythrocyte P antigen). N Engl J Med. 1994;330:1192–1196.
24. Liu JM, Green SW, Shimada T, Young NS. A block in full-length transcript maturation in cells nonpermissive for B19 parvovirus. J Virol. 1992;66:4686–4692.
25. Anderson MJ, Higgins PG, Davis LR, et al. Experimental parvoviral infection in humans. J Infect Dis. 1985;152:257–265.
26. Field AM, Cohen BJ, Brown KE, et al. Detection of B19 parvovirus in human fetal tissues by electron microscopy. J Med Virol. 1991;35:85–95.
27. Porter HJ, Heryet A, Quantrill AM, et al. Combined non-isotopic in situ hybridisation and immunohistochemistry on routine paraffin wax embedded tissue: Identification of cell type infected by human parvovirus and demonstration of cytomegalovirus DNA and antigen in renal infection. J Clin Pathol. 1990;43:129–132.
28. Naides SJ, Weiner CP. Antenatal diagnosis and palliative treatment of non-immune hydrops fetalis secondary to fetal parvovirus B19 infection. Prenat Diagn. 1989;9:105–114.
29. Frickhofen N, Abkowitz JL, Safford M, et al. Persistent B19 parvovirus infection in patients infected with human immunodeficiency virus type 1 (HIV-1): A treatable cause of anemia in AIDS. Ann Intern Med. 1990;113:926–933.
30. Moffatt S, Tanaka N, Tada K, et al. A cytotoxic nonstructural protein, NS1, of human parvovirus B19 induces activation of interleukin-6 gene expression. J Virol. 1996;70:8485–8491.
31. Cohen BJ, Buckley MM. The prevalence of antibody to human parvovirus B19 in England and Wales. J Med Microbiol. 1988;25:151–153.
32. Koch WC, Adler SP. Human parvovirus B19 infections in women of childbearing age and within families. Pediatr Infect Dis J. 1989;8:83–87.
33. Schwarz TF, Gürtler LG, Zoulek G, et al. Seroprevalence of human parvovirus B19 infection in Sao Tomé and Principe, Malawi and Mascarene Islands. Int J Med Microbiol. 1989;271:231–236.
34. de Freitas RB, Wong D, Boswell F, et al. Prevalence of human parvovirus (B19) and rubella virus infections in urban and remote rural areas in northern Brazil. J Med Virol. 1990;32:203–208.
35. Cohen BJ, Field AM, Gudnadottir S, et al. Blood donor screening for parvovirus B19. J Virol Methods. 1990;30:233–238.
36. McOmish F, Yap PL, Jordan A, et al. Detection of parvovirus B19 in donated blood: A model system for screening by polymerase chain reaction. J Clin Microbiol. 1993;31:323–328.
37. Anderson MJ, Cohen BJ. Human parvovirus B19 infections in United Kingdom 1984–86 (Letter). Lancet. 1987;1:738–739.
38. Serjeant GR, Serjeant BE, Thomas PE, et al. Human parvovirus infection in homozygous sickle cell disease. Lancet. 1993;341:1237–1240.
39. Chorba T, Coccia P, Holman RC, et al. The role of parvovirus B19 in aplastic crisis and erythema infectiosum (fifth disease). J Infect Dis. 1986;154:383–393.
40. Gillespie SM, Cartter ML, Asch S, et al. Occupational risk of human parvovirus B19 infection for school and day-care personnel during an outbreak of erythema infectiosum. JAMA. 1990;263:2061–2065.
41. Lauer BA, MacCormack JN, Wilfert C. Erythema infectiosum: An elementary school outbreak. Am J Dis Child. 1976;130:252–254.
42. Woolf AD, Campion GV, Chishick A, et al. Clinical manifestations of human parvovirus B19 in adults. Arch Intern Med. 1989;149:1153–1156.
43. Adler SP, Manganello AM, Koch WC, et al. Risk of human parvovirus B19 infections among school and hospital employees during endemic periods. J Infect Dis. 1993;168:361–368.
44. Koziol DE, Kurtzman G, Ayub J, et al. Nosocomial human parvovirus B19 infection: Lack of transmission from a chronically infected patient to hospital staff. Infect Control Hosp Epidemiol. 1992;13:343–348.
45. Evans JP, Rossiter MA, Kumaran TO, et al. Human parvovirus aplasia: Case due to cross infection in a ward. BMJ. 1984;288:681.

46. Lyon DJ, Chapman CS, Martin C, et al. Symptomatic parvovirus B19 infection and heat-treated factor IX concentrate (Letter). Lancet. 1989;1:1085.
47. Azzi A, Ciappi S, Zakvrzewska K, et al. Human parvovirus B19 infection in hemophiliacs first infused with two high-purity, virally attenuated factor VIII concentrates. Am J Hematol. 1992;39:228–230.
48. Williams MD, Cohen BJ, Beddall AC, et al. Transmission of human parvovirus B19 by coagulation factor concentrates. Vox Sang. 1990;58:177–181.
49. Balfour HH. Erythema infectiosum (fifth disease): Clinical review and description of 91 cases seen in an epidemic. Clin Pediatr (Phila). 1969;8:721–727.
50. Cheinisse L. Une cinquième maladie éruptive: le mégal-érythème épidémique. Semin Med. 1905;25:205–207.
51. Anderson MJ, Jones SE, Fisher-Hoch SP, et al. Human parvovirus, the cause of erythema infectiosum (fifth disease)?(Letter). Lancet. 1983;1:1378.
52. Naides SJ, Piette W, Veach LA, et al. Human parvovirus B19-induced vesiculopustular skin eruption. Am J Med. 1988;84:968–972.
53. Halasz CL, Cormier D, Den M. Petechial glove and sock syndrome caused by parvovirus B19. J Am Acad Dermatol. 1992;27:835–838.
54. Bagot M, Revuz J. Papular-purpuric "gloves and socks" syndrome: Primary infection with parvovirus B19? (Letter; comment). J Am Acad Dermatol. 1991;25:341–342.
55. Vargas-Diez E, Buezo GF, Aragues M, et al. Papular-purpuric gloves-and-socks syndrome. Int J Dermatol. 1996;35:626–632.
56. Shiraishi H, Umetsu K, Yamamoto H, et al. Human parvovirus (HPV/B19) infection with purpura. Microbiol Immunol. 1989;33:369–372.
57. Evans LM, Grossman ME, Gregory N. Koplik spots and a purpuric eruption associated with parvovirus B19 infection. J Am Acad Dermatol. 1992;27:466–467.
58. Lobkowicz F, Ring J, Schwarz TF, et al. Erythema multiforme in a patient with acute human parvovirus B19 infection. J Am Acad Dermatol. 1989;20:849–850.
59. Frank R, Glander HJ, Haustein UF. [Dermatologic symptoms of parvovirus B19 infections]. Hautarzt. 1996;47:365–368.
60. Garcia-Tapia AM, Fernandez-Gutierrez del Alamo C, Giron JA, et al. Spectrum of parvovirus B19 infection: Analysis of an outbreak of 43 cases in Cadiz, Spain. Clin Infect Dis. 1995;21:1424–1430.
61. Jacks TA. Pruritus in parvovirus infection. J R Coll Gen Pract. 1987;37:210–211.
62. Ginsburg SM. Acute erythroid aplasia (erythroblastopenia) and vascular purpura in an otherwise hematologically normal child. Ann Intern Med. 1961;55:317–321.
63. Luzzi GA, Kurtz JB, Chapel H. Human parvovirus arthropathy and rheumatoid factor (Letter). Lancet. 1985;1:1218.
64. White DG, Woolf AD, Mortimer PP, et al. Human parvovirus arthropathy. Lancet. 1985;1:419–421.
65. Dijkmans BA, van Elsacker-Niele AM, Salimans MM, et al. Human parvovirus B19 DNA in synovial fluid. Arthritis Rheum. 1988;31:279–281.
66. Kandolf R, Kirschner P, Hofschneider PH, et al. Detection of parvovirus in a patient with "reactive arthritis" by in situ hybridization. Clin Rheumatol. 1989;8:398–401.
67. Soderlund M, von Essen R, Haapasaari J, et al. Persistence of parvovirus B19 DNA in synovial membranes of young patients with and without chronic arthropathy (See comments). Lancet. 1997;349:1063–1065.
68. Pattison JR, Jones SE, Hodgson J, et al. Parvovirus infections and hypoplastic crisis in sickle-cell anaemia. Lancet. 1981;1:664–665.
69. Serjeant GR, Topley JM, Mason K, et al. Outbreak of aplastic crisis in sickle cell anaemia associated with parvovirus-like agent. Lancet. 1981;2:595–597.
70. Young N. Hematologic and hematopoietic consequences of B19 parvovirus infection. Semin Hematol. 1988;25:159–172.
71. Hamon MD, Newland AC, Anderson MJ. Severe aplastic anaemia after parvovirus infection in the absence of underlying haemolytic anaemia (Letter). J Clin Pathol. 1988;41:1242.
72. Conrad ME, Studdard H, Anderson LJ. Aplastic crisis in sickle cell disorders: Bone marrow necrosis and human parvovirus infection. Am J Med Sci. 1988;295:212–215.
73. Anderson MJ, Davis LR, Hodgson J, et al. Occurrence of infection with a parvovirus-like agent in children with sickle cell anaemia during a two-year period. J Clin Pathol. 1982;35:744–749.
74. Saunders PW, Reid MM, Cohen BJ. Human parvovirus induced cytopenias: A report of five cases (Letter). Br J Haematol. 1986;63:407–410.
75. Inoue S, Kinra NK, Mukkamala SR, et al. Parvovirus B-19 infection: Aplastic crisis, erythema infectiosum and idiopathic thrombocytopenic purpura. Pediatr Infect Dis J. 1991;10:251–253.
76. Foreman NK, Oakhill A, Caul EO. Parvovirus-associated thrombocytopenic purpura (Letter). Lancet 1988;2:1426–1427.
77. Lefrère JJ, Courouce AM, Muller JY, et al. Human parvovirus and purpura (Letter). Lancet. 1985;2:730.
78. Frickhofen N, Raghavachar A, Heit W, et al. Human parvovirus infection (Letter). N Engl J Med. 1986;314:646.
79. McClain K, Estrov Z, Chen H, et al. Chronic neutropenia of childhood: Frequent association with parvovirus infection and correlations with bone marrow culture studies. Br J Haematol. 1993;85:57–62.
80. Hartman KR, Brown KE, Green SW, et al. Lack of evidence for parvovirus B19 viraemia in children with chronic neutropenia (Letter). Br J Haematol. 1994;84:895–896.
81. Pont J, Puchhammer-Stöckl E, Chott A, et al. Recurrent granulocytic aplasia as clinical presentation of a persistent parvovirus B19 infection. Br J Haematol. 1992;80:160–165.
82. Young NS, Mortimer PP, Moore JG, et al. Characterization of a virus that causes transient aplastic crisis. J Clin Invest. 1984;73:224–230.
83. Frickhofen N, Young NS. Persistent parvovirus B19 infections in humans. Microb Pathog. 1989;7:319–327.
84. Kurtzman GJ, Cohen B, Meyers P, Amunullah A, et al. Persistent B19 parvovirus infection as a cause of severe chronic anaemia in children with acute lymphocytic leukaemia. Lancet. 1988;2:1159–1162.
85. Abkowitz JL, Brown KE, Wood RW, et al. Clinical relevance of parvovirus B19 as a cause of anemia in patients with human immunodeficiency virus infection. J Infect Dis. 1997;176:269–273.
86. Koch WC, Massey G, Russell CE, et al. Manifestations and treatment of human parvovirus B19 infection in immunocompromised patients. J Pediatr. 1990;116:355–359.
87. Risdall RJ, McKenna RW, Nesbit ME, et al. Virus-associated hemophagocytic syndrome. Cancer. 1979;44:993–1002.
88. Reiner AP, Spivak JL. Hematophagic histiocytosis: A report of 23 new patients and a review of the literature. Medicine (Baltimore). 1988;67:369–388.
89. Hanada T, Yamamura H, Isobe T, et al. Pure red cell aplasia in association with malignant histiocytosis. Cancer. 1986;57:2325–2328.
90. Shirono K, Tsuda H. Parvovirus B19-associated haemophagocytic syndrome in healthy adults. Br J Haematol. 1995;89:923–926.
91. Warsof SL, Nicolaides KH, Rodeck C. Immune and non-immune hydrops. Clin Obstet Gynecol. 1986;29:533–542.
92. Porter HJ, Khong TY, Evans MF, et al. Parvovirus as a cause of hydrops fetalis: Detection by in situ DNA hybridisation. J Clin Pathol. 1988;41:381–383.
93. Miller E, Fairley CK, Cohen BJ, et al. Immediate and long term outcome of human parvovirus B19 infection in pregnancy. Br J Obstet Gynaecol. 1998;105:174–178.
94. Rodis JF, Rodner C, Hansen AA, et al. Long-term outcome of children following maternal human parvovirus B19 infection. Obstet Gynecol. 1998;91:125–128.
95. Weiland HT, Vermey-Keers C, Salimans MM, et al. Parvovirus B19 associated with fetal abnormality (Letter). Lancet. 1987;1:682–683.
96. Katz VL, McCoy MC, Kuller JA, et al. An association between fetal parvovirus B19 infection and fetal anomalies: A report of two cases. Am J Perinatol. 1996;13:43–45.
97. Brown KE, Green SW, Antunez de Mayolo J, et al. Congenital anaemia after transplacental B19 parvovirus infection. Lancet. 1994;343:895–896.
98. Watanabe T, Satoh M, Oda Y. Human parvovirus B19 encephalopathy (Letter). Arch Dis Child. 1994;70:71.
99. Cassinotti P, Schultze D, Schlageter P, et al. Persistent human parvovirus B19 infection following an acute infection with meningitis in an immunocompetent patient. Eur J Clin Microbiol Infect Dis. 1993;12:701–704.
100. Okumura A, Ichikawa T. Aseptic meningitis caused by human parvovirus B19. Arch Dis Child. 1993;68:784–785.
101. Suzuki N, Terada S, Inoue M. Neonatal meningitis with human parvovirus B19 infection (Letter). Arch Dis Child. 1995;73:F196–F197.
102. Koduri PR, Naides SJ. Aseptic meningitis caused by parvovirus B19. Clin Infect Dis. 1995;21:1053.
103. Denning DW, Amos A, Rudge P, et al. Neuralgic amyotrophy due to parvovirus infection (Letter). J Neurol Neurosurg Psychiatry. 1987;50:641–642.
104. Walsh KJ, Armstrong RD, Turner AM. Brachial plexus neuropathy associated with human parvovirus infection. BMJ. 1988;296:896.
105. Faden H, Gary GW Jr, Korman M. Numbness and tingling of fingers associated with parvovirus B19 infection (Letter). J Infect Dis. 1990;161:354–355.
106. Saint-Martin J, Choulot JJ, Bonnaud E, et al. Myocarditis caused by parvovirus (Letter; comment). J Pediatr. 1990;116:1007–1008.
107. Knisely AS, O'Shea PA, Anderson LJ, et al. Parvovirus B19 infection, myocarditis, and death in a 3-year-old boy (Abstract). Pediatr Pathol. 1988;8:665.
108. Borreda D, Palomera S, Gilbert B, et al. [Twenty-four cases of human parvovirus B19 infection in children]. Ann Pediatr (Paris). 1992;39:543–549.
109. Enders G, Dötsch J, Bauer J, et al. Life-threatening parvovirus B19-associated myocarditis and cardiac transplantation as possible therapy: Two case reports. Clin Infect Dis. 1998;26:355–358.
110. Chia JK, Jackson B. Myopericarditis due to parvovirus B19 in an adult. Clin Infect Dis. 1996;23:200–201.
111. Orth T, Herr W, Spahn T, et al. Human parvovirus B19 infection associated with severe acute perimyocarditis in a 34-year-old man (Letter). Eur Heart J. 1997;18:524–525.
112. Respondek M, Bratosiewicz J, Pertynski T, et al. Parvovirus particles in a fetal-heart with myocarditis: Ultrastructural and immunohistochemical study. Arch Immunol Ther Exp (Warsz). 1997;45:465–470.
113. Morey AL, Keeling JW, Porter HJ, et al. Clinical and histopathological features of parvovirus B19 infection in the human fetus. Br J Obstet Gynaecol. 1992;99:566–574.
114. Yoto Y, Kudoh T, Haseyama K, et al. Human parvovirus B19 infection associated with acute hepatitis. Lancet. 1996;347:868–869.
115. Langnas AN, Markin RS, Cattral MS, et al. Parvovirus B19 as a possible causative agent of fulminant liver failure and associated aplastic anemia. Hepatology. 1995;22:1661–1665.
116. Schwarz TF, Bruns R, Schröder C, et al. Human parvovirus B19 infection associated with vascular purpura and vasculitis (Letter). Infection. 1989;17:170–171.
117. Li Loong TC, Coyle PV, Anderson MJ, et al. Human serum parvovirus associated vasculitis. Postgrad Med J. 1986;62:493–494.
118. Corman LC, Dolson DJ. Polyarteritis nodosa and parvovirus B19 infection (Letter). Lancet. 1992;339:491.
119. Leruez-Ville M, Lauge A, Morinet F, et al. Polyarteritis nodosa and parvovirus B19 (Letter). Lancet. 1994;344:263–264.
120. Finkel TH, Torok TJ, Ferguson PJ, et al. Chronic parvovirus B19 infection and

systemic necrotising vasculitis: Opportunistic infection or aetiological agent?. Lancet. 1994;343:1255–1258.
121. Yoto Y, Kudoh T, Haseyama K, et al. Human parvovirus B19 infection in Kawasaki disease (Letter). Lancet. 1994;344:58–59.
122. Cohen BJ. Human parvovirus B19 infection in Kawasaki disease (Letter). Lancet. 1994;344:59.
123. Anderson LJ, Tsou C, Parker RA, et al. Detection of antibodies and antigens of human parvovirus B19 by enzyme-linked immunosorbent assay. J Clin Microbiol. 1986;24:522–526.
124. Erdman DD, Usher MJ, Tsou C, et al. Human parvovirus B19 specific IgG, IgA, and IgM antibodies and DNA in serum specimens from persons with erythema infectiosum. J Med Virol. 1991;35:110–115.
125. Kurtzman GJ, Cohen BJ, Field AM, et al. Immune response to B19 parvovirus and an antibody defect in persistent viral infection. J Clin Invest. 1989;84:1114–1123.
126. Rosenfeld SJ, Young NS, Alling D, et al. Subunit interaction in B19 parvovirus empty capsids. Arch Virol. 1994;136:9–18.
127. von Poblotzki A, Gerdes C, Reischl U, et al. Lymphoproliferative responses after infection with human parvovirus B19. J Virol. 1996;70:7327–7330.
128. Cohen BJ, Mortimer PP, Pereira MS. Diagnostic assays with monoclonal antibodies for the human serum parvovirus-like virus (SPLV). J Hyg (Lond). 1983;91:113–130.
129. Patou G, Pillay D, Myint S, et al. Characterization of a nested polymerase chain reaction assay for detection of parvovirus B19. J Clin Microbiol. 1993;31:540–546.
130. Musiani M, Zerbini M, Gentilomi G, et al. Parvovirus B19 clearance from peripheral blood after acute infection. J Infect Dis. 1995;172:1360–1363.
131. Cassinotti P, Burtonboy G, Fopp M, et al. Evidence for persistence of human parvovirus B19 DNA in bone marrow. J Med Virol. 1997;53:229–232.
132. Goldstein AR, Anderson MJ, Serjeant GR. Parvovirus associated aplastic crisis in homozygous sickle cell disease. Arch Dis Child. 1987;62:585–588.
133. Smith MA, Shah NR, Lobel JS, et al. Severe anemia caused by human parvovirus in a leukemia patient on maintenance chemotherapy. Clin Pediatr (Phila). 1988;27:383–386.
134. Fairley CK, Smoleniec JS, Caul OE, et al. Observational study of effect of intrauterine transfusions on outcome of fetal hydrops after parvovirus B19 infection. Lancet. 1995;346:1335–1337.
135. Garner JS. Guideline for isolation precautions in hospitals. The Hospital Infection Control Practices Advisory Committee. Infect Control Hosp Epidemiol. 1996;17:53–80.
136. Pillay D, Patou G, Hurt S, et al. Parvovirus B19 outbreak in a children's ward. Lancet. 1992;339:107–109.
137. Torok TJ, Pavia AT, Anderson LJ. Efficacy of immune globulin for prevention of human parvovirus B19 infection. (Abstract 8). Sixth Parvovirus Workshop, Montpellier, France, 1995; P6.
138. Bansal GP, Hatfield J, Dunn FE, et al. Immunogenicity studies of recombinant human parvovirus B19 proteins. In: Brown F, Chanock RM, Ginsberg HS, et al, eds. Vaccines92. Cold Spring Harbor, NY: Cold Spring Harbor Laboratory Press; 1992:315–319.

RNA VIRUSES

Reoviridae

Chapter 137

Orthoreoviruses and Orbiviruses

THEODORE F. TSAI

The family Reoviridae comprises viruses of plants, fish, insects, and other terrestrial animals in nine genera; among them, some orthoreoviruses, rotaviruses, orbiviruses, and coltiviruses infect humans.[1, 2] The rotaviruses (see Chapter 139) and Colorado tick fever virus (see Chapter 138), after which the last genus is named, are discussed separately; others are described here.

Virions are 60 to 80 nm in diameter and icosahedral but may appear spheric. The inner core, containing 10 to 12 segments of linear double-stranded RNA in equimolar proportions, is surrounded by two or more protein layers but no lipid envelope. Individual genomic segments encode RNA polymerase and other nonstructural proteins, and structural inner or outer capsid proteins that serve in cell attachment and, for some viruses, hemagglutination, and that define group and type-specific antigens. Antigenic relationships between viruses in different genera have not been observed.

ORTHOREOVIRUSES

Reoviruses 1 through 3 are ubiquitous and infect a broad range of mammals including humans, although their role in human disease has been considered unclear.[3] Infections are cosmopolitan and occur at an early age such that antibody prevalence rises from approximately 30% in the second year of life to over 80% by the age of 60 years.[4] Most infections probably are inapparent or result in mild respiratory or gastrointestinal symptoms. The viruses, which are stable over a broad pH range and in aerosols, often are recovered from sewage and environmental sources and presumably are transmitted to humans by fecal-oral and airborne routes. Because infections are so widespread, the causal connection between a clinical syndrome and infection has often been difficult to establish, as underscored by the virus's name, an acronym for *respiratory, enteric, orphan virus.*[3]

Mild respiratory illness with low-grade fever, malaise, rhinorrhea, and pharyngitis with mild diarrhea has been described in children in outbreaks and has been produced in experimental infections of adult volunteers.[3, 5–8] A maculopapular or vesicular exanthem frequently has accompanied illnesses in children, and in one case a measles-like illness with conjunctivitis, photophobia, lymphadenopathy, and a confluent morbilliform rash was reported.[7, 9–11] More serious cases of interstitial or confluent pneumonia and fatal systemic illness have been described.[10, 11]

Culture-proven neurologic infections have been reported in patients with aseptic meningitis and disseminated encephalomyelitis.[12, 13] Concurrent hepatitis and encephalitis also were reported in three cases.[10]

The role of reovirus type 3 in the etiology of biliary atresia has been suggested by a mouse model of the disease, but results of human studies have been mixed.[3, 14] Several serologic studies and examination of tissues of patients with extrahepatic biliary atresia or choledochal cysts for reoviral RNA have produced contradictory results.[15, 16] Other viruses—cytomegalovirus, Epstein-Barr virus, respiratory synctial virus, and rotavirus—have also been implicated in the etiology of congenital cholestatic liver disease. This disorder, and at least in the United States, has a seasonal clustering that suggests an environmental factor, which could be infectious.[14] A sporadic case of congenital biliary, anorectal, and esophageal atresia with an early switch of fetal to adult hemoglobin production has also been attributed to reovirus 3 infection.[17] The results of studies to date remain difficult to interpret, but a contributory role of reovirus infection under a two-hit hypothesis has been proposed.

ORBIVIRUSES

Virions of 80 nm comprise outer and inner capsid layers surrounding a core and genome of 10 RNA segments.[1, 18] Outer capsid VP2 and core surface VP7 proteins define type-specific and group-specific antigens, respectively. The fourth largest genomic segment of Kemerovo virus has been associated with mouse neurovirulence.[19] The more than 100 cataloged orbiviruses are principally vector-borne (transmitted by ticks, mosquitoes, midges, and gnats), and many are important diseases of livestock animals (e.g., bluetongue, epizootic hemorrhagic fever of deer, and African horse sickness viruses) in which hematopoietic infection may occur. Several cause severe congenital anomalies, such as aqueductal stenosis, hydrocephalus, and arthrogryposis in animals, and have been proposed for models of these human disorders. Seven orbiviruses have been implicated in human disease, one in the United States.

A trio of tick-borne orbiviruses transmitted in central Europe and Russia, and all members of the Kemerovo antigenic complex, have been implicated with varied strength of evidence in cases of neurologic infection.[20–22] Kemerovo virus was isolated from cerebrospinal fluid or implicated serologically in 12 encephalitis cases, in which Russian spring-summer encephalitis was excluded, in the Kemerovo region of Russia. For Lipovnik virus, serologic evidence of infection with that virus alone or with concurrent tick-borne encephalitis virus was shown in meningoencephalitis patients in the former Czechoslovakia. Serologic evidence of infection with Lipovnik or Tribec virus was also demonstrated in patients with polyradiculitis from the same geographic region. All three viruses have been isolated from *Ixodes* ticks that also transmit neurotropic infections due to tick-borne encephalitis and Lyme disease in overlapping areas of Europe, so their respective roles in the etiology of acute and subacute neurologic disease in these locations should be interpreted cautiously. Acute infection can be diagnosed serologically, preferably by demonstrating viral-specific IgM in cerebrospinal fluid.

In the southwestern United States, infection with a virus antigenically related to Kemerovo-group orbiviruses is suspected to cause an acute febrile illness with myalgia, vomiting, and abdominal pain, accompanied by leukopenia, thrombocytopenia, and anemia.[23] The observation comes from a study of Oklahoma and Texas patients with tick exposure in whom Rocky Mountain spotted fever was ruled out and who demonstrated antibody seroconversions to Lipovnik and Six Gun City (another orbivirus) viruses, suggesting infection with a related agent. No virus was recovered from acute blood specimens, and the relationship of the infection to clinical illness is undetermined. A Kemerovo-related orbivirus of rabbits and large animals has also been reported in the Midwest, but its pathogenic potential for humans is unknown.[24]

Two orbiviruses in Africa and one in South America have been associated with nonspecific febrile illnesses.[25–27] Orungo virus has been isolated in East, Central, and West Africa and has been implicated in sporadic cases and outbreaks of acute illness with myalgias and headache. However, infections, probably transmitted between humans by anopheline mosquitoes, are highly prevalent, and their role in these clinical illnesses is unclear. Lebombo virus was isolated from blood of a Nigerian child and also from mosquitoes and rodents, and Changuinola virus was isolated from a mosquito catcher in Panama.

REFERENCES

1. Virus taxonomy, classification and nomenclature of viruses. Sixth report of the International Committee on Taxonomy of Viruses. Arch Virol. 1995;S10.
2. Reoviridae I and II. Curr Top Microbiol Immunol. 1998; 233.
3. Cherry JD. Reoviruses. In: Feigin RD, Cherry JD. Textbook of Pediatric Infectious Diseases, 4th ed. Philadelphia: WB Saunders; 1998:1893–1897.
4. Selb B, Weber B. A study of human reovirus IgG and IgA antibodies by ELISA and Western blot. J Virol Methods. 1994;47:15–26.
5. Hilleman MR, Hamparian VV, Ketler A, et al. Acute respiratory illnesses among children and adults. JAMA. 1962;180:445–453.
6. Rosen L, Hovis JF, Mastrota FM, et al. An outbreak of infection with a type 1 reovirus among children in an instritution. Am J Hyg. 1960;71:266–274.
7. Lerner AM, Cherry JD, Klein JO, et al. Infections with reoviruses. N Engl J Med. 1962;267:947–952.
8. Rosen L, Evans HE, Spickard A. Reovirus infections in human volunteers. Am J Hyg. 1963;77:29–37.
9. El-Rai FM, Evans AS. Reovirus infections in children and young adults. Arch Environ Health. 1963;7:700–704.
10. Joske RA, Keall DD, Leak PJ, et al. Hepatitis-encephalitis in humans with reovirus infection. Arch Intern Med. 1964;113:811–816.
11. Tillotson JR, Lerner AM. Reovirus type 3 associated with fatal pneumonia. N Engl J Med. 1967;276:1060–1063.
12. Hugo Johansson PJ, Sveger T, Ahlfors K, et al. Reovirus type 1 associated with meningitis. Scand J Infect Dis. 1996;28:117–120.
13. Krainer L, Aronson BE. Disseminated encephalomyelitis in humans with recovery of hepatoencephalitis virus (HEV). J Neuropathol Exp Neurol. 1969;18:339–342.
14. Yoon PW, Bresee JS, Olney RS, et al. Epidemiology of biliary atresia: A population-based study. Pediatrics. 1997;99:376–382.
15. Tyler KL, Sokol RJ, Oberhaus SM, et al. Detection of reovirus RNA in hepatobiliary tissues from patients with extrahepatic biliary atresia and choledochal cysts. Hepatology. 1998;27:1475–1482.
16. Steele MI, Marshall CM, Lloyd RE, Randoph VE. Reovirus 3 not detected by reverse transcriptase–mediated polymerase chain reaction analysis of preserved tissue from infants with cholestatic liver disease. Hepatology 1995;21:697–702.
17. Dessanti A, Massarelli G, Piga MT, et al. Biliary, anorectal and esophageal atresia: A new entity? Tohoku J Exp Med. 1997;181:49–55.
18. Gould AR, Hyatt AD. The orbivirus genus. Diversity, structure, replication and phylogenetic relationships. Comp Immunol Microbiol Infect Dis. 1994;17:163–188.
19. Nuttall PA, Jacobs SC, Jones LD, et al. Enhanced neurovirulence of tick-borne orbiviruses resulting from genetic modulation. Virology. 1992;187:407–412.
20. Chumakov MP, Karpovich LG, Sarmanova ES, et al. Report on the isolation from *Ixodes persulcatus* ticks and from patients in western Siberia of a virus differing from the agent of tick-borne encephalitis. Acta Virol. 1963;7:82–83.
21. Libikova H, Heinz F, Ujhazyova D, Stunzner D. Orbiviruses of the Kemerovo complex and neurological disease. Med Microbiol Immunol. 1978;116:255–263.
22. Malkova D, Holubova J, Kolman JM, et al. Antibodies against some arboviruses in persons with various neuropathies. Acta Virol. 1980;24:298.
23. Tsai TF. Arboviral infections in the United States. Infect Dis Clin North Am. 1991;5:73–102.
24. Theil KW. McCloskey CM, Scott DP. Serologic evidence for rabbit syncytium virus in eastern cottontail rabbits (*Sylvilagus floridanus*) in Ohio. J Wildlife Dis. 1993:29:470–474.
25. Tomori O, Fabiyi A. Orungo virus: A new agent from mosquitoes and man in Uganda and Nigeria. Nigerian Med J. 1966;7:5–8.
26. Familusi JB. Moore DL, Fomufod AK, Causey OR. Vurs isolates from children with febrile convulsions in Nigeria. A correlation study of clinical and laboratory observations. Clin Pediatr. 1972;11:272–276.
27. Karabatsos N, ed. Internation Catalogue of Arboviruses 1985, Including Certain Other Viruses of Vertebrates. 3rd ed. San Antonio, Texas: American Society of Tropical Medicine and Hygiene; 1987:198.

Chapter 138

Coltiviruses (Colorado Tick Fever)

THEODORE F. TSAI

GENERAL

Coltiviruses are morphologically and structurally similar to the orbiviruses (Chapter 137) but contain 12 RNA segments. The seven viruses all appear to be tick- or mosquito-borne. Colorado tick fever (CTF), the type species; Salmon River virus, isolated from a patient with a CTF-like illness in Idaho; Eyach virus, isolated in Germany and France; and isolate S6-14-03, recovered from a hare in California, are antigenically related and are either proved or suspected to cause human disease (see next section).[1, 2] Three other antigenically distinct coltiviruses, Banna, Beijing, and Gansu viruses, isolated in China, have been implicated in neurologic infection.[3–5]

Banna virus, a tick-associated orbivirus, was first isolated from cerebrospinal fluid of two encephalitis patients and from serum of 25 patients with nonspecific febrile illness in Yunnan province in southern China and subsequently from 8 febrile illness patients in Xinjiang province, in the the far western part of China.[3, 4] Beijing virus, which is antigenically distinct and exhibits a different RNA electrophoretic pattern, was isolated in 1991 from serum or cerebrospinal fluid, or both, of 33 viral encephalitis patients hospitalized at the Beijing Childrens Hospital and subsequently from mosquitoes captured near the city.[5] Another antigenically and electrophoretically distinct coltivirus, isolated from *Culex tritaeniorhychus* mosquitoes in Gansu province, has been linked serologically to encephalitis cases occurring in Henan and Jiangsu provinces. However, a small serosurvey suggested a high level of endemic transmission, and the role of the infection in these cases is uncertain. Neutralization and enzyme-linked immunosorbent assays have been employed in antigenic characterization of the isolates and in serologic studies. A coltivirus, antigenically similar to a strain previously recovered from mosquitoes in Indonesia, was also isolated from an encephalitis patient in the 1997 EV71 outbreak in Malaysia, but its role in the patient's illness still is unclear.[6] In conclusion, several distinct vector-borne coltiviruses appear to cause neurologic infection in Asia, but clinical features of the infections, their epidemiology, and their transmission patterns are undefined.

COLORADO TICK FEVER

CTF is an acute self-limited febrile illness with the unusual feature that marrow erythrocytic precursors are infected, leading to prolonged viremia lasting the life span of infected red cells. The virus is transmitted in the western United States and Canada by the wood tick, *Dermacentor andersoni*, which is distributed in mountainous terrain from 4000- to 10,000-foot elevations.[7] This area also corresponds to the virus's distribution, principally in the U.S. and Canadian Rocky Mountains, Wasatch and Sierra Nevada Ranges, and Black Hills, and nearly all patients give a history of exposure to these locations, usually while hiking, fishing, or camping (Fig. 138–1). Patients presenting with the illness in other states have been diagnosed by astute clinicians who have elicited a travel and tick exposure history. In addition, several cases have occurred in persons who did not travel to an enzootic location but were infected by ticks carried on clothing, on equipment, or in the automobile of a returned household member–traveler. One transfusion-acquired case has also been reported.[8] Transmission is seasonal, from March to September, with the peak period of risk in Colorado occurring between April and June.[9]

The virus is transmitted transtadially (between stages) in the tick, from its larval, nymphal, and adult forms, and horizontally, between the infected ticks and their mammalian hosts—rodents and other small mammals in the case of the immature forms, and larger mammals, including deer and humans, in the case of the adult.[7] The virus is not transmitted transovarially in the tick, however. Most human infections are acquired from adult ticks. South-facing dry and rock-covered slopes, supporting open stands of ponderosa pine and juniper and sagebrush underbrush, favor the viral transmission cycle by providing sufficient humidity for the tick, and cover and burrows for ground squirrels, chipmunks, marmots, and other small mammals that are the principal tick and viral-amplifying hosts.[10]

Sporadic cases of serologically diagnosed CTF have been reported from areas of California outside the range of *D. andersoni* (e.g., Contra Costa county). *Dermacentor variabilis* is suspected to be the vector, and a CTF-related virus (S1-14-03) isolated from a ground squirrel and hare in California may be the etiologic agent in these cases.[2] A second antigenically distinct virus, recovered from blood of a patient who acquired a CTF-like illness while rafting on the middle fork of the Salmon River, Idaho, appears to be responsible for the majority of CTF cases in Montana and Idaho (T. F. Tsai and N. Karabatsos, unpublished observations). Successive infections with this or another unrecognized related coltivirus could account for sporadic cases of repeated CTF-like illnesses. In Europe, yet another antigenically related virus, Eyach virus, isolated from *Ixodes ricinus* and *Ixodes ventalloi* ticks in Germany and France, has been implicated in cases of neurologic illness in the former Czechoslovakia.[1]

A discrete history of tick bite or exposure in 90% of cases has allowed estimation of a mean incubation period of 3 to 4 days (range zero to 14 days).[9] The onset usually is abrupt with fever, chills, intense headache, severe generalized myalgias, and hyperesthetic skin, leading to profound weakness and prostration.[9, 11, 12] Nausea, vomiting, and abdominal symptoms are not prominent, and compared with other febrile illnesses occurring in the same season, upper respiratory symptoms are significantly less common. Patients usually confine themselves to bed and appear weak and indifferent; in previous years, as many as 14% of patients were hospitalized. There are

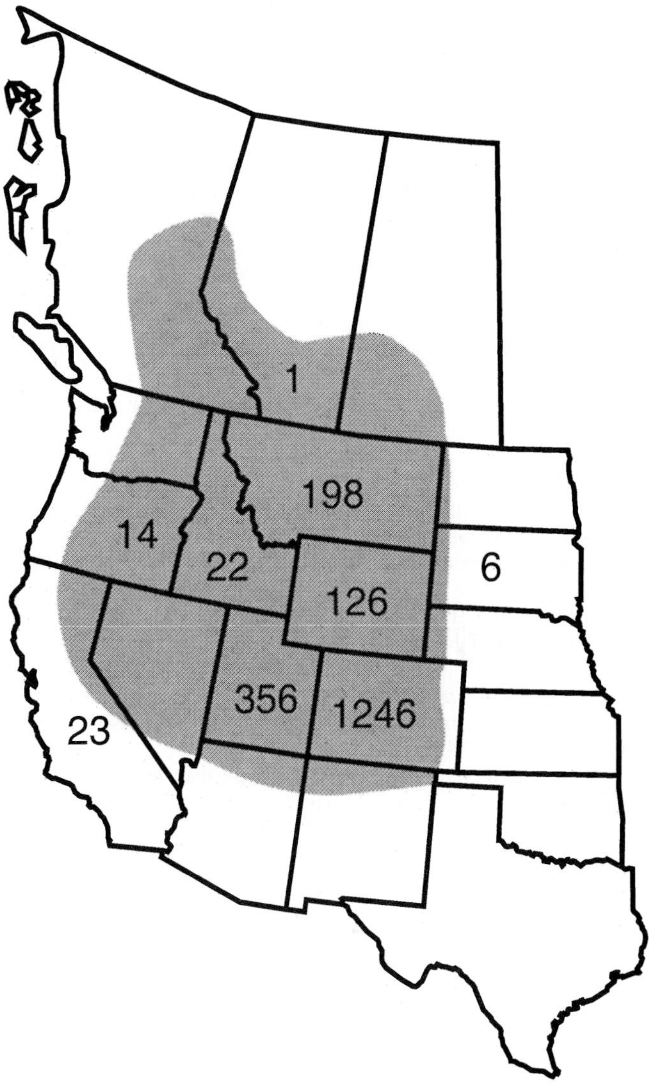

FIGURE 138–1. Geographic distribution of *Dermacentor andersoni* (wood ticks) and reported cases of Colorado tick fever, 1990–1996, United States and Canada.

few specific physical findings: the conjunctivae may be injected, and examination of the oral cavity may disclose an erythematous pharynx and palatal enanthem; lymphadenopathy and a slightly enlarged tender spleen may be present. A maculopapular or petechial rash may be seen in 15% of patients, and this can suggest Rocky Mountain spotted fever.

Acute symptoms generally resolve within a week, but their remission is followed in half of the cases by recurrent symptoms 2 to 3 days later, giving rise to a diphasic or saddleback fever curve. A third recrudescence rarely may occur. Although the acute toxic phase of the illness may be brief, extreme weakness, lassitude, and asthenia persist for weeks and even months. The duration of convalescence is age-dependent, with continued fatigue after 3 weeks in 70% of patients older then 30 years and full recovery in 1 week or less in patients younger than 20 years.[9]

In children, illness is complicated by aseptic meningitis or encephalitis in 5 to 10% of cases, and fatal cases with generalized hemorrhage and shock rarely have been reported.[11–13] However, the unrecognized contribution of dual *Rickettsia rickettsie* infection could not be discounted in some cases. Epididymoorchitis, pneumonia, hepatitis, and myocarditis also have been reported to complicate cases in adults.[14, 15] The possibility of vertically transmitted fetal infection has been suggested by cases of spontaneous abortion, occurring 2 weeks after infection in a pregnant woman, and of perinatal illness with leukopenia in a 3-day-old infant whose mother had developed CTF 6 days before delivery.

Leukopenia is characteristic, reaching a mean nadir count of 3900/mm^3 5 to 6 days after the onset of illness, often with the initial remission of symptoms.[16] The decline reflects an absolute decline in circulating neutrophils, often accompanied by a left shift, atypical lymphocytes, and a relative lymphocytosis. A moderate decrease in the platelet count also is usual. Examination of the bone marrow reveals a maturational arrest of granulocytic cells with a reduction in mature cells and increased numbers of metamyelocytes and myelocytes, and also a reduction in megakaryocytes. The virus infects eythroblasts and primitive CD34$^+$ stem cells, but although cells remain infected as they pass through their maturational stages and are released into the peripheral circulation, persistent infection in marrow cells has not been demonstrated.[17] The duration of viremia parallels the survival of infected red cells and persists for 4 weeks after the onset of illness in approximately one half of the cases.

The virus can be recovered easily from the peripheral blood or from stored refrigerated clots, up to 6 weeks after the onset, in Vero or BHK-21 cells or in suckling mice; but a laboratory diagnosis is accessible by identifying infected red cells in a peripheral smear by indirect immunofluorescence.[18] Viral genomic products in acute blood have been identified by polymerase chain reaction, but serologic diagnosis by IgM-capture enzyme-linked immunosorbent assay, neutralization, or complement fixation is the usual method of laboratory confirmation.[19, 20]

No specific therapy is available, although the sensitivity of most coltiviruses and orbiviruses to ribavirin suggests the potential utility of that drug. Bed rest, fluids, and antipyretics—avoiding aspirin, which could exacerbate the hemorrhagic diathesis associated with thrombocytopenia—are recommended as symptomatic therapy. Patients should not donate blood until at least 6 months after recovery.

Tick-avoidance measures may be effective in preventing the disease. Walking over open spaces, avoiding grassy, vegetated areas; wearing long pants with overlapping socks, preferably of a light color to facilitate the discovery of adherent ticks; conducting periodic tick checks; spraying clothing and gear with permethrin (a repellent and acaricide); and applying diethyltoluamide-containing repellent on uncovered skin are recommended to reduce tick exposure and bites. A secular decline in CTF cases in Colorado in the last 2 decades at the same time that populations and park visitations have increased, has suggested that increased public awareness of tick-avoidance measures may have had some effect on reducing the incidence of the disease.

REFERENCES

1. Chastel C, Main AJ, Couatarmanac HA, et al. Isolation of Eyach virus (Reoviridae, Colorado tick fever group) from *Ixodes ricinus* and *Ixodes ventalloi* ticks in France. Arch Virol. 1984;82:161–167.
2. Lane RS, Emmons RW, Devlin V, et al. Survey for evidence of Colorado tick fever virus outside of the known endemic area in California. Am J Trop Med Hyg. 1982;31:837–843.
3. Chen BQ, Tao SJ. Arbovirus survey in China in recent ten years. Chin Med J. (Engl). 1996;109:13–15.
4. Li QP. First isolation of 8 strains of new orbivirus (Banna) from patients with innominate fever in Xinjiang. Endemic Dis Bull. 1992;7:77–81.
5. Zhao ZJ, Huang YJ, Zhou YT, et al. Isolation and identification of a kind of new virus from patients with viral encephalitis in Beijing. Chin J Virol. 1994;8:297–299.
6. Brown SE. Gorman BM, Tesh RB, Knudson DL. Coltiviruses isolated from mosquitoes collected in Indonesia. Virology. 1993;196:363–367.
7. Burgdorfer W. Tick-borne disease in the United States: Rocky Mountain spotted fever and Colorado tick fever. Acta Trop. 1977;34:103–126.
8. Centers for Disease Control. Transmission of Colorado tick fever virus by blood transfusion—Montana. MMWR. 1975;24:422–427.
9. Goodpasture HC, Poland JD, Francy DB, et al. Colorado tick fever: Clinical epidemiologic and laboratory aspects of 228 cases in Colorado in 1973–74. Ann Intern Med. 1973;131:288–293.
10. McLean RG, Shriner RB, Polorny KS, et al. The ecology of Colorado tick fever in Rocky Mountain National Park in 1974. III. Habitats supporting the virus. Am J Trop Med Hyg. 1989;40:86.
11. Spruance SL, Bailey A. Colorado tick fever. Arch Intern Med. 1973;131:288–293.
12. Silver HK, Meiklejohn G, Kempe CH. Colorado tick fever. Am J Dis Child. 1961;101:56–62.
13. Fraser CH, Schiff DW. Colorado tick fever encephalitis. Pediatrics. 1962;29:187–190.
14. Loge RV. Acute hepatitis associated with Colorado tick fever. West J Med. 1985;142:91.
15. Emmons RW, Schade HI. Colorado tick fever simulating acute myocardial infraction. JAMA. 1972;222:87–88.
16. Anderson Rd, Entringe MA, Roginson WA. Virus-induced leukopenia: Colorado tick fever as a human model. J Infect Dis. 1985;151:449.
17. Phillip CS, Callaway C, Chu MC, et al. Replication of Colorado tick fever virus within human hematopoietic progenitor cells. J Virol. 1993;67:2389–2395.
18. Emmons RW, Lennette EH. Immunofluorescent staining in the laboratory diagnosis of Colorado tick fever. J Lab Clin Med. 1966;68:923–929.
19. Calishser CH, Poland JD, Calisher SB, et al. Diagnosis of Colorado tick fever by enzune immunoassays for immunoglobulin M and G antibodies. J Clin Microbiol. 1985;2:84.
20. Johnson AJ, Karabatsos N, Lanciotti RS. Detection of Colorado tick fever virus by using reverse transcriptase PCR and application of the technique in laboratory diagnosis. J Clin Microbiol. 1997;35:1203–1208.

Chapter 139

Rotavirus

PAUL A. OFFIT
H. FRED CLARK

Viral gastroenteritis is an important cause of disease and death worldwide. Each year in Asia, Africa, and Latin America, an estimated 3 to 5 billion cases of gastroenteritis account for 5 to 10 million deaths.[1] A number of viruses, including caliciviruses, adenoviruses, Norwalk and Norwalk-like viruses astroviruses, and nonclassified small round viruses (see Chapters 163 and 164), are associated with disease. However, since their identification as a human pathogen in 1973, rotaviruses have been found to be the most important cause of gastroenteritis in infants and young children in both developed and developing countries.[2–4] In developing countries, rotaviruses account for 10 to 20% of gastroenteritis-associated deaths.[1, 5] Each year in the United States, rotavirus infections account for 3.5 million cases of diarrhea, 500,000 physician visits, 50,000 hospitalizations, and 20 deaths among children younger than 5 years of age.[6–8] Virtually all children in both developed and developing countries are infected with rotaviruses by 2 to 3 years of age.[9, 10]

The devastating impact of this disease has created interest in disease prevention by immunization. A candidate rotavirus vaccine was submitted to the U.S. Food and Drug Administration for licensure in January 1997 and was approved and recommended for use in all children in August 1998.

DESCRIPTION OF VIRUS

Rotavirus is a genus within the family Reoviridae.[11] By electron microscopy, the viruses are seen to be about 70 nm in size and look like wheels (*rota* is derived from the Latin word for "wheel") with short spokes radiating from a wide central hub (Fig. 139–1). The viral genome consists of 11 separate segments of double-stranded RNA ranging in molecular weight from 2×10^5 to 2.2×10^6 Da. Coinfection of cells in vitro with two different rotavirus strains may result in progeny virions that contain RNA gene segments from each of the parent strains (reassortants). For the most part, each gene segment codes for a single rotavirus protein. Rotaviruses are nonenveloped and consist of an outer capsid and a core. Two proteins

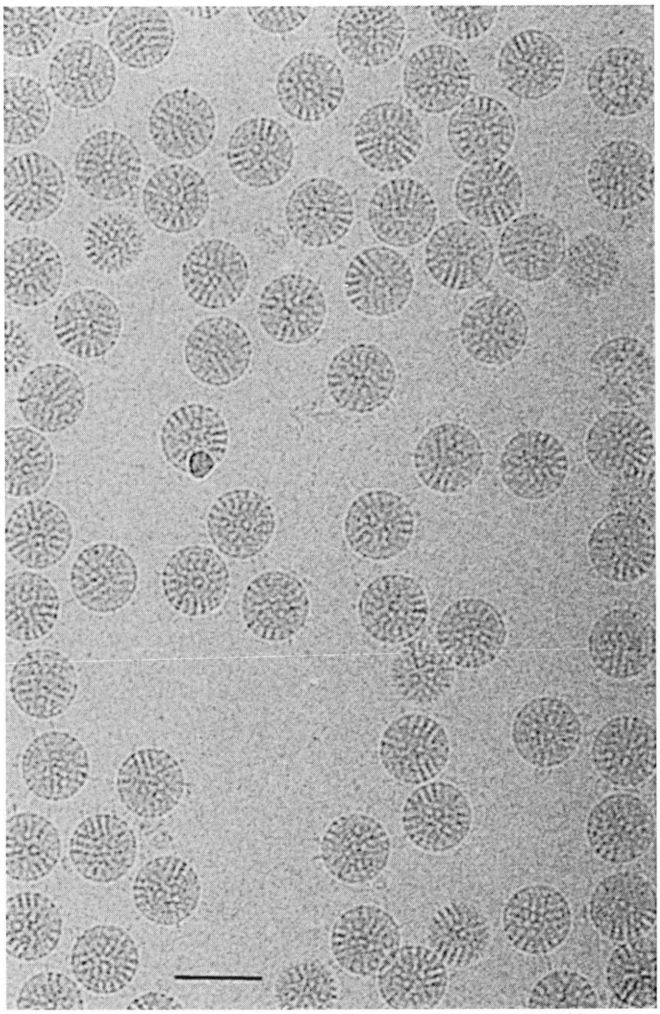

FIGURE 139–1. Electron micrograph of rotavirus particles embedded in vitreous ice (bar = 10,000 Å). (Courtesy of Dr. B. V. V. Prasad, Baylor College of Medicine, Houston, Tex.)

(viral protein 4 [vp4] and vp7) make up the rotavirus outer capsid. Vp4 is an 88-kD protein that is the virus hemagglutinin and probable cell attachment protein. Vp4 projects as a spike from the virus surface and makes up approximately 2.5% of the viral mass. Cleavage of vp4 by trypsin into two smaller proteins is associated with virus entry into cells. Vp7 is a 37-kD glycoprotein that makes up the smooth outer capsid and represents approximately 30% of the viral mass. Four proteins (vp1, vp2, vp3, and vp6) make up the virus core, with vp6 accounting for 50% of the viral mass and 80% of the viral core. Six nonstructural proteins (NS53, NS34, NS35, NS28, NS26, and NS12) are also produced during rotavirus infection.

There are three rotavirus groups (A, B, and C) that cause disease in humans. These groups are distinguished by antigenic differences on the virus core and differences in migration of RNA gene segments.[12] Although both group B and group C rotaviruses can cause disease in young children and adults,[13–15] virtually all rotavirus outbreaks in developed and developing countries are caused by group A rotaviruses.

In animals inoculated with reassortant rotaviruses, both vp4 and vp7 independently evoke antibodies that neutralize virus infectivity in vitro (i.e., determine serotype).[16, 17] Therefore, in a manner analogous to the influenza virus hemagglutinin and neuraminidase, categorization of rotavirus serotypes includes a description of both the vp4 (protease-sensitive protein [P]) and the vp7 (glycoprotein [G]) type. At least nine G types have been isolated from humans. G types 1 through 4 are most commonly isolated, whereas G types 5, 6, 8, 9, 10, and 12 are far less common.[12, 18–20] Distinction of rotavirus P types is based on gene sequence differences or differential recognition of strains by polyclonal or monoclonal antibody preparations.[12, 21–24] There are at least six different human rotavirus P types. P type 1a, the most common, is usually associated with G types 1, 3, or 4: P type 1b is usually associated with G type 2.

Rotaviruses are relatively resistant to commonly used hard-surface disinfectants and hygienic hand-washing agents but are susceptible to inactivation by compounds containing chlorine or chlorine dioxide.[25, 26] Rotaviruses are inactivated by levels of acid normally found in the human stomach (i.e., pH 2.0) independent of the presence of pepsin.[27–29] The capacity of rotaviruses to survive for long periods on hard surfaces, in potable and recreational waters, on human hands, and at pH values between 3.0 and 10.0 is consistent with the high nosocomial infection rate observed in hospitals.[25, 30]

PATHOGENESIS

Rotaviruses replicate in mature villous epithelial cells that line the small intestine.[2, 31] Rotavirus outer capsid protein vp4 (cleaved in the presence of trypsin) attaches to glycolipids on the host cell surface[32, 33] and enters the cytoplasm by direct plasma membrane penetration.[34–36] The mechanism by which rotaviruses induce diarrhea is not completely understood, but it is in part mediated by the relative loss of absorptive villus tip epithelial cells in relation to secretory crypt epithelial cells. In addition, there is a loss of intestinal permeability to macromolecules (including lactose) associated with decreased levels of intestinal disaccharidases.[37–39] Rotavirus-induced lactase deficiency may last 10 to 14 days.[38]

One of the rotavirus nonstructural proteins, NSP4 (NS26), has been found to act as an enterotoxin. Suckling mice exposed to purified NSP4 (NS26) developed diarrhea. Diarrhea was possibly mediated by excess chloride secretion by a calcium-dependent signalling pathway.[40]

EPIDEMIOLOGY

As determined by surveys of antibody prevalence in children's sera throughout the world, almost all children are infected with rotavirus within the first 3 years of life.[9, 10] Unlike the experience with bacterial enteropathogens (e.g., enterotoxigenic *Escherichia coli*), there is little evidence that risk of exposure to rotavirus is less in developed than in developing nations. Although infection is ubiquitous in both situations, rotavirus disease is relatively much more common in hygienically advanced locales, where it is often the most common cause of infant diarrhea.

The basic questions of epidemiology of rotavirus disease—the explanations for the age of susceptibility, seasonality of disease, and interepidemic reservoirs—remain largely unresolved. The maximum incidence of rotavirus gastroenteritis is commonly between 6 and 24 months of age.[41] However, clinical disease, sometimes severe, can occur at younger ages. Also, as much as 25% of disease leading to hospitalization occurs in children older than 2 years of age. The onset of maximum susceptibility is probably correlated with the decline of maternally acquired immune factors. Serum immunoglobulin G (IgG) of maternal origin tends to disappear at about 5 months of age.[9] However, there is no clear correlation between decline of maternally acquired milk or serum antibodies and onset of susceptibility. Despite numerous studies, it has *not* been clearly demonstrated that breast-feeding significantly affects the incidence or severity of rotavirus disease.[42–44] A possible role for maturational changes in gut epithelium in mediating the age of susceptibility has been suggested but not demonstrated.

Although severe rotavirus disease occasionally occurs in newborns, young infants (<2 months old) are relatively resistant to rotavirus disease and to active immunization with rotavirus vaccines.[45] A high incidence of rotavirus fecal shedding unaccompanied by disease was first identified in a newborn nursery in Melbourne.[46] In this situation it was determined that a single strain, identified by electropherotype, circulated in the nursery year after year and was unrelated to various community strains[46] and that infants infected in nurseries experienced less severe disease when subsequently infected with rotavirus at a later age.[47] Nurseries with endemic rotavirus infection were later identified in Europe and in South America,[48, 49] but not in the United States.

Investigators determined that nursery rotavirus isolates from several continents shared similar gene 4 base sequences.[49] A "nursery" genotype has been defined by these data, although the P protein phenotype (P type 2)[51] is difficult to distinguish with polyclonal reference antisera. The "nursery" P type may be associated with G serotypes 1, 2, 3, or 4. Although the "nursery" P type was thought to be invariably associated with attenuation, it is now apparent that P type 2 rotaviruses can be associated with severe gastroenteritis.[52]

Susceptibility to rotavirus infection and disease continues throughout life. The most severe disease appears to be associated with the infant's initial infection, and the highest proportion of rotavirus disease occurs in the first two rotavirus seasons (in temperate climates). Some studies have found high proportions of infant infections to be asymptomatic,[53, 54] but others have generally found attack rates of 20 to 30% in each of the first two rotavirus seasons, for a cumulative disease prevalence of at least 50%.[55–58]

Early reports of rotavirus disease outbreaks in institutionalized populations of elderly persons[59] have not been followed by substantial evidence that rotavirus is a major geriatric problem. Rotavirus has occasionally been reported as a cause of disease in military populations[60] and in hospital workers[61] and as a cause of travellers' diarrhea.[62] By far the most common setting for adult disease is that associated with parenting of infected infants. Approximately 50% of parents experience rotavirus infection at the time of infant rotavirus disease; one third of these adult infections are symptomatic.[41]

The mode of transmission of rotavirus infection is assumed to be primarily fecal-oral, although respiratory transmission has also been postulated. Clearly, infected infants shed virus in feces in high concentration at the onset of disease and for 4 to 7 days afterward; the handling of infants in diapers and the casual hygienic habits of toddlers allow for easy dissemination of virus. Nevertheless, rotavirus generally is not, except in daycare situations,[63] associated with common-source outbreaks of gastroenteritis. Rather, in temperate climates, rotavirus disease acts as a seasonal pandemic of repeatable onset and duration. In 8 of 10 consecutive years of observation in Philadelphia, the "rotavirus season" began in mid-January (Clark HF, unpublished data).

In North America, seasonal urban epidemics begin in the south (late summer in Mexico City), progressing later to the north and east, and culminating in epidemics beginning in late winter in the Maritime Provinces of Canada.[6, 64] These regional outbreaks typically last 4 or 5 months and are followed by a summer respite, characterized by virtually no rotavirus disease. The reason for this seasonality is unknown. In the tropics such patterns are not observed: disease incidence may occur in several seasonal peaks or throughout the year.

The reservoir for persistence of rotavirus between the annual winter epidemics is also unknown. It is possible that healthy adults or partially immune children shed virus chronically in low titer. This has been determined to be the case for cattle and swine.[65, 66] Public water supplies are another possible reservoir of infection.[67, 68] Because adult volunteer studies have indicated that the human infectious dose may be less than 1 plaque-forming unit (pfu),[69] a waterborne reservoir of rotavirus infection might be efficient even if virus were present in low concentration.

The role of serotype in epidemiology is unclear. Rotavirus G types 1 through 4 predominate worldwide, with G type 1 occurring most commonly. The reasons for the continued dominance of serotype 1 in most populations are unknown. Occasional infections with rotavirus G types 5, 6, 8, 9, and 10 are of unknown significance. There is no evidence that severity of rotavirus disease is associated with serotype.[70, 71] The description of human G type 3 isolates with similarities to rotavirus of animal origin suggests that interspecies infections occasionally occur.[72–74]

Seroprevalence studies indicate that most children acquire antibody to G types 1 through 4, but it is unclear whether all are infected with these serotypes or whether antibody profiles represent a progressive broadening of the immune response to repeated infections with one or a few serotypes.[75]

In a given year in a community, the seasonal outbreak usually consists of only one or two serotypes and a limited number of different "strains" as defined by electropherotype. From year to year in a community, a given serotype may persist but the "strains" appear to be constantly shifting, with a given electropherotype rarely persisting for longer than a season or two.

CLINICAL MANIFESTATIONS

Infants and young children most commonly have fever, vomiting, diarrhea, and occasionally dehydration. In children admitted to the hospital with moderate to severe dehydration, fever and vomiting most commonly persist for 2 to 3 days and diarrhea for 4 to 5 days; dehydration is usually isotonic.[76–79] Children admitted with rotavirus-induced diarrhea are more likely to have associated vomiting, severe dehydration, and a prolonged hospital stay, compared with those with infectious diarrhea induced by other agents.[78, 79] Diarrhea is watery without blood or mucus; leukocytes may be detected in the feces of a small percentage of patients.[79] Although coryza and cough often precede gastrointestinal symptoms, there is no evidence that replication of rotaviruses in the upper respiratory tract is important in the spread of infectious virus.[76, 77, 79]

Rotavirus infections have been associated with aseptic meningitis,[80, 81] necrotizing enterocolitis,[82, 83] acute myositis,[84] hepatic abscess,[85] pneumonia,[86] Kawasaki disease,[87] sudden infant death syndrome,[88] and Crohn's disease.[89] However, it is not surprising that a virus that affects virtually every child by 3 years of age is associated with many diseases found in this age group. There remains no clear evidence that rotavirus replication is supported by cells other than those that line the small intestine or that viremia is an important component in the pathogenesis of rotavirus-induced disease.

Children with immunodeficiency syndromes may develop rotavirus-induced gastroenteritis lasting many weeks or months.[90–92] Rota-viruses shed from immunodeficient hosts often have abnormal migration patterns of double-stranded RNA gene segments.[93, 94] The relation between these unusual viruses and persistent disease in immunodeficient hosts remains unclear.

IMMUNE RESPONSE

The humoral immune response of infants and young children to rotavirus infection is well characterized.[95–98] Within the first week of illness, rotavirus-specific IgM is detected in the duodenal fluid and serum. At 1 and 4 months after infection, rotavirus-specific IgG and IgA are detected in the duodenal fluid and rotavirus-specific IgG and monomeric IgA in the serum. One year after infection, rotavirus-specific IgG but not IgA is detected in the serum, and neither is detected at the mucosal surface. Because of its persistence in serum after natural infection, circulating rotavirus-specific IgG provides an excellent marker for previous exposure to rotavirus in older infants and children. In addition, fecal or duodenal IgA provides an excellent marker for recent infection (either primary infection or reinfection) because of the relatively rapid disappearance of this isotype from the intestinal mucosal surface.[99] The P and G type specificities of the humoral immune response after natural infection remain unclear.

Neonates infected within the first 2 weeks of life are protected against relatively severe disease but not against reinfection.[47] In addition, whereas symptomatic reinfection 1 year after primary infection (even with the same serotype) is commonly described,[47–69, 100–110] symptomatic reinfection within 4 months is unusual. Therefore, protection against reinfection by natural infection may be short-lived and incomplete. Protection against rotavirus disease is probably best predicted by the immunologic response occurring at the intestinal mucosal surface. High levels of fecal, rotavirus-specific IgA correlate with protection against disease.[111, 112] Although some studies have reported that the quantity of serotype-specific neutralizing antibodies directed against the challenge virus in serum is directly correlated with protection against disease,[102] this has not been a consistent finding.[113]

DIAGNOSIS

Rotavirus was not known to infect humans until 1973,[2] even though it causes a ubiquitous infection characterized by many days of shedding of virus in high concentration in feces and it was well known as a major etiologic agent of diarrhea in cattle as early as 1969.[114] Undoubtedly, identification of rotavirus was "missed" because so many cytopathic enteroviruses were readily isolated from feces that there was little incentive to look for enteric viruses by means other than virus isolation in cell culture. In addition, rotaviruses of human origin proved to be much more difficult to propagate in cell culture than rotavirus strains of bovine, porcine, or simian origin.

Although rotavirus is by far the most common cause of severe dehydrating winter diarrhea of infants in the developed world, there is no pathognomonic symptomatology. Diagnosis requires identification of the etiologic agent. Despite anecdotal reports of rotavirus in respiratory secretions, routine diagnosis is universally based on identification of rotavirus in feces or suspensions of rectal swabs.

The original "gold standard" test of electron microscopy to visualize rotavirus particles has been almost completely replaced by an enzyme-linked immunosorbent assay (ELISA) test for rotavirus-specific antigen. A number of reliable ELISA test kits are marketed commercially. The kits are based on capture antibodies (either polyclonal or monoclonal antibody preparations) that are primarily directed against the core protein vp6 (antigenically conserved among group A rotavirus strains). The sensitivity of ELISA tests is equal to that of electron microscopy.[115–117] However, false-positive reactions (especially during summer months) have been reported.[118]

For rapid diagnosis, a number of latex agglutination kits have been produced. These tests may be completed in a few minutes with no special equipment. They have a high degree of specificity but somewhat less sensitivity than alternative methods.[119, 120]

In laboratories equipped to routinely perform gel electrophoresis, the application of polyacrylamide gel electrophoresis with silver stain (PAGE-SS) to diagnose rotavirus infection offers attractive advantages. By this technique, rotavirus-containing specimens analyzed on polyacrylamide gels reveal the characteristic rotavirus pattern of 11 segments of double-stranded RNA. In different laboratories, PAGE-SS analysis was found to be as sensitive or slightly less sensitive than ELISA for diagnosis. The PAGE-SS sensitivity may be enhanced by phenol-chloroform extraction of the diagnostic specimen.[121, 122]

PAGE-SS diagnosis has the great advantage that there are no false-positives. Furthermore, the identification of specific double-stranded RNA gel patterns (electropherotypes) is of special utility in identifying strain-identical infections; this may be invaluable in tracing nosocomial transmission of rotavirus infection. PAGE-SS is also the only routinely available diagnostic test that can differentiate non–group A from group A rotaviruses.[123]

Determination of serotype is not normally of clinical importance in the diagnosis of rotavirus disease, because no virulence correlates of serotype have been consistently identified. However, serotype determination may be of great interest in epidemiologic studies and in investigations of the efficacy of vaccines or other prophylactic or therapeutic interventions. Serotyping of rotavirus directly from fecal specimens by ELISA with monoclonal antibodies to the four major G types is now possible with a commercially available kit. However, the identification of monoclonal antibodies with strict specificity for the major human P types has been difficult, and such reagents are not now commercially available.

The polymerase chain reaction technique presently exhibits the most promise for simply and accurately identifying the major prevalent types of rotavirus G and P antigens.[21, 123–125]

TREATMENT

The cornerstone of therapy for rotavirus-induced diarrhea is replacement of fluids and electrolytes lost during infection. Fluid replacement therapy using a solution provided by the World Health Organization and the United Nations International Children's Emergency Fund has been used successfully in children with mild, moderate, or severe dehydration and has saved millions of lives in developing countries. The solution contains glucose (111 mmol/liter), sodium (90 mmol/liter), potassium (20 mmol/liter), chloride (80 mmol/liter), and base (provided as trisodium citrate or sodium bicarbonate at 10 mmol/liter), at an osmolarity of 330 mmol/liter. The carbohydrate-sodium ratio of 1.2:1 takes best advantage of the coupled transport of sodium and glucose across the intestinal mucosal surface and offers an efficient means of providing calories, replacing electrolyte losses, and increasing uptake of water.[126] In the United States, oral rehydration solutions are recommended for all children with vomiting or diarrhea during the rehydration phase of therapy, except for those with severe dehydration, severe carbohydrate malabsorption, or fluid losses in stool greater than 10 ml/kg per hour. Feeding should begin within 24 hours of illness and should include breast milk or diluted formula or milk in infants, or lactose-free, carbohydrate-rich foods in older children. Feeding early in the course of diarrhea promotes enterocyte regeneration and diminishes intestinal permeability.[127–131] Because of their high glucose content, low sodium content, and high osmolarity, fruit juices and soft drinks are not recommended for use in the management of childhood diarrhea.

The Committee on Nutrition of the American Academy of Pediatrics recommends the use of feeding within 24 hours after onset of illness and the use of oral rehydration fluids in children with mild or moderate dehydration. However, these recommendations often are not followed by physicians.[132] In the United States, rehydration with intravenous fluids is often used in place of oral rehydration therapy. However, the cost, trauma, and potential risk of nosocomial infections associated with hospitalization clearly outweigh the time it takes to teach parents how to administer oral fluids properly.

Neither antibiotics, antisecretory drugs (e.g., bismuth subsalicylate), antimotility drugs (e.g., diphenoxylate, atropine, loperamide), absorbents (e.g., kaolin), nor antiemetics (e.g., phenothiazines) play a role in amelioration of acute infection, prevention of reinfection, or reduction of fluid losses during rotavirus-induced gastroenteritis.

Amelioration of acute disease in infants is not afforded by passive administration of bovine milk antibodies containing high titers of human rotavirus–specific neutralizing antibodies.[133] Because multiple cycles of rotavirus replication occur before the onset of clinical disease, administration of antibodies at the time of illness is probably too late to alter the clinical course. On the other hand, in children with immunodeficiency disorders (in whom rotavirus replication may occur over many weeks or months), rotavirus-specific immunoglobulin preparations administered orally may abate shedding and ameliorate disease.[134] Although ribavirin has been found to alter virus replication in vitro,[135, 136] there is no evidence that ribavirin alters clinical disease in vivo.

PREVENTION

Given the infant mortality associated with rotavirus gastroenteritis in the developing world, prevention of disease by vaccination is an important goal. The prevalence of rotavirus morbidity, including hospitalizations, in developed nations also indicates that an efficient vaccine against rotavirus disease would be cost-effective. Attempts to develop a rotavirus vaccine for infants were initiated soon after the discovery of human rotavirus and continue to be actively pursued.

Vaccine development has not been based on any clear understanding of the critical immunoprotective antigenic components of rotavirus, nor on knowledge of the critical protective components of the host immune response. Rather, development has been largely empirical.

Animal-Origin Rotavirus Vaccines

Rotaviruses of animal origin have been proposed and evaluated as live vaccine candidates for humans. The first of these was Nebraska calf diarrhea virus (NCDV), a bovine (G type 6) rotavirus.[137–140] After adaptation to growth in primate cell cultures, this virus, now designated RIT 4237, was administered orally to adults and infants without significant toxicity and with little shedding of virus in feces.[43, 141, 142] Placebo-controlled studies in Finnish infants demonstrated protection rates of 50 to 88% against rotavirus diarrhea of varying severity,[143] but other studies have shown limited protection[144] or no protection[145–147] against rotavirus disease. Another bovine-origin rotavirus vaccine candidate, WC3,[56, 148–150] is also G type 6 but has a P type distinct from that of NCDV. WC3, like NCDV, exhibits little or no toxicity for infants. WC3 has conferred protection (rates of 50 to 76%) in some clinical efficacy trials but has been ineffective in others.[56, 58, 150]

The most extensively studied animal-origin rotavirus vaccine is rhesus rotavirus (RRV), which is a G type 3 rotavirus whose vp7 is nevertheless distinguishable from human G type 3.[151–153] RRV is more immunogenic and more reactogenic than bovine rotaviruses.[154–156] However, placebo-controlled trials have yielded inconsistent results, with efficacy rates from 0 to 67%.[45, 147, 157–160]

Both the bovine-origin rotavirus vaccines and RRV induce almost exclusively homotypic G-specific antibody responses in seronegative infants. Each of these vaccines, however, induces a more broadly cross-reactive antibody response in infants with evidence of previous rotavirus infection.

Human-Animal Reassortant Rotavirus Vaccines

The approach to the development of rotavirus vaccines that is currently receiving most attention is the generation of reassortants of animal and human rotaviruses. The reassortants contain a gene coding for human virus G protein (vp7), or in one case a gene for a human P protein (vp4), and the remaining genome of the animal virus. The intention is to provide a vaccine that is attenuated because of its animal origin but expresses a human serotype protein on its surface and therefore induces a human type-specific humoral immune response. Reassortants bearing human G type specificities have been prepared from both simian (RRV) and bovine (WC3) rotaviruses.[161–163]

RRV reassortants expressing the vp7 of human G types 1, 2, and 4 have been developed and have been formulated as a tetravalent vaccine in which RRV provides the G type 3 component. RRV reassortants retain the characteristic of RRV of inducing transient fevers in some infants.[164] In clinical efficacy trials, both univalent and tetravalent (RRV-TV) reassortant vaccines have provided protection against rotavirus disease.

Univalent G1 vaccine has provided a protection rate in a natural G1 challenge season as high as 77% against all disease.[158] The RRV-TV vaccine has been tested in extensive clinical efficacy trials in the United States, Venezuela, Brazil, and Finland.[165–170] Protection rates for all rotavirus disease with this vaccine have ranged from 49 to 66%. Although type G1–specific antibody responses and protection against type G1 rotavirus disease appear to be slightly reduced in RRV-TV compared with the G1-univalent RRV vaccine, the utility of including non-G1 serotypes has been demonstrated. In an efficacy trial in a Native American population in the United States in which the natural challenge was predominantly G3 rotavirus, administration of RRV-TV was associated with 50% protection against all rotavirus disease, whereas the univalent G1 reassortant of RRV induced only 29% protection.[167] In most efficacy trials, RRV-TV has provided levels of protection against severe rotavirus disease that exceeded those against total rotavirus disease (i.e., of any severity). Protection rates against severe rotavirus disease have ranged from 57% in Brazil to 91% in Finland.[169, 170] In two large U.S. trials, the rates were 80 and 82%, although the rates of protection against all rotavirus disease were only 57 and 49%, respectively.[165, 166]

RRV-TV was licensed for use in the United States in August 1998. Recommendation is for administration of three doses of RRV-TV (4.0×10^5 pfu each) concomitant with other childhood vaccines to infants at approximately 2, 4 and 6 months of age.

A WC3 reassortant vaccine with human G type 1 has been shown to retain the nonreactogenic properties of its bovine-origin rotavirus parent.[162] In three efficacy trials conducted in Rochester, New York, and Philadelphia, Pennsylvania, this reassortant induced rates of protection against all rotavirus disease ranging from 63 to 100%, with protection against severe rotavirus disease exceeding 85% in each trial.[171, 172] A reassortant of WC3 containing the P protein (vp4) of the most common human serotype (P1a) was also constructed. In an immunogenicity trial, a combination of P1a and G1 reassortants in infants was found to give a more vigorous immune response than either reassortant alone.[173] Subsequently, a quadrivalent vaccine was constructed containing G1, G2, G3, and P1 reassortants of WC3. In a multicenter efficacy trial in the United States, this vaccine induced 67% protection against all rotavirus disease. No fevers were associated with vaccine, but a slight excess of mild diarrheas occurred after administration of the first dose.[174] Clinical trials are continuing to establish the ideal combination of WC3 reassortants for protection and safety.

Human-Origin Rotavirus Vaccines

Limited attempts to develop human-origin rotavirus vaccines have been undertaken. The first candidate to receive attention was a "nursery" strain, M37 (P type 2, G type 1).[175] This "vaccine strain" was inefficient in induction of G type 1 specific antibodies and in one study did not provide protection against rotavirus disease.[176]

More recently, clinical trials have been initiated with a human serotype P1aG1 rotavirus isolate, designated strain 89-12. This virus was attenuated by serial passage in African green monkey kidney cells.[177] Given to infants as two doses of 10^5 pfu each, the vaccine appeared to be safe, although there was a slight excess of watery stools in vaccinees compared with placebo recipients. A majority of infants exhibited rotavirus-specific serum IgA (90%) and fecal IgA (71%) responses, but only 33% had a serum-neutralizing antibody response to the vaccine strain virus. Efficacy trials of this vaccine candidate are in progress.

The orally administered reassortant rotavirus vaccines currently offer the most promise, but it appears that, at best, they will be less than 100% protective. Therefore, it is likely that in the future novel immunization strategies will explore other routes of antigen administration and innovative delivery systems for virion or subvirion rotavirus components. Such approaches may be employed to enhance responses to primary immunization with reassortant rotavirus vaccines.

REFERENCES

1. Walsh J, Warren K. Selective primary health care: An interim strategy for disease control in developing countries. N Engl J Med. 1979;301:967–974.
2. Bishop R, Davidson G, Holmes I, et al. Virus particles in epithelial cells of

duodenal mucosa from children with acute non-bacterial gastroenteritis. Lancet. 1973;2:1281–1283.

3. Black R, Merson M, Rahman A, et al. A two-year study of bacterial, viral, and parasitic agents associated with diarrhea in rural Bangladesh. J Infect Dis. 1980;142:660–664.
4. Kapikian A, Kim H, Wyatt R, et al. Human reovirus-like agent as the major pathogen associated with "winter" gastroenteritis. N Engl J Med. 1976;295:965–972.
5. Snyder J, Merson M. The magnitude of the global problem of acute diarrheal disease: A review of active surveillance data. Bull World Health Organ. 1982;60:605–613.
6. Glass R, Kilgore P, Holman R, et al. The epidemiology of rotavirus diarrhea in the United States: Surveillance and estimates of disease burden. J Infect Dis. 1996;174(Suppl 1):S5–S11.
7. Ho M, Glass R, Pinsky P, et al. Diarrheal diseases in American children: Are they preventable? JAMA. 1988;260:3281–3285.
8. Matson D, Estes M. Impact of rotavirus infection at a large pediatric hospital. J Infect Dis. 1990;162:598–604.
9. Urasawa S, Urasawa T, Taniguchi K, et al. Serotype determination of human rotavirus isolates and antibody prevalence of pediatric population in Hokkaido, Japan. Arch Virol. 1984;81:1–12.
10. Yolken R, Wyatt R, Zissis G. Epidemiology of human rotavirus types 1 and 2 as studied by enzyme-linked immunosorbent assay. N Engl J Med. 1978;299:1156–1161.
11. Bellamy R, Both G. Molecular biology of rotaviruses. Adv Virus Res. 1990;38:1–43.
12. Estes M, Cohen J. Rotavirus gene structure and function. Microbiol Rev. 1989;53:410–449.
13. Hung T, Chen G, Wand C, et al. Waterborne outbreak of rotavirus diarrhea in adults in China caused by a novel rotavirus. Lancet. 1984;1:1139–1142.
14. Fang Z, Ye Q, Ho M, et al. Investigation of an outbreak of adult diarrhea rotavirus in China. J Infect Dis. 1989;160:948–953.
15. Peñaranda M, Cubitt W, Sinarachatanant P, et al. Group C rotavirus infections in patients with diarrhea in Thailand, Nepal and England. J Infect Dis. 1989;160:392–397.
16. Hoshino Y, Sereno M, Midthun K, et al. Independent segregation of two antigenic specificities (vp3 and vp7) involved in neutralization of rotavirus infectivity. Proc Natl Acad Sci U S A. 1985;82:8701–8704.
17. Offit P, Blavat G. Identification of the two rotavirus genes determining neutralization specificities. J Virol. 1986;57:376–378.
18. Browning G, Fitzgerald T, Chalmers R, et al. A novel group A rotavirus G serotype: Serological and genomic characterization of equine isolate F123. J Clin Microbiol. 1991;29:2043–2046.
19. Taniguchi K, Urasawa T, Kobayashi N, et al. Nucleotide sequence of vp4 and vp7 genes of human rotaviruses with subgroup I specificity and long RNA pattern: Implication for new G serotype specificity. J Virol. 1990;64:5640–5644.
20. Beards G, Xu L, Ballard A, et al. A serotype 10 human rotavirus. J Clin Microbiol. 1992;30:1432–1435.
21. Gentsch J, Glass R, Woods P, et al. Identification of group A rotavirus gene 4 types by polymerase chain reaction. J Clin Microbiol. 1992;30:1365–1373.
22. Gorziglia M, Larralde G, Kapikian A, et al. Antigenic relationships among human rotaviruses as determined by outer capsid protein vp4. Proc Natl Acad Sci U S A. 1990;87:7155–7159.
23. Coulson B. Typing of human rotavirus vp4 by an enzyme immunoassay using monoclonal antibodies. J Clin Microbiol. 1993;31:1–8.
24. Padilla-Noriega L, Werner-Eckert R, Mackow E, et al. Serologic analysis of human rotavirus serotypes P1A and P2 by using monoclonal antibodies. J Clin Microbiol. 1993;31:622–628.
25. Ansari S, Springthorpe V, Sattar S. Survival and vehicular spread of human rotaviruses: Possible relation to seasonality of outbreaks. Rev Infect Dis. 1991;13:448–461.
26. Berman D, Hoff J. Inactivation of simian rotavirus SA11 by chlorine, chlorine dioxide, and monochloramine. Appl Environ Microbiol. 1984;48:317–323.
27. Weiss C, Clark H. Rapid inactivation of rotaviruses by exposure to acid buffer or acidic gastric juice. J Gen Virol. 1985;66:2725–2730.
28. Estes M, Graham D, Smith E, et al. Rotavirus stability and inactivation. J Gen Virol. 1979;43:403–409.
29. Meng Z, Birch C, Heath R, et al. Physiochemical stability and inactivation of human and simian rotaviruses. Appl Environ Microbiol. 1987;53:727–730.
30. Keswick B, Pickering L, Dupont H, et al. Survival and detection of rotaviruses on environmental surfaces in day care centers. Appl Environ Microbiol. 1983;46:813–816.
31. Davidson G, Goller J, Bishop R, et al. Immunofluorescence in duodenal mucosa of children with acute enteritis due to a new virus. J Clin Pathol. 1975;28:263–266.
32. Willoughby R, Yolken R, Schnaar R. Rotaviruses specifically bind to the neutral glycosphingolipid asialo-GM1. J Virol. 1990;64:4830–4835.
33. Srnka C, Tiemeyer M, Gilbert J. Cell surface ligands for rotavirus: Mouse intestinal glycolipids and synthetic carbohydrate analogs. Virology. 1992;190:794–805.
34. Suzuki H, Kitaoka S, Sato T, et al. Further investigation on the mode of entry of human rotavirus into cells. Arch Virol. 1986;91:135–144.
35. Fukuhara N, Yoshie O, Kitaoka S, et al. Evidence for endocytosis-independent infection by human rotavirus. Arch Virol. 1987;97:93–99.
36. Kaljot K, Shaw R, Rubin D, et al. Infectious rotavirus enters cells by direct cell membrane penetration, not by endocytosis. J Virol. 1988;62:1136–1144.
37. Mavromichalis J, Evans N, McNeish A, et al. Intestinal damage in rotavirus and adenovirus gastroenteritis assessed by D-xylose malabsorption. Arch Dis Child. 1977;52:589–591.
38. Hyams J, Krause P, Gleason P. Lactose malabsorption following rotavirus infection in young children. J Pediatr. 1981;99:916–918.
39. Stintzing G, Johansen K, Magnusson K, et al. Intestinal permeability in small children during and after rotavirus diarrhoea assessed with different-size polyethyleneglycols (PEG 400 and PEG 1000). Acta Paediatr Scand. 1986;75:1005–1009.
40. Ball J, Tian P, Zeng C, et al. Age-dependent diarrhea induced by a rotavirus nonstructural glycoprotein. Science 1996; 272:101–104.
41. Brandt CD, Kim HW, Yolken RH, et al. Comparative epidemiology of two rotavirus serotypes and other viral agents associated with pediatric gastroenteritis. Am J Epidemiol. 1979;110:243–254.
42. Gurwith M, Wenman W, Gurwith D, et al. Diarrhea among infants and young children in Canada: A longitudinal study in three northern communities. J Infect Dis. 1983;147:685–692.
43. Weinberg RJ, Tipton G, Klish WJ, et al. Effect of breast feeding on morbidity in rotavirus gastroenteritis. Pediatrics. 1984;74:250–253.
44. Duffy LC, Byers TE, Riepenhoff-Talty M, et al. The effects of infant feeding on rotavirus-induced gastroenteritis: A prospective study. Am J Public Health. 1986;76:259–263.
45. Vesikari T, Ruuska T, Delem A, et al. Neonatal rotavirus vaccination with RIT 4237 bovine rotavirus vaccine: A preliminary report. Pediatr Infect Dis J. 1987;6:164–169.
46. Rodger SM, Bishop RF, Birch C, et al. Molecular epidemiology of human rotaviruses in Melbourne, Australia, from 1973 to 1979, as determined by electrophoresis of genome ribonucleic acid. J Clin Microbiol. 1981;13:272–278.
47. Bishop RF, Barnes GL, Cipriani E, et al. Clinical immunity after neonatal rotavirus infection: A prospective longitudinal study in young children. N Engl J Med. 1983;309:72–76.
48. Garbarg-Chenon A, Brussieux J, Boisivon A, et al. Epidemiology of human rotaviruses in a maternity unit as studied by electrophoresis of genomic RNA. Eur J Epidemiol. 1985;1:33–36.
49. Perez-Schael I, Daoud G, White L, et al. Rotavirus shedding by newborn children. J Med Virol. 1984;14:127–136.
50. Flores J, Midthun K, Hoshino Y, et al. Conservation of the fourth gene among rotaviruses recovered from asymptomatic newborn infants and its possible role in attenuation. J Virol. 1986;60:972–979.
51. Larralde G, Flores J. Identification of gene 4 alleles among human rotaviruses by polymerase chain reaction–derived probes. Virology. 1990;179:469–473.
52. Santos N, Gouvea V, Li B, et al. VP4 typing of human rotavirus in the USA. ASV Scientific Program and Abstracts. 1993;A109.
53. Walther FJ, Bruggeman C, Daniels-Bosman MSM, et al. Symptomatic and asymptomatic rotavirus infections in hospitalized children. Acta Paediatr Scand. 1983;72:659–663.
54. Champsaur H, Questiaux E, Prevot J, et al. Rotavirus carriage, asymptomatic infection, and disease in the first two years of life: I. Virus shedding. J Infect Dis. 1984;149:667–674.
55. Rodriguez WJ, Kim HW, Brandt CD, et al. Longitudinal study of rotavirus infection and gastroenteritis in families served by a pediatric medical practice: Clinical and epidemiologic observations. Pediatr Infect Dis J. 1987;6:170–176.
56. Clark HF, Borian FE, Bell LM, et al. Protective effect of WC3 vaccine against rotavirus diarrhea in infants during a predominantly serotype 1 rotavirus season. J Infect Dis. 1988;158:570–587.
57. Clark HF, Borian F, Plotkin SA. Immune protection of infants against rotavirus gastroenteritis by a serotype 1 reassortant of bovine rotavirus WC3. J Infect Dis. 1990;161:1099–1104.
58. Bernstein DI, Smith VE, Sander DS, et al. Evaluation of WC3 rotavirus vaccine and correlates of protection in healthy infants. J Infect Dis. 1990;162:1055–1062.
59. Hrdy DB. Epidemiology of rotaviral infection in adults. Rev Infect Dis. 1987;9:461–469.
60. Meurman OH, Laine MJ. Rotavirus epidemic in adults. N Engl J Med. 1977;296:1298–1299.
61. Hjelt K, Grauballe P, Henrickson L, et al. Rotavirus infections among the staff of a general paediatric department. Acta Paediatr Scand. 1985;74:617–618.
62. Vollett JJ, Ericsson CD, Gibson G, et al. Human rotavirus in an adult population with travelers' diarrhea and its relationship to the location of food consumption. J Med Virol. 1979;4:81–87.
63. Bartlett AV III, Reves RR, Pickering LK. Rotavirus in infant-toddler day care centers: Epidemiology relevant to disease control strategies. J Pediatr. 1988;113:435–441.
64. Gouvea V, Ho M-S, Glass R, et al. Serotypes and electropherotypes of human rotavirus in the United States: 1987–1989. J Infect Dis. 1990; 162:362–367.
65. Goto Y, Kurogi H, Inaba Y, et al. Sequential isolation of rotavirus from individual calves. Vet Microbiol. 1986;11:177–184.
66. Banfield DA, Stotz I, Moore R, et al. Shedding of rotavirus in feces of sows before and after farrowing. J Clin Microbiol. 1982;16:186–190.
67. Rao VC, Metcalf TG, Melnick JL. Development of a method for concentration of rotavirus and its application to recovery of rotaviruses from estuarine waters. Appl Environ Microbiol. 1986;52:484–488.
68. Gerba CP, Keswick BH, DuPont HL, et al. Isolation of rotavirus and hepatitis A virus from drinking water. Monogr Virol. 1984;15:119–125.
69. Ward R, Bernstein D, Young E, et al. Human rotavirus studies in volunteers: Determination of infectious dose and serological response to infection. J Infect Dis. 1986;154:871–880.

70. Barnes G, Unicomb L, Bishop R. Severity of rotavirus infection in relation to serotype, monotype and electropherotype. J Paediatr Child Health. 1992;28:54–57.
71. Bern C, Unicomb L, Gentsch J, et al. Rotavirus diarrhea in Bangladeshi children: Correlation of disease severity with serotypes. J Clin Microbiol. 1992;30:3234–3238.
72. Li B, Clark HF, Gouvea V. Human cytopathic rotavirus (HCR3) is closely related to animal rotaviruses. ASV Scientific Program and Abstracts. 1993;A109.
73. Nakagomi O, Mochizuki M, Aboudy Y, et al. Hemagglutination by a human rotavirus isolate as evidence for transmission of animal rotaviruses to humans. J Clin Microbiol. 1992;30:1011–1013.
74. Nakagomi O, Kaga E, Gerna G, et al. Subgroup I serotype 3 human rotavirus strains with long RNA pattern as a result of naturally occurring reassortment between members of the bovine and AU-1 genogroups. Arch Virol. 1992;126:337–342.
75. Brussow H, Werchau H, Liedtke W, et al. Prevalence of antibodies to rotavirus in different age-groups of infants in Bochum, West Germany. J Infect Dis. 1988;157:1014–1022.
76. Tallett S, MacKenzie C, Middleton P, et al. Clinical, laboratory, and epidemiologic features of a viral gastroenteritis in infants and children. Pediatrics. 1977;60:217–222.
77. Carr M, McKendrick D, Spyridakis T. The clinical features of infantile gastroenteritis due to rotavirus. Scand J Infect Dis. 1978;8:241–243.
78. Kovacs A, Chan L, Hotrakitya C, et al. Rotavirus gastroenteritis: Clinical and laboratory features and use of the rotazyme test. Am J Dis Child. 1987;141:161–166.
79. Rodriguez W, Kim H, Arrobio J, et al. Clinical features of acute gastroenteritis associated with human reovirus-like agent in infants and young children. J Pediatr. 1977;91:188–193.
80. Salmi T, Arstilla P, Koivikko A. Central nervous system involvement in patients with rotavirus gastroenteritis. Scand J Infect Dis. 1978;10:29–31.
81. Wong C, Price Z, Bruckner D. Aseptic meningitis in an infant with rotavirus gastroenteritis. Pediatr Infect Dis J. 1984;3:244–266.
82. Rotbart H, Levin M, Yolken R, et al. An outbreak of rotavirus-associated necrotizing enterocolitis. J Pediatr. 1983;103:454–459.
83. Rotbart H, Nelson W, Glade M, et al. Neonatal rotavirus-associated necrotizing enterocolitis: Case control study and prospective surveillance during an outbreak. J Pediatr. 1988;112:87–93.
84. Hattori H, Torii S, Nagafuji H, et al. Benign acute myositis associated with rotavirus gastroenteritis. J Pediatr. 1992;121:748–749.
85. Grunow J, Dunton S, Waner J. Human rotavirus-like particles in a hepatic abscess. J Pediatr. 1985;106:73–76.
86. Santosham M, Yolken R, Quiroz E, et al. Detection of rotavirus in respiratory secretions of children with pneumonia. J Pediatr. 1983;103:583–585.
87. Matsuno S, Utagawa E, Sugiura A. Association of rotavirus infection with Kawasaki syndrome. J Infect Dis. 1983;148:177.
88. Yolken R, Murphy M. Sudden infant death syndrome associated with rotavirus infection. J Med Virol. 1982;10:291–296.
89. Whorwell P, Beeken W, Phillips C, et al. Isolation of reovirus-like agents from patients with Crohn's disease. Lancet. 1977;1:1169–1171.
90. Saulsbury F, Winkelstein J, Yolken R. Chronic rotavirus infection in immunodeficiency. J Pediatr. 1980;97:61–65.
91. Wood D, David T, Chrystie I, et al. Chronic enteric virus infection in two T-cell immunodeficient children. J Med Virol. 1988;24:435–444.
92. Gilger M, Matson D, Conner M, et al. Extraintestinal rotavirus infections in children with immunodeficiency. J Pediatr. 1992;120:912–917.
93. Pedley S, Hundley F, Chrystie I, et al. The genomes of rotaviruses isolated from chronically infected immunodeficient children. J Gen Virol. 1984;65:1141–1150.
94. Hundley F, McIntyre M, Clark B, et al. Heterogeneity of genome rearrangements in rotaviruses isolated from a chronically infected immunodeficient child. J Virol. 1987;61:3365–3372.
95. Davidson G, Hogg R, Kirubakaran C. Serum and intestinal immune response to rotavirus enteritis in children. Infect Immun 1983;40:447–452.
96. Riepenhoff-Talty M, Bogger-Goren S, Li P, et al. Development of serum and intestinal antibody response to rotavirus after naturally acquired rotavirus infection in man. J Med Virol. 1981;8:215–222.
97. Grimwood K, Lund J, Coulson B, et al. Comparison of serum and mucosal antibody responses following severe acute rotavirus gastroenteritis in young children. J Clin Microbiol. 1988;26:732–738.
98. Aiyar J, Ban M, Bhandari N, et al. Rotavirus-specific antibody response in saliva of infants with rotavirus diarrhea. J Infect Dis. 1990;162:1383–1384.
99. Coulson B, Grimwood K, Masendycz P, et al. Comparison of rotavirus immunoglobulin: A coproconversion with other indices of rotavirus infection in a longitudinal study in childhood. J Clin Microbiol. 1990;28:1367–1374.
100. Black R, Greenberg H, Kapikian A, et al. Acquisition of serum antibody to Norwalk virus and rotavirus in relation to diarrhea in a longitudinal study of young children in rural Bangladesh. J Infect Dis. 1982;145:483–489.
101. Mata L, Simhon A, Urratia J, et al. Epidemiology of rotaviruses in a cohort of 45 Guatemalan Mayan Indian children observed from birth to the age of three years. J Infect Dis. 1983;148:452–461.
102. Chiba S, Nakata S, Urasawa T, et al. Protective effect of naturally acquired homotypic and heterotypic rotavirus antibodies. Lancet. 1986;417–421.
103. Ward R, Bernstein D, Shukla R, et al. Effects of antibody to rotavirus on protection of adults challenged with a human rotavirus. J Infect Dis. 1989;159:79–88.
104. Linares A, Gabbay Y, Mascarenhas J, et al. Epidemiology of rotavirus subgroups and serotypes in Belem, Brazil: A three-year study. Ann Inst Pasteur/Virol. 1988;139:89–99.
105. Georges-Courbet M, Monges J, Beraud-Cassel A, et al. Prospective longitudinal study of rotavirus infections in children from birth to two years of age in Central Africa. Ann Inst Pasteur/Virol. 1988;139:421–428.
106. Friedman M, Gaul A, Sarov B, et al. Two sequential outbreaks of rotavirus gastroenteritis: Evidence for symptomatic and asymptomatic reinfection. J Infect Dis. 1988;158:814–822.
107. Grinstein S, Gomez J, Bercovich J, et al. Epidemiology of rotavirus infection and gastroenteritis in prospectively monitored Argentine families with young children. Am J Epidemiol. 1989;130:300–308.
108. Reves R, Hossain M, Midthun K, et al. An observational study of naturally-acquired immunity to rotavirus diarrhea in a cohort of 363 Egyptian children. Am J Epidemiol. 1989;130:981–988.
109. O'Ryan M, Matson D, Estes M, et al. Molecular epidemiology of rotavirus in young children attending day care centers in Houston. J Infect Dis. 1990;162:810–816.
110. De Champs C, Laveran H, Peigue-Lafeville H, et al. Sequential rotavirus infections: Characterization of serotypes and electropherotypes. Res Virol. 1991;142:39–45.
111. Coulson B, Grimwood K, Hudson I, et al. Role of coproantibody in clinical protection of children during reinfection with rotavirus. J Clin Microbiol. 1992;30:1678–1694.
112. Matson D, O'Ryan M, Herrera I, et al. Fecal antibody responses to symptomatic and asymptomatic rotavirus infections. J Infect Dis. 1993;167:577–583.
113. Ward R, Clemens J, Knowlton D, et al. Evidence that protection against rotavirus diarrhea after natural infection is not dependent on serotype-specific neutralizing antibody. J Infect Dis. 1992;166:1251–1257.
114. Mebus CA, Underdahl NR, Rhodes MB, et al. Calf diarrhea (scours): Reproduced with a virus from a field outbreak. Univ Nebraska Res Bull. 1969;233:1–16.
115. Brandt CD, Kim HW, Rodriguez WJ, et al. Comparison of direct electron microscopy, immune electron microscopy and rotavirus enzyme-linked immunosorbent assay for detection of gastroenteritis viruses in children. J Clin Microbiol. 1981;13:976–981.
116. Rubenstein AS, Miller MF. Comparison of enzyme immunoassay with electron microscopy procedures for detecting rotavirus. J Clin Microbiol. 1982;15:938–944.
117. Bridger JC. Novel rotaviruses in animals and man. In: Diarrhea Viruses, Ciba Foundation Symp 128. Chichester: John Wiley & Sons; 1987;5–23.
118. Chrystie IL, Totterdell BM, Banatvala JE. False positive Rotazyme tests on faecal samples from babies. Lancet. 1983;2:1028.
119. Doern GV, Herrman JE, Henderson P, et al. Detection of rotavirus with a new polyclonal antibody enzyme immunoassay (Rotazyme II) and commercial latex agglutination test (Rotalex): Comparison with a monoclonal antibody enzyme immunoassay. J Clin Microbiol. 1986;23:226–229.
120. Sanders RC, Campbell AD, Jenkins AF. Routine detection of human rotavirus by latex agglutination: Comparison with latex agglutination, electron microscopy and polyacrylamide gel electrophoresis. J Virol Methods. 1986;13:285–290.
121. Dolan KT, Twist EM, Horton-Slight P, et al. Epidemiology of rotavirus electropherotypes determined by a simplified diagnostic technique with RNA analysis. J Clin Microbiol. 1985;21:753–758.
122. Kalica AR, Garon CF, Wyatt RG, et al. Differentiation of human and calf reovirus-like agents associated with diarrhea using polyacrylamide gel electrophoresis of RNA. Virology. 1976;74:86–92.
123. MacRae MA. Nucleic acid based analysis of non-group A rotaviruses. In: Novel Diarrhea Viruses, Ciba Foundation Symp 128. Chichester: John Wiley & Sons; 1987;24–48.
124. Gouvea V, Glass RI, Woods P, et al. PCR amplification and typing of rotavirus nucleic acid from stool specimens. J Clin Microbiol. 1990;28:276–282.
125. Gorziglia M, Green K, Nishikawa K, et al. Sequence of the fourth gene of human rotaviruses recovered from asymptomatic or symptomatic infections. J Virol. 1988;62:2978–2984.
126. Avery ME, Snyder JD. Oral therapy for acute diarrhea: The underused simple solution. N Engl J Med. 1990;323:891–894.
127. Santosham M, Foster S, Reid R, et al. Role of soy-based, lactose-free formula during treatment of acute diarrhea. Pediatrics. 1985;76:292–298.
128. Santosham M, Goepp J, Burns B, et al. Role of soy-based, lactose-free formula in the outpatient management of diarrhea. Pediatrics. 1991;87:619–622.
129. Brown HO, Levine ML, Lipkin M. Inhibition of intestinal cell renewal and migration induced by starvation. Am J Physiol. 1963;205:868–872.
130. Isolauri E, Juntunen M, Wiren S, et al. Intestinal permeability changes in acute gastroenteritis: Effects of clinical factors and nutritional management. J Pediatr Gastroenterol Nutr. 1989;8:466–473.
131. Brown KH, Gastanaduy AS, Saavedra JM, et al. Effect of continued oral feeding on clinical and nutritional outcomes of acute diarrhea in children. J Pediatr. 1988;112:191–200.
132. Bezerra JA, Stathos TH, Duncan B, et al. Treatment of infants with acute diarrhea: What's recommended and what's practiced. Pediatrics. 1992;90:1–4.
133. Hilpert H, Brussow H, Mietens C, et al. Use of bovine milk concentrate containing antibody to rotavirus to treat rotavirus gastroenteritis in infants. J Infect Dis. 1987;156:158–165.
134. Guarino A, Guandalini S, Albano F, et al. Enteral immunoglobulins for treatment of protracted rotaviral diarrhea. Pediatr Infect Dis J. 1991;10:612–614.
135. Schoub BD, Prozesky OW. Antiviral activity of ribavirin in rotavirus gastroenteritis of mice. Antimicrob Agents Chemother. 1977;12:543–544.
136. Smee DF, Sidwell RW, Clark SM, et al. Inhibition of rotaviruses by selected

antiviral substances: Mechanisms of viral inhibition and in vivo activity. Antimicrob Agents Chemother. 1982;21:66–73.
137. Mebus CA, White RG, Bass EP, et al. Immunity to neonatal calf diarrhea virus. J Am Vet Med Assoc. 1973;163:880–883.
138. Mebus CA, White RG, Stair FL, et al. Neonatal calf diarrhea: Results of a field trial using a reo-like virus vaccine. Vet Med Am Clin. 1972;67:173–174.
139. Thurber ET, Bass EP, Beckenhauer WH. Field trial evaluation of a reocoronavirus calf diarrhea vaccine. Can J Comp Med. 1977;41:131–136.
140. Acres SD, Radostits OM. The efficacy of a modified live reo-like virus vaccine and an *E. coli* bacteria for prevention of acute neonatal diarrhea of beef calves. Can Vet J. 1976;17:197–212.
141. Vesikari T, Isolauri E, Delem A, et al. Immunogenicity and safety of life oral attenuated bovine rotavirus vaccine strain RIT 4237 in adults and young children. Lancet. 1983;11:807–811.
142. Vesikari T, Isolauri E, D'Hondt E, et al. Protection of infants against rotavirus diarrhoea by RIT 4237 attenuated bovine rotavirus strain vaccine. Lancet. 1984;1:977–980.
143. Vesikari T, Isolauri E, Delem A, et al. Clinical efficacy of the RIT 4237 live attenuated bovine rotavirus vaccine in infants vaccinated before a rotavirus epidemic. J Pediatr. 1985;107:189–194.
144. Lanata CF, Black RE, deAguila R, et al. Protection of Peruvian children against rotavirus diarrhea of specific serotypes by one, two or three doses of the RIT 4237 attenuated bovine rotavirus vaccine. J Infect Dis. 1989;159:452–459.
145. Hanlon P, Hanlon K, Marsh V, et al. Trial of an attenuated bovine rotavirus vaccine (RIT 4237) in Gambian infants. Lancet. 1987;1:1342–1345.
146. DeMol P, Zissis G, Butzler JP, et al. Failure of live, attenuated oral rotavirus vaccine. Lancet. 1986;2:108.
147. Santosham M, Letson GW, Wolff M, et al. A field study of the safety and efficacy of two candidate rotavirus vaccines in a native American population. J Infect Dis. 1991;163:483–487.
148. Clark HF, Furukawa T, Bell LM, et al. Immune response of infants and children to low passage bovine rotavirus (strain WC3). Am J Dis Child. 1986; 140: 350–356.
149. Garbag-Chenon A, Fontaine J-L, Lasfargues G, et al. Reactogenicity and immunogenicity of rotavirus WC3 vaccine in 5- to 12-month-old infants. Ann Inst Pasteur/Virol. 1989;140:207–217.
150. Georges-Courbot MC, Monges J, Siopathis MR, et al. Evaluation of the efficacy of a low passage bovine rotavirus vaccine (strain WC3) in children in Central Africa. Res Virol. 1991;142:405–411.
151. Stuker G, Oshiro LS, Schmidt NJ. Antigenic comparisons of two new rotaviruses from rhesus monkeys. J Clin Microbiol. 1980;11:202–203.
152. Nishikawa K, Hoshino Y, Taniguchi K, et al. Rotavirus vp7 neutralization epitopes of serotype 3 strains. Virology. 1989;171:503–515.
153. Kapikian AZ, Midthun K, Hoshino Y, et al. Rhesus rotavirus: A candidate vaccine for prevention of human rotavirus disease. In: Lerner RA, Chanock RM, Brown F (eds). Molecular and Chemical Basis of Resistance to Parasitic, Bacterial, and Viral Diseases. Cold Spring Harbor: Cold Spring Harbor Laboratory; 1985:357–367.
154. Vesikari T, Kapikian AZ, Delem A, et al. A comparative trial of rhesus monkey (RRV-1) and bovine (RIT 4237) oral rotavirus vaccines in young children. J Infect Dis. 1986;153:832–839.
155. Losonsky GA, Rennels MB, Kapikian AZ, et al. Safety, infectivity, transmissibility and immunogenicity of rhesus rotavirus vaccine (MMU18006) in infants. Pediatr Infect Dis J. 1986;5:25–29.
156. Wright PF, Tajima T, Thompson J, et al. Candidate rotavirus vaccine (rhesus rotavirus strain) in children: An evaluation. Pediatrics. 1987;80:473–480.
157. Christy C, Madore HP, Pichichero ME, et al. Field trial of rhesus rotavirus vaccine in infants. Pediatr Infect Dis J. 1988;7:647–650.
158. Madore HP, Christy C, Pichichero M, et al. Field trial of rhesus rotavirus or human-rhesus rotavirus reassortant vaccine of vp7 serotype 3 or 1 specificity in infants. J Infect Dis. 1992;166:235–243.
159. Gothefors L, Wadell G, Juto P, et al. Prolonged efficacy of rhesus rotavirus vaccine in Swedish children. J Infect Dis. 1989;159:753–757.
160. Perez-Schael I, Garcia D, Gonzalez M, et al. A prospective study of diarrheal diseases in Venezuelan children to evaluate the efficacy of rhesus rotavirus vaccine. J Med Virol. 1990;30:219–229.
161. Midthun K, Greenberg H, Hoshino Y, et al. Reassortant rotaviruses as potential live rotavirus vaccine candidates. J Virol. 1985;53:949–954.
162. Clark HF, Borian FE, Modesto K, et al. Serotype 1 reassortant of bovine rotavirus WC3, strain WI79-9, induces a polytypic antibody response in infants. Vaccine. 1990;8:327–332.
163. Perez-Schael I, Blanco M, Vilar M, et al. Clinical studies of a quadrivalent rotavirus in Venezuelan infants. J Clin Microbiol. 1990;28:553–558.
164. Vesikari T, Ruuska T, Green K, et al. Protective efficacy against serotype 1 rotavirus diarrhea by live oral rhesus-human reassortant rotavirus vaccines with human rotavirus vp7 serotype 1 or 2 specificity. Pediatr Infect Dis J. 1992;11:535–542.
165. Sack D. Efficacy of rhesus rotavirus monovalent or tetravalent oral vaccines in US children. Interscience Conference on Antimicrobial Agents and Chemotherapy. 1992;344.
166. Borian FE, Clark HF, Plotkin SA. Immune response of infants to sequential dosing regimens of WC3 and WI79-9 oral rotavirus vaccines. Interscience Conference on Antimicrobial Agents and Chemotherapy. 1990;1226.
167. Santosham M, Moulton LH, Reid R, et al. Efficacy and safety of high-dose rhesus-human reassortant rotavirus vaccine in Native American populations. J Pediatr. 1997;131:632–638.
168. Perez-Schael I, Guntinas MJ, Perez M, et al. Efficacy of the rhesus rotavirus-based quadrivalent vaccine in infants and young children in Venezuela. N Engl J Med. 1997;337:1181–1187.
169. Linhares AC, Gabbay YB, Mascarenhas JDP, et al. Immunogenicity, safety, and efficacy of tetravalent rhesus-human, reassortant rotavirus vaccine in Belem, Brazil. Bull World Health Organ. 1996;74:491–500.
170. Joensuu J, Koskenniemi E, Pang X, and Vesikari T. Randomized placebo-controlled trial of rhesus-human reassortant rotavirus vaccine for prevention of severe rotavirus gastroenteritis. Lancet. 1997;350:1205–1209.
171. Clark HF, Borian FE, Plotkin SA. Immune protection of infants against rotavirus gastroenteritis by a serotype 1 reassortant of bovine rotavirus WC3. J Infect Dis. 1990;161:1099–1104.
172. Treanor J, Clark HF, Pichichero M, et al. Evaluation of the protective efficacy of a serotype 1 bovine-human rotavirus reassortant vaccine in infants. Pediatr Infect Dis J. 1995;14:301–307.
173. Clark HF, Welsko D, Offit P. Infant responses to bovine rotavirus WC3 reassortants containing human rotavirus vp7, vp4, or vp7 + vp4. Interscience Conference on Antimicrobial Agents and Chemotherapy. 1992;1394.
174. Clark HF, Offit P, Ellis R, et al. The development of multivalent bovine rotavirus (strain WC3) reassortant vaccine for infants. J Infect Dis. 1996;174(Suppl):S73–S80.
175. Midthun K, Halsey NA, Jett-Goheen M, et al. Safety and immunogenicity of human rotavirus vaccine strain M37 in adults, children and infants. J Infect Dis. 1991;164:792–796.
176. Vesikari T, Ruuska T, Koivu H-P, et al. Evaluation of the M37 human rotavirus vaccine in 2-to-6-month-old infants. Pediatr Infect Dis J. 1991;10:912–917.
177. Bernstein DI, Smith VE, Sherwood JR, et al. Safety and immunogenicity of live, attenuated human rotavirus vaccine 89-12. Vaccine. 1998;16:381–387.

Togaviridae

Chapter 140

Alphaviruses

LEWIS MARKOFF

All of the medically important alphaviruses are vector-borne. Most have hosts in nature other than humans and vectors that are crucial to the virus life cycle. Three alphaviruses currently cause human disease in the United States: eastern equine encephalitis (EEE), western equine encephalitis (WEE), and Venezuelan equine encephalitis (VEE) viruses. These are among the "New World" alphaviruses, defined by their antigenic and nucleotide sequence relatedness, as well as by their occurrence in North America or South America. "Old World" alphaviruses of major importance include chikungunya virus (in Africa and Asia), O'nyong-nyong virus (in Africa), Mayaro virus (in South America), Ross River virus (in Australia, Oceania), Sindbis virus (in Africa, Scandinavia, the countries of the former Soviet Union, Asia), and Barmah Forest virus (in Australia). The Old World alphaviruses primarily cause fever, rash, and arthropathy.

HISTORICAL OVERVIEW

WEE and EEE viruses were initially recovered from the brains of horses with encephalitis in California, in 1930, and in New Jersey, in 1933, respectively. By 1938, both of these agents had been established as causes of encephalitis in humans.[1] Similarly, VEE virus was first isolated from the brains of horses in Venezuela during an epidemic of encephalitis in 1938.[2] The first reports of VEE infection in humans were from laboratories in which equine isolates were being studied, in 1943. Apparently this outbreak was due to the aerosol spread of infectious virus to laboratory workers. Naturally acquired human illness due to VEE was first reported from Colombia in 1952 in association with an epizootic disease in equines.[3] The first reports of VEE virus infection in humans in the United States were published in 1968.[4]

Retrospective analysis of historical accounts suggests that chikungunya virus caused epidemics of the fever-rash-arthralgia syndrome in Indonesia (1779), East Africa (1823, 1870), India (1824, 1871, 1901, 1923), the Far East (1901), West Africa (1925), and possibly the southeastern United States (1827). The virus was first isolated during an epidemic in Tanzania in 1952 and 1953.[5]

PATHOGENS

The alphaviruses constitute a genus in the family Togaviridae. The genus *Rubivirus*, which includes a single species, rubella virus, is grouped in the same family.[6] Formerly, alphaviruses were known as "group A arboviruses" (*ar*thropod-*bo*rne viruses).[7] Alphaviruses are lipid-enveloped virions with a diameter of 50 to 60 nm. The alphavirus genome is an 11- to 12-kilobase positive-stranded RNA. In virus particles, genomic RNA is complexed with the virus-coded core protein in an icosahedral nucleocapsid structure. Two glycoproteins, E1 and E2, are inserted in the lipid membrane surrounding the nucleocapsid and project outward from the membrane. E1 and E2 appear to form both hetero- and homodimers, which are responsible for the structural stability of the virus particle.[8] An additional small viral structural protein, the 6K protein, is also associated with membranes and is heavily acylated.[9] E2 appears primarily responsible for attachment of virus to the cell surface. E2 antibodies, but not generally E1 antibodies, can neutralize virus infectivity. E1 has hemagglutinin activity.

Alphaviruses enter cells by receptor-mediated endocytosis. A laminin-binding protein was recently identified as a specific receptor for VEE in cultured mosquito cells.[10] After entry into the cell and uncoating, four viral nonstructural proteins are derived by translation of the 5′-terminal two thirds of genomic RNA. These nonstructural proteins include a viral protease and an RNA-dependent RNA polymerase required for further steps in virus replication. The structural proteins are encoded by a subgenomic messenger RNA (mRNA) copy of the 3′-terminal one third of the genome; it is separately transcribed from a full-length negative-stranded RNA template under control of a subgenomic promoter. The structural protein E2 is derived from cleavage of a 62-kilodalton precursor polypeptide. E2 and E1 are initially inserted in the plasma membrane of infected cells and are acquired along with the lipid envelope by nucleocapsid structures during budding to form nascent virions. The 6K protein is also inserted in the membrane and is required for the specific interaction of E2, E1, and the nucleocapsid.[11] Like that of other positive-stranded RNA viruses, the alphavirus genome is infectious when transfected into susceptible cells. Full-length complementary DNA (cDNA) copies of alphavirus genomes have been constructed, and RNA transcribed in vitro from such cDNAs is also uniformly infectious.[12–16]

Nucleotide sequencing of alphavirus genomes has permitted the phylogenetic subgrouping of the alphaviruses. By that analysis, O'nyong-nyong and Ross River viruses are grouped with Semliki Forest virus (SFV) in the SFV subgroup. The EEE subgroup includes EEE and VEE. Sindbis virus and related viruses, including WEE, constitute a third subgroup.[17] Nucleotide sequence analysis also showed that the WEE genome is recombinant: the nonstructural and core protein genes are derived from an EEE-like ancestral genome, whereas the structural glycoproteins E1 and E2 are derived from the genome of a Sindbis-like virus.[18]

Complement fixation and hemagglutination inhibition (HAI) tests define seven distinct alphavirus antigenic complexes. EEE, VEE, and WEE are prototype viruses for each of three such complexes.[19] Chikungunya, O'nyong-nyong, and Ross River viruses are grouped with SFV in a fourth complex. Middelburg, Nduma, and Barmah Forest virus (BFV), respectively, constitute the single species in each of the three additional alphavirus serogroups. BFV is a cause of epidemic polyarthritis in northern Australia.[20]

Species within an antigenic complex are distinguished from each other by the plaque reduction neutralization assay. Within the EEE antigenic complex, two North American subtypes and one South American subtype are thus defined. The WEE antigenic complex includes New World viruses—WEE, Buggy Creek, Highlands J, Fort Morgan, and Aura—and Old World viruses—Sindbis and the Sindbis subtypes Babanki, Ockelbo, Kyzylagh, and Whataroa. Nucleotide sequence analysis shows that, as for the prototype WEE genome, the New World virus genomes, except the Aura virus genome, were derived by a recombination event between ancestral Sindbis-like and EEE-like genomes.[21] Five subtypes of VEE are recognized. Subtype I occurs in tropical America and is medically most important. Five geographic variants of subtype I are distinguishable. Variants IAB and IC were associated with equine epizootics and human epidemics that occurred between the 1920s and the early 1970s. Variants ID and IE and subtype II (Everglades virus) are less virulent and are associated with enzootic disease.

EPIDEMIOLOGY

Alphaviruses Causing Encephalitis

Alphaviruses all are limited in their geographic spread by the range of their respective arthropod vectors. EEE virus infection occurs focally along the eastern and Gulf coasts of the United States, and documented cases have occurred as far north as southern Canada and as far south as northern areas of South America and the Caribbean.[22] EEE is a summertime disease, occurring most frequently in children and the elderly.[23] A few human cases occur each year. Although the disease is relatively rare, an outbreak is usually noteworthy because of the high case-fatality rate (50 to 70%). The incidence of equine cases greatly exceeds that of human cases, and outbreaks resulting in the deaths of hundreds of horses have been reported in the northeastern United States and in Florida.[22]

In North America, the principal enzootic vector for EEE is the mosquito *Culiseta melanura*, which breeds in freshwater swamps and feeds on passerine birds. Avian infection may result in death in some cases or may be without apparent consequence in others. Regardless of the severity of the illness, it results in viremia of sufficient magnitude and frequency to maintain a reservoir of infected mosquitoes.[24] In the United States, EEE has caused major epidemics of hemorrhagic enterocolitis in emus, which are bred for meat and other by-products, thus providing a reservoir of infected birds in close contact with humans. The illness is associated with high-titer viremia and may result in death. Transmission from birds to horses and humans is mediated by mosquitoes other than *C. melanura*, which is highly ornithophilic. Possible vectors include *Aedes* and *Coquillettidia* spp.[25] Infection of horses and humans results in low or undetectable levels of viremia. Therefore, these hosts do not serve as reservoirs for further spread of virus. In summary, conditions for EEE epizootics include the presence of *C. melanura* and susceptible bird populations coincident with vector mosquitoes capable of feeding on both birds and the horses or humans in the vicinity. In temperate climates, maintenance of epizootics is further interdicted by winter, which is not suitable for survival of the vector population. This may account for the relative rarity of these epidemics. It is also surprising that virus can be isolated from the same endemic foci in successive years. Despite extensive investigation, the mechanism of virus persistence or "overwintering" is not understood.

The WEE viruses are distributed primarily in the Americas. Sindbis virus and its subtypes are found in the former Soviet Union, Europe, Scandinavia, and New Zealand. A subtype of WEE, isolated in Argentina, is presumed to be representative of endemic strains in South America.[26] In North America, WEE is a summertime disease of horses and humans in states west of the Mississippi and in corresponding Canadian provinces. The vector is *Culex tarsalis*. Risk factors for infection include rural residence, outdoor employment in farming (because the vector favors irrigated areas), and male gender. Since 1955, the annual incidence of disease has varied, ranging from 0 to 200 cases per year. Peaks occur in years of epizootic or epidemic activity. The most extensive epidemic recorded occurred on the western plains of the United States and Canada in 1941, resulting in 300,000 cases of encephalitis in horses and mules and 3336 cases of encephalitis in humans.[27] For WEE, during an epidemic seroconversion will occur in a very high percentage of the adult population, but the case-infection ratio ranges from less than 1:1000 in older adults to nearly 1:1 in infants. Thus, encephalitis is most frequent in infants less than 1 year old. However, encephalitis is most severe in older adults. Case-fatality rates are 3 to 4%. In contrast, EEE infection rates are low in an epidemic, but the case-infection ratio is higher than for WEE and is highest in the young. As previously mentioned, in a high proportion of cases, full-blown encephalitis due to EEE is fatal.[28]

The incidence of alphavirus encephalitis has been declining in the United States during the last 12 years. Of 148 cases of encephalitis due to "arbovirus" infection reported to the Centers for Disease Control and Prevention in 1987, 41 were attributed to WEE. In contrast, only two reported cases of encephalitis were proved to be related to alphavirus infection in 1992 (both due to EEE). These cases occurred in Massachusetts and Florida. This incidence represented a 30-year low, despite increased surveillance of birds, horses, and potential-vector mosquitoes for infection. During 1996 and 1997, a total of 284 cases of arbovirus encephalitis were reported. Nineteen of these illnesses were due to EEE virus; five of them were fatal. Most EEE cases occurred in Florida, Georgia, Louisiana, or South Carolina. No human cases of WEE have been reported since 1994. For comparison, LaCrosse virus, a member of the California serogroup of bunyaviruses, accounted for 250 cases of arboviral encephalitis during the same time span.[29]

VEE infections in South America and Central America, caused primarily by the epizootic strains (subtypes IAB and IC), have been associated with tens of thousands of both equine and human cases.[30] For epizootic viruses, equines play an important role in maintenance, because they become viremic. At least 10 mosquito species, including *Culex, Aedes, Mansonia, Psorophora*, and *Deinocerites* spp., have been identified as probable epidemic vectors.[31] Epizootics have been documented in Venezuela, Colombia, Ecuador, and Peru at intervals of 10 years or less since the 1930s. Typically, epizootics begin in areas of tropical forest during the rainy season. In the center of an epizootic, transmission usually continues until all horses are dead or immune. Spread may be to contiguous areas or may be sporadic. In Venezuela, in 1962 through 1964, 32,000 human cases were reported, with a fatality rate of 0.6%. In 1971, the spread of epidemic VEE into Texas resulted in the deaths of more than 10,000 horses. Increased incidence of human disease typically follows that of equine disease by 1 to 2 weeks. Severe human disease with encephalitis is most common in children. Like horses, humans also develop a viremia of sufficient magnitude to infect mosquitoes. However, humans have never been implicated in epidemic transmission. Similarly, although VEE can be isolated from throat washings, person-to-person transmission has not been documented.[32]

Molecular studies comparing epizootic strains and commonly isolated enzootic ones originally suggested that these sets of VEE subtypes were highly unrelated. In fact, the common vector for enzootic strains of VEE, *Culex melanconion*, was found to be refractory to oral infection with epizootic virus.[33] Therefore, the mechanism for persistence of epizootic strains between epidemics was sought. Recent comparisons of the nucleotide sequences of newly emerging (IC-like) epizootic viruses in South America suggest that they evolved from a group of ID-like viruses by spontaneous mutation.[34]

Horses are not amplifying hosts for enzootic strains of VEE (subtypes ID, IE, and II). These viruses are principally maintained by their mosquito vector and rodents that thrive in tropical and subtropical swamps and forests. Humans living in these areas manifest a high prevalence of antibody. These viruses cause encephalitis sporadically in Central America (subtypes ID and IE) and Florida (subtype II).

Alphaviruses Causing Fever, Rash, and Polyarthritis

Chikungunya means "that which bends up," in reference to the crippling manifestations of the disease. *Aedes* mosquitoes of subgenera *Stegomyia* are the principal vectors in Africa, and the virus seems to be maintained by transmission to nonhuman primates. Humans in appropriate concentrations may also provide a reservoir for the infection of mosquitoes. *Aedes aegypti* is implicated as a vector in urban epidemics in Africa and in Asia. Serologic survey of native populations using the HAI assay suggests that epidemics occur periodically, when the youngest group of inhabitants of an endemic area are susceptible. Otherwise, disease occurrence is sporadic. From 20 to more than 90% of the population of tropical and subtropical Africa show serologic evidence of infection. Because *Aedes* mosquitoes are increasingly prevalent in North America and South America, where the population would be uniformly susceptible to infection, the possibility for epidemics is evident.[5]

O'nyong-nyong virus is antigenically related to chikungunya virus. Disease due to O'nyong-nyong virus initially appeared in Uganda in the form of an epidemic that involved 2 million people in its final extent by the mid- to late 1960s. Risk factors included residence in rural villages, where the vector *Anopheles* mosquitoes congregate. A nonhuman primate reservoir of infection is not known.

Sindbis virus is transmitted among birds by *Culex* mosquitoes. Studies in South Africa show that extensive human disease occurs in parallel with years of abundant rainfall, in association with flooding of usually arid regions. Thus, infected mosquitoes and susceptible humans are presumably brought into proximity. Infection rates may approach 15% during a major transmission season. Sindbis virus and the flavivirus West Nile virus share the avian–*Culex* mosquito hosts. In South Africa, the Nile Valley of Egypt, and Israel, people with antibodies to Sindbis virus frequently also have antibodies to West Nile virus. In Europe, symptomatic disease is recognized in the region between 60 and 65 degrees north latitude in Sweden, Finland, and the Commonwealth of Independent States. Sindbis virus infection is a disease of adults who work or vacation in forested areas. The virus has been isolated from *Culiseta, Aedes*, and *Culex* mosquitoes. Little is known about alternative natural hosts that might provide a reservoir for virus in this region.[35]

Ross River virus is a cause of epidemic polyarthritis in Australia in areas of heavy rainfall. Joint symptoms are especially intense and may be of prolonged duration, for up to 3 years after fever and rash have abated.[36] Recently, spread of the virus to the Pacific Islands has been documented. The facts that this virus has been isolated from mosquitoes and that human disease is seasonal are clues to its dependence on vector transmission.

Mayaro virus was first isolated in the Caribbean in the 1950s in association with an epidemic of febrile illness with rash and occasional arthropathy. It has since been documented to have caused epidemics in Brazil and Bolivia. The virus has been isolated from *Haemagogus* mosquitoes and from marmosets as well as other nonhuman primates.[37] These may provide a reservoir for virus in the natural setting.

For a large number of alphaviruses, including Bebaru, Cabassou, Getah, Kyzylagach, Middelburg, Nduma, Pixuna, Sagiyama, Semliki Forest, Una, and Whataroa viruses, either the virus is not known to cause human disease, or disease is of the fever-arthropathy type and is rare.

PATHOGENESIS

The locus of virus replication in the mosquito is the midgut epithelium. This is generally thought to be a lifelong persistent productive infection, although alphavirus infection may cause necrotic changes in the midgut in certain instances.[38] Alphavirus infections of humans are initiated by the bite of an infected mosquito, which results in the deposition of virus in subcutaneous and possibly cutaneous tissues. At least one alphavirus, VEE, is also highly infectious for humans when contacted by aerosol, as evidenced by outbreaks among laboratory workers. The initial phase of infection is marked by viremia and a febrile response signaling the replication of virus in non-neural tissues. The earliest measurable evidence of a VEE immune response is the presence of antibody directed against a virion surface component that is non-neutralizing but mediates viral clearance. This is followed by the advent of neutralizing antibodies with E2 specificity. Prior to central nervous system (CNS) invasion in experimental animals, VEE replicates in lymphoid tissues, resulting in necrotic changes, and in bone marrow, resulting in lymphopenia. Lymphoid infection in mice is followed by high-titer viremia, during which the peripheral CNS is seeded, mainly through the olfactory system.[39] VEE also replicates in the pancreas and salivary glands of experimental animals but does not appear to have a diabetogenic effect in humans who have survived encephalitis. Infection of neurons by VEE in animals leads to an acute encephalitis with necrosis, mild to moderate neutrophilic infiltrate, gliosis, and perivascular cuffing with involvement of Purkinje cells.[40] Associated neuronal cell death is by apoptosis.[41] EEE causes lesions throughout the brain and spinal cord, most severely involving the cerebral cortex and basal ganglia. WEE causes focal necrosis in the striatum, globus pallidus, cerebral cortex, thalamus, pons, and meninges. Transplacental spread of VEE and WEE may affect the fetus, resulting in massive cerebral necrosis.[23, 30]

During self-limited infection with a non-neurotropic alphavirus, such as chikungunya virus, the level of viremia closely parallels the fever curve. As viremia fades and fever subsides, HI and neutralizing antibody titers start to rise, suggesting that these immune responses curtail infection. Biopsy specimens of skin involved in the maculopapular to macular rash of chikungunya virus infection show lymphocytic perivascular cuffing and extravasation of erythrocytes from superficial capillaries.[42] Arthralgia may accompany early symptoms of fever and malaise, as in infection due to chikungunya virus, or may be slightly delayed and quite severe, leading to frank arthritis, as in Ross River virus infection. The joint fluid in the latter cases is inflammatory and contains viral antigens but no infectious virus.

Although it does not commonly invade the human CNS, Sindbis virus causes a fatal encephalitis in neonatal mice. This constitutes a basis for the study of CNS invasion by neurotropic alphaviruses. The initial event appears to be infection of capillary endothelial cells, allowing virus to access neuronal cells through the microvasculature or through transport across vessel walls into the brain parenchyma.[43] Once infected, mature neurons are more resistant to apoptotic cell death caused by Sindbis virus than are immature neurons, both in culture and in vivo. The outcome seems related to the cell's ability to produce mediators of apoptosis or antagonists of apoptosis in response to infection. More mature mice or older neuronal cell cultures appear to resist cell death by increasing production of inhibitors of apoptosis.[44]

Studies in mice also bear on the possible mechanisms for clearance of infection. Certain Sindbis virus–specific monoclonal antibodies can induce viral clearance from the CNS in the mouse by restricting viral gene expression. Thus, the presence of antibody with the proper specificity can attenuate entirely the intracellular processes necessary for virus replication. Despite the complete cessation of viral replication, viral RNA can be shown to persist in infected neurons for several months. Removal of antibody results in recrudescence of infection.[45] This phenomenon is completely independent of a cell-mediated immune response and suggests a mechanism for persistence of alphavirus infections in the CNS. Although neurologic symptoms may be among the sequelae of infection with the neurotropic flaviviruses, and although arthritis of several years' duration may follow Ross River virus infection, persistence of infectious alphaviruses in humans has not been documented.

As previously suggested, E2-specific antibodies are readily shown to protect against infection, probably by neutralization of virus infectivity. Other studies have led to the identification of a domain within E2 that induces protection without inducing neutralizing antibodies. The "LMN cassette," representing amino acids 297 to 352 in the case of the Sindbis virus E2, elicits non-neutralizing antibodies that appear to protect mice via antibody-dependent complement-mediated cytolysis of infected cells.[46]

A role for cytotoxic T cells in viral clearance or protection is suggested by animal experiments: mice immunized with the Sindbis nonstructural protein nsp-2 do not develop a protective humoral immune response but do recover from paralysis caused by Sindbis replication in the CNS, whereas unimmunized mice do not. Nsp-2–immunized mice that were depleted of T cells exhibited the unimmunized phenotype; they did not clear virus or recover from paralysis.[47]

CLINICAL MANIFESTATIONS

Alphavirus Infections Causing Encephalitis

EEE and WEE infections are heralded by headache, high fever, chills, nausea, and vomiting. Vertigo and sore throat with respiratory symptoms are also common in WEE infection. In cases in which CNS involvement is seen, initial symptoms are followed by mental confusion and somnolence within a few days, which may progress to coma. The incidence of focal or generalized seizures or convulsions is inversely related to age. Physical examination may reveal nuchal rigidity, depressed or hyperactive reflexes, tremors, muscle twitching, and spastic paralysis. Infants may develop bulging fontanelles.[48, 49] Complete blood count usually reveals a leukocytosis, of greater degree in EEE infection than in WEE infection. Cerebrospinal fluid (CSF) protein is elevated, and cells are present. Typical cell counts in WEE infection are 50 to 500/mm^3 and in EEE infection are 600 to 2000/mm^3. Lymphocytes are the predominant cell type in CSF. Neurologic sequelae (most severe after EEE infection) include mental retardation, behavioral changes, convulsive disorders, and paralysis. These may occur, respectively, in 30% of infants recovering from WEE infection and in 70% of those recovering from EEE infection. Sequelae are less frequent in older age groups, but parkinsonism may occur in adults following WEE.

The most common clinical manifestation of epizootic VEE infection is a febrile illness with malaise occurring after an incubation period of 1 to 6 days. Chills, myalgia, and headache with or without photophobia, hyperesthesia, and vomiting are common. Occasionally, patients complain of a sore throat. Fever may remit in a short time, with recrudescence the next day. About 4% of children and less than 1% of adults progress to severe encephalitis, which usually occurs after a few days to a week of the prodromal illness.[31] Features of encephalitis include nuchal rigidity, ataxia, convulsions, coma, and paralysis, in ascending order of severity. Laboratory studies characteristically reveal lymphopenia, sometimes accompanied by neutropenia and mild thrombocytopenia within a day or two of onset. Serum aspartate transaminase and lactate dehydrogenase enzymes are typically elevated. CSF examination reveals a few hundred lymphocytes. The overall case-fatality rate is less than 1% but approaches 20% of cases that progress to encephalitis. Nearly all persons in endemic areas contract enzootic VEE infection, as suggested by the results of serologic surveys.[31] Most seem to have experienced the influenza-like prodromal illness or to have been asymptomatic.

Alphavirus Infections Causing Fever, Rash, and Polyarthritis

Chikungunya fever is taken as the prototype of the diseases caused by the large group of alphaviruses causing fever, rash, and polyarthritis. Chikungunya fever is an acute viral infection characterized by a rapid transition from health to illness that includes severe arthralgia and fever.[50] The incubation period ranges from 1 to 12 days. The fever is characterized by a rapid rise in temperature to as high as 40°C and is often accompanied by shaking chills. After a few days, fever may abate, with subsequent recrudescence, giving rise to a "saddle-back" fever curve. Arthralgia is polyarticular, favoring the small joints and sites of previous injury, and is most intense on arising. Patients typically avoid movement as much as possible. Joints may swell without significant fluid accumulation. These symptoms may last for from 1 week to several months and are accompanied by myalgia. The rash characteristically appears on the first day of illness, but onset may be delayed. It usually presents as a flush over the face and neck, which evolves to a maculopapular or macular form that may be pruritic. The latter lesions appear on the trunk, limbs, face, palms, and soles, in that order of frequency. Petechial skin lesions have also been noted. Headache, photophobia, retro-orbital pain, sore throat with objective signs of pharyngitis, nausea, and vomiting also occur in this setting. Laboratory tests may reveal mild leukopenia with relative lymphocytosis. The erythrocyte sedimentation rate is usually markedly elevated, and the C-reactive protein assay is positive.[51] Severe arthritic involvement is most commonly seen in adults, whereas children occasionally present with symptoms referable to the CNS, including seizures and convulsions. Long-term joint involvement has been reported in association with HLA-B27.[42]

DIAGNOSIS

The epidemiology of each of the disease entities caused by alphaviruses is highly specific and provides a major clue to diagnosis. Thus, knowledge of the recent travel and outdoor exposure history of the patient is of vital importance. In certain situations, during epidemic spread of a disease, the diagnosis will be obvious. In the United States, the initial signs and symptoms of EEE or WEE infection may mimic those of infections due to enteroviruses. Encephalitis due to the flavivirus St. Louis encephalitis (SLE) virus may occur in the same setting as for encephalitis due to WEE, although clinical disease due to SLE is more common in the elderly than in infants. Ultimately, definitive diagnosis depends on obtaining appropriate acute and convalescent specimens for virologic and serologic testing. For EEE, the virus can be isolated from serum during the prodrome,[48] but most cases are diagnosed by testing paired sera in HAI assays or in a neutralization assay. Convalescing patients may manifest high titers of complement-fixing antibodies, and immunoglobulin M (IgM) antibodies can be detected on enzyme-linked immunosorbent assay (ELISA).[52] Virus may be isolated from brain post mortem. Magnetic resonance imaging may be of value; EEE causes focal radiographic changes involving the basal ganglia and thalamus, which distinguished EEE disease from herpes encephalitis in one study.[53] Results of diagnostic testing for WEE follow a similar pattern, except that viremia is usually not detectable. The presence of WEE in a specimen may be documented by inoculating suckling mice or embryonated eggs. In contrast, sera taken from patients with VEE infection within 48 hours of onset almost always test positive for virus. However, sera from patients with full-blown encephalitis usually test negative, and the diagnosis may be made by complement fixation testing. ELISA for VEE-specific IgM in sera and CSF is available. IgM and IgG ELISAs using attenuated VEE as antigen are the most sensitive diagnostic tests but should be followed by the plaque reduction neutralization assay to prove specificity.[54]

The presentation of chikungunya virus infection may be indistinguishable from that of Mayaro, O'nyong-nyong, Ross River, or Sindbis virus infection. In addition, parvovirus infection, the prodrome of hepatitis B, juvenile rheumatoid arthritis, and rubella may also be confused with chikungunya fever or with the other alphavirus infections. Patients with chikungunya fever are usually viremic for the first 48 hours, and the virus is easily isolated by in vivo or in vitro methods. Viremia may be so intense (with titers of $>10^7$) as to yield measurable amounts of hemagglutinating activity from sera.[55] Consequently, virus in sera can also often be detected by ELISA directly.[56] As previously mentioned, the decline in level of viremia parallels a rapid rise in titers of HAI and neutralizing antibodies. ELISA testing for virus-binding antibodies may detect cross-reactive immune responses to other alphaviruses.

TREATMENT AND PREVENTION

There is no specific treatment for any of the alphavirus infections. For encephalitis, supportive measures and intensive nursing care are indicated. Ribavirin and other nucleoside analogues have some in vitro activity against these viruses in tissue culture but are not in use clinically.

Prevention of WEE and EEE depends primarily on control of vector mosquito populations. During outbreaks, susceptible persons engaged in high-risk activities should be advised to avoid exposure as much as is practicable, by the use of effective mosquito repellents and netting, by wearing of full-length trousers and long-sleeved shirts, and by avoiding outdoor activities at least during periods of maximal mosquito activity. Inactivated vaccines against EEE and WEE are available for limited human use. Similar veterinary vaccines are used against EEE in horses and birds and against WEE in horses. The inactivated EEE vaccine is derived from a North American virus isolate and may not be efficacious in the prevention of disease caused by the South American antigenic variant of EEE virus.[57]

Both formalin-inactivated and live attenuated vaccines to prevent VEE infection are in limited use in humans. Efficacy of the formalin-inactivated vaccine was greatly enhanced in mice when antigens were microencapsulated in biodegradable microspheres.[58] The live attenuated VEE strain is used in the diagnostic ELISA, and large-scale vaccination of horses with this strain is the major approach to the interdiction of VEE epizootics. A live attenuated vaccine against chikungunya fever has been shown to be safe in humans. One study in which live attenuated VEE and chikungunya fever vaccines were sequentially administered to human volunteers indicates that preexisting alphavirus immunity interferes with a subsequent neutralizing antibody response to a heterologous vaccine virus.[59]

The existing live VEE vaccine candidate is a temperature-sensitive mutant virus derived several years ago by conventional virologic methods. Newer approaches to the development of vaccines to prevent alphavirus infections have involved the use of recombinant DNA technology; attenuating mutations are inserted into full-length cDNA copies of the viral genome. RNA transcribed from such mutant constructs produces infectious attenuated virus when transfected into cells. VEE virus has been one focal point of this approach to vaccine development. A viable mutant virus derived from VEE cDNA that contained mutations affecting cleavage of the viral structural proteins was avirulent in mice and conferred a protective immune response.[60] This vaccine produced solid mucosal immunity in mice, possibly as a consequence of the tropism of VEE for lymphoid tissues.[61] This property of VEE is now viewed as a basis for efficacy of VEE cDNA-based vaccines designed to induce immunity to foreign viral antigens,[13, 15, 16] especially in situations in which mucosal immune responses are considered to be of crucial importance for protection, such as against human immunodeficiency virus.[16]

REFERENCES

1. Fothergill LD, Dingle JH, Farber S, et al. Human encephalitis caused by a virus of eastern variety of equine encephalitis. N Engl J Med. 1983;219:411.
2. Beck CG, Wyckof RWG. Venezuelan equine encephalitis. Science. 1938;88:530.
3. San Martin-Barberi C, Groot H, Osborn-Mesa E. Human epidemic in Colombia caused by the Venezuelan equine encephalitis virus. Am J Trop Med Hyg. 1954;3:283.
4. Ehrenkranz NJ, Ventura AK. Venezuelan equine encephalitis virus infection in man. Annu Rev Med. 1974;25:9.
5. Peters CJ, Dalrymple JM. Alphaviruses. In: Fields BN, Knipe DM, eds. Virology. 2nd ed. New York: Raven Press; 1990:713–761.

6. Francki RIB, Fauquet CM, Knudson DL, Brown F. Classification and nomenclature of viruses. Arch Virol. 1991;2(Suppl):223.
7. Calisher CH, Karabatsos N. Arbovirus serogroups: Definition and geographic distribution. In: Monath TP, ed. The Arboviruses: Epidemiology and Ecology, v. 1. Boca Raton, Fla: CRC Press; 1988:19–57.
8. Anthony RP, Brown DT. Protein-protein interactions in an alphavirus membrane. J Virol. 1991;65:1187–1194.
9. Gaedigk-Nitschko K, Schlesinger MJ. The Sindbis virus 6K protein can be detected in virions and is acylated with fatty acids. Virology. 1990;175:274–281.
10. Ludwig GV, Kondig JP, Smith JF. A putative receptor for Venezuelan equine encephalitis virus from mosquito cells. J Virol. 1996;70:5592–5599.
11. Yao JS, Strauss EG, Strauss JH. Interactions between PE2, E1, and 6K required for assembly of alphaviruses studied with chimeric viruses. J Virol. 1996;70:7910–7920.
12. Rice CM, Lewis R, Strauss JH, et al. Production of infectious transcripts from Sindbis virus cDNA clones: Mapping of lethal mutations, rescue of a temperature-sensitive marker and in vitro mutagenesis to generate defined mutants. J Virol. 1987;61:3809–3819.
13. Davis NL, Brown KW, Johnston RE. A viral vaccine vector that expresses foreign genes in lymph nodes and protects against mucosal challenge. J Virol. 1996;70:3781–3787.
14. Xiong C, Levis R, Shen P, et al. Sindbis virus: An efficient broad host range vector for gene expression in animal cells. Science. 1989;243:1188–1191.
15. Pushko P, Parker M, Ludwig GV et al. Replicon-helper systems from attenuated Venezuelan equine encephalitis virus: Expression of heterologous genes in vitro and immunization against heterologous pathogens in vivo. Virology. 1997;239:389–401.
16. Carey IJ, Betts MR, Irlbeck DM, et al. Humoral, mucosal, and cellular immunity in response to a human immunodeficiency virus type 1 immunogen expressed by a Venezuelan equine encephalitis virus vaccine vector. J Virol. 1997;71:3031–3038.
17. Levinson RS, Strauss JH, Strauss EG. Complete sequence of the genomic RNA of O'nyong-nyong virus and its use in the construction of alphavirus phylogenetic trees. Virology. 1990;175:110–123.
18. Hahn CS, Lustig S, Strauss EG, et al. Western equine encephalitis virus is a recombinant virus. Proc Natl Acad Sci U S A. 1988;85:5997–6001.
19. Calisher CH, Shope RE, Brandt WE, et al. Proposed antigenic classification of registered arboviruses. I. Togaviridae. Alphavirus Intervirol. 1980;14:229–232.
20. Mackenzie JS, Smith DW. Mosquito-borne viruses and epidemic polyarthritis. Med J Aust. 1996;164:90–93.
21. Weaver SC, Kang W, Shirako Y, et al. Recombinational history and molecular evolution of Western equine encephalitis complex alphaviruses. J Virol. 1997;71:613–623.
22. Monath TP. Arthropod-borne encephalitides in the Americas. Bull WHO. 1979;57:513–533.
23. Tsai TF, Monath TP. Viral diseases in North America transmitted by arthropods or from vertebrate reservoirs. In: Feigin RD, Cherry JD, eds. Textbook of Pediatric Infectious Diseases. 2nd ed. Philadelphia: WB Saunders; 1988:1417.
24. Shope RE, de Andrade AHP, Bensabeth G, et al. The epidemiology of EEE, WEE, SLE, and Tralock viruses. Am J Epidemiol. 1966;84:467–477.
25. Chamberlain RW. Vector relationship of the arthropod-borne encephalitides in North America. Ann N Y Acad Sci. 1958;70:312–319.
26. Reisen WK, Monath TP. Western equine encephalomyelitis. In: Monath TP, ed. The Arboviruses: Epidemiology and Ecology, v. V. Boca Raton, Fla: CRC Press; 1989:90–137.
27. Reeves WC, Hammon W. Epidemiology of the arthropod-borne encephalitides in Kern County, California, 1943–52. Univ Calif Pub Public Health. 1962;4:257.
28. Feemster RF. Equine encephalitis in Massachusetts. N Engl J Med. 1957;257:701–704.
29. Centers for Disease Control and Prevention. Arboviral disease in the United States, 1996–1997. MMWR Morb Mort Wkly Rep. 1998. In press.
30. Groot H. The health and economic impact of Venezuelan equine encephalitis. In: Venezuelan Encephalitis, Proceedings of the Workshop-Symposium on Venezuelan Encephalitis Virus. Washington, DC: Pan American Health Organization; 1972:244.
31. Johnson KM, Martin DH. Venezuelan equine encephalitis. Adv Vet Sci Comp Med. 1974;18:79.
32. Bowen GS, Fashinell TR, Dean PB, et al. Clinical aspects of human Venezuelan equine encephalitis in Texas. Bull Pan Am Health Org. 1976;10:46–57.
33. Scherer WF, Cupp EW, Dziem GM, et al. Mesenteronal infection threshold of an epizootic strain of Venezuelan equine encephalitis virus in *Culex (melanconion) taeniopus* mosquitoes and its implication to the apparent disappearance of this virus from an enzootic habitat in Guatemala. Am J Trop Med Hyg. 1982;31:1030–1037.
34. Powers AM, Obserste MS, Brault AC, et al. Repeated emergence of epidemic/epizootic Venezuelan equine encephalitis from a single genotype of enzootic subtype ID virus. J Virol. 1997;71:6697–6705.
35. Niklasson B. Sindbis and Sindbis-like viruses. In: Monath TP, ed. The Arboviruses: Epidemiology and Ecology, v. IV. Boca Raton, Fla: CRC Press; 1988:167–176.
36. Mudge PR. Clinical features of epidemic polyarthritis. Arbovirus Res Aust. 1982:158–166.
37. Pinheiro FP, LeDuc JW. Mayaro virus disease. In: Monath TP, ed. The Arboviruses: Epidemiology and Ecology, v. III. Boca Raton, Fla: CRC Press; 1988:137–150.
38. Weaver SC, Lorenz LH, Scott TW. Pathologic changes in the midgut of *Culex tarsalis* following infection with Western equine encephalomyelitis virus. Am J Trop Med Hyg. 1992;47:691–701.
39. Charles PC, Walters E, Margolis F, et al. Mechanism of neuro-invasion of Venezuelan equine encephalitis virus in the mouse. Virology. 1995;208:662–671.
40. Gorelkin L. Venezuelan equine encephalitis in an adult animal host. Am J Pathol. 1973;73:425–432.
41. Jackson AC, Rossiter JP. Apoptotic cell death is an important cause of neuronal cell injury in Venezuelan equine encephalitis virus infection of mice. Acta Neuropathol. 1997;93:349–353.
42. Fourie ED, Morrison JGL. Rheumatoid arthritis syndrome after chikungunya fever. S Afr Med J. 1979;56:130–132.
43. Dropulic B, Masters CL. Entry of neurotropic arboviruses into the central nervous system: An in vitro study using mouse brain endothelium. J Infect Dis. 1990;161:685–691.
44. Griffin DE, Hardwick JM. Regulators of apoptosis on the road to persistent alphavirus infection. Annu Rev Microbiol. 1997;51:565–592.
45. Levine B, Griffin DE. Persistence of viral RNA in mouse brains after recovery from acute alphavirus encephalitis. J Virol. 1992;66:6429–6435.
46. Grosfeld H, Lustig S, Gozes Y, et al. Divergent envelope E2 alphavirus sequences spanning amino acids 297 to 352 induce in mice virus-specific immunity and antibodies with complement-mediated cytolytic activity. Virology. 1992;66:1084–1090.
47. Gorrell MD, Lemm JA, Rice CM, Griffin DE. Immunization with nonstructural proteins promotes functional recovery of alphavirus-infected neurons. J Virol. 1997;71:3415–3419.
48. Clarke DH. Two nonfatal human infections with the virus of eastern encephalitis. Am J Trop Med Hyg. 1961;10:67–70.
49. Baker AB. Western equine encephalitis. Clinical features. Neurology. 1958;8:880–881.
50. Deller JJ, Russell PK. Chikungunya disease. Am J Trop Med Hyg. 1968;17:1007–1011.
51. Kennedy AC, Fleming J, Solomon L. Chikungunya viral arthropathy: A clinical description. J Rheumatol. 1980;7:231–236.
52. Calisher CH, El-Kafrawi AO, Al-Deen Mahmud MI, et al. Complex-specific immunoglobulin M antibody patterns in humans infected with alphaviruses. J Clin Microbiol. 1986;23:155–159.
53. Deresiewicz RL, Thaler SJ, Zamani AA. Clinical and neuroradiographic manifestations of eastern equine encephalitis. N Engl J Med. 1997;336:1867–1874.
54. Coates DM, Makh SR, Jones N, et al. Assessment of assays for the serodiagnosis of Venezuelan equine encephalitis. J Infect Dis. 1992;25:279–289.
55. Carey DE, Myers RM, DeRanitz CM, el al. The 1964 chikungunya epidemic at Vellore, South India, including observations about concurrent dengue. Trans R Soc Trop Med Hyg. 1969;63:434–435.
56. Tan R, Meegan J, LeDuc J, et al. Enzyme-linked immunosorbent assay for diagnosis of chikungunya disease. Presented at the Thirty-fourth Annual Meeting of the American Society of Tropical Medicine and Hygiene, Miami, Fla, November 3–7, 1985.
57. Strizki JM, Repik PM. Differential reactivity of immune sera from human vaccinees with field strains of equine encephalitis virus. Am J Trop Med Hyg. 1995;53:564–570.
58. Greenway TE, Eldridge JH, Ludwig G, et al. Enhancement of protective immune responses to Venezuelan equine encephalitis virus with micro-encapsulated vaccine. Vaccine. 1995;13:1411–1420.
59. McClain DJ, Pittman PR, Ramsburg HH, et al. Immunologic interference from sequential administration of live attenuated alphavirus vaccines. J Infect Dis. 1998;177:634–641.
60. Davis NL, Brown KW, Greenwald GF, et al. Attenuated mutants of Venezuelan equine encephalitis virus containing lethal mutations in the PE2 cleavage signal combined with a second site suppressor mutation in E1. Virology. 1995;212:102–110.
61. Charles PC, Brown KW, Davis NL, et al. Mucosal immunity induced by immunization with a live attenuated Venezuelan equine encephalitis vaccine candidate. Virology. 1997;228:153–160.

Chapter 141

Rubella Virus (German Measles)

ANNE A. GERSHON

Rubella is an acute exanthematous viral infection of children and adults. The clinical illness is characterized by rash, fever, and lymphadenopathy and resembles a mild case of measles (rubeola). Although many infections with the agent are subclinical, this virus has the potential to cause fetal infection with resultant birth defects and, uncommonly in adults, various forms of arthritis.

Rubella virus was first isolated in 1962 by Parkman and colleagues[1] and by Weller and Neva.[2] Rubella virus is classified in the

Togaviridae family[3, 4] on the basis of its RNA genome, icosahedral capsid, and lipoprotein envelope. Rubella virus is closely related to the alphaviruses, but in contrast to alphaviruses, no vector is required for transmission of rubella, and it is serologically distinct from alphaviruses.[4] Therefore, rubella virus has been placed in a separate genus, *Rubivirus*.

On electron microscopy, rubella virus is roughly spherical. Its envelope, which has short surface projections, has a diameter of about 60 nm. The envelope surrounds the nucleocapsid, which has a diameter of about 30 nm; it is composed of a helix of protein and RNA. Rubella virus matures by budding from the cell membrane.[5]

Three structural polypeptides associated with rubella virus are termed E1, E2, and C. Nonstructural proteins that are related to replication and transcription probably also exist. E1 and E2 are transmembrane glycoproteins, and C is the capsid protein that surrounds the RNA of the virion. Hemagglutinin and complement-fixing antigens are composed of varying proportions and mixtures of E1, E2, and C.[6–8]

The rubella virus is relatively unstable, and it is inactivated by lipid solvents, trypsin, formalin, ultraviolet light, and extremes of pH and heat and is inhibited by amantadine.[9] Cytopathic effects may not be noted in all cell lines in which rubella virus replicates. However, cytopathic effects are readily observed in the rabbit kidney cell line RK-13 and in primary African green monkey cell.[6]

EPIDEMIOLOGY

Rubella was not distinguished clinically from certain other exanthematous infections until the late 19th century. It was at one time termed *third* disease, measles and scarlet fever being *first* and *second*, respectively.[10] Because postnatal rubella is such a mild illness, the disease was considered to be of only minor importance for many years. However, in 1941, when Gregg[11] recognized the link between maternal rubella and certain congenital defects, a more complete picture of disease due to rubella virus began to emerge.

The incidence of clinical cases of postnatal rubella is highest in the spring, and it was traditionally recognized to be most common in children 5 to 9 years of age.[12] However, some evidence suggests that rubella is now being seen with increasing frequency in an older age group because of the widespread use of rubella vaccine.[13] Rubella is only a moderately contagious illness, in contrast to measles. Thus, in the prevaccine era only 80 to 90% of adults were immune to rubella, whereas 98% were immune to measles.[12]

Epidemics of rubella of minor proportions used to occur in the prevaccine era every 6 to 9 years, with the occurrence of epidemics at intervals of up to 30 years. The most recent major epidemic in the United States occurred in 1964, during which some 12,500,000 persons were infected.[14] Since the licensure of a live attenuated rubella vaccine in 1969, there have been no subsequent large rubella epidemics in countries where the vaccine is widely used. Limited outbreaks have continued to occur, however, in settings such as schools and military camps where groups of susceptible individuals have close contact with each other.[13]

Transmission of Rubella

Rubella virus is spread in droplets that are shed from the respiratory secretions of infected persons. Patients are most contagious when the rash is erupting, but they may shed virus from the throat from 10 days before the onset of the rash to 15 days after its onset. Patients with subclinical cases of illness may also transmit the infection to others.[9]

Infants with congenital rubella shed large quantities of virus from body secretions for many months. They may thus transmit the infection to those who care for them. These babies continue to excrete rubella virus despite high titers of neutralizing antibody, a puzzling phenomenon that has yet to be explained.[15]

Persons who have received rubella vaccine do not transmit rubella to others, although the virus may be isolated from the pharynx. It may be that the quantity of virus shed is too small to be infectious.[16–18]

Maintenance of Immunity to Rubella

After an attack of rubella, lifelong protection against the disease develops in most persons. However, the factors responsible for this protection are not precisely understood. It is known that antibody titers to rubella virus develop, but the significance of declining antibody titers with time remains unclear. Cell-mediated immunity to rubella virus due to $CD4^+$ and $CD8^+$ T lymphocytes has also been detected by in vitro assays[6, 19] months to years after an attack of rubella. The persistence of humoral and cellular immunity to rubella in a group of cloistered nuns who had no opportunity for reexposure to rubella virus has been documented.[20] The persistence of specific antibody as long as 14 years after immunization has also been demonstrated.[21, 22]

Nevertheless, despite the presence of specific immunity to rubella virus, it appears that reinfection with rubella virus can occur. This had been long suspected on clinical grounds alone.[23, 24] Rubella reinfections have been documented by detection of a significant boost in rubella antibody titer in naturally immune persons after reexposure to the virus. The overwhelming majority of reinfections are asymptomatic.[25] It is likely that the virus can multiply locally in the upper respiratory tract but that viremia occurs infrequently because the host's immune response eradicates the virus before it can invade the blood. However, occasionally, patients with proven rubella reinfection years after natural rubella and with symptoms indicative of viremia such as arthritis and rash have been described.[26]

Rubella reinfection occurring months or years after the receipt of rubella vaccine has also been observed. Several investigators have documented reinfections in up to 80% of persons who had received rubella vaccine previously and who were subsequently exposed to rubella during an epidemic.[25, 27, 28] Most of these reinfections have not been characterized by clinical illness but were identified only by a boost in antibody titer. Viremia is probably extremely rare in such cases,[27, 29, 30] although rubella virus has been recovered from throat secretions in reinfections.[25, 29] In one study of eight seronegative adult vaccinees who were experimentally challenged with wild-type rubella virus, replication in the respiratory tract was found in seven and viremia was present in two.[31] These subjects, however, also experienced only a mild illness or remained asymptomatic.[31]

Reinfections have been more common in vaccinees than in persons who had natural rubella, and reinfections are most common in persons with hemagglutination inhibition (HAI) antibody titers of 1:64 or less.[25, 27, 29] It has been suggested that there may also be qualitative differences in antibody between persons with vaccine-induced immunity and those with natural immunity, because in one study, even with similar HAI titers, vaccinees were 10 times more likely to be reinfected than were those with natural immunity to rubella.[25]

Whether rubella reinfection that occurs during pregnancy can result in transmission of the virus to the fetus has been the subject of much debate. Several case reports in the older literature ascribing fetal defects to maternal rubella reinfection were actually primary maternal infections in all likelihood.[32–34] Viremia has been documented in one woman with detectable rubella antibody before immunization.[35] Boué and colleagues studied a small number of women with documented subclinical cases of rubella reinfection during pregnancy who carried their babies to term; all the babies were found to be normal.[36] In a number of other case reports of rubella reinfection during pregnancy, babies born (at term) to the affected mothers had symptoms suggestive of congenital rubella.[37–42] Most of these reinfections occurred years after the natural infection, although some occurred years after immunization.[41, 42] However, these transmissions are acknowledged to be extremely rare events, particularly as reflected by the exceedingly low incidence of congenital rubella in the United States today (see later on).

In summary, it appears that persons immune to rubella, by virtue either of having had the natural infection or of having received rubella vaccine, may be reinfected when reexposed. However, this infection is usually asymptomatic and detectable only by serologic means. Viremia in reinfection appears, fortunately, to be a rare event.

It was at one time hoped that the presence of large numbers of immune people in a community could prevent rubella epidemics from occurring, so-called herd immunity. However, it has been documented that herd immunity does not eliminate the spread of rubella.[42]

PATHOGENESIS

The incubation period for rubella ranges from 12 to 23 days, with an average of 18 days. As in measles (see Chapter 149), a primary and a secondary viremia are believed to accompany rubella. Rubella virus has been detected in leukocytes of patients as much as 1 week before the onset of symptoms.[44] As measles, the rubella rash appears as immunity develops and the virus disappears from the blood,[6] suggesting that the rash is immunologically mediated. Although circulating immune complexes are detectable during rubella, they do not seem to contribute to the development of rash.[6, 45] Rubella virus has been isolated from involved skin,[46] but this does not preclude the possibility that the rash is secondary to an immune response to the virus.

CLINICAL MANIFESTATIONS

Age is the most important determinant of the severity of rubella. Postnatally acquired rubella is generally an innocuous infection, and as is true for many viral illnesses, children are apt to have milder disease than are adults. In contrast, the fetus is at high risk to develop severe rubella with serious sequelae if infected transplacentally during maternal rubella in early pregnancy.

Postnatal Rubella

Many if not most cases of postnatal rubella are subclinical.[14, 47] Among those patients who are symptomatic, children do not experience a prodromal phase, but adults may have a prodrome of malaise, fever, and anorexia for several days. The major clinical manifestations of postnatal rubella are adenopathy, which may last several weeks, and rash. The lymph nodes involved include the posterior auricular, posterior cervical, and suboccipital chains; on occasion, splenomegaly also occurs.[48] These symptoms are not specific for rubella, and the disease may resemble measles, toxoplasmosis, scarlet fever, roseola, parvovirus B19 infection, and certain enterovirus infections.

The rash of rubella begins on the face and moves down the body. It is maculopapular but not confluent, may desquamate during convalescence, and may be absent in some cases. An enanthem consisting of petechial lesions on the soft palate (Forscheimer spots) has been described for rubella, but unlike Koplik spots in measles, this enanthem is not diagnostic for rubella. The rash may be accompanied by mild coryza and conjunctivitis. Usually the rash lasts 3 to 5 days. Fever, if present, rarely lasts beyond the first day of rash.

Complications of Postnatal Rubella

In contrast to the case with measles (rubeola), complications of postnatal rubella are uncommon. Bacterial superinfection after rubella is rare.

Arthritis or arthralgia has been reported in as many as one third of women with rubella; of interest, this complication is less frequent in children and men.[49] This arthritis tends to involve the fingers, wrists, and knees, and it occurs either as the rash is appearing or soon afterward. It may be rather slow to resolve, and take as long as a month. Rarely does chronic arthritis develop.

The pathogenesis of rubella arthritis is not entirely understood. The frequency of detection and the quantity of circulating immune complexes are higher in rubella vaccinees reporting joint complaints than in those with no joint involvement.[45, 50] Rubella virus has been isolated from joint effusions in cases of acute and recurrent rubella arthritis associated either with previous natural infection or with vaccination.[51–59] Rubella virus has also been isolated from peripheral blood mononuclear cells in patients with chronic arthritis.[58, 60] A persistent rubella virus infection of human synovial cells cultured in vitro has also been reported, which has been advanced as an explanation for the pathogenesis of chronic forms of rubella arthritis.[61]

Hemorrhagic manifestations occur as a complication in approximately 1 in 3000 cases of rubella.[48, 62] In contrast to other complications of rubella, this occurs more often in children than in adults. This complication may be secondary to both thrombocytopenia and vascular damage, and it is probably immunologically mediated.[62] Some investigators have proposed that mild thrombocytopenia often goes undetected in apparently "uncomplicated" rubella.[63] Thrombocytopenia may last from weeks to months and may cause serious problems if bleeding into vital areas such as the brain, kidney, or eye occurs.[48] Thrombocytopenic purpura as the single clinical manifestation of rubella in children has also been reported.[62]

Encephalitis is an extremely uncommon complication of rubella; it has been reported, during an epidemic, to occur in 1 of 5000 cases. It occurs more frequently in adults than in children, and it is associated with a mortality of 20 to 50%.[48, 64, 65] Survivors usually have no sequelae.[6] A fatal case of rubella encephalitis in a 2-month-old child whose mother had rubella in the last week of pregnancy has been reported.[66]

Mild hepatitis has been described as an unusual complication of rubella.[67]

Congenital Rubella

Rubella can be a disastrous disease in early gestation and lead to fetal death, premature delivery, and an array of congenital defects.

The incidence of congenital rubella in a given population is quite variable, depending on the number of susceptible individuals, the circulation of virus in the community, and in recent times, the use of rubella vaccine. The rubella epidemic of 1964 left 30,000 affected infants in its wake. Between 1969 and 1979, however, an average of 39 cases per year was reported to the Centers for Disease Control and Prevention (CDC).[68, 69] Since then, an all-time low of only an average of 10 cases per year has been reported in the United States.[69]

The effects of rubella virus on the fetus are, to a large extent, dependent on the time of infection; generally the younger the fetus when infected, the more severe the illness. During the first 2 months of gestation, the fetus has a 65 to 85% chance of being affected, with an outcome of either multiple congenital defects and/or spontaneous abortion.[6] Rubella during the third month of fetal life has been associated with a 30 to 35% chance of developing a single defect such as deafness or congenital heart disease. Fetal infection during the fourth month carries a 10% risk of a single congenital defect. Occasionally fetal damage (deafness alone) is seen if rubella occurs up to the 20th week of gestation.[70]

The specific signs and symptoms of congenital rubella may be classified as temporary such as low birth weight, permanent such as deafness, and developmental such as myopia.[68] The most common manifestations are deafness, cataract or glaucoma, congenital heart disease, and mental retardation; a list of the major clinical manifestations is presented in Table 141–1.[68]

Prospective studies of the congenital rubella syndrome suggest that it should not be thought of as a static disease. Some children whose mothers had rubella during pregnancy and who, at birth, were considered normal were found to have manifestations of congenital rubella on reaching school age.[71, 72] Diabetes mellitus appearing in

14. Horstmann DM. Rubella: The challenge of its control. J Infect Dis. 1971;123:640.
15. Cooper LZ, Green RH, Krugman S, et al. Neonatal thrombocytopenic purpura and other manifestations of rubella contracted in vitro. Am J Dis Child. 1965;110:416.
16. Halstead SB, Diwan AR. Failure to transmit rubella vaccine virus. JAMA. 1971;215:634.
17. Scott HD, Byrne EB. Exposure of susceptible pregnant women to rubella vaccines. JAMA. 1971;215:609.
18. Fleet WF, Schaffner W, Lefkowitz LB, et al. Exposure of susceptible teachers to rubella vaccinees. Am J Dis Child. 1972;123:28.
19. Steele RW, Hensen SA, Vincent MM, et al. A ^{51}Cr microassay technique for cell-mediated immunity to viruses. J Immunol. 1973;110:1502.
20. Rossier E, Phipps PH, Weber JM, et al. Persistence of humoral and cell-mediated immunity to rubella virus in cloistered nuns and in schoolteachers. J Infect Dis. 1981;144:137–141.
21. Horstmann D, Schluederberg A, Emmons JE, et al. Persistence of vaccine-induced immune responses to rubella: Comparison with natural infection. Rev Infect Dis. 1985;7(Suppl):80–85.
22. Plotkin S, Buser F. History of RA27/3 rubella vaccine. Rev Infect Dis. 1985;7(Suppl):77–78.
23. Hillenbrand FKM. Rubella in a remote community. Lancet. 1956;2:64.
24. Fry J, Dillane JB, Fry L. Rubella 1962. Br Med J. 1962;2:833.
25. Horstmann DM, Liebhaber H, Le Bouvier GL, et al. Rubella: Reinfection of vaccinated and naturally immune persons exposed in an epidemic. N Engl J Med. 1970;283:771.
26. Wilkins J, Leedom JM, Salvotore MA, et al. Clinical rubella with arthritis resulting from reinfection. Ann Intern Med. 1972;77:930.
27. Davis WJ, Larson HE, Simsarian JP, et al. A study of rubella immunity and resistance to infection. JAMA. 1971;215:600.
28. Chang TW, Des Rosiers S, Weinstein L. Clinical and serologic studies of an outbreak of rubella in a vaccinated population. N Engl J Med. 1970;283:246.
29. Wilkins J, Leidom JM, Portnoy B, et al. Reinfection with rubella virus despite live vaccine-induced immunity. Am J Dis Child. 1969;118:275.
30. Forrest JM, Menser MA, Honeyman MC, et al. Clinical rubella eleven months after vaccination. Lancet. 1972;2:399.
31. Schiff G, Young B, Stefanovic GM, et al. Challenge with rubella virus after loss of detectable vaccine-induced immunity. Rev Infect Dis. 1985;7(Suppl): 156–163.
32. Northrop RL, Gardner WM, Guttmann WF. Rubella reinfection during early pregnancy. A case report. Obstet Gynecol. 1972;39:524.
33. Banatvala JE, Best JM. Rubella infections. Lancet. 1973;1:1452.
34. Biano S, Cochran W, Herrmann KL, et al. Rubella reinfection during pregnancy. Am J Dis Child. 1975;129:1353.
35. Balfour HH, Groth KE, Edelman CK. Rubella viraemia and antibody responses after rubella vaccination and reimmunization. Lancet. 1981;1:1078.
36. Boué A, Nicolas A, Montagron B. Reinfection with rubella in pregnant women. Lancet. 1971;1:2151.
37. Eilard T, Strannegard O. Rubella reinfection in pregnancy followed by transmission to the fetus. J Infect Dis. 1974;129:594.
38. Levine JB, Berkowitz CD, St Geme JW. Rubella virus reinfection during pregnancy leading to late-onset congenital rubella syndrome. J Pediatr. 1982;100:589.
39. Fosgren M, Carlson G, Strongert K. Case of congenital rubella after maternal reinfection. Scand J Infect Dis. 1979;11:81–93.
40. Partridge JW, Flewett TH, Whitehead JEM. Congenital rubella affecting an infant whose mother had rubella antibodies before conception. Br Med J. 1981;282:187–188.
41. Bott LM, Eizenberg DH. Congenital rubella after successful vaccination. Med J Aust. 1982;1:514–515.
42. Robinson J, Lemay M, Vaudry WL. Congenital rubella after anticipated maternal immunity: Two cases and a review of the literature. Pediatr Infect Dis J. 1994;13:812–815.
43. Klock LE, Rachelfsky GS. Failure of rubella herd immunity during an epidemic. N Engl J Med. 1973;288:69.
44. Heggie AD, Robbins FC. Rubella in naval recruits. N Engl J Med. 1964;271:231.
45. Coyle PK, Wolinsky JS, Buimovici-Klein E, et al. Rubella-specific immune complexes after congenital infection and vaccination. Infect Immun. 1982;36:498–503.
46. Heggie AD. Pathogenesis of rubella exanthem. Isolation of rubella virus from skin. N Engl J Med. 1971;285:664.
47. Buescher EL. Behavior of rubella virus in adult populations. Arch Gesamte Virusforsch. 1965;16:470.
48. Heggie AD, Robbins FC. Natural rubella acquired after birth. Am J Dis Child. 1969;118:12.
49. Johnson RE, Hall AP. Rubella arthritis. N Engl J Med. 1958;258:743.
50. Vergani D, Morgan-Capner P, Davies ET, et al. Joint symptoms, immune complexes and rubella. Lancet. 1980;1:321–322.
51. Hildebrandt HM, Maasab HF. Rubella synovitis in a one-year-old patient. N Engl J Med. 1966;274:1428.
52. Phillips CA, Behbehani AM, Johnson LW, et al. Isolation of rubella virus: An epidemic characterized by rash and arthritis. JAMA. 1965;191:615.
53. Ogra PL, Herd JK. Arthritis associated with induced rubella infection. J Immunol. 1971;107:810–813.
54. Smith CA, Petty RE, Tingle AJ. Rubella virus and arthritis. Rheum Dis Clin North Am. 1987;13:265–274.
55. Grahame R, Armstrong R, Simmons NA, et al. Isolation of rubella virus from synovial fluid in five cases of seronegative arthritis. Lancet. 1981;2:649–651.
56. Grahame R, Armstrong R, Simmons NA, et al. Chronic arthritis associated with the presence of intrasynovial rubella virus. Ann Rheum Dis. 1983;42:2–13.
57. Fraser JR, Cunningham AL, Hayes K, et al. Rubella arthritis in adults. Isolation of virus, cytology, and other aspects of synovial infection. Clin Exp Rheumatol. 1983;1:287–293.
58. Chantler JK, Tingle AJ, Petty RE. Persistent rubella virus infection associated with chronic arthritis in children. N Engl J Med. 1985;313:1117–1123.
59. Chantler JK, da Roza DM, Bonnie ME, et al. Sequential studies on synovial lymphocyte stimulation by rubella antigen, and rubella virus isolation in an adult with persistent arthritis. Ann Rheum Dis. 1985;44:564–568.
60. Chantler JK, Ford DK, Tingle AJ. Persistent rubella infection and rubella-associated arthritis. Lancet. 1982;1:1323–1325.
61. Cunningham AL, Fraser JRE. Persistent rubella virus infection of human synovial cells cultured in vitro. J Infect Dis. 1985;151:638–645.
62. Ozsoyla S, Kanra G, Savas G. Thrombocytopenic purpura related to rubella infection. Pediatrics. 1978;62:567.
63. Boyer WL, Sherman FE, Michaels RH, et al. Purpura in congenital and acquired rubella. N Engl J Med. 1965;273:1362.
64. Steen E, Torp KH. Encephalitis and thrombocytopenic purpura after rubella. Arch Dis Child. 1956;31:470.
65. Sherman FE, Michaels RH, Kenny FM. Acute encephalopathy (encephalitis) complicating rubella. JAMA. 1965;192:675.
66. Sheinis M, Sarov I, Maor E, et al. Severe neonatal rubella following maternal infection. Pediatr Infect Dis J. 1985;4:202–203.
67. Zeldis JB, Miller JG, Dienstag JL. Hepatitis in an adult with rubella. Am J Med. 1985;79:515–516.
68. Cooper LZ. Congenital rubella in the United States. In: Krugman S, Gershon A, eds. Infections of the Fetus and the Newborn Infant. New York: Alan R. Liss; 1975:1.
69. Centers for Disease Control and Prevention. Increase in rubella and congenital rubella—United States. MMWR Morb Mortal Wkly Rep. 1991;40:93–99.
70. Marshall WC. Rubella: Current problems and recent developments. Br J Clin Pract. 1976;30:56.
71. Menser MA, Forrest JM. Rubella: High incidence of defects in children considered normal at birth. Med J Aust. 1974;1:123.
72. Peckham CS. Clinical and laboratory study of children exposed in utero to maternal rubella. Arch Dis Child. 1972;47:571.
73. Norris JM, Dorman JS, Rewers M, Porte RE. The epidemiology and genetics of insulin-dependent diabetes mellitus. Arch Pathol Lab Med. 1987;111:905–909.
74. Menser MA, Forrest JM, Honeyman MC, et al. Diabetes, HLA antigens and congenital rubella. Lancet. 1974;2:1508–1509.
75. Ginsberg-Felner F, Witt ME, Fedun B, et al. Diabetes mellitus and auto-immunity in patients with the congenital rubella syndrome. Rev Infect Dis. 1985;7(Suppl):170–176.
76. Townsend JJ, Baringer JR, Wolinsky JS, et al. Progressive rubella panencephalitis: Late onset after congenital rubella. N Engl J Med. 1975;292:990.
77. Weil MC, Itabashi HH, Cremer NE, et al. Chronic progressive panencephalitis due to rubella virus simulating subacute sclerosing panencephalitis. N Engl J Med. 1975;292:994.
78. McIntosh ED, Menser MA. A fifty-year follow-up of congenital rubella. Lancet. 1992;340:414–415.
79. Alford CA, Neva FA, Weller TH. Virologic and serologic studies on human products of conception after maternal rubella. N Engl J Med. 1964;271:1275.
80. Hardy JB, Sever JL, Gilkeson MR. Declining antibody titers in children with congenital rubella. J Pediatr. 1969;75:213.
81. Doege TC, Kim KK. Studies of rubella and its prevention with gamma globulin. JAMA. 1967;200:584.
82. Fuccillo DA, Steele RW, Hensen SA, et al. Impaired cellular immunity to rubella virus in congenital rubella. Infect Immun. 1974;9:81.
83. Naeye RL, Blanc W. Pathogenesis of congenital rubella. JAMA. 1965;194:1277.
84. Driscoll SG. Histopathology of gestational rubella. Am J Dis Child. 1969;118:49.
85. Tondury G, Smith DW. Fetal rubella pathology. J Pediatr. 1966;68:867.
86. Plotkin SA, Vaheri A. Human fibroblasts infected with rubella virus produce a growth inhibitor. Science. 1967;154:659.
87. Nusbacher J, Hirschhorn K, Cooper LZ. Chromosomal abnormalities in congenital rubella. N Engl J Med. 1967;276:1409.
88. Rabinowe SL, George KL, Loughlin R, et al. Congenital rubella. Monoclonal antibody–defined T cell abnormalities in young adults. Am J Med. 1986;81:779–782.
89. Cherry JD. Newer viral exanthems. Prog Med Virol. 1973;16:269.
90. Bell EF, Ross CA, Grist NR. ECHO 9 infection in pregnant women with suspected rubella. J Clin Pathol. 1975;28:267.
91. Black JB, Durigon E, Kite-Powell K, et al. Seroconversion to human herpesvirus 6 and human herpesvirus 7 among Brazilian children with clinical diagnoses of measles or rubella. Clin Infect Dis. 1996;23:1156–1158.
92. Levin MJ, Oxman MN, Moore MG, et al. Diagnosis of congenital rubella in utero. N Engl J Med. 1974;290:1187.
93. Chernesky M, Wyman L, Mahoney J, et al. Clinical evaluation of the sensitivity and specificity of a commercially available enzyme immunoassay for detection of rubella virus–specific immunoglobulin M. J Clin Microbiol. 1984;20:400–404.
94. Field PR, Gong CM. Diagnosis of postnatally acquired rubella by use of three enzyme-linked immunoadsorbent assays for specific immunoglobulins G, and M and single radial hemolysis for specific immunoglobulin G. J Clin Microbiol. 1944;20:951–958.
95. Wittenburg RA, Roberts M, Elliott L, et al. Comparative evaluation of commercial rubella virus antibody kits. J Clin Microbiol. 1985;21:161–163.

96. Hedman K, Salonen E, Keski-Oja J, et al. Single-serum radial hemolysis to detect recent rubella infection. J Infect Dis. 1986;154:1018–1023.
97. Ferraro MJ, Kallas WM, Welch KP, et al. Comparison of a new, rapid enzyme immunoassay with a latex agglutination test for qualitative detection of rubella antibodies. J Clin Microbiol. 1987;25:1722–1724.
98. Morgan-Capner P, Hodgson J, Hambling MH, et al. Detection of rubella-specific IgM in subclinical reinfection in pregnancy. Lancet. 1985;244–246.
99. Belin E, Safyer S, Braslow C. False positive IgM-rubella enzyme-linked immunoassay in three first trimester pregnant patients. Pediatr Infect Dis J. 1990;9:671–672.
100. Terry GM, Ho TL, Warren RC, et al. First trimester prenatal diagnosis of congenital rubella: A laboratory investigation. Br Med J. 1986;292:930–933.
101. Bosma TJ, Corbett KM, Eckstein MB, et al. Use of PCR for prenatal and postnatal diagnosis of congenital rubella. J Clin Microbiol. 1995;33:2881–2887.
102. Daffos F, Forestier F, Grangeot-Keros L, et al. Prenatal diagnosis of congenital rubella. Lancet. 1984;2:1–3.
103. Grose C, Itani O, Weiner C. Prenatal diagnosis of fetal infection: Advances from aminocentesis to cordocentesis—congenital toxoplasmosis, rubella, cytomegalovirus, varicella virus, parvovirus and human immunodeficiency virus. Pediatr Infect Dis J. 1989;8:459–468.
104. Schiff GM. Titered lots of immune globulin. Efficacy in the prevention of rubella. Am J Dis Child. 1969;118:322.
105. Parkman PD, Meyer HM, Kirschstein RL, et al. Attenuated rubella virus I. Development and laboratory characterization. N Engl J Med. 1966;275:569.
106. Ewert DP, Frederick PD, Moscola L. Resurgence of congenital rubella syndrome in the 1990s. Report on missed opportunities and failed prevention policies among women of childbearing age. JAMA. 1992;267:2616–2620.
107. Watson JC, Hadler SC, Dykewicz CA, et al. Measles, mumps, and rubella—Vaccine use and strategies for elimination of measles, rubella, and congenital rubella syndrome and control of mumps: Recommendations of the Advisory Committee on Immunization Practices (ACIP). MMWR Morb Mortal Wkly Rep. 1998;47(RR-8):1–57.
108. Plotkin SA, Farquhar JD, Katz M, et al. Attenuation of RA 27/3 rubella virus in W1-38 human diploid cells. Am J Dis Child. 1969;118:178.
108. LeBouvier GL, Plotkin SA. Precepitin responses to rubella vaccine RA 27/3. J Infect Dis. 1971;123:220.
109. Ogra PL, Kerr-Grant D, Umana G, et al. Antibody response in serum and nasopharynx after naturally acquired and vaccine-induced infection with rubella virus. N Engl J Med. 1971;285:1333.
110. Modlin JF, Brandling-Bennett AD, Witte JJ, et al. A review of 5 years' experience with rubella vaccine in the United States. Pediatrics. 1975;55:20.
111. Tingle AJ, Chantler JK, Pot KH, et al. Postpartum rubella immunization: Association with development of prolonged arthritis, neurological sequelae, and chronic rubella viremia. J Infect Dis. 1985;152:606–612.
112. Cooper LZ, Ziring PR, Weiss HJ, et al. Transient arthritis after rubella vaccination. Am J Dis Child. 1969;118:218.
113. Horstmann DM, Liebhaber H, Kohorn EI. Postpartum vaccination of rubella-susceptible women. Lancet. 1970;2:1003.
114. Monto AS, Cavallero JJ, Whale EH. Frequency of arthralgia in women receiving one of three rubella vaccines. Arch Intern Med. 1970;126:635.
115. Lerman ST, Nankervis GA, Heggie AD, et al. Immunologic response, virus excretion and joint reactions with rubella vaccine. A study of adolescent girls and young women given live attenuated virus vaccine (HPV-77 DE5). Ann Intern Med. 1971;74:67.
116. Howson CP, Katz M, Johnston RB Jr, et al. Chronic arthritis after rubella vaccination. Clin Infect Dis. 1992;15:307–312.
117. Mitchell LA, Tingle AJ, MacWilliam L, et al. HLA-DR Class II associations with rubella vaccine–induced joint manifestations. J Infect Dis. 1998;177:5–12.
118. Miki NPH, Chantler JK. Differential ability of wild-type and vaccine strains of rubella virus to replicate and persist in human joint tissue. Clin Exp Rheumatol. 1992;10:3–12.
119. Dennehy PH, Saracen CL, Peter G. Seroconversion rates to combined measles-mumps-rubella-varicella vaccine of children with upper respiratory infection. Pediatrics. 1994;94:514–516.
120. Centers for Disease Control and Prevention. Rubella vaccination during pregnancy 1971–1986. MMWR Morb Mortal Wkly Rep. 1987;36:457–461.
121. Phillips CA, Maeck JVS, Rogers WA, et al. Intrauterine rubella infection following immunization with rubella vaccine. JAMA. 1970;213:624.
122. Vahieri A, Vesikari T, Oker-Blum N, et al. Isolation of attenuated rubella-vaccine virus from human products of conception and uterine cervix. N Engl J Med. 1972;286:1071.
123. Wyll SA, Herrmann K. Inadvertent rubella vaccination of pregnant women. Fetal risk in 215 cases. JAMA. 1973;225:1472.
124. Modlin JF, Herrmann K, Brandling-Bennett AD, et al. Risk of congenital abnormality after inadvertent rubella vaccination of pregnant women. N Engl J Med. 1976;294:972.
125. Fleet WF, Benz EW, Karzon DT, et al. Fetal consequences of maternal rubella immunization. JAMA. 1974;227:621.

Flaviviruses

Chapter 142

Flaviviruses (Yellow Fever, Dengue, Dengue Hemorrhagic Fever, Japanese Encephalitis, St. Louis Encephalitis, Tick-Borne Encephalitis)

THEODORE F. TSAI

The Flavivirus genus comprises more than 68 principally arthropod transmitted or zoonotic viruses, of which 30 are known to cause human disease.[1] Some among the remainder are "orphans" that have an unknown pathogenic potential but that have infected humans. The agents are classified in the family Flaviviridae (from *flavus,* Latin for "yellow" and for *yellow fever virus,* the type species) with viruses in the Pestivirus genus (which are of veterinary importance) and those in the genus of hepatitis C–like viruses on the basis of similar morphologic characteristics and genomic structures.[2] No antigenic relationships, however, have been demonstrated between viruses in the respective genera.

From a global perspective, the public health burdens of flaviviral infections such as dengue, yellow fever, Japanese encephalitis, and tick-borne encephalitis have been of sufficient magnitude to stimulate, at an early stage, the development of vaccines to control the diseases.[3–5] For the latter three diseases, the licensure and distribution of effective vaccines for more than 60, 30, and 20 years, respectively, have led to significant reductions in incidence and, in some locations, the effective disappearance of cases; dengue vaccines are under active development. Many of the other flaviviruses cause considerable morbidity, but their appearance as individual cases or outbreaks are infrequent or are too local in impact to have stimulated a concerted approach to prevention and control.

Flaviviral infections are important considerations in the differential diagnosis of central nervous system (CNS) infection, hemorrhagic fever, and acute febrile illnesses with arthropathy or rash, especially in returned travellers.[6] By evaluating the epidemiologic history, including the places and dates of travel, activities and immunizations, in conjunction with clinical features of the illnesses and their incubation periods, the clinician can obtain important clues to pursue or exclude a diagnosis. Those diseases of chief importance are described later.

HISTORY

Yellow Fever

Although the historical record and molecular taxonomic studies of viral strains have indicated an African origin of yellow fever (YF), the disease was first recognized in an outbreak occurring in the New World in 1648. The virus was probably introduced by *Aedes aegypti*–infested slave-trading vessels from West Africa, and, through the next 2 centuries, similar outbreaks spread by introduction to port cities in the New World and in Europe. Their calamity was illustrated by the 1793 Philadelphia epidemic in which one tenth of the city's population died and by the 1878 Mississippi Valley epidemic of

100,000 cases, the cost of which equaled the national budget. Sanitary measures, especially the introduction of piped water, unwittingly diminished transmission of the disease, although its mosquito-borne route of spread was not demonstrated until 1900 and its viral cause until after 1928. Theiler's development of the attenuated 17D vaccine strain in the 1930s was recognized by a Nobel Prize, but more than 60 years later, vaccine implementation in areas with endemic transmission remains fragmentary, and outbreaks recur periodically.

Dengue

Because of dengue's nonspecific clinical features, the interpretation of historical records for evidence of past epidemics is open to speculation; however, Benjamin Rush's description of the 1780 Philadelphia epidemic was the earliest description in English of breakbone fever. Sporadic outbreaks appeared worldwide through the early decades of this century, the last in the United States occurring in Florida in 1934 and New Orleans in 1945. Clinical descriptions of dengue complicated by hemorrhages, shock, and death were reported in outbreaks in Australia in 1897, in Greece in 1928, and in Formosa in 1931. Mosquito-borne transmission of the infection by *A. aegypti* was demonstrated in 1903. While isolating the virus in 1944, Sabin demonstrated the failure of two viral strains to cross-protect humans, thus establishing the existence of dengue viral serotypes. Hammon characterized two more serotypes in 1956. After World War II, the start of a pandemic with intensified transmission of multiple viral serotypes began in Southeast Asia, leading to outbreaks of dengue hemorrhagic fever–dengue shock syndrome (DHF-DSS). In the last 2 decades, a similar pattern of intensified viral transmission and increased DHF-DSS incidence has been established in Southwest Asia, the Americas, and Oceania, fueled by secular changes toward urbanization, population growth, and increased mobility.

Japanese Encephalitis

Japanese encephalitis (JE) virus was isolated from a patient in a fatal case in Japan in 1934, but summertime encephalitis outbreaks leading to thousands of cases previously had been characterized and called Japanese *B* encephalitis to differentiate the disease from Von Economo's encephalitis lethargica (the qualifying *B* has fallen into disuse). Mosquito-borne transmission of the virus was established in 1938. The burden of annual epidemics led to the introduction in the mid-1960s of vaccines that effectively eliminated the disease in Japan, Korea, and Taiwan and reduced the annual incidence in China by 10-fold, from 160,000 cases in 1966 to 16,000 in 1996. Since the 1970s, the incidence of the disease has increased in countries of Southeast Asia, India, Nepal, and Sri Lanka, probably due to changes in agricultural productivity and increased recognition rather than to viral spread. However, novel introductions of the virus to northern Australia in 1995 and twice to western Pacific islands have been documented. Childhood immunization programs now have been established in Thailand and areas of Vietnam and Sri Lanka.

St. Louis Encephalitis

St. Louis encephalitis (StLE) was first reported as an epidemic of unknown cause in St. Louis, Missouri, in 1933. A U.S. Public Health Service investigation identified its viral cause and on the basis of epidemiologic features, surmised a mosquito-borne mode of transmission that subsequently was proved by viral isolations from *Culex* mosquitoes in outbreaks in the Yakima Valley, Washington. With the occurrence of more than 10,000 cases in over 50 outbreaks through 1990, the disease has been regarded as the most important cause of epidemic viral encephalitis in the United States. However, since the last and largest series of outbreaks between 1974 and 1977, in which an estimated 3000 cases were recognized in Ontario, Manitoba, and all but eight states, the frequency and scale of outbreaks have diminished. Outbreaks in Houston, New Orleans, and Dallas have underscored homelessness and, possibly, human immunodeficiency virus (HIV) infection as novel risk factors for acquiring the disease.

Tick-Borne Encephalitis

Tick-borne encephalitis (TBE) was described clinically in Austria in 1927, but isolation of the virus responsible for central European encephalitis (CEE) was not reported until 1948. An investigation of cases in the far eastern part of Russia in 1932 led to descriptions of Russian spring-summer encephalitis (RSSE) and in 1937, isolation of the virus from the blood of patients and from *Ixodes* tick vectors. CEE virus or closely related strains have subsequently been isolated from most areas of continental Europe, including Scandinavia, the Iberian peninsula, Turkey, and Greece and related louping ill virus, from the British Isles. Oral transmission from the milk of infected livestock was confirmed in a common source epidemic leading to 660 cases in Czechoslovakia in 1951. The annual occurrence of several hundred cases in Austria led to the distribution of an inactivated vaccine to high-risk groups beginning in 1973; general distribution has led to a significant decline in disease incidence.

Powassan virus, considered a North American analogue, was isolated from a patient in a fatal case in Ontario in 1958, but human cases and viral isolations subsequently have been reported from Russia. Fewer than 50 cases have been recognized in total.

PATHOGENS

Virions are spheric, 40 to 60 nm in diameter, and consist of a lipid envelope covered densely with surface projections comprising M (membrane) and E (envelope) glycoproteins.[1, 2, 7] The latter are organized as dimers, paired horizontally head to tail, on the virion surface. The viruses are unstable in the environment and sensitive to heat, ultraviolet radiation, disinfectants, including alcohol and iodine, and acid pH. The nucleocapsid joins the capsid (C) protein to a single strand of positive-sense RNA of 11 kilobases, which includes a 10-kilobase open reading frame for a single polyprotein precursor, flanked by noncoding regions at either end. The order of protein gene products from the 5′ end is C, premembrane (preM, a precursor of the mature M protein), E, and a series of seven nonstructural proteins needed in the viral replicative process: NS1, NS2A, NS2B, NS3, NS4A, NS4B, NS5.

The E protein exhibits important biologic properties, including viral-cellular attachment, endosomal membrane fusion, and the display of sites mediating hemagglutination and viral neutralization. Its carboxy terminus provides a membrane anchor, and on the virion surface, it is folded into three structural and corresponding antigenic domains, including an immunoglobulin-like motif that may be involved in receptor binding. Viral neutralizing epitopes are scattered on its surface, which because the protein is folded, are nonlinear and conformationally dependent. PreM protein chaperones the E protein in the cell secretory pathway, preventing its misfolding, before it is cleaved to its M form in the mature virion. NS1 is expressed on the surface of infected cells and is also excreted as a complement-fixing antigen. Although antibodies to NS1 do not neutralize the virus, they provide protective immunity, probably by complement and cell-mediated responses against infected cells.[8] Aside from their replicative functions, NS1, NS2a, NS3, and NS5 display epitopes mediating viral serotype and flaviviral cross-reactive HLA-restricted lymphocytic responses.[9–11]

Viral attachment to unidentified cellular receptors is followed by endocytic uptake of virus-containing vesicles where acidic-induced changes of the viral envelope lead to fusion activity, uncoating of the nucleocapsid, and viral RNA release into the cytoplasm. Glycosaminoglycans and proteoglycans have been implicated as receptors in some studies, but coreceptors may also be involved, and viral binding evidently varies with cell type.[12] The viral polyprotein is processed by repeated passage through the rough endoplasmic reticulum, providing the replicative complex for further viral RNA and protein synthesis and the assembly of nascent virions that mature through the Golgi and trans-Golgi network. Immature virions collect in the highly proliferated endoplasmic reticulum and secretory vesicles before release, although intracellular nucleocapsid accumulations have been observed in some virus-cell systems.

Flaviviruses are adapted to grow in a wide variety of insect, tick, and vertebrate cells and at temperatures spanning the normal temperatures of their arthropod, reptilian, mammalian, and avian hosts. Cytopathologic changes and plaque formation develop in Vero LLCMK2, BHK-21, PS, and primary chick and duck embryo cells, whereas infection of mosquito cell lines (e.g., C6/36 and AP61) is typically nondestructive and may persist.

A wide range of vertebrates, including mammals, birds, and reptiles, are naturally infected as amplifying hosts in the transmission cycle of alternating arthropod and vertebrate infection.[1, 6] These infections are usually asymptomatic, but individual viruses may be pathogenic for domesticated or wild animals; for example, several neurotropic flaviviruses, JE, StLE, West Nile, Kunjin, CEE, and Powassan viruses, produce encephalitis in horses, and certain CEE viral strains are neurotropic for dogs, sheep, and goats; JE virus is an important cause of swine abortion; louping ill is a manifestation of encephalitis in sheep; and YF and Kyasanur Forest disease are lethal in some monkey species. Laboratory rodents are generally susceptible to infection, with sensitivity inversely related to age.

With few exceptions, the flaviviruses can be classified by cross-neutralization assays into eight antigenic groups, of which the most important are the JE complex, consisting of JE, StLE, West Nile, and Murray Valley encephalitis viruses; the dengue complex of dengue 1 through 4 viruses; the tick-borne virus complex, including CEE, RSSE, louping ill, Powassan, Kyasanur Forest disease, and Omsk hemorrhagic fever viruses; YF virus; and a complex of non–vector-borne rodent- and bat-associated viruses.[1, 2, 6] Genetic studies largely support the antigenic classification and suggest the evolution of non–vector-borne flaviviruses from a hypothetic progenitor with the further sequential evolution of tick-borne and mosquito-borne viruses.[13] Genomic sequencing studies of specific viruses have facilitated the tracking of viral movements historically and in epidemics. For example, YF viral strains have been divided into East African, West African, and New World genotypes, with a close relationship between the latter two supporting the hypothesis that YF virus was introduced to the Western Hemisphere from Africa.[14] Genotypic markers have been of particular help in understanding the emergence of dengue and JE epidemics in the wake of viral introductions from other regions.[15, 16] Genotypes also have been correlated with viral biologic characteristics that underlie their transmission patterns. For example, StLE viral genotypes from the eastern and western United States exhibit distinct neurovirulence and transmission characteristics that are consistent with epidemiologic observations.[17]

EPIDEMIOLOGY

Yellow Fever

YF is transmitted in areas of sub-Saharan Africa and South America (Fig. 142–1). The disease has never been documented in Asia, but, in principle, anthroponotic (vector-borne person-to-person) transmission of the virus could occur there and in other *A. aegypti*–infested locations, including the southern United States.[4, 6] Epidemic (*urban*) yellow fever is transmitted by *A. aegypti* mosquitoes that are infected after feeding on viremic humans and then spread the infection in subsequent feeding attempts. The threat of epidemic transmission arises when a person with a forest-acquired infection travels to an *A. aegypti*–infested location while viremic.

The fluctuating global incidence of YF has been dominated by epidemics in Africa that, between 1986 and 1991 produced 20,424 reported cases and 5447 deaths (see Fig. 142–1). Official reports, however, considerably underestimated the true magnitude of those epidemics, which field studies estimated as 50-fold greater or over a million cases.[18, 19] Epidemic attack rates ranged as high as 30 in 1000, with case-fatality ratios of 20 to 50%. Two countries have reported their first outbreaks ever. In 1992, an outbreak of 26 among rural villagers in the Kerio Valley of Kenya was the first outbreak in East Africa in 50 years. In Gabon, a 1994 outbreak in a forest mining camp that spread to nearby *A. aegypti*–infested villages was an example of the potentially virulent transition to epidemic YF. The declining size and number of epidemics in recent years probably reflects cyclic changes in viral activity, increased human immunity acquired in recent epidemics, and emergency vaccination campaigns.[20]

In South America, an annual mean of approximately 100 cases was reported in the last 25 years, reflecting the occurrence of forest-acquired cases occurring in the greater Magdalena, Orinoco, and Amazon river basins.[18] In its *jungle cycle,* the virus is transmitted from tree-hole *Haemagogus* and *Sabethes* mosquitoes to forest monkeys in wandering epizootics following the movement of the animals and of the virus to susceptible populations. Cases predominate between January and March among males 15 to 45 years who are bitten incidentally by infected mosquitoes while employed as agricultural and forestry workers, soldiers, and settlers. An intensification of enzootic viral transmission frequently produces clusters of monkey deaths, which is accepted as evidence of an increased transmission risk to humans. The last urban outbreak in the Western Hemisphere was reported in Trinidad in 1954, but the growth of urban areas and their reinfestation by *A. aegypti* have renewed concern for the emergence of epidemics, especially in cities bordering forested areas. Since 1995, several patients with jungle-acquired disease have been hospitalized in Brazilian cities and in Santa Cruz, Bolivia, without epidemic spread, but the threat prompted mass vaccination campaigns and other control measures.[21]

In the moist savanna of Africa, a variety of tree-hole–breeding mosquitoes transmit infections among humans and monkeys during the end of the rainy season, leading to early infections in children and sporadic cases that are typically unrecognized. Annual infections in the range of 1% are estimated in areas of West Africa, which suggests that more than 200,000 endemic cases may occur annually.[22] Infections are spread readily by migration, with the potential for involvement of *A. aegypti* in urban areas and in dry locations where stored water provides breeding sites. During the dry season, the virus survives in infected mosquito eggs that are resistant to desiccation.

Dengue and Dengue Hemorrhagic Fever

Four serotypes of dengue virus are transmitted in the tropics, in an area roughly between 35 degrees north and 35 degrees south latitude, corresponding to the distribution of *A. aegypti,* the principal mosquito vector (Fig. 142–2).[23] *Aedes albopictus* and *Aedes polynesiensis* can transmit the infection in specific circumstances. Although enzootic transmission among forest monkeys in Asia and Africa has been described, anthroponotic viral transmission is sufficient to maintain the virus, and these animal infections could represent either epiphenomena or potentially a vestigial sylvatic cycle. The intensification of dengue transmission in tropical cities, where growing populations live under crowded conditions, can be understood in view of the close relationship of *A. aegypti* to humans.[24–27] After the virus feeds on a viremic person, viral replication in the mosquito over 1–2 weeks (extrinsic incubation period) is required before it can transmit the virus on subsequent feeding attempts, which may number several times a day depending on the availability of hosts, over its lifetime of 1 to 4 weeks. *A. aegypti* is adapted to breed around human dwellings, where the insects oviposit in uncovered water storage containers as well as miscellaneous containers holding water such as vases, flower dishes, cans, automobile tires, and other discarded objects. Adult mosquitoes shelter indoors and bite during 1- to 2-

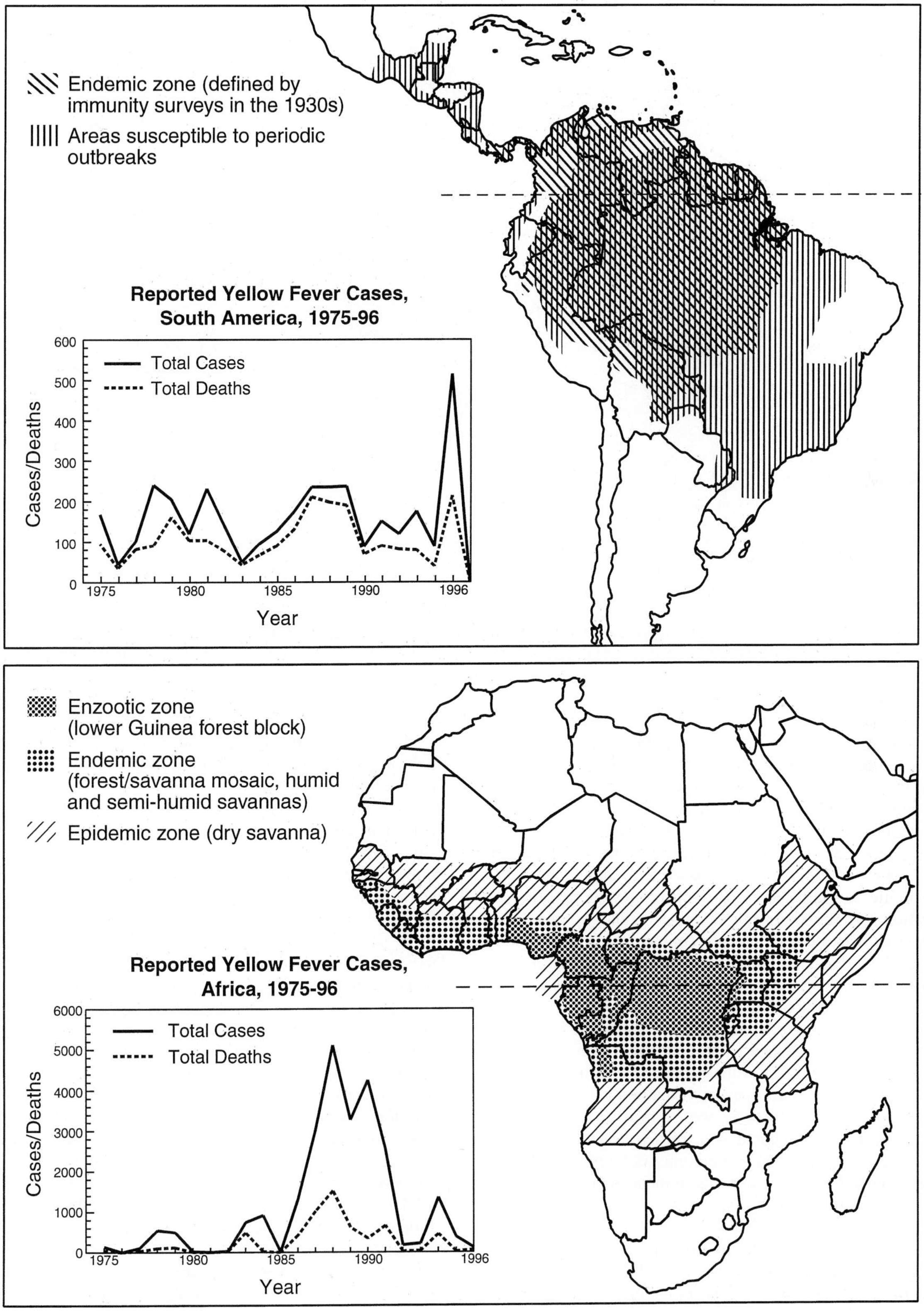

FIGURE 142–1. Geographic areas at risk for endemic and epidemic yellow fever, South America and Africa, and yellow fever cases reported to the World Health Organization, 1975–1996.

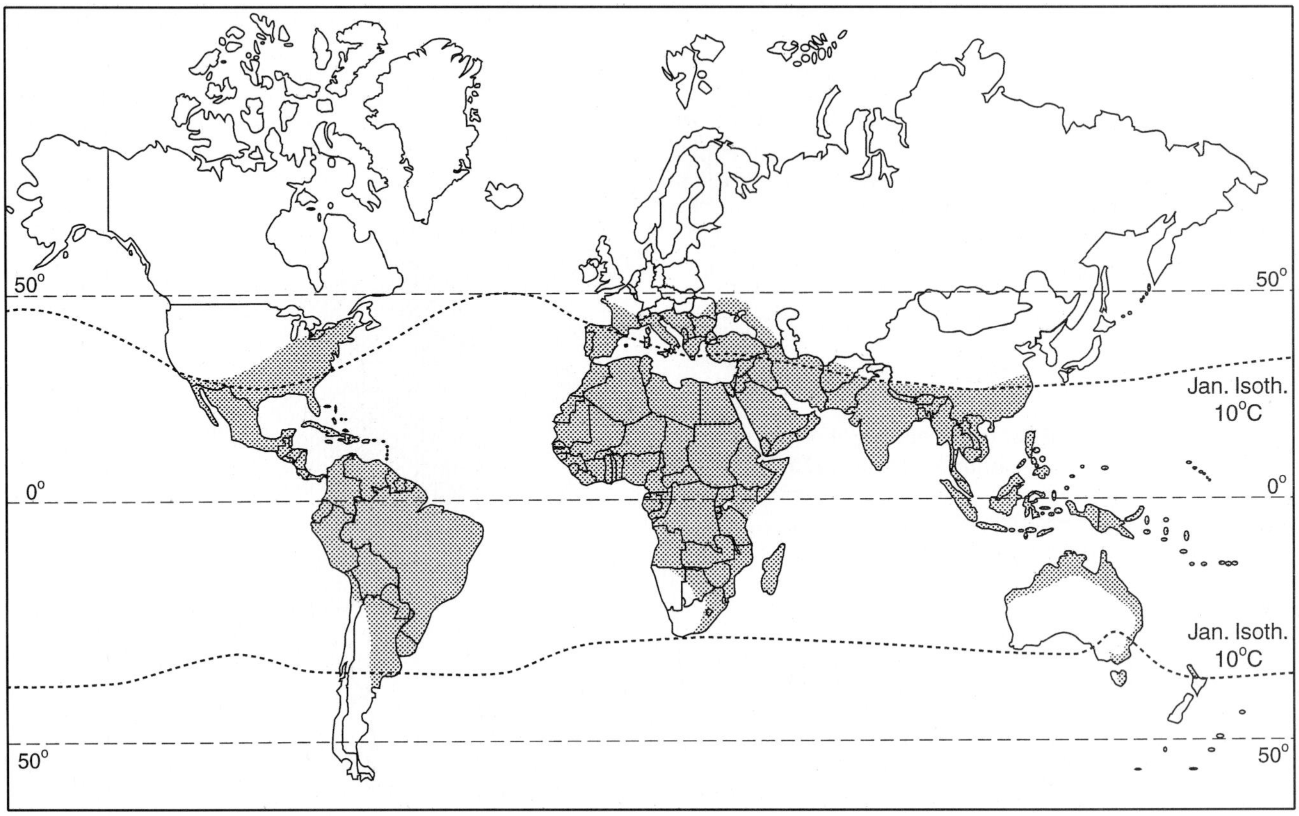

FIGURE 142–2. Approximate actual and potential distribution of *Aedes aegypti.* The band between the 10°C isotherms represents potential distribution. (From World Health Organization. Technical Guide for Diagnosis, Treatment, Surveillance, Prevention, and Control of Dengue Haemorrhagic Fever. 2nd ed. Geneva: World Health Organization; 1997.)

hour intervals in the morning and late afternoon. In areas with endemic transmission, 1 of every 20 houses may contain an infected mosquito.[27] Cases often cluster in households, and human movements and the mosquito's peregrinations within a range of 800 m rapidly spread the infection.[28] In tropical areas, transmission is maintained throughout the year and intensifies during the rainy season, when infected vector mosquitoes are more abundant as higher humidity lengthens their lifespan and increased temperatures shorten the extrinsic incubation period.

When the virus is introduced into susceptible populations, usually by viremic travelers, epidemic attack rates have reached 50 to 70%. Because cross-protective immunity among the serotypes is limited, epidemic transmission recurs with the introduction of novel types. Furthermore, because secondary infections predispose to dengue hemorrhagic fever (DHF, see later), the concurrent transmission of multiple viral serotypes establishes the necessary conditions for endemic DHF. Under these circumstances, virtually all DHF cases are in children with secondary infections, with a relative risk of developing DHF in secondary compared with primary infection as high as 100.[29–32] The central role of prior immunity is illuminated by the phenomenon of DHF in infants born to immune mothers who are infected for the first time before 1 year of age. In these cases, the age distribution parallels the expected decline of passively acquired maternal antibodies.[33, 34] Outbreaks in Cuba in 1981 and 1997, in which DHF cases occurred only in the age cohort exposed during the last epidemic period, older than 3 years and older than 17 years, respectively (see later), further underscore secondary infection as a critical precondition for DHF.[35, 36] Anecdotal DHF cases in persons with primary infections have been reported, however, pointing to the contributory roles of viral strain and host factors.[37, 38] Race and specific HLA haplotypes have been implicated in the risk of acquiring DHF, and a variable predominance of cases has been observed in girls and in children with good nutrition, indicating the contributions of both genetic and acquired host factors to susceptibility to the syndrome.[36, 39, 40]

Intensified dengue transmission in Asia after World War II evolved in the previously described pattern, resulting in novel epidemics of DHF beginning in the 1950s. Dengue infection rates in Southeast Asian areas with hyperendemic transmission are now in the range of 5 to 10%, with DHF incidence rates of 10 to 300 in 100,000.[24, 25] In Thailand, dengue accounts for one third of acute febrile illnesses in children seeking medical attention.[29, 41] Although DHF still is principally a disease of children younger than 15 years, the peak age of risk has risen as dengue virus transmission has declined. In the Western Hemisphere, a higher proportion of severe dengue fever and DHF cases has been reported in adults.[42] Globally, 3 billion people reside in areas at risk for dengue fever, among whom 100 million dengue fever and 500,000 DHF cases are estimated annually.

Epidemics recently have emerged or intensified in southern China, Taiwan, India, the East Coast of Africa, Oceania, and the Middle East. Of note, because of their location in a developed country, were smoldering dengue-2 and dengue-3 virus outbreaks between 1996 and 1998 in Queensland, Australia.[43, 44] The most dramatic ascendance of dengue and DHF, however, has occurred in the Caribbean and Latin America where *A. aegypti* has become widely reestablished since its near eradication in YF-control efforts ending in the 1970s.[24–26, 42] Before 1977, only dengue-2 and dengue-3 viruses were transmitted in the hemisphere, and DHF was virtually nonexistent. Introductions of dengue-1 virus in 1977 and dengue-4, 4 years later were followed by their rapid spread broadly in the region. The subsequent introduction in 1981 of a novel dengue-2 viral strain to Cuba, possibly from Southeast Asia, produced the first major DHF epidemic in the hemisphere, resulting in 116,143 hospitalizations,

10,000 for shock; resurgent transmission after a period of intense mosquito control led to another outbreak in 1997.[35, 36] Since 1989, recurrent DHF outbreaks have been reported in an enlarging area within the region, including Venezuela, Colombia, Brazil, Guyana, French Guiana, Nicaragua, Honduras, Costa Rica, Puerto Rico, and Mexico, resulting in several thousand DHF cases each year and nearly 12,000 cases in 1998 (unpublished Pan American Health Organization report). The introduction of a novel dengue-3 strain to Central America in 1994 has been anticipated as an accelerant for increased dengue incidence and severity in the region.

The dissemination of dengue viruses by viremic travelers has been facilitated by the increased mobility of people living within endemic areas and internationally by burgeoning air travel. Between 1986 and 1994, 203 anecdotal dengue cases were confirmed among travelers returning to the United States.[45] Incidence rates in American soldiers assigned temporarily to Sudan and Haiti were in the range of 1 in 1000 per month, but exposure and risk in travelers may differ.[46] In one study, dengue was diagnosed in 5% of febrile returned travelers, but in specific instances, attack rates in aid workers in tropical countries have exceeded 50%.[47] Small numbers of autochthonous cases acquired in Texas towns bordering Mexico were recognized in 1980, 1986, and 1995.[48]

Infection was transmitted from a viremic patient by accidental needlestick in one case and from a bone marrow donor who was incubating the disease in another (J Rigau, personal communication). The high incidence of infection in endemic areas suggests that transfusion-associated cases could occur frequently, but in these same populations, immunity in recipients is also high and differentiating a transfusion-transmitted case from a natural infection would be difficult.

Japanese Encephalitis

JE is transmitted in Asia over an area spanning one third of the world circumference, from Pakistan at the westernmost edge of the viral distribution to far eastern Russia (Table 142–1). The disease is endemic and periodically epidemic in Southeast Asia, China, and the subcontinent.[3, 6, 49] Sporadic cases are reported in tropical Asia, including the Indonesian and Philippine archipelagoes, but field studies suggest a higher incidence.[50] Twice, in 1947 and 1990, the virus was introduced to the western Pacific, resulting in outbreaks on Guam and Saipan. In 1995, the virus invaded the Torres Strait islands of Australia and in 1998, its mainland, arousing fears that the virus may have become established.[16, 51, 52]

Worldwide, 160,000 cases were reported to the World Health Organization in 1966 and 16,000 cases in 1996, the 10-fold decline reflecting widespread childhood immunization in China, Japan, Korea, and Taiwan, as well as regional economic development and a declining emphasis on agriculture. In the latter three countries, few cases are reported currently, although enzootic viral transmission persists. In areas with endemic transmission, an annual incidence of 2.5 in 10,000 in children younger than 15 years is estimated, with a case-fatality rate of 25% and disability in 45% of surviving patients.[3, 6, 49] Extrapolated to the 700 million children younger than 15 years in the region, an estimated 175,000 JE cases, 45,000 deaths, and 78,000 disabled children would occur annually in the absence of immunization. In an era when polio has declined to the point of eradication, JE is now preeminent among causes of pediatric central nervous system infections in the region.

Within temperate areas, JE is transmitted sporadically from July to September, at a relatively low incidence and with periodic seasonal epidemics. In subtropical Asia, viral transmission extends from March to October in a hyperendemic pattern, resulting in higher incidence rates. Year-round transmission in tropical Asia (e.g., Indonesia) fluctuates with irrigation schedules, resulting in cases throughout the year and the absence of easily detected seasonal epidemics. The scarcity of pigs in Islamic Indonesia and Malaysia and the circulation of naturally attenuated JE viral strains have also been cited as contributing factors to the relative paucity of recognized cases.

The virus is transmitted by *Culex tritaeniorhynchus* and related ground-pool–breeding mosquitoes to pigs and aquatic birds, which are the principal viral-amplifying hosts.[53] Viremic adult pigs are asymptomatic, but infected pregnant sows abort or deliver stillbirths. Infected horses and humans are symptomatic but incidental hosts. Rice paddies provide favorable breeding habitats for vector mosquitoes; consequently, the risk of infection is highest in rural areas. However, both pigs and rice paddies are found at the edges of some Asian cities, resulting in isolated cases and rarely, urban outbreaks. The mosquito vectors chiefly feed outdoors, in the evenings, and prefer animal to human hosts.

More than 99% of infections are subclinical; consequently, in areas with endemic transmission, naturally acquired infections at an early age result in immunity of over 80% of young adults. Cases occur chiefly in children between 2 and 10 years of age with a slight predominance of boys. In Japan, Korea, and Taiwan, where children are protected by immunization, cases occur principally in elderly persons, reflecting waning immunity or other biologic factors associated with senescence.[54]

Expatriate and traveler cases have been recognized since 1932, and outbreaks among American, British, and Australian soldiers in World War II, Korea, and Vietnam were considered militarily important. Since 1978, 12 cases have been recognized in American travelers, soldiers, or their family members.[55] Travelers of all ages without naturally acquired protective antibodies are at risk for acquiring the illness. However, the risk is slight, estimated to be 1 in 150,000 person-months of exposure, reflecting low vector mosquito infection rates (0.5%) and the small case/infection ratio (0.3%).

St. Louis Encephalitis

Outbreak-associated cases of StLE have been reported from virtually all U.S. states, Ontario and Manitoba provinces, and Sonora State, Mexico, whereas only sporadic cases have been reported from Argentina, Brazil, Panama, Trinidad, French Guiana, Surinam, Curacao, Jamaica, and the Dominican Republic (Fig. 142–3). Enzootic viral transmission has also been recognized in Alberta, British Columbia, Ecuador, Guatemala, and Haiti and may occur elsewhere in the hemisphere.[56–58]

In the United States, the virus is transmitted to birds in three distinct cycles: by *Culex pipiens* and *Culex quinquefasciatus* in the midwest and eastern states; *Culex nigripalpus* in Florida; and *Culex tarsalis* in the Great Plains and farther west. Humans are infected incidentally from the enzootic cycle. Characteristics of the vectors and their respective transmission cycles define epidemiologic features in each location.[56–58]

In the East, StLE is transmitted periodically in localized and regional outbreaks at lengthy intervals without significant transmission in intervening years. Outbreaks in the late summer and fall occur in urban areas, often in older neighborhoods, where polluted wastewater provides breeding habitat for *C. pipiens* and *C. quinquefasciatus*—the northern and southern house mosquitoes, respectively. More than 50 epidemics have been recognized in small towns or cities, including Houston, Dallas, Memphis, New Orleans, Chicago, and Detroit. In three outbreaks since 1991, disproportionate risk was reported in homeless HIV-infected persons, probably reflecting their increased vulnerability to mosquito bites in the evening, when the vectors are most active.[59] Outbreaks in Florida occur more diffusely in suburban and urban locations where swales and ground pools provide breeding sites for *C. nigripalpus*. In 1990, 222 cases were reported from 28 counties with incidence rates ranging from less than 1 to 21 in 100,000. Slightly higher risk has been reported in males, possibly reflecting increased outdoor exposure in the crepuscular period at dawn and dusk. The 1990 epidemic extended from July through the first 2 weeks of the next year. In the West, StLE is transmitted perennially and at a low level in rural areas, frequently

TABLE 142-1 Risk of Japanese Encephalitis by Country, Region, and Season*

Country	Affected Areas or Jurisdictions	Transmission Season	Comments
Bangladesh	Few data, probably widespread	Possibly July–December, as in northern India	Outbreak reported from Tangail district, Dacca division; sporadic cases in Rājshāhi division
Bhutan	No data	No data; presumed to be similar to Nepal	
Brunei	Presumed to be sporadic-endemic, as in Malaysia	Presumed year-round transmission	
Myanmar (Burma)	Presumed to be endemic-hyperendemic countrywide	Presumed to be May–October	Outbreaks in Shan State, Chiang Mai Valley
Cambodia	Probably endemic-hyperendemic countrywide	Presumed to be May–October	Some JE cases confirmed in epidemics of uncertain cause October–December, 1993–1998
Democratic Republic of Korea	Presumed countrywide, chiefly in rural areas <800 m	July–October	Epidemics reported in 1970s; few recent data
India	Reported cases from all states, except Arunāchal, Dādra, Damān, Diu, Gujarāt, Himāchal, Jammu, Kashmīr, Lakshadweep, Meghālaya, Nagar Haveli, Orissa, Punjab, Rājasthān, and Sikkim	*South India:* May–October in Goa; October–January in Tamil Nādu; August–December in Karnātaka; second peak, April–June in Mandya district *Andrha Pradesh:* September–December *North India:* July–December	Outbreaks in West Bengal, Bihār, Karnātaka, Tamil Nādu, Andrha Pradesh, Assam, Uttar Pradesh, Manipur, Mahārāshtra, and Goa; urban cases reported, e.g., Lucknow
Indonesia	Kalimantan, Bali, Nusa Tenggara, Sulawesi, Moluccas, West Irian, Java, Lombok	Probably year-round risk; varies by island; peak risks associated with rainfall, rice cultivation, and presence of pigs; peak period of risk, November–March, June–July in some years	Hyperendemic on Bali; sporadic cases recognized elsewhere; vaccine not recommended if travel is to major cities only
Japan†	Rare—sporadic cases on all islands except Hokkaidō	June–September except Ryukyu; islands (Okinawa) April–October	Vaccine not routinely recommended if travel is to major cities only; enzootic transmission without human cases observed on Hokkaidō
Laos	Presumed to be endemic-hyperendemic countrywide	Presumed to be May–October	
Malaysia	Sporadic—endemic in all states of peninsula, Sarawak, and probably Sabah	November–January peak on peninsula	Vaccine not recommended if travel is to major cities only
Nepal	Hyperendemic in southern lowlands (Terai); sporadic cases now recognized in Kāthmāndāū valley.	July–December	Vaccine recommended for travelers to lowlands
Papua New Guinea	Transmission or sporadic cases reported from D'Entrecasteaux Islands, Gulf, Milne Bay, South Highland, West Sepik, Western Provinces	Unknown	Vaccine not routinely recommended
People's Republic of China	Cases in all provinces except Xizang (Tibet), Xinjiang, and Qinghai; hyperendemic in southern China; endemic–periodically epidemic in temperate areas; rare cases in Hong Kong New Territories	*Northern China:* May–September *Southern China:* April–October (Guangxi, Yunnan, Guangdong, and Southern Fujian, Sichuan, Guizhou, Hunan, and Jiangxi provinces)	Vaccine not routinely recommended for travelers to major cities only, including Hong Kong
Pakistan	May be transmitted in central deltas	Presumed to be June–January	Cases reported near Karāchi; endemic areas overlap those for West Nile virus
Philippines	Presumed to be endemic on all islands	Uncertain; speculations based on locations and agroecosystems *West Luzon, Mindoro, Negro Palowan:* April–November *Elsewhere:* Year-round; greatest risk, April–January	Outbreaks described in Nueva Écija, Luzon, and Manila
Republic of Korea	Rare sporadic cases	July–October	Last major outbreaks in 1982–1983; vaccine not recommended if travel is to major cities only
Russia	Far Eastern maritime areas south of Khabarousk	Peak period, July–September	Rare human cases reported
Singapore	Rare cases—last indigenous case in 1992	Year-round transmission no longer detected	Vaccine not routinely recommended
Sri Lanka	Endemic in all but mountainous areas; periodically epidemic in northern and central provinces	October–January; secondary peak of enzootic transmission, May–June	Outbreaks in central (Anuradhapura) and northwestern provinces
Taiwan†	Sporadic cases except in central mountains	April–October; June peak	Cases in and around Taipei
Thailand	Hyperendemic in north; sporadic-endemic in south	May–October	Annual outbreaks in Chiang Mai Valley; sporadic cases in Krung Thep (Bangkok) suburbs
Vietnam	Endemic-hyperendemic in all provinces	May–October	Highest rates in and near Ha Noi (Hanoi)
Western Pacific and Australia	Discrete epidemics reported on Guam, Saipan (Northern Mariana Islands); sporadic cases in Torres Strait and Cape York, Australia	Uncertain; possibly September–January in Pacific; February–April in far northern Australia	Enzootic cycle may not be sustainable; epidemics may follow viral introductions; single Australian mainland case (Cape York peninsula) reported in 1998

*Assessments are based on publications, surveillance reports, and personal correspondence. Extrapolations have been made from available data. Transmission patterns may change. Consult CDC ([303] 221-6400) or other public health authorities for latest trends.

†Reported human cases may not accurately reflect risks to nonimmune visitors because of high immunization rates in local populations. Humans are incidental to the transmission cycle. High levels of viral transmission may occur in the absence of human disease.

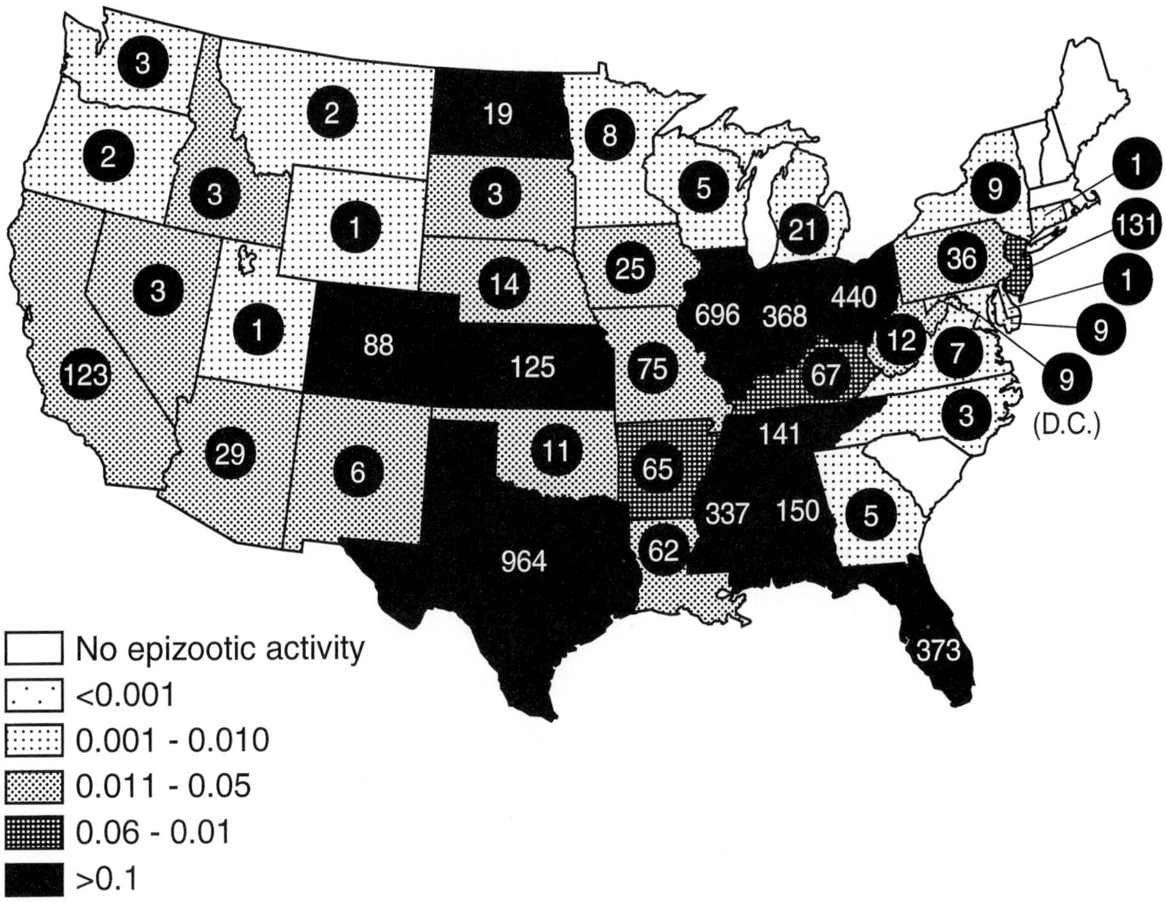

FIGURE 142–3. Reported St. Louis encephalitis cases and incidence per 10,000, United States, 1964–1996.

in association with irrigated farms and pastures. The low fatality rate among these cases has suggested that the disease may be milder due to the circulation of relatively attenuated strains. Forty years ago, outbreaks in agricultural areas occurred at regular intervals, but more recently, cases have been more sporadic and frequently have involved avocational exposures or have occurred in proximity to cities. Small urban outbreaks occurred in southern California in 1984, in western Colorado in 1985, and on the Colorado Front Range in 1987. The decline in cases has been attributed to secular changes in land use, air-conditioned residences, and other factors leading to reduced exposure. Diminished exposure to infection has been confirmed in rural California populations in whom seroprevalence rates now range from 0.1 to 11%.

The risk of illness is associated most strongly with advanced age, but a slightly elevated risk is also seen in infants. The importance of age is reflected in the declining ratio of asymptomatic to symptomatic infection, ranging from 800:1 in children to 85:1 in adults older than 60 years (Fig. 142–4).[56, 60]

Tick-Borne Encephalitis

Several related neurotropic tick-borne viruses are transmitted across the Holarctic, with some evidence for their dissemination from an Asian source.[6, 13, 61, 62] RSSE virus is transmitted in eastern Russia, Korea, China, and Japan; CEE and related viral strains in Scandinavia, Europe, and eastern states of the former Soviet Union; louping ill virus in the British Isles; and Powassan and a related deer tick virus of unknown pathogenicity in North America.[63, 64] CEE has been recognized throughout Europe except Portugal and the Benelux countries, but as suggested by the disease name, endemic transmission is most intense in Austria, areas of Germany, Poland, Hungary, the former Yugoslavia, Czechoslovakia, and western Russia (Fig. 142–5). In these countries, incidence rates in unvaccinated populations have approached 50 in 100,000, but risk is highly focal. In Austria, national vaccination has reduced the incidence of disease to less than 1 in 100,000. Sporadic cases are reported from France, Liechtenstein, Sweden, Switzerland, Italy, and Greece. In the Far East, RSSE cases occur principally among people working or living in sylvatic locations in Russia, Korea, northern China, and Hokkaido Island, Japan.

The viruses are transmitted horizontally between ticks and vertebrates and through the winter by vertical transmission in the ticks and by latent infections in hibernating animals. The virus passes transovarially and transtadially, from egg to larva, nymph, and adult, so all stages of the tick and both male and female ticks transmit infections to animals and humans. Larval and nymphal ticks feed principally on birds and small mammals, and adult ticks on larger mammals such as roe deer; deer; domestic goats; sheep; cows; dogs; cats; and humans. Human infections are incidental to the transmission cycle. Animal movements can spread ticks and the virus to new foci.

Within the ranges of *Ixodes ricinus* and *Ixoders persulcatus,* the principal tick vectors of CEE and RSSE, respectively, the ticks are distributed focally in sheltered microhabitats with high humidity and moderate temperatures, limited to elevations below 1000 m. Landscape ecology studies have characterized forest ecotones to fields or meadows, and low stands of deciduous trees and brush with a thick canopy as high-risk biotopes that correlate with foci of human cases.[65] Transmission foci tend to be highly stable but are subject to human environmental modifications. In central Europe, cases occur

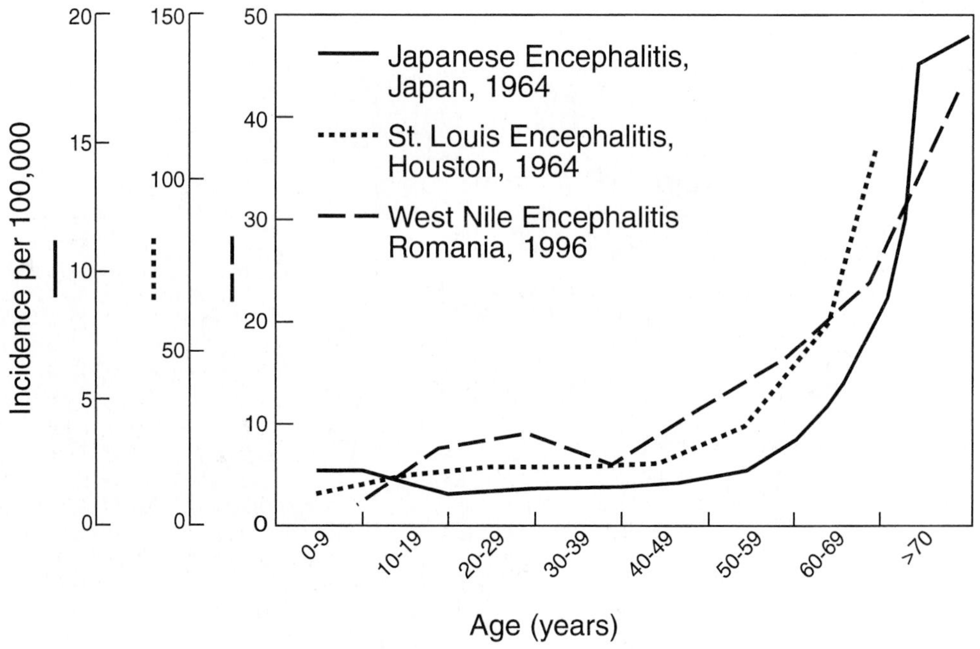

FIGURE 142–4. Age-specific incidence of St. Louis encephalitis, West Nile encephalitis, and Japanese encephalitis. (Data from refs. 54, 60, and 128.)

from April until November, peaking in June-July with a secondary rise in October.

Cases have predominated in adults, 20 to 50 years of age, with a male predominance, reflecting occupational exposure in forestry and farming. But children at outdoor play and persons with avocational exposure while hiking, berry picking, or mushroom gathering also may be at risk, depending on the location and season. Risk among most persons with short-term exposures, however, is low. Among American soldiers stationed in central Europe, no cases and one seroconversion were detected in 3297 person-months of exposure.[66] Louping ill is principally an occupational disease of veterinarians, sheep herders, and butchers.[67]

CEE virus is stable at acid pH, and consumption of unpasteurized milk or mild products from infected goats, sheep, or cows previously accounted for 10 to 20% of CEE cases. Small outbreaks still occur, and the possibility that Powassan virus could be transmitted from raw milk products in the United States has been suggested.[68] Slaughter or butchering infected animals or meat is a principal mode of transmission for louping ill virus to humans and also has been reported in CEE and in a Kyasanur Forest disease-related illness (see later).[69] Infection has also been acquired from infected ticks carried to households on fomites.

In addition to CEE virus, *I. ricinus* also transmits several borrelia responsible for Lyme disease (and also *Ehrlichia phagocytophila* and several species of rickettsia), but in at-risk areas, Lyme disease is far more common than the other diseases. This difference reflects the low proportion, 0.1 to 5%, of virus-infected ticks and the 10-fold higher borrelia infection rates of ticks in the same location. This distinction may result from the brevity of viremias in animal hosts, providing an opportunity for tick infection of only a few days, whereas persistent borrelia infections of rodents offer a higher likelihood of tick infection during feeding. An analogous situation obtains in the United States, where *Ixodes scapularis* transmits Lyme disease, babesiosis, granulocytic ehrlichiosis, and in experimental studies was shown to be competent to transmit Powassan virus.[70] However, *Ixodes cookei* ticks, the principal vector of Powassan virus, and *I. scapularis* differ somewhat in their host range, which may further limit opportunities for the viral and borrelial transmission cycles to intersect.

PATHOGENESIS

Yellow Fever

Early stages of YF infection can be inferred from vaccine studies. Two days after inoculation of the attenuated 17d vaccine, levels of tumor necrosis factor-α (TNF-α), interleukin-1 receptor antagonist (IL-1ra), and to a lesser extent interleukin-6 (IL-6) rise with a secondary TNF-α peak 7 days later.[71, 72] The cytokines are synthesized in response to local spread of the vaccine, and again as a response to viremia that peaks between days 5 and 6.[73] TNF-α elevations correspond to declines in the lymphocyte count. After wild-type viral infection, the grippe phase of early YF presumably is associated with a similarly timed elaboration of cytokines. In experimentally inoculated rhesus monkeys, the virus replicates initially in local lymph nodes followed by blood-borne spread and further replication in liver, lung, and adrenal glands, and most prolifically in regional lymph tissue, spleen, and bone marrow.[74] Infection by mosquito feeding, which introduces cytokines from their saliva, is believed to differ from experimental needle inoculation in the outcome of local viral replication and distribution, but the importance of these factors in modulating human flaviviral infections is unknown.

Pathologic changes are most pronounced in the liver and kidneys, but widespread hemorrhages are found on mucosal surfaces, in the skin, and within various organs. Numerous petechial hemorrhages and erosion of the gastric mucosa contribute to the hematemesis that typically introduces the illness. Hepatocellular damage is characterized by a patchy midzonal distribution, sparing cells around the central vein and portal triad. The extent of lobular necrosis is variable, with an average of 60%, but even with confluent lobular necrosis, the reticular architecture is preserved. Early changes consist of glycogen depletion and cloudy swelling, followed by accumulations of fat and of ceroid pigment. Necrotic cells finally undergo coagulation with the formation of characteristic eosinophilic Councilman's bodies that may correspond to apoptotic cells. A minimal mononuclear inflammatory response is seen in the liver and other organs. Viral antigen is identified initially in Kupffer cells and appears later in hepatocytes, Councilman's bodies, and endothelial cells.[75–77] Healing occurs without fibrosis.

Albuminuria and renal insufficiency reflect prerenal factors, in-

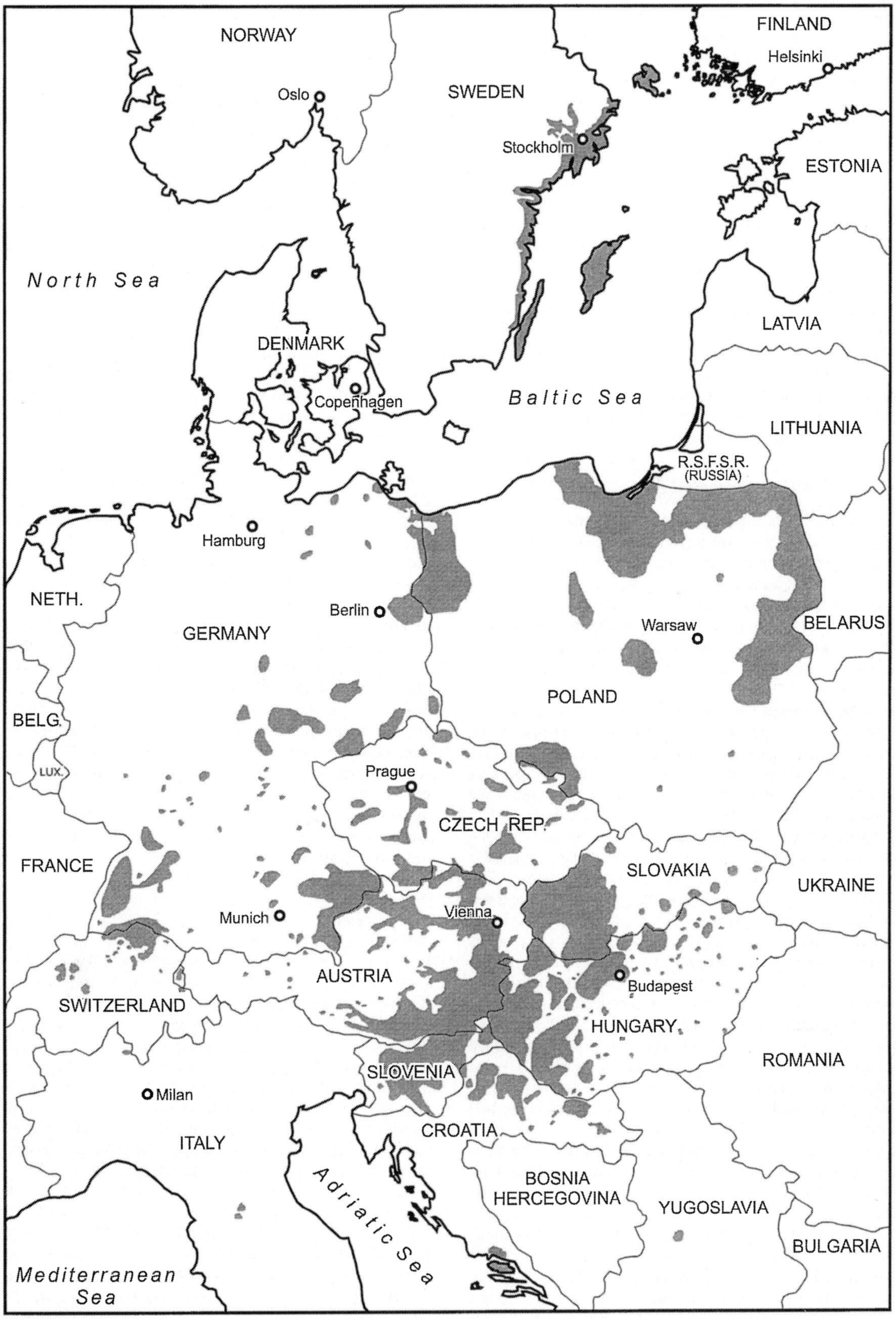

FIGURE 142–5. Recognized endemic foci of tick-borne encephalitis in Europe.

cluding vomiting and myocarditis, as well as parenchymal invasion, and in advanced illness, acute tubular necrosis.[78] Viral antigen can be identified in the kidney and also in the heart, in which degenerative fatty infiltration of the myocardium and of the conduction system contribute to decreased output and to arrhythmias.[77] Neurologic findings probably reflect metabolic disturbances, cerebral edema, and hemorrhages rather than encephalitis. The cause of the bleeding diathesis is ill-defined but probably represents a combination of reduced hepatic synthesis of clotting factors, intravascular coagulation, thrombocytopenia, and endothelial and platelet dysfunction. A combination of direct parenchymal damage and a systemic inflammatory response–like syndrome appear to contribute to shock and a fatal outcome. Neutralizing antibodies elaborated within the first week of illness clear the virus, and recovery is followed by lifelong immunity.

Heterologous flaviviral immunity (e.g., previous dengue) is believed to provide partial protection against infection, which may contribute to the absence of YF in Asia.[79] But unlike DHF, antibody-mediated immune enhancement does not result. Genetic selection has been described in survivors of YF epidemics, and youth and advanced age have both been implicated as risk factors for symptomatic illness.[4, 6, 80, 81] Hepatitis B carriage, which is prevalent in areas of Africa with endemic YF, is not a risk factor for symptomatic disease.[82]

Dengue and Dengue Hemorrhagic Fever

Self-limited dengue fever is the usual clinical outcome of infection, but an immunopathologic response in some patients, usually in the setting of heterologous immunity, produces the syndrome of DHF-DSS (Fig. 142–6).[6, 23, 33, 83]

After an infectious mosquito bite, the virus replicates in local lymph nodes and within 2 to 3 days disseminates via the blood to various tissues. Virus circulates in the blood typically for 4 to 5 days in infected monocytes, B cells, and T cells and replicates several days longer in peripheral sites. Nearly all patients are viremic at the point of clinical presentation with fever and clear the virus from the blood within a day after defervescence.[84] Malaise and grippe symptoms that typify dengue probably reflect the patient's cytokine response; however, myalgia, a cardinal feature of the illness, may also indicate pathologic changes in muscle, typified by a moderate perivascular mononuclear infiltrate with lipid accumulation and in some cases, mitochondrial changes, muscle necrosis, and creatine phosphokinase level elevations.[85, 86] Musculoskeletal pain (breakbone fever) conceivably could reflect viral infection of bone marrow elements, including dendritic (CD11b/CD18 [MAC-1])-positive and adventitial reticular (nerve growth factor receptor–positive) cells.[87] Local suppression of erythrocytic, myelocytic, and thrombocytic poiesis within 4 to 5 days is reflected in peripheral cytopenias. Hemophagocytosis has been described in anecdotal cases.[88] Histopathologic examination of skin from patients with rash discloses a minor degree of lymphocytic dermal vasculitis and variably, viral antigen.[89] Elevated hepatic transaminase levels have been reported in over 80% of dengue fever cases, with no relationship to coincident hepatitis B or C infection.[86] In fatal cases, histopathologic findings resemble those of early mild YF, with Kupffer cell hypertrophy; focal ballooning and necrosis of hepatocytes in a midzonal distribution with occasional Councilman's body formation; mild fatty changes; and a scant periportal mononuclear cell response.[90] Viral antigen has been demonstrated in hepatocytes, Kupffer cells, and endothelia. In vitro studies suggest an early induction of apoptosis in infected hepatocytes. Neurologic complications have been attributed chiefly to cerebral edema, metabolic alterations, and focal and sometimes massive intracranial hemorrhages, but anecdotal cases have indicated the possibility of viral CNS invasion and encephalitis.[91] Intrathecal viral-specific immunoglobulin M (IgM) antibodies have been detected in some patients, and viral antigen or genomic sequences in neurons, astrocytes, microglia, and endothelial cells in others.[92–93]

Shock in DHF-DSS follows the sudden extravasation of plasma into extravascular sites including the pleural and abdominal cavities, usually with the defervescence of fever.[6, 23, 41, 83] The extensive increase in vascular permeability is associated with elevated levels of plasma soluble tumor necrosis factor receptor (sTNFR/75), IL-8, interferon-γ, and other mediators, and local endothelial production of IL-8 RANTES with apoptotic endothelial cell death.[94–99] In addition, immune complex formation activates the complement system with increases in C3a and C5a.[100] IL-6 and intercellular adhesion molecule 1 levels are depressed in parallel with hypoalbuminemia and the general loss of serum proteins. The rapid predictable reversibility of the syndrome within 48 hours and the paucity of histopathologic correlates—usually perivascular edema with diapedesis of red cells and widespread focal hemorrhages—suggest that the inflammatory response produces a vasculopathy. Reduced cardiac output further contributes to shock.[101] The hemorrhagic diathesis is complex and not well understood, reflecting a combination of cytokine action and vascular injury, viral antibodies binding to platelets or cross-reactive with plasminogen and other clotting factors, reduced platelet function and survival, and a mild consumptive coagulopathy.[102, 103]

The increased frequency of DHF in secondary dengue infections has suggested a role of heterologous antibodies in enhancing viral uptake and replication in Fc receptor–bearing cells (antibody-mediated immune enhancement).[34, 104–107] Simultaneously, levels of TNF-α, soluble CD8, and soluble IL-2 that are higher in DHF than in dengue fever patients indicate an activation of cross-reactive memory $CD4^+$ and $CD8^+$ T cells in response to a second infection. The resulting production of IL-2, interferon-γ, and other lymphokines is reinforced by the increased abundance of infected target cells due to interferon-γ–mediated upregulation of Fc receptors and flaviviral-induced expression of major histocompatibility complex I and II molecules that further activate T lymphocytes.[108] Activated infected monocytes and endothelia produce and release with their lysis TNF-α, IL-1, platelet activating factor (PAF), IL-8, and RANTES, which act in synergy with lymphokines, histamine, and viral immune complex–induced C3a and C5a to produce the temporary vascular endothelial dysfunction leading to plasma leakage. Novel cytotoxic and cytokine-inhibiting factors elaborated by infected mononuclear cells have been reported, but their pathogenetic role is uncertain.[109]

Although infection with any of the serotypes can produce DHF, there is some indication for a greater propensity after second infections with dengue-2 or -3 viruses or with specific strains of putatively greater virulence. Trends toward an increased or fluctuating severity of illness during prolonged outbreaks have been attributed to the evolution of viral quasispecies.[110]

The rise of levels of serum neutralizing antibodies is correlated with the clearance of viremia, but immunity is associated with both humoral and cellular immune responses.[84] The latter are mediated by $CD4^+$ and $CD8^+$ cells recognizing serotype-specific, dengue serotype–cross-reactive epitopes and flaviviral–cross-reactive epitopes.[9–11, 94] The stimulation of cross-protective immunity from infection with one dengue viral serotype must be limited and brief because infection with a second type during the same transmission season is not uncommon. Illness after infection with two serotypes, namely, a third bout of dengue, occurs infrequently, and after three infections, virtually never. Repeated episodes of DHF have been recognized rarely, presumably because immune factors that promote immunopathologic responses are outweighed by immune responses that clear the infection (B. Innis, personal communication).

Flaviviral Encephalitis

The variable and potentially lengthy incubation period of 4 to 21 days (usually 1 week) reflects the interval for viral replication locally and in peripheral sites, with a subsequent brief viremia before the virus invades the CNS.[6] Virus rarely can be recovered from blood, no longer than 1 week after the onset of illness and before the onset of neurologic symptoms. The large proportion of infections that are asymptomatic, approximately 300 for each symptomatic case, is

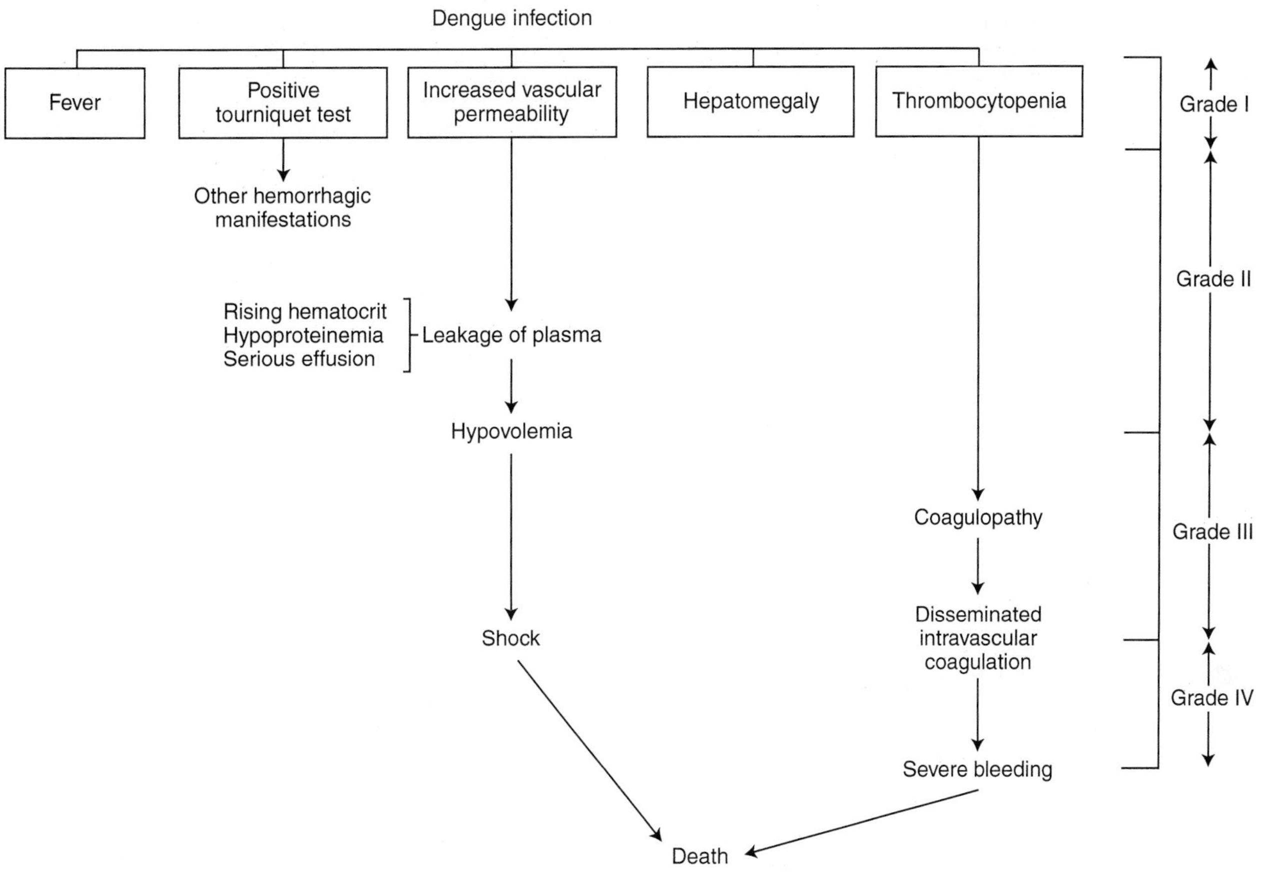

FIGURE 142–6. Clinical spectrum, pathophysiology, and classification of dengue hemorrhagic fever. At the top are key clinical findings; in the center, pathophysiologic mechanisms; and on the side, the World Health Organization classification of cases:

Grade 1: Fever accompanied by nonspecific constitutional symptoms; the only hemorrhagic manifestation is a positive tourniquet test result easy bruising, or both.

Grade 2: Spontaneous bleeding in addition to the manifestations of grade I patients, usually in the forms of skin or other hemorrhages.

Grade 3: Circulatory failure manifested by a rapid, weak pulse and narrowing of pulse pressure or hypotension, with the presence of cold clammy skin and restlessness.

Grade 4: Profound shock with undetectable blood pressure or pulse.

(From World Health Organization. Technical Guide for Diagnosis, Treatment, Surveillance, Prevention, and Control of Degue Hemorrhagic Fever. 2nd ed. Geneva: World Health Organization; 1997.)

striking and remarkably consistent among StLE, JE, and West Nile encephalitis. Subclinical infection presumably reflects the peripheral clearance of virus before neuroinvasion. The virus enters the CNS from the blood by growing through vascular endothelial cells to the parenchymal side or, alternatively, through the olfactory epithelium.[111–112] Within the brain, virions spread from cell to cell. Pathologic changes consist of meningeal congestion and inflammation, brain edema, and a widespread encephalitis with a predilection for the hippocampus and temporal cortex, thalamus, substantia nigra, cerebellum, periventricular areas of the brain stem, and anterior spinal cord. Poliomyelitis with destruction of motor neuron nuclei in the brain stem and cervical and upper lumbar cord is frequently seen in TBE, more so in the far eastern form of the disease and less often in JE and StLE. Focal neuronal degeneration and necrosis with neuronophagia evolve to the formation of glial nodules, and with healing, spongiform changes. Viral antigen appears in neuronal bodies and their processes and later in phagocytic cells.[113, 114] Perivascular inflammatory infiltrates consist of activated T cells and macrophages; within the cerebrospinal fluid (CSF), T cells predominate above their proportion in serum, with a correspondingly lower ratio of B and natural killer cells. T-cell activation is evidenced by the expression of HLA-DR followed by CD25 (IL2-R) and CD71 (transferrin receptor) and elevated CSF levels of neopterin and β_2-microglobulin.[115–117]

The rare recovery of virus from CSF, usually in patients with fulminant and fatal disease, is associated with the absence of intrathecal antibodies, indicating an important role of viral neutralization in recovery.[118] On the other hand, intrathecal immune-complex formation and antineurofilament and anti–myelin basic protein antibodies have also been reported in association with a poor outcome, suggesting immunopathologic injury.[119, 120] Although cell-mediated responses to infected cells aid in clearing the virus, limited studies have not correlated cellular proliferative responses with the outcome.

The biphasic and relatively prolonged course of illness in TBE is reflected in CSF neopterin, β_2-microglobulin, and intrathecal IgG synthesis that remain elevated for 6 weeks and pleocytosis that persists considerably longer than in other CNS infections, consistent with a protracted inflammatory reaction.[121] Although this time course alludes to a postinfectious process, pathologic changes with viral antigen in neurons, focal and perivascular infiltrates, and the recovery of virus from patients with fatal cases are consistent with a primary encephalitis.[122] Delayed CNS clearance of JE virus has also been suggested by the presence of infectious virus, antigen, or IgM antibodies in CSF several weeks after the onset of illness. JE viral antigen has been detected in peripheral blood mononuclear cells months after clinical recovery.[123–124] Clinically, subacute and progressive paralysis of the limb musculature and chronic epilepsy are well-known features of RSSE, suggesting CNS viral persistence.[125] Similar chronic symptomatic infections have been modeled in RSSE and West Nile virus–infected monkeys.

Advanced age is preeminent among the risk factors for developing neurologic infection. In susceptible populations, illness rates steeply with age whereas infections uniformly attack persons of all ages, specifying age-related host factors rather than increased exposure as the risk factor (Fig. 142–7).[51, 58, 60, 126–128] The biologic basis for the age-related susceptibility is ill defined. Although it may simply reflect immunosenescence, other observations indicate roles for functional or structural CNS changes facilitating neuroinvasion. As examples, neurocysticercosis is more prevalent in fatal JE cases than in patients dying of other conditions, and hypertension was associated with an increased risk of fatal StLE.[129, 130] The interaction of concurrent viral, bacterial, or parasitic infections has been reported to alter expected outcomes of tick-borne encephalitis and JE, either from facilitated neuroinvasion or immune factors.[131, 132] Heterologous dengue immunity has been associated with a better outcome of StLE and JE.[133, 134]

CLINICAL FEATURES

Yellow Fever

YF illness ranges in severity from an undifferentiated self-limited grippe to hemorrhagic fever that is fatal in 50% of cases.[6, 74, 78] In addition, from 5 to 50% of infections are inapparent. After an incubation period of 3 to 6 days, fever, headache, and myalgias begin abruptly, accompanied by few physical findings except conjunctival injection, facial flushing, and a relative bradycardia (Faget's sign), and on laboratory examination, leukopenia. In the majority of cases, resolution of this *period of infection* concludes the illness, but in others, the remission of fever for a few hours to several days is followed by renewed symptoms, high fever, headache, lumbosacral back pain, nausea, vomiting, abdominal pain, and somnolence *(period of intoxication)*. The illness is dominated by icteric hepatitis and a hemorrhagic diathesis with prominent gastrointestinal bleeding and hematemesis, epistaxis, gum bleeding, and petechial and purpuric hemorrhages. Weakness and prostration are compounded by poor intake of food and protracted vomiting. Albuminuria is a constant feature that aids in the differentiation of YF from other causes of viral hepatitis. Deepening jaundice and elevations in transaminase levels continue for several days at the same time that azotemia and progressive oliguria ensue. Direct bilirubin levels rise to 5 to 10 mg/dl, whereas alkaline phosphatase levels are only slightly raised; not infrequently, aspartate aminotransferase levels may be elevated above alanine aminotransferase levels because of myocardial damage.[135] Ultimately, hypotension, shock, and metabolic acidosis develop, compounded by myocardial dysfunction and arrhythmias as late events and acute tubular necrosis in some patients. Confusion, seizures, and coma distinguish the late stages of illness, but CSF examination discloses an elevated protein level without pleocytosis, consistent with cerebral edema or encephalopathy. Death usually occurs within 7 to 10 days after onset. If the patient survives the critical period of illness, secondary bacterial infections resulting in pneumonia or sepsis are frequent complications. Recovery has not been followed by chronic hepatitis.

Clinically, severe YF resembles other viral hemorrhagic fevers occurring in Africa and South America, so laboratory confirmation is required to make the diagnosis. Early exclusion of other causes with the potential for person-to-person spread is important to prevent nosocomial transmission. Other forms of viral hepatitis, particularly hepatitis E, which frequently presents in outbreaks, leptospirosis, malaria, typhoid, typhus, relapsing fever, acute fatty liver of pregnancy and toxin-related hepatitis, have presented alternative diagnoses.

Dengue Fever and Dengue Hemorrhagic Fever

Dengue fever is an acute febrile disease with headaches, musculoskeletal pain, and rash, but the severity of illness and clinical manifestations vary with age. Infection is asymptomatic in 80% of infants and children, and illness—consisting of fever, malaise or irritability, pharyngeal injection, upper respiratory symptoms, and rash—cannot be readily differentiated from other common childhood infections. The illness is more severe and begins more acutely in adults. After an incubation period of 4 to 7 days, fever—often with chills, severe frontal headache, and retro-orbital pain—develops abruptly with a rapid progression to prostration, severe musculoskeletal and lumbar back pain, and abdominal tenderness. Anorexia, nausea, vomiting, hyperesthesia of the skin, and dysgeusia are frequent complaints. Initially, the skin appears flushed, but within 3 to 4 days and the lysis of fever, an indistinct macular and sometimes scarlatiniform rash develops, sparing the palms and soles. As the rash fades or desquamates, localized clusters of petechiae on the extensor surfaces of the limbs may remain. A second episode of fever and symptoms may ensue in a saddleback pattern. Recovery is followed by a prolonged period of listlessness, easy fatiguability, and even depression.

Although virtually all cases are uncomplicated, minor bleeding from mucosal surfaces, usually epistaxis, bleeding from the gums, hematuria, and metrorrhagia, are not uncommon, and gastrointestinal

FIGURE 142–7. St. Louis encephalitis cases by age and clinical syndrome, Chicago, Ill. Although illness severity increases with age, more than half of cases in children result in encephalitis. (Adapted from Zweighaft RM, Rasmussen C, Brolnitsky O, et al. St. Louis encephalitis: The Chicago experience. Am J Trop Med Hyg. 1979; 28:114.)

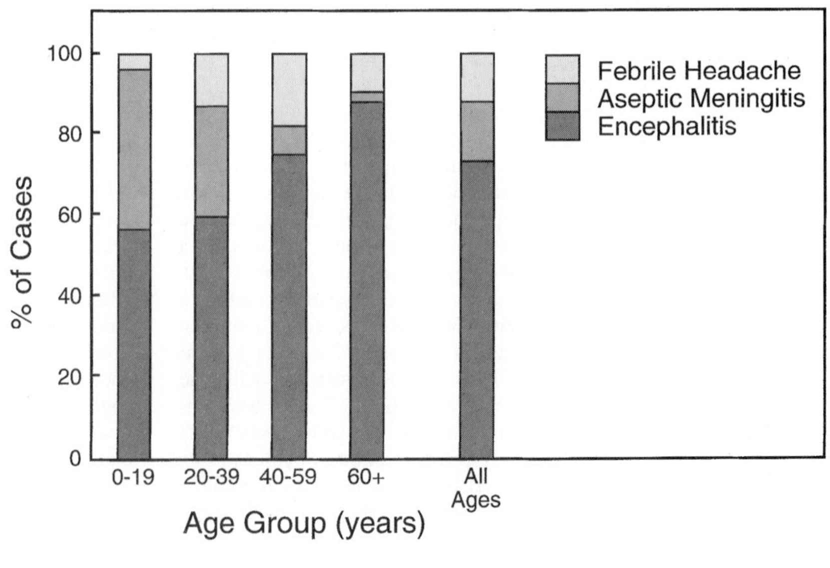

hemorrhage and hemoptysis can occur (see Fig. 142–6).[136] In patients with preexisting peptic ulcer disease, severe, even fatal, gastric bleeding can be precipitated.[137] Subcapsular splenic bleeding and rupture, uterine hemorrhage resulting in spontaneous abortion, and severe postpartum bleeding have also been reported.[138, 139] It is important to differentiate these phenomena from the bleeding diathesis that accompanies the life-threatening syndrome of hypotension and circulatory failure in DHF-DSS.

Hepatitis frequently complicates dengue fever.[86] In Taiwan, transaminase levels raised 10-fold above normal were observed in 11% of cases, with rare deaths due to hepatic failure. Neurologic symptoms associated with dengue fever have been reported sporadically and attributed to hemorrhages or cerebral edema, but recovery of virus from the CSF, intrathecal viral-specific IgM, and immunohistochemical evidence of infection in the brain indicate the possibility of primary dengue encephalitis in some cases.[91–93]

Vertical transmission of dengue virus to neonates whose mothers had an onset of primary or secondary dengue fever zero to 8 days before delivery has resulted in acute neonatal dengue manifesting as fever, cyanosis, apnea, mottling, hepatomegaly, and reduced platelet counts as low as 16,000/mm^3.[139] One baby died of intracerebral hemorrhage, but others, although ill, did not have other signs of DHF, and they recovered without incident. Dengue virus was isolated from the neonates in some cases. The outcome of infection acquired earlier in pregnancy has not been addressed satisfactorily. Anecdotal reports have described spontaneous abortion (see earlier) and a variety of birth defects and, in a postepidemic investigation, an increase of neural tube defects.[140] Another investigation found no increases in abnormal pregnancy outcomes.[141] In a study of cord blood samples from infants delivering 5 to 9 months after an outbreak, 4 of 59 had viral-specific IgM, but all the infants appeared normal.[142]

The central clinical features of DHF-DSS are hemorrhagic phenomena and hypovolemic shock due to increased vascular permeability and plasma leakage.[6, 23, 83, 143, 144] The early clinical features of children who ultimately develop DHF-DSS are indistinguishable from those of ordinary dengue fever, namely, fever, malaise, headache, musculoskeletal pain, facial flushing, anorexia, nausea, and vomiting. However, with the defervescence of fever 2 to 7 days later, reduced perfusion and early signs of shock are manifested by central cyanosis, restlessness, diaphoresis, and cool, clammy skin and extremities. Abdominal pain is a frequent complaint. In cases with a benign course of illness, blood pressure and pulse may be maintained, but a rapid and weak pulse, narrowing of the pulse pressure to less than 20 mmHg, and, in the most extreme cases, an unobtainable blood pressure establish the shock syndrome. The platelet count declines, and petechiae appear in widespread distribution with spontaneous ecchymoses. Bleeding occurs at mucosal surfaces, from the gastrointestinal tract, and at venipuncture sites. The liver is palpably enlarged in up to 75% of patients, with variable splenomegaly. Elevated amylase levels and sonographic evidence of pancreatic enlargement are found in up to 40% of patients. Pleural effusions can be detected in more than 80% of cases if a decubitus film is taken, and, in combination with an elevated hematocrit and hypoalbuminemia, reflecting hemoconcentration, these studies provide objective measures of plasma loss. However, ultrasonography has been more sensitive in detecting pleural effusions, ascites, and gallbladder edema in more than 95% of severe cases; para- and perirenal effusions in 77%; and also hepatic and splenic subcapsular and pericardial effusions.[145] The presence of pleural and peritoneal effusions is associated with severe disease. Adult respiratory distress syndrome may develop with capillary-alveolar leakage.[146] In untreated patients, hypoperfusion complicated by myocardial dysfunction and reduced ejection fractions results in metabolic acidosis and organ failure. With support through the critical period of illness, spontaneous resolution of vasculopathy and circulatory failure usually can be expected within 2 to 3 days, with complete recovery afterward. The duration of illness ranges from 7 to 10 days in most cases. Fatality rates have reached 50% in underserved populations, but in experienced centers, less than 1% of cases are fatal. Encephalopathy, often reflecting CNS hemorrhage, prolonged shock, or hepatic or renal failure, infrequently complicate the illness, but they are associated with a poor prognosis. As would be expected in areas where dengue infects 10% of children a year, concurrent infection with bacteria, parasites, and other viral pathogens occur frequently. Dual infections, principally gram-negative sepsis, have been reported in 1 of 200 children hospitalized with dengue, resulting in prolonged fever and hospitalization.[147] Reactivation of herpes virus 6 infection has been reported in two thirds of DHF patients.

Attempts to differentiate dengue fever clinically from other acute febrile illnesses are unlikely to be successful, although the diagnosis is aided if laboratory examination indicates leukopenia, neutropenia, thrombocytopenia, or mildly elevated aspartate aminotransferase levels.[41, 110] Even when facial flushing was included as a selective criterion in a study that also included DHF patients, the only differentiating symptoms were anorexia, nausea, and vomiting. A positive tourniquet test, a requirement in the DHF case definition, is obtained more often than in children with other febrile illnesses, but its specificity is low. In comparison to chikungunya, another epidemic *A. aegypti*–borne infection, dengue patients are less likely to have conjunctivitis, rash, and musculoskeletal pain.[148] The difficulty of differentiating dengue from rubella, measles, and even influenza has been underscored by the early misrecognition of entire epidemics. The clinical differentiation of DHF from YF and other viral hemorrhagic fevers is also difficult, and diagnosis requires laboratory confirmation.

Clinical or laboratory differentiation, at the time of first presentation, of children destined to develop DHF would facilitate intervention before the sudden onset of shock. In one study, aspartate aminotransferase elevations greater than 60 U/ml, leukocyte counts less than 5000/ml, and absolute neutrophil counts less than 3000/ml had higher predictive values than the tourniquet test in differentiating dengue from other febrile illnesses.[41, 110] In another study, an elevated s-TNFR-75 level had a sensitivity of 93% and a negative predictive value of 95% in foretelling shock.[95] Although the specificity was 34%, the choice of a 55 pg/ml cutoff errs conservatively. Elevated IL-8 levels may also have prognostic value.[99] Studies to discover the pathogenic role of other cytokines are in progress.

Japanese Encephalitis

Infection is symptomatic in less than 1% of cases of JE, but the illness is usually a severe encephalitis, leading frequently to coma and to a fatal outcome in 25% of cases. The spectrum of clinical illness is probably broader than is appreciated from an evaluation of hospitalized patients. JE cases are found among hospitalized children with acute pyrexia of undetermined origin, and, undoubtedly, many patients with febrile illnesses and headache or aseptic meningitis do not present to a hospital. Studies have drawn attention to patients presenting with spinal paralysis without encephalitic signs, initially misdiagnosed as poliomyelitis cases, and conversely, acute behavioral changes mimicking psychosis without motor signs.[149–151] The earliest symptoms are lethargy and fever and, frequently, headache, abdominal pain, nausea, and vomiting. Lethargy increases over several days when uncharacteristic behaviors associated with an agitated delirium, unsteadiness, and abnormal motor movements may develop, advancing to progressive somnolence and coma. Although the prodrome may evolve over several days to a week, some children present with a sudden convulsion after a brief febrile illness.

The chief findings are high fever and altered consciousness, ranging from mild disorientation or a subtle personality change to a severe state of confusion, delirium, and coma.[3, 6, 49, 152] Mutism has been a presentation in some cases. Nuchal rigidity is a variable finding, present in one third to two thirds of the cases. Cranial nerves palsies resulting in facial paralysis and dysconjugate gaze are detected in one third of the cases. Muscular weakness can be associated with decreased or increased tone and can be generalized or asymmetric, with hemiparesis or unusual distributions of flaccid and spastic paralysis. Hyperreflexia, ankle clonus, and other abnormal reflexes may be elicited. Disordered movements such as nonstereotypical flailing, ataxia, or tremor may be present initially, and not uncommonly, choreoathetosis, rigidity, masked facies, and other extrapyramidal signs appear later in the illness. Focal or generalized seizures develop in 50 to 75% of cases. Signs of increased intracranial pressure such as papilledema and hypertension are detected in a minority of patients, although some fatal cases show evidence of uncal or tentorial herniation. More than one third of patients in coma need ventilatory support. Fulminant cases may be rapidly fatal, but more typically, improvement can be expected after a week with the defervescence of fever. Neurologic function is regained gradually over several weeks, with further recovery after hospital discharge over intervals of months to years. Infections from stasis ulcers, urinary tract infection, pneumonia, and bacteremia frequently complicate the lengthy recovery from coma and paralysis and may be secondary causes of death. The virulence of the infection is underscored by contemporary fatality rates of 25% in locations with intensive care facilities. Neurological abnormalities such as seizure disorders, motor and cranial nerve paresis, cortical blindness, and movement disorders persist in up to one third of cases after 5 years, whereas a greater proportion, perhaps even 75% of recovered children, exhibit behavioral and psychologic abnormalities. Anecdotal cases of clinical relapse weeks after hospital discharge with recovery of virus from peripheral blood have alluded to delayed viral clearance or persistence, but the significance of these observations is uncertain.[124] In illness acquired in the first or second trimesters of pregnancy, the virus can infect the fetal-placental unit and precipitate abortion.[153] Cases acquired in the third trimester have not been reported to interrupt pregnancy. Congenital infections have been reported only when the virus was newly introduced to a susceptible adult population, since nearly all women in endemic areas have acquired immunity. Nonimmune travelers are also at risk.

Laboratory studies disclose peripheral leukocytosis, as high as 30,000/mm^3 with a left shift, and hyponatremia. The CSF is usually not under pressure. Pleocytosis ranges from less than 10 to several thousand per cubic millimeter, with a median of several hundred cells of a predominantly lymphocytic composition.[152] CSF protein is typically normal, and when it is elevated, levels rarely exceed 100 mg/dl. The electroencephalogram discloses a pattern of diffuse delta-wave activity and rarely, spike and seizure discharges. Brain imaging reveals diffuse white matter edema and abnormal signals mainly in the thalamus—often with evidence of hemorrhage—basal ganglia, cerebellum, midbrain, pons, and spinal cord.[154, 155] Thalamic involvement is consistent with the electroencephalogram pattern of slowing. Neurogenic electromyogram patterns are consistent with anterior horn cell destruction.

In rural Asia, tuberculous and pyogenic meningitis and lead encephalopathy (where children are occupied by recycling batteries) are the principal alternative diagnoses. Typhoid fever with tremors and ataxia, cerebral malaria, dengue infection with encephalopathy, heat stroke, and enterovirus 71 encephalitis have been confused with JE, the latter two when they have occurred in outbreaks. Encephalitis due to Nipah virus, a newly isolated paramyxovirus spread directly from pigs, initially was mistaken for JE because of its occurrence in rural residents who have contact with pigs; the virus' geographic distribution outside of Malaysia, where it was discovered, is unknown (see also Chapter 149). In areas where the disease is endemic, JE is the cause of 25 to 65% of hospitalized encephalitis cases.

St. Louis Encephalitis

StLE has been classified into syndromes of fever with constitutional symptoms and headache, aseptic meningitis, and fatal encephalitis.[6, 127, 156] The proportion of cases in each category is age-dependent, with increasing proportions of encephalitis and fatal cases in adults, especially in the elderly (see Figs. 142–3 and 142–4). The illness usually begins with a febrile prodrome of malaise, fever, headache, and myalgias, sometimes with upper respiratory or abdominal symptoms, that evolves over several days to more than a week with progressive lethargy, periods of confusion, and the onset of tremor, clumsiness, and ataxia. Vomiting and diarrhea are common, and some patients complain of dysuria, urgency, and incontinence.

Altered consciousness, marked by confusion, delirium, or somnolence, is the predominant presenting feature, and generalized motor weakness is more usual than are focal signs. Indications of meningeal irritation are inconstant and elicited more often in children. Mental clouding may be subtle and manifested only by slight disorientation. Most patients do not progress to deep coma. Tremulousness involving the eyelids, tongue, lips, and extremities is usual, and cerebellar signs, including ataxia in ambulatory patients, are common. One fourth of patients display a facial or other cranial nerve palsy. Pathologic reflexes are elicited irregularly. Various abnormal movements may be present, including myoclonic jerks, nystagmus, and, in rare cases, opsoclonus. Convulsions are infrequent and signal a poor prognosis, except in children. In the usual course of events, fever declines over several days, accompanied by general improvement and clearing of the sensorium. However, pneumonia, thrombophlebitis and pulmonary embolism, stroke, gastrointestinal hemorrhage, and nosocomial infection can complicate recovery. Illness is fatal in 8% of cases overall and in 20% of cases in persons older than 60 years. In recovered adults, asthenia, emotional lability, anxiety, irritability, forgetfulness, tremor, dizziness, and unsteadiness may persist for months, accompanied by tremor, asymmetric deep tendon reflexes, and visual disturbances.[157] Clinical relapses or progressive illness have not been described. Infants and young children frequently exhibit significant neurologic sequelae when discharged, but psychomotor function is usually recovered on later follow-up.[158] Little is known of the risk or outcome of congenital infection. Pregnancy and delivery progressed normally in one case acquired during the third trimester (T. F. Tsai, unpublished observation). HIV infection has not complicated the clinical course of illness in several anecdotal cases (J. Luby, unpublished observations).

The peripheral white blood cell count may be slightly elevated. Proteinuria and abnormalities of the urinary sediment are detected in some patients. Hyponatremia appears in more than one third of patients, and alanine aminotransferase and creatine phosphokinase levels may be slightly elevated. The CSF is under pressure in the range of 200 to 250 mmH_2O in one third of cases, and CSF protein exceeds 45 mg/100 ml in over two thirds of cases. A principally monocytic CSF pleocytosis of 5 to several hundred cells is usual. The typical electroencephalogram pattern of diffuse generalized slowing with delta-wave activity rarely is superimposed with focal discharges and spike activity.[156] Few reports of imaging studies are available. Only premorbid abnormalities are present in most cases, without cortical edema, pathologic enhancement, or a mass effect; however, specific abnormal signals have been seen in the substantia nigra of a few patients (J. Luby, unpublished observations).

The diagnosis should be suspected if the case is one of a cluster in the summer or early fall, especially if the patient is an elderly or homeless person. A cerebral ischemic event, heat stroke, medication or drug toxicity, or other cause of delirium or encephalopathy has frequently been the initial diagnosis in confirmed cases. Other infectious causes of acute encephalitis cannot be distinguished easily on a clinical basis.

Tick-Borne Encephalitis

Infection leads to symptoms of TBE in only 1 in 250 persons. Because the illness is biphasic and neurologic infection develops in the second phase in only 5 to 30% of patients, neurologic cases form a minority of all infections.[6, 121, 159] Conversely, the initial phase may have been inapparent in some patients presenting with neurologic symptoms. After an incubation period as long as 28 days, illness begins with a nonspecific grippe of fever, malaise, headache, myalgias, nausea, and vomiting. Within a week, these symptoms resolve spontaneously, concluding the illness in the majority of cases. But in others who progress to neurologic infection, the remission of symptoms is temporary, usually 2 to 8 days (range 1 to 20), when illness with high fever, headache, and vomiting resumes. The second phase may be limited to aseptic meningitis (commonly in children), or it can manifest as encephalitis, myelitis, radicular neuritis, or their combinations, with severe cases occurring more often in elderly persons. Early prodromal symptoms may be undetected in children, whose illness in greater than two thirds of cases is uncomplicated by encephalitis or myelitis. Altered consciousness, ataxia, tremor, paresthesias, focal signs, and, less often, seizures characterize the presentation with encephalitis. Limb weakness and paralysis usually represent lower motor neuron lesions from myelitis or radicular neuritis; paresis may be transient or evolve to permanent weakness and muscular atrophy. The shoulder girdle and upper limb musculature are affected most frequently, and urinary bladder continence and other autonomic functions can also be disturbed. Bulbar involvement, most often of cranial nerves III, VII, IX, X, and XI, produces gaze and peripheral facial paralysis, dysphagia, dysarthria, and, rarely, respiratory distress. The outcome generally is good, especially in children, but the prognosis varies with age. Approximately 1% of cases are fatal, and these cases or residual neurologic deficits occur most often in elderly persons. Sequelae are reported in up to 40% of patients, most frequently consisting of psychologic disturbances such as asthenia, headache, memory loss and decreased concentration, anxiety, and emotional lability but also ataxia and incoordination, tremor, dysphasia, and, in less than 5%, specific cranial or spinal muscular paralysis.[121, 160] Rarely, recovery is complicated by persistent convulsions, although EEG abnormalities may persist silently in a larger proportion of cases. Pneumonia, heart failure, and other complications associated with prolonged hospitalization have been reported. A rare case of hemorrhagic fever occurred in a laboratory-acquired louping ill infection.[67]

The far eastern form of the disease is more severe, with fatalities occurring in 20% of hospitalized cases and residual neurologic sequelae in up to 60% of recovered patients.[125] As in CEE, the neurologic presentation is variable, relecting a diffuse encephalitis. The illness is monophasic, however, presenting with hectic fever, violent headache, vomiting, photophobia, nuchal rigidity, stupor, focal deficits, seizures, and coma. Poliomyelitic involvement of the brain stem and upper spinal cord produces cranial nerve palsies, respiratory and cardiac disturbances, and a characteristic syndrome of brachial plexus and neck weakness with residual atrophy. A variety of serious neurologic sequelae may result, including progressive motor weakness and epilepsia partialis continua, reflecting a chronic encephalitis.

Powassan encephalitis is a severe encephalitis with focal features in more than 50% of reported cases; in one patient, the clinical presentation with olfactory hallucinations and temporal lobe seizures mimicked herpes encephalitis.[161, 162] Among 16 reported cases, 2 were fatal and 7 had significant residua of hemi- or quadriplegia or aphasia. Spinal paralysis with residual muscular wasting is similar to the poliomyelitis associated with RSSE and CEE.[163]

Examination of the peripheral blood discloses leukopenia in the initial phase of illness, leukocytosis up to 20,000/mm^3 during the second phase, with a transition to leukopenia again before recovery. The C reactive protein level and the erythrocyte sedimentation rate are usually elevated. Thrombocytopenia, elevated alanine and aspartate aminotransferase levels, and electrocardiographic abnormalities have been reported anecdotally.[164] The CSF pleocytosis average of less than 100/mm^3 is significantly lower than that in other CNS infections, and its lymphocytic composition increases to 85% by the ninth day of illness. The CSF protein level, although normal at the onset of neurologic symptoms, rises during the next 6 weeks with an increase in both the IgG index, indicating intrathecal synthesis, and the albumin index, indicating disturbed blood-brain barrier permeability, until it returns to normal 1 year later.[121] The distribution of CSF lymphocyte cell markers in TBE, $CD3^+CD25^+$, differs from the $CD3^+CD71^+$, $CD19^+$ distribution in patients dually infected with *Borrelia burgdorferi.* This distinction has been proposed as an approach to rapidly identify neuroborreliosis patients, who should be treated with antibiotics.[116, 117] Anecdotal reports indicate abnormal magnetic resonance imaging signals in the thalami and basal ganglia.[165]

Although a history of tick bite is given in only half of the cases, exposure to an endemic focus during the transmission season should trigger suspicion. TBE is transmitted under the same circumstances as *B. burgdorferi,* and clinically, their radicular and aseptic meningitis syndromes can overlap. Anecdotal observations suggest that neurologic symptoms of Lyme disease may occur more often in the context of concurrent TBE, and conversely, that TBE may be more severe in a dual infection.[117, 131, 132] TBE results in a more prolonged course of illness and hospitalization than other acute encephalitides of presumed viral origin; this pattern and the presence of spinal paralysis may aid in making the diagnosis. Myelitis cases can mimic Guillain-Barré syndrome or poliovirus infection.

LABORATORY DIAGNOSIS

Viral isolation is relevant to the diagnosis of suspected YF and dengue because patients may present while still viremic and viral infectivity titers in blood are sufficiently high that attempts may be successful. Identifying the infective dengue viral serotype is important chiefly for public health reasons, but an individual patient also may benefit because future exposure to other serotypes places the patient at higher risk for DHF. Neurotropic flaviviruses can occasionally be isolated from blood taken within the first week after the onset of illness and before the onset of neurologic symptoms. In general, viral recovery from blood is successful only before an antibody response develops. Contrary to expectation, the isolation of neurotropic viruses from the CSF is usually unsuccessful except in the early stages of fulminant illness.

Tissue samples, whether from biopsy or autopsy, ideally should be divided into aliquots that are frozen at −70°C for viral isolation and fixed in buffered formalin and glutaraldehyde for light and electron microscopy. Viscerotomy liver samples are frequently taken after death as a means of postmortem YF diagnosis, but because pathologic changes are not pathognomonic, a purely histologic diagnosis should be considered presumptive and supplemented with immunohistochemical staining using viral-specific antibodies. Liver biopsy should never be attempted from suspected YF patients, who are at risk of fatal hemorrhage. StLE, RSSE, and JE viruses have been isolated from brain, lung, liver, spleen, and kidney with varied success, depending on the duration of illness and the day of death. Diverse areas of the brain and spinal cord should be sampled. StLE virus was also isolated from vitreous humor in one case. Suckling mice and C6/36 or AP61 mosquito cell cultures are the most sensitive systems for viral isolation, but Vero, $LLCMK_2$, PS and other continuous vertebrate cell lines are also used.[166]

Multiplex polymerase chain reaction assays in various formats that simultaneously identify the presence of dengue virus and its serotype in serum samples are used only in specialized laboratories in the United States and several Asian and South American countries.[167, 168] YF virus genomic sequences have also been detected in blood, but clinical experience is limited. In the few reported evaluations, polymerase chain reaction has been insensitive in detecting flaviviral genomic sequences in the CSF of encephalitis patients, a trend consistent with the usual difficulty of viral isolation from CSF; however, one study suggested that viral nucleic acid may be detected with greater sensitivity in acute-phase serum samples.[169, 170]

Laboratory diagnosis of most cases, especially in travelers who come to clinical attention after viremia has cleared, depends principally on the serologic testing of serum and in the case of neurologic infections, also CSF.[171, 172] IgM detection by antibody capture enzyme-linked immunosorbent assay (ELISA) is the preferred technique, although some laboratories successfully detect IgM and IgG antibodies by indirect immunofluorescence assay. The assay is more than 95% sensitive when serum specimens from 7 to 10 days after the onset are tested. In secondary flaviviral infections, a combination of IgM and IgG ELISA is 100% sensitive as early as 4 to 5 days after the onset of illness. Both CSF and serum should be examined in cases of flaviviral encephalitis because IgM may appear earlier in CSF. When both specimens are tested, nearly all patients are positive by 10 days after the onset of illness, with a 10% increase in cumulative positivity per day, as a rule of thumb (Fig. 142–8).[172] Serum IgM in dengue infection declines to undetectable levels within 60 days, but antibodies persist for up to 9 months in recovered StLE and TBE cases and for more than 2 months in more than 50% of West Nile encephalitis patients, potentially limiting the specificity of tests (see later). Heterologous reactions with other flaviviruses are problematic where numerous flaviviruses cocirculate, but in tropical Asia, where only JE and dengue viruses infect humans, the infections are easily distinguished.[171] Circumstances are more complex in Africa and even in Australia, where early infections with a greater number of flaviviruses are prevalent. Fractionation of IgM before hemagglutination inhibition testing and competitive epitope-blocking ELISAs improve the specificity, but among sera from African patients, all serologic approaches frequently fail to resolve previous and recent infections. Heterologous flaviviral antibodies have become an issue even among specimens submitted in the United States for arboviral diagnosis. Previous dengue infection, reflecting prior exposures in persons who had resided abroad, is now the most frequent arboviral diagnosis in the New York State laboratory (L. Grady, personal communication). These heterologous dengue antibodies frequently pose difficulties in the interpretation of tests for StLE and Powassan encephalitis. Although neutralization tests provide the greatest specificity, they are time-consuming, are expensive to perform, and are offered only in specialized laboratories. Hemagglutination inhibition and complement fixation tests are now used infrequently, but they still have utility under some circumstances. Complement fixation antibodies are relatively specific in distinguishing between antigenic complexes, and because they rise rather late, often 4 to 6 weeks after the onset and decline with a half-life of 3 years, positive reactions indicate infection in the intermediate period after the disappearance of IgM antibodies. Hemagglutination inhibition and neutralizing antibodies can persist for decades after infection. Rapid immunochromatographic tests formatted as small folders to detect dengue and JE IgM and IgG have demonstrated high sensitivity and specificity in field evaluations (100 and 90%, respectively, for the dengue test) and should facilitate laboratory confirmation of cases in clinical facilities.[173]

In a patient with a compatible illness, a case is confirmed by a fourfold change in the serum antibody titer or, alternatively in encephalitis patients, by the demonstration of viral-specific IgM in CSF, reflecting intrathecal immune response. An elevated serum IgM antibody level alone is considered presumptive evidence of recent infection when high IgM prevalence rates in the population prevail from frequent asymptomatic infections and antibody persistence through the transmission season.

Serologic testing for StLE, dengue, and other selected arboviruses is performed at several private laboratories, at most state laboratories, and at Centers for Disease Control and Prevention, U.S. Army Medical Research Institute for Infectious Diseases, and other reference laboratories. In addition, an indirect immunofluorescence assay kit for the domestic arboviruses that includes a StLE antigen can be purchased in the United States and a TBE ELISA kit in Europe. Dengue immunochromatographic folders and ELISA kits are sold in Asia and Australia.

PREVENTION AND THERAPY

Yellow Fever

Hospitalization in an intensive care facility where the patient can be sequestered from mosquitoes is recommended to provide close clinical monitoring and supportive care and to prevent anthroponotic transmission. Blood in the acute phase of illness is potentially infectious. No antiviral therapy is available, and specific supportive interventions have not been evaluated. General support with oxygen, fluids, and pressors are indicated to treat and prevent hypotension and metabolic acidosis. H_2-receptor antagonists and sucralfate may be of value in preventing or ameliorating gastric bleeding. Avoidance of sedatives and drugs dependent on hepatic metabolism is prudent, and the medication-dosing intervals should be adjusted with reduced renal function. Encephalopathy should be investigated for treatable metabolic causes, particularly hypoglycemia. Fresh-frozen plasma and vitamin K have been administered to replenish clotting factors. The effect of heparin therapy is unproved. Secondary infections should be pursued and treated.

YF is vaccine-preventable with the attenuated 17D vaccine that produces immunity in more than 95% of recipients and long-term, possibly lifelong, protection with a single 0.5-ml subcutaneous dose.[4] Vaccination has been associated with anaphylaxis in 1 in 116,000 doses, in recipients with egg allergy, since the vaccine is produced in chick embryos or, possibly, with allergy to gelatin that is added as a vaccine stabilizer. Its most serious side effect, however, is potentially fatal vaccine-associated encephalitis, which in 12 of 21 known cases has occurred in infants younger than 4 months. For this reason, the vaccine is contraindicated in infants younger than 4 months and is recommended for 4- to 9- month-old infants only under situations of high risk. YF and measles vaccines are coadministered at the 9-month Expanded Programme of Immunization visit under World Health Organization–United Nations Children's Fund

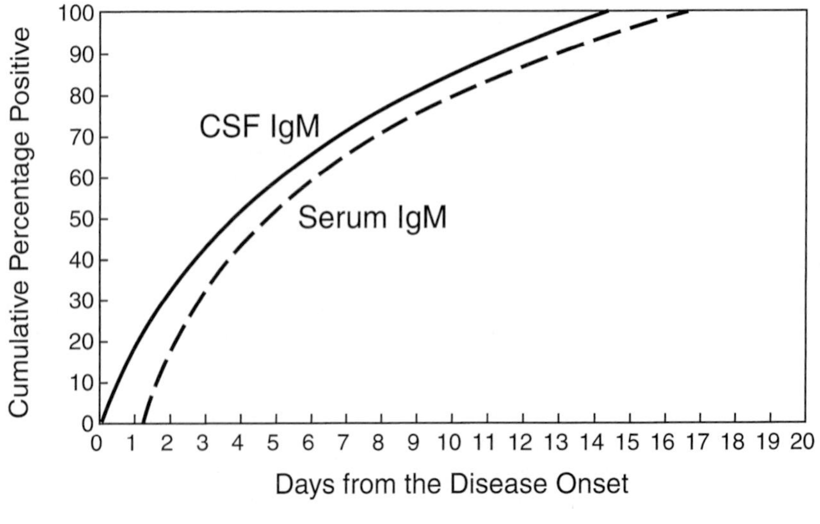

FIGURE 142–8. Cumulative percentage positivity of anti–West Nile viral IgM and IgG ELISA antibodies in cerebrospinal fluid by day after illness onset. (Adapted from Tardei G, Ruta S, Chitu V, et al. Evaluation of IgM and IgG enzyme immunoassays in the serologic diagnosis of West Nile virus infection. J Clin Microbiol. In press.)

recommendations in 35 African countries; however, compliance is low. A virologically proven case of vaccine-associated encephalitis in an elderly recipient stimulated a study that indicated a higher risk of serious vaccine side effects in persons older than 65 years, but the findings are considered preliminary (T. F. Tsai, unpublished observations). The vaccine's risk in pregnancy has not been established. Cord blood IgM viral antibodies indicating congenital infection were reported in one case without evidence of birth defects.[174, 175] In small studies, the vaccine was less immunogenic in pregnant women, asymptomatic HIV-infected adults (77% antibody response), and HIV-infected infants (17% antibody response); no adverse events, however, were reported in the latter two groups.[175–177]

Travelers to at-risk South American and African countries should receive the vaccine at 10-year intervals to meet international requirements. The vaccine can be given concurrently with measles, oral polio, hepatitis A or B, meningococcal polysaccharide, oral or intramuscular typhoid, or oral cholera vaccines; chloroquine; or immune serum globulin.

Prevention of epidemic *A. aegypti*–borne YF follows the approach for dengue control with the reduction of peridomestic breeding sites. In dry savanna and urban locations where drinking water frequently must be stored, the simple expedient of covering the containers or reservoirs eliminates a principal source of breeding. Surveillance of viral activity by monitoring viral infection rates in sylvatic mosquitoes has been proposed as an early warning system for West and Central Africa, where outbreaks frequently emerge in a regionwide distribution. The discovery of intensified viral activity, even in a small number of sentinel sites, may be a sufficiently sensitive predictor of viral activity in a broader area to trigger timely and effective mass immunization. In South America, surveys to detect dead monkeys on the forest floor are conducted to monitor viral transmission and risk of its spillover to humans.

Dengue and Dengue Hemorrhagic Fever

Antipyretics may help to relieve the symptoms of dengue fever, but to avert Reye's syndrome and hemostatic complications, aspirin should not be used. Oral rehydration is indicated to replace losses from vomiting and high fever. Attentive clinical monitoring of suspected DHF-DSS cases and anticipatory and supportive care are lifesaving and have reduced fatality rates by 50- to 100-fold. A treatment algorithm and a detailed protocol for monitoring patients by clinical and laboratory markers have been published by the World Health Organization.[23] The critical activities are monitoring circulation and vascular leakage every 1 to 2 hours by serial clinical assessments of pulse, blood pressure, skin perfusion, urine output, and hematocrit, to trigger intravenous fluid therapy. A greater than 20% hematocrit increase (e.g., from 35 to 42%) indicates a significant loss of intravascular volume and the urgent need for fluid resuscitation. Normal saline is administered to maintain circulation and, under continued monitoring, for recurrent shock. Shock necessitates rapid intervention with isotonic crystalloid solutions or, if needed, plasma or whole-blood transfusions. Neither high-dose methylprednisolone (30 mg/kg) nor AC-17 (carbazochrome sodium sulfonate), which was believed to reduce vascular permeability, was beneficial in controlled trials.[178, 179] In some locations, intravenous gamma globulin has been used empirically but no benefit has been established in a controlled evaluation. Because vascular integrity is usually restored spontaneously in 48 hours, overhydration resulting in pulmonary edema is a risk, and positive-pressure ventilation with positive end-expiratory pressure may be needed. As a result of the opposing dangers of adult respiratory distress syndrome due to capillary leakage and excessive fluid administration, DHF-DSS has been reported to be the third most common cause of adult respiratory distress syndrome in hospitalized children in Malaysia.[146] Whole-blood, platelet, and fresh-frozen plasma transfusions may be needed in cases with significant hemorrhages, but caution is indicated in the administration of heparin except in cases with clear signs of disseminated intravascular coagulopathy. Invasive procedures should be minimized to avoid hemorrhagic complications. Secondary and concurrent infections should be investigated and treated.

Dengue prevention currently relies on public health and community-based *A. aegypti* control programs to remove and destroy mosquito-breeding sites.[28, 180] The ubiquity of containers that potentially provide breeding habitats in urban neighborhoods and individual houses makes this a formidable challenge even with strict legal enforcement and concerted public action under strong governments (e.g., in Singapore and Cuba). Insecticidal fogging is considered unhelpful, but in sealed houses, indoor insecticidal sprays should be effectual. Several approaches to vaccine development are being pursued. The most advanced is a tetravalent combination of attenuated dengue strains that is under phase II clinical evaluation.[5] Travelers can protect themselves by using repellents and insecticidal sprays indoors.

Flaviviral Encephalitis

No specific therapy for flaviviral encephalitis has been developed, but the anecdotal use of interferon-alfa in the prophylaxis and treatment of JE cases has been reported.[181] A mixture of JE-virus–neutralizing monoclonal antibodies was reportedly beneficial in a clinical trial in China, but considerable experience with TBE immune globulin therapy has underscored the potential hazards of immunotherapy.[182, 183] Passive immunization has been associated with exacerbation of the disease, and its use, even within the recommended interval of 96 hours after a tick bite, should be undertaken with due caution. Corticosteroid therapy of TBE resulted in a more rapid reduction of fever but prolonged hospitalization.

Supportive care should focus on controlling seizures, ventilatory support of respiratory failure, and monitoring and reducing cerebral edema. In many Asian centers, mannitol is given routinely in JE cases, but a controlled trial of dexamethasone therapy found no benefit or harm from its administration.[184] Fluid and electrolyte administration should balance circulatory needs, the avoidance of cerebral edema, and inappropriate antidiuretic hormone secretion. Secondary infections should be anticipated and treated.

Three JE vaccines are licensed, but the inactivated cell culture–derived P-3 strain vaccine and live-attenuated SA14-14-2 vaccines are distributed only in China. Three and two doses, respectively, are administered in spring campaigns to children older than 1 year followed by a variable number of boosters with the killed vaccine. The live vaccine, however, is highly immunogenic after even one dose.[185, 186] Both vaccines have been safe, and their respective efficacies are 85% and 98%. An inactivated mouse brain–derived vaccine produced in Japan, Korea, Taiwan, Thailand, and Vietnam is administered in early childhood in two primary doses with 4 to 6 additional boosters at various intervals until 15 years. The efficacy is 91%. The vaccine is distributed internationally to military personnel and travelers in three 1-ml doses, administered subcutaneously, on days zero, 7, and 30. Angioedema and generalized urticaria with an onset up to 3 days after vaccination occur in 0.3% of vaccinees, so in travelers, the series should be completed a week before departure.[187, 188] Anecdotal cases of acute disseminated encephalomyelitis temporally related to vaccination have been reported. Recommendations for vaccination are conservative because of vaccine side effects and the slight risk of acquiring the disease during travel. Vaccination is not recommended routinely and is reserved for expatriates in Asia, persons with a high risk of exposure, and travelers spending more than 30 days during the transmission season in an endemic area (see Table 142–1). Others should avoid outdoor exposure at dusk and use mosquito repellents and mosquito bed nets. Novel inactivated, attenuated, and genetically engineered vaccines are under study.[5]

Two inactivated TBE vaccines derived from infected chick embryo cells are licensed in Europe and distributed with considerable uptake rates in areas with a high transmission risk.[189, 190] Administration in three doses over a year with an additional booster 3 years later has been highly effective in reducing rates of disease. An abbreviated zero-7, and 21-day immunization schedule is also immunogenic.[191] Cross-protection against RSSE virus has been shown in animals, but clinical efficacy against the disease has not been reported. Sensitivity to thimerosol and local side effects occur frequently. Several temporally related cases of Guillain-Barré syndrome have been reported, albeit without a proven causal association. The vaccine is not licensed in the United States, but it has been distributed as an investigational new drug by the U.S. Army. For most travelers, the risk of acquiring the disease is extremely low, and personal protective measures, such as the avoidance of risky habitats, protective clothing, and repellents, are appropriate. Expatriates may choose to be immunized abroad, and for the exceptional short-term traveler with high-risk activities, preexposure prophylaxis with TBE immune globulin, 0.05 ml/kg intramuscularly, is an alternative, although its efficacy is unproven. A promising naked DNA vaccine is under study.

Vector control is impractical as a means of JE prevention because of the extensive areas that must be treated. Pig immunization effectively prevents abortions in sows and can modulate the transmission of disease to humans, but widescale implementation is impractical. Emergency truck-mounted or aerial applications of adulticides are routinely administered in response to StLE epidemics, usually in conjunction with programs of avian or mosquito surveillance that provide early warning of increased viral transmission. Public health warnings to avoid outdoor activities in the evening and rescheduling evening high school football games and Halloween trick-or-treat activities to daylight hours were shown to reduce the risk of acquiring the disease in central Florida. In the absence of effective therapies or prophylaxis, public health interventions are the only available preventative measures. Control of TBE in defined locations by the area application of acaricides has been effective in reducing vector ticks, but widespread implementation is impractical.

OTHER FLAVIVIRAL INFECTIONS

West Nile Fever

West Nile virus is related antigenically to JE and StLE viruses, but clinically, infection usually produces a simple febrile illness, often with rash, lymphadenopathy, and polyarthropathy. Infections with the three viruses are similar, however, in their high infection/case ratio of 300:1 and the heightened severity of illness with age.[128] Various viscerotropic presentations have been reported, notably, hepatitis, pancreatitis, and myocarditis; however, neurologic infection is the most serious complication. Encephalitis, myelitis, or aseptic meningitis leads to a fatal outcome in 5% of cases, usually in elderly patients. The virus is one of the most widely distributed of arboviruses, causing endemic and occasionally epidemic infections in Africa, the Middle East, southern Europe, and South Asia.[192] A viral subtype, Kunjin virus, is transmitted in Southeast Asia and Australia.[193] The virus is spread between various *Culex* mosquito vectors and birds; *Culex univittatus* is the principal vector in Africa and Asia, and in Europe, *Culex modestus* and *C. pipiens* have been implicated as enzootic and epidemic vectors, respectively. Dissemination of the virus by migratory birds probably underlies its widespread distribution. Recent outbreaks of encephalitis in Romania and Algeria, equine encephalitis in Italy and Morocco, and recovery of the virus in Portugal are evidence of increased transmission in Europe and the Mediterranean littoral. Supportive care may be lifesaving in neurologic cases. An experimental inactivated vaccine has been developed.

Murray Valley Encephalitis

The Murray Valley encephalitis virus is a member of the antigenic complex of JE, StLE, and West Nile viruses, and like those viruses, it is transmitted in a mosquito-avian cycle, chiefly by *Culex annulirostris*. Foci of perennial viral transmission are maintained in western Australia, where sporadic cases and small outbreaks occur. At infrequent intervals since the initial recognition of the disease in 1917, the virus has spread to the heavily populated southeastern river valleys, where it has produced larger outbreaks, the most recent in 1981. Sporadic cases have also been recognized in Papua New Guinea. Approximately 350 cases have been reported in total, with a case-fatality rate of 20% in the most recent outbreak. The onset of encephalitis is preceded by a prodrome of headache, nausea, vomiting, photophobia, and neck stiffness, followed within 2 to 5 days by changes in sensorium, stupor, and motor signs.[194] Coma, limb paralysis, and respiratory depression necessitating ventilatory support develop in severe cases. Recovery is followed by motor paralysis in severe cases and by milder motor disturbances and emotional and psychologic symptoms in a higher proportion of survivors. Serologic diagnosis is potentially encumbered by cross-reactive antibodies to Kunjin, Kokobera, JE, Edge Hill, Alfuy, Sepik, dengue, and other flaviviruses in the region. Supportive treatment has spared mortality and morbidity. Regional surveillance of sentinel chicken infections is maintained as an early warning system.

Rocio Encephalitis

Rocio encephalitis was recognized to be the novel cause of a series of encephalitis outbreaks that occurred from 1975 to 1977 in the Ribiera Valley and Santista lowlands in coastal Šao Paulo and Paraná-states, Brazil.[195] More than 1000 cases were identified, chiefly in fishermen and others with outdoor occupations. The virus was isolated from human brain, and its relationship to StLE virus was shown antigenically and more recently by genomic sequencing. The virus is transmitted from *Psorophora* mosquitoes to birds, and human infections are incidental. Sporadic asymptomatic infections have been detected in field studies, but outbreaks have not recurred. In 1996, serologic evidence of infection was reported in Bahia State, far to the north, but the virus has not been isolated outside the original focus. A prodrome of fever, headache, malaise, vomiting, and conjunctivitis precedes the onset of altered consciousness, motor weakness, and, frequently, cerebellar signs. Neurologic infection progresses to coma in one third of cases and death in 10%. Neurologic and psychologic sequelae have been reported in 20% of survivors. Supportive treatment is potentially lifesaving. Emergency insecticidal applications have been implemented in outbreak control.

Kyasanur Forest Disease

The report of an outbreak of monkey deaths and hemorrhagic fever with jaundice in 1957 in the Kyasanur Forest of Mysore (now Karnataka) State, India triggered an investigation of what was suspected to be the much-feared introduction of yellow fever to Asia.[196, 197] The virus, isolated from dead langur monkeys and *Haemaphysalis* ticks, turned out to be a novel member of the antigenic complex of tick-borne flaviviruses and was shown to be transmitted between various ixoidid ticks and forest rodents, insectivores, and monkeys. That epidemic and subsequent sporadic cases and outbreaks occurred during the dry season in peasants clearing the forest for pasture, and the endemic area has gradually spread and enlarged in the state with those activities. Serologic evidence of infection has also been reported in northwestern India and from the Andaman Islands. Between 1982 and 1988, 1847 cases were reported. The incubation period is 3 to 8 days, after which illness begins abruptly with fever, headache, chills, vomiting, myalgia, photophobia, and conjunctival suffusion. Facial and conjunctival hyperemia, lymphadenopathy, hepatospenomegaly, and petechiae are found on examination. Diffuse hemorrhages from the nares, gums, and gastrointestinal tract develop with hemorrhagic pulmonary edema in 40% of cases and renal failure in severe cases. After defervescence and a remission of symptoms for as long as 1 to 3 weeks, a second phase of illness develops, with

TABLE 142-2 Less Commonly Recognized Flaviviral Infections

Virus and Reference	Clinical Syndrome	Geographic Distribution	Transmission Cycle	Mode of Transmission
Alma-Arasan[198]	Febrile illness, meningitis	Kazakhstan	*Ixodes persulcatus*–?	V
Apoi	Encephalitis	Japan	Rodent–?	L
Banzi[199]	Nonspecific febrile illness	South, East Africa	*Culex rubinotus*–rodent	M
Bussuquara[200]	Fever, arthralgias	Brazil, Colombia, Panama	*Culex melaconion* spp.—rodent	M
Edge Hill[201]	Fever, polyarthritis	Australia	*Aedes vigilax*–marsupial	M
Ilhéus[202]	Fever, myalgia, encephalitis	Argentina, Brazil, Colombia, Guatemala, Panama, Trinidad	*Psorophora ferox*–bird	M, E
Karshi[198]	Nonspecific febrile illness	Uzbekistan	Various ticks–rodent	T
Kokobera[203]	Fever, polyarthralgia	Australia, Papua New Guinea	*Culex annulirostris*–? marsupial	M
Koutango	Fever, rash, arthralgia	West and Central Africa	Tick–rodent	L
Kunjin[193]	Fever, polyarthralgia, encephalitis	Australia, Malaysia, Thailand	*Culex annulirostris*–bird	M
Langat[204]	Fever, encephalitis	Malaysia, Thailand, Russia	*Ixodes* tick–rodent	T
Modoc[205]	Aseptic meningitis	Western United States, Canada	Rodent–rodent	Z
Negishi[206]	Encephalitis	Japan, China, Russia	Tick–unknown	L, T
Rio Bravo[207]	Nonspecific febrile illness, meningitis	Western United States, Canada	Bat–bat	Z, L
Sepik[208]	Nonspecific febrile illness	Papua New Guinea	*Mansonia* spp.–?	M
SPH 16111–related viruses[209]	Pneumonia, encephalitis, lymphadenopathy, rash	São Paulo, Brazil	Unknown	U
Spondweni[210]	Fever, arthralgia, rash	South and West Africa	*Aedes* spp.–?	L, M
Usutu[211]	Fever, rash	South and Central Africa	*Culex* spp.–bird	M
Wesselsbron[212]	Fever, arthralgia, rash, encephalitis	Sub-Saharan Africa, Thailand	*Aedes* spp.–?	M, L, DC
Zika[213]	Fever, rash, arthralgia	West, East, and Central Africa; Indonesia, Malaysia	*Aedes* spp.–monkey	M

Abbreviations: DC, Contact with infected sheep; E, experimental infection; L, laboratory-acquired infection; M, mosquito-borne infection; T, tick-borne infection; U, unknown; V, vector-borne; Z, zoonotic infection.

neurologic symptoms in 15 to 50% of patients. Laboratory findings are similar to those of DHF, with leukopenia, thrombocytopenia, an elevated hematocrit reflecting hemoconcentration, and elevated hepatic transminase levels. Patients have detectable viremias up to 12 days after the onset of illness. From 5 to 10% of cases are fatal, and iridokeratitis has been reported in survivors. An inactivated chick embryo–derived vaccine is produced locally and is distributed in response to epidemics. A related virus was recently isolated from abattoir workers in Saudi Arabia who developed a similar illness. The virus's origin and reservoir are unknown, but it is speculated that infection may have been transmitted from imported viremic sheep at slaughter or from their infected ticks.[69]

Omsk Hemorrhagic Fever

The Omsk hemorrhagic fever virus is transmitted between *Dermacentor* ticks and small mammals in forest-steppe zones of the Omsk, Novosibirsk, Kurgan, and Tjumen' regions of western Siberia, but the disease emerged in significant form only after muskrats were introduced to the region to establish a fur industry.[197] Outbreaks between 1945 and 1958 led to muskrat epizootics and 1500 human cases, chiefly in trappers, their family members, and laboratory workers. Infection is transmitted directly from infected animal tissues or by tick bite, in a spring–early summer peak and again in autumn. The illness resembles Kyasanur Forest disease, but neuropsychiatric sequelae have been reported more often. The case-fatality rate is less than 3%. Inactivated TBE vaccine (produced in Russia) has been reported to offer cross-protection against the disease.

Less Commonly Recognized Flaviviral Infections

Small numbers or even single cases of the diseases listed in Table 142–2 have been reported. In some instances, experimental human infection (evaluated as cancer therapy) provides the only knowledge of their pathogenicity.

REFERENCES

1. Monath TP, Heinz FX. Flaviviruses. In: Fields BN, Knipe DM, Howley PM, eds. Virology. 3rd ed. New York: Raven; 1995:961.
2. Murphy FA, Fauquet CM, Bishop DHL, et al eds. Virus taxonomy. Sixth International Report of the International Committee on Taxonomy of Viruses. Arch Virols, Suppl 10, 1995.
3. Tsai TF, Chang GJ, Yu YX. Japanese encephalitis vaccines. In: Plotkin SA, Orenstein WA, eds. Vaccines. 3rd ed. Philadelphia: WB Saunders; 1999:672.
4. Monath TP. Yellow fever vaccine. In: Plotkin SA, Orenstein WA, eds. Vaccines. 3rd ed. Philadelphia: WB Saunders; 1999:815–880.
5. Kanesa-Thasan N, Putnak R, Hoke CH. New and improved vaccines for dengue, Japanese encephalitis, and yellow fever viruses. In: Levine MM, Woodrow GC, Kaper JB, Cobon GS, eds. New Generation Vaccines. 2nd ed. New York: Marcel-Dekker; 1997:587.
6. Monath TP, Tsai TF. Flaviviruses. In: Richman DD, Whitley RJ, Hayden FG, eds. Clinical Virology. New York: Churchill-Livingstone; 1997:1133.
7. Chambers TJ, Hahn CS, Galler R, Rice CM. Flavivirus genome organization, expression, and replication. Ann Rev Microbiol. 1990;44:649.
8. Schlesinger JJ, Foltzer M, Chapman S. The Fc portion of antibody to yellow fever virus NS1 is a determinant of protection against YF encephalitis in mice. Virology. 1993;192:132.
9. Brinton MA, Kurane I, Mathew A, et al. Immune mediated and inherited defenses against flaviviruses. Clin Diagn Virol. 1998;10:129.
10. Mathew A, Kurane I, Green S, et al. Predominance of HLA-restricted cytotoxic T-lymphocyte responses to serotype-cross-reactive epitopes on nonstructural proteins following natural secondary dengue virus infection. J Virol. 1998;72:3999.
11. Kurane I, Zeng L, Brinton MA, Ennis FA. Definition of an epitope on NS3 recognized by human $CD4^+$ cytotoxic T lymphocyte clones cross-reactive for dengue virus types 2, 3, and 4. Virology. 1998;240:169.
12. Bielefeldt-Ohmann, H. Analysis of antibody-independent binding of dengue viruses and dengue virus envelope protein to human myelomonocytic cells and B lymphocytes. Virus Res. 1998;57:63–79.
13. Kuno G, Chang WJ, Tsuchiya KR, et al. Phylogeny of the genus Flavivirus. J Virol. 1998;72:73.
14. Chang GJ, Cropp BC, Kinney RM, et al. Nucleotide sequence variation of the envelope protein gene identifies two distinct genotypes of yellow fever virus. J Virol. 1995;69:5773.
15. Rico-Hesse R, Harrison LM, Salas RA, et al. Origins of dengue type 2 viruses associated with increased pathogenicity in the Americas. Virology. 1997;230:244.
16. Hanna JN, Ritchie SA, Phillips DA, et al. An outbreak of Japanese encephalitis in the Torres Strait, Australia, 1995. Med J Aust. 1996;165:256.
17. Trent DW, Monath TP, Bown GS, et al. Variation among strains of St Louis encephalitis virus: Basis for a genetic, pathogenic and epidemiologic classification. Ann N Y Acad Sci. 1980;354:219.
18. Robertson SE, Hull BP, Tomori O, et al. Yellow fever: A decade of reemergence. JAMA. 1996;276:1157.
19. Monath TP: Yellow fever: Victor, victoria? Conqueror, conquest? Epidemics and research in the last forty years and prospects for the future. Am J Trop Med Hyg. 1991;45:1.
20. World Health Organization. Yellow fever, 1996–1997. Part 1. Wkly Epidemiol Rec. 1998;46:354.
21. Vasconcelos PFC, Rodrigues SG, Degallier N, et al. An epidemic of sylvatic yellow fever in the southeast region of Maranhao state, Brazil, 1993–1994: Epidemiologic and entomologic findings. Am J Trop Med Hyg. 1997;57:132–137.

22. Monath TP, Nasidi A. Should yellow fever vaccine be included in the expanded program of immunization in Africa? A cost-effectiveness analysis for Nigeria. Am J Trop Med Hyg. 1993;48:274.
23. World Health Organization. Technical Guide for Diagnosis, Treatment, Surveillance, Prevention, and Control of Dengue Haemorrhagic Fever. 2nd ed. Geneva: World Health Organization, 1997.
24. Gubler DJ. Dengue and dengue hemorrhagic fever. Clin Microbiol Rev. 1998;11:480.
25. Halstead SB. The XXth century dengue pandemic: Need for surveillance and research. World Health Stat Q. 1992;45:292.
26. Monath TP. Yellow fever and dengue – the interactions of virus, vector and host in the re-emergence of epidemic disease. Virology. 1994; 5:133–145.
27. Kuno G. Factors influencing the transmission of dengue viruses. In: Gubler DJ, Kuno G, eds. Dengue and Dengue Hemorrhagic Fever. New York: CAB International; 1997:61.
28. Reiter P, Gubler DJ. Surveillance and control of urban dengue vectors. In: Gubler DJ, Kuno G, eds. Dengue and Dengue Hemorrhagic Fever. New York: CAB International 1997:425.
29. Burke DS, Nisalak A, Johnson DE, et al. A prospective study of dengue infections in Bangkok. Am J Trop Med Hyg. 1988;38:172.
30. Sangkawhibha N, Rohanasuphor S, Ahandrik S, et al. Risk factors in dengue shock syndrome: A prospective study in Rayong, Thailand. I. The 1980 outbreak. Am J Epidemiol. 1984;120:653.
31. Thein S, Aung MM, Shwe TN, et al. Risk factors in dengue shock syndrome. Am J Trop Med Hyg. 1997;56:566.
32. Halstead SB. Dengue and hemorrhagic fevers of southeast Asia. Yale J Biol Med. 1965;37:434.
33. Halstead SB. Pathogenesis of dengue: Challenges to molecular biology. Science. 1988;239:476.
34. Kliks S, Nisalak A, Brandt WE, et al. Evidence that maternal dengue antibodies are important in the development of dengue hemorrhagic fever in infants. Am J Trop Med Hyg. 1988;38:411.
35. Kouri GP, Guzman MG, Bravo JR, et al. Dengue haemorrhagic fever/dengue shock syndrome: Lessons from the Cuban epidemic. Bull World Health Organ. 1989;67:375.
36. Bravo JR, Guzman MG, Louri GP. Why dengue hemorrhagic fever in Cuba? 1. Individual risk factors for dengue hemorrhagic fever/dengue shock syndrome. Trans R Soc Trop Med Hyg. 1987;81:816.
37. Gubler DJ, Suharyono W, Lubis I, et al. Epidemic dengue 3 in central Java, associated with low viremia in man. Am J Trop Med Hyg. 1981;30:1094.
38. Scott RMcN, Nimmanitya S, Bancroft WH, et al. Shock syndrome in primary dengue infections. Am J Trop Med Hyg. 1976;25:866.
39. Thisyakorn U, Nimmanitya S. Nutritional status of children with dengue hemorrhagic fever. Clin Infect Dis. 1993;16:295.
40. Chiewslip P, Scott RM, Bhamarapravati N. Histocompatibility antigens and dengue hemorrhagic fever. Am J Trop Med Hyg. 1981;30:1100.
41. Kalayanarooj S, Vaughn DW, Nimmannitya S, et al. Early clinical and laboratory indicators of acute dengue illness. J Infect Dis. 1997;176:313.
42. Ramirez-Ronda CH, Garcia CD. Dengue in the Western Hemisphere. Infect Dis Clin North Am. 1994;8:107.
43. Hanna JN, Ritchie SA, Merritt AD, et al. Two contiguous outbreaks of dengue type 2 in north Queensland. Med J Aust. 1998;168:221.
44. Tropical Public Health Unit. Dengue 3 in Cairns: The story so far. Commun Dis Intell. 1998;22.
45. Imported dengue—United States, 1996. MMWR. 1998;47:544.
46. Trofa AF, DeFraites RF, Smoak BL, et al. Dengue in US military personnel in Haiti. JAMA. 1997;277:1546.
47. Steffen R, Ciurea-Loechel A, Charoenvit Y, et al. Pilot study on seroconversions in febrile travelers after a visit to a developing country (Abstract). Fifth International Society for Travel Medicine, Montreal. In press.
48. Rawlings JA, Hendricks KA, Burgess CR, et al. Dengue surveillance in Texas, 1995. Am J Trop Med Hyg. 1998;59:95.
49. Rojanasuphot S, Tsai TF, eds. Regional Workshop on Control Strategies for Japanese Encephalitis. Southeast Asian J Trop Med Public Health. 1995;26:S3.
50. Cardosa MJ, Hooi TP, Kaur P. Japanese encephalitis virus is an important cause of encephalitis among children in Penang. Southeast Asian J Trop Med Public Health. 1995;26:272–275.
51. Paul WS, Moore PS, Karabatsos N, et al. Outbreak of Japanese encephalitis on the island of Saipan, 1990. J. Infect Dis. 1993;167:1053.
52. Anonymous. Japanese encephalitis on the Australian mainland. Commun Dis Intell. 1998;22.
53. Rosen L. The natural history of Japanese encephalitis virus. Ann Rev Microbiol. 1986;40:395.
54. Kitaoka M. Shift of age distribution of cases of Japanese encephalitis in Japan during the period 1950 to 1967. In: Hammon WMcD, Kitaoka M, Downs WG, eds. Immunization for Japanese Encephalitis. Tokyo: Igaku-Shoin; 1972:287–291.
55. Immunization Practices Advisory Committee (ACIP). Inactivated Japanese encephalitis virus vaccine: Recommendations of the ACIP. MMWR Morb Mortal Wkly Rep. 1993;42(RR-1):1–15.
56. Monath TP. Epidemiology. In: Monath TP, ed. St Louis Encephalitis. Washington, DC: American Public Health Association, 1980:239.
57. Monath TP, Tsai TF. ST Louis encephalitis: Lessons from the last decade. Am J Med Hyg. 1987;37:40S.
58. Luby JP. St. Louis encephalitis. Epidemiol Rev. 1979;1:55.
59. Okhuysen PC, Crane JK, Pappas J. St. Louis encephalitis in patients with human immunodeficiency virus infection. Clin Infect Dis. 1993;17:140.
60. Luby JP, Miller G, Gardner P, et al. The epidemiology of St Louis encephalitis in Houston, Texas, 1964. Am J Epidemiol. 1967;86:584.
61. Gresikova M, Calisher CH. Tick-borne encephalitis. In: Monath TP, ed. The Arboviruses: Ecology and Epidemiology, v. 4. Boca Raton, Fla: CRC; 1988:177.
62. Zanotto PM, Gao GF, Gritsun T, et al: An arbovirus cline across the Northern Hemisphere. Virology. 1995;210:152.
63. Kunz C. Tick borne encephalitis in Europe. Acta Leidensia. 1992;2:1.
64. Telford SR III, Armstrong PM, Katavolos P, et al. A new tick-borne encephalitis-like virus infecting New England deer ticks, *Ixodes dammini.* Emerg Infect Dis. 1997;3:165.
65. Daniel M, Kolar J, Zeman P, Pavelka K, Sadlo J. Predictive map of *Ixodes ricinus* high-incidence habitats and a tick-borne encephalitis risk assessment using satellite data. Exp Appl Acarol. 1998;22:417.
66. McNeil JG, Lednar WM, Stansfield SK, et al. Central European tick-borne encephalitis: Assessment of risk for persons in the armed services and vacationers. J Infect Dis. 1985;152:650.
67. Davidson MM, Williams H, MacLoed JA. Louping ill in man: A forgotten disease. J Infect. 1991;23:241.
68. Woodall JP, Roz A. Experimental milk-borne transmission of Powassan virus in the goat. Am J Trop Med Hyg. 1977;26:190.
69. Zaki AM. Isolation of a flavivirus related to the tick-borne encephalitis complex from human cases in Saudi Arabia. Transact R Soc Trop Med Hyg. 1997;91:179.
70. Costero A, Grayson MA: Experimental transmission of Powassan virus (Flaviviridae) by *Ixodes scapularis* ticks (Acari: Ixodidae). Am J Trop Med Hyg. 1996;55:536.
71. Hacker UT, Jelinek T, Erhardt S, et al. In vivo synthesis of tumor necrosis factor-α in healthy humans after live yellow fever vaccination. J Infect Dis. 1998;177:774.
72. Bonnevie-Nielsen V, Heron I, Monath TP, Calisher CH: Lymphocytic 2′,5′-oligoadenylate synthetase activity increases prior to the appearance of neutralizing antibodies and immunoglobulin M and immunoglobulin G antibodies after primary and secondary immunization with yellow fever vaccine. Clin Diagn Lab Immunol. 1995;2:302–306.
73. Wheelock EF, Sibley WA. Circulating virus, interferon and antibody after vaccination with the 17-D strain of yellow fever virus. N Engl J Med. 1965;273:194–198.
74. Strode GK, ed. Yellow Fever. New York: McGraw-Hill; 1951.
75. Monath TP, Ballinger ME, Miller BR, Salaun JJ: Detection of yellow fever viral RNA by nucleic acid hybridization and viral antigen by immunocytochemistry in fixed human liver. Am J Trop Med Hyg. 1989;40:663.
76. Deubel V, Huerre M, Cathomas G, et al. Molecular detection and characterization of yellow fever virus in blood and liver specimens of a non-vaccinated fatal human case. J Med Virol. 1997;53:212.
77. DeBrito T, Sigueira SAC, Santos RTM, et al. Human fatal yellow fever—Immunohistochemical detection of viral antigens in the liver, kidney and heart. Pathol Res Pract. 1992;188:177.
78. Monath TP. Yellow fever: A medically neglected disease. Rev Infect Dis. 1987;9:165.
79. Monath TP. The absence of yellow fever in Asia: Hypotheses. A cause for concern? Virus Inform Exch Newslett. 1989;6:106–107.
80. Martin M, Letteau L, Steele S, et al. Advanced age as a risk factor for serious adverse events due to yellow fever vaccine (Abstract). Fifth International Society for Travel Medicine, Montreal. In press.
81. DeVries RRP, Meera Khan P, Bernini LF, et al. Genetic control of survival in epidemics. J Immunogenet. 1979;6:271–287.
82. Monath TP, Hadler SC. Type B hepatitis and yellow fever infections in West Africa. Trans R Soc Trop Med Hyg. 1987;18:172–173.
83. Halstead SB. Antibody, macrophages, dengue virus infection, shock and hemorrhage: A pathogenetic cascade. Rev Infect Dis. 1989;11:S830.
84. Vaughn DW, Green S, Kalayanarooj S, et al. Dengue in the early febrile phase: Viremia and antibody responses. J Infect Dis. 1997;176:322.
85. Malheiros SMF, Oliveira ASB, Schmidt B, et al. Dengue: Muscle biopsy findings in 15 patients. Arq Neuropsiquiatr. 1993;51:159.
86. Kuo C-H, Tai D-I, Chang-Chien C-S, et al. Liver biochemical tests and dengue fever. Am J Trop Med Hyg. 1992;47:265.
87. Rothwell SW, Putnak R, La Russa VF. Dengue-2 virus infection of human bone marrow: Characterization of dengue-2 antigen–positive stromal cells. Am J Trop Med Hyg. 1996;54:503.
88. Ramanathan M, Duraisamy G. Haemophagocytosis in dengue haemorrhagic fever: A case report. Ann Acad Med. 1991;20:803.
89. Desruelles F, Lamaury I, Roudier M, et al. Cutaneo-mucous manifestations of dengue (in French). Ann Dermatol Venereol. 1997;124:237.
90. Bhamarapravati N, Toochinda P, Boonyapaknavik V. Pathology of Thailand hemorrhagic fever. V. A study of 100 autopsy cases. Ann Trop Med Parasitol. 1967;61:500.
91. Lum LCS, Lam SK, Choy YS, et al. Dengue encephalitis: A true entity? Am J Trop Med Hyg. 1996;54:256.
92. Hommel D, Talarmin A, Deubel V, et al. Dengue encephalitis in French Guinea. Res Virol. 1998;149:235.
93. Ramos C, Sanchez G, Pando RH, et al. Dengue virus in the brain of a fatal case of hemorrhagic dengue fever. J Neurovirol. 1998;4:465.
94. Kurane I, Ennis FA. Cytokines in dengue virus infections: Role of cytokines in the pathogenesis of dengue hemorrhagic fever. Semin Virol. 1994;5:443.
95. Bethell DB, Flobbe K, Phuong CXT, et al. Pathophysiologic and prognostic role of cytokines in dengue hemorrhagic fever. J Infect Dis. 1998;177:778.

96. Avirutnan P, Malasit P, Seliger B, et al. Dengue virus infection of human endothelial cells leads to chemokine production, complement activation, and apoptosis. J Immunol. 1998;161:6338.
97. Kurane I, Innis BL, Nimmannitya S, et al. Activation of T lymphocytes in dengue virus infections: High levels of soluble interleukin 2 receptor, soluble CD4, soluble CD8, interleukin 2, and interferon-γ in sera of children with dengue. J Clin Invest. 1991;88:1473.
98. Hober D, Poli L, Roblin B, et al. Serum levels of tumor necrosis factor-α (TNF-α), interleukin-6 (IL-6), and interleukin-1β (IL-1β) in dengue-infected patients. Am J Trop Med Hyg. 1993;48:324.
99. Raghupathy R, Chaturvedi UC, Al-Sayer H, et al. Elevated levels of IL-8 in dengue hemorraghic fever. J Med Virol. 1998;56:280.
100. Bokisch VA, Top FH Jr, Russel PK, et al. The potential pathogenic role of complement in dengue hemorrhagic shock syndrome. N Engl J Med. 1973;289:996.
101. Kabra SK, Juneja R, Madhulika, et al. Myocardial dysfunction in children with dengue haemorrhagic fever. Natl Med J India. 1998;11:59.
102. Chungue E, Poli L, Roche C, et al. Correlation between detection of plasminogen cross-reactive antibodies and hemorrhage in dengue virus infection. J Infect Dis. 1994;170:1304.
103. Falconar AKI. The dengue virus nonstructural-1 protein (NS1) generates antibodies to common epitopes on human blood clotting, integrin/adhesin proteins and binds to human endothelial cells: Potential implications in haemorrhagic fever pathogenesis. Arch Virol. 1997;142:897.
104. Kliks SC, Nisalak A, Brandt WE, et al. Antibody dependent enhancement of dengue virus growth in human monocytes as a risk factor for dengue hemorrhagic fever. Am J Trop Med Hyg. 1989;40:444.
105. Morens DM. Antibody-dependent enhancement of infection and the pathogenesis of viral disease. Clin Infect Dis. 1994;19:500.
106. Halstead SB, Nimmannitya S, Cohen SN. Observations related to pathogenesis of dengue haemorrhagic fever. IV. Relation of disease severity to antibody response and virus recovered. Yale J Biol Med. 1970;42:311.
107. Halstead SB, O'Rourke EJ. Dengue viruses and mononuclear phagocytes. I. Infection enhancement by non-neutralizing antibody. J Exp Med. 1977;146:201.
108. Mullbacher A, Lobigs M. Up-regulation of MHC class I by flavivirus-induced peptide translocation into the endoplasmic reticulum. Immunity. 1995;3:207.
109. Chang D-M, Shaio M-F. Production of Interleukin-1 (IL-1) and IL-1 inhibitor by human monocytes exposed to dengue virus. J Infect Dis. 1994;170:811.
110. Deparis X, Murgue B, Roche C, et al. Changing clinical and biological manifestations of dengue during the dengue-2 epidemic in French Polynesia in 1996/97—description and analysis in a prospective study. Trop Med Int Health. 1998;3:859.
111. Dropulic B, Masters CL. Entry of neurotropic arboviruses into the central nervous system: An in vitro study using mouse brain endothelium. J Infect Dis. 1990;161:685.
112. Monath TP, Cropp CB, Harrison AK. Mode of entry of a neurotropic arbovirus into the central nervous system: Reinvestigation of an old controversy. Lab Invest. 1983;48:399.
113. Johnson RT, Burke DS, Elwell M, et al. Japanese encephalitis: Immunocytochemical studies of viral antigen and inflammatory cells in fatal cases. Ann Neurol. 1985;18:567.
114. Desai A, Shankar SK, Ravi V, et al. Japanese encephalitis virus antigen in the human brain and its topographic distribution. Acta Neuropathol. 1995;89:368.
115. Johnson RT, Intralawan P, Puapanwatton S. Japanese encephalitis: Identification of inflammatory cells in cerebrospinal fluid. Ann Neurol. 1986;20:691.
116. Tomazic J, Ihan A. Flow cytometric analysis of lymphocytes in cerebrospinal fluid in patients with tick-borne encephalitis. Acta Neurol Scand. 1997;95:29.
117. Tomazic J, Ihan A, Strle F, et al. Immunological differentiation between tickborne encephalitis with and without concomitant neuroborreliosis. Eur J Clin Microbiol Infect Dis. 1997;16:920.
118. Leake CJ, Burke DS, Nisalak A, Hoke CH. Isolation of Japanese encephalitis virus from clinical specimens using a continuous mosquito cell line. Am J Trop Med Hyg. 1986;35:1045–1050.
119. Desai A, Ravi V, Guru SC, et al. Detection of autoantibodies to neural antigens in the CSF of Japanese encephalitis patients and correlation of findings with the outcome. J Neurol Sci. 1994;122:109.
120. Desai A, Ravi V, Chandramuki A, Gourie-Devi M. Proliferative response of human peripheral blood mononuclear cells to Japanese encephalitis virus. Microbiol Immunol. 1995;39:269.
121. Gunther G, Haglund M, Lindquist L, et al. Tick-borne encephalitis in Sweden in relation to a septic meningo-encephalitis of other etiology: A prospective study of clinical course and outcome. J Neurol. 1997;244:230.
122. Tomazic J, Poljak M, Popovi M, et al. Tick-borne encephalitis: Possibly a fatal disease in its acute stage. PCR amplification of TBE RNA from postmortem brain tissue (Case report). Infection. 1997;25:41.
123. Ravi V, Desai AS, Shenoy PK, et al. Persistence of Japanese encephalitis virus in the human nervous system. J Med Virol. 1993;40:326.
124. Sharma S, Mathur A, Prakash R, et al. Japanese encephalitis virus latency in peripheral blood lymphocytes and recurrence of infection in children. Clin Exp Immunol. 1991;85:85.
125. Silber LA, Soloviev VD. Far Eastern tick-borne spring-summer (spring) encephalitis. In: Davis BD, Fisher SH, eds. American Review of Soviet Medicine. New York: America-Soviet Medical Society; 1946:1.
126. Ogawa M, Okubo H, Tsuji Y, et al. Chronic progressive encephalitis occurring 13 years after Russian spring-summer encephalitis. J Neurol Sci. 1973;19:363.
127. Zweighaft RM, Rasmussen C, Brolnitsky O, et al. St Louis encephalitis: The Chicago experience. Am J Trop Med Hyg. 1979;28:114.
128. Tsai TF, Popovici F, Cernescu C, et al. West Nile encephalitis epidemic in southeastern Romania. Lancet. 1998;352:767.
129. Desai A, Shankar SK, Jayakumar PN, et al. Co-existence of cerebral cysticercosis with Japanese encephalitis: A prognostic modulator. Epidemiol Infect. 1997;118:165.
130. Broun GO. Relationship ofhypertensive vaxcular disease to mortality in cases of St Louis encephalitis. Med Bull St. Louis Univ. 1952;4:32.
131. Cimperman J, Maraspin V, Lotri-Furlan S, et al. Concomitant infection with tick-borne encephalitis virus and *Borrelia burgdorferi sensu latu* in patients with acute meningitis or meningoencephalitis. Infection. 1998;26:160.
132. Oksi J, Viljanen MK, Kalimo H, et al. Fatal encephalitis caused by concomitant infection with tick-borne encephalitis virus and *Borrelia burgdorferi.* Clin Infect Dis. 1993;16:392.
133. Edelman R, Schneider RJ, Chieowanich P, et al. The effect of dengue virus infection on the clinical sequelae of Japanese encephalitis: A one year follow-up study in Thailand. Southeast Asian J Trop Med Public Health. 1975;6:308.
134. Bond JO, Hammon WMcD. Epidemiologic studies of possible cross protection between dengue and St Louis encephalitis arboviruses in Florida. Am J Epidemiol. 1970;92:321–329.
135. Francis TI, Moore DL, Edington GM, Smith JA. A clinicopathological study of human yellow fever. Bull World Health Organ. 1972;46:659.
136. Thisyakorn U, Thisyakorn C. Dengue infections with unusual manifestations. J Med Assoc Thai. 1994;77:410.
137. Tsai JC, Juo CH, Chen PC. Upper gastrointestinal bleeding in dengue fever. Am J Gastroenterol. 1991;86:33.
138. Imbert P, Sordet D, Hovette P, Touze JE. Spleen rupture in a patient with dengue fever. Trop Med Parasitol. 1993;44:327.
139. Chye JK, Lim CT, Ng KB, et al. Vertical transmission of dengue. Clin Infect Dis. 1997;25:1374.
140. Sharma JB, Gulati N. Potential relationships between dengue fever and neural tube defects in a northern district of India. Int J Gynecol Obstet. 1992;39:291–295.
141. Mirovsky J, Holub J, Nguyen BC. Influence de la dengue sur la grossesse et le foetus. Gynecol Obstet (Paris). 1965;65:673.
142. Fernandez R, Rodriguez T, Borbonet F, et al: Study of the relationship dengue-pregnancy in a group of Cuban-mothers (in Spanish). Rev Cubana Med Trop. 1994;46:76.
143. Cohen SN, Halstead SB. Shock associated with dengue infection. I. The clinical and physiologic manifestations of dengue hemorrhagic fever in Thailand, 1964. J Pediatr. 1966;68:448.
144. Kautner I, Robinson MJ, Kuhnle U. Dengue virus infection: Epidemiology, pathogenesis, clinical presentation, diagnosis and prevention. J Pediatr. 1997;131:516.
145. Setiawan MW, Samsi TK, Wulur H, et al. Dengue haemorrhagic fever: Ultrasound as an aid to predict the severity of the disease. Pediatr Radiol. 1998;28:1.
146. Lum LCS, Thong MK, Cheah YK, Lam SK. Dengue-associated adult respiratory distress syndrome. Ann Trop Paediatr. 1995;15:335.
147. Pancharoen C, Thisyakorn U. Coinfections in dengue patients. Pediatr Infect Dis J. 1998;17:81.
148. Halstead SB, Nimmannitya S, Margiotta MR. Dengue and chikungunya virus infection in man in Thailand. II. Observations on disease in outpatients. Am J Trop Med Hyg. 1969;18:972.
149. Solomon T, Kneen R, Dung NM, et al. Poliomyelitis-like illness due to Japanese encephalitis virus. Lancet. 1998;351:1094.
150. Srikanth S, Ravi V, Poornima S, et al. Viral antibodies in recent onset, nonorganic psychoses: Correspondence with symptomatic severity. Soc Biol Psychiatry. 1994;36:517.
151. Misra UK, Kalita J. Anterior horn cells are also involved in Japanese encephalitis. Acta Neurol Scand. 1997;96:114.
152. Dickerson RB, Newton JR, Hansen JE. Diagnosis and immediate prognosis of Japanese B encephalitis. Am J Med. 1952;12:227.
153. Chaturvedi UC, Mathur A, Chandra A, et al. Transplacental infection with Japanese encephalitis virus. J Infect Dis. 1980;141:712.
154. Kimura K, Dosaka A, Hashimoto Y, et al. Single-photon emission CT findings in acute Japanese encephalitis. AJNR. 1997;18:465.
155. Misra UK, Kalita J, Jain SK, Mathur A. Radiological and neurophysiological changes in Japanese encephalitis. J Neurol Neurosurg Psychiatry. 1994;57:1484.
156. Brinker KR, Paulson G, Monath TP, et al. St Louis encephalitis in Ohio, September 1975. Clinical and EEG studies in 16 cases. Arch Intern Med. 1979;139:561.
157. Azar GJ, Bond JO, Chappell GL, Lawton AH. Follow-up studies of St Louis encephalitis in Florida: Sensorimotor findings. Am J Public Health. 1966;56:1074.
158. Palmer RJ, Finley KH. Sequelae of encephalitis. Report of a study after the California epidemic. Calif Med. 1956;84:98–100.
159. Wahlberg P, Saikku G, Grummer-Korvenkontio M. Tick-borne viral encephalitis in Finland: The clinical features of Kumlinge disease during 1959–1987. J Intern Med. 1989;225:173.
160. Haglund M, Forsgren M, Lindh G, Lindquist L. A 10-year follow-up study of tick-borne encephalitis in the Stockholm area and a review of the literature: Need for a vaccination strategy. Scand J Infect Dis. 1996;28:217.
161. Artsob H. Powassan encephalitis. In: Monath TP, ed. The Arboviruses: Ecology and Epidemiology, v. 4. Boca Raton, Fla: CRC Press; 1988:29.
162. Embil J, Camfield P, Artsob H, et al. Powassan virus encephalitis resembling herpes simplex encephalitis. Arch Intern Med. 1983;143:341.
163. Conway D, Rossier E, Spence L, et al. Powassan virus encephalitis with shoulder girdle involvement. Can Dis Weekly Rep. 1976;85:2.

164. Lotric-Furlan S, Strle F: Thrombocytopenia: A common finding in the initial phase of tick-borne encephalitis. Infection. 1995;23:203.
165. Lorenzi S, Pfister HW, Padovan C, Yousry T. MRI abnormalities in tick-borne encephalitis. Lancet. 1996;347:698.
166. Tsai TF. Arboviruses. In: Murray PR, Baron EJ, Pfaller MA, et al, eds. Manual of Clinical Microbiology. 7th ed. Washington, DC: American Society of Microbiology. In press.
167. Sudiro TM, Ishiko H, Rothman AL, et al. Microplate-reverse hybridization method to determine dengue virus serotype. J Virol Methods. 1998;73:229.
168. Harris E, Roberts TG, Smith L, et al. Typing of dengue viruses in clinical specimens and mosquitoes by single-tube multiplex reverse transcriptase PCR. Clin Microbiol. 1998;36:2634.
169. Puchhammer-Stockl E, Kunz C, Mandl CW, Heinz FX. Identification of tick-borne encephalitis virus ribonucleic acid in tick suspensions and in clinical specimens by a reverse transcription–nested polymerase chain reaction assay. Clin Diagn Virol. 1995;4:321.
170. Meiyu F, Huosheng C, Cuihua C, et al. Detection of flaviviruses by reverse transcriptase–polymerase chain reaction with the universal primer set. Microbiol Immunol. 1997;41:209.
171. Innis BL, Nisalak A, Nimmannitya S, et al. An enzyme-linked immunosorbent assay to characterize dengue infections where dengue and Japanese encephalitis co-circulate. Am J Trop Med Hyg. 1989;40:418.
172. Tardei G, Ruta S, Chitu V, et al. Evaluation of IgM and IgG enzyme immunoassays in the serologic diagnosis of West Nile virus infection. J Clin Microbiol. In press.
173. Berry N, Chakravarti A, Gur R, Mathur MD. Serological investigation of a febrile outbreak in Delhi, India, using a rapid immunochromatographic test. J Clin Microbiol. 1998;36:2795.
174. Tsai TF, Raul R, Lynberg MC, Letson GW. Congenital yellow fever virus infection after immunization in pregnancy. J Infect Dis. 1993;168:1520.
175. Nasidi A, Monath TP, Vandenberg J, et al. Yellow fever vaccine and pregnancy: A four year prospective study. Trans R Soc Trop Med Hyg. 1993;87:337.
176. Goujon C, Tohr M, Feuillie V, et al. Good tolerance and efficacy of yellow fever vaccine among subjects carriers of human immunodeficiency virus (Abstract). Fourth International Conference on Travel Medicine, April 23–27, 1995, Acapulco, Mexico. p 63.
177. Sibailly TS, Wiktor SZ, Tsai TF, et al. Poor antibody response to yellow fever vaccination in children infected with human immunodeficiency virus type 1. Pediatr Infect Dis J. 1997;16:1177.
178. Tassniyom S, Vasanawathana S, Dhiensiri T, et al. Failure of carbazochrome sodium sulfonate (AC-17) to prevent dengue vascular permeability or shock: A randomized, controlled trial. J Pediatr. 1997;131:525.
179. Tassniyom S, Vasanawathana S, Chirawatkul A, Rojanasuphot S: Failure of high-dose methylprednisolone in established dengue shock syndrome: A placebo-controlled, double-blind study. Pediatrics. 1993;92:111.
180. Gubler DJ. *Aedes aegypti* and *Aedes aegypti*–borne disease control in the 1990's: Top down or bottom up. Am J Trop Med Hyg. 1989;40:571.
181. Harinasuta C, Nimmanitya S, Titsyakorn U. The effect of interferon alpha A on two cases of Japanese encephalitis in Thailand. Southeast Asian J Trop Med Public Health. 1985;16:332–336.
182. Arras C, Fescharek R, Gregersen JP. Do specific hyperimmunoglobulins aggravate clinical course of tick-borne encephalitis? Lancet. 1996;347:1331.
183. Kluger G, Schottler, Waldvogel K, et al. Tickborne encephalitis despite specific immunoglobulin prophylaxis. Lancet. 1995;346:1502.
184. Hoke CH Jr, Vaughn DW, Nisalak A, et al. Effect of high-dose dexamethasone on the outcome of acute encephalitis due to Japanese encephalitis virus. J Infect Dis. 1992;165:631.
185. Hennessy S, Zhengle L, Tsai TF, et al. Effectiveness of live-attenuated Japanese encephalitis vaccine (SA14-14-2): A case-control study. Lancet. 1996;347:1583.
186. Sohn YM, Park MS, Rho HO, et al. Primary and booster immune responses to SA14-14-2 Japanese encephalitis vaccine in Korean infants. Vaccine. In press.
187. Berg SW, Mitchell BS, Hanson RK, et al. Systemic reactions in US Marine Corps personnel who received Japanese encephalitis vaccine. Clin Infect Dis. 1997;24:265.
188. Plesner A-M, Ronne T. Allergic mucocutaneous reactions to Japanese encephalitis vaccine. Vaccine. 1997;15:1239.
189. Kunz C, Heinz FX, Hofmann H. Immunogenicity and reactigenicity of a highly purified vaccine against tick-borne encephalitis. J Med Virol. 1980;6:103.
190. Kunz C, Hofmann H, Stary A. Field studies with a new tick-borne encephalitis (TBE) vaccine. Zentralbl Bakt I Orig A. 1976;243:141.
191. Harabacz I, Bock H, Jungst Ch, et al. A randomized phase II study of a new tick-borne encephalitis vaccine using three different doses and two immunization regimens. Vaccine. 1992;10:145.
192. McIntosh BM, Jupp PG, Dos Santos I, et al. Epidemics of West Nile and Sindbis viruses in South Africa with *Culex (Culex) univittatus* Theobold as vector. S Afr J Sci. 1970;72:295.
193. Muller D, McDonald M, Stallman N, et al. Kunjin virus encephalomyelitis. Med J Aust. 1986;144:41.
194. Bennett N McK. Murray Valley encephalitis, 1974: Clinical features. Med J Aust. 1976;2:446.
195. Lopes O, Sacchetta L de A, Coimbra TLM, et al. Emergence of a new arbovirus disease in Brazil. II. Epidemiologic studies on 1975 epidemic. Am J Epidemiol. 1978;108:394.
196. Pavri K. Clinical, clinicopathologic, and hematologic features of Kyasanur Forest disease. Rev Infect Dis Suppl. 1989;4S:854.
197. Prabha A, Prabhu MG, Raghuvcer CV, et al. Clinical study of 100 cases of Kyasanur Forest disease with clinicopathological correlation. Indian J Med Sci. 1993;47:124.
198. Lvov DK: Arboviral zoonoses of northern Eurasia (Eastern Europe and The Commonwealth of Independent States). In: Beran GW, ed. Handbook of Zoonoses. 2nd ed. Boca Raton, Fla: CRC; 1994:237.
199. Smithburn KC, Paterson HE, Heymann CS, et al. An agent related to Uganda S virus from man and mosquitoes in South Africa. S Afr Med J. 1959;33:959.
200. Srihongse S, Johnson CM. The first isolation of Bussuquara virus from man. Trans R Soc Trop Med Hyg. 1971;65:541.
201. Aaskov JG, Phillips DA, Wiemers MA. Possible clinical infection with Edge Hill virus. Trans R Soc Trop Med Hyg. 1993;87:452.
202. Southam CM, Moore AE. West Nile, Ilheus, and Bunyamwera infections in man. Am J Trop Med. 1951;31:724.
203. Boughton CR, Hawkes RA, Naim HM. Illness caused by a Kokobera-like virus in southeastern Australia. Med J Aust. 1986;145:90.
204. Webb HE. Leukaemia and neoplastic processes treated with Langat and Kyasanur Forest disease viruses: A clinical and laboratory study of 28 patients. BMJ. 1966;5482:258.
205. Reeves WC. Epidemiology and Control of Mosquito-Borne Arboviruses in California, 1943–1987. Sacramento, Calif: California Mosquito Vector Control Association; 1990.
206. Okuno T, Oya A, Ho T. The identification of Negishi virus: A presumably new member of Russian spring-summer encephalitis virus family isolated in Japan. Jpn J Med Sci Biol. 1961;14:51.
207. Sulkin SE, Burns KF, Shelton DF, Wallis C. Bat salivary gland virus: Infections of man and monkey. Tex Rep Biol Med. 1962;20:113.
208. Woodroofe GM, Marshall ID. Arboviruses from the Sepik district of New Guinea. In: John Curtin School of Medical Research Annual Report. Australian National University; 1971:90.
209. Nassar ES, Coimbra TLM, Rocco IM, et al. Human disease caused by an arbovirus closely related to Ilheus virus: Report of five cases. Intervirology. 1997;40:247.
210. Wolfe MS, Calisher CH, McGuire K. Spondweni virus infection in a foreign resident of Upper Volta. Lancet. 1982;2:1306.
211. Rapport annuel du Centre Collaborateur OMS de Reference et de Recherche pours les Arbovirus. Dakar: Institut Pasteur; 1983.
212. Heymann CS, Kokernot RH, De Meillon B. Wesselsbron virus infections in man. S Afr Med J, 1958;32:543–545.
213. Digoutte J-P, Salaun J-J, Robin Y, et al. Les arboviroses mineures en Afrique centrale et occidentale. Med Trop (Mars). 1980;40:523–533.

Chapter 143

Hepatitis C

DAVID L. THOMAS
STANLEY M. LEMON

HISTORY OF NON-A, NON-B VIRAL HEPATITIS AND HEPATITIS C

Hepatitis C is an acute or chronic necroinflammatory disease of the liver that is due to infection with a unique hepatotropic flavivirus. The major clinical manifestation is progressive hepatic fibrosis, which leads to cirrhosis and an increased risk of hepatocellular carcinoma. The disease was first recognized in the early 1970s, when serologic tests for hepatitis A virus (HAV) and hepatitis B virus (HBV) became generally available. It was noted at that time that most cases of transfusion-associated hepatitis were not caused by either of these viruses, leading to the term *non-A, non-B hepatitis*.[1,2] Studies in chimpanzees confirmed that blood-borne non-A, non-B hepatitis was transmissible and due to a relatively small, lipid-enveloped virus.[3,4] In the late 1980s, Michael Houghton's laboratory at Chiron Corporation, working with Daniel Bradley's laboratory at the Centers for Disease Control and Prevention, identified a virally encoded antigen associated with non-A, non-B hepatitis and called the agent *hepatitis C virus* (HCV).[5] This finding rapidly led to the molecular cloning of the complete viral genome[6] and other major discoveries, including recognition of the proclivity of this virus to establish persistent infection, and its strong association with chronic hepatitis, cirrhosis, and hepatocellular carcinoma.

HEPATITIS C VIRUS

Virion Properties and Classification

HCV is a spheric, enveloped, positive-strand RNA virus approximately 50 nm in diameter (Fig. 143–1).[7,8] Its structure, genomic organization, and replication cycle are similar to those of members of the family Flaviviridae, yet sufficiently distinct to merit classification within a separate, novel genus, Hepacivirus. Related genera include the genus Flavivirus (e.g., yellow fever virus and dengue viruses) and the genus Pestivirus (e.g., bovine viral diarrhea virus and classic swine fever virus). Several "GB" viruses (including GB virus C, which is often inappropriately referred to as a "hepatitis" virus, that is, hepatitis G virus)[9,10] (see Chapter 144) are also in the Flaviviridae family, although they have not yet been assigned to a particular genus. Of these viruses, GB virus B has the highest level of relatedness to HCV. Sucrose-gradient studies of infectious plasma and sera suggest that HCV may associate with low-density lipoproteins and, in some samples, with antibody in high-density complexes.[11–14] Both high- and low-density fractions may have similar viral RNA content as determined by reverse transcription–polymerase chain reaction (RT–PCR) assays. However, the high-density fractions are generally less infectious for chimpanzees, suggesting that infectivity is reduced by the association of the virus with immunoglobulins.[11]

Organization of the Hepatitis C Virus Genome

Nontranslated RNA Segments

The genome of HCV is a positive-sense, single-stranded RNA molecule approximately 9.7 Kilobases in length. The RNA contains a single large (approximately 3000 amino acids) open reading frame flanked by highly conserved 5′ and 3′ untranslated regions (UTRs) (Fig. 143–2).[6] The nature of the 5′ terminus of the genome is uncertain, but available evidence suggests that it is not likely to have a conventional 5′ cap structure. The HCV 5′ UTR is approximately 341 nucleotides in length. It demonstrates extensive secondary and tertiary RNA structure and contains an approximately 300 nucleotide segment that acts as an *internal ribosomal entry site* directing the cap-independent translation of the viral open reading frame.[15–19] Although early evidence suggested that this internal ribosomal entry site extends in a 3′ direction past the initiating AUG into the sequence of the open reading frame, more recent work disputes this claim. The HCV 5′ UTR and the closely related 5′ UTRs of pestiviruses are unique among eukaryotic RNAs in that they are capable of binding directly to the 40-S ribosome subunit in the absence of any protein translation initiation factor.[20] The binary complex formed by the 5′ UTR RNA and the 40-S subunit appears to involve specific macromolecular interactions around the initiator AUG codon of HCV.[21] Thus, HCV initiates the translation of its proteins via a unique prokaryotic-like mechanism that is likely to be a useful target for future antiviral drug development.

The 3′ UTR consists of a relatively variable 30-nucleotide segment downstream of the termination codon that is followed by a highly variable polyU(C) tract of approximately 100 nucleotides but apparently variable in length. Downstream of the polyU(C) tract, there is a highly conserved 98-base sequence (so called 3′-X sequence).[22–24] This highly structured 3′-terminal 98-base sequence is the most conserved segment of the HCV genome, and it is required for viral replication. It is likely to serve as a replicase recognition site during the initiation of minus-strand RNA synthesis.

Polyprotein

The approximately 9 Kilobase open reading frame encodes a polyprotein that is cotranslationally processed into at least 10 proteins. These include, from the amino terminus, four structural proteins (the viral nucleocapsid or *core* protein; the envelope proteins E1 and E2; and a short, possibly transmembrane, protein, p7 or NS2A) and six nonstructural proteins that are involved in replication of the viral RNA (see Fig. 142–2). Processing of the polyprotein is directed by both cellular and viral proteinases. Four distinct signal sequences within the amino third of the polyprotein direct the translocation of the nascent protein into the endoplasmic reticulum, with the result that signal peptidase cleaves the polyprotein at the C–E1, E1–E2, E2–NS2A, and NS2A–NS2B junctions.

Structural Proteins

The first 191 amino acids of the HCV polyprotein are cleaved from the nascent polypeptide by signal peptidase, forming the highly basic

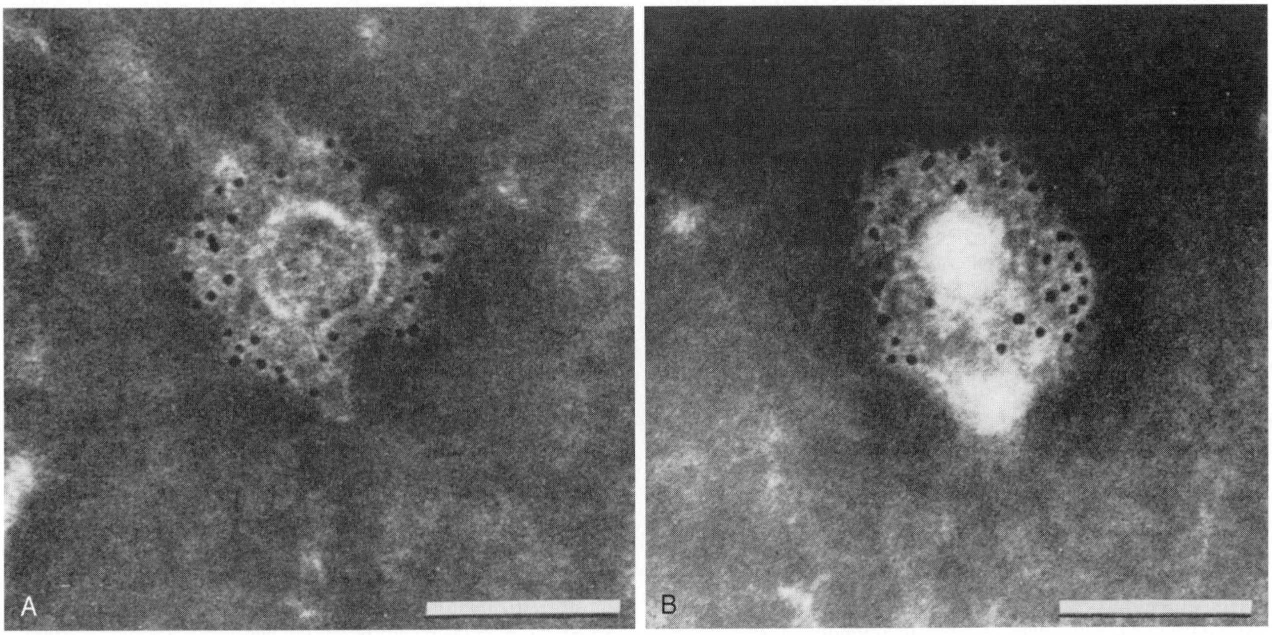

FIGURE 143–1. Electron microscopic images of hepatitis C virus (HCV) virions concentrated from human plasma by high-speed centrifugation. The virions are identified by staining with gold-labeled antibodies to the HCV envelope proteins. (From Kaito M, Watanabe S, Tsukiyama-Koham K, et al. Hepatitis C virus particle detected by immunoelectron microscopic study. J Gen Virol. 1994;75:1755–1760.)

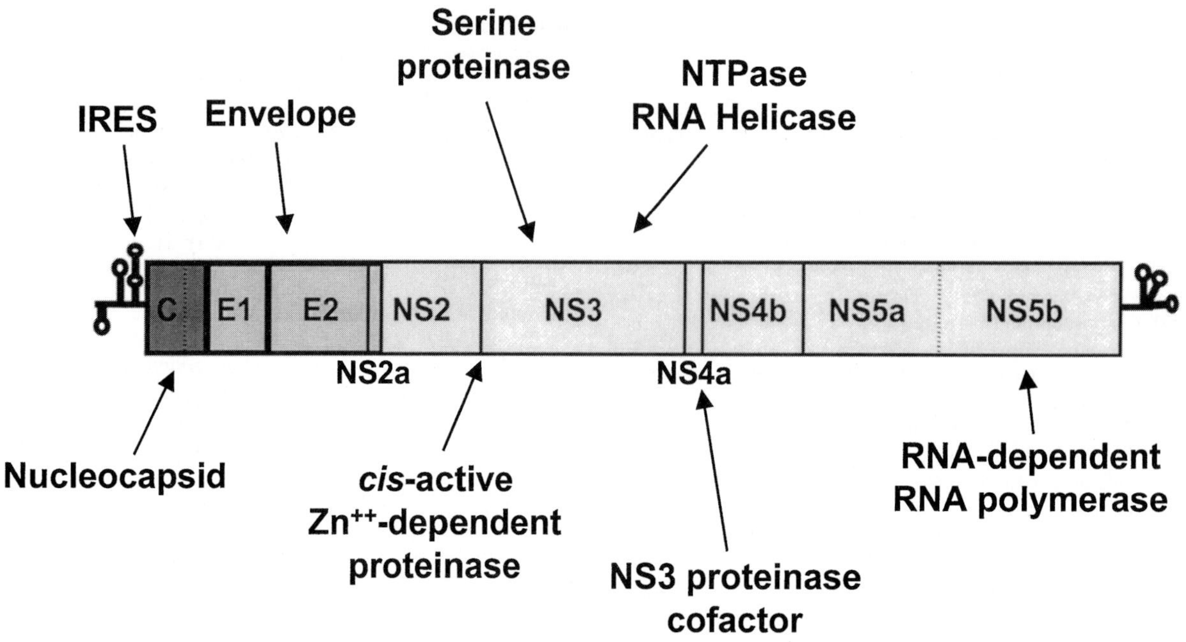

FIGURE 143–2. Organization of the hepatitis C virus genome. The large rectangular box represents the open reading frame, within which vertical lines indicate sites of proteolytic cleavage by cellular and viral proteinases. Individual proteins and their major functions and enzymatic activities are labeled. The solid lines at each end of the open reading frame represent the 5′ and 3′ (left and right, respectively) untranslated segments of the genome. See text for details.

core protein.[25–28] This protein has RNA-binding activity and may undergo a subsequent internal cleavage by an unspecified proteinase. Some studies suggest that the large, amino-terminal product of this cleavage is then translocated to the nucleus. A number of biologic activities have been associated with the core protein, including suppression of HBV replication; alterations in regulation of the cell cycle and transcription of cellular protooncogenes; either induction or suppression of apoptosis; and transformation of rat embryo fibroblasts.[29–38] Interestingly, several different lines of evidence suggest that the core protein binds the cytoplasmic tail of several cellular receptors belonging to the tumor necrosis factor receptor family, particularly tumor necrosis factor receptor-1 and the lymphotoxin-β receptor, and that it may modulate signal transduction through these receptors.[34, 35, 37] However, because HCV does not replicate well in any type of cultured cell, these data are derived from studies in which the core protein has been expressed from recombinant complementary DNA (cDNA). It is not clear whether similar biologic activity is associated with the protein during replication of the virus within the liver. The core protein is immunogenic, and antibody to it is typically present in infected individuals (see "Diagnosis of Hepatitis C Virus").

Yellow fever virus and other members of the genus Flavivirus have a single major envelope protein and a glycosylated, cell-associated NS1 protein that can elicit neutralizing antibodies. However, HCV has two major envelope glycoproteins (E1 and E2) and no comparable NS1 protein. Signal peptidases direct cleavage of the HCV polyprotein at amino acid residues 383 and 746, producing the E1 and E2 proteins, respectively.[26] These are secreted into the endoplasmic reticulum (ER) as type 1 membrane proteins, remaining anchored to the membrane by a hydrophobic carboxy-terminal anchor sequence. An additional cleavage appears to produce the putative NS2A (p7) protein.[39] The function of this short polypeptide is unknown, but it is highly hydrophobic and also likely to remain associated with the membrane.[39, 40] The E1 and E2 proteins are heavily glycosylated, with sugar moieties representing about 50% of the mature mass of each. The two major envelope proteins associate with each other as a noncovalent heterodimeric complex; covalently linked complexes have also been identified but are thought to arise from misfolded forms of the proteins.[41] When expressed from recombinant heterologous viruses, E1 and E2 remain localized to the ER compartment and are not secreted to the cell surface.[42, 43] This suggests that HCV particles assemble and exit the cell by budding into the ER during replication of the virus. The envelope proteins have been reported to interact with the core protein, as well as lactoferrin.[41, 44] The significance of the latter interaction, if any, is unknown.

A highly variable segment approximately 30 amino acid residues in length near the amino terminus of E2 has been called the *hypervariable region 1* (HVR-1).[45–47] It is the most variable segment of the envelope proteins and is assumed to exist as a polypeptide loop on the surface of the virion. Infected persons frequently have antibodies that react with synthetic peptides representing the HVR-1 sequences of the virus with which they are infected. The appearance of such antibodies results in the selection of variant viruses with HVR-1 sequences that are less reactive. This suggests that the HVR-1 harbors a neutralization epitope and that it is a site of mutations causing immune escape (see "Genetic Diversity").[48–50] The extent of sequence heterogeneity within the HVR-1 indicates that there are few sequence-related constraints on its function. Hypothetically, this may be to mask a deeper, more highly conserved structure within the envelope, such as a recognition site for the cellular receptor.

E2 has also been reported to interact with protein kinase R, which is induced by interferon, a possible mechanism for overcoming the antiviral activity.[50a]

Nonstructural Proteins

The NS2B protein is cleaved from the remainder of the polyprotein by a cis-active, zinc-dependent metalloproteinase activity that is localized to the peptide sequence spanning the NS2B–NS3 cleavage site. This activity resides within residues 827 through 1207 of the polyprotein, a segment including the carboxy terminus of NS2B and the amino terminus of NS3. NS2B is a transmembrane protein, but its role in replication of the virus (other than participating in directing the NS2B–NS3 cleavage) is not known.[51, 52]

The NS3 protein has serine proteinase activity localized to its amino-terminal third, and an RNA helicase with nucleoside triphosphatase activity in its carboxy-terminal domain. Atomic-level resolution structures have recently been solved for both these functional domains, and both are promising targets for antiviral development.[53–56] The NS3 serine proteinase activity is responsible for the NS3–NS4, NS4A–NS4B, NS4B–NS5A, and NS5A–NS5B cleavages. It is located within the amino-terminal 181 amino acid residues of the NS3 protein and includes the catalytic triad His-1083, Asp-1107, and Ser-1165.[57, 58] Substitutions at any of these residues abrogate downstream cleavage.[57] Thus, although the NS2-NS3 metalloproteinase mediates the NS2–NS3 cleavage in cis, the NS3 serine proteinase is responsible for all downstream polyprotein-processing events, which occur largely in trans. The mature, fully active NS3 proteinase is formed by the noncovalent association of NS3 with the NS4A protein, which becomes an integral part of the proteinase structure.[53, 59–61] Also important to NS3 conformation and function is zinc, which is bonded to four residues, mutations of which markedly affect enzyme activity.

The carboxy-terminal 465 amino acids of NS3 have both nucleoside triphosphatase and RNA helicase activity. There is evidence that the helicase has 3′ to 5′ directionality and binds to the 3′ poly(U) sequence.[62, 63] A pathogenic role has also been proposed, since NS3 expression has been shown to transform NIH 3T3 cells and to induce tumors in nude mice.[64] However, the primary role of the helicase is unquestionably the unwinding of duplex RNA molecules during the replication of the viral genome. No cleavage site has been identified between the NS3 proteinase and helicase, suggesting functional interdependence.[65]

NS4A is a relatively small protein that is an important component of the NS3 serine proteinase, as described earlier. It has a hydrophobic extension that is likely to anchor the proteinase-helicase to intracellular membranes during replication of the virus. The functional role of NS4B is not known, but it is suspected to be part of the viral RNA replicase complex. The NS5A protein is also likely to play a role in replication, but its function remains obscure. NS5A phosphorylation depends on NS4A.[66, 67] Sequence polymorphisms within a short segment of NS5A (the *interferon sensitivity determining region*) have been correlated with resistance to interferon therapy, and, as with the E2 protein, this may be mediated by the interaction of NS5A with the catalytic domain of interferon-induced protein kinase R.[68–70] Inactivation of protein kinase R by NS5A would mitigate both the antiviral and antiproliferative activities of interferon. However, the association between interferon sensitivity determining region polymorphisms and interferon resistance has been questioned and may be genotype-specific. Furthermore, there is no direct proof that NS5A expression alters protein kinase R function during replication of the virus, nor is it certain that the stochiometry would allow this.

The NS5B protein is highly conserved and contains a Gly-Asp-Asp motif that is characteristic of RNA-dependent RNA polymerases. NS5B proteins expressed from recombinant cDNA have been shown to have polymerase activity in vitro, although it has not been possible to demonstrate specificity for HCV RNA as template.[71–73] As with the enzymatic activities of the NS3 protein, there are hopes that the NS5B RNA polymerase may prove to be a suitable target for antiviral drug development.

Replication

Little is known about details of the HCV replication cycle because there is no permissive cell culture system in which this process can be studied directly. However, analogies with other positive-strand RNA viruses suggest the following scenario (Fig. 143–3). The virus is likely to enter the cell through an interaction with a specific cell surface receptor molecule. Although further evidence is required before it can be considered to be a viral receptor, there is strong evidence that E2 binds specifically to CD81, a cell surface molecule that is widely expressed in many different tissues including the liver.[74] After attachment, penetration, and uptake into the cellular endosome, it is likely that the acidic pH alters the conformation of the envelope proteins, which fuse with the endosomal membrane. The viral RNA is released into the cytoplasm, where it acts as messenger RNA directing the cap-independent translation of the viral polyprotein. The ability to rescue infectious virus by intrahepatic inoculation of synthetic, genome-length RNA in chimpanzees provides strong proof for this step in the replication cycle.[75, 76] Viral translation occurs in association with the rough ER, and segments of the polyprotein are secreted into the lumen of the ER as it undergoes a series of cotranslational proteolytic cleavages, as described in the preceding section.

The core protein remains within the cytoplasm, likely anchored to the ER membrane at its carboxy terminus, whereas E1 and E2 are secreted into the lumen of the ER and become heavily glycosylated. The RNA-dependent RNA polymerase, NS5B, recognizes the 3′ end of the input genomic RNA and directs the synthesis of a negative-strand copy of the genome. In directing the transcription of the viral RNA, NS5B probably acts as part of a macromolecular replicase complex containing NS3, NS4A, NS4B, or NS5A, or all of these. The resulting duplex RNA would then serve as a template for the subsequent synthesis of multiple copies of the positive-strand genomic RNA. It is very likely that specific RNA structures at the 5′ and 3′ ends of the viral RNA serve as promoters for these transcriptional events, which probably occur in close association with intracellular membranes. The genomic RNA is packaged into new viral particles, which likely are extruded into the ER leading to the release of the virus via the vesicular secretory pathway.

The foregoing description of HCV replication is highly speculative. Few of these details have been confirmed experimentally due to the technical difficulties that beset the field: the absence of both permissive cell lines and a readily available small-animal model. Furthermore, there is much speculation but little hard data concerning the impact of HCV protein expression on the biology of the hepatocyte.

Genetic Diversity

The liver is usually presumed to be the primary source of virus present in blood, but there are few data that directly support this conjecture. HCV-specific antigens and both negative- and positive-strand HCV RNA have been identified within hepatocytes, indicating that replication does occur in this cell type via a negative-strand intermediate as outlined earlier.[7, 77, 78] However, additional data suggest that the virus may also replicate within peripheral mononuclear cells of lymphoid or perhaps bone marrow origin (see next section).[79, 80] Mathematical models of viral kinetics suggest a half-life of approximately 2.5 hours for virions in the blood stream and suggest that up to 1.0×10^{12} virions may be produced each day in a chronically infected human.[81, 82] This rate exceeds comparable estimates of the production of human immunodeficiency virus (HIV) by more than an order of magnitude.

The Hepatitis C Virus Quasispecies

The high level of virion turnover, coupled with the absence of proofreading by the NS5B RNA polymerase, results in relatively rapid accumulation of mutations within the viral genome. Multiple HCV variants can be recovered from the plasma and liver of an infected individual at any time. Thus, like many RNA viruses, HCV exists in each infected person as a quasispecies, or "swarm" of closely related but distinct genetic sequences.[47, 83] For example, in the blood of a recently infected individual, up to 85% of cDNA clones recovered from viral RNAs may represent unique genetic variants.[84] During RNA replication, mutations occur in a random fashion throughout the genome. Which mutations are propagated within the quasispecies population depends on whether the nucleotide substitution affects viral replication by altering essential protein or RNA structures.

Immunologic responses also appear to be important selective forces. For example, viral RNAs containing spontaneous mutations within the HVR-1 segment of the E2 protein (see "Structural Pro-

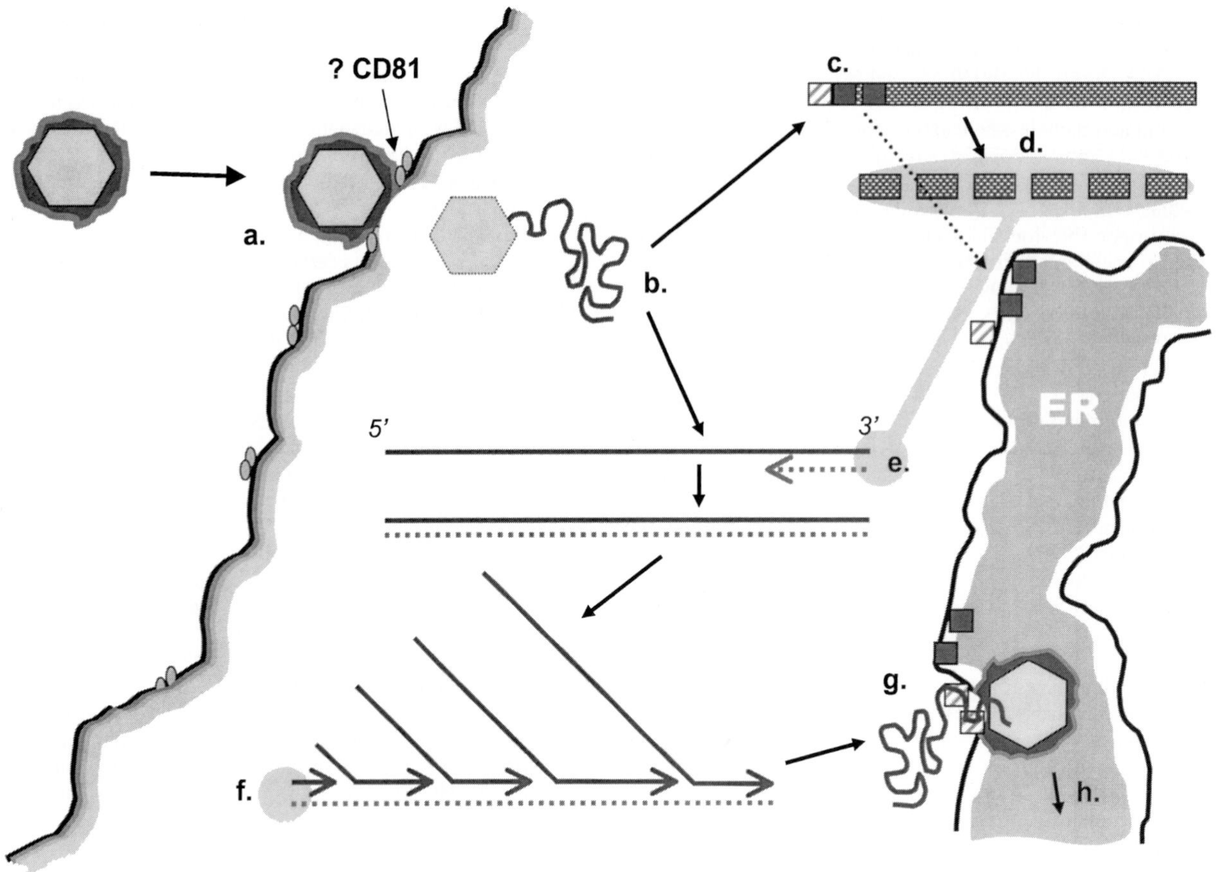

FIGURE 143–3. Speculative scheme for major events in the replication of hepatitis C virus. Specific steps include: (a) attachment and penetration of the virion into the hepatocyte; (b) release of viral RNA into cytoplasm, possibly secondary to a fusion of the viral envelope with the endosomal membrane (not shown); (c) cap-independent translation, and (d) processing of the viral polyprotein resulting in production of the core protein *(striped symbols)*, envelope protein *(shaded symbols)*, and at least seven nonstructural proteins *(stippled symbols)*; (e) assembly of the replicase complex at the 3′ end of the virion RNA followed by synthesis of a minus-strand replicative intermediate RNA *(dotted line)*; (f) synthesis of multiple positive-strand copies of the RNA from a duplex RNA template; (g) assembly of virus particles in the late ER, early Golgi compartments; and (h) release from the cell. These events are based largely on current understanding of other positive-strand viruses, and many of these details have yet to be confirmed by direct experimental evidence. See text for further details.

teins") may be favored for survival in the host because they reduce the binding of preexisting neutralizing antibodies to the viral envelope.[85–88] Significantly, agammaglobulinemic patients have a slower evolution of amino acid sequence changes within HVR-1.[89, 90] There is also evidence that cellular immune responses may drive the selection of specific variants.[91] Thus, the variants recovered from blood reflect the balance of production and selective forces.

Although the nucleotide substitutions identified in the blood represent only a fraction of all mutations generated during viral replication, these mutations are estimated to accumulate at an overall rate of 0.9 to 1.92×10^{-3} base substitutions/site/year.[92–94] The diversity of an HCV quasispecies swarm can be described either in terms of the number of nucleotide differences between variants (i.e., *genetic distance*) or in terms of the number of distinct variants (i.e., *genetic complexity*). There is considerable interest in determining the clinical correlates of these parameters. Although much remains to be learned, it appears that genetic complexity is linked to the extent of disease and the duration of infection.[95] This is consistent with the hypothesis that immunologic responses affect both the extent of disease progression and the generation of sequence diversity. Differences in the HCV quasispecies present in the blood and liver have been described, suggesting that differences in tissue tropism may also influence genetic variation (see later).[80, 96, 97]

The extent of genetic diversity varies markedly throughout the HCV genome, being highest in the segment that encodes the amino terminus of the second envelope protein, E2, within the so-called HVR-1.[85–88] High conservation at some loci suggests functional constraint (mutations there may be lethal or sufficiently disadvantageous to replication to be undetectable among surviving viral populations). The clinical-pathologic significance of HCV quasispecies is considered in greater detail later.

Hepatitis C Virus Genotypes

In addition to the impressive heterogeneity that often exists among HCV sequences present in a single infected individual (i.e., quasispecies variation), there is also remarkable genetic heterogeneity and divergence among HCV sequences recovered from different individuals (i.e., strain and genotype variation). Phylogenetic evaluation of HCV sequences recovered from multiple geographic regions suggests that there are at least six major genotypes (Fig. 143–4).[98] Depending on the genomic region evaluated, HCV sequences assigned to different genotypes may have less than 60% nucleotide sequence identity. Significantly, this level of nucleotide sequence divergence usually correlates with substantial serotypic differences among other RNA viruses (e.g., poliovirus type 1 versus poliovirus type 2, which are not cross-neutralizable in assays of antibody-mediated neutralization). Virtually nothing is known, however, of the existence or extent of serotypic variation among HCV strains.

Within individual HCV genotypes, strains can be further grouped into subgenotypes (subtypes) that generally share 75 to 85% nucleotide sequence identity within the core, E1, and NS5 regions of the genome.[98, 99] In contrast, the variants that exist within the quasispecies of a single person generally have 91 to 99% identity in these regions.[100] The phylogenetic grouping of HCV strains appears to be largely independent of the segment of the genome that is analyzed.[98, 101]

The geographic distribution of HCV genotypes is not fully characterized, but some trends are apparent. Within the United States, the majority of isolates are genotype 1a (60%) and 1b (20%) (Fig. 143–5).[102, 103] In contrast, genotype 4 infections are prevalent throughout Africa and the Middle East.[104] For example, more than 90% of the viral sequences recovered in an Egyptian survey were of genotype 4.[105] Types 5 and 6 have been reported in Southeast Asia and South Africa.[106–108] Genotype 3 occurs in Asia but has been linked in other geographic regions to illicit drug use.[109] Differences between early proposals for genotype nomenclature may cause some confusion in interpreting such studies. However, at present there is general acceptance of a uniform nomenclature.[110]

Viral Tropism

There is little doubt that HCV replicates within the hepatocyte. However, replication may also occur in other cell types. Some studies have suggested the presence of negative-strand HCV RNA in T cells, B cells, and monocytes, especially in patients with chronic infection.[111–115] However, others have suggested that this occurs

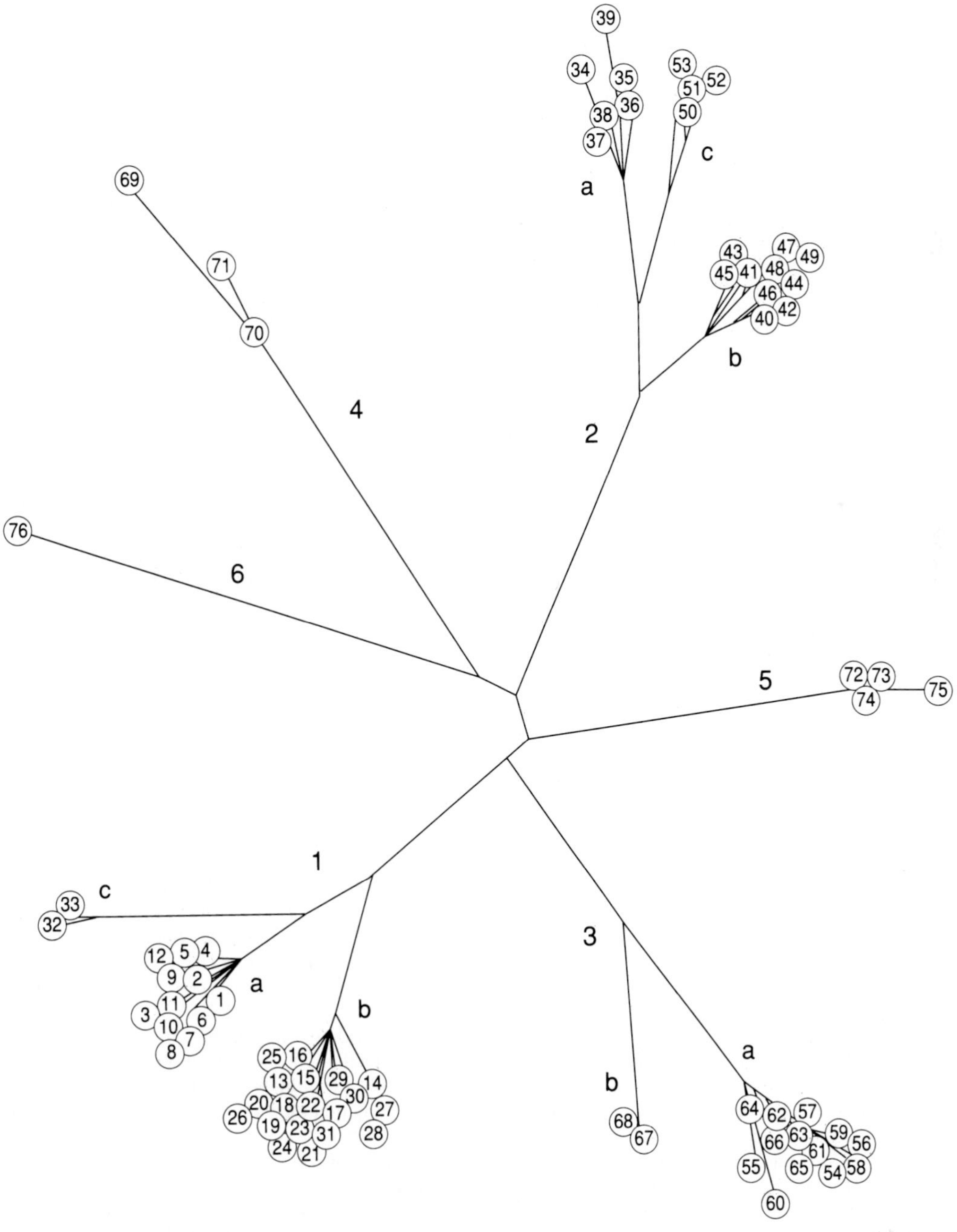

FIGURE 143–4. A phylogenetic tree demonstrating sequence diversity in the NS-5 region in 76 different strains of hepatitis C virus (HCV). This analysis shows three levels of sequence diversity (represented by the distance of individually numbered strains of HCV from one another within the tree), and six distinct clusters of related strains ("genotypes"). According to this analysis, the prototype American strain (HCV-1) is classified in genotype 1a, whereas most Japanese strains are in genotype 1b. (From Simmonds P, Holmes EC, Cha T-A, et al. Classification of hepatitis C virus into six major genotypes and a series of subtypes by phylogenetic analysis of the NS-5 region. J Gen Virol. 1993; 74:2391–2399.)

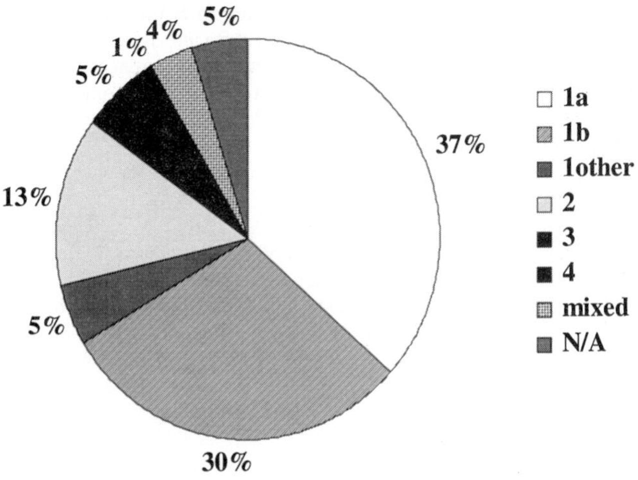

FIGURE 143–5. Distribution of hepatitis C virus genotypes in 438 patients seen at tertiary referral centers in the United States.[103] Genotypes were inferred by line probe assay.

rarely[79] or not at all.[116, 117] Interestingly, in one study the HCV quasispecies detected in peripheral blood mononuclear cells was genetically more similar to that from liver than to that from blood.[113] Other studies have suggested that certain lymphocytotropic variants may be favored for replication in lymphoid cells, both in chimpanzees and in cell culture.[80] Mutations within the 5′ UTR of these lymphoid-adapted variants selectively increase internal ribosomal entry site–directed, cap-independent translation in cultured lymphoid cell lines, but not in cells derived from hepatocytes (H Lerat and S Lemon, unpublished data). Although further information is needed, these observations point to possible differences in the tissue tropism of quasispecies variants. Since the specificity of polymerase chain reaction assays for negative-strand RNA is often suspect, these latter data provide a more persuasive case for replication of the virus in lymphoid cells.

HCV RNA also has been detected in cutaneous lesions of persons with HCV-related cryoglobulinemia and vasculitis,[118] in renal biopsies of patients with HCV-associated membranoproliferative glomerulonephritis,[119] and (with variable success) in various body fluids including saliva, semen, tears, urine, and ascitic fluid.[120–124] Unlike HBV, HCV does not replicate through a DNA intermediate and does not have the ability to integrate its genetic information into chromosomal DNA. Because of this, the detection of HCV sequences in these tissues and fluids is likely to reflect the presence of infectious virus.

Experimental Models

Cell Culture Systems

No cell culture system has yet been developed that permits substantial HCV replication. High-level subgenomic replication has been generated in a human hepatoma cell line.[124a] Low-level HCV replication has been demonstrated in lymphoid cell lines, including a murine retrovirus-infected human T-cell line (HPB-Ma), a human T-lymphotropic virus type I–infected line (MT-2), a human B-cell line (Daudi), and others.[125–128] In these cell lines, replication has been shown to be sensitive to exogenous interferon, and strong evidence has been presented for transmission of the virus between cells.[129, 130] The genetic diversity of the viral inoculum declines over time in such cultures, suggesting the selection of a particular variant that is favored for replication (see preceding section). Furthermore, a chimpanzee has been successfully infected with culture supernatant harvested from Daudi cells 58 days after their inoculation with virus.[131] Low-level HCV replication also has been demonstrated in human hepatocytes immortalized with simian virus 40, primary chimpanzee hepatocytes, and primary human hepatocytes.[132, 133] However, no one has yet recovered infectious virus after transfection of synthetic genome-length RNA into any type of cell culture, although HCV can be rescued by inoculation of the RNA into the liver of a chimpanzee.[75, 76, 134]

Animal Models

The chimpanzee, *Pan troglodytes,* is the only nonhuman animal species that has been demonstrated conclusively to be permissive for HCV replication. Percutaneous inoculation of HCV RNA-positive plasma, and in one instance saliva, has resulted in HCV infection.[135–137] Also, as noted previously, chimpanzees have been infected by intrahepatic inoculation of synthetic genome-length RNA derived from cDNA clones.[75, 76, 134] Thus, the chimpanzee represents a valuable model for HCV infection. There is, however, generally much less evidence for HCV-related disease in infected chimpanzees than in infected humans, and there may also be differences in the frequency of viral persistence and in the nature of the immunologic response.[137]

Several lines of transgenic mice have been established that express transgenes encoding all or some HCV proteins under the control of liver-specific promoters.[138–141] None of these transgenes contains the complete HCV genome, and thus HCV gene expression is not associated with the production of infectious virus. However, because these animals have immunologic tolerance to the HCV proteins they express, they are useful in determining the effect of viral protein expression on hepatocyte function in the absence of an immune response. Although some of these transgenic mouse lineages appear to be free of disease, at least three mouse lines that were established in two different laboratories develop age-related hepatic steatosis and hepatocellular carcinoma.[139–140a] These phenotypic effects appear specific for expression of the core protein, and they suggest that nonimmune mechanisms play a role in the pathogenesis of HCV-related liver injury. In addition, salivary gland lesions similar to those observed with Sjögren's syndrome have been noted in transgenic mice expressing the envelope proteins of HCV.[142] Finally, a 1998 report describes the construction of a transgenic mouse with an inducible HCV transgene.[143] Induction of HCV gene expression led to an immune-mediated hepatitis in mice derived from this lineage, suggesting that it may be a useful model for investigating the immune response to HCV proteins in vivo.

NATURAL HISTORY AND PATHOGENESIS

Viral Persistence

In experimentally infected chimpanzees and in humans, HCV RNA can be detected in plasma within weeks of exposure.[135, 144–146] Viremia persists in as many as 85% of acutely infected persons.[145, 147–152] After the first year of infection, HCV RNA is usually continuously detected, and the quantity of virus in plasma or serum remains fairly constant.[135, 145, 148, 153] HCV RNA may be intermittently undetectable in some persons with chronic infection, especially during the first year of infection and in those with low baseline levels of viremia.[135, 145, 148] However, unlike clearance of HBV, spontaneous clearance of HCV is rare after chronic infection becomes established.

In at least 15% of acutely infected humans, viremia is transient and is no longer detected 3 to 24 months after infection. Viral clearance is not correlated with the antibody response detected in clinical assays, indicating that these assays are unlikely to measure neutralizing antibodies.[148] HCV antibody and HCV-specific T-cell proliferative responses may persist for years after viremia is cleared.[147, 148, 154] However, in chimpanzees, both HCV RNA and antibody can be cleared within a few years of inoculation.[137, 155]

Persons who clear the infection spontaneously are not at risk for cirrhosis.

In the early stages of the infection, it is not possible to predict whether the infection will be self-limited. In one study, individuals with self-limited infection had lower peak levels of plasma HCV RNA and were more likely to have jaundice or be white.[148] However, HCV RNA can be transiently undetectable in individuals who ultimately develop persistent infection, and it may be present for up to 24 months in those who go on to clear the virus. Thus, a long-term pattern of undetectable HCV RNA and normal serum alanine aminotransferase (ALT) levels on multiple occasions are necessary to conclude that the infection has terminated.

Because of limitations in experimental models and the infrequent recognition of natural acute infection, the mechanisms of viral clearance are poorly understood. Host differences have been described such as the presence of certain class 2 major histocompatibility alleles.[156] Clearance of viremia has also been associated with a strong $CD4^+$ T-cell response, especially to NS3, which has an epitope that reacts with 10 common HLA class II alleles and has a relatively conserved sequence.[157–160] A helper T-cell-1 phenotype and the associated cytokine profile also are associated with self-limited viremia.[161]

Cytotoxic T lymphocytes (CTLs) are likely to play an important role in suppressing the infection, and the intensity of this immune response may affect the level of viremia. The CTL response to infection is vigorous and directed at epitopes in multiple HCV proteins.[162, 163] Stronger polyclonal CTL responses in the peripheral blood and liver have been associated with lower levels of circulating HCV RNA.[164, 165] HCV-specific CTLs have also been found in persons who were exposed to HCV but never were known to have had HCV antibody or viremia.[166, 167] However, viremia generally persists despite HCV-specific CTLs, suggesting that this cellular immune response is not sufficient to clear viremia. Similarly, viremia persists despite a broad humoral immune response to HCV epitopes, although earlier antibody response to the E2 HVR-1 domain was associated with clearance.[168]

The failure to eliminate the infection despite what appears to be a vigorous immune response remains unexplained. It has been suggested that HCV sequence variation may contribute to viral persistence. Mutations may alter the amino acid sequences of critical epitopes, leading to the escape of a new variant from a previously suppressive immune response, either cellular or humoral.[50, 91, 169] Viral escape from a CTL clone has been reported in a persistently infected chimpanzee and was shown to correlate with a single NS3 amino acid substitution.[91] Variants may also antagonize CTLs, and an antagonist NS3 peptide has been reported in chronic HCV infection.[170] In one study, acutely infected persons who developed persistent infection had a more complex quasispecies.[171] In addition, viral persistence has been associated with a greater proportion of nonsynonymous amino acid substitutions in the HVR-1 segment of E2, suggesting that immune pressure on HVR-1 epitopes was advantageous to viral survival.[171] However, given that the immune response to HCV is directed against multiple epitopes simultaneously, it seems much more likely that quasispecies diversity results from, rather than acts as a primary cause of, viral persistence.

The high frequency with which HCV establishes persistent infection in nonimmunocompromised adults contrasts sharply with the pattern of HBV infection and suggests that HCV has evolved one or more specific mechanisms to evade immune responses. The highly glycosylated nature of the viral envelope may protect it against antibody-mediated neutralization. Furthermore, the envelope may have evolved a structure (namely the putative E2 HVR-1 polypeptide loop) that allows it to decoy antibodies and to protect an otherwise vulnerable, conserved receptor-binding ligand from antibody attack. In addition, the virus may regulate replication to a level that is too low to disrupt cellular homeostasis and that generates only meager amounts of viral antigens. It has been suggested that this may occur at the level of viral translation.[21]

The HCV core protein binds to the cytoplasmic tail of the tumor necrosis factor-α receptor and the lymphotoxin-β receptor.[34, 35, 37] This binding occurs immediately adjacent to the death domain and may modulate signal transduction through the receptor. Although the biologic effects of this interaction remain controversial, it is possible that it protects the infected cell against tumor necrosis factor-α–mediated apoptotic cell death. Alternatively, the E2NS5A proteins have been shown to bind to the catalytic domain of protein kinase R, and this interaction may block the antiproliferative and antiviral effects of this interferon-induced kinase.[50a, 70] It seems likely that many factors contribute to the HCV persistence and that even more interactions of HCV proteins with immune effector mechanisms will be uncovered.

Progression of Disease

Although HCV infection leads to hepatic inflammation and steatosis, the major pathologic consequence of persistent HCV infection is the development of hepatic fibrosis, which may progress to life-threatening cirrhosis and a greatly increased risk of hepatocellular carcinoma. These long-term complications generally occur more than 20 years after the onset of infection, though more rapid progression has been reported.[172–174] There are wide estimates (5 to 25%) of the probability of cirrhosis occurring 10 to 20 years after infection.[151, 174–178] In a study of women infected in Ireland by contaminated Rh immune globulin, the incidence of cirrhosis during 15 to 20 years of follow-up was very low (<5%).[179] This is a best-case scenario, however, as all the infected persons in this cohort were female and relatively young at the time of infection, and few reported excessive alcohol consumption. These are all factors associated with less severe disease (see later).

A more representative view of the natural history of HCV infection comes from a large retrospective-prospective study by Seeff and coworkers, who evaluated mortality and morbidity in a cohort of patients at a mean of 18 years after post-transfusion hepatitis.[178, 180] These individuals were compared with control patients who were similarly transfused but had not developed recognizable hepatitis. Overall mortality was high, reflecting the severity of underlying conditions, but not increased in HCV-infected patients. Liver-related mortality was slightly higher in patients with post-transfusion hepatitis (3%) than controls (1.5%), and it was estimated that approximately 10% of patients with post-transfusion hepatitis had cirrhosis 20 years later.[178] Other studies of post-transfusion hepatitis have suggested a higher rate of progression to cirrhosis.[172, 174] Once cirrhosis occurs, the rates of progression to liver failure (decompensated cirrhosis) and hepatocellular carcinoma are approximately 2 to 4 and 1 to 7% per year, respectively.[181–183]

This variability in the estimated frequency of life-threatening liver injury relates to the study setting and the relative contributions of environmental, host, and viral factors (Table 143–1). Studies in tertiary care facilities generally predict higher rates of progression because they include a greater proportion of symptomatic subjects (referral bias). The leading environmental determinant appears to be alcohol ingestion.[184–188] Although excessive alcohol ingestion and HCV infection independently may cause cirrhosis, combined exposure has a synergistic effect.[185, 187, 189] This is especially true with very heavy alcohol ingestion (more than 50 to 125 g/day), which in one study increased the risk of cirrhosis approximately 100-fold.[185] The mechanism underlying this synergy with an environmental toxin remains obscure, but both alcohol and HCV infection may cause microvesicular steatosis, suggesting a common pathway involving mitochondrial injury.

Coinfection with HBV may also accelerate the progression of disease, but persistent GB virus C (so-called hepatitis G virus) infection does not affect hepatitis C.[190–194] HIV infection increases the level of HCV viremia and is associated with more rapid progression of liver disease.[195–200] Increased progression of liver disease

TABLE 143-1 Factors Associated with Cirrhosis in Persons with Hepatitis C Infection

Factor	Comment
Environmental	
Alcohol use	Importance of moderate use (<20 g daily) has not been established
Host	
HIV infection	Demonstrated in hemophiliacs and appears to be increasingly important as HIV-related survival improves
Infection duration	Cirrhosis is rare before 10 years
HLA type	HLA B54 with cirrhosis; DRB1*0301 with lack of cirrhosis
Viral	
Quasispecies complexity	Cross-sectional studies cannot assess causality, and complexity is related to duration of infection
HCV genotype 1	Type 1b in some but not other studies; 1b infections may be of longer duration confounding this association
HCV RNA level	Weak association sometimes lost in multivariate analysis

Abbreviations: HCV, Hepatitis C virus; HIV, human immunodeficiency virus.

also has been reported with immunosuppression associated with agammaglobulinemia and transplantation.[201–203]

Very little is known about the natural history of HCV infection in children, but both extremes (asymptomatic infection and liver failure) may occur.[204–207] There is some evidence that the progression of disease is increased in elderly persons, and males appear to be at greater risk for cirrhosis as well as liver cancer.[208]

Host genetics and the immune response are likely to affect the outcome of persistent infection. Specific HLA alleles have been associated with differences in the progression of disease.[209–212] As described earlier, persistently infected persons have CTLs directed against a myriad of epitopes. The activity of the CTL response appears to correlate with the serum ALT level and the hepatic inflammatory score, suggesting that they promote injury, probably by apoptosis as well as the elaboration of cytokines that recruit nonspecific inflammatory cells to the site of infection.[163, 213] In the livers of patients with chronic hepatitis C, HCV-specific helper T cells are found principally in the periportal zone and secrete helper T cell-1 cytokines like interleukin-2 and interferon-γ, whereas interleukin-10 levels are decreased.[214] Apoptotic cell death can occur in association with the expression of HCV core protein.[215] Notably, the T-cell subpopulations in the liver differ from those in peripheral blood, emphasizing the importance of liver-derived cells in studies of pathogenesis. In addition, an exceptionally large proportion of the lymphocytes that are present within the liver are nonconventional *natural T* cells or γδ T cells. The functions of these cells and their roles in the pathogenesis of hepatitis C are not understood.

Viral determinants of hepatitis C progression have also been proposed. In some but not all clinical studies, cirrhosis was associated with infection with genotype 1b virus, the presence of a greater complexity of the HCV quasispecies, and higher levels of viremia.[95, 102, 216–218] However, whether the presence of these viral factors early in disease can predict the long-term outcome has not been evaluated carefully, and the level of viremia is clearly not as strongly related to progression of the disease as in HIV infection. In this context, it is important to note that steatosis and hepatocellular carcinoma have both been observed in immunotolerant transgenic mice expressing the core protein of HCV.[139, 140]

There is some evidence that the route of inoculation may affect the progression of HCV infection. In several studies, injection drug users had a less severe hepatic histologic appearance than those infected by transfusion.[219, 220] It is not known whether this relates to the inoculum size or to unidentified host factors.

Hepatocellular Carcinoma

There is a strong association between HCV infection and hepatocellular carcinoma in most populations, but there is considerable variation in the fraction of hepatocellular carcinoma cases that are attributable to HCV infection worldwide.[221–224] Chronic HBV infection remains the leading factor in the development of hepatocellular carcinoma in many countries. However, in Japan, Korea, and southern Europe, 50 to 75% of cases of hepatocellular carcinoma are associated with HCV infection.[225] In one Italian study, HCV infection was found in 71% of patients with liver cancer, and HBV infection in only 15%.[224] A study in Japan reported a threefold increased incidence of hepatocellular carcinoma in HCV-infected persons, compared with those with chronic hepatitis B.[225] The mortality rate due to hepatocellular carcinoma in Japan increased approximately twofold during the 1980s, and this increase could be attributed entirely to an increased incidence of HCV-associated liver cancer.[226] Evidence also exists for an association between HCV infection and hepatocellular carcinoma in the United States, where serologic evidence of HCV infection is present in 13 to 50% of patients with hepatocellular carcinoma.[227, 228]

Relatively little is known about how chronic HCV infection leads to cancer. The HCV genome is not reverse-transcribed to DNA, nor does it integrate into host cell chromosomes. However, transforming activities have been associated with the core and NS3 proteins.[33, 64] Strong evidence in favor of a direct or indirect transforming action of the core protein comes from studies of transgenic mice that develop such tumors in the absence of an immune response (H. Lerat and S. M. Lemon, unpublished data).[139] In addition, it is possible that NS5A promotes the development of tumors by repressing the antitumor activity of protein kinase R.[70] However, chronic hepatic inflammation is by itself sufficient to cause hepatocellular carcinoma. This hypothesis has been proved in a transgenic mouse model.[229] In this setting, liver cancer probably occurs as a result of increased hepatocyte turnover, dysregulation of pro-apoptotic and anti-apoptotic cellular signaling pathways, the generation of free hydroxyl radicals that are capable of damaging cellular DNA or all of these. An inflammatory mechanism is consistent with the observation that HCV-related hepatocellular carcinoma usually (but not always) occurs in association with cirrhosis and that the risk of hepatocellular carcinoma is also increased in cirrhosis due to other causes.[230]

Several cofactors have been proposed in the development of HCV-associated hepatocellular carcinoma. HBV coinfection appears to increase the risk of hepatocellular carcinoma in HCV-infected persons.[191, 231] Infection with genotype 1b virus also has been associated with hepatocellular carcinoma, but this may reflect a longer duration of infection.[223, 227, 232] Alcohol and tobacco use, older age, and male gender are associated with hepatocellular carcinoma among HCV-infected persons.[191, 223]

CLINICAL MANIFESTATIONS OF HEPATITIS C VIRUS INFECTION

Acute Hepatitis C

Acute HCV infection may cause malaise, nausea, and right upper quadrant pain, followed by dark urine and jaundice. It is clinically indistinguishable in the individual patient from other types of acute viral hepatitis. Based on studies of transfusion recipients,[233, 234] the incubation period for acute hepatitis C averages about 7 weeks and is thus intermediate between that of hepatitis A and that of hepatitis B. HCV RNA can be detected in blood within 2 weeks of exposure and is followed by elevations in serum levels of the liver-specific aminotransferases, ALT and aspartate aminotransferase, and in some cases bilirubin. Clinical symptoms and elevations of aminotransferase levels are generally less severe than with acute hepatitis A or B. Prospective studies of transfusion recipients and injection drug users show that over 75% of acute hepatitis C infections are anicteric and would be missed without careful screening for ALT-level elevation or seroconversion.[148, 233] Extrahepatic manifestations are not prominent in acute HCV infection.

Fulminant Hepatitis C

Approximately 20% of all cases of fulminant hepatitis that are thought to be caused by infectious agents are not due to HAV or HBV. Although this would suggest a role for HCV, the frequency with which HCV causes fulminant hepatitis is controversial. HCV infection has been associated with 40 to 60% of fulminant non-A, non-B hepatitis in Japan, but it is a very uncommon cause of fulminant liver disease in western countries.[235–237] This discordance has never been explained but might arise from variation either in host factors or viral strains, or both. There appears to be an increased likelihood of fulminant liver disease after acute HAV infection in persons with underlying chronic hepatitis C.[238]

Chronic Hepatitis C

Approximately 85% of persons with acute hepatitis C infection develop persistent viremia, as described in the previous section "Viral Persistence" (Fig. 23–6). Thus, although only one in six cases of symptomatic acute viral hepatitis is due to HCV infection, HCV is the leading infectious cause of chronic liver disease in the United States. Persistently infected individuals tend to have few symptoms that are clearly caused by HCV infection (e.g., fatigue or malaise), leading some to question if hepatitis C is of any consequence in the majority of patients who never develop cirrhosis.[177] However, preliminary research now suggests that many quality-of-life indices are reduced in HCV-infected patients, even in the absence of cirrhosis, and that they improve with successful therapy.[239]

HCV infection usually persists for decades, during which time serum ALT levels typically fluctuate independently of symptoms, whereas serum HCV RNA levels remain fairly constant.[147, 172, 240, 241] The inflammation detected on liver biopsy also varies over time.[173, 242] Some individuals develop fibrosis, which typically begins in portal triads but can bridge between triads or central veins and ultimately destroy the hepatic architecture, progressing to cirrhosis.[243] There is a poor correlation between necroinflammatory liver injury, serum ALT levels, serum HCV RNA levels, and the extent of fibrosis.[244] Once established, 10 to 20% of HCV-infected persons with cirrhosis decompensate clinically within 5 years, as evidenced by esophageal varices, ascites, coagulopathy, encephalopathy, or hepatocellular carcinoma.[181–183]

However, it is not possible to predict which HCV-infected patient will develop cirrhosis and which will go on to clinically decompensated liver disease. Cirrhosis is uncommon in persons with persistently normal ALT levels, but the magnitude and frequency of elevation of the ALT levels correspond poorly with the extent of fibrosis.[244] The HCV genotype and RNA level are weak indicators of the outcome of the disease, at best (see the earlier section "Progression of Disease").

Histologic examination of the liver remains the best indicator of the stage of disease (see "Liver Biopsy"). Hepatic histologic examination can be especially helpful when the duration of infection is known. For example, patients who have been infected for more than 25 years but have little inflammation and no more than mild portal fibrosis are exceedingly unlikely to develop cirrhosis in the ensuing 5 years. This information can be useful if there are relative contraindications to treatment or if serious adverse reactions occur. However, for most patients, the duration of infection is unknown and histologic examination of the liver shows intermediate amounts of fibrosis and inflammation. Too little is known about the natural history of disease for such patients to reliably predict the prognosis with a single biopsy.

Hepatocellular Carcinoma

Primary hepatocellular carcinoma is typically a late complication of chronic hepatitis C, usually occurring in patients with cirrhosis.[223, 224] HCV-related liver cancer has been particularly evident in Japan and Italy, where it typically occurs after 2 or more decades of infection (see earlier). Clinical findings can include a sudden worsening of prior symptoms and signs of cirrhosis (fatigue, ascites, jaundice), often in association with right upper quadrant pain. However, small, asymptomatic hepatocellular carcinomas are not uncommonly detected at the time of liver transplantation. Serum α-fetoprotein levels are often very high. Ultrasonography or computerized tomography reveal an intrahepatic mass, but a specific diagnosis requires liver biopsy.

Extrahepatic Manifestations of Hepatitis C Virus Infection

HCV infection is strongly associated with essential mixed cryoglobulinemia, membranoproliferative glomerulonephritis, and porphyria cutanea tarda. Up to half of HCV-infected persons have circulating cryoglobulins. However, only a small percentage develop the vasculitic syndrome of essential cryoglobulinemia (type II or type III, with circulating polyclonal IgG and IgM immune complexes).[245, 246] Membranoproliferative glomerulonephritis may occur in association with HCV-related cryoglobulinemia, generally in the absence of vasculitis.[246, 247] Chronic HCV infection has also been found in 60 to 80% of persons with sporadic (but not familial) porphyria cutanea tarda.[248–250] To a lesser extent, HCV infection has been associated with Mooren's corneal ulcers, Sjögren's syndrome, lichen planus, and idiopathic pulmonary fibrosis.[251] The pathogenesis of such conditions remains unknown. However, sialadenitis resembling that occurring in Sjögren's syndrome has been observed in transgenic mice expressing HCV envelope proteins.[142] Thyroid autoantibodies, Hashimoto's

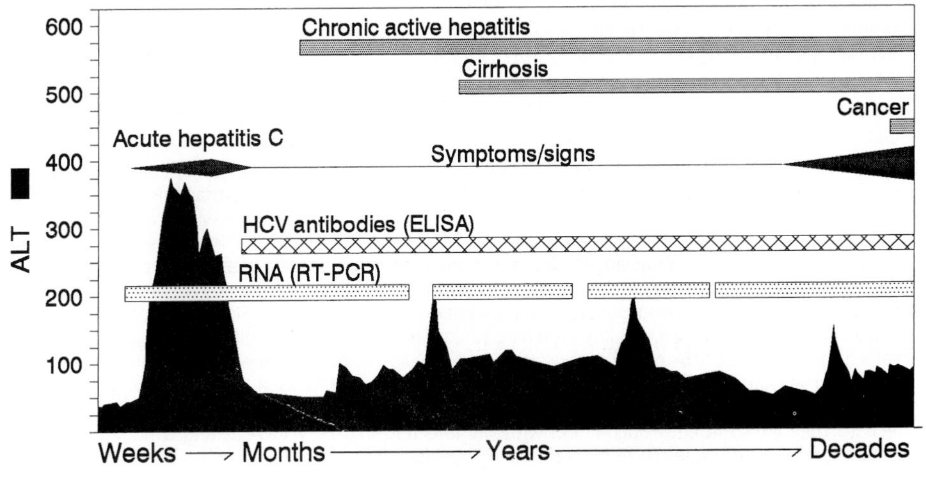

FIGURE 143–6. The natural history of hepatitis C virus infection.

thyroiditis, and hypothyroidism have been associated with chronic hepatitis C in women.[252]

DIAGNOSIS OF HEPATITIS C VIRUS INFECTION

Serologic Examination

The laboratory diagnosis of HCV infection is based principally on the detection of antibodies to recombinant HCV peptides. The first-generation enzyme immunoassay (EIA) measured antibodies directed against a recombinant protein involving primarily the NS4 sequence (see Fig. 143–2) fused to bacterial superoxide dismutase (so-called c100-3 antigen).[253] The second-generation EIA included additional synthetic antigens from the core ("c22-3") and NS3 ("c33-C" or "c200").[254–256] The third-generation EIA that is used today includes an additional antigen from the NS5 region of the polyprotein and, more importantly, a reconfiguration of the core and NS3 antigens. The sensitivity of the third-generation assay is estimated to be 97%, and it can detect HCV antibody within 6 to 8 weeks of exposure.[257, 258] These assays are measures of HCV infection, not immunity. Tests for viral-neutralizing antibody are not available, for reasons described previously (see "Natural History and Pathogenesis"). Assays for immunoglobulin M (IgM) HCV antibodies are not clinically useful.

So-called confirmatory tests are commonly used to evaluate a positive EIA result. The U.S. Food and Drug Administration (FDA) has licensed the recombinant immunoblot assay (RIBA) (Ortho Diagnostic Systems, Raritan, N.J.) as a supplemental test. First-, second-, and third-generation variations of this test employ plastic strips coated with individual bands of each recombinant antigen used in the EIA.[259, 260] The RIBA generally identifies the specific antigens to which antibodies are reacting in the EIA and may be positive (two antigens or more), indeterminate (one antigen), or negative. EIA- and RIBA-positive sera usually contain HCV RNA, as indicated by direct detection (see next section) and by lookback studies of donations that caused infection after transfusion.[259, 261, 262] EIA-positive, RIBA-indeterminate sera may also contain HCV RNA, especially if the reactivity was to core or NS3 antigens (the c22-3 and c33-c bands). The third-generation RIBA appears to reduce the frequency of indeterminate results.[263]

It is important to note that the EIA has been configured to optimize sensitivity, as the primary use of the assay is for screening for HCV infection. As with all tests, the predictive value of the EIA is directly related to the prevalence of infection in the population screened. Among injection drug abusers, HCV RNA can be detected in approximately 85% of second-generation EIA-positive sera. More than 98% of EIA-positive, RNA-negative sera from these injection drug abusers are RIBA-positive, indicating that most EIA-reactive samples among drug abusers are true positive results (D. L. Thomas, unpublished data). At the other extreme, up to half of all third-generation EIA-positive blood donations do not have detectable HCV RNA or a positive RIBA.[263]

Detection of Viral RNA

HCV RNA can be detected in plasma and serum by RT-PCR and by branched DNA (bDNA) assays. In the former assay, RNA extracted from the sample is reverse-transcribed to virus-specific cDNA, which is amplified in a PCR using oligonucleotide primers specific for conserved genomic segments. There are many "home-brew" RT-PCR assays, and Roche Diagnostic Systems (Branchburg, N.J.) markets an RT-PCR kit (AMPLICOR HCV Detection Kit). The bDNA assay (Quantiplex HCV-RNA assay, Chiron Corp., Emeryville, Calif.) is a direct hybridization assay, using a branch-chained DNA probe and enzymatic amplification of the hybridization signal.[264] These assays vary in their ability to detect HCV RNA, but RT-PCR assays are generally more sensitive than the bDNA assay. In some studies, home-brew assays and a modification of the Roche AMPLICOR have been capable of detecting 100 genome equivalents/ml. However, the true relative sensitivities are difficult to establish and may vary from specimen to specimen because of the presence of inhibitors.[265] Fortunately, the analytic sensitivity of RT-PCR usually exceeds the HCV RNA level of most untreated patients.

Detection of HCV RNA indicates ongoing infection, whereas clearance of serum HCV RNA either spontaneously or after treatment correlates with ALT normalization and improvement in the liver histologic appearance. However, as of Feburary 1999, no RNA detection assays had yet been approved by the FDA for diagnosis of HCV infection, and their reliability has been questioned. In one study, only 16% of 31 laboratories accurately identified all samples in a standardized panel.[266]

Diagnosis

The possible inaccuracy of HCV RNA assays underscores the importance of clinical judgment and follow-up in establishing the diagnosis. A single negative test for viral RNA does not exclude HCV infection in an EIA-positive patient with an elevated ALT level and a risk factor. Conversely, many blood donors with a positive EIA test do not have HCV infection. Several diagnostic algorithms are reasonable and may vary according to local resources (Fig. 143–7). The first test should generally be an EIA. In a patient with significant risk factors or clinical findings of liver disease, RNA detection could be used for confirmation, whereas in low-risk populations, supplemental RIBA tests are preferred. This approach has practical merit and is based on the principle that after the first 6 months of infection, antibody testing is stable and reproducible, whereas RNA test results may vary.

Because even a positive third-generation EIA has a low predictive value in a low-risk setting, the possibility of infection can often be resolved with a single negative RIBA, whereas a single negative HCV PCR would require further testing. Conversely, in a high-risk setting, the predictive value of the HCV EIA is sufficiently high that further testing may not be warranted. If a confirmatory test is desired, RNA testing is preferred since the expected positive result not only "confirms" the EIA but also indicates that the infection is ongoing.

FIGURE 143–7. Algorithms for pretreatment diagnosis of hepatitis C virus (HCV) infection. HCV RNA testing should be done by a sensitive, reproducible assay. Medical follow-up means evaluation by a clinician with experience in managing HCV infection. *Dotted lines* indicate a medically acceptable alternative diagnostic approach. *Abbreviations:* ALT, Alanine aminotransferase, which is considered positive if greater than the upper limit of normal; EIA, enzyme immunoassay; RIBA, recombinant immunoblot assay.[1] Data are insufficient to define the frequency with which this testing should be repeated. Negative results obtained on two occasions over 6 months are reassuring; depending on the sensitivity of the assay and the presence of absence of other indicators of infection (e.g., elevated ALT), additional testing may be needed. *A, Low prevalence* means HCV infection is not suspected, such as with screening of blood donations or candidates for life insurance. Screening for acute HCV infection after exposure or because of symptoms is considered high prevalence. RIBA is preferred to confirm positive EIA results in low prevalence populations because the negative predictive value is greater than with HCV RNA or ALT testing (see text). *B, High prevalence* means HCV infection is suspected by exposure history or clinical status (e.g., unexplained elevated liver enzymes). HCV RNA testing is preferred as a confirmatory test when infection is suspected because a positive result differentiates ongoing from convalescent infection.[2] False-negative EIA results have been associated with agammaglobulinemia, renal dialysis, and HIV infection. They are sufficiently uncommon with HIV infection that HCV RNA testing is not routinely recommended in HCV EIA negative persons unless infection is otherwise suggested (e.g., elevated ALT levels).

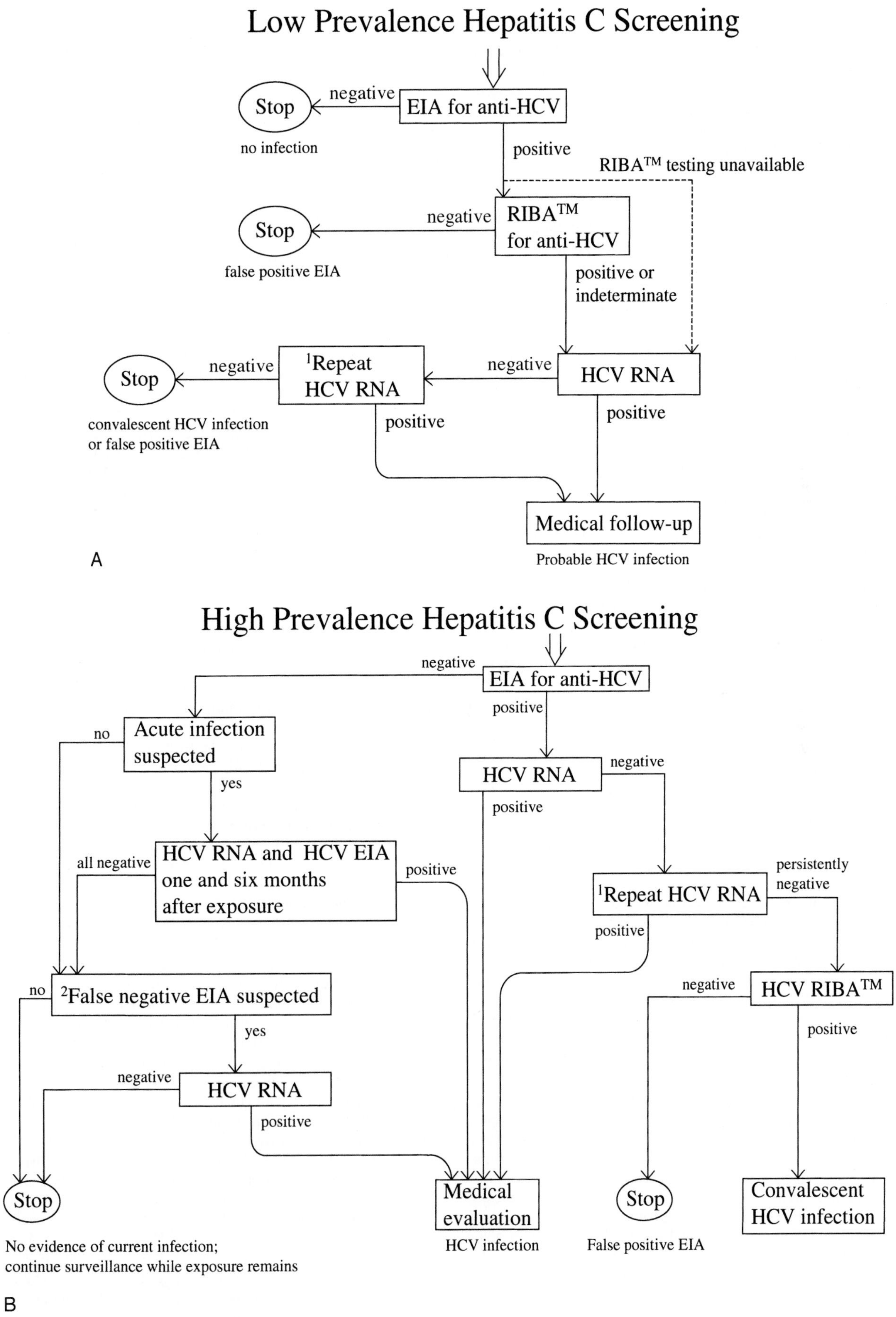

FIGURE 143–7. *See legend on opposite page*

Quantification

The quantity of HCV RNA in serum and plasma is several orders of magnitude less than that in liver tissue. Nonetheless, it is generally considered an accurate reflection of viral replication,[267, 268] although this relationship has been questioned.[269] There are several methods for HCV RNA quantification, but none is FDA-approved as of February 1999. The bDNA test is relatively precise and, although its sensitivity is limited, detects RNA in most untreated patients.[264, 270, 271] Another commercially available quantitative assay, the AMPLICOR HCV Monitor Test Kit (Roche Diagnostic Systems), amplifies HCV RNA along with a known quantity of labeled template.[272] Serial dilution and competitive RT-PCR are also used to quantify HCV RNA, and "real-time" RT-PCR assays have been developed and appear particularly promising.[271, 273, 274]

Because of the variation among different assays, it is important to use the same test (performed by one laboratory) when obtaining serial measurements of viremia in individual patients. It is difficult to compare HCV RNA assays because of the absence of quantitative standards, different reporting units, and the lack of a "gold standard" aside from chimpanzee infectivity.[270, 271] In addition to the assay used, a number of factors may affect the estimate of HCV quantity including the time to centrifugation, storage temperature, collection tube, and testing laboratory.[272, 275] In an untreated individual, it is uncommon for the quantity of HCV RNA in the blood to change more than 10-fold over an interval of 1 to 5 years.[276, 277]

Genotype

Various methods have been utilized to determine the genotype of a viral strain. The most commonly used tests detect subtype-specific point mutations in PCR-amplified cDNA. These include the line probe assay, which is based on reverse dot-blot hybridization (Innogenetics, Zwijnaarde, Belgium), restriction fragment length polymorphism assays, and RT-PCR using subtype-specific primers.[278–281] Phylogenetic analysis of cDNA sequence is the gold standard for evaluating HCV genotypes. A serologic method for establishing genotype (but not subtype) has also been developed (Chiron Corp.).

Liver Biopsy

Liver biopsy remains the best method for assessing the severity of hepatitis C. The histologic hepatic examination may exclude other liver diseases, such as alcohol-induced liver injury or hemochromatosis, and it provides information concerning four distinct HCV-related processes: periportal necrosis (piecemeal necrosis), parenchymal injury, portal inflammation, and fibrosis.[242, 243, 282] A numeric grading system, the histologic activity index or *Knodell's score,* has been developed in an effort to standardize the evaluation of liver biopsies. This provides an index of the extent of disease ranging from zero to 22, calculated as the sum of scores for each category.[282] However, the extent of fibrosis is likely to be the most important finding in patients with chronic hepatitis C. In an alternative system, separate scores are given for the inflammatory and fibrotic components of the disease.[283]

Although biopsy is the best index of the stage of hepatitis C, there may be differences in the histologic appearance when samples from different sections of the liver are taken at autopsy. Furthermore, there is variation between observers in interpreting the histologic picture, and approximately 0.3% of biopsies lead to significant complications such as hemorrhage.[284, 285] In addition, the histologic "snapshot" of the current state of inflammation and fibrosis does not always predict the future course of disease. Thus, although liver biopsy provides far more information than noninvasive tests like the ALT or HCV RNA levels, the decision to biopsy warrants careful consideration.

In a recent survey of more than 1000 members of the American Gastroenterological Association, over 90% indicated they would obtain a liver biopsy on a patient with HCV infection and an elevated ALT level, whereas only 46% said they would do so if the ALT level were normal. Closely linked to the use of biopsy is the treatment perspective. For many clinicians, the histologic appearance of the liver substantially influences the decision of whom to treat and whether to continue treatment in patients with non–life-threatening adverse reactions. In view of improved treatment outcomes, others have recently suggested that it is more cost effective to treat all patients without contraindications and perform biopsies only on those without sustained responses. Although the current guidelines for use of biopsy are controversial, as therapy becomes more successful and safer, it is likely that HCV-infected persons will routinely be started on therapy without biopsy. Current contraindications to liver biopsy include severe coagulopathy and clinical evidence of decompensated cirrhosis.

EPIDEMIOLOGY OF HEPATITIS C

HCV is most often transmitted by percutaneous exposure to blood. However, the predominant modes of transmission may change over time and differ between and even within countries. In economically developed countries, most new HCV infections are related to illicit injection drug use, though blood transfusions were once important sources of infection. HCV may also be transmitted between sexual partners and from a mother to her infant, though these are relatively uncommon compared with transmission of HBV.

Prevalence of Hepatitis C Virus

HCV infection has been reported in virtually every country in which has been carefully evaluated, suggesting that HCV, unlike HIV, has a long-standing global distribution. Although there are only a few regions of the world in which prevalence data are representative, it is estimated that more than 170 million persons are infected worldwide.[286] In developed nations, the HCV prevalence is typically 1 to 2% in the general population and less than 0.5% among blood donors. An accurate estimate of hepatitis C prevalence in the United States is available from the Third National Health and Nutrition Examination Survey. Overall, the results of this survey indicate that approximately 3.9 million individuals have been infected with HCV in the United States, or 1.8% of the general population, and an estimated 2.7 million have persistent infection.[287] The prevalence of HCV infection in the United States is higher among racial minorities than in white Americans, and greater in African Americans than in Mexican Americans. However, these racial trends are chiefly due to socioeconomic status, which is strongly inversely associated with HCV infection. In this survey, most HCV infections could be attributed to high-risk drug use or sexual behaviors.

Although the prevalence of HCV is remarkably similar in many parts of the world, there are a few distinct geographic regions in which infection is especially common. In Egypt, for example, HCV infection occurs in 10 to 30% of the general population.[288–293] Similarly high rates of infection have been found in certain geographic regions of Japan, Taiwan, and Italy. In such areas, HCV infection is generally more prevalent among persons older than 40 years and uncommon in those younger than 20 years.[294–297] This cohort effect suggests that transmission occurred through a practice that has been discontinued, such as traditional folk remedies or reuse of needles for injection.[294, 295, 297–299] Although not confirmed, it is suspected that a national campaign to treat schistosomiasis infections was responsible for many infections in Egypt. Injection therapy for schistosomiasis was administered to entire villages until the 1970s, and needles were frequently reused. In the isolated Arahiro region of Japan, 45% of individuals older than 41 years of age were found to have HCV infection.[300] In contrast, in another area of Japan the prevalence was 2% in this age group. Folk remedies including acupuncture and cutting of the skin with nonsterilized knives were likely transmission modes.

A high prevalence of HCV infection also has been reported in some urban areas of developed countries. In Baltimore, Maryland, HCV infection was found in 18% of patients attending an inner-city emergency department and in 15% of persons attending a nearby clinic for sexually transmitted diseases.[301, 302] A high prevalence of HCV infection (20 to 40%) also has been noted among incarcerated prisoners in California, Maryland, and Texas. Undoubtedly, in these settings, prior illicit injection drug use is chiefly responsible for the acquisition of the infection.

Incidence of Hepatitis C Virus Infection

In the 1980s, the annual incidence of HCV infection in the United States was approximately 15 in 100,000, but since then it has declined significantly.[303, 304] The Centers for Disease Control and Prevention has estimated that at least two thirds of all community-acquired HCV infections are related to illicit injection drug use (Fig. 143–8). Approximately 38% of persons with acute hepatitis C admit to such drug use within the 6 months before their illness.[305, 306] An additional 44% admit to the illicit use of noninjected drugs or have other indicators of illicit injection drug use. Sexual or household exposure to HCV is detected in approximately 10 to 15% of individuals with acute HCV infection, whereas transfusions, occupational exposures, and other factors are infrequently identified (<4%).[307]

Transmission of Hepatitis C Virus

Biologic Basis of Transmission

HCV transmission requires that infectious virions contact susceptible cells that are permissive for replication. However, with the technologies available at present, it is difficult to ascertain which body fluids contain infectious hepatitis C particles. Using sensitive techniques, HCV RNA can be detected in blood (including serum and plasma), saliva, tears, seminal fluid, ascitic fluid, and cerebrospinal fluid.[120–124] HCV RNA–containing blood is infectious when administered intravenously, for example, by transfusion or experimental inoculation of chimpanzees. In addition, a chimpanzee has been infected by the intravenous inoculation of saliva.[136] However, there is very little information available regarding the potential infectivity of other body fluids. Furthermore, it is not clear how the virus reaches its primary site of replication within the liver without direct percutaneous inoculation into the blood stream. It is possible that the virus is able to infect and replicate within some peripheral blood mononuclear cells.[79] However, there is little direct evidence for a primary site of replication outside the liver. Nonetheless, sexual transmission appears to occur (see later), and infection has been reported after conjunctival exposure to blood.[308]

Percutaneous Transmission

Infection occurs in more than 90% of seronegative recipients who are transfused with blood from HCV-antibody–positive donors.[262, 309] Thus, there is a high prevalence of HCV infection in multiply transfused thalassemic and hemophilic patients.[195, 310–312] Before the introduction of nonspecific surrogate tests (serum ALT levels and antibody to HBV core protein) as well as specific EIA assays for the detection of HCV infection in blood donations, approximately 17% of HCV infections in the United States were caused by transfusion.[313] With the introduction of the EIA test, the risk of transfusion-transmitted hepatitis C has been reduced substantially.[314, 315] Transmission may still occur rarely from donors with recent infection who have not yet developed detectable antibodies.[316] It is much more difficult to estimate how often infection may result from the transfusion of blood from infectious donors who have lost or never developed HCV antibody, but this is also likely to be a rare event. Accordingly, blood transfusion now causes less than 4% of HCV infections in the United States, a risk estimated to be less than 1 in 100,000.[306, 317]

HCV also has been transmitted by the administration of contaminated blood products. Many hemophilic patients were infected by contaminated clotting factor concentrates, and there have been several large outbreaks related to the administration of contaminated intravenous immune globulin.[201, 318–323] The risk of transmission by these products has been greatly diminished by the introduction of solvent-detergent and other viral inactivation procedures. Transplantation of organs from HCV-infected donors almost always results in HCV infection in seronegative recipients[324–326] and in seropositive recipients may lead to superinfection with a second distinct viral strain.[327]

Use of contaminated needles and other paraphernalia associated with illicit drug use accounts for the majority of HCV infections in most developed countries. Since 1992, at least two thirds of new HCV infections in the United States have been associated with illicit drug use.[306] Worldwide, 50 to 95% of persons acknowledging drug use have HCV infection.[328–333] HCV infection generally occurs within months of initiating the illicit use of injected drugs. In one cohort, 80% of subjects acknowledging 2 or more years of injection use were infected with the virus, a prevalence that was higher than that of HIV or HBV infection.[328, 334] HCV infection is more rapidly acquired by drug users than hepatitis B because adults generally clear HBV infection. Thus, the experienced users, who "initiate" novice users through needle sharing, are 10-fold more likely to be HCV carriers. HCV infection occurring in the context of drug use but without a history of direct injection of drugs may be due to other, undetected percutaneous blood exposures. For example, it has been suggested that the sharing of contaminated straws for intranasal

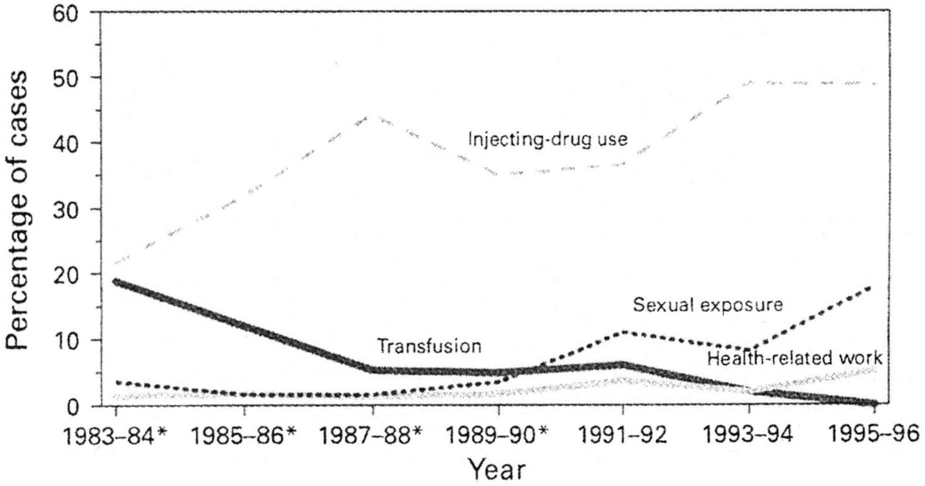

FIGURE 143–8. Reported cases of acute hepatitis C by selected risk factors—United States, 1983–1996. (From Centers for Disease Control and Prevention. Recommendations for prevention and control of hepatitis C virus [HCV] infection and HCV-related chronic disease. MMWR Morb Mortal Wkly Rep. 1998; 47:1–39.)

use of cocaine may lead to HCV infection.[240] However, unacknowledged injection use is difficult to exclude.

In the United States, there appears to have been a significant reduction in the incidence of HCV associated with illicit drug use since the late 1980s.[304] Although needle-exchange programs have been associated with a reduction in HCV infection in some (but not all) studies, these programs are not sufficiently available to account for this nationwide trend.[335, 336]

HCV may be transmitted by other percutaneous exposures that are not associated with drug use but that occur too infrequently to be detected in many studies. For example, tattooing has been associated with HCV infection in some studies.[337, 338] Human bite and folk remedies, such as acupuncture and scarification rituals, may also be associated with HCV infection.[339]

Nosocomial Infection

In developed nations, nosocomial HCV transmission is uncommon and typically involves a break in infection control protocols. An example of patient-to-patient transmission of HCV was documented when two patients were found to have HCV infection 8 to 10 weeks after a colonoscopic procedure that had been performed with an instrument used hours earlier on an HCV-infected patient.[340] The HCV strains infecting all three patients shared a high level of nucleotide sequence identity within a variable segment of the genome, strongly suggesting a common source of infection. In this instance, the instrument was not properly scrubbed after each use. The nosocomial transmission of HCV within hemodialysis units and in other hospital settings has also been suggested by the identification of clusters of patients infected with closely related strains of the virus.[341–345] Infection control breaks were recognized in some outbreaks and are the most likely explanation for the sporadic occurrence of infections in this setting.

Transmission of HCV to health care workers occurs after 2 to 8% of accidental needlestick exposures to HCV-infected patients.[346–348] Studies of such accidents indicate that the risk of HCV transmission is intermediate (~3% per documented exposure) between that of HIV (~0.3%) and HBV (~30%) transmission.[346, 348, 349] Although hollow bore needlestick exposures account for most documented instances of HCV transmission, HCV infection has also been reported from blood splashed on the conjunctiva and from a solid bore needlestick.[308] Despite these risks, the prevalence of HCV infection among dental and medical health care workers is commonly less than or similar to that of the general population.[350–356]

HCV may also be transmitted from health care providers to patients.[357] However, in community-based studies in the United States, patients with acute HCV infection rarely report recent interaction with a health care provider, and work restrictions are not routinely required for HCV-infected health care workers.[304]

In contrast to developed nations, in economically developing areas of the world nosocomial HCV transmission is common, occurring both following traditional (Western) and nontraditional medical care. Thus, it is likely that nosocomial practices are the leading source of HCV transmission worldwide.

Sexual Transmission

Although transmission of HCV during sexual intercourse has not been proved, there is mounting circumstantial evidence that it occurs. HCV RNA has been detected in semen and saliva,[120, 122, 123] and persons with multiple sexual partners and commercial sex workers have a high HCV prevalence.[301, 358–362] Acute HCV infection has also been reported in instances where sexual, but not other, exposures were recognized.[363, 364] In multiple studies of families of HCV-infected patients carried out in Japan and in Europe, sexual partners generally have been the only household contacts at increased risk for infection, a risk that increases with the duration of the relationship.[365–368] HCV strains recovered from sexual partners often show a high level of nucleotide sequence identity.[358, 366, 368, 369] However, although these observations are consistent with sexual transmission, other common exposures such as sharing razors or needles cannot be ruled out.

Some studies of patients attending STD clinics and some studies of commercial sex workers indicate that sexual behavior and numbers of partners may influence the risk of acquiring HCV infection.[301, 361, 370, 371] In general, however, the association between sexual behavior and HCV infection is much weaker than with HBV or HIV infections. Moreover, a number of studies indicate that sexual transmission is not common. Studies of long-term sexual partners of HCV-infected hemophiliac patients and transfusion recipients generally show little or no evidence for HCV transmission, even if there has been unprotected sexual intercourse.[372–375] In addition, HCV prevalence among homosexual men also is generally lower than for other infections such as HIV and HBV infection and syphilis, for which sexual transmission is well established.[376–379] In one study, only 4.6% of a cohort of homosexual men were infected with HCV, whereas 58% had been infected with HBV.[376]

Thus, the available data suggest that HCV is transmitted infrequently during sexual intercourse. It is not known whether the relative infrequency of sexual transmission is due to a paucity of infectious virions in seminal or vaginal fluids or to insufficient numbers of susceptible cells within the genital mucosa. Nonetheless, individuals in long-term monogamous relationships should be informed of the low risk of future transmission and, according to recent U.S. Public Health Service guidelines, encouraged to discuss this risk and the use of barrier precautions with their sexual partners.[304]

Maternal-to-Infant Transmission

HCV is uncommonly transmitted from mother to infant. Estimates of the perinatal transmission frequency vary but range from 0 to 8% in larger studies.[380–388] The timing of transmission is not known. However, HCV RNA has been detected within a month of birth in non–breast-fed infants delivered by cesarean section, suggesting that transmission occurs in utero in at least some instances.[387, 388] Because of the passive transfer of maternal HCV antibodies, the diagnosis of infant HCV infection must be based on the detection of viral RNA or the persistence of antibody after 18 months of age. Because viremia can be intermittent in the first years of life and some HCV RNA–positive infants never develop HCV antibody, infant infection can only be excluded by repeated HCV RNA testing.

HCV RNA has been detected in breast milk.[389] However, in most studies, the risk of HCV transmission is similar in breast-fed and bottle-fed babies.[382, 383, 386, 390–395] Neither the CDC nor the American Academy of Pediatrics recommends that HCV-infected mothers bottle-feed to prevent HCV transmission.[304, 396]

Transmission Cofactors

Seropositive individuals who do not have detectable HCV RNA in their blood appear to be much less infectious than those who do. In a recent review of 2022 parenteral, sexual, and perinatal HCV exposures, HCV was transmitted only by individuals with detectable viremia.[397] Moreover, nonparenteral (e.g., perinatal) transmission of HCV is very rare when the level of viremia is low.[388] Thus, the magnitude of HCV viremia appears to be an important factor in determining the risk of transmission. Some but not all studies indicate that infection with HIV may be an important cofactor for both sexual and maternal-to-infant transmission.[383, 384, 392, 398] It is likely that this association reflects an increase in the level of HCV viremia, probably due to HIV-related immunosuppression.[196, 199, 399–401]

TREATMENT OF CHRONIC HEPATITIS C (also see Chapter 102)

There is intense interest in developing therapeutic regimens that are capable of inhibiting HCV replication and improving the natural history of the disease. Treatment with interferon appears to do both but is expensive, associated with significant adverse reactions, and effective in only a minority of treated persons. Recently, the combination of ribavirin and interferon was shown to be better than interferon monotherapy for both initial treatment and re-treatment of patients who have relapsed after interferon therapy.

Interferon Therapy

Mechanism of Action

Interferons, a heterogenous group of cytokines that are expressed in response to viral infection, induce the expression of multiple genes that have antiviral or antiproliferative activity, or both. These include, among others, RNase L, 2′-5′ oligoadenylate synthetase, M proteins, and protein kinase R. Interferons are normally induced by the presence of double-stranded RNA. They suppress the replication of many viruses and also exert an antiproliferative effect on the cell. There is strong evidence for a direct antiviral effect following the administration of interferon to HCV-infected persons.[82] However, interferons also act as immunomodulators and, for example, upregulate the level of expression of histocompatibility antigens on the surface of hepatocytes (also see Chapter 37).

Efficacy

Recombinant interferons have been used widely for the treatment of chronic hepatitis C. Recombinant interferon alfa-2b was the first drug approved by the FDA for treatment of hepatitis C. The first large-scale clinical trials compared 3 million units of interferon-alfa-2b given subcutaneously three times a week for 6 months versus placebo.[403, 404] Normalization of the ALT level (a biochemical response) at the end of treatment *(end-of-treatment response)* was achieved in almost half of those receiving interferon. However, relapse was common, and less than 20% still had normal ALT levels 6 months after discontinuation of drug *(sustained response).* When clearance of plasma HCV RNA was considered *(virologic response)* the outcomes were slightly worse. Extension of the length of therapy to 12 to 18 months did not change the end-of-treatment response but, more importantly, improved the virologic and biochemical sustained response to 20 to 30%.[405] In several of the early placebo-controlled trials, liver biopsies were carried out before and after a 6-month course of interferon therapy. Histologic improvement (e.g., a decrease in the Knodell score) was observed in the majority of treated persons but was rare in those receiving placebo. Interestingly, histologic improvement occurred in many treated patients who did not have biochemical or virologic end-of-treatment responses.[403, 404, 406–408]

A large number of clinical studies have examined the factors influencing the efficacy of interferon treatment for chronic hepatitis C, including patient variables as well as the use of alternative regimens involving higher individual doses, daily dosing, and the use of an induction and maintenance schedule. A detailed discussion of these studies is provided in Chapter 102. However, several generalizations can be made here. Patients infected with genotype 1 viruses have a lower overall response than patients with genotype 2 or 3 viruses, as do those with more extensive fibrosis or cirrhosis, higher intrahepatic iron stores, and higher baseline levels of viremia (Table 143–2). Other factors associated in some studies with a sustained response include a short duration of infection, young age, female gender, a low hepatic iron level, low viral genetic complexity, and an interferon dose of 3 million units or greater.

Daily dosing, particularly induction dosing with initial daily doses of up to 10 million units per day, results in more rapid and complete declines in the quantity of circulating virus.[82] However, higher doses are associated with more frequent adverse reactions, and whether they result in greater long-term efficacy is not known.

In addition to interferon-alfa-2b, several other interferon formulations have been used for treatment of chronic hepatitis C. These include a recombinant consensus interferon, interferon-alfa-2a, and interferon-alfa-2b-n1 (lymphoblastoid interferon).[409–411] These products generally have safety profiles similar to those of interferon-alfa-2b, and although they may have some advantages over interferon-alfa-2b,[412] studies of comparative efficacy are still under way. Long-acting formulations such as pegylated interferon are also under evaluation and may increase the availability of interferon therapy for certain patient groups (see Chapter 103).

TABLE 143–2 Predictors of Sustained Virologic Response after Interferon-alfa and Ribavirin Therapy as Initial Treatment for Hepatitis C: Two Large Trials

Factor	HITG[420]	IHIT[423]
Interferon and ribavirin vs. interferon alone	Yes	Yes
HCV genotype 2 or 3	Yes	Yes
Low plasma HCV RNA level	Yes	Yes
Young age	No	Yes
Low fibrosis score on biopsy	Yes	Yes
Female	No	Yes

Abbreviations: HCV, Hepatitis C virus; HITG, Hepatitis Interventional Therapy Group; IHIT, International Hepatitis Interventional Therapy.

The long-term impact of interferon therapy on the slowly progressive natural history of chronic hepatitis C is difficult to evaluate since there are few studies with "hard" clinical end points, such as survival or even the development of cirrhosis. More than 90% of those who achieve a sustained response remain free of liver disease and have undetectable plasma HCV RNA for 5 years.[413] A randomized, controlled, prospective study did demonstrate a reduction in the incidence of hepatocellular carcinoma in Japanese patients with well-compensated cirrhosis who were given relatively high dose interferon therapy (6 million units of interferon twice a week for 12 to 24 weeks).[414] Additional studies suggest that patients treated with interferon have a lower risk of developing decompensated cirrhosis and hepatocellular carcinoma, a benefit that is greater for but not limited to those with sustained responses.[407, 408, 415]

Interferon therapy is generally reserved for those patients who have chronic HCV infection (detectable viral RNA in their blood) and evidence of active necroinflammatory liver disease with persistent ALT-level elevations.[416] Documentation of at least moderate inflammatory disease and staging of fibrosis by liver biopsy before therapy remain a generally accepted standard of practice, although some experienced clinicians are beginning to question the need for this invasive procedure (see "Liver Biopsy" earlier).

Pharmacokinetics and Adverse Reactions

The pharmacokinetics of interferon-alfa-2b are poorly understood. In serum, interferon-alfa-2b levels peak approximately 6 hours after subcutaneous dosing and are undetectable by 16 hours. The drug is removed principally by renal catabolism and has an estimated half-life of approximately 2 hours. The correlation between the serum level and the biologic activity is poorly understood. Decreases in the quantity of circulating HCV RNA can be detected within 8 hours of the initiation of therapy; an approximately 90% reduction in the level of viremia may be evident within 48 hours with high doses of interferon-alfa-2b.[82]

Adverse reactions to interferon-alfa-2b are common.[417] Flulike symptoms are experienced by most persons within 6 hours of the first dose but generally diminish after 1 to 2 weeks. Fatigue, depression, and cognitive changes may occur. These side effects can be unacceptable, leading to discontinuation of the drug, although therapy can often be continued with counseling and antidepressant administration. Hair thinning is a common late complication of therapy. Asymptomatic retinal abnormalities occur, but their significance is not known.[418] Interferon-alfa-2b also commonly causes mild-to-moderate transient bone marrow suppression, manifested by anemia, thrombocytopenia, and especially neutropenia. These hematologic reactions may require dose reduction or administration of medications that stimulate blood cell production, or both.

Serious, but generally reversible, adverse events occur in approximately 1% of patients receiving interferon therapy and include thyroid disease, autoimmune disease, psychosis, diabetes mellitus, seizures, and cardiovascular disease. Life-threatening and irreversible adverse events are associated with interferon therapy in 0.1% of patients and include liver failure, sepsis with neutropenia, and suicide.

Combination Therapy with Ribavirin and Interferon

Ribavirin is a guanosine analogue with high oral bioavailability and exceptionally broad antiviral activity. It is a potent inhibitor of cellular inosine monophosphate dehydrogenase, but its precise mechanism of antiviral action is controversial. The use of orally administered ribavirin in combination with interferon-alfa-2b significantly enhances the rate of sustained response with minimal additional toxicity.[419, 420] How it does this is uncertain. However, the failure of ribavirin monotherapy to significantly influence levels of HCV viremia has led to the suggestion that its effect on hepatitis C may be through modulation of the immune response.[422, 423] The principal adverse reaction is hemolytic anemia, which occurs in the first week of use, peaks at 1 month, and requires dose reduction in 15% of patients.[420, 421]

When administered alone, ribavirin therapy was associated with a biochemical end-of-treatment response in 21 to 43% of patients, and improvement in the histologic appearance of the liver in some ALT responders.[424–426] However, HCV RNA levels were significantly reduced in only a few percent of ribavirin-treated patients. In combination with interferon-alfa-2b, however, ribavirin has a dramatic effect on the frequency of sustained-treatment responses, both in those who have relapsed after interferon monotherapy and those who have never been treated.[419–421, 427] As initial treatment, 48 weeks of therapy with ribavirin and interferon-alfa-2b was associated with a sustained virologic response of 38%, compared with only 13% for interferon alone.[420] Compared with the 48-week regimen, virologic sustained-response rates are slightly lower overall (31 versus 38%) with 24 weeks of combination therapy, but the difference was found only in patients with genotype 1 infections.[421] In fact, in patients with genotype 2 or 3, the virologic sustained-response rates appear to be similar with 24 and 48 weeks of ribavirin–interferon-alfa-2b combination therapy, suggesting that the shorter duration could be considered in patients with these genotypes. Histologic improvement was also more substantial with combination therapy, especially when given for 48 weeks.[420, 421] The magnitude in improvement in histologic activity and the proportion who improve are greater among patients with a virologic sustained response, but improvements (albeit small) can also be seen in up to 39% of those with persistent viremia.[420]

With interferon monotherapy, a successful ALT or HCV RNA response after 8 to 12 weeks of therapy strongly predicts the eventual likelihood of a successful end-of-treatment response (approximately 90%) and sustained response (approximately 70%).[428, 429] Thus, if there is no response to monotherapy by 12 weeks, it may be reasonable to discontinue treatment. However, with combination ribavirin–interferon-alfa-2b therapy, viremia was not cleared until after 12 weeks of therapy in some patients who ultimately achieved a virologic sustained response.[420] Thus, the early-response rule does not seem to hold with combination therapy. It is not known whether the extent of reduction in the level of viremia (versus complete clearance of the viral RNA) can be used as an alternative indicator of the ultimate response.

Combination therapy appears to be more efficacious than interferon monotherapy in all patient groups, although factors that predict a poor response to interferon monotherapy (genotype 1, high-level viremia, and extensive baseline fibrosis) also predict a reduced response to the combination.[420, 421] Adverse reactions resulted in discontinuation of the combination therapy in 21% of patients, almost half of which were reductions in hemoglobin levels related to the administration of ribavirin. Although the combination of ribavirin and interferon-alfa-2b offers the greatest efficacy of any therapeutic regimen tested to date, it is important to note that 50 to 60% of patients undergoing primary therapy with this combination still fail to achieve a sustained response. In addition, less than 10% of those who initially failed to respond to a course of interferon monotherapy (interferon nonresponders) achieve a virologic sustained response with ribavirin-interferon therapy, indicating that its chief advantage is reducing the frequency of virologic relapse.

Other Therapies

Iron-reduction therapy has been associated with normalization of serum ALT activities and a better response to interferon therapy, but it has not gained general acceptance. Parenteral thymosin-α_1 given in combination with interferon has been associated with an improved sustained response.[430] Oral amantadine, *N*-acetylcysteine, and ursodiol have also been used in HCV infections, but there are no controlled data supporting their use.

It is hoped that safer and more effective therapeutic agents will become available in the future. The x-ray crystallographic solution of structures of several crucial viral enzymes raises the possibility that more potent and selective antiviral agents can be developed. Especially important targets are the NS3 helicase and proteinase, the RNA-dependent polymerase, and the internal ribosomal entry site.

Screening for Hepatitis C

Most HCV infections are not recognized by patients and health care providers. Improved treatment outcomes and the capacity to prevent long-term disease complications underscore the importance of better recognition of the infection. Although therapy is not indicated for all HCV-infected persons, guidelines for HCV screening have been published (Table 143–3).[304]

PREVENTION

Preexposure Prevention

The key to reducing the incidence of HCV infection is decreasing exposure to contaminated blood. The incidence of post-transfusion HCV infection has been reduced to very low levels by screening blood donations for HCV antibody as well as surrogate markers of

TABLE 143–3 Persons Who Should Be Screened for Hepatitis C Infection*

High Prevalence	Postexposure Testing
Persons who ever injected illegal drugs	Persons with percutaneous or heavy mucosal exposure to HCV-positive blood
Persons with elevated aminotransferase levels	Children born to HCV-infected women
Persons on hemodialysis	Sexual partners of HCV-infected persons, who should consider HCV screening, though the risk of transmission through intercourse is low
Persons who received transfusions or organ transplants including clotting factor concentrates produced before 1987 or either a transfusion or organ transplant before July 1992	
Persons in settings with demonstrated high HCV prevalence and where risk factor ascertainment may be poor, e.g., inmates, patients attending inner-city clinics for sexually transmitted diseases, and patients attending some university emergency departments†	

*See 1998 Public Health Service guidelines for full recommendations regarding HCV screening.[304]
†Screening may be useful for such individuals in settings in which there are resources to counsel and manage infections.
Abbreviation: HCV, Hepatitis C virus.

HCV infection.[314, 315] Although the impact is more difficult to measure, nosocomial HCV transmission in developing countries should decrease with worldwide adherence to universal precautions. There is conflicting evidence that needle-exchange programs reduce HCV transmission among illicit drug users.[335, 336] More work is clearly necessary to prevent transmission in this setting.

Efforts to develop an HCV vaccine are complicated by the extensive genetic and possible antigenic diversity among HCV strains, as well as the absence of solid immunity after natural infections, as discussed earlier. Nonetheless, a candidate vaccine containing recombinant envelope glycoproteins was found to protect chimpanzees against low-level intravenous challenge with the virus from which the envelope protein sequences were derived. Such immunization also may attenuate infection due to heterologous strains of the virus.[431] Phase I human studies of a related vaccine began in 1998, but complete protection against multiple HCV isolates is not anticipated in the near future.

Postexposure Prevention

Early studies provide conflicting data about the extent to which HCV infection is modified by the administration of pooled human immune globulin.[432–434] However, since HCV-seropositive donations are no longer included in the plasma pools from which immune globulin is manufactured, no benefit would be expected from products on the market today. Administration of immune globulin is not recommended in U.S. Public Health Service guidelines after exposure to HCV.[304]

An individual who has a documented exposure (e.g., a health care worker sustaining a needlestick from a patient who is known to be infected) should be screened for HCV antibodies and have an ALT test as soon as possible after exposure to exclude prior infection. Serologic and ALT testing should be repeated at least once 6 months later. Some authorities also test for HCV RNA 2 to 4 weeks after exposure, because there is anecdotal evidence interferon-alfa-2b may be more effective when used early in the course of infection rather than years later. However, this may be unnecessary because it is not known whether therapy begun 1 month after exposure is more effective than that initiated at 6 months. In addition, it is not possible to predict whether the infection will persist at this early stage.

REFERENCES

1. Feinstone SM, Kapikian AZ, Purcell RH, et al. Transfusion-associated hepatitis not due to viral hepatitis type A or B N Engl J Med. 1975;292:767–770.
2. Prince AM, Brotman B, Grady GF, et al. Long-incubation post-transfusion hepatitis without serological evidence of exposure to hepatitis-B virus. Lancet. 1974;2:241–246.
3. Tabor E, Gerety RJ, Drucker JA, et al. Transmission of non-A, non-B hepatitis from man to chimpanzee. Lancet. 1978;1:463–466.
4. Alter HJ, Purcell RH, Holland PV, et al. Transmissible agent in non-A, non-B hepatitis. Lancet. 1978;1:459–463.
5. Choo Q-L, Kuo G, Weiner AJ, et al. Isolation of a cDNA clone derived from a blood-borne non-A, non-B viral hepatitis genome. Science. 1989;244:359–364.
6. Choo Q-L, Richman KH, Han JH, et al. Genetic organization and diversity of the hepatitis C virus. Proc Natl Acad Sci U S A. 1991;88:2451–2455.
7. Shimizu YK, Feinstone SM, Kohara M, et al. Hepatitis C virus: Detection of intracellular virus particles by electron microscopy. Hepatology. 1996;23:205–209.
8. Kaito M, Watanabe S, Tsukiyama-Kohara K, et al. Hepatitis C virus particle detected by immunoelectron microscopic study. J Gen Virol. 1994;75:1755–1760.
9. Simons JN, Leary TP, Dawson GJ, et al. Isolation of novel virus-like sequences associated with human hepatitis. Nat Med. 1995;1:564–569.
10. Theodore D, Lemon SM. GB virus C, hepatitis G virus, or human orphan flavivirus? Hepatology. 1997;25:1285–1286.
11. Hijikata M, Shimizu YK, Kato H, et al. Equilibrium centrifugation studies of hepatitis C virus: Evidence for circulating immune complexes. J Virol. 1993;67:1953–1958.
12. Kanto T, Hayashi N, Takehara T, et al. Buoyant density of hepatitis C virus recovered from infected hosts: Two different features in sucrose equilibrium density-gradient centrifugation related to degree of liver inflammation. Hepatology. 1994;19:296–302.
13. Choo SH, So HS, Cho JM, et al. Association of hepatitis C virus particles with immunoglobulin: A mechanism for persistent infection. J Gen Virol. 1995;76:2337–2341.
14. Miyamoto H, Okamoto H, Sato K, et al. Extraordinarily low density of hepatitis C virus estimated by sucrose density gradient centrifugation and the polymerase chain reaction. J. Gen. Virol. 1992;73:715–718.
15. Brown EA, Zhang H, Ping LH, et al. Secondary structure of the 5′ nontranslated regions of hepatitis C virus and pestivirus genomic RNAs. Nucleic Acids Res. 1992;20:5041–5045.
16. Bukh J, Purcell RH, Miller RH. Sequence analysis of the 5′ noncoding region of hepatitis C virus. Proc Natl Acad Sci U S A. 1992;89:4942–4946.
17. Kamoshita N, Tsukiyama-Kohara K, Kohara M, et al. Genetic analysis of internal ribosomal entry site on hepatitis C virus RNA: Implication for involvement of the highly ordered structure and cell type–specific transacting factors. Virology. 1997;233:9–18.
18. Han JH, Shyamala V, Richman KH, et al. Characterization of the terminal regions of hepatitis C viral RNA: Identification of conserved sequences in the 5′ untranslated region and poly (A) tails at the 3′ end. Proc Natl Acad Sci U S A. 1991;88:1711–1715.
19. Honda M, Ping LH, Rijnbrand RC, et al. Structural requirements for initiation of translation by internal ribosome entry within genome-length hepatitis C virus RNA. Virology. 1996;222:31–42.
20. Pestova TV, Shatsky IN, Fletcher SP, et al. A prokaryotic-like mode of cytoplasmic eukaryotic ribosome binding to the initiation codon during internal translation initiation of hepatitis C and classical swine fever virus RNAs. Genes Dev. 1998;12:67–83.
21. Honda M, Brown EA, Lemon SM. Stability of a stem-loop involving the initiator AUG controls the efficiency of internal initiation of translation on hepatitis C virus RNA. RNA. 1996;2:955–968.
22. Yamada N, Tanihara K, Takada A, et al. Genetic organization and diversity of the 3′ noncoding region of the hepatitis C virus genome. Virology. 1996;223:255–261.
23. Kolykhalov AA, Feinstone SM, Rice CM. Identification of a highly conserved sequence element at the 3′ terminus of hepatitis C virus genome RNA. J Virol. 1996;70:3363–3371.
24. Tanaka T, Kato N, Cho MJ, et al. Structure of the 3′ terminus of the hepatitis C virus genome. J Virol. 1996;70:3307–3312.
25. Grakoui A, Wychowski C, Lin C, et al. Expression and identification of hepatitis C virus polyprotein cleavage products. J Virol. 1993;67:1385–1395.
26. Hijikata M, Kato N, Ootsuyama Y, et al. Gene mapping of the putative structural region of the hepatitis C virus genome by in vitro processing analysis. Proc Natl Acad Sci U S A. 1991;88:5547–5551.
27. Barba G, Harper F, Harada T, et al. Hepatitis C virus core protein shows a cytoplasmic localization and associates to cellular lipid storage droplets. Proc Nat Acad Sci U S A. 1997;94:1200–1205.
28. Yasui K, Wakita T, Tsukiyama-Kohara K, et al. The native form and maturation process of hepatitis C virus core protein. J Virol. 1998;72:6048–6055.
29. Chang SC, Yen J-H, Kang H-Y, et al. Nuclear localization signals in the core protein of hepatitis C virus. Biochem Biophys Res Commun. 1994;205:1284–1290.
30. Santolini E, Migliaccio G, La Monica N. Biosynthesis and biochemical properties of the hepatitis C virus core protein. J Virol. 1994;68:3631–3641.
31. Suzuki R, Matsuura Y, Suzuki T, et al. Nuclear localization of the truncated hepatitis C virus core protein with its hydrophobic C terminus deleted. J Gen Virol. 1995;76:53–61.
32. Ray RB, Meyer K, Ray R. Suppression of apoptotic cell death by hepatitis C virus core protein. Virology. 1996;226:176–182.
33. Ray RB, Lagging LM, Meyer K, et al. Hepatitis C virus core protein cooperates with ras and transforms primary rat embryo fibroblasts to tumorigenic phenotype. J Virol. 1996;70:4438–4443.
34. Chen CM, You LR, Hwang LH, et al. Direct interaction of hepatitis C virus core protein with the cellular lymphotoxin-β receptor modulates the signal pathway of the lymphotoxin-β receptor. J Virol. 1997;71:9417–9426.
35. Matsumoto M, Hsieh TY, Zhu NL, et al. Hepatitis C virus core protein interacts with the cytoplasmic tail of lymphotoxin-β receptor. J Virol. 1997;71:1301–1309.
36. Ray RB, Steele R, Meyer K, et al. Transcriptional repression of p53 promoter by hepatitis C virus core protein. J Biol Chem. 1997;272:10,983–10,986.
37. Zhu NL, Khoshnan A, Schneider R, et al. Hepatitis C virus core protein binds to the cytoplasmic domain of tumor necrosis factor (TNF) receptor 1 and enhances TNF-induced apoptosis. J Virol. 1998;72:3691–3697.
38. Shrivastava A, Manna SK, Ray R, et al. Ectopic expression of hepatitis C virus core protein differentially regulates nuclear transcription factors. J Virol. 1998;72:9722–9728.
39. Lin C, Lindenbach BD, Pragai BM, et al. Processing in the hepatitis C virus E2-NS2 region: Identification of p7 and two distinct E2-specific products with different C termini. J Virol. 1994;68:5063–5073.
40. Mizushima H, Hijikata M, Asabe S, et al. Two hepatitis C virus glycoprotein E2 products with different C termini. J Virol. 1994;68:6215–6222.
41. Yi M, Kaneko S, Yu DY, et al. Hepatitis C virus envelope proteins bind lactoferrin. J Virol. 1997;71:5997–6002.
42. Dubuisson J, Hsu HH, Cheung RC, et al. Formation and intracellular localization of hepatitis C virus envelope glycoprotein complexes expressed by recombinant vaccinia and Sindbis viruses. J Virol. 1994;68:6147–6160.
43. Ralston R, Thudium K, Berger K, et al. Characterization of hepatitis C virus envelope glycoprotein complexes expressed by recombinant vaccinia viruses. J Virol. 1993;67:6753–6761.
44. Lo SY, Selby MJ, Ou JH. Interaction between hepatitis C virus core protein and E1 envelope protein. J Virol. 1996;70:5177–5182.

45. Weiner AJ, Brauer MJ, Rosenblatt J, et al. Variable and hypervariable domains are found in the regions of HCV corresponding to the flavivirus envelope and NS1 proteins and the pestivirus envelope glycoproteins. Virology. 1991;180:842–848.
46. Kato N, Ootsuyama Y, Ohkoshi S, et al. Characterization of hypervariable regions in the putative envelope protein of hepatitis C virus. Biochem Biophys Res Commun. 1992;189:119–127.
47. Kato N, Ootsuyama Y, Tanaka T, et al. Marked sequence diversity in the putative envelope proteins of hepatitis C viruses. Virus Res. 1992;22:107–123.
48. Farci P, Shimoda A, Wong D, et al. Prevention of hepatitis C virus infection in chimpanzees by hyperimmune serum against the hypervariable region 1 of the envelope 2 protein. Proc Natl Acad Sci U S A. 1996;93:15,394–15,399.
49. Kato N, Sekiya H, Ootsuyama Y et al. Humoral immune response to hypervariable region 1 of the putative envelope glycoprotein (gp70) of hepatitis C virus. J Virol. 1993;67:3923–3930.
50. Weiner AJ, Geysen HM, Christopherson C, et al. Evidence for immune selection of hepatitis C virus (HCV) putative envelope glycoprotein variants: Potential role in chronic HCV infections. Proc Natl Acad Sci U S A. 1992;89:3468–3472.
50a. Taylor DR, Shi ST, Romano PR, et al. Inhibition of the interferon-inducible protein kinase PKR by HCV E2 protein. Science. 1999;285:107–110.
51. Grakoui A, McCourt DW, Wychowski C, et al. A second hepatitis C virus–encoded proteinase. Proc Natl Acad Sci U S A. 1993;90:10,583–10,587.
52. Santolini E, Pacini L, Fipaldini C, et al. The NS2 protein of hepatitis C virus is a transmembrane polypeptide. J Virol. 1995;69:7461–7471.
53. Kim JL, Morgenstern KA, Lin C, et al. Crystal structure of the hepatitis C virus NS3 protease domain complexed with a synthetic NS4A cofactor peptide. Cell. 1996;87:343–355.
54. Yao NH, Hesson T, Cable M, et al. Structure of the hepatitis C virus RNA helicase domain. Nat Struct Biol. 1997;4:463–467.
55. Kim JL, Morgenstern KA, Griffith JP, et al. Hepatitis C virus NS3 RNA helicase domain with a bound oligonucleotide: The crystal structure provides insights into the mode of unwinding. Structure. 1998;6:89–100.
56. Yao NH, Hesson T, Cable M, et al. Structure of the hepatitis C virus RNA helicase domain. Nat Struct Biol. 1997;4:463–467.
57. Kolykhalov AA, Agapov EV, Rice CM. Specificity of the hepatitis C virus NS3 serine protease: Effects of substitutions at the 3/4A, 4A/4B, 4B/5A, and 5A/5B cleavage sites on polyprotein processing. J Virol. 1994;68:7525–7533.
58. Tomei L, Failla C, Santolini E, et al. NS3 is a serine protease required for processing of hepatitis C virus polyprotein. J Virol. 1993;67:4017–4026.
59. Tanji Y, Hijikata M, Satoh S, et al. Hepatitis C virus–encoded nonstructural protein NS4A has versatile functions in viral protein processing. J Virol. 1995;69:1575–1581.
60. Failla C, Tomei L, De Francesco R. Both NS3 and NS4A are required for proteolytic processing of hepatitis C virus nonstructural proteins. J Virol. 1994;68:3753–3760.
61. Lin C, Pragai BM, Grakoui A, et al. Hepatitis C virus NS3 serine proteinase: Trans-cleavage requirements and processing kinetics. J Virol. 1994;68:8147–8157.
62. Tai CL, Chi WK, Chen DS, et al. The helicase activity associated with hepatitis C virus nonstructural protein 3 (NS3). J Virol. 1996;70:8477–8484.
63. Kim DW, Kim J, Gwack Y, et al. Mutational analysis of the hepatitis C virus RNA helicase. J Virol. 1997;71:9400–9409.
64. Sakamuro D, Furukawa T, Takegami T. Hepatitis C virus nonstructural protein NS3 transforms NIH 3T3 cells. J Virol. 1995;69:3893–3896.
65. Morgenstern KA, Landro JA, Hsiao K, et al. Polynucleotide modulation of the protease, nucleoside triphosphatase, and helicase activities of a hepatitis C virus NS3-NS4A complex isolated from transfected COS cells. J Virol. 1997;71:3767–3775.
66. Asabe SI, Tanji Y, Satoh S, et al. The N-terminal region of hepatitis C virus–encoded NS5A is important for NS4A-dependent phosphorylation. J Virol. 1997;71:790–796.
67. Kaneko T, Tanji Y, Satoh S, et al. Production of two phosphoproteins from the NS5A region of the hepatitis C viral genome. Biochem Biophys Res Commun. 1994;205:320–326.
68. Enomoto N, Sakuma I, Asahina Y, et al. Comparison of full-length sequences of interferon-sensitive and resistant hepatitis C virus 1b. Sensitivity to interferon is conferred by amino acid substitutions in the NS5A region. J Clin Invest. 1995;96:224–230.
69. Enomoto N, Sakuma I, Asahina Y, et al. Mutations in the nonstructural protein 5A gene and response to interferon in patients with chronic hepatitis C virus 1b infection. N Engl J Med. 1996;334:77–81.
70. Gale MJJ, Korth MJ, Tang NM, et al. Evidence that hepatitis C virus resistance to interferon is mediated through repression of the PKR protein kinase by the non-structural 5A protein. Virology. 1997;230:217–227.
71. Ferrari E, Wright-Minogue J, Fang JWS, et al. Characterization of soluble hepatitis C virus RNA-dependent RNA polymerase expressed in *escherichia coli.* J Virol. 1999;73:1649–1654.
72. Lohmann V, Körner F, Herian U, et al. Biochemical properties of hepatitis C virus NS5B RNA-dependent RNA polymerase and identification of amino acid sequence motifs essential for enzymatic activity. J Virol. 1997;71:8416–8428.
73. Yamashita T, Kaneko S, Shirota Y, et al. RNA-dependent RNA polymerase activity of the soluble recombinant hepatitis C virus NS5B protein truncated at the C-terminal region. J Biol Chem. 1998;273:15,479–15,486.
74. Pileri P, Uematsu Y, Campagnoli S, et al. Binding of hepatitis C virus to CD81. Science. 1998;282:938–941.
75. Kolykhalov AA, Agapov EV, Blight KJ, et al. Transmission of hepatitis C by intrahepatic inoculation with transcribed RNA. Science. 1997;277:570–574.
76. Yanagi M, Purcell RH, Emerson SU, et al. Transcripts from a single full-length cDNA clone of hepatitis C virus are infectious when directly transfected into the liver of a chimpanzee. Proc Natl Acad Sci U S A. 1997;94:8738–8743.
77. Negro F, Pacchioni D, Shimizu Y, et al. Detection of intrahepatic replication of hepatitis C virus RNA by in situ hybridization and comparison with histopathology. Proc Natl Acad Sci U S A. 1992;89:2247–2251.
78. Krawczynski K, Beach MJ, Bradley DW, et al. Hepatitis C antigens in hepatocytes. Immuno-morphologic detection and identification. Gastroenterology. 1992;103:622–629.
79. Lerat H, Berby F, Trabaud MA, et al. Specific detection of hepatitis C virus minus strand RNA in hematopoietic cells. J Clin Invest. 1996;97:845–851.
80. Shimizu YK, Igarashi H, Kanematu T, et al. Sequence analysis of the hepatitis C virus genome recovered from serum, liver, and peripheral blood mononuclear cells of infected chimpanzees. J Virol. 1997;71:5769–5773.
81. Lam NP, Neumann AU, Gretch DR, et al. Dose-dependent acute clearance of hepatitis C genotype 1 virus with interferon alfa-2b. Hepatology. 1997;26:226–231.
82. Neumann AU, Lam NP, Dahari H, et al. Hepatitis C viral dynamics in vivo and the antiviral efficacy of interferon-alpha therapy. Science. 1998;282:103–107.
83. Martell M, Esteban Ji, Quer J, et al. Hepatitis C virus (HCV) circulates as a population of different but closely related genomes: Quasispecies nature of HCV genome distribution. J Virol. 1992;66:3225–3229.
84. Wang Y, Ray SC, Laeyendecker O, et al. Assessment of hepatitis C virus sequence complexity by the electrophoretic mobility of both single- and double-stranded DNA. J Clin Micro. 1998;36:2982–2989.
85. Kurosaki M, Enomoto N, Marumo F, et al. Rapid sequence variation in the hypervariable region of hepatitis C virus during the course of chronic infection. Hepatology. 1993;18:1293–1299.
86. Kao J-H, Chen P-J, Lai M-Y, et al. Quasispecies of hepatitis C virus and genetic drift of the hypervariable region in chronic type C hepatitis. J Infect Dis. 1995;172:261–264.
87. Kato N, Ootsuyama Y, Sekiya H, et al. Genetic drift in hypervariable region 1 of the viral genome in persistent hepatitis C virus infection. J Virol. 1994;68:4776–4784.
88. Van Doorn L-J, Capriles I, Maertens G, et al. Sequence evolution of the hypervariable region in the putative envelope region E2/NS1 of hepatitis C virus is correlated with specific humoral immune responses. J Virol. 1995;69:773–778.
89. Odeberg J, Yun ZB, Sönnerborg A, et al. Variation of hepatitis C virus hypervariable region 1 in immunocompromised patients. J Infect Dis. 1997;175:938–943.
90. Booth JC, Kumar U, Webster D, et al. Comparison of the rate of sequence variation in the hypervariable region of E2/NS1 region of hepatitis C virus in normal and hypogammaglobulinemic patients. Hepatology. 1998;27:223–227.
91. Weiner A, Erickson AL, Kansopon J, et al. Persistent hepatitis C virus infection in a chimpanzee is associated with emergence of a cytotoxic T lymphocyte escape variant. Proc Natl Acad Sci U S A. 1995;92:2755–2759.
92. Ogata N, Alter HJ, Miller RH, et al. Nucleotide sequence and mutation rate of the H strain of hepatitis C virus. Proc Natl Acad Sci U S A. 1991;88:3392–3396.
93. Abe K, Inchauspe G, Fujisawa K. Genomic characterization and mutation rate of hepatitis C virus isolated from a patient who contracted hepatitis during an epidemic of non-A, non-B hepatitis in Japan. J Gen Virol. 1992;73:2725–2729.
94. Okamoto H, Kojima M, Okada S, et al. Genetic drift of hepatitis C virus during an 8.2-year infection in a chimpanzee: Variability and stability. Virology. 1992;190:894–899.
95. Honda M, Kaneko S, Sakai A, et al. Degree of diversity of hepatitis C virus quasispecies and progression of liver disease. Hepatology. 1994;20:1144–1151.
96. Cabot B, Esteban JI, Martell M, et al. Structure of replicating hepatitis C virus (HCV) quasispecies in the liver may not be reflected by analysis of circulating HCV virions. J Virol. 1997;71:1732–1734.
97. Maggi F, Fornai C, Vatteroni ML, et al. Differences in hepatitis C virus quasispecies composition between liver, peripheral blood mononuclear cells and plasma. J Gen Virol. 1997;78:1521–1525.
98. Simmonds P, Holmes EC, Cha T-A, et al. Classification of hepatitis C virus into six major genotypes and a series of subtypes by phylogenetic analysis of the NS-5 region. J Gen Virol. 1993;74:2391–2399.
99. Bukh J, Purcell RH, Miller RH. Sequence analysis of the core gene of 14 hepatitis C virus genotypes. Proc Natl Acad Sci U S A. 1994;91:8239–8243.
100. Bukh J, Miller RH, Purcell RH. Genetic heterogeneity of hepatitis C virus: Quasispecies and genotypes. Semin Liver Dis. 1995;15:41–63.
101. Simmonds P, Smith DB, McOmish F, et al. Identification of genotypes of hepatitis C virus by sequence comparisons in the core, E1 and NS-5 regions. J Gen Virol. 1994;75:1053–1061.
102. Zein NN, Rakela J, Krawitt EL, et al. Hepatitis C virus genotypes in the United States: Epidemiology, pathogenicity, and response to interferon therapy. Ann Intern Med. 1996;125:634–639.
103. Lau JYN, Davis GL, Prescott LE, et al. Distribution of hepatitis C virus genotypes determined by line probe assay inpatients with chronic hepatitis C seen at tertiary referral centers in the United States. Ann Intern Med. 1996;124:868–876.
104. Dusheiko GM, Schmilovitz-Weiss H, Brown D, et al. Hepatitis C virus genotypes: An investigation of type-specific differences in geographic origin and disease. Hepatology. 1994;19:13–18.
105. Ray SC, Arthur R, Carella AV, Bukh J, Thomas DL. Genetic epidemiology of hepatitis C virus throughout Egypt. Presented at Fifth International Meeting on hepatitis C and related viruses, Venice, June 25, 1998.
106. Simmonds P. Variability of hepatitis C virus. Hepatology. 1995;21:570–583.
107. Mellor J, Walsh EA, Prescott LE, et al. Survey of type 6 group variants of hepatitis C virus in southeast Asia by using core based genotyping assay. J Clin Microbiol. 1996;34:417–423.
108. Simmonds P, Mellor J, Sakuldamrongpanich T, et al. Evolutionary analysis of

variants of hepatitis C virus found in South-East Asia: Comparison with classifications based upon sequence similarity. J Gen Virol. 1996;77:3013–3024.
109. Pawlotsky J-M, Tsakiris L, Roudot-Thoraval F, et al. Relationship between hepatitis C virus genotypes and sources of infection in patients with chronic hepatitis C. J Infect Dis. 1995;171:1607–1610.
110. Lau JYN, Mizokami M, Kolberg JA, et al. Application of six hepatitis C virus genotyping systems to sera from chronic hepatitis C patients in the United States. J Infect Dis. 1995;171:281–289.
111. Chang TT, Young KC, Yang YJ, et al. Hepatitis C virus RNA in peripheral blood mononuclear cells: Comparing acute and chronic hepatitis C virus infection. Hepatology. 1996;23:977–981.
112. Moldvay J, Deny P, Pol S, et al. Detection of hepatitis C virus RNA in peripheral blood mononuclear cells of infected patients by in situ hybridization. Blood. 1994;83:269–273.
113. Navas S, Martín J, Quiroga JA, et al. Genetic diversity and tissue compartmentalization of the hepatitis C virus genome in blood mononuclear cells, liver, and serum from chronic hepatitis C patients. J Virol. 1998;72:1640–1646.
114. Ounanian A, Gueddah N, Rolachon A, et al. Hepatitis C virus RNA in plasma and blood mononuclear cells in patients with chronic hepatitis C treated with alpha-interferon. J Med Virol. 1995;45:141–145.
115. Zehender G, Meroni L, De Maddalena C, et al. Detection of hepatitis C virus RNA in CD19 peripheral blood mononuclear cells of chronically infected patients. J Infect Dis. 1997;176:1209–1214.
116. Lanford RE, Chavez D, Von Chisari F, et al. Lack of detection of negative-strand hepatitis C virus RNA in peripheral blood mononuclear cells and other extrahepatic tissues by the highly strand-specific rTth reverse transcriptase PCR. J Virol. 1995; 69:8079–8083.
117. Laskus T, Radkowski M, Wang LF, et al. Hepatitis C virus negative strand RNA is not detected in peripheral blood mononuclear cells and viral sequences are identical to those in serum: A case against extrahepatic replication. J Gen Virol. 1997;78:2747–2750.
118. Agnello V, Abel G. Localization of hepatitis C virus in cutaneous vasculitic lesions in patients with type II cryoglobulinemia. Arthritis Rheum. 1997;40:2007–2015.
119. Johnson RJ, Gretch DR, Yamabe H, et al. Membranoproliferative glomerulonephritis associated with hepatitis C virus infection. N Engl J Med. 1993;328:465–470.
120. Liou TC, Chang TT, Young KC, et al. Detection of HCV RNA in saliva, urine, seminal fluid, and ascites. J Med Virol. 1992;37:197–202.
121. Chen M, Yun Z-B, Sällberg M et al. Detection of hepatitis C virus RNA in the cell fraction of saliva before and after oral surgery. J Med Virol. 1995;45:223–226.
122. Wang JT, Wang TH, Sheu JC, et al. Hepatitis C virus RNA in saliva of patients with posttransfusion hepatitis and low efficiency of transmission among spouses. J Med Virol. 1992;36:28–31.
123. Fiore RJ, Potenza D, Monno L, et al. Detection of HCV RNA in serum and seminal fluid from HIV-1 co-infected intravenous drug addicts. J Med Virol. 1995;46:364–367.
124. Mendel I, Muraine M, Riachi G, et al. Detection and genotyping of the hepatitis C RNA in tear fluid from patients with chronic hepatitis C. J. Med. Virol. 1997;51:231–233.
124a. Lohmann V, Korner F, Koch J-O, et al. Replication of subgenomic hepatitis C virus RNAs in a hepatoma cell line. Science. 1999;285:110–113.
125. Shimizu YK, Iwamoto A, Hijikata M, et al. Evidence for in vitro replication of hepatitis C virus genome in a human T-cell line. Proc Natl Acad Sci U S A. 1992;89:5477–5481.
126. Nakajima N, Hijikata M, Yoshikura H, et al. Characterization of long-term cultures of hepatitis C virus J Virol. 1996;70:3325–3329.
127. Shimizu YK, Purcell RH, Yoshikura H. Correlation between the infectivity of hepatitis C virus in vivo and its infectivity in vitro. Proc Natl Acad Sci U S A. 1993;90:6037–6041.
128. Yoo BJ, Selby MJ, Choe J, et al. Transfection of a differentiated human hepatoma cell line (Huh7) with in vitro–transcribed hepatitis C virus (HCV) RNA and establishment of a long-term culture persistently infected with HCV. J Virol. 1995;69:32–38.
129. Mizutani T, Kato N, Ikeda M, et al. Long-term human T-cell culture system supporting hepatitis C virus replication. Biochem Biophys Res Commun. 1996;227:822–826.
130. Mizutani T, Kato N, Hirota M, et al. Inhibition of hepatitis C virus replication by antisense oligonucleotide in culture cells. Biochem Biophys Res Commun. 1995;212:906–911.
131. Shimizu YK, Igarashi H, Kiyohara T, et al. Infection of a chimpanzee with hepatitis C virus grown in cell culture. J Gen Virol. 1998;79:1383–1386.
132. Ito T, Mukaigawa J, Zuo J, et al. Cultivation of hepatitis C virus in primary hepatocyte culture from patients with chronic hepatitis C results in release of high titre infectious virus. J Gen Virol. 1996;77:1043–1054.
133. Lanford RE, Sureau C, Jacob JR, et al. Demonstration of in vitro infection of chimpanzee hepatocytes with hepatitis C virus using strand-specific RT/PCR. Virology. 1994;202:606–614.
134. Beard MR, Abell G, Honda M, et al. An infectious molecular clone of a Japanese genotype 1b hepatitis C virus. Hepatology. 1999;30:316–324.
135. Farci P, Alter HJ, Wong D, et al. A long-term study of hepatitis C virus replication in non-A, non-B hepatitis. N Engl J Med. 1991;325:98–104.
136. Abe K, Inchauspe G. Transmission of hepatitis C by saliva. Lancet. 1991;337:248–248.
137. Bassett SE, Brasky KM, Lanford RE. Analysis of hepatitis C virus–inoculated chimpanzees reveals unexpected clinical profiles. J Virol. 1998;72:2589–2599.
138. Kawamura T, Furusaka A, Koziel MJ, et al. Transgenic expression of hepatitis C virus structural proteins in the mouse. Hepatology. 1997;25:1014–1021.
139. Moriya K, Fujie H, Shintani Y, et al. The core protein of hepatitis C virus induces hepatocellular carcinoma in transgenic mice. Nat Med. 1998;4:1065–1067.
140. Moriya K, Yotsuyanagi H, Shintani Y, et al. Hepatitis C virus core protein induces hepatic steatosis in transgenic mice. J Gen Virol. 1997;78:1527–1531.
140a. Lerat H, Honda M, Gosert R, et al. Transgenic mice expressing HCV proteins develop microvesicular steatosis and hepatocellular carcinoma. Abstract. Presented at the Fifth International Meeting on Hepatitis C and Related Viruses. Bethesda, Md., June 1999.
141. Pasquinelli C, Shoenberger JM, Chung J, et al. Hepatitis C virus core and E2 protein expression in transgenic mice. Hepatology. 1997;25:719–727.
142. Koike K, Moriya K, Ishibashi K, et al. Sialadenitis histologically resembling Sjögren syndrome in mice transgenic for hepatitis C virus envelope genes. Proc Natl Acad Sci U S A. 1997;94:233–236.
143. Wakita T, Taya C, Katsume A, et al. Efficient conditional transgene expression in hepatitis C virus cDNA transgenic mice mediated by the Cre/loxP system. J Biol Chem. 1998;273:9001–9006.
144. Shimizu YK, Weiner AJ, Rosenblatt J, et al. Early events in hepatitis C virus infection of chimpanzees. Proc Natl Acad Scix U S A. 1990;87:6441–6444.
145. Prince AM, Brotman B, Inchauspe G, et al. Patterns and prevalence of hepatitis C virus infection in posttransfusion non-A, non-B hepatitis. J Infect Dis. 1993;167:1296–1301.
146. Abe K, Inchauspe G, Shikata T, et al. Three different patterns of hepatitis C virus infection in chimpanzees. Hepatology. 1992;15:690–695.
147. Alter MJ, Margolis HS, Krawczynski K, et al. The natural history of community acquired hepatitis C in the United States. N Engl J Med. 1992;327:1899–1905.
148. Villano SA, Vlahov D, Nelson KE, et al. Persistence of viremia and the importance of long-term follow-up after acute hepatitis C infection. Hepatology. 1999;29:908–914.
149. Di Bisceglie A, Goodman ZD, Ishak KG, et al. Long-term clinical and histopathological follow-up of chronic post-transfusion hepatitis. Hepatology. 1991;14:969–974.
150. Barrera JM, Bruguera M, Ercilla MG, et al. Persistent hepatitis C viremia after acute self-limiting posttransfusion hepatitis C. Hepatology. 1995;21:639–644.
151. Mattsson L, Sonnerborg A, Weiland O. Outcome of acute symptomatic non-A, non-B hepatitis: A 13-year follow-up study of hepatitis C virus markers. Liver. 1993;13:274–278.
152. Puoti M, Zonaro A, Ravaggi A, et al. Hepatitis C virus RNA and antibody response in the clinical course of acute hepatitis C virus infection. Hepatology. 1992;16:877–881.
153. Thomas DL, Rai R, Anania F, et al. A prospective investigation of hepatitis C viral load. Hepatology. 1998;28:568A.
154. Haydon GH, Jarvis LM, Blair CS, et al. Clinical significance of intrahepatic hepatitis C virus levels in patients with chronic HCV infection. Gut. 1998;42:570–575.
155. Bassett SE, Thomas DL, Brasky KM, et al. Viral persistence, antibody to E1 and E2 and HVR-1 sequence stability in hepatitis C virus–inoculated chimpanzees. J Virol. 1998;73:1118–1126.
156. Minton EJ, Smillie D, Neal KR, et al. Association between MHC class II alleles and clearance of circulating hepatitis C virus. J Infect Dis. 1998;178:39–44.
157. Missale G, Bertoni R, Lamonaca V, et al. Different clinical behaviors of acute hepatitis C virus infection are associated with different vigor of the anti-viral cell-mediated immune response. J Clin Invest. 1996;98:706–714.
158. Lechmann M, Ihlenfeldt HG, Braunschweiger I, et al. T- and B-cell responses to different hepatitis C virus antigens in patients with chronic hepatitis C infection and in healthy anti-hepatitis C virus-positive blood donors without viremia. Hepatology. 1996;24:790–795.
159. Diepolder HM, Gerlach JT, Zachoval R, et al. Immunodominant $CD4^+$ T-cell epitope within nonstructural protein 3 in acute hepatitis C virus infection. J Virol. 1997;71:6011–6019.
160. Diepolder HM, Zachoval R, Hoffmann RM, et al. Possible mechanism involving T-lymphocyte response to non-structural protein 3 in viral clearance in acute hepatitis C virus infection. Lancet. 1995;346:1006–1007.
161. Tsai SL, Liaw YF, Chen MH, et al. Detection of type 2-like T-helper cells in hepatitis C virus infection: Implications for hepatitis C virus chronicity. Hepatology. 1997;25:449–458.
162. Koziel MJ, Dudley D, Afdhal N, et al. Hepatitis C virus (HCV)-specific cytotoxic T lymphocytes recognize epitopes in the core and envelope proteins of HCV. J Virol. 1993;67:7522–7532.
163. Koziel MJ, Dudley D, Wong JT, et al. Intrahepatic cytotoxic T lymphocytes specific for hepatitis C virus in persons with chronic hepatitis (published erratum appears in J Immunol. 1993; 150:2563). J Immunol. 1992;149:3339–3344.
164. Nelson DR, Marousis CG, Davis GL, et al. The role of hepatitis C virus–specific cytotoxic T lymphocytes in chronic hepatitis C. J Immunol. 1997;158:1473–1481.
165. Rehermann B, Chang KM, McHutchison JG, et al. Quantitative analysis of the peripheral blood cytotoxic T lymphocyte response in patients with chronic hepatitis C virus infection. J Clin Invest. 1996;98:1432–1440.
166. Bronowicki JP, Vetter D, Uhl G, et al. Lymphocyte reactivity to hepatitis C virus (HCV) antigens shows evidence for exposure to HCV in HCV-seronegative spouses of HCV-infected patients. J Infect Dis. 1997;176:518–522.
167. Koziel MJ, Wong DKH, Dudley D, et al. Hepatitis C virus–specific cytolytic T lymphocyte and T helper cell responses in seronegative persons. J Infect Dis. 1997;176:859–866.
168. Zibert A, Meisel H, Kraas W, et al. Early antibody response against hypervariable region 1 is associated with acute self-limiting infections of hepatitis C virus. Hepatology. 1997;25:1245–1249.
169. Shimizu YK, Hijikata M, Iwamoto A, et al. Neutralizing antibodies against hepati-

tis C virus and the emergence of neutralization escape mutant viruses. J Virol. 1994;68:1494–1500.

170. Chang KM, Rehermann B, McHutchison JG, et al. Immunological significance of cytotoxic T lymphocyte epitope variants in patients chronically infected by the hepatitis C virus. J Clin Invest. 1997;100:2376–2385.
171. Ray SC, Wang YM, Laeyendecker O, et al. Acute hepatitis C virus structural gene sequences as predictors of persistent viremia: Hypervariable region 1 as decoy. J Virol. 1999;73:2938–2946.
172. Tong MJ, El-Farra NS, Reikes AR, et al. Clinical outcomes after transfusion-associated hepatitis C. N Engl J Med. 1995;332:1463–1466.
173. Kiyosawa K, Sodeyama T, Tanaka E, et al. Interrelationship of blood transfusion, non-A, non-B hepatitis and hepatocellular carcinoma: Analysis by detection of antibody to hepatitis C virus. Hepatology. 1990;12:671–675.
174. Hopf U, Moller B, Kuther D, et al. Long-term follow-up of posttransfusion and sporadic chronic hepatitis non-A, non-B and frequency of circulating antibodies to hepatitis C virus (HCV). J Hepatol. 1990;10:69–76.
175. Di Bisceglie AM, Goodman ZD, Ishak KG, et al. Long-term clinical and histopathological follow-up of chronic posttransfusion hepatitis. Hepatology. 1991;14:969–974.
176. Tremolada F, Casarin C, Alberti A, et al. Long-term follow-up of non-A, non-B (type C) post-transfusion hepatitis. J Hepatol. 1992;16:273–281.
177. Koretz RL, Abbey H, Coleman E, et al. Non-A, non-B post-transfusion hepatitis. Looking back in the second decade. Ann Intern Med. 1993;119:110–115.
178. Seeff LB. Natural history of hepatitis C. Hepatology. 1997;26:21S–28S.
179. Kenny-Walsh E. Clinical outcomes after hepatitis C infection from contaminated anti-D immune globulin. Irish Hepatology Research Group. N Engl J Med. 1999;340:1228–1233.
180. Seeff LB, Buskell-Bales ZB, Wright EC, et al. Long-term mortality after transfusion-associated non-A, non-B hepatitis. N Engl J Med. 1992;327:1906–1911.
181. Fattovich G, Giustina G, Degos F, et al. Morbidity and mortality in compensated cirrhosis C: A follow-up study of 384 patients. Gastroenterology. 1997;112:463–472.
182. Colombo M, De Franchis R, Del Ninno E, et al. Hepatocellular carcinoma in Italian patients with cirrhosis. N Engl J Med. 1991;325:675–680.
183. Tsukuma H, Hiyama T, Tanaka S, et al. Risk factors for hepatocellular carcinoma among patients with chronic liver disease. N Engl J Med. 1993;328:1797–1801.
184. Coelho-Little ME, Jeffers LJ, Bernstein DE, et al. Hepatitis C virus in alcoholic patients with and without clinically apparent liver disease. Alcohol. 1995;19:1173–1176.
185. Corrao G, Aricò S. Independent and combined action of hepatitis C virus infection and alcohol consumption on the risk of symptomatic liver cirrhosis. Hepatology. 1998;27:914–919.
186. Fong TL, Kanel GC, Conrad A, et al. Clinical significance of concomitant hepatitis C infection in patients with alcoholic liver disease. Hepatology. 1994;19:554–557.
187. Ostapowicz G, Watson KJR, Locarnini SA, et al. Role of alcohol in the progression of liver disease caused by hepatitis C virus infection. Hepatology. 1998;27:1730–1735.
188. Pessione F, Degos F, Marcellin P, et al. Effect of alcohol consumption on serum hepatitis C virus RNA and histological lesions in chronic hepatitis C. Hepatology. 1998;27:1717–1722.
189. Schiff ER. Hepatitis C and alcohol. Hepatology. 1997;26:39S–42S.
190. Fong T-L, Di Bisceglie AM, Waggoner JG, et al. The significance of antibody to hepatitis C virus in patients with chronic hepatitis B. Hepatology. 1991;14:64–67.
191. Chiba T, Matsuzaki Y, Abei M, et al. The role of previous hepatitis B virus infection and heavy smoking in hepatitis C virus–related hepatocellular carcinoma. Am J Gastroenterol. 1996;91:1195–1203.
192. Benvegnù L, Fattovich G, Noventa F, et al. Concurrent hepatitis B and C virus infection and risk of hepatocellular carcinoma in cirrhosis: A prospective study. Cancer. 1994;74:2442–2448.
193. Enomoto M, Nishiguchi S, Fukuda K, et al. Characteristics of patients with hepatitis C virus with and without GB virus C/hepatitis G virus co-infection and efficacy of interferon alfa-2b. Hepatology. 1998;27:1388–1393.
194. Laskus T, Radkowski M, Wang LF, et al. Lack of evidence for hepatitis G virus replication in the livers of patients coinfected with hepatitis C and G viruses. J Virol. 1997;71:7804–7806.
195. Eyster ME, Diamondstone LS, Lien JM, et al. Natural history of hepatitis C virus infection in multitransfused hemophiliacs: Effect of coinfection with human immunodeficiency virus. The Multicenter Hemophilia Cohort Study. J Acquir Immune Defic Syndr. 1993;6:602–610.
196. Thomas DL, Shih JW, Alter HJ, et al. Effect of human immunodeficiency virus on hepatitis C virus infection among injecting drug users. J Infect Dis. 1996;174:690–695.
197. Sherman KE, O'Brien J, Gutierrez AG, et al. Quantitative evaluation of hepatitis C virus RNA in patients with concurrent human immunodeficiency virus infections. J Clin Microbiol. 1993;31:2679–2682.
198. Bierhoff E, Fischer HP, Willsch E, et al. Liver histopathology in patients with concurrent chronic hepatitis C and HIV infection. Virchows Arch Int. J Pathol. 1997;430:271–277.
199. Darby SC, Ewart DW, Giangrande PL, et al. Mortality from liver cancer and liver disease in haemophilic men and boys in UK given blood products contaminated with hepatitis C. Lancet. 1997;350:1425–1431.
200. García-Samaniego J, Soriano V, Castilla J, et al. Influence of hepatitis C virus genotypes and HIV infection on histological severity of chronic hepatitis C. Am J Gastroenterol. 1997;92:1130–1134.
201. Bjoro K, Froland SS, Yun Z, et al. Hepatitis C infection in patients with primary hypogammaglobulinemia after treatment with contaminated immune globulin. N Engl J Med. 1994;331:1607–1611.
202. Gretch DR, Bacchi CE, Corey L, et al. Persistent hepatitis C virus infection after liver transplantation: Clinical and virological features. Hepatology. 1995;22:1–9.
203. Collier J, Heathcote J. Hepatitis C viral infection in the immunosuppressed patient. Hepatology. 1998;27:2–6.
204. Bortolotti F, Resti M, Giacchino R, et al. Hepatitis C virus infection and related liver disease in children of mothers with antibodies to the virus. J Pediatr. 1997;130:990–993.
205. Chang M-H, Ni Y-H, Hwang L-H, et al. Long term clinical and virologic outcome of primary hepatitis C virus infection in children: A prospective study. Pediatr Infect Dis J. 1994;13:769–773.
206. Kage M, Fujisawa T, Shiraki K, et al. Pathology of chronic hepatitis C in children. Child Liver Study Group of Japan. Hepatology. 1997;26:771–775.
207. Ni YH, Chang MH, Lin KH, et al. Hepatitis C viral infection in thalassemic children: Clinical and molecular studies. Pediatr Res. 1996;39:323–328.
208. Poynard T, Bedossa P, Opolon P. Natural history of liver fibrosis progression in patients with chronic hepatitis C. Lancet. 1997;349:825–832.
209. Aikawa T, Kojima M, Onishi H, et al. HLA DRB1 and DQB1 alleles and haplotypes influencing the progression of hepatitis C. J Med Virol. 1996;49:274–278.
210. Higashi Y, Kamikawaji N, Suko H, et al. Analysis of HLA alleles in Japanese patients with cirrhosis due to chronic hepatitis C. Gastroenterol Hepatol. 1996;11:241–246.
211. Kuzushita N, Hayashi N, Katayama K, et al. Increased frequency of HLA DR13 in hepatitis C virus carriers with persistently normal ALT levels. J Med Virol. 1996;48:1–7.
212. Kuzushita N, Hayashi N, Moribe T, et al. Influence of HLA haplotypes on the clinical courses of individuals infected with hepatitis C virus. Hepatology. 1998;27:240–244.
213. Hiramatsu N, Hayashi N, Katayama K, et al. Immunohistochemical detection of Fas antigen in liver tissue of patients with chronic hepatitis C. Hepatology. 1994;19:1354–1359.
214. Napoli J, Bishop GA, McGuinness PH, et al. Progressive liver injury in chronic hepatitis C infection correlates with increased intrahepatic expression of Th1-associated cytokines. Hepatology. 1996;24:759–765.
215. Ruggieri A, Harada T, Matsuura Y, et al. Sensitization to Fas-mediated apoptosis by hepatitis C virus core protein. Virology. 1997;229:68–76.
216. Nousbaum J-B, Pol S, Nalpas B, et al. Hepatitis C virus type 1b (II) infection in France and Italy. Ann Intern Med. 1995;122:161–168.
217. Koizumi K, Enomoto N, Kurosaki M, et al. Diversity of quasispecies in various disease stages of chronic hepatitis C virus infection and its significance in interferon treatment. Hepatology. 1995;22:30–35.
218. Gretch D, Corey L, Wilson J, et al. Assessment of hepatitis C virus RNA levels by quantitative competitive RNA polymerase chain reaction: High titer viremia correlates with advanced stage of disease. J Infect Dis. 1994;169:1219–1225.
219. Gordon SC, Elloway RS, Long JC, et al. The pathology of hepatitis C as a function of mode of transmission: Blood transfusion vs. intravenous drug use. Hepatology. 1993;18:1338–1343.
220. Roudot-Thoraval F, Bastie A, Pawlotsky JM, et al. Epidemiological factors affecting the severity of hepatitis C virus–related liver disease: A French survey of 6,664 patients. The Study Group for the Prevalence and the Epidemiology of Hepatitis C Virus. Hepatology. 1997;26:485–490.
221. Saito I, Miyamura T, Ohbayashi A, et al. Hepatitis C virus infection is associated with the development of hepatocellular carcinoma. Proc Natl Acad Sci U S A. 1990;87:6547–6549.
222. Bukh J, Miller RH, Kew MC, et al. Hepatitis C virus RNA in southern African blacks with hepatocellular carcinoma. Proc Natl Acad Sci U S A. 1993;90:1848–1851.
223. Bruno S, Silini E, Crosignani A, et al. Hepatitis C virus genotypes and risk of hepatocellular carcinoma in cirrhosis: A prospective study. Hepatology. 1997;25:754–758.
224. Simonetti RG, Camma C, Fiorello F, et al. Hepatitis C virus infection as a risk factor for hepatocellular carcinoma in patients with cirrhosis. Ann Intern Med. 1992;116:97–102.
225. Edamoto Y, Tani M, Kurata T, et al. Hepatitis C and B virus infections in hepatocellular carcinoma—*Analysis of direct detection of viral genome in paraffin embedded tissues.* Cancer. 1996;77:1787–1791.
226. Kiyosawa K, Furuta S. Hepatitis C virus and hepatocellular carcinoma. Curr Stud Hematol Blood Transfus. 1994;61:98–120.
227. Zein NN, Poterucha JJ, Gross JB Jr, et al. Increased risk of hepatocellular carcinoma in patients infected with hepatitis C genotype 1b. Am J Gastroenterol. 1996;91:2560–2562.
228. Yu MC, Yuan JM, Ross RK, et al. Presence of antibodies to the hepatitis B surface antigen is associated with an excess risk for hepatocellular carcinoma among non-Asians in Los Angeles county, California. Hepatology. 1997;25:226–228.
229. Nakamoto Y, Guidotti LG, Kuhlen CV, et al. Immune pathogenesis of hepatocellular carcinoma. J Exp Med. 1998;188:341–350.
230. Di Bisceglie AM. Hepatitis C and hepatocellular carcinoma. Hepatology. 1997;26:34S–38S.
231. Kew MC, Yu MC, Kedda MA, et al. The relative roles of hepatitis B and C viruses in the etiology of hepatocellular carcinoma in southern African blacks. Gastroenterology. 1997;112:184–187.
232. Silini E, Bottelli R, Asti M, et al. Hepatitis C virus genotypes and risk of hepatocellular carcinoma in cirrhosis: A case-control study. Gastroenterology. 1996;111:199–205.
233. Aach RD, Stevens CE, Hollinger FB, et al. Hepatitis C virus infection in post-transfusion hepatitis. N Engl J Med. 1991;325:1325–1329.

234. Alter HJ, Purcell RH, Shih JW, et al. Detection of antibody to hepatitis C virus in prospectively followed transfusion recipients with acute and chronic non-A, non-B, hepatitis. N Engl J Med. 1989;321:1494–1500.
235. Yanagi M, Kaneko S, Unoura M, et al. Hepatitis C virus in fulminant hepatic failure (letter). N Engl J Med. 1991;324:1895–1896.
236. Farci P, Alter HJ, Shimoda A, et al. Hepatitis C virus–associated fulminant hepatic failure. N Engl J Med. 1996;335:631–634.
237. Wright TL, Hsu H, Donegan E, et al. Hepatitis C virus not found in fulminant non-A, non-B hepatitis. Ann Intern Med. 1991;115:111–112.
238. Vento S, Garofano T, Renzini C, et al. Fulminant hepatitis associated with hepatitis A virus superinfection in patients with chronic hepatitis C. N Engl J Med. 1998;338:286–290.
239. Foster GR, Goldin RD, Thomas HC. Chronic hepatitis C virus infection causes a significant reduction in quality of life in the absence of cirrhosis. Hepatology. 1998;27:209–212.
240. Conry-Cantilena C, Vanraden MT, Gibble J, et al. Routes of infection, viremia, and liver disease in blood donors found to have hepatitis C virus infection. N Engl J Med. 1996;334:1691–1696.
241. Inglesby TV, Rai RM, Astemborski J, et al. A prospective community-based evaluation of liver enzymes in individuals with hepatitis C. Hepatology. 1998;29:590–596.
242. Perrillo RP. The role of liver biopsy in hepatitis C. Hepatology. 1997;26:57S–61S.
243. Goodman ZD, Ishak KG. Histopathology of hepatitis C virus infection. Semin. Liver Dis. 1995;15:70–81.
244. Shakil AO, Conry-Cantilena C, Alter HJ, et al. Volunteer blood donors with antibody to hepatitis C virus: Clinical, biochemical, virologic, and histologic features. Ann. Intern. Med. 1995;123:330–337.
245. Agnello V, Chung RT, Kaplan LM. A role for hepatitis C virus infection in type II cryoglobulinemia. N. Engl. J. Med. 1992;327:1490–1495.
246. Misiani R, Bellavita P, Fenili D, et al. Hepatitis C virus infection in patients with essential mixed cryoglobulinemia. Ann Intern Med. 1992;117:573–577.
247. Johnson RJ, Gretch DR, Yamabe H, et al. Membranoproliferative glomerulonephritis associated with hepatitis C virus infection. N. Engl. J. Med. 1993;328:465–470.
248. Fargion S, Piperno A, Cappellini MD, et al. Hepatitis C virus and porphyria cutanea tarda: Evidence of a strong association. Hepatology. 1992;16:1322–1326.
249. Herrero C, Vicente A, Bruguera M, et al. Is hepatitis C virus infection a trigger of porphyria cutanea tarda? Lancet. 1993;341:788–789.
250. DeCastro M, Sanchez J, Herrera JF, et al. Hepatitis C virus antibodies and liver disease in patients with porphyria cutanea tarda. Hepatology. 1993;17:551–557.
251. Gumber SC, Chopra S. Hepatitis C: A multifaceted disease—review of extrahepatic manifestations. Ann. Intern. Med. 1995;123:615–620.
252. Tran A, Quaranta JF, Benzaken S, et al. High prevalence of thyroid autoantibodies in a prospective series of patients with chronic hepatitis C before interferon therapy. Hepatology. 1993;18:253–257.
253. Kuo G, Choo Q-L, Alter HJ et al. An assay for circulating antibodies to a major etiologic virus of human non-A, non-B hepatitis. Science. 1989;244:362–364.
254. McHutchinson JG, Person JL, Govindarajan S, et al. Improved detection of hepatitis C virus antibodies in high-risk populations. Hepatology. 1992;15:19–25.
255. Nakatsuji Y, Matsumoto A, Tanaka E, et al. Detection of chronic hepatitis C virus infection by four diagnostic systems: First-generation and second-generation enzyme-linked immunosorbent assay, second-generation recombinant immunoblot assay and nested polymerase chain reaction analysis. Hepatology. 1992;16:300–305.
256. Chien DY, Choo QL, Tabrizi A, et al. Diagnosis of hepatitis C virus (HCV) infection using an immunodominant chimeric polyprotein to capture circulating antibodies: Reevaluation of the role of HCV in liver disease. Proc Natl Acad Sci U S A. 1992;89:10,011–10,015.
257. Courouсé A-M, Le Marrec N, Girault A, et al. Anti-hepatitis C virus (anti-HCV) seroconversion in patients undergoing hemodialysis: Comparison of second- and third-generation anti-HCV assays. Transfusion. 1994;34:790–795.
258. Gretch DR. Diagnostic tests for hepatitis C. Hepatology. 1997;26:43S–47S.
259. Van der Poel CL, Cuypers HTM, Reesink HW, et al. Confirmation of hepatitis C virus infection by new four-antigen recombinant immunoblot assay. Lancet. 1991;337:317–319.
260. Buffet C, Charnaux N, Laurent-Puig P, et al. Enhanced detection of antibodies to hepatitis C virus by use of a third-generation recombinant immunoblot assay. J Med Virol. 1994;43:259–261.
261. McGuinness PH, Bishop GA, Lien A, et al. Detection of serum hepatitis C virus RNA in HCV antibody–seropositive volunteer blood donors. Hepatology. 1993;18:485–490.
262. Vrielink H, van der Poel CL, Reesink HW, et al. Look-back study of infectivity of anti-HCV ELISA-positive blood components. Lancet. 1995;345:95–96.
263. Damen M, Zaaijer HL, Cuypers HTM, et al. Reliability of the third-generation recombinant immunoblot assay for hepatitis C virus. Transfusion. 1995;35:745–749.
264. Lau JY, Davis GL, Kniffen J, et al. Significance of serum hepatitis C virus RNA levels in chronic hepatitis C. Lancet. 1993;341:1501–1504.
265. Abdel-Hamid M, Edelman R, Constantine N. Optimization, assessment and proposed use of a direct nested reverse transcription-polymerase chain reaction protocal of the detection of hepatitis C virus. Hum Virol. 1997;1:58–65.
266. Zaaijer HL, Cuypers HTM, Reesink HW, et al. Reliability of polymerase chain reaction for detection of hepatitis C virus. Lancet. 1993;341:722–724.
267. Adinolfi LE, Andreana A, Utili R, et al. HCV RNA levels in serum, liver, and peripheral blood mononuclear cells of chronic hepatitis C patients and their relationship to liver injury. Am J Gastroenterol. 1998;93:2162–2166.
268. Martin J, Navas S, Quiroga JA, et al. Quantitation of hepatitis C virus in liver and peripheral blood mononuclear cells from patients with chronic hepatitis C virus infection. J Med Virol. 1998;54:265–270.
269. Terrault NA, Dailey PJ, Ferrell L, et al. Hepatitis C virus: Quantitation and distribution in liver. J Med Virol. 1997;51:217–224.
270. Bresters D, Cuypers HT, Reesink HW, et al. Comparison of quantitative cDNA-PCR with the branched DNA hybridization assay for monitoring plasma hepatitis C virus RNA levels in haemophilia patients participating in a controlled interferon trial. J Med Virol. 1994;43:262–268.
271. Gretch DR, Dela Rosa C, Carithers RL Jr, et al. Assessment of hepatitis C viremia using molecular amplification technologies: Correlations and clinical implications. Ann Intern Med. 1995;123:321–329.
272. Miskovsky EP, Carella AV, Gutekunst K, et al. Clinical characterization of a competitive PCR assay for quantitative testing of hepatitis C virus. J Clin Microbiol. 1996;34:1975–1979.
273. Morris T, Robertson B, Gallagher M. Rapid reverse transcription–PCR detection of hepatitis C virus RNA in serum by using the TaqMan fluorogenic detection system. J Clin Microbiol. 1996;34:2933–2936.
274. Kaneko S, Murakami S, Unoura M, et al. Quantitation of hepatitis C virus RNA by competitive polymerase chain reaction. J Med Virol. 1992;37:278–282.
275. Davis GL, Lau JYN, Urdea MS, et al. Quantitative detection of hepatitis C virus RNA with a solid-phase signal amplification method: Definition of optimal conditions for specimen collection and clinical application in interferon-treated patients. Hepatology. 1994;19:1337–1341.
276. Gordon SC, Dailey PJ, Silverman AL, et al. Sequential serum hepatitis C viral RNA levels longitudinally assessed by branched DNA signal amplification. Hepatology. 1998;28:1702–1706.
277. Nguyen TT, Sedghi-Vaziri A, Wilkes LB, et al. Fluctuations in viral load (HCV RNA) are relatively insignificant in untreated patients with chronic HCV infection. J Viral. Hepat. 1996;3:75–78.
278. Stuyver L, Rossau R, Wyseur A et al. Typing of hepatitis C virus isolates and characterization of new subtypes using a line probe assay. J Gen Virol. 1993;74:1093–1102.
279. Stuyver L, Wyseur A, Van Arnhem W, et al. Second-generation line probe assay for hepatitis C virus genotyping. J Clin Microbiol. 1996;34:2259–2266.
280. Thiers V, Jaffredo F, Tuveri R, et al. Development of a simple restriction fragment length polymorphism (RFLP) based assay for HCV genotyping and comparative analysis with genotyping and serotyping tests. J Virol Methods. 1997;65:9–17.
281. Widell A, Shev S, Mansson S, et al. Genotyping of hepatitis C virus isolates by a modified polymerase chain reaction assay using type specific primers: Epidemiological applications. J Med Virol. 1994;44:272–279.
282. Knodell RG, Ishak KG, Black WC, et al. Formulation and application of a numerical scoring system for assessing histological activity in asymptomatic chronic active hepatitis. Hepatology. 1981;1:431–435.
283. Desmet VJ, Gerber M, Hoofnagle JH, et al. Classification of chronic hepatitis: Diagnosis, grading and staging. Hepatology. 1994;19:1513–1520.
284. Goldin RD, Goldin JG, Burt AD, et al. Intra-observer and inter-observer variation in the histopathological assessment of chronic viral hepatitis. J Hepatol. 1996;25:649–654.
285. McGill DB, Rakela J, Sinsmeister AR, et al. A 21-year experience with major hemorrhage after percutaneous liver biopsy. Gastroenterology. 1990;99:1392–1400.
285a. Everhart JE, Stolar M, Hoofnagle JH. Management of hepatitis C: A national survey of gastroenterologists and hepatologists. Hepatology. 1997;26:78S–82S.
286. World Health Organization. Hepatitis C: Global prevalence. Wkly Epidemiol Rec. 1997;341–348.
287. Alter MJ, Kruszon-Moran D, Nainan OV, et al. The prevalence of hepatitis C virus infection in the United States, 1988 through 1994. N Engl J Med. 1999;341:556–562.
288. Arthur RR, Hassan NF, Abdallah MY, et al. Hepatitis C antibody prevalence in blood donors in different governorates in Egypt. Trans R Soc Trop Med Hyg. 1997;91:271–274.
289. Abdel-Wahab MF, Zakaria S, Kamel M, et al. High seroprevalence of hepatitis C infection among risk groups in Egypt Am J Trop Med Hyg. 1994;51:563–567.
290. Kamel MA, Ghaffar YA, Wasef MA, et al. High HCV prevalence in Egyptian blood donors (Letter; Comment). Lancet. 1992;340:427–427.
291. Darwish MA, Raouf TA, Rushdy P, et al. Risk factors associated with a high seroprevalence of hepatitis C virus infection in Egyptian blood donors. Am J Trop Med Hyg. 1993;49:440–447.
292. Hibbs RG, Corwin AL, Hassan NF, et al. The epidemiology of antibody to hepatitis C in Egypt (Letter). J Infect Dis. 1993;168:789–790.
293. El-Sayed NM, Gomatos PJ, Rodier GR, et al. Seroprevalence survey of Egyptian tourism workers for hepatitis B virus, hepatitis C virus, human immunodeficiency virus, and *Treponema pallidum* infections: Association of hepatitis C virus infections with specific regions of Egypt. Am J Trop Med Hyg. 1996;55:179–184.
294. Osella AR, Misciagna G, Leone A, et al. Epidemiology of hepatitis C virus infection in an area of southern Italy. J Hepatol. 1997;27:30–35.
295. Chiaramonte M, Stroffolini T, Lorenzoni U, et al. Risk factors in community-acquired chronic hepatitis C virus infection: A case-control study in Italy. J Hepatol. 1996;24:129–134.
296. Nakashima K, Ikematsu H, Hayashi J, et al. Intrafamilial transmission of hepatitis C virus among the population of an endemic area of Japan. JAMA. 1995;274:1459–1461.
297. Guadagnino V, Stroffolini T, Rapicetta M, et al. Prevalence, risk factors, and genotype distribution of hepatitis C virus infection in the general population: A community-based survey in southern Italy. Hepatology. 1997;26:1006–1011.
298. Prati D, Capelli C, Silvani C, et al. The incidence and risk factors of community-acquired hepatitis C in a cohort of Italian blood donors. Hepatology. 1997;25:702–704.

299. Noguchi S, Sata M, Suzuki H, et al. Routes of transmission of hepatitis C virus in an endemic rural area of Japan—Molecular epidemiologic study of hepatitis C virus infection. Scand. J Infect Dis. 1997;29:23–28.
300. Kiyosawa K, Tanaka E, Sodeyama T, et al. Transmission of hepatitis C in an isolated area in Japan: Community-acquired infection. Gastroenterology. 1994;106:1596–1602.
301. Thomas DL, Cannon RO, Shapiro C, et al. J Infect Dis. 1994;169:990–995.
302. Kelen GD, Green GB, Purcell RH, et al. Hepatitis B and hepatitis C in emergency department patients. N Engl J Med. 1992;326:1399–1404.
303. Alter MJ. Epidemiology of hepatitis C in the West. Semin Liver Dis. 1995;15:5–14.
304. Centers for Disease Control and Prevention. Recommendations for prevention and control of hepatitis C virus (HCV) infection and HCV-related chronic disease. MMWR Morb Mortal Wkly Rep. 1998;47:1–39.
305. Alter MJ, Hadler SC, Judson FN, et al. Risk factors for acute non-A, non-B hepatitis in the United States and association with hepatitis C virus infection. JAMA. 1990;264:2231–2235.
306. Alter MJ. Epidemiology of hepatitis C. Hepatology. 1997;26:62S–65S.
307. Alter MJ, Mast EE, Moyer LA, et al. Hepatitis C. Infect Dis Clin North Am. 1998;12:13–26.
308. Sartori M, La Terra G, Aglietta M, et al. Transmission of hepatitis C via blood splash into conjunctiva. Scand J Infect Dis. 1993;25:270–271.
309. Esteban JI, Lopez-Talavera JC, Genesca J, et al. High rate of infectivity and liver disease in blood donors with antibodies to hepatitis C virus. Ann Intern Med. 1991;115:443–449.
310. Lai ME, Mazzoleni AP, Argiolu F, et al. Hepatitis C virus in multiple episodes of acute hepatitis in polytransfused thalassaemic children. Lancet. 1994;343:388–390.
311. De Montalembert M, Costagliola DG, Lefrere JJ, et al. Prevalence of markers for human immunodeficiency virus types 1 and 2, human T-lymphotropic virus type I, cytomegalovirus, and hepatitis B and C virus in multiply transfused thalassemia patients. The French Study Group on Thalassaemia. Transfusion. 1992;32:509–512.
312. Brettler DB, Alter HJ, Dienstag JL, et al. Prevalence of hepatitis C virus antibody in a cohort of hemophilia patients. Blood. 1990;76:254–256.
313. Centers for Disease Control and Prevention. Public Health Service interagency guidelines for screening blood, plasma, organs, tissue and semen for evidence of hepatitis B and C. MMWR. 1991;40:1–23.
314. Donahue JG, Munoz A, Ness PM, et al. The declining risk of post-transfusion hepatitis C virus infection. N Engl J Med. 1992;327:369–363.
315. Blajchman MA, Bull SB, Feinman SV. Post-transfusion hepatitis: Impact of non-A, non-B hepatitis surrogate tests. Lancet. 1995;345:21–25.
316. Widell A, Elmud H, Persson MH, et al. Transmission of hepatitis C via both erythrocyte and platelet transfusions from a single donor in serological window–phase of hepatitis C. Vox Sang. 1996;71:55–57.
317. Schreiber GB, Busch MP, Kleinman SH, et al. The risk of transfusion-transmitted viral infections. The Retrovirus Epidemiology Donor Study. N Engl J Med. 1996;334:1685–1690.
318. Blanchette V, Walker I, Gill P, et al. Hepatitis C infection in patients with hemophilia: Results of a national survey. Canadian Hemophilia Clinic Directors Group. Transfus Med Rev. 1994;8:210–217.
319. Kinoshita T, Miyake K, Okamoto H, et al. Imported hepatitis C virus genotypes in Japanese hemophiliacs (Letter). J Infect Dis. 1993;168:249–250.
320. Morfini M, Mannucci PM, Ciavarella N, et al. Prevalence of infection with the hepatitis C virus among Italian hemophiliacs before and after the introduction of virally inactivated clotting factor concentrates: A retrospective evaluation. Vox Sang. 1994;67:178–182.
321. Yap PL, McOmish F, Webster ADB, et al. Hepatitis C virus transmission by intravenous immunoglobulin. J Hepatol. 1994;21:455–460.
322. Power JP, Lawlor E, Davidson F. Hepatitis C viraemia in recipients of Irish intravenous anti-D immunoglobulin. Lancet. 1994;344:1166–1167.
323. Bresee JS, Mast EE, Coleman FJ, et al. Hepatitis C virus infection associated with administration of intravenous immune globulin—a cohort study. JAMA. 1996;276:1563–1567.
324. Pereira BJG, Milford EL, Kirkman RL, et al. Prevealence of hepatitis C virus RNA in organ donors positive for hepatitis C antibody and in the recipients of their organs. N Engl J Med. 1992;327:910–915.
325. Terrault NA, Wright TL. Hepatitis C virus in the setting of transplantation. Semin Liver Dis. 1995;15:92–100.
326. Pereira BJG, Milford EL, Kirkman RL, et al. Transmission of hepatitis C virus by organ transplantation. N Engl J Med. 1991;325:454–460.
327. Konig V, Bauditz J, Lobeck H, et al. Hepatitis C virus reinfection in allografts after orthotopic liver transplantation. Hepatology. 1992;16:1137–1143.
328. Thomas DL, Vlahov D, Solomon L, et al. Correlates of hepatitis C virus infections among injection drug users in Baltimore. Medicine. 1995;74:212–220.
329. Bolumar F, Hernandez-Aguado I, Ferrer L, et al. Prevalence of antibodies to hepatitis C in a population of intravenous drug users in Valencia, Spain, 1990–1992. Int J Epidemiol. 1996;25:204–209.
330. Girardi E, Zaccarelli M, Tossini G, et al. Hepatitis C virus infection in intravenous drug users: Prevalence and risk factors. Scand J Infect Dis. 1990;22:751–752.
331. Bell J, Batey RG, Farrell GC, et al. Hepatitis C virus in intravenous drug users. Med J Aust. 1990;153:274–276.
332. Van Ameijden EJ, van den Hoek JA, Mientjes GH, et al. A longitudinal study on the incidence and transmission patterns of HIV, HBV and HCV infection among drug users in Amsterdam. Eur J Epidemiol. 1993;9:255–262.
333. Patti AM, Santi AL, Pompa MG, et al. Viral hepatitis and drugs: A continuing problem. Int J Epidemiol. 1993;22:135–139.
334. Garfein RS, Vlahov D, Galai N, et al. Viral infections in short-term injection drug users: The prevalence of the hepatitis C, hepatitis B, human immunodeficiency, and human T-lymphotropic viruses. Am J Public Health. 1996;86:655–661.
335. Hagan H, Jarlais DCD, Friedman SR, et al. Reduced risk of hepatitis B and hepatitis C among injection drug users in the Tacoma syringe exchange program. Am J Public Health. 1995;85:1531–1537.
336. Hagan H, McGough JP, Thiede H, et al. Syringe exchange and risk of infection with hepatitis B and C viruses. Am J Epidemiol. 1999;149:203–213.
337. Ko YC, Ho MS, Chiang TA, et al. Tattooing as a risk of hepatitis C virus infection. J Med Virol. 1992;38:288–291.
338. Sun DX, Zhang FG, Geng YQ, et al. Hepatitis C transmission by cosmetic tattooing in women. Lancet. 1996;347:541–541.
339. Dusheiko GM, Smith M, Scheuer PJ. Hepatitis C virus transmission by human bite. Lancet. 1990;336:503–504.
340. Bronowicki JP, Venard V, Botté C, et al. Patient-to-patient transmission of hepatitis C virus during colonoscopy. N Engl J Med. 1997;337:237–240.
341. Allander T, Gruber A, Naghavi M, et al. Frequent patient-to-patient transmission of hepatitis C virus in a haematology ward. Lancet. 1995;345:603–607.
342. Schvarcz R, Johansson B, Nyström B, et al. Nosocomial transmission of hepatitis C virus. Infection. 1997;25:74–77.
343. Munro J, Biggs JD, McCruden EAB. Detection of a cluster of hepatitis C infections in a renal transplant unit by analysis of sequence variation of the *NS5a* gene. J Infect Dis. 1996;174:177–180.
344. Stuyver L, Claeys H, Wyseur A, et al. Hepatitis C virus in a hemodialysis unit: Molecular evidence for nosocomial transmission. Kidney Int. 1996;49:889–895.
345. Sampietro M, Badalamenti S, Salvadori S, et al. High prevalence of a rare hepatitis C virus in patients treated in the same hemodialysis unit: Evidence for nosocomial transmission of HCV. Kidney Int. 1995;47:911–917.
346. Kiyosawa K, Sodeyama T, Tanaka E, et al. Hepatitis C in hospital employees with needlestick injuries. Ann Intern Med. 1991;115:367–369.
347. Ridzon R, Gallagher K, Ciesielski C, et al. Simultaneous transmission of human immunodeficiency virus and hepatitis C virus from a needle-stick injury. N Engl J Med. 1997;336:919–922.
348. Mitsui T, Iwano K, Masuko K, et al. Hepatitis C virus infection in medical personnel after needlestick accident. Hepatology. 1992;16:1109–1114.
349. Seeff LB, Wright EC, Zimmerman HJ, et al. Type B hepatitis after needle-stick exposure: Prevention with hepatitis B immune globulin. Ann Intern Med. 1978;88:285–293.
350. Thomas DL, Gruninger SE, Siew C, et al. Occupational risk of hepatitis C infections among general dentists and oral surgeons in North America. Am J Med. 1996;100:41–45.
351. Thomas DL, Factor S, Kelen G, et al. Hepatitis B and C in health care workers at the Johns Hopkins Hospital. Arch Intern Med. 1993;153:1705–1712.
352. Gerberding JL, Incidence and prevalence of human immunodeficiency virus, hepatitis B virus, hepatitis C virus, and cytomegalovirus among health care personnel at risk for blood exposure: Final report from a longitudinal study. J Infect Dis. 1994;170:1410–1417.
353. Kuo MY, Hahn LJ, Hong CY, et al. Low prevalence of hepatitis C virus infection among dentists in Taiwan. J Med Virol. 1993;40:10–13.
354. Campello C, Majori S, Poli A, et al. Prevalence of HCV antibodies in health-care workers from northern Italy. Infection. 1992;20:224–226.
355. Polish LB, Tong MJ, Co RL, et al. Risk factors for hepatitis C virus infection among health care personnel in a community hospital. Am J Infect Control. 1993;21:196–200.
356. Puro V, Petrosillo N, Ippolito G, et al. Occupational hepatitis C virus infection in Italian health care workers. Am J Public Health. 1995;85:1272–1275.
357. Esteban JI, Gómez J, Martell M, et al. Transmission of hepatitis C virus by a cardiac surgeon. N Engl J Med. 1996;334:555–560.
358. Thomas DL, Zenilman JZ, Alter HJ, et al. Sexual transmission of hepatitis C virus among patients attending Baltimore sexually transmitted diseases clinics—an analysis of 309 sexual partnerships. J Infect Dis. 1995;171:768–775.
359. Van Doornum GJJ, Hooykaas C, Cuypers MT, et al. Prevalence of hepatitis C virus infections among heterosexuals with multiple partners. J Med Virol. 1991;35:22–27.
360. Petersen EE, Clemens R, Bock HL, et al. Hepatitis B and C in heterosexual patients with various sexually transmitted diseases. Infection. 1992;20:128–131.
361. Nakashima K, Kashiwagi S, Hayashi J, et al. Sexual transmission of hepatitis C virus among female prostitutes and patients with sexually transmitted diseases in Fukuoka, Kyushu, Japan. Am J Epidemiol. 1992;136:1132–1137.
362. Utsumi T, Hashimoto E, Okumura Y, et al. Heterosexual activity as a risk factor for the transmission of hepatitis C virus. J Med Virol. 1995;46:122–125.
363. Capelli C, Prati D, Bosoni P, et al. Sexual transmission of hepatitis C virus to a repeat blood donor. Transfusion. 1997;37:436–440.
364. Healey CJ, Smith DB, Walker JL, et al. Acute hepatitis C infection after sexual exposure. Gut. 1995;36:148–150.
365. Akahane Y, Kojima M, Sugai Y, et al. Hepatitis C virus infection in spouses of patients with type C chronic liver disease. Ann Intern Med. 1994;120:748–752.
366. Kao JH, Chen PJ, Yang PM, et al. Intrafamilial transmission of hepatitis C virus: The important role of infections between spouses. J Infect Dis. 1992;166:900–903.
367. Kao JH, Hwang YT, Chen PJ, et al. Transmission of hepatitis C virus between spouses: The important role of exposure duration. Am J Gastroenterol. 1996;91:2087–2090.
368. Chayama K, Kobayashi M, Tsubota A, et al. Molecular analysis of intraspousal transmission of hepatitis C virus. J Hepatol. 1995;22:431–439.
369. Piazza M, Sagliocca L, Tosone G, et al. Sexual transmission of the hepatitis C

virus and efficacy of prophylaxis with intramuscular immune serum globulin—A randomized controlled trial. Arch Intern Med. 1997;157:1537–1544.
370. Nakashima K, Kashiwagi S, Hayashi J, et al. Prevalence of hepatitis C virus infection among female prostitutes in Fukuoka, Japan. J Gastroenterol. 1996;31:664–668.
371. Wu JC, Lin HC, Jeng FS, et al. Prevalence, infectivity, and risk factor analysis of hepatitis C virus infection in prostitutes. J Med Virol. 1993;39:312–317.
372. Bresters D, Mauser-Bunschoten ED, Reesink HW, et al. Sexual transmission of hepatitis C. Lancet. 1993;342:210–211.
373. Everhart JE, Di Bisceglie AM, Murray LM, et al. Risk for non-A, non-B (Type C) hepatitis through sexual or household contact with chronic carriers. Ann Intern Med. 1990;112:544–555.
374. Brettler DB, Mannucci PM, Gringeri A, et al. The low risk of hepatitis C virus transmission among sexual partners of hepatitis C infected hemophilic males: An international, multicenter study. Blood. 1992;80:540–543.
375. Gordon SC, Patel AH, Kulesza GW, et al. Lack of evidence for the heterosexual transmission of hepatitis C. Am J Gastroenterol. 1992;87:1849–1851.
376. Melbye M, Biggar RJ, Wantzin P, et al. Sexual transmission of hepatitis C virus: Cohort study (1981–9) among European homosexual men. BMJ. 1990;301:210–212.
377. Osmond DH, Charlebois E, Sheppard HW, et al. Comparison of risk factors for hepatitis C and hepatitis B virus infection in homosexual men. J Infect Dis. 1993;167:66–71.
378. Bodsworth NJ, Cunningham P, Kaldor J, et al. Hepatitis C virus infection in a large cohort of homosexually active men: Independent associations with HIV-1 infection and injecting drug use but not sexual behaviour. Genitourin Med. 1996;72:118–122.
379. Donahue JG, Nelson KE, Munoz A, et al. Antibody to hepatitis C virus among cardiac surgery patients, homosexual men, and intravenous drug users in Baltimore, Maryland. Am J Epidemiol. 1991;134:1206–1211.
380. Roudot Thoraval F, Pawlotsky JM, Thiers V, et al. Lack of mother-to-infant transmission of hepatitis C virus in human immunodeficiency virus-seronegative women: A prospective study with hepatitis C virus RNA testing. Hepatology. 1993;17:772–777.
381. Reinus JF, Leikin EL, Alter HJ, et al. Failure to detect vertical transmission of hepatitis C virus. Ann Intern Med. 1992;117:881–886.
382. Ohto H, Terazawa S, Nobuhiko S, et al. Transmission of hepatitis C virus from mothers to infants. N Engl J Med. 1994;330:744–750.
383. Zanetti AR, Tanzi E, Paccagnini S, et al. Mother-to-infant transmission of hepatitis C virus. Lancet. 1995;345:289–291.
384. Lam JPH, McOmish F, Burns SM, et al. Infrequent vertical transmission of hepatitis C virus. J Infect Dis. 1993;167:572–576.
385. Novati R, Thiers V, Monforte AD, et al. Mother-to-child transmission of hepatitis C virus detected by nested polymerase chain reaction. J Infect Dis. 1992;165:720–723.
386. Wejstal R, Widell A, Mansson A-S, et al. Mother-to-infant transmission of hepatitis C virus. Ann Intern Med. 1992;117:887–890.
387. Resti M, Azzari C, Mannelli F, et al. Mother to child transmission of hepatitis C virus: Prospective study of risk factors and timing of infection in children born to women seronegative for HIV-1. Tuscany Study Group on Hepatitis C Virus Infection. BMJ. 1998;317:437–441.
388. Thomas DL, Villano SA, Reister K, et al. Perinatal transmission of hepatitis C virus from human immunodeficient virus type 1–infected mothers. J Infect Dis. 1998;177:1480–1488.
389. Ogasawara S, Kage M, Kosai K, et al. Hepatitis C virus RNA in saliva and breastmilk of hepatitis C carrier mothers. Lancet. 1993;341:561–561.
390. Resti M, Azzari C, Lega L, et al. Mother-to-infant transmission of hepatitis C virus. Acta Paediatr. 1995;84:251–255.
391. Lin H-H, Kao J-H, Hsu H-Y, et al. Absence of infection in breast-fed infants born to hepatitis C virus–infected mothers. J Pediatr. 1995;126:589–591.
392. Manzini P, Saracco G, Cerchier A, et al. Human immunodeficiency virus infection as risk factor for mother-to-child hepatitis C virus transmission; persistence of anti-hepatitis C virus in children is associated with the mother's anti-hepatitis C virus immunoblotting pattern. Hepatology. 1995;21:328–332.
393. Paccagnini S, Principi N, Massironi E, et al. Perinatal transmission and manifestation of hepatitis C virus infection in a high risk population. Pediatr Infect Dis J. 1995;14:195–199.
394. Ohto H, Okamoto H, Mishiro S. Vertical transmission of hepatitis C virus (Reply). N Engl J Med. 1994;331:400–400.
395. Kumar RM, Shahul S. Role of breast-feeding in transmission of hepatitis C virus to infants of HCV-infected mothers. J Hepatol. 1998;29:191–197.
396. Hepatitis C virus infection. American Academy of Pediatrics. Committee on Infectious Diseases. Pediatrics. 1998;101:481–485.
397. Dore GJ, Kaldor JM, McCaughan GW. Systematic review of role of polymerase chain reaction in defining infectiousness among people infected with hepatitis C virus. BMJ. 1997;315:333–337.
398. Eyster ME, Alter HJ, Aledort LM, et al. Heterosexual co-transmission of hepatitis C virus (HCV) and human immunodeficiency virus (HIV). Ann Intern Med. 1991;115:764–768.
399. Telfer PT, Brown D, Devereux H, et al. HCV RNA levels and HIV infection: Evidence for a viral interaction in haemophilic patients. Br J Haematol. 1994;88:397–399.
400. Sherman KE, O'Brien J, Gutierrez G, et al. Quantitative evaluation of hepatitis C virus RNA in patients with concurrent human immunodeficiency virus infections. J Clin Microbiol. 1993;31:2679–2682.
401. Eyster ME, Fried MW, Di Bisceglie AM, et al. Increasing hepatitis C virus RNA levels in hemophiliacs: Relationship to human immunodeficiency virus infection and liver disease. Blood. 1994;84:1020–1023.
402. Beld M, Penning M, Lukashov V, et al. Evidence that both HIV and HIV-induced immunodeficiency enhance HCV replication among HCV seroconverters. Virology. 1998;244:504–512.
403. Davis GL, Balart LA, Schiff ER, et al. Treatment of chronic hepatitis C with recombinant interferon alfa-2b. N Engl J Med. 1989;321:1501–1506.
404. Di Bisceglie AM, Martin P, Kassianides C, et al. Recombinant interferon alfa-2b therapy for chronic hepatitis C. N Engl J Med. 1989;321:1506–1510.
405. Poynard T, Bedossa P, Chevallier M, et al. A comparison of three interferon alfa-2b regimens for the long-term treatment of chronic non-A, non-B hepatitis. N Engl J Med. 1995;332:1457–1462.
406. Saez-Royuela F, Porres JC, Moreno A, et al. High doses of recombinant alpha-interferon or gamma-interferon for chronic hepatitis C: A randomized, controlled trial. Hepatology. 1991;13:327–331.
407. Kasahara A, Hayashi N, Mochizuki K, et al. Risk factors for hepatocellular carcinoma and its incidence after interferon treatment in patients with chronic hepatitis C. Hepatology. 1998;27:1394–1402.
408. Serfaty L, Aumaître H, Chazouillères O, et al. Determinants of outcome of compensated hepatitis C virus-related cirrhosis. Hepatology. 1998;27:1435–1440.
409. Keeffe EB, Hollinger FB, Bailey R, et al. Therapy of hepatitis C: Consensus interferon trials. Hepatology. 1997;26:101S–107S.
410. Farrell GC. Therapy of hepatitis C: Interferon alfa-2b-n1 trials. Hepatology. 1997;26:96S–100S.
411. Lee WM. Therapy of hepatitis C: Interferon alfa-2a trials. Hepatology. 1997;26:89S–95S.
412. Tong MJ, Reddy KR, Lee WM, et al. Treatment of chronic hepatitis C with consensus interferon: A multicenter, randomized, controlled trial. Consensus Interferon Study Group. Hepatology. 1997;26:747–754.
413. Marcellin P, Boyer N, Gervais A, et al. Long-term histologic improvement and loss of detectable intrahepatic HCV RNA in patients with chronic hepatitis C and sustained response to interferon-α therapy. Ann Intern Med. 1997;127:875–881.
414. Nishiguchi S, Kuroki T, Nakatani S, et al. Randomised trial of effects of interferon-α on incidence of hepatocellular carcinoma in chronic active hepatitis C with cirrhosis. Lancet. 1995;346:1051–1055.
415. Mazzella G, Accogli E, Sottili S, et al. Alpha interferon treatment may prevent hepatocellular carcinoma in HCV-related liver cirrhosis. J Hepatol. 1996;24:141–147.
416. National Institutes of Health consensus development conference panel statement: Management of hepatitis C. Hepatology. 1997;26:2S–10S.
417. Dusheiko G. Side effects of alpha interferon in chronic hepatitis C. Hepatology. 1997;26:112S–121S.
418. Manesis EK, Moschos M, Brouzas D, et al. Neurovisual impairment: A frequent complication of alpha-interferon treatment in chronic viral hepatitis. Hepatology. 1998;27:1421–1427.
419. Davis GL, Esteban-Muir R, Rustgi VK, et al. Interferon alfa-2b alone or in combination with ribavirin for the treatment of relapse of chronic hepatitis C. N Engl J Med. 1998;339:1493–1499.
420. McHutchison JG, Gordon SC, Schiff ER, et al. Interferon alfa-2b alone or in combination with ribavirin as initial treatment for chronic hepatitis C. N Engl J Med. 1998;339:1485–1492.
421. Patterson JL, Fernandez-Larson R. Molecular mechanisms of action of ribavirin. Rev Infect Dis. 1990;12:1139–1146.
422. Ning Q, Brown D, Parodo J, et al. Ribavirin inhibits viral-induced macrophage production of TNF, IL-1, the procoagulant fgl2 prothrombinase and preserves Th1 cytokine production but inhibits Th2 cytokine response. J Immunol. 1998;160:3487–3493.
423. Poynard T, Marcellin P, Lee SS et al. Randomised trial of interferon alfa-2b ribavirin for 48 weeks or for 24 weeks versus interferon alfa-2b plus placebo for 48 weeks for treatment of chronic infection with hepatitis C virus. Lancet. 1998;352:1426–1432.
424. Bodenheimer HCJ, Lindsay KL, Davis GL, et al. Tolerance and efficacy of oral ribavirin treatment of chronic hepatitis C: A multicenter trial. Hepatology. 1997;26:473–477.
425. Dusheiko G, Main J, Thomas H, et al. Ribavirin treatment for patients with chronic hepatitis C: Results of a placebo-controlled study. J Hepatol. 1996;25:591–598.
426. Di Bisceglie AM, Conjeevaram HS, Fried MW, et al. Ribavirin as therapy for chronic hepatitis C—a randomized, double-blind, placebo-controlled trial. Ann Intern Med. 1995;123:897–903.
427. Reichard O, Norkrans G, Frydén A, et al. Randomised, double-blind, placebo-controlled trial of interferon α-2b with and without ribavirin for chronic hepatitis C. Lancet. 1998;351:83–87.
428. Lee WM, Reddy KR, Tong MJ, et al. Early hepatitis C virus RNA responses predict interferon treatment outcomes in chronic hepatitis C. Hepatology. 1998;28:1411–1415.
429. Tong MJ, Blatt LM, McHutchison JG, et al. Prediction of response during interferon alfa-2b therapy in chronic hepatitis C patients using viral and biochemical characteristics: A comparison. Hepatology. 1997;26:1640–1645.
430. Sherman KE, Sjogren M, Creager RL, et al. Combination therapy with thymosin α1 and interferon for the treatment of chronic hepatitis C infection: A randomized, placebo-controlled double-blind trial. Hepatology. 1998;27:1128–1135.
431. Choo QL, Kuo G, Ralston R, et al. Vaccination of chimpanzees against infection by the hepatitis C virus. Proc Natl Acad Sci U S A. 1994;91:1294–1298.
432. Seeff LB, Zimmerman JH, Wright EL, et al. A randomized double-blind controlled trial of the efficacy of immune serum globulin for the prevention of post-transfusion hepatitis. A Veterans Administration Cooperative Study. Gastroenterology. 1977;72:111–121.

433. Sanchez-Quijano A, Pineda JA, Lissen E, et al. Prevention of post-transfusion non-A, non-B hepatitis by nonspecific immunoglobulin in heart surgery patients. Lancet. 1988;1:1245–1249.
434. Krawczynski K, Alter MJ, Tankersley DL, et al. Effect of immune globulin on the prevention of experimental hepatitis C virus infection. J Infect Dis. 1996;173:822–828.

Chapter **144**

Hepatitis G Virus and TT Virus

HARVEY J. ALTER

DISCOVERY OF THE HEPATITIS G VIRUS AND THE GB AGENT

The "blind" cloning of the hepatitis C virus (HCV)[1] established a new paradigm for viral discovery. With that discovery and others since that time, molecular biology transformed classic virology—allowing for the characterization of agents that have never been visualized, serologically identified, grown in culture, or molecularly defined. Minute quantities of unknown virus can now be vastly amplified with random primers, blindly cloned, and then detected by immunoscreening, as in the case of HCV, the hepatitis E virus (HEV), and the hepatitis G virus (HGV), or by representational difference analysis, as in the case of the GB virus (GBV) types A, B, and C.

The development of sensitive serologic assays to detect antibodies to HCV allowed for wide-scale testing of sera from previously pedigreed cases of transfusion-associated or community-acquired hepatitis that had been classified by exclusion as non-A, non-B hepatitis. It was shown that HCV was the major etiologic agent in these cases, but that 10 to 20% of cases could not be explained on this etiologic basis.[2, 3] This suggested the existence of an additional human hepatitis virus, tentatively designated non-ABC. Further clinical investigations revealed that approximately 30% of the cases of chronic hepatitis[4] and the vast majority of the cases of fulminant hepatitis[5] and hepatitis-associated aplastic anemia[6] were classified by serologic and molecular exclusion as non-ABC hepatitis cases. The designations non-ABC and non–A–E have been used interchangeably in the literature. The more inclusive term, non–A–E, indicating serologic exclusion of the five established hepatitis viruses, will be used henceforth in this chapter.

With this clinical background, two independent teams initiated viral discovery programs to find and characterize the non–A–E agent(s). Workers at the Abbott laboratories in North Chicago, Illinois, began their investigations with a specimen designated the *GB agent*—"GB" being the initials of a surgeon who had developed acute hepatitis in the 1960s; his serum had been inoculated into marmosets and appeared to transmit hepatitis in that model.[7] However, controversy existed over whether the observed hepatitis was due to a transmissible human agent or represented reactivation of an endogenous marmoset hepatitis virus. The controversy was never resolved, and the GB agent lay dormant in frozen storage until resurrected by the Abbott team in the 1990s. They began their experiments using serum from the 11th passage of the GB agent in marmosets. Employing representational difference analysis (RDA), a form of subtractive cloning, they essentially amplified RNA from pre- and postinoculation marmoset sera and performed "molecular subtraction" by hybridization.[8] Sequences that were common to the pre- and postinoculation specimens were excluded from further analysis, and sequences present only in the postinoculation sample were further investigated to determine if they were exogenous to marmoset, human, and bacterial species and if they contained sequences that were novel to the gene bank. An exogenous and novel sequence was identified, and by using overlapping clones, the full genome of the new agent was characterized.[8, 9] It soon became apparent that two novel agents were present in the GB-infected marmoset sera, and these agents were designated *GBV-A* and *GBV-B*. Using molecular amplification and GB-specific serology, it was shown that GBV-A was an endogenous marmoset agent that did not appear to be associated with hepatitis, that GBV-B was the probable causative agent of marmoset hepatitis, and that neither GBV-A nor GBV-B could be detected in human non-ABC hepatitis cases. The investigators then used degenerate primers deduced from shared sequences in GBV-A, GBV-B, and HCV and discovered a third agent, designated *GBV-C,* which has been proposed as a human agent causing non–A–E hepatitis.[10]

HGV was discovered by investigators at Genelabs, Inc. (Redwood City, California), in collaboration with investigators at the Centers for Disease Control and Prevention (CDC) and the National Institutes of Health (NIH).[11] The approach used in these investigations was more akin to that used for the cloning of HCV. The cloning source was serum both from humans with presumed non–A–E hepatitis and from chimpanzees that had been inoculated with such sera. Using sequence-independent single primer amplification (SISPA), an amplification technology that does not require prior knowledge of the genomic sequence, these investigators amplified complementary DNA (cDNA), cut restriction fragments, and then cloned the fragments using an expression vector whose protein product was detected by immunoscreening.[11] As with GBV, the genome of the relevant clone was shown to be exogenous and novel to sequences stored in the gene bank. The full genomic sequence was derived by "walking the genome" using overlapping clones.[12] The nucleic acid sequence in characteristic conserved regions and the general genomic organization identified the agent as a flavivirus. Subsequent analysis showed HGV to have greater than 95% global sequence and amino acid homology with GBV-C; thus, these two agents were virtually identical, representing strain variants of a common agent.[13] In contrast, HGV and GBV-C had less than 25% homology with any other known member of the Flaviviridae family, including HCV, yellow fever virus, and dengue fever virus, and hence represented a new genus within that family.[13]

Because the HGV–GBV-C agent was found during investigations seeking a new hepatitis virus and because the cloning sources were patients or animals with hepatitis, it was assumed that these were hepatitis agents. The hepatitis G virus was so named because an enterically transmitted hepatitis F virus had been reported and G was the next letter available in the hepatitis alphabet. However, the hepatitis F virus was never confirmed and appears to have been spuriously classified, and the hepatitis G virus has not been conclusively shown to cause hepatitis (see later on).

In summary, two novel members of the family Flaviviridae have been independently cloned and individually named (HGV and GBV-C), and both have been reported as a cause of non–A–E hepatitis. Results of subsequent studies have shown these agents to be virtually identical and have cast some doubt on whether they are actually hepatitis agents. Nonetheless, HGV and GBV-C are prevalent agents with a high carrier rate among volunteer blood donors and in the general population. Although the precise transmission rate is unknown, it is apparent that HGV/GBV-C is readily transmitted by blood transfusion and that it frequently leads to persistent viremia in the infected recipient. Beyond these observations, there are many unresolved issues including the role of nonparenteral transmission mechanisms, hepatotropism, and hepatic and extrahepatic pathogenicity. A more fundamental issue is whether this is a hepatitis virus and a significant agent in the causation of non–A–E (cryptogenic) acute and chronic hepatitis. In essence, the long-range clinical significance of the HGV/GBV-C discovery is yet to be determined. To some extent, we are now victims of the inordinate sensitivity of molecular technology. These powerful methodologies are double-edged swords because they uncover agents of unknown clinical significance, as well as established pathogens.

STRUCTURE, GENOMIC ORGANIZATION, AND VIROLOGY

HGV/GBV-C is a single-stranded, positive-sense RNA virus of approximately 9.4 kilobases coding for 3100 amino acids.[12, 13] It is an enveloped virus and thus susceptible to solvent detergent inactivation. Its genomic organization is similar to that of the flaviviruses, and the agent is distantly related to HCV (25% homology), the yellow fever virus, and the pestiviruses including bovine diarrhea virus. It is, however, sufficiently distinct from all these agents to be considered a new genus within the Flaviviridae family. HGV/GBV-C shares with other members of the Flaviviridae family a genomic structure that includes a 5′ non-coding region, followed by the structural domains for the viral envelope and then a series of nonstructural genes that extend to a 3′ non-coding region. The nonstructural genes code for proteins with enzymatic functions including helicase, serine protease, and RNA-dependent RNA polymerase. A feature unique to HGV/GBV-C is that the core (nucleocapsid) domain, so important to HCV structure and function, either does not exist or exists in a severely truncated form.[14] It is interesting to speculate that the absence of the nucleocapsid may be responsible for the low pathogenicity of this agent.

HGV/GBV-C, like other members of the Flaviviridae family, exists as a series of closely related variants, or quasispecies, but the extent of quasispecies formation is markedly less than that for HCV, which may explain why this agent is more readily contained by the immune system, such that viral clearance occurs in the majority of infected persons. HGV/GBV-C isolates fall into four main genotypes.[15] They can be used for epidemiologic investigations but do not appear to have clinical relevance.

DETECTION OF HEPATITIS G VIRUS/GB VIRUS-C

Most published data on HGV/GBV-C are based on the detection of viral RNA by polymerase chain reaction (PCR) assay. Originally, primers from nonstructural regions were used (NS-3 and NS-5), but these regions were less well conserved and therefore less sensitive targets than the highly conserved 5′ noncoding region. Primers from the 5′ noncoding region are now routinely employed for detection of HGV/GBV-C RNA. Although the presence of viral RNA is an accurate index of viremia and transmissibility, assays for its detection are not practical for the screening of blood donors or other mass screening programs. Thus, considerable effort has been expended to develop an antibody assay that would indirectly reflect the presence of virus. This proved to be unexpectedly difficult, and no antibody has been found that could reliably distinguish HGV/GBV-C carriers from the background population. This is in sharp contrast to HCV infection, in which infected persons readily develop antibodies to proteins expressed along the entire HCV genome, and in which any of these antibodies can distinguish HCV carriers from controls. The reason for this disparity in the immune response to these two genomically similar members of the Flaviviridae family is unknown.

Whereas reliable serologic markers that coexist with viremia have been difficult to develop, antibody to the envelope protein, E2, can be easily detected and appears to be an excellent marker of recovery from HGV/GBV-C infection and a powerful epidemiologic tool.[16] Hence, during acute or chronic HGV/GBV-C infection, the only marker of that infection is the detection of viral RNA by PCR assay or another molecular amplification technique. However, after the clearance of HGV/GBV-C RNA, antibody to the E2 envelope protein can be measured. Aside from a brief overlap period during recovery, HGV/GBV-C RNA and anti-E2 antibody are mutually exclusive, the former indicating ongoing viremia and the latter recovery from prior infection.[17] In combination, these two markers reflect HGV/GBV-C exposure and provide a fuller profile of the occurrence of this infection than would either marker alone. The relationship between HGV/GBV-C RNA and anti-E2 antibody is similar to the relationship between hepatitis B surface antigen (HBsAg) and anti-surface antibody (anti-HBs) in hepatitis B virus (HBV) infection. There is, however, no detectable HGV/GBV-C antigen that could substitute for measurement of RNA.

PREVALENCE AND PERSISTENCE OF HEPATITIS G VIRUS/GB VIRUS C

HGV/GBV-C prevalence in eligible U.S. volunteer blood donors ranges from 1 to 2% in most studies but has been as high as 4% in some reports.[18] Similar frequencies have been reported throughout the world. It is important to reemphasize that these rates are derived from PCR measurements of viremia and not simply from detection of antibody. Such occurrence rates of viremia are 5- to 10-fold higher than the prevalence of HCV viremia (0.3%) estimated when HCV testing was first introduced. Using a combination of HGV/GBV-C RNA and anti-E2 antibody assays, the exposure rate as well as the active infection rate can be estimated. The exposure rate among volunteer donors has been found to be 3 to 6 times the rate of viremia, and the rates of exposure and of viremia are considerably higher among paid blood donors.[16] In persons at high risk for parenteral exposure, such as hemophiliacs and intravenous drug abusers, the viremia rate may be as high as 15 to 20% and the exposure rate 60 to 80%.[19] The large difference between the exposure rate and the active infection rate suggests that approximately three quarters of HGV/GBV-C carriers eventually clear the virus, a proportion vastly greater than in HCV infection. Indeed, the levels of persistent viremia compared with recovery rates from infection for HCV and HGV appear to be the converse of each other. In HCV infection, 15% of the patients recover and 85% become long-term carriers, whereas in HGV infection, 15% appear to be long-term carriers and nearly 85% recover, though recovery may take several years.

EPIDEMIOLOGY OF HEPATITIS G VIRUS/GB VIRUS C

HGV/GBV-C is predominantly spread through parenteral routes, principally intravenous drug abuse and blood transfusion. However, any percutaneous exposure represents a potential means of transmitting this agent, as well as other established parenterally transmitted agents including HCV, HBV, and human immunodeficiency virus (HIV). Hence, tattooing, acupuncture, folk medicine practices, accidental needlestick among health care workers, and renal dialysis are among the many potential modes of inadvertent parenteral exposure. Although the reuse of needles without proper intervening sterilization is no longer practiced in most industrialized nations, such practice is a relevant concern in the developing world. Furthermore, because agents such as HGV/GBV-C and HCV can persist for a lifetime, many infected persons detected at present may have been exposed in the 1940s through the 1960s, when disposable needles and instruments were not uniformly used even in industrialized societies. In those years, it is quite possible that viruses were disseminated by dental instruments, barbers' razors, manicurists' tools, mass vaccinations, and immune globulin or other drug administration. For example, it is known that HBV infected more than 50,000 soldiers from a contaminated preparation of yellow fever vaccine.[20] It is suspected that schistosomiasis vaccination and treatment may account for the high frequency of HCV infection currently observed in Egypt and that contaminated lots of Rh immune globulin accounted for outbreaks of hepatitis C in Ireland,[21] while folk-medicine practitioners have been shown to spread HCV in Japan.[22] These are documented examples of HCV transmission by subtle parenteral routes, and there is no reason to think that HGV would not also be spread by each of these modalities. More recently, cocaine snorting has been proposed as a still more cryptic form of parenteral transmission. A high frequency of cocaine snorting has been observed among HCV carriers who denied intravenous drug use or other established means of parenteral exposure.[23] It has been hypothesized that shared snorting devices may deposit minute amounts of one person's blood onto another's nasal membranes that have been denuded by repeated cocaine use. This mechanism of viral spread has not been proved for HCV and has not been tested for HGV/GBV-C, but it exemplifies the covert means by which blood may be spread from person to person.

The fact that HGV/GBV-C is up to five times more prevalent than HCV suggests that it may be spread by additional nonparenteral routes, particularly sexual. Hence, HGV/GBV-C has been sought in populations at high risk for sexually transmitted diseases. In a study of prostitutes, it was found that the frequency of HGV infection was 11%, a rate much higher than the background prevalence and equivalent to the rates of HBV and HCV infection in this same population.[24] It was also shown that the prevalence of HGV/GBV-C increased in proportion to the duration of prostitution. Although such studies suggest sexual transmission, they do not establish it, because of the overlap with intravenous drug use in sexually promiscuous populations and because of the difficulty in obtaining accurate drug use history in such populations. A limited number of studies have been performed among the spouses of HGV-infected persons. In one study in Taiwan,[25] the spouses of 100 index cases with hepatitis C, 12 of whom were also infected with HGV/GBV-C, were tested; 14% of partners were HCV-infected, compared with 42% (5/12) who were HGV/GBV-C–infected. Nucleotide sequence comparison and phylogenetic tree analysis of the genome in HGV/GBV-C–infected couples revealed the isolates in each partner to be closely related. These results suggested sexual transmission of HGV/GBV-C and also indicated that sexually exposed persons were at higher risk of developing HGV/GBV-C infection than HCV infection. Although it is probable that HGV/GBV-C infection is a sexually transmitted as well as parenterally transmitted infection, the number of partners studied is relatively small, and it is always difficult to exclude covert means of shared parenteral exposure among spouses or other long-term sexual partners. Hence, in Japan, it was found that partners shared folk medicine practitioners who were using contaminated instruments,[22] and in other geographic areas, partners may share razor blades or toothbrushes capable of transmitting small but infectious quantities of blood. Additional large, well-controlled studies are required to firmly establish sexual transmission of HGV/GBV-C. Although the genomic similarities among the isolates from sexual partners constitute convincing evidence for sexual transmission, identical viral isolates may also be acquired when partners share a common parenteral source. The latter possibility emphasizes the difficulty in establishing proof of sexual transmission when the transmission may be real but inefficient and when the background prevalence is high. This dilemma has hampered the interpretation of data regarding the sexual transmission of HCV, and the issue remains unresolved after nearly a decade of investigation.

The data for vertical transmission of HGV/GBV-C are stronger. In a study in Germany,[26] it was shown that 10 of 18 (56%) babies born to HGV/GBV-C–positive mothers were infected with HGV/GBV-C. In contrast, in this same population of women who were intravenous drug abusers, only 1 of 19 (5%) infants born to HCV-infected mothers were infected with HCV. Sequence homology in the NS-5 region of the HGV/GBV-C isolates from 10 mother-infant pairs showed sufficient identity to confirm vertical transmission. All 10 babies remained HGV/GBV-C–positive throughout a follow-up period of 2 to 12 months, but none had any clinical or biochemical signs of liver disease.

There is no evidence for household or other casual transmission of HGV/GBV-C infection in the absence of overt or covert parenteral exposures, and there are no recommendations to change behavior patterns within the household or workplace based solely on HGV/GBV-C positivity.

CLINICAL RELEVANCE OF HEPATITIS G VIRUS/GB VIRUS C

Although it is clear that HGV/GBV-C is a ubiquitous agent that is readily transmitted by blood transfusion and other parenteral means and that can cause persistent infection, its clinical significance is largely unknown and the source of considerable controversy. Because HGV/GBV-C was found during the course of investigations to uncover new hepatitis agents, and because it was found in patients and animals with unexplained hepatitis, an etiologic link between HGV/GBV-C and the coexistent hepatitis was a logical assumption. However, because the agent is so prevalent, very carefully selected controls are required to establish a causal relationship. It is thus relevant to examine in more detail the diseases for which HGV/GBV-C has been proposed as the etiologic agent. These diseases include acute and chronic non–A–E hepatitis (transfusion-associated and community-acquired), fulminant hepatitis, hepatitis-associated aplastic anemia, and hepatocellular carcinoma.

Relationship of Hepatitis G Virus/GB Virus C to Non–A–E Hepatitis

Cumulative data from studies throughout the world indicate that HGV/GBV-C RNA is found in 10 to 20% of patients with non–A–E hepatitis.[27–29] Thus, at best, HGV/GBV-C accounts for the minority of such cases. More important, in the few studies with appropriate controls, it has been shown that HGV/GBV-C is no more common in non–A–E hepatitis than it is in patients with hepatitis B or C or in patients with nonviral liver diseases, such as autoimmune hepatitis and alcoholic liver disease.[29, 30] Thus, the agent has not demonstrated appropriate specificity for non–A–E (cryptogenic) hepatitis, and whether HGV/GBV-C plays an etiologic role in these cases has been difficult to ascertain. Analyses of these cryptogenic cases, prospectively followed transfusion recipients,[31] and cases of community-acquired hepatitis[32] each suggest that there is a background agent (non–A–G) that is 3- to 10-fold more prevalent than HGV/GBV-C. The potential existence of an unmeasurable but prevalent background agent makes it extremely difficult to evaluate what is at best a weak association between HGV/GBV-C and viral hepatitis and to exclude the possibility that HGV/GBV-C is merely an innocent bystander in a process due to an as-yet undiscovered infectious agent or of some noninfectious cause.

In a prospective study of transfusion recipients conducted at NIH,[31] it was found that HGV/GBV-C accounted for at most 4% of transfusion-associated hepatitis cases. However, even in this small number, causality was not established, because there was a dissociation between HGV/GBV-C RNA levels and serum alanine aminotransferase (ALT) levels (Fig. 144–1), and because cases of unknown etiology (non–A–G hepatitis) were four times more common than cases presumed related to HGV/GBV-C. It was also shown in the NIH study[31] that of all the HGV/GBV-C infections (N = 82) in prospectively followed transfusion recipients (Fig. 144–2), 73% were not associated with any serum ALT elevation, 16% were associated with such minor and isolated serum ALT elevations that they did not meet the study criteria for hepatitis diagnosis, and 7% were HGV-HCV coinfections, in which the hepatitis was presumed to be due to HCV. Hence, only 4% of isolated HGV/GBV-C infections were associated with hepatitis, but even here causality was unlikely in view of the inconsistent relationship between serum ALT elevations and HGV/GBV-C RNA levels (see Fig. 144–1). Prospective studies in Taiwan[32] also failed to reveal an association between HGV/GBV-C and transfusion-associated hepatitis; among 25 recipients acutely infected with HGV/GBV-C in the absence of HCV, the mean peak serum ALT was only 31 U/liter; 20 had persistently normal serum ALT levels, and the others had only low-grade, isolated serum ALT elevations insufficient to establish the diagnosis of hepatitis.

HGV/GBV-C is infrequently associated with community-acquired hepatitis. In the CDC "sentinel counties" study,[33] only 9% of the patients with acute, community-acquired non–A–E hepatitis were HGV/GBV-C–seropositive. By serologic exclusion, the vast majority of cases that were not due to HCV infection were classified as non–A–G hepatitis. The ratio of non–A–G cases to possible HGV/GBV-C cases was 10:1. Furthermore, in the few cases in which HGV/GBV-C seropositivity was demonstrated, the acute hepatitis resolved, while HGV/GBV-C persisted, suggesting that the patients

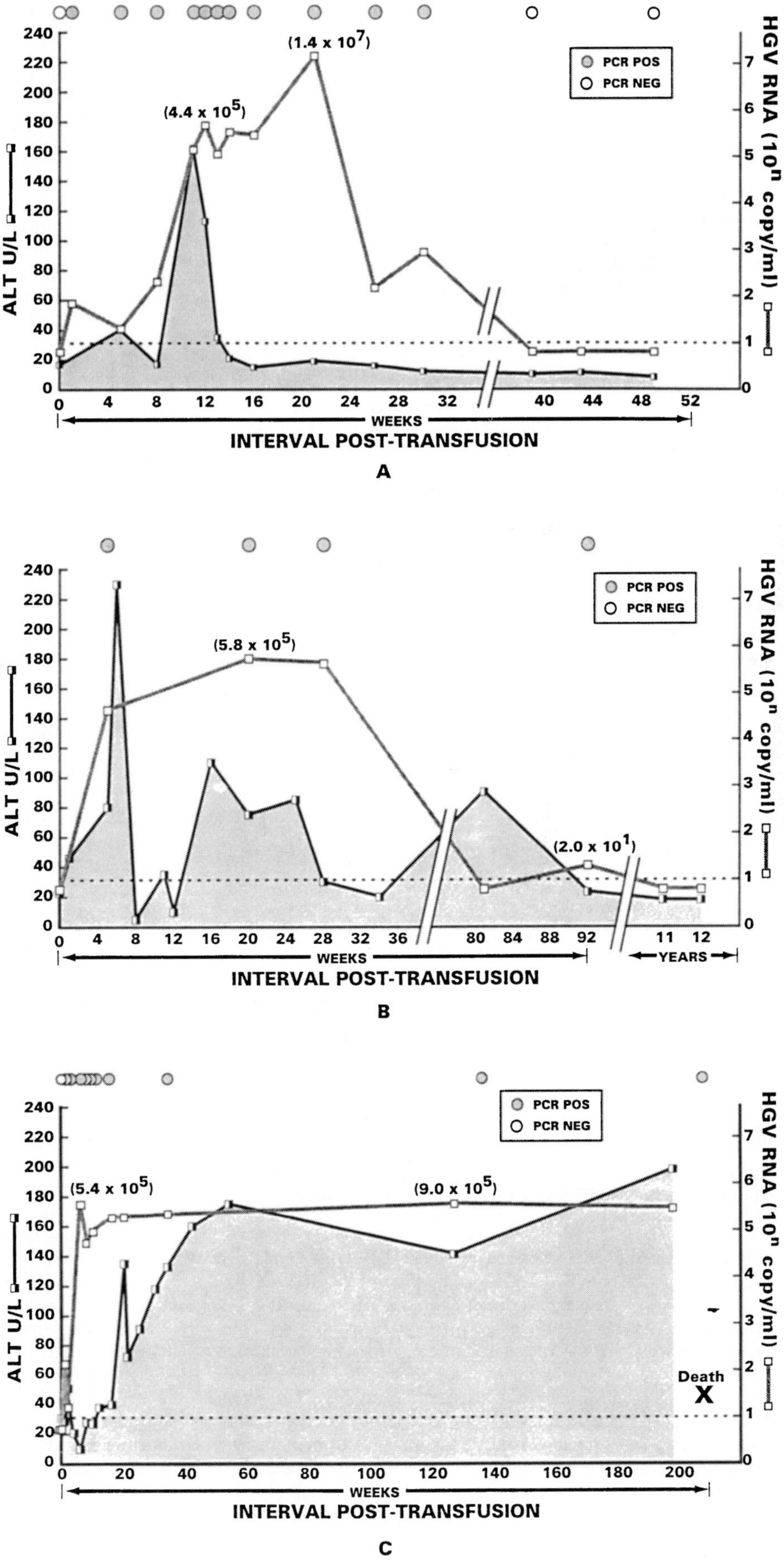

FIGURE 144–1. Hepatitis G virus (HGV) infection in three patients with transfusion-associated hepatitis. Levels of alanine aminotransferase (ALT; *shaded areas*) and HGV RNA *(squares)* in three patients infected only with HGV are shown plotted against the time since transfusion. Qualitative results of polymerase chain reaction for HGV RNA (positive, *shaded circles*; negative, *open circles*) are shown above each panel. The *dashed lines* indicate the limit of detection of HGV RNA. In each patient, the relation between the HGV RNA and ALT levels was inconsistent. In one patient *(panel A)*, HGV RNA continued to increase despite the normalization of ALT levels, and RNA remained detectable for at least 20 weeks after the ALT level had decreased to normal. In the second patient *(panel B)*, HGV RNA was elevated at week 28, when the ALT level was normal and it was undetectable at week 80, when the ALT level was rising. In the third patient *(panel C)*, 20 weeks elapsed from the first appearance of HGV RNA to the first elevation of ALT. The numbers inside the panels show the values for HGV RNA in copies per milliliter. (From Alter HJ, Nakatsuji Y, Melpolder J, et al. The incidence of transfusion-associated hepatitis G virus infection and its relation to liver disease. N Engl J Med. 1997;336:747. Copyright © 1997 Massachusetts Medical Society. All rights reserved.)

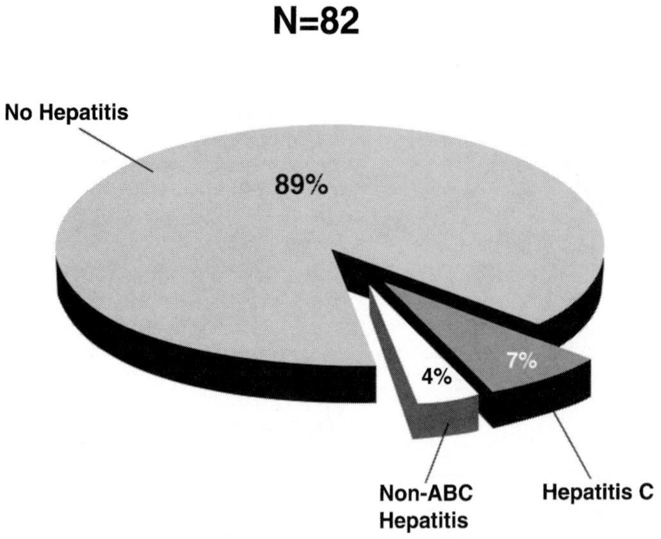

FIGURE 144–2. Clinical outcome of acute transfusion-associated hepatitis G virus (HGV) infection. In a prospective National Institutes of Health study of transfusion-transmitted HGV infection, 35 acute HGV infections were detected among 357 transfusion recipients tested. A statistical extrapolation was then made to project the number of infections that would have been observed if the entire recipient population of 965 subjects had been tested (see ref. 31 for details of the statistical analysis). The total number of HGV infections was projected to be 82. Among the 82 subjects acutely infected with HGV, 89% did not develop hepatitis (73% with no alanine aminotransferase [ALT] elevations and 16% with isolated, minor ALT elevations that did not meet the study criteria for hepatitis diagnosis), 7% had coexistent hepatitis C virus infection that was considered to be the cause of the hepatitis, and only 4% (3 patients) had non-ABC hepatitis in which HGV/GB virus type C (GBV-C) was the only virus identified. However, in these three patients, the level of HGV RNA generally did not correlate with the level of ALT (see Fig. 144–1) and HGV/GBV-C did not appear to be the causative agent.

were chronic HGV/GBV-C carriers with a superimposed acute hepatitis of undefined etiology. Thus, neither in sporadic, community-acquired hepatitis cases nor in transfusion-associated hepatitis cases has there been strong evidence to support HGV/GBV-C as the causal agent, although that possibility cannot be excluded.

Further evidence against HGV/GBV-C as a hepatitis agent stems from the poor correlation between serum ALT level and the presence of HGV/GBV-C RNA in virtually every population tested, including blood donors,[31] blood recipients,[31] dialysis patients,[34] hemophiliacs, and intravenous drug abusers.[35] This is in contrast to findings in persons with hepatitis C or hepatitis B infections; in these populations, the presence of viremia closely correlates with biochemical and histologic evidence of hepatitis.

Hepatitis G Virus/GB Virus C and Hepatitis C Virus Coinfection

Although it is difficult to assess whether HGV/GBV-C plays a primary role in the causation of hepatitis, the role of HGV/GBV-C in determining the clinical severity of coexistent HCV infection can be examined. Among HCV-infected persons, 10 to 20% are coinfected with HGV/GBV-C, presumably through common routes of exposure. Numerous studies[31, 36, 37] have shown that HGV/GBV-C has no impact on the course of coexistent hepatitis C. Peak serum ALT level, peak bilirubin level, histologic severity, severity of viremia, frequency of chronic hepatitis, and response to interferon are virtually identical in patients with combined HGV/GBV-C and HCV infection and in those with HCV infection alone. The lack of influence of HGV/GBV-C on the clinical, biochemical, histologic, or virologic course of coexistent HCV infection has been so uniform from study to study and the number of studies (more than 30) so large that this conclusion appears unequivocal.

Role in Fulminant Hepatitis

Of those cases of fulminant hepatitis thought to be of viral origin, only a small number are due to hepatitis virus A (HAV), HBV, and HCV, and the vast majority of cases have remained etiologically undefined. Early studies of HGV/GBV-C prevalence in patients with fulminant hepatitis showed very high rates of infection; in one study from Japan, 50% of patients with fulminant hepatitis were HGV/GBV-C–positive.[38] However, subsequent reports from other areas of the world and additional studies from Japan showed much lower rates of HGV/GBV-C infection, and several studies of fulminant hepatitis showed that no cases were HGV/GBV-C–related.[39] This dichotomy may be explained by the fact that patients with fulminant hepatitis have generally received multiple transfusions before being tested for HGV/GBV-C. In these patients, the administration of fresh-frozen plasma to correct abnormalities in clotting function is common, and it appears that such transfusions were in most cases given prior to HGV/GBV-C testing in most studies that reported a very high prevalence of this agent. Given the high prevalence of HGV/GBV-C among blood donors and the large number of fresh-frozen plasma units transfused to patients with clotting disorders associated with fulminant hepatic failure, there is a high probability that such patients would become HGV-infected as the result, rather than the cause, of their liver failure. No study has shown a strong association between HGV/GBV-C and fulminant hepatic failure when a history of pre-test transfusion has been reliably excluded.

Hepatitis-Associated Aplastic Anemia

The entity of hepatitis-associated aplastic anemia, in which severe marrow aplasia generally occurs 1 to 2 months after an episode of acute hepatitis, has been thought to be related to a single agent that could simultaneously or sequentially infect both the liver and the bone marrow and impair their respective functions. When HCV was discovered, it was an intriguing candidate for the causative agent of hepatitis-associated aplastic anemia, because another flavivirus, dengue fever virus, was known to infect hematopoietic stem cells in culture. Hence, the concept that a hepatotropic flavivirus, HCV, might also infect the bone marrow and impair hematopoiesis had inherent logic. However, this did not prove to be the case, and no specific association between HCV and hepatitis-associated aplastic anemia was found.[40] The subsequent discovery of HGV/GBV-C invoked the same deductive sequence, and extensive studies were undertaken in Neal Young's laboratory at the NIH. The initial findings were promising, as a high proportion of hepatitis-associated aplastic anemia patients were infected with HGV/GBV-C. However, it was shown subsequently that the presence of HGV/GBV-C in such patients was probably related to transfusions received after the onset of aplasia.[41] The rare patients who had not received transfusions prior to testing were found to be HGV/GBV-C–negative, and the rate of HGV/GBV-C in the aplastic anemia patients was no different from that in other similarly transfused hematologic populations.[41] Hence, the association between hepatitis and bone marrow failure remains unexplained. The association may be due to a single, as-yet unidentified agent that infects both the liver and the bone marrow, or the aplasia may be immunologically mediated and independent of direct viral attack on hematopoietic cells. In the latter scenario, a hepatitis agent could initiate immune complex disease that would target the marrow or could contain cross-reactive antigens that would make the marrow a cotarget of the antiviral immune response. Alternatively, both the hepatitis and the aplasia may be immunologically mediated, and the inciting event may or may not be viral infection. One clinical observation favoring an immunologic basis for the marrow aplasia is that it responds to immunosuppressive therapies in a manner similar to that observed with idiopathic aplastic anemia, a disease now considered to be immune-mediated.

Relationship to Hepatocellular Carcinoma

Both HCV and HBV show a significant association with hepatocellular carcinoma (HCC); indeed, infection with these two agents may be the primary underlying cause of HCC throughout the world. Epidemiologic investigations generally have failed to establish a similar association between HGV/GBV-C and HCC. A case-control study in Africa[42] compared 167 South African blacks who had HCC and 167 race-, age-, and sex-matched hospital-based controls. Persons infected with HGV/GBV-C did not have an increased relative risk of developing HCC (relative risk of 0.9), nor did infection with HGV/GBV-C increase the risk of tumor development in persons coinfected with HBV or HCV. A case-control study in Italy[43] showed a significant association between HGV/GBV-C and HCC, but the possible role of HGV/GBV-C in HCC causation seemed modest at best, because the population-attributable risk was only 4%, compared with 22% for HBV, 36% for HCV, and 52% for heavy alcohol intake. In Japan, where rates of HCC are high, the frequency of HGV/GBV-C infection was similar among patients with HCC (10%), patients with cirrhosis who did not have HCC (10%), and patients with neither HCC nor cirrhosis who were HCV-infected (13%).[44] It was concluded that HGV/GBV-C was unlikely to be a major etiologic agent of HCC in Japan. A similar conclusion was reached in England.[45] Thus, in geographic regions with a generally high incidence of HCC, data do not support an important role for HGV/GBV-C in cancer causation.

Hepatitis G Virus/GB Virus C in the Liver Transplant Setting

HGV/GBV-C has been found in 10 to 30% of patients undergoing liver transplantation for cryptogenic cirrhosis.[46] Similar high rates of occurrence are found in patients who received liver transplantion for hepatitis C– or alcohol-associated cirrhosis; thus, there is no specific association between HGV/GBV-C infection and cryptogenic forms of end-stage liver disease. The high frequency of HGV/GBV-C infection in these patients is thought to reflect the frequency of prior parenteral exposures in patients who develop cirrhosis, irrespective of the etiology of that cirrhosis. Even more striking is the fact that up to 70% of liver transplant recipients may test HGV/GBV-C–positive after transplantation.[47] It is probable that this high rate merely reflects additional exposure to blood products in the peritransplant period, but the possibility of reactivation of latent HGV/GBV-C infection secondary to transplant-associated immunosuppression cannot be excluded.

Despite the high frequency of viremia in this patient population, it has been repeatedly shown that HGV/GBV-C infection does not influence either the frequency or the severity of post–liver transplant hepatitis, nor does this frequent infection affect overall graft or patient survival.[46, 47]

REPLICATION OF HEPATITIS G VIRUS/GB VIRUS C IN THE LIVER

Because the cumulative observations presented suggest that the relationship between HGV/GBV-C and non–A–E hepatitis is tenuous, and because the agent does not worsen the course of coexistent hepatitis C or B or make liver disease worse even in immunocompromised transplant patients, the appropriateness of the appellation "hepatitis virus" could be questioned. In this regard, HGV/GBV-C has not been shown conclusively to replicate in the liver, though this issue remains unresolved. Several studies have reported finding HGV/GBV-C RNA in liver tissue using PCR assay as the method of detection.[48, 49] Madejon and colleagues[50] found genomic GBV-C RNA in 7 of 7 liver samples from patients with serum GBV-C RNA and also found antigenomic (negative-strand) RNA in 6 of these 7 liver specimens. In contrast, Laskus and associates[51] studied serum and liver HGV/GBV-C RNA in 10 patients, 9 of whom were coinfected with HCV. Negative-strand HGV/GBV-C RNA was not found in the liver of any patient, whereas negative-strand HCV RNA was found in 7 of 9 livers from the coinfected patients. Pessoa and coworkers[52] studied HGV/GBV-C– and HCV-coinfected patients in the transplant setting and compared liver and serum RNA titers; their results did not provide evidence for hepatic replication. Studies using in situ hybridization have been limited, with generally negative results, but Mushahwar and colleagues[53] have recently reported finding HGV/GBV-C in hepatocytes by both in situ hybridization and immunohistochemical staining. Thus, the issue of whether this agent resides in and replicates in the liver remains controversial and constitutes an important area for further investigation.

A final observation on hepatotropism is that two laboratories have transmitted HGV/GBV-C to chimpanzees.[54, 55] In neither study did the animals develop hepatitis, and no virus was found within the liver, even when serum titers were at their peak.

FUTURE PERSPECTIVES ON HEPATITIS G VIRUS/GB VIRUS C

Perhaps the most significant clinical observation countermanding a role for HGV/GBV-C in liver disease is that despite the continued transfusion of HGV/GBV-C to at least 1% and possibly up to 4% of transfusion recipients, there is no apparent hepatitis burden associated with that transmission; post-transfusion hepatitis rates continue to decline globally and, in prospective studies in the United States and Japan, now approach zero.[56] Thus, the designation "hepatitis virus" may have been premature, and further well-controlled clinical, molecular, and histologic studies are needed to place this virus in proper clinical perspective.

The debate over the clinical relevance and hepatotropism of HGV/GBV-C has broader implications because the proliferation and sophistication of molecular biology will continue to uncover new infectious agents. Each will be tested for their prevalence in blood donors and for their potential to be transmitted to blood recipients. Some may have disease associations, and others, such as HGV/GBV-C, may not have discernible disease outcomes. At present, HGV/GBV-C is a virus in search of a disease and a virus whose primary site of replication is unknown. Despite the absence of a proven disease association, its high prevalence, its persistence, and its ease of transmission by parenteral and probably nonparenteral routes dictate continued study of this agent and its potential clinical implications.

The key features of HGV/GBV-C infection are summarized in Table 144–1.

TABLE 144–1 Features of Hepatitis G Virus/GB Virus–C Infection

Feature	Comment/Description
Taxonomic classification of agent	New genus in family Flaviviridae
Epidemiology	Globally distributed (frequency 3 to 15%)
	Viremia in 1 to 2% of healthy donors
Replication of virus in liver	Controversial
Disease associations	
Cryptogenic hepatitis or cirrhosis	Most studies have shown no relationship
Fulminant hepatitis	Early studies suggested a relationship, but not confirmed in later studies
Coinfection with hepatitis C virus	No effect on hepatitis C clinical course
Transfusion-associated hepatitis	Insignificant role

TT VIRUS

A new "hepatitis" agent has been reported from Japan.[57] This agent, designated the TT virus (TTV), is a nonenveloped, single-stranded, circular DNA virus of relatively high density (1.31 to 1.32 g/cm^3). These physical characteristics suggest that it is a member of the family Circoviridae. It was discovered by RDA in the serum of a patient (whose name had the initials TT) who had transfusion-associated hepatitis. The initial report by Nishizawa and colleagues[57] investigated five cases of transfusion-associated hepatitis and found the acute appearance of TTV in three of the five patients so affected. There was a general correlation between DNA level and serum alanine (ALT) level, but there were time periods during which these levels diverged. Each of the three patients had mild hepatitis (peak serum ALT <200 U/L), and all recovered from their hepatitis. It was subsequently shown that TTV had a wide range of sequence divergence, allowing classification into genotypes 1 and 2, each of which divide into subtypes a and b.[58] Subsequent studies have shown TTV to be very prevalent in Japan and to be distributed throughout the world.[59] TTV DNA has been found in at least 12% of Japanese blood donors, indicating an extraordinarily high carrier rate. TTV DNA has been found in 3 to 7.5% of U.S. blood donors—a rate near triple that of HGV. TTV is clearly transmitted by blood transfusion and is highly prevalent in populations with frequent parenteral exposures; it has been found in up to 68% of hemophiliacs, 46% of dialysis patients, and 40% of intravenous drug abusers.[60] The very high prevalence of this agent in the general population suggests that nonparenteral means of transmission may also exist. Recently, Okamoto and associates[61] have reported the finding of TTV DNA in the bile and feces of persons with high-level viremia. Hence, this agent may be spread by the fecal-oral route.

As with HGV, the key questions are whether TTV is a primary hepatitis virus and whether it can account for cryptogenic cases of fulminant hepatitis, chronic hepatitis, and cirrhosis. The answers to these questions are not conclusive at this time. In Japan, TTV has been found in up to 45% of patients with acute or chronic non–A–G hepatitis.[60] Although this rate is significantly higher than that in the donor population, it does not prove causality, as is evident in the case of HGV/GBV-C infection. These rates must be compared with those for persons of similar age and similar parenteral exposure history who have nonviral liver disease or liver disease due to established hepatitis agents and for persons without liver disease. These data will be forthcoming in future studies, allowing the issues of hepatotropism and liver disease causation to be more accurately assessed. It is of interest that TTV has been found in the liver by PCR assay at titers 10 to 100 times that of the corresponding serum.[61]

One of the strongest arguments against a role for TTV as a primary agent of hepatitis is that the high prevalence in the donor population would ensure that almost all persons who receive multiple transfusions would be exposed to this agent, and yet transfusion-associated hepatitis rates continue to decline and are now approaching zero. Hence, there is a dissociation between the number of exposures and the number of hepatitis cases, although antibody data are not yet available to assess the number of susceptible persons in the recipient population. Finally, although the data are conflicting, there has been generally poor correlation between the presence of TTV and elevated serum ALT levels. Clearly, further studies are needed before TTV can claim its place as the next hepatitis virus.

REFERENCES

1. Choo QL, Kuo G, Weiner AJ, et al. Isolation of a cDNA clone derived from a blood-borne non-A, non-B viral hepatitis genome. Science. 1989;244:359.
2. Alter HJ, Purcell RH, Shih JW, et al. Detection of antibody to hepatitis C virus in prospectively followed transfusion recipients with acute and chronic non-A, non-B hepatitis. N Engl J Med. 1989;321:1494.
3. Alter MJ, Margolis HS, Krawczynski K, et al. The natural history of community-acquired hepatitis C in the United States. N Engl J Med. 1989;327:1899.
4. Fiordalisi G, Zanella I, Mantero G, et al. High prevalence of GB virus C infection in a group of Italian patients with hepatitis of unknown etiology. J Infect Dis. 1996;174:181.
5. Wright TL, Hsu H, Donegan E, et al. Hepatitis C virus not found in fulminant non-A, non-B hepatitis. Ann Intern Med. 1991;115:111.
6. Zeldis JB, Dienstag JL, Gale RP. Aplastic anemia and non-A, non-B hepatitis. Am J Med. 1983;74:64.
7. Deinhardt F, Holmes AW, Capps RB, Popper H. Studies on the transmission of disease of human viral hepatitis to marmoset monkeys. I. Transmission of disease, serial passage and description of liver lesions. J Exp Med. 1967;125:673.
8. Simons JH, Pilot-Matias TJ, Leary TP, et al. Identification of two flavivirus-like genomes in the GB hepatitis agent. Proc Natl Acad Sci U S A 1995;92:3401.
9. Schlauder GG, Dawson GJ, Simons JN, et al. Molecular and serologic analysis in the transmission of the GB hepatitis agents. J Med Virol. 1995;46:81.
10. Simons JN, Leary TP, Dawson GJ, et al. Isolation of novel virus-like sequences associated with human hepatitis. Nature Med. 1995;1:564.
11. Linnen J, Wages J Jr, Zhang-Keck Z-Y, et al. Molecular cloning and disease association of hepatitis G virus: A transmissible agent. Science. 1996;271:505.
12. Okamoto H, Nakao H, Inoue T, et al. The entire nucleotide sequences of two GB virus C/hepatitis G virus isolates of distinct genotypes from Japan. J Gen Virol. 1997;78:737.
13. Erker JC, Simons JN, Muerhoff AS, et al. Molecular cloning and characterization of a GB virus C isolate from a patient with non–A–E hepatitis. J Gen Virol. 1996;77:2713.
14. Simons JN, Desai SM, Schultz DE, et al. Translation initiation in GB viruses A and C: Evidence for internal ribosome entry and implications for genome organization. Virology. 1996;70:6126.
15. Muerhoff AS, Simons JN, Leary TP, et al: Sequence heterogeneity within the 5′-terminal region of the hepatitis GB virus C genome and evidence for genotypes. J Hepatol. 1996;25:379.
16. Tacke M, Schmolke S, Schlueter V, et al. Humoral immune response to the E2 protein of hepatitis G virus is associated with long-term recovery from infection and reveals a high frequency of hepatitis G virus exposure among healthy blood donors. Hepatology. 1997;26:1626.
17. Tanaka E, Kiyosawa K, Shimoda K, et al. Evolution of hepatitis G virus infection and antibody response to envelope protein in patients with transfusion-associated non-A, non-B hepatitis. J Viral Hep. 1998;5:153.
18. Feucht HH, Zollner B, Polywka S, et al. Prevalence of hepatitis G viremia among healthy subjects, individuals with liver disease, and persons at risk for parenteral transmission. J Clin Microbiol. 1997;35:767.
19. Aikawa T, Sugai Y, Okamoto H. Hepatitis G infection in drug abusers with chronic hepatitis C. N Engl J Med. 1996;334:195.
20. Seef LB, Beebe GW, Hoofnagle JH, et al. A serologic follow-up of the 1942 epidemic of post-vaccination hepatitis in the United States Army. N Engl J Med. 1987;316:965.
21. Power JP, Lawlor E, Davidson F, et al. Hepatitis C viraemia in recipients of Irish intravenous anti-D immunoglobulin. Lancet. 1994;344:1166.
22. Kiyosawa K, Tanaka E, Sodeyama T, et al. Transmission of hepatitis C in an isolated area in Japan; community-acquired infection. Gastroenterology. 1994;106:1596.
23. Conroy-Cantilena C, VanRaden M, Gibble J, et al. Routes of infection, viremia, and liver disease in blood donors found to have hepatitis C virus infection. N Engl J Med. 1996;334:1691.
24. Kao JH, Chen W, Chen PJ et al. GB virus-C/hepatitis G virus infection in prostitutes; possible role of sexual transmission. J Med Virol. 1997;52:381.
25. Kao JH, Liu CJ, Chen PJ, et al. Interspousal transmission of GB virus-C/hepatitis G virus: a comparison with hepatitis C virus. J Med Virol. 1997;53:348.
26. Viazov S, Riffelmann M, Sarr S, et al. Transmission of GBV-C/HGV from drug-addicted mothers to their babies. J Hepatol. 1997;27:85.
27. Laskus T, Wang LF, Radkowski M, et al. Hepatitis G virus infection in American patients with cryptogenic cirrhosis: No evidence for liver replication. J Infect Dis. 1997;176:1491.
28. Sugai Y, Nakayama H, Fukuda M, et al. Infection with GB virus C in patients with chronic liver disease. J Med Virol. 1997;51:175.
29. Colombatto P, Ranone A, Civitico G, et al. A new hepatitis C virus–like flavivirus in patients with cryptogenic liver disease associated with elevated GGT and alkaline phosphatase serum levels. J Viral Hepat 1997;4(Suppl 1):55.
30. Guilera M, S'aiz JC, L'opez-Labrador FX, et al. Hepatitis G virus infection in chronic liver disease. Gut. 1998;42:107.
31. Alter HJ, Nakatsuji Y, Melpolder J, et al. The incidence of transfusion-associated hepatitis G virus infection and its relation to liver disease. N Engl J Med. 1997;336:747.
32. Wang JT, Tsai FC, Lee CZ, et al. A prospective study of transfusion-transmitted GB virus C infections: Similar frequency but different clinical presentation compared with hepatitis C virus. Blood. 1996;88:1881.
33. Alter MJ, Gallagher M, Morris TT, et al. Acute non–A–E hepatitis in the United States and the role of hepatitis G virus infection. N Engl J Med. 1997;336:741.
34. Tribl B, Oesterreicher C, Pohanka E, et al. GBV-C/HGV in hemodialysis patients: Anti-E2 antibodies and GBV-C/HGV-RNA in serum and peripheral blood mononuclear cells. Kidney Int. 1998;53:212.
35. Gerolami V, Halfon P, Chambost H, et al. Prevalence of hepatitis G virus RNA in a monocentric population of French haemophiliacs. Br J Haematol. 1997;99:209.
36. Pawlotsky JM, Roudot-Thoraval F, Muerhoff AS, et al. GB virus C (GBV-C) infection in patients with chronic hepatitis C. Influence on liver disease and on hepatitis virus behavior: Effect of interferon alpha therapy. J Med Virol. 1998;54:26.

37. Tanaka E, Alter HJ, Nakatsuji Y, et al. Effects of hepatitis G virus infection on chronic hepatitis C. Ann Intern Med. 1996;125:740.
38. Yoshiba M, Okamoto H, Mishiro S. Detection of the GBV-C hepatitis virus genome in serum from patients with fulminant hepatitis of unknown aetiology. Lancet. 1995;346:1131.
39. Hadziyannis SJ. Fulminant hepatitis and the new G/GBV-C flavivirus. J Viral Hepat. 1997;4:15.
40. Hibbs JR, Frickhofer N, Rosenfeld SJ, et al. Aplastic anemia and viral hepatitis. Non-A, non-B, non-C? JAMA. 1992;267:2051.
41. Brown KE, Wong S, Young NS. Prevalence of GBV-C/HGV, a novel 'hepatitis' virus, in patients with aplastic anaemia. Br J Haematol. 1997;97:492.
42. Lightfoot K, Skelton M, Kew MC, et al. Does hepatitis GB virus-C infection cause hepatocellular carcinoma in black Africans? Hepatology. 1997;26:740.
43. Tagger A, Donato F, Ribero ML, et al. A case-control study on GB virus C/hepatitis G virus infection and hepatocellular carcinoma. Brescia HCC Study. Hepatology. 1997;26:1653.
44. Kubo S, Nishiguchi S, Kuroki T, et al. Poor association of GBV-C viremia with hepatocellular carcinoma. J Hepatol. 1997;27:91.
45. Hollingsworth RC, Minton EJ, Fraser-Moodie C, et al. Hepatitis G infection: Role in cryptogenic chronic liver disease and primary liver cell cancer in the UK. J Viral Hepat. 1998;5:165.
46. Karayiannis P, Brind AM, Pickering J. Hepatitis G virus does not cause significant liver disease after liver transplantation. J Viral Hepat. 1998;5:35.
47. Berenguer M, Terrault NA, Piatak M, et al. Hepatitis G virus infection in patients with hepatitis C virus infection undergoing liver transplantation. Gastroenterology. 1996;111:1569.
48. Saito S, Tanaka K, Kondo M, et al. Plus and minus-stranded hepatitis G virus RNA in liver tissue and in peripheral blood mononuclear cells. Biochem Biophys Res Comm. 1997;237:288.
49. Kanda T, Yokosuka O, Tagawa M, et al. Quantitative analysis of GBV-C RNA in liver and serum by strand-specific reverse transcription-polymerase chain reaction. J Hepatol. 1998;29:707.
50. Madejon A, Fogeda M, Bartolome J, et al. GB virus C RNA in serum, liver, and peripheral blood mononuclear cells from patients with chronic hepatitis B, C and D. Gastroenterology. 1997;113:573.
51. Laskus T, Radkowski M, Wang LF, et al. Lack of evidence for hepatitis G virus replication in the livers of patients coinfected with hepatitis C and G viruses. J Virol. 1997;71:7804.
52. Pessoa MG, Terrault NA, Detmer J, et al. Quantitation of hepatitis G and C viruses in the liver: Evidence that hepatitis G virus is not hepatotropic. Hepatology. 1998;27:877.
53. Mushahwar IK, Erker JC, Muerhoff AS, et al. Tissue tropism of GBV-C and HCV in immunocompromised patients and protective immunity of antibodies to GB virus C second envelope (GBV-C E2) glycoprotein. Hepatologia Clinica 1998;6(Suppl 1):23.
54. Bukh J, Kim JP, Govindarajan S, et al. Experimental infection of chimpanzees with hepatitis G virus and genetic analysis of the virus. J Infect Dis. 1998;177:855.
55. Krawczynski K. Novel hepatitis agents: The significance of clinical and experimental studies. An overview. J Gastroenterol Hepatol. 1997;12:S193.
56. Alter HJ. Posttransfusion hepatitis in the United States. In: Nishioka K, Suzuki H, Mishiro S, Oda T, eds. Viral Hepatitis and Liver Disease. Tokyo: Springer-Verlag; 1994:551.
57. Nishizawa T, Okamoto H, Konishi K, et al. A novel DNA virus (TTV) associated with elevated transaminase levels in posttransfusion hepatitis of unknown etiology. Biochem Biophys Res Comm. 1997;241:92.
58. Okamoto H, Nishizawa T, Kato N, et al. Molecular cloning and characterization of a novel DNA virus (TTV) associated with posttransfusion hepatitis of unknown etiology. Hepatol Res. 1998;10:1.
59. Simmonds P, Davidson F, Lycett C, et al. Detection of a novel DNA virus (TTV) in blood donors and blood products. Lancet. 1998;352:191.
60. Naoumov NV, Petrova EP, Thomas MG, Williams R. Presence of a newly described human DNA virus (TTV) in patients with liver disease. Lancet. 1998;352:195.
61. Okamoto H, Akahane Y, Ukita M, et al. Fecal excretion of a nonenveloped DNA virus (TTV) associated with posttransfusion non–A–G hepatitis. J Med Virol. 1998;56:128.

Coronaviridae

Chapter 145

Coronaviruses

KENNETH McINTOSH

In 1965 Tyrrell and Bynoe were able to passage a virus obtained from the respiratory tract of an adult suffering from a common cold by serially culturing nasal wash fluids in human embryonic tracheal organ cultures.[1] The medium from these cultures consistently produced colds in volunteers. The agent involved, however, failed to grow in tissue culture. It was ether-sensitive but not related to any of the known myxo- or paramyxoviruses. Subsequently, electron microscopy of fluids from infected organ cultures revealed particles that resembled the infectious bronchitis virus of chickens.[2] The particles were medium sized (80 to 150 nm), pleomorphic, membrane coated, and covered with widely spaced club-shaped surface projections. At about the same time, Hamre and Procknow recovered a cytopathic agent in tissue culture from medical students with colds.[3] This agent was also unrelated to known myxo- and paramyxoviruses and was ether-sensitive. Subsequent electron microscopy revealed similar or identical particles.[2]

After this, McIntosh and others reported the recovery of multiple strains of ether-sensitive agents from the human respiratory tract; all of them had the typical morphology of infectious bronchitis virus.[4] At much the same time a number of previously unclassified animal viruses including mouse hepatitis virus and transmissible gastroenteritis virus of swine were shown to have the same characteristic morphology by electron microscopy.[5, 6] Very shortly thereafter the name *coronavirus* (the prefix *corona* denoting the crownlike appearance of the surface projections) was chosen to signify a new genus for this group of viruses.[7]

The number and importance of animal coronaviruses quickly grew, with the eventual inclusion of viruses causing diseases in rats, mice, chickens, turkeys, calves, dogs, cats, rabbits, and pigs. The organ systems involved in these diseases include the respiratory and gastrointestinal tracts, the central nervous system, the kidneys, and the liver. The variety of animal species infected and the multiplicity of systems involved have made this one of the most important veterinary viral genera.

In view of the prominence of enteric coronaviruses in animal diseases, it is not surprising that coronavirus-like particles (CVLPs) have also been described in human fecal materials. During the past 10 to 15 years, reports of such particles have been numerous. It has been difficult to grow them reproducibly in vitro, however, and knowledge about them is limited.

DESCRIPTION OF THE PATHOGEN

The coronavirus nucleic acid is RNA, and the viral particle contains either three or four protein species: a surface glycoprotein (the S protein) that forms the petal-shaped surface projections and is probably responsible for the stimulation of neutralizing antibody; a shorter hemagglutinin-esterase protein, also on the surface but occurring only on OC43 and certain animal coronaviruses; a membrane glycoprotein contained within the trilamellar membrane; and a nucleocapsid protein complexed with the RNA. The RNA is of positive sense, single stranded, polyadenylated, and infectious, and it has a molecular weight of about 6×10^6. The strategy of replication of coronaviruses is unique in that all messenger RNAs form a nested set with common polyadenylated 3′ ends, with only the unique portion of the 5′ end being translated.[8]

All coronaviruses develop exclusively in the cytoplasm of infected cells. They bud into cytoplasmic vesicles from membranes of the endoplasmic reticulum. These virus-filled vesicles then are either extruded by reverse pinocytosis or released from the cell when the cell is destroyed.[9] The resultant virus particles have a diameter of 60 to 220 nm and are pleomorphic, with widely spaced, petal-shaped projections 20 nm long. Viral antigens appear on the surface of the cell during replication.[10]

A cellular receptor for coronavirus 229E, human aminopeptidase N, has been described.[11] An animal coronavirus, mouse hepatitis virus, which is related to strain OC43, uses as its receptor a member of the carcinoembryonic antigen family.[12] OC43 itself may use one of several cell surface molecules, including 9-*O*-acetylated neuraminic acid and the HLA-I molecule.[13]

Two human coronavirus strains, 229E and OC43, have been best studied because of their successful adaptation to growth in tissue culture or animals. There are probably other strains, but their characterization has been severely limited because they have been grown only in human embryonic tracheal organ culture.[4] Most of the strains isolated from the human respiratory tract are antigenically related to either 229E or OC43.[14] These two strains are antigenically distinct.[15] It appears likely, moreover, that there are complex antigenic interrelationships between them and the other human coronavirus serotypes. Some volunteers infected with several of the types for which serologically useful antigens are not available develop antibody titer rises to both 229E and OC43.[16]

Coronavirus strain 229E and some closely related strains grow in human diploid cell lines (Figs. 145–1 and 145–2). Recovery from clinical specimens often requires blind subpassage. All other human respiratory coronaviruses have been recovered from clinical specimens only in organ cultures from human embryonic tracheal or nasal epithelium. Strains OC43 and OC38, antigenically identical to each other, were subsequently adapted first to growth in suckling mouse brain and then to tissue culture.

Tissue culture–grown OC43 and 229E serve as antigens for serosurveys of disease and infection in various human populations.[17, 18]

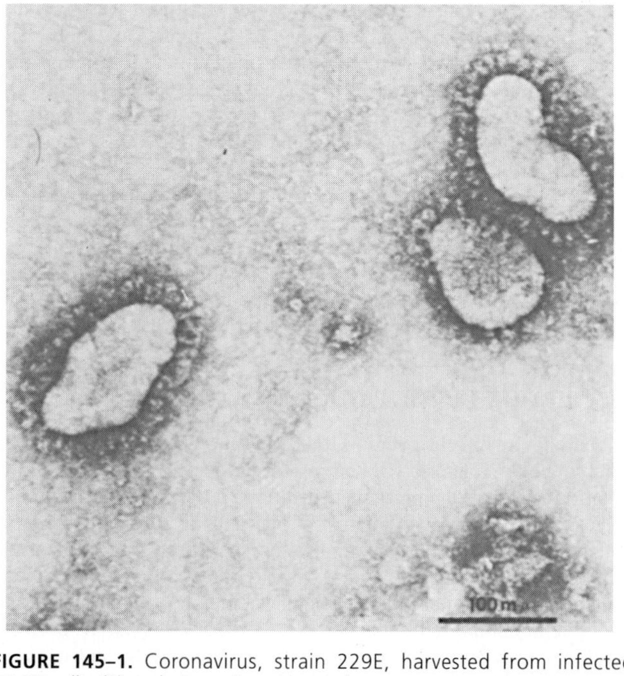

FIGURE 145–1. Coronavirus, strain 229E, harvested from infected WI-38 cells. (Phosphotungstic acid stain.)

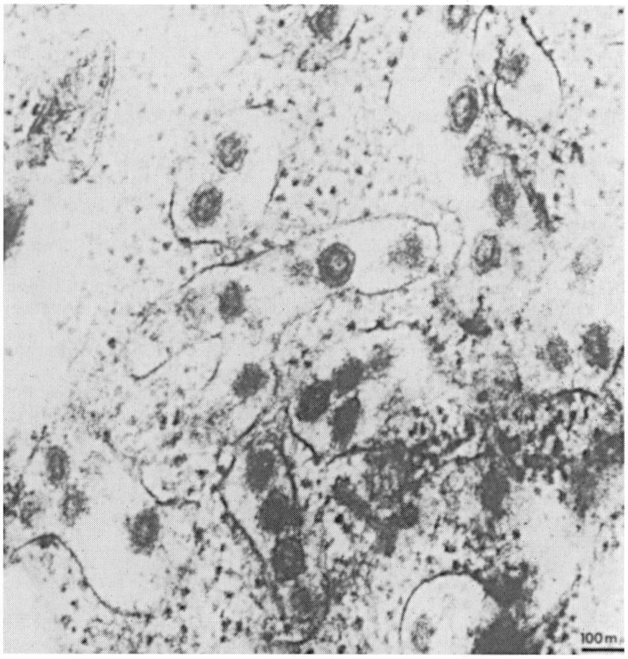

FIGURE 145–2. Coronavirus strain 229E in WI-38 cells.

Virus diagnosis from respiratory specimens can be accomplished either by antigen detection[19, 20] or, with likely greater sensitivity, by reverse transcriptase–polymerase chain reaction.[21]

Enteric coronaviruses have also been difficult to cultivate in vitro. All but a few strains have been detected only by electron microscopy of human fecal material.[22–26] Some strains have been antigenically characterized by immune electron microscopy of particles in stool and found to be related to the respiratory coronavirus OC43.[27] Several strains have been propagated in intestinal organ culture.[28, 29] Two strains obtained from an outbreak of necrotizing enterocolitis in Texas and passaged in intestinal organ cultures were found to contain four or five antigenically active proteins separable on polyacrylamide gels.[29] These proteins migrated with apparent molecular weights similar to those of well-studied coronaviruses. Antigenic relatedness to OC43 or other coronaviruses was not, however, demonstrable. The accumulating evidence favors the view that these strains and strains antigenically related to OC43[27] are members of the family Coronaviridae. The less well studied strains, characterized only by their distinctive morphology on electron microscopy and called, for lack of a better name, *coronavirus-like particles*, may also be coronaviruses, but the evidence is less compelling.

CLINICAL MANIFESTATIONS

The human respiratory coronaviruses have been proved to cause colds in adults, and most strains were originally recovered from adults during upper respiratory tract illness. Almost all the antigenically distinct respiratory coronavirus strains have been administered to volunteers, and all these produce illness with similar characteristics.[14] A summary of these characteristics is shown in Table 145–1, in which a comparison is made with colds produced by rhinoviruses in similarly inoculated volunteers. The incubation period of coronavirus colds was longer and their duration somewhat shorter, but the symptoms were very similar. Low-grade fever was present in about one volunteer in five, and malaise after coronavirus inoculation was frequent. Asymptomatic infection was sometimes seen and, indeed, has been a feature of serologic surveys of natural infection of children and adults. The mechanism of respiratory tract symptoms is not clear but is probably more closely related to a release of mediators[30]

TABLE 145-1 Clinical Features of Colds Produced by Experimental Infection with Four Viruses

	Coronaviruses		Rhinoviruses	
Feature	*229E*	*B814*	*Type 2 (HGP or PK)*	*DC*
No. of volunteers inoculated	26	75	213	251
No. getting colds	13 (50%)	34 (45%)	78 (37%)	77 (31%)
Incubation period (days)				
Mean	3.3	3.2	2.1	2.1
Range	2–4	2–5	1–5	1–4
Duration (days)				
Mean	7	6	9	10
Range	3–18	2–17	3–19	2–26
Maximum no. of handkerchiefs used daily				
Mean	23	21	14	18
Range	8–105	8–120	3–38	33–60
Malaise (%)	46	47	28	25
Headache (%)	85	53	56	56
Chill (%)	31	18	28	15
Pyrexia (%)	23	21	14	18
Mucopurulent nasal discharge (%)	0	62	83	80
Sore throat (%)	54	79	87	73
Cough (%)	31	44	68	56
No. of volunteers with colds of indicated severity				
Mild	10 (77%)	24 (71%)	63 (80%)	36 (47%)
Moderate	2 (15%)	7 (20%)	12 (15%)	28 (36%)
Severe	1 (8%)	3 (9%)	4 (5%)	13 (17%)

From Bradburne AF, Bynoe ML, Tyrrell DAJ. Effects of a "new" human respiratory virus in volunteers. BMJ. 1967;3:767–769. Reproduced by permission of the BMJ.

than to cell injury. It is likely that the colds produced in volunteers are similar to those produced in adults by natural infection.[31, 32]

More serious, lower respiratory tract illness is probably on occasion caused by coronavirus infection. Several strains resembling 229E have been recovered from infants with pneumonia,[33] and antibody titer rises also have been found with a frequency of 3 to 8% in this group.[33, 34] An extensive survey of hospitalized children in England failed to uncover a single instance of coronavirus infection.[19] Surveys of hospitalized children using more sensitive methods, such as reverse transcriptase–polymerase chain reaction, have not been performed, however.

Coronavirus infection in marine recruits has been associated with pneumonia or pleural reaction in about one third, and it is possible that lower respiratory tract disease can, under special circumstances, occur in adults.[35] The association of coronavirus infection with bouts of wheezing in asthmatic children or children with recurrent wheezy bronchitis has also been described.[36, 37] Finally, six separate longitudinal serologic studies of adults with chronic pulmonary disease or asthma have each shown a significant association of coronavirus infection with exacerbations of respiratory symptoms.[18, 38–42] Elderly persons are also subject to more severe respiratory disease during coronavirus infection.[43]

The nature of the illness associated with enteric coronavirus infection is much less clear. One study significantly associated gastroenteritis in infants 2 to 12 months of age with the presence of CVLPs in the stool.[27] Another study, confined to infants in a neonatal intensive care unit, found highly significant associations between the presence of CVLPs in the stool and the presence of water-loss stools, bloody stools, abdominal distention, and bilious gastric aspirates.[25] A further study of symptomatic babies shedding CVLPs pointed to possible differences between rotavirus diarrhea and CVLP-associated diarrhea: although fever and vomiting were of very similar incidence, stools were more often occult blood–positive (18 versus 0%), less often watery (66 versus 92%), and more often mucoid (32 versus 8%).[44] Finally, coronaviruses have been associated with at least three outbreaks of necrotizing enterocolitis in newborns,[24, 25, 29] and the best-characterized strains[29] were isolated from infants with this illness.

Like many other viruses, coronaviruses have been sought as possible etiologic agents in multiple sclerosis. The search has been stimulated by the capacity of JHM, a well-studied strain of mouse hepatitis virus, to produce in mice and rats a chronic demyelinating encephalitis histologically similar to multiple sclerosis.[45] Evidence of viruses related to mouse hepatitis virus, OC43,[46, 47] and 229E[48] has been found by virus isolation,[46] in situ hybridization, immunohistology,[47] and polymerase chain reaction.[48] Moreover, T-cell lines established from patients with multiple sclerosis by stimulation with myelin basic protein or 229E were found to be cross-reactive with the opposite antigen, suggesting that molecular mimicry might be a possible pathogenic mechanism for the disease association.[49] Nevertheless, compelling evidence is lacking to establish an etiologic or pathogenetic association of coronaviruses with central nervous system disease in humans.

EPIDEMIOLOGY

Like all other known respiratory virus infections, coronavirus infections have been found wherever they have been sought. This includes North America, South America, Europe, and Asia.

In temperate climates, respiratory coronavirus infections occur more often in the winter and spring than in the summer and fall. The contribution of coronavirus infections to the total number of upper respiratory illnesses may be as high as 35% during times of peak viral activity. Overall, the proportion of adult colds produced by coronaviruses may be reasonably estimated at 15%.

In the United States, the two strains that have been extensively studied, OC43 and 229E, have demonstrated periodicity, with large epidemics occurring at 2- to 3-year intervals.[50] Strain 229E tends to be epidemic throughout the United States, whereas strain OC43 tends to appear in localized outbreaks. The proportion of those infected (as judged by a rise in antibody titer) who become ill is about one half. Reinfection appears to be common and may be due to the rapid diminution of antibody levels after infection.[51] Infection occurs at all ages but is most common in children.

Enteric coronaviruses (or CVLPs) have been most frequently associated with gastrointestinal disease in neonates and infants younger than 12 months. Particles have been found in the stools of adults with the acquired immunodeficiency syndrome.[52, 53] Asymptomatic shedding is common, particularly in tropical climates[54] and in populations living in poor hygienic conditions.[55] They are apparently shed for prolonged periods[23, 25, 43] and have little or no seasonality.[56]

PROSPECTS FOR PREVENTION AND AREAS IN WHICH FUTURE STUDIES ARE NEEDED

It seems unlikely that coronaviruses will become the target of a large preventive campaign as long as the traditional modes of immunoprophylaxis are used. Multiple antigenic strains exist, and reinfection is common. The prospects of control by immunization therefore appear dim. It is likely, however, that because of their unique biology and their prominence in veterinary medicine, methods of control through chemotherapy will be developed. If these are sufficiently nontoxic, it may be possible to apply them to respiratory disease in humans.

REFERENCES

1. Tyrrell DAJ, Bynoe ML. Cultivation of a novel type of common-cold virus in organ cultures. BMJ. 1965;1:1467–1470.
2. Almeida JD, Tyrrell DAJ. The morphology of three previously uncharacterized human respiratory viruses that grow in organ culture. J Gen Virol. 1967;1:175–178.
3. Hamre D, Procknow JJ. A new virus isolated from the human respiratory tract. Proc Soc Exp Biol. 1966;121:190–193.
4. McIntosh K, Dees JH, Becker WB, et al. Recovery in tracheal organ cultures of novel viruses from patients with respiratory disease. Proc Natl Acad Sci U S A. 1967;57:933–940.

5. McIntosh K, Becker WB, Chanock RM. Growth in suckling mouse brain of "IBV-like" viruses from patients with upper respiratory tract disease. Proc Natl Acad Sci U S A. 1967;58:2268–2273.
6. Witte KH, Tajima M, Easterday BC. Morphologic characteristic and nucleic acid type of transmissible gastroenteritis virus of pigs. Arch Ges Virusforsch. 1968;23:53–70.
7. Tyrrell DAJ, Almeida JD, Berry DM, et al. Coronaviruses. Nature. 1968;220:650.
8. Holmes KV, Lai MMC: Coronaviridae and their replication. In: Fields B, Knipe D, Howley P, eds. Fields Virology. 3rd ed. Philadelphia: Lippincott-Raven; 1996:1075.
9. Becker WB, McIntosh K, Dees JH, et al. Morphogenesis of avian infectious bronchitis virus and a related human virus (strain 229E). J Virol. 1967;1:1019–1027.
10. Gerna G, Battaglia M, Cereda PM, et al. Reactivity of human coronavirus OC43 and neonatal calf diarrhea coronavirus membrane-associated antigens. J Gen Virol. 1982;60:385–390.
11. Yeager CL, Ashmun RA, Williams RK, et al. Human aminopeptidase N is a receptor for human coronavirus 229E. Nature. 1992;357:420–422.
12. Williams RK, Jiang GS, Holmes KV. Receptor for mouse hepatitis virus is a member of the carcinoembryonic antigen family of glycoproteins. Proc Natl Acad Sci U S A. 1991;88:5533–5536.
13. Collins AR. HLA class I antigen serves as a receptor for human coronavirus OC43. Immunol Invest 1993;22:95–103.
14. Macnaughton MR, Madge MH, Reed SE. Two antigenic groups of human coronaviruses detected by using enzyme-linked immunosorbent assay. Infect Immun. 1981;33:734–737.
15. Schmidt OW. Antigenic characterization of human coronaviruses 229E and OC43 by enzyme-linked immunosorbent assay. J Clin Microbiol. 1984;20:175–180.
16. Bradburne AF, Somerset BA. Coronavirus antibody titres in sera of healthy adults and experimentally infected volunteers. J Hyg (Camb). 1972;70:235–244.
17. Kraaifeveld CA, Reed SE, Macnaughton MR. Enzyme-linked immunosorbent assay for detection of antibody in volunteers experimentally infected with human coronavirus strain 229E. J Clin Microbiol. 1980;12:493–497.
18. Gill EP, Dominguez EA, Greenberg SB, et al. Development and application of an enzyme immunoassay for coronavirus OC43 antibody in acute respiratory illness. J Clin Microbiol. 1993;32:2372–2376.
19. McIntosh K, McQuillin J, Reed SE, et al. Diagnosis of human coronavirus infection by immune fluorescence: Method and application to respiratory disease in hospitalized children. J Med Virol. 1978;2:341–346.
20. Lina B, Valette M, Foray S, et al. Surveillance of community-acquired viral infections due to respiratory viruses in Rhone-Alpes (France) during winter 1994 to 1995. J Clin Microbiol. 1996;34:3007–3011.
21. Myint S, Johnston S, Sanderson G, Simpson H. Evaluation of nested polymerase chain methods for the detection of human coronaviruses 229E and OC43. Mol Cell Probes. 1994;8:357–364.
22. Mathan M, Mathan VI, Swaminathan SP, et al. Pleomorphic virus-like particles in human faeces. Lancet. 1975;1:1068–1069.
23. Baker SJ, Mathan M, Mathan VI, et al. Chronic enterocyte infection with coronavirus: One possible cause of the syndrome of tropical sprue? Dig Dis Sci. 1983;27:1039–1043.
24. Chany C, Moscovici O, Lebon P, et al. Association of coronavirus infection with neonatal necrotizing enterocolitis. Pediatrics. 1982;69:209–214.
25. Vaucher YE, Ray CG, Minnich LL, et al. Pleomorphic, enveloped, virus-like particles associated with gastrointestinal illness in neonates. J Infect Dis. 1982;145:27–36.
26. Maass G, Baumeister HG, Freitag N. Viren als Ursache der akuten Gastroenteritis bei Sauglingen und Kleinkindern. Munch Med Wochenschr. 1977;119:1029–1034.
27. Gerna G, Passarani N, Battaglia M, et al. Human enteric coronaviruses: Antigenic relatedness to human coronavirus OC43 and possible etiologic role in viral gastroenteritis. J Infect Dis. 1985;151:796–803.
28. Caul EO, Egglestone SI. Further studies on human enteric coronaviruses. Arch Virol. 1977;54:107–117.
29. Resta S, Luby JP, Rosenfeld CR, et al. Isolation and propagation of a human enteric coronavirus. Science. 1985;229:978–981.
30. Linden M, Greiff L, Andersson M, et al. Nasal cytokines in common cold and allergic rhinitis. Clin Exp Allergy. 1995;25:166–172.
31. Bradburne AF, Bynoe ML, Tyrrell DAJ. Effects of a "new" human respiratory virus in volunteers. BMJ. 1967;3:767–769.
32. Hendley JO, Fishburne HB, Gwaltney JM Jr. Coronavirus infections in working adults: Eight-year study with 229E and OC43. Am Rev Respir Dis. 1972;105:805–811.
33. McIntosh K, Chao RK, Krause HE, et al. Coronavirus infections in acute lower respiratory tract disease in infants. J Infect Dis. 1974;130:502–507.
34. McIntosh K, Kapikian AZ, Turner HC, et al. Seroepidemiologic studies of coronavirus infection in adults and children. Am J Epidemiol. 1970;91:585–592.
35. Wenzel RP, Hendley JO, Davies JA, et al. Coronavirus infections in military recruits: Three-year study with coronavirus strains OC43 and 229E. Am Rev Respir Dis. 1976;109:621–624.
36. McIntosh K, Ellis EF, Hoffman LS, et al. The association of viral and bacterial respiratory infections with exacerbations of wheezing in young asthmatic children. J Pediatr. 1973;82:578–593.
37. Mertsola J, Ziegler T, Ruuskanen O, et al. Recurrent wheezy bronchitis and viral respiratory infections. Arch Dis Child. 1991;66:124–129.
38. Gump DW, Phillips A, Forsyth BR, et al. Role of infection in chronic bronchitis. Am Rev Respir Dis. 1976;113:465–474.
39. Buscho RO, Saxtan D, Shultz PS, et al. Infections with viruses and *Mycoplasma pneumoniae* during exacerbations of chronic bronchitis. J Infect Dis. 1978;137:377–383.
40. Smith CB, Golden CA, Kanner RE, et al. Association of viral and *Mycoplasma pneumoniae* infections with acute respiratory illness in patients with chronic obstructive pulmonary diseases. Am Rev Respir Dis. 1980;121:225–232.
41. Nicholson KG, Kent J, Ireland DC. Respiratory viruses and exacerbations of asthma in adults. BMJ. 1993;307:982–986.
42. Wiselka MJ, Kent J, Cookson JB, Nicholson KG. Impact of respiratory virus infection in patients with chronic chest disease. Epidemiol Infect. 1993;111:337–346.
44. Falsey AR, McCann RM, Hall WJ, et al. The "common cold" in frail older persons: Impact of rhinovirus and coronavirus in a senior daycare center. J Am Geriatr Soc. 1997;45:706–711.
44. Mortensen ML, Ray CG, Payne CM, et al. Coronaviruslike particles in human gastrointestinal disease. Epidemiologic, clinical, and laboratory observations. Am J Dis Child. 1985;139:928–934.
45. Nagashima K, Wege H, Meyermann R, et al. Coronavirus induced subacute demyelinating encephalitis in rats. A morphological analysis. Acta Neuropathol. 1978;44:63–70.
46. Burks JS, DeVald BL, Jankovsky LD, et al. Two coronaviruses isolated from central nervous system tissue of two multiple sclerosis patients. Science. 1980;209:933–934.
47. Murray RS, Brown B, Brian D, et al. Detection of coronavirus RNA and antigen in multiple sclerosis brain. Ann Neurol. 1992;31:525–533.
48. Stewart JN, Mounir S, Talbot PJ. Human coronavirus gene expression in the brains of multiple sclerosis patients. Virology. 1992;191:502–505.
49. Talbot PJ, Paquette JS, Ciurli C, et al. Myelin basic protein and human coronavirus 229E cross-reactive T cells in multiple sclerosis. Ann Neurol. 1996;39:233–240.
50. Monto AS. Medical reviews, coronaviruses. Yale J Biol Med. 1974;47:234–251.
51. Callow KA, Parry HF, Sergeant M, et al. The time course of the immune response to experimental coronavirus infection in man. Epidemiol Infect. 1990;105:435–446.
52. Kern P, Muller G, Schmitz H, et al. Detection of coronavirus-like particles in homosexual men with acquired immunodeficiency and related lymphadenopathy syndrome. Klin Wocheschr. 1985;63:68–72.
53. Schmidt W, Schneider T, Heise W, et al. Stool viruses, coinfections, and diarrhea in HIV-infected patients. Berlin Diarrhea/Wasting Syndrome Study Group. J Acquir Immune Defic Syndr Hum Retrovirol. 1996;13:33–38.
54. Marshall JA, Birch CJ, Williamson HG, et al. Coronavirus-like particles and other agents in the faeces of children in Efate, Vanuatu. J Trop Med Hyg. 1982;85:213–215.
55. Marshall JA, Thompson WL, Gust ID. Coronavirus-like particles in adults in Melbourne, Australia. J Med Virol. 1989;29:238–243.
56. Payne CM, Ray CG, Borduin V, et al. An eight-year study of the viral agents of acute gastroenteritis in humans: Ultrastructural observations and seasonal distribution with a major emphasis on coronavirus-like particles. Diagn Microbiol Infect Dis. 1986;5:39–54.

Paramyxoviridae

Chapter 146

Parainfluenza Viruses

PETER F. WRIGHT

HISTORY

The five parainfluenza viruses[1–3] were first isolated from humans among the flurry of new viruses identified in the late 1950s. Initially described in association with laryngotracheobronchitis (croup) in hospitalized children, parainfluenza viruses were identified as viruses that had the property of hemadsorbtion of red blood cells. Subsequently, their important role in human respiratory disease in childhood and more recently in immunocompromised patients was well described. In the 1960s, mucosal IgA antibody was shown to have a protective role against parainfluenza viruses; they remain the viruses for which mucosal immune protection has been most clearly demonstrated. Advances in reverse genetics have led to characterization of the role of individual parainfluenza viral proteins and the rational design of vaccine candidates for prevention of human respiratory disease caused by these viruses.[4, 5]

DESCRIPTION OF VIRUSES

Classification and Structure

Human parainfluenza viruses are members of the genera *Paramyxovirus* (parainfluenza types 1 and 3) and *Rubulavirus* (parainfluenza types 2, 4A, and 4B) and belong to the Paramyxoviridae family.[6, 7] They have a lipid bilayer envelope derived from the host cell, are roughly spherical with a diameter of 150 to 200 nm, have glycoprotein spikes extending from the envelope surface, and have a single-stranded, nonsegmented, negative-sense RNA genome. The human pathogens included in this family are the five parainfluenza viruses (designated parainfluenza types 1, 2, 3, 4A, and 4B), mumps, measles, and respiratory syncytial virus. Significant animal pathogens within the family include Sendai virus, simian virus type 5, Newcastle disease virus, canine distemper virus, and rinderpest. In 1994, a fatal illness occurred in horses in two isolated outbreaks in Australia that also killed two humans who had worked closely with the horses. The virus, formerly called equine morbillivirus but now named Hendra virus, has recently been shown to fit best within the Paramyxoviridae family.[8] The natural host for Hendra virus appears to be the fruit bat. Recently, a Hendra-like paramyxovirus, referred to as Nipah virus, which infects pigs, has been reported to cause outbreaks of disease in Malaysia and Singapore in humans who have been in contact with swine (see also Chapter 149).[8a]

Replication

Parainfluenza viruses attach to sialic acid–containing cellular molecules via the hemagglutinin-neuraminidase (HN) protein.[6] Sialic acid–expressing cells are widespread, and thus the specificity of attachment does not explain the respiratory tract tropism of parainfluenza viruses. The HN protein is coupled with the activated fusion (F) protein to allow cell entry of the virus.[9, 10] Activation of the F protein is by proteolytic cleavage, which is mediated by cellular serine proteases. In the case of Sendai virus, F-protein cleavage occurs by a protease that is unique to a subset of respiratory cells called Clara cells. The unique localization of the protease may be a factor in localization of the replication of parainfluenza viruses to the respiratory tract. Differences in tropism are striking between closely related viruses, as for example, the respiratory localization of parainfluenza viruses contrasted to the preference of mumps for acinar tissue. Parainfluenza viruses do not appear to enter or unfold in the acid environment of the endosome as occurs with influenza viruses. The nucleocapsid complex consists of the viral RNA and three internal proteins—nucleocapsid protein (NP), polymerase protein (L), and phosphorylated nucleocapsid–associated protein (P)—that initiate a primary transcription event to generate the messenger RNA from which viral proteins are translated. In addition, a full-length antigenome with positive-sense RNA is formed from which the genome is replicated. Diversity in expression of the P-gene–coded products leads to additional regulatory proteins whose functions are not fully defined. Still within the cytoplasm, virion assembly takes place in several steps. The new NP protein assembles with the genomic RNA to form a helical structure. The P- and L-protein complexes then join to form the nucleocapsid. After being synthesized in the endoplasmic reticulum and traveling a secretory pathway in the cell, the envelope proteins assemble at the cell surface with a polarity that favors the apical surface of the cell. The other major structural protein, matrix protein, plays a role in virus assembly and release from the cell surface by budding. The neuraminidase component of the HN protein may aid in release from the cell and prevention of virus aggregation by cleaving sialic acid residues to which the virus would otherwise reattach. The entire process is not efficient in that many incomplete noninfectious particles are formed that can interfere with the yield of infectious virus.

PATHOGENESIS

Tropism

Parainfluenza viruses cause acute respiratory infections. The peak of illness is associated with peak virus shedding based on observations in children infected with a partially attenuated parainfluenza type 3 vaccine candidate.[11] Parainfluenza viruses replicate exclusively in cells of the respiratory epithelial layer.[7] The epithelial layer is a complex mixture of cell types that vary as one traverses to different depths of the upper and lower respiratory tract. Clinically, parainfluenza viruses most typically cause illness in the large airways of the lower respiratory tract manifested as laryngotracheobronchitis, or croup.[12] The reasons for this particular localization are not known. The best evidence is that parainfluenza viruses replicate in the ciliated epithelial cells that line much of the upper and lower respiratory tract.[13, 14] Not only do they grow in these superficial cells, but they are also released by budding only from the apical surface of the cell back into the mucin layer above the epithelium.[15]

As with influenza viruses, a surface protein of parainfluenza viruses, the fusion or F protein, is cleaved by a serine protease, a process required for replication of the virus. With Sendai virus, a murine virus closely related to parainfluenza virus type 1, mutations in the F protein that allow more ready cleavage lead to a mutant that will replicate throughout the body.[16] Conversely, mutants of Sendai virus that are no longer cleaved by trypsin are highly attenuated.[17] In rodent models, a protease produced by the Clara cells of the respiratory tract has been identified that mediates this cleavage in Sendai and influenza viruses.[18, 19] Clara cells are secretory cells that release this protease into the respiratory tract, where it presumably acts in a paracrine fashion to cleave virus in the extracellular environment or in the process of budding from cells.[20] Early in Sendai infection, Clara cells secrete an abundance of tryptase Clara. The enzyme is found overlying the adjoining ciliated cells in which parainfluenza is replicating.[21] The human counterpart of this protein has not been identified, but serine protease activity is demonstrable in human secretions.[22]

Some of the parainfluenza viruses cause cell fusion and syncytia formation. The precise role of syncytia formation in disease is not known. It could potentially allow cell-to-cell spread without virus being exposed to neutralizing antibody in the extracellular environment.

Immune Response

Serum neutralizing antibodies directed toward epitopes on the HN and F surface proteins of parainfluenza virus are found after infection.[7, 23–25] Monoclonal antibodies are preferentially formed to epitopes on the HN virus.[26] In experimental animals, antibodies raised to an HN vaccinia construct were considerably more protective than antibodies to protein F.[27] After several infections, antibodies may develop that cross-neutralize different parainfluenza strains. Cytotoxic T-cell epitopes are primarily found on the internal nucleoprotein.[28]

In spite of these effective immune targets, children and adults are repeatedly infected with parainfluenza viruses over the course of a lifetime. Reinfection is more likely to solely involve the upper respiratory tract with sparing of the lower respiratory tract after the first or second exposure in immunocompetent individuals.[29, 30] Antigenic variation occurs, but it is not progressive[31]; thus, reinfection probably reflects a waning of immunity over time rather than antigenic drift of the virus.[32] This pattern is in obvious contrast to influenza virus, where progressive antigenic drift is one of the major ways in which the virus escapes immune surveillance.

Immunity to parainfluenza viruses, no matter how poorly sustained, can be demonstrated. Prior infection in animal models blocks virus recovery on subsequent challenge. Experimental infection of adults with wild-type viruses is modulated by the level of immunity,[33] and it is more difficult to infect seropositive children with live-attenuated vaccines than readily infect immunologically naive children.[34] In both adults and children, recovery of virus is dramatically lowered by recent past exposure to the virus.

The most important component of resistance appears to be mucosal immunity. In animal models, greater protection is afforded by intranasal than by systemic administration of parainfluenza type 3 glycoproteins.[35] In addition, passive IgA antibody delivered into the respiratory tract of mice provides greater protection than does IgG.[36] In adults after an experimental parainfluenza type 1 challenge, reisolation of virus was inversely correlated with the detection of local neutralizing antibody in secretions and not with serum antibody[37] (Fig. 146–1). In children, prior natural infection blocks the replication of live-attenuated, intranasally administered virus vaccines, which replicate freely in naive children, including children in the first 6 months of life with passively acquired maternal serum antibody. However, in children the mechanisms of protection against parainfluenza viruses are less well defined than in adults. Symptomatic disease with lower respiratory tract involvement can be seen after reinfection with parainfluenza type 3.[38]

IgA antibody has the property of being transcytosed across epithelial cells from the basolateral surface to release at the apical surface into the respiratory tract.[39] It has been proposed that antibody and virus may colocalize within cells and result in intracellular inhibition of virus assembly and release.[40] Evidence that this mechanism may occur with IgA monoclonal antibodies to Sendai virus has been published.[41]

In addition to prevention of reinfection, immunity is involved in terminating primary infection. In animal models, the role of $CD8^+$ T cells is critical in virus clearance. Lymphoid cells, some of which are virus specific and some of which are bystanders, accumulate in the regional peribronchial lymph nodes during acute infection. The bystander lymphoid cells presumably contribute to the establishment of immunologic memory. The cells active in cytotoxic destruction of virally infected cells appear to accumulate in the airways and can be found in bronchoalveolar lavage fluid.[42] The severity of disease in individuals with T-cell deficits (see "Clinical Manifestations," later) suggests the importance of T-cell immunity in clearance of infection. It has been shown that parainfluenza virus type 3 can downregulate granzyme B, one of the perforins that mediates cytotoxicity, thus suggesting a mechanism for immune modulation by parainfluenza viruses.[43]

EPIDEMIOLOGY

A number of studies have examined the impact of respiratory viral infections in pediatric practice.[38, 44, 45] Parainfluenza type 3 is the most frequently recovered of the parainfluenza virus types in longitudinal studies of respiratory illness in children. Roughly half as many parainfluenza type 1 isolates are found as parainfluenza type 3 isolates and one quarter as many isolates of parainfluenza type 2 as type 3[38] (Table 146–1). Parainfluenza viruses vary in their seasonal epidemiology by type. Parainfluenza type 3 virus is endemic, with isolation throughout the year; however, a distinct peak is seen in the spring months of April and May.[38, 45] Parainfluenza virus types 1 and 2 cause annual fall epidemics of disease and often alternate in years, so an individual type may be seen only every 2 years. Parainfluenza virus types 4A and 4B are isolated so seldomly that their seasonality is not well described.[46, 47]

In the unique environment of overwintering on the South Pole where 20 people were isolated for a 6-month period, parainfluenza virus types 1 and 3 were repeatedly isolated through the quarantine period, which suggests that persistent or repeated infection was spread in this small cohort.[48] In tissue culture cells, persistent parainfluenza virus type 3 infection can also be established.[49]

The early age at which parainfluenza type 3 virus is first recovered is another trait that distinguishes it from types 1 and 2. Parainfluenza type 3 virus, like respiratory syncytial virus, is commonly

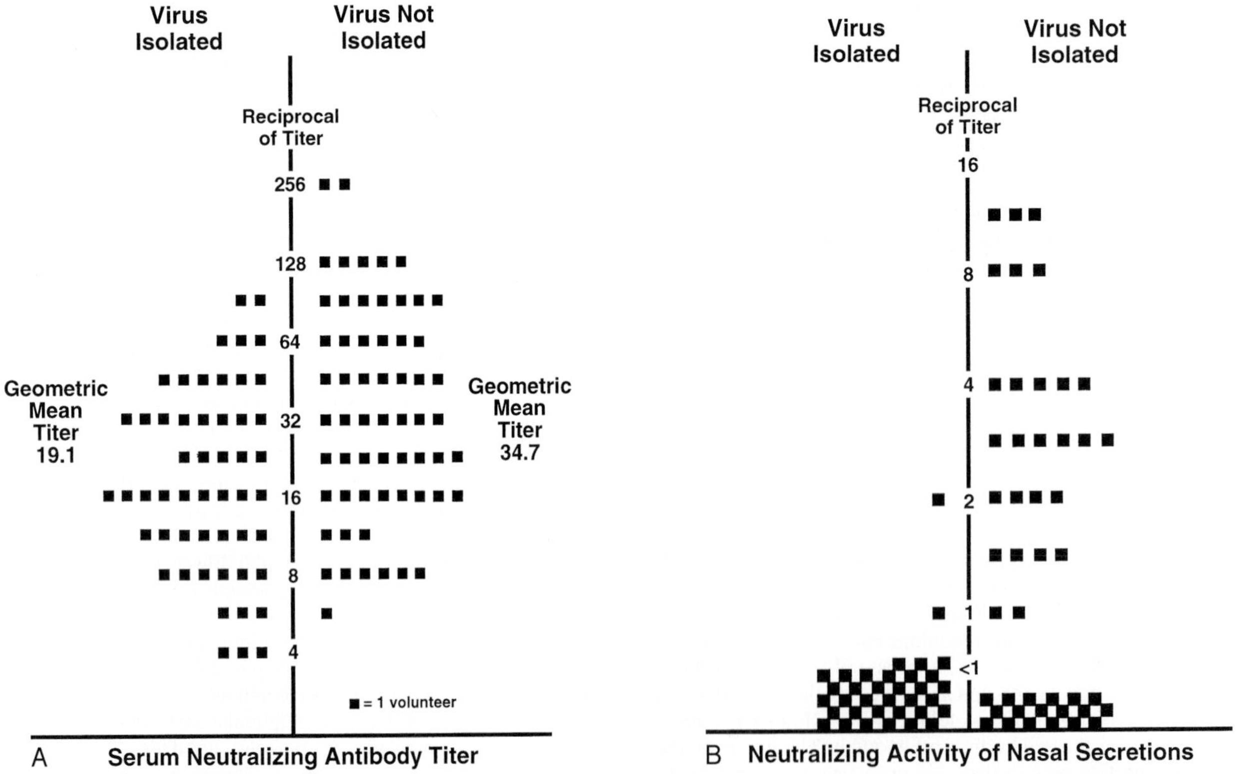

FIGURE 146–1. *A*, Serum neutralizing antibody titer before challenge with parainfluenza type 1 virus. *B*, Neutralizing activity of nasal secretions before challenge with parainfluenza type 1 virus. (From Smith CB, Purcell RH, Bellanti JA, et al. Protective effect of antibody to parainfluenza type I virus. N Engl J Med. 1966;275:1145–1152.)

TABLE 146–1 Diagnoses, Signs, and Symptoms in Patients from Whom Parainfluenza Viruses Were Isolated

	Type				
No. of Isolates	*1 (n = 77)*	*2 (n = 33)*	*3 (n = 157)*	*Other (n = 19)*	*p**
Diagnosis					
Acute otitis	38†	30	52	32	.03
Croup	16	6	5	21	.01
Bronchiolitis	1	9	6	0	
Signs and Symptoms					
Cough	73	67	81	77	
Hoarseness	28	18	11	39	.001
Rales/rhonchi	6	15	15	11	
Wheezing	9	12	4	5	
Temperature >38°C	33	16	38	6	.004
Irritability	47	30	54	72	.02

*Fisher's exact test for null hypothesis that all types are alike.
†Values are percentages of patients with the finding.
Data from ref. 38.

seen in the first 6 months of life,[50] an age at which most viral infections are prevented or attenuated by maternal antibody. By age 5, almost all children have experienced infection with all three parainfluenza types. The impact of parainfluenza virus infections is best reflected by the peaks of hospitalization for croup that occur during biannual type 1 epidemics, which have been estimated to cause 18,000 hospitalizations nationwide.[51] In all croup cases from which virus can be isolated, about 60% of the isolates are parainfluenza.[38, 45, 52] The cost of a typical parainfluenza type 1 and 2 fall epidemic was estimated at $190 milllon for emergency room use and hospitalization.[53] Parainfluenza type 3 virus is more endemic and less associated with the distinctive clinical finding of croup, but it causes more hospitalizations for lower respiratory tract illness than does either parainfluenza type 1 or 2. Although the best studies are now 35 years old, the role of parainfluenza viruses as the second leading contributor to pediatric hospitalization for respiratory disease, after respiratory syncytial virus, is unlikely to have changed.[54] One report described 10 hospitalizations associated with isolation of parainfluenza virus type 4.[55] Nosocomial spread of parainfluenza viruses among hospitalized patients has been shown to occur.[56, 57]

In adults, parainfluenza viruses have been implicated in about 10% of acute respiratory illnesses.[58] Disease is also seen in the elderly, but without the impact of respiratory syncytial virus or influenza.[59] Definition of the role of parainfluenza viruses in the elderly may require sensitive assays such as polymerase chain reaction[60] to detect the low-level shedding that typically accompanies viral infections in the elderly. Studies to date implicate parainfluenza viruses in less than 5% of acute respiratory infections in the elderly.[61, 62] Nevertheless, a nursing home outbreak has been described.[63]

CLINICAL MANIFESTATIONS

Parainfluenza viruses cause a spectrum of respiratory illnesses.[64] In healthy children, the majority of illnesses are upper respiratory, although 30 to 50% are associated with otitis media[65] (see Table 146–1). In a 20-year epidemiologic study at Vanderbilt, 15% of parainfluenza isolates were associated with lower respiratory tract disease.[38] Lower respiratory tract disease was manifested as either bronchiolitis, with types 2 and 3, or croup, with type 1.[38] Croup is characterized by a barking cough, a hoarse voice, and stridor. Radiographically, croup is distinguished by the "steeple sign" of progressive subglottic narrowing. In some children, repeated episodes of "spasmodic" croup may occur. It is unclear whether these episodes are separate illnesses. Among the virus isolates obtained from cases of croup, about 60% are parainfluenza.[38, 45, 52] In immunocompetent adults, clinical manifestations are primarily those of an upper respiratory tract infection.

Parainfluenza infections cause severe disease in both adult and pediatric bone marrow and lung transplant recipients.[66–69] In bone marrow transplant recipients at the University of Texas M. D. Anderson Hospital, 56% of 61 parainfluenza isolates were associated with uncomplicated upper respiratory illness; however, pneumonia developed in the remaining patients, with a mortality of 37%.[69] Similar data were reported from the University of Minnesota, which documented 27 parainfluenza infections among 1253 bone marrow transplant recipients, 6 of which were fatal.[66] In four cases the virus could be isolated only with bronchoalveolar lavage. Ten percent of lung transplant patients from the same institution suffered parainfluenza infections.[67] Other immunosuppressed patients can have prolonged shedding of parainfluenza viruses, particularly parainfluenza type 3.[70] Fatal pneumonias have been described in children with severe combined immunodeficiency syndrome.[71] Rarely, parainfluenza virus types 2 and 3 have been isolated from cerebrospinal fluid in association with aseptic meningitis[72, 73]

Parainfluenza viruses have not been strongly associated with asthma in adults.[74] However, in children an IgE-mediated pathway leading to recurrent wheezing after parainfluenza infection has been proposed.[75]

DIAGNOSIS

As with many viruses, three approaches to the diagnosis of parainfluenza virus infection are currently used: viral culture, detection of viral antigen or nucleic acid, and serologic analysis. The gold standard remains the isolation of virus in tissue culture. Parainfluenza viruses are rarely isolated from healthy children, so the finding of parainfluenza virus in association with an acute respiratory illness is strong proof of an association. The sensitivity of the method is greatest in primary infection, where 4 to 5 $\log_{10}$ of virus can be recovered per milliliter of nasal secretions for up to 10 days after the onset of illness.[76] In adults and older children undergoing repeated infections, the height and duration of virus shedding are much lower. In suspected lower respiratory tract disease in an immunocompromised host or transplant recipient, direct sampling of the lower respiratory tract by lung biopsy or lavage may be necessary to recover the agent.

Sensitive cell lines for parainfluenza virus include primary rhesus or cynomolgus monkey kidney cells and a monkey kidney line, LLC-MK2.[77] After primary isolation and identification by hemadsorption, the putative parainfluenza virus must be typed via immunofluorescence or hemadsorption inhibition. With parainfluenza type 2, hemadsorption cannot be relied on to identify all isolates, and immunofluorescence must be used to detect growth.[78] Critical to the success of isolating parainfluenza viruses is the way in which the specimen is collected (optimally by nasal wash or nasal aspiration), and the specimen must be kept at 4°C and transported promptly to the laboratory. Rapid diagnosis does not have the sensitivity of tissue culture and entails direct immunofluorescence of exfoliated cells and enzyme-linked immunosorbent assay (ELISA) capture techniques. No commercial ELISA kits are currently available. Polymerase chain reaction amplification has been described for parainfluenza type 3 virus[79] and will distinguish type 3 from types 1 and 2 in a single multiplex assay.[60] Serologic tests can be used to track the age-related acquisition of infection in infancy, and comparison of antibody titers in closely timed paired sera during and after an illness is a moderately sensitive and specific, although slow way of making a diagnosis. An acute serum specimen should be obtained within 4 days of the onset of illness and a convalescent serum specimen within 2 weeks of the illness.

THERAPY

The effectiveness of specific antivirals for parainfluenza virus infection has not been established. The use of ribavirin as an aerosolized or intravenous preparation has been reported after heart and bone marrow transplantation in anecdotal cases,[80, 81] but controlled studies are lacking. Aerosolized aprotinin, a protease inhibitor, reduced the mortality associated with Sendai virus infection in mice from 90% in the untreated group to 10% in the aprotinin-treated group. Inhibition of tryptase Clara by surfactant and other airway protease inhibitors is another theoretical antiviral approach.[82, 83] A similar effect was seen with an antibody to tryptase Clara.

In children, the weight of opinion is that aerosolized steroids have a role to play in the management of croup as a clinical illness.[84–86] In a recent study,[87] nebulized budesonide was compared with intramuscular dexamethasone and placebo in moderately severe croup in 144 children seen in the emergency room. All received racemic epinephrine and cool mist. Viral cultures were done in 133 of the patients, with parainfluenza viruses recovered from 46 of the children, 29 of whom had parainfluenza type 1. Only seven viruses other than parainfluenza were identified. Seventy-one percent of the placebo group required hospitalization versus 38% in the budesonide group and 23% in the dexamethasone group. The results in each group were significantly different from each other, and systemic steroids would seem to be the current treatment of choice. Nebulized epinephrine provides short-term relief, but return to the baseline obstruction occurs within 2 hours.[88] Its use in combination with either oral or intramuscular dexamethasone seems indicated. The value of cool mist has not been demonstrated in small controlled trials, but the clinical impression is one of improvement of children in the shower or during a ride to the hospital with exposure to cool air.[89]

PREVENTION

An inactivated whole-virus parainfluenza type 3 vaccine was explored in the late 1960s, but it was immunogenic and not protective. This vaccine was evaluated in parallel with an inactivated respiratory syncytial virus vaccine that resulted in enhanced illness. Because the parainfluenza type 3 vaccine did not enhance illness, development of inactivated and subunit vaccines has continued. Several subunit vaccines have been developed,[90, 91] but none have entered clinical testing.

Two live-attenuated, intranasally administered parainfluenza type 3 vaccines are in development.[92] One is derived from a bovine parainfluenza type 3 virus.[93] This vaccine protects against a challenge with human parainfluenza type 3 virus in chimpanzees.[94] The bovine strain has been evaluated in phase I trials in adults, children, and infants.[94–96] It appears to be safe and immunogenic and is undergoing commercial development. In parallel, a cold-adapted parainfluenza type 3 virus vaccine was attenuated by multiple passages in tissue culture.[97] At passage 12, the virus was still insufficiently attenuated in young children.[98] After 45 passages in tissue culture cells, it was evaluated for protection in a chimpanzee challenge model[99] and subsequently in stepwise studies in young children.[100] The safety and immunogenicity profile of the cold-passaged virus are comparable to that of the bovine strain,[34] and it is also undergoing further clinical evaluation. The potential for using attenuated parainfluenza type 3 strains to generate parainfluenza type 1 and 2 vaccines on the same genetic background as the type 3 strains is now being explored.[101] Critical questions that must still be answered are whether these vaccines can enable infants to mount an immune response, whether interference between strains occurs, and what degree of protection or amelioration of illness is provided by such vaccine approaches.

REFERENCES

1. Chanock RM. Association of a new type of cytopathogenic myxovirus with infantile croup. J Exp Med. 1956;104:555–576.
2. Chanock RM, Parrott RH, Cook K, et al. Newly recognized myxovirus in children with respiratory diseases. N Engl J Med. 1958;258:207–213.
3. Andrews CH, Bang FB, Chanock RM, et al. Parainfluenza viruses 1, 2, and 3: Suggested names for recently described myxoviruses. Virology. 1959;8:129–130.
4. Durbin AP, Siew JW, Murphy BR, et al. Minimum protein requirements for transcription and RNA replication of a minigenome of human parainfluenza virus type 3 and evaluation of the rule of six. Virology. 1997;234:74–83.
5. Durbin AP, Hall SL, Siew JW, et al. Recovery of infectious human parainfluenza virus type 3 from cDNA. Virology. 1997;235:323–332.
6. Lamb RA, Kolakofsky D. Paramyxoviridae: The viruses and their replication. In: Fields BN, Knipe DM, Howley PM, eds. Virology. Philadelphia: Lippincott-Raven; 1996:1177–1204.
7. Collins PL, Chanock RM, McIntosh K. Parainfluenza viruses. In: Fields BN, Knipe DM, Howley PM, eds. Virology. Philadelphia: Lippincott-Raven; 1990:1205–1241.
8. Wang LF, Michelski WP, Yu M, et al. A novel P/V/C gene in the new member of the member of the Paramyxoviridae family, which causes lethal infection in humans, horses, and other animals. J Virol. 1998;72:1482–1490.
8a. Centers for Disease Control and Prevention. Outbreak of Hendra-like virus—Malaysia and Singapore, 1998–1999. MMWR Morb Mortal Wkly Rep. 1999;48:265–269.
9. Yao Q, Hu X, Compans RW. Association of the parainfluenza virus fusion and hemagglutinin-neuraminidase glycoproteins on cell surfaces. J Virol. 1997;71:650–656.
10. Lamb RA. Paramyxovirus fusion: A hypothesis for changes. Virology. 1993;197;1–11.
11. Wright PF. Parainfluenza viruses 342–50. In: Belshe RB, ed. Textbook of Human Virology. 2nd ed. St. Louis: Mosby–Year Book; 1991.
12. Parrott RH, Vargosko AJ, Kim HW, et al. Clinical features of infection with hemadsorption viruses. N Engl J Med. 1959;260:731–738.
13. Heath RB. The pathogenesis of respiratory viral infection. Postgrad Med J. 1979;55:122–127.
14. Massion PP, Funari P, Ikeda S, et al. Parainfluenza (Sendai) virus infects ciliated cells and secretory cells but not basal cells of rat tracheal epithelium. Am J Respir Cell Mol Biol. 1993;9:361–370.
15. Blau DM, Compans RW. Polarization of viral entry and release in epithelial cells. Semin Virol. 1996;7:245–253.
16. Tashiro M, Yokogoshi M, Tobita K, et al. Organ tropism of Sendai virus in mice; proteolytic activation of the fusion glycoprotein in mouse organs and budding site at the bronchial epithelium. J Virol. 1990;64:3627–3634.
17. Tashiro M, Seto JT, Choosakul S, et al. Changes in specific cleavability of the Sendai virus fusion protein: Implications for pathogenicity in mice. J Virol. 1992;73:1575–1579.
18. Tashiro M, Yokogoshi Y, Tobita K, et al. Tryptase Clara, an activating protease for Sendai virus in rat lungs, is involved in pneumopathogenicity. J Virol. 1992;66:7211–7216.
19. Kido H, Yokogoshi Y, Sakai K, et al. Isolation and characterization of a novel trypsin-like protease found in rat bronchial Clara cells. J Biol Chem. 1992;267:13573–13579.
20. Sakai K, Kawaguchi Y, Kishino Y, et al. Electron immunohistochemical localization in rat bronchiolar epithelial cells of tryptase Clara, which determines the pneumotropism and pathogenes of Sendai virus and influenza virus. J Histochem Cytochem. 1993;41:89–93.
21. Sakai K, Kohri T, Tashiro M, et al. Sendai virus infection changes the subcellular localization of tryptase Clara in rat bronchiolar epithelial cells. J Eur Respir. 1994;7:686–692.
22. Morel-Barbey CL, Oeltmann TN, Edwards KM, et al. Role of respiratory tract protease in infectivity of influenza virus. J Infect Dis. 1987;155;667–672.
23. Kasel JA, Frank AL, Keitel WA, et al. Acquisition of serum antibodies to specific viral glycoproteins of parainfluenza virus 3 in children. J Virol. 1984;52:828–832.
24. Ray R, Glaze BJ, Compans RW. Role of individual glycoproteins of human parainfluenza virus type 3 in the induction of a protective immune response. J Virol. 1988;62:783–787.
25. Spriggs MK, Collins PL, Tierney E, et al. Immunization with vaccinia virus

recombinates that express the surface glycoproteins of human parainfluenza virus type 3 (PIV3) protects patas monkeys against PIV3 infection. J Virol. 1988;62:1293–1296.
26. Cole GA, Katz JM, Hogg TL, et al. Analysis of the primary T-cell response to Sendai virus infection in C57BL/6 mice: CD4+ T-cell recognition is directed predominantly to the hemagglutinin-neuraminidase glycoprotein. J Virol. 1994; 68:6863–6870.
27. Spriggs MK, Murphy BR, Prince GA, et al. Expression of the F and HN glycoproteins of human parainfluenza virus type 3 by recombinant vaccinia viruses: Contribution of the individual proteins to host immunity. J Virol. 1987;61:3416–3423.
28. Al-ahdal MN, Nakamura L, Flanagan TD. Cytotoxic T-lymphocyte reactivity with individual Sendai virus glycoproteins. J Virol. 1985;54:53–57.
29. Welliver R, Wong DT, Choi TS, et al. Natural history of parainfluenza virus infection in childhood. J Pediatr. 1982;101:180–187.
30. Glezen WP, Frank AL, Taber LH, et al. Parainfluenza virus type 3: Seasonality and risk of infection and reinfection in young children. J Infect Dis. 1984;150:851–857.
31. Hetherinton SV, Watson AS, Scroggs RA, et al. Human parainfluenza virus type 1 evolution combines cocirculation of strains and development of geographically restricted lineages. J Infect Dis. 1994;169:248–252.
32. van Wyke Coelingh KL, Winter C, Murphy BR. Antigentic variation in the hemagglutinin-neuraminidase protein of human parainfluenza type 3 virus. Virology. 1985;143:569–582.
33. Kapikian AZ, Chanock RM, Bethseda MD. et al. Inoculation of human volunteers with parainfluenza virus type 3. JAMA. 1961;178:537–541.
34. Karron RA, Wright PF, Newman FK, et al. A live human parainfluenza type 3 virus is attenuated and immunogenic in healthy infants and children. J Infect Dis. 1995;172:1445–1450.
35. Ray R, Glaze BJ, Moldoveanu Z, et al. Intranasal immunization of hampsters with envelope glycoproteins of human parainfluenza virus type 3. J Infect Dis. 1988;157:648–654.
36. Manzanec MB, Lamm ME, Lyn D, et al. Comparison of IgA versus IgG monoclonal antibodies for passive immunization of the murine respiratory tract. Virus Res. 1992;23:1–12.
37. Smith CB, Purcell RH, Bellanti JA, et al. Protective effect of antibody to parainfluenza type 1 virus. N Engl J Med. 1966;275:1145–1152.
38. Reed G, Jewett PH, Thompson J, et al. Epidemiology and clinical impact of parainfluenza virus infections in otherwise healthy infants and young children <5 years old. J Infect Dis. 1997;175:807–813.
39. Mazanec MB, Coudret CL, Fletcher DR. Intracellular neutralization virus by immunoglobulin A anti-hemoagglutination monoclonal antibodies. J Virol. 1995;69:1339–1343.
40. Mazanec MB, Nerud JG, Kaetzel CS, et al. A three-tiered view of the role of IgA mucosal defense. Immunol Today. 1993;14:430–435.
41. Mazanec MB, Nerud JG, Lamm ME. Immunoglobulin A monoclonal antibodies protect against Sendai virus. J Virol. 1987;61:2624–2626.
42. Hou S, Doherty PC. Clearance of Sendai virus $CD8^+$ T cells requires direct targeting to virus-infected epithelium. Eur J Immunol. 1995;25:111.
43. Sieg S, Xia L, Huang Y, et al. Specific inhibition of granzyme B by parainfluenza virus type 3. J Virol. 1995;69:3538–3541.
44. Glezen WP, Loda FA, Clyde WA, et al. Epidemiologic patterns of acute lower respiratory disease of children in a pediatric group practice. J Pediatr. 1971;78:397–406.
45. Knott AM, Long CE, Hall CB. Parainfluenza viral infections in pediatric outpatients: Seasonal patterns and clinical characteristics. Pediatr Infect Dis J. 1994;13:269–273.
46. Gardner SD. The isolation of parainfluenza 4 sub-types A and B in England and serological studies of their prevalence. J Hyg (Lond). 1969;67:540–545.
47. Kilgore GE, Dowdle WR. Antigenic characterization of parainfluenza 4A and 4B by the hemagglutination-inhibition test and distribution of HI antibody in human sera. Am J Epidemiol. 1970;91:306–316.
48. Muchmore HG, Parkinson AJ, Humphries JE, et al. Persistent parainfluenza virus shedding during isolation at the South Pole. Nature. 1981;289:187–189.
49. Moscona A, Galinski MS. Characterization of human parainfluenza virus type 3 persistent infection in cell culture. J Virol. 1990;64:3212–3218.
50. Moisiuk SE, Robson D, Klass L, et al. Outbreak of parainfluenza virus type 3 in an intermediate care neonatal nursery. J Pediatr Infect Dis. 1998;17:49–53.
51. Marx A, Torok TJ, Holman RC, et al. Pediatric hospitalizations for croup (laryngotracheobronchitis): Biennial increases associated with human parainfluenza virus 1 epidemics. J Infect Dis. 1997;176:1423–1427.
52. Denny FW, Murphy TF, Clyde WA Jr, et al. Croup: An 11 year study in a pediatric practice. Pediatrics. 1983;71:871–876.
53. Hendrickson KJ, Kuhn SM, Savatski LL. Epidemiology and cost of infection with human parainfluenza virus types 1 and 2 in young children. Clin Infect Dis. 1994;18:770–779.
54. Chanock RM, Parrott RH. Acute respiratory disease in infancy and childhood: Present understanding and prospects for prevention. J Pediatr. 1965;36:21–30.
55. Rubin EE, Wuennec P, McDonald JC. Infections due to parainfluenza virus type 4 in children. Clin Infect Dis. 1993;17:998–1002.
56. Karron RA, O'Brien KL, Froehlich JL, et al. Molecular epidemiology of parainfluenza type 3 virus outbreak on a pediatric ward. J Infect Dis. 1993;167:1441–1445.
57. Mufson MA, Mocega HE, Krause HE. Acquisition of parainfluenza 3 virus infection by hospitalized children I. Frequencies, rates, and temporal data. J Infect Dis. 1973;128:141–147.
58. Tumova B, Heinz F, Syrucek L, et al. Occurence and aetiology of acute respiratory diseases; results of a longterm surveillance programme. Acta Virol. 1988;33:50–62.
59. Nicholson KG, Kent J, Hammersley V, et al. Acute viral infections of upper respiratory tract in elderly people living in the community: Comparative, prospective, population based study of disease burden. BMJ. 1997;315:1060–1064.
60. Echevarria JE, Erdman DD, Swierkosz EM, et al. Simultaneous detection and identification of human parainfluenza viruses 1, 2 and 3 from clinical samples by multiplex PCR. J Clin Microbiol. 1998;36:1388–1391.
61. Falsey AR, McCann RM, Hall WJ, et al. Acute respiratory tract infection in daycare centers for older persons. JAGS. 1995;43:30–36.
62. Orr PH, Peeling RW, Brunka J, et al. Serology study of responses to selected pathogens causing respiratory tract infection in the institutionalized elderly. J Clin Infect Dis. 1996;23:1240–1245.
63. Glasgow KW, Tamblyn SE, Blair G. A respiratory outbreak due to parainfluenza virus type 3 in a home for the aged—Ontario. Can Commun Dis Rep. 1995;21(7):57–61.
64. Denny FW. The clinical impact of human respiratory virus infections. J Respir Crit Care Med. 1995;152(Suppl):S4–S12.
65. Henderson FW, Collier AM, Sanyal MA, et al. A longitudinal study of respiratory viruses and bacteria in the etiology of acute otitis media with effusion. N Engl J Med. 1982;306:1377–1384.
66. Wendt CH, Weisdorf DJ, Jordan CM, et al. Parafluenza virus respiratory infection after bone marrow transplantion. N Engl J Med. 1992;326:921–926.
67. Wendt C, Fox JMK, Hertz M. Paramyxovirus infection in lung transplant recipients. J Heart Lung Transplant. 1995;14:479–485.
68. Apalsch AM, Green M, Ledesma-Medina J, et al. Parainfluenza and influenza virus infections in pediatric organ transplant recipients. Clin Infect Dis. 1995;20:394–399.
69. Lewis VA, Champlin R, Englund J, et al. Respiratory disease due to parainfluenza virus in adult bone marrow transplant recipients. J Clin Infect Dis. 1996;23:1033–1037.
70. Scully RE, Mark EJ, McNeeley WF, et al. Case records of the Massachusetts General Hospital. N Engl J Med. 1996;335:1133–1140.
71. Jarvis WR, Middleton PJ, Gelfand EW. Parainfluenza pneumonia in severe combined immunodeficiency disease. J Pediatr. 1979;93:423–425.
72. Arisoy ES, Demmler GJ, Thakar S, et al. Meningitis due to parainfluenza virus type 3: Report of two cases and review. Clin Infect Dis. 1993;17:995–997.
73. Jantausch BA, Wiedermann BL, Jeffries B. Parainfluenza virus type 2 meningitis and parotitis in an 11-year-old child. South Med J. 1995;88:230–231.
74. Sokhandan M, McFadden R, Huang YT, et al. The contribution of respiratory viruses to severe exacerbations of asthma in adults Chest. 1995;107:1570–1575.
75. Welliver RC, Wong DT, Middleton E Jr, et al. Role of parainfluenza virus–specific IgE in pathogens of croup and wheezing subsequent to infection. J Infect Dis. 1982;101:889–896.
76. Frank AL, Taber LH, Wells CR, et al. Patterns of shedding of myxoviruses and paramyxoviruses in children. J Infect Dis. 1981;144:433–441.
77. Frank AL, Couch RB, Griffis CA, et al. Comparison of different tissue cultures for isolation and quantitation of influenza and parainfluenza viruses. J Clin Microbiol. 1979;10:32–36.
78. Henrickson KJ, Kuhn SM, Savatski, LL, et al. Recovery of human parainfluenza virus types one and two. J Virol Methods. 1994;46:189–205.
79. Karron RA, Froehlich JL, Bobo L, et al. Rapid detection of parainfluenza virus type 3 RNA in respiratory specimens: Use of reverse transcription–PCR–enzyme immunoassay. J Clin Microbiol. 1994;32:484–488.
80. Sparrelid LP, Ekelof-Andstrom E, Aschais J, et al. Ribavirin therapy in bone marrow transplant recipients with viral respiratory tract infection. Bone Marrow Transplant. 1997;19:905–908.
81. Cobian L, Houston S, Greene J, et al. Parainfluenza virus respiratory infection after heart transplantation: Successful treatment with ribavirin. Clin Infect Dis. 1995;21:1040–1041.
82. Kido H, Sakai K, Hishino Y, et al. Pulmonary surfactant is a potential endogenous inhibitor of proteolytic activation of Sendai virus and influenza A virus. FEBS Lett. 1993;322:115–119.
83. Beppu Y, Imamura Y, Tashiro M, et al. Human mucus protease inhibitor in airway fluids is a potential defensive compound against infection with influenza A and Sendai viruses. J Biochem. 1997;121:309–316.
84. Jaffee DM. The treatment of croup with glucocorticoids. N Engl J Med. 1998;339:553–554.
85. Klassen TP, Feldman ME, Watters LK, et al. Nubulized budesonide for children with mild-to-moderate croup. N Engl J Med. 1994;331:285–290.
86. Geelhoed G. Croup. Pediatr Pulmonol. 1997;23:370–374.
87. Johnson DA, Jacobson S, Edney PC, et al. A comparison of nebulized budesonide, intramuscular dexamethasone, and placebo for moderately severe croup. N Engl J Med. 1998;339:498–503.
88. Skolnik NS. Treatment of croup: A critical review. Am J Dis Child. 1989;143:1045–1049.
89. Bourchier D, Dawson KP, Fergusson DM. Humidification in viral croup: A controlled trial. Aust Paediatr J. 1984;20:289–291.
90. Homa FL, Brideau RJ, Lehman DJ, et al. Development of a novel subunit vaccine that protects cotton rats against both human respiratory syncytial virus and human parainfluenza virus type 3. J Gen Virol. 1993;74:1995–1999.
91. Ray R, Brown VE, Compans RW. Glycoproteins of human parainfluenza virus type 3: Characterization and evaluation as a subunit vaccine. J Infect Dis. 1985;152:1219–1230.
92. Murphy BR, Collins PL. Current status of respiratory syncytial virus (RSV) and parainfluenza virus type 3 (PIV3) vaccine development: Memorandum from a joint WHO/NIAID meeting. Bull World Health Organ. 1997;75:307–313.

93. van Wyke CL, Tierney EL, London WT, et al. Attenuation of bovine parainfluenza virus type 3 in nonhuman primates and its ability to confer immunity to human parainfluenza virus type 3 challenge. J Infect Dis. 1988;157:655–662.
94. Clements ML, Belshe RB, King J, et al. Evaluation of bovine, cold-adapted human, and wild-type human parainfluenza type 3 viruses in adult volunteers and in chimpanzees. J Clin Microbiol. 1991;29:1175–1182.
95. Karron RA, Wright PF, Hall SL, et al. A live attenuated bovine parainfluenza virus type 3 vaccine is safe, infectious, immunogenic, and phenotypically stable in infants and children. J Infect Dis. 1995;171:1107–1114.
96. Karron RA, Makene M, Gay K, et al. Evaluation of a live attenuated bovine parainfluenza type 3 vaccine in two- to six-month-old infants. Pediatr Infect Dis J. 1996; 15:650–654.
97. Belshe RB, Hissom FK. Cold adaption of parainfluenza virus type 3: Induction of three phenotypic markers. J Med Virol. 1982;10:235–242.
98. Choppin S, Richardson CD, Merz O, et al. The functions and inhibition of the membrane glycoproteins of paramyxoviruses and myxoviruses and the role of the measles virus M protein in subacute sclerosing panecephalitis. J Infect Dis. 1981;143:352–362.
99. Hall SL, Sarris CM, Tierney EL, et al. A cold-adapted mutant of parainfluenza virus type 3 is attenuated and protective in chimpanzees. J Infect Dis. 1993;167:958–962.
100. Belshe RB, Karron RA, Newman FK, et al. Evaluation of a live attenuated, cold-adapted parainfluenza virus type 3 vaccine in children. J Clin Microbiol. 1992;30:2064–2070.
101. Tao T, Durbin AP, Whitehead SS, Davoodi F, et al. Recovery of a fully viable chimeric human parainfluenza virus (PIV) type 3 in which the hemagglutinin-neuraminidase and fusion glycoproteins have been replaced by those of PIV type 1. J Virol. 1998;72:2995–2961.

Chapter 147

Mumps Virus

STEPHEN G. BAUM
NATHAN LITMAN

Mumps is an acute generalized viral infection that occurs primarily in school-aged children and adolescents. The most prominent manifestation of this disease is nonsuppurative swelling and tenderness of the salivary glands, with one or both parotid glands involved in most cases. The disease is benign and self-limited, with one third of affected persons having subclinical infection. Meningitis and epididymo-orchitis represent the two most important of the less frequent manifestations of this disease. As is characteristic of many viral infections, mumps is usually a more severe illness in persons past the age of puberty than in children and more commonly leads to extrasalivary gland involvement in these older patients.

HISTORY

Hippocrates described mumps and its contagious characteristics in the fifth century BC. In the late 1700s, Hamilton emphasized the occurrence of orchitis as a manifestation of mumps. The experimental production of the disease in monkeys by Johnson and Goodpasture in 1934[1] provided the evidence that a filterable virus was present in the saliva of patients with mumps. In 1945, Habel reported the cultivation of mumps virus in the chick embryo.[2] Enders and colleagues described the skin test and the development of complement-fixing antibodies after mumps in humans.[3] A killed virus vaccine used in the early 1950s on human subjects achieved limited success,[4] and in 1966 Buynak and Hilleman reported the development of an effective live virus vaccine.[5]

The etymology of the word *mumps* is unclear. It may arise from the English noun *mump*, meaning a lump, or from the English verb *to mump*, defined as "to be sulky"—a description of the characteristic facial expression. Alternatively, the term *mumps* has been ascribed to the mumbling speech pattern of the affected person. In the older literature, mumps may be called "epidemic parotitis."

THE AGENT

Mumps virus is a member of the Paramyxoviridae family, which includes the following genera: *Rubulavirus* (mumps virus, New Castle disease virus, human parainfluenza virus types 2, 4a, and 4b), *Paramyxovirus* (human parainfluenza virus types 1 and 3), *Morbillivirus* (measles), and *Pneumovirus* (human respiratory syncytial virus). The complete mumps virion has an irregular spherical shape, with a diameter ranging from 90 to 300 nm and averaging about 200 nm. The nucleocapsid is enclosed by an envelope that has three layers and is about 10 nm thick.[6] The external surface is regularly studded with glycoproteins possessing hemagglutinin, neuraminidase, and cell-fusion activity. The viral (V) antigen, antibodies to which are detected late in infection by the complement fixation test, is associated with this layer. The middle component of the envelope is a lipid bilayer that is acquired from the host cell as the virus buds off the cytoplasmic membrane. The innermost surface of the envelope is a nonglycosylated membrane protein that maintains the outer structure of the virus. The genome of the virus is contained in a nucleocapsid that is a helical structure composed of a continuous linear molecule of single-stranded RNA surrounded by symmetrically repeating protein subunits. The capsid protein carries RNA polymerase activity. The nucleocapsid represents the soluble (S) antigen, antibodies to which are detectable early in infection by the complement fixation test. Only one serotype of mumps virus is known.

Mumps virus is ether-sensitive by virtue of its lipid envelope. It is stable at 4°C for several days and at −65°C for months to years; however, repeated freezing and thawing may diminish viral activity.

The virus replicates in a variety of cell cultures as well as in embryonated hens' eggs.[7] In routine diagnostic virology, monkey kidney, human embryonic kidney, or HeLa cell cultures are used for primary isolation. Cytopathic effects such as the appearance of intracytoplasmic eosinophilic inclusions, rounding of cells, or the fusion of cells into giant multinucleate syncytia may be noted.[8] The presence of mumps virus is usually confirmed by the hemagglutination inhibition (HAI) test, which uses convalescent serum after mumps infection to inhibit the adsorption of chick erythrocytes added to mumps-infected epithelial cells.

EPIDEMIOLOGY

Mumps is endemic throughout the world. In the United States, before the licensing of live attenuated mumps vaccine in 1967, epidemics occurred every 2 to 5 years.[9] Although the disease occurred throughout the year, the peak incidence was between January and May.[10] Epidemics have been reported in military populations and other closed communities such as prisons, boarding schools, ships, and remote islands.[11, 12] Meyer demonstrated that mumps is spread through the community by children in schools, with secondary spread to family members.[13] There has been more than a 99% decline in the annual U.S. incidence of mumps since 1967, with only 751 cases reported to the Centers for Disease Control and Prevention (CDC) in 1996; the seasonal variation that was evident in earlier years is no longer apparent.[14]

Mumps is uncommon in infants younger than 1 year of age. Resistance to infection in this age group is on the basis of passive immunity acquired by the placental transfer of maternal antibody. In the prevaccine era, more than 50% of the cases occurred in the 5- to 9-year-old age group, and 90% of the cases occurred in children younger than 14 years of age. In 1996, more than a third of infections were reported in persons older than 15 years of age. In the prevaccine era, 80 to 90% of adults older than 20 years of age in the United States were immune to mumps on the basis of natural infection. At present in the United States, immunity to mumps among children and most young adults relies on prior vaccination. Men and women have the same frequency of development of parotitis with mumps infection.[15]

Humans are the only known natural host; however, monkeys

and other laboratory animals have been experimentally infected.[1] Although persistent infections in cultured cells are commonly established by mumps virus,[16] a carrier state is not known to exist in humans.

PATHOGENESIS

The virus is naturally transmitted via direct contact, droplet nuclei, or fomites and enters through the nose or mouth. More intimate contact is needed to transmit mumps than for either measles or varicella. The period of peak contagion is just before or at the onset of parotitis.

Experimental mumps infection has been produced in humans and monkeys by direct instillation of the virus into Stensen's duct.[1] However, the incubation period in this experimental model is shorter than in naturally occurring disease, and initial infection of the parotid gland does not explain the fact that meningitis or other manifestations of mumps infection may occur before the onset of parotitis. It has been suggested that during the incubation period the virus proliferates in the upper respiratory tract epithelium and that viremia ensues, with secondary dissemination and localization to glandular and neural tissue.[17, 18]

PATHOLOGY

Salivary glands from patients infected with mumps are rarely available for pathologic examination because of the benign course in the great majority of the cases. When parotid glands have been examined, diffuse interstitial edema has been found, along with a serofibrinous exudate consisting primarily of mononuclear leukocytes. Neutrophils and necrotic debris accumulate within the ductal lumen, and the ductal epithelium shows degenerative changes. The glandular cells are relatively spared, but they may also be involved with edema and overflow of the inflammatory reaction from the interstitial tissues. The multinucleate syncytia and intracytoplasmic eosinophilic inclusions that are occasionally seen in mumps-infected tissue culture are not present in vivo. When the pancreas or the testis is involved, the microscopic picture is quite similar to that seen in the salivary glands, except that interstitial hemorrhage and polymorphonuclear leukocytes are more frequently noted in orchitis. Local areas of infarction may occur because the vascular supply is compromised by increased pressure due to edema within an inelastic tunica albuginea. When the process has been particularly severe, atrophy of the germinal epithelium may result, with accompanying hyalinization and fibrosis.

The description of brain involvement in mumps encephalitis has most often been that of a postinfectious encephalitis characterized by perivenous demyelinization, perivascular mononuclear cuffing, and a generalized increase in microglial cells with relative sparing of neurons.[19] However, descriptions of what appears to be a primary mumps encephalitis have been reported that show widespread neuronolysis but without evidence of demyelinization.[20]

CLINICAL MANIFESTATIONS

The incubation period of mumps averages 16 to 18 days, with a range of 2 to 4 weeks. Characteristically, the prodromal symptoms are nonspecific and include low-grade fever, anorexia, malaise, and headache. Within a day, the nature of the illness becomes apparent when the patient complains of an earache, and tenderness can be elicited by palpation of the ipsilateral parotid. The involved gland is soon visibly enlarged and progresses to a maximum size over the next 2 to 3 days. The most severe pain accompanies the period of rapid enlargement. At its height, parotitis results in lifting of the ear lobe upward and outward. Lesser degrees of enlargement can more readily be appreciated by viewing the patient from behind. The enlarged parotid gland obscures the angle of the mandible, whereas cervical adenopathy does not hide this anatomic landmark. Usually, one parotid gland enlarges a couple of days after the other; however, mumps results in unilateral parotitis alone in one quarter of patients with salivary gland involvement. The orifice of Stensen's duct is frequently edematous and erythematous. Trismus may result from the parotitis, and the patient may have difficulty with pronunciation and mastication. Ingestion of citrus fruits or juices typically exacerbates the pain. During the first 3 days of illness, the patient's temperature may range from normal to 40°C. After parotid swelling has reached its peak, pain, fever, and tenderness rapidly resolve, and the parotid gland returns to normal size within a week. Complications of parotitis are rare but are reported to include sialectasia resulting in recurrent acute and chronic sialadenitis.[21]

Involvement of the other salivary glands may occur in conjunction with parotitis in up to 10% of the cases but is rare as the sole manifestation of mumps infection (Table 147–1). Submandibular gland involvement mimics signs of anterior cervical lymphadenopathy. The sublingual glands are the least frequently inflamed during mumps infection; when involvement occurs, it is usually bilateral and may be associated with swelling of the tongue. Presternal pitting edema develops in 6% of patients with mumps, most commonly in those who have submandibular adenitis.[22] The proposed mechanism for the involvement of the tongue and presternal area is obstruction of the lymphatic drainage of those regions by enlarged salivary glands.

Central nervous system involvement is the most common extrasalivary gland manifestation of mumps. As documentation of the remarkable neurotropism of this virus, Bang and Bang[23] reported the presence of cerebrospinal fluid (CSF) pleocytosis in 51% of 255 patients with mumps but without other evidence of meningitis. Clinical meningitis occurs in 1 to 10% of persons with mumps parotitis,[24] on the other hand, only 40 to 50% of the patients with mumps meningitis, confirmed by serology or viral isolation, have parotitis.[24–27] Meningeal symptoms, like any of the other manifestations of mumps infection, may occur before, during, after, or in the absence of parotitis. Its onset averages 4 days after the appearance of salivary gland involvement but may be as early as 1 week before or as late as 2 weeks after parotitis.[23–26] Men are afflicted three times as often as women,[24–27] but the age distribution is the same as for uncomplicated mumps. Ritter noted that mumps meningitis with parotitis is most frequent in the spring, whereas meningitis without parotitis is most frequent in summer.[25] The typical clinical features associated with viral meningitis are present, that is, headache, vomiting, fever, and nuchal rigidity. Lumbar puncture yields CSF containing 10 to 2000 white blood cells (WBC) per mm^3. The predominating cells are usually lymphocytes, but 20 to 25% of the patients have a polymorphonuclear leukocyte predominance.[26] Protein levels are normal to mildly elevated, and 90 to 95% of the patients have a CSF protein content of less than 70 mg/100 ml.[26, 27] Hypoglycorrhachia (CSF

TABLE 147–1 Frequency of Common Clinical Manifestations of Mumps

Manifestation	Frequency (%)
Glandular	
Parotitis	60–70
Submandibular and/or sublingual sialadenitis	10
Epididymo-orchitis*	25 (postpubertal men)
Oophoritis*	5 (postpubertal women)
Neural	
CSF pleocytosis	50
Meningitis	1–10
Encephalitis	0.1
Transient high-frequenty deafness	4
Other	
ECG abnormalities	5–15
Renal function abnormalities (mild)	>60

*Rare before puberty and usually unilateral.
Abbreviations: CSF, Cerebrospinal fluid; ECG, electrocardiogram.

glucose concentration of <40 mg/100 ml) is reported in 6 to 30% of the patients[26–28] and appears to be more common than in other viral meningitides. These CSF abnormalities may persist for 5 weeks or longer.[25, 28] The finding of a depressed CSF sugar level with a moderate to marked pleocytosis may cause the physician to consider bacterial meningitis in the differential diagnosis, especially if neutrophils predominate, as they may early in the disease. As in other cases of meningitis, when mononuclear cells prevail in the CSF, tuberculous and fungal disorders should be considered.

Abatement of fever by lysis and resolution of symptoms generally occur 3 to 10 days after the onset of illness. The meningitis is benign, with complete recovery and an absence of sequelae. Before the introduction of the live attenuated mumps vaccine in 1967, mumps accounted for approximately 10% of the cases of aseptic meningitis in the United States. At present, aseptic meningitis is rarely attributed to mumps.

Encephalitis is reported to occur in from 1 in 6000[29] to 1 in 400[30] cases of mumps. The former ratio probably represents a more accurate estimate. There appears to be a bimodal distribution of cases according to the time of onset: an early group in which onset that coincides with the presence of parotitis and a larger, late group in which the condition develops 7 to 10 days after the onset of parotitis. As noted in the section on pathology, early-onset encephalitis represents direct damage to neurons as a result of viral invasion, whereas late-onset disease is a postinfectious demyelinating process related to the host response to infection. These two processes probably represent the ends of a continuum of disease. Some patients die after the primary viral invasion of the brain, and some of those who survive produce antibodies to the virus or neural breakdown products and develop an "autoimmune" reaction. The clinical features are generally those of a nonfocal encephalitis; in addition to marked changes in the level of consciousness, neurologic findings may include convulsions, paresis, aphasia, and involuntary movements. CSF values are similar to those in uncomplicated meningitis. Fever is quite high, and characteristically temperatures of 40 to 41°C are present. Neurologic manifestations and fever gradually resolve over a period of 1 to 2 weeks. Sequelae such as psychomotor retardation and convulsive disorders are reported,[25–27] but their frequency cannot be determined from the available data. Death occurs in 1.4% of the reported cases.[30]

Through the mid-1960s, mumps was the leading recognized cause of viral encephalitis in the United States, being responsible for 20 to 30% of cases. However, by 1981, it represented only 0.5% of cases of viral encephalitis nationwide, and by the 1990s, mumps encephalitis was rare. The major factor accounting for this change was an effective mumps immunization program.

The term *meningoencephalitis* is frequently used in describing patients with various degrees of central nervous system involvement.[20, 24, 25, 28, 31] This term should be eliminated in reference to mumps because it confuses a common and essentially benign condition (meningitis) with a relatively uncommon and serious illness (encephalitis) that may result in neurologic residua or death. Clearly, many patients with mumps meningitis may have lethargy, as may a large percentage of persons with any viral infection such as influenza. However, the presence of profound changes in the level of consciousness or other findings suggestive of supratentorial involvement indicate the clear diagnosis of encephalitis as distinct from the ambiguous designation of meningoencephalitis. Although nuchal rigidity and CSF pleocytosis may be present in patients with encephalitis, the meningeal component is a trivial aspect of this illness.

Transient high-frequency-range deafness has been reported in 4.4% of the cases of mumps in a military population.[32] Permanent unilateral deafness occurs in 1 in 20,000 cases of mumps.[33] The onset of otologic symptoms may be gradual or abrupt; vertigo is frequently present. On subsequent testing, vestibular function has been normal.

Other neurologic syndromes rarely associated with, mumps include cerebellar ataxia,[34] facial palsy,[35] transverse myelitis,[36] ascending polyradiculitis (Guillain-Barré syndrome),[37] and a poliomyelitis-like syndrome.[38] There are now several well-documented cases of aqueductal stenosis and hydrocephalus developing after central nervous system infection caused by mumps.[39–41] Experimental and clinical reports clearly implicate mumps as the probable causative disorder.[42–44]

Epididymo-orchitis is the most common extrasalivary gland manifestation in the adult. It develops in 20 to 30% of postpubertal males undergoing mumps infection and is bilateral in one of six of those with testicular involvement.[45, 46] Although it has been reported in infancy, it is rare before puberty. Two thirds of cases occur during the first week of parotitis, and another one quarter arise during the second week.[45] However, gonadal involvement may precede parotitis or occur as the only manifestation of mumps. The onset is abrupt, with temperatures in the range of 39 to 41°C, chills, headache, vomiting, and testicular pain. Genital examination reveals warmth, swelling, and tenderness of the involved testicle and erythema of the scrotum. Epididymitis is present in 85% of the cases and usually precedes the orchitis. The testis may be enlarged to three to four times its normal size. Constitutional complaints and fever generally parallel the severity of gonadal involvement. Fever resolves in 84% of the patients in 5 days or less. Pain and swelling resolve shortly after defervescence. However, tenderness may persist for longer than 2 weeks in 20% of the cases.[45] Early in convalescence, a loss of turgor may be appreciated. When testes are examined months to years later, some degree of atrophy is noted in 50% of the patients.

The anxiety engendered by mumps orchitis is difficult to allay. The psychological fears of sexual impotence and sterility far outweigh the potential debility from testicular atrophy. Clearly, most men who have unilateral orchitis need fear nothing other than a possible cosmetic imbalance. Even those with bilateral involvement should be assured that impotence (other than psychogenic) is not a sequela and that sterility is rare. In large surveys of infertile men, mumps is infrequently implicated as the causative disorder. Twenty-eight cases of testicular malignancy in men with atrophy of the testis due to mumps orchitis have been reported.[47]

Oophoritis develops in 5% of postpubertal women with mumps. Symptoms include fever, nausea, vomiting, and lower abdominal pain. Impaired fertility and premature menopause have been reported as a consequence of ovarian involvement but must be considered to be rare.[48]

Joint involvement during mumps is noted infrequently in adults and rarely in children.[49, 50] Migratory polyarthritis is the most frequently described clinical form. Monoarticular arthritis and arthralgia have also been reported; both large and small joints are involved. Symptoms most commonly start 10 to 14 days after the onset of parotitis and may last up to 5 weeks. The process resolves spontaneously without residual joint damage.

Pancreatitis is manifested by severe epigastic pain and tenderness accompanied by fever, nausea, and vomiting. It is uncommon as a severe illness; however, many affected persons may complain of mild degrees of upper abdominal discomfort.

Electrocardiographic changes appear in up to 15% of patients with mumps; the most common abnormalities are depressed ST segments, flattened or inverted T waves, and prolonged P–R intervals.[51, 52] Clinically manifested myocarditis is rare; however, deaths associated with myocarditis have been reported both during the acute illness and after a chronically progressive deteriorating course.[51, 52]

Utz and colleagues[53] prospectively evaluated renal function in 20 young adult Navy servicemen admitted with mumps. These investigators discovered transient mild to moderate abnormalities of urinary concentration, creatinine clearance, and phenolsulfonphthalein excretion in most of this group. Hughes and associates have reported two deaths related to mumps-associated nephritis.[54]

A variety of other manifestations have accompanied mumps infection, but the following must be considered extremely rare: thyroiditis,[55] mastitis,[56] prostatitis,[57] hepatitis,[58] and thrombocytopenia.[59]

COMPLICATIONS

Gestational viral infections have been extensively investigated in a controlled cohort study by Siegel and coworkers.[60–62] They observed excess fetal deaths when mumps developed during the first trimester; second- and third-trimester mumps infections were not associated with increased fetal mortality.[60] Low birth weight (<2500 g) was identified in 7.7% of infants born to mumps-infected mothers, compared with 3.3% of a control group; this is not, however, a statistically significant difference. Although the number of cases was small, when the data were analyzed with respect to the onset of infection, the effect on birth weight was greatest when mumps occurred in the first trimester.[61] A variety of congenital malformations have been described in pregnancies complicated by maternal mumps[63]; however, these anomalies are described in single case reports without comparison with an uninfected control population. As reported by Siegel and colleagues,[62] occurrence rates of major congenital defects were equal in both mumps and control newborn populations; even when the data were analyzed by trimester, no trends could be established. Similar results have been obtained by a British team after reviewing 500 pregnancies complicated by maternal mumps.[64]

St. Geme and others have suggested an "embryopathic" relationship between intrauterine mumps infection and endocardial fibroelastosis (EFE) on the basis of the presence of skin test reactivity to mumps antigen in a high percentage of the EFE patients.[65] Experimentally induced infection of the chick embryo has added histopathologic support to this association.[66] Although some observers have disputed that mumps plays an etiologic role[67], recent studies using polymerase chain reaction (PCR) techniques have demonstrated mumps viral RNA in more than 70% of samples of myocardium from patients with autopsy-proven EFE.[68] There has been a marked decline in the incidence of EFE in the last 2 decades.

A similar controversy exists over the possible role of mumps in the etiology of juvenile diabetes mellitus. Diabetes, either transient or permanent, which developed soon after mumps, has been the subject of a number of case reports.[69, 70] However, it is not clear whether this is simply coincidental. Epidemiologic studies have demonstrated a 7-year periodicity in the incidence of both mumps and childhood diabetes, with a 3- to 4-year lag time between their respective peaks.[71] Coxsackievirus B4 has also been epidemiologically linked to diabetes.[72] Although the frequency of EFE has declined in recent years, there has not been a decline in the frequency of juvenile diabetes mellitus coincident with the decreasing frequency of mumps after introduction of the mumps vaccine.

IMMUNOLOGY

After clinical or subclinical mumps infection, a variety of immunologic responses can be demonstrated. Complement-fixing antibodies directed against the S antigen appear rapidly; sometimes they are present at the onset of clinically apparent illness. Anti-V antibody titers rise more slowly and peak about 2 to 4 weeks after the beginning of disease.[73] However, anti-S antibody titers decline rapidly over a period of several months to undetectable levels, whereas anti-V antibody titers drop more slowly and persist for years. This pattern of response provides the possibility of a serologic diagnosis of mumps from a single serum specimen. An acute-phase serum demonstrating a high anti-S–low anti-V titer or a high anti-S–high anti-V titer can be interpreted as evidence of current or very recent infection, respectively. The presence in serum of only anti-V antibodies would indicate a more remote infection with mumps.

Neutralizing antibodies appear during convalescence, and detectable titers persist for years. Although assays for these antibodies constitute the most reliable test to determine whether a person is immune to mumps, such assays are cumbersome and not routinely performed. Assays for HAI antibodies, which also develop after the onset of mumps, are the simplest of the serologic studies, but results are unreliable because of potential cross-reactions with other paramyxoviruses. Enzyme-linked immunosorbent assays (ELISAs) for antibody to mumps have been developed[74, 75] and are widely available.

Delayed hypersensitivity to an intradermally administered mumps skin test antigen develops between 3 weeks and 3 months after mumps.[3] The skin test was widely used as a measure of immunity to mumps as well as a test for the competence of delayed hypersensitivity. The use of mumps skin test antigen to determine immunity to mumps has been abandoned because of the variability of lots of the skin test antigen, and because of false-positive and false-negative results.

Transplacental transfer of maternal mumps complement-fixing, HAI, and neutralizing antibodies has been demonstrated.[76] Titers in maternal and cord serum are nearly identical. Neutralizing antibodies persist for several months and account for the rarity of mumps in young infants, as well as for the lack of response to immunization in this age group. One attack of mumps, whether inapparent or clinically manifested, confers lifelong immunity.

DIAGNOSIS

In most instances, the diagnosis of mumps is made on the basis of a history of exposure and of parotid swelling and tenderness accompanied by mild to moderate constitutional symptoms.

Either the WBC and differential counts in mumps are normal, or there may be a mild leukopenia with a relative lymphocytosis. When meningitis, orchitis, or pancreatitis is present, leukocytosis with a shift to the left is most commonly encountered. The serum amylase level is elevated in the presence of parotitis and may remain abnormal for 2 to 3 weeks. Serum amylase levels may also be elevated in the absence of clinical salivary gland involvement. Mumps pancreatitis also increases amylase levels; differentiation from salivary gland amylase may be achieved by isoenzyme analysis or serum pancreatic lipase determinations.

The typical CSF findings in mumps meningitis have been described previously. Similar although less marked CSF abnormalities are present in half of the patients with mumps parotitis but without apparent central nervous system involvement. In a patient with aseptic meningitis, an elevated serum amylase level should suggest mumps infection.

Laboratory confirmation of typical mumps is unnecessary. However, when parotitis is absent or recurrent, when extrasalivary gland manifestations are prominent, or when documentation of the presence of a specific viral disorder is desired, a variety of diagnostic aids can be used.

The definitive diagnosis of mumps depends on serologic studies or viral isolation. The presence of IgM antibodies as determined by ELISA or a fourfold rise between acute and convalescent sera on complement fixation, HAI, ELISA, or neutralization testing confirms the diagnosis. The HAI test can be affected by heterologous antibody responses to parainfluenza virus infection. Because parotitis can be caused by parainfluenza 3 virus,[77] serologic testing and virus isolation studies for parainfluenza 3 virus should be undertaken if the HAI test is used in the diagnosis of mumps. Immunity to mumps is usually assessed by ELISA. This assay combines ease of performance with reliability.

Virus is usually present in saliva for about 1 week, from 2 to 3 days before to 4 to 5 days after the onset of parotitis. However, virus has been isolated from saliva as early as 6 days before and as late as 9 days after the first signs of salivary gland involvement. In addition, virus may be recovered from the saliva of persons with inapparent infection or those who manifest only extrasalivary gland signs.[78] The virus is frequently isolated from the CSF in patients with clinical meningitis during the first 3 days of meningeal symptoms[24] and is present as late as the sixth day of central nervous system disease. Viruria has been detected during the first 2 weeks of illness: in one study, 72% of urine specimens during the first 5 days of illness yielded a positive culture.[53] Viremia has rarely been detected and has been found only during the first 2 days of illness.[17, 18]

DIFFERENTIAL DIAGNOSIS

A variety of entities may simulate mumps but can be easily differentiated from mumps on the basis of chronicity or associated symptoms. Infectious processes involving parotid glands are most likely to be confused with mumps because of their acute onset and associated fever. Parainfluenza 3 virus, coxsackieviruses, and influenza A viruses have been reported to cause acute parotitis.[77, 79, 80] These entities can be differentiated from mumps only by viral culture or serology. Bilateral parotid swelling is often seen in children with human immunodeficiency virus (HIV) infection. Suppurative parotitis, most often caused by *Staphylococcus aureus* or gram-negative organisms, usually occurs in the postoperative period, in premature newborns, or in debilitated patients with poor oral intake. The gland is warm, hard, and extremely tender; the overlying skin is erythematous. Massage of the parotid expresses purulent drainage from Stensen's duct.

Parotid enlargement caused by drugs or metabolic disorders is usually bilateral and asymptomatic. Phenylbutazone, thiouracil, iodides, and phenothiazines have been implicated in this condition.[57] Diabetes mellitus, malnutrition, cirrhosis, and uremia are among the metabolic disorders that can cause parotid swelling.[57]

Tumors, cysts, and obstruction caused by stones or structure are usually unilateral. Rare conditions that may mimic mumps include Mikulicz's syndrome, Parinaud's syndrome, uveoparotid fever of sarcoidosis, and Sjögren's syndrome.

THERAPY

Therapy for mumps parotitis is symptomatic and supportive. Treatment with analgesic-antipyretics such as aspirin or acetaminophen relieves pain caused by salivary gland inflammation and reduces fever. Topical application of warm or cold packs to the parotid may also relieve discomfort. Intravenous fluid administration may be necessary for patients with meningitis or pancreatitis who have persistent vomiting. Lumbar puncture may relieve the headache associated with meningitis.

Management of orchitis is purely symptomatic. Bed rest, narcotic analgesics, support of the inflamed testis with a "bridge," and ice packs make the patient feel more comfortable. An anesthetic block of the spermatic cord with 1% procaine hydrochloride may alleviate severe pain.[81] There is no convincing evidence that the use of steroids or diethylstilbestrol or incision of the tunica albuginea produces more rapid resolution of the orchitis or prevents subsequent atrophy. Interferon-alfa-2b administered to four men with bilateral mumps orchitis resulted in prompt resolution of symptoms, with no evidence of testicular atrophy or oligospermia during follow-up study.[82] Further investigation to establish the efficacy of this treatment is needed.

Gellis[83] and colleagues have shown that 20 ml of mumps immune globulin administered intramuscularly to adult men with mumps reduces the incidence of orchitis from 27.4% to 7.8%. However, mumps immune globulin is no longer commercially available.

PREVENTION

Recommendations for the management of patients with mumps include isolation until the parotid swelling has resolved to prevent the spread of infection to susceptible persons. This measure may be of little value, particularly in closed populations such as schools or hospitals,[84] because virus is present in saliva days before parotitis develops and because persons with clinically inapparent infection can shed virus.

Passive protection to exposed susceptible persons may have been afforded by mumps immune globulin, available in the past. However, Reed and colleagues[12] report that use of mumps immune globulin during an epidemic in Alaska did not reduce clinical parotitis or inapparent infection rates and did not diminish the incidence of meningitis and orchitis.

Active immunization with the Jeryl Lynn strain of attenuated mumps virus vaccine has been available in the United States since December 1967. The vaccine is prepared in chick embryo cell culture.[5] A single subcutaneous immunization produces protective levels of mumps-neutralizing antibodies in more than 95% of vaccines.[5] Although the antibody levels produced are lower than after natural infection, adequate titers are maintained for at least 10.5 years.[85] Adverse reactions to the vaccine are uncommon; transient suppression of tuberculin-delayed hypersensitivity has been reported. Vaccine virus is not present in secretions of immunized children. In Japan, aseptic meningitis associated with mumps vaccine virus occurred in 0.05 to 0.3% of recipients of the Urabe AM 9 mumps vaccine; manifestations began 2 to 4 weeks after immunization.[86, 87] Studies in the United States did not reveal evidence of an increased risk of aseptic meningitis after administration of the Jeryl Lynn strain of mumps vaccine.[88]

All children older than 12 months of age should be immunized. Vaccination should take place at 12 to 15 months of age and again at 5 to 12 years of age, as part of immunization with the combined live measles-mumps-rubella virus vaccine (MMR). Most states now require evidence of immunity to mumps (i.e., documented immunization, physician-diagnosed disease, or antibody studies) for school entrance and attendance (see Chapter 312). Immunization should also be considered for male adolescents and adults without a history of mumps. Male medical personnel who have no neutralizing antibodies to mumps should be immunized. Immunization after exposure may not provide protection from natural infection.

As with other live virus vaccines, mumps vaccine should not be administered to pregnant women, patients receiving immunosuppressive therapy, or persons with severe febrile illnesses, advanced malignancies, or congenital or acquired immunodeficiencies. Serious reactions to the mumps component of MMR have not been reported in limited studies in HIV-infected patients. However, a fatal case of measles pneumonitis occurred in a 21-year-old man with advanced HIV disease who was vaccinated with MMR; therefore, MMR should not be administered to such patients[89] (see Chapter 312).

REFERENCES

1. Johnson CD, Goodpasture EW. An investigation of the etiology of mumps. J Exp Med. 1934;59:1.
2. Habel K. Cultivation of mumps virus in the developing chick embryo and its application to the studies of immunity to mumps in man. Pub Health Rep. 1945;60:201.
3. Enders JF, Cohen S, Kane LW. Immunity in mumps. II. The development of complement fixing antibody and dermal hypersensitivity in human beings following mumps. J Exp Med. 1945;81:119.
4. Habel K. Vaccination of human beings against mumps; vaccine administered at the start of an epidemic. I. Incidence and severity of mumps in vaccinated and control groups. Am J Hyg. 1951;54:295.
5. Buynak EB, Hilleman MR. Live attenuated mumps virus vaccine. I. Vaccine development. Proc Soc Exp Biol Med. 1966;123:768.
6. Kleiman MB. Mumps virus. In: Lennette EH, ed. Laboratory Diagnosis of Viral Infections. 2nd ed. New York: Marcel Dekker; 1992:549.
7. Deinhardt FW, Shramek GJ. Mumps virus. In: Lennette EH, Spaulding EH, Truant JP, eds. Manual of Clinical Microbiology. Washington, DC: American Society for Microbiology; 1974:703.
8. Henle G, Deinhardt F, Girardi A. Cytolytic effects of mumps virus in tissue cultures of epithelial cells. Proc Soc Exp Biol Med. 1954;87:386.
9. Centers for Disease Control and Prevention. Mumps Surveillance 1973. MMWR. 1974;23:431.
10. Centers for Disease Control and Prevention. Summary of notifiable diseases, United States, 1991. MMWR. 1991;40:3.
11. Philip RN, Reinhard KR, Lackman DB. Observations on a mumps epidemic in a "virgin" population. Am J Hyg. 1959;69:91.
12. Reed D, Brown G, Merrick R, et al. A mumps epidemic on St. George Island, Alaska. JAMA. 1967;199:967.

13. Meyer MG. An epidemiologic study of mumps; its spread in schools and families. Am J Hyg. 1962;75:259.
14. Centers for Disease Control and Prevention. Summary of notifiable diseases, United States, 1996. MMWR 1996;45(53):1–88.
15. Centers for Disease Control and Prevention. Mumps surveillance, Report No. 1. January 1968.
16. Truant AL, Hullum JV. A persistent infection of baby hamster kidney—21 cells with mumps virus and the role of temperature sensitive variants. J Med Virol. 1977;1:49.
17. Kilham L. Isolation of mumps virus from the blood of a patient. Proc Soc Exp Biol Med. 1948;69:99.
18. Overman Jr. Viremia in human mumps infection. Arch Intern Med. 1958;102:354.
19. Donohue WL, Playfair FD, Whitaker L. Mumps encephalitis. J Pediatr. 1955;47:395.
20. Taylor FB, Toreson WE. Primary mumps meningo-encephalitis. Arch Intern Med. 1963;112:216.
21. Travis LW, Hecht DW. Acute and chronic inflammatory diseases of the salivary glands, diagnosis and management. Otolaryng Clin North Am 1977;10:329.
22. Gellis SS, Peters M. Mumps with presternal edema. Bull Johns Hopkins Hosp. 1944;75:241.
23. Bang HO, Bang J. Involvement of the central nervous system in mumps. Acta Med Scand. 1943;113:487.
24. McLean DM, Bach RD, Larke RPB, et al. Mumps meningoencephalitis, Toronto, 1963. Can Med Assoc J. 1964;90:458.
25. Ritter BS. Mumps meningoencephalitis in children. J Pediatr. 1958;52:424.
26. Levitt LP, Rich TA, Kinde SW, et al. Central nervous system mumps. Neurology (NY). 1970;20:829.
27. Johnstone JA, Ross CAC, Dunn M. Meningitis and encephalitis associated with mumps infection. Arch Dis Child. 1972;47:647.
28. Wilfert CM. Mumps meningoencephalitis with low cerebrospinal-fluid glucose, prolonged pleocytosis and elevation of protein. N Engl J Med. 1969;280:855.
29. Russell RR, Donald JC. The neurological complications of mumps. Br Med J. 1958;2:27.
30. Centers for Disease Control. Mumps surveillance, January 1977–December 1982. Issued September 1984.
31. Azimi PH, Shaban S, Hilty MD, et al. Mumps meningoencephalitis prolonged abnormality of cerebrospinal fluid. JAMA. 1975;234:1161.
32. Vuori M, Lahikainen EA, Peltonen T. Perceptive deafness in connection with mumps. Acta Otolaryngol. 1962;55:231.
33. Everberg G. Deafness following mumps. Acta Otolaryngol. 1957;48:397.
34. Cohen HA, Ashkenazi A, Nussinovitch M, et al. Mumps-associated acute cerebellar ataxia. Am J Dis Child. 1992;146:930–931.
35. Beardwell A. Facial palsy due to the mumps virus. Br J Clin Pract. 1969;23:37.
36. Nussinovitch M, Brand N, Frydman M, et al. Transverse myelitis following mumps in children. Acta Paediatr. 1992;81:183–184.
37. Ghosh S. Guillain-Barré syndrome complicating mumps. Lancet. 1967;1:895.
38. Lennette EH, Caplan GE, Magoffin RL. Mumps virus infection simulating paralytic poliomyelitis. Pediatrics. 1960;25:788.
39. Timmons GD, Johnson KP. Aqueductal stenosis and hydrocephalus after mumps encephalitis. N Engl J Med. 1970;283:1505.
40. Bray PF. Mumps: A cause of hydrocephalus? Pediatrics. 1972;49:446.
41. Oran B, Ceri A, Yilmaz H, et al. Hydrocephalus in mumps meningoencephalitis: Case report. Pediatr Infect Dis J. 1995;14:724–725.
42. Johnson RT, Johnson KP. Hydrocephalus following viral infection. The pathology of aqueductal stenosis developing after experimental mumps virus infection. J Neuropathol Exp Neurol. 1968;27:591.
43. Herndon RM, Johnson RT, Davis LE, et al. Ependymitis in mumps virus meningitis. Arch Neurol. 1974;30:475.
44. Uno M, Takano T, Yamano T, et al. Age-dependent susceptibility in mumps-associated hydrocephalus: Neuropathologic features and brain barriers. Acta Neuropathol (Berl). 1997;94:207–215.
45. Candel S. Epididymitis in mumps, including orchitis: Further clinical studies and comments. Ann Intern Med. 1951;34:20.
46. Lambert B. The frequency of mumps and of mumps orchitis. Acta Genet Stat Med. 1951;2(Suppl 1):1–166.
47. Kaufman JJ, Bruce PT. Testicular atrophy following mumps, a cause of testis tumour? J Urol. 1963;35:67.
48. Morrison JC, Givens JR, Wiser WL. Mumps oophoritis: A cause of premature menopause. Fertil Steril. 1975;26:655.
49. Appelbaum E, Kohn J, Steinman RE, et al. Mumps arthritis. Arch Intern Med. 1952;90:217.
50. Caranasos GJ, Felder JR. Mumps arthritis. Arch intern Med. 1967;119:394.
51. Kussy JC, Fatal mumps myocarditis. Minn Med. 1974;57:285.
52. Roberts WC, Fox SM. Mumps of the heart, clinical and pathologic features. Circulation. 1965;32:342.
53. Utz JP, Houk VN, Alling DW. Clinical and laboratory studies of mumps. IV. Viruria and abnormal renal function. N Engl J Med. 1964;270:1283.
54. Hughes WT, Steigman AJ, Delong HF. Some implications of fatal nephritis associated with mumps. Am J Dis Child. 1966;111:297.
55. Eylan E, Zmucky R, Sheba C. Mumps virus and subacute thyroiditis: Evidence of a causal association. Lancet. 1957;1:1062.
56. Krugman S, Katz SL, Gershon AA, et al. Mumps (epidemic parotitis). In: Infectious Diseases of Children. 9th ed. St. Louis: Mosby–Year Book; 1992:260.
57. Pomeroy C, Jordan MC. Mumps. In: Hoeprich PD, Jordan MC, eds. Infectious Diseases. 4th ed. Philadelphia: JB Lippincott; 1989:801.
58. Petersdorf RG, Bennett IL. Treatment of mumps orchitis with adrenal hormones: Report of 23 cases with a note on the hepatic involvement in mumps. Arch Intern Med. 1957;99:222.
59. Graham DY, Brown CH, Benrey J, et al. Thrombocytopenia: A complication of mumps. JAMA. 1974;227:1162.
60. Siegel M, Fuerst HT, Peress NS. Comparative fetal mortality in maternal virus diseases: A prospective study on rubella, measles, mumps, chickenpox and hepatitis. N Engl J Med. 1966;274:768.
61. Siegel M, Fuerst HT. Low birth weight and maternal virus diseases: A prospective study of rubella, measles, mumps, chickenpox and hepatitis. JAMA. 1966;197:680.
62. Siegel MS. Congenital malformations following chickenpox, measles, mumps, and hepatitis. Results of a cohort study. JAMA. 1973;226:1521.
63. Gershon AA. Chickenpox, measles and mumps. In: Remington JS, Klein JO, eds. Infectious Disease of the Fetus and Newborn. Philadelphia: WB Saunders: 1990:395.
64. Manson MM, Logan WPD, Loy RM. Rubella and other virus infections in pregnancy. Reports on Public Health and Medical Subjects, No. 101. London: Ministry of Health; 1960.
65. St Geme JW, Noren GR, Adams P. Proposed embryopathic relation between mumps virus and primary endocardial fibroelastosis. N Engl J Med. 1966;275:339.
66. St Geme JW, Peralta H, Farias E, et al. Experimental gestational mumps virus infection and endocardial fibroelastosis. Pediatrics. 1971;48:821.
67. Gersony WM, Katz SL, Nadas AS. Endocardial fibroelastosis and the mumps virus. Pediatrics. 1966;37:430.
68. Ni J, Bowles NE, Kim YH, et al. Viral infection of the endocardium in endocardial fibroelastosis. Molecular evidence for the role of mumps virus as an etiologic agent. Circulation. 1997;95:133–139.
69. Dacou-Voutetakis C, Constantinidis M, Moschos A, et al. Diabetes mellitus following mumps: Insulin reserve. Am J Dis Child. 1974;127:890.
70. Hinden E. Mumps followed by diabetes. Lancet. 1962;1:1138.
71. Sultz HA, Hart BA, Zielezny M, et al. Is mumps virus an etiologic factor in juvenile diabetes mellitus? J Pediatr. 1975;86:654.
72. Gamble DR, Kinsley ML, Fitzgerald MG, et al. Viral antibodies in diabetes mellitus. Br Med J. 1969;3:627.
73. Henle G, Harris S, Henle W. The reactivity of various human sera with mumps complement fixation antigens. J Exp Med. 1948;88:133.
74. Nigro G, Nanni F, Midulla M. Determination of vaccine-induced and naturally acquired class-specific antibodies by two indirect ELISAs. J Virol Methods. 1986;13:91–106.
75. Doern GV, Robbie L, St Amand R. Comparison of the Vidas and Bio-Whittaker enzyme immunoassays for detecting IgG reactive with varicella-zoster virus and mumps virus. Diagn Microbiol Infect Dis. 1997;28:31–34.
76. Hodes D, Brunell PA. Mumps antibody placental transfer and disappearance during the first year of life. Pediatrics. 1970;45:99.
77. Zollar LM, Mufson MA. Acute parotitis associated with parainfluenza 3 virus infection. Am J Dis Child. 1970;119:147.
78. Henle G, Henle W, Wendell KK, et al. Isolation of mumps virus from human beings with induced apparent or inapparent infections. J Exp Med. 1948;88:223.
79. Howlett JG, Somlo F, Kalz F. A new syndrome of parotitis with herpangina caused by the coxsackie virus. Can Med Assoc J. 1957;77:5.
80. Brill SJ, Gilfillan RF. Acute parotitis associated with influenza type. A. N Engl J Med. 1977;296:1391.
81. Lyon RP, Bruyn HB. Mumps epididymo-orchitis: Treatment by anesthetic block of the spermatic cord. JAMA. 1966;196:736.
82. Erpenbach KH. Systemic treatment with interferon-alpha 2B: An effective method to prevent sterility after bilateral mumps orchitis. J Urol. 1991;146:54.
83. Gellis SS, McGuiness AC, Peters M. A study on the prevention of mumps orchitis with gamma globulin. Am J Med Sci. 1945;210:661.
84. Brunell PA, Brickman A, O'Hare D, et al. Ineffectiveness of isolation of patients as a method of preventing the spread of mumps. N Engl J Med 1968;279:1357.
85. Weibel RE, Buynak EB, McLean AA, et al. Persistence of antibody in human subjects following administration of combined liver attenuated measles, mumps, and rubella vaccines. Proc Soc Exp Biol Med. 1980;165:260.
86. Fuginaga T, Youichi M, Tamura H, et al. A prefecture-wide survey of mumps meningitis associated with measles, mumps and rubella vaccine. Pediatr Infect Dis J. 1991;10:204.
87. Sugiura A, Yamada A. Aseptic meningitis as a complication of mumps. Pediatr Infect Dis J. 1991;10:209.
88. Black S, Shinfeld H, Ray P, et al. Risk of hospitalization because of aseptic meningitis after measles-mumps-rubella vaccination in one to two year old children: An analysis of the Vaccine Safety Datalink (VSD) Project. Pediatr Infect Dis J. 1997;16:500–503.
89. Angel JA, Walpita P, Lerch RA, et al. Vaccine-associated measles pneumonitis in an adult with AIDS. Ann Intern Med. 1998;129:104.

Chapter 148

Respiratory Syncytial Virus

CAROLINE BREESE HALL
CAROL A. McCARTHY

Were we but able to explain
The fiefdom of the microbe—
Why one man is his serf,
Another is his lord
When all are his domain. . . .
C. B. H.

Respiratory syncytial virus (RSV) is the major cause of lower respiratory tract illness in young children.[1–5] Its presence may be witnessed in most communities in this country by the yearly upsurge of pneumonia, bronchiolitis, and tracheobronchitis in the very young. So effectively does RSV spread that essentially all persons have experienced infection with this agent within the first few years of life. Immunity, however, is not complete, and reinfection is common. Although life-threatening infections generally occur only during the first couple of years of life, RSV infections contribute an appreciable share of the morbidity due to acute upper respiratory tract infections and exacerbations of wheezing and bronchitis in older children and adults. The health care costs associated with these outpatient infections add appreciably to the Institute of Medicine's estimated cost of $300 million for hospitalized infants with RSV infection.[6]

HISTORY

The major agent that causes outbreaks of bronchiolitis occurring in the winter or spring was discovered in 1956 when Morris and coworkers[7] isolated a new virus from one of 14 chimpanzees suffering from colds. They entitled this new agent *chimpanzee coryza agent.* Whether this agent was also able to infect humans was not then known but was suspected since one laboratory worker developed a specific antibody to chimpanzee coryza agent. Subsequently, Chanock and colleagues[8] confirmed that the agent caused respiratory illness in humans when they obtained two isolates from children that were indistinguishable from chimpanzee coryza agent. These isolates were recovered from the throat swabs of a child with bronchopneumonia (Long's strain) and from a child with laryngotracheobronchitis (Snyder's strain). Chanock and Finberg[9] subsequently detected rises of specific neutralizing antibody to chimpanzee coryza agent in children with respiratory illnesses and also discovered that such antibody was present in most children by the time they reached school age. The inappropriateness of calling this virus chimpanzee coryza agent became apparent, and it was renamed *respiratory syncytial virus* to denote its clinical and laboratory manifestations. Multiple studies soon followed to support RSV's current claim as the major agent causing outbreaks of lower respiratory disease in infants.[10–20]

DESCRIPTION

Classification

RSV belongs to the Paramyxoviridae family, which consists of four genera, three of which form the subfamily, Paramyxovirinae, consisting of *Paramyxovirus,* containing human parainfluenza types 1 and 3 viruses; *Rubulavirus,* containing mumps and human parainfluenza viruses types 2 and 4 among others; and *Morbillivirus,* represented by measles virus. RSV belongs to the fourth genus, *Pneumovirus* of the Pneumovirinae subfamily. Within this same genus are the morphologically and biologically similar pneumonia virus of mice, bovine RSV, ovine RSV, caprine RSV, and turkey rhinotracheitis virus. Distinctive features of RSV include the number and order of genes and lack of hemagglutinin and neuraminidase activity.[21]

Characteristics

RSV is an enveloped, medium-sized (120 to 300 nm) virus. Its genome is a single strand of negative-sense RNA that is associated with viral proteins throughout its length, forming the nucleocapsid. The viral envelope is a bilipid layer derived from the plasma membrane of the host cells and has the appearance of a thistle with transmembrane surface glycoprotein spikes 11 to 12 nm in length and 6 to 10 nm apart. Electron microscopy of ultrathin sections of infected tissue reveals RSV as pleomorphic, round or filamentous particles budding from the cytoplasmic membrane that are fringed by the glycoprotein projections.[22]

Ten quintessential viral proteins have now been determined for RSV, and the complete gene sequence of the A2 strain has been described (Fig. 148–1).[6, 21, 23] The viral RNA consists of 15,222 nucleotides that are transcribed into 10 monocistronic polyadenylated messenger RNAs, each of which encodes for a major polypeptide chain. Three of the proteins (N, P, and L) are associated with the nucleocapsid. Of the five associated with the envelope, three, F, G, and SH, are glycosylated transmembrane surface proteins, and two, M and M2 are nonglycosylated matrix proteins. Two proteins, NS1 and NS2, are nonstructural proteins of the virion (Fig. 148–1). The two glycosylated surface proteins, the F and G proteins, appear integral and important in the infectivity and pathogenesis of the virus. The fusion, or F protein, bears a structural similarity to the fusion protein of the paramyxoviruses, consisting of two disulfide-linked fragments (F1 and F2). The F protein initiates viral penetration by fusing viral and cellular membranes and promotes viral spread by melding infected to adjacent uninfected cells, thereby resulting in the characteristic syncytia. Efficient fusion, however, appears to require the coexpression of all three of the surface glycoproteins, F, G, and SH.[24] The largest glycoprotein, the G protein, appears to mediate attachment of the virus to the host cells.

RSV withstands changes in temperature and pH relatively poorly. Only 10% of RSV remained after exposing the virus to 55°C for 5 minutes.[25] At 37°C the virus was stable for 1 hour, but only 10% of the infectivity remained after 24 hours. At 25°C, 10% infectivity was present after 48 hours, and at 4°C, 1% of the infectivity remained after 7 days.[25] RSV does not tolerate slow freezing and thawing. Complete loss of infectivity occurs when the virus is slowly frozen at −30°C and then thawed.[11] When slowly frozen at −65°C, the infectivity titer fell by approximately 0.5 log.[25] RSV also withstands an acid medium poorly, and the optimal pH is 7.5.[25] The virus is inactivated quickly by ether, chloroform, and a variety of detergents such as 0.1% sodium deoxycholate, sodium dodecyl sulfate, and Triton X-100. Storage of RSV can be enhanced by flash freezing in an alcohol and dry ice bath and by adding glycerin or sucrose.[26]

At room temperature, RSV in the secretions of patients may survive on nonporous surfaces, such as countertops, for 3 to 30 hours, depending on the humidity.[27] On porous surfaces, such as cloth and paper tissue, survival is generally shorter, usually less than 1 hour. The infectivity of RSV on the hands is variable from person to person but is usually less than 1 hour. The survival of RSV in the environment appears to depend in part on the drying time as well as the humidity.[27, 28]

Laboratory Propagation

RSV grows well in several human cell lines and may be adapted to a number of others. For primary isolation, human heteroploid cells,

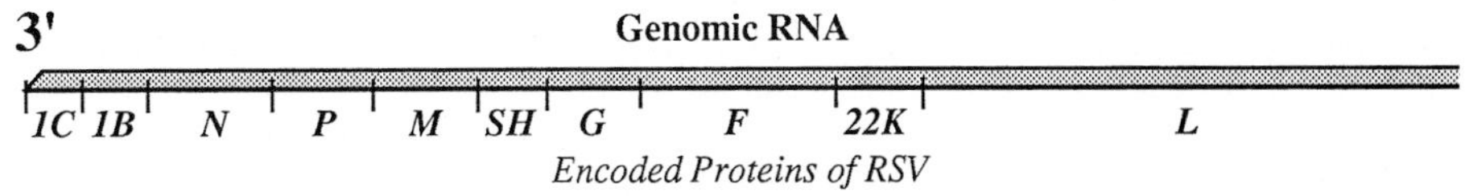

FIGURE 148–1. Simplified representation of the genomic structure of respiratory syncytial virus (RSV).

such as HEp-2 and HeLa cells, are usually preferred. Other cell lines that may be used but are usually less sensitive include human kidney, amnion, and diploid fibroblastic cells, and monkey kidney cells.[11, 29] The sensitivity of all these cell lines, including the heteroploid human lines, for the growth of RSV is variable and must be monitored. The presence of RSV in infected cell cultures is detected by its characteristic syncytial appearance (Fig. 148–2). However, the degree of syncytial formation depends on the type of cell culture, the heaviness of the cell sheet, the medium, the strain of virus, the multiplicity of infection, and its laboratory adaptation. Induction of syncytia and the amount of fusion protein have also been shown to depend on the presence of calcium in the media in HEp-2 cultures.[30] On primary isolation in sensitive heteroploid cell cultures, the characteristic cytopathic effect of RSV may be first detected after an average 3 to 5 days.[31] With strains of RSV that are adapted to tissue culture, new infectious virus may first be detected 10 to 12 hours after inoculation, but the typical syncytia do not develop until 10 to 24 hours later. The syncytia progress until the cell sheet is completely destroyed, which usually occurs within 4 days. A variable proportion of the cell sheet may also show rounding of the cells without fusion, especially in some primary cell lines.

About 90% of the inoculum is absorbed within 2 hours by standard sensitive cell lines. The viral surface glycoproteins may be detected by immunofluorescence 7 to 10 hours after inoculation.[32] Cell-free virus subsequently may be demonstrated in the culture medium, but up to 90% of the virus remains cell-associated. When the virus has been subjected to repeated high passage, persistent infection may occur.[33] The amount of cell-free virus then diminishes, and the characteristic cytopathic effect is lost when persistent infection is established. Production of defective interfering particles, which is dependent on the multiplicity of infection, may also occur and results in less infectious virus and fewer cytopathologic findings.

Antigenic Variation

Antigenic variation among strains of RSV previously was believed to be minor based on cross-neutralization assays in experimental animals. Monoclonal antibodies made it possible to detect appreciable strain differences and allowed RSV isolates to be divided into two major groups, A and B (initially designated 1 and 2), and into subtypes within each group.[34–45] Group A is represented by the A2 strain and group B by the 18537 strain. Overall, the antigenic relatedness for the two strain groups is 25%[21, 39, 40, 41, 46] The major diversity between group A and group B resides with the G, F, SH, and NS1 proteins.[21, 39, 44, 47–51] The strain heterogenicity is even greater when analyzed genetically. G, the attachment protein, possesses the greatest genetic variability, and second is the SH protein. This is reflected in the relative antigenic relatedness of the G protein of each group of only 1 to 7% in comparison with 50% for the F proteins. Furthermore, the amino acid diversity of the G proteins within each group is appreciable, from 12% for group B to 20% for group A. The F, N, P, M2, NS1, and NS2 proteins are more highly conserved, demonstrating an amino acid homology of more than 87% and a nucleotide homology of more than 75%.

Strains of both groups circulate simultaneously during outbreaks, but the proportions that are A and B vary, as do the subtypes.[36, 38, 42, 43, 44, 52, 53] Antigenic and molecular analyses of the relatedness of strains circulating concurrently in a single locale, as well as in multiple areas worldwide, indicate that the strains within both groups possess genetic diversity. Even in widely separated geographic areas, the cocirculating strains may have similar genotypes and parallel evolutionary lineages. Analyses of the G protein of strains collected over decades and from diverse areas suggest that the pressure of the population's immunity may play a role in the slow accumulation of the amino acid substitutions that result in strain evolution.[44, 54–56]

Infection in Animals

A variety of animal species may be experimentally infected with RSV,[57] but natural infection with human RSV strains is limited mostly to humans and chimpanzees. Bovine strains of RSV (BRSV) have been recovered from cows with respiratory illness, potentially providing a natural animal model for the study of human RSV

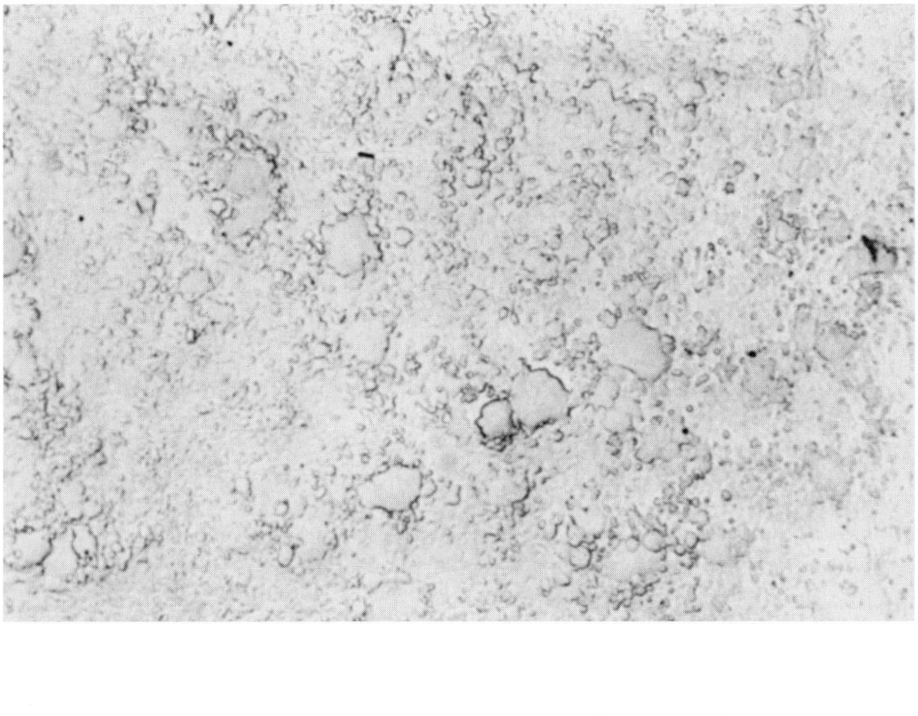

FIGURE 148–2. HEp-2 culture 4 days after inoculation with a nasal wash from an infant hospitalized with pneumonia. Multiple foci of the characteristic refractile syncytial cytopathic effect of RSV are apparent.

infection, and BRSV has been investigated as a possible candidate for a human vaccine.[58–61] BRSV is antigenically and genetically closely related to human RSV.[62–64] Antibodies directed against the F, N, P, and M proteins of either virus recognize the heterologous virus. BRSV strains also appear to consist of two major antigenic subgroups.[63] Ovine and caprine strains of RSV have also been recovered, but genetic analysis suggests that these strains are closely enough related to BRSV that they and BRSV may not be different, host-specific viruses, but antigenic subgroups.[65, 66] The development of an animal model for infant RSV infection has been perplexing and problematic.[57] In general, animal models do not develop similar symptomatic lower respiratory tract disease. Infection of the upper and lower respiratory tracts has been accomplished in a number of animal models, but, with the exception of the chimpanzee, RSV replication in the lung is generally poor or limited, and the pulmonary abnormality is often inconsistent or absent. Chimpanzees infected with RSV may develop respiratory illness and shed virus. However, they do not usually develop lower respiratory tract involvement similar to that of infants and generally exhibit poor permissiveness to RSV replication on challenge.[7, 67, 68] Pneumonia has been induced in the cebus monkey, and the African green monkey has been used as a model for enhanced lung abnormality induced by the formalin-inactivated vaccine.[67, 69, 70] A potential lamb model has been developed after challenge with ovine, bovine, or human RSV strains.[71–73] When human RSV was inoculated intratracheally or intranasally, tachypnea and fever were observed more frequently than in lambs given placebo.[73] Infection in ferrets has been associated with some histopathologic changes in the upper respiratory tract and in the lower respiratory tract in infant ferrets.[74] Various rodents have been utilized, particularly cotton rats and mice, but even in these most commonly used models, replication of RSV is only semipermissive.[75] Graham and colleagues[76] have developed a mouse model that develops clinical illness and appreciable lung abnormality. A number of other animals may be infected asymptomatically, including other primates, guinea pigs, minks, and chinchillas.[67]

EPIDEMIOLOGY

Distribution

In every geographic area studied, evidence of infection with RSV has been found. In areas of widely differing climates, RSV infection appears to have similar characteristics of ubiquity, and primary infection occurs in the very young.[3, 5, 19, 20, 77, 78]

Seasonal Occurrence

Outbreaks of RSV infection occur yearly. Indeed, RSV is the only viral respiratory agent that may be relied on to produce a sizable crop of infection each year.[3–5, 79] The outbreaks usually occur in the winter or spring. In Washington, D.C., and in Chapel Hill, North Carolina, the epidemics have been noted to occur in "long and short" cycles, alternating between appearances in the winter and spring.[1, 3, 4, 80] In other areas with colder climates, RSV has tended to appear at regular yearly intervals in the winter, with the peak prevalence falling in January through March.[81, 82] Wherever the area, RSV appears to have an unusually predictable and regular pattern. Annual outbreaks of RSV in the United States from 1992 to 1997 monitored by the National Respiratory and Enteric Virus Surveillance System of the Centers for Disease Control and Prevention showed that widespread activity began each November, peaking in most areas in January and February and continuing until April to mid-May for an average of 22 weeks.[82] In the Southeast, however, the peak of RSV activity tended to be 2 to 3 months earlier.

Epidemiologic Manifestations

The spread of RSV infection within a community produces such characteristic ramifications that the presence of RSV often may be deduced without specific viral diagnosis. Characteristically, RSV produces a rise in the number of cases of bronchiolitis and pediatric pneumonia in the community and a rise in the number of hospital admissions of young children with acute lower respiratory tract disease.[4, 19, 80, 81] The size of the outbreaks of RSV infection in general does not vary enough to change these barometers in most temperate climates, but milder outbreaks may be observed, frequently to be followed the next season by an outbreak of greater than usual severity.

Acquisition of Infection According to Age

Experience with RSV is so universal at a young age that virtually all children have been infected in the first several years of life. All newborns passively acquire specific neutralizing antibody and antibody to the major surface glycoproteins of the virus from their mothers.[5, 83, 84] Without natural infection, the level of antibody falls over the next 6 to 7 months such that little is detectable.[5] But by 2 years of age, 95% or more of children have become seropositive.[85]

Prevalence and Incidence

The importance of RSV in causing respiratory illness in children is illustrated in Table 148–1. It is the major agent recovered from young children with pneumonia and bronchiolitis. The proportion of cases that are identified as caused by RSV varies according to the population examined and the methods used. During the peak period of an epidemic, RSV may be isolated from up to 89% of the young children admitted to the hospital with acute lower respiratory tract disease.[31] In contrast, RSV is rarely isolated from children without respiratory disease (see Table 148–1).[4, 12]

From their studies in Washington, D.C., Parrott and colleagues[1, 4, 5] have estimated that about one half of the infants followed longitudinally were infected during their first RSV epidemic and that essentially all had become infected after experiencing two RSV epidemics. Furthermore, in 40% of these first infections, a febrile pneumonitis developed. The yearly attack rate for RSV lower respiratory tract disease has been estimated to be 23 per 1000 children younger than 1 year in middle-income families in North Carolina and 9 per 1000 in families in a Seattle prepaid medical practice.[80, 96] During the second year of life, the rates were approximately the same. In children 2 to 3 years of age, the attack rates declined to 15 per 1000 in Chapel Hill and 7 per 1000 in Seattle. In 4- and 5-year-old children, the yearly attack rates were estimated to be 8 and 5 per 1000, respectively. Prospective studies suggest that the frequency of lower respiratory tract infection with RSV is actually much higher. In groups of infants followed closely, the attack rate for RSV lower respiratory tract diseases varied from 15 to 50%.[80, 91, 97–99] Even higher rates have been detected in a day care center in which the children were examined almost daily. Under these circumstances, which would detect the mildest illnesses, the rate in children 6 months of age or younger was 115 per 1000 children per year.[87]

Age, sex, and socioeconomic factors appear to influence the expression of RSV disease.[100] The most severe illness occurs in the

TABLE 148–1 Proportion of Respiratory Illnesses Caused by Respiratory Syncytial Virus in Children

Syndrome	Percentage Caused by RSV	References
Bronchiolitis	43–90	1, 4, 86, 87, 88, 89
Pneumonia	5–40	1–3, 12, 79, 90–95
Tracheobronchitis	10–30	4, 91
Croup	3–10	3, 4, 11, 79, 86, 91, 93
Asymptomatic	0.3	4

Abbreviation: RSV, Respiratory syncytial virus.

youngest infants (Fig. 148–3). Boys appear to have a higher incidence of lower respiratory tract disease. In Chapel Hill, boys younger than 6 years had a rate of RSV lower respiratory tract disease of 2.4 per 100, compared with 1.5 per 100 for girls.[3, 79] That boys get more severe disease is also suggested by the preponderance of boys admitted to the hospital with lower respiratory tract disease.[5, 31, 100] A greater proportion of hospitalized children are from lower socioeconomic areas.[3, 80, 87] In a middle-income practice in Chapel Hill, approximately 1 of every 1000 patients with RSV infection required hospitalization.[79, 80] In contrast, in lower-income populations the risk of hospitalization is fivefold to 10-fold higher.[4, 101, 102] In Washington, D.C., the need for hospitalization has been estimated to occur for 1 of every 100 RSV infections.[4, 101] Gender and socioeconomic factors, however, do not appear to influence the attack rate, but rather the severity of the infection.[80, 87]

Incidence of Repeated Infections

Repeated infections with RSV are common, and no age group appears protected. In a Chapel Hill day care center, 98% of children first exposed to RSV became infected.[103] A second exposure resulted in 74% of the children becoming infected, and a third exposure only reduced the attack rate to 65%. In urban Rochester, New York, 44% of the families with young children became infected with RSV during the winter months when it was prevalent in the community.[104] Of the exposed family members, 46% became infected. Although the attack rate was highest in infants, between 38 and 47% of older children and adults acquired RSV infection. In the Houston family study in which children were followed from birth, the infection rate was 68.8 per 100 children in the first year of life, and during the second year at least half were reinfected.[99]

PATHOGENESIS

In adult volunteers, experimental infection occurs after an average incubation of 5 days.[105, 106] Most studies confirm this as the average incubation period with a range of 2 to 8 days.[14, 107, 108] Inoculation of the virus may occur through the nose or eye, and both appear to be equally sensitive portals of entry, whereas the mouth is a much less sensitive means of inoculation.[109] RSV infection is generally confined to the respiratory tract, and spread of the virus may occur from the upper passageways to involve the entire lower respiratory tract.

Initially in bronchiolitis, the pathologic findings are a lymphocytic peribronchiolar infiltration with some edema of the walls and surrounding tissue.[18, 110, 111] Subsequently, the characteristic proliferation and necrosis of the epithelium of the bronchioles develop. The lumens of these small airways become obstructed from the sloughed epithelium and from the increased mucus secretion. Impedance to the flow of air occurs during both inspiration and expiration but is greater in the latter when the lumen is narrowed further by the positive expiratory pressure. Hyperinflation, therefore, results from the trapping of air peripheral to the sites of partial occlusion. With complete obstruction, trapped air eventually becomes absorbed, resulting in the characteristic multiple areas of atelectasis. Young infants are particularly prone to develop such areas of atelectasis as the collateral channels that maintain alveolar expansion in the presence of airway obstruction are not yet well developed. An increase in lung volume and expiratory resistance, therefore, occurs in bronchiolitis.[112–114]

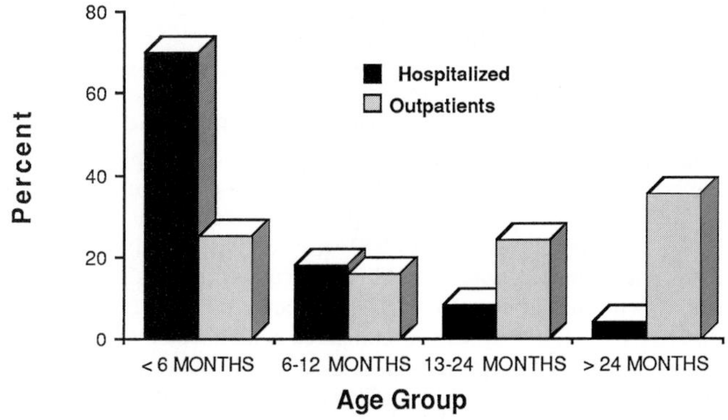

FIGURE 148–3. Difference in the age distribution of inpatients and outpatients with RSV infection in Rochester, New York, illustrates the effect of age on the severity of infection. Seventy percent of infants requiring hospitalization were younger than 6 months. In comparison, 25% of the children treated as outpatients were younger than 6 months and 38% were older than 2 years.

Infants with lower respiratory tract disease from RSV often have pathologic evidence of both pneumonia and bronchiolitis. Pneumonia patients demonstrate an interstitial infiltration of mononuclear cells that may be accompanied by edema and necrotic areas that lead to alveolar filling.[110, 115]

Some histologic evidence of recovery is present in most patients with of bronchiolitis within the first week of illness and is marked by the beginning regeneration of the bronchiolar epithelium.[110] Ciliated cells may not be present for weeks, and other morphologic alterations may persist indefinitely.[116]

Theories of Pathogenesis

How RSV engenders these pathogenic findings remains mostly a mystery. RSV produces its most devastating illness at the time when specific antibody, maternally derived, is invariably and abundantly present. The severity of RSV infection in the young infant and in those children with high levels of circulating antibody induced by an inactivated RSV vaccine has suggested that immunologic mechanisms may contribute to the pathogenesis of the disease in infants.[98, 117, 118]

In the late 1960s, trials of the first RSV vaccine, a formalin-inactivated RSV vaccine (lot 100), were initiated.[98, 117, 118] Infants who received the vaccine produced both complement-fixing and neutralizing antibodies to RSV. When exposed subsequently to natural RSV infection, however, immunized children were not protected from RSV infection and some developed an exaggerated illness characterized by severe lower respiratory tract disease requiring hospitalization. A variety of immune mechanisms have been proposed to explain the augmented disease in the vaccinees as well as the lower respiratory tract disease seen in infants with natural infection. Much attention has been given to the role of antibody in the pathogenesis, including the hypothesis that an immune complex reaction may occur between the virus and passively acquired immunoglobulin G (IgG) antibody in the infant's lung, especially when the local defense of secretory antibody is absent.[119, 120] Additional hypotheses have suggested that the manifestations of RSV lower respiratory tract disease may result from RSV-specific IgE-mediated disease, from a detrimental T-cell response, or mostly from the immunologic immaturity of the young infant.

Alternatively, severe RSV infection in infancy may be explained without involving any immunologic mechanism. Exposure to large doses of virus coupled with the small lumen of the infant's airway may be sufficient to produce the severe disease seen in the young baby. The airway of the young infant is particularly vulnerable to any degree of inflammation and obstruction, since resistance to the flow of air is related inversely to the cube of the radius. Infection in the small peripheral airways of the infant, therefore, results in greater physiologic changes than in the older child, and mechanisms of compensation are less well developed.[116, 121]

Immunity

Naturally acquired immunity to RSV infection is incomplete. Repeated infections are common, but severe disease rarely occurs after the primary encounter. Lower respiratory tract involvement may occur with repeated infections, but it is generally confined to those at either end of the age spectrum.[87, 99, 103, 122, 123]

The relative contributions of antibody and T lymphocytes in the response to either a primary or recurrent exposure is unclear. Their significance in the pathogenesis of natural disease or that seen after immunization with the formalin-inactivated vaccine is also the subject of investigation.

The role of serum antibody in immunity to RSV still requires further clarification. In general, the level of serum antibody has not been predictive of the risk of infection, the severity of illness, or recovery in children or adults.[5, 124, 125] Clearly, maternal antibody does not provide complete protection during infancy. However, several studies have suggested that high levels of maternal antibody correlate with lower infection rates[84, 126–128] and with less severity of illness in some studies[127, 129] but not in others.[5, 124]

Data from studies in mice depleted of B cells suggest that serum antibody is not required for the clearance of RSV in a primary infection but appears to be a factor in protection from reinfection.[130] During both a primary infection and a rechallenge, however, these B-cell–depleted mice exhibited greater clinical illness compared with control animals. These investigators concluded that antibody has an illness-sparing affect in RSV infection.[130]

Recent studies have further defined antibody responses to specific RSV proteins and have failed to implicate humoral immunity in the pathogenesis of RSV disease, but rather have increasingly shown the potential benefit and protective effects of specific humoral antibody. Animal studies have supported the integral role of the F and G surface glycoproteins in the immune response to RSV. Monoclonal antibodies to F and G proteins passively administered or immunization with F and G proteins has resulted in nearly complete protection against RSV challenge in the lung, but not the upper respiratory tract.[68, 131–134] Trials of hyperimmune RSV globulin in young children also have demonstrated that higher antibody levels protect against more severe RSV disease.[135, 136]

Studies attempting to explain the phenomenon of the enhanced disease associated with the formalin-inactivated vaccine have contributed to the understanding of the significance of the antibody response to RSV infection. Two decades after the trials of the formalin-inactivated vaccine, Murphy and colleagues[137] measured neutralizing and enzyme-linked immunosorbent titers to the F and G proteins in the stored sera from the children immunized with the lot 100 vaccine. The vaccinees had produced enzyme-linked immunosorbent antibodies to both proteins, but younger infants had poor or absent responses to the G glycoprotein. This pattern of antibody response was similar to that of unvaccinated (control) infants with natural infection. Neutralizing antibody responses, however, were low in both older and younger vaccinees and differed significantly from the response of the age-matched control infants after natural infection. Indeed, the ratio of levels of neutralizing antibody to enzyme-linked immunosorbent F antibody was significantly lower in the vaccinees. This suggested that the formalin may have altered important epitopes on the RSV proteins resulting in an imbalance or excess of nonprotective antibody. Further investigation demonstrated that the antibody response of vaccinees was also deficient in fusion inhibition activity.[138]

Whether strain variation is a significant factor in determining the immune or clinical response is not yet clear. In infants with primary infection, the homologous and heterologous antibody responses to the F proteins of the two major subgroups appear to be similar. Relatively little heterologous response, however, occurs to the G protein.[46] Some evidence, nevertheless, exists to suggest that prior infection with a group A strain virus provides more protection against reinfection with either a homologous or a heterologous strain.[139, 140]

Local antibody production may be important in RSV infection since the virus spreads from cell to cell, and in animal studies circulating antibody does not prevent viral replication in the nasal passages.[131, 132, 141] A number of studies have identified neutralizing activity in the nasal secretions of children with RSV infection, but a correlation with protection or the severity of illness often could not be made.[98, 119, 124, 142–144] The presence of this neutralizing activity in the secretions was associated with diminished viral shedding, but it was also present at the time of hospital admission in the secretions of infants with primary infections.[119, 143–145] McIntosh and coworkers[144] have defined the nonspecific nature of this neutralizing activity and have demonstrated that a specific IgA-antibody response does occur in infants recovering from RSV infection. Although this specific IgA antibody does not neutralize the virus, its presence is correlated with diminished titers of virus. Specific IgM, IgG, and IgE antibodies may also be found in the secretions of children with RSV infections.[143, 146–148] The IgM antibody appears early and disappears, and IgG appears later. The infant's secretory response to the F and G proteins is similar to their serum response in that the response is diminished in younger infants and is lower to the G protein.[149, 150] The F protein also appears to elicit a response more favorable ratio of IgA to IgE.[150]

Most children with RSV infection produce a transient response to specific IgE or IgG antibody in the respiratory tract.[146, 147] The length and magnitude of the specific IgE response and of the concentrations of histamine in the nasopharyngeal secretions have been correlated with wheezing during the acute illness and with subsequent episodes of bronchospasm. The IgE response may initiate a cascade of mediators that produce the inflammatory response in the infant's lung.[151] Indeed, the respiratory secretions of infants with RSV bronchiolitis have been shown to contain not only histamine, but also increased levels of the leukotriene LTC4 and eosinophil cationic protein, both of which may play a role in airway bronchospasm and inflammation.[152–154]

Cell-mediated immunity is likely to be pivotal in the response to infection and recovery. This is supported by the observations that adults and children with deficiencies of cellular immunity, as well as experimentally immunosuppressed animals, have more severe disease and prolonged shedding.[155–159]

Cellular immunity has been evaluated to a limited degree in humans, and to a much greater degree in the mouse model. Early measurement of cell-mediated immunity performed in the 1970s suggested that the severe illness observed in both natural infection and that following immunization with formalin-inactivated vaccine was related to an exaggerated lymphoproliferative response.[160, 161]

RSV-specific class I major histocompatibility complex–restricted cytotoxic T lymphocytes (CTLs) initially identified in the lungs and spleen of mice were detected subsequently in the peripheral blood of adults not acutely infected with RSV.[162–164] This CTL response has been shown to be associated with an ameliorated clinical course in RSV-infected adult volunteers.[165] Infants with primary RSV infection may also exhibit specific CTL reactivity, usually within 10 days after infection.[166, 167] The N, F, and M2 proteins have been shown to be targets for CTLs in both mice and humans.[164, 168–171] Human CTLs also recognize SH, M, and NS2 proteins.[171] The method of priming appears to influence the specificity of CTLs.[168, 172]

The response of helper T (Th) cells to RSV has also been studied in mice and humans.[173, 174] Adult human peripheral blood lymphocytes depleted of $CD8^+$ T cells proliferate when challenged with whole RSV as well as with the F, G, M2, and P proteins.[174] The type of Th-cell response to RSV may be influenced by the kind of priming immunization.[175, 176] Mice infected with RSV after initial priming with inactivated RSV produced increased interleukin-4 messenger RNA (IL-4) expression compared with that of interferon-γ, suggestive of a Th2-type response. In contrast, initial priming with live RSV was associated with a relative decrease in IL-4 messenger RNA expression compared with that of interferon-γ, suggestive of a Th1-type response.[175] The T-cell lines specific for the F protein contain $CD4^+$ cells with Th1 characteristics and some $CD8^+$ cells, whereas T-cell lines specific for the G protein are primarily $CD4^+$ cells with a Th2-cytokine profile.[176] Manipulation of experimental design to favor a Th1-type cytokine response has been shown to be desirable in RSV infection.[177] $CD8^+$ cells may have a critical influence on the regulation of the elicited Th-cell response.[177, 178]

Adoptive transfer experiments have shown that CTLs can enhance the clearing of RSV from the mouse lung.[179–181] Some studies have found increased morbidity and abnormality associated with the clearance of RSV by CTLs[179, 181] whereas others have not observed enhanced illness with CTL transfer.[180] Similarly, Th cells can enhance the clearance of RSV from the lungs of RSV-infected mice. In these studies, transfer of Th cells was also associated with increased abnormality.[181] Whether T cells produce a beneficial or a detrimental effect may depend on the timing, numbers, specificity, and types of T cells present.

The production of RSV-induced cytokines by different cells, including epithelial cells, macrophages, and peripheral blood mononuclear cells has been evaluated.[182–188] Recent investigation of the interaction of RSV with respiratory epithelial cells has shown that RSV infection of human bronchial epithelial cells is associated with production of IL-6, IL-8, and granulocyte-macrophase colony-stimulating factor.[183] IL-6 and IL-8 as well as tumor necrosis factor-α, IL-1α, IL-1β, and IL-11 are produced by RSV infection of the pulmonary epithelial cell line A549, which has features of type II alveolar epithelial cells.[184–186] Nasal lavage fluid, taken from children 3 to 54 months of age, revealed increased IL-1β, IL-8, IL-6, and tumor necrosis factor-α during upper respiratory tract infections from RSV as well as from other pathogens.[189] These cytokines may initiate or augment local inflammatory responses.[190] RSV infection upregulates the expression of intercellular adhesion molecule 1 in respiratory epithelial cells, which may increase adhesion and infiltration of inflammatory cells.[186, 191] Modification of such responses is an important target area for new therapeutic agents.

CLINICAL MANIFESTATIONS

Infection in Young Children

Primary infections with RSV may be manifested as lower respiratory tract diseases, pneumonia, bronchiolitis, tracheobronchitis, or upper respiratory tract illness, often accompanied by fever and otitis media. Rarely is the infection asymptomatic.[4, 12, 15, 91, 103, 192] The risk of lower respiratory tract involvement occurring with the first infection appears high. Pneumonia or bronchiolitis has been estimated to occur in 30 to 71%.[5, 14, 97, 99, 103] In closed populations of infants, the proportion developing lower respiratory tract disease may be even higher, up to 89%.[108, 193] Even in previously healthy outpatients, the proportion who develop lower respiratory tract disease is appreciable (Fig. 148–4).

Of the lower respiratory tract syndromes, pneumonia and bronchiolitis are the most frequent in infants.[3, 4, 91, 192] Croup is the least common form of clinical illness and usually accounts for less than 5 to 10% of the cases.[91] Pneumonia and bronchiolitis are often difficult to differentiate, and many infants may appear to have both syndromes. Wheezing, rhonchi, rales, and infiltrates on chest roentgenograms may be present in both syndromes.[80, 86] In bronchiolitis, the infiltrates are due to atelectasis, but these often cannot be differentiated from the inflammatory shadows of pneumonia. Bronchiolitis is characterized by the two classic signs of wheezing and hyperaeration of the lung.

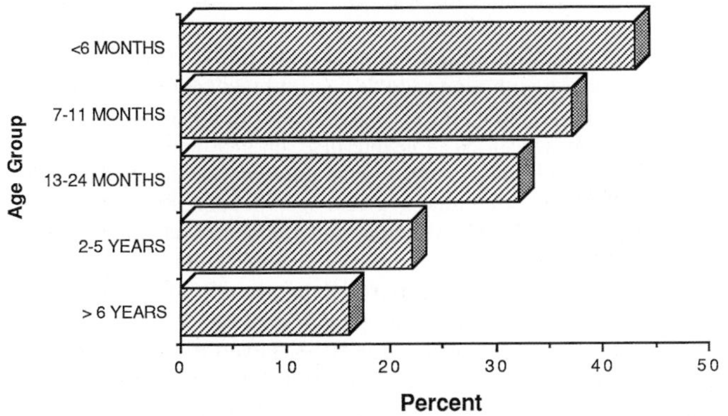

FIGURE 148–4. Proportion of outpatients according to age in Rochester, New York, 1977–1987, who were infected with RSV and developed lower respiratory tract disease.

Lower respiratory tract disease is usually heralded by an upper respiratory tract infection with nasal congestion and often pharyngitis. Fever occurs in most young children, with temperatures ranging from 38 to 40°C. Fever is usually present for 2 to 4 days. The height or duration of the fever does not correlate with the severity of the disease and is frequently absent at the time of admission to the hospital.[108, 194] Cough is frequent and often a predominant sign. It may be paroxysmal and associated with vomiting, but not with a "whoop" typical of pertussis.[17, 194–196] Laryngitis or hoarseness is not a common feature. Usually after several days of upper respiratory tract signs and a deepening cough, the lower respiratory tract involvement may become evident by the onset of dyspnea, an increased respiratory rate, and retractions of the intercostal muscles. In bronchiolitis, expiration tends to be prolonged, and the respiratory rate may be remarkably elevated. Intercostal retractions are also prominent in bronchiolitis, which emphasizes that inspiratory obstruction of the lower airway exists as well as the more obvious expiratory obstruction. On auscultation, the infant may have crackles and wheezing, which may be present intermittently and may fluctuate in intensity.[17, 197]

The chest roentgenogram may show a variety of findings, most typically multiple areas of interstitial infiltration and hyperinflation of the lung.[198–202] These abnormalities, however, may be minimal, and the severity of the child's illness appear out of proportion to the roentgenographic findings. Hyperaeration has been shown to be especially indicative of RSV infection and occurs in over half the children hospitalized with RSV infection. Hyperaeration was commonly present with peribronchial thickening, but in 15%, hyperaeration was the only abnormality. Consolidation, which may be from atelectasis, has been noted in about 20 to 25% of the children, particularly in younger infants, and most commonly is subsegmental in the right upper or middle lobe.[198–199, 201] Pleural fluid is rarely demonstrated, although one study states its occurrence at 5%.[198] Certain signs such as hyperinflation and right upper or middle lobe consolidation may be indicative of RSV infection, but roentgenographic differentiation from infection by other viruses, and sometimes by bacteria, is often not possible.

Cyanosis is rarely evident in infants hospitalized with RSV lower respiratory tract disease despite hypoxemia, which may be profound.[197, 203, 204] In one group of hospitalized infants, the mean arterial oxygen saturation on admission was 87% percent, a range of 74 to 95%. The degree of hypoxemia and thus the severity of the illness are difficult to assess clinically, indicating the need for measurement of the infant's arterial oxygen saturation.[203, 205, 206] Clinical findings vary on the same child over short periods of time, and the assessment of severity by the degree of auscultatory sounds, retractions, and respiratory rate has generally been unreliable.[263, 205–207] Abnormalities in the arterial oxygen saturation tend to be prolonged beyond the time of discharge, which correlates with the prolonged viral shedding of these infants.[203, 208] In most infants, the duration of illness is 7 to 21 days, and hospitalization, if required, averages 3 to 7 days.[194, 203, 209, 210]

Otitis Media

RSV has been demonstrated to replicate in the middle ear of experimentally infected animals, and otitis media is a common complication of RSV infection in young children.[14, 17, 104, 194, 211–222] It may accompany both primary and secondary infection, but it is most frequent in infants. By polymerase chain reaction, RSV has been detected in 75% of middle ear effusions in children with documented RSV infection.[216] RSV may be recovered from the ear as the sole pathogen or more often in conjunction with a bacterial pathogen, usually *Streptococcus pneumoniae*.[212, 216, 218, 219] Clinical and experimental evidence now suggests that coinfection of RSV with a bacterial pathogen may worsen the outcome of otitis media, resulting in a greater chance of treatment failure with antibiotics and persistent effusion.[216–221, 223]

Infections in Older Children and Adults

Repeated or secondary infections occurring after the first 3 years of life are most commonly manifested as an upper respiratory tract illness or tracheobronchitis, or infrequently they may be asymptomatic.[91, 99, 104] However, lower respiratory tract illness may occur.

When families infected with RSV have been studied, repeated infection is rarely 1st citation for 194 (change to 224) found to be asymptomatic, even in previously normal adults.[104, 224, 225–227] Most family members develop signs of upper respiratory tract infection, with nasal congestion and cough as the most common signs (Table 148–2). Fever and earache are more common in young children than in older family members. Although RSV infections may mimic the common cold, they tend to be more severe and prolonged than are other upper respiratory tract infections.[104, 221, 228] Illnesses caused by RSV are associated with a greater frequency of fever and conjunctivitis, usually mild, in the acute phase of the illness and with more prolonged nasal congestion, cough, and earache (Table 148–2). In one prospective study, 1 week after the start of their upper respiratory tract illness from RSV, only 32% of the family members had recovered, compared with 74% of those with upper respiratory tract illnesses not caused by RSV. The family members with RSV upper respiratory tract infections remained symptomatic for an average of 9 days, with a range of 1 to 32 days.[104]

TABLE 148–2 Frequency of Signs and Symptoms in 119 Respiratory Illnesses in Family Members: Comparison of 37 Illnesses from Respiratory Syncytial Virus with 82 Illnesses Not Associated with the Virus

Sign or Symptom	RSV-Associated Illness (%)	RSV-Negative Illness (%)	*p* Value*
Nasal congestion			
Acute†	91.9	83	NS
Late‡	59.5	26	>.001
Cough			
Acute	81.1	78	NS
Late	45.9	21	<.01
Hoarseness			
Acute	35.1	26	NS
Late	2.7	4	NS
Sore Throat			
Acute	32.4	37	NS
Late	2.7	5	NS
Fever			
Acute	27.0	13	>.05 to <.10
Late	5.4	1	NS
Conjunctivitis			
Acute	24.3	12	>.05 to <.10
Late	0.0	2	NS
Earache			
Acute	18.9	13	NS
Late	13.5	2	<.05
Rash			
Acute	8.1	4	NS
Late	5.4	1	NS
Asymptomatic			
Acute	—	—	NS

*Probability is derived from the chi-square test.
†Acute RSV illness is defined as occurring on the day RSV was first isolated plus 1 culture day before or after isolation; acute RSV-negative illness is defined as starting on the first day of symptoms plus the next culture day.
‡Late RSV illness is defined as occurring on the first day after the acute phase until the first asymptomatic day; late RSV-negative illness is defined as occurring on the first day after the acute phase to the first asymptomatic day.
Abbreviation: NS, Not significant; RSV, respiratory syncytial virus.
From Hall CB, Geiman JM, Biggar R, et al. Respiratory syncytial virus infections within families. N Engl J Med. 1976; 294:414–417.

TABLE 148–3 Clinical Manifestations of Respiratory Syncytial Virus Infection in 74 Normal, Healthy Adults Aged 20 to 62 Years

	Total Subjects with RSV Infection (%) (n = 74)	Subjects with Proven RSV Infection in Past 18 Mo (%) (n = 37)
Symptomatic infection	85	78
	Symptomatic Subjects (%) (n = 63)	**Symptomatic Subjects with Proven RSV Infection in Past 18 Mo (%) (n = 29)**
Type of illness		
Upper respiratory tract	79	86
With fever ≥37.8°C	57	41
No known fever	22	45
Tracheobronchitis or bronchitis	16	10
Reactive airway disease	5	4
Complications (otitis, sinusitis)	22	10
Work absence	51	24

Abbreviation: RSV, Respiratory syncytial virus.

Natural RSV infection in young adults has been studied probably most closely in hospital and medical personnel, including nursing and medical students, who generally are young, healthy adults with close exposure to infected infants.[224, 229–232] Most of these young adults are symptomatic with their RSV infection (Table 148–3). In about half, the illness may be severe enough to cause some incapacitation. A relatively high proportion develop prolonged coughing and signs leading to the diagnosis of tracheobronchitis or bronchitis, sometimes with otitis, emphasizing RSV's propensity to cause more severe and prolonged illness in adults than other common viral respiratory tract agents such as rhinoviruses (see Tables 148–2 and 148–3). As shown in Table 148–3, recent RSV infection tends to ameliorate the symptoms of RSV infection, but repetitive infection still occurs despite the patient's having had a symptomatic RSV infection within the previous 18 months. Viral shedding can occur for an average of 3 to 6 days, with a range of 1 to 12 days. Serial pulmonary function testing has been performed in young adults with moderate clinical symptoms.[194] In all those tested, the total pulmonary resistance was elevated, and hyperreactivity of the airway to cholinergic stimulus was demonstrated for 8 weeks after the onset of illness (Fig. 148–5).[224] This prolonged hyperreactivity has been postulated to result from the epithelial inflammation and damage caused by the virus. With destruction of the normal epithelium, sensitization of the rapidly adapting sensory receptors of the airways may occur.

Although respiratory disease from RSV in elderly persons, especially those institutionalized, has been recognized for some time, only recently has the impact of RSV infection on the health care burden of older healthy individuals been appreciated. In institutionalized elderly populations, RSV infection has often been nosocomially acquired and has resulted in severe disease, including pneumonia in 5 to 50% of the cases with a fatal outcome in up to 20%.[233–241] Outbreaks of RSV infection have also been documented occasionally in younger, institutionalized adults and frequently as a major cause of exacerbations of chronic bronchitis, mainly in elderly individuals, but also in younger, ambulatory patients.[240, 242–249]

Overall, the proportion of hospital admissions for pneumonia in adults that were proved to be from RSV infection has ranged from 2 to 6%.[226, 239, 240, 243, 246, 250] A recent study in two counties in Ohio from December 1990 through May 1992 examined the causes for community-acquired lower respiratory tract infection in 1195 adults admitted with a clinical diagnosis of pneumonia during the RSV seasons; 4.4% had serologic evidence of RSV infection (Table 148–

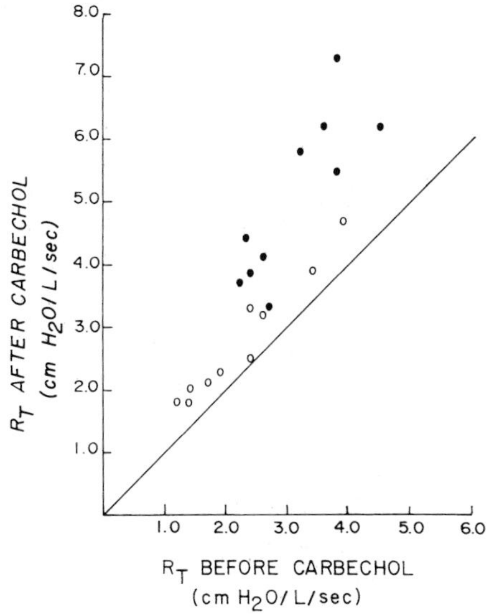

FIGURE 148–5. Relationship between total pulmonary resistance (R_T) before and after carbachol aerosol inhalation in 10 normal adults with acute RSV infection. Closed circles are values obtained in initial testing; open circles, at testing 16 weeks later. The line is the line of identity. The increased airway reactivity demonstrated on the initial testing was prolonged beyond the time of the clinical symptoms and lasted for at least 8 weeks. (Data from Hall and colleagues.[194])

4).[226] RSV was one of the four most common pathogens identified, although the cause was not suspected in any patient. Patients with pneumonia from RSV had some clinical features that distinguished them from patients with pneumonia due to other causes, most characteristic of which were the presence of wheezing and rhonchi (Table 148–5). Furthermore, the chest roentgenogram had pneumonia or consolidation in 40% of those with RSV infection, and in 35% it was lobar. Although in this surveillance study RSV was among the four most common causes of community-acquired pneumonia in hospitalized adults, this was probably an underestimation, as the means of diagnosis was serologic, which is an insensitive method in adults.[226, 239, 240]

TABLE 148–4 Percentage of Patients Hospitalized for Lower Respiratory Tract Infection in Two Ohio Counties Who Were Infected with Respiratory Syncytial Virus, by 10-Year Age Group

Age Group (Yr)	No. RSV-Infected / No. Tested	RSV-Infected (%)
18–29	5/99	5.1
30–39	3/150	2.0
40–49	5/168	3.0
50–59	5/199	2.5
60–69	23/362	6.4
70–79	7/388	1.8
80–89	8/191	4.2
≥90	1/25	4.0

Abbreviation: RSV, Respiratory syncytial virus.

Uncommon Manifestations of Infection

A variety of nonrespiratory manifestations have been associated with RSV infection in case reports. The role of RSV in producing any of these associated disorders is unclear. Central nervous system disorders, including meningitis, myelitis, ataxia, and hemiplegia, have been reported rarely.[251, 252] A neuropathic strain of RSV in mice, however, has been adapted to produce encephalitis in the suckling mouse by intracerebral inoculation.[253] RSV has also been associated with cardiac abnormalities, including myocarditis and arrhythmias[18] along with a variety of exanthems involving the trunk or face, or both.[18, 251, 252, 254–257]

Nosocomial Infection

The characteristics of RSV make it a particularly frequent and potentially hazardous nosocomial infection, which often is not recognized.[107, 229–232, 241, 258–273] RSV produces outbreaks each year with widespread infection in both children and adults, including medical personnel, who may have mild enough illness as to not cause absences from work. Furthermore, the spread of the virus is facilitated by the number of young infants admitted during an outbreak who tend to shed high titers of virus for prolonged periods.[209] Introduction onto a ward is almost inevitable, and a susceptible population is always present since repeated infections are common.

In 1941, Adams[274] described an outbreak of pneumonia that

TABLE 148–5 Clinical Presentation of Adults Hospitalized with Lower Respiratory Infections*

Clinical Feature	RSV (%) (*n* = 57)	Influenza (%) (*n* = 65)†	Bacterial (%) (*n* = 93)‡	Atypical (%) (*n* = 89)§	All non-RSV (%) (*n* = 1528)
Reported cough	88	78**	73†	83	79**
Reported fever	61	75**	77†	67	64
Reported shortness of breath	82	80	73**	76	78
Reported runny nose	58	57	40†	51	50
Reported sinus pain	33	31	31	30	26
Reported ear pain	19	22	20	16	16
Reported sore throat	42	40	35	39	35
Reported wheezing	79	68**	47†	63†	62*
Wheeze on physical exam	53	31*	19†	18†	28†
Wheeze on exam or report	93	74*	56†	68†	70†
Rhonchi on physical exam	46	29**	20†	26*	28*
Crackles on physical exam	42	52	57**	58†	50
Chest radiograph "pneumonia"	40	25**	54**	60†	44
Chest radiograph "clear"	27	38	16**	10**	20
WBC count <12,000	67	78**	40†	55**	54**

*RSV-infected patients are compared with those having documented infections with influenza virus, "typical" bacterial agents, and "atypical" pneumonia agents and entire group of RSV-negative patients.
†Influenza A and B virus.
‡*Streptococcus pneumoniae, Haemophilus influenzae, Streptococcus pyogenes, Neisseria meningitidis, Staphylococcus aureus, Escherichia coli,* and *Klebsiella* species.
§*Legionella pneumophilia, Mycoplasma pneumoniae,* and *Chlamydia pneumoniae.*
‖$.001 < p \leq .01$ vs. RSV-positive group.
¶$.01 < p \leq .05$ vs. RSV-positive group.
**$.05 < p < .20$ vs. RSV-positive group.
†† $p \leq .001$ vs. RSV-positive group.
Abbreviation: RSV, Respiratory syncytial virus; WBC, white blood cell.

affected young hospitalized infants and resulted in the death of 28%. This was probably the first description of a nosocomial outbreak of RSV infection, but only some 20 years later was RSV implicated as the cause when Adams and his coworkers[10, 275] observed a similar outbreak of illness in infants that could then be identified as being caused by RSV. Although recent nosocomial outbreaks of RSV in infants have not been associated with such a high mortality, fatal infection may still occur, especially in those with underlying diseases.[229, 231, 264, 265, 269, 272, 276] Nosocomial infections acquired by infants and older patients with underlying diseases, especially immunocompromised conditions, are almost always symptomatic, ranging from a febrile upper respiratory tract illness to severe lower respiratory tract involvement and death.[229–231, 241, 264, 265, 269, 276, 277]

How RSV spreads so effectively on hospital wards is not entirely clear. Antigenic and genomic fingerprinting of specific strains of RSV is a powerful tool in tracing the origins of nosocomial RSV outbreaks. A method using reverse transcriptase–polymerase chain reaction to detect RSV in air samples has been developed that may be able to delineate further the pattern of spread on hospital wards.[270, 278] Studies using such methods have indicated that frequently more than one strain and origin of RSV erupt into a single nosocomial outbreak.[270] Hospital staff and sometimes visitors appear to be important in the spread of the virus.[229–231, 258–265, 270, 271] During these nosocomial outbreaks, close to one half of the hospital personnel have acquired RSV infection.[229–231, 258, 259, 264, 271] Transmission of the virus appears to occur not only through the staff's becoming infected but also possibly by the spread of contaminated secretions from infected patients to other patients by staff. This mode of spread appears feasible because RSV in the secretions of an infected infant can survive on countertops for more than 24 hours, and on hospital gowns, paper, tissues, and skin for 15 to 60 minutes.[27] Furthermore, infectious virus may be recovered from hands that have contacted these contaminated surfaces, and fomites have been implicated as a mode of spread.[263] Volunteers have been exposed to infected infants in one of three ways that may allow spread to occur: (1) close contact, (2) fomites with subsequent self-inoculation, or (3) small-particle aerosol.[263] Volunteers exposed by either of the first two, but not the last method, became infected. This suggests that small-particle aerosol is less important in the spread of RSV than direct contact with infectious secretions via fomites or large-particle aerosols that generally traverse no more than about 3 feet.

Infection control procedures are described in the subsequent section on prevention.

COMPLICATIONS

Patients at High Risk for Severe Infection

Children with Underlying Diseases

Complicated RSV infection is most likely to occur in young infants and those with underlying diseases, especially those with cardiopulmonary and congenital disorders (Table 148–6).[18, 155, 156, 211, 279–281] An estimated one quarter to two thirds of the fatal RSV infections occur in children with such underlying diseases.[18, 110, 111, 155, 279, 280] Groups of children who clearly have been identified as being at high risk for complicated or fatal RSV infection are those with underlying pulmonary disease, including those with prematurity or bronchopulmonary dysplasia[279, 282–286] and cystic fibrosis,[279, 287, 288] infants with congenital heart disease,[279, 280, 289] patients of all ages with immunocompromised conditions,[155, 159, 279, 290–301] and children with other underlying generalized conditions, such as neurologic diseases and nephrotic syndrome.[300, 301]

Prematurity is the most frequently identified risk factor (see Table 148–6). Infants with very low birth weight and with subsequent chronic lung disease are at particular risk for rehospitalization with RSV infection and complicated and sometimes fatal disease.[282–286, 302, 303] This risk continues into the second and third year of life.[284]

In prospective studies conducted over a 16-year period, 60% of children hospitalized with RSV lower respiratory tract disease had an underlying high-risk condition if children aged 6 weeks or younger are included (see Table 148–6). Over a 3-year period, a retrospective review of high-risk pediatric patients hospitalized with RSV disease in 12 tertiary care centers in Canada showed similar findings.[279] The longest periods of hospitalization were required by immunocompromised patients, but the highest mortality rates were in children with chronic lung disease (3.5%) and with congenital heart disease (3.4%). Of the children with congenital heart disease, the highest mortality was in those with pulmonary hypertension, as shown in an earlier study in Rochester, New York.[280] However, in the Rochester study of a decade earlier, twice as many patients had pulmonary hypertension, and the mortality in this subgroup of patients was 73% compared with 9.4% in the Canadian study, suggesting that advances in surgical and medical care have markedly improved the prognosis. Another Canadian study conducted in 1993–1995 in patients with RSV lower respiratory tract disease and underlying heart disease showed that the morbidity and mortality from RSV in these patients varied according to the type and severity of the heart disease, but that those with pulmonary hypertension had the most complicated courses.[281]

Immunocompromised Patients

Increasing numbers of immunosuppressed patients are being recognized as having complications resulting from RSV infection, and many of these infections are acquired nosocomially.[155, 159, 276, 279, 290–298, 304–306] Suppression of cell-mediated immunity appears to be the major, but not the only, factor in the extensive and severe disease of these patients.[156, 306] Children with congenital combined immunodeficiency diseases are at particular risk.[155, 307] Patients with transplants and malignancy undergoing suppressive chemotherapy usually demonstrate not only extensive pulmonary infection but prolonged shedding of the virus, and the clinical manifestations are similar in adults and in children. A diffuse interstitial process on a chest roentgenogram is the most frequent finding, but lobar infiltrates and pleural effusions also have been observed.[269] Since the differential diagnosis of such

TABLE 148–6 Proportions of Different Types of Underlying Conditions in 1532 Children Hospitalized with Lower Respiratory Tract Disease from Respiratory Syncytial Virus, Strong Memorial Hospital, Rochester, New York, 1976–1996

	Percentage of All Children Hospitalized with RSV Infection with Underlying Conditions of							
Years	*Prematurity (<36 wk)*	*Cardiac Condition*	*Chronic Lung Condition*	*Immuno-compromise*	*Multiple Congenital Abnormalities*	*Other Conditions*	*Age ≤6 wk*	*Total with One or More Underlying Conditions*
1976–1984	21	11	3	2	5	6	26	63
1985–1992	20	7	8	2	5	3	25	57
1993–1996	28	10	9	3	4	5	24	67
1976–1996	25	8	8	2	5	5	25	63

Abbreviations: RSV, Respiratory syncytial virus.

pulmonary findings is broad, RSV is often not considered, especially in adult patients. Yet recent studies suggest that RSV is the most frequent pathogen. At the M. D. Anderson Cancer Center in Houston, surveillance of adults with leukemia or recent bone marrow transplant with respiratory illness yielded a respiratory virus in 27%, and RSV was recovered most often.[306] RSV also accounted for the majority of community-acquired infections in bone marrow transplant recipients cared for at The Fred Hutchinson Cancer Research Center in Seattle.[295] Lung transplant patients have been reported as having the highest incidence of such infections.[299] Mortality rates are consistently high in these compromised patients, frequently around 50%, but range from 20 to 100%.[269, 294, 297, 306]

The frequency and extent of morbidity associated with RSV in patients infected with human immunodeficiency virus have not been well delineated.[296, 308] In the relatively small number of patients infected with human immunodeficiency virus in whom this has been examined, RSV appears primarily to cause pneumonia, rather than bronchiolitis, and results in prolonged viral shedding, sometimes for months.

In immunocompromised patients, specimens obtained by bronchoalveolar lavage may be preferable to sputum or throat culture samples for the rapid diagnosis of RSV. In one series, specimens from bronchoalveolar lavage were positive for RSV in a median of 2 days compared with a median of 8 days for sputum or throat samples.[159] In another study among pediatric patients, a combination of a rapid antigen-detection test and 48 hour shell vial culture on all submitted respiratory specimens gave a sensitivity of 97% and a positive result in most in 48 hours.[309] Tissue obtained by open lung biopsy may also be diagnostic when submitted for viral isolation or for antigen identification and may allow the detection of multinucleated giant cells on histologic examination. The role of serologic examination is especially limited in the management of these patients because of inconsistent antibody responses as well as the time required for seroconversion.

Aerosolized ribavirin therapy in these immunosuppressed patients may be beneficial, if started early, and when combined with careful infection control procedures has resulted in diminished morbidity from nosocomial infection in bone marrow transplant units.[269, 273, 293–295, 298, 306, 310] Intravenous ribavirin as sole therapy in these patients did not result in significant improvement in one study.[295] Although further studies are needed, a combination of antiviral and immunoglobulin therapy may be a preferable option.[298, 306]

Because of the high risk of death in RSV-infected recipients of bone marrow transplants, some units employ a policy of having a culture for RSV performed on all patients before the initiation of transplantation.[311] If RSV is found, treatment with ribavirin has been recommended before bone marrow transplantation.[311] Others do not feel that routine surveillance cultures are indicated because of the short incubation period for RSV and the time required for the virus to become positive in culture but would prefer prompt evaluation for RSV in patients with respiratory symptoms.[293] In addition, sinus roentgenograms have been suggested for all febrile patients along with cultures of sinus specimens for RSV in patients with sinus abnormalities on the roentgenograms.

Acute Complications

The acute complications of RSV infection in infants include apnea, respiratory failure, and rarely secondary bacterial infection. Apnea has been demonstrated to occur in about 20% of the infants hospitalized with RSV infection.[312–314] Infants who appear particularly at risk for this complication are those in the first couple of months of life, those who were premature, and those developing moderate to severe hypoxemia.[312–314] RSV infection has also been associated, as a contributing factor, with the sudden infant death syndrome, particularly in infants older than 3 months, but the evidence is circumstantial.[315–318] Progressive hypercarbia, respiratory failure, and apnea are the major factors leading to assisted ventilation. Although hypoxemia is very common in hospitalized infants, progressive hypercarbia is uncommon.[198, 204] Secondary bacterial infection is unusual in RSV infection.[17, 110, 300] In a 9-year prospective study of infants hospitalized with RSV lower respiratory tract disease, secondary bacterial pneumonia occurred in less that 1% but appeared to be more frequent in infants who had been treated with broad-spectrum antibiotics.[300] In another recent study of young febrile children with and without bronchiolitis, bacteremia occurred in none of the 156 patients with bronchiolitis compared with 2.7% of the controls.[319]

Long-Term Complications

The long-term complications of RSV infections are difficult to delineate. Whether hypoxemia, prolonged or unrecognized, in infancy affects the infant's later pulmonary development is unknown. Even less clear is RSV's role in the high rate of wheezing and pulmonary function abnormalities that have been shown by numerous epidemiologic and clinical studies to occur subsequently in those hospitalized in infancy with bronchiolitis and RSV lower respiratory tract disease.[320–333] More recent evidence suggests that children with early wheezing who subsequently have recurrent hyperreactivity of the airways can be differentiated into two groups by their subsequent clinical courses.[334–339] The larger group of these infants has diminished lung function at birth, the anatomic basis of which is not delineated, but these infants appear normal. Nevertheless, they may be at greater risk of developing chronic pulmonary abnormalities as older adults. The other, smaller group of early wheezers are those with an atopic predisposition who are more likely to develop asthma in later childhood.

DIAGNOSIS

The diagnosis of RSV infection often may be made with reasonable accuracy on the basis of clinical and epidemiologic findings in infants with lower respiratory tract disease, but the findings are less specific in adults. A specific diagnosis may be made by viral isolation or by one of the expanding number of new rapid diagnostic tests. A nasal wash is the usually preferred specimen to be obtained for viral isolation since it produces the highest rate of viral recovery.[31] Alternatively, a swab of the nasopharynx and one of the throat combined together in one vial of medium can be used. Since RSV is a relatively labile virus, especially when subjected to temperature and pH changes, the specimen should be inoculated onto the proper cell lines as soon as possible.[11, 25, 340–344] The characteristic cytopathic effect of RSV is usually present within 3 to 7 days, and the use of shell vials may enhance the speed of identification.[340, 343, 344]

The plethora of rapid techniques for diagnosing RSV infections include immunofluorescent assays, enzyme immunoassay radioimmunoassays, DNA-RNA hybridization, and RNA polymerase chain reaction.[340, 341, 345–352] Kellogg[341] has analyzed the relative advantages of culture, direct and indirect fluorescent antibody techniques, and enzyme immunoassays. The reported sensitivities of the rapid techniques compared with cell culture are in part dependent on the technical expertise and cell lines in the laboratory performing the viral isolation. Low recovery of RSV from cultures enhances the reported sensitivity of the rapid technique to which it is being compared.[341, 345, 353] The reported sensitivity of cell culture compared with various rapid techniques has thus ranged from 57 to 90% or more.[341, 345, 353] Cell cultures, however, have the major advantage of detection of copathogens and ideally should be used in addition to a rapid technique to diagnose RSV.

Serologic diagnosis of RSV infection has been more useful for epidemiologic studies than for patient management because of the delay required to obtain convalescent sera. Furthermore, young infants, older individuals with repeated infections, and immunocompromised patients may not produce a significant rise in antibody titer, depending on the assay used.[13, 42, 105, 149, 226, 342, 348, 354] Current means of serologic diagnosis include the complement fixation test, which is generally less sensitive than enzyme immunoassays, immunofluorescent assays, and neutralization assays.[23, 355] Also utilized are immunoprecipitation, fusion inhibition, and Western blot assays, which along with enzyme immunoassays and immunofluorescent assays may detect class-specific antibodies directed to specific viral proteins.[23, 348, 356] Secretory class–specific antibodies to RSV in nasopharyngeal secretions may also be detected by enzyme immunoassays.[357] Since these secretory antibodies may be present earlier in infection than humoral antibodies, their detection has been used as an adjunct to diagnosis by antigen detection.[357] Detection of RSV-specific antibody in urine samples is another potential diagnostic tool.[358]

TREATMENT

Good supportive care along with careful monitoring is of the utmost importance in the management of severely ill infants and may be credited with the appreciable decrease in morbidity and mortality in recent years in infants with RSV infection, especially in infants with underlying cardiopulmonary conditions.[279, 280]

Supplemental oxygen should be administered to the hypoxemic patient to maintain an oxygen saturation level of at least 92%. Other frequently employed therapies, such as mist and chest physiotherapy, have been shown to be of no benefit.[359, 360] In infants with severe RSV infection and respiratory failure, newer therapies that appear promising based on limited studies include heliox, inhaled nitric oxide, and the intratracheal instillation of natural surfactant.[361–363]

Bronchodilating agents, corticosteroids, and antibiotics have been evaluated as therapy in children with RSV infection, especially in those with wheezing. Controlled studies have indicated that for most of these children these agents are of limited or no benefit, and their use should be highly selective. Despite this, these agents appear to be administered to the majority of children hospitalized with RSV infection.[364, 365–367] A variety of bronchodilating agents and routes of administration have been studied in children with RSV infection. The results have generally been inconsistent or conflicting.[367–372] Most have indicated minimal or no clinical benefit. This may be related to the obstruction of the airways in infants being caused primarily by the inflammation of the RSV infection.[367–370] Recent studies evaluating aerosols of epinephrine, however, suggest that these agents produce more consistent beneficial effect than albuterol.[372–375] Corticosteroid therapy administered in a variety of routes in controlled studies to children with RSV infection or bronchiolitis, or both, has shown no significant benefit.[376–385] One study reported greater initial improvement with oral prednisolone, but the duration of hospitalization was not shortened.[386] The potential benefit of corticosteroid therapy in children with underlying chronic pulmonary conditions, including bronchopulmonary dysplasia, and RSV infection has not been evaluated adequately.

Bacterial infection complicating RSV lower respiratory tract disease is relatively rare, especially in previously normal infants.[366, 387] The frequent administration of unnecessary antibiotics to children hospitalized with RSV lower respiratory tract infection arises in part from the difficulty in differentiating it from a bacterial pneumonia, the common roentgenographic appearance of a subsegmental consolidated area, and the young age of infants hospitalized with RSV infection.[388] Since broad-spectrum antibiotics administered parenterally to such infants may result in a greater likelihood of secondary bacterial infection and potential antibiotic resistance of organisms, their use should be reserved for proven bacterial infection and highly selected cases.[366, 387]

Ribavirin, a synthetic nucleoside that is a broad-spectrum antiviral agent, is the only currently approved specific treatment for RSV lower respiratory tract disease in hospitalized infants.[389–391] The drug is administered as a small-particle aerosol into a tent, Oxy-Hood, mask, or ventilator for a period of 8 to 20 hours each day, usually for 2 to 5 days, depending on the time to improvement. Shorter and intermittent periods of treatment may be as beneficial.[392]

Ribavirin therapy generally should be considered for patients at high risk for complicated or severe disease, such as those with underlying cardiac, pulmonary, and immunosuppressive conditions.[393] Clinical benefit and greater improvement in oxygen saturation levels have been shown in a number of controlled studies with relatively small numbers of patients, but improvement in certain outcome measures, such as a shortened duration of hospitalization, have not been proved.[394–405] This and the current expense of ribavirin and its administration indicate that its use should be restricted to selected high-risk cases.

Infants treated with ribavirin have been shown to have in their secretions diminished levels of RSV-specific IgE and IgA antibodies, which have been associated with more severe clinical illness.[153, 406] Ribavirin has not been associated with viral resistance or adverse effects in treated patients. The long-term outcome of children treated with ribavirin when hospitalized with RSV infection during infancy has now been evaluated in several controlled studies.[407–411] Children who had received ribavirin therapy when followed with clinical and pulmonary evaluations have been shown to fare as well as or better than controls. Trends toward a beneficial effect were noted in tests of pulmonary function, which were significant in one study when the groups were adjusted for the initial severity of the RSV illness. In another study, with a follow-up of only 1 year from hospitalization with RSV bronchiolitis, the prevalence of reactive airway disease and number of episodes were significantly less in those receiving ribavirin compared with controls.[411]

Vitamin A as therapy for children hospitalized with RSV infection also has been evaluated.[412–414] Serum levels of vitamin A in these hospitalized children tended to be low, especially in those more severely ill. Vitamin A administered as therapy, nevertheless, provided no significant clinical benefit, and in one study vitamin A recipients had significantly longer hospital stays than placebo recipients.[413]

Interferon-alfa-2a has been examined as therapy in a limited number of RSV-infected infants and of volunteers with experimental RSV infection,[415, 416] but the results were not promising.

PREVENTION

The viper's venom,
the serpent's spell
Daunts not the tortoise
beneath his shell. . . .
C. B. Hall

Infection Control

Prevention rather than treatment is the preferable, but yet-unattained, goal for the control of RSV infection. The very young age at which RSV first attacks makes prophylactic intervention problematic. Breast-feeding appears to offer the infant some protection against RSV lower respiratory tract infection. Some epidemiologic studies have suggested that the risk of acquiring RSV infection that requires hospitalization is less in infants who are breast-fed.[80, 417–419]

Prevention of infection through interruption of the transmission of the virus is probably impossible at home. On hospital wards, however, attempts to prevent transmission of the virus are warranted. RSV may be spread by close contact and by direct inoculation of droplets of the secretions from an infected person. In addition, RSV may possibly be spread indirectly from hands that touch infectious secretions that contaminate surfaces in the environment.[27, 229, 230, 263, 271] Hence, careful hand washing by all personnel is of particular importance. The use of eye-nose goggles has been shown to diminish appreciably the nosocomial infection rate, presumably by decreasing self-inoculation of the virus into the eyes and nose.[258, 259] In two studies, the use of gowns and masks has not been shown to be of further benefit.[232, 420] In other studies, increasing compliance with a policy of glove and gown isolation precautions significantly reduced the nosocomial infection rate.[260, 421] Infected patients should be isolated or cohorted, especially on wards with high-risk patients, such as those who are immunosuppressed.[273, 309] During RSV outbreaks, staff with respiratory illnesses should not care for those most at risk for complicated RSV infection.[230–232] Newer rapid diagnostic techniques for RSV have enhanced the efficacy of infection control procedures, especially on bone marrow units, and potentially may reduce the cost of such procedures.[273, 309]

Use of Respiratory Syncytial Virus Antibody

The use of immune globulin, both for therapy and prophylaxis, has become of increasing interest.[136, 422–428] Intraperitoneal and intranasal human immune globulin with high titers of neutralizing antibodies of RSV administered to experimental animals has resulted in protection of the lower respiratory tract against RSV challenge.[423, 429–431] Immune globulin therapy also appeared to have a synergistic effect when administered with ribavirin.[432] A small, therapeutic, placebo-controlled, study was subsequently conducted in children hospitalized with RSV disease. Intravenous immune globulin with high titers of RSV-neutralizing antibody administered therapeutically was associated with reduced viral shedding and improved oxygenation, but no shortening of the hospital stay.[433] After an interval of 10 years, two more therapeutic trials were conducted with RSV immune globulin (RSVIG), which had recently been licensed for prophylaxis in high-risk infants.[424, 425] These controlled studies in high-risk infants and in previously healthy infants showed RSVIG therapy to be safe but without significant clinical benefit. In the treatment trial of normal infants, beneficial trends existed in the number of days of hospitalization, intensive care, and mechanical ventilation. Significant reductions in titers of RSV cultured from the airways also occurred.

RSVIG administered prophylactically once a month to high-risk infants in controlled studies, however, resulted in significant reductions in the severity and number of hospitalizations for RSV infection, as well as for respiratory illnesses not associated with RSV.[135, 136, 434] Licensure of RSVIG (RespiGam) was subsequently issued for the prophylaxis against RSV for high-risk infants, those who are high risk because of prematurity and underlying pulmonary disease. According to the American Academy of Pediatrics,[393] the patients for whom RSVIG prophylaxis should be considered are children younger than 2 years with bronchopulmonary dysplasia who are currently receiving or have received oxygen therapy within the 6 months before the anticipated RSV season. Infants with the gestational age of 32 weeks or less without bronchopulmonary dysplasia and who do not meet these criteria still were acknowledged as potentially benefiting from RSVIG prophylaxis, especially those with the youngest gestational age at birth and chronologic age at the beginning of the RSV season.[393] RSVIG was not approved, however, for children with chronic heart disease, especially those with cyanotic heart disease, as they had appeared not to benefit and possibly do worse with RSVIG prophylaxis than the controls.[135, 434]

Topically administered immune globulin for the prophylaxis and treatment of RSV has been evaluated in animal models and in preliminary trials in infants.[426, 435, 436] Immune globulin with high titers against RSV administered intranasally or aerosolized into the respiratory tract of the cotton rat model resulted in protection. In five pediatric centers in Switzerland, however, an initial trial of aerosolized immune globulin for therapy of hospitalized infants with RSV infection provided no substantial beneficial effect on the clinical illness.[426]

Monoclonal antibodies raised against RSV are now being evaluated for therapy and prophylaxis,[437–440] and a chimeric mouse-human IgG monoclonal antibody (palivizumab or Synagis) has been approved for the same indications as the human immuno globulin noted previously. Monoclonal antibody offers the potential advantages of ease of administration, since it may be administered intramuscularly, and for therapy directed toward epitopes important in immunity to RSV.

Although RSVIG is not approved for use in immunosuppressed patients, a number of reports exist of its use for such patients, especially for those who have received transplants.[295, 296, 298, 310, 306, 436] Immune globulin therapy has been combined with ribavirin therapy in some of these patients. No controlled trials are yet available to determine the efficacy of immunotherapy with or without ribavirin in immunosuppressed patients.

Immunization

Control of RSV infections has been cited as a priority for national and world health programs for a number of years. Concurrently has come the recognition that this goal cannot be achieved without the development of a successful vaccine.

Notable barriers to the development of a safe and effective vaccine against RSV exist, however. Many of these arise because of the singular characteristics of RSV infection. A successful vaccine must be able to protect against illness at a time when specific maternal antibody is abundantly present and must overcome the potential dampening effect passive antibody may have on the infant's immature immune response. Furthermore, the ideal vaccine should provide better protection than natural disease, which confers only limited protection against subsequent infection. Because the components of an optimal immune response to RSV remain a conundrum, the design and evaluation of a vaccine remain difficult. The importance of a vaccine eliciting each of the various components of the systemic immune response, as well as of local and mucosal immunity, needs further definition. In addition, whether any component of the current candidate vaccines could elicit a detrimental response similar to that observed with the use of the original formalin-inactivated vaccine remains a concern and hampers vaccine development.

The initial alum-precipitated formalin-inactivated vaccine developed in the 1960s produced excellent levels of serum antibody but was followed by the unfortunate event of augmented disease in the vaccinees during subsequent natural infection,[98, 117, 118, 129] as discussed previously. This past experience, however, spurred the investigation into the immunopathogenesis of the abnormal response and has suggested some potential criteria for the future development of safe and successful candidate vaccines.[137, 138, 441–443] The immune response appears to be affected by the type of immunizing agent. Experimental evidence suggests that the formalin-inactivated vaccine induced a Th2-type response, indicating that if the initial immune response to RSV is to be via immunization, the vaccine should produce a Th1-type response with both CD4 and CTL cells.[175, 177, 178] Initial live candidate vaccines were developed using cold-adapted strains from temperature-sensitive mutants. Despite promising results in adult volunteers, subsequent studies proved these initial strains to be unsuitable for a vaccine in young children. They resulted in unacceptable degrees of illness, were overattenuated and not protective, or were genetically unstable with reversion to wild-type virus, which was shed.[422, 444–447] Continued research, however, has produced more promising candidate mutant strains.[422, 448, 451] The previously tested, but unsuccessful, cp-RSV mutant has been modified by introducing additional mutations. The cp-RSV mutants produced by chemical mutagenesis and prolonged passage in cell culture have produced more suitable restriction of temperature and viral replication, genetic stability, attenuation, and yet immunogenicity in animal models.[449, 450, 452–454] In volunteers, initial studies of these vaccines have been promising.[454]

The recent advances in molecular techniques have led to vaccine candidates generated from specific viral proteins. Efforts have been focused on the two major surface glycoproteins, F and G,[68, 133, 455–460] which have been prepared as purified proteins, alone or in combination.[458, 460–462] One subunit vaccine, composed primarily of the F protein, has been evaluated in trials in adults and in children with a prior history of RSV infection.[451, 458, 460, 464–467] In these studies, the vaccine has appeared safe and immunogenic as measured by antibody responses. In elderly individuals, it was less immunogenic than in children. In a small controlled trial in seropositive children with cystic fibrosis, reduction in the mean number of lower respiratory tract illnesses was observed but no protection against infection from RSV.[464] In a small study of children with bronchopulmonary dysplasia, this vaccine appeared to be protective.[467] It is also being evaluated for immunization of women during pregnancy with the goal of providing the infant protection through humoral and breast milk antibody.[468]

Genes coding for RSV proteins have also been incorporated into viral vectors, including vaccinia, baculovirus, and adenovirus.[455, 457, 459, 469] The G glycoprotein has also been synthesized in *Salmonella typhimurium* cells.[470] In a number of experimental animals, immunization with these types of vaccines has been encouraging. The response, however, has varied according to the immunizing protein, the type of vector, and the animal model.[455, 471, 472] Issues related to the safety of the vector, particularly in individuals who may be immunocompromised, also are of consideration in the development of a live recombinant vaccine.[473]

Recent investigations have produced a generation of peptide vaccines representing selected epitopes that stimulate protective B- and T-cell responses.[462] This strategy has the advantage of specifically targeting a desired immune response. Because this type of vaccine does not induce a strong CTL response, which may be important in the protection and recovery from RSV, different types of adjuvant systems are being explored for vaccine development.[474] Among those currently being evaluated for immunization against RSV are cholera toxin, ISCOMS, and saponin.[475–477] Recent studies of peptide mimotopes offer another potential approach to RSV prevention.[478]

REFERENCES

1. Brandt CD, Kim HW, Arrobio JO, et al. Epidemiology of respiratory syncytial virus infection in Washington, DC. III. Composite analysis of eleven consecutive yearly epidemics. Am J Epidemiol. 1973;98:355–364.
2. Chanock RM, Parrott RH. Acute respiratory disease in infancy and childhood: Present understanding and prospects for prevention. Pediatrics. 1965;36:21–39.
3. Glezen WP, Denny FW. Epidemiology of acute lower respiratory disease in children. N Engl J Med. 1973;288:498–505.
4. Kim HW, Arrobio JO, Brandt CD, et al. Epidemiology of respiratory syncytial virus infection in Washington DC. I. Importance of the virus in different respiratory tract disease syndromes and temporal distribution of infection. Am J Epidemiol. 1973;98:216–225.
5. Parrott RH, Kim HW, Arrobio JO, et al. Epidemiology of respiratory syncytial virus infection in Washington, DC. II. Infection and disease with respect to age, immunologic status, race and sex. Am J Epidemiol. 1973;98:289–300.
6. Heilman CA. Respiratory syncytial and parainfluenza viruses. J Infect Dis. 1990;161:402–406.
7. Morris JA, Blount RE, Savage RE. Recovery of cytopathogenic agent from chimpanzees with coryza. Proc Soc Exp Biol Med. 1956;92:544–549.
8. Chanock R, Roizman B, Myers R. Recovery from infants with respiratory illness of a virus related to chimpanzee coryza agent (CCA). I. Isolation, properties and characterization. Am J Hyg. 1957;66:281–290.
9. Chanock RM, Finberg L. Recovery from infants with respiratory illness of a virus related to chimpanzee coryza agent (CCA). II. Epidemiologic aspects of infection in infants and young children. Am J Hyg. 1957;66:291–300.
10. Adams JM, Imagawa DT, Zike K. Epidemic bronchiolitis and pneumonitis related to respiratory syncytial virus. JAMA. 1961;176:1037–1039.
11. Beem M, Wright FH, Hamre D, et al. Association of the chimpanzee coryza agent with acute respiratory disease in children. N Engl J Med. 1960;263:523–530.
12. Chanock RM, Kim HW, Vargosko AJ, et al. Respiratory syncytial virus. I. Virus recovery and other observations during 1960 outbreak of bronchiolitis pneumonia, and minor respiratory diseases in children. JAMA. 1961;176:647–653.
13. Hamre D, Procknow JJ. Viruses isolated from natural common colds in the USA. BMJ. 1961;2:1382–1385.
14. Kapikian AZ, Bell JA, Mastrota FM, et al. An outbreak of febrile illness and pneumonia associated with respiratory syncytial virus infection. Am J Hyg. 1961;74:234–248.
15. McClelland L, Hilleman MR, Hamparian VV, et al. Studies of acute respiratory illnesses caused by respiratory syncytial virus. N Engl J Med. 1961;264:1169–1175.
16. Parrott RH, Vargosko AJ, Kim HW, et al. Respiratory syncytial virus. II. Serologic studies over a 34-month period of children with bronchiolitis, pneumonia, and minor respiratory diseases. JAMA. 1961;176:653–657.
17. Reilly CM, Stokes J Jr, McClelland L, et al. Studies of acute respiratory illness caused by respiratory syncytial virus. 3. Clinical and laboratory findings. N Engl J Med. 1961;264:1176–1182.
18. Gardner PS, Turk DC, Aherne WA, et al. Deaths associated with respiratory tract infection in childhood. BMJ. 1967;4:316–320.
19. Grist NR, Ross CAC, Stott EJ. Influenza, respiratory syncytial virus, and pneumonia in Glasgow, 1962–1965. BMJ. 1967;1:456–457.
20. Suto T, Yano N, Ikeda M, et al. Respiratory syncytial virus infection and its serologic epidemiology. Am J Epidemiol. 1965;82:211–224.
21. Collins PL, McIntosh K, Chanock RM. Respiratory syncytial virus. In: Fields BN, McIntosh K, Chanock RM, eds. Fields Virology. 3rd ed, v. 1. Philadelphia: Lippincott-Raven; 1995:1313–1351.
22. Arslanagic E, Matsumoto M, Suzuki K, et al. Maturation of respiratory syncytial virus within HEP-2 cell cytoplasm. Acta Virol. 1996;40:209–214.
23. Walsh E, Hall C: Approaches to a vaccine for respiratory syncytial virus. In: Meyers RA, ed. Encyclopedia of Molecular Biology and Molecular Medicine. Weinheim, Germany: VCH; 1996:286–296.
24. Heminway BR, Yu W, Tanaka Y, et al. Analysis of respiratory syncytial virus F, G, and SH proteins in cell fusion. Virology. 1994;200:801–805.
25. Hambling MH. Survival of the respiratory syncytial virus during storage under various conditions. Br J Exp Pathol. 1964;45:647–655.
26. Berthiaume L, Joncas J, Pavilanis V. Comparative structure, morphogenesis, and biological characteristics of the respiratory syncytial (RS) virus and the pneumonia virus of mice (PVM). Arch Gesamte Virusforsch. 1974;45:39–51.
27. Hall CB, Geiman JM, Douglas RG Jr. Possible transmission by fomites of respiratory syncytial virus. J Infect Dis. 1980;141:98–102.
28. Rechsteiner J, Winkler KC. Inactivation of respiratory syncytial virus in aerosol. J Gen Virol. 1969;5:405–410.
29. Walsh EE, Hall CB. Respiratory syncytial virus. In: Schmidt NJ, Emmons RW, eds. Diagnostic Procedures for Viral and Rickettsial Infections. New York: American Public Health Association; 1989:693–712.
30. Shahrabadi MS, Lee PWK. Calcium requirement for syncytium formation in HEp-2 cells by respiratory syncytial virus. J Clin Microbiol. 1988;26:139–141.
31. Hall CB, Douglas RG Jr. Clinically useful method for the isolation of respiratory syncytial virus. J Infect Dis. 1975;131:1–5.
32. Routledge EG, Wilcocks MM, Morgan L, et al. Expression of the respiratory syncytial virus 22K protein on the surface of infected HeLa cells. J Gen Virol. 1987;68:1217–1222.
33. Senterfit LB. Persistent infection of RSV. In: RSV Workshop, July 20–21, 1977. Washington, DC: National Institutes of Health.
34. Anderson LJ, Hierholzer JC, Tsou C, et al. Antigenic characterization of respiratory syncytial virus strains with monoclonal antibodies. J Infect Dis. 1985;151:626–633.
35. Mufson MA, Orvell C, Rafnar B, Norrby E. Two distinct subtypes of human respiratory syncytial virus. J Gen Virol. 1985;66:2111–2124.
36. Hendry RM, Talis AL, Godfrey E, et al. Concurrent circulation of antigenically distinct strains of respiratory syncytial virus during community outbreaks. J Infect Dis. 1986;153:291–297.
37. Norrby E, Mufson MA, Hooshmand S. Structural differences between subtype A and B strains of respiratory syncytial virus. J Gen Virol. 1986;67:2721–2729.
38. Akerlind B, Norrby E. Occurrence of respiratory syncytial virus subtypes A and B strains in Sweden. J Med Virol. 1986;19:241–247.
39. Johnson PR, Spriggs MK, Olmsted RA, Collins PL. The G glycoprotein of human respiratory syncytial viruses of subgroups A and B: Extensive sequence divergence between antigenically related proteins. Proc Natl Acad Sci U S A. 1987;84:5625–5629.
40. Walsh EE, Brandriss MW, Schlesinger JJ. Immunological differences between the envelope glycoproteins of two strains of human respiratory syncytial virus. J Gen Virol. 1987;68:2169–2176.
41. Johnson PR, Olmsted RA, Prince GA, et al. Antigenic relatedness between glycoproteins of human respiratory syncytial virus subgroups A and B: Evaluation of the contributions of F and G glycoproteins to immunity. J Virol. 1987;10:3163–3166.
42. Hall CB, Walsh EE, Schnabel KC, et al. Occurrence of groups A and B of respiratory syncytial virus over 15 years: Associated epidemiologic and clinical characteristics in hospitalized and ambulatory children. J Infect Dis. 1990;162:1283–1290.
43. Anderson LJ, Hendry RM, Pierik LT, et al. Multicenter study of strains of respiratory syncytial virus. J Infect Dis. 1991;163:687–692.
44. Storch GA, Anderson LJ, Park CS, et al. Antigenic and genomic diversity within group A respiratory syncytial virus. J Infect Dis. 1991;163:858–861.
45. Mufson MA, Åkerlind-Stopner B, Örvell C, et al. A single-season epidemic with respiratory syncytial virus subgroup B2 during 10 epidemic years, 1978 to 1988. J Clin Microbiol. 1991;29:162–165.
46. Hendry RM, Burns JC, Walsh EE, et al. Strain-specific serum antibody responses in infants undergoing primary infection with respiratory syncytial virus. J Infect Dis. 1988:157:640–647.
47. Johnson PR, Collin PL. The A and B subgroups of human respiratory syncytial virus: Comparison of intergenic and gene-overlap sequences. J Gen Virol. 1988; 69:2901–2906.
48. Johnson PR, Collins PL. The fusion glycoprotein of human respiratory syncytial viruses of subgroups F and B; sequence conservation provides a structural basis for antigenic relatedness. J Gen Virol. 1988;69:2623–2628.
49. Johnson PR, Collins PL. Sequence comparison of the phosphoprotein mRNAs of

antigenic subgroups A and B of human respiratory syncytial virus identifies a highly divergent domain in the predicted protein. J Gen Virol. 1990;71:481–485.
50. Johnson PR, Collins PL. The 1B (NS2), 1C (NS1), and N proteins of human respiratory syncytial virus (RSV) of antigenic subgroups A and B: Sequence conservation and divergence within RSV genomic RNA. J Gen Virol. 1989;70:1539–1547.
51. Sullender WM, Mufson MA, Anderson LJ, Wertz GW. Genetic diversity of the attachment protein of subgroup B respiratory syncytial viruses. J Virol. 1991;65:5425–5434.
52. Morgan LA, Routledge EG, Willcocks MM, et al. Strain variations of respiratory syncytial virus. J Gen Virol. 1987;68:2781–2788.
53. Mufson MA, Belshe RB, Orvell C, Norrby E. Respiratory syncytial virus epidemics: Variable dominance of subgroups A and B strains among children, 1981–1986. J Infect Dis. 1988;157:143–148.
54. Cane PA, Pringle CR. Evolution of subgroup A respiratory syncytial virus: Evidence for progressive accumulation of amino acid changes in the attachment protein. J Virol. 1995;69:2918–2925.
55. Cane PA, Pringle CR. Molecular epidemiology of human respiratory syncytial virus. Semis Virol. 1995;6:371–378.
56. Cane PA, Pringle CR. Analysis of linear epitopes recognized by the primary human antibody response to a variable region of the attachment (G) protein of respiratory syncytial virus. J Med Virol. 1997;51:297–304.
57. Byrd LG, Prince GA. Animal models of respiratory syncytial virus infection. Clin Infect Dis J. 1997;25:1363–1368.
58. Kinman TG, Westenbrink F, Schreuder BEC, Straver PJ. Local and systemic antibody response to bovine respiratory syncytial virus infection and reinfection in calves with and without maternal antibodies. J Clin Microbiol. 1987;25:1097–1106.
59. Piazza RM, Johnson, SA, Darnell MER, et al. Bovine respiratory syncytial virus protects cotton rats against human respiratory syncytial virus infection. J Virol. 1993;67:1503–1510.
60. Baker JC, Werdin RE, Ames TR, et al. Study on the etiologic role of bovine respiratory syncytial virus in pneumonia of dairy calves. J Am Vet Med Assoc. 1986;189:66–70.
61. Kinman TG, Westenbrink F. Immunity to human and bovine respiratory syncytial virus (Review). Arch Virol. 1990;112:1–25.
62. Amann VL, Lerch RS, Anderson K, Wertz GW. Bovine respiratory syncytial virus nucleocapsid protein: mRNA sequence analysis and expression from recombinant vaccinia virus vectors. J Gen Virol. 1992;73:999–1003.
63. Baker JC, Wilson EG, McKay GL, et al. Identification of subgroups of bovine respiratory syncytial virus. J Clin Microbiol. 1992;30:1120–1126.
64. Beeler JA, Coelingh K. Neutralization epitopes of respiratory syncytial virus: Effect of mutation upon fusion function. J Virol. 1989;63:2941–2950.
65. Alansari H, Potgeiter LN. Nucleotide sequence analysis of the ovine respiratory syncytial virus G glycoprotein gene. Virology. 1993;196:873–877.
66. Bastien N, Simard C, Trudel M. Partial nucleotide sequence of the genes encoding the fusion and attachment glycoproteins from a caprine respiratory syncytial virus isolate. In: Abstracts of the IX International Congress of Virology 1993;171:P12–P27.
67. Belshe RB, Richardson LS, London WT, et al. Experimental respiratory syncytial virus infection of four species of primates. J Med Virol. 1977;1:157–162.
68. Collins PL, Purcell RH, London WT, et al. Evaluation in chimpanzees of vaccinia virus recombinants that express the surface glycoproteins of human respiratory syncytial virus. Vaccine. 1990;8:164–168.
69. Richardson LS, Belshe RB, London WT, et al. Evaluation of five temperature sensitive mutants of respiratory syncytial virus in primates. I. Viral shedding, immunologic response, and associated illness. J Med Virol. 1978;3:91–100.
70. Kakuk TJ, Soike K, Brideau RJ, et al. A human respiratory syncytial virus (RSV) primate model of enhanced pulmonary pathology induced with a formalin-inactivated RSV vaccine but not a recombinant FG subunit vaccine. J Infect Dis. 1993;167:533–561.
71. Wagner MH, Evermann JF, Gaskin J, et al. Subacute effects of respiratory syncytial virus infection on lung function in lambs. Pediatr Pulmonol. 1991;11:56–64.
72. Sharma R, Woldehiwet Z. Pathogenesis of bovine respiratory syncytial virus in experimentally infected lambs. Vet Microbiol. 1990;23:267–272.
73. Lapin CD, Hiatt PW, Langston C, et al. A lamb model for human respiratory syncytial virus infection. Pediatr Pulmonol. 1993;15:151–156.
74. Prince GA, Porter DD. The pathogenesis of respiratory syncytial virus infection in infant ferrets. Am J Pathol. 1976;82:339–352.
75. Murphy BR, Prince GA, Lawrence LA, et al. Detection of respiratory syncytial virus (RSV) infected cells by in situ hybridization in the lungs of cotton rats immunized with formalin-inactivated virus or purified RSV F and G glycoprotein subunit vaccine and challenged with RSV. Virus Res. 1990;16:153–162.
76. Graham BS, Perkins MD, Wright PF, Karzon DT. Primary respiratory syncytial virus infection in mice. J Med Virol. 1988;26:153–162.
77. Berman S. Epidemiology of acute respiratory infections in children of developing countries. Rev Infect Dis. 1991;13:S454–S462.
78. McIntosh K. Pathogenesis of severe acute respiratory infections in the developing world: Respiratory syncytial virus and parainfluenza virus. Rev Infect Dis. 1991;13(Suppl):S492–S500.
79. Glezen WP, Loda FA, Clyde WA Jr, et al. Epidemiologic patterns of acute lower respiratory disease of children in a pediatric group practice. J Pediatr. 1971;78:397–406.
80. Glezen WP. Pathogenesis of bronchiolitis epidemiologic considerations. Pediatr Res. 1977;11:239–243.
81. Hall CB, Douglas RG Jr. Respiratory syncytial virus and influenza: Practical community surveillance. Am J Dis Child. 1976;130:615–620.
82. Centers for Disease Control. Update: Respiratory Syncytial Virus Activity—United States, 1997–98 Season. MMWR. 1997;46:1163–1165.
83. Beem M, Egerer R, Anderson J. Respiratory syncytial virus neutralizing antibodies in persons residing in Chicago, Illinois. Pediatrics. 1964;34:761–770.
84. Ward KA, Lambden PR, Ogilvie MM, Watt PJ. Antibodies to respiratory syncytial virus polypeptides and their significance in human infection. J Gen Virol. 1983;64:1867–1876.
85. LaVia WV, Marks MI, Stutman HR. Respiratory syncytial virus puzzle: Clinical features, pathophysiology, treatment, and prevention. J Pediatr. 1992;121:503–510.
86. Gardner PS. How etiologic, pathologic, and clinical diagnoses can be made in a correlated fashion. Pediatr Res. 1977;11:254–261.
87. Denny FW, Collier AM, Henderson FW, et al. The epidemiology of bronchiolitis. Pediatr Res. 1977;11:234–236.
88. Jackson GG, Muldoon RL. Viruses causing common respiratory infections in man. III. Respiratory syncytial viruses and coronaviruses. J Infect Dis. 1973;128:674–692.
89. Henderson FW, Clyde WA Jr, Collier AM, et al. The etiologic and epidemiologic spectrum of bronchiolitis in pediatric practice. J Pediatr. 1979;95:183–190.
90. Murphy TF, Henderson FW, Clyde WA Jr, et al. Pneumonia: An eleven-year study in a pediatric practice. Am J Epidemiol. 1981;113:12–21.
91. Denny FW, Clyde WA Jr. Acute lower respiratory tract infections in nonhospitalized children. J Pediatr. 1986;108:635–646.
92. Coates HV, Chanock RM. Clinical significance of respiratory syncytial virus. Postgrad Med. 1964;35:460–465.
93. Loda FA, Clyde WA, Glezen WP, et al. Studies of the role of viruses, bacteria, and *M. pneumoniae* as causes of lower respiratory tract infections in children. J Pediatr. 1968;72:161–176.
94. Macasaet FF, Kidd PA, Bolano CR, et al. The etiology of acute respiratory infections. III. The role of viruses and bacteria. J Pediatr. 1968;72:829–839.
95. Maletzky AJ, Cooney MK, Luce R, et al. Epidemiology of viral and mycoplasmal agents associated with childhood lower respiratory illness in a civilian population. J Pediatr. 1971;78:407–414.
96. Foy HM, Cooney MK, Maletzky AJ, et al. Incidence and etiology of pneumonia, croup, and bronchiolitis in preschool children belonging to a prepaid medical care group over a four-year period. Am J Epidemiol. 1973;97:80–92.
97. Loda FA, Glezen WP, Clyde WA Jr. Respiratory disease in group day care. Pediatrics. 1972;49:428–437.
98. Kim HW, Canchola JG, Brandt CD, et al. Respiratory syncytial virus disease in infants despite prior administration of antigenic inactivated vaccine. Am J Epidemiol. 1969;89:422–434.
99. Glezen WP, Taber LH, Frank AL, Kasel JA. Risk of primary infection and reinfection with respiratory syncytial virus. Am J Dis Child. 1986;140:543–546.
100. Holberg CJ, Wright AL, Martinez FD, et al. Risk factors for respiratory syncytial virus–associated lower respiratory illnesses in the first year of life. Am J Epidemiol. 1991;133:1135–1151.
101. Parrott RH, Kim HW, Brandt CD, et al. Respiratory syncytial virus in infants and children. Prev Med. 1974;3:473–480.
102. Glezen WP. Incidence of respiratory syncytial and parainfluenza type 3 viruses in an urban setting. Pediatr Virol. 1987;2:1–4.
103. Henderson FW, Collier AM, Clyde WA Jr, Denny FW. Respiratory syncytial virus infections, reinfections and immunity. A prospective, longitudinal study in young children. N Engl J Med. 1979;300:530–534.
104. Hall CB, Geiman JM, Biggar R, et al. Respiratory syncytial virus infections within families. N Engl J Med. 1976;294:414–419.
105. Johnson KM, Chanock RM, Rifkind D, et al. Respiratory syncytial virus. IV. Correlation of virus shedding, serologic response, and illness in adult volunteers. JAMA. 1961;176:663–667.
106. Kravetz HM, Knight V, Chanock RM, et al. Respiratory syncytial virus. III. Production of illness and clinical observations in adult volunteers. JAMA. 1961;176:657–663.
107. Gardner PS, Court SDM, Brocklebank JT, et al: Virus cross-infection in paediatric wards. BMJ. 1973;2:571–575.
108. Sterner G, Wolontis S, Bloth B, et al. Respiratory syncytial virus. An outbreak of acute respiratory illness in a home for infants. Acta Paediatr Scand. 1966;55:273–279.
109. Hall CB, Douglas RG Jr, Schnabel KC, Geiman JM. Infectivity of respiratory syncytial virus by various routes of inoculation. Infect Immun. 1981;33:779–783.
110. Aherne W, Bird T, Court SDM, et al. Pathological changes in virus infections of the lower respiratory tract in children. J Clin Pathol. 1970;23:7–18.
111. Urquhart GED, Gibson AAM. RSV infections and infant deaths. BMJ. 1970;3:110.
112. Phelan PD, Williams HE, Freeman M. The disturbances of ventilation in acute viral bronchiolitis. Aust Paediatr J. 1968;4:96–104.
113. Wohl MEB. Present capacity to evaluate pulmonary function relevant to bronchiolitis. Pediatr Res. 1977;11:252–253.
114. Wohl MEB, Stigol LC, Mead J. Resistance of the total respiratory system in healthy infants and infants with bronchiolitis. Pediatrics. 1969;43:495–509.
115. Neilson KA, Yunis EJ. Demonstration of respiratory syncytial virus in an autopsy series. Pediatr Pathol. 1990;10:491–502.
116. Reid L. Influence of the pattern of structural growth of lung on susceptibility to specific infectious diseases in infants and children. Pediatr Res. 1977;11:210–215.
117. Fulginiti VA, Eller JJ, Sieber OF, et al. Respiratory virus immunization. I. A field trial of two inactivated respiratory virus vaccines; an aqueous trivalent parainflu-

enza virus vaccine, and an alum-precipitated respiratory syncytial virus vaccine. Am J Epidemiol. 1969;89:435–448.
118. Kapikian AZ, Mitchell RH, Chanock RM, et al. An epidemiologic study of altered clinical reactivity to respiratory syncytial (RS) virus infection in children previously vaccinated with an inactivated RS virus vaccine. Am J Epidemiol. 1969;89:405–421.
119. Chanock RM. Control of acute mycoplasmal and viral respiratory tract disease. Science. 1970;169:248–256.
120. Chanock RM, Kapikian AZ, Mills J. Influence of immunological factors in respiratory syncytial virus disease of the lower respiratory tract. Arch Environ Health. 1970;21:347–355.
121. Hogg JC, Williams J, Richardson JB, et al. Age as a factor in the distribution of lower-airway conductance and in the pathologic anatomy of obstructive lung disease. N Engl J Med. 1970;282:1283–1287.
122. Hall CB, Walsh EE, Long CE, Schnabel KC. Immunity to and frequency of reinfection with respiratory syncytial virus. J Infect Dis. 1991;163:693–698.
123. Black-Payne C. Respiratory syncytial virus infection among families and within hospitals: Infancy to the aged. Schumpert Med Q. 1992;9:203–219.
124. Bruhn FW, Yeager AS. Respiratory syncytial virus in early infancy. Am J Dis Child. 1977;131:145–148.
125. Toms GL, Scott R. Respiratory syncytial virus and the infant immune response. Arch Dis Child. 1987;62:544–546.
126. Ogilvie MM, Vatheneo S, Radford M, et al. Maternal antibody and respiratory syncytial virus infection in infancy. J Med Virol. 1981;7:263–271.
127. Glezen WP, Paredes A, Allison JE, et al. Risk of respiratory syncytial virus infection for infants from low-income families in relationship to age, sex, ethnic group and maternal antibody level. J Pediatr. 1981;98:708–715.
128. Fernald GW, Almond JR, Henderson FW. Cellular and humoral immunity in recurrent respiratory syncytial virus infections. Pediatr Res. 1983;17:753–758.
129. Lamprecht CL, Krause HE, Mufson MA. Role of maternal antibody in pneumonia and bronchiolitis due to respiratory syncytial virus. J Infect Dis. 1976;134:211–217.
130. Graham BS, Bunton LA, Rowland J, et al. Respiratory syncytial virus infection in anti-μ treated mice. J Virol. 1991;65:4936–4942.
131. Taylor G, Stott EJ, Bew M, et al. Monoclonal antibodies protect against respiratory syncytial virus infection in mice. Immunology. 1984;52:137–142.
132. Walsh EE, Schlesinger JJ, Brandriss MW. Protection from respiratory syncytial virus infection in cotton rats by passive transfer of monoclonal antibodies. Infect Immun. 1984;43:756–758.
133. Walsh EE, Hall CB, Briselli M, et al. Immunization with glycoprotein subunits of respiratory syncytial virus to protect cotton rats against viral infection. J Infect Dis. 1987;155:1198–1203.
134. Olmsted RA, Elango N, Prince GA, et al. Expression of the F glycoprotein of respiratory syncytial virus by a recombinant vaccinia virus: Comparison of the individual contributions of the F and G glycoproteins to host immunity. Proc Natl Acad Sci U S A. 1986;83:7462–7466.
135. Groothuis JR, Simoes EA, Levin MJ, et al. Prophylactic administration of respiratory syncytial virus immune globulin to high-risk infants and young children. The RSVIG Study Group. N Engl J Med. 1993;329:1524–1530.
136. The Prevent Study Group. Reduction of respiratory syncytial virus hospitalization among premature infants and infants with bronchopulmonary dysplasia using respiratory syncytial virus immune globulin prophylaxis. Pediatrics. 1997;99:93–99.
137. Murphy BR, Prince GA, Walsh EE, et al. Dissociation between serum neutralizing antibody responses of infants and children who received inactivated respiratory syncytial virus vaccine. J Clin Microbiol. 1986;24:197–202.
138. Murphy BR, Walsh EE. Formalin-inactivated respiratory syncytial virus vaccine induces antibodies to the fusion glycoprotein that are deficient in fusion-inhibiting activity. J Clin Microbiol. 1988;26:1595–1597.
139. Mufson MA, Belshe R, Orvell C, Norrby E. Subgroup characteristics of respiratory syncytial virus strains recovered from children with two consecutive infections. J Clin Microbiol. 1987;25:1535–1539.
140. Muelenaer PM, Henderson FW, Hemming VG, et al. Group-specific serum antibody responses in children with primary and recurrent respiratory syncytial virus infections. J Infect Dis. 1991;164:15–21.
141. Prince GA, Horswood RL, Chanock RM. Quantitative aspects of passive immunity to respiratory syncytial virus infection in infants cotton rats. J Virol. 1985;55:517–520.
142. Scott R, Gardner PS. Respiratory syncytial virus neutralizing activity in nasopharyngeal secretions. J Hyg (Lond). 1970;68:581–588.
143. Kaul TN, Welliver RC, Wong DT, et al. Secretory antibody response to respiratory syncytial virus infection. Am J Dis Child. 1981;135:1013–1016.
144. Mclntosh K, Masters HB, Orr I, et al. The immunologic response to infection with respiratory syncytial virus in infants. J Infect Dis. 1978;138:24–32.
145. Mills JV, Van Kirk JE, Wright PF, et al. Experimental respiratory syncytial virus infection of adults. Possible mechanisms of resistance to infection and illness. J Immunol. 1971;107:123–130.
146. Welliver RC, Kaul TN, Ogra PL. The appearance of cell-bound IgE in respiratory-tract epithelium after respiratory-syncytial-virus infection. N Engl J Med. 1980;303:1198–1202.
147. Welliver RC, Wong DT, Sun M, et al. The development of respiratory syncytial virus–specific IgE and the release of histamine in naso-pharyngeal secretions after infection. N Engl J Med. 1981;305:841–846.
148. Gardner PS. Immunologic studies of RS infections. Workshop on Respiratory Syncytial and Parainfluenza Viruses, July 21, 1977. Bethesda, Md: National Institutes of Health.
149. Murphy BR, Graham BS, Prince GA, et al. Serum and nasal-wash immunoglobulin G and A antibody response of infants and children to respiratory syncytial virus F and G glycoproteins following primary infection. J Clin Microbiol. 1986;23:1009–1014.
150. Welliver RC, Sun M, Hildreth SW, et al. Respiratory syncytial virus–specific antibody responses in immunoglobulin A and E isotypes to the F and G proteins and to intact virus after natural infection. J Clin Microbiol. 1989;27:295–299.
151. Welliver RC, Kaul TJ, Sun M, Ogra PL. Defective regulation of immune responses in respiratory syncytial virus infection. J Immunol. 1984;133:1925–1930.
152. Volovitz B, Faden H, Ogra PL. Release of leukotriene C_4 in respiratory tract during acute viral infection. J Pediatr. 1988;112:218–222.
153. Volovitz B, Welliver RC, de Castro G, et al. The release of leukotrienes in the respiratory tract during infection with respiratory syncytial virus: Role in obstructive airway disease. Pediatr Res. 1988;24:504–507.
154. Garofalo R, Kimpen JLL, Welliver RC, Ogra PL. Eosinophil degranulation in the respiratory tract during naturally acquired respiratory syncytial virus infection. J Pediatr. 1992;120:28–32.
155. Hall CB, Powell KR, MacDonald NE, et al. Respiratory syncytial virus infection in children with compromised immune function. N Engl J Med. 1986;315:77–81.
156. Ogra PL, Patel J. Respiratory syncytial virus infection and the immunocompromised host. Pediatr Infect Dis J. 1988;7:246–249.
157. Johnson RA, Prince GA, Suffin SC, et al. Respiratory syncytial virus infection in cyclophosphamide-treated cotton rats. Infect Immun. 1982;37:369–373.
158. Graham BS, Bunton LA, Wright PF, Karzon DT. Role of T lymphocyte subsets in the pathogenesis of primary infection and rechallenge with respiratory syncytial virus in mice. J Clin Invest. 1991;88:1026–1033.
159. Englund JA, Sullivan CJ, Jordan C, et al. Respiratory syncytial virus infection in immunocompromised adults. Ann Intern Med. 1988;109:203–208.
160. Scott R, Kaul A, Scott M, et al. Development of in-vitro correlates of cell mediated immunity to respiratory syncytial infection in humans. J Infect Dis. 1978;137:810–817.
161. Kim HW, Leikin SL, Arrobio J, et al. Cell-mediated immunity to respiratory syncytial virus induced by inactivated vaccine or by infection. Pediatr Res. 1976;10:75–78.
162. Taylor G, Stott EJ, Hayle AJ. Cytotoxic lymphocytes in the lungs of mice infected with respiratory syncytial virus. J Gen Virol. 1985;66:2533–2538.
163. Bangham CRM, Cannon MJ, Karzon DT, Askonas BA. Cytotoxic T-cell response to respiratory syncytial virus in mice. J Virol. 1985;56:55–59.
164. Bangham CRM, Openshaw PJM, Ball LA, et al. Human and murine cytotoxic T cells specific to respiratory syncytial virus recognize the viral nucleoprotein (N), but not the major glycoprotein (G), expressed by vaccinia virus recombinants. J Immunol. 1986;137:3973–3977.
165. Isaacs D, MacDonald NE, Bangham CRM, et al. The specific cytotoxic T-cell response in adult volunteers to infection with respiratory syncytial virus. Immunol Infect Dis. 1991;1:5–12.
166. Isaacs D, Bangham CRM, McMichael AJ. Cell-mediated cytotoxic response to respiratory syncytial virus in infants with bronchiolitis. Lancet. 1987;2:769–771.
167. Chiba Y, Higashidato Y, Suga K, et al. Development of cell-mediated cytotoxic immunity to respiratory syncytial virus in human infants following naturally acquired infection. J Med Virol. 1989;28:133–139.
168. Cannon MJ, Bangham CRM. Recognition of respiratory syncytial virus fusion protein by mouse cytotoxic T cell clones and a human cytotoxic T cell line. J Gen Virol. 1989;70:79–87.
169. Nicholas JA, Rubino KL, Levely ME, et al. Cytolytic T-lymphocyte responses to respiratory syncytial virus: Effector cell phenotype and target proteins. J Virol. 1990;64:4232–4241.
170. Openshaw PJM, Anderson K, Wertz GW, Askonas BA. The 22,000-kilodalton protein of respiratory syncytial virus is a major target for K^d-restricted cytotoxic T lymphocytes from mice primed by infection. J Virol. 1990;64:1683–1689.
171. Cherrie AH, Anderson K, Wertz GW, Openshaw PJM. Human cytotoxic T cells stimulated by antigen on dendritic cells recognize the N, SH, F, M, 22K, and 1b proteins of respiratory syncytial virus. J Virol. 1992;66:2102–2110.
172. Pemberton RM, Cannon MJ, Openshaw PJM, et al. Cytotoxic T cell specificity for respiratory syncytial virus proteins: Fusion protein is an important target antigen. J Gen Virol. 1987;68:2177–2182.
173. Openshaw PJM, Pemberton RM, Ball LA, et al. Helper T cell recognition of respiratory syncytial virus in mice. J Gen Virol. 1988;69:305–312.
174. Anderson JJ, Harrop JA, Peers H, et al. Recognition of respiratory syncytial (RS) virus proteins by human and BALB/c CD4+ lymphocytes. J Med Virol. 1991;35:165–173.
175. Graham BS, Henderson GS, Tang YW, et al. Priming immunization determines T helper cytokine mRNA expression patterns in lungs of mice challenged with respiratory syncytial virus. J Immunol. 1993;151:2032–2040.
176. Alwan WH, Record FM, Openshaw PJ. Phenotypic and functional characterization of T-cell lines specific for individual respiratory syncytial virus proteins. J Immunol. 1993;1250:5211–5218.
177. Tang YW, Neuzil KM, Fischert JE, et al. Deteminants and kinetics of cytokine expression patterns in lungs of vaccinated mice challenged with respiratory syncytial virus. Vaccine. 1997;15:597–602.
178. Srikiatkhachorn A, Braciale TL. Virus-specific CD8+ T lymphocytes downregulate T helper cells type 2 cytokine secretion and pulmonary eosinphilia during experimental murine respiratory syncytial virus infection. J Exp Med. 1997;186:421–432.
179. Cannon MJ, Openshaw PJM, Askonas BA. Cytotoxic T cells clear virus but augment lung pathology in mice infected with respiratory syncytial virus. J Exp Med. 1988;163:1163–1168.

180. Muñoz JL, McCarthy CA, Clark ME, Hall CB. Respiratory syncytial virus infection in C57BL/6 mice: Clearance of virus from the lungs with virus-specific cytotoxic T cells. J Virol. 1991;65:4494–4497.
181. Alwan WH, Record FM, Openshaw PJ. CD4+ T cells clear virus but augment disease in mice infected with respiratory syncytial virus. Comparison with the effects of CD8+ T cells. Clin Exp Immunol. 1992;88:527–536.
182. Kimpen JL, Garofalo R, Welliver RC, et al: An ultrastructural study of the interaction of human eosinophils with respiratory syncytial virus. Pediatr Allergy Immunol. 1996;7:48–53.
183. Noah TL, Becker S. Respiratory syncytial virus–induced cytokine production by a human bronchial epithelial cell line. Am J Physiol 1993;265(Lung Cell Mol Physiol 9):L472–L478.
184. Arnold R, Humbert B, Werchau H, et al. Interleukin-8, interleukin-6, and soluble tumour necrosis factor receptor type I release from a human pulmonary epithelial cell line (A549) exposed to respiratory syncytial virus. Immunology. 1994;84:126–133.
185. Elias JA, Zheng T, Einarsson O, et al. Epithelial interleukin-11. Regulation by cytokines, respiratory syncytial virus, and retinoic acid. J Biol Chem. 1994;269:22,261–22,268.
186. Patel JA, Kunimoto M, Sim TC, et al. Interleukin-1α mediates the enhanced expression of intercellular adhesion molecule-1 pulmonary epithelial cells infected with respiratory syncytial virus. Am J Respir Cell Mol Biol. 1995;13:602–609.
187. Midulla F, Villani A, Panuska JR, et al. Respiratory syncytial virus lung infection in infants: Immunoregulatory role of infected alveolar macrophages. J Infect Dis. 1993;168:1515–1519.
188. Roberts NJ Jr, Prill AH, Mann TN. Interleukin 1 and interleukin 1 inhibitor production by human macrophages exposed to influenza virus or respiratory syncytial virus. J Exp Med. 1986;163:511–519.
189. Noah TL, Henderson FW, Wortman IA, et al. Nasal cytokine production in viral acute upper respiratory infection of childhood. J Infect Dis. 1995;171:584–592.
190. Levine SJ. Bronchial epithelial cell-cytokine interactions in airway inflammation. Ann Intern Med. 1995;123:288–304.
191. Stark JM, Godding V, Sedgwick JB, Busse WW. Respiratory syncytial virus infection enhances neutrophil and eosinophil adhesion to cultured respiratory epithelial cells. J Immunol. 1996;156:4774–4782.
192. Chapman RS, Henderson FW, Clyde WA Jr, et al. The epidemiology of tracheobronchitis in pediatric practice. Am J Epidemiol. 1981;114:786–797.
193. Lee GC-Y, Funk GA, Chen ST, et al. An outbreak of respiratory syncytial virus infection in an infant nursery. J Formos Med Assoc. 1973;72:39–46.
194. Berglund B. Studies on respiratory syncytial virus infection. Acta Paediatr Scand Suppl. 1967;176:1.
195. Tyrrell DAJ. Discovering and defining the etiology of acute respiratory disease. Am Rev Respir Dis. 1963;88:77–84.
196. Gardner PS. Respiratory syncytial virus infections. Postgrad Med J. 1973;49:788–791.
197. Wohl MEB. Bronchiolitis. Pediatr Ann. 1986;15:307–313.
198. Rice RP, Loda F. A roentgenographic analysis of respiratory syncytial virus pneumonia in infants. Radiology. 1966;87:1021–1027.
199. Simpson W, Hacking PM, Court SDM, et al. The radiological findings in respiratory syncytial virus infection in children. II. The correlation of radiological categories with clinical and virological findings. Pediatr Radiol. 1974;2:155–160.
200. Khamapirad T, Glezen WP. Clinical and radiographic assessment of acute lower respiratory tract disease in infants and children. Semin Respir Infect. 1987;2:130–144.
201. Friis B, Eiken M, Hornsleth A, Jensen A. Chest x-ray appearances in pneumonia and bronchiolitis. Acta Paediatr Scand. 1990;79:219–225.
202. Davies HD, Wang EEL, Manson D, et al. Reliability of the chest radiograph in the diagnosis of lower respiratory illness in young children. Pediatr Infect Dis J. 1996;15:600–604.
203. Hall CB, Hall WJ, Speers DM. Clinical and physiological manifestations of bronchiolitis and pneumonia: Outcome of respiratory syncytial virus. Am J Dis Child. 1979;133:798–802.
204. Reynolds EOR. Arterial blood gas tensions in acute disease of lower respiratory tract in infancy. BMJ. 1963;1:1192–1195.
205. Mulholland EK, Olinsky A, Shann FA. Clinical findings and severity of acute bronchiolitis. Lancet. 1990;335:1259–1261.
206. Shaw KN, Bell LM, Sherman NH. Outpatient assessment of infants with bronchiolitis. Am J Dis Child. 1991;145:151–155.
207. Alario AS, Lewander WJ, Dennehy P, et al. The relationship between oxygen saturation and the clinical assessment of acutely wheezing infants and children. Pediatr Emerg Care. 1995;11:331–339.
208. Hall CB, Douglas RG Jr, Geiman JM. Respiratory syncytial virus infections in infants: Quantitation and duration of shedding. J Pediatr. 1976;89:11–15.
209. Hall CB, Douglas RG Jr, Geiman JM. Quantitative shedding patterns of respiratory syncytial virus in infants. J Infect Dis. 1975;132:151–156.
210. McMillan JA, Tristram DA, Weiner LB, et al. Prediction of the duration of hospitalization in patients with respiratory syncytial virus: Use of clinical parameters. Pediatrics. 1988;81:22–26.
211. Berglund B, Kortekangas AE, Lauren P. Experimental inoculation of guinea pigs' middle ear with respiratory syncytial virus. Acta Otolaryngol (Stockh). 1966;224(Suppl):268.
212. Gronroos JA, Vihma L, Salmivalli A, et al. Co-existing viral (respiratory syncytial) and bacterial (pneumococcus) otitis media in children. Acta Otolaryngol. 1968;65:505–517.
213. Klein BS, Dollete FR, Yolken RH. The role of respiratory syncytial virus and other viral pathogens in acute otitis media. J Pediatr. 1982;101:16–20.
214. Henderson FW, Collier AM, Sanyal MA, et al. A longitudinal study of respiratory viruses and bacteria in the etiology of acute otitis media with effusion. N Engl J Med. 1982;306:1377–1383.
215. Chonmaitree T, Howie VM, Truant AL. Presence of respiratory viruses in middle ear fluids and nasal wash specimens from children with otitis media. Pediatrics. 1986;77:698–702.
216. Chonmaitree T, Owen MJ, Patel JA, et al. Effect of viral respiratory tract infection on outcome of acute otitis media. J Pediatr. 1992;120:856–862.
217. Okamoto Y, Kudo K, Shirotori K, et al. Detection of genomic sequences of respiratory syncytial virus in otitis media with effusion in children. Ann Otol Rhinol Laryngol Suppl. 1992;157:7–10.
218. Harsten G, Prellner K, Löfgren B, Kalm O. Serum antibodies against respiratory tract viruses in episodes of acute otitis media. J Laryngol Otol. 1991;105:337–340.
219. Andrade MA, Hoberman A, Glustein J, et al. Acute otitis media in patients with bronchiolitis. Pediatrics. 1998;101:617–619.
220. Arola J, Ziegler T, Ruuskanen O, et al. Respiratory syncytial virus infection as a cause of prolonged symptoms in acute otitis media. J Pediatr. 1990;116:697–701.
221. Arola J, Ruuskanen O, Ziegler T, et al. Clinical role of respiratory syncytial virus infection in acute otitis media. Pediatrics. 1990;86:848–855.
222. Uhari M, Hietala J, Tuokko H. Risk of acute otitis media in relation to the viral etiology of infections in children. Clin Infect Dis. 1995;20:521–524.
223. Patel J, Faden H, Sharma S, Ogra PL. Effect of respiratory syncytial virus on adherence, colonization and immunity of non-typable *Haemophilus influenzae:* Implications for otitis media. Int J Pediatr Otorhinolaryngol. 1992;23:15–23.
224. Hall WJ, Hall CB, Speers DM. Respiratory syncytial virus infections in adults: Clinical, virologic, and serial pulmonary function studies. Ann Intern Med. 1978;88:203.
225. Finger R, Anderson LJ, Dicker RC, et al. Epidemic infections caused by respiratory syncytial virus in institutionalized young adults. J Infect Dis. 1987;155:1335–1339.
226. Dowell SF, Anderson LJ, Gary HE Jr. Respiratory syncytial virus is an important cause of community-acquired lower respiratory infection among hospitalized adults. J Infect Dis. 1996;174:456–462.
227. Mlinaric-Galinovic G, Falsey AR, Walsh EE. Respiratory syncytial virus infection in the elderly. Eur J Clin Microbiol Infect Dis. 1996;15:777–781.
228. Monto AS, Cavallaro JJ. The Tecumseh study of respiratory illness. II. Patterns of occurrence of infection with respiratory pathogens, 1965–1969. Am J Epidemiol. 1971;94:280–289.
229. Hall CB, Douglas RG Jr, Geiman JM, et al. Nosocomial respiratory syncytial virus infections. N Engl J Med. 1975;293:1343–1346.
230. Hall CB, Geiman JM, Douglas RG Jr, et al. Control of nosocomial respiratory syncytial viral infections. Pediatrics. 1978;62:728–731.
231. Hall CB, Kopelman A, Douglas RG Jr. Neonatal respiratory syncytial viral infections. N Engl J Med. 1979:300:393–396.
232. Hall CB, Douglas RG Jr. Nosocomial respiratory syncytial virus infections: The role of gowns and masks on prevention. Am J Dis Child. 1981;135:512–515.
233. Osterweil D, Norman D. An outbreak of an influenza-like illness in a nursing home. J Am Geriatr Soc. 1990;38:659–662.
234. Gross PA, Rodstein M, LaMontagne JR, et al. Epidemiology of acute respiratory illness during an influenza outbreak in a nursing home: A prospective study. Arch Intern Med. 1988;148:559–561.
235. Sorvillo FJ, Huie SF, Strassburg MA, et al. An outbreak of respiratory syncytial virus pneumonia in a nursing home for the elderly. J Infect. 1984;9:252–256.
236. Hart RJC. An outbreak of respiratory syncytial virus in an old people's home. J Infect. 1984;8:259–261.
237. Garvie DG, Gray J. Outbreak of respiratory syncytial virus infection in the elderly. BMJ. 1980;281:1253–1254.
238. Mathur U, Bentley DW, Hall CB. Concurrent outbreaks of respiratory syncytial virus and influenza A/Texas/77 infection in the institutionalized elderly and chronically ill. Ann Intern Med. 1980;93:49–52.
239. Falsey AR, Treanor JJ, Betts RG, Walsh EE. Viral respiratory infections in the institutionalized elderly: Clinical and epidemiologic findings. J Am Geriatr Soc. 1992;40:115–119.
240. Falsey AR, Cunningham CK, Barker WH, et al. Respiratory syncytial virus and influenza A infection in the hospitalized elderly. J Infect Dis. 1995;172:389–394.
241. Guidry GG, Black-Payne CA, Payne DK, et al. Respiratory syncytial virus infection among intubated adults in a university medical intensive care unit. Chest. 1991;100:1377–1384.
242. Morales F, Calder MA, Inglis JM, et al. A study of respiratory infections in the elderly to assess the role of respiratory syncytial virus. J Infect. 1983;7:236–247.
243. Fransen H, Sterner G, Forsgren M, et al. Acute lower respiratory illness in elderly patients with respiratory syncytial virus infection. Acta Med Scand. 1967; 182:323–330.
244. Finger R, Anderson LJ, Dicker RC, et al. Epidemic infections caused by respiratory syncytial virus in institutionalized young adults. J Infect Dis. 1987;155:1335–1339.
245. Takimoto CH, Cram DL, Root RK. Respiratory syncytial virus infections on an adult medical ward. Arch Intern Med. 1991;151:706–708.
246. Vikefors T, Gandien M, Olcen P. Respiratory syncytial virus infections in adults. Am Rev Respir Dis. 1987;136:561–564.
247. Spelman DW, Stanley PA. Respiratory syncytial virus pneumonia in adults. Med J Aust. 1983;1:430–431.
248. Sommerville RG. Respiratory syncytial virus in acute exacerbations of chronic bronchitis. Lancet. 1963;2:1247–1248.

249. Carilli AD, Gohd RS, Gordon W. A virologic study of chronic bronchitis. N Engl J Med. 1964;270:123–127.
250. Zaroukian MH, Kashyap GH, Wentworth BB. Respiratory syncytial virus infection: A cause of respiratory distress and pneumonia in adults. Am J Med Sci. 1988;295:218–222.
251. Cappel R, Thirty L, Clinet G. Viral antibodies in the CSF after acute CNS infections. Arch Neurol. 1975;32:629–631.
252. Wallace SJ, Zealley H. Neurological, electroencephalgraphic, and virological findings in febrile children. Arch Dis Child. 1970;45:611–623.
253. Cavallaro JJ, Maassab HF, Abrams GD. An immunofluorescent and histopathological study of respiratory syncytial virus (RSV) encephalitis in suckling mice. Proc Soc Exp Biol Med. 1967;124:1059–1064.
254. Giles TD, Gohd RS. Respiratory syncytial virus and heart disease. JAMA. 1976;236:1128–1130.
255. Berkovich S, Kibrick S. Exanthem associated with respiratory syncytial virus infection. J Pediatr. 1964;65:368–370.
256. Moss PD. Serological studies with respiratory syncytial virus. Lancet. 1963;1:298–300.
257. Bairan AC, Cherry JD, Fagan LF, Codd JE Jr. Complete heart block and respiratory syncytial virus. Am J Dis Child. 1974;127:264–265.
258. Gala CL, Hall CB, Schnabel KC, et al. The use of eye-nose goggles to control nosocomial respiratory syncytial virus infection. JAMA. 1986;256:2706–2708.
259. Agah R, Cherry JD, Garakian AJ, Chapin M. Respiratory syncytial virus (RSV) infection rate in personnel caring for children with RSV infections. Am J Dis Child. 1987;141:695–697.
260. Leclair JM, Freeman J, Sullivan BF, et al. Prevention of nosocomial respiratory syncytial virus infections through compliance with glove and gown isolation precautions. N Engl J Med. 1987;317:329–334.
261. Snydman DR, Greer C, Mesner HC, McIntosh K. Prevention of nosocomial transmission of respiratory syncytial virus in a newborn nursery. Infect Control Hosp Epidemiol. 1988;9:105–108.
262. Sims DG, Downham MAPS, Webb JKG, et al. Hospital cross-infection on children's wards with respiratory syncytial virus and the role of adult carriage. Acta Paediatr Scand. 1975;64:541–545.
263. Hall CB, Douglas RG Jr. Modes of transmission of respiratory syncytial virus. J Pediatr. 1981;99:100–103.
264. Hall CB. Nosocomial viral respiratory infections: Perennial weeds on pediatric wards. Am J Med. 1981;70:670–676.
265. Hall CB. The nosocomial spread of respiratory syncytial virus infections. Annu Rev Med. 1983;34:311–319.
266. Isaacs D, Dickson H, O'Callaghan C, et al. Handwashing and cohorting in prevention of hospital acquired infections with respiratory syncytial virus. Arch Dis Child. 1991;66:227–231.
267. Krasinski K, LaCouture R, Holzman RS, et al. Screening for the respiratory syncytial virus and assignment to a cohort at admission to reduce nosocomial transmission. J Pediatr. 1990;116:894–898.
268. Madge P, Paton JY, McColl JH, Mackie PLK. Prospective controlled study of four infection-control procedures to prevent nosocomial infection with respiratory syncytial virus. Lancet. 1992;340:1079–1083.
269. Harrington RD, Hooton TM, Hackman RC, et al. An outbreak of respiratory syncytial virus in a bone marrow transplant center. J Infect Dis. 1992;165:987–993.
270. Storch GA, Hall CB, Anderson LJ, et al. Antigenic and nucleic acid analysis of nosocomial isolates of respiratory syncytial virus. J Infect Dis. 1993;167:562–566.
271. Nosocomial infection with respiratory syncytial virus. Lancet. 1992;340:1071–1072.
272. Langley JM, LeBlanc JC, Wang EEL, et al. Nosocomial respiratory syncytial virus infection in Canadian pediatric hospitals: A pediatric investigators collaborative network on infections in Canada study. Pediatrics. 1997;100:943–946.
273. Garcia R, Raad I, Abi-Said D, et al. Nosocomial respiratory syncytial virus infections: Prevention and control in bone marrow transplant patients. Infect Control Hosp Epidemiol. 1997;18:412–416.
274. Adams JM. Primary virus pneumonitis with cytoplasmic inclusion bodies; a study of an epidemic involving thirty-two infants with nine deaths. JAMA. 1941;116:925–933.
275. Adams JM, Imagawa DT, Zike K. Relationship of pneumonitis in infants to respiratory syncytial virus. Lancet. 1961;81:502–506.
276. Englund JA, Anderson LJ, Rhame FS. Nosocomial transmission of respiratory syncytial virus in immunocompromised adults. J Clin Microbiol. 1991;29:115–119.
277. Agius G, Dindinaud G, Biggar RJ, et al. An epidemic of respiratory syncytial virus in elderly people: Clinical and serological findings. J Med Virol. 1990;30:117–127.
278. Rana-Singh MA, Krilov LR, Ginocchio CC, et al. RT-PCR methodology to detect RSV in air samples from hospital rooms of patients with RSV infection. Abstracts of Infectious Diseases Society of America, 34th Annual Meeting, New Orleans, September 18–20, 1996;52:98A.
279. Navas L, Wang E, de Carvalho V, Robinson J. Improved outcome of respiratory syncytial virus infection in a high-risk hospitalized population of Canadian children. J Pediatr. 1992;121:348–354.
280. MacDonald NE, Hall CB, Suffin SC, et al. Respiratory syncytial viral infection in infants with congenital heart disease. N Engl J Med. 1982;307:397–400.
281. Mahant S, Robinson JL, Wang EEL. Hospital morbidity in patients with RSV lower respiratory illness (LFI) and underlying heart disease: Analysis of PICNIC RSV database (Abstracted). Washington, DC: Academy of Pediatrics Society; May 1997;41(4, pt 2):78A.
282. Cunningham CK, McMillan JA, Gross SJ. Rehospitalization for respiratory illness in infants of less than 32 weeks' gestation. Pediatrics. 1991;88:527–532.
283. Groothuis JR, Gutierrez KM, Lauer BA. Respiratory syncytial virus infection in children with bronchopulmonary dysplasia. Pediatrics. 1988;82:199–203.
284. Groothuis JR, Salbenblatt CK, Lauer BA. Severe respiratory syncytial virus infection in older children. Am J Dis Child. 1990;144:346–348.
285. Meert K, Heidemann S, Abella B, Sarnaik A. Does prematurity alter the course of respiratory syncytial virus infection? Crit Care Med. 1990;18:1357–1359.
286. Tammela OK. First-year infections after initial hospitalization in low birth weight infants with and without bronchopulmonary dysplasia. Scand J Infect Dis. 1992;24:515–524.
287. Hordvik NL, König P, Hamory B, et al. Effects of acute viral respiratory tract infections in patients with cystic fibrosis. Pediatr Pulmonol. 1989;7:217–222.
288. Abman SH, Ogle JW, Butler-Simon N, et al. Role of respiratory syncytial virus in early hospitalizations for respiratory distress of young infants with cystic fibrosis. J Pediatr. 1988;113:826–830.
289. De Zegher F, DeBoeck K, Devlieger H, et al. Respiratory syncytial virus infection in infants with unequal pulmonary perfusion. N Engl J Med. 1991;324:1066–1067.
290. Craft AW, Reid MM, Gardner PS, et al. Virus infections in children with acute lymphoblastic leukemia. Arch Dis Child. 1979;54:755–769.
291. Pohl C, Green M, Wald ER, Ledesma-Medina J. Respiratory syncytial virus infections in pediatric liver transplant recipients. J Infect Dis. 1992;165:166–169.
292. Anderson DJ, Jordan MC. Viral pneumonia in recipients of solid organ transplant (Review). Semin Respir Infect. 1990;5:38–49.
293. Hertz MI, Englund JA, Snover D, et al. Respiratory syncytial virus–induced acute lung injury in adult patients with bone marrow transplants: A clinical approach and review of the literature. Medicine. 1989;68:269–281.
294. Whimbey E, Champlin RE, Couch RB, et al. Community respiratory virus infections among hospitalized adult bone marrow transplant recipients. Clin Infect Dis J. 1996;22:778–782.
295. Bowden RA. Respiratory virus infections after marrow transplant: The Fred Hutchinson Cancer Research Center experience. Am J Med. 1997;102:27–30.
296. King JC Jr. Community respiratory viruses in individuals with human immunodeficiency virus infection. Am J Med. 1997;102:19–24.
297. Ljungman P. Respiratory virus infections in bone marrow transplant recipients: The European perspective. Am J Med. 1997;102:44–47.
298. Whimbey E, Englund JA, Couch RB. Community respiratory virus infections in immunocompromised patients with cancer. Am J Med. 1997;102:10–18.
299. Wendt CH. Community respiratory viruses: Organ transplant recipients. Am J Med. 1997;102:31–36.
300. Hall CB, Powell KR, Schnabel KC, et al. The risk of secondary bacterial infection in infants hospitalized with respiratory syncytial viral infection. J Pediatr. 1988;113:266–271.
301. MacDonald NE, Wolfish N, McLaine P, et al. Role of respiratory viruses in exacerbations of primary nephrotic syndrome. J Pediatr. 1986;108:378–382.
302. Stevens TP, Hall CB, Maniscalo WM, Sinkin RA. Risk of RSV-associated hospitalization (RSV-hosp) and economic impact of RSV prophylaxis for premature infants born ≤ 32 weeks gestation (Abstract 1348). Pediatr Res. 1997;41.
303. Nachman SA, Navaie-Waliser M, Qureshi MZ. Rehospitalization with respiratory syncytial virus after neonatal intensive care unit discharge: A 3-year follow-up. Pediatrics. 1997;100:e8.
304. Whimbey E, Bodey GP. Viral pneumonia in the immunocompromised adult with neoplastic disease: The role of common community respiratory viruses. Semin Respir Infect. 1992;7:122–131.
305. Miller RB, Chavers BM. Respiratory syncytial virus infections in pediatric and renal transplant recipients. Pediatr Nephrol. 1996;10:213–215.
306. Couch RB, Englund JA, Whimbey E. Respiratory viral infections in immunocompetent and immunocompromised persons. Am J Med. 1997;102:2–9.
307. Gelfand EW, McCurdy D, Rao CP, Middleton PJ. Ribavirin treatment of viral pneumonitis in severe combined immunodeficiency disease. Lancet. 1983;2:732–733.
308. Chandwani S, Borkowsky W, Krasinski K, et al. Respiratory syncytial virus infection in human immunodeficiency virus-infected children. J Pediatr. 1990;117:251–254.
309. Beekman SE, Engler HD, Collins AS, et al. Rapid identification of respiratory viruses: Impact on isolation practices and transmission among immunocompromised pediatric patients. Infect Control Hosp Epidemiol. 1996;17:581–586.
310. Englund JA, Piedra PA, Whimbey E. Prevention and treatment of respiratory syncytial virus and parainfluenza viruses in immunocompromised patients. Am J Med. 1997;102:61–70.
311. Fouillard L, Mouthon L, Laporte JP, et al. Severe respiratory syncytial virus pneumonia after autologous bone marrow transplantation: A report of three cases and review. Bone Marrow Transplant. 1992;9:97–100.
312. Bruhn FW, Mokrohisky ST, McIntosh K. Apnea associated with respiratory syncytial virus infection in young infants. J Pediatr. 1977;90:382–386.
313. Anas NG, Boettrich C, Hall CB, Brooks JG. The association of apnea and respiratory syncytial virus infection in infants. J Pediatr. 1982;101:65–68.
314. Church NR, Anas NG, Hall CB, et al. Respiratory syncytial virus–related apnea in infants: Demographics and outcome. Am J Dis Child. 1984;138:247–250.
315. Downham MAPS, Gardner PS, McQuillin J, et al. Role of respiratory viruses in childhood mortality. BMJ. 1975;1:235–239.
316. Ferris JAJ, Aherne WA, Locke WS, et al. Sudden and unexpected deaths in infants: Histology and virology. BMJ. 1973;2:439–442.
317. Williams AL, Uren EC, Bretherton L. Respiratory viruses and sudden infant death. BMJ. 1984;288:1491–1493.
318. Southall DP. Role of apnea in the sudden infant death syndrome: A personal view. Pediatrics. 1988;81:73–84.

319. Kuppermann N, Bank DE, Walton EA, et al. Risks for bacteremia and urinary tract infections in young febrile children with bronchiolitis. Arch Pediatr Adolesc Med. 1997;151:1207–1214.
320. Burrows B, Lebowitz MD, Knudson RJ. Epidemiologic evidence that childhood problems predispose to airway disease in the adult (an association between adult and pediatric respiratory disorders). Pediatr Res. 1977;11:218–220.
321. Burrows B, Knudson RJ, Lebowitz MD. The relationship of childhood respiratory illness to adult obstructive airway disease. Am Rev Respir Dis. 1977;115:751–760.
322. Eisen AH, Bacal HL. The relationship of acute bronchiolitis to bronchial asthma. A 4- to 14-year follow-up. Pediatrics. 1963;31:859–861.
323. Rooney JC, Williams HE. The relationship between proved viral bronchiolitis and subsequent wheezing. J Pediatr. 1971;79:744–747.
324. Zweiman B, Schoenwetter WF, Hildreth EA. The relationship between bronchiolitis and allergic asthma. J Allerg. 1966;37:48–53.
325. Kattan M, Klens TG, Lapierre JG, et al. Pulmonary function abnormalities in symptom-free children after bronchiolitis. Pediatrics. 1977;59:683–688.
326. Gurwitz D, Mindorff C, Levison H. Increased incidence of bronchial reactivity in children with a history of bronchiolitis. J Pediatr. 1981;98:551–555.
327. Stokes GM, Milner AD, Hodges IGC, Groggins RC. Lung function abnormalities after acute bronchiolitis. J Pediatr. 1981;98:871–874.
328. Twiggs JT, Larson LA, O'Connell EJ, et al. Respiratory syncytial virus infection: Ten year follow-up. Clin Pediatr. 1981;20:187–190.
329. Sims DG, Downham MAPS, Gardner PS, et al. Study of 8-year-old children with a history of respiratory syncytial virus bronchiolitis in infancy. BMJ. 1978;1:11–14.
330. Sims DG, Gardner PS, Weightman D, et al. Atopy does not predispose to RSV bronchiolitis or post bronchiolitic wheezing. BMJ. 1981;282:2086–2088.
331. Pullan CR, Hey EN. Wheezing, asthma and pulmonary dysfunction 10 years after infection with respiratory syncytial virus in infancy. BMJ. 1982;284:1665–1669.
332. Hall CB, Hall WJ, Gala CL, et al. A long term prospective study of children following respiratory syncytial virus infection. J Pediatr. 1984;105:358–364.
333. Sly PD, Hibbert ME. Childhood asthma following hospitalization with acute viral bronchiolitis in infancy. Pediatr Pulmonol. 1989;7:153–158.
334. Martinez FD, Morgan WJ, Wright AL, et al. Diminished lung function as a predisposing factor for wheezing respiratory illness in infants. N Engl J Med. 1988;319:1112–1117.
335. Martinez FD, Stern DA, Wright AL, et al. Association of non-wheezing lower respiratory tract illnesses in early life with persistently diminished serum IgE levels. Thorax. 1995;50:1067–1072.
336. Martinez FD. Viral infections and the development of asthma. Am J Respir Crit Care Med. 1995;151:1644–1647.
337. Martinez FD, Wright AL, Taussig LM, et al. Asthma and wheezing in the first six years of life. N Engl J Med. 1995;332:133–138.
338. Dodge R, Martinez FD, Cline MG, et al. Early childhood respiratory symptoms and the subsequent diagnosis of asthma. J Allergy Clin Immunol. 1994;24:48–54.
339. Wilson N. The significance of early wheezing. Clin Exper Allergy 1994;24:522–529.
340. Walsh EE, Hall CB. Respiratory syncytial virus. In: Schmidt NJ, Emmons RW, eds. Diagnostic Procedures for Viral and Rickettsial Infections. New York: American Public Health Association; 1989:693–712.
341. Kellogg JA. Culture vs direct antigen assays for detection of microbial pathogens from lower respiratory tract specimens suspected of containing the respiratory syncytial virus. Arch Pathol Lab Med. 1991;115:451–458.
342. Falsey AR, McCann RM, Hall WJ, Criddle MM. Evaluation of four methods for the diagnosis of respiratory syncytial virus infection in older adults. J Am Geriatr Soc. 1996;44:71–73.
343. Rabalais GP, Stout GG, Ladd KL, Cost KM. Rapid diagnosis of respiratory viral infections by using a shell vial assay and monoclonal antibody pool. J Clin Microbiol. 1992;30:1505–1508.
344. Engler HD, Preuss J. Laboratory diagnosis of respiratory syncytial virus infection in 24 hours of utilizing shell vial cultures. J Clin Microbiol. 1997;35:2165–2167.
345. Halstead DC, Todd S, Fritch G. Evaluation of five methods for respiratory syncytial virus detection. J Clin Microbiol. 1990;28:1021–1025.
346. Paton AW, Paton JC, Lawrence AJ, et al. Rapid detection of respiratory syncytial virus in nasopharyngeal aspirates by reverse transcription and polymerase chain reaction amplification. J Clin Microbiol. 1992;30:901–904.
347. Cubie HA, Inglis JM, McGowan AM. Detection of respiratory syncytial virus antigen and nucleic acid in clinical specimens using synthetic oligonucleotides. J Virol Methods. 1991;34:27–35.
348. Erdman DD, Anderson LJ. Monoclonal antibody-based capture enzyme immunoassays for specific serum immunoglobulin G (IgG), IgA, and IgM antibodies to respiratory syncytial virus. J Clin Microbiol. 1990;28:2744–2749.
349. Van Milaan AJ, Sprenger MJW, Rothbarth PH, et al. Detection of respiratory syncytial virus by RNA-polymerase chain reaction and differentiation of subgroups with oligonucleotide probes. J Med Virol. 1994;44:80–87.
350. Tristram DA, Welliver RC. Respiratory syncytial virus. In: Murray PR, Baron EJ, Pfaller MA, et al. Manual of Clinical Microbiology. 6th ed. Washington, DC: ASM Press; 1995;93:2–9.
351. Freymuth F, Vabret A, Galateau-Salle F, et al. Detection of respiratory syncytial virus, parainfluenza virus 3, adenovirus, and rhinovirus sequences in respiratory tract of infants by polymerase chain reaction and hybridization. Clin Diagn Virol. 1997;8:31–40.
352. Valassina M, Cuppone AM, Cusi MG, Valensin PE. Rapid detection of different RNA respiratory virus species by multiplex RT-PCR: Application to clinical specimens. Clin Diagn Virol. 1996;8:227–232.
353. Woodin KA, Menegus MA. Rapid diagnosis of respiratory syncytial virus infection. Pediatr Virol. 1991;6:1, 5–8.
354. Murphy BR, Alling DW, Snyder MH, et al. Effect of age and preexisting antibody on serum antibody response of infants and children to the F and G glycoproteins during respiratory syncytial viral infection. J Clin Microbiol. 1986;24:894–898.
355. Tristram DA, Welliver RC. Respiratory syncytial virus. In: Murray PR, Baron EJ, Pfaller MA, et al. Manual of Clinical Microbiology. 6th ed. Washington, DC: ASM Press; 1995;93:2–9.
356. Meddens MJM, Herbrink P, Lindeman J, et al. Serodiagnosis of respiratory syncytial virus (RSV) infection in children as measured by detection of RSV-specific immunoglobulins G, M, and A, with enzyme-linked immunoabsorbent assay. J Clin Microbiol. 1990;28:152–155.
357. Jensen IP, Thisted E, Glikmann G, et al. Secretory IgM and IgA antibodies to respiratory syncytial virus in nasopharyngeal aspirates: A diagnostic supplement to antigen detection. Clin Diagn Virol. 1997;8:219–226.
358. Ireland DC, Nicholson KG. Diagnosis of respiratory virus infections using GACELISA of urinary antibodies. J Immunol Methods. 1996;195:73–80.
359. Taussig LM. Mists and aerosols: New studies, new thoughts (Editorial). J Pediatr. 1974;84:619–622.
360. Webb MSC, Martin GA, Cartlidge PHT, et al. Chest physiotherapy in acute bronchiolitis. Arch Dis Child. 1985;60:1078–1079.
361. Paret G, Dekel B, Vardi A, et al. Heliox in respiratory failure secondary to bronchiolitis: A new therapy. Pediatr Pulmonol. 1996;22:322–323.
362. Hoehn T, Krause M, Hentschel P. Improvement of oxygenation in an infant with bronchopulmonary dysplasia and acute respiratory syncytial virus pneumonia by the use of inhaled nitric oxide during high-frequency ventilation (Abstract). Pediatr Res. 1997;41:255A.
363. Vos G, Rijtemamn MN, Blanco C. Treatment of respiratory failure due to respiratory syncytial virus pneumonia with natural surfactant. Pediatr Pulmonol. 1996;22:412–415.
364. Law B, Carvalho VD. Respiratory syncytial virus infections in hospitalized Canadian children: Regional differences in patient populations and management practices. Pediatr Infect Dis J. 1993;12:659–663.
365. Kimpen JLL, Schaad UB. Treatment of respiratory syncytial virus bronchiolitis: 1995 poll of members of the European Society for Paediatric Infectious Diseases. Pediatr Infect Dis J. 1997;16:479–481.
366. Samson LM, Cooke C, MacDonald NE. Analysis of antibiotic use and misuse in children hospitalized with RSV infection (Abstract). Pediatr Res. 1996;653:111A.
367. Dobson JV, Stephens-Groff SM, McMahon SR, et al. The use of albuterol in hospitalized infants with bronchiolitis. Pediatrics. 1998;101:361–368.
368. Flores G, Horwitz RI. Efficacy of β2-agonists in bronchiolitis: A reappraisal and meta-analysis. Pediatrics. 1997;100:233–239.
369. Kellner JD, Ohlsson A, Gadomski AM, Wang EEL. Efficacy of bronchodilator therapy in bronchiolitis. Arch Pediatr Adolesc Med. 1996;150:1166–1172.
370. Mahesh VK, Taussig LM. The wheezing infant: Acute and long-term management. J Respir Dis. 1990;11:799–810.
371. Klassen TP, Rowe PC, Sutcliffe T, et al. Randomized trial of salbutamol in acute bronchiolitis. J Pediatr. 1991;118:807–811.
372. Hickey RW, Gochman RF, Chande V, David HW. Albuterol delivered via metered-dose inhaler with spacer for outpatient treatment of young children with wheezing. Arch Pediatr Adolesc Med. 1994;148:189–194.
373. Sanchez I, DeKoster J, Powell RE, et al. Effect of racemic epinephrine and salbutamol on clinical score and pulmonary mechanics in infants with bronchiolitis. J Pediatr. 1993;122:145–151.
374. Menon K, Sutcliffe T, Klassen TP. A randomized trial comparing the efficacy of epinephrine with salbutamol in the treatment of acute bronchiolitis. J Pediatr. 1995;126:1004–1007.
375. Kristjansson S, Carlsen KCL, Wennergren G, et al. Nebulised racemic adrenaline in the treatment of acute bronchiolitis in infants and toddlers. Arch Dis Child. 1993;69:650–654.
376. Connolly JH, Field CMB, Glasgow JFT, et al. A double blind trial of prednisone in epidemic bronchiolitis due to respiratory syncytial virus. Acta Paediatr Scand. 1969;58:116–120.
377. Leer JA, Green JL, Heimlich EM, et al. Corticosteroid treatment in bronchiolitis. A controlled collaborative study in 297 infants and children. Am J Dis Child. 1969;117:495–503.
378. Yaffe SJ, Weiss CF, Cann HM, et al. Should steroids be used in treating bronchiolitis? Pediatrics. 1970;46:640–642.
379. Springer C, Bar-Yishay E, Uwayyed K, et al. Corticosteroids do not affect the clinical or physiological status of infants with bronchiolitis. Pediatr Pulmonol. 1990;9:181–185.
380. Maayan C, Itzhaki T, Bar-Yishay E, et al. The functional response of infants with persistent wheezing to nebulized beclamethasone dipropionate. Pediatr Pulmonol. 1986;2:9–14.
381. Carlsen K-H, Leegaard J, Larsen S, Orstavik I. Nebulized beclomethasone dipropionate in recurrent obstructive episodes after acute bronchiolitis. Arch Dis Child. 1988;63:1428–1433.
382. Klassen TP. Recent advances in the treatment of bronchiolitis and laryngitis. Pediatr Clin North Am. 1997;44(1):249–261.
383. Roosevelt G, Sheehan K, Grupp-Phelan J, et al. Dexamethasone in bronchiolitis: A randomized controlled trial. Lancet. 1996;348:292–295.
384. DeBenedictis FM, Canny GJ, Levison H. The role of corticosteroids in respiratory diseases of children. Pediatr Pulmonol. 1996;22:44–57.
385. De Boeck K, Van der Aa N, Van Lierde S, et al. Respiratory syncytial virus

bronchiolitis: A double-blind dexamethasone efficacy study. J Pediatr. 1997;131:919–921.

386. Van Woensel JBM, Wolfs TFW, Van Aalderen WMC, et al. Randomised double blind placebo controlled trial of prednisolone in children admitted to hospital with respiratory syncytial virus bronchiolitis. Thorax. 1997;52:634–637.
387. Hall CB, Powell KR, Schnabel KC, et al. The risk of secondary bacterial infection in infants hospitalized with respiratory syncytial viral infection. J Pediatr. 1988;113:266–271.
388. Rice RP, Loda F. A roentgenographic analysis of respiratory syncytial viral pneumonia in infants. Radiology. 1996;87:1021–1027.
389. Knight V, Gilbert BE. Chemotherapy of respiratory viruses. Adv Intern Med. 1986;31:95–118.
390. Rodriguez WJ, Parrott RH. Ribavirin aerosol treatment of serious respiratory syncytial virus infection in infants (Review). Infect Dis Clin North Am. 1987;1:425–439.
391. Knight V, Yu CP, Gilbert BE, Orr R. Ribavirin aerosol treatment: Emerging technology and clinical summary. London, New York: Royal Society of Medicine Services Limited; International Congress and Symposium Series. 1988;145:69–84.
392. Englund JA, Piedra PA, Jefferson LS, et al. High-dose, short-duration ribavirin aerosol therapy in children with suspected respiratory syncytial virus infection. J Pediatr. 1990;117:313–320.
393. Report of the Committee of Infectious Diseases: Respiratory syncytial virus. In: Peter G, ed. Redbook. 24th ed. Elk Grove Village, Ill: American Academy of Pediatrics; 1997:443–447.
394. Barry W, Cockburn F, Cornall R, et al. Ribavirin aerosol for acute bronchiolitis. Arch Dis Child. 1986;61:593–594.
395. Groothuis JR, Woodin KA, Katz R, et al. Early ribavirin treatment of respiratory syncytial viral infection in high-risk children. J Pediatr. 1990;117:792–798.
396. Hall CB, McBride JT, Gala CL, et al. Ribavirin aerosol treatment of respiratory syncytial viral infection in infants with underlying cardiac and pulmonary disease. JAMA. 1985;254:3047–3051.
397. Hall CB, McBride JT, Walsh EE, et al. Aerosolized ribavirin treatment of infants with respiratory syncytial viral infection. N Engl J Med. 1986;308:1443–1447.
398. Hall CB, Walsh EE, Hruska JF, et al. Ribavirin aerosol treatment of experimental respiratory syncytial viral infection in young adults: A controlled double blind study. JAMA. 1983;249:2666–2670.
399. Knight V, Yu CP, Gilbert BE, et al. Ribavirin aerosol treatment: Emerging technical and clinical summary. Royal Society of Medicine Services Limited. International Congress and Symposium Series, No. 145, 1988:69–84.
400. Liss HP, Bernstein J. Ribavirin aerosol in the elderly. Chest. 1988;93:1239–1241.
401. Rodriguez WJ, Kim HW, Brandt CD, et al. Aerosolized ribavirin in the treatment of patients with respiratory syncytial virus disease. Pediatr Infect Dis J. 1987;6:159–163.
402. Rodriguez WJ, Parrott RH. Ribavirin aerosol treatment of serious respiratory syncytial virus infection in infants. Infect Dis Clin North Am. 1987;1:425–439.
403. Smith DW, Frankel LR, Mathers LH, et al. A controlled trial of aerosolized ribavirin in infants receiving mechanical ventilation for severe respiratory syncytial virus infection. N Engl J Med. 1991;325:24–29.
404. Taber LH, Knight V, Gilbert BE, et al. Ribavirin aerosol treatment of bronchiolitis due to respiratory syncytial virus infection in infants. Pediatrics. 1983;72:613–618.
405. Randolph A, Wang EE. Ribavirin for respiratory syncytial virus lower respiratory tract infection. Arch Pediatric Adolesc Med. 1996;150:942–947. In: Redbook. 24th ed. Elk Grove Village, Ill: American Association of Pediatrics; 1997:443–447.
406. Rosner IK, Welliver RC, Edelson PJ, et al. Effect of ribavirin therapy on respiratory syncytial virus-specific IgE and IgA responses after infection. J Infect Dis. 1987;155:1043–1047.
407. Krilov L, Mandel F, Barone S, Fagin J. The Bronchiolitis Study Group. Follow-up of children with respiratory syncytial virus bronchiolitis in 1986 and 1987: Potential effect of ribavirin on long term pulmonary function. Pediatr Infect Dis J. 1997;16:273–276.
408. Long C, Voter K, Barker W, Hall C. Long term follow-up of children hospitalized with respiratory syncytial virus lower respiratory tract infection and randomly treated with ribavirin or placebo. Pediatr Infect Dis J. 1997;16:1023–1028.
409. Voter KZ, Long C, Hall CB. Respiratory illnesses and lung function following ribavirin therapy in infancy. Abstract 2334. Pediatr Res. 1996;39:392A.
410. Rodriguez WJ, Arrobio J, Fink R, et al. Prospective (7 yrs) follow up (FU) and pulmonary functions (PFT) from A placebo (P) controlled randomized trial of ribavirin (R) in RSV bronchiolitis (B). Abstract 1086. Pediatr Res. 1996;39:183A.
411. Edell D, Bruce E, Hale K, et al. Reduced long-term respiratory morbidity after treatment of respiratory syncytial virus bronchiolitis with ribavirin in previously healthy infants: A preliminary report. Pediatr Pulmonol. 1998;25:154–158.
412. Dowell S, Papic Z, Bresee J, et al. Treatment of respiratory syncytial virus infection with vitamin A: A randomized, placebo-controlled trial in Santiago, Chile. Pediatr Infect Dis J. 1996;15:782–786.
413. Bresee J, Fischer M, Dowell S, et al. Vitamin A therapy for children with respiratory syncytial virus infection: A multicenter trial in the United States. Pediatr Infect Dis J. 1996;15:777–782.
414. Quinlan KP, Hayani KC. Vitamin A and respiratory syncytial virus infection: Serum levels and supplementation trial. Arch Pediatr Adolesc Med. 1996;150:25–30.
415. Higgins PG, Barrow GI, Tyrrell DA, et al. The efficacy of intranasal interferon alpha-2a in respiratory syncytial virus infection in volunteers. Antiviral Res. 1990;14:3–10.
416. Chipps BE, Sullivan WF, Portnoy JM. Alpha-2a-interferon for treatment of bronchiolitis caused by respiratory syncytial virus. Pediatr Infect Dis J. 1993;12:653–658.
417. Sims DG, Downham MAPS, McQuillin J, et al. Respiratory syncytial virus infection in northeast England. BMJ. 1976;2:1095–1098.
418. Downham MAPS, Scott R, Sims DG, et al. Breast-feeding protects against respiratory syncytial virus infections. BMJ. 1976;2:274–276.
419. Pullan CR, Toms GL, Martin AJ, et al. Breast feeding and respiratory syncytial virus infection. BMJ. 1980;281:1034–1036.
420. Murphy D, Todd JK, Chao RR, et al. The use of gowns and masks to control respiratory illness in pediatric personnel. J Pediatr. 1981;99:746.
421. Madge P, Paton JY, McColl JH, Mackie PLK. Prospective controlled study of four infection-control procedures to prevent nosocomial infection with respiratory syncytial virus. Lancet. 1992;340:1079–1083.
422. Chanock RM, Parrott RH, Connors M, et al. Serious respiratory tract disease caused by respiratory syncytial virus: Prospects for improved therapy and effective immunization. Pediatrics. 1992;90:137–143.
423. Hemming VG, Prince GA. Respiratory syncytial virus: Babies and antibodies. Infect Agents Dis. 1992;1:24–32.
424. Rodriguez W, Gruber W, Groothuis J, et al. Respiratory syncytial virus immune globulin treatment of RSV lower respiratory tract infection in previously healthy children. Pediatrics. 1997;100:937–946.
425. Rodriguez W, Gruber W, Welliver R, et al. Respiratory syncytial virus immune globulin intravenous therapy for RSV lower respiratory tract infection in infants and young children at high risk for severe RSV infections. Pediatrics. 1997;99:454–461.
426. Rimensberger P, Burek-Kozlowski A, Morell A, et al. Aerosolized immunoglobulin treatment of respiratory syncytial virus infection in infants. Pediatr Infect Dis J. 1996;15:209–216.
427. Meissner H, Groothuis JR. Immunoprophylaxis and the control of RSV disease. Pediatrics. 1997;100:260–263.
428. Meissner H, Welliver R, Chartrand S, et al. Prevention of respiratory syncytial virus infection in high risk infants: Consensus opinion on the role of immunoprophylaxis with respiratory syncytial virus hyperimmune globulin. Pediatr Infect Dis J. 1996;15:1059–1068.
429. Prince GA, Hemming VG, Horswood RL, et al. Effectiveness of topically administered neutralizing antibodies in experimental immunotherapy of respiratory syncytial virus infection in cotton rats. J Virol. 1987;61:1851–1854.
430. Hemming VG, Prince GA, London WT, et al. Topically administered immunoglobulin reduces pulmonary respiratory syncytial virus shedding in owl monkeys. Antimicrob Agents Chemother. 1988;32:1269–1270.
431. Hemming V, Prince G, Groothuis J, Siber G. Hyperimmune globulins in prevention and treatment of respiratory syncytial virus infection. Clin Microbiol Rev. 1995;8:22–33.
432. Gruber WC, Wilson SZ, Throop BJ, Wyde PR. Immunoglobulin administration and ribavirin therapy: Efficacy in respiratory syncytial virus infection in the cotton rat. Pediatr Res. 1987;21:270–274.
433. Hemming VG, Rodriguez W, Kim HW, et al. Intravenous immunoglobulin treatment of respiratory syncytial virus infections in infants and young children. Antimicrob Agents Chemother. 1987;31:1882–1886.
434. Simoes EAF, Sondheimer HM, Meissner HC, et al. Respiratory syncytial virus immunoglobulin as prophylaxis against respiratory syncytial virus in children with congenital heart disease. Pediatr Res. 1996;662:113A.
435. Faverio L, Piazza F, Johnson S, et al. Immunoprophylaxis of group B respiratory syncytial virus infection in cotton rats. J Infect Dis. 1997;175:932–934.
436. DeVincenzo J, Montana J, Krishnamurthy G, et al. Aerosolized respiratory syncytial virus (RSV) antibody treatment of RSV infected cotton rats. In: Abstracts of the Infectious Diseases Society of America, 34th Annual Meeting, New Orleans, La 1996:54:101A.
437. Weltzin R, Traina-Dorge K, Soike J-Y, et al. Intranasal monoclonal IgA antibody to respiratory syncytial virus protects rhesus monkeys against upper and lower respiratory tract infection. J Infect Dis. 1996;174:256–261.
438. Subramanian KNS, Weisman L, Rhodes T, et al. Safety, tolerance and pharmacokinetics of a humanized monoclonal antibody to respiratory syncytial virus in premature infants and infants with bronchopulmonary dysplasia. MEDI-493 Study Group. Pediatr Infect Dis J. 1998;17:110–115.
439. Johnson S, Oliver C, Prince GA, et al. Development of a humanized monoclonal antibody (MEDI-493) with potent in vitro and in vivo activity against respiratory syncytial virus. J Infect Dis. 1997;176:1215–1224.
440. Everitt DE, Davis CB, Thompson K, et al. The pharmacokinetics, antigenicity, and fusion-inhibition activity of RSHZ19, a humanized monoclonal antibody to respiratory syncytial virus, in healthy volunteers. J Infect Dis. 1996;174:463–469.
441. Connors M, Giese NA, Kulkarni AB, et al. Enhanced pulmonary histopathology induced by respiratory syncytial virus (RSV) challenge of formalin-inactivated RSV-immunized BALB/c mice is abrogated by depletion of interleukin-4 (IL-4) and IL-10. J Virol. 1994;68:5321–5325.
442. Connors M, Kulkarni AB, Firestone CY, et al. Pulmonary histopathology induced by respiratory syncytial virus (RSV) challenge of formalin-inactivated RSV-immunized BALB/c mice is abrogated by depletion of $CD4^+$ T cells. J Virol. 1992;66:7444–7451.
443. Prince GA, Jenson BA, Hemming VG, et al. Enhancement of respiratory syncytial virus pulmonary pathology in cotton rats by prior intramuscular inoculation of formalin-inactivated virus. J Virol. 1986;57:721–728.
444. Kim HW, Arrobio JO, Pyles G, et al. Clinical and immunological responses of infants and children to administration of low-temperature adapted respiratory syncytial virus. Pediatrics. 1971;48:745–755.

445. Kim HW, Arrobio JO, Brandt CD, et al. Safety and antigenicity of temperature sensitive (ts) mutant respiratory syncytial virus (RSV) in infants and children. Pediatrics. 1973;52:56–63.
446. Wright PF, Bleshe RB, Kim HW, et al. Administration of a highly attenuated, live respiratory syncytial virus vaccine to adults and children. Infect Immun. 1982;37:397–400.
447. McKay E, Higgins P, Tyrrell D, Pringle C. Immunogenicity and pathogenicity of temperature-sensitive modified respiratory syncytial virus in adults volunteers. J Med Virol. 1988;25:411–421.
448. Watt PJ, Robinson BS, Pringle CR, Tyrrell DA. Determinants of susceptibility to challenge and the antibody response of adult volunteers given experimental respiratory syncytial virus vaccines. Vaccine. 1990;8:231–236.
449. Crowe JE Jr, Bui PT, Firestone CV, et al. Live subgroup B respiratory syncytial virus vaccines that are attenuated, genetically stable, and immunogenic in rodents and nonhuman primates. J Infect Dis. 1996;173:829–839.
450. Firestone C, Whitehead S, Collins P, et al. Nucleotide sequence analysis of the respiratory syncytial virus subgroup A cold-passaged (cp) temperature sensitive (ts) cpts-248/404 live attenuated virus vaccine candidate. Virology. 1996;225:419–422.
451. Tristram DA, Welliver RC. A vaccine for RSV: Is it possible? Contemp Pediatr. 1996;13(3):47–63.
452. Crowe JE Jr, Bui PT, Davis AR, et al. A further attenuated derivative of a cold-passaged temperature-sensitive mutant of human respiratory syncytial virus (RSV cpts-248) retains immunogenicity and protective efficacy against wild-type challenge in seronegative chimpanzees. Vaccine. 1994;12:783–790.
453. Crowe JE Jr, Bui PT, London WT, et al. Satisfactorily attenuated and protective mutants derived from a partially attenuated cold passaged respiratory syncytial virus mutant by introduction of additional attenuating mutations during chemical mutagenesis. Vaccine. 1994;12:691–699.
454. Pringle CR, Filipiuk AH, Robinson VS, et al. Immunogenicity and pathogenicity of a triple temperature-sensitive modified respiratory syncytial virus in adult volunteers. Vaccine. 1993;11:473–478.
455. Wertz GW, Sullender WM. Approaches to immunization against respiratory syncytial virus. Biotechnology. 1992;20:151–176.
456. Stott EJ, Taylor G, Ball LA, et al. Immune and histopathological responses in animals vaccinated with recombinant vaccinia virus that express individual genes of human respiratory syncytial virus. J Virol. 1987;61:3855–3861.
457. Hsu K-H L, Lubeck MD, Davis AR, et al. Immunogenicity of recombinant adenovirus-respiratory syncytial virus vaccines with adenovirus types 4, 5, and 7 vectors in dogs and a chimpanzee. J Infect Dis. 1992;166:769–775.
458. Tristram DA, Welliver RC, Mohar CK, et al. Immunogenicity and safety of respiratory syncytial virus subunit vaccine in seropositive children 18–36 months old. J Infect Dis. 1993;167:191–195.
459. Wathen MW, Brideau RJ, Thomsen DR. Immunization of cotton rats with the human respiratory syncytial virus F glycoprotein produced using a baculovirus vector. J Infect Dis. 1989;159:255–264.
460. Welliver RC, Tristram DA, Batt K, et al. Respiratory syncytial virus–specific cell-mediated immune responses after vaccination with a purified fusion protein subunit vaccine. J Infect Dis. 1994;170:425–428.
461. Brideau RJ, Wathen MW. A chimeric glycoprotein of human respiratory syncytial virus termed FG induces T-cell mediated immunity in mice. Vaccine. 1991;9:863–864.
462. Trudel M, Nadon F, Séguin C, Binz H. Protection of BALB/c mice from respiratory syncytial virus infection by immunization with a synthetic peptide derived from the G glycoprotein. Virology. 1991;185:749–757.
463. Brandt C, Power UF, Plotnicky-Gilquin H, et al. Protective immunity against respiratory syncytial virus in early life after murine maternal or neonatal vaccination with the recombinant G fusion protein BBG2Na. J Infect Dis. 1997;176:884–891.
464. Piedra P, Grace S, Jewell A, et al. Purified fusion protein vaccine protects against lower respiratory tract illness during respiratory syncytial virus season in children with cystic fibrosis. Pediatr Infect Dis J. 1996;15:23–31.
465. Falsey A, Walsh E. Safety and immunogenicity of a respiratory syncytial virus subunit vaccine (PFP-2) in the institutionalized elderly. Vaccine. 1997;15:1130–1132.
466. Falsey A, Walsh E. Safety and immunogenicity of a respiratory syncytial virus subunit vaccine (PFP-2) in ambulatory adults over age 60. Vaccine. 1996;14:1214–1218.
467. Groothuis JR, King SJ, Hogerman DA, et al. Safety and immunogenicity of a purified F protein respiratory syncytial virus (PFP-2) vaccine in seropositive children with bronchopulmonary dysplasia. J Infect Dis. 1998;177:467–469.
468. Englund J, Piedra P, Kasel J, et al. IgG and IgA antibody (Ab) in breast milk (BrM) following postpartum immunization with respiratory syncytial virus (RSV) purified fusion protein vaccine (PFP-2) or trivalent inactivated influenza virus vaccine (TIV). Infectious Diseases Society of America, 34th Annual Meeting, New Orleans, La, September 18–20, 1996;48:67A.
469. Connors M, Collins PL, Firestone CY, et al. Cotton rats previously immunized with a chimeric RSV FG glycoprotein develop enhanced pulmonary pathology when infected with RSV, a phenomenon not encountered following immunization with vaccinia–RSV combinants or RSV. Vaccine. 1992;10:475–484.
470. Martin-Gallardo A, Fleischer E, Doyle SA, et al. Expression of the G glycoprotein of human respiratory syncytial virus in *Salmonella typhimurium*. J Gen Virol. 1993;74:453–458.
471. Collins PL, Purcell RH, London WT, et al. Evaluation in chimpanzees of vaccinia virus recombinants that express the surface glycoproteins of human respiratory syncytial virus. Vaccine. 1990;8:164–168.
472. Crowe JE Jr, Collins PL, London WT, et al. A comparison in chimpanzees of the immunogenicity and efficacy of live attenuated respiratory syncytial virus (RSV) temperature-sensitive mutant vaccines and vaccinia virus recombinants that express the surface glycoproteins of RSV. Vaccine. 1993;11:1395–1404.
473. Hruby DE. Vaccinia virus vectors: New strategies for producing recombinant vaccines. Clin Microbiol Rev. 1990;3:153–170.
474. Rouse BT, Norley S, Martin S. Antiviral cytotoxic T lymphocyte induction and vaccination. Rev Infect Dis. 1988;10:16–33.
475. Trudel M, Nadon F, Séguin C, et al. Initiation of cytotoxic T-cell response and protection of Balb/c mice by vaccination with an experimental ISCOMs respiratory syncytial virus subunit vaccine. Vaccine. 1992;10:107–112.
476. Reuman PD, Keely SP, Schiff GM. Similar subclass antibody responses after intranasal immunization with UV-inactivated RSV mixed with cholera toxin or live RSV. J Med Virol. 1991;35;192–197.
477. Hancock GE, Speelman DJ, Frenchick PJ, et al. Formulation of the purified fusion protein of respiratory syncytial virus with the saponin QS-21 induces protective immune responses in BALB c mice that are similar to those generated by experimental infection. Vaccine. 1995;13:391–400.
478. Chargelegue D, Obeid OE, Hsu SC, et al. A peptide mimic of a protective epitope of respiratory syncytial virus selected from a combinatorial library induces virus-neutralizing antibodies and reduces viral load in vivo. J Virol. 1998;72:2040–2046.

Chapter 149

Measles Virus (Rubeola)

ANNE A. GERSHON

Measles is an acute infection caused by the rubeola virus. It is a highly contagious disease that is usually seen in children. The illness is characterized by cough, coryza, fever, and a maculopapular rash that begins several days after the initial symptoms appear. There is a characteristic enanthem, Koplik's spots, that is specific for measles and that also precedes the onset of rash. Recovery from measles is the rule, but serious complications of the respiratory and central nervous systems may occur. Measles in the United States overall has been dramatically controlled since the introduction of live attenuated measles vaccine in 1963, but it remains a serious problem in developing countries.

Measles virus belongs to the genus *Morbillivirus* of the family Paramyxoviridae. Measles virus is closely related to the viruses causing canine and phocine distemper, rinderpest of cattle, and peste des petits ruminants of goats and sheep. Although each is a distinct agent, certain antigens are shared.[1, 2] Wild measles virus is pathogenic only for primates. Recently, Hendra and Hendra-like (Nipah) viruses, which are newly recognized viruses of the family Paramyxoviridae, have been implicated as causes of serious respiratory and encephalitic diseases in humans (see later discussion).

DESCRIPTION OF THE PATHOGEN

Morphology

On electron microscopy, measles virions are pleomorphic spheres with a diameter of 100 to 250 nm. Virions consist of an inner nucleocapsid that is a coiled helix of protein and RNA and an envelope that bears two types of short surface projections.[2, 3] These projections (peplomers) include the conical-shaped hemagglutinin (H) peplomer and the dumbbell-shaped fusion (F) peplomer. The molecular weight of the single-stranded RNA has been reported to be 4.5×10^6.[2] The entire genome has been sequenced, and therefore it is possible to differentiate between wild measles virus and vaccine-type virus.[2]

Chemical and Antigenic Composition

Measles virus is composed of six structural proteins.[2] Three are complexed with RNA; the nucleoprotein (N), the polymerase protein (P), and the large protein (L). Three are associated with the viral envelope. The membrane envelope contains the M protein, a nonglycosylated protein associated with the inner lipid bilayer, and two glycoproteins designated H and F.[4] The H glycoprotein is responsible for the adsorption of virus to receptors on the host cell, the first step in infection. The complement regulatory protein CD46, which is widely distributed in primate tissues, serves as a receptor for the H glycoprotein of measles virus.[2, 5] The H glycoprotein also constitutes the antigen that mediates hemagglutination. Hemagglutination of red blood cells from Old World monkeys forms a major serologic test for measuring antibody to measles virus, the hemagglutination inhibition (HI) test. The F glycoprotein is responsible for the membrane fusion of virus and host cell, penetration of the virus into the host cell, and hemolysis. Unlike many other paramyxoviruses, neuraminidase is not found on the envelope of measles virus.[6] Genetic and antigenic variation of measles virus is now recognized; the sequence of genes coding for H and N is the most variable.[7] Eight genotypes have been described.[8] The measles virus antigens and their now-recognized role in human disease[4, 9] are discussed later.

Growth of Measles Virus in Tissue Culture

Measles virus was first successfully isolated in the laboratory by Enders and Peebles in 1954.[10] The virus was initially propagated in primary human renal cells, but later it was found that the virus could also be cultivated in kidney cell cultures of simian origin. Wild measles virus is rather difficult to propagate in vitro because it is slow growing and only a limited number of types of cell cultures are permissive for the virus.

Typically, the cytopathic effects produced by measles virus in tissue cultures consist of stellate cells with increased refractility and, especially on passage, multinucleated syncytial giant cells containing intranuclear inclusions. In the absence of cytopathic effects, virus replication can also be detected by hemadsorption of rhesus monkey erythrocytes. Presumptive isolates of measles virus are identified by typing with monoclonal antibodies by immunofluorescence or plaque reduction tests.[2, 11]

Host Range

Humans are the only natural host for wild measles virus, but monkeys may also be infected with the virus. In general the illness caused by measles virus in monkeys is milder than that in humans.[12] It has not been possible to infect small laboratory animals such as rodents with wild measles virus. However, newborn and suckling rodents may be infected with vaccine strains administered by the intracerebral route.[13, 14]

Epidemiology

Measles has been recognized as a disease for some 2000 years, but the infectious nature of the illness was not recognized until about 150 years ago. In 1846, Panum[15] studied an epidemic of measles in the Faroe Islands and noted that the disease was contagious, that there was an incubation period of about 2 weeks, and that infection appeared to lead to lifelong immunity.

The next major advance in the understanding of measles did not occur until 1954, when Enders and Peebles[10] reported successful propagation of wild measles virus in primary human renal tissue culture cells. Their success led directly to the development of live measles vaccine, which was licensed for use in the United States in 1963.

Measles is seen in every country in the world. Without the use of vaccine, epidemics of measles lasting 3 to 4 months would be predicted to occur every 2 to 5 years. Countries in which measles vaccine is widely used have experienced a marked decrease in the incidence of disease. For example, for many years 200,000 to 500,000 cases of measles were reported annually in the United States. Since 1963, when the vaccine was licensed, the incidence of measles in the United States has decreased by almost 99%.[16, 17] This decrease has been especially pronounced since the enactment in the early 1980s of laws requiring proof of immunity to measles for school entry. The yearly incidence of measles in the United States reached a nadir in 1983, when 1497 cases were reported to the Centers for Disease Control and Prevention (CDC) in Atlanta. In the late 1980s and early 1990s, however, there was an increase in the incidence of measles that was brought under control by an increased rate of immunization and institution of the routine use of two doses of measles vaccine for all children.[18–20] In 1990 more than 25,000 cases of measles and 89 measles-associated deaths were reported to the CDC.[21] In 1991, however, the number of reported cases dropped significantly, to 9643.[22] Between 1993 and 1996, fewer than 1000 annual cases in the United States were reported to the CDC.[23] Using molecular techniques, it was demonstrated that interruption of transmission of indigenous measles occurred in 1993. Since that time, most cases of measles in the United States were the result of international importations of measles virus.[8]

Measles now has been reported in preschool children, many of whom are too young to be vaccinated.[22] Measles has also been reported, but to a lesser extent, in vaccinated school-aged children. About half of these cases have a history of prior vaccination; most of these are thought to be the result of primary vaccine failure.[20, 24] At present there continues to be minimal evidence that immunity induced by measles vaccine wanes with time.[19, 24–28] The major reasons that measles has not been eliminated from the United States continue to be a failure to immunize all persons who qualify for vaccination, primary vaccine failure, and importations of measles to the United States from other countries.[8, 27–30]

Spread of Infection

The measles virion is a very labile agent that is sensitive to acid, proteolytic enzymes, strong light, and drying.[2] The virus, however, remains infective in droplet form in air for several hours, especially under conditions of low relative humidity. This latter fact may account for the increased incidence of measles in winter.[31]

Measles, an airborne virus, is spread by direct contact with droplets from respiratory secretions of infected persons. It is one of the most communicable of the infectious diseases. Patients with measles are most infectious during the late prodromal phase of the illness, when cough and coryza are at their peak[12]; however, the disease is probably contagious from several days before until several days after the onset of rash. Measles virus has been isolated from respiratory secretions of patients with measles only up to 48 hours after the onset of rash.[32] Airborne spread of measles in physicians' offices[33, 34] and in a sports complex[35] have been observed.

Additional Diseases Associated with Measles Virus

Diseases other than measles that have been associated with measles virus include subacute sclerosing panencephalitis (SSPE), multiple sclerosis, Crohn's disease, Paget disease of bone, and systemic lupus erythematosus. SSPE is a chronic degenerative neurologic disease that occurs several to many years after an attack of measles, particularly in children who had measles before 2 years of age. The disease was at one time more common in the rural southeast than in other areas of the United States. A few children who received measles vaccine and who had no prior history of measles have been observed to develop SSPE. However, it is unknown whether these children might have had a subclinical case of measles before receiving vaccine. The incidence of SSPE has declined since the introduction of measles vaccine.[16, 36]

Patients with SSPE have unusually high measles antibody titers both in their serum and in their cerebrospinal fluid.[37] SSPE is caused by a persistent infection with a measles-related virus in the central nervous system (CNS) that occurs despite a vigorous immune response on the part of the host. The pathogenesis of SSPE is extremely complex and has been ascribed to a combination of host factors and viral replicative phenomena. Although a measles-like virus has occasionally been isolated, with the use of cocultivation techniques, from the brains of patients with SSPE at autopsy,[38, 39] the infection is usually characterized by an inability to produce viral progeny.[40] This inability may be a result of defects in the formation of gene products arising from genomic mutations caused by errors of RNA replication. Originally the inability to replicate was ascribed to failure of the infective virus to produce measles M protein.[41] Later, it was realized that this failure was related to mutations of the gene encoding this protein.[40] Now it is recognized that defects in enveloped gene products H and F also occur as a result of other genomic mutations of the causative virus.[40] Host factors such as defective immunity and the ability of specific antibodies to confine the virus to intracellular multiplication are also postulated to play a role in the pathogenesis of SSPE.[40–45] Measles virus RNA was demonstrated by the combination of in situ reverse transcriptase–polymerase chain reaction (RT-PCR) in neurons, astrocytes, oligodendrocytes, and vascular endothelial cells in the brain of a patient who died from SSPE.[46]

Multiple sclerosis, Crohn's disease, and SLE have a much more tenuous etiologic link with measles virus than does SSPE[47–49] and are probably unrelated. An etiologic role for measles virus in Paget's disease of bone has been raised as a possibility but as yet is unproved.[50–53]

PATHOGENESIS

Measles virus infects by invasion of the respiratory epithelium. Studies on volunteers inoculated with live measles virus indicate that infection may occur after instillation of virus at any point from the nose to the lower parts of the respiratory tract.[50]

Based on Fenner's mousepox model for exanthems[51] and a monkey model of measles infection,[52] it has been suggested[12] that local multiplication at the respiratory mucosa leads to a primary viremia, during which the virus spreads in leukocytes to the reticuloendothelial system. As a result of necrosis of infected reticuloendothelial cells, an increased amount of virus is released, and reinvasion of leukocytes (secondary viremia) occurs.

Measles virus has been isolated from the leukocytes of patients with clinical measles.[54] The virus has also been propagated in vitro in human T and B lymphocytes and in monocytes.[55] The major infected cell in the blood is the monocyte.[2, 56] Both endothelial and epithelial cells are infected. Infected tissues include thymus, spleen, lymph nodes, liver, skin, conjunctiva, and lung.[2]

After the secondary viremic phase of measles occurs, the entire respiratory mucosa becomes involved with the disease. This accounts for the cough and coryza that are classic signs of measles. In addition, measles may directly cause croup, bronchiolitis, and pneumonia. It has also been postulated that damage to the respiratory tract from, for example, edema and a loss of cilia predisposes to secondary invasion resulting in such complications as bacterial otitis media and pneumonia.[12]

Within a few days after generalized involvement of the respiratory tract has occurred, Koplik's spots appear and are followed by the development of a rash. Both manifestations are believed to result from similar pathologic mechanisms. On microscopic examination of skin and mucous membranes, multinucleate giant cells and other similar histologic changes are observed in both the epidermis and the oral epithelium.[57]

It has long been recognized that the appearance of the measles rash coincides temporally with the appearance of serum antibody and the termination of communicability of the disease. Therefore, it has been postulated that the skin and mucous membrane manifestations of measles actually represent hypersensitivity of the host to the virus. Measles virus antigen has been demonstrated in the involved skin and mucous membranes by immunofluorescence.[57–59] Measles virus has also been isolated from the rash in its early stages.[52] If hypersensitivity is the actual cause of the rash, however, it is probably mediated by cellular rather than humoral immunity,[60] and therefore patients with agammaglobulinemia who contract measles develop a rash. Patients with deficiencies in cell-mediated immunity, on the other hand, may develop measles giant cell pneumonia (Hecht's) without a rash after an exposure to measles or if measles vaccine is given.[61, 62]

Immunity

Immunity to measles after an attack of the disease appears to be lifelong. After measles vaccination, immunity is similarly of many years' duration and is probably lifelong in most persons.[16] It remains unknown why measles antibody persists for years after infection. One possible explanation is that measles virus becomes latent after the acute infection and, while latent, provides an immunologic stimulus to antibody formation. However, latent measles virus has not been demonstrated in humans or in experimental animals. An alternative explanation for the persistence of measles antibody is that reexposure to the virus results in an antigenic boost and continued antibody synthesis. It is known that reinfection with measles can occur and that reinfection is almost always asymptomatic even though it is detectable by a boost in antibody titer.[63] Cellular immunity to measles virus probably also plays a role in the prevention of recurrent measles, because patients with agammaglobulinemia do not have multiple attacks of measles. A cell-mediated response to measles antigen in the absence of detectable measles antibody was reported in two physicians in whom no disease developed despite repeated exposures to measles.[64] Therefore, when humoral antibodies to measles are absent or of low magnitude, cellular immunity to the virus may protect against subsequent illness. Cellular immunity to measles virus in peripheral blood of persons with a history of measles has been shown by in vitro lymphocyte stimulation after exposure to measles antigen[65] and by demonstration of measles-specific class I and II cytotoxic T cells.[66–68] A complex interplay of cellular immunity and cytokines occurs before, during, and after measles infection in healthy patients.[69]

During infection, CD8 and CD4 T cells are activated and probably participate in clearance of virus and development of rash. During recovery, suppression of cell-mediated responses occurs, with elevation of suppressive cytokines such as interleukin-4, which may be responsible for such phenomena as depressed delayed-type hypersensitivity to tuberculin in tuberculin-positive persons.[2, 70] Effects of vaccine on the immune system that resemble natural measles have also been described.[71]

CLINICAL MANIFESTATIONS

The incubation period of measles is 10 to 14 days; it is often somewhat longer in adults than in children. A prodromal phase lasting several days begins after the incubation period. This phase probably coincides with the secondary viremia.[12] It is manifested by malaise, fever, anorexia, conjunctivitis, and respiratory symptoms such as cough and coryza and may resemble a severe upper respiratory tract infection. Toward the end of the prodrome, just before the appearance of the rash, Koplik's spots appear.

Koplik's spots are pathognomonic of measles. First noted by Koplik in 1896,[72] they consist of bluish gray specks on a red base. They have also been likened to grains of sand, and without examination of the buccal mucosa in good light they may be overlooked. Most often they appear on the mucosa opposite the second molars. However, in severe cases the entire mucous membrane of the mouth may be involved. This enanthem persists for several days and begins to slough as the rash appears.

The rash of measles usually begins on the face and proceeds down the body to involve the extremities last, including the palms and soles (Fig. 149–1). During the healing phase, the involved areas (except palms and soles) may desquamate. The rash is erythematous and maculopapular; as it progresses it becomes confluent, especially on the face and the neck. The rash usually lasts about 5 days and starts to clear first on the skin that was first involved. The patient with measles is usually most ill during the first or second day of the rash. Several days after the appearance of the rash the fever abates and the patient begins to feel better. The entire uncomplicated illness from late prodrome to resolution of the fever and rash lasts 7 to 10 days; cough may be the last symptom to disappear.

Complications

The most common complications of measles involve the respiratory tract and the CNS. Involvement of the respiratory tract is part of the virus infection itself. In addition, bacterial superinfection may occur in any area of the respiratory tract, including the middle ear. Superinfection may be secondary to local tissue damage inflicted by the virus and depression of cellular immunity. Pneumonia accompanying measles may be caused either by direct viral invasion of the lungs or by bacterial superinfection.[73] Roentgenographic evidence of pneumonia is not uncommon even during apparently uncomplicated measles.[12] Pneumonia accounts for about 60% of complications deaths in infants dying of measles, whereas death from complications of acute encephalitis is more often observed in children 10 to 14 years of age.[74, 75]

Encephalitis after measles in normal hosts may be acute or chronic (e.g., SSPE). Acute measles encephalitis manifests with a resurgence of fever during convalescence and frequently with headaches, seizures, and changes in the state of consciousness. Up to 50% of the patients with measles and no symptoms suggesting cerebral involvement may have abnormalities detected by electroencephalography,[76] so it is believed that viral invasion of the CNS is a common feature of measles. However, only 1 in 1000 to 2000 patients with measles develops clinical signs of encephalitis. Measles encephalitis ranges from mild to severe, with a high proportion of patients who recover being left with neurologic sequelae.

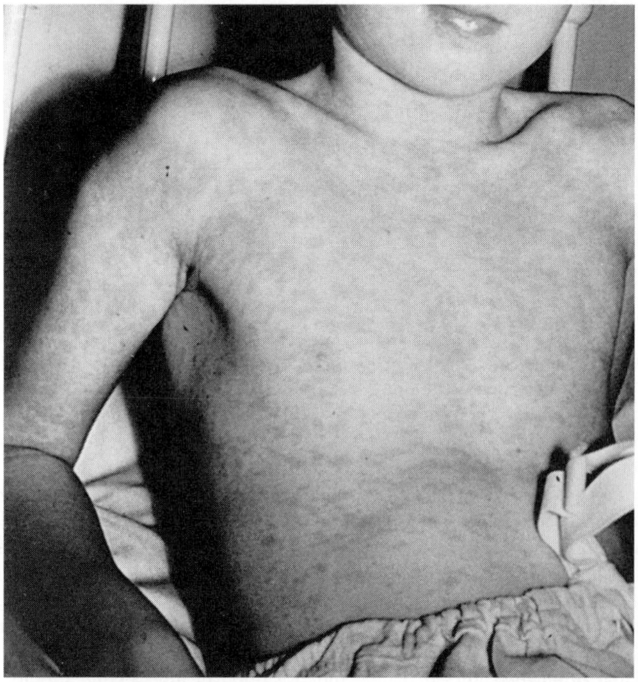

FIGURE 149–1. Typical rash in a case of measles.

Measles virus has been isolated from the brains of several persons dying of measles encephalitis.[77–80] However, virus isolation is uncommon and usually requires special virologic techniques such as cocultivation. It is hypothesized that acute measles encephalitis is caused by hypersensitivity to virus in brain tissue. Both viral antigens and host antigens are present on the surface of measles-infected cells in vitro.[81] Therefore, the hypersensitivity may be directed against both viral and host (brain) antigens, thus accounting for the encephalitic symptoms. Demyelination, vascular cuffing, gliosis, and infiltration of fat-laden macrophages near blood vessel walls are noted on pathologic specimens of brain from patients with measles encephalitis.[2] In a laboratory study of serum and cerebrospinal fluid from 19 patients with postinfectious measles encephalitis, similarities between experimental allergic encephalomyelitis (e.g., immune responses to myelin basic protein, early destruction of myelin) were demonstrated in about 50%. There was no evidence of intrathecal synthesis of antibody against measles virus, suggesting the importance of the immune response, rather than viral multiplication in the pathogenesis of measles encephalitis.[82]

Transient hepatitis has also been reported during acute measles.[83]

Modified Measles

An extremely mild form of measles has been observed in persons with some degree of passive immunity to the virus. This includes some babies younger than 1 year of age who have passively acquired maternal antibody to measles virus and susceptible persons who have received γ-globulin after an exposure to measles.

The symptoms of modified measles are variable, and certain classic symptoms such as the prodromal period, conjunctivitis, Koplik's spots, and rash may be absent. The incubation period may be prolonged. At times the infection is subclinical, and with a great degree of passively acquired immunity the infection may be prevented completely.[63]

Atypical Measles

This syndrome has been described in persons who received killed measles vaccine (or killed vaccine followed soon afterward by live vaccine) and who, several years later, were exposed to wild measles virus.[84, 85] In the face of an undetectable or a very low measles antibody titer, these patients have developed unusual manifestations of measles followed by the appearance of extremely high measles antibody titers (e.g., 1:100,000) in their serum.[86]

After a prodrome of fever and pain for 1 to 2 days, the rash appears. Unlike classic measles, it begins peripherally and may be urticarial, maculopapular, hemorrhagic, vesicular, or some combination of these types. The disease may be misdiagnosed as varicella, Rocky Mountain spotted fever, Henoch-Schönlein purpura, drug eruption, or toxic shock syndrome. The patient has a high fever, edema of the extremities, interstitial pulmonary infiltrates, hepatitis, and, on occasion, a pleural effusion. The disease tends to be severe with a somewhat more prolonged course than regular measles. At least one fatality has been reported. No specific therapy is available. Measles virus has not been isolated from these patients, and they do not appear to transmit measles to others.[85]

The pathogenesis of this syndrome is believed to be one of hypersensitivity to measles virus in a partially immune host. Whether cell-mediated or humoral immune mechanisms, or both, are involved remains controversial.[85, 87, 88]

One hypothesis concerning pathogenesis is that killed measles vaccine lacks the antigen that stimulates the antibody responsible for preventing the entry of measles virus into cells, thereby allowing measles infection to occur in the face of partial immunity derived from killed vaccine.[89, 90] It has been shown that killed measles vaccine does not induce antibody to the F protein, an antigen that facilitates spread of the virus from one cell to another by inducing cell fusion. This further explains the paradox of severe measles infection despite partial immunity.[4, 90]

Recurrences of atypical measles have not been reported. Therefore, persons who received killed measles vaccine (or killed vaccine followed soon afterward by live vaccine) in the past should be reimmunized with live measles vaccine. It is important that persons who have received killed vaccine be made aware that severe local reactions can follow an injection of live vaccine.[91, 92] Usually the reaction consists of tenderness and erythema around the injection site. However, severe local edema and high fever may also occur. Immunization with live vaccine is recommended because the associated risk is lower than the risk of being exposed to the wild-type virus.[93]

Measles in Immunocompromised Patients

Severe measles may occur in persons with compromised or deficient cellular immunity, such as those being treated for malignant disease and children with the acquired immunodeficiency syndrome (AIDS) or any form of congenital immunodeficiency.[61, 94–96] In a report of measles cases occurring in immunocompromised patients in 1989–1990, combined with some recorded in the literature, the case-fatality rate for severe measles in children and young adults was calculated to be 70% in 40 oncology patients and 40% in 11 patients infected with the human immunodeficiency virus (HIV). Of the oncology patients, 40% had no rash, 58% had pneumonitis, and 20% had encephalitis. Of the HIV-infected patients, 27% had no rash and 82% had pneumonia.[97] Should immunocompromised patients be inadvertently exposed to measles, they may develop giant cell pneumonia without evidence of a rash.[61, 94, 97] In such instances, the clinical diagnosis of measles may be difficult or impossible to make. Because these children may also have poor antibody responses, virus isolation from infected tissue (or identification of measles antigen by immunofluorescence) may be the only means for diagnosis. A chronic form of encephalitis resembling SSPE, often with a concomitant pneumonia, has also been reported in persons with deficient cellular immunity.[42, 43] This entity has been classified as subacute measles encephalitis and may be confirmed by the presence of measles RNA or infectious virus in brain tissue.[98]

Malnourished children, especially in developing countries, have also been reported to develop severe measles. This may be related to poor cell-mediated immune responses secondary to malnutrition.[99] Intense exposure to the virus secondary to crowding may also play a role in the severity of measles in developing countries.[100, 101]

Immunocompromised patients with no history of clinical measles who are exposed to the infection should be passively immunized with immunoglobulin, even if they have previously been immunized (see later discussion).

Measles in Pregnant Women and Their Offspring

Measles (rubeola) during pregnancy, in contrast to German measles (rubella), is not known to cause congenital anomalies of the fetus.[102] However, measles in pregnancy has been associated with spontaneous abortion and premature delivery.[12] Measles can be severe in pregnancy. During 1988–1991, when there was a resurgence of measles in the United States, a number of pregnant women developed measles. Of 13 such women hospitalized in Houston, Texas, 54% had respiratory complications requiring admission to the intensive care unit, and one died.[103] These women were thought to have primary measles pneumonia. Measles in the offspring of mothers with measles ranges from mild to severe.[104, 105] It is therefore recommended that infants born to women with active measles be passively immunized with immunoglobulin at birth.

Measles in Persons with Tuberculosis

It has long been thought that tuberculosis is aggravated in persons who contract natural measles, presumably secondary to a depression of cell-mediated immunity by measles virus.[2] For example, the tuberculin test has been reported to become negative for about 1 month after measles or measles vaccination.[12] It seems prudent to defer measles vaccination in persons with known tuberculosis until antituberculosis therapy is underway. In geographic areas and populations where tuberculosis is rare, it is not mandatory to perform a tuberculin test on an infant before administering measles vaccine.[106]

Measles in Adults

Measles has long been regarded as an illness of childhood. When it occurs in adults, it is often a more severe illness. In a series of 3220 young adult military recruits with measles between 1976 and 1979, about 3% developed pneumonia requiring hospitalization. Bacterial superinfection of the respiratory tract occurred in 30%, and 17% had evidence of bronchospasm. In addition, 31% had laboratory evidence of hepatitis, 29% had otitis media, and 25% had sinusitis.[107] Among patients with measles reported to the CDC in 1991, the incidence of complications was higher in those older than 20 years of age than in children.[21]

DIAGNOSIS

Classic measles with cough, coryza, conjunctivitis, Koplik's spots, and a maculopapular rash beginning on the face is easily diagnosed clinically. Often there is a striking leukopenia, perhaps related to the infection and death of leukocytes. A laboratory diagnosis of measles is helpful when the clinician is unfamiliar with the illness owing to the decline in cases of clinical measles since the introduction of measles vaccine. A laboratory diagnosis may also be helpful in cases of possible atypical measles or when unexplained pneumonia or encephalitis occurs in an immunocompromised patient.

Measles may be diagnosed in the laboratory by virus isolation, by the identification of measles antigen in infected tissues, or by the demonstration of a significant serologic response to measles virus. Virus isolation is technically difficult, and facilities for isolation are not always available. It is particularly useful in patients with fatal pneumonia and in patients with an immunodeficiency, in whom an antibody response may be minimal. Immunofluorescent examination of cells from nasal exudates or from urinary sediment for the presence of measles antigen may be useful for a rapid diagnosis of measles.[102, 108] A sensitive RT-PCR method to demonstrate measles virus RNA has been described.[109]

The most frequently used method of laboratory diagnosis is the serologic response to the virus. A fourfold or greater increase in measles antibody titer in acute and convalescent serum specimens is considered diagnostic for measles. A number of methods are available, usually through hospital or state health department laboratories, including neutralization, complement fixation, enzyme-linked immunosorbent assay (ELISA), and HI. Neutralization, which requires propagation of the virus in vitro, is technically difficult. Therefore, this test, although sensitive, is infrequently used. Complement fixation is not an overly sensitive technique, but it is adequate for the diagnosis of acute measles. It is not useful, however, for determining the immune status to measles.

The HI test is slightly less sensitive than virus neutralization, but generally there is good correlation between the two tests. Antibodies detectable by this test persist for many years, so immune status to measles may also be determined by HI. For the diagnosis of acute or atypical measles, two serum specimens, acute and convalescent, are required. SSPE may also be diagnosed by the demonstration of high measles HI titers in serum and cerebrospinal fluid in the presence of a compatible illness.[108]

The ELISA is more sensitive and simpler to perform than

HI.[110, 111] This assay can also be adapted to detect specific IgM antibody,[112] and it is therefore useful for the diagnosis of acute measles on one serum sample. An HI test that uses capillary blood collected on filter paper from finger- or heel-stick specimens has also been described and is used by some state health department laboratories.[113]

PREVENTION

Since the development and use of live measles vaccine, methods to prevent measles have changed dramatically. Prevention today is ideally carried out long before an anticipated exposure to measles by the administration of live vaccine during the early part of the second year of life. However, there are rare occasions when passive immunization against measles with γ-globulin must be used.

Included in the group of persons for whom passive immunization is recommended are those who are at high risk to develop severe or fatal measles, who are susceptible, and who have been exposed to the infection. Such persons include children with malignant disease, particularly if they are receiving chemotherapy or radiotherapy or both, and children with significant deficits in cell-mediated immunity, including patients with AIDS. Babies younger than 1 year of age (including newborns whose mothers have measles) are also at increased risk after an exposure to measles. Because measles has been reported even after vaccination in HIV-infected children, it has been recommended that they also be passively immunized with immunoglobulin after a recognized exposure.[96, 97, 106, 114] To be effective, passive immunization must be given within 6 days after an exposure; administration after 6 days would not be expected to influence the course of the disease.

For a healthy infant younger than 1 year of age who has been exposed to measles, the modifying dose of immunoglobulin is 0.25 ml/kg intramuscularly. An infant passively immunized in this fashion should be given live measles vaccine at the age of 15 months.[106] For immunocompromised, exposed children, a larger dose of immunoglobulin is required. These children should be given immunoglobulin, 0.5 mg/kg intramuscularly, with a maximum of 15 ml.[106]

Active immunization against measles was developed in the early 1960s. Live and killed measles vaccines were licensed for use in the United States in 1963. Killed vaccine was withdrawn from the market in 1967, after the recognition of atypical measles in recipients of this vaccine. The first marketed live measles vaccine was the Edmonston B strain. This vaccine was associated with a fairly high incidence of moderately severe side reactions such as rash and fever, and it was therefore often administered along with a dose of immunoglobulin. Subsequently, more attenuated vaccines were developed (Schwarz and Attenuvax), and, because the incidence of vaccine reactions is low with these vaccines, immunoglobulin is no longer given along with measles vaccine.

In 1976 it was recommended that all healthy children be given live measles vaccine at 15 months of age. At present, it is recommended that children be immunized between the ages of 12 to 15 months.[106] Two doses of measles vaccine given at 15 months and again in childhood (usually as measles-mumps-rubella vaccine [MMR]) are now routinely recommended.[93, 106] Properly administered measles vaccine has been associated with persistence of immunity to measles for many years.[115, 116] In one study, although measles HI antibodies were no longer detectable in some subjects, antibodies were demonstrated by neutralization and revaccination was associated with a classic booster antibody response.[115] In the general population, 95% of properly immunized children can be expected to respond serologically to measles vaccine.

Vaccination is not usually recommended for infants younger than 12 months of age because the induction of immunity may be suppressed by residual transplacentally acquired antibodies. In situations in which the incidence of natural measles before the age of 1 year is high, live measles vaccine may be given at 6 to 9 months of age but should be followed by additional routine doses.[106] Measles antibody titers are lower in women vaccinated as children than in women who have had natural measles, and the offspring of vaccinated women often lose transplacentally acquired measles antibodies before 1 year of age.[117, 118] Therefore vaccination can be routinely given as early as 12 months of age, because most women of childbearing years today were vaccinated as children.

Transient fever and rash develop about 1 week after vaccination in 5 to 15% of children.[106] In a 1986 study of 1162 twins who were given either MMR or placebo, there were side effects (fever, irritability, drowsiness, conjunctivitis) in 0.5 to 4%.[119] Symptoms of CNS dysfunction after measles vaccine are exceedingly rare.[120] Because measles may be severe in adults, immunization of adults who were not vaccinated previously, who have no history of measles, and who were born after 1956 is recommended by the CDC.[93] A 1986 Chicago study of hospital employees, however, indicated that only 1 (0.03%) of 266 was susceptible to measles; about one third were born after 1957.[121]

A number of reasons for apparent primary vaccine failures of measles vaccine have been proposed.[16] These include improper storage of vaccine at temperatures exceeding 4°C, failure to use the proper diluent for the lyophilized vaccine, exposure of the vaccine to light or heat, and vaccination in the presence of low levels of passive antibody. The latter may occur if infants are immunized at 12 months of age or younger, if children are vaccinated 1 or 2 months after receiving an injection of immunoglobulin, if the more attenuated vaccines are given with immunoglobulin, or if live measles vaccine is administered soon after killed measles vaccine. No deleterious effects have been associated with measles revaccination. Although it is probably unusual, sustained transmission of measles has been reported in secondary schools even when 95% of the students were immune and more than 99% were immunized.[122, 123]

Live measles vaccine is contraindicated in persons with deficits in cell-mediated immunity and in pregnant women. Fatal measles in children with AIDS has been reported.[114, 124] Although the potential risks of measles vaccine in these children are unknown, they may be less than the disease itself. It is currently recommended that children with known asymptomatic HIV infection receive measles vaccine at the age of 15 months.[95, 106] The use of measles vaccine should also be *considered* for children with known HIV infection who manifest symptoms if their CD4 T-cell levels are relatively well preserved, especially if they live in locations where there is transmission of measles, such as certain inner-city areas.[106] One case of fatal measles resulting from vaccine virus in a teenaged vaccinated boy has been described.[96] Children who have been treated for malignant disease may be given measles vaccine 3 months after they have completed their course of therapy.[106]

Serious hypersensitivity reactions to measles vaccine in persons allergic to egg protein have been reported.[125] Persons with a history of anaphylactic reactions after the ingestion of eggs should be vaccinated only with extreme caution.[125, 126]

Susceptible persons who are exposed to measles, with the exception of young babies, pregnant women, and immunocompromised persons, may be given live measles vaccine to prevent disease as an alternative to immunoglobulin. If the vaccine is given shortly after exposure, clinical cases of measles may be prevented, because the incubation period of measles vaccine is about 7 days, compared with 10 days for clinical measles.[12]

An experimental measles vaccine, a derivative of the original Edmonston B vaccine strain termed Edmonston-Zagreb, administered at a dose 10 to 100 times higher than usual, proved to be immunogenic in 4- to 6-month-old infants.[127] Despite its short-term safety, however, the rate of mortality from causes other than measles in these vaccinees in Senegal was significantly higher than in children who received standard vaccine.[128] Therefore this vaccine is no longer in use.

TREATMENT

The patient should be given supportive therapy such as antipyretics and fluids as indicated. Bacterial superinfection should be promptly treated with appropriate antimicrobials, but prophylactic antibiotics to prevent superinfection are of no known value and are therefore not recommended.

Vitamin A, 200,000 IU administered orally to children for 2 days, has been used successfully to decrease the severity of measles.[129–131] Side effects include transient vomiting and headache.

Administration of vitamin A has been reported to reduce seroconversion in vaccinees and should therefore be avoided at or after immunization.[132] The efficacy of ribavirin administered intravenously or by aerosol for treatment of severe measles is unproven.[103, 114, 133]

HENDRA AND HENDRA-LIKE (NIPAH) VIRUSES

Hendra virus, formerly called equine morbillivirus, has been recently described as a cause of outbreaks of respiratory illness in horses and humans in Hendra[134, 135] and Mackay,[136] Queensland, Australia. Hendra virus is a member of the Paramyxoviridae family, whose natural host appears to be fruit bats of the *Pteropus* species.[137] Human infection has been acquired through contact with blood, bodily fluids, or excretions of infected horses.

In April 1999, an outbreak of 229 cases of encephalitis, of which 48% were fatal, was reported from Malaysia in which a previously unrecognized Hendra-like virus (Nipah) was implicated as the causative agent.[138] A smaller outbreak involving nine cases of encephalitis and two cases of respiratory illness associated with the Hendra-like virus was reported from Singapore. Humans appear to have acquired infection from infected pigs, and most cases occurred among men working on pig farms in Malaysia. The cases in Singapore occurred among men who handled swine imported from Malaysia.

In the outbreak in Malaysia, illness in humans consisted of 3 to 14 days of fever, followed by drowsiness and confusion, and in some cases, progression to coma within 24 to 48 hours.[138] Some patients manifested respiratory illness. Preliminary nucleotide sequencing indicates that Hendra and Hendra-like (Nipah) viruses are related but distinct. Diagnosis of infection can be made by detection of IgM antibodies in blood and cerebrospinal fluids.

REFERENCES

1. Imagawa DT. Relationships among measles, canine distemper and rinderpest viruses. Prog Med Virol. 1968;10:160.
2. Griffin, DE, Bellini WJ. Measles. In: Fields BN, ed. Virology. New York: Raven Press; 1996:1267–1312.
3. Waterson AP. Measles virus. Arch Ges Virusforsch. 1965;16:57.
4. Choppin PW, Richardson CD, Merz DC, et al. The functions and inhibition of the membrane glycoproteins of paramyxoviruses and myxoviruses and the role of the measles virus M protein in subacute sclerosing panencephalitis. J Infect Dis. 1981;143:352.
5. Naniche D, Varior-Krishnsnan G, Cervoni F, et al. Human membrane cofactor protein (CD46) acts as a cellular receptor for measles virus. J Virol. 1993;67:6025–6032.
6. Howe C, Schluederberg A. Neuraminidase associated with measles virus. Biochem Biophys Res Commun. 1970;40:606.
7. Rota JS, Rota PA, Redd SB, et al. Genetic analysis of measles viruses isolated in the United States, 1995–1996. J Infect Dis. 1998;177:204–208.
8. Bellini WJ, Rota PA. Genetic diversity of wild-type measles viruses: Implications for global measles elimination programs. Emerg Infect Dis. 1998;4:29–35.
9. Hall WW, Choppin PW. Measles-virus proteins in the brain tissue of patients with subacute sclerosing panencephalitis. Absence of the M protein. N Engl J Med. 1981;304:1152.
10. Enders JF, Peebles TC. Propagation in tissue cultures of cytopathogenic agents from patients with measles. Proc Soc Exp Biol Med. 1954;86:277.
11. Enders JF. Measles virus, historical review, isolation and behavior in various systems. Am J Dis Child. 1962;103:282.
12. Kempe CH, Fulginiti VA. The pathogenesis of measles virus infection. Arch Ges Virusforsch. 1965;16:103.
13. Burnstein T, Frankel JW, Jensen JH. Adaptation of measles virus to suckling hamsters. Fed Proc. 1958;17:507.
14. Imagawa DT, Adams JM. Propagation of measles virus in suckling mice. Proc Soc Exp Biol Med. 1958;98:567.
15. Panum P. Observations made during the epidemic of measles on the Faroe Islands in the year 1846. Med Classics. 1938–9;3:829.
16. Krugman S. Present status of measles and rubella immunization in the United States: A medical progress report. J Pediatr. 1977;90:1.
17. Centers for Disease Control and Prevention. Measles—United States, 1991. MMWR Morb Mortal Wkly Rep. 1992;41:1–12.
18. Schlenker TL, Bain C, Baughman AL, et al. Measles herd immunity. Association of attack rates with immunization rates in preschool children. JAMA. 1992;267:823–826.
19. Frank J, Orenstein W, Bart K, et al. Major impediments to measles elimination. Am J Dis Child. 1985;139:881.
20. Hutchins S, Markowitz L, Atkinson W, et al. Measles outbreaks in the United States 1987 through 1990. Pediatr Infect Dis J. 1996;15:31–38.
21. Public Sector Vaccination Efforts. MMWR Morb Mortal Wkly Rep. 1992;41:522.
22. Centers for Disease Control and Prevention. Measles vaccination levels among selected groups of preschool-aged children—United States. MMWR Morb Mortal Wkly Rep. 1991;40:36.
23. Centers for Disease Control and Prevention. Measles: United States. MMWR Morb Mortal Wkly Rep. 1995;45:305–307.
24. Markowitz LE, Preblud SR, Fine PE, et al. Duration of live measles vaccine–induced immunity. Pediatr Infect Dis J. 1990;9:101–110.
25. Krugman S. Further-attenuated measles vaccine: Characteristics and use. Rev Infect Dis. 1983;5:477–481.
26. Mathias RG, Meekison WG, Arcand TA, et al. The role of secondary vaccine failures in measles outbreaks. Am J Public Health. 1989;79:475–477.
27. Gindler JS, Atkinson W, Markowitz LE, et al. Epidemiology of measles in the United States in 1989 and 1990. Pediatr Infect Dis J. 1992;841–846.
28. Anders JF, Jacobson RM, Poland G, et al. Secondary failure rates of measles vaccines: A metaanalysis of published studies. Pediatr Infect Dis J. 1996;15:62–66.
29. Frank JA, Orenstein WA, Bart KJ, et al. Major impediments to measles elimination. Am J Dis Child. 1985;39:881–888.
30. Bennish M, Arnow PM, Beem MO, et al. Epidemic measles in Chicago in 1983. Sustained transmission in the preschool population. Am J Dis Child. 1986;140:341–344.
31. De Jong JG. The survival of measles virus in air, in relation to the epidemiology of measles. Arch Ges Virusforsch. 1965;16:97.
32. Ruckle G, Rogers KD. Studies with measles virus II: Isolation of virus and immunologic studies in persons who have had the natural disease. J Immunol. 1957;78:341.
33. Bloch AB, Orenstein W, Ewing WM, et al. Measles outbreak in a pediatric practice: Airborne transmission in an office setting. Pediatrics. 1985;75:767–783.
34. Remington PL, Hall W, Davis IH, et al. Airborne transmission of measles in a physician's office. JAMA. 1985;253:1574–1577.
35. Ehresmann KR, Hedberg CW, Grimm MB, et al. An outbreak of measles at an international sporting event with airborne transmission in a domed stadium. J Infect Dis. 1995;171:679–683.
36. Modlin JF, Jabbour JT, Witte JJ, et al. Epidemiologic studies of measles, measles vaccine, and subacute sclerosing panencephalitis. Pediatrics. 1977;59:505.
37. Connolly JH, Allen IV, Hurwitz LJ, et al. Measles-virus antibody and antigen in subacute sclerosing panencephalitis. Lancet. 1967;1:542.
38. Barbosa LH, Fuccillo DA, Sever JL, et al. Subacute sclerosing panencephalitis: Isolation of measles virus from a brain biopsy. Nature. 1969;221:974.
39. Payne FE, Baublis JV, Itabashi HH. Isolation of measles virus from cell cultures of brain from a patient with subacute sclerosing panencephalitis. N Engl J Med. 1969;281:585.
40. Cattaneo R, Schmidt A, Billeter MA, et al. Multiple viral mutations rather than host factors cause defective measles virus gene expression in a subacute sclerosing panencephalitis line. J Virol. 1988;62:1388–1397.
41. Hall WW, Lamb RA, Choppin PW. Measles and subacute sclerosing panencephalitis virus proteins: Lack of antibodies to the M protein in patients with subacute sclerosing panencephalitis. Proc Soc Natl Acad Sci U S A. 1979;76:2047–2051.
42. Aicardi J, Goutieres F, Arsenio-Nunes ML, et al. Acute measles encephalitis in children with immunosuppression. Pediatrics. 1977;59:232.
43. Breitfeld V, Hashida Y, Sherman FE, et al. Fatal measles infection in children with leukemia. Lab Invest. 1973;28:279.
44. Gerson KL, Haslam HA. Subtle immunologic abnormalities in four boys with subacute sclerosing panencephalitis. N Engl J Med. 1971;285:78.
45. Sever JL. Persistent measles infection of the central nervous system: Subacute sclerosing panencephalitis. Rev Infect Dis. 1983;4:467–473.
46. Isaacson SH, Asher DM, Goded MS, et al. Widespread, restricted low-level measles virus infection of brain in a case of subacute sclerosing panencephalitis. Acta Neuropathol. 1996;91:135–139.
47. Adams JM, Imagawa DT. Measles antibodies in multiple sclerosis. Proc Soc Exp Biol Med. 1962;111:562.
48. Tannenbaum M, Hsu K, Buda J, et al. Electron microscopic virus-like material in systemic lupus erythematosus: With preliminary immunologic observations on presence of measles antigen. J Urol. 1971;105:615.
49. Feeney M, Winwood P, Snook J. A case-control study of measles vaccination and inflammatory bowel disease. Lancet. 1997;350:764–766.
50. Kress S, Schluederberg AE, Hornick RB, et al. Studies with live attenuated measles-virus vaccine. Am J Dis Child. 1961;101:701.
51. Fenner F. The pathogenesis of the acute exanthems. Lancet. 1948;2:915.
52. Sergiev PS, Ryazantseva NE, Shroit IG. The dynamics of pathological processes in experimental measles in monkeys. Acta Virol (Engl). 1960;4:265.
53. Siris ES. Seeking the elusive etiology of Paget disease: A progress report. J Bone Miner Res. 1996;11:1599–1601.
54. Gresser I, Chany C. Isolation of measles virus from the washed leucocytic fraction of blood. Proc Soc Exp Biol Med. 1963;113:695.

55. Joseph BS, Lampert PW, Oldstone MBA. Replication and persistence of measles virus in defined subpopulations of human leukocytes. J Virol. 1975;16:1638.
56. Esolen IM, Ward BJ, Moench TR, et al. Infection of monocytes during measles. J Infect Dis. 1993;168:47–52.
57. Suringa DWR, Bank LJ, Ackerman AB. Role of measles virus in skin lesions and Koplik's spots. N Engl J Med. 1970;283:1139.
58. Kimura A, Tosaka K, Nakao T. Measles rash I: Light and electron microscopic study of skin eruptions. Arch Virol. 1975;47:295.
59. Kimura A, Tosaka K, Nakao T. An immunofluorescent and electron microscopic study of measles skin eruptions. Tohoku J Exp Med. 1975;117:245.
60. Lackmann PJ. Immunopathology of measles. Proc R Soc Med. 1974;67:12.
61. Enders JF, McCarthy K, Mitus A, et al. Isolation of measles virus at autopsy in case of giant cell pneumonia without rash. N Engl J Med. 1959;261:875.
62. Mitus A, Holloway A, Evans AE, et al. Attenuated measles vaccine in children with acute leukemia. Am J Dis Child. 1962;103:413.
63. Krugman S, Giles JP, Friedman H, et al. Studies on immunity to measles. J Pediatr. 1965;66:471.
64. Ruckdeschel JC, Graziano KD, Mardiney MR. Additional evidence that the cell-associated immune system is the primary host defense against measles (rubeola). Cell Immunol. 1975;17:11.
65. McFarland HF, Pedone CA, Mingioli ES, et al. The response of human lymphocyte subpopulations to measles, mumps, and vaccinia virus antigens. J Immunol. 1980;125:221–225.
66. Kreth HW, ter Mulen V, Eckert G. Demonstration of HLA restricted killer cells in patients with acute measles. Med Microbiol Immunol. 1979;165:203–214.
67. Lucas CJ, Biddison WE, Nelson ID, et al. Killing of measles virus infected cells by human cytotoxic T cells. Infect Immunol. 1982;38:226–232.
68. Jacobson S, Rose JW, Flerlage ML, et al. Induction of measles virus-specific human cytotoxic T cells by purified measles virus nucleocapsid and hemagglutinin polypeptides. Viral Immunol. 1987;1:153–162.
69. Griffin DE, Ward BJ, Jauregui E, et al. Immune activation in measles. N Engl J Med. 1989;320:1667–1672.
70. Smithwick EM, Berkovich S. In vitro suppression of the lymphocyte response to tuberculin by live measles virus. Proc Soc Exp Biol Med. 1966;123:276.
71. Hussey GD, Goddard EA, Hughes J, et al. The effect of Edmonston-Zagreb and Schwartz measles vaccines on immune responses in infants. J Infect Dis. 1996;173:1320–1326.
72. Koplik H. The diagnosis of the invasion of measles from a study of the exanthemata as it appears on the buccal mucous membranes. Arch Pediatr. 1896;13:918.
73. Quiambao BP, Gatchalian SR, Halonen P, et al. Coinfection is common in measles-associated pneumonia. Pediatr Infect Dis J. 1998;17:89–93.
74. Barkin RM. Measles mortality: A retrospective look at the vaccine era. Am J Epidemiol. 1975;102:341–349.
75. Barkin RM. Measles mortality. Analysis of the primary cause of death. Am J Dis Child. 1975;129:307–309.
76. Gibbs FA, Gibbs EL, Carpenter PR, et al. Electroencephalographic changes in "uncomplicated" childhood diseases. JAMA. 1959;171:1050.
77. McLean DM, Best JM, Smith PA, et al. Viral infections of Toronto children during 1965: II. Measles encephalitis and other complications. Can Med Assoc J. 1966;94:905.
78. Meulen VT, Müller D, Käckell Y, et al. Isolation of infectious measles virus in measles encephalitis. Lancet. 1972;2:1172.
79. Scott TF. Postinfectious and vaccinial encephalitis. Med Clin North Am. 1967;51:701.
80. Shaffer MF, Rake G, Hodes HL. Isolation of virus from a patient with fatal encephalitis complicating measles. Am J Dis Child. 1942;64:815.
81. Drzenick R, Rott R. Host-specific antigens of lipid-containing RNA viruses: Viruses as a carrier of cell-specific antigens. Int Arch Allergy. 1969;36(Suppl):146.
82. Johnson RT, Griffin D, Hirsch R, et al. Measles encephalomyelitis: Clinical and immunologic studies. N Engl J Med. 1984;310:137–141.
83. McLellan RK, Gleiner JA. Acute hepatitis in an adult with rubeola. JAMA. 1982;247:2000.
84. Rauh LW, Schmidt R. Measles immunization with killed virus vaccine. Am J Dis Child. 1965;109:232.
85. Fulginiti VA, Eller JJ, Downie AW, et al. Altered reactivity to measles virus. JAMA. 1967;202:1075.
86. Frey HM, Krugman S. Atypical measles syndrome: Unusual hepatic, pulmonary, and immunologic aspects. Am J Med. 1981;281:55.
87. Lennon RG, Isacson P, Rosales T, et al. Skin tests with measles and poliomyelitis vaccines in recipients of inactivated measles virus vaccine: Delayed dermal hypersensitivity. JAMA. 1967;200:275.
88. Bellanti JA, Sanga RL, Klutinis B, et al. Antibody responses in serum and nasal secretions of children immunized with inactivated and attenuated measles-virus vaccines. N Engl J Med. 1969;280:628.
89. Norrby E, Ruckle GE, Meulen VT. Differences in the appearance of antibodies to structural components of measles virus after immunization with inactivated and live virus. J Infect Dis. 1975;132:262.
90. Annunziato D, Kaplan M, Hall WW, et al. Atypical measles syndrome: Pathologic and serologic features. Pediatrics. 1982;70:203–209.
91. Scott TJ, Bonanno DE. Reactions to live-measles virus vaccine in children previously inoculated with killed-virus vaccine. N Engl J Med. 1967;277:248.
92. Stetler HC, Gens RD, Seastrom GR. Severe local reactions to live measles virus vaccine following an immunization program. Am J Public Health. 1983;73:899–900.
93. Centers for Disease Control and Prevention. General recommendations on immunization: Recommendations of the Immunization Practices Advisory Committee (ACIP). MMWR Morb Mortal Wkly Rep. 1994:43(RR-1).
94. Mitus A, Enders JF, Craig JM, et al. Persistence of measles virus and depression of antibody formation in patients with giant cell pneumonia after measles. N Engl J Med. 1959;261:882.
95. Centers for Disease Control and Prevention. Recommendations of the Immunization Practices Advisory Committee: Immunization of children infected with human immunodeficiency virus. Supplementary ACIP statement. MMWR Morb Mortal Wkly Rep. 1988;37:181–183.
96. Centers for Disease Control and Prevention. Measles pneumonitis following M-M-R vaccination of a patient with HIV infection. MMWR Morb Mortal Wkly Rep. 1996;45:603–606.
97. Kaplan LJ, Daum RS, Smaron M, et al. Severe measles in immunocompromised patients. JAMA. 1992;267:1237–1241.
98. Mustafa MM, Weitman SD, Winick NJ, et al. Subacute measles encephalitis in the young immunocompromised host: Report of two cases diagnosed by polymerase chain reaction and treated with ribavirin and review of the literature. Clin Infect Dis. 1993;16:654–660.
99. Katz M, Stiehm ER. Host defense in malnutrition. Pediatrics. 1977;59:490.
100. Aaby P, Bukh J, Lisse IM, et al. Measles mortality, state of nutrition, and family structure: A community study for Guinea-Bissau. J Infect Dis. 1983;147:693–701.
101. Aaby P, Bukh J, Hoff G, et al. High measles mortality in infancy related to intensity of exposure. J Pediatr. 1986;109:40–44.
102. Gershon A, Young N. Chickenpox, measles, and mumps. In: Remington J, Klein J, eds. Infectious Diseases of the Fetus and Newborn Infants. Philadelphia: WB Saunders; 1994;591–602.
103. Atmar RL, Englund JA, Hammill H. Complications of measles during pregnancy. Clin Infect Dis. 1992;14:217–226.
104. Bloch AB, Orenstein WA, Hinman AR. Comment. J Infect Dis. 1981;143:753–754.
105. Gazala E, Karplus M, Liberman JR, et al. The effect of maternal measles on the fetus. Pediatr Infect Dis J. 1985;4:203–204.
106. Report of the Committee on Infectious Diseases. 24th ed. Evanston, Il.: American Academy of Pediatrics ("The Red Book"); 1997.
107. Gremillion DH, Crawford GE. Measles pneumonia in young adults. An analysis of 106 cases. Am J Med. 1981;71:539–542.
108. Schiff GM. Measles (rubeola). In: Lennette EH, ed. Laboratory Diagnosis of Viral Infections. 2nd ed. New York: Marcel Dekker; 1992;535–547.
109. Matsuzono Y, Narita M, Ishiguro N, et al. Detection of measles virus from clinical samples using polymerase chain reaction. Arch Pediatr Adolesc Med. 1994;148:289–293.
110. Rice GPA, Casali P, Oldstone MBA. A new solid-phase enzyme-linked immunosorbent assay for specific antibodies to measles virus. J Infect Dis. 1983;147:1055–1059.
111. Weigle K, Murphy D, Brunell P. Enzyme-linked immunosorbent assay for evaluation of immunity to measles virus. J Clin Microbiol. 1984;19:376.
112. Mayo DR, Brennan T, Cormier DP, et al. Evaluation of a commercial measles virus immunoglobulin M enzyme immunoassay. J Clin Microbiol. 1991;29:2865.
113. Wassilak S, Bernier R, Herrmann K, et al. Measles seroconfirmation using dried capillary blood specimens in filter paper. Pediatr Infect Dis J. 1984;3:117–121.
114. Krasinski K, Borkowsky W. Measles and measles immunity in children infected with human immunodeficiency virus. JAMA. 1989;261:2512–2516.
115. Krugman S. Further-attenuated measles vaccine: Characteristics and use. Rev Infect Dis. 1983;5:477–481.
116. Pederson IR, Mordhorst CH, Ewald T, et al. Long-term antibody response after measles vaccination in an isolated arctic society in Greenland. Vaccine. 1986;4:173–178.
117. Chui L, Marusyk RG, Pabst HF. Measles virus specific antibody in infants in a highly vaccinated society. J Med Virol. 1991;33:199–204.
118. Johnson CE, Nalin DR, Chui LW, et al. Measles vaccine immunogenicity in 6- versus 15-month old infants born to mothers in the measles vaccine era. Pediatrics. 1994;93:939–943.
119. Peltola H, Heinonen O. Frequency of true adverse reactions to measles-mumps-rubella vaccine. Lancet. 1986;1:939–944.
120. Weibel RE, Caserta V, Benor DE, et al. Acute encephalopathy followed by permanent brain injury or death associated with further attenuated measles vaccines: A review of claims submitted to the National Vaccine Injury Compensation Program. Pediatrics. 1998;101:383–387.
121. Chou T, Weil D, Arnow P. Prevalence of measles antibodies in hospital personnel. Infect Cont. 1986;7:309–311.
122. Wassilak S, Orenstein W, Strickland P, et al. Continuing measles transmission in students despite a school-based outbreak control program. Am J Epidemiol. 1985;122:208–217.
123. Gustafson T, Lievens A, Brunell P, et al. Measles outbreak in a fully immunized secondary-school population. N Engl J Med. 1987;316:771–774.
124. Centers for Disease Control and Prevention. Measles in HIV-infected children, United States. MMWR Morb Mortal Wkly Rep. 1988;37:183–186.
125. Herman JJ, Radin R, Schneiderman R. Allergic reactions to measles (rubeola) vaccine in patients hypersensitive to egg protein. J Pediatr. 1983;102:196.
126. James JM, Burks AW, Robertson P, et al. Safe administration of the measles vaccine to children allergic to eggs. N Engl J Med. 1995;332:1262–1266.
127. Whittle HC, Mann G, Eccles M, et al. Immunisation of 4–6 month old Gambian infants with Edmonston-Zagreb measles vaccine. Lancet. 1984;2:834–837.
128. Garenne M, Leroy O, Beau J-P, et al. Child mortality after high-titre measles vaccines: Prospective study in Senegal. Lancet. 1991;338:903–908.

129. Arrieta C, Zaleska M, Stutman H, et al. Vitamin A levels in children with measles in Long Beach, California. J Pediatr. 1992;121:75–78.
130. Frieden TR, Sowell AL, Henning K, et al. Vitamin A levels and severity of measles. Am J Dis Child. 1992;146:182–186.
131. Hussey GD, Klein M. A randomized, controlled trial of vitamin A in children with severe measles. N Engl J Med. 1990;323:160–164.
132. Semba RD, Munasir Z, Beeler J, et al. Reduced seroconversion to measles in infants given vitamin A with measles vaccination. Lancet. 1995;345:1330–1332.
133. Forni AL, Schluger NW, Roberts RB. Severe measles pneumonitis in adults: Evaluation of clinical characteristics and therapy with intravenous ribavirin. Clin Infect Dis. 1994;19:454–462.
134. Murray K, Selleck P, Hooper P, et al. A morbillivirus that caused fatal disease in horses and humans. Science. 1995;268:94–97.
135. Selvey LA, Wells RM, McCormack JG, et al. Infection of humans and horses by a newly described morbillivirus. Med J Australia 1995;162:642–645.
136. Hooper PT, Gould AR, Russell GM, et al. The retrospective diagnosis of a second outbreak of equine morbillivirus infection. Australian Vet J. 1996;74:244–265.
137. Philbey AW, Kirkland PD, Ross AD, et al. An apparently new virus (family Paramyxoviridae) infectious for pigs, humans and fruit bats. Emerg Infect Dis. 1998;4:269–271.
138. Centers for Disease Control and Prevention. Outbreak of Hendra-like virus–Malaysia and Singapore, 1998–1999. MMWR Morb Mortal Wkly Rep. 1999; 48:265–269.

Rhabdoviridae

Chapter 150

Vesicular Stomatitis and Related Viruses

STEVEN M. FINE

Vesicular stomatitis virus (VSV) most prominently causes a vesicular disease in domestic animals that resembles foot-and-mouth disease. Outbreaks within domestic animal herds decrease production and result in restrictions on the transport and sale of animals and animal products, which results in significant economic losses. VSV infects a high percentage of people who live in endemic areas, but VSV-associated disease in humans is generally mild, although significant morbidity can occur. In addition, since the VSV-G protein can bind to numerous cell types, VSV has earned a major role in molecular biology research involving the transduction of genetic material into cells.

CLASSIFICATION AND MORPHOLOGY

VSV is enveloped and contains a single strand of negative-sense RNA that encodes five structural proteins; the glycoprotein (G), membrane (or matrix) protein (M), nucleoprotein (N), and two internal proteins (L and P).[1, 2] It belongs to the family Rhabdoviridae, genus *Vesiculovirus*[3] and assumes the bullet morphology characteristic of the Rhabdoviridae. Approximately 1200 identical copies of the G protein cover its surface in an ordered, densely packed array of spikes, which present only one antigenic determinant accessible to neutralizing antibodies.[4, 5] Of the 16 distinct *Vesiculovirus* serotypes discovered thus far (see Table 150–1), six cause animal or human disease: VS–New Jersey (VS-NJ), VS-Indiana (VS-I), VS-Alagoas, Chandipura, Isfahan, and Piry.[6–9]

MOLECULAR BIOLOGY

The VSV-G protein binds to the surface of most cell types. Thus, molecular biologists often replace the envelope proteins in other viral vectors with VSV-G in order to expand the host range of the vector. Viruses produced in cell lines expressing the VSV-G protein are thus *pseudotyped* with VSV-G on their surfaces. They can infect a large variety of cells and are therefore tremendously useful for gene transduction.[10, 11] Likewise, replacing the G protein of VSV with CD4 and a human immunodeficiency virus (HIV) coreceptor (CXCR4) enabled a VSV vector to selectively infect and kill HIV-infected T cells by binding to the HIV-gp120 expressed on the surface of HIV-infected cells.[12]

EPIDEMIOLOGY

Epizootic

In North America, VSV disease caused by VS-NJ or VS-I appears in sporadic, epizootic outbreaks in domesticated horses and cattle, mainly in the central and southwestern United States and Canada and in Mexico. Outbreaks of VS-I occurred in 1942, 1956, 1964, 1965, and 1997 and of VS-NJ in 1944, 1949, 1957, 1963, 1982, 1985, 1995, and 1997.[13] They typically begin in late spring, spread to adjacent or remote herds, and abate after heavy frost. The vector is not known, although insects are suspected. VSV was isolated from a mosquito during an epizootic outbreak in New Mexico[14] and from biting midges and black flies that may be responsible for long-distance transport of the virus.[15] The 1995 epizootic episode in the southwestern United States began in May, in horses in New Mexico, and by October had spread to 367 premises in Arizona, Colorado, New Mexico, Utah, and Wyoming. Seventy-eight percent of cases were in horses and 22% in cattle, and one case was in a llama. Production losses, quarantines, and restrictions on livestock shows, auctions, and rodeos cost an estimated $50 to $100 million.[16]

Enzootic

In parts of Central and South America and in the United States on Ossabaw Island, Georgia, outbreaks of disease from enzootic VS-NJ predictably appear near the beginning of the dry season (November) and last through March. Farms located near forests as well as those with poultry experience higher rates of attack.[17] One year in Costa Rica, 9 to 11% of cattle on affected farms developed disease, which constituted 2.6% of cattle overall.[17, 18] Lactation and a high acute VSV antibody titer increase the risk of disease for a given animal, but other diseases do not predispose to VSV disease.[17] The reservoirs

TABLE 150–1 Vesiculoviruses

Serotype	Location of Isolation
VS-Indiana	United States
VS–New Jersey	United States
VS-Alagoas	Brazil[6]
VS-Carajas	Brazil[8]
Maraba	Brazil[8]
Jurona	Brazil
Piry	Brazil
Calchaqui	Argentina
Cocal	Trinidad[13]
La Joya	Panama
Chandipura	India[53, 54]
Isfahan	Iran[7]
Perinet	Madagascar[55]
Porton-S	Sarawak
Keuraliba	Senegal
Jug Bogdanovac	Yugoslavia[56]

Adapted from Travassos da Rosa AP, Tesh RB, Travassos da Rosa JF, et al. Carajas and Maraba viruses, two new vesiculoviruses isolated from phlebotomine sand flies in Brazil. Am J Trop Med Hyg. 1984; 33:999–1006.

and vectors for enzootic disease are not known, but phlebotomine sand flies harbor virus in enzootic areas.[6–8, 19–21] They can also transmit VSV to animals as well as transovarially to a new generation of sand flies in which it can also replicate.[20, 22, 23] Mosquitoes can also harbor VSV and can transmit infection to animals in a laboratory setting.[24] The high prevalence of VS-NJ antibodies in cows in enzootic areas of Costa Rica (82% for VS-NJ and 17.7% for VS-I)[18] indicates a high lifetime probability of infection, many of which infections are probably subclinical. Wild animals in enzootic areas also have VS-I and VS-NJ antibodies, VS-I mainly in arboreal and semiarboreal species and VS-NJ in bats, Carnivora, and some rodents.[25, 26]

Animal Disease

VSV infection causes an acute vesicular disease in horses, cattle, swine, goats, llamas, and some wild animals.[16, 27] Excess salivation, with fever and blisters or vesicles in and around the mouth, nose, hooves, or teats, appears after a 2- to 8-day incubation period. Vesicles may burst and the epithelium may slough, leaving large, contiguous areas exposed and irritated. Secondary bacterial infection leading to mastitis may complicate the course, and lameness can develop. A debilitating, nonvesicular manifestation with systemic symptoms, such as fever and weight loss, also sometimes occurs. Most animals recover after 2 to 3 weeks,[17, 28] but viral sequences may persist.[29]

Human Disease

Humans usually contract VSV during close contact with infected animals.[30, 31] Human infection with VSV is usually asymptomatic or causes mild illness but is not always benign. Of eight animal handlers who contracted VS-I during a 1965 epizootic episode in cattle, seven reported an illness that included fever, malaise, myalgias, emesis, and pharyngitis, and two of them developed oral vesicular lesions in 24 to 48 hours. Although most had mild illnesses that quickly resolved, one otherwise healthy male experienced pharyngeal and buccal lesions, lymphadenopathy, and a 20-pound weight loss over 3 weeks.[28] In another case, 30 hours after self-inoculation with VS-I, a laboratory worker developed fever, chills, retroorbital pain, myalgias, nausea, emesis, and diarrhea, which resolved in 3 days.[32] VSV is neurotropic in baby mice,[33] and two cases of VSV meningoencephalitis have been reported in children. In one, a 3-year-old boy from Panama infected with VS-I developed fever, chills, emesis, and generalized tonic-clonic seizures and remained neurologically impaired at discharge.[9]

The vast majority of human VSV infections go unrecognized, indicating either mild or subclinical illness. In an area of Iran enzootic for Isfahan, all residents over 5 years old were seropositive in one study,[7] and in a VS-Alagoas–endemic area of Columbia, 62 to 83% of people were seropositive,[6] indicating previous infection. This relatively high rate of seropositivity, which increases with age, also occurs with other serotypes in their respective enzootic areas.[19, 25, 31, 34]

DIAGNOSIS

VSV causes lesions that look like those of the more dangerous foot-and-mouth disease; therefore, VSV outbreaks demand urgent diagnosis. Current diagnostic methods include complement fixation, serum neutralization, enzyme-linked immunosorbent assay (ELISA), or viral isolation in tissue culture.[16] Recently developed assays, using reverse transcription and the polymerase chain reaction, ease the collection of samples, can identify viral RNA from lesions previously treated with toxic substances, and are being adapted for general use.[35]

HOST RESPONSE AND TREATMENT

Studies in mice showed that the presence of B cells and antibody responses was associated with recovery and the development of resistance to VSV; however, $CD4^+$ T cells also contribute to long-term survival, and secretion of interleukin-12 may be beneficial.[36–38] Antibody-mediated neutralization blocks virus-to-cell binding and requires 200 to 500 VSV-G-protein–specific immunoglobulin G molecules per virus particle.[2, 4] Neutralizing antibodies bind to the same G-protein epitope and protect against infection with the same strain.[5, 39]

Human infections with VSV are usually mild and generally do not require treatment. No specific treatments exist, and antiviral agents have not been evaluated in vivo. Interferon-α, β and interferon-γ inhibit VSV growth in vitro[40–42] and protect newborn mice from lethal VSV infection.[43] Prostaglandins A1 and A2,[44, 45] ribavirin,[46, 47] and some experimental compounds[48–50] inhibit VSV in vitro. In animals, secondary bacterial infections of the mouth, teats, and hooves should be treated appropriately, and a mild, antiseptic mouthwash may relieve pain from blisters.[51] Nutritional support may help animals that stop eating.

PREVENTION AND VACCINATION

Experimental vaccination with a recombinant vaccinia vector expressing the VSV-G protein stimulated neutralizing antibody production and protected mice against lethal VSV disease after intravenous challenge. In cattle, protection was incomplete, but correlated with high antibody titer.[52] The U.S. Department of Agriculture has approved a killed vaccine for animals, but its efficacy is unknown.[16]

REFERENCES

1. Banerjee AK, Barik S. Gene expression of vesicular stomatitis virus genome RNA. Virology. 1992;188:417–428.
2. Dietzschold B, Schneider LG, Cox JH. Serological characterization of the three major proteins of vesicular stomatitis virus. J Virol. 1974;14:1–7.
3. Knudson DL. Rhabdoviruses. J Gen Virol. 1973;20(Suppl) :105–130.
4. Kelley JM, Emerson SU, Wagner RR. The glycoprotein of vesicular stomatitis virus is the antigen that gives rise to and reacts with neutralizing antibody. J Virol. 1972;10:1231–1235.
5. Bachmann MF, Rohrer UH, Kundig TM, et al. The influence of antigen organization on B cell responsiveness. Science. 1993;262:1448–1451.
6. Tesh RB, Boshell J, Modi GB, et al. Natural infection of humans, animals, and phlebotomine sand flies with the Alagoas serotype of vesicular stomatitis virus in Colombia. Am J Trop Med Hyg. 1987;36:653–661.
7. Tesh R, Saidi S, Javadian E, et al. Isfahan virus, a new vesiculovirus infecting humans, gerbils, and sandflies in Iran. Am J Trop Med Hyg. 1977;26:299–306.
8. Travassos da Rosa AP, Tesh RB, Travassos da Rosa JF, et al. Carajas and Maraba viruses, two new vesiculoviruses isolated from phlebotomine sand flies in Brazil. Am J Trop Med Hyg. 1984;33:999–1006.
9. Quiroz E, Moreno N, Peralta PH, et al. A human case of encephalitis associated with vesicular stomatitis virus (Indiana serotype) infection. Am J Trop Med Hyg. 1988;39:312–314.
10. Arai T, Matsumoto K, Saitoh K, et al. A new system for stringent, high-titer vesicular stomatitis virus G protein–pseudotyped retrovirus vector induction by introduction of Cre recombinase into stable prepackaging cell lines. J Virol. 1998;72:1115–1121.
11. Yee JK, Friedmann T, Burns JC. Generation of high-titer pseudotyped retroviral vectors with very broad host range. Methods Cell Biol. 1994;43:99–112.
12. Schnell MJ, Johnson JE, Buonocore L, et al. Construction of a novel virus that targets HIV-1-infected cells and controls HIV-1 infection [See comments]. Cell. 1997;90:849–857.
13. Jonkers AH. The epizootiology of the vesicular stomatitis viruses: A reappraisal. Am J Epidemiol. 1967;86:286–291.
14. Sudia WD, Fields BN, Calisher CH. The isolation of vesicular stomatitis virus (Indiana strain) and other viruses from mosquitoes in New Mexico, 1965. Am J Epidemiol. 1967;86:598–602.
15. Cupp EW, Mare CJ, Cupp MS, et al. Biological transmission of vesicular stomatitis virus (New Jersey) by *Simulium vittatum* (Diptera: Simuliidae). J Med Entomol. 1992;29:137–140.
16. Bridges VE, McCluskey BJ, Salman MD, et al. Review of the 1995 vesicular stomatitis outbreak in the western United States. J Am Vet Med Assoc. 1997;211:556–560.
17. Vanleeuwen JA, Rodriguez LL, Waltner-Toews D. Cow, farm, and ecologic risk factors of clinical vesicular stomatitis on Costa Rican dairy farms. Am J Trop Med Hyg. 1995;53:342–350.
18. Rodriguez LL, Vernon S, Morales AI, et al. Serological monitoring of vesicular stomatitis New Jersey virus in enzootic regions of Costa Rica. Am J Trop Med Hyg. 1990;42:272–281.

19. Shelokov A, Peralta PH. Vesicular stomatitis virus, Indiana type: An arbovirus infection of tropical sandflies and humans? Am J Epidemiol. 1967;86:149–157.
20. Comer JA, Tesh RB, Modi GB, et al. Vesicular stomatitis virus, New Jersey serotype: Replication in and transmission by *Lutzomyia shannoni* (Diptera: Psychodidae). Am J Trop Med Hyg. 1990;42:483–90.
21. Corn JL, Comer JA, Erickson GA, et al. Isolation of vesicular stomatitis virus New Jersey serotype from phlebotomine sand flies in Georgia. Am J Trop Med Hyg. 1990;42:476–482.
22. Tesh RB, Chaniotis BN, Johnson KM. Vesicular stomatitis virus, Indiana serotype: Multiplication in and transmission by experimentally infected phlebotomine sandflies (*Lutzomyia trapidoi*). Am J Epidemiol. 1971;93:491–495.
23. Tesh RB, Chaniotis BN. Transovarial transmission of viruses by phlebotomine sandflies. Ann N Y Acad Sci. 1975;266:125–134.
24. Calisher CH, Monath TP, Sabattini MS, et al. A newly recognized vesiculovirus, Calchaqui virus, and subtypes of Melao and Maguari viruses from Argentina, with serologic evidence for infections of humans and horses. Am J Trop Med Hyg. 1987;36:114–119.
25. Tesh RB, Peralta PH, Johnson KM. Ecologic studies of vesicular stomatitis virus. I. Prevalence of infection among animals and humans living in an area of endemic VSV activity. Am J Epidemiol. 1969;90:255–261.
26. Johnson KM, Tesh RB, Peralta PH. Epidemiology of vesicular stomatitis virus: Some new data and a hypothesis for transmission of the Indian serotype. J Am Vet Med Assoc. 1969;155:2133–2140.
27. Green SL. Vesicular stomatitis in the horse. Vet Clin North Am Equine Pract. 1993;9:349–353.
28. Fields BN, Hawkins K. Human infection with the virus of vesicular stomatitis during an epizootic. N Engl J Med. 1967;277:989–994.
29. Letchworth GJ, Barrera JC, Fishel JR, et al. Vesicular stomatitis New Jersey virus RNA persists in cattle following convalescence. Virology. 1996;219:480–484.
30. Reif JS, Webb PA, Monath TP, et al. Epizootic vesicular stomatitis in Colorado, 1982: Infection in occupational risk groups. Am J Trop Med Hyg. 1987;36:177–182.
31. Brody JA, Fischer GF, Peralta PH. Vesicular stomatitis virus in Panama. Human serologic patterns in a cattle raising area. Am J Epidemiol. 1967;86:158–161.
32. Johnson KM, Vogel JE, Peralta PH. Clinical and serological response to laboratory-acquired human infection by Indiana type vesicular stomatitis virus (VSV). Am J Trop Med Hyg. 1966;15:244–246.
33. Bi Z, Barna M, Komatsu T, et al. Vesicular stomatitis virus infection of the central nervous system activates both innate and acquired immunity. J Virol. 1995;69:6466–6472.
34. Cline BL. Ecological associations of vesicular stomatitis virus in rural Central America and Panama. Am J Trop Med Hyg. 1976;25:875–883.
35. Rodriguez LL, Fitch WM, Nichol ST. Ecological factors rather than temporal factors dominate the evolution of vesicular stomatitis virus. Proc Natl Acad Sci U S A. 1996;93:13030–13035.
36. Bachmann MF, Kalinke U, Althage A, et al. The role of antibody concentration and avidity in antiviral protection. Science. 1997;276:2024–2027.
37. Thomsen AR, Nansen A, Andersen C, et al. Cooperation of B cells and T cells is required for survival of mice infected with vesicular stomatitis virus. Int Immunol. 1997;9:1757–1766.
38. Komatsu T, Barna M, Reiss CS. Interleukin-12 promotes recovery from viral encephalitis. Viral Immunol. 1997;10:35–47.
39. Bachmann MF, Hengartner H, Zinkernagel RM. T helper cell–independent neutralizing B cell response against vesicular stomatitis virus: Role of antigen patterns in B cell induction? Eur J Immunol. 1995;25:3445–3451.
40. Witter F, Barouki F, Griffin D, et al. Biologic response (antiviral) to recombinant human interferon alpha 2a as a function of dose and route of administration in healthy volunteers. Clin Pharmaco Ther. 1987;42:567–575.
41. Maheshawari RK, Friedman RM. Interferon induced inhibition of enveloped viruses. Prog Clin Biol Res. 1985;202:297–305.
42. Baxt B, Sonnabend JA, Bablianian R. Effects of interferon on vesicular stomatitis virus transcription and translation. J Gen Virol. 1977;35:325–334.
43. DeClercq E, De Somer P. Protective effect of interferon and polyacrylic acid in newborn mice infected with a lethal dose of vesicular stomatitis virus. Life Sci. 1968;7:925–933.
44. Pica F, Rossi A, Santirocco N, et al. (1996) Effect of combined alpha IFN and prostaglandin A1 treatment on vesicular stomatitis virus replication and heat shock protein synthesis in epithelial cells. Antiviral Res. 1996;29:187–198.
45. Parker J, Ahrens PB, Ankel H. Antiviral effects of cyclopentenone prostaglandins on vesicular stomatitis virus replication. Antiviral Res. 1995;26:83–96.
46. Fernandez-Larsson R, O'Connell K, Koumans E, Patterson JL. Molecular analysis of the inhibitory effect of phosphorylated ribavirin on the vesicular stomatitis virus in vitro polymerase reaction. Antimicrob Agents Chemother. 1989;33:1668–1673.
47. Toltzis P, Huang AS. Effect of ribavirin on macromolecular synthesis in vesicular stomatitis virus–infected cells. Antimicrob Agents Chemother. 1986;29:1010–1016.
48. Shuto S, Obara, T, Saito Y, et al. New neplanocin analogues. 6. Synthesis and potent antiviral activity of 6′-homoneplanocin A1. J Med Chem. 1996;39:2392–2399.
49. Spinu K, Vorozhbit V, Grushko T, et al. Antiviral activity of tomatoside from *Lycopersicon esculentum* Mill. Adv Exp Med Biol. 1996;404:505–509.
50. Muller-Decker K, Amtmann E, Sauer, G. Inhibition of the phosphorylation of the regulatory non-structural protein of vesicular stomatitis virus by an antiviral xanthate compound. J Gen Virol. 1987;68:3045–3056.
51. APHIS. Precautions for Horses Diagnosed with Vesicular Stomatitis. Colorado Department of Agriculture Animal Industry Division; 1998.
52. Mackett M, Yilma T, Rose JK, et al. Vaccinia virus recombinants: Expression of VSV genes and protective immunization of mice and cattle. Science. 1985;227:433–435.
53. Fontenille D, Traore-Lamizana M, Trouillet J, et al. First isolations of arboviruses from phlebotomine sand flies in West Africa. Am J Trop Med Hyg. 1994;50:570–574.
54. Bhatt PN, Rodrigues FM. Chandipura: A new arbovirus isolated in India from patients with febrile illness. Indian J Med Res. 1967;55:1295–1305.
55. Clerc Y, Rodhain F, Digoutte JP, et al. The Perinet virus, rhabdoviridae, of the vesiculovirus type isolated in Madagascar from Culicidae (in French). Arch Inst Pasteur Madagascar. 1982;49:119–129.
56. Vesenjak-Hirjan J, Punda-Polic V, Dobe M. Geographical distribution of arboviruses in Yugoslavia. J Hyg Epidemiol Microbiol Immunol. 1991;35:129–140.

Chapter **151**

Rabies Virus

THOMAS P. BLECK
CHARLES E. RUPPRECHT

Rabies is a viral disease producing an almost uniformly fatal encephalitis in humans and most other mammals. It has been present throughout recorded history and literature and likely predates the evolution of humans. Rabies remains one of the most common viral causes of death in the developing world. Exposure to the virus also has profound medical and economic implications throughout the world, with as many as 4 million people annually receiving postexposure treatment (PET) to prevent rabies.[1] Although current technology can produce safe agents for PET, the expense involved often leads to the use of older, more dangerous vaccines in the developing world, with their attendant risk of catastrophic neurologic complications.

Rabies, Latin for "madness," derives from *rabere,* "to rave," and is related to the Sanskrit word for violence, *rabhas.* The Greek term for rabies, *lyssa,* also means "madness" and provides the genus name (Lyssavirus). The Babylon Eshnuna code contains the first known mention of rabies in the 23rd century BC.[2] Democritus provided a clear description of animal rabies in about 500 BC. Wound cauterization was the preferred treatment in the first century AD and remained the only real therapy until Pasteur introduced immunization in 1885. Wound cautery was recommended for the management of rabid animal bites until the mid 20th century.[2] Another remedy that remains part of popular culture (with little recognition of its origin) was the hair of the dog that bit the patient.[3]

Rabies in the Western Hemisphere predates Columbus but remained rare due to a low population density.[4] Bats spread the disease among cattle and humans in Central America in the early 16th century.[5] Rabies epizootics began in the northern and eastern United States in the 19th century, reflecting the importation of foxes for hunting.[6]

Rabies was only diagnosed clinically until 1903, when Adelchi Negri described the cytoplasmic inclusions that bear his name.[7] These were the only pathologic marker before the development of the fluorescent antibody test in 1958.[8]

VIROLOGY

Classification

The Rhabdoviridae are negatively stranded RNA viruses; two genera infect animals (*Lyssavirus* and *Vesiculovirus*) and one infects plants. Rabies virus (serotype 1) is the type species of *Lyssavirus*[6] and vesicular stomatitis virus that of *Vesiculovirus*. Rabies is enzootic, and sometimes epizootic, in a variety of mammals. The five other members of the *Lyssavirus* genus rarely cause human disease (Table

TABLE 151–1 Members of the Lyssavirus Genus

Virus	Serotype	Reservoir
Rabies	1	Found worldwide except for Australia, a few other island nations, and Antarctica
Lagos bat	2	Probably enzootic in fruit bats; no reported human cases.
Mokola	3	Probably an insectivore or rodent species limited to parts of Africa; a few domestic animal and two human cases reported
Duvenhage	4	Probably insectivorous bats; cases identified in South Africa, Zimbabwe, and Senegal
European bat lyssavirus 1	5	European insectivorous bats (probably *Eptesicus serotinus*)
European bat lyssavirus 2	6	European insectivorous bats (probably *Myotis dasycneme*)

Data from ref. 6.

TABLE 151–2 Rhabdoviral Genes and Products

Gene	Synonyms	Size (kD)	Function
N (nucleocapsid)		50	
NS (nonstructural)	M_1, *P*	40	Originally thought to encode nonstructural protein but now known to produce structural protein that is phosphorylated by kinases in host cell and joins with L
M (matrix)	M_2	26	Responsible for assembly and budding of bullet-shaped particles, in concert with G protein attachment to host cell receptors
G (glycoprotein)		65	
L (large)		160–190	RNA-dependent RNA polymerase; required for transcription of negatively stranded viral RNA; appears to form complex with NS

Data from refs. 15–22.

151–1). The taxonomy of the newly described Australian bat lyssavirus (see later) remains to be determined.

Vesiculoviruses share many of the virologic characteristics of the lyssaviruses. They infect a large number of animal and insect species; humans occasionally are infected by contact with animals, typically via respiratory secretions (see Chapter 150).[9] Seven vesiculoviruses are known occasionally to infect humans.[10] A related virus, borna, produces central nervous system infection in birds and primates and is suggested by some authors to be related to human psychiatric disorders. In contrast to the rhabdoviruses, however, it replicates in the nucleus rather than in the cytoplasm. Its taxonomy remains uncertain.

Composition

Lyssaviruses (Fig. 151–1) are bullet-shaped, with an average length of 180 nm and an average diameter of 75 nm.[11] The complete virus includes a helical nucleocapsid with 30 and 35 coils between 4.2 and 4.6 nm in length.[12] This is enclosed in a lipoprotein envelope 7.5- to 10-nm thick, from which glycoprotein (G protein) spikes project 10 nm.[13] These spikes cover the surface of the virus except at the blunt end.

The rabies genome is a single, negatively stranded RNA molecule with a mass of 4.6×10^3 kD,[14] encoding five genes: *N*, *NS* (or M_1), *M* (or M_2), *G*, and *L* (Table 151–2).[15] Phosphorylation of the N nucleoprotein regulates replication of the viral RNA[16] and is potentially immunogenic.[17] It is probably required to switch from the transcription of gene products to the production of a full-length positively stranded RNA.[18] The NS phosphoprotein may control the L protein, an RNA-dependent RNA polymerase.[19, 20] The M, or matrix, protein is located between the nucleocapsid and lipoprotein envelope[21]; and is responsible for the assembly and budding of bullet-shaped particles, in concert with the G protein.[22]

The G protein is involved in cellular reception and is the antigen inducing neutralizing antibodies; variability in this protein is responsible for serotypic differences among lyssaviruses,[23] and mutations at position 333 (substituting glutamine or isoleucine for arginine) disrupt virulence.[24] This arginine residue appears to be essential for fusion of the viral envelope with neurons.[25] Molecular modifications of the G protein can increase its antigenicity.[26]

Replication Strategy

Neuronal attachment is probably mediated by more than one mechanism, including binding to a ganglioside,[27] and independently to the

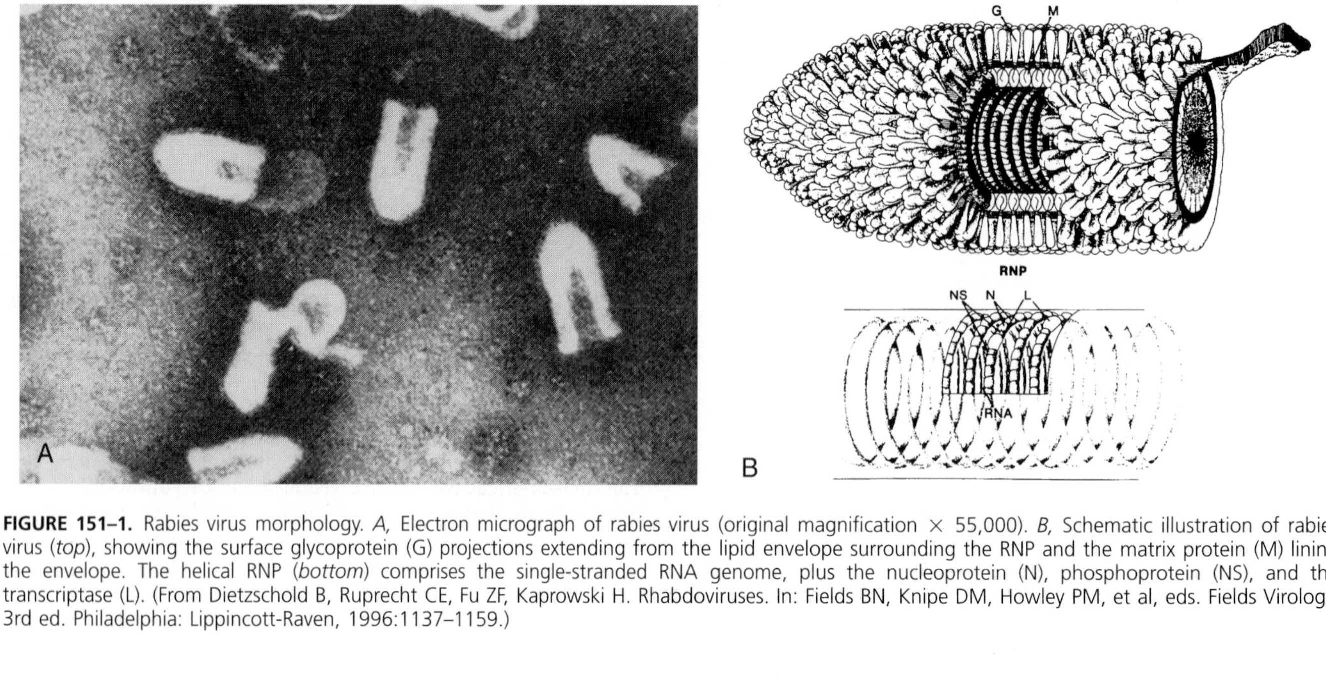

FIGURE 151–1. Rabies virus morphology. *A*, Electron micrograph of rabies virus (original magnification × 55,000). *B*, Schematic illustration of rabies virus (*top*), showing the surface glycoprotein (G) projections extending from the lipid envelope surrounding the RNP and the matrix protein (M) lining the envelope. The helical RNP (*bottom*) comprises the single-stranded RNA genome, plus the nucleoprotein (N), phosphoprotein (NS), and the transcriptase (L). (From Dietzschold B, Ruprecht CE, Fu ZF, Kaprowski H. Rhabdoviruses. In: Fields BN, Knipe DM, Howley PM, et al, eds. Fields Virology. 3rd ed. Philadelphia: Lippincott-Raven, 1996:1137–1159.)

neural cell adhesion molecule (CD56).[28] In muscle, the virus binds to the nicotinic acetylcholine receptor.[29] Once bound to the receptor, the virus is probably internalized by receptor-mediated endocytosis. This forms a coated pit, which then fuses with a lysosome, from which the nucleocapsid escapes into the cytosol.[30] The viral envelope forms from host membranes into which the G and M proteins are inserted.[31] The envelope includes small amounts of host proteins.[20]

The virus does not tolerate a pH below 3 or above 11 and is inactivated by ultraviolet light, sunlight, desiccation, and exposure to formalin, phenol, ether, trypsin, β-propiolactone, and detergents.

EPIDEMIOLOGY

Rabies is currently distributed worldwide except for Antarctica and a few island nations. In 1996 (the last year for which global data are available), 106 nations reported the presence of rabies, and 44 reported its absence.[32] Worldwide, dogs account for 54% of animal rabies, terrestrial wildlife 42%, and bats 4%.[32] Recent reports from Australia describe a rabies virus variant in the Ballina region that infects flying foxes.[33] Animals and humans dying from Ballina virus encephalitis have the typical neuropathologic changes of rabies,[34] and the disease appears to be preventable by standard rabies vaccines.[35]

Human Rabies

The epidemiology of human rabies reflects that of local animal rabies.[36] In developing areas in which canine rabies remains common, most human cases result from dog bites. In regions where dogs are immunized, most human cases follow exposure to rabid wild animals.

Throughout the world in 1996, 33,209 cases of human rabies were reported to the World Health Organization.[32] These reports probably represent an underestimate of the worldwide incidence of the disease, which may cause as many as 100,000 deaths annually.[6] An estimated 4 million persons receive PET annually, with the vast majority of persons being treated with vaccine types carrying a risk of neurologic complications.[37] In the United States, one or two cases were reported annually in the 1990s. After several years of zero to three cases per year, however, the total for 1994 was six cases, five in 1995, three in 1996, and two in 1997 (Fig. 151–2). In countries of very low prevalence, an increasing percentage of cases are imported, occur after very long incubation periods, or lack a known source of exposure. In the United States, the sources of human cases have changed from predominantly domestic animals (1945 to 1965) to largely unknown sources (1976 to present). However, molecular biologic studies of these unknown cases indicate that most are of bat origin. An example of this was reported in 1999.[38] A 29-year-old man died of encephalitis, and a rabies virus with strong homology to bat rabies virus was identified. He had no bat or other animal exposure history.

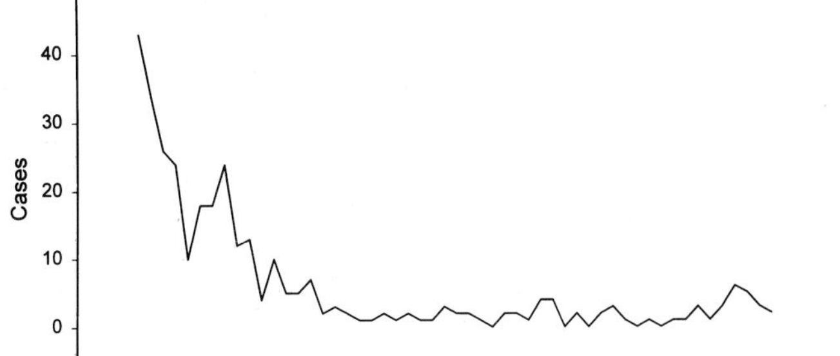

FIGURE 151–2. Reported cases of human rabies in the United States by year. (Data from the CDC Annual Summaries of Notifiable Diseases.)

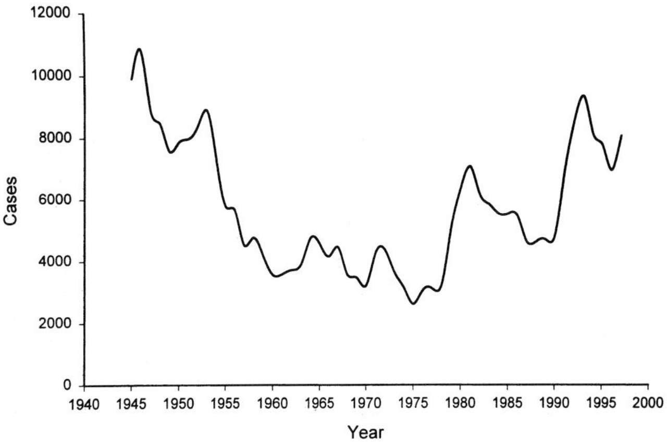

FIGURE 151–3. Reported cases of animal rabies in the United States by year. (Data from the CDC Annual Summaries of Notifiable Diseases.)

Animal Rabies

In the developing world, rabies is predominantly a problem of domestic and feral animals. The developed nations have largely eliminated rabies from domestic animals, leaving wild animals as the major affected group. In the United States, the incidence of animal rabies has been increasing during the past 2 decades (Fig. 151–3).

A resurgence of raccoon rabies in the United States began in 1977 near the Virginia–West Virginia border and in the ensuing 2 decades has expanded to involve most of the eastern states. More than 20,000 cases of raccoon rabies have been reported, with several thousand secondary cases in dogs and other animals.[39] In the state of New York, the number of humans receiving PET increased from 84 in 1989 to over 1000 in 1992.[40] The median cost per patient in Massachusetts was $2376 in 1995, with estimates of the total cost to the state as high as $6.4 million.[41] Rabies is also increasing among previously rarely affected species in other parts of the United States, such as coyotes.[42]

Bats are increasingly the source of human rabies in the United States.[43] The epizoology of bat rabies is changing from typical reservoirs (e.g., the common big brown bat) to include previously rarely affected species (e.g., the silver-haired bat).[44] Ten of the 15 human rabies cases known to have been contracted from bats in the United States since 1980 involve silver-haired bat rabies virus.[45] Molecular epidemiologic evidence reinforces the importance of avoiding contact with downed bats or other wildlife.[46, 47]

PATHOGENESIS

Rabies infection begins with centripetal spread of the virus via peripheral nerves to the central nervous system (CNS), proliferation within the CNS, and centrifugal spread via peripheral nerve to many tissues.[27, 48] After entering through a break in the skin, across a mucosal surface, or through the respiratory tract, virus replicates in muscle cells and in so doing infects the muscle spindle. It then infects the nerve that innervates the spindle and moves centrally within the axons of these neurons. Replication occurs in peripheral neurons, but not usually in glia, either peripheral or central. Virus is present in dorsal root ganglia within 60 to 72 hours of inoculation and before its arrival in spinal cord neurons, confirming its transport within sensory neurons.

Other studies suggest that the neuromuscular junction is also a major site of neuronal invasion,[49] and blocking acetylcholine receptors inhibits viral attachment.[50] Partial sequence homology exists between rabies virus glycoprotein and several snake neurotoxins binding to this receptor.[51]

Natural rabies infection appears to require a period of local viral replication, perhaps to increase the inoculum, before nervous system infection occurs. Timely administration of antirabies immunoglobulin and active immunization are able to prevent spread of the virus into the nervous system, thereby preventing disease. Once the virus has entered peripheral nerve, current therapeutic techniques do not prevent subsequent replication and spread, and it quickly moves centrally via retrograde axoplasmic flow.[52, 53] In contrast, herpes simplex virus and tetanus toxin make use of microtubular transport systems and therefore move much more rapidly.[54] After reaching the spinal cord, the rabies virus spreads throughout the CNS, following established patterns of synaptic connectivity.[55] Virtually every neuron is infected.[31]

After CNS infection, virus spreads to the rest of the body via peripheral nerves. The high concentration of virus in saliva results from viral shedding from sensory nerve endings in the oral mucosa[31] as well as replication in the salivary glands.

The mechanisms by which rabies damages the CNS are obscure, since pathologic evidence of neuronal necrosis is frequently minimal or absent. It may interfere with neurotransmission[56] and with endogenous opioid systems,[57] and the almost 30-fold increase in local nitric oxide production[58] suggests an excitotoxic mechanism. There is an inverse relationship between the concentration of G protein produced and the pathogenicity of different viral strains, and a monotonic relationship between pathogenicity and the induction of apoptosis.[59]

Pathology

The brain in furious rabies usually appears unremarkable grossly,[60] except for the vascular congestion. The microscopic pathologic appearance of rabies is typically an encephalitis with Negri bodies. However, not all autopsy specimens show the perivascular lymphocytic cuffing and necrosis that characterize encephalitis, and some cases appear histologically as meningitis.[61] Negri bodies are concentrated in hippocampal pyramidal cells, and less frequently in cortical neurons and cerebellar Purkinje cells.[60] They are round or oval, usually eosinophilic cytoplasmic inclusions between 1 and 7 μm across and contain viral nucleocapsids.[62] The acidophilic lyssa body is ultrastructurally identical to the Negri body.[63]

Paralytic rabies primarily affects the spinal cord, with severe inflammation and necrosis.[64] The brain stem is involved to a lesser extent. A few patients have cortical Negri bodies. Segmental demyelination occurs in the peripheral nerves, resembling acute inflammatory poly-neuropathy (the Guillain-Barré syndrome).

The systemic abnormality is most remarkable for the presence of myocarditis.[65] This cardiac disorder resembles the myocarditis that occurs in hypercatecholaminergic states such as pheochromocytoma, subarachnoid hemorrhage, and tetanus.[54] Negri bodies are found in the hearts of some patients, suggesting a direct viral role in this condition.[66] Atrial ganglioneuritis suggests that the virus reaches the myocardium via spread from the nervous system.[67]

Immune Responses

The immune response to natural rabies infection is insufficient to prevent disease. Rabies can produce immunosuppression,[68] and only a minority of unvaccinated patients develop a measurable antibody response.[69] Patients developing a cellular immune response tend to have the encephalitic (furious) form rather than the paralytic form and die faster than those who do not mount such a response.[70] Some investigators believe that interleukin-1 production in the CNS may explain the immunosuppressive effect of the virus.[71] The virus may persist in macrophages and may later emerge to produce disease.[72] This may explain some cases with very long incubation periods.

CLINICAL MANIFESTATIONS

Human Rabies

Several variables affect the risk of rabies and the rate of development of clinical disease after exposure to a rabid animal.[73] The viral inoculum is important, reflected by the relationship of the extent of exposure to the saliva to the rapidity of progression. A bite with prominent salivary contamination (e.g., through exposed skin) is more likely to produce rabies than one through thick clothing that removes saliva from the animal's teeth. Multiple bites are more likely to transmit the disease than a single bite. The location of the bite also influences the risk of rabies; bites on the face are more likely to result in disease than those on the extremities. Salivary contamination of a preexisting wound can transfer virus, as can exposure of mucous membranes or the respiratory tract to aerosolized virus.[74] Transmission between humans has been documented only in corneal transplantation.[75] One recipient received standard PET plus interferon and did not develop rabies.[76] The reported incubation period for rabies varies from a few days to more than 19 years, although 75% of patients become ill in the first 90 days after exposure.

The initial symptoms of rabies resemble those of other systemic viral infections, including fever, headache, malaise, and disorders of the upper respiratory and gastrointestinal tracts (Table 151–3).[77] Initial neurologic symptoms may include subtle changes in personality and cognition, and paresthesiae or pain near the exposure site. Rabies is rarely considered early in the differential diagnosis. In one series, physicians considered rabies in only 3 of 21 patients on their first visit, despite an exposure history in many.[77] The prodrome typically lasts about 4 days, but up to 10 days may elapse before more specific symptoms and signs supervene.[78]

Myoedema (mounding of part of the muscle struck with a reflex hammer, which then disappears in a few seconds) is present during the prodrome and persists throughout the disease.[79]

Human rabies infections are divided into two forms: *furious* (or *encephalitic*) and *paralytic* (or *dumb*). The furious form presents with the hydrophobia, delirium, and agitation that form the common picture of rabies. About a fifth of patients present with the paralytic form and have little clinical evidence of cerebral involvement until late in their course. The spinal cord and brain stem bear the brunt of the illness in the paralytic form. The pathogenetic distinction between the two types of rabies is unclear; it does not appear to be based on virologic or antigenic differences.[80] In either form, the symptomatic

TABLE 151–3 Durations of Different Stages of Rabies

Stage	Type (% of Cases)	Duration (% of Cases)	Associated Findings
Incubation period		<30 d (25) 30–90 d (50) 90 d to 1 y (20) >1 yr (5)	None
Prodrome and early symptoms		2–10 d	Paresthesias or pain at wound site; fever; malaise; anorexia; nausea and vomiting
Acute neurologic disease	Furious rabies (80)	2–7 d	Hallucinations; bizarre behavior; anxiety; agitation; biting; hydrophobia; autonomic dysfunction; syndrome of inappropriate antidiuretic hormone
	Paralytic rabies (20)	2–7 d	Ascending flaccid paralysis
Coma		0–14 d	
Death*			

*Rare recoveries have been reported.
Data from ref. 66.

course usually runs 2 to 14 days before coma supervenes. Death occurs an average of 18 days after the onset of symptoms but the range is broad.[77] Intensive support can prolong survival by about 50%.[81]

Furious Rabies

Hydrophobia is the symptom most identified with furious rabies. Sir William Gowers provides a seminal description of hydrophobia and its sequelae, including:[82]

> *. . .Some discomfort about the throat, an occasional sense of choking, or a little difficulty in swallowing liquids. . . . The attempt to drink occasions some spasm in the pharynx, which increases in the course of a few hours, and spreads to the muscles of respiration, causing a short, quick inspiration, a "catch in the breath. . . ." This increases in severity to a strong inspiratory effort, in which the extraordinary muscles of respiration, sternomastoid, scaleni, etc., and even the facial muscles, take part; the shoulders are raised, and the angles of the mouth drawn outwards. As the intensity of the spasm increases, so does the readiness with which it is excited. It may be caused by the mere contact of water with the lips, and a state of cutaneous hyperæsthesia develops, so that various impressions, such as a draught of air, which normally excite a respiratory effort, bring on the spasm. The mere movement of air caused by raising the bedclothes may be sufficient. The patient is often unable to swallow the saliva, which is usually abundant and viscid, so that it hangs about the mouth and is expelled with difficulty. . . . Vomiting is common. . . . The attacks of spasm are very distressing to the patient; the mental state which they occasion increases the readiness with which they are produced; and in some cases the mere sight of water or the sound of dropping water will cause an attack. It may even be excited by visual impressions which cause a similar sensation, as the reflection from a looking glass, or even a strong light. The sufferer's horror and dread of these excitants becomes intense. Thus the disturbance in the act of swallowing liquids, which constitutes . . . the first symptom and keynote of the disease, spreads, on the one hand, to mental disturbance, and on the other to extensive muscular spasm. In each of these directions further symptoms develop. The spasm, at first confined to the muscles of deglutition and respiration, spreads to the other muscles of the body, and the paroxysms, at first respiratory, afterwards become general, and assume a convulsive character, although still excited by the same causes. The convulsions may consist of general muscular rigidity, sometimes tetanoid in character, with actual opisthotonus. . . . Actual delusions occasionally supervene, and there may even be wild delirium. The mental derangement is most intense during the paroxysms of spasms, and the frenzied patient may spit his saliva at those about him, and often attempts to bite them with his teeth, making occasional strange sounds in his throat which have been thought to resemble the barking of a dog.*

Hydrophobia represents an exaggerated irritant reflex of the respiratory tract, possibly arising from the nucleus ambiguus.[83] Other findings include episodic hyperactivity, seizures, and aerophobia. Hyperventilation is frequently present. Along with coma, evidence of pituitary dysfunction often develops, especially disordered water balance (either inappropriate antidiuresis or diabetes insipidus). Hyperventilation gives way to forms of periodic and ataxic respiration,[83] and eventually apnea supervenes. Cardiac arrhythmias are common, predominantly supraventricular tachycardias and bradycardias, reflecting either brain stem dysfunction or myocarditis.[84] Autonomic dysfunction is common, including pupillary dilation, anisocoria, piloerection, markedly increased salivation and sweating, and, rarely, priapism[85] or spontaneous ejaculation.[86]

With the exception of some rare reports, patients entering coma generally die within 1 to 2 weeks despite maximal supportive care. Furious rabies patients who receive maximal intensive care support and survive for a longer-than-expected period appear to pass into the paralytic phase before death.[81]

TABLE 151–4 Susceptibility of Various Animal Species to Rabies

Very High	High	Moderate	Low
Wolves	Hamsters	Dogs	Opossums
Foxes	Skunks	Primates	
Coyotes	Raccoons		
Kangaroo rats	Domestic cats		
Cotton rats	Rabbits		
Jackals	Bats		
Voles	Cattle		

Data from ref. 89.

Paralytic ("Dumb") Rabies

In contrast to the furious form, paralytic rabies patients lack hydrophobia, aerophobia, hyperactivity, or seizures. Their initial findings suggest an ascending paralysis, resembling acute inflammatory polyneuropathy (the Guillain-Barré syndrome), or a symmetric quadriparesis. Weakness may be more severe in the extremity where the virus was introduced. Meningeal signs (headache, neck stiffness) may be prominent despite a normal sensorium. As the disease progresses, the patient becomes confused and then declines into coma.

Nonneurologic Findings

In addition to the cardiac arrhythmias mentioned earlier, the systemic complications of rabies are similar to those of other critically ill patients. The virus disseminates to many organs, but proof of its role in other organ dysfunction is lacking. Hypotension is usually due to volume depletion but may reflect brain stem involvement. Gastrointestinal disturbances include bleeding, vomiting, diarrhea, and ileus.[87] Death is usually due to myocarditis, with cardiac arrhythmia or congestive heart failure as mechanisms.[88]

Animal Rabies

A complete description of the behavioral effects of rabies in all the species that may be infected is beyond the scope of this text. World Health Organization studies have established a crude ranking of rabies susceptibility, which is summarized in Table 151–4.[89]

Descriptions of the behavioral changes of rabid animals are available elsewhere.[90, 75]

DIAGNOSIS

General

The diagnosis of rabies poses little difficulty in a nonimmunized patient presenting with hydrophobia after a bite by a known rabid animal. The presentation in areas in which domestic animals are immunized is seldom this straightforward. During the incubation period, no diagnostic studies in the patient are useful; recognition of an exposure to a potentially rabid animal should prompt prophylactic treatment. When symptoms begin, standard laboratory testing does not reliably distinguish rabies from other encephalitides. The cerebrospinal fluid (CSF) is abnormal in a minority, with a lymphocytic pleocytosis (5 to 30 cells mm^3), a normal glucose level, and a modest protein level elevation (less than 100 mg/dl).[91] Imaging studies, although rarely reported, are typically normal[92] unless hypoxia has intervened.

Direct fluorescent antibody staining of biopsy or necropsy (animal or human) tissue remains the standard for the diagnosis of rabies. In humans, the procedure of choice is direct fluorescent antibody analysis of a skin biopsy obtained from the nape of the neck, above the hairline.[93] The virus tends to localize in hair follicles. During the first week of symptoms, about 50% of samples reveal rabies virus, with an increasing percentage thereafter.[94] The reverse transcriptase–polymerase chain reaction test is emerging as the diagnostic procedure of choice in suspected rabies, especially in human cases.[95] This test can be performed on CSF or saliva of patients, or on tissue. The reverse transcriptase–polymerase chain reaction test allows more specific determination of the geographic and host species origin of a particular rabies virus.[96, 97] It can be successfully performed on decomposed brain material,[98] a situation in which older techniques failed.[99] The older corneal impression test[100] is no longer in common use.

The rapid fluorescent focus inhibition test is a serologic test for neutralizing antirabies antibody.[101] A few untreated patients have detectable antibody by day 6 of clinical illness, 50% by day 8, and usually 100% by day 15. Any CSF levels are diagnostically valuable, even in patients who have received PET. CSF may also be examined for the presence of specific oligoclonal bands not found in the serum as a method of confirming CNS infection.[102]

Differential Diagnosis

When furious rabies is considered, the major differential consideration is another viral encephalitis. In the absence of exposure to a rabid animal, and if hydrophobia and hyperactivity are not prominent, it may be difficult to distinguish among these possibilities.[103] Since the CSF and electroencephalographic findings in rabies may mimic those of herpes simplex encephalitis, some patients receive empirical therapy with acyclovir while awaiting a more secure diagnosis (e.g., polymerase chain reaction).

Tetanus is occasionally confused with rabies, because opisthotonic posturing may be seen in either.[54] However, the other symptoms of rabies, such as hydrophobia, are not seen in tetanus, and the CSF and electroencephalogram are normal in tetanus. Strychnine poisoning should be considered and may be excluded by laboratory testing.

Paralytic rabies may resemble acute inflammatory polyneuropathy, transverse myelitis, or poliomyelitis. Electromyographic studies may be useful in the distinction of rabies from polyneuropathy. In transverse myelitis, pain at the level of the lesion may be helpful, as may the finding of a high T-2 signal lesion. A sensory level is characteristic of transverse myelitis, whereas in rabies sensory function is typically normal.[84] Fever usually precedes weakness in poliomyelitis, and the resolution of fever with the onset of neurologic findings favors this diagnosis. A history of poliomyelitis immunization should be sought.

The sometimes prolonged incubation period of rabies recalls the slow infections of the CNS caused by conventional viruses (e.g., progressive multifocal leukoencephalopathy).[104] However, rabies requires neither a defect in host immunity nor a mutation in the virus to produce disease, distinguishing it from the agents in this group. Spongiform changes in brain tissue in rabies[105] may resemble those of the prion diseases.[106]

Although CNS reactions to the rabies vaccines available in developed countries are exceptionally rare, patients receiving older vaccine forms containing myelin determinants occasionally develop acute disseminated encephalomyelitis (ADEM; also called postvaccinial encephalomyelitis; see "Prophylaxis," later). ADEM is a syndrome with many precipitants other than rabies vaccine. ADEM resembles encephalitis, or occasionally presents as a mass lesion resembling a brain abscess. It typically begins 10 to 14 days after vaccine exposure, which would constitute an unusually brief incubation period for rabies. In the absence of viral isolation, a high rapid fluorescent focus inhibition test titer in spinal fluid is evidence for rabies rather than ADEM even in patients who have been immunized,[107] as is a positive reverse transcriptase–polymerase chain reaction test. ADEM produces high-T2 lesions visible by magnetic resonance imaging.[108]

Patients potentially exposed to rabies may develop a psychological reaction termed *rabies hysteria.*[109] They may refuse to attempt to drink water; in contrast, the patient with rabies, at least initially, attempts to drink but is halted by pharyngeal spasms.

PREVENTION

Prophylaxis

Although the control of animal rabies is central to the prevention of human disease, few nations have eliminated it, and these usually maintain quarantine procedures lest the disease reappear. Therefore, prophylactic procedures (for domestic animals and selected humans) and PET for humans remain essential. Prophylaxis for cats and dogs in many countries is required by law; in the United States, the use of 1- or 3-year vaccines is permitted, although only the 3-year vaccines are recommended.[110] Vaccination should be performed or supervised by a veterinarian; improper administration can lead to a lack of immunity.[111] Measurement of animal seroconversion rates may be considered to ensure protection,[112] and immunization of livestock is recommended in areas of increasing rabies prevalence.

Vaccination of wild animals is an effective public health measure.[113] The use of vaccines effective after ingestion allows immunization of wild animals.[114] An intensive 4-year campaign in Belgium nearly eliminated rabies from the fox population.[115] This approach may also be effective in dogs.[116] Veterinary vaccines cost about $0.50 per dose in the United States. In contrast, Semple-type (grown in sheep brain cultures) human vaccines cost about $5 per course; Vero cell vaccine in France about $160 per course; and human diploid cell vaccine in the United States more than $500 per course.[117]

Preexposure prophylaxis is confined to people with a relatively high risk of rabies exposure, such as veterinarians, laboratory workers using rabies virus, spelunkers, and people planning to visit countries of high dog rabies prevalence in which access to appropriate medical care is limited. Current recommendations for international travelers are available at the Centers for Disease Control and Prevention web site (http://www.cdc.gov/epo/mmwr/mmwr_rr.html). A series of three intramuscular or intradermal injections (days zero, 7, and 21 or 28) is sufficient; antibody response determination is not required in normal hosts. Booster doses every 2 to 3 years are usually recommended for individuals frequently at risk of exposure. An adequate antibody response is generally considered to be complete neutralization at the 1:5 level by rapid fluorescent focus inhibition test, which is equivalent to the 0.5 IU/ml concentration suggested by the World Health Organization.

Postexposure Treatment

The cornerstone of rabies prevention is wound care, potentially reducing the risk of rabies by 90%.[118] Thorough washing with a 20% soap solution is as effective as the formerly recommended quaternary ammonium compounds.[119] Irrigation with a virucidal agent such as povidone-iodine is advisable.[120] After wound care, the clinician must decide whether to institute passive or active immunization. Prompt consultation with public health officials is advised, because this decision is based on the current incidence of rabies in the animal species involved in the exposure.[121] Recommendations according to the type of animal species and type of exposure involved are presented in Table 151–5.[122] The most recent recommendations of the Advisory Committee on Immunization Practices for adminstration of PET are presented in Table 151–6.[122]

A healthy dog or cat in countries of low prevalence who has bitten, or otherwise transferred saliva to, a human is observed for 10 days. If the animal's behavior remains normal, the patient need not receive PET beyond proper wound care. If the animal's behavior changes, it should undergo immediate pathologic examination for evidence of rabies infection. If infection is confirmed, there is adequate time to institute PET. Wild mammal exposure, especially if the

TABLE 151–5 Rabies Postexposure Prophylaxis Guide—United States, 1999

Animal Type	Evaluation and Disposition of Animal	Postexposure Prophylaxis Recommendations
Dogs, cats, and ferrets	Healthy and available for 10 days' observation	Persons should not begin prophylaxis unless animal develops clinical signs of rabies*
	Rabid or suspected rabid	Immediately vaccinate
	Unknown (e.g., escaped)	Consult public health officials
Skunks, raccoons, foxes, and most other carnivores; bats	Regarded as rabid unless animal proved negative by laboratory tests†	Consider immediate vaccination
Livestock, small rodents, lagomorphs (rabbits and hares), large rodents (woodchucks and beavers), and other mammals	Consider individually	Consult public health officials Bites of squirrels, hamsters, guinea pigs, gerbils, chipmunks, rats, mice, other small rodents, rabbits, and hares almost never require antirabies postexposure prophylaxis

*During the 10-day observation period, begin postexposure prophylaxis at the first sign of rabies in a dog, cat, or ferret that has bitten someone. If the animal exhibits clinical signs of rabies, it should be euthanized immediately and tested.
†The animal should be euthanized and tested as soon as possible. Holding for observation is not recommended. Discontinue vaccine if immunofluorescence test results of the animal are negative.
From Advisory Committee on Immunization Practices. Rabies prevention—United States, 1999: Recommendations of the Immunization Practices Advisory Committee (ACIP). MMWR. 1999;48. Available at ftp://ftp.cdc.gov/pub/Publications/mmwr/rr/rr4801.pdf.

animal exhibits uncharacteristic behavior, warrants PET in most circumstances. If the animal is available for pathologic examination, and pathologic examination of the brain does not indicate the presence of rabies virus, PET may be discontinued. An algorithm for the approach to PET is presented in Figure 151–4. PET appears safe in pregnant women and should not be withheld when an indication exists.[123]

Rabies immune globulin is available in human and equine forms (pooled antiserum of equine origin and purified antirabies serum of equine origin). These immune globulins are purified from the sera of hyperimmunized donors. Two human preparations are available in the United States: Imogam Rabies-HT (Pasteur-Mérieux) and BayRab (Bayer). Human rabies immune globulin is given in a dose of 20 IU/kg. Previous recommendations called for half of the dose to be injected in the vicinity of the wound, and the remainder injected intramuscularly in the gluteal region. However, the most recent World Health Organization and Centers for Disease Control and Prevention recommendations call for the entire dose to be infiltrated into the wound if anatomically feasible.[122, 124] The recommended dose of purified antirabies serum of equine origin is 40 IU/kg. Failure to infiltrate wounds with rabies immune globulin, or surgical closure of wounds before immune globulin infiltration, has been associated with the development of rabies in patients despite otherwise proper PET.[125]

Many different forms of rabies vaccine have been produced since Pasteur's original success in 1882. In some developing nations, Semple-type vaccine is still employed, but it carries a risk of central and peripheral neurologic complications in the range of 1 in 200 to 1 in 1600 vaccinees.[78] The production of vaccine in sheep CNS, a common method of Semple-type vaccine production, also carries the theoretical risk of transmitting the scrapie prion.[126] Suckling mouse brain vaccine is effective and safer, with a neurologic complication rate of approximating 1 in 8000.

The currently available vaccines for human use in the United States include human diploid cell vaccine (Imovax Rabies), vaccine grown in rhesus monkey diploid cell cultures (rabies vaccine, adsorbed), and purified chick embryo cell vaccine (Rab Avert). These vaccines are remarkably safe and immunogenic. Local reactions (pain, swelling, or induration) are common, but systemic complaints (fever, headache, malaise, nausea, abdominal pain, or adenopathy) occur in a minority of patients. Serious reactions have been exceedingly rare, with the Guillain-Barré syndrome reported very rarely.[127] To report a vaccine reaction, one should call the appropriate number: for human diploid cell vaccine, Connaught Laboratories, Inc., at 800-VACCINE; for rabies vaccine, adsorbed, the BioPort Corporation at 517-335-8120; and for purified chich embryo cell vaccine, Chiron Corporation at 800-244-7668. Corticosteroids should only be given to patients experiencing a life-threatening vaccine reaction, because they interfere with the development of immunity. Immunocompromised patients may not respond adequately to vaccination, and antibody titers should be measured 2 to 4 weeks after immunization.[122]

In other countries, other PET vaccines (e.g., vaccines grown in chick embryos or Vero cell cultures)[128] and regimens are often employed. Consultation with the rabies officer of the state health department may be helpful for the management of patients in whom

TABLE 151–6 Rabies Postexposure Prophylaxis Schedule—United States, 1999

Vaccination Status	Treatment	Regimen*
Not previously vaccinated	Wound cleansing	All postexposure treatment should begin with immediate thorough cleansing of all wounds with soap and water. If available, virucidal agent such as povidone-iodine solution should be used to irrigate wounds.[73]
	RIG	Administer 20 IU/kg body weight. If anatomically feasible, *full dose* should be infiltrated around the wounds and any remaining volume should be administered IM at anatomic site distant from vaccine administration. Also, RIG should not be administered in same syringe as vaccine. Because RIG might partially suppress active production of antibody, no more than recommended dose should be given.
	Vaccine	HDCV, RVA, or PCEC 1 ml, IM (deltoid area†), one each on days 0‡, 3, 7, 14, and 28.
Previously vaccinated§	Wound cleansing	All postexposure treatment should begin with immediate thorough cleansing of all wounds with soap and water. If available, virucidal agent such as povidone-iodine solution should be used to irrigate wounds.[73]
	RIG	RIG should *not* be administered.
	Vaccine	HDCV, RVA, or PCEC 1 ml, IM (deltoid area†), one each on days 0‡ and 3.

*These regimens are applicable for all age groups, including children.
†The deltoid area is the only acceptable site of vaccination for adults and older children. For younger children, the outer aspect of the thigh may be used. Vaccine should never be administered in the gluteal area.
‡Day 0 is the day the first dose of vaccine is administered.
§Any person with a history of preexposure vaccination with HDCV, RVA or PCEC; prior postexposure prophylaxis with HDCV, RVA, or PCEC; or previous vaccination with any other type of rabies vaccine and a documented history of antibody response to the prior vaccination.
Abbreviations: HDCV, Human diploid cell vaccine; PCEC, purified chick embryo cell vaccine; RIG, rabies immune globulin; RVA, rabies vaccine adsorbed.
From Advisory Committee on Immunization Practices. Rabies prevention—United States, 1999: Recommendations of The Immunization Practices Advisory Committee (ACIP). MMWR Morb Mortal Wkly Rep. 1999;48. Available at ftp://ftp.cdc.gov/pub/Publications/mmwr/rr/rr4801.pdf.

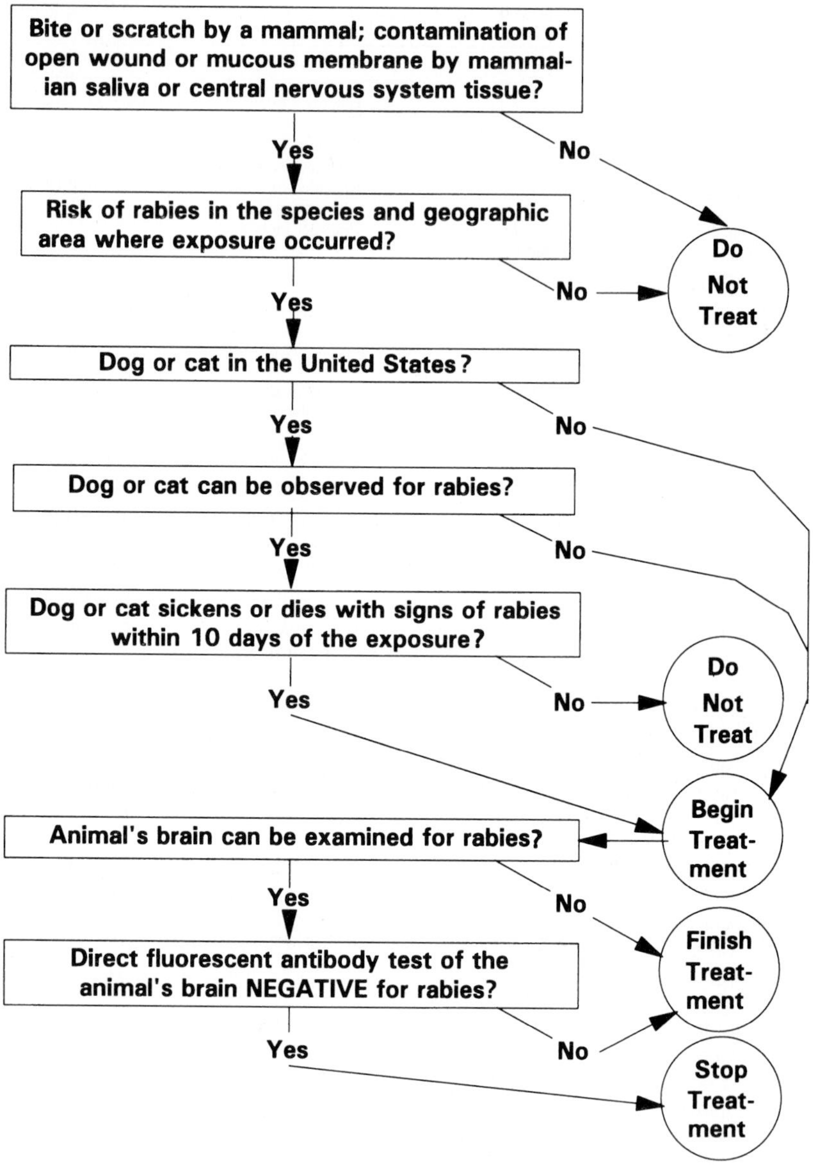

FIGURE 151–4. Algorithm for human rabies postexposure prophylaxis. In highly suspect animals, treatment should be started immediately and discontinued if fluorescent antibody test results of the animal brain are negative. In some cases when the risk is low, treatment may be delayed for up to 48 hours pending the result of fluorescent antibody testing. (From Fishbein DB, Bernard KW. Rabies virus. In:Mandell GL, Bennett JL, Dolin R, eds. Principles and Practice of Infectious Diseases. 4th ed. New York: Churchill Livingstone; 1995:1527.)

PET has been initiated with a vaccine not approved for use in the United States.

The usual dose of human diploid cell vaccine or rabies vaccine, adsorbed, for postexposure prophylaxis is 1 ml intramuscularly on the day of exposure (or as soon as possible thereafter), repeated on days 3, 7, 14, and 28. Other schedules are available for use; physicians not familiar with their use should consult local public health authorities and review the most recent World Health Organization and Centers for Disease Control and Prevention recommendations.[122, 124] The varying immunogenicity of different regimens, and their interaction with the response to immune globulin,[129] raises the possibility of treatment failure if the recommendations are not carefully followed. If possible, the vaccine should be administered in the deltoid muscle. Gluteal injections, which may miss the muscle, have been associated with some vaccine failures. In small children, the vaccine may be given in the lateral thigh. The vaccine must not be given in the same region as the immune globulin. Intradermal vaccine administration (0.1 ml) was previously only recommended for preexposure prophylaxis, but in 1996 the World Health Organization recommended it as an alternative for PET. Patients who have been previously vaccinated receive 1 ml intramuscularly on days zero and 3 only, without rabies immune globulin.

A single case of a transient false-positive enzyme-linked immunosorbent assay for human immunodeiciency virus after human diploid cell vaccine immunization was reported in 1994.[130] Subsequent screening of samples from 50 patients recently immunized against rabies revealed no similar cases,[131] but in view of similar phenomena with other vaccines, physicians should be aware of this possibility.

Personnel caring for rabies patients should practice standard universal and respiratory precautions. In addition, they should receive a preexposure immunization sequence and maintain a serum antirabies antibody titer of 0.5 IU/ml.[132] Exposures to potentially contaminated secretions or tissues should lead to standard PET.

TREATMENT

There is no established, specific treatment for rabies once symptoms have begun. Despite excellent intensive care, almost all patients succumb to the disease or its complications within a few weeks of onset. The three patients in the 1970s who survived, two of whom made apparently complete recoveries,[133–135] represent very unusual occurrences. Each of these patients had undergone some form of PET, and it seems likely that this treatment modified their course. Another case with partial recovery was reported in 1994 in a child who received rabies vaccine without immune globulin.[102] Trials of many agents have been undertaken in clinical rabies, including interferons, interferon-inducing agents, ribavirin, and cytosine arabinoside, without beneficial effects.[132]

REFERENCES

1. Meslin F-X, Fishbein DB, Matter HC. Rationale and prospects for rabies elimination in developing countries. In: Rupprecht CE, Dietzschold B, Koprowski H, eds. Lyssaviruses. Berlin: Springer-Verlag; 1994:1–26.
2. Baer GM. Rabies — an historical perspective. Infect Agents Dis. 1994;3:168–180.
3. Fleming G. Rabies and hydrophobia. London: Chapman & Hall; 1872:7.
4. Blancou J, Aubert MFA, Artois M. Fox rabies. In: Baer GM, ed. The Natural History of Rabies. 2nd ed. Boca Raton, Fla: CRC Press; 1991:257–290.
5. Baer GM. Vampire bat and bovine paralytic rabies. In: Baer GM, ed. The Natural History of Rabies 2nd ed. Boca Raton Fla: CRC Press; 1991:389–403.
6. Rupprecht CE, Smith JS, Fekadu M, Childs JE. The ascension of wildlife rabies: A cause for public health concern or intervention? Emerging Infect Dis. 1995;1:107–114.
7. Negri A. Zur Aetiologie der Tollwuth. Die Diagnose der Tollwuth auf Grund der neuen Befunde. Z Hyg Infectionskr 1903;44:519–540.
8. Goldwasser RA, Kissling RE. Fluorescent antibody staining of street and fixed rabies virus antigens. Proc Soc Exp Biol Med. 1958;98:219–223.
9. Reif JS, Webb PA, Monath TP, et al. Epizootic vesicular stomatitis in Colorado, 1982: Infection in occupational risk groups. Am J Trop Med Hyg. 1987;36:17–82.
10. Stoeckle MY. Rhabdoviridae. In: Mandell GM, Bennett JE, Dolin R, eds. Principles and Practice of Infectious Diseases. New York: Churchill Livingstone; 1994:1526–1527.
11. Wunner WH. The chemical composition and molecular structure of rabies viruses. In: Baer GM, ed. The natural history of rabies. 2nd ed. Boca Raton, Fla: CRC Press; 1991:31–67.
12. Sokol F, Schlumberger HD, Wiktor TK, et al. Biochemical and biophysical studies on the nucleocapsid and on the RNA of rabies virus. Virology. 1969;38:651–665.
13. Dietzschold B, Rupprecht CE, Fu ZF, Koprowski H. Rhabdoviruses. In: Fields BN, Knipe DM, Howley PM, et al, eds. Fields Virology. 3rd ed. Philadelphia: Lippincott-Raven; 1996:1137–1159.
14. Tordo N, Poch O, Ermine A, et al. Walking along the rabies genome: Is the large G-L intergenic region a remnant gene? Proc Natl Acad Sci U S A 1986;83:3914–3918.
15. Bleck TP, Rupprecht CE. Rabies. In: Richman DD, Whitley RJ, Hayden FG, eds. Clinical Virology. New York: Churchill Livingstone; 1997:879–897.
16. Yang J, Koprowski H, Dietzschold B, Fu ZF. Phosphorylation of rabies virus nucleoprotein regulates viral RNA transcription and replication by modulating leader RNA encapsidation. J Virol. 1999;73:1661–1664.
17. Goto H, Minimoto N, Ito H, et al. Expression of the nucleoprotein of rabies virus in *Escherichia coli* and mapping of antigenic sites. Arch Virol. 1995;140:1061–1074.
18. Blumberg BM, Giorgi C, Kolakofsky D. N protein of vesicular stomatitis virus selectively encapsidates leader RNA in vitro. Cell. 1983;32:559–567.
19. Tordo N, Poch O, Ermine A, et al. Completion of the rabies virus genome sequence determination: Highly conserved domains among the L (polymerase) proteins of unsegmented negative-strand RNA viruses. Virology. 1988;165:565–576.
20. Levy JA, Fraenkel-Conrat H, Owens RA. Virology. Englewood Cliffs, NJ: Prentice-Hall; 1994:77–85.
21. Coll JM. The glycoprotein G of rhabdoviruses. Arch Virol. 1995;140:827–851.
22. Mebatsion T, Weiland F, Conzelmann KK. Matrix protein of rabies virus is responsible for the assembly and budding of bullet-shaped particles and interacts with the transmembrane spike glycoprotein G. J Virol. 1999;73:242–250.
23. Rupprecht CE, Dietzschold B, Wunner WH, Koprowski H. Antigenic relationships of lyssaviruses. In: Baer GM, ed. The Natural History of Rabies. 2nd ed. Boca Raton: CRC; 1991:69–100.
24. Seif I, Coulon P, Rollin PE, Flamand A. Rabies virulence: Effect on pathogenicity and sequence characterization of rabies virus mutations affecting antigenic site III of the glycoprotein. J Virol. 1985;53:926–934.
25. Morimoto K, Ni Y-J, Kawai A. Syncytium formation is induced in the murine neuroblastoma cell cultures which produce pathogenic G proteins of the rabies virus. Virology. 1992;189:203–216.
26. Otvos L, Krivulka GR, Urge L, et al. Comparison of the effects of amino acid substitutions and the β-*N*- vs α-*O*-glycosylation on the T-cell stimulatory activity and conformation of an epitope on the rabies virus glycoprotein. Biochim Biophys Acta. 1995;1267:55–64.
27. Kawai A, Morimoto K. Functional aspects of lyssavirus proteins. In: Rupprecht CE, Dietzschold B, Koprowski H eds. Lyssaviruses. Berlin: Springer-Verlag; 1994: 27–42.
28. Thoulouze MI, Lafage M, Schachner M, et al. The neural cell adhesion molecule is a receptor for rabies virus. J Virol. 1998;72:7181–7190.
29. Burrage TG, Tignor GH, Smith AL. Rabies virus binding at neuromuscular junctions. *Virus Res.* 1985;2:273–289.
30. Gosztonyi G. Reproduction of lyssaviruses: Ultrastructural composition of lyssaviruses and functional aspects of pathogenesis. In: Rupprecht CE, Dietzschold B, Koprowski H, eds. Lyssaviruses. Berlin: Springer-Verlag; 1994:43–68.
31. Murphy FA, Bauer SP, Harrison AK, Winn WC. Comparative pathogenesis of rabies and rabies-like viruses. Infection of the central nervous system and centrifugal spread to peripheral tissues. Lab Invest. 1973;29:1–16.
32. World Health Organization. World Survey of Rabies No. 32 for the Year 1996. Geneva: World Health Organization; 1998. Available at http://www.who.int/emc-documents/rabies/whoemczdi984c.html.
33. Speare R, Skerratt L, Foster R, et al. Australian bat lyssavirus infection in three fruit bats from north Queensland. Commun Dis Intell. 1997;21:117–120.
34. Samaratunga H, Searle JW, Hudson N. Non-rabies Lyssavirus human encephalitis from fruit bats: Australian bat Lyssavirus (pteropid Lyssavirus) infection. Neuropathol Appl Neurobiol. 1998;24:331–335.
35. Torvaldsen S, Watson T. Rabies prophylaxis in Western Australia: The impact of Australian bat lyssavirus. Commun Dis Intell. 1998;22:149–152.
36. Turner GS. A review of the world epidemiology of rabies. Trans R Soc Trop Med Hyg. 1976;70:175–178.
37. Meslin F-X, Fishbein DB, Matter HC. Rationale and prospects for rabies elimination in developing countries. In: Rupprecht CE, Dietzschold B, Koprowski H, eds. Lyssaviruses. Berlin: Springer-Verlag; 1994:1–26.
38. Human rabies—Virginia, 1998. MMWR Morb Mortal Wkly Rep. 1999;48:95–97.
39. Rupprecht CE, Smith JS. Raccoon rabies: The re-emergence of an epizootic in a densely populated area. Semin Virol. 1994;5:155–164.
40. Centers for Disease Control. Extension of the raccoon rabies epizootic—United States, 1992. MMWR 1992;41:661–664.
41. Kreindel SM, McGuill M, Meltzer M, et al. The cost of rabies postexposure prophylaxis: One state's experience. Public Health Rep. 1998;113:247–251.
42. Clark KA, Neill SU, Smith JS, et al. Epizootic canine rabies transmitted by coyotes in south Texas. J Am Vet Med Assoc. 1994;204:536–540.
43. Krebs JW, Strine TW, Smith JS, et al. Rabies surveillance in the United States during 1994. J Am Vet Med Assoc. 1995;297:1562–1575.
44. Childs JE, Trimarchi CV, Krebs JW. The epidemiology of bat rabies in New York State, 1988–92. Epidemiol Infect. 1994; 113:501–511.
45. Centers for Disease Control and Prevention. Human rabies—Connecticut, 1995. MMWR. 1996;45:207–209.
46. Centers for Disease Control and Prevention. Human rabies—Alabama, Tennessee, and Texas, 1994. MMWR Morb Mortal Wkly Rep. 1995;44:269–272.
47. Schmida TO. Resurgence of rabies. Arch Pediatr Adolesc Med. 1995;149:1043.
48. Murphy FA, Bauer SP, Harrison AK, Winn WC. Comparative pathogenesis of rabies and rabies-like viruses. Virus infection and transit from inoculation site to the central nervous system. Lab Invest. 1973;28:361–376.
49. Watson HD, Tignor GH, Smith AL. Entry of rabies virus into the peripheral nerves of mice. J Gen Virol. 1981;56:371–382.
50. Lentz TL, Burrage TG, Smith AL, et al. Is the acetylcholine receptor a rabies virus receptor? Science. 1982;215:182–184.
51. Lentz TL, Wilson PT, Hawrot E, Speicher DW. Amino acid sequence similarity between rabies virus glycoprotein and snake venom curaremimetic neurotoxins. Science 1984;226:847–848.
52. Ceccaldi PE, Gillet JP, Tsiang H. Inhibition of the transport of rabies virus in the central nervous system. J Neuropathol Exp Neurol. 1989;48:620–630.
53. Tsiang H. Pathogenesis of rabies virus infection of the nervous system. In: Maramorsch K, Murphy FA, Shatkin AJ. eds. Advances in virus research. v. 42. New York: Academic; 1992:375–412.
54. Bleck TP, Brauner JS. Tetanus. In: Scheld WM, Whitley RJ, Durack DT, eds. Infections of the central nervous system. 2nd ed. New York: Raven; 1997: 629–653.
55. Ugolini G. Specificity of rabies virus as a transneuronal tracer of motor networks: Transfer from hypoglossal motoneurons to connected second-order and higher order central nervous system cell groups. J Comp Neurol. 1995;356:457–480.
56. Charlton KM. The pathogenesis of rabies and other lyssaviral infections: Recent studies. In: Rupprecht CE, Dietzschold B, Koprowski H, eds. Lyssaviruses. Berlin: Springer-Verlag; 1994:95–119.
57. Koschel K, Munzel P. Inhibition of opiate receptor-mediated signal transmission by rabies virus in persistently infected NG-108-15 mouse neuroblastoma–rat glioma hybrid cells. Proc Natl Acad Sci U S A. 1984;81:950–954.
58. Hooper DC, Ohnishi ST, Kean R, et al. Local nitric oxide production in viral and autoimmune diseases of the central nervous system. Proc Natl Acad Sci U S A. 1995;92:5312–5316.
59. Morimoto K, Hooper DC, Spitsin S, et al. Pathogenicity of different rabies virus variants inversely correlates with apoptosis and rabies virus glycoprotein expression in infected primary neuron cultures. J Virol. 1999;73:510–518.
60. Esiri MM, Kennedy PGE. Virus diseases. In: Adams JH, Duchen LW, eds. Greenfield's neuropathology. New York: Oxford University Press; 1992:335–399.
61. Dupont JR, Earle KM. Human rabies encephalitis. A study of forty-nine fatal cases with a review of the literature. Neurology. 1965; 15:1023–1034.
62. De Brito T, Araujo MD, Tiriba A. Ultrastructure of the Negri body in human rabies. J Neurol Sci. 1973;20:363–372.
63. Sung JH, Hayano M, Mastri AR, Okagaki T. A case of human rabies and ultrastructure of the Negri body. J Neuropathol Exp Neurol. 1976; 35:541–559.
64. Chopra JS, Banerjee AK, Murthy JMK, Pal SR. Paralytic rabies: A clinicopathologic study. Brain. 1980; 103:789–802.
65. Cohen SL, Gardner S, Lanyi C, et al. A case of rabies in man: Some problems of diagnosis and management. BMJ. 1976; 1:1041–1042.
66. Fishbein DB. Rabies in humans. In: Baer GM, ed. The Natural History of Rabies. 2nd ed. Boca Raton, Fla: CRC Press; 1991:519–549.
67. Metze K, Feiden W. Rabies virus ribonucleoprotein in the heart. N Engl J Med. 1991;324:1814–1815.
68. Wiktor TJ, Doherty PC, Koprowski H. Suppression of cell mediated immunity by street rabies virus. J Exp Med. 1977;145:1617–1622.

69. Kasempimolporn S, Hemachuda T, Khawplod P, Manatsathit S. Human immune response to rabies nucleocapsid and glycoprotein antigens. Clin Exp Immunol. 1991;84:195–199.
70. Hemachuda T, Phanuphak P, Sriwanthana B. Immunologic study of human encephalitic and paralytic rabies. A preliminary study of 16 patients. Am J Med. 1988;84:673–677.
71. Haour F, Marquette C, Ban E, et al. Receptors for interleukin-1 in the central nervous system and neuroendocrine systems. Ann Endocrinol (Paris). 1995;56:173–179.
72. Ray NB, Ewalt LC, Lodmell DL. Rabies virus replication in primary murine bone marrow macrophages and in human and murine macrophage-like cell lines: Implications for viral persistence. J Virol. 1995;69:764–772.
73. Whitley RJ, Middlebrooks M. Rabies. In: Scheld WM, Whitley RJ, Durack DT, eds. Infections of the central nervous system. New York: Raven; 1991:127–144.
74. Constantine DG. Rabies Transmission by Air in Bat Caves. Washington, DC: United States Public Health Service; 1967.
75. Bleck TP, Rupprecht CE. Rabies. In: Richman DD, Whitley RJ, Hayden FG, eds, Clinical Virology. New York: Churchill Livingstone; 1997:879–897.
76. Sureau P, Portnoi D, Rollin D, et al. Prévention de la transmission inter-humaine de la rage greffe de cornée. C R Séances Acad Sci. 1981;293:689–692.
77. Anderson LJ, Nicholson KG, Tauxe RV, Winkler WG. Human rabies in the United States, 1960 to 1979: Epidemiology, diagnosis, and prevention. Ann Intern Med. 1984;100:728–735.
78. Fishbein DB, Bernard KW. Rabies virus. In: Mandell GM, Bennett JE, Dolin R, eds. Principles and practice of infectious diseases. New York: Churchill Livingstone; 1994:1527–1543.
79. Hemachudha T, Phanthumchinda K, Phanuphak P, Manatsathit S. Myoedema as a clinical sign in paralytic rabies. Lancet. 1987;1:1210.
80. Lopez A, Miranda P, Tejada E, Fishbein DB. Outbreak of human rabies in the Peruvian jungle. Lancet. 1992;339:408–411.
81. Gode GR, Saksena R, Batra RK, et al. Treatment of 54 clinically diagnosed rabies patients with two survivals. Indian J Med Res. 1988;88:564–566.
82. Gowers WR. A manual of diseases of the nervous system. Philadelphia: P Blakiston; 1888:1237–1254.
83. Warrell DA, Davisdon NM, Pope HM, et al. Pathophysiologic studies in human rabies. Am J Med. 1976;60:180–190.
84. Cheetham HD, Hart J, Coghill NF, Fox B. Rabies with myocarditis. Two cases in England. Lancet. 1970; 1:921–922.
85. Hemachuda T. Human rabies: Clinical aspects, pathogenesis, and potential therapy. In: Rupprecht CE, Dietzschold B, Koprowski H, eds. Lyssaviruses. Berlin: Springer-Verlag; 1994:121–143.
86. Dutta JK. Rabies presenting with priapism (Letter). J Assoc Physicians India 1994;42:430.
87. Bhatt DR, Hattwick MAW, Gerdson R, et al. Human rabies: Diagnosis, complications, and prognosis. Am J Dis Child. 1974;127:862–869.
88. Warrel DA. The clinical picture of rabies in man. Trans R Soc Trop Med Hyg. 1976;701:188–195.
89. World Health Organization. Sixth Report of the Expert Committee on Rabies. Technical report series 523. Geneva: World Health Organization, 1973.
90. Baer GM, ed. The natural history of rabies. 2nd ed. Boca Raton: CRC; 1991.
91. Hemachuda T. Rabies. In: McKendall RR, ed. Viral diseases, v. 56/12: Vinken PJ, Bruyn GW, Klawans HL, series eds. Handbook of Clinical Neurology. Amsterdam: Elsevier Science; 1989:383–404.
92. Houff SA, Burton RC, Wilson RW, et al. Human-to-human transmission of rabies virus by corneal transplant. N Engl J Med. 1979;300:603–604.
93. Bryceson AD, Greenwood BM, Warrell DA, et al. Demonstration during life of rabies antigen in humans. J Infect Dis. 1975;131:71–74.
94. Blenden DC, Creech W, Torres-Anjel MJ. Use of immunofluorescence examination to detect rabies virus in the skin of humans with clinical encephalitis. J Infect Dis. 1986;154:698–701.
95. Crepin P, Audry L, Rotivel Y, et al. Intravitam diagnosis of human rabies by PCR using salvia and cerebsospinal fluid. J Clin Microbiol. 1998;36:1117–1121.
96. Arai YT, Yamada K, Kameoka Y, et al. Nucleoprotein gene analysis of fixed and street rabies virus variants using RT-PCR. Arch Virol. 1997;142:1787–1796.
97. Nadin-Davis SA. Polymerase chain reaction protocols for rabies virus discrimination. J Virol Methods. 1998;75:1–8.
98. Whitby JE, Johnstone P, Sillero-Zubiri C. Rabies virus in the decomposed brain of an Ethiopian wolf detected by nested reverse transcription–polymerase chain reaction. J Wildl Dis. 1997;33:912–915.
99. Albas A, Ferrari CI, da Silva LH, et al. Influence of canine brain decomposition on laboratory diagnosis of rabies. Rev Soc Bras Med Trop. 1999;32:19–22.
100. Zaidman GW, Billingsley A. Corneal impression test for the diagnosis of acute rabies encephalitis. Ophthalmology. 1998;105:249–251.
101. Smith JS, Yager PA, Baer GM. A rapid reproducible test for determining rabies neutralizing antibody. Bull World Health Organ. 1973;48:535–541.
102. Alvarez L, Fajardo R, Lopez E, et al. Partial recovery from rabies in a nine-year-old boy. Pediatr Infect Dis J. 1994;13:1154–1155.
103. Whitley RJ. Viral encephalitis. N Engl J Med. 1990; 323:242–250.
104. Johnson RT. Slow infections of the central nervous system caused by conventional viruses. In Björnsson J, Carp, RI, Löve A, Wisniewski HM, eds. Slow infections of the central nervous system. Ann NY Acad Sci. 1994;724:6–13.
105. Bundza A, Charlton KM. Comparison of spongiform lesions in experimental scrapie and rabies in skunks. Acta Neuropathol. 1988;3:275–280.
106. Bleck TP, Alston SR. Prion diseases. In: Bleck TP, ed. Central Nervous System and Ocular Infections, v. II: Mandell GM (series ed.). Atlas of Infectious Diseases. New York: Churchill Livingstone; 1995:11.1–11.16.
107. Warrell MJ, Looareesuwan S, Manatsathit S, et al. Rapid diagnosis of rabies and post-vaccinal encephalitides. Clin Exp Immunol. 1988;71:229–234.
108. Murthy JM. MRI in acute disseminated encephalomyelitis following Semple antirabies vaccine. Neuroradiology. 1998;40:420–423.
109. Fishbain DA, Barsky S, Goldberg M. Monosymptomatic hypochondriacal psychosis: Belief of contracting rabies. Int J Psychiatry Med. 1992;22:3–9.
110. Centers for Disease Control and Prevention. Compendium of animal rabies control, 1999. J Am Vet Med Assoc. 1999;214:198–202.
111. Conti LA, Tucker G, Heston S. Rabies in a dog vaccinated by its owner (Letter). J Am Vet Med Assoc. 1994;205:1250.
112. Eng TR, Fishbein DB, Talamante HE, et al. Immunogenicity of rabies vaccines used during an urban epizootic of rabies in Mexico. Vaccine. 1994;12:1259–1306.
113. Schneider LG. Rabies virus vaccines. Dev Biol Stand. 1995;84:49–54.
114. Rupprecht CE, Hanlon CA, Niezgoda M, et al. Recombinant rabies vaccines: Efficacy assessment in free-ranging animals. Onderstepoort J Vet Res. 1993; 60:463–468.
115. Brochier B, Boulanger D, Costy F, Pastoret P-P. Toward rabies elimination in Belgium by fox vaccination using a vaccinia-rabies glycoprotein recombinant virus. Vaccine. 1994;12:1368–1371.
116. Matter HC, Kharmachi H, Haddad N, et al. Test of three bait types for oral immunization of dogs against rabies in Tunisia. Am J Trop Med Hyg. 1995;52:489–495.
117. Petricciani JC. Ongoing tragedy of rabies. Lancet. 1993; 342:1067–1068.
118. Dean DJ. Pathogenesis and prophylaxis of rabies in man. N Y State J Med. 1963; 63:3507–3513.
119. Anderson LJ, Winkler WG. Aqueous quaternary ammonium compounds and rabies treatment. J Infect Dis. 1979; 139:494–495.
120. Griego RD, Rosen T, Orengo IF, Wolf JE. Dog, cat, and human bites: A review. J Am Acad Dermatol. 1995;33:1019–1029.
121. Mann JM, Burkhart MJ, Rollag OJ. Anti-rabies treatment in New Mexico: Impact of a comprehensive consultations-biologics system. Am J Public Health. 1980; 70:128–132.
122. ACIP. Rabies prevention—United States, 1999: Recommendations of the Immunization Practices Advisory Committee (ACIP). MMWR Morb Mortal Wkly Rep. 1999;48(RR-1):1–21. Available at ftp://ftp.cdc.gov/pub/Publications/mmwr/rr/rr4801.pdf.
123. Chutivongse S, Wilde H, Benjavongkulchai M, et al. Postexposure rabies vaccination during pregnancy: Effect on 202 women and their infants. Clin Infect Dis. 1995;20:818–820.
124. World Health Organization. WHO Recommendations on Rabies Post-exposure Treatment and the Correct Technique of Intradermal Immunization against Rabies. Geneva: World Health Organization; 1997. Available at http://www.who.int/emc-documents/rabies/whoemczoo966c.htm.
125. Wilde H, Sirikawin S, Sabcharoen A, et al. Failure of post-exposure treatment of rabies in children. Clin Infect Dis. 1996; 22:228–232.
126. Arya SC. Transmissible spongiform encephalopathies and sheep-brain derived rabies vaccines (Letter). Biologicals. 1994;22:73.
127. Bernard KW, Smith PW, Kader FJ, Moran MJ. Neuroparalytic illness and human diploid cell rabies vaccine. JAMA. 1982; 248:3136–3138.
128. Hemachuda T, Mitrabhakdi E, Wilde H, et al. Additional reports of failure to respond to treatment after rabies exposure in Thailand. Clin Infect Dis. 1999;28:143–144.
129. Lang J, Simanjuntak GH, Soerjosembodo S, Koesharyono C. Suppressant effect of human or equine rabies immunoglobulins on the immunogenicity of postexposure rabies vaccination under the 2-1-1 regimen: A field trial in Indonesia. MAS054 Clinical Investigator Group. Bull World Health Organ. 1998;76:491–495.
130. Pearlman E, Ballas S. False-positive human immunodeficiency virus screening test related to rabies vaccination. Arch Pathol Lab Med. 1994;118:805–806.
131. Plotkin SA, Loupi E, Blondeau C. False-positive human immunodeficiency virus screening test related to rabies vaccination (Letter). Arch Pathol Lab Med. 1995;119:679.
132. Dutta JK, Dutta TK. Treatment of clinical rabies in man: Drug therapy and other measures. Clin Pharmacol Ther. 1994;32:594–597.
133. Hattwick MA, Weis TT, Stechschulte CJ, et al. Recovery from rabies. A case report. *Ann Intern Med.* 1972; 76:931–942.
134. Porras C, Barboza JJ, Fuenzalida E, et al. Recovery from rabies in man. *Ann Intern Med.* 1976;85:44–48.
135. Rabies in a laboratory worker—New York. MMWR Morb Mortal Wkly Rep. 1977;26:183.

Filoviridae

Chapter 152

Marburg and Ebola Virus Hemorrhagic Fevers

C. J. PETERS

Filoviruses are rarely encountered and little is known about their natural history. However, because of the serious human disease they cause and our lack of predictive information about them, they demand our attention. These agents cause a severe, unrelenting viral hemorrhagic fever with high mortality. The identification of Marburg in 1967 was the first of only 15 independent isolations of Marburg virus or the related Ebola viruses from humans.[1] Each episode has been characterized by the mysterious emergence of a filovirus with no traces of its origin detectable. Primates (humans and monkeys) are the only disease targets involved to date, but they are not thought to serve as reservoirs. Viral epidemics have originated from Africa and apparently from a single source in the Philippines. The name of the viral family comes from their characteristic threadlike (*filo,* Latin "filament") morphology, and this has made their recognition in tissues or clinical samples unusually readily achieved with the electron microscope.

VIRAL CHARACTERIZATION

Filoviruses are elongated structures 80 nm in diameter. The basic length of the replicative form is 790 nm for Marburg and 970 nm for Ebola viruses, but long, branching convoluted structures are often formed.[2, 3] The 50-nm helical nucleocapsid is surrounded by a spike-studded membrane formed as the virus buds from the host cell. Inclusions of nucleocapsid aggregates can be visualized in electron microscopy of thin sections and are often visible as magenta-staining cytoplasmic structures in ordinary pathologic sections.

The virion genetic material is a single strand of negative-sense RNA of 4.2×10^6 Da that produces monocistronic messages during infection. These properties, the gene organization, virion structure, and viral sequence information place these viruses in a distinct family, Filoviridae in the order Mononegavirales. The glycoprotein gene codes for the 125- (Ebola) or 170- (Marburg) kDa transmembrane spike protein that is highly glycosylated and is antigenically most characteristic for each virus.[2, 3] Other virion proteins include a polymerase (180 kD), nucleocapsid protein (96 to 104 kD), matrix protein (40 kD), and three smaller proteins. Ebola viruses also code for a truncated glycoprotein species that is produced in soluble form.[4]

There are four known subtypes of Ebola that differ significantly from one another,[4] and a second Marburg subtype has been recognized.[5] Comparison of 1172 nucleotides from the *GP* gene shows more than a 40% difference between any pair of the three subtypes from Sudan, Zaire, Côte d'Ivoire, and Reston. Marburg viral strains differ from Ebola viruses in their genome organization, the size of their structural proteins, glycosylation patterns, and virion length, suggesting the possibility of the existence of two genera within the family.[3]

No serologic cross-reactivity has been demonstrated between the Marburg and Ebola viruses. The Ebola subtypes share varied degrees of cross-reactivity by the commonly used indirect fluorescent antibody or the enzyme-linked immunosorbent assay (ELISA) test.[3, 6] No hemagglutinin has been demonstrated. An unusual biologic feature of filoviruses has been the difficulty in demonstrating neutralization in cell culture or animals by convalescent sera.

All material in this chapter is in the public domain, with the exception of any borrowed figures or tables.

EPIDEMIOLOGY

Basic Ecology

There is no viral family with such a mysterious natural history. Each filovirus case or epidemic has been investigated seeking the source of the virus without success. In the case of epidemics, it has usually been possible to trace the epidemic back to a human or nonhuman primate index case, but no further. Suspects have included spiders, soft ticks, bats, and monkeys, but there is no field evidence to incriminate any of these.[1] Growth of the virus has been most commonly achieved in mammalian cells, not arthropods or their cell culture.[3, 7] Prolonged infection has been demonstrated in bats, suggesting the need for further study.[8]

Marburg Virus

In 1967, African green monkeys were brought from Uganda to Europe for use in vaccine production and biomedical research. They were infected with a "new" virus that resulted in deaths among the monkeys and transmission to humans. Seven deaths occurred among the 25 primary and 6 secondary human cases.[9] In 1980, a French engineer working in western Kenya 200 to 300 km from the site where the monkeys were shipped in 1967 developed Marburg virus disease, infecting one of the physicians caring for him[10]; and again in 1987, a visitor to the same region died from Marburg virus infection.[5] The only authenticated Marburg virus circulation outside this area occurred in a traveler in Zimbabwe, who infected two persons during his medical care in South Africa.[11]

Ebola Virus (Zaire, Sudan, and Côte d'Ivoire Subtypes)

Ebola virus was first recognized in 1976, when two unrelated epidemics occurred in northern Zaire and 850 km away in southern Sudan; 88% of the patients in 318 recognized cases died in the former, and 53% of 284 in the latter.[12, 13] Disease recurred in the same area of the Sudan in 1979,[14] and the Zaire subtype virus was isolated from a patient in a solitary case in northwestern Zaire in 1977.[15] Ebola hemorrhagic fever was not recognized again for almost 2 decades. Then in 1995–1996, an additional Ebola subtype (Côte d'Ivoire) was isolated from a human patient,[16] three separate Zaire subtype epidemics were recognized in Gabon,[17] and a major epidemic (315 cases, 81% case-fatality rate) from the Zaire subtype occurred in Kikwit, Zaire.[18] Notably, one Gabon patient made his way from the forest village where he fell ill to the capital and thence to South Africa, transmitting fatal infection to a nurse there.

Ebola Virus (Reston Subtype)

In 1989–1991, another subtype was discovered in Reston, Virginia, among dying cynomolgus monkeys imported from Manila, Philippines.[19] This virus proved to be highly virulent for macaques, but the four animal caretakers who were infected suffered no overt disease. Fortunately, the quarantine regulations put in place after Marburg virus was first recognized in 1967 prevented the movement of infected animals outside the receiving facility. Other episodes occurred in Italy in 1992 and in the United States in 1996.[20] All these events were traced to the facility of a single exporter, but the ultimate source of the virus has never been ascertained, although Mindanao was the origin of the monkeys taken for conditioning and resale.[21] Four humans have been observed to seroconvert, and several humans have been found to be seropositive by immunoglobulin G (IgG) ELISA with no history of disease.[19, 21]

Transmission to Humans

In the original Marburg, Germany, importation, close contact with monkey blood or with cell cultures was present in all primary cases. Secondary cases were mainly among hospital staff and were associated with blood exposure.[19] The 1976 Zaire Ebola epidemic in particular was driven by the use of improperly sterilized needles and syringes, resulting in much of the geographic spread of infection. Interhuman spread of Ebola virus in the African epidemics was very extensive among medical staff, often resulting in closure of hospitals and clinics. Transmission to household contacts ranged between 3 and 17%, involved up to five generations of infection, and was associated with close contact with sick patients and their body fluids. The epidemics subsided with the use of properly sterilized equipment, closure of hospitals, education of the populace, and institution of mask-gown-glove precautions.[12, 13, 18, 22] In the Reston, Virginia, epizootic among imported monkeys, there was transmission by droplet and possibly small-particle aerosol; spread to three of the humans caring for them was thought to be by droplets or small-particle aerosols, and a fourth suffered a scalpel accident during a monkey necropsy.[19]

The exact routes by which filoviruses may be spread are not intimately known. Parenteral inoculation with contaminated needles or syringes has been efficient and carries an enhanced mortality.[12] Skin or mucous membrane contact with virus-laden materials has probably been responsible for most recognized human infections. In addition to high titers of virus in blood, the skin of patients is extensively infected, including fibroblasts and other dermal structures[23]; this probably accounts for the additional risk to those participating in traditional burial preparation of the cadaver[12] and mourners touching the cadaver.[22] Experimental studies of filoviruses establish that they are stable[24] and highly infective[25] in small-particle aerosols, and observations of intermonkey transmission have suggested aerosol transmission. In addition, virions have been visualized in alveoli of humans and aerosol-infected monkeys.[19, 26] Nevertheless, airborne infection plays a minor role, if any, in interhuman spread.

CLINICAL MANIFESTATIONS

Filovirus hemorrhagic fevers have an incubation period of 5 to 10 days (range 2 to 19) and begin with the abrupt onset of fever usually accompanied by myalgia and headache.[9, 11–13, 18, 22, 27] The fever is joined by some combination of nausea and vomiting, abdominal pain, diarrhea, chest pain, cough, and pharyngitis. Other common features include photophobia, lymphadenopathy, conjunctival injection, jaundice, and pancreatitis. Central nervous system involvement is often manifested by somnolence, delirium, or coma. As the disease progresses, wasting becomes evident, and bleeding manifestations such as petechiae, hemorrhages and ecchymoses around needle puncture sites, and mucous membrane hemorrhages occur in half or more of the patients. Around day 5, most patients develop a maculopapular rash, prominent on the trunk. In the second week, the patient defervesces and improves markedly or dies in shock with multiorgan dysfunction, often accompanied by disseminated intravascular coagulation, anuria, and liver failure. Convalescence may be protracted and accompanied by arthralgia, orchitis, recurrent hepatitis, transverse myelitis, or uveitis.[9, 28]

The mortality of Marburg infection is approximately one in four, Ebola Sudan subtype one in two, and Ebola Zaire subtype 80 to 90%. Studies during epidemics suggest that subclinical infections with these viruses are uncommon, although a small percentage of the normal population has antibodies reactive in the IgG ELISA.[22, 29] The limited number of Ebola Reston subtype infections observed have been subclinical.

PATHOGENESIS AND PATHOLOGY

Filovirus disease has similar findings in human patients and nonhuman primate models. The viremia persists throughout the acute period, and its disappearance coincides with clinical improvement and usually the appearance of antibodies in blood.[30] The effective immune response is probably not humoral since passive convalescent antibody transfer does not protect against experimental inoculation.[3, 28, 31] Possible explanations for the failure to mount an effective immune response in fatal cases include the presence of a putatively immunosuppressive amino acid sequence in the filovirus glycoprotein,[32] the secretion of a soluble glycoprotein by Ebola virus–infected cells,[4] and the extensive lymphoid damage evident in postmortem examination.[26] In addition, Ebola-infected cells have a deficient response to interferon induction of the antiviral state or gene activation.[7, 33]

Important morphologic lesions include focal necrosis in many organs, particularly the liver, where Councilman's bodies are present, and the lymphoid organs, where prominent follicular necrosis occurs.[12, 13, 26] Necrotic lesions are found in conjunction with antigen and viral particles in endothelial, mononuclear, and parenchymal cells of virtually all organs. In addition to the morphologic basis for the multiorgan functional defects, cytokines are extensively activated in sick humans[34] or isolated, infected human mononuclear cells.[35] In contrast, inflammatory cell infiltrates are minimal. Disseminated intravascular coagulation may be important in some situations but is not usually the dominant mechanism of vascular damage.[3, 11]

DIAGNOSIS

Travel to rural sub-Saharan Africa (and now perhaps the Philippines) or exposure to nonhuman primates is a historical clue. The presence of thrombocytopenia and leukopenia with elevated transaminase levels (aspartate aminotransferase levels higher than alanine aminotransferase levels) is characteristic of filoviruses and some other viral hemorrhagic fevers, but a severe progressive course with abdominal pain and diarrhea should lead to suspicion of a filovirus. The rash is not seen with other viral hemorrhagic fevers.

Culture is positive during the acute stages, and seroconversion occurs around day 8 to 12. Antigen detection or polymerase chain reaction amplification of reverse transcription products provides a practical and sensitive method of diagnosis.[29, 30] Negative stains of serum and thin sections of buffy coat or fixed tissue (liver, kidney) are helpful, but careful measurement of the putative virions and their internal structure is necessary to exclude artefacts.

In convalesence, virus has been isolated from semen for several weeks and from anterior chamber fluid in a case of late uveitis. Negative semen cultures should be obtained from patients before they resume unprotected sexual activity.

IgM antibodies detected in capture ELISA are useful in early convalesence.[30] IgG serologic testing has not been reliable. False-positives and unreproducible results are quite common when the indirect fluorescent antibody test is applied. For this reason, confirmation even of apparent seroconversions is desirable; only cases verified by viral isolation or from viral-isolation–verified epidemics have been included in the previous discussion. The IgG ELISA appears to have decreased this problem but still requires further verification.[6, 28, 29]

PREVENTION AND TREATMENT

Although some drugs have shown promise in animal studies, no antivirals are available, nor does convalescent plasma hold much promise.[28] Interferon has not been effective and may lead to fever and other symptoms that would complicate management. Whole-blood transfusions from recent convalescents were used in the 1995 Zaire epidemic, but a lack of concomitant controls precluded evaluation of their efficacy and retrospective analysis taking into account the day of initial treatment and other variables suggested they were not useful.[36] A DNA vaccine induces protective cellular immunity in guinea pigs.[31]

Prevention of epidemics rests on early recognition of initial cases and prompt institution of barrier nursing.[18] Increased clinical awareness should lead to the institution of barrier nursing, which can be done with means appropriate to the African health care setting.[37] Fatal cases can be recognized readily by immunohistochemical staining of postmortem skin samples, obviating the need for cold preservation of samples and providing a safe inexpensive diagnostic modality in these high-mortality diseases.[23]

Management of the patient should be supportive with minimal

trauma and careful maintenance of hydration, realizing the possibility of myocardial compromise and increased lung vascular permeability. Replacement of coagulation factors and platelets is indicated. Heparin or other treatment of disseminated intravascular coagulation should be undertaken only if laboratory evidence of disseminated intravascular coagulation is present, and if adequate hematologic support is available.

At the community level, properly sterilized injection equipment, protection from body fluids and skin contact during preparation of the dead, and routine barrier nursing precautions are probably adequate in most cases.[18, 37] In the United States, where more aggressive therapeutic procedures may be practiced, strict isolation, barrier nursing, staff training to avoid parenteral exposures, and, when practical, respirator protection should be routine.[38]

Extensive quarantine precautions are now in place to prevent the movement of infected monkeys into the United States as well as contamination of vaccines or cell cultures. Nevertheless, the potential for the emergence of filoviruses as a significant public health problem may exist,[1] and concern by the clinician in this country is warranted when suspicious cases with an epidemiologic link to Africa or nonhuman primates occur.

Note: Useful sources for information of the basic biology of filoviruses are the books that followed the Marburg outbreak[9] and the 1976 Ebola outbreak[39]; a 1999 journal supplement with much of the 1975 Kikwit, Zaire, outbreak and other data[28] (available at http://www.journals.uchicago.edu/JID/journal/contents/v179nS1.html); and a 1999 review volume.[2] These compendia have been referenced freely here to limit the size of the reference list.

REFERENCES

1. Murphy FA, Peters CJ. Ebola virus: Where does it come from and where is it going? In: Krause RM, ed. Emerging Infections. New York: Academic Press; 1998:375–410.
2. Klenk H-D, ed. Marburg and Ebola Viruses. Curr Top Microbiol Immunol. 1999; 235:1–225.
3. Peters CJ, Sanchez A, Rollin PE, et al. Filoviridae: Marburg and Ebola viruses. In: Fields BN, Knipe DN, eds. Virology. 3rd ed. New York: Raven; 1999:1161–1176.
4. Sanchez A, Trappier SG, Mahy BWJ, et al. The virion glycoproteins of Ebola viruses are encoded in two reading frames and are expressed through transcriptional editing. Proc Natl Acad Sci U S A. 1996;93:3602.
5. Sanchez A, Trappier SG, Ströher U, et al. Variation in the glycoprotein and *VP35* genes of Marburg virus strains. Virology. 1998;240:138.
6. Ksiazek TG, Rollin PE, Jahrling PB, Peters CJ. Enzyme-linked immunosorbent assays for the detection of antibodies to Ebola viruses. J Infect Dis. 1999; 179 (Suppl 1):S192–S198.
7. Van der Groen G, Webb P, Johnson K, et al. Growth of Lassa and Ebola viruses in different cell lines. In: Pattyn SR, ed. Ebola Virus Haemorrhagic Fever. Amsterdam: Elsevier North-Holland Biomedical; 1978:255.
8. Swanepoel R, Leman PA, Burt FJ, et al. Experimental inoculation of plants and animals with Ebola virus. Emerging Infect Dis. 1996; 2:321–325.
9. Martini GA, Siegert R, eds. Marburg Virus Disease. Berlin: Springer-Verlag; 1971:1–230.
10. Smith DH, Johnson BK, Isaacson M, et al. Marburg virus disease in Kenya. Lancet. 1982;1:816–820.
11. Gear JSS, Cassel GA, Gear AJ, et al. Outbreak of Marburg virus disease in Johannesburg. BMJ. 1975;4:489–493.
12. World Health Organization. Ebola haemorrhagic fever in Zaire, 1976. Report of an international commission. Bull World Health Organ. 1978;56:271–293.
13. World Health Organization. Ebola haemorrhagic fever in Sudan, 1976. Report of a WHO/international study team. Bull World Health Organ. 1978;56:247–270.
14. Baron RC, McCormick JB, Zubeir OA. Ebola hemorrhagic fever in southern Sudan: Hospital dissemination and intrafamilial spread. Bull World Health Organ. 1983;6:997–1003.
15. Heymann DL, Weisfeld JS, Webb PA, et al. Ebola hemorrhagic fever: Tandala, Zaire, 1977–1978. J Infect Dis. 1980;142:372–376.
16. Formenty P, Hatz C, Stoll A, et al. Human infection due to Ebola Côte d'Ivoire: Clinical and biological presentation. J Infect Dis. 1999;179(Suppl 1):S48–S53.
17. Georges A, Leroy EB, Renaut AA, et al. Recent Ebola outbreaks in Gabon from 1994 to 1997: Epidemiological and health control issues. J Infect Dis. 1999; 179(Suppl 1):S65–S75.
18. Khan AS, Kweteminga TF, Heymann DH, et al. The reemergence of Ebola hemorrhagic fever (EHF), Zaire, 1995. J Infect Dis. 1999;179(Suppl 1):S76–S86.
19. Peters CJ, Johnson ED, Jahrling PB, et al. Filoviruses. In: Morse S, ed. Emerging Viruses. New York: Oxford University Press; 1991:159–175.
20. Rollin PE, Williams J, Bressler D, et al. Ebola (subtype Reston) virus among quarantined non-human primates recently imported from the Philippines to the United States. J Infect Dis. 1999;179(Suppl 1):S108–S114.
21. Miranda ME, Ksiazek TG, Retuya TJ, et al. Epidemiology of Ebola (subtype Reston) virus in the Philippines, 1996. J Infect Dis. 1999;179(Suppl 1):S115–S119.
22. Dowell SF, Mukunu R, Ksiazek TG, et al. Transmission of Ebola hemorrhagic fever: A study of risk factors in family members, Kikwit, Zaire 1995. J Infect Dis. 1999;179(Suppl 1):S87–S91.
23. Zaki S, Greer PW, Shieh WJ, et al. A novel immunohistochemical assay for detection of Ebola virus in skin: Implications for diagnosis and surveillance of Ebola hemorrhagic fever. J Infect Dis. 1999;179(Suppl 1):S36–S37.
24. Belanov YF, Muntyanov VP, Kryuk VD, et al. Retention of Marburg virus infecting capability on contaminated surfaces and in aerosol particles (in Russian). Vopr Virusol. 1996;41(1):32–34.
25. Bazhutin NB, Belanov EF, Spiridonov VA, et al. The influence of the methods of experimental infection with Marburg virus on the features of the disease process in green monkeys. Vopr Virusol. 1992;37:153–156.
26. Zaki SR, Goldsmith CS. Pathologic features of filovirus infections in humans. Curr Top Microbiol Immunol. 1999;235:97–116.
27. Bwaka MA, Bonnet M, Calain P, et al. Ebola hemorrhagic fever in Kikwit, Democratic Republic of Congo (former Zaire): Clinical observations. J Infect Dis. 1999; 179(Suppl 1):S1–S7.
28. Peters CJ, LeDuc JW, ed. Ebola: The virus and the disease. J Infect Dis. 1999; 179(Suppl 1):S1–S288.
29. Busico KM, Marshall KL, Ksiazek TG, et al. Prevalence of IgG antibodies to Ebola virus in individuals during an Ebola outbreak, Democratic Republic of the Congo, 1995. J Infect Dis. 1999;179(Suppl 1):S102–S107.
30. Ksiazek TG, Rollin PE, Williams AJ, et al. Clinical virology of Ebola hemorrhagic fever (EHF): Virus, virus antigen, and IgG and IgM antibody findings among EHF patients in Kikwit, Democratic Republic of the Congo, 1995. J Infect Dis. 1999;179(Suppl 1):S177–S187.
31. Xu L, Sanchez A, Yang Z, et al. Genetic immunization for Ebola virus infection. Nat Med. 1998;4:37.
32. Volchkov VE, Blinov VM, Netesov SV. The envelope glycoprotein of Ebola virus contains an immunosuppressive-like domain similar to oncogenic retroviruses. FEBS Lett. 1992;305:181–184.
33. Harcourt BH, Sanchez A, Offerman MK. Ebola virus selectively inhibits responses to interferons, but not to IL-1beta in endothelial cells. J Virol. 1999;73:3491–3496.
34. Villinger F, Rollin PE, Brar SS, et al. Markedly elevated levels of IFN-gamma/alpha, IL-2, IL-10 and TNF-alpha associated with fatal Ebola virus infection. J Infect Dis. 1999;179(Suppl 1):S188–S191.
35. Schnittler HJ, Feldmann H. Molecular pathogenesis of filovirus infections: Role of macrophages and endothelial cells. In: HD Klenk, ed. Marburg and Ebola Viruses. New York: Springer; 1999:175–204.
36. Sadek RF, Kilmarx PH, Khan AS, et al. Outbreak of Ebola hemorrhagic fever, Zaire, 1995. A closer numerical look. J Infect Dis. 1999;179(Suppl 1):S24–S27.
37. Lloyd ES, Zaki SR, Rollin PE, et al. Long-term disease surveillance in Bandundu region, democratic republic of the Congo: A model for early detection and prevention of Ebola hemorrhagic fever. J Infect Dis. 1999;179(Suppl 1):S274–S280.
38. Centers for Disease Control and Prevention. Update: Management of patients with suspected viral hemorrhagic fever–United States. MMWR. 1995;44:475–479.
39. Pattyn SR, ed. Ebola Virus Haemorrhagic Fever. Amsterdam: Elsevier North-Holland; 1978.

Orthomyxoviridae

Chapter 153

Influenza Virus

JOHN J. TREANOR

Influenza is an acute, usually self-limited febrile illness caused by infection with influenza type A or B virus that occurs in outbreaks of variable severity almost every winter. The attack rates during such outbreaks may be as high as 10 to 40% over a 5- to 6-week period.

This chapter was based on a chapter by Robert Betts in the fourth edition of this text.

The most common clinical manifestations are fever, myalgia, and cough. Infection with other respiratory viruses such as respiratory syncytial virus and adenovirus may produce clinical manifestations indistinguishable from those of the characteristic systemic illness with cough that results from influenza virus infection, but such infections do not occur in epidemics. The two most important features of influenza are the epidemic nature of the disease and the mortality that results in part from its pulmonary complications.

HISTORICAL OVERVIEW

Influenza virus has been causing recurrent epidemics of febrile respiratory disease every 1 to 3 years for at least the past 400 years.[1, 2] Although the disease is not associated with a characteristic manifestation such as rash, the high attack rate, the explosive nature of the epidemic, and the frequency of cough allow the identification of some past epidemics. For example, Sydenham's account of an epidemic that occurred in 1679 is a clear description of influenza.[3] Hirsch tabulated 299 outbreaks occurring at an average interval of 2.4 years between 1173 and 1875.[1] As discussed later on, severe epidemics of worldwide scope occur less often and are referred to as pandemics. The first recorded pandemic that clearly fits the description of influenza occurred in 1580, although others may have occurred earlier. Since then, 31 pandemics have been described. The greatest pandemic in recorded history occurred in 1918–1919 when, during three "waves" of influenza, 21 million deaths were recorded worldwide, 549,000 of these in the United States.[4]

The modern era of understanding of influenza was ushered in by Smith and associates when they isolated influenza A virus in ferrets in 1933.[5] Influenza B virus was isolated by Francis in 1939[6] and influenza C virus by Taylor in 1950.[7] The discovery by Burnet in 1936 that influenza virus could be grown in embryonated hens' eggs allowed extensive study of the properties of the virus and the development of inactivated vaccines.[8] Animal cell culture systems for the growth of influenza viruses were developed in the 1950s.[9] The phenomenon of hemagglutination, which was discovered by Hirst in 1941, led to simpler and inexpensive methods for the measurement of virus and specific antibody.[10] Studies using hemagglutination and testing of serum specimens obtained at specified times from elderly persons who were alive during historical outbreaks (so-called serologic archaeology) have helped to characterize the antigenic nature of viruses associated with epidemics that occurred before the identification of influenza virus.[11, 12] Preliminary characterization of the virus responsible for the 1918 epidemic has been accomplished by polymerase chain reaction (PCR) amplification of viral RNA recovered from pathology specimens.[13]

Evidence of the protective efficacy of inactivated vaccines was developed in the 1940s.[14, 15] Vaccines have been in widespread use in various parts of the world since, but usually only for selected segments of a population. The first attempt at immunization of an entire population was made in 1976 in the United States with the National Immunization Program against swine influenza, but it was not possible to estimate its efficacy because an epidemic did not occur. More recently, under the aegis of Medicare,. communities increased their use of vaccine dramatically. The impact of this program on the incidence of influenza and of complications secondary to influenza can now be assessed. Two antiviral agents have been approved for therapy and prophylaxis of influenza A in the United States: amantadine in the mid-1960s and rimantadine in 1993. Both are approved for all influenza A virus subtypes but are not active against influenza B or C virus.

THE VIRUSES

Classification

Influenza viruses belong to the family Orthomyxoviridae and are classified into three distinct types—influenza A virus, influenza B virus, and influenza C virus—on the basis of major antigenic differences. In addition, there are significant differences in genetic organization, structure, host range, and epidemiologic and clinical characteristics between the three influenza virus types (Table 153–1). However, all three viruses share certain features that are fundamental to their biologic behavior, including the presence of a host cell–derived envelope, envelope glycoproteins of critical importance in virus entry and egress from cells, and a segmented genome of negative-sense (i.e., opposite of message-sense), single-stranded RNA. The standard nomenclature for influenza viruses includes the influenza type, place of initial isolation, strain designation, and year of isolation. For example, the influenza A virus isolated by Francis[16] from a patient in Puerto Rico in 1934 is given the strain designation A/Puerto Rico/8/34, sometimes referred to as "PR8" virus.

Morphologic Characteristics

The morphologic characteristics of all influenza virus types, subtypes, and strains are similar. Electron microscopic studies estimate these viruses to be 80 to 120 nm in diameter and show them to be enveloped viruses covered with surface projections or spikes. They may exist as spherical or elongated filamentous particles as well (Figs. 153–1 and 153–2). The latter shape predominates in newly isolated strains, whereas most laboratory-adapted strains consist almost entirely of spherical particles. The filamentous forms vary in length but may be up to 40 nm long.

Eight structural proteins have been identified in influenza A viruses. The surface spikes are glycoproteins that possess either hemagglutinin (HA) or neuraminidase (NA) activity. The rod-shaped HA spikes each measure approximately 4 nm in diameter by 14 nm in length. They can be removed from the intact virion by sodium dodecyl sulfate, by bromelain, or by chymotrypsin. Each spike is a trimer composed of three HA polypeptides, each with molecular weights of 75,000 to 80,000, resulting in a trimer with a molecular weight of approximately 224,640.[17] The HA is synthesized as a monomer (HA_0) that is cleaved by host cell proteases into HA_1 and HA_2 components, which remain linked together. Antigenic sites and sites for binding to cells are located in the globular head of the molecule.

The viral NA is an enzyme that catalyzes the removal of terminal

TABLE 153–1 Differences among Influenza A, B, and C Viruses

Feature	Influenza A	Influenza B	Influenza C
Genetics	8 gene segments	8 gene segments	7 gene segments
Structure	10 viral proteins M2 unique	11 viral proteins NB unique	9 viral proteins HEF unique
Host range	Humans, swine, equine, avian, marine mammals	Humans only	Humans and swine
Epidemiology	Antigenic shift and drift Drift is generally linear	Antigenic drift only More than one variant may cocirculate	Antigenic drift only Multiple variants
Clinical features	May cause large pandemics with significant mortality in affected young people	Severe disease generally confined to elderly or high risk, pandemics not seen	Mild disease without seasonality

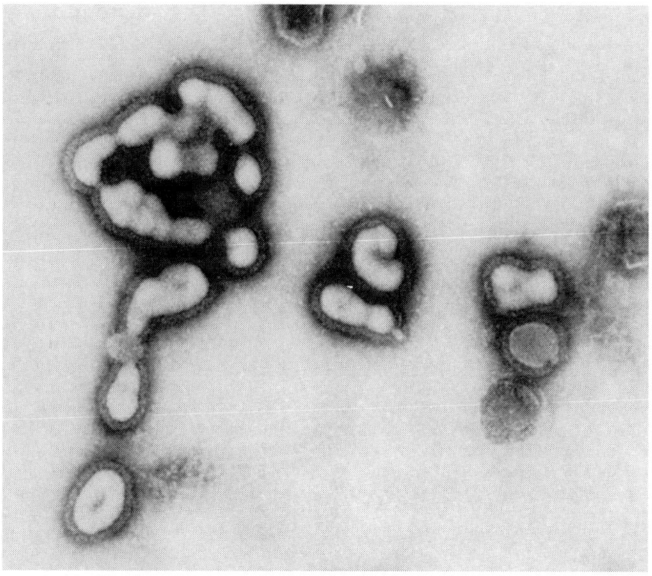

FIGURE 153–1. Electron micrograph of influenza A/USSR/77 H1N1 (×189,000).

sialic acids (*N*-acetylneuraminic acid) from sialic acid–containing glycoproteins. The NA spike is shaped like a mushroom rather than a rod (see Fig. 153–2) and has a molecular weight of 240,000. The intact NA consists of a tetramer of NA polypeptides, each with a molecular weight of 58,000. As in the HA, antigenic sites, as well as the enzyme active site, are located in the mushroom-shaped head.

At least 15 highly divergent, antigenically distinct HAs have been described in influenza A viruses (H1 to H15) as well as at least 9 distinct NAs (N1 to N9). A third integral membrane protein, the M2 protein, is also present in small amounts on the viral envelope.

Interior to the envelope is the matrix, or M1, protein.[18] This protein is believed to provide stability to the virion. Within the envelope are eight physically discrete nucleocapsid segments (Table 153–2). Each nucleocapsid is composed of a single segment of genomic RNA intimately associated with the viral nucleoprotein (NP), with the three polymerase proteins PB1, PB2, and PA bound to one end. These so-called "internal" viral proteins are important targets for cross-reactive, virus-specific cytotoxic T lymphocytes (CTLs). Two nonstructural viral proteins, NS1 and NS2, are also found within infected cells.

EPIDEMIOLOGY

Disease Impact

Influenza epidemics are regularly associated with excess morbidity and mortality,[19] usually expressed in the form of excess rates of pneumonia and influenza-associated hospitalizations and deaths during epidemics.[19, 20] Pneumonia and influenza deaths fluctuate annually in a predictable fashion, with peaks in the winter and troughs in the summer, as depicted in Figure 153–3. In this type of representation, observed pneumonia- and influenza-related death rates are compared with an expected baseline derived from a time-series regression model,[21] which allows calculation of excess mortality due to influenza epidemics. Estimated excess pneumonia and influenza deaths (i.e., deaths in which specific ICD-9 codes [of the World Health Organization's International Classification of Diseases] are recorded as the cause of death) attributable to influenza epidemics[22] are shown in Table 153–3, alongside the estimated percentage of isolates that

FIGURE 153–2. Schematic model for the influenza virus virion.

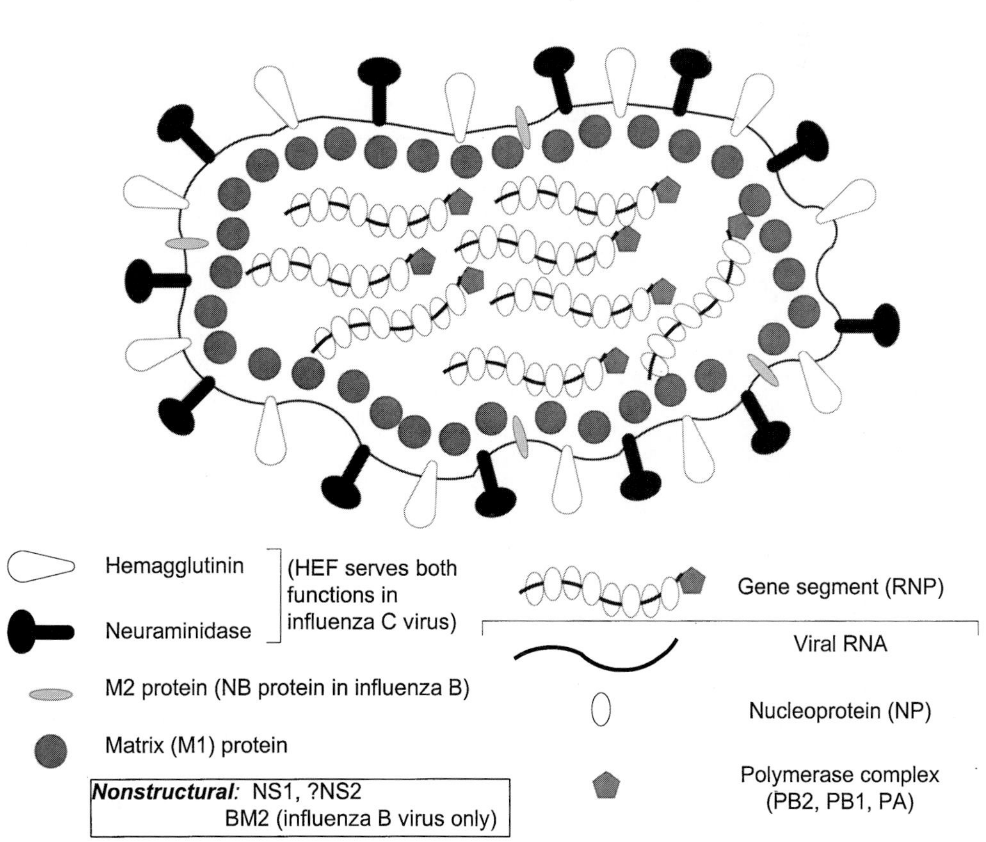

TABLE 153-2 Genes and Protein Products of Influenza A Virus

RNA Segment Number	Gene Product Description	Name of Protein	Proposed Function(s)
1	PB1	Basic polymerase 1	RNA transcriptase
2	PB2	Basic polymerase 2	Cap binding, endonucleolytic cleavage
3	PA	Acidic polymerase	Unknown
4	HA	Hemagglutinin	Viral attachment to cell membranes; membrane fusion
5	NA	Neuraminidase	Cleaves sialic acid from cell surface, released from membranes; prevents aggregation.
6	NP	Nucleoprotein	Encapsidates RNA, regulation of transcription/replication
7	M	Matrix	Surrounds viral core; controls nuclear transport
	M2	Matrix 2	Ion channel, regulates pH in endosome
8	NS1	Nonstructural	Regulation of messenger RNA transport from nucleus
	NS2	Nonstructural 2	Mutations result in increased production of defective-interfering particles

FIGURE 153–3. Pneumonia-influenza deaths. The observed and expected ratios of deaths attributed to pneumonia and influenza in 121 cities are presented as determined by the time-series method.

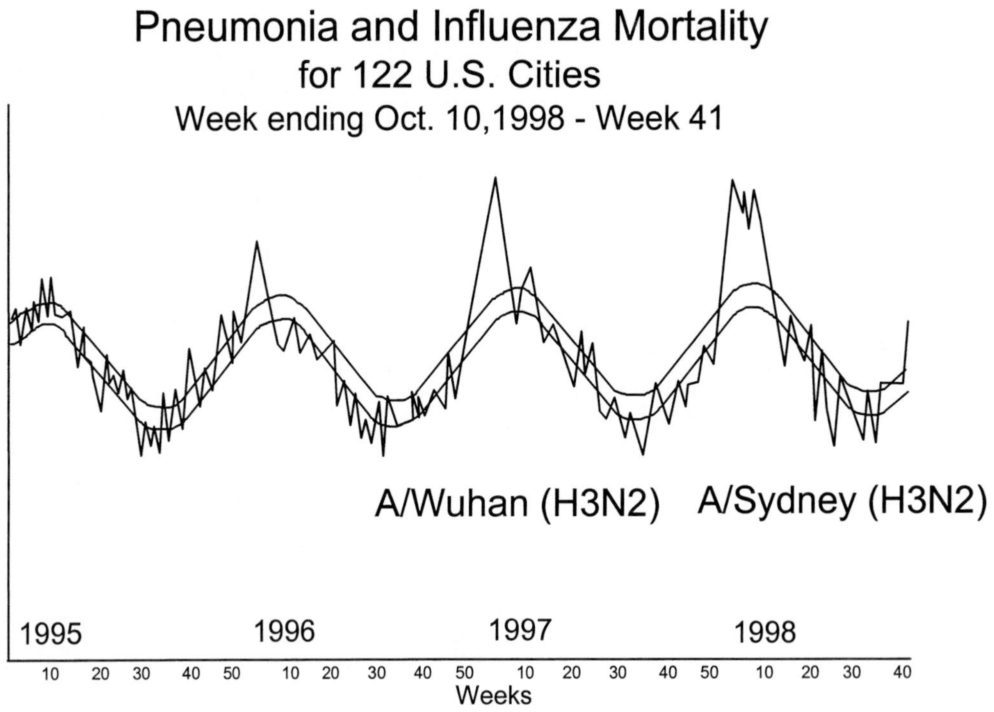

TABLE 153-3 Estimated Excess Pneumonia- and Influenza-Related Deaths and Excess Mortality from All Causes during Influenza Epidemics

Year	Frequency of Isolate Subtypes (%) *H3N2*	*H1N1*	*B*	Pneumonia- and Influenza-Related Excess Deaths (range)	All-Cause Excess Deaths (range)
1972–73	90	0	10	7900 (5500–10,300)	18,300 (1200–35000)
1973–74	20	0	80	0	0
1974–75	100	0	0	6500 (4100–8900)	15,100 (0–32,100)
1975–76	70	0	30	11,800 (9200–14,400)	24,600 (3,400–45,900)
1976–77	5	0	95	0	0
1977–78	60	26	14	8300 (6000–10,500)	46,200 (19,800–72,700)
1978–79	0	98	2	0	0
1979–80	2	1	97	5100 (3500–6700)	17,300 (600–34,100)
1980–81	77	23	0	11,700 (9100–14,200)	47,200 (27,800–66,600)
1981–82	1	24	75	2100 (600–3700)	0
1982–83	79	10	11	4700 (2800–6700)	9600 (0–19,200)
1983–84	5	50	45	3500 (1600–5400)	8200 (0–17,600)
1984–85	97	0	3	8100 (6600–9600)	36,200 (17,700–54,700)
1985–86	24	0	76	6700 (4900–8500)	34,000 (6,800–61,200)
1986–87	—	—	—	1800 (1100–2500)	16,800 (1900–31,700)
1987–88	0	80	20	7400 (5600–9100)	33,400 (12,900–53,800)
1988–89	45	45	10	5100 (3600–6600)	10,500 (800–20,200)
1989–90	90	1	9	10,100 (8500–11,700)	43,600 (27,600–59,600)
1990–91	4	3	93	4200 (2400–6100)	23,000 (0–46,000)
1991–92	19	81	0	6600 (5600–7700)	41,700 (19,600–63,700)

Data from Chapter 141 by Robert Betts in the previous edition of this text and from Simonsen et al.[22]

were typed as influenza A (H3N2), A (H1N1), or B in each year. Significant levels of excess mortality are reported in most years. Generally, the level of excess mortality is highest in years when influenza A (H3N2) viruses predominate, but influenza B and to a lesser extent influenza A H1N1 viruses also can be associated with excess mortality. Because not all influenza-related deaths are manifested as pneumonia, the pneumonia and influenza mortality statistics probably underestimate the true impact of influenza on the population. Table 153–3 also lists the all-cause excess mortality, defined as the number of deaths due to any cause above a similarly derived baseline that occur during periods of influenza epidemic activity. Although less precise than the pneumonia- and influenza-related deaths, all-cause mortality probably is a more accurate reflection of the total burden of influenza. Mortality is only the most severe manifestation of influenza impact, and similar techniques can be used to estimate excess morbidity due to influenza epidemics.[23] Data from the Tecumseh Community Health Study has been used to estimate that influenza is responsible for 13.8 to 16.0 million excess respiratory illnesses per year in the United States among young people (less than 20 years of age), and for 4.1 to 4.5 million excess illnesses in older persons.[23]

Influenza is usually associated with a U-shaped epidemic curve. Attack rates are generally highest in the young, whereas mortality is generally highest in the elderly[19, 24] (Fig. 153–4). Excess morbidity and mortality are particularly high in persons with certain high-risk medical conditions, including adults and children with cardiovascular and pulmonary conditions such as asthma, or those requiring regular medical care because of chronic metabolic disease, renal dysfunction, hemoglobinopathies, or immunodeficiency.[25, 26] Recent reports also suggest that influenza may result in more severe disease and prolonged symptoms in persons with human immunodeficiency virus (HIV) infection,[27] and in those with iatrogenic immunosuppression.[28] It should be recognized that although complication rates are higher in the elderly and debilitated, the majority of persons hospitalized during influenza epidemics were ambulatory and leading productive lives prior to the acute illness.[25]

Much of the impact of influenza is related to the malaise and consequent disability that it produces, even in young, healthy people. It has been estimated that a typical case of influenza, on average, is associated with 5 to 6 days of restricted activity, 3 to 4 days of bed disability, and about 3 days lost from work or school.[29, 30] The average number of medical visits for cases in which medical attention was sought was from 1.1 to 3.6 visits, depending on year of the outbreak and age of the patient. It is worth noting that direct medical costs of illness account for only about 20% or the total expenses of a case of influenza, with a major proportion (30 to 50%) of the economic impact related to loss of productivity. Influenza is also associated with decreased job performance in working adults[31, 32] and with reduced levels of independent functioning in older adults.[33]

Epidemic Influenza

An epidemic is an outbreak of influenza confined to one location, such as a city, town, or country. In a given community, epidemics of influenza A virus infection have a characteristic pattern. A graphic description of an epidemic due to an A/Victoria/75/H3N2-like virus that occurred in 1976 in Houston, Texas, is shown in Figure 153–5. Such localized epidemics begin rather abruptly, reach a sharp peak in 2 to 3 weeks, and last 5 to 6 weeks.[34] Reports of increased numbers of children with febrile respiratory illness are often the first indication of influenza, although on occasion, an outbreak in a nursing home may be the very first indication of influenza in a community. Outbreaks in children are usually soon followed by the occurrence of influenza-like illnesses among adults. The next event is increased hospital admissions for patients with pneumonia, exacerbation of chronic obstructive pulmonary disease (COPD), croup, and congestive heart failure. Increased school and industrial absenteeism also occurs, but these events are insensitive and late indicators of influenza in a community.[34] Although an increased number of deaths due to pneumonia is a highly specific indicator of influenza, it invariably lags behind the other indicators because of two factors: (1) the time from the onset of illness to time of death and (2) the delay involved in reporting deaths to public health officials.[35] During epidemics, average overall attack rates are estimated to be 10 to 20%, but in selected populations or age groups, attack rates of 40 to 50% are not unusual.[36] The factors that lead to termination of an outbreak in any given location are unclear, because usually the outbreak ceases long before the supply of susceptible persons is exhausted.

In temperate climates in either hemisphere, epidemics occur almost exclusively in the winter months (generally October to April in the Northern Hemisphere and May to September in the Southern Hemisphere), whereas influenza may be seen year-round in the tropics. Outbreaks in the Southern Hemisphere may predict the type of virus that will occur in the Northern Hemisphere the following winter. The reasons for these seasonal changes are not entirely clear. Modeling studies suggest that the effect can mostly be explained by postulating seasonal effects on virus transmissibility.[37] Such effects could be the result of more favorable environmental conditions for virus survival,[38] or of behavioral changes that increase transmission, such as indoor crowding. In large countries such as the United States and Australia, regional differences in the time occurrence

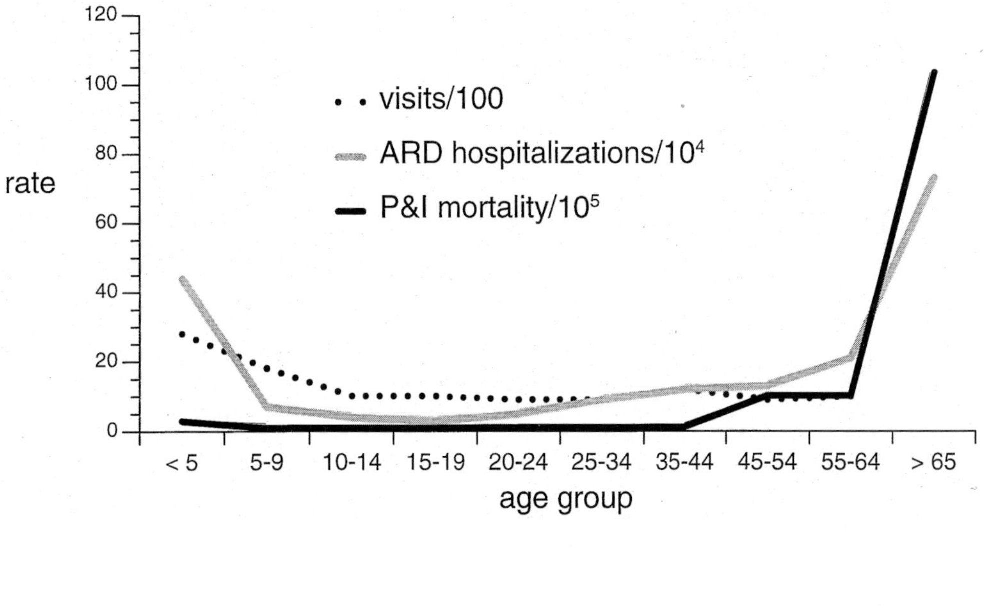

FIGURE 153–4. Typical epidemic curve in the interpandemic era, showing the rates of medically attended illness, hospitalizations for acute respiratory disease, and pneumonia- and influenza-related mortality by age for several seasons of influenza in Houston, Texas. Attack rates and hospitalizations occur at both extremes of age, but mortality occurs largely in those older than 65. (Data from ref. 24.)

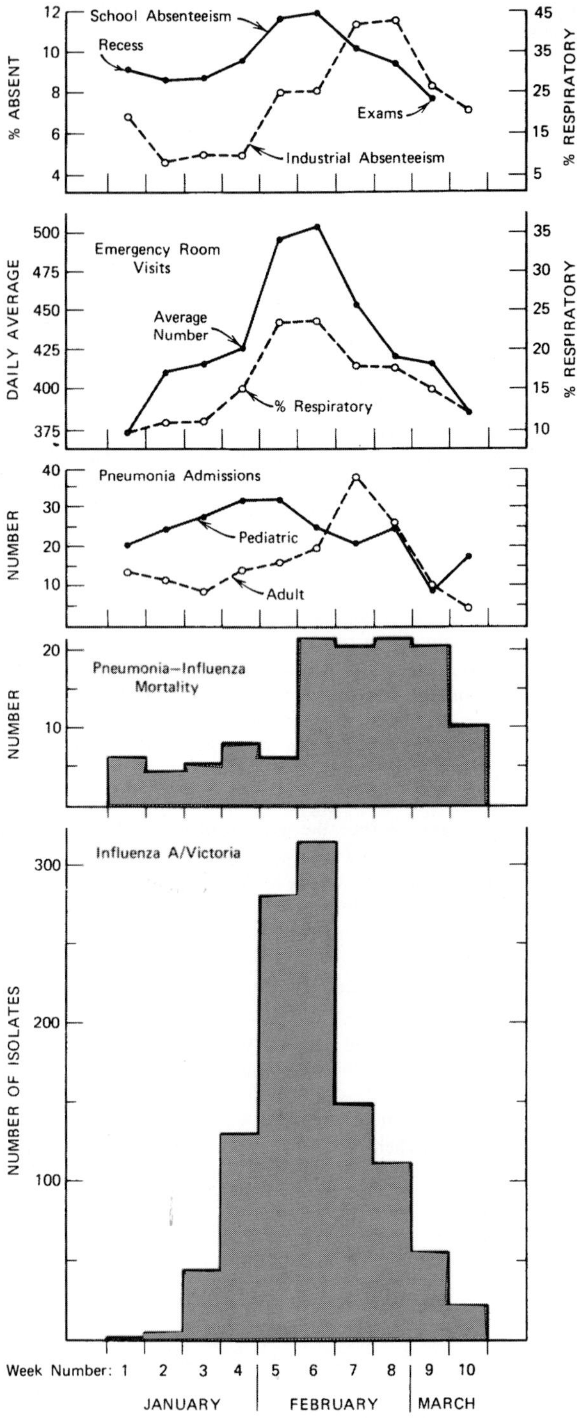

FIGURE 153–5. Correlation of the nonvirologic indexes of epidemiologic influenza with the number of isolates of A/Victoria virus according to week, Houston, 1976 (industrial absenteeism is indicated by the percentage with respiratory complaints). (From Glezen WP, Couch RB. Interpandemic influenza in the Houston area, 1974–1976. N Engl J Med. 1978;298:587–593.)

of influenza outbreaks are also apparent. Not uncommonly, major outbreaks occur in some communities or regions while others are experiencing modest or no activity whatsoever.

For many years, it had been noted that during an epidemic of influenza, a single strain of influenza virus prevailed and that other respiratory viruses diminished in frequency or disappeared.[36, 39] However, in recent years, it has been recognized that two different strains within a single subtype (e.g., A/Victoria/3/75/H3N2 and A/Texas/1/77/H3N2)[40] or that two differing influenza A subtypes (H1N1 and H3N2) can circulate simultaneously. Furthermore, concomitant outbreaks of influenza A and influenza B and simultaneous outbreaks of influenza A and respiratory syncytial virus infection have been demonstrated.[41] In many years, the end of the influenza epidemic season is characterized by a brief spike in cases due to a new strain. These limited outbreaks, which have been referred to as a "herald wave," often predict the predominant strain in the next influenza season.[42]

Pandemic Influenza

In contrast to the familiar pattern of epidemic influenza, pandemics are severe outbreaks that rapidly progress to involve all parts of the world, associated with the emergence of a new virus to which the overall population possesses no immunity. Characteristics of pandemics include extremely rapid transmission with concurrent outbreaks worldwide; the occurrence of diseases outside the usual seasonality, including the summer months; high attack rates in all age groups, with high levels of mortality particularly in healthy young adults[43]; and multiple waves of disease immediately before and after the main outbreak. The interval between pandemics is quite variable and unpredictable, but it is likely that pandemics of influenza will continue to occur in the future.

Antigenic Variation

One of the unique and most remarkable features of influenza virus is the frequency with which changes in antigenicity occur; these changes are referred to as antigenic variation. Alteration of the antigen structure of the virus leads to infection with variants to which little or no resistance may be present in the population at risk. The phenomenon of antigenic variation helps explain why influenza continues to be a major epidemic disease of humans.

Antigenic variation involves principally the two external glycoproteins of the virus, the HA and the NA, and is referred to as *antigenic drift* or *antigenic shift,* depending on whether the variation is small or great, respectively.

Antigenic Drift

Antigenic drift refers to relatively minor antigenic changes that occur frequently (every year or every few years) within the HA or the NA, or both, of the virus. The mechanism of antigenic drift has been studied most intensively for the HA, and it is generally accepted that the mechanism is one of gradual accumulation of amino acid changes in one or more of the five identified major antigenic sites on the HA molecule.[44, 45] Because antibody generated by exposure to previous strains does not neutralize the antigenic variant as effectively, immunologic selection takes place, and the variant supplants previous strains as the predominant virus in the epidemic. Support for this thesis comes from experimental work demonstrating that antigenic variants (representing drift) can be produced in cell cultures in the presence of limiting amounts of antibody, and these variants have similar single amino acid sequence in the HA.[46–49]

Comparison of the HA gene sequences of influenza viruses isolated in successive years reveals differences in the patterns of evolution of the HA between influenza A, B, and C viruses. Generally, a single lineage or relatively few lineages of HA circulate in humans, and the accumulation of point mutations is linear, with each strain replacing the previously circulating one. In contrast, multiple lineages of influenza C virus cocirculate, as indicated by sequence comparisons with the HEF gene. The evolution of influenza B viruses is somewhere between these two examples, with relatively few lineages, but more than one, of HA gene cocirculating.[50] Relatively less

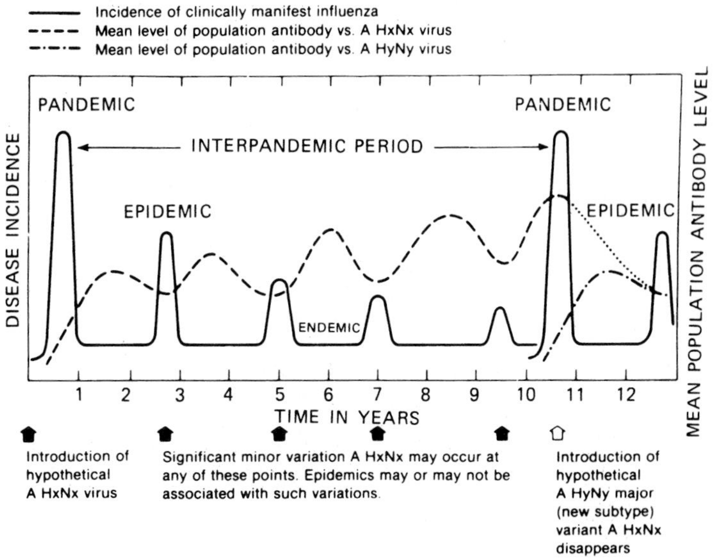

FIGURE 153–6. Schema of the occurrence of influenza pandemics and epidemics in relation to the level of immunity in the population. AXxNx and AHyNy represent influenza viruses with completely different hemagglutinins and neuraminidases. (Modified from Kilbourne ED. The epidemiology of influenza. In Kilbourne ED, ed. Influenza Viruses and Influenza. New York: Academic Press; 1975:483.)

information is available regarding the evolution of NA gene sequences, but these appear to follow a similar pattern.[51] Generally, in the first years after a new subtype appears, antigenic drift occurs infrequently. Thereafter, new variants appear more and more frequently as the end of an era approaches.

Antigenic Shift

The major antigenic shifts that herald pandemic influenza presumably result from a different mechanism. The viruses involved are "new" viruses to which the population has no immunity. There is very little or no serologic relationship between the HA or NA antigens of the "old" and those of the "new" viruses; hence, in nomenclature, each receives a different designation. A schema is shown in Figure 153–6 that ties together the concepts of antigenic shift and antigenic drift in relation to population immunity. When a new virus subtype, here called HxNx, to which antibody is lacking, is introduced into a population, pandemic influenza results. After one or more waves of pandemic influenza, the level of immunity in the population increases, which makes the emergence of a variant with antigenic drift more likely, because the level of immunity to it will be less than to the original strain. This phenomenon is repeated with subsequent epidemics due to strains of influenza A HxNx that exhibit some antigenic drift. After 10 to 30 years of circulation of variants with this given subtype, the level of immunity in the population to all variants within the subtype is very high, and the conditions for the spread of a new virus subtype, HyNy, become favorable, with the subsequent emergence of a new pandemic of influenza.

The pattern of replacement of HA and NA subtypes during the most recent century of pandemics is shown in Table 153–4, based both on virus isolation and on seroarcheology. Serologic studies suggest that the pandemic of 1889 was associated with viruses of an H2N2 subtype, followed by a pandemic in 1901 due to an H3N8 subtype.[12] As noted previously, the Spanish pandemic of 1918 was due to an H1N1 virus, which in turn was supplanted in the Asian pandemic of 1957 with H2N2 viruses. In 1968, the Hong Kong pandemic was caused by viruses of the H3N2 subtype. In 1977, viruses of the H1N1 subtype were reintroduced through an unknown mechanism. These viruses are genetically identical to H1N1 viruses that were circulating in 1950. Since 1977, influenza A viruses of both the H1N1 and H3N2 subtypes have cocirculated.

The degree of genetic difference between subtypes, 30% or greater, precludes their arising by simple point mutation, and the origin of new pandemic strains has been the subject of intense interest and study, for obvious reasons. The most plausible explanation for their origin takes into account three features of this phenomenon: (1) that the virus has a segmented genome, (2) that pandemics occur only with influenza A viruses, and (3) that influenza A viruses, but not other influenza viruses, maintain a large reservoir of genetic diversity in animals.

Influenza A viruses infect a variety of species, including humans, swine, horses, marine mammals, and, in particular, birds. In fact, no fewer than 15 unique HA subtypes (H1 to H15)[52] and 9 NA subtypes (N1 to N9)[53] have been identified in avian influenza viruses. Fortunately, avian influenza A viruses themselves appear to be relatively restricted in their ability to replicate in humans. The precise molecular mechanisms responsible for the host range preferences of avian influenza A viruses are not completely known, but several factors probably play a role. The divergent evolution of the genes of these viruses in avian hosts could have resulted in less efficient interactions

TABLE 153–4 Antigenic Subtypes of Influenza A Virus Associated with Pandemic Influenza

Year	Interval between Pandemics (yr)	Designation	Extent of Antigenic Change in Surface Protein*	Severity of Pandemic
1889	—	H2N2	?	Severe
1901	12	H3N8	H+ + + N+ + +	Moderate
1918	29	H1N1	H+ + + N+ + +	Severe
1957	39	H2N2	H+ + + N+ + +	Severe
1968	11	H3N2	H+ + + N–	Moderate
1977	9	H1N1	H+ + + N+ + +	Mild

*+, Minor change; + +, moderate change; + + +, major change; –, no change.

between undefined viral and mammalian host cell components. The relative attenuation of avian-human influenza reassortants for humans[54] supports a role for non-HA genes in this restriction. In addition, the HAs of avian and mammalian influenza viruses display a different host cell receptor specificity, with avian viruses preferring receptors containing sialic acid–galactose linkages of the $\alpha 2 \rightarrow 3$ variety and mammalian viruses preferring $\alpha 2 \rightarrow 6$ linkages.

Extensive sequence analysis has suggested at least two mechanisms by which avian viruses can circumvent these barriers to interspecies transmission. These studies have shown significant sequence similarity between the HA, NA, and PB1 gene segments of the pandemic H2N2 virus and avian viruses,[55, 56] and between the H3 and PB1 gene segments of the pandemic H3N2 virus and avian viruses,[55, 57] suggesting that in some circumstances, new pandemic viruses arise by reassortment between avian viruses, which provide novel surface glycoproteins, and human viruses, which provide genes allowing efficient replication. Reassortment would be facilitated by the presence of a third species that is susceptible to infection with both avian and human viruses, and pigs meet this requirement. This is an especially attractive concept because it would explain the observation that new pandemics often arise in the Far East, where humans, pigs, and aquatic fowl live in close proximity. There have been several recent intriguing observations suggesting interspecies transmission in the Far East,[58, 59] as well as demonstration of naturally occurring avian-human reassortant viruses in pigs.[60]

A second mechanism would involve direct adaptation to the human host and is supported by sequence analysis showing that the 1918 pandemic was probably due to direct introduction of a swine influenza A virus into humans.[13] Recently, it has been shown that avian H1N1 viruses introduced into swine populations are evolving in these animals and have switched receptor specificity to a more mammalian type.[61] This type of evolution is probably facilitated by the presence of both types of receptors in pig tracheal epithelia.[61] It is likely, however, that such events occur rarely.

There is obviously great interest in predicting the possibilities for a new pandemic influenza, a disease that can be considered the prototype of an emerging (or reemerging) infection.[62] The serologic observation that infection in humans appears to be limited to viruses of the H1, H2, and H3 subtype HA and of the N1, N2, and possibly N8 subtype NA suggests that there may be limitations on the possible makeup of such a virus.[63] However, a recent outbreak in humans of infection due to influenza viruses of the H5N1 subtype[64] in Hong Kong casts some doubt on this hypothesis. Although the virus in this outbreak was clearly of avian origin,[64, 65] severe and even fatal disease was seen.[66] Clear-cut evidence of person-to-person transmission of this virus has not been found, so that it remains possible that the localized outbreak of H5N1 infections in humans in Hong Kong was related to the unique circumstances of exposure to large numbers of infected birds on the island.

The failure of the H5N1 virus to transmit out of Hong Kong, similar to the failure of the H1N1 "swine flu" virus to transmit out of Fort Dix in 1976, points out the difficulties inherent in making predictions about pandemic influenza. Although both viruses possessed antigenic characteristics that would have facilitated rapid spread through the population at that time, this did not occur. Other factors that are not currently well characterized probably are crucial in determining the pandemic potential of such viruses. It is possible that viruses like these will eventually develop these characteristics, if allowed to evolve in the human host. The final answer to the question is unclear; in the meantime, considerable planning is under way for the almost inevitable occurrence of the next pandemic.[67]

PATHOGENESIS AND HOST RESPONSE

Cellular Pathogenesis

Influenza virus infection is acquired by a mechanism involving the transfer of virus-containing respiratory secretions from an infected person to a susceptible person.[68] A number of lines of evidence indicate that dispersion of virus in small-particle aerosols (<10 μm in mass median diameter) is the predominant factor in such person-to-person transmission. First, large amounts of virus are present in respiratory secretions of infected persons at the time of illness and are thus available for dispersion in small-particle aerosols created by sneezing, coughing, and talking.[68] Second, the explosive nature and simultaneous onset in many persons suggest that a single infected person can transmit virus to a large number of susceptible persons. Furthermore, influenza virus type A has been shown to be relatively stable in small-particle aerosols at a variety of relative humidities and temperatures, but survival appears to be favored by low relative humidity and low environmental temperature.[69] In experimental influenza in volunteers, inoculation with small-particle aerosols produces an illness that more closely mimics natural disease than does inoculation with large drops into the nose.[70, 71] Finally, in such experimental infections, doses of 137 to 300 times the median tissue culture infective dose ($TCID_{50}$) are required to infect by nasal drops, whereas 0.6 to 3.0 $TCID_{50}$ (i.e., a 100-fold-higher dose) is infectious by the aerosol route.[70, 71]

Once virus is deposited on the respiratory tract epithelium, it can attach to and penetrate columnar epithelial cells if not prevented from doing so by specific secretory antibody (immunoglobulin A [IgA]), by nonspecific mucoproteins to which virus may attach, or by the mechanical action of the mucociliary apparatus. After adsorption, virus replication begins, leading to cell death through several mechanisms. There is a dramatic shutoff of host cell protein synthesis, which occurs at several levels. Newly synthesized cellular messenger RNAs (mRNAs) are degraded, probably because cleavage by the virus cap endonuclease renders these transcripts susceptible to hydrolysis by cellular nuclease,[72] while translation of already synthesized cytoplasmic mRNAs is blocked at both initiation and elongation.[73] Finally, expression of the influenza virus acidic polymerase protein has been shown to induce generalized degradation of coexpressed proteins through an unknown mechanism.[74] Ultimately, the loss of critical cellular proteins probably contributes to cell death.

In addition to effects leading to cell necrosis, there is increasing evidence that infection of cells with influenza A and B viruses may cause cell death by apoptosis,[75, 76] a form of cell death characterized by fragmentation of nuclear DNA. Bronchiolar epithelial and alveolar cells harvested from experimentally infected mice also exhibit apoptotic changes, suggesting that this mechanism of cell death may be important in the pathogenesis of influenza in vivo.[77] The specific mechanism by which influenza virus induces apoptosis is unclear but may be related to induction of Fas antigen by double-stranded RNA during virus replication.[78]

Virus release continues for several hours before cell death ensues. Released virus then may initiate infection in adjacent and nearby cells, so within a few replication cycles, a large number of cells in the respiratory tract are releasing virus and dying because of virus replication. The duration of the incubation period to the onset of illness and virus shedding ranges from 18 to 72 hours, depending in part on the inoculum size.[68, 79]

Influenza virus infection of peripheral blood mononuclear cells, including polymorphonuclear leukocytes (PMLs), lymphocytes, and monocytes, is nonproductive but associated with measurable defects in cellular function that may be relevant to the pathogenesis of influenza-related infectious complications. These include defects in PML chemotaxis and phagocytosis,[80] as well as decreased proliferation and costimulation by mononuclear cells.[81, 82] The effects are mediated by virus replication and also possibly by a direct toxic effect of certain virus proteins, including the HA, the NA,[83, 84] and the NP.[85] It has been noted that the short portion of the sequence of the influenza A virus NP is homologous with a naturally occurring peptide found in normal bronchoalveolar lavage fluid that inhibits polymorphonuclear neutrophil (PMN) chemotaxis and oxidative burst.[86]

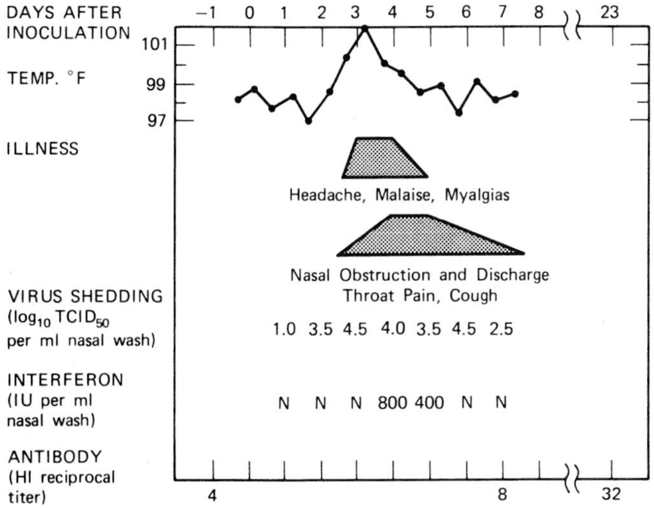

FIGURE 153–7. A case report of a volunteer inoculated by nose drops with 300 $TCID_{50}$ A/Aichi/69/H3N2. N, Negative.

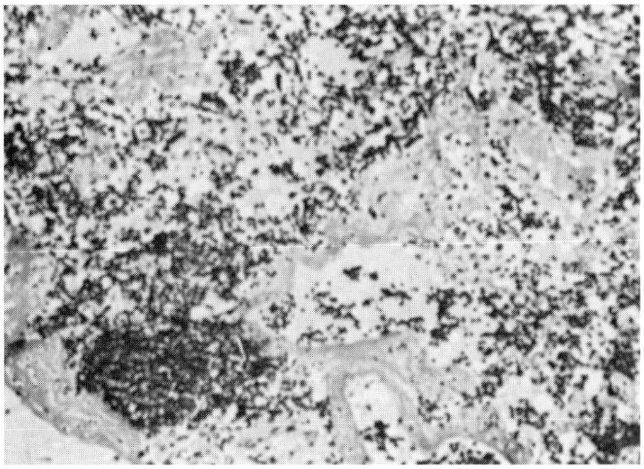

FIGURE 153–9. Lung parenchyma in primary influenza viral pneumonia shows extensive hemorrhage, acellular hyaline membrane lining alveolar ducts and alveoli, and a paucity of inflammatory cells within the alveoli (H&E, ×400). (Courtesy of I. D. Stuard, Reading, Pa.)

Virus Shedding

Quantitation of virus in respiratory tract specimens reveals a characteristic pattern (Fig. 153–7). Virus is first detected just before the onset of illness (within 24 hours), rapidly rises to a peak of 3.0 to 7.0 $\log_{10}$ $TCID_{50}$/ml, remains elevated for 24 to 48 hours, and then rapidly decreases to low titers.[68] Usually, influenza virus is no longer detectable after 5 to 10 days of virus shedding. In young children, shedding of high titers of virus is prolonged.[87]

The severity of illness correlates temporally with quantities of virus shed in experimental influenza in volunteers, thus suggesting that a major mechanism in the production of illness is cell death resulting from viral replication.[68] It is not known whether such a correlation holds for natural influenza. However, some severely ill persons shed only small amounts of virus. The occurrence of systemic illness and fever suggests dissemination of virus via the blood stream, but infectious virus in the blood has only rarely been detected.[88]

Histopathology

Bronchoscopy in persons with typical, uncomplicated acute influenza reveals diffuse inflammation of the larynx, trachea, and bronchi, with mucosal injection and edema.[89, 90] Biopsy in these cases has revealed a range of histologic findings, from vacuolization of columnar cells with cell loss, to extensive desquamation of the ciliated columnar epithelium down to the basal layer of cells[90, 91] (Fig. 153–8). Individual cells show shrinkage, pyknotic nuclei, and a loss of cilia. Viral antigen can be demonstrated in epithelial cells but is not seen in the basal cell layer.[92] Generally, the tissue response becomes more prominent in more distal segments of the airway.[90] Epithelial damage is accompanied by cellular infiltrates composed primarily of lymphocytes and histiocytes.[90] Histologic features at autopsy in more severe cases are those of extensive necrotizing tracheobronchitis, with ulceration and sloughing of the bronchial mucosa,[91, 93] extensive hemorrhage, hyaline membrane formation, and a paucity of polymorphonuclear cell infiltration (Fig. 153–9). Patients with secondary bacterial pneumonia have the changes characteristic of bacterial pneumonia in addition to the tracheobronchial features of influenza (Fig. 153–10). Recovery is associated with rapid regeneration of the epithelial cell layer and pseudometaplasia.

Pathophysiology

Abnormalities of pulmonary function are frequently demonstrated in otherwise healthy, nonasthmatic young adults with uncomplicated

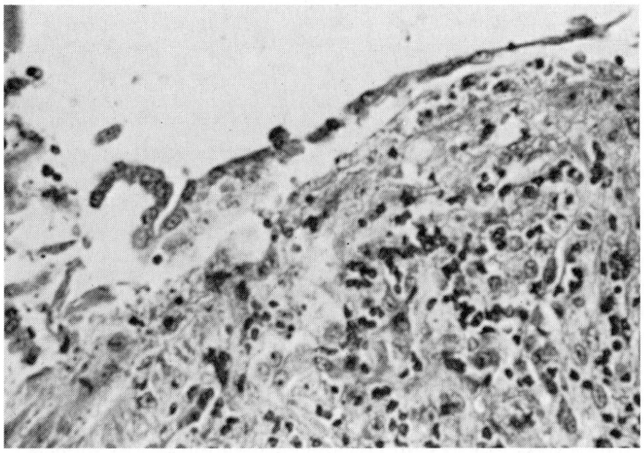

FIGURE 153–8. A small bronchus in acute influenza A infection shows ulceration and attempted regeneration of epithelium (H&E, ×100). (Courtesy of I. D. Stuard, Reading, Pa.)

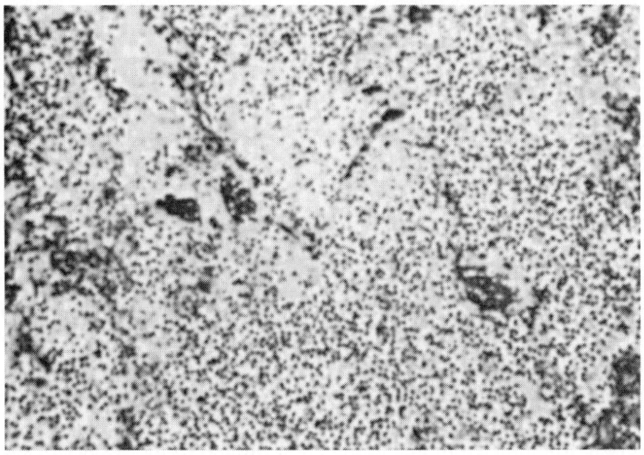

FIGURE 153–10. Lung parenchyma in secondary bacterial infection *(Streptococcus pneumoniae)* complicating influenza A virus infection. Note the marked intra-alveolar polymorphonuclear cell exudate (H&E, ×400). (Courtesy of I. D. Stuard, Reading, Pa.)

(nonpneumonic) acute influenza. Demonstrated defects include diminished forced flow rates, increased total pulmonary resistance, and decreased density-dependent forced flow rates, consistent with generalized increased resistance in airways less than 2 mm in diameter,[94, 95] as well as increased responses to bronchoprovocation.[94] In addition, abnormalities of carbon monoxide diffusing capacity[96] and increases in the alveolar-arterial oxygen gradient[97] have been seen. Of note, pulmonary function defects can persist for weeks after clinical recovery. Influenza in asthmatics[98] or patients with chronic obstructive disease[99] with influenza may result in acute declines in forced vital capacity (FVC) or the forced expiratory volume in 1 second (FEV_1). Persons with acute influenza may be more susceptible to bronchoconstriction from air pollutants such as nitrates.[100]

Primary viral pneumonia is an uncommon but frequently severe complication of acute influenza. In this situation, virus infection reaches the lung either by contiguous spread from the upper respiratory tract or by inhalation. The trachea and bronchi contain bloody fluid, and the mucosa is hyperemic.[101] Changes consistent with tracheitis, bronchitis, and bronchiolitis are seen, with loss of normal ciliated epithelial cells. Submucosal hyperemia, focal hemorrhage, edema, and cellular infiltrate are present. The alveolar spaces contain variable numbers of neutrophils and mononuclear cells admixed with fibrin and edema fluid. The alveolar capillaries may be markedly hyperemic with intra-alveolar hemorrhage. Acellular, hyaline membranes line many of the alveolar ducts and alveoli.[101] Pathologic findings seen by biopsy of lung in nonfatal cases are similar to those described in fatal cases.[102]

Bacterial superinfection is a well-recognized complication of viral pneumonia and accounts for a large proportion of the morbidity and mortality of viral lower respiratory tract disease, especially in adults. Consequently, the spectrum of disease and pathophysiology of bacterial superinfection has been studied intensively, and a number of factors identified in viral respiratory disease which could play a role in increasing the risk of bacterial infection.[103] Uncomplicated influenza is associated with significant abnormalities in ciliary clearance mechanisms.[104, 105] In addition, increased adherence of bacteria to virus-infected epithelial cells has been demonstrated.[106, 107] The disruption of the normal epithelial cell barrier to infection and loss of mucociliary clearance undoubtedly contribute to the enhancement of bacterial pathogenesis.[90, 108] Alterations in PMLs and mononuclear cells, as described previously, may also contribute to enhanced bacterial infection.[81, 109, 110] Finally, bacteria themselves may enhance the replication of some viruses such as influenza viruses by the release of proteases that cleave the viral HA.[111]

Viral Factors Influencing Pathogenicity

Clinical characteristics of illness during the 1918 influenza pandemic differed from those of subsequent pandemics, with higher mortality rates in young adults. Because the virus responsible for this pandemic is not available for further study, it is impossible to know what viral factors, if any, might have been responsible for this pathogenic behavior. Since that time, there has been little direct evidence for major inherent differences in viral strains that would affect pathogenic potential in humans. Recent H1N1 viruses appear to cause relatively milder illness than that due to recent H3N2 viruses.[112, 113] However, for the most part, the severity of most epidemics is probably determined largely by the status of immunity in the population.

An essential feature of influenza A virus replication is that proteolytic cleavage of the HA is required for generation of infectious virus, and this plays a part in the most clear-cut demonstration of the role of an individual influenza virus protein in pathogenicity. Infection of fowl with avian influenza viruses can result in a relatively avirulent asymptomatic infection limited to the respiratory and gastrointestinal mucosa, or in a virulent, rapidly progressive, fatal systemic infection with involvement of the brain and visceral organs. Comparison of the HAs of virulent and avirulent strains of H5 and H7 subtype influenza A viruses has shown that the structure of the HA cleavage site is crucial in determining the virulence phenotype in this model. Proteases capable of cleaving the HA of avirulent viruses, such as tryptase Clara,[114] are restricted in distribution to cells of the respiratory and gastrointestinal mucosa, thereby limiting replication to these areas. However, the addition of several basic amino acids to the cleavage site,[115] coupled with the absence of a nearby glycosylation site,[116] renders the HA capable of being cleaved by ubiquitous cellular furin-like proteases[117] and allows these viruses to escape the confines of the mucosa and replicate systemically.[118] Variability in HA cleavage has not as yet been demonstrated to be a factor in the pathogenicity of influenza viruses in humans, but severe cases of influenza have recently been reported in persons infected with an avian influenza virus possessing a highly cleavable HA.[66] Evaluation of the nucleotide sequence of the HA from the 1918 pandemic virus did not reveal this virus to have the highly cleavable type of HA,[13] so an explanation for the enhanced pathogenicity of this virus remains lacking.

Numerous additional animal models have been described in which it is possible to generate influenza viruses with altered levels of pathogenicity. A variety of classic genetic and molecular biologic techniques have been used to evaluate the role of specific viral genes or gene products in determining the virulence of influenza viruses in these models. An exhaustive review of these studies is beyond the scope of this chapter, but the studies have generally shown that virulence is a multigenic trait whose specific basis varies among virus strains and the models used.[119–121]

Immunology

Epidemiologic and experimental observations in humans have shown that infection with influenza virus results in long-lived resistance to reinfection with the homologous virus.[122] In addition, variable degrees of cross-protection within a subtype have been observed, but infection induces essentially no protection across subtypes,[123] or between types A and B. Infection induces both systemic and local antibody and also cytotoxic T-cell responses, each of which plays a role in recovery from infection and resistance to reinfection.

Antibody Responses

Systemic Antibody Responses

Infection with influenza virus results in the development of antibody to the influenza virus envelope glycoproteins HA and NA, as well as to the structural M and NP proteins. Some people may develop antibody to the M2 protein as well.[124] As measured by enzyme-linked immunosorbent assay (ELISA), serum IgM, IgA, and IgG antibodies to the HA appear simultaneously within 2 weeks of inoculation of virus.[125] The antibody response is more rapid after reinfection. The development of anti-NA antibodies parallels that of HA antibodies.[126] However, whereas responses to the HA develop after primary infection, responses to the NA appear to require previous infection.[123] Peak antibody responses are seen at 4 to 7 weeks after infection and decline slowly thereafter; titers can still be detected years after infection even without reexposure.

Antibody to the HA can be measured by standard HA inhibition (HAI) tests or a variety of ELISAs and neutralizes virus infectivity.[127] Because of the cost of the HA neutralization test and its requirement for cell cultures, the HAI test is the primary method of detecting antigenic relatedness among HAs of influenza viruses. Anti-HA antibody protects against both disease and infection with the homologous virus.[128] Although there is no exact correlation, serum HAI titers of 1:40 or greater, or serum neutralizing titers of 1:8 or greater, are associated with protection against infection; HAI titers of 1:20 or 1:10 are associated with lesser degrees of protection. More recent data suggest that for the elderly, a serum HAI antibody titer above 1:80 is required for complete protection.[129]

Protection in clinical studies has been shown to be primarily strain-specific, but some degree of protection is present against strains showing antigenic drift within a subtype, depending on the degree of drift.[130, 131] For example, Foy and associates showed that influenza A vaccine (A/Hong Kong/68/H3N2) induced protection against the drift variant A/England/72/H3N2 virus subtype, which persisted for 3 years.[130] Generally, antibody that is present in low quantity, or that is directed primarily against a heterologous strain of influenza, may only modify the severity of illness and may not prevent infection.

Antibody to the NA can be measured by NA inhibition or ELISA. In contrast to anti-HA antibody, anti-NA antibody does not neutralize virus infectivity but instead reduces efficient release of virus from infected cells, resulting in decreased plaque size in in vitro assays[132] and reductions in the magnitude of virus shedding in infected animals.[133, 134] Observations on the relative protection of persons with anti-N2 antibody during the A/Hong Kong/68 (H3N2) pandemic,[126, 135] as well as experimental challenge studies in humans,[136] have shown that anti-NA antibody can be protective against disease and results in decreased virus shedding and severity of illness but is infection-permissive.[137] Passive transfer studies in mice have also suggested that antibody to the M2 protein of influenza A viruses may have an effect similar to that of anti-NA antibody.[138]

Antibodies to internal viral proteins such as M or NP can be measured by the complement fixation (CF) test. These antibodies are cross-reactive among type A viruses but are non-neutralizing and do not appear to play a role in protective immunity. They disappear much more rapidly (weeks to months) than do neutralizing HA or anti-NA antibodies, primarily because they are predominantly IgM rather than IgG; therefore, they may be useful for diagnosis of recent infection.

Mucosal Antibody Responses

The majority of studies of mucosal responses to influenza in humans have concentrated on measurement of HA responses by ELISA or by neutralization tests, because nonspecific inhibitors of hemagglutination present in nasal mucus interfere with the standard HAI test. These studies have demonstrated significant mucosal responses to infection with wild-type virus or live attenuated influenza vaccines. Both IgA and IgG are found in nasal secretions. Nasal HA-specific IgG is predominantly IgG_1, and its levels correlate well with serum levels of HA-specific IgG_1, suggesting that nasal IgG originates by passive diffusion from the systemic compartment.[139] Nasal HA-specific IgA is predominantly polymeric IgA_1, suggesting local synthesis. Serum HA-specific IgA is also mostly polymeric IgA_1. The origin of serum IgA after mucosal infection is unclear, but it may derive from seeding of peripheral lymphoid tissue by memory cells derived from the mucosa.[128]

Studies in mice and ferrets have emphasized the importance of local IgA antibody in resistance to infection, particularly in protection of the upper respiratory tract. Polymeric IgA was shown to be specifically transported into the nasal secretions of mice and to protect against nasal challenge. Protection could be abrogated by intranasal administration of antiserum against IgA but not IgM or IgG.[140] Local antibody has also been shown to play a role in protection against antigenic variants in mice.[141] Studies in humans have also suggested that the resistance to reinfection induced by virus infection is mediated predominantly by local HA-specific IgA, whereas that induced by parenteral immunization with inactivated virus also depends on systemic IgG.[136, 142] Almost all persons with nasal neutralizing antibody titers of 1:4 or greater are protected against influenza.[143, 144] Of importance, either mucosal or systemic antibody alone can be protective if present in high enough concentrations, and optimal protection occurs when both are present.[145]

Cellular Responses

Antibody responses to the HA are T cell–dependent,[146–148] and class II major histocompatibility complex (MHC)–restricted $CD4^+$ cells provide help (as T helper [Th] cells) to B cells for production of antibody to the HA and the NA. Both $CD4^+$ cells that recognize epitopes on the HA molecule and $CD4^+$ cells recognizing epitopes on M, NP, or PB2 may provide help for HA antibody production.[149, 150] The epitopes on HA recognized by Th cells are distinct from those recognized by neutralizing antibody[151] and may be cross-reactive within a subtype. Influenza-specific Th cells also promote the generation of virus-specific $CD8^+$ CTLs.[152, 153]

Recently, it has been recognized that Th responses can be further classified as type 1 (Th1) or type 2 (Th2) responses based on the profile of cytokines produced upon in vitro challenge. Influenza virus infection in mice generates a strong Th1-type response.[154] Th2-type cytokines (interleukins IL-4, IL-5, IL-6, and IL-10) have been also described in the lungs of mice infected with influenza virus.[155, 156] Circumstantial evidence suggests that protective immune responses to influenza are associated with Th1-type responses. Adoptive transfer of anti-influenza T-cell clones secreting cytokines of the Th2 type fails to promote viral clearance,[157] and administration of interferon-γ delays viral clearance and development of CTLs in influenza virus infected mice.[158] Of note, blockade of interferon-γ by interferon antibody does not effect development of CTL responses but results in reduced migration of PMNs to the lung in the murine model.[159] In addition, administration of IL-4 to infected mice promotes Th2-type responses and results in markedly delayed viral clearance.[160]

Influenza virus–infected cells can be lysed by antibody in the presence of complement, by the effects of antibody-dependent cellular cytotoxicity,[161] or by the action of cytotoxic T lymphocytes (CTLs). Generally, CTLs express CD8 and are class I MHC–restricted. Such cells may recognize either HA or internal proteins such as M, NP, or PB2.[162] Therefore, CTLs may be subtype-specific or, in the case of those that recognize internal proteins, may be broadly cross-reactive, lysing cells infected with influenza A but not influenza B virus.[163, 164] In addition, class II–restricted cells may exhibit cytotoxic activity similar to that shown by class I–restricted cells.[164]

Extensive adoptive transfer experiments have shown that virus-specific CTLs can mediate recovery from influenza virus infection,[165–170] including both HA-specific and cross-reactive Tc lymphocytes. However, studies in mice lacking class I MHC have shown that CTLs are not absolutely required for recovery.[171–173]

CTL responses to influenza also develop in humans following influenza virus infections, generally peaking on about day 14 after infection.[174] Although not studied extensively, the presence of virus-specific pre-challenge class I–restricted CTLs has been shown to correlate with reductions in the duration and level of virus replication in adults with low levels of serum HA and NA antibody who were challenged with influenza A virus.[175] The role of CTLs directed against internal viral proteins in protection against severe disease in humans is unclear, as the internal virus proteins were shared between viruses causing the pandemics of 1957 and 1968 and the viruses in circulation immediately prior to these pandemics.[56, 63] Memory CTL responses may play a role in ameliorating the severity of disease and in speeding recovery following infection, as suggested by the finding of more severe influenza in persons with severe defects in cell-mediated immunity.[28]

Interferon is frequently detected in respiratory tract specimens and serum specimens from patients or volunteers with influenza virus infection and illness.[176, 177] Usually, shedding of virus precedes the appearance of interferon in both nasal secretions and serum by 1 to 2 days. The time of the appearance of interferon, between days 3 and 6, correlates with abatement of symptoms and a decrease in viral titers, which suggests that interferon may be active in the recovery process before serum or secretory antibody is detected. Recent studies have demonstrated that a wealth of additional cytokines are also elaborated during uncomplicated influenza in humans;[178] the role these cytokines play in pathogenesis or recovery from disease is unclear.

CLINICAL FINDINGS IN INFLUENZA

Uncomplicated Influenza

Typical uncomplicated influenza often begins with an abrupt onset of symptoms after an incubation period of 1 to 2 days. Many patients can pinpoint the hour of onset.[68, 179–181] Initially, systemic symptoms predominate and include fever, chills (which may be frank shaking chills), headaches, myalgia, malaise, and anorexia. In more severe cases, prostration is observed. Usually, myalgia and headaches are the most troublesome symptoms, and the severity is related to the magnitude of the febrile responses. Myalgia may involve the extremities or the long muscles of the back. In children, calf muscle myalgia may be particularly prominent. Severe pain in the eye muscles can be elicited by gazing laterally, and arthralgia but not frank arthritis is commonly observed. Other ocular symptoms include tearing and burning. The systemic symptoms usually persist for 3 days, the usual duration of fever.

Respiratory symptoms—particularly a dry cough, severe pharyngeal pain, and nasal obstruction and discharge—are usually also present at the onset of illness but are overshadowed by the systemic symptoms. The predominance of systemic symptoms is a major feature distinguishing influenza from other viral upper respiratory tract infections. Hoarseness and a dry or sore throat may also be present, but these symptoms tend to appear as systemic symptoms diminish, and thus they become more prominent as the disease progresses, persisting 3 to 4 days after the fever subsides. Cough is the most frequent and troublesome of these symptoms and may be accompanied by substernal discomfort or burning. Elderly individuals may present with only high fever, lassitude, and confusion without the characteristic respiratory manifestations, which may not occur at all. In addition, there is a wide range of symptoms in healthy adults, ranging from those of classic influenza to mild illness or asymptomatic infection.

Fever is the most important physical finding. The temperature usually rises rapidly to a peak of 100 to 104°F and occasionally to 106°F within 12 hours of onset, concurrent with the development of systemic symptoms. Fever is usually continuous but may be intermittent, especially if antipyretics are administered. On the second and third days of illness, the temperature elevation is usually 0.5 to 1.0° lower than on the first day, and as the fever subsides, the systemic symptoms diminish. Typically, the duration of fever is 3 days, but it may last 4 to 8 days. In a small number of cases, a second fever spike occurs on the third or fourth day, resulting in a biphasic fever curve.

Early in the course of illness, the patient appears toxic, the face is flushed, and the skin is hot and moist. The eyes are watery and reddened. A clear nasal discharge is common, but nasal obstruction is uncommon. The mucous membranes of the nose and throat are hyperemic, but exudate is not observed. Moderate enlargement and tenderness of cervical lymph nodes are often present. Transient scattered rhonchi or localized areas of rales are found in fewer than 20% of cases. A convalescent period of 1, 2, or more weeks to full recovery then ensues. Cough, lassitude, and malaise are the most frequent symptoms during this period.

Available data suggest that illness associated with influenza B virus infection closely resembles that described for influenza A, although some authorities have suggested that influenza B illness may be somewhat milder than influenza A illness.[182, 183] In contrast, influenza C infection, when it occurs, causes afebrile common colds and rarely, if ever, produces the influenza syndrome.[184] It does not occur in epidemics.

At the extremes of age, there are prominent differences in the epidemiologic and clinical characteristics. Influenza attack rates are higher in children than in adults.[24, 185] Maximal temperatures tend to be higher among children, and cervical adenopathy is more frequent among children than among adults.[79] Croup associated with influenza virus infection occurs only among children.[186–188] Among elderly persons, fever remains a very frequent finding, although the magnitude of the febrile response may be lower than among children and young adults. Pulmonary complications are far more frequent in the elderly than in any other age group.

Complications of Influenza

Pulmonary Complications

Two manifestations of pneumonia associated with influenza are well recognized: primary influenza viral pneumonia and secondary bacterial infection (Table 153–5). In addition, less distinct and milder pulmonic syndromes often occur during an outbreak of influenza that may represent tracheobronchitis, localized viral pneumonia, or possibly mixed viral and bacterial pneumonia. Comparative features of these clinical syndromes are shown in Table 153–4. Studies to determine the interaction between virus and bacteria have helped researchers understand the different clinical patterns.[189]

Primary Influenza Viral Pneumonia

The syndrome of primary influenza viral pneumonia was first well documented in the 1957–1958 outbreak.[89, 101] However, it is clear that many of the deaths in the 1918–1919 outbreak were due to the occurrence of this syndrome among young healthy adults. In outbreaks since 1918, primary influenza viral pneumonia has occurred predominantly among persons with cardiovascular disease, especially rheumatic heart disease with mitral stenosis, and to a lesser extent in others with chronic cardiovascular and pulmonary disorders. The illness begins with a typical onset of influenza, followed quickly by

TABLE 153–5 Comparative Features of Pulmonary Complications of Influenza

Feature	Primary Viral Pneumonia	Secondary Bacterial Pneumonia	Mixed Viral-Bacterial Pneumonia	Localized Viral Pneumonia
Setting	Cardiovascular disease Pregnancy Young adult (Hsw1N1)	Age >65 yr Pulmonary disease	Any associated with influenza A or B	?Normal
Clinical history	Relentless progression from classic 3-day influenza	Improvement, then worsening after 3-day influenza	Picture of influenza A or B	Continuation of classic 3-day syndrome
Physical examination	Bilateral findings, no consolidation	Consolidation	Consolidation	Area of rales
Sputum bacteriologic findings	Normal flora	Pneumococci *Staphylococcus* *Haemophilus influenzae*	Pneumococci *Staphylococcus* *H. influenzae*	Normal flora
Chest x-ray infiltrate	Bilateral findings	Consolidation	Consolidation	Segmental
White blood cell count	Leukocytosis with shift to the left	Leukocytosis with shift to the left	Leukocytosis with shift to the left	Usually normal
Isolation of influenza virus	Yes	Yes/no	Yes	Yes
Response to antibiotics	No	Yes	Often	No
Mortality	High	Low	Variable	Very low

a rapid progression of fever, cough, dyspnea, and cyanosis. Physical examination and chest x-ray studies reveal bilateral features consistent with the adult respiratory disease syndrome but no consolidation. Blood gas studies show marked hypoxia, Gram stain of the sputum fails to reveal significant bacteria, and bacterial culture yields sparse growth of normal flora, whereas viral cultures yield high titers of influenza A virus. Affected patients do not respond to antibiotics; the mortality is high. At autopsy, findings consist of tracheitis, bronchitis, diffuse hemorrhagic pneumonia, hyaline membranes lining alveolar ducts and alveoli, and a paucity of inflammatory cells within the alveoli (see Figs. 153–9 and 153–10). At present, late in the interpandemic era, severe primary influenza viral pneumonia is very rare.

Secondary Bacterial Pneumonia

Secondary bacterial pneumonia often produces a syndrome that is clinically indistinguishable from that occurring in the absence of influenza (Table 153–6).[190, 191] The patients, who most often are elderly or have chronic pulmonary, cardiac, and metabolic or other disease, have a classic influenza illness followed by a period of improvement lasting usually 4 to 14 days. Recrudescence of fever is associated with symptoms and signs of bacterial pneumonia such as cough, sputum production, and an area of consolidation detected on physical examination and chest film. Gram staining and culture of sputum reveal a predominance of a bacterial pathogen, most often *Streptococcus pneumoniae* or *Haemophilus influenzae* (see Table 153–6). *Staphylococcus aureus* is seen less frequently now than it was in the 1957–1958 outbreak. Such patients usually respond to specific antibiotic therapy. Analysis of different radiographic patterns of pneumonia indicates that a variety of abnormalities can occur[192, 193] in all age groups.

Other Clinical Patterns of Pneumonia

During an outbreak of influenza, many cases are observed that do not clearly fit into either of the aforementioned categories.[194] The disease is not relentlessly progressive, yet the fever pattern may not be biphasic. These patients may have primary viral, secondary bacterial, or mixed viral and bacterial infection of the lung. In more recent epidemics in which surveillance cultures of specimens from hospitalized patients have been obtained, most patients with pneumonia and influenza presented early, while they were still culture-positive for influenza virus. Most responded to antibiotics without the use of antivirals. In addition, milder forms of influenza viral pneumonia involving only one lobe or segment ("localized viral pneumonia") have been described that do not invariably lead to death, and that are more likely to be confused with pneumonia due to *Mycoplasma pneumoniae* than to pneumonia produced by bacterial infection.

TABLE 153-6 Etiology of Bacterial Pneumonia During and Preceding Influenza Outbreak

Etiologic Agent	Frequency: No. of Patients — *During Influenza Outbreak* 1968–1969*	*During Preceding Year† (No Influenza)*
Pneumococci	52 (48%)	103 (62%)
Staphylococcus	21 (19%)	10 (6%)
Staphylococcus and others	7 (7%)	7 (4%)
Haemophilus influenzae	12 (11%)	14 (8%)
Other gram-negative species	16 (15%)	32 (20%)
Total	108	167

*Three-week period only.
†Twelve-month period.
From Schwarzmann SW, Adler JL, Sullivan RFJ, Marine WM. Bacterial pneumonia during the Hong Kong influenza epidemic of 1968–1969. Arch Intern Med. 1971;127:1037–1041. With permission.

In children, pneumonia may occur, but it is less common than in adults. Bronchitis may also occur as a manifestation of influenza A or B virus infection, but respiratory syncytial virus and parainfluenza virus type 3 are more important causes of bronchiolitis.

Pulmonary Complications in Immunosuppressed Patients

In patients with HIV infection, influenza has not been recognized as a major clinical problem, although disease of greater severity has been noted in some patients,[27] and pneumonic complications of influenza have occurred. Additional studies are required to better define the importance of influenza virus infection in HIV-infected patients.

Influenza has been noted to cause severe disease with an increased incidence of pneumonia in immunosuppressed children with cancer, compared with age-matched persons without immunosuppression.[195] Severe disease associated with pneumonia and death has been reported, particularly in bone marrow transplant recipients and patients with leukemia.[28, 196, 197] Persons with relatively greater degrees of immunosuppression early after transplantation appear to be at greatest risk.[197] However, for reasons that are not completely clear, influenza has not appeared to be quite the problem in this population that other respiratory viruses, particularly paramyxoviruses, are. Influenza virus shedding can be quite prolonged in immunosuppressed children,[198] particularly those with HIV infection and low $CD4^+$ counts.[199] Because of the prolonged, unchecked replication of influenza viruses in these patients, resistance to antiviral drugs eventually occurs in many of those who have received treatment with these agents.[198, 200]

Other Pulmonary Complications

In addition to pneumonia, other pulmonary complications of influenza have been recognized.

Croup

Significant numbers of cases of croup occur in influenza A and B outbreaks.[186, 187] Croup associated with influenza A virus appears to be more severe but less frequent than that associated with parainfluenza virus type 1 or 3 or respiratory syncytial virus infections (see Chapter 49).

Exacerbation of Chronic Pulmonary Disease

Acute exacerbation of chronic bronchitis, a phenomenon that is associated with infection by other respiratory viruses and bacteria,[201–203] is common. Studies by Monto and Ross have shown that such infections can result in a permanent loss of pulmonary function.[204] Another major illness that is exacerbated is asthma. Often, stable asthma will worsen to status asthmaticus owing to influenza.[205, 206] Another illness exacerbated by influenza is cystic fibrosis. In children afflicted with this entity, influenza infections may lead to severe complications.[207]

Frequency of Pulmonary Involvement

The findings of persistent physiologic changes in the lower respiratory tract with uncomplicated influenza discussed earlier suggest that viral invasion of the lower respiratory tract is common in uncomplicated influenza and may help to explain the relatively long convalescence. The frequency of overt involvement of the respiratory tract has been answered in part by Fry.[192, 193, 208] In five successive epidemics, he showed that the overall rate of chest complications (tracheobronchitis or pneumonia) was 9.5%. From the ages of 5 to 50 years, the rate was low (4 to 8%), but it increased progressively after the age of 60 to a level of 73% in persons over 70 years of age. Foy and coworkers studied seven successive epidemics of influenza A infection and showed that six of the seven were associated with at least a doubling of pneumonia rates among adults.[209] Still other investigators have studied rates of admission to hospital and have shown a lower effect on hospitalization.[209–211]

Nonpulmonary Complications

Most of the complications of influenza have been evaluated in years when there were sizable outbreaks.[101, 212–214] However, as antigenic variation of a subtype evolves and as the exposure of the population to vaccine and to virus occurs, the full-blown influenza syndrome becomes a less frequent manifestation. Nonetheless, infection rates may remain high, and consequences of infection in severely debilitated elderly patients remain significant.

Myositis

Myositis and myoglobinuria with tender leg muscles and elevated serum creatine kinase (CK) levels have been reported mostly in children after influenza A or influenza B infection, most commonly after the latter,[215–218] but can occur in adults as well. Symptoms may be sufficiently severe to interfere with walking, but neurologic changes are not evident.

Cardiac Complications

Both myocarditis and pericarditis have been rarely associated with influenza A or B virus infection.[219] Some investigators have associated influenza with myocardial infarction. However, neither myocarditis nor pericarditis is commonly observed at autopsy among patients who died of primary influenza viral pneumonia.[101] In patients with cardiac disease, influenza virus infection carries a significant risk of death.[213, 220, 221]

Toxic Shock Syndrome

In recent outbreaks of influenza A or B, a toxic shock–like syndrome has occurred in previously healthy children or adults. The presumed pathogenic mechanism was a virus-effected change in colonization and replication characteristics of the toxin-producing staphylococcus.[222, 223]

Central Nervous Complications

Guillain-Barré syndrome has been reported to occur after influenza A infection, as it has after numerous other infections, but no definite etiologic relationship has been established. In addition, cases of transverse myelitis and encephalitis have occurred rarely.[224, 225] An etiologic association of these disorders with influenza virus infection has only infrequently been proved, and influenza infection at most accounts for only a small proportion of cases of each of these entities.

Reye's Syndrome

Reye's syndrome, first described in 1963, is a complication associated with influenza, with varicella, and with many other virus infections in children.[226–229]

Reye's syndrome can occur several days after a typical upper respiratory, gastrointestinal, or chickenpox infection. The classic manifestation of Reye's syndrome is a change in mental status.[230] Manifestations range from lethargy to delirium, obtundation, seizures, and respiratory arrest (Table 153–7). Lumbar puncture reveals normal protein values and normal cell counts, confirming the presence of encephalopathy rather than encephalitis or meningoencephalitis. The most frequent laboratory abnormality is elevation of the blood ammonia level, which occurs in almost all patients. Hypoglycemia is present most often in patients with antecedent varicella or gastrointestinal illness (37%), as compared with those who had upper respiratory illness (15%). Serum aspartate aminotransferase (AST), serum alanine aminotransferase (ALT), and bilirubin values are commonly elevated, as are CK and lactic dehydrogenase (LDH) levels. The prothrombin time is usually increased. Coma (stage 4 or 5) on admission is evidence of increased intracranial pressure, and a blood ammonia level greater than 300 μg/dl is significantly associated with mortality.

TABLE 153–7 Reye's Syndrome: Clinical Characteristics

Characteristic	Frequency among Affected Patients (%)
Antecedent illness*	
Upper respiratory tract illness	89
Varicella	7
Gastrointestinal illness	4
Central nervous system manifestations	
Stage of coma on admission	
0 Alert	2
1 Lethargy, follows verbal commands	26
2 Stupor, combativeness, conjugate deviation	42
3 Coma, decortication	17
4 Coma, decerebration, loss of oculocephalic reflexes	10
5 Coma, absent pupillary reaction, flaccidity	3
Laboratory data	
Blood glucose <50 mg/dl	15
Blood ammonia†	
>48 μg/dl (upper limit of normal)	98
>100 μg/dl	76
>200 μg/dl	46
>500 μg/dl	13

*Interval between onset of the antecedent illness and hospitalization (mean, 5.7 days).
Data from Corey et al.[228] and Consensus Development Conference.[231]

The striking feature is the absence of inflammatory changes.[229, 230] On microscopic examination, the chief finding is fatty infiltration of hepatocytes. The main ultrastructural feature is alteration of the hepatocyte mitochondria including swelling and pleomorphism. The pathologic features most often detected in the brain have been those of cerebral edema and anoxic neuronal degeneration, but no gross inflammation.

General supportive measures include hemodynamic monitoring with careful attention to fluid and electrolyte balance and to the provision of assistance for ventilation with intubation when needed. Intravenous glucose is infused to correct hypoglycemia. Modalities such as dialysis and amino acid and phosphate and insulin infusions to correct specific metabolic abnormalities have not altered the outcome.[231–233] Because the major cause of death is cerebral edema, monitoring intracranial pressure[234] with therapy directed at lowering increased intracranial pressure (such as mannitol and glycerol) constitutes a reasonable approach.

The recognition of the connection between administration of acetylsalicyclic acid (aspirin) and Reye's syndrome led to recommendations to avoid aspirin in viral infections, and the syndrome has largely disappeared.[235–237] The American Academy of Pediatrics has recommended that another antipyretic agent be substituted for aspirin in children with fevers due to influenza or varicella.[231, 237]

DIAGNOSIS

Virus Isolation

Virus isolation or detection of viral antigen in respiratory secretions is the technique of greatest utility in the setting of acute illness. Virus can be isolated readily from nasal swab specimens, throat swab specimens, nasal washes, or combined nose-and-throat swab specimens. There is a general consensus that throat swab alone is probably less sensitive for detection than other samples. Virus can be isolated directly from sputum samples, if sputum is being produced.[238] Samples should be placed into containers of viral transport medium and transported to the laboratory as soon as possible, although the virus survives overnight if the specimen is kept on ice. Specimens for influenza are inoculated onto rhesus monkey kidney, cynomolgus monkey kidney, or Madin-Darby canine kidney cell cultures, where virus is detected by cytopathic effect or hemadsorption. About two thirds of the positive cultures can be detected within 3 days of inoculation and the remainder by 5 to 7 days. Many hospital viral diagnostic laboratories and most state health laboratories can detect influenza virus by these cell culture techniques or, less commonly, by the inoculation of embryonated hens' eggs.

Rapid Diagnosis

A variety of techniques have been employed in order to speed the process. Centrifugation of samples directly onto cells in shell vials with detection of the production of viral antigens by immunofluorescence (IF) studies or ELISA can reduce the time needed to detect virus to 1 or 2 days.[239] Rapid detection of viral antigen directly in respiratory secretions can be accomplished by a variety of techniques including IF studies,[240] time-resolved immunofluoresence assay (TRFIA),[241] radioenzyme immunoassay,[242] and ELISA.[243] The most rapid of the ELISAs can produce results in less than 1 hour, with sensitivity and specificity approaching those of cell culture under optimal conditions. Available formats include filter immunoassays (Directigen flu A)[244] and microtiter plate assays (Enzygnost A and B).[245] The sensitivity of such tests may be higher with nasopharyngeal washes and swabs than with other samples.[246] Recently, PCR techniques have been described for rapid detection of influenza virus RNA in clinical samples.[247, 248] Such techniques may also be useful for direct characterization of viral genes without alterations introduced by virus isolation techniques.[249]

Serologic Testing

Serologic tests comparing acute and convalescent sera, although sensitive and specific, do not yield data in time to affect clinical decisions. For serologic diagnosis, CF or HAI tests are most commonly used. Paired serum specimens, consisting of an acute and a convalescent serum specimen obtained 10 to 20 days after the acute-phase serum specimen, should be submitted for testing. Fourfold or greater rises in titer are considered diagnostic of infection.[250]

Epidemiologic Diagnosis

A diagnosis can also be made on epidemiologic grounds. That is, when influenza virus is confirmed in a region or community by the local or state health department or by the Centers for Disease Control and Prevention (CDC), persons with fever, muscle aches, and cough probably have influenza. In fact, several studies have shown the accuracy of a clinical diagnosis in the setting of an influenza outbreak to be as high as 85%.[251–256] However, this may not be the case in institutional settings, in which respiratory syncytial virus infection can mimic influenza.[257]

TREATMENT

Uncomplicated Influenza

Amantadine and Rimantadine

The antiviral drugs amantadine and rimantadine are active against all strains of influenza A virus in a variety of cell culture systems and animal models.[258] In cell culture, inhibitory levels for influenza A virus range from 0.2 to 0.4 μg/ml for amantadine and from 0.1 to 0.4 μg/ml for rimantadine.[259] Both drugs are active against influenza A virus only at clinically achievable levels. The antiviral activity of these drugs is due to interaction with the M2 protein of susceptible viruses, as indicated by analysis of drug-resistant mutants.[260–262] Binding of these drugs to the M2 protein interferes with the function of M2 as an ion channel, which can be measured by in vitro assays of channel activity.[263] In turn, this inhibits the pH-dependent release of ribonucleoproteins (RNPs), manifested by inhibition of uncoating in cell culture assays.[264–267] The drugs may also effect HA maturation of certain strains of virus.

There are pharmacokinetic differences between amantadine and rimantadine.[268] Amantadine does not undergo metabolism and is excreted unchanged in the urine, with a half-life of 12 to 18 hours. These characteristics lead to rapid accumulation of amantadine in two settings: in patients with renal failure and in the elderly with reduced renal function due to age. In the elderly, it is recommended that the dosage of amantadine be reduced to no more than 100 mg daily and perhaps even to 100 mg every other day after the first few days, although extensive evidence of the efficacy for these lower doses is not available. By contrast, rimantadine undergoes extensive metabolism. Less than 15% of drug is excreted in the urine unchanged, and the remainder is excreted as metabolic products.[269] However, rimantadine accumulates only very slowly, which may explain the development of side effects in the prophylactic studies but not in the treatment studies. The recommended dose of rimantadine in the elderly is also 100 mg per day. The mechanisms of action of these drugs and their pharmacokinetics are described in more detail in Chapter 36.

Both amantadine and rimantadine are active in the treatment of experimentally induced and naturally acquired influenza A, with most studies showing a reduction in clinical symptom scores, a more rapid reduction of fever, and a reduction in the levels and duration of virus shedding compared with placebo.[255, 270] Amantadine was also shown to be slightly more effective than aspirin in the reduction of clinical symptoms of naturally acquired influenza A in young adults.[256] In addition, treatment with amantadine results in significantly more rapid improvement in small airways dysfunction in healthy adults with uncomplicated influenza (Fig. 153–11).[94, 271] Rimantadine has also been evaluated in the treatment of influenza A in children and was shown to reduce the level of virus shedding early in infection, whereas acetaminophen did not.[272, 273] More variable effects on clinical symptom scores have been seen, with one study showing a decrease in scores and fever compared with acetaminophen[272] and with another, in which illness was relatively mild, showing no significant difference.[273] In both studies, virus shedding was relatively prolonged in persons receiving rimantadine, and resistant virus was shed late in the course of illness. Illness associated with shedding of resistant virus was similar to that associated with drug-sensitive virus. As discussed later on, comparative studies of the efficacy of amantadine or rimantadine in the treatment of more complicated influenza infection—for example, in hospitalized patients or those with pneumonia—have not been reported. However, most authorities support the use of amantadine in the treatment of complicated influenza A virus infection, even late in the course of illness.[274] Amantadine is currently licensed in both the United States and Canada for treatment of influenza in adults and children, Rimantadine is licensed in the United States for treatment in adults.

Neither drug has been subjected to extensive efficacy evaluation in high-risk subjects. One placebo-controlled blinded study carried out in nursing home patients showed more rapid reduction in fever and in symptoms in rimantadine recipients. Furthermore, physicians who were caring for these patients, but who were blinded to the study drug status, prescribed significantly fewer antipyretics, antitussives, and antibiotics and obtained fewer chest radiographs for the rimantadine recipients.[275]

The major side effects of amantadine are minor, reversible central nervous system (CNS) side effects such as insomnia, dizziness, or difficulty in concentrating.[255, 271, 276] These side effects may be more troublesome in the elderly, in whom a dose reduction to 100 mg per day is recommended. In addition, amantadine use has been associated with seizures in persons with a prior seizure disorder. Rimantadine is associated with a considerably reduced rate of CNS side effects, but the dose of rimantadine should be reduced to 100 mg per day in the elderly as well.

Antiviral drug resistance has been one factor that has limited the

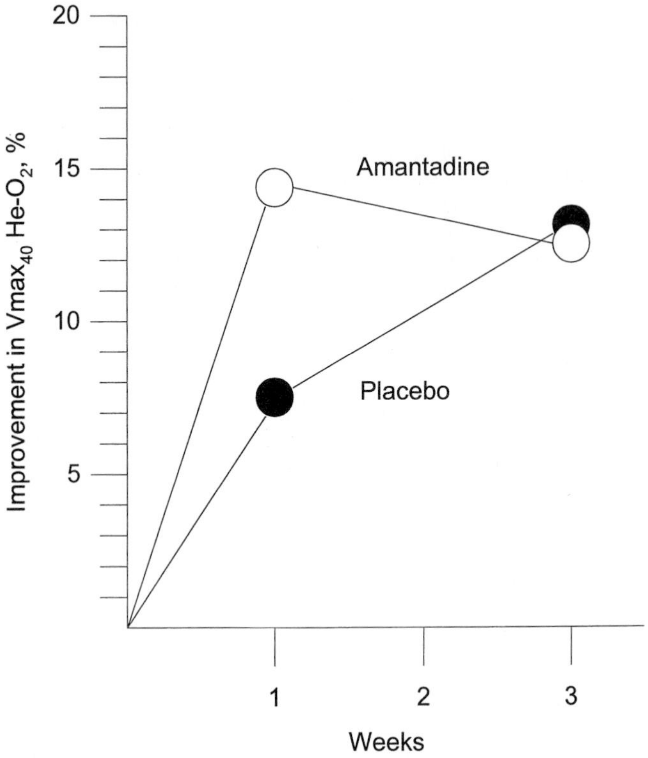

FIGURE 153–11. Improvement in pulmonary function with amantadine treatment of uncomplicated influenza A in young adults. There was a statistically significant difference between amantadine and placebo recipients in the degree of improvement of pulmonary function after 1 week. (Modified from Little J, Hall W, Douglas RGJ, et al. Amantadine effect on peripheral airways abnormalities in influenza. Ann Intern Med. 1976;85:177–182.)

more widespread use of these drugs.[277] Amantadine- and rimantadine-resistant viruses emerge fairly frequently in persons receiving treatment with these drugs,[278, 279] although resistant virus is seen infrequently in unexposed persons.[280] Resistant virus can be transmitted to and cause disease in susceptible contacts,[278, 279, 281] and drug-resistant virus retains full pathogenic potential in experimental animals.[282, 283] Although the use of combined vaccination and amantadine can decrease the generation and transmission of resistant viruses,[284, 285] the problem of drug resistance remains an important consideration that may limit the more widespread use of these agents. However, the M2 protein remains an attractive target for development of antiviral agents because it is specific for influenza virus and because highly accurate in vitro screening assays are available.[286]

Other Antiviral Compounds with Activity against Influenza

The determination of the crystal structure of the NA complexed with its substrate, sialic acid,[287] has allowed the development of a series of sialic acid analogues with NA-inhibiting activity.[288] The first of these compounds to see clinical use, 4-guanidino-2,4-dideoxy-2,3-dehydro-*N*-acetylneuraminic acid (4-guanidino-Neu5Ac2en, zanamivir), is a highly potent and selective inhibitor of the NA of influenza A and B viruses. Zanamivir has significant antiviral activity against a wide variety of laboratory and clinical influenza A and B isolates in cell culture and in the mouse and ferret models.[288, 289] The drug is not bioavailable when given orally; therefore, effective use of this agent requires local administration. Intranasal zanamivir has been shown to be effective in the therapy of influenza in the adult challenge model in which both early treatment (beginning 26 to 32 hours after challenge) and late treatment (beginning 50 hours after challenge) were effective in reducing virus shedding compared with placebo, and early treatment also reduced symptom scores and reduced the frequency of middle ear abnormalities.[290, 291] Subsequently, inhaled zanamivir was shown to be active in the early treatment of naturally acquired acute influenza A and B in humans, resulting in an approximately 24-hour decrease in the duration of symptoms when administered within the first 48 hours of illness.[292] Zanamivir also reduced the frequency of complications in a small number of high-risk subjects.[293] This drug is therefore the first antiviral with clear-cut clinical efficacy against both influenza A and B in humans. Oral anti-NA inhibitors, such as the experimental compound GS4104, are also in development. Studies in the human challenge model[294] and in natural infection[295] have demonstrated similar levels of efficacy. In field trials, treatment in otherwise healthy adults within 36 hours of onset of symptoms resulted in an approximately 50% reduction in the rate of complications, primarily sinusitis and bronchitis.[295] It is very likely that a number of NA inhibitors will be licensed for the treatment of influenza A and B in the near future.

Because zanamavir interacts with highly conserved residues within the influenza virus NA, it was hoped that antiviral resistance would be a limited problem. In fact, truly resistant viruses have not been isolated from humans who received zanamavir in clinical trials to date, although a resistant virus has been reported in an immunosuppressed child receiving zanamivir under a compassionate use protocol.[200]

Viruses resistant to the in vitro antiviral activity of zanamavir have been isolated after passage in cell culture. Analysis of these viruses has revealed two basic mechanisms of resistance and illustrate the interactive roles of the viral HA and NA in attachment to and release from infected cells. Mutations within the catalytic framework of the NA that abolish binding of the drugs have been described.[296, 297] Depending on the location of the mutation, these viruses may be specifically resistant to only one inhibitor. Resistance mutations in the NA may be associated with altered characteristics of the enzyme with significantly reduced activity.[298, 299]

A second type of mutation associated with drug-resistant viruses identified in cell culture involves mutations in the receptor binding region of the HA. In order to understand these mutations, it is necessary to recall that the major function of the NA is to cleave sialic acid receptors from the host cell, thereby allowing the virus to leave and spread to other cells.[300, 301] HA mutations associated with resistance to NA inhibitors reduce the affinity of the HA for its receptor, allowing cell-to-cell spread of virus in the absence of NA activity.[296, 302] It is even possible to generate inhibitor-dependent viruses, in which the affinity for the receptor is apparently so low that NA activity must be inhibited in order to allow the virus to bind at all. Resistant viruses with HA mutations exhibit cross-resistance to these drugs in cell culture but may retain susceptibility in animal models. Many of these viruses also exhibit reduced virulence in animals.

The antiviral drug ribavirin (1β-D-ribofuranosyl-1,2,3-triazole-3-carboxamide) is active against influenza A and B virus in human challenge models when administered by small particle aerosol.[303, 304] However, the relatively limited efficacy of the drug[305] and the cumbersome method of administration have limited its utility in this situation. An anecdotal report suggested that intravenous ribavirin may be useful for the treatment of influenza virus–associated acute myocarditis.[306]

Other Treatment Modalities

Acutely ill febrile patients should be at bed rest, and fluid intake should be adequate. Acetylsalicylic acid (0.6 to 0.9 g every 3 to 4 hours) is effective in reducing fever.[256] However, antipyretics other than aspirin are recommended for children.[307] Nasal obstruction may be relieved by phenylephrine (0.25%) or oxymetazoline hydrochloride (0.05%; 0.025% in younger children) nasal spray or drops, and cough may be reduced with cold water vaporization or guaifenesin cough syrup containing dextromethorphan, 1 to 3 teaspoons every 3 to 4 hours (lower dose in young children).

Pulmonary Complications

There have been no controlled studies of amantadine, rimantadine, or ribavirin treatment of influenza viral pneumonia, so the use of these agents in this condition is based on extrapolation from anecdotal case reports of benefit and on data indicating an effect of amantadine on peripheral airway resistance in uncomplicated influenza (see Fig. 153–11).[94, 271]

Supportive care is important, including fluid and electrolyte management. Supplemental oxygen, intubation, tracheotomy, assisted ventilation, and the use of positive end-expiratory pressure may have a role depending on the severity of the illness.[308] For patients with proven or suspected bacterial supra-infection, appropriate antibiotics for the specific organism should be administered. Because of the rapidly progressive illness in many cases of pneumonia occurring during an influenza epidemic, therapy effective against the potential pathogens, including *S. pneumoniae, H. influenzae,* and possibly *S. aureus,* is indicated if an etiologic diagnosis cannot be made from a Gram stain of the sputum.

Other Complications

There is no specific therapy for cardiac, CNS, or other complications. A discussion of the treatment of Reye's syndrome is presented in the section on that illness.

PREVENTION

Vaccines

Both inactivated vaccines and live attenuated virus vaccines have been developed to stimulate humoral and, to a lesser extent, cellular immunity to influenza. The major focus of influenza immunization has generally been the stimulation of local and systemic antibodies to the HA and NA.[309] Inactivated influenza vaccines have been in use since the late 1940s and represent the main control measure for influenza available today. More recently, considerable progress has been made in the development of live attenuated vaccines.

Inactivated Influenza Vaccine

At present, inactivated influenza vaccines—either whole-virus vaccines, detergent-treated "split-product" vaccines, or subunit HA/NA vaccines—are licensed for the prevention of influenza. Because disease due to influenza A (H1N1), A (H3N2), and influenza B viruses may occur in a single season, a trivalent vaccine is currently used.

Vaccine Composition, Dosage, and Administration

The process of selecting the particular strains to be included in the vaccine represents an educated guess regarding the viral antigenic variants likely to be causing disease in the coming season. New strains are collected worldwide on a continuous basis and subjected to careful molecular and antigenic characterization. These data, along with evaluation of the antibody responses to previous vaccines, current epidemiologic trends, and the growth characteristics in eggs of candidate strains, are used by the U.S. Public Health Advisory Committee on Immunization Practices to make recommendations with regard to the composition of the vaccine. Because of the time required to actually produce the vaccine, this decision must be made approximately 6 to 9 months prior to distribution of the final product.

The dose-response curve for standard inactivated vaccine appears to be fairly flat,[310, 311] with an increase in local reactions seen with higher doses.[312] Therefore, vaccine is currently standardized at a concentration of 30 μg/mL as determined by immunodiffusion. A dose of 0.5 ml (15 μg), administered by intramuscular injection, is given to children 3 years of age and older, and younger children should receive 0.25 ml. Adults and older children should receive vaccine in the deltoid, whereas younger children are generally vaccinated in the anterolateral aspect of the thigh. Only a single dose of vaccine is required in persons who have been previously vaccinated or who have experienced prior infection with a related virus subtype, but a two-dose schedule is required in children younger than 9 years of age who are receiving influenza vaccine for the first time and in other "unprimed" persons.[310, 313] Use of a second dose of vaccine in adults does not provide any benefit.[314]

Vaccine-Related Side Effects

Randomized, placebo-controlled trials of modern influenza vaccines have demonstrated these vaccines to be well tolerated in all age groups. One quarter to one half of vaccine recipients feel some discomfort at the vaccine site 8 to 24 hours after vaccination, but only about 5% have moderately severe transient local pain and swelling. Systemic symptoms, such as malaise, headache, or myalgias, occur at a low rate, similar to that noted for placebo.[310, 315, 316] Reactions to whole-virus and split-product vaccines at current doses are similar in adults,[311] but whole-virus vaccines were associated with a higher rate of fever in children[313] and are not recommended for those younger than 12 years of age, in whom subvirion or split-product vaccines should be used.

During the 1976 National Immunization Program against swine influenza, 45 million persons received influenza vaccine. In the first 4 to 6 weeks after vaccination, an excess rate of cases of Guillain-Barré syndrome (GBS) occurred among vaccinees, compared with that in persons who did not receive the vaccine.[317] The estimated risk of acquiring GBS during that vaccination program was 1 in 100,000 vaccinations; the mortality for persons with GBS was 5% (i.e., 1 in 2 million vaccinations), and another 5 to 10% had some residual neurologic abnormality.[317] The relationship between inactivated influenza vaccines other than the Swine/New Jersey/76 vaccine and GBS is less clear-cut. National surveillance conducted since 1976 has generally not identified increased rates of this syndrome following vaccination. However, very slight increases in the risk of GBS were seen following the 1992–1993 and 1993–1994 vaccines, representing an excess of slightly more than 1 case per 1 million persons vaccinated.[318]

Concern has been raised that influenza vaccination can be associated with severe drug toxicity in patients receiving warfarin or theophylline, owing to vaccine-induced depression of the metabolic activity of the hepatic cytochrome p-450 enzyme system.[319] However, two subsequent studies failed to support the initial observations. A prospective study of residents (155 receiving theophylline and 48 receiving warfarin) in 52 nursing homes during the 1982–1983 influenza season failed to reveal evidence of warfarin or theophylline toxicity in the 30-day period after vaccination.[320] Similar findings were obtained in other studies.[321, 322]

Recent influenza vaccination has been associated with false-positive results on ELISA testing for antibody to HIV, human T-lymphotropic virus type I (HTLV-1), and hepatitis C virus.[323] Results on Western blot antibody testing remain negative. This phenomenon is infrequent (occurring in 0.6 to 1.7% of blood donors who received influenza vaccination) and appears to be of relatively short duration, at least for HIV and HTLV-1 serologic studies. It is believed that this false-positive reaction is caused by an early nonspecific IgM response after influenza vaccination.[323]

Immunogenicity in Healthy Adults

Inactivated influenza vaccines are immunogenic when administered at the currently recommended dose of approximately 15 μg of each HA antigen in healthy adults and result in increases in HA-inhibiting antibody in about 90% of recipients.[311, 315, 316] Antibody to the NA is seen less frequently, partly because of the relative lability of the NA during the inactivation process. In addition, animal studies have suggested that anti-NA responses are impaired when this antigen is presented in association with an HA to which the animal is "primed" (so-called intravirionic competition).[324, 325] Both systemic and local antibody responses have been observed.[143, 326] Previous exposure significantly affects the magnitude of the serum antibody response.[327] Generally, the responses of children with high-risk conditions are similar to those of age-matched controls.[328–331]

Safety and Immunogenicity in High-Risk Persons

Individuals with chronic renal disease may respond less well to influenza vaccine,[332] although not all studies have reported such an effect.[333, 334] The response in patients undergoing hemodialysis is similar to that in normal persons.[332–334] Diminished immune responses to vaccination may occur in renal transplant recipients.[335–337] Such impaired responses are associated with increased degrees of both azotemia and immunosuppression.[335, 338] Cyclosporine, a potent suppressor of T cells, is associated with significantly more impaired immune responses to vaccination.[338, 339] Of importance, adverse effects from vaccines are no more frequent than are those that occur in control subjects, and renal function is not adversely affected.

Influenza vaccination is safe and immunogenic in persons with rheumatoid arthritis[340] and systemic lupus erythematosus[341, 342] and is not associated with exacerbations of disease. The immune response to vaccination in HIV-infected persons is related to the degree of immunosuppression.[343] It has been suggested that the immune activation associated with influenza immunization may transiently stimulate HIV replication, with some studies showing transient, minor increases in viral load after immunization[344, 345] and others showing no effect.[346] The clinical significance of these observations is unclear, and the potential benefits of vaccination argue against withholding vaccine for these considerations.

Most patients with chronic lung disease respond reasonably well to vaccination, and steroids at doses commonly used to treat reactive airways disease do not appear to preclude vaccine responses.[347, 348] Of importance, vaccination is safe and is not associated with worsening pulmonary function.[348, 349]

Other patients at risk for pulmonary complications of influenza but who may have a greater potential to develop side effects from vaccine administration (e.g., patients with neurologic disease) have not been studied extensively. One study in patients with multiple sclerosis[350] showed no deleterious effects, and response rates were comparable with those for healthy persons. Because persons with a history of GBS have a higher risk of spontaneously developing GBS again, many physicians avoid administering inactivated influenza vaccine to such persons, particularly if the GBS occurred within 6 weeks after a previous influenza vaccination.

Protective Efficacy

Inactivated influenza vaccine was effective in the prevention of influenza A in several randomized or semirandomized controlled studies conducted in young adults, with levels of protection of 70 to 90% when there was a good antigenic match between vaccine and epidemic viruses.[131, 351, 352] However, when the antigenic relatedness of the vaccine strain and the epidemic strain is low, the effectiveness of inactivated vaccine is considerably less.[351, 353, 354] Studies suggest that vaccines reduce the frequency of severe illness to a greater degree than the frequency of infection, both in young adults and in the elderly.[129, 355, 356] Vaccination of healthy adults is associated with decreased absenteeism[357] from work or school and is significantly cost-saving.[358]

Relatively few prospective trials of protective efficacy have been conducted in high-risk populations. In one recent randomized, placebo-controlled trial in an elderly population, inactivated vaccine was approximately 58% effective in preventing laboratory-documented influenza.[359] In addition, numerous retrospective case-control studies are available that have documented the effectiveness of inactivated influenza vaccines in this age group.[25, 354, 355, 360–364] A recent meta-analysis of published cohort observational trials derived a very similar estimate of 56% for the level of vaccine efficacy against respiratory illness in the elderly.[365] Vaccine is protective against influenza- and pneumonia-related hospitalization in the elderly and is even accompanied by a decrease in all-cause mortality.[366] A recently conducted Medicare demonstration project indicated that vaccine usage had a beneificial effect on reduction of hospital admissions associated with laboratory-documented influenza A or B infection.[367] It has been estimated that among elderly persons living in the community, influenza vaccination is associated with a direct savings of $117 per year per person vaccinated.[368] It has also been suggested that vaccination of staff members in long-term care facilities can have a major impact on mortality among elderly residents of these institutions.[369]

Despite studies that support the use of inactivated vaccines in the elderly, the protective efficacy of vaccination appears to be lower in persons older than 65 years of age than in younger adults,[354, 359, 362, 370–372] possibly because of decreased antibody responsiveness to influenza vaccine in this age group.[316, 373–377] The specific factors in aging that result in decreased immune responses to vaccination have not been identified with certainty. Aged animals clearly have diminished responses to vaccination compared with those in young animals. However, in human studies, multiple factors may be involved. Not all studies have shown diminished responses to vaccination in the elderly, with the effect of the specific antigen outweighing any effect of age.[378] The effect of age may be primarily in affecting the subclass of HA-specific IgG produced,[379] consistent with an effect of aging on numbers of naive T cells. In some studies, the presence of chronic disability, rather than age per se, appears better able to predict lack of responsiveness.[380] Malnutrition, also a common problem in the disabled elderly, does not appear to play an important role.[381] Some studies have suggested that whole-virus vaccines are more immunogenic in the elderly, but this finding has not been consistent with all formulations of vaccine.[382, 383]

Live Attenuated Vaccines

Live virus vaccines for influenza have also been intensively evaluated in humans but are not currently licensed for clinical use. The use of live attenuated viruses as influenza vaccines offers several potential advantages over parenteral inactivated vaccines, including induction of a mucosal immune response that closely mimics that induced by natural influenza virus infection.[384] In addition, the superiority of such vaccines in protection of the upper respiratory tract[385] could potentially be useful in strategies to limit the spread of virus within the population.[386] In practical terms, the use of a nasal rather than parenteral route of administration might be more acceptable to patients, particularly those in younger age groups.

A key requirement for the development of attenuated influenza vaccines is the ability to rapidly attenuate new antigenic variants. The most widely used approach takes advantage of the segmented nature of the influenza virus genome to generate reassortant viruses in which the gene segments encoding attenuation are derived from a well-characterized master donor vaccine virus, and the gene segments encoding the HA and NA are derived from the new antigenic variant.[387, 388] In the past, extensive studies were performed to evaluate the use of temperature-sensitive[389] or avian[390] influenza viruses as donors of attenuating genes. However, these approaches were not successful, because of either genetic instability[391] or unreliable attenuation.[392, 393] Of importance, such deficiencies in the safety profile of these approaches to live attenuated influenza vaccine were detected only when studies were performed in young children, who are generally most susceptible to infection by the vaccine viruses.

Cold-Adapted Influenza Vaccines

The most promising approach to the development of a master donor virus has been the use of cold-adapted *(ca)* viruses. The process of cold adaptation refers to the repetitive passage of a virus at gradually decreasing temperatures until a virus is isolated that replicates efficiently at a low temperature at which the replication of the original wild-type virus is significantly restricted.[394] During this process, additional mutant phenotypes are frequently acquired.

The *ca* influenza A/Ann Arbor/6/60 virus[394] has been extensively evaluated as a donor of attenuating genes for the generation of *ca* vaccine viruses. A large number of *ca* A/AA/60 reassortant influenza A viruses has been evaluated in young adults, children, and high-risk groups and found to be attenuated and immunogenic (reviewed by Murphy.[395] Of importance, genetic reversion to virulence has not been demonstrated, even in seronegative young children. Lack of reversion is likely because the genetic basis of attenuation resides on at least three gene segments, the PB1, PB2, and PA gene segments.[396, 397] In addition, because none of these gene segments would be expected to interact with the HA or NA of the wild-type donor virus, the attenuation of *ca* reassortant viruses would not be expected to vary significantly from reassortant to reassortant. A similarly derived *ca* influenza B/Ann Arbor/1/66 virus has been used as a donor of attenuating genes for the generation of *ca* influenza B vaccine viruses.[394]

Reassortant *ca* monovalent influenza A[142, 385] and B[398, 399] viruses or trivalent preparations of *ca* viruses[400] provide protection against homologous wild-type challenge in susceptible young adults at least equal to that provided by inactivated vaccines. Reassortant *ca* viruses have also been shown to protect against natural wild-type influenza infection in randomized, controlled field trials in children.[401, 402] In a recent study conducted in over 1600 children ages 18 to 72 months, a two-dose schedule of intranasal live trivalent *ca* vaccine was shown to be well tolerated and to have greater than 90% efficacy in prevention of illness due to influenza A (H3N2) and B viruses (H1N1 infections did not occur during the study).[403] In a field trial conducted in more than 5000 adults, the level of protection afforded by a bivalent cold-adapted influenza A vaccine was approximately equal to that of inactivated vaccine.[404] Because of the multiple exposures to influenza virus that accumulate with aging, *ca* vaccine viruses tend to manifest relatively limited replication and immunogenicity in the elderly.[405–407] However, the combinations of intranasal cold-adapted influenza A vaccine and parenteral inactivated vaccine provided enhanced protection against influenza A in a small study conducted among debilitated patients residing in a nursing home.[408] In summary, current evidence suggests that live cold-adapted vaccine will be particularly useful in small children and will serve as an acceptable option for vaccination of healthy adults. In elderly persons, the combination of live and inactivated vaccine may provide enhanced protection.

Other Live Vaccines

A variety of additional live attenuated influenza viruses have been evaluated. Perhaps the most intriguing, novel approach has utilized techniques for the reverse genetic engineering of specific mutations in the genome of influenza A and B viruses.[409–411] An influenza A virus in which the 3′ and 5′ ends of the NA gene segment were replaced by the corresponding regions of an influenza B virus was recently shown to replicate and to manifest attenuated virulence in a murine model.[412] Attenuation has also been achieved by manipulation of the stalk of the NA,[413, 414] and by direct introduction of attenuating mutations into the PB2 gene.[415] Further development of such viruses may lead to a second generation of potential live virus vaccine candidates, as well as providing a vector for the administration of additional immunogenic epitopes.[416, 417]

DNA Vaccines

A potential advantage of live viral vaccines is that they result in endogenous, intracellular synthesis of viral antigen and presentation in the context of class I MHC. An alternative means to induce intracellular synthesis of viral antigens is the delivery of the genes encoding the antigen of interest by a heterologous foreign vector. Recently, it has been recognized that under certain circumstances, foreign DNA could be delivered directly to the cells of an intact animal, taken up, and expressed, and that the animal would manifest an immune response to the foreign gene product.[418] Immunization of mice with DNA encoding the HA, as well as the internal M and NP proteins, of influenza A induces long-lived humoral and cellular immune responses[419, 420] that are protective against viral infection and disease. Recently, immunization of African green monkeys with DNA encoding a combination of three HAs and other influenza virus genes was shown to induce serum antibody against all three HAs.[421]

Recommendations for Vaccine Use

Inactivated influenza vaccines remain the only vaccines currently available for prevention of influenza. Recommendations for the use of inactivated vaccine[422] are based on the strategy that immunization efforts should be concentrated on two groups: (1) persons at increased risk for the development of influenza-related complications, and (2) persons who can transmit influenza to those at high risk for complications. Groups for whom such efforts should be targeted are shown in Table 153–8.

Vaccine should usually be administered in the fall to allow time for the development of protective immunity prior to the influenza season. However, adults who have been vaccinated numerous times previously can have a measurable increase in antibody only a few days after vaccination. Influenza vaccine can be given at the same time as pneumococcal vaccine, which has a similar target population but is administered once.[423] There is a much higher frequency of hospitalization for influenza among persons who have been hospitalized within the previous 3 months.[424] Therefore, physicians should consider vaccinating such persons prior to hospital discharge if there is any doubt about medical follow-up.

The only contraindication to vaccination is hypersensitivity to hens' eggs, in which the vaccine virus is grown. Generally, if the person to be vaccinated can eat eggs or egg-containing products, vaccination is safe. Although vaccine is usually not administered to patients with a genuine anaphylactic hypersensitivity to egg products, such persons can be desensitized and safely vaccinated if necessary.[425, 426]

Special attention needs to be given to the timing of vaccine administration in patients who are receiving cytotoxic drugs. Studies in children[427] and in adults[428] who are receiving treatment for malignancy show that a significantly lower proportion of patients produce antibody (50% of adults or children) when vaccine is administered simultaneously with chemotherapy than when vaccine is administered at the nadir of the white cell count response or when no chemotherapy is given. Over 95% of the adults or children with malignancies responded to A/New Jersey/76 if chemotherapy was not being administered at the time vaccine was given.[427, 428]

Except for the influenza pandemics of 1918–1919 and 1957–

TABLE 153–8 Target Groups for Influenza Immunization

Groups at increased risk for influenza-related complications
Persons 65 years of age and older
Residents of nursing homes and other chronic care facilities that house persons of any age who have chronic conditions
Adults and children who have chronic disorders of the pulmonary or cardiovascular system, including children with asthma
Children and teenagers (aged 6 months to 18 years) who are receiving long-term aspirin therapy
Women who will be in the second or third trimester of pregnancy during the influenza season
Occupational groups with increased potential for transmission of influenza to persons at high risk
Physicians, nurses, and other health care personnel
Employees of nursing homes and other chronic care facilities who have patient contact
Providers of home care and household contacts of persons at high risk

From Centers for Disease Control and Prevention. Prevention and control of influenza: Recommendations of the Advisory Committee on Immunization Practices (ACIP). MMWR Morb Mortal Wkly Rep. 1998;47(RR-6):1–26.

1958, influenza in pregnancy has not been associated with increased mortality or fetal loss.[429] However, the increased physiologic demands of pregnancy could be associated with enhanced severity of influenza, and recent studies suggest that there is a significant increase in hospitalizations for cardiorespiratory conditions among women in the third trimester of pregnancy during influenza season.[430] Experience with the use of influenza vaccine in pregnancy has been considerable, and it appears to be safe in this situation. Therefore, current recommendations are to administer vaccine to women who will be in the second or third trimester of pregnancy (i.e., >14 weeks of gestation) during influenza season.[422] A secondary potential benefit of this strategy is the provision of antibody to the infant, depending on the timing of maternal immunization.[431] Because of the high rate of spontaneous fetal loss during the first trimester, vaccination should generally be avoided during this period, unless the pregnant woman has other high-risk medical conditions, in which case vaccine should be administered regardless of the stage of pregnancy.

The duration of protective immunity appears to be limited, particularly in the elderly,[432] and in most years, one or more of the vaccine components are updated to keep pace with antigenic drift in circulating viruses. Thus, current inactivated vaccines must be administered yearly. In some situations, yearly administration has been reported to result in decreased effectiveness.[433] Recent studies suggest that prior immunization does not adversely affect immune responses to vaccination or the protection afforded by inactivated vaccine, at least in healthy adults.[356]

Chemoprophylaxis

Amantadine and rimantadine are approved for use as prophylactic agents against influenza. Their level of efficacy is about 75 to 90%,[275, 276, 434–439] and protection may be additive to that of vaccine. In a study evaluating prophylaxis against influenza in young adults, rimantadine was compared with amantadine and placebo.[276] Both drugs were significantly more effective in preventing clinical influenza than was placebo; however, rimantadine was associated with a lower incidence of toxic side effects than that noted with amantadine. In fact, side effects in rimantadine recipients were similar in frequency to those in placebo recipients. More recently, rimantadine administered for prophylaxis to 60 people older than 65 years of age was as well tolerated as placebo and yielded a lower incidence of clinical influenza than did placebo.[440] In one study, lower doses of rimantadine (100 mg/day) were found to be effective as prophylaxis against influenza A.[441] Taken together, these data suggest that if both drugs are available, there may be an improved benefit/risk ratio with use of rimantadine compared with amantadine.

Because of the cost, requirements for prolonged administration of drugs, and potential for side effects, mass chemoprophylaxis against influenza in the general population is impractical at present. Amantadine or rimantadine can be considered for prophylaxis for selected persons for a 5- to 7-week period during an outbreak of influenza, particularly for those rare, high-risk persons who have an absolute contraindication to vaccine.[442] Chemoprophylaxis may also be used to supplement protection offered by vaccine in patients who might be expected have a suboptimal response to vaccination.[440] Mass chemoprophylaxis could be considered in the event of emergence of an antigenic variant for which vaccine would be ineffective, such as in a pandemic situation, although the logistic problems inherent in this approach are daunting.

There are several other situations in which shorter courses of chemoprophylaxis may be useful. High-risk patients who are not vaccinated until after the epidemic has already begun can receive chemoprophylaxis for 2 weeks after vaccination to prevent influenza until the antibody responses to vaccination mature. Amantadine and rimantadine have no effect on the antibody response to vaccination with inactivated vaccines. Chemoprophylaxis can also be considered after a known exposure to a case of influenza. Such contact prophylaxis has been evaluated in family studies and in institutional outbreaks. In the family setting, rates of influenza A are reduced in family contacts as long as the index case is not treated at the same time.[443] However, when both the index case as well as those due to family contacts are treated, prophylaxis generally fails and is associated with the development and transmission of drug-resistant virus within the family.[278] Illness caused by resistant virus in this situation is similar to that caused by sensitive virus.

Amantadine or rimantadine or both are currently recommended for use during institutional outbreaks of influenza A, a situation that has been compared to an outbreak in a large family.[277] Although no placebo-controlled, randomized trials have been done to evaluate the use of amantadine under these circumstances, retrospective analyses of such outbreaks support this recommendation.[442, 444] These studies have suggested efficacy of amantadine during nosocomial outbreaks among high-risk patients in hospitals, as well as in multiple outbreaks in nursing homes. Amantadine-resistant virus has also been isolated under these circumstances, with person-to-person transmission, which suggests that patients receiving treatment should be separated from those receiving prophylaxis in institutional outbreaks.[281, 445] In some situations, especially when vaccination rates are low, prophylaxis in staff members may also be useful to control an outbreak.[258, 439, 446]

Nosocomial Influenza

Nosocomial influenza has produced major problems in several epidemics in the past and continues to do so.[447] This is not surprising, because hospitals include a concentration of patients at risk for complications and mortality related to influenza. Thus, special attention to the prevention of nosocomial spread of influenza should be undertaken when an epidemic is identified in the community. Factors that seem appropriate include encouragement of vaccination, supplemented with amantadine or rimantadine for hospital staff members.[439, 446, 448] If staff members develop illness, they should be required to stay home from work, if at all possible. Visitors with any illness should be prohibited. Patients with acute illness should be isolated in single rooms or in groups, and staff members should be divided into groups to provide care either for patients with suspected influenza or for patients thought not to have influenza. It may be prudent to place special emphasis on chemoprophylaxis for staff members providing care for acutely ill patients. Wearing gowns and masks and hand washing are a logical part of the isolation procedure for influenza. It may also be wise to postpone elective surgery when nosocomial influenza is apparent, because anesthesia may add to the risk of pulmonary complications associated with influenza. Strictly speaking, the value of these procedures has not been proved. However, nosocomial influenza has produced disastrous consequences, and reasonable and logical efforts to curtail it seem justified.[439, 446, 448]

REFERENCES

1. Hirsch A. Handbook of Geographical and Historical Pathology, v. 1. London: New Syndenham Society; 1883.
2. Thomson D, Thomson R. Influenza. New York: Ann Pickett-Thomas Research Labs; 1933.
3. Syndenham T. Influenza: Of the epidemic diseases. In: Major RH, ed. Classical Descriptions of Disease. Springfield, Ill: Charles C Thomas; 1955:201.
4. Crosby AW. Epidemic and Peace, 1918, part IV. Westport, CT: Greenwood Press; 1976.
5. Smith W, Andrewes CH, Laidlaw PP. A virus obtained from influenza patients. Lancet. 1933;2:66–68.
6. Francis T Jr. A new type of virus from epidemic influenza. Science. 1940;92:405–408.
7. Taylor RM. A further note on 1233 ("influenza C") virus. Arch Gesamte Virusforsch. 1951;4:485–495.
8. Burnet FM. Influenza virus on the developing egg. I. Changes associated with the development of an egg-passage strain of virus. Br J Exp Pathol. 1936;17:282–295.
9. Mogabgab WJ, Green IJ, Dierkhising OC. Primary isolation and propagation of

influenza virus in cultures of human embryonic renal tissue. Science. 1954;120:320–321.
10. Hirst GK. The agglutination of red cells by allantoic flid of chick embryos infected with influenza virus. Science. 1941;94:22–23.
11. Schoenbaum SC, Coleman MT, Dowdle WR, Mostow SR. Epidemiology of influenza in the elderly: Evidence of virus recycling. Am J Epidemiol. 1976;103:166–173.
12. Masurel N, Marine WM. Recycling of Asian and Hong Kong influenza A virus hemagglutinins in man. Am J Epidemiol. 1973;97:44–49.
13. Taubenberger JK, Reid AH, Krafft AE, et al. Initial genetic characterization of the 1918 "Spanish" influenza virus. Science. 1997;275:1793–1796.
14. Francis T Jr, Salk JE, Pearson HE, Brown PN. Protective effect of vaccination against influenza A. Proc Soc Exp Biol Med. 1944;55:104–105.
15. Francis T Jr, Pearson HE, Salk JE, Brown PN. Immunity in human subjects artifically infected with influenza virus type B. Am J Pub Health. 1944;34:317–334.
16. Francis T Jr. Transmission of influenza by a filterable virus. Science. 1934;80:457–459.
17. Wilson IA, Skehel JJ, Wiley DG. Structure of the hemagglutinin membrane glycoprotein of influenza virus at 3Å resolution. Nature. 1981;289:366.
18. Kendal AP, Galphin JC, Palmer EL. Replication of influenza virus at elevated temperature: Production of virus-like particles with reduced matrix protein content. Virology. 1977;76:186.
19. Glezen WP. Serious morbidity and mortality associated with influenza epidemics. Epidemiol Rev. 1982;4:24–44.
20. Perrotta DM, Decker M, Glezen WP. Acute respiratory disease hospitalizations as a measure of impact of epidemic influenza. Am J Epidemiol. 1985;122:468–476.
21. Liu KJ, Kendal AP. Impact of influenza epidemics on mortality in the United States from October 1972 to May 1985. Am J Public Health. 1987;77:712–716.
22. Simonsen L, Clarke MJ, Williamson DW, et al. The impact of influenza epidemics on mortality: Introducing a severity index. Am J Pub Health. 1997;87:1944–1950.
23. Sullivan KM, Monto AS, Longini IM. Estimates of the US health impact of influenza. Am J Pub Health. 1993;83:1712–1716.
24. Glezen WP, Keitel WA, Taber LH, et al. Age distribution of patients with medically-attended illnesses caused by sequential variants of influenza A/H1N1: Comparison to age-specific infection rates, 1978–1989. Am J Epidemiol. 1991;133:296–304.
25. Barker WH, Mullooly JP. Impact of epidemic type A influenza in a defined adult population. Am J Epidemiol. 1980;112:798–813.
26. Centers for Disease Control and Prevention. Prevention and control of influenza: Recommendations of the Immunization Practices Advisory Committee (ACIP). MMWR Morb Mortal Wkly Rep. 1992;41:1–17.
27. Safrin S, Rush JD, Mills J. Influenza in patients with human immunodeficiency virus infection. Chest. 1990;98:33–37.
28. Whimbey E, Eling LS, Couch RB, et al. Influenza A virus infection among hospitalized adult bone marrow transplant recipients. Bone Marrow Transplant. 1994;13:437–440.
29. Schoenbaum SC. Impact of influenza in persons and populations. In: Brown LE, Hampson AW, Webster RG, eds. Options for the Control of Influenza III. New York: Elsevier Science B.V.; 1996;17–25.
30. Kavet J. A perspective on the significance of pandemic influenza. Am J Pub Health. 1977;67:1063–1070.
31. Keech M, Scott AJ, Ryan PJJ. The impact of influenza and influenza-like illness on productivity and healthcare resource utilization in a working population. Occup Med. 1998;48:85–90.
32. Smith AP, Thomas M, Brockman P, et al. Effect of influenza B virus infection on human performance. BMJ. 1993;306:760–761.
33. Barker WH, Borisute H, Cox C. A study of the impact of influenza on the functional status of frail older people. Arch Intern Med. 1998;158:645–650.
34. Glezen WP, Couch RB. Interpandemic influenza in the Houston area, 1974–1976. N Engl J Med. 1978;298:587–593.
35. Glezen WP, Payne AA, Snyder DN, Downs TD. Mortality and influenza. J Infect Dis. 1982;146:313–321.
36. Monto AS, Kioumehr F. The Tecumseh study of respiratory illness. IX. Occurrence of influenza in the community, 1966–1971. Am J Epidemiol. 1975;102:553–559.
37. Yorke MA, Nathanson N, Pianigiani G, Martin J. Seasonality and the requirements for perpetuation and eradication of viruses in populations. Am J Epidemiol. 1979;109:103–123.
38. Schaffer FL, Soergel ME, Straube DC. Survival of airborne influenza virus: Effects of propagating host, relative humidity, and composition of spray fluids. Arch Virol. 1976;54:263–273.
39. Hall CB, Douglas RG Jr. Respiratory syncytial virus and influenza: Practical community surveillance. Am J Dis Child. 1976;130:615–620.
40. Kendal AP, Schieble J, Cooney MK, et al. Co-circulation of two influenza A (H3N2) antigenic variants detected by virus surveillance in individual communities. Am J Epidemiol. 1978;108:308–311.
41. Falsey AR, Cunningham CK, Barker WH, et al. A comparison of respiratory syncytial virus and influenza infection in the hospitalized elderly. Presented at the Thirty-first Annual Meeting of the Infectious Disease Society of America, New Orleans, September 1993.
42. Glezen WP, Couch RB, Six HR. The influenza herald wave. Am J Epidemiol. 1982;116:589–598.
43. Simonsen L, Clarke MJ, Schonberger LB, et al. Pandemic versus epidemic influenza mortality: A pattern of changing age distribution. J Infect Dis. 1998;178:53–60.
44. Stevens DJ, Douglas AR, Skehel JJ, Wiley DC. Antigenic and amino acid sequence analysis of the variants of H1N1 influenza virus in 1986. Bull WHO. 1987;65:177–180.
45. Webster RG, Kendal AP, Gerhard W. Analysis of antigenic drift in recently isolated influenza A (H1N1) viruses using monoclonal antibody preparations. Virology. 1979;96:258–264.
46. Webster RG, Laver WG, Air GM, et al. The mechanism of antigenic drift in influenza viruses: analysis of Hong Kong (H3N2) variants with monoclonal antibodies to the hemagglutinin molecule. Ann N Y Acad Sci. 1980;354:142–161.
47. Lai CJ, Markoff LJ, Sveda MM, et al. Genetic variation of influenza A viruses as studied by recombinant DNA techniques. Ann N Y Acad Sci. 1980;354:162–171.
48. Hauptmann R, Clarke LD, Mountford RC, et al. Nucleotide sequence of the haemagglutinin gene of influenza virus A/England/321/77. J Gen Virol. 1983;64:215–220.
49. Webster RG, Laver WG. Determination of the number of nonoverlapping antigenic areas on Hong Kong (H3N2) influenza virus hemagglutinin with monoclonal antibodies and the selection of variants with potential epidemiological significance. Virology. 1980;104:139–148.
50. Yamashita M, Krystal M, Fitch WM, Palese P. Influenza B virus evolution: Co-circulating lineages and comparison of evolutionary patterns with those of influenza A and C viruses. Virology. 1988;163:112–122.
51. Xu X, Cox NJ, Bender CA, et al. Genetic variation in the neuraminidase genes of influenza A (H3N2) viruses. Virology. 1996;224:175–183.
52. Rohm C, Zhou N, Suss J, et al. Characterization of a novel influenza hemagglutinin, H15: Criteria for determination of influenza A subtypes. Virology. 1996;217:508–515.
53. Colman PM, Ward CW. Structure and diversity of influenza virus neuraminidase. Curr Top Microbiol Immunol. 1985;11:177–255.
54. Murphy BR, Sly DL, Tierney EL, et al. Reassortant virus derived from avian and human influenza A viruses is attenuated and immunogenic in monkeys. Science. 1982;218:1330–1332.
55. Kawaoka Y, Krauss S, Webster RG. Avian-to-human transmission of the PB1 gene of influenza A viruses in the 1957 and 1968 pandemics. J Virol. 1989;63:4603–4608.
56. Treanor J, Kawaoka Y, Miller R, et al. Nucleotide sequence of the avian influenza A/Mallard/NY/6750 virus polymerase genes. Virus Res. 1989;14:257–270.
57. Bean WJ, Schell M, Katz J, et al. Evolution of the H3 hemagglutinin from human and nonhuman hosts. J Virol. 1992;66:1129–1138.
58. Shu LL, Zhou NN, Sharp GB, et al. An epidemiological study of influenza viruses among Chinese farm families with household ducks and pigs. Epidemiol Infect. 1996;117:179–188.
59. Zhou N, He S, Zhang T, et al. Influenza infection in humans and pigs in southeastern China. Arch Virol. 1996;141:649–661.
60. Castrucci MR, Donatelli I, Sidoli I, et al. Genetic reassortment between avian and human influenza A viruses in Italian pigs. Virology. 1993;193:503–506.
61. Ito T, Couceiro JN, Kelm S, et al. Molecular basis for the generation in pigs of influenza A viruses with pandemic potential. J Virol. 1998;72:7367–7373.
62. Webster RG, Wright SM, Castrucci MR, et al. Influenza—a model of an emerging virus disease. Intervirology. 1993;35:16–25.
63. Treanor JJ, Murphy B. Genes involved in the restriction of replication of avian influenza A viruses in primates. In: Kurstak E, ed. Virus Variability, Epidemiology, and Control, v. 2. New York: Plenum Publishing; 1990:159–176.
64. Subbarao K, Klimov A, Katz J, et al. Characterization of an avian influenza A (H5N1) virus isolated from a child with a fatal respiratory illness. Science. 1998;279:393–396.
65. Suarez DL, Perdue ML, Cox N, et al. Comparisons of highly virulent H5N1 influenza A viruses isolated from humans and chickens from Hong Kong. J Virol. 1998;72:6678–6688.
66. Yuen KY, Chan PKS, Peiris M, et al. Clinical features and rapid viral diagnosis of human disease associated with avian influenza A H5N1 virus. Lancet. 1998;351:467–471.
67. Shortridge KF. The next pandemic influenza virus? Lancet 1995;346:1210–1212.
68. Douglas RG Jr. Influenza in man. In: Kilbourne ED, ed. The Influenza Viruses and Influenza. New York: Academic Press; 1975:395–447.
69. Hemmes HJ, Winkler DC, Kool SM. Virus survival as a seasonal factor in influenza and poliomyelitis. Nature. 1960;188:430.
70. Alford RH, Kasel JA, Gerone PJ, Knight V. Human influenza resulting from aerosol inhalation. Proc Soc Exp Biol Med. 1966;122:800–804.
71. Little JW, Douglas RG Jr, Hall WJ, Roth FK. Attenuated influenza produced by experimental intranasal inoculation. J Med Virol. 1979;3:177–188.
72. Katze M, Krug R. Metabolism and expression of RNA polymerase II transcripts in influenza virus infected cells. Mol Cell Biol. 1984;4:2198–2206.
73. Katze M, DeCorato D, Krug R. Cellular mRNA translation is blocked at both initiation and elongation after infection by influenza virus or adenovirus. J Virol. 1986;60:1027–1039.
74. Sanz-Esquerro JJ, De La Luna S, Ortin J, Nieto A. Individual expression of the influenza virus PA protein induces degradation of coexpressed proteins. J Virol. 1995;69:2420–2426.
75. Hinshaw VS, Olsen CW, Dybdahl-Sissoko N, Evans D. Apoptosis: A mechanism of cell killing by influenza A and B viruses. J Virol. 1994;68:3667–3673.
76. Takizawa T, Shigeru M, Higuchi Y, et al. Induction of programmed cell death (apoptosis) by influenza virus infection in tissue culture cells. J Gen Virol. 1993;74:2347–2355.
77. Mori I, Komatsu T, Takeuchi K, et al. In vivo induction of apoptosis by influenza virus. J Gen Virol. 1995;76:2869–2873.
78. Takizawa T, Fukuda R, Miyawaki T, et al. Activation of the apoptotic Fas antigen-

encoding gene upon influenza virus infection involving spontaneously produced beta-interferon. Virology 1995;209:288–296.
79. Jordan WS, Denny FW, Badger GF. A study of illness in a group of Cleveland families. XVII. The occurrence of Asian influenza. Am J Hyg. 1958;68:160.
80. Larson HE, Parry RP, Tyrrell DAJ. Impaired polymorphonuclear leucocyte chemotaxis after influenza virus infection. Br J Dis Chest. 1980;74:56–62.
81. Roberts NJ, Steigbigel RT. Effect of in vitro virus infection on response of human monocytes and lymphocytes to mitogen stimulation. J Immunol. 1978;121:1052–1058.
82. Roberts NJ, Prill AH, Mann TN. Interleukin 1 and interleukin 1 inhibitor production by human macrophages exposed to influenza virus or respiratory syncytial virus: Respiratory syncytial virus is a potent inducer of inhibitory activity. J Exp Med. 1986;163:511–519.
83. Suzuki H, Kurita T, Kakinuma K. Effects of neuraminidase on O_2 consumption and release of O_2 and H_2O_2 from phagocytosing human polymorphonuclear leukocytes. Blood. 1982;60:446–453.
84. Cassidy LF, Lyles DS, Abramson JS. Depression of polymorphonuclear leukocyte functions by purified influenza virus hemagglutinin and sialic acid–binding lectins. J Immunol. 1989;142:4401–4406.
85. Cooper JA Jr, Carcelen R, Culbreth R. Effects of influenza A nucleoprotein on polymorphonuclear neutrophil function. J Infect Dis. 1996;173:279–284.
86. Cooper JA Jr, Culbreth RR. Characterization of a neutrophil inhibitor peptide harvested from human bronchiolar lavage: Homology to influenza A nucleoprotein. Am J Respir Cell Mol Biol. 1996;15:207–215.
87. Hall CB, Douglas RGJ. Nosocomial influenza infection as a cause of intercurrent fevers in infants. Pediatrics. 1975;55:673.
88. Stanley ED, Jackson GG. Viremia in asian influenza. Trans Assoc Am Physicians. 1966;79:376–387.
89. Martin CM, Kunin CM, Gottlieb LS, et al. Asian influenza A in Boston, 1957–1958. Arch Intern Med. 1959;103:516–531.
90. Walsh JJ, Dietlein LF, Low FN, et al. Bronchotracheal response in human influenza. Arch Intern Med. 1961;108:376–388.
91. Hers JFP, Mulder J, Masurel N, et al. Studies on the pathogenesis of influenza virus pneumonia in mice. J Pathol Bacteriol. 1962;83:207–217.
92. Mulder J, Hers JF. Influenza. Groningen, Netherlands: Wolters-Noordhoff; 1979.
93. Oseasohn R, Adelson L, Kaji M. Clinicopathologic study of 33 fatal cases of Asian influenza. N Engl J Med. 1959;260:509.
94. Little JW, Hall WJ, Douglas RG Jr, et al. Airway hyperreactivity and peripheral airway dysfunction in influenza A infection. Am Rev Respir Dis. 1978;118:295–303.
95. Hall WJ, Douglas RG Jr, Hyde RW, et al. Pulmonary mechanics after uncomplicated influenza A infection. Am Rev Respir Dis. 1976;113:141–147.
96. Horner GJ, Gray FD Jr. Effect of uncomplicated, presumptive influenza on the diffusing capacity of the lung. Am Rev Respir Dis. 1973;108:866–869.
97. Johanson WGJ, Pierce AK, Sanford JP. Pulmonary function in uncomplicated influenza. Am Rev Respir Dis. 1969;100:141–146.
98. Kondo S, Abe K. The effects of influenza virus infection on FEV_1 in asthmatic children. Chest. 1991;100:1235–1238.
99. Smith CB, Kanner RE, Goldern CA, et al. Effect of viral infections on pulmonary function in patients with chronic obstructive pulmonary diseases. J Infect Dis. 1980;141:271–279.
100. Utell MJ, Aquilina AT, Hall WJ, et al. Development of airway reactivity to nitrates in subjects with influenza. Am Rev Respir Dis. 1980;121:233–241.
101. Louria DB, Blumenfeld HL, Ellis JT, et al. Studies on influenza in the pandemic of 1957–1958. II. pulmonary complications of influenza. J Clin Invest. 1959;38:213–265.
102. Yelandi AV, Colby TV. Pathologic features of lung biopsy specimens from influenza pneumonia cases. Hum Pathol. 1994;25:47–53.
103. Greenberg SB. Viral pneumonia. Infect Dis Clin North Am. 1991;5:603–621.
104. Levandowski RA, Gerrity TR, Garrard CS. Modifications of lung clearance mechanisms by acute influenza A infection. J Lab Clin Med. 1985;106:428–432.
105. Camner P, Jarstrand C, Philipson K. Tracheobronchial clearance in patients with influenza. Am Rev Respir Dis. 1973;108:131–135.
106. George RC, Broadbent DA, Drasar BS. The effect of influenza virus on the adherence of *Haemophilus influenzae* to human cells in tissue culture. Br J Exp Pathol. 1983;64:655–659.
107. Babiuk LA. Viral-bacterial synergistic interactions in respiratory infections in applied virology. In: Kurstak E, Al-Nakib W, Kurstak C, eds. Applied Virology. New York: Academic Press; 1984:431.
108. Ramphal R, Fischschweiger W, Shands JWJ, Small PA. Murine influenzal tracheitis: A model for the study of influenza and tracheal epithelial repair. Am Rev Respir Dis. 1979;120:1313–1324.
109. Cassidy LF, Lyles DS, Abramson JS. Synthesis of viral proteins in polymorphonuclear leukocytes infected with influenza A virus. J Clin Microbiol. 1988;26:1267–1270.
110. Abramson JS, Wheeler JG, Parce JW, et al. Suppression of endocytosis in neutrophils by influenza A virus in vitro. J Infect Dis. 1986;154:456–463.
111. Akaike T, Molla A, Ando M, et al. Molecular mechanism of complex infection by bacteria and virus analyzed by a model using *Serratia* protease and influenza virus in mice. J Virol. 1989;63:2252–2259.
112. Frank AL, Taber LH, Wells JM. Comparison of infection rates and severity of illness for influenza A subtypes H1N2 and H3N2. J Infect Dis. 1985;151:73–80.
113. Wright PF, Thompson J, Karzon DT. Differing virulence of H1N1 and H3N2 influenza strains. Am J Epidemiol. 1980;112:814–819.
114. Kido H, Yokogoshi Y, Sakai K, et al. Isolation and characterization of a novel trypsin-like protease found in rat bronchiolar Clara cells: A possible activator of the viral fusion glycoprotein. J Biolog Chem. 1992;267:13573–13579.
115. Kawaoka Y, Webster RG. Sequence requirements for cleavage activation of influenza virus hemagglutinin expressed in mammalian cells. Proc Natl Acad Sci U S A. 1988;85:324–328.
116. Kawaoka Y, Webster RG. Interplay between carbohydrate in the stalk and the length of the connecting peptide determined the cleavability of influenza virus hemagglutinin. J Virol. 1989;63:3296–3300.
117. Stieneke-Grober A, Vey M, Angliker H, et al. Influenza virus hemagglutinin with multibasic cleavage site is activated by furin, a subtilisin-like endoprotease. EMBO J. 1992;11:2407–2414.
118. Horimoto T, Kawaoka Y. Reverse genetics provides direct evidence for a correlation of hemagglutinin cleavability and virulence of an avian influenza A virus. J Virol. 1994;68:3120–3128.
119. Brown EG. Increased virulence of a mouse-adapted variant of influenza A/FM/1/47 virus is controlled by mutations in genome segments 4, 5, 7, and 8. J Virol. 1990;64:4523–4533.
120. Li S, Schulman J, Itamura S, Palese P. Glycosylation of neuraminidase determines the neurovirulence of influenza A/WSN/33 virus. J Virol. 1993;67:6667–6673.
121. Schlesinger RW, Bradshaw GL, Barbone F, et al. Role of hemagglutinin cleavage and expression of M1 protein in replication of A/WS/33, A/PR/8/34, and WSN influenza viruses in mouse brain. J Virol. 1989;63:1695–1703.
122. Noble GR. Epidemiologic and clinical aspects of influenza. In: Beare AS, ed. Basic and Applied Influenza Research. Boca Raton, Fla: CRC Press, 1982:1179.
123. Couch RB, Kasal JA. Immunity to influenza in man. Annu Rev Microbiol. 1983;37:529–549.
124. Black RA, Rota PA, Gorodkova N, et al. Antibody response to the M2 protein of influenza A virus expressed in insect cells. J Gen Virol. 1993;74:143–146.
125. Murphy BR, Nelson DL, Wright PF, et al. Secretory and systemic immunologic response in children infected with live attenuated influenza A virus. Infect Immun. 1982;36:1102–1108.
126. Murphy BR, Kasel JA, Chanock RM. Association of serum antineuraminidase antibody with resistance to influenza in man. N Engl J Med. 1972;286:1329–1332.
127. Virelizier J-L. Host defenses against influenza virus: The role of anti-hemagglutinin antibody. J Immunol. 1975;115:434–439.
128. Murphy BR, Clements ML. The systemic and mucosal immune response of humans to influenza A virus. Curr Top Microbiol Immunol. 1989;146:107–116.
129. Betts RF, O'Brien D, Menegus M, et al. A comparison of the protective benefit of influenza (FLU) vaccine in reducing hospitalization of patients infected with FLU A or FLU B. Clin Infect Dis. 1993;17:573 (A257).
130. Foy HM, Cooney MK, McMahan R, et al. Single-dose monovalent A2 Hong Kong influenza vaccine. Efficacy 14 months after immunization. JAMA. 1971;217:1067–1071.
131. Meiklejohn G, Eickhoff TC, Graves P, IJ. Antigenic drift and efficacy of influenza virus vaccines, 1976–1977. J Infect Dis. 1978;138:618–624.
132. Webster RG, Reay PA, Laver WG. Protection against lethal influenza with neuraminidase. Virology. 1988;164:230–237.
133. Schulman JL, Khakpour M, Kilbourne ED. Protective effects of specific immunity to viral neuraminidase on influenza virus infection of mice. J Virol. 1968;2:778–786.
134. Schulman JL, Khakpour M, Kilbourne ED. Protective effects of hemagglutinin and neuraminidase antigens on influenza virus: Distinctiveness of hemagglutinin antigens of Hong Kong–68 virus. J Virol. 1968;2:778.
135. Monto AS, Kendal AP. Effect of neuraminidase antibody on Hong Kong influenza. Lancet 1973;1:623–625.
136. Clements ML, Betts RF, Tierney EL, Murphy BR. Serum and nasal wash antibodies associated with resistance to experimental challenge with influenza A wild-type virus. J Clin Microbiol. 1986;24:157–160.
137. Johansson BE, Grajower B, Kilbourne ED. Infection-permissive immunization with influenza virus neuraminidase prevents weight loss in infected mice. Vaccine. 1993;11:1037–1039.
138. Treanor JJ, Tierney EL, Zebedee SL, et al. Passively transferred monoclonal antibody to the M2 protein inhibits influenza A virus replication in mice. J Virol. 1990;64:1375–1377.
139. Wanger DK, Clements ML, Reimer CB, et al. Analysis of immunoglobulin G antibody responses after administration of live and inactivated influenza A vaccine indicates that nasal wash immunoglobulin G is a transudate from serum. J Clin Microbiol. 1987;25:559–562.
140. Renegar KB, Small PAJ. Passive transfer of local immunity to influenza virus by IgA antibody. J Immunol. 1991;146:1972–1978.
141. Liew FY, Russell SM, Appleyard G, et al. Cross-protection in mice infected with influenza A virus by the respiratory route is correlated with local IgA antibody rather than serum antibody or cytotoxic T cell activity. Eur J Immunol. 1984;14:409–413.
142. Clements ML, Betts RF, Tierney EL, Murphy BR. Resistance of adults to challenge with influenza A wild-type virus after receiving live or inactivated virus vaccine. J Clin Microbiol. 1986;23:73–76.
143. Wenzel RP, Hendley JO, Sande MA, Gwaltney JM Jr. Revised (1972–1973) bivalent influenza vaccine: Serum and nasal antibody responses to parenteral vaccination. JAMA. 1973;226:435–438.
144. Kilbourne ED, Butler WT, Rossen RD. Specific immunity in influenza—summary of influenza workshop III. J Infect Dis. 1973;127:220.
145. Couch RB, Douglas RGJ, Rossen R, et al. Role of secretory antibody in influenza. In: Dayton DHJ, Jr, Small PA Jr, Chanock RM, et al, eds. The Secretory Immunologic System. Washington, DC: US General Printing Office; 1969:93.

146. Virelizier J-L, Allison AC, Shild GC. Antibody responses to antigenic determinants of influenza virus hemagglutinin. II. Original antigenic sin: A bone marrow–derived lymphocyte memory phenomenon modulated by thymus-derived lymphocytes. J Exp Med. 1974;140:1571–1578.
147. Burns WH, Billups LC, Notkins AL. Thymus dependence of viral antigens. Nature. 1975;256:654–656.
148. Lucas SJ, Barry DW, Kind P. Antibody production and protection against influenza in immunodeficient mice. Infect Immun. 1978;20:115–119.
149. Russell SM, Liew FY. T cells primed by influenza virion internal components can cooperate in the antibody response to haemagglutinin. Nature. 1979;280:147–148.
150. Lamb JR, Woody JN, Hartzman RJ, Eckels DD. In vitro influenza virus–specific antibody production in man: Antigen-specific and HLA-restricted induction of helper activity mediated by cloned human T lymphocytes. J Immunol. 1982;129:1465–1470.
151. Hackett CJ, Deitzschold B, Gerhard W, et al. Influenza virus site recognized by a murine helper T cell specific for H1 strains: Localization to a nine amino acid sequence in the hemagglutinin molecule. J Exp Med. 1983;158:294–302.
152. Biddison WE, Sharrow SO, Shearer GM. T cell subpopulations required for the human cytotoxic T lymphocyte response to influenza virus: Evidence for T cell help. J Immunol. 1981;127:487–491.
153. Reiss CS, Burakoff SJ. Specificity of the helper T cell for the cytotoxic T lymphocyte response to influenza viruses. J Exp Med. 1981;154:541.
154. Topham DJ, Tripp RA, Sarawar SR, et al. Immune CD4+ T cells promote the clearance of influenza virus from major histocomptibility complex class II –/– respiratory epithelium. J Virol. 1996;70:1288–1291.
155. Baumgarth N, Brown L, Jackson D, Kelso A. Novel features of the respiratory tract T-cell response to influenza virus infection: Lung T cells increase expression of gamma interferon mRNA in vivo and maintain high levels of mRNA expression for interleukin-5 (IL-5) and IL-10. J Virol. 1994;68:7575–7581.
156. Sarawar SR, Carding SR, Allan W, et al. Cytokine profiles in bronchoalveolar lavage cells from mice with influenza pneumonia: Consequences of CD4+ and CD8+ T cell depletion. Reg Immunol. 1993;5:142–150.
157. Graham MB, Braciale VL, Braciale TJ. Influenza virus–specific CD4+ T helper type 2 T lymphocytes do not promote recovery from experimental virus infection. J Exp Med. 1994;180:1273–1282.
158. Sarawar SR, Sangster M, Coffman RL, Doherty PC. Administration of anti–IFN-γ antibody to β_2-microglobulin–deficient mice delays influenza virus clearance but does not switch the response to a T helper cell 2 phenotype. J Immunol. 1994;153:1246–1253.
159. Baumgarth N, Kelso A. In vivo blockade of gamma interferon affects the influenza virus–induced humoral and the local cellular immune response in lung tissue. J Virol. 1996;70:4411–4418.
160. Moran TM, Isobe H, Fernandez-Sesma A, Shulman JL. Interleukin-4 causes delayed virus clearance in influenza virus–infected mice. J Virol. 1996;70:5230–5235.
161. Hashimoto G, Wright PF, Karzon DT. Antibody-dependent cell-mediated cytotoxicity against influenza virus–infected cells. J Infect Dis. 1983;148:785–794.
162. Fleischer B, Becht H, Rott R. Recognition of viral antigens by human influenza A virus–specific T lymphocyte clones. J Immunol. 1985;165:2800–2804.
163. Braciale TJ. Immunologic recognition of influenza virus–infected cells. II. Expression of influenza A matrix protein on the infected cell surface and its role in recognition by cross-reactive cytotoxic T cells. J Exp Med. 1977;146:673–689.
164. Yewdell JW, Hackett CJ. The specificity and function of T lymphocytes induced by influenza A viruses. In: Krug R, ed. The Influenza Viruses. New York: Plenum Press; 1989:361–429.
165. Lin Y-L, Askonas BA. Biologic properties of an influenza A virus–specific killer T cell clone. Inhibition of virus replication in vivo and induction of delayed-type hypersensitivity reactions. J Exp Med. 1981;154:225–234.
166. Lukacher AE, Braciale VL, Braciale TJ. In vivo effector function of influenza virus–specific cytotoxic T lymphocyte clones is highly specific. J Exp Med. 1984;160:814–826.
167. Taylor PM, Askonas BA. Influenza nucleoprotein–specific cytotoxic T-cell clones are protective in vivo. Immunology. 1986;58:417–420.
168. Yap KL, Ada GL, McKenzie IFC. Transfer of specific cytotoxic T lymphocytes protects mice inoculated with influenza virus. Nature. 1978;273:238–239.
169. MacKenzie CD, Taylor PM, Askonas BA. Rapid recovery of lung histology correlates with clearance of influenza virus by specific CD8+ cytotoxic cells. Immunology. 1989;67:375–381.
170. Reiss CS, Schulman JL. Cellular immune responses of mice to influenza virus infection. Cell Immunol. 1980;56:502–506.
171. Eichelberger M, Allan W, Zijlstra M, et al. Clearance of influenza virus respiratory infection in mice lacking class I major histocompatibility complex–restricted T cells. J Exp Med. 1991;174:875–880.
172. Scherle PA, Palladino G, Gerhard W. Mice can recover from pulmonary influenza virus infection in the absence of class I–restricted cytotoxic T cells. J Immunol. 1992;148:212–217.
173. Epstein SL, Misplon JA, Lawson CM, et al. Beta 2-microglobulin–deficient mice can be protected against influenza A infection by vaccination with vaccinia-influenza recombinants expressing hemagglutinin and neuraminidase. J Immunol. 1993;150:5484–5493.
174. Ennis FA. Some newly recognized aspects of resistance against and recovery from influenza. Arch Virol. 1982;73:207–217.
175. McMichael AJ, Gotch FM, Noble GR, Beare PAS. Cytotoxic T-cell immunity to influenza. N Engl J Med. 1983;309:13–17.
176. Murphy BR, Baron S, Chalhub EG, et al. Temperature-sensitive mutants of influenza virus IV. Induction of interferon in the nasopharynx by wild-type and a temperature-sensitive recombinant virus. J Infect Dis. 1973;128:488–493.
177. Jao RL, Wheelock EF, Jackson GG. Production of interferon in volunteers infected with Asian influenza. J Infect Dis. 1970;121:419–426.
178. Hayden FG, Fritz R, Lobo MC, et al. Local and systemic cytokine responses during experimental human influenza A virus infection. Relation to symptom formation and host defense. J Clin Invest. 1998;101:643–649.
179. Jordan WS, Gordon I, Dorrance WR. A study of illness in a group of Cleveland families. VII. Transmission of acute nonbacterial gastroenteritis to volunteers: Evidence for two different etiologic agents. J Exp Med. 1953;98:461–475.
180. Kilbourne ED, Loge JP. Influenza A prime: a clinical study of an epidemic caused by a new strain of virus. Ann Intern Med. 1950;33:371–382.
181. Stuart-Harris CH. Twenty years of influenza epidemics. Am Rev Respir Dis. 1961;83:54–75.
182. Nigg C, Ecklund CM, Wilson DE. Study of epidemics of influenza B. Am J Hyg. 1942;35:265–275.
183. Blaine WB, Luby JP, Martin SM. Severe illness with influenza B. Am J Med. 1980;68:181–189.
184. Mogabgab WJ. Virus association with upper respiratory illnesses in adults. Ann Intern Med. 1963;59:306–311.
185. McIntosh K, Halonon P, Ruuskanen O. Report of a workshop on respiratory viral infection: Epidemiology, diagnosis, treatment and prevention. Clin Infect Dis. 1993;16:151–164.
186. Glezen WP, Loda FA, Clyde WA Jr, et al. Epidemiologic patterns of acute lower respiratory disease of children in a pediatric group practice. J Pediatr. 1971;78:397–406.
187. Howard JB. Influenza A2 virus as a cause of croup requiring tracheostomy. J Pediatr. 1972;81:1148–1150.
188. Glezen WP, Paredes A, Taber LH. Influenza in children. JAMA. 1980;243:1345–1349.
189. Scheiblauer H, Reinacher M, Tashiro M, Rott R. Interactions between bacteria and influenza A virus in the development of influenza pneumonia. J Infect Dis. 1992;166:783–791.
190. Schwarzmann SW, Adler JL, Sullivan RFJ, Marine WM. Bacterial pneumonia during the Hong Kong influenza epidemic of 1968–1969. Arch Intern Med. 1971;127:1037–1041.
191. Bisno AL, Griffin JP, VanEpps KA. Pneumonia and Hong Kong influenza: A prospective study of the 1968–1969 epidemic. Am J Med Sci. 1971;261:251–274.
192. Fry J. Lung involvement in influenza. Br Med J. 1951;2:1374.
193. Fry J. Influenza A (Asian) 1957: Clinical and epidemiological features in a general practice. Br Med J. 1958;1:259.
194. Kay D, Rosenbluth M, Hook EW. Endemic influenza II. The nature of the disease in the post-pandemic period. Am Rev Respir Dis. 1962;85:9.
195. Kempe A, Hall CB, MacDonald NE, et al. Influenza in children with cancer. J Pediatr. 1989;115:33–39.
196. Hirschhorn LR, McIntosh K, Anderson KG, Dermody TS. Influenzal pneumonia as a complication of autologous bone marrow transplantation (Letter). Clin Infect Dis. 1992;14:786–787.
197. Yousuf HM, Englund J, Couch R, et al. Influenza among hospitalized adults with leukemia. Clin Infect Dis. 1997;24:1095–1099.
198. Klimov AI, Rocha E, Hayden FG, et al. Prolonged shedding of amantadine-resistant influenzae A viruses by immunodeficient patients: Detection by polymerase chain reaction–restriction analysis. J Infect Dis. 1995;172:1352–1355.
199. Evans KM, Kline MW. Prolonged influenza A infection responsive to rimantadine therapy in a human immunodeficiency virus–infected child. Pediatr Infect Dis J. 1995;14:332–334.
200. Gubareva LV, Matrosovich MN, Brenner MK, et al. Evidence for zanamivir resistance in an immunocompromised child infected with influenza B virus. J Infect Dis. 1998;178:1257–1262.
201. Carilli AD, Gohd RS, Grodon W. A virologic study of chronic bronchitis. N Engl J Med. 1964;270:123.
202. Stark JE, Heath RB, Curwen MP. Infection with influenza and parainfluenza viruses in chronic bronchitis. Thorax. 1965;20:124.
203. Stenhouse AC. Rhinovirus infection in acute exacerbation of chronic bronchitis: A controlled prospective study. Br Med J. 1967;3:461.
204. Monto AS, Ross HW. The Tecumseh study of respiratory illness. Am J Epidemiol. 1978;107:57.
205. Clementsen P, Jensen CB, Hannoun C, et al. Influenza A virus potentiates basophil histamine release caused by endotoxin-induced complement activation. Examination of normal individuals and patients with intrinsic asthma. Allergy. 1988;43:93–99.
206. Lin CY, Kuo YC, Liu WT, Lin CC. Immunomodulation of influenza virus infection in the precipitating asthma attack. Chest. 1988;93:1234–1238.
207. Ferson MJ, Morton JR, Robertson PW. Impact of influenza on morbidity in children with cystic fibrosis. J Paediatr Child Health. 1991;27:308–311.
208. Fry J. Influenza, 1959: The story of an epidemic. Br Med J. 1959;2:135–147.
209. Foy HM, Cooney MK, Allan I, Kenny GE. Rates of pneumonia during influenza epidemics in Seattle, 1964 to 1975. JAMA. 1979;241:253–258.
210. Jones A, MacFarlane J, Pugh S. Antibiotic therapy. Clinical features and outcome of 36 adults presenting to hospital with proven influenza: Do we follow guideline? Postgrad Med J. 1991;67:988–990.
211. Fedson DS, Wajda A, Nicol JP, Roos LL. Disparity between influenza vaccination rates and risks for influenza-associated hospital discharge and death in Manitoba in 1982–1983. Ann Intern Med. 1992;116:550–555.

212. Tillett HE, Smith JWG, Clifford RE. Excess morbidity and mortality associated with influenza in England and Wales. Lancet. 1980;1:793.
213. Barker WH, Mullooly JP. Pneumonia and influenza deaths during epidemics: Implications for prevention. JAMA. 1982;142:85–89.
214. Choi K, Thacker SB. Mortality during influenza epidemics in the United States, 1967–1978. Am J Public Health. 1982;72:1280–1287.
215. Middleton PJ, Alexander RM, Szymanski MT. Severe myositis during recovery from influenza. Lancet. 1970;2:533.
216. Simon NM. Acute myoglobinuria associated with type A2 influenza. JAMA. 1970;212:1704–1707.
217. Dietzman DE, Schaller JG, Ray CG, Reed ME. Acute myositis associated with influenza B infection. Pediatrics. 1976;57:255–258.
218. Minow RA, Gorbach S, Johnson BL Jr, Dornfeld L. Myoglobinuria associated with influenza A infection. Ann Intern Med. 1974;80:359–361.
219. Greco TP, Askenase PW, Kashgarian M. Postviral myositis: Myxovirus-like structures in affected muscle. Ann Intern Med. 1977;86:193–198.
220. Glezen WP, Decker M, Perrotta DM. Survey of underlying conditions of persons hospitalized with acute respiratory disease during influenza epidemics in Houston, 1978–1981. Am Rev Respir Dis. 1987;136:550–555.
221. Bainton D, Jones GR, Hole D. Influenza and ischemic heart disease: A possible trigger for acute myocardial infarction. Int J Epidemiol. 1978;7:231.
222. MacDonald KL, Osterholm MT, Hedberg CW, et al. Toxic shock syndrome: A newly recognized complication of influenza and influenza like illness. JAMA. 1987;257:1053–1058.
223. Sperber SJ, Francis JB. Toxic shock during an influenza outbreak. JAMA. 1987;257:1086–1089.
224. Edelen JS, Bender TR, Chin TDY. Encephalopathy and pericarditis during an outbreak of influenza. Am J Epidemiol. 1974;100:79–83.
225. Bayer WH. Influenza B encephalitis. West J Med. 1987;147:466–468.
226. Varma RR, Riedel DR, Komorouski RA. Reye's syndrome in non-pediatric age groups. JAMA. 1979;242:1373.
227. Corey L, Rubin RJ, Hattwick MA, et al. A nationwide outbreak of Reye's syndrome: Its epidemiologic relationship to influenza B. Am J Med. 1976;61:615.
228. Corey L, Rubin RJ, Bregman D, et al. Diagnostic criteria for influenza B–associated Reye's syndrome: Clinical vs. pathologic criteria. Pediatrics. 1977;60:602.
229. Chaves-Carballo E, Gomez MR, Sharbrough FW. Encephalopathy and fatty infiltration of the viscera (Reye-Johnson syndrome): A 17-year experience. Mayo Clin Proc. 1975;50:209.
230. Schiff GM. Reye's syndrome. Ann Rev Med. 1976;27:447.
231. Consensus Development Conference. Diagnosis and treatment of Reye's syndrome. JAMA. 1981;246:2441.
232. Hottenlocher PR. Reye's syndrome: Relation of outcome to therapy. J Pediatr. 1970;80:845.
233. Trey C, Burns DG, Saunder SJ. Treatment of hepatic coma by exchange blood transfusion. N Engl J Med. 1966;294:473.
234. Kindt GW, Waldman J, Kohl S, et al. Intracranial pressure in Reye's syndrome: Monitoring and control. JAMA. 1975;231:473.
235. Waldman RJ, Hall WN, McGee H, Van Amburg G. Aspirin as a risk factor in Reye's syndrome. JAMA. 1982;247:3089–3094.
236. Halpin TJ, Holtzhauer FJ, Campbell RJ, et al. Reye's syndrome and medication use. JAMA. 1982;248:687–691.
237. Starks KM, Ray G, Dominguez LB. Reye's syndrome and salicylate use. Pediatrics 1980;66:859.
238. Kimball AM, Foy HM, Cooney MK, et al. Isolation of respiratory syncytial and influenza viruses from the sputum of patients hospitalized with pneumonia. J Infect Dis. 1983;147:181–184.
239. Espy MJ, Smith TF, Harmon MW, Kendal AP. Rapid detection of influenza virus by shell vial assay with monoclonal antibodies. J Clin Microbiol. 1986;24:677–679.
240. Daisy JA, Lief FS, Friedman HW. Rapid diagnosis of influenza A infection by direct immunofluorescence of nasopharyngeal aspirates in adults. J Clin Microbiol. 1979;9:688–692.
241. Walls HH, Johansson KH, Harmon MW, et al. Time-resolved fluoroimmunoassay with monoclonal antibodies for rapid diagnosis of influenza infections. J Clin Microbiol. 1986;24:907–912.
242. Coonrod JD, Betts RF, Linnemann CC Jr, Hsu LC. Etiologic diagnosis of influenza A virus by enzymatic radioimmunoassay. J Clin Microbiol. 1984;19:361–365.
243. Harmon MW, Pawlik KM. Enzyme immunoassay for direct detection of influenza type A and adenovirus antigens in clinical specimens. J Clin Microbiol. 1982;15:5–11.
244. Waner JL, Todd SJ, Shalaby H, et al. Comparison of directigen FLU-A with viral isolation and direct immunofluorescence for the rapid detection and identification of influenza A virus. J Clin Microbiol. 1991;29:479–482.
245. Doller G, Schuy W, Tjhen KY, et al. Direct detection of influenza virus antigen in nasopharyngeal specimens by direct enzyme immunoassay in comparison with quantitating virus shedding. J Clin Microbiol. 1992;30:866–869.
246. Ryan-Pourier KA, Katz JM, Webster RG, Kawaoka Y. Application of directagen FLU-A for the detection of influenza A virus in human and non-human specimens. J Clin Microbiol. 1992;30:1072–1075.
247. Class ECJ, Sprenger MJW, Kleter GEM, et al. Type-specific identification of influenza viruses A, B, and C by the polymerase chain reaction. J Virol Methods. 1992;39:1–13.
248. Pisareva M, Bechtereva T, Plyusnin A, et al. PCR-amplification of influenza A virus–specific sequences. Arch Virol. 1992;125:313–318.
249. Katz JM, Wang M, Webster RG. Direct sequencing of the HA gene of influenza (H3N2) reveals sequence identity with mammalian cell-grown virus. J Virol. 1990;64:1808–1811.
250. Dowdle WN, Kendal AP, Noble GR. Influenza viruses. In: Lenette EH, Schmidt NJ, eds. Diagnostic Procedures for Viral, Rickettsial, and Chlamydial Infections. Washington, DC: American Public Health Association; 1979:603–605.
251. Rabinovich S, Baldini JT, Bannister R. Treatment of influenza: The therapeutic efficacy of rimantadine HC1 in a naturally occurring influenza A2 outbreak. Am J Med Sci. 1969;257:328–335.
252. Wingfield WL, Pollack D, Grunert RR. Therapeutic efficacy of amantadine HC1 and rimantadine HC1 in naturally occurring influenza A2 respiratory illness in man. N Engl J Med. 1969;281:579–584.
253. Knight V, Fedson D, Baldini J, et al. Amantadine therapy of epidemic influenza A2 (Hong Kong). Infect Immun. 1970;1:200–204.
254. Galbraith AW, Oxford JS, Schild GC, et al. Therapeutic effect of 1-adamantanamine hydrochloride in naturally occurring influenza A2/Hong Kong infection. Lancet. 1971;1:113–115.
255. Van Voris LP, Betts RF, Hayden FG, et al. Successful treatment of naturally occurring influenza A/USSR/77 H1N1. JAMA. 1981;245:1128–1131.
256. Younkin SW, Betts RF, Roth FK, Douglas RG Jr. Reduction in fever and symptoms in young adults with influenza A/Brazil/78 H1N1 infection after treatment with aspirin or amantadine. Antimicrob Agents Chemother. 1983;23:577–582.
257. Falsey AR, Walsh EE, Betts RF. Serologic evidence of respiratory syncytial virus infection in nursing home patients. J Infect Dis. 1990;162:568–569.
258. Dolin R. Antiviral chemotherapy and chemoprophylaxis. Science. 1985;227:1296–1303.
259. Douglas RG Jr. Prophylaxis and treatment of influenza. N Engl J Med. 1990;322:443–450.
260. Lubeck MD, Schulman JL, Palese P. Susceptibility of influenza A viruses to amantadine is influenced by the gene coding for the M protein. J Virol. 1978;28:710–716.
261. Hay AJ, Wolstenholme AJ, Skehel JJ, Smith MH. The molecular basis of the specific anti-influenza action of amantadine. EMBO J. 1985;4:3021–3024.
262. Belshe RB, Smith MH, Hall CB, et al. Genetic basis of resistance to rimantadine emerging during treatment of influenza virus infection. J Virol. 1988;62:1508–1512.
263. Pinto LH, Holsinger LJ, Lamb RA. Influenza virus M2 protein has ion channel activity. Cell. 1992;69:517–528.
264. Richman DD, Yazaki P, Hostetler KY. The intracellular distribution and antiviral activity of amantadine. Virology. 1981;112:81–90.
265. Richman DD, Hostetler KY, Yazaki PJ, Clark S. Fate of influenza A virion proteins after entry into subcellular fractions of LLC cells and the effect of amantadine. Virology. 1986;151:200–210.
266. Bukrinskaya AG, Vorkunova NK, Kornilayeva GV, et al. Influenza virus uncoating in infected cells and effect of rimantadine. J Gen Virol. 1982;60:49–59.
267. Ruigrok RWH, Hirst EMA, Hay AJ. The specific inhibition of influenza A virus maturation by amantadine: An electron microscopic examination. J Gen Virol. 1991;72:191–194.
268. Hayden FG, Minocha A, Spyker DA, Hoffman HE. Comparative single-dose pharmacokinetics of amantadine hydrochloride and rimantadine hydrochloride in young and elderly adults (published erratum appears in Antimicrob Agents Chemother. 1986;30:579). Antimicrob Agents Chemother. 1985;28:216–221.
269. Wills RJ, Farolino DA, Choma N, Keigher N. Rimantadine pharmacokinetics after single and multiple doses. Antimicrob Agents Chemother. 1987;31:826–828.
270. Hayden FG, Monto AS. Oral rimantadine hydrochloride therapy of influenza A virus H3N2 subtype infection in adults. Antimicrob Agents Chemother. 1986;29:339–341.
271. Little J, Hall W, Douglas RGJ, et al. Amantadine effect on peripheral airways abnormalities in influenza. Ann Intern Med. 1976;85:177–182.
272. Hall CB, Dolin R, Gala CL, et al. Children with influenza A infection: Treatment with rimantadine. Pediatrics. 1987;80:275–282.
273. Thompson J, Fleet W, Lawrence E, et al. A comparison of acetaminophen and rimantadine in the treatment of influenza A infection in children. J Med Virol. 1987;21:249–255.
274. Douglas RG Jr. Treatment of influenza (Letter). N Engl J Med. 1992;322:1753.
275. Betts RF, Treanor J, Braman P, et al. Antiviral agents to prevent or treat influenza in the elderly. J Respir Dis. 1987;8(Suppl):S56–S59.
276. Dolin R, Reichman RC, Madore HP, et al. A controlled trial of amantadine and rimantadine in the prophylaxis of influenza A in humans. N Engl J Med. 1982;307:580–584.
277. Monto AS, Arden NH. Implications of viral resistance to amantadine in control of influenza A. Clin Infect Dis. 1992;15:362–367.
278. Hayden FG, Belshe RB, Clover RD, et al. Emergence and apparent transmission of rimantadine-resistant influenza A virus in families. N Engl J Med. 1989;321:1696–1702.
279. Hayden FG, Sperber SJ, Belshe RB, et al. Recovery of drug-resistant influenza A virus during therapeutic use of rimantadine. Antimicrob Agents Chemother. 1991;35:1741–1747.
280. Belshe RB, Burk B, Newman F, et al. Resistance of influenza A virus to amantadine and rimantadine: Results of one decade of surveillance. J Infect Dis. 1989;159:430–435.
281. Degelau J, Somani SK, Cooper SL, et al. Amantadine-resistant influenza A in a nursing facility. Arch Intern Med. 1992;152:390–392.
282. Bean WJ, Threlkeld SC, Webster RG. Biologic potential of amantadine-resistant influenza A virus in an avian model. J Infect Dis. 1989;159:1050–1056.

283. Sweet C, Hayden FG, Jakeman KJ, et al. Virulence of rimantadine-resistant human influenza A (H3N2) viruses in ferrets. J Infect Dis. 1991;164:969–972.
284. Webster RG, Kawaoka Y, Bean WJ, et al. Chemotherapy and vaccination: A possible strategy for the control of highly virulent influenza virus. J Virol. 1985;55:173–176.
285. Webster RG, Kawaoka Y, Bean WJ. Vaccination as a strategy to reduce the emergence of amantadine- and rimantadine-resistant strains of A/Chick/Pennsylvania/83 (H5N2) influenza virus. J Antimicrob Chemother. 1986;18:157–164.
286. Tu Q, Pinto LH, Luo G, et al. Characterization of inhibition of M2 ion channel activity by BL-1743, an inhibitor of influenza A virus. J Virol. 1996;70:4246–4252.
287. Varghese JN, Laver WG, Colman PM. Structure of the influenza glycoprotein antigen neuraminidase at 2.9Å resolution. Nature. 1983;303:35–40.
288. von Itzstein M, Wu W-Y, Kok GB, et al. Rational design of potent sialidase-based inhibitors of influenza virus replication. Nature. 1993;363:418–423.
289. Woods JM, Bethell RC, Coates JAV, et al. 4-Quanidino-2,4-dideoxy-2,3-dehydro-*N*-acetylneuraminic acid is a highly effective inhibitor both of the sialidase (neuraminidase) and of growth of a wide range of influenza A and B viruses in vitro. Antimicrob Agents Chemother. 1993;37:1473–1479.
290. Hayden FG, Treanor JJ, Betts RF, et al. Safety and efficacy of the neuraminidase inhibitor GG167 in experimental human influenza. JAMA. 1996;275:295–299.
291. Walker JB, Hussey EK, Treanor JJ, et al. Effects of the neuraminidase inhibitor zanamivir on otologic manifestations of experimental human influenza. J Infect Dis. 1997;176:1417–1422.
292. Hayden FG, Osterhaus ADME, Treanor JJ, et al. Efficacy and safety of the neuraminidase inhibitor zanamivir in the treatment of influenza virus infections. N Engl J Med. 1997;337:874–880.
293. MIST. Randomised trial of efficacy and safety of inhaled zanamivir in treatment of influenza A and B virus infections. Lancet. 1998;352:1877–1881.
294. Hayden FG, Treanor JJ, Lobo M, et al. Randomized, double-blind studies of the oral neuraminidase inhibitor GS4104 (Ro64-0796) in experimental human influenza. JAMA. In press.
295. Treanor JJ, Vrooman PS, Hayden FG, et al. Efficacy of oral GS4104 in treating acute influenza. Presented at the Thirty-eighth Interscience Conference on Antimicrobial Agents and Chemotherapy. Abstract LB-4. San Diego, Calif, September 1998.
296. Gubareva LV, Bethell R, Hart GJ, et al. Characterization of mutants of influenza A selected with the neuramindase inhibitor 4-guanidino-Neu5Ac2en. J Virol. 1996;70:1818–1827.
297. Gubareva LV, Robinson MJ, Bethell RC, Webster RG. Catalytic and framework mutations in the neuraminidase active site of influenza viruses that are resistant to 4-guanidino-neu5ac2en. J Virol. 1997;71:3385–3390.
298. McKimm-Breschkin JL, Sahasrabudhe A, Blick TJ, et al. Mutations in a conserved residue in the influenza virus neuraminidase active site decreases sensitivity to neu5acen-derived inhibitors. J Virol. 1998;72:2456–2462.
299. Goto H, Bethell RC, Kawaoka Y. Mutations affecting the sensitivity of the influenza virus neuraminidase to 4-guanidino-2,4-dideoxy-2,3-dehydro-*N*-acetylneuraminic acid. Virology. 1997;238:265–272.
300. Garcia-Sastre A, Palese P. The cytoplasmic tail of the neuraminidase protein of influenza A virus does not play an important role in the packaging of this protein into viral envelopes. Virus Res. 1995;37:37–47.
301. Mitnaul LJ, Castrucci MR, Murti KG, Kawaoka Y. The cytoplasmic tail of influenza A virus neuraminidase (NA) affects NA incorporation into virions, virion morphology, and virulence in mice but is not essential for virus replication. J Virol. 1996;70:873–879.
302. Blick TJ, Sahasrabudhe A, McDonald M, et al. The interaction of neuraminidase and hemagglutinin mutations in influenza virus in resistance to 4-guanidino-neu5ac2en. Virology. 1998;246:95–103.
303. Gilbert BE, Wilson SZ, Knight V, et al. Ribavirin small-particle aerosol treatment of infections caused by influenza virus strains A/Victoria/7/83 (H1N1) and B/Texas/1/84. Antimicrob Agents Chemother. 1985;27:309–313.
304. Wilson SZ, Gilbert BE, Quarles JM, et al. Treatment of influenza A (H1N1) virus infection with ribavirin aerosol. Antimicrob Agents Chemother. 1984;26:200–203.
305. Bernstein DI, Reuman PD, Sherwood JR, et al. Ribavirin small-particle aerosol treatment of influenza B virus infection. Antimicrob Agents Chemother. 1988;32:761–764.
306. Ray CG, Icenogle TB, Minnich LL, et al. The use of intravenous ribavirin to treat influenza virus–associated acute myocarditis. J Infect Dis. 1989;159:829–836.
307. Fulginiti V. Committee on Infectious Diseases Special Report: Aspirin and Reye's syndrome. Pediatrics. 1983;69:810.
308. Winterbauer RH, Ludwig WR, Hammer SP. Clinical course, management, and long-term sequelae of respiratory failure due to influenza viral pneumonia. Johns Hopkins Med J. 1977;141:148.
309. Kilbourne ED. Comparative efficacy of neuraminidase-specific and conventional influenza virus vaccines in induction of antibody to neuraminidase in humans. J Infect Dis. 1976;134:384–394.
310. Wright PF, Cherry JD, Foy HM, et al. Antigenicity and reactogenicity of influenza A/USSR/77 virus vaccine in children—a multicentered evaluation of dosage and toxicity. Rev Infect Dis. 1983;5:758–764.
311. LaMontagne JR, Noble GR, Quinnan GV, et al. Summary of clinical trials of inactivated influenza vaccine-1978. Rev Infect Dis. 1983;5:723–736.
312. Mostow RA, Schoenbaum SC, Dowdle WR, et al. Studies on inactivated influenza vaccine II effect of increasing dosage on antibody response and adverse reactions in man. Am J Epidemiol. 1970;92:248–256.
313. Wright PF, Thompson J, Vaughn WT, et al. Trials of influenza A/New Jersey/76 virus vaccine in normal children: An overview of age-related antigenicity and reactogenicity. J Infect Dis. 1977;136(Suppl):S731–S741.
314. Gross PA, Weksler ME, Quinnan GVJ, et al. Immunization of elderly people with two doses of influenza vaccine. J Clin Microbiol. 1987;25:1763–1765.
315. Cate TR, Couch RB, Parker D, Baxter B. Reactogenicity, immunogenicity, and antibody persistence in adults given inactivated influenza virus vaccines—1978. Rev Infect Dis. 1983;5:737–747.
316. Quinnan GV, Schooley R, Dolin R, et al. Serologic responses and systemic reactions in adults after vaccination with monovalent A/USSR/77 and trivalent A/USSR/77, A/Texas/77, B/Hong Kong/72 influenza vaccines. Rev Infect Dis. 1983;5:748–757.
317. Schonberger LB, Bregman DJ, Sullivan-Bolyai JZ, et al. Guillain-Barré syndrome following vaccination in the national influenza immunization program, United States, 1976–1977. Am J Epidemiol. 1979;110:105–123.
318. Lasky T, Tarracciano GJ, Magder L, et al. The Guillain-Barré syndrome and the 1992–1993 and 1993–1994 influenza vaccines. N Engl J Med. 1998;339:1797–1802.
319. Kramer P, McClain CJ. Depression of aminopyrine metabolism by influenza vaccination. N Engl J Med. 1981;305:1262–1264.
320. Patriarca PA, Kendal AP, Stricof RL, et al. Influenza vaccination and warfarin or theophylline toxicity in nursing-home residents (Letter). N Engl J Med. 1983;308:1601–1602.
321. Hannan SE, May JJ, Pratt DS, et al. The effect of whole virus influenza vaccination on theophylline pharmacokinetics. Am Rev Respir Dis. 1988;137:903–906.
322. Bussey HI, Saklad JJ. Effect of influenza vaccine on chronic warfarin therapy. Drug Intell Clin Pharm. 1988;22:198–201.
323. MacKenzie WR, Davis JP, Peterson DE, et al. Multiple false-positive serologic tests for HIV, HTLV-1, and hepatitis C following influenza vaccination, 1991. JAMA. 1992;268:1015–1017.
324. Johansson BE, Moran TM, Bona CA, Kilbourne DE. Immunologic response to influenza virus neuraminidase is influenced by prior experience with the associated viral hemagglutinin. III. Reduced generation of neuraminidase-specific helper T cells in hemagglutinin-primed mice. J Immunol. 1987;139:2015–2019.
325. Johansson BE, Kilbourne ED. Dissociation of influenza virus hemagglutinin and neuraminidase eliminates their intravirionic antigenic competion. J Virol. 1993;67:5721–5723.
326. Clements ML, Murphy BR. Development and persistence of local and systemic antibody responses in adults given live attenuated or inactivated influenza A virus vaccine. J Clin Microbiol. 1986;23:66–72.
327. Levandowski RA, Regnery HL, Staton E, et al. Antibody responses to influenza B viruses in immunologically unprimed children. Pediatrics. 1991;88:1031–1036.
328. Allison JE, Glezen WP, Taber LH, et al. Reactogenicity and immunogenicity of bivalent influenza A and monovalent influenza B virus vaccines in high-risk children. J Infect Dis. 1977;136(Suppl):S672–S676.
329. Hillman BC, Jamison RM, Kirkpatrick CJ. Reactivity and antibody response to vaccination with bivalent influenza A/Victoria/75-A/New Jersey/76 vaccines in children with chronic pulmonary diseases. J Infect Dis. 1977;136(Suppl):S638–S644.
330. Hall CB, Modlin JF, Hilman BC, et al. Response of children with cardiac disease to the bivalent influenza A vaccines. J Infect Dis. 1977;136(Suppl):S632–S637.
331. Groothuis JR, Levin MJ, Rabalais GP, et al. Immunization of high-risk infants younger than 18 months of age with split-product influenza vaccine. Pediatrics. 1991;87:823–828.
332. Pabico RC, Douglas RG Jr, Betts RF, et al. Influenza vaccination of patients with glomerular diseases: Effects on creatinine clearance, urinary protein excretion, and antibody response. Ann Intern Med. 1974;81:171–177.
333. Osanloo EO, Berlin BS, Popli S, et al. Antibody responses to influenza vaccination in patients with chronic renal failure. Kidney Int. 1978;14:614–618.
334. Jordan MC, Rousseau WE, Tegtmeier GE, et al. Immunogenicity of inactivated influenza virus vaccine in chronic renal failure. Ann Intern Med. 1973;79:790–794.
335. Pabico RC, Douglas RG Jr, Betts RF, et al. Antibody response to influenza vaccination in renal transplant patients: Correlation with allograft function. Ann Intern Med. 1976;85:431–436.
336. Stiver HG, Graves P, Meiklejohn G, et al. Impaired serum antibody response to inactivated influenza A and B vaccine in renal transplant recipients. Infect Immun. 1977;16:738–741.
337. Kumar SS, Ventura AK, VanderWerf B. Influenza vaccination in renal transplant recipients. JAMA. 1978;239:840–842.
338. Versluis DJ, Beyer WE, Masurel N, et al. Impairment of the immune response to influenza vaccination in renal transplant recipients by cyclosporine, but not azathioprine. Transplantation. 1986;42:376–379.
339. Huang KL, Armstron JA, Ho M. Antibody response after influenza immunization in renal transplant patients receiving cyclosporin A or azathioprine. Infect Immun. 1983;40:421–424.
340. Chalmers A, Scheifele D, Patterson C, et al. Immunization of patients with rheumatoid arthritis against influenza: A study of vaccine safety and immunogenicity. J Rheumatol 1994;21:1203–1206.
341. Brodman R, Gilfillan R, Glass D, Schur PH. Influenzal vaccine response in systemic lupus erythematosus. Ann Intern Med. 1978;88:735–740.
342. Williams GW, Steinberg AD, Reinertsen JL, et al. Influenza immunization in systemic lupus erythematosus: A double-blind trial. Ann Intern Med. 1978;88:729–734.
343. Nelson KE, Clements ML, Miotti P, et al. The influence of human immunodeficiency virus (HIV) infection on antibody responses to influenza vaccines. Ann Intern Med. 1988;109:383–388.

344. O'Brien WA, Ferbas-Grovit K, Namazi A, et al. Human immunodeficiency virus–type 1 replication can be increased in peripheral blood of seropositive patients after influenza vaccination. Blood. 1995;86:1082–1089.
345. Tasker SA, O'Brien WA, Treanor JJ, et al. Effects of influenza vaccination in HIV-infected adults: A double-blind, placebo-controlled trial. Vaccine. 1998;16:1039–1042.
346. Glesby MJ, Hoover DR, Farzadegan H, et al. The effect of influenza vaccination on human immunodeficiency virus type 1 load: A randomized, double-blind, placebo-controlled study. J Infect Dis. 1996;174:1332–1336.
347. Kubiet MA, Gonzalez-Rothi RJ, Cottey R, Bender BS. Serum antibody response to influenza vaccine in pulmonary patients receiving corticosteroids. Chest. 1996;110:367–370.
348. Park CL, Frank AL, Sullivan M, et al. Influenza vaccination of children during acute asthma exacerbation and concurrent prednisone therapy. Pediatrics. 1996;98:196–200.
349. Stenius-Aarniala B, Huttunen JK, Pyhala R, et al. Lack of clinical exacerbations in adults with chronic asthma after immunization with killed influenza virus. Chest. 1986;89:786–789.
350. Sibley WA, Bamford CR, Laguna JF. Influenza vaccination in patients with multiple sclerosis. JAMA. 1976;236:1965–1966.
351. Meiklejohn G. Viral respiratory disease at Lowry Air Force Base in Denver, 1952–1982. J Infect Dis. 1983;148:775–783.
352. Ruben FL. Prevention and control of influenza: Role of vaccine. Am J Med. 1987;82:31–33.
353. Barker WH, Mullooly JP. Influenza vaccination of elderly persons: Reduction in pneumonia and influenza hospitalizations and deaths. JAMA. 1980;244:2547–2549.
354. Ruben FL, Johnston F, Streiff EJ. Influenza in a partially immunized population: Effectiveness of killed Hong Kong vaccine against infection with the England strain. JAMA. 1974;230:863–866.
355. Gross PA, Quinnan GV, Rodstein M, et al. Association of influenza immunization with reduction in mortality in an elderly population: A prospective study. Arch Intern Med. 1988;148:562–565.
356. Keitel WA, Cate TR, Couch RB. Efficacy of sequential annual vaccination with inactivated influenza virus vaccine. Am J Epidemiol. 1988;127:353–364.
357. Leighton L, Williams M, Aubery D, Parker SH. Sickness absence following a campaign of vaccination against influenza in the workplace. Occup Med. 1996;46:146–150.
358. Nichol KL, Lind A, Margolis KL, et al. The effectiveness of vaccination against influenza in healthy, working adults. N Engl J Med. 1995;333:889–893.
359. Govaert TM, Thijs CT, Masurel N, et al. The efficacy of influenza vaccination in elderly individuals. A randomized double-blind placebo-controlled trial. JAMA. 1994;270:1956–1961.
360. Paul WS, Cowan J, Jackson GG. Acute respiratory illness among immunized and nonimmunized patients with high-risk factors during a split season of influenza A and B. J Infect Dis. 1988;157:633–639.
361. Patriarca PA, Weber JA, Parker RA, et al. Efficacy of influenza vaccine in nursing homes: Reduction in illness and complications during an influenza A (H3N2) epidemic. JAMA. 1985;253:1136–1139.
362. Saah AJ, Neufeld R, Rodstein M, et al. Influenza vaccine and pneumonia mortality in a nursing home population. Arch Intern Med. 1986;146:2353–2357.
363. Patriarca PA, Weber JA, Parker RA, et al. Risk factors for outbreaks of influenza in nursing homes: A case-control study. Am J Epidemiol. 1986;124:114–119.
364. Betts RF, Dolin R, Treanor JJ, et al. Inactivated influenza vaccine reduces frequency and severity of illness in the elderly. Presented at the Twenty-fourth Interscience Conference on Antimicrobial Agents and Chemotherapy, Washington, DC, September 1984. American Society for Microbiology.
365. Gross PA, Hermogenes AW, Sacks HS, et al. The efficacy of influenza vaccine in elderly persons: A meta-analysis and review of the literature. Ann Intern Med. 1995;123:518–527.
366. Fedson DS, Wajda A, Nicol JP, et al. Clinical effectiveness of influenza vaccination in Manitoba. JAMA. 1993;270:1956–1961.
367. Bennett NM, Lewis B, Doniger AS, et al. A coordinated, community wide program in Monroe County, New York, to increase influenza immunization rates in the elderly. Arch Intern Med. 1994;154:1741–1745.
368. Nichol KL, Margolis KL, Wuorenma J, Von Sternberg T. The efficacy and cost effectiveness of vaccination against influenza among elderly persons living in the community. N Engl J Med. 1994;331:778–784.
369. Potter J, Stott DJ, Roberts MA, et al. Influenza vaccination of health care workers in long-term-care hospitals reduces the mortality of elderly patients. J Infect Dis. 1997;175:1–6.
370. Carter ML, Renzulio PO, Helgerson SD, et al. Influenza outbreaks in nursing homes: How effective is influenza vaccine in the institutionalized elderly? Infect Control Hosp Epidemiol. 1986;11:473–478.
371. Arden NH, Patriarca PA, Kendal AP. Experiences in the use and efficacy of inactivated influenza vaccine in nursing homes. In: UCLA Symposia on Molecular and Cellular Biology, Options for the Control of Influenza, v. 36. Keystone, Colo: Alan R Liss; 1986.
372. Arroyo JC, Postic B, Brown A, et al. Influenza A/Philippines/2/82 outbreak in a nursing home: Limitations of influenza vaccination in the aged. Am J Infect Control. 1984;12:329–334.
373. Powers DC, Belshe RB. Effect of age on cytotoxic T lymphocyte memory as well as serum and local antibody responses elicited by inactivated influenza vaccine. J Infect Dis. 1993;197:584–592.
374. Nicholson KG, Baker DJ, Chakraverty P, et al. Immunogenicity of inactivated influenza vaccine in residential homes for elderly people. Age Ageing. 1992;21:182–188.
375. Coles FB, Balzano GJ, Morse DL. An outbreak of influenza A(H3N2) in a well immunized nursing home population. J Am Geriatr Soc. 1992;40:589–592.
376. Remarque EJ, van Beek WC, Ligthart GJ, et al. Improvement of the immunoglobulin subclass response to influenza vaccine in elderly nursing-home residents by the use of high-dose vaccines. Vaccine. 1993;11:649–654.
377. Treanor J, Dumyati G, O'Brien D, et al. Evaluation of cold-adapted, reassortant influenza B virus vaccines in elderly and chronically ill adults. J Infect Dis. 1994;169:402–407.
378. Glathe H, Bigl S, Grosche A. Comparison of humoral immune responses to trivalent influenza split vaccine in young, middle-aged and elderly people. Vaccine. 1993;11:702–705.
379. Powers DC. Effect of age on serum immunoglobulin G subclass antibody responses to inactivated influenza virus vaccine. J Med Virol. 1994;43:57–61.
380. Gross PA, Quinnan GV, Weksler ME, et al. Relation of chronic disease and immune response to influenza vaccine in the elderly. Vaccine. 1989;7:303.
381. Pozzetto B, Odelin MF, Bienvenu J, et al. Is there a relationship between malnutrition, inflammation, and post-vaccinal antibody response to influenza viruses in the elderly? J Med Virol. 1993;41:39–43.
382. McElhaney JE, Meneilly GS, Lechelt KE, et al. Antibody response to whole-virus and split-virus influenza vaccines in successful ageing. Vaccine. 1993;11:1055–1060.
383. McElhaney JE, Meneilly GS, Lechelt KE, Bleackley RC. Split-virus influenza vaccines: Do they provide adequate immunity in the elderly? J Gerontol. 1994;49:M37–M43.
384. Johnson PR, Feldman S, Thompson JM, et al. Immunity to influenza A virus infection in young children: A comparison of natural infection, live cold-adapted vaccine, and inactivated vaccine. J Infect Dis. 1986;154:121–127.
385. Clements ML, Betts RF, Murphy BR. Advantage of live attenuated cold-adapted influenza A virus over inactivated vaccine for A/Washington/80 (H3N2) wild-type virus infection. Lancet. 1984;1:704–708.
386. Rudenko LG, Slepushkin AN, Monto AS, et al. Efficacy of live attenuated and inactivated influenza vaccines in schoolchildren and their unvaccinated contacts in Novgorod, Russia. J Infect Dis. 1993;168:881–887.
387. Chanock RM, Murphy BR. Use of temperature-sensitive and cold-adapted mutant viruses in the immunoprophylaxis of acute respiratory tract disease. Rev Infect Dis. 1980;2:421–432.
388. Wright PF, Karzon DT. Live attenuated influenza vaccines. Prog Med Virol. 1987;34:70–88.
389. Murphy BR, Wood FT, Massicot JG, et al. Temperature-sensitive mutants of influenza virus. XV. The genetic and biologic characterization of a recombinant influenza virus containing two *ts* lesions produced by mating two complementing, single lesion *ts* mutants. Virology. 1978;88:231–243.
390. Murphy BR, Buckler-White AJ, London WT, et al. Avian-human reassortant influenza A viruses derived by mating avian and human influenza A viruses. J Infect Dis. 1984;150:841–850.
391. Tolpin MD, Massicot JG, Mullinix MG, et al. Genetic factors associated with loss of the temperature-sensitive phenotype of the influenza A/Alaska/77-*ts*-1A2 recombinant during growth in vivo. Virology. 1981;112:505–517.
392. Steinhoff MC, Halsey NA, Wilson MH, et al. Comparison of live, attenuated cold-adapted and avian-human influenza A/Bethesda/85 (H3N2) reassortant virus vaccines in infants and children. J Infect Dis. 1990;162:394–401.
393. Steinhoff MC, Halsey NA, Wilson MH, et al. The A/Mallard/6750/78 avian-human, but not the A/Ann Arbor/6/60 cold-adapted, influenza A/Kawasaki/(H1N1) reassortant virus vaccine retains partial virulence for infants and children. J Infect Dis. 1991;165:1023–1028.
394. Maassab HF, DeBorde DC. Development and characterization of cold-adapted viruses for use as live virus vaccines. Vaccine. 1985;3:335–369.
395. Murphy BR. Use of live, attenuated cold-adapted influenza A reassortant virus vaccines in infants, children, young adults, and elderly adults. Infect Dis Clin Pract. 1993;2:176–181.
396. Snyder MH, Betts RF, DeBorde D, et al. Four viral genes independently contribute to attenuatiion of live influenza A/Ann Arbor/6/60 (H2N2) cold-adapted reassortant virus vaccines. J Virol. 1988;62:488–495.
397. Subbarao EK, Perkins M, Treanor JJ, Murphy BR. The attenuation phenotype conferred by the M gene of the influenza A/Ann Arbor/6/60 cold-adapted virus (H2N2) on the A/Korea/82 (H3N2) reassortant virus results from a gene constellation effect. Virus Res. 1992;25:37–50.
398. Keitel WA, Couch RB, Cate TR, et al. Cold-recombinant influenza B/Texas/1/84 virus vaccine: Attenuation, immunogenicity, and efficacy against homotypic challenge. J Infect Dis. 1990;161:22–26.
399. Clements ML, Snyder MH, Sears SD, et al. Evaluation of the infectivity, immunogenicity, and efficacy of live cold-adapted influenza B/Ann Arbor/1/86 reassortant virus in adult volunteers. J Infect Dis. 1990;161:869–877.
400. Treanor JJ, Betts RF, Kotloff K, et al. Efficacy of trivalent, live, cold-adapted influenza vaccine (CAIV-T) in prevention of virus infection and illness following challenge of adults with wild-type influenza A (H1N1), A (H3N2), and B viruses. J Infect Dis. 1998. In press.
401. Piedra PA, Glezen WP. Influenza in children: Epidemiology, immunity, and vaccines. Semin Pediatr Infect Dis. 1992;2:140–146.
402. Gruber WC, Belshe RB, King JC, et al. Evaluation of live attenuated influenza vaccines in children 6–18 months of age: Safety, immunogenicity, and efficacy. J Infect Dis. 1996;173:1313–1319.
403. Belshe RB, Mendelman PM, Treanor J, et al. The efficacy of live attenuated cold-

adapted trivalent, intranasal influenzavirus vaccine in children. N Engl J Med. 1998;358:1405–1412.
404. Edwards KM, Dupont WD, Westrich MK, et al. A randomized controlled trial of cold-adapted and inactivated vaccines for the prevention of influenza A disease. J Infect Dis. 1994;169:68–76.
405. Powers DC, Fries LF, Murphy BR, et al. In elderly persons live attenuated influenza A virus vaccines do not offer an advantage over inactivated virus vaccine in inducing serum or secretory antibodies or local immunologic memory. J Clin Microbiol. 1991;29:498–505.
406. Gorse GJ, Belshe RB, Munn NJ. Local and systemic antibody responses in high-risk adults given live attenuated and inactivated influenza A virus vaccines. J Clin Microbiol. 1988;26:911–918.
407. Powers DC, Sears SD, Murphy BR, et al. Systemic and local antibody responses in elderly subjects given live or inactivated influenza A virus vaccines. J Clin Microbiol. 1989;27:2666–2671.
408. Treanor JJ, Mattison HR, Dumyati G, et al. Protective efficacy of combined live intranasal and inactivated influenza A virus vaccines in the elderly. Ann Intern Med. 1992;117:625–633.
409. Enami M, Luytjes W, Krystal M, Palese P. Introduction of site-specific mutations into the genome of influenza virus. Proc Natl Acad Sci U S A. 1990;87:3802–3805.
410. Luytjes W, Krystal M, Enami M, et al. Amplification, expression, and packaging of a foreign gene by influenza virus. Cell. 1989;59:1107–1113.
411. Barclay WS, Palese P. Influenza B viruses with site-specific mutation introduced into the HA gene. J Virol. 1995;69:1275–1279.
412. Muster T, Sabbarao EK, Enami M, et al. An influenza A virus containing influenza B virus 5′ and 3′ noncoding regions on the neuraminidase gene is attenuated in mice. Proc Natl Acad Sci U S A. 1991;88:5177–5181.
413. Castrucci MR, Bilsel P, Kawaoka Y. Attenuation of influenza A virus by insertion of a foreign epitope into the neuraminidase. J Virol. 1992;66:4647–4653.
414. Castrucci MR, Kawaoka Y. Biologic importance of neuraminidase stalk length in influenza A viruses. J Virol. 1993;67:759–764.
415. Subbarao EK, Park EJ, Lawson CM, et al. Sequential addition of temperature-sensitive missense mutations into the PB2 gene of influenza A transfectant viruses can effect an increase in temperature sensitivity and attenuation and permits the rational design of a genetically engineered live influenza A virus vaccine. J Virol. 1995;69:5969–5977.
416. Li S, Polonis V, Isobe H, et al. Chimeric influenza virus induces neutralizing antibodies and cytotoxic T cells against human immunodeficiency virus type 1. J Virol. 1993;67:6659–6666.
417. Muster T, Ferko B, Klima A, et al. Mucosal model of immunization against human immunodeficiency virus type 1 with a chimeric influenza virus. J Virol. 1995;69:6678–6686.
418. Wolff JA, Malone RW, Williams P, et al. Direct gene transfer into mouse muscle in vivo. Science. 1990;247:1465–1468.
419. Ulmer JB, Donnelly JJ, Parker SE, et al. Heterologous protection against influenza by injection of DNA encoding a viral protein. Science. 1993;259:1745–1749.
420. Robinson HL, Hunt LA, Webster RG. Protection against a lethal influenza virus challenge by immunization with a haemagglutinin-expressing plasmid DNA. Vaccine. 1993;11:957–960.
421. Donnelly JJ, Friedman A, Martinez D, et al. Preclinical efficacy of a prototype DNA vaccine: Enhanced protection against antigenic drift in influenza virus. Nat Med. 1995;1:583–587.
422. Centers for Disease Control and Prevention. Prevention and control of influenza: Recommendations of the Advisory Committee on Immunization Practices (ACIP). MMWR Morb Mortal Wkly Rep. 1998;47(RR-6):1–26.
423. DeStefano F, Goodman RA, Noble GR, et al. Simultaneous administration of influenza and pneumococcal vaccines. JAMA. 1982;247:2551–2554.
424. Fedson DS. Influenza prevention and control: Past practices and future prospects. Am J Med. 1987;82:42–47.
425. Davies R, Pepys J. Egg allergy, influenza vaccine, and immunoglobulin E antibody. J Allergy Clin Immunol. 1976;57:373–383.
426. Murphy DR, Strunk RC. Safe administration of influenza vaccine in asthmatic children hypersensitive to egg proteins. J Pediatr. 1985;106:931–933.
427. Gross PA, Lee H, Wolff JA, et al. Influenza immunization in immunosuppressed children. J Pediatr. 1978;92:30–35.
428. Ortbals DW, Liebhaber H, Presant CA, et al. Influenza immunization of adult patients with malignant diseases. Ann Intern Med. 1977;87:552–557.
429. Freeman DW, Barno A. Deaths from Asian influenza associated with pregnancy. Am J Obstet Gynecol. 1959;78:1172–1175.
430. Neuzil KM, Reed GW, Mitchel EF, et al. The impact of influenza on acute cardiopulmonary hospitalizations in pregnant women. Am J Epidemiol. 1998. In press.
431. Englund JA, Mbawuike IN, Hammill H, et al. Maternal immunization with influenza or tetanus toxoid vaccine for passive antibody protection in young infants. J Infect Dis. 1993;168:647–656.
432. MacKenzie JS. Influenza subunit vaccine: Antibody response to one and two doses of vaccine and length of response, with particular reference to the elderly. Br Med J. 1977;1:200–202.
433. Hoskins TW, Davies JR, Smith AJ, et al. Assessment of inactivated influenza A vaccine after three outbreaks of influenza A at Christ's Hospital. Lancet. 1979;1:33–35.
434. Monto AS, Gunn RA, Bandyk MG, King CL. Prevention of Russian influenza by amantadine. JAMA. 1979;241:1003–1007.
435. Jackson GG, Muldoon RL, Akers LW. Serologic evidence for prevention of influenza infections by an anti-influenzal drug adamantanamine hydrochloride. Antimicrob Agents Chemother. 1963;1963:703–707.
436. Togo Y, Hornick RB, Dawkins ATJ. Studies on induced influenza in man. I. Double-blind studies designed to assess prophylactic efficacy of amantadine hydrochloride against A2/Rockville/1/65 strain. JAMA. 1968;203:1089.
437. Smorodintsev AA, Zlydnikov DM, Kiseleva AM, et al. Evaluation of amantadine in artificially induced A2 and B influenza. JAMA. 1970;213:1448–1454.
438. Smorodintsev AA, Karpuchin GI, Zlydikov DM. The prospect of amantadine for prevention of influenza A2 in humans (effectiveness of amantadine during influenza A2/Hong Kong epidemics in January–February, 1969, in Leningrad). Ann N Y Acad Sci. 1970;173:44.
439. O'Donoghue J, Ray CG, Terry DW Jr, Beaty HN. Prevention of nosocomial influenza infection with amantadine. Am J Epidemiol. 1973;97:276–282.
440. Monto AS, Ohmit SE, Hornbuckle K, Pearce CL. Safety and efficacy of long-term use of rimantadine for prophylaxis of type A influenza in nursing homes. Antimicrob Agents Chemother. 1995;39:2224–2228.
441. Brady MT, Sears SD, Pacini DL, et al. Safety and prophylactic efficacy of low-dose rimantadine in adults during an influenza A epidemic. Antimicrob Agents Chemother. 1990;34:1633–1636.
442. Arden NH, Patriarca PA, Fasano MB, et al. The roles of vaccination and amantadine prophylaxis in controlling an outbreak of influenza A (H3N2) in a nursing home. Arch Intern Med. 1988;148:865–868.
443. Galbraith AW, Oxford JS, Schild GC. Protective effect of 1-adamantanamine hydrochloride on influenza A2 in the family environment. Lancet. 1969;2:1026–1028.
444. Atkinson WL, Arden NH, Patriarca PA, et al. Amantadine prophylaxis during an institutional outbreak of type A (H1N1) influenza. Arch Intern Med. 1986;146:1751–1756.
445. Mast EE, Harman MW, Gravenstein S, et al. Emergence and possible transmission of amantadine-resistant viruses during nursing home outbreaks of influenza A(H3N2). Am J Epidemiol. 1991;134:988–997.
446. Douglas RG, Betts RF, Hruska JF, et al. Epidemiology of nosocomial viral infections. In: Weinstein L, ed. Seminars in Infectious Diseases. New York: Stratton; 1979:98–144.
447. Everts RJ, Hanger HC, Jennings LC, et al. Outbreaks of influenza A among elderly hospital patients. N Z Med J. 1996;109:272–274.
448. Weingarten S, Staniloff H, Ault M, et al. Do hospital employees benefit from influenza vaccine? J Gen Intern Med. 1988;3:32.

Bunyaviridae

Chapter 154

California Encephalitis, Hantavirus Pulmonary Syndrome, and Bunyavirid Hemorrhagic Fevers

C. J. PETERS

The family Bunyaviridae comprises more than 200 animal viruses classified into four major genera (Bunyavirus, Phlebovirus, Nairovirus, and Hantavirus) readily distinguished by genetic, morphologic, biochemical, and immunologic characteristics.[1] The circulation of the viruses in nature via arthropod-vertebrate cycles or chronic infection of vertebrates leads to disease distributions that are determined by ecologic circumstances, can be highly focal, and depend on weather and climatic variables. Caused by a virus in the genus Bunyavirus, California encephalitis (CE) is the commonest childhood central nervous system (CNS) disease reported every year, making CE second in importance only to St. Louis encephalitis among the mosquito-borne viral diseases in the United States. La Crosse (LAC)

All material in this chapter is in the public domain, with the exception of any borrowed figures or tables.

virus is responsible for most cases of CE, although a number of other antigenically related viruses compose the CE group, including California and Jamestown Canyon viruses. Although not endemic in the Americas, Rift Valley fever (RVF), Crimean-Congo hemorrhagic fever (CCHF), and Hantaan (HTN) viruses cause serious and fatal acute disease with hemorrhagic manifestations on other continents.[2–4] In addition, relatives of HTN virus, isolated initially in Korea in 1978,[5] are present in wild rodents in the Americas (for example, Sin Nombre virus [SNV]), and are implicated as causes of severe pulmonary edema and shock.[4, 6] Salient features of these agents including genus assignment and associated diseases are summarized in Table 154–1. Emphasis in the following presentation is given primarily to LAC and SNV viruses with comparative properties for HTN, RVF, and CCHF viruses where appropriate. A few emerging agents are mentioned.

VIRAL CHARACTERIZATION

Structure, Genetics, Antigenic Relationships

Bunyaviridae are spheric, lipid membrane–enclosed viruses 90 to 110 nm in diameter. They contain three negative-sense RNA segments that code for six or fewer proteins. The molecular weights of the proteins and RNA vary by genus, but the small RNA codes for a viral nucleoprotein and the middle RNA for two glycosylated envelope proteins.[7] Nonstructural proteins are usually found, and the large RNA is thought to encode a viral polymerase encapsidated with the virus. In general, the G1 or G2 protein, or both, are responsible for viral neutralization, fusion of infected cells, and hemagglutination.[8, 9] The nucleocapsid protein is thought to be the most important source of immunologic relationships observed within and across genera of the family. In general, the fluorescent antibody (FA) test is the most cross-reactive with hemagglutination-inhibition and particularly the neutralization tests providing greater specificity. The latter is of greatest use in distinguishing individual viruses. Increasingly enzyme-linked immunosorbent assay (ELISA) tests are used for diagnosis of acute or resolving (immunoglobulin M [IgM]) or retrospective (IgG) infections.

Morphogenesis

Viral morphogenesis usually occurs intracellularly, with virions maturing by budding from the Golgi complex and endoplasmic reticulum into vesicles. Exceptions include RVF virus, which also buds through the outer cell membrane of hepatocytes,[10] and SNV, which matures at the cytoplasmic membrane.[11]

EPIDEMIOLOGY

Basic Ecology and Distribution

California Encephalitis Viruses

LAC virus is medically the most significant CE virus in the United States, and its principal vector is *Aedes triseriatus,* a forest-dwelling, treehole-breeding mosquito of the north-central and northeastern regions of the country. LAC virus is maintained in this mosquito by transovarial transmission supplemented by intraspecific venereal transmission and amplification during summer by mosquitoes feeding on viremic chipmunks, squirrels, foxes, and woodchucks.[12, 13]

Female mosquitoes infected by any of these mechanisms are capable of transmitting virus by biting. The virus survives during the winter in mosquito eggs.[14] LAC virus and human encephalitis were first recognized in the upper Mississippi and Ohio River valleys. Most cases have been reported from Wisconsin, Minnesota, Iowa, Indiana, Ohio, and Illinois.[1] However, recognition of the disease in West Virginia[15] and Georgia[16] has led to an understanding that viral transmission occurs throughout the eastern United States. Other vectors are not of major importance except focally. The recently introduced Asian mosquito *Aedes albopictus* is an efficient vector and is capable of horizontal transmission in the laboratory.[17] Its strongly anthropophilic biting habits and its documented extension into areas where LAC virus is endemic raise concern.[18]

Other CE viruses have distinct ecologic cycles based on an element of transovarial transmission in mosquitoes, and human disease is generally mild or uncommon.

Rift Valley Fever and Crimean-Congo Hemorrhagic Fever

RVF virus is maintained in sub-Saharan Africa by transovarial transmission in certain floodwater-breeding *Aedes* mosquitoes, notably *Aedes mcintoshi.*[19] Infected eggs can remain dormant but viable in soil for years while awaiting heavy rains for subsequent hatching. Other mosquitoes are important during epizootics and epidemics; large domestic ungulates such as sheep or cattle serve as amplifiers because they experience high viremia during infection.[20] In 1977, the virus was introduced into Egypt, producing widespread epidemic disease in humans and domestic animals; it has reappeared in the 1990s. It is likely that other receptive areas such as North America could suffer the same fate if an introduction should occur.[2]

CCHF virus is transmitted by ticks. The principal vectors belong to the genus *Hyalomma.* Immature stages feed on hares, hedgehogs, and ground-feeding birds, whereas adults parasitize large wild and domestic animals. This virus is widely distributed in the southwestern Soviet Union, the Balkans, the Middle East, and Africa.[3]

Hantaviruses

These agents are fundamentally parasites of wild rodents and perhaps insectivores.[4] As such, hantaviruses are the exception to the general rule that Bunyaviridae members are arthropod-borne viruses. Although many rodent species worldwide have been shown to harbor antibodies, antigens, nucleic acids, or infectious viruses, or all of these, each of the presently recognized viral species has a single major rodent host species. Rodents become chronically infected despite an immune response that eliminates viremia, and they excrete virus in urine and saliva for weeks or months.[21, 22] Mechanisms of intraspecific transmission depend largely on horizontal transmission between sexually mature animals.[4, 23] HTN virus, the cause of severe hemorrhagic fever with renal syndrome (HFRS) in Korea, China, and eastern Russia is carried by the striped field mouse, *Apodemus agrarius.*[5] *Apodemus agrarius* is found in or near cultivars of humans; rodent breeding seasons and human agricultural practices result in fall and spring disease peaks.[24] Dobrava virus associated with *Aedes flavicollis* is the major cause of severe HFRS in the Balkans.

Bank voles, *Clethrionomys glareolus,* are the reservoir-vectors of Puumala virus, the cause of a milder form of HFRS termed *nephropathia epidemica* in Scandinavia, the western Soviet Union, and Europe. These small rodents are found in forests and agricultural hedgerows, have highly fluctuating populations, and disperse into rural and suburban gardens and dwellings particularly in the fall and winter of years when their populations reach peaks.[25, 26]

Another hantavirus, Seoul virus, is found worldwide in *Rattus norvegicus.* Seoul virus in Asia causes HFRS resembling the disease from HTN virus, except the course is milder and more prominent hepatic involvement is seen. Continuous intraspecific transmission of the virus during a 5-year period has been documented in Baltimore, Maryland.[23]

Many native North and South American rodents (family Muridae, subfamily Sigmodontinae) host phylogenetically distinct hantaviruses associated with hantavirus pulmonary syndrome (HPS).[27] The most important North American virus is SNV. The reservoir of SNV is the deer mouse, *Peromyscus maniculatus,* a species that is widespread in the United States and readily enters homes and other structures. On

TABLE 154–1 Some Characteristics of Severe Diseases Caused by Bunyaviridae

Disease	Genus and Viruses	Vector	Transmission to Humans	Disease Pattern and Annual Incidence	Major Clinical Features
California encephalitis	*Bunyavirus* La Crosse California encephalitis Jamestown Canyon	*Aedes triseriatus* Transovarial transmission, amplification by chipmunks	Mosquito bite	Summer-fall Northern U.S.: 60–130 cases	Meningoencephalitis, seizures, cerebral edema
Rift Valley fever	*Phlebovirus* Rift Valley fever	*Aedes mcintoshi* Transovarial transmission. Horizontal transmission in other arthropods	Mosquito bite. Aerosol or contact with fresh carcasses, domestic animals	Endemic in rainy season sub-Saharan Africa: hundreds of cases. Occasional epidemics associated with exceptional rainfall	Acute febrile illness with occasional retinitis, hemorrhagic fever, or encephalitis
Crimean-Congo hemorrhagic fever	*Nairovirus* Crimean-Congo hemorrhagic fever	*Hyalomma* ticks Amplified by hares, domestic animals	Tick bite, contact with blood of humans or domestic animals	Spring-summer. Former Soviet Union, Middle East, Africa: 50–200 cases	Severe hemorrhagic fever
Hemorrhagic fever with renal syndrome	*Hantavirus* Hantaan Dobrava Seoul Puumala	Chronic infection of striped field mouse, yellow-necked mouse, rat, or bank vole	Aerosols from rodent excreta	Endemic and epidemic. Season depends on local conditions. Asia, Europe: 100,000 cases	Fever, shock, bleeding, renal failure
Hantavirus pulmonary syndrome	*Hantavirus* Sin Nombre Others	Chronic infection of deer mouse	Aerosols from rodent excreta	Discovered 1993. Dozens of cases annually in North and South America	Fever, shock, pulmonary edema

the East Coast, the closely related New York virus is a chronic infection of the white-footed mouse, *Peromyscus leucopus*. Somewhat more distantly related viruses are Bayou and Black Creek Canal viruses found in the southern United States and Florida, respectively, and associated with a degree of renal failure in their clinical picture.

Transmission to Humans

California Encephalitis Viruses

LAC virus transmission occurs through the bite of female mosquitoes that have viral infection of their salivary glands. Human infection occurs mainly during the summer and early fall in persons entering forested areas for recreation or those living near forests. *Aedes triseriatus* will range a considerable distance from forest across open terrain in search of a blood meal and breeds effectively in some manufactured containers such as abandoned tires, bringing the mosquito range closer to human habitation.[28]

Rift Valley Fever and Crimean-Congo Hemorrhagic Fever

RVF in Africa has two main modes of transmission. It is recognized as a disease of farmers, veterinarians, and abattoir workers who have close contact with blood shed from sick domestic livestock or fresh carcasses containing a high concentration of virus.[20] However, another major route of transmission to humans is from mosquito bite, particularly during epidemics. Infrequent years of heavy precipitation trigger the dormant transovarially infected eggs, and other secondary vectors widely disseminate virus.[2] CCHF virus infects humans principally by the bite of adult *Hyalomma* ticks. Milkers and shepherds are frequent victims. Asymptomatically viremic sheep and cattle have been implicated in transmission to abattoir workers, even outside known endemic areas,[29] and crushing infected ticks may also be hazardous. Highly infectious blood from patients also has caused several alarming nosocomial hospital outbreaks with fatalities in medical personnel, particularly when the correct diagnosis of the index case was not suspected.[30, 31]

Hantaviruses

Aerosols of virus-contaminated rodent urine or perhaps feces are thought to represent the principal vehicle for the transmission of hantaviruses; disease has also followed the bite of infected rodents (saliva contains virus).[24, 32] Infections from *Apodemus* or *Clethrionomys* are acquired principally by persons visiting or working in forests and on farms. Depending on the circumstances, the incidence may be highest in summer or in fall and early winter. Disease is maximal in "high-rodent" years, when suburban residents may be exposed to dispersing infected rodents.[4, 24–26, 33]

Infection with Seoul virus from *R. norvegicus* may occur on farms and in residential areas. Cases of HFRS were thus traced to nontraveling residents of urban Seoul, Korea. Rat-borne disease has striking seasonal prevalence (winter-spring) in China.[33] In addition, infection, human disease, and even death have been linked to infected laboratory rats in Korea, Japan, Belgium, France, and the United Kingdom.[32] Rat colonies are apparently infected by the introduction of infected laboratory rats or by contact with wild rats bearing the virus. The United States has been spared this problem because rat stocks imported for research are cesarean delivered and barrier maintained.

Deer mice are numerous and readily enter human dwellings and outbuildings, particularly when mouse populations are high or in autumn when food and cover are scarce. Abundant rodent populations were present in the southwestern United States in summer 1993 when the virus was first discovered. By the end of 1993, cases had been identified in most of the western states as well as retrospective cases from as long ago as 1979.[4]

CLINICAL MANIFESTATIONS

California Encephalitis Viruses

Infection of humans by CE viruses is most commonly asymptomatic. After an incubation period of 3 to 7 days, however, individuals may suffer mild febrile illness, encephalitis, or meningoencephalitis. More than 90% of acute CNS disease caused by LAC virus occurs in children younger than 15 years; males are affected more often than females, and the mortality in acute CNS disease is about 1%.[1, 15, 34, 35] Clinically and pathologically, CE is difficult to distinguish from other acute viral infections of the CNS. It can range in severity from mild aseptic meningitis to a severe disease mimicking herpes encephalitis. Computed tomographic scans are abnormal in a minority of cases, magnetic resonance imaging is sometimes positive, and either can yield focal images[15]; the electroencephalogram is usually abnormal and often focally so, even with periodic lateralizing epileptiform discharges that lead to a suspicion of herpes encephalitis.[50] Fever, headache, nausea, and vomiting are present in most patients. Lethargy, aphasia, incoordination, and focal motor abnormalities, even paralysis, may be present, but the outstanding serious finding is convulsions, which occurs in about one half of cases. The spinal fluid generally shows a modest pleocytosis (<100 white blood cells/mm^3) that occasionally is largely granulocytic and exhibits a normal or slightly increased protein concentration. Peripheral leukocytosis in excess of 15,000 white blood cells/mm^3 is not uncommon. Although most patients make uneventful recoveries, abnormal electroencephalographic findings 1 to 5 years later are present in 75%, emotional lability is persistent in 10%, and epilepsy is a chronic problem in 6 to 10% of all diagnosed cases. Thus, the residua of CE may be more serious than is generally appreciated.

Rift Valley Fever and Crimean-Congo Hemorrhagic Fever

RVF infection in humans causes undifferentiated febrile disease in the great majority of instances. Perhaps 10% of patients experience macular and perimacular retinitis and vasculitis that may cause a permanent loss of vision. In as much as 1% of infections, fulminant disease with hemorrhage, jaundice, and hepatitis may develop at the end of a 3- to 6-day febrile episode; half these patients die. Other infections (<1%) lead to severe, frequently fatal encephalitis directly related to viral invasion of the CNS.

CCHF is a severe hemorrhagic fever with shock, disseminated intravascular coagulation, frequent extensive bleeding, and severe thrombocytopenia. The virus infects the reticuloendothelial system and frequently involves hepatocytes extensively, leading to icteric hepatitis.[36] Mortality ranges from 20 to 50%.

Hantaviruses: Hemorrhagic Fever with Renal Syndrome

The hallmarks of clinical infection by HTN, Dobrara, Seoul, and Puumala viruses are fever, thrombocytopenia, and acute renal insufficiency pathologically typical of acute interstitial nephritis. The incubation period, typically 2 weeks, may vary from 5 to 42 days. In the severe Asian form of HFRS due to HTN virus, patients who survive full-blown disease progress through febrile (toxic), hypotensive, oliguric, and polyuric clinical stages and may require weeks or months to recover from general asthenia.

In the toxic phase, patients complain of headache, abdominal and lower back pain, dizziness, and, often, blurred vision.[37–39] Conjunctival injection and petechiae occur over the upper trunk and soft palate. An erythematous flush that blanches on pressure is characteristically seen on the torso and face. Leukocyte levels are normal or more likely elevated, often exceeding 20,000/mm^3. The differential count shows a left shift, immature myeloid cells, and atypical lymphocytes as well, confirming the decreased thrombocyte count. At the end of the febrile period (4 to 7 days), many patients experience severe clinical shock. Those surviving then must endure varied grades of renal insufficiency that can include anuria, oliguria, mucosal bleeding diathesis, electrolyte and acid-base abnormalities, hypertension, and pneumonitis complicated by pulmonary edema. After 3 to 10 days, polyuria begins with its attendant stresses on the fluid and electrolyte balance. The fatality rate in Asian HFRS averages about 5%: one third during the shock phases and two thirds (cerebrovascular accidents and pulmonary edema) during the renal phases of illness. Hemodynamic changes result from massive acute capillary leak syndrome of uncertain cause and equally poorly understood shock-inducing mechanisms. The renal lesions, predominantly in medullary tubules, are possibly related to systemic and intrarenal hemodynamic factors and the influence of immunopathologically released kinins and cytokines.[40]

The milder form of HFRS caused by Puumala virus and often referred to as *nephropathia epidemica* is rarely hemorrhagic and is fatal in less than 1% of clinical cases. Abdominal pain and hyposphenuria may be manifestations. Up to 90% of Puumala virus infections are asymptomatic. Proteinuria, creatinine level elevation, and leukocytosis, although common, are much less severe than for HTN virus infection.

Seoul virus also causes a mild to moderately severe HFRS in Asia. Although the virus is found wherever the reservoir sewer rat occurs, disease has rarely been described in the United States. However, there is epidemiologic evidence linking Seoul virus antibodies to chronic hypertensive renal failure.[41]

Hantaviruses: Hantavirus Pulmonary Syndrome

HPS begins with a febrile prodrome followed by a severe increase in pulmonary vascular permeability and shock.[42, 43] If hypoxia is managed and shock is not fatal, the vascular leak reverses in a few days and recovery is apparently complete. The first symptoms are fever of sudden onset and generalized myalgia. This prodrome resembles the initial phases of HFRS and may also be accompanied by abdominal pain and gastrointestinal disturbances.[40] About 4 to 5 days later (range 1 to 10 days), the patient presents with respiratory symptoms, which usually consist of modest cough and dyspnea. Examination may be unrevealing, but generally fever, tachycardia, and tachypnea are present, perhaps with mild hypotension. Laboratory abnormalities commonly found at this time or developing within 1 to 2 days thereafter are an elevated hematocrit; leukocytosis or left shift, or both; abnormal lymphocytes and immature myeloid cells on smear; mild thrombocytopenia; a prolonged activated partial thromboplastin time; and mildly elevated aspartate aminotransferase or lactate dehydrogenase levels. Mild increases in serum creatinine levels and proteinuria occur in some cases,[27] but the severe renal lesions seen in HFRS are not a regular feature of this syndrome.[40] Respiratory involvement can progress from mild desaturation and interstitial pulmonary edema to florid pulmonary edema with respiratory failure in a matter of hours.[44] HPS should be suspected when an otherwise healthy adult develops unexplained pulmonary edema or is suspected of adult respiratory distress syndrome without one of the known causes of adult respiratory distress syndrome being present; thrombocytopenia or a falling platelet count are particularly useful findings early in the course.[40]

The histopathologic findings of interstitial infiltrates of T lymphocytes and alveolar pulmonary edema without marked necrosis or polymorphonuclear leucocyte involvement correlates with the rapid resolution of the lesion and suggests that the major abnormality may be the induction of a functional vascular permeability increase via an immunopathologic mechanism.[45]

DIAGNOSIS

The diagnosis of CE is immunologic because virus is not present in blood or secretions during the phase of clinical CNS disease. The diagnosis can be rapidly and specifically achieved by ELISA tests for antiviral IgM antibodies in blood and cerebrospinal fluid, usually, but not always, positive at the time of admission.[46] A licensed indirect FA test is available for IgG and IgM antibodies to LAC and is useful in the diagnosis.[15] Virtually all hantavirus patients have both IgM and IgG ELISA antibodies present when admitted to the hospital.[4, 6, 40] Hantaviruses can be recovered only with difficulty in cell culture or animal hosts,[24] but the agent can be detected in tissue by reverse transcription and polymerase chain reaction or by immunohistochemical staining.[6, 45]

RVF and CCHF viruses are readily recovered from the blood of acutely ill patients in cell cultures or suckling mice. Antigen detection ELISA is useful in diagnosis, particularly of severe cases. Although there is less experience with the polymerase chain reaction, it seems to provide additional sensitivity with no loss of specificity. Antibodies detectable by a variety of methods generally appear within 5 to 14 days of onset and coincide with clinical improvement. ELISA detection of IgM antibodies is a reliable definitive method.[20, 29, 30, 45] Because of the aerosol hazard to laboratory personnel, acute samples must be handled with care, and attempts to isolate these two agents should be restricted to facilities with maximal containment.

PREVENTION AND TREATMENT

With the exception of RVF, for which there is an investigational inactivated vaccine,[47] prevention of these diseases is only accomplished by personal means (avoidance of rodent contact; mosquito and tick repellents) and perhaps in the case of CE by the elimination of manufactured containers leading to mosquito breeding together with aerial spraying of slow-release insecticides over forested areas of known high *A. triseriatus* reproduction.[48]

Ribavirin, a guanosine analogue, was effective in the treatment of HFRS in a double-blind placebo-controlled study in China using the intravenous dosing regimen established for Lassa fever (Chapter 155). Studies in vitro and in laboratory animals suggest that ribavirin also might be effective in the treatment of severe RVF and CCHF, and clinical experience with the drug in CCHF supports its use.[49] An open-label trial of ribavirin failed to show any marked efficacy in HPS patients, perhaps because death typically occurs within 24 to 48 hours of hospitalization.[27, 45] A controlled trial of ribavirin in HPS is under way.

Effective supportive medicine is important in all of the severe bunyavirid diseases. Careful management of coma, cerebral edema, and seizures is critical in CE patients; there is danger in too vigorous use of phenobarbital in children with status epilepticus.[50, 51] LAC virus is sensitive in vitro to ribavirin, and treatment of one unusual case diagnosed with brain biopsy has been reported.[15] Early management of hantavirus patients should avoid excessive administration of fluids in these febrile, hemoconcentrated, hypotensive patients. Vascular leak leads to extravasation into retroperitoneal tissues (HFRS) or lung (HPS); cardiatonic drugs should be used early because of the hemodynamic profile of decreased cardiac output and increased systemic vascular resistance.[40] Patients with Asian HFRS may require hemodialysis or peritoneal dialysis during the oliguric phase, and plasma protein or whole blood, or both, may be useful in treating hemorrhage and/or shock in this and other hemorrhagic fevers. Heparin is not recommended for the treatment of presumptive or incipient disseminated intravascular coagulation. Patients with mild HFRS due to Puumala virus rarely require dialysis.

OTHER BUNYAVIRIDAE OF CONCERN

Jamestown Canyon Virus

This California group Bunyavirus is more important than was previously recognized and has been implicated in encephalitis in several adults.[52] Antibodies are not often sought in encephalitis patients and cross-react with other CE antigens in some tests. It is distributed widely across North America and is transmitted by *Culiseta inornata* and several species of *Aedes* mosquitoes, and often-burgeoning populations of white-tailed deer are suspected as the vertebrate amplifier.[53]

Oropouche Virus

Another Bunyavirus (Simbu group) has caused epidemics in towns and cities of Brazil, Panama, and Peru but also has a much wider distribution in the forest.[54, 55] Infection of humans results in an abrupt onset of fever, chills, headache, myalgia, and often vomiting and arthralgia. Aseptic meningitis has been reported in some cases. The disease is self-limiting, but prolonged asthenia and arthralgia may occur. The natural forest cycle is unknown, but in urban areas rainy season leads to breeding of biting midges, and epidemics involve thousands of humans.

Toscana Virus

The classic sand fly fevers (Sicilian and Naples viruses) are acute febrile illnesses with headache and myalgias and were common in the broad European and Asian range of their vector, *Phlebotomus papatasi* until DDT campaigns against malaria virtually eliminated this sand fly in much of Europe. Another sand fly, *Phlebotomus perniciosus*, spreads the related but distinct Phlebovirus Toscana, which appears to be an important cause of febrile disease, aseptic meningitis, and mild encephalitis in both adults and children who are residents or travelers in the European Mediterranean.[56] Infections in vacationers have been reported from Cyprus to Portugal. Two sites in central Italy identified 155 cases of CNS disease over a 10-year period, principally in the summer months.[57]

REFERENCES

1. Peters CJ, Le Duc JW. Bunyaviridae: Bunyaviruses, phleboviruses, and related viruses. In: Belshe RB, ed. Textbook of Human Virology. St Louis: Mosby–Year Book; 1991:571.
2. Peters CJ. Emergence of Rift Valley fever. In: Saluzzo JF, Dodet B, eds. Factors in the Emergence of Arbovirus Diseases. Paris: Elsevier; 1997:253.
3. Hoogstraal H. The epidemiology of tick-borne Crimean-Congo hemorrhagic fever in Asia, Europe, and Africa. J Med Entomol. 1979;15:304.
4. Peters CJ, Mills JN, Spiropoulou C, et al. Hantaviruses. In: Tropical Infectious Diseases: Principles, Pathogens, and Practice. Guerrant RL, Walker DH, Weller PF, eds. New York: WB Saunders; 1999:1189–1212.
5. Lee HW, Lee PW, Johnson KM. Isolation of the agent of Korean hemorrhagic fever. J Infect Dis. 1978;137:298.
6. Nichol ST, Spiropoulou CF, Morzunov S, et al. Genetic identification of a hantavirus associated with an outbreak of acute respiratory illness. Science. 1993;262:914–917.
7. Schmaljohn CS. Bunyaviridae: The viruses and their replication. In: Fields BN, Knipe DM, Howley PM, eds. Fields Virology. 3rd ed. Philadelphia: Lippincott-Raven; 1996:1447.
8. Dantas JR, Okuno Y, Tanishira O, et al. Viruses causing hemorrhagic fever with renal syndrome (HFRS) grouped by immunoprecipitation and hemagglutination inhibition. Intervirology. 1987;27:161.
9. Gonzales-Scarano F, Jansen RS, Najjar JA, et al. An avirulent G1 glycoprotein variant of La Crosse bunyavirus with defective fusion function. J Virol. 1985;54:757.
10. Anderson GW Jr, Smith JF. Immunoelectron microscopy of Rift Valley fever viral morphogensis in primary rat hepatocytes. Viriology. 1987;161:91.
11. Goldsmith CS, Elliott LH, Peters CJ, Zaki SR. Ultrastructural characteristics of Sin Nombre virus, causative agent of hantavirus pulmonary syndrome. Arch Virol. 1995;140:2107.
12. Thompson WH: Vector-virus relationship. In: Calisher CH, Thompson WH, eds. California Serogroup Viruses, Proceedings of an International Symposium. New York: Alan R Liss; 1983:57.
13. Yuill TM. The role of mammals in the maintenance and dissemination of La Crosse virus. In: Calisher CH, Thompson WH, eds. California Serogroup viruses, Proceedings of an International Symposium. New York: Alan R Liss; 1983:77.
14. Watts DM, Thompson WH, Yuill TM, et al. Overwintering of La Crosse virus in *Aedes triseriatus*. Am J Trop Med Hyg. 1974;23:694.
15. McJunkin JE, Khan RR, Tsai TF. California–La Crosse encephalitis. Infect Dis Clin North Am. 1998;12:83.
16. Sikes RK, Calisher CH, Smith JD. Human infections with La Crosse virus in Georgia, 1982. South Med J. 1984;77:972.
17. Cully JF, Streit TG, Geard PB. Transmission of La Crosse virus by four strains of *Aedes albopictus* and from the eastern chipmunk (*Tamias striatus*). J Am Mosquito Control Assoc. 1992;8:237.
18. Kitron U, Swanson J, Crandell M, et al. Introduction of *Aedes albopictus* into a La Crosse virus–enzootic site in Illinois. EID. 1998;4:627.
19. Lithicum KJ, Davies FG, Kairo A, et al. Rift Valley fever virus (family Bunyaviridae, genus Phlebovirus). Isolation from Diptera collected during an interepizootic period in Kenya. J Hyg (Lond). 1985;95:197.
20. Swanepoel R, Coetzer JAW. Riff Valley fever. In: Coetzer JAW, Thomson GR, Tustin RC, eds. Infectious Diseases of Livestock with Special Reference to Southern Africa. Cape Town: Oxford University Press; 1994:688.
21. Lee HW, Lee PW, Baek LJ, et al. Intraspecific transmission of Hantaan virus, etiotogic agent of Korean hemorrhagic fever, in the rodent *Apodemus agrarius*. Am J Trop Med Hyg. 1981;30:1106.
22. Hutchinson KL, Rollin PE, Peters CJ. Pathogenesis of a North American hantavirus, Black Creek Canal virus, in experimentally infected *Sigmodon hispidus*. Am J Trop Med Hyg. 1998;59:58.
23. Childs JE, Glass GE, Korch GW, LeDuc JW. The ecology and epizootiology of hantaviral infections in small mammal communities of Baltimore: A review and synthesis. Bull Soc Vector Ecol. 1988;13:113.
24. Lee HW. Korean hemorrhagic fever. Prog Med Virol. 1982;28:96.
25. Korpela H, Lahdevirta J. The role of small rodents and patterns of living in the epidemiology of nephropathia epidemica. Scand J Infect Dis. 1978;10:303.
26. Niklasson B, Hornfeldt B, Lindkvist A, et al. Temporal dynamics of Puumala virus antibody prevalence in voles and of nephropathia epidemica incidence in humans. Am J Trop Med Hyg. 1995;53:134.
27. Peters CJ. Hantavirus Pulmonary Syndrome in the Americas In: Scheld WM, Craig WA, Hughes JM, eds. Emerging Infections II. Washington, DC: ASM Press; 1998:7–64.
28. Mather TN, DeFoliart GR. Dispersion of gravid *Aedes triseriatus* (Diptera: Culcicidae) from woodlands into open terrain. J Med Entmol. 1984;21:384.
29. Rodriguez LL, Maupin GO, Ksiazek TG, et al. Molecular investigation of a multi-source outbreak of Crimean-Congo hemorrhagic fever in the United Arab Emirates. Am J Trop Med Hyg. 1997;57:512.
30. Burney MI, Ghafoor A, Saleen M, et al. Nosocomial outbreak of viral hemorrhagic fever–Congo virus in Pakistan, January 1976. Am Trop Med Hyg. 1980;29:941.
31. Van Eeden PJ, Joubert JR, van de Wal BW, et al. A nosomial outbreak of Crimean-Congo haemorrhagic fever at Tygerberg hospital. I. Clinical features. S Afr Med J. 1985;68:711
32. Kawamata J, Yamanouchi T, Dohmae K, et al. Control of laboratory acquired hemorrhagic fever with renal syndrome (HFRS) in Japan. Lab Anim Sci. 1987;37:431.
33. Chen HX, Qiu FX, Dong BJ, et al. Epidemiologic studies in hemorrhagic fever with renal syndrome in China. J Infect Dis. 1986;154:394.
34. Young DJ. California encephalitis virus. Report of three cases and review of the literature. Ann Intern Med. 1966;65:419.
35. Johnson KP, Lepow ML, Johnson RT. California encephalitis. I. Clinical and epidemiologic studies. Neurology (NY). 1968;89:250.
36. Burt FJ, Swanepoel R, Shieh W-J, et al. Immunohistochemical and in situ localization of Crimean-Congo hemorrhagic fever virus in human tissues and pathogenic implications. Arch Pathol Lab Med. 1997;121:839.
37. Lee JS, Cho BY, Lee MC, et al. Clinical features of serologically proven Korean hemorrhagic fever patients. Seoul J Med. 1980;21:163.
38. Earle DP. Symposium on epidemic hemorrhagic fever. Am J Med. 1954;16:617.
39. Bruno P, Harrison HL, Brown J, et al. The protean manifestations of hemorrhagic fever with renal syndrome. A retrospective review of 26 cases from Korea. Ann Intern Med. 1990;113:385.
40. Peters CJ, Simpson G, Levy H. Spectrum of hantavirus infection: Hemorrhagic fever with renal syndrome and hantavirus pulmonary syndrome. Annu Rev Med. 1999;50:531–545.
41. Glass GE, Watson AJ, LeDuc JW, et al. Infection with a ratborne hantavirus in US residents is consistently associated with hypertensive renal disease. J Infect Dis. 1993;167:694.
42. Duchin JS, Koster F, Peters CJ, et al. Hantavirus pulmonary syndrome: Clinical description of disease caused by a newly recognized hemorrhagic fever virus in the southwestern United States. N Engl J Med. 1994;330:949.
43. Moolenaar RL, Dalton C, Lipman HB, et al. Clinical features that differentiate hantavirus pulmonary syndrome from three other acute respiratory illnesses. Clin Infect Dis. 1995;21:643.
44. Ketai LH, Williamson MR, Telepak RJ, et al. Hantavirus pulmonary syndrome: Radiographic findings in 16 patients. Radiology. 1994;191:665.
45. Zaki SR, Greer PW, Coffield LM, et al. Hantavirus pulmonary syndrome: Pathogenesis of an emerging infectious disease. Am J Pathol. 1995 146:552.
46. Calisher CH, Pretzman CI, Muth DJ, et al. Serodiagnosis of La Crosse virus infections in humans by detection of immunoglobulin M class antibodies. J Clin Microbiol. 1986;12:667.
47. Niklasson B, Peters CJ, Bentsson E, et al. Rift Valley fever virus vaccine trial. Study of neutralizing antibody response in humans. Vaccine. 1985;3:123.
48. Francy DB. Mosquito control for prevention of California (La Crosse) encephalitis. In: Calisher CH, Thompson WH, eds. California Serogroup Viruses. Proceedings of an International Symposium. New York: Alan R Liss; 1983:365.
49. Peters CJ, Reynolds JA, Slone TW, et al. Prophylaxis of Rift Valley fever with antiviral drugs, immune serum, an interferon inducer, and a macrophage activator. Antiviral Res. 1986;6:285.
50. Deering WM. Neurological aspects and treatment of La Crosse encephalitis. In: Calisher CH, Thompson WH, eds. California Serogroup Viruses. Proceedings of an International Symposium. New York: Alan R Liss; 1983:187.
51. McJunkin JE, Khan R, de los Reyes EC, et al. Treatment of severe La Crosse

encephalitis with intravenous ribavirin following diagnosis by brain biopsy. Pediatrics. 1997;99:261.
52. Deibel R, Srihongse S, Grayson M, et al. Jamestown Canyon virus: The etiologic agent of an emerging human disease. In: Calisher CH, Thompson WH, eds. California Serogroup Viruses, Proceedings of an International Symposium. New York: Alan R Liss; 1983:313.
53. Fulhorst CF, Hardy JL, Eldridge BF, et al. Ecology of Jamestown Canyon virus (Bunyaviridae: California serogroup) in coastal California. Am J Trop Med Hyg. 1996;55:185.
54. Watts DM, Phillips I, Callahan JD, et al. Oropouche virus transmission in the Amazon River basin of Peru. Am J Trop Med Hyg. 1997;56:148.
55. Pinheiro FP, Travassos da Rosa APA, Vasconcelos PFC. An overview of Oropouche fever epidemics in Brazil and neighbouring countries. In: Travassos da Rosa APA, Vasconcelos PFC, Travassos da Rosa JFX, eds. An Overview of Arbovirology in Brazil and Neighboring Countries. Belem, Brazil: Instituto Evandro Chagas; 1998;187.
56. Nicoletti L, Ciufolini MG, Verani P. Sandfly fever viruses in Italy (Review). Arch Virol. 1996;Suppl 11:41.
57. Nicoletti L, Verani P, Caciolli S, et al. Central nervous system involvement during infection by Phlebovirus Toscana of residents in natural foci in central Italy (1977–1988). Am J Trop Med Hyg. 1991;45:429.

Arenaviridae

Chapter 155

Lymphocytic Choriomeningitis Virus, Lassa Virus, and the South American Hemorrhagic Fevers

C. J. PETERS

The a renaviruses are a family possessing single-stranded RNA, a unique morphology, and a predilection for rodents as virus reservoirs. They include lymphocytic choriomeningitis (LCM) virus, Lassa virus, and the genetically and antigenically related Tacaribe complex of viruses. The Tacaribe complex is primarily associated with American rodents (family Muridae, subfamily Sigmodontinae), whereas LCM, Lassa, and their close relatives are from Old World rodents (family Muridae, subfamily Murinae), suggesting their long association and coevolution with rodents.[1, 2] Significant human disease is associated with several of the viruses (Table 155–1). The family prototype, LCM virus, was first isolated in 1933 during serial monkey passage of human material obtained from a fatal infection in the first documented epidemic of St. Louis encephalitis.[3] Junin, Machupo, Lassa, Guanarito, and Sabia viruses were first recovered during investigations of human disease in 1958,[4] 1963,[5] 1969,[6] 1989,[7] and 1990,[8] respectively.

VIRAL CHARACTERIZATION

Virions are round, oval, or pleomorphic particles averaging about 110 to 130 nm in diameter but ranging from 50 to 300 nm.[9] The viral envelope is formed by budding from the viral glycoprotein–bearing host plasma membrane. The surface of the particle bears 6- to 10-nm spikes, and the interior shows variable numbers of characteristic dense granules, 20 to 25 nm in diameter, which have been shown to be host cell ribosomes (Fig. 155–1). These unique structures resembling grains of sand are responsible for the family name (Latin, *arenosos*, or "sandy"). Arenaviruses contain a segmented RNA genome with 31 and 22-S strands. Host ribosomal RNA of 28, 18, and 4 to 6 S is also present but apparently is not biologically functional.[10, 11]

The S, or small, RNA of arenaviruses codes for three virion proteins in a unique manner.[11] The 60- to 70-kD nucleocapsid protein (N) is read first in a conventional negative sense, and later a glycoprotein precursor polypeptide (GPC) is transcribed from genomic sense messenger RNA. This pattern has been termed *ambisense*.[12] The GPC protein is then glycosylated and cleaved to form the spike glycoproteins G1 and G2, typically of molecular weights 35 to 45 and 40 to 60 kD.[13] Arenavirus L, or large, RNA is also ambisense and codes for a viral polymerase of about 200 kD and a zinc-finger protein.[2]

Epitopes mediating neutralization and antibody-complement cell lysis have been localized to the glycoproteins, particularly G1, which is also more genetically and antigenically variable among viral species.[13, 14] The most serologically cross-reactive protein is N, which is usually measured in the diagnostic indirect fluorescent antibody (IFA) test. Protective T-cell epitopes are coded by the genes for N and GPC and probably other proteins as well.[15] Viruses attach to host cells via α-dystroglycan or possibly other receptors, or both, fuse, interiorize, and uncoat within an acidic compartment.[13, 16] Replication is usually not accompanied by overt cytopathic effects.

EPIDEMIOLOGY AND EPIZOOTOLOGY

Arenaviruses are parasites of rodents. They exhibit high species specificity, and a single rodent species is the reservoir for a given agent. Chronic viral infection without obvious disease occurs with the release of virus into excreta, especially urine, resulting in transmission to humans. Among rodents, both vertical transmission and horizontal intraspecific spread are important to varied degrees.[2] Thus, human arenaviral disease is determined by viral pathogenicity, by the geographic distribution of a particular reservoir rodent, and by rodent-human ecologic factors that permit contact with excreted virus.

Lymphocytic Choriomeningitis

Although LCM virus infection may occur worldwide, human infection has been conclusively demonstrated only in Europe and the Americas.[17] Moreover, in regions where the virus is known to exist, infection in the two closely related nonoverlapping reservoir species *Mus domesticus* and *Mus musculus* is highly focal. Studies conducted in Baltimore, Boston, and Washington, D.C., revealed a spotty distribution of virus-positive mice in houses.[18, 19] Similarly, in Germany, much higher murine infection rates prevail in the west-central than in the southern or northern portions of the country.[20]

Human cases of LCM are most common in autumn. This pattern is the result of seasonal population densities of rodents and the movement of mice into homes and barns with cold weather. In addition, seasonal variation in infection rates of *Mus* or differential survival of excreted virus related to the temperature and relative humidity may be involved. It has been shown that aerosolized arenaviruses survive better at lower humidity.[21] Situations associated with wild mouse infection of humans include substandard housing such as mobile homes or inner-city dwellings, the cleaning of rodent-infested barns or outbuildings, and the autumn entry of wild mice into dwellings. Most human LCM infections occur among young adults, although persons of all ages have been affected.

The mode of transmission in most sporadic human infections is not definitely known; however, experimental and epidemiologic observations implicate aerosols, direct contact with rodents, and rodent bites in that order as the most likely vehicles.[3, 18, 22, 23] The incubation period of human LCM disease is variable, but it most

All material in this chapter is in the public domain, with the exception of any borrowed figures or tables.

TABLE 155–1 Arenaviruses and Human Disease

Virus	Disease	Geography	Reservoir	Pathogenesis	Specific Therapy	Prevention
Lymphocytic choriomeningitis	Aseptic meningitis; other organ involvement	North and South America, Europe, and wherever *Mus* is introduced	*Mus domesticus* and *Mus musculus* (house mice)	Systemic infection; when CNS invasion occurs, immunopathologic CNS disease follows	None	House mouse control and avoidance, particularly pregnant women; monitor mouse and hamster suppliers
Lassa	Lassa fever	West Africa, particularly Sierra Leone, Guinea, Liberia, and Nigeria	*Mastomys huberti, Mastomys erythroleucus* (multimammate mouse)	Vascular leak, multiorgan dysfunction, shock; bleeding and CNS involvement occur but not as common as in South American diseases	Intravenous ribavirin	Rodent avoidance and control in houses may be of ancillary benefit; strict isolation of hospitalized patients
Junin	Argentine HF	Argentine pampas	*Calomys musculinis*	As Lassa fever, except encephalopathy and thrombocytopenia are common, as is hemorrhage	Convalescent plasma Ribavirin probably efficacious	Effective live-attenuated vaccine
Machupo	Bolivian HF	Bolivia, Beni Department	*Calomys callosus*	As Argentine HF	Ribavirin or convalescent plasma	Elimination of rodents from home; laboratory evidence for cross-protection by Junin vaccine
Guanarito	Venezuelan HF	Venezuela, Portuguesa State	*Zygodontomys brevicauda*	As Argentine HF	Unknown; ribavirin or convalescent plasma suggested	Unknown; rodent control?
Sabia	Brazilian HF	Brazil	Unknown	Resembles Argentine HF; patient in single naturally occurring case had severe hepatitis	Unknown; ribavirin suggested	Unknown

Abbreviations: CNS, Central nervous system; HF, hemorrhagic fever.

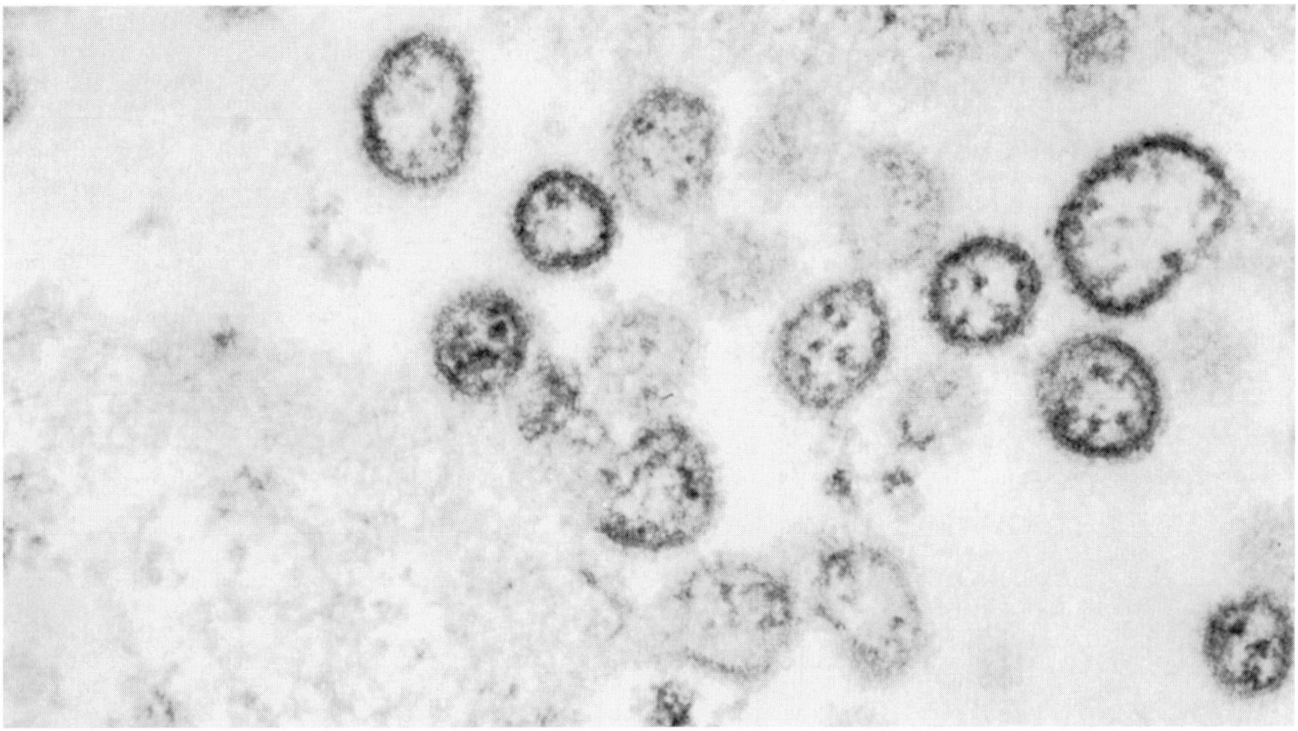

FIGURE 155–1. Electron micrograph of Lassa virus in the first Vero cell passage envelope, and electron-dense interior granules can be seen. (×121,000.)

often ranges from 5 to 10 days. Patients not seeking medical care for the nonspecific febrile illness that begins at this time, but who may later present with acute meningitis, generally are found to have been exposed 2 to 3 weeks before the onset of nervous system signs.

Although most sporadic LCM cases are attributed to contact with infected wild mice, outbreaks of disease have been traced to infected laboratory mice or Syrian hamsters *(Mesocricetus auratus)*. Several of these were the result of the introduction of LCM virus into hamsters through infected tumor cell lines.[23] A recent epidemic resulted from chronic infection of nude, athymic mice by stored infected hamster tumors.[24] Other outbreaks in the United States and Europe resulted from exposure in the home to pet hamsters obtained from breeders with infected stock.[25, 26]

Lassa Fever

Lassa fever is a disease of West Africa; however, with the contemporary ease of international travel, it may occur anywhere in the world. This disease is distinguished from other arenaviral diseases by its occasional ability to spread from person to person. Lassa fever was initially recognized in a Nigerian hospital where three nurses developed illness successively.[27] Since then, nosocomial outbreaks have been reported from Nigeria, Liberia, and Sierra Leone. Lassa virus has been recovered from patients in Guinea, and serologic studies have shown its presence in every country of West Africa from Nigeria to Senegal. West Africa, however, represents only a small part of the range of *Mastomys* rodents, which serve as viral reservoirs, and different species of these are found throughout the continent south of the Sahara Desert. Further work is needed to define the species of the genus *Mastomys*, but clearly at least two species are infected in Sierra Leone,[28, 29] probably *Mastomys huberti* and *Mastomys erythroleucus*. Isolation of Lassa-like viruses of reduced pathogenicity for laboratory animals and presumably for humans from related rodents elsewhere in Africa may provide a partial explanation for the observed regional boundaries of Lassa fever, through understanding of rodent-virus genetic interactions.

Most of the nosocomial outbreaks of Lassa fever have occurred during the dry season (January to April). Endemic transmission occurs throughout the year, with more cases during dry than wet periods.[28, 30] All ages and both sexes are infected equally; in some villages in Sierra Leone, infection rates may reach 10 to 20% per year. Based on serologic data, there may be 20 mild or inapparent infections for each hospitalized case.[28] In contrast, retrospective studies among white missionaries suggest, but do not yet prove, that moderately severe or even fatal illness usually follows infection.[31] Outbreaks typically include health care workers because of their direct exposure to patients and infectious body fluids.

The modes of Lassa virus transmission are not precisely known, but they are almost certainly multiple. Endemic transmission is related to infected rodents by aerosol and direct contact, and most probably to person-to-person spread in homes. *Mastomys* are common rodents in houses and in the nearby bush, and control campaigns cannot be expected to prevent the disease, although model intensive efforts in a village in Sierra Leone resulted in a temporary fourfold reduction in transmission to humans. During nosocomial outbreaks, parenteral inoculation of body fluids (e.g., surgery or autopsy accidents), contact with infected body fluids, and aerosols generated by patients have all been incriminated.[30] Tertiary and quaternary cases in outbreaks are less numerous than are secondary cases, which suggests that only the unusual patient is very infectious.

The incubation period varies from 3 to 16 days (usually 7 to 12) when infection is transmitted from person to person. It is assumed to be similar in rodent-transmitted infection.

South American Hemorrhagic Fevers

The South American hemorrhagic fevers (HFs) are local public health problems in Argentina, Bolivia, and Venezuela and are caused by Junin, Machupo, and Guanarito viruses. Another lethal arenavirus, Sabia virus, has been discovered in Brazil, but its health impact and reservoir are not yet known.[8]

In Argentina, the principal reservoir rodent is *Calomys musculinus*.[32] Argentine HF occurs mainly in an expanding zone within the rich agricultural pampas of northern Buenos Aires province. *Calomys* populations reach their highest density in the cornfields during the austral fall (February to May); the disease thus affects principally men engaged in harvesting corn. Roughly 200 to 2000 cases are reported annually, and the numbers have not changed substantially despite a reduction in exposure through the change from manual to mechanized harvesting techniques. Infectious aerosols are thought to be the most common mode of transmission, although food contamination and the direct contact of abraded fingers with blood and tissues of rodents crushed by machinery may also occur.

Bolivian HF is restricted to the tropical savannah of the Beni Department in northeastern Bolivia. The small reservoir rodent *Calomys callosus*[33] freely enters homes and gardens in this region, and most infections are house acquired. The incidence of cases is greatest from April to July (late rainy and early dry season), but the dominant feature of the epidemiologic pattern is that of small outbreaks in different villages and ranches with several years of quiescence thereafter. In town epidemics, all ages and both sexes are equally affected. On remote ranches and in fields, adult male patients predominate. Transmission is thought to occur by aerosols from infected rodents or possibly by contact with food contaminated by infectious rodent urine. Both nosocomial[34] and person-to-person[35] transmission have occurred, although these routes are not usual.

The annual variations in both Bolivian and Argentine HF incidence may be related to fluctuations in rodent populations brought about by the infertility of chronic viremic animals limiting *Calomys* numbers[36] when horizontal spread reaches high levels.[37]

In Portuguesa State of Venezuela, cases of HF were noted in September 1989. The causative agent, named *Guanarito virus* for the municipality where most of the cases were found,[7] has the cane mouse *(Zygodontomys brevicauda)*[38] as reservoir. The main affected population was settlers moving into cleared forest areas to practice smallhold agriculture. The carrier rodents are well adapted to open grasslands and readily invaded fields, pastures, and peridomestic habitats.

Sabia virus has caused a single natural human infection that was fatal, as well as two laboratory infections.[8, 39]

After parenteral exposures, the incubation period of South American HF may be only 2 to 6 days. The estimated interval after natural exposure to either Junin or Machupo viruses (and presumably Guanarito and Sabia viruses as well) ranges from 5 to 19 days, with a mode of 7 to 12 days.

Other Arenaviruses

Several African viruses related to Lassa and LCM viruses have been discovered (Mopeia, Mobala, Ippy), but no human disease, and in many cases no human infection, has been identified.[1, 2, 40] Similarly, there is a growing group of viruses in the Tacaribe complex that have not been associated with human disease in both South (Amapari, Flexal, Latino, Oliveros, Parana, Pichinde, Pirital) and North America (Tamiami and Whitewater Arroyo).[1,2,41] Some have caused human infections in the laboratory without inducing disease (Pichinde virus), but most are under continuing study, including the Whitewater Arroyo virus in the western United States.[41]

PATHOGENESIS

Rodents

Arenavirus infection of rodent hosts is chronic but clinically benign. The age of the host, route of infection, and strain of virus are important variables. In natural murine infections with LCM virus, the newborn or fetal animal becomes chronically viremic but has normal growth and fertility; in spite of widespread infection of many organs, there is no inflammatory response. Peripheral inoculation of adult mice results in a transient immunizing infection.

Laboratory-manipulated strains of LCM virus exhibit different pathogenicity for inbred strains of laboratory mice, and this infection has been extremely important in studying viral immunopathology and $CD8^+$ T-cell function. Infection of newborn mice results in chronic viremic infection in which T-cell immunity is suppressed. Depending on the murine genotype, different quantities of antiviral antibodies are produced and complex with viral antigens, leading to the development of chronic glomerulonephritis.[42] The artificial intracerebral inoculation of adult mice produces an acute fatal choriomeningitis with extensive mononuclear cell infiltrate mediated by immune cytotoxic T cells.[43]

The responses of natural reservoir *Calomys* rodents experimentally infected with Junin or Machupo virus resemble the mouse-LCM virus outcomes.[2, 34, 36] The differences are that lethal infection is not inducible by any route at any age, that antigen-antibody complexes are not demonstrable, and that some adult rodents develop chronic infection exactly like that observed in very young mice. In addition, chronic infection with Machupo virus induces a microcytic hemolytic anemia (Coombs negative) that results in chronic splenomegaly.

Mastomys rodents infected with Lassa virus similarly show no acute signs, do not develop inflammatory responses, and exhibit chronic infection or an effective immune response depending on age.[44] Chronic infection is marked by persistent immunofluorescent antibodies, but few observations regarding late immune complex disease have been made.

Arenavirus infection of nonreservoir rodents results in benign, self-limited infection and immunity. Guinea pigs, however, may suffer severe acute disease and provide useful models for arenaviral HF.[40]

Nonhuman Primates

Monkeys are good but not perfect models for the pathogenesis and experimental therapy of arenavirus infections in humans.[3, 21, 40, 44–46] Macaque monkeys are readily infected by the inhalation of LCM virus, and the resulting disease resembles HF rather than central nervous system disease. Marmosets are also susceptible to fatal disease from LCM virus, including zoo animals fed infected newborn mice.[45]

Lassa virus induces a fatal disease in rhesus monkeys infected by small-particle aerosols, establishing the aerosol infectivity of the virus; the monkeys also have a pathologic appearance similar to that of humans.[21] Machupo and Junin viruses are also pathogenic for nonhuman primates, and these models as well as the more tractable guinea pig models have provided considerable information on the pathogensis of human HF.[40, 46, 47]

Humans

Few data are available regarding the histopathology of fatal cases of human LCM infection, which is uncommonly lethal. Two fatal cases associated with early studies of the virus in monkeys displayed hemorrhagic necrosis much more typical of other arenavirus HFs[48]; they are regarded as aberrant human responses to this agent. A single fatal human encephalitis case was particularly well studied, and the patient showed a marked neuronal pattern of viral infection.[49]

Fatal Lassa virus infection in humans shows relatively few lesions. Variable necrosis with little or no inflammatory response has been observed in liver, spleen, and adrenal glands.[50] Focal liver necrosis is always found, but in no instance was the hepatic abnormality sufficient to cause death.[51] The degree of histologic change rarely seems sufficient to explain the clinical severity of the disease on a morphologic basis. Studies in animal models suggest that direct viral infection of endothelial cells as well as mediators possibly released from infected macrophages may be extremely important in causing the vascular dysfunction and shock of these viral HFs.[47, 52] Immunopathologic events seem less likely to be involved because immunosuppression fails to ameliorate the disease in animal models.[52]

Patients dying of Argentine or Bolivian HF have few prominent findings. There is no vasculitis and virtually no inflammatory response in any organ, but a pattern of small focal hemorrhages is present, primarily in mucosal surfaces. Hepatic necrosis, on the average, is more severe in Lassa than in Junin or Machupo infections, but Councilman-like bodies are readily discernible in all three diseases. Bronchopneumonia, either primary viral or secondary bacterial, is a common finding in these diseases as well.

Argentine HF virus patients exhibit extremely high concentrations of circulating endogenous interferon-alfa that reach a maximum at 6 to 12 days of illness. The highest levels were observed in fatal cases.[53] Experimental and clinical studies support the concept that interferons may prove to be detrimental rather than beneficial in arenavirus infections.[54] High levels of circulating proinflammatory cytokines are present as well.[55]

At autopsy, tissues of humans and monkeys infected by Lassa, Junin, or Machupo virus contain large amounts of virus, viral antigen, and in some instances virions as in liver in Lassa infection. Spleen, nodes, and bone marrow are major replication sites for Junin and Machupo viruses, whereas Lassa virus is found in many viscera and, notably, in the placentas of pregnant women. Prominent infection of mesothelial surfaces may well be important in the frequent development of serous effusions.[2, 56]

CLINICAL MANIFESTATIONS

Clinically apparent infections with all the arenaviruses are similar in presenting manifestations. Fever is typically insidious in onset and is accompanied by headache and significant myalgia and malaise. Relative bradycardia is common, as is dysesthesia, particularly hyperesthesia of the skin. Thereafter, the various diseases pursue different courses.

Lymphocytic Choriomeningitis Virus

LCM virus infections are most commonly febrile illnesses with headache and systemic symptoms and are associated with leukopenia and thrombocytopenia.[3, 22, 23, 25, 57, 58] After 3 to 5 days of nonspecific illness, occasionally with lymphadenopathy and a maculopapular rash, the fever subsides, but it frequently recurs in 2 to 4 days with several days of even more severe headache. Patients may exhibit frank meningitis during this second febrile period. There may be papilledema; cerebrospinal fluid (CSF) pressure usually is elevated, the protein concentration ranges from 50 to 300 mg/dl, and several hundred lymphocytes/mm^3 are commonly observed. Hypoglycorrachia is found in less than one third of the cases. Encephalomyelitic infection may present as encephalitis, psychosis, paraplegia, or disturbances of cranial, sensory, or autonomic nervous function. Ependymal inflammation has resulted in transient aqueductal stenosis.

Occasionally, patients develop orchitis, myocarditis, arthritis, or alopecia. Orchitis develops 1 to 3 weeks after the onset of the illness; it is usually unilateral and painful and resolves within 2 weeks. Myocarditis is revealed by electrocardiographic changes and labile tachycardia during and after the second febrile period. Arthritis occurs during convalescence, principally affects the metacarpophalangeal and proximal interphalangeal joints, and is marked by minimal swelling and redness; it generally resolves within a few weeks.

The second febrile episode as well as some of the complications of convalescence have long been thought to represent immunopathologic phenomena. Antibodies detectable by immunofluorescence appear at about this time, and the lymphocytes in the CSF presumably are analogues of the T lymphocytes that cause LCM disease in the intracerebrally inoculated adult mouse.[58]

Lassa Fever

Most Lassa virus infections in Africa are mild or subclinical.[41] Severe multisystem disease occurs only in 5 to 10% of infections. Case-fatality rates in hospitalized patients average 15 to 25%.[51, 59] In a case-control study of patients hospitalized with Lassa fever in Sierra Leone, the frequencies of selected findings (percentages) were as follows: retrosternal chest pain, 74%; sore throat, 60%; back pain, 62%; cough, 62%; abdominal pain, 50%; vomiting, 49%; diarrhea, 26%; conjunctivitis, 25%; facial edema, 10% and proteinuria, 43%. Mucosal bleeding at any time was noted in just 17% of patients. These findings were present in many febrile patients not infected with Lassa virus, which rendered a clinical diagnosis in many instances impossible. A combination of fever, pharyngitis, retrosternal pain, and proteinuria correctly predicted 70% of laboratory-confirmed Lassa fever cases and 80%, by exclusion, of the control illnesses.[60] Central nervous system involvement has been described with encephalopathy, encephalitis, meningeal signs, and convalescent cerebellar syndromes.[61]

Lassa virus infection also causes serious disease and death in children, although manifestations may be even more protean or clinically confusing than among adults.[62] Four cases (three fatal) of a distinctive syndrome consisting of severe generalized edema, abdominal distention, and bleeding were recorded in children younger than 2 years in Liberia.[63]

Concentrations of virus and serum aspartate transaminase in the blood at admission are highly reliable, objective predictors of the outcome of infection. Patients having at least 10^3 median tissue culture infective doses of virus per milliliter and 150 IU/liter of aspartate transaminase experienced 78% mortality, whereas 83% of those with lower values survived.[64, 65] The clinical manifestations associated with death, however, generally occur during the second week of illness. These consist of hypotension, peripheral vasoconstriction, reduced urinary output, facial and pulmonary edema, and in some cases, pleural effusions and ascites. These events, often accompanied by minor hemorrhages from mucosal surfaces, strongly suggest a lesion of diffuse capillary leakage. Myocardial depression may contribute to the circulatory defect.

Patients who do not develop a capillary leak syndrome may experience other complications during the second or third week of illness. Chief among these is eighth-nerve deafness, which may be unilateral or bilateral and has been seen in almost one third of hospitalized cases.[66] Some of the patients have mild lesions or will improve, but village surveys confirm a major impact of Lassa infection on hearing loss in the community. About 3 to 5% of male patients suffer pericarditis detected by auscultation that resolves clinically in 7 to 10 days; all such patients survive. Less common complications include uveitis and orchitis. Many hospitalized Lassa fever patients undergo some degree of transient alopecia during convalescence.

South American Hemorrhagic Fevers

Argentine and Bolivian HFs are remarkably similar clinically, and the mortality rate in each is about 15 to 30%.[32, 67, 68] Reported Venezuelan HF cases have been somewhat more severe, although this probably reflects case ascertainment.[7] The onset of the illness is insidious, with progressive fever, malaise, and myalgia often centered over the lower back. There may be epigastric pain, retro-orbital pain, dizziness, photophobia, and constipation. Conjunctival injection, flushing of the face and upper portion of the trunk, and orthostatic hypotension also are common. An enanthem consisting of petechiae or small vesicles, or both, on the palate and fauces is present in most patients, as are skin petechiae, particularly in the axilla, and generalized lymphadenopathy.

Fever is unremitting, and some patients become progressively ill with one of a combination of syndromes of vascular or neurologic disease. Vascular disease consists of (1) increasing evidence of a capillary leak syndrome; (2) proteinuria, rising hematocrit, and the onset of gingival, gastrointestinal, nasal, and other membrane hemorrhages; (3) narrowing pulse pressure; and (4) vasoconstriction and clinical shock.[68] There may be signs of pulmonary infiltration due to a vascular leak or to secondary bacterial infection, which is a common complication, or both. Such patients are extremely difficult to manage. Plasma expanders may precipitate refractory pulmonary edema. Neurologic disease is common and is heralded by the development of hyporeflexia followed by gait abnormalities, palmomental reflex, tremors of the tongue and upper extremities, and other cerebellar signs. If these changes are followed by clonic seizures and coma, the prognosis is extremely grave.

Convalescence requires several weeks but occurs without sequelae. Alopecia and nail furrows are very common, as is postural hypotension for 1 to 2 weeks.

Intrauterine Infection

Arenaviruses readily invade the fetus, whether in their natural reservoir, laboratory animals, or humans. In Lassa fever, pregnant women often abort and suffer a high mortality,[69] and similar observations have been made in Argentine and Bolivian HFs. LCM virus infection of pregnant women leads to fetal infection, hydrocephalus, microcephaly, or chorioretinitis, or all of these.[70–72] More than a dozen cases have now been recognized in the United States (L. L. Barton and M. B. Metz, personal communication, 1999). Because viral antibody rates indicate that about 5% of adults in large cities of the United States have been infected with LCM virus, congenital infection may be more common than appreciated.[1, 73]

DIAGNOSIS

The diagnosis of past infection with arenaviruses is best done through serologic tests with enzyme-linked immunosorbent assay (ELISA) because of the sensitivity of the test. Until more data are obtained confirming ELISA specificity, cell culture plaque-reduction neutralization tests should be used as a supplement because of their known sensitivity and specificity.

The diagnosis of acute illness, by contrast, has features unique to each agent. In the case of LCM, virus is found in the blood early and in the CSF late in disease. The most sensitive test is to inoculate young adult mice in the brain.[17] Fluorescent immunostaining of inoculated cell cultures reveals virus earlier than mouse inoculation in most instances. IgM ELISA of serum and CSF is an effective method of diagnosis and is supplanting IFA and other serologic tests.[74]

Virus can be recovered from the blood of acutely ill patients in all arenavirus HFs, but titers are highest in Lassa fever. The viremic interval ranges from 3 to 20 days, with Lassa fever being the most persistent. Throat swabs are frequently positive as well, and late shedding (second to third week) in urine is observed in Lassa infection. Patients with LCM and Lassa fever who exhibit meningeal signs have increased protein, leukocytes, and virus in spinal fluids.[18, 61]

Lassa fever virus is easily isolated from blood during the first 7 to 10 days of illness by inoculating cell cultures.[64] Junin virus was recovered from 96% of patients by cocultivation of patients' blood mononuclear cells with Vero cell cultures, whereas cell cultures or suckling mice were only about 50% positive when whole blood was tested.[75] Isolation of some strains of Machupo virus is difficult, but others are readily recovered in cell culture.[5, 34] Throat swabs may be positive in some patients with Lassa fever and LCM, and urine may contain virus up to 67 days in Lassa fever patients.[76] Biopsy or autopsy specimens of lymphoid tissues, marrow, and liver usually yield virus, often in concentrations greatly exceeding those found in blood.[34, 50]

Serodiagnosis of Lassa fever by detection of IgM antibodies by IFA or ELISA is rapid and quite sensitive.[64, 77] In Sierra Leone, 75% of patients were IFA-positive on admission (mean duration of illness, 8.5 days). In recent studies, either Lassa antigen or IgM antibodies were detectable in the blood of virtually all acutely ill patients, and the degree of antigenemia was correlated with poor prognosis (T. G. Ksiazek, P. E. Rollin, and C. J. Peters, unpublished observations). Antibodies detectable by IFA appear about 2 weeks after the onset of LCM illness.[74]

Reverse transcription of extracted RNA followed by polymerase chain reaction amplification has been used successfully in limited numbers of patients, but more experience is needed to ensure sensitivity and broad reactivity of primers among different virus strains.[1, 78]

PREVENTION AND TREATMENT

Arenavirus infection may be prevented by interdicting transmission from rodents to humans, from person to person, and from infected specimens to laboratory workers or by passive or active immunization. Community rodent control completely halted a major outbreak of Bolivian HF[79]; elimination of infected laboratory hamsters controlled LCM outbreaks.[22, 25] A household rodent control study of Lassa infection, however, gave disappointing results.[80]

Person-to-person spread within hospitals has been a problem with Lassa fever. In endemic situations such as in Sierra Leone, partial spatial isolation of patients and the use of "enteric precautions" such as gloves, gowns, and careful disposal of patient wastes and fomites have generally served to prevent the spread of infection. Segregation of patients on the basis of the risk of death and likely content of virus in blood and body fluids by measuring aspartate transaminase levels should be of value. Some hospital outbreaks, particularly in Nigeria, appear to have been caused by infectious aerosols.[30, 34] Thus, wherever practical, it is advisable to place patients in single rooms with isolated negative-pressure airflow, and to provide medical staff with goggles and with positive-pressure filtered air respirators or absolute filter respirators.[81] All potentially contaminated refuse or specimens should be double-bagged and the outer bag rinsed with 0.6% sodium hypochlorite before removal from the patient's room. Isolation of patients should continue until multiple blood and urine specimens are virus negative. Condoms should be used for a period in convalescence because of the occasional sexual transmission of arenavirus HF. In the recognized cases of Lassa fever that have been exported from Africa, no secondary transmission has yet been detected in contacts or in medical staff, indicating that a conservative approach to isolation provides a reasonable standard of safe care in most cases.

Laboratory-acquired infection is a major problem because all arenaviruses are infectious as aerosols. Several infections, some fatal, have occurred in laboratory workers. Thus, it is imperative that work with all arenaviruses except LCM be conducted in special laboratories having maximal biologic containment. Clinical pathologic tests, particularly in Lassa fever patients, also present problems. Aerosols must be minimized or contained. Acid treatment inactivates virus for leukocyte counts, and alcohol fixation is useful for blood smears; heating serum at 60°C for 1 hour is feasible for measuring heat-stable substances.[82]

There are no licensed arenavirus vaccines. However, field trials with a live-attenuated Argentine HF vaccine showed greater than 95% efficacy and virtually no side effects.[83] More than 170,000 doses have been used in the endemic area. Work in laboratory animals suggests the Junin vaccine would be efficacious against Machupo, but not Guanarito or Sabia viruses. Vaccinia-vectored Lassa genes have given protection to experimental animals and suggest the possibility of such a vaccine for use in humans,[84] but the immunology of the Old World arenaviruses is complicated, and additional work is required.[36]

Convalescent human plasma was proved effective in the treatment of Argentine HF (16% placebo versus 1% treated mortality) provided adequate amounts of neutralizing antibodies were given before the ninth day of illness.[85] Cerebellar signs, usually transient and possibly the result of virus multiplication in the central nervous system, occurred in 10% of those receiving this treatment. Immune plasma treatment of Lassa fever has not been as successful, and experiments in animals suggest that this may be related to the fact that neutralizing antibodies after Lassa virus infection appear weeks after recovery and are generally of low titer and avidity.[36, 74]

Ribavirin, a purine nucleoside having broad-spectrum antiviral properties, was found to be highly effective in monkeys lethally infected with Lassa and other arenaviruses.[40] The intravenous administration of this compound to Lassa patients admitted to the hospital in Sierra Leone with aspartate transaminase elevations of at least 150 IU reduced the mortality from 55 to 5% if treatment was begun before day 7 of the disease.[65] A positive effect on survival was achieved, however, at all stages of infection. After a 30-mg/kg loading dose, patients were given, 15 mg/kg every 6 hours for 4 days and then 7.5 mg/kg three times daily for 6 additional days. Reversible anemia, not requiring transfusions, was the only adverse effect associated with treatment. Close contacts of patients with Lassa fever should be monitored for the appearance of fever, and if any indications of Lassa fever are present, ribavirin therapy should be begun expectantly. Ribavirin has been used with apparent success in aborting a Sabia laboratory infection,[39] in treating Bolivian HF patients,[35] and in late therapy of Argentine HF patients.[85] Given the similarities to Lassa virus and similar preclinical test efficacy, the drug should be considered for any overwhelming arenavirus infection.

Supportive care may be lifesaving in HF. Fluid balance should be maintained orally as long as possible. Cautious volume replacement therapy with the judicious use of colloid should be started before the appearance of clinical shock, and electrolyte balance should be maintained.

REFERENCES

1. Bowen MD, Peters CJ, Nichol ST. The phylogeny of New World (Tacaribe complex) arenaviruses. Virology. 1996;219:285–290.
2. Enria D, Bowen M, Mills JN, et al. Arenaviruses. In: Guerrant RL, Walker DH, Weller PF, eds. Tropical Infectious Diseases: Principles, Pathogens, and Practice. Philadelphia: Churchill Livingstone; 1999:Chapter 111.
3. Armstrong C, Lillie RD. Experimental lymphocytic choriomeningitis of monkeys and mice produced by a virus encountered in studies of the 1933 St Louis encephalitis epidemic. Public Health Rep. 1934;49:1019–1027.
4. Parodi AS, Greenway DJ, Rugiero HR. Sobre la etiologia del brote epidemico de Junin. El Dia Medico. 1958;30:2300–2301.
5. Johnson KM, Wiebenga NH, Mackenzie RB, et al. Virus isolations from human cases of hemorrhagic fever in Bolivia. Proc Soc Exp Biol Med. 1965;118:113–118.
6. Buckley SM, Casals J. Lassa fever, a new virus disease of man from West Africa. III. Isolation and characterization of the virus. Am J Trop Med Hyg. 1970;19:680–691.
7. Salas R, de Manzione N, Tesh RB, et al. Venezuelan hemorrhagic fever. Lancet. 1991;338:1033–1036.
8. Coimbra TLM, Nassar ES, Burattini MN, et al. New arenavirus isolated in Brazil. Lancet. 1994;343:391–392.
9. Murphy FA, Whitfield SG. Morphology and morphogenesis of arenaviruses. 1975; Bull World Health Organ. 52:409–419.
10. Rawls WE, Leung WC. Arenaviruses. In: Fraenkel-Conrat H, Wagner RR, eds. Comprehensive Virology, v. 14. New York: Plenum; 1979:157–192.
11. Bishop DHL, Auperin DD. Gene structure and organization in arenaviruses. Curr Top Microbiol Immunol. 1987;133:5–18.
12. Auperin D, Romanowski V, Galinsky M, et al. Sequencing studies of Pichinde virus sRNA indicates a novel coding strategy, an ambisense viral sRNA. J Virol. 1984;52:897.
13. Burns JW, Buchmeier MJ. Glycoproteins of the arenaviruses. In: Salvato MS, ed. The Arenaviridae. New York: Plenum; 1993:17–31.
14. Howard CR. Antigenic diversity among the arenaviruses. In: Salvato MS, ed. The Arenaviridae. New York: Plenum; 1993:37–50.
15. Klavinskas LS, Whitton JL, Oldstone MBA. Molecular anatomy of the cytotoxic T-lymphocyte responses to lymphocytic choriomeningitis virus. In: Salvato MD, ed. The Arenaviridae. New York: Plenum; 1993:225–242.
16. Cao W, Henry MD, Borrow P, et. al. Identification of alpha-dystroglycan as a receptor for lymphocytic choriomeningitis virus and lassa fever virus. Science. 1998;282:2079–2081.
17. Lehmann-Grube F. Lymphocytic Choriomeningitis Virus. New York: Springer; 1971.
18. Farmer TW, Janeway CA. Infection with the virus of lymphocytic choriomeningitis. Medicine (Baltimore). 1942;2:11.
19. Childs JC, Glass GE, Korch GW, et al. Lymphocytic choriomeningitis virus infection and house mouse *(Mus musculus)* distribution in urban Baltimore. Am J Trop Med Hyg. 1992;47:27–34.
20. Ackermann R, Bloedhorn H, Kupper B, et al. Über die Verbreiting des Virus der lymphocytaren Choriomeningitis unter den Mausen in Westdeutschland. I. Utersuchungen uberwiegend an Hausmauden *(Mus musculus)*. Zentrabl Bakteriol. 1964;194:407.
21. Stephenson EH, Larson EW, Dominik JW. Effect of environmental factors on aerosol induced Lassa virus infection. J Med Virol. 1984;14:295.
22. Hinman AR, Fraser DW, Douglas RG, et al. Outbreak of lymphocytic choriomeningitis virus infection in medical center personnel. Am J Epidemiol. 1975;101:103.
23. Baum SG, Lewis AM, Rowe WP, et al. Epidemic nonmeningitic lymphocytic choriomeningitis virus infection. N Engl J Med. 1966;274:934.
24. Dykewitz CA, Dato VM, Fisher-Hoch SF, et al. Lymphocytic choriomeningitis outbreak associated with nude mice in a research institute, JAMA. 1992;267:1349–1353.
25. Biggar RJ, Woodall JP, Walter PD, et al. Lymphocytic choriomeningitis outbreak associated with pet hamsters: Fifty-seven cases from New York State. JAMA. 1975;232:494.
26. Ackermann R, Stille W, Blumenthal W, et al. Syrische Goldhamster als Ubertrager von lymphozytarer Choriomeningitis. Dtsch Med Wochenschr. 1972;97:1725.
27. Frame JD, Baldwin JM Jr, Gocke DJ, et al. Lassa fever, a new virus disease of man from West Africa. I. Clinical description and pathological findings. Am J Trop Med Hyg. 1970;19:670.
28. McCormick JB, Webb PA, Krebs JW, et al. A prospective study of the epidemiology and ecology of Lassa fever. J Infect Dis. 1987;155:437.
29. Robbins CB, Van Der Straeten E. Comments on the systematics of *Mastomys* Thomas 1915 with the description of a new West African species. Senckenbergiana Biologica. 1989;69:1– 14.
30. Monath TP. Lassa fever: Review of epidemiology and epizootology. Bull World Health Organ. 1975;52:577.
31. Frame JD. Surveillance of Lassa fever in missionaries stationed in West Africa. Bull World Health Organ. 1975;52:593.
32. Sabattini MS, Maiztegui JI. Fiebre hemorrhagica argentina. Medicina (Buenos Aires). 1970;30(Suppl):111.
33. Johnson KM, Kuns ML, Mackenzie RB, et al. Isolation of Machupo virus from wild rodent *Calomys callosus*. Am J Trop Med Hyg. 1966;15:103.
34. Peters CJ, Kuehne RW, Mercado R, et al. Hemorrhagic fever in Cochabamba, Bolivia, 1971. Am J Epidemiol. 1974;99:425–433.
35. Kilgore PE, Peters CJ, Mills JN, et al. Prospects for the control of Bolivian hemorrhagic fever. Emerg Infect Dis. 1995;1:97–100.
36. Webb P, Justines G, Johnson KM. Infection of wild and laboratory animals with Machupo and Latino viruses. Bull World Health Organ. 1975;52:493.
37. Mills JN, Ellis BA, McKee KT, et al. A longitudinal study of Junin virus activity in the rodent reservoir of Argentine hemorrhagic fever. Am J Trop Med Hyg. 1992;47:749–763.
38. Fulhorst CF, Bowen MD, Salas RA, et al. Isolation and characterization of Pirital virus, a newly discovered South American arenavirus. Am J Trop Med Hyg. 1997;56:548–553.
39. Barry M, Russi M, Armstrong L, et al. Treatment of a laboratory-acquired Sabia virus infection. N Eng J Med. 1995;333:294– 296.
40. Peters CJ, Jahrling PB, Liu CT, et al. Experimental studies of arenaviral hemorrhagic fevers. Curr Top Microbiol Immunol. 1987;134:5.
41. Fulhorst CF, Bowen MD, Ksiazek TG, et al. Isolation and characterization of Whitewater Arroyo virus, a novel North American arenavirus. Virology. 1996;224:114–120.
42. Oldstone MBA, Dixon FJ. Pathogenesis of chronic disease associated with persistent lymphocytic choriomeningitis infection. II. Relationship of the antilymphocytic choriomeningitis virus immune response to tissue injury in chronic lymphocytic choriomeningitis disease. J Exp Med. 1970;131:1.
43. Nathanson N, Monjan AA, Panitch HS, et al. Virus-induced cell-mediated immunopathological disease. In: Notkins AL, ed. Viral Immunology and Immunopathology. New York: Academic Press; 1975:357–391.
44. Walker DH, Wulff H, Lange JV, et al. Comparative pathology of Lassa virus infection in monkeys, guinea pigs, and *Mastomys natalensis*. Bull World Health Organ. 1975;52:523.
45. Montali RJ, Scanga CA, Perkikoff D, et al. A common-source outbreak of callitrichid hepatitis in captive tamarins and marmosets. J Infect Dis. 1993;167:946–950.
46. McKee KT Jr, Mahlandt BG, Maiztegui JI, et al. Experimental Argentine hemorrhagic fever in rhesus monkeys: Viral strain-dependent clinical response. J Infect Dis. 1985;152:218.
47. Peters CJ. Pathogenesis of viral hemorrhagic fevers. In: Nathanson N, Ahmed R, Gonzalez-Scarano F, et al, eds. Viral Pathogenesis. Philadelphia: Lippincott-Raven; 1997:779–799.
48. Smadel JE, Green RH, Paltauf RM, et al. Lymphocytic choriomeningitis: Two human fatalities following an unusual febrile illness. Proc Soc Exp Biol Med. 1942;49:683.
49. Warkel RL, Rinaldi CF, Bancroft WH, et al. Fatal acute meningoencephalitis due to lymphocytic choriomeningitis virus. Neurology. 1973;23:198–202.
50. Walker DH, McCormick JB, Johnson KM, et al. Pathologic and virologic study of fatal Lassa fever in man. Am J Pathol. 1982;107:349.
51. McCormick JB, Walker DB, King IJ, et al. Lassa virus hepatitis: A study of fatal Lassa fever in humans. Am J Trop Med Hyg. 1986;35:401.
52. Kenyon RH, Green DE, Peters CJ. Effect of immuno-suppression on experimental Argentine hemorrhagic fever in guinea pigs. J Virol. 1985;53:75–80.
53. Levis SC, Saavedra MC, Ceccoli C, et al. Correlation between endogenous interferon and the clinical evolution of patients with Argentine hemorrhagic fever. J Interferon Res. 1985;5:383.
54. Vilcek J. Adverse effects of interferon in virus infections, autoimmune diseases and acquired immunodeficiency. Prog Med Virol. 1984;30:62.

55. Marta RF, Montero VF, Hack CE, et al. Proinflammatory cytokines and elastase-alpha-1antitrypsin in Argentine hemorrhagic fever. Am J Trop Med Hyg. 1999;60:85–89.
56. Zaki SR, Peters CJ. Viral hemorrhagic fevers. In: Connor DH, Chandler FW, Schwartz DA, et al, eds. The Pathology of Infectious Diseases. Norwalk, Conn: Appleton & Lange; 1997:347–364.
57. Vanzee BE, Douglas RG, Betts RF, et al. Lymphocytic choriomeningitis in university hospital personnel. Am J Med. 1975;58:803–807.
58. Peters CJ. Arenavirus diseases. In: Porterfield JS, ed. Kass Handbook of Infectious Diseases. Exotic Viral Infections. New York: Chapman and Hall Medical; 1995:227–246.
59. Monson MH, Frame JD, Jahrling PB, et al. Endemic Lassa fever in Liberia. I. Clinical and epidemiological aspects of Curran Lutheran Hospital, Zorzor, Liberia. Trans R Soc Trop Med Hyg. 1984;78:549.
60. McCormick JB, King IJ, Webb PA, et al. A case-control study of the clinical diagnosis and course of Lassa fever. J Infect Dis. 1987;155:445.
61. Solbrig MV. Lassa virus and central nervous system diseases. In: Salvato MS, ed. The Arenaviridae. New York: Plenum; 1993:325–330.
62. Webb PA, McCormick JB, King IJ, et al. Lassa fever in children in Sierra Leone, West Africa. Trans R Soc Trop Med Hyg. 1986;80:577.
63. Monson MH, Cole AK, Frame JD, et al. Pediatric Lassa fever: A review of 33 Liberian cases. Am J Trop Med Hyg. 1987;36:408.
64. Johnson KM, McCormick JB, Webb PA, et al. Clinical virology of Lassa fever in hospitalized patients. J Infect Dis. 1987;155:456.
65. McCormick JB, King IB, Webb PA, et al. Lassa fever: Effective therapy with ribavirin. N Engl J Med. 1986;314:20.
66. Cummins D, McCormick JB, Bennett D, et al. Acute sensorineural deafness in Lassa fever. JAMA. 1990;264:2093–2096.
67. Maiztegui JI. Clinical and epidemiological patterns of Argentine haemorrhagic fever. Bull World Health Organ. 1975;52:567.
68. Stinebaugh BJ, Schloeder FX, Johnson KM, et al. Bolivian hemorrhagic fever: A report of four cases. Am J Med. 1966;40:217.
69. Price ME, Fisher-Hoch SP, Craven RB, et al. A prospective study of maternal and fetal outcome in acute Lassa fever infection during pregnancy. BMJ. 1988;297:584–587.
70. Barton LL, Budd SC, Morfitt WS, et al. Congenital lymphocytic choriomeningitis virus infection in twins. Pediatr Infect Dis J. 1993;12:942–946.
71. Ackermann R, Korver G, Turss R, et al. Pranatale Infektion mit dem Virus der lymphozytaren Choriomeningitis. Dtsch Med Wochenschr. 1974;99:629–632.
72. Wright R, Johnson D, Neumann M, et al. Congenital lymphocytic choriomeningitis virus syndrome: A disease that mimics congenital toxoplasmosis or cytomegalovirus infection. Pediatrics. 1997;100:E9.
73. Childs JE, Glass GE, Ksiazek TG, et al. Human-rodent contact and infection with lymphocytic choriomeningitis and Seoul viruses in an inner-city population. Am J Trop Med Hyg. 1991;44:117–121.
74. Lehmann-Grube F, Kallay M, Ibscher B, Schwartz R. Serologic diagnosis of human infections with lymphocytic choriomeningitis virus: Comparative evaluation of seven methods. J Med Virol 1979;4:125–136.
75. Ambrosio AM, Enria DA, Maiztegui JI. Junin virus isolation from lymphomononuclear cells of patients with Argentine hemorrhagic fever. Intervirology. 1986;25:97.
76. Emond RTD, Bannister B, Lloyd G, et al. A case of Lassa fever: Clinical and virological findings. BMJ. 1982;285:1001.
77. Nicklasson BS, Jahrling PB, Peters CJ. Detection of Lassa virus antigens and Lassa virus-specific immunoglobulins G and M by enzyme-linked immunosorbent assay. J Clin Microbiol. 1984;20:239.
78. Park JY, Peters CJ, Rollin PE, et al. Development of an RT-PCR assay for diagnosis of lymphocytic choriomeningitis virus (LCMV) infection and its use in a prospective surveillance study. J Med Virol. 1997;51:107–114.
79. Mackenzie RB. Epidemiology of Machupo virus infection. I. Pattern of human infection, San Joaquin, Bolivia, 1962–1965. Am J Trop Med Hyg. 1965;14:808.
80. Keenlyside RA, McCormick JB, Webb PA, et al. Case-control study of *Mastomys natalensis* and humans in Lassa virus–infected households in Sierra Leone. Am J Trop Med Hyg. 1983;32:829–837.
81. CDC (1995) update: Management of patients with suspected viral hemorrhagic fever—United States. MMWR Morb Mortal Wkly Rep. 44:475–479.
82. Mitchell SW, McCormick JB. Physicochemical inactivation of Lassa, Ebola, and Marburg viruses and effect on clinical laboratory analyses. J Clin Microbiol. 1984;20:486.
83. Auperin DD. Construction and evaluation of recombinant virus vaccines for Lassa fever. In: Salvato MS, ed. The Arenaviridae. New York: Plenum; 1993:259–280.
84. Maiztegui JI, McKee KT, Barrera Oro JG, et al. Protective efficacy of a live attenuated vaccine against Argentine hemorrhagic fever. J Infect Dis. 1998;177;277–283.
85. Enria D, Maiztegui JI. Antiviral treatment of Argentine hemorrhagic fever. Antivir Res. 1994;23:23–31.

Retroviridae

Chapter 156

Human T-Cell Lymphotropic Virus Types I and II

JAINULABDEEN J. IFTHIKHARUDDIN
JOSEPH D. ROSENBLATT

The International Committee on the Taxonomy of Viruses classifies the human T-cell lymphotropic virus types I and II (HTLV-I and HTLV-II)—as well as bovine leukemia virus (BLV)—in the family Retroviridae on the basis of nucleotide sequence and genome structure. On the basis of pathogenicity, these viruses were previously classified in the oncovirus subfamily.[1–3] Morphologically, HTLV-I and HTLV-II are type-C viruses, which, along with simian T-cell lymphoma virus (STLV), make up a group of retroviruses known as the primate T-cell leukemia/lymphoma viruses. They differ from other leukemia and sarcoma retroviruses in that they do not contain cell-derived oncogenes and require neither active viremia nor a conserved site of provirus integration for transformation or leukemogenesis.[4] The biologic properties of these viruses and their molecular genetic structure distinguish them from human immunodeficiency virus type 1 (HIV-1) and type 2 (HIV-2), which are members of the lentivirus group of retroviruses. Both oncoviruses and lentiviruses are capable of prolonged asymptomatic infection in vivo. However, in vitro, HIV-1 and HIV-2 have cytopathic effects on human T cells and monocytes, whereas HTLV-1 and HTLV-II are capable of transforming T cells, resulting in immortalized T-cell lines. HTLV-I has been implicated in the pathogenesis of adult T-cell leukemia/lymphoma (ATL) as well as a unique form of progressive neurologic disease called HTLV-I–associated myelopathy (HAM). HTLV-II is less clearly linked to human diseases but has been associated with scattered cases of leukemia as well as neurologic disease.

HISTORICAL OVERVIEW

HTLV-I, the first recognized human retrovirus, was described in 1980 by Poiesz and colleagues,[5] who isolated retroviral particles with characteristic type C morphology and budding from fresh and cultured lymphocytes of a 28-year-old black man with a diagnosis of cutaneous T-cell lymphoma. In 1977, Japanese workers described the syndrome of adult T-cell leukemia, a T-cell malignancy, afflicting persons born in the islands of southern Japan.[6] In 1981, Hinuma and associates[7] reported type C retroviral particles in cell lines from patients with ATL, and they named this putative agent *adult T-cell leukemia virus* (ATLV). Subsequent work in many laboratories confirmed that HTLV-I and ATLV were one and the same virus and that HTLV-I is the etiologic agent of ATL. Association of HTLV-I with neurologic disease is credited to Gessain and colleagues in 1985, who reported high levels of antibody to HTLV-I in patients with tropical spastic paraparesis (TSP) in Martinique.[8] This disorder—also known as HTLV-I–associated myelopathy (HAM), or chronic progressive myelopathy (CPM)—has since been recognized in other populations in which HTLV-I is endemic.

A related retrovirus was found by Kalyanaraman and coworkers,[9] in 1982, in a T-cell line established from the spleen of a 37-year-old white man (Mo) who had an unusual T-cell variant of hairy cell leukemia. Although serum from Mo contained antibodies to the major internal core protein (p24) of previous HTLV isolates, immunologic cross-reactivity tests of p24 revealed significant differences. Labeled HTLV-II, this virus has been linked anecdotally to human hematologic malignancies and neurologic disease. However, epidemiologic evidence confirming that HTLV-II is the etiologic agent in these cases is lacking.

STRUCTURE AND MOLECULAR ORGANIZATION

HTLV-I and HTLV-II virions are spheric, 100 nm in diameter, and composed of an internal core of structural proteins (nucleocapsid, capsid, and matrix—also named p15, p24, and p19 *gag* proteins) surrounding the viral RNA and polymerase and an outer layer of viral envelope glycoproteins (surface and transmembrane glycoproteins—named gp46 and gp21, respectively) anchored in a lipid membrane.[4] Though sharing the same overall genetic organization, the viruses show some diversity at the nucleotide level, exhibiting a variable degree of amino acid homology between viral capsid and envelope proteins. There is 65% overall nucleotide homology between sequenced HTLV-I and HTLV-II isolates. Homology is lowest within the long terminal repeat sequences (30%) and is highest within the 3′ *tax/rex* regulatory genes (75 to 80%).[10–12]

The proviral genome of HTLV-I and HTLV-II encodes *gag*, *pol*, and *env* genes characteristic of all known retroviruses.[13] Both ends of the genome are flanked by noncoding direct-repeat sequences known as long terminal repeats (LTRs). The LTRs mediate proviral integration and contain cis-acting regulatory elements important for viral transcription, viral mRNA processing, and reverse transcription. In addition, there is a unique region at the 3′ end of the genome, called pX, that contains four small open reading frames (ORFs): X-I, X-II, X-III, and X-IV.[14] The ORFs X-III and X-IV encode the regulatory genes *tax* and *rex*, respectively. Despite similar function, the *tax*- and *rex*-encoded proteins bear little amino acid homology with the corresponding proteins encoded by the transcriptional and post-transcriptional regulators, *tat* and *rev*, in HIV-1 and HIV-2, respectively. The HTLV-I/II genome is graphically represented in Figure 156–1. Readers may wish to refer to the article by Franchini[15] for an extensive review of the molecular biology of HTLV.

Tax

HTLV-I Tax is a 40-kilodalton (kD) protein (p40^{tax}), while HTLV-II Tax is a 37-kD protein (p37^{tax}).[16, 17] These proteins localize primarily to the nucleus of infected cells, although small amounts of Tax have been found in the cytoplasm. The Tax proteins of HTLV-I and HTLV-II are crucial to the viral life cycle and are essential for transformation of human T lymphocytes.[18]

Tax is a trans-activating nuclear phosphoprotein that regulates viral transcription by interacting with Tax-responsive elements—called TRE-1 and TRE-2—located in the U3 region of the proviral LTR.[19–21] Tax does not bind directly to the DNA; rather, it appears to mediate its effect by activating other transcription factors that bind to TRE-1 and TRE-2.[22–24] Members of the cyclic adenosine monophosphate (cAMP)-responsive element–binding protein (CREB) and activating transcription factor (ATF) family (CREB/ATF) have been shown to interact with TRE-1 (a 21–base-pair (bp) repeated element).[22, 24–26] Tax interacts indirectly with three highly homologous regulatory elements known as 21-bp repeats in the HTLV LTR via binding to the KIX domain of CREB, resulting in a stable ternary complex that can recruit coactivators such as CREB-binding protein (CBP).[27–30] TRE-2 appears to interact with a variety of other transcriptional factors including Sp1, TIF-1, Ets1, Myb, and THP.[23, 31–34] Following activation by Tax, these transcription factors can bind to and induce transcription from many other cellular genes including interleukins IL-1 and IL-2, IL-3, IL-6, granulocyte-macrophage colony–stimulating factor (GM-CSF), *c-fos*, *c-sis*, *c-myc*, vimentin, parathyroid hormone–related protein (PTHrP), transforming growth factor β1 (TGF-β1), major histocompatibility complex class I, nuclear factor κB (NF-κB), nerve growth factor, and tumor necrosis factor β.[15] This "promiscuous" transactivation by *tax* of several cellular genes via multiple transcriptional pathways probably plays an important role in neoplastic transformation as well as viral replica-

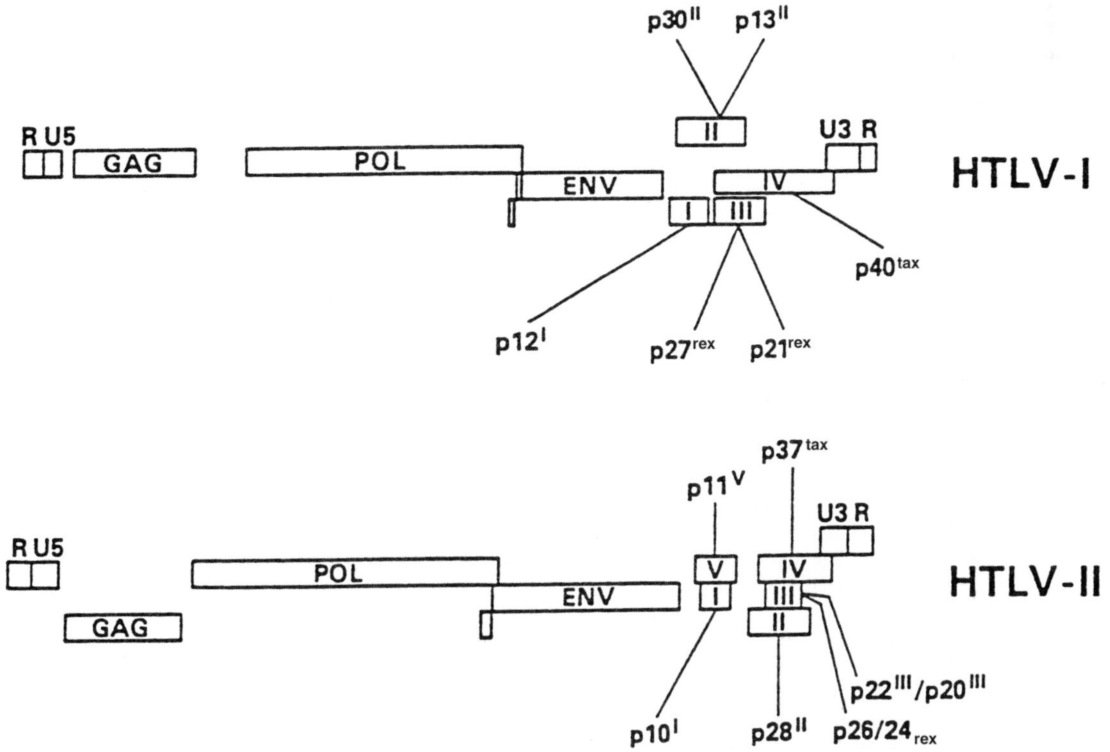

FIGURE 156–1. Schematic representation of the genomic structure of HTLV-I and HTLV-II. (From Franchini G. Molecular mechanisms of human T-cell leukemia/lymphotropic virus type I infection. Blood. 1995;86:3619–3639.)

tion. The only gene known to be negatively regulated by *tax* is the β-polymerase gene, a host DNA repair enzyme.[35]

Tax transactivation of cellular genes appears to occur by at least two other pathways: the NF-κB/Rel proteins and the serum response factor (SRF). The NF-κB proteins are involved in transactivation of IL-2, TGF-β, GM-CSF, IL-2R α-chain, *c-myc*, and vimentin.[15, 34] Tax binds directly to several NF-κB proteins. Tax also binds to NF-κB precursor proteins, facilitating their translocation to the nucleus.[36–40] In addition, Tax has been shown to bind the NF-κB inhibitor protein IκB-α and to dissociate IκB/NF-κB complexes. This may lead to enhanced transcription of NF-κB–regulated genes.[41] Tax activation of IL-6 via NF-κB has been shown to cause Jak 2 phosphorylation and subsequent activation.[42] Jak kinases and STAT (signal transducer and activation of transcription) proteins (Jak-STAT pathway) have been shown to be constitutively activated in some but not all HTLV-I–transformed T-cells.[43] Overexpression of the high-affinity IL-2R, presumably due to Tax, is a persistent feature of ATL cells as well as of HTLV-transfected cells. Tax interaction with serum response factors (SRFs) can also activate the serum responsive element (SRE), causing aberrant induction of the immediate-early genes *c-fos, egr-1*, and *egr-2*.[44]

Stabilization and inactivation of the function of the tumor suppressor gene p53, by HTLV-I Tax, has been recently demonstrated.[45] Tax has also been shown to transactivate the intercellular adhesion molecule 1 (ICAM-1).[46, 47] ICAM-1 is the counterreceptor for leukocyte function–associated antigen 1 (LFA-1). These adhesion molecules play important roles in cell-cell interactions and signal transduction. In theory, upregulation of ICAM-1 could facilitate transmission of HTLV, by promoting adhesion between infected T cells and target T cells and also by inducing T-cell proliferation.

Rex

The *rex* gene of HTLV-I and HILV-II encodes two protein species in each virus. In HTLV-I, a 27-kD Rex protein and a 21-kD Rex protein appear to result from the use of alternative initiator methionine codons, but in HTLV-II, a 26-kD Rex protein appears to be formed by phosphorylation of a serine residue in a 24-kD protein.[48] The Rex proteins of HTLV-I and HTLV-II play an important role in regulating viral mRNA processing and are essential for export of full-length *gag/pol* and single-spliced *env* mRNA from nucleus to cytoplasm.[49, 50] This function is analogous to that of Rev in HIV-1 and HIV-2.[51, 52] Rex localizes to the nucleus and specifically to the nucleoli of infected cells.[53, 54] Phosphorylated Rex binds with high affinity to *cis*-acting RNA sequences, called Rex-responsive elements (RxREs), in the viral mRNA.[55–60] This interaction appears to facilitate the exit of mRNA from the nucleus to the cytoplasm. Rex binding may also inhibit mRNA splicing by preventing early steps in spliceosome assembly.[61] A suppressive effect on nuclear transport conferred by the *cis*-acting repressive sequences (CRSs) in the LTR may be relieved upon the binding of Rex to RxRE.[62] Rex also appears to partially enhance expression of the IL-2R α-chain[63] and has also been shown to bind prothymosin-alpha, a nuclear protein thought to be associated with cellular proliferation.[64] As a consequence of the accumulation of Rex in the cell, there is an accumulation of unspliced and single-spliced mRNA, favoring the production of viral structural *(gag)* and *env* proteins. This is accompanied by a decrease in the levels of double-spliced messenger RNA (mRNA) encoding Tax and Rex. Rex accumulation may also inhibit *tax*, thus slowing viral transcription.[65] A fine balance between *tax* and *rex* expression and function may dictate the rate of viral replication within infected cells.

Other Proteins Encoded by the pX Region

Several other proteins—p12^{I}, p13^{II}, and p30^{II}/tof—are also encoded from the X region, located between the end of the envelope gene and the beginning of *tax/rex*.[66] Of these, p12^{I} has been well characterized and is a 12-kD, 99-amino-acid protein, encoded by both double- and single-spliced mRNAs in ORF X-I (see Fig 156–1). This protein is highly hydrophobic and displays two putative transmembrane domains that account for more than half of its size. Repetitive motifs of unknown significance, LLFL, are scattered through the protein, and at least four putative Snc homology region 3 (SH3)-binding motifs can be recognized.[67, 68] The p12^{I} protein is considered to be a weak oncogene, because it structurally resembles the bovine papilloma virus E5 protein and cooperates with the latter in oncogenic transformation of murine fibroblast cells. Both proteins mainly localize to the cellular endomembranes and interact with another very hydrophobic protein, the 16-kD subunit of H^+ vacuolar H^+ ATPase, which is involved in proton transport into cellular organelles.[69, 70] The p12^{I} protein also interacts with and downregulates the β and γ_c chains of IL-2R. This may alter cellular responses to IL-2 and other cytokines and thereby play a role in T-cell transformation.[71]

In summary, the HTLV genome contains a variety of trans-regulatory proteins that appear to be important in viral regulation as well as in dysregulation of cellular gene expression. However, the exact role played by these proteins in T-cell transformation and oncogenesis remains to be clarified.

GENETIC VARIABILITY

Human T-Cell Lymphotropic Virus Type I

HTLV-I isolates from different parts of the world show a high degree of nucleotide sequence conservation, in contrast to HIV-1, in which considerable genomic variability occurs. Isolates of HTLV-I from Japan, the West Indies, the Americas, and Africa share 97% or greater homology.[72–74] Even the most divergent HTLV-I variant, isolated in Melanesia, is 92% homologous with a prototypic Japanese isolate.[75] The majority of these nucleotide differences are single-point mutations and do not correlate with specific disease patterns.[73] Rather, this genetic variability appears to reflect the geographic origin and, hence, possibly the migration patterns of ancient populations carrying the virus. Phylogenetic analysis has been used to classify HTLV-I into five major molecular and geographic subtypes, or "clades"[76]: (1) a cosmopolitan (C) subtype isolated all over the world, (2) a Japanese (J) subtype, (3) a West African (WA) subtype, (4) a Central African (CA) subtype, and (5) a Melanesian (M) subtype.

Some species of nonhuman primates harbor viruses genetically related to HTLV-I,[77] and it is believed that nonhuman primates constitute the natural reservoir of HTLVs. Phylogenetic analysis supports the concept of interspecies transmission among nonhuman primates, as well as between nonhuman primates and humans, with independent evolution of HTLV-I in Southeast Asia and in Africa and with dissemination of HTLV-I by forced or voluntary movements of human populations.[78]

The high degree of genetic conservation between various isolates of HTLV-I may be explained by differences between HTLV and HIV life cycles, kinetics, and underlying molecular events. One hypothesis is that the HTLV-I reverse transcriptase (RT) functions with increased fidelity compared with the corresponding HIV-1 RT. This would result in fewer alterations to the DNA provirus, and thus in the progeny virions, with each cycle of replication. Alternatively, reduced variability may merely reflect the significantly lower levels of HTLV-I and HTLV-II viral replication in infected persons, as compared with replication of HIV-1. Owen and coworkers[79] recently cloned a 60- to 65-kD protein with RT activity from HTLV-I. This is the first report of a cloned protein from HTLV-I displaying RT activity and may lead to further characterization of its biochemical properties.

Human T-Cell Lymphotropic Virus Type II

Based on relative divergence of the nucleotide sequences of the *env* (4.3%), *gag* (3.8%), and LTR (5.7%) regions,[80–82] HTLV-II was initially classified into two subtypes: HTLV-IIa (previously known as HTLV-II Mo) and HTLV-IIb (formerly HTLV-II NRA). The Tax protein of HTLV-IIb is 25 amino acids longer and is a more potent transactivator of the HTLV-II LTR than the corresponding HTLV-IIa protein.[82, 83] The in vivo significance of this functional difference is not known. In 1996, Eiraku and coworkers demonstrated the existence of a third subtype, HTLV-IIc, in urban Brazilian and Indian populations.[83] HTLV-IIc has LTR and *env* sequences related to HTLV-IIa and *tax* sequences similar to those of HTLV-IIb.

Molecular epidemiologic studies have shown that while HTLV-IIa infection is the predominant infection in intravenous drug users (IVDUs) in urban North America,[84] HTLV-IIb is the predominant subtype in Indian groups in Panama, Colombia, and Argentina.[85]

EPIDEMIOLOGY OF HUMAN T-CELL LYMPHOTROPIC VIRUS TYPES I AND II

Geographic Distribution

HTLV-I infection is present in widely scattered, apparently unrelated populations in the world (Fig. 156–2). The two best-studied areas are the islands of southwestern Japan, where approximately 20% of adults are seropositive,[86] and the Caribbean basin, where 2 to 5% of black adults are seropositive. The endemic areas in the Caribbean basin include the West Indies, northern South America, and the southeastern United States.[87–93] The infection has also been demonstrated in well-studied immigrant populations originating from such areas, such as West Indians living in England, Japanese immigrants in Hawaii, and blacks from the southern United States in New York City.[94–96] In addition, HTLV-I infection has been reported to be endemic in several other regions of the world including Central and West Africa,[97, 98] Melanesia,[99] parts of South America,[100] the Middle East,[101] and India.[102]

HTLV-II is reported mainly in IVDUs and their sexual contacts and in certain Native American populations. HTLV-II is generally more frequently identified than HTLV-I in IVDUs and has been shown to be endemic in IVDUs in the United States and in Europe, South America (Brazil), and Southeast Asia (Vietnam).[103–106] In 1986, the prevalence of HTLV-II infection in IVDUs in the borough of Queens in New York City, was shown to be 18%.[107] The presence of HTLV-II infection in culturally and geographically distinct Indian groups in North America (New Mexico and Florida),[108] Central America (Panama),[109] and South America (Argentina, Brazil, Colombia, and Chile)[110–113] led to speculation that HTLV-II may have originated in the New World. However, the degree of homology between HTLV-I and HTLV-II, as well as the recent demonstration of HTLV-II infection among pygmies in Africa,[114–117] supports a common geographic origin in Africa.

The prevalence of HTLV-I and HTLV-II increases with age in endemic populations.[86, 118, 119] This may reflect historical changes in the transmission of the virus, acquisition of disease in adulthood, or possibly, delayed seroconversion in persons with latent infection.[120–122]

Transmission

Modes of viral transmission have been well established for HTLV-I. The available evidence suggests that routes of transmission of HTLV-II are similar to those of HTLV-I. A discrete cellular receptor for both HTLV-I and HTLV-II has yet to be isolated but appears to reside on chromosome 17.[123, 124] The three major reported routes of HTLV-I transmission are sexual intercourse, administration of blood products, and mother-to-child transfer. In endemic areas, seropositive persons are clustered around families, reflecting the predominance of mother-to-child and male-to-female transmission. Prolonged close contact between people and transfer of infected T cells are probably required. The available evidence indicates that infection with HTLV-I and HTLV-II is lifelong and is asymptomatic in most affected persons.

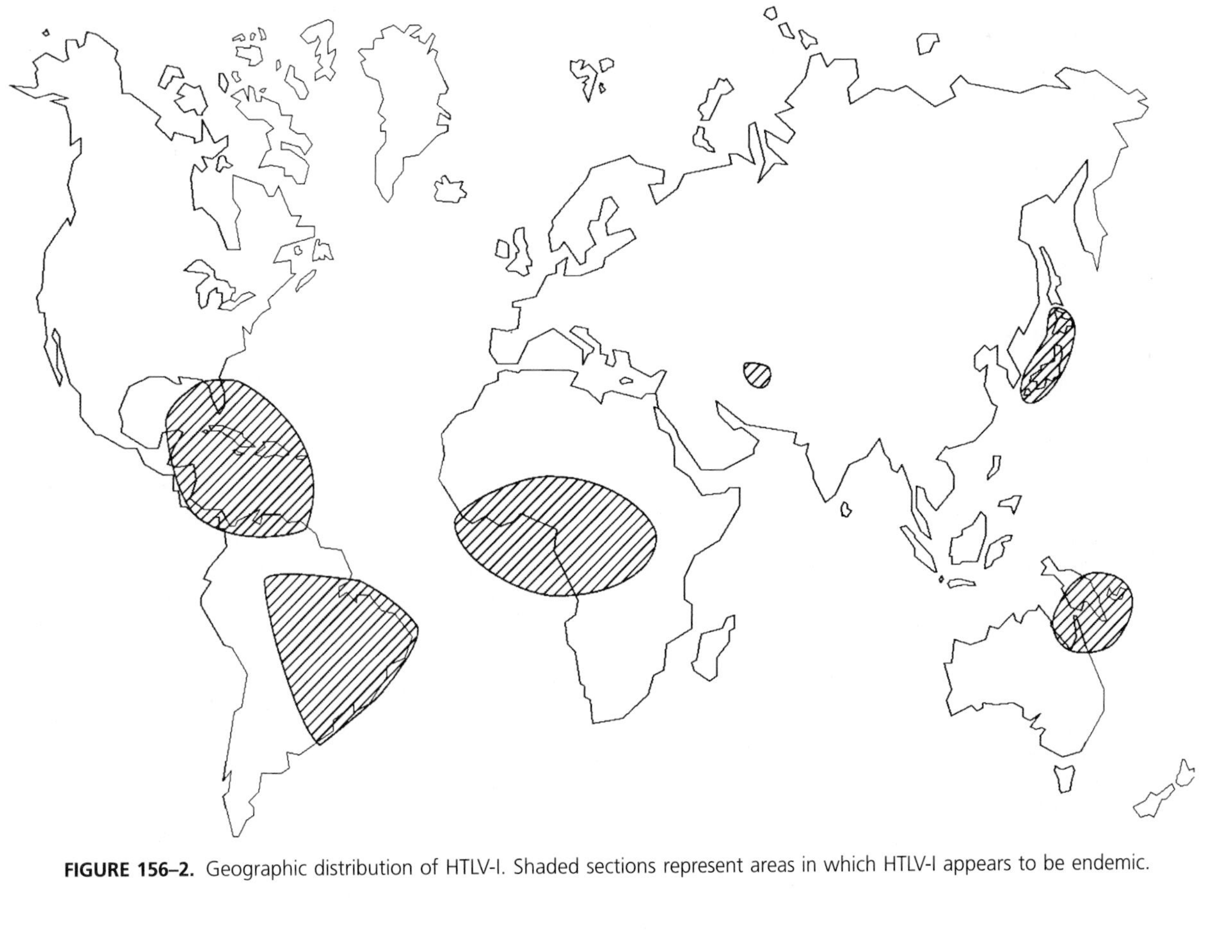

FIGURE 156–2. Geographic distribution of HTLV-I. Shaded sections represent areas in which HTLV-I appears to be endemic.

Mother-to-Child Transfer

In contrast to the mode of perinatal transmission of HIV-1 and HIV-2, breast-feeding is the predominant route of mother-to-child HTLV-I and HTLV-II transmission and occurs through ingestion of infected milk-borne lymphocytes.[125] Fifteen to 20% of children of seropositive mothers acquire HTLV-I through breast-feeding.[126, 127] Intrauterine transfer of HTLV-I has been documented very rarely.[128] Follow-up studies indicate that seroconversion typically occurs in infants at the age of 1 to 3 years.[129, 130] Children with seropositive fathers and seronegative mothers generally do not acquire the infection. Seroconversion is unusual in infants who are not breast-fed. Virus-positive lymphocytes are abundant in breast milk, and infection can be transmitted to animals by feeding infected breast milk. Abstaining from breast-feeding or even a shorter duration of breast-feeding may break the cycle of viral transmission in endemic areas. In one study, the prevalence of infection was the same in infants breast-fed for less than 7 months as in those not breast-fed.[131] Maternal anti-HTLV-I IgG is present in cord blood of virtually all infants born to seropositive mothers, but anti-HTLV-I IgM and virus-positive lymphocytes are not found, consistent with the lack of prenatal transmission.[132] The risk of transmission in breast-fed babies is higher with increased viral load and increased antibody titers in the mother.[125, 133, 134] Transmission of HTLV-I has been shown to be inhibited by passive immunization with antibody against HTLV-I.[135, 136]

Sexual Transmission

Sexual transmission of HTLV-I is bidirectional. However, male-to-female transmission occurs far more frequently than the reverse. After 10 years of sexual contact with an infected partner, a woman has a 61% likelihood of being infected, as opposed to only 0.4% for a man.[127] The presence of genital ulcers increases the risk of viral transmission.[137] Other risk factors associated with viral sexual transmission include high viral load and high titers of anti-HTLV antibodies.[137, 138] Virus-positive mononuclear cells have been detected in semen.[139] This finding, coupled with the low rate of female-to-male viral transmission, suggests that semen is the major vehicle of viral transmission. Condoms may therefore prevent sexual transmission of HTLV-I.

The prevalence of HTLV infection in male homosexuals in the United States and Europe, although higher than in the general population, is relatively low (0.3 to 0.4%).[140, 141] A study from Trinidad showed that the seroprevalence of HIV-1 among homosexual men was three times higher than that of HTLV-I (40% versus 15%).[142] These findings suggest that HTLV-I is less efficiently transmitted by homosexual contact than is HIV-1.

Transfusion of Blood Products

HTLV-I is readily transmitted by transfusion of cellular blood components (such as whole blood, packed cells, and platelet concentrates) but not by transfusion of the plasma fraction or plasma derivatives. This finding reflects the facts that the virus is highly cell-associated and that the infectious titer in plasma is extremely low. Seroconversion rates of 44 to 63% have been reported in recipients of HTLV-I–infected cellular components in HTLV-I endemic areas.[143, 144] HTLV seroprevalence is generally low among persons who have hemophilia unless they were also multiply transfused with cellular blood products before institution of routine screening.[145, 146] Storage of red cell units prior to transfusion significantly decreases the risk of HTLV-I and HTLV-II transmission. In one study, the rate of transmission fell to zero when blood was stored for more than 14 days, compared with 47% for a storage period of 14 days or less.[147] This finding has been ascribed to depletion of infected cells, presumably T lymphocytes during storage. Although rare, HTLV-I transmission by blood products can lead to rapid development of HTLV-I–associated myelopathy, within 6 months of transmission.[148] This may relate in part to viral load at the time of transmission. Transfusion-associated ATL, however, has rarely been reported. In recognition of this risk, testing of donated blood for HTLV-I has been routine in the United States since 1988.[149] In developing countries without a mandatory serologic screening program, blood transfusion remains a major risk factor for HTLV-I infection.[150, 151] Routine screening of donated blood in the United States led to the recognition that HTLV infection is more common than was previously thought. A seropositivity rate of 0.05% was noted in two large studies of more than 600,000 U.S. volunteers.[152, 153] Specific typing indicated that approximately 60% of HTLV-seropositive persons were actually infected with HTLV-II. The high degree of amino acid homology between HTLV-I and HTLV-II is responsible for the antigenic cross-reactivity. Interviews with donors revealed that HTLV-I infection was principally associated with donor origin from endemic regions, whereas intravenous drug use was the major risk factor for HTLV-II infection.[152]

The Centers for Disease Control and Prevention issued guidelines for counseling persons infected with HTLV-I and HTLV-II in 1993.[154] Seropositive persons are advised not to donate blood, semen, body organs, or other tissues and not to share needles or syringes, not to breast-feed infants, and to use latex condoms to prevent sexual transmission. They are also advised to communicate their HTLV-positive status to their physician. Although the risk of accidental transmission to health care workers is low,[155] universal precautions as recommended for contact with all patients should be observed.[156]

DIAGNOSIS

The most commonly used screening test for HTLV-I and HTLV-II infection is an enzyme-linked immunosorbent assay (ELISA) using inactivated HTLV-I whole-virus lysate antigen, which appears to detect most HTLV-II infections as well.[157] After initial reactivity on ELISA, supplemental testing, generally by the Western blot technique, is conducted to confirm the presence of HTLV-I or HTLV-II antibodies. Other supplemental tests that have been used include indirect fluorescent-antibody assay, radioimmunoprecipitation assay (RIPA), line immunoassay (LIA), and polymerase chain reaction (PCR).[157–159] Owing to the high degree of amino acid homology, most supplemental serologic assays also cannot distinguish between HTLV-I and HTLV-II. Methods generally used to distinguish HTLV-I from HTLV-II include PCR[159, 160] and enzyme immunoassays using virus-specific synthetic peptides derived from either HTLV-I or HTLV-II.[161]

DISEASES ASSOCIATED WITH HUMAN T-CELL LYMPHOTROPIC VIRUS TYPE I

Adult T-Cell Leukemia

Adult T-cell leukemia/lymphoma (ATL, formerly ATLL) is a proliferative disorder of T cells characterized by lymphadenopathy, hypercalcemia, lytic bone lesions, skin involvement, and hepatosplenomegaly.[162] The skin lesions seen in ATL are varied and include localized or diffuse papules, nodules (Fig. 156–3), plaques, erythematous patches, and diffuse erythroderma. Abnormal lymphocytes with convoluted nuclei—so-called "flower cells" (Fig. 156–4)—are seen in the blood.

The malignant T cells of ATL are mature (terminal deoxynucleotide transferase–negative [TdT^-]) and $CD4^+/CD8^-$ and have increased IL-2R α-chain (CD25/TAC antigen) expression.[163–166] Integration of the HTLV-I provirus into the cellular genome is monoclonal,[167, 168] indicating that the malignant T cells are monoclonal and originate from a single HTLV-I–infected T cell. The site of integration, although constant for a given patient, varies between individual patients and does not appear to be important in the pathogenesis of ATL. The virus appears to be latent in neoplastic cells, and Tax expression in ATL cells has not been shown convincingly.

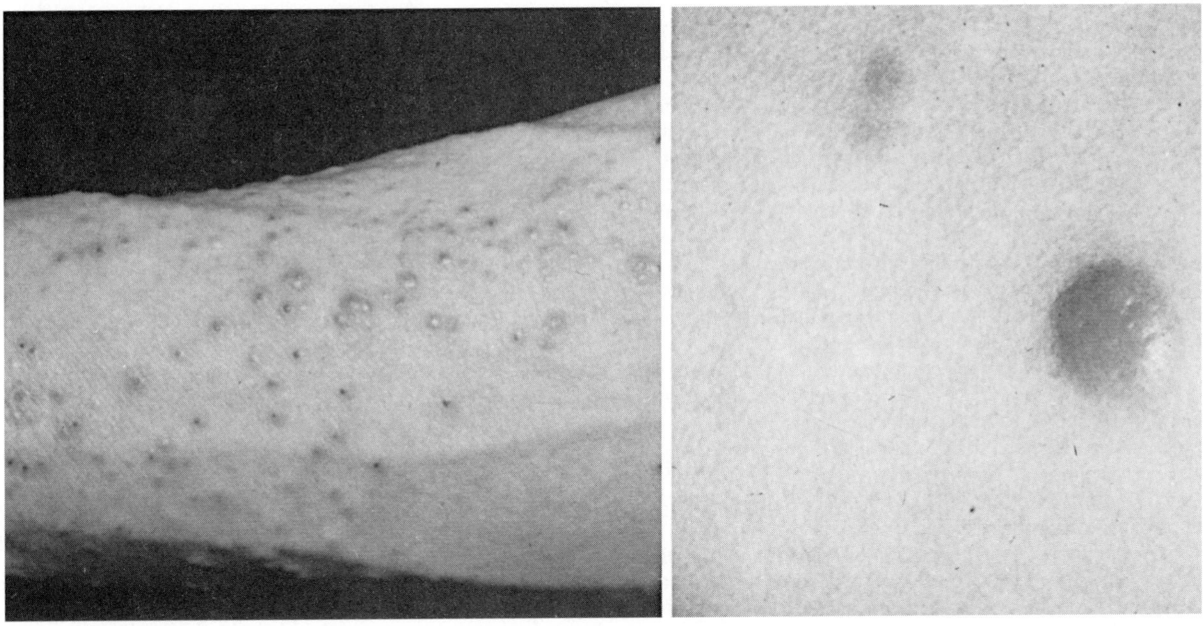

FIGURE 156–3. Skin papules and nodules in a patient with adult T-cell leukemia/lymphoma. (Courtesy of M. Tomonaga.)

The lifetime risk of development of ATL in HTLV-I carriers is estimated at 1 to 4%.[169] This suggests that although the initiating event is the retroviral infection, at least two or more "hits" may be required for leukemic transformation. The latent period from infection to actual development of disease is estimated to be 30 to 50 years.[169, 170] Most persons with ATL appear to have acquired the infection in childhood.

On the basis of clinical presentation, ATL has been classified by Shimoyama into four subtypes[171]:

1. *Smoldering ATL*—characterized by 5% or more abnormal T cells in the peripheral blood with a normal total lymphocyte count, the presence of skin lesions, and occasionally, pulmonary involvement. There is no hypercalcemia, lymphadenopathy, or other visceral involvement. Serum lactate dehydrogenase (LDH) levels may be elevated. This phase is often indolent and can last for years.

2. *Chronic ATL*—characterized by an absolute lymphocytosis (4×10^9/liter or more) with a T-cell lymphocytosis (more than 3.5×10^9/liter). LDH may be increased up to twice the normal limit. Patients may have lymphadenopathy, hepatomegaly, splenomegaly, skin, and pulmonary involvement. No hypercalcemia, ascites, pleural effusion, or involvement of the central nervous system, bone, or gastrointestinal tract is present in this subtype of ATL. The median survival time for patients with the chronic subtype is 24 months.[171]

3. *Lymphomatous ATL*—characterized by lymphadenopathy in the absence of lymphocytosis. Lymph node involvement with ATL must be histologically proved. The median survival time for these patients is short: 10 months.[171]

4. *Acute ATL*—includes the remaining patients and may present as a leukemia or a high-grade non-Hodgkin's lymphoma with circulating leukemic cells. Hypercalcemia, lytic bone lesions, and visceral involvement are common. Acute ATL has a poor prognosis, with a median survival time of 6.2 months.[171] Transformation from the smoldering or chronic phase to the acute form can occur at any point in the disease course.

ATL is associated with lymphomas of several histologic subtypes (Fig. 156–5) but most frequently has features of a diffuse large cell lymphoma.[172] There does not appear to be a significant correlation between histopathologic grade and clinical course.[172] Biopsy of skin

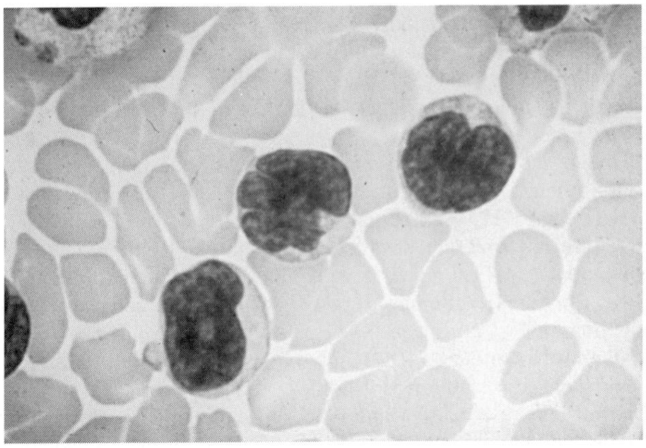

FIGURE 156–4. Blood smear showing atypical lymphocyte (center) with convoluted nucleus—so-called flower cell. (Courtesy of M. Tomonaga.)

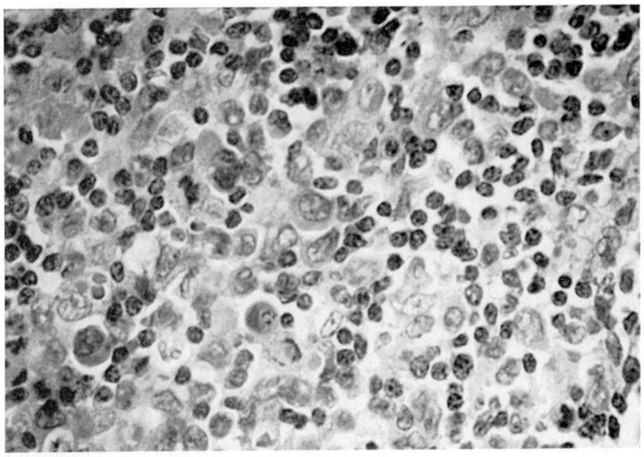

FIGURE 156–5. Histopathologic appearance of a lymph node in a patient with adult T-cell leukemia/lymphoma, showing diffuse infiltration by neoplastic lymphoid cells. (Courtesy of M. Tomonaga.)

lesions reveals dermal or epidermal infiltration with malignant lymphocytes. So-called Pautrier's microabscesses may also be noted in the dermis, as in mycosis fungoides. Biopsy of bony lytic lesions reveals osteoclast activation and bone resorption, often without infiltration by ATL cells. Levels of parathyroid hormone are usually normal. It has been suggested that Tax transactivation and production of various cytokines (e.g., PTHrP, various interleukins) is responsible for the hypercalcemia, osteoclast activation, and lytic bone lesions seen in this disorder.[173]

Multiple cytogenetic abnormalities have been reported in ATL, including frequent abnormalities of chromosome 14 involving the T-cell receptor locus.[174] Survival has shown correlation with the complexity of the karyotypic abnormality in some studies.[175]

Patients with ATL are immunocompromised, and opportunistic infections are frequent. *Pneumocystis carinii* pneumonia, cryptococcal meningitis, and disseminated fungal infections have been described,[91] as well as viral infections (cytomegalovirus, herpes zoster, generalized herpes simplex). *Strongyloides stercoralis* appears to be a common concurrent infection.[176–179] A Japanese study showed that 58.3% of patients with strongyloidiasis were HTLV-I–positive, and of these, 66.6% had monoclonal integration of HTLV-I proviral DNA in their blood lymphocytes.[177] This has provoked speculation that *Strongyloides* infection may be a cofactor in the development of ATL. Leukemic cells have been reported to suppress B-cell immunoglobulin secretion by a complex mechanism involving induction of suppressor cells after activation of normal suppressor cell precursors.[164]

Immunity may be impaired in otherwise asymptomatic HTLV-I carriers. Bacterial and fungal skin infections occur frequently,[180–182] and cutaneous anergy has been reported.[183] Concomitant infection with HIV-1 and HTLV-I has been described, but it is not clear if this accelerates progression to AIDS.[184–186]

Considerations in the differential diagnosis of ATL include other T-cell malignancies such as non-Hodgkin's lymphoma, mycosis fungoides, and Sézary's syndrome. ATL should be suspected in any adult patient from an endemic population with a T-cell malignancy. The presence of circulating "flower cells," hypercalcemia, and skin lesions is highly suggestive. On immunophenotyping, the leukemic cells are characteristically TdT^- and $CD4^+$ and $CD25^+$. The diagnosis can be confirmed by testing for anti-HTLV-I antibody or demonstrating monoclonal integration of proviral DNA in the malignant cells by Southern blotting.

Most patients with acute ATL are managed with combination chemotherapy using a regimen that includes an anthracycline, such as CHOP (cyclophosphamide, doxorubicin, vincristine, and prednisone). Treatment-related toxicity may outweigh any benefit in the case of indolent disease. A complete remission (CR) rate of 35.8% was reported by Taguchi and colleagues,[187] using CHOP followed by etoposide, vindesine, ranimustine, and mitoxantrone with granulocyte colony–stimulating factor support. However, durable remissions are rare,[188] and most patients experience relapse within 6 to 12 months. The nucleoside analogue deoxycoformycin may benefit some patients with this disease.[189] Expression of the multidrug resistance gene MDR-1 has been demonstrated in ATL cells, particularly following relapse, and may be mediated by Tax.[190, 191] This may partly account for the poor responses seen with conventional chemotherapy. There are insufficient data regarding the role of high-dose chemotherapy and autologous or allogeneic bone marrow or stem cell transplantation in the treatment of ATL. Spontaneous regression of ATL has been reported rarely.[192]

Interferons (INFs) have inhibitory effects on HTLV-I in vitro[193] but produce CR in less than 10% of cases in vivo.[194–196] The addition of the antiretroviral drug zidovudine to INF-α has been reported to produce CR in 26% of cases.[197, 198] This combination was shown to be effective in some patients in whom combination chemotherapy had previously failed. Why an antiretroviral should affect ATL, which is not thought to depend on active viral replication, is unclear. Monoclonal antibodies (anti-Tac coupled with yttrium 90) targeting the IL-2R α-chain, constitutively expressed by ATL cells, were reported to result in CR in 2 of 16 patients and partial remission in 7 of 16 patients, along with normalization of serum calcium levels and improvement in liver function.[165, 199]

Human T-Cell Lymphotropic Virus Type I–Associated Myelopathy

HTLV-I–associated myelopathy, also known as tropical spastic paresis or chronic progressive myelopathy, is a chronic progressive demyelinating disease that affects the spinal cord and white matter of the central nervous system (CNS).[200–202] The lifetime incidence of HAM in HTLV-I carriers is estimated to be less than 5%.[203] Typical time of onset of HAM is in the fourth decade of life, with a female-to-male ratio of 2:1.[204] Coexistence of both HAM and ATL in the same patient has been reported rarely.[205–207]

Gait disturbance and weakness and stiffness of the lower limbs are common presenting signs and symptoms of HAM.[204, 208] Lower extremities are affected to a much greater degree than upper extremities. Spasticity may be moderate to severe, and low back pain is common. As the disease progresses, bladder and bowel dysfunction can occur.[209–211] Sensory involvement is generally mild and can result in a variable degree of sensory loss and dysesthesias. Disease progression is variable. In one series, after a mean period of 14.4 years (range, 1 to 30 years), 34% of patients could walk with minor difficulty, 40% of patients could walk with difficulty using a cane or crutches, and 26% of patients were bedridden.[212]

Results of magnetic resonance imaging may be normal, or the scans show atrophy of the spinal cord and nonspecific lesions in the brain.[209, 210, 213–215] Protein and immunoglobulin levels are moderately increased in the cerebrospinal fluid (CSF), and oligoclonal bands are frequently seen.[204, 208] Atypical lymphocytes resembling ATL "flower cells" may be found in the CSF and in the peripheral blood.[208]

Considerations in the differential diagnosis of HAM include multiple sclerosis,[216] toxic neuropathies (cassava neurotoxicity or lathyrism in tropical countries), malnutrition,[217] infections such as HIV infection and syphilis, and other spinal cord or CNS disorders.

Pathologic findings consist of a perivascular and parenchymal infiltration of mononuclear lymphoid cells accompanied by myelin and axonal destruction.[200, 218] This process results in degeneration of the white matter, most conspicuously in the thoracic spinal cord.[204, 208] Varying degrees of brain parenchymal degeneration have also been described, with reactive astrocytosis and perivascular mononuclear cell infiltration. These mononuclear cells are predominantly $CD8^+$ lymphocytes,[201, 213, 219] suggesting that an immune mechanism may play a role in the development of HAM. Jacobson and coworkers[220] have described a high frequency of cytolytic T cells in HAM with a specificity directed against MHC-I–restricted epitopes derived from the Tax protein, suggesting that the response to Tax may be important in the pathogenesis of this disorder.

As opposed to lymphocytes in ATL, HTLV-I–infected lymphocytes in HAM are oligoclonal or polyclonal, rather than monoclonal. It is believed that HTLV-I causes neurologic disease by indirect mechanisms. Investigators have so far been unable to demonstrate that the virus can infect and replicate in cells of the CNS in vivo. Two major models of pathogenesis of HAM have been postulated: an autoimmune model and a cytotoxic model.[221] The former model postulates that HTLV-I infection activates autoreactive T cells, which then cause autoimmune destruction within the CNS.[222] The latter model invokes HTLV-I infection of glial cells, which subsequently induces a cytotoxic immune response against these cells, leading to demyelination.[219]

There is no effective treatment for HAM. Corticosteroids,[202, 208] plasmapheresis,[223] cyclophosphamide,[224] and INF-α[225, 226] may produce transient responses. Danazol,[227] an anabolic steroid, has been reported to improve gait and bladder function; its mechanism of action is poorly understood. Other treatment modalities described in the literature include the use of anti-TAC antibodies[228] directed against the CD25 IL-2R α-chain and zidovudine.[229, 230] At present, treatment with Danazol or corticosteroids is most often used in the absence of an experimental protocol.

Other Diseases Associated with Human T-Cell Lymphotropic Virus Type I

HTLV-I has been implicated in several other disorders (Table 156–1) including an inflammatory arthropathy,[231] uveitis,[232] polymyositis,[233] infectious dermatitis in children,[234] pulmonary disorders,[235] and Sjögren's syndrome.[236] HTLV-I *env*-pX transgenic rats are affected by a wide spectrum of collagen vascular diseases and have been shown to develop a number of autoantibodies including rheumatoid factor, in high titers, and anti–double-stranded DNA.[237] HTLV-I–like Tax, Rex, and Pol sequences as well as virus-like particles have been described in peripheral blood mononuclear cells of patients with mycosis fungoides and Sézary's syndrome who are otherwise seronegative for viral infection.[238–240] Pancake and colleagues reported the presence of antibody against HTLV-I Tax in patients with mycosis fungoides who were seronegative for antibodies to viral structural proteins.[241] These provocative findings have resulted in speculation linking mycosis fungoides to a "seronegative" HTLV-I infection but have not been confirmed by other investigators.[242]

DISEASES ASSOCIATED WITH HUMAN T-CELL LYMPHOTROPIC VIRUS TYPE II

HTLV-II has been shown to possess a broad tropism for peripheral blood mononuclear cells.[243] It was previously thought that the in vivo cellular tropism of HTLV-II was restricted to $CD8^+$ T cells.[244] In contrast, HTLV-I predominantly infects $CD4^+$ T cells, although some infected $CD8^+$ cells are also found.[245, 246] HTLV-II has been associated with certain rare hematologic malignancies including atypical hairy cell leukemia,[9, 247] and with some cases of large granular lymphocytic leukemia[248] and mycosis fungoides.[242] However, evidence confirming an etiologic role of HTLV-II in these disorders is lacking. In at least one instance, oligoclonal integration of HTLV-II into $CD8^+$ cells of a patient with atypical T-cell malignancy was confirmed.[247] An epidemiologic study conducted in an HTLV-II–endemic population found no increase in the incidence of hairy cell leukemia, mycosis fungoides, or chronic lymphocytic leukemia.[249]

HTLV-II has also been linked with neurodegenerative disorders characterized by spastic paraparesis and variable degrees of ataxia.[250, 251] The virus has been isolated from a patient with a chronic progressive neurologic disease indistinguishable from HAM/TSP.[252] A progressive spastic myelopathy was also reported in a patient coinfected with HIV-1 and HTLV-II.[253]

Elevated serum creatine kinase levels, suggesting underlying myositis, were reported in a cohort of HTLV-II–infected IVDUs.[254] HTLV-II–infected persons may be at increased risk for a variety of infections, including pneumonia, minor fungal infections, abscesses, lymphadenopathy, and bladder or kidney infections, consistent with a degree of underlying immunologic impairment.[255, 256]

TABLE 156–1 Clinical Syndromes Reported in Association with Human T-Cell Lymphotropic Virus Types I and II (HTLV-I and HTLV-II)

HTLV-I	HTLV-II
Adult T-cell leukemia/lymphoma	Atypical hairy cell leukemia? Large granular lymphocytic leukemia?
HTLV associated myelopathy	Myelopathy, cerebellar ataxia
Mycosis fungoides?	Mycosis fungoides?
Increased susceptibility to infections	Increased susceptibility to infections
Polymyositis	Myositis
Uveitis	
Arthropathy	
Sjögren's syndrome	
Pulmonary syndrome, alveolitis	
Infectious dermatitis	

SUMMARY

HTLV-I and HTLV-II are complex retroviruses with unique regulatory genes. Whereas HTLV-I has been shown to be the etiologic agent in ATL and HAM, HTLV-II has yet to be definitively linked to a specific human disorder. The pathogenesis of diseases induced by these viruses remains unclear, and no effective therapy exists. Approximately 10 to 20 million people are estimated to be infected by HTLV-I.[15] Preventive strategies such as screening of blood products and avoidance of breast-feeding remain the mainstay of the global approach to this virus, but such measures may not always be readily applicable in all developing countries.

REFERENCES

1. Coffin JM. Structure and classification of retroviruses. In: Levy JA, ed. The Retroviridae. New York: Plenum Press; 1992:19–50.
2. Murphy FA, Fauquet CM, Bishop DHL, et al. Virus taxonomy: Sixth Report of the International Committee on the Taxonomy of Viruses. New York: Springer-Verlag; 1995.
3. Teich N. Taxonomy of retroviruses. In: Weiss R, Teich N, Varmus H, Coffin J, eds. RNA Tumor Viruses. Cold Spring Harbor, NY: Cold Spring Harbor Laboratory; 1985:1–16.
4. Wong-Staal F, Gallo RC. Human T-lymphotropic retroviruses. Nature. 1985;317:395–403.
5. Poiesz BJ, Ruscetti FW, Gazdar AF, et al. Detection and isolation of type C retrovirus particles from fresh and cultured lymphocytes of a patient with cutaneous T-cell lymphoma. Proc Natl Acad Sci U S A. 1980;77:7415–7419.
6. Uchiyama T, Yodoi J, Sagawa K, et al. Adult T-cell leukemia: Clinical and hematologic features of 16 cases. Blood. 1977;50:481–492.
7. Hinuma Y, Nagata K, Hanaoka M, et al. Adult T-cell leukemia: Antigen in an ATL cell line and detection of antibodies to the antigen in human sera. Proc Natl Acad Sci U S A. 1981;78:6476–6480.
8. Gessain A, Barin F, Vernant JC, et al. Antibodies to human T-lymphotropic virus type-I in patients with tropical spastic paralysis. Lancet. 1985;2:407–410.
9. Kalyanaraman VS, Sarngadharan MG, Robert-Guroff M, et al. A new subtype of human T-cell leukemia virus (HTLV-II) associated with a T-cell variant of hairy cell leukemia. Science. 1982;218:571–573.
10. Shimotohno K, Takahashi Y, Shimizu N, et al. Complete nucleotide sequence of an infectious clone of human T-cell leukemia virus type II: An open reading frame for the protease gene. Proc Natl Acad Sci U S A. 1985;82:3101–3105.
11. Haseltine WA, Sodroski J, Patarca R, et al. Structure of 3′ terminal region of type II human T lymphotropic virus: Evidence for new coding region. Science. 1984;225:419–421.
12. Shimotohno K, Wachsman W, Takahashi Y, et al. Nucleotide sequence of the 3′ region of an infectious human T-cell leukemia virus type II genome. Proc Nat Acad Sci U S A. 1984;81:6657–6661.
13. Seiki M, Hattori S, Yoshida M. Human adult T-cell leukemia virus: Molecular cloning of the provirus DNA and the unique terminal structure. Proc Natl Acad Sci U S A. 1982;79:6899–6902.
14. Seiki M, Hattori S, Hirayama Y, Yoshida M. Human adult T-cell leukemia virus: Complete nucleotide sequence of the provirus genome integrated in leukemia cell DNA. Proc Natl Acad Sci U S A. 1983;80:3618–3622.
15. Franchini G. Molecular mechanisms of human T-cell leukemia/lymphotropic virus type I infection. Blood. 1995;86:3619–3639.
16. Slamon DJ, Shimotohno K, Cline MJ, et al. Identification of the putative transforming protein of the human T-cell leukemia viruses HTLV-I and HTLV-II. Science. 1984;226:61–65.
17. Lee TH, Coligan JE, Sodroski JG, et al. Antigens encoded by the 3′-terminal region of human T-cell leukemia virus: Evidence for a functional gene. Science. 1984;226:57–61.
18. Ross TM, Pettiford SM, Green PL. The tax gene of human T-cell leukemia virus type 2 is essential for transformation of human T lymphocytes. J Virol. 1996;70:5194–5202.
19. Cann AJ, Rosenblatt JD, Wachsman W, et al. Identification of the gene responsible for human T-cell leukemia virus transcriptional regulation. Nature. 1985;318:571–574.
20. Felber BK, Paskalis H, Kleinman-Ewing C, et al. The p*X* protein of HTLV-I is a transcriptional activator of its long terminal repeats. Science. 1985;229:675–679.
21. Sodroski JG, Rosen CA, Haseltine WA. Trans-acting transcriptional activation of the long terminal repeat of human T lymphotropic viruses in infected cells. Science. 1984;225:381–385.
22. Jeang KT, Boros I, Brady J, et al. Characterization of cellular factors that interact with the human T-cell leukemia virus type I p40x–responsive 21-base-pair sequence. J Virol. 1988;62:4499–4509.
23. Marriott SJ, Boros I, Duvall JF, Brady JN. Indirect binding of human T-cell

leukemia virus type I *tax 1* to a responsive element in the viral long terminal repeat. Mol Cell Biol. 1989;9:4152–4160.
24. Suzuki T, Fujisawa JI, Toita M, Yoshida M. The trans-activator tax of human T-cell leukemia virus type I (HTLV-I) interacts with cAMP-responsive element (CRE) binding and CRE modulator proteins that bind to the 21-base-pair enhancer of HTLV-I. Proc Natl Acad Sci U S A. 1993;90:610–614.
25. Willems L, Kettmann R, Chen G, et al. A cyclic AMP–responsive DNA-binding protein (CREB2) is a cellular transactivator of the bovine leukemia virus long terminal repeat. J. Virol. 1992;66:766–772.
26. Adam E, Kerkhofs P, Mammerickx M, et al. Involvement of the cyclic AMP–responsive element binding protein in bovine leukemia virus expression in vivo. J Virol. 1994;68:5845–5853.
27. Kwok RP, Laurance ME, Lundblad JR, et al. Control of cAMP-regulated enhancers by the viral transactivator Tax through CREB and the co-activator CBP. Nature. 1996;380:642–646.
28. Yin MJ, Gaynor RB. HTLV-I 21 bp repeat sequences facilitate stable association between Tax and CREB to increase CREB binding affinity. J Mol Biol. 1996;264:20–31.
29. Giebler HA, Loring JE, vanOrden K, et al. Anchoring of CREB binding protein to the human T-cell leukemia virus type 1 promoter: A molecular mechanism of Tax transactivation. Mol Cell Biol. 1997;17:5156–5164.
30. Lenzmeier BA, Giebler HA, Nyborg JK. Human T-cell leukemia virus type 1 Tax requires direct access to DNA for recruitment of CREB binding protein to the viral promoter. Mol Cell Biol. 1998;18:721–731.
31. Bosselut R, Duvall JF, Gegonne A, et al. The product of the c-ets-1 proto-oncogene and the related Ets2 protein act as transcriptional activators of the long terminal repeat of human T-cell leukemia virus HTLV-1. EMBO J. 1990;9:3137–3144.
32. Bosselut R, Lim F, Romond PC, et al. Myb protein binds to multiple sites in the human T-cell lymphotropic virus type 1 long terminal repeat and transactivates LTR-mediated expression. Virology. 1992;186:764–769.
33. Marriott SJ, Lindholm PF, Brown KM, et al. A 36-kilodalton cellular transcription factor mediates an indirect interaction of human T-cell leukemia/lymphoma virus type I TAX 1 with a responsive element in the viral long terminal repeat. Mol Cell Biol. 1990;10:4192–4201.
34. Yoshida M. HTLV-I oncoprotein Tax deregulates transcription of cellular genes through multiple mechanisms. J Cancer Res Clin Oncol. 1995;121:521–528.
35. Jeang KT, Widen SG, Seemes OJ, Wilson SH. HTLV-I transactivator protein, Tax, is a trans-repressor of the human β-polymerase gene. Science. 1990;247:1082–1084.
36. Suzuki T, Hirai H, Fujisawa J, et al. A transactivator Tax of human T-cell leukemia virus type 1 binds to NF-κB p50 and serum response factor (SRF) and associates with enhancer DNAs of the NF-κB site and CArG box. Oncogene. 1993;8:2391–2397.
37. Hirai H, Suzuki T, Fujisawa J, et al. Tax protein of human T-cell leukemia virus type I binds to the ankyrin motifs of inhibitory factor κB and induces nuclear translocation of transcription factor NF-κB proteins for transcriptional activation. Proc Natl Acad Sci U S A. 1994;91:3584–3588.
38. Hirai H, Fujisawa J, Suzuki T, et al. Transcriptional activator Tax of HTLV-I binds to the NF-κB precursor p105. Oncogene. 1992;7:1737–1742.
39. Beimling P, Moelling K. Direct interaction of CREM protein with 21 bp Tax-response elements of HTLV-I LTR. Oncogene. 1992;7:257–262.
40. Beraud C, Sun SC, Ganchi P. Human T-cell leukemia virus type I Tax associates with and is negatively regulated by the NF-kappa B2 p100 gene product: Implications for viral latency. Mol Cell Biol. 1994;14:1374–1382.
41. Suzuki T, Hirai H, Murakami T, Yoshida M. Tax protein of HTLV-I destabilizes the complexes of NF-kappa B and I kappa B-alpha and induces nuclear translocation of NF-kappa B for transcriptional activation. Oncogene. 1995:10:1199–1207.
42. Xu X, Kang SH, Heidenreich O, et al. Constitutive activation of different Jak tyrosine kinases in human T-cell leukemia virus type I (HTLV-I) tax protein or virus-transformed cells. J Clin Invest. 1995;96:1548–1555.
43. Migone TS, Lin JX, Cereseto A, et al. Constitutively activated Jak-STAT pathway in T-cells transformed with HTLV-I. Science. 1995;269:79–81.
44. Fujii M, Tsuchiya H, Chuhjo T, et al. Interaction of HTLV-I Tax 1 with p67SRF causes the aberrant induction of cellular immediate-early genes through CArG boxes. Genes Dev. 1992;6:2066–2076.
45. Pise-Masison CA, Choi KS, Radonovich M, et al. Inhibition of p53 transactivation function by the human T-cell lymphotropic virus type I Tax protein. J Virol. 1998;72:1165–1170.
46. Tanaka Y, Hayashi M, Takagi S, Yoshie O. Differential transactivation of the intercellular adhesion molecule 1 gene promoter by Tax1 and Tax2 of human T-cell leukemia viruses. J Virol. 1996;70:8508–8517.
47. Owen SM, Rudolph DL, Dezzutti CS, et al. Transcriptional activation of the intercellular adhesion molecule 1 (CD54) gene by human T lymphotropic virus types I and II Tax is mediated through a palindromic response element. AIDS Res Hum Retroviruses. 1997;13:1429–1437.
48. Green PL, Xie YM, Chen IS. The Rex proteins of human T-cell leukemia virus type II differ by serine phosphorylation. J Virol. 1991;65:546–550.
49. Kiyokawa T, Seiki M, Iwashita S, et al. $P27^{X-III}$ and $p21^{X-III}$ proteins encoded by the pX sequence of human T-cell leukemia virus type I. Proc Natl Acad Sci U S A. 1985;82:8359–8363.
50. Rosenblatt JD, Cann AJ, Slamon DJ, et al. HTLV-II *trans*-activation is regulated by the overlapping tax/rex nonstructural genes. Science. 1988;240:916–919.
51. Hanly SM, Rimsky LT, Malim MH, et al. Comparative analysis of the HTLV-I rex and HIV-I rev trans-regulatory proteins and their RNA response elements. Genes Dev. 1989;3:1534–1544.
52. Itoh M, Inoue J, Toyoshima H, et al. HTLV-I rex and HIV-I rev act through similar mechanisms to relieve suppression of unspliced RNA expression. Oncogene. 1989;4:1275–1279.
53. Nosaka T, Siomi H, Adachi Y, et al. Nucleolar targeting signal of human T-cell leukemia virus type I rex-encoded protein is essential for cytoplasmic accumulation of unspliced viral mRNA. Proc Natl Acad Sci U S A. 1989;86:9798–9802.
54. Siomi H, Shida H, Nam SH, et al. Sequence requirements for nucleolar localization of human T-cell leukemia virus type I pX protein which regulates viral RNA processing. Cell. 1988;55:197–209.
55. Black AC, Ruland CT, Yip MT, et al. Human T-cell leukemia virus type II Rex binding and activity require an intact splice donor site and a specific RNA secondary structure. J Virol. 1991;65:6645–6653.
56. Bogerd HP, Tiley LS, Cullen BR. Specific binding of the human T-cell leukemia virus type I Rex protein to a short RNA sequence located within the Rex-response element. J Virol. 1992;66:7572–7575.
57. Grassman R, Berchtold S, Aepinus C, et al. In vitro binding of human T-cell leukemia virus rex proteins to the rex-response element of viral transcripts. J Virol. 1991;65:3721–3727.
58. Yip MT, Dynan WS, Green PL, et al. Human T-cell leukemia virus (HTLV) type II rex protein binds specifically to RNA sequences of the HTLV long terminal repeat but poorly to the human immunodeficiency virus type I Rev-responsive elements. J Virol. 1991;65:2261–2272.
59. Seiki M, Inoue J, Hidaka M, Yoshida M. Two cis-acting elements responsible for post-transcriptional trans-regulation of gene expression of human T-cell leukemia virus type I. Proc Natl Acad Sci U S A. 1988;85:7124–7128.
60. Ballaun C, Farrington GK, Dubrovnik M, et al. Functional analysis of human T-cell leukemia virus type I rex-response element: Direct RNA binding of Rex protein correlates with in vivo activity. J Virol. 1991;65:4408–4413.
61. Bakker A, Li X, Ruland CT, et al. Human T-cell leukemia virus type II Rex inhibits pre-mRNA splicing in vitro at an early state of spliceosome formation. J Virol. 1996;70:5511–5518.
62. Black AC, Chen IS, Arrigo S, et al. Regulation of HTLV-II gene expression by Rex involves positive and negative cis-acting elements in the 5′ long terminal repeat. Virology. 1991;181:433–444.
63. Kanamori H, Suzuki N, Siomi H, et al. HTLV-I p27rex stabilizes human interleukin-2 receptor alpha chain mRNA. EMBO J. 1990;9:4161–4166.
64. Kubota S, Adachi Y, Copeland TD, Oroszlan S. Binding of human prothymosin alpha to the leucine-motif/activation domains of HTLV-I Rex and HIV-I Rev. Eur J Biochem. 1995;233:48–54.
65. Watanabe CT, Rosenblatt JD, Bakker A, et al. Negative regulation of gene expression from the HTLV-II long terminal repeat by Rex: Functional and structural dissociation from positive post-transcriptional regulation. AIDS Res Hum Retroviruses. 1996;12:535–546.
66. Koralnik IJ, Fullen J, Franchini G. The $p12^{I}$; $p13^{II}$, and $p30^{II}$ proteins encoded by human T-cell leukemia/lymphotropic virus type I open reading frames I and II are localized in three different cellular compartments. J Virol. 1993;67:2360–2366.
67. Pawson T. Protein modules and signalling networks. Nature. 1995;373:573–580.
68. Alexandropoulos K, Cheng G, Baltimore D. Proline-rich sequences that bind to Src homology 3 domains with individual specificities. Proc Natl Acad Sci U S A. 1995;92:3110–3114.
69. Schlegel R, Wade-Glass M, Rabson MS, Yang YC. The E5 transforming gene of bovine papillomavirus encodes a small hydrophobic polypeptide. Science. 1986;233:464–467.
70. Franchini G, Mulloy JC, Koralnik IJ, et al. The human T-cell leukemia/lymphotropic virus type I $p12^{I}$ protein cooperates with the E5 oncoprotein of bovine papilloma virus in cell transformation and binds the 16-kilodalton subunit of the vacuolar H^{+} ATPase. J Virol. 1993;67:7701–7704.
71. Mulloy JC, Crownley RW, Fullen J, et al. The human T-cell leukemia/lymphotropic virus type I $p12^{I}$ protein binds the interleukin-2 receptor β and γ_c chains and affects their expression on the cell surface. J Virol. 1996;70:3599–3605.
72. Gessain A, Gallo RC, Franchini G. Low degree of human T-cell leukemia/lymphoma virus type I genetic drift in vivo as a means of monitoring viral transmission and movement of ancient human populations. J Virol. 1992;66:2288–2295.
73. Komurian F, Pelloquin F, de The G. In vivo genomic variability of human T-cell leukemia virus type I depends more upon geography than upon pathologies. J Virol. 1991;65:3770–3778.
74. Malik KT, Even J, Karpas A. Molecular cloning and complete nucleotide sequence of an adult T-cell leukemia virus/human T-cell leukemia virus type I (ATLV/HTLV-I) isolate of Caribbean origin: Relationship to other members of the ATLV/HTLV-I subgroup. J Gen Virol. 1988;69:1695–1710.
75. Gessain A, Yanagihara R, Franchini G, et al. Highly divergent molecular variants of human T-lymphotropic virus type I from isolated populations in Papua New Guinea and the Solomon Islands. Proc Natl Acad Sci. U S A. 1991;88:7694–7698.
76. Vidal AU, Gessain A, Yoshida M, et al. Phylogenetic classification of human T-cell leukemia/lymphoma virus type I genotypes in five major molecular and geographical subtypes. J Gen Virol. 1994;75:3655–3666.
77. Watanabe T, Seiki M, Tsujimoto H, et al. Sequence homology of the simian retrovirus genome with human T-cell leukemia virus type 1. Virology. 1985;144:59–65.
78. Yanagihara R, Saitou N, Nerurkar VR, et al. Molecular phylogeny and dissemination of human T-cell lymphotropic virus type I viewed within the context of primate evolution and human migration. Cell Mol Biol. 1995;41(Suppl 1):S145–S161.
79. Owen SM, Lal RB, Ikeda RA. Cloning and expression of a human T-lymphotropic virus type 1 protein with reverse transcriptase activity. J. Virol. 1998;72:5279–5284.

80. Lee H, Idler KB, Swanson P, et al. Complete nucleotide sequence of HTLV-II isolate NRA: Comparison of envelope sequence variation of HTLV-II isolates from US blood donors and US and Italian IV drug users. Virology 1993;196:57–69.
81. Takahashi H, Zhu SW, Ijichi S, et al. Nucleotide sequence analysis of human T cell leukemia virus. Type II (HTLV-II) isolates. AIDS Res Hum Retroviruses. 1993;9:721–732.
82. Pardi D, Kaplan JE, Coligan JE, et al. Identification and characterization of an extended tax protein in human T-cell lymphotropic virus type II subtype b isolates. J Virol. 1993;67:7663–7667.
83. Eiraku N, Novoa P, da Costa Ferreira M et al. Identification and characterization of a new and distinct molecular subtype of human T-cell lymphotropic virus type II. J Virol. 1996;70:1481–1492.
84. Switzer WM, Pieniazek D, Swanson P, et al. Phylogenetic relationship and geographic distribution of multiple human T-cell lymphotropic virus type II subtypes. J Virol. 1995;69:621–632.
85. Hall WW, Kubo T, Ijichi S, et al. Human T-cell leukemia/lymphoma virus, type II (HTLV-II): Emergence of an important newly recognized pathogen. Sem Virol. 1994;5:165–178.
86. Hinuma Y, Komoda H, Chosa T, et al. Antibodies to adult T-cell leukemia-virus–associated antigen (ATLA) in sera from patients with ATL and controls in Japan: A nation-wide seroepidemiologic study. Int J Cancer. 1982;29:631–635.
87. Schupbach J, Kalyanaraman VS, Sarngadharan MG, et al. Antibodies against three purified proteins of the human type C retrovirus, human T-cell leukemia-lymphoma virus, in adult T-cell leukemia-lymphoma patients and healthy blacks from the Caribbean. Cancer Res. 1983;43:886–891.
88. Schaffar-DesHayes L, Chavance M, Monplaisir N, et al. Antibodies to HTLV-I p24 in sera of blood donors, elderly people and patients with hemopoietic diseases in France and in French West Indies. Int J Cancer. 1984;34:667–670.
89. Miller GJ, Pegram SM, Kirkwood BR, et al. Ethnic composition, age and sex, together with location and standard of housing, as determinants of HTLV-I infection in an urban Trinidadian community. Int J Cancer. 1986;38:801–808.
90. Roman GC. The neuroepidemiology of tropical spastic paralysis. Ann Neurol. 1988;23(Suppl):S113–S120.
91. Bunn PA Jr, Schechter GP, Jaffe E, et al. Clinical course of retrovirus-associated adult T-cell lymphoma in the United States. N Engl J Med. 1983;309:257–264.
92. Blayney DW, Blattner WA, Robert-Guroff M, et al. The human T-cell leukemia-lymphoma virus in the southeastern United States. JAMA. 1983;250:1048–1052.
93. Centers for Disease Control and Prevention. Adult T-cell leukemia/lymphoma associated with human T-lymphotropic virus type I (HTLV-I) infection—North Carolina. MMWR Morb Mortal Wkly Rep. 1987;36:804–812.
94. Catovsky D, Greaves MF, Rose M, et al. Adult T-cell lymphoma-leukemia in blacks from the West Indies. Lancet. 1982;1:639–643.
95. Blattner WA, Nomura A, Clark JW, et al. Modes of transmission and evidence for viral latency from studies of human T-cell lymphotropic virus type I in Japanese migrant populations in Hawaii. Proc Natl Acad Sci U S A. 1986;83:4895–4898.
96. Dosik H, Denic S, Patel N, et al. Adult T-cell leukemia/lymphoma in Brooklyn. JAMA. 1988;259:2255–2257.
97. Wiktor SZ, Piot P, Mann JM, et al. Human T-cell lymphotropic virus type I (HTLV-I) among female prostitutes in Kinshasa, Zaire. J Infect Dis. 1990; 161:1073–1077.
98. Delaporte E, Dupont A, Peeters M, et al. Epidemiology of HTLV-I in Gabon (Western Equatorial Africa). Int J Cancer. 1988;42:687–689.
99. Yanagihara R, Jenkins CL, Alexander SS, et al. Human T lymphotropic virus type I infection in Papua New Guinea: High prevalence among the Hagahai confirmed by Western analysis. J Infect Dis. 1990;162:649–654.
100. Nogueira CM, Cavalcanti M, Schechter M, Ferreira OC Jr. Human T lymphotropic virus type I and II infections in healthy blood donors from Rio de Janeiro, Brazil. Vox Sang 1996;70:47–48.
101. Meytes D, Schochat B, Lee H, et al. A serological and molecular survey for HTLV-Iinfection in a high-risk Middle Eastern group. Lancet. 1990;336:1533–1535.
102. Singhal BS, Lalkaka JA, Sonoda S, et al. Human T-lymphotropic virus type I infections in Western India. AIDS. 1993;7:138–139.
103. Lee H, Swanson P, Shorty VS, et al. High rate of HTLV-II infection in seropositive IV drug abusers from New Orleans. Science. 1989;244:471–475.
104. Krook A, Blomberg J. HTLV-II among injecting drug users in stockholm. Scand J Infect Dis. 1994;26:129–132.
105. Gabbai AA, Bordin JO, Vieira-Filho JP, et al. Selectivity of human T-lymphotropic virus type-1 (HTLV-I) and HTLV-II infection among different populations in Brazil. Am J Trop Med Hyg. 1993;49:664–671.
106. Fukushima Y, Takahashi H, Hall WW, et al. Extraordinary high rate of HTLV type II seropositivity in intravenous drug abusers in South Vietnam. AIDS Res Human Retroviruses. 1995;11:637–645.
107. Robert-Guroff M, Weiss SH, Giron JA, et al. Prevalence of antibodies to HTLV-I, -II, and -III in intravenous drug abusers from an AIDS endemic region. JAMA. 1986;255:3133–3137.
108. Levine PH, Jacobson S, Elliott R, et al. HTLV-II infection in Florida Indians. AIDS Res Hum Retroviruses. 1993;9:123–127.
109. Feigenbaum F, Fang C, Sandler SG. Human T-lymphotropic virus type II in Panamanian Guaymi Indians. Transfusion. 1994;34:158–161.
110. Biglione M, Gessain A, Quiruelas S, et al. Endemic HTLV-II infection among Tobas and Matacos Amerindians from North Argentina. J Acquir Immun Defic Syndr. 1993;6:631–633.
111. Lal RB, Povoa M, Lai AA. Seroprevalence of HTLV-II in Paragaminos, State of Para, Brazil. J Acquir Immun Defic Syndr. 1992;5:634–636.
112. Fujiyama C, Fujiyoshi T, Miura T, et al. A new endemic focus of human T lymphotropic virus type II carriers among Orinoco natives in Colombia. J Infect Dis. 1993;168:1075–1077.
113. Cartier L, Araya F, Castillo JL, et al. Southernmost carriers of HTLV-I/II in the world. Jpn J Cancer Res. 1993;84:1–3.
114. Goubau P, Desmyter J, Ghesquiere J, Kasereka B. HTLV-II among pygmies. Nature. 1992;359:201.
115. Froment A, Delaporte E, Dazza MC, Larouze B. HTLV-II among pygmies from Cameroon. AIDS Res Hum Retroviruses. 1993;9:707.
116. Goubau P, Liu HF, DeLange GG, et al. HTLV-II seroprevalence in pygmies across Africa since 1970. AIDS Res Hum Retroviruses. 1993;9:709–713.
117. Goubau P, Vandamme A, Beuselinck K, Desmyter J. Proviral HTLV-I and HTLV-II in the Efe pygmies of northeastern Zaire. J Acquir Immune Defic Syndr Hum Retrovirol. 1996;12:208–209.
118. Lee HH, Weiss SH, Brown LS, et al. Patterns of HIV-1 and HTLV-I/II in intravenous drug abusers from the middle Atlantic and central regions of the USA. J Infect Dis. 1990;162:347–352.
119. Khabbaz RF, Hartel D, Lairmore M, et al. Human T lymphotropic virus type II (HTLV-II) infection in a cohort of New York intravenous drug users: An old infection? J Infect Dis. 1991;163:252–256.
120. Oguma S, Imamura Y, Kusumoto Y, et al. Accelerated declining tendency of human T-cell leukemia virus type I carrier rates among younger blood donors in Kumamoto, Japan. Cancer Res. 1992;52:2620–2623.
121. Morofuji-Hirata M, Kajiyama W, Nakashima K, et al. Prevalence of antibody to human T-cell lymphotropic virus type I in Okinawa, Japan, after an interval of 9 years. Am J Epidemiol. 1993;137:43–48.
122. Ueda K, Kusuhara K, Tokugawa K, et al. Mother-to-child transmission of human T-lymphotropic virus type I (HTLV-I): An extended follow-up study on children between 18 and 22–24 years old in Okinawa, Japan. Int J Cancer. 1993;53:597–600.
123. Sommerfelt MA, Williams BP, Clapham PR, et al. Human T-cell leukemia viruses use a receptor determined by human chromosome 17. Science. 1988;242:1557–1559.
124. Tajima Y, Tashiro K, Camerini D. Assignment of the possible HTLV receptor gene to chromosome 17q21–q23. Somat Cell Mol Genet. 1997;23:225–227.
125. Wiktor SZ, Pate EJ, Murphy EL, et al. Mother-to-child transmission of human T-cell lymphotropic virus type I (HTLV-I) in Jamaica: Association with antibodies to envelope glycoprotein (gp46) epitopes. J Acquir Immune Defic Syndr. 1993;6:1162–1167.
126. Kajiyama W, Kashiwagi S, Ikematsu H, et al. Intrafamilial transmission of adult T-cell leukemia virus. J Infect Dis. 1986;154:851–857.
127. Ando Y, Nakano S, Saito K, et al. Transmission of adult T-cell leukemia retrovirus (HTLV-I) from mother to child: Comparison of bottle-fed with breast-fed babies. Jpn J Cancer Res. 1987;78:322–324.
128. Komuro A, Hayami M, Fujii H, et al. Vertical transmission of adult T-cell leukemia virus. Lancet. 1983;i:240.
129. Nyambi PN, Ville Y, Louwagie J, et al. Mother-to-child transmission of human T-cell lymphotropic virus types I and II (HTLV-I/II) in Gabon: A prospective follow-up of 4 years. J Acquir Immune Defic Syndr Hum Retrovirol. 1996;12:187–192.
130. Kusuhara K, Sonoda S, Takahashi K, et al. Mother-to-child transmission of human T-cell leukemia virus type I (HTLV-I): A fifteen-year follow-up study in Okinawa, Japan. Int J Cancer. 1987;40:755–757.
131. Oki T, Yoshinaga M, Otsuda H, et al. A sero-epidemiological study on mother-to-child transmission of HTLV-I in southern Kyushu, Japan. Asia Oceania J Obstet Gynaecol. 1992;18:371–377.
132. Hino S, Yamaguchi K, Katamine S, et al. Mother-to-child transmission of human T-cell leukemia virus type-I. Jpn J Cancer Res. 1985;76:474–480.
133. Hino S, Katamine S, Miyamoto T, et al. Association between maternal antibodies to the external envelope glycoprotein and vertical transmission of human T-lymphotropic virus type I. Maternal anti-env antibodies correlate with protection in non–breast-fed children. J Clin Invest. 1995;95:2920–2925.
134. Hino S, Sugiyama H, Doi H, et al. Breaking the cycle of HTLV-I transmission via carrier mothers' milk. Lancet. 1987;ii:158–159.
135. Sawada T, Iwahara Y, Ishii K, et al. Immunoglobulin prophylaxis against milkborne transmission of human T-cell leukemia virus type I in rabbits. J Infect Dis. 1991;164:1193–1196.
136. Takahashi K, Takezaki T, Oki T, et al. Inhibitory effect of maternal antibody on mother-to-child transmission of human T-lymphotropic virus type I. The Mother-to-Child Transmission Study Group. Int J Cancer. 1991;49:673–677.
137. Murphy EL, Figueroa JP, Gibbs WN, et al. Sexual transmission of human T-lymphotropic virus type I (HTLV-I). Ann Intern Med. 1989;111:555–560.
138. Kaplan JE, Khabbaz RF, Murphy EL, et al. Male-to-female transmission of human T-cell lymphotropic virus types I and II: Association with viral load. The Retrovirus Epidemiology Donor Study Group. J Acquir Immune Defic Syndr Hum Retrovirol. 1996;12:193–201.
139. Nakano S, Ando Y, Ichijo M, et al. Search for possible routes of vertical and horizontal transmission of adult T-cell leukemia virus. Jpn J Cancer Res. 1984;75:1044–1045.
140. Meyer RD, Moudgil T, Detels R, et al. Seroprevalence of human T-cell leukemia viruses in selected populations of homosexual men. J Infect Dis. 1990;162:1370–1372.
141. Goudsmit J, deWolf F, van de Wiel B, et al. Spread of human T-cell leukemia virus (HTLV-I) in the Dutch homosexual community. J Virol. 1987;23:115–121.
142. Bartholomew C, Saxinger WC, Clark JW, et al. Transmission of HTLV-1 and HIV among homosexual men in Trinidad. JAMA 1987;257:2604–2608.

143. Okochi K, Sato H, Hinuma Y. A retrospective study on transmission of adult T-cell leukemia virus by blood transfusion: Seroconversion in recipients. Vox Sang. 1984;46:245–253.
144. Kamihira S, Nakasima S, Oyakawa Y, et al. Transmission of human T-cell lymphotropic virus type I by blood transfusion before and after mass screening of sera from seropositive donors. Vox Sang. 1987;52:43–44.
145. Dekaban G, Inwood M, Waters D, et al. Absence of human T-lymphotropic virus types I and II infection in an Ontario hemophilia population. Transfusion. 1992;32:513–516.
146. Canavaggio M, Leckie G, Allain JP, et al. The prevalence of antibody to HTLV-I/II in United States plasma donors and in United States and French hemophiliacs. Transfusion. 1990;30:780–782.
147. Kleinman S, Swanson P, Allain JP, Lee H. Transfusion transmission of human T-lymphotropic virus types I and II: Serologic and polymerase chain reaction results in recipients identified through look-back investigations. Transfusion. 1993;33:14–18.
148. Gout O, Baulac M, Gessain A, et al. Rapid development of myelopathy after HTLV-I infection acquired by transfusion during cardiac transplantation. N Engl J Med. 1990;322:383–387.
149. Licensure of screening tests for antibody to human T-lymphotropic virus type I. MMWR Morb Mortal Wkly Rep. 1988;37:736–740, 745–747.
150. Delaporte E, Peeters M, Bardy JL, et al. Blood transfusion as a major risk factor for HTLV-I infection among hospitalized children in Gabon (Equatorial Africa). J Acquir Immune Defic Syndr. 1993;6:424–428.
151. Frery N, Chavance M, Valette I, et al. HTLV-I infection in French West Indies: A case-control study. Eur J Epidemiol. 1991;7:175–182.
152. Lee HH, Swanson P, Rosenblatt, JD, et al. Relative prevalence and risk factors of HTLV-I and HTLV-II infection in US blood donors. Lancet. 1991;337:1435–1439.
153. Eble BE, Busch MP, Guiltinan AM, et al. Determination of human T lymphotropic virus type by polymerase chain reaction and correlation with risk factors in northern California blood donors. J Infect Dis. 1993;167:954–957. [Published erratum appears in J Infect Dis. 1993;168:262.]
154. Centers for Disease Control and Prevention and the U.S.P.H.S. Working Group. Guidelines for counseling persons infected with human T-lymphotropic virus type I (HTLV-I) and type II (HTLV-II). Ann Intern Med. 1993;118:448–454.
155. Amin RM, Jones B, Rupert M, et al. Risk of retroviral infection among retrovirology laboratory and health care workers. Abstract T-20. Presented at the Ninety-second General Meeting of the American Society for Microbiology, New Orleans, La, May 26–30, 1992.
156. Anon. Recommendations for prevention of HIV transmission in healthcare settings. MMWR Morb Mortal Wkly Rep. 1987;36(Suppl):S3–S18.
157. Update: Serologic testing for human T-lymphotropic virus type I—United States. 1989 and 1990. MMWR Morb Mortal Wkly Rep. 1992;41:259–262.
158. Constantine NT. Serologic tests for the retroviruses: Approaching a decade of evolution. AIDS 1993;7:1–13.
159. Rosenblatt JD, Zack JA, Chen IS, Lee H. Recent advances in detection of human T-cell leukemia viruses type I and II infection. Nat Immun Cell Growth Regul. 1990;9:143–149.
160. Ehrlich GD, Glaser JB, LaVigne K, et al. Prevalence of human T-cell leukemia/lymphoma virus (HTLV) type II infection among high-risk individuals: Type-specific identification of HTLVs by polymerase chain reaction. Blood. 1989;74:1658–1664.
161. Viscidi RP, Hill PM, Li SJ, et al. Diagnosis and differentiation of HTLV-I and HTLV-II infection by enzyme immunoassays using synthetic peptides. J Acquir Immune Defic Syndr. 1991;4:1190–1198.
162. Takatsuki K, Yamaguchi K, Kawano F, et al. Clinical aspects of adult T-cell leukemia/lymphoma. Curr Top Microbiol Immunol. 1985;115:89–97.
163. Hattori T, Uchiyama T, Toibana T, et al. Surface phenotype of Japanese adult T-cell leukemia cells characterized by monoclonal antibodies. Blood. 1981;58:645–647.
164. Waldmann TA, Greene WC, Sarin PS, et al. Functional and phenotypic comparison of human T-cell leukemia/lymphoma virus positive adult T-cell leukemia with human T-cell leukemia/lymphoma virus negative Sézary leukemia, and their distinction using anti-Tac monoclonal antibody identifying the human receptor for T-cell growth factor. J Clin Invest. 1984;73:1711–1718.
165. Waldmann TA, White JD, Goldman CK, et al. The interleukin-2 receptor: A target for monoclonal antibody treatment of human T-cell lymphotrophic virus I–induced adult T-cell leukemia. Blood. 1993;82:1701–1712.
166. Depper JM, Leonard WJ, Kronke M, et al. Augmented T-cell growth receptor expression in HTLV-I–infected human leukemic T-cells. J Immunol. 1984;133:1691–1695.
167. Kinoshita K, Amagasaki T, Ikeda S, et al. Preleukemic state of adult T-cell leukemia: Abnormal T lymphocytosis induced by human adult T-cell leukemia lymphoma virus. Blood. 1985; 66:120–127.
168. Yoshida M, Seiki M, Yamaguchi K, Takatsuki K. Monoclonal integration of human T-cell leukemia provirus in all primary tumors of adult T-cell leukemia suggests causative role of human T-cell leukemia virus in the disease. Proc Natl Acad Sci U S A. 1984;81:2534–2537.
169. Tajima K, Kuroishi T. Estimation or rate of incidence of ATL among ATLV (HTLV-I) carriers in Kyushu, Japan. Jpn J Clin Oncol. 1985;15:423–430.
170. Murphy EL, Hanchard B, Figueroa JP, et al. Modelling the risk of adult T-cell leukemia/lymphoma in persons infected with human T-lymphotropic virus type I. Int J Cancer. 1989;43:250–253.
171. Shimoyama M. Diagnostic criteria and classification of clinical subtypes of adult T-cell leukaemia-lymphoma. A report from the Lymphoma Study Group (1984–87). Br J Haematol. 1991;79:428–437.
172. Davey FR, Hutchison RE. Pathology and immunology of adult T-cell leukemia/lymphoma. Curr Opin Oncol. 1991;3:13–20.
173. Ejima E, Rosenblatt JD, Ou J, Prager D. Parathyroid hormone–related protein gene expression and human T-cell leukemia virus-1 infection. Miner Electrolyte Metab. 1995;21:143–147.
174. Berger R. Chromosomal abnormalities in T-cell malignant lymphoma. Bull Cancer. 1991;78:283–290.
175. Sanada I, Tanaka R, Kumagai E, et al. Chromosomal aberrations in adult T-cell leukemia: Relationship to the clinical severity. Blood. 1985;65:649–654.
176. Newton RC, Limpuangthip P, Greenberg S, et al. Strongyloides stercoralis hyperinfection in a carrier of HTLV-I virus with evidence of selective immunosuppression. Am J Med. 1992;92:202–208.
177. Nakada K, Yamaguchi K, Furugen S, et al. Monoclonal integration of HTLV-I proviral DNA in patients with strongyloidiasis. Int J Cancer. 1987;40:145–148.
178. Plumelle Y, Gonin C, Edouard A, et al. Effect of *Strongyloides stercoralis* infection and eosinophilia on age at onset and prognosis of adult T-cell leukemia. Am J Clin Pathol. 1997;107:81–87.
179. Sato Y, Shiroma Y. Concurrent infections with *Strongyloides* and T-cell leukemia virus and their possible effect on immune responses of host. Clin Immunol Immunopathol. 1989;52:214–224.
180. Yamaguchi K, Nishimura H, Kohrogi H, et al. A proposal for smoldering adult T-cell leukemia: A clinicopathological study of five cases. Blood. 1983;62:758–766.
181. Kawano F, Yamaguchi K, Nishimura H, et al. Variation in the clinical courses of adult T-cell leukemia. Cancer. 1985;55:851–856.
182. LaGrenade L, Harnchar B, Fletcher V, et al. Infective dermatitis of Jamaican children: A marker for HTLV-I infection. Lancet. 1990;336:1345–1347.
183. Murai K, Tachibana N, Shiori S, et al. Suppression of delayed-type hypersensitivity to PPD and PHA in elderly HTLV-I carriers. J Acquir Immune Defic Syndr. 1990;3:1006–1009.
184. Bartholomew C, Blattner W, Cleghorn F. Progression to AIDS in homosexual men co-infected with HIV and HTLV-I in Trinidad. Lancet. 1987;2:1469.
185. Gotuzzo E, Escamilla J, Phillips IA, et al. The impact of human T-lymphotropic virus type I/II infection on the prognosis of sexually acquired cases of acquired immune deficiency syndrome. Arch Intern Med. 1992;152:1429–1432.
186. Cleghorn FR, Blattner WA. Does human T-cell lymphotropic virus type I and human immunodeficiency virus type I co-infection accelerate acquired immune deficiency syndrome? Arch Intern Med. 1992;152:1372–1373.
187. Taguchi H, Kinoshita KI, Takatsuki K, et al. An intensive chemotherapy of adult T-cell leukemia/lymphoma: CHOP followed by etoposide, vindesine, ranimustine, and mitoxantrone with granulocyte colony–stimulating factor support. J Acquired Immune Defic Syndr Hum Retrovirol. 1996;12:182–186.
188. Tsukasaki K, Ikeda S, Murata K, et al. Characteristics of chemotherapy-induced clinical remission in long survivors with aggressive adult T-cell leukemia/lymphoma. Leuk Res. 1993;17:157–166.
189. Daenen S, Rojer RA, Smit JW, et al. Successful chemotherapy with deoxycoformycin in adult T-cell lymphoma-leukemia. Br J Haematol. 1984;58:723–727.
190. Kuwazuru Y, Hanada S, Furukawa T, et al. Expression of P-glycoprotein in adult T-cell leukemia cells. Blood. 1990;76:2065–2071.
191. Chuang SE, Doong SI, Lin MT, Cheng AL. Tax of the human T-lymphotropic virus type I transactivates promoter of the MDR-1 gene. Biochem Biophys Res Commun. 1997;238:482–486.
192. Shimamoto Y, Kikuchi M, Funai N, et al. Spontaneous regression in adult T-cell leukemia/lymphoma. Cancer. 1993;72:735–740.
193. Koyama Y, Tanaka Y, Oda S, et al. Antiviral and antiproliferative activities of recombinant human interferon alpha 2, beta and gamma on HTLV-I and ATL cells in vitro. Sangyo Ika Daigaku Zasshi. 1990;12:149–161.
194. Matsushima M, Yoneyama A, Nakamura T, et al. A first case of complete remission of beta-interferon sensitive adult T-cell leukemia. Eur J Haematol. 1987;39:282–287.
195. Tamura K, Makino S, Araki Y, et al. Recombinant interferon beta and gamma in the treatment of adult T-cell leukemia. Cancer. 1987;59:1059–1062.
196. Saigo K, Shiozawa S, Shiozawa K, et al. Alpha-interferon treatment for adult T-cell leukemia: Low levels of circulating alpha-interferon and its clinical effectiveness. Blut. 1988;56:83–86.
197. Gill PS, Harrington W Jr, Kaplan MH, et al. Treatment of adult T-cell leukemia-lymphoma with a combination of interferon alfa and zidovudine. N Engl J Med. 1995;332:1744–1748.
198. Hermine O, Bouscary D, Gessain A, et al. Brief report: Treatment of adult T-cell leukemia-lymphoma with zidovudine and interferon alfa. N Engl J Med. 1995;332:1749–1751.
199. Waldmann TA, White JD, Carrasquillo JA, et al. Radioimmunotherapy of interleukin-2R alpha–expressing adult T-cell leukemia with yttrium-90-labeled anti-Tac. Blood. 1995;86:4063–4075.
200. Akizuki S, Setoguchi M, Nakazato O, et al. Case studies: An autopsy case of human T-lymphotropic virus type-I–associated myelopathy. Hum Pathol. 1988;19:988–990.
201. Bhigjee AI, Wiley CA, Wachsman W, et al. HTLV-I–associated myelopathy: Clinicopathologic correlation with localization of provirus to spinal cord. Neurology. 1991;41:1990–1992.
202. Ohama E, Horikawa Y, Shimizu T, et al. Demyelination and remyelination in spinal cord lesions of human lymphotropic virus type I–associated myelopathy. Acta Neuropathol. 1990;81:78–83.
203. Kaplan JE, Osame M, Kubota H, et al. The risk of development of HTLV-

I–associated myelopathy/tropical spastic paraparesis among persons infected with HTLV-I. J Acquir Immun Defic Syndr. 1990;3:1096–1101.
204. Vernant JC, Maurs L, Gessain A, et al. Endemic tropical spastic paraparesis associated with human T-lymphotropic virus type I: A clinical and seroepidemiological study of 25 cases. Ann Neurol. 1987;21:123–130.
205. Kawai H, Nishida Y, Takagi M, et al. HTLV-I associated myelopathy with adult T-cell leukemia. Neurology. 1989;39:1129–1131.
206. Lee JW, Fox EP, Rodgers-Johnson P, et al. T-cell lymphoma, tropical spastic paraparesis, and malignant fibrous histiocytoma in a patient with human T-cell lymphotropic virus, type I. Ann Intern Med. 1989;110:239–241.
207. Yasui C, Fukaya T, Koizumi H, et al. HTLV-I–associated myelopathy in a patient with adult T-cell leukemia. J Am Acad Dermatol. 1991;24:633–637.
208. Osame M, Matsumoto M, Usuku K, et al. Chronic progressive myelopathy associated with elevated antibodies to human T-lymphotropic virus type I and adult T-cell leukemia like cells. Ann Neurol. 1987;21:117–122.
209. Gessain A, Gout O. Chronic myelopathy associated with human T-lymphotropic virus type I (HTLV-I). Ann Intern Med. 1992;117:933–946.
210. Gout O, Gessain A, Bolgert F, et al. Chronic myelopathies associated with human T-lymphotropic virus type I. A clinical, serologic, and immunovirologic study of ten patients in France. Arch Neurol. 1989;46:255–260.
211. Shibasaki H, Endo C, Kuroda Y, et al. Clinical picture of HTLV-I associated myelopathy. J Neurol Sci. 1988;87:15–24.
212. Roman GC, Roman LN. Tropical spastic paraparesis. A clinical study of 50 patients from Tumaco (Colombia) and review of the worldwide features of the syndrome. J Neurol Sci. 1988;87:121–138.
213. Levin MC, Lehky TJ, Flerlage AN, et al. Immunologic analysis of a spinal cord-biopsy specimen from a patient with human T-cell lymphotropic virus type I–associated neurologic disease. N Engl J Med. 1997;336:839–845.
214. Rodgers-Johnson P, Morgan OS, Mora C, et al. The role of HTLV-I in tropical spastic paraparesis in Jamaica. Ann Neurol. 1988;23(Suppl):S121–S126.
215. Tournier-Lasserve E, Gout O, Gessain A, et al. HTLV-I, brain abnormalities on magnetic resonance imaging, and relation with multiple sclerosis. Lancet. 1987;ii:49–50.
216. Godoy AJ, Kira J, Hasuo K, Goto I. Characterization of cerebral white matter lesions of HTLV-I associated myelopathy/tropical spastic paraparesis in comparison with multiple sclerosis and collagen-vasculitis: A semiquantitative MRI study. J Neurol Sci. 1995;133:102–111.
217. Roman GC, Spencer PS, Schoenberg BS. Tropical myeloneuropathies: The hidden endemias. Neurology. 1985;35:1158–1170.
218. Iwasaki Y. Pathology of chronic myelopathy associated with HTLV-I infection (HAM/TSP). J Neurol Sci. 1990;96:103–123.
219. Moore GR, Traugott U, Scheinbert LC, Raine CS. Tropical spastic paraparesis: A model of virus-induced, cytotoxic T-cell–mediated demyelination? Ann Neurol. 1989;26:523–530.
220. Koenig S, Woods RM, Brewah YA, et al. Characterization of MHC class I restricted cytotoxic T cell responses to tax in HTLV-1 infected patients with neurological disease. J Immunol. 1993;151:3874–3883.
221. Hollsberg P, Hafler DA. What is the pathogenesis of human T-cell lymphotropic virus type I–associated myelopathy/tropical spastic paraparesis? Ann Neurol. 1995;37:143–145.
222. Hollsberg P, Hafler DA. Seminars in medicine of the Beth Israel Hospital, Boston. Pathogenesis of diseases induced by human lymphotropic virus type I infection. N Engl J Med. 1993;328:1173–1182.
223. Matsuo H, Nakamura T, Tsujihata M, et al. Plasmapheresis in treatment of human T-lymphotropic virus type-I associated myelopathy. Lancet. 1988;ii:1109–1113.
224. Matsuo H, Nakamura T, Shibayama K, et al. Long-term follow-up of immunomodulation in treatment of HTLV-I associated myelopathy. Lancet. 1989;i:790.
225. Izumo S, Goto I, Itoyama Y, et al. Interferon-alpha is effective in HTLV-I associated myelopathy: A multicenter, randomized, double-blind, controlled trial. Neurology. 1996;46:1016–1021.
226. Shibayama K, Nakamura T, Nagasato K, et al. Interferon-alpha treatment in HTLV-Iassociated myelopathy. Studies of clinical and immunological aspects. J Neurol Sci. 1991;106:186–192.
227. Harrington WJ Jr, Sheremata WA, Snodgrass SR, et al. Tropical spastic paraparesis/HTLV-I associated myelopathy (TSP/HAM): Treatment with an anabolic steroid danazol. AIDS Res Hum Retroviruses. 1991;7:1031–1034.
228. Tendler CL, Greenberg SJ, Blattner WA, et al. Transactivation of interleukin 2 and its receptor induces immune activation in human T-cell lymphotropic virus type I–associated myelopathy: Pathogenic implications and a rationale for immunotherapy. Proc Natl Acad Sci U S A. 1990;87:5218–5222.
229. Gout O, Gessain A, Iba-Zizen M, et al. The effect of zidovudine on chronic myelopathy associated with HTLV-I. J Neurol. 1991;238:108–109.
230. Sheremata WA, Benedict D, Squilacote DC, et al. High-dose zidovudine induction in HTLV-I–associated myelopathy: Safety and possible efficacy. Neurology. 1993;43:2125–2129.
231. Nishioka K, Nakajima T, Hasunuma T, Sato K. Rheumatic manifestation of human leukemia virus infection. Rheum Dis Clin North Am. 1993;19:489–503.
232. Mochizuki M, Tajima K, Watanabe T, Yamaguchi K. Human T lymphotropic virus type 1 uveitis. Br J Ophthalmol. 1994;78:149–154.
233. Morgan OS, Rodgers-Johnson P, Mora C, Char G. HTLV-I and polymyositis in Jamaica. Lancet. 1989;ii:1184–1187.
234. LaGrenade L, Schwartz RA, Janniger CK. Childhood dermatitis in the tropics: With special emphasis on infective dermatitis, a marker for infection with human T-cell leukemia virus-I. Cutis. 1996;58:115–118.
235. Maruyama I, Mori S, Kawabata M, Osame M. Bronchopneumonopathy in HTLV-I associated myelopathy (HAM) and non-HAM HTLV-I carriers. Nippon Kyobu Shikkan Gakkai Zasshi. 1992;30:775–779.
236. Nakamura H, Eguchi K, Nakamura T, et al. High prevalence of Sjögren's syndrome in patients with HTLV-I associated myelopathy. Ann Rheum Dis. 1997;56:167–172.
237. Yamazaki H. Development of collagen vascular diseases and production of autoantibodies in HTLV-I env-pX transgenic rats (Japanese). Hokkaido Igaku Zasshi. 1996;71:325–343.
238. Ghosh SK, Abrams JT, Terunuma H, et al. Human T-cell leukemia virus type I tax/rex DNA and RNA in cutaneous T-cell lymphoma. Blood. 1994;84:2663–2671.
239. Pancake BA, Zucker-Franklin D, Coutavas EE. The cutaneous T-cell lymphoma, mycosis fungoides, is a human T-cell lymphotropic virus–associated disease. A study of 50 patients. J Clin Invest. 1995;95:547–554.
240. Zucker-Franklin D, Coutavas EE, Rush MG, Zouzias DC. Detection of human T-lymphotropic virus–like particles in cultures of peripheral blood lymphocytes from patients with mycosis fungoides. Proc Natl Acad Sci U S A. 1991;88:7630–7634.
241. Pancake BA, Wassef EH, Zucker-Franklin D. Demonstration of antibodies to human T-cell lymphotropic virus-I tax in patients with the cutaneous T-cell lymphoma, mycosis fungoides, who are seronegative for antibodies to the structural proteins of the virus. Blood. 1996;88:3004–3009.
242. Zucker-Franklin D, Hooper WC, Evatt BL. Human lymphotropic retroviruses associated with mycosis fungoides: Evidence that human T-cell lymphotropic virus type I (HTLV-II) as well as HTLV-I may play a role in the disease. Blood. 1992;80:1537–1545.
243. Lal RB, Owen SM, Rudolph DL, et al. In vivo cellular tropism of human T-lymphotropic virus II is not restricted to CD8+ cells. Virology. 1995;210:441–447.
244. Ijichi S, Ramundo MB, Takahashi H, Hall WW. In vivo cellular tropism of human T-cell leukemia virus type II (HTLV-II). J Exp Med. 1992;176:293–296.
245. Popovic M, Lange-Wantzin G, Sarin PS, et al. Transformation of human umbilical cord blood T-cells by human T-cell leukemia/lymphoma virus. Proc Natl Acad Sci U S A. 1983;80:5402–5406.
246. Richardson JH, Edwards AJ, Cruickshank JK, et al. In vivo cellular tropism of human T-cell leukemia virus type 1. J Virol. 1990;64:5682–5687.
247. Rosenblatt JD, Golde DW, Wachsman W, et al. A second isolate of HTLV-II associated with atypical hairy-cell leukemia. N Engl J Med. 1986;315:372–377.
248. Loughran TP Jr, Coyle T, Sherman MP, et al. Detection of human T-cell leukemia/lymphoma virus, Type II, in a patient with large granular lymphocytic leukemia. Blood. 1992;80:1116–1119.
249. Hjelle B, Mills R, Swenson S, et al. Incidence of hairy cell leukemia, mycosis fungoides, and chronic lymphocytic leukemia in first known HTLV-II–endemic population. J Infect Dis 1991;163:435–440.
250. Harrington WJ Jr, Sheremata W, Hjelle B, et al. Spastic ataxia associated with human T-cell lymphotropic virus type II infection. Ann Neurol. 1993;33:411–414.
251. Hjelle B, Appenzeller O, Mills R, et al. Chronic neurodegenerative disease associated with HTLV-II infection. Lancet. 1992;339:645–646.
252. Jacobson S, Lehky T, Nishimura M, et al. Isolation of HTLV-II from a patient with chronic, progressive neurological disease clinically indistinguishable from HTLV-I–associated myelopathy/tropical spastic paraparesis. Ann Neurol. 1993;33:392–396.
253. Rosenblatt JD, Tomkins P, Rosenthal M, et al. Progressive spastic myelopathy in a patient co-infected with HIV-I and HTLV-II: Autoantibodies to the human homologue of rig in blood and cerebrospinal fluid. AIDS. 1992;6:1151–1158.
254. Rosenblatt JD, Plaeger-Marshall S, Giorgi JV, et al. A clinical, hematologic, and immunologic analysis of 21 HTLV-II–infected intravenous drug users. Blood. 1990;76:409–417. (Erratum published in Blood. 1990;76:1901.)
255. Modahl LE, Young KC, Varney KF, et al. Are HTLV-II–seropositive injection drug users at increased risk of bacterial pneumonia, abscess, and lymphadenopathy? J Acquir Immune Defic Syndr Hum Retrovirol. 1997;16:169–175.
256. Murphy EL, Glynn SA, Fridey J, et al. Increased prevalence of infectious diseases and other adverse outcomes in human T lymphotropic virus types I– and II–infected blood donors. Retrovirus Epidemiology Donor Study (REDS) Study Group. J Infect Dis. 1997;176:1468–1475.

Chapter 157

Human Immunodeficiency Viruses

HOWARD Z. STREICHER
MARVIN S. REITZ, JR.
ROBERT C. GALLO

The acquired immunodeficiency syndrome (AIDS) was recognized in the United States in 1981 with a sudden outbreak of opportunistic infections, *Pneumocystis carinii* pneumonia, and Kaposi's sarcoma (KS).[1–3] On the basis of the epidemiologic features, association with the loss of CD4$^+$ lymphocytes and immunosuppression, and likely infectious etiology, a new human retrovirus was pursued as a causal agent. The field of retrovirology had opened just a decade earlier with the description of reverse transcriptase (RT) and with the discovery of human T cell leukemia/lymphoma virus type I and type II (HTLV-I and HTLV-II), the first two known human retroviruses, in 1979 and 1981 (reported in 1980 and 1982, respectively).[4, 5]

By 1984, the detection, isolation, and propagation of the human immunodeficiency virus type 1 (HIV-1), the third human retrovirus, had led to the development of a diagnostic test, an increasingly detailed understanding of the molecular biology of this virus, and, most important, the beginning of rational antiviral therapy.[6–12] After a long era of expanding research, new therapeutic combinations (RT and protease inhibitors), combined with the ability to measure circulating viral RNA, have led to a dramatically improved clinical course for persons fortunate enough to have access to therapy. Within a brief period, technological advances have brought a clear understanding of viral dynamics and the disease process, focusing attention on viral replication, host immune responses, and T-cell dynamics while at the same time confirming the causal role of the virus. Equally dramatic has been the elucidation of how HIV enters cells utilizing both the CD4 molecule and a chemokine receptor as a dual receptor system, as well as the recent solution of the three-dimensional structure of the viral envelope protein. Contemporary retrovirology is largely devoted to the study of HIV-1 and of HIV-associated diseases. The molecular and cellular biology of this virus is now better understood than that of almost any other in history; yet there remains much to be done in the areas of prevention, therapy, vaccines, and immune reconstitution.

Viruses are obligate intracellular parasites, and every aspect of the virus is in some way relevant to virus-host relationships. This chapter outlines the life cycle, the molecular and cellular biology, and the structure of HIV-1, with emphasis on the pathogenesis and therapy of AIDS and associated neurologic diseases and tumors. Although the division of the chapter into sections is useful for organization of the information presented, in reality the subjects cannot be separated from one another; from the perspective of both virus and host, the process of infection is a continuous series of connected interactions.

BACKGROUND

Retroviruses constitute a large and diverse family of enveloped RNA viruses that use as a replication strategy the transcription of virion RNA into linear double-stranded DNA with subsequent integration into the host genome. The characteristic enzyme used for this process, an RNA-dependent DNA polymerase that reverses the flow of genetic information, is known as reverse transcriptase. The unique lifestyle of the retrovirus involves two forms, a DNA provirus and an RNA-containing infectious virion. The basic structure, genetic organization, and life cycle of HIV-1 are similar to those of most retroviruses, but with some additional features.

As RNA viruses, retroviruses have the survival advantage of great genetic diversity. As viruses with a DNA intermediate in their replication cycle, they also have the advantage of latency, as do many DNA viruses, but even more so because the DNA provirus is integrated into the chromosomal DNA. As a CD4$^+$ T-cell– and macrophage-tropic virus, HIV has the advantage of reducing the effectiveness of host immune attacks.

Retroviruses are typically 100 nm in diameter and contain two single strands of RNA, which permits recombination between the strands (Fig. 157–1). The typical genome is 10 kilobases (Kb) in size and contains three major structural genes, namely, *gag, pol,* and *env.* HIV-1 also contains several additional genes; similar "extra" genes—first described in HTLV-I—are essential to viral replication. These complicated genomes are characteristic of human retroviruses. Although sharing T-cell tropism, genomic complexity, and functional similarities, the four known human retroviruses—HIV-1 and -2 and HTLV-I and-II—and related animal viruses belong to two different groups.

Retroviruses have been classified by a number of different biologic features, and at present, infectious retroviruses are grouped into at least seven genera.[13] The human retroviruses include lentiviruses (HIV-1 and -2), *onc* viruses (HTLV-I and -II), and human endogenous virus (HERV-K).[14]

Oncogenic retroviruses occur in all classes of vertebrates. The first infectious agents that produced cancer in chickens were isolated by Ellerman and Bang (1908) and by Peyton Rous (1911).[15, 16] These workers were considerably ahead of their time, and their work produced little immediate impact. Rous won a Nobel prize in 1966. The pioneering work of Ludwig Gross in the 1950s stimulated renewed interest by demonstrating that oncogenic viruses could produce tumors in mammals.[17]

The study of retroviral infection at the cellular level has made continuing contributions to the development of molecular biology and medicine. Experimental observation and vision led to a hypothesis that challenged the "central dogma" of molecular biology—namely, that genetic information must necessarily flow from DNA to RNA.[18, 19] The discovery of the crucial enzyme for this process, RT, helped to initiate the modern era of molecular biology.[20, 21] The discovery that a retroviral transforming gene, v-*src*, was also present in the host cellular genome, c-*src*, demonstrated the cellular origin of retroviral oncogenes and opened oncology to the molecular exploration of the control of cell growth. Despite the common occurrence of these viruses in a number of mammalian species, it once seemed unlikely that any human retroviruses existed. This picture was changed with the discovery of HTLV-I, which was causally associated first with adult T-cell leukemia, an aggressive T-cell lymphoma,[5] and later with a neurologic disease, tropical spastic paraparesis (TSP).[22] Although there is little variation among HTLV-I isolates, HTLV-II, the second human retrovirus, is 50% identical to HTLV-I at the genomic level.[4] Similarly, HIV-2, the fourth human retrovirus, was identified as a serologic variant of HIV-1, the third human retrovirus, and later was isolated from patients in western Africa.[23, 24] Some types of simian immunodeficiency virus (SIV) are so closely related to HIV-2 that they may form an overlapping continuum with recent common ancestors. HIV-2 may infect several monkey species, and SIV has been detected as a human infection in several laboratory workers. SIVs have been used extensively to study animal models of immunodeficiency.[25] Other species, including cats (feline leukemia virus [FeLV] and feline immunodeficiency virus [FIV]) and cattle (bovine leukemia virus [BLV] and bovine immunodeficiency virus [BIV]), harbor related viruses. The lentivirus family also includes the ungulate viruses, maedi-visna virus, caprine arthritis-encephalitis virus, and equine infectious anemia virus.

In addition to infectious and endogenous retroviruses, a number of other elements that utilize RT have been described. These "retro"

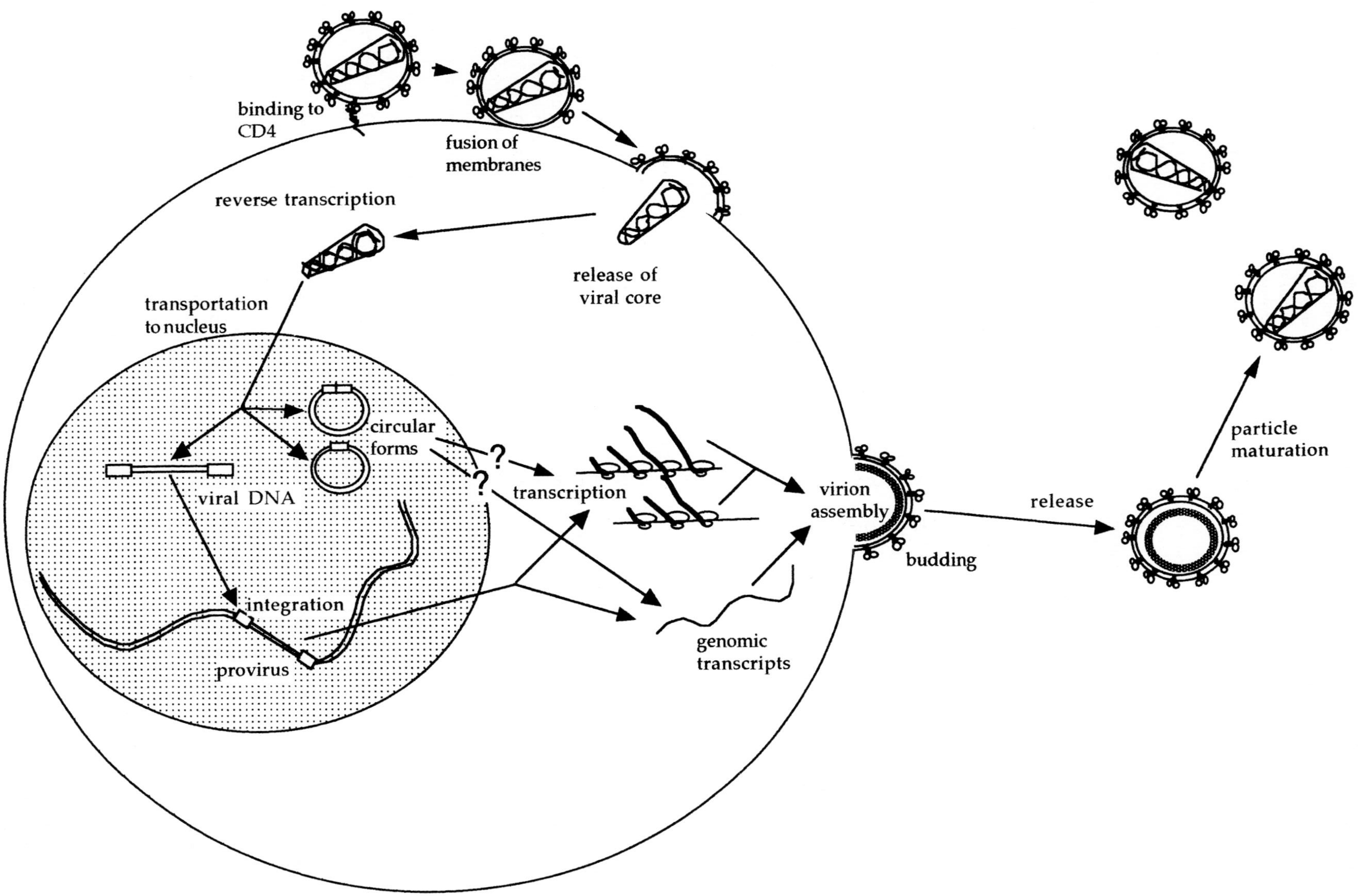

FIGURE 157–1. The life cycle of HIV-1. The life cycle begins with the binding of the virus to CD4 on the cell surface, followed by fusion of the viral envelope with the cell membrane and release of the viral core into the cytoplasm. The process of reverse transcription is completed, and the viral DNA is integrated into the host cell genome to form the provirus. In the presence of appropriate host cell stimulation, the viral 5′ LTR (long terminal repeat) is transcriptionally active and viral mRNA transcripts are produced. These are initially spliced to give short messages coding for the viral proteins Tat, Rev, and Nef, but Rev influences the cellular splicing machinery and/or RNA transport system to produce unspliced mRNAs that code for the structural proteins as well as provide a source of genomic transcripts for new viral particles.

elements also constitute a diverse group of related entities that inhabit the genomes of all eukaryotic and many prokaryotic organisms. It is possible or at least compelling to think of all of these elements evolving from one ancient RT gene, as proposed by Temin. These include retroposons (Alu-like sequences and processed pseudogenes), which function as mobile DNA elements that may jump to other regions of the genome; retrotransposon-containing LINE elements; long terminal repeat (LTR)–containing elements; pararetroviruses (hepadnavirus) that use RT; and endogenous retroviruses. Large-scale genomic sequencing has revealed that a huge fraction of many eukaryote genomes consists of transposable elements.[26] These mobile DNA sequences range in size from hundreds to thousands of base pairs—SINEs or LINEs—and may "jump" from one location to another. As-yet unknown mechanisms must be present to control these elements. A number of diseases have been associated in humans with gene disruption by insertion.[27] A comprehensive review of the expanse of retrovirus biology has recently been published.[28]

VIRAL TRANSMISSION AND LIFE CYCLE

Transmission

The infectious life cycle of HIV can be described both at the molecular, single-cell level and at the level of an organism infected with a "swarm" of closely related viral species. The infectious cycle of HIV begins with host exposure to the virus. The most common mode of infection is sexual transmission at the genital or colonic mucosa, exposure to other infected fluids such as blood or blood products, from mother to infant, or occasionally accidental occupational exposure. Acute HIV infection is often manifested as a transient symptomatic illness associated with high-titer virus replication and a robust immunologic response. Transmitted viruses typically utilize the interaction of the viral glycoprotein gp120 with the cellular receptor CD4 and the chemokine receptor CCR5 to gain cell entry, thus selecting for macrophage-tropic *non–syncytia-forming* variants.[29] This may explain the remarkable discovery that persons who lack a functional CCR5 receptor are relatively resistant to infection by sexual transmission. Non–macrophage-tropic strains, also called *syncytia-inducing* or SI, are typically found late in infection. These strains use another chemokine receptor, CXCR4, to facilitate entry and are apparently not readily transmitted from person to person. In a model of acute infection in the macaque, the first cellular targets of intravaginal inoculation of the virus are Langerhans cells, tissue dendritic cells in the lamina propria, which then fuse with lymphocytes. Infected cells can be found in draining lymph nodes within 2 days and in plasma by 5 days.[30]

In HIV-1–infected persons, there is a rapid rise in the degree of plasma viremia, with high viral titers and widespread dissemination, probably targeting lymphoid organs and the central nervous system (CNS). This phase is followed by a marked reduction in virus to steady-state levels, probably owing to vigorous antivirus cellular responses. The immune response, as well as the marked plasma viremia, probably accounts for the mononucleosis-like acute syndrome seen in half of the patients. Initially, perhaps within hours of infection, at least three inhibitory chemokines may be produced. As is the case for many infections with viruses that establish chronic infections, this response is at least partially successful in controlling replication. Levels of HIV-1–specific cytotoxic T lymphocyte(s) (CTLs) are inversely correlated with plasma viral RNA levels.[31] High levels of potent CTL virus-specific cells targeted to the viral Env protein, and soluble factors (notably chemokines) produced by these cells early in infection may correlate with the decline of virus, even before a neutralizing antibody can be detected.[32]

A great deal of variability in peak viral RNA plasma levels is seen during the first 120 days after infection. By 4 to 6 months, viral levels decline to reach a temporary steady state, sometimes called a viral setpoint. This level is highly correlated with disease progression. Thus, early in the course of infection, virus-host interactions are established that are often predictive of subsequent disease.[33]

Intervention to control infection during this initial period has been shown to decrease the risk of subsequent infection in health care workers after percutaneous exposure. Treatment in mothers and exposed neonates has also shown a dramatic effect in decreasing the incidence of maternal-fetal transmission.[34] The theory underlying the use of prophylaxis following sexual exposure is biologically plausible but lacks direct proof of efficacy.[35]

Life Cycle

The life cycle of HIV-1 can be considered in two distinct phases (see Fig. 157–1). The initial early events occur within a short time and include viral attachment, entry, reverse transcription, entry into the nucleus, and integration of the double-stranded DNA (the provirus). The second phase occurs over the lifetime of the infected cell as viral and cellular proteins regulate the production of viral proteins and new infectious virions.

Infection is initiated by the binding of the virion gp120 Env protein to the CD4 molecule found on some T cells, macrophages, and microglial cells. Both SIV and HIV-2 also utilize this molecule. CD4 was first shown to be a viral receptor in a number of studies showing the susceptibility of CD4-bearing cells to infection and the ability to block infection with anti-CD4 monoclonal antibodies in culture. Transfection of human $CD4^-$ HeLa cells with CD4 DNA rendered them permissive for infection.[36] Successful in vitro experiments blocking this interaction with soluble CD4 utilized laboratory strains adapted to cell lines and led to therapeutic attempts using immunoglobulin CD4, which were not successful. Subsequent experiments showed that primary isolates were not sensitive to soluble CD4 and highlighted the necessity of using primary rather than laboratory-adapted isolates in studying virus-host interactions.

Early experiments demonstrated that, as with other lentiviruses, macrophages could also be infected with HIV, but strains differed in their ability to infect either T-cell lines or monocytes.[37] Binding to CD4 is not sufficient for entry of HIV into either human or nonhuman cells, and the fact that small changes in the V3 loop of envelope gp120 (see later on) could determine tropism of the virus for either macrophage or T-cell lines suggested that a second receptor was present. The first important clue for the basis of this tropism was the unexpected finding that a group of chemokines isolated from $CD8^+$ T cells inhibited macrophage-tropic but not T-cell line–adapted strains.[38] This discovery at once explained the nature of a long-sought CD8 viral suppressor factor and suggested a previously unexpected role for chemokine receptors. The independent identification of an orphan chemokine receptor, CXCR4, as the second receptor for T-cell line–tropic strains[39] resulted in a rapid series of reports demonstrating CCR5 to be the principal second receptor for macrophage-tropic strains, and CXCR4, for T-cell line–adapted strains.[40–44] Crystallographic evidence indicates that CD4 binds in a recessed pocket on gp120 and includes a deep cavity that binds to phenylalanine-43 of CD4. Previous mutagenesis studies had shown this to be a crucial residue for binding.[45] Recent studies also indicate a role for sugar molecules, glycosaminoglycans, in the binding of gp120, which influences interactions with the chemokine receptor.[46]

Events that occur immediately after viral entry—collectively, the disassembly process—are not simply the reverse of viral assembly. For example, recent studies have shown that HIV-1 must incorporate a cellular protein, cyclophilin A, which binds to viral capsid protein p17. Failure to incorporate this cellular protein results in profound post-entry block during the next viral entry. Coincidentally, cyclophilin (peptidyl-prolyl isomerase) is the binding protein for cyclosporine, an inhibitor of T-cell activation, suggesting that activation-related cellular processes may be enlisted in viral disassembly.[47, 48] In addition, Vif and Nef, accessory viral proteins, may also be required.[49]

The process of reverse transcription begins in the cytoplasm as DNA synthesis is initiated from the transfer RNA primer bound to the viral genomic RNA just downstream of the 5′ LTR. Reverse transcription proceeds in an orderly fashion in a similar manner in all retroviruses.[50] Briefly, the transcription complex begins at the 5′ end, copies the U5 and R regions of the 5′ LTR, and then jumps to the 3′ end of the RNA, where the newly synthesized R region DNA binds to the R region of the 3′ LTR. Reverse transcription continues through the U3 region of the 3′ LTR and then the remainder of the viral RNA, which gives a complete minus strand of DNA. The RNA is degraded by the viral ribonuclease H, except for two resistant purine-rich tracts in the middle and toward the 3′ end of the viral RNA. These then serve as the primers for formation of the plus strand.[51]

Retroviruses are positive-stranded RNA viruses. No viral message is encoded directly from virion RNA; the virus particle lacks cellular RNA polymerase and transcriptional factors, and during the process of reverse transcription, the positive-strand RNA produced from the viral genomic template is destroyed by the RNase H function of the RT. Because reverse transcription takes place in the cytoplasm, local concentrations of nucleotides may be a limiting factor, particularly in nondividing cells. This is the rationale for using the ribonucleoside reductase inhibitor hydroxyurea to limit viral replication.[52, 53]

During the formation of double-stranded DNA, the uncoated nucleoprotein complex, sometimes termed the pre-integration complex, is imported into the nucleus.[54] This is an energy-requiring process that uses nuclear localization signals present on viral Gag, Vpr, and integrase proteins. Unlike most retroviruses, which integrate into the host cellular DNA as the nuclear membrane is disrupted during cell division, HIV-1 can be imported into the nucleus and integrate into nondividing cells. This may be especially important in the infection of monocytes and macrophages, which are essentially nondividing cells (and possibly for use of HIV as a gene delivery vector).

Integrase (IN)-negative mutants of HIV do not integrate and do not produce infectious virus.[55, 56] Integration does not appear to be site-directed. However, virus may preferentially integrate into or near two repeated DNA elements, L1 and Alu, that move throughout the genome as retrotransposons.[57] Integration of the provirus appears to be an essential step in every replication cycle. In eukaryotes, integration is typical only of retroviruses and retrotransposable elements.[13] Unintegrated viral DNA may survive, particularly in quiescent cells; the highest levels of unintegrated virus are found in the brain tissue of patients with HIV-associated encephalitis, probably most or all in microglial cells. This may provide a stable intermediate in cells that are temporarily not permissive for infection; if cell activation occurs when these forms are present, viral infection may then proceed to completion.

Integration of viral DNA establishes a linear copy of the viral genome in the genome of the cell and replication occurs along with the cell. Synthesis of new viral RNA genomes and proteins is accomplished in a highly regulated manner utilizing host cell enzymes. Integration is generally for the life of the cell and, with the cell and its progeny, for the life of the organism. Until this point, most retroviruses follow a similar molecular plan. It is at this point in the life cycle that differences in the natural history of different viruses emerge. HIV infection may be unique in that a high level of viral production from several different cellular compartments is maintained throughout the course of infection. The high number of replication cycles that occur in a single infection allows for the generation of variants and selection by drugs or the immune system.

Once integration has occurred, virus production depends on the presence of cellular and viral factors required for activation of viral promoters. External factors, including infection and production of inflammatory cytokines, and cellular activation may enhance viral replication.[58] The molecular mechanisms regulating virus production include cellular pathways involving factors, such as the nuclear factor-kappa B (NF-κB) family of inducible transcription factors, that result in a cascade of events leading to viral genome expression.[59, 60]

A unique feature of HIV-1 is that expression of different viral RNA species is temporally regulated. Using cellular enzymes, such as RNA polymerase II, transcription of the provirus is initiated at the viral promoter, at the junction of the U3-R regions in the LTR, as a single complete message. The viral messenger RNA (mRNA) and genomic RNA transcripts, processed by cellular machinery, are spliced, capped, polyadenylated, and transported to the cytoplasm for translation into viral proteins (Fig. 157–2). Differential splicing of this complete RNA, controlled in part by the viral protein Rev, determines the type of message and protein that is produced. Early after infection, activated cells produce 2-Kb mRNAs for viral regulatory proteins that can be detected by Northern blot analysis[61]; using even more sensitive RT-polymerase chain reaction (PCR) techniques, expression can be detected within 6 hours.[62] These messages represent the unique doubly spliced RNA for Tat, Rev, and Nef proteins. The Tat protein induces a markedly enhanced activity of the viral promoter, chiefly by increasing RNA elongation, resulting in further increased RNA and protein production. The Rev protein serves to decrease the production of double-spliced messages. With the accumulation of Rev protein, there is a switch to enhanced expression of unspliced and singly spliced mRNAs that code for the late viral proteins. These proteins include the virion proteins Gag, Pol, and Env and Vpu, Vpr, and Vif, as well as genomic RNA. The delayed transit from early to late viral genes is probably due to the requirement for a threshold amount of Rev needed to bind and form multimers of the protein complexed with the Rev regulatory element (RRE) located in all of the incompletely spliced mRNAs. Packaging of the genomic RNA within a virus particle requires the presence of a specific packaging signal located between the major splice donor at the 5′ end of the genome and the initiation codon for Gag. In the absence of this signal, mature particles are formed that are devoid of RNA. The incorporation of genomic RNA requires two "zinc finger" domains found in the p7 Gag protein. Assembly of mature viral particles occurs at the cell membrane with the association of matrix protein p17 with the cytoplasmic domain of envelope transmembrane protein gp41, which in turn binds to the viral gp120 on the outer surface. Assembled virions include the viral envelope proteins, cell membrane and associated cellular proteins, a matrix composed mainly of Gag p17, and an inner core containing RNA, RT, integrase (IN), and core proteins p7 and p24, as well as Vpr and p6 proteins. The mature viral particle characteristically buds from the cell surface into the surrounding media, completing the life cycle of the virus.

THE PATHOGEN

Virus Structural and Regulatory Proteins

The mature infectious virus particle buds from a cell membrane forming a sphere with an outer lipid bilayer and a nucleocapsid with a dense, cone-shaped core (Fig. 157–3). The core appears to be attached to the viral outer envelope at its narrow end.[63] The outer membrane contains 72 spiked knobs, which are assembled as trimers of the outer envelope protein gp120 bound to the transmembrane portion, gp41. The viral membrane is cholesterol-rich and includes cellular proteins.[64]

Each mature virion is composed of two molecules of single-stranded RNA surrounded by three *gag* gene cleavage products: the p17 outer matrix protein; the p24 major capsid protein, which forms the capsid shell; and the p7 nucleoprotein, which binds tightly to the viral RNA. The nucleocapsid is composed of a p17 myristoylated outer-matrix protein sandwiched between the membrane-bound envelope and p24 capsid protein of the core. The p7 protein binds the two positive-strand copies of complete viral RNA attached at the packaging site, and it also binds to p24. A number of other viral proteins required for the early phases of infection are incorporated with the virion: protease, which is essential for viral assembly; RT and IN, which are needed after entry for viral DNA synthesis and integration; $tRNA^{lys}$ at the 5′ end of the RNA, which serves as the primer for initiation of negative-strand DNA synthesis; and Vpr.

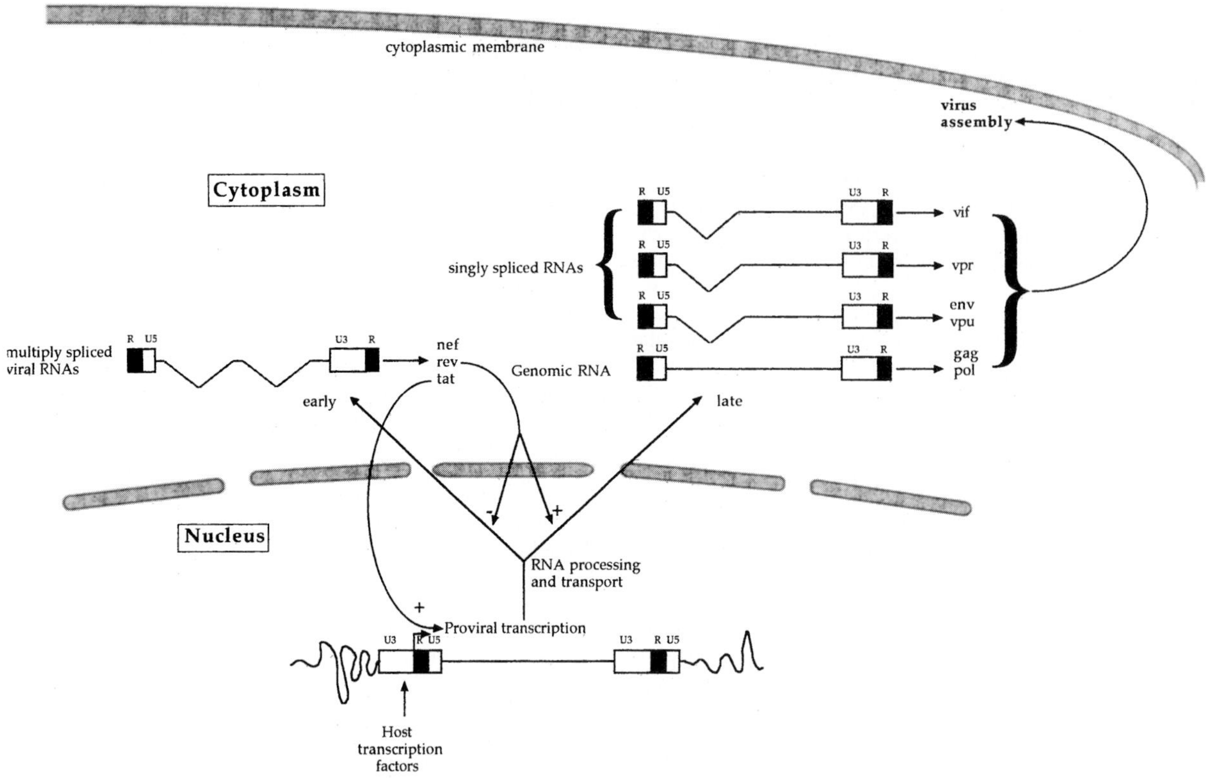

FIGURE 157–2. The role of RNA splicing in the life cycle of HIV-1. The early mRNA transcripts of HIV-1 are doubly spliced and produce viral regulatory proteins Tat, Rev, and Nef. The function of HIV Rev is to facilitate the expression of the late transcripts of HIV-1. These can be divided into two categories: unspliced and singly spliced. The unspliced HIV-1 mRNA has two functions: it is translated into the structural precursor polyproteins for the *gag* and *pol* gene products and is incorporated into virions as genomic RNA. The different singly spliced mRNAs of HIV-1 are translated into the envelope proteins gp120 and gp41, as well as Vif and Vpr,[148] and Vpu.

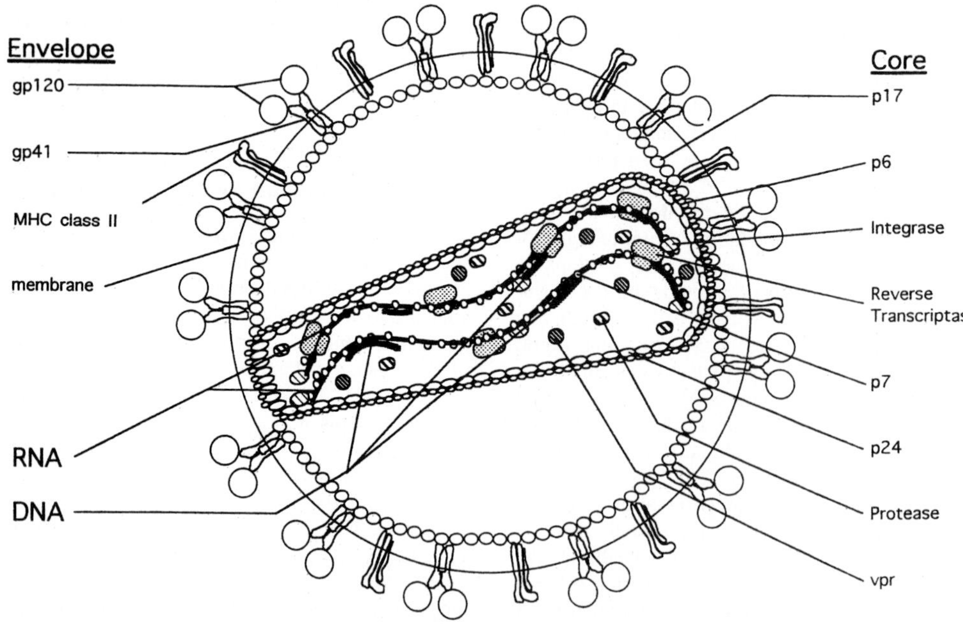

FIGURE 157–3. Structure of the HIV-1 virion. The viral envelope is formed from the host cell membrane, into which the HIV-1 envelope proteins gp41 and gp120 have been inserted and may include several host cell proteins, most significantly the major histocompatibility complex class II proteins. The matrix between the envelope and the core is formed predominantly from Gag protein p17. The core contains the viral RNA, closely associated with Gag protein p7, in addition to RT and integrase. It has also been shown that virions contain complementary DNA, as shown, synthesized by the RT. The major structural proteins of the core are Gag proteins p24 and p6. Also present within the virion is the protease and two cleavage products from the Gag precursor protein (p1 and p2, not shown) of undetermined position within the virion. Vpr is also packaged in the virion and is thought to be localized within the core, as shown.

TABLE 157–1 Genes and Gene Products of Human Immunodeficiency Virus Types 1 and 2

Gene	Protein(s)	Size (kD)	Function/Properties
gag	p17		Matrix protein; interacts with gp41
	p24		Core protein
	p6		Core protein; binds to Vpr
	p7		Nucleocapsid; binds to RNA
	p1		
	p2		
pol	Protease	10	Proteolytic cleavage of Gag and Pol
	Reverse transcriptase	66, 51	Polymerase and RNase H activity (p66 only)
	Integrase	32	Integration into chromosome
env	gp120		Envelope; viral entry into cell
	gp41		Transmembrane protein; cell fusion
vif	Virion infectivity protein	23	Efficient cell-free transmission
vpr	Viral protein R	15	Enhances viral replication in primary cells, virion-associated protein; G_2/M phase arrest; nuclear localization
tat	*Trans*-activator of transcription	14	Major viral *trans*-activator
rev	Regulator of expression of virion protein	19	Enhances expression of unspliced and singly spliced RNAs
*vpu**	Viral protein U	15–16	Enhances virion release from cells; downregulates CD4
nef	Negative regulatory factory	27	Inhibits or enhances viral replication depending on strain and cell type Downregulates CD4; MHC class I
vpx†	Virion protein X	25	Packaged into the virion

*HIV-1 only.
†HIV-2 only.
Abbreviations: HIV, Human immunodeficiency virus; MHC, major histocompatibility complex.

This last protein is a small protein that contains a nuclear localization signal and is associated with the nucleocapsid in large quantities. The virus also encodes at least five regulatory and accessory genes of diverse function, some of which have been discussed already, that are present in the infected cell but not in the mature virion. A list of viral proteins is presented in Table 157–1.

Genetic Organization

The HIV-1 proviral DNA integrated into the host cell is 9.7 Kb in length and follows the basic genomic structure common to most retroviruses: *gag-pol-env* genes flanked by two complete viral LTRs (Fig. 157–4). The provirus is symmetrically flanked at either end by the viral LTR and by cellular sequences representing the site of integration. These LTRs contain transcriptional regulatory sequences, RNA processing signals, packaging sites, and the integration sites. The 5′ end begins with the *gag* gene, which encodes core and matrix proteins; the *pol* gene, which begins in an overlapping frame encoding viral protease, RT, and IN; and then the *env* gene, which encodes the outer and transmembrane envelope proteins. One group of accessory genes is located between the *pol* and *env* sequences and a second group at the 3′ end of the virus (Fig. 157–5).

Transcription of a single unspliced RNA is initiated at the 5′ end by the cellular RNA polymerase II. The unspliced mRNA serves as a template for translation of the Gag and Gag-Pol precursor polypeptides. This message is also spliced to produce single-spliced transcripts for Vif, Vpr, and Vpu proteins and the Env precursor polypeptide. The precursor polyproteins are then cleaved by cellular or viral

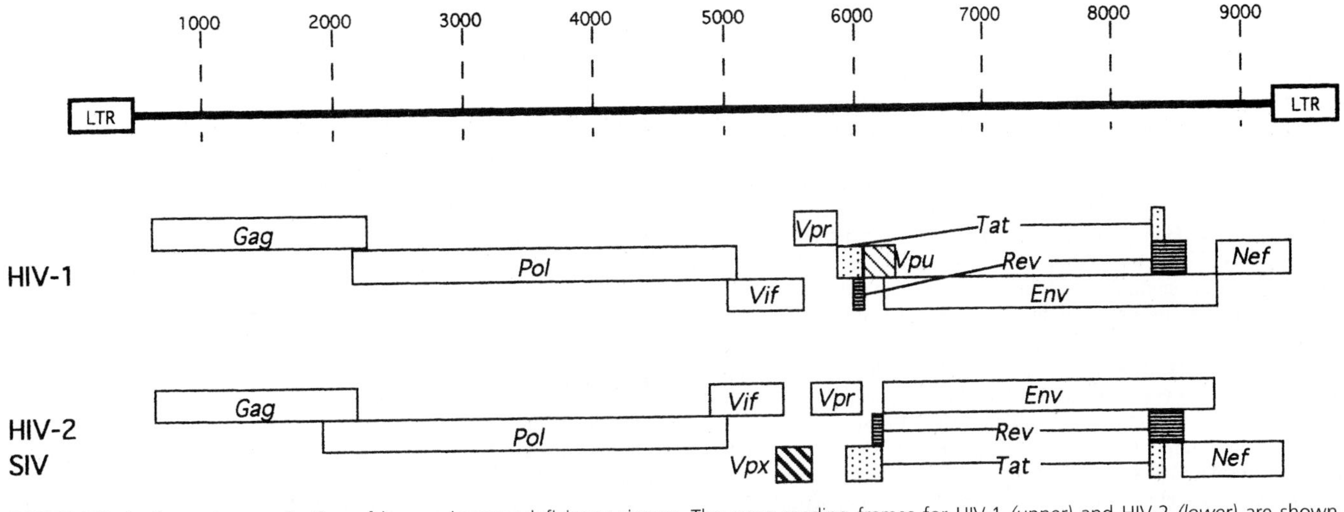

FIGURE 157–4. Genomic organization of human immunodeficiency viruses. The open reading frames for HIV-1 *(upper)* and HIV-2 *(lower)* are shown. The different genes are represented on three levels corresponding to the three alternate reading frames of the nucleic acid. In this way, the different viral proteins are shown in the correct reading frame relative to each other. The map of HIV-1 is based on the infectious molecular clone HXB2, corrected for truncations in the *vpr* and *nef* reading frames, as well as the loss of *vpu* owing to a mutated start codon. The map of HIV-2 is based on the infectious molecular clone isy/sbl, corrected for an extended open *rev* reading frame due to a mutated stop codon.[147]

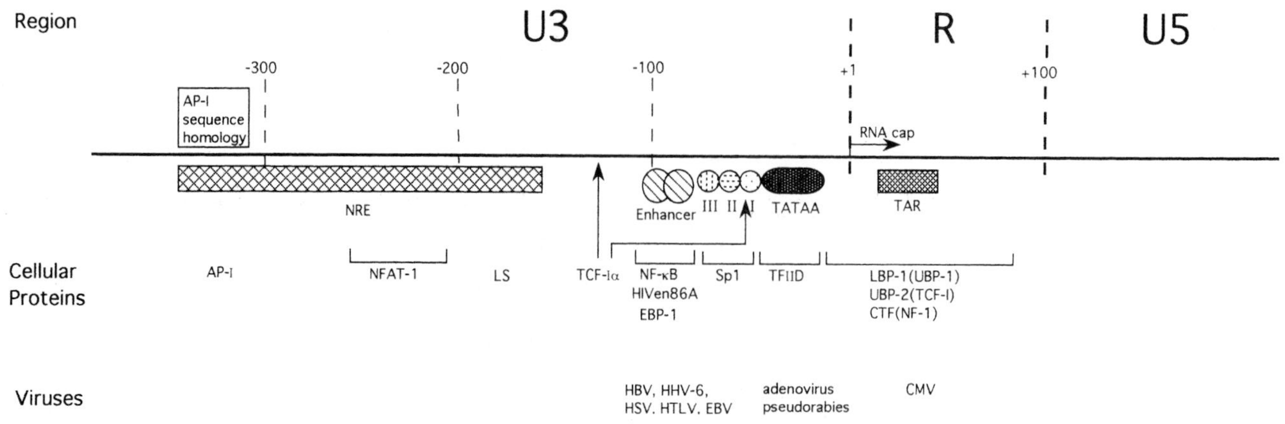

FIGURE 157–5. The HIV-1 long terminal repeat (LTR). Like other retroviruses, the LTR of HIV-1 is composed of three regions: U3, R, and U5. Integrated proviral DNA is flanked by two complete LTRs, whereas genomic viral RNA transcripts contain partial LTRs at either end, the 5′ end containing the R and U5 regions, and the 3′ end containing the U3 and R regions. The untranslated 5′ (U3) region contains the major regulatory domains of the LTR, including an NRE and the major binding sites for cellular enhancers of HIV-1 transcription, NF-κB and SP1. A number of cellular as well as viral proteins interact directly or indirectly with the LTRs. The R region of the LTR includes the TAR, which (as RNA) binds the HIV-1 transcriptional activator, Tat, and a number of cellular factors that also enhance transcriptional activity.

enzymes; the Gag and Gag-Pol precursors are cleaved by the viral protease, which is itself transcribed from the unspliced viral message. The Env precursor polypeptide is cleaved by cellular proteases.

VIRION STRUCTURAL PROTEINS

Gag Proteins

The cleavage of the Gag precursor protein by viral protease produces the structural components of the virus that interact with other viral proteins, RNA, and cellular proteins. To form the virus capsid structure, one large protein is made from the viral mRNA. This 55-kilodalton (kD) polyprotein—a Gag precursor protein sometimes called p55—is cleaved into at least five structural proteins by the viral 34-Kb protease encoded at the 5′ end of the *pol* gene. Lack of protease function, either through inhibition by drugs or following transfection of the p55 gene into a cell that lacks protease, results in the formation of noninfectious viral particles.[65]

The p55 protein can be seen on Western blot preparations made from whole cell lysates but not on those made from mature virions. During or shortly after self-assembly, the viral protease is activated and the precursor is cleaved into three principal proteins and two smaller peptides. These proteins undergo extensive post-translational modification by cellular enzymes. After translation, the initiating methionine residue is removed, and p17 is myristoylated; p17 and p24 are phosphorylated by cellular kinases; p7 (the nucleocapsid protein, or NC) binds to two zinc ions to form the "zinc fingers" that bind to RNA. Although the virus depends on cellular systems for many functions, it requires the virally encoded protease for the cleavage of the Gag proteins. Gag proteins are sufficient to form particles when expressed from transfected cells. These self-assembled particles are noninfectious but may be combined with recombinant Env proteins or other immunogenic proteins and used as immunogens.

The p17 matrix protein, MA (molecular weight 17,000), contains about 130 amino acids and is myristoylated on a glycine at its N-terminus by the host cell enzyme *N*-myristoyl transferase.[66] The first 31 amino acids target the myristoylated protein to the cell membrane, and non-myristoylated proteins form noninfectious capsids. In addition to viral assembly at the cell surface, MA may function as part of the preintegration complex determining cell tropism and targeting viral DNA to the cell nucleus.[67] The p24 capsid protein, CA, is produced by two cleavages to form a 240-amino-acid hydrophobic protein that forms the major subunits of the viral capsid and self-associates to form dimers and higher-order structures. This protein binds the cellular cyclophilins.[68] A major homology region of 29 amino acids is shared with many retroviruses.[69, 70] P24 Gag is typically the easiest protein to detect using sera from infected patients, and serologic detection in infected animals gave the name *group antigen* (Gag) to these proteins. The C-terminal sequences encode a 70-amino-acid hydrophilic protein, NC, that binds both viral RNA and the capsid p24 protein, intertwining approximately one molecule with 4 to 6 nucleotides of RNA.[71] A "zinc finger" domain binds RNA, while the NC recognizes the packaging site on Gag.[72, 73] Two small proteins of unknown function, p2 and p1, are found in the viral core.

Viral Enzymes

Pol Gene Products

The *pol* gene encodes three enzymes: protease, RT, and IN. These proteins are synthesized from the same mRNA as the Gag proteins through a ribosomal translational frameshift. The cleavage of the 160-kD precursor polyprotein is essential for viability. It has been estimated that there are about 2000 copies of each Gag protein and 100 copies of each Pol protein in each virion.

Protease

The protease is a 10-kD 99-amino-acid protein that is fully active as a dimer. It is autocatalytically cleaved from the precursor protein during the viral assembly process. Site-specific mutagenesis has demonstrated that noninfectious particles containing uncleaved Gag and Gag-Pol proteins are produced if this enzyme is inactivated. The similarity of viral protease to other aspartyl proteases such as angiotensin-converting enzyme (ACE) greatly facilitated the design of potent antiviral drugs, including inhibitors of dimerization and molecules that bind to the active catalytic site.[65, 74]

Reverse Transcriptase

Viral RT is an RNA-dependent DNA polymerase. This highly versatile enzyme is capable of synthesizing DNA copies from both RNA and DNA templates and degrading viral RNA from RNA-DNA hybrids. RT and its RNase H activity are indispensable for viral replication. The protein is first cleaved from the precursor polyprotein to form a p66 homodimer and after a second cleavage to form a p66-p51 heterodimer with identical N-terminal ends.

The structure of the RT heterodimer has been used to reveal the enzymatic mechanism of reverse transcription and the molecular basis of resistance to antiviral drugs.[75] The p66 and p51 assemble in an unusual head-to-tail heterodimer. Four domains of the p66 protein are similar in shape to a clenched right hand and are designated as the fingers, palm, and thumb. These are joined to the RNase H domain. The cleft between them contains the highly conserved catalytic site Tyr-Met-Asp-Asp. The p51 subunit, although derived from the same protein, maintains a different conformation.[76, 77]

RT plays a major role in the generation of diversity in retroviruses. The fidelity of the enzyme has been determined for a variety of retroviruses by measuring misincorporation rates on defined templates. For HIV-1, this rate ranges from 1/1700 to 1/4000 misincorporations per nucleotide per replication, somewhat higher than for other retroviruses and considerably greater than for the host cell polymerases. For the 9.7-Kb HIV-1 genome, the in vivo error rate is estimated to be one misincorporation per replication cycle.[78]

Variants produced by RT generate sequence diversity, may emerge under the selective pressure of immune responses or antiviral drugs, and may allow virus to change cell tropism. However, the same lack of fidelity also allows nucleoside analogues to be preferentially incorporated into viral rather than cellular DNA.[79, 80]

Integrase

IN is a 288-amino-acid, 32-kD viral enzyme that mediates the linkage of double-stranded viral DNA into the host cell genome. Integration occurs following the translocation of a large complex derived from the viral core from the cytoplasm into the nucleus. IN is part of this complex and catalyzes the cleavage of viral DNA and ligation to host cell DNA.[81] A large central acidic domain of IN is highly conserved in retroviruses and retrotransposons. Once integrated, the provirus can be considered for most purposes to be a stable genetic element remaining for the life of the cell and, through cellular replication, for the life of the individual.

Envelope Glycoproteins and Viral Fusion

The *env* gene of HIV-1 encodes a single-spliced viral RNA transcript that encodes both Vpu and a 160-kD precursor that is synthesized in the late stages of viral replication; this 850-amino-acid polyprotein is cleaved by cellular proteases at amino acids 512 and 513 to form the external gp120 and the transmembrane gp41. Proteolytic cleavage is essential for viral infectivity. There is extensive *N*-linked glycosylation on asparagine residues with high-mannose complex oligosaccharide groups. Nonglycosylated virus does not bind to CD4, and selective removal of glycosylation sites reduces infectivity. Attempts to alter glycosylation by mutagenesis in order to enhance viral immunogenicity have resulted in viruses that either retain virulence or have lost potency and fail to evoke immune responses.

The extensive variation among different strains of HIV-1 and the ability of the virus to evolve during the course of a single infection and to rapidly adapt to drugs and immunologic attack present problems in therapy and vaccine development. Most of the variability among strains of HIV occurs in the envelope sequence in five variable domains of gp120, designated V1 through V5 (comprising amino acids 128 to 152, 182 to 195, 300 to 330, 395 to 415, and 460 to 467, respectively).[82] The third variable region, called the V3 loop (formed by joining two cysteine residues), is a dominant antibody-neutralizing domain of gp120 and plays an important role in determining viral tropism. Four regions that are relatively invariant have been designated C1 through C4 (amino acids 33 to 60, 87 to 126, 231 to 276, and 460 to 467). These regions presumably maintain essential viral structures.

Although some structure-function relationships have been deduced from secondary structure, biochemical, mutagenic, and immunologic analysis, the solution of the crystal structure of the gp120 protein and of part of the gp41 protein has literally put a new face on the virus, with implications for cell fusion mechanisms and immune evasion. The crystal structure of gp120 at 2.5-Å resolution reveals a cavity-laden gp120–CD4 interface and a conserved binding site for the chemokine receptor with evidence for a conformational change upon CD4 binding. Gp120 is visualized as two domains joined by a bridge. The V3 loop, together with conserved regions that remain unexposed until CD4 binding occurs, is the principal determinant of chemokine receptor variability. An understanding of the structural basis that enables HIV to evade humoral responses while maintaining function may help in vaccine design.[83–85]

Viral-Cell Fusion

The viral envelope ultimately must be understood as a fusion machine allowing viral entry into target cells. Fusion depends on the sequential binding of gp120 to the CD4 and chemokine receptors, but the fusogenic machinery is located in gp41. The fusion peptide that is inserted into the target cell membrane is formed at the new amino terminus created by proteolytic cleavage of the gp160 precursor protein.[86] However, this hydrophobic tip must be kept in an inactive state until juxtaposed to the target cell membrane. Premature triggering of the fusion peptide would result in an inactive virus. Recently, the core structure of gp41 has been crystallized from peptide fragments.[87]

The core structure that mediates the fusion-active state between virus and cell is formed from a trimer of gp41 molecules composed of two α-helical regions within gp41 that form a six-helix bundle characteristic of "coiled coils." The crystallized complex shows striking structural homology with the low pH–induced fusogenic conformation of the influenza virus hemagglutinin protein (HA), which contains three antiparallel helices packed in a central trimeric coiled coil. The conformational change in HIV-1 is not mediated by endocytic uptake into the low pH compartment as it is for HA, however. Probably, the binding to the second receptor triggers the conformational change, which leads to cell fusion and virus uptake. The transition from a loop structure to a coiled-coil state is the basis for the "spring-loaded" model of activation for membrane fusion. The fusion-active state has been identified using synthetic viral peptides to block fusion following triggering.[88] Synthetic peptides that span all or part of these domains can inhibit HIV cell fusion and infection.[89]

Viral Regulatory and Accessory Genes

In addition to the structural genes, HIV has six accessory genes: *tat* (coding for the *trans*-activator of transcription); *rev* (encoding the regulator of viral expression); *vif* (encoding the virion infectivity factor); *vpr* (encoding the viral protein R); *vpu* (encoding viral protein U); and *nef* (encoding the negative regulatory factor). These genes enable the virus to manipulate host cell processes and to achieve efficient replication under host selective pressure, thus contributing to disease progression.[49]

Of these genes, only *tat* and *rev* are necessary for high levels of viral expression in culture. Tat protein augments viral RNA by increasing transcription, primarily by permitting elongation of otherwise blocked short nascent RNA chains. Rev regulates the splicing and transport of RNA. Vif appears to be required for efficient cell-free transmission of virus. Nef has been found to be crucial to viral virulence and immune evasion and downregulates surface expression of CD4, presumably to allow efficient expression of gp120 on the cell surface. Vpr also downregulates surface expression of CD4. Vpr is the only accessory protein found abundantly in the mature virion.

As a presumed example of convergent evolution, *tax* and *rex* genes present in HTLV-I (and related viruses) encode two proteins, Tax (*trans*-activator of transcription) and Rex (regulatory of viral expression); these genes function analogously to *tat* and *rev*. Similar genes are present in HIV-2, which lacks *vpu* but has *vpx*, which encodes a unique protein Vpx (viral protein X). Accessory genes that are formed by complex splicing arrangements are not generally found in all retroviruses, suggesting that retroviruses should be classified as either simple or complex, depending on the presence or absence of these genes.[13]

Early in infection, a *rev*-independent pathway removes "introns" from the viral transcript. The multiply spliced messages of *tat* and *rev* are transported and translated and as proteins are shuttled back to the nucleus. As Tat acts and Rev accumulates in the nucleus, additional unspliced and single-spliced messages for *gag, gag-pol,* and *env* and viral accessory genes *vpu, vpr,* and *vif* are transported out of the nucleus.[89a]

Tat

The Tat protein is translated from a transcript that contains three exons. The *tat* reading frame overlaps both the *rev* and *env* genes. Tat is a small nuclear (14 to 16 kD) protein that varies in size, containing 86 to 102 amino acids, depending on the strain of HIV-1. The first 72 amino acids contained in the first exon are required for full activity, while all of the length variation occurs at the C-terminal end of the protein.[90] Tat binds to the Tat activation response element (TAR) region found in all HIV-1 mRNAs, in conjunction with cellular factors, to stabilize the nascent mRNA and enhance its rate of elongation up to 1000-fold. However, Tat activation is downregulated after periods of several hours, suggesting that these cellular cofactors may be present in limited amounts and that negative regulatory factors may down-modulate Tat function.

The Tat protein has three functional domains. A highly conserved cysteine-rich domain between amino acids 22 and 37 contains seven cysteine residues and two "zinc finger" motifs, as is characteristic of a number of DNA-binding proteins. Loss of any one of six cysteines results in loss of activity. The interaction of Tat with TAR is mediated through a basic domain between nucleic acids 48 and 56. One requirement for Tat activity is the CDC2-like kinase CD9, which phosphorylates the carboxyl-terminal domain of RNA polymerase II. However, Tat must first interact with a host cell factor, which is cell-specific and limits Tat activation in nonhuman cells. This factor, encoded on chromosome 12, has been identified as a novel 87-kD cyclin C–related protein named cyclin T.[91] Overexpression of this protein, along with CD4 and chemokine receptors, may permit virus infection and expression in nonpermissive cells.

Tat also contains an RGD (arginine-glycine-aspartate) motif at amino acids 78 to 80 that is common to proteins that bind to integrin receptors. This feature is consistent with the finding that Tat may be secreted by cells into the media and act as an extracellular growth factor. Binding of HIV-1 Tat to cells derived from KS lesions, mediated in part through the RGD motif, enhances the growth of these cells. Extracellular Tat by itself has been shown to induce KS-like lesions in nude mice.[92]

All three functional domains of Tat are highly conserved among HIV-1 isolates. HIV-2/SIV Tat has an additional 30 amino acids in the N-terminal sequence but lacks the RGD region. Tat should be an inviting target for blocking viral replication, although in some instances cellular factors may allow virus to be expressed without Tat.[93] Extracellular Tat may also be immunosuppressive.[94]

Tat can effect the expression of heterologous and cellular genes, including the promoters of the human polyomaviruses, human papillomaviruses, and cytokines, such as tumor necrosis factor-α (TNF-α), and interleukin-2 (IL-2). The first exon of Tat has been shown to downregulate major histocompatibility complex (MHC) class I expression. Recently, the demonstration that another viral protein, Nef, also functions to downregulate this protein suggests that these proteins are important because the immune system is exerting significant selective pressure on the virus. It also illustrates how single viral proteins may have multiple or complex functions.

Rev

The *rev* gene encodes a serine phosphorylated protein, Rev, that ranges in size from 106 to 123 amino acids but is most commonly 116 amino acids in length, with a molecular weight of 19 kD. This protein is translated from a unique doubly spliced mRNA, with the second splice acceptor located downstream of the Tat translation initiation site.[95] Expression of Rev results in the accumulation of viral structural proteins encoded by the Gag, Pol, Env, Vpu, Vpr, and Vif mRNAs. In contrast, multiple-spliced viral messages for Tat, Rev, and Nef are efficiently expressed without Rev protein. In the absence of Rev, most viral mRNAs are processed to the double-spliced form, thereby limiting the production of virions. Rev protein accumulates in the nucleolus and shuttles back and forth to the cytoplasm. Although it binds to unspliced genomic RNA, it does not appear in the mature virion. Rev binds to a unique RNA element located in the Env coding region of HIV-1 RNA. This Rev regulatory element, RRE, is found in all unspliced and singly spliced mRNAs.

Rev contains at least two functional domains: an arginine-rich region* at amino acids 35 to 50, which is conserved and required for nucleolar localization and specific RRE binding, and a multimerization domain. After initial RRE binding, multiple additional Rev molecules bind to each other, and this oligomerization is required for activity.[96]

Nef

The *nef* gene product is a 206-amino-acid myristoylated protein that inserts into the cell membrane. The Nef protein may have many different properties that depend in part on the experimental methodology used to analyze them. The original observation that T-cell–tropic, Nef-deleted viruses replicated to high levels led to the name *negative factor.* Downregulation of CD4 requires myristoylation and membrane targeting of Nef to the cytoplasmic domain of CD4 and increases CD4 endocytosis. The protection of HIV-1–infected cells by Nef protein against killing by CTL correlates with downregulation of MHC class I.[97] Nef appears to be important to maintain high virus loads associated with rapid progression to immunodeficiency.

Viruses with Nef deleted appear to be less virulent than wild-type viruses but equally infectious, both in tissue culture and in rhesus macaques. The possible role of Nef as a virulence factor has led to the use of Nef-deleted virus as a potential live vaccine in rhesus macaques. These "attenuated" viruses were able to protect against infection by challenge with other virulent SIV strains. However, the Nef-deleted viruses are not entirely benign and are themselves able to cause disease in both newborn animals and adults.

The immune response to Nef may exert considerable selection pressure. When T cells capable of CTL activity against Nef were transferred to HIV-infected patients, a Nef-deleted variant emerged, and although there was apparent successful immunologic intervention, the patient's disease progressed.[98] Nef-deleted viruses detected in several human clusters have been associated with little or no disease, raising the possibility that they represent less virulent viruses.[99] Whether or not these viruses could be used as either protective vaccines or therapeutic vaccines remains a subject of controversy, but in our view, such an approach appears to present unacceptable risks.

Vif

Vif is a 193-amino-acid viral protein of 23 to 27 kD with no *N*-linked glycosylation sites. The infectivity of Vif deletion mutants is decreased up to 1000-fold in some cell lines compared with that of wild-type virus. The deleted virus is capable of cell entry and initiating reverse transcription, but double-stranded DNA is not produced. Accordingly, Vif may govern an early phase in the formation of the preintegration complex. Because the protein has not been found in the mature virion, it presumably effects a crucial step in viral assembly.[100]

Vpr

Vpr is a 96-amino-acid protein translated from a single-spliced mRNA and, like Vif, is dependent on Rev function. Vpr is abun-

*RQARRNRRRRWRRERQR.

dantly present in the mature virion associated with capsid protein. Expression of p55 Gag and Vpr in transfected cells is sufficient for incorporation and export of viral proteins. The protein plays a role in the nuclear localization of the preintegration complex.[101] In addition, in transfected human muscle cells, Vpr blocks proliferation and induces differentiation, suggesting a nuclear role for Vpr in regulation of gene expression. Vpr causes arrest of cell cycle progression at the G_2/M interface, presumably through an effect on cyclin CDC2 activity, which correlates with the ability to activate HIV transcription.[102, 103] A gene encoding a second homologous protein, VpX, is found in HIV-2 and several SIV strains but not in nonprimate lentiviruses.

Vpu

Vpu is an amphipathic integral membrane protein.[104] The first 27 amino acids are hydrophobic, while the remainder of this small, 81-amino-acid 16-kD protein is hydrophilic. A single-spliced message overlaps with the *env* gene in a different reading frame.[105] The protein forms oligomeric complexes localized to the perinuclear region. Cells infected with Vpu-defective mutants show large accumulations of intracellular vesicles, in contrast with those infected with wild-type virus. Vpu along with Nef is associated with the rapid degradation of CD4, which may in part eliminate CD4–gp160 intracellular complexes that interfere with virus production. The CD4 cytoplasmic tail is required for targeting the degradation of CD4 by Vpu. Vpu has structural similarities to the influenza virus M2 protein, an ion channel protein that modulates the pH of the *trans*-Golgi.[106]

Virus Regulation and the Long Terminal Repeat

The LTR of all retroviruses is located at each end of the provirus as a direct repeat containing U3, R, and U5 region. It functions as a eukaryotic transcription unit (see Fig. 157–4). The U3 region contains the viral promoter and enhancer elements; the R region includes the mRNA initiation site (+1) used by all viral messages and ends at the polyadenylation site. The function of the U5 region is not well understood. It separates the R region from the tRNA primer binding site used to initiate reverse transcription. HIV-1 uses $tRNA^{lys}$ as a primer. Once the virus has formed a double-stranded DNA copy, it depends entirely on cellular machinery for transcription and translation.

However, the control of virus expression results from a complex set of interactions between viral elements and cellular proteins. Small changes in these regions may result in profound differences in virus behavior. *Cis*-acting control elements of the virus (TAR, TATAA, SP1, and enhancer and negative regulatory regions, located within the U3 and R regions) interact with cellular and viral proteins. These interactions, which occur at both the DNA and the RNA levels, are crucial in controlling the level of viral expression in both resting and activated cells.[107]

The TATAA box, located at -27 (relative to the RNA initiation site), binds the critical cellular transcription factor TFIID to initiate transcription. The promoter region, the binding site of the cellular polymerase, lies further 5′ (between -45 and -77) and contains three binding sites for the cellular SP1 transcription factor.[108]

An enhancer element is still further 5′, mapping to nucleotides -82 to -105, and contains a consensus sequence also found in the κ-immunoglobulin, IL-2, and IL-2R enhancer regions. This region binds an inducible cellular transcription factor, NF-κB. Although originally described in B lymphocytes, this factor or family of factors is also expressed in activated T cells and stimulates HIV expression.[59, 60]

In addition to NF-κB, other factors have been shown to increase HIV-1 promoter activity by interactions in the region. These include cellular cytokines, such as TNF-α and IL-1, and heterologous viral proteins, such as HTLV-I Tax. Such observations indicate molecular mechanisms by which other viruses could interact with HIV; however, the relevance of such interactions in vivo is not known.

Further 5′ are the binding sites for additional cellular factors (AP-1, NFAT-1) that lie within a negative regulatory element (NRE). Removing this region from a functional provirus enhances virus expression, again suggesting that viral production is carefully modulated in both a negative and positive manner.

The R region of the LTR codes for the 5′ untranslated leader sequence shared by all HIV-1 mRNAs and for the Tat-responsive element (TAR), essential for the activity of the potent virally coded HIV-1 *trans*-activating protein, Tat. The TAR is available in the LTR transcript as a unique stem loop structure. Of interest, the structure of the HIV-2 LTR is significantly different from that of the HIV-1 LTR and may contribute to distinctly different biologic activities of these two human retroviruses.

VIRUS-HOST INTERACTIONS

Viral Receptors, Chemokines, Receptors, and Tropism

Chemokines and their receptors constitute a complex signaling system essential for orchestrating inflammatory responses. Over 40 chemokines are grouped into two principal families, C-C and C-X-C; there are at least 14 known seven-transmembrane spanning, pertussis toxin–sensitive, G protein–coupled chemokine receptors. These molecules have been exploited by bacterial and viral pathogen receptors to gain entry or activate cells, and virally encoded antagonists often subvert chemokine function.[109, 110]

The revelation that chemokine receptors are essential for HIV cell fusion brings together several distinct areas of viral research: how $CD8^+$ cell–derived factors suppress HIV-1 replication; the mechanisms of cell entry and viral tropism; and host genetic determinants of infection. Three C-C cytokines released by $CD8^+$ T cells—RANTES, MIP-1α, and MIP-1β—bind to the CCR5 receptor and potently suppress HIV macrophage tropic virus.[38, 111] The first coreceptor identified, the CXCR4 molecule, known at the time only as an "orphan receptor," was discovered using a complementary DNA (cDNA) screening approach for receptor activity mediating cell-cell fusion.[39] A group of reports followed, showing that a recently identified receptor, CCR5, that could utilize as ligands the identified suppressor molecules, was the main coreceptor for primary isolates and macrophage tropic strains.[40–44] The number of receptors that may function as coreceptors continues to expand. Dual tropic strains are able to use both coreceptors. The role of other receptors, such as CX3CR1, expressed in the brain, or CCR8, expressed in the thymus, is not known. Some strains of monocyte-tropic virus may use CCR2 or CCR3. Chemokine coreceptor use may be a determinant of viral virulence and disease progression.[112]

A mutant CCR5 gene that codes for a receptor that is unable to bind virus has been found in exposed but uninfected persons, strongly suggesting that a functional CCR5 protein is required for infection.[113] Homozygosity for this mutant is a strong protective factor, but infections by CCR5-independent viruses have been documented in a person with hemophilia and in another person following sexual transmission. Heterozygous adults and children are not protected from infection but may take a longer time to develop disease.[114, 115]

Pathogenesis, T-Cell Depletion, and Viral Load

Understanding the rates of HIV-1 production and associated loss of T cells has been dramatically advanced by the ability to measure the changes produced by potent new drug combinations. HIV-1 production and T-cell turnover constitute a continuous dynamic process.[116, 117] Mathematical modeling of virus production has suggested that a continuous battle is being waged. Production of billions of virions and T-cell turnover estimated at a billion cells per day may help to account for the very rapid emergence of viral variants and the fluctuating and progressive nature of T-cell depletion. Virus may be distributed across different cellular compartments with different rates of turnover and production. Even in the steady state that may occur during periods of clinical latency, hordes of virus freshly infecting T cells lead to a highly activated immune system that is attempting both to control virus replication and to renew itself.[118] The increase in $CD4^+$ cells with highly active antiretroviral therapy (HAART) is probably due to a combination of initial redistribution of memory T cells and a continuous but slow repopulation with newly produced naive T cells.[119]

Although no similar measure of T-cell turnover in uninfected individuals is available, bromodeoxyuridine labeling of $CD4^+$ and $CD8^+$ populations in SIV-infected macaques suggested a generalized state of activation and rapid T-cell turnover compared with uninfected animals.

The mathematical models that have been proposed, while useful, probably grossly oversimplify the real dynamics of infection. Several pathologic mechanisms, including direct viral killing and activation-induced apoptosis, have been suggested. For example, circulating Tat protein, along with abnormally high levels of α-interferon in HIV-infected people, appears to suppress cell-mediated immunity.[94] Uninfected $CD8^+$ cells turn over as rapidly as $CD4^+$ cells but are not initially depleted.[120] The eventual loss of noninfected $CD8^+$ T cells may be mediated by gp120 binding to CXCR4.[121] Eventually, viral escape from immune control and emergence of T-cell–tropic viruses utilizing CXCR4 may lead to immunodeficiency.[122] All of these models incorporate two common assumptions: a demonstrated quantitative association between virus production and T-cell depletion and a compartmentalization of virus production and cell turnover at different rates.

The significance of virus integration for the natural history of HIV-1 infection has been vividly demonstrated by the effects of combination therapy on virus production from different populations of cells and has helped to define what is meant by latent infection. Potent antiretroviral regimens that include a combination of RT and protease inhibitors can produce sustained reductions of plasma viral RNA to below detectable limits.[123] Patients with detectable viral plasma RNA, even if the level is greatly reduced, have viral loads in their lymph nodes similar to those in the nodes of patients who did not receive treatment, reflecting ongoing viral replication and emergence of drug resistance.[124] However, even in persons with no detectable plasma RNA, viral DNA could be detected in lymph nodes and peripheral blood mononuclear cells (PBMCs), and virus could be grown from PBMCs after removal of $CD8^+$ cells and activation. Furthermore, no new mutations associated with drug resistance were detected from these isolates recovered after 2 years of therapy. This strongly suggests that virus persisted in a long-lived and latently infected T-cell population. This pool of latently infected cells is probably established very early during primary HIV-1 infection. Even though plasma viremia could be suppressed, initiation of HAART therapy as early as 10 days after onset of symptoms did not prevent generation of latently infected $CD4^+$ lymphocytes.[125] Although the frequency of these cells is low, on the order of 16 per million PBMCs, the fact that virus may survive by hiding out in these cells may represent a significant factor in long-term therapy and shape strategies to eliminate virus.[126, 127]

Viral Variation: Genetic and Phenotypic Variation

One of the most striking characteristics of HIV-1 is its remarkable variability contributing to phenotype diversity, resulting in altered cell tropism, immune escape, and resistance to RT and protease inhibitors.[128] As a consequence of the underlying variation by mutation, high rates of virus turnover and selection of viral variants cause viral evolution in individual hosts with time, as well as among populations of infected individuals. On the basis of phylogenetic analysis, HIV strains can be separated into genetic subgroups A-J and a more distant group O. In an individual case, the initial infection transmits a limited range of variants, generally of a single group, and subsequent exposure following infection rarely results in infection with a second variant. Therefore, most affected persons appear to be infected with a single strain that evolves into a swarm of related viruses or quasispecies during the course of infection.[129] By the time a person has been infected for several years, viruses emerge that are able to use the CXCR4 receptor. This phenotypic change is associated with progressive disease. Most of the variation is neutral and not adaptive. Although the mutation rate per base pair per cycle is presumed to be equal throughout the genome, diversity is greatest within distinct regions of the envelope gp120, presumably owing to selection. Neutral variation has resulted in grouping of the viruses into clades that may represent geographic distribution and transmission of virus rather than functional differences. HIV is going through rapid epidemiologic change even as the virus is being studied. Thus, genetic relatedness of viruses can be used to track transmission of the virus as well as the relatedness of different viruses. This information is often presented in the form of a viral phylogenetic tree.[130, 130a]

HUMAN IMMUNODEFICIENCY VIRUS–RELATED NEUROLOGIC DISEASE

Approximately half of all HIV-infected patients, including children, will develop neurologic disease during the course of infection. Disease may be caused directly by HIV infection of the nervous system or secondarily by infection or tumors associated with immunodeficiency. Primary neurologic disease can occur anytime during the course of infection and anywhere along the CNS neuraxis; the AIDS dementia complex, vacuolar neuropathy, and peripheral neuropathy are the most frequent presentations[131, 132] (see Chapter 110).

AIDS-dementia complex is a progressive disorder that can be manifested as signs and symptoms of behavioral, cognitive, or motor dysfunction in any combination. Examination of brain tissue and spinal cord shows high levels of HIV-1 mRNA and expression of viral proteins in microglial cells and macrophages in 90% of symptomatic patients. The extent of virus expression correlates with the severity of clinical disease and increases with time. Viral levels measured in the cerebrospinal fluid (CSF) reflect active production of virus. High levels ($>10^6$ copies/ml) suggest high viral loads in the CNS and may be independent of levels found in the peripheral circulation.[133] Vacuolar myelopathy is a unique degeneration of the spinal cord that may be found in 20% of AIDS patients. Although the etiology and role of the virus are still unclear, the disorder is associated with dementia and bears the same pathologic hallmark of multinucleated cells. HIV-1 is also associated with a diverse group of peripheral neuropathies, and the virus can be demonstrated in the dorsal root ganglia and peripheral nerves.

In vitro studies of human brain cultures have shown that HIV-1 is efficiently expressed only in microglial cells and that the ability to infect these cells is the same as for the macrophage. Infection of microglial cells, probably derived from circulating macrophages, requires binding to CD4 and the presence of a chemokine receptor (CCR3 or CCR5) that mediates fusion with macrophage tropic strains.[134] Of great interest, neurologic symptoms and virologic evidence of CSF infection can be found during primary HIV infection prior to seroconversion. This suggests that the CNS is seeded with virus very early and possibly continually during the course of infection.

The pathologic mechanism responsible for neurologic degeneration is not known. However, several mechanisms have been proposed. Most of these involve toxicity associated with HIV-1 proteins or release of cellular products from infected cells. For example, gp120 has been shown to be toxic to neurons in vitro, and TNF-α is toxic to oligodendrocytes, the myelin-forming cells of the CNS. Tat and Nef have also been shown to be neurotoxic. It should be noted that the damage seen in AIDS dementia is not cell type–specific but, rather, is generalized, affecting all of the cells within a given area of the brain, and that the lesions are widely distributed. Clusters of HIV-1–infected microglial cells form nodules and characteristic multinucleated syncytia, with loss of surrounding tissue, resulting in spongiform lesions. Imaging often demonstrates a degree of brain atrophy.[135] Antiviral therapy can produce a dramatic reversal of dementia, particularly in children. Therapy has been chiefly directed to prevention of opportunistic infections and antiretroviral therapy. Zidovudine, which crosses the blood-brain barrier, has been effective, sometimes dramatically so, in both children and adults. The effect of current combined therapy on clinical and virologic CNS disease is not yet known.[136]

MALIGNANCIES AND HUMAN IMMUNODEFICIENCY VIRUS

Although cancer is not common in the young adults that are most frequently exposed to HIV, KS was recognized as a defining clinical presentation of AIDS. Previously known as a rare and usually indolent vascular tumor, the incidence in patients with HIV infection may be 10 to 20%, more than 10,000 times than that in the general population. Several forms of KS have been described: classic KS; endemic KS, not HIV-associated; transplantation-associated KS; and AIDS-associated KS. The tumor appears to be a vascular proliferation characterized by the presence of spindle cells, vascular channels, and a mixed cellular infiltrate.[137] The "malignant" cell is most likely a population of activated endothelial cells which are sometimes clonal and sometimes not. These cells themselves and factors produced from these cells, such as basic fibroblast growth factor (bFGF) and vascular endothelial cell growth factor (VEGF), can induce vascular lesions in nude mice. The HIV protein Tat can bind to KS spindle cells and stimulate their growth.[138] Although the importance of immunodeficiency and viral proliferation in the etiology of KS is well established, the mechanism is not certain, and KS may occur early in the course of HIV infection. Within the group of HIV-infected individuals, KS occurs predominantly in homosexuals and bisexuals, leading to the hypothesis that a previously undescribed infectious agent might cause KS. Using modern culture techniques, two new human herpesviruses—HHV-6 and HHV-7—were isolated from T cells in 1986. In 1994, using DNA subtraction hybridization, DNA representing a novel herpesvirus was obtained from KS lesions, which led to the isolation of HHV-8[139] (see Chapter 129). Also known as KS herpesvirus (KSHV), it is related to other gamma herpesviruses such as Epstein-Barr virus (EBV). HHV-8 has also been identified in an EBV-transformed B-cell line and from a unique form of B-cell lymphoma known as body cavity lymphoma. This large virus contains many genes that interact with host cells, including several chemokine and cytokine homologues that can induce vascular growth.[140] Seroepidemiologic studies have made a strong association between this virus and KS. Virus was found to be associated with all forms of KS, and seroconversion precedes the appearance of KS in HIV-infected persons. The prevalence of HHV-8 is far greater than the incidence of KS, however, and the relationship of the virus to the disease is not likely to be simple. A recent review discusses this and other aspects of KS that are not clear at present.[141] Although the incidence of KS appears to be decreasing and established lesions may respond to antiviral therapy, clinicians are still faced with the challenge of treating a cancer with considerable morbidity.

Non-Hodgkin's lymphoma occurs at a rate over 200-fold higher in HIV-infected patients, affecting about 10% of those with $CD4^+$ counts of less than 200. These tumors are predominantly extranodal and often of high grade, with small cell non-cleaved histologic features[142, 143] (see Chapter 111). EBV is found in almost all primary CNS tumors, but high rates of dysregulated B-cell turnover may account for increased cellular turnover, which predisposes to lymphoma.[144] Several other rare tumors, including leiomyosarcoma, have been reported as well.[145] Cervical cancer, almost universally associated with human papillomavirus infection, is accepted as an AIDS-defining illness.[146] However, the incidence of common cancers does not appear to be greatly increased. Most of the cancers seen appear to be associated directly or indirectly with viral proliferation, so that the role of the immune system may be more directly related to viral expression than to immune control of tumor.

CONCLUSION

Antiretroviral therapy directed at HIV-1 has continued to change as rapidly as anything in medicine. Significant advances in the ability to treat individual cases, propelled by an understanding of the biology of the virus, have led to the control of viral replication and have altered the course of disease progression. At present, patients have been maintained on combination therapy for several years, with a low rate of relapse due to development of resistance and low viral burdens. Immune restoration and long-term control or complete eradication of the viral burden with minimal toxicity remain elusive challenges, while intense efforts continue to focus on new anti-HIV therapies. As we have learned, retroviral disease has a social aspect that, as much as viral biology, determines the extent of viral transmission and the dimensions of the epidemic, resulting in a series of epidemics, each with a unique sociobiology. Moreover, despite remarkable progress, the full social and economic effects of the global HIV epidemic are just starting to materialize, with devastating losses of population and productivity (see Chapter 104). Renewed emphasis on an anti-HIV vaccine that might either stem an ongoing epidemic or ameliorate the course of disease has produced encouraging results in primates and the beginning of human trials (see Chapter 117). The long history of retrovirology has been filled with remarkable, often unexpected discoveries based on scientific imagination supported by technological advances. There is every reason to expect that continued advances will deepen our understanding of fundamental biologic processes and that we will meet the challenges presented by HIV and the inevitability of the emergence of new pathogens.

REFERENCES

1. Masur H, Michelis MA, Greene JB, et al. An outbreak of community-acquired *Pneumocystis carinii* pneumonia: Initial manifestations of cellular immune dysfunction. N Engl J Med. 1981;305:1431.
2. Gottlieb MS, Schroff R, Schanker HM, et al. *Pneumocystis carinii* pneumonia and mucosal candidiasis in previously healthy homosexual men: Evidence of a new acquired cellular immunodeficiency. N Engl J Med. 1981;305:1425.
3. Durack DT. Opportunistic infections and Kaposi's sarcoma in homosexual men. N Engl J Med. 1981;305:1465.
4. Kalyanaraman VS, Sarngadharan MG, Robert-Guroff M, et al. A new subtype of human T-cell leukaemia virus (HTLV-II) associated with a T-cell variant of hairy cell leukaemia. Science. 1982;218:571.
5. Poiesz BJ, Ruscetti FW, Reitz MS, et al. Isolation of a new type-C retrovirus (HTLV) in primary uncultured cells of a patient with Sézary T-cell leukaemia. Nature. 1981;294:268.
6. Gallo RC, Montagnier L. AIDS in 1988. Sci Am. 1988;259:41.
7. Barre-Sinoussi F, Chermann JC, Rey F, et al. Isolation of a T-lymphotrophic retrovirus from a patient at risk for acquired immune deficiency syndrome (AIDS). Science. 1983;220:868.
8. Gallo RC, Salahuddin SZ, Popovic M, et al. Human T-lymphotropic retrovirus, HTLV-III, isolated from AIDS patients and donors at risk for AIDS. Science. 1984;224:500.
9. Popovic M, Sarngadharan MG, Read E, et al. A method for the detection, isolation, and continuous production of cytopathic human T-lymphotropic retroviruses of the HTLV family (HTLV-III) from patients with AIDS and pre-AIDS. Science. 1984;224:497.
10. Schupbach J, Popovic M, Gilden RV, et al. Serological analysis of a subgroup of human T-lymphotropic retroviruses (HTLV-III) associated with AIDS. Science. 1984;224:503.
11. Sarngadharan MG, Popovic M, Bruch L, et al. Antibodies reactive with human T-lymphotropic retroviruses (HTLV-III) in the serum of patients with AIDS. Science. 1984;224:506.
12. Mitsuya H, Weinhold KJ, Furman PA, et al. 3′-Azido-2′-deoxythymidine (BW A509U): An antiviral agent that inhibits the infectivity and cytopathic effect of human T-lymphotrophic virus type III/lymphadenopathy associated virus in vitro. Proc Natl Acad Sci U S A. 1985;82:7096.
13. Coffin J. Retrovirology: An overview. In: Wormser G, ed. AIDS and Other Manifestations of HIV Infection. Philadelphia: Lippincott-Raven; 1998:41.
14. Boller K, Konig H, Sauter M, et al. Evidence that HERV-K is the endogenous retrovirus sequence that codes for the human teratocarcinoma-derived retrovirus HTDV. Virology. 1993;196:349.

15. Ellerman V, Bang O. Experimentelle leukamie bei huhnem. Centralbl Bacteriol. 1908;46:595.
16. Rous P. Transmission of a malignant new growth by means of a cell-free filtrate. JAMA. 1911;56:198.
17. Gross L. Development and serial cell-free passage of a highly potent strain of mouse leukemia virus. Proc Soc Exp Biol Med. 1957;76:27.
18. Temin HM. The effects of actinomycin D on growth of Rous sarcoma virus in vitro. Virology. 1963;20:577.
19. Temin HM. The participation of DNA in Rous sarcoma virus production. Virology. 1964;23:486.
20. Temin H, Mizutani S. RNA-dependent DNA polymerase in virions of Rous sarcoma virus. Nature. 1970;226:1211.
21. Baltimore D. Viral RNA–dependent DNA polymerase. Nature. 1970;226:1209.
22. Gessain A, Barin F, Vernanat J. Antibodies to human T-lymphotropic virus type-I in patients with tropical spastic paraparesis. Lancet. 1985;2:407.
23. Kanki PJ, Barin F, M'Boup M, et al. New human T-lymphotropic retrovirus related to simian T-lymphotropic retrovirus type III (STLV-III). Science. 1986;232:238.
24. Clavel F, Guetard D, Brun-Vezinet F, et al. Isolation of a new human retrovirus from West African patients with AIDS. Science. 1986;233:343.
25. Weiss R. Retroviral zoonoses. Nat Med. 1998;4:391.
26. Kidwell MG, Lisch DR. Hybrid genetics: Transposons unbound. Nature. 1998;393:22.
27. Kobayashi K, Nakahori Y, Miyake M, et al. An ancient retrotransposal insertion causes Fukuyama-type congenital muscular dystrophy. Nature. 1998;394:388.
28. Coffin J, Hughs S, Varmus H. Retroviruses. Cold Spring Harbor, NY: Cold Spring Harbor Laboratory Press; 1998.
29. Miedema F, Meyaard L, Koot M, et al. Changing virus-host interactions in the course of HIV-1 infection. Immunol Rev. 1994;140:35.
30. Kahn JO, Walker BD. Acute human immunodeficiency virus type 1 infection. N Engl J Med. 1998;339:33.
31. Ogg GS, Jin X, Bonhoeffer S, et al. Quantitation of HIV-1–specific cytotoxic T lymphocytes and plasma load of viral RNA. Science. 1998;279:2103.
32. Musey L, Hughes J, Schacker T, et al. Cytotoxic T-cell responses, viral load, and disease progression in early human immunodeficiency virus type 1 infection. N Engl J Med. 1997;337:1267.
33. Schacker TW, Hughes JP, Shea T, et al. Biological and virologic characteristics of primary HIV infection. Ann Intern Med. 1998;128:613.
34. Cardo DM, Culver DH, Ciesielski CA, et al. A case-control study of HIV seroconversion in health care workers after percutaneous exposure. (Centers for Disease Control and Prevention Needle-stick Surveillance Group.) N Engl J Med. 1997;337:1485.
35. Katz MH, Gerberding JL. The care of persons with recent sexual exposure to HIV. Ann Intern Med. 1998;128:306.
36. Maddon PJ, McDougal JS, Clapham PR, et al. HIV infection does not require endocytosis of its receptor, CD4. Cell. 1988;54:865.
37. Gartner S, Markovits P, Markovitz DM, et al. The role of mononuclear phagocytes in HTLV-III/LAV infection. Science. 1986;233:215.
38. Cocchi F, DeVico AL, Garzino-Demo A, et al. Identification of RANTES, MIP-1α, and MIP-1β as the major HIV-suppressive factors produced by CD8^{+}T cells. Science. 1995;270:1811.
39. Feng Y, Broder CC, Kennedy PE, Berger EA. HIV-1 entry cofactor: Functional cDNA cloning of a seven-transmembrane, G protein–coupled receptor. Science. 1996;272:872.
40. Deng H, Liu R, Ellmeirer W, et al. Identification of a major co-receptor for primary isolates of HIV-1. Nature. 1996;381:661.
41. Choe H, Farzan M, Sun Y, et al. The β-chemokine receptors CCR3 and CCR5 facilitate infection by primary HIV-1 isolates. Cell. 1996;85:1135.
42. Dragic T, Litwin V, Allaway GP, et al. HIV-1 entry into CD4+ cells is mediated by the chemokine receptor CC-CKR-5. Nature. 1996;381:667.
43. Alkhatib G, Combadiere C, Broder CC, et al. CC CKR5: A RANTES, MIP-1α, MIP-1β receptor as a fusion cofactor for macrophage-tropic HIV-1. Science. 1996;272:1955.
44. O'Brien S. AIDS: A role for host genes. Hosp Pract. 1998;33:53.
45. Wyatt R, Sodroski J. The HIV-1 envelope glycoprotein: Fusogens, antigens, and immunogens. Science. 1998;280:1884.
46. Reitter JN, Means RE, Desrosiers RC. A role for carbohydrates in immune evasion in AIDS. Nat Med. 1998;4:679.
47. Sherry B, Zybarth G, Alfano M, et al. Role of cyclophilin A in the uptake of HIV-1 by macrophages and T lymphocytes. Proc Natl Acad Sci U S A. 1998;95:1758.
48. Braaten D, Franke EK, Luban J. Cyclophilin A is required for an early step in the life cycle of human immunodeficiency virus type 1 before the initiation of reverse transcription. J Virol. 1996;70:3551.
49. Emerman M, Malim MH. HIV-1 regulatory/accessory genes: Keys to unraveling viral and host cell biology. Science. 1998;280:1880.
50. Wong-Staal F. Human immunodeficiency viruses and their replication. In: Fields BN, ed. Virology. 2nd ed. New York: Raven Press; 1990:1529.
51. Peliska JA, Benkovic SJ. Mechanism of DNA strand transfer reactions catalyzed by HIV-1 reverse transcriptase. Science. 1992;258:1112.
52. Lori F, Malykh A, Cara A, et al. Hydroxyurea as an inhibitor of human immunodeficiency virus-type 1 replication. Science. 1994;266:801.
53. Rutschmann O, Opravil M, Iten A, et al. A placebo-controlled trial of didanosine plus stavudine, with and without hydroxyurea, for HIV infection. AIDS. 1998;12:F71.
54. Farnet CM, Hasseltine WA. Determination of viral proteins present in the human immunodeficiency virus type 1 preintegration complex. J Virol. 1991;65:1910.
55. Wiskerchen M, Muesing MA. Human immunodeficiency virus type 1 integrase: Effects of mutations on viral ability to integrate direct viral gene expression from unintegrated viral DNA templates, and sustain propagation in primary cells. J Virol. 1995;69:376.
56. Cara A, Cereseto A, Lori F, Reitz MS Jr. HIV-1 protein expression from synthetic circles of DNA mimicking the extrachromosomal forms of viral DNA. J Biol Chem. 1996;271:5393.
57. Stevens SW, Griffith JD. Human immunodeficiency virus type 1 may preferentially integrate into chromatin occupied by L1Hs repetitive elements. Proc Natl Acad Sci U S A. 1994;91:5557.
58. Honda Y, Rogers L, Nakata K, et al. Type I interferon induces inhibitory 16-kD CCAAT/enhancer binding protein (C/EBP) beta, repressing the HIV-1 long terminal repeat in macrophages: Pulmonary tuberculosis alters C/EBP expression, enhancing HIV-1 replication. J Exp Med. 1998;188:1255.
59. Kawakami K, Scheidereit C, Roeder RG. Identification and purification of a human immunoglobulin enhancer-binding protein (NF-κB) that activates transcription from a human immunodeficiency virus type 1 promoter in vitro. Proc Natl Acad Sci U S A. 1988;85:4700.
60. Nabel G, Baltimore D. An inducible transcription factor activates expression of human immunodeficiency virus in T cells. Nature. 1987;326:711.
61. Kim SY, Byrn R, Groopman J, Baltimore D. Temporal aspects of DNA and RNA synthesis during human immunodeficiency virus infection: Evidence for differential gene expression. J Virol. 1989;63:3708.
62. Klotman ME, Kim S, Buchbinder A, et al. Kinetics of expression of multiply spliced RNA in early human immunodeficiency virus type 1 infection of lymphocytes and monocytes. Proc Natl Acad Sci U S A. 1991;88:5011.
63. Hoglund S, Ofverstedt LG, Nilsson A, et al. Spatial visualization of the maturing HIV-1 core and its linkage to the envelope. AIDS Res Hum Retroviruses. 1992;8:1.
64. Arthur LO, Bess JW Jr, Sowder RC II, et al. Cellular proteins bound to immunodeficiency viruses: Implications for pathogenesis and vaccines. Science. 1992;258:1935.
65. Flexner C. HIV-protease inhibitors. N Engl J Med. 1998;338:1281.
66. Bryant M, Ratner L. Myristoylation-dependent replication and assembly of human immunodeficiency virus I. Proc Natl Acad Sci U S A. 1990;87:523.
67. Bukrinsky MI, Haggerty S, Dempsey MP, et al. A nuclear localization signal within HIV-1 matrix protein that governs infection of non-dividing cells. Nature. 1993;365:666.
68. Luban J, Bossolt KL, Franke EK, et al. Human immunodeficiency virus type 1 Gag protein binds to cyclophilins A and B. Cell. 1993;73:1067.
69. Mammano F, Ohagen A, Hoglund S, Gottlinger HG. Role of the major homology region of human immunodeficiency virus type 1 in virion morphogenesis. J Virol. 1994;68:4927.
70. Dorfman T, Bukovsky A, Ohagen A, et al. Functional domains of the capsid protein of human immunodeficiency virus type 1. J Virol. 1994;68:8180.
71. Karpel RL, Henderson LE, Oroszlan S. Interactions of retroviral structural proteins with single-stranded nucleic acids. J Biol Chem. 1987;262:4961.
72. South TL, Blake PR, Sowder RC III, et al. The nucleocapsid protein isolated from HIV-1 particles binds zinc and forms retroviral-type zinc fingers. Biochemistry. 1990;29:7786.
73. Sakaguchi K, Zambrano N, Baldwin ET, et al. Identification of a binding site for the human immunodeficiency virus type 1 nucleocapsid protein. Proc Natl Acad Sci U S A. 1993;90:5219.
74. Roberts NA, Martin JA, Kinchington D, et al. Rational design of peptide-based HIV proteinase inhibitors. Science. 1990;248:358.
75. Huang H, Chopra R, Verdine G, Harrison S. Structure of a covalently trapped catalytic complex of HIV-1 reverse transcriptase: Implications for drug resistance. Science. 1998;282:1669.
76. Arnold E, Jacobo-Molina A, Nanni R, et al. Structure of HIV-1 reverse transcriptase/DNA complex at 7 Å resolution showing active site locations. Nature. 1993;357:85.
77. Kohlstaedt L, Wang JM, Friedman J, et al. The structure of HIV-1 reverse transcriptase. In: Skalka A, Goff S, eds. Reverse Transcriptase. Cold Spring Harbor, NY: Cold Spring Harbor Laboratory Press; 1993:223.
78. Lukashov VV, Goudsmit J. HIV heterogeneity and disease progression in AIDS: A model of continuous virus adaptation. AIDS. 1998;12:S43.
79. Pavlakis G. The molecular biology of human immunodeficiency virus type 1. In: DeVita V, Hellman S, Rosenberg S, eds. AIDS: Biology, Treatment, and Prevention. Philadelphia: Lippincott-Raven; 1997:45.
80. Varmus H. Retroviruses. Science. 1988;240:1427.
81. Bukrinsky MI, Sharova N, McDonald TL, et al. Association of integrase, matrix, and reverse transcriptase antigens of human immunodeficiency virus type 1 with viral nucleic acids following acute infection. Proc Natl Acad Sci U S A. 1993;90:6125.
82. Starcich BR, Hahn BH, Shaw GM, et al. Identification and characterization of conserved and variable regions in the envelope gene of HTLV-III/LAV, the retrovirus of AIDS. Cell. 1986;45:637.
83. Kwong PD, Wyatt R, Robinson J, et al. Structure of an HIV gp120 envelope glycoprotein in complex with the CD4 receptor and a neutralizing human antibody. Nature. 1998;393:648.
84. Wyatt R, Kwong PD, Desjardins E, et al. The antigenic structure of the HIV gp120 envelope glycoprotein. Nature. 1998;393:705.
85. Balter M. Revealing HIV's T cell passkey. Science. 1998;280:1833.
86. White JM. Membrane fusion. Science. 1992;258:917.
87. Chan DC, Fass D, Berger JM, Kim PS. Core structure of gp41 from the HIV envelope glycoprotein. Cell. 1997;89:263.

88. Furuta RA, Wild CT, Weng Y, Weiss CD. Capture of an early fusion-active conformation of HIV-1 gp41 (Published erratum: Nat Struct Biol. 1998;5:612). Nat Struct Biol. 1998;5:276.
89. Wild CT, Shugars DC, Greenwell TK, et al. Peptides corresponding to a predictive alpha-helical domain of human immunodeficiency virus type 1 gp41 are potent inhibitors of virus infection. Proc Natl Acad Sci U S A 1994;91:9770.
89a. Garrett ED, Tiley LS, Cullen BR. Rev activates expression of the human immunodeficiency virus type 1 *vif* and *vpr* gene products. J Virol. 1991;65:1653.
90. Fischer AG, Feinberg MB, Josephs SF, et al. The trans-activator gene of HTLV-III is essential for virus replication. Nature. 1986;320:367.
91. Wei P, Garber ME, Fang SM, et al. A novel CDK-9–associated C-type cyclin interacts directly with HIV-1 Tat and mediates its high-affinity, loop-specific binding to TAR RNA. Cell. 1998;92:451.
92. Ensoli B, Gendelman R, Markham P, et al. Synergy between basic fibroblast growth factor and HIV-1 Tat protein in induction of Kaposi's sarcoma. Nature. 1994;371:674.
93. Luznik L, Kraus G, Guatelli J, et al. Tat-independent replication of human immunodeficiency viruses. J Clin Invest. 1995;95:328.
94. Zagury D, Lachgar A, Chams V, et al. Interferon alpha and Tat involvement in the immunosuppression of uninfected T cells and C-C chemokine decline in AIDS. Proc Natl Acad Sci U S A. 1998;31:3581.
95. Sodroski J, Goh WC, Rosen C, et al. A second post-transcriptional trans-activator gene required for HTLV-III replication. Nature. 1986;321:412.
96. Malim MH, Bohnlein S, Hauber J, Cullen BR. Functional dissection of the HIV Rev trans-activator-derivation of a trans-dominant repressor of Rev function. Cell. 1989;58:205.
97. Collins KL, Chen BK, Kalams SA, et al. HIV-1 Nef protein protects infected primary cells against killing by cytotoxic T lymphocytes. Nature. 1998;391:397.
98. Koenig S, Conley AJ, Brewah YA, et al. Transfer of HIV-1–specific cytotoxic T lymphocytes to an AIDS patient leads to selection for mutant HIV variants and subsequent disease progression. Nat Med. 1995;1:330.
99. Deacon NJ, Tsykin A, Solomon A, et al. Genomic structure of an attenuated quasispecies of HIV-1 from a blood transfusion donor and recipients. Science. 1995;270:988.
100. Oberste MS, Gonda MA. Conservation of amino-acid sequence motifs in lentivirus Vif proteins. Virus Genes. 1992;6:95.
101. Heinzinger NK, Bukinsky MI, Haggerty SA, et al. The Vpr protein of human immunodeficiency virus type 1 influences nuclear localization of viral nucleic acids in non-dividing host cells. Proc Natl Acad Sci U S A. 1994;91:7311.
102. Felzien LK, Woffendin C, Hottiger MO, et al. HIV transcriptional activation by the accessory protein, VPR, is mediated by the p300 co-activator. Proc Natl Acad Sci U S A. 1998;95:5281.
103. Poon B, Grovit-Ferbas K, Stewart SA, Chen ISY. Cell cycle arrest by Vpr in HIV-1 virions and insensitivity to antiretroviral agents. Science. 1998;281:266.
104. Maldarelli F, Chen MY, Willey RL, Strebel K. Human immunodeficiency virus type 1 Vpu protein is an oligomeric type I integral membrane protein. J Virol. 1993;67:5056.
105. Schwartz S, Felber BK, Fenyo EM, Pavlakis GN. Env and Vpu proteins of human immunodeficiency virus type 1 are produced from multiple bicistronic mRNAs. J Virol. 1990;64:5448.
106. Pinto LH, Holsinger LJ, Lamb RA. Influenza virus M2 protein has ion channel activity. Cell. 1992;69:517.
107. Fan H. Influences of the long terminal repeats on retrovirus pathogenicity. Semin Virol. 1990;1:165.
108. Jones KA, Peterlin BM. Control of RNA initiation and elongation at the HIV-1 promoter. Annu Rev Biochem. 1994;63:717.
109. Pease JE, Murphy P. Microbial corruption of the chemokine system: An expanding paradigm. Semin Immunol. 1998;10:169.
110. Premack BA, Schall TJ. Chemokine receptors: Gateways to inflammation and infection. Nat Med. 1996;2:1174.
111. Garzino-Demo A, DeVico AL, Cocchi F, Gallo RC. Beta-chemokines and protection from HIV type 1 disease. AIDS Res Hum Retroviruses. 1998;14:S177.
112. Connor RI, Sheridan KE, Ceradini D, et al. Change in co-receptor use correlates with disease progression in HIV-1–infected individuals. J Exp Med. 1997;185:621.
113. Liu R, Paxton WA, Choe S, et al. Homozygous defect in HIV-1 co-receptor accounts for resistance of some multiply-exposed individuals to HIV infection. Cell. 1996;86:367.
114. O'Brien TR, Goedert JJ. Chemokine receptors and genetic variability: Another leap in HIV research. JAMA. 1998;279:317.
115. Misrahi M, Teglas JP, N'Go N, et al. CCR5 chemokine receptor variant in HIV-1 mother-to-child transmission and disease progression in children (French Pediatric HIV Infection Study Group). JAMA. 1998;279:277.
116. Wei X, Ghosh SK, Taylor ME, et al. Viral dynamics in human immunodeficiency virus type 1 infection. Nature. 1995;373:117.
117. Ho DD, Neumann AU, Perelson AS, et al. Rapid turnover of plasma virions and $CD4^+$ lymphocytes in HIV-1 infection. Nature. 1995;373:123.
118. Coffin JM. HIV population dynamics in vivo: Implications for genetic variation, pathogenesis, and therapy. Science. 1995;267:483.
119. Pakker NG, Notermans DW, deBoer RJ, et al. Biphasic kinetics of peripheral blood T cells after triple combination therapy in HIV-1 infection: A composite of redistribution and proliferation. Nat Med. 1998;4:208.
120. Mohri H, Bonhoeffer S, Monard S, et al. Rapid turnover of T lymphocytes in SIV-infected rhesus macaques. Science. 1998;279:1223.
121. Herbein G, Mahlnecht U, Batliwalla F, et al. Apoptosis of CD8+ T cells is mediated by macrophages through interaction of HIV gp120 with chemokine receptor CXCR4. Nature. 1998;395:189.
122. Zagury D. A naturally unbalanced combat. Nat Med. 1997;3:156.
123. Gulick RM, Mellors JW, Havlir D, et al. Treatment with indinavir, zidovudine, and lamivudine in adults with human immunodeficiency virus infection and prior antiretroviral therapy. N Engl J Med. 1997;337:734.
124. Wong JK, Gunthard HF, Havlir DV, et al. Reduction of HIV-1 in blood and lymph nodes following potent antiretroviral therapy and the virologic correlates of treatment failure. Proc Natl Acad Sci U S A. 1997;94:12574.
125. Chun TW, Engel D, Berrey MM, et al. Early establishment of a pool of latently infected, resting $CD4^+$ T cells during primary HIV-1 infection. Proc Natl Acad Sci U S A. 1998;95:8869.
126. Wong JK, Hezareh M, Gunthard HF, et al. Recovery of replication-competent HIV despite prolonged suppression of plasma viremia. Science. 1997;278:1291.
127. Finzi D, Hermankova M, Pierson T, et al. Identification of a reservoir for HIV-1 in patients on highly active antiretroviral therapy. Science. 1997;278:1295.
128. Wong-Staal F, Shaw GM, Hahn BH, et al. Genomic diversity of human T-lymphotropic virus type III (HTLV-III). Science. 1985;229:759.
129. Wolinsky SM, Wike CM, Korber BT, et al. Selective transmission of human immunodeficiency virus type-1 variants from mothers to infants. Science. 1992;225:1134.
130. Korber B, Theiler J, Wolinsky S. Limitations of a molecular clock applied to considerations of the origin of HIV-1. Science. 1998;280:1868.
130a. Meyers G, Berzofsky JA, Korber B, et al. Human Retroviruses and AIDS. Los Alamos National Laboratory, New Mexico, 1992.
131. Glass JD, Johnson RT. Human immunodeficiency virus and the brain. Annu Rev Neurosci. 1996;19:1.
132. Berger J, Levy R. AIDS and the Nervous System. Philadelphia: Lippincott-Raven; 1997.
133. Wiley CA, Soontornniyomkij V, Radhakrishnan L, et al. Distribution of brain HIV loads in AIDS. Brain Pathol. 1998;8:277.
134. Westmoreland SV, Rottman JB, Williams KC, et al. Chemokine receptor expression on resident and inflammatory cells in the brain of macaques with simian immunodeficiency virus encephalitis. Am J Pathol. 1998;152:659.
135. Budka H. Neuropathology of human immunodeficiency virus infection. Brain Pathol. 1991;1:163.
136. Foudranine N, Hoetelmans R, Lange J, et al. Cerebrospinal-fluid HIV-1 RNA and drug concentrations after treatment with lamivudine plus zidovudine or stavudine. Lancet. 1998;351:1547.
137. Safai B. Tumors in HIV infection. In: Wormser G, ed. AIDS and Other Manifestations of HIV Infection. Philadelphia: Lippincott-Raven; 1998:295.
138. Ensoli B, Barillari G, Salahuddin SZ, et al. Tat protein of HIV stimulates growth of cells derived from Kaposi's sarcoma lesions of AIDS patients. Nature. 1990;345:84.
139. Chang Y, Cesarman E, Pessin MS, et al. Identification of herpesvirus-like DNA sequences in AIDS-associated Kaposi sarcoma. Science. 1994;266:1865.
140. Arvanitakis L, Geras-Raaka E, Varma A, et al. Human herpesvirus KSHV encodes a constitutively active G-protein–coupled receptor linked to cell proliferation. Nature. 1997;385:347.
141. Gallo RC. The enigmas of Kaposi's sarcoma. Science. 1998;282:1837.
142. Cote TR, Biggar RJ, Rosenberg PS, et al. Non-Hodgkin's lymphoma among people with AIDS: Incidence, presentation and public health burden. Int J Cancer. 1997;73:645.
143. Beral V, Peterman T, Berkelman R, Jaffe H. AIDS-associated non-Hodgkin's lymphoma. Lancet. 1991;337:805.
144. Flinn I, Ambinder R: AIDS primary central nervous system lymphoma. Curr Opin Oncol. 1966;8:373.
145. McClain KL, Leach CJ, Jenson HB et al: Association of Epstein-Barr virus with leiomyosarcomas in young people with AIDS. N Engl J Med. 1995;332:12.
146. Williams AB, Darragh TM, Vranizan K, et al. Anal and cervical human papillomavirus infection and risk of anal and cervical intraepithelial abnormalities in human immunodeficiency virus-infected women. Obstet Gynecol. 1994;83:205.

Picornaviridae

Chapter 158

Introduction to Picornaviridae

JOHN F. MODLIN

CHARACTERISTICS OF PICORNAVIRUSES

The sigla of the coined word picornavirus (pico, "very small"; RNA, nucleic acid type) describe the hallmarks of this large family of animal viruses.[1] Picornaviruses are icosahedral, approximately 30 nm in diameter, and nonenveloped. The virion capsid is composed of 60 structural subunits that are formed from four polypeptides with an aggregate molecular weight of 80 to 140 kD. The capsid encloses a linear, single-stranded RNA genome approximately 7.5 kilobases in length. The RNA is infectious and either may serve as a template for the synthesis of additional RNA or may be encapsidated to form progeny virions. The RNA also functions as a monocistronic messenger whose translational product, a "polyprotein" of molecular weight 250 kD, is coded for by a single open reading frame involving about 90% of the entire genome. The polyprotein subsequently undergoes specific cleavages to form the structural polypeptides, an RNA replicase, viral-coded proteases, and additional polypeptides necessary for intracellular replication.

Lacking a lipid envelope, picornaviruses are resistant to ether, chloroform, and alcohol. However, they are readily inactivated by ionizing radiation, formaldehyde, and phenol.[1]

CLASSIFICATION OF PICORNAVIRUSES

The family Picornaviridae can be separated into five genuses according to aligned VP1 sequence information: (1) aphthoviruses, (2) cardioviruses, (3) enteroviruses, (4) rhinoviruses, and (5) heparnaviruses. The cardioviruses and aphthoviruses are prominent pathogens of mice and cloven-hoofed farm animals, respectively. In addition, there are other enteroviruses and rhinoviruses whose natural hosts are monkeys, cattle, horses, swine, and insects. Hepatitis A virus is the sole representative of the Heparnavirus genus.

The subclassification of the human enteroviruses and rhinoviruses is shown in Table 158–1. These two classes are morphologically identical but can be distinguished on the basis of several clinical, epidemiologic, and biophysical properties. Enteroviruses are stable at pH 3 to 10, whereas rhinoviruses are unstable below pH 6. After initial replication in the oropharynx, enteroviruses, unlike rhinoviruses, survive transit through the acidic environment of the stomach and reach the lower intestinal tract, where they replicate more extensively. The buoyant density of enteroviruses in cesium chloride is 1.32 to 1.35 g/cm^3, whereas that of rhinoviruses is 1.39 to 1.45 g/cm^3. The optimal temperature for the replication of enteroviruses is 37°C; in contrast, the 33°C optimum for rhinoviruses reflects their adaptation to the lower temperatures of the nasal passages. Picornaviruses are rapidly inactivated at temperatures in excess of 50°C. The stability of enteroviruses at ambient temperatures exceeds that of rhinoviruses. Molar $MgCl_2$ reduces the thermolability of enteroviruses across a wide range of temperatures, allowing live, attenuated oral poliomyelitis vaccines to maintain potency when refrigeration is suboptimal or unavailable.

Rhinoviruses are covered in Chapter 162. The remaining sections of this chapter focus on the biological characteristics of the human enteroviruses.

Subclassification of Enteroviruses

The enteroviruses historically have been divided into subgroups (i.e., polioviruses, group A coxsackieviruses, group B coxsackieviruses, and echoviruses) according to differences in host range and pathogenicity, and further subdivided into serotypes on the basis of serum neutralization (see Table 158–1). Overall, 72 serotypes have been identified, but this number has been reduced to 67 distinct serotypes because of redundancy or mistaken classification. Several enteroviruses have biologic properties bridging the major subgroups, which make it difficult to categorize them unambiguously (see the later section "Newer Enteroviruses"). Newly recognized enteroviruses, including serotypes 68 and higher, have therefore been sequentially numbered and classified simply as enteroviruses.[2] The distinctive characteristics of the major enterovirus subgroups are outlined in the following sections.

Polioviruses

Polioviruses generally replicate only in primates or primate cell cultures, although rare strains such as the type 2 Lansing strain have been adapted to rodents. Although polioviruses multiply in the alimentary tract of some subhuman primates, the hallmark of these viruses is the characteristic histopathologic lesions produced by direct inoculation of the central nervous system. Three serotypes are recognized by cross-neutralization tests.

Coxsackieviruses

Coxsackieviruses, unlike polioviruses, produce paralysis and death in experimentally infected suckling mice. This property enabled their

TABLE 158–1 Classification and Host Range of Human Picornaviruses

		Experimental Host Range		
Subgroup	**Serotypes**	***Primates***	***Newborn Mice***	***Cell Culture***
Polioviruses	1–3	+ +	0*	+ +
Coxsackieviruses A	1–24†	0‡	+ + +	±§
Coxsackieviruses B	1–6	0	+ + +	+ +
Echoviruses	1–34‖	0	0¶	+ +
Enteroviruses	68–72**	Variable	Variable	+
Rhinoviruses	1–100	0	0	+ +

*Rare strains (e.g., Lansing strain of poliovirus 2) have been adapted to mice.
†Coxsackievirus A23 has been reclassified as echovirus 9, which leaves 23 coxsackieviruses in group A. Antigenic interrelationships exist between coxsackievirus types A3 and A8, A11 and A15, and A13 and A18.
‡Coxsackievirus A7 is pathogenic for the central nervous system of primates.
§Most coxsackievirus serotypes of group A are not readily isolated in cell cultures, but exceptions exist (e.g., types A9 and A16); additional serotypes have been adapted to cell cultures.
‖Echovirus 10 has been reclassified as reovirus 1 and echovirus 28 as rhinovirus 1A. Echovirus 34 is a variant of coxsackievirus A24; 31 serotypes of echovirus therefore remain from the original 34. Antigenic interrelationships exist between echovirus types 1 and 8, 12 and 29, and 6 and 30. Echoviruses 22 and 23 may be reclassified to the novel genus Paraenterovirus.
¶Except echovirus 21.
**Hepatitis A virus is classified as enterovirus 72 but is genetically distinct from all other enteroviruses.

recognition as a distinct class of agents when they were first recovered in 1948 from the feces of two children suffering from a poliomyelitis-like syndrome in the town of Coxsackie, New York.[3] When additional serologically distinct agents were discovered, it was soon recognized that some (group A coxsackieviruses) produce generalized myositis of skeletal muscle that results in flaccid paralysis of suckling mice, whereas others (group B coxsackieviruses) produce focal myositis but a more generalized infection of the myocardium, brown fat, pancreas, and central nervous system that results in spastic paralysis.[4] Moreover, the group B coxsackieviruses, like polioviruses, usually could also be propagated in cultured primate cells, whereas most of the group A coxsackieviruses grew poorly or not at all in cell culture. Eventually 23 serotypes of group A coxsackieviruses and 6 serotypes of group B coxsackieviruses were recognized.

Echoviruses

With the development of cell culture technology, additional viruses were discovered in fecal specimens of healthy children.[5, 6] These agents produce cytopathic effects in primate cell culture but are immunologically distinct from polioviruses and generally nonpathogenic for suckling mice or for the central nervous system of primates. Initially unassociated with any illness, these "orphan" viruses were named ECHO (enteric cytopathic human orphan) viruses, subsequently simplifed to echoviruses. Although 31 echovirus serotypes are currently recognized, serotypes 22 and 23 are likely to be reclassified as a distinct picornaviral genus (proposed name: Paraenterovirus) becuase they substantially diverge genetically from the other enteroviruses.[7, 9]

Newly Identified Enteroviruses

Several of the first 63 numbered serotypes defied precise classification, although they had all the physicochemical properties of enteroviruses. For example, coxsackievirus A9 could regularly be isolated in cultured primate cells, although its pathogenicity for mice was typical of group A coxsackieviruses. Some isolates of echovirus 9 were discovered that are antigenically identical to the prototype strain but are pathogenic for mice. Because of these biologic and serologic ambiguities, newly recognized human enteroviral serotypes are designated by serial numbers only.[2] Since adoption of this simplified taxonomic scheme in 1970, four new serotypes have been discovered (enteroviruses 68 to 71). Hepatitis A virus was briefly classified as enterovirus 72, until genetic sequence data led to reclassification of this virus as a heparnavirus.[10]

Despite some overlap in the types of illness produced by viral groups of the original classification, the association of a particular group with a specific syndrome (for example, group B coxsackieviruses with myocarditis and pericarditis) is sufficiently distinctive to justify the continued use of the older scheme for the first 63 serotypes. Moreover, comparison of genetic sequences of polioviruses, coxsackieviruses, and echoviruses support the validity of the original classification.[11] Serotypes within a specific subgroup maintain RNA sequence homology of greater than 65% within the region coding for capsid protein, whereas the relatedness between viruses representing different subgroups is generally less.[11, 12]

MOLECULAR BIOLOGY OF ENTEROVIRUSES AND THEIR REPLICATION

The RNA genomes of naturally occurring polioviruses, attenuated polioviruses, and many nonpolio enteroviruses have been fully sequenced, and the replication of polioviruses in primate cells has been studied in extensive detail.[12] Poliovirus type 1 RNA has been reverse transcribed and the complementary DNA sequences cloned and transfected into cultured cells, resulting in progeny virions.[13, 14] The molecular structure and intracellular replicative events appear to be very similar for all the human enteroviruses.

The enteroviral genome incorporates approximately 7450 nucleotides divided into three regions: a 5′ end region of 743 nucleotides, a continuous-coding region of about 6625 nucleotides, and a 3′ polyA end region of variable length. The 5′ terminus is covalently linked to a small virus-coded protein of approximately 7 kD (VPg) that is required for the initiation of RNA synthesis. Removal of the polyA 3′ terminus renders the RNA noninfectious. The most conserved regions of the genome are the 5′ noncoding region and those coding for the VPg protein and the RNA polymerase.[15] The regions coding for the structural proteins are less conserved, and there is considerable variation with the regions that code for epitopes that bind neutralizing antibody.

Host cell susceptibility to enteroviral infection is defined by the presence of specific membrane receptor proteins that bind enteroviral serotypes along taxonomic lines (Table 158–2).[16, 17] The three poliovirus serotypes share a common receptor, a molecule of unknown function resembling members of the immunoglobulin superfamily that is coded on human chromosome 19.[18–20] Both decay-accelerating factor (DAF, or CD55), a known complement regulatory protein, and intercellular adhesion molecule 1 play a role in coxsackie A21 virus cell entry.[21] The group B coxsackieviruses also interact with two different cell membrane proteins, coxsackievirus-adenovirus receptor, which is a 49-kd protein of unknown function, and DAF.[22, 23] The presence of coxsackievirus-adenovirus receptor permits binding and cell entry by all six coxsackie B virus serotypes,[23] whereas antibodies to DAF block binding and infection by serotypes 1, 3, and 5.[22, 24, 25] DAF also appears to be a major echovirus receptor, binding many echovirus serotypes,[26, 27] whereas echovirus serotypes 1 and 8 bind to the α_2-subunit of the very late antigen (VLA) integrin molecule.[28, 29]

Penetration, uncoating, and release of the nucleic acid into the cytoplasm occur within minutes at 37°C. RNA synthesis begins about 30 minutes after infection and results in the exponential increase of complementary and progeny RNA until 2.5 hours after infection, when there is a switch to a linear accumulation of mainly progeny RNA. Each cell synthesizes about 2×10^5 molecules of progeny RNA, 50% of which is used as messenger RNA by the cell. RNA synthesis is regulated by a viral RNA–dependent RNA polymerase. A polyprotein with a molecular mass of about 250 kD is synthesized

TABLE 158–2 Enterovirus Cell Membrane Receptors Identified to Date

Virus	Serotypes	Receptor Protein	Family
Polio	1–3	Poliovirus receptor	Immunoglobulin
Coxsackie A	13, 18, 21	Intercellular adhesion molecule 1	Immunoglobulin
Coxsackie B	1–6	Coxsackie adenovirus receptor	Immunoglobulin
Coxsackie B	1, 3, 5	Decay-accelerating factor	Complement regulator
Echovirus	1, 8	Very late antigen 2 ($\alpha_2\beta_1$)	Integrin
Echovirus	6, 7, 11, 12, 13, 20, 21, 29, 33	Decay-accelerating factor	Complement regulator
Enterovirus	70	Decay-accelerating factor	Complement regulator

from the open reading frame, which is initially cleaved into three polypeptides. The 5′ product, P1, undergoes subsequent cleavages to form four capsid proteins. Cleavage of P2 and P3 results in eight nonstructural proteins whose known functions include promotion of viral RNA synthesis, proteolytic cleavage of the translational products, and inhibition of host cell protein synthesis.

The complete virion contains 60 copies of each of the four structural proteins. Synthesis of the capsid proceeds by aggregation of five copies each of VP1, VP3, and VP0 (a precursor of VP2 and VP4) into subunits, and assembly of 12 of these pentamers into the complete dodecahedral capsid shell. Encapsidation of the viral RNA is associated with a final cleavage of the VP0 protein to VP2 and VP4. The latter is an internal protein closely associated with the RNA. For polioviruses, VP1 is the dominantly exposed protein, containing at least two epitopes that induce neutralizing antibodies. VP2 and VP3 are partially exposed and antigenic.

Host protein and RNA synthesis are severely compromised by 3 hours after infection. After about 6 to 7 hours, virions are visible by electron microscopy within the cytoplasm, and they are subsequently released by lysis of the cell, which results in a yield of 10^4 to 10^5 virions per cell. The number of infectious virions is 10 to 1000-fold lower.

PATHOGENESIS AND IMMUNITY IN ENTEROVIRAL INFECTIONS

Pathogenesis

The pathogenesis of infection is best understood for polioviruses, which have been extensively investigated both in primates experimentally infected with neurovirulent strains and in humans infected with vaccine strains.[30–33] Available information supports the essential similarity of the pathogenetic events for the nonpolio enteroviruses except for the principal target organs affected after viremia.

Studies of coxsackievirus infection in subprimate mammals, principally mice, have produced much information about the influence of various host and environmental factors on the ability of the virus to replicate in target organs and about the mechanism of vertical transmission of enteroviruses from infected pregnant animals to their offspring.

Enteroviruses infect humans primarily as a result of the ingestion of fecally contaminated material. Ingested virus implants and replicates in susceptible tissues of the pharynx or distal part of the gut. The precise site of viral entry and initial replication in the gastrointestinal tract is not established, although enteroviruses have been demonstrated within the mucosal M cells, which are implicated in the uptake from the lumen of gastrointestinal reoviruses.[34] Enteroviral replication in ileal lymphoid tissue is detectable 1 to 3 days after the ingestion of virus. Humans ingesting more than 10^6 times the median tissue culture infective dose ($TCID_{50}$) of attenuated poliovirus regularly shed virus in both oropharyngeal secretions and feces, whereas lower infecting doses ($<10^5$ $TCID_{50}$) result only in fecal shedding.[30] Moreover, the quantity of virus recoverable from the tonsils is much less than that in Peyer's patches, where it may reach 10^7 to 10^8 $TCID_{50}/g$. The maximal duration of viral excretion is 3 to 4 weeks from the pharynx and 5 to 6 weeks or even longer in the feces. These observations suggest that polioviruses replicate most efficiently in the lower intestines, especially the distal portion of the small bowel.

After multiplication in submucosal lymphatic tissues, enteroviruses pass to regional lymph nodes (cervical, mesenteric) and give rise to a "minor viremia" that is transient and not usually detectable. During this low-grade viremia, virus spreads to reticuloendothelial tissue such as the liver, spleen, bone marrow, and deep lymph nodes. In subclinical infections, which are the most common, viral replication at this point ceases or is contained by host defense mechanisms. However, in a minority of infected persons, further replication of virus occurs in these reticuloendothelial sites leading to a sustained ("major") viremia that coincides with the onset of the "minor illness" of poliomyelitis and probably the nonspecific febrile illnesses associated with other enterovirus infections. Prodromal viremia has been demonstrated with wild strains of poliovirus[33, 35] and echovirus 9[36] but is uncommon with Sabin vaccine strains except for type 2.[37]

The major viremia results in dissemination to target organs such as the central nervous system, heart, and skin. In these tissues, necrosis and inflammatory lesions are observed, whereas histopathologic lesions are generally not seen in the gut and lymphoreticular tissues associated with earlier replicative events. In target organs, the degree of inflammatory change and tissue necrosis corresponds to the titer of infectious virus present. The severity of infection in experimental animals can be enhanced by induced exercise, cold exposure, malnutrition, pregnancy, and immunosuppression with corticosteroids or radiation.

Mutation of Enteroviruses during Natural Infection

Enteroviruses undergo a high rate of mutation during replication in the human gastrointestinal tract. Transcription errors of the single-stranded RNA genome occur with a frequency of 1 per 10^4 bases, approximately one error per genome. Single-site mutations are commonly observed in the 5′ noncoding region of attenuated polioviruses within days of feeding to young infants, a change associated with longer excretion and increased neurovirulence.[38, 39] Oligonucleotide fingerprinting of serial polio vaccine virus and nonpolio enteroviral isolates from children with agammaglobulinemia has confirmed that these viruses undergo continuous genetic variation during replication in the gastrointestinal tract over a period of months to years.[40, 41]

Dual infection of the same cell with different enteroviral strains may produce recombinant progeny virus, especially when the parent strains share the same serotype. Intertypic recombinants are less frequent but can be demonstrated in 1 per 10^4 to 1 per 10^5 infectious virions in vitro,[42] and also in the feces of infants fed trivalent oral poliovirus vaccine.[43]

Immunity and the Immune Response

Immunity to enteroviral infections is serotype-specific. Antibody-mediated immune mechanisms operate both in the alimentary tract to prevent mucosal infection and in the blood to prevent dissemination to target organs. Circulating antibodies play the most important role in preventing enteroviral disease. Small concentrations of type-specific neutralizing antibodies prevent poliovirus viremia and paralysis in experimentally infected primates.[44] Passive immunity to paralytic disease in humans can be achieved by the administration of immune serum globulin before exposure to neurovirulent polioviruses.[45, 46] However, passively administered immune globulin does not modify the outcome of established central nervous system poliovirus disease[47]; at this late stage of infection, patients invariably have indigenous circulating antibodies. There is no proven role for immune globulin treatment of other systemic enterovirus infections. Immunoglobulin A (IgA) antibody appears in nasal secretions 2 to 4 weeks after the administration of live-attenuated oral poliovirus vaccine and persists for at least 15 years.[32] The intranasal administration of inactivated poliovirus vaccine induces low, transient secretory IgA levels. Alimentary immunity is relative. On reexposure to infectious virus, high titers of oropharyngeal secretory IgA antibodies prevent or substantially reduce poliovirus shedding. With lower titers of IgA antibodies, there is more extensive oropharyngeal replication of virus and more prolonged shedding.[32] A similar inhibition of viral replication by IgA antibodies has been shown in the lower gastrointestinal tract. The elaboration of virus-specific IgA antibodies by the small intestine appears to depend on local immunocompetent tissues, not those of the pharynx. This principle was elegantly demonstrated by experiments in which infants with double-barrel colostomies were fed live-attenuated poliovirus through the colostomy. Although they developed serum IgA, IgG, and IgM antibodies to poliovirus, secretory IgA antibodies were elaborated only in the distal loop of the colostomy and not in the pharynx or proximal loop. When subsequently challenged with oral poliovirus vaccine orally, they shed virus from the pharynx but not from the distal segment of the bowel and then proceeded to develop IgA antibodies in pharyngeal secretions.[48] Antibodies to enteroviruses are present in the colostrum and milk of immune women, and this may interfere with the replication of OPV virus given to breast-fed neonates.[49] Maternal antibodies passively acquired either transplacentally or via milk modify enteroviral infections of early infancy either by preventing infection or by causing subclinical but nonetheless immunizing infection.[49, 50]

As early as 1 to 3 days after enteroviral challenge, IgM humoral antibodies are produced that predominate in serum during the first month and disappear within 2 to 3 months.[32] IgG antibody, which is generally detected by 7 to 10 days after infection, is mostly of the IgG_1 and IgG_3 subtypes.[51] Neutralizing IgG antibodies in serum persist for life after natural infection with enteroviruses. Humoral antibodies have an important role in the recovery from enteroviral infection, as evidenced by the development of persistent infections in persons with significant B-cell immunodeficiency.[52] Nonetheless, there is both clinical and laboratory evidence that humoral antibody alone is not sufficient to limit enteroviral replication in target organs. Data from several laboratories indicate that macrophage function is also a critical component of the immune response to enteroviral infection.[53, 54] Selective ablation of macrophage function in experimental animals markedly enhances the severity of coxsackievirus B infections,[53] whereas inhibition of T-lymphocyte function has little effect.[55]

Persons with abnormal cell-mediated immunity are not predisposed to serious or prolonged enterovirus infections unless they have accompanying B-cell dysfunction. Even though T lymphocytes do not contribute to the inhibition of enteroviral replication, there is growing evidence that certain immunopathologic events after enterovirus infection are mediated by T-cell activity. In the murine model of coxsackievirus B3–induced myocarditis, a late phase of the inflammatory response appears to be secondary to virus-induced cytotoxic T-cell destruction of myocytes, a process that is partially controlled by the major histocompatibility genetic locus in the mouse.[56]

EPIDEMIOLOGY OF ENTEROVIRAL INFECTIONS

Endemic and Epidemic Behavior

Enteroviruses are distributed worldwide. Infection rates vary with the season, geography, and age and socioeconomic status of the population sampled. Enteroviral infections occur throughout the year, but in temperate climates infections are strikingly more prevalent in the summer and autumn months (June to October in the Northern Hemisphere).[57] This seasonal periodicity, which has never been satisfactorily explained, is repeatedly observed each year in cities of the northern United States but is less pronounced in Atlanta and Miami and disappears altogether in the tropics, where enteroviruses are endemic the year round. Climate also affects the frequency and abundance of enteroviruses isolated from the feces of healthy children. For example, several surveys of southern and southwestern cities of the United States have indicated that 7 to 15% of children sampled during the year excreted enteroviruses, whereas comparable populations in New York, Buffalo, and Minneapolis had annual excretion rates less than 5%.[58]

Age and Socioeconomic Status

Three quarters of enteroviral infections reported to the World Health Organization occur in children younger than 15 years.[59] In the United States, attack rates for both infection and illness with nonpolio enteroviruses are highest in infants younger than 1 year.[60, 61] During the annual peak period of enteroviral transmission in Rochester, New York, the incidence of infection was found to be 12.8% during the first month of life.[62] Rates of symptomatic enteroviral infection drop after the second month of life[63] but remain higher for infants and toddlers compared with older children and adults. Enteroviral infections are more prevalent among lower-socioeconomic class children than among children of the upper or middle classes, a fact probably explained by crowding, poor hygiene, and opportunities for fecal contamination. Simultaneous infection by more than one serotype is common under these circumstances. A study of infants in Karachi, Pakistan, revealed that 80% yielded rectal swabs with at least one enterovirus. Of the positives, nearly half yielded two enteroviruses and occasional subjects as many as four.[64]

The frequency with which particular serotypes of enteroviruses cause infection varies markedly. Wild-type polioviruses now circulate only in a diminishing number of developing countries (see Chapter 159), whereas vaccine strains are commonly isolated throughout the world because of widespread oral poliovirus vaccine use. In urban areas of the United States, usually one to three nonpolio enteroviral serotypes predominate each season, and these vary from one region to another. Some serotypes are isolated with low frequency in the same locality in sequential years, whereas others have produced epidemics only to disappear the following season and for years thereafter. Occasional epidemics are almost global, such as the one caused by echovirus 9 in the late 1950s and the explosive pandemics of acute hemorrhagic conjunctivitis due to enterovirus 70 and coxsackievirus A24 that have occurred over the past 3 decades. During the 4-year period 1993 through 1996, the 10 most common serotypes of nonpolio enteroviral isolates submitted from state and local public health laboratories to the Enterovirus Surveillance Program of the Centers for Disease Control and Prevention accounted for 59 to 81% of all isolates within a given year.[65]

Echoviruses represent slightly less than half of these clinical isolates, and group B coxsackieviruses represent about one fourth (Table 158–3).[66] It is likely that group A coxsackieviruses are considerably underrepresented in these data because only a few serotypes such as A9 and A16 grow readily in cell culture.[67] The prevalent serotypes change little from year to year,[57, 65, 66] although occasional serotypes may emerge, or reemerge after years of relative inactivity, such as occurred with echovirus 30 in the early 1990s.[68] Infection with some serotypes, such as coxsackievirus B6 and enteroviruses 68 and 69, is rarely recognized.

There may be several reasons why individual serotypes of enteroviruses appear and disappear and behave as either endemic or epidemic pathogens. Some epidemic strains such as echovirus 9 may spread rapidly and exhaust susceptible individuals in the population

TABLE 158–3 Most Common Serotypes Identified among Enterovirus Isolates Submitted to the Centers for Disease Control and Prevention, 1993–1996

Serotype	Percentage
Echovirus 9	12.7
Coxsackievirus B5	11.5
Echovirus 30	9.5
Coxsackievirus A9	6.6
Coxsackievirus B2	6.2
Echovirus 6	5.1
Echovirus 11	4.5
Echovirus 7	4.4
Coxsackievirus B4	4.4
Coxsackievirus B3	4.0
Unknown	3.8
Echovirus 17	2.7
Echovirus 22	2.2
Enterovirus 71	2.1
All others	20.3

Data from ref. 66.

beyond a "critical mass" necessary for continued transmission, whereas those strains appearing endemically over several years may be less contagious. Periodic reappearances of the same enteroviral serotype occur in which the new strain is poorly neutralized by antisera to earlier strains[69, 70] or varies significantly from earlier strains by certain well-characterized genetic markers.[71]

Molecular Epidemiology

The study of enteroviral epidemiology has been augmented by the application of several molecular genetic methods including two-dimensional oligonucleotide gel electrophoresis of viral RNA *(fingerprinting)*, analysis of viral RNA with labeled complementary DNA (cDNA) probes, and amplification and identification of defined RNA sequences with the polymerase chain reaction (PCR). These methods have been used to unambiguously differentiate live vaccine and naturally occurring poliovirus strains[72, 73] and to trace the routes of spread of poliovirus type 1,[74] coxsackievirus A24,[75] and enterovirus 70[76, 77] by determining the degree of RNA relatedness among epidemiologically distinct isolates. Hamby and associates used RNA fingerprinting to demonstrate the reemergence of an epidemic coxsackievirus B5 strain in 1983 that had remained dormant in the United States for 16 years.[71]

Genomic RNA sequencing has proved the most adept in characterizing the evolutionary relationships among poliovirus isolates of the same serotype. "Genotypes" are distinguished from one another by the divergence of more than 15% among the RNA nucleotides in the homologous portions of the genome that are sequenced.[73] This technique has demonstrated the relatedness of the outbreak of poliovirus type 1 in Finland in 1984–1985 to strains circulating in the Mediterranean region[78]; and has traced the pandemic spread of acute hemorrhagic conjunctivitis caused by both enterovirus 70 and coxsackievirus A24 in the 1980s.[75, 76, 79]

Transmission

Because viral shedding from the gastrointestinal tract is more prolonged than is shedding from the upper respiratory tract, the fecal-oral route is thought to be the predominant mode of enteroviral transmission. Notable exceptions to this pattern occur, however. Coxsackievirus A21, which especially causes upper respiratory infections, is probably spread by respiratory secretions,[80] whereas enterovirus 70, the agent of acute hemorrhagic conjunctivitis, appears to be spread by fomites, fingers, and ophthalmologic instruments contaminated with virus in tears.[81] Respiratory-oral spread has been postulated to play a role in the transmission of poliovirus in settings of good hygiene and also in the spread of coxsackieviruses, which are frequently shed simultaneously from both the upper respiratory tract and in the feces.[82] Although direct spread of enteroviruses from person to person is likely, the mechanisms of transmission by direct or indirect contact have not been studied under experimental conditions. Vigorous washing with soap and water reduces but does not eliminate infectious poliovirus from the hands.[83] Although enteroviruses have been isolated from flies, cockroaches, food exposed to naturally infected flies, and dog feces, transmission by these vehicles has never been demonstrated. Sampling of sewage in most cities, especially in summer months, usually yields several enteroviral serotypes.[84] Clams in seawater polluted by sewage concentrate enteroviruses 10- to 60-fold. Nevertheless, except for hepatitis A, waterborne epidemics of enteroviral diseases attributed to shellfish ingestion have never been demonstrated.

Longitudinal studies have shown clustering of enterovirus infections in families.[82] Once the virus has been introduced into the household, secondary attack rates for infection among susceptible family members (those lacking type-specific antibody) are 90 to 100% for wild-type polioviruses and approximately 75% for coxsackieviruses.[82] Secondary attack rates for echoviruses are less than 50%, probably because these viruses tend to be shed only in feces and for shorter periods. Infants in diapers who shed virus in the feces are the most efficient disseminators of infection. Mothers and infant siblings are at greater risk of acquiring infection than are fathers and teenaged siblings.[82] For all enteroviruses, the period of maximal contagiousness corresponds to the period of maximal viral excretion in the feces.

Reinfections (viral excretion by a person with preexisting antibodies to a given serotype) occur, but they are not associated with illness. The duration of excretion of virus is considerably shorter than in the primary infection.[82, 85]

Incidence of Infection and Illness

Approximately 95% of infections due to wild-type polioviruses and at least 50 to 80% of nonpolio enteroviral infections are completely asymptomatic. Even symptomatic infections usually produce undifferentiated febrile illnesses lasting but a few days, often accompanied by symptoms of upper respiratory tract infection.[86] These illnesses may be caused by virtually any enteroviral serotype and are clinically indistinguishable from infection by many other viral agents. Disease syndromes considered characteristic of enteroviruses, such as aseptic meningitis or pericarditis, are in fact unusual manifestations of infection; a 4-year longitudinal family-based study in New York City detected 291 enteroviral infections, none with "characteristic" illnesses, and only 6 with exanthems.[82]

The risk of certain enterovirus-related clinical syndromes varies with age and sex. Aseptic meningitis is most commonly recognized in very young infants, whereas some other illnesses such as pleurodynia and myopericarditis are recognized predominantly in adolescents and young adults. Symptomatic enteroviral infections in elderly persons are uncommon. Among young children, boys are at greater risk of illness (but not infection) than are girls.[61] Aseptic meningitis and poliomyelitis occur nearly twice as often in boys. After puberty, the reverse is true, perhaps because women have greater exposure than men to children shedding virus.[82, 87] Pregnancy also appears to enhance the severity of enteroviral infections. The incidence of paralytic poliomyelitis was two to three times higher in pregnant women than in age-matched nonpregnant women in Boston before the control of poliomyelitis.[88] There are also clinical and epidemiologic data that suggest that enteroviral illnesses are more frequent[89] and more severe[90] in persons who exercise vigorously before the onset of symptoms. Although these data are anecdotal, they are supported by considerable evidence that exercise enhances the severity of coxsackievirus B infection in the murine model.

Although the incidence and prevalence of nonpolio enteroviral infections have been accurately measured in selected populations and they are undeniably common, the overall incidence in the United States is unknown. Viral isolations tend to be reported only from patients with symptomatic illness, especially the "characteristic" syndromes, for which reporting is incomplete. Serologic surveys encompassing all 67 enteroviral serotypes are not feasible. Antibody prevalence rates measured for a few serotypes indicate that after the decline of passively acquired maternal antibodies after the age of 6 months, the fraction of immune persons in the population rises progressively with age until 15 to 90% of the adult population have type-specific neutralizing antibodies for each serotype tested, depending on the serotype and the socioeconomic class of the population surveyed.[61, 82]

Incubation Period and Period of Communicability

The incubation period for illness due to enteroviral infections can rarely be determined precisely. Because the source of infection is often an asymptomatic person who transmits virus as readily as one who is ill, the time of exposure is usually unknown. Although the incubation period may range from 2 days to 2 weeks, it is usually 3 to 5 days. Patients with enteroviral illnesses typically excrete virus in throat secretions or feces for several days before the onset of symptoms and continue to excrete virus in feces for several weeks thereafter. The period of communicability is therefore potentially long. However, the period of maximal communicability is believed to be early in illness, when viral shedding is greatest.

LABORATORY DIAGNOSIS OF ENTEROVIRAL INFECTIONS

The laboratory diagnosis of enteroviral infection is accomplished by cell culture, PCR, or retrospectively by serologic methods.

Viral Isolation

Cell culture remains the most widely used method, and the method to which other techniques are compared. The opportunity to recover a virus in cell culture is optimized by sampling of multiple sites. Late in the course of enteroviral illnesses, viral cultures of feces are useful because the lower intestine may be the only site from which the agent is still being excreted. An etiologic diagnosis can be confirmed by the isolation of virus from cerebrospinal fluid, pericardial fluid, tissue, or blood, depending on the clinical syndrome. Isolation of virus from the upper respiratory tract or stool is considered by some to be less definitive, because intercurrent asymptomatic infections etiologically unrelated to the observed illness may produce a false-positive result. However, background rates of asymptomatic infection are generally low enough that isolation of an enterovirus from a throat or stool specimen is strong evidence of causation. Conversely, late in the course of enteroviral illnesses, viral cultures of feces are useful because the lower intestine may be the only site from which the agent is still being excreted.

With the identification of a characteristic cytopathic effect in any of three or four appropriately chosen cell lines, a presumptive diagnosis of enteroviral infection can usually be reported by the laboratory within 2 to 5 days.[91] The primary monkey kidney cell lines and the human embryonic fibroblast cell lines used routinely in diagnostic virology laboratories support the growth of most polioviruses, group B coxsackieviruses, and echoviruses. The inclusion of buffalo green monkey kidney cells and human rhabdomyosarcoma cells enhances the recovery of group B coxsackieviruses and echoviruses, respectively.[91] Only a few serotypes of the group A coxsackieviruses (e.g., A9, A16) grow readily in routinely used cell lines. Although the use of specialized cell lines such as rhabdomyosarcoma[92] or guinea pig embryo[93] may aid the recovery of some group A coxsackieviruses in cell culture, inoculation of newborn mice remains the method of choice for recovery of this subgroup of enteroviruses.[67] The serotype of an enterovirus isolated in cell culture is most often determined with the use of the Lim Benyesh–Melnick intersecting antiserum pools,[94] an assay that is performed mainly by research and reference laboratories. Because the equine sera that constitute the Lim Benyesh–Melnick pools were harvested against enterovirus strains prevalent more than 30 years ago, their ability to identify contemporary isolates has modestly diminished.[95] In the future, it is likely that enterovirus strains will be characterized by genomic sequencing.

Polymerase Chain Reaction

Reverse transcriptase–PCR is a rapid, sensitive, and specific method of detecting enterovirus RNA in clinical specimens. Most reported PCR protocols amplify a highly conserved portion of the 5′ nontranslated region of the genome, enabling the detection of most enteroviruses except for echovirus serotypes 22 and 23.[96, 97] Subgroup-specific primers that distinguish the polioviruses have also been described.[98, 99] With cerebrospinal fluid specimens from patients with aseptic meningitis, PCR detects enteroviral RNA in 66 to 86%, compared with viral isolation rates of approximately 30%.[100–102] Experience with non–cerebrospinal fluid specimens is more limited. PCR has detected enteroviral RNA from throat swabs, serum, urine, and stool. At least two reports suggest that the sensitivity with urine specimens is somewhat lower than with other specimens.[103, 104] PCR has detected enteroviral RNA in a minority of endomyocardial biopsy specimens from cases of acute myopericarditis.[105, 106]

Serology

The microneutralization test is the most widely employed method for the determination of antibodies to enteroviruses. Because microneutralization is serotype-specific, it has limited usefulness in the routine diagnosis of nonpolio enteroviral infections because of the low feasibility of testing with multiple live viral antigens, and because methods based on neutralization are relatively insensitive, poorly standardized, and labor-intensive. Type-specific immunoassays are more versatile methods that are now offered in commercial laboratories for assay of antibodies against the more common enteroviral serotypes. Serum IgM antibody to the group B coxsackieviruses can often be detected early in the course of illness, but positive test results are not serotype-specific and may occur during infections with enteroviruses of other classes.[107] Epitopes on capsid proteins have been described that are common to many different enteroviral serotypes,[108] and a monoclonal antibody is reported to detect a VP1 capsid antigen common to many enteroviruses.[109] However, identification of a common antigen that is sufficiently immunogenic to form the basis of a broadly reactive serologic assay has not been reported.

TREATMENT AND PREVENTION OF ENTEROVIRAL INFECTIONS

Some immunocompromised patients with persistent enteroviral infections have been successfully treated with immune globulins. Although effective antiviral therapy is not yet approved, a variety of antiviral and immunomodulating agents have shown activity against enteroviruses and rhinoviruses in vitro, in animal models, and in early clinical trials.[110–113] Among the most promising of these are antiviral drugs represented by a class of compounds that bind avidly to a pocket in the viral capsid, altering viral attachment and uncoating.[114] One of these compounds, pleconaril, is an orally administered drug with a favorable pharmacokinetic and toxicity profile that has been shown to reduce the duration of illness among adults with enteroviral aseptic meningitis.[115]

The preexposure administration of immune globulin is known to reduce the risk of paralytic poliomyelitis.[45] It is very likely that immune globulin would also prevent nonpolio enteroviral disease as well, but this strategy is rarely applicable to clinical practice. The successful vaccine approach against paralytic poliomyelitis is detailed in Chapter 159. In the setting of a community epidemic or a patient hospitalized with enteroviral illness, simple hygienic measures such as hand washing and careful disposal or autoclaving of potentially infected feces and secretions should be practiced. Gown and mask procedures or isolation of the patient except in the newborn nursery are unwarranted. Pregnant women, especially those near term, should be advised to avoid contact with patients suspected of having enteroviral illness.

REFERENCES

1. Melnick JL. Portraits of viruses: The picornaviruses. Intervirology. 1983;20:61–100.
2. Rosen L, Melnick J, Schmidt NJ, et al. Subclassification of enteroviruses and ECHO virus type 34. Arch Ges Virusforsch. 1970;30:89.
3. Dalldorf G, Sickles G. An unidentified, filtrable agent isolated from the feces of children with paralysis. Science. 1948;108:61.
4. Melnick JL, Shaw EW, Curnen EC. A virus from patients diagnosed as non-paralytic poliomyelitis or aseptic meningitis. Proc Soc Exp Biol Med. 1949;71:344.
5. Ramos-Alvarez M, Sabin AB. Characteristics of poliomyelitis and other enteric

viruses recovered in tissue culture from healthy American children. Proc Soc Exp Biol Med. 1954;87:655.
6. Melnick JL, Agren K. Poliomyelitis and coxsackie viruses isolated from normal infants in Egypt. Proc Soc Exp Biol Med. 1952;81:621.
7. Coller B-AG, Chapman NM, Beck MA, et al. Echovirus 22 is an atypical enterovirus. J Virol. 1990;64:2692–2701.
8. Hyypia T, Horsnell C, Maaronen M, et al. A distinct picornavirus group identified by sequence analysis. Proc Natl Acad Sci U S A. 1992;89:8847–8851.
9. Auvinen P, Hyypia T. Echoviruses include genetically distinct serotypes. J Gen Virol. 1990;71:2133–2139.
10. Cohen JI, Ticehurst JR, Purcell RH, et al. Complete nucleotide sequence of wild-type hepatitis A virus: Comparison with different strains of hepatitis A and other picornaviruses. J Virol. 1987;61:50–59.
11. Palmenberg AC. Sequence alignments of picornavirus capsid proteins. In: Semler B, Ehrenfeld E, eds. Molecular Aspects of Picornavirus Infection and Detection. Washington, DC: ASM Press; 1988:211–241.
12. Rueckert RR. Picornaviridae and their replication. In: Fields BN, Knipe DM, eds. Virology. 2nd ed. New York: Raven; 1990:507–548.
13. Racaniello VR, Baltimore D. Cloned poliovirus complentary DNA is infectious in mammalian cells. Science. 1981;214:916.
14. Racaniello VR, Baltimore D. Molecular cloning of poliovirus cDNA and determination of the complete nucleotide sequence of the viral genome. Proc Natl Acad Sci U S A. 1981;78:4887–4891.
15. Werner G, Rosenwirth B, Bauer E, et al. Molecular cloning and sequence determination of the genomic regions encoding protease and genome-linked protein of three picornaviruses. J Virol. 1986;57:1084–1093.
16. Rotbart HA, Kirkegaard K. Picornavirus pathogenesis: Viral access, attachment and entry into susceptible cells. Semin Virol. 1992;3:483–499.
17. Holland JJ. Receptor affinities as major determinants of enterovirus tissue tropisms in humans. Virology. 1961;15:312–326.
18. Miller DA, Miller OJ, Vaithilingam GD, et al. Human chromosome carries a poliovirus receptor gene. Cell. 1974;1:167–173.
19. Mendelsohn CL, Johnson B, Lionetti KA, et al. Transformation of a human poliovirus receptor gene into mouse cells. Proc Natl Acad Sci U S A. 1986;83:7845–7849.
20. Mendelsohn CL, Wimmer E, Racaniello VR. Cellular receptor for poliovirus: Molecular cloning, nucleotide sequence, and expression of a new member of the immunoglobulin super family. Cell. 1989;56:855–865.
21. Shafren DR, Dorahy DJ, Ingham RA, Burns GF, Barry RD. Coxsackieviruses A21 binds to decay-accelerating factor but requires intracellular adhesion molecule 1 for cell entry. J Virol. 1997;71:4736–4743.
22. Shafren DR, Bates RC, Agrez MV, et al. Coxsackieviruses B1, B3, and B5 use decay accelerating factor as a receptor for cell attachment. J Virol. 1995;69:3873–3877.
23. Bergelson JM, Cunningham JA, Droguett G, et al. Isolation of a common receptor for coxsackie B viruses and adenoviruses 2 and 5. Science. 1997;275:1320–1323.
24. Crowell RL, Field AK, Schleif WA, et al. Monoclonal antibody that inhibits infection of HeLa and rhabdomyosarcoma cells by selected enteroviruses through receptor blockade. J Virol. 1986;57:438–445.
25. Hsu K-HL, Lonberg-Holm K, Alstein B, Crowell RL. A monoclonal antibody specific for the cellular receptor for the group B coxsackieviruses. J Virol. 1988;62:1647–1652.
26. Modlin JF. Unpublished data.
27. Bergelson JM, Chan M, Solomon K, et al. Decay-accelerating factor (CD55), a glycosylphosphatidylinositol-anchored complement regulatory protein, is a receptor for several echoviruses. Proc Natl Acad Sci U S A. 1994;91:6245–6248.
28. Bergelson JM, Shepley MP, Chan BMC, et al. Identification of the integrin VLA-2 as a receptor for echovirus 1. Science. 1992;255:1718–1720.
29. Bergelson JM, St. John N, Kawaguchi S, et al. Infection by echoviruses 1 and 8 depends on the α_2 subunit of human VLA-2. J Virol. 1993;67:6847–6852.
30. Sabin AB. Behavior of chimpanzee-avirulent poliomyelitis viruses in experimentally infected human volunteers. Am J Med Sci. 1955;230:1.
31. Sabin AB. Pathogenesis of poliomyelitis: Reappraisal in light of new data. Science. 1956;123:1151–1157.
32. Ogra PL, Karzon DT. Formation and function of poliovirus antibody in different tissues. Prog Med Virol. 1971;13:157.
33. Horstmann DM, McCollum RW. Poliomyelitis virus in human blood during the "minor illness" and the asymptomatic infection. Proc Soc Exp Biol Med. 1953;82:434.
34. Wolf JL, Rubin DH, Finberg R, et al. Intestinal M cells: A pathway for entry of reovirus into the host. Science. 1981;212:471–472.
35. Davis DC, Melnick JL. Two additional examples of viremia in asymptomatic poliomyelitis infection. Pediatrics. 1957;20:975.
36. Yoshioka I, Horstmann DM. Viremia in infection due to echo virus type 9. N Engl J Med. 1961;262:224–228.
37. Horstmann DM, Opton EM, Klemperer R, et al. Viremia in infants vaccinated with oral poliovirus vaccine (Sabin). Am J Hyg. 1964;79:47.
38. Minor PD, John A, Ferguson M, Icenogle JP. Antigenic and molecular evolution of the vaccine strain of type 3 poliovirus during the period of excretion by a primary vaccinee. J Gen Virol. 1986;67:693–706.
39. Jameson BA, Bonin J, Wimmer E, et al. Natural variants of the Sabin type 1 vaccine strains of poliovirus and correlation with a poliovirus neutralization site. Virology. 1985;143:337–341.
40. Yoneyama T, Hagiwara A, Hara M, et al. Alteration in oligonucleotide fingerprint patterns of the viral genome in poliovirus type 2 isolated from paralytic patients. Infect Immun. 1982;37:46–53.
41. O'Neil KM, Pallansch MA, Winkelstein JA, et al. Chronic group A coxsackievirus infection in agammaglobulinemia: Demonstration of genomic variation of serotypically identical isolates persistently excreted from the same patient. J Infect Dis. 1988;157:183–186.
42. Tolskaya EA, Romanova LI, Kolesnikova MS, et al. Intertypic recombination in poliovirus: Genetic and biochemical studies. Virology. 1983;124:121–132.
43. Kew OM, Nottay BK, eds. Evolution of the oral poliovaccine strains in humans occurs by both mutation and intramolecular recombination. In: Chanock R, Lerner R, eds. Modern Approaches to Vaccines. Cold Spring Harbor, NY: Cold Spring Harbor Laboratory Press; 1985:357–362.
44. Bodian D, Nathanson N. Inhibitory effect of passive antibody on virulent poliovirus excretion and on immune response in chimpanzees. Bull Johns Hopkins Hosp. 1960;107:143.
45. Stevens KM. Estimate of molecular equivalent of antibody required for prophylaxis and therapy of poliomyelitis. J Hyg. 1959;57:198–201.
46. Hammon WM, Coriell LI, Stokes J Jr. Evaluation of Red Cross gamma globulin as a prophylactic agent for poliomyelitis. JAMA. 1952;150:139.
47. Bahlke AM, Perkins JE. Treatment of preparalytic poliomyelitis with gamma globulin. JAMA. 1945;129:1146.
48. Ogra PL, Karzon DT. Distribution of poliovirus antibody in serum, nasopharynx, and alimentary tract following segmental immunization of the lower alimentary tract with poliovaccine. J Immunol. 1969;102:1423.
49. Warren RJ, Lepow ML, Bartsch GE, Robbins FC. The relationship of maternal antibody, breast feeding, and age to the susceptibility of newborn infants to infection with attenuated poliovirus. Pediatrics. 1964;34:4–13.
50. Modlin JF, Polk BF, Horton P, et al. Perinatal echovirus 11 infection: Risk of transmission during a community outbreak. N Engl J Med. 1981;305:368–371.
51. Torfason EG, Reimer CB, Keyserling HL. Subclass restriction of human enterovirus antibodies. J Clin Microbiol. 1987;25:1376–1379.
52. McKinney RE, Katz SL, Wilfert CM. Chronic enteroviral meningoencephalitis in agammaglobulinemic patients. Rev Infect Dis. 1987;9:334–356.
53. Rager-Zisman B, Allison AC. The role of antibody and host cells in the resistance of mice against infection by coxsackie B-3 virus. J Gen Virol. 1973;19:329–338.
54. Woodruff J. Lack of correlation between neutralizing antibody production and suppression of coxsackie B-3 replication in target organs: Evidence for involvement of mononuclear inflammatory cells in host defense. J Immunol. 1979;123:31.
55. Woodruff JF, Woodruff JJ. Involvement of T lymphocytes in the pathogenesis of coxsackievirus B3 heart disease. J Immunol. 1974;113:1726–1734.
56. Rose NR, Wolfgram LJ, Herskowitz A, et al. Postinfectious autoimmunity: Two distinct phases of coxsackievirus B3–induced myocarditis. Ann N Y Acad Sci. 1986;475:146–156.
57. Moore M. Enteroviral disease in the United States, 1970–1979. J Infect Dis. 1979;146:103.
58. Gelfand HM, Holgium AH, Marchetti GE, et al. A continuing surveillance of enterovirus infections in healthy children in six United States cities. I. Viruses isolated during 1960 and 1961. Am J Hyg. 1963;78:358.
59. Grist NR, Bell EJ, Assad F. Enteroviruses in human disease. Prog Med Virol. 1978;24:114–157.
60. Dagan R, Powell KR, Hall CB, Menegus MA. Identification of infants unlikely to have serious bacterial infection although hospitalized for suspected sepsis. J Pediatr. 1985;107:855–860.
61. Froeschle JE, Feorino PM, Gelfand HM, et al. A continuing surveillance of enterovirus infections in healthy children in six United States cities. II. Surveillance enterovirus isolates from cases of acute central nervous system disease. Am J Epidemiol. 1966;83:455.
62. Jenista JA, Dalzell LE, Davidson PW, Menegus M. Outcome studies of neonatal enterovirus infection. Pediatr Res 1984;18(2):230A.
63. Rorabaugh ML, Berlin LE, Heldrich F, et al. Aseptic meningitis among infants less than two years of age: Acute illness and neurologic complications. Pediatrics. 1993;92:206–211.
64. Parks WP, Queiroga LT, Melnick JL. Studies of infantile diarrhea in Karachi, Pakistan. II. Multiple virus isolations from rectal swabs. Am J Epidemiol. 1967;85:469.
65. Strikas RA, Anderson LJ, Parker RA. Temporal and geographic patterns of isolates of nonpolio enteroviruses in the United States. J Infect Dis. 1986;153:346–351.
66. Centers for Disease Control and Prevention. Nonpolio enterovirus surveillance—United States, 1993–1996. Morb Mortal Wkly Rep. 1997;46:748–750.
67. Lipson SM, Walderman R, Costello P, et al. Sensitivity of rhabdomyosarcoma and guinea pig embryo cell cultures to field isolates of difficult-to-cultivate group A coxsackieviruses. J Clin Microbiol. 1986;26:1298–1303.
68. Centers for Disease Control and Prevention. Enterovirus surveillance—United States, 1990. MMWR. 1990;39:788–789.
69. Hovi T, Cantell K, Houvilainen A, et al. Outbreak of paralytic poliomyelitis in Finland: Widespread circulation of antigenically altered poliovirus type 3 in a vaccinated population. Lancet. 1986;1:1427–1432.
70. Huovilainen A, Hovi T, Kinnunen L, et al. Evolution of poliovirus during an outbreak: Sequential type 3 poliovirus isolates from several persons show shifts of neutralization determinants. J Gen Virol. 1987;68:1373–1378.
71. Hamby BB, Pallansch MA, Kew OM. Reemergence of an epidemic coxsackie B5 genotype. J Infect Dis. 1987;156:288–292.
72. Yang CF, De L, Holloway BP, et al. Detection and identification of vaccine-related polioviruses by the polymerase chain reaction. Virus Res. 1991;20:159–179.

73. Kew OM. Applications of Molecular Epidemiology to the Surveillance of Poliomyelitis. Poliomyelitis Vaccines: Re-evaluating Policy Options. Washington, DC: National Academy of Sciences, 1988.
74. Hatch MH, Marchetti GE, Nottay BK, et al. Strain characterization studies of poliovirus type 1 isolates from poliomyelitis cases in the United States in 1979. Dev Biol Stand. 1981;47:307–315.
75. Lin K-H, Wang H-L, Sheu M-M, et al. Molecular epidemiology of a variant of coxsackievirus A24 in Taiwan: Two epidemics caused by phylogenetically distinct viruses from 1985 to 1989. J Clin Microbiol. 1993;31:1160–1166.
76. Takeda N, Miyamura K, Ogino T, et al. Evolution of enterovirus type 70: Oligonucleotide mapping analysis of RNA genome. Virology. 1984;134:375–388.
77. Miyamura K, Tanimura M, Takeda N, et al. Evolution of enterovirus 70 in nature: All isolates were recently derived from a common ancestor. Arch Virol. 1986;89:1–14.
78. Poyry T, Kinnunen L, Kapsenberg J, et al. Type 3 poliovirus/Finland/1984 is genetically related to common Mediterranean strains. J Gen Virol. 1990;71:2535–2541.
79. Ishiko H, Takeda N, Miramura K, et al. Phylogenetically different strains of a variant of coxsackievirus A24 were repeatedly introduced but discontinued circulating in Japan. Arch Virol. 1992;126:179–193.
80. Couch RB, Douglas RG, Lindgren KM, et al. Airborne transmission of respiratory infection with coxsackievirus A type 21. Am J Epidemiol. 1970;91:78–86.
81. Hierholzer JC, Hilliard KA, Esposito JJ. Serosurvey for "acute hemorrhagic conjunctivitis" virus (enterovirus 70) antibodies in the southeastern United States, with review of the literature and some epidemiologic implications. Am J Epidemiol. 1975;102:533.
82. Kogon A, Spigland I, Frothingham TE, et al. The Virus Watch Program: A continuing surveillance of viral infections in metropolitan New York families. Am J Epidemiol. 1969;89:51.
83. Schurmann W, Eggers HJ. An experimental study on the epidemiology of enteroviruses: Water and soap washing of poliovirus 1–contaminated hands, its effectiveness and kinetics. Med Microbiol Immunol. 1985;174:221–236.
84. Horstmann DM, Emmons J, Gimpel L, et al. Enterovirus surveillance following a communitywide oral poliovirus vaccination program: A seven year study. Am J Epidemiol. 1973;97:173.
85. Fox JP. Epidemiology of poliomyelitis in populations before and after vaccination with inactivated viruses. Fourth International Poliomyelitis Conference. Philadelphia: JB Lippincott; 1958:136.
86. Johnson KM, Bloom HH, Forsyth B, et al. The role of enteroviruses in respiratory disease. Am Rev Respir Dis. 1963;88:240.
87. Siegel M, Greenberg M, Bodian J. Presence of children in the household as a factor in the incidence of paralytic poliomyelitis in adults. N Engl J Med. 1957;257:958.
88. Weinstein L, Aycock WL, Feemster RF. Relation of sex, pregnancy, and menstruation to susceptibility in poliomyelitis. N Engl J Med. 1951;245:54–58.
89. Baron RC, Hatch MH, Kleeman K, et al. Aseptic meningitis among members of a high school football team. An outbreak associated with echovirus 16 infection. JAMA. 1982;248:1724.
90. Josselson J, Pula T, Sadler JH. Acute rhabdomyolysis associated with echovirus 9 infection. Arch Intern Med. 1980;140:1671.
91. Dagan R, Menegus MA. A combination of four cell types for rapid detection of enteroviruses in clinical specimens. J Med Virol. 1986;19:219–228.
92. Schmidt NJ, Ho H, Lennette EH. Propagation and isolation group A coxsackieviruses in RD cells. J Clin Microbiol. 1975;2:183.
93. Landry ML, Madore HP, Fong CKY, et al. Use of guinea pig embryo cell cultures for isolation and propagation of group A coxsackieviruses. J Clin Microbiol. 1981;13:588.
94. Melnick JL, Wimberly IL. Lyophilized combination pools of enterovirus equine antisera. New LBM pools prepared from reserves of antisera stored frozen for two decades. Bull World Health Organ. 1985;63:543–550.
95. Modlin JF, Pallansch M. Unpublished experience.
96. Rotbart HA, Sawyer MH, Fast S, et al. Diagnosis of enteroviral meningitis by using PCR with a colorimetric microwell detection assay. J Clin Microbiol. 1994;32:2590–2592.
97. Halonen P, Rocha E, Hierholzer J, et al. Detection of enteroviruses and rhinoviruses in clinical specimens by PCR and liquid-phase hybridization. J Clin Microbiol. 1995;33:648–653.
98. Abraham R, Chonmaitree T, McCombs J, et al. Rapid detection of poliovirus by reverse transcription and polymerase chain amplification: Application for differentiation between poliovirus and non-poliovirus enteroviruses. J Clin Microbiol. 1993;31:395–399.
99. Kilpatrick DR, Nottay B, Yang C-F, et al. Group-specific identification of polioviruses by PCR using primers containing mixed-base or deoxyinosine residues at positions of codon degeneracy. J Clin Microbiol. 1996;34:2990–2996.
100. Sawyer M, Holland D, Aintablian N, et al. Diagnosis of enteroviral central nervous system infection by polymerase chain reaction during a large community outbreak. Pediat Infect Dis J. 1994;13:177–182.
101. Yerly S, Gervaix A, Simonet V, et al. Rapid and sensitive detection of enteroviruses in specimens from patients with aseptic meningitis. J Clin Microbiol. 1996;34:199–201.
102. Pozo F, Casas I, Tenorio A, et al. Evaluation of a commercially available reverse transcription–PCR assay for diagnosis of enteroviral infection in archival and prospectively collected cerebrospinal fluid specimens. J Clin Microbiol. 1998;36:1741–1745.
103. Nielsen LP, Modlin JF, Rotbart HA. Detection of enteroviruses by polymerase chain reaction in urine samples from patients with aseptic meningitis. Pediatr Infect Dis J. 1996;15:625–627.
104. Rotbart HA, Ahmed A, Hickey S, et al. Diagnosis of enterovirus infection by PCR of multiple specimen types. Pediatr Infect Dis J. 1997;16:409–411.
105. Weiss LM, Movahed LA, Billingham ME, Cleary ML. Detection of coxsackievirus B3 RNA in myocardial tissues by polymerase chain reaction. Am J Pathol. 1991;138:497–503.
106. Jin O, Sole MJ, Butany JW, et al. Detection of enterovirus RNA in myocardial biopsies from patients with myocarditis and cardiomyopathy using gene amplification by polymerase chain reaction. Circulation. 1990;82:8–16.
107. Pozzetto B, Gaudin OG, Aouni M, Ros A. Comparative evaluation of immunoglobulin M neutralizing antibody response in acute-phase sera and virus isolation for the routine diagnosis of enterovirus infection. J Clin Microbiol. 1989;27:705–708.
108. Romero JR, Putnak JR, Wimmer E. Enteroviral capsid protein VP3 as a group antigen for the enteroviruses. Pediatr Res. 1988;23:380A.
109. Yousef GE, Brown IN, Mowbray JF. Derivation and biochemical characterization of an enterovirus group-specific monoclonal antibody. Intervirology. 1987;28:163–170.
110. Stansfield SK, de la Pena W, Koenig S, et al. Human leukocyte interferon in the treatment and prophylaxis of acute hemorrhagic conjunctivitis. J Infect Dis. 1984;149:822–823.
111. Matsumori A, Crumpacker CS, Abelmann WH. Prevention of viral myocarditis with recombinant human leukocyte interferon alpha A/D in a murine model. Am J Coll Cardiol. 1987;9:1320–1325.
112. McKinlay MA, Steinberg BA. Oral efficacy of WIN 51711 in mice infected with human poliovirus. Antimicrob Agents Chemother. 1986;29:30–32.
113. Korant BD, Towatari T, Ivanoff L, et al. Viral therapy: Prospects for protease inhibitors. J Cell Biochem. 1986;32:91–95.
114. Zhang A, Nanni RG, Oren DA, et al. Three-dimensional structure-activity relationships for antiviral agents that interact with picornavirus capsids. Semin Virol. 1992;3:453–471.
115. Weiner LB, Rotbart HA, Gilbert DL, et al. Treatment of "enterovirus" meningitis with pleconaril (VP 63843), an antipicornavirus agent. 37th Interscience Conference on Antimicrobial Agents and Chemotherapy. Toronto: American Society for Microbiology, 1997.

Chapter 159

Poliovirus

JOHN F. MODLIN

Polioviruses are the cause of poliomyelitis, a systemic infectious disease of widely differing severity that prominently affects the central nervous system (CNS) and sometimes is complicated by paralysis. The name of the disease (*polios,* "gray"; *myelos,* "marrow" or "spinal cord"), now commonly shortened to polio, is descriptive of the pathologic lesions that involve neurons in the gray matter, especially in the anterior horn of the spinal cord. Older, less commonly used names for the disease include *infantile paralysis* and *Heine-Medin disease.*

Paralytic poliomyelitis has been completely controlled in the United States and other developed countries by the continuous, universal use of two vaccines, inactivated poliovirus vaccine (IPV) and live-attenuated oral poliovirus vaccine (OPV). Furthermore, the eradication of poliovirus infection from the entire world is anticipated to occur early in the 21st century.

HISTORY

Evidence of poliomyelitis exists from antiquity, and reports of the clinical features of sporadic cases appeared as early as 1840.[1] However, there is little record of epidemic poliomyelitis until the late 19th century, when outbreaks were first recorded in northern Europe and the United States. Medin characterized the natural history and neurologic complications of poliomyelitis in 1890 after an outbreak in Scandinavia, and Caverly wrote the first description of epidemic poliomyelitis in the United States, an outbreak of 132 cases near Rutland, Vermont, in 1894.[2]

Major progress in understanding poliomyelitis was signaled by the demonstration of its infectious nature by Landsteiner and Popper, who in 1908 transmitted the disease to monkeys by inoculation of human spinal cord homogenates. Progress remained limited until the landmark discovery in 1949 by Enders, Weller, and Robbins that poliovirus could be propagated in vitro in cultures of human embryonic tissues of nonneural origin.[3] This discovery facilitated experimental investigation of the pathogenesis of the disease and the development of vaccines. Bodian and colleagues first recognized the three distinct serotypes of poliovirus.[4] By 1952, Bodian and Horstmann had independently discovered that viremia occurred early in infection, which explained the systemic phase of the illness and supported the hypothesis that virus spreads to the CNS by nonneural pathways.[5–7]

Salk and associates reported in 1953 that human subjects could be successfully immunized with formalin-inactivated poliovirus,[8] which rapidly led to extensive field trials and licensure of vaccines in 1955. Because of the ensuing dramatic decline in paralytic poliomyelitis, the development of the vaccine has rightfully been hailed as one of the great accomplishments of medical science. Meanwhile, Sabin, Koprowski, Melnick, and others developed live-attenuated poliovirus vaccines,[9] which led to still further reductions in disease incidence after their licensure in 1962. Universal polio immunization ultimately resulted in eradication of disease due to naturally occurring *(wild-type)* polioviruses in the United States by 1979, and, under the aegis of the Pan American Health Organization, in the entire Western Hemisphere by 1991. Although endemic and epidemic poliomyelitis remains an important cause of lameness in sub-Saharan Africa and some parts of the Indian subcontinent, disease due to polioviruses has been targeted for complete eradication within the next decade as a result of a dedicated World Health Organization global program.[10–12]

INFECTIOUS AGENTS

General

Polioviruses are members of the genus Enterovirus, family Picornaviridae, whose properties are described in Chapter 158. Three serotypes are distinguished from one another on the basis of neutralization tests. Infection confers type-specific, lifelong immunity to disease but little or no immunity to infection or disease caused by heterologous serotypes.[13] Before the introduction of poliovirus vaccines, most paralytic disease was caused by type 1.[14, 15] Naturally occurring or live-attenuated vaccine strains, or both, may circulate in various populations, depending on the regional usage of OPV and whether endemic transmission of virulent polioviruses has been eliminated.

Host Range and Virulence

Humans are the only natural host and reservoir of polioviruses, although experimental infections and disease can be produced in other primates, and polioviruses can be adapted to replicate in subprimate mammals. Naturally occurring strains vary over a 10 million–fold range in neurovirulence.[16] Rhesus and cynomolgus monkeys are readily paralyzed by most naturally occurring strains, although much higher doses or more virulent strains are required to paralyze chimpanzees and humans. In contrast, polioviruses are more infectious for the human gut than for the gut of lower primates.

Vaccine strains are occasionally able to paralyze rhesus and cynomolgus monkeys, but only when injected in high doses directly into the CNS. In addition to low neurovirulence, vaccine strains can often be distinguished from naturally occurring strains by their temperature sensitivity and by subtle antigenic differences. The genomes for each of the attenuated Sabin vaccine strains have been fully sequenced as well as the genomes of each of the naturally occurring parental strains. The RNA sequences of the vaccine strains differ from the sequences of their naturally occurring parents by less than 1%, the smallest difference occurring between the type 3 vaccine and parent strains. For all three serotypes, analogous nucleotide substitutions in the 5′-noncoding region appear to be associated with diminished ability to replicate in the gastrointestinal tract, and with reduced neurovirulence.[17–19] Attenuating mutations also map to capsid proteins for individual serotypes.

PATHOGENESIS

General

The early events in the pathogenesis of poliomyelitis and other enterovirus infections, described in Chapter 158, include implantation and replication of virus in the gut and adjacent lymphoid tissues. After spread to deep lymph nodes, a "minor viremia," may disseminate virus to susceptible reticuloendothelial tissues. In asymptomatic infections, the virus is contained at this point and elicits the formation of type-specific antibodies. In a few persons, however, replication in the reticuloendothelial system gives rise to a "major viremia," which corresponds temporally with the "minor illness" also known as abortive poliomyelitis. At this point, the course of poliomyelitis deviates from other enteroviral diseases in the capacity of polioviruses to cause extensive necrosis of neurons in the gray matter of the brain and spinal cord. The preponderance of evidence indicates that viremia precedes paralysis in both experimental primates and humans.[20, 21] The exact routes by which the CNS then becomes infected remains uncertain and controversial. A study in transgenic mice expressing the human poliovirus receptor suggests that polioviruses spread from muscle to CNS via peripheral nerve fibers, rather than directly from the blood stream.[22] Neuropathologic studies and animal experiments indicate that spread is neural once the virus reaches the CNS.[23, 24]

Pathologic Features

Poliovirus principally affects motor and autonomic neurons. Neuronal destruction is accompanied by an inflammatory infiltrate of polymorphonuclear leukocytes, lymphocytes, and macrophages. These lesions are characteristically distributed throughout the gray matter of the anterior horn of the spinal cord and the motor nuclei of the pons and medulla.[25] Involved less severely are neurons of the mesencephalon, cerebellar roof nuclei, and precentral gyrus of the cerebral cortex. Clinical symptoms depend on the severity of lesions rather than on their distribution, which is similar in essentially all cases; almost all fatal cases have involvement of both the spinal cord and the cranial nerve nuclei and brain stem, even in the absence of bulbar signs. The dorsal root ganglia are commonly involved pathologically, but this does not result in sensory deficits. Viral replication in the spinal cord is maximal during the first few days after the onset of paralysis and generally becomes undetectable by a week, but inflammatory lesions may persist for months.

EPIDEMIOLOGY

General

Epidemiologic features of poliovirus infections are similar to those caused by other enteroviruses (see Chapter 158), but certain features of poliomyelitis are distinctive. The disease was predominantly sporadic before the late 1800s, when epidemics were first recognized in Scandinavia, western Europe, and the United States. In the developed countries, the first half of the 20th century witnessed sporadic epidemic disease occurring every few years without regular periodicity. By the early 1950s, epidemic polio occurred regularly in the United States with approximately 25 cases per 100,000 population reported annually. Accompanying the increased incidence was a shift in the affected age groups. In 1920, 90% of the cases occurred in infants younger than 5 years ("infantile paralysis"). In the early 1950s, the peak incidence was in 5- to 9-year-olds and more than one third of the cases occurred in persons older than 15 years. Abundant epidemiologic evidence supports the explanation that in the endemic period before 1900, polioviruses were ubiquitous and resulted in mostly inapparent infections that conferred widespread immunity in early childhood; with rising standards of hygiene in the 20th century, infection frequently was delayed until a later age, when the pool of susceptible people was large enough to permit the spread of epidemic disease. This concept presupposes that the appearance of epidemics of paralytic poliomyelitis was a result of a higher ratio of paralysis to inapparent infections among children old enough to have lost the protection of passively acquired maternal antibody.[26]

The introduction of IPVs in 1955 and live-attenuated OPVs in 1962 produced sudden, dramatic reductions in the incidence of paralytic poliomyelitis in the developed countries of the world. In the United States, the attack rate fell from 17.6 cases of poliomyelitis (paralytic and nonparalytic) per 100,000 population in 1955 to 0.4 case per 100,000 in 1962. During the next 2 decades, the rate of disease continued to fall until 1979, when the last case of endemic, naturally occurring poliomyelitis was reported, indicating that indigenous transmission of naturally occurring polioviruses has completely ceased in the United States.[27] This fade-out of naturally occurring strains has been attributed to the widespread use of OPV and to a reduction in the number of susceptible persons to a level insufficient to allow perpetration of wild-type strains during periods when transmission is naturally low (i.e., winter and spring).[26]

Vaccine-Associated Paralytic Poliomyelitis

After 1979, when the last case of naturally occurring poliomyelitis occurred, approximately eight to nine cases of paralytic poliomyelitis occurred annually in the United States, caused by live-vaccine viruses.[28] Recent evidence indicates that fewer cases have occurred since 1997, when IPV was incorporated into the routine polio immunization schedule. Vaccine-associated disease has occurred in both recipients of the vaccine and their contacts. Recipient cases occur predominantly in children younger than 4 months, 25 to 30% of whom have B-cell disorders. Most recipient cases occur 7 to 21 days after the administration of OPV. In contrast, disease in contacts occurs mostly in young adults, with the onset usually 20 to 29 days after the administration of vaccine. More than 80% of both recipient and contact cases are associated with the first dose of OPV.[29] OPV virus types 3 and 2 are more common causes of vaccine-associated paralysis than type 1; however, more than one type has been isolated from clinical specimens in some cases.[29] The overall risk of OPV-related disease is estimated to be 1 case per 2.6 million doses of OPV distributed.[29] The morbidity and mortality of vaccine-associated paralytic poliomyelitis appear to differ little from disease caused by naturally occurring polioviruses. Immunodeficient cases may have a worse prognosis because of prolonged infection.

CLINICAL FEATURES

Incubation Period

Best estimates of the incubation period of poliomyelitis are 9 to 12 days (range: 5 to 35 days) measured from presumed contact until the onset of the prodrome, and 11 to 17 days (range: 8 to 36 days) until the onset of paralysis.[30] The lower limits of these ranges are suspect, because even in instances of presumed single exposures, both the presumed index case and the contact may have had prior exposure to other asymptomatically infected persons. Poliovirus has been detected in the feces up to 19 days before the onset of paralysis.[31]

Clinical Manifestations of Infection

The manifestations of infection by polioviruses range from inapparent illness to severe paralysis and death. Usual estimates of the ratio of inapparent to clinically recognized polio infection vary between 60:1 and 1000:1.[26, 32] Figure 159–1 depicts the time of onset for the various clinical manifestations of poliovirus infection. At least 95% of infections are asymptomatic or inapparent and can be recognized only by the isolation of poliovirus from feces or oropharynx or by a rise in antibody titer. Abortive poliomyelitis, which occurs in 4 to 8% of infections, is characterized by a 2- to 3-day period of fever, headache, sore throat, listlessness, anorexia, vomiting, and abdominal pain, along with a normal neurologic examination. Abortive poliomyelitis is not clinically distinguishable from many other viral infections and can only be suspected clinically during an epidemic. Nonparalytic poliomyelitis differs from abortive poliomyelitis by the presence of signs of meningeal irritation. The disease is indistinguishable from aseptic meningitis caused by other enteroviruses. The systemic manifestations of nonparalytic poliomyelitis are generally more severe than in abortive poliomyelitis.

Spinal Paralytic Poliomyelitis

Frank paralysis occurs in roughly 0.1% of all poliovirus infections. In children there is frequently a biphasic course with *minor* and *major* illnesses.[33] The minor illness, coinciding with viremia, corresponds with the symptoms of abortive poliomyelitis and lasts 1 to 3 days. The patient then appears to be recovering and remains symptom-free for 2 to 5 days before the abrupt onset of the major illness. The preparalytic symptoms and signs of the major illness are those of meningitis, with headache, fever, malaise, vomiting, neck stiffness, and cerebrospinal fluid (CSF) pleocytosis. The temperature is generally 37°C to 39°C and is often is accompanied by chills, but rarely by rigors. This biphasic pattern (seen in perhaps one third of the children) is rarely observed in adults, who usually have a single phase but a more prolonged prodrome of symptoms before the more gradual onset of paralysis.[33, 34] Paralysis is rarely the first manifestation of illness. Severe myalgias herald the onset of the major illness, especially in older persons. Localized cutaneous hyperesthesia, paresthesias, involuntary muscle spasm, and muscular fasciculations are occasionally observed during this phase.

Meningismus and accompanying muscle pain generally are present for 1 to 2 days before frank weakness and paralysis ensue. The severity of the disease varies from weakness of a single portion of one muscle to complete quadriplegia. The paralysis is flaccid; stretch reflexes are initially hyperactive and then become absent. The most characteristic feature of the paralysis is its asymmetric distribution, which affects some muscle groups while sparing others. Proximal muscles of the extremities tend to be more involved than distal muscles, the legs are more commonly involved than the arms, and the large muscle groups of the hand are at greater risk than the small ones. Any combination of limbs may be paralyzed, but the most common pattern is involvement of one leg, followed by one arm, or both legs and both arms. Quadriplegia is almost never observed in infants.[34] Although occasional cases progress from the onset of weakness to complete quadriplegia and bulbar involvement in a few hours, more commonly the paralysis extends over 2 to 3 days. Progression of paralysis almost invariably halts when the patient becomes afebrile.[33] Paralysis of the bladder is usually associated with paralysis of the legs. It occurs in about one quarter of the adults but is uncommon in children. Sensory loss in poliomyelitis is very rare,[35] and its occurrence should strongly suggest some other diagnosis (e.g., Guillain-Barré syndrome).

Bulbar Paralytic Poliomyelitis

Bulbar poliomyelitis consists of paralysis of muscle groups innervated by cranial nerves, especially those of the soft palate and pharynx, resulting in dysphagia, nasal speech, and sometimes dyspnea. The ninth and tenth cranial nerves are by far the most frequently involved,[36] and pharyngeal paralysis often is the only obvious

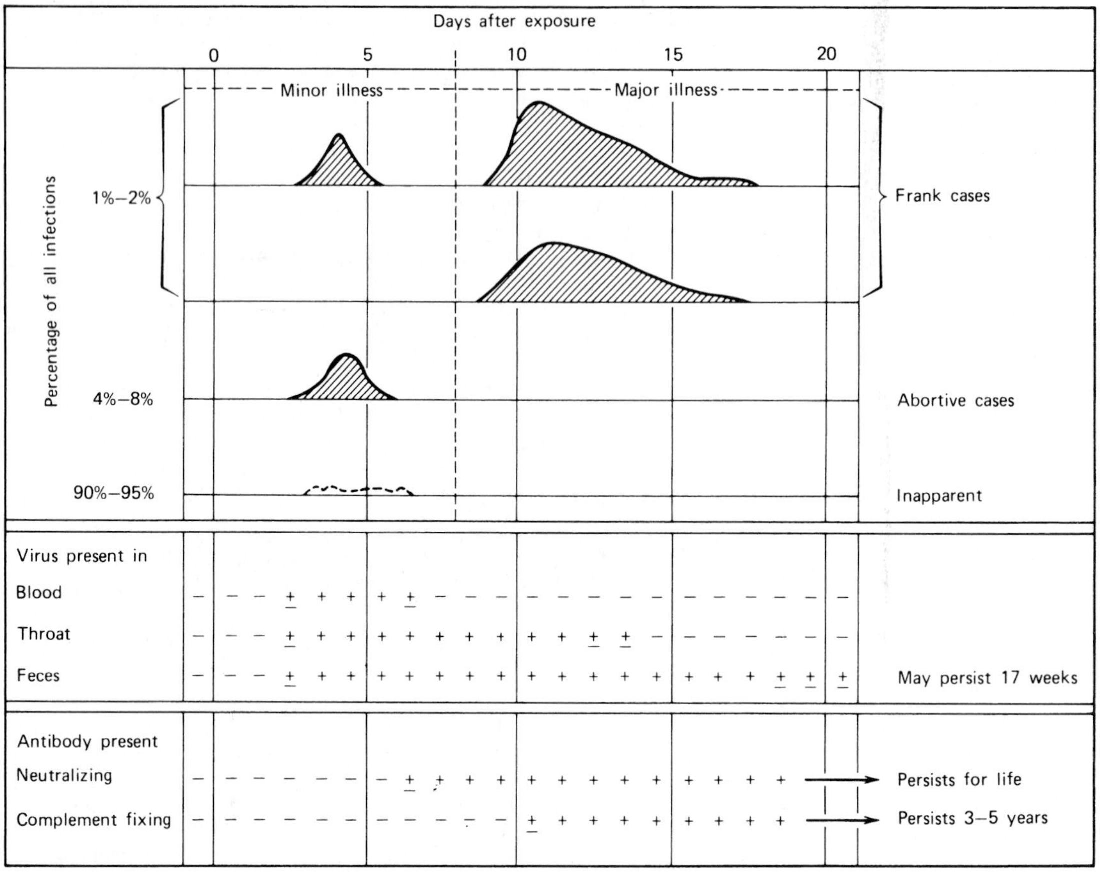

FIGURE 159–1. Schema of the clinical and subclinical forms of poliomyelitis, showing presence of virus and antibodies in relation to the development and persistence of the infection. (From Paul JR. History of Poliomyelitis. New Haven, Conn: Yale University Press; 1971.)

sign. Pooling of secretions occurs, and patients usually are extremely anxious and agitated about their inability to swallow and breathe. The prognosis becomes ominous when there is involvement of the circulatory and respiratory centers of the medulla. The frequency of the bulbar form of the disease has varied in different epidemics from 5 to 35% of paralytic cases. It is more common in adults.[34] Mixed bulbar and spinal involvement is common, with pure bulbar poliomyelitis accounting for not more than about 10% of paralytic poliomyelitis.

Polioencephalitis

Encephalitis, manifested primarily by confusion and disturbances of consciousness, is an uncommon form of poliomyelitis occurring principally in infants. It is the only type of poliomyelitis in which seizures are common. In contrast to spinal paralytic polio, there may be spastic paralysis, which reflects the presence of upper motor neuron involvement. The illness is not clinically distinguishable from many other infections that cause encephalitis.

Complications

The most important complication of paralytic poliomyelitis is respiratory compromise caused by paralysis of the respiratory muscles including the diaphragm and intercostal muscles, by airway obstruction from involvement of the cranial nerve nuclei, or by lesions of the respiratory center.[37] Pharyngeal paralysis typically results in noisy respirations because of pooling of secretions. Myocarditis has been documented by viral isolation and histologic lesions at autopsy,[38, 39] but it is rarely diagnosed clinically. Gastrointestinal events such as hemorrhage, paralytic ileus, and gastric dilatation may complicate acute paralysis.[40] Catheter-associated urinary tract infections and ureteral stones are common complications of prolonged bed rest and immobility in patients with residual paralysis.[41]

Risk Factors

Several preexisting factors and provocative events are known to influence the likelihood that an individual, once infected with poliovirus, will develop paralysis.

Age, Sex, and Pregnancy

Before puberty, poliovirus infections occur equally in boys and girls, although paralysis is more common in boys.[42] Among adults, women are at greater risk of infection but are not necessarily at greater risk of paralysis.[43, 44] Clinical data suggest that both the incidence and the severity of poliomyelitis may be increased in pregnant women.[44, 45] Not only are women of childbearing age more likely to be exposed to infections in young children,[43] but late pregnancy may be associated with increased susceptibility to more serious illness.

Immunodeficiency

Persons with congenital and acquired B-cell immunodeficiency have a markedly increased risk of OPV-vaccine–associated paralytic poliomyelitis (VAPP). Approximately 29% of the 89 VAPP cases reported to occur between 1985 and 1997 were immunodeficient.[46] Two thirds of immunodeficient VAPP cases have occurred among infant OPV recipients. The remaining immunodeficient patients, who are mostly adults, have acquired VAPP via exposure to infants recently fed OPV. The risk of VAPP among newborn infants with a congenital B-cell immunodeficiency disorder is estimated to be 2000-fold higher than for an immunocompetent infant.[29] There is little evidence that immunodeficiency states that predominately affect T-cell function, rather than B-cell function, increase the risk of VAPP. Although one Romanian infant infected with human immunodeficiency virus (HIV) is reported to have developed VAPP,[47] there has been no evidence of any neurologic complication among thousands of HIV-infected infants known to have received OPV in the United States and elsewhere.[48, 49] Similarly, VAPP is not known to complicate hematologic malignancies, bone marrow transplantation, or solid organ transplantation.

Some clinical features distinguish VAPP in immunodeficient patients from VAPP in those who are immunocompetent. The incubation period after the ingestion of OPV is unusually long, ranging from 30 to 120 days. The illness is protracted, and it may be associated with progression of paralysis over several weeks, chronic meningitis, and progressive neurologic dysfunction that includes both upper and lower motor neuron signs.[50, 51] Immunodeficient VAPP patients have a significantly higher risk of dying as a result of the infection than do immunocompetent VAPP patients.[46] Fecal excretion of virus in surviving cases has been estimated to occur for as long as 9 years in one immunodeficient patient.[52] The majority of VAPP cases in immunocompromised children and adults have been associated with type 2 OPV virus.[53]

Other Factors

Strenuous exercise substantially increases both the incidence and the severity of paralytic poliomyelitis.[54, 55] Exercise during the minor illness or the prodrome has no effect, but it is detrimental when it occurs during the first 3 days of the major illness.[55]

Both epidemiologic[56, 57] and experimental studies[58, 59] have confirmed that poliomyelitis tends to localize in a limb that has been the site of an intramuscular injection or injury within 2 to 4 weeks before the onset of infection. This association holds for both naturally occurring disease and vaccine-associated paralytic poliomyelitis.[60]

Tonsillectomized persons have a risk of acquiring bulbar poliomyelitis that is approximately eight times the risk in persons with intact tonsils. At risk are individuals with the onset of infection shortly before or after tonsillectomy and those whose tonsillectomy was performed in the remote past.[61, 62] Because the ninth and tenth cranial nerves supply the fauces, the spread of virus from damaged nerve endings may explain the acute effect.

Differential Diagnosis

Many diseases may mimic the nonspecific signs and symptoms of abortive poliomyelitis. Also, the aseptic meningitis caused by polioviruses is clinically indistinguishable from meningitis due to many other viral causes (see Chapters 71 and 160).

Few diseases, however, are likely to be confused with paralytic poliomyelitis. The most important is the Guillain-Barré syndrome. The patient with poliomyelitis is febrile, has signs of meningeal irritation, and appears acutely ill. The paralysis is characteristically asymmetric and virtually never accompanied by sensory loss. In contrast, in Guillain-Barré syndrome, there is symmetric, ascending paralysis with loss of sensation in approximately 80% of the cases. Facial diplegia occurs in about half of the patients with Guillain-Barré syndrome but is very uncommon even in bulbar poliomyelitis. In poliomyelitis, continued extension of paralysis beyond 3 to 4 days is unusual, whereas in Guillain-Barré syndrome the paralysis may spread in successive stages over a period of up to 2 weeks. Paresthesias are uncommon in poliomyelitis but common in Guillain-Barré syndrome. Characteristics of the CSF are useful in distinguishing the two conditions. In acute poliomyelitis, pleocytosis and a minimally elevated protein concentration are present, whereas in Guillain-Barré syndrome the protein level is elevated with absent or minimal pleocytosis (albuminocytologic dissociation).

Laboratory Diagnosis

Abnormalities of the CSF are not distinguishable from those of other viral diseases that cause aseptic meningitis. Polioviruses usually can be isolated from throat secretions in the first week of illness, and from feces often for several weeks. However, unlike many other enteroviruses causing aseptic meningitis, polioviruses rarely are isolated from the CSF. In sporadic cases of poliomyelitis occurring in areas of low incidence, it is important to characterize virus isolates as either wild type (naturally occurring strains) or vaccine-like; this methodology is available only in public health reference laboratories. Isolation from CSF (or brain and spinal cord in fatal cases), although uncommon, is especially valuable in evaluating vaccine-associated disease, because recovery of fecal virus is expected in this situation and only a CNS virus isolate with vaccine characteristics provides conclusive evidence of the etiologic association.

In the absence of a viral isolate, the diagnosis of poliovirus infection can be established serologically by testing paired acute and convalescent sera by neutralization against antigens of the three serotypes. Serologic tests cannot distinguish between wild-type virus and vaccine virus infection.

Prognosis

Available mortality figures date from the era of epidemic poliomyelitis when critical care medicine was not as sophisticated as it is today. During this period, the overall mortality of paralytic poliomyelitis was 5 to 10% but was substantially higher (20 to 60%) with bulbar involvement.[63] A varied degree of permanent weakness is observed in approximately two thirds of patients with paralytic poliomyelitis. Complete recovery is less likely when acute paralysis is severe, and patients requiring mechanical ventilation because of spinal respiratory paralysis rarely recover without some sequelae. Curiously, although bulbar poliomyelitis causes the greatest threat to life in the first week of illness, it is rarely responsible for permanent damage in surviving patients. Recovery from pharyngeal paralysis usually is evident by 10 days and eventually complete. Muscular paralysis in poliomyelitis usually progresses or extends for only 1 to 3 days after its onset, but occasionally for as long as 1 week.[64] Some estimate of the eventual outcome can be made after 1 month, when most reversible damage will have disappeared. Very little additional return of function can be expected beyond 9 months, although surviving muscles can be reeducated to perform additional tasks.

Postpoliomyelitis Syndrome

Some patients who partially or fully recover from paralytic poliomyelitis experience a new onset of muscle weakness, pain, atrophy, and fatigue many years after the acute illness.[65] Typically, the involved muscles are the same as those affected during the original illness, but weakness may also occur in previously unaffected limb muscles. Progression of new symptoms is gradual, and, as a result, affected individuals are seldom disabled.[66] Population-based studies suggest that the syndrome affects 20 to 30% of previously paralyzed patients.[67] The risk of postpoliomyelitis syndrome peaks between 25 and 35 years after acute poliomyelitis.[67] Although the cause is unknown, some authorities believe that late progression of muscle weakness is a result of physiologic attrition of motor units innervating muscles and muscle groups already less innervated as a result of earlier acute infection.[68]

Management

Specific antiviral agents for the treatment of poliomyelitis are not yet available. Management, therefore, is supportive and symptomatic.

In the acute phase of paralytic poliomyelitis, patients should be hospitalized. Bed rest is essential to prevent augmentation or extension of paralysis. Hot moist packs applied to muscles are very helpful in relieving pain and spasm. Physical therapy should be initiated once the progression of paralysis has ceased.

Paralysis of the respiratory muscles necessitates mechanical ventilation before hypoxia develops, generally when the vital capacity falls to less than 50%. Tank respirators used in the past to treat this form of paralysis are available in few hospitals; despite their advantage of avoiding tracheal intubation, they have been replaced by positive-pressure ventilators, which permit easier access to the patient. Pooling of secretions in the pharynx in mild bulbar poliomyelitis, if it is unaccompanied by spinal respiratory paralysis, can be managed with postural drainage and suction. Severe bulbar paralysis necessitates tracheal intubation. Weakness or paralysis of the bladder may necessitate catheterization.

Management of long-term physical and psychiatric sequelae of paralytic poliomyelitis is beyond the scope of this book. The reader is referred to excellent older references on these topics.[69, 70]

POLIOVIRUS IMMUNIZATION

Poliovirus Vaccines

Both IPV and live-attenuated OPV have been used effectively for more than 30 years in controlling paralytic poliomyelitis. The introduction of Salk IPV in 1955 led to an immediate and dramatic reduction in both epidemic and endemic poliomyelitis. The IPV available for the first several years possessed relatively low potency, accounting for the observation that as many as 17% of children with paralytic poliomyelitis in 1959 had received three or more doses of IPV.[71] Meanwhile live-attenuated OPV strains were developed by multiple passage of polioviruses in monkey kidney cell culture and selection of mutants with low virulence for primates.[72] Successful field trials of the Sabin OPV vaccine strains were carried out in the United States and many foreign countries from 1955 to 1959, and OPV was introduced for routine use in 1962 as separate monovalent vaccines; the trivalent product became available in 1964. OPV was quickly accepted by the pediatric and public health community because of several perceived advantages, including superior immunogenicity; lower cost; ease of administration; spread of vaccine virus to unimmunized, susceptible persons; and induction of gastrointestinal immunity.

Inactivated Poliovirus Vaccine

IPV is prepared by the inactivation of poliovirus seed strains by the method originally developed by Jonas Salk, that is, 1:1000 formalin treatment for 12 to 14 days at 37°C. The potency of IPV has been "enhanced" in the past 2 decades by the adoption of continuous cell lines and microcarrier systems for vaccine production. Enhanced-potency IPV was introduced in Europe and Canada in the early 1980s and licensed in the United States in 1987. The preparation now available (IPOL, Pasteur Mérieux Connaught) is produced in monkey kidney cells and contains 40-, 8-, and 32-Da antigen units, respectively, for poliovirus serotypes 1, 2, and 3. Four doses of IPV are recommended at 2 months, 4 months, 6 to 18 months, and 4 to 6 years of age.[73]

The currently licensed IPV is more immunogenic than the formulations available before 1987. Seroconversion rates are equal to, and mean antibody titers are superior to, those of OPV when given according to the same schedule. Neutralizing antibodies are detectable to all three types in 99% of recipients after two doses, and 100% after the third dose.[74, 75] A large boost in antibody titer follows the third dose.[74] After three doses, mean titers to types 1 and 3 are higher than in OPV-immunized children, whereas mean titers to type 2 are equivalent. Detectable antibody persists at protective levels for at least 5 years, although mean titers decline considerably.[76] The efficacy of IPV after one or two doses may be lower than for an equivalent number of OPV doses. A case-control study in Senegal indicated protection rates of 36 and 89% for recipients of one and two doses, respectively.[77]

IPV-immunized children develop little or no measurable secretory antibody.[78] When challenged with live polioviruses, IPV-immunized children shed the challenge virus in their feces at a higher rate, higher titer, and for a longer period than do OPV-immunized children,[79, 80] indicating a greater potential for asymptomatic infection and transmission of circulating polioviruses to unimmunized contacts. Although this is widely considered to be a disadvantage of IPV, there is evidence that the universal use of IPV results in partial protection that extends to unvaccinated persons in the community, albeit less than the protection provided by OPV.[81–84]

Live-Attenuated Poliovirus Vaccine

The trivalent OPV (Orimune, Wyeth-Lederle Vaccines and Pediatrics, Inc.) distributed in the United States contains sufficient live virus to exceed by approximately $\log_{10}$ the Food and Drug Administration's minimal potency standards of $10^{5.5}$, $10^{4.5}$, and $10^{5.2}$ median tissue culture infective dose ($TCID_{50}$) for poliovirus types 1, 2, and 3, respectively.[85] Because the more efficient replication of type 2 OPV virus regularly interferes with the replication of types 1 and 3,[86] a primary series of three doses is required to ensure seroconversion to all three serotypes.

Complete immunization with OPV includes four doses routinely given at 2 months, 4 months, 6 to 18 months, and 4 to 6 years of age.[73] Seroconversion rates after one OPV dose are 50, 85, and 30% to serotypes 1, 2, and 3, respectively.[87] Two months after the second dose, more than 86% of infants have serum antibody to all three poliovirus serotypes, and 2 months after the third dose, the prevalence of antibody to all three types is more than 96%.[74, 88] Detectable serum antibody to all three types persists in 84 to 98% of vaccinees 5 years after primary immunization.[89] Reexposure to vaccine viruses probably aids the maintenance of antibody levels in the population.[90, 91] Secretory immunoglobulin A poliovirus antibody appears in oropharyngeal and duodenal secretions 1 to 3 weeks after OPV immunization[78] and persists for at least 5 to 6 years.[92] Challenge studies suggest that the intestinal immunity induced by OPV is similar to intestinal immunity after natural infection.[93]

Although the true efficacy of OPV has never been tested under conditions of exposure to natural polioviruses in the United States, it is estimated to be very high on the basis of over 3 decades of general use. OPV efficacy evaluated during a type 1 poliovirus outbreak in Taiwan was estimated to be 82, 96, and 98% for 1, 2, and 3 or more doses, respectively.[94]

Nonimmune OPV recipients shed vaccine viruses in the feces for 1 to 6 weeks and from the oropharynx for 1 to 3 weeks. The spread of OPV virus to unimmunized children is considered to be advantageous, especially in areas in which vaccine acceptance levels are low. The importance of this "back door" method of protecting the community is uncertain. A seroprevalence study in Houston and Detroit found that 11 to 42% of 11- to 35-month-old children had antibody, despite receiving no prior OPV.[95]

The only disadvantage of OPV is the very rare occurrence of VAPP. Up to 1997, an average of eight cases of VAPP have been reported annually in the United States.[29, 96, 97] Approximately 45% of VAPP cases are recent OPV vaccinees[29]; most of these are infants, and most (80 to 90%) occur after the first feeding of OPV. A similar number of VAPP cases (approximately 48%) occur among direct contacts of recent OPV recipients[29] who are generally parents, other family members, baby-sitters, or other associates of the family who have close contact with a recent OPV vaccinee.

Approximately 22% of reported VAPP cases have occurred in children and adults who are immune-deficient.[53] Most patients have either isolated B-cell immunodeficiency or severe combined immunodeficiency syndrome.[53] VAPP associated with HIV infection has been reported in one Romanian infant[47] but is not known to have occurred in the United States. The majority of infections in immunocompromised children and adults have been associated with type 2 OPV virus.[29]

The mechanism by which the OPV viruses cause rare cases of paralytic disease is not fully understood. It is well known that OPV virus readily undergoes mutation during the brief period of intestinal replication, and that isolates can be recovered that are neurovirulent for primates.[98] Most OPV recipients shed polioviruses that have reverted to the naturally occurring genotype at a specific locus in the 5′ noncoding region of the genome that is strongly associated with attenuation for each of the three OPV serotypes.[99] However, because the attenuated Sabin strains differ from their virulent parent strains at multiple genetic loci, other mutational events probably contribute to reversion to full neurovirulence.[100–104]

U.S. Poliovirus Immunization Strategy

The United States relied on OPV alone for routine polio immunization from 1963 until 1997. During this period, both endemic and epidemic wild-type poliomyelitis were completely eradicated and the risk of imported poliomyelitis continued to decline with increasing control beyond the borders of the United States. Because even an extremely low risk of VAPP could not be tolerated in this climate, both the American Academy of Pediatrics and the Centers for Disease Control Advisory Committee on Immunization Practices (ACIP) have moved in several steps during the 1990s toward greater use of IPV.[105] In June 1999, the ACIP recommended exclusive use of IPV in the U.S. childhood immunization schedule, while permitting OPV only for travel to polio-endemic regions for persons for whom only one dose of polio vaccine can be given before protection is required (see also Chapter 312).[106]

POLIOMYELITIS IN DEVELOPING NATIONS AND GLOBAL ERADICATION

The existence of poliomyelitis was ignored for many years in developing countries because polio was considered to be an epidemic disease of wealthier nations. In the 1960s and 1970s, lameness surveys of schoolchildren in more than 20 nations revealed lower limb paralysis prevalence rates of 2 to 11 per 1000, figures that reflect poliomyelitis incidence rates that equal or exceed those of the peak epidemic years in the United States.[107, 108] Most cases of paralytic poliomyelitis in developing countries occur in children between the ages of 6 months and 2 years. The majority of cases are caused by type 1 poliovirus. Although approximately 80% of the world's children have received three or more OPV doses by 5 years of age,[12] many children remain unprotected because current poliomyelitis immunization programs fail to reach them or because of failure of administered polio vaccines to produce adequate immunity to all three poliovirus serotypes.

Use of Poliomyelitis Vaccines in the Developing World

OPV is used almost exclusively in underdeveloped nations because of its lower cost and ease of administration. The superior secretory immunity in the gastrointestinal tract induced by OPV is considered an advantage because of high rates of exposure to wild-type polioviruses. Transmission of OPV virus from immunized to nonimmune contacts, an event that is thought to be aided by poor sanitation and crowded living conditions, is also considered an advantage of OPV. During the past 2 decades, a uniform recommendation of three OPV doses in the first year of life (at 6, 10, and 14 weeks of age) has supplanted the variable immunization schedules previously practiced in developing countries. In 1985, the EPI schedule was amended to include a dose of trivalent OPV given shortly after birth; this practice provides an opportunity to administer at least one dose of vaccine to a child that may not present for routine health maintenance.[109] Even though the passively acquired maternal antibody to polioviruses present in the infant's circulation and in maternal colostrum reduces vaccine virus replication in the gastrointestinal tract and therefore blunts the immune response in some infants, infants who receive OPV at birth are more likely to have antibody to all three poliovirus types at 4 months of age.[110]

Unfortunately, in many tropical countries, the full recommended series of OPV may fail to produce active immunity to all three poliovirus serotypes in a significant proportion of infants. Low seroconversion rates to three OPV doses have been documented in many locations,[111–116] averaging 73, 90, and 70% for types 1, 2, and 3, respectively.[85] In Israel and Brazil, the poor response has been cited as a contributing factor to outbreaks of poliomyelitis despite relatively high immunization rates existing before the appearance of epidemic disease.[116–118] Although the reasons for the lower potency of OPV in tropical areas remains incompletely understood, both vaccine formulation and the effect of concurrent diarrheal illnesses have emerged as important factors. The OPV vaccines distributed to most developing countries only marginally meet the 1988 Expanded Programme of Immunization minimal potency standards of 10^6, 10^5, and $10^{5.5}$ $TCID_{50}$ for types 1, 2, and 3, respectively. Patriarca and colleagues demonstrated that a twofold increase in the type 3 component increased the seroconversion rate from 16 to 42% among type 3–seronegative Brazilian children given one dose of trivalent OPV.[118] Diarrheal disease at the time of immunization also reduces seroconversion rates to OPV. Studies conducted in Brazil and Gambia[119] and in Bangladesh[120] have shown reduced seroconversion rates to types 2 and 3 OPV among infants with diarrhea at the time of OPV feeding, whereas the response to type 1 was not affected. The impact of diarrhea on seroconversion persists despite the administration of three or four OPV doses.

Although IPV has been shown to be highly immunogenic among children in developing areas,[121, 122] the costs associated with production and delivery, and the requirement for injection, have made the sole use of IPV an undesirable alternative for use in developing countries. However, IPV has been used as a supplement to OPV immunization in Israel, where type 1 poliovirus continued to cause epidemic disease in the Gaza Strip despite relatively good rates of OPV coverage,[116, 123] and in Côte d'Ivoire, where IPV administered at 9 months markedly enhanced seroconversion rates among infants given OPV at 2, 3, and 4 months of age.[124]

Global Eradication

In 1974, the World Health Organization founded the Expanded Programme on Immunization to provide monetary and technical support for basic immunization against several childhood diseases worldwide. The programs have produced substantial progress by applying several strategies to the control of poliomyelitis, including routine immunization programs, National Immunization Days, and intensified surveillance and response to outbreaks.[10, 11] The adoption of pulse immunization in epidemic areas via National Immunization Days in which all children receive live oral vaccine regardless of polio immunization history has been an effective approach in many locations.[125, 126] Seroconversion rates during mass campaigns are higher than for routine immunization,[127] possibly because of the spread of OPV virus, or because they are conducted during the dry season, when diarrheal disease is less prevalent.

By 1983, an international conference in Bellagio, Italy, articulated the vision of worldwide poliomyelitis eradication[128]; and in 1985, the Pan American Health Organization resolved to eradicate poliomyelitis from the Western Hemisphere, a goal that was achieved by 1991. By 1997, the reported incidence of poliomyelitis had steadily declined to approximately 4000 cases/year (compared with an estimated 600,000 cases annually in the prevaccine era).[11, 12] Despite this progress, wild-type polioviruses continue to circulate and cause disease in many developing nations. Sub-Saharan Africa and South Asia remain regions with high rates of endemic disease. The Expended Programme on Immunization recommendations are intended to be universal, but polio vaccines fail to reach many children because of interrupted vaccine supplies, problems in delivery from central stores to the final locations for immunization, and disruptions in the cold chain necessary to maintain the potency of OPV. In addition, continued civil strife, poor political support, and inadequate funding continue to hamper efforts to control poliomyelitis and represent the major obstacles to the World Health Assembly goal of worldwide eradication of poliomyelitis by the year 2000.[11, 129]

REFERENCES

1. Paul JR. History of Poliomyelitis. New Haven, Conn: Yale University Press; 1971.
2. Vermont State Department of Public Health. Infantile paralysis in Vermont. Brattleboro: Vermont Printing Co; 1924.
3. Enders JF, Weller TH, Robbins FC. Cultivation of the Lansing strain of poliomyelitis virus in cultures of various human embryonic tissue. Science. 1949;109:85–87.
4. Bodian D, Morgan IM, Howe HA. Differentiation of three types of poliomyelitis virus. III. The grouping of fourteen strains into three immunological types. Am J Hyg. 1949;49:234.
5. Bodian D. Pathogenesis of poliovirus in normal and passively immunized primates after virus feeding. Fed Proc. 1952;11:462.
6. Horstmann DM. Poliomyelitis in the blood of orally infected monkeys and chimpanzees. Proc Soc Exp Biol Med. 1952;79:417.
7. Horstmann DM, McCollum RW. Poliomyelitis virus in human blood during the "minor" illness and asymptomatic infection. Proc Soc Exp Biol Med. 1953;82:434–437.
8. Salk JE. Studies in human subjects on active immunization against poliomyelitis. I. A preliminary report of experiments in progress. JAMA. 1953;151:1081–1098.
9. Anonymous. Live Poliovirus Vaccines. First and Second International Conferences on Live Poliovirus Vaccines. Washington, DC: World Health Organization; 1959 and 1960.
10. Wright PF, Kim-Farley RJ, de Quadros CA, et al. Strategies for the global eradication of poliomyelitis by the year 2000. N Engl J Med. 1991;325:1774–1779.
11. Hull HF, Ward NA, Hull BP, et al. Paralytic poliomyelitis: Seasoned strategies, disappearing disease. Lancet. 1994;343:1331–1337.
12. Centers for Disease Control and Prevention. Progress toward global eradication of poliomyelitis, 1997. MMWR Morb Mortal Wkly Rep. 1998;47:414–419.
13. Bodian D. Second attacks of paralytic poliomyelitis in human beings in relation to immunity, virus types and virulence. Am J Hyg. 1951;54:174.
14. Shelokov A, Habel K, McKinstry DW. Relation of poliomyelitis virus types to clinical disease and geographic distribution: A preliminary report. Ann N Y Acad Sci. 1955;61:998.
15. Centers for Disease Control. Neurotropic Diseases Surveillance. Annual Poliomyelitis Summary, 1971. Atlanta: Centers for Disease Control; 1973.
16. Sabin AB. Properties and behavior of orally administered attenuated polio virus vaccine. In: Fourth International Poliomyelitis Conference. Philadelphia: JB Lippincott; 1958:124.
17. Westrop GD, Wareham KA, Evans D, et al. Genetic basis of attenuation of the Sabin type 3 oral poliovirus vaccine. J Virol. 1989;63:1338–1344.
18. Pollard SR, Dunn G, Cammack N, et al. Nucleotide sequence of a neurovirulent variant of the type 2 oral poliovirus vaccine. J Virol. 1989;63:4949–4951.
19. Omata T, Kohara M, Kuge S, et al. Genetic analysis of the attenuation phenotype of poliovirus type 1. J Virol. 1986;58:348–358.
20. Bodian D. Viremia in experimental poliomyelitis. I. General aspects of infection after intravascular inoculation with strains of high and low invasiveness. Am J Hyg. 1954;60:339.
21. Bodian D. Emerging concept of poliomyelitis infection. Science. 1955;122:105.
22. Ren R, Racaniello VR. Poliovirus spreads from muscle to the central nervous system by neural pathways. J Infect Dis. 1992;166:747–752.
23. Jubelt B, Gallez-Hawkins G, Narayan O, Johnson RT. Pathogenesis of human poliovirus infection in mice. II. Age dependency of paralysis. J Neuropathol Exp Neurol. 1980;39:138–148.
24. Bodian D, Howe HA. An experimental study of the role of neurones in the dissemination of poliomyelitis virus in the nervous system. Brain. 1940;63:135.
25. Bodian D. Histopathological basis of clinical findings in poliomyelitis. Am J Med. 1949;6:563–578.
26. Nathanson N, Martin JR. The epidemiology of poliomyelitis: Enigmas surrounding its appearance and disappearance. Am J Epidemiol. 1979;110:672.
27. Kim-Farley RJ, Bart KJ, Schonberger LB, et al. Poliomyelitis in the USA: Virtual elimination of disease caused by wild virus. Lancet. 1984;2:1315–1317.
28. Centers for Disease Control and Prevention. Paralytic poliomyelitis—United States, 1980–1994. MMWR Morb Mortal Wkly Rep. 1997;46:79–83.
29. Strebel PM, Sutter RW, Cochi SL, et al. Epidemiology of poliomyelitis in the United States one decade after the last reported case of indigenous wild virus–associated disease. Clin Infect Dis. 1992;14:568–579.
30. Horstmann DM, Paul JR. The incubation period in human poliomyelitis and its implications. JAMA. 1947;135:11.
31. Brown GC, Francis Jr T, Pearson HE. Rapid development of carrier state and detection of poliomyelitis virus in stool nineteen days before onset of paralytic disease. JAMA. 1945;129:121.
32. Melnick JL, Ledinko N. Social serology: Antibody levels in a normal young population during an epidemic of poliomyelitis. Am J Hyg. 1951;54:354.
33. Horstmann DM. Clinical aspects of acute poliomyelitis. Am J Med. 1949;6:592.
34. Weinstein L, Shelokov A, Seltser R, Winchell GD. A comparison of the clinical features of poliomyelitis in adults and children. N Engl J Med. 1952;246:297–302.
35. Plum F. Sensory loss with poliomyelitis. Neurology. 1956;6:166.
36. Baker AB. Bulbar poliomyelitis: Its mechanism and treatment. Am J Med. 1949;6:614.
37. Ibsen B. The clinical diagnosis and evaluation of respiratory problems in patients with acute poliomyelitis. In: Fourth International Poliomyelitis Conference. Philadelphia: JB Lippincott; 1958:483–487.
38. Galpine JF, Wilson WCM. Occurrence of myocarditis in paralytic poliomyelitis. BMJ. 1959;2:1379.
39. Weinstein L. Cardiovascular disturbances in poliomyelitis. Circulation. 1957;15:735.
40. Neu H. Gastrointestinal complications in poliomyelitis. In: Fourth International Poliomyelitis Conference. Philadelphia: JB Lippincott; 1958:546.
41. Plum F. Prevention of urinary calculi after paralytic poliomyelitis. JAMA. 1958;168:1302–1306.
42. Abramson H, Greenberg M. Acute poliomyelitis in infants under one year of age: Epidemiological and clinical features. Pediatrics. 1955;16:477.
43. Siegel M, Greenberg M, Bodian J. Presence of children in the household as a factor in the incidence of paralytic poliomyelitis in adults. N Engl J Med. 1957;257:958.
44. Weinstein L, Aycock WL, Feemster RF. Relation of sex, pregnancy, and menstruation to susceptibility in poliomyelitis. N Engl J Med. 1951;245:54.
45. Anderson GW, Anderson G, Skaar A, Sandler F. Poliomyelitis in pregnancy. Am J Hyg. 1952;55:127–139.
46. Prevots R. Personal communication.
47. Ion-Neldescu N, Dobrescu A, Strebel PM, Sutter RW. Vaccine-associated paralytic poliomyelitis and HIV infection (Letter). Lancet. 1994;343:51–52.
48. Von Reyn CF, Clements CJ, Mann JM. Human immunodeficiency virus infection and routine childhood immunisation. Lancet. 1987;2:669–672.
49. Onorato IM, Markowitz LE, Oxtoby MJ. Childhood immunization, vaccine-preventable diseases and infection with human immunodeficiency virus. Pediatr Infect Dis J. 1988;7:588–595.
50. Davis LE, Bodian D, Price D, et al. Chronic progressive poliomyelitis secondary to vaccination of an immunodeficient child. N Engl J Med. 1977;297:241–245.
51. Wyatt HV. Poliomyelitis in hypogammaglobulinemics. J Infect Dis. 1973;128:802.
52. Kew OM, Sutter RW, Nottay BK, et al. Prolonged replication of a type 1 vaccine–derived poliovirus in an immunodeficient patient. J Clin Microbiol. 1998;36:2893–2899.
53. Sutter RW, Prevots DR. Vaccine-associated paralytic poliomyelitis among immunodeficient persons. Infect Med. 1994;11:426, 429–430, 435–438.
54. Russell WR. Paralytic poliomyelitis: The early symptoms, and the effect of physical activity on the course of disease. BMJ. 1949;1:465.
55. Horstmann DM. Acute poliomyelitis. Relation of physical activity at the time of onset to the course of the disease. JAMA. 1950;142:236.
56. Greenberg M, Abramson H, Cooper HM, Solomon HE. The relation between recent injections and paralytic poliomyelitis in children. Am J Public Health. 1952;42:142–152.
57. Sutter RW, Patriarca PA, Suleiman AM, et al. Attributable risk of DTP (diphtheria and tetanus toxoids and pertussis vaccine) injection in provoking paralytic poliomyelitis during a large outbreak in Oman. J Infect Dis. 1992;165:444–449.
58. Bodian D. Viremia in experimental poliomyelitis. II. Viremia and the mechanism of the "provoking" effect of injections or trauma. Am J Hyg. 1954;60:358.
59. Trueta J, Hodes R. Provoking and localizing factors in poliomyelitis. Lancet. 1954;1:998.
60. Strebel PM, Nedelcu N-I, Baughman AL, et al. Intramuscular injections within 30 days of immunization with oral poliovirus vaccine—a risk factor for vaccine-associated paralytic poliomyelitis. N Engl J Med. 1995;332:500–506.
61. Eley RC, Flake CG. Acute anterior poliomyelitis following tonsillectomy and adenoidectomy: With special reference to the bulbar form. J Pediatr. 1938;13:63.
62. Paffenbarger RS. The effect of prior tonsillectomy on incidence and clinical type of acute poliomyelitis. Am J Hyg. 1957;66:131.
63. Ferris BG Jr, Auld PAM, Cronkhite L, et al. Life threatening poliomyelitis, Boston, 1955. N Engl J Med. 1960;262:371.
64. Russell WR, Fischer-Williams M. Recovery of muscular strength after poliomyelitis. Lancet. 1954;1:330.
65. Dalakas MC, Sever JL, Madden DL, et al. Late postpoliomyelitis muscular atrophy: Clinical, virologic, and immunologic studies. Rev Infect Dis. 1984;6:S562–S567.
66. Dalakas MC, Elder G, Hallet M, et al. A long-term follow-up study of patients with post-poliomyelitis neuromuscular symptoms. N Engl J Med. 1986;314:959–963.
67. Ramlow J, Alexander M, LaPorte R, et al. Epidemiology of the post-polio syndrome. Am J Epidemiol. 1992;136:769–786.
68. Johnson RT. Late progression of poliomyelitis paralysis: Discussion of pathogenesis. Rev Infect Dis. 1984;6:S568–S569.
69. Bennett RI. Care of the after effects of poliomyelitis. Am J Med. 1949;6:620.
70. Weinstein L. Diagnosis and treatment of poliomyelitis. Med Clin North Am. 1948;32:1377.
71. Melnick JL. Advantages and disadvantages of killed and live poliomyelitis vaccines. Bull World Health Organ. 1978;56:21.
72. Sabin AB. Oral polio vaccine: History of its development and use and current challenge to eliminate poliomyelitis from the world. J Infect Dis. 1985;151:420–436.

73. Centers for Disease Control and Prevention. Poliomyelitis prevention in the United States: Introduction of a sequential vaccination schedule of inactivated poliovirus vaccine followed by oral poliovirus vaccine. Recommendations of the Advisory Committee on Immunization Practices (ACIP). MMWR Morb Mortal Wkly Rep. 1997;46:1–25.
74. McBean AM, Thoms ML, Albrecht P, et al. The serologic response to oral polio vaccine and enhanced potency inactivated polio vaccines. Am J Epidemiol. 1988;128:615–628.
75. Simoes EA, John TJ. The antibody response of seronegative infants to inactivated poliovirus vaccine of enhanced potency. Dev Biol Stand. 1986;14:127–131.
76. Swartz TA, Roumiantzeff M, Peyron L, et al. Use of a combined DTP-polio vaccine in a reduced schedule. Dev Biol Stand. 1986;65:159–166.
77. Robertson SE, Traverso HP, Drucker JA, et al. Clinical efficacy of a new, enhanced-potency, inactivated poliovirus vaccine. Lancet. 1988;1:897–899.
78. Ogra PL, Karzon DT, Righthand F. Immunoglobulin response in serum and secretions after immunization with live and inactivated poliovaccine and natural infection. N Engl J Med. 1968;279:893–900.
79. Onorato IM, Modlin JF, McBean AM, et al. Mucosal immunity induced by enhanced potency IPV and OPV. J Infect Dis. 1991;163:1–6.
80. Modlin JF, Halsey NA, Thoms ML, et al. Humoral and mucosal immunity in infants induced by three sequential IPV-OPV immunization schedules. J Infect Dis. 1997;75(Suppl 1):S228–S234.
81. Fox JP, Elveback L, Scott W, et al. Herd immunity: Basic concept and relevance to public health immunization practices. Am J Epidemiol. 1971;94:179–189.
82. Stickle G. Observed and expected poliomyelitis in the United States, 1958–1961. Am J Public Health. 1964;54:1222–1229.
83. Bijkerk H. Poliomyelitis epidemic in the Netherlands. Dev Biol Stand. 1979;43:195–206.
84. Schaap GJP, Bijkerk H, Coutinho RA, et al. The spread of wild poliovirus in the well-vaccinated Netherlands in connection with the 1978 epidemic. Prog Med Virol. 1984;29:124–140.
85. Patriarca PA, Wright PF, John TJ. Factors affecting the immunogenicity of oral poliovirus vaccine in developing countries. Rev Infect Dis. 1991;13:926–939.
86. Robertson HE, Acker MS, Dillenberg HO, et al. Community-wide use of a "balanced" trivalent oral poliovirus vaccine (Sabin). Can J Public Health. 1962;53:179–191.
87. Cohen-Abbo A, Culley BS, Reed GW, et al. Seroresponse to trivalent oral poliovirus vaccine as a function of dosage interval. Pediatr Infect Dis J. 1995;14:100–106.
88. Hardy GE, Hopkins CC, Linneman CC, et al. Trivalent oral poliovirus vaccine: A comparison of two infant immunization schedules. Pediatrics. 1970;45:444–448.
89. Krugman RD, Hardy GE, Sellers C. Antibody persistence after primary immunization with trivalent oral poliovirus vaccine. Pediatrics. 1977;60:80–82.
90. Bass JW, Halsted SB, Fischer GW, et al. Oral polio vaccine: Effect of booster vaccination one to 14 years after primary series. JAMA. 1978;239:2252–2255.
91. Nishio O, Ishihara Y, Sakae K, et al. The trend of acquired immunity with live poliovirus vaccine and the effect of revaccination: Follow-up of vaccinees for ten years. Dev Biol Stand. 1984;12:1–10.
92. Ogra PL. Mucosal immune response to poliovirus vaccines in childhood. Rev Infect Dis. 1984;6:S361–S368.
93. Ghendon YUZ, Sanakoyeva II. Comparison of the resistance of the intestinal tract to poliomyelitis virus (Sabin's strains) in person after naturally and experimentally acquired immunity. Acta Virol. 1961;5:265–273.
94. Kim-Farley RJ, Rutherford G, Lichfield P, et al. Outbreak of paralytic poliomyelitis, Taiwan. Lancet. 1984;2:1322–1324.
95. Chen R, Hanfling M, Hausinger S. Extent of secondary spread of oral polio vaccine virus spread in inner-city pre-school children. 32nd Interscience Conference on Antimicrobial Agents and Chemotherapy, Anaheim, Calif, 1992.
96. Nkowane BM, Wassilak SCF, Orenstein WA, et al. Vaccine-associated paralytic poliomyelitis: United States: 1973 through 1984. JAMA. 1987;257:1335–1340.
97. Prevots DR, Sutter RW, Strebel PM, et al. Completeness of reporting for paralytic poliomyelitis, United States, 1980 through 1991. Arch Pediatr Adolesc Med. 1994;148:479–485.
98. Sabin AB. Properties and behavior of orally administered attenuated poliovirus vaccine. JAMA. 1957;164:1216–1223.
99. Minor P, Dunn G, Begg N, et al. Poliovirus vaccination schedules and reversion to virulence. Presented at 33rd Conference on Antimicrobial Agents and Chemotherapy, New Orleans, La, 1993.
100. Almond JW. The attenuation of poliovirus neurovirulence. Annu Rev Microbiol 1987;41:154–180.
101. Minor PD, John A, Ferguson M, Icenogle JP. Antigenic and molecular evolution of the vaccine strain of type 3 poliovirus during the period of excretion by a primary vaccinee. J Gen Virol. 1986;67:693–706.
102. Stanway G, Hughes PJ, Mountford RC, et al. Comparison of the complete nucleotide sequences of the genomes of the neurovirulent poliovirus P3/Leon/37 and its attenuated Sabin vaccine derivative P3/Leon 12a1b. Proc Natl Acad Sci U S A. 1984;81:1539–1543.
103. Almond JW, Westrop GD, Evans DM, et al. Studies on the attenuation of the Sabin type 3 oral polio vaccine. J Virol Methods. 1987;17:183–189.
104. Evans DM, Dunn G, Minor PD, et al. Increased neurovirulence associated with a single nucleotide change in a noncoding region of the Sabin type 3 poliovaccine genome. Nature. 1985;314:548–550.
105. Centers for Disease Control and Prevention: Use of sequential IPV/OPV schedule. MMWR Morb Mortal Wkly Rep. 1998;47:1017–1019.
106. Centers for Disease Control and Prevention. Recommendations of the Advisory Committee on Immunization Practices: Revised Recommendations for Routine Poliomyelitis Vaccination. MMWR Morb Mortal Wkly Rep. 1999;48:590.
107. Ofusu-Amaah S. The challenge of poliomyelitis in tropical Africa. Rev Infect Dis. 1984;6:318–320.
108. Henderson RH. The Expanded Programme on Immunization of the World Health Organization. Rev Infect Dis. 1984;6:475–479.
109. Expanded Programme on Immunization Global Advisory Group. Wkly Epidemiol Rec. 1985;60:13–16.
110. Dong D-X, Hu X-M, Liu W-J, et al. Immunization of neonates with trivalent oral poliomyelitis vaccine (Sabin). Bull World Health Organ. 1986;64:853–860.
111. John TJ, Jayabal P. Oral polio vaccination of children in the tropics. I. The poor seroconversion rates and the absence of viral interference. Am J Epidemiol. 1972;96:263–269.
112. Domok I, Balayan MS, Fayinka OA, et al. Factors affecting the efficacy of live poliovirus vaccine in warm climates. Bull World Health Organ. 1974;51:333–347.
113. John TJ, Christopher S. Oral polio vaccination of children in the tropics. II. Antibody response in relation to vaccine virus infection. Am J Epidemiol. 1975;102:414–421.
114. Hanlon P, Hanlon L, Marsh V, et al. Serological comparisons of approaches to polio vaccination in the Gambia. Lancet. 1987;1:800–801.
115. De Brito Bastos NC, de Carvalho ES, Schatzmayr H, et al. Antipoliomyelitis program in Brazil: A serologic study of immunity. Bull Pan Am Health Organ. 1974;8:54–65.
116. Lasch EE, Abed Y, Abdulla K, et al. Successful results of a program combining live and inactivated poliovirus vaccines to control poliomyelitis in Gaza. Rev Infect Dis. 1984;6:467–470.
117. Melnick JL. Combined use of live and killed vaccines to control poliomyelitis in tropical areas. Dev Biol Stand. 1981;47:265–273.
118. Patriarca PA, Laender F, Palmeira G, et al. Randomised trial of alternative formulations of oral poliovaccine in Brazil. Lancet. 1988;1:429–433.
119. WHO Collaborative Study Group on Oral Poliovirus Vaccine. Effect of diarrhea on seroconversion to oral poliovirus vaccine. 32nd Interscience Conference on Antimicrobial Agents and Chemotherapy, Anaheim, Calif, 1992.
120. Myaux JA, Unicomb L, Besser RE, et al. Effect of diarrhea on the humoral response to oral polio vaccination. Pediatr Infect Dis J. 1996;15:204–209.
121. Swartz TA, Ben-Porath E, Ben-Yshai Z, et al. A controlled trial with inactivated poliovaccine. Dev Biol Stand. 1981;47:199–206.
122. Simoes EAF, Padmini B, Steinhoff MC, et al. Antibody response of infants to two doses of inactivated poliovirus vaccine of enhanced potency. Am J Dis Child. 1985;139:977–980.
123. Lasch EE, Abed Y, Marcus O, et al. Combined live and inactivated poliovirus vaccine to control poliomyelitis in a developing country—five years after. Dev Biol Stand. 1986;65:137–143.
124. Morinere BJ, van Loon FPL, Rhodes PH, et al. Immunogenicity of a supplemental dose of oral versus inactivated poliovirus vaccine. Lancet. 1993;341:1545–1550.
125. John TJ. Poliomyelitis in India: Prospects and problems of control. Rev Infect Dis. 1984;6:438–441.
126. Sabin AB. Strategies for elimination of poliomyelitis in different parts of the world with use of oral poliovirus vaccine. Rev Infect Dis. 1984;6:391–396.
127. Richardson G, Linkins R, Eames M, et al. Immunogenicity of oral poliovirus vaccine (OPV) given in mass campaigns versus routine immunization programs. Presented at 33rd Conference on Antimicrobial Agents and Chemotherapy, New Orleans, La, 1993.
128. Rockefeller Foundation. Protecting the world's children: Vaccines and immunization. Bellagio, Italy: Rockefeller Foundation, 1984.
129. World Health Organization. Global eradication of poliomyelitis by the year 2000. Wkly Epidemiol Rec. 1988;63:161–162.

Chapter 160

Coxsackieviruses, Echoviruses, and Newer Enteroviruses

JOHN F. MODLIN

This chapter covers human disease caused by the group A coxsackieviruses, group B coxsackieviruses, echoviruses, and newer enteroviruses, which as members of the genus Enterovirus, share many characteristics with polioviruses, including structure, physicochemical properties, mode of replication, pathogenesis, and epidemiology (described in Chapter 159). More than 90% of infections caused by the nonpolio enteroviruses are asymptomatic or result only in undifferentiated febrile illness.[1] When disease occurs, the spectrum and severity of clinical manifestations vary with the age, gender, and immune status of the host and with the subgroup, serotype, and even the intratypic enterovirus strain.

Some clinical syndromes (viral meningitis and some exanthems) are caused by many enterovirus serotypes, some are predominately caused by certain enterovirus subgroups (e.g., pleurodynia and myocarditis by the group B coxsackieviruses), and other diseases are mostly associated with individual enterovirus serotypes (Table 160–1). Infections caused by the taxonomically separate "newer enteroviruses" are considered at the end of this chapter (see Table 160–2).

CENTRAL NERVOUS SYSTEM INFECTIONS

Acute Aseptic Meningitis

Acute aseptic meningitis is a syndrome characterized by signs and symptoms of meningeal irritation and cerebrospinal fluid (CSF) pleocytosis in the absence of bacteria or fungi. The numerous causes of aseptic meningitis are listed in Chapter 71. Most community-acquired cases are caused by viruses; of these, group B coxsackieviruses and echoviruses together cause more than 90% of cases.[2] Group A coxsackieviruses cause relatively fewer cases.[2] Although many enterovirus serotypes are reported to cause aseptic meningitis, group B coxsackievirus serotypes 2 through 5 and echovirus serotypes 4, 6, 9, 11, 16, and 30 are the most frequently implicated. Furthermore, infection with certain serotypes, particularly the group B coxsackieviruses and echovirus 30, is more likely to be accompanied by aseptic meningitis than is infection with other common enterovirus serotypes.[3]

Clinical Manifestations

Infants younger than 3 months have the highest rates of clinically recognized aseptic meningitis, in part because lumbar punctures are routinely performed for evaluation of fever in this age group.[4] Only a minority of these infants have clinical manifestations suggestive of neurologic disease.[3]

The severity of disease in older children and adults with aseptic meningitis varies widely. The onset may be gradual or abrupt, and the typical patient has a brief prodrome of fever and chills. Headache is usually a prominent complaint. Meningismus, when present, varies from mild to severe. Kernig's and Brudzinski's signs are present in only about one third of patients. Pharyngitis and other symptoms of upper respiratory tract infections are often present. The illness is sometimes biphasic, as in poliomyelitis; in these patients, fever and myalgia are present for a few days, followed by defervescence and absence of symptoms for 2 to 10 days before the sudden reappearance of fever and headache signals the onset of meningitis. Complications such as febrile seizures, complex seizures, lethargy, coma, and movement disorders occur early in the course of aseptic meningitis in 5 to 10% of patients.[4, 5] Adults may experience a more prolonged period of fever and headache than infants and children do, and some adult patients may take weeks to return to normal activity.[6]

Laboratory Diagnosis

The clinical diagnosis of aseptic meningitis depends on routine examination of CSF. The CSF is clear and under normal or mildly increased pressure. The total CSF cell count is usually 10 to 500/mm^3 but may occasionally exceed 1000/mm^3, although cell counts less than 10/mm^3 may occur in a small minority of cases.[2, 7–10] Differential cell counts of the CSF often reveal an increased proportion of neutrophils, but the differential invariably shifts to a predominance of lymphocytes during the initial 1 to 2 days of illness. By 24 hours after the initial evaluation, the CSF differential should have fewer than 50% neutrophils.[11, 12] In general, the CSF glucose concen-

TABLE 160–1 Clinical Spectrum of Infection with Coxsackieviruses and Echoviruses*

	Group A Coxsackieviruses	Group B Coxsackieviruses	Echoviruses
Illness associated with many enteroviruses	Asymptomatic infection Febrile illness with or without respiratory symptoms Aseptic meningitis (1–11, 14, 16–18, 22, 24) Encephalitis (2, 5, 6, 7, 9) Paralysis (4, 6, 7, 9, 11, 14, 21)	Asymptomatic infection Febrile illness with or without respiratory symptoms Aseptic meningitis (1–6) Encephalitis (1–3, 5, 6) Paralysis (1–6)	Asymptomatic infection Febrile illness with or without respiratory symptoms Aseptic meningitis (all except 24, 26, 29, 32) Encephalitis (2–4, 6, 7, 9, 11, 14, 17–19, 25) Paralysis (1–4, 6, 7, 9, 11, 14, 16, 18, 19, 30)
Illness more characteristic of particular groups or serotypes	Herpangina (2–6, 8, 10, 22) Hand-foot-and-mouth syndrome (5, 7, 9, 10, 16) Lymphonodular pharyngitis (10) Exanthem (2, 4, 5, 9, 16) Epidemic conjunctivitis (24)	Exanthem (1, 3, 4, 5) Pleurodynia (1–5) Pericarditis (1–5) Myocarditis (1–5) Generalized disease of newborn (1–5)	Exanthem (especially 9, 16 but also 1–8, 11, 14, 18, 19, 25, 30, 32, 33) Generalized disease of newborn (4, 6, 7, 9, 11, 12, 14, 19, 21, 51) Neonatal diarrhea (11, 14, 18) Chronic meningoencephalitis in agammaglobulinemics (2, 3, 5, 9, 11, 19, 24, 25, 30, 33)
Etiologic role undefined or uncertain	Diarrhea Hemolytic-uremic syndrome (4) Myositis (9) Guillain-Barré syndrome (2, 5, 9) Reye's syndrome Mononucleosis-like syndrome (5, 6) Infectious lymphocytosis	Diarrhea Myositis (2, 6) Diabetes mellitus Hemolytic-uremic syndrome (2, 4) Mononucleosis-like syndrome (5) Reye's syndrome	Diarrhea Hemolytic-uremic syndrome (22) Reye's syndrome Myositis (9, 11) Guillain-Barré syndrome (6, 22) Infectious lymphocytosis (25)

*Implicated serotypes designated in parentheses.

tration is normal and the CSF protein concentration is normal or slightly elevated. However, the glucose content may be lower than normal in 18 to 33% of cases,[13–15] and values less than 40 mg/dl may occur.[4, 15] Uncommonly, it may be difficult to exclude bacterial meningitis on the basis of the CSF profile alone. In some cases, the CSF findings may closely mimic those of tuberculous meningitis.[16]

Enteroviruses can be detected in CSF and other specimens by cell culture and by polymerase chain reaction (PCR) genomic amplification. Cell culture remains more widely available and yields an isolate that can be further serotyped for clinical or epidemiologic purposes. However, culture requires multiple cell lines, is labor intensive, and typically requires 3 to 7 days to yield a viral isolate.[17, 18] The overall sensitivity of virus isolation from the CSF of patients with aseptic meningitis is 30 to 35%,[2, 19–23] although higher figures have been reported during some echovirus outbreaks.[7, 9, 24] Concomitant culture of serum, upper respiratory secretions, urine, and stool will enhance the likelihood of virus recovery. The introduction of PCR has improved the speed and sensitivity of enterovirus detection in CSF.[25] For confirmed or suspected enteroviral meningitis cases, PCR sensitivity ranges from 66 to over 90%.[23, 26–28]

Differential Diagnosis

Partially treated bacterial meningitis is the most important condition to be distinguished from enteroviral aseptic meningitis. Although some clinical features of bacterial meningitis incompletely treated with antimicrobials may overlap with those of enteroviral aseptic meningitis when therapy has been instituted before lumbar puncture, several studies have demonstrated that pretreatment of bacterial meningitis alters the CSF minimally; even when some parameters are altered by therapy (i.e., change from polymorphonuclear to lymphocytic pleocytosis), others continue to indicate bacterial disease (i.e., low glucose or high protein concentration).[29–31] The arboviruses, lymphocytic choriomeningitis virus, leptospirosis, Lyme borreliosis, and acute human immunodeficiency virus syndrome account for most of the remaining cases of infectious aseptic meningitis. Mumps virus infection was a common cause of aseptic meningitis before the introduction of mumps vaccine in the United States. Aseptic meningitis also occurs with other infectious and noninfectious diseases (see Chapter 71), but the etiology is usually apparent because of other clinical features.

Management and Prognosis

Although hospitalization is not necessary for all cases and indeed may not be feasible during summer epidemics of enterovirus infections, it is advisable when disturbances in consciousness, muscle weakness, or a petechial rash suggests the possibility of a more serious illness. Pyogenic bacterial meningitis should be excluded by lumbar puncture. When bacterial meningitis cannot be excluded because of prior antibiotic treatment, administration of appropriate antimicrobials is advisable after performing Gram stains and bacterial cultures. CSF PCR testing is useful in deciding whether continued administration of antimicrobials is indicated, especially when results are available within 1 to 2 days.

In most cases, treatment consists only of relief of symptoms. Analgesics are usually given to older children and adults to alleviate headache. Pleconaril, an orally administered enteroviral capsid–stabilizing drug, significantly reduces the duration of headache and other symptoms but is not yet licensed by the Food and Drug Administration[32] (see Chapter 36). Antiviral therapy may provide significant symptomatic relief to adults and older children, who may experience lassitude and easy fatigability for weeks after the acute illness.[6] In one large study of enteroviral aseptic meningitis, subtle disturbances in motor function such as limitation of passive motion, muscle spasm, and poor coordination were observed during convalescence.[5] These abnormalities slowly resolve and are rarely detectable 1 year after infection. In young children, fever and signs of meningeal irritation subside in a few days to 1 week. Infants younger than 3 months may have fewer symptoms of illness and fewer complications than older infants do.[4] Although some investigators have suggested that enteroviral meningitis in the first year of life may result in permanent neurologic sequelae,[33, 34] studies of larger numbers of children that use more rigorous methods indicate that the long-term prognosis for the youngest infants is also excellent.[35, 36]

Encephalitis

Encephalitis is a well-described, although unusual manifestation of coxsackievirus and echovirus central nervous system (CNS) infection. Symptoms of encephalitis sometimes complicate the course of aseptic meningitis. Rarely, full-blown encephalitis dominates the clinical illness in the presence or absence of meningeal involvement. The enteroviruses, including poliovirus, account for only 11 to 22% of all cases of encephalitis that are proved to be viral; this prevalence ranks behind arboviruses, herpes simplex virus, and lymphocytic choriomeningitis virus.[19, 37] Numerous serotypes have been implicated as causes of encephalitis; coxsackievirus types A9, B2, and B5 and echovirus types 6 and 9 are the serotypes reported most often. The evidence linking each of these serotypes to encephalitis is highly variable. In a minority of cases, a specific etiology has been proved by isolating virus from brain tissue or CSF; in others, the cause of encephalitis has been inferred by isolating virus from a non-neurologic site or by serology.

In perinatally acquired enterovirus infection, encephalitis may be one manifestation of generalized viral infection. Beyond the neonatal period, children and young adults have been most frequently affected. Clinical manifestations have ranged from lethargy, drowsiness, and personality change to seizures, paresis, and coma. Children with focal encephalitis present with partial motor seizures, hemichorea, and acute cerebellar ataxia,[38–42] features that in some cases have suggested a diagnosis of herpes simplex virus encephalitis.[39, 43] Group A coxsackieviruses have been conspicuous among the agents isolated from infants and children with focal enteroviral encephalitis.[39]

The CSF findings in enteroviral encephalitis are similar to those found in aseptic meningitis. Abnormalities on an electroencephalogram usually reflect the extent and severity of brain involvement. Most patients with coxsackievirus and echovirus encephalitis beyond the neonatal period recover fully, although static neurologic sequelae and rare deaths occur.[19, 38, 44, 45]

Paralysis and Other Neurologic Complications of Coxsackievirus and Echovirus Infections

Sporadic cases of flaccid motor paralysis have been associated with several coxsackievirus and echovirus serotypes and with enterovirus 71. Coxsackievirus A7, which is neuropathogenic in monkeys, and enterovirus 71 have each caused disease with sufficient frequency to be recognized as the etiologic agent in outbreaks of paralysis.[46–49] Coxsackievirus A9 was found to be the etiology of 3.1% of poliomyelitis cases in New Delhi, India, over a period of 7 years.[50] In sporadic cases, the serotypes that are most often implicated have been coxsackieviruses A7, A9, and B1 to B5 and echoviruses 6 and 9. Less frequently implicated serotypes are coxsackieviruses A4, A5, and A10 and echoviruses 1 to 4, 7, 11, 14, 16 to 18, and 30.[51–54]

Paralytic disease caused by the nonpolio enteroviruses is characteristically less severe than poliovirus-associated paralysis. In fact, muscle weakness is more common than flaccid paralysis, and the paresis is not usually permanent. Cranial nerve involvement has occasionally resulted in complete unilateral oculomotor palsy.[55] Rare cases of fatal bulbar involvement have been reported.[56]

Guillain-Barré syndrome has been reported in a small number of patients in association with coxsackievirus serotypes A2, A5, and

A9 and with echovirus serotypes 6 and 22.[20, 57, 58] In a few cases, the implicated virus has been isolated from CSF or the brain stem.[58] Transverse myelitis has been reported in one patient who had a rise in neutralizing antibody to coxsackievirus B4[57] and in another who had echovirus 5 recovered from CSF.[59] Systemic coxsackievirus B2 disease has been reported with many of the clinical features of Reye's syndrome.[60] Furthermore, several children with well-documented Reye's syndrome have had a variety of enteroviruses isolated concurrently from multiple sites, including the brain and CSF[61, 62]; however, a clear etiologic or epidemiologic link between enterovirus infection and Reye's syndrome has not been established. Opsoclonus-myoclonus, or the "dancing eyes" syndrome, has been reported in two children with concurrent coxsackievirus B3 infection.[63]

EXANTHEMS

Coxsackieviruses and echoviruses cause a variety of exanthems, which are sometimes associated with enanthems. With the exception of hand-foot-and-mouth (HFM) disease, these eruptions are not sufficiently distinctive to permit a reliable etiologic diagnosis on clinical grounds alone. Virus can be isolated from the vesicular lesions of patients with HFM disease, and therefore these lesions appear to be a direct result of viral invasion of the skin after viremia. No attempts at isolation of virus from the skin in cases of maculopapular and petechial exanthems have been reported; consequently, it is not known whether these lesions are also caused by the virus directly or by immunopathologic mechanisms.

Enteroviral exanthems themselves cause little morbidity. They are important as sentinels of the prevalence of coxsackieviruses and echoviruses in the community and because they are often confused with other infective exanthems, some of which have more serious implications. Rashes caused by enteroviruses may be grouped according to the type of exanthem that they mimic: (1) rubelliform or morbilliform, (2) roseoliform, (3) vesicular, and (4) petechial. Some overlap between these types of exanthems may be observed in different patients infected with the same enterovirus or even among different morphologic lesion types in the same patient.

Rubelliform and Morbilliform Exanthems

Fine maculopapular rashes resembling rubella but occurring during summer epidemics are common manifestations of echovirus infection. High attack rates have been noted with echovirus 9, the most common serotype associated with rubelliform rash. In one epidemic, 57% of persons younger than 5 years with illness caused by echovirus 9 had rash, 41% of those 5 to 9 years old had rash, but rash affected only 6% of those older than 10 years.[24] The rash, which characteristically appears simultaneously with fever, begins on the face and then spreads to the neck, chest, and extremities. Usually, innumerable faint pink macules 1 to 3 mm in diameter that do not itch or desquamate are present. The exanthem is most likely to be confused with rubella,[64] but helpful distinguishing features include the absence of pruritus and posterior cervical lymphadenopathy.[65] In occasional patients with an enanthem resembling Koplik spots and a blotchy eruption, the disease may be confused with measles, but the coryza and conjunctivitis characteristic of that disease are absent.[66] Other serotypes associated with rubelliform rash include echoviruses 2, 4, 11, 19, and 25 and coxsackievirus A9.

Roseoliform Exanthems

These enterovirus exanthems are distinctive not in their appearance, but in their timing; as in roseola, the rash does not appear until defervescence. The prototype is the "Boston exanthem," the first of the enterovirus exanthems to be recognized and now known to be caused by echovirus 16.[67, 68] Multiple cases often occur sequentially in families, rash developing in as many as one quarter of the children in a household. The mean age of those affected is 3 years. Most children are mildly ill with low-grade fever and pharyngitis. The fever lasts 24 to 36 hours and then declines simultaneously with the appearance of discrete, nonpruritic, salmon-pink macules and papules approximately 1 cm in diameter on the face and upper part of the chest. The extremities are less commonly involved. The duration of the lesions is 1 to 5 days. Other enterovirus serotypes (coxsackievirus B1 and B5 and echovirus 11 and 25) have also been associated with roseola-like illness.[69–71] Exanthem subitum (roseola infantum) is a common, nonseasonal exanthem in which the rash typically develops as the fever declines; it is now known to be caused by human herpesvirus 6 (see Chapter 129).

Herpetiform Exanthems

Hand-Foot-and-Mouth Disease

Coxsackievirus A16 (less commonly A5, A7, A9, A10, B2, and B5) is the etiologic agent of a distinctive vesicular eruption known as HFM disease or vesicular stomatitis with exanthem.[72–74] HFM disease may also be caused by enterovirus 71, sometimes in association with CNS disease. Children younger than 10 years are often affected, and spread to other family members occurs commonly. Most patients complain of sore throat or sore mouth, and affected young children may refuse to eat. Temperatures of 38°C to 39°C last 1 to 2 days and are accompanied in essentially all cases by vesicles in the oral cavity occurring chiefly on the buccal mucosa and tongue. Several lesions may coalesce to form bullae, which frequently ulcerate by the time that they are seen by a physician. Peripherally distributed cutaneous lesions occur in roughly 75% of patients.[75] These lesions are most common on the hands and feet, where either the extensor surfaces or the palms and soles may be involved. They also occur more proximally on the extremities and sometimes on the buttocks or genitalia. Disseminated lesions have been described in an infant with preexisting atopic eczema and have been given the sobriquet "eczema coxsackium" by analogy with eczema herpeticum and eczema vaccinatum.[76]

The skin lesions of HFM disease are tender and consist of mixed papules and clear vesicles with a surrounding zone of erythema. Skin biopsy demonstrates that the lesions are located subepidermally and are accompanied by mixed lymphocytic and polymorphonuclear inflammation and extensive acantholysis of the overlying epidermis.[77] Eosinophilic nuclear inclusions and intracytoplasmic picornavirus particles can be seen microscopically within cells surrounding dermal vessels.[78]

The vesicular lesions of HFM disease superficially resemble those caused by herpes simplex or varicella-zoster virus. Patients with HFM disease invariably have lesions of the oral mucosa. In contrast, oral lesions are less common in patients with chickenpox; moreover, these patients generally appear more ill, and their cutaneous lesions are more extensive and centrally distributed, generally with sparing of the palms and soles. Patients with primary herpetic gingivostomatitis also usually appear more ill and have a higher fever and cervical lymphadenopathy; lesions are usually confined to the oral cavity and do not involve the extremities. The enanthem of herpangina also resembles HFM disease, but it occurs more posteriorly and typically involves the fauces and soft palate.

Other Herpetiform Exanthems

Generalized vesicular eruptions are reported to be caused by coxsackievirus A9[79] and echovirus 11.[80] The eruptions caused by coxsackievirus A9 are similar to the lesions of HFM disease, but they occur in crops on the head, trunk, and extremities. Unlike chickenpox, the vesicles do not evolve to form pustules and scabs. The vesicular eruptions caused by echovirus 11 have occurred in immunocompromised adult patients.[80] An acute eruption resembling dermatomal zoster in which echovirus 6 was isolated from the bullous lesions has been reported.[81]

Petechial Exanthems and Other Cutaneous Manifestations

Petechial and purpuric rashes have been described with echovirus 9[24, 82] and coxsackievirus A9[83] infections. When these rashes have a hemorrhagic component, the illness is easily confused with meningococcal disease, especially if aseptic meningitis occurs simultaneously. Occasionally, cutaneous eruptions of coxsackievirus A9 disease have an urticarial nature.[79] One child has been reported to have papular acrodermatitis (Gianotti-Crosti syndrome) in association with coxsackievirus A16 infection.[84]

ACUTE RESPIRATORY DISEASE

Many enterovirus serotypes cause undifferentiated febrile illnesses ("summer grippe") with sore throat and occasionally cough or coryza. Enteroviruses account for most viruses recovered from children with summertime upper respiratory tract infections.[85] Enterovirus upper respiratory tract illnesses are generally clinically indistinguishable from disease caused by other agents such as rhinoviruses and *Mycoplasma pneumoniae,* unless accompanied by aseptic meningitis, exanthem, or other clinical features suggesting enterovirus infection. In experimentally infected volunteers and occasionally in individuals with naturally acquired disease, some coxsackieviruses and echoviruses appear capable of causing lower respiratory tract disease. However, the role of enteroviruses in lower respiratory illness is not clearly defined; at present, they must be considered rare causes of nonbacterial pneumonia.

The best characterized enteroviral respiratory pathogens are coxsackieviruses A21 and A24, which produce illness resembling the common cold, except (perhaps) for a higher incidence of fever.[86, 87] Outbreaks of coxsackievirus A21 illness are reported predominantly in military populations. Although epidemics in civilians have not been recognized, sporadic infections presumably account for antibody prevalence rates of 70% in persons older than 50 years.[87] Unlike most other enteroviruses, coxsackievirus A21 is more readily recovered from throat swabs than from feces. In volunteers receiving small-particle aerosols of the virus, illness has included not only coryza and sore throat but also tracheobronchitis and pneumonia.[88]

Among the echoviruses, serotype 11 is the most firmly established and (possibly) the most common cause of respiratory disease,[87] although serotypes 4, 8, 9, 20, 22, and 25 appear to be responsible for similar illnesses. Echovirus 11 produces sore throat, coryza, cough, and sometimes fever. It has also been associated with croup. The spectrum of group B coxsackievirus disease includes coryza, laryngotracheobronchitis, bronchiolitis, and pneumonia.[57, 89] Pneumonia, which may be interstitial or a patchy bronchopneumonia, has occurred in children[90] and rarely in adults.[91]

Herpangina

Herpangina (herpes = vesicular eruption; angina = quinsy, or inflammation of the throat) is a well-characterized vesicular enanthem of the fauces and soft palate that is accompanied by fever, sore throat, and pain on swallowing. Herpangina is usually seen in the setting of summer outbreaks involving children 3 to 10 years old and, less commonly, adolescents and young adults. Sporadic illnesses are less common. Group A coxsackieviruses (serotypes 1 to 10, 16, and 22) are the most common viruses recovered from patients with herpangina. Other serotypes that have been isolated far less commonly from persons with herpangina include group B coxsackieviruses 1 to 5 and echoviruses 3, 6, 9, 16, 17, 25, and 30.[92]

Clinical Manifestations

The illness begins suddenly with temperatures of 37.7°C to 40.5°C. Vomiting, myalgia, and headache are common at the onset but generally do not persist. Sore throat and pain on swallowing are the most prominent symptoms and precede appearance of the enanthem by several hours to a day. Casual inspection of the throat reveals erythema and mild exudate of the tonsils, which leads to a diagnosis of pharyngitis or tonsillitis if the characteristic enanthem is missed. The enanthem begins as punctate macules, which evolve over a 24-hour period to 2- to 4-mm erythematous papules that vesiculate and then ulcerate centrally. The lesions, which usually number two to six but rarely a dozen, are moderately painful. They are located on the soft palate, most frequently on the free-hanging margin between the tonsils and the uvula. Less commonly, they are on the tonsils, the posterior pharyngeal wall, or the buccal mucosa. The fever subsides in 2 to 4 days, but the ulcers may persist for up to a week. Patients with herpangina do not appear very ill and require only symptomatic treatment for sore throat. Prompt recovery occurs in all cases.

A variant of the syndrome, acute lymphonodular pharyngitis, has been described in association with coxsackievirus A10 infection.[93] Lesions occur in the same distribution as herpangina but consist of tiny nodules of packed lymphocytes that eventually recede without undergoing vesiculation or ulceration.

Differential Diagnosis

Herpangina is most often confused with bacterial tonsillitis or other viral causes of pharyngitis, but these infections do not produce vesicular lesions. Furthermore, the lesions of herpangina occur in the posterior of the oral cavity, whereas other vesicular enanthems such as primary herpetic gingivostomatitis and HFM disease characteristically occur in the anterior of the oral cavity, especially on the inner aspects of the lips, the buccal mucosa, and the tongue. Gingivitis, prominent systemic toxicity, and cervical lymphadenitis are additional features of primary herpes simplex infection that are not seen in herpangina. In HFM disease, lesions also occur on the extremities in most cases. Aphthous stomatitis is characterized by larger ulcerative lesions of the lips, tongue, and buccal mucosa; a history of multiple recurrences is common, and the disease usually occurs in older children, adolescents, and adults.

Smears of scrapings of the lesions do not reveal the giant cells or intranuclear inclusions that are characteristic of herpes simplex. Typical cases can be confidently diagnosed on clinical grounds, but confirmation may be obtained by isolation of the etiologic agent from the throat or feces.

Epidemic Pleurodynia

Epidemic pleurodynia is an acute infections disease characterized by fever and sharp, spasmodic pain in the chest or upper part of the abdomen. The name *pleurodynia* (pleura = rib or side; odyne = pain) calls attention to the common symptom of a "stitch" in the intercostal region and does not connote disease of the pleura.

History and Etiology

Pleurodynia was first described in 1872 by Daae and by Homann during an outbreak of "acute muscular rheumatism spread by contagion" in Norway. Other reports subsequently appeared in Scandinavia; in particular, Ejnar Sylvest, a Danish general practitioner, in 1933 described his experience with the disease on the island of Bornholm in the Baltic Sea. His monograph received worldwide attention after it was translated into English in 1934.[94] Over the years, many synonyms for the disease have been used, among which are epidemic myalgia, epidemic benign dry pleurisy, devil's grippe, Drangedal disease, Bamle disease, Bornholm disease, and Sylvest's disease. Little has been added to Sylvest's descriptions of the disease and its epidemiology, pathogenesis, and complications.

The etiologic role of group B coxsackieviruses, the most important cause of epidemic pleurodynia, was established in 1949.[95, 96]

Other agents rarely implicated in pleurodynia include echoviruses 1, 6, 9, 16, and 19 and group A coxsackieviruses 4, 6, 9, and 10.[53, 54, 97, 98]

Epidemiology

Major epidemics have been reported at infrequent intervals, often 10 to 20 years. Attack rates during epidemics of pleurodynia have been higher in sparsely populated areas than in cities. It is probable that the disease occurs worldwide, but published reports have come primarily from Europe and North America. Persons with pleurodynia are somewhat older than those with most other diseases caused by coxsackieviruses and echoviruses. Multiple family members may be attacked almost simultaneously or in rapid succession separated by several days.

Pathogenesis

Pleurodynia is a disease of muscle, not of the pleura or peritoneum. Although pleurodynia probably results from direct viral invasion of muscles after viremia, direct virologic evidence supporting this hypothesis is lacking. Tenderness mimicking spontaneously occurring pain can be elicited by pressure on affected muscles in most cases; in addition, palpable, often visible muscle swelling is a subtle finding in some cases.[94] A pleural friction rub has been rare or absent in most epidemics, although this sign has occasionally been noted in 7% or more of those afflicted.[99, 100]

Clinical Manifestations

Pleurodynia usually has no prodrome and begins with an abrupt onset of spasmodic pain, typically over the lower part of the rib cage or the upper abdominal region. Febrile temperatures of 38°C to 39.5°C peak within 1 hour after the onset of each paroxysm and subside as the pain recedes. Sore throat and headache may occur, but cough and catarrhal symptoms are notably absent. Aseptic meningitis and orchitis occur in a small number of patients with pleurodynia, generally less than 10%.[94, 101, 102] Pericarditis and pneumonia are rare.[100]

The intensity of the pain varies considerably. It is variously described as sticking, a "stitch" in the side, lancinating, stabbing, constricting, or viselike. Patients asked to localize the pain are likely to indicate a broad area with the palm of the hand rather than a specific point with the finger. The most common location is the vicinity of the costal margin on one or both sides or occasionally the subxiphoid region. Approximately half the patients, especially adults, have pain primarily in muscles of the thorax, especially the intercostals, the trapezius, and occasionally the erector spinae or pectoralis major. In the other half, pain is primarily in the upper part of the abdomen, especially the hypochondrium (internal and external obliques and transversus abdominis) or the epigastrium (rectus abdominis). Periumbilical pain and pain in the lower abdominal quadrants are also seen, especially in children, in whom abdominal localization of pain is the rule.[86, 99] A few patients experience pain in neither the chest nor the abdomen but instead in the neck or limbs[102]; in these cases, the diagnosis can be made only by association with other typical cases in the family. Whatever the localization of the pain, it is usual for an individual patient to experience this pain in only one or two areas of the body.

Although the location and severity vary, it is the spasmodic and paroxysmal character of the pain that is its hallmark. If the pain is mild and the patient ambulatory, the patient stoops forward or leans to the side to splint the chest. With more severe pain, the patient lies still in bed and appears acutely ill and apprehensive. Chest pain limits deep inspiration, so respirations are shallow and rapid. Auscultation of the chest reveals no abnormalities. Motion also produces pain, and patients resist being turned in bed.

Pain can be elicited by pressure on the involved muscles in most patients. Swelling is seen or felt only occasionally and by careful, sequential observations; it is detected most readily when the rectus abdominis or erector spinae is involved. Involvement of the muscles of the hypochondrium does not cause discrete swelling, but spasm of these muscles leads to loss of the upper superficial abdominal reflexes.

Most patients are ill for 4 to 6 days. Children have milder disease than adults do, and adults are often confined to bed. The first paroxysm is the most severe, and subsequent paroxysms are shorter and accompanied by less fever. Although dull aching of involved muscles usually persists between bouts of sharp pain, the patient may look and feel entirely healthy between paroxysms. About one quarter of patients experience multiple recurrences, often after they have been free of pain for a day or more and have felt well enough to return to work or school.[94, 102] In about half of these persons, recurrence of pain is at the same site; in the remainder, a new site is attacked. Late relapses occur in some patients after they have been free of symptoms for a month or more.[102]

Diagnosis

The severity, location, and other characteristics of the pain are so protean that pleurodynia is readily confused with many other illnesses. Pain in the chest may mimic pneumonia, pulmonary infarction, myocardial ischemia, and the preeruptive phase of zoster. Abdominal pain in epidemic pleurodynia may resemble a variety of causes of acute abdomen. Normal auscultatory examination of the chest, together with the characteristic spasmodic and relapsing character of the pain, is helpful in excluding pneumonia. A negative chest radiographic film is also helpful, although pleural effusions may rarely be present.

Management and Prognosis

Analgesics and the application of heat to affected muscles are useful in relieving pain in most cases; in some, opiate analgesics are required for adequate pain control. Despite the distressing tendency of the disease to relapse, all patients eventually recover completely. Debility out of all proportion to the apparent severity of the illness is occasionally observed for several months during convalescence.[94, 101]

MYOPERICARDITIS

Because enteroviruses rarely, if ever attack the pericardium alone without involving the subepicardial myocardium, the term *myopericarditis* therefore best describes the disease caused by these viruses when they affect the heart[103] (see Chapter 68). Clinically, however, the signs of either myocarditis or pericarditis often predominate. In older children and adults, the severity of myopericarditis varies from asymptomatic cardiac involvement to fulminant disease with intractable heart failure and death. The myocarditis that occurs with generalized enterovirus infection in the newborn is discussed separately in the later section on neonatal infections.

An epidemic of coxsackievirus B5 myopericarditis occurred in Finland in autumn 1965 when 18 patients were admitted to a single hospital.[104] Epidemic myopericarditis appears to be exceptional, however, and most reported cases beyond the neonatal period have been sporadic, probably because involvement of the heart is a relatively uncommon manifestation of illness even during substantial enterovirus epidemics.

Etiology and Pathogenesis

Enteroviruses appear to be the most common viral agents and account for at least half of all cases of acute myopericarditis.[105–108] However, the strength of the evidence linking a given enterovirus serotype with myopericarditis varies considerably. Proof of causation exists for all group B coxsackievirus serotypes, group A coxsackievirus types 4 and 16, and echovirus types 9 and 22 by demonstration of infectious virus or viral antigen in myocardium or pericardial fluid.[54, 109–113] The evidence is less substantive for group A coxsackievirus types 1, 2, 5, 8, and 9 and echovirus types 1 to 4, 6 to 8, 11, 14, 19, 25, and 30.[108–110, 112–122] These serotypes have been recovered from noncardiac sources during an episode of acute myopericarditis, some with a significant increase in antibody titer to the homotypic virus.

Many other viruses have been associated with myopericarditis, although adenovirus,[123–125] influenza A virus,[126] mumps virus,[127] and vaccinia virus[128] are the principal nonenterovirus agents that have been detected directly in pericardial fluid or myocardial tissue. The weight of clinical evidence suggests that *M. pneumoniae,* respiratory syncytial virus, Epstein-Barr virus, varicella-zoster virus, and measles virus also cause myopericarditis.

Group B coxsackieviruses and other enteroviruses reach the heart during the viremia that follows replication in the gastrointestinal or respiratory tract (see Chapter 158). Experimental studies in a murine model strongly suggest that virus replication occurs in myofibers and results in scattered myofiber necrosis followed by focal infiltration of polymorphonuclear leukocytes, lymphocytes, plasma cells, and macrophages.[129] A chronic inflammatory response persists for weeks to months when replicating virus is no longer present in the heart, and this lingering response has been the subject of keen interest. Some investigators consider the late-phase inflammatory response to be due to virus-induced, cytotoxic T-lymphocyte destruction of myocytes.[130] Others have postulated the development of a myocardial neoantigen[131] or cross-reactivity between viral and myocardial cell antigens.[132] Healing is accompanied by a variable degree of interstitial fibrosis and evidence of myocyte loss.

Clinical Manifestations

Enteroviral myocarditis occurs at all ages but has a special predilection for physically active adolescents and young adults. The incidence in males is at least twice that in females.[106, 108] In two thirds of cases, an upper respiratory tract illness precedes the onset of cardiac manifestations by 7 to 14 days.[108] The most common symptoms are dyspnea, chest pain, fever, and malaise, each of which occurs in about 60 to 90% of cases.[104, 108, 133–135] Pain in the precordial area is usually dull, but it may resemble angina pectoris or be sharp, pleuritic, and aggravated by recumbency when pericarditis is present. A pericardial friction rub, often transient, has been observed in 35 to 80% of cases. Enlargement of the cardiac silhouette on chest radiograph films, present in about 50%, may be due to either pericardial effusion or cardiac dilatation. A gallop rhythm and other signs of frank congestive heart failure are observed in roughly 20%.[133, 135]

Electrocardiographic abnormalities are invariably present. With pericarditis or mild myocarditis, which are the most common, these abnormalities consist of ST-segment elevations or nonspecific ST-segment and T-wave abnormalities. More severe myocardial disease may lead to the development of Q waves, ventricular tachyarrhythmias, and all degrees of heart block. Echocardiography may confirm the presence of acute ventricular dilatation or a diminished cardiac ejection fraction. Serum levels of myocardial enzymes are frequently elevated. Other clinical manifestations of systemic enteroviral disease sometimes occur with myopericarditis and include aseptic meningitis, pleurodynia, hepatitis, and orchitis.

Acute myocardial infarction associated with chest pain, arrhythmias, and congestive heart failure may be difficult to distinguish from myopericarditis. Patients suspected of having acute myocardial infarction sometimes have evidence of concurrent group B coxsackievirus infection,[136–138] and focal myocarditis has been proved in at least one case of acute coxsackievirus B5 infection.[139] Furthermore, some patients presenting with suspected myocardial infarction who have normal coronary angiographic studies have been shown to have myocarditis based on radiolabeled anti–myosin antibody cardiac scanning.[140]

Diagnosis

Although coxsackieviruses have been isolated on numerous occasions from pericardial fluid or heart muscle at autopsy[106] or by open biopsy procedures,[141, 142] in practice these specimens are rarely available. Diagnosis by virus isolation from myocardium obtained by percutaneous, transvenous biopsy of the right ventricle is theoretically feasible but has not yet been reported. Cardiac tissue infrequently yields a viral isolate when cultured, and only a small number of specimens yield a positive PCR result for enteroviral RNA.[143, 144] In the absence of identification of virus in cardiac tissue, the diagnosis often rests on circumstantial evidence provided by recovery of the agent from the oropharynx or feces or on serologic evidence of recent infection by a group B coxsackievirus.

Management

Supportive treatment includes standard management of pericardial pain, pericardial effusion, arrhythmias, and heart failure. Bed rest is recommended during the acute stage because evidence in experimentally infected mice indicates that exercise augments the mortality associated with coxsackievirus myocarditis (see Chapter 158).

Intravenous immune globulin (IGIV) may have beneficial immunomodulatory effects.[145] One study using historical controls found improved cardiac function and a trend toward increased survival in children with acute myopericarditis treated with IGIV.[146] However, randomized, controlled trials have not been reported.

Immunosuppressive treatment of acute myopericarditis has been recommended largely on the basis of anecdotal and uncontrolled reports of the use of corticosteroids, sometimes in combination with other immunosuppressive agents.[147–152] However, experimental evidence of adverse rather than beneficial effects has made clinicians wary of steroid use in patients with acute myopericarditis.[153] Furthermore, a large prospective trial of prednisone combined with either cyclosporine or azathioprine showed no difference in outcome between treated patients and patients randomized to receive only supportive treatment.[154]

Course and Prognosis

Most children and adults recover uneventfully. Fatalities during the acute disease occur in only 0 to 4% of cases and are essentially restricted to those in whom severe myocarditis predominates over pericarditis. Persistent electrocardiographic abnormalities (10 to 20%), cardiomegaly (5 to 10%), and chronic congestive heart failure are indications of permanent myocardial injury that occur overall in about one third of patients identified with acute myopericarditis; these abnormalities may ultimately lead to a diagnosis of dilated cardiomyopathy.[108, 133, 135] Chronic constrictive pericarditis has occurred after intervals of 5 weeks to 1 year.[155–157]

Dilated Cardiomyopathy

Chronic dilated cardiomyopathy, which is second only to ischemic heart disease as a cause of chronic congestive heart failure, is the final result of multiple infectious and noninfectious cardiac insults,[158] including up to one third of cases of acute myopericarditis and, in some instances, unrecognized past enterovirus infection.[108, 133, 135] Some investigators have detected enterovirus RNA in cardiac tissue months to years after the onset of dilated cardiomyopathy, but others who have searched with similar methods have not detected enteroviral RNA.[159–165] The persistence of enteroviral RNA in tissue from an immunologically normal host, whether as a result of ongoing viral replication or another mechanism, is a concept that challenges our current understanding of enterovirus biology and should therefore be regarded with skepticism until more definitive data are generated.

COXSACKIEVIRUS AND ECHOVIRUS DISEASE IN THE NEWBORN INFANT

The human neonate is uniquely susceptible to coxsackievirus and echovirus disease. Although many enterovirus serotypes cause the same self-limited clinical syndromes in neonates as they do in older persons (e.g., aseptic meningitis, exanthems), some serotypes are capable of producing fulminant, frequently fatal disease in the newborn infant. Group B coxsackievirus serotypes 2 to 5 and echovirus 11 are most frequently associated with overwhelming systemic neonatal infections. Rare cases of serious neonatal disease are reported with group A coxsackievirus serotypes 3, 9, and 16.[166–168]

Epidemiology

Although most neonatal enteroviral infections are acquired directly from the mother, some infections are transmitted nosocomially. The first description of group B coxsackievirus disease in newborn infants followed outbreaks occurring in newborn nurseries in South Africa, Zimbabwe, and The Netherlands.[169] Many nursery outbreaks of neonatal echovirus infection have been recorded, with the severity of neonatal disease varying according to the viral serotype.[170] Introduction of infection into the nursery has been traced to an infected mother or to ill hospital personnel. Infant-to-infant spread within nurseries probably occurs via the hands of personnel engaged in mouth care, gavage feeding, and other activities requiring close direct contact.[171]

Because most neonatal enterovirus infections are sporadic rather than nosocomial, the incidence and severity of neonatal enteroviral infection generally reflect the occurrence of enteroviral disease in the community. Although many cases occur sporadically during the enterovirus season, clusters of vertically transmitted neonatal infection sometimes occur during community outbreaks with a single enterovirus serotype.[172, 173]

Pathophysiology

Most newborns with life-threatening enterovirus disease are infected via vertical transmission from the infected mother in the perinatal period.[170, 174] Approximately 60 to 70% of women who bear infected infants have a febrile illness during the last week of pregnancy.[8, 170] Ample experimental evidence indicates that the fetus is relatively protected by the placenta during maternal infection,[174] but the newborn has a high risk of infection,[175, 176] perhaps as a result of exposure to either virus-positive cervical secretions[177, 178] or viremic maternal blood.[179] Although most vertically transmitted enterovirus infections are probably acquired during delivery, some infants are infected before delivery as evidenced by the recovery of virus from cord blood[178] and the development of disease within the first 2 days of life.[170, 180]

Once a newborn infant is infected, it is presumed that enteroviruses spread systemically via the blood stream. Tropism for and replication within specific organs of the neonatal host appear to depend on both virus and host factors. Experimental evidence suggests that some neonatal tissues are innately more susceptible to infection with some enteroviruses than the corresponding tissues from an adult host.[181] In addition, the neonatal immune system is insufficient to control the replication and spread of virulent enteroviruses. Both premature and term human infants respond adequately to enterovirus infection with humoral neutralizing antibody.[182] However, macrophage function, which does not sufficiently mature until several weeks of age in the human neonate, is necessary to limit initial enteroviral replication.[183, 184]

The outcome of neonatal infection is also strongly influenced by the presence or absence of passively acquired maternal antibody specific for the infecting enterovirus serotype.[175, 185, 186] Thus, the timing of maternal infection in relation to the development of maternal IgG antibody and delivery of the infant may be the most critical factor in determining the outcome of neonatal enterovirus infection.

Clinical Manifestations

Symptoms develop in most neonates with generalized coxsackievirus and echovirus disease between 3 and 7 days of life.[170, 180] A small number have signs of illness in the delivery room or within the first 1 to 2 days of life[170, 180]; conversely, the onset of fatal infection has been documented in infants as old as 3 months.[187] Male infants and premature infants are overrepresented among infants with serious illness. Early symptoms are generally mild and nonspecific and include listlessness, anorexia, and transient respiratory distress. Fever may or may not be present. Approximately one third of cases have a biphasic illness with a period of 1 to 7 days of apparent well-being interspersed between the initial symptoms and the appearance of more serious manifestations.

Generalized enterovirus disease in the newborn most often occurs in one of two characteristic clinical syndromes, either myocarditis or fulminant hepatitis. Neonatal myocarditis, which is often accompanied by encephalitis and sometimes by hepatitis, is characteristically a manifestation of group B coxsackievirus infection[54, 169] and less commonly echovirus 11 infection.[120, 188] Fulminant hepatitis is characterized by hypotension, profuse bleeding, jaundice, and multiple organ failure. Echovirus 11 is responsible for a large proportion of cases, but well-documented cases of severe hepatitis in neonates have resulted from echovirus serotypes 4, 6, 7, 9, 12, 14, 19, 20, 21, and 31.[170, 189–193]

Myocarditis

Signs of neonatal myocarditis include rapid onset of heart failure, respiratory distress, tachycardia often exceeding 200 beats per minute, cardiomegaly, systolic murmurs, and electrocardiographic evidence of myocardial injury and arrythmias. Cyanosis and circulatory collapse rapidly develop in severely affected infants. Fatal cases are often accompanied by disseminated viral infection involving other organs in a pattern resembling that seen in experimentally infected suckling mice; these organs, in order of frequency, are the CNS, liver, pancreas, and adrenal gland. Most affected neonates are lethargic, but seizures, a bulging fontanelle, and CSF pleocytosis indicate the presence of meningoencephalitis. Enlargement of the liver is more often due to congestive heart failure than to viral hepatitis.

Although initial reports suggested that most cases of neonatal coxsackievirus myocarditis ended fatally, accumulated experience now indicates that the mortality is less than 50%. Death usually occurs within 1 week of onset. Myocardial function rapidly improves in surviving infants after defervescence, generally by 1 week, although in a few infants convalescence is prolonged for several weeks. Pathologic data are limited to information obtained at postmortem examination. Infants dying of myocarditis have enlarged, dilated hearts, extensive myonecrosis, and a variable degree of cardiac inflammation. Lymphocytic infiltration of the brain, meninges, lungs, liver, pancreas, and adrenal glands may also be found.

Hepatitis

The initial symptoms of severe neonatal hepatitis syndrome are lethargy, poor feeding, and increasing jaundice. These nonspecific symptoms may initiate an evaluation and therapy for bacterial sepsis. However, within 1 to 2 days, the jaundice progresses and ecchymoses, bleeding from puncture sites, and signs of metabolic acidosis develop. From this stage, most infected infants rapidly progress downhill with uncontrollable hemorrhage, hepatic failure, acute renal failure, and generalized seizures. Hepatic transaminases rise rapidly to extremely high levels. Thrombocytopenia is generally profound; markedly prolonged prothrombin times and partial thromboplastin times are indicative of profound hepatic failure.

More than half of infants with severe neonatal echovirus hepatitis die within days after the onset of symptoms despite therapy with blood products and intensive supportive care. Some ultimately fatal cases survive for 2 to 3 weeks with supportive care.[172] Postmortem findings include massive hepatic necrosis and extensive hemorrhage into the cerebral ventricles, pericardial sac, renal medullae, and interstitial spaces of many solid organs.[194] Inflammation is commonly limited to the liver and adrenal glands, with sparing of the heart, brain, meninges, and other organs. The long-term prognosis for surviving infants is not well known, although hepatic fibrosis and chronic hepatic insufficiency develop in some early in life.

Pneumonia

Several cases of enterovirus pneumonia occurring in the first few days of life have been reported, all of them fatal and caused by echovirus types 6,[195] 9,[196] and 11[197] and group A coxsackievirus type 3.

Diagnosis and Differential Diagnosis

The diagnosis of neonatal coxsackievirus and echovirus infection is most rapidly made by detection of viral RNA by PCR or isolation of virus in cell culture. Virus is usually present in the infected neonate in high titer, so recovery from oropharyngeal secretions, feces, and urine is relatively rapid; virus may also be recovered from blood, CSF, ascitic fluid, and multiple tissues obtained at biopsy or autopsy. Because infected infants make humoral antibody to the virus, the diagnosis can also be made by serologic means when a specific enterovirus serotype is suspected.

Neonatal myocarditis is sometimes mistaken for congenital heart disease because in both conditions murmurs and evidence of congestive heart failure may be present. However, fever and electrocardiographic evidence of acute myocardial injury are absent in patients with congenital heart disease. The early features of myocarditis and severe hepatitis resemble those of bacterial sepsis. Because of liver and CNS involvement in either syndrome, visceral dissemination with perinatally acquired herpes simplex virus in the absence of cutaneous lesions may be suspected.

Management

Management of neonatal enteroviral disease is supportive. Infants in congestive heart failure require judicious fluid management and administration of ionotropic agents and diuretics. The profuse bleeding and coagulopathy that result from hepatic failure necessitate frequent replacement therapy with packed red blood cells, platelets, and fresh frozen plasma. Vitamin K should be administered intravenously in pharmacologic doses. Large doses of IGIV, which have been reported to improve outcome in at least one case,[198] may be justified given the extremely poor prognosis. Pleconaril, an orally administered experimental antipicornavirus drug, is undergoing evaluation in infants with serious enteroviral infections.[199] It is available on a compassionate-use basis from the manufacter, ViroPharma, Inc., Exton, Pennsylvania.

CHRONIC MENINGOENCEPHALITIS IN AGAMMAGLOBULINEMIC AND OTHER IMMUNOCOMPROMISED PATIENTS

The enteroviruses have been responsible for persistent, sometimes fatal infections of the CNS in patients with hereditary or acquired defects in B-lymphocyte function; most reported patients are children with X-linked agammaglobulinemia.[200] Persistent skeletal muscle involvement causes a dermatomyositis-like syndrome in more than half of these patients, and many also have chronic hepatitis.

Etiologic Agents

Most cases have been caused by echoviruses; single cases caused by group A coxsackievirus serotypes 4, 11, and 15 and by group B coxsackievirus serotypes 2 and 3 are recorded.[200, 201] Several enterovirus infections have been detected by PCR testing of CSF and other specimens when the serotype could not be identified.[202, 203]

Clinical Manifestations

Nervous system manifestations may be totally absent, or mild nuchal rigidity, headache, lethargy, papilledema, seizure disorders, motor weakness, tremors, and ataxia may be present. These neurologic abnormalities may fluctuate in severity, disappear, or steadily progress. The CSF exhibits lymphocytic pleocytosis and a higher protein concentration than is usually seen in cases of acute enteroviral aseptic meningitis. An enterovirus can be repeatedly recovered from the CSF over a period of months to years, usually in high titer. In some cases, virus is isolated only intermittently from the CSF or detected only by PCR. For unknown reasons, it is usually more difficult to find virus in the feces than in the CSF. Enteroviruses have been recovered from many other sites in these patients, including the brain, lung, liver, spleen, kidney, myocardium, pericardial fluid, skeletal muscle, and bone marrow.[200] Some patients have been infected with more than one enterovirus serotype, either concurrently[204] or sequentially.[200, 201] The etiology of the chronic muscle and soft tissue inflammation is not fully understood, but recovery of echovirus from muscle in one case suggests a role for direct virus infection.[205]

In many persons, possibly most, the disease ends fatally. Autopsy findings have included chronic meningitis and encephalitis, with lymphocytic perivascular cuffing, focal loss of neurons, and gliosis of both gray and white matter. However, widespread destruction of motor neurons such as that seen in poliomyelitis has not been observed.

Prophylaxis and Therapy

Prophylactic use of standard immune serum globulin does not completely prevent chronic enterovirus infection. IGIV, which has now replaced immune serum globulin for routine replacement therapy for patients with B-cell immunodeficiency, may prove more effective because much higher serum IgG concentrations can be maintained.

Use of IGIV in the treatment of chronic enterovirus meningitis has been ineffective, even when using IGIV lots with relatively high concentrations of specific antibody. Some patients have experienced clinical improvement when IGIV has been injected directly into the ventricles,[200] but relapse of infection may occur even after long-term intraventricular IGIV therapy.

Infections in Bone Marrow Transplant Recipients

Bone marrow allograft recipients have profoundly suppressed immunologic responses during the immediate post-transplant period, including suppression of the ability to mount a humoral immune response. In some recipients, enterovirus infections have developed in the post-transplant period that were disseminated, prolonged, and contributed to fatal outcomes.[206–208] In addition, Townsend and colleagues observed considerable morbidity and mortality during an outbreak of coxsackievirus A1 diarrheal illness in a bone marrow transplantation unit.[209] During this outbreak, viral-induced diarrhea was difficult to distinguish from graft-versus-host enteropathy.

ACUTE HEMORRHAGIC CONJUNCTIVITIS

Acute hemorrhagic conjunctivitis (AHC) is a contagious ocular infection characterized by pain, swelling of the eyelids, and subconjunctival hemorrhage that generally resolves spontaneously within a week. Epidemic or pandemic disease has now occurred in most parts of the world.

Etiologic Agents

Enterovirus 70 has been responsible for tens of millions of cases of AHC since 1969. A variant of coxsackievirus A24 causes a similar, but geographically more restricted disease that has afflicted hundreds of thousands of persons. Some epidemics of conjunctivitis in the Far East have involved both viruses sequentially or concurrently. Although the relative contribution of these two agents has not always been defined, it is clear that enterovirus 70 has accounted for greater total morbidity.

Epidemiology

Since the emergence of AHC as an apparently new disease in 1969, its explosive, pandemic spread has been without parallel among viral infections other than influenza. The disease was first recognized almost simultaneously in Ghana and Indonesia, and from these two foci it spread rapidly.[210] During 1970 to 1972, the epidemic reached westward and northward along the coast of Africa to Liberia, Sierra Leone, Morocco, and Egypt; southeastward to Nigeria; and ultimately to the Democratic Republic of Congo and South Africa. In Europe, small outbreaks in 1971 to 1973 occurred in England, former Soviet Union, Holland, France, and Yugoslavia. Enterovirus 70 was the cause of these epidemics,[211, 212] but an antigenically distinct virus, subsequently shown to be a variant of coxsackievirus A24, was identified as the etiologic agent of more than 60,000 cases of AHC in Singapore in 1970.[213–215] In 1971 the disease again appeared in Singapore, but this time the epidemic was caused by enterovirus 70. Smaller outbreaks caused by enterovirus 70 continued in Singapore until 1974 to 1975, when coxsackievirus A24 once again emerged as the epidemic strain. During at least two epidemics (Hong Kong in 1971 and India in 1975), both viruses circulated simultaneously.[216, 217] AHC has since been epidemic in most of the Far East and India. Enterovirus 70 was responsible in 1971 alone for an estimated 1 million cases in Calcutta[218] and 500,000 in Bombay.[219] Other regions of Asia and the Far East where AHC has been epidemic include Vietnam, Bangladesh, Thailand, Sri Lanka, Taiwan, the Philippines, American Samoa, and Japan.

Thus far, the Western Hemisphere has been spared the widespread epidemic disease experienced in Asia and Africa. Most disease in the West has been confined to seasonal outbreaks in Central America and the Caribbean. AHC did not appear in the United States until September 1981, when enterovirus 70 disease was first noted in Key West, Florida. Within weeks, approximately 2500 cases occurred, largely among disadvantaged blacks in Miami.[220] However, this outbreak was brief, and AHC activity has not been noted in the United States since 1981, with the exception of a few imported cases.[221] Coxsackievirus A24 AHC cases first appeared in the Western Hemisphere in Trinidad, Jamaica, St. Croix, Panama, and Mexico in 1986.[222] Approximately 31,000 cases occurred in Puerto Rico in 1987.[223]

Although the geographic distribution of AHC is wide, large-scale epidemics have occurred predominantly in crowded coastal areas of tropical countries during the hot, rainy season.[224] Outbreaks in economically developed countries and temperate climates have been much more limited.

Patterns of Transmission

Unlike most other enterovirus infections, AHC is probably transmitted primarily from fingers or fomites directly to the eye rather than by respiratory secretions or fecal contamination. Both enterovirus 70 and coxsackievirus A24 can be regularly recovered from the conjunctiva early in the illness but only infrequently from throat secretions or feces. Both appear to be naturally occurring, temperature-sensitive viruses whose optimal replication at 33°C to 35°C probably reflects their adaptation to the temperature of the conjunctiva.[225, 226] Not only is virus shedding quantitatively greater from the eye than from the gut, but rapid serial transmission at approximately 24-hour intervals is more consistent with direct spread of virus from hand to eye rather than with fecal-oral spread because fecal shedding would probably be delayed for several days after implantation of virus.

AHC is highly contagious and spreads rapidly. During a 1980 enterovirus 70 outbreak in Singapore, the secondary attack rate within affected households was 72.6%.[227] Contagion is favored by crowding and unsanitary living conditions. AHC occurs substantially more often among the poor than among others living in the same country.[228, 229] Reuse of water for bathing and sharing of towels are implicated as factors contributing to the spread of infection. Limited outbreaks of AHC in Europe have been primarily nosocomial, particularly in ophthalmology clinics, where infection appears to have been spread directly by physicians' fingers or by instruments.

Postepidemic antibody prevalence rates of nearly 50% have been observed in Ghana and Indonesia but only 6% in affected populations of Japan. These findings are consistent with less explosive spread of AHC in economically developed regions. Antibody prevalence rates are highest in children younger than 10 years, whereas attack rates for clinical disease are greatest in young adults, which indicates that many infections in children must be inapparent or mild.[230, 231]

Clinical Manifestations

AHC begins abruptly, and the illness reaches its peak on the first day. It usually occurs first in one eye and then a few hours later in the other. The main symptoms are a burning, foreign body sensation, ocular pain, photophobia, swelling of the eyelids, and watery discharge.[220] Constitutional symptoms such as fever, malaise, and headache are observed in 20% of cases. The most distinctive sign is subconjunctival hemorrhage, which is present in 70 to 90% of patients with AHC caused by enterovirus 70,[231] but it is much less frequent in cases caused by coxsackievirus A24.[214, 215, 217] The hemorrhages may be pinpoint or occupy the entire bulbar conjunctiva and are precipitated by everting the upper lid or by rubbing the eyes (Fig. 160–1). Conjunctival edema is said to be more common in the elderly; hemorrhage is more profuse in young patients.[231] Small

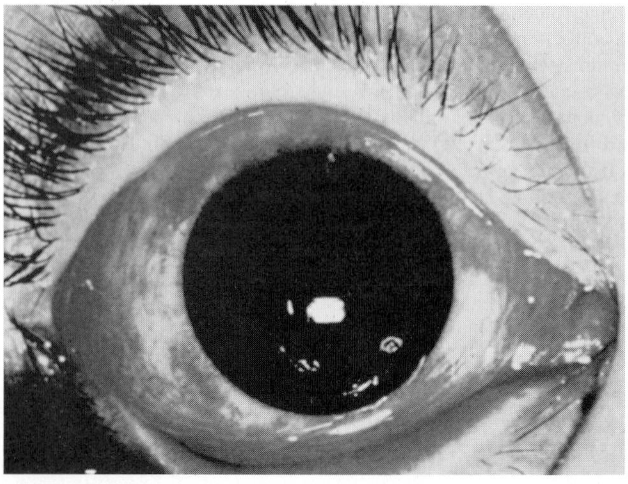

FIGURE 160–1. Acute hemorrhagic conjunctivitis due to enterovirus 70. (From Kono R, Uchida Y. Acute hemorrhagic conjunctivitis. Ophthalmol Dig. 1977; 39:14.)

follicles appear on the tarsal conjunctiva after 3 to 5 days in 90% of patients. In most cases, corneal erosion or a fine punctate epithelial keratitis can be demonstrated by slit-lamp examination after staining with fluorescein. The ocular discharge is serous or seromucoid and contains abundant neutrophils in the first 24 hours. Preauricular lymph nodes are often enlarged and tender by the second day of illness. Recovery is usually noticeable by the second or third day and is complete in most cases in 10 days, although discoloration from the hemorrhages sometimes persists for many days.

Complications

In severe cases of AHC, keratitis occasionally persists for several weeks but almost never leads to permanent scarring. Iritis has not been reported. Conjunctivitis may be complicated by secondary bacterial infection.

Motor paralysis occurs in persons who have recently recovered from AHC. Although more than 200 cases of this important complication have now been reported from India, Thailand, Formosa, and Senegal,[219, 233–236] paralysis is rare when compared with the enormous number of cases of AHC. The disease is clinically indistinguishable from poliomyelitis except for its temporal association with AHC, which it generally follows by 2 to 5 weeks (range, 5 to 60 days). A "minor illness" with fever and constitutional symptoms usually precedes the onset of neurologic manifestations by 1 to 3 days. Radicular pain and paresthesias are prominent early symptoms preceding the onset of asymmetric paralysis of the limbs. Bulbar paralysis complicates as many as one half of cases; respiratory failure has been observed rarely. The CSF abnormalities are those of aseptic meningitis.

Neurologic complications of AHC have been reported only during epidemics caused by enterovirus 70 and not those caused by coxsackievirus A24. Enterovirus 70 has not been recovered from the CSF and only once from feces.[233] However, high titers of specific neutralizing antibody to enterovirus 70 have been demonstrated in the CSF of virtually all patients with motor paralysis but not in patients with AHC alone.[235] The neuroparalytic potential of enterovirus 70 is also supported by reproduction of poliomyelitis clinically and pathologically after inoculation of the agent into monkey spinal cords.[237]

Differential Diagnosis

AHC is not likely to be confused with other causes of conjunctivitis during major epidemics. Small outbreaks or sporadic cases may be mistaken for adenovirus infection causing epidemic keratoconjunctivitis (see Chapter 132). The incubation period of epidemic keratoconjunctivitis is longer, usually 5 to 7 days as compared with 1 day for AHC. In AHC, the conjunctivitis reaches its peak several hours after onset and lasts less than 1 week, whereas symptoms from epidemic keratoconjunctivitis are maximal after several days and sometimes last for 2 or 3 weeks. Early in the illness, pain and subconjunctival hemorrhage are characteristic of AHC but are uncommon in epidemic keratoconjunctivitis. Follicular deposits on the conjunctiva are much more prominent in epidemic keratoconjunctivitis, as are subepithelial corneal opacities persisting after the conjunctivitis has subsided. Bacterial and chlamydial causes of conjunctivitis generally do not cause extensive outbreaks with abrupt onset after a short incubation period.

Laboratory Diagnosis

Enterovirus 70 and coxsackievirus A24 can be recovered from conjunctival swabs or scrapings of patients with AHC during the first 3 days of illness.[212, 238] Isolation rates exceeding 90% from conjunctival scrapings have been reported for coxsackievirus A24, but recovery rates for enterovirus 70 have been somewhat lower.[228] Less than 5% of fecal specimens or throat swabs have been positive for either virus. Rising antibody titers can be demonstrated in paired sera from patients with conjunctivitis.

Treatment and Prevention

Treatment of conjunctivitis is symptomatic. Antimicrobial agents are not indicated unless bacterial suprainfection is present. Contagion can be prevented by careful hand washing, use of separate towels, and sterilization of ophthalmologic instruments.

ILLNESSES IN WHICH THE ETIOLOGIC ROLE OF ENTEROVIRUSES IS MINOR, UNCERTAIN, OR POORLY DEFINED

Coxsackieviruses and echoviruses, possibly as a result of their replication in the small bowel, are frequently cited as causes of nonbacterial diarrhea or gastroenteritis. However, conflicting results have been obtained in several studies that compared rates of enteroviral isolation from children with acute diarrheal illness versus matched healthy control subjects.[54, 239–241] The consensus of these reports favors a variable, generally small excess of enteroviral infections in subjects with diarrhea. Evidence is somewhat stronger that certain echoviruses, particularly types 11, 14, and 18, have occasionally been responsible for epidemic diarrhea of young infants.[54, 241, 242] Most of these studies were performed before the discovery of toxigenic *Escherichia coli,* rotaviruses, enteric adenoviruses, and caliciviruses, now established as major causes of diarrheal illness. In light of this new knowledge, additional epidemiologic investigations encompassing all these agents will be required before the contribution of enteroviruses to diarrheal disease can be accurately assessed. Nonetheless, their role is probably minor.

The hemolytic-uremic syndrome has been temporally associated with coxsackieviruses A4, B2, and B4 and with echovirus 22.[243–245] Similarly, coxsackievirus B5 has been reported in association with acute renal failure in five patients.[246] Although it has been speculated that immune complexes or a nonimmunologic Shwartzman-like reaction is triggered by enterovirus infection, an etiologic relationship is unlikely now that a strong link between enterohemorrhagic *E. coli* infection and the hemolytic-uremic syndrome has been made.

Enteroviruses have been implicated as a cause of acute myositis in some patients,[187, 247–254] although the diagnosis has rarely been proved virologically. Echovirus 11 has been recovered from clinically involved skeletal muscle of a 3-month-old infant with a fatal systemic infection.[187] In other cases, coxsackievirus A9, group B coxsackievirus types 2 and 6, and echovirus 9 have been etiologically linked to myositis on the basis of serology, recovery of virus from the throat or feces, or demonstration of viral antigen in muscle by immunofluorescence. Both generalized polymyositis and focal myositis have been noted, the latter sometimes localized to the thighs. Clinical myositis is manifested by fever, chills, weakness, hypotonia, tenderness, and edema of the involved muscle groups. Myoglobinemia, myoglobinuria, and an elevated creatine phosphokinase level are often found. Most reported patients have recovered rapidly. The syndrome of acute pleurodynia, which is clearly related to group B coxsackievirus infection, is caused by localized myositis of the chest and abdominal wall muscles (see earlier).

Hepatitis has been associated with enterovirus infections, especially group B coxsackieviruses. Generally, hepatitis has been part of severe multisystem disease in neonates or, rarely, adults.[255–260] An etiologic association between coxsackievirus infection and isolated hepatitis has not been established.

Pancreatitis has been reported in patients with group B coxsackievirus type 1 to 5 and echovirus type 6, 11, 22, and 30 infections.[261–264] Prospective studies of acute pancreatitis have demonstrated concurrent enterovirus infection in 2 to 20% of cases.[263, 264] Orchitis has been observed in adolescent boys during infection with coxsackievirus A9, group B coxsackieviruses 2, 4, and 5, and echovirus 6,[265–269] including coxsackievirus B5 isolation from a testicular biopsy specimen in one case.[265]

Lymphadenopathy has been described in a few outbreaks of illness caused by coxsackieviruses and echoviruses, but it has not been prominent.[54] Splenomegaly and a heterophil-negative, mononucleosis-like syndrome have also been reported.[54] Echoviruses have been associated with acute arthritis; echovirus 11 was recovered from synovial fluid in one case.[270, 271] In separate case reports, echovirus 25[272, 273] and an untyped enterovirus resembling a group A coxsackievirus[273] have been recovered from the gastrointestinal tracts of children with acute infectious lymphocytosis; however, further evidence of an etiologic association is lacking.

Diabetes Mellitus

A gradually accumulating body of epidemiologic, clinical, and experimental evidence suggests an intriguing link between the group B coxsackieviruses and type 1 insulin-dependent diabetes mellitus (IDDM). The reader is referred to several excellent reviews for more detailed analyses.[262, 274–278]

The observation that new-onset IDDM cases occur in seasonal patterns[279, 280] and sometimes in clusters or small outbreaks[278, 281, 282] has been cited as evidence for the role of viral disease in the pathophysiology of IDDM. The peak occurrence of new IDDM cases is late in the calendar year, 1 to 2 months later than peak enterovirus activity. However, the occurrence of enterovirus infection and IDDM during the same season could be independent, and at least two studies found no increase in new onset of IDDM after outbreaks of group B coxsackievirus disease.[283, 284] Cross-sectional studies in which the prevalence of group B coxsackievirus antibody has been compared in children with IDDM and controls are inconclusive. In general, studies that used hospital or neighborhood controls have found a positive association, whereas those using sibling controls have not.[274, 277]

Two major theories on the pathophysiology of virus-induced IDDM exist and are not necessarily mutually exclusive. The "direct hit" hypothesis, which posits destruction of pancreatic islets by direct virus infection, derives support from murine studies in which enteroviruses cause specific destruction of β-cells in the islets of Langerhans,[262, 285] from detection of enterovirus RNA in serum at the onset of IDDM,[286, 287] and from postmortem isolation of coxsackievirus serotypes B4[288] and B5[289] from the pancreatic tissue of children dying of ketoacidosis as their initial manifestation of IDDM. Demonstration of group B coxsackievirus IgM antibody in the serum of children with recent-onset IDDM supports the direct-infection hypothesis, although inconsistency regarding this finding has been noted across different studies.[290–294]

A second theory focuses on acute viral infection as a trigger for an autoimmune response to pancreatic islet cells; the autoimmune response is induced by the similarity between viral and islet cell antigens, which may be related to a past viral insult, genetic predisposition, or both.[295] This concept is supported by the induction of chronic islet cell inflammation in genetically susceptible mice by enterovirus infection,[296] by the observation that most children with IDDM have humoral anti–islet cell antibodies at diagnosis, and by one study demonstrating a temporal association between the development of islet cell antibodies and seroconversion to group B coxsackievirus infection.[297] Recent investigations suggest that molecular mimicry between a nonstructural coxsackievirus protein and a β-cell enzyme may permit autoimmune destruction of pancreatic islet cell tissue.[298] Although persistent enterovirus infection is also considered a possible mechanism of islet cell damage, no evidence is widely accepted that enteroviruses are capable of persisting in an immunocompetent human host.

INFECTIONS CAUSED BY THE NEWER ENTEROVIRUSES

Four new enteroviruses, serotypes 68 to 71 (Table 160–2), have been recognized since adoption of the simplified classification scheme described in Chapter 158. Enterovirus 68, recovered from the stool of an asymptomatic child, has yet to be associated with a disease and is therefore considered an "orphan" virus.[299] Enterovirus 69 has been isolated from the throat secretions of infants with bronchiolitis and pneumonia.[300] These two viruses have been little studied, and only a handful of isolates from California and Mexico have been recovered. Enterovirus 70 is recognized as the major cause of AHC, a distinctive infection affecting persons in warm, humid coastal areas in many parts of the world (see earlier). Enterovirus 71, the most recently discovered enterovirus serotype, has been recognized as a cause of cutaneous and CNS disease in scattered locations throughout the world since 1969.

Enterovirus 71 Infections

Enterovirus 71, initially recognized as the cause of outbreaks of aseptic meningitis and encephalitis in California between 1969 and 1972,[301] has subsequently been isolated in many parts of the world. Most recognized infections have occurred in patients with aseptic meningitis or HFM disease. However, a significant proportion of patients with enterovirus 71 infections have had more serious CNS complications, especially acute paralytic manifestations similar to poliomyelitis.[48, 49, 302–304]

Etiologic Agent

Enterovirus 71 is an acid-stable picornavirus that is pathogenic for suckling mice and produces a myositis characteristic of the group A coxsackieviruses. A poliomyelitis-like disease can be produced by oral or parenteral challenge in cynomolgus monkeys.[305, 306] Neurovirulence in monkeys appears to be related to the ability of enterovirus 71 strains to replicate at higher temperatures.[306] The antigenic relatedness of several strains isolated in different parts of the world has been demonstrated by neutralization with type-specific antisera.[307]

Epidemiology

Enterovirus 71 was initially isolated from young children with encephalitis and aseptic meningitis in California in 1969.[301] This virus was not isolated outside California until 1972, when enterovirus 71 CNS infections were diagnosed nearly simultaneously in the state of New York[308] and in Melbourne, Australia.[309] In both locations, cutaneous manifestations were a prominent feature of the illness in many patients. Subsequently, clusters of enterovirus 71 disease have been reported in Sweden, Australia, Japan, Hong Kong, Bulgaria, Hungary, France, and many locations in the United States.[309–315]

Enterovirus 71 is unique among the nonpolio enteroviruses as a cause of epidemic paralysis. Localized outbreaks of paralytic disease have involved small numbers of patients over several years,[301–303, 309] and regional epidemics have involved hundreds to thousands of persons within a single season.[48, 311, 312] The largest outbreaks of serious CNS disease occurred in Bulgaria and Hungary, where significant numbers of poliomyelitis-like cases and numerous deaths were noted.[49, 316]

The mode of transmission is presumed to be predominantly through fecal-oral spread. Most symptomatic infections occur in children younger than 6 years, and very young children have a disproportionately high number of cases of encephalitis and motor paralysis.

Clinical Manifestations

Because the literature contains few data from individual patients,[302] only a general summary of the clinical features of enterovirus 71 infection can be given. Furthermore, most reports of enterovirus 71 infection have come from central reference virus laboratories; thus, patients who have only mild or nonspecific symptoms or signs are

TABLE 160-2 Geographic Distribution and Types of Infection or Illness Associated with Newer Enteroviruses

	Enterovirus Immunotype			
	68	*69*	*70*	*71*
Type of Infection or Illness	*California*	*Mexico*	*Global Except Australia*	*California, New York, Sweden, Australia, Japan, Bulgaria, Hungary, France*
Asymptomatic	+	+	+	+
Fever and respiratory disease	+		+	+
Meningitis/encephalitis			+	+
Paralysis			+	+
Acute hemorrhagic conjunctivitis			+	
Hand-foot-and-mouth disease				+
Maculopapular exanthem				+
Myopathy				+

likely to be underrepresented in the literature. Regardless, it is apparent that the spectrum of clinical illness has varied considerably among outbreaks of infection reported from different locations. During outbreaks of enterovirus 71 infection in Australia, Sweden, and Japan, most patients had either typical HFM disease or aseptic meningitis, usually after a prodrome of 1 to 3 days of fever[309, 310, 312, 313]; serious CNS disease was not observed. In contrast, HFM disease was not seen in the 1975 Bulgarian epidemic of enterovirus 71 aseptic meningitis,[49] although an acute paralytic syndrome indistinguishable from poliomyelitis developed in 21% of recognized cases. Paralytic complications tended to develop rapidly, often within 10 to 30 hours after the onset of symptoms. Approximately half of those with paralysis had evidence of encephalitis or cranial nerve involvement (bulbar syndrome). The overall mortality for those with documented infection was 6.2%, including 29.5% in patients with paralytic disease and 65% in patients with bulbar involvement.[49] The occurrence of HFM syndrome and serious CNS disease is not mutually exclusive because both features of enterovirus 71 infection have been noted during outbreaks in Rochester, New York,[302] Japan,[317] Hong Kong,[303] and Australia.[48] Other less common manifestations attributed to enterovirus 71 infection include generalized maculopapular rash,[309] myocarditis,[49] infectious polyneuritis,[309] and upper respiratory tract disease.[49, 309]

Differential Diagnosis

Infections caused by enterovirus 71 may be clinically indistinguishable from infections caused by certain other enterovirus serotypes. The principal cause of HFM disease is coxsackievirus A16, although a variety of other enterovirus serotypes may also be responsible, as noted earlier. Epidemic paralytic disease has virtually always been attributed to the polioviruses, although rare cases of sporadic motor paresis or paralysis have been caused by other enterovirus serotypes.

Laboratory Diagnosis

Enterovirus 71 has been isolated from a number of clinical specimens, including vesicle fluid, feces, oropharyngeal secretions, urine, and CSF. Isolation rates are highest from vesicle swabs and lowest from the CSF.[48, 49, 318] Primary isolation has been most successful in African green monkey kidney cell culture and in suckling mice. Even under optimal conditions, a cytopathic effect may take 5 to 8 days to develop and then progresses slowly and incompletely. Because standard enterovirus antiserum pools do not contain antiserum to enterovirus 71, isolates of this serotype may be reported as "nontypable enterovirus."

Treatment and Prevention

Treatment of enterovirus 71 infection is symptomatic and supportive. Widespread distribution of oral polio vaccine during the Bulgarian epidemic was postulated to have dampened the spread of enterovirus 71 disease by virtue of gastrointestinal interference, but proof of a significant effect of oral polio vaccine is lacking. A killed enterovirus 71 vaccine was prepared for use during this epidemic but not administered to humans.

REFERENCES

1. Kogon A, Spigland I, Frothingham TE, et al. The Virus Watch Program: A continuing surveillance of viral infections in metropolitan New York families. Am J Epidemiol. 1969;89:51.
2. Berlin LE, Rorabaugh ML, Heldrich F, et al. Aseptic meningitis in infants less than two years of age: Diagnosis and etiology. J Infect Dis. 1993; 168:888–892.
3. Dagan R, Jenista J, Menegus MA. Association of clinical presentation, laboratory findings, and virus serotypes with the presence of meningitis in hospitalized infants with enterovirus infection. J Pediatr. 1988;113: 975–978.
4. Rorabaugh ML, Berlin LE, Heldrich F, et al. Aseptic meningitis among infants less than two years of age: Acute illness and neurologic complications. Pediatrics. 1993;92:206–211.
5. Lepow ML, Coyne N, Thompson LB, et al. A clinical, epidemiologic and laboratory investigation of aseptic meningitis during the four-year period, 1955–1958. II. The clinical disease and its sequelae. N Engl J Med. 1962;266:1188–1193.
6. Rotbart H, Brennan PJ, Fife KH, et al. Enterovirus meningitis in adults. Clin Infect Dis. 1998;27:896–898.
7. Haynes RE, Cramblett HG, Kronfol HJ. Echovirus 9 meningoencephalitis in infants and children. JAMA. 1969;208:1657.
8. Lake AM, Lauer BA, Clark JC, et al. Enterovirus infections in neonates. J Pediatr. 1976;89:787–791.
9. Wilfert CM, Lauer BA, Cohen M, et al. An epidemic of echovirus 18 meningitis. J Infect Dis. 1975;131:75–78.
10. Wenner HA, Abel D, Olson LC, et al. A mixed epidemic associated with echovirus types 6 and 11. Am J Epidemiol. 1981;114:369.
11. Amir J, Harel L, Frydman M, Handsher R, Varsano I. Shift in cerebrospinal polymorphonuclear cell percentage in the early stage of aseptic meningitis. J Pediatr. 1991;119:938–941.
12. Feigin RD, Shackelford PG. Value of repeat lumbar puncture in the differential diagnosis of meningitis. N Engl J Med. 1973;289:571.
13. Avner E, Satz J, Plotkin SA. Hypoglycorrhachia in young infants with viral meningitis. J Pediatr. 1975;87:883.
14. Sumaya CV, Corman LI. Enteroviral meningitis in early infancy: Significance in community outbreaks. Pediatr Infect Dis. 1982;3:151–154.
15. Singer JI, Mauer PR, Riley JP, Smith PB. Management of central nervous system infections during an epidemic of enteroviral aseptic meningitis. J Pediatr. 1980;96:559–563.
16. Malcom BS, Eiden JJ, Hendley JO. Echovirus type 9 meningitis simulating tuberculous meningitis. Pediatrics. 1980;65:725.
17. Chonmaitree T, Ford C, Sanders C, Lucia HL. Comparison of cell cultures for rapid isolation of enteroviruses. J Clin Microbiol. 1988;26:2576–2580.
18. Dagan R, Menegus MA. A combination of four cell types for rapid detection of enteroviruses in clinical specimens. J Med Virol. 1986;19:219–228.
19. Lennette EH, Magoffin R, Knouf EG. Viral central nervous system disease: An etiologic study conducted at the Los Angelos County General Hospital. JAMA. 1962;179:687.
20. Lepow ML, Carver DH, Wright HT, et al. A clinical, epidemiologic and laboratory investigation of aseptic meningitis during the four-year period, 1955–1958. I. Observations concerning etiology and epidemiology. N Engl J Med. 1962;266:1181–1187.
21. Marier R, Rodriguez W, Chloupek RJ, et al. Coxsackievirus B5 infection and aseptic meningitis in neonates and children. Am J Dis Child. 1975;129:321–325.
22. Torphy DE, Ray GC, Thompson RS, et al. An epidemic of aseptic meningitis due

to echovirus type 30: Epidemiologic features and clinical and laboratory findings. Am J Public Health. 1970;60:1447.
23. Yerly S, Gervaix A, Simonet V, et al. Rapid and sensitive detection of enteroviruses in specimens from patients with aseptic meningitis. J Clin Microbiol. 1996;34:199–201.
24. Sabin AB, Krumbiegel ER, Wigand R. ECHO type 9 virus disease. Am J Dis Child. 1958;96:197.
25. Rotbart HA. Nucleic acid detection systems for enteroviruses. Clin Microbiol Rev. 1991;4:156–168.
26. Schlesinger Y, Sawyer MH, Storch GA. Enteroviral meningitis in infancy: Potential role for polymerase chain reaction in patient management. Pediatrics. 1994;94:157–162.
27. Sawyer M, Holland D, Aintablian N, et al. Diagnosis of enteroviral central nervous system infection by polymerase chain reaction during a large community outbreak. Pediatr Infect Dis J. 1994;13:177–182.
28. Rotbart HA, Sawyer MH, Fast S, et al. Diagnosis of enteroviral meningitis by using PCR with a colorimetric microwell detection assay. J Clin Microbiol. 1994;32:2590–2592.
29. Mandal BK. The dilemma of partially treated bacterial meningitis. Scand J Infect Dis. 1976;8:185.
30. Converse GM, Gwaltney JMJ, Strasburg DA, et al. Alteration of cerebrospinal fluid findings by partial treatment of bacterial meningitis. J Pediatr. 1973;83:220.
31. Dalton HP, Allison MJ. Modification of laboratory results by partial treatment of bacterial meningitis. Am J Clin Pathol. 1968;49:410.
32. Weiner LB, Rotbart HA, Gilbert DL, et al. Treatment of "enterovirus" meningitis with pleconaril (VP 63843), an antipicornavirus agent. Presented at the Thirty-seventh Interscience Conference on Antimicrobial Agents and Chemotherapy, Toronto, 1997.
33. Farmer K, MacArthur BA, Clay MM. A follow-up study of 15 cases of neonatal meningoencephalitis due to coxsackie virus B5. J Pediatr. 1975;87:568–571.
34. Sells CJ, Carpenter RL, Ray CG. Sequelae of central-nervous-system enterovirus infections. N Engl J Med. 1975;293:1–4.
35. Bergman I, Painter MJ, Wald ER, et al. Outcome in children with enteroviral meningitis during the first year of life. J Pediatr. 1987;110:705–709.
36. Rorabaugh ML, Berlin LE, Rosenberg L, et al. Absence of Neurodevelopmental Sequelae from Aseptic Meningitis. Baltimore: Society for Pediatric Research; 1992.
37. Meyer HM, Johnson RT, Crawford IP, et al. Central nervous system syndromes of viral etiology. A study of 713 cases. Am J Med. 1960;29:334–337.
38. Chalhub E, Devivo D, Siegel BA, et al. Coxsackie A9 focal encephalitis associated with acute infantile hemiplegia and porencephaly. Neurology. 1977;27:574.
39. Modlin JF, Dagan R, Berlin LE, et al. Focal encephalitis with enterovirus infections. Pediatrics. 1991;88:841–845.
40. Peters ACB, Vielvoye GJ, Versteeg J, et al. Echo 25 focal encephalitis and subacute hemichorea. Neurology. 1979;29:676–681.
41. Roden VJ, Cantor HE, O'Connor DM, et al. Acute hemiplegia of childhood associated with coxsackie A9 viral infection. J Pediatr. 1975;86:56.
42. Morens DM. Enteroviral disease in early infancy. J Pediatr. 1978;92:374–377.
43. Whitley RJ, Cobbs CG, Alford CA, et al. Diseases that mimic herpes simplex encephalitis. JAMA. 1989;262:234–239.
44. Klapper PE, Bailey AS, Longson M, et al. Meiningoencephalitis caused by coxsackievirus group B type 2: Diagnosis confirmed by measuring intrathecal antibody. J Infect. 1984;8:227–231.
45. Price RA, Garcia JH, Rightsel WA. Choriomeningitis and myocarditis in an adolescent with isolation of coxsackie B5 virus. Am J Clin Pathol. 1970;53:825.
46. Voroshilova MK, Chumakov MP. Poliomyelitis-like properties of AB-IV-coxsackie A7 group of viruses. Prog Med Virol. 1959;2:106.
47. Grist NR, Bell EJ. Enteroviral etiology of the paralytic poliomyelitis syndrome. Arch Environ Health. 1970;21:382.
48. Gilbert GL, Dickson KE, Waters M-J, et al. Outbreak of enterovirus 71 infection in Victoria, Australia, with a high incidence of neurologic involvement. Pediatr Infect Dis J. 1988;7:484–488.
49. Shindarov LM, Chumakov MP, Voroshilova MK, et al. Epidemiological, clinical, and pathophysiological characteristics of epidemic poliomyelitis-like disease caused by enterovirus 71. J Hyg Epidemiol Microbiol Immunol. 1979;23:284.
50. Santhanam S, Choudhury DS. Coxsackie A-9 in the etiology of poliomyelitis-like diseases. Indian J Pediatr. 1985;52:405–408.
51. Assaad F, Cockburn WC. Four year study of WHO virus reports on enteroviruses other than poliovirus. Bull World Health Organ. 1972;46:329.
52. Godtfredsen A, Hansen B. A case of mild paralytic disease due to ECHO virus type 11. Acta Pathol Microbiol Scand. 1961;53:111.
53. Grist NR, Bell EJ. The epidemiology of enteroviruses. Scot Med J. 1975;20:27.
54. Kibrick S. Current status of coxsackie and ECHO viruses in human disease. Prog Med Virol. 1964;6:27.
55. Hertenstein JR, Sarnat HB, O'Connor DM. Acute unilateral oculomotor palsy associated with ECHO 9 viral infection. J Pediatr. 1976;89:79.
56. Steigman AJ, Lipton MM. Fatal bulbospinal paralytic poliomyelitis due to ECHO 11 virus. JAMA. 1960;174:178.
57. Dery P, Marks MI, Shapera R. Clinical manifestations of coxsackievirus infections in children. Am J Dis Child. 1974;128:464.
58. Geer J. Coxsackie virus infections in Southern Africa. Yale J Biol Med. 1961;34:289.
59. Barak Y, Schwartz JF. Acute transverse myelitis associated with ECHO type 5 infection (Letter). Am J Dis Child. 1988;142:128.
60. Kaul A, Cohen ME, Broffman G, et al. Reye-like syndrome associated with coxsackie B2 virus infection. J Pediatr. 1979;94:67.
61. Alvira MM, Mendoza M. Reye's syndrome: A viral myopathy? N Engl J Med. 1975;292:1297.
62. Brunberg JA, Bell WE. Reye syndrome. Arch Neurol. 1974;30:304.
63. Kuban KC, Ephros MA, Freeman RL, et al. Syndrome of opsoclonus-myoclonus caused by coxsackie B3 infection. Ann Neurol. 1983;13:69–71.
64. Bell EJ, Ross CAC, Grist NR. Echo 9 infection in pregnant women with suspected rubella. J Clin Pathol. 1975;28:267.
65. Lerner AM, Klein JO, Levin HS, et al. Infections due to coxsackie virus group A, type 9, in Boston, 1959, with special reference to exanthems and pneumonia. N Engl J Med. 1960;263:1265.
66. Annunziato D. Koplik spots and echo 9 virus (Letter). N Y State J Med. 1987;87:667.
67. Neva FA. A second outbreak of Boston exanthem disease in Pittsburgh during 1954. N Engl J Med. 1956;254:838.
68. Neva FA, Femster RF, Gorbach IJ. Clinical and epidemiological features of an unusual epidemic exanthem. JAMA. 1954;155:544.
69. Hall CB, Cherry JD, Hatch MH, et al. The return of Boston exanthem: Echovirus 16 infections in 1974. Am J Dis Child. 1977;131:323.
70. Cherry JD, Lerner AM, Klein JO, et al. Coxsackie B5 infections with exanthems. Pediatrics. 1963;31:455.
71. Moritsugu Y, Sawada K, Hinohara M, et al. An outbreak of type 25 echovirus infection with exanthem in an infant home near Tokyo. Am J Epidemiol. 1968;87:599.
72. Hughes RO, Roberts C. Hand, foot, mouth disease associated with coxsackie A9 virus. Lancet. 1972;2:751.
73. Lindenbaum JE, Van Dyck PC, Allen RG. Hand, foot and mouth disease associated with coxsackievirus group B. Scand J Infect Dis. 1975;7:161.
74. Robinson CR, Doane FW, Rhodes AJ. Report of an outbreak of febrile illness with pharyngeal lesions and exanthem. Can Med Assoc J. 1958;79:615.
75. Adler JL, Mostow SR, Mellin II, et al. Epidemiologic investigation of hand, foot, and mouth disease: Infection caused by coxsackievirus A16 in Baltimore, June through September 1968. Am J Dis Child. 1970;120:309.
76. Nahmias AJ, Froeschle JE, Feorino PM, et al. Generalized eruption in a child with eczema due to coxsackievirus A16. Arch Dermatol. 1968;97:147.
77. Miller GD. Hand-foot-and-mouth disease. JAMA. 1968;203:827.
78. Kimura A, Abe M, Nakao T. Light and electron microscopic study of skin lesions in patients with hand, foot, and mouth disease. Tohoku J Exp Med. 1977;122:237.
79. Cherry JD, Lerner AM, Klein JO, et al. Coxsackie A9 infections with exanthems with particular reference to urticaria. Pediatrics. 1963;31:819.
80. Deseda-Tous J, Byatt PH, Cherry JD. Vesicular lesions in adults due to echovirus 11 infections. Arch Dermatol. 1977;113:1705.
81. Meade RH, Chang TW. Zosterlike eruption due to echovirus 6. Am Dis Child. 1979;133:283–284.
82. Frothingham TE. ECHO virus type 9 associated with three cases simulating meningococcemia. N Engl J Med. 1958;259:484.
83. Cherry JD, Jahn CL. Virologic studies of exanthems. J Pediatr. 1966;68:204.
84. James WD, Odom RB, Hatch MH. Gianotti-Crosti–like eruption associated with coxsackievirus A16 infection. J Am Acad Dermatol. 1982;6:862.
85. Kepfer P, Hable DA, Smith TF. Viral isolation rates during summer from children with acute upper respiratory tract disease and healthy children. Am J Clin Pathol. 1974;61:1–5.
86. Johnson KM, Bloom HH, Forsyth B, et al. The role of enteroviruses in respiratory disease. Am Rev Respir Dis. 1963;88:240.
87. Jackson GG, Muidoon RL. Viruses causing common respiratory infections in man. II. Enteroviruses and paramyxoviruses. J Infect Dis. 1973;128:387.
88. Couch RB, Cate TR, Gerone PJ, et al. Production of illness with a small particle aerosol of coxsackie A21. J Clin Invest. 1965;44:535.
89. Eckert HL, Portnoy B, Salvatore MA, et al. Group B coxsackie virus infection in infants with acute lower respiratory disease. Pediatrics. 1967;39:526.
90. Flewett TH. Histological study of two cases of coxsackie B virus pneumonia in children. J Clin Pathol. 1965;18:743.
91. Jahn CL, Felton OL, Cherry JD. Coxsackie B1 pneumonia in an adult. JAMA. 1964;189:236.
92. Cherry JD, Jahn CL. Herpangina. The etiologic spectrum. Pediatrics. 1965;36:632.
93. Steigman AJ, Lipton MM, Braspennickx H. Acute lymphonodular pharyngitis: A newly described condition due to coxsackie A virus. J Pediatr. 1962;61:331.
94. Sylvest E. Epidemic Myalgia: Bornholm Disease. London: Oxford University; 1934.
95. Weller TH, Enders JF, Buckingham M, Finn JJ Jr. Etiology of epidemic pleurodynia: Study of two viruses isolated from typical outbreak. J Immunol. 1950;65:337–346.
96. Curnen EC, Shaw EW, Melnick JL. Disease resembling nonparalytic poliomyelitis associated with virus pathogenic for infant mice. JAMA. 1949;141:894–901.
97. Bell EJ, Grist NR. ECHO viruses, carditis, and acute pleurodynia. Am Heart J. 1971;82:133.
98. Madhaven HN, Bedninath S, Chanraseker S. A case of pleurodynia associated with coxsackie virus type A9. J Assoc Physicians India. 1977;25:491.
99. Disney ME, Howard EM, Wood BSB. Bornholm disease in children. BMJ. 1953;1:1351–1354.
100. Bain HW, McLean DM, Walker SJ. Epidemic pleurodynia (Bornholm disease) due to coxsackie B-5 virus: The interrelationship of pleurodynia, benign pericarditis, and aseptic meningitis. Pediatrics. 1961;27:889–903.
101. Gordon RB, Lennette EH, Sandrock RS. The varied clinical manifestations of coxsackie viral infections. Arch Intern Med. 1959;103:63–75.

102. Warin JF, Davies JBM, Sanders FK, Vizoso AD. Oxford epidemic of Bornholm disease, 1951. BMJ. 1953;1:1345–1351.
103. Smith WG. Adult heart disease due to the coxsackie virus group B. Br Heart J. 1966;28:204.
104. Helin M, Savola J, Lapinleimu K. Cardiac manifestations during a coxsackie B5 epidemic. BMJ. 1968;2:97.
105. Grist NR, Bell EJ. A six-year study of coxsackievirus B infections in heart disease. J Hyg. 1974;73:165.
106. Grist NR. Coxsackie virus infections of the heart. In: Waterson AP, ed. Recent Advances in Clinical Virology, v. 1. Edinburgh: Churchill Livingstone; 1977:141.
107. Ayuthya PSN, Jayavasu JJ, Pongpanich B. Coxsackie group B virus and primary myocardial disease in infants and children. Am Heart J. 1974;88:311.
108. Sainani GS, Krompotic E, Slodki SJ. Adult heart disease due to the coxsackie virus B infection. Medicine (Baltimore). 1968;47:133.
109. Russell SJM, Bell EJ. Echoviruses and carditis. Lancet. 1970;1:784.
110. Grist NR, Bell EJ. Coxsackieviruses and the heart. Am Heart J. 1969;77:295.
111. Woodruff JF. Viral myocarditis. Am J Pathol. 1980;101:427–484.
112. Lerner AM, Wilson FM. Virus myocardiopathy. Prog Med Virol. 1973;15:63.
113. Meehan WF, Bertrand CA. Ventricular tachycardia associated with echovirus infection. JAMA. 1970;212:1701.
114. Grist NR, Bell EJ. Coxsackie virus and heart diseases. BMJ. 1968;3:556.
115. Grist NR, Bell EJ, Assad F. Enteroviruses in human disease. Prog Med Virol. 1978;24:114–157.
116. Schleissner LA, Fiala M, Imagawa DT, et al. Application of systolic time intervals to acute cardiomyopathy with echovirus 2. Chest. 1976;69:563.
117. Kanra G, Dogruel N, Tinaztepe K, et al. Myocarditis caused by echovirus 11 virus. Turk J Pediatr. 1978;20:24.
118. Lewes D, Rainford DJ, Lane WF. Symptomless myocarditis and myalgia in viral and *Mycoplasma pneumoniae* infections. Br Heart J. 1974;36:924.
119. Van Loon GR, Masson AM. Viral pericarditis. Can Med Assoc J. 1968;99:163.
120. Berkovich S, Rodriguez-Torres R, Lin J-S. Virologic studies in children with acute myocarditis. Am J Dis Child. 1968;115:207.
121. Bell EJ, Grist NR. Echoviruses, carditis, and acute pleurodynia. Lancet. 1970;1:326.
122. Johnson RT, Portnoy B, Rogers NG, et al. Acute benign pericarditis: Virologic study of 34 patients. Arch Intern Med. 1961;108:823.
123. Shimizu C, Rambaud C, Cheron G, et al. Molecular identification of viruses in sudden infant death associated with myocarditis and pericarditis. Pediatr Infect Dis J. 1995;14:584–588.
124. Martin AB, Webber S, Fricker FJ, et al. Acute myocarditis. Rapid diagnosis by PCR in children. Circulation. 1994;90:330–339.
125. Lozinski GM, Davis GG, Krous HF, et al. Adenovirus myocarditis: Retrospective diagnosis by gene amplification from formalin-fixed, paraffin-embedded tissues. Hum Pathol. 1994;25:831–834.
126. Hildebrandt HM, Massab HF, Willis PW. Influenza virus pericarditis. Am J Dis Child. 1962;104:579.
127. Centers for Disease Control. Fatal mumps myocarditis in England. MMWR Morb Mort Wkly Rep. 1980;27:425.
128. Caldera R, Sarrut S, Mallet R, et al. Existetil des complications cardiaques de la vaccine? Sem Hop Paris. 1961;37:1281.
129. Woodruff JF, Woodruff JJ. Involvement of T lymphocytes in the pathogenesis of coxsackievirus B3 heart disease. J Immunol. 1974;113:1726–1734.
130. Rose NR, Wolfgram LJ, Herskowitz A, et al. Postinfectious autoimmunity: Two distinct phases of coxsackievirus B3–induced myocarditis. Ann N Y Acad Sci. 1986;475:146–156.
131. Paque RE, Strauss DC, Nealon TJ, Gauntt CJ. Fractionation and immunologic assessment of KCl-extracted cardiac antigens in coxsackievirus B3 viral-induced myocarditis. J Immunol. 1979;123:358–365.
132. Gauntt CJ, Arizpe HM, Higdon AL, et al. Anti–coxsackievirus B3 neutralizing antibodies with pathological potential. Eur Heart J. 1991;12 (Suppl D): S124–S129.
133. Smith WG. Coxsackie B myopericarditis in adults. Am Heart J. 1970;80:34.
134. Sainani GS, Dekate MP, Rao CP. Heart disease caused by coxsackievirus B infection. Br Heart J. 1975;37:819.
135. Koontz CH, Ray CG. The role of coxsackie group B virus infections in sporadic myopericarditis. Am Heart J. 1971;82:750.
136. Woods JD, Nimmo MJ, MacKay-Scollay EM. Acute transmural myocardial infarction associated with active coxsackie virus B infection. Am Heart J. 1975;89:283.
137. Griffiths PD, Hannington G, Booth JC. Coxsackie B virus infection and myocardial infarction. Lancet. 1980;1:1387.
138. Lau RC. Coxsackie B virus–specific IgM responses in coronary care unit patients. J Med Virol. 1986;18:193–198.
139. Desaneto A, Bullington JD, Bullington RH, et al. Coxsackie B5 heart disease. Demonstration of inferolateral wall myocardial necrosis. Am J Med. 1980;68:295.
140. Narula J, Khaw BA, Dec GW, et al. Brief report: Recognition of acute myocarditis masquerading as acute myocardial infarction. N Engl J Med. 1993;328:100–104.
141. Sutton GC, Harding HB, Truehart RP, et al. Coxsackie B4 myocarditis in an adult: Successful isolation of virus from ventricular myocardium. Aerospace Med. 1967;38:66.
142. Sutton GC, Tobin JR, Fox RT, et al. Study of the pericardium and ventricular myocardium: Exploratory mediastinoscopy and biopsy in unexplained heart disease. JAMA. 1963;185:786.
143. Jin O, Sole MJ, Butany JW, et al. Detection of enterovirus RNA in myocardial biopsies from patients with myocarditis and cardiomyopathy using gene amplification by polymerase chain reaction. Circulation. 1990;82:8–16.
144. Weiss LM, Movahed LA, Billingham ME, Cleary ML. Detection of coxsackievirus B3 RNA in myocardial tissues by polymerase chain reaction. Am J Pathol. 1991;138:497–503.
145. Weller AH, Hall M, Huber SA. Polyclonal immunoglobulin therapy protects against cardiac damage in experimental coxsackievirus-induced myocarditis. Eur Heart J. 1992;13:115–119.
146. Drucker NA, Colan SD, Lewis AB, et al. γ-Globulin treatment of acute myocarditis in the pediatric population. Circulation. 1994;89:252–257.
147. Ainger LE. Acute aseptic myocarditis: Corticosteroid therapy. J Pediatr. 1964;64:716–723.
148. Segal JP, Harvey WP, Gurel T. Diagnosis and treatment of primary myocardial disease. Circulation. 1965;32:837–844.
149. Voigt GC. Steroid therapy in viral myocarditis. Am Heart J. 1968;75:575–576.
150. Mason JW, Billingham ME, Ricci DR. Treatment of acute inflammatory myocarditis assisted by endomyocardial biopsy. Am J Cardiol. 1980;45:1037–1044.
151. Jones SSR, Herskowitz A, Hutchins GM, Baughman KL. Effects of immunosuppressive therapy in biopsy-proved myocarditis and borderline myocarditis on left ventricular function. Am J Cardiol. 1991;68:370–376.
152. Mortensen SA, Baandrup U, Buch J, et al. Immunosuppressive therapy of biopsy proven myocarditis: Experiences with corticosteroids and cyclosporin. Int J Immunother. 1985;1:35–45.
153. Kilbourne ED, Wilson CB, Perrier D. The induction of gross myocardial lesions by a Coxsackie (pleurodynia) virus and cortisone. J Clin Invest. 1956;35:362–370.
154. Mason JW, O'Connell JB, Herskowitz A, et al. A clinical trial of immunosuppressive therapy for myocarditis. N Engl J Med. 1995;333:269–275.
155. Gibbons JE, Goldbloom RB, Dobell ARC. Rapidly developing pericardial constriction in childhood following acute nonspecific pericarditis. Am J Cardiol. 1965;15:863.
156. Howard EJ, Maier HC. Constrictive pericarditis following acute coxsackie viral pericarditis. Am Heart J. 1968;75:247.
157. Matthews JD, Cameron SJ, George M. Constrictive pericarditis following coxsackie virus infection. Thorax. 1970;25:624.
158. Codd MB, Sugrue DD, Gersh BJ, Melton L III. Epidemiology of idiopathic dilated and hypertrophic cardiomyopathy. A population-based study in Olmsted County, Minnesota, 1975–1984. Circulation. 1989;80:564–572.
159. Weiss LM, Liu XF, Chang KL, Billingham ME. Detection of enteroviral RNA in idiopathic dilated cardiomyopathy and other human cardiac tissues. J Clin Invest. 1991;90:156–159.
160. Andreoletti L, Hober D, Decoene C, et al. Detection of enteroviral RNA by polymerase chain reaction in endomyocardial tissue of patients with chronic cardiac diseases. J Med Virol. 1996;48:53–59.
161. Giacca M, Severini GM, Mestroni L, et al. Low frequency of detection by nested polymerase chain reaction of enterovirus ribonucleic acid in endomyocardial tissue of patients with idiopathic dilated cardiomyopathy. J Am Coll Cardiol. 1994;24:1033–1040.
162. de Leeuw N, Melchers WJG, Balk AHMM, et al. No evidence for persistent enterovirus infection in patients with end-stage idiopathic dilated cardiomyopathy. J Infect Dis. 1998;178:256–259.
163. Griffin LD, Kearney D, Ni J, et al. Analysis of formalin-fixed and frozen myocardial autopsy samples for viral genome in childhood myocarditis and dilated cardiomyopathy with endocardial fibroelastosis using polymerase chain reaction (PCR). Cardiovasc Pathol. 1995;4:3–11.
164. Grasso M, Arbustini E, Silini E, et al. Search for coxsackievirus B3 RNA in idiopathic dilated cardiomyopathy using gene amplification by polymerase chain reaction. Am J Cardiol. 1992;69:658–664.
165. Muir P, Nicholson F, Illavia SJ, et al. Serological and molecular evidence of enterovirus infection in patients with end-stage dilated cardiomyopathy. Heart. 1996;76:243–249.
166. Baker DA, Phillips CA. Maternal and neonatal infection with coxsackievirus. Obstet Gynecol. 1980;55 (Suppl):S12–S15.
167. Talsma M, Vegting M, Hess J. Generalized Coxsackie A9 infection in a neonate presenting with pericarditis. Br Heart J. 1984;52:683–685.
168. Wright HT, Landing BH, Lennette EH, et al. Fatal infection in an infant associated with coxsackie virus group A, type 16. N Engl J Med. 1963;268:1041.
169. Gear JHS, Measroch V. Coxsackievirus infection of the newborn. Prog Med Virol. 1973;15:42–62.
170. Modlin JF. Perinatal echovirus infection: Insights from a literature of 61 cases of serious infection and 16 outbreaks in nurseries. Rev Infect Dis. 1986;8:918–926.
171. Kinney JS, McCray E, Kaplan JE, et al. Risk factors associated with echovirus 11 infection in a newborn nursery. Pediatr Infect Dis J. 1986;5:192–197.
172. Modlin JF. Fatal echovirus 11 disease in premature neonates. Pediatrics. 1980;66:775–780.
173. Piraino FF, Sedmak G, Raab K. Echovirus 11 infections of newborns with mortality during the 1979 enterovirus season in Milwaukee, Wis. Public Health Rep. 1982;97:346.
174. Modlin JF, Kinney JS. Perinatal enterovirus infections. In: Aronoff SC, Hughes WT, Kohl S, et al, eds. Advances in Pediatric Infectious Diseases, v. 2. Chicago: Year Book; 1987.
175. Modlin JF, Polk BF, Horton P, et al. Perinatal echovirus 11 infection: Risk of transmission during a community outbreak. N Engl J Med. 1981;305:368–371.
176. Cherry JL, Soriano F, Jahn CL. Search for perinatal enterovirus infection. Am J Dis Child. 1968;116:245–250.
177. Reyes MP, Ostrea EM, Roskamp J, Lerner AM. Disseminated neonatal echovirus 11 disease following antenatal maternal infection with a virus-positive cervix and virus-negative gastrointestinal tract. J Med Virol. 1983;12:155–159.

178. Jones MJU, Kolb M, Votava HJ, et al. Intrauterine echovirus type 11 infection. Mayo Clin Proc. 1980;55:509–512.
179. Yoshioka I, Horstmann DM. Viremia in infection due to echo virus type 9. N Engl J Med. 1961;262:224–228.
180. Kaplan MH, Klein SW, McPhee J, Harper RG. Group B coxsackievirus infections in infants younger than three months of age: A serious childhood illness. Rev Infect Dis. 1983;5:1019–1032.
181. Kunin CM. Virus-tissue union and the pathogenesis of enterovirus infections. J Immunol. 1962;88:556–569.
182. Eichenwald HF, Kotsevalov O. Immunologic responses of premature and full-term infants to infection with certain viruses. Pediatrics. 1960;25:829–839.
183. Rager-Zisman B, Allison AC. The role of antibody and host cells in the resistance of mice against infection by coxsackie B-3 virus. J Gen Virol. 1973;19:329–338.
184. Woodruff J. Lack of correlation between neutralizing antibody production and suppression of coxsackie B-3 replication in target organs: Evidence for involvement of mononuclear inflammatory cells in host defense. J Immunol. 1979;123:31.
185. Modlin JF, Bowman M. Perinatal transmission of coxsackie B3 virus in a murine model. J Infect Dis. 1987;156:21–25.
186. Berry PJ, Nagington J. Fatal infection with echovirus 11. Arch Dis Child. 1982;57:22–29.
187. Halfon N, Spector SA. Fatal echovirus type 11 infections. Am J Dis Child. 1981;135:1017.
188. Drew JH. Echo 11 virus outbreak in a nursery associated with myocarditis. Aust J Pediatr. 1973;9:90.
189. Georgieff MK, Johnson DE, Thompson TR, et al. Fulminant hepatic necrosis in an infant with perinatally acquired echovirus 21 infection. Pediatr Infect Dis J. 1987;6:71–73.
190. Spector SA, Straube RC. Protean manifestations of perinatal enterovirus infection. West J Med. 1983;138:847–851.
191. Speer ME, Yawn DH. Fatal hepatoadrenal necrosis in the neonate associated with echovirus types 11 and 12 presenting as a surgical emergency. J Pediatr Surg. 1984;19:591–593.
192. Wreghitt TG, Gandy GM, King A, et al. Fatal neonatal echo 7 virus infection (Letter). Lancet 1984;2:465.
193. Chambon M, Delage C, Bailly J-L, et al. Fatal hepatic necrosis in a neonate with echovirus 20 infection: Use of the polymerase chain reaction to detect enterovirus in liver tissue. Clin Infect Dis. 1997;24:523–524.
194. Mostoufizadeh G, Lack EE, Gang DL, et al. Postmortem manifestations of echovirus 11 sepsis in five newborn infants. Hum Pathol. 1983;14:819–823.
195. Boyd MT, Jordan SW, Davis LE. Fatal pneumonitis from congenital echovirus type 6 infection. Pediatr Infect Dis J. 1987;6:1138–1139.
196. Cheeseman SH, Hirsch MS, Keller EW, et al. Fatal neonatal pneumonia caused by echovirus type 9 (Letter). Am J Dis Child. 1977;131:1169.
197. Toce SS, Keenan WJ. Congenital echovirus 11 pneumonia in association with pulmonary hypertension. Pediatr Infect Dis J. 1988;7:360–362.
198. Johnston JM, Overall JC. Intravenous immunoglobulin in disseminated neonatal echovirus 11 infection. Pediatr Infect Dis J. 1989;8:254–256.
199. Rotbart HA. Pleconaril therapy of potentially life-threatening enterovirus infections. Presented at the Thirty-sixth Annual Meeting of the Infectious Disease Society of America, Denver, 1998.
200. McKinney RE, Katz SL, Wilfert CM. Chronic enteroviral meningoencephalitis in agammaglobulinemic patients. Rev Infect Dis. 1987;9:334–356.
201. O'Neil KM, Pallansch MA, Winkelstein JA, et al. Chronic group A coxsackievirus infection in agammaglobulinemia: Demonstration of genomic variation of serotypically identical isolates persistently excreted from the same patient. J Infect Dis. 1988;157:183–186.
202. Rotbart HA, Kinsella JP, Wasserman RL. Persistent enterovirus infection in culture-negative meningoencephalitis: Demonstration by enzymatic amplification. J Infect Dis. 1990;161:787–791.
203. Webster ADB, Rotbart HA, Warner T, et al. Diagnosis of enterovirus brain disease in hypogammaglobulinemic patients by polymerase chain reaction. Clin Infect Dis. 1993;17:657–661.
204. Webster ADB. Echovirus disease in hypogammaglobulinaemic patients. Clin Rheum Dis. 1984;10:189–203.
205. Mease PJ, Ochs HD, Wedgewood RJ. Successful treatment of echovirus meningoencephalitis and myositis-fasciitis with intravenous immune globulin therapy in a patient with X-linked hypogammaglobulinemia. N Engl J Med. 1981;304:1278.
206. Biggs DD, Toorkey BC, Carrigan DR, et al. Disseminated echovirus infection complicating bone marrow transplantation. Am J Med. 1990;88:421–425.
207. Aquino VM, Farah RA, Lee ME, Sandler ES. Disseminated coxsackie A9 infection complicating bone marrow transplantation. Pediatr Infect Dis J. 1996;15:1053–1054.
208. Galama JMD, de Leeuw N, Wittebol S, et al. Prolonged enteroviral infection in a patient who developed pericarditis and heart failure after bone marrow transplantation. Clin Infect Dis. 1996;22:1004–1008.
209. Townsend TR, Bolyard EA, Yolken RH, et al. Outbreak of coxsackie A1 gastroenteritis: A complication of bone-marrow transplantation. Lancet. 1982;1:820.
210. Kono R. Apollo 11 disease or acute hemorrhagic conjunctivitis: A pandemic of a new enterovirus infection of the eyes. Am J Epidemiol. 1975;101:383.
211. Kono R, Sasagawa A, Ishii K, et al. Pandemic of new type of conjunctivitis. Lancet. 1972;2:1191.
212. Mirkovic RR, Kono R, Yin-Murphy M, et al. Enterovirus type 70: The etiologic agent of pandemic acute hemorrhagic conjunctivitis. Bull World Health Organ. 1973;49:341.
213. Mirkovic RR, Schmidt NJ, Yin-Murphy M, et al. Enterovirus etiology of the 1970 Singapore epidemic of acute conjunctivitis. Intervirology. 1974;4:119.
214. Yin-Murphy M, Lim KH. Picornavirus epidemic conjunctivitis Singapore. Lancet. 1972;2:857.
215. Yin-Murphy M, Lim KH, Yo YM. A coxsackievirus type A24 epidemic of acute conjunctivitis. Southeast Asian J Trop Med Public Health. 1976;7:1.
216. Higgins PG, Scott RJ, Davies PM, et al. A comparative study of viruses associated with acute hemorrhagic conjunctivitis. J Clin Pathol. 1974;27:292.
217. Christopher S, Theogaraj S, Godbole S, et al. An epidemic of acute hemorrhagic conjunctivitis due to coxsackievirus A24. J Infect Dis. 1982;146:16–19.
218. Ray I, Roy IS, Sarkhar JK, et al. Laboratory investigations of an epidemic of conjunctivitis in Calcutta: A preliminary report. Bull Calcutta Sch Trop Med. 1972;20:1.
219. Kono R, Miyamura K, Tajiri E, et al. Neurologic complications associated with acute hemorrhagic conjunctivitis virus infection and its serologic confirmation. J Infect Dis. 1974;129:590.
220. Sklar VE, Patriarca PA, Onorato IM, et al. Clinical findings and results of treatment in an outbreak of acute hemorrhagic conjunctivitis in southern Florida. Am J Ophthalmol. 1983;95:45.
221. Kuritsky JN, Weaver JH, Bernard KW, et al. An outbreak of acute hemorrhagic conjunctivitis in central Minnesota. Am J Ophthalmol. 1983;96:449–452.
222. Centers for Disease Control. Acute hemorrhagic conjunctivitis caused by coxsackievirus A24—Caribbean. MMWR Morb Mortal Wkly Rep. 1987;36:245–251.
223. Centers for Disease Control. Acute hemorrhagic conjunctivitis caused by coxsackievirus A24 variant—Puerto Rico. MMWR Morb Mortal Wkly Rep. 1988;37:123–124.
224. Hierholzer JC, Hilliard KA, Esposito JJ. Serosurvey for "acute hemorrhagic conjunctivitis" virus (enterovirus 70) antibodies in the southeastern United States, with review of the literature and some epidemiologic implications. Am J Epidemiol. 1975;102:533.
225. Miyamura K, Yamazaki S, Tajiri E, et al. Growth characteristics of acute hemorrhagic conjunctivitis (AHC) virus in monkey kidney cells. Intervirology.1974;4:279.
226. Stanton GJ, Langford MP, Baron S. Effect of interferon, elevated temperature, and cell type on replication of acute hemorrhagic conjunctivitis viruses. Infect Immun. 1977;18:370.
227. Goh KT, Doraisingham S, Yin-Murphy M. An epidemic of acute conjunctivitis caused by enterovirus-70 in Singapore in 1980. Southeast Asian J Trop Med Public Health. 1981;12:473.
228. Arnow PM, Hierholzer JC, Higbee J, et al. Acute hemorrhagic conjunctivitis: A mixed virus outbreak among Vietnamese refugees on Guam. Am J Epidemiol. 1977;105:69.
229. Onorato IM, Morens DM, Schonberger LB, et al. Acute hemorrhagic conjunctivitis caused by enterovirus type 70: An epidemic in American Samoa. Am J Trop Med Hyg. 1985;34:984–991.
230. Kono R, Sasagawa A, Miyamura K, et al. Serologic characterization and seroepidemiologic studies on acute hemorrhagic conjunctivitis (AHC) virus. Am J Epidemiol. 1975;101:444.
231. Kono R, Uchida Y. Acute hemorrhagic conjunctivitis. Ophthalmol Dig. 1977;39:14.
232. Kono R, Sasagawa A, Yamazaki S. Seroepidemiologic studies of acute hemorrhagic conjunctivitis virus (enterovirus type 70) in West Africa: III. Studies with animal sera from Ghana and Senegal. Am J Epidemiol. 1981;114:362.
233. Kono R, Miyamura K, Tajiri E, et al. Virological and serological studies of neurological complications of acute hemorrhagic conjunctivitis in Thailand. J Infect Dis. 1977;135:706.
234. Hung TS, Sung SM, Liang HC, et al. Radiculomyelitis following acute hemorrhagic conjunctivitis. Brain. 1976;99:771.
235. Wadia NH, Katrak SM, Misra VP, et al. Polio-like motor paralysis associated with acute hemorrhagic conjunctivitis in an outbreak in 1981 in Bombay. J Infect Dis. 1983;147:660.
236. Katiyar BC, Misra S, Singh RB, et al. Adult Polio-like syndrome following enterovirus 70 conjunctivitis (natural history of the disease). Acta Neurol Scand. 1983;67:263–274.
237. Kono R, Uchida N, Sasagawa A, et al. Neurovirulence of acute hemorrhagic conjunctivitis virus in monkeys. Lancet. 1973;1:61.
238. Yin-Murphy M. Simple tests for the diagnosis of picornavirus epidemic conjunctivitis (acute haemorrhagic conjunctivitis). Bull World Health Organ. 1976;54:675.
239. Ramos-Alverez M, Olarte J. Diarrheal diseases of children. Am J Dis Child. 1964;107:218.
240. Yow DM, Melnick JL, Blattner JR, et al. Enteroviruses in infantile diarrhea. Am J Hyg. 1963;77:283.
241. Steinhoff MC. Viruses and diarrhea—a review. Am J Dis Child. 1978;132:302.
242. Patel JR, Daniel J, Mathan VI. An epidemic of acute diarrhoea in rural southern India associated with echovirus type 11 infection. J Hyg. 1985;95:483–492.
243. Oregan S, Robitaille P, Mongeau J, et al. The hemolytic-uremic syndrome associated with echo 22 infection. Clin Pediatr (Phila). 1980;19:125.
244. Ray CG, Tucker VL, Harris DJ, et al. Enteroviruses associated with the hemolytic-uremic syndrome. Pediatrics. 1970;46:378.
245. Glasgow LA, Balduzzi P. Isolation of coxsackie virus group A, type 4, from a patient with hemolytic-uremic syndrome. N Engl. J Med. 1965;273:754.
246. Aronson MD, Phillips CA. Coxsackievirus B5 infections in acute oliguric renal failure. J Infect Dis. 1975;132:303.
247. Fukuyama Y, Ando T, Yokota J. Acute fulminant myoglobinuric polymyositis with picornavirus-like crystals. J Neurol Neurosurg Psychiatry. 1977;40:775.

248. Gyorkey F, Cabral GA, Gorkey PK, et al. Coxsackievirus aggregates in muscle cells of polymyositis patient. Intervirology. 1978;10:69.
249. Schiraldi O, Iandolo E. Polymyositis accompanying coxsackie virus B2 infection. Infection. 1978;6:32.
250. Josselson J, Pula T, Sadler JH. Acute rhabdomyolysis associated with echovirus 9 infection. Arch Intern Med. 1980;140:1671.
251. Jehn UW, Fink MW. Myositis, myoglobinemia, and myoglobinuria associated with enterovirus echo 9 infection. Arch Neurol. 1980;33:457.
252. Bowles NE, Dubowitz V, Sewry CA, Archard LC. Dermatomyositis, polymyositis, and coxsackie-B-virus infection. Lancet. 1987;1:1004–1007.
253. Kuroda Y, Neshige R, Oda K, et al. Chronic polymyositis: Presence of coxsackievirus A9 antigen in muscle. Jpn J Med. 1986;25:191–194.
254. De Renck J, De Coster W, Inderadjaja N. Acute viral polymyositis with predominant diaphragm involvement. J Neurol Sci. 1977;33:453.
255. Lansky LL, Krugman S, Huq G. Anicteric coxsackie B hepatitis. J Pediatr. 1979;94:64.
256. Leggiadro RJ, Chwatsky DN, Zucker SW. Echovirus 3 infection associated with anicteric hepatitis. Am J Dis Child. 1982;136:744.
257. O'Shaughnessey WJ, Buechner HA. Hepatitis associated with a coxsackie B5 virus infection during late pregnancy. JAMA. 1962;179:71.
258. Morris JA, Elisberg BL, Pond WL, et al. Hepatitis associated with coxsackie virus group A, type 4. N Engl J Med. 1962;267:1230.
259. Sun NC, Smith VM. Hepatitis associated with myocarditis: Unusual manifestation of infection with coxsackie virus group B, type 3. N Engl J Med. 1966;274:190.
260. Gregor GR, Geller SA, Walker GF, et al. Coxsackie hepatitis in an adult with ultrastructural demonstration of the virus. Mt Sinai J Med. 1975;42:575.
261. Ursing B. Acute pancreatitis in coxsackie B infection. BMJ. 1973;3:524.
262. Craighead JE. The role of viruses in the pathogenesis of pancreatic disease and diabetes mellitus. Prog Med Virol. 1975;19:162.
263. Arnesjo B, Eden T, Ihse I, et al. Enterovirus infections in acute pancreatitis—a possible etiologic connection. Scand J Gastroenterol. 1976;11:645.
264. Imrle CW, Ferguson JC, Sommerville RG. Coxsackie and mumps virus infection in a prospective study of acute pancreatitis. Gut. 1977;18:53.
265. Craighead JE, Mahoney EM, Carver DH, et al. Orchitis due to coxsackie virus group B, type 5. N Engl J Med. 1962;267:498.
266. Welliver RC, Cherry JD. Aseptic meningitis and orchitis associated with echovirus 6 infection. J Pediatr. 1978;92:239.
267. Ager EA, Felsenstein WC, Alexander ER, et al. An epidemic of illness due to coxsackie virus group B, type 2. JAMA. 1964;187:251.
268. Willems WR, Hornig C, Bauer H, et al. A case of coxsackie A9 virus infection with orchitis. J Med Virol. 1978;3:137–140.
269. Murphy AM, Simmul R. Coxsackie B4 virus infections in New South Wales during 1962. Med J Aust. 1964;2:443.
270. Blotzer JW, Myers AR. Echovirus associated polyarthritis. Report of a case with synovial fluid and synovial histologic characterization. Arthritis Rheum. 1978;21:978.
271. Kujala G, Newman JH. Isolation of echovirus type 11 from synovial fluid in acute monocytic arthritis. Arthritis Rheum. 1985;28:98–99.
272. Van der Sar A. Acute infectious lymphocytosis with echovirus type 25. West Indian Med J. 1979;28:185.
273. Norwitz MS, Moore GT. Acute infectious lymphocytosis: An etiologic study of an outbreak. N Engl J Med. 1968;279:399.
274. Barrett-Connor E. Is insulin-dependent diabetes mellitus caused by coxsackievirus B infection? A review of the epidemiologic evidence. Rev Infect Dis. 1985;7:207–215.
275. Yoon JW. The role of viruses and environmental factors in the induction of diabetes. Curr Top Microbiol Immunol. 1990;164:95–123.
276. Craighead JE, Huber SA, Sriram S. Animal models of picornavirus-induced autoimmune disease: Their possible relevance to human disease. Lab Invest. 1990;63:432–446.
277. Banatvala JE. Insulin-dependent (juvenile-onset, type 1) diabetes mellitus coxsackie B viruses revisited. Prog Med Virol. 1987;34:33–54.
278. Rewers M, Atkinson M. The possible role of enteroviruses in diabetes mellitus. In: Rotbart HA, ed. Human Enterovirus Infections. Washington, DC: American Society for Microbiology; 1995:353–385.
279. Gleason RE, Kahn CB, Funk IB, Craighead JE. Seasonal incidence of insulin-dependent diabetes in Massachusetts, 1964–1973. Int J Epidemiol. 1982;11:39–45.
280. Gamble DR, Taylor KW. Seasonal incidence of diabetes mellitus. BMJ. 1969;3:631–633.
281. Huff JC, Hierholzer JC, Farris WA. An "outbreak" of juvenile diabetes mellitus: Consideration of a viral etiology. Am J Epidemiol. 1974;100:277–287.
282. Rewers M, LaPorte R, Walczak M, et al. Apparent epidemic of insulin-dependent diabetes mellitus in midwestern Poland. Diabetes. 1987;36:106–113.
283. Hierholzer JC, Farris WA. Follow-up of children infected in a coxsackievirus B3 and B4 outbreak: No evidence of diabetes mellitus. J Infect Dis. 1974;129:741–746.
284. Dippe SE, Bennett PH, Miller M, et al. Lack of causal association between coxsackie B4 virus infection and diabetes. Lancet. 1975;1:1314–1317.
285. Hartig PC, Madge GE, Webb SR. Diversity within a human isolate of coxsackie B4: Relationship to viral-induced diabetes mellitus. J Med Virol. 1983;11:23–30.
286. Clements GB, Galbraith DN, Taylor KW. Coxsackie B virus infection and onset of childhood diabetes. Lancet. 1995;346:221–223.
287. Andreoletti L, Hober D, Hober-Vandenberghe C, et al. Detection of coxsackie B virus RNA sequences in whole blood samples from adult patients at the onset of type I diabetes mellitus. J Med Virol. 1997;52:121–127.
288. Yoon JW, Austin M, Onodera T, Notkins AL. Virus-induced diabetes mellitus: Isolation of a virus from the pancreas of a child with diabetic ketoacidosis. N Engl J Med. 1979;300:1173–1179.
289. Gladish R, Hofmann W, Waldherr R. Myocarditis and insulitis in coxsackievirus infection. Z Kardiol. 1976;65:835–849.
290. Helfand RF, Gary HE Jr, Freeman CY, et al. Serologic evidence of an association between enteroviruses and onset of type 1 diabetes mellitus. J Infect Dis. 1995;172:1206–1211.
291. D'Alessio DJ. A case-control study of group B coxsackievirus immunoglobulin M antibody prevalence and HLA-DR antigens in newly diagnosed cases of insulin-dependent diabetes mellitus. Am J Epidemiol. 1992;135:1331–1338.
292. Gamble DR, Cumming H. Coxsackie B virus and juvenile-onset diabetes. Lancet. 1985;2:455–456.
293. Tuvemo T, Dahlquist G, Frisk G, et al. The Swedish childhood diabetes study. III. IgM against coxsackie B viruses in newly diagnosed type 1 (insulin-dependent) diabetic children—no evidence of increased antibody frequency. Diabetologia. 1989;32:745–747.
294. Frisk G, Fohlman J, Kobbah M, et al. High frequency of coxsackie-B-virus specific IgM in children developing type I diabetes during a period of high diabetes morbidity. J Med Virol. 1985;17:219–227.
295. Oldstone MBA. Molecular mimicry and autoimmune disease. Cell. 1987;50:819–820.
296. See DM, Tilles JG. Pathogenesis of virus-induced diabetes in mice. J Infect Dis. 1995;171:1131–1138.
297. Hiltunen M, Hyoty H, Knip M, et al. Islet cell antibody seroconversion in children is temporally associated with enterovirus infections. J Infect Dis. 1997;175:554–560.
298. Solimena M, De Camilli P. Coxsackieviruses and diabetes. Nat Med. 1995;1:25–26.
299. Rosen L, Schmidt NJ, Kern J. Toluca-1, a newly recognized enterovirus. Arch Ges Virusforsch. 1973;40:132.
300. Schieble JH, Fox VL, Lennette EH. A probable new human picornavirus associated with respiratory disease. Am J Epidemiol. 1967;85:297.
301. Schmidt NJ, Lennette EH, Ho HH. An apparently new enterovirus isolated from patients with disease of the central nervous system. J Infect Dis. 1974;129:304.
302. Chonmaitree T, Menegus MA, Schervish-Swierkosz EM, et al. Enterovirus 71 infection: Report of an outbreak with two cases of paralysis and a review of the literature. Pediatrics. 1981;67:489.
303. Samuda GM, Chang WK, Yeung CY, et al. Monoplegia caused by enterovirus 71:An outbreak in Hong Kong. Pediatr Infect Dis J. 1987;6:206–208.
304. Centers for Disease Control. Case of paralytic illness associated with enterovirus 71 infection. MMWR Morb Mortal Wkly Rep. 1988;37:108.
305. Hashimoto I, Hagiwara A, Kodama H. Neurovirulence in cynomolgus monkeys of enterovirus 71 isolated from a patient with hand, foot, and mouth disease. Arch Virol. 1978;56:257.
306. Hagiwara A, Yoneyama T, Takami S, et al. Genetic and phenotypic characteristics of enterovirus 71 isolates from patients with encephalitis and with hand, foot, and mouth disease. Arch Virol. 1984;79:273–283.
307. Melnick JL, Schmidt NJ, Minkovic RR, et al. Identification of Bulgarian strain 258 of enterovirus 71. Intervirology. 1980;12:297.
308. Deibel R, Gross L, Collins DN. Isolation of a new enterovirus. Proc Soc Exp Biol Med. 1975;148:203.
309. Kennett ML, Birch CJ, Lewis FA, et al. Enterovirus type 71 infection in Melbourne. Bull World Health Organ. 1974;51:609.
310. Tagaya I, Takayama R, Hagiwara A. A large-scale epidemic of hand, foot and mouth disease associated with enterovirus 71 infection in Japan in 1978. Jpn J Med Sci Biol. 1981;34:191.
311. Miwa C, Ohtani M, Watanabe H, et al. Epidemic of hand, foot and mouth disease in Gifu prefecture in 1978. Jpn J Med Sci Biol. 1980;33:167.
312. Hagiwara A, Tagaya I, Yoneyama T. Epidemic of hand, foot, and mouth disease associated with enterovirus 71 infection. Intervirology. 1978;9:60.
313. Bloomberg J, Lycke E, Ahlfors K, et al. New enterovirus type associated with epidemic of aseptic meningitis and/or hand, foot, and mouth disease. Lancet. 1974;2:122.
314. Moses EB, Narian JP, Hatch MH, et al. Isolation of echovirus type 11 and enterovirus type 71 in a day care winter outbreak. J Ark Med Soc. 1987;83:469–471.
315. Sohier R. Enterovirus type 71 surveillance: France. World Health Organ Wkly Epidemiol Rec. 1979;54:219.
316. Nagy G, Takatsy S, Kukan E, et al. Virological diagnosis of enterovirus type 71 infections: Experiences gained during an epidemic of acute CNS diseases in Hungary in 1978. Arch Virol. 1982;71:217.
317. Ishimaru Y, Nakano S, Yamaoka K, Takami S. Outbreaks of hand, foot, and mouth disease by enterovirus 71: High incidence of complication disorders of central nervous system. Arch Dis Child. 1980;55:583.
318. Chumakov MP, Voroshilova MK, Shindarov L, et al. Enterovirus 71 isolated from cases of poliomyelitis-like disease in Bulgaria. Arch Virol. 1979;60:329.

Chapter 161

Hepatitis A Virus

STEPHEN M. FEINSTONE
IAN D. GUST

Hepatitis A is generally an acute, self-limiting infection of the liver by an enterically transmitted picornavirus, hepatitis A virus (HAV). Infection may be asymptomatic or result in acute hepatitis. Rarely, fulminant hepatitis can ensue. Although the duration and severity of symptoms vary widely, hepatitis A infections never cause chronic liver disease.

HISTORY

The earliest accounts of contagious jaundice are found in ancient China.[1] Although the symptoms that were described are similar to those currently found in people with hepatitis A, it should be remembered that a number of other infections produce similar symptoms. The earliest outbreaks of hepatitis that were almost certainly hepatitis A were documented in Europe in the 17th and 18th centuries, especially during periods of war. From 1855, the disease became known as "catarrhal jaundice" because the pathologists Bamberger and Virchow believed that the disease was caused by blockage of the common bile duct by a plug of inspissated mucus.[2] The first suggestion that the disease was caused by an infectious agent was made by McDonald, who unable to demonstrate the involvement of enteric bacteria, suggested that the infection might be caused by a virus.[3] Shortly thereafter, Cockayne proposed that the sporadic and the epidemic forms of jaundice were manifestations of the same disease.[4] In 1923, Blumer analyzed a large number of epidemics of hepatitis in the United States and identified its predilection for young adults and children and peak incidence in winter and fall.[5] The first indication of the existence of a second form of hepatitis came in 1833, when an outbreak of hepatitis was observed in shipyard workers who were vaccinated against smallpox with a particular batch of human glycerinated lymph.[6] The disease, which became known as "serum hepatitis," was assumed to be due to a blood-borne infectious agent. During the 1920s and 1930s, other outbreaks that appeared to be associated with the administration of serum or blood were described.[7]

Analysis of epidemics of hepatitis during World War II confirmed the existence of two epidemiologically and etiologically distinct forms of the disease that MacCallum called infectious hepatitis and serum hepatitis.[8–10] Experimental transmission studies in volunteers soon clarified the major features of the two diseases. Hepatitis A had an incubation period of between 15 and 49 days and was transmitted by the fecal-oral route.[9, 11, 12] Later studies demonstrated that the virus could be detected in feces or blood during the acute infection, that infection could be transmitted experimentally by both the oral and parenteral routes, and that infection was followed by long-term immunity and could be prevented by prior administration of normal human immune globulin (IG).[5, 8, 13] In addition, the disease was shown to be associated with a filterable agent resistant to heating at 56°C for 30 minutes and resistant to diethyl ether. In the 1950s and 1960s, Krugman and colleagues expanded these observations by a series of studies in human volunteers that further defined the incubation period, period of infectivity, and period of viremia, and they developed standardized reagents representing hepatitis A and hepatitis B.[14] In 1973, Feinstone and colleagues detected 27-nm virus-like particles in the stools of volunteers infected with hepatitis A and demonstrated that they were aggregated by convalescent but not by preinfection serum, thus indicating that the particles represented the etiologic agent of the disease.[15] The identification of HAV, transmission of the disease to marmosets and chimpanzees, propagation of HAV in cell culture, and molecular cloning of the viral genome ushered in a new era of research that culminated almost 2 decades later in the development and licensing of effective vaccines.[16–22]

CLASSIFICATION AND PHYSICOCHEMICAL AND BIOLOGIC PROPERTIES OF HEPATITIS A VIRUS

HAV is a member of the Picornaviridae family, which includes the enteroviruses and rhinoviruses of humans, as well as the apthoviruses (foot-and-mouth disease viruses) of hoofed animals and cardioviruses (encephalomyocarditis virus) of mice. Although originally classified as Enterovirus type 72,[23, 24] HAV now has its own genus, Heparnavirus, within the Picornaviridae family.[25]

Structure

HAV is a 27- to 28-nm spherical, nonenveloped virus[15] (Fig. 161–1) with a surface structure suggesting icosahedral symmetry[26] (Table 161–1).

Purification of virus from clinical samples or tissue culture yields three distinct populations of particles[27]: mature hepatitis A virus virions that band at 1.32 to 1.34 g/cm^3 in CsCl and sediment at approximately 160 S (similar to enteroviruses and cardioviruses), a lower-density fraction that bands at about 1.27 g/cm^3 in CsCl and sediments at 70 to 80 S and may represent empty capsids or particles with incomplete genomes (see Table 161–1), and a high-density fraction (1.4 g/cm^3) that may represent particles with a more open virion structure that allows increased penetration and binding of CsCl to the viral particle.[28] These high-density particles have been shown to contain RNA but tend to be less stable than mature virions.[29–31]

Resistance to Physical and Chemical Agents

HAV is more resistant to heat than other picornaviruses are.[32] It is stable after incubation at 56°C, will remain viable for many years if stored at −20°C, and even in a dried form at room temperature, maintains its infectivity for several weeks.[33] The virus is destroyed by boiling for 5 minutes, whereas incubation at 60°C for 10 to 12 hours results in only partial inactivation. In experiments evaluating HAV infectivity in susceptible cells, complete inactivation was observed after 4 minutes at 70°C, after 5 seconds at 80°C, and virtually instantly at 85°C (see Table 161–1). Outbreaks of hepatitis A have been reported after the ingestion of partially cooked shellfish, which suggests that steaming may be insufficient to destroy the virus.[34, 35] Infectivity has been detected for days to months in live oysters, waste water, freshwater, seawater, soil, or marine sediment.[36] The ability of the virus to survive relatively high temperatures and solvent inactivation highlights the need for meticulous care when handling feces in the hospital or laboratory setting and for disinfection of potentially contaminated surfaces.

HAV is stable at pH 3 for 3 hours at room temperature and resistant to diethyl ether, chloroform, and up to 50% trichlorotrifluoroethane.[37–39] This property is useful in preparing bacteria-free inocula for cell culture.

HAV can be inactivated by autoclaving (121°C for 30 minutes) and exposure to chlorine (15 minutes at concentrations of 1.5 to 2.5 mg/liter).[40] Although chlorine is the most commonly used agent for water decontamination, iodine (3 mg/liter for 5 minutes) and potassium permanganate (30 mg/liter for 5 minutes) are probably also effective. HAV is also inactivated by high dilutions of formalin (1:4000 for 72 hours at 37°C or 3% for 5 minutes at 25°C) or by ultraviolet irradiation (ultraviolet at 1.1 W at a depth of 0.9 cm for 60 seconds and especially ultraviolet irradiation at 60°C).[39] As a

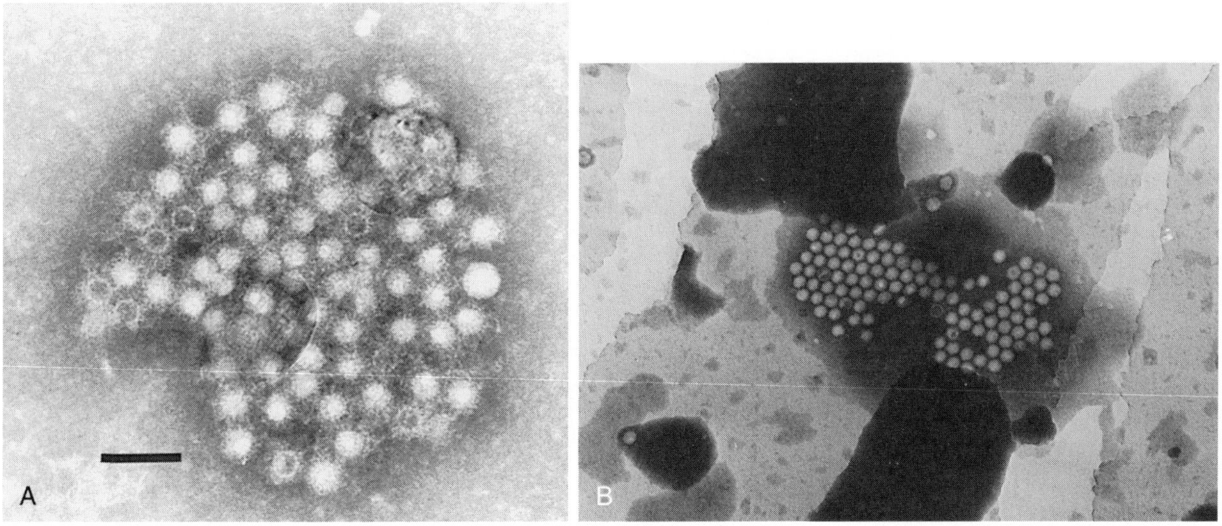

FIGURE 161–1. Electron micrographs of hepatitis A virus particles *(A)* aggregated by antibody, 27–28 nm in diameter; *B,* highly concentrated, purified hepatitis A virus from human feces.

result of several outbreaks of hepatitis A in hemophiliacs who received factor VIII that had been treated by a solvent detergent method for inactivation of lipid-enveloped viruses, interest has focused on techniques capable of inactivating nonenveloped viruses without compromising the biologic activity of the proteins of interest.[41] Currently, the most promising techniques are dry heat (80°C for 24 hours), ultraviolet irradiation (>0.1 J/cm^2), or γ-irradiation (25 kCi).[42, 43]

Hepatitis A Genome and Proteins

The first evidence that the HAV genome consisted of RNA was provided by Provost and colleagues, who showed that purified virus stained orange-red with acridine orange.[39] Consistent with this evidence was the fact that HAV particles and antigen were found exclusively in the cytoplasm of infected cells.[44] The RNA nature of the genome was confirmed by others using enzymatic technologies.[21, 45] Molecular cloning and sequence analysis demonstrated that the HAV genome is composed of single-stranded, positive-sense linear RNA of 7478 nucleotides (strain HM175) and a molecular weight of approximately 2.25×10^6, which is similar to the genomes of other picornaviruses.[46, 47] Sequence analysis also revealed that the HAV genome has a structure and gene order similar to that of other picornaviruses. However, some differences in detail place HAV into its own genus.

As in other picornaviruses, the 5′ end of the genome does not have a cap structure but instead has a small, covalently bound protein termed VPg.[48] The nucleotide sequence of the HAV genome begins at the 5′ end with the UU typical of picornaviruses, followed by an additional 732 bases before the AUG translation start codon[47] (Fig. 161–2). This AUG codon begins a single long open reading frame of 6681 nucleotides that encodes a polyprotein 2227 amino acid residues in length. The coding region of picornaviruses has been arbitrarily divided into three parts termed P1, P2, and P3, and the peptides that are ultimately cleaved from the translation products of these regions are referred to as 1A, 1B, 1C, 2A, 2B, 2C, and so forth, in order of translation from the 5′ to the 3′ end of the genome.[49] The HAV genome ends with a 3′ noncoding region of 63 nucleotides that is followed by a poly(A) tail. The four capsid proteins are coded by the first 2373 nucleotides (P1) and the nonstructural proteins by the remainder (P2 and P3).

HAV is composed of four capsid polypeptides as detected first by sodium dodecyl sulfate–polyacrylamide gel electrophoresis and by molecular cloning and nucleic acid sequencing. By analogy with other picornaviruses, these proteins, which are coded within the P1 (see earlier) region, are referred to as virion proteins (VP): VP1 = peptide 1D (molecular weight 32,800 Da), VP2 = 1B (24,800 Da), VP3 = 1C (27,300 Da), and VP4 = 1A (2500 Da).[50–53] In addition, a polypeptide with a molecular weight of approximately 40,000 Da has been described and is thought to represent a precursor to VP1 that is a fusion between the 1D peptide and the 2A peptide.[54] A VP0 peptide that is the precursor to VP4 and VP2 can also be detected, especially in immature virions.[55] The predicted VP4 molecule has never been experimentally determined to be within the virion particle and, at just 23 amino acids, is about one third the size of the VP4 proteins of other picornaviruses.

TABLE 161–1 Major Features of Hepatitis A Virus

Virion	Nonenveloped (naked), spherical particles, surface structure suggesting icosahedral symmetry
Diameter	27–28 nm
Nucleic acid	Single-stranded linear RNA, positive polarity, 7478 nucleotides (strain HM 175)
Molecular weight	Approximately 2.25×10^6
Density in CsCl	Mature: 1.32 to 1.34 g/cm^3 Empty capsids, particles with incomplete genome: 1.27 g/cm^3 Less stable particles with a more open virion structure: 1.4 g/cm^3
Proteins	VP1 (MW, 32,800), VP2 (24,800), VP3 (27,300), VP4 (2500); VPO, precursor to VP4 and VP2

Stability Condition	Stable	Reduction of Infectivity	Complete Inactivation
Heat	56°C for 30 min Room temp for 1 wk 25°C for 30 d (in dried feces)	60°C for 12 h	70°C for 4 min 80°C for 5 sec 85°C for 1 sec Autoclaving, 121°C for 30 min
Acid	pH 3, room temp, 3 h		
Solvents	Ether, chloroform, Freon		
UV			1.1 W, 0.9 cm, 1 min
Formalin		1 : 350, room temp, 60 min	1 : 4000, 37°C, 72 h
Chlorine		0.5–1.0 mg HOCl/L, 60 min	1.5–2.5 mg HOCl/L, 15 min

Abbreviation: VP, Virion protein.

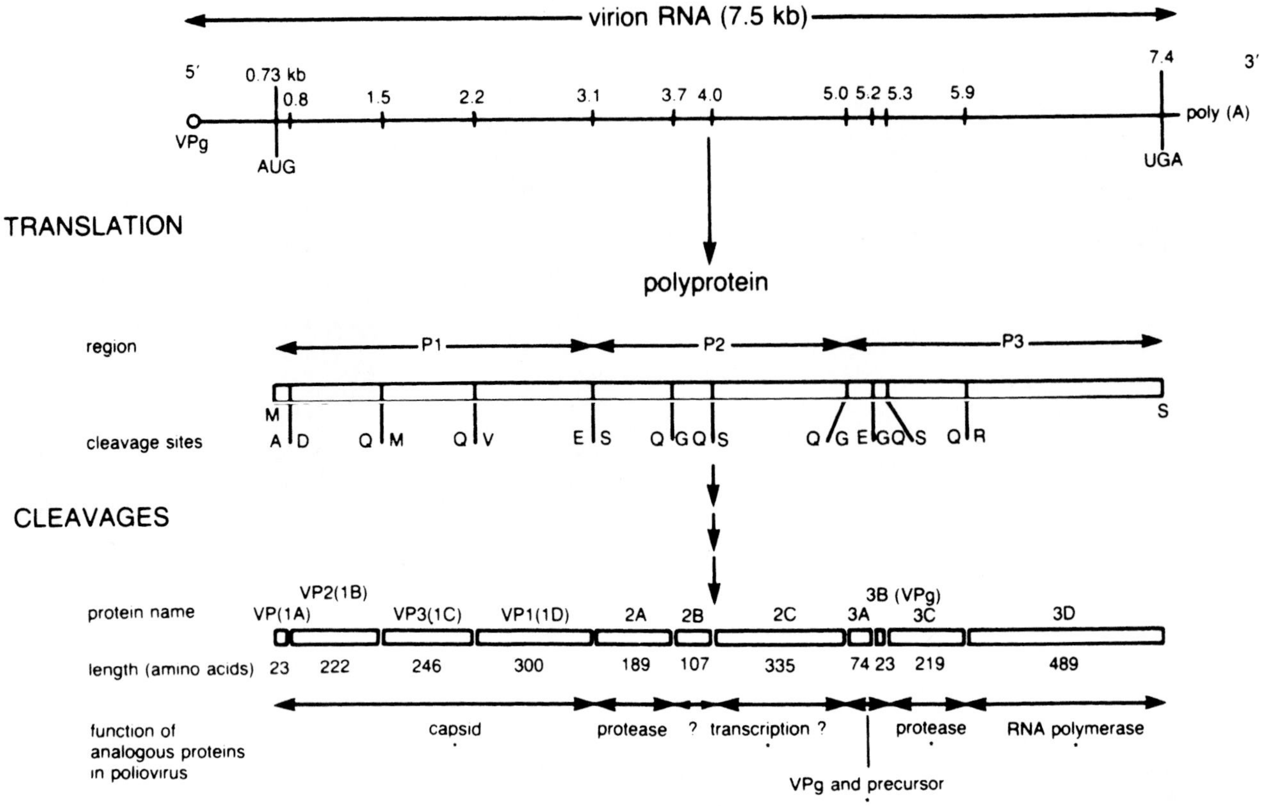

FIGURE 161–2. Organization of the RNA genome of hepatitis A virus and protein cleavage. Covalently attached VPg protein (5′ end; *top*) start codons at 0.73 kb, gene start/end positions (small vertical marks and stop codons at 7.4 kb), and poly(A) at the 3′ terminus. Hepatitis A virus RNA is probably translated *(large vertical arrow)* into a precursor polyprotein *(middle)* that is cleaved by viral proteases in several steps *(small vertical arrows)* to generate mature proteins. Regions of the polyprotein are indicated according to standard nomenclature, as are predicted residues at the amino and carboxy termini of mature proteins. Names, lengths, and proposed functions in poliovirus are indicated in the lower diagram along with hepatitis A virus proteins. Hepatitis A virus is composed of four capsid polypeptides that are coded within the P1 region. These proteins are referred to as virion proteins (VP1, VP2, VP3, and VP4). Nonstructural proteins are coded within the P2 and P3 region. *Abbreviations:* A, Alanine; D, aspartate; E, glutamate; G, glycine; M, methionine; Q, glutamine; R, arginine; S, serine; V, Valine. (From Ticehurst JR. Hepatitis A virus: Clones, cultures, and vaccines. Semin Liver Dis. 1986;6:46.)

Antigenic Composition

Although a variety of genotypes of HAV have been identified by analysis of genome sequences (Fig. 161–3), there appears to be only one serotype.[56–58] This view is supported by the observation that immune serum globulin prepared in developed countries and monovalent vaccines prepared from strains originating in Australia, Central America, or Europe protect travelers from disease equally well irrespective of their destination.

Neutralization sites for HAV are located primarily on the structural proteins VP1 and VP3, with possibly a minor contribution from VP2.[56, 58] The binding characteristics of eight neutralizing monoclonal antibodies have been analyzed by competition assays. These antibodies seemed to recognize epitopes within a closely related antigenic site.[57]

Although many strains of HAV have been described on the basis of different growth characteristics, nucleotide sequence, or geographic origin,[59, 60] strain HM175 is the most widely used laboratory strain and has the widest range of cell culture–adapted variants.[20]

Polyclonal and monoclonal antibodies directed against the major antigenic determinant appear to be capable of detecting strains of HAV isolated in different parts of the world, thus confirming the presence of only one major serotype.[56–58] Comparison of nucleic acid sequences in the region around the VP1/2A junction (Fig. 161–3) from viruses isolated in different parts of the world indicates that HAV strains can be differentiated into four genotypes (I, II, III, and VII). Three additional types (IV, V, and VI) have been identified in monkeys and may be viruses of simian origin.[57, 61–63] Strains recovered from patients in the United States were closely related to each other, whereas viruses recovered in Western Europe belonged to three genotypes, thus suggesting importation from other geographic regions.[47, 64] Although individual strains of HAV have differences at the molecular level that may be useful for epidemiologic studies, a high degree of identity in nucleic acid (up to 90%) and amino acid sequence (up to 98%) is generally seen between strains.[65]

Biology of Hepatitis A Virus in Cell Culture

HAV was first propagated in marmoset liver explant cultures and a cloned line of fetal rhesus monkey kidney cells (FRhK-6) with a strain of virus (CR326) that had been adapted by multiple passages in *Saguinus mystax* and *Saguinus labiatus* marmosets.[18] Many HAV strains have subsequently been isolated from clinical material, although the procedure may take several weeks. Until recently, only epithelial or fibroblast cells of primate origin have been shown to support growth of the virus.[19, 20, 66] However, in a systematic search for cells that would support HAV replication, growth was detected in cells of guinea pig, dolphin, and porcine origin.[67]

The major characteristics of HAV in cell culture are slow growth and low yields relative to other picornaviruses.[68] In addition, the virus remains largely cell associated, does not usually produce a cytopathic effect, and readily leads to persistently infected cell lines.[69] Rapidly replicating variants of HAV have been selected that

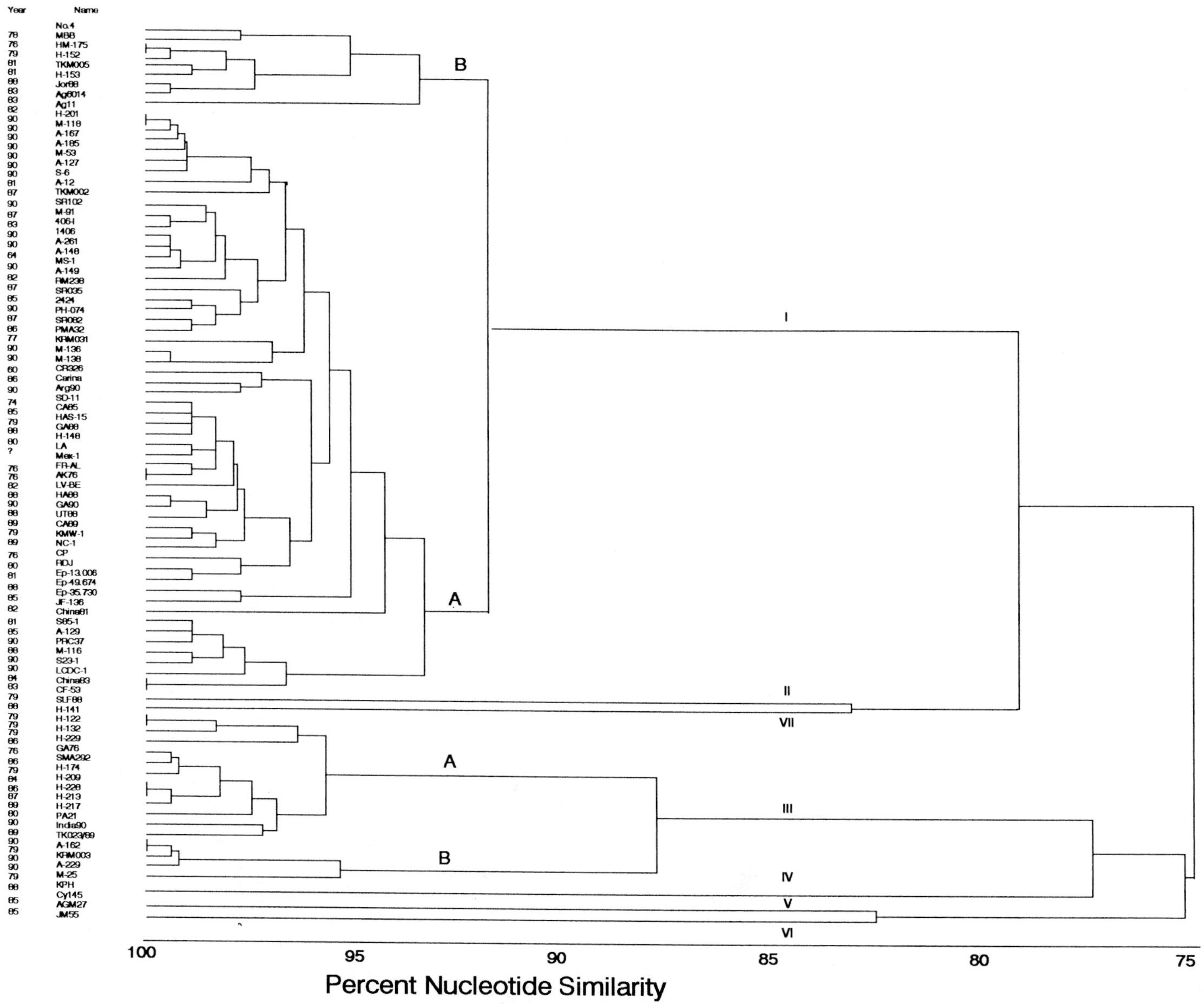

FIGURE 161–3. Relationship among hepatitis A virus strains determined by the sequence of the VP1/2A region. Nucleotide sequence alignments of 92 isolates were compared. The genotypes were divided into groups I–VII and groups I and III were divided into subgroups A and B. (Courtesy of S. M. Lemon, Galveston, Tex.)

induce cytopathic effects in some cell lines; these variants have proved extremely useful for virus titrations and studies of inactivation kinetics.[70, 71]

Although a number of HAV strains have been adapted to cell culture,[59, 60, 72–74] the process is unreliable, so in vitro cultivation has not been used for confirmation of diagnosis in environmental studies. A variety of methods are used for detection and quantitation, including immunofluorescence or immunoperoxidase staining of infected cells, radioimmunoassay or enzyme immunoassay of culture harvests, radioimmunofocus assay, plaque assay using a cytopathic strain of HAV, molecular hybridization assay, and polymerase chain reaction (PCR).[64, 74–76] Studies of the replication of HAV in cell culture revealed that new viral RNA can be detected within 2 to 6 hours and at least 10 virus-specific proteins within 3 to 6 hours of inoculation. The virus appears in the cytoplasm within 12 to 18 hours,[76a] and the amount of hepatitis A antigen increases steadily for 4 days and then declines over the next few weeks. In contrast to the experience with other picornaviruses, no inhibition of host cell macromolecular synthesis has been observed in HAV-infected cell culture systems.[76b, c]

The morphologic changes in cells infected by virus are minimal. Hepatitis A antigen can be detected by appropriate staining and is most prominent in the region surrounding the nucleus. Persistently infected B-SC-1 cells are essentially normal when examined by electron microscopy, except that the cytoplasm is more vacuolated and less dense and contains more lysozyme-like bodies than uninfected cells do.[77]

Repeated passage in cell culture has been used to apply mutation pressure to HAV to alter the phenotype. For example, HAV variants have been selected that grow more rapidly or are resistant to neutralization by monoclonal antibodies.[58, 71, 78, 79] Attenuated strains of HAV have been selected by multiple tissue culture passages, and cold adaptation has been achieved by passage at reduced temperature.[80–82] Some of the mutations responsible for these altered phenotypes have been identified by molecular cloning and sequencing of the mutant. Mutations within the 5′ untranslated region and mutations within the 2B and 2C coding regions of HAV RNA have been shown to enhance virus replication in vitro.[73, 79, 83]

Although evidence of extrahepatic viral replication in humans in tissues other than the liver is sparse, some cells of the gastrointestinal tract are probably susceptible to HAV.[84] Animal studies have demonstrated some evidence of replication in the oropharynx or tonsillar tissue and the upper portion of the small intestine.[84, 85]

Most viruses initiate infection by first binding to a specific cell surface receptor molecule. There had been some suggestion that HAV did not bind to a specific receptor. The virus has a relatively hydrophobic capsid and it is known to nonspecifically adhere to most cells in culture. However, recently the cellular receptor molecule has been identified by Kaplan and colleagues first in cells of simian origin[86] and later in human cells.[87] This molecule is a novel mucin-like class I integral membrane glycoprotein of 451 amino acids. Because this molecule is expressed on cells from many tissues, differential expression of the receptor does not account for the organ tropism of HAV. Further work with this receptor will undoubtedly shed light on some of the unique features of HAV replication.

Host Range

Humans are considered to be the only important reservoir of HAV. However, the existence of extrahuman reservoirs of infection remains possible. In 1961, Hillis described an outbreak of hepatitis A among chimpanzee handlers who apparently contracted the infection from the chimpanzees.[88, 89] Epidemiologic data suggested that the animals had become infected during captivity, but before their importation into the United States. Interestingly, although epidemics of hepatitis were recognized in American primate handlers, the disease was rarely seen in Africa, presumably because most handlers were already immune.

In 1962, Deinhardt and colleagues demonstrated liver function abnormalities in chimpanzees that were inoculated with human feces or acute-phase sera known to have transmitted hepatitis A to humans.[90] In 1967, they inoculated tamarins (*Saguinus nigricollis*) with sera from patients who were judged to have hepatitis A and were able to transmit infection.[91] These results were confirmed in other species of tamarins and later in chimpanzees.[92–95]

Widespread screening of nonhuman primates has revealed antibodies to HAV in chimpanzees, gorillas, orangutans, gibbons, macaques, owl monkeys, pig tail monkeys, rhesus monkeys, and several species of South American tamarin monkeys.[95–98] The presence of antibodies in some species (such as stump-tailed monkeys) at the time of capture may indicate the existence of an animal reservoir of hepatitis A infection or the presence of cross-reactive viruses in nature.[96]

EPIDEMIOLOGY

Surveillance Data for Hepatitis A: Major Patterns of Infection

Hepatitis A has a worldwide distribution and, like other enteric infectious diseases, is typically an infection of childhood that is more common under conditions of crowding and poor hygiene (Table 161–2). The fall in incidence of hepatitis A in developed countries in recent decades (Fig. 161–4) is associated with access to high-quality water and improved facilities for handling and treating human waste.[99, 100] The epidemiology of hepatitis A in many parts of the world is changing rapidly, so data obtained in the 1960s and 1970s may not be valid today.[101] The lowest prevalence of anti-HAV in adults is observed in the relatively closed population of Switzerland and in Scandinavia,[102–104] whereas in the United States, Japan, Australia, and many European countries, some 40 to 70% of the adult population have antibody to HAV.[103, 105–107] Although the age of exposure to hepatitis A has been increasing in the United States, children and young adults remain the primary target[105] (Table 161–3). Virtually all adults living in some areas of the Mediterranean basin, Africa, and many parts of Asia or other developing parts of the world show evidence of past infection.[105, 108–110]

In most countries, underreporting results in a gross underestimate of the incidence of the disease.[100] In 1995, 31,582 cases of hepatitis A were reported in the United States. However, the Centers for Disease Control and Prevention (CDC) estimates that probably at least 94,000 cases and 180,000 infections occurred in that year.[111] The CDC has reported that the number of cases of hepatitis A reported in the United States has been increasing for the 4 years ending with 1995, especially in the western states (Figs. 161–5 and 161–6), although it remains unclear if whether this increase represents better reporting or an actual increase in cases.

Age-Specific Prevalence. Three distinct patterns of age-stratified prevalence of antibody to hepatitis A can be defined in different

TABLE 161–2 Global Patterns of Hepatitis A Virus Transmission

Endemicity	Disease Rate	Peak Age of Infection	Transmission Patterns
High	Low to high	Early childhood	Person to person; outbreaks uncommon
Moderate	High	Late childhood/ young adults	Person to person; foodborne and waterborne outbreaks
Low	Low	Young adults	Person to person; foodborne and waterborne outbreaks
Very low	Very low	Adults	Travelers; outbreaks uncommon

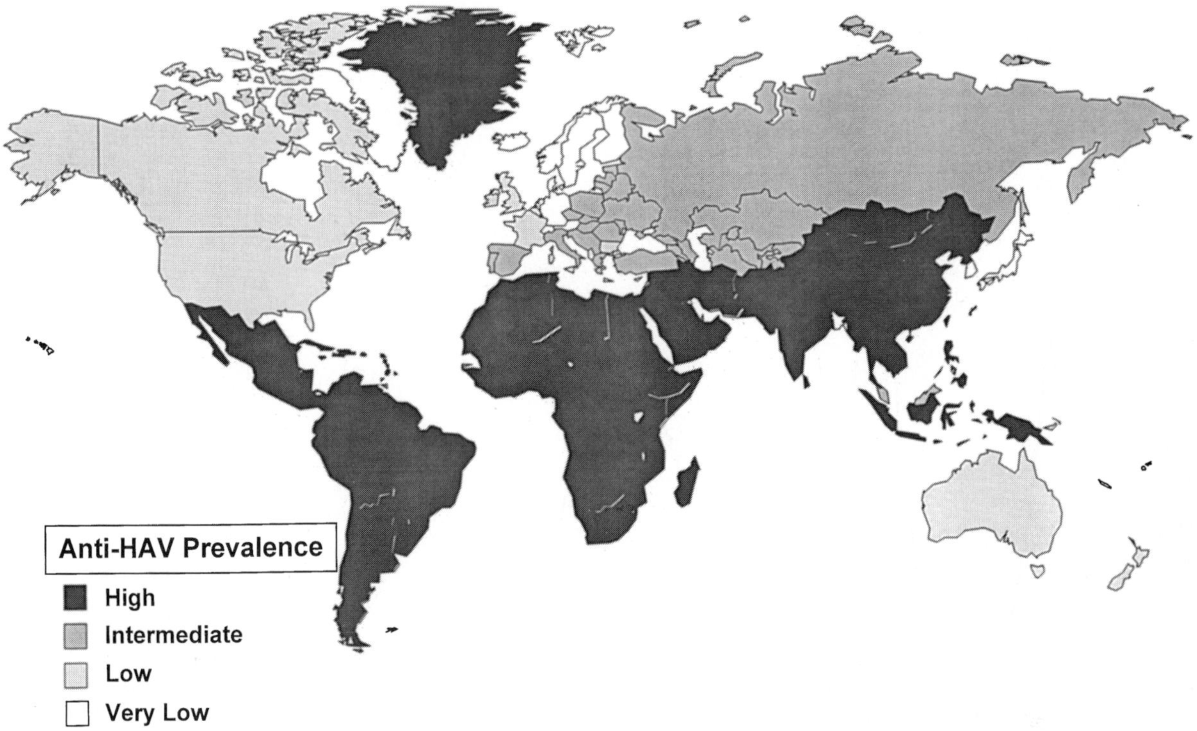

FIGURE 161–4. Endemicity patterns of hepatitis A virus infection generalized by country. Infection patterns may vary significantly within a country. (From Centers for Disease Control and Prevention. MMWR Morb Mortal Wkly Rep. 1996;45:7.)

populations[112] (Fig. 161–7). Pattern A is seen in developing countries where hepatitis A is hyperendemic, and virtually all children are infected while younger than 10 years, but disease is rare.[100] The cases of hepatitis A that are observed in these countries usually occur in visitors such as missionaries, voluntary aid workers, and tourists. In one study, the attack rate among foreign missionaries in Africa was 2% per year, with higher rates in individuals younger than 30 years.[102, 113]

In countries in which steady improvement in hygiene and sanitation has taken place over a number of years, an increase in the mean age of exposure has been observed, as well as a decline in the total rate of infection.[101, 114, 115] In these populations, the age-specific prevalence of anti-HAV has a sigmoidal shape (pattern B). This pattern is seen in Scandinavian countries, Japan, parts of Western Europe, North America, and Australia. In these countries the rate of exposure to HAV is very low in children and increases slowly during early adult life.[116] The relatively high prevalence of antibody in the older population of developed countries is probably due to exposure to the virus during childhood, when the disease was more common.[117] Paradoxically, as living standards improve and the proportion of nonimmune individuals in the adolescent and adult population increases, the incidence of clinical disease may actually rise, and under these circumstances, hepatitis A may become a public health problem.[118, 119]

TABLE 161-3 Age Distribution of Hepatitis A

Age Group	No. of Cases	Rate per 100,000
Total	31,582*	
<5	2,053	10.42
5–14	6,666	17.99
15–24	6,382	18.00
25–44	12,160	14.85
45–64	2,801	5.65
>64	1,042	3.18

*Age not reported = 478.

In 1988, a large epidemic associated with the ingestion of contaminated shellfish occurred in Shanghai, China, where 310,746 cases of hepatitis A were reported between January and May (Table 161–4).[120, 121] Disease was most common in adults between the ages of 20 and 40 years, presumably because the older population was largely immune and clinical disease was uncommon in young children.

The third pattern of age-specific prevalence of anti-HAV (see Fig. 161–7, pattern C) is occasionally seen in closed communities in which an epidemic of hepatitis A has occurred in the past. Lacking any means of maintaining itself, the disease disappears until the virus is subsequently reintroduced. When reintroduction occurs, the resulting outbreak is confined to children born since the previous outbreak and susceptible adults who did not reside in the community at the time.[100, 122–124]

Although it is convenient to think of these patterns as mutually exclusive, in many large countries all three exist in different groups of the population.

Relation of Age and Gender to Infection. Because hepatitis A is enterically transmitted when the virus is present, infections are common in young children.[125] Where overcrowding, lack of clean water, or inadequate systems for removal and treatment of sewage are factors, childhood exposure to HAV is almost universal. Because infection in children is usually mild or inapparent, hepatitis A is not a public health issue other than among tourists or long-term visitors.[126–129] As levels of hygiene and sanitation improve, the mean age of exposure rises.[130] In 1969 and 1970, 49% of patients with hepatitis A in Melbourne, Australia, were younger than 15 years and only 18% were older than 30. By 1975, although the incidence of the disease had declined, the major burden had shifted to young adults, with 61% of cases being in the 15- to 29-year-old age group.[130]

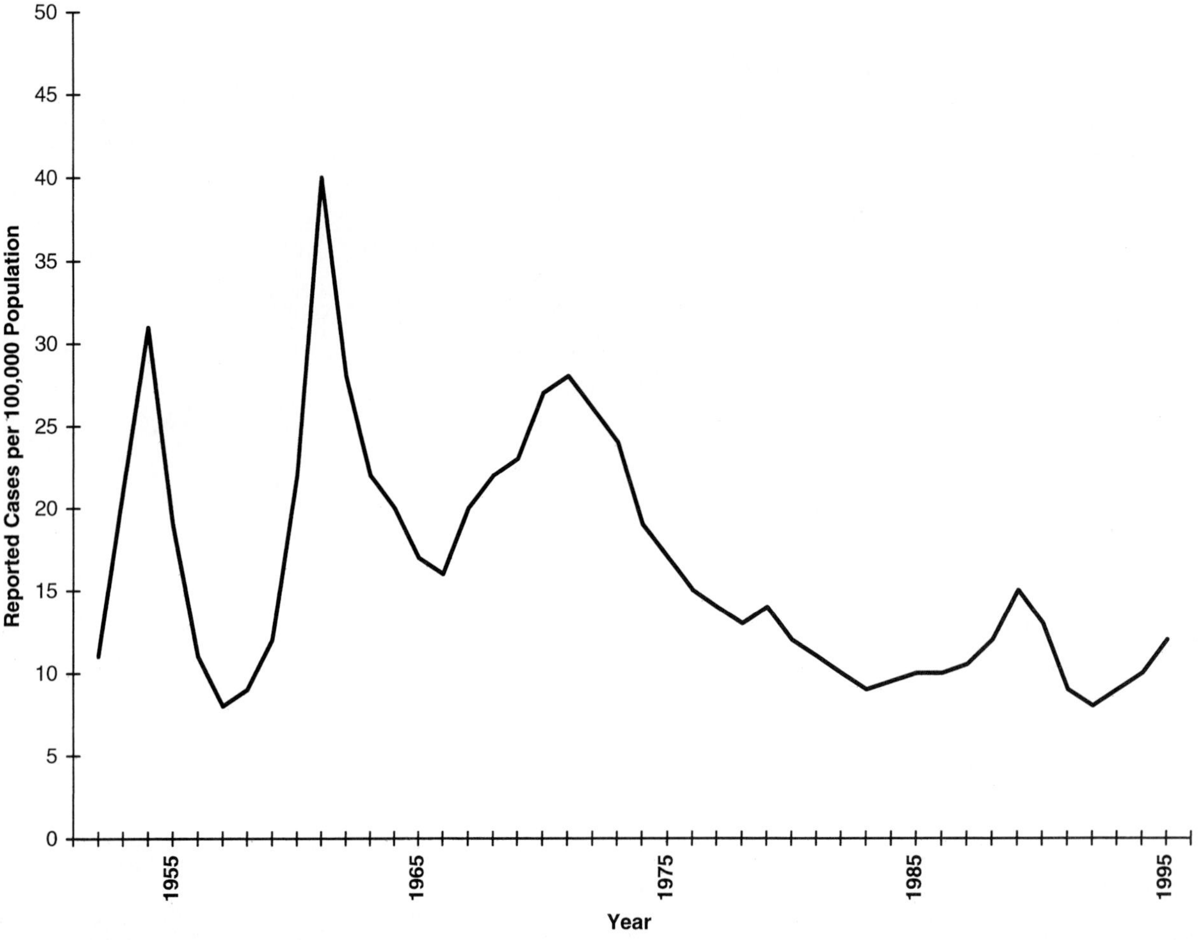

FIGURE 161–5. Reported incidence of hepatitis A, 1952–1995, United States. (From National Notifiable Diseases Surveillance System, Centers for Disease Control and Prevention, Atlanta, Ga; courtesy of Dr. C. N. Shapiro, Atlanta, Ga.)

Hepatitis A seems to be equally common in men and women, except where occupation (e.g., sewage workers, child care workers) or other factors (male homosexuality, intravenous drug use) are involved.[131]

Epidemic Patterns. Cyclic patterns of disease with peaks every 5 to 10 years have been noted in some developed countries with temperate climates.[105, 111, 132] In the United States and Canada, major waves of disease occurred in 1954, 1961, and the early 1970s (see Fig. 161–5); in Australia in 1956 and 1961; in Denmark in the immediate postwar period and again in the mid-1950s; and in the Netherlands in 1954 and 1960. In recent decades, declining rates of infection have been associated with a loss of periodicity of the disease in many countries.[105]

Socioeconomic and Other Factors. Many studies demonstrate a higher prevalence of infection in people who live in overcrowded conditions in many parts of the world, including the United States.

TABLE 161–4 Clinical Spectrum of Hepatitis A in a 1988 Shanghai Epidemic

	310,746 Cases Identified from January to May 1988
Case-fatality rate	0.015%, 47 deaths during hepatitis A: 25, fulminant hepatitis; 15, hepatitis A with underlying chronic liver disease; 7, miscellaneous diseases
	Clinical Manifestations of 8647 Hospitalized Patients
Age	12–71 yr, 90.8% between the ages of 20 and 40 yr
Incubation period	21.6 d (range, 12–36)

Symptom or Sign	%	Clinical Findings	%	Complications	%
Jaundice	84	Hepatomegaly	87	Cholestasis	1.6–5.3
Weight loss	82	Splenomegaly	9	Upper gastrointestinal bleeding	0.5–1.2
Malaise	80	Skin rashes	3	Thrombocytopenic purpura	<0.1 (6 cases)
Fever	76	Mild edema	2	Guillain-Barré syndrome	<0.1 (4 cases)
Nausea	69	Petechia	2	Pure red cell aplasia	<0.1 (3 cases)
Vomiting	47	Cardiac arrhythmias	0.8	Autoimmune hemolytic anemia	<0.1 (2 cases)
Abdominal pain	37			Transverse myelitis, optic neuritis	<0.1 (1 case each)
Arthralgia	6				

Data from Yao G. Clinical spectrum and natural history of viral hepatitis A in a 1988 Shanghai epidemic. In: Hollinger FB, Lemon SM, Margolis HS, eds. Viral Hepatitis and Liver Disease. Baltimore: Williams & Wilkins; 1991.

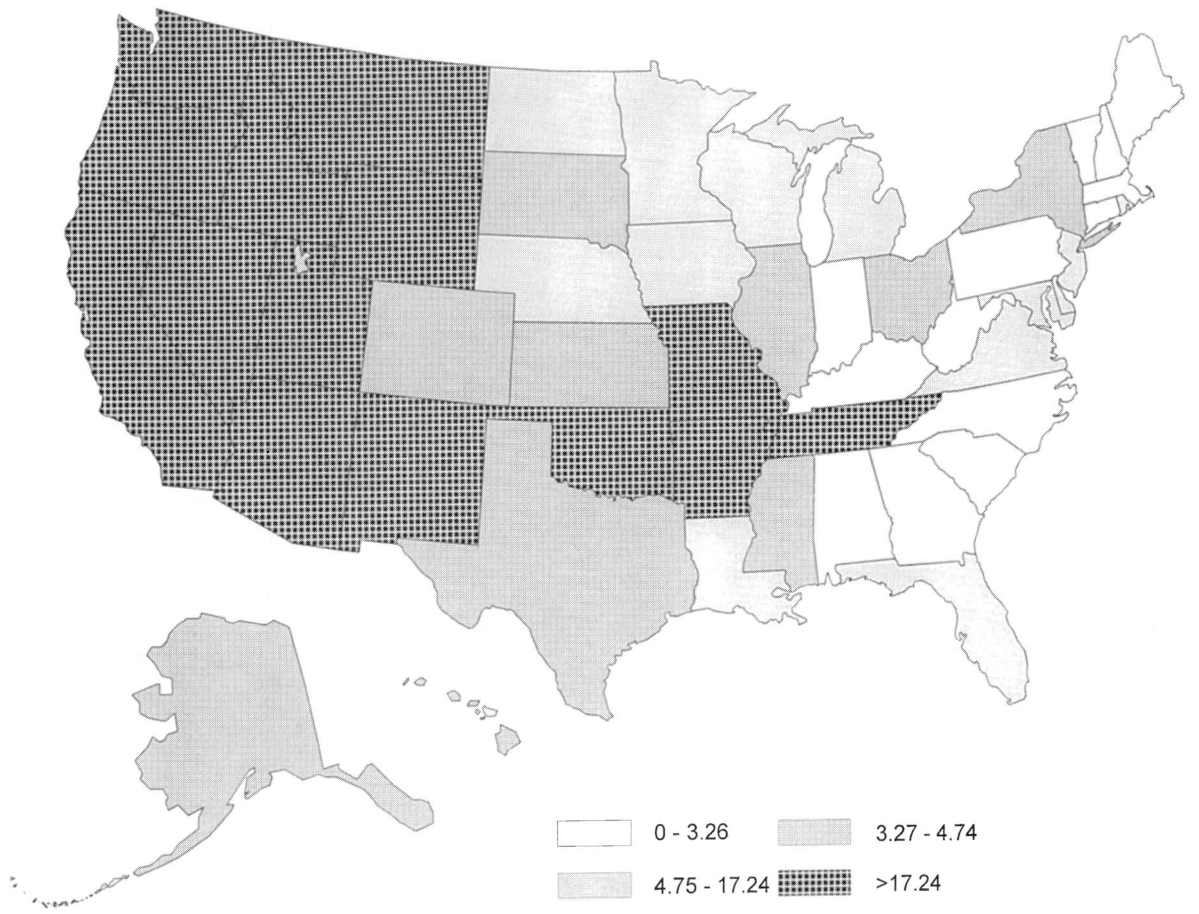

FIGURE 161–6. Reported cases of hepatitis A, per 100,000 population, within the United States generalized by state, 1995. There has been an increase in cases reported, especially in the western states, over the 4-year period through 1995. (From Centers for Disease Control and Prevention. Summary of notifiable diseases, United States, 1995. MMWR Morb Mortal Wkly Rep. 1996;44: No. 53.)

In a study done in the Israeli army, for example, the highest prevalence of hepatitis A seropositivity was in those of North African origin, followed by those of Asian, native Israeli, and Western origin.[100, 105, 133, 134]

Groups at Risk. In developed countries, certain groups are at increased risk of infection[99] (Table 161–5), including (1) patients and staff of institutions for the intellectually handicapped, where it is difficult to maintain high standards of hygiene[99, 135]; (2) staff and children attending daycare centers, especially large centers open to children in diapers[136, 137]; (3) homosexual men who engage in anal-oral contact[138, 139]; (4) intravenous drug users[140, 141]; and (5) travelers from low-risk areas to endemic areas, particularly if they stay for extended periods.[102, 126, 142] Travelers may return home while incubating the disease and spread it to their families. In a study of American Peace Corps personnel before the licensure of hepatitis A vaccine, a strictly regulated policy of immune serum globulin at 4-month intervals reduced the rate of hepatitis A from 1.6 to 2.1 cases per 100 person-years to 0.1 to 0.3 cases; U.S. foreign service personnel, for whom no immune serum globulin was mandated, had hepatitis A rates of 0.06 to 0.16 per 100 person-years, depending on the area of the world. Symptomatic hepatitis A develops in Western European travelers to developing countries in Africa, Asia, and Latin American, as well as in travelers to infrequently visited countries in Eastern Europe, at the rate of 3 cases per 1000 people per month of stay. Those who eat and drink under poor hygienic conditions have an

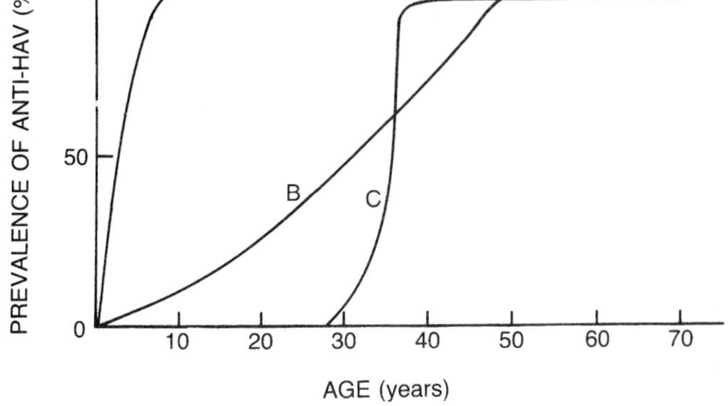

FIGURE 161–7. Different patterns *(A–C)* of age-specific prevalence of anti–hepatitis A virus.

TABLE 161–5 Risk Factors Associated with Acute Hepatitis A

Risk Factor	Percent of Total Cases
Personal contact	24.0
Daycare associated	15.1
Foreign travel	5.5
Outbreak associated	4.7
Male homosexuality	3.8
Parenteral drug use	2.4
Unknown	44.5

even higher risk, 20 cases per 1000 people per month. With an estimated 14 million such travelers each year, it has been proposed that hepatitis A is the most common vaccine-preventable illness among travelers.[113] Others at increased risk are military personnel, especially when deployed in endemic areas, and possibly workers who have direct contact with sewage containing human waste.[143, 144] Despite these well-known risks, around 40% of hepatitis A cases in the United States are not associated with any identifiable risk factor.[99] Person-to-person contact with infected family members incubating hepatitis A or with subclinical disease is probably the most important way that hepatitis A infection is acquired.[99]

MODE OF TRANSMISSION

Duration of Infectivity

Shedding of Virus in the Feces. Data on the infectivity of patients with hepatitis A are based largely on studies in human volunteers supplemented by epidemiologic observations and, to a limited extent, by animal studies. Infectious HAV has been detected in feces collected 14 to 21 days before and 8 days after the onset of jaundice.[145, 146] HAV particles or antigen has been detected in feces at least 5 days before the onset of biochemically confirmed hepatitis.[147, 148] The concentration of virus was shown to decline rapidly over the first 7 days of illness, and particles were rarely detected more than 14 days after the onset of dark urine.[149] Failure to detect virus particles by immune electron microscopy or viral antigen by radioimmunoassay cannot be taken as evidence of the absence of infectious virus because both techniques have limited sensitivity.

In general, the virus is capable of maintaining endemicity only in large populations with a continuing supply of new susceptible individuals. In relatively isolated populations such as in Greenland, Alaska, or the Pacific island of Funafuti, hepatitis A occurs in epidemics many years apart and disappears in the intervening years.[122, 129, 150] Similar disease patterns have been observed in institutions for the mentally handicapped; the pattern of disease suggests introduction of the virus by new patients or staff.[135, 151]

Viremia. HAV can be detected in the blood during the incubation period of the disease and probably remains in the blood after the onset of symptoms and even after the appearance of antibody. In orally infected owl monkeys, the viremia was shown to last from day 10 postinoculation until day 35,[152] and in orally infected chimpanzees, the duration of the viremia was from day 14 through day 28.[84] In early human volunteer studies, infection was documented in individual specimens collected as early as 25 days and in pools of sera collected 14 to 21 days and 3 to 7 days before the appearance of jaundice.[14] By using a sensitive reverse transcriptase-PCR assay, HAV RNA was detected in the blood in most patients only before alanine aminotransferase (ALT) reached peak levels. However, the viral genome was observed in some patients' sera even after ALT reached peak levels and in a few after seroconversion to HAV antibody.[153] It has also been shown that acute-phase (postjaundice) serum containing low levels of antibody remains infectious when intravenously inoculated into susceptible tamarin monkeys.[154] Nevertheless, in contrast to hepatitis B and C, only a few accounts of transmission of HAV by blood transfusion have appeared.[155] The low rate of transmission by blood transfusions is probably due to several factors: (1) the relatively short viremia, (2) absence of a carrier state, and (3) cotransfusion of neutralizing antibodies and a relatively high rate of preexisting antibody in many patients requiring transfusion. Blood-borne infections seem to play little role in the transmission of HAV in nature, and blood donors are not routinely tested for the presence of the virus.

Nevertheless, outbreaks have occurred that were caused by HAV contamination of human serum or plasma. In one instance, acute hepatitis A developed in a high proportion of cancer patients treated with interleukin-2 and lymphokine-activated killer cells that had been cultured in the presence of pooled human serum. The most probable source of contamination was the pooled "normal" human serum used to supplement the medium in which the lymphokine-activated killer cells were maintained.[156] Several reports of hepatitis A transmission by factor VIII concentrates have appeared.[41] These concentrates are prepared from large pools of plasma containing more than 10,000 donations. The resultant products were "virologically inactivated" by either heat or a solvent detergent process. Because HAV is relatively heat stable and has no essential lipids, these treatments may not be effective in eliminating infectious HAV. Nevertheless, it is not recommended that source plasma be screened for HAV because no practical test for the presence of infectious virus is available. The occurrence of these events is still unusual, and the disease does not produce long-term sequelae. Immunization is now recommended for any susceptible person who receives pooled plasma products routinely. Regulatory authorities are beginning to require manufacturers of plasma products to ensure that the products are produced or treated in such a way that HAV is eliminated or inactivated.

Other Modes of Transmission. Although HAV may occasionally be detected in saliva, urine, and nasopharyngeal secretions, no evidence has proved that its presence in those sites is of major epidemiologic significance.[84]

Routes of Infection

Person to Person. The most important means of transmission is from person to person via the fecal-oral route. Transmission is generally limited to close contacts,[99] especially in families with young children, because infections in children are often unnoticed and their standards of hygiene are poor.[99, 137, 157] Family studies indicate that most household cases occur one incubation period or more after the index case, which implies that the patient is most infectious just before the onset of symptoms.[158, 159]

Hepatitis A is rarely spread by casual contact, and the need for prophylaxis of school contacts is often debated. It has been said that play contacts are more important than those in the classroom, although transmission within schools can clearly happen.[160, 161] Outbreaks have also been reported in association with neonatal intensive care units,[162, 163] the major features of which are a low incidence of disease in the babies and a high rate of infection in family members. Vertical transmission has been reported in association with an outbreak in a neonatal intensive care unit but appears to be extremely rare. Prenatal transmission appears to have occurred when maternal blood containing HAV entered the fetal circulation as a result of placental abruption.[163]

Although point-source outbreaks caused by contaminated food are often explosive and are followed about one incubation period later by some secondary cases, most epidemics are spread person to person, which results in much slower development of the epidemic. An excellent example occurred in 1982–1983 in the tiny Pacific island of Kosrae. After a long period of absence, hepatitis A was recognized in June 1982; the number of cases increased gradually, peaking after 5 to 6 months and declining over the next 5 to 6 months.[164]

Foodborne and Waterborne. Common-vehicle epidemics of hepatitis A resulting from the consumption of contaminated food have been reported on numerous occasions. Two mechanisms are recognized for foodborne spread of hepatitis A: clean food may be contaminated by a food handler who is incubating hepatitis A, or the food may have been contaminated at its source, such as may occur with shellfish. In many countries, an important mechanism of transmission is the consumption of raw or partially cooked shellfish (e.g., oysters harvested from waters that have been contaminated with human sewage).[120, 165–167] Shellfish are particularly likely to transmit hepatitis A because they may filter 60 to 100 liters of water a day to obtain adequate supplies of food and oxygen, with the virus being concentrated more than 10,000-fold. Shellfish are often eaten raw or after gentle steaming, which is sufficient to cause the shell to open but inadequate to inactivate the virus.[35, 168] The massive epidemic of hepatitis A in Shanghai (see Table 161–4) was attributed to the ingestion of raw clams.[120]

Processed food can also be contaminated at its source. A multistate outbreak of hepatitis A occurred from contaminated frozen strawberries.[169] This contamination may take place when the berries are picked or in the processing plant, and the outbreak can be spread over the entire area of distribution of the processed food. A recent second outbreak of hepatitis A associated with frozen strawberries is believed to have been due to contamination at the time of picking the berries.[170] Because HAV is stable in a range of environmental conditions, virtually any food can be contaminated during processing. Cooked foods may still be contaminated after cooking.

Food handlers at the point of preparation are the other source of foodborne outbreaks. Despite the fact that in the United States an estimated 1000 food handlers are infected with hepatitis A each year, the number of food handler–associated outbreaks reported to the CDC is no more than four or five per year.[171] In most outbreaks, transmission of infection can be traced to a food handler who failed to observe hand-washing procedures. When such outbreaks occur, they tend to consume significant resources.[172]

The first waterborne epidemic of hepatitis A was described in 1920, and since then, many other episodes have been documented.[173] However, waterborne outbreaks of hepatitis A are uncommon in developed countries and account for less than 1% of all cases in the United States. Drinking water supplies in the United States are very safe, but localized outbreaks have been reported from contaminated well water.[174, 175] Even when the water supply is contaminated by raw sewage, cases do not always appear because hepatitis A is not always present in a given community. An investigation of a town whose water supply had become contaminated with sewage found essentially no cases among a sample of 213 susceptible residents.[176] Heavily contaminated water can be rendered safe for hepatitis A by the addition of high levels of chlorine or by boiling.

PATHOGENESIS

Although HAV shares many virologic characteristics with enteroviruses, it has several differentiating features that influence the pathogenesis and clinical expression of the disease. HAV is resistant to heat, solvents, and acid and grows slowly in living cells, where it has been shown to be relatively noncytolytic and to have little effect on the rate of host protein synthesis.

Incubation Period

Determination of the incubation period of disease is imprecise because the early symptoms of hepatitis are often vague and nonspecific. Jaundice may not be noticed by the patient, so the most useful marker of the onset of the disease is a change in urine color, which is almost always recognized by the patient and is the most common reason for seeking medical attention. The range of incubation is between 2 and 7 weeks, with a mean of about 4 weeks. In the large shellfish-associated epidemic in Shanghai, where the time of exposure could be well documented, the range of incubation was 12 to 36 days, with a mean of about 22 days[121] (see Table 161–4). Although HAV can be transmitted orally or parenterally, the incubation period is independent of the route of inoculation.[177] Experiments in primates and observations in humans suggest that the incubation period is dependent on the infectious dose.[178] The incubation period in marmosets was increased by approximately 1 week for each $\log_{10}$ reduction in dose. The shortest incubation period, less than 1 week, was observed after the inoculation of 10^8 infectious doses, and the longest was 7 weeks, after inoculation of one infectious dose (Fig. 161–8).

Viral Replication

HAV is generally transmitted by the fecal-oral route. Because the virus is acid resistant, it probably passes through the stomach, replicates lower in the intestine,[85, 152, 179] and is then transported to the liver, which is the major site of replication.[85, 180, 181] Evidence of replication in the oropharynx has been obtained in chimpanzees.[84] HAV, like many other picornaviruses, is highly organ specific with little evidence of significant replication outside the liver. Virus is shed from infected liver cells into the hepatic sinusoids and canaliculi, passes into the intestine, and is excreted in feces. In humans as well as in nonhuman primates, HAV has been detected in the liver, bile, and feces.[182–184] The first indirect evidence that virus may replicate in the gut was the detection of coproantibodies in the feces,[185, 186] followed by the demonstration of hepatitis A antigen in duodenal lining cells.[85] Nonetheless, the major pathology is restricted to the liver.

Pathogenesis

HAV is generally not cytopathic in cell culture, and histopathologic findings in experimental animals and humans do not show widespread hepatocyte necrosis, although the vast majority of hepatocytes at the peak of viral replication appear to be infected by immunohistochemical staining. Therefore, immune mechanisms have been invoked to explain the pathogenesis of the disease.[187] It has been postulated that liver cell damage occurs through a cell-mediated immune response, whereas circulating antibodies are probably more important in limiting the spread of virus to uninfected liver cells and other organs. This hypothesis is consistent with observations in animal models and humans. For example, intravenous inoculation of marmosets with a large dose of HAV resulted in mildly abnormal liver function test results (Fig. 161–9) and detectable hepatitis A antigen in hepatocytes within 1 week. Enzyme levels stabilized or

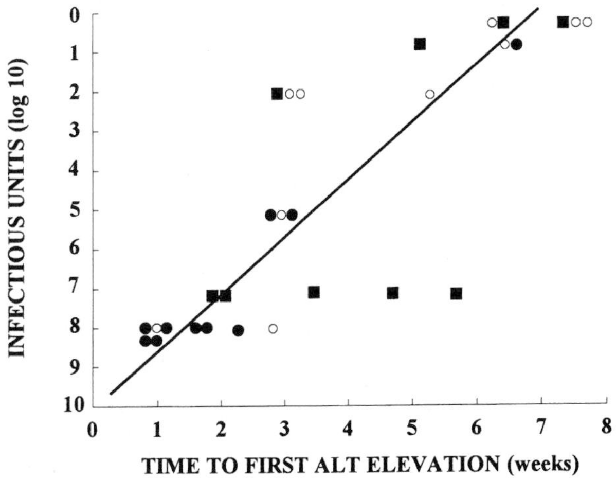

FIGURE 161–8. Inverse relationship between dose of hepatitis A virus and incubation period in marmosets *(filled markers)* and chimpanzees *(open markers)* measured from the time of intravenous inoculation to the first elevation of alanine aminotransferase. Different strains of hepatitis A virus were used. HM-175; MS-1. (From Purcell RH, Feinstone SM, Ticehurst JR, et al. Hepatitis A virus. In: Vyas GN, Dienstag JL, Hoofnagle JH, eds. Viral Hepatitis and Liver Disease. Orlando, Fla: Grune & Stratton; 1984:9.)

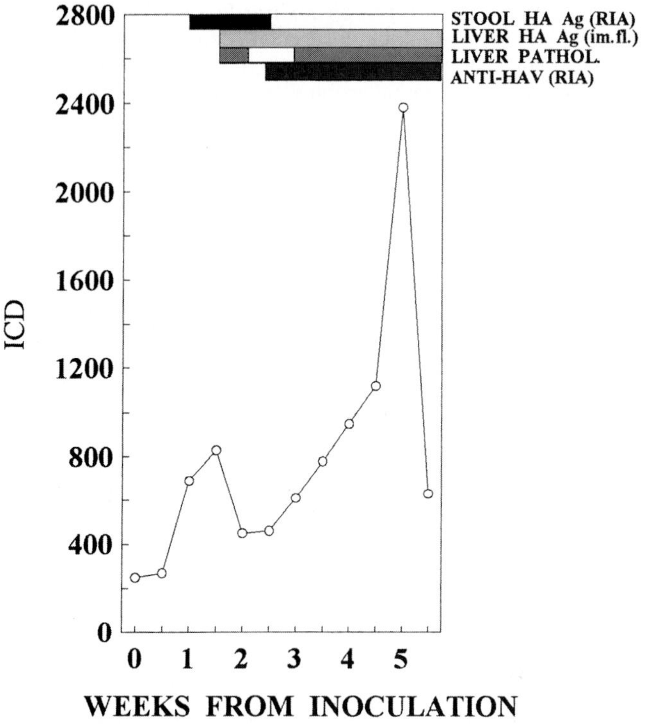

FIGURE 161–9. Biphasic enzyme elevation in a marmoset inoculated with 10^8 infectious units of hepatitis A virus. The second enzyme elevation occurs at about the time of the appearance of serum antibody. *Abbreviation:* ICD, Isocitrate dehydrogenase. (From Feinstone SM, Gust ID. Hepatitis A infection: Clinical aspects. In: Seeff LB, Lewis JH, eds. Current Perspectives in Hepatology. New York: Plenum;1989:3.)

even declined until the third week after inoculation, when a second, higher peak was observed coincident with the appearance of serum antibodies.[188] One explanation is that the early mild hepatitis was due to a direct viral effect but the second, more severe episode was due to an immune response. The presence of large quantities of virus in hepatocytes before the onset of hepatitis also argues against a major direct cytopathic effect of HAV.[44, 152] It has been suggested that virally elicited T cells target infected liver cells and induce immunopathology. In human studies, Vallbracht found that lymphocytes from convalescing patients produced cytotoxic effects against autologous epidermal cell lines infected with HAV and that $CD8^+$ T-cell clones demonstrated cytotoxic activity against autologous fibroblasts infected with hepatitis A. These findings are consistent with the hypothesis that $CD8^+$ T lymphocytes mediate liver cell damage.[187, 189] Furthermore, natural killer cells have been demonstrated to be capable of lysing HAV-infected tissue culture cells.[190]

Although liver damage occurs at the time that circulating antibodies become detectable, it has not been proved that the pathology is antibody dependent.[191] Circulating immune complexes containing HAV and specific IgM antibodies have been found during infection. However, immunoglobulin and complement deposits were not found at the sites of liver cell damage, and resolution of disease occurred even when antibody levels were rising and hepatitis A antigen could still be detected in the liver.[192, 193]

CLINICAL FEATURES

Hepatitis A is an acute or subclinical infection of the liver.[194] Although the clinical expression of infection varies widely, the disease is usually self-limited and mild. The most important determinant of the severity of illness is age. The ratio of anicteric to icteric cases has been reported to vary from 12:1 to 1:3.5, depending on the age at which infection occurs.[195] Between 1983 and 1989 the CDC estimated that about 9% of the hepatitis A cases occurred in people older than 50 years but that about 72% of the deaths caused by hepatitis A occurred in that age group (Table 161–6).

Over 90% of infections in children younger than 5 years are silent, and the proportion of symptomatic infections increases with age. In the Greenland epidemic of 1970–1974, the frequency of clinically recognizable hepatitis increased from 1% in children younger than 1 year to 24% in 15-year-olds.[122, 123] Similar low rates of clinical symptoms have been noted in children involved in outbreaks in daycare centers in the United States[196, 197]; however, adults infected in these outbreaks usually became jaundiced.

In a major study from China, adults and children older than 8 years who were close family contacts of patients involved in a waterborne outbreak of hepatitis A were studied. Of those with serologic evidence of infection, 34.3% were asymptomatic and had normal liver function test results, 45.7% had subclinical infections (elevated liver enzyme levels without jaundice), and only 20% were jaundiced. No significant difference was noted in the clinical attack rate between children older than 8 years and adults.[198]

Symptoms

Patients with hepatitis A often describe a mild illness—the prodrome (Fig. 161–10)—that appears 1 to 7 days before the onset of dark urine, although longer periods have been recorded.[194] These symptoms are not usually severe enough to cause the patient to seek medical attention or to stay home from work. In the early stages, flulike symptoms are common; fever (up to 40°C) may be accompanied by chills, mild headache, malaise, and fatigue. Loss of appetite is a common symptom, with patients reporting that the sight or smell of food, especially fatty foods, is nauseating.[199] Vomiting may occur but is neither severe nor protracted, and weight loss is common. In addition, patients with hepatitis A often lose their taste for tobacco. Occasionally, hepatitis A may be manifested atypically with symptoms such as diarrhea, cough, coryza, or arthralgia. Such manifestations are more common in children.[188, 200] A rarely described symptom is urticaria without cholestasis.[201]

The first specific sign of disease and the one that causes most patients to seek medical attention is the onset of dark urine. Bilirubinuria is usually followed within a few days by pale or clay-colored feces and yellow discoloration of the sclera, skin, and mucous membranes. The return of color to the stool occurs 2 or 3 weeks after the onset of illness and is an indication of resolution of disease. Itching, a sign of cholestasis, occurs in less than 50% of patients but may be severe enough to require antipruritics.

On physical examination, the patient's liver may be enlarged and sometimes tender. In adults the liver can be enlarged up to 14 cm in the vertical axis and has a firm consistency. The spleen is palpable in 5 to 15% of patients. Spider nevi may appear on the trunk and usually disappear during convalescence. Other physical findings occur rarely.

The duration of illness varies, but by the third week most patients feel better, have lost their hepatomegaly, and have normal or nearly normal levels of serum ALT and aspartate aminotransferase (AST).

TABLE 161–6 Age-Related Death Rate in Hepatitis A

Age Group	No. Cases (%)	No. Deaths (%)	Case Fatality/1000
<5	6,165 (5.3)	9 (2.4)	1.5
5–14	22,548 (19.5)	1 (0.3)	0.004
15–29	49,642 (43)	28 (7.3)	0.57
30–49	26,961 (23.3)	67 (17.6)	2.5
>49	10,235 (8.8)	276 (72.4)	27
Total	115,551	381	3.3

From Centers for Disease Control Viral Hepatitis Surveillance Program, 1983–1989.

FIGURE 161–10. Clinical, virologic, and serologic events associated with viral hepatitis.

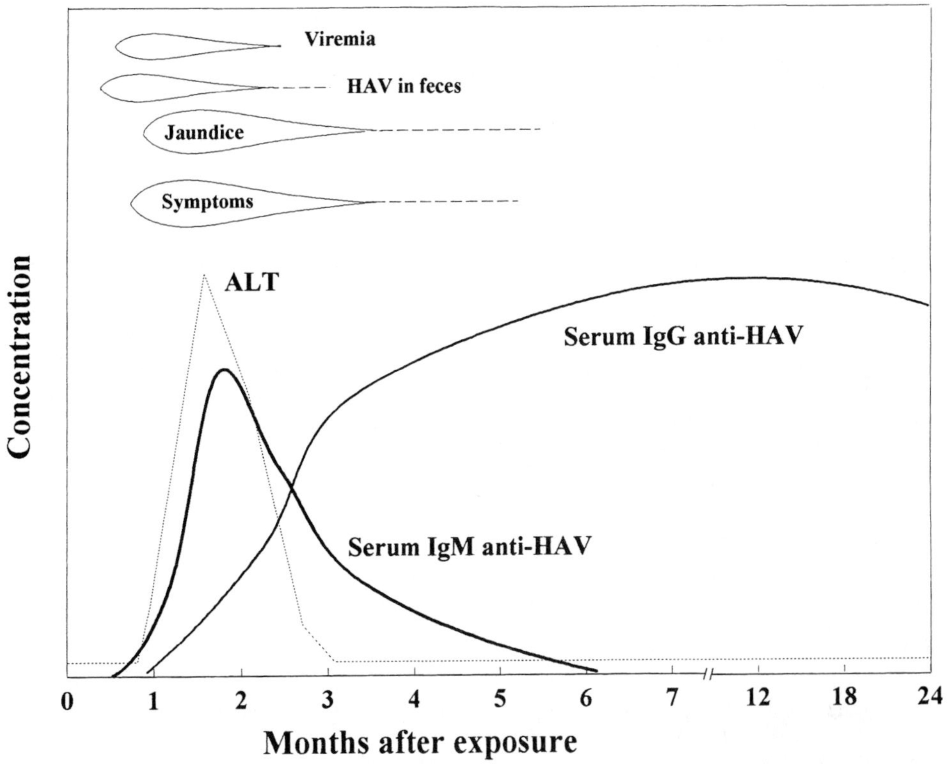

In many patients the appearance of jaundice is associated with rapid resolution of symptoms. In a study of 59 patients in the United States, about two thirds recovered within 2 months, 85% within 3 months, and nearly all by 6 months.[202]

The clinical course and histologic findings do not differ in pregnancy.[203] No transmission of HAV to the fetus could be documented, nor were any specific consequences on fetal health or survival detected.[204] Likewise, no evidence has suggested more severe infection or subsequent loss of immunity in the presence of human immunodeficiency virus infection.[205] Recently it has been proposed that hepatitis A infection in chronic carriers of hepatitis C virus may be more severe and more likely to result in fulminant hepatitis A.[206] It should be noted that this finding is in conflict with several other studies.[207–209]

Complications

Recognized complications of hepatitis A include cholestasis, prolonged and relapsing disease, fulminant hepatitis, triggering of chronic active autoimmune hepatitis, and autoimmune extrahepatic disease.

Cholestatic hepatitis, characterized by fever, pruritus, and prolonged jaundice, has been reported as an occasional complication. Cholestasis developed in 4 of 59 (7%) patients in a hospital-based study.[202] In a detailed description of six patients, peak serum bilirubin levels of 12 to 29 mg/dl were recorded, and jaundice lasted for 12 to 18 weeks. In each case, peak ALT levels were below 500 IU/liter.[210] Liver biopsies revealed centrilobular cholestasis and portal inflammation. Although the prognosis is universally favorable, a short, rapidly tapered course of corticosteroids may be used to reduce symptoms and hasten resolution.

Relapsing disease has been reported as an occasional complication in both adults and children.[211–213] Tong and associates reported that 12% of the 59 patients he studied suffered a relapse.[202] Typically, the second peak of disease is milder than the first. In the study of Tong and colleagues, the mean ALT level was 3500 mIU/ml and the mean bilirubin level was 4.9 mg/dl during the first peak and 1554 mIU/ml and 2.5 mg/dl, respectively, during the second. In another study of patients with relapses, HAV was detected in stool samples during the second episode.[211] However, it is not known whether excretion of HAV ever stopped or whether this relapse was a reactivation of the original infection. Although the pathogenesis of relapses has not been elucidated, it is important to recognize that each case resolved without sequela.

Extrahepatic manifestations of hepatitis A rarely include cardiac involvement, although patients with acute hepatitis may have bradycardia and electrocardiograms may show prolongation of the PR interval and some mild T wave depression. These changes resolve rapidly during convalescence.[201] HAV infection rarely causes pathology of other organs, but occasional cases of postviral encephalitis, Guillain-Barré syndrome, cholecystitis, acute pancreatitis, acute renal failure secondary to interstitial nephritis, aplastic or hemolytic anemia, agranulocytosis, thrombocytopenic purpura, or pancytopenia have been reported.[214–217] Several cases of arthritis, vasculitis, and cryoglobulinemia have also been reported.[193, 218, 219] Some patients may become depressed, and, occasionally the depression may be severe enough to require treatment, but it is usually mild and self-limited.

Hepatitis A is mostly benign, although severity increases with age,[196, 220] and long-term sequelae in recovered patients are unknown. Death from hepatitis A is well documented, but unusual. In the Shanghai epidemic, 47 deaths were registered among 310,746 cases[121] (see Table 161–4). The CDC estimated 94,000 cases of hepatitis A in the United States in 1995 with more than 150 deaths for a case-fatality rate of at least 0.16%.[111]

The most serious complication of hepatitis A is fulminant hepatic failure, defined by the appearance of severe acute liver disease with hepatic encephalopathy in a previously healthy person.[221] Fulminant hepatitis is a rare occurrence in hepatitis A, but about 8% of the estimated 2000 yearly cases of fulminant hepatic failure in the United States are believed to be due to hepatitis A.[221] However, not all deaths associated with hepatitis A are due to fulminant hepatic failure. Of the 47 deaths recorded in the large Shanghai epidemic, 25 were judged to be due to fulminant hepatitis A, 15 patients had underlying chronic liver disease, and 7 had other nonhepatic causes of death. Presently, about 7% of orthotopic liver transplants are performed for fulminant hepatic failure, and about 7% of these are for hepatitis A–associated liver failure.[221] Mortality in fulminant hepatitis A appears to be correlated with age, and survival without a transplant is rare in persons older than 50 years. Danger signs include excitability, irritability, insomnia, confusion, and severe vomiting. Laboratory and clinical evidence of deteriorating liver function, especially prolonged prothrombin times, correlates with the histologic picture of almost complete destruction of the hepatic parenchyma, with only a reticulin framework and portal tracts remaining. Occasionally, small groups of surviving hepatocytes can be seen close to the portal tracts, which may represent foci of regeneration. Surprisingly, little indication of a vigorous inflammatory response has been noted.

LABORATORY DIAGNOSIS

Hepatitis A is not clinically distinguishable from other forms of viral hepatitis, although the diagnosis may be suspected in a patient with typical symptoms during an outbreak. Liver function tests (see Fig. 161–10), especially serum levels of ALT and AST, are sensitive measures of parenchymal liver damage but are not specific for hepatitis A. In the study by Tong and coworkers, the peak mean ALT level was 1952 mIU/ml and the mean peak AST was 1442 mIU/ml, with the highest ALT level being 9711 mIU/ml, although values greater than 20,000 mIU/ml have been observed.[202] The ALT levels returned to normal by a mean of 7.4 weeks (range, 1 to 29 weeks). Although elevated ALT levels are detected in patients with severe hepatitis, high levels are not necessarily correlated with an adverse outcome. Alkaline phosphatase levels are usually only mildly elevated, and persisting elevated levels suggest hepatitis-associated cholestasis.[210] The highest bilirubin level in the Tong study was 38 mg/dl and the peak levels of serum bilirubin were positively correlated with age.

Elevated levels of total serum IgM, a mild lymphocytosis, and occasional atypical mononuclear cells are commonly found in patients with acute hepatitis A but are not diagnostic of the disease.[202, 222]

The diagnosis of acute hepatitis A is most commonly confirmed by detection of specific IgM in a single acute-phase serum sample.[223–225] The hepatitis A–specific IgM antibody is usually present at the initial evaluation and may be detectable at the time of the first rise in ALT. Although several types of IgM assay have been developed, the most widely used are capture radioimmunoassays and enzyme immunoassays.[224, 226, 227] IgM anti-HAV can be detected in nearly 100% of patients with acute hepatitis A at their first clinical examination and remains positive in most for 3 to 6 months and for 12 months in up to 25% of patients.[225] False-positive tests are rare and should be suspected when IgM anti-HAV is found to persist for more than a year. Assay for total antibody to the virus is of little diagnostic value because IgG persists for many years and may be related to a past infection. Although a fourfold rise in titer of total antibody in two consecutive serum specimens would be considered diagnostic of acute hepatitis A infection, the commercial IgM assay is the primary diagnostic tool, and it is possible that by the time the patient seeks medical attention, the total antibody level would have reached a plateau.

Antibodies to naturally acquired HAV are primarily directed against the virion and do not react well with the individual peptides that make up the virion capsid. Low levels of antibodies to nonstructural proteins are found in the serum of convalescing patients and may be used to distinguish the antibody response to natural infection from the response to a killed or subunit vaccine.[228, 229]

HAV or viral antigen can be detected in the stools of patients 1 to 2 weeks before symptoms develop, but such detection has little place in routine clinical diagnosis because the tests are not widely available and shedding is often complete before the patient seeks medical attention.[75, 76, 230] Molecular-based diagnostic techniques, including hybridization and especially PCR, have been used in research laboratories when a highly sensitive test for the presence of HAV is required. PCR has been very useful in the study of environmental samples.[231, 232]

Routine cell culture of HAV is difficult, expensive, and too slow to be useful for clinical diagnosis. Molecular hybridization or PCR to detect the RNA genome of HAV overcomes the potential problem of interference by antibody and, although more sensitive than antigen detection (by a factor of 10^3 to 10^4), is still not sufficiently sensitive for all circumstances.[233, 234]

Liver biopsy is rarely indicated to establish a diagnosis in acute hepatitis because this procedure is associated with a small, but finite risk and the histopathology is not usually diagnostic. In one study done in Japan, where biopsy for acute hepatitis has been routine, 86 patients with serologically established acute hepatitis A were evaluated for quantitative and qualitative light microscopic features, together with biopsies from 78 patients with acute hepatitis B and from 76 patients with acute hepatitis non-A, non-B. Hepatitis A was characterized by more pronounced portal inflammation than was hepatitis non-A, non-B, but less conspicuous parenchymal changes such as focal necrosis, Kupffer cell proliferation, acidophil bodies, and ballooning. Nonspecific reactive hepatitis with slightly raised serum transaminase levels was often seen during recovery from hepatitis A and needs to be distinguished from the longer-lasting cases of acute hepatitis B and C.[235, 236] Hepatitis A antigen and HAV particles can be detected in the cytoplasm of infected cells by immunofluorescence, immunoperoxidase staining, or thin-section electron microscopy.[182, 237, 238]

IMMUNITY

The high prevalence of antibody in older individuals in countries that have a low incidence of hepatitis A suggests that anti-HAV IgG usually persists for life. Second attacks of hepatitis A have not been documented in the field and have not been induced experimentally. In two sets of experiments involving a total of 19 volunteers, reinoculation with HAV 6 to 9 months after the initial illness failed to induce disease.[5, 239]

It is known that passive immunization with immune serum globulin can provide complete protection against hepatitis A, which indicates that serum antibody alone is sufficient to prevent infection. It has been difficult to judge the effect of mucosal immunity because IgA antibodies in saliva or feces are either not detected or are present at very low levels.[240] The antibody response to HAV infection is generally brisk and high titered. Both IgG and IgM can usually be detected at the time of the first expression of clinical illness (see Fig. 161–10). Neutralizing antibody as measured by in vitro tissue culture assays can also be detected early in disease. Because HAV is not usually cytopathic, a radioimmunofocus reduction test was devised that is equivalent to a plaque reduction assay.[241] This highly sensitive test was shown to correlate closely, although about 100-fold more sensitively, with total antibody radioimmunoassay. With this assay, IgM and IgG have been shown to possess neutralizing activity. It has also been demonstrated that patients convalescing from hepatitis A may have very high titers of in vitro neutralizing antibody. Serum dilutions of 1:100,000 to 1:500,000 or more are not uncommon.

The role of T lymphocytes in protection from HAV infection has not been elucidated. However, it is known from studies of passive immunization with IG that antibody alone is sufficient to protect from infection. Undoubtedly, T-cell responses do occur, and $CD8^+$ cytotoxic T lymphocytes and possibly natural killer cells are important in pathogenesis.[190, 242, 243]

PREVENTION

The most effective method of controlling hepatitis A and other enteric infections is through improved standards of hygiene and sanitation, especially the provision of clean water. Good hygienic practices with particular emphasis on hand washing and restriction of activities of workers who are ill are of primary importance in the food preparation industry. These general measures are most important to prevent hepatitis A transmission from person to person in families and hospitals. Nosocomial infections have been reported but are not common.[244, 245] Hence, hospitalized patients need only enteric isolation (see Chapter 294). Private rooms, gowns, and masks are not necessary unless the patient is incontinent.[246] Gloves should be worn when handling any material potentially contaminated with feces. Frequent hand washing, whether gloves are worn or not, should be emphasized. Hospital personnel in general do not have a higher prevalence of antibody to HAV than matched controls do.[247] However, several outbreaks of hepatitis A in hospital nurseries have been reported with transmission to staff.[162, 163, 248, 249]

Travelers to developing countries should be advised to eat only properly cooked food and be careful of uncooked vegetables and shellfish. Even in the vaccine era, the maxim to prevent traveler's diarrhea, "boil it, cook it, peel it, or forget it," also applies to hepatitis A prevention.[250]

Improvements in sanitary systems, although technologically possible, may not be practical in large parts of the world. In more developed areas, sudden deterioration in living conditions because of war or political or economic instability can rapidly degrade sanitary systems. In the developed world, hepatitis A remains a risk associated with travel to exotic areas. Therefore, considerable effort has been expended in the development of hepatitis A vaccines.

Passive Immunization

Before the licensing of hepatitis A vaccines, the mainstay of hepatitis A immunoprophylaxis had been passive immunization with pooled IG, which has been known in the past as gamma globulin or immune serum globulin. Even with the availability of vaccines, IG still has importance in hepatitis A prophylaxis. IG has proved useful for the prevention of hepatitis A in travelers, Peace Corps volunteers, and military personnel and even in postexposure prophylaxis in common-source or family outbreaks. However, IG has never been successful in altering the epidemiology of hepatitis in a high-risk community because of the transient nature of the protection, coverage rates, and perhaps lack of herd immunity.

IG is manufactured from large pools of plasma collected from tens of thousands of donors. Because the prevalence of antibody to HAV in the population has been declining, concern has been voiced that antibody levels against HAV in IG preparations might drop below effective levels. Although no standard for anti-HAV levels exists in IG preparations in the United States even though prophylaxis against hepatitis A is the primary use for this product, anti-HAV levels remain adequate at this time to provide short-term protection.[251] Eventually, consideration may need to be given to the manufacture of IG from selected antibody-positive donors to the development of a hyperimmune globulin for hepatitis A prevention analogous to other agent-specific hyperimmune globulins.[252] With the recent licensure of inactivated hepatitis A vaccines, the use of IG for preexposure prophylaxis has been largely eliminated, but IG still has a role in the prevention of hepatitis A after exposure has already occurred, when an exposure is expected before the vaccine would become effective, and in children younger than 2 years, for whom the vaccine has not been approved.

The efficacy of IG was first demonstrated in an outbreak at a summer camp[253] in 1944 and has been confirmed many times since.[254] Several studies have demonstrated the effectiveness of IG in preexposure settings such as travelers, military personnel,[255] and Peace Corps workers.[256] The rate of HAV infections in Peace Corps volunteers dropped from 1.6 to 2.1 cases per 100 per year before mandatory IG every 4 months to 0.1 to 0.3 cases per 100 per year after the institution of a mandatory program.[256] Active prophylaxis with the recently licensed killed vaccines has largely supplanted the use of IG in this setting. Nevertheless, IG is still recommended for postexposure prophylaxis. If administered within 2 weeks of exposure, IG is effective in eliminating or attenuating the severity of clinical disease, but actual infection might still occur. Passive/active immunization often results from the use of IG in the postexposure setting. IG is useful for limiting the spread of hepatitis in small, defined outbreaks. However, it has not been highly effective in preventing large community-wide long-term epidemics of hepatitis A.[257]

TABLE 161–7 Recommendations for Preexposure Hepatitis A Immunoprophylaxis

Age (yr)	Exposure Duration	Recommended Prophylaxis
<2	Short term (<3 mo)	IG, 0.02 ml/kg
<2	3–5 mo	IG, 0.06 ml/kg
<2	>5 mo	IG, 0.06 ml/kg repeated every 5 mo
>2	Short or long term	HAV vaccine HAV vaccine + IG as above if exposure is expected in less than 2 wk Substitute IG as above if vaccine is contraindicated or refused

Abbreviations: HAV, Hepatitis A virus; IG, immune globulin.

Tables 161–7 and 161–8 outline the recommended use of IG for the prevention of hepatitis A. In general, IG is recommended for postexposure prophylaxis and for unvaccinated individuals who expect to be in a high-risk situation in less than 2 weeks. IG is also recommended for preexposure prophylaxis for anyone who cannot take the vaccine, usually because of known allergy to one of its components. IG is also recommended for children younger than 2 for whom the vaccine has not yet been approved. Cost analysis studies have also shown that individuals such as travelers who expect to have no more than two short-term exposures to hepatitis A over a 10-year period could more economically be protected by IG than by vaccine. Vaccine becomes more cost-effective for those who expect to travel three or more times in a 10-year period or stay in an endemic area more than 6 months.[258] As the cost for vaccine is reduced and that for IG increases, these analyses may need to be redone.

Postexposure prophylaxis is recommended for those known to have been exposed less than 2 weeks before immunization. In many postexposure situations it is often too late for prophylaxis to be effective by the time that the index case is discovered (see Table 161–8). Close personal contacts of persons thought to be incubating hepatitis A should be immunized with IG. Casual contacts such as school classmates who have not had physical contact usually do not require IG prophylaxis. The proper use of IG can limit a defined outbreak or a family outbreak of hepatitis A. However, IG has not generally been successful in controlling larger epidemic situations. In these instances, exposure is too broad and the immunity may not last long enough for the virus to be eliminated from the population.

The usual dose of IG is a single intramuscular injection of 0.02 or 0.06 ml/kg (see Tables 161–7 and 161–8). The lower dose is

TABLE 161–8 Recommendations for Postexposure Hepatitis A Prophylaxis

Age (yr)	Timing of Exposure	Recommended Prophylaxis
All ages	<2 wk since exposure	IG, 0.02 ml/kg
All ages	>2 wk since exposure	None
>2	>2 wk since exposure and long-term or repeated exposure likely	IG, 0.02 ml/kg, + HAV vaccine
<2	<2 wk since exposure or for preexposure prophylaxis	IG, 0.06 ml/kg repeated every 5 mo during period of exposure
>2	>2 wk since exposure but future exposure likely	HAV vaccine

Abbreviations: HAV, Hepatitis A virus; IG, immune globulin.

adequate to provide protection for up to 3 months and the higher dose is effective for up to 6 months.[251] Intramuscular preparations of IG should never be given intravenously, and intravenous preparations of IG are not intended for routine HAV prophylaxis; they are used for patients with immune deficiencies and are formulated at a lower globulin concentration.

Active Immunization

Active Immunization with hepatitis A vaccines has developed along classic lines similar to the path followed for polio vaccines. Like poliovirus, the initial breakthrough came with the in vitro cultivation of HAV in cell lines suitable for vaccine production.[18] Formalin-inactivated, cell culture–produced, whole-virus vaccines have now been approved in much of the world. Live-attenuated vaccines based on the CR326 and the HM175 strains have also been tested in primates and to a limited extent in humans, and the H2 strain has been used in extended clinical trials in China.[80, 82, 259, 260]

Two HAV killed vaccines have been approved for use in the United States and widely throughout the world. A third vaccine has now been licensed in Europe, and several other similar inactivated vaccines have been developed and registered, at least in their country of manufacture.[261, 262] Both widely licensed vaccines are produced from highly cell culture–adapted virus strains that have also been shown to be highly attenuated in humans, which gives them an extra measure of safety.[260, 263] The entire nucleotide sequences of both the wild-type and the vaccine variant of strain HM175 have been determined.[46, 47] A full-length, infectious cDNA clone of the cell culture–adapted virus was made,[264] and the mutations responsible for cell culture adaptation and attenuation have been determined by the molecular construction of chimeric viruses.[73, 83, 265] It was found that substitutions and deletions in the 5′ noncoding region and substitutions in the 2B/2C coding regions are highly important for cell culture adaptation and attenuation of virulence. However, mutations throughout the genome contributed to improved in vitro replication.[79]

Both vaccines are grown in MRC-5 cells, purified, inactivated by formalin, and formulated with alum as an adjuvant. Both vaccines begin to be effective about 2 weeks after a single intramuscular dose. For individuals who expect repeated exposure or require long-term protection, a booster dose is recommended 6 to 12 months after the initial vaccination.

Clinical trials indicate that inactivated hepatitis A vaccines are safe and highly immunogenic and provide durable protection against infection; the protection is expected to last at least 10 years for those receiving the primary vaccine plus the booster.[261, 266–268] In one study, 1037 healthy seronegative children 2 to 16 years of age in a community experiencing yearly outbreaks of hepatitis A received either a single dose of formalin-inactivated vaccine or placebo. No cases of hepatitis occurred in the vaccinated group, except for a few that appeared within 3 weeks of vaccination. These cases represented patients who were already incubating the infection at the time of vaccination. In the placebo group, 34 cases of hepatitis A were observed during the 3 weeks after vaccination, thus indicating a 100% vaccine protective efficacy.[267, 269] In a large field trial of an inactivated vaccine involving over 40,000 children in Thailand, the vaccine was found to be at least 80% effective in comparison to placebo and was without serious adverse reactions.[268]

The licensed inactivated hepatitis A vaccines have all been shown to be highly and rapidly immunogenic. They induce seroconversions to protective levels of antibody in as little as 2 weeks after the initial dose.[270, 271] Therefore, travelers, military personnel, or others who had no previous vaccine could be vaccinated as little as 2 weeks before their expected exposure instead of receiving IG.[272] The level of antibody after vaccination varies with the dose and schedule of the vaccine. However, after a single dose of vaccine, antibody titers are higher than titers produced by known protective levels of IG but are generally lower than titers measured after natural infection.[106, 273–275] The quality of the antibody response after vaccination has also been studied. With similar radioimmunoassay titers of HAV antibody, the IG recipients had higher neutralization titers but negligible radioimmunoprecipitation titers when compared with the group that was vaccinated.[275] However, it has also been shown that IG prepared from the serum of vaccinees could protect a chimpanzee from HAV challenge when the titer of antibody achieved in the chimpanzee was similar to that found in humans receiving IG prophylaxis.[276]

The common recommended schedule of a single dose followed by a booster dose 6 to 12 months later produces very high levels of antibody, although still below the titers sometimes seen after natural infection.[106, 273] However, based on titers achieved after passive immunization with IG that are known to be effective in the prevention of hepatitis A, it appears that only very low levels of serum antibody are required for protection. After the booster dose, it is estimated that protective levels of antibody will persist for 10 to 30 years. Because the incubation period for hepatitis A is usually 4 weeks and the anamnestic responses observed after the 12-month booster are rapid and robust, it has been suggested that vaccinees who have seroconverted will be protected even if their antibody levels have fallen below protective levels.[266] Long-term follow-up studies will have to be performed to confirm this hypothesis.

Inactivated hepatitis A vaccine is indicated for anyone 2 years of age or older who is at increased risk of exposure to hepatitis A and does not have preexisting antibody. It is not generally cost-effective to screen children for anti-HAV before vaccination unless they spent part of their childhood in a highly endemic area or had a history of exposure. Depending on the local epidemiologic situation, prescreening of adults who would be predicted to have greater than a 50% chance of being anti-HAV positive should be considered if time permits. Vaccination of persons with preexisting antibody has not been shown to carry any risk. Those considered to be at risk for preexposure prophylaxis include travelers to countries where HAV is endemic, military personnel, certain ethnic or geographic populations that have high rates of hepatitis C virus, homosexual or bisexual men, intravenous drug users, those routinely receiving plasma fractionation products such as factor VIII, and those engaged in high-risk employment such as primate handlers or laboratory workers who handle HAV. In addition, vaccine should be considered for certain individuals who although not at higher risk of infection, carry special risks if infected.

Travelers. The risk of hepatitis A in Europeans traveling to Africa, Asia, or South America was 3/1000 per month of stay and 20/1000 per month for those living under local conditions.[113] Between 1985 and 1990 the number of travel-related cases of hepatitis A in Sweden remained constant at about 140 per year. However, as a proportion of the total cases in Sweden, it has risen from about 20% to about 55% in 1990, the largest single cause of hepatitis A cases in that country.[277] Among seronegative American missionaries to sub-Saharan Africa in the prevaccine era, 28% were infected by HAV within 2 years and over 90% were seropositive after 20 years of service.[278] As of 1992, before the vaccine was licensed, foreign travel accounted for 5.5% of U.S. cases.[279] Protection rates in vaccinated travelers are estimated to exceed 97%.[126]

Military Personnel. Hepatitis A has caused morbidity and affected the outcome in wars throughout recorded history. Military personnel deployed in high-risk areas are at special risk because of their field living conditions. The long-term protection afforded by vaccine over IG is a considerable advantage for the military, where the logistics of administering IG every few months limited its utility.[272]

High-Risk Ethnic or Geographic Populations. Many Native American and Alaskan people have experienced cyclic epidemics of hepatitis A and have a continuing endemic problem. It has been recommended that vaccine programs be established to prevent HAV infections in these groups and to break the cycles of epidemics. The vaccines have been shown to perform well in these high-risk Native American populations.[257, 280, 281]

Male Homosexuals. Surveillance data have found that male homosexuals account for 3.8% of the hepatitis A cases reported in the United States.[279] This figure could be due to multiple partners or sexual practices. Vaccination of this group should reduce the rate quickly and could possibly have a herd immunity effect in the homosexual community.

Intravenous Drug Users. Drug users also have a high rate of HAV infection because of either sharing of needles with an individual who is viremic or possibly lifestyle factors. Vaccine is indicated for this group, although drug users are notoriously hard to reach for immunizations.

Regular Recipients of Blood or Plasma-Derived Products. The risk of hepatitis A from a blood transfusion or from plasma derivatives is extremely low, but both have been reported.[41, 282] Individuals who receive these products regularly should be immunized against diseases transmitted via blood-borne means with available vaccines. Many recipients of factor VIII, for instance, have been infected by hepatitis C virus or even hepatitis B virus, and they should not undergo another infection of their liver. Presently, these products are treated by a viral inactivation process often based on solvents or heat. Because HAV is resistant to organic solvents and is relatively resistant to heat, cases of hepatitis A associated with factor VIII have caused the manufacturers to begin to develop new methods that would eliminate infectious HAV from their products. Nevertheless, vaccination of this group remains prudent.

High-Risk Employment. Several occupations carry at least a potential for HAV exposure. Certain employees of institutions for developmentally challenged individuals have in the past been at risk. Staff of daycare centers, especially those that care for children before bowel training, may also be at risk. These centers have been involved in outbreaks over recent years. However, it is difficult to show that individual staff members are at higher risk because these outbreaks generally remain uncommon in comparison to the total number of such centers. Some studies have shown that sewer workers have a higher rate of HAV infections than the general population, which seems reasonable. However, these findings have not been confirmed in every study.[283] Health care personnel have not been shown to be at increased risk, and most patients with hepatitis A are not admitted to the hospital. If a community has a particular problem, it may be prudent to vaccinate the health care personnel who are expected to be in contact with those infected.

Individuals Who Do Not Have Increased Risk but Should Consider Vaccination. Persons with chronic liver disease of any etiology should be vaccinated. Although the risk for any individual is low, an HAV infection superimposed on chronic liver disease can be very serious and may result in death. Food handlers are another special category where the risk of infection may be no higher than that of the general population; however, if infected, they have the potential to transmit the disease to a large number of people.

Administration of inactivated hepatitis A vaccine concomitantly with IG to produce both immediate and long-term immunity has been studied several times. The rate of seroconversion in these instances has not been reduced by coadministration of IG. However, antibody titers are generally lower than when vaccine is given alone. Because titers induced by the vaccine far exceed those needed for protection, these reductions are not considered clinically significant.[284–286] Inasmuch as hepatitis A vaccine is indicated for travelers to countries with a high rate of hepatitis A, the use of HAV vaccine with other common traveler vaccines has been studied. Neither the titer nor the reactogenicity rate of hepatitis A vaccine was affected when administered concurrently with hepatitis B, yellow fever vaccine, or typhoid vaccines.[287–289]

Control of community outbreaks of hepatitis A may be one of the most important uses for the vaccine and provides the clearest evidence of its effectiveness. A vaccine program was initiated in schoolchildren in two adjoining villages with 5000 inhabitants in Slovakia that were experiencing a community-wide outbreak of hepatitis A. Eight cases of hepatitis occurred in the 157 susceptible children (5.1%) who were not vaccinated and 1 case in the 404 children (0.25%) who received at least one dose of vaccine. Soon after the vaccine program was initiated in the students, no new cases were reported in the general population of the villages.[290]

Large outbreaks of hepatitis A have been reported in rural Alaska every 8 to 12 years since the 1960s. McMahon and colleagues have studied these outbreaks and tried to control them in the past with IG. Although massive immunization campaigns using IG were able to temporarily reduce the number of cases reported, the effect never lasted, and the epidemics always returned and spread.[257] In August 1992, an outbreak of hepatitis A began in the Tok/Glennallen area and another outbreak began in the Kotzebue area and began to spread to adjoining areas. During the next 12 months, 529 clinical cases were reported from these regions with a population of 22,629 despite the liberal administration of IG to household contacts. After serologic survey of a population sample from an affected village and analysis of previously collected sera from other regions, it was decided to offer vaccine to all persons 40 years of age and younger, to all seronegative persons older than 40 residing in the Tok/Glennallen region, to all individuals younger than 20 years, and to all seronegatives between 20 and 34 years of age in the other areas. The overall seroconversion rate was about 90% after a single dose of vaccine. Of 2826 persons eligible for vaccination in the Kotzebue area, 1829 were vaccinated. The hepatitis A infection rate within 60 weeks of initiation of the vaccine program was 2.1% in the vaccinees, 12% in nonvaccinated eligibles, and 0.1% in nonvaccinated ineligibles. Most of the cases among the vaccinees occurred soon after vaccine administration. The vaccine program did not completely eliminate hepatitis A in the city of Kotzebue, where only about 50% of the eligibles were vaccinated. However, in the outlying villages, where vaccine coverage was about 80% of the eligibles, hepatitis was virtually eliminated within 8 weeks of initiation of the vaccination program.[257]

Disease Control Strategies. Experience gained from vaccination programs intended to interdict ongoing broad-based outbreaks of hepatitis A in some groups of Native Americans and communities of observant Jews living in New York, as well as other urban outbreaks, indicates that such vaccine programs, especially when targeted to children, can dramatically control the outbreaks.[220, 257, 281] The Advisory Committee for Immunization Practices has recommended that in communities experiencing high rates of hepatitis A, routine vaccination of children begin at age 2 and an accelerated vaccination program be implemented for older unvaccinated children until the vaccine coverage among children exceeds 70% (Table 161–9). In communities with an intermediate rate of hepatitis A, it is recommended that local surveillance and epidemiologic data determine the best vaccine strategy. Because these communities are often in large metropolitan areas, the most feasible and cost-effective strategy may be to target certain areas or groups that have the highest rates of disease.[220] If such a strategy is contemplated, the sensitivities of the local communities must be considered before acceptance of such a program. Targeting risk groups such as daycare centers and male homosexuals in these communities may also be beneficial if surveillance data indicate that these groups could be a substantial source of infection.

Strategies for the use of hepatitis A vaccine depend on the goal. Some groups will require vaccination even if cost-benefit analyses are not favorable. For instance, the military clearly sees an importance for the use of this vaccine in certain troops, and they will determine the strategy that best fits their needs even though the results of a strict cost analysis might not be favorable.[272, 291] Persons who are in high-risk groups could individually benefit from vaccination, and cost-effectiveness analyses may be favorable.[258, 292] How-

TABLE 161-9 Advisory Committee on Immunization Practices Recommendations for Use of Hepatitis A Virus Vaccine and Immune Globulin

Preexposure Prophylaxis

At present the ACIP recommends HAV vaccine for persons older than 2 yr who are at increased risk for infection and for any person wishing to obtain immunity

Populations at increased risk of HAV infection or the adverse consequences of infection

- Persons traveling or working in countries with high or intermediate endemicity should be vaccinated or receive IG before departure. IG is recommended for children <2 yr old because the vaccine is not yet licensed for this group. Ideally, travelers should be vaccinated at least 4 wk before departure. Those who elect not to be immunized should be offered IG, which provides effective protection for up to 3 mo
- Children in communities that have high rates of disease and periodic outbreaks
- Men who have sex with men. Prevaccination testing may be warranted in men older than 40 yr
- Users of illegal drugs: Immunization is indicated for both injecting and noninjecting drug users if local epidemiologic observations suggest that they have an increased risk of infection
- Persons who have an occupational risk for infection. Although only those who work directly with the virus have been shown to be at increased risk, it seems prudent to consider vaccination of other groups, e.g., sewage workers, plumbers, primate handlers, medical and nursing staff, and the staff of daycare centers
- Persons with chronic liver disease or clotting factor deficiencies requiring infusions of clotting factor concentrates
- Consideration should be given to vaccination of food handlers if an appropriate health, economic, or other benefit can be obtained

Outbreaks

- Communities with high rates of hepatitis A. Routine immunization of children 2 yr of age and accelerated vaccination of older children who have not previously been vaccinated should be rapidly implemented
- Communities with intermediate rates of hepatitis A. If subgroups with a high incidence of disease can be identified, they should be immunized, provided that high rates of coverage can be attained rapidly
- Outbreaks in daycare centers, hospitals, institutions for the intellectually disabled, etc., have traditionally been controlled by widespread use of IG

Postexposure Prophylaxis

The ACIP still recommends the use of IG for individuals who have been exposed to HAV in the past 14 d and who are believed to be susceptible to the disease

- Household and sexual contacts of known cases
- Staff and attendees of daycare centers or homes after one or more cases have occurred in children or employees or two or more attendee households
- Fellow food handlers and, under some circumstances, consumers of food prepared by a food handler in whom hepatitis A develops
- Schools, hospitals, and work settings. IG prophylaxis is not recommended for persons with a casual contact with a single case. Under outbreak situations, IG would be recommended for persons thought to be exposed

From Centers for Disease Control and Prevention. Prevention of hepatitis A through active or passive immunization: Recommendations of the Advisory Committee on Immunization Practices (ACIP). MMWR Morb Mortal Wkly Rep. 1996;45:1.

ever, from a public health point of view, it is not likely that a strategy based only on vaccination of risk groups will be useful in controlling hepatitis A in the general population.[279] It is possible that the aggressive use of vaccine in high-rate and intermediate-rate communities will alter the rates of disease in the country as a whole. However, if the goal is to significantly reduce the national incidence of hepatitis A, the only strategy that is likely to work would be to include the vaccine in the routine childhood vaccination schedule.[293]

The use of hepatitis A vaccine in developing countries where infection in early childhood is nearly universal but disease is uncommon is not contemplated. As standards of living improve in these areas, greater problems with hepatitis A often arise. Although vaccine strategies could be devised for parts of these countries that have good water and sanitation facilities, the cost of such a program today may not make it a high priority when compared with other major health problems encountered in developing countries.

THERAPY AND GENERAL MANAGEMENT

At present, no specific therapy is available for hepatitis A, and management is supportive. In the rare event of fulminant hepatitis, hospitalization and symptomatic supportive treatment become necessary.[221] Identification of patients requiring liver transplantation is difficult because as many as 60% of patients, especially children, with fulminant hepatic failure caused by hepatitis A survive.[294] Transplantation is used for the management of carefully selected patients who have a poor prognosis with medical management alone. The survival rate is reported to be 80%, although reinfection has been reported.[295, 296]

In most patients with hepatitis A, admission to the hospital is not indicated, provided that patients have access to good care. If hospitalized, fecally incontinent patients, patients with diarrhea, and small children should be given a separate room and toilet. The necessity for bed rest seems to have been overstated because no objective evidence has been provided that bed rest or restriction of physical activity affects the outcome of disease. Dietary restrictions, including prohibition of even modest amounts of alcohol, also seem to have little effect on outcome. Nevertheless, recommendation of abstention from alcohol has become conventional because alcohol has been linked with relapse of jaundice.[297]

It is crucial, however, to recognize that all cases of hepatitis A, except the rare event of fulminant hepatitis A, will resolve without any chronic sequelae.

REFERENCES

1. Zuckerman AJ. The history of viral hepatitis from antiquity to the present. In: Deinhardt F, Deinhardt J, eds. Viral Hepatitis: Laboratory and Clinical Science. New York: Marcel Dekker; 1983:3.
2. Virchow R. Ueber das Vorkommen und den Nachweis des Hepatogenen, Insbesondere des katarrhalischen Icterus. Virchows Arch. 1865;32:117.
3. McDonald S. Acute yellow atrophy of the liver. Edin Med J. 1907;1:83.
4. Cockayne EA. Catarrhal jaundice, sporadic and epidemic, and its relation to acute yellow atrophy of the liver. Q J Med. 1912;6:1.
5. Havens WP Jr. Immunity in experimentally induced infectious hepatitis. J Exp Med. 1946;84:403.
6. Lurmann A. Eine Ikterusepidemie. Berl Klin Wochenschr. 1885;22:20.
7. Anonymous. Eine nosokomiale ikterus-epidemie. Beta Med Scand. 1926;16:544.
8. Havens WP Jr, Paul JP. Prevention of infectious hepatitis with gamma globulin. JAMA. 1997;129:270.
9. Neefe JR, Gellis SS, Stokes J. Homologous serum hepatitis and infectious (epidemic) hepatitis; studies in volunteers bearing on immunological and other characteristics of the etiological agents. Am J Med Sci. 1946;1:3–22.
10. MacCallum FO. Early studies on viral hepatitis. Br Med Bull. 1972;28:105.
11. Havens WP Jr, Ward R, Drill VA, et al. Experimental production of hepatitis by feeding icterogenic materials. Proc Soc Exp Biol Med. 1944;57:206.
12. MacCallum FO, Bradley WH. Transmission of infective hepatitis to human volunteers. Lancet. 1944;2:228.
13. Gellis SS, Stokes J Jr, Brother GM, et al. The use of immune globulin (gamma globulin) in infectious (epidemic) hepatitis in the Mediterranean theatre of operations. JAMA. 1945;128:1062.
14. Krugman S. Viral hepatitis: Overview and historical perspectives. Yale J Biol Med. 1976;49:199.
15. Feinstone SM, Kapikian AZ, Purceli RH. Hepatitis A: Detection by immune electron microscopy of a viruslike antigen associated with acute illness. Science. 1973;182:1026.
16. Maynard JE, Lorenz D, Bradley DW, et al. Review of infectivity studies in nonhuman primates with virus-like particles associated with MS-1 hepatitis. Am J Med Sci. 1975;270:81.
17. Dienstag JL, Feinstone SM, Purcell RH, et al. Experimental infection of chimpanzees with hepatitis A virus. J Infect Dis. 1975;132:532.
18. Provost PJ, Hilleman MR. Propagation of human hepatitis A virus in cell culture in vitro. Proc Soc Exp Biol Med. 1979;160:213.
19. Frosner GG, Deinhardt F, Scheid R, et al. Propagation of human hepatitis A virus in a hepatoma cell line. Infection. 1979;7:303.
20. Daemer RJ, Feinstone SM, Gust ID, et al. Propagation of human hepatitis A virus in African green monkey kidney cell culture: Primary isolation and serial passage. Infect Immun. 1981;32:388.
21. Ticehurst JR, Racaniello VR, Baroudy BM, et al. Molecular cloning and characterization of hepatitis A virus cDNA. Proc Natl Acad Sci U S A. 1983;80:5885.
22. Andre FE, D'Hondt E, Delem A, et al. Clinical assessment of the safety and efficacy of an inactivated hepatitis A vaccine: Rationale and summary of findings. Vaccine. 1992;10(Suppl 1):S160–S168.
23. Melnick JL. Classification of hepatitis A virus as enterovirus type 72 and of hepatitis B virus as hepadnavirus type 1. Intervirology. 1982;18:105.
24. Melnick JL. Properties and classification of hepatitis A virus. Vaccine. 1992;10(Suppl 1):S24–S26.
25. Pringle CR. The universal system of virus taxonomy of the International Committee on Virus Taxonomy (ICTV), including new proposals ratified since publication of the Sixth ICTV Report in 1995 [published erratum appears in Arch Virol 1998;143(3):630]. Arch Virol. 1998;143:203.
26. Luo M, Rossmann MG, Palmenberg AC. Prediction of three-dimensional models for foot-and-mouth disease virus and hepatitis A virus. Virology. 1988;166:503.

27. Coulepis AG, Locarnini SA, Westaway EG, et al. Biophysical and biochemical characterization of hepatitis V virus. Intervirology. 1982;18:107.
28. Anonymous. Differences in the physical properties of dense and standard poliovirus particles. J Gen Virol. 1977;34:465.
29. Lemon SM, Jansen RW, Newbold JE. Infectious hepatitis A virus particles produced in cell culture consist of three distinct types with different buoyant densities in CsCl. J Virol. 1985;54:78.
30. Siegl G, Frosner GG. Characterization and classification of virus particles associated with hepatitis A. II. Type and configuration of nucleic acid. J Virol. 1978;26:48.
31. Shorrock C, Neuberger J. The changing face of liver transplantation. Gut. 1993;34:295.
32. Parry JV, Mortimer PP. The heat sensitivity of hepatitis A virus determined by a simple tissue culture method. J Med Virol. 1984;14:277.
33. McCaustland KA, Bond WW, Bradley DW, et al. Survival of hepatitis A virus in feces after drying and storage for 1 month. J Clin Microbiol. 1982;16:957.
34. Koff RS, Sears HS. Internal temperature of steamed clams. N Engl J Med. 1967;276:737.
35. Millard J, Appleton H, Parry JV. Studies on heat inactivation of hepatitis A virus with special reference to shellfish. Part 1. Procedures for infection and recovery of virus from laboratory-maintained cockles. Epidemiol Infect. 1987;98:397.
36. Sobsey MD. Survival and persistence of hepatitis A virus in environmental samples. In: Zuckerman AJ, ed. Viral Hepatitis and Liver Disease. New York: Alan R Liss; 1988:124.
37. Provost PJ, Wolanski BS, Miller WJ, et al. Biophysical and biochemical properties of CR326 human hepatitis A virus. Am J Med Sci. 1975;270:87.
38. Siegl G, Weitz M, Kronauer G. Stability of hepatitis A virus. Intervirology. 1984;22:218.
39. Provost PJ, Wolanski BS, Miller WJ, et al. Physical, chemical and morphologic dimensions of human hepatitis A virus strain CR326 (38578). Proc Soc Exp Biol Med. 1975;148:532.
40. Peterson DA, Hurley TR, Hoff JC, et al. Effect of chlorine treatment on infectivity of hepatitis A virus. Appl Environ Microbiol. 1983;45:223.
41. Mannucci PM, Gdovin S, Gringeri A, et al. Transmission of hepatitis A to patients with hemophilia by factor VIII concentrates treated with organic solvent and detergent to inactivate viruses. The Italian Collaborative Group. Ann Intern Med. 1994;120:1.
42. Hart HF, Hart WG, Crossley J, et al. Effect of terminal (dry) heat treatment on non-enveloped viruses in coagulation factor concentrates. Vox Sang. 1994;67:345.
43. Chin S, Williams B, Gottlieb P, et al. Virucidal short wavelength ultraviolet light treatment of plasma and factor VIII concentrate: Protection of proteins by antioxidants. Blood. 1995;86:4331.
44. Mathiesen LR, Feinstone SM, Purcell RH, et al. Detection of hepatitis A antigen by immunofluorescence. Infect Immun. 1977;18:524.
45. Feinstone SM, Moritsugu Y, Shih JW, et al. Characterization of HAV. In: Vyas GN, Cohen SN, Schmid R, eds. Viral Hepatitis. Philadelphia: Franklin Institute Press; 1978:41–48.
46. Cohen JI, Rosenblum B, Ticehurst JR, et al. Complete nucleotide sequence of an attenuated hepatitis A virus: Comparison with wild-type virus. Proc Natl Acad Sci U S A. 1987;84:2497.
47. Cohen JI, Ticehurst JR, Purcell RH, et al. Complete nucleotide sequence of wild-type hepatitis A virus: Comparison with different strains of hepatitis A virus and other picornaviruses. J Virol. 1987;61:50.
48. Weitz M, Baroudy BM, Maloy WL, et al. Detection of a genome-linked protein (VPg) of hepatitis A virus and its comparison with other picornaviral VPgs. J Virol. 1986;60:124.
49. Ruckert RR, Wimmer E. Systematic nomenclature of picornavirus proteins. J Virol. 1984;50:957.
50. Tratschin JD, Siegl G, Frosner GG, et al. Characterization and classification of virus particles associated with hepatitis A. III. Structural proteins. J Virol. 1981;38:151.
51. Wheeler CM, Robertson BH, Van Nest G, et al. Structure of the hepatitis A virion: Peptide mapping of the capsid region. J Virol. 1986;58:307.
52. Gauss-Muller V, Lottspeich F, Deinhardt F. Characterization of hepatitis A virus structural proteins. Virology. 1986;155:732.
53. Updike WS, Tesar M, Ehrenfeld E. Detection of hepatitis A virus proteins in infected BS-C-1 cells. Virology. 1991;185:411.
54. Jia XY, Summers DF, Ehrenfeld E. Primary cleavage of the HAV capsid protein precursor in the middle of the proposed 2A coding region. Virology. 1993;193:515.
55. Kusov YY, Kazachkov YA, Dzagurov GK, et al. Identification of precursors of structural proteins VP1 and VP2 of hepatitis A virus. J Med Virol. 1992;37:220.
56. Lemon SM, Chao SF, Jansen RW, et al. Genomic heterogeneity among human and nonhuman strains of hepatitis A virus. J Virol. 1987;61:735.
57. Stapleton JT, Lemon SM. Neutralization escape mutants define a dominant immunogenic neutralization site on hepatitis A virus. J Virol. 1987;61:491.
58. Lemon SM, Binn LN. Antigenic relatedness of two strains of hepatitis A virus determined by cross-neutralization. Infect Immun. 1983;42:418.
59. Binn LN, Lemon SM, Marchwicki RH, et al. Primary isolation and serial passage of hepatitis A virus strains in primate cell cultures. J Clin Microbiol. 1984;20:28.
60. Siegl G, deChastonay J, Kronauer G. Propagation and assay of hepatitis A virus in vitro. J Virol Methods. 1984;9:53.
61. Robertson BH, Khanna B, Nainan OV, et al. Epidemiologic patterns of wild-type hepatitis A virus determined by genetic variation. J Infect Dis. 1991;163:286.
62. Robertson BH, Jansen RW, Khanna B, et al. Genetic relatedness of hepatitis A virus strains recovered from different geographical regions. J Gen Virol. 1992;73:1365.
63. Brown EA, Jansen RW, Lemon SM. Characterization of a simian hepatitis A virus (HAV): Antigenic and genetic comparison with human HAV. J Virol. 1989;63:4932.
64. Jansen RW, Siegl G, Lemon SM. Molecular epidemiology of human hepatitis A virus defined by an antigen-capture polymerase chain reaction method. Proc Natl Acad Sci U S A. 1990;87:2867.
65. Jansen RW, Siegl G, Lemon SM. Molecular epidemiology of hepatitis A virus (HAV). In: Hollinger FB, Lemon SM, Margolis HS, eds. Viral Hepatitis and Liver Disease. Baltimore: Williams & Wilkins; 1991:58.
66. Gauss-Muller V, Frosner GG, Deinhardt F. Propagation of hepatitis A virus in human embryo fibroblasts. J Med Virol. 1981;7:233.
67. Dotzauer A, Feinstone SM, Kaplan G. Susceptibility of nonprimate cell lines to hepatitis A virus infection [published erratum appears in J Virol 1994 Oct;68(10):6829]. J Virol. 1994;68:6064.
68. Siegl G: Replication of hepatitis A virus and processing of proteins. Vaccine. 1992;10(Suppl 1):S32–S35.
69. de Chastonay J, Siegl G. Replicative events in hepatitis A virus–infected MRC-5 cells. Virology. 1987;157:268.
70. Cromeans T, Sobsey MD, Fields HA. Development of a plaque assay for a cytopathic, rapidly replicating isolate of hepatitis A virus. J Med Virol. 1987;22:45.
71. Cromeans T, Fields HA, Sobsey MD. Replication kinetics and cytopathic effect of hepatitis A virus. J Gen Virol. 1989;70:2051.
72. Cohen JI, Rosenblum B, Feinstone SM, et al. Attenuation and cell culture adaptation of hepatitis A virus (HAV): A genetic analysis with HAV cDNA. J Virol. 1989;63:5364.
73. Emerson SU, Huang YK, McRill C, et al. Molecular basis of virulence and growth of hepatitis A virus in cell culture. Vaccine. 1992;10(Suppl 1):S36–S39.
74. Mathiesen LR, Fauerholdt L, Moller AM, et al. Immunofluorescence studies for hepatitis A virus and hepatitis B surface and core antigen in liver biopsies from patients with acute viral hepatitis. Gastroenterology. 1979;77:623.
75. Hollinger FB, Bradley DW, Maynard JE, et al. Detection of hepatitis A viral antigen by radioimmunoassay. J Immunol. 1975;115:1464.
76. Purcell RH, Wong DC, Moritsugu Y, et al. A microtiter solid-phase radioimmunoassay for hepatitis A antigen and antibody. J Immunol. 1976;116:349.
76a. Locarnini SA, Coulepis AG, Westaway EG, et al. Restricted replication of human hepatitis A virus in cell culture: Intracellular biochemical studies. J Virol. 1981;37:216–225.
76b. Wheeler CM, Fields HA, Schable CA, et al. Adsorption, purification, and growth characteristics of hepatitis A virus strain HAS-15 propagated in fetal rhesus monkey kidney cells. J Clin Microbiol. 1986;23:434–440.
76c. Anderson DA, Locarnini SA, Gust ID. Replication of hepatitis A virus. In: Zuckerman AJ, ed. Viral Hepatitis and Liver Disease. New York: Alan R Liss; 1988:8–11.
77. Kiernan RE, Marshall JA, Coulepis AG, et al. Cellular changes associated with persistent hepatitis A infection in vitro. Arch Virol. 1987;94:81.
78. Tedeschi V, Purcell RH, Emerson SU. Partial characterization of hepatitis A viruses from three intermediate passage levels of a series resulting in adaptation to growth in cell culture and attenuation of virulence. J Med Virol. 1993;39:16.
79. Emerson SU, Huang YK, Purcell RH. 2B and 2C mutations are essential but mutations throughout the genome of HAV contribute to adaptation to cell culture. Virology. 1993;194:475.
80. Karron RA, Daemer R, Ticehurst J, et al. Studies of prototype live hepatitis A virus vaccines in primate models. J Infect Dis. 1988;157:338.
81. Provost PJ, Banker FS, Giesa PA, et al. Progress toward a live, attenuated human hepatitis A vaccine. Proc Soc Exp Biol Med. 1982;170:8.
82. Mao JS, Dong DX, Zhang HY, et al. Primary study of attenuated live hepatitis A vaccine (H2 strain) in humans. J Infect Dis. 1989;159:621.
83. Funkhouser AW, Purcell RH, D'Hondt E, et al. Attenuated hepatitis A virus: Genetic determinants of adaptation to growth in MRC-5 cells. J Virol. 1994;68:148.
84. Cohen JI, Feinstone S, Purcell RH. Hepatitis A virus infection in a chimpanzee: Duration of viremia and detection of virus in saliva and throat swabs. J Infect Dis. 1989;160:887.
85. Karayiannis P, Jowett T, Enticott M, et al. Hepatitis A virus replication in tamarins and host immune response in relation to pathogenesis of liver cell damage. J Med Virol. 1986;18:261.
86. Kaplan G, Totsuka A, Thompson P, et al. Identification of a surface glycoprotein on African green monkey kidney cells as a receptor for hepatitis A virus. EMBO J. 1996;15:4282.
87. Feigelstock D, Thompson P, Mattoo P, et al. The human homolog of HAVcr-1 codes for a hepatitis A virus cellular receptor. J Virol. 1998;72:6621.
88. Hillis WD. An outbreak of infectious hepatitis among chimpanzee handlers at a United States Air Force base. Am J Hyg. 1961;73:316.
89. Hillis WD. Viral hepatitis: A vulnerable foe. Mil Med. 1978;143:86.
90. Deinhardt F, Courtois F, Dherte P. Studies of liver function tests in chimpanzees after inoculation with human infectious hepatitis virus. Am J Hyg. 1962;75:311.
91. Deinhardt F, Holmes AW, Capps RB, et al. Studies on the transmission of human viral hepatitis to marmoset monkeys. J Exp Med. 1967;125:673.
92. Holmes AW, Wolfe L, Rosenblate H, et al. Hepatitis in marmosets: Induction of disease with coded specimens from a human volunteer study. Science. 1969;165:816.
93. Lorenz D, Barker LF, Stevens D, et al. Hepatitis in marmosets: Induction of disease with coded specimens from a human volunteer study. Proc Soc Exp Biol Med. 1970;135:348.
94. Maynard JE, Bradley DW, Gravelle CR, et al. Preliminary studies of hepatitis A in chimpanzees. J Infect Dis. 1975;131:194.
95. Maynard JE, Lorenz D, Bradley DW, et al. Review of infectivity studies in nonhuman primates with virus-like particles associated with MS-1 hepatitis. Am J Med Sci. 1975;270:81.
96. Coursaget P, Levesque B, Gretillat E, et al. Hepatitis A in primates outside captivity (Letter). Lancet. 1981;2:929.

97. LeDuc JW, Escajadillo A, Lemon SM: Hepatitis A virus among captive Panamanian owl monkeys (Letter). Lancet. 1981;2:1427.
98. Provost PJ, Villarejos VM, Hilleman MR. Suitability of the rufiventer marmoset as a host animal for human hepatitis A virus. Proc Soc Exp Biol Med. 1977;155:283.
99. Shapiro CN, Coleman PJ, McQuillan GM, et al. Epidemiology of hepatitis A: Seroepidemiology and risk groups in the USA. Vaccine. 1992;10(Suppl 1):S59–S62.
100. Shapiro CN, Margolis HS. Worldwide epidemiology of hepatitis A virus infection. J Hepatol. 1993;18(Suppl 2):S11–S14.
101. Poovorawan Y, Vimolkej T, Chongsrisawat V, et al. The declining pattern of seroepidemiology of hepatitis A virus infection among adolescents in Bangkok, Thailand. Southeast Asian J Trop Med Public Health. 1997;28:154.
102. Studer S, Joller-Jemelka HI, Steffen R, et al. Prevalence of hepatitis A antibodies in Swiss travellers. Eur J Epidemiol. 1993;9:50.
103. Frosner GG, Papaevangelou G, Butler R, et al. Antibody against hepatitis A in seven European countries. I. Comparison of prevalence data in different age groups. Am J Epidemiol. 1979;110:63.
104. Regan CM, Syed Q, Corkery A. Hepatitis A vaccine (Letter). BMJ. 1991;303:414.
105. Shapiro CN, Shaw FE, Mandel EJ, et al. Epidemiology of hepatitis A in the United States. In: Hollinger FB, Lemon SM, Margolis HS, eds. Viral Hepatitis and Liver Disease. Williams & Wilkins; Baltimore: 1991:71.
106. Fujiyama S, Odoh K, Kuramoto I, et al. Current seroepidemiological status of hepatitis A with a comparison of antibody titers after infection and vaccination. J Hepatol. 1994;21:641.
107. Boughton CR, Hawkes RA, Ferguson V. Viral hepatitis A and B: A seroepidemiological study of a non-hepatitic Sydney population. Med J Aust. 1980;1:177.
108. Utili R, Galanti B, Da Villa G, et al. Hyperendemicity of viral hepatitis in the Neapolitan area: An epidemiological study. Boll Ist Sieroter Milan. 1983;62:145.
109. Mele A, Stroffolini T, Palumbo F, et al. Incidence of and risk factors for hepatitis A in Italy: Public health indications from a 10-year surveillance. SEIEVA Collaborating Group. J Hepatol. 1997;26:743.
110. DeFraites RF, Feighner BH, Binn LN, et al. Immunization of US soldiers with a two-dose primary series of inactivated hepatitis A vaccine: Early immune response, persistence of antibody, and response to a third dose at 1 year. J Infect Dis. 1995;171(Suppl 1):S61–S69.
111. Centers for Disease Control and Prevention. Notifiable disease reports. MMWR Morb Mortal Wkly Rep. 1995;44:974.
112. Gust ID, Feinstone SM. Hepatitis A. Boca Raton, Fla: CRC Press; 1998.
113. Steffen R: Hepatitis A in travelers: The European experience. J Infect Dis. 1995;171(Suppl 1):S24–S28.
114. Innis BL, Snitbhan R, Hoke CH, et al. The declining transmission of hepatitis A in Thailand. J Infect Dis. 1991;163:989.
115. Stroffolini T, D'Amelio R, Matricardi PM, et al. The changing epidemiology of hepatitis A in Italy. Ital J Gastroenterol. 1993;25:372.
116. Akbar SM, Onji M, Kanaoka M, et al. The seroepidemiology of hepatitis A and B in a Japanese town. Asia Pac J Public Health. 1992;6:26.
117. Taylor-Wiedeman J, Moritsugu Y, Miyamura K, et al. Seroepidemiology of hepatitis A virus in Japan. Jpn J Med Sci Biol. 1987;40:119.
118. Stroffolini T, De Crescenzo L, Giammanco A, et al. Changing patterns of hepatitis A virus infection in children in Palermo, Italy. Eur J Epidemiol. 1990;6:84.
119. Perez-Trallero E, Cilla G, Urbieta M, et al. Falling incidence and prevalence of hepatitis A in northern Spain. Scand J Infect Dis. 1994;26:133.
120. Halliday ML, Kang LY, Zhou TK, et al. An epidemic of hepatitis A attributable to the ingestion of raw clams in Shanghai, China. J Infect Dis. 1991;164:852.
121. Yao G. Clinical spectrum and natural history of viral hepatitis A in a 1988 Shanghai epidemic. In: Hollinger FB, Lemon SM, Margolis HS, eds. Viral Hepatitis and Liver Disease. Baltimore: Williams & Wilkins; 1991:76.
122. Skinhoj P. Natural history of viral hepatitis in Greenland. Am J Med Sci. 1975;270:305.
123. Skinhoj P, Mikkelsen F, Hollinger FB. Hepatitis A in Greenland: Importance of specific antibody testing in epidemiologic surveillance. Am J Epidemiol. 1977;105:140.
124. Wong DC, Purcell RH, Rosen L. Prevalence of antibody to hepatitis A and hepatitis B viruses in selected populations of the South Pacific. Am J Epidemiol. 1979;110:227.
125. Smith PF, Grabau JC, Werzberger A, et al. The role of young children in a community-wide outbreak of hepatitis A. Epidemiol Infect. 1997;118:243.
126. Steffen R, Kane MA, Shapiro CN, et al. Epidemiology and prevention of hepatitis A in travelers. JAMA. 1994;272:885.
127. Smalligan RD, Lange WR, Frame JD, et al. The risk of viral hepatitis A, B, C, and E among North American missionaries. Am J Trop Med Hyg. 1995;53:233.
128. Gust ID, Lehmann NI, Dimitrakakis M. A seroepidemiologic study of infection with HAV and HBV in five Pacific Islands. Am J Epidemiol. 1979;110:237.
129. Gust ID, Lehmann NI, Dimitrakakis M, et al. Seroepidemiology of infection with hepatitis A and B viruses in an isolated Pacific population. J Infect Dis. 1979;139:559.
130. Gust ID, Lehmann NI, Lucas CR. Relationship between prevalence of antibody to hepatitis A antigen and age: A cohort effect (Letter)? J Infect Dis. 1978;138:425.
131. Naruto H, Shimizu Y, Iwata K, et al. Incidence of hepatitis A virus infection among Japanese volunteers staying in developing countries. Jpn J Exp Med. 1983;53:135.
132. Centers for Disease Control and Prevention. Summary of notifiable diseases, United States. MMWR Morb Mortal Wkly Rep. 1994;43(53):6.
133. Cilla G, Perez-Trallero E, Marimon JM, et al. Prevalence of hepatitis A antibody among disadvantaged gypsy children in northern Spain. Epidemiol Infect. 1995;115:157.
134. Green MS, Tsur S, Slepon R. Sociodemographic factors and the declining prevalence of anti–hepatitis A antibodies in young adults in Israel: Implications for the new hepatitis A vaccines. Int J Epidemiol. 1992;21:136.
135. Bell JC, Crewe EB, Capon AG. Seroprevalence of hepatitis A antibodies among residents of a centre for people with developmental disabilities. Aust N Z J Med. 1994;24:365.
136. Hadler SC, Erben JJ, Francis DP, et al. Risk factors for hepatitis A in day-care centers. J Infect Dis. 1982;145:255.
137. Shapiro CN, Hadler SC. Hepatitis A and hepatitis B virus infections in day-care settings. Pediatr Ann. 1991;20:435.
138. Corey L, Holmes KK. Sexual transmission of hepatitis A in homosexual men: Incidence and mechanism. N Engl J Med. 1980;302:435.
139. Stewart T, Crofts N. An outbreak of hepatitis A among homosexual men in Melbourne. Med J Aust. 1993;158:519.
140. Widell A, Hansson BG, Moestrup T, et al. Increased occurrence of hepatitis A with cyclic outbreaks among drug addicts in a Swedish community. Infection. 1983;11:198.
141. Villano SA, Nelson KE, Vlahov D, et al. Hepatitis A among homosexual men and injection drug users: More evidence for vaccination. Clin Infect Dis. 1997;25:726.
142. Mele A, Sagliocca L, Palumbo F, et al. Travel-associated hepatitis A: Effect of place of residence and country visited. J Public Health Med. 1991;13:256.
143. Heng BH, Goh KT, Doraisingham S, et al. Prevalence of hepatitis A virus infection among sewage workers in Singapore. Epidemiol Infect. 1994;113:121.
144. Cadilhac P, Roudot-Thoraval F. Seroprevalence of hepatitis A virus infection among sewage workers in the Parisian area, France. Eur J Epidemiol. 1996;12:237.
145. Krugman S, Ward R, Giles JP. Infectious hepatitis: Detection of virus during the incubation period and in clinically inapparent infection. N Engl J Med. 1959;261:729.
146. Havens WPJ. Period of infectivity of patients with experimentally induced infectious hepatitis. J Exp Med. 1946;83:251.
147. Dienstag JL, Feinstone SM, Kapikian AZ, et al. Faecal shedding of hepatitis-A antigen. Lancet. 1975;1:765.
148. Dienstag JL, Routenberg JA, Purcell RH, et al. Foodhandler-associated outbreak of hepatitis type A. An immune electron microscopic study. Ann Intern Med. 1975;83:647.
149. Coulepis AG, Locarnini SA, Lehmann NI, et al. Detection of hepatitis A virus in the feces of patients with naturally acquired infections. J Infect Dis. 1980;141:151.
150. Maynard JE. Infectious hepatitis at Fort Yukon, Alaska—report of an outbreak, 1960–61. Am J Public Health. 1963;53:31.
151. Lehmannn NI, Sharma DL, Gust ID. Prevalence of antibody to the hepatitis A virus in a large institution for the mentally retarded. J Med Virol. 1978;2:335.
152. ASHER LVS, Binn LN, Mensing TL, et al. Pathogenesis of hepatitis A in orally inoculated owl monkeys (*Aotus trivirgatus*). J Med Virol. 1995;47:260.
153. Yotsuyanagi H, Iino S, Koike K, et al. Duration of viremia in human hepatitis A viral infection as determined by polymerase chain reaction. J Med Virol. 1993;40:35.
154. Barker LF, Dienstag JL, Lorenz DE, et al. Serologic and animal inoculation studies of a communal outbreak of viral hepatitis, type A. Am J Med Sci. 1977;274:247.
155. Lemon SM. The natural history of hepatitis A: The potential for transmission by transfusion of blood or blood products. Vox Sang. 1994;67(Suppl 4):19, 24–26.
156. Weisfuse IB, Graham DJ, Will M, et al. An outbreak of hepatitis A among cancer patients treated with interleukin-2 and lymphokine-activated killer cells. J Infect Dis. 1990;161:647.
157. Shaw FE Jr, Shapiro CN, Welty TK, et al. Hepatitis transmission among the Sioux Indians of South Dakota. Am J Public Health. 1990;80:1091.
158. Roumeliotou A, Papachristopoulos A, Alexiou D, et al. Intrafamilial clustering of hepatitis A. Infection. 1994;22:96.
159. Frosner GG, Overby LR, Flehmig B, et al. Seroepidemiological investigation of patients and family contacts in an epidemic of hepatitis A. J Med Virol. 1977;1:163.
160. Rajaratnam G, Patel M, Parry JV, et al. An outbreak of hepatitis A: School toilets as a source of transmission. J Public Health Med. 1992;14:72.
161. Papaevangelou G, Mosley JW, Kyriakidou A, et al. Viral hepatitis: Lack of transmission in an Athenian school. Int J Epidemiol. 1978;7:341.
162. Rosenblum LS, Villarino ME, Nainan OV, et al. Hepatitis A outbreak in a neonatal intensive care unit: Risk factors for transmission and evidence of prolonged viral excretion among preterm infants. J Infect Dis. 1991;164:476.
163. Watson JC, Fleming DW, Borella AJ, et al. Vertical transmission of hepatitis A resulting in an outbreak in a neonatal intensive care unit. J Infect Dis. 1993;167:567.
164. Gust ID: The epidemiology of viral hepatitis. In: Vyas GN, Dienstag JL, Hoofnagle JH, eds. Hepatitis and Liver Disease. Orlando, Fla: Grune & Stratton; 1984:415.
165. Enriquez R, Frosner GG, Hochstein-Mintzel V, et al. Accumulation and persistence of hepatitis A virus in mussels. J Med Virol. 1992;37:174.
166. Cromeans TL, Nainan OV, Margolis HS. Detection of hepatitis A virus RNA in oyster meat. Appl Environ Microbiol. 1997;63:2460.
167. Dienstag JL, Gust ID, Lucas CR, et al. Mussel-associated viral hepatitis, type A: Serological confirmation. Lancet. 1976;1:561.
168. Peterson DA, Wolfe LG, Larkin EP, et al. Thermal treatment and infectivity of hepatitis A virus in human feces. J Med Virol. 1978;2:201.
169. Niu MT, Polish LB, Robertson BH, et al. Multistate outbreak of hepatitis A associated with frozen strawberries. J Infect Dis. 1992;166:518.
170. Centers for Disease Control and Infection. Hepatitis A associated with consumption of frozen strawberries—Michigan, March 1997. MMWR Morb Mortal Wkly Rep. 1997;46(13):288.
171. Carl M, Francis DP, Maynard JE. Food-borne hepatitis A: Recommendations for control. J Infect Dis. 1983;148:1133.

172. Dalton CB, Haddix A, Hoffman RE, et al. The cost of a food-borne outbreak of hepatitis A in Denver, Colo. Arch Intern Med. 1996;156:1013.
173. Mosley JW. Water-borne infectious hepatitis. N Engl J Med 1959;261:703.
174. Bowen GS, McCarthy MA. Hepatitis A associated with a hardware store water fountain and a contaminated well in Lancaster County, Pennsylvania, 1980. Am J Epidemiol. 1983;117:695.
175. Bloch AB, Stramer SL, Smith JD, et al. Recovery of hepatitis A virus from a water supply responsible for a common source outbreak of hepatitis A. Am J Public Health. 1990;80:428.
176. Thornton L, Fogarty J, Hayes C, et al. The risk of hepatitis A from sewage contamination of a water supply. Commun Dis Rep CDR Rev. 1995;5:R1–R4.
177. Krugman S, Giles JP, Hammond J. Infectious hepatitis: Evidence for two distinctive clinical, epidemiological and immunological types of infection. JAMA. 1967;200:365.
178. Purcell RH, Feinstone SM, Ticehurst JR, et al. Hepatitis A virus. In: Vyas GN, Dienstag JL, Hoofnagle JH, eds. Viral Hepatitis and Liver Disease. Orlando, Fla: Grune & Stratton; 1984:9.
179. Mathiesen LR, Moller AM, Purcell RH, et al. Hepatitis A virus in the liver and intestine of marmosets after oral inoculation. Infect Immun. 1980;28:45.
180. Taylor GM, Goldin RD, Karayiannis P, et al. In situ hybridization studies in hepatitis A infection. Hepatology. 1992;16:642.
181. Taylor M, Goldin RD, Ladva S, et al. In situ hybridization studies of hepatitis A viral RNA in patients with acute hepatitis A. J Hepatol. 1994;20:380.
182. Mathiesen LR, Drucker J, Lorenz D, et al. Localization of hepatitis A antigen in marmoset organs during acute infection with hepatitis A virus. J Infect Dis. 1978;138:369.
183. Krawczynski KK, Bradley DW, Murphy BL, et al. Pathogenetic aspects of hepatitis A virus infection in enterally inoculated marmosets. Am J Clin Pathol. 1981;76:698.
184. Shimizu YK, Shikata T, Beninger PR, et al. Detection of hepatitis A antigen in human liver. Infect Immun. 1982;36:320.
185. Locarnini SA, Coulepis AG, Kaldor J, et al. Coproantibodies in hepatitis A: Detection by enzyme-linked immunosorbent assay and immune electron microscopy. J Clin Microbiol. 1980;11:710.
186. Yoshizawa H, Itoh Y, Iwakiri S, et al. Diagnosis of type A hepatitis by fecal IgA antibody against hepatitis A antigen. Gastroenterology. 1980;78:114.
187. Vallbracht A, Fleischer B. Immune pathogenesis of hepatitis A. Arch Virol Suppl. 1992;4:3.
188. Feinstone SM, Gust ID. Hepatitis A infection: Clinical aspects. In: Seeff LB, Lewis JH, eds. Current Perspectives in Hepatology. New York: Plenum; 1989:3.
189. Fleischer B, Vallbracht A. Demonstration of virus-specific cytotoxic T lymphocytes in liver tissue in hepatitis A—a model for immunopathological reactions. Behring Inst Mitt. 1991;89:226.
190. Baba M, Hasegawa H, Nakayabu M, et al. Cytolytic activity of natural killer cells and lymphokine activated killer cells against hepatitis A virus infected fibroblasts. J Clin Lab Immunol. 1993;40:47.
191. Gabriel P, Vallbracht A, Flehmig B. Lack of complement-dependent cytolytic antibodies in hepatitis A virus infection. J Med Virol. 1986;20:23.
192. Margolis HS, Nainan OV. Identification of virus components in circulating immune complexes isolated during hepatitis A virus infection. Hepatology. 1990;11:31.
193. Inman RD, Hodge M, Johnston ME, et al. Arthritis, vasculitis, and cryoglobulinemia associated with relapsing hepatitis A virus infection. Ann Intern Med. 1986;105:700.
194. Koff RS. Clinical manifestations and diagnosis of hepatitis A virus infection. Vaccine. 1992;10(Suppl 1):S15–S17.
195. Mathiesen LR. The hepatitis A virus infection. Liver. 1981;1:81.
196. Hadler SC, McFarland L. Hepatitis in day care centers: Epidemiology and prevention. Rev Infect Dis. 1986;8:548.
197. Hadler SC, Webster HM, Erben JJ, et al. Hepatitis A in day-care centers. A community-wide assessment. N Engl J Med. 1980;302:1222.
198. Yang NY, Yu PH, Mao ZX, et al. Inapparent infection of hepatitis A virus. Am J Epidemiol. 1988;127:599.
199. Smith FR, Henkin RI, Dell RB. Disordered gustatory acuity in liver disease. Gastroenterology. 1976;70:568.
200. Gust ID. Acute viral hepatitis. Aust Fam Physician. 1978;7:535.
201. Scully LJ, Ryan AE. Urticaria and acute hepatitis A virus infection. Am J Gastroenterol. 1993;88:277.
202. Tong MJ, el-Farra NS, Grew MI. Clinical manifestations of hepatitis A: Recent experience in a community teaching hospital. J Infect Dis. 1995;171(Suppl 1):S15–S18.
203. Mishra L, Seeff LB. Viral hepatitis, A though E, complicating pregnancy. Gastroenterol Clin North Am. 1992;21:873.
204. Zhang RL, Zeng JS, Zhang HZ. Survey of 34 pregnant women with hepatitis A and their neonates. Chin Med J (Engl). 1990;103:552.
205. McNair AN, Main J, Thomas HC. Interactions of the human immunodeficiency virus and the hepatotropic viruses. Semin Liver Dis. 1992;12:188.
206. Vento S, Garofano T, Renzini C, et al. Fulminant hepatitis associated with hepatitis A virus superinfection in patients with chronic hepatitis C. N Engl J Med 1998;338:286.
207. Leino T, Pebody R, Leinikki P. Hepatitis associated with hepatitis A superinfection in patients with chronic hepatitis C (Letter). N Engl J Med. 1998;338:1772.
208. Battegay M, Naef M, Bucher HC. Hepatitis associated with hepatitis A superinfection in patients with chronic hepatitis C (Letter). N Engl J Med. 1998;338:1771.
209. Mele A, Tosti ME, Stroffolini T. Hepatitis associated with hepatitis A superinfection in patients with chronic hepatitis C (Letter). N Engl J Med. 1998;338:1771.
210. Gordon SC, Reddy KR, Schiff L, et al. Prolonged intrahepatic cholestasis secondary to acute hepatitis A. Ann Intern Med. 1984;101:635.
211. Sjogren MH, Tanno H, Fay O, et al. Hepatitis A virus in stool during clinical relapse. Ann Intern Med. 1987;106:221.
212. Cobden I, James OF. A biphasic illness associated with acute hepatitis A virus infection. J Hepatol. 1986;2:19.
213. Chiriaco P, Guadalupi C, Armigliato M, et al. Polyphasic course of hepatitis type A in children (Letter). J Infect Dis. 1986;153:378.
214. Davis LE, Brown JE, Robertson BH, et al. Hepatitis A post-viral encephalitis. Acta Neurol Scand. 1993;87:67.
215. Davis TV, Keeffe EB. Acute pancreatitis associated with acute hepatitis A. Am J Gastroenterol. 1992;87:1648.
216. Geltner D, Naot Y, Zimhoni O, et al. Acute oliguric renal failure complicating type A nonfulminant viral hepatitis. A case presentation and review of the literature. J Clin Gastroenterol. 1992;14:160.
217. Mourani S, Dobbs SM, Genta RM, et al. Hepatitis A virus–associated cholecystitis. Ann Intern Med. 1994;120:398.
218. Ilan Y, Hillman M, Oren R, et al. Vasculitis and cryoglobulinemia associated with persisting cholestatic hepatitis A virus infection. Am J Gastroenterol. 1990;85:586.
219. Dan M, Yaniv R. Cholestatic hepatitis, cutaneous vasculitis, and vascular deposits of immunoglobulin M and complement associated with hepatitis A virus infection. Am J Med. 1990;89:103.
220. Centers for Disease Control and Prevention: Prevention of hepatitis A through active or passive immunization: Recommendations of the Advisory Committee on Immunization Practices (ACIP). MMWR Morb Mortal Wkly Rep. 1996;45:1.
221. Hoofnagle JH, Carithers RLJ, Shapiro C, et al. Fulminant hepatic failure: Summary of a workshop. Hepatology. 1995;21:240.
222. Norkrans G, Nilsson LA, Frosner G, et al. Serum immunoglobulin levels in hepatitis non-A, non-B: A comparison with hepatitis A and B. Infection. 1980;8:98.
223. Hoofnagle JH, Di Bisceglie AM: Serologic diagnosis of acute and chronic viral hepatitis. Semin Liver Dis. 1991;11:73.
224. Bradley DW, Maynard JE, Hindman SH, et al. Serodiagnosis of viral hepatitis A: Detection of acute-phase immunoglobulin M anti–hepatitis A virus by radioimmunoassay. J Clin Microbiol. 1977;5:521.
225. Decker RH, Kosakowski SM, Vanderbilt AS, et al. Diagnosis of acute hepatitis A by HAVAB-M, a direct radioimmunoassay for IgM anti-HAV. Am J Clin Pathol. 1981;76:140.
226. Locarnini SA, Ferris AA, Lehmann NI, et al. The antibody response following hepatitis A infection. Intervirology. 1977;8:309.
227. Flehmig B, Ranke M, Berthold H, et al. A solid-phase radioimmunoassay for detection of IgM antibodies to hepatitis A virus. J Infect Dis. 1979;140:169.
228. Robertson BH, Jia XY, Tian H, et al. Antibody response to nonstructural proteins of hepatitis A virus following infection. J Med Virol. 1993;40:76.
229. Summers DF, Ehrenfeld E. Host antibody response to viral structural and nonstructural proteins after hepatitis A virus infection. J Infect Dis. 1992;165:273.
230. Mathiesen LR, Feinstone SM, Wong DC, et al. Enzyme-linked immunosorbent assay for detection of hepatitis A antigen in stool and antibody to hepatitis A antigen in sera: Comparison with solid-phase radioimmunoassay, immune electron microscopy, and immune adherence hemagglutination assay. J Clin Microbiol. 1978;7:184.
231. Tsai YL, Sobsey MD, Sangermano LR, et al. Simple method of concentrating enteroviruses and hepatitis A virus from sewage and ocean water for rapid detection by reverse transcriptase–polymerase chain reaction. Appl Environ Microbiol. 1993;59:3488.
232. Le Guyader F, Dubois E, Menard D, et al. Detection of hepatitis A virus, rotavirus, and enterovirus in naturally contaminated shellfish and sediment by reverse transcription–seminested PCR. Appl Environ Microbiol. 1994;60:3665.
233. Fan X, Zhang Z. Increased tumour necrosis factor alpha production by neutrophils in patients with hepatitis B. J Clin Pathol. 1994;47:616.
234. Normann A, Graff J, Flehmig B. Detection of hepatitis A virus in a factor VIII preparation by antigen capture/PCR. Vox Sang. 1994;67(Suppl 1):57, 61.
235. Abe H, Beninger PR, Ikejiri N, et al. Light microscopic findings of liver biopsy specimens from patients with hepatitis type A and comparison with type B. Gastroenterology. 1982;82:938.
236. Kobayashi K, Hashimoto E, Ludwig J, et al. Liver biopsy features of acute hepatitis C compared with hepatitis A, B, and non-A, non-B, non-C. Liver. 1993;13:69.
237. Shimizu YK, Mathiesen LR, Lorenz D, et al. Localization of hepatitis A antigen in liver tissue by peroxidase-conjugated antibody method: Light and electron microscopic studies. J Immunol. 1978;121:1671.
238. Huang SN, Lorenz D, Gerety RJ. Electron and immunoelectron microscopic study on liver tissues of marmosets infected with hepatitis A virus. Lab Invest. 1979;41:63.
239. Neefe JR, Stokes J Jr, Gellis SS. Homologous serum hepatitis and infectious (epidemic) hepatitis: Experimental study of immunity and cross immunity in volunteers; preliminary report. Am J Med Sci. 1945;210:561.
240. Stapleton JT, Lange DK, LeDuc JW, et al. The role of secretory immunity in hepatitis A virus infection. J Infect Dis. 1991;163:7.
241. Lemon SM, Binn LN. Serum neutralizing antibody response to hepatitis A virus. J Infect Dis. 1983;148:1033.
242. Baba M, Fukai K, Hasegawa H, et al. The role of natural killer cells and lymphokine activated killer cells in the pathogenesis of hepatic injury and hepatitis A. J Clin Lab Immunol. 1992;38:1.
243. Kurane I, Binn LN, Bancroft WH, et al. Human lymphocyte responses to hepatitis A virus–infected cells: Interferon production and lysis of infected cells. J Immunol. 1985;135:2140.

244. Reed CM, Gustafson TL, Siegel J, et al. Nosocomial transmission of hepatitis A from a hospital-acquired case. Pediatr Infect Dis. 1984;3:300.
245. Goodman RA, Carder CC, Allen JR, et al. Nosocomial hepatitis A transmission by an adult patient with diarrhea. Am J Med. 1982;73:220.
246. American Academy of Pediatrics. Hepatitis A. In: Peter G, ed. Red Book: Report of the Committee on Infectious Diseases. 24th ed. Elk Grove, Ill: American Academy of Pediatrics; 1997:237.
247. Chiaramonte M, Trivello R, Moschen ME, et al. The risk of hepatitis A virus infection for hospital staff. Boll 1st Sieroter Milan. 1983;62:304.
248. Lee KK, Vargo LR, Le CT, et al. Transfusion-acquired hepatitis A outbreak from fresh frozen plasma in a neonatal intensive care unit. Pediatr Infect Dis J. 1992;11:122.
249. Centers for Disease Control and Prevention. Outbreak of viral hepatitis in the staff of a pediatric ward. MMWR Morb Mortal Wkly Rep. 1977;26:77.
250. Kozicki M, Steffen R, Schar M. 'Boil it, cook it, peel it or forget it': Does this rule prevent travellers' diarrhoea? Int J Epidemiol. 1985;14:169.
251. Lerman Y, Shohat T, Ashkenazi S, et al. Efficacy of different doses of immune serum globulin in the prevention of hepatitis A: A three-year prospective study. Clin Infect Dis. 1993;17:411.
252. Smallwood LA, Tabor E, Finlayson JS, et al. Antibodies to hepatitis A virus in immune serum globulin (Letter). Lancet. 1980;2:482.
253. Stokes N. The prevention and attenuation of infectious hepatitis by gamma globulin. JAMA. 1945;127:144.
254. Stapleton JT. Passive immunization against hepatitis A. Vaccine. 1992;10(Suppl 1):S45–S47.
255. Weiland O, Niklasson B, Berg R, et al. Clinical and subclinical hepatitis A occurring after immunoglobulin prophylaxis among Swedish UN soldiers in Sinai. Scand J Gastroenterol. 1981;16:967.
256. Pierce PF, Cappello M, Bernard KW. Subclinical infection with hepatitis A in Peace Corps volunteers following immune globulin prophylaxis. Am J Trop Med Hyg. 1990;42:465.
257. McMahon BJ, Beller M, Williams J, et al. A program to control an outbreak of hepatitis A in Alaska by using an inactivated hepatitis A vaccine. Arch Pediatr Adolesc Med. 1996;150:733.
258. Van Doorslaer E, Tormans G, van Damme P. Cost-effectiveness analysis of vaccination against hepatitis A in travellers. J Med Virol. 1994;44:463.
259. Mao JS. Development of live, attenuated hepatitis A vaccine (H2-strain). Vaccine. 1990;8:523.
260. Cho MW, Ehrenfeld E. Rapid completion of the replication cycle of hepatitis A virus subsequent to reversal of guanidine inhibition. Virology. 1991;180:770.
261. Vidor E, Fritzell B, Plotkin S. Clinical development of a new inactivated hepatitis A vaccine. Infection. 1996;24:447.
262. Gluck R, Mischler R, Brantschen S, et al. Immunopotentiating reconstituted influenza virus virosome vaccine delivery system for immunization against hepatitis A. J Clin Invest. 1992;90:2491.
263. Sjogren MH, Purcell RH, McKee K, et al. Clinical and laboratory observations following oral or intramuscular administration of a live attenuated hepatitis A vaccine candidate. Vaccine. 1992;10(Suppl 1):S135–S137.
264. Cohen JI, Ticehurst JR, Feinstone SM, et al. Hepatitis A virus cDNA and its RNA transcripts are infectious in cell culture. J Virol. 1987;61:3035.
265. Cohen JI, Rosenblum B, Feinstone SM, et al. Attenuation and cell culture adaptation of hepatitis A virus (HAV): A genetic analysis with HAV cDNA. J Virol. 1989;63:5364.
266. Nalin DR, Kuter BJ, Brown L, et al. Worldwide experience with the CR326F-derived inactivated hepatitis A virus vaccine in pediatric and adult populations: An overview. J Hepatol. 1993;18(Suppl 2):S51–S55.
267. Werzberger A, Mensch B, Kuter B, et al. A controlled trial of a formalin-inactivated hepatitis A vaccine in healthy children. N Engl J Med. 1992;327:453.
268. Innis BL, Snitbhan R, Kunasol P, et al. Protection against hepatitis A by an inactivated vaccine. JAMA. 1994;271:1328.
269. Werzberger A, Kuter B, Shouval D, et al. Anatomy of a trial: A historical view of the Monroe inactivated hepatitis A protective efficacy trial. J Hepatol. 1993;18(Suppl 2):S46–S50.
270. Shouval D, Ashur Y, Adler R, et al. Safety, tolerability, and immunogenicity of an inactivated hepatitis A vaccine: Effects of single and booster injections, and comparison to administration of immune globulin. J Hepatol. 1993;18(Suppl 2):S32–S37.
271. van Damme P, Mathei C, Thoelen S, et al. Single dose inactivated hepatitis A vaccine: Rationale and clinical assessment of the safety and immunogenicity. J Med Virol. 1994;44:435.
272. Hoke CH Jr, Binn LN, Egan JE, et al. Hepatitis A in the US Army: Epidemiology and vaccine development. Vaccine. 1992;10(Suppl 1):S75–S79.
273. Zaaijer HL, Leentvaar-Kuijpers A, Rotman H, et al. Hepatitis A antibody titres after infection and immunization: Implications for passive and active immunization. J Med Virol. 1993;40:22.
274. Fujiyama S, Iino S, Odoh K, et al. Time course of hepatitis A virus antibody titer after active and passive immunization. Hepatology. 1992;15:983.
275. Lemon SM, Murphy PC, Provost PJ, et al. Immunoprecipitation and virus neutralization assays demonstrate qualitative differences between protective antibody responses to inactivated hepatitis A vaccine and passive immunization with immune globulin. J Infect Dis. 1997;176:9.
276. Purcell RH, D'Hondt E, Bradbury R, et al. Inactivated hepatitis A vaccine: Active and passive immunoprophylaxis in chimpanzees. Vaccine. 1992;10(Suppl 1):S148–S151.
277. Nordenfelt E. Hepatitis A in Swedish travellers. Vaccine. 1992;10(Suppl 1):S73–S74.
278. Lange WR, Frame JD. High incidence of viral hepatitis among American missionaries in Africa. Am J Trop Med Hyg. 1990;43:527.
279. Lemon SM, Shapiro CN. The value of immunization against hepatitis A. Infect Agents Dis. 1994;3:38.
280. Newcomer W, Rivin B, Reid R, et al. Immunogenicity, safety and tolerability of varying doses and regimens of inactivated hepatitis A virus vaccine in Navajo children. Pediatr Infect Dis J. 1994;13:640.
281. Welty TK, Darling K, Dye S, et al. Guidelines for prevention and control of hepatitis A in American Indian and Alaska Native communities. S D J Med. 1996;49:317.
282. Hollinger FB, Khan NC, Oefinger PE, et al. Posttransfusion hepatitis type A. JAMA. 1983;250:2313.
283. Maguire H. Hepatitis A virus infection. Risk to sewage workers unproved (Letter). BMJ. 1993;307:561.
284. Zanetti A, Pregliasco F, Andreassi A, et al. Does immunoglobulin interfere with the immunogenicity to Pasteur Merieux inactivated hepatitis A vaccine? J Hepatol. 1997;26:25.
285. Wagner G, Lavanchy D, Darioli R, et al. Simultaneous active and passive immunization against hepatitis A studied in a population of travellers. Vaccine. 1993;11:1027.
286. Leentvaar-Kuijpers A, Coutinho RA, Brulein V, et al. Simultaneous passive and active immunization against hepatitis A. Vaccine. 1992;10(Suppl 1):S138–S141.
287. Ambrosch F, Andre FE, Delem A, et al. Simultaneous vaccination against hepatitis A and B: Results of a controlled study. Vaccine. 1992;10(Suppl 1):S142–S145.
288. Gil A, Gonzalez A, Dal-Re R, et al. Interference assessment of yellow fever vaccine with the immune response to a single-dose inactivated hepatitis A vaccine (1440 EL.U.). A controlled study in adults. Vaccine. 1996;14:1028.
289. Bienzle U, Bock HL, Kruppenbacher JP, et al. Immunogenicity of an inactivated hepatitis A vaccine administered according to two different schedules and the interference of other "travellers" vaccines with the immune response. Vaccine. 1996;14:501.
290. Prikazsky V, Olear V, Cernoch A, et al. Interruption of an outbreak of hepatitis A in two villages by vaccination. J Med Virol. 1994;44:457.
291. Jefferson TO, Behrens RH, Demicheli V. Should British soldiers be vaccinated against hepatitis A? An economic analysis. Vaccine. 1994;12:1379.
292. Behrens RH, Roberts JA. Is travel prophylaxis worth while? Economic appraisal of prophylactic measures against malaria, hepatitis A, and typhoid in travellers. BMJ. 1994;309:918.
293. Margolis HS, Shapiro CN. Considerations for the development of recommendations for the use of hepatitis A vaccine. J Hepatol. 1993;18(Suppl 2):S56–S60.
294. O'Grady J. Management of acute and fulminant hepatitis A. Vaccine. 1992;10(Suppl 1):S21–S23.
295. Fagan E, Yousef G, Brahm J, et al. Persistence of hepatitis A virus in fulminant hepatitis and after liver transplantation. J Med Virol. 1990;30:131.
296. Gane E, Sallie R, Saleh M, et al. Clinical recurrence of hepatitis A following liver transplantation for acute liver failure. J Med Virol. 1995;45:35.
297. Mijch AM, Gust ID. Clinical, serologic, and epidemiologic aspects of hepatitis A virus infection. Semin Liver Dis. 1986;6:42.

Chapter 162

Rhinovirus

JACK M. GWALTNEY, JR.

Since antiquity, people have been plagued with colds[1]; however, it was only in 1914 that the first direct evidence of the infectious nature of colds was reported by Kruse. He produced colds in volunteers by intranasal instillation of bacteria-free filtrates of secretions from cold sufferers.[2] In the 1940s and 1950s, Dingle and colleagues[3] and a British research team headed by Andrewes[4] examined many facets related to the etiology and epidemiology of colds. At a later date, the nasal secretions used by Andrewes and Tyrrell for human transmission studies were shown to contain rhinoviruses.

Pelon and associates[5] and Price[6] independently isolated a new virus in 1956, which was later designated rhinovirus 1A. Another significant advance in the isolation and characterization of a number of rhinoviruses was the use by Ketler and coworkers[7] of the highly sensitive human embryonic lung cells developed by Hayflick and Moorhead.[8] By 1963, the number of known immunotypes had increased so rapidly that no single laboratory could characterize the rhinovirus group. Beginning in 1967, a collaborative program directed by Kapikian and associates[9] established a uniform classification system for the known rhinovirus immunotypes 1 to 55. In 1971 other immunotypes were added, which brought the total to 89,[10] and in 1986 the addition of 11 new immunotypes increased the number to 100.[11] The viral genome[12–14] and the x-ray crystallographic structure of the viral shell[15] were characterized in 1984 and 1985, respectively.

Epidemiologic studies have shown that rhinoviruses are the major known cause of the common cold.[16–18] There is also evidence that they have a role in acute sinus infections,[19] otitis media,[20] exacerbations of chronic bronchitis,[21–23] and attacks of asthma.[24, 25] Discovery of the rhinoviruses established that the common cold is a complex syndrome produced by a large number of antigenically distinct viruses and that controlling colds with vaccines is not feasible. Recent work in the field has focused on the role that inflammatory mediators play in rhinovirus pathogenesis and on developing new methods of chemoprophylaxis and chemotherapy.

DESCRIPTION OF THE PATHOGEN

Classification

Rhinoviruses are one of five genera of the picornavirus family[26] and share basic properties with enteroviruses, including 40 to 60% homology between their genomes.[27] Rhinoviruses are distinguished from enteroviruses by their susceptibility to inactivation by acid and a higher density in cesium chloride gradients.[28, 29]

Morphology and Structure

The overall size of the virus is 20 to 27 nm[28, 29] (Table 162–1). Like other picornaviruses, rhinovirus contains four structural proteins (VP1, VP2, VP3, and VP4), that form a nonenveloped capsid with icosahedral symmetry. The high degree of cesium binding suggests that the capsid structure is less densely packed than in other picornaviruses. Examination of the atomic structure of the viral shell has revealed that it is composed of 60 repeated subunits (protomers) organized as 12 pentamers and containing the four viral proteins (Fig. 162–1). A deep cleft on the viral surface separates the five VP1 subunits clustered about the pentamer axis from the adjacent VP2 and VP3 subunits. This cleft, the structure of which is highly conserved among immunotypes, is the site of viral attachment to the cellular receptor.[30] When an IgG molecule binds to the surface of the virus in a position spanning the cleft, it blocks viral attachment to the cellular receptor. At the base of the cleft lies a pocket that is the binding site for a class of capsid-binding antiviral compounds.

Rhinoviruses have been found to use one of three cellular receptors.[31] The "major group," which contains 91 of the viral immunotypes, uses the intercellular adhesion molecule 1 (ICAM-1) receptor.[32] The remaining types, with one exception, use the low-density lipoprotein receptor.[33] Attachment of type 87 is inhibited by treatment with neuraminidase, and its receptor is believed to be a sialoprotein.

TABLE 162–1 Characteristics of Rhinovirus

Size: 20–27 nm
Shape: nonenveloped capsid with icosahedral symmetry constructed from 60 repeated protomers
Molecular weight: 8.16 × 10^6 Da
Density: higher in cesium chloride gradient than other members of the picornavirus group are, which suggests a more open capsid structure
Nucleic acid: single-stranded RNA with positive polarity containing approximately 7000 nucleotides
Optimal growth temperature 33°C–35°C; growth restricted at 37°C
Replication: virus synthesis and maturation in cell cytoplasm
Antigenicity: type specific

The rhinovirus genome contains a single strand of positive (sense) RNA about 7200 bases long that is organized in essentially the same way as that of poliovirus.[35] Rhinovirus RNA has genes that code for the four capsid proteins, VPg, a small protein at the 5′ end, an RNA polymerase, and a protease. The virus is ether resistant but labile in an acid environment of pH 3 to 5. Virus synthesis and maturation occur in the cytoplasm.

Biologic Characteristics

Heating, ultraviolet light, and desiccation cause rhinovirus to lose its native antigenicity and acquire a new set of surface determinants called the coreless or heated antigen.[36] Rhinovirus is sensitive to acidic pH less than 5 and to alkaline pH exceeding 9. Capsid-binding drugs such as chalcones stabilize rhinovirus against heat inactivation.

Native human rhinovirus will infect only humans and higher primates and grows in cell cultures derived from these species. The optimal temperature for rhinovirus replication, 33°C to 35°C, corresponds to the temperature found in the nose and large airways.[37] At a core body temperature of 37°C, virus yields fall by as much as 90% of maximum.[38] The relatively low temperature range for optimal rhinovirus growth may explain why generalized infection as manifested by viremia has not been observed with rhinovirus.[39, 40] Also, temperature may be one of the factors inhibiting viral replication in the intestinal tract. Gastrointestinal secretions may likewise have an adverse effect on virus survival.[41] In humans, the growth of rhinovirus takes place primarily in the cells of the upper airway.[42] Evidence suggests that the adenoidal area is an important location for initiation of infection.[43] In support is the finding that lymphoepithelial cells located in the crypts of the adenoid have been shown by immunohistochemistry to contain heavy concentrations of ICAM-1.[44] Infection also spreads to the ciliated epithelial cells of the nasal passages but appears to be spotty in location.[43, 45, 46] In some patients, the virus may also replicate in the large airways.[37] Rhinovirus survives on skin and environmental surfaces for at least several hours after contamination of these sites.[47]

Antigenic Characteristics

Four major immunogenic neutralization sites are present within each rhinovirus protomer.[28, 29] Rhinoviruses have been numbered 1 to 100 and subtype 1A on the basis of these surface antigens.[9–11] Identification is based on neutralization of viral growth with hyperimmune animal antiserum containing 20 units of antibody. The native antigenic structure of the virus can be altered by exposure to pH 5 at 56°C or to 2 mol/liter urea.[48] The configurational change in the capsid that results from such treatments produces an altered state of antigenicity characterized by reactivity with heterologous rhinovirus types. The altered, or C-antigenic, state does not stimulate protective antibody.

With antisera against the 100 numbered rhinovirus immunotypes, it has been possible to identify most strains recovered in recent field studies.[11, 49, 50] Thus, it does not appear that new immunotypes of rhinovirus are emerging at a rapid rate. However, antigenic differences have been found in strains of the same type recovered several years apart[51, 52]; also, intertypes have been discovered,[53] which suggests that some antigenic drift of rhinoviruses does take place. With a cloned stock of rhinovirus type 2 it has been shown that escape from neutralization by monoclonal antibody can occur with a single amino acid substitution in the viral shell.[54]

EPIDEMIOLOGY

Distribution and Prevalence

Rhinoviruses have a worldwide distribution. In a given geographic area, the different antigenic types circulate in a random fashion with no pattern other than for current types to be slowly replaced by

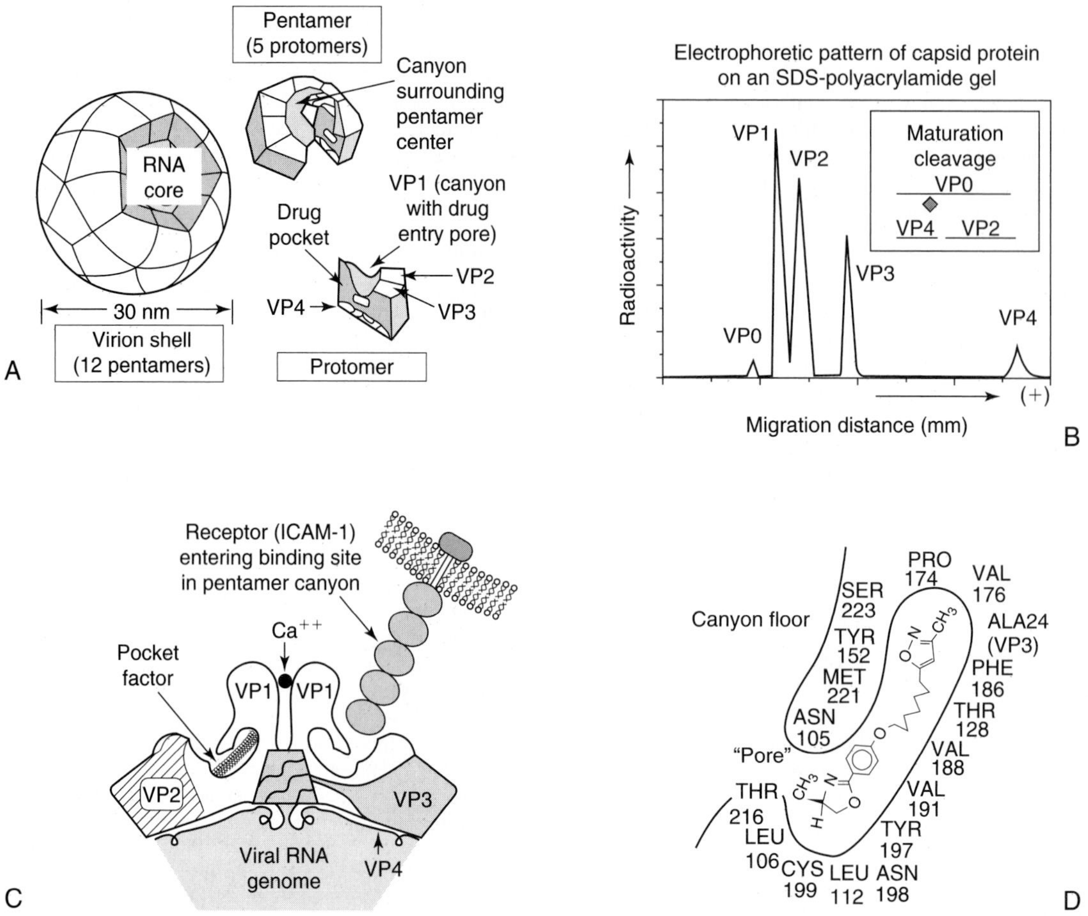

FIGURE 162–1. Key features of a human rhinovirus. *A,* The virion shell consists of 12 pentamers, one of which has been removed to show the approximate location of the RNA packed tightly into a central cavity. Each pentamer, in turn, consists of five wedge-shaped subunits, called protomers. The canyon (*stippled*) is shown in only one of the 12 pentamers. *B,* The virion contains four major proteins (VP1, 2, 3, and 4) plus traces of another, VP0, representing residual precursor following the maturation cleavage (*see inset*) required for acquisition of infectivity. *C,* Transverse section through the center of a pentamer depicting entry of its cellular receptor (ICAM-1) and the location of the drug-binding pocket just beneath the canyon floor. An ion, located at each pentamer center in HRV-1A, 14, and 16, is tentatively identified as calcium, which is necessary for attachment of some rhinoviruses. *D,* Detail showing orientation of a capsid binder (WIN 52084) and identity of amino acid residues lining the canyon floor and drug-binding pocket in a single protomer. In HRV14 the drug prevents attachment of its receptor, intercellular adhesion molecule-1 (ICAM-1). (Courtesy of Dr. Roland R. Ruckert.)

strains of different antigenic types.[55] Infections begin to occur in early childhood and continue throughout life.[56–58] Studies of the prevalence of rhinovirus antibody show rapid acquisition of antibody during childhood and adolescence, with a peak prevalence in young adults,[59] probably reflecting their exposure to young children. Antibody prevalence then declines slightly and remains relatively constant throughout adulthood. A slight decrease in the prevalence of antibody in older adults probably results from lessened viral exposure. Rhinoviruses are also encountered in military populations, where they are a cause of respiratory disease in military recruits.[60–62]

Seasonal Pattern of Infection

In temperate climates, rhinoviruses have a well-established seasonal pattern, with fall and spring peaks of infection. Most characteristic in the United States is an early fall outbreak of rhinovirus colds, which annually initiates the respiratory disease season.[17, 63] In adults with colds in the eastern United States, rhinovirus infection rates are highest in September. In some years and some locations, however, a fall rhinovirus outbreak has not been observed.[50] A second, less prominent peak of rhinovirus infection occurs in March, April, and May. Rhinoviruses also account for a relatively high proportion of summer colds. In the winter months, rhinovirus activity is low; coronaviruses and possibly undiscovered agents are thought to account for most colds at that time. In tropical areas, rhinovirus outbreaks have been encountered in the rainy season[56] and, in the arctic, during cold weather.[64] The reasons for the seasonal pattern of rhinovirus infection are not known. Volunteers exposed to thermal cold have not shown increased susceptibility to experimental rhinovirus colds.[65] Seasonal changes in living conditions, such as the opening of schools and crowding indoors, may be important in initiating fall rhinovirus outbreaks. Also, rhinoviruses survive better under conditions of high relative humidity, which occurs from late spring to midfall in temperate areas.[66]

Infection and Illness Rates

Rhinovirus colds are one of the most common infections in humans. In longitudinal studies, rhinovirus has been recovered in cell culture from 25% of adults with colds[17] and detected by culture combined with polymerase chain reaction in 50%.[67] Infection rates range from 1.2 infections per person-year in children younger than 1 year[68] to 0.7 in young adults.[17, 69] Infection rates in men and women are similar. In illness surveillance studies at the workplace, not in persons seeking medical care, cigarette smokers had rhinovirus illness rates similar to those of nonsmokers, although their illnesses were more severe.[17, 70] From 70 to 88% of rhinovirus infections are associated with symptomatic respiratory illness, for an apparent-to-inapparent infection ratio of approximately 3:1.[17, 61, 69, 71, 72]

Serum neutralizing antibody is a major factor in determining rhinovirus infection rates. The relative risk of infection in persons with serum antibody titers of less than 1:2 is 174 when compared with persons with titers of 1:32 or 1:64. Lack of antibody also increases the risk of illness, but to a lesser degree. Recent work has also shown that chronic stress[73] and the number of social ties[74] also affect the risk of rhinovirus illness. However, in antibody-free subjects (<1:2), lack of chronic stress or the presence of abundant social ties did not protect against infection after rhinovirus challenge.

Transmission

A major site for rhinovirus transmission is the home,[75–77] and the most frequent introducer of infection is a schoolchild. Secondary infections are most common in young siblings and mothers. One- to 5-day intervals are seen between the onset of cases occurring in families. Secondary attack rates in family members have ranged from 25 to 70% and have varied with the immune status of the person exposed to the invading virus. Equally important locations for rhinovirus spread are schools and daycare centers.[78, 79] In some outbreaks, up to 77% of children in a nursery school became infected when a new serotype was introduced into the classroom.[80] Mixing of different rhinovirus types in a school population provides an efficient way for the virus to be disseminated in a community.

Epidemiologic observations suggest that efficient rhinovirus transmission depends on some type of close contact that allows exposure to infectious secretions over a short distance. Studies in volunteers have shown that spread of infectious nasal secretions from hand to hand, followed by autoinoculation of the nasal and conjunctival mucosa, is an efficient means of viral transmission.[81] Contamination of the hands with nasal secretions containing rhinovirus is a common occurrence in people with natural colds. These individuals may then pass virus to the hands of others with whom they have contact. Finger-to-nose and finger-to-eye contact occurs frequently in the course of normal behavior and provides a means for accidental self-inoculation of susceptible persons. Also, rhinovirus has been recovered from objects in the homes of persons with colds,[81] and infection has been transmitted to volunteers by means of contaminated plastic tiles.[82] In one field study entailing regular treatment of the hands with a virucidal lotion, persons using the active treatments had fewer rhinovirus colds than did those using a placebo lotion.[83] The findings of that study provide direct evidence that the hand contamination/self-inoculation route of rhinovirus transmission occurs under natural conditions.

Experimental rhinovirus infection has also been transmitted through the air in either large- or small-particle aerosols.[84] The development of a reliable aerosol model demonstrates the feasibility of that route of rhinovirus transmission. Further studies designed to interrupt spread of natural infection by the different routes are needed to determine their relative importance.[83]

PATHOGENESIS

A basic feature of rhinovirus pathogenicity is the susceptibility of the nose of nonimmune individuals to the virus. Under experimental conditions, one median tissue culture infective dose ($TCID_{50}$) of rhinovirus placed in the nose will lead to infection and illness.[85] Virus can be recovered from the nasal secretions of a volunteer 8 to 10 hours after nasal inoculation.[39, 85, 86] Viral shedding increases to peak levels on the second and third day, at which time nasal secretions contain 10 to 1000 $TCID_{50}$/ml of virus. Clinical manifestations of illness appear as early as 8 to 10 hours after viral inoculation into the nose[86, 87] and reach a peak on the second and third day after challenge.[85, 88, 89] During the acute illness, large quantities of protein are released from the mucous membrane of the nose. Over the first 5 days of experimental rhinovirus infection, mean (±SD) nasal secretions weighed 23 (±22) g.[89] Also at this time, ciliated epithelial cells containing rhinovirus antigen are present in nasal mucus, but their numbers are low and do not correlate with the severity of illness in individual cases.[46]

The specific mechanisms by which rhinovirus produces disease have only recently been investigated. Histologic examination of nasal biopsy specimens from volunteers with experimental infections has failed to show consistent pathologic changes.[88, 90] These studies suggest that damage to the epithelium is slight and that the infection might serve as a trigger for the release of chemical mediators and activation of neurologic reflexes, which are the ultimate cause of the clinical illness. The role of inflammatory pathways in the pathogenesis of rhinovirus colds is being investigated by measuring mediator concentrations in respiratory secretions, by blocking mediator and reflex activity by specific compounds, and by challenging volunteers with selected mediators applied to the upper airway. By these approaches, several mediators, including bradykinin and lysyl-bradykinin,[86, 91] prostaglandin,[91, 92] histamine,[91, 93, 94] and interleukin-1, interleukin-6, and interleukin-8, have been associated with symptom development in rhinovirus colds (Table 162–2). Also, parasympathetic[95] and α-adrenergic[96] pathways have been implicated in contributing to some of the symptoms of rhinovirus colds.

IMMUNITY

Rhinovirus infection stimulates the appearance of serum neutralizing antibody in up to 80% of persons with natural colds.[70, 97] The neutralizing activity is associated with serum fractions containing IgA and IgG.[98, 99] After recent experimental infections, rhinovirus-neutralizing activity has also been associated with serum IgM. In addition, neutralizing activity is present in nasal secretions, where it is associated primarily with IgA's 9S and 11S fractions.[100] During rhinovirus colds, transudation of considerable amounts of serum immunoglobulin occurs in nasal secretions.[101, 102]

After an infection in which antibody has been stimulated, most persons appear to be immune to reinfection with the same serotype.[70, 76, 103] Longitudinal studies have shown the persistence of serum antibody for years,[57] and it is probable that most rhinovirus colds confer long-lasting immunity. Antibody responses do not follow all infections, however. Also, in volunteers, protection associated with preexisting antibody can be overcome by a large virus challenge.[104] Therefore, it is evident that recurrent infections with the same rhinovirus type do occur.

It has been suggested that the primary immune mechanism in rhinovirus infection is the neutralizing antibody present in nasal secretions rather than that in serum. However, because nasal and serum antibody are found in close association,[98, 105] it has been difficult to provide a definite answer to this question.[106–108]

CLINICAL MANIFESTATIONS

Signs and Symptoms of Rhinovirus Colds

Rhinoviruses produce a typical common cold. The median length of illness in young adults is 7 days, but symptoms last up to 2 weeks in one quarter of cases.[70] Complaints fall into nasal, pharyngeal, lower respiratory tract, and general categories. As observed in a group of patients, the symptoms of rhinovirus colds have a consistent pattern[109] (Fig. 162–2). However, wide variations occur in individual patients, and it is not possible to distinguish rhinovirus infections from other causes of upper respiratory illness on clinical grounds alone.

In an adult with an uncomplicated rhinovirus cold, fever is uncommon, and other systemic complaints are of low-grade severity. In most cases, rhinorrhea and nasal obstruction are the most prominent complaints. A sore or scratchy throat is also frequently present.

TABLE 162–2 Possible Inflammatory Pathways in Rhinovirus Colds

Mediator	Physiologic Actions That May Be Responsible for Cold Symptoms	Possible Links to Pathogenesis
Histamine	Dilatation of small vessels Increased permeability of postcapillary venules Stimulation of secretion of exocrine glands (goblet cells) Stimulation of nerve endings	Intranasal inhalation causes sneezing, rhinorrhea, nasal obstruction, and sore throat Increased histamine levels in nasal secretions from experimental colds First-generation antihistamines reduce sneezing and rhinorrhea in natural and experimental rhinovirus colds
Kinins	Vasodilatation (arterioles) Increased permeability of small venules Stimulation of pain nerve endings Stimulation of the release of histamine from mast cells	Intranasal inhalation causes rhinorrhea, nasal obstruction, and sore throat Increased kinin levels in nasal secretions from natural and experimental rhinovirus colds
Prostaglandins	E and D_2 cause vasodilatation E_2 causes pain when injected intradermally E_1 and E_2 act synergistically with bradykinin and histamine to increase vascular permeability $F_{2\alpha}$ causes bronchoconstriction (especially in asthmatics)	Intranasal inhalation causes rhinorrhea (D_2, $F_{2\alpha}$), nasal obstruction (D_2), sore throat ($F_{2\alpha}$), cough ($F_{2\alpha}$) Increased levels of stable metabolite of prostacyclin, 6-keto-PGF_1, in nasal secretions from experimental rhinovirus colds (preliminary data) Naproxen reduces headache, malaise, myalgia, and cough in experimental rhinovirus colds
Interleukin-1	Recruitment of inflammatory cells (neutrophils and lymphocytes) Increased responsiveness of some cells to bradykinin Increased vascular permeability Release of prostanoids, platelet-activating factor, and other inflammatory mediators	Increased interleukin-1 levels in nasal secretions from experimental rhinovirus colds
Interleukin-8	Recruitment of neutrophils	Increased interleukin-8 levels in nasal secretions from experimental rhinovirus colds
Interleukin-6	Stimulates acute-phase response Causes fever	Increased interleukin-6 levels in nasal secretions from experimental rhinovirus colds
Parasympathetic nervous system	Stimulates secretion of seromucous glands	Intranasal and oral treatment with parasympatholytic compounds reduces nasal secretions in experimental rhinovirus colds

Cough and hoarseness occur in approximately 30 and 20% of cases, respectively. In cigarette smokers, the frequency and duration of cough are prolonged. In the average case, nasal and pharyngeal symptoms subside rapidly during the third and fourth day of illness.

On examination, the end of the nose may have a red color, and clear or mucoid nasal secretions are frequently present. Nasal obstruction is often more obvious to the patient than to the physician unless special methods are used to measure resistance to nasal airflow. A glistening appearance of the nasal membrane is often seen. The pharyngeal mucosa may show mild edema and erythema, but marked inflammation or exudate does not occur. Rhonchi may be heard on examination of the chest. In many patients with a moderate degree of subjective discomfort, the nose and throat show few objective changes at the time of examination.

Rhinoviruses also cause the common cold in children. Available evidence is conflicting on the role of rhinoviruses in viral pneumonia, croup, and bronchiolitis. The prevailing opinion is that rhinoviruses do not commonly cause these illnesses in children.[110–113] Rhinovirus infections are associated with a modest increase in circulating neutrophils and a moderate elevation of the erythrocyte sedimentation rate.[103]

Complications of Rhinovirus Colds

Bacterial Sinusitis. Bacterial sinusitis has been reported to complicate 0.5 to 2.2% of common respiratory diseases.[3, 114] In recent studies, experimental[115] and natural[116] rhinovirus colds have been associated with acute reversible abnormalities of the ostiomeatal complex and sinus cavities. Also, in studies in adults with acute sinusitis, rhinovirus has been recovered from aspirates obtained by direct puncture of the maxillary sinus.[19] In some cases, virus was obtained alone, but in most cases, bacterial pathogens, including *Streptococcus pneumoniae* and unencapsulated strains of *Haemophilus influenzae,* were also recovered. Presumably, the viral sinusitis leads to entrapment of bacteria in the sinus cavity and subsequently to bacterial sinusitis.

Bacterial Otitis Media. Two percent of common respiratory disease is complicated by bacterial otitis media.[3] Respiratory viruses have been implicated in the pathogenesis of this disease by creating inflammatory obstruction of the eustachian tube and abnormal middle ear pressure.[20, 94, 117] Also, respiratory viruses, including rhinovirus, have been recovered directly from the middle ear fluid of patients with otitis media.[118, 119] In some cases, bacteria were recovered in combination with the virus. Bacteria presumably become trapped in the middle ear as a result of the virus-associated changes.

Acute Infectious Episodes in Patients with Chronic Bronchitis. Rhinoviruses have been implicated in acute infectious exacerbations in patients with chronic bronchitis.[21–23] It is not known whether rhinovirus invades the bronchial tree directly, but a study[37] using a sampling device designed to minimize upper airway contamination of specimens suggests that such invasion can occur. Mild alterations in ventilation have been reported in some chronic bronchitics with rhinovirus infection.[120] Secondary bacterial infection may also play a role in this condition.

Precipitation of Asthma. Rhinovirus infection is an important cause of attacks of asthma in children and adults.[121] Asthmatic children experience a significantly greater number of viral respiratory infections than do nonasthmatic control subjects.[122] Rhinoviruses have been recovered from these patients at the onset of an asthmatic attack, which suggests that the virus may be an initiating factor in the illness.[24, 25] Experimental rhinovirus infection leads to a decrease in forced expiratory volume in 1 second and an increase in histamine sensitivity in some but not all young adults with mild to moderate asthma.[123] Evidence now indicates that rhinovirus infection induces bronchial inflammation and hyperresponsiveness, and work on pathogenic mechanisms is in progress.[121]

Diagnosis

Viral Isolation. Rhinoviruses grow well in several cell culture systems, particularly human embryonic lung (WI-38 and MRC-5 strains) and M-HeLa cells. However, unexplained variation in the sensitivity of these cells can cause problems in testing if not recognized.[124, 125] Viral growth is optimum at 33°C to 34°C, and cultures must be incubated in a roller drum to achieve maximum cytopathic change. Rhinovirus cytopathic effect is usually evident in 2 to 6 days (Fig. 162–3). Because the specificity of the viral antigen of each type prevents serologic identification of members of the group as a whole, culture has been the only practical method of diagnosis. Recently,

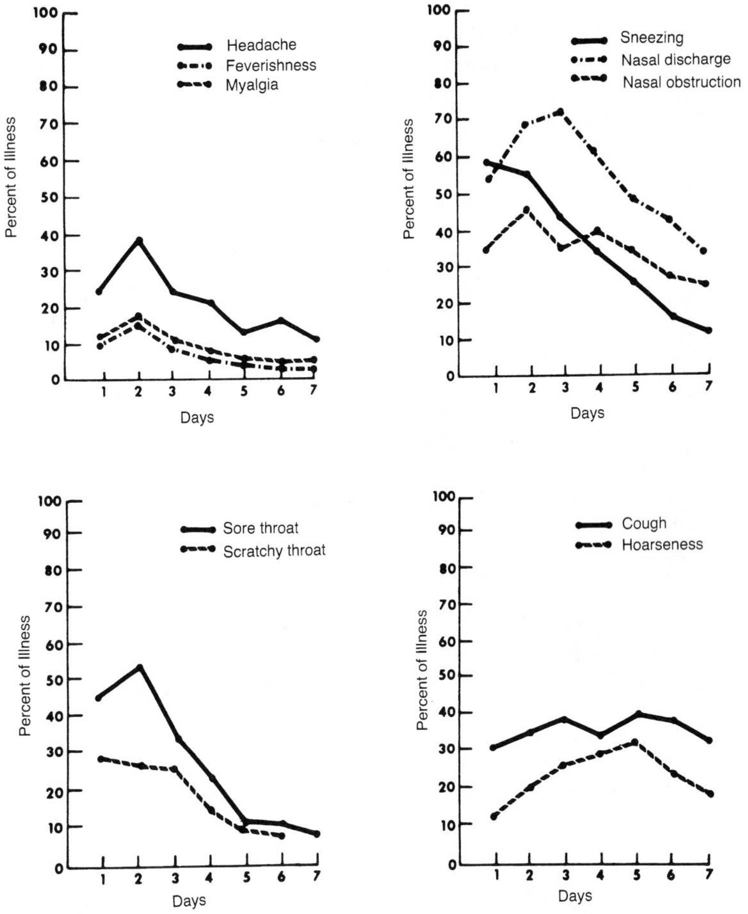

FIGURE 162–2. Rhinovirus cold symptoms (139 adults with natural infection).

polymerase chain reaction with nucleic acid probes has been adapted to detect rhinovirus.[126, 127]

Identification of the antigenic type of an unknown rhinovirus by neutralization requires a large battery of antisera, and it is best accomplished with a system of intersecting antiserum pools.[128] A microtitration system can be used for preliminary identification.[129, 130] Final proof of antigenic type is demonstrated by neutralization of the $TCID_{10-300}$ of virus by 20 units of antibody using monovalent hyperimmune animal serum.

Serology. A neutralization test can be used for the serodiagnosis of rhinovirus infection if the infecting type is known. However, the multiplicity of rhinovirus types prevents the use of serologic techniques for routine diagnosis. For measuring neutralizing antibody in human serum, it is necessary to use small doses of virus ($TCID_{3-30}$) if the test is to have satisfactory sensitivity.[131]

TREATMENT AND PREVENTION

Symptomatic Therapy (See Chapter 46)

A combination of a first-generation antihistamine and a nonsteroidal anti-inflammatory compound is effective treatment for rhinovirus colds. Treatment should be started as early as symptoms are recognized and continued every 12 hours for 4 to 5 days. Penicillin and other antibiotics have no place in therapy because they neither ameliorate the viral illness nor reduce the frequency of bacterial complications.

Rest, hydration, nasal decongestants, saline gargles, and cough suppressants may also be useful. If needed, oral decongestants may be used on a regular basis during the acute stage of illness. Nasal decongestants tend to cause "rebound" nasal obstruction and sore throat. The regular application of a petrolatum-based ointment helps prevent painful maceration of the nares. Patients with secondary bacterial sinusitis or otitis media require appropriate antimicrobial therapy.

Prospects for Vaccines and Antivirals

Studies of the molecular structure of the rhinovirus shell[28, 29] confirm that rhinovirus is not a good candidate for vaccine development. The most conserved region of the viral capsid lies in the bottom of the surface cleft, where it is inaccessible to antibody. Experimental rhinovirus vaccines made against one immunotype of virus have reduced the rate of symptomatic illness and viral shedding, but not the overall rate of infection of volunteers given an experimental challenge with rhinovirus.[105, 132, 133] Because of the large number of rhinovirus immunotypes, the prospects for an effective rhinovirus vaccine are not good.

Chemical compounds with in vitro activity against rhinovirus continue to be discovered.[134] However, most of those reaching the stage of testing in humans have, unfortunately, shown little, if any effectiveness. The most promising results have been obtained with recombinant interferon-α2 applied topically in the nose. Given prophylactically in doses of approximately 5 million units or greater a day, interferon-α2 has been highly effective in preventing experimental infection and illness.[135] When used for contact prophylaxis in two field studies in families, topical interferon-α2 reduced the overall rate of colds in treated persons by 40% and virtually eliminated colds caused specifically by rhinovirus.[136, 137] When used for the treatment of experimental rhinovirus colds, interferon-α2 reduced viral shedding substantially but had only a modest effect on symptomatic illness.[135] After chronic administration, topical interferon-α2

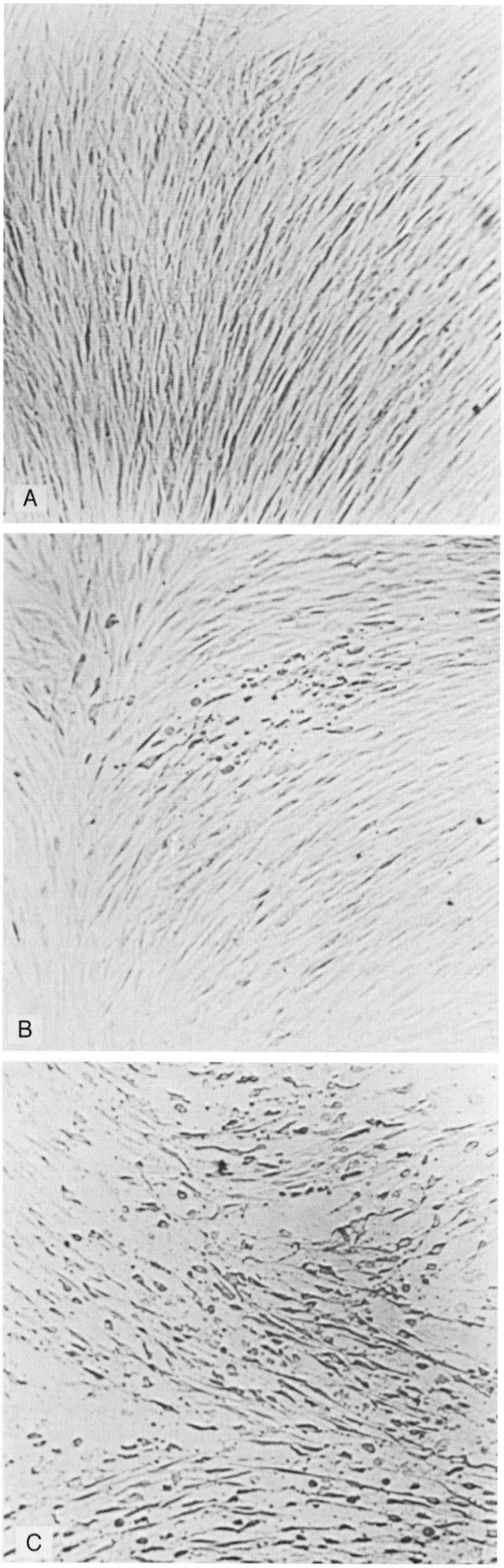

FIGURE 162–3. Rhinovirus cytopathic effect in human embryonic lung cells (WI-38). *A*, Uninfected cell cultures (× 160). *B*, Cytopathic effect of rhinovirus type 39 at 48 hours. *C*, Cytopathic effect at 72 hours.

causes local side effects consisting of nasal irritation and stuffiness and pinpoint mucosal ulcerations, thus limiting its use to short-term administration for contact prophylaxis and therapy.

Considerable work has been done on a group of compounds called "capsid binders" that bind to a pocket in VP1 below the canyon. Although these compounds have potent antirhinovirus activity in cell culture and reduce viral shedding in volunteers, their effectiveness in treatment has been disappointing.[138, 139] Also, the emergence of drug resistance is a problem with some compounds in this group. Another approach that is receiving attention is to block viral attachment either with monoclonal antibody to cellular (ICAM-1) receptor or with artificial soluble ICAM-1 to bind virus before it reaches natural receptor. When given 7 hours before or 12 hours after rhinovirus challenge, ICAM-1 had a moderate effect in blocking symptoms.[140] Monoclonal antibody to ICAM-1 has also shown promise when used prophylactically in the rhinovirus challenge model.[141]

Combined Antiviral-Antimediator Treatment

A new experimental approach to the treatment of rhinovirus colds is based on the observed failure of potent antivirals such as interferon and capsid binders to have therapeutic efficacy when given alone and on an understanding of the role of inflammatory mediators in pathogenesis. The treatment consists of a combination of an antiviral agent for reducing viral replication and selected compounds that block inflammatory pathways. In one controlled trial, subjects with experimental rhinovirus colds were given interferon-α2b and ipratropium into the nose simultaneously with oral naproxen at the onset of symptoms.[142] With the combined therapy, viral shedding and progression of illness were reduced in the treated group, and treated subjects who met the diagnostic criteria for colds had significantly lower symptom scores than controls did.

Environmental Measures to Control Infection

If the hand contact/self-inoculation route is one means by which rhinovirus spreads under natural conditions, persons can protect themselves by hand washing and avoiding finger-eye and finger-nose contact. Until further knowledge is gained on this question, it seems expedient to take such precautions, particularly when a member of the household has a respiratory illness. It may be possible to develop additional approaches to hand[83] and environmental[82] disinfection that might be effective in interrupting the spread of rhinovirus colds if the natural route of spread is by this means. Because aerosol spread may be another route of rhinovirus transmission,[84] covering coughs and sneezes with disposable nasal tissues is also recommended.

REFERENCES

1. Gwaltney JM Jr. Historical eras of the common cold. In: Sande MA, Root RK, eds. Contemporary Issues in Infectious Diseases, v. 10, Viral Infections: Diagnosis, Treatment and Prevention. New York: Churchill Livingstone; 1992:1–13.
2. Kruse W. Die Erreger von Husten and Schupfen. Munchen Med Wochenschr. 1914;61:1547.
3. Dingle JH, Badger GF, Jordan WS Jr. Illness in the Home. A Study of 25,000 Illnesses in a Group of Cleveland Families. Cleveland: Western Reserve University; 1964.
4. Andrewes C. The Common Cold. New York: WW Norton; 1965.
5. Pelon W, Mogabgab WJ, Phillips IA, et al. A cytopathogenic agent isolated from naval recruits with mild respiratory illness. Proc Soc Exp Biol Med. 1957;94:262.
6. Price WH. The isolation of a new virus associated with respiratory clinical disease in humans. Proc Natl Acad Sci U S A. 1956;42:892.
7. Ketler A, Hamparian VV, Hilleman MR. Characterization and classification of ECHO 28–rhinovirus–coryzavirus agents. Proc Soc Exp Biol Med. 1962;110:821.
8. Hayflick L, Moorhead PS. The serial cultivation of human diploid cell strains. Exp Cell Res. 1961;25:585.
9. Kapikian AZ, Conant RM, Hamparian VV, et al. Rhinoviruses: A numbering system. Nature. 1967;213:761.
10. Kapikian AZ, Conant RM, Hamparian VV, et al. A collaborative report: Rhinoviruses—extension of the numbering system. Virology. 1971;43:524.

11. Hamparian VV, Colonno RJ, Cooney MK, et al. A collaborative report: Rhinoviruses—extension of the numbering system from 89 to 100. Virology. 1987;159:191.
12. Callahan PL, Mizutani S, Colonno RJ. Molecular cloning and complete sequence determination of RNA genome of human rhinovirus 14. Proc Natl Acad Sci U S A. 1985;82:732.
13. Stanway G, Hughes PJ, Mountford RC, et al. The complete nucleotide sequence of a common cold virus; human rhinovirus 14. Nucleic Acids Res. 1984;12:7859.
14. Skern T, Sommergruber W, Blaas D, et al. Human rhinovirus 2: Complete nucleotide sequence and proteolytic processing signals in the capside protein region. Nucleic Acids Res. 1985;12:2111.
15. Rossmann MG, Arnold E, Erickson JW, et al. The structure of a human common cold virus (rhinovirus 14) and its functional relations to other picornaviruses. Nature. 1985;317:145.
16. Hamre D, Procknow JJ. Viruses isolated from natural common colds among young adult medical students. Am Rev Respir Dis. 1963;88:277.
17. Gwaltney JM Jr, Hendley JO, Simon G, et al. Rhinovirus infections in an industrial population. I. The occurrence of illness. N Engl J Med. 1966;275:1261.
18. Monto AS, Ullman BM. Acute respiratory illness in an American community: The Tecumseh study. JAMA. 1974;227:164.
19. Evans FO, Sydnor JB, Moore WEC, et al. Sinusitis of the maxillary antrum. N Engl J Med. 1975;293:735.
20. Buchman CA, Doyle WJ, Skoner D, et al. Otologic manifestations of experimental rhinovirus infection. Laryngscope. 1994;104:1295–1299.
21. Eadie MB, Stott EJ, Grist RN. Virological studies in chronic bronchitis. BMJ. 1966;2:671.
22. McNamara MJ, Phillips IA, Williams OB. Viral and *Mycoplasma pneumoniae* infections in exacerbations of chronic lung disease. Am Rev Respir Dis. 1969;100:19.
23. Stenhouse AC. Rhinovirus infection in acute exacerbations of chronic bronchitis: A controlled prospective study. BMJ. 1967;3:461.
24. Hilleman MR, Reilly CM, Stokes J Jr, et al. Clinical epidemiologic findings in coryzavirus infections. Am Rev Respir Dis. 1963;88(Suppl):S274.
25. Minor TE, Dick EC, DeMeo AN, et al. Viruses as precipitants of asthmatic attacks in children. JAMA. 1974;227:292.
26. Wildy P. Classification and nomenclature of viruses. In: Melnick JL, ed. Monographs in Virology. Basel: Karger; 1971.
27. Palmenberg AC. Sequence alignments of picornaviral capsid proteins. In: Semler BL, Ehrenfeld E, eds. Molecular Aspects of Picornavirus Infection and Detection. Washington, DC: American Society for Microbiology; 1987:211–241.
28. Couch RB. Rhinoviruses. In: Fields BN, Knipe DM, Chanock RM, et al, eds. Virology. New York: Raven; 1985:795.
29. Gwaltney JM Jr, Colonno RJ, Hamparian VV, et al. Rhinovirus. In: Schmidt NJ, Emmons K, eds. Diagnostic Procedures for Viral, Rickettsial and Chlamydial Infections. 6th ed. Washington, DC: American Public Health Association; 1989:579.
30. Smith TJ, Olson NH, Cheng RH, et al. Structure of human rhinovirus complexed with Fab fragments from a neutralizing antibody. J Virol. 1993;67:1148–1158.
31. Colonno RJ. Virus receptors: The Achilles' heel of human rhinovirus. Adv Exp Med Biol. 1992;312:61–70.
32. Piela-Smith TH, Broketa G, Hand A, Korn JH. Regulation of ICAM-1 expression and function in human dermal fibroblasts by IL-4. J Immunol. 1992;148:1375–1381.
33. Hofer F, Gruenberger M, Howalski H, et al. Members of the low density lipoprotein receptor family mediate cell entry of a minor-group common cold virus. Proc Natl Acad Sci U S A. 1994;91:1839–1841.
34. Uncapher CR, DeWitt CM, Colonno RJ. The major and minor group receptor families contain all but one human rhinovirus serotype. Virology. 1991;180:814–817.
35. Skern T, Duechler M, Sommergruber W, et al. The molecular biology of human rhinoviruses. Biochem Soc Symp. 1987;53:63–73.
36. Gwaltney JM Jr, Ruckert RR. Rhinovirus. In Richman DD, Whitley RJ, Hayden FG, eds. Clinical Virology. New York: Churchill Livingstone; 1997:1025–1047.
37. Halperin SA, Eggleston PA, Hendley JO, et al. Pathogenesis of lower respiratory tract symptoms in experimental rhinovirus infection. Am Rev Respir Dis. 1983;128:806.
38. Stott EJ, Killington RA. Rhinoviruses. Annu Rev Microbiol. 1972;26:503.
39. Douglas RG Jr, Cate TR, Gerone PJ, et al. Quantitative rhinovirus shedding patterns in volunteers. Am Rev Respir Dis. 1966;94:159.
40. Douglas RG Jr, Rossen RD, Butler WT, et al. Rhinovirus neutralizing antibody in tears, parotid saliva, nasal secretions and serum. J Immunol. 1967;99:297.
41. Cate TR, Douglas RG Jr, Johnson KM, et al. Studies on the inability of rhinovirus to survive and replicate in the intestinal tract of volunteers. Proc Soc Exp Biol Med. 1967;124:1290.
42. Gwaltney JM Jr. Epidemiology of the common cold. Ann N Y Acad Sci. 1980;353:54.
43. Winther B, Gwaltney JM Jr, Mygind N, et al. Sites of rhinovirus recovery after point inoculation of the upper airway. JAMA. 1986;256:1763.
44. Winther B, Greve JM, Gwaltney JM Jr, et al. Surface expression of intercellular adhesion molecule 1 on epithelial cells in the human adenoid. J Infect Dis. 1997;25:574–583.
45. de Arruda E III, Mifflin TE, Gwaltney JM Jr, et al. Localization of rhinovirus replication in vitro with in situ hybridization. J Med Virol. 1991;34:38–44.
46. Turner RB, Hendley JO, Gwaltney JM Jr. Shedding of infected ciliated epithelial cells in rhinovirus colds. J Infect Dis. 1982;145:849–853.
47. Hendley JO, Wenzel RP, Gwaltney JM Jr. Transmission of rhinovirus colds by self-inoculation. N Engl J Med. 1973;288:1361.
48. Lonberg-Holm K, Yin FH. Antigenic determinants of infective and inactivated human rhinoviruses type 2. J Virol. 1973;12:114.
49. Krilov L, Pierik L, Keller E, et al. The association of rhinoviruses with lower respiratory tract disease in hospitalized patients. J Med Virol. 1986;19:345.
50. Monto AS, Bryan ER, Ohmit S. Rhinovirus infections in Tecumseh, Michigan: Illness frequency and number of serotypes. J Infect Dis. 1987;156:43.
51. Schieble JH, Lennette EH, Fox VL. Antigenic variation of rhinovirus type 22. Proc Soc Exp Biol Med. 1970;133:329.
52. Stott EJ, Walker M. Antigenic variation among strains of rhinovirus type 51. Nature. 1969;224:1311.
53. Halfpap LM, Cooney MK. Isolation of rhinovirus intertypes related to either rhinoviruses 12 and 78 or 36 and 58. Infect Immun. 1983;40:213.
54. Speller SA, Sanger DV, Clarke BE, Rowlands DJ. The nature and spatial distribution of amino acid substitutions conferring resistance to neutralizing monoclonal antibodies in human rhinovirus type 2. J Gen Virol. 1993;74:193–200.
55. Hamre D. Rhinoviruses. In: Melnick JL, ed. Monographs in Virology 1. Basel: Karger; 1968.
56. Monto AS, Johnson KM. A community study of respiratory infections in the tropics. II. The spread of six rhinovirus isolates within the community. Am J Epidemiol. 1968;88:55.
57. Taylor-Robinson D. Studies on some viruses (rhinoviruses) isolated from common colds. Arch Ges Virusforsch. 1963;13:281.
58. Tyrrell DAJ. Rhinoviruses. In: Gard S, Hallauer C, Myer KF, eds. Virology Monographs 2. New York: Springer-Verlag; 1968.
59. Hamparian VV, Conant RM, Thomas DC. Rhinovirus Reference Laboratory, Annual Contract Progress Report to the National Institute of Allergy and Infectious Diseases. Contract No. 69-2062. National Institutes of Health; Bethesda, MD: Dec 1, 1969–Nov 30, 1970.
60. Forsyth BR, Bloom HH, Johnson KM, et al. Patterns of illness in rhinovirus infection of military personnel. N Engl J Med. 1963;269:602.
61. Johnson KM, Bloom HH, Forsyth BR, et al. Relationship of rhinovirus infection to mild upper respiratory disease. II. Epidemiologic observations in male military trainees. Am J Epidemiol. 1965;81:131.
62. Rosenbaum MJ, DeBerry P, Sullivan EJ, et al. Epidemiology of the common cold in military recruits with emphasis on infections by rhinovirus type 1A, 2, and two unclassified rhinoviruses. Am J Epidemiol. 1971;93:183.
63. Monto AS, Cavallaro JJ. The Tecumseh study of respiratory illness. II. Patterns of occurrence of infection with respiratory illness pathogens, 1965–1969. Am J Epidemiol. 1971;94:280.
64. Wulff H, Nobel GR, Maynard JE, et al. An outbreak of respiratory infection in children associated with rhinovirus types 16 and 29. Am J Epidemiol. 1969;90:304.
65. Douglas RG Jr, Lindgren KM, Couch RB. Exposure to cold environment and rhinovirus common cold: Failure to demonstrate effect. N Engl J Med. 1968;279:743.
66. Gwaltney JM Jr, The Jeremiah Metzger Lecture. Climatology and the common cold. Trans Am Clin Climatolog Assoc. 1984;96:159–175.
67. Mäkelä MJ, Puhakka T, Ruuskanen O, et al. Viruses and bacteria in the etiology of the common cold. J Clin Microbiol. 1998;36:539–542.
68. Cooney MK, Hall CE, Fox JP. The Seattle virus watch. 3. Evaluation of isolation methods and summary of infections detected by virus isolations. Am J Epidemiol. 1972;96:286.
69. Hamre D, Connelly AP Jr, Procknow J. Virologic studies of acute respiratory disease in young adults. IV. Virus isolations during four years of surveillance. Am J Epidemiol. 1966;83:238.
70. Gwaltney JM Jr, Hendley JO, Simon G, et al. Rhinovirus infections in an industrial population. II. Characteristics of illness and antibody response. JAMA. 1967;202:494.
71. Fox JP, Hall CE, Cooney MK, et al. The Seattle virus watch. II. Objectives, study population and its observation, data processing and summary of illnesses. Am J Epidemiol. 1972;96:270.
72. Mufson MA, Bloom HH, Forsyth BR, et al. Relationship of rhinovirus to mild upper respiratory disease. III. Further epidemiologic observations in military personnel. Am J Epidemiol. 1966;83:379.
73. Cohen S, Gwaltney JM Jr, Doyle WJ, et al. State and trait negative affect as predictors of objective and subjective symptoms of a common cold. J Personality Soc Psychol. 1995;68:159–169.
74. Cohen S, Doyle WJ, Skoner DP, et al. Social ties and susceptibility to the common cold. JAMA. 1997;227:1940–1944.
75. Dick EC, Blumer CR, Evans AS. Epidemiology of infections with rhinovirus types 43 and 55 in a group of University of Wisconsin student families. Am J Epidemiol. 1967;86:386.
76. Hendley JO, Gwaltney JM Jr, Jordan WS Jr. Rhinovirus infections in an industrial population. IV. Infections within families of employees during two fall peaks of respiratory illness. Am J Epidemiol. 1969;89:184.
77. Monto AS. A community study of respiratory infections in the tropics. III. Introduction and transmission of infections within families. Am J Epidemiol. 1968;88:69.
78. Periera MA, Andrews BE, Gardner SD. A study on the virus aetiology of mild respiratory infections in the primary school child. J Hyg. 1967;64:475.
79. Kendall EJC, Bynoe ML, Tyrrell DAJ. Virus isolations from common colds occurring in a residential school. BMJ. 1962;2:82.
80. Beem MO. Acute respiratory illness in nursery school children: A longitudinal study of the occurrence of illness and respiratory viruses. Am J Epidemiol. 1969;90:30.

81. Gwaltney JM Jr, Moskalski PB, Hendley JO. Hand to hand transmission of rhinovirus colds. Ann Intern Med. 1978;88:463.
82. Gwaltney JM Jr, Hendley JO. Transmission of experimental rhinovirus infection by contaminated surfaces. Am J Epidemiol. 1982;116:828.
83. Hendley JO, Gwaltney JM Jr. Mechanisms of transmission of rhinovirus infections. Epidemiol Rev. 1988;10:242.
84. Dick EC, Jennings LC, Mink KA, et al. Aerosol transmission of rhinovirus colds. J Infect Dis. 1987;156:442.
85. Douglas RG Jr. Pathogenesis of rhinovirus common colds in human volunteers. Ann Otol Rhinol Laryngol. 1970;79:563.
86. Naclerio RM, Proud D, Kagey-Sobotka A, et al. Kinins are generated during experimental rhinovirus colds. J Infect Dis. 1988;157:133–142.
87. Gwaltney JM Jr. Sinusitis: Pathogenesis and antimicrobial resistance. Hosp Med. 1997;33(Suppl):35–39.
88. Douglas RG Jr, Alford BR, Couch RB. Atraumatic nasal biopsy for studies of respiratory virus infection in volunteers. Antimicrob Agents Chemother. 1968;8:340.
89. Parekh HH, Cragun KT, Hayden FG, et al. Nasal mucus weights in experimental rhinovirus infection. Am J Rhinol. 1992;6(3):107–110.
90. Winther B, Farr B, Turner RB, et al. Histopathologic examination and enumeration of polymorphonuclear leukocytes in the nasal mucosa during experimental rhinovirus colds. Acta Otolaryngol Suppl (Stockh). 1984;413:19.
91. Doyle WJ, Boehm S, Skoner DP. Physiologic responses to intranasal dose-response challenges with histamine, methacholine, bradykinin, and prostaglandin in adult volunteers with and without nasal allergy. J Allergy Clin Immunol. 1990;86:924–935.
92. Sperber SJ, Hendley JO, Hayden FG, et al. Effects of naproxen on experimental rhinovirus colds. A randomized, double-blind, controlled trial. Ann Intern Med. 1992;117:37–41.
93. Gaffey MJ, Gwaltney JM Jr, Sastre A, et al. Intranasal and oral antihistamine treatment of experimental rhinovirus colds. Am Rev Respir Dis. 1987;136:556–560.
94. Doyle WJ, McBride TP, Skoner DP, et al. A double-blind, placebo-controlled clinical trial of the effect of chlorpheniramine on the response of the nasal airway, middle ear and eustachian tube to provocative rhinovirus challenge. Pediatr Infect Dis J. 1988;7:229–238.
95. Gaffey MJ, Hayden FG, Boyd JC, et al. Ipratropium bromide treatment of experimental rhinovirus infection. Antimicrob Agents Chemother. 1988;32:1644–1647.
96. Sperber SJ, Sorrentino JV, Riker DK, et al. Evaluation of an alpha agonist alone and in combination with a nonsteroidal anti-inflammatory agent in the treatment of experimental rhinovirus cold. Bull N Y Acad Med. 1989;65:145–160.
97. Gwaltney JM Jr, Jordan WS Jr. Rhinoviruses and respiratory disease. Bacteriol Rev. 1964;28:409.
98. Cate TR, Rossen RD, Douglas RG Jr, et al. The role of nasal secretion and serum antibody in the rhinovirus common cold. Am J Epidemiol. 1966;84:352.
99. Rossen RD, Douglas RG Jr, Cate TR, et al. The sedimentation behavior of rhinovirus neutralizing activity in nasal secretion and serum following the rhinovirus common cold. J Immunol. 1966;97:532.
100. Knopf HLS, Perkins JC, Bertran DM, et al. Analysis of the neutralizing activity in nasal wash and serum following intranasal vaccination with inactivated type 13 rhinovirus. J Immunol. 1970;104:566.
101. Butler WT, Waldmann TA, Rossen RD, et al. Changes in IgA and IgG concentrations in nasal secretions prior to the appearance of antibody during viral respiratory infection in man. J Immunol. 1970;105:584.
102. Rossen RD, Kasel JA, Couch RB. The secretory immune system: Its relation to respiratory viral infection. In: Melnick JL, ed. Progress in Medical Virology. Basel: Karger; 1971:194.
103. Cate TR, Couch RB, Johnson KM. Studies with rhinoviruses in volunteers: Production of illness, effect of naturally acquired antibody, and demonstration of a protective effect not associated with serum antibody. J Clin Invest. 1964;43:56.
104. Hendley JO, Edmondson WP Jr, Gwaltney JM Jr. Relation between naturally acquired immunity and infectivity of two rhinoviruses in volunteers. J Infect Dis. 1971;125:243.
105. Mufson MA, Ludwig WM, James HD Jr, et al. Effect of neutralizing antibody on experimental rhinovirus infection. JAMA. 1963;186:578.
106. Perkins JC, Tucker DN, Knopf HLS, et al. Comparison of protective effect of neutralizing antibody in serum and nasal secretions in experimental rhinovirus type 13 illness. Am J Epidemiol. 1969;90:519.
107. Perkins JC, Tucker DN, Knopf HLS, et al. Evidence for protective effect of an inactivated rhinovirus vaccine administered by the nasal route. Am J Epidemiol. 1969;90:319.
108. Gwaltney JM Jr. Rhinoviruses. In: Evans AS, ed. Viral Infections of Humans: Epidemiology and Control. 3rd ed. New York: Plenum; 1989:593–615.
109. Rao SR, Hendley JO, Hayden FG, Gwaltney JM Jr. Symptom expression in natural and experimental rhinovirus colds. Am J Rhinol. 1995;9:49–52.
110. Bloom HH, Forsyth BR, Johnson KM, et al. Relationship of rhinovirus infection to mild upper respiratory disease. 1. Results of a survey in young adults and children. JAMA. 1963;186:38.
111. Glezen WP, Loda FA, Clyde WA, et al. Epidemiologic patterns of acute lower respiratory disease of children in a pediatric group practice. J Pediatr. 1971;78:397.
112. Mufson MA, Krause HE, Mocega HE, et al. Viruses, *Mycoplasma pneumoniae* and bacteria associated with lower respiratory tract disease among infants. Am J Epidemiol. 1970;91:192.
113. Portnoy B, Eckert HL, Salvatore MA. Rhinovirus infection in children with acute lower respiratory disease: Evidence against etiological importance. Pediatrics. 1965;35:899.
114. Gwaltney JM Jr. Acute community-acquired sinusitis. Clin Infect Dis. 1996;23:1209–1223.
115. Turner BW, Cail WS, Hendley JO, et al. Physiologic abnormalities in the paranasal sinuses during experimental rhinovirus colds. J Allergy Clin Immunol. 1992;90:474–478.
116. Gwaltney JM Jr, Phillips CD, Miller RD, et al. Computed tomographic study of the common cold. N Engl J Med. 1994;330:25–30.
117. McBride TP, Doyle WJ, Hayden FG, et al. Alterations of eustachian tube, middle ear and nose in rhinovirus infections. Arch Otolaryngol Head Neck Surg. 1989;115:1054–1059.
118. Gwaltney JM Jr. Virology of middle ear. Ann Otol Rhinol Laryngol. 1971;80:365.
119. Arola M, Ruuskanen O, Ziegler T, et al. Clinical role of respiratory virus infection in acute otitis media. Pediatrics. 1990;86:848.
120. Smith CB, Kanner RE, Golden CA, et al. Effect of viral infections on pulmonary function in patients with chronic obstructive pulmonary diseases. J Infect Dis. 1980;141:271.
121. Folkerts G, Busse WW, Nijkamp FP, et al. Virus-induced airway hyperresponsiveness and asthma. Am J Respir Crit Care Med. 1998;157:1708–1720.
122. Minor TE, Baker JW, Dick EC, et al. Greater frequency of viral respiratory infections in asthmatic children as compared with their nonasthmatic siblings. J Pediatr. 1974;85:472.
123. Halperin SA, Eggleston PA, Beasley P, et al. Exacerbations of asthma in adults during experimental rhinovirus infection. Am Rev Respir Dis. 1985;132:976.
124. Brown PK, Tyrrell DAJ. Experiments on the sensitivity of strains of human fibroblasts to infection with rhinovirus. Br J Exp Pathol. 1964;45:571.
125. Gwaltney JM Jr, Edmondson WP Jr. Etiology and Epidemiology of Acute Respiratory Disease. Annual Progress Report to the Commission on Acute Respiratory Disease of the Armed Forces Epidemiological Board. Contract No. DADA 49-007-MD-1000, September 15, 1968.
126. Johnston SL, Sanderson G, Pattemore PK, et al. Use of polymerase chain reaction for diagnosis of picornavirus infection in subjects with and without respiratory symptoms. J Clin Microbiol. 1993;31:111–117.
127. Arruda E, Hayden FG. Detection of human rhinovirus RNA in nasal washings by PCR. Mol Cell Probes 1993;7:373–379.
128. Kenny GE, Cooney MK, Thompson DJ. Analysis of serum pooling schemes for identification of large numbers of viruses. Am J Epidemiol. 1970;91:439.
129. Gwaltney JM Jr. Micro-neutralization test for identification of rhinovirus serotypes. Proc Soc Exp Biol Med. 1966;122:1137.
130. Kriel RL, Wulff H, Chin TDY. Micro-neutralization test for determination of rhinovirus and coxsackievirus A antibody in human diploid cells. Appl Microbiol. 1969;17:611.
131. Douglas RG Jr, Fleet WF, Cate TR, et al. Antibody to rhinovirus in human sera. I. Standardization of a neutralization test. Proc Soc Exp Biol Med. 1968;127:497.
132. Andrewes C, Tyrrell DAJ, Stones PB, et al. Prevention of colds by vaccination against a rhinovirus: A report by the scientific committee on common cold vaccines. BMJ. 1965;1:1344.
133. Douglas RG Jr, Couch RB. Parenteral inactivated rhinovirus vaccine: Minimal protective effect. Proc Soc Exp Biol Med. 1972;139:899.
134. Sperber SJ, Hayden FG. Minireview. Chemotherapy of rhinovirus colds. Antimicrob Agents Chemother. 1988;19:409–419.
135. Hayden FG. Use of interferons for prevention and treatment of respiratory viral infections. In: Mills J, Corey L, eds. Antiviral Chemotherapy: New Directions for Clinical Application and Research. New York: Elsevier; 1986:28.
136. Hayden FG, Albrecht JK, Kaiser DL, et al. Prevention of natural colds by contact prophylaxis with intranasal alpha$_2$-interferon. N Engl J Med. 1986;314:71.
137. Douglas RM, Moore BW, Miles HB, et al. Prophylactic efficacy of intranasal alpha$_2$-interferon against rhinovirus infections in the family setting. N Engl J Med. 1986;314:65.
138. Al-Nakib W, Higgins PG, Barrow GI, et al. Suppression of colds in human volunteers challenged with rhinovirus by a new synthetic drug (R61837). Antimicrob Agents Chemother. 1989;33:522–525.
139. Hayden FG, Andries K, Janssen PAJ. Safety and efficacy of intranasal pirodavir (R77975) in experimental rhinovirus infection. Antimicrob Agents Chemother. 1992;36:727–732.
140. Turner RB, Wecker MT, Pohl G, et al. Efficacy of tremacamra, a soluble intercellular adhesion molecule-1, for experimental rhinovirus infection: A randomized clinical trial. JAMA. 1999;281:1797–1804.
141. Hayden FG, Gwaltney JM Jr, Colonno RJ. Modification of experimental rhinovirus colds by receptor blockade. Antiviral Res. 1988;9:233–247.
142. Gwaltney JM Jr. Combined antiviral and antimediator treatment of rhinovirus colds. J Infect Dis. 1992;166:776–782.

Caliciviridae and Other Gastroenteritis Viruses

Chapter 163

Norwalk Virus and Other Caliciviruses

JOHN J. TREANOR
RAPHAEL DOLIN

Acute gastrointestinal disease is an exceedingly common and widespread illness throughout the world. According to the National Health Interview Survey in the United States, the incidence of such disease is 11.2% per year, with an estimated 23.7 to 26.0 days lost from work or school per 100 persons annually.[1] In a survey of families in the Cleveland area, acute "nonbacterial," or viral, gastroenteritis was second in frequency only to the common cold as a disease among families.[2] Worldwide, it has been estimated that acute diarrheal disease accounts for nearly 5 million deaths in children younger than 5 years.[3] Although the etiology of much of this disease remains unknown, recent evidence suggests that many cases result from viral infections.[4, 5] Two new virus families, the Caliciviridae and the Astroviridae (see Chapter 164) have emerged as important causes of gastroenteritis in adults and children.

HISTORY

Failure to isolate causative agents, bacterial or viral, from apparently infectious outbreaks of diarrhea and vomiting led to the widely held assumption that undetected viruses were responsible for such disease. In 1945, Reimann and coworkers[6] transmitted disease to volunteers by administering bacteria-free filtrates of throat washings, stool filtrates, or both from naturally occurring cases. Gordon and colleagues[7] and Jordan and coworkers[8] induced disease in normal volunteers with bacteria-free material. These studies described two transmissible agents of sub-bacterial size, the Marcy and FS agents, that appeared to be antigenically distinct. However, these workers were unable to detect viral agents in vitro with the techniques available at that time. Despite extensive virologic investigations in laboratories throughout the world, relatively little progress was made in this area until 1972, when the Norwalk virus, the prototype of this group, was described and partially characterized.[9, 10] This virus was initially detected in diarrheal stools obtained from people during an outbreak of gastroenteritis in Norwalk, Ohio, that involved students in an elementary school and family contacts. Subsequently, additional viruses with similar properties were described, including the Hawaii,[11] Montgomery County,[12] Taunton,[13] and Snow Mountain[14] viruses, whose names were based on the geographic region in which they were first recognized. All these viruses had a similar small round-structured morphology by electron microscopy, had similar size and density, did not grow in any in vitro propagation system, and were responsible for acute gastroenteritis, commonly in epidemic form with high secondary attack rates.[4] At the same time, viruses with more readily identifiable morphology by electron microscopy, referred to as human caliciviruses,[15] were observed in the stools of individuals, primarily children, with gastroenteritis. Subsequent molecular studies have clearly identified all these viruses as members of the Caliciviridae family.

CLASSIFICATION

The name *calicivirus* is derived from the characteristic appearance of the viral particles under the electron microscope, which consists of a scalloped border with "cuplike" indentations on its surface (Fig. 163–1) from which the Latin name *chalice* or *calyx* is derived.[16, 17] Caliciviruses have been detected in a variety of animal species, including marine mammals, swine, felines, and rabbits, as well as humans. Caliciviruses currently recognized as pathogens in humans include the Norwalk virus and other human caliciviruses responsible for gastroenteritis that are discussed in this chapter. Hepatitis E virus,[18] which causes enterically transmitted non-A, non-B hepatitis, has features of its genome that are similar to those of caliciviruses, but it is currently unclassified (see Chapter 165).

VIROLOGY

Although many animal caliciviruses replicate efficiently in cell culture, no practical in vitro method has been described for the propagation of human caliciviruses responsible for gastroenteritis. Therefore, grouping of these viruses together was originally based on physical properties determined by electron microscopic visualization or physicochemical manipulation of infectious inocula. Because of the small numbers of virions characteristically found in stool samples, visualization of the particles by electron microscopy is usually enhanced by the addition of immune serum, which obscures the typical features of calicivirus morphology (Fig. 163–2). The virions are 26 to 34 nm in diameter, have cubic symmetry, lack envelopes, and have a buoyant density in CsCl of 1.34 to 1.41 g/cc. When examined, these viruses appear to be relatively heat and acid stable and ether resistant.[10] In addition, immunoprecipitation of virions purified from stool samples established that the Norwalk[19] virus contains a single structural polypeptide 59 to 62 kD in molecular mass, characteristic of the *Caliciviridae.*[20] Similar results were obtained with the Snow Mountain virus,[21] as well as with a Japanese strain of human calicivirus.[22]

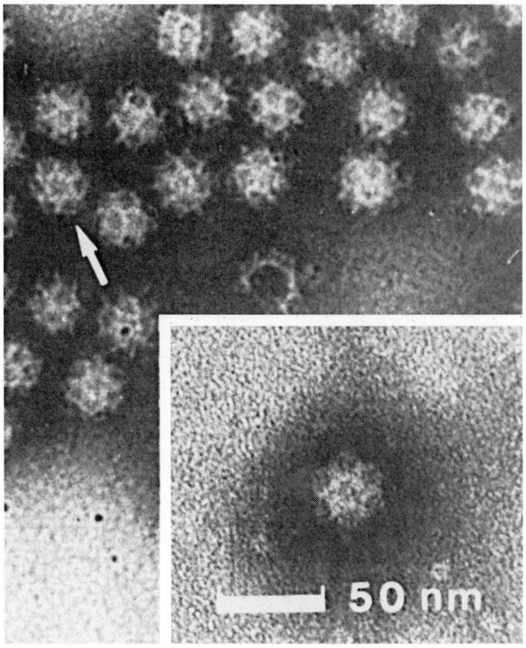

FIGURE 163–1. Calicivirus particles *(arrow)* in a fecal extract from a child with gastroenteritis. (Inset is higher magnification of particle indicated by arrow.) (From Chiba S, Sakuma Y, Kogasaka R, et al. An outbreak of gastroenteritis associated with calcivirus in an infant home. J Med Virol. 1979;4:249–254. Reprinted by permission of Wiley-Liss, Inc., a division of John Wiley & Sons, Inc.)

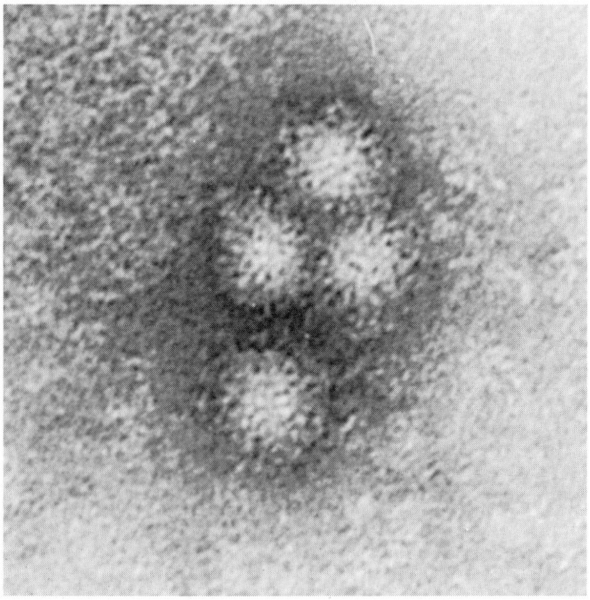

FIGURE 163–2. Snow Mountain agent in stool filtrate from a volunteer with experimentally induced disease as visualized by immune electron microscopy. Particles are 27 nm in diameter and are stained with 2% phosphotungstic acid.

The development of polymerase chain reaction (PCR) techniques allowed cloning[23, 24] and sequencing[25] of the Norwalk virus genome and subsequent establishment of this virus as a member of the Caliciviridae. The Norwalk virus contains a single-stranded positive-sense RNA genome of 7654 nt with a polyadenlyated 3′ tail.[25, 26] The genomic organization of the Norwalk virus is shown in Figure 163–3.[25] Three long open reading frames are present. The first open reading frame encodes a protein approximately 57 kD in molecular mass. It has been suggested that this protein is the viral RNA polymerase, as well as having helicase and protease functions, on the basis of sequence homology with other RNA viruses.[25] The second open reading frame encodes a viral capsid protein 58 kD in molecular mass.[27] From work done with animal caliciviruses, it is likely that this protein is encoded by a subgenomic mRNA in infected cells. When expressed in insect cells by a recombinant baculovirus, viral capsid protein spontaneously assembles into virion-like structures that are immunogenic and react specifically with convalescent human sera.[27] The three-dimensional structure of these empty capsids has been studied by electron cryomicroscopy, which suggests that the capsid has icosahedral symmetry with T = 3.[28] Finally, the third open reading frame encodes a protein predicted to be 22.5 kD in molecular mass that currently has no known function.[25]

With the widespread utilization of molecular diagnostic techniques, viruses structurally similar to the Norwalk virus continue to be detected in diarrheal stools during outbreaks of gastroenteritis throughout the world. Generally, the convention of geographic naming has been maintained, which has led to the Southampton,[29] Toronto,[30] Mexico,[31] and Lordsdale[32] viruses, among others. No consensus naming scheme has yet been accepted, but one proposed system includes the type of virus, strain designation, year of isolation, and country of isolation.[33] By this system, the Norwalk virus, which was first detected in an outbreak in Ohio in 1968, would be known as HuCV/NV/8FIIa/68/US.

The genomes of many of these viruses have been determined to have an organization similar to that of Norwalk virus.[29, 34–36] However, complete sequencing of the Sapporo strain of human calicivirus has suggested that the genome of this virus is organized slightly differently from that of Norwalk virus, with the open reading frame encoding the capsid being in frame with the nonstructural polyprotein.[37]

Sequence data and more limited antigenic analysis have shown that a significant degree of both genotypic and antigenic variability exists within these viruses. The widespread application of PCR techniques for the detection of virus in stool samples has resulted in the identification and partial nucleotide sequence analysis of a large number of these viruses. By comparison of sequences within the putative RNA-dependent RNA polymerase regions, they can be broadly divided into three main genogroups, with genogroup 1 represented by the Norwalk virus and group 2 represented by the Hawaii and Snow Mountain viruses.[38–41] Alignment studies have shown approximately 80 to 95% similarity within groups and approximately 60 to 65% similarity between groups 1 and 2 within the polymerase

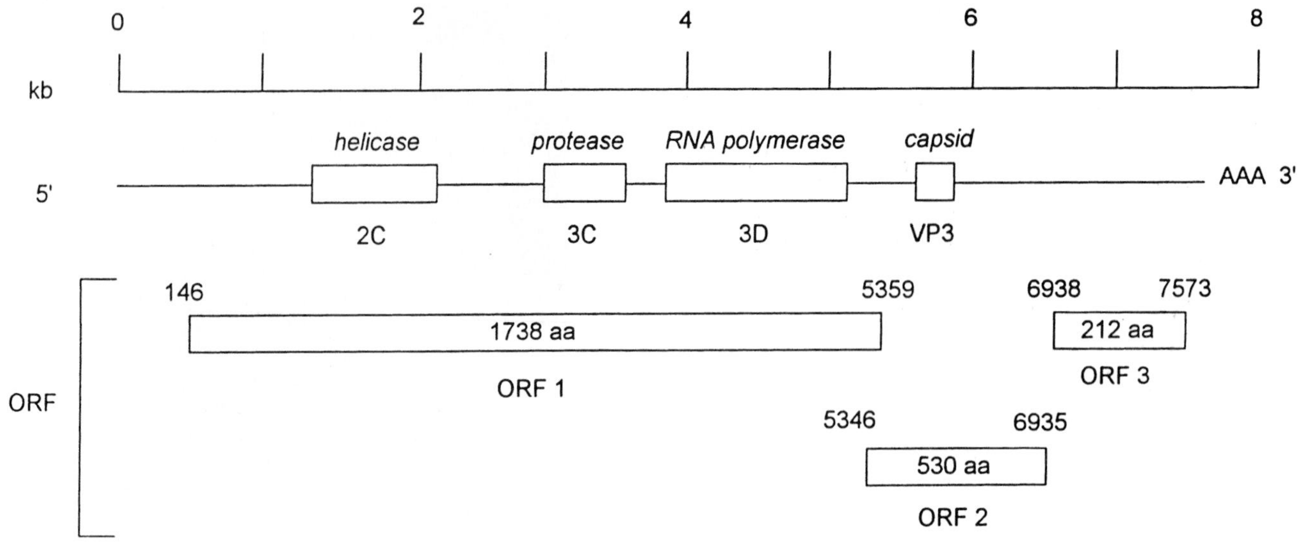

FIGURE 163–3. Genomic organization of the Norwalk virus. The three open reading frames (ORF) present on the positive strand are shown with the predicted sizes of their polypeptide products. Above this map are indicated regions of amino acid similarity to domains of known function in the picornavirus genome. The size of the genome in kilobases is shown at the top. (From Jiang X, Wang M, Wang K, Estes MK. Sequence and genomic organization of Norwalk virus. Virology. 1993;195:51–61.)

region.[38, 39] Groups 1 and 2 may also be further divided into subgroups as more extensive information becomes available.[36, 42, 43] Caliciviruses with so-called "classic" morphology by electron microscopy such as the Sapporo virus, have a significantly divergent genetic sequence and constitute a third genogroup.[44, 45] Analysis of sequence homologies in the polymerase region of the Sapporo virus and similar enteric caliciviruses suggests that they are more closely related to animal caliciviruses such as feline calicivirus than they are to genogroup 1 or 2 Norwalk-like viruses, with approximately 21 to 27% homology to genogroup 1 and 2 viruses and 40% homology to feline calicivirus.[44] Relatively less information regarding capsid sequences is available. Generally, the amino acid homology within the capsid region is less than that within the polymerase region. The degree of sequence divergence varies within the capsid sequences, with sequences in the middle of the capsid region having the most diversity[39] and those at the amino and carboxy termini being less divergent. Phylogenetic trees based on capsid sequence have a slightly different structure than those based on polymerase structure.[46]

Because of the lack of a convenient in vitro propagation system, antigenic characterization of these viruses is less straightforward. The most clear-cut distinction is between the Norwalk and Hawaii viruses because these agents have been compared by cross-challenge experiments in human subjects.[47] In these studies, infection with the Norwalk virus provided short-term protection against rechallenge with the Norwalk virus and closely related Montgomery County agent, but not against the Hawaii agent, and vice versa. Because this type of experiment is the closest analogue to virus neutralization that is available, this study provides evidence of at least two distinct Norwalk serotypes, roughly corresponding to the two genotypes just described.

Additional differences can be detected by using carefully chosen postinfection human sera in immune electron microscopy or solid-phase immunoassay techniques. The Norwalk, Hawaii, and Snow Mountain viruses are antigenically distinct by these techniques.[12, 14, 48–51] Some antigenic cross-reactivity has been described between Japanese small round-structured viruses and the Norwalk and Hawaii viruses.[52, 53] In addition, at least two and possibly four serovarieties of human calicivirus have been described from outbreaks in the United Kingdom that are distinct from those detected in Japan.[54]

Virus-like particles have been generated by expression of the capsid regions of the Norwalk[27] and Desert Shield[35] viruses belonging to genogroup 1; the MX,[36] Lordsdale,[32] Snow Mountain,[46] Hawaii,[55] and Toronto[30] viruses belonging to genogroup 2; and the Sapporo[56] virus belonging to genogroup 3. As additional capsid regions are expressed, it is likely that more clear-cut antigenic distinctions between these viruses can be drawn. However, definitive serotyping of these viruses awaits the development of a practical neutralization assay.

EPIDEMIOLOGY

The clinical syndromes in which the Norwalk viruses have been implicated appear to be exceedingly widespread and common. Disease can occur throughout the year and affects all age groups in both open and closed populations.

Experimental induction of illness in normal volunteers suggests that the major route of person-to-person transmission is fecal-oral. Epidemiologic reports have also implicated vomitus as a vehicle of transmission,[57, 58] and virus has been detected in vomitus by electron microscopy[59] and PCR.[60] Airborne transmission has also occasionally been implicated,[61, 62] but limited attempts to experimentally transmit virus with nasopharyngeal washings from an ill volunteer were unsuccessful.[10]

Norwalk and related viruses were first recognized in association with point-source outbreaks of gastroenteritis, and such outbreaks remain the most common situation in which Norwalk viruses have been implicated as etiologic agents. Several features are characteristics of such outbreaks and may be useful in empirical diagnosis. These features include a short-lived illness of 2 to 3 days' duration with vomiting as a prominent symptom in most affected individuals, an incubation period of 24 to 48 hours, high secondary attack rates, and lack of identifiable pathogens on routine examination of stool samples.[63] Thirty-four to 42 percent of outbreaks of acute gastroenteritis meeting these criteria were etiologically associated with the Norwalk virus,[64] and additional outbreaks may have been associated with other related viruses for which assays were not as readily available.

Almost any type of food that has contact with contaminated water may serve as a vehicle for outbreaks of Norwalk-related gastroenteritis. Also included are drinking contaminated water and even swimming in pools or lakes in which ill individuals have been swimming,[65, 66] which is an indication of the highly infectious nature of these viruses. Of note, these viruses appear to be relatively resistant to inactivation by chlorine.[58] Because products such as shellfish or contaminated commercial ice[67] can be distributed to multiple sites, such outbreaks may be exceedingly widespread.[68] Contamination of foodstuffs has been traced to both presymptomatic[69] and postsymptomatic[70] food handlers, thus complicating infection control recommendations.

Shellfish such as clams and oysters are filter feeders and efficiently concentrate microorganisms from contaminated water. When consumed, these foods are very frequently implicated in the transmission of enteric viruses in general and Norwalk-like gastroenteritis in particular.[71] It has been possible in some cases to document transmission via the practice of dumping diarrheal stools overboard in the same areas that shellfish are harvested.[72, 73] Norwalk viruses appear to be somewhat resistant to heat inactivation, and even thorough cooking of shellfish does not entirely eliminate the risk of transmission.[73, 74]

Outbreaks of Norwalk-related gastroenteritis are particularly common in closed settings such as in hospitals, nursing homes, ships, and the military.[75–77] Secondary transmission is a prominent feature of such outbreaks. Although most of these outbreaks will terminate spontaneously after 1 to 2 weeks, some may be quite prolonged. For example, it is very common to have recurrent outbreaks on cruise ships despite stringent attempts to determine the source and disinfect the ship between cruises.

Recommendations for evaluation and control of nosocomial outbreaks[78] include identification and elimination of common sources, as well as hand washing and barrier methods to prevent secondary transmission. Exclusion of ill employees may be important in limiting the spread of nosocomial outbreaks.[79] These methods have generally been found to be more effective in limiting the spread of outbreaks from unit to unit within an institution than in terminating an outbreak in an individual unit once it has begun.[80, 81] The Viral Gastroenteritis Section, Centers for Disease Control and Prevention, is available for advice regarding such outbreaks (404-639-3577).

Studies of serum antibody to Norwalk viruses suggest that infection with these viruses is exceedingly widespread. In developed countries, serum antibody to the Norwalk virus is first noted at ages 3 to 4, and antibody prevalence gradually rises to greater than 50% by the fifth decade of life.[82] Similar findings have been seen with the Snow Mountain virus.[49] Studies using recombinant Norwalk antigen have suggested that significant increases in antibody prevalence occur in infancy, upon entry into primary schools, and in young adulthood.[83] Antibody appears to be acquired more rapidly in developing countries.[82] Seroepidemiologic studies of human caliciviruses carried out in Japan and in the United Kingdom indicate that antibody is acquired in early childhood and can be detected in up to 90% of older children and adults.[54, 84] Infection with human caliciviruses also appears to be widely prevalent in Southeast Asia.[85] The age when serum antibody is acquired as assessed by assays using recombinant Norwalk capsid antigen appears to be similar in other developed countries such as Sweden[86] and Japan.[87] Antibody appears to be acquired more rapidly in developing countries[82] and may be rare or nonexistent in some isolated populations.[82, 88]

Although the Norwalk viruses have most commonly been associated with outbreaks predominantly involving adults, recognition of the role of these viruses as causes of gastroenteritis in children in various parts of the world has increased.[15, 16, 89–93] Most illness reported with the "classic" human caliciviruses has been in young children. Calicivirus-like particles were first described in the stools of children with gastroenteritis[94] in 1976 and have subsequently been detected in community-wide, daycare,[95] and nosocomial outbreaks of gastroenteritis in children,[96] as well as in sporadic cases in various parts of the world.[15, 16, 89–91] Toronto virus has been reported to be the second most common virus detected in the stools of young children with gastroenteritis.[97] The frequency of Norwalk-like gastroenteritis appears to be approximately one tenth that of rotavirus in children when direct comparison has been done.[98] In one study, 49% of prospectively monitored Finnish infants and children seroresponded to Norwalk virus over a 2-year period.[99] Additional studies with newer, more sensitive, and widely available diagnostic tests are likely to expand recognition of the potential role of the Norwalk viruses as causes of sporadic gastroenteritis in children.

The role of antigenic variation in the epidemiology of these viruses remains an area of continued investigation. Generally, antibody to viruses within genogroup 2 appears to be more common than within genogroup 1.[100] Within any geographic region, significant variation may be seen from year to year in the predominant genotypes of viruses associated with illness.[101, 102]

PATHOGENESIS

Because convenient animal models for gastroenteritis induced by the Norwalk viruses are not available, information about the pathogenesis of this illness is based largely on studies of experimentally induced disease in healthy volunteers. Acute infection with Norwalk and Hawaii viruses results in a reversible histopathologic lesion in the jejunum,[11, 103–105] with apparent sparing of the stomach[106] and rectum (Fig. 163–4). The villi are blunted, but the mucosa is otherwise intact. Round cell and polymorphonuclear leukocytic infiltration is seen in the lamina propria. By electron microscopy, the epithelial cells are similarly intact, microvilli are shortened, and widened intercellular spaces are noted. These histopathologic changes appear within 24 hours after virus challenge, are present at the height of illness, and persist for a variable period after the illness. The histopathologic changes have generally cleared within 2 weeks after the onset of illness, although some jejunal changes have been noted as late as 6 weeks after challenge. Histopathologic changes have been described in both clinical and subclinical cases of infection[104, 105] and appear to be indistinguishable in both Norwalk and Hawaii virus–induced disease.

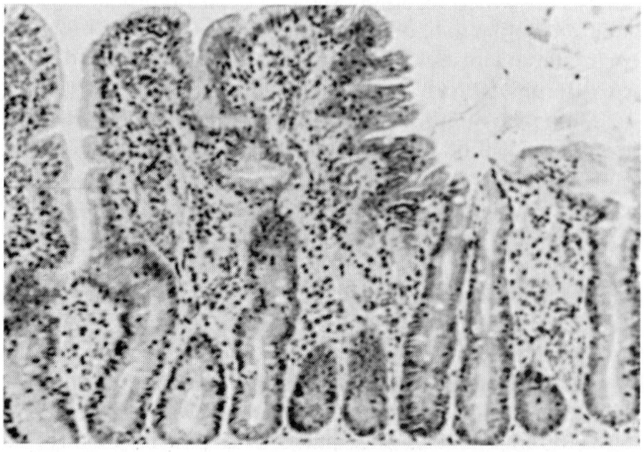

FIGURE 163–4. Light micrograph of a jejunal mucosal biopsy specimen from a volunteer with Hawaii-induced disease 48 hours after challenge. Blunted villi and inflammatory cell infiltrate in the lamina propria are present. (Hematoxylin and eosin, ×140.)

Diarrhea induced by the Norwalk virus is associated with transient malabsorption of D-xylose and fat[107] and with decreased activity of brush-border enzymes, including alkaline phosphatase and trehalase.[103] Absorption and brush-border enzyme levels return to normal values within 2 weeks after challenge. During acute illness, a variable amount of intestinal fluid is produced, but infection with the Norwalk and Hawaii agents has not been associated with detectable enterotoxin production. Adenylate cyclase levels in jejunal biopsy specimens appear to be normal during infection.[108] Thus, the precise mechanisms of viral-induced diarrhea and vomiting remain unknown at present. Little is known regarding the pathogenesis of illness associated with other human caliciviruses. Calicivirus infections of animals have been associated with atrophy of the small intestinal mucosa along with a mild inflammatory infiltrate in the lamina propria.[109, 110]

Virus shedding in stools as detected by immune electron microscopy or radioimmunoassay is maximal over the first 24 to 48 hours after illness.[12, 14] In volunteer studies, virus has been rarely detected beyond 72 hours after the onset of vomiting or diarrhea[12, 14] by these techniques. However, more prolonged shedding of virus after challenge has been detected by sensitive enzyme-linked immunosorbent assay (ELISA) techniques using hyperimmune animal sera[111] or PCR. The clinical significance of the prolonged detection of virus in stools is unclear, but epidemiologic data have implicated individuals who are postsymptomatic in transmission of illness.[70]

IMMUNE RESPONSES

Infection with the Norwalk virus results in the induction of virus-specific serum IgG, IgA, and IgM antibody,[112–115] even in the presence of previous exposure. IgA and IgM responses appear to be relatively short lived, whereas elevations in Norwalk-specific serum IgG persist for months.[114, 115] In addition to recognizing the infecting strain of calicivirus, serum antibody produced in response to infection may also recognize related strains of virus, although generally to lower titer. Such heterologous antibody responses are more common within a genogroup than between genogroups.[113, 116] Serum IgM and IgA antibody may be more specific for the infecting strain of virus.[113] By using baculovirus-expressed capsid proteins it has been demonstrated that responses to viruses within genogroup 1 may be more specific than responses to infection with viruses within genogroup 2.[43] Heterologous responses have also been seen in individuals infected with genogroup 3 viruses.[54] These broad responses are in contrast to the extremely specific antibody response of animals hyperimmunized with capsid antigen[40] and may in part reflect the extensive prior exposure of most adults to related viruses. It is not clear that such heterologous responses are significant from the point of view of protection against reinfection; however, they do complicate the process of assigning a specific agent on the basis of serologic grounds alone.

Mucosal immune responses have not been studied extensively, but jejunal IgA synthesis has been shown to be elevated in biopsy specimens obtained 2 weeks after challenge with the Norwalk agent,[117] and fecal IgA responses after Norwalk virus infection have also been reported.[118] Limited studies of cell-mediated immune responses in these infections indicate that acute illness is associated with a transient lymphopenia that involves thymus-derived, bone marrow–derived, and null cell subpopulations.[119]

Parameters defining protective immunity to the Norwalk viruses are poorly understood. After infection with Norwalk virus, most individuals manifest resistance to reinfection that persists for at least 4 to 6 months.[120, 121] Multiple exposure appears to increase this resistance.[121] This short-term resistance does not seem to extend to other, antigenically distinct viruses.[47] Infection-induced resistance eventually wanes, and after 2 to 3 years such individuals are susceptible to reinfection with the same virus.[120] In addition, some individuals manifest a poorly defined long-term resistance to infection and consistently remain well despite repeated challenge with virus.[120]

Studies of the role of serum antibody in mediating this protection have yielded conflicting results. In most studies in adults, infection and illness induced by Norwalk-like agents occur in the presence of a wide range of preexisting serum antibody levels, which thus correlate poorly with protection.[113, 121] However, after repeated experimental exposure of adults[121] and in epidemiologic studies conducted in children in developing countries,[122, 123] better correlation has been noted between the presence of serum antibody and protection from illness. Protection may be related to other host defense factors such as a local mucosal antibody analogous to the role played by secretory IgA in poliovirus infection.[124] However, direct measurements of intestinal antibody have failed to show a correlation with protection from Norwalk-induced illness,[125] and the presence of prechallenge Norwalk-specific fecal IgA was also not protective against challenge.[126] The parameters of immunity to genogroup 3 human caliciviruses in children have not been well studied. In a study of an outbreak that occurred in an orphanage in Japan, the presence of preexisting serum antibody was associated with a lower likelihood of the development of illness.[127]

CLINICAL MANIFESTATIONS

The clinical characteristics of illness induced by the Norwalk agent appear to be similar in both naturally occurring and experimentally induced disease (Fig. 163–5). Incubation periods are generally 24 to 48 hours, although ranges of 18 to 72 hours have been observed. The onset of symptoms can be either gradual or abrupt, and most persons complain first of abdominal cramps with or without nausea. Generally, both vomiting and diarrhea occur, although either can be present alone. Myalgias, malaise, and occasional headaches are also seen. Low-grade fever (with temperatures of 101°F to 102°F) occurs in approximately half the cases. Disease manifestations generally last 48 to 72 hours and remit without sequelae.

Diarrheal stool is generally moderate in amount, with four to eight stools being produced over a period of 24 hours. Stools are characteristically nonbloody, lack mucus, and may be loose to watery. Fecal leukocytes are not seen in Norwalk-induced disease. Illnesses induced by each of the Norwalk-like agents appear to be clinically indistinguishable. Illness induced by the morphologically characteristic human caliciviruses, that is, genogroup 3 viruses, appears to be similar but is generally seen in a younger population.

DIAGNOSIS

A clinical diagnosis of Norwalk-like illness can be suspected on the basis of epidemiologic information and by the absence of other documented pathogens. However, the signs and symptoms of illness are not sufficiently characteristic to enable a diagnosis to be made on clinical grounds alone. Routine laboratory tests are also generally not helpful in making a specific diagnosis of Norwalk-like infection. Peripheral white blood cell counts are normal or slightly elevated with a relative polymorphonuclear leukocytosis and lymphopenia but with otherwise unremarkable white cell morphology. The results of liver function tests, blood urea nitrogen and creatinine determinations, and urinalysis are generally within normal limits. The absence of fecal leukocytes, as determined by microscopic examination of stools stained with methylene blue,[128] is a useful tool with which to exclude infection with enteroinvasive pathogens such as *Shigella.*

Specific diagnosis requires laboratory confirmation, which is currently available only as a research technique. Because these agents currently cannot be cultivated in vitro, a variety of methods have been developed to detect virus directly in stool samples. Immune electron microscopy, in which immune sera are used to aggregate and highlight virions in stool suspensions (see Fig. 163–2), was the method used to originally identify these viruses.[14, 129] The technique has the advantage of being readily adaptable to the detection of new virus types and can be used both for the detection of virus and for antibody determination, but it cannot be conveniently used for routine screening. Therefore, immunoassays have been developed for detection of specific viruses. Because animal hyperimmune sera were not available, initial immunoassays for the detection of Norwalk,[48] Snow Mountain,[50] and Hawaii[51] viruses used postinfection sera from human volunteers as reagents. Expression of the capsid antigens by recombinant DNA techniques provided a way to generate high-titered animal hyperimmune sera for diagnostic purposes. Antigen detection immunoassays using such reagents have been reported for the Norwalk and other similar viruses. An antigen detection ELISA for human calicivirus using hyperimmune animal sera has also been reported.[130] Preliminary results using such assays suggest that they are extremely sensitive for detection of homologous virus but lack sensitivity for detection of even slight antigenic variants,[40] which has limited their application.

Nucleic acid detection techniques such as PCR have also been used extensively for Norwalk virus detection.[131–134] The success of this strategy depends on the ability to remove inhibitors of reverse transcription from the samples and the choice of primers in relatively

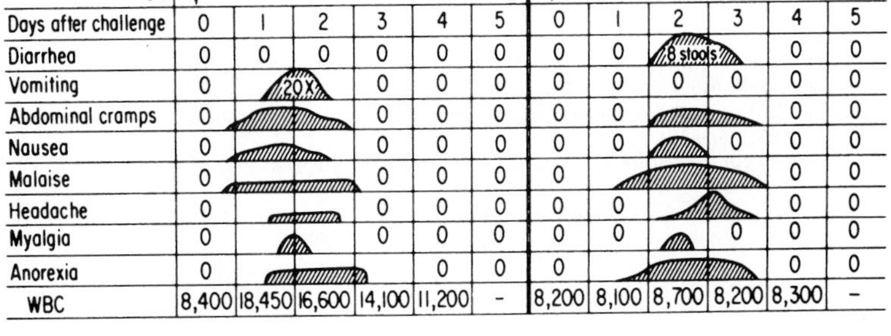
A. Volunteer 1
B. Volunteer 2
ORAL TEMPERATURE (F°)
102
101
100
99
98
97
Challenge
Challenge
Days after challenge 0 1 2 3 4 5 0 1 2 3 4 5
Diarrhea 0 0 0 0 0 0 0 0 8 stools 0 0
Vomiting 0 20X 0 0 0 0 0 0 0 0 0
Abdominal cramps 0 0 0 0 0 0 0 0
Nausea 0 0 0 0 0 0 0 0 0
Malaise 0 0 0 0 0 0 0
Headache 0 0 0 0 0 0 0 0
Myalgia 0 0 0 0 0 0 0 0 0 0
Anorexia 0 0 0 0 0 0
WBC 8,400 18,450 16,600 14,100 11,200 - 8,200 8,100 8,700 8,200 8,300 -

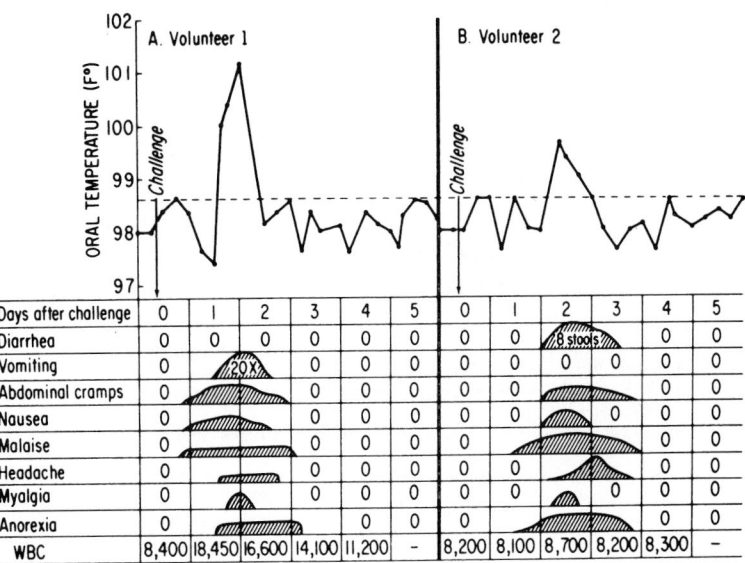

FIGURE 163–5. Clinical response of two healthy volunteers after the oral administration of the Norwalk agent. The height of the shaded curve is proportional to the severity of the sign or symptom. (From Dolin R, Treanor J, Madore HP. Novel agents of viral enteritis in humans. J Infect Dis. 1987;155:365–375.)

conserved regions of the genome to widen the scope of viruses detected. Conversely, carefully selected primers within relatively more divergent capsid regions can be used to differentiate virus strains genotypically.[42] Highly sensitive molecular techniques such as PCR may be particularly useful for detecting contamination of food and environmental samples.[60, 135–138]

Immunoassay techniques have also been adapted for the detection of antibody to these viruses and are useful for the serologic diagnosis of infection. Because virus excretion in stools is limited and collection of stool samples in outbreaks can be problematic, serologic techniques are more often used for diagnostic purposes.[139] Serum antibody titer rises can be detected within 10 to 14 days after the onset of illness, and a specific viral diagnosis can thus be established, although the possibility of heterologous antibody responses should be kept in mind.

TREATMENT AND PREVENTION

Disease induced by the Norwalk-like agents is generally self-limited and resolves without specific treatment, although occasionally the disease may be somewhat more severe in debilitated hosts. Oral fluid replacement with isotonic liquids as tolerated by the patient is generally adequate to replace fluid losses. Rarely, parenteral intravenous therapy may be required if severe vomiting and diarrhea develop. Symptomatic treatment of headache, myalgias, and nausea with analgesics and antiemetics may provide relief. In one study, the administration of bismuth subsalicylate reduced gastrointestinal symptoms in Norwalk-induced disease in normal volunteers but had no effect on the number or character of stools or on virus shedding.[140] Although antiperistaltic agents are frequently prescribed to control diarrhea, their effect on the disease course and on excretion of virus has not been rigorously evaluated.

Recent reports of the development of immune responses after oral administration of Norwalk virus capsids provide an interesting possible approach to immunization against these viruses.[141] Because of the tendency of these viruses to form virus-like particles when expressed in heterologous systems and their relatively simple structure, Norwalk virus has also proved to be an excellent model to evaluate expression of vaccine antigens in plants as a method for oral immunization.[142] However, development of effective vaccines to prevent Norwalk or human calicivirus gastroenteritis may be a daunting task if current data suggesting that effective long-term immunity is not induced after infection prove true. In addition, the apparent presence of multiple antigenic types may also present a challenge to vaccine development. These illnesses also appear to be reasonable targets for the application of broadly protective antiviral measures such as antiviral chemoprophylaxis and therapy. Because outbreaks are often associated with waterborne or foodborne spread, efforts to reduce potential sources of contamination are also important control measures.

REFERENCES

1. Current estimates from the Health Interview Survey—1972. United States Department of Health, Education, and Welfare, 1973.
2. Dingle JH, Badger GF, Feller AE, et al. A study of illness in a group of Cleveland families. I. A plan of study and certain general observations. Am J Hyg. 1953;58:16–37.
3. Snyder SD, Merson MH. The magnitude of the global problem of acute diarrheal disease: A review of active surveillance data. Bull World Health Organ. 1982;60:605–613.
4. Dolin R, Treanor J, Madore HP. Novel agents of viral enteritis in humans. J Infect Dis. 1987;155:365–375.
5. Blacklow NR, Greenberg HB. Viral gastroenteritis. N Engl J Med. 1991;325:252–264.
6. Reimann HA, Price AH, Hodges JH. The cause of epidemic diarrhea, nausea, and vomiting (viral dysentery?). Proc Soc Exp Biol Med. 1945;59:8–9.
7. Gordon I, Ingraham HS, Korns RF. Transmission of epidemic gastroenteritis to human volunteers by oral administration of fecal filtrate. J Exp Med. 1947;86: 409–422.
8. Jordan WS, Gordon I, Dorrance WR. A study of illness in a group of Cleveland families. VII. Transmission of acute nonbacterial gastroenteritis to volunteers: Evidence for two different etiologic agents. J Exp Med. 1953;98:461–475.
9. Kapikian AZ, Gerin JL, Wyatt RG, et al. Density in cesium chloride of the Norwalk agent: Determination by ultracentrifugation and immune electron microscopy. Proc Soc Exp Biol Med. 1973;142:874–877.
10. Dolin R, Blacklow NR, DuPont H, et al. Biological properties of Norwalk agent of acute infectious nonbacterial gastroenteritis. Proc Soc Exp Biol Med. 1972;140:578–583.
11. Dolin R, Levy AG, Wyatt RG, et al. Viral gastroenteritis induced by the Hawaii agent: Jejunal histopathology and serologic response. Am J Med. 1975;59:768–771.
12. Thornhill TS, Wyatt RG, Kalica AR, et al. Detection by immune electron microscopy of 26–27 nm virus-like particles associated with two family outbreaks of gastroenteritis. J Infect Dis. 1977;138:20–27.
13. Caul EO, Ashley C, Pether JVS. Norwalk-like particle in epidemic gastroenteritis in the U.K. Lancet. 1979;2:1292.
14. Dolin R, Reichman RC, Roessner KD, et al. Detection by immune electron microscopy of the Snow Mountain agent of acute viral gastroenteritis. J Infect Dis. 1982;146:184–189.
15. Flewett TH, Davies H. Caliciviruses (Letter). Lancet. 1976;1:311.
16. Chiba S, Sakuma Y, Kogasaka R, et al. An outbreak of gastroenteritis associated with calicivirus in an infant home. J Med Virol. 1979;4:249–254.
17. Chiba S, Sakuma Y, Kagasaka R, et al. Fecal shedding of virus in relation to the days of illness in infantile gastroenteritis due to calicivirus. J Infect Dis. 1980;142:247–249.
18. Tam AW, Smith MM, Guerra ME, et al. Hepatitis E virus (HEV): Molecular cloning and sequencing of the full-length viral genome. Virology. 1991;185:120–131.
19. Greenberg HB, Valdesuso J, Kalica AR. Proteins of Norwalk virus. J Virol. 1981;37:994–999.
20. Schaffer FL, Bachrach HL, Brown F, et al. Caliciviridae. Intervirology. 1980;14:1–6.
21. Madore HP, Treanor J, Dolin R. Characterization of the Snow Mountain agent of viral gastroenteritis. J Virol. 1986;58:487–492.
22. Terashima H, Chiba S, Sakuma Y, et al. The polypeptide of a human calicivirus. Arch Virol. 1983;78:1–7.
23. Jiang X, Graham DY, Wang K, et al. Norwalk virus genome cloning and characterization. Science. 1990;250:1580–1583.
24. Matsui S, Kim JP, Greenberg HB, et al. The isolation and characterization of a Norwalk virus–specific cDNA. J Clin Invest. 1991;87:1456–1461.
25. Jiang X, Wang M, Wang K, et al. Sequence and genomic organization of Norwalk virus. Virology. 1993;195:51–61.
26. Hardy ME, Estes MK. Completion of the Norwalk virus genome sequence. Virus Genes. 1996;12:287–290.
27. Jiang X, Wang M, Graham DY, et al. Expression, self-assembly, and antigenicity of the Norwalk virus capsid protein. J Virol. 1992;66:6527–6532.
28. Prasad BV, Rothnagel R, Jiang X, et al. Three-dimensional structure of baculovirus-expressed Norwalk virus capsids. J Virol. 1994;68:5117–5125.
29. Lambden PR, Caul ED, Ashley CR, et al. Sequence and genome organization of a human small round-structured (Norwalk-like) virus. Science. 1993;259:516–519.
30. Leite JP, Ando T, Noel JS, et al. Characterization of Toronto virus capsid protein expressed in baculovirus. Arch Virol. 1996;141:865–875.
31. Jiang X, Matson DO, Velazquez FR, et al. Study of Norwalk-related viruses in Mexican children. J Med Virol. 1995;47:309–316.
32. Dingle KE, Lambden PR, Caul EO, et al. Human enteric *Caliciviridae:* The complete genome sequence and expression of virus-like particles from a genetic group II small round structured virus. J Gen Virol. 1995;76:2349–2355.
33. Estes MK, Atmar RL, Hardy ME. Norwalk and related diarrhea viruses. In: Richman DD, Whitley RJ, Hayden FG, eds. Clinical Virology. New York: Churchill Livingstone; 1997:1073–1095.
34. Lew JF, Petric M, Kapikian AZ, et al. Identification of minireovirus as a Norwalk-like virus in pediatric patients with gastroenteritis. J Virol. 1994;68:3391–3396.
35. Lew JF, Kapikian AZ, Jiang X, et al. Molecular characterization and expression of the capsid protein of a Norwalk-like virus recovered from a Desert Shield troop with gastroenteritis. Virology. 1994;200:319–325.
36. Jiang X, Matson DO, Ruiz-Palacios GM, et al. Expression, self-assembly, and antigenicity of a Snow Mountain agent–like Calicivirus capsid protein. J Clin Microbiol. 1995;33:1452–1455.
37. Liu BL, Clarke IN, Caul EO, et al. Human enteric caliciviruses have a unique genome structure and are distinct from the Norwalk-like viruses. Arch Virol. 1995;140:1345–1356.
38. Wang J, Jiang X, Madore HP, et al. Sequence diversity of small, round-structured viruses in the Norwalk virus group. J Virol. 1994;68:5982–5990.
39. Lew JF, Kapikian AZ, Valdesuso J, et al. Molecular characterization of the Hawaii virus and other Norwalk-like viruses: Evidence for genetic polymorphism among human caliciviruses. J Infect Dis. 1994;170:535–542.
40. Jiang X, Wang J, Estes MK. Characterization of SRSVs using RT-PCR and a new antigen ELISA. Arch Virol. 1995;140:363–374.
41. Ando T, Mulders MN, Lewis DC, et al. Comparison of the polymerase region of small round structured virus strains previously classified in three antigenic types by solid-phase immune electron microscopy. Arch Virol. 1994;135:217–226.
42. Ando T, Monroe SS, Gentsch JR, et al. Detection and differentiation of antigenically distinct small round-structured viruses (Norwalk-like viruses) by reverse transcription–PCR and southern hybridization. J Clin Microbiol. 1995;33:64–71.
43. Noel JS, Ando T, Leite JP, et al. Correlation of patient immune responses with

genetically characterized small round-structured viruses involved in outbreaks of nonbacterial acute gastroenteritis in the United States, 1990 to 1995. J Med Virol. 1997;53:372–383.
44. Matson DO, Zhong W-M, Nakata S, et al. Molecular characterization of a human calicivirus with sequence relationships closer to an animal calicivirus than other known human caliciviruses. J Med Virol. 1995;45:215–222.
45. Lambden PR, Caul EO, Ashley CR, et al. Human enteric caliciviruses are genetically distinct from small round structured viruses. Lancet. 1994;343:666–667.
46. Hardy ME, Kramer SF, Treanor JJ, et al. Human calicivirus genogroup II capsid sequence diversity revealed by analysis of the prototype Snow Mountain agent. Arch Virol. 1997;142:1469–1479.
47. Wyatt RG, Dolin R, Blacklow NR, et al. Comparison of three agents of acute infectious nonbacterial gastroenteritis by virus challenge in volunteers. J Infect Dis. 1974;129:709–714.
48. Greenberg HB, Wyatt RG, Valdesuso J, et al. Solid phase microtiter radioimmunoassay for detection of the Norwalk strain of acute non-bacterial epidemic gastroenteritis virus and its antibodies. J Med Virol. 1978;2:97–108.
49. Dolin R, Roessner KD, Treanor J, et al. Radioimmunoassay for detection of Snow Mountain agent of viral gastroenteritis. J Med Virol. 1985;19:11–18.
50. Madore HP, Treanor JJ, Pray KA, et al. Enzyme-linked immunosorbent assays for Snow Mountain and Norwalk agents of viral gastroenteritis. J Clin Microbiol. 1986;24:456–459.
51. Treanor JJ, Madore HP, Dolin R. Development of an enzyme immunoassay for the Hawaii agent of viral gastroenteritis. J Virol Methods. 1988;22:207–214.
52. Hayashi Y, Ando T, Utagawa E, et al. Western blot (immunoblot) assay of small, round-structured virus associated with an acute gastroenteritis outbreak in Tokyo. J Clin Microbiol. 1989;27:1728–1733.
53. Okada S, Lekine S, Ando T, et al. Antigenic characterization of small, round-structured viruses by immune electron microscopy. J Clin Microbiol. 1990;28:1244–1248.
54. Cubitt WD, Blacklow NR, Herrmann JE. Antigenic relationships between human caliciviruses and Norwalk virus. J Infect Dis. 1987;156:806–814.
55. Green KY, Kapikian AZ, Valdesuso J, et al. Expression and self-assembly of recombinant capsid protein from the antigenically distinct Hawaii human calicivirus. J Clin Microbiol. 1997;35:1909–1914.
56. Numata K, Hardy ME, Nakata S, et al. Molecular characterization of morphologically typical human calicivirus Sapporo. Arch Virol. 1997;142:1537–1552.
57. Chadwick PR, McCann R. Transmission of a small round structured virus by vomiting during a hospital outbreak of gastroenteritis. J Hosp Infect. 1994;26:251–259.
58. Patterson W, Haswell P, Fryers PT, et al. Outbreak of small round structured virus gastroenteritis arose after kitchen assistant vomited. Commun Dis Rep CDR Rev. 1997;7:R101–R103.
59. Greenberg HB, Wyatt RG, Kapikian AZ. Norwalk virus in vomitus. Lancet. 1979;1:55.
60. Kilgore PE, Belay ED, Hamlin DM, et al. A university outbreak of gastroenteritis due to a small round-structured virus. Application of molecular diagnostics to identify the etiologic agent and patterns of transmission. J Infect Dis. 1996;173:787–793.
61. Sawyer LA, Murphy JJ, Kaplan JE, et al. 25- to 30-nm virus particle associated with a hospital outbreak of acute gastroenteritis with evidence for airborne transmission. Am J Epidemiol. 1988;127:1261–1271.
62. Caul EO. Small round structured viruses: Airborne transmission and hospital control. Lancet. 1994;343:1240–1242.
63. Kaplan JE, Feldman R, Campbell DS, et al. The frequency of a Norwalk-like pattern of illness in outbreaks of acute gastroenteritis. Am J Public Health. 1982;72:1329–1332.
64. Kaplan JE, Gary GW, Barron RC, et al. Epidemiology of Norwalk gastroenteritis and the role of Norwalk virus in outbreaks of acute nonbacterial gastroenteritis. Ann Intern Med. 1982;96:756–761.
65. Baron RC, Murphy FD, Greenberg HB. Norwalk gastrointestinal illness—an outbreak associated with swimming in a recreational lake with secondary person-to-person transmission. Am J Epidemiol. 1982;115:163–172.
66. Koopman JS, Eckert EA, Greenberg HB. Norwalk virus enteric illness acquired by swimming exposure. Am J Epidemiol. 1982;115:173–177.
67. Cannon RO, Poliner JR, Hirschhorn RB, et al. A multistate outbreak of Norwalk virus gastroenteritis associated with consumption of commercial ice. J Infect Dis. 1991;164:860–863.
68. Hedberg CW, Osterholm MT. Outbreaks of food-borne and waterborne viral gastroenteritis. Clin Microbiol Rev. 1993;6:199–210.
69. Lo SV, Connolly AM, Palmer SR, et al. The role of the pre-symptomatic food handler in a common source outbreak of food-borne SRSV gastroenteritis in a group of hospitals. Epidemiol Infect. 1994;113:513–521.
70. Patterson T, Hutching P, Palmer S. Outbreak of SRSV gastroenteritis at an international conference traced to food handled by a post-symptomatic caterer. Epidemiol Infect. 1993;111:157–162.
71. Stafford R, Strain D, Heymer M, et al. An outbreak of Norwalk virus gastroenteritis following consumption of oysters. Commun Dis Intell. 1997;21:317–320.
72. Kohn MH, Farley TA, Ando T, et al. An outbreak of Norwalk virus gastroenteritis associated with eating raw oysters. Implications for maintaining safe oyster beds. JAMA. 1995;273:466–471.
73. McDonnell S, Kirkland KB, Hlady WG, et al. Failure of cooking to prevent shellfish-associated viral gastroenteritis. Arch Intern Med. 1997;157:111–116.
74. Kirkland KB, Meriwether RA, Leiss JK, et al. Steaming oysters does not prevent Norwalk-like gastroenteritis. Public Health Rep. 1996;111:527–530.
75. Khan AS, Moe CL, Glass RI, et al. Norwalk virus–associated gastroenteritis traced to ice consumption aboard a cruise ship in Hawaii: Comparison and application of molecular method–based assays. J Clin Microbiol. 1994;31:318–322.
76. Bourgeois AL, Gardiner CH, Thornton SA, et al. Etiology of acute diarrhea among United States military personnel deployed to South America and west Africa. Am J Trop Med Hyg. 1993;48:243–248.
77. Hyams KC, Bourgeois AL, Merrell BR, et al. Diarrheal disease during Operation Desert Shield. N Engl J Med. 1991;325:1423–1428.
78. Centers for Disease Control. Viral agents of gastroenteritis: Public health importance and outbreak management. MMWR Morb Mortal Wkly Rep. 1990;39:1–24.
79. Rodriguez EM, Parrott C, Rolka H, et al. An outbreak of viral gastroenteritis in a nursing home: Importance of excluding ill employees. Infect Control Hosp Epidemiol. 1996;17:587–592.
80. Augustin AK, Simor AE, Shorrock C, et al. Outbreaks of gastroenteritis due to Norwalk-like virus in two long-term care facilities for the elderly. Can J Infect Control 1995;10:111–113.
81. Russo PL, Spelman DW, Harrington GA, et al. Hospital outbreak of Norwalk-like virus. Infect Control Hosp Epidemiol 1997;18:576–579.
82. Greenberg HB, Valdesuso J, Kapikian AZ, et al. Prevalence of antibody to the Norwalk virus in various countries. Infect Immun. 1979;26:270–273.
83. Gray JJ, Jiang X, Morgan-Capner P, et al. Prevalence of antibodies to Norwalk virus in England: Detection by enzyme-linked immunosorbent assay using baculovirus-expressed Norwalk virus capsid antigen. J Clin Microbiol. 1993;31:1022–1025.
84. Sakuma Y, Chiba S, Kogasaka R, et al. Prevalence of antibody to human calicivirus in general population of northern Japan. J Med Virol. 1981;7:221–225.
85. Nakata S, Chiba S, Terashima H, et al. Prevalence of antibody to human calicivirus in Japan and Southeast Asia determined by radioimmunoassay. J Clin Microbiol. 1985;22:519–521.
86. Hinkula J, Ball JM, Lofgren S, et al. Antibody prevalence and immunoglobulin IgG subclass pattern to Norwalk virus in Sweden. J Med Virol. 1995;47:52–57.
87. Numata K, Nakata S, Jiang X, et al. Epidemiologic study of Norwalk virus infections in Japan and Southeast Asia by enzyme-linked immunosorbent assays with Norwalk virus capsid protein produced by the baculovirus expression system. J Clin Microbiol. 1994;32:121–126.
88. Gabbay YB, Glass RI, Monroe SS, et al. Prevalence of antibodies to Norwalk virus among Amerindians in isolated Amazonian communities. Am J Epidemiol. 1994;139:728–733.
89. Kjeldsberg E. Small spherical viruses in faeces from gastroenteritis patients. Acta Pathol Microbiol Immunol Scand. 1977;85:351–354.
90. Spatt HC, Marks MI, Gomersall M, et al. Nosocomial infantile gastroenteritis associated with mini-rotavirus and calicivirus. J Pediatr. 1978;93:922–926.
91. Oishi I, Maeda A, Yamazaki K, et al. Calicivirus detected in outbreaks of acute gastroenteritis in school children. Biken J. 1980;23:163–168.
92. Steele AD, Phillips J, Smit TK, et al. Snow Mountain–like virus identified in young children with winter vomiting disease in South Africa. J Diarrhoeal Dis Res. 1997;15:177–182.
93. Levett PN, Gu M, Luan B, et al. Longitudinal study of molecular epidemiology of small round-structured viruses in a pediatric population. J Clin Microbiol. 1996;34:1497–1501.
94. Madeley CR, Cosgrove BP. Caliciviruses in man (Letter). Lancet. 1976;1:199–200.
95. Grohmann G, Glass RI, Gold J, et al. Outbreak of human calicivirus gastroenteritis in a day-care center in Sydney, Australia. J Clin Microbiol. 1991;29:544–550.
96. Struve J, Bennet R, Ehrnst A, et al. Nosocomial calicivirus gastroenteritis in a pediatric hospital. Pediatr Infect Dis J. 1994;13:882–885.
97. Middleton PJ, Szymanski MT, Petric M. Viruses associated with acute gastroenteritis in young children. Am J Dis Child. 1977;131:733.
98. Wolfaardt M, Taylor MB, Booysen HF, et al. Incidence of human calicivirus and rotavirus infection in patients with gastroenteritis in South Africa. J Med Virol. 1997;51:290–296.
99. Lew JF, Valdesuso J, Vesikari T, et al. Detection of Norwalk virus or Norwalk-like virus infections in Finnish infants and young children. J Infect Dis. 1994;169:1364–1367.
100. Cubitt WD, Green KY, Payment P. Prevalence of antibodies to the Hawaii strain of human calicivirus as measured by a recombinant protein based immunoassay. J Med Virol. 1998;54:135–139.
101. Lewis DC, Hale A, Jiang X, et al. Epidemiology of Mexico virus, a small round-structured virus in Yorkshire, United Kingdom, between January 1992 and March 1995. J Infect Dis. 1997;175:951–954.
102. Vinje J, Altena SA, Koopmans MP. The incidence and genetic variability of small round-structured viruses in outbreaks of gastroenteritis in The Netherlands. J Infect Dis. 1997;176:1374–1378.
103. Agus SG, Dolin R, Wyatt RG, et al. Acute infectious nonbacterial gastroenteritis: Intestinal histopathology. Ann Intern Med. 1973;79:18–25.
104. Schreiber DS, Blacklow NR, Trier JS. The mucosal lesion of the proximal small intestine in acute infectious nonbacterial gastroenteritis. N Engl J Med. 1973;288:1318–1323.
105. Schreiber DS, Blacklow NR, Trier JS. The small intestinal lesion induced by Hawaii agent acute infectious nonbacterial gastroenteritis. J Infect Dis. 1974;129:705–708.
106. Widerlite L, Trier J, Blacklow N, et al. Structure of the gastric mucosa in acute infectious nonbacterial gastroenteritis. Gastroenterology. 1975;70:321–325.
107. Blacklow NR, Dolin R, Feson DS, et al. Acute infectious nonbacterial gastroenteritis: Etiology and pathogenesis. Ann Intern Med. 1972;76:993–1000.

108. Levy AG, Widerlite L, Schwartz CJ, et al. Jejunal adenylate cyclase activity in human subjects during viral gastroenteritis. Gastroenterology. 1976;70:321–325.
109. Woode GN, Bridger JC. Isolation of small viruses resembling astroviruses and caliciviruses from acute enteritis of calves. J Med Microbiol. 1978;11:441–452.
110. Saif LJ, Bohl EH, Theil KW, et al. Rotavirus-like, calicivirus-like, and 23-nm virus-like particles associated with diarrhea in young pigs. J Clin Microbiol. 1980;12:105–111.
111. Graham DY, Jian X, Tanaka T, et al. Norwalk virus infection of volunteers: New insights based on improved assays. J Infect Dis. 1994;170:34–43.
112. Cukor G, Nowak NA, Blacklow NR. Immunoglobulin M responses to the Norwalk virus of gastroenteritis. Infect Immun. 1982;37:463–468.
113. Treanor JJ, Jiang X, Madore HP, et al. Subclass-specific serum antibody responses to recombinant Norwalk virus capsid antigen (rNV) in adults infected with Norwalk, Snow Mountain, or Hawaii viruses. J Clin Microbiol. 1993;31:1630–1634.
114. Erdman DD, Gary GW, Anderson LJ. Development and evaluation of an IgM capture enzyme immunoassay for diagnosis of recent Norwalk virus infection. J Virol Methods. 1989;24:57–66.
115. Erdmann DD, Gary GW, Anderson LJ. Serum immunoglobulin A response to Norwalk virus infection. J Clin Microbiol. 1989;27:1417–1418.
116. Madore HP, Treanor JJ, Buja R, et al. Antigenic relatedness among the Norwalk-like agents by serum antibody rises. J Med Virol. 1990;32:96–101.
117. Agus S, Falchuk ZM, Sessoms CS, et al. Increased jejunal IgA synthesis in vitro during acute infectious nonbacterial gastroenteritis. Am J Dig Dis. 1974;19:127–131.
118. Okhuysen P, Jiang X, Tenjaria G, et al. Detection of Norwalk specific fecal IgA in challenged volunteers utilizing ELISA with baculovirus expressed Norwalk particles as coating antigens. Abstract 1392. Presented at the Thirty-second Interscience Conference on Antimicrobial Agents and Chemotherapy, Anaheim, Calif, 1992.
119. Dolin R, Reichman RC, Fauci AS. Lymphocyte populations in acute viral gastroenteritis. Infect Immun. 1976;14:422–428.
120. Parrino TA, Schreiber DS, Trier JS, et al. Clinical immunity in acute gastroenteritis caused by Norwalk agent. N Engl J Med. 1977;291:86–89.
121. Johnson PC, Mathewson JJ, DuPont HL, et al. Multiple-challenge study of host susceptibility to Norwalk gastroenteritis in US adults. J Infect Dis. 1990;161:18–21.
122. Black RE, Greenberg HB, Kapikian AZ, et al. Acquisition of serum antibody to Norwalk virus and rotavirus and relation to diarrhea in a longitudinal study of young children in rural Bangladesh. J Infect Dis. 1982;145:483–489.
123. Ryder RW, Singh N, Reeves WC, et al. Evidence of immunity induced by naturally acquired rotavirus and Norwalk virus infection on two remote Panamanian islands. J Infect Dis. 1985;135:20–27.
124. Ogra PL, Karzon DT. Formation and function of poliovirus antibody in different tissues. Prog Med Virol. 1971;13:156–193.
125. Greenberg HB, Wyatt RG, Kalica AR, et al. New insights in viral gastroenteritis. Perspect Virol. 1981;11:163–187.
126. Okhuysen PC, Jiang X, Ye L, et al. Viral shedding and fecal IgA response after Norwalk virus infection. J Infect Dis. 1995;171:566–569.
127. Nakata S, Chiba A, Terashima H, et al. Humoral immunity in infants with gastroenteritis caused by human calicivirus. J Infect Dis. 1985;152:274–279.
128. Harris JC, DuPont HL, Hornick RB. Fecal leukocytes in diarrheal illness. Ann Intern Med. 1972;76:697–703.
129. Kapikian Z, Wyatt RG, Dolin R, et al. Visualization of 27 nm particle associated infectious nonbacterial gastroenteritis. J Virol. 1972;10:1075–1081.
130. Nakata S, Chiba S, Terashima H, et al. Microtiter solid-phase radioimmunoassay for detection of human calicivirus in stools. J Clin Microbiol. 1983;17:198–201.
131. Jiang X, Wang J, Graham DY, et al. Detection of Norwalk virus in stool by polymerase chain reaction. J Clin Microbiol. 1992;30:2529–2534.
132. De Leon R, Matsui SM, Baric RS, et al. Detection of Norwalk virus in stool specimens by reverse transcriptase–polymerase chain reaction and nonradioactive oligoprobes. J Clin Microbiol. 1992;30:3151–3157.
133. Willcocks MM, Silcock JG, Carter MJ. Detection of Norwalk virus in the UK by the polymerase chain reaction. FEMS Microbiol Lett. 1993;112:7–12.
134. Moe CL, Gentsch J, Ando T, et al. Application of PCR to detect Norwalk virus in fecal specimens from outbreaks of gastroenteritis. J Clin Microbiol. 1994;32:642–648.
135. Atmar RL, Metcalf TG, Neill FH, et al. Detection of enteric viruses in oysters by using the polymerase chain raction. Appl Environ Microbiol. 1993;59:631–635.
136. Gouvea V, Santos N, Timenetsky M, et al. Identification of Norwalk virus in artificially seeded shellfish and selected foods. J Virol Methods. 1994;8:177–187.
137. Beller M, Ellis A, Lee SH, et al. Outbreak of viral gastroenteritis due to a contaminated well. International consequences. JAMA. 1997;278:563–568.
138. Le Guyader F, Neill FH, Estes MK, et al. Detection and analysis of a small round-structured virus strain in oysters implicated in an outbreak of acute gastroenteritis. Appl Environ Microbiol. 1996;62:4268–4272.
139. Gary GW, Anderson LJ, Keswick BH, et al. Norwalk virus antigen and antibody response in an adult volunteer study. J Clin Microbiol. 1987;25:2001–2003.
140. Steinhoff MC, Douglas RG Jr, Greenberg HB, et al. Bismuth subsalicylate therapy of viral gastroenteritis. Gastroenterology. 1980;78:1495–1499.
141. Ball JM, Hardy ME, Atmar RL, et al. Oral immunization with recombinant Norwalk virus–like particles induces a systemic and mucosal immune response in mice. J Virol. 1998;72:1345–1353.
142. Mason HS, Ball MM, Shi J-J, et al. Expression of Norwalk virus capsid in transgenic tobacco and potato and its oral immunogenicity in mice. Proc Natl Acad Sci U S A. 1996;93:5335–5340.

Chapter **164**

Astroviruses, Toroviruses, and Picobirnaviruses

JOHN J. TREANOR
RAPHAEL DOLIN

In addition to the caliciviruses (see Chapter 163), several other viruses have been implicated as agents of gastroenteritis in adults and children. The strongest evidence exists for the role of astroviruses, but toroviruses and picobirnaviruses have also been implicated as possible causes of gastroenteritis.

ASTROVIRUSES

Astroviruses are members of a new virus family, the Astroviridae, and are now recognized as important causes of gastroenteritis in children and adults. Together with the Caliciviridae, these small RNA viruses are probably responsible for the bulk of presumably viral gastroenteritis that had previously been of unknown etiology.

Virology

Astroviruses are small RNA viruses found in a wide variety of animal species, including humans. The virions are nonenveloped, display cubic symmetry, and are approximately 28 to 30 nm in diameter. Under the electron microscope, the particles in stool samples have a characteristic morphology that consists of round smooth edges with multiple triangular electron-lucent areas and an electron-dense center, which results in the appearance of a five- or six-pointed star from which the virus derives its name[1–3] (Fig. 164–1). Analysis of virus grown in cell culture has shown the virus particles to exhibit a layer of 10-nm spikelike projections on the surface.[4] The human astroviruses have a density of 1.35 to 1.37 g/cc in CsCl and contain a positive-sense, single-stranded 35S RNA genome with a 3′ poly-adenylated tail.[5] The genomic organization includes three open reading frames: ORF1a encodes the protease region, ORF1b encodes the polymerase, and ORF2 encodes the capsid protein(s).[6, 7] The capsid is translated from a subgenomic polyadenylated RNA in infected cells.[8, 9] The number of viral structural proteins appears to vary with the serotype, with between one and three reported for the human viruses,[10, 11] possibly reflecting differences in processing of the capsid precursor.[12] Generation of an infectious cDNA clone has recently been reported[13] and will probably add significantly to studies of the molecular biology of these viruses.

Astrovirus serotypes can be distinguished by immunofluorescence or plaque neutralization techniques,[14, 15] whereas considerable cross-reactivity exists by enzyme immunoassay[16] because of the presence of a group antigen. At least seven serotypes of human astroviruses have been recognized[14, 16–18] and are denoted HAstV-1 to HAstV-7. All seven serotypes are widely distributed throughout the world.[18] Further characterization of these viruses has been greatly enhanced by the development of methods for their adaptation to and propagation in cell culture systems.[14, 16, 19–21]

Epidemiology

Astroviruses have been detected in the stools of between 2 and 9% of children with diarrhea brought to medical attention in a variety of settings (Table 164–1). Outbreaks have been described in schools, daycare settings, and pediatric wards.[1, 2, 23, 27–29] Illness has most often

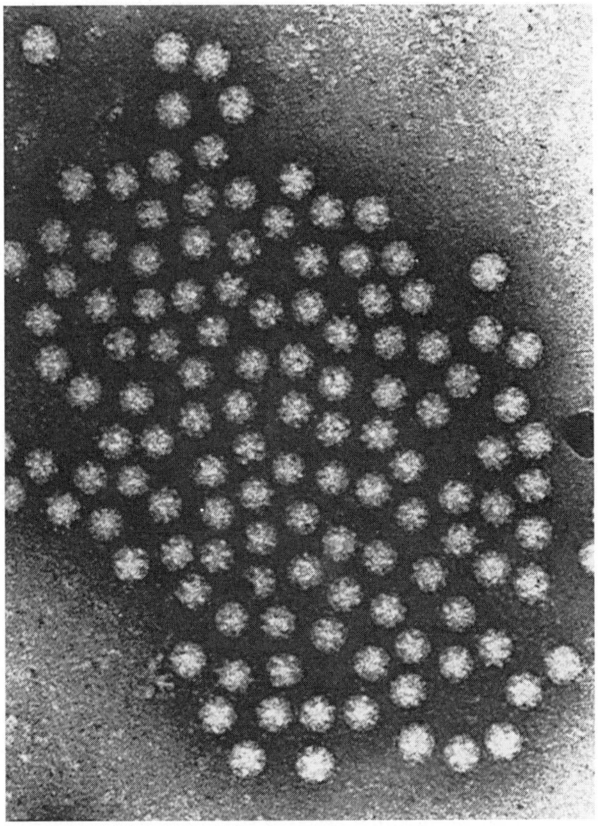

FIGURE 164–1. Astrovirus in the intestinal contents of gnotobiotic lambs. Particles are 30 nm in diameter. (From Snodgrass DR, Gray W. Detection and transmission of 30 nm virus particles [astroviruses] in the faeces of lambs with diarrhoea. Arch Virol. 1977;55:287–291.)

been seen in individuals younger than 3 years, although outbreaks in healthy adults[30, 31] and in elderly populations[32] have also been described. Astroviruses have been detected in the stools of immunosuppressed patients with diarrhea, including human immunodeficiency virus (HIV)-infected patients,[33] and after bone marrow transplantation.[34] A winter predilection has been noted in temperate climates,[11, 35] whereas infection occurs throughout the year in tropical climates,[25] similar to the pattern reported for rotaviruses. Transmission is presumably by the fecal-oral route. Seroprevalence studies in the United Kingdom have shown that 75% of children between 3 and 4 years of age have detectable serum antibody,[36] thus suggesting that infection, largely asymptomatic, is common. Serosurveys of this type have generally identified antibody to HAstV-1 more commonly than to the other serotypes.[37, 38]

Pathogenesis

The pathogenesis of astrovirus-induced illness is not well understood. Astrovirus infections in animals have been associated with small intestinal villus shortening and with mild inflammatory infiltrates in the lamina propria.[39, 40] Astrovirus infection may result in decreased intestinal disaccharidase activity and subsequent osmotic diarrhea,[41] similar to the mechanism postulated for rotavirus. Stool filtrates that contain astroviruses readily infect volunteers after oral administration but induce illness very infrequently,[10, 42] which suggests that astroviruses may be less "pathogenic" in adults than are the Norwalk viruses.

TABLE 164–1 Detection of Astroviruses in Children with Diarrhea

Geographic Location	% of Samples in Which Astroviruses Were Detected in Subjects	
	With Illness	*Without Illness*
Baltimore[22]	2.7	1.4
Phoenix[23]	4.0	2.4
Thailand[24]	8.6	2.0
Guatemala[25]	7.3	2.4
Korea[26]	1.9	2.2
Peru[26]	2.9	2.5

Clinical Illness

Illness attributed to astroviruses consists primarily of diarrhea, headache, malaise, and nausea, whereas vomiting appears to be less common. In general, the symptoms are similar to those seen in rotavirus infection in children, but they are more mild. Low-grade fever is frequently present. The incubation period of illness has been estimated to be 3 to 4 days, and in the absence of coexisting pathogens, disease manifestations usually last 5 days or less, with occasional longer duration. The duration of virus shedding as assessed by polymerase chain reaction may be longer than by enzyme immunoassay—as long as 35 days.[43]

Diagnosis and Treatment

In contrast to other recently described viral agents of gastroenteritis, astroviruses are often shed in large amounts in stool and can be readily detected by electron microscopy even without immune aggregation. Detection of astroviruses in cell culture has been carried out by immune electron microscopy or by immunofluorescence, and an enzyme immunoassay technique[44] that detects the astrovirus group antigen has been used widely in epidemiologic studies. Nucleic acid hybridization[45] and polymerase chain reaction–based[46] detection techniques have also been reported. Polymerase chain reaction is significantly more sensitive than enzyme immunoassay.[43]

Illness associated with these agents is generally self-limited, and treatment, if required at all, is supportive and directed at maintaining hydration and electrolyte balance.

TOROVIRUSES

Toroviruses are enveloped, single-stranded, positive-sense RNA viruses that are classified as members of the Torovirus genus in the family Coronaviridae. Toroviruses are well-established intestinal pathogens of horses (Berne virus) and cattle (Breda virus). Particles with similar morphology have been detected by electron microscopy in diarrheal stools of humans but are not sufficiently distinctive in appearance to allow definitive identification as toroviruses. Recently, the development of immunologic reagents has allowed identification of these fringed virus particles in stool samples as toroviruses.[47, 48] The role of these viruses as causative agents of gastroenteritis is still emerging. In one study, toroviruses were detected significantly more often in the stools of children with diarrhea than in controls, although often in association with other enteric pathogens.[49]

PICOBIRNAVIRUSES

The picobirnaviruses are small, icosahedral viruses with a segmented double-stranded RNA genome with either two or three segments. Their exact taxonomic position is unclear. They derive their name from the observation that they have a segmented double-stranded RNA genome similar to the bisegmented genome of the Birnaviridae, but are smaller (pico), with a virion size of 30 to 40 nm.[50] They were first observed in the stools of humans[51] in the course of studies using polyacrylamide gel electrophoresis to detect rotavirus. Picobirnaviruses have been found in the stools of a variety of animals and in children and adults with diarrhea, including HIV-infected adults.[33, 52, 53] However, the role of these viruses as causative agents of gastroenteritis is unclear because the prevalence of picobirnaviruses in stools of individuals with and without diarrhea is similar.[54]

REFERENCES

1. Madeley CR, Cosgrove BP. 28 nm particles in faeces in infantile gastroenteritis (Letter). Lancet. 1975;2:451.
2. Ashley CR, Caul EO, Paver WK. Astrovirus-associated gastroenteritis in children. J Clin Pathol. 1978;31:939–943.
3. Snodgrass DR, Gray W. Detection and transmission of 30 nm virus particles (astroviruses) in the faeces of lambs with diarrhoea. Arch Virol. 1977;55:287–291.
4. Risco C, Carrascosa JL, Pedregosa AM, et al. Ultrastructure of human astrovirus serotype 2. J Gen Virol. 1995;76:2075–2080.
5. Herring AJ, Gray EW, Snodgrass DR. Purification and characterization of bovine astrovirus. J Gen Virol. 1981;53:47–55.
6. Jiang B, Monroe SS, Koonin EV, et al. RNA sequence of astrovirus: Distinctive genomic organization and a putative retrovirus-like ribosomal frameshifting signal that directs the viral replicase synthesis. Proc Nat Acad Sci U S A. 1993;90:10539–10543.
7. Willcocks MM, Brown TDK, Madeley CR, et al. The complete sequence of a human astrovirus. J Gen Virol. 1994;75:1785–1788.
8. Monroe SS, Stine SE, Gorelkin L, et al. Temporal synthesis of proteins and RNAs during human astrovirus infection of cultured cells. J Virol. 1991;65:641–648.
9. Matsui SM, Kim JP, Greenberg HB, et al. Cloning and characterization of human astrovirus immunoreactive epitopes. J Virol. 1993;67:1712–1715.
10. Midthun K, Greenberg HB, Kurtz JB, et al. Characterization and seroepidemiology of a type 5 astrovirus associated with an outbreak of gastroenteritis in Marin County, California. J Clin Microbiol. 1993;31:955–962.
11. Monroe SS, Glass RI, Noah N, et al. Electron microscopic reporting of gastrointestinal viruses in the United Kingdom, 1985–1987. J Med Virol. 1991;33:193–198.
12. Belliot G, Laveran H, Monroe SS. Capsid protein composition of reference strains and wild isolates of human astroviruses. Virus Res. 1997;49:49–57.
13. Geigenmuller U, Ginzton NH, Matsui SM. Construction of a genome-length cDNA clone for human astrovirus serotype 1 and synthesis of infectious RNA transcripts. J Virol. 1997;71:1713–1717.
14. Kurtz JB, Lee TW. Human astrovirus serotypes (Letter). Lancet. 1984;2:1405.
15. Hudson RW, Herrmann JE, Blacklow NR. Plaque quantitation and virus neutralization assays for human astroviruses. Arch Virol. 1989;108:33–38.
16. Herrmann JE, Hudson RW, Perron-Henry DM, et al. Antigen characterization of cell-cultivated astrovirus serotypes and development of astrovirus-specific monoclonal antibodies. J Infect Dis. 1988;158:182–185.
17. Lee TW, Kurtz JB. Prevalence of human astrovirus serotypes in the Oxford region 1976–1992, with evidence for two new serotypes. Epidemiol Infect. 1994;112:187–193.
18. Noel JS, Lee TW, Kurtz JB, et al. Typing of human astroviruses from clinical isolates by enzyme immunoassay and nucleotide sequencing. J Clin Microbiol. 1995;33:797–801.
19. Lee TW, Kurtz JB. Serial propagation of astrovirus in tissue culture with the aid of trypsin. J Gen Virol. 1981;57:421–424.
20. Willcocks MM, Carter MJ, Laidler FR, et al. Growth and characterisation of human faecal astrovirus in a continuous cell line. Arch Virol. 1990;113:73–81.
21. Yamashita T, Kobayashi S, Sakae K, et al. Isolation of cytopathic small round viruses with BS-C-1 cells from patients with gastroenteritis. J Infect Dis. 1991;164:954–957.
22. Kotloff KL, Herrmann JE, Blacklow NR, et al. The frequency of astrovirus as a cause of diarrhea in Baltimore children. Pediatr Infect Dis J. 1992;11:587–589.
23. Lew JF, Moe CL, Monroe SS, et al. Astrovirus and adenovirus associated with diarrhea in children in day care settings. J Infect Dis. 1991;164:673–678.
24. Herrmann JE, Taylor DN, Echeverria P, et al. Astroviruses as a cause of gastroenteritis in children. N Engl J Med. 1991;324:1757–1760.
25. Cruz JR, Bartlett AV, Herrmann JE, et al. Astrovirus-associated diarrhea among Guatemalan ambulatory rural children. J Clin Microbiol. 1992;30:1140–1144.
26. Moe CL, Allen JR, Monroe SS, et al. Detection of astrovirus in pediatric stool samples by immunoassay and RNA probe. J Clin Microbiol. 1991;29:2390–2395.
27. Kurtz JB, Lee TW, Pickering D. Astrovirus associated gastroenteritis in a children's ward. J Clin Pathol. 1977;30:948–952.
28. Konno T, Suzuki H, Ishida N, et al. Astrovirus-associated epidemic gastroenteritis in Japan. J Med Virol. 1982;9:11–17.
29. Esahli H, Breback K, Bennet R, et al. Astroviruses as a cause of nosocomial outbreaks of infant diarrhea. Pediatr Infect Dis J. 1991;10:511–515.
30. Oishi I, Yamazaki K, Kimoto T, et al. A large outbreak of acute gastroenteritis associated with astrovirus among students and teachers in Osaka, Japan. J Infect Dis. 1994;170:439–443.
31. Belliot G, Laveran H, Monroe SS. Outbreak of gastroenteritis in military recruits associated with serotype 3 astrovirus infection. J Med Virol. 1997;51:101–106.
32. Gray JJ, Wreghitt TG, Cubitt WD, et al. An outbreak of gastroenteritis in a home for the elderly associated with astrovirus type 1 and human calicivirus. J Med Virol. 1987;23:377–381.
33. Grohmann GS, Glass RI, Pereira HG, et al. Enteric viruses and diarrhea in HIV-infected patients. Enteric Opportunistic Infections Working Group. N Engl J Med. 1993;329:14–20.
34. Cox GJ, Matsui SM, Lo RS, et al. Etiology and outcome of diarrhea after marrow transplantation: A prospective study. Gastroenterology. 1994;107:1398–1407.
35. Lew JF, Glass RI, Petric M, et al. Six-year retrospective surveillance of gastroenteritis viruses identified at ten electron microscopy centers in the United States and Canada. Pediatr Infect Dis J. 1990;9:709–714.
36. Kurtz J, Lee TW. Astrovirus gastroenteritis age distribution of antibody. Med Microbiol Immunol. 1978;166:227–230.
37. Kriston S, Willcocks MM, Carter MJ, et al. Seroprevalence of astrovirus types 1 and 6 in London, determined using recombinant virus antigen. Epidemiol Infect. 1996;117:159–164.
38. Koopmans MP, Bijen MH, Monroe SS, et al. Age-stratified seroprevalence of neutralizing antibodies to astrovirus types 1 to 7 in humans in The Netherlands. Clin Diagn Lab Immunol. 1998;5:33–37.
39. Snodgrass DR, Angus KW, Gray EW, et al. Pathogenesis of diarrhoea caused by astrovirus infection in lambs. Arch Virol. 1979;60:217–226.
40. Woode GN, Bridger JC. Isolation of small viruses resembling astroviruses and caliciviruses from acute enteritis of calves. J Med Microbiol. 1978;11:441–452.
41. Thouvenelle ML, Haynes JS, Sell JL, et al. Astrovirus infection in hatchling turkeys: Alterations in intestinal maltase activity. Avian Dis. 1995;39:343–348.
42. Kurtz JB, Lee TW, Craig JW, et al. Astrovirus infection in volunteers. J Med Virol. 1979;3:221–230.
43. Mitchell DK, Monroe SS, Jiang X, et al. Virologic features of an astrovirus diarrhea outbreak in a day care center revealed by reverse transcriptase–polymerase chain reaction. J Infect Dis. 1995;172:1437–1444.
44. Herrmann JE, Nowak NA, Perron-Henry DM, et al. Diagnosis of astrovirus gastroenteritis by antigen detection with monoclonal antibodies. J Infect Dis. 1990;161:226–229.
45. Willcocks MM, Carter MJ, Silcock JG, et al. A dot-blot hybridization procedure for the detection of astrovirus in stool samples. Epidemiol Infect. 1991;107:405–410.
46. Major ME, Eglin RP, Easton AJ. 3′ terminal nucleotide sequence of human astrovirus type 1 and routine detection of astrovirus nucleic acid and antigens. J Virol Methods. 1992;39:217–225.
47. Koopmans M, Petric M, Glass RI, et al. Enzyme-linked immunosorbent assay reactivity of torovirus-like particles in fecal specimens from humans with diarrhea. J Clin Microbiol. 1993;31:2738–2744.
48. Duckmanton L, Luan B, Devenish J, et al. Characterization of torovirus from human fecal specimens. Virology. 1997;239:158–168.
49. Koopmans MP, Goosen ES, Lima AA, et al. Association of torovirus with acute and persistent diarrhea in children. Pediatr Infect Dis J. 1997;16:504–507.
50. Chandra R. Picobirnavirus, a novel group of undescribed viruses of mammals and birds: A minireview. Acta Virol. 1997;41:59–62.
51. Pereira HG, Fialho AM, Flewett TH, et al. Novel viruses in human faeces. Lancet. 1988;2:103–104.
52. Giordano MO, Martinez LC, Rinaldi D, et al. Detection of picobirnavirus in HIV-infected patients with diarrhea in Argentina. J Acquir Immune Defic Syndr Hum Retrovirol 1998;18:380–383.
53. Gonzalez GG, Pujol FH, Liprandi F, et al. Prevalence of enteric viruses in human immunodeficiency virus seropositive patients in Venezuela. J Med Virol. 1998;55:288–292.
54. Gallimore CI, Appleton H, Lewis D, et al. Detection and characterisation of bisegmented double-stranded RNA viruses (picobirnaviruses) in human faecal specimens. J Med Virol. 1995;45:135–140.

Unclassified Viruses

Chapter 165

Hepatitis E Virus

ROBERT H. PURCELL
SUZANNE U. EMERSON

Hepatitis E virus (HEV) causes an acute, self-limiting hepatitis. This unclassified virus is enterically transmitted, although other routes of transmission may exist. Infection with HEV may be asymptomatic or may cause hepatitis varying in degree of severity from mild to fulminant disease. Fulminant hepatitis E has been reported most frequently in pregnant women. Hepatitis E is the most common form of acute hepatitis in adults in highly endemic regions of Asia,

All material in this chapter is in the public domain, with the exception of any borrowed figures or tables.

but the disease is rarely diagnosed in industrialized countries, including the United States.

HISTORY

Evidence for an enterically transmitted form of viral hepatitis distinct from viral hepatitis A came from serologic studies of waterborne epidemics of hepatitis in India in the late 1970s. Khuroo, and Wong and colleagues, demonstrated that patients involved in such epidemics of hepatitis in the Kashmir region and in Delhi, India, respectively, lacked serologic evidence of recent hepatitis A virus (HAV) infection.[1, 2] In fact, all the patients were found to have immunoglobulin G (IgG)-class but not IgM-class antibodies to HAV, indicating that they had been infected with HAV in the past and were presumably immune to reinfection. Therefore, they concluded that another agent must have caused the hepatitis. Three years later, Balayan and coworkers confirmed the existence of a new hepatitis virus by transmitting hepatitis to a volunteer from a patient involved in an outbreak of enterically transmitted non-A, non-B hepatitis in central Asia.[3] The volunteer (one of the authors of the paper), who had preexisting antibody to HAV, developed a severe hepatitis, shed virus-like particles in his feces, and developed antibodies to the virus-like particles during convalescence. Balayan and coworkers also inoculated cynomolgus monkeys with the new virus and again demonstrated hepatitis, virus-like particles, and an immune response to the particles in this primate species.[3]

The new form of non-A, non-B hepatitis came to be known as epidemic non-A, non-B hepatitis or enterically transmitted non-A, non-B hepatitis. Subsequently, the name of the disease was changed to *hepatitis E* to conform with the accepted nomenclature for the other types of viral hepatitis and the virus was designated *hepatitis E virus*.[4–6]

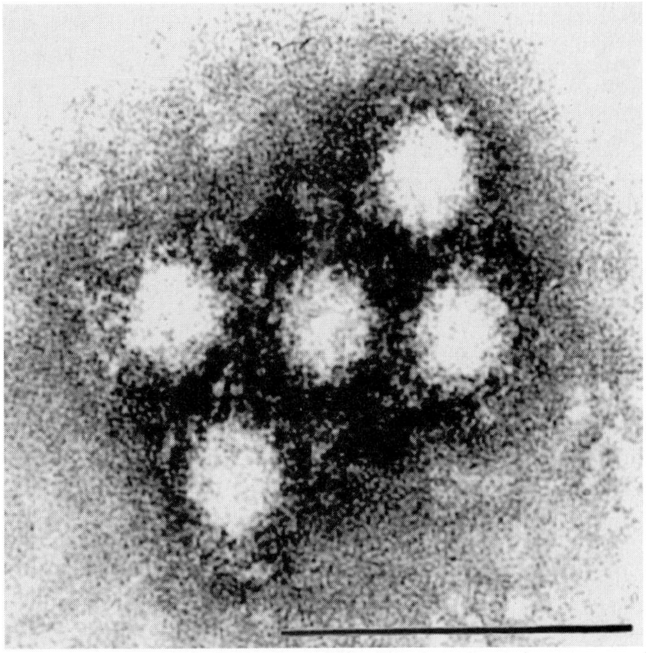

FIGURE 165–1. Antibody-coated hepatitis E virus particles detected in the feces of a patient with hepatitis E in Pakistan (immune electron microscopy). (Modified from Ticehurst J, Popkin TJ, Bryan JP, et al. Association of hepatitis E virus with an outbreak of hepatitis in Pakistan: Serologic responses and pattern of virus excretion. J Med Virol. 1992;36:84–92.)

VIRUS

Morphology

HEV is a spherical, nonenveloped particle that is approximately 30 to 32 nm in diameter (Fig. 165–1).[7, 8] It has an indefinite surface structure that is intermediate between that of the Norwalk agent (a member of the Caliciviridae family) and that of HAV (a member of the Picornaviridae family).[9] It is believed to have an icosahedral symmetry.[8]

Physicochemical Characteristics

The buoyant density of HEV is 1.35 to 1.40 g/cm^3 in CsCl.[3, 10] Its sedimentation coefficient is 183 S.[11] The virus appears to be relatively stable to environmental and chemical agents.[12] HEV contains an RNA genome enclosed within a capsid that is composed of one or possibly two proteins, but direct analysis of purified virions has not been possible to date.[13]

Genome Organization

The genome of HEV is a single-stranded positive-sense RNA molecule approximately 7.2 kilobases in length followed by a polyA tract (Fig. 165–2).[13, 14] The genome consists of a short 5′ nontranslated region that is capped,[14a] three open reading frames (ORFs), each in a different coding frame, and a short 3′ nontranslated region that is terminated by a stretch of adenosine residues. ORF1, the largest ORF, is believed to encode the nonstructural protein or proteins of the virus. Based on the identification of characteristic amino acid motifs,[15] the following genetic elements have been identified, in order, from the 5′ to the 3′ end of the ORF: a methyl transferase, presumably involved in capping the 5′ end of the viral genome; the "Y" domain, a sequence of unknown function that is found in certain other viruses, including rubella virus; a papain-like cysteine protease, a type of protease found predominantly in alphaviruses and rubella virus[16]; a proline-rich "hinge" that may provide flexibility and that contains a region of hypervariable sequence[17, 18]; an "X" domain of unknown function that has been found adjacent to papain-like protease domains in the polyproteins of other positive-strand RNA viruses[16]; a domain containing helicase-like motifs similar to those found in viruses containing type I (superfamily 3) helicases[19, 20]; and an RNA-dependent polymerase, with motifs most closely related to those found in viruses containing an RNA polymerase of superfamily 3.[21] ORF2, approximately 2000 nucleotides in length, begins approximately 40 nucleotides 3′ of the termination of ORF1 and consists of a 5′ signal sequence, a 300-nucleotide region rich in codons for arginine, probably representing an RNA-binding site,[13] and three potential glycosylation sites.[22] Although glycosylation of one or more of these sites has been demonstrated in vitro, it has not been established whether they are glycosylated in the mature virus.[23] The protein encoded by ORF2 appears to be the capsid protein of HEV. ORF3, less than 400 nucleotides in length, overlaps ORF1 by one nucleotide at its 5′ end and overlaps ORF2 by over 300 nucleotides at its 3′ end. The function of ORF3 is unknown,[17] but it has been reported to be a phosphoprotein.[24]

Classification

Because the morphology and genomic organization of HEV resemble those of the caliciviruses, it was classified as a member of the family Caliciviridae.[25] However, the sequence of HEV is not closely related to that of any other virus, including the caliciviruses. In fact, it most closely resembles the sequence of rubella virus, a member of the virus family Togaviridae, as well as the sequence of beet necrotic yellow vein virus, a plant furovirus.[26] In addition, its codon usage most closely resembles that of rubella virus, and the sequences of the putative RNA polymerase and helicase of HEV resemble those of superfamily 3 viruses (rubella, other alphaviruses, and so forth)

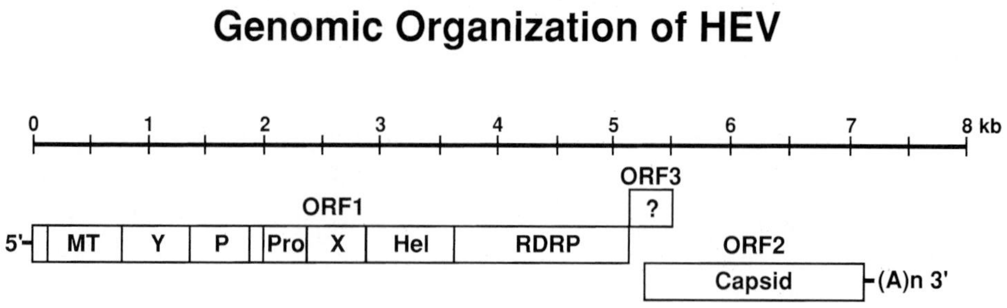

FIGURE 165–2. Organization of hepatitis E virus genome. The approximately 7.2-kilobase genome encodes three open reading frames (ORFs). The nonstructural proteins are probably encoded within the large 5′ ORF (ORF 1); see the text for details. The capsid protein is thought to be encoded by the 3′ ORF (ORF 2). The small, overlapping third ORF (ORF 3) encodes an immunogenic protein of unknown function. (Courtesy of X-J Meng.)

rather than those of superfamily 1 (caliciviruses, picornaviruses, and so forth).[13] For these and other reasons, HEV has been removed from the family Caliciviridae and is presently unclassified.[27]

Geographic Distribution and Genetic Variation

Hepatitis E has been clinically important primarily in developing countries of Southeast and Central Asia, the Middle East, and North Africa.[5, 28] Epidemic hepatitis E has also been reported in Mexico.[29] Individual cases of hepatitis E have been reported occasionally in industrialized countries, including the United States.[30] Strains of HEV recovered from within one geographic region generally are genetically similar and characteristic of that region and differ from strains indigenous to other regions.[31–38] However, the overall heterogeneity of HEV strains is not great, and all strains recovered to date appear to belong to the same serotype.[7, 8, 11, 39–42] The genomes of several HEV strains from Asia, North Africa, Mexico, and the United States have been entirely or partially sequenced.[13, 14, 18, 31–36, 38, 43–47] On the basis of analysis of these sequences, HEV strains can be classified into three major genotypes: Asian-African strains, a Mexican strain, and U.S. and swine strains (Fig. 165–3).[35, 38] The Asian-African strains can be subdivided into closely related Northern and Central Asian strains, Southeast and Southern Asian strains, and North African strains.[31–33] The Asian strains are more closely related to one another than they are to the African strains. The Mexican and U.S. strains of HEV are significantly different from the Asian strains and from each other, whereas swine HEV and U.S. human isolates

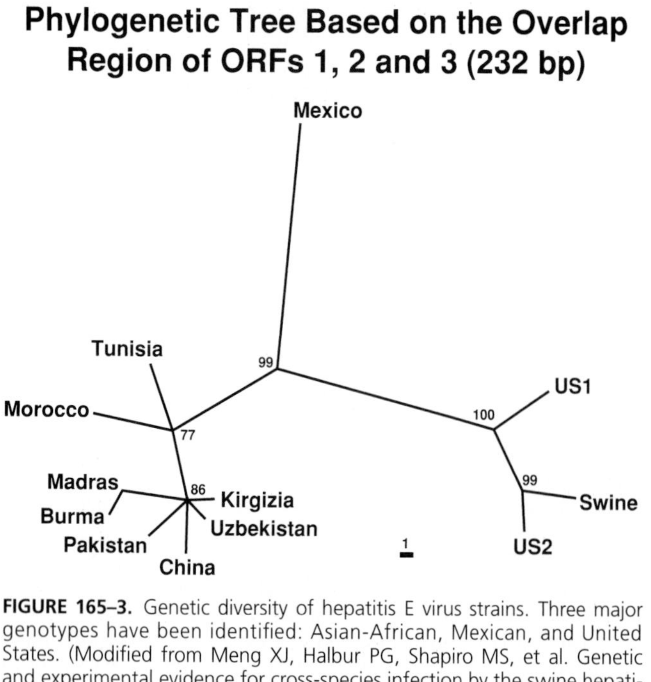

FIGURE 165–3. Genetic diversity of hepatitis E virus strains. Three major genotypes have been identified: Asian-African, Mexican, and United States. (Modified from Meng XJ, Halbur PG, Shapiro MS, et al. Genetic and experimental evidence for cross-species infection by the swine hepatitis E virus. J Virol. 1998;72:9714–9721.)

of HEV are closely related.[35, 38] In addition, each of these three major genetic groups has nucleotide deletions or insertions, or both, that are unique to the respective group.[38] The ORF1 sequences of the three major genotypes differ from each other in nucleotide sequence identity by about 20%, whereas sequence identity within each group differs by no more than 5 to 10%.[31, 32, 35, 38] Thus, genetic heterogeneity appears to be regionally distributed, suggesting that HEV is an ancient virus. The strains of HEV with sequences resembling those of Southern and Southeast Asian strains have been recovered in North Africa, South Africa, the Middle East and the Mediterranean region, but these are thought to have been introduced, as in other regions of the world, from Asia in recent times by recreational travelers, religious pilgrims, or laborers.[48–52]

Recently, a fourth major genotype of HEV was discovered in Asia, and other new variants were identified in Europe.[52a, b] Undoubtedly, the genetic complexity of HEV will continue to expand as new data are collected.

Antigenic Composition

HEV encodes multiple antigens that are reactive in a variety of assays, including immunoelectronmicroscopy,[3] immunofluorescence,[53, 54] enzyme-linked immunosorbent assay (ELISA),[41, 55] and Western blot.[41, 56–60] The virus was first visualized and antibody to it first detected by immunoelectronmicroscopy.[3] Although cumbersome and difficult to interpret, immunoelectronmicroscopy provided important serodiagnostic and epidemiologic information until other tests were developed, after the cloning of the HEV genome in 1991 and expression of recombinant viral antigens.[13] On the basis of antibody mapping with synthetic peptides, a number of linear epitopes have been identified on HEV-encoded proteins.[59, 61–64] At least 12 such epitopes have been identified among the nonstructural proteins encoded by ORF1; these were concentrated in the protein believed to encode the RNA polymerase.[63] Of greater diagnostic importance are epitopes encoded by the other two ORFs. Three major epitopes, found respectively in the amino-terminal, central, and carboxy-terminal regions of the gene product of ORF2 (capsid protein) have been reported.[63, 65] One immunoreactive epitope has been localized to the carboxy-terminal region (approximate position between amino acid 592 and the end of the protein at amino acid 660). Similarly, a major epitope is found in the carboxy-terminal 30 amino acids of the gene product of ORF3.[65] Although epitopes located in ORF2 are relatively highly conserved among different HEV strains, the epitope in ORF3 is relatively poorly conserved. Thus, diagnostic tests based on ORF2 epitopes appear to be more broadly reactive than those based on ORF3 epitopes, but this has not been a universal finding.[57, 61, 66–71] Although synthetic peptides based on the demonstrated linear epitopes of ORFs 2 and 3 have been useful in diagnostic tests,[62] longer recombinant proteins, especially those expressed from ORF2, have proved to be more sensitive for detecting anti-HEV in natural infections of humans and experimental infections of nonhuman primates.[41, 55, 71–74] Specifically, antibodies detected with large expressed ORF2 proteins appear to be longer lasting than antibodies detected with synthetic peptides, especially those peptides representing ORF3.[75, 76] This is probably because large expressed proteins of ORF2, which can form virus-like particles, detect antibodies to conformational epitopes.[41, 77] However, full-length protein expressed from ORF2 was found to detect acute-phase anti-HEV better than late convalescent antibody.[78] An artificial mosaic protein containing selected epitopes of ORF2 and ORF3 coupled together may be an exception because it provides a sensitive detection assay.[79] Neutralizing antibody to HEV appears to be directed against epitopes of ORF2 that have yet to be identified. Neutralization assays have been reported but are difficult to perform.[80]

Host Range, Experimental Transmission to Animals

Chimpanzees, Old World monkeys (rhesus, cynomolgus, pigtail macaques, African green monkeys), New World monkeys (owl monkeys, squirrel monkeys, tamarins),[8, 39, 41, 81] swine,[82–85] rodents,[86–88] and sheep[89] have been reported to be susceptible to experimental infection with HEV. Extensive studies in primates have confirmed the utility of these animals, especially chimpanzees, rhesus monkeys, and cynomolgus monkeys, for experimental transmission of human strains of HEV. The susceptibility of swine, rats, and mice to infection with human HEV strains has been difficult to confirm.[83, 90–92] However, a unique HEV strain indigenous to swine has been discovered.[93] This strain of HEV is distinct from previously reported strains of HEV. Swine HEV is transmissible to nonhuman primates, including rhesus monkeys and chimpanzees, suggesting that the host range of this virus is greater than that of other HEV strains.[38] Interestingly, two isolates of HEV from patients with apparently endemic hepatitis E in Minnesota and Tennessee were very closely related to swine HEV isolates from the same general geographic area; one of these was subsequently transmitted both to nonhuman primates and to swine, suggesting that swine HEV may occasionally infect humans under natural conditions.[35, 38]

Captive rhesus monkeys within North American breeding colonies acquire antibody to HEV in a pattern strongly suggestive of endemic infection.[94, 95] However, a virus has not yet been recovered from these animals, and it is not clear whether rhesus monkeys are infected with a unique simian HEV or whether human strains of HEV are circulating in the breeding colonies. Seronegative rhesus monkeys and cynomolgus monkeys as well as chimpanzees are highly susceptible to experimental infection with human strains of HEV. The course of infection in experimentally infected primates is similar to that in humans. The incubation period to peak liver enzyme levels is generally 3 to 8 weeks but can be quite variable, depending on the dose of virus administered.[39, 41, 96, 97] Peak viremia and peak shedding of virus in the feces occur during the incubation period and early acute phase of disease.[3, 40, 98, 99] The detection of HEV antigens in the liver parallels the detection of viremia in the serum and feces,[53, 98] and histologic changes in the liver generally parallel biochemical evidence of hepatitis.[99] As in humans, hepatitis E in nonhuman primates is acute and self-limiting. Unlike experimental hepatitis caused by the other human hepatitis viruses, experimental hepatitis E is dose-dependent: high doses of virus are associated with histologic and biochemical evidence of hepatitis, whereas lower doses of virus (<1000 infectious doses) are more likely to be associated with a normal histologic appearance and normal serum liver enzyme values.[72] As in hepatitis A, the immune response in primates to HEV appears during the late incubation period or early acute phase of infection and is characterized by a brisk IgM and IgG anti-HEV response. Viremia may persist after the appearance of anti-HEV, suggesting that the virus coexists with antibody in immune complexes in the blood.[100] Infection with HEV protects nonhuman primates from hepatitis E after reexposure to the virus.[41, 101, 102]

Epidemiology

HEV is an important human pathogen in Southeast and Central Asia, the Middle East, and North and West Africa. Epidemic hepatitis E has been reported in Mexico, and rare to occasional cases of hepatitis E have been identified in a number of industrialized countries, including the United States.[35] The more spectacular form of the disease, epidemic hepatitis E, is actually a relatively uncommon occurrence, and by far the majority of the cases occur as endemic or sporadic disease.[3, 29, 49, 56, 58, 69, 103–137] Endemic hepatitis E is limited to a band of developing countries, often in tropical or subtropical regions. In much of Asia, HEV is the single most frequent cause of acute hepatitis in adults[138]; in parts of the Middle East and North Africa, it is second only to hepatitis B.[49, 127] Most of the cases reported in industrialized countries occur in travelers recently returned from an endemic area.[30, 49, 111, 139–153] However, rare cases of hepatitis E that appear to have been contracted locally do occur in industrialized countries (see later).

Although there are still questions about the relative sensitivity and specificity of serologic tests for anti-HEV, a more complete picture of the worldwide distribution and seroprevalence of HEV infection is emerging. Surprisingly, the prevalence of antibody to HEV in developing and documented endemic regions is much lower than expected (3 to 27%),[59, 68, 69, 114, 152, 154–187] with a few exceptions, and the prevalence of anti-HEV in nonendemic regions has been much higher than anticipated (1 to 28%).[59, 68, 113, 133, 188–199] In many, but not all, studies, the prevalence of anti-HEV in infants and children has been much lower than expected for a virus transmitted by the fecal-oral route.[69, 113, 114, 154] The greatest incremental increase in the prevalence of anti-HEV has generally been found among young adults, the age group at the highest risk of clinical disease (Figs. 165–4 and 165–5).[69, 113, 154, 200, 201] In older adults, the prevalence of anti-HEV is relatively constant (10 to 40%), with little or no difference in the prevalence between men and women.[69, 113, 154] Although such a pattern of age-specific anti-HEV might suggest a cohort effect representing the disappearance of HEV from endemic regions as was seen for HAV previously,[5] similar age-specific anti-HEV patterns have been reported for sera collected 10 years apart from the same population residing in an area that is highly endemic for HEV (see Fig. 165–4).[154] Thus, HEV appears to have epidemiologic characteristics that are quite different from those of most viruses, such as HAV, that are transmitted by the fecal-oral route.

Young children are susceptible to infection with HEV, because clinical disease has occurred with a similar frequency in all age groups in some epidemics[114] and sporadic clinical hepatitis E in children has been reported.[58, 81, 107, 108, 110, 114, 200, 202–205] A male preponderance of cases has been observed in some, but not all, epidemics.[206] In areas where the disease is endemic, waterborne epidemics of hepatitis E are more likely to occur during the rainy season, when

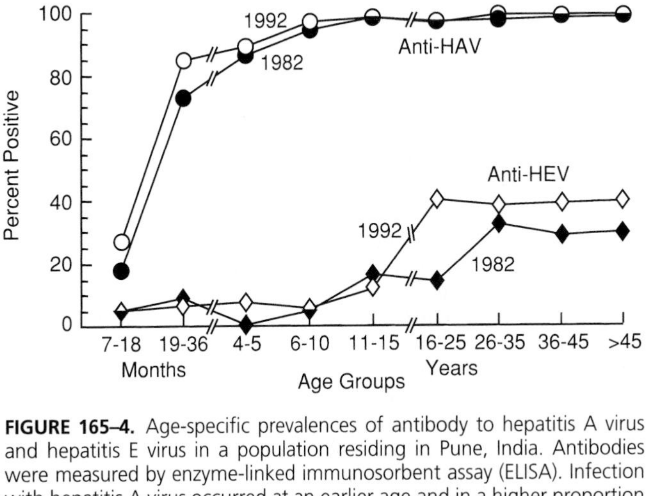

FIGURE 165–4. Age-specific prevalences of antibody to hepatitis A virus and hepatitis E virus in a population residing in Pune, India. Antibodies were measured by enzyme-linked immunosorbent assay (ELISA). Infection with hepatitis A virus occurred at an earlier age and in a higher proportion of the population than infection with hepatitis E virus. (Modified from Arankalle VA, Tsarev SA, Chadha MS, et al. Age-specific prevalence of antibodies to hepatitis A and E viruses in Pune, India, 1982 and 1992. J Infect Dis. 1995;171:447–450.)

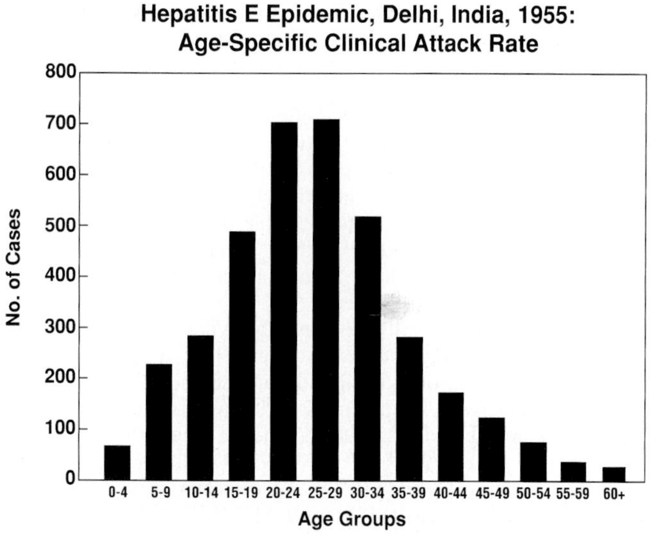

FIGURE 165–5. The age-specific clinical attack rate of hepatitis in a large, waterborne epidemic of hepatitis in Delhi, India, 1955–1956. The epidemic was caused by hepatitis E virus. (Modified from Viswanathan R. Epidemiology. Indian J Med Res. 1957;45:1–29.)

flooding of rivers occurs.[200] The famous Delhi epidemic of hepatitis E, occurring in the winter of 1955–1956, resulted from rechanneling of the flooded Yamuna river, causing raw sewage from a drainage ditch to be drawn into the intake pipes of a malfunctioning water treatment plant.[206] In the Kashmir region of India, epidemics of hepatitis E have followed the spring thaws, when the feces accumulated over the winter have been washed into melting rivers.[207]

Prevalence of Anti–Hepatitis E Virus in Animal Species

Antibody to HEV has been detected in several species of wild and domestic animals, including wild cynomolgus, rhesus and bonnet macaques, and langurs[208, 209]; captive rhesus monkeys[94]; domestic swine[210]; and wild rats and mice.[87, 211] Although earlier reports were from countries in which HEV is endemic, a high prevalence of antibody to HEV has been reported in domestically raised rhesus monkeys and swine and wild rats in the United States.[92–94] Such antibody levels increased with age; most young animals tested negative, but 80 to 100% of adults had antibody to HEV.

Hepatitis E Virus Infection of Animals

In addition to the transmission of human strains of HEV to nonhuman primates, its transmission to swine, rats, mice, and sheep has also been reported.[82, 84–86, 88, 89] Although reported in the literature, the transmission of human strains of HEV to domestic swine and laboratory rats and mice has been difficult to confirm.[83, 90–92] In contrast, an HEV strain isolated from young domestic swine was experimentally transmissible to other swine and, furthermore, to nonhuman primates.[38, 83] This virus was genetically distinct from all previously recovered human strains and probably represents the first recognized nonhuman strain of HEV.[93] Interestingly, two isolates of HEV from human hepatitis E patients in Tennessee and Minnesota, respectively, were shown to be closely related to swine HEV, and one of these was experimentally transmitted to swine.[35, 38, 212] Because swine HEV and the two human U.S. isolates were genetically very similar (including sharing specific nucleotide insertions), and because they came from the same geographic region, it is possible that all three of the viruses are of swine origin.

Modes of Transmission

Most epidemics of hepatitis E have been waterborne,[1, 2, 29, 103, 116, 120, 172, 173, 201, 206, 213–219] but a few foodborne epidemics have been reported from China,[220–223] and cases of suspected hepatitis E have been epidemiologically linked to the consumption of raw or uncooked shellfish.[224] The epidemiologic risk factors associated with most sporadic cases of hepatitis E have not been identified. Person-to-person spread from patients to contacts appears to be relatively uncommon, at least in most studies.[107, 110, 225, 226] However, one hospital-related outbreak has been reported.[227] The relatively rapid acquisition of anti-HEV during puberty raises the question of whether HEV might be sexually transmitted. However, there is no direct evidence for this. The duration of infectivity after exposure to HEV is not fully known, but viral RNA can be detected in the feces as early as 1 week and as late as 5 weeks after inoculation in experimental infections of nonhuman primates,[18] and protracted viremia of up to 45 to 112 days has been detected by polymerase chain reaction (PCR) in naturally infected patients.[228, 229] HEV was detected in the feces of one experimentally infected volunteer as early as 4 weeks after exposure and persisted for 2.5 weeks, disappearing at approximately the time of onset of jaundice.[3] Viremia was detected as early as day 22 in a second volunteer, approximately 1 week earlier than the virus was detected in feces.[230]

Thus, there is a relatively long period of viremia and fecal shedding of HEV, principally during the period before the onset of disease.[228, 229] Transmission of the other enterically transmitted hepatitis virus, HAV, by contaminated blood or blood products has been reported to occur occasionally,[231] suggesting that similar transmission of HEV might occur if blood or plasma were donated during the incubation period of hepatitis E. However, there is no conclusive seroepidemiologic evidence for the transmission of HEV by blood or blood products.[161, 232–247]

Zoonoses

Zoonosis (the transmission of diseases from animals to humans) is a well-recognized phenomenon. Because the epidemiology of HEV is somewhat unusual and because antibodies to HEV have been discovered in several species of animals, it has been proposed that animals may serve as a reservoir for HEV[87] and that environmental conditions can expose humans to animal feces containing HEV. The discovery that two HEV strains recovered from patients with hepatitis E in the United States were very closely related to swine HEV that was endemic to the same geographic region[35, 38, 93] supports the hypothesis that zoonoses of HEV may occur occasionally. However, the failure to prove conclusively the transmission of bona fide human strains of HEV to animals makes this an unlikely explanation for most cases of hepatitis E, whether epidemic or endemic.

Xenozoonoses

Xenozoonosis (the transmission of animal viruses to humans via transplantation of animal organs and tissues to humans) is a potential threat. The prospects for such transmissions have been greatly increased with improvements in procedures to control immediate and delayed rejection of animal organs by the human immune system. With the control of rejection a possibility, there is growing interest in the xenotransplantation of animal organs and tissues because of the shortage of suitable clinical materials of human origin. Swine are currently the donors of choice, although these animals harbor a number of viruses.[38, 248] The discovery of swine HEV has added another virus to the list of viruses that must be excluded from swine herds before tissues and organs from those herds can be considered for xenotransplantation.

PATHOGENESIS

Incubation Period

The incubation period from exposure to the onset of clinical disease is approximately 28 to 40 days, based on analysis of waterborne epidemics in which the time of exposure was identified.[206] In experimental HEV transmission studies in humans, liver enzyme values peaked 42 to 46 days after ingestion of the virus.[3] In experimental infection of pregnant rhesus monkeys, the incubation period in one study was as short as 1 to 2 weeks,[249] but this was not observed in another similar study in which the incubation period averaged 4 to 5 weeks.[94] An incubation period of 4 to 6 weeks is in good agreement with the results of numerous experimental infections of nonhuman primates. The first appearance of viremia, detected by reverse transcription–polymerase chain reaction (RT-PCR), occurred 3 weeks after ingestion of the virus in one volunteer,[230] but viremia after intravenous exposure of nonhuman primates has been as short as 9 days.[18]

Viral Replication

HEV has been reported to replicate in cell culture.[80, 86, 250, 251] However, because HEV does not replicate well in cell culture, its replicative pathway is not fully understood. The mechanisms of attachment to susceptible cells, entry, and uncoating are unknown, but it is assumed that the virus attaches to receptor sites on hepatocytes and possibly cells in the intestinal tract. After uncoating, the positive-sense, polyadenylated genome of HEV is probably directly translated via cellular mechanisms that recognize capped RNA. Translated ORF1 is probably cleaved by cellular proteases. The motif of a papain-like protease has been detected in the sequence of ORF1,[15] but a functional protease has not been demonstrated. Replicative intermediate negative-strand RNA is probably synthesized by the viral RNA polymerase that is thought to be encoded by the 3′ region of ORF1. The viral polymerase probably also synthesizes subsequent strands of positive-sense full-length RNA, as well as at least two subgenomic messenger RNAs of 3.7- and 2.0-kilobase length, respectively.[13] Assembly and transport of HEV out of the cell are poorly understood. The gene product of ORF2 has been tentatively identified as the capsid protein; it contains hydrophobic, signal-like sequences at its amino-terminal end[17] as well as an arginine-rich region that probably binds the genomic RNA.[13] The gene product of ORF3 also contains a hydrophobic, signal-like sequence at its amino-terminal end, but it is not known whether this small immunogenic protein is incorporated into the virion.[17] Nothing is known about whether release of the virus from infected cells is an active process or the result of virus-mediated cell death, but virus is found in the bile during the acute phase of infection, and bile may be the principal source of HEV in the feces.[18, 249, 252]

Pathology

Although all viral hepatitis is histologically similar, the histologic changes in the liver of patients with hepatitis E are somewhat characteristic.[215] Histologic changes include focal necrosis associated with minimal infiltration. The lesions are not localized to a particular zone of the lobule. Inflammation is modest and consists of Kupffer cells and polymorphonuclear leukocytes in focal lesions that resemble drug-associated toxic hepatitis. Cholestatic hepatitis is a frequent finding and is characterized by ballooning hepatocytes, cytoplasmic cholestasis, and focal cytolytic necrosis. "Pseudoglandular" modification of the hepatocyte plates has been a prominent finding in some epidemics (Fig. 165–6). The lack of a temporal relationship between viral replication in the liver and histopathologic and biochemical evidence of hepatitis suggests that HEV, like the other hepatitis viruses, is not cytopathic and that the pathogenesis of hepatitis E is immunologically mediated, but this remains speculative.[253]

The average severity of HEV infections is somewhat greater than that of hepatitis A infections. Thus, the mortality of hepatitis E has been reported to be as high as 1%, whereas hepatitis A has a mortality of up to 0.2%.[254] However, the mortality of hepatitis E in pregnant women has been as high as 20%, with incremental increases in the mortality rate with each succeeding trimester of pregnancy.[119, 255–258] In one study, the mortality rate in the first, second, and third trimesters of pregnancy were 1.5, 8.5, and 21.0%, respectively.[122] However, although frequently reported, a high mortality among pregnant women has not been detected in all studies, suggesting that the observation may be in part artifactual.[259, 260] Nevertheless, none of the other four recognized hepatitis viruses appears to cause such severe hepatitis in pregnancy[261] except for hepatitis B.[262, 263] Acute hepatitis E superimposed on chronic hepatitis B has also been reported in pregnant and nonpregnant patients with fulminant hepatitis.[131] Fulminant non-A, non-B hepatitis occurring in nonendemic areas appears not to be caused by HEV.[264]

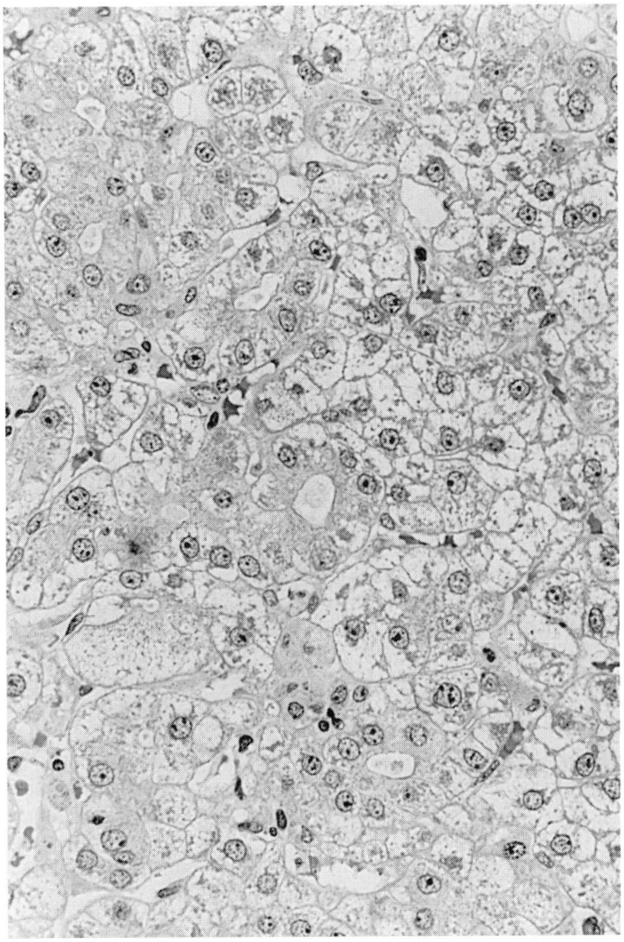

FIGURE 165–6. Liver biopsy from a 30-year old Pakistani patient with acute hepatitis E (hematoxylin and eosin, ×100). The specimen demonstrates acinar transformation ("pseudoglandular" alteration) and cholestasis within the lumen. Hepatocytes demonstrate "ballooning" and degeneration. (Courtesy of M. Sjögren.)

Immune Response

Specific IgM and IgG immune responses to HEV occur early in the infection, usually by the onset of clinical illness. In this respect, hepatitis E resembles hepatitis A, and a serologic diagnosis usually can be made at the time of presentation of the patient. IgM anti-HEV disappears after several months, whereas IgG anti-HEV persists.[104] IgG anti-HEV appears to diminish in titer at a more rapid rate than antibody to hepatitis A, raising questions about the duration of immunity after hepatitis E. However, anti-HEV has been detected as long as 13 to 14 years after infection.[71, 265] Anti-HEV of the IgA class has also been detected in the serum of naturally infected individuals.[266] The significance of such antibody is unknown. All isolates of HEV to date are serologically related, and convalescent antibody produced in response to infection with one strain of HEV probably protects against subsequent exposure to all other strains.[7, 8, 11, 39–42] Little is known about the cell-mediated immune response to HEV in humans.

CLINICAL MANIFESTATIONS

Symptoms

Hepatitis E cannot be differentiated from other types of viral hepatitis on the basis of clinical presentation (Fig. 165–7).[5, 49, 58] Clinically, the severity of HEV infections may range from inapparent to fulminant.[5, 104, 207, 226, 267] However, most patients experience abdominal pain and tenderness, nausea, vomiting, and fever.[268] Serologic tests have confirmed that clinical disease can occur in individuals of all ages, including children.[58, 107, 109, 110, 114, 202] Hepatitis E never progresses to chronicity, but prolonged persistence of IgM anti-HEV (21 months) was reported in one patient.[69] Recurrent (bimodal) hepatitis E has not been reported, except in experimentally infected nonhuman primates.[209] In contrast, recurrent hepatitis A is relatively common.[269]

In experimental infections of nonhuman primates, the clinical presentation of hepatitis E is dose-dependent: the severity of infection is directly related to the infectivity titer of challenge virus.[72] This is in contrast to results of challenge studies of nonhuman primates with the other human hepatitis viruses: a single infectious dose can cause hepatitis as severe as that following massive exposure.[270, 271] The minimal dose of HEV causing hepatitis in nonhuman primates is approximately a thousand times greater than the minimal dose causing infection.[72] It is not known whether such a clinical–infectious dose relationship exists for naturally infected humans, but if so, it could explain how HEV can be maintained in a population with little or no clinical disease.

Complications

The only complications of hepatitis E are those related to severe hepatitis in pregnancy. In addition to the apparent high mortality of infected pregnant women, a high incidence of fetal wastage has been reported.[119, 272–274] In one study of 10 consecutive pregnant women presenting with hepatitis E, 6 developed fulminant hepatitis and 2 died.[275] Of the eight infants available for study, two died and one of these had massive hepatic necrosis. Five of the infants had elevated levels of liver enzymes and HEV viremia in cord blood or early postnatal serum samples, as detected by RT-PCR. This study suggests that intrauterine infection with HEV can be a cause of perinatal morbidity and mortality. Similar evidence for fetal wastage was detected in one but not in a second study of experimental HEV infection of pregnant rhesus monkeys.[94, 249]

LABORATORY DIAGNOSIS

Hepatitis E is the most likely cause of waterborne epidemics of hepatitis occurring in developing countries in which HAV infection is still highly endemic. However, in countries in which improved public health has resulted in a high prevalence of young adults who remain susceptible to HAV infection, waterborne epidemics may be caused by HAV or HEV. In such epidemics, unusually severe hepatitis in pregnant women should suggest hepatitis E. Clinical hepatitis E is rare in industrialized countries and is usually associated with recent travel from a region in which hepatitis E is endemic.[30] However, two cases of hepatitis E in the United States, from which a virus very closely related to swine HEV was recovered, suggests that HEV must be considered as a possible, albeit rare cause in all cases of acute viral hepatitis.[35, 38, 93, 212]

Serologic Tests

As with all types of viral hepatitis, serologic tests are necessary to establish a diagnosis. Hepatitis E can usually be diagnosed by the detection of anti-HEV of the IgM class in a serum sample obtained during the acute phase of disease. Antibody of the IgG class may also be present (see Fig. 165–7).

Commercial tests for IgM and IgG are available in Europe, Asia, and Canada but not in the United States. A number of experimental assays for anti-HEV have been reported. These include tests based on ELISA and Western blot technology and utilize synthetic peptides or recombinant antigens expressed from ORF2 or ORF3, or both, of the viral genome. Many of these assays have been compared in a test of coded samples prepared in a joint study by the Centers for Disease Control and Prevention and the National Institutes of Health.[71] The assays varied widely in sensitivity and specificity. In general, assays based on antigens derived from ORF2 of the virus, with or without antigens from ORF3, were much better than assays based solely on antigens derived from ORF3. Tests based on ELISA

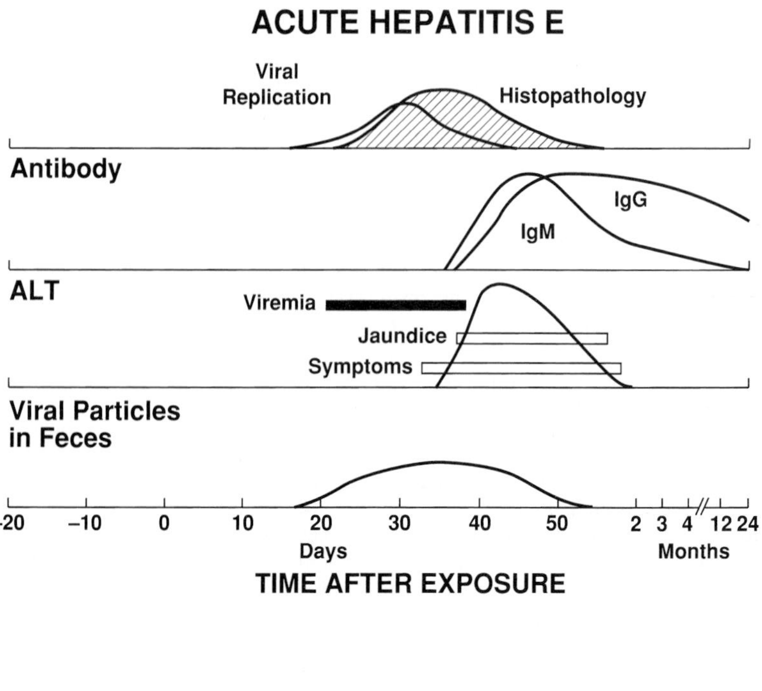

FIGURE 165–7. Diagram of clinical and serologic events in a typical case of acute hepatitis E. Antibody patterns are based on enzyme-linked immunosorbent assay (ELISA) results; viremia and fecal shedding are based on polymerase chain reaction data. (Modified from Purcell RH, Hoofnagle JH, Ticehurst J, et al. Hepatitis viruses. In: Schmidt NJ, Emmons RW, eds. Diagnostic Procedures for Viral, Rickettsial and Chlamydial Infections. 6th ed. Washington, DC: American Public Health Association; 1989:957–1065.)

methods were slightly better than Western blot assays. Based on field studies with the best of these assays, IgM anti-HEV can be detected in up to 96% of acute infections if a serum sample is obtained 1 to 4 weeks after the onset of disease.[56, 75, 79, 104, 109, 114, 276] By 3 months after the onset of the acute phase, IgM anti-HEV is no longer detectable in at least 50% of hepatitis E patients.[103, 114, 132] Anti-HEV of the IgM class reaches peak titers (1:1000 to 1:10,000) during the first 4 weeks of disease.[103, 104] A rising titer of IgG anti-HEV is also diagnostic. Peak titers of IgG anti-HEV (1:1000 to 1:100,000) are detected 2 to 4 weeks after the onset of disease and diminish relatively rapidly thereafter.[68, 103, 104] Thus, a very high titer of IgG anti-HEV may also suggest recent infection.[70] Some cases of hepatitis E appear not to have a serologic response to the virus: acute-phase feces from well-studied seronegative cases of viral hepatitis associated with waterborne epidemics of hepatitis E have transmitted HEV to nonhuman primates (R. H. Purcell and S. U. Emerson, unpublished data). The infected primates had hepatitis E with a typical serologic response to the virus. It is not known why these patients remained seronegative or whether they would be susceptible to a second case of hepatitis E after reexposure to the virus.

Molecular Tests

Molecular approaches to studying the epidemiology of HEV are promising. Molecular epidemiology is rapidly augmenting, and in some cases replacing, seroepidemiology as a tool for understanding infectious diseases, especially for infections in which the etiologic agent is present at levels too low to be detected directly by serologic means. PCR and RT-PCR have revolutionized epidemiology and diagnostics. However, because HEV does not cause chronic infections, the value of molecular approaches has been limited to the study of acute infections.[229, 263, 277–279] After serologic identification of the involvement of swine in the epidemiology of HEV infections, RT-PCR was invaluable for identifying the virus in acutely infected animals and for selecting suitable specimens for attempts to transmit the virus to susceptible animals.[93] Molecular tools such as RT-PCR have also been useful for identifying modes of transmission and estimating the duration of infectivity in cases of hepatitis E.[18, 52, 228–230] However, a positive result for HEV RNA by RT-PCR is not the equivalent of infectivity, because RT-PCR is generally more sensitive than infectivity for measuring HEV.

Genomic RNA of HEV can be detected in acute-phase feces and blood by RT-PCR in most naturally infected humans and experimentally infected nonhuman primates during the acute phase of the disease (see Fig. 165–7).[18, 229] The virus can often be detected in the bile at this time.[6, 18, 81, 249, 280] HEV may be detected in blood and feces of primates for up to 5 weeks after the onset of disease.[18] Primers for RT-PCR must be selected carefully because HEV is genetically heterogeneous. Primers located in highly conserved regions of the genome or degenerate primers must be used to ensure detection of all recognized variants of HEV.

IMMUNITY

Because the immunopathogenesis of hepatitis E is poorly understood, the role of immunity in preventing reinfection is speculative. It has been suggested that infection with HEV during childhood results in an inapparent infection with subsequent rapid loss of anti-HEV and immunity and that clinical disease results from reexposure of such individuals as young adults.[204] This can be neither confirmed nor refuted at present. However, when nonhuman primates that are convalescent from experimental hepatitis E are rechallenged with the same or distantly related HEV strains, they are protected against a second case of hepatitis E.[7, 8, 11, 39–42] Furthermore, a correlation was found between the presence of IgG anti-HEV and resistance to clinical hepatitis in cohorts exposed to HEV in a waterborne epidemic.[104, 217] Finally, the success of passive and active immunoprophylaxis under experimental conditions (see later) argues for antibody-mediated immunity after HEV infection.

PREVENTION

General Sanitation

The role of improved sanitation and public hygiene in the control of hepatitis E is somewhat hard to assess. Clearly, industrialized countries with a generally high level of public sanitation do not experience epidemics of waterborne hepatitis E or significant endemic or sporadic disease, although hepatitis A continues to be an important cause of clinical disease in some of these countries, for example, the United States. In developing countries, even where the prevalence of antibody to HAV is extremely high, the prevalence of antibody to HEV is much lower.[164, 170, 174, 177, 178, 181, 184, 198, 281] These observations suggest that HEV is either much less readily spread or much less stable than HAV in the environment or that other factors are involved. It is difficult at present to assess the importance of animal reservoirs for the maintenance of HEV in the environment, but this clearly needs to be studied. Regardless of mechanisms of transmission, however, improved sanitation is important in controlling all infectious diseases that have fecal-oral transmission as a prominent part of their epidemiology.

Immunoprophylaxis

Passive Immunoprophylaxis

Attempts to prevent hepatitis E by the administration of normal immune globulin have generally been unsuccessful or uncertain, even when the immune globulin was manufactured from pooled plasma obtained from areas endemic for hepatitis E.[29, 216, 226, 282, 283] Failure of such globulin to protect may be related to the relatively low prevalence and titer of anti-HEV in such populations. One study failed to demonstrate protection of nonhuman primates after they were administered convalescent serum obtained from a volunteer who had been experimentally infected with HEV 4 years earlier, but the authors failed to demonstrate anti-HEV in the infused monkeys at the time of challenge with HEV and they employed a very large but unquantified intravenous dose of challenge virus.[284] Such a study may have little relevance to predicting the efficacy of immune globulin with a high titer of anti-HEV administered to individuals with exposure to relatively small doses of HEV acquired by the natural route of infection. In contrast, infusion of nonhuman primates with convalescent serum or plasma from other primates experimentally infected with HEV has protected them against hepatitis E.[100, 285] However, infection was not necessarily prevented, probably because relatively large doses of HEV were administered intravenously. These studies suggest that passively acquired anti-HEV does modify hepatitis E and may be useful for passive immunoprophylaxis in pregnant women during epidemics.

Active Immunoprophylaxis

There are no commercially available vaccines for the prevention of hepatitis E. However, attempts to protect primates against experimental hepatitis E by vaccination with recombinant HEV-derived proteins have yielded encouraging results.[100, 286–289] Among the most extensively tested are proteins expressed from baculovirus in insect cells. The full-length (72-kD) protein encoded by ORF2 is spontaneously processed in insect cells to a protein of approximately 50 to 60 kD by proteolytic cleavage of the amino- and carboxy-terminal portions of the protein.[41, 74, 77, 290–292] The resultant protein is more soluble than the full-length protein, can form virus-like particles, and is highly immunogenic in nonhuman primates.[41, 77, 287–289] It is also useful as an antigen for ELISA.[41, 77] This protein, when combined with alum adjuvant, has been shown to protect against hepatitis E after challenge with homologous or heterologous HEV.[100, 287–289] However, the vaccine generally did not protect against infection, possibly because the challenge virus was administered intravenously and at a high dose. Clinical trials of a candidate hepatitis E vaccine are in progress, but a commercial vaccine is not expected to be available until early in the 21st century.

THERAPY

There is no specific therapy for hepatitis E. Patients should be treated symptomatically as for hepatitis A. Because neither hepatitis A nor hepatitis E progress to chronicity, attempts to treat with antiviral agents are not warranted.

REFERENCES

1. Khuroo MS. Study of an epidemic of non-A, non-B hepatitis. Possibility of another human hepatitis virus distinct from post-transfusion non-A, non-B type. Am J Med. 1980;68:818–824.
2. Wong DC, Purcell RH, Sreenivasan MA, et al. Epidemic and endemic hepatitis in India: Evidence for non-A/non-B hepatitis virus etiology. Lancet. 1980;2:876–878.
3. Balayan MS, Andjaparidze AG, Savinskaya SS, et al. Evidence for a virus in non-A, non-B hepatitis transmitted via the fecal-oral route. Intervirology. 1983;20:23–31.
4. Bradley DW. Hepatitis non-A, non-B viruses become identified as hepatitis C and E viruses. In: Melnick JL, ed. Progress in Medical Virology. Basel: Karger; 1990:101–135.
5. Purcell RH, Ticehurst JR. Enterically transmitted non-A, non-B hepatitis: Epidemiology and clinical characteristics. In: Zuckerman A, ed. Viral Hepatitis and Liver Disease. New York: Alan R Liss; 1988:131–137.
6. Reyes GR, Purdy MA, Kim JP, et al. Isolation of a cDNA from the virus responsible for enterically transmitted non-A, non-B hepatitis. Science. 1990;247:1335–1339.
7. Bradley DW. Enterically-transmitted non-A, non-B hepatitis. Br Med Bull. 1990;46:442–461.
8. Ticehurst J. Identification and characterization of hepatitis E virus. In: Hollinger FB, Lemon SM, Margolis H, eds. Hepatitis and Liver Disease. Baltimore: Williams & Wilkins; 1991:501–513.
9. Kapikian AZ, Chanock RM. Norwalk group of viruses. In: Fields BN, ed. Virology. New York: Raven; 1985:1495–1517.
10. Favorov MO, Goldberg EZ, Gurov AV, et al. Some physicochemical properties of non-A, non-B hepatitis virus with the fecal-oral mechanism of transmission and specific diagnosis of the disease (in Russian). Vopr Virusol. 1989;1:47–50.
11. Bradley DW, Andjaparidze AG, Cook EH Jr, et al. Etiologic agent of enterically-transmitted non-A, non-B hepatitis. J Gen Virol. 1988;69:731–738.
12. Jothikumar N, Aparna K, Kamatchiammal S, et al. Detection of hepatitis E virus in raw and treated wastewater with the polymerase chain reaction. Appl Environ Microbiol. 1993;59:2558–2562.
13. Tam AW, Smith MM, Guerra ME, et al. Hepatitis E virus (HEV): Molecular cloning and sequencing of the full-length viral genome. Virology. 1991;185:120–131.
14. Huang C-C, Nguyen D, Fernandez J, et al. Molecular cloning and sequencing of the Mexico isolate of hepatitis E virus (HEV). Virology. 1992;191:550–558.

14a. Kabrane-Lazizi Y, Meng XJ, Purcell RH, Emerson SU. Evidence that the genomic RNA of hepatitis E virus is capped. J Virol. 1999. In press.

15. Koonin EV, Gorbalenya AK, Purdy MA, et al. Computer-assisted assignment of functional domains in the nonstructural polyprotein of hepatitis E virus: Delineation of an additional group of positive-strand RNA plant and animal viruses. Proc Natl Acad Sci U S A. 1992;89:8259–8263.
16. Gorbalenya AK, Koonin EV, Lai MM-C. Putative papain-related proteases of positive-strand RNA viruses. FEBS Lett. 1991;288:201–205.
17. Reyes GR, Huang C-C, Yarbough PO, et al. Hepatitis E virus. J Hepatol. 1991;13:S155–S161.
18. Tsarev SA, Emerson SU, Reyes GR, et al. Characterization of a prototype strain of hepatitis E virus. Proc Natl Acad Sci U S A. 1992;89:559–563.
19. Gorbalenya AK, Koonin EV, Donchenko AP, et al. Two related superfamilies of putative helicases involved in replication, recombination, repair and expression of DNA and RNA genomes. Nucleic Acids Res. 1989;17:4713–4730.
20. Gorbalenya AK, Koonin EV, Donchenko AP, et al. A novel superfamily of nucleoside triphosphate–binding motif-containing proteins which are probably involved in duplex unwinding in DNA and RNA replication and recombination. FEBS Lett. 1988;239:16–24.
21. Koonin EV. The phylogeny of RNA-dependent RNA polymerases of positive-strand RNA viruses. J Gen Virol. 1991;72:2197–2206.
22. Bradley DW, Purdy MA. Molecular and serological characteristics of hepatitis E virus. In: Nishioka K, Suzuki H, Mishiro S, et al, eds. Viral Hepatitis and Liver Disease. Tokyo: Springer-Verlag; 1993:42–45.
23. Jameel S, Zafrullah M, Ozdener MH, et al. Expression in animal cells and characterization of the hepatitis E virus structural proteins. J Virol. 1996;70:207–216.
24. Zafrullah M, Ozdener MH, Panda SK, et al. The ORF3 protein of hepatitis E virus is a phosphoprotein that associates with the cytoskeleton. J Virol. 1997;71:9045–9053.
25. Cubitt W, Bradley D, Carter M, et al. Caliciviridae. Arch Virol Suppl. 1995;10:359–363.
26. Fry KE, Tam AW, Smith MM, et al. Hepatitis E virus (HEV): Strain variation in the nonstructural gene region encoding consensus motifs for an RNA-dependent RNA polymerase and an ATP/GTP binding site. Virus Genes. 1992;6:173–185.
27. Pringle CR. Virus Taxonomy—San Diego 1998. Arch Virol. 1998;143:1449–1459.
28. Mast EE, Alter MJ. Epidemiology of viral hepatitis: An overview. Semin Virol. 1993;4:273–283.
29. Velázquez O, Stetler HC, Avila C, et al. Epidemic transmission of enterically transmitted non-A, non-B hepatitis in Mexico, 1986–1987. JAMA. 1990;263:3281–3285.
30. CDC. Hepatitis E among US travelers, 1989–1992. MMWR Morb Mortal Wkly Rep. 1993;42:1–4.
31. Chatterjee R, Tsarev S, Pillot J, et al. African strains of hepatitis E virus that are distinct from Asian strains. J Med Virol. 1997;53:139–144.
32. Van Cuyck-Gandré H, Zhang HY, Tsarev SA, et al. Characterization of hepatitis E virus (HEV) from Algeria and Chad by partial genome sequence. J Med Virol. 1997;53:340–347.
33. Gouvea V, Snellings N, Cohen SJ, et al. Hepatitis E virus in Nepal: Similarities with the Burmese and Indian variants. Virus Res. 1997;53:87–96.
34. Huang R, Nakazono N, Ishii K, et al. Existing variations on the gene structure of hepatitis E virus strains from some regions of China. J Med Virol. 1995;47:303–308.
35. Schlauder GG, Dawson GJ, Erker JC, et al. The sequence and phylogenetic analysis of a novel hepatitis E virus isolated from a patient with acute hepatitis reported in the United States. J Gen Virol. 1998;79:447–456.
36. Yin SR, Purcell RH, Emerson SU. A new Chinese isolate of hepatitis E virus: Comparison with strains recovered from different geographical regions. Virus Genes. 1994;9:23–32.
37. Yin SR, Tsarev SA, Purcell RH, et al. Partial sequence comparison of eight new Chinese strains of hepatitis E virus suggests the genome sequence is relatively stable. J Med Virol. 1993;41:230–241.
38. Meng XJ, Halbur PG, Shapiro MS, et al. Genetic and experimental evidence for cross-species infection by the swine hepatitis E virus. J Virol. 1998;72:9714–9721.
39. Bradley DW, Krawczynski K, Cook EH, et al. Enterically transmitted non-A, non-B hepatitis: Serial passage of disease in cynomolgus macaques and tamarins and recovery of disease-associated 27- to 34-nm viruslike particles. Proc Natl Acad Sci U S A. 1987;84:6277–6281.
40. Bradley DW, Krawczynski K, Cook EH Jr, et al. Enterically transmitted non-A, non-B hepatitis: Etiology of disease and laboratory studies in nonhuman primates. In: Zuckerman AJ, ed. Viral Hepatitis and Liver Disease. New York: Alan R Liss; 1988:138–147.
41. Tsarev SA, Tsareva TS, Emerson SU. ELISA for antibody to hepatitis E virus (HEV) based on complete open-reading frame-2 protein expressed in insect cells: Identification of HEV infection in primates. J Infect Dis. 1993;168:369–378.
42. Yin S, Bao Z, Tian X, et al. Protection of rhesus monkeys from challenge with hepatitis E virus. Bull Acad Mil Med Sci. 1992;16:115–118.
43. Aye TT, Uchida T, Ma XZ, et al. Complete nucleotide sequence of a hepatitis E virus isolated from the Xinjiang epidemic (1986–1988) of China. Nucl Acids Res. 1992;20:3512.
44. Aye TT, Uchida T, Ma X, et al. Sequence comparison of the capsid region of hepatitis E virus isolated from Myanmar and China. Microbiol Immunol. 1992;36:615–621.
45. Aye TT, Uchida T, Ma X, et al. Sequence and gene structure of the hepatitis E virus isolated from Myanmar. Virus Genes. 1993;7:95–110.
46. Bi SL, Purdy MA, McCaustland KA, et al. The sequence of hepatitis E virus isolated directly from a single source during an outbreak in China. Virus Res. 1993;28:233–247.
47. Hsieh SY, Yang PY, Ho YP, et al. Identification of a novel strain of hepatitis E virus responsible for sporadic acute hepatitis in Taiwan. J Med Virol. 1998;55:300–304.
48. Al-Kandari S, Nordenfelt E, Al-Nakib B, et al. Acute non-A, non-B hepatitis in Kuwait. Scand J Infect Dis. 1987;19:611–616.
49. Ghabrah T, Strickland T, Tsarev S, et al. Acute viral hepatitis in Saudi Arabia: Seroepidemiological analysis, risk factors, clinical manifestations, and evidence for a sixth hepatitis agent. Clin Infect Dis. 1995;21:621–627.
50. Glynn MJ, Rashid A, Antao AJO, et al. Imported epidemic non-A, non-B hepatitis in Qatar. J Med Virol. 1985;17:371–375.
51. Skidmore SJ, Yarbough PO, Gabor KA, et al. Imported hepatitis E in UK. Lancet. 1991;337:1541.
52. Pina S, Jofre J, Emerson SU, et al. Characterization of a strain of infectious hepatitis E virus isolated from sewage in a non-endemic area. Appl Environ Microbiol. 1998;64:4485–4488.

52a. Hsieh SY, Yang PY, Ho YP, et al. Identification of a novel strain of hepatitis E virus responsible for sporadic acute hepatitis in Taiwan, J Med Virol. 55:300–304.

52b. Schlauder GG, Desai SM, Zanetti AR, et al. Novel hepatitis E virus (HEV) isolates from Europe: Evidence for additional genotypes of HEV. J Med Virol. 1999;57:243–251.

53. Krawczynski K, Bradley DW. Enterically transmitted non-A, non-B hepatitis: Identification of virus-associated antigen in experimentally infected cynomolgus macaques. J Infect Dis. 1989;159:1042–1049.

54. Purdy MA, Carson D, McCaustland KA, et al. Viral specificity of hepatitis E virus antigens identified by fluorescent antibody assay using recombinant HEV proteins. J Med Virol. 1994;44:212–214.
55. Yarbough PO, Tam AW, Gabor K, et al. Assay development of diagnostic tests for hepatitis E. Viral Hep Liv Dis. 1994;367–370.
56. Favorov MO, Fields HA, Purdy MA, et al. Serologic identification of hepatitis E virus infections in epidemic and endemic settings. J Med Virol. 1992;36:246–250.
57. He J, Tam AW, Yarbough PO, et al. Expression and diagnostic utility of hepatitis E virus putative structural proteins expressed in insect cells. J Clin Microbiol. 1993;31:2167–2173.
58. Hyams KC, Purdy MA, Kaur M, et al. Acute sporadic hepatitis E in Sudanese children: Analysis based on a new Western blot assay. J Infect Dis. 1992;165:1001–1005.
59. Paul DA, Knigge MF, Ritter A, et al. Determination of hepatitis E virus seroprevalence by using recombinant fusion proteins and synthetic peptides. J Infect Dis. 1994;169:801–806.
60. Purdy MA, McCaustland KA, Krawczynski K, et al. Expression of a hepatitis E virus (HEV)-trpE fusion protein containing epitopes recognized by antibodies in sera from human cases and experimentally infected primates. Arch Virol. 1992;123:335–349.
61. Coursaget P, Buisson Y, Depril N, et al. Mapping of linear B cell epitopes on open reading frames 2– and 3–encoded proteins of hepatitis E virus using synthetic peptides. FEMS Microbiol Lett. 1993;109:251–256.
62. Favorov MO, Khudyakov YE, Fields HA, et al. Enzyme immunoassay for the detection of antibody to hepatitis E virus based on synthetic peptides. J Virol Methods. 1994;46:237–250.
63. Kaur M, Hyams KC, Purdy MA, et al. Human linear B-cell epitopes encoded by the hepatitis E virus include determinants in the RNA-dependent RNA polymerase. Proc Natl Acad Sci U S A. 1992;89:3855–3858.
64. Qi Z, Cui D, Pan W, et al. Synthesis and application of hepatitis E virus peptides to diagnosis. J Virol Methods. 1995;55:55–66.
65. Yarbough PO, Tam AW, Fry KE, et al. Hepatitis E virus: Identification of type-common epitopes. J Virol. 1991;65:5790–5797.
66. Khudyakov YE, Khudyakova NS, Fields HA, et al. Epitope mapping in proteins of hepatitis E virus. Virology. 1993;194:89–96.
67. Khudyakov YE, Khudyakova NS, Jue DL, et al. Comparative characterization of antigenic epitopes in the immunodominant region of the protein encoded by open reading frame 3 in Burmese and Mexican strains of hepatitis E virus. J Gen Virol. 1994;75:641–646.
68. Dawson GJ, Chau KH, Cabal CM, et al. Solid-phase enzyme-linked immunosorbent assay for hepatitis E virus IgG and IgM antibodies utilizing recombinant antigens and synthetic peptides. J Virol Methods. 1992;38:175–186.
69. Lee S-D, Wang Y-J, Lu R-H, et al. Seroprevalence of antibody to hepatitis E virus among Chinese subjects in Taiwan. Hepatology. 1994;19:866–870.
70. Ghabrah TM, Tsarev S, Yarbough PO, et al. Comparison of tests for antibody to hepatitis E virus. J Med Virol. 1998;55:134–137.
71. Mast EE, Alter MJ, Holland PV, et al. Evaluation of assays for antibody to hepatitis E virus by a serum panel. Hepatology. 1998;27:857–861.
72. Tsarev SA, Tsareva TS, Emerson SU, et al. Infectivity titration of a prototype strain of hepatitis E virus in cynomolgus monkeys. J Med Virol. 1994;43:135–142.
73. He J, Ching WM, Yarbough P, et al. Purification of a baculovirus-expressed hepatitis E virus structural protein and utility in an enzyme-linked immunosorbent assay. J Clin Microbiol. 1995;33:3308–3311.
74. Zhang Y, McAtee P, Yarbough P, et al. Expression, characterization, and immunoreactivities of a soluble hepatitis E virus putative capsid protein species expressed in insect cells. Clin Diagn Lab Immunol. 1997;4:423–428.
75. Koshy A, Grover S, Hyams K, et al. Short-term IgM and IgG antibody responses to hepatitis E virus infection. Scand J Infect Dis. 1996;28:439–441.
76. Li F, Zhuang H, Kolivas S, et al. Persistent and transient antibody responses to hepatitis E virus detected by Western immunoblot using open reading frame 2 and 3 and glutathione S-transferase fusion proteins. J Clin Microbiol. 1994;32:2060–2066.
77. Li TC, Yamakawa Y, Suzuki K, et al. Expression and self-assembly of empty virus-like particles of hepatitis E virus. J Virol. 1997;71:7202–7213.
78. Li F, Torresi J, Locarnini S, et al. Amino-terminal epitopes are exposed when full-length open reading frame 2 of hepatitis E virus is expressed in *Escherichia coli*, but carboxy-terminal epitopes are masked. J Med Virol. 1997;52:289–300.
79. Favorov MO, Khudyakov YE, Mast EE, et al. IgM and IgG antibodies to hepatitis E virus (HEV) detected by an enzyme immunoassay based on an HEV-specific artificial recombinant mosaic protein. J Med Virol. 1996;50:50–58.
80. Meng J, Dubreuil P, Pillot J. A new PCR-based seroneutralization assay in cell culture for diagnosis of hepatitis E. J Clin Microbiol. 1997;35:1373–1377.
81. Jameel S, Durgapal H, Habibullah CM, et al. Enteric non-A, non-B hepatitis: Epidemics, animal transmission, and hepatitis E virus detection by the polymerase chain reaction. J Med Virol. 1992;37:263–270.
82. Balayan MS, Usmanov RK, Zamyatina NA, et al. Brief report: Experimental hepatitis E infection in domestic pigs. J Med Virol. 1990;32:58–59.
83. Meng XJ, Halbur PG, Haynes JS, et al. Experimental infection of pigs with the newly identified swine hepatitis E virus (swine HEV), but not with human strains of HEV. Arch Virol. 1998;143:1405–1415.
84. Usmanov RK, Balaian MS, Dzhumalieva DI, et al. Experimental hepatitis E infection in piglets (in Russian). Vopr Virusol. 1991;36:212–216.
85. Usmanov RK, Balaian MS, Kazachkov I, et al. Further study of experimental hepatitis E in piglets (in Russian). Vopr Virusol. 1994;39:208–212.
86. Huang RT, Li DR, Wei J, et al. Isolation and identification of hepatitis E virus in Xinjiang, China. J Gen Virol. 1992;73:1143–1148.
87. Karetnyi YV, Dzhumalieva DI, Usmanov RK, et al. Probable involvement of rodents in the spread of viral hepatitis E. Zh Mikrobiol Epidemiol Immunobiol. 1993;4:52–56.
88. Maneerat Y, Clayson E, Myint K, et al. Experimental infection of the laboratory rat with the hepatitis E virus. J Med Virol. 1996;48:121–128.
89. Usmanov RK, Balaian MS, Dvoinikova OV, et al. Experimental infection of lambs with hepatitis E virus (in Russian). Vopr Virusol. 1994;39:165–168.
90. Bradley DW. Hepatitis E: Epidemiology, aetiology and molecular biology. Rev Med Virol. 1992;2:19–28.
91. Platt KB, Yoon K-J, Zimmerman JJ. Susceptibility of swine to hepatitis E virus and its significance to human health. Swine Research Report. Ames, Iowa: Iowa State University Press; 1998;125–126.
92. Kabrane-Lazizi Y, Fine JB, Elm J, et al. Evidence for wide-spread infection of wild rats with hepatitis E virus in the United States. Am J Trop Med Hygiene. 1999;61(5).
93. Meng X-J, Purcell RH, Halbur PG, et al. A novel virus in swine is closely related to the human hepatitis E virus. Proc Natl Acad Sci U S A. 1997;94:9860–9865.
94. Tsarev SA, Tsareva TS, Emerson SU, et al. Experimental hepatitis E in pregnant rhesus monkeys: Failure to transmit hepatitis E virus (HEV) to offspring and evidence of naturally acquired antibodies to HEV. J Infect Dis. 1995;172:31–37.
95. Purcell RH, Tsarev SA. Seroepidemiology of hepatitis E. In: Buisson Y, Coursaget P, Kane M, eds. Enterically-Transmitted Hepatitis Viruses. Joué-lès-Tours, France: La Simarre; 1996:153–166.
96. Ticehurst J, Rhodes LL, Krawczynski K, et al. Infection of owl monkeys (*Aotus trivirgatus*) and cynomolgus monkeys (*Macaca fascicularis*) with hepatitis E virus from Mexico. J Infect Dis. 1992;165:835–845.
97. Uchida T, Win KM, Suzuki K, et al. Serial transmission of a putative causative virus of enterically transmitted non-A, non-B hepatitis to *Macaca fascicularia* and *Macaca mulatta*. Jpn J Exp Med. 1990;60:13–21.
98. Longer CF, Denny SL, Caudill JD, et al. Experimental hepatitis E: Pathogenesis in cynomolgus macaques (*Macaca fascicularis*). J Infect Dis. 1993;168:602–609.
99. Tsarev SA, Emerson SU, Tsareva TS, et al. Variation in course of hepatitis E in experimentally infected cynomolgus monkeys. J Infect Dis. 1993;167:1302–1306.
100. Tsarev SA, Tsareva TS, Emerson SU, et al. Successful passive and active immunization of cynomolgus monkeys against hepatitis E. Proc Natl Acad Sci U S A. 1994;91:10,198–10,202.
101. Arankalle VA, Favorov MO, Chadha MS, et al. Rhesus monkeys infected with hepatitis E virus (HEV) from the former USSR are immune to subsequent challenge with an Indian strain of HEV. Acta Virol. 1993;37:515–518.
102. Arankalle VA, Chadha MS, Chobe LP, et al. Cross-challenge studies in rhesus monkeys employing different Indian isolates of hepatitis E virus. J Med Virol. 1995;46:358–363.
103. Arankalle VA, Chadha MS, Tsarev SA, et al. Seroepidemiology of water-borne hepatitis in India and evidence for a third enterically-transmitted hepatitis agent. Proc Natl Acad Sci U S A. 1994;91:3428–3432.
104. Bryan JP, Tsarev SA, Iqbal M, et al. Epidemic hepatitis E in Pakistan: Patterns of serologic response and evidence that antibody to hepatitis E virus protects against disease. J Infect Dis. 1994;170:517–521.
105. Chauhan A, Dilawari JB, Jameel S, et al. Common aetiological agent for epidemic and sporadic non-A, non-B hepatitis. Lancet. 1992;339:1509–1510.
106. Coursaget P, Krawczynski K, Buisson Y, et al. Hepatitis E and hepatitis C virus infections among French soldiers with non-A, non-B hepatitis. J Med Virol. 1993;39:163–166.
107. El-Zimaity DMT, Hyams KC, Imam IZE, et al. Acute sporadic hepatitis E in an Egyptian pediatric population. Am J Trop Med Hyg. 1993;48:372–376.
108. Favorov MO, Kuzin SN, Yashina TL, et al. Characteristics of viral non-A non-B hepatitis with fecal-oral mode of infection transmission in Southern Uzbekistan (in Russian). Vopr Virusol. 1988;34:436–442.
109. Goldsmith R, Yarbough PO, Reyes GR, et al. Enzyme-linked immunosorbent assay for diagnosis of acute sporadic hepatitis E in Egyptian children. Lancet. 1992;339:328–331.
110. Hyams KC, McCarthy MC, Kaur M, et al. Acute sporadic hepatitis E in children living in Cairo, Egypt. J Med Virol. 1992;37:274–277.
111. Koshy A, Richards AL, Al-Mufti S, et al. Acute sporadic hepatitis E in Kuwait. J Med Virol. 1994;42:405–408.
112. Krawczynski K, Bradley D, Ajdukiewicz A, et al. Virus-associated antigen and antibody of epidemic non-A, non-B hepatitis: Serology of outbreaks and sporadic cases. In: Shikata T, Purcell RH, Uchida T, eds., Viral hepatitis C, D, and E. New York: Elsevier Science; 1991:229–236.
113. Lok ASF, Kwan W-K, Moeckli R, et al. Seroepidemiological survey of hepatitis E in Hong Kong; by recombinant-based enzyme immunoassays. Lancet. 1992;340:1205–1208.
114. Mushahwar IK, Dawson GJ, Bile KM, et al. Serological studies of an enterically transmitted non-A, non-B hepatitis in Somalia. J Med Virol. 1993;40:218–221.
115. Saguanwongse S, Pojanagaroon B, Jayavasu C. Detection of 27–32 nm virus-like particles in stools of non-A, non-B hepatitis patients in Thailand by immunoelectron microscopy. Southeast Asian J Trop Med Public Health. 1990;21:265–268.
116. Skidmore SJ, Yarbough PO, Gabor KA, et al. Hepatitis E virus: The cause of a waterbourne hepatitis outbreak. J Med Virol. 1992;37:58–60.
117. Song DY, Zhuang H, Li Z, et al. Hepatitis E in Hetian city: Analysis of 562 cases. Chung Hua Nei Ko Tsa Chih. 1992;31:275–277.
118. Ticehurst J, Popkin TJ, Bryan JP, et al. Association of hepatitis E virus with an

outbreak of hepatitis in Pakistan: Serologic responses and pattern of virus excretion. J Med Virol. 1992;36:84–92.
119. Tsega E, Hansson B-G, Krawczynski K, et al. Acute sporadic viral hepatitis in Ethiopia: Causes, risk factors, and effects on pregnancy. Clin Infect Dis. 1992;14:961–965.
120. Uchida T, Aye TT, Ma X, et al. An epidemic outbreak of hepatitis E in Yangon of Myanmar: Antibody assay and animal transmission of the virus. Acta Pathol Japonica. 1993;43:94–98.
121. Zaaijer HL, Yin MF, Lelie PN. Seroprevalence of hepatitis E in the Netherlands. Lancet. 1992;340:681.
122. Zhuang H, Cao X-Y, Liu C-B, et al. Enterically transmitted non-A, non-B hepatitis in China. In: Shikata T, Purcell RH, Uchida T, eds. Viral hepatitis C, D, and E. New York: Elsevier Science; 1991:277–285.
123. Tsai JF, Jeng JE, Chang WY, et al. Antibodies to hepatitis E virus among Chinese patients with acute hepatitis in Taiwan. J Med Virol. 1994;43:341–344.
124. Tan D, Im S, Yao J, et al. Acute sporadic hepatitis E virus infection in southern China. J Hepatol. 1995;23:239–245.
125. Jardi R, Buti M, Rodriguez-Frias F, et al. Hepatitis E infection in acute sporadic hepatitis in Spain. Lancet. 1993;341:1355–1356.
126. John R, Abraham P, Kurien G, et al. Sporadic hepatitis E in southern India. Trans R Soc Trop Med Hyg. 1997;91:392.
127. Gomatos P, Mounir M, Arthur R, et al. The etiology of community-acquired viral hepatitis in Cairo, Egypt: Diagnosis of HEV infections. Egypt J Med Microbiol. 1996;5:223–229.
128. Gunaid AA, Nasher TM, el-Guneid AM, et al. Acute sporadic hepatitis in the Republic of Yemen. J Med Virol. 1997;51:64–66.
129. Cacopardo B, Russo R, Preiser W, et al. Acute hepatitis E in Catania (Eastern Sicily) 1980–1994. The role of hepatitis E virus. Infection. 1997;25:313–316.
130. Corwin A, Dai T, Duc D, et al. Acute viral hepatitis in Hanoi, Viet Nam. Trans R Soc Trop Med Hyg. 1996;90:647–648.
131. Coursaget P, Buisson Y, N'gawara MN, et al. Role of hepatitis E virus in sporadic cases of acute and fulminant hepatitis in an endemic area (Chad). Am J Trop Med Hyg. 1998;58:330–334.
132. Chow WC, Lee AS, Lim GK, et al. Acute viral hepatitis E: Clinical and serological studies in Singapore. J Clin Gastroenterol. 1997;24:235–238.
133. Buti M, Jardí R, Cotrina M, et al. Hepatitis E virus infection in acute hepatitis in Spain. J Virol Methods. 1995;55:49–54.
134. Arif M, Qattan I, Ramia S. Possible aetiological role of hepatitis E virus in acute non-A, non-B, non-C hepatitis in Saudi Arabia. Trans R Soc Trop Med Hyg. 1996;90:645–646.
135. Lynch M, O'Flynn N, Cryan B, et al. Hepatitis E in Ireland. Eur J Clin Microbiol Infect Dis. 1995;14:1109.
136. Heath T, Burrow J, Currie B, et al. Locally acquired hepatitis E in the Northern Territory of Australia. Med J Aust. 1995;162:318–319.
137. Hyams KC, Yarbough PO, Gray S, et al. Hepatitis E virus infection in Peru. Clin Infect Dis. 1996;22:719–720.
138. Pattanayak S. Magnitude of the problem of hepatitis and directions for research, prevention and control. New Delhi: World Health Organization, WHO Regional Office for South-East Asia; 1986:1–13.
139. Smalley D, Brewer S, Dawson G, et al. Hepatitis E virus infection in an immigrant to the United States. South Med J. 1996;89:994–996.
140. Skidmore SJ, Sherratt LM. Hepatitis E infection in the UK. J Viral Hepat. 1996;3:103–105.
141. Wu JC, Sheen IJ, Chiang TY, et al. The impact of travelling to endemic areas on the spread of hepatitis E virus infection: Epidemiological and molecular analyses. Hepatology. 1998;27:1415–1420.
142. Smalligan R, Lange W, Frame J, et al. The risk of viral hepatitis A, B, C and E among North American missionaries. Am J Trop Med Hyg. 1995;53:233–236.
143. Jänisch T, Preiser W, Berger A, et al. Emerging viral pathogens in long-term expatriates (I): Hepatitis E virus. Trop Med Int Health. 1997;2:885–891.
144. Gambel JM, Drabick JJ, Seriwatana J, et al. Seroprevalence of hepatitis E virus among United Nations Mission in Haiti (UNMIH) peacekeepers, 1995. Am J Trop Med Hyg. 1998;58:731–736.
145. Drabick J, Gambel J, Gouvea V, et al. A cluster of acute hepatitis E infection in United Nations Bangladeshi Peacekeepers in Haiti. Am J Trop Med Hyg. 1997;57:449–454.
146. Clayson E, Innis B, Myint KS, et al. Short report: Relative risk of hepatitis A and E among foreigners in Nepal. Am J Trop Med Hyg. 1995;52:506–507.
147. Burans J, Sharp T, Wallace M, et al. Threat of hepatitis E virus infection in Somalia during Operation Restore Hope. Clin Infect Dis. 1994;18:100–102.
148. Alecci A, Bonciani M, Tola T. Prevalence of anti-HEV among Italian soldiers sent in East Africa for "Restore Hope" mission. Eur J Epidemiol. 1997;13:735.
149. De Cock KM, Bradley DW, Sandford NL, et al. Epidemic non-A, non-B hepatitis in patients from Pakistan. Ann Intern Med. 1987;106:227–230.
150. Fletcher J. A traveler returning from Nepal with hepatitis E. Med J Aust. 1993;159:563.
151. Moaven LD, Fuller AJ, Doultree JC, et al. A case of acute hepatitis E in Victoria. Med J Aust. 1993;159:124–125.
152. Roberts JK, Whitlock RT. Hepatitis E in a traveler to Bangladesh. Ann Intern Med. 1992;117:93.
153. Zaaijer HL, Kok M, Lelie PN, et al. Hepatitis E in the Netherlands: Imported and endemic. Lancet. 1993;341:826.
154. Arankalle VA, Tsarev SA, Chadha MS, et al. Age-specific prevalence of antibodies to hepatitis A and E viruses in Pune, India, 1982 and 1992. J Infect Dis. 1995;171:447–450.
155. Pujol FH, Favorov MO, Marcano T, et al. Prevalence of antibodies against hepatitis E virus among urban and rural populations in Venezuela. J Med Virol. 1994;234–236.
156. Thomas DL, Mahley RW, Badur S, et al. Epidemiology of hepatitis E virus infection in Turkey. Lancet. 1993;341:1561–1562.
157. Tsega E, Krawczynski K, Hansson B-G, et al. Outbreak of acute hepatitis E virus infection among military personnel in Northern Ethiopia. J Med Virol. 1991;34:232–236.
158. Pawlotsky JM, Bélec L, Grésenguet G, et al. High prevalence of hepatitis B, C, and E markers in young sexually active adults from the Central African Republic. J Med Virol. 1995;46:269–273.
159. Rioche M, Dubreuil P, Kouassi-Samgare A, et al. [Incidence of sporadic hepatitis E in Ivory Coast based on still problematic serology] (in French). Bull World Health Organ. 1997;75:349–354.
160. Focaccia R, Sette H Jr, Conce ičao OJG. Hepatitis E in Brazil. Lancet. 1995;346:1165.
161. Cengiz K, Özyilkan E, Coar AM, et al. Seroprevalence of hepatitis E in hemodialysis patients in Turkey. Nephron. 1996;74:730.
162. Blitz-Dorfman L, Monsalve F, Atencio R, et al. Serological survey of markers of infection with viral hepatitis among the Yukpa Amerindians from western Venezuela. Ann Trop Med Parasitol. 1996;90:655–657.
163. Arif M, Qattan I, Al-Faleh F, et al. Epidemiology of hepatitis E virus (HEV) infection in Saudi Arabia. Ann Trop Med Parasitol. 1994;88:163–168.
164. Aubry P, Niel L, Niyongabo T, et al. Seroprevalence of hepatitis E virus in an adult urban population from Burundi. Am J Trop Med Hyg. 1997;57:272–273.
165. Aubry P, Larouze B, Niyongabo T, et al. [Markers of hepatitis C and E virus in Burundi] (in French). Bull Soc Pathol Exot. 1997;90:150–152.
166. Abdelaal M, Zawawi TH, al Sobhi E, et al. Epidemiology of hepatitis E virus in male blood donors in Jeddah, Saudi Arabia. Isr J Med Sci. 1998;167:94–96.
167. Brahm J, Hurtado C, Moraga M, et al. [Hepatitis E virus infection in Chile: preliminary report] (in Spanish). Rev Med Chil. 1996;124:947–949.
168. Bernal MC, Leyva A, Garcia F, et al. Seroepidemiological study of hepatitis E virus in different population groups. Eur J Clin Microbiol Infect Dis. 1995;14:954–958.
169. Benjelloun S, Bahbouhi B, Bouchrit N, et al. Seroepidemiological study of an acute hepatitis E outbreak in Morocco. Res Virol. 1997;148:279–287.
170. Cruells MR, Mescia G, Gaibisso R, et al. [Epidemiological study of hepatitis A and E viruses in different populations in Uruguay]. Gastroenterol Hepatol. 1997;20:295–298.
171. Chow WC, Ng HS, Lim GK, et al. Hepatitis E in Singapore—a seroprevalence study. Singapore Med J. 1996;37:579–581.
172. Corwin A, Putri M, Winarno J, et al. Epidemic and sporadic hepatitis E virus transmission in west Kalimantan (Borneo), Indonesia. Am J Trop Med Hyg. 1997;57:62–65.
173. Corwin A, Jarot K, Lubis I, et al. Two years' investigation of epidemic hepatitis E virus transmission in West Kalimantan (Borneo), Indonesia. Trans R Soc Trop Med Hyg. 1995;89:262–265.
174. Darwish MA, Faris R, Clemens JD, et al. High seroprevalence of hepatitis A, B, C, and E viruses in residents in an Egyptian village in The Nile Delta: A pilot study. Am J Trop Med Hyg. 1996;54:554–558.
175. Grabow WOK, Favorov MO, Khudyakova NS, et al. Hepatitis E seroprevalence in selected individuals in South Africa. J Med Virol. 1994;44:384–388.
176. Ibarra H, Reidemann S, Reinhardt G, et al. [Prevalence of hepatitis E virus antibodies in blood donors and other population groups in southern Chile] (in Spanish). Rev Med Chil. 1997;125:275–278.
177. Ibarra H, Reidemann S, Siegel F, et al. Hepatitis E virus in Chile. Lancet. 1994;344:1501.
178. Kamel M, Troonen H, Kapprell HP, et al. Seroepidemiology of hepatitis E virus in the Egyptian Nile Delta. J Med Virol. 1995;47:399–403.
179. Langer BCA, Frösner GG, von Brunn A. Epidemiological study of viral hepatitis types A, B, C, D, and E among Inuits in West Greenland. J Viral Hepat. 1997;4:339–349.
180. Poovorawan Y, Theamboonlers A, Chumdermpadetsuk S, et al. Prevalence of hepatitis E virus infection in Thailand. Ann Trop Med Parasitol. 1996;90:189–196.
181. Perez OM, Morales W, Paniagua M, et al. Prevalence of antibodies to hepatitis A, B, C, and E viruses in a healthy population in Leon, Nicaragua. Am J Trop Med Hyg. 1996;55:17–21.
182. Parana R, Cotrim HP, Cortey-Boennec ML, et al. Prevalence of hepatitis E virus IgG antibodies in patients from a referral unit of liver diseases in Salvador, Bahia, Brazil. Am J Trop Med Hyg. 1997;57:60–61.
183. Tucker T, Kirsch R, Louw S, et al. Hepatitis E in South Africa: Evidence for sporadic spread and increased seroprevalence in rural areas. J Med Virol. 1996;50:117–119.
184. Talarmin A, Kazanji M, Cardoso T, et al. Prevalence of antibodies to hepatitis A, C, and E viruses in different ethnic groups in French Guiana. J Med Virol. 1997;52:430–435.
185. Mouzin E, Beilke M. Hepatitis E virus infection in Peru. Clin Infect Dis. 1996;22:719–720.
186. Ritter A, Flacke H, Vornwald A, et al. A seroprevalence study of hepatitis E in Europe and the Middle East. Viral Hepat Liver Dis. 1994;432–434.
187. Pang L, Alencar FEC, Cerutti C, et al. Hepatitis E infection in the Brazilian Amazon. Am J Trop Med Hyg. 1995;52:347–348.
188. Zanetti AR, Dawson GJ. The Study Group of Hepatitis E. Hepatitis type E in Italy: A seroepidemiological survey. J Med Virol. 1994;42:318–320.
189. Mast E, Kuramoto I, Favorov M, et al. Prevalence of and risk factors for antibody

to hepatitis E virus seroreactivity among blood donors in northern California. J Infect Dis. 1997;176:34–40.
190. Thomas DL, Yarbough P, Vlahov D, et al. Seroreactivity to hepatitis E virus in areas where the disease is not endemic. J Clin Microbiol. 1997;35:1244–1247.
191. Bernal Reyes R, Licona Solís JE. Seroepidemiología de la hepatitis E en el Estado de Hidalgo. Rev Gastroenterol Mex. 1996;61:233–238.
192. Bernal W, Smith HM, Williams R. A community prevalence study of antibodies to hepatitis A and E in inner-city London. J Med Virol. 1996;49:230–234.
193. Peng CF, Lin MR, Chue PY, et al. Prevalence of antibody to hepatitis E virus among healthy individuals in Southern Taiwan. Microbiol Immunol. 1995;39:733–736.
194. Pazdiora P, Nemecek V, Topolcan O. [Initial results of monitoring hepatitis E virus antibodies in selected population groups in the West Bohemia region] (in Czech). Epidemiol Mikrobiol Imunol. 1996;45:117–118.
195. Queiros L, Condeco J, Tender A, et al. [The seroprevalence for hepatitis E viral antibodies in the northern region of Portugal] (in Portuguese). Acta Med Port. 1997;10:447–453.
196. Quiroga J, Cotonat T, Castillo I, et al. Hepatitis E virus seroprevalence in acute viral hepatitis in a developed country confirmed by a supplemental assay. J Med Virol. 1996;50:16–19.
197. Stroffolini T, Menchinelli M, Dambruoso V, et al. Prevalence of hepatitis E in a central Italian town at high endemicity for hepatitis C virus. Ital J Gastroenterol. 1996;28:523–525.
198. Trautwein C, Kiral G, Tillmann HL, et al. Risk factors and prevalence of hepatitis E in German immigrants from the former Soviet Union. J Med Virol. 1995;45:429–434.
199. Moaven L, Asten M, Crofts N, et al. Seroepidemiology of hepatitis E in selected Australian populations. J Med Virol. 1995;45:326–330.
200. Clayson E, Shrestha M, Vaughn D, et al. Rates of hepatitis E virus infection and disease among adolescents and adults in Kathmandu, Nepal. J Infect Dis. 1997;176:763–766.
201. Clayson E, Vaughn D, Innis B, et al. Association of hepatitis E virus with an outbreak of hepatitis at a military training camp in Nepal. J Med Virol. 1998;54:178–182.
202. Arankalle VA, Chadha MS, Mehendale SM, et al. Outbreak of enterically transmitted non-A, non-B hepatitis among schoolchildren. Lancet. 1988;2:1199–1200.
203. Schlauder G, Dawson G, Mushahwar I, et al. Viraemia in Egyptian children with hepatitis E virus infection. Lancet. 1993;341:378.
204. Aggarwal R, Shahi H, Naik S, et al. Evidence in favour of high infection rate with hepatitis E virus among young children in India. J Hepatol. 1997;26:1425–1430.
205. Ripabelli G, Sammarco ML, Campo T, et al. Prevalence of antibodies against enterically transmitted viral hepatitis (HAV and HEV) among adolescents in an inland territory of central Italy. Eur J Epidemiol. 1997;13:45–47.
206. Viswanathan R. Epidemiology. Indian J Med Res. 1957;45:1–29.
207. Khuroo MS. Hepatitis E. The enterically transmitted non-A, non-B hepatitis. Indian J Gastroenterol. 1991;10:96–100.
208. Arankalle VA, Goverdhan MK, Banerjee K. Antibodies against hepatitis E virus in Old World monkeys. J Viral Hepat. 1994;1:125–129.
209. Balayan MS. HEV infection: Historical perspectives, global epidemiology, and clinical features. In: Hollinger FB, Lemon SM, Margolis H, eds. Viral Hepatitis and Liver Disease. Baltimore: Williams & Wilkins; 1991:498–501.
210. Clayson E, Innis B, Myint K, et al. Detection of hepatitis E virus infections among domestic swine in the Kathmandu Valley of Nepal. Am J Trop Med Hyg. 1995;53:228–232.
211. Clayson ET, Snitbhan R, Ngarmpochana M, et al. Evidence that the hepatitis E virus (HEV) is a zoonotic virus: Detection of natural infections among swine, rats, and chickens in an area endemic for human disease. In: Buisson Y, Coursaget P, Kane M, eds. Enterically-Transmitted Hepatitis Viruses. Joué-lès-Tours, France: La Simarre; 1996:329–335.
212. Kwo P, Schlauder G, Carpenter H, et al. Acute hepatitis E by a new isolate acquired in the United States. Mayo Clin Proc. 1997;72:1133–1136.
213. Rab MA, Bile MK, Mubarik MM, et al. Water-borne hepatitis E virus epidemic in Islamabad, Pakistan: A common source outbreak traced to the malfunction of a modern water treatment plant. Am J Trop Med Hyg. 1997;57:151–157.
214. Iqbal M, Ahmed A, Qamar A, et al. An outbreak of enterically transmitted non-A non-B hepatitis in Pakistan. Am J Trop Med Hyg. 1989;40:438–443.
215. Ramalingaswami V, Purcell R. Waterborne non-A, non-B hepatitis. Lancet. 1988;1:571–573.
216. Tandon BN, Joshi YK, Jain SK, et al. An epidemic of non-A non-B hepatitis in north India. Indian J Med Res. 1982;75:739–744.
217. Viswanathan R. Infectious hepatitis in Delhi (1955–1956): A critical study; epidemiology. Indian J Med Res. 1957;45:1–29.
218. Coursaget P, Buisson Y, Enogat N, et al. Outbreak of enterically-transmitted hepatitis due to hepatitis A and hepatitis E viruses. J Hepatol. 1998;28:745–750.
219. Corwin A, Khiem H, Clayson E, et al. A waterborne outbreak of hepatitis E virus transmission in southwestern Viet Nam. Am J Trop Med Hyg. 1996;54:559–562.
220. Bai F, Zhaorigetai, Wu BR. A foodborne outbreak of non-A, non-B hepatitis. Neimenggu Med J. 1987;7:157–158.
221. Meng H, Yiang XC, He SC, et al. A food-borne outbreak of non-A, non-B hepatitis. Chin J Prevent Med. 1987;21:28–30.
222. Qin SM, Wang HL, Chen LY, et al. A preliminary report of an out-break of non-A, non-B hepatitis. Chin J Infect Dis. 1984;2:272–273.
223. Shi GR, Li SQ, Qian L, et al. The epidemiolgical study on a food-borne outbreak of non-A, non-B hepatitis. J Chin Med Univ. 1987;16:150–151.
224. Caredda F, Antinori S, Re T, et al. Clinical features of sporadic non-A, non-B hepatitis possibly associated with faecal-oral spread. Lancet. 1985;2:414–145.
225. Aggarwal R, Naik SR. Hepatitis E: Intrafamilial transmission versus waterborne spread. J Hepatol. 1994;21:718–723.
226. Cao X-Y, Ma X-Z, Liu Y-Z, et al. Epidemiological and etiological studies on enterically transmitted non-A, non-B hepatitis in the south part of Xinjiang. In: Shikata T, Purcell RH, Uchida T, eds. Viral Hepatitis C, D, and E. New York: Elsevier Science; 1991:297–312.
227. Robson SC, Adams S, Brink N, et al. Hospital outbreak of hepatitis E. Lancet. 1992;339:1424–1425.
228. Nanda SK, Ansari IH, Acharya SK, et al. Protracted viremia during acute sporadic hepatitis E virus infection. Gastroenterology. 1995;108:225–230.
229. Clayson E, Myint KS, Snitbhan R, et al. Viremia, fecal shedding, and IgM and IgG responses in patients with hepatitis E. J Infect Dis. 1995;172:927–933.
230. Chauhan A, Jameel S, Dilawari JB, et al. Hepatitis E virus transmission to a volunteer. Lancet. 1993;341:149–150.
231. Mannucci PM, Gdovin SL, Gringeri A, et al. Transmission of hepatitis A to patients with hemophilia by factor VIII concentrates treated with organic solvent and detergent to inactivate viruses. Ann Intern Med. 1994;120:1–7.
232. Mannucci PM, Gringeri A, Santagostino E, et al. Low risk of transmission of hepatitis E virus by large-pool coagulation factor concentrates. Lancet. 1994;343:597–598.
233. Klarmann D, Kreuz W, Kornhuber B. Low prevalence of hepatitis E virus antibodies in hepatitis C virus–positive patients with coagulation disorders. Transfusion. 1995;35:969–970.
234. Psichogiou M, Tzala E, Boletis J, et al. Hepatitis E virus infection in individuals at high risk of transmission of non-A, non-B hepatitis and sexually transmitted diseases. Scand J Infect Dis. 1996;28:443–445.
235. Barzilai A, Schulman S, Karetnyi Y, et al. Hepatitis E virus infection in hemophiliacs. J Med Virol. 1995;46:153–156.
236. Zaaijer HL, Mauser-Bunschoten EP, Veen JH, et al. Hepatitis E virus antibodies among patients with hemophilia, blood donors, and hepatitis patients. J Med Virol. 1995;46:244–246.
237. Wang CW, Tschen SY, Schalasta G, et al. Anti-hepatitis E virus markers in hemodialysis patients. Nephron. 1996;72:343–345.
238. Psichogiou M, Tassopoulos N, Papatheodoridis G, et al. Hepatitis E virus infection in a cohort of patients with acute non-A, non-B hepatitis. J Hepatol. 1995;23:668–673.
239. Pohjanpelto P, Ebeling F, Rasi V, et al. Hepatitis E virus: No evidence of parenteral transmission in Finland. Thromb Haemost 1995;74:1379–1387.
240. Psichogiou M, Vaindirli E, Tzala E, et al. Hepatitis E virus (HEV) infection in haemodialysis patients. Nephrol Dial Transplant. 1996;11:1093–1095.
241. Knodler B, Hiller J, Loliger CC, et al. [Hepatitis E antibodies in blood donors, hemodialysis patients and in normal people] (in German). Beitr Infusionsther Transfusionsmed. 1994;32:124–127.
242. Gessoni G, Manoni F. Hepatitis E virus infection in north-east Italy: Serological study in the open population and groups at risk. J Viral Hepat. 1996;3:197–202.
243. Fabrizi F, Lunghi G, Bacchini G, et al. Hepatitis E virus infection in haemodialysis patients: A seroepidemiological survey. Nephrol Dial Transplant. 1997;12:133–136.
244. Dalekos GN, Zervou E, Elisaf M, et al. Antibodies to hepatitis E virus among several populations in Greece: Increased prevalence in an hemodialysis unit. Transfusion. 1998;38:589–595.
245. Wang C-H, Flehmig B, Jahn G, et al. Hepatitis E virus in haemodialysis (Letter to Editor). Vox Sang. 1997;73:54–55.
246. Sylvan S, Jacobson S, Christenson B. Prevalence of antibodies to hepatitis E virus among hemodialysis patients in Sweden. J Med Virol. 1998;54:38–43.
247. Buffet C, Laurent-Puig P, Chandot S, et al. A high hepatitis E virus seroprevalence among renal transplantation and haemophilia patient populations. J Hepatol. 1996;24:122–125.
248. Weiss RA. Transgenic pigs and virus adaptation. Nature. 1998;391:327–328.
249. Arankalle VA, Chadha MS, Banerjee K, et al. Hepatitis E virus infection in pregnant rhesus monkeys. Indian J Med Res. 1993;97:4–8.
250. Tam AW, White R, Yarbough PO, et al. In vitro infection and replication of hepatitis E virus in primary cynomolgus macaque hepatocytes. Virology. 1997;238:94–102.
251. Kazachkov YA, Balayan MS, Ivannikova TA, et al. Hepatitis E virus in cultivated cells. J Arch Virol. 1992;127:399–402.
252. Humphrey C, Cook EH, McCaustland K, et al. Enterically-transmitted non-A, non-B hepatitis (ET-NANBH): Isolation of infectious virus from gall bladder bile. Abstract FP4. The II International Symposium on Viral Hepatitis and Hepatocellular Carcinoma. Taipei, Taiwan, ROC, 1988.
253. Soe S, Uchida T, Suzuki K, et al. Enterically transmitted non-A, non-B hepatitis in cynomolgus monkeys: Morphology and probable mechanism of hepatocellular necrosis. Liver. 1989;9:135–145.
254. Purcell RH, Hoofnagle JH, Ticehurst J, et al. Hepatitis viruses. In: Schmidt NJ, Emmons RW eds. Diagnostic Procedures for Viral, Rickettsial and Chlamydial Infections. 6th ed. Washington, DC: American Public Health Association; 1989:957–1065.
255. Hamid SS, Jafri MW, Khan H, et al. Fulminant hepatic failure in pregnant women: Acute fatty liver or acute viral hepatitis? J Hepatol. 1996;25:20–27.
256. Khuroo MS, Teli MR, Skidmore S, et al. Incidence and severity of viral hepatitis in pregnancy. Am J Med. 1981;70:252–255.
257. Jaiswal SB, Chitnis DS, Asolkar MV, et al. Aetiology and prognostic factors in hepatic failure in central India. Trop Gastroenterol. 1996;17:217–220.

258. Kar P, Budhiraja S, Narang A, et al. Etiology of sporadic acute and fulminant non-A, non-B viral hepatitis in north India. Indian Soc Gastroenterol. 1997;16:43–45.
259. Hussaini SH, Skidmore SJ, Richardson P, et al. Severe hepatitis E infection during pregnancy. J Viral Hepat. 1997;4:51–54.
260. Arankalle VA, Chadha MS, Dama BM, et al. Role of immune serum globulins in pregnant women during an epidemic of hepatitis E. J Viral Hepat. 1998;5:199–204.
261. Mishra L, Seeff LB. Viral hepatitis, A through E, complicating pregnancy. Gastroenterol Clin North Am. 1992;21:873–887.
262. Nayak NC, Panda SK, Datta R, et al. Aetiology and outcome of acute viral hepatitis in pregnancy. J Gastroenterol Hepatol. 1989;4:345–352.
263. Acharya SK, Dasarathy S, Kumer TL, et al. Fulminant hepatitis in a tropical population: Clinical course, cause, and early predictors of outcome. Hepatology 1996;23:1448–1455.
264. Kuwada SK, Patel VM, Hollinger FB, et al. Non-A, non-B fulminant hepatitis is also non-E and non-C. Am J Gastroenterol. 1994;89:57–61.
265. Khuroo MS, Kamili S, Dar MY, et al. Hepatitis E and long-term antibody status. Lancet. 1993;341:1355.
266. Chau KH, Dawson GJ, Bile KM, et al. Detection of IgA class antibody to hepatitis E virus in serum samples from patients with hepatitis E virus infection. J Med Virol. 1993;40:334–338.
267. Balayan MS. New form of hepatitis with fecal-oral mode of spread. Soc Med Rev E Virol. 1987;2:235–261.
268. Mast EE, Purdy MA, Krawczynski K. Hepatitis E. Baillieres Clin Gastroenterol. 1996;10:227–242.
269. Glikson M, Galun E, Oren R, et al. Relapsing hepatitis A: Review of 14 cases and literature survey. Medicine. 1992;71:14–23.
270. Barker LF, Maynard JE, Purcell RH, et al. Hepatitis B virus infection in chimpanzees: Titration of subtypes. J Infect Dis. 1975;132:451–458.
271. Purcell RH, Feinstone SM, Ticehurst JR, et al. Hepatitis A virus. In: Vyas GN, Dienstag J, Hoofnagle J, eds. Viral Hepatitis and Liver Disease. Proceedings 1984 Viral Hepatitis Symposium, San Francisco, California, March 8–10, 1984. Orlando, Fla: Grune & Stratton; 1984:9–22.
272. Malkani PK, Grewal AK. Observations on infectious hepatitis in pregnancy. Indian J Med Res. 1957;Jan:77–84.
273. Song D-Y, Zhuang H, Kang X-C, et al. Hepatitis E in Hetian city: A report of 562 cases. In: Hollinger FB, Lemon SM, Margolis H, eds. Viral Hepatitis and Liver Disease. Baltimore: Williams & Wilkins; 1991:528–529.
274. Reyes GR. Overview of the epidemiology and biology of the hepatitis E virus. In: Willson RA, ed. Viral Hepatitis. New York: Marcel Dekker; 1997:239–258.
275. Khuroo MS, Kamili S, Jameel S. Vertical transmission of hepatitis E virus. Lancet. 1995;345:1025–1026.
276. Ke WM, Tan D, Li JG, et al. Consecutive evaluation of immunoglobulin M and G antibodies against hepatitis E virus. J Gastroenterol. 1996;31:818–822.
277. Chobe LP, Chadha MS, Banerjee K, et al. Detection of HEV RNA in faeces, by RT-PCR during the epidemics of hepatitis E in India (1976–1995). J Viral Hepat. 1997;4:129–133.
278. Van Cuyck-Gandre H, Caudill JD, Zhang HY, et al. Short report: Polymerase chain reaction detection of hepatitis E virus in north African fecal samples. Am J Trop Med Hyg. 1996;54:134–135.
279. Ray R, Aggarwal R, Salunke PN, et al. Hepatitis E virus genome in stools of hepatitis patients during large epidemic in north India. Lancet. 1991;338:783–784.
280. Uchida T, Suzuki K, Komatsu K, et al. Occurrence and character of a putative causative virus of enterically-transmitted non-A, non-B hepatitis in bile. Jpn J Exp Med. 1990;60:23–29.
281. Arif M. Enterically transmitted hepatitis in Saudi Arabia: An epidemiological study. Ann Trop Med Parasitol. 1996;90:197–201.
282. Joshi YK, Babu S, Sarin S, et al. Immunoprophylaxis of epidemic non-A non-B hepatitis. Indian J Med Res. 1985;81:18–19.
283. Khuroo MS, Dar MY. Hepatitis E: Evidence for person-to-person transmission and inability of low dose immune serum globulin from an Indian source to prevent it. Indian J Gastroenterol. 1992;11:113–116.
284. Chauhan A, Dilawari JB, Sharma R, et al. Role of long-persisting human hepatitis E virus antibodies in protection. Vaccine. 1998;16:755–756.
285. Pillot J, Türkoglu S, Dubreuil P, et al. Cross-reactive immunity against different strains of the hepatitis E virus transferable by simian and human sera. C R Acad Sci III. 1995;318:1059–1064.
286. Purdy MA, McCaustland KA, Krawczynski K, et al. Preliminary evidence that a trpE-HEV fusion protein protects cynomolgus macaques against challenge with wild-type hepatitis E virus (HEV). J Med Virol. 1993;41:90–94.
287. Fuerst TR, Yarbough PO, Zhang Y, et al. Prevention of hepatitis E using a novel ORF-2 subunit vaccine. In: Buisson Y, Coursaget P, Kane M, eds. Enterically-Transmitted Hepatitis Viruses. Joué-les-Tours, France: La Simarre; 1996:384–392.
288. Tsarev SA, Tsareva TS, Emerson SU, et al. Recombinant vaccine against hepatitis E: Dose response and protection against heterologous challenge. Vaccine. 1997;15:1834–1838.
289. Tsarev SA, Tsareva TS, Emerson SU, et al. Prospects for prevention of hepatitis E. In: Buisson Y, Coursaget P, Kane M, eds. Enterically-Transmitted Hepatitis Viruses. Proceedings of the International Symposium on Enterically-Transmitted Hepatitis Viruses, Paris, France, October 1995. Joué-les-Tours, France: La Simarre; 1996:373–383.
290. Robinson R, Burgess W, Emerson SU, et al. Structural characterization of recombinant hepatitis E virus ORF2 proteins in baculovirus-infected insect cells. Protein Expr Purif. 1998;12:75–84.
291. McAtee C, Zhang Y, Yarbough P, et al. Purification of a soluble hepatitis E open reading frame 2–derived protein with unique antigenic properties. Protein Expr Purif. 1996;8:262–270.
292. McAtee C, Zhang Y, Yarbough P, et al. Purification and characterization of a recombinant hepatitis E protein vaccine candidate by liquid chromatography-mass spectrometry. J Chromatogr B Biomed Sci Appl. 1996;685:91–104.

SECTION B

PRION DISEASES

Chapter 166

Prions and Prion Diseases of the Central Nervous System (Transmissible Neurodegenerative Diseases)

KENNETH L. TYLER

The concept of "atypically slow infections" was introduced in 1954 by Sigurdsson,[1] based on his observations of the naturally occurring diseases of visna, maedi, and scrapie in sheep. He suggested that these "slow infections" were progressive pathologic processes caused by a transmissible agent that remained clinically silent during a prolonged incubation period lasting months to years, after which progressive clinical disease appeared, usually ending in profound disability or death.

After the initial reports describing the clinical and pathologic features of kuru appeared (see later on), Hadlow remarked on the similarities in the neuropathology of kuru and scrapie, thereby triggering the search for the potential transmissibility of kuru, as had been demonstrated previously for scrapie. The key features linking kuru and scrapie that drew Hadlow's attention were the presence in both disorders of profound neuronal degeneration and intense reactive astrogliosis in the absence of an associated inflammatory response.[2]

Kuru became the prototype of a new group of human neurologic disorders that have been linked by (1) common pathologic features, (2) the capability of infected brain material to transmit the disease, and (3) molecular and genetic data indicating that the accumulation of abnormal host proteins—prions—is central to their pathogenesis. This group of diseases now includes the human diseases Creutzfeldt-Jakob disease (CJD), Gerstmann-Straüssler-Scheinker syndrome (GSS), and fatal familial insomnia (FFI), as well as the animal diseases of scrapie, bovine spongiform encephalopathy (BSE), transmissible mink encephalopathy, chronic wasting disease of elk and deer, feline spongiform encephalopathy, and exotic ungulate encephalopathy.[3–16] These disorders are frequently referred to as *transmissible neurodegenerative diseases* or *prion diseases.*

In 1982 Prusiner proposed the name *prion* for the agent responsible for the transmissible neurodegenerative diseases.[17] The term *prion* was initially chosen to emphasize the hypothesis that the causative agents in these diseases were *pro*teinaceous *i*nfectious particles that could be distinguished from viruses and viroids by their apparent lack of nucleic acid.[17, 18] Subsequently, a prion has been defined as a "small infectious pathogen containing protein" that is "resistant to procedures that modify or hydrolyze nucleic acids."[19]

Human prion diseases share a number of fundamental properties. First, their major pathologic manifestations are confined almost exclusively to the central nervous system (CNS). Second, the diseases typically have long incubation times that, at least in the case of kuru, may even exceed 30 years.[8, 20, 21] Third, the diseases appear to be inexorably progressive and ultimately fatal. Fourth, the neuropathologic hallmarks of the prion diseases are surprisingly similar to, although not identical with, cardinal features that include a reactive astrocytosis with little inflammatory response and typically, but not invariably, small vacuoles (spongiform change) within the neuropil. Finally, each of these diseases appears to be associated with aberrant metabolism and results in accumulation of the prion protein (PrP).

MOLECULAR BIOLOGY AND PROPERTIES OF PRIONS

The bulk of investigations of prions have involved the scrapie agent, which can be taken as the unofficial prototype for the group. Purification of material from brains of animals infected with scrapie resulted in the identification of a protease-resistant protein, designated the prion protein, PrP. PrP appears to be the major, and possibly exclusive, component of prions, the agents responsible for prion diseases. Systematic studies of the resistance and susceptibility of prions to a wide variety of physical and chemical agents have been undertaken in an effort to glean information concerning its fundamental composition and structure (see refs. 13, 16, and 22–24 for review). Prions are extraordinarily resistant to inactivation by agents that hydrolyze, modify, or shear nucleic acids, including nucleases, ultraviolet radiation, and nucleophiles.[25, 26] Hybridization studies using probes derived from the PrP gene sequence (see later on) also indicate that there are fewer than 0.004 PrP gene sequence per median infective dose (ID_{50}) unit of prion infectivity.[24, 27] These results have been interpreted as indicating that prions do not contain nucleic acid, although some investigators continue to insist that it remains possible for prions to contain an extremely small amount (e.g., <50 nucleotides) of nucleic acid, or nucleic acid protected within a densely packed protein shell.[12, 28–32] Salient properties of prions are summarized in Table 166–1.

In contradistinction to the difficulty in inactivating scrapie prions with manipulations that alter or hydrolyze nucleic acids is the relative ease in reducing infectivity of prions with agents that digest, denature, or chemically modify proteins.[18] These include a variety of proteolytic enzymes, denaturing agents, detergents, organic solvents, chaotropic salts, and urea. These studies suggest that protein is an integral component of prions and is required for their infectivity.

Initial attempts to characterize prions were severely hampered by the difficulty in conducting bioassays to measure infectivity, and the fact that studies required the use of large animals such as sheep or goats. Subsequent purification of prions has been greatly facilitated by the transmission of scrapie and other prion diseases to small rodents, including mice[33] and Syrian hamsters,[34] and by the development of improved bioassays.[35] One of the most commonly employed bioassays, the incubation time interval assay, is based on the assumption that as the infective dose of prions in a test inoculum increases, the incubation time to the development of illness decreases.[36, 37] Although the accuracy of this type of assay has been questioned,[38] its use dramatically facilitated development of improved purification procedures for prions.

Using a variety of purification strategies, it has been possible to increase the specific infectivity (ID_{50} units per mg of protein) in scrapie preparations more than 4000-fold over the initial starting material.[39] As noted previously, the major, and perhaps exclusive, component in these purified preparations is a hydrophobic protein with a molecular mass of 27 to 30 kD, which has been designated PrP 27–30.[24, 40, 41] It was subsequently shown that PrP 27–30 is the protease-resistant core generated by removal of approximately 67 amino acids from the amino-terminus of a larger protein of molecular mass 33 to 35 kD, designated PrP 33–35 or PrP^{Sc} (see later on).[27, 42]

TABLE 166-1 Properties of Cellular (PrP^c) and Scrapie (PrP^{Sc}) Prion Proteins

Feature	Protein: PrP^c *(Normal Isoform)*	Protein: PrP^{Sc} *(Scrapie Isoform)*
Protease K digestion	Sensitive	Resistant
Detergent extraction	Soluble	Forms rods, fibrils
Secondary structure	α-Helix (42%) β-Sheet (3%)	α-Helix (30%) β-Sheet (43%)
Predominant cellular localization	Cell surface	Vesicles (acidic compartment)
Presence in normal brain	Yes	No
Presence in scrapie-infected brain	+	+ + +
Synthesis rate ($T_{1/2}$)	Rapid (<0.1 h)	Slow (1–3 h)
Degradation rate ($T_{1/2}$)	Rapid (5 h)	Slow (>24 h)

After Johnson RT. Viral Infections of the Nervous System. 2nd ed. Philadelphia, Lippincott-Raven, 1998. With permission.

A protein similar to PrP^{Sc}, designated PrP^C, is present in the brains of normal (uninfected) animals. PrP^{Sc} differs from the PrP^C in a number of biologic and chemical properties including increased resistance to protease digestion and capacity to polymerize into abnormal structures referred to as prion rods or scrapie-associated fibrils (SAFs)—investigators disagree as to whether these are identical.[16, 43–46]

Purification of PrP^{Sc} from the brains of scrapie-infected animals allowed the amino acid sequence of its amino-terminal amino acids to be determined. This sequence was used to generate a series of oligonucleotide probes that were used to screen a cDNA library containing 150,000 colonies derived from scrapie-infected hamster brain. This strategy ultimately led to the cloning and sequencing of the gene encoding PrP (reviewed in ref. 23). This was a crucial discovery, because it indicated that the PrP was encoded by a host gene rather than contained within the infectious agent itself.[24] The PrP gene has been mapped to the short arm of human chromosome 20 and the homologous region of mouse chromosome 2.[47] The PrP gene is either identical to or extremely closely linked to genes *(Prn-i, Sinc)* that control the incubation time to onset of illness in inbred strains of mice infected with scrapie.[23, 24, 48, 49] This provides additional evidence for the key role played by PrP in the pathogenesis of prion diseases.

The PrP gene[11, 23, 24, 27, 50, 51] begins with a guanine-cytosine (GC)–rich promoter region. After a 10-kilobase intron, there is a long open reading frame (ORF) contained within a single exon. This ORF encodes a large 253-amino-acid (human) or 254-amino-acid (mouse, hamster) protein[27, 50] that encompasses PrP 33–35. The carboxyl-terminal 23 amino acids of PrP are removed during biosynthesis, and a phosphatidylinositol glycolipid anchor is added.[52] An amino-terminal signal sequence of 22 amino acids is also removed by host cell proteases, presumably within either the rough endoplasmic reticulum or lysosomes.[53] There are two asparagine-linked oligosaccharides, which are subsequently sialylated within the Golgi apparatus, and a single disulfide bond.[54] No differences have been detected in the organization of the PrP gene in normal and scrapie-infected animals.[55]

The topologic orientation of PrP^C in the cell membrane remains to be definitively established, because the protein contains both two transmembrane-spanning domains[56] and a glycosyl phosphatidylinositol (GPI)[52] anchor. Most models of PrP^C suggest that it is attached to the cell surface by the GPI anchor. The half-life of surface PrP^C is about 6 hours.[57] The protein is degraded after endocytosis,[58] although some PrP^C may be recycled to the cell surface.[59] A secreted form of PrP^C has also been found in cell cultures[60] and may be present in cerebrospinal fluid (CSF).[61]

PrP^{Sc} accumulates within cells, rather than being located on the cell surface like its normal counterpart. PrP^{Sc} is found in cytoplasmic vacuoles and secondary lysosomes.[23, 24, 51, 53, 57, 62] It has recently been suggested that conversion of PrP^C to PrP^{Sc} occurs in caveolae-like membranous domains.[63] A key step in the synthesis of the abnormal isoform PrP^{Sc} may occur during transit of PrP between the Golgi apparatus, where the protein is sialylated, and its subsequent entry into lysosomes.[53]

Various forms of PrP may be synthesized at the endoplasmic reticulum. It has been suggested that some of these topologic isoforms may be neurotoxic, and indeed, expression of some forms in transgenic mice can lead to neurodegenerative disease.[64] However, the exact mechanisms by which accumulation of PrP^{Sc} results in neuronal dysfunction remain to be clarified.

Rodent neuronal cultures exposed to peptides encompassing part or all of amino acids 106 to 126 of the PrP undergo apoptotic cell death, suggesting that PrP or its derivatives may be neurotoxic.[65, 66] This neurotoxicity does not occur in cells devoid of PrP^C.[67] Future studies of scrapie infection in persistently infected neuronal cell cultures may help clarify the mechanisms of PrP^{Sc} neurotoxicity.[68, 69]

Levels of mRNA encoding PrP^C appear to vary during development, and amounts of the protein differ in different tissues. Levels of PrP are greatest in the CNS and are substantially higher in neurons than in glial cells.[70] These results suggest that PrP^C may play a role in neuronal development; however, the function of PrP^C in normal cells remains unknown. It was previously suggested that the chicken prion protein copurified with a protein having acetylcholine receptor–inducing activity (ARIA),[71, 72] but recent evidence indicates that PrP and ARIA are distinct from one another.[73]

Transgenic mice with a disrupted PrP gene show normal early development and do not have detectable abnormalities in the CNS or elsewhere.[74–76] These mice may show alterations in circadian rhythms and sleep-wake cycles[77] and may develop progressive ataxia associated with loss of cerebellar Purkinje cells as they age.[78] These findings are of interest given the prominence of insomnia in the human prion disease fatal familial insomnia (FFI), and of cerebellar disease in patients with Gerstmann-Straüssler-Scheinker syndrome (GSS), kuru, and some forms of Creutzfeldt-Jakob disease (CJD) (see later on). Older mice harboring high copy numbers of wild-type PrP transgenes develop neurologic illness characterized clinically by truncal ataxia, hindlimb paralysis, and tremors, and pathologically by necrotizing myopathy, demyelinating polyneuropathy, and focal CNS vacuolization.[79]

The expression of the PrP gene does not differ between normal and scrapie-infected animals.[27, 50] Despite this fact, PrP^{Sc} clearly accumulates in scrapie-infected animals. Although expression of PrP^C messenger RNA (mRNA) does increase during normal development, the PrP gene is constitutively expressed in adult animals,[27, 50] and PrP^C levels do not increase during adult life in uninfected animals. These findings, combined with differences in the biologic properties of PrP^C and PrP^{Sc}, have led to the conclusion that in infected animals, PrP^C undergoes a post-translational modification resulting in its conversion to the abnormal PrP^{Sc} isoform.[55] The conformational change that results from the conversion of the normal cellular prion protein (PrP^C) to the abnormal disease-associated isoform (PrP^{Sc}) is associated with a marked decrease in the protein's α-helical content and a corresponding increase in the amount of β-pleated sheet.[16, 80–82] Recent evidence suggests that this conversion occurs predominantly within certain subcellular compartments including caveolae-like membranous domains.[63]

The identification of specific mutations in patients with familial prion diseases (see later on) provided the impetus to develop transgenic mice expressing mutant forms of the *PRNP* gene. Transgenic mice with the proline to leucine (P102L) mutation found in GSS syndrome patients within the mouse *PRNP* gene (MoPrP–P101L) develop spongiform changes in the CNS, gliosis, neuronal loss, and PrP^+ plaques.[83] These mice develop clinical features of scrapie. When brain extracts from these diseased mice are inoculated into transgenic mice, these mice develop neuropathologic changes consistent with scrapie but not overt clinical disease.[84, 85]

Transgenic mice with a variety of additional mutations in codons 113, 115, and 118 of the PRNP gene also develop spontaneous neurodegeneration that can be transmitted to hamsters and transgenic mice.[13] Transgenic mice have also been created carrying transgenes with deletions in individual regions of the *PRNP* gene encoding areas of putative important secondary structure in PrP.[86] Transgenic mice with transgene deletions in the amino-terminal part of PrP remain healthy, whereas those with deletions in either of the two carboxyl-terminal α-helices develop neurodegenerative disease. However, their disease differs from typical prion disease and is characterized by enlarged neurons with prominent cytoplasmic inclusions.

Studies with transgenic mice have also led to the hypothesis that there is another, as yet unidentified host factor—"protein X"—that binds to PrP^C and facilitates its conversion to PrP^{Sc}.[87, 88] It has been suggested that PrP^C and PrP^{Sc} molecules bind together through a site in the amino-terminal portion of PrP, whereas the X factor binds near the carboxyl terminus of PrP.[13, 88, 89] Studies using conformation-sensitive monoclonal antibodies and Fab fragments suggest that it is at the amino-terminal amino acid residues (amino acids 90 to 112) of PrP that the most striking conformational changes occur during its conversion to PrP^{Sc}.[13, 90, 91] Overexpression of a PrP with deletions in a nearby region (amino acids 114 to 121) inhibits accumulation of PrP^{Sc} in scrapie-infected neuroblastoma cells—effectively behaving as a dominant negative mutant.[92] Three mutations in patients with familial prion diseases (GSS syndrome) are known to occur within these regions (e.g., P102L, P105L, A117V), but the majority do not. This suggests that mutations elsewhere in the protein may also influence PrP^C to PrP^{Sc} conversion, perhaps by destabilizing PrP structure.[13]

The accumulation of PrP^{Sc} in infected animals following experimental inoculation and in spontaneously occurring prion disease clearly indicates that prions are capable of replication. The mechanism by which PrP replicates, and therefore by which scrapie infectivity increases, remains unknown, although a number of possibilities have been suggested.[13, 16, 23, 24, 51] It has been proposed that the combination of a single PrP^{Sc} molecule with a single PrP^C molecule results in a heterodimeric intermediate that is subsequently transformed into two PrP^{Sc} molecules. This interaction is consistent with data from studies of transgenic mice.[93, 94] This process continues through successive cycles in which newly created PrP^{Sc} combines in exponentially increasing numbers with PrP^C molecules.[22–24, 51] A number of additional models of prion replication have also been proposed (see refs. 24, 51, and 95).

A number of studies indicate that once inoculated into the CNS, PrP^{Sc} disseminates by spreading within the axons of nerve cells,[96–103] possibly by slow axonal transport. Intriguing recent studies suggest that B cells may play a crucial role in the neuroinvasion of scrapie, although the mechanism by which this occurs remains unclear. Immunodeficient mice with defects in B cells but not isolated T-cell defects fail to develop scrapie after intraperitoneal challenge.[104] It has been suggested that following peripheral inoculation, prions may undergo an initial period of replication in lymphoreticular tissues[104] prior to neuroinvasion, which as noted appears to occur via axonal transport.

PRION DISEASES

Kuru

Kuru was the first of the human prion diseases to be studied in detail[7, 105–115] (Table 166–2). It was originally endemic within the Fore linguistic tribal group of the Eastern Highlands of Papua New Guinea. Epidemiologic studies suggested that the disease may have

TABLE 166–2 Clinical and Epidemiologic Features of Human Prion Diseases

Disease	Typical Symptoms	Route of Acquisition	Distribution	Span of Overt Illness
Kuru	Loss of coordination, often followed by dementia	Infection (probably through cannibalism, which stopped by 1958)	Known only in highlands of Papua New Guinea; some 2600 cases have been identified since 1957	Three months to 1 year
Creutzfeldt-Jakob disease	Dementia, followed by loss of coordination, although sometimes the sequence is reversed	Usually unknown (in "sporadic" disease) Sometimes (in 10 to 15% of cases) inheritance of a mutation in the gene coding for the prion protein (PrP) Rarely, infection as an inadvertent consequence of a medical procedure	*Sporadic form:* 1 person per million worldwide *Inherited form:* some 100 extended families have been identified *Infectious form:* about 80 cases have been identified	Typically about 1 year; range is 1 month to more than 10 years
Gerstmann-Sträussler-Scheinker syndrome	Loss of coordination, often followed by dementia	Inheritance of a mutation in the PrP gene	Some 50 extended families have been identified	Typically 2 to 6 years
Fatal familial insomnia	Trouble sleeping and disturbance of autonomic nervous system, followed by insomnia and dementia	Inheritance of a mutation in the PrP gene	Nine extended families have been identified	Typically about 1 year

From Prusiner SB. The prion diseases. Sci Am. 1995;268:48–57.

been transmitted through the practice of ritual cannibalism,[8, 113] and no one born since the cessation of this practice has developed kuru.[8] The disease typically begins insidiously with a prodromal phase of headaches and arthralgia. This is followed by the development of an inexorably progressive neurologic disease resulting in death within 3 months to 2 years of onset.[8] The cardinal clinical features include cerebellar ataxia, action tremor, and involuntary movements (choreoathetosis, myoclonic jerks, and coarse fasciculations), followed in the later stages of the illness by progressively worsening dementia. Cranial nerve abnormalities, motor weakness, and sensory loss remain absent or occur only in the late stages of the disease.

Laboratory tests are rarely helpful in making the diagnosis.[8] The CSF profile is unremarkable, and the electroencephalogram does not show the characteristic periodic sharp wave complexes typical of CJD (see later on).[114] In a study of brain material derived from 18 patients with kuru, 95% of the tissue preparations transmitted the infection to primates.[7]

Histologic examination of kuru brains shows neuronal loss and astrogliosis with the accumulation of PrP^{Sc}.[8, 112, 116] One of the pathologic hallmarks of kuru is the presence of PrP^{Sc}-reactive plaques, predominantly in cerebellar tissue. These plaques are usually unicentric, located in the granular layer of the cerebellum, and often associated with microglial cells.[117] Molecular analyses of the gene encoding the prion protein *(PRNP)* and of the characteristics of the PrP^{Sc} derived from brain material from kuru patients are limited. To date, there have been no reports of mutations in the *PRNP* gene in kuru patients. However, patients with kuru may show a higher-than-expected incidence of homozygosity at a polymorphic codon, 129, of the *PRNP* gene[9, 116] (see later on).

Creutzfeldt-Jakob Disease

Although CJD remains a rare disease, with a prevalence and incidence of approximately 1 case per million population worldwide, it is the most commonly encountered of the human prion diseases and has been responsible for much of our current knowledge concerning the clinical, pathologic, and laboratory features of these diseases[3–5, 7, 9–11, 14] (see Table 166–2). The overwhelming majority (85 to 95%) of cases are sporadic. Familial cases, although accounting for only a minority of patients, have proved to be invaluable in establishing the role played by the PrP gene in the pathogenesis of this disease (see later on). Familial CJD is typically inherited in autosomal dominant fashion, although the penetrance may be variable.

CJD shows no gender predilection. Mean age at onset is between 57 and 62 years, although patients as young as 17 to 20 years of age[118–120] and over 80 years of age with classic CJD have been reported.[118, 121] Early onset of CJD should prompt a thorough search for iatrogenic sources of infection, such as administration of cadaveric human growth or gonadotropic hormone or the transplantation of potentially infected human material, and is also a characteristic of some cases of so-called new variant CJD (vCJD) (see later on).

Despite fears to the contrary, CJD is not contagious. Examples of iatrogenic person-to-person spread are exceedingly rare,[122, 123] but such spread has followed transplantation of dural grafts,[124–132] corneal transplantation,[133–135] liver transplantation,[136] use of dura mater material in radiographic embolization procedures,[137, 138] and use of contaminated neurosurgical instruments or stereotactic depth electrodes.[139–141] In the case of dura mater grafts, the vast majority of implicated grafts have been the products of a single commercial producer. For example, a review of Japanese experience with CJD identified 43 cases of dural graft–associated CJD during the period 1979 to 1996. Of these 43 cases, 41 had received dura mater grafts from the same processor.[132]

Nearly 100 cases of iatrogenic CJD have been reported in young patients who received cadaveric human growth hormone (HGH) for the treatment of endocrine disorders including panhypopituitarism[123, 142–149] or cadaveric pituitary gonadotropin for infertility,[150, 151] practices that have now fortunately been discontinued. Patients with HGH-associated CJD typically received injections of GH, prepared from pools of up to 15,000 pituitary glands, several times weekly for several years. CJD developed after a variable incubation period (range, 3 to 22 years), and patients often presented with a clinical picture reminiscent of kuru. Ataxia and associated incoordination and extrapyramidal features are often prominent, and dementia may be minimal or absent in the early stages. There have been only two reported cases of gonadotropin-associated CJD, but the clinical features appear similar to those described in GH-associated CJD.

Animal transmission studies suggest that whole blood, serum, or buffy coat derived from patients with CJD or animals experimentally inoculated with prions can contain low levels of infectivity.[152, 153] This has raised legitimate concerns about the risk of transmitting CJD via transfusion of blood or blood products.[154] However, despite fears to the contrary, there have been no documented cases in which CJD has been transmitted by transfusion of blood or blood products,[155] nor does a history of preceding transfusion appear to increase the risk for CJD in epidemiologic studies.[156]

Isolated cases of CJD have occurred in approximately 24 physicians and other health care workers,[157] including 2 neurosurgeons,[158, 159] 1 pathologist,[160] 9 nurses,[118, 158] and 2 histology technicians.[161, 162] Despite the natural concern these reports produce among some health care professionals, it is important to recognize that the incidence of CJD in this group does not exceed what would be expected by chance alone. There have been no documented reports of clear-cut transmission of disease from patients to hospital or mortuary staff. Similarly, although isolated cases of conjugal CJD have been reported, there does not appear to be any increased risk to spouses or other family members from exposure to CJD. As noted earlier, the presence of familial cases of CJD appears invariably to result from genetic factors rather than person-to-person spread of illness.

A recent report suggested that CJD cases in rural Kentucky might be associated with eating squirrel brains.[163] Perhaps the most surprising aspect of this report was the finding that 27% of a group of age-matched controls without neurologic disease living in western Kentucky also reported eating squirrel brains, either scrambled with eggs or as part of a meat and vegetable stew! The importance of squirrel brain ingestion as a risk factor for CJD remains to be confirmed, but this practice is unlikely to be a significant risk factor for the majority of patients.

Epidemiologic studies have tried to calculate odds ratios for various potential risk factors for CJD.[156] The two most important risk factors appear to be a family history of CJD (adjusted odds ratio of 19.1) and a medical history of psychotic disease (adjusted odds ratio of 9.9). Although several other potential risk factors were associated with adjusted odds ratios of 1.0 or higher, none achieved statistical significance. Among these risk factors (with adjusted odds ratios indicated in parentheses) were a medical history of poliomyelitis (3.9), a family history of dementia (1.9) or Parkinson's disease (1.7), occupational exposure to cows or sheep (1.6 to 1.7), occupation as a health care professional (1.5), and dietary exposure to liver (1.3). Odds ratios were not elevated in patients who had undergone neurosurgical or non-neurosurgical procedures or blood transfusion or who had a history of dietary exposure to brain or kidney meat.[156] Another recent case control study suggested that multiple surgical procedures (odds ratio 2.1) or more than 10 years' duration living or working on a farm (odds ratio 2.7) significantly increased the risk of developing CJD. In this study, having a relative with dementia did not increase the risk for CJD nor did blood transfusions.[156a]

CJD typically presents as a rapidly progressive dementia with associated myoclonus, although these characteristics are hardly apparent in the original descriptions of the disease.[164–167] There is a great deal of variability in the clinical manifestations of CJD, and this has led to attempts to describe a variety of clinical subtypes, including those with predominance of visual (Heidenhain[168]), cerebellar (Brownell-Oppenheimer[169]), thalamic (Stern[170]), and striatal (Garcin and coworkers[171]) features (see ref. 172 for review). The primary importance of these syndromes is that they indicate that CJD may predominantly affect particular brain regions disproportionately.

In the majority of patients, CJD begins with mental deterioration, which may be manifested as dementia, behavioral disturbances, or other deficits in higher cortical function.[173, 174] In about a third of the patients, predominant initial visual or cerebellar symptoms may overshadow dementia. Mental deterioration is typically rapidly progressive, and the average duration of illness from onset of symptoms to death is 7 to 9 months. Unusual cases of longer duration have been described.[175] In addition to profound and rapidly progressive mental deterioration, another almost invariant feature of the disease is the presence of myoclonus. This is frequently aggravated or induced by startle. Extrapyramidal symptoms and signs including hypokinesia and rigidity and cerebellar signs and symptoms including nystagmus, tremor, and ataxia ultimately develop in about two thirds of patients. About 40 to 80% of patients will have signs of corticospinal tract dysfunction, including hyperreflexia, spasticity, and extensor plantar responses. Fifty percent of CJD patients will have prominent visual disturbances, which can include visual field cuts, cortical blindness, and visual agnosia. Rare cases have been reported in which isolated myoclonic alien hand syndrome has been the initial manifestation of CJD and has preceded the appearance of dementia and startle myoclonus.[176]

Certain neurologic disturbances only rarely occur as prominent features in CJD, and their presence should prompt consideration of other diagnostic possibilities. Although seizures occur in 10 to 20% of cases, they are rarely a dominant feature and are typically amenable to therapy. Some patients have vague sensory complaints, but prominent sensory signs are unusual except in vCJD (discussed later on). Cranial nerve involvement is never prominent, although isolated cases with involvement of the pupils, extraocular movements, and trigeminal, auditory, and vestibular systems have been reported.[177] CJD does not typically affect the peripheral nervous system to any significant degree; however, demyelinating peripheral neuropathy does occur in transgenic mice overexpressing wild-type PrP.[79] Neuropathy has been described in rare patients with familial CJD and the E200K mutation,[178] as well as in rare cases of sporadic CJD.[179] Nonetheless, the presence of significant peripheral neuropathy should not be attributed to CJD until other possibilities have been carefully excluded.

Rare cases of CJD have also been reported in which the clinical features were indicative of prominent autonomic nervous system involvement. These included hypohidrosis, bowel dysfunction, abnormal pupillary responses to autonomic drugs, abnormal diurnal blood pressure variation, and electrocardiographic abnormalities.[180]

A subgroup of patients (10%) develop prominent lower motor neuron signs and symptoms, including prominent muscular atrophy and fasciculations.[181] These patients frequently have a slowly progressive illness of longer duration—atypical for classic CJD. Unlike classic CJD[182, 183] this "amyotrophic" variant of CJD is only rarely transmissible to primates, suggesting that most cases are not truly cases of prion disease but are probably more closely related to syndromes of amyotrophic lateral sclerosis plus dementia (ALS-dementia complex).

Routine laboratory and diagnostic tests are rarely of help in establishing the diagnosis of CJD but may be useful in excluding other diagnostic possibilities. The blood count, differential count, and sedimentation rate all are normal. A few patients have had abnormalities in liver function.[183, 184] It has recently been suggested that some patients have elevated serum levels of S100 protein[185] (see later discussion).

The CSF is acellular, with a normal glucose level and a normal or mildly elevated protein content. The presence of a significant pleocytosis or hypoglycorrachia should prompt a search for other diagnostic possibilities.

Several studies have suggested that the presence of specific proteins in CSF may serve as useful diagnostic tests for CJD. This was first suggested when abnormalities were noted in the CSF protein profile of patients with CJD after two-dimensional isoelectric focusing.[186–188] One of the abnormal CSF proteins is the "14–3–3" protein. Specific Western immunoblot assays for CSF 14–3–3 protein have been developed.[189, 190] Elevated 14–3–3 protein has been reported in 95% of patients with definite sporadic CJD and in 93% of patients with probable sporadic CJD.[190] The test may be less sensitive for the diagnosis of familial CJD than for that of sporadic CJD. In one recent report, only 5 of 10 patients with familial disease had elevated CSF 14–3–3 protein,[190] although in another report of Libyan patients with familial CJD and the E200K mutation (see later on), symptomatic cases were detected but not "healthy carriers."[191]

Elevations in CSF 14–3–3 protein also occur in patients with herpes encephalitis, metabolic encephalopathy, intracerebral metastatic cancer, and hypoxic encephalopathy.[190] These generate "false-positive" results when the 14–3–3 assay is used as a diagnostic test for CJD. Despite this fact, initial reports suggest that the test appears to have high overall sensitivity and specificity for the diagnosis of CJD.[190]

Levels of a variety of proteins including neuron-specific enolase, S100 glial protein, tau protein, creatinine kinase BB, and ubiquitin[192–196] may be elevated in the CSF, although it remains to be seen if these abnormalities are characteristic enough to be clinically useful. It has been suggested that finding elevations of CSF neuron-specific enolase (>35 ng/mL) or S100 (>8 ng/mL) in combination with the 14–3–3 protein may add to the sensitivity and specificity of the 14–3–3 test.[194] The CSF S100 protein assay alone (>8 ng/mL) has been reported to have 84% specificity and 91% sensitivity for the diagnosis of sporadic CJD.[195] PrP^C has been detected in human CSF, but as yet there is no available CSF-based diagnostic test for the presence of PrP^{Sc}.

Recently, a serum version of the S100 test has been developed and has been reported in an initial study to have a sensitivity of 78% and a specificity of 81% for the diagnosis of CJD using a cut-off value of 213 pg/mL or greater.[185] Like other surrogate markers of CJD, this test suffers from the problem that elevated values can be found in a variety of neurologic diseases including Alzheimer's disease, Parkinson's disease, multi-infarct dementia, meningoencephalitis, hypoxic brain injury, multiple sclerosis, and Wernicke's disease.[185]

Computed tomography (CT) scans may be abnormal in CJD, but the changes are nonspecific and nondiagnostic.[197, 198] However, the presence of profound and rapidly progressive dementia in association with a CT scan without evidence of significant atrophy should suggest the possibility of CJD, as patients with advanced Alzheimer's disease typically have prominent atrophy. In some patients with CJD, serial CT scans[199, 200] may show rapidly progressing cerebral atrophy and associated ex vacuo ventricular enlargement. This type of rapidly evolving CT scan changes is only rarely encountered in other forms of dementia.

Magnetic resonance imaging (MRI) appears to be more sensitive than CT in detecting abnormalities in patients with CJD. A number of reports describe MRI findings in isolated cases or in small series of patients.[167, 201–209] Abnormally increased T2 signals in the striatum and thalamus are commonly reported. Less commonly seen are signal abnormalities limited to peripheral cortex.[210] Diffusion-weighted images may show symmetric increases in signal intensity in the basal ganglia, thalamus, cingulate gyrus, and parts of the frontal cortex.[208, 211] Despite the profusion of case reports on the subject of neuroimaging studies in patients with CJD, the sensitivity and specificity of these techniques have never been established. Experience suggests that although the presence of typical abnormalities in the appropriate clinical setting may enhance suspicion for CJD, neuroimaging studies are relatively insensitive,[209] and the absence of CT or MRI abnormalities does not significantly decrease the diagnostic likelihood of CJD.

Studies evaluating other imaging techniques, such as positron emission tomography (PET)[212, 213] and single photon emission computed tomography (SPECT),[213, 214] are too few to determine the sensitivity or specificity of these tests. [^{18}F]fluorodeoxyglucose PET typically shows decreased glucose utilization in involved cortical areas, and SPECT shows decreased perfusion that may be either global or confined to involved brain regions.

Patients with CJD often have characteristic abnormalities on electroencephalography (EEG),[141, 199, 215–220] and this test may be extremely helpful as a diagnostic tool.[220] The classic EEG pattern, which ultimately appears in 67 to 95% of patients, consists of a slow background interrupted by generalized bilaterally synchronous biphasic or triphasic periodic sharp wave complexes (PSWCs).[215, 216, 220, 221] These occur at intervals of 0.5 to 2.5 seconds and have a duration of 100 to 600 msec. PSWCs may be absent early in disease, may disappear in the terminal stages, and are often more dramatic during periods of alertness, but they may disappear during sleep or under the influence of certain drugs including barbiturates, benzodiazepines, and methylphenidate.[222] It has been suggested that the presence of PSWCs, identified according to strict criteria in blinded EEG readings, has a sensitivity of 67% and a specificity of 86% for the diagnosis of CJD.[220] During sleep, many patients will have almost complete absence of the rapid eye movement (REM) stage, as well as other disturbances in sleep architecture.[223] Obtaining serial electroencephalograms in patients suspected of CJD may be extremely useful if PSWCs are absent on an initial EEG study.[200, 217, 218] Lack of this typical EEG pattern in a patient whose illness has lasted for more than 4 months should cast doubt on the diagnosis of CJD. However, it is important to recognize that typical EEG abnormalities may be absent in cases of familial CJD[224] and are not generally seen in GSS, FFI, or vCJD (see later on).

For definitive diagnosis of sporadic cases, examination of brain material remains the "gold standard." Neuropathologic features of neuronal loss, reactive gliosis, and neuronal vacuolation (spongiform change), with an absence of inflammatory changes, are typically present in such cases and are consistent with the diagnosis. It is important to recognize that CJD may occasionally coexist with Alzheimer's disease or another form of dementia.[225, 226]

The availability of monoclonal and polyclonal antibodies against prion proteins[227, 228] has allowed for the identification of PrP^{Sc} by Western immunoblot assay in brain material obtained at autopsy or by biopsy.[229] Immunologic tests appear to be both sensitive and specific[230, 231] and have largely replaced demonstration of transmissibility to animals as the standard for diagnosis. A variety of techniques have been developed to immunostain for PrP^{Sc} in paraffin-embedded brain material[232] or in cryostat preparations blotted onto nitrocellulose membranes ("histoblots"). Hydrolytic autoclaving or proteolysis disrupts the normal PrP^{C} isoform but leaves abnormal and still immunoreactive PrP^{Sc}. With these techniques, a variety of PrP staining patterns have been identified in CJD brain tissue. Such tissue may show positive PrP staining limited to plaques or a more diffuse pattern of staining that colocalizes with synaptic markers (e.g., synaptophysin) throughout the gray matter, or a combination of both patterns.[232] In cases of familial CJD, distinct neuropathologic and immunostaining features often correlate with particular PrP gene mutations (see later on).

There have been several attempts to utilize the various available clinical, laboratory, and neuropathologic tests to develop diagnostic criteria for sporadic CJD.[233, 234] It has been suggested that patients exhibiting appropriate clinical signs and symptoms including EEG abnormalities can be classified on this basis alone as having "probable" CJD. To achieve a "definite" diagnosis, these features must be combined with morphologic evidence of CJD including (1) typical neuropathologic findings on light microscopic examination of frozen or formalin-fixed brain tissue (e.g., spongiform degeneration, neuronal loss, astrogliosis, PrP^{Sc+} plaques), (2) positive immunohistochemical staining for PrP^{Sc} after appropriate pretreatment of tissue with guanidine thiocyanate, autoclaving, or related techniques, or (3) positive histoblotting of tissue for PrP^{Sc} after proteinase K treatment. Although no longer employed with any frequency, demonstration of animal transmission from brain material can also be accepted as evidence for definite CJD. Finally, in patients with the appropriate clinical manifestations, demonstration of a *PRNP* gene mutation can be taken as definitive evidence of CJD (see later on). However, it is crucial to recognize that *PRNP* mutations occur only in the relatively small minority (<10%) of familial prion diseases (familial CJD, GSS, FFI; see later on). Genetic techniques are therefore highly specific but very insensitive when used for diagnosis of isolated cases of prion disease.

Genetics of Creutzfeldt-Jakob Disease

Mutations in the gene encoding the prion protein *(PRNP)* are virtually never found in patients with sporadic (nonfamilial) CJD or the rare cases of sporadic GSS.[235] The only exception has been a single Japanese case of apparently sporadic CJD, in which a double mutation involving codons 180 and 232 was found[236] (Table 166–3). A number of reports suggest that polymorphisms at codon 129 of the PrP gene may play a role in disease expression in sporadic CJD, new variant CJD, and iatrogenic CJD. For example, although 51% of normal persons will exhibit methionine-valine heterozygosity at codon 129 of the PrP gene (Met/Val), with the remainder demonstrating homozygosity for methionine or valine (37% Met/Met, 12% Val/Val), it has been reported that up to 95% of patients who develop sporadic (nonfamilial) CJD and 100% of patients with new variant CJD will exhibit homozygosity at this locus.[237] Similarly, five of seven studied cases of GH-related CJD showed homozygosity for valine or methionine at codon 129 (four Val/Val, one Met/Met).[238] Particular patterns of codon 129 polymorphism in patients with sporadic CJD may also be associated with specific patterns of PrP^{Sc} immunostaining in brain tissues.[232] It has also been suggested that a protein designated "Y," encoded by a locus near but distinct from *PRNP,* may also act to influence both the topographic distribution of PrP^{Sc} in the brain and the associated pattern of vacuolation.[16]

There has been an explosion of reports identifying over 20 distinct mutations in the *PRNP* gene associated with the inherited prion diseases, including familial CJD, GSS syndrome, and FFI (see refs. 8, 9, 13, 16, 239, and 240 for review; see also Table 166–3). One of the most interesting features of these cases is that specific mutations in the PrP gene are frequently but not invariably associated with particular clinical and pathologic disease phenotypes. It appears that particular mutations may influence the age at onset and duration of disease; the prominence of certain clinical features including dementia, myoclonus, and ataxia; the presence of typical EEG abnormalities; the degree of spongiform neuropathologic change; and the regional distribution and pattern of accumulation of PrP^{Sc} within the brain.

Perhaps the most commonly encountered mutation in familial CJD is a lysine-for–glutamic acid substitution in codon 200 (E200K). This mutation has been found in geographic clusters of familial CJD in Slovakia and Chile and among Sephardic Jews in Greece, Libya, Tunisia, and Israel.[9, 241–245] At least one family with this particular mutation presented with a disease resembling progressive supranuclear palsy that was not associated with myoclonus or EEG abnormalities typical of CJD.[246] It has been reported that immunostaining for PrP^{Sc} in familial CJD cases with this mutation tends to show PrP accumulation in a dense synaptic pattern in the gray matter rather than within plaques.[232]

Additional mutations reported in familial CJD include an asparagine-for–aspartic acid mutation in codon 178 (D178N)[247] and an isoleucine-for-valine substitution in codon 210 (V210I).[13] The D178N mutation has been described in kindreds from Finland and Europe.[247, 248] Some of these patients have had disease characterized by earlier age at onset, longer duration of illness, and absence of typical periodic EEG changes.[249] Mutations in this codon have also been described in patients with GSS and FFI (see later on). It has recently been suggested that the phenotype expression of the codon 178 mutation may be influenced by the nature of the associated codon 129 polymorphism. Patients with homozygosity for Val at

TABLE 166-3 Common *PRNP* Gene Point Mutations Associated with Human Prion Diseases

Codon Number†	Mutation Designation	Normal Amino Acid	Mutant Amino Acid	Common Clinical Phenotype
102	P102L	Pro	Leu	GSS
105	P105L	Pro	Leu	GSS
117	A117V	Ala	Val	GSS
145	Y145*	Tyr	STOP	GSS
178	D178N	Asp	Asn	CJD, FFI‡
180	V180I	Val	Ile	CJD
183	T183A	Thr	Ala	FT D
198	F198S	Phe	Ser	GSS (+ NFT)
200	E200K	Glu	Lys	CJD
208	R208H	Arg	His	CJD
210	V200I	Val	Ile	CJD
217	Q217R	Glu	Arg	GSS (+ NFT)
232	M232R	Met	Arg	CJD

†Note: Octapeptide repeat inserts between codons 51 and 91 are also associated with CJD. Homozygosity for valine or methionine at polymorphic codon 129 is associated with an increased susceptibility to iatrogenic CJD, new variant CJD, and sporadic CJD.
‡In the presence of the D178N mutation, valine homozygosity at polymorphic codon 129 is associated with CJD and methionine homozygosity at codon 129 with FFI.
Abbreviations: CJD, Creutzfeldt-Jakob disease; FFI, fatal familial insomnia; FTD, autosomal dominant frontotemporal dementia; GSS, Gerstmann-Sträussler-Scheinker syndrome; NFT, neurofibrillary tangles.
See the article by Prusiner[13] and text discussion for details.

codon 129 present with familial CJD, whereas those with homozygosity for Met at codon 129 present with FFI (see later on). In addition to mutations resulting in amino acid substitutions in the PrP gene, a number of base-pair insertions have been described within the PrP gene in cases of familial CJD.[9, 35, 250, 251]

New Variant Creutzfeldt-Jakob Disease

Beginning in 1995, 23 cases of a "new variant" of CJD were reported from the United Kingdom,[72, 252–254] as well as a single additional case from France.[255, 256] A total of 39 cases had been diagnosed by the end of 1998. The epidemiologic, clinical, and pathologic features of these cases set them apart from typical sporadic CJD (sCJD).[253, 254, 257] Patients with vCJD have been considerably younger than patients with sCJD, with a mean age at onset of 29 years (range, 16 to 48 years), compared with 65 years for sCJD. The duration of illness in vCJD is longer (average 14 months) than that in sCJD (4.5 months). The patients with vCJD frequently presented with sensory disturbances and psychiatric manifestations, both of which are unusual in sCJD. Among the sensory symptoms were pain, dysesthesias, or paresthesias involving the face, hands, feet, and legs or in a hemisensory distribution. Only one of five patients who underwent electromyography (EMG) and nerve conduction studies was found to have abnormalities, and these consisted of mild denervation in the tibialis anterior and an absent peroneal F wave. The single French patient did, however, have clear clinical and neurophysiologic evidence of a polyneuropathy.[255] Psychiatric manifestations were frequently present early in these patients with vCJD and included psychosis, depression, and anxiety. Symptoms of depression included apathy, withdrawal, weight loss, and insomnia and often prompted an initial diagnosis of psychiatric illness. As disease progressed, the most frequent neurologic signs included pyramidal signs (in 93% of the patients), myoclonus (in 86%), rigidity (in 86%), cerebellar signs (in 79%), and akinetic mutism (in 79%). Half the patients eventually exhibited chorea and up-gaze paresis, and 21% had cortical blindness.

In a more detailed analysis of the psychiatric symptoms in these patients,[258] it was noted that psychiatric symptoms were a consistent and early clinical feature in vCJD. Psychiatric symptoms persisted until they were obscured by dementia. Most patients were found to have depression, personality change, withdrawal, and insomnia. Anorexia and weight loss accompanied depressive symptoms. Twelve of 14 patients had transient delusions. These often occurred near the onset of illness, were detailed and complex in nature, and transient in duration (lasting hours or 1 to 2 days). Auditory hallucinations occurred in 5 of 14 cases and visual hallucinations in 8 of 14. Psychiatric medication was not of sustained benefit, although in 3 of 14 patients, transient improvement was noted.

Neuroimaging studies were not particularly informative in these patients. The findings on 8 of 11 CT scans and 8 of 14 MRI scans were essentially normal. Three additional patients had mild cerebral atrophy as their only MRI abnormality. Two of the 23 patients had increased T2 signal in the posterior thalamus, as did the French patient.[254, 255] SPECT was performed in two patients, both of whom had abnormal areas of cerebral perfusion.[254] Widespread areas of decreased cerebral perfusion were also reported in two other cases of vCJD.[259] PET findings were normal in the only patient tested.[254] None of the 21 patients tested showed the characteristic PSWCs seen in sCJD.[254] Most patients had nonspecific abnormalities including slowing, which worsened as the disease progressed. It is important to recognize that initial EEG findings were normal in 29% (4/14) of patients and remained so in 3 patients despite the presence of impressive cognitive and neurologic abnormalities.[254] The CSF was tested for 14–3–3 protein in five cases; two of which were positive. This may have been an underestimate, as the CSF specimen was thought to be "suboptimal" owing to prolonged nonrefrigerated storage in all three negative cases.[254] None of the 14 cases tested had mutations in the *PRNP* gene, but all showed homozygosity for methionine at polymorphic codon 129.[254] Homozygosity for methionine or valine at this codon has been previously reported to occur with increased frequency in both sCJD and iatrogenic CJD (discussed previously).

The neuropathologic features of vCJD are also strikingly different than those of sCJD.[253] The most characteristic differences between the neuropathology of vCJD and sCJD appear to be the prominent involvement of the cerebellum in almost all cases of vCJD, as compared with only a subset of cases with sCJD (Brownell-Oppenheimer variant and GSS syndrome cases). New variant CJD cases also show typical spongiform change, neuronal loss, and astrogliosis in cortex, basal ganglia, and thalamus, but these do not distinguish vCJD from sCJD. New variant CJD cases also had prominent ("florid") PrP^{Sc+} amyloid plaques distributed throughout the cerebrum and cerebellum and, to a lesser extent, the basal ganglia and thalamus. These plaques had a dense eosinophilic center and pale periphery and were surrounded by spongiform change in the neuropil. The plaques stain strongly positive for PrP^{Sc}.[253] In many respects, the vCJD plaques share similarities with but are not identical to the plaques seen in kuru and GSS syndrome. Patients with vCJD also appear to have a consistent pattern of electrophoretic mobility of their PrP^{Sc} protein that is distinct from the mobility patterns encountered in sCJD and is similar to that seen in bovine spongiform encephalopathy (BSE) PrP^{Sc}.[256, 260, 261]

Additional evidence for a BSE-vCJD link comes from the close neuropathologic similarities ("signature") between the two diseases, including the presence of florid PrP^{Sc+} plaques throughout the brain, and the distribution and intensity of vacuolation in different brain regions ("lesion profile").[262] It is important to emphasize that these various pieces of evidence are suggestive rather than conclusive of a BSE-vCJD association.

It has been proposed that vCJD is the result of bovine-to-human transmission of BSE.[260, 262–264] Evidence for this proposal is suggestive but not yet conclusive. From an epidemiologic viewpoint, cases of vCJD followed a massive epidemic of BSE in the United Kingdom with a lag period that is consistent with the known inoculation period of prions. During the BSE epidemic, whose first cases were retrospectively recognized as early as April 1985, it was estimated that several hundred thousand BSE-infected cattle might have entered the human food chain.[257, 265–267] The number of BSE-infected cattle peaked during 1992 to 1993 and has subsequently declined steadily. This decline has been attributed to bans on using ruminant protein for ruminant feeds (July 1988) and on using bovine brain, spinal cord, and other specified offals as feed for nonruminant animals and poultry (September 1990). A third ban prohibited use of certain bovine tissues for human consumption (November 1989).[257, 265, 266] It has been suggested that the BSE epidemic was triggered by changes in the rendering process, particularly the abandonment of the use of organic solvents.[257, 268]

The PrP^{Sc} protein isolated from the brains of vCJD patients has the same glycosylation pattern as that of BSE PrP^{Sc} and a pattern distinct from that of PrP^{Sc} found in GSS, FFI, and previous cases of sporadic (nonvariant) CJD.[256, 260, 261] A variety of studies have suggested that transmission of BSE to humans, if it in fact occurs, may be a rare event. Among factors that may reduce the likelihood of bovine-to-human transmission of BSE are (1) the relatively low levels of BSE PrP^{Sc} present in bovine tissues humans are most frequently exposed to, (2) the inefficiency of the oral route of transmission, (3) the species barrier, and (4) the inefficiency of conversion of human PrP^{C} to PrP^{Sc} by BSE PrP^{Sc} (see refs. 13, 265, and 269–272).

To date, definitive diagnosis of vCJD has depended on neuropathologic analysis of brain tissue obtained at necropsy or by brain biopsy. Because PrP is distributed outside the CNS, most prominently in lymphoreticular tissue, it has been suggested that analysis of PrP from extraneural lymphoreticular tissue, such as the tonsil, might provide a less invasive method for diagnosis of vCJD.[273] Tonsil tissue obtained at necropsy from a patient who had confirmed vCJD showed abnormal PrP staining in germinal centers. PrP isolated from tonsil tissue showed protease-resistant PrP by Western immunoblot assay, and the PrP^{Sc} protein had a glycosylation pattern similar to that described with vCJD. Similar efforts to identify abnormal PrP in lymphoreticular tissues from patients with GSS were not successful.[274] In a recent study, tonsil biopsy and biopsy of spleen or lymph node was positive for Prp^{sc} in all patients (8–10 tested) with vCJD and no patients with sporadic CJD.[274a] If subsequent studies confirm the sensitivity and specificity of tonsil and lymphoreticular tissue biopsy for diagnosis of vCJD, this may become an important diagnostic tool.

Gerstmann-Straüssler-Scheinker Syndrome

GSS syndrome is an exceedingly rare human prion disease, with an incidence of 1 to 10 cases per 100 million population per year (see Table 166–2). The majority of reported cases are familial, with an autosomal dominant pattern of inheritance and virtually complete penetrance. Approximately two dozen independent kindreds have been identified worldwide to date.

The basic clinical features are those of a midlife progressive spinocerebellar degeneration with associated dementia.[275–278] The average duration of disease is 5 years, with mean age at onset of 43 to 48 years (range, 24 to 66 years). In typical cases, cerebellar features dominate the clinical picture, with dementia a late or minor accompaniment. In most patients, when dementia does occur the features are those of a global dementia with impairment in intelligence, memory, attention, and cognitive skills.[279, 280] Cerebellar dysfunction manifests as incoordination, clumsiness, and difficulty walking. Associated clinical findings include ataxia, dysmetria, tremor, nystagmus, and dysarthria. Some families have more prominent dementia, spasticity, extrapyramidal signs, or other findings.[278, 281] In contrast to CJD, myoclonus is only rarely a prominent feature in GSS syndrome and is often entirely absent. Much of the clinical heterogeneity of the disease may be the result of the variable phenotypic effects of different PrP gene mutations associated with the disease (see later on).

Laboratory tests are rarely helpful in the diagnosis but may be of value in excluding other diagnostic possibilities. As in kuru and vCJD, but unlike in sCJD, the electroencephalogram in GSS does not show PSWCs.[276] CT scans may show evidence of cerebellar or brain stem atrophy, and MRI studies have been limited,[276, 282] but some patients have had decreased T_2 signal in the striatum, substantia nigra, and red nucleus. PET studies using fluoro-2-deoxyglucose (FDG) have been performed in some affected persons. Typical findings include decreased FDG uptake in temporoparietal cortices in patients with dementia and in cerebellar cortices in patients with prominent ataxia.[283]

Definitive diagnosis requires the examination of brain material. Like the other prion diseases, the GSS syndrome may be transmitted to animals by brain material from infected cases,[284] although the frequency of transmission appears to be considerably lower than that reported for kuru and sporadic CJD.[7] Neuropathologic findings are typical of other prion diseases, except that virtually all patients have amyloid plaques reminiscent of those of kuru (kuru plaques) found throughout the brain, but in largest concentration within the cerebellum. Within the cerebellum, plaques are typically found in the molecular layer, are often multicentric, and are associated with a microglial reaction.[117] In some families, spongiform changes are minimal or absent. Atypical kindreds have been reported in which prion amyloid plaques are prominent throughout the telencephalon and not limited to the cerebellum and in which neurofibrillary tangles are prominent.[285] Cases of this type may have been previously mischaracterized as familial Alzheimer's disease. The availability of immunostaining now allows the amyloid plaques associated with prion diseases to be clearly distinguished from the senile plaques characteristic of Alzheimer's disease. Prion plaques immunostain with antibodies against PrP^{Sc} and do not stain with antibodies to β-amyloid protein, whereas senile plaques have the opposite characteristics.[4, 286]

A number of PrP gene mutations have been identified in patients with familial GSS syndrome[8, 9, 35, 239, 240, 287, 288] (see Table 166–3). The most common appears to be a leucine-for-proline substitution on codon 102 (P102L).[228, 287, 289–291] This mutation was found in descendants of the original family described by Gerstmann, Straüssler, and Scheinker.[292–294] Transgenic mice with this codon 102 mutation spontaneously develop a neurodegenerative disease indistinguishable from scrapie,[84, 85, 295] providing additional evidence that PrP gene mutations are responsible for familial GSS syndrome. In the case of the GSS P102L mutation, the phenotype may also be influenced by the nature of the amino acids present at the polymorphic codon 129. The clinical presentation of patients with P102L may differ between patients who have associated methionine or valine homozygosity at codon 129 (P102L–M129, P102L–V129),[291] although such a correlation is not invariably found.[296] Affected families have been described with leucine-for-proline mutations at codon 105 (P105L),[278, 281] valine-for-alanine mutations in codon 117 (A117V), double mutations involving codons 117 and 129,[297] a stop (amber) mutation in place of a tyrosine at codon 145 (Y145STOP),[278, 298] serine-for-phenylalanine mutations in codon 198 (F198S),[299] mutations in codon 217 (Q217R),[278] leucine-for-glutamic acid mutations in codon 219 (E219L),[283] and base-pair inserts.[300] It has been suggested that GSS associated with the P102L mutation may present predominantly as ataxia[289] with severe spongiform degeneration,[278] whereas patients with GSS A117V, Y145STOP, and F198S mutations may have more prominent dementia associated with neurofibrillary degeneration. It is important to recognize that many of the clinical and pathologic phenotypes show significant variation and heterogeneity not only between families with similar mutations but also among members of the same family.[283, 296, 301]

Fatal Familial Insomnia

FFI is a newly recognized familial human prion disease,[302–304] although there is some clinical and pathologic overlap between FFI and cases previously described as "thalamic dementia"[305] (see Table 166–2). Onset of disease is in middle or late life (35 to 61 years), with an average disease duration of 13 (range, 7 to 25) months.[303] There is one report of a 60-year-old woman with FFI whose son died at the age of 20 from a rapidly progressive dementia without associated insomnia.[306] Inheritance follows an autosomal dominant pattern.[303] Although the initial reports described Italian kindreds, families with FFI have subsequently been reported from the United States, France, England, Australia, and Japan, indicating the disease is probably distributed worldwide. In this unusual disorder, patients present with progressive insomnia, dysautonomia (hyperhidrosis, hyperthermia, tachycardia, and hypertension), and motor disturbances that can include ataxia, myoclonus, spasticity, hyperreflexia, and dysarthria.[302, 303, 307, 308] Monitoring of daily rest-activity patterns in affected patients often shows a loss of normal circadian rest-activity rhythm.[309] Mental status abnormalities can include hallucinations, delirium, confusion, memory deficits, and decreased attention, but frank dementia is rarely encountered.[307] Early impairment of attention, vigilance, and memory and a progressive dreamlike or confusional state are characteristic neurobehavioral deficits.[310] These features appear to be distinct from the typical features of classic cortical and subcorticol dementias and the Wernicke-Korsakoff syndrome.[310] Many patients have endocrine disturbances, including decreased adrenocorticotropic hormone secretion, increased cortisol secretion, and loss of the normal circadian pattern of growth hormone, prolactin, and melatonin secretion.

Neuropathologic changes including neuronal loss and gliosis are found consistently in the anterior ventral and mediodorsal nuclei of the thalamus and occasionally in the olivary nucleus and cerebellar and cerebral cortex.[302, 303, 310, 311] Within the thalamus, there is a correlation between the functional properties of specific thalamic relay nuclei and the severity of neuronal loss. For example, neuronal loss appears greatest in those nuclei subserving associative and motor functions.[312] Spongiform changes have been reported in only a single case. Immunostaining of brain material for PrP^{Sc} is positive,[302] although the concentrations of protein appear to be among the lowest encountered in the human prion diseases.[313]

PSWCs on the electroencephalogram, characteristic of CJD, have been described in only one patient. Sleep studies show an early reduction in sleep spindles and K complexes, drastic reduction in total sleep time, and disruption of normal sleep architecture. Non-REM sleep may be entirely absent, and persisting REM sleep may not be associated with atonia.[314] PET scans using FDG show severely reduced glucose utilization in the thalamus and, to a lesser extent, in the cingulate gyrus, the hypometabolism correlating with regions of greatest neuronal loss.[315, 316]

Like the other human prion diseases, FFI is also transmissible to experimental animals.[317] Virtually all reported cases have been associated with an asparagine-for-aspartic acid substitution in codon 178 (D178N)[302, 311, 318] (see Table 166–3). As discussed earlier, polymorphism at codon 129 appears to determine the phenotypic expression of D178N mutations. Patients who exhibit homozygosity for methionine at codon 129 (M129) develop FFI, those who exhibit heterozygosity develop an FFI-like illness with longer symptom duration, and those who show homozygosity for valine develop familial CJD.[311, 316, 319–323] There is one report of a patient with a lysine mutation at codon 200 and associated homozygosity for methionine at codon 129 who developed CJD associated with severe insomnia.[324] At autopsy, this patient was found to have FFI-like pathologic changes in the thalamus, supporting the idea that these changes are responsible for the dysregulation in sleep patterns. Of interest, mice with knockout mutations in the *PRNP* gene show altered circadian activity rhythms and patterns, suggesting that PrP may play a role in the normal regulation of these processes.[77]

TREATMENT OF PRION DISEASES

Kuru, CJD, GSS, and FFI appear to be invariably fatal diseases from which there is virtually no hope of recovery. On patient with documented CJD has apparently recovered, but all other confirmed cases have ended fatally. There is no known effective form of therapy. Treatments with agents such as idoxuridine[325, 326] acyclovir,[327, 328] interferon,[329] polyanions,[330] and amphotericin B[331] all have been unsuccessful. Anecdotal reports of stabilization or improvement following treatment with amantadine,[332–335] vidarabine,[336] and methisoprinol[337] have not been confirmed by other studies[338] or in unpublished trials in individual patients.

The availability of both animal models of prion disease and cell culture systems including neuroblastoma cells permanently infected with prions may provide better models for screening new anti-prion drugs.[339] For example, the anion Congo red has been shown to delay disease onset in rodent models of prion disease and to reduce the accumulation of PrP^{Sc} in infected neuroblastoma cells.[339, 340] The anthracycline IDX inhibits prion disease in Syrian hamsters,[341] and molecular chaperones including glycerol and dimethyl sulfoxide interfere with the formation of PrP^{Sc} in cell culture.[342]

As the pathogenesis of prion diseases is better understood at a molecular level, new opportunities for therapeutic intervention may be identified.[13] Possible targets for intervention include the conversion of PrP^{C} to PrP^{Sc}.[13, 343] This might result from stabilization of PrP^{C} or from prevention of binding of PrP^{Sc} with PrP^{C} or of the binding of protein X.

HANDLING OF POTENTIALLY INFECTIOUS MATERIAL

As noted earlier, there is no evidence that prion diseases are contagious in the usual sense of the term, although instances of person-to-person spread have been documented. Almost without exception these iatrogenic cases have required the direct inoculation, implantation, or transplantation of infectious material. Kuru appears to have been transmitted by ingestion, and this has been suggested as a possible route of infection in cases of vCJD. Kuru, CJD, and BSE have been transmitted to primates and rodents by the oral route, although this route is quite inefficient.[269, 344] As might be expected, repeated oral inoculations are more effective in transmitting infection than single doses.[345] Nonetheless, there is no evidence that ingestion is an important route of spread for CJD, GSS, or FFI, and its importance in vCJD remains to be established.

On the basis of studies in animals,[5, 7, 265] it can be expected that the highest concentrations of the infectious agent in human tissues occur in the brain, spinal cord, and eye. Other organs or body fluids occasionally found to contain infectious material include CSF, lymphoreticular organs, kidney, and lung. The infectious agent is almost never found in blood or urine, and no cases of blood transfusion–associated CJD have been documented, nor does transfusion appear to be a major risk factor for the acquisition of CJD in epidemiologic studies.[154, 155, 156a, 346] There are no reported isolations of infectious material from human feces, saliva, sputum, vaginal secretions, or milk.[5, 7]

From a practical viewpoint, it appears that the universal system of precautions now widely employed in most health care settings is more than adequate for dealing with patients suspected of having prion diseases. Gloves should be worn for handling blood, CSF, urine, feces, and material soiled by these fluids and for the performance of invasive procedures including venipuncture and lumbar puncture. Masks, gowns, and protective eyewear should be worn if extensive exposure to blood, CSF, body fluids, or neural tissue is anticipated. Gloves should be discarded after single patient use, and hands should be thoroughly washed. Potentially infectious material should be placed in appropriate containers, bagged to reduce the risk of accidental spills, and clearly marked. Persons transporting this material should wear gloves. Care should be taken to avoid self-inoculation with needles, surgical instruments, or other sharp objects. Specific guidelines and precautions have also been suggested for special situations such as the performance of neuropathologic autopsies in suspected cases of CJD.[347]

Controversy continues concerning the best procedures for fully sterilizing instruments, tissues, or other materials known to contain prions. The Committee on Health Care Issues of the American Neurological Association has suggested either steam autoclaving (1 hour at 132°C) or immersion into 1 N NaOH (1 hour at room temperature).[348] Prusiner and Hsiao[6] and Prusiner and colleagues[3] have suggested more rigorous decontamination protocols for steam autoclaving (4.5 hours at 121°C and 15 pounds per square inch) or 1 N NaOH immersion (three treatments of 30 minutes each). Prion infectivity is not reliably reduced by exposure to ultraviolet light, alcohol solutions, phenol, bleach, or formalin.[349–351] Recent studies have suggested that concentrated (≥3 M) guanidine thiocyanate solutions may be highly effective as disinfectants.[352]

REFERENCES

1. Sigurdsson B. Rida, a chronic encephalitis of sheep: With general remarks on infections which develop slowly and some of their special characteristics. Br Vet J. 1954;110:341–354.
2. Hadlow WJ. Neuropathology and the scrapie-kuru connection. Brain Pathol. 1995;5:27–31.
3. Prusiner SB, Hsiao KK, Bredesen DE, DeArmond SJ. Prion disease. In: McKendall RR, ed. Viral Disease. Handbook of Clinical Neurology, 12/56). Amsterdam: Elsevier; 1989:543–580.
4. Prusiner SB. Prions and neurodegenerative diseases. N Engl J Med. 1987;317:1571–1581.
5. Asher DM. Slow viral infections. In: Scheld WM, Whitley RJ, Durack DT, eds. Infections of the Central Nervous System. 2nd ed. New York: Lippincott-Raven; 1997:199–221.
6. Prusiner SB, Hsiao KK. Prions causing transmissible neurodegenerative diseases. In: Schlossberg D, ed. Infections of the Nervous System. New York: Springer-Verlag; 1990:153–168.
7. Brown P, Gibbs CJ Jr, Rodgers-Johnson P, et al. Human spongiform encephalopathy: The National Institutes of Health series of 300 cases of experimentally transmitted disease. Ann Neurol. 1994;35:513–529.
8. Gajdusek CD. Infectious amyloids: Subacute spongiform encephalopathies as transmissible cerebral amyloidoses. In: Fields BN, Knipe DM, Howley PM, eds. Fields Virology. 3rd ed. New York: Lippincott-Raven; 1996:2851–2900.
9. Hsiao KK, Prusiner SB. Inherited human prion diseases. Neurology. 1990;40:1820–1827.
10. Ravilochan K, Tyler KL. Human transmissible neurodegenerative diseases (prion diseases). Semin Neurol. 1992;12:178–192.
11. Prusiner SB. Genetic and infectious prion diseases. Arch Neurol. 1993;50:1129–1153.
12. Haywood AM. Transmissible spongiform encephalopathies. N Engl J Med. 1997;337:1821–1828.
13. Prusiner SB. Prion diseases and the BSE crisis. Science. 1997;278:245–251.
14. Prusiner SB. Molecular biology and pathogenesis of prion diseases. Trends Biochem Sci 1997;21:482–487.
15. Goldfarb LG, Brown P. The transmissible spongiform encephalopathies. Annu Rev Microbiol. 1995;46:57–65.
16. Prusiner SB. Prions. In: Fields BN, Knipe DM, Howley PM, eds. Fields Virology. 3rd ed. New York: Lippincott-Raven; 1996:2901–2950.
17. Prusiner SB. Novel proteinaceous infectious particles cause scrapie. Science. 1982;216:136–144.
18. Prusiner SB. The prion hypothesis. In: Prusiner SB, McKinley MP, eds. Prions. San Diego: Academic Press; 1987:17–36.
19. Prusiner SB. Terminology. In: Prusiner SB, McKinley MP, eds. Prions. San Diego: Academic Press; 1987:37–53.
20. Klitzman RL, Alpers MP, Gajdusek DC. The natural incubation period of kuru and the episodes of transmission in three clusters of patients. Neuroepidemology. 1985;3:3–20.
21. Prusiner SB, Gajdusek DC, Alpers MP. Kuru with incubation periods exceeding two decades. Ann Neurol. 1982;12:1–9.
22. Prusiner SB. Scrapie prions. Annu Rev Microbiol. 1989;43:345–374.
23. Prusiner SB. Chemistry and biology of prions. Biochemistry. 1992;31:12277–12288.
24. Prusiner SB. Molecular biology and genetics of neurodegenerative diseases caused by prions. Adv Virus Res. 1992;41:241–280.
25. Bellinger-Kawahara C, Diener TO, McKinley MP, et al. Purified scrapie prions resist inactivation by procedures that hydrolyze, modify, or shear nucleic acids. Virology. 1987;160:271–274.
26. Bellinger-Kawahara C, Cleaver JE, Diener TO, et al. Purified scrapie prions resist inactivation by UV irradiation. Virology. 1987;61:159–166.
27. Oesch B, Westaway D, Walchli M, et al. A cellular gene encodes scrapie PrP 27-30 protein. Cell. 1985;40:735–746.
28. Kimberlin RH, Hope J. Genes and genomes in scrapie. Trends Genet. 1987;3:117–118.
29. Kimberlin RH, Walker CA. Scrapie: How much do we really understand? Neuropath Appl Neurobiol. 1986;12:131–147.
30. Bruce ME, Dickinson AG. Biological evidence that scrapie agents has an independent genome. J Gen Virol. 1987;68:79–89.
31. Rohwer RG. The scrapie agent: "A virus by any other name." Curr Top Microbiol Immunol 1991;172:195–232.
32. Narang HK, Asher DM, Gajdusek DC. Evidence that DNA is present in abnormal tubulofilamentous structures found in scrapie. Proc Natl Acad Sci U S A. 1988;85:3575–3579.
33. Chandler RL. Encephalopathy in mice produced by inoculation with scrapie brain material. Lancet. 1961;1:1378–1379.
34. Manuelidis EE, Manuelidis L, Pincus IH, Collins WF. Transmission, from man to hamster, of Creutzfeldt-Jakob disease with clinical recovery (Letter). Lancet. 1978;2:40–42.
35. Prusiner SB, McKinley MP, Bolton DC, et al. Methods for assay, purification and characterization. In: Maramorosch K, Koprowski H, eds. Methods in Virology, v 8). New York: Academic Press; 1984:293–345.
36. Prusiner SB, Groth DF, Cochran SP, et al. Molecular properties, partial purification and assay by incubation time period measurements of the hamster scrapie agent. Biochemistry. 1980;19:4883–4891.
37. Prusiner SB, Cochran SP, Groth DF, et al. Measurement of the scrapie agent using an incubation time interval assay. Ann Neurol. 1982;11:353–358.
38. Lax AJ, Millson GC, Manning EF. Can scrapie titres be calculated accurately from incubation periods? J Gen Virol. 1983;64:971–973.
39. Gabizon R, McKinley MP, Groth D, Prusiner SB. Immunoaffinity purification and neutralization of scrapie prion infectivity. Proc Natl Acad Sci U S A. 1988;85:6617–6621.
40. McKinley MP, Bolton DC, Prusiner SB. A protease-resistant protein is a structural component of the scrapie prion. Cell. 1983;35:57–62.
41. Bolton DC, McKinley MP, Prusiner SB. Molecular characteristics of the major scrapie prion protein. Biochemistry. 1984;23:5898–5905.
42. Meyer RK, McKinley MP, Bowman KA, et al. Separation and properties of cellular and scrapie prion proteins. Proc Natl Acad Sci U S A. 1986;83:2310–2314.
43. Merz PA, Rohwer RG, Kascsak R, et al. Infection-specific particle from the unconventional slow virus diseases. Science. 1984;225:437–440.
44. Prusiner SB, McKinley MP, Bowman KA, et al. Scrapie prions aggregate to form amyloid-like birefringent rods. Cell. 1983;35:349–358.
45. Merz PA, Kascsak R, Rubenstein R, et al. Antisera to scrapie-associated fibril protein and prion protein decorate scrapie-associated fibrils. J Virol. 1987;61:42–49.
46. Merz PA, Somerville RA, Wisniewski HM, et al. Scrapie associated fibrils in Creutzfeldt-Jakob disease. Nature. 1983;306:474–478.
47. Sparkes RS, Simon M, Cohn VH, et al. Assignment of the human and mouse prion protein genes to homologous chromosomes. Proc Natl Acad Sci U S A. 1986;83:7358–7362.
48. Westaway D, Goodman P, Mirenda C, et al. Distinct prion proteins in short and long scrapie incubation period mice. Cell. 1987;51:651–662.
49. Carlson GA, Kingsbury DT, Goodman P, et al. Linkage of prion protein and scrapie incubation time genes. Cell. 1986;46:503–511.
50. Chesebro B, Race R, Wehrly K, et al. Identification of scrapie prion protein–specific mRNA in scrapie-infected and uninfected brain. Nature. 1985;315:331–333.
51. Prusiner SB. Molecular biology of prion diseases. Science. 1991;252:1515–1522.
52. Stahl N, Borchelt DR, Hsiao KK, Prusiner SB. Scrapie prion protein contains a phosphatidylinositol glycolipid. Cell. 1987;51:229–240.
53. Taraboulos A, Raeber AJ, Borchelt DR, Serban D, Prusiner SB. Synthesis and trafficking of prion proteins in cultured cells. Mol Biol Cell. 1992;3:851–863.
54. Bolton DC, Meyer RK, Prusiner SB. Scrapie PrP 27-30 is a sialoglycoprotein. J Virol. 1985;53:596–606.
55. Basler K, Oesch B, Scott M, et al. Scrapie and cellular PrP isoforms are encoded by the same chromosomal gene. Cell. 1986;46:417–428.
56. Hay B, Barry RA, Leberburg I, et al. Biogenesis and transmembrane orientation of the cellular isoform of the scrapie prion protein. Mol Cell Biol. 1987;7:914–920.
57. Borchelt DR, Scott M, Taraboulos A, et al. Scrapie and cellular prion proteins differ in their kinetics of synthesis and topology in cultured cells. J Cell Biol. 1990;110:743–752.
58. Shyng SL, Heuser JE, Harris DA. A glycolipid-anchored prion protein is endocytosed via clathrin-coated pits. J Cell Biol. 1994;125:1239–1250.
59. Shyng SL, Huber MT, Harris DA. A prion protein cycles between the cell surface and an endocytic compartment in cultured neuroblastoma cells. J Biol Chem. 1993;21:15922–15928.
60. Hay B, Prusiner SB, Lingappa VR. Evidence of a secretory form of the cellular prion protein. Biochemistry. 1987;26:8110–8115.
61. Tagliavini F, Prelli F, Porro M, et al. A soluble form of prion protein in human cerebrospinal fluid: Implications for prion-related encephalopathies. Biochem Biophys Res Commun. 1992;184:1398–1404.

62. Borchelt DR, Taraboulos A, Prusiner SB. Evidence for synthesis of scrapie prion proteins in endocytic pathway. J Biol Chem. 1992;267:16188–16199.
63. Vey M, Pikuhn S, Wille H, et al. Subcellular colocalization of the cellular and scrapie prion protein in caveolae-like membranous domains. Proc Natl Acad Sci U S A. 1996;93:14945–14949.
64. Hegde RS, Mastrianni J, Scott M, et al. A transmembrane form of the prion protein in neurodegenerative disease. Science. 1998;279:827–834.
65. Forloni G, Angeretti N, Chiesa R, et al. Neurotoxicity of a prion protein fragment. Nature. 1993;362:543–546.
66. Brown DR, Schmidt B, Kretzschmar HA. Role of microglia and host prion protein in neurotoxicity of a prion protein fragment. Nature. 1996;380:345–347.
67. Brandner S, Isenmann S, Raeber A, et al. Normal host prion protein necessary for scrapie-induced neurotoxicity. Nature. 1996;379:339–343.
68. Taraboulos A, Serban D, Prusiner SB. Scrapie prion proteins accumulate in the cytoplasm of persistently infected cultured cells. J Cell Biol. 1990;110:2117–2132.
69. Rogers M, Yehiely F, Scott M, Prusiner SB. Conversion of truncated and elongated prion proteins into the scrapie isoform in cultured cells. Proc Natl Acad Sci U S A. 1993;90:3182–3186.
70. Kretzschmar HA, Prusiner SB, Stowring LE, DeArmond SJ. Scrapie prion proteins are synthesized in neurons. Am J Pathol. 1986;122:1–5.
71. Harris DA, Falls DL, Johnson FA, Fischbach GD. A prion-like protein from chicken brain copurifies with an acetylcholine receptor–inducing activity. Proc Natl Acad Sci U S A. 1991;88:7664–7668.
72. Harris DA, Lele P, Snider WD. Localization of the mRNA for a chicken prion protein by in situ hydridization. Proc Natl Acad Sci U S A. 1993;90:4309–4313.
73. Falls DL, Rosen KM, Corfas G, et al. ARIA, a protein that stimulates acetylcholine receptor synthesis, is a member of the neu ligand family. Cell. 1993;72:801–815.
74. Bueler H, Fischer M, Lang Y, et al. Normal development and behavior of mice lacking the normal cell surface PrP protein. Nature. 1992;356:577–582.
75. Bueler H, Aguzzi A, Sailer A, et al. Mice devoid of PrP are resistant to scrapie. Cell. 1993;73:1339–1347.
76. Prusiner SB, Groth D, Serban A, et al. Ablation of the prion protein (PrP) gene in mice prevents scrapie and facilitates production of anti-PrP antibodies. Proc Natl Acad Sci U S A. 1993;90:10608–10612.
77. Tobler I, Gaus SE, Deboer T, et al. Altered circadian activity rhythms and sleep in mice devoid of prion protein. Nature. 1996;380:639–642.
78. Sakaguchi S, Katamine S, Nishida N, et al. Loss of cerebellar Purkinje cells in aged mice homozygous for a disrupted PrP gene. Nature. 1996;380:528–531.
79. Westaway D, DeArmond SJ, Cayetano-Canlas J, et al. Degeneration of skeletal muscle, peripheral nerves, and the central nervous system in transgenic mice overexpressing wild-type prion proteins. Cell. 1994;76:117–129.
80. Pan KM, Baldwin M, Nguyen J, et al. Conversion of alpha-helices into beta-sheets features in the formation of the scrapie prion proteins. Proc Natl Acad Sci U S A. 1993;90:10962–10966.
81. Bamborough P, Wille H, Telling GC, et al. Prion protein structure and scrapie replication: Theoretical, spectroscopic, and genetic investigations. Cold Spring Harb Symp Quant Biol. 1996;61:495–509.
82. Riek R, Hornemann S, Wider G, et al. NMR structure of the mouse prion protein domain PrP(121–231). Nature. 1996;382:180–182.
83. Hsiao KK, Scott M, Foster D, et al. Spontaneous neurodegeneration in transgenic mice with mutant prion protein [see comments]. Science. 1990;250:1587–1590.
84. Hsiao KK, Groth D, Scott M, et al. Serial transmission in rodents of neurodegeneration from transgenic mice expressing mutant prion protein. Proc Natl Acad Sci U S A. 1994;91:9126–9130.
85. Telling GC, Haga T, Torchia M, et al. Interactions between wild-type and mutant prion proteins modulate neurodegeneration in transgenic mice. Genes Dev 1996;10:1736–1750.
86. Muramoto T, DeArmond SJ, Scott M, et al. Heritable disorder resembling neuronal storage disease in mice expressing prion protein with deletion of an alpha-helix. Nature Med. 1997;3:750–755.
87. Telling GC, Scott M, Mastrianni J, et al. Prion propagation in mice expressing human and chimeric PrP transgenes implicates the interaction of cellular PrP with another protein. Cell. 1995;83:79–90.
88. Kaneko K, Zulianello L, Scott M, et al. Evidence for protein X binding to a discontinous epitope on the cellular prion protein during scrapie prion propagation. Proc Natl Acad Sci U S A. 1997;94:10069–10074.
89. Kaneko K, Vey M, Scott M, et al. COOH-terminal sequence of the cellular prion protein directs subcellular trafficking and controls conversion into the scrapie isoform. Proc Natl Acad Sci U S A. 1997;94:2333–2338.
90. Peretz D, Williamson RA, Matsunaga Y, et al. A conformational transition at the N terminus of the prion protein features in formation of the scrapie isoform. J Mol Biol. 1997;273:614–622.
91. Kocisco DA, Lansbury PT, Caughey B. Partial unfolding and refolding of scrapie-associated prion protein: Evidence for a critical 16-kDa C-terminal domain. Biochemistry. 1996;35:13434–13442.
92. Holscher C, Delius H, Burkle A. Overexpression of the nonconvertible PrPC D114–121 in scrapie-infected mouse neuroblastoma cells leads to *trans*-dominant inhibition of wild-type PrPSc accumulation. J Virol. 1998;72:1153–1159.
93. Prusiner SB, Scott M, Foster M, et al. Transgenetic studies implicate interaction between homologous PrP isoforms in scrapie prion replication. Cell. 1990;63:673–686.
94. Scott M, Groth D, Foster D, et al. Propagation of prions with artificial properties in transgenic mice expressing chimeric PrP genes. Cell. 1993;73:979–988.
95. Weissmann C. A 'unified theory' of prion propagation. Nature. 1991;352:679–683.
96. Kimberlin RH, Walker CA. Pathogenesis of mouse scrapie: Evidence for neural spread of infection to the CNS. J Gen Virol. 1980;51:183–187.
97. Fraser H. Neuronal spread of scrapie agent and targeting of lesions within the retino-tectal pathway. Nature. 1982;295:149.
99. Gajdusek DC. Hypothesis: Interference with axonal transport of neurofilament as a common pathogenic mechanism in certain diseases of the central nervous system. N Engl J Med. 1985;312:714–719.
100. Kimberlin RH, Hall S, Walker C. Pathogenesis of mouse scrapie: Evidence for direct neural spread of infection to the CNS after injection of the sciatic nerve. J Neurol Sci. 1983;61:315–325.
101. Taraboulos A, Jendroska K, Serban D, et al. Regional mapping of prion proteins in brain. Proc Natl Acad Sci U S A. 1992;89:7620–7624.
102. DeArmond SJ, Yang SL, Lee A, et al. Three scrapie prion isolates exhibit different accumulation patterns of the prion protein scrapie isoform. Proc Natl Acad Sci U S A. 1993;90:6449–6453.
103. Beekes M, McBride PA, Baldauf E. Cerebral targeting indicates vagal spread of infection in hamsters fed with scrapie. J Gen Virol. 1998;79:601–607.
104. Klein MA, Frigg R, Flechsig E, et al. A crucial role for B cells in neuroinvasive scrapie. Nature. 1997;390:687–690.
105. Zigas V. Laughing Death. The Untold Story of Kuru. Clifton, NJ: Humana Press; 1990.
106. Zigas V, Gajdusek DC. Kuru: Clinical study of a new syndrome resembling paralysis agitans in natives of the Eastern Highlands of Australian New Guinea. Med J Aust. 1957;2:745–754.
107. Gajdusek DC, Gibbs CJ Jr, Alpers MP. Experimental transmission of a kuru syndrome to chimpanzees. Nature. 1966;209:794–796.
108. Gajdusek DC, Zigas V. Degenerative disease of the central nervous system in New Guinea. The endemic occurrence of "kuru" in the native population. N Engl J Med. 1957;257:974–978.
109. Gajdusek DC, Zigas V. Clinical, pathological and epidemiological study of an acute progressive degenerative disease of the central nervous system among natives of the Eastern Highlands of New Guinea. Am J Med. 1959;26:442–469.
110. Scrimgeour EM, Masters CL, Alpers MP, et al. A clinico-pathologic study of a case of kuru. J Neurol Sci. 1983;59:265–275.
111. Hornabrook RW. Kuru: A subacute cerebellar degeneration—the natural history and clinical features. Brain. 1968;91:53–74.
112. Klatzo I, Gajdusek DC, Zigas V. Pathology of kuru. Lab Invest. 1959;8:799–847.
113. Alpers MP. Epidemiology and ecology of kuru. In: Prusiner SB, Hadlow WJ, eds. Slow Transmissible Diseases of the Nervous System. New York: Academic Press; 1979:67–90.
114. Cobb WA, Hornabrook RW, Sanders S. The EEG of kuru. Electroencephalogr Clin Neurophysiol. 1973;34:419–427.
115. Kuru: Forty years later, a historical note. Brain Pathol. 1997;7:555–560.
116. Hainfellner JA, Liberski PP, Guiroy DC, et al. Pathology and immunocytochemistry of a kuru brain. Brain Pathol. 1997;7:547–553.
117. Guiroy DC, Wakayama I, Liberski PP, Gajdusek DC. Relationship of microglia and scrapie amyloid-immunoreactive plaques in kuru, Creutzfeldt-Jakob disease and Gerstmann-Straüssler syndrome. Acta Neuropathol. 1994;87:526–530.
118. Brown P, Cathala F, Rabertas RB, et al. The epidemiology of Creutzfeldt-Jakob disease. Conclusions of a 15 year investigation in France and review of the world literature. Neurology. 1987;37:895–909.
119. Packer RJ, Cornblath DR, Gonatas NK, et al. Creutzfeldt-Jakob disease in a 20-year-old women. Neurology. 1980;30:492–496.
120. Monreal J, Collins GH, Masters CL, et al. Creutzfeldt-Jakob disease in an adolescent. J Neurol Sci. 1981;52:341–350.
121. de Silva R, Findlay C, et al. Creutzfeldt-Jakob disease in the elderly. Postgrad Med J 1997;73:557–559.
122. Brown P. Iatrogenic Creutzfeldt-Jakob disease. Aust N Z J Med. 1990;20:633–635.
123. Brown P, Preece MA, Will RG. "Friendly fire" in medicine: Hormones, homografts, and Creutzfeldt-Jakob disease. Lancet. 1992;340:24–27.
124. Thadani V, Penar PL, Partington J, et al. Creutzfeldt-Jakob disease probably acquired from a cadaveric dural graft. J Neurosurg. 1988;69:766–769.
125. Nisbet TJ, MacDonaldson I, Bishara SN. Creutzfeldt-Jakob disease in a second patient who received a cadaveric dura mater graft. JAMA. 1989;261:1118.
126. Masullo C, Pocchiari M, Macchi G, et al. Transmission of Creutzfeldt-Jakob disease by dural cadaveric graft (Letter). J Neurosurg. 1989;71:954–955.
127. Willison HJ, Gale AN, McLaughlin JE. Creutzfeldt-Jakob disease following cadaveric dura mater graft (Letter). J Neurol Neurosurg Psychiatry. 1991;54:940.
128. Harvey I, Coyle E. Creutzfeldt-Jakob disease after non-commercial dura mater graft (Letter). Lancet. 1992;340:615.
129. Pocchiari M, Masullo C, Salvatore M, et al. Creutzfeldt-Jakob disease after non-commercial dura mater graft (Letter). Lancet. 1992;340:614–615.
130. Weber T, Tumani H, Holdorff B, et al. Transmission of Creutzfeldt-Jakob disease by handling of dura mater graft (Letter). Lancet. 1993;341:123–124.
131. Miyashita K, Inuzuka T, Kondo H, et al. Creutzfeldt-Jakob disease in a patient with a cadaveric dural graft. Neurology. 1991;41:940–941.
132. Creutzfeldt-Jakob disease associated with cadaveric dura mater grafts—Japan, January 1979–May 1996. MMWR Morb Mortal Wkly Rep. 1998;46:1066–1069.
133. Duffy P, Wolf J, Collins G, et al. Possible person to person transmission of Creutzfeldt-Jakob disease (Letter). N Engl J Med. 1974;290:692–693.
134. Allan B, Tuft S. Transmission of Creutzfeldt-Jakob disease in corneal grafts. BMJ. 1997;315:1553–1554.
135. Heckmann JG, Lang CJ, Petruch F, et al. Transmission of Creutzfeldt-Jakob disease via a corneal transplant. J Neurol Neurosurg Psychiatry. 1997;63:388–390.

136. Creange A, Gray F, Cesaro P, et al. Creutzfeldt-Jakob disease after liver transplantation. Ann Neurol. 1995:38:269–272.
137. Antoine JC, Michel D, Bertholon P, et al. Creutzfeldt-Jakob disease after extracranial dura mater embolization for nasopharyngeal angiofibroma. Neurology. 1997;48:1451–1453.
138. Defebvre L, Destee A, Caron J, et al. Creutzfeldt-Jakob disease after embolization of intercostal arteries with cadaveric dura mater suggesting a systemic transmission of the prion agent. Neurology. 1997;48:1470–1471.
139. Will RG, Matthews WB. Evidence for case-to-case transmission of Creutzfeldt-Jakob disease. J Neurol Neurosurg Psychiatry. 1982;45:235–238.
140. Nevin S, McMenemy WH, Behrman S, Jones DP. Subacute spongiform encephalopathy—a subacute form of enceophalopathy attributable to vascular dysfunction (spongiform cerebral atrophy). Brain. 1960;83:519–564.
141. Jones DP, Nevin S. Rapidly progressive cerebral degeneration (subacute vascular encephalopathy) with mental disorder, focal disturbances, and myoclonic epilepsy. J Neurol Neurosurg Psychiatry. 1954;17:148–159.
142. Gibbs CJ Jr, Joy A, Heffner R, et al. Clinical and pathological features and laboratory confirmation of Creutzfeldt-Jakob disease in a recipient of pituitary derived human growth hormone. N Engl J Med. 1985;313:734–738.
143. Brown P, Gajdusek DC, Gibbs CJ Jr, Asher DM. Potential epidemic of Creutzfeldt-Jakob disease from human growth hormone therapy. N Engl J Med. 1985;313:728–731.
144. Brown P. The decline and fall of Creutzfeldt-Jakob disease associated with human growth hormone therapy. Neurology. 1988;38:1135–1137.
145. Ellis CJ, Katifi H, Weller RO. A further British case of growth hormone induced Creutzfeldt-Jakob disease. J Neurol Neurosurg Psychiatry. 1992;55:1200–1202.
146. Gibbs CJjr, Asher DM, Brown PW, et al. Creutzfeldt-Jakob disease infectivity of growth hormone derived from human pituitary glands (Letter). N Engl J Med. 1993;328:358–359.
147. Markus HS, Duchen LW, Parkin EM, et al. Creutzfeldt-Jakob disease in recipients of human growth hormone in the United Kingdom: A clinical and radiographic study. Q J Med. 1992;82:43–51.
148. Frasier SD. The not-so-good old days: Working with pituitary growth hormone in North America, 1956 to 1985. J Pediatr. 1997;131:S1–S4.
149. Villemeur TB, Deslys J-P, Pradel A, et al. Creutzfeldt-Jakob disease from contaminated growth hormone extracts in France. Neurology. 1996;47:690–695.
150. Cochius JI, Hyman N, Esiri MM. Creutzfeldt-Jakob disease in a recipient of human pituitary-derived gonadotrophin: A second case. J Neurol Neurosurg Psychiatry. 1992;55:1094–1095.
151. Dumble JL, Klein RD. Creutzfeldt-Jakob legacy for Australian women treated with human pituitary gonadotrophins (Letter). Lancet. 1992;340:847–878.
152. Manuelidis EE, Kim JH, Mericangas JR, Manuelidis L. Transmission to animals of Creutzfeldt-Jakob disease from human blood. Lancet. 1985;2:896–897.
153. Manuelidis EE, Gorgacs EJ, Manuelidis L. Viremia in experimental Creutzfeldt-Jakob disease. Science. 1978;200:1069–1071.
154. Ricketts MN. Is Creutzfeldt-Jakob disease transmitted in the blood? Is the absence of evidence of risk evidence of the absence of risk? CMAJ. 1997;157:1389–1392.
155. Brown P. Can Creutzfeldt-Jakob disease be transmitted by transfusion? Curr Opin Hematol. 1995;2:472–477.
156. Wientjens DPWM, Davinipour Z, Hofman A, et al. Risk factors for Creutzfeldt-Jakob disease: A reanalysis of case-controlled studies. Neurol. 1996;46:1287–1291.
156a. Collins S, Law MG, Fletcher A, et al. Surgical treatment and risk of sporadic Creutzfeldt-Jakob disease: A case-control study. Lancet. 1999;353:693–697.
157. Berger JR, David NJ. Creutzfeldt-Jakob disease in a physician: A review of the disorder in health care workers. Neurology. 1993;43:205–206.
158. Masters CL, Harris JO, Gajdusek DC, et al. Creutzfeldt-Jakob disease: Patterns of worldwide occurrence and significance of familial and sporadic clustering. Ann Neurol. 1979;5:177–188.
159. Schoene WC, Masters CL, Gibbs CJ Jr, et al. Transmissible spongiform encephalopathy (Creutzfeldt-Jakob disease): Atypical clinical and pathological findings. Arch Neurol. 1981;38:473–477.
160. Gorman DG, Benson DF, Vogel DG, Vinters HV. Creutzfeldt-Jakob disease in a pathologist (Letter). Neurol. 1992;42:463.
161. Sitwell L, Lach B, Atack E, et al. Creutzfeldt-Jakob disease in a histopathology technician (Letter). N Engl J Med. 1988;31:854.
162. Miller DC. Creutzfeldt-Jakob disease in histopathology technicians (Letter). N Engl J Med. 1988;318:853–854.
163. Berger JR, Weisman E, Weisman B. Creutzfeldt-Jakob disease and eating squirrel brains. Lancet. 1997;350:642.
164. Creutzfeldt HG. Über eine eigenartige herdformige Erkrankung des Zentralnervensystems (Vorlaufuge Mitteilung). Z ges Neurol Psychiat. 1920;57:1–18.
165. Creutzfeldt HG. On a particular focal disease of the central nervous system (preliminary communcation). In: Rottenberg DA, Hochberg FH, eds. Neurological Classics in Modern Translation. New York: Hafner; 1977:97–112.
166. Jakob A. Über eigenartige Erkrankungen des Zentralnervensystems mit bemerkenswetem anatomischen Befunde (spastiche Pseudosklerose-Encephalomyelopathie mit disseminierten Degenerationsherden). Deutsch Z Nervenheilk. 1921;70:132–146.
167. Gertz H-J, Henkes H, Cerros-Navarro J. Creutzfeldt-Jakob disease: Correlation of MRI and neuropathological findings. Neurology. 1988;38:1481–1482.
168. Heidenhain A. Klinische und anatomische Untersuchungen über eine eigenartige Erkrankung des Zentralnervensystems im Praesenium. Zeitschrift für die gesamte Neurologie und Psychiatrie. 1929;118:49–114.
169. Brownell B, Oppenheimer DR. An ataxic form of subacute presenile polioencephalopathy (Creutzfeldt-Jakob disease). J Neurol Neurosurg Psychiatry. 1965;28:350–361.
170. Stern K. Severe dementia associated with bilateral symmetrical degeneration of the thalamus. Brain. 1939;62:157–171.
171. Garcin R, Brion S, Khochneviss AA. Le syndrome de Creutzfeldt-Jakob et les syndromes corticostries du presenium (a l'occasion de 5 observations anatomo-cliniques). Rev Neurol (Paris). 1963;109:419–441.
172. Kirschbaum WR. Jakob-Creutzfeldt Disease. New York: Elsevier; 1968.
173. Brown P, Cathala F, Castaigne P, Gajdusek DC. Creutzfeldt-Jakob disease: Clinical analysis of a consecutive series of 230 neuropathologically verified cases. Ann Neurol. 1986;20:597–602.
174. Cathala F, Baron H. Clinical aspects of Creutzfeldt-Jakob disease. In: Prusiner SB, McKinley MP, eds. Prions: Novel Infectious Pathogens Causing Scrapie and Creutzfeldt-Jakob Disease. Orlando: Academic Press; 1987:467–509.
175. Brown P, Rodgers-Johnson P, Cathala F, et al. Creutzfeldt-Jakob disease of long duration: Clinicopathological characteristics, transmissibility, and differential diagnosis. Ann Neurol. 1984;16:295–304.
176. MacGowan DJ, Delanty N, Petito F, et al. Isolated myoclonic alien hand as the sole presentation of pathologically established Creutzfeldt-Jakob disease: A report of two patients. J Neurol Neurosurg Psychiatry. 1997;63:404–407.
177. Guiroy DC, Shankar SK, Gibbs CJ, et al. Neuronal degeneration in the trigeminal ganglia in Creutzfeldt-Jakob disease. Ann Neurol. 1989;25:102–106.
178. Antoine JC, Laplanche JL, Mosnier JF, et al. Demyelinating peripheral neuropathy with Creutzfeldt-Jakob disease and mutation at codon 200 of the prion protein gene. Neurol. 1996;46:1123–1127.
179. Esiri MM, Gordon WI, Collinge J, Patten JS. Peripheral neuropathy in Creutzfeldt-Jakob disease. Neurology. 1997;48:784.
180. Nomura E, Harada T, Kurokawa K, et al. Creutzfeldt-Jakob disease associated with autonomic nervous system dysfunction in the early stage. Intern Med. 1997;36:492–496.
181. Salazar AM, Masters CL, Gajdusek DC, Gibbs CJ Jr. Syndromes of amyotrophic lateral sclerosis and dementia: Relation to transmissible Creutzfeldt-Jakob disease. Ann Neurol. 1983;14:17–26.
182. Gibbs CJ Jr, Gajdusek DC, Asher DM, et al. Creutzfeldt-Jakob disease (spongiform encephalopathy): Transmission to chimpanzee. Science. 1968;161:388–389.
183. Roos R, Gajdusek DC, Gibbs CJ Jr. The clinical characteristics of transmissible Creutzfeldt-Jakob disease. Brain. 1973;96:1–20.
184. Tanaka M, Iizuko O, Yuasa T. Hepatic dysfunction in Creutzfeldt-Jakob disease. Neurology. 1992;42:1249.
185. Otto M, Wiltfang J, Schutz E, et al. Diagnosis of Creutzfeldt-Jakob disease by measurement of S100 protein in serum: Prospective case-control study. BMJ. 1998;316:577–582.
186. Blisard KS, Davis LE, Harrington MG, et al. Pre-mortem diagnosis of Creutzfeldt-Jakob disease by detection of abnormal cerebrospinal fluid proteins. J Neurol Sci. 1990;99:75–81.
187. Harrington MG, Merril CR, Asher DM, Gajdusek DC. Abnormal proteins in the cerebrospinal fluid of patients with Creutzfeldt-Jakob disease. N Engl J Med. 1986;315:279–283.
188. Zerr I, Bodemer M, Otto M, et al. Diagnosis of Creutzfeldt-Jakob disease by two-dimensional electrophoresis of cerebrospinal fluid. Lancet. 1996;348:846–849.
189. Hsich G, Kenney K, Gibbs CJ, et al. The 14-3-3 brain protein in cerebrospinal fluid as a marker for transmissible spongiform encephalopathies. N Engl J Med. 1996;335:924–930.
190. Zerr I, Bodemer M, Gefeller O, et al. Detection of 14-3-3 protein in the cerebrospinal fluid supports the diagnosis of Creutzfeldt-Jakob disease. Ann Neurol. 1998;43:32–40.
191. Roseman H, Meiner Z, Kahana E, et al. Detection of 14-3-3 protein in the CSF of genetic Creutzfeldt-Jakob disease. Neurol. 1997;49:593–595.
192. Jimi T, Wakayama Y, Shibuya S, et al. High levels of nervous system–specific proteins in cerebrospinal fluid in patients with early stage Creutzfeldt-Jakob disease. Clin Chim Acta. 1992;21:37–46.
193. Manaka H, Kato T, Kurita K, et al. Marked increase in cerebrospinal fluid ubiquitin in Creutzfeldt-Jakob disease. Neurosci Lett. 1992;139:47–49.
194. Weber T, Otto M, Bodemer M, Zerr I. Diagnosis of Creutzfeldt-Jakob disease and related human spongiform encephalopathies. Biomed Pharmacother 1997;51:381–387.
195. Otto M, Stein H, Szudra A, et al. S-100 protein concentration in the cerebrospinal fluid of patients with Creutzfeldt-Jakob disease. J Neurol. 1997;244:566–570.
196. Otto M, Wiltfang J, Tumani H, et al. Elevated levels of tau-protein in the cerebrospinal fluid of patients with Creutzfeldt-Jakob disease. Neurosci Lett. 1997;225:210–212.
197. Galvez S, Cartier L. Computed tomographic findings in 15 cases of Creutzfeldt-Jakob disease with histological verification. J Neurol Neurosurg Psychiatry. 1984;47:1244–1246.
198. Berciano J, Diez C, Polo JM, et al. CT appearance of panencephalopathic and ataxic type of Creutzfeldt-Jakob disease. J Comput Assit Tomogr. 1991;15:332–334.
199. Hayashi R, Hanyu N, Kuwabara T, Moriyama S. Serial computed tomographic and electroencephalographic studies in Creutzfeldt-Jakob disease. Acta Neurol Scand. 1992;85:161–165.
200. Schelnska GK, Walter GF. Serial computed tomography findings in Creutzfeldt-Jakob disease. Neuroradiology. 1989;31:303–306.
201. Kovanen J, Erkinjuntti T, Livanainen M, et al. Cerebral MR and CT imaging in Creutzfeldt-Jakob disease. J Comp Assist Tomogr. 1985;9:125–128.

202. Milton WJ, Atlas SW, Lavi E, Mollman JE. Magnetic resonance imaging of Creutzfeldt-Jakob disease. Ann Neurol. 1991;29:438–440.
203. Rother J, Schwartz A, Harle M, Wentz KU, Berlit P, Hennerici M. Magnetic resonance imaging follow-up in Creutzfeldt-Jakob disease. J Neurol. 1992;239:404–406.
204. Esmonde TFG, Will RG. Magnetic resonance imaging in Creutzfeldt-Jakob disease (Letter). Ann Neurol. 1992;31:230–231.
205. Johns DW, Drazkowski JF, Drayer BP, Lieberman AN. Appearance of striatal signal hyperintensity on MRI preceding classic symptoms in ataxic Creutzfeldt-Jakob disease: Case report. Barrow Neurol Inst Q. 1993;9:14–17.
206. Yamamoto K, Morimatsu M. Increased signal in basal ganglia and white matter on magnetic resonance imaging in Creutzfeldt-Jakob disease. Ann Neurol. 1992;32:114.
207. Finkenstaedt M, Szudra A, Zerr I, et al. MR imaging of Creutzfeldt-Jakob disease. Radiology. 1996;199:793–798.
208. Bahn MM, Kido DK, Lin W, Pearlman AL. Brain magnetic resonance diffusion abnormalities in Creutzfeldt-Jakob disease. Arch Neurol. 1997;54:1411–1415.
209. Zeidler M, Will RG, Ironside JW, et al. Magnetic resonance imaging is not a sensitive test for Creutzfeldt-Jakob disease. BMJ. 1996;312:844.
210. Falcone S, Quencer RM, Bowen B, et al. Creutzfeldt-Jakob disease: Focal symmetrical cortical involvement demonstrated by MR imaging. AJNR Am J Neuroradiol. 1992;13:403–406.
211. Demaerel P, Baert AL, Vanopdenbosch L, Dom R. Diffusion-weighted magnetic resonance imaging in Creutzfeldt-Jakob disease. Lancet. 1997;349:847–848.
212. Holthoff VA, Sandmann J, Pawlik G, et al. Positron emission tomography in Creutzfeldt-Jakob disease. Arch Neurol. 1990;47:1035–1038.
213. Grunwald F, Pohl C, Bender H, et al. 18F-deoxyglucose PET and ^{99m}Tc-bicisate-SPECT in Creutzfeldt-Jakob disease. Ann Nucl Med. 1996;10:131–134.
214. Watanabe N, Seto H, Shimuzu M, et al. Brain SPECT of Creutzfeldt-Jakob disease. Clin Nucl Med 1996;21:236–241.
215. Levy RS, Chiappa KH. Clinical neurophysiology. In: Bastian FO, ed. Creutzfeldt-Jakob Disease and Other Transmissible Spongiform Encephalopathies. St. Louis: Mosby; 1991:185–202.
216. Levy RS, Chiappa KH, Burke CJ, Young RR. Early evolution and incidence of electroencephalographic abnormalities in Creutzfeldt-Jakob disease. J Clin Neurophysiol. 1986;3:1–21.
217. Aguglia U, Farnarier G, Tinuper P, et al. Subacute spongiform encephalopathy with periodic paroxysmal activities: Clinical evolution and serial EEG findings in 20 cases. Clin Electroencephalogr. 1987;18:147–158.
218. Chiofalo N, Fuentes A, Galvez S. Serial EEG findings in 27 cases of Creutzfeldt-Jakob disease. Arch Neurol. 1980;37:143–145.
219. Burger LJ, Rowan AJ, Goldensohn ES. Creutzfeldt-Jakob disease. An electroencephalographic study. Arch Neurol. 1972;26:428–433.
220. Steinhoff BJ, Racker S, Herrendorf G, et al. Accuracy and reliability of periodic sharp wave complexes in Creutzfeldt-Jakob disease. Arch Neurol. 1996;53:162–166.
221. Traub RD, Pedley TA. Virus induced electrotonic coupling: Hypothesis on the mechanism of periodic EEG discharges in Creutzfeldt-Jakob disease. Ann Neurol. 1981;10:405–410.
222. Elliott F, Gardner-Thorpe C, Barwick DD, Foster JB. Jakob-Creutzfeldt disease: Modification of clinical and electroencephalographic activity with methylphenidate and diazepam. J Neurol Neurosurg Psychiatry. 1974;37:879–887.
223. Donnet A, Farnarier G, Gambarelli D, et al. Sleep electroencephalogram at the early stage of Creutzfeldt-Jakob disease. Clin Electroencephalogr. 1992;23:118–125.
224. Tietjen GE, Drury I. Familial Creutzfeldt-Jakob disease without periodic EEG activity. Ann Neurol. 1990;28:585–588.
225. Brown P, Jannotta F, Gibbs CJ Jr, et al. Coexistence of Creutzfeldt-Jakob disease and Alzheimer's disease in the same patient. Neurology. 1990;40:226–228.
226. Muramoto T, Kitamoto T, Koga H, Tateishi J. The coexistence of Alzheimer's disease and Creutzfeldt-Jakob disease in a patient with dementia of long duration. Acta Neuropathol. 1992;84:686–689.
227. Barry RA, Prusiner SB. Monoclonal antibodies to the cellular and scrapie prion proteins. J Infect Dis. 1986;154:518–521.
228. Bendheim PE, Barry RA, DeArmond SJ, et al. Antibodies to a scrapie prion protein. Nature. 1984;310:418–421.
229. Castellani R, Parchi P, Madoff L, et al. Biopsy diagnosis of Creutzfeldt-Jakob disease by Western blot: A case report. Brain Pathol. 1997;28:623–626.
230. Bockman JM, Kingsbury DT, McKinley MP, et al. Creutzfeldt-Jakob disease prion proteins in human brains. N Engl J Med. 1985;312:73–78.
231. Brown P, Coker-Vann M, Pomeroy K, et al. Diagnosis of Creutzfeldt-Jakob disease by Western blot identification of a marker protein in human brain tissue. N Engl J Med. 1986;314:547–551.
232. Kitamoto T, Doh-ura K, Muramoto T, et al. The primary structure of the prion protein influences the distribution of abnormal prion protein in the central nervous system. Am J Pathol. 1992;141:271–277.
233. Budka H, Aguzzi A, Brown P, et al. Neuropathological diagnostic criteria for Creutzfeldt-Jakob disease (CJD) and other human spongiform encephalopathies (prion diseases). Brain Pathol. 1995;5:459–466.
234. Kretzschmar H, Ironside J, DeArmond SJ, Tateishi J. Diagnostic criteria for sporadic Creutzfeldt-Jakob disease. Arch Neurol. 1996;53:913–920.
235. Goldfarb LG, Brown P, Goldgaber D, et al. Creutzfeldt-Jakob disease and kuru patients lack a mutation consistently found in the Gerstmann-Straüssler-Scheinker syndrome. Exp Neurol. 1990;108:247–250.
236. Hitoshi S, Nagura H, Yamagouchi H, Kitamoto T. Double mutations at codon 180 and codon 232 of the PrP gene in an apparently sporadic case of Creutzfeldt-Jakob disease. J Neurol Sci. 1993;93:208–212.
237. Palmer MS, Dryden AJ, Hughes JT, Collinge J. Homozygous prion protein genotype predisposes to sporadic Creutzfeldt-Jakob disease (Letter). Nature. 1991;352:340–342.
238. Collinge J, Palmer MS, Dryden AJ. Genetic predisposition to iatrogenic Creutzfeldt-Jakob disease. Lancet. 1991;337:1441–1442.
239. Brown P. The phenotypic expression of different mutations in transmissible human spongiform encephalopathy. Rev Neurol (Paris). 1992;148:317–327.
240. Collinge J. Inherited prion diseases. Adv Neurol. 1993;61:155–165.
241. Hsiao KK, Meiner Z, Kahana E, et al. Mutation of the prion protein in Libyan Jews with Creutzfeldt-Jakob disease. N Engl J Med. 1991;324:1091–1097.
242. Brown P, Galvez S, Goldfarb LG, et al. Familial Creutzfeldt-Jakob disease in Chile associated with the codon 200 mutation of the PRNP amyloid precursor gene on chromosome 20. J Neurol Sci. 1992;112:65–67.
243. Goldfarb LG, Mitrova E, Brown P, et al. Mutation in codon 200 of scrapie amyloid protein in two clusters of Creutzfeldt-Jakob disease in Slovakia (Letter). Lancet. 1990;336:514–515.
244. Goldfarb LG, Korczyn AD, Brown P, et al. Mutation in codon 200 of scrapie amyloid precursor gene linked to Creutzfeldt-Jakob disease in Sephardic Jews of Libyan and non-Libyan origin (Letter). Lancet. 1990;336:637–638.
245. Meiner Z, Gabizon R, Prusiner SB. Familial Creutzfeldt-Jakob disease. Codon 200 prion disease in Libyan Jews. Medicine. 1997;76:227–237.
246. Bertoni JM, Brown P, Goldfarb LG, et al. Familial Creutzfeldt-Jakob disease (codon 200 mutation) with supranuclear palsy. J Am Med Assoc. 1992;268:2413–2415.
247. Goldfarb LG, Brown P, Haltia M, et al. Creutzfeldt-Jakob disease cosegregates with codon 178 Asn PRNP mutation in families of European origin. Ann Neurol. 1992;31:274–281.
248. Goldfarb LG, Haltia M, Brown P, et al. New mutation in scrapie amyloid precursor gene (at codon 178) in Finnish Creutzfeldt-Jakob disease kindred (Letter). Lancet. 1991;337:425.
249. Brown P, Goldfarb LG, Kovanen J, et al. Phenotypic characteristics of familial Creutzfeldt-Jakob disease associated with the codon 178 Asn PRNP mutation. Ann Neurol. 1992;31:282–285.
250. Brown P, Goldfarb LG, McCombie WR, et al. Atpyical Creutzfeldt-Jakob disease in an American family with an insert mutation in the PRNP amyloid precursor gene. Neurology. 1992;42:422–427.
251. Collinge J, Brown J, Hardy J, et al. Inherited prion disease with a 144 base pair gene insertion. 2. Clinical and pathological features. Brain. 1992;115:687–710.
252. Britton TC, Al-Sarraj S, Shaw C, et al. Sporadic Creutzfeldt-Jakob disease in 1 16-year-old in the UK. Lancet. 1995;346:1155.
253. Will RG, Ironside JW, Zeidler M, et al. A new variant of Creutzfeldt-Jakob disease in the UK. Lancet. 1996;347:921–925.
254. Zeidler M, Stewart GE, Barraclough CR, et al. New variant Creutzfeldt-Jakob disease: Neurological features and diagnostic tests. Lancet. 1997;350:903–907.
255. Chazot G, Broussolle E, Lapras CL, et al. New variant Creutzfeldt-Jakob disease in a 26-year-old French man. Lancet. 1996;347:1181.
256. Delys J-P, Lasmezas CI, Streichenberger N, et al. New variant Creutzfeldt-Jakob disease in France. Lancet. 1997;349:30–31.
257. Schonberger L. New variant Creutzfeldt-Jakob disease and bovine spongiform encephalopathy. Infect Dis Clin North Am. 1998;12:111–121.
258. Zeidler M, Johnstone EC, Bamber RWK, et al. New variant Creutzfeldt-Jakob disease: Psychiatric features. Lancet. 1997;350:908–910.
259. deSilva, R, Patterson J, Hadley D, et al. Single photon emission computed tomography in the identification of new variant Creutzfeldt-Jakob disease: Case reports. BMJ. 1998;316:593–594.
260. Collinge J, Sidle KCL, Meads J, et al. Molecular analysis of prion strain variation and the aetiology of 'new variant' CJD. Nature. 1996;383:685–690.
261. Parchi P, Capellari S, Chen SG, et al. Typing prion isoforms. Nature. 1997;386:232.
262. Bruce ME, Will RG, Ironside JW, et al. Transmissions to mice indicate that 'new variant' CJD is caused by BSE agent. Nature. 1997;389:498–501.
263. Hill AF, Desbruslais M, Joiner S, et al. The same prion strain causes vCJD and BSE. Nature. 1997;389:448–450.
264. Lasmezas CI, Deslys J-P, Demalmay R, et al. BSE transmission to macaques. Nature. 1996;381:743–744.
265. Collee JG, Bradley R. BSE: A decade on—part 2. Lancet. 1997;349:715–721.
266. Collee JG, Bradley R. BSE: A decade on—part 1. Lancet. 1997;349:636–641.
267. Anderson RM, Donnelly CA, Ferguson NM, et al. Transmission dynamics and epidemiology of BSE in British cattle. Nature. 1996;382:779.
268. Nathanson N, Wilesmith J, Griot C. Bovine spongiform encephalopathy (BSE): Causes and consequences of a common source epidemic. Am J Epidemiol. 1997;145:959.
269. Kimberlin RH, Walker CA. Pathogenesis of scrapie in mice after intragastric infection. Virus Res. 1989;12:213–220.
270. Collinge J, Palmer MS, Sidle KCL, et al. Unaltered susceptibility to BSE in transgenic mice expressing human prion protein. Nature. 1995;378:779–783.
271. Raymond GJ, Hope J, Kocisko DA, et al. Molecular assessment of the potential transmissibilities of BSE and scrapie to humans. Nature. 1997;388:285–288.
272. Tyler KL. Risk of human exposure to bovine spongiform encephalopathy. Br Med J. 1995;311:1420–1421.
273. Hill AF, Zeidler M, Ironside J, Collinge J. Diagnosis of new variant Creutzfeldt-Jakob disease by tonsil biopsy. Lancet. 1997;349:99–100.
274. Kawashima T, Furukawa H, Doh-ura K, Iwaki T. Diagnosis of new variant Creutzfeldt-Jakob disease by tonsil biopsy. Lancet. 1997;350:68–69.

274a. Hill AF, Butterworth RJ, Joiner S, et al. Investigation of variant Cruetzfeldt-Jakob disease and other human prion diseases with tonsil biopsy samples. Lancet. 1999;353:183–189.

275. Brown P, Goldfarb LG, Brown WT, et al. Clinical and molecular genetic study of a large German kindred with Gerstmann-Sträussler-Scheinker syndrome. Neurology. 1991;41:375–379.

276. Farlow MR, Yee Rd, Dlouhy SR, et al. Gerstmann-Straüssler-Scheinker disease. I. Extending the clinical spectrum. Neurology. 1989;39:1446–1452.

277. Kuzuhara S, Kanazawa I, Sasaki H, et al. Gerstmann-Straüssler-Scheinker's disease. Ann Neurol. 1983;14:216–225.

278. Ghetti B, Dlouhy SR, Giaccone G, et al. Gerstmann-Straüssler-Scheinker disease and the Indiana kindred. Brain Pathol. 1995;5:61–75.

279. Unverzagt FW, Farlow MR, Norton J, et al. Neuropsychological function in patients with Gerstmann-Straüssler-Scheinker disease from the Indiana kindred (F198S). J Int Neuropsychol Soc 1997;3:169–178.

280. Lyketsos CG, Kraus M. The dementia of Gerstmann-Straüssler-Scheinker syndrome: Clinical variability demonstrated by two case reports. J Neuropsychiat Clin Neurosci 1995;7:239–242.

281. Itoh Y, Yamada M, Hayakawa M, et al. A variant of Gerstmann-Straüssler-Scheinker disease carrying codon 105 mutation with codon 129 polymorphism of the prion protein gene: A clinicopathological study. J Neurol Sci. 1994;127:77–86.

282. Wimberger D, Uranitsch K, Schindler E, Kramer J. Gerstmann-Straüssler-Scheinker syndrome: MR findings. J Comput Assist Tomogr. 1993;17:326–327.

283. Tanaka Y, Minematsu K, Moriyasu H, et al. A Japanese family with a variant of Gerstmann-Straüssler-Scheinker disease. J Neurol Neurosurg Psychiatry. 1997;62:454–457.

284. Masters CL, Gajdusek DC, Gibbs CJ Jr. Creutzfeldt-Jakob disease virus isolations from the Gerstmann-Straüssler-Scheinker syndrome. With an analysis of the various forms of amyloid plaque deposition in the virus-induced spongiform encephalopathies. Brain. 1981;104:559–588.

285. Amano N, Yagishita S, Yokoi S, et al. Gerstmann-Straüssler syndrome—a variant type: Amyloid plaques and Alzheimer's neurofibrillary tangles in cerebral cortex. Acta Neuropathol. 1992;84:15–23.

286. Nolchin D, Sumi SM, Bird TD, et al. Familial dementia with PrP positive amyloid plaques: A variant of Gerstmann-Straüssler syndrome. Neurology. 1989;39:910–918.

287. Hsiao KK, Baker HF, Crow TJ, et al. Linkage of prion protein missense variant to Gerstmann-Straüssler syndrome. Nature. 1989;338:342–345.

288. Hsiao KK, Cass C, Schellenberg GD, et al. A prion protein variant in a family with the telencephalic form of Gerstmann-Straüssler-Scheinker syndrome. Neurol. 1991;41:681–684.

289. Kretzschmar HA, Kufer P, Riethmuller G, et al. Prion protein mutation at codon 102 in an Italian family with Gerstmann-Straüssler-Scheinker syndrome. Neurology. 1992;42:809–810.

290. Young K, Clark HB, Piccardo P, et al. Gerstmann-Straüssler-Scheinker disease with the PRNP P102L mutation and a valine at codon 129. Brain Res. 1997;44:147–150.

291. Young K, Jones CK, Piccardo P, et al. Gerstmann-Straüssler-Scheinker disease with a mutation at codon 102 and methionine at codon 129 of PRNP in previously unreported patients. Neurol. 1995;45:1127–1134.

292. Gerstmann J, Straüssler E, Scheinker I. Über eine eigenarte hereditär-familiäre Erkrankung des Zentralnervensystems. Zugleich ein Beitrag zur Frage des vorzeitgen lokalen Alterns. Zeitschrift für die gesamte Neurologie und Psychiatrie. 1936;154:736–762.

293. Kretzschmar HA, Honold G, Seitelberger F, et al. Prion protein mutation in family first described by Gerstmann, Straüssler, Scheinker (Letter) Lancet. 1991;337:1160.

294. Hainfellner JA, Brantner-Inthaler S, Cervenakova L, et al. The original Gerstmann-Straüssler-Scheinker family of Austria: Divergent clinicopathological phenotypes but constant PrP genotype. Brain Pathol. 1995;5:201–211.

295. Hsiao KK, Scott M, Foster D, et al. Spontaneous neurodegeneration in transgenic mice with mutant prion protein. Science. 1990;250:1587–1590.

296. Barbanti P, Fabbrini G, Salvatore M, et al. Polymorphism at codon 129 or codon 219 of PRNP and clinical heterogeneity in a previously unrecognized family with Gerstmann-Straüssler-Scheinker disease (PrP-P102L mutation). Neurology. 1996;47:734–741.

297. Tranchant C, Doh-ura K, Warter JM, et al. Gerstmann-Straüssler-Scheinker disease in an Alsatian family: Clinical and genetic studies. J Neurol Neurosurg Psychiatry. 1992;55:185–187.

298. Kitamoto T, Iizuka R, Tateishi J. An amber mutation of prion protein in Gerstmann-Straüssler syndrome with mutant PrP plaques. Biochem Biophys Res Commun. 1993;192:525–531.

299. Piccardo P, Seiler C, Dlouhy SR, et al. Proteinase-K–resistant prion protein isoforms in Gerstmann-Straüssler-Scheinker (GSS) disease (Indiana kindred). J Neuropath Exp Neurol. 1996;55:1157–1163.

300. Goldfarb LG, Brown P, Vrbovska A, et al. An insert mutation in the chromosome 20 amyloid precursor gene in a Gerstmann-Straüssler-Scheinker family. J Neurol Sci. 1992;111:189–194.

301. Tranchant C, Sergeant N, Wattez A, et al. Neurofibrillary tangles in Gerstmann-Straüssler-Scheinker syndrome with the A117V prion gene mutation. J Neurol Neurosurg Psychiatry. 1997;63:240–246.

302. Medori R, Tritschler H-J, LeBlanc A, et al. Fatal familial insomnia, a prion disease with a mutation at codon 178 of the prion protein gene. N Engl J Med. 1992;326:444–449.

303. Manetto V, Medori R, Cortelli P, et al. Fatal familial insomnia: Clinical and pathologic study of five new cases. Neurology. 1992;42:312–319.

304. Lugaresi E, Medori R, Montagna P, et al. Fatal familial insomnia and dysautonomia with selective degeneration of thalamic nuclei. N Engl J Med. 1986;315:997–1003.

305. Petersen BB, Tabaton M, Berg L, et al. Analysis of the prion protein gene in thalamic dementia. Neurology. 1992;42:1859–1863.

306. Silburn P, Cervenakova L, Varghese P, et al. Fatal familial insomnia: A seventh family. Neurol. 1996;47:1326–1328.

307. Galassi R, Morreale A, Montagna P, et al. Fatal familial insomnia: A neuropsychological study of a disease with thalamic degeneration. Cortex. 1992;28:175–187.

308. Nagayama M, Shinohara Y, Furukawa H, Kitamoto T. Fatal familial insomnia with a mutation at codon 178 of the prion protein gene: First report from Japan. Neurology. 1996;47:1313–1316.

309. Plazzi G, Schutz Y, Cortelli P, et al. Motor overactivity and loss of motor circadian rhythm in fatal familial insomnia. Sleep. 1997;20:739–742.

310. Gallassi R, Morreale A, Montagna P, et al. Fatal familial insomnia: Behavioral and cognitive features. Neurol. 1996;46:935–939.

311. McLean CA, Storey E, Gardner RJ, et al. The D178N (cis-129M) "fatal familial insomnia" mutation associated with diverse clinicopathologic phenotypes in an Australian kindred. Neurology. 1997;49:552–558.

312. Macchi G, Rossi G, Abbamondi AL, et al. Diffuse thalamic degeneration in fatal familial insomnia. A morphometric study. Brain Res. 1997;771:154–158.

313. Brown P, Kenney K, Little BW, et al. Intracerebral distribution of infectious amyloid protein in spongiform encephalopathy. Ann Neurol. 1995;38:245–253.

314. Sforza E, Montagna P, Tinuper P, et al. Sleep-wake cycle abnormalities in fatal familial insomnia. Evidence of the role of the thalamus in sleep regulation. Electroencephalogr Clin Neurophysiol. 1995;94:398–405.

315. Perani D, Cortelli P, Lucignani G, et al. [18F]FDG PET in fatal familial insomnia: The functional effects of thalamic lesions. Neurology. 1993;43:2565–2569.

316. Cortelli P, Perani D, Parchi P, et al. Cerebral metabolism in fatal familial insomnia: Relation to duration, neuropathology, and distribution of protease-resistant prion protein. Neurology. 1997;49:126–133.

317. Tateishi J, Brown P, Kitamoto T, et al. First experimental transmission of fatal familial insomnia. Nature. 1995;376:434–435.

318. Medori R, Montagna P, Tritschler HJ, et al. Fatal familial insomnia: A second kindred with mutation of prion protein gene at codon 178. Neurology. 1992;42:669–670.

319. Goldfarb LG, Petersen RB, Tabaton M, et al. Fatal familial insomnia and familial Cruetzfeldt-Jakob disease: Disease phenotype determined by a DNA polymorphism. Science. 1992;258:806–880.

320. Monari L, Chen SG, Brown P, et al. Fatal familial insomnia and familial Creutzfeldt-Jakob disease: Different prion proteins determined by a DNA polymorphism. Proc Natl Acad Sci U S A. 1994;91:2839–2842.

321. Gambetti P, Parchi P, Petersen RB, et al. Fatal familial insomnia and familial Creutzfeldt-Jakob disease: Clinical, pathological and molecular features. Brain Pathol. 1995;5:43–51.

322. Gambetti P. Fatal familial insomnia and familial Creutzfeldt-Jakob disease: A tale of two diseases with the same genetic mutation. Curr Top Microbiol Immunol 1996;207:19–25.

323. Parchi P, Castellani R, Cortelli P, et al. Regional distribution of protease-resistant prion protein in fatal familial insomnia. Ann Neurol. 1995;38:21–29.

324. Chapman J, Arlazoroff A, Goldfarb LG, et al. Fatal insomnia in a case of familial Creutzfeldt-Jakob disease with the codon 200(Lys) mutation. Neurology. 1996;46:758–761.

325. Herishanu Y. Antiviral drugs in Jakob-Creutzfeldt disease. J Am Geriatr Soc. 1973;21:229–231.

326. Goldhammer Y, Bubis JJ, Sarova-Pinhas I, Braham J. Subacute spongiform encephalopathy and its relation to Creutzfeldt-Jakob disease: Report on six cases. J Neurol Neurosurg Psychiatry. 1972;35:1–10.

327. Newman PK. Acyclovir in Creutzfeldt-Jakob disease (Letter). Lancet. 1984;1:793.

328. David AS, Grant R, Ballantyne JP. Unsuccessful treatment of Creutzfeldt-Jakob disease with acyclovir. Lancet. 1984;1:512–513.

329. Kovanen J, Haltia M, Cantell K. Failure of interferon to modify Creutzfeldt-Jakob disease. Br Med J 1980;280:902.

330. Brown P. Biologic and chemotherapeutic forays into the field of unconventional viruses. In: DeClercq E, Walker RT, eds. Targets for the Design of Antiviral Agents. New York: Plenum Press; 1984;131–157.

331. Masullo C, Macchi G, Xi YG, Pocchiari M. Failure to ameliorate Creutzfeldt-Jakob disease with amphotericin B therapy (Letter). J Infect Dis. 1992;165:784–785.

332. Braham J. Jakob-Creutzfeldt disease: Treatment by amantadine. Br Med J. 1971;4:212–213.

333. Sanders WL, Dunn TL. Creutzfeldt-Jakob disease treated with amantadine. J Neurol Neurosurg Psychiatry. 1973;36:581–584.

334. Sanders WL. Creutzfeldt-Jakob disease treated with amantadine. J Neurol Neurosurg Psychiat. 1979;42:960–961.

335. Terzano MG, Montanari E, Calzetti S, et al. The effect of amantadine on arousal and EEG patterns in Creutzfeldt-Jakob disease. Arch Neurol. 1983;40:555–559.

336. Furlow TW Jr, Whitley RJ, Wilmes FJ. Repeated suppression of Creutzfeldt-Jakob disease with vidarabine. Lancet. 1982;2:564–556.

337. Villa G, Caltagirone C, Macchi G. Unusual clinical course in a case of Creutzfeldt-Jakob disease. Ital J Neurol Sci. 1982;3:155–158.

338. Ratcliffe J, Rittman A, Wolf S, Verity MA. Creutzfeldt-Jakob disease with focal onset unsuccessfully treated with amantadine. Bull LA Neurol Soc. 1975;40:18–20.

339. Priola SA, Caughey B. Inhibition of scrapie-associated PrP accumulation. Mol Neurobiol. 1994;8:113–120.

340. Caspi S, Halimi M, Yanai A, et al. The anti-prion activity of Congo red. Putative mechanism. J Biol Chem. 1998;273:3484–3489.

341. Tagliavini F, McArthur RA, Canciani B, et al. Effectiveness of anthracycline against experimental prion disease in Syrian hamsters. Science. 1997;276:1119–1122.
342. Tatzelt J, Prusiner SB, Welch WJ. Chemical chaperones interfere with the formation of scrapie prion protein. EMBO J. 1996;15:6363–6373.
343. Cohen FE, Pan K-M, Huang Z, et al. Structural clues to prion replication. Science. 1994;264:530–531.
344. Gibbs CJ Jr, Amyx HL, Bacote A, et al. Oral transmission of kuru, Creutzfeldt-Jakob disease and scrapie to non-human primates. J Infect Dis. 1980;142:205–208.
345. Diringer H, Roehmel J, Beekes M. Effect of repeated oral infection of hamsters with scrapie. J Gen Virol. 1998;79:609–612.
346. Esmonde TF, Will RG, Slattery JM, et al. Creutzfeldt-Jakob disease and blood transfusion. Lancet. 1993;341:205–207.
347. Ironside J, Bell JE. The "high risk" neuropathological autopsy in AIDS and Creutzfeldt-Jakob disease: Principles and practice. Neuropath Appl Neurobiol. 1996;22:388–393.
348. Committee on Health Care Issues ANA. Precautions in handling tissues, fluids and other contaminated materials from patients with documented or suspected Creutzfeldt-Jakob disease. Ann Neurol. 1986;19:75–77.
349. Brown P, Gibbs CJ Jr, Amyx HL, et al. Chemical disinfection of Creutzfeldt-Jakob disease virus. N Engl J Med. 1982;306:1279–1282.
350. Brown P, Rohwer RG, Gajdusek DC. Newer data on the inactivation of scrapie virus or Creutzfeldt-Jakob disease virus in brain tissue. J Infect Dis. 1986;153:1145–1148.
351. Brown P, Wolff A, Liberski PP, Gajdusek DC. Resistance of scrapie infectivity to steam autoclaving and formaldehyde fixations and limited survival after ashing at 360°C: Practical and theoretical implications. J Infect Dis. 1989;161:467–472.
352. Manuelidis L. Decontamination of Creutzfeldt-Jakob disease and other transmissible agents. J Neurovirol. 1997;3:62–65.

SECTION C

CHLAMYDIAL DISEASES

Chapter 167

Introduction to Chlamydial Diseases

ROBERT B. JONES
BYRON E. BATTEIGER

Chlamydiae are obligate intracellular parasites with a unique biphasic life cycle.[1] They are classified in the order Chlamydiales, which contains only one family, the Chlamydiaceae, and one genus, *Chlamydia.* Within this genus four species are recognized currently, *C pecorum,*[2] *C. psittaci, C. trachomatis,* and *C. pneumoniae.* All except *C. pecorum* have been associated with human disease (Table 167–1). Although the chlamydiae have been classified taxonomically on the basis of their phenotypic properties, sequence data of their ribosomal RNA firmly establish them as a unique class of bacteria that are closely related to each other but only distantly to other eubacteria.[3] Based on ribosomal RNA sequencing, the current species *C. psittaci* contains four distinct genetic groups of strains that may be proposed in the future as separate species.[4, 5] DNA sequence homology confirms these insights.[6, 7] The multiple strains of *C. psittaci* exhibit from less than 10 to 60% homology with each other and from less than 5 to approximately 20% with *C. trachomatis* strains. The human strains of *C. trachomatis* are almost 100% homologous with each other and approximately 30% with the mouse biovar. The latter does not cause human disease, and it has also been suggested that the mouse biovar should be classified as a separate species.[5, 6] *Chlamydia pneumoniae* shows 10% or less homology with either of the other two species and so far appears to consist of only a single strain, TWAR.[8, 9]

Chlamydia trachomatis has been most extensively studied because of its association with ocular trachoma and its prevalence as a sexually transmitted pathogen. Three biovars have been identified. The trachoma biovar is associated with oculogenital disease and contains at least 12 strains or serovars. The lymphogranuloma venereum biovar contains three distinct strains. A combination of monoclonal antibody typing and genotyping by DNA sequence analysis has identified a number of additional isolates in these two biovars that represent either variants of existing strains or new strains.[10] In addition, minor variants have been found by polymerase chain reaction amplification and nucleotide sequencing of the *omp1* gene that encodes the antigenically variable major outer membrane protein.[11, 12] The mouse pneumonitis biovar appears to contain only a single strain. *Chlamydia pneumoniae* may be as prevalent a human pathogen as *C. trachomatis,* but it was only recognized in 1992,[13] and the full extent and spectrum of disease remain to be defined. There are multiple strains of *C. psittaci,* which primarily infect birds and other nonhuman hosts. Transmission to humans occasionally occurs, usually after exposure to avian strains.[14]

Chlamydiae are prokaryotes. They exhibit morphologic and structural similarities to gram-negative bacteria including a trilaminar outer membrane (Fig. 167–1), which contains lipopolysaccharide and several membrane proteins that are structurally and functionally analogous to proteins found in *Escherichia coli.* Chlamydiae appear to lack classic peptidoglycan,[1, 15] a macromolecule that provides most prokaryotes with structural rigidity and osmotic stability, although the chlamydial genome contains all the genes necessary for peptidoglycan synthesis.[16] Instead, the extracellular form, the elementary body (EB), exhibits extensive disulfide cross-linking between cysteine residues both within and between outer membrane proteins.[17, 18] The result is an almost sporelike structure that is metabolically inert.

The life cycle is initiated when an EB attaches to a susceptible epithelial cell. A number of candidates for chlamydial adhesins have been proposed, and putative membrane protein candidates have been identified via the Chlamydia Genome Project,[16] but the identity of adhesins and associated epithelial cell receptors remain uncertain (reviewed by Wyrick[19]). The EB enters the epithelial cell by receptor-mediated endocytosis via clathrin-coated pits,[6, 20] but evidence exists for other mechanisms, including pinocytosis via noncoated pits.[19] It is likely that chlamydiae exploit several adhesin-ligand pairs and entry mechanisms. Lysosomal fusion is inhibited by undefined mechanisms allowing EB to reside in a protected membrane-bound vesicle called an *inclusion.* The EB, which is approximately 350 nm in diameter, then undergoes reorganization into the much larger replicative form, the reticulate body (RB), which is about 800 to 1000 nm in diameter.[21] The initial event triggering this reorganization has not been defined precisely, but early events include new synthesis of chlamydial proteins,[6] reduction of disulfide bonds so that membrane proteins are no longer cross-linked,[18] and activation of an adenosine

TABLE 167–1 Chlamydial Species

Species	Biovars (Strains)	Method of Spread	Natural Host	Associated Human Diseases
C. pecorum	Many	?Aerosol, sexual in animal hosts	Swine, ruminants, marsupials (koala)	None known
C. psittaci	Many	Aerosol, sexual in animal hosts	Birds, sheep, cats, etc.	Pneumonia, endocarditis, abortions
C. trachomatis	LGV (L_1, L_2, L_3)	Sexual	Humans	Lymphogranuloma venereum
	Trachoma (A, B, Ba, C)	Hand to eye fomites, flies	Humans	Ocular trachoma
	(B, Ba, D–K)	Sexual, hand to eye, neonatal	Humans	Oculogenital disease in adults and children, infant pneumonia
	Mouse pneumonitis	?Aerosol	Mouse	None
C. pneumoniae	TWAR	?Aerosol	Humans	Bronchitis, pneumonia, ?coronary artery disease

Abbreviation: TWAR, TW = 183 and AR = 39.

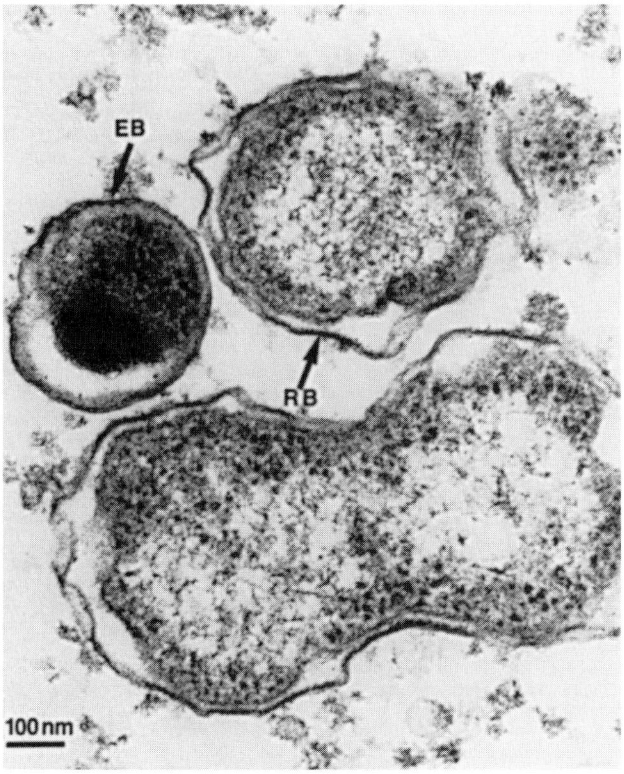

FIGURE 167–1. Electron photomicrograph of *Chlamydia trachomatis,* serovar A, growing in tissue culture. The larger reticular bodies (RBs) have more diffuse chromatin. One of the RBs appears to be dividing, and the trilaminar outer membrane is evident in some areas. *Abbreviations:* EB, elementary body. (Photo courtesy of Ms. Wandy L. Beatty, Madison, Wis.)

triphosphatase.[22] During growth and replication, chlamydiae obtain high-energy phosphate compounds from the host cell.[23] Consequently, they are considered energy parasites. They also require some amino acids and are able to synthesize others, although specific requirements vary among strains and species.[6] RBs are osmotically unstable and incapable of infecting another cell. They divide by binary fission to produce an ever-enlarging inclusion (Fig. 167–2). The intracellular regulatory signals that control EB-to-RB and RB-to-EB conversion are not known, but the relative concentrations of the cyclic nucleotides cyclic adenosine monophosphate and cyclic guanosine monophosphate appear to be important.[24] Condensation of RBs into EBs leads to a reduction in size with extensive shedding of membrane blebs containing lipopolysaccharide[25] and compaction of the chromatin into an electron-dense nucleoid. The latter is mediated by a histone-like protein and is associated with a general decrease in transcription.[26] Depending on the species, the cell membrane proteins are cross-linked either during condensation or later during cell lysis and release.[6] Release of the organisms from infected cells can be accomplished by cell lysis,[27] extrusion of intact inclusions,[28] or a process resembling exocytosis.[29] The release of the infectious elementary bodies permits infection of new cells and continuation of the life cycle.

The mechanisms of intracellular survival and growth of chlamydiae within host cells are likely to be clarified, given advances in cell biology and the genome sequence of *C. trachomatis* serovar D reported in 1998.[16] *Chlamydia trachomatis* inhibits apoptosis in epithelial cells when induction is attempted using a variety of signals.[30] From the point of view of the intracellular parasite, preventing programmed cell death until the developmental cycle is complete is a crucial determinant of survival. Chlamydiae express proteins that localize in the cytoplasmic surface of the inclusion membrane, the prototype of which is IncA.[31] Such exported proteins may be involved in the trafficking of inclusions into the exocytic pathway,[32, 33] the trafficking of host cell lipids into chlamydial membranes,[34] and the inhibition of apoptosis.[30] Such proteins are hypothesized to enter the host cell from the inclusion by type III secretion,[35] used by *Yersinia* and other species to inject effector proteins into eukaryotic cells. *Chlamydia trachomatis* has been shown to possess type III secretion genes,[16, 35] including potential effectors like phosphatases and kinases used by other bacteria to influence eukaryotic cell signaling. Chlamydial forms possess surface projections[36] that are outwardly similar to structures in *Salmonella* known to be composed of type III secretion components. It is speculated that the surface projections of chlamydiae may constitute the chlamydial type III secretion apparatus.[37]

In host-defense cells, such as macrophages, some strains of *C. psittaci* exhibit productive growth.[38] Conversely, macrophages restrict the growth of both the lymphogranuloma venereum and trachoma biovars of *C. trachomatis* although they are more permissive for lymphogranuloma venereum.[39] Human polymorphonuclear leukocytes ingest and destroy *C. trachomatis* and *C. psittaci* fairly efficiently. However, a small proportion of organisms remain viable and potentially able to perpetuate infection.[40]

Phenotypically, the four species differ antigenically, metabolically, and in host cell preference, antibiotic susceptibility, and inclu-

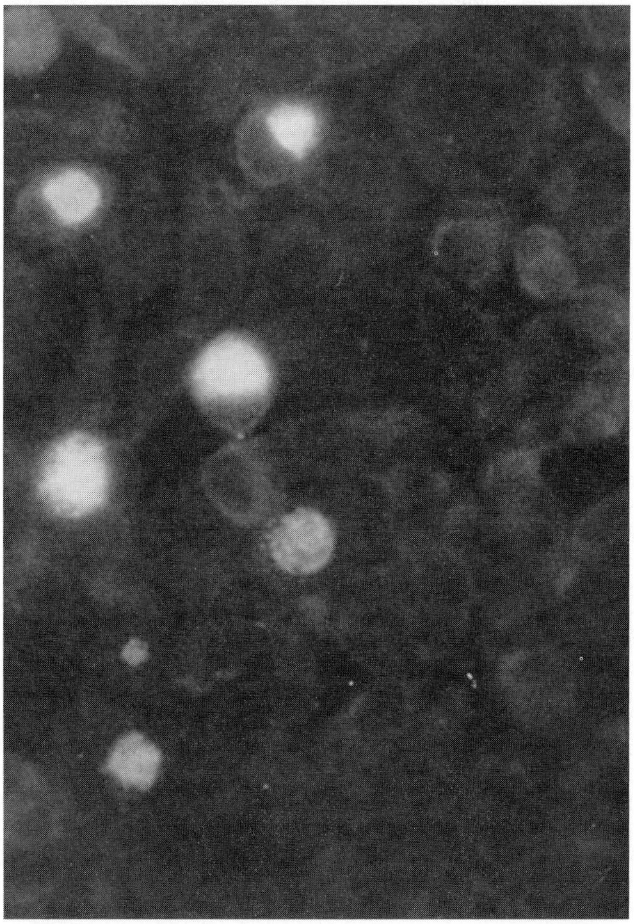

FIGURE 167–2. *Chlamydia trachomatis* inclusions in a McCoy cell monolayer stained with a genus reactive mouse monoclonal antibody followed by fluorescein conjugated rabbit anti-mouse immunoglobulin. (From Jones RB, VanDer Pol B, Katz BP. Effect of differences in specimen processing and passage technique on recovery of *Chlamydia trachomatis.* J Clin Microbiol. 1989;27:894–898. Photo courtesy of Ms. B. Van Der Pol, Indiana University School of Medicine, Indianapolis, Ind.)

sion morphology. Shared antigenic determinants are present in the lipopolysaccharide and some of the membrane proteins.[1,8] In addition, several outer-membrane proteins contain species and subspecies determinants. Strain-specific determinants reside primarily in the major outer-membrane protein.[41] All strains of *C. trachomatis* are sensitive to sulfonamides, whereas *C. pneumoniae* and most strains of *C. psittaci* are not. The morphology of the elementary and reticulate bodies of *C. psittaci* and *C. trachomatis* are very similar to each other. Also, the RBs of all four species appear identical. However, the elementary bodies of *C. pneumoniae* are often pear shaped, with a relatively large periplasmic space that contains some electron-dense structures that are not seen in the other two species and whose function is unknown.[8] *Chlamydia psittaci* forms multiple small inclusions in a single infected cell with each infective elementary body forming its own inclusion. In cells infected with multiple *C. trachomatis* EBs, the organism-containing vesicles often fuse so that each infected cell contains only one or two inclusions.[25] However, nonfusogenic variants of *C. trachomatis* have been described (Walter Stamm, unpublished data, June 1998) whose inclusions appear to lack IncA. The inclusions of *C. pneumoniae* resemble those of *C. psittaci* but are less variable in shape. Only *C. trachomatis* accumulates glycogen in its inclusions, a property that allows their staining with iodine.

The chlamydial genome has a molecular mass of only 660×10^6 daltons, which is smaller than that of any other prokaryote except *Mycoplasma* spp.[1] The Chlamydia Genome Project has completed the complete genome sequence of *C. trachomatis* serovar D, which is 1.043 million base pairs.[16] Based on examination of the sequence, certain metabolic pathways are missing, including amino acid and purine-pyrimidine biosynthesis, anaerobic fermentation, and transformation competence proteins. Complete glycolytic and glycogen-degrading pathways are present, and a full synthetic capacity for fatty acids, phospholipids, lipopolysaccharide, and peptidoglycan is represented.[16]

Chlamydia pneumoniae does not appear to contain any extrachromosomal genetic material,[8] whereas some strains of *C. psittaci*[42] and most strains of *C. trachomatis* contain a plasmid of approximately 7.5 kb. Slight sequence variations exist between plasmids from different strains within *C. trachomatis* and more extensive variations among the plasmids from *C. psittaci.*[43] Although the extensive conservation implies a critical function and, based on sequence homology with *E. coli* genes, it has been suggested that it may play a role in DNA replication,[44] the function of the plasmid remains unknown.

Chlamydia trachomatis and *C. pneumoniae* appear to be exclusively human pathogens, except for the mouse pneumonitis biovar of *C. trachomatis,* which does not infect humans. Lymphogranuloma venereum strains of *C. trachomatis* as well as those associated with oculogenital disease are generally spread by sexual contact, during birth, or by autoinoculation of the eye with infected genital secretions. The strains associated with ocular trachoma are spread by fingers, by fomites, and on the feet of flies. Transfer of respiratory secretions by aerosol or hand is probably the primary mode of transmission of *C. pneumoniae.*[13]

The natural history of chlamydial infections is unknown or only poorly defined in most cases. However, a growing body of data suggests that chronic asymptomatic or persistent infections are frequent. This appears to be the case for *C. psittaci* in animals[6] and for both *C. trachomatis*[45–47] and *C. pneumoniae*[48] in humans. Moreover, serologic and anatomic data suggest that chronic *C. pneumoniae* infections may play a role in atherosclerosis and coronary artery disease.[13,49]

REFERENCES

1. Moulder JW. Looking at chlamydiae without looking at their hosts. Am Soc Microbiol News. 1984;50:353–362.
2. Fukushi H, Hirai K. 1989. Proposal of *Chlamydia pecorum* sp. nov. for *Chlamydia* strains derived from ruminants. Int J Syst Bacteriol. 1992;42:306–308.
3. Weisburg WG, Hatch TP, Woese CR. Eubacterial origin of chlamydiae. J Bacteriol. 1986;167:570–574.
4. Everett KDE, Andersen AA. The ribosomal intergenic spacer and domain I of the 23S rRNA gene are phylogenetic markers for *Chlamydia* spp. Int J Syst Bacteriol. 1997;47:461–473.
5. Pudjiatmoko, Fukushi H, Ochiai Y, et al. Phylogenetic analysis of the genus *Chlamydia* based on 16S rRNA gene sequences. Int J Syst Bacteriol. 1997;47:425–431.
6. Moulder JW. Interaction of chlamydiae and host cells in vitro. Microbiol Rev. 1991;55:143–190.
7. Herring AJ. The molecular biology of chlamydia—a brief overview. J Infect. 1992;25(Suppl I):1–10.
8. Grayston JT, Kuo C-C, Campbell LA, et al. *Chlamydia pneumoniae* sp. nov. for *Chlamydia* sp. strain TWAR. Int J Syst Bacteriol. 1989;39:88–90.
9. Pettersson B, Andersson A, Leitner T, et al. Evolutionary relationships among members of the genus *Chlamydia* based on 16S ribosomal DNA analysis. J Bacteriol. 1997;179:4195–4205.
10. Lampe MF, Suchland RJ, Stamm WE. Nucleotide sequence of the variable domains within the major outer membrane protein gene from serovariants of *Chlamydia trachomatis*. Infect Immun. 1993;61:213–219.
11. Stothard DR, Boguslawski G, Jones RB. Phylogenetic analysis of the *Chlamydia trachomatis* major outer membrane protein and examination of potential pathogenic determinants. Infect Immun. 1998;66:3618–3625.
12. Dean D, Millman K. Molecular and mutation trends analyses of *omp1* alleles for serovar E of *Chlamydia trachomatis*. J Clin Invest. 1997;99:475–483.
13. Grayston JT. Infections caused by *Chlamydia pneumoniae* strain TWAR. Clin Infect Dis. 1992;15:757–763.
14. Yung AP, Grayson ML. Psittacosis—a review of 135 cases. Med J Aust. 1988;148:228–233.
15. Fox A, Robers JC, Gilbart J, et al. Muramic acid is not detectable in *Chlamydia psittaci* or *Chlamydia trachomatis* by gas chromatography–mass spectrometry. Infect Immun. 1990;58:835–837.
16. Stephens RS, Kalman S, Lammel C, et al. Genome sequence of an obligate intracellular pathogen of humans: *Chalmydia trachomatis*. Science. 1998;282:754–759.
17. Newhall WJV, Jones RB. Disulfide-linked oligomers of the major outer membrane protein of chlamydiae. J Bacteriol. 1983;154:998–1001.
18. Hatch TP, Miceli M, Sublett JE. Synthesis of disulfide-bonded outer membrane proteins during the developmental cycle of *Chlamydia psittaci* and *Chlamydia trachomatis*. J Bacteriol. 1986;165:379–385.
19. Wyrick PB. Cell biology of chlamydial infection. In: Stephens RS, Byrne GI, Christiansen G, et al, eds. Chlamydial Infections: Proceedings of the 9th International Symposium on Human Chlamydial Infection. International Chlamydial Symposium, San Francisco. 1998;69–78.
20. Wyrick PB, Choong J, Davis CH, et al. Entry of genital *Chlamydia trachomatis* into polarized human epithelial cells. Infect Immun. 1989;57:2378–2389.
21. Schachter J, Caldwell HD. Chlamydiae. Ann Rev Microbiol. 1980;34:285–309.
22. Peeling R, Peeling J, Brunham R. High-resolution ^{31}P nuclear magnetic resonance study of *Chlamydia trachomatis:* Induction of ATPase activity in elementary bodies. Infect Immun. 1989;57:3338–3344.
23. Hatch TP, Al-Hossainy E, Silverman JA. Adenine nucleotide and lysine transport in *Chlamydia psittaci.* J Bacteriol. 1982;150:662–670.
24. Kaul R, Wenman WM. Cyclic AMP inhibits developmental regulation of *Chlamydia trachomatis.* J Bacteriol. 1986;168:722–777.
25. Stirling P, Richmond SJ. Production of outer membrane blebs during chlamydial replication. FEMS Microbiol Lett. 1980;9:103–105.
26. Barry CE, Hayes SF, Hackstadt T. Nucleoid condensation in *Escherichia coli* that express a chlamydial histone homolog. Science. 1992;256:377–379.
27. Todd WJ, Storz J. Ultrastructural cytochemical evidence for the activation of lysosomes in the cytocidal effect of *Chlamydia psittaci.* Infect Immun. 1975;12:638–646.
28. De la Maza LM, Peterson EM. Scanning electron microscopy of McCoy cells infected with *Chlamydia trachomatis.* Exp Mol Pathol. 1982;36:217–226.
29. Todd WJ, Caldwell HD. The interaction of *Chlamydia trachomatis* with host cells: Ultrastructural studies of the mechanism of release of a biovar II strain from HeLa 229 cells. J Infect Dis. 1985;151:1037–1044.
30. Fan T, Lu H, Hu H, et al. Inhibition of apoptosis in chlamydia-infected cells: Blockade of mitochondrial cytochrome c release and caspase activation. J Exp Med. 1998;187:487–496.
31. Rockey DD, Grosenbach D, Hruby DE, et al. *Chlamydia psittaci* IncA is phosphorylated by the host cell and is exposed on the cytoplasmic face of the developing inclusion. Mol Microbiol. 1997;24:217–228.
32. Hackstadt T, Scidmore MA, Rockey DD. Lipid metabolism in *Chlamydia trachomatis*–infected cells: Directed trafficking of Golgi-derived sphingolipids to the chlamydial inclusion. Proc Natl Acad Sci U S A. 1995;92:4877–4881.
33. Heinzen RA, Scidmore MA, Rockey DD, Hackstadt T. Differential interaction with endocytic and exocytic pathways distinguish parasitophorous vacuoles of *Coxiella burnetii* and *Chlamydia trachomatis*. Infect Immun. 1996;64:796–809.
34. Wylie JL, Hatch GM, McClarty G. Host cell phospholipids are trafficked to and then modified by *Chlamydia trachomatis*. J Bacteriol. 1997;179:7233–7242.
35. Hsia R-C, Pannekoek Y, Ingerowski E, Bavoil PM. Type III secretion genes identify a putative virulence locus of *Chlamydia*. Mol Microbiol. 1997;25:351–359.
36. Matsumoto A. Structural characteristics of chlamydial bodies. In: Barron AL, ed. Microbiology of Chlamydia. Boca Raton, Fla: CRC Press;1998:21–46.
37. Bavoil PB, Hsia R-C. Type III secretion in *Chlamydia*: A case of déjà vu? Mol Microbiol. 1998;28:860–862.

38. Wyrick PB, Brownridge EA. Growth of *Chlamydia psittaci* in macrophages. Infect Immun. 1978;19:1054–1060.
39. Kuo C-C. Cultures of *Chlamydia trachomatis* in mouse peritoneal macrophages: Factors affecting organism growth. Infect Immun. 1978;20:439–445.
40. Register KB, Morgan PA, Wyrick PB. Interaction between *Chlamydia* spp. and human polymorphonuclear leukocytes in vitro. Infect Immun. 1986;52:664–670.
41. Stephens RS, Sanchez-Pescador R, Wagar EA, et al. Diversity of *Chlamydia trachomatis* major outer membrane protein genes. J Bacteriol. 1987;169:3879–3885.
42. McClenaghan M, Honeycombe JR, Bevan BJ, et al. Distribution of plasmid sequences in avian and mammalian strains of *Chlamydia psittaci.* J Gen Microbiol. 1988;134:559–565.
43. Comanducci M, Ricci S, Cevenini R, et al. Diversity of the *Chlamydia trachomatis* common plasmid in biovars with different pathogenicity. Plasmid. 1990;23:149–154.
44. Hatt C, Ward ME, Clarke IN. Analysis of the entire nucleotide sequence of the cryptic plasmid of *Chlamydia trachomatis* serovar L1. Evidence for involvement in DNA replication. Nucleic Acids Res. 1988;16:4053–4067.
45. Dan M, Rotmensch HH, Eylan E, et al. A case of lymphogranuloma venereum of 20 years' duration. Br J Vener Dis. 1980;56:344–346.
46. Campbell LA, Patton DL, Moore DE, et al. Detection of *Chlamydia trachomatis* deoxyribonucleic acid in women with tubal infertility. Fertil Steril. 1993;59:45–50.
47. Shepard MK, Jones RB. Recovery of *Chlamydia trachomatis* from endometrial and fallopian tube biopsies in women with infertility of tubal origin. Fertil Steril. 1989;52:232–238.
48. Hammerschlag MR, Chirgwin K, Roblin PM, et al. Persistent infection with *Chlamydia pneumoniae* following acute respiratory illness. Clin Infect Dis. 1992;14:178–182.
49. Ridker P. Inflammation, infection and cardiovascular risk: How good is the clinical evidence? Circulation. 1998;97: 1671.

Chapter 168

Chlamydia trachomatis (Trachoma, Perinatal Infections, Lymphogranuloma Venereum, and Other Genital Infections)

ROBERT B. JONES
BYRON E. BATTEIGER

One of the diseases caused by *Chlamydia trachomatis*—ocular trachoma—has been recognized since antiquity. Therapy for trachoma and its complications was described in China in the 27th century BC and in Egypt in the 19th century BC.[1] However, the organism's role in genital tract infections was not appreciated until the early part of the 20th century. Before the introduction of perinatal ocular prophylaxis for gonorrhea, it was assumed that all neonatal conjunctivitis was gonococcal in origin. However, even after prophylaxis was introduced, neonatal conjunctivitis continued to occur, and in 1909 conjunctival scrapings from neonates with conjunctivitis were shown to contain cells with cytoplasmic inclusions identical to those seen in patients with ocular trachoma.[2] Subsequently, inclusions were demonstrated in cells from the cervix of the mother and the urethra of the father of an infected infant,[3] and in urethral scrapings from men with nongonococcal urethritis (NGU).[4]

C. trachomatis infections impose a significant burden on humans globally. It has been estimated that worldwide 500 million people are affected by ocular trachoma with some 7 to 9 million blind as a result.[5] Ocular trachoma is considered the most common cause of potentially preventable blindness. Furthermore, genital tract infections are even more prevalent and have as major complications acute pelvic inflammatory disease, ectopic pregnancy, infertility, and infant pneumonia. Because of a lack of universal testing and reporting, reliable prevalence data are not available. However, the Centers for Disease Control and Prevention (CDC) has estimated that there are approximately 4 million new *C. trachomatis* infections per year in the United States.[6] Based on selective screening of target populations of sexually active women, the proportion infected ranges from 8 to 40%, with a median of about 15%.[7] Approximately 10% of sexually active asymptomatic men are infected.[8, 9]

LIFE CYCLE

As discussed in the preceding chapter, chlamydiae have a complex biphasic life cycle (Fig. 168–1). The extracellular infectious form, the elementary body, attaches to a susceptible epithelial cell. Neither the eukaryotic receptors nor the chlamydial surface structures responsible have been fully defined, although possible candidates have been identified.[10–13]

C. trachomatis can enter cells by phagocytosis, pinocytosis, or receptor-mediated endocytosis. The last is the pathway by which eukaryotic cells internalize and transport macromolecules to specific sites within the cell. Convincing data that receptor-mediated endocytosis is also the pathway primarily used by the trachoma biovar of *C. trachomatis* come from experiments using polarized human genital epithelial cells.[14] In this model, infecting chlamydial elementary bodies are found predominantly in clathrin-coated pits and vesicles that are associated with receptor-mediated endocytosis.[15] The clathrin-coated pit invaginates and becomes an endocytic vesicle containing the chlamydial elementary body.[14]

The elementary body has stores of adenosine triphosphate (ATP) and an adenosine triphosphatase (ATPase)[16] that is activated in the presence of reducing agents.[17] ATPase activation and reduction of the disulfide bonds that cross-link membrane proteins are early events in reorganization of elementary bodies into reticulate bodies.[17, 18] The major outer membrane protein is a porin that is extensively cross-linked by disulfide bonds both internally and with two other cysteine-rich membrane proteins in elementary bodies but not in reticulate bodies.[19, 20] Reduction of these bonds may be a key factor in initiation of reorganization.

The reticulate body is the replicative form. As it divides it fills the endosome, now a cytoplasmic inclusion, with its progeny and with glycogen. When an epithelial cell is infected with more than one elementary body of *C. trachomatis,* the endosomes usually fuse so that each cell contains only one inclusion. The yield of new infectious units per host cell ranges from less than 100 to more than 1000,[21] representing the equivalent of 8 to 12 doublings of a single organism. Synthesis of specific proteins is cycle dependent. Proteins thought to be associated with conversion of elementary to reticulate bodies are synthesized early,[22] followed by the major outer membrane protein and then late in the cycle by the other cysteine-rich proteins[20] and DNA-binding proteins.[23] Regulation of the cycle appears to be at a transcriptional level. Growth cycle–specific mRNA has been identified[24] and multiple promoters for several different genes described.[25] Binding of subunits of RNA polymerase to the different promoters may serve as a key regulatory mechanism.[25] Two of the DNA-binding proteins of *C. trachomatis* have extensive sequence homology with eukaryotic histone H1. They are expressed concomitantly with nucleoid condensation and cessation of transcription as the reticulate body forms an elementary body. They may provide global regulation of gene expression rather than conventional transcriptional regulation.[26]

In tissue culture the life cycle takes between 48 and 72 hours, with some strains or serovars growing faster than others. In particular, strains of the lymphogranuloma venerum (LGV) biovar usually complete their life cycle more rapidly than those of the trachoma biovar. At the end of the cycle, an inclusion containing elementary bodies of the LGV biovar ruptures inside the cell, causing cell lysis and death with release of the elementary bodies.[21] The same sequence of events can occur with trachoma biovar strains, but their inclusions also can be released intact without killing the host cell by a process similar to exocytosis.[27, 28] This difference in effect on host cells is paralleled by more efficient cell-to-cell spread by LGV strains in

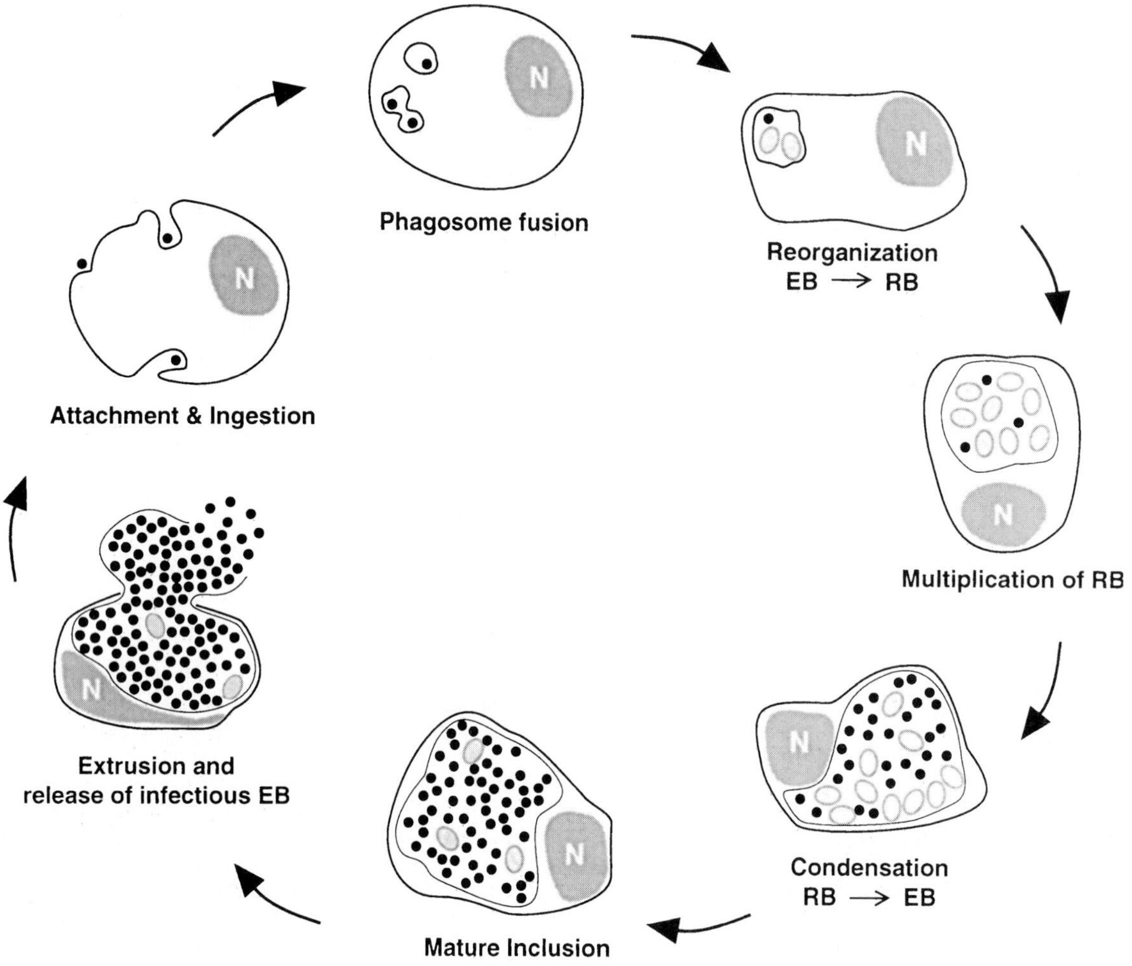

FIGURE 168–1. Life cycle of *Chlamydia trachomatis* in tissue culture. *Abbreviations:* EB, Elementary bodies; N, nucleus; RB, reticulate bodies.

tissue culture and their propensity to cause more invasive disease in vivo.[28]

ANTIGENIC AND CHEMICAL COMPOSITION

Isolates of *C. trachomatis* from the LGV and trachoma biovars were originally classified into 1 of 15 serovars (see Chapter 167, Table 167–1) based on antigenic cross-reactivity in the microimmunofluorescence test of Wang and Grayston.[29] Three serovars, L_1, L_2, and L_3, were associated with clinical LGV and only rarely recovered under other circumstances. The remaining 12 serovars were associated with oculogenital disease: strains A, B, Ba, and C with ocular trachoma and strains D through K with inclusion conjunctivitis and genital tract disease. Occasionally, serovars B and Ba have been isolated from the genital tract, but A and C have not. Cross-reactivity patterns revealed two subspecies subgroups: B complex (B, Ba, D, E, L_1, and L_2) and C complex (C, J, H, I, A, K, and L_3). Serovars F and G bridge the two complexes, although they are more closely related to the B complex.[29] These relationships were confirmed and further defined by monoclonal antibodies that identified genus-, species-, subspecies-, and serovar (strain)-specific antigens.[30, 31] In addition, they led to recognition of three additional serovars (Da, Ia, and L_{2a}).[32]

The epitopes reactive with species-, subspecies-, and serovar-specific antibodies are located in four variable sequence regions of the major outer membrane protein.[33, 34] The serovar-specific epitopes are found mostly in variable sequence regions 1 and 2, whereas the more broadly shared epitopes clustered in variable region 4.[33] However, some serovars are known to contain more than one serovar-specific epitope, and serovar-specific epitopes are found in variable region 4 as well.[35] More recently, classification of strains based on nucleotide sequencing of the major outer membrane protein gene (*OMP*1) has revealed variation within serovars[36, 37] that may reflect immunologic pressure[38] and that is useful in defining the molecular epidemiology of trachoma[39] and genital infection.[40] Genus-reactive epitopes have been demonstrated in the major outer membrane protein,[41] the 60-kD cysteine-rich protein,[41] and in a 60-kD heat shock protein (HSP60).[42] However, the immunodominant genus-reactive epitope is in lipopolysaccharide. Chlamydial lipopolysaccharide is closely related to the lipopolysaccharide of other gram-negative bacteria, in particular the deep rough (Re) mutants of *Salmonella minnesota* and *Salmonella typhimurium.* However, it contains a 3-deoxy-D-manno-octulosonic acid trisaccharide in a 2, 4, and 2, 8 linkage, with the latter being unique to the genus *Chlamydia.*[43]

The chlamydial genome of serovar D has been sequenced, and the data are available on the Internet.[44] Previously, a number of genes had been cloned and sequenced, including the genes for the major outer membrane protein,[33, 45] the 60-kD cysteine-rich outer membrane protein,[46] the 60-kD heat shock protein,[42] enzymes involved in lipopolysaccharide synthesis,[43] and the S7 and S12 ribosomal proteins.[47] Information derived from comparative analysis includes confirmation of the antigenic relationships predicted by serologic and monoclonal antibody studies[48] and a molecular basis for some of the antigenic variation observed within serovars.[49, 50] In addition, sequence analysis of 16S ribosomal RNA genes has confirmed the eubacterial nature of chlamydiae and established their singularity.[51] By this measure their closest relatives are the *Planctomyces*, an obscure group of bacteria that also lack peptidoglycan.

PATHOGENESIS

The mechanisms by which *C. trachomatis* induces inflammation and tissue destruction are only partially understood. The LGV biovar of *C. trachomatis* gains entrance through breaks in the skin or infects epithelial cells of the mucous membranes of the genital tract or rectum. It is then carried by lymphatic drainage to the regional lymph nodes, where it multiplies inside mononuclear phagocytes.[52] The characteristic histopathology is that of granuloma formation with development of small abscesses that may become necrotic or coalesce into suppurative foci.[53]

The target cells of the trachoma biovar of *C. trachomatis* are the squamocolumnar epithelial cells of the endocervix and upper genital tract in women and the conjunctiva, urethra, and rectum in men and women. In men the epididymis and perhaps the prostate can be infected, whereas in infants the columnar epithelial cells of the respiratory tract are also commonly infected.[52] Regardless of the site, the initial response to infection appears to be primarily a polymorphonuclear leukocyte response.[54–56] Infected epithelial cells in vitro produce interleukin 8 and other proinflammatory cytokines, leading to the initial neutrophilic response.[57] Lipopolysaccharide may be the predominant chlamydial antigen capable of inducing proinflammatory cytokines.[58]

The initial neutrophilic infiltration is followed by tissue infiltration with lymphocytes, macrophages, plasma cells, and eosinophils.[52] In ocular and genital infections, plasma cells may be present in large numbers,[59, 60] whereas in infant pneumonia, eosinophils and neutrophils predominate.[55] In ocular and genital disease with the trachoma biovar, lymphoid follicles form as the acute inflammation begins to subside. Lymphoid follicles are aggregates of lymphocytes and macrophages in the submucosa. There is thinning or loss of epithelium overlying them and they may become necrotic as the disease progresses.[52] They are clinically apparent in the conjunctiva as raised avascular lesions.[1] Epithelial proliferation leads to formation of papillae and papillary hypertrophy. Then as the infection begins to resolve, fibrosis and scarring occur.

Initial infection in the eye in humans[52] and in the eye[60] and genital tract in monkeys[61] resolves with little or no residual tissue damage. However, in both settings recurrent infection produces an accelerated and more intense inflammatory response with scarring and tissue damage. The potential role of reinfection in chlamydial disease was first recognized during human trachoma vaccine trials in which volunteers were immunized and then subsequently challenged with live organisms.[62, 63] In these and other studies in humans and monkeys, limited serovar-specific protection against infection could be induced. However, when infection did occur after immunization, it was more severe, and the increased severity was not serovar-specific.[1, 63]

Multiple, recurrent, or persistent infection is required for development of ocular trachoma, and much of the inflammation and tissue damage appears to be due to the host immune response to the organism.[63] In nonendemic areas, adults can develop trachoma after sensitization by genital tract infection.[63] Marked inflammation can be induced in the eyes of previously infected monkeys by application of an extract of *C. trachomatis* containing the chlamydial 60-kD heat shock protein (cHSP60).[64] Furthermore, the presence of serum antibodies reactive with HSP60 are associated with ectopic pregnancy and infertility in women.[65–67] There is considerable sequence homology between cHSP60 and analogous proteins from other species including humans,[68, 69] and human sera reactive with cHSP60 also react with an analogous human protein.[68, 70] Consequently, it has been suggested that the pathogenesis of chlamydial disease in part may be autoimmune, with cHSP60 the sensitizing antigen.[69–71] In mice the antibody response to HSP60 is restricted at the major histocompatibility locus,[72] that is, the genetic background of the mouse regulates the response. If the same is true in humans, it might explain some of the variability observed both in the antibody response and morbidity in infected individuals.[72] More recent data have confirmed the relationship between antibody response to cHSP60 and risk of pelvic inflammatory disease[73] and scarring trachoma.[74]

Chlamydiae are able to induce cytokine production, one consequence of which is the production of interferon-α (IFN-α).[75] IFN-α inhibits chlamydial replication[76] and in animal models shortens duration of infection.[77] In vitro it induces a persistent infection in which synthesis cHSP60 continues out of proportion to structural membrane components.[78] However, removal of the IFN-α allows infectious organisms to be recovered. If such persistent infections occur in people (see later discussion), then cyclic changes in inhibitory cytokines, chlamydial replication, antigen production, and hypersensitivity response could explain the chronic inflammation and scarring often associated with chlamydial infections.[78]

IMMUNITY

Natural infection with *C. trachomatis* appears to confer very little protection against reinfection, and the protection conferred is short lived. Multiple or persistent infections are an essential factor in the pathogenesis of ocular trachoma.[79] Moreover, recurrent infection rates are quite high in sexually active individuals with genital tract infections: 29% over a 3½-year period in men and women attending a sexually transmitted disease clinic[80] and 38.4% in adolescent women who were followed prospectively for up to 2 years.[81] However, some data suggest that genital tract infections confer at least partial immunity against reinfection. In women with endocervical infection, secretory immunoglobulin A correlates inversely with numbers of organisms shed.[82] Men experiencing their first episode of NGU are more likely to have *C. trachomatis* recovered from their urethra than are men with a prior history of NGU.[83] Also, individuals at risk for a chlamydial infection who have either a prior history of any sexually transmitted disease or a documented chlamydial infection within the preceding 6 months are at lower risk for a chlamydial infection than those without such a history.[84] In the trachoma vaccine trials mentioned earlier, partial serovar-specific immunity could be elicited, but protection lasted only for 1 to 2 years.[63, 79]

In mouse models, CD4 lymphocytes of the Th1 type that traffic to the genital mucosa are crucial for restriction of intracellular growth and resolution of infection,[85] and antibodies directed at epitopes on the major outer membrane protein may play a role in reducing acquisition of infection.[86] Antibodies may also influence the severity of upper genital tract pathology in the mouse.[87] Both antibody and cell-mediated mechanisms are important in protective immunity in the guinea pig model.[88] It is possible that antigen presentation in natural mucosal infection may be relatively ineffective in producing strong protective immunity, because dendritic cells pulsed in vitro with inactivated chlamydiae are capable of conferring protective immunity in the mouse model.[89] Because of the combination of protective and deleterious effects seen with whole organism infection or vaccination, present vaccine development efforts are directed at defining relevant epitopes that could be used as components in some form of a synthetic or genetically engineered vaccine.[90] Early studies of DNA vaccines based on the omp1 gene of the mouse pneumonitis strain of *C. trachomatis* show reduced organism burden and mortality in a mouse pneumonia model.[91] However, similar studies have been unable to demonstrate an influence on the course of experimental genital infection in mice.[92]

LABORATORY DIAGNOSIS

Among *C. trachomatis* infections, only classic trachoma can be diagnosed on clinical grounds alone, and then only in the proper epidemiologic setting. Other chlamydial infections require laboratory confirmation for definitive diagnosis. Laboratory procedures of value include cytologic examination for intracytoplasmic inclusions, isolation of *C. trachomatis* in tissue culture, demonstration of chlamydial antigen by enzyme-linked immunosorbent assay or by immunofluorescent staining, or demonstration of nucleic acid by direct hybridization or by amplification techniques. These techniques are the subject of a recent in-depth review.[93]

Cytologic Diagnosis

In infant inclusion conjunctivitis and in ocular trachoma, typical intracytoplasmic inclusions can often be identified in Giemsa-stained cell scrapings from the conjunctiva. The technique is relatively insensitive in mild disease, although inclusion-bearing cells may be found in 10 to 30% of scrapings collected from patients with active trachoma.[94] Stained scrapings are positive in infants with neonatal conjunctivitis and in adults with inclusion conjunctivitis in as many as 90% and 50%, respectively. Cytology also has been used to evaluate endocervical scrapings, including those obtained for Papanicolaou smears. Interpretation is difficult, and sensitivity and specificity have been low.[95]

Isolation in Cell Culture

C. trachomatis grows well in a variety of cell lines that can be maintained in tissue culture. Most commonly used are McCoy or HeLa cells, which are grown either on glass cover slips in 12-mm diameter vials or on the bottom of polystyrene microtiter plate wells.[96] Incubation in tissue culture is from 40 to 72 hours, depending on the cell type and biovar. Intracytoplasmic inclusions can be detected after staining with Giemsa, Macchiavellos, or Gimenez stains or by immunofluorescence. Inclusions can also be detected in McCoy cells by staining with iodine, which stains glycogen.[94] However, immunofluorescent staining with monoclonal antibodies is the most sensitive and specific means of detecting inclusions (see Chapter 167, Fig. 167–2).[97] The quantity of infectious chlamydiae in a specimen is usually expressed as inclusion-forming units. A requirement for proper handling of clinical specimens before tissue culture inoculation is critical for optimal recovery of organisms but limits its utility.[98] For example, specimens must be maintained at 4°C and inoculated into tissue culture within 24 hours from the time they are obtained.[99] Alternatively, they can be frozen and stored at −70°C before inoculation, but this results in loss of some organisms and in false-negative results in some specimens containing a small number of inclusion-forming units.[100] Sensitivity of culture is also enhanced by blind passage of monolayers after incubation or by inoculation of multiple monolayers with a single specimen.[98] Although its specificity approaches 100%, even under optimal conditions, the sensitivity of culture is less than 100%. It has been estimated at between 70 and 90% in experienced laboratories.[101] These estimates have proved to be accurate in studies comparing the results of culture and more sensitive nucleic acid amplification tests.[93] Because of its high specificity, cell culture is the only test that should be used to establish the presence or absence of infection in situations with legal implications (e.g., rape or sexual abuse).[6]

The numbers of viable organisms shed by infected individuals and the isolation rates parallel each other. Both are affected by the clinical presentation.[102] For example, the highest isolation rates and numbers of recoverable inclusion-forming units are found in ocular infections such as active trachoma and neonatal or adult inclusion conjunctivitis. Rates are lower in mild or chronic ocular disease. Also, in infected individuals more organisms are recovered from the endocervix than from the male urethra, and even fewer are recovered from the female urethra.[103] However, when women at risk for infection are cultured at both the endocervix and urethra, as opposed to the endocervix alone, the increase in identification of infected women is approximately 20%,[103] that is, 20% of infected women have positive urethral and negative endocervical cultures. In LGV, the organism can be recovered from bubo pus in approximately 30% of cases and less frequently from sites such as the cervix or the urethra.[104] In appropriate clinical settings, *C. trachomatis* has been recovered from the nasopharynx and rectum,[105] bronchoalveolar lavage fluid and lung biopsy tissue,[106, 107] endometrium, fallopian tubes,[108] epididymis,[109] peritoneal cavity,[110] and donor semen.[111]

Antigen Detection and Nucleic Acid Hybridization

Several tests that do not require culture for detection of chlamydiae are commercially available. Recommendations as to when these tests are acceptable alternatives to culture are outlined in Table 168–1, and are based on a review[6] of published evaluations of their performance characteristics. The tests themselves are based on either (1) antigen detection by direct fluorescent antibody (DFA) staining, (2) antigen detection by enzyme-linked immunosorbent assay, or (3) detection of chlamydial ribosomal RNA by hybridization with a DNA probe. Published evaluations have been based primarily on MicroTrak DFA (Syva Co., Palo Alto, Calif.) and Chlamydiazyme (Abbott Laboratories, North Chicago, Ill.), although a number of similar tests have been approved by the Food and Drug Administration.[6] Most studies evaluating such tests have reported sensitivities greater than 70% and specificities of 97 to 99% in populations of men and women with a prevalence of infection of 5% or more.[6] These performance characteristics offer acceptable positive and negative predictive values for most diagnostic purposes.[6] In general, nonculture tests are more reliable in patients who are symptomatic and shedding large numbers of organisms than in patients who are asymptomatic and may be shedding fewer numbers of organisms.[102, 112]

In low-prevalence populations (i.e., less than 5% infected), a significant proportion of positive test results will be false positives. For example, if 1000 patients have a prevalence of 3%, then 30 are infected. A test with a sensitivity of 80% and a specificity of 99% will detect 24 of the infected people but will falsely identify 10 (1% of 1000) uninfected as infected. Consequently, the interpretation of a positive test result must be handled with care in counseling patients, and verification may be desirable. Verification of a positive test result can be by (1) culture, (2) a second nonculture test that identifies a different chlamydial antigen or nucleic acid sequence than the first test, or (3) a blocking antibody or competitive probe.[6] However, as noted earlier, only culture should be used if there are potential legal consequences associated with misdiagnosis of a chlamydial infection.[6]

Each format has its own advantages and disadvantages. DFA allows assessment of the quality of the specimen in addition to the presence or absence of organisms but requires a highly skilled microscopist for proper interpretation[112] (Fig. 168–2). Tests using antibodies directed against the major outer membrane protein are

TABLE 168–1 Use of Nonculture Tests for Diagnosis of *Chlamydia trachomatis* Infection

Population	Specimen	Prevalence	Acceptable Nonculture Test	Verification Required
Women	Endocervical	High†	Yes	No
		Low	Yes	Yes
Men	Urethra	High		No‡
		Low	Yes	?§
Women and men	Rectal	Any	No	—
Infants	Genital/rectal	Any	No	—
	Nasopharyngeal	Any	No	—
	Conjunctival	Any	Yes	No

*Verification of positive test result always required if adverse social or legal effects would result from a patient being misdiagnosed as having a sexually transmitted chlamydial infection.
†High = ≥5%.
‡Only Chlamydiazyme EIA or MicroTrak DFA; not enough data for other tests.
§Insufficient data.
Adapted from Centers for Disease Control and Prevention. Recommendations for the prevention and management of *Chlamydia trachomatis* infections. MMWR Morb Mortal Wkly Rep. 1993; 42:1–39.

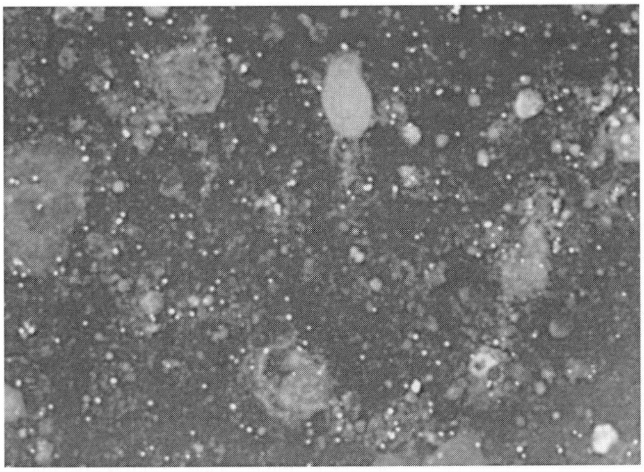

FIGURE 168–2. Immunofluorescent staining of a urethral specimen from a man heavily infected with *Chlamydia trachomatis.* Hundreds of stained organisms are seen against the dark background (×400). (Courtesy of Ms. Barbara Van Der Pol, Indianapolis, Ind.)

species specific, whereas those using antilipopolysaccharide antibodies can cross react with other bacteria, including other species of chlamydiae.[6] Performance of the enzyme immunoassay tests requires personnel with fewer skills but these tests generally take longer to perform. To differentiate false-positive from true-positive reactions, some manufacturers provide reagents for the test to be repeated on the same specimen with blocking antibody present.[113] The DNA hybridization techniques are relatively easy to perform and interpret. Although considerably fewer comparative data have been published on the DNA hybridization techniques than on the other formats, their sensitivity and specificity appear similar to those of the enzyme immunoassay tests.[114, 115]

Amplification Tests

Amplification tests based on the detection of chlamydial DNA using polymerase chain reaction (PCR) or ligase chain reaction (LCR) or specific chlamydial rRNA using transcription-mediated amplification are now available. A review of recent studies establish that these tests are more sensitive than culture and are nearly as specific.[93, 116–119] The three tests that are currently commercially available are the Roche Amplicor PCR, the Abbott LCx LCR, and the GenProbe TMA. More data are available for PCR and LCR, and published comparisons indicate that the two tests are equivalent in sensitivity and specificity.[93] Moreover, both detect *C. trachomatis* in urine or in self-administered vaginal swab specimens,[120] with a sensitivity comparable to that obtained with urogenital swab specimens, and make noninvasive testing for chlamydial infections possible.[119, 121] Several studies of military recruits,[122] adolescents,[123] high school students,[124] and juvenile detainees[125] indicate the utility of these tests in diagnosing infection without pelvic examination or swab specimens and outside traditional screening sites. What remains to be determined is the most cost-effective way of employing amplification tests in screening situations to have the greatest impact on the public health consequences of undiagnosed chlamydial infections.

The choice of the most appropriate test depends on the clinical setting, the facilities available, and the relative cost.

Serology

A complement fixation test is commercially available that measures antibodies against group reactive antigens (i.e., lipopolysaccharide) in people infected with *C. trachomatis* or *Chlamydia psittaci.* Virtually, 100% of individuals with LGV or psittacosis will have complement fixing antibody titers greater than 1:16.[126] However, the test lacks specificity because approximately 50% of adults with inclusion conjunctivitis, 15% of men with urethritis, and 45% of women with endocervical infection also have titers 1:16 or greater, and almost 10% of women with chlamydial cervicitis have titers 1:64 or greater.[126] Titers this high are rare in men with uncomplicated urethritis. Patients with LGV often present 3 to 4 weeks after the onset of their illness, by which time their antibody titer is stable. Consequently, in an appropriate clinical setting a complement fixation titer of 1:64 or greater is strongly supportive of a diagnosis of LGV, although confirmation requires a fourfold or greater titer rise between acute and convalescent specimens.[126]

The other test that has been used extensively in the United States is the microimmunofluorescence test. In its most common format, elementary bodies from each of the 15 serovars are employed as antigens, and antibodies against cell wall components of the organisms are detected.[29] This test is far more sensitive than the complement fixation test and is positive in 99% or more of women with cervicitis, 80 to 90% of men with urethritis, and 100% of adults with inclusion conjunctivitis.[29, 126] Infected men who are seronegative are usually men who are experiencing their first episode of urethritis and have not yet had time to develop antibody.

The test also detects anti-*Chlamydia* IgG in 100% of infants with pneumonia or inclusion conjunctivitis, but this may reflect passively transferred maternal antibody. Anti-*Chlamydia* IgM is present in approximately 30% of infants with neonatal inclusion and in 100% with chlamydial pneumonia.[126] Consequently, an IgM titer of 1:32 or greater in the microimmunofluorescence test can be diagnostic of infant chlamydial pneumonia in an appropriate clinical setting. The test also allows distinction between reactivity against *C. trachomatis* and *Chlamydia pneumoniae* and between reactivity to LGV as opposed to a trachoma biovar strain.

Anti-*Chlamydia* IgM is uncommon in adults with genital tract infection. The prevalence of anti-*Chlamydia* IgG is high in sexually active adults, even in those who do not have an active infection, and is likely due to past infection. There is a statistically significant association between chlamydia-specific serum IgA and active disease. However, the sensitivity, specificity, and predictive values are not high enough to make it clinically useful in the diagnosis of active disease.[127] Thus, chlamydial serologies are not recommended for diagnosis of active disease except in suspected cases of LGV, psittacosis, and infants with pneumonia.

CLINICAL MANIFESTATIONS

C. trachomatis infections can be divided into four clinical categories: (1) classic ocular trachoma, (2) LGV, (3) other oculogenital diseases in adults, and (4) perinatal infections.

Ocular Trachoma

In areas endemic for trachoma, the first infection usually occurs early in life, and active disease persists for several years. Although initial infections tend to resolve spontaneously, they are frequently complicated by reinfection or by superimposed bacterial conjunctivitis. In its initial stages, trachoma manifests as a chronic follicular conjunctivitis with papillary hypertrophy and inflammatory infiltration. As the disease progresses, scarring of the conjunctiva occurs, and there is involvement of the cornea. In addition, as the inner surface of the lids become scarred, the eyelashes turn in and abrade the cornea, resulting in ulceration, scarring, and visual loss. Some children with only mild disease are left with some conjunctival scarring and pannus formation (fibrovascular infiltrate), whereas others develop badly scarred conjunctivas and corneas, although the latter may not occur until well into adult life.[1, 128] The World Health Organization's simplified grading scheme for trachoma[129] is presented in Table 168–2.

TABLE 168-2 WHO Simplified Grading Scheme

1. Trachomatous inflammation—Follicular (TF): There are five or more follicles in the upper tarsal conjunctiva (follicles must be at least .05 mm in diameter).
2. Trachomatous inflammation—intense (TI): Pronounced inflammatory thickening of the tarsal conjunctiva, which obscures half of the normal deep tarsal vessels.
3. Trachomatous conjunctival scarring (TS): The presence of easily visible scars in the tarsal conjunctiva.
4. Trachomatous trichiasis (TT): At least one eyelash rubs on the eyeball. Evidence of recent removal of inturned lashes was also graded as trichiasis.
5. Corneal opacity (CO): Easily visible corneal opacity present over the pupil, which was so dense that at least part of the pupil margin was blurred when seen through the opacity.

Adapted from Thylefors B, Dawson CR, Jones BR, et al. A simple system of the assessment of trachoma and its complications. Bull World Health Organ. 1987; 65:477–483.

Treatment. In endemic areas, the primary reservoir is children with ocular infection. Transmission is by hand-to-eye contact between children and their caregivers or by contact with the feet of flies who feed on the exudate from children with active conjunctivitis.[130, 131] Hygienic factors that seem to be particularly important in control of disease include facial cleanliness and reduction of household fly density. Topical antibiotic therapy is of marginal benefit,[128] perhaps, in part, because extraocular sites, such as the nasal pharynx and rectum, are colonized in children with trachoma.[132] Systemic antibiotic therapy is effective in individuals and may be in communities in which the incidence of disease is relatively low.[128] However, compliance with erythromycin is poor, and doxycycline is contraindicated in young children. Preliminary results of trials of mass treatment with azithromycin at the village level indicate that both infection and clinical disease are markedly decreased at 6 and 12 months after treatment.[133–135] Programs involving lid surgery teams for the prevention of blindness due to lid deformities that cause continuing corneal damage also are of value.[128] Because of the hygienic factors, there is a strong historic link between improvement in socioeconomic conditions and disappearance of endemic trachoma.

Lymphogranuloma Venereum

LGV is a sexually transmitted disease caused by the LGV serovars of *C. trachomatis.* It is endemic in Africa, India, Southeast Asia, South America, and the Caribbean and occurs as a sporadic disease elsewhere. There are three distinct stages.

The first stage is formation of a primary lesion, usually on genital mucosa or adjacent skin. *C. trachomatis* cannot infect squamous epithelial cells, and when the primary lesion occurs on the external genitalia or in the vagina the organism probably gains entry through minute lacerations or abrasions.[104] The primary lesion is usually a small papule or herpetiform ulcer that produces few or no symptoms and is generally not noticed. It appears between 3 and 30 days after acquisition of infection[53] and heals rapidly without leaving a scar. It also can be intraurethral, producing a symptomatic urethritis.

The secondary stage occurs days to weeks after the primary lesion and is characterized by lymphadenopathy and systemic symptoms. The lymph nodes involved are those that drain the primary lesion and thus depend on its location. In men the primary lesion is usually on the penis or in the urethra, and the inguinal lymph nodes are the main ones affected. Lymphadenopathy is unilateral in two thirds of patients.[53] Similarly, when the site of primary infection is vulvar, then inguinal and femoral nodes are affected. When it is rectal, the affected nodes are the deep iliac, and when it is upper vaginal or cervical, the obturator and iliac nodes are infected.[104]

Inguinal lymphadenopathy, however, is the most characteristic manifestation of the secondary stage and the one most frequently recognized. Initially the lymph nodes are discrete and tender with overlying erythema, but because of extensive periadenitis the inflammatory process spreads from the lymph nodes into the surrounding tissue, forming an inflammatory mass. Abscesses within the mass coalesce, forming a bubo that may rupture spontaneously with development of loculated abscesses, fistulas, or sinus tracts.[136]

Systemic manifestations associated with this phase include fever, headache, and myalgias. Meningitis may occur, and in some cases, the organism has been recovered from blood or cerebrospinal fluid.[104] Rupture of the fluctuant inflammatory mass (bubo) relieves pain and fever,[104] although sinus tracts may continue to drain thick, yellowish pus for several weeks or months before fully resolving.[136] Excised inguinal nodes often have a characteristic inflammatory response, with central stellate coalescing abscesses that contain neutrophils and necrotic debris surrounded by a zone of palisaded epithelioid cells, macrophages, and occasional multinucleated giant cells. Surrounding this, there is an outer layer of lymphocytes and plasma cells. With time, nodal architecture is effaced and replaced by progressive fibrosis. This histopathology is suggestive of the diagnosis of LGV or cat-scratch disease but is not unique to these entities.

Healing leaves some scarring in the inguinal region but does not result in significant sequelae in most cases. Relapse occurs in approximately 20% of untreated cases.[104] Only about one third of buboes become fluctuant and rupture. The others harden and form inguinal masses, which gradually involute over time.[136] Femoral nodes are also frequently affected, and the division between the femoral and inguinal nodes by the inguinal ligament produces the "groove" in the groove sign described as characteristic of LGV.[104] Inguinal or femoral lymphadenopathy may be misdiagnosed as inguinal hernia, whereas deep iliac node involvement may raise a question of appendicitis.

Only 20 to 30% of women present with inguinal lymphadenopathy as their primary manifestation. Other common presentations are symptoms consistent with proctitis, proctocolitis, or complaints of lower abdominal and back pain due to involvement of deep pelvic and lumbar lymph nodes.[136] In the third stage, complications include *esthiomene* (Greek meaning, "eating away"), which refers to hypertrophic chronic granulomatous enlargement with ulceration of the external genitalia (either the vulva or scrotum and penis).[136] Lymphatic obstruction also may lead to elephantiasis of the male or female genitalia.

The differential diagnosis of inguinal lymphadenopathy in the age group likely to be infected includes herpes simplex virus, syphilis, chancroid, and occasionally lymphoma.[137] Mild leukocytosis, with an increase in monocytes and eosinophils, frequently accompanies early bubonic and anogenital rectal LGV.[104] Significant polymorphonuclear leukocytosis suggests bacterial adenitis or superinfection with pyogenic bacteria. The diagnosis can be made based on a positive chlamydial serology, isolation of LGV from infected tissue, or sometimes histopathology. A skin test (Frei test) has been used in the past but is not currently available.[104, 138] *C. trachomatis* can be recovered from bubo aspirates, genital tissue, or rectal tissue in only about 30% of cases.[104] Histopathologic changes in LGV are not specific but when combined with serologic results in an appropriate clinical setting, they are usually sufficient to make a presumptive diagnosis.

LGV manifesting as inguinal lymphadenopathy can be distinguished from genital herpes by the presence of the multiple painful ulcers at the site of the primary herpes infection, in contrast to the painless primary lesion of LGV, and by matting of the lymph nodes in LGV. Also, lymphadenopathy is frequently bilateral in herpes but not in LGV. A diagnosis of syphilis is suggested by a primary lesion with indurated margins (chancre) and bilateral and nontender inguinal lymphadenopathy. Large ulcers that are multiple and extremely tender in association with lymphadenopathy suggest chancroid. The pseudobuboes, which occur in granuloma inguinale, are nodules in the skin and subcutaneous tissue, with lymph node involvement being the result of secondary infection.[53] However, the clinical presentation of sexually transmitted agents causing inguinal lymphadenopathy clearly overlaps, and appropriate laboratory tests usually are required to distinguish among them. When an ulcer is present, a darkfield examination should be performed for *Treponema pallidum* and serologic tests for syphilis obtained.[53, 104, 137]

Treatment of Lymphogranuloma Venereum. Although sulfonamides have in vitro activity against *C. trachomatis* and some clinical efficacy, they do not produce bacteriologic cures reliably.[138] Tetracycline, doxycycline, minocycline, chloramphenicol, erythromycin, and rifampin have been used with good effect in the treatment of primary and secondary stages of LGV.[104, 139, 140] Few comparative data are available, but current recommendations by the CDC are for 21 days of doxycycline, 100 mg twice daily, with erythromycin or sulfisoxazole listed as alternative regimens.[141] In addition, fluctuant buboes should be aspirated to prevent rupture and sinus tract formation.[104] Antibiotic therapy results in rapid abatement of constitutional symptoms but has only a limited effect on bubo resolution.[104] Effects on late complications such as strictures are variable.[53, 104]

Oculogenital Disease in Adults

Inclusion Conjunctivitis. In the adult, chlamydial eye infection manifests as an acute follicular conjunctivitis, often with a foreign body sensation in the eye. Symptoms are usually unilateral. The clinical picture in the first 2 weeks is dominated by hyperemia and a mucoid discharge that becomes purulent.[142] This is followed by lymphoid follicle formation (frequently with corneal lesions and epithelial keratitis[143, 144]), as well as invasion of the cornea by blood vessels (pannus), and is indistinguishable from early ocular trachoma. Preauricular lymphadenopathy and otitis media may be present.[143] Untreated or improperly treated, the condition may persist for many months, and scarring similar to that seen in mild trachoma may occur, although usually the infection resolves without complications.[145]

Slightly more than half of adults with inclusion conjunctivitis have concurrent genital tract infections with *C. trachomatis.*[145, 146] In such individuals, the presumed mode of transmission is autoinoculation with infected genital secretions or, in some cases, direct inoculation from an infected partner. More difficult to explain is the acquisition of infection by individuals who do not have concurrent genital tract infections. Spread between individuals from eye to eye by transfer of infected secretions without sexual contact is probably more frequent than is generally appreciated.[146] Although as many as 9% of patients with keratoconjunctivitis who are 16 to 20 years of age have chlamydial ocular infection, eye involvement still is seen in less than 1% of individuals with proven genital tract infection.[145, 146]

The differential diagnosis is primarily conjunctivitis caused by adenovirus or other viruses.[144] A definitive diagnosis can be made only by demonstration of the organism. The condition responds promptly to the administration of appropriate systemic antibiotics, with decrease in discharge, hyperemia, and symptoms from keratitis within 48 hours.[142]

Urogenital Infections. Reliable estimates do not exist for the risk of transmission of *C. trachomatis* with a single episode of sexual intercourse. However, it appears to be substantially less than that for the transmission of *Neisseria gonorrhoeae.*[147] Based on extrapolation of data from partner notification programs and from couples with discordant cell culture–proven infection, the transmission probability has been estimated at 0.39 from men to women and at 0.32 from women to men.[148] More recently, transmission probability has been estimated at approximately 0.68 in both directions, based on results of a more sensitive diagnostic test, PCR.[149] However, these estimates are based on average frequency of intercourse among pairs rather than a single encounter. Partners of asymptomatic individuals identified through a screening program are less likely to be infected than partners of symptomatic individuals,[150] and in one study, recent exposure to a new partner was much more strongly associated with gonococcal than with chlamydial infection.[151] Furthermore, in adolescents, chlamydial infection is strongly associated with frequency of intercourse, both in those reporting only one lifetime partner and in those reporting more than one lifetime partner.[152] Thus, in contrast to gonococcal infections, genital infections with *C. trachomatis* have more characteristics of a prevalent than an incident disease. Most individuals infected with *N. gonorrhoeae* develop symptoms and seek care quickly, whereas many men and most women infected with *C. trachomatis* are either asymptomatic or minimally symptomatic and present for diagnosis as a result of screening or because a contact is symptomatic.[151]

C. trachomatis is recovered more often from women who acquire gonorrhea than from similarly exposed women who do not acquire gonorrhea.[153] In individuals with gonorrhea the recurrence rate of *C. trachomatis* infection with the same serovar is significantly greater than can be explained by variables related to likely exposure.[154] Furthermore, individuals infected with both *C. trachomatis* and *N. gonorrhoeae* shed larger numbers of *C. trachomatis* than those infected with *C. trachomatis* alone.[102] These data suggest that acquisition of a gonococcal infection either reactivates a persistent chlamydial infection or increases the susceptibility of the host to acquisition of chlamydiae.

Urethritis. There is little information on the natural history of untreated urethral infection. Only one of eight infected men who were followed without treatment for a minimum of 21 days developed symptomatic urethritis.[155] Although asymptomatic infections are common in men, *C. trachomatis* is also the cause of between 30 and 50% of cases of symptomatic NGU and an even higher proportion of cases of postgonococcal urethritis.[156] A differential clinical response to antimicrobials active against *Ureaplasma urealyticum* as opposed to *C. trachomatis* suggests that 10 to 20% of cases of NGU are caused by *U. urealyticum,*[157] and another 10% appear to be due to infection with *Trichomonas vaginalis.*[158] *C. trachomatis* also can be recovered from approximately 20% of men with gonococcal urethritis.[159] When men who are dually infected are treated only with single-dose therapy for their gonorrhea, most will develop postgonococcal urethritis, which manifests as a persistence or recurrence of their urethritis. In the United States the incidence of NGU exceeds that of gonococcal urethritis by ratios greater than 2 to 1 in most sexually transmitted diseases clinics, with even higher ratios in many private practice settings.[7] Risk factors for chlamydial urethritis in men include age younger than 20 years, black race, and heterosexual orientation.[160]

The incubation period for symptomatic chlamydial urethritis is usually between 7 and 14 days, in contrast to gonococcal urethritis, which is approximately 4 days. Patients present with dysuria and urethral discharge, which tends to be white, gray, or sometimes clear, in contrast to the more purulent discharge observed with gonococcal urethritis.[160] The discharge may be so slight as to be demonstrable only after penile stripping and then only in the morning. Some patients may deny the presence of discharge but may note stained underwear ("peter tracks") in the morning resulting from scant discharge overnight. However, there is sufficient overlap between the signs and symptoms of gonococcal and nongonococcal urethritis so that a reliable distinction between them cannot be made on clinical grounds alone. An average of four or more polymorphonuclear leukocytes per oil immersion field (1000×) in a Gram stain of an endourethral swab specimen establishes a diagnosis of urethritis.[161] The absence of organisms with the morphology of *N. gonorrhoeae* and the subsequent failure to culture *N. gonorrhoeae* establishes a diagnosis of NGU. In adolescent males, more than 10 leukocytes per high-power field in the initial 15 to 20 ml of a first-catch urine specimen is also strongly suggestive of urethritis,[162] as is a positive urine leukocyte esterase test result.[163] The primary complications of chlamydial urethritis in men are (1) epididymitis; (2) sexually reactive arthritis, including Reiter's syndrome; and (3) transmission to women.

Epididymitis and Prostatitis. *C. trachomatis* and *N. gonorrhoeae* are the most frequent causes of epididymitis in men younger than 35 years, whereas enterobacteriaceae (primarily *Escherichia coli*) are the usual pathogens in men older than 35.[164] In younger men urethritis also is usually present, but its absence does not exclude chlamydial infection or gonorrhea as the etiologic agent. Chlamydial epididymitis is often associated with oligospermia in the acute phase,[164] but long-term follow-up has not been performed and it is uncertain whether future fertility is impaired. However, epididymitis is usually unilateral, and attempts to correlate chlamydial infections with male factor infertility have been unsuccessful.[165] Although some investigators have recovered *C. trachomatis* from prostatic expressate or biopsies, convincing evidence that it plays a role in chronic or abacterial prostatitis has yet to be developed.[166]

Proctitis and Proctocolitis. Although asymptomatic rectal carriage of *C. trachomatis* occurs in both infants[105] and adults,[167] *C. trachomatis* is a fairly common cause of proctitis and proctocolitis in homosexual men.[168] Proctocolitis can result from direct inoculation of the rectum in either men or women through anal intercourse, or as a result of lymphatic spread from the cervix and posterior vaginal wall in LGV.[104, 169] In either situation the more severe disease is caused by the LGV serovars. The primary symptoms are anal pruritus and a mucous rectal discharge that becomes mucopurulent. The mucosa becomes ulcerated, and a chronic inflammatory process occurs in the bowel wall, with noncaseating granulomas and crypt abscesses.

As the disease progresses, muscle layers are replaced by fibrous tissue, which contracts to form rectal strictures. Sinus tract formation can lead to rectovaginal fistulas in women.[136, 169] Patients with proctocolitis experience fever, rectal pain, and tenesmus. The inflammatory process as seen on sigmoidoscopy may be localized to one segment or may occur at several different levels concurrently. Involvement of distal rectal mucosa can lead to perirectal abscesses and anal fissures. Outgrowths of lymphatic tissue resembling hemorrhoids occur as a result of lymphatic obstruction.

The clinical and histologic similarity to other inflammatory bowel diseases, such as Crohn's disease, can lead to misdiagnosis and inappropriate therapy.[168] Infection with serovars of the trachoma biovar produce much milder disease, which can range from asymptomatic infection to acute proctitis with rectal pain, mucopurulent discharge, abdominal pain, diarrhea, and bleeding. Leukocytes usually are present on rectal Gram stain even in asymptomatic patients.[168, 170]

Sexually Reactive Arthritis. Reactive arthritis appears to be an immune-mediated inflammatory response to an infection that occurs at a site distant from the primary infection.[171] Although enteric infections can provoke reactive arthritis, chlamydial infections appear to be the most common triggering event. Approximately 1% of men presenting with NGU develop an acute aseptic arthritis syndrome referred to as sexually reactive arthritis. One third of these have the full complex of Reiter's syndrome.[172] In men with untreated Reiter's syndrome who have urethritis, *C. trachomatis* can be recovered from the urethra in as many as 69% at the onset of the acute arthritis.[173] Reiter's syndrome patients have elevated synovial and serum antibody levels to *C. trachomatis,*[173] and it has been reported that patients who develop Reiter's syndrome following chlamydial urethritis have antibodies in sera and synovial fluid directed against chlamydial HSP60.[174] Approximately 80% of Reiter's syndrome patients also have the histocompatibility marker HLA-B27.[172] Furthermore, in addition to Reiter's syndrome, there appears to be an association among chlamydial infection, HLA-B27, and undifferentiated oligoarthritis.[175]

Synovial lymphocytes from Reiter's syndrome patients show a higher proliferative response in vitro to chlamydial antigens than peripheral blood lymphocytes from the same patients or synovial fluid lymphocytes from control patients.[171] These and other data suggest that *C. trachomatis* may be present in the joints of afflicted patients but in a form that either cannot be cultured or is very difficult to culture. Early reports suggested that *C. trachomatis* could be recovered by culture from synovial membranes of patients with Reiter's syndrome,[176, 177] but more recent studies have not confirmed this even with improvements in isolation technique.[171] Organisms with morphology consistent with *Chlamydia* have been identified in the synovium of Reiter's syndrome patients by electron microscopy, immunocytochemical staining,[171, 173] and molecular hybridization and amplification techniques,[171] suggesting that *Chlamydia* may persist in some form in synovial membranes of patients with Reiter's syndrome. More recently, chlamydial DNA was found in synovial biopsies together with mRNA detected by reverse transcriptase PCR, suggesting that detectable forms and DNA represent viable, persistent organisms.[178] These persistent chlamydiae exhibit aberrant gene expression, with no *OMP1* mRNA detected, but with detectable cHSP60 mRNA.[178] A double-blind study comparing lymecycline (tetracycline-L-methylene lysine) and placebo in patients with reactive arthritis suggested that 3 months of treatment was efficacious in arthritis associated with chlamydial infection but not in reactive arthritis associated with other causes.[179] Furthermore, when patients with Reiter's syndrome were treated for genitourinary infections with antichlamydial antibiotics, the incidence of arthritic relapses was significantly reduced compared with that in patients left untreated or treated with penicillin.[180] These data have led some to suggest that patients with Reiter's syndrome should receive prompt antichlamydial therapy for arthritic recurrences and any genitourinary complaints suggestive of a chlamydial infection.[181]

Genital Infection in Women. Although most infected women are asymptomatic, it is women who suffer the most serious consequences of genital chlamydial infections. Risk factors for infection vary in different population groups, but in most circumstances being a sexual partner of a man with either gonococcal or nongonococcal urethritis confers a risk of infection in excess of 30%.[7, 159] In the United States higher prevalence rates in sexually active individuals have been associated with younger age, black race, unmarried status, low socioeconomic conditions, and oral contraceptive use.[6, 7, 182] Young age is strongly associated with increased risk of chlamydial infection among sexually active females. In addition, young age is associated with increased risk of repeated infection,[183] with an associated increased risk of pelvic inflammatory disease (PID), ectopic pregnancy, and infertility.[184] Oral contraceptives may increase susceptibility or ease of detection because of an increase in cervical ectopy and thus in exposed susceptible cells. Alternatively, oral contraceptive use may be a surrogate marker for increased sexual activity.[182] In some studies,[185] but not others,[151] a recent change of sexual partners and increased numbers of partners also have been associated with increased prevalence.

The natural history of endocervical infection with *C. trachomatis* in women is not known. In most animal models, including primates, an immune response is mounted after infection or reinfection, and the organism is eventually eradicated.[186] It is likely that this occurs in a substantial proportion of infected women as well, or the women may inadvertently receive effective antichlamydial therapy for some other indication. However, some data suggest that chlamydiae can persist for a prolonged period of time in the female genital tract. In 14 infected college women who were followed for a minimum of 15 months without specific treatment, 7 remained infected.[187] Likewise 68 of 85 (80%) infected adolescent women who remained asymptomatic were still infected when reevaluated 2 months or more after their initial evaluation.[188] Other examples of persistent infection in humans include a case of LGV from which the organism was recovered after 20 years,[189] persistence of organisms in the synovium of patients with Reiter's syndrome,[171, 178] detection of chlamydial DNA in fallopian tube biopsy specimens from infertile women,[190] infants persistently infected for up to 28 months,[191] and recovery of *C. trachomatis* from the fallopian tubes and endometrium of infertile women in circumstances in which recent acquisition of infection was unlikely.[108]

Cervicitis and Urethritis. Approximately 70% of women with endocervical infection are without symptoms or have only mild symptoms such as vaginal discharge, bleeding, mild abdominal pain, or dysuria.[7] Dysuria may reflect concurrent urethral infection, whereas a vaginal discharge may be due to endocervical rather than vaginal infection in the adult. *C. trachomatis* cannot infect the squamous epithelium of the adult vagina. However, it can cause vaginitis before puberty when the vagina is lined with transitional cell epithelium.[192] On examination the cervix may appear normal or exhibit edema, erythema, and hypertrophy with a mucopurulent discharge from the os[54] (Fig. 168–3). Studies employing colposcopy emphasize the follicular nature of the cervicitis as well as erythema and ectopy.[193]

The acute urethral syndrome is defined as dysuria and frequency with fewer than 10^5 organisms per ml of urine.[194] In one study of 59 women with this syndrome, 42 also had pyuria and 11 of those 42 were infected with *C. trachomatis,* as were 3 of 66 women without symptoms and 1 of 35 with cystitis. Most of the remainder of the women with pyuria had low urine concentrations of coliform bacteria or *Staphylococcus saprophyticus* demonstrated by suprapubic aspiration.[194] Women with this clinical syndrome respond to appropriate antibiotics such as doxycycline. *C. trachomatis* has also been isolated from Bartholin's glands in women with bartholinitis. Although case control studies found an association between cervical dysplasia or neoplasia and *C. trachomatis* infection,[195, 196] in prospective studies of women with human papillomavirus infections concurrent chlamydial infection had no effect on the course of their cervical lesions.[197] Further investigation is required, but it appears that *C. trachomatis* does not play a significant role in the development of cervical neoplasia.

Of potentially far greater concern is the recently reported association between chlamydial cervicitis and acquisition of human immunodeficiency virus (HIV) infection by women.[198] In a case control study of female prostitutes in Zaire, the adjusted odds ratio for HIV seroconversion for *C. trachomatis* infection was 3.6 with a 95% confidence interval of 1.4 to 9.1. For gonorrhea it was 4.8 with a 95% confidence interval of 2.4 to 9.8. More recent data support the idea that infections due to *C. trachomatis* and other sexually transmitted agents increase shedding of HIV in genital secretions.[199] That infection with agents that produce genital mucosal inflammation could increase the risk of acquisition of HIV is not surprising and has substantial public health implications for control of the spread of HIV among heterosexuals.[199]

Endometritis and Salpingitis. The proportion of women with endocervical *C. trachomatis* infections who develop acute salpingitis has been estimated at 8%.[7] Eighteen of 109 (16.5%) infected asymptomatic adolescent women followed for 2 months or more became symptomatic, but only 2 (1.8%) developed clinical PID.[188] However, when women infected with both *C. trachomatis* and *N. gonorrhoeae* were treated for gonorrhea with penicillin only, 6 of 20 (30%) developed acute salpingitis during a 7-day follow-up interim.[200] The broader term *pelvic inflammatory disease* is preferable to *salpingitis,* as it encompasses clinically suspected endometritis or salpingitis, or both, that has not been confirmed pathologically or by direct visual inspection of the fallopian tubes (e.g., laparoscopically).[201] The proportion of women presenting with acute PID from whom chlamydiae can be isolated from the urogenital tract ranges between 5 and 51%, depending on the population studied and the techniques used, but is most often approximately 20%.[7] Histologic evidence of plasma cell endometritis is present in most cases of laparoscopically verified salpingitis.[202] Endometritis is also present in 40% of women with mucopurulent cervicitis and presumably progresses to salpingitis if untreated.[59] The spectrum of PID associated with *C. trachomatis* infection ranges from acute, severe disease, with perihepatitis and ascites, to asymptomatic or "silent" salpingitis.[203] Subclinical, undiagnosed salpingitis appears to be far more common than acute disease. When women with chlamydial salpingitis are compared with women with gonococcal or with nongonococcal nonchlamydial salpingitis, the former are more likely to experience a chronic, subacute course with a longer duration of abdominal pain before seeking medical care. Yet, they have as much or more tubal inflammation at laparoscopy.[204] Routine screening of asymptomatic women for chlamydial infection and treating those identified as infected has been shown to reduce the incidence of PID in a health maintenance organization setting.[205]

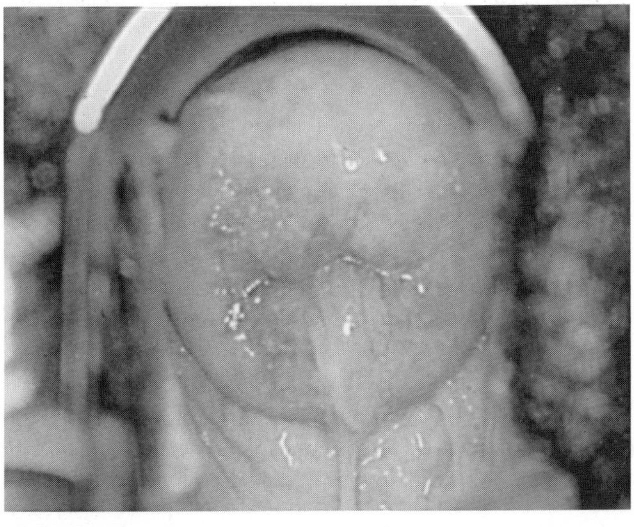

FIGURE 168–3. Colposcopy of a woman with mucopurulent cervicitis and purulent discharge from endocervical os. (Courtesy of Dr. David Soper, Richmond, Va.)

Infertility and Ectopic Pregnancy. The long-term consequences of both acute PID and silent, subclinical disease are tubal infertility, ectopic pregnancy, and chronic pelvic pain syndrome.[203] In developed countries, infertility affects approximately one in six couples, with tubal occlusion being a factor in 10 to 30%.[201] The mechanisms responsible for the tubal occlusion are not understood. In the case of *Chlamydia,* presumably they relate to a combination of chronic inflammation and scarring with either recurrent or persistent infection. Repeated endocervical infections followed by a direct tubal inoculation of *C. trachomatis* in monkeys produces peritubular adhesions as well as plasma cell endometritis.[206] Furthermore, women with nongonococcal salpingitis are more likely to have an adverse reproductive outcome than women with gonococcal salpingitis.[207]

In a prospective study of women who underwent laparoscopy for suspected PID, those with verified salpingitis were followed for a mean of 94 months. Sixteen percent of the patients and 2.7% of the controls failed to conceive. Ten percent of patients and none of the control subjects had confirmed tubal factor infertility. Tubal factor infertility increased with severity of infection as judged at the time of the index laparoscopy from 0.6% after a case of mild PID to 21.4% after a case of severe PID, and it increased with number of episodes of PID from 8% after one episode to 19% after two, and 40% after three. The ectopic pregnancy rate was 9.1% among patients versus 1.4% among controls.[208]

Most women with infertility due to tubular disease do not have a prior history of a sexually transmitted disease or of PID. However, a strong association between tubal infertility and serologic evidence of prior chlamydial infection has been a consistent observation in multiple studies.[7] Furthermore, *Chlamydia* has been recovered from fallopian tube biopsies in women undergoing microtuboplasty for surgical correction of damaged tubes,[108, 110] and chlamydial DNA and antigens have been demonstrated by in situ hybridization in the fallopian tubes of infertile women from whom *Chlamydia* could not be recovered by culture.[209]

Case control studies also have shown a strong association between ectopic pregnancy and serologic evidence of past chlamydial infection,[7] and in one study 22% of women experiencing ectopic pregnancy had histologic evidence of plasma cell salpingitis as well as antichlamydial antibodies.[210] Moreover, 81% of women experiencing ectopic pregnancy who had high titers of antichlamydial antibodies had specific antibody to cHSP60,[67] suggesting that hypersensitivity to this protein may play a role in tubal damage. In addition, presence of cHSP60 antibodies predict a two- to threefold increased risk of PID.[73] However, a recent attempt to detect chlamydial DNA in tubal tissue from women with ectopic pregnancies by polymerase chain amplification was unsuccessful,[211] and the role of persistent, as opposed to prior, infection in ectopic pregnancy remains to be defined.

Pregnancy Complications. Women experiencing recurrent spontaneous abortions were found to have high titers of antichlamydial IgG but negative endocervical cultures for *C. trachomatis,*[212] raising the possibility that prior or persistent *C. trachomatis* infection of the endometrium may be associated with some spontaneous abortions. Existing data on the effect of *C. trachomatis* infections on pregnancy outcome are conflicting. Several studies[213] found no association between adverse outcome and *C. trachomatis* infection, although a subset of women with IgM antibody against *C. trachomatis* (indicating recent infection) had lower birth weight infants than women lacking specific IgM.[214] Other investigators found an association between chlamydial infection and prematurity and premature rupture of the membranes.[215, 216]

In the largest published treatment study, an analysis of pregnancy outcomes was carried out in 1110 women who were infected with *C. trachomatis* but not treated, 1323 infected women who were treated with erythromycin, and 9111 uninfected, untreated women.[217] Comparison of these groups revealed a significant association between treatment and a decrease in premature rupture of the membranes with an odds ratio of 0.56 (0.37 to 0.85). In addition, there was a trend toward increased perinatal survival with an odds ratio of 2.21 (0.89 to 5.49, $p < 0.08$).

Pregnancy outcomes have also been compared in 244 treated women who were cured of a *C. trachomatis* infection and 79 treated women who had a persistent or recurrent infection.[218] Successful treatment was found to decrease the frequency of premature rupture of the membranes and small-for-gestational-age infants.

These studies suggest that treatment of *C. trachomatis* infection in pregnancy is likely to improve pregnancy outcome as well as prevent infant infection. However, more definitive data are needed.

Other Infections. Pneumonia due to *C. trachomatis* is primarily a disease of infants, although there have been isolated reports of *C. trachomatis* pneumonia in immunocompromised patients.[219, 220] In addition, pulmonary infection in laboratory workers exposed to relatively high concentrations of LGV serovars has occurred with resultant pneumonitis, lymphadenitis, or pleural effusion[107] (R. Jones, unpublished observations). Previously reported serologic associations with community-acquired pneumonia[221] probably reflect cross-reacting antibody with then-unrecognized *C. pneumoniae. C. trachomatis* also has been associated serologically with meningoencephalitis,[222] myocarditis,[223] and endocarditis.[224]

Treatment of Genital and Ocular Infections in Adults. The antibiotics that have activity against *Chlamydia* include the tetracyclines, macrolides and related compounds, rifampin, and some of the fluoroquinolones.[225] Although chlamydiae lack peptidoglycan, ampicillin and penicillin, both of which penetrate eukaryotic cells to a limited degree, have some activity, whereas cephalosporins and aminocyclitols do not. Considerable clinical data are available on the treatment of uncomplicated urogenital tract infections in both men and women. These data have been reviewed recently, and guidelines for the prevention and management of *C. trachomatis* infections have been published.[6] For several years standard therapy for uncomplicated genital tract infection has been doxycycline, 100 mg orally, twice daily for 7 days, with erythromycin as the first alternative. However, azithromycin given as a single 1-g dose, has been found to be as effective as a 7-day course of doxycycline[226] and is one of the recommended regimens in the most recent guidelines for the treatment of sexually transmitted diseases from the CDC. This is the only antimicrobial agent effective against *C. trachomatis* infection as single-dose therapy, which eliminates lack of compliance as a source of treatment failure. However, recent studies indicate that early recurrences of chlamydial infection occur in adolescents treated with azithromycin in as many as 5 to 13%.[227, 228] Reinfection is likely in some, but not all, of these early recurrences and suggests persistent infection despite treatment in some cases.[228] Azithromycin has also been shown to be effective in the treatment of the nongonococcal urethritis syndrome, whether due to *C. trachomatis,* genital mycoplasmas, or neither.[229] Ofloxacin at a dose of 300 mg twice daily for 7 days has been approved by the U.S. Food and Drug Administration for uncomplicated *C. trachomatis* infections. However, it should not be used in adolescents younger than 18 years of age or in pregnant women.[6] Relative costs should be a consideration in choice of therapy, given the excellent efficacy achieved with doxycycline in compliant patients.

Pregnant women unable to tolerate erythromycin at the standard dose of 500 mg four times a day for 7 days can be treated with 250 mg four times a day for 14 days or amoxicillin, 500 mg orally, three times a day for 7 to 10 days. There are fewer treatment failures in women who are able to complete a full course of erythromycin in women who take than amoxicillin.[230, 231] However, amoxicillin appears to be more effective overall because of a lower frequency of side effects and better compliance.[231, 232] Clindamycin is only partially effective in eradicating *C. trachomatis* in men with NGU,[233] but it appears to be as efficacious as erythromycin in both pregnant[234] and nonpregnant women.[235] Doxycycline and ofloxacin are contraindicated in pregnancy. Azithromycin has not been approved for use in pregnancy, and its safety and efficacy have not yet been established. However, a small trial of azithromycin versus erythromycin in pregnancy suggests that it may be effective and well-tolerated.[236]

Clinical conditions in which the likelihood of a chlamydial infection is high enough to warrant presumptive treatment for *C. trachomatis* in both the patient and any sexual partners are NGU (heterosexual men), PID, epididymitis in men younger than age 35, and gonococcal infection in either men or women.[6] Presumptive treatment of mucopurulent cervicitis alone is more controversial, and current guidelines suggest diagnostic testing with treatment based on test results as a reasonable approach.[141]

Proctitis in homosexual men and the acute urethral syndrome in women may be managed either presumptively or based on test results. Empirical therapy of both proctitis and epididymitis should include treatment for gonorrhea, for example, ceftriaxone, 250 mg intramuscularly, in a single dose, followed by 7 to 10 days of doxycycline, 100 mg orally twice daily.[141] When chlamydial infection is proven or strongly suspected, partners with whom the person has had recent sexual contact should be treated.[6]

The management of PID, even when gonorrhea is present, should always include therapy directed against *C. trachomatis,* as well as *N. gonorrhoeae* and anaerobic bacteria. Some experts recommend that initial therapy should be parenteral, followed by oral administration after initial improvement.[141] Recommended regimens include cefoxitin or cefotetan along with doxycycline, with the latter continued for a total of 14 days, or, alternatively, clindamycin and an aminoglycoside, again followed by doxycycline to complete a total of 14 days of therapy. An alternative to doxycycline is to continue clindamycin orally at a dose of 450 mg four times a day to complete 14 days of therapy.[141] Outpatient regimens include initial, single-dose, intramuscular therapy with a second- or third-generation cephalosporin plus 14 days of doxycycline. Alternatively, ofloxacin, 400 mg orally twice daily, plus oral metronidazole may be given.[141]

Few comparative data exist on the treatment of adult inclusion conjunctivitis, but tetracycline and its congeners (e.g., doxycycline) are effective when given for a 2- to 3-week period of time.[237] Erythromycin is an effective alternative.

Perinatal Infections

Neonatal Inclusion Conjunctivitis. Infant infection usually is acquired during passage through an infected birth canal. Exceptions include occasional infants who seem to have acquired an infection perinatally in spite of birth by cesarean section[238] and infants who acquire the organism postnatally from an infected caregiver by hand-to-eye contact. Between 22 and 44% of infants born to infected women develop neonatal conjunctivitis, although approximately 60% have serologic evidence of infection.[239] The usual incubation period is 5 to 12 days from birth, although the onset may be as late as 6 weeks of age.[240] Typically, a watery ocular discharge appears, which becomes progressively more purulent. The eyelids swell and the conjunctivae become erythematous and thickened. At birth, the conjunctiva lacks a lymphoid layer, and so follicles do not develop initially but may become apparent after 3 to 6 weeks.

The progression of the disease is very similar to that described for adults with spontaneous resolution occurring in most untreated infants after 3 to 12 months.[241] However, mild or subclinical infection may persist for several years,[191] and late sequelae such as scars and corneal lesions occur in a small proportion of cases.[242] A mucopurulent rhinitis, and in female infants vulvovaginitis, is often associated with the conjunctivitis. The primary differential diagnosis in a newborn is gonococcal ophthalmia, which is uncommon in children who receive ocular prophylaxis at birth but still does occur.[243] Ocular prophylaxis does not seem to be effective against *C. trachomatis* infection even when erythromycin or tetracycline is applied topically.[243]

Infant Pneumonia. Between 11 and 20% of infants born to infected mothers develop pneumonia due to *C. trachomatis.*[244] Infected infants usually become symptomatic before 8 weeks of age with nasal obstruction and/or discharge, tachypnea, and cough.[245] Presentation for care is usually between 4 and 11 weeks, and, characteristically, the infants have been symptomatic for 3 or more weeks before presentation. Most are only moderately ill and are afebrile.[246] A history of conjunctivitis is present in approximately one half of infants and middle ear abnormalities in more than half.[245] Paroxysms of staccato coughing that interfere with sleeping and eating are sometimes present. Auscultation may reveal scattered crackles, but breath sounds are usually good and wheezing absent. Chest x-rays show bilateral interstitial infiltrates with hyperinflation[245] (Fig. 168–4). Peripheral eosinophilia, arterial hypoxemia, and elevated serum immunoglobulins are characteristics.[245–247] *C. trachomatis* can usually be recovered from nasopharyngeal swab specimens and antichlamydial IgM titers are elevated.[244]

Untreated, the course is protracted, lasting weeks to months.[246] Especially in very young infants the initial respiratory manifestations of *C. trachomatis* infection may be more severe and include prolonged spells of apnea or respiratory failure.[248, 249] Although published reports emphasize more serious disease, it is likely that most patients with *C. trachomatis* infant pneumonia are treated as outpatients, often without laboratory confirmation of diagnosis. However, follow-up for as long as 8 years of children who had chlamydial pneumonia in the first 6 months of life has demonstrated a higher-than-normal frequency of obstructive airway disease (by pulmonary function testing) and of physician-diagnosed asthma.[250, 251] Thus, long-term respiratory sequelae may be significant.

Perinatally acquired *C. trachomatis* infection may persist in the nasopharynx, urogenital tract, or rectum for more than 2 years.[191] Consequently, differentiating infection acquired at birth from infection due to sexual abuse may be particularly difficult in younger children. In older children, infection with *C. trachomatis* needs to be differentiated from that with *C. pneumoniae.* For this reason and because of problems with specificity with the nonculture tests, only tissue culture using *C. trachomatis*–specific fluorescent antibody to detect inclusions should be used for diagnosis of infections in the genitalia, rectum, or pharynx in children.[141]

Prevention and Treatment of Infant Infections. Topical treatment of inclusion conjunctivitis is not recommended primarily because of difficulty in application and failure to eliminate concurrent nasopharyngeal carriage.[252] The latter can result in either recurrent conjunctivitis, pneumonia, or both.[252] Recommended therapy is oral erythromycin in doses of 50 mg/kg of body weight per day in four divided doses for 10 to 14 days. The efficacy of therapy is approximately 80%, and a second course may be required.[253] The course of therapy for *C. trachomatis* pneumonia is the same as that for conjunctivitis, and the efficacy is also approximately 80%. Mothers of infants with *C. trachomatis* should be evaluated and treated appropriately.

Prenatal screening for chlamydia and treatment of infected women is approximately 90% effective in preventing their infants from acquiring infection.[253] However, in populations at high risk for reinfection, particularly adolescents, reacquisition of infection after the first trimester is frequent,[254] and repeated prenatal screening may be warranted in this population.

PREVENTION STRATEGIES

Primary prevention strategies involve (1) attempting to induce behavioral changes that reduce the risk of acquisition of chlamydial infections, as well as other sexually transmitted diseases, and (2) identification and treatment of persons with genital infection before they can transmit the infection.

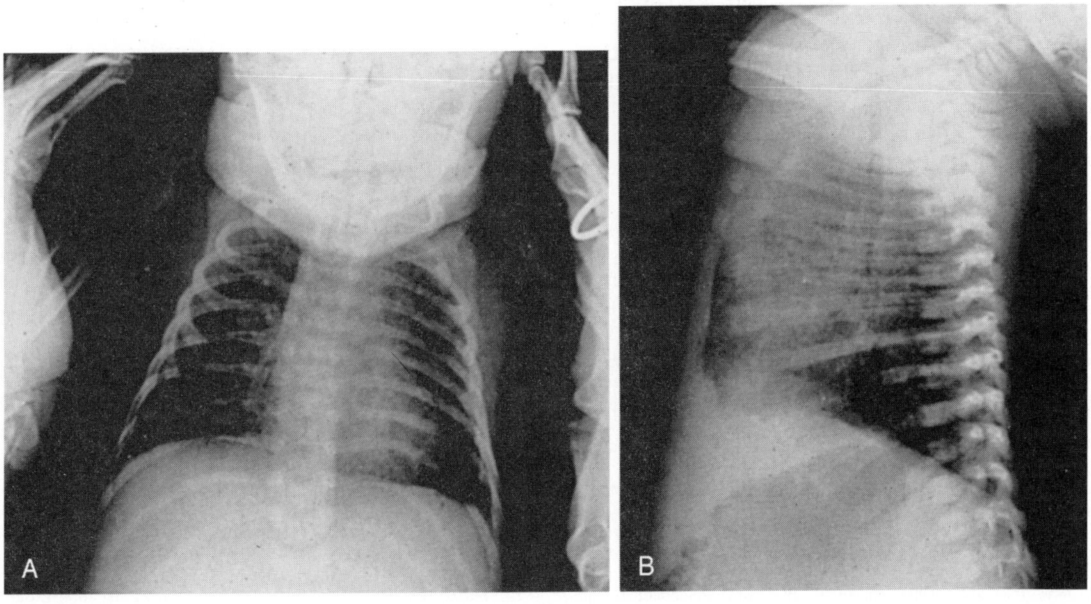

FIGURE 168–4. *A* and *B*, Chest radiographs of a 2-month-old infant with *Chlamydia trachomatis* pneumonia demonstrate typical patchy interstitial infiltrates and flattened diaphragms. (Courtesy of Dr. John Gaebler, Indianapolis, Ind.)

TABLE 168–3 Indications for Screening Women for *Chlamydia trachomatis* Infection

Special circumstances
Admission to detention facility
Presentation for induced abortion
Routine pelvic examination including prenatal or family planning visit*
Mucopurulent cervicitis
Sexually active and younger than 20 years of age
Persons 20–24 years of age who either (1) admit inconsistent use of barrier contraceptives or (2) have had a new or more than one sex partner in the preceding 3 months
Persons older than 24 years of age with both of risk factors (1) and (2)

*Any pelvic examination if younger than 20 years of age unless sexual activity since last test has been limited to a single mutually monogamous partner. Otherwise, annually.
Adapted from Centers for Disease Control and Prevention. Recommendations for the prevention and management of *Chlamydia trachomatis* infections. MMWR Morb Mortal Wkly Rep. 1993; 42:1–39.

Behaviors that reduce risk of infection include delaying age of first intercourse, decreasing numbers of partners, use of condoms, and use of vaginal sponges containing the spermicide nonoxynol 9.[6, 255–257] Nonoxynol 9 has some in vitro activity against *C. trachomatis*[258] and in two controlled trials was shown to reduce male-to-female transmission.[255, 256] A more recent controlled trial showed that nonoxynol 9 did not reduce the rate of male-to-female new chlamydia infection.[259] Nonoxynol 9 exhibits in vitro toxicity to cervical cells[258] and increases the likelihood of vaginal yeast infection.[256]

Programs that appear effective in reducing transmission include screening of high-risk populations for asymptomatic infections and partner notification and treatment. Indications for screening women are summarized in Table 168–3.

Because of the frequency of repeated chlamydial infections within the first several months following treatment of an initial infection,[228, 260] more frequent (e.g., every 6 months) screening of asymptomatic sexually active adolescents may be necessary.[261] The feasibility of employing noninvasive screening (urine testing) of sexually active young men and women has been proven using nucleic acid amplification tests (PCR, LCR), particularly in nontraditional settings such as high schools, military intake centers, juvenile detention centers, and other nonclinic sites in the community.[122–124] Also promising is the potential use of the leukocyte esterase test to identify asymptomatic adolescent men with pyuria for further evaluation with more expensive amplification tests.[163, 262, 263]

Notification and treatment of sexual partners also is effective in reducing infection and can be shown to be cost effective in spite of the resources required.[264, 265] In Sweden, where there is an extensive educational and control program using the previously mentioned elements, there has been a dramatic decline in chlamydial infections over the last decade.[265, 266] In addition, in selected areas in the United States that have many of these elements in place, such as the states of Washington[267] and Wisconsin[257] and the city of Indianapolis,[268] significant declines in the prevalence of *C. trachomatis* infection have been observed.

REFERENCES

1. Schachter J, Dawson CR. Human Chlamydial Infections. Littleton, Mass: PSG Publishing; 1978:63–96.
2. Halberstaedter L, von Prowazek S. Über chlamydozoenbefunde bei blennorrhoea neonatorum non gonorrhoica. Klin Wochenschr. 1909;46:1839–1840.
3. Heymann B. Über die fundorte der Powazek' schen korperchen. Berl Klin Wochenschr. 1910;47:663–666.
4. Lindner K. Zur atiologie der gonokokkenfreien urethritis. Wien Klin Wochenschr. 1910;23:283–284.
5. Thylefors B. Development of trachoma control programs and the involvement of national resources. Rev Infect Dis. 1985;7:774–776.
6. Centers for Disease Control and Prevention. Recommendations for the prevention and management of *Chlamydia trachomatis* infections, 1993. MMWR Morb Mortal Wkly Rep. 1993;42:1–39.
7. Cates W Jr, Wasserheit JN. Genital chlamydial infections: Epidemiology and reproductive sequelae. Am J Obstet Gynecol. 1991;164:1771–1781.
8. Podgore JK, Holmes KK, Alexander ER. Asymptomatic urethral infections due to *Chlamydia trachomatis* in male U.S. military personnel. J Infect Dis. 1982;146:828.
9. Karam GH, Martin DH, Flotte TR, et al. Asymptomatic *Chlamydia trachomatis* infections among sexually active men. J Infect Dis. 1986;154:900–903.
10. Wyrick PB. Cell biology of chlamydial infection. In: Stephens RS, Byrne GI, Christiansen G, et al, eds. Chlamydial Infections: Proceedings of the 9th International Symposium on Human Chlamydial Infection, International Chlamydia Symposium, San Francisco, 1998:69–78.
11. Joseph TD, Bose SK. Surface components of HeLa cells that inhibit cytadherence of *Chlamydia trachomatis*. FEMS Microbiol Lett. 1992;70:177–180.
12. Joseph TD, Bose SK. A heat-labile protein of *Chlamydia trachomatis* binds to HeLa cells and inhibits the adherence of chlamydiae. Proc Natl Acad Sci U S A. 1991;88:4054–4058.
13. Su H, Watkins NG, Zhang YX, et al. *Chlamydia trachomatis* host cell interactions: Role of the chlamydial major outer membrane protein as an adhesion. Infect Immun. 1990;58:1017–1025.
14. Wyrick PB, Choong J, Davis CH, et al. Entry of genital *Chlamydia trachomatis* into polarized human epithelial cells. Infect Immun. 1989;57:2378–2389.
15. Hodinka RL, Davis CH, Choong J, et al. Ultrastructural study of endocytosis of *Chlamydia trachomatis* by McCoy cells. Infect Immun. 1988;56:1456–1463.
16. Tipples G, McClarty G. The obligate intracellular bacterium *Chlamydia trachomatis* is auxotrophic for three of the four ribonucleoside triphosphates. Mol Microbiol. 1993;8:1105–1114.
17. Peeling R, Peeling J, Brunham R. High-resolution ^{31}P nuclear magnetic resonance study of *Chlamydia trachomatis:* Induction of ATPase activity in elementary bodies. Infect Immun. 1989;57:3338–3344.
18. Hatch TP, Miceli M, Sublett JE. Synthesis of disulfide-bonded outer membrane proteins during the developmental cycle of *Chlamydia psittaci* and *Chlamydia trachomatis.* J Bacteriol. 1986;165:379–385.
19. Bavoil P, Ohlin A, Schachter J. Role of disulfide bonding in outer membrane structure and permeability in *Chlamydia trachomatis.* Infect Immun. 1984;44:479–485.
20. Newhall WJ 5th. Biosynthesis and disulfide cross-linking of outer membrane components during the growth cycle of *Chlamydia trachomatis.* Infect Immun. 1987;55:162–168.
21. Moulder JW. Interaction of chlamydiae and host cells in vitro. Microbiol Rev. 1991;55:143–190.
22. Lundemose AG, Birklund S, Larsen PM, et al. Characterization and identification of early proteins in *Chlamydia trachomatis* serovar L2 by two-dimensional gel electrophoresis. Infect Immun. 1990;58:2378–2386.
23. Wagar EA, Stephens RS. Developmental form-specific DNA-binding proteins in *Chlamydia* spp. Infect Immun. 1988;56:1678–1684.
24. Crenshaw RW, Fahr MJ, Wichlan DG, et al. Developmental cycle-specific host-free RNA synthesis in *Chlamydia* spp. Infect Immun. 1990;58:3194–3201.
25. Herring AJ. The molecular biology of chlamydia: A brief overview. J Infect. 1992;25(Supp I):1–10.
26. Barry CE, Hayes SF, Hackstadt T. Nucleoid condensation in *Escherichia coli* that express a chlamydial histone homolog. Science. 1992;256:377–379.
27. de la Maza LM, Peterson EM. Scanning electron microscopy of McCoy cells infected with *Chlamydia trachomatis.* Exp Mol Pathol. 1982;36:217–326.
28. Todd WJ, Caldwell HD. The interaction of *Chlamydia trachomatis* with host cells: Ultrastructural studies of the mechanism of release of a biovar II strain from HeLa 229 cells. J Infect Dis. 1985;151:1037–1044.
29. Wang SP, Grayston JT. Microimmunofluorescence antibody responses in *Chlamydia trachomatis* infection, a review. In: Mardh PA, Holmes KK, Oriel JD, et al, eds. Chlamydial Infections. Amsterdam: Elsevier Biomedical Press; 1982:301–316.
30. Wang SP, Kuo CC, Barnes RC, et al. Immunotyping of *Chlamydia trachomatis* with monoclonal antibodies. J Infect Dis. 1985;152:791–800.
31. Newhall WJ 5th, Terho P, Wilde CE 3rd, et al. Serovar determination of *Chlamydia trachomatis* isolates by using type-specific monoclonal antibodies. J Clin Microbiol. 1986;23:333–338.
32. Wang SP, Grayston JT. Three new serovars of *Chlamydia trachomatis:* Da, Ia, and L2a. J Infect Dis. 1991;163:403–405.
33. Baehr W, Zhang YX, Joseph T, et al. Mapping antigenic domains expressed by *Chlamydia trachomatis* major outer membrane protein genes. Proc Natl Acad Sci U S A. 1988;85:4000–4004.
34. Stephens RS, Wagar EA, Schoolnik GK. High-resolution mapping of serovar-specific and common antigenic determinants of the major outer membrane protein of *Chlamydia trachomatis.* J Exp Med. 1988;167:817–831.
35. Batteiger BE. The major outer membrane protein of a single *Chlamydia trachomatis* serovar can possess more than one serovar-specific epitope. Infect Immun. 1996;64:542–547.
36. Dean D, Millman K. Molecular and mutation trends analyses of omp1 alleles for serovar E of *Chlamydia trachomatis.* J Clin Invest. 1997;99:475–483.
37. Stothard DR, Boguslawski G, Jones RB. Phylogenetic analysis of the *Chlamydia trachomatis* major outer membrane protein and examination of potential pathogenic determinants. Infect Immun. 1998;66:3618–3625.
38. Brunham RC, Plummer FA, Stephens RS. Bacterial antigenic variation, host immune response, and pathogen-host coevolution. Infect Immun. 1993;61:2273–2276.
39. Hayes LJ, Pecharatana S, Bailey RL, et al. Extent and kinetics of genetic change in the omp1 gene of *Chlamydia trachomatis* in two villages with endemic trachoma. J Infect Dis. 1995;172:268–272.
40. Brunham RC, Kimani J, Bwayo J, et al. The epidemiology of *Chlamydia trachomatis* within a sexually transmitted diseases core group. J Infect Dis. 1996;173:950–956.

41. Mondesire RR, Maclean IW, Shewen PE, et al. Identification of genus-specific eptiopes on the outer membrane complexes of *Chlamydia trachomatis* and *Chlamydia psittaci* immunotypes 1 and 2. Infect Immun. 1989;57:2914–2918.
42. Yuan Y, Lyng K, Zhang YX, et al. Monoclonal antibodies define genus-specific, species-specific and cross-reactive epitopes of the chlamydial 60-kilodalton heat shock protein (hsp60): Specific immunodetection and purification of chlamydial hsp60. Infect Immun. 1992;60:2288–2296.
43. Belunis CJ, Mdluli KE, Raetz CRH, et al. A novel 3-deoxy-D-manno-octulosonic acid transferase from *Chlamydia trachomatis* required for expression of the genus-specific eptiope. J Biol Chem. 1992;267:18702–18707.
44. Stephens RS, Kalman S, Fenner C, Davis R. *Chlamydia* Genome Project. http://chlamydia-www.berkeley.edu:4231. 1998.
45. Stephens RS, Mullenbach G, Sanchez Pescador R, et al. Sequence analysis of the major outer membrane protein gene from *Chlamydia trachomatis* serovar L2. J Bacteriol. 1986;168:1277–1282.
46. Allen JE, Stephens RS. Identification by sequence analysis of two-site posttranslational processing of the cysteine-rich outer membrane protein 2 of *Chlamydia trachomatis* serovar L2. J Bacteriol. 1989;171:285–291.
47. Wagar EA, Pang M. The gene for the S7 ribosomal protein of *Chlamydia trachomatis:* Characterization within the chlamydial str operon. Mol Microbiol. 1992;6:327–335.
48. Yuan Y, Zhang YX, Watkins NG, et al. Nucleotide and deduced amino sequences for the four variable domains of the major outer membrane proteins of the 15 *Chlamydia trachomatis* serovars. Infect Immun. 1989;57:1040–1049.
49. Dean D, Patton M, Stephens RS. Direct sequence evaluation of the major outer membrane protein gene variant regions of *Chlamydia trachomatis* subtypes D′, I′, and L2′. Infect Immun. 1991;59:1579–1582.
50. Lampe MF, Schland RJ, Stamm WE. Nucleotide sequence of the variable domains within the major outer membrane protein gene from serovariants of *Chlamydia trachomatis.* Infect Immun. 1993;61:213–219.
51. Weisburg WG, Hatch TP, Woese CR. Eubacterial origin of chlamydiae. J Bacteriol. 1986;167:570–574.
52. Kuo CC. Host response. In: Barron AL, ed. Microbiology of Chlamydia. Boca Raton, Fla: CRC Press; 1988:193–208.
53. Schachter J, Dawson CR. Human Chlamydial Infections. Littleton, Mass: PSG Publishing; 1978:45–62.
54. Brunham RC, Paavonen J, Stevens CE, et al. Mucopurulent cervicitis: The ignored counterpart in women of urethritis in men. N Engl J Med. 1984;311:1–6.
55. Griffin M, Pushpanathan C, Andrews W. *Chlamydia trachomatis* pneumonitis: A case study and literature review. Pediatr Pathol. 1990;10:843–852.
56. Braley AE. Inclusion blenorrhea. Am J Ophthalmol. 1938;21:1203–1207.
57. Rasmussen SJ, Eckmann L, Quayle AJ, et al. Secretion of proinflammatory cytokines by epithelial cells in response to *Chlamydia* infection suggests a central role for epithelial cells in chlamydial pathogenesis. J Clin Invest. 1997;99:77–87.
58. Ingalls RR, Rice PA, Qureshi N, Takayama K, Lin JS, Golenbock DT. The inflammatory cytokine response to Chlamydia trachomatis infection is endotoxin mediated. Infect Immun. 1995;63:3125–3130.
59. Paavonen J, Kiviat N, Brunham RC, et al. Prevalence and manifestations of endometritis among women with cervicitis. Am J Obstet Gynecol. 1985;152:280–286.
60. Patton DL, Taylor HR. The histopathology of experimental trachoma: Ultrastructural changes in the conjunctival epithelium. J Infect Dis. 1986;153:870–878.
61. Patton DL, Kuo CC, Wang SP, et al. Distal tubal obstruction induced by repeated *Chlamydia trachomatis* salpingeal infections in pigtailed macaques. J Infect Dis. 1987;155:1292–1299.
62. Grayston JT, Wang SP, Lin HM, et al. Trachoma vaccine studies in volunteer students of the National Defense Medical Center. II. Response to challenge eye inoculation of egg grown trachoma virus. Chin Med J (Republic of China). 1961;8:312–318.
63. Grayston JT, Wang S. New knowledge of chlamydiae and the diseases they cause. J Infect Dis. 1975;132:87–105.
64. Taylor HR, Maclean IW, Brunham RC, et al. Chlamydial heat shock proteins and trachoma. Infect Immun. 1990;58:3061–3063.
65. Brunham RC, Peeling R, Maclean I, et al. *Chlamydia trachomatis*–associated ectopic pregnancy: Serologic and histologic correlates. J Infect Dis. 1992;165:1076–1081.
66. Brunham RC, Maclean IW, Binns B, et al. *Chlamydia trachomatis:* Its role in tubal infertility. J Infect Dis. 1985;152:1275–1282.
67. Wagar EA, Schachter J, Bavoil P, et al. Differential human serologic response to two 60,000 molecular weight *Chlamydia trachomatis* antigens. J Infect Dis. 1990;162:922–927.
68. Cerrone MC, Ma JJ, Stephens RS. Cloning and sequence of the gene for heat shock protein 60 from *Chlamydia trachomatis* and immunological reactivity of the protein. Infect Immun. 1991;59:79–90.
69. Morrison RP, Belland RJ, Lyng K, et al. Chlamydial disease pathogenesis: 57 kD chlamydial hypersensitivity antigen is a stress response protein. Exp Med. 1989;170:1271–1283.
70. Yi Y, Zhong G, Brunham RC. Continuous B cell epitopes in *Chlamydia trachomatis* heat shock protein 60. Infect Immun. 1993;61:1117–1120.
71. Domeika M, Domeika K, Paavonen J, et al. Humoral immune response to conserved epitopes of *Chlamydia trachomatis* and human 60-kDa heat-shock protein in women with pelvic inflammatory disease. J Infect Dis. 1998;177:714–719.
72. Zhong G, Brunham RC. Antibody responses to chlamydial heat shock proteins hsp60 and hsp70 are H2 linked. Infect Immun. 1992;60:3143–3149.
73. Peeling RW, Kimani J, Plummer F, et al. Antibody to chlamydial hsp60 predicts an increased risk for chlamydial pelvic inflammatory disease. J Infect Dis. 1997;175:1153–1158.
74. Peeling RW, Bailey RL, Conway DJ, et al. Antibody response to the 60-kDa chlamydial heat-shock protein is associated with scarring trachoma. J Infect Dis. 1998;177:256–259.
75. Zhong G, Peterson EM, Czarniecki CW, et al. Role of endogenous gamma interferon in host defense against *Chlamydia trachomatis* infections. Infect Immun. 1989;57:152–157.
76. Rothermel CD, Byrne GI, Havell EA. Effect of interferon on the growth of *Chlamydia trachomatis* in mouse fibroblasts (L cells). Infect Immun. 1983;39:362–370.
77. Rank RG, Ramsey KH, Pack EA, et al. Effect of gamma interferon on resolution of murine chlamydial genital infection. Infect Immun. 1992;60:4427–4429.
78. Beatty WL, Byrne GI, Morrison RP. Morphologic and antigenic characterization of interferon-gamma–mediated persistent *Chlamydia trachomatis* infection in vitro. Proc Natl Acad Sci U S A. 1993;90:1–5.
79. Grayston JT, Wang SP, Yeh LJ, et al. Importance of reinfection in the pathogenesis of trachoma. Rev Infect Dis. 1985;7:717–725.
80. Katz BP, Caine VA, Batteiger BE, et al. A randomized trial to compare 7- and 21-day tetracycline regimens in the prevention of recurrence of infection with *Chlamydia trachomatis.* Sex Transm Dis. 1991;18:36–40.
81. Blythe MJ, Katz BP, Batteiger BE, et al. Recurrent genitourinary chlamydial infections in sexually active female adolescents. J Pediatr. 1992;121:487–493.
82. Brunham RC, Kuo CC, Cles L, et al. Correlation of host immune response with quantitative recovery of *Chlamydia trachomatis* from the human endocervix. Infect Immun. 1983;39:1491–1494.
83. Alani MD, Darougar S, Burns DC, et al. Isolation of *Chlamydia trachomatis* from the male urethra. Br J Vener Dis. 1977;53:88–92.
84. Katz BP, Batteiger BE, Jones RB. Effect of prior sexual transmitted disease on the isolation of *Chlamydia trachomatis.* Sex Transm Dis. 1987;14:160–164.
85. Igietseme JU, Ramsey KH, Magee DM, et al. Resolution of murine chlamydial genital infection by the adoptive transfer of a biovar-specific, Th1 clone. Reg Immunol. 1994;5:317–324.
86. Su H, Feilzer K, Caldwell HD, Morrison RP. *Chlamydia trachomatis* genital tract infection of antibody-deficient gene knockout mice. Infect Immun. 1997;65:1993–1999.
87. Cotter TW, Meng Q, Shen ZL, et al. Protective efficacy of major outer membrane protein specific immunoglobulin A (IgA) and IgG murine monoclonal antibodies in a murine model of *Chlamydia trachomatis* genital tract infection. Infect Immun. 1995;63:4704–4714.
88. Rank RG. Role of the immune response. In: Barron AL, ed. Microbiology of chlamydia. Boca Raton, FL: CRC Press; 1988:217–234.
89. Su H, Messer R, Whitmire W, et al. Vaccination against chlamydial genital tract infection after immunization with dendritic cells pulsed ex vivo with nonviable Chlamydiae. J Exp Med. 1998;188:809–818.
90. Ward ME. Chlamydial vaccines future trends. J Infect. 1992;25(Suppl 1):11–26.
91. Zhang D, Yang X, Berry J, et al. DNA vaccination with the major outer membrane protein gene induces acquired immunity to Chlamydia trachomatis (mouse pneumonitis) infection. J Infect Dis. 1997;176:1035–1040.
92. Pal S, Barnhart KM. Abai AM, et al. Immunization of mice with expression plasmids containing DNA sequences corresponding to the C. trachomatis MOPN MOMP failed to protect against a genital challenge. In: Stephens RS, Byrne GI, Christiansen G, et al, eds. Chlamydial Infections: Proceedings of the Ninth International Symposium on Human Chlamydial Infection. International Chlamydial Symposium, San Francisco, 1998:438–441.
93. Black CM. Current methods of laboratory diagnosis of *Chlamydia trachomatis* infections. Clin Microbiol Rev. 1997;10:160–184.
94. Schachter J, Dawson CR. Human Chlamydial Infections. Littleton, Mass: PSG Publishing; 1978:181–219.
95. Dorman SA, Danos LM, Wilson DJ, et al. Detection of chlamydial cervicitis by Papanicolaou-stained smears and culture. Am J Clin Pathol. 1983;79:421–425.
96. Yoder BL, Stamm WE, Koester CM, et al. Microtest procedure for isolation of *Chlamydia trachomatis.* J Clin Microbiol. 1981;13:1036–1039.
97. Stamm WE, Tam M, Koester M, et al. Detection of *Chlamydia trachomatis* inclusions in McCoy cell cultures with fluorescein-conjugated monoclonal antibodies. J Clin Microbiol. 1983;17:666–668.
98. Jones RB, Van Der Pol B, Katz BP. Effect of differences in specimen processing and passage technique on recovery of *Chlamydia trachomatis.* J Clin Microbiol. 1989;27:894–898.
99. Mahony JB, Chernesky MA. Effect of swab type and storage temperature on the isolation of *Chlamydia trachomatis* from clinical specimens. J Clin Microbiol. 1985;22:865–867.
100. Lin JL, Jones WE, Yan L, et al. Underdiagnosis of *Chlamydia trachomatis* infection: Diagnostic limitations in patients with low-level infection. Sex Transm Dis. 1992;19:259–265.
101. Schachter J. Biology of *Chlamydia trachomatis.* In: Holmes KK, Mardh PA, Sparling PF, et al. eds. Sexually Transmitted Diseases. New York: McGraw-Hill; 1984:243–257.
102. Barnes RC, Katz BP, Rolfs RT, et al. Quantitative culture of endocervical *Chlamydia trachomatis.* J Clin Microbiol. 1990;28:774–780.
103. Jones RB, Katz BP, Van Der Pol PB, et al. Effect of blind passage and multiple sampling on recovery of *Chlamydia trachomatis* from urogenital specimens. J Clin Microbiol. 1986;24:1029–1033.
104. Perine PL, Osoba AO. Lymphogranuloma venereum. In: Holmes KK, Mardh PA,

Sparling PF, et al. eds. Sexually Transmitted Diseases. 2nd ed. New York: McGraw-Hill; 1990:195–204.

105. Schachter J, Grossman M, Holt J, et al. Infection with *Chlamydia trachomatis:* Involvement of multiple anatomic sites in neonates. J Infect Dis. 1979;139:232–234.
106. Moncada JV, Schachter J, Wofsy C. Prevalence of *Chlamydia trachomatis* lung infection in patients with acquired immune deficiency syndrome. J Clin Microbiol. 1986;23:986.
107. Bernstein DI, Hubbard T, Wenman WM, et al. Mediastinal and supraclavicular lymphadenitis and pneumonitis due to *Chlamydia trachomatis* serovars L1 and L2. N Engl J Med. 1984;311:1543–1546.
108. Shepard MK, Jones RB. Recovery of *Chlamydia trachomatis* from endometrial and fallopian tube biopsies in women with infertility of tubal origin. Fertil Steril. 1989;52:232–238.
109. Berger RE, Alexander ER, Monda GD, et al. *Chlamydia trachomatis* as a cause of acute "idiopathic" epididymitis. N Engl J Med. 1978;298:301–304.
110. Henry-Suchet J, Catalan F, Loffredo V, et al. *Chlamydia trachomatis* associated with chronic inflammation in abdominal specimens from women selected for tuboplasty. Fertil Steril. 1981;36:599–605.
111. Sherman JK, Jordan GW. Cryosurvival of *Chlamydia trachomatis* during cryopreservation of human spermatozoa. Fertil Steril. 1985;43:664–666.
112. Stamm WE. Diagnosis of *Chlamydia trachomatis* genitourinary infections. Ann Intern Med. 1988;108:710–717.
113. Moncada J, Schachter J, Bolan G, et al. Confirmatory assay increases specificity of the Chlamydiazyme test for *Chlamydia trachomatis* infection of the cervix. J Clin Microbiol. 1990;28:1770–1773.
114. Clarke LM, Sierra MF, Daidone BJ, et al. Comparison of the Syva MicroTrak enzyme immunoassay and genprobe PACE 2 with cell culture for diagnosis of cervical *Chlamydia trachomatis* infection in a high-prevalence female population. J Clin Microbiol. 1993;31:968–971.
115. Chapin-Robertson K. Use of molecular diagnostics in sexually transmitted diseases. Critical assessment. Diagn Microbiol Infect Dis. 1993;16:173–184.
116. Ossewaarde JM, Rieffe M, Rozenberg-Arska M, et al. Development and clinical evaluation of polymerase chain reaction test for detection of *Chlamydia trachomatis.* J Clin Microbiol. 1992;30:2122–2128.
117. Viscidi RP, Bobo L, Hook EW, et al. Transmission of *Chlamydia trachomatis* among sex partners assessed by polymerase chain reaction. J Infect Dis. 1993;168:488–492.
118. Dille BJ, Butzen CC, Birkenmeyer LG. Amplification of *Chlamydia trachomatis* by ligase chain reaction. J Clin Microbiol. 1993;31:729–731.
119. Mahony JB, Luinstra KE, Waner J, et al. Interlaboratory agreement study of a double set of PCR plasmid primers for detection of *Chlamydia trachomatis* in a variety of genitourinary specimens. J Clin Microbiol. 1994;32:87–91.
120. Hook EW III, Smith K, Mullen C, et al. Diagnosis of genitourinary *Chlamydia trachomatis* infections by using the ligase chain reaction on patient-obtained vaginal swabs. J Clin Microbiol. 1997;35:2133–2135.
121. Bauwens JE, Clark AM, Loeffelholz MJ, et al. Diagnosis of *Chlamydia trachomatis* urethritis in men by polymerase chain reaction assay of first-catch urine. J Clin Microbiol. 1993;31:3013–3016.
122. Gaydos CA, Howell MR, Pare B, et al. *Chlamydia trachomatis* infections in female military recruits. N Engl J Med. 1998;339:739–744.
123. Rietmeijer CA, Yamaguchi KJ, Ortiz CG, et al. Feasibility and yield of screening urine for *Chlamydia trachomatis* by polymerase chain reaction among high-risk male youth in field-based and other nonclinic settings. Sex Transm Dis. 1997;24:429–435.
124. Miller ME, Dyer IE, Richwald GA, et al. *Chlamydia* screening of Los Angeles high school students using urine ligase chain reaction assay. In: Stephens RS, Byrne GI, Christiansen G, et al, eds. Chlamydial Infections: Proceedings of the Ninth International Symposium on Human Chlamydial Infections. International Chlamydia Symposium, San Francisco, 1998:289–292.
125. Dyer IE, Miller ME, Richwald GA, et al. *Chlamydia* screening in juvenile custody facilities. In: Stephens RS, Byrne GI, Christiansen G, et al, eds. Chlamydial Infections: Proceedings of the Ninth International Symposium on Human Chlamydial Infections. International Chlamydia Symposium, San Francisco, 1998:293–296.
126. Schachter J. Chlamydiae. In: Rose NR, Friedman H, eds. Manual of Clinical Immunology. 2nd ed. Washington, DC: American Society for Microbiology; 1980:700–706.
127. Mattila A, Miettinen A, Heinonen PK, et al. Detection of serum antibodies to *Chlamydia trachomatis* in patients with chlamydial and nonchlamydial pelvic inflammatory disease by the IPAzyme chlamydia enzyme immunoassay. J Clin Microbiol. 1993;31:998–1000.
128. Dawson CR, Schachter J. Strategies for treatment and control of blinding trachoma: Cost effectiveness of tropical or systemic antibiotics. Rev Infect Dis. 1985;7:768–773.
129. Thylefors B, Dawson CR, Jones BR, et al. A simple system for the assessment of trachoma and its complications. Bull WHO. 1987;65:477–483.
130. Taylor HR, Siler JA, Mkocha HA, et al. The natural history of endemic trachoma: A longitudinal study. Am J Trop Med Hyg. 1992;46:552–559.
131. Forsey T, Darougar S. Transmission of chlamydiae by the housefly. Br J Ophthalmol. 1981;65:147–150.
132. Malaty R, Zaki S, Said ME, et al. Extraocular infections in children in areas with endemic trachoma. J Infect Dis. 1981;143:853.
133. Schachter J, West S, Mabey D, et al. Azithromycin in control of trachoma 3. Effect of treatment on *Chlamydia trachomatis* infection in trachoma. In: Stephens RS, Byrne GI, Christiansen G, et al, eds. Chlamydial Infections: Proceedings of the Ninth International Symposium on Human Chlamydial Infection. International Chlamydia Symposium, San Francisco, 1998:347–350.
134. Mabey D, Bailey R, Faal H, et al. Azithromycin in control of trachoma 2. Community based treatment of trachoma with oral azithromycin: A one year follow-up study in The Gambia. In: Stephens RS, Byrne GI, Christiansen G, et al, eds. Chlamydial Infections: Proceedings of the Ninth International Symposium on Human Chlamydial Infections. International Chlamydia Symposium, San Francisco, 1998:351–354.
135. Dawson CR, Sheta A, Sallam S, et al. Azithromycin in the control of trachoma 5: Oral azithromycin compared to topical oxytetracycline for active trachoma in Egypt. In: Stephens RS, Byrne GI, Christiansen G, et al, eds. Chlamydial Infections: Proceedings of the Ninth International Symposium on Human Chlamydial Infections. International Chlamydia Symposium, San Francisco, 1998:355–358.
136. D'Aunoy R, von Haam E. General reviews: Venereal lymphogranuloma. Arch Pathol. 1939;27:1032–1082.
137. Piot P, Plummer FA. Genital ulcer adenopathy syndrome. In: Holmes KK, Mardh PA, Sparing PF, et al, eds. Sexually Transmitted Diseases. 2nd ed. New York: McGraw-Hill; 1990:711–716.
138. Coutts WE. Lymphogranuloma venereum: A general review. Bull WHO. 1950;2:545–562.
139. Greenblatt RB. Antibiotics in treatment of lymphogranuloma venereum and granuloma inguinale. Ann N Y Acad Sci. 1952;55:1082–1089.
140. Greaves AB, Hilleman MR, Taggart SR, et al. Chemotherapy in bubonic lymphogranuloma venereum: A clinical and serological evaluation. Bull WHO. 1957;16:277–289.
141. Centers for Disease Control and Prevention. 1998 guidelines for treatment of sexually transmitted diseases. MMWR Morb Mortal Wkly Rep. 1998;47 (No. RR-1):1–116.
142. Schachter J, Dawson CR. Human Chlamydial Infections. Littleton, Mass: PSG Publishing; 1978:97–109.
143. Dawson CR, Schachter J. TRIC agent infections of the eye and genital tract. Am J Ophthalmol. 1967;63 (Suppl):1288–1298.
144. Stenson S. Adult inclusion conjunctivitis: Clinical characteristics and corneal changes. Arch Ophthalmol. 1981;99:605–608.
145. Rönnerstam R, Persson K, Hansson H, et al. Prevalence of chlamydial eye infection in patients attending an eye clinic, a VD clinic, and in healthy persons. Br J Ophthalmol. 1985;69:385–388.
146. Stenberg K, Mardh PA. Genital infection with *Chlamydia trachomatis* in patients with chlamydial conjunctivitis: Unexplained results. Sex Transm Dis. 1991;18:1–4.
147. Lycke E, Löwhagen GB, Hallhagen G, et al. The risk of transmission of genital *Chlamydia trachomatis* infection is less than that of genital *Neisseria gonorrhoeae* infection. Sex Transm Dis. 1980;7:6–10.
148. Katz BP, Caine VA, Jones RB. Estimation of transmission probabilities for chlamydial infection. In: Bowie WR, Caldwell HD, Jones RP, et al, eds. Chlamydial Infections. Cambridge: Cambridge University Press; 1990:567–570.
149. Quinn TC, Gaydos C, Shepherd M, et al. Epidemiologic and microbiologic correlates of *Chlamydia trachomatis* infection in sexual partnerships. JAMA. 1996;276:1737–1742.
150. Ramstedt K, Forssman L, Giesecke J, et al. Epidemiologic characteristics of two different populations of women with *Chlamydia trachomatis* infection and their male partners. Sex Transm Dis. 1991;18:205–210.
151. Hook EW 3d, Reichart CA, Upchurch DM, et al. Comparative behavioral epidemiology of gonococcal and chlamydial infections among patients attending a Baltimore, Maryland, sexually transmitted disease clinic. Am J Epidemiol. 1992;136:662–672.
152. Blythe MJ, Katz BP, Orr DP, et al. Historical and clinical factors associated with *Chlamydia trachomatis* genitourinary infection in female adolescents. J Pediatr. 1988;112:1000–1004.
153. Oriel JD, Ridgway GL. Studies of the epidemiology of chlamydial infection of the human genital tract. In: Mardh PA, Holmes KK, Piot P, et al, eds. Chlamydial Infections. Amsterdam: Elsevier Biomedical Press; 1982:425–428.
154. Batteiger BE, Fraiz J, Newhall WJ, et al. Association of recurrent chlamydial infection with gonorrhea. J Infect Dis. 1989;159:661–669.
155. Stamm WE, Cole B. Asymptomatic *Chlamydia trachomatis* urethritis in men. Sex Transm Dis. 1986;13:163–165.
156. Bowie WR, Alexander ER, Holmes KK. Etiologies of postgonococcal urethritis in homosexual and heterosexual men: Roles of *Chlamydia trachomatis* and *Ureplasma urealyticum.* Sex Transm Dis. 1978;5:151–154.
157. Bowie WR, Wang SP, Alexander ER, et al. Etiology of nongonococcal urethritis. Evidence for *Chlamydia trachomatis* and *Ureaplasma urealyticum.* J Clin Invest. 1977;59:735–742.
158. Krieger JN, Verdon M, Siegel N, et al. Risk assessment and laboratory diagnosis of trichomoniasis in men. J Infect Dis. 1992;166:1362–1366.
159. Nettleman MD, Jones RB, Roberts SD, et al. Cost effectiveness of culturing for *Chlamydia trachomatis.* A study in a clinic for sexually transmitted diseases. Ann Intern Med. 1986;105:189–196.
160. Stamm WE, Koutsky LA, Benedetti JK, et al. *Chlamydia trachomatis* urethral infections in men. Prevalence, risk factors, and clinical manifestations. Ann Intern Med. 1984;100:47–51.
161. Bowie WR. Approach to men with urethritis and urologic complications of sexually transmitted diseases. Med Clin North Am. 1990;74:1543–1557.
162. Adger H, Sweet RL, Shafer MA, et al. Screening for *Chlamydia trachomatis* and *Neisseria gonorrhoeae* in adolescent males: Value of first-catch urine examination. Lancet. 1984;2:944–945.
163. Shafer MA, Schachter J, Moscicki AB, et al. Urinary leukocyte esterase screening

test for asymptomatic chlamydial and gonococcal infections in males. JAMA. 1989;262:2562–2566.
164. Berger RE, Alexander ER, Harnisch JP, et al. Etiology, manifestations and therapy of acute epididymitis: Prospective study of 50 cases. J Urol. 1979;121:750–754.
165. Ruijs GJ, Kauer FM, Jager S, et al. Is serology of any use when searching for correlations between *Chlamydia trachomatis* infection and male infertility? Fertil Steril. 1990;53:131–136.
166. Shortliffe LMD, Sellers RG, Schachter J. The characterization of the nonbacterial prostatitis: Search for an etiology. J Urol. 1992;148:1461–1466.
167. Jones RB, Rabinovitch RA, Katz BP, et al. Recovery of *Chlamydia trachomatis* from the pharynx and rectum of heterosexual patients at risk for genital infection. Ann Intern Med. 1985;6:757–762.
168. Quinn TC, Goodell SE, Mkrtichian E, et al. *Chlamydia trachomatis* proctitis. N Engl J Med. 1981;305:195–200.
169. Annamunthodo H. Rectal lymphogranuloma venereum in Jamaica. Ann Roy Coll Surg Engl. 1961;28:141–159.
170. Stamm WE, Holmes KK. *Chlamydia trachomatis* infections of the adult. In: Holmes KK, Mardh PA, Sparling PF, et al, eds. Sexually Transmitted Diseases. 2nd ed. New York: McGraw-Hill; 1990:181–193.
171. Rahman MU, Hudson AP, Schumacher HR Jr. *Chlamydia* and Reiter's syndrome (reactive arthritis). Rheum Dis Clin North Am. 1992;18:67–79.
172. Keat A, Thomas BJ, Taylor-Robinson D. Chlamydial infection in the aetiology of arthritis. Br Med Bull. 1983;39:168–174.
173. Keat A. Extragenital *Chlamydia trachomatis* infection as sexually-acquired reactive arthritis. J Infect. 1992;25:(Suppl 1):47–49.
174. Inman RD, Morrison RP. Immunoblot analysis of reactivity to chlamydial 57-kD heat shock protein in Reiter's syndrome (Abstract). Arthritis Rheum. 1990;33:S26.
175. Sieper J, Braun J, Brandt J, et al. Pathogenetic role of *Chlamydia, Yersinia* and *Borrelia* in undifferentiated oligoarthritis. J Rheumatol. 1992;19:1236–1242.
176. Schachter J. Isolation of bedsoniae from human arthritis and abortion tissues. Am J Ophthalmol. 1967;63:1082/56–6/60.
177. Vilppula AH, Yli-Kerttula UI, Ahlroos AK, Terho PE. Chlamydial isolation and serology in Reiter's syndrome. Scan J Rheumatol. 1981;10:181–185.
178. Gerard HC, Branigan PJ, Schumacher HR Jr, Hudson AP. Synovial *Chlamydia trachomatis* in patients with reactive arthritis/Reiter's syndrome are viable but show aberrant gene expression. J Rheumatol. 1998;25:734–742.
179. Lauhio A, Leirisalo-Repo M, Lähdevirta J, et al. Double-blind, placebo-controlled study of three-month treatment with lymecycline in reactive arthritis, with special reference to *Chlamydia* arthritis. Arthritis Rheum. 1991;34:6–14.
180. Bardin T, Enel C, Cornelis F, et al. Antibiotic treatment of veneral disease and Reiter's syndrome in a Greenland population. Arthritis Rheum. 1992;35:190–194.
181. Bardin T, Schumacher HR. Should we treat postvenereal Reiter's syndrome by antibiotics (Editorial)? J Rheumatol. 1991;18:1780–1782.
182. Washington AE, Gove S, Schachter J, et al. Oral contraceptives, *Chlamydia trachomatis* infection, and pelvic inflammatory disease. JAMA. 1985;253:2246–2250.
183. Hillis SD, Nakashima A, Marchbanks PA, et al. Risk factors for recurrent *Chlamydia trachomatis* infections in women. Am J Obstet Gynecol. 1994;170:801–806.
184. Hillis SD, Owens LM, Marchbanks PA, et al. Recurrent chlamydial infections increase the risks of hospitalization for ectopic pregnancy and pelvic inflammatory disease. Am J Obstet Gynecol. 1997;176:103–107.
185. Handsfield HH, Jasman LL, Roberts PL, et al. Criteria for selective screening for *Chlamydia trachomatis* infection in women attending family planning clinics. JAMA. 1986;255:1730–1734.
186. Wolner-Hanssen P, Patton DL, Holmes KK. Protective immunity in pigtailed macaques after cervical infection with *Chlamydia trachomatis*. Sex Transm Dis. 1991;18:21–25.
187. McCormack WM, Alpert S, McComb DE, et al. Fifteen-month follow-up study of women infected with *Chlamydia trachomatis*. N Engl J Med. 1979;300:123–125.
188. Rahm VA, Gnarpe H, Odlind V. *Chlamydia trachomatis* among sexually active teenage girls. Lack of correlation between chlamydial infection, history of the patient and clinical signs of infection. Br J Obstet Gynaecol. 1988;95:916–919.
189. Dan M, Rotmensch HH, Eylan E, et al. A case of lymphogranuloma venereum of 20 years' duration. Br J Vener Dis. 1980;56:344–346.
190. Campbell LA, Patton DL, Moore DE, et al. Detection of *Chlamydia trachomatis* deoxyribonucleic acid in women with tubal infertility. Fertil Steril. 1993;59:45–50.
191. Bell TA, Stamm WE, Wang SP, et al. Chronic *Chlamydia trachomatis* infections in infants. JAMA. 1992;267:400–402.
192. Bump RC. *Chlamydia trachomatis* as a cause of prepubertal vaginitis. Obstet Gynecol. 1985;65:384–388.
193. Dunlop EMC, Garner A, Darougar S, et al. Colposcopy, biopsy, and cytology results in women with chlamydial cervicitis. Genitourin Med. 1989;65:22–31.
194. Stamm WE, Wagner KF, Amsel R, et al. Causes of the acute urethral syndrome in women. N Engl J Med. 1980;303:409–415.
195. Hare MJ, Taylor-Robinson D, Cooper P. Evidence for an association between *Chlamydia trachomatis* and cervical intraepithelial neoplasia. Br J Obstet Gynaecol. 1982;89:489–492.
196. Schachter J, Hill EC, King EB, et al. *Chlamydia trachomatis* and cervical neoplasia. JAMA. 1982;248:2134–2138.
197. Yliskoski M, Tervahauta A, Saarikoski S, et al. Clinical course of cervical human papillomavirus lesions in relation to coexistent cervical infections. Sex Transm Dis. 1992;19:137–139.
198. Laga M, Manoka A, Kivuvu M, et al. Nonulcerative sexually transmitted diseases as risk factors for HIV-1 transmission in women: Results from a cohort study. AIDS. 1993;7:95–102.
199. Centers for Disease Control and Prevention. HIV prevention through early detection and treatment of other sexually transmitted diseases—United States. MMWR Morb Mortal Wkly Rep. 1998;47(No. RR-12):2–4.
200. Stamm WE, Guinan ME, Johnson C, et al. Effect of treatment regimens for *Neisseria gonorrhoeae* on simultaneous infection with *Chlamydia trachomatis*. N Engl J Med. 1984;310:545–549.
201. Cates W Jr, Rolfs RT Jr, Aral SO. Sexually transmitted diseases, pelvic inflammatory disease, and infertility: An epidemiologic update. Epidemiol Rev. 1990;12:199–220.
202. Paavonen J, Aine R, Teisala K, et al. Comparison of endometrial biopsy and peritoneal fluid cytologic testing and laparoscopy in the diagnosis of acute pelvic inflammatory disease. Am J Obstet Gynecol. 1985;151:645–650.
203. Paavonen J. Genital *Chlamydia trachomatis* infections in the female. J Infect. 1992;25(Suppl 1):39–45.
204. Svenssen L, Westrom L, Ripa KT, et al. Differences in some clinical and laboratory parameters in acute salpingitis related to culture and serologic findings. Am J Obstet Gynecol. 1980;138:1017–1021.
205. Scholes D, Stergachis A, Heidrich FC, et al. Prevention of pelvic inflammatory disease by screening for cervical chlamydial infection. N Engl J Med. 1996;334:1362–1366.
206. Patton DL, Wölner-Hanssen P, Cosgrove SJ, et al. The effects of *Chlamydia trachomatis* on the female reproductive tract of the *Macaca nemestrina* after a single tubal challenge following repeated cervical inoculations. Obstet Gynecol. 1990;76:643–650.
207. Brunham RC, Binns B, Guijon F, et al. Etiology and outcome of acute pelvic inflammatory disease. J Infect Dis. 1988;158:510–517.
208. Weström L, Joesoef R, Reynolds G, et al. Pelvic inflammatory disease and fertility: A cohort study of 1,844 women with laparoscopically verified disease and 657 control women with normal laparoscopic results. Sex Transm Dis. 1992;19:185–192.
209. Campbell LA, Patton DL, Moore DE, et al. Detection of *Chlamydia trachomatis* deoxyribonucleic acid in women with tubal infertility. Fertil Steril. 1993;59:45–50.
210. Brunham RC, Binns F, McDowell J, et al. *Chlamydia trachomatis* infection in women with ectopic pregnancy. Obstet Gynecol. 1986;67:722–726.
211. Osser S, Persson K. Chlamydial antibodies and deoxyribonucleic acid in patients with ectopic pregnancy. Fertil Steril. 1992;57:578–582.
212. Witkin SS, Ledger WJ. Antibodies to *Chlamydia trachomatis* in sera of women with recurrent spontaneous abortions. Am J Obstet Gynecol. 1992;167:135–139.
213. McGregor JA, French JI. *Chlamydia trachomatis* infection during pregnancy. Am J Obstet Gynecol. 1991;164:1782–1789.
214. Berman SM, Harrison HR, Boyce WT, et al. Low birth weight, prematurity, and postpartum endometritis: Association with prenatal cervical *Mycoplasma hominis* and *Chlamydia trachomatis* infections. JAMA. 1987;257:1189–1194.
215. Gravett MG, Nelson HP, DeRouen T, et al. Independent associations of bacterial vaginosis and *Chlamydia trachomatis* infection with adverse pregnancy outcome. JAMA. 1986;256:1899–1903.
216. Martius J, Krohn MA, Hillier SL, et al. Relationships of vaginal *Lactobacillus* species, cervical *Chlamydia trachomatis,* and bacterial vaginosis to preterm birth. Obstet Gynecol. 1988;71:89–95.
217. Ryan GM, Jr, Abdella TN, McNeeley SG, et al. *Chlamydia trachomatis* infection in pregnancy and effect of treatment on outcome. Am J Obstet Gynecol. 1990;162:34–39.
218. Cohen I, Vielle JC, Calkins BM. Improved pregnancy outcome following successful treatment of chlamydial infection. JAMA. 1990;263:3160–3163.
219. Ito JI, Comess KA, Alexander ER, et al. Pneumonia due to *Chlamydia trachomatis* in an immunocompromised adult. N Engl J Med. 1982;307:95–98.
220. Meyers JD, Hackman RC, Stamm WE. *Chlamydia trachomatis* infection as a cause of pneumonia after human marrow transplantation. Transplantation. 1983;36:130–134.
221. Komaroff AL, Aronson MD, Schachter J. *Chlamydia trachomatis* infection in adults with community-acquired pneumonia. JAMA. 1981;245:1319–1322.
222. Myhre EB, Mardh PA. *Chlamydia trachomatis* infection in a patient with meningoencephalitis. N Engl J Med. 1981;304:910–911.
223. Grayston JT, Mordhorst CH, Wang SP. Childhood myocarditis associated with *Chlamydia trachomatis* infection. JAMA. 1981;246:2823–2837.
224. van der Bel-Kahn JM, Watanakunakorn C, Menefee MG, et al. *Chlamydia trachomatis* endocarditis. Am Heart J. 1978;95:627–636.
225. Ehret JM, Judson FN. Susceptibility testing of *Chlamydia trachomatis:* From eggs to monoclonal antibodies. Antimicrob Agents Chemother. 1988;32:1295–1299.
226. Martin DH, Mroczkowski TF, Dalu ZA, et al. A controlled trial of a single dose of azithromycin for the treatment of chlamydial urethritis and cervicitis. N Engl J Med. 1992;327:921–925.
227. Hillis SD, Coles B, Litchfield B, et al. Doxycycline and azithromycin for prevention of chlamydial persistence or recurrence one month after treatment in women: A use-effectiveness study in public health settings. Sex Transm Dis. 1998;25:5–11.
228. Katz BP, Fortenberry D, Orr DP. Factors affecting chlamydial persistence or recurrence one and three months after treatment. In: Stephens RS, Byrne GI, Christiansen G, et al, eds. Chlamydial Infections: Proceedings of the Ninth International Symposium on Human Chlamydial Infections. International Chlamydia Symposium, San Francisco, 1998:35–38.
229. Stamm WE, Hicks CB, Martin DH, et al. Azithromycin for empirical treatment of the nongonococcal urethritis syndrome in men: A randomized double-blind study. JAMA. 1995;274:545–549.
230. Bell TA, Sandstrom IK, Eschenbach DA, et al. Treatment of *Chlamydia tracho-*

matis in pregnancy with amoxicillin. In: Mardh PA, Holmes KK, Oriel JD, et al, eds. Chlamydial Infections. Amsterdam: Elsevier Biomedical Press; 1982:221–224.
231. Magat AH, Alger LS, Nagey DA, et al. Double-blind randomized study comparing amoxicillin and erythromycin for the treatment of *Chlamydia trachomatis* in pregnancy. Obstet Gynecol. 1993;81:745–749.
232. Crombleholme WR, Schachter J, Grossman M, et al. Amoxicillin therapy for *Chlamydia trachomatis* in pregnancy. Obstet Gynecol. 1990;75:752–756.
233. Bowie WR, Yu JS, Jones HD. Partial efficacy of clindamycin against *Chlamydia trachomatis* in men with nongonococcal urethritis. Sex Transm Dis. 1986;13:76–80.
234. Alger LS, Lovchik JC. Comparative efficacy of clindamycin versus erythromycin in eradication of antenatal *Chlamydia trachomatis*. Am J Obstet Gynecol. 1991;165:375–381.
235. Campbell WF, Dodson MG. Clindamycin therapy for *Chlamydia trachomatis* in women. Am J Obstet Gynecol. 1990;162:343–347.
236. Wehbeh HA, Ruggeirio RM, Shahem S, et al. Single-dose azithromycin for *Chlamydia* in pregnant women. J Reprod Med. 1998;43:509–514.
237. Viswalingam ND, Daroughar S, Yearsley P. Oral doxycycline in the treatment of adult chlamydial ophthalmia. Br J Ophthalmol. 1986;70:301–304.
238. Shariat H, Young M, Abedin M. An interesting case presentation: A possible new route for perinatal acquisition of chlamydia. J Perinatol. 1992;12:300–302.
239. Harrison HR, Alexander ER. Chlamydial infections in infants and children. In: Holmes KK, Mardh PA, Sparling PF, et al, eds. Sexually Transmitted Diseases. 2nd ed. New York: McGraw-Hill; 1990;811–820.
240. Chandler JW, Alexander ER, Pheiffer TA, et al. *Ophthalmia neonatorum* associated with maternal chlamydial infections. Trans Am Acad Ophthalmol Otolaryngol. 1977;83:302–308.
241. Schachter J, Dawson CR. Human Chlamydial Infections. Littleton, Mass: PSG Publishing; 1978:111–120.
242. Persson K, Rönnerstam R, Svanberg L, et al. Neonatal chlamydial eye infection: An epidemiological and clinical study. Br J Ophthalmol. 1983;67:700–704.
243. Hammerschlag MR, Cummings C, Roblin PM, et al. Efficacy of neonatal ocular prophylaxis for the prevention of chlamydial and gonococcal conjunctivitis. N Engl J Med. 1989;320:769–772.
244. Schachter J, Grossman M, Sweet RL, et al. Prospective study of perinatal transmission of *Chlamydia trachomatis*. JAMA. 1986;255:3374–3377.
245. Tipple MA, Beem MO, Saxon EM. Clinical characteristics of the afebrile pneumonia associated with *Chlamydia trachomatis* infection in infants less than six months of age. Pediatrics. 1979;63:192–197.
246. Beem MO, Saxon EM. Respiratory tract colonization and a distinctive pneumonia syndrome in infants infected with *Chlamydia trachomatis*. N Engl J Med. 1977;296:306–310.
247. Harrison HR, English MG, Lee CK, et al. *Chlamydia trachomatis* infant pneumonitis: Comparison with matched controls and other infant pneumonitis. N Engl J Med. 1978;288:702–708.
248. Wheeler WB, Kurachek SC, Lobas JG, et al. Acute hypoxemic respiratory failure caused by *Chlamydia trachomatis* and diagnosed by flexible bronchoscopy. Am Rev Respir Dis. 1990;142:471–473.
249. Broadbent R, O'Leary L. Chlamydial infections in young infants—a cause for concern. N Z Med J. 1988;101:44–45.
250. Brasfield DM, Stagno S, Whitley RJ, et al. Infant pneumonitis associated with cytomegalovirus, *Chlamydia, Pneumocystis,* and *Ureaplasma:* Follow-up. Pediatrics. 1987;79:76–83.
251. Weiss SG, Newcomb RW, Beem MO. Pulmonary assessment of children after chlamydial pneumonia of infancy. J Pediatr. 1986;108:659–664.
252. Heggie AD, Jaffe AC, Stuart LA, et al. Topical sulfacetamide vs oral erythromycin for neonatal chlamydial conjunctivitis. Am J Dis Child. 1985;139:564–566.
253. Pereira LH, Embil JA, Haase DA, et al. Cytomegalovirus infection among women attending a sexually transmitted disease clinic: Association with clinical symptoms and other sexually transmitted diseases. Am J Epidemiol. 1990;131:683–692.
254. Oh MK, Cloud GA, Baker SL, et al. Chlamydial infection and sexual behavior in young pregnant teenagers. Sex Transm Dis. 1993;20:45–50.
255. Louv WC, Austin H, Alexander WJ, et al. A clinical trial of nonoxynol 9 for preventing gonococcal and chlamydial infections. J Infect Dis. 1988;158:518–523.
256. Rosenberg MJ, Rojanapithayakorn W, Feldblum PJ, et al. Effect of contraceptive sponge on chlamydial infection, gonorrhea, and candidiasis. A comparative clinical trial. JAMA. 1987;257:2308–2312.
257. Addiss DG, Vaughn ML, Ludka D, et al. Decreased prevalence of *Chlamydia trachomatis* infection associated with a selective screening program in family planning clinics in Wisconsin. Sex Transm Dis. 1993;20:28–35.
258. Patton DL, Wang SK, Kuo CC. In vitro activity of nonoxynol 9 on HeLa 229 cells and primary monkey cervical epithelial cells infected with *Chlamydia trachomatis*. Antimicrob Agents Chemother. 1992;36:1478–1482.
259. Roddy RE, Zekeng L, Ryan KA, et al. A controlled trial of nonoxynol 9 film to reduce male-to-female transmission of sexually transmitted diseases. N Engl J Med. 1998;339:504–510.
260. Burstein GR, Gaydos CA, Diener-West M, et al. Incident *Chlamydia trachomatis* infection among inner-city adolescents. JAMA. 1998;280:521–526.
261. Orr DP, Fortenberry JD. Screening adolescents for sexually transmitted infections. JAMA. 1998;280:654–655.
262. Sellors JW, Mahony JB, Pickard L, et al. Screening urine with a leukocyte esterase strip and subsequent chlamydial testing of asymptomatic men attending primary care practitioners. Sex Transm Dis. 1993;20:152–156.
263. Bowden FJ. Reappraising the value of urine leukocyte esterase testing in the age of nucleic acid amplification. Sex Transm Dis. 1998;25:322–326.
264. Katz BP, Danos CS, Quinn TS, et al. Efficiency and cost effectiveness of field follow-up for patients with *Chlamydia trachomatis* infection in a sexually transmitted diseases clinic. Sex Transm Dis. 1988;15:11–16.
265. Ripa T. Epidemiologic control of genital *Chlamydia trachomatis* infections. Scand J Infect Dis. 1990;69(Suppl):157–167.
266. Herrmann BF, Johansson AB, Mardh PA. A retrospective study of efforts to diagnose infections by *Chlamydia trachomatis* in a Swedish county. Sex Transm Dis. 1991;18:233–237.
267. DeLisle S, Fine D, Kaetz S, et al. A multistate model for the prevention and control of sexually transmitted chlamydia infections. Abstract 162. Tenth International Meeting of the International Society for STD Research, Helsinki, Finland, 1993.
268. Jones RB. Treatment of *Chlamydia trachomatis* infections of the urogenital tract. In: Bowie WR, Caldwell HD, Jones RP, et al, eds. Chlamydial Infections. Cambridge: Cambridge University Press; 1990;509–518.

Chapter 169

Chlamydia psittaci (Psittacosis)

DAVID SCHLOSSBERG

Psittacosis is a systemic infection that frequently causes pneumonia. Its relationship to bird exposure has been known for more than a hundred years. In 1879 Ritter studied an outbreak in Switzerland and called it *pneumotyphus*.[1] Morange applied the term *psittacosis* (from the Greek word for parrot) in 1892 after studying cases associated with sick parrots. In 1930 the organism was identified in several laboratories, by Bedson in the United Kingdom, Kromwede in the United States, and Levinthal in Germany.[2]

The name psittacosis has persisted, even though the term *ornithosis* more accurately depicts the potential for all birds to spread this infection. In fact, even mammals, including humans, are rare sources of psittacosis.

The causative agent of psittacosis is *Chlamydia psittaci*, one of the four species of *Chlamydia*. The others are *Chlamydia trachomatis* (which causes trachoma and genitourinary infection), *Chlamydia pneumoniae* (a cause of pneumonia and possibly coronary disease), and *Chlamydia pecorum* (at present considered an animal pathogen).

EPIDEMIOLOGY

C. psittaci is common in birds and domestic animals. Infection is therefore a hazard to pet owners, pet shop employees, poultry farmers (turkey-associated psittacosis has the highest attack rate in psittacosis epidemics), workers in abattoirs and processing plants (psittacosis is the most common abattoir-associated pneumonia), and veterinarians. However, anyone in contact with an infected bird or animal is at risk. Human cases occur both sporadically and as outbreaks.[4–6]

Most patients with psittacosis have had some contact with birds, usually as a pet. In fact, importation of exotic birds (sometimes illegal) has been correlated with an increase in human psittacosis in the United States, Sweden, England, and Wales.[7] Often the bird was recently acquired or was ill. Bird contact may achieve surprising levels of intimacy. Patients have acquired psittacosis by kissing their parrot or by performing mouth-to-mouth resuscitation on a dying bird. Other patients have had more trivial or transient exposure, such as visits to public bird parks, transporting pigeons by car, passing through a room in which infected birds were sitting, sharing a stage with a parrot, or guarding crates of pigeons at a railroad depot. Still, some patients (25%) have had no avian exposure.[8, 9]

Birds transmit the infection to their nestlings, which in turn shed the organism during periods of both illness and good health. In bird populations studied, there is a baseline prevalence of 5 to 8% of *C. psittaci* carriage. This may increase to 100% when birds are subjected to the stress of shipping, crowding, and breeding.[2, 9]

It is likely that all birds are susceptible. More than 130 avian species have been documented as hosts of *C. psittaci*.[2] These include members of the parrot family (macaws, cockatoos, parakeets, budgerigars), finches (canaries, bullfinches, goldfinches, sparrows), poultry (hens, ducks, geese, turkeys), and pigeons, pheasants, egrets, seagulls, and puffins.

Infection may appear in birds years after exposure. Infected birds may be asymptomatic or obviously sick. In the latter case, birds may exhibit shivering, depression, anorexia, emaciation, dyspnea, and diarrhea, frequently with closed eyes and ruffled feathers. Spontaneous relapse and remittance of the illness may occur, although it is during periods of illness that infected birds excrete the largest numbers of organisms. Discharge from their beaks and eyes and feces and urine are all infective; their feathers and the dust around their cage become contaminated.[10]

Thus, the infection is generally spread by the respiratory route, by direct contact or aerosolization of infective discharges or dust. Rarely, the bird may spread the infection by a bite. If untreated, 10% of infected birds become chronic asymptomatic carriers.[8, 9]

Strains from turkeys and psittacine birds are the most virulent for humans.[8] Although most human exposure comes from avian strains of *C. psittaci*, disease has occurred in ranchers after exposure to infected tissues from parturient cows, goats, and sheep. Endocarditis has been attributed to avian and nonavian strains, and cats have spread feline pneumonitis to humans and other mammals.

Human-to-human transmission is rare, and it is therefore thought unnecessary to isolate patients in the hospital or to give antibiotic prophylaxis to contacts. However, cases acquired from humans tend to be more severe than avian-acquired disease. Environmental sanitation is important because the organism is resistant to drying and can remain viable for months at room temperature.[2, 9]

CLINICAL FINDINGS

The disease begins after an incubation period of 5 to 15 days. Onset may be insidious or abrupt, and the clinical manifestations tend to be nonspecific. Several syndromes may result. The infection may be subclinical, or it may resemble a nonspecific viral illness with fever and malaise, or a mononucleosis-like syndrome with fever, pharyngitis, hepatosplenomegaly, and adenopathy. A typhoidal form manifests as fever, bradycardia, malaise, and splenomegaly. Finally, the presentation most suggestive of the etiology is that of atypical pneumonia, with nonproductive cough, fever, headache, and chest film abnormalities more dramatic than would be suggested by the physical findings. The illness ranges in severity from an inapparent or mild disease to a fatal systemic illness with prominent respiratory symptoms.

Because many patients have an illness with nonspecific findings, the list of initial diagnoses for which patients have been referred to hospitals is extensive. This list reflects the various organ systems that may be involved in *C. psittaci* infection and includes the diagnoses of pneumonia, meningitis, gastroenteritis, hepatitis, urinary tract infection, endocarditis, vasculitis, septicemia, malaria, brucellosis, fever of unknown origin, pulmonary embolism, myocardial infarction, tonsillitis, pancreatic carcinoma, and polymyositis.[6, 11]

The most common symptom is fever, occurring in 50 to 100% of patients. Cough has been reported in 50 to 100%, but it often appears late in the illness and is not present initially. Headache, myalgias, and chills are reported in 30 to 70% of patients. The nonspecificity of these signs and symptoms may be puzzling until cough supervenes. Even then, the long list of other signs and symptoms that occur in less than half the patients may be particularly confusing: diaphoresis, photophobia, tinnitus, ataxia, deafness, anorexia, nausea and vomiting, abdominal pain, diarrhea, constipation, sore throat, dyspnea, hemoptysis, epistaxis, arthralgia, and rash. Chest soreness is reported, but true pleuritic pain is rare.[6, 9, 11, 12]

The signs most frequently reported are fever, pharyngeal erythema, rales or other abnormalities on chest auscultation, and hepatomegaly. These occur in more than half of the cases. Fewer than half the patients show the signs of somnolence, confusion, tachycardia, relative bradycardia, pleural rub, splenomegaly (this occurs toward the end of the first week and is extremely helpful diagnostically), adenopathy, palatal petechiae, herpes labialis, Horder's spots (see later on), and muscle tenderness.[6, 9, 11]

Specific end-organ involvement reflects the systemic nature of psittacosis. The organ most commonly involved in humans is the lung. This is manifested clinically by cough, dyspnea, and a variety of nonspecific auscultatory findings on physical examination. Cardiac complications include pericarditis (rarely with effusion and tamponade), myocarditis, and "culture-negative" endocarditis. *C. psittaci* infection is associated with preexisting heart disease and may cause valvular destruction.[13, 14] Arterial embolism to major vessels occurs rarely. The source of these emboli and the mechanism are unknown; some are attributed to endocarditis or mural thrombi.[15]

Hepatitis may develop, sometimes with jaundice.[16] Anemia may result from hemolysis (both Coombs' test positivity and cold agglutinins are reported) and from a reactive hemophagocytosis, in which case pancytopenia may be present. Disseminated intravascular coagulation (DIC) also complicates psittacosis.[17–19] Reactive arthritis occurs 1 to 4 weeks after the initial illness. Although most of the described cases are polyarticular, monoarticular arthritis has also been described.[20]

Neurologic abnormalities include cranial nerve palsy (including sensorineural hearing loss), cerebellar involvement, transverse myelitis, confusion, meningitis, encephalitis, transient focal neurologic signs, and seizures. Results of cerebrospinal fluid examination on lumbar puncture are usually normal; a small number of white cells (predominantly lymphocytes) may be seen, and the protein on occasion is greatly elevated.[21–25]

Dermatologic phenomena include Horder's spots, which occur in a pink blanching maculopapular eruption resembling the rose spots of typhoid fever. Also described are erythema multiforme, erythema marginatum, erythema nodosum, and urticaria, as well as acrocyanosis, subungual splinter hemorrhages, and superficial venous thromboses.[26, 27] The kidney may develop an acute glomerulonephritis or acute tubulointerstitial nephritis, as well as acute tubular necrosis.[28–30] Psittacosis has severe consequences in pregnancy and often causes DIC, hepatic dysfunction, and placentitis with fetal compromise.[31, 32]

Also noted as complications of psittacosis are phlebitis, pancreatitis, and thyroiditis. Bacteremia has been demonstrated in a patient with a sarcoid-like illness.[33]

There is no documented protection after infection, and second infections have been seen in spite of elevated levels of complement-fixing antibodies.[2] Treated birds can be reinfected also.

LABORATORY FINDINGS

The total white blood cell count is usually normal or slightly elevated. Two thirds of patients have a leftward shift. Eosinophilia has been seen in convalescence. Results on liver function testing are mildly abnormal in 50% of cases, and may suggest cholestasis. Culture of the organism is possible from blood in the first 4 days of illness and from sputum in the first 2 weeks. However, although the organism can be isolated in cell culture and by animal inoculation, these methods are dangerous, and serologic diagnosis is preferred (see later).

Appearance on the chest film is abnormal in approximately 75% of patients (range 50 to 90%) and is usually more abnormal than auscultation would predict. The most frequent finding is consolidation in a single lower lobe, seen in 90% of the abnormal chest films. However, a variety of patterns have been reported, including a homogeneous ground-glass appearance, a patchy reticular pattern radiating from the hila, segmental or lobar consolidation with or without atelectasis, a miliary pattern, and unilateral or bilateral hilar enlargement. These chest film findings may take as long as 20 weeks to resolve, with the occurrence of resolution by 6 weeks on average.

Pleural effusions are seen in up to 50% of cases but are usually small and asymptomatic.[6, 34, 35] As noted, hilar enlargement may be present but never as the sole manifestation of disease.[35]

PATHOLOGIC FINDINGS

Birds show involvement predominantly in the liver, spleen, and pericardium, but in humans the lung is most frequently and characteristically involved. The trachea and bronchi become inflamed, with widespread mucous plugging. The inflammation spreads from respiratory bronchioles to the alveoli in a lobular pattern. Alveolar and then interstitial exudate accumulates; this is composed of mononuclear cells with a few polymorphonuclear leukocytes, red blood cells, epithelial cells, and fibrin. There is hyperplasia, proliferation, and desquamation of alveolar lining cells, which contain basophilic intracytoplasmic inclusions. Hilar lymph nodes swell, and the lungs become rubbery and solid. The classic sequence of congestion, edema, and red and then gray hepatization is seen.[36]

The brain is congested and edematous, with diffuse arachnoiditis. Meningeal exudate contains macrophages with intracytoplasmic inclusions. The heart shows monocytic infiltration, edema, fatty degeneration, and subendocardial hemorrhage. The pathologic findings in acute glomerulonephritis include hyaline glomerular occlusion, with subepithelial electron-dense deposits on electron microscopy. The liver may show nonspecific hepatitis or granulomas.[10, 16, 20] Infected placental tissue shows intervillositis with trophoblastic cytoplasmic inclusions.[31] In emboli, polymorphonuclear leukocytes, platelets, and fibrin are seen, but not organisms or chlamydial antigen.[19]

DIAGNOSIS

Culture is dangerous, and newer techniques such as polymerase chain reaction and antigen detection by direct fluorescence antibody testing or enzyme-linked immunosorbent assay (ELISA) are promising but remain investigational.[37, 38] Thus, diagnosis of psittacosis is currently established by demonstrating complement-fixing or microimmunofluorescent antibodies in serum. Usually the titer is 1:64 or higher. For surveillance purposes, the Centers for Disease Control and Prevention (CDC) considers a *confirmed* case one with a positive culture result or associated with clinical illness compatible with psittacosis plus a fourfold or greater change in antibody titer to at least 1:32 or IgM by microimmunofluorescence (MIF) testing of at least 1:16; a *probable* case is one associated with psittacosis-compatible illness linked epidemiologically with a confirmed case or a titer of at least 1:32 in a single specimen. There are false-positive and false-negative reactions. Also, the complement fixation test is only genus-specific and does not distinguish *C. psittaci* from *C. trachomatis* or *C. pneumoniae*, both of which are common pathogens. MIF testing has greater sensitivity and specificity and can measure both IgM and IgG, but cross-reactions still occur. Thus, serologic testing remains imperfect. In addition, antibiotic therapy can delay or diminish the antibody response.[39]

TREATMENT

The treatment of choice is tetracycline hydrochloride, 500 mg PO qid, or doxycycline, 100 mg PO bid, for 10 to 21 days. Some observers recommend the longer course to prevent relapse, but this is controversial. Erythromycin therapy is the alternative treatment but may be less efficacious in severe cases.

Most patients respond within 24 hours subjectively. Without treatment, the fatality rate is approximately 20%; with treatment, it drops to 1%. The best therapy for endocarditis is valve replacement and prolonged antimicrobial therapy.[5, 9, 10, 15]

PREVENTION

Infected birds should be treated with tetracycline, chlortetracycline, or doxycycline for at least 45 consecutive days. The U.S. Department of Agriculture (USDA) requires that imported birds be quarantined for 30 days to prevent introduction of Newcastle disease. During this period birds are treated with chlortetracycline. The USDA recommends that importers continue treatment for an additional 15 days, but this is not always done, and if treated for fewer than 45 days, some infected birds will continue to shed the organism.[9, 10, 38]

DIFFERENTIAL DIAGNOSIS

The list of considerations in the differential diagnosis is extensive, and the diagnostic possibilities depend on the presentation. A typhoidal picture suggests one of the etiologies of the mononucleosis syndrome, typhoid fever, brucellosis, tularemia, influenza, or subacute bacterial endocarditis. Respiratory signs and symptoms plus headache and myalgias should orient the clinician to causes of atypical pneumonia, such as viral pneumonia, Q fever, legionellosis, and infection with mycoplasma and *C. pneumoniae*.[35]

Helpful clues to a diagnosis of psittacosis, when present, are relative bradycardia, rash, hemoptysis, epistaxis, and splenomegaly.

REFERENCES

1. Harris RL, Williams TW. Contribution to the Question of Pneumotyphus: A discussion of the original article by J. Ritter in 1880. Rev Infect Dis. 1985;7:119–122.
2. Macfarlane JT, Macrae AD. Psittacosis. Med Bull. 1983;39:163–167.
3. Sheehy N, Markey B, Gleeson M, et al. Differentiation of *Chlamydia psittaci* and *C. pecorum* strains by species specific PCR. J Clin Microbiol. 1996;34:3175–3179.
4. Esposito AL. Pulmonary infections acquired in the workplace. Clin Chest Med. 1992;13:355–365.
5. Crosse B. Psittacosis: A clinical review. J Infect. 1990;21:251–259.
6. Schlossberg D, Delgado J, Moore MM, et al. An epidemic of avian and human psittacosis. Arch Intern Med. 1993;153:2594–2596.
7. Reeve RVA, Carter LA, Taylor N, et al. Respiratory tract infections and importation of exotic birds. Lancet. 1988;829–830.
8. Psittacosis (Editorial). BMJ. 1972;1:1–2.
9. Centers for Disease Control and Prevention. Compendium of Psittacosis (Chlamydiosis) Control 1997. Issued July 18, 1997. No. RR-13.
10. Grimes JE. Zoonoses acquired from pet birds. Vet Clin. 1987;17:209–218.
11. Yung AP, Grayson ML. Psittacosis—a review of 135 cases. Med J Aust. 1988;148:228–233.
12. Schaffner W, Drutz DJ, Duncan GW, et al. The clinical spectrum of endemic psittacosis. Arch Intern Med. 1967;119:433–443.
13. Shapiro DS, Kenney SC, Johnson M, et al. Brief report: *Chlamydia psittaci* endocarditis diagnosed by blood culture. N Engl J Med. 1992;326:1192–1195.
14. Page SR, Stewart JT, Bernstein JJ. A progressive pericardial effusion caused by psittacosis. Br Heart J. 1988;60:87–89.
15. Patel RT, Jekinson LR, Wheeler MH, et al. Arterial embolism associated with psittacosis. J Royal Soc Med. 1991;84:374–375.
16. Samra Z, Pik A, Guidetti-Sharon A, et al. Hepatitis in a family infected by *Chlamydia psittaci*. J Royal Soc Med. 1991;84:347–348.
17. Timmerman R, Bieger R. Haemolytic anemia due to cold agglutinins caused by psittacosis. Neth J Med. 1989;34:306–309.
18. Hamilton DV. Short reports—psittacosis and disseminated intravascular coagulation. BMJ. 1975;17:370.
19. Wong KF, Chan JKC, Chan CH, et al. Psittacosis-associated hemophagocytic syndrome. Am J Med. 1991;91:204–205.
20. Tsapas G, Klonizakis I, Casakos K, et al. Psittacosis and arthritis. Chemotherapy. 1991;37:143–145.
21. Zumla A, Lipscomb G, Lewis D. Sixth cranial nerve palsy complicating psittacosis. J Neurol Neurosurg Psychiatry. 1988;51:1462.
22. Newton P, Lalvani A, Conlon CP. Psittacosis associated with bilateral 4th cranial nerve palsies. J Infect. 1996;32:63–65.
23. Crook T, Bannister B. Acute transverse myelitis associated with *Chlamydia psittaci* infection. J Infect. 1996;32:151–152.
24. Brewis C, McFerran J. Farmer's ear: Sudden sensorineural hearing loss due to *Chlamydia psittaci* infection. J Laryngol Otol. 1997;111:855–857.
25. Shee CD. Cerebellar disturbance in psittacosis. Postgrad Med J. 1988;64:382–383.
26. Green ST, Hamlet NW, Willocks L, et al. Psittacosis presenting with erythema-marginatum-like lesions—a case report and a historical review. Clin Exp Dermatol. 1990;225–227.
27. Semel J. Cutaneous findings in a case of psittacosis. Arch Dermatol. 1984;120:1227–1229.
28. Jeffrey RF, More IAR, Carrington MB, et al. Acute glomerulonephritis following infection with *Chlamydia psittaci*. Am J Kidney Dis. 1992;1:94–96.
29. Mason AB, Jenkins P. Acute renal failure in fulminant psittacosis. Respir Med. 1994;88:239–240.
30. Branley P, Speed B. Acute interstitial nephritis due to *Chlamydia psittaci*. Aust N Z J Med. 1995;25:365.

31. Hyde SR, Benirschke K. Gestational psittacosis: Case report and literature review. Mod Pathol. 1997;10:602–607.
32. Jorgensen DM. Gestational psittacosis in a Montana sheep rancher. Emerg Infect Dis. 1997;3:191–194.
33. Harris AA, Pottage JC, Kessler HA, et al. Psittacosis bacteremia in a patient with sarcoidosis. Ann Intern Med. 1984;101:502–504.
34. Sahn SA. Pleural effusions in the atypical pneumonias. Semin Respir Infect. 1988;3:322–334.
35. Fraser RG, Paré JAP, Paré PD, et al. Diagnosis of Diseases of the Chest. Philadelphia: WB Saunders; 1991.
36. Strano A. Psittacosis. In: Connor DH, Chandler FW, eds. Pathology of Infectious Diseases. Stamford, Conn: Appleton & Lange, 1997.
37. Messmer TO, Skelton SK, Moroney JF, et al. Application of a nested multiplex PCR to psittacosis outbreaks. J Clin Microbiol. 1997;35:2043–2046.
38. Oldach DW, Gaydos CA, Mundy LM, et al. Rapid diagnosis of *Chlamydia psittaci* pneumonia. Clin Infect Dis. 1993;17:338–343.
39. Schacter J. Chlamydiae. In: Rose NR, de Macario EL, Folds JD, et al., eds. Manual of Clinical Laboratory Immunology. Washington, DC: American Society for Microbiology; 1997.

Chapter 170

Chlamydia pneumoniae

LISA A. JACKSON
J. THOMAS GRAYSTON

Chlamydia pneumoniae (TWAR), the most recently identified of the three chlamydial species pathogenic for humans, shares with *Chlamydia trachomatis* and *Chlamydia psittaci* the unique chlamydial developmental cycle but differs from those two species in several important characteristics. Unlike *C. trachomatis, C. pneumoniae* is not sexually transmitted but is spread via respiratory secretions, and unlike *C. psittaci*, it has no bird or animal reservoir. *C. pneumoniae* isolates show very little genotypic or phenotypic variation and to date only a single serovar or strain of *C. pneumoniae* has been identified; thus, the strain name, TWAR, is synonymous with that species designation. *C. pneumoniae* is a common cause of community-acquired acute respiratory infection and more recently has also been associated with atherosclerotic cardiovascular disease.

HISTORICAL OVERVIEW

The organism was first isolated in 1965, from a conjunctival swab obtained from a child enrolled in a trachoma vaccine trial in Taiwan.[1] Another isolate, also obtained from a conjunctival swab specimen, from a child in Iran in 1968, was later shown to be *C. pneumoniae*. Despite the conjunctival source of these isolates, *C. pneumoniae* has not been serologically associated with eye disease or identified as a cause of ocular infection. These two isolates were obtained by inoculation of the yolk sacs of embryonated chicken eggs, which was the only method then available for growth of chlamydiae, but which is not optimal for morphologic characterization of isolates. It was not until 1971, when cell culture methods became available, that the Taiwan isolate—designated TW-183—was observed to form round, dense inclusions in host cells. These inclusions were more similar in appearance to those of *C. psittaci* than to those of *C. trachomatis* and, unlike *C. trachomatis* inclusions, did not stain with iodine; therefore, the isolate was believed to be a variant of *C. psittaci*.[1]

Based on this assumption, further explorations of a possible association with respiratory infection were initiated. Serologic testing, for antibodies directed against the TW-183 organism, of banked serum specimens from a 1977 epidemic of mild pneumonia in northern Finland suggested that the TW-183 organism was the etiologic agent.[2] The role of *C. pneumoniae* as a human pathogen was more firmly established in 1983, when the first respiratory isolate—designated AR-39—was obtained from a throat swab specimen from a Seattle university student with pharyngitis.[3] The strain name TWAR (TW + AR) was derived from the laboratory designations of the first conjunctival and respiratory isolates. Since that time, studies incorporating isolation, molecular detection methods, and serologic testing have further defined the epidemiology and spectrum of acute respiratory infection due to TWAR. In 1989, DNA sequence analysis, as well as morphologic study by electron microscopy, established TWAR as a separate species of *Chlamydia*, designated *C. pneumoniae*.[4]

MICROBIOLOGY

As described in Chapter 169, chlamydiae are obligate intracellular bacteria that have a unique biphasic developmental cycle. Chlamydiae have cell walls, replicate by binary fission, and contain DNA, RNA, and ribosomes. They synthesize some proteins; they cannot, however, synthesize adenine triphosphate (ATP) or guanosine triphosphate (GTP) and must rely on the host cell for energy sources. The small, dense *elementary body* is the metabolically inactive infectious form of the organism. Elementary bodies have a rigid cell wall resulting from disulfide cross-linking of envelope proteins, allowing survival outside the host cell. After infection of a susceptible host eukaryotic cell by receptor-mediated endocytosis, the elementary bodies differentiate into *reticulate bodies*, which constitute the larger, metabolically active form of the organism. Inside the host cell, the reticulate bodies divide by binary fission, forming a microcolony, referred to as a *chlamydial inclusion*, that is visible by light or electron microscopy (Fig. 170–1). During this process, chlamydial antigens are released onto the surface of the host cell, stimulating a host immune response.[5] After a period of growth and division, the reticulate bodies reorganize and condense to form new elementary bodies, which are released from the host cell to initiate new infectious cycles.

As demonstrated in Figure 170–1, *C. pneumoniae* has a characteristic pear-shaped elementary body surrounded by a periplasmic space that is morphologically distinct from the round elementary body of *C. trachomatis*. It is assumed that this shape indicates that the *C. pneumoniae* elementary body has a less rigid cell wall than that in the other chlamydial species. The pear shape may also have functional

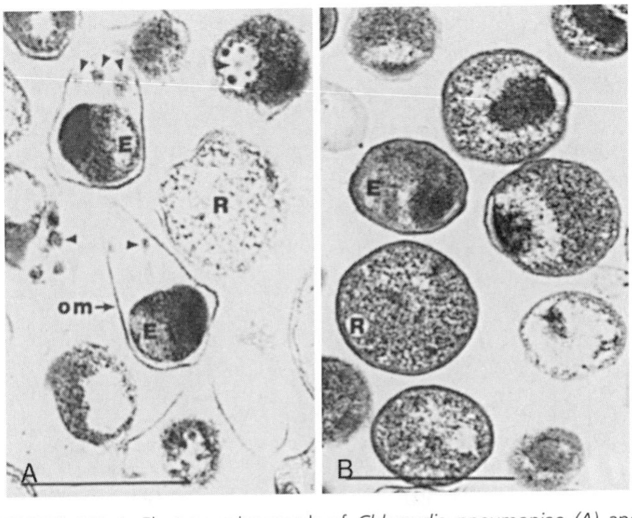

FIGURE 170–1. Electron micrograph of *Chlamydia pneumoniae (A)* and *Chlamydia trachomatis (B)* (bar = 0.5 μm). *Abbreviations*: E, Elementary body; R, reticulate body; om, outer membrane; arrowhead, small electron-dense bodies of undetermined function. (From Grayston JT, Kuo C-C, Campbell LA, et al. *Chlamydia pneumoniae* sp. nov. for *Chlamydia* sp. strain TWAR. Int J Syst Bacteriol. 1989;39:88–90.)

significance, as ultrastructural studies have demonstrated that the *C. pneumoniae* elementary bodies first attach to host cells by the pointed end and then secure other binding sites on the host cells by forming cell wall protrusions, enter host cells by invaginating the host cell membrane, and form vacuolated endocytic vesicles.[6] By electron microscopy, small, electron-dense bodies of unknown function have also been identified in the periplasmic space.

C. pneumoniae isolates have 94 to 100% DNA homology with each other but less than 10% with *C. trachomatis* or *C. psittaci*.[7] All *C. pneumoniae* isolates tested are immunologically similar; representative strains from different countries have been examined by molecular fingerprinting and found to be identical; and major outer membrane proteins of strains from the United States, Japan, and Finland have been sequenced and found to be identical.[8, 9] In contrast to the other *Chlamydia* species, at this time *C. pneumoniae* has only one immunotype or serovar.

EPIDEMIOLOGY

Seroprevalence and Seroconversion

Much of the current information on the epidemiology of *C. pneumoniae* infection is derived from serologic studies using the microimmunofluorescence test for detection of *C. pneumoniae*–specific antibodies. These studies indicate that *C. pneumoniae* is a common cause of infection throughout the world, with seroprevalence rates of over 50% among adults in the United States and many other countries.[10–19] Although *C. pneumoniae* was not identified as a respiratory pathogen until the 1980s, testing of banked serum specimens indicates that it has been a cause of acute respiratory infection since at least 1958.[20] Retrospective testing of stored sera also indicates that at least in some instances, such as an epidemic of "ornithosis" in northern Europe in the 1980s[21, 22] and an outbreak of respiratory illness in a school in England in 1983,[23] *C. pneumoniae* was the cause of respiratory infections previously attributed to *C. psittaci* on the basis of the *Chlamydia* complement fixation serologic test, which does not distinguish between infection with the two species.

As shown in Figure 170–2, seropositivity rates are very low among children under 5 years of age and then rise rapidly during the school-age years.[18] By early adulthood, approximately 50% of persons are seropositive. This rate continues to gradually increase with age, reaching approximately 75% in the elderly. Because antibody titers decline with time, the persistently high seropositivity rates documented in the older age groups suggests that "boosting" of the antibody response by reinfection is common.[24]

Studies of age-specific rates of seroconversion show a similar trend. Testing of banked sera samples from a long-term study of Seattle families indicated that children in the 5- to 9-year-old age group had the highest rate of a fourfold or higher rise in antibody titer between consecutive specimens, with the next highest rate seen among children in the 10- to 14-year-old age group (Table 170–1).[25] The available clinical information suggested that many antibody conversions were asymptomatic. Reinfection was also documented, in that some persons had a fourfold or greater antibody rise in more than one set of paired specimens obtained during the course of the study. In addition, most of the antibody rises were in adults. A study of children in Sweden showed a similar pattern, with annual seroconversion rates of 8.0% in children ages 8 through 12 years and 5.9% in children ages 12 through 16.[26]

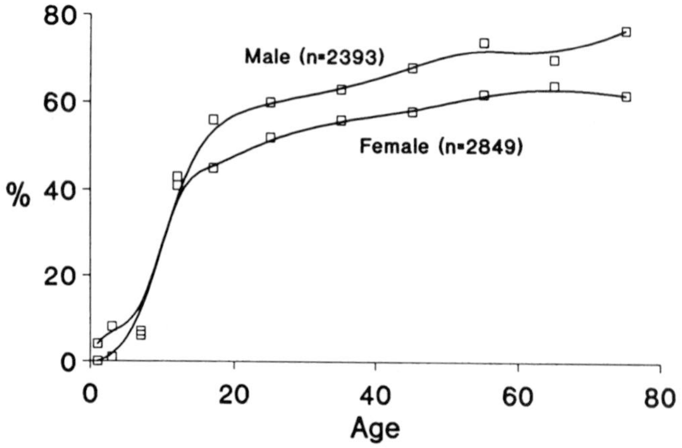

FIGURE 170–2. *Chlamydia pneumoniae* age-specific microimmunofluorescence seropositivity (IgG titer ≥8) rates among 5242 persons in Seattle. (From Grayston JT. Infections caused by *Chlamydia pneumoniae* strain TWAR. Clin Infect Dis. 1992;15:757–763.)

TABLE 170–1 Age and Rate of Serologic Evidence of Acute Infection with *Chlamydia pneumoniae*

Age Group (yr)	No. of Acute Rises*	No. of Person-Years	Incidence† of Infection
0–4	0	27	—
5–9	14	151	9.3
10–14	15	242	6.2
15–19	2	91	2.2
>19	6	394	1.5

*Defined as a fourfold or greater rise in antibody titer between consecutive specimens.
†Rate per 100 person-years at risk.
Adapted from Aldous MB, Grayston JT, Wang S-P, et al. Seroepidemiology of *Chlamydia pneumoniae* TWAR infection in Seattle families, 1966–1979. J Infect Dis. 1992;166:646–649.

Gender-specific seropositivity rates are approximately equal in children; however, among adults, rates among males are significantly higher than among females (see Fig. 170–2). Although this finding has been replicated in studies of numerous other populations,[15, 16, 18, 25, 27, 28] a satisfactory explanation for this difference has not been elucidated to date.

Acute Respiratory Infection

C. pneumoniae is a significant cause of pneumonia in both the hospital and outpatient settings. Results of hospital-based studies have indicated that the organism accounts for approximately 7 to 10% of cases of community-acquired pneumonia among adults.[29–35] These estimates are corroborated by findings from a population-based active surveillance study of adults hospitalized with community-acquired pneumonia in Ohio, which identified *C. pneumoniae* as the etiologic agent, using standard serologic criteria (Table 170–2), in 8.9% of cases.[36] In that study, the incidence of community-acquired pneumonia requiring hospitalization overall and that of such cases of pneumonia specifically attributed to *C. pneumoniae* were estimated to be 266.8 and 23.8 per 100,000 population, respectively. *C. pneumoniae* was therefore estimated to cause between 36,700 and 49,700 hospitalized pneumonia cases within the U.S. noninstitutionalized population annually. When serologic criteria restricted to a fourfold or greater change in titer between paired specimens were used, the highest rate of pneumonia due to *C. pneumoniae* was found

TABLE 170–2 Serologic Criteria for Acute Infection with *Chlamydia pneumoniae*

Fourfold or greater rise in *C. pneumoniae*–specific IgG or IgM titer between acute and convalescent* specimens

OR

Single IgG titer ≥512†

OR

Single IgM titer ≥16

*Convalescent specimens are optimally obtained at least 3 weeks after the acute specimen.
†IgG titers of ≥16 and <512 indicate past infection.

to be among the 65- to 79-year-old age group (Fig. 170–3); however, the organism accounted for the highest proportion of cases among the 18- to 34-year-old age group (Fig. 170–4). Unlike with *Streptococcus pneumoniae*, which demonstrated peak rates of infection in the winter months, rates of *C. pneumoniae* infection did not vary significantly by season, which is consistent with other reports.[33, 37]

Most respiratory infections due to *C. pneumoniae* do not result in hospitalization; therefore, higher rates of infection are found in the ambulatory setting. Testing of sera obtained during a study of children and adults with pneumonia at Group Health Cooperative of Puget Sound during 1963 through 1975, in which over 80% of the cases were not hospitalized,[38] identified *C. pneumoniae* as the etiologic agent in 8% of cases,[18] with a corresponding incidence of 100 per 100,000 population. Within that population, the highest rates of pneumonia due to *C. pneumoniae* were among the elderly; this pattern differed from that seen with *Mycoplasma pneumoniae* infection, with peak rates among children. In that study, *M. pneumoniae* was identified, by serologic criteria or isolation of the organism from pharyngeal swab specimens, or both, in 15% of cases, for an incidence of 180 per 100,000 population.

C. pneumoniae is infrequently documented as a cause of acute lower respiratory tract in infants,[18, 39–41] but as described above, it is an important cause of pneumonia among older children, especially in the outpatient setting.[18, 39, 42–45] Up to 28% of cases of pneumonia among school-aged children have been attributed to *C. pneumoniae*.[42, 43] Among children with moderate to severe acute lower respiratory tract infection, coinfections with *C. pneumoniae* and other agents, such as *Streptococcus pneumoniae* or influenza A virus, have been reported.[42–45] Coinfection, particularly with *S. pneumoniae*, is also not uncommon among adults hospitalized with pneumonia.[34]

C. pneumoniae is also a significant cause of bronchitis and upper respiratory infections. Among adults, *C. pneumoniae* accounts for approximately 5% of cases of bronchitis[37, 46] and sinusitis[37] but is a less frequent cause of pharyngitis, generally accounting for only approximately 1% of cases.[37]

The limited available data indicate that *C. pneumoniae* is also a significant cause of morbidity among elderly nursing home residents.

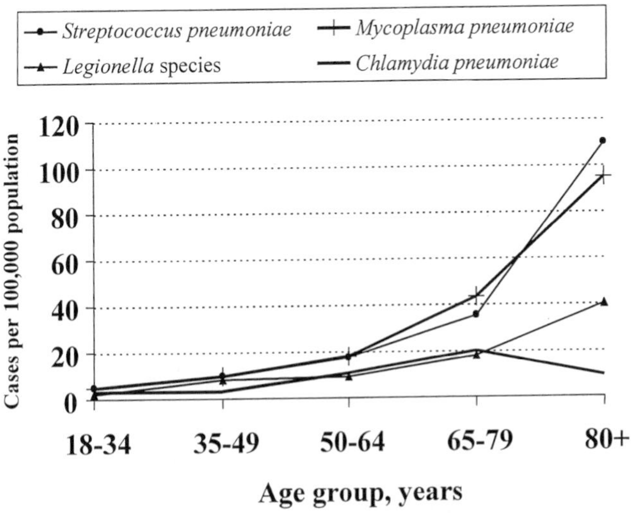

FIGURE 170–3. Age-specific rates of hospital admissions for community-acquired pneumonia due to *Chlamydia pneumoniae, Mycoplasma pneumoniae, Streptococcus pneumoniae*, and *Legionella*, from a population-based study. *C. pneumoniae* infection was defined by a fourfold or greater rise in titer between acute and convalescent sera specimens. (Adapted from Marston BJ, Plouffe JF, File TM, et al. Incidence of community-acquired pneumonia requiring hospitalization: Results of a population-based active surveillance study in Ohio. Arch Intern Med. 1997; 157:1709–1718.)

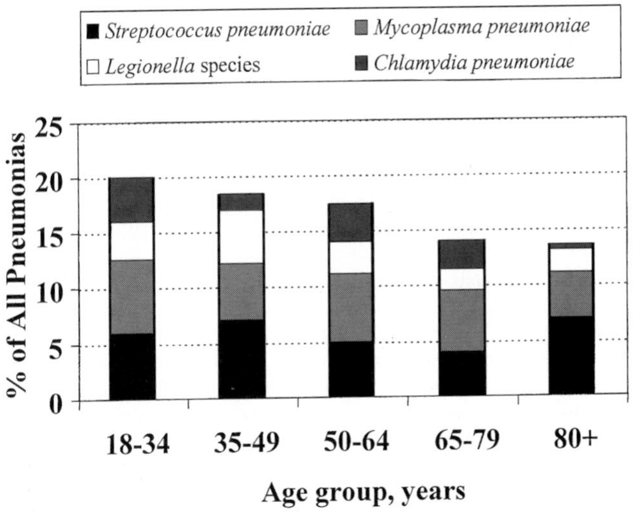

FIGURE 170–4. Percentage of hospital admissions for community-acquired pneumonia attributed to *Chlamydia pneumoniae, Mycoplasma pneumoniae, Streptococcus pneumoniae*, and *Legionella*, by age group, from a population-based study. *C. pneumoniae* infection was defined by a fourfold or greater rise in titer between acute and convalescent sera specimens. (Adapted from Marston BJ, Plouffe JF, File TM, et al. Incidence of community-acquired pneumonia requiring hospitalization: Results of a population-based active surveillance study in Ohio. Arch Intern Med. 1997;157:1709–1718.)

In one nursing home study, *C. pneumoniae* was associated with 9.4% of febrile illness episodes by serologic criteria and, among residents with clinically diagnosed respiratory infection, accounted for 12% of cases of acute bronchitis and 17% of cases of pneumonia.[47] Serologic response to a second agent (*Haemophilus influenzae*, influenza A virus, respiratory syncytial virus, or parainfluenza 3 virus) was identified in 33% of those cases.

Epidemic Disease

C. pneumoniae is primarily a cause of endemic disease; however, outbreaks of respiratory infection have been reported in nursing homes[48] and schools,[23] among military recruits,[49, 50] and within families.[51–53] More sustained increases, persisting for months to years, in rates of respiratory infection due to *C. pneumoniae* among members of communities[2] or countries[22, 54] have also been reported.

CLINICAL MANIFESTATIONS

Pneumonia and bronchitis are the most common clinical syndromes associated with *C. pneumoniae* infection. Upper respiratory infections, including sinusitis and pharyngitis, may also occur, either in isolation or in conjunction with a lower respiratory infection. Detection of the organism from pharyngeal swab specimens obtained from asymptomatic persons,[55–58] as well as the high seropositivity rates present among populations studied, also suggests that clinically inapparent infection is common and that respiratory carriers may serve as reservoirs for dissemination of the organism. The incubation period of infection due to *C. pneumoniae* is about 21 days, which is longer than the incubation period for many other respiratory pathogens.[53, 59]

As with the other bacterial causes of atypical pneumonia, *M. pneumoniae* and *Legionella pneumophila*, the clinical manifestations of acute respiratory infection due to *C. pneumoniae* are nonspecific.[37, 46, 60] Upper respiratory signs and symptoms, such as rhinitis, sore throat, or hoarseness, may be reported initially. These signs and symptoms may then subside over days to weeks, followed by the onset of cough, which is a predominant feature of *C. pneumoniae* respiratory infections—thus in some cases resulting in a biphasic pattern of illness symptoms.

The duration from onset of symptoms to presentation for medical evaluation tends to be longer for infections due to *C. pneumoniae* than for those caused by other respiratory agents.[37, 46, 60–62] Patients with *C. pneumoniae* infection are also reported to be less likely to give a history of fever, or to have an elevated temperature at the initial clinical evaluation than patients with respiratory infection due to other agents.[37, 46, 62]

In addition to having a gradual onset, symptoms due *C. pneumoniae* respiratory infections may be of prolonged duration, with persistance of cough and malaise for several weeks or months despite appropriate antibiotic therapy.[46] In one study of adult patients presenting to an emergency department with cough of at least 2 weeks in duration, 20% were found to have serologic evidence of acute infection with *C. pneumoniae*.[63]

A single, subsegmental, patchy infiltrate is the classic radiographic feature associated with atypical pneumonias and is commonly seen with *C. pneumoniae* infection[64] (Fig. 170–5). However, this pattern is also common in cases of pneumonia due to typical bacterial pathogens, including *S. pneumoniae*.[64] In addition, other radiographic features such as lobar or sublobar consolidation, interstitial infiltrates, bilateral involvement, pleural effusion, and hilar adenopathy may also be demonstrated with *C. pneumoniae* infection, although less frequently.[64–67] Therefore, the pattern of infiltrates on the chest radiograph is not a reliable indicator of the probable etiologic agent for cases of community-acquired pneumonia.[64, 66] As with other atypical pathogens, the white blood cell count is usually not elevated with *C. pneumoniae* infection,[37, 60] and other laboratory findings are nonspecific.

The immunologic response to primary infection with *C. pneumoniae* is at best partially protective, and reinfection with the organism may occur. Reinfection is usually associated with a different pattern of antibody response and tends to be clinically less severe than primary infection.[46, 49]

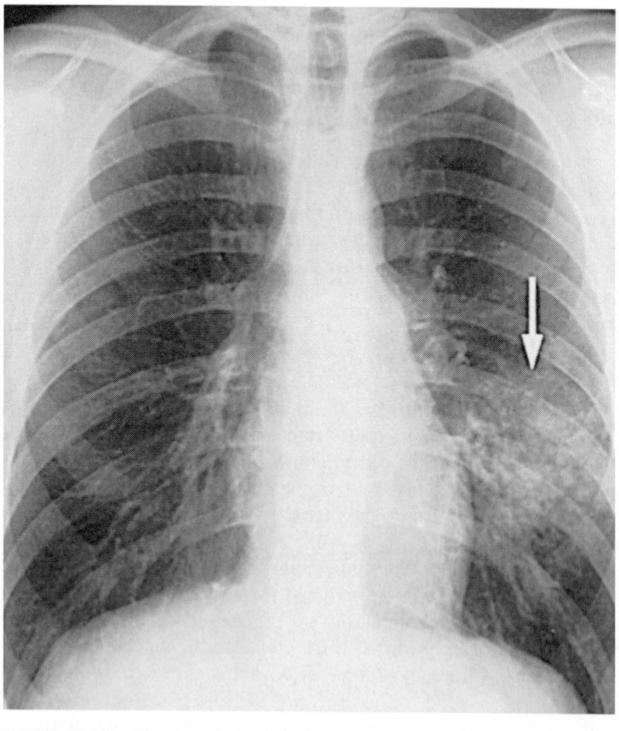

FIGURE 170–5. Chest radiograph of a 17-year-old male with pneumonia due to *Chlamydia pneumoniae* (TWAR) showing "atypical" pneumonitis in the left lower lobe *(arrow)*. (From Grayston JT, Kuo C-C, Wang S-P, et al. A new *Chlamydia psittaci* strain, TWAR, isolated in acute respiratory tract infections. N Engl J Med. 1986;315:161–168. Copyright © 1986 Massachusetts Medical Society. All rights reserved.)

Infection in Hosts with Altered Defense Mechanisms

C. pneumoniae has been identified as a cause of lower respiratory infection in immunocompromised patients, including persons infected with human immunodeficiency virus (HIV).[68–71] However, whether immunocompromised persons are at increased risk of infection with *C. pneumoniae*, or of more severe disease as a consequence of infection, is not well defined. *C. pneumoniae* has also been identified as a cause of acute respiratory exacerbations in patients with cystic fibrosis[72] and has been associated with acute chest syndrome in children with sickle cell disease.[73]

Other Syndromes

C. pneumoniae has been serologically associated with the development of adult-onset asthma[74–76] as well as with acute exacerbations among adults with asthma[74, 77] and has been associated with reactive airway disease in children.[57, 78] The organism has been isolated from adults and children with otitis media,[79–82] often in conjunction with isolation of other bacterial pathogens.[81, 82] Other reported clinical syndromes include endocarditis,[83, 84] lumbosacral meningoradiculitis,[85] and erythema nodosum.[86, 87] A case of Guillain-Barré syndrome following infection with *C. pneumoniae* has been reported.[88] The organism has been associated serologically with encephalitis in children[89] and adults.[90] A multisystem febrile illness in a 10-year-old boy with pneumonia, pericarditis, pleuritis, and hepatosplenomegaly was documented to be due to *C. pneumoniae* by serologic study and by polymerase chain reaction (PCR) detection of the organism in lymph node and liver biopsy samples.[62]

Several chronic diseases have been presumptively associated with *C. pneumoniae* infection, the best example of which is atherosclerotic cardiovascular disease, as further described later on. *C. pneumoniae* has been associated with sarcoidosis in serologic studies[91] and was detected by PCR or immunocytochemistry in three sarcoid skin granuloma specimens[92]; however, it was not detected by PCR in lung biopsy specimens from 33 patients with sarcoid in another report.[93] *C. pneumoniae* has also been implicated in reactive arthritis,[94] and a serologic association with lung cancer has been reported.[95]

DIAGNOSIS

A number of specific laboratory tests for detection of infection due to *C. pneumoniae* have been developed, but most are used primarily for research purposes. Some hospital and commercial clinical laboratories perform serologic testing, which is the method most often used for documentation of clinical infection.

Serologic Testing

The microimmunofluorescence test[96] detects *C. pneumoniae*–specific antibodies and is the standard serologic assay for this organism. The serologic criteria for the diagnosis of acute infection with *C. pneumoniae* in our laboratory at the University of Washington are shown in Table 170–3. Because the rise in antibody titer following acute infection may be delayed, a 3- to 4-week interval is recommended for obtaining the second, convalescent serum specimen. False-positive IgM reactions may occur in the presence of circulating rheumatoid factor; therefore, absorption of sera with an anti–human IgG reagent prior to testing is recommended.[97]

In contrast to the microimmunofluorescence test, the chlamydial complement fixation test, which detects antibodies against chlamydial lipopolysaccharides, does not differentiate between infection caused by *C. pneumoniae, C. psittaci*, or *C. trachomatis*.

The pattern of antibody response following reinfection with *C.*

TABLE 170-3 Timing of Antibody Appearance after Illness Onset in First Infection and Reinfection with *Chlamydia pneumoniae*

	Time to Antibody Appearance	
Antibody	***First Infection***	***Reinfection***
IgM	2–4 wk	May not appear, or only at low titers
IgG	6–8 wk	1–3 wk, often rising to greater than 512

Abbreviation: CF, Complement fixation.

pneumoniae differs from that following first infection. In first infection, a prompt chlamydial complement fixation antibody response is seen and *C. pneumoniae*–specific IgM antibody appears later, about 3 weeks after the onset of illness. A *C. pneumoniae*–specific IgG antibody response is produced but may not appear until 6 to 8 weeks after onset of illness. In reinfection, complement fixation and IgM antibody may not appear, or may appear only at low titers, while the IgG antibody response occurs relatively quickly, often in 1 to 2 weeks, and IgG may reach titers of 512 or higher.

Although in most cases, detection of the organism by isolation or PCR testing of pharyngeal swabs is associated with a rise in serologic titer, *C. pneumoniae* has been detected in pharyngeal swab specimens from persons reported to be persistently seronegative.[42, 57] Pharyngeal carriage of the organism may result in a less pronounced immune response than that seen in acute respiratory infection.

Isolation

C. pneumoniae can be isolated in cell culture,[98] a method that has been enhanced by the development of a *C. pneumoniae*–specific monoclonal antibody conjugated with fluorescein, which improves detection of the few inclusions generally present. The organism is fastidious and slow-growing, however; therefore, isolation is not usually attempted for documentation of infection in the clinical setting but can be useful for research purposes.

Oropharyngeal swab specimens are preferred for isolation, and detection rates are equivalent to those for nasopharyngeal specimens. Sputum is toxic to cell cultures and therefore is not a suitable specimen for isolation. Pharyngeal swabs should be placed in chlamydial transport medium (sucrose–phosphate–glutamic acid [SPG] buffer solution) and refrigerated at 4°C as soon as possible and then kept at that temperature for 1 to 4 hours before freezing to −65°C, as more rapid freezing decreases the titer of viable organisms.[99]

Polymerase Chain Reaction Testing

PCR techniques using various *C. pneumoniae*–specific primers have been developed and used for detection of the organisms in pharyngeal swab, bronchoalveolar lavage, and sputum specimens.[70, 100–106] The PCR method is somewhat more sensitive than isolation for detection of the organism from these specimens and may ultimately be useful as a rapid diagnostic test. This method has also been used to detect *C. pneumoniae* in pathologic tissue specimens.

TREATMENT

Erythromycin, tetracycline, and doxycycline are active in vitro against *C. pneumoniae* and have traditionally been recommended as first-line therapeutic agents.[107–109] Newer macrolide-like antibiotics, such as azithromycin and clarithromycin, are also active in vitro and achieve high intracellular concentrations.[108, 109] These agents are better tolerated than erythromycin and therefore may be considered as either first-line agents or as alternates to erythromycin and the tetracyclines for treatment of infections believed to be due to *C. pneumoniae*. Some quinolones also appear active in vitro.[108, 110] The organism is not susceptible to penicillin, ampicillin, or sulfa drugs.[107, 109]

Limited data on the efficacy of antibiotic treatment for *C. pneumoniae* respiratory infections are available from clinical trials. A randomized trial of clarithromycin versus erythromycin among children 3 to 12 years of age with radiographically documented pneumonia indicated that both agents were greater than 90% clinically effective in the treatment of infection due to *C. pneumoniae*.[42] A randomized trial of levofloxacin for treatment of community-acquired pneumonia in adults reported a 98% clinical success rate in treatment of *C. pneumoniae* infections.[111]

High rates of respiratory infections occur among military recruits during basic training, and in this setting, weekly azithromycin prophylaxis was estimated to be 58% effective (95% confidence interval of 15 to 79%) in preventing infections by *C. pneumoniae*.[112]

Clinical reports indicate that symptoms may persist or recur after conventional or longer courses of treatment with erythromycin, doxycycline, or tetracycline.[37, 49, 113] Therefore, if these agents are used, a minimum of 10 to 14 days of treatment is recommended. If azithromycin or clarithromycin is used, the standard course of therapy indicated for treatment of respiratory infections is recommended. If symptoms persist despite treatment, a second course with a different antibiotic may be effective.

CHLAMYDIA PNEUMONIAE AND ATHEROSCLEROSIS

C. pneumoniae has been associated with atherosclerotic cardiovascular disease by the results of seroepidemiologic studies, by detection of the organism in atherosclerotic plaque specimens, by experimental in vitro cell culture studies, by animal model studies, and, most recently, by two small secondary prevention antibiotic treatment trials. The first study to suggest an association was reported from Finland in 1988 and indicated that patients hospitalized for coronary artery disease were significantly more likely to have serologic evidence of past infection with *C. pneumoniae* than were population-matched controls.[114] Subsequently, multiple seroepidemiologic studies have been reported from Europe and the United States demonstrating significant associations with coronary artery[115–120] as well as cerebrovascular[121–123] disease.

C. pneumoniae has been detected by immunologic staining or PCR in a high proportion, ranging in most studies from 40% to up to 100%, of atheromatous specimens from coronary,[92, 124–130] carotid,[131–134] femoral, and popliteal[135] arteries and the aorta.[136–138] In contrast, the organism has not been detected in more limited studies of coronary[126] or carotid arteries[133] without atheromatous changes. The organism has also been isolated from a carotid endarterectomy specimen,[131] the coronary artery of a recipient's heart removed prior to heart transplantation,[127] and, in one report, coronary artery specimens from 16% (11/70) of patients undergoing coronary artery bypass graft surgery.[128]

C. pneumoniae has been shown to readily infect human vascular smooth muscle, endothelial, and monocyte-macrophage cell lines.[139–142] Infection of human monocyte-derived macrophages with *C. pneumoniae* exposed to native low-density lipoprotein (LDL) has been demonstrated to induce transformation of those cells into lipid-laden foam cells.[143] Furthermore, exposure of the infected macrophages to both LDL and heparin, which binds to LDL and interferes with its uptake via the macrophage native LDL receptor, blocks this transformation, suggesting that *C. pneumoniae*–induced foam cell formation results from dysregulation of native LDL uptake or metabolism, or both. *C. pneumoniae* infection of cultured endothelial cells has also been shown to stimulate tissue factor (procoagulant) activity and to enhance platelet adhesion.[141]

The seroepidemiologic findings and the reports of detection of the organism in atherosclerotic plaque specimens suggest an association between *C. pneumoniae* and atherosclerotic disease; however, these results are not sufficient to determine whether the organism plays a causal role in this process. Animal experimental models in development have the potential to provide more direct evidence of causality as well as insight into potential pathogenic mechanisms.

Results of studies using ApoE-deficient knockout mice, which spontaneously develop atherosclerosis on a normal diet, indicate that *C. pneumoniae* can be detected in aortic plaque specimens after intranasal inoculation, that the organism persists in aortic plaque for at least 20 weeks following initial infection, and that infection appears to accelerate the progression of the atherosclerotic process in these animals.[144, 145] Studies of New Zealand white rabbits, which do not typically develop atherosclerosis on a normal diet, found that animals infected intranasally with *C. pneumoniae* later showed changes in the aorta consisting of intimal thickening or fibrolipid plaques, and that *C. pneumoniae* could be detected in those plaque specimens by immunocytochemistry studies.[146, 147]

Another study of New Zealand white rabbits, which were fed a slightly cholesterol-enhanced diet to enhance atherosclerotic lesion development and then intranasally inoculated with either *C. pneumoniae* or saline and randomized to a 7-week course of treatment with azithromycin or to no treatment, found that the infected, untreated animals had significantly larger areas of plaque involvement of the thoracic aorta than those seen in the uninfected controls.[148] In contrast, the infected, azithromycin-treated rabbits did not demonstrate this increase, with mean areas of plaque involvement that were not significantly different from those in the uninfected controls, suggesting that treatment with azithromycin ameliorated the infection-induced acceleration in atherosclerotic plaque development.

Last, two small secondary prevention human clinical trials of antibiotic therapy directed against *C. pneumoniae* have reported a reduction in the risk of cardiac outcome events among patients with known coronary artery disease. The first study, of 80 male outpatients with a history of myocardial infarction who were seropositive for *C. pneumoniae*, found that treatment with either one or two 3-day courses of 500 mg per day of azithromycin led to a reduction in the risk of cardiac outcome events during the approximately 18-month follow-up period compared with the risk of such events in a predominantly nonrandomized composite group of untreated patients (odds ratio of 0.2; 95% confidence limit of 0.05–0.8).[149] The second study randomized 202 patients hospitalized for unstable angina or non–Q-wave myocardial infarction to roxithromycin (a macrolide-like agent not available in the United States), 150 mg twice daily for 30 days, or placebo. Preliminary results reported after the first 31 days of the 6-month follow-up period indicated a lower rate of cardiac outcome events among the treated group (1/93 [1%] versus 9/93 [10%]; p = .02).[150] These two studies are the first to suggest a possible protective effect of treatment with antibiotics active against *C. pneumoniae* on cardiac outcomes. Larger, randomized controlled studies with longer follow-up periods are needed to confirm and extend these findings: at present, several such studies are under way or are in the planning stages.

REFERENCES

1. Kuo C-C, Chen H-H, Wang S-P, Grayston JT. Identification of a new group of *Chamydia psittaci* strains called TWAR. J Clin Microbiol 1986;24:1034–1037.
2. Saikku P, Wang S-P, Kleemola M, et al. An epidemic of mild pneumonia due to an unusual strain of *Chlamydia psittaci*. J Infect Dis. 1985;151:161–168.
3. Grayston JT, Kuo C-C, Wang S-P, et al. A new *Chlamydia psittaci* strain, TWAR, isolated in acute respiratory tract infections. N Engl J Med. 1986;315:161–168.
4. Grayston JT, Kuo C-C, Campbell LA, et al. *Chlamydia pneumoniae* sp. nov. for *Chlamydia* sp. strain TWAR. Int J Syst Bacteriol. 1989;39:88–90.
5. Caldwell HD, Kromhout J, Schachter J. Purification and partial characterization of the major outer membrane protein of *Chlamydia trachomatis*. Infect Immun. 1981;31:1161–1176.
6. Kuo C-C, Chi EY, Grayston JT. Ultrastructural study of entry of *Chlamydia* strain TWAR into HeLa cells. Infect Immun. 1988;56:1668–1672.
7. Cox RL, Kuo C-C, Grayston JT, Campbell LA. Deoxyribonucleic acid relatedness of *Chlamydia* sp. strain TWAR to *Chlamydia trachomatis* and *Chlamydia psittaci*. Int J Syst Bacteriol. 1988;38:265–268.
8. Perez Melgosa M, Kuo C-C, Campbell LA. Outer membrane complex proteins of *Chlamydia pneumoniae*. FEMS Microbiol Letters. 1993;112:199–204.
9. Kaltenboeck B, Kousoulas KG, Storz J. Structures of and allelic diversity and relationships among the major outer membrane protein *(ompA)* genes of the four chlamydial species. J Bacteriol. 1993;175:487–502.
10. Forsey T, Darougar S, Treharne HD. Prevalence in human beings of antibodies to *Chlamydia* IOL-207, an atypical strain of *Chlamydia*. J Infect. 1986;12:145–152.
11. Kanamoto Y, Ouchi K, Mizui M, et al. Prevalence of antibody to *Chlamydia pneumoniae* TWAR in Japan. J Clin Microbiol. 1991;29:816–818.
12. Marton A, Károlyi A, Szalka A. Prevalence of *Chlamydia pneumoniae* antibodies in Hungary. Eur J Clin Microbiol Infect Dis. 1992;11:139–142.
13. Montes M, Cilla G, Alcorta M, Pérez-Trallero E. High prevalence of *Chlamydia pneumoniae* infection in children and young adults in Spain. Pediatr Infect Dis J. 1992;11:972–973.
14. Wang S-P, Grayston JT. Microimmunofluorescence serological studies with the TWAR organism. In: Oriel JD, Ridgway G, Schachter J, et al, eds. Chlamydial Infections. Cambridge, England: Cambridge University Press; 1986:329–332.
15. Wang S-P, Grayston JT. Population prevalence antibody to *Chlamydia pneumoniae*, strain TWAR. In: Bowie WR, Caldwell HD, Jones RP, et al., eds. Chlamydial Infections. Cambridge, England: Cambridge University Press; 1990:402–405.
16. Paltiel O, Kark JD, Leinonen M, Saikku P. High prevalence of antibodies to *Chlamydia pneumoniae*; determinants of IgG and IgA seropositivity among Jerusalem residents. Epidemiol Infect. 1995;114:465–473.
17. Einarsson S, Sigurdsson HK, Magnusdottir SD, et al. Age specific prevalence of antibodies against *Chlamydia pneumoniae* in Iceland. Scand J Infect Dis. 1994;26:393–397.
18. Grayston JT. Infections caused by *Chlamydia pneumoniae* strain TWAR. Clin Infect Dis. 1992;15:757–763.
19. Ni AP, Lin GY, Yang L, et al. A seroepidemiologic study of *Chlamydia pneumoniae, Chlamydia trachomatis* and *Chlamydia psittaci* in different populations on the mainland of China. Scand J Infect Dis. 1996;28:553–557.
20. Karvonen M, Tuomilehto J, Naukkarinen A, Saikku P. The prevalence and regional distribution of antibodies against *Chlamydia pneumoniae* (strain TWAR) in Finland in 1958. Int J Epidemiol. 1992;21:391–398.
21. Frydén A, Kihlström E, Maller R, et al. A clinical and epidemiological study of "ornithosis" caused by *Chlamydia psittaci* and *Chlamydia pneumoniae* (strain TWAR). Scand J Infect Dis. 1989;21:681–691.
22. Grayston JT, Mordhorst CH, Bruu AL, et al. Countrywide epidemics of *Chlamydia pneumoniae*, strain TWAR, in Scandinavia, 1981–1983. J Infect Dis. 1989;159:1111–1114.
23. Pether JVS, Wang S-P, Grayston JT. *Chlamydia pneumoniae*, strain TWAR, as the cause of an outbreak in boys' school previously called psittacosis. Epidemiol Infect. 1989;103:395–400.
24. Patnode D, Wang S-P, Grayston JT. Persistence of *Chlamydia pneumoniae*, strain TWAR microimmunofluorescent antibody. In: Bowie WR, Caldwell HD, Jones RP, et al, eds. Chlamydial Infections. Cambridge, England: Cambridge University Press; 1990;406–409.
25. Aldous MB, Grayston JT, Wang S-P, et al. Seroepidemiology of *Chlamydia pneumoniae* TWAR infection in Seattle families, 1966–1979. J Infect Dis. 1992;166:646–649.
26. Haidl S, Sveger T, Persson K. Longitudinal pattern of antibodies to *Chlamydia pneumoniae* in children. In: Orfila J, Byrne GI, Cherneskey MA, et al, eds. Chlamydial Infections—1994. Bologna: Societa Editrice Esculapio; 1994:189–192.
27. Kese D, Hren-Vencelj H, Socan M, et al. Prevalence of antibodies to *Chlamydia pneumoniae* in Slovenia. Eur J Clin Microbiol Infect Dis. 1994;13:523–524.
28. Karvonen M, Tuomilehto J, Pitkaniemi J, et al. Importance of smoking for *Chlamydia pneumoniae* seropositivity. Int J Epidemiol. 1994;23:1315–1321.
29. Steinhoff D, Lode H, Ruckdeschel G, et al. *Chlamydia pneumoniae* as a cause of community-acquired pneumonia in hospitalized patients in Berlin. Clin Infect Dis. 1996;22:958–964.
30. Fang GD, Fine M, Orloff J, et al. New and emerging etiologies for community-acquired pneumonia with implications for therapy: A prospective multicenter study of 359 cases. Medicine. 1990;69:307–316.
31. Marrie TJ, Durant H, Yates L. Community-acquired pneumonia requiring hospitalization: 5-year prospective study. Rev Infect Dis. 1989;11:586–599.
32. Bates JH, Campbell GD, Barren AL, et al. Microbial etiology of acute pneumonia in hospitalized patients. Chest. 1992;101:1005–1112.
33. Porath A, Schlaffer F, Lieberman D. The epidemiology of community-acquired pneumonia among hospitalized adults. J Infect. 1997;34:41–48.
34. Grayston JT, Diwan VK, Cooney M, et al. Community- and hospital-acquired pneumonia associated with *Chlamydia* TWAR infection demonstrated serologically. Arch Intern Med. 1989;149:169–173.
35. Marrie TJ, Grayston JT, Wang S-P, et al. Pneumonia associated with the TWAR strain of *Chlamydia*. Ann Intern Med. 1987;106:507–511.
36. Marston BJ, Plouffe JF, File TM, et al. Incidence of community-acquired pneumonia requiring hospitalization: Results of a population-based active surveillance study in Ohio. Arch Intern Med. 1997;157:1709–1718.
37. Thom DH, Grayston JT, Wang S-P, et al. *Chlamydia pneumoniae* strain TWAR, *Mycoplasma pneumoniae* and viral infections in acute respiratory disease in a university student health clinic population. Am J Epidemiol. 1990;132:248–256.
38. Foy HM, Kenny GE, Cooney MK, et al. Long-term epidemiology of infections with *Mycoplasma pneumoniae*. J Infect Dis. 1979;139:681–687.
39. Jantos CA, Wienpahl B, Schiefer HG, et al. Infection with *Chlamydia pneumoniae* in infants and children with acute lower respiratory tract disease. Pediatr Infect Dis J. 1995;14:117–122.
40. Yeung SM, McLeod K, Wang SP, et al. Lack of evidence of *Chlamydia pneumoniae*

infection in infants with acute lower respiratory tract disease. Eur J Clin Microbiol Infect Dis. 1993;12:850–854.

41. Forgie IM, O'Neill KP, Lloyd-Evans N, et al. Etiology of acute lower respiratory tract infections in Gambian children: I. Acute lower respiratory tract infections in infants presenting at the hospital. Pediatr Infect Dis J. 1991;10:33–34.
42. Block S, Hedrick J, Hammerschlag MR, et al. *Mycoplasma pneumoniae* and *Chlamydia pneumoniae* in pediatric community-acquired pneumonia: Comparative efficacy and safety of clarithromycin vs. erythromycin ethylsuccinate. Pediatr Infect Dis J. 1995;14:471–477.
43. Chirgwin K, Roblin PM, Gelling M, et al. Infection with *Chlamydia pneumoniae* in Brooklyn. J Infect Dis. 1991;163:757–761.
44. Forgie IM, O'Neill KP, Lloyd-Evans N, et al. Etiology of acute lower respiratory tract infections in Gambian children: II. Acute lower respiratory tract infection in children ages one to nine years presenting at the hospital. Pediatr Infect Dis J. 1991;10:42–47.
45. Saikku P, Ruutu P, Leinonen M, et al. Acute lower-respiratory-tract infection associated with chlamydial TWAR antibody in Filipino children. J Infect Dis. 1988;158:1095–1097.
46. Thom DH, Grayston JT, Campbell LA, et al. Respiratory infection with *Chlamydia pneumoniae* in middle-aged and older adult outpatients. Eur J Clin Microbiol Infect Dis. 1994;13:785–792.
47. Orr PH, Peeling RW, Fast M, et al. Serological study of responses to selected pathogens causing respiratory tract infection in the institutionalized elderly. Clin Infect Dis. 1996;23:1240–1245.
48. Troy CJ, Peeling RW, Ellis AG, et al. *Chlamydia pneumoniae* as a new source of infectious outbreaks in nursing homes. JAMA. 1997;277:1214–1218.
49. Ekman M-R, Grayston JT, Visakorpi R, et al. An epidemic of infections due to *Chlamydia pneumoniae* in military conscripts. Clin Infect Dis. 1993;17:420–425.
50. Kleemola M, Saikku P, Visakorpi R, et al. Epidemics of pneumonia caused by TWAR, a new *Chlamydia* organism, in military trainees in Finland. J Infect Dis. 1988;157:230–236.
51. Blasi F, Cosentini R, Denti F, Allegra L. Two family outbreaks of *Chlamydia pneumoniae* infection. Eur Respir J. 1994;7:102–104.
52. Mordhorst CH, Wang S-P, Grayston JT. Outbreak of *Chlamydia pneumoniae*, strain TWAR infection in four farm families. Eur J Clin Microbiol Infect Dis. 1992;11:617–620.
53. Mordhorst CH, Wang A-P, Grayston JT. Transmission of *C. pneumoniae* (TWAR). In: Orfila J, Byrne GI, Cherneskey MA, et al, eds. Chlamydial Infections—1994. Bologna: Societa Editrice Esculapio; 1994:488–491.
54. Myhra W, Mordhorst CH, Wang S-P, Grayston JT. Clinical features of *Chlamydia pneumoniae*, strain TWAR, infection in Denmark 1975–1987. In: Bowie WR, Caldwell HD, Jones RP, et al, eds. Chlamydial Infections. Cambridge, England: Cambridge University Press; 1990:422–425.
55. Gnarpe J, Gnarpe H, Sundelöf B. Endemic prevalence of *Chlamydia pneumoniae* in subjectively healthy persons. Scand J Infect Dis. 1991;23:387–388.
56. Hyman CL, Roblin PM, Gaydos CA, et al. Prevalence of asymptomatic nasopharyngeal carriage of *Chlamydia pneumoniae* in subjectively healthy adults: Assessment by polymerase chain reaction–enzyme immunoassay and culture. Clin Infect Dis. 1995;20:1174–1178.
57. Emre U, Roblin PM, Gelling M, et al. The association of *Chlamydia pneumoniae* infection and reactive airway disease in children. Arch Pediatr Adolesc Med. 1994;148:727–732.
58. Hyman CL, Augenbraun MH, Roblin PM, et al. Asymptomatic respiratory tract infection with *Chlamydia pneumoniae* TWAR. J Clin Microbiol. 1991;2082–2083.
59. Kishimoto T, Kimura M, Kubota Y, et al. An outbreak of *C. pneumoniae* infection in households and schools. In: Orfila J, Byrne GI, Cherneskey MA, et al, eds. Chlamydial Infections—1994. Bologna: Societa Editrice Esculapio; 1994:465–468.
60. Kauppinen MT, Saikku P, Kujala P, et al. Clinical picture of community-acquired *Chlamydia pneumoniae* pneumonia requiring hospital treatment: A comparison between chlamydial and pneumococcal pneumonia. Thorax. 1996;51:185–189.
61. Grayston JT, Aldous MB, Easton A, et al. Evidence that *Chlamydia pneumoniae* causes pneumonia and bronchitis. J Infect Dis. 1993;168:1231–1235.
62. Grayston JT. *Chlamydia pneumoniae* (TWAR) infections in children. Pediatr Infect Dis J. 1994;13:675–685.
63. Wright SW, Edwards KM, Decker MD, et al. Prevalence of positive serology for acute *Chlamydia pneumoniae* infection in emergency department patients with persistent cough. Acad Emerg Med. 1997;4:179–183.
64. Kauppinen MT, Lähde S, Syrjälä H. Roentgenographic findings of pneumonia caused by *Chlamydia pneumoniae*: A comparison with *Streptococcus pneumoniae*. Arch Intern Med. 1996;156:1851–1856.
65. Cosentini R, Blasi F, Raccanelli R, et al. Severe community-acquired pneumonia: A possible role for *Chlamydia pneumoniae*. Respiration. 1996;63:61–65.
66. McConnell CT Jr, Plouffe JF, File TM, et al. Radiographic appearance of *Chlamydia pneumoniae* (TWAR strain) respiratory infections. Radiology. 1994;192:819–824.
67. Augenbraun MH, Roblin PM, Mandel LJ, et al. *Chlamydia pneumoniae* pneumonia with pleural effusion: Diagnosis by culture. Am J Med. 1991;91:437–438.
68. Augenbraun MH, Roblin MR, Chirwing K, et al. Isolation of *Chlamydia pneumoniae* from lungs of patients infected with the human immunodeficiency virus. J Clin Microbiol. 1991;29:401–402.
69. Clark R, Mushatt D, Fazal B. Case report: *Chlamydia pneumoniae* pneumonia in an HIV-infected man. Am J Med Sci. 1991;302:155–156.
70. Gaydos CA, Fowler CL, Gill VJ, et al. Detection of *Chlamydia pneumoniae* by polymerase chain reaction–enzyme immunoassay in an immunocompromised population. Clin Infect Dis. 1993;17:718–723.
71. Comandini UV, Maggi P, Santopadre P, et al. *Chlamydia pneumoniae* respiratory infections among patients infected with the human immunodeficiency virus. Eur J Clin Microbiol Infect Dis. 1997;16:720–726.
72. Emre U, Bernius M, Roblin PM, et al. *Chlamydia pneumoniae* infection in patients with cystic fibrosis. Clin Infect Dis. 1996;22:819–823.
73. Miller ST, Hammerschlag MR, Chirgwin K, et al. Role of *Chlamydia pneumoniae* in acute chest syndrome of sickle cell disease. J Pediatr. 1991;118:30–33.
74. Hahn DL, Dodge RW, Golubjatnikov R. Association of *Chlamydia pneumoniae* (strain TWAR) infection with wheezing, asthmatic bronchitis, and adult-onset asthma. JAMA. 1991;266:225–230.
75. Hahn DL, Golubjatnikov R. Asthma and chlamydial infection: A case series. J Fam Pract. 1994;38:589–595.
76. Hahn DL, Anttila T, Saikku P. Association of *Chlamydia pneumoniae* IgA antibodies with recently symptomatic asthma. Epidemiol Infect. 1996;117:513–517.
77. Allegra L, Blasi F, Centanni S, et al. Acute exacerbations of asthma in adults: Role of *Chlamydia pneumoniae* infection. Eur Respir J. 1994;7:2165–2168.
78. Emre U, Sokolovskaya N, Roblin PM, et al. Detection of anti–*Chlamydia pneumoniae* IgE in children with reactive airway disease. J Infect Dis. 1995;172:256–257.
79. Ogawa H, Fujisawa T, Kazuyama Y. Isolation of *Chlamydia pneumoniae* from middle ear aspirates of otitis media with effusion: A case report. J Infect Dis. 1990;162:1000–1001.
80. Ogawa H, Hashiguchi K, Kazuyama Y. Recovery of *Chlamydia pneumoniae* in six patients with otitis media and effusion. J Laryngol Otol. 1992;106:490–492.
81. Block SL, Hammerschlag MR, Hedrick J, et al. *Chlamydia pneumoniae* in acute otitis media. Pediatr Infect Dis J. 1997;16:858–862.
82. Storgaard M, Østergaard L, Jensen JS, et al. *Chlamydia pneumoniae* in children with otitis media. J Infect Dis. 1997;25:1090–1093.
83. Marrie TJ, Harczy M, Mann OE, et al. Culture-negative endocarditis probably due to *Chlamydia pneumoniae*. J Infect Dis. 1990;161:127–129.
84. Norton R, Scheqetluk S, Kok TW. *Chlamydia pneumoniae* pneumonia with endocarditis (Letter). Lancet. 1995;345:1376–1377.
85. Michel D, Antoine JC, Pozzetto B, et al. Lumbosacral meningoradiculitis associated with *Chlamydia pneumoniae* infection. J Neurol Neurosurg Psychiatry. 1992;55:511.
86. Erntell M, Ljunggren K, Gadd T, Persson K. Erythema nodosum—a manifestation of *Chlamydia pneumoniae* (strain TWAR) infection. Scand J Infect Dis. 1989;21:693–696.
87. Sundelof B, Gnarpe H, Gnarpe J. An unusual manifestation of *Chlamydia pneumoniae* infection: Meningitis, hepatitis, iritis and atypical erythema nodosum. Scand J Infect Dis. 1993;25:259–261.
88. Haidl S, Ivarsson S, Bjerre I, Persson K. Guillain-Barré syndrome after *Chlamydia pneumoniae* infection. N Engl J Med. 1992;326:576–577.
89. Koskiniemi M, Korppi M, Mustonen K, et al. Epidemiology of encephalitis in children: A prospective multicentre study. Eur J Pediatr. 1997;156:541–545.
90. Koskiniemi M, Gencay M, Salonen O, et al. *Chlamydia pneumoniae* associated with central nervous system infections. Eur Neurol. 1996;36:160–163.
91. Puolakkainen M, Campbell LA, Kuo C-C, et al. Serological response to *Chlamydia pneumoniae* in patients with sarcoidosis. J Infect. 1996;33:199–205.
92. Jackson LA, Campbell LA, Schmidt RA, et al. Frequency of detection of *Chlamydia pneumoniae* in cardiovascular atheroma: Evaluation of the innocent bystander hypothesis. Am J Pathol. 1997;150:1785–1790.
93. Blasi F, Rizzato G, Gambacorta M, et al. Failure to detect the presence of *Chlamydia pneumoniae* in sarcoid pathology specimens. Eur Respir J. 1997;10:2609–2611.
94. Braun J, Laitko S, Treharne J, et al. *Chlamydia pneumoniae*—a new causative agent of reactive arthritis and undifferentiated oligoarthritis. Ann Rheum Dis. 1994;53:100–105.
95. Laurila AL, Anttila T, Laara E, et al. Serological evidence of an association between *Chlamydia pneumoniae* infection and lung cancer. Int J Cancer. 1997;74:31–34.
96. Wang S-P, Grayston JT. Immunologic relationship between genital TRIC, lymphogranuloma venereum, and related organisms in a new microtiter indirect immunofluorescence test. Am J Ophthalmol. 1970;70:367–374.
97. Verkooyen RP, Hazenberg MA, Van Haaren GH, et al. Age-related interference with *Chlamydia pneumoniae* microimmunofluorescence serology due to circulating rheumatoid factor. J Clin Microbiol. 1992;30:1287–1290.
98. Kuo C-C, Grayston JT. A sensitive cell line, HL cells, for isolation and propagation of *Chlamydia pneumoniae* strain TWAR. J Infect Dis. 1990;162:755–758.
99. Kuo C-C, Grayston JT. Factors affecting viability and growth in HeLa 229 cells of *Chlamydia* sp. strain TWAR. J Clin Microbiol. 1988;26:812–815.
100. Campbell LA, Perez-Melgosa M, Hamilton DJ, et al. Detection of *Chlamydia pneumoniae* by polymerase chain reaction. J Clin Microbiol. 1992;30:434–439.
101. Gaydos CA, Quinn TC, Eiden JJ. Identification of *Chlamydia pneumoniae* by DNA amplification of the 16S rRNA gene. J Clin Microbiol. 1992;30:796–800.
102. Gaydos CA, Eiden JJ, Oldach D, et al. Diagnosis of *Chlamydia pneumoniae* in patients with community acquired pneumonia by polymerase chain reaction enzyme immunoassay. Clin Infect Dis. 1994;19:157–160.
103. Gaydos CA, Roblin PM, Hammerschlag MR, et al. Diagnostic utility of PCR–enzyme immunoassay, culture, and serology for detection of *Chlamydia pneumoniae* in symptomatic and asymptomatic patients. J Clin Microbiol. 1994;32:903–905.
104. Tong CYW, Sillis M. Detection of *Chlamydia pneumoniae* and *Chlamydia psittaci* in sputum samples by PCR. J Clin Pathol. 1993;45:313–317.
105. Dalhoff K, Maass M. *Chlamydia pneumoniae* pneumonia in hospitalized patients:

Clinical characteristics and diagnostic value of polymerase chain reaction detection in BAL. Chest. 1996;110:351–356.
106. Ramirez JA, Ahkee S, Tolentino A, et al. Diagnosis of *Legionella pneumophila, Mycoplasma pneumoniae*, or *Chlamydia pneumoniae* lower respiratory infection using the polymerase chain reaction on a single throat swab specimen. Diagn Microbiol Infect Dis. 1996;24:7–14.
107. Kuo C-C, Grayston JT. In vitro drug susceptibility of *Chlamydia* sp. strain TWAR. Antimicrob Agents Chemother. 1988;32:257–258.
108. Kuo C-C, Jackson LA, Lee A, Grayston JT. *In vitro* activities of azithromycin, clarithromycin, and other antibiotics against *C. pneumoniae*. Antimicrob Agents Chemother. 1996;40:2669–2670.
109. Hammerschlag MR, Qumei KK, Roblin PM. In vitro activities of azithromycin, clarithromycin, L-ofloxacin, and other antibiotics against *Chlamydia pneumoniae*. Antimicrob Agents Chemother. 1992;36:1573–1574.
110. Hammerschlag MR, Hyman CL, Roblin PM. In vitro activities of five quinolones against *Chlamydia pneumoniae*. Antimicrob Agents Chemother. 1992;36:682–683.
111. File TM Jr, Segreti J, Dunbar L, et al. A multicenter, randomized study comparing the efficacy and safety of intravenous and/or oral levofloxacin versus ceftriaxone and/or cefuroxime axetil in treatment of adults with community-acquired pneumonia. Antimicrob Agents Chemother. 1997;41:1965–1972.
112. Gray GC, McPhate DC, Leinonen M, et al. Weekly oral azithromycin as prophylaxis for agents causing acute respiratory disease. Clin Infect Dis. 1998;26:103–110.
113. Hammerschlag MR, Chirgwin K, Roblin PM, et al. Persistent infection with *Chlamydia pneumoniae* following acute respiratory illness. Clin Infect Dis. 1992;14:178–182.
114. Saikku P, Leinonen M, Mattila K, et al. Serological evidence of an association of a novel *Chlamydia*, TWAR, with chronic coronary heart disease and acute myocardial infarction. Lancet. 1988;2:983–986.
115. Saikku P, Leinonen M, Tenkanen L, et al. Chronic *Chlamydia pneumoniae* infection as a risk factor for coronary heart disease in the Helsinki Heart Study. Ann Intern Med. 1992;116:273–278.
116. Thom DH, Grayston JT, Siscovick DS, et al. Association of prior infection with *Chlamydia pneumoniae* and angiographically demonstrated coronary artery disease. JAMA. 1992;268:68–72.
117. Thom DH, Wang S-P, Grayston JT, et al. *Chlamydia pneumoniae* strain TWAR antibody and angiographically demonstrated coronary heart disease. Arterioscler Thromb. 1991;11:547–551.
118. Linnanmäki E, Leinonen M, Mattila K, et al. *Chlamydia pneumoniae*–specific circulating immune complexes in patients with chronic coronary heart disease. Circulation. 1993;87:1130–1134.
119. Mendall MA, Carrington D, Strachan D, et al. *Chlamydia pneumoniae*: Risk factors for seropositivity and association with coronary heart disease. J Infect. 1995;30:121–128.
120. Patel P, Mendall MA, Carrington D, et al. Association of *Helicobacter pylori* and *Chlamydia pneumoniae* infections with coronary heart disease and cardiovascular risk factors. BMJ. 1995;311:711–714.
121. Melnick SL, Shahar E, Folsom AR, et al. Past Infection by *Chlamydia pneumoniae* strain TWAR and asymptomatic carotid atherosclerosis. Am J Med. 1993;95:499–504.
122. Wimmer ML, Sandmann-Strupp R, Saikku P, Haberl RL. Association of chlamydial infection with cerebrovascular disease. Stroke. 1996;27:2207–2210.
123. Cook PJ, Honeybourne D, Lip GY, et al. *Chlamydia pneumoniae* antibody titers are significantly associated with acute stroke and transient cerebral ischemia: The West Birmingham Stroke Project. Stroke. 1998;29:404–410.
124. Campbell LA, O'Brien ER, Cappuccio AL, et al. Detection of *Chlamydia pneumoniae* (TWAR) in human coronary atherectomy tissues. J Infect Dis. 1995;172:585–588.
125. Kuo C-C, Shor A, Campbell LA, et al. Demonstration of *Chlamydia pneumoniae* in atherosclerotic lesions of coronary arteries. J Infect Dis. 1993;167:841–849.
126. Kuo C-C, Grayston JT, Campbell LA, et al. *Chlamydia pneumoniae* (TWAR) in coronary arteries of young (15 to 35 year) adults. Proc Natl Acad Sci U S A. 1995;92:6911–6914.
127. Ramirez JA and the *Chlamydia pneumoniae*/Atherosclerosis Study Group. Isolation of *Chlamydia pneumoniae* from the coronary artery of a patient with coronary atherosclerosis. Ann Intern Med. 1996;125:979–982.
128. Maass M, Bartels C, Engel PM, et al. Endovascular presence of viable *Chlamydia pneumoniae* is a common phenomenon in coronary artery disease. J Am Coll Cardiol. 1998;31:827–832.
129. Mühlestein JB, Hammond EH, Carlquist JF, et al. Increased incidence of *Chlamydia* species within the coronary arteries of patients with symptomatic atherosclerotic versus other forms of cardiovascular disease. J Am Coll Cardiol. 1996;27:1555–1561.
130. Shor A, Kuo C-C, Patton DL. Detection of *Chlamydia pneumoniae* in coronary arterial fatty streaks and atheromatous plaques. S Afr Med J. 1992;82:158–161.
131. Jackson LA, Campbell LA, Kuo CC, et al. Isolation of *Chlamydia pneumoniae* from a carotid endarterectomy specimen. J Infect Dis. 1997;176:292–295.
132. Chiu B, Viira E, Tucker W, Fong IW. *Chlamydia pneumoniae*, cytomegalovirus, and herpes simplex virus in atherosclerosis of the carotid artery. Circulation. 1997;96:2144–2148.
133. Grayston JT, Kuo C-C, Coulson AS, et al. *Chlamydia pneumoniae* (TWAR) in atherosclerosis of the carotid artery. Circulation. 1995;92:3397–3400.
134. Yamashita K, Ouchi K, Shirai M, et al. Distribution of *Chlamydia pneumoniae* infection in the atherosclerotic carotid artery. Stroke. 1998;29:773–778.
135. Kuo C-C, Coulson AS, Campbell LA, et al. Detection of *Chlamydia pneumoniae* in atherosclerotic plaques of the artery of lower extremities from patients undergoing bypass operation for arterial obstruction. J Vasc Surg. 1997;26:1–3.
136. Kuo C-C, Gown AM, Benditt EP, Grayston JT. Detection of *Chlamydia pneumoniae* in aortic lesions of atherosclerosis by immunocytochemical stain. Arterioscler Thromb: 1993;13:1501–1504.
137. Blasi F, Denti F, Erba M, et al. Detection of *Chlamydia pneumoniae* but not *Helicobacter pylori* in atherosclerotic plaques of aortic aneurysms. J Clin Microbiol. 1996;34:2766–2769.
138. Juvonen J, Juvonen T, Laurila A, et al. Demonstration of *Chlamydia pneumoniae* in the walls of abdominal aortic aneurysms. J Vasc Surg. 1997;25:499–505.
139. Knoebel E, Vijayagopal P, Gifueroa JE, Martin DH. In vitro infection of smooth muscle cells by *Chlamydia pneumoniae*. Infect Immun. 1997;65:503–506.
140. Gaydos CA, Summersgill JT, Sahney NN, et al. Replication of *Chlamydia pneumoniae* in vitro in human macrophages, endothelial cells, and aortic artery smooth muscle cells. Infect Immun. 1996;64:1614–1620.
141. Fryer RH, Schwobe EP, Woods ML, Rodgers GM. *Chlamydia* species infect human vascular endothelial cells and induce procoagulant activity. J Investig Med. 1997;45:168–174.
142. Godzik KL, O'Brien ER, Wang S-K, Kuo C-C. In vitro susceptibility of human vascular wall cells to infection with *Chlamydia pneumoniae*. J Clin Microbiol. 1995;33:2411–2414.
143. Kalayoglu MV, Byrne GI. Induction of macrophage foam cell formation by *Chlamydia pneumoniae*. J Infect Dis. 1998;177:725–729.
144. Moazed TC, Kuo C, Grayston JT, Campbell LA. Murine models of *Chlamydia pneumoniae* infection and atherosclerosis. J Infect Dis. 1997;175:883–890.
145. Moazed TC, Campbell LA, Rosenfeld ME, et al. *Chlamydia pneumoniae* infection accelerates the progression of atherosclerosis in apolipoprotein (Apo-E)–deficient mice. In: Stephens RS, Byrne GI, Christiansen G, et al, eds. Chlamydial Infection. Berkeley, Calif: University of California Printing Services; 1998:426–429.
146. Fong IW, Chiu B, Viira E, et al. Rabbit model for *Chlamydia pneumoniae* infection. J Clin Microbiol. 1997;35:48–52.
147. Laitinen K, Laurila A, Pyhälä L, et al. *Chlamydia pneumoniae* infection induces inflammatory changes in the aortas of rabbits. Infect Immun. 1997;65:4832–4835.
148. Mühlestein JB, Anderson JL, Hammond EH, et al. Infection with *Chlamydia pneumoniae* accelerates the development of atherosclerosis and treatment with azithromycin prevents it in a rabbit model. Circulation. 1998;97:633–636.
149. Gupta S, Leatham EW, Carrington D, et al. Elevated *Chlamydia pneumoniae* antibodies, cardiovascular events, and azithromycin in male survivors of myocardial infarction. Circulation. 1997;96:404–407.
150. Gurfinkle E, Bozovich G, Daroca A, et al. Randomised trial of roxithromycin in non–Q-wave coronary syndromes: ROXIS pilot study. Lancet. 1997;350:404–407.

S E C T I O N   D

MYCOPLASMA DISEASES

Chapter 171

Introduction to *Mycoplasma* Diseases

STEPHEN G. BAUM

Mycoplasmas are ubiquitous as pathogens and colonizing agents in the plant and animal kingdoms. They represent the smallest known free-living forms, but because they have fastidious growth requirements, they are often difficult to culture on a cell-free medium. On the other hand, the presence of several species of *Mycoplasma* as commensals in animals and on human oral and genital mucosa has in the past produced frequent contamination of cell cultures.[1] Such contamination has in turn led to the false implication of mycoplasmas as causative agents in many human diseases, both trivial and life threatening. Knowledge of the true range of diseases that these organisms cause is, however, expanding rapidly with the advent of immunohistochemical and nucleic acid probe techniques used to detect mycoplasmas directly in tissue specimens.

DESCRIPTION OF THE ORGANISM

Mycoplasmas are prokaryotes that lack a cell wall. They are bounded by a cell membrane containing sterols, substances not found in either bacteria or viruses. Because of their small size (150 to 250 nm) and deformable membrane, they are able to pass through filters with pore sizes that retain bacteria.[2] Therefore, when first discovered, they were thought to be viruses.[3] However, their ability to grow in cell-free medium and the fact that they contain both RNA and DNA clearly sets them apart from this class of microorganisms. For a time, mycoplasmas were thought to be L (Lister) forms of bacteria, which like mycoplasmas, do not have cell walls. However, like the bacteria from which they derive, L-forms lack sterols in their membranes and under certain conditions can be made to revert to their walled parental forms.[4] DNA homology studies have failed to demonstrate any significant relationship between mycoplasmas and known bacteria (Table 171–1).

The small size of these organisms would suggest that they require many exogenous nutrients for growth, including vitamins, amino acids, nucleic acid precursors, and most especially, lipids. The latter are provided by the addition of serum or cholesterol to growth medium. Energy is supplied by carbohydrate metabolism. Some nonfermenting mycoplasmas derive energy from amino acid (arginine) metabolism. As its name implies, *Ureaplasma* can split urea, but it is unclear whether urea splitting is the sole source of energy for these organisms.[5]

Most mycoplasmas grown on agar form colonies with a dense central zone and a less dense peripheral zone. The resultant colony has been likened to the shape of a fried egg (Fig. 171–1 *A*). An important exception is *Mycoplasma pneumoniae,* the most significant human pathogen of the genus. This mycoplasma forms no peripheral halo, and colonies have been likened to a mulberry (Fig. 171–1 *B*).

Other characteristics of *Mycoplasma* growth in vitro include absorption of erythrocytes from a number of animal species and hemolysis of erythrocytes in blood agar through the elaboration of hydrogen peroxide.

TAXONOMY AND DISTRIBUTION

Mycoplasmas have now been assigned taxonomically to their own class, Mollicutes, which has three main families: Mycoplasmataceae, which encompasses organisms infecting and colonizing humans and animals; Spironoplasmataceae, the plant mycoplasmas; and Acholeplasmataceae, most of which are isolated primarily from birds. A fourth family, Anaeroplasmataceae, consists of strict anaerobes that have been isolated from cattle and birds. They are not known to infect humans.

The family Mycoplasmataceae is composed of two genera responsible for human infection: *Mycoplasma* and *Ureaplasma;* the genus *Mycoplasma* has at least 13 species that infect humans, as listed in Figure 171–2.[6] Ureaplasmas were previously referred to as T-strain mycoplasmas because of the tiny colonies that they formed on agar.[7]

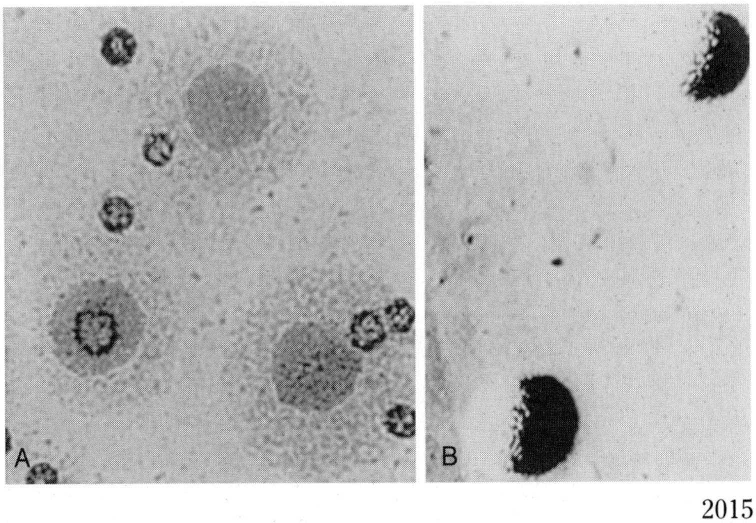

FIGURE 171–1. Photomicrograph of colonies of mycoplasma growing on agar medium. *A, Mycoplasma salivarium* colonies growing with "fried egg" appearance. *B, Mycoplasma pneumoniae* colonies with "mulberry" colony formation.

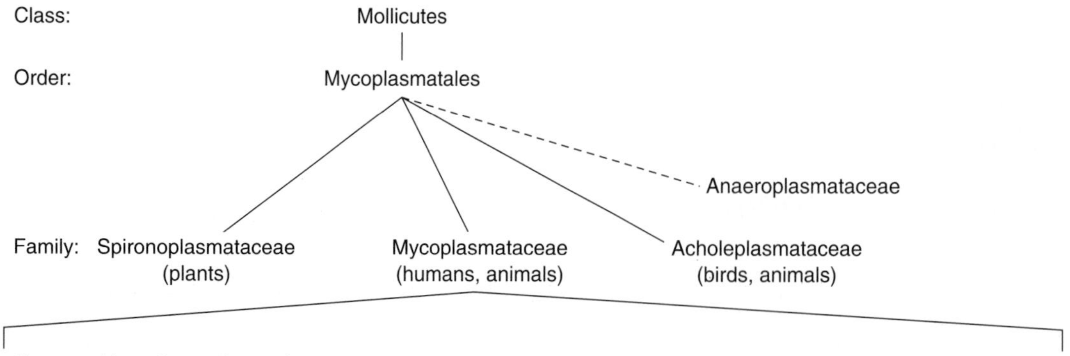

Genus: *Mycoplasma* (human)

Subgroup	Sites of isolation	Occurrence	Diseases
M. hominis	GU tract (F>M) Conjunctiva (neonate) Blood (peripartum) Surgical wounds, joints	Common	Cervicitis, vaginitis, ? prostatitis Conjunctivitis Peripartum sepsis Sternotomy infection, arthritis, especially in immunocompromised
M. orale	Oropharynx	Common	?
M. pneumoniae	Respiratory tract	Common	URI, pneumonia
M. salivarium	Oropharynx, gingiva	Common	? Periodontal disease
M. buccale	Oropharynx	Uncommon	?
M. faucium	Oropharynx	Uncommon	?
M. fermentans (*incognitus* str.)	GU tract Blood, tissues	Uncommon Uncommon	? ? Fulminant multisystem disease in patients with AIDS and healthy individuals
M. genitalium	GU tract	Uncommon	Urethritis
M. lipophilum	Oropharynx	Rare	?
M. primatum	Oropharynx, GU tract	Rare	?
M. pirum	Blood (HIV+)	Rare	?
M. spermatophilum	GU tract	Rare	?
M. penetrans	GU tract (M>F)	Rare	?
Genus: *Ureaplasma*			
Subgroup *U. urealyticum*	GU tract (F>M)	Common	Urethritis, upper GU infection, ? prematurity

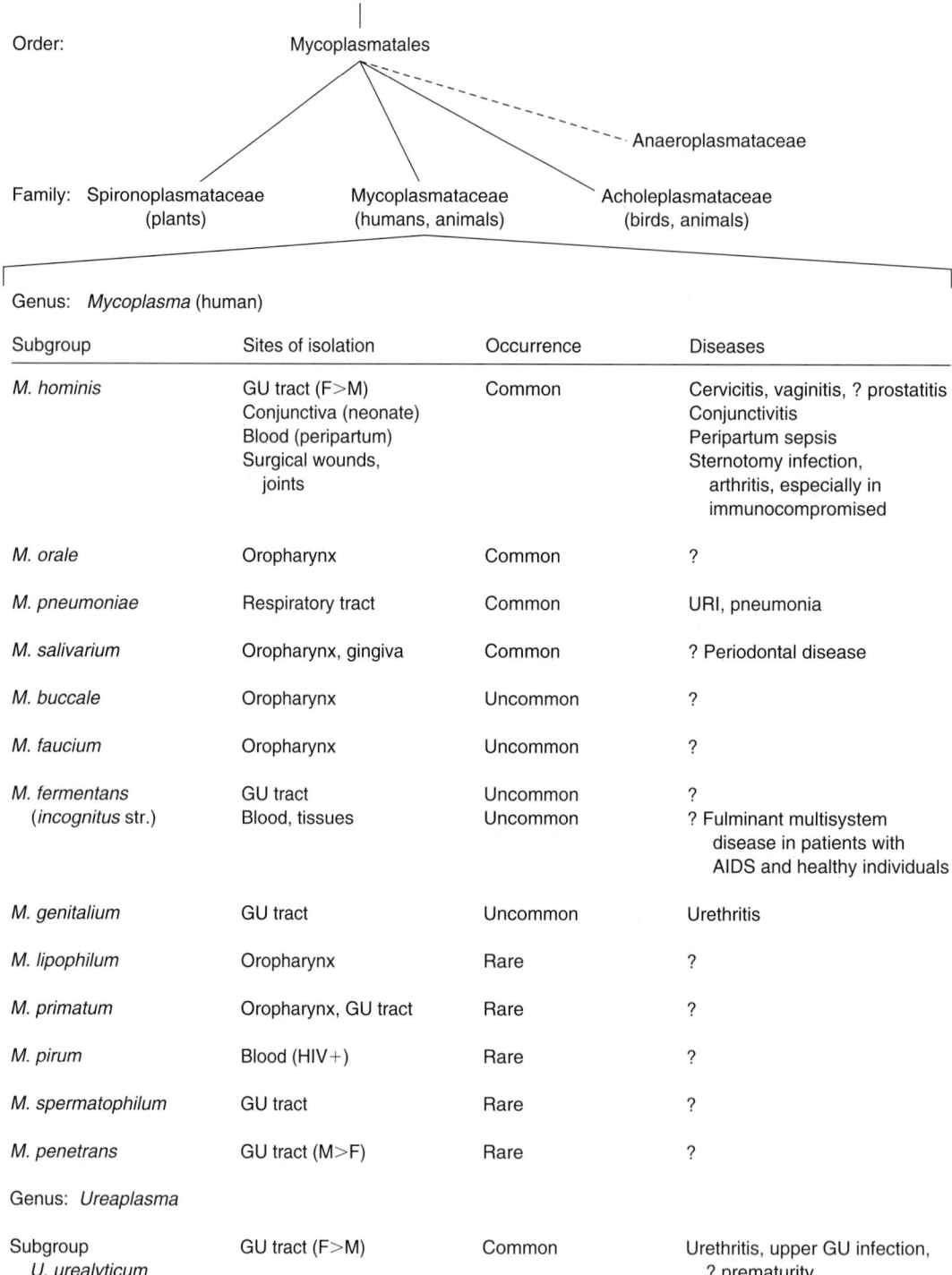

FIGURE 171–2. Taxonomy and distribution of the class Mollicutes. *Abbreviations*: AIDS, Acquired immunodeficiency syndrome; F, female; GU, genitourinary; HIV, human immunodeficiency virus; M, male; URI, upper respiratory infection. (Modified from Somerson NL, Cole BC. The mycoplasma flora of human and nonhuman primates. In: Tully JG, Whitcomb RF, eds. The Mycoplasmas. V. 2. New York: Academic Press; 1979:191–216.)

TABLE 171-1 Characteristics Defining Mycoplasmas

General
Prokaryotic
Small size: 150–250 nm
No cell wall
Trilayered cell membrane
Most are aerobic
Fastidious growth requirements
Form "fried egg" colonies on agar
Differentiation from bacteria and L-forms
Sterols in membrane
No DNA homology with known bacteria
Low guanine + cytosine content
Low-molecular-weight genome (4.5×10^8–1×10^9 Da)
No reversion to walled forms
Differentiation from viruses
Contain both DNA and RNA
Free living: cell-free growth on defined media in vitro
Extracellular parasitism in vivo

Modified from Couch RB. *Mycoplasma* diseases: Introduction. In: Mandell GL, Douglas RG Jr, Bennett JE, eds. Principles and Practice of Infectious Diseases. New York: Churchill Livingstone; 1990:1445–1446.

PATHOGENESIS

Mycoplasmas appear to cause infection primarily as extracellular parasites. They attach to the surface of ciliated and nonciliated epithelial cells. Subsequent events are unclear but may include direct cytotoxicity of such elaborated substances as hydrogen peroxide,[8] or they may cause cytolysis via an inflammatory response mediated through chemotaxis of mononuclear cells or antigen-antibody reactions.

Mycoplasmas are very common contaminants of tissue cultures.[1, 9] In this situation they are most often intracellular parasites. This fact may contribute to the difficulty in eradicating mycoplasmas from contaminated cultures. Their presence has been shown to markedly alter both cellular and viral molecular events, a fact that has prompted some to question many of the molecular biologic results derived from tissue culture experiments.[1]

MYCOPLASMAS NEWLY ASSOCIATED WITH HUMAN DISEASE

Mycoplasma fermentans (*incognitus* Strain)

Mycoplasma incognitus, a variant of *M. fermentans, Mycoplasma penetrans,* and *Mycoplasma pirum* have been associated with severe disease in healthy peoply and those with acquired immunodeficiency syndrome (AIDS).[10, 11] *M. fermentans* was first isolated by Lo and colleagues from the blood, organs, and Kaposi's sarcoma lesions of patients with AIDS and has since been reported to cause fulminant multisystem infection in presumably healthy patients.[11] The organism was first believed to be a virus,[10] then was identified as the mycoplasma *M. penetrans,*[12] and was ultimately shown by immunohistochemistry, DNA homology, electron microscopy, and in situ hybridization to be a mycoplasma closely related to *M. fermentans.*[13, 14] The organism has been identified at the advancing margins of lesions in the liver, brain, spleen, lymph nodes, and thymus of infected patients.[15] *M. penetrans* has been isolated from the urogenital tract and *M. pirum* from the blood of patients with human immunodeficiency virus (HIV).[11]

Cultivation of these organisms directly from patient material on cell-free medium has proved to be difficult, and prior animal and tissue culture passage is required. This difficulty in direct culturing has fueled a controversy over whether these organisms are pathogens or contaminants in these patients. A further controversy exists regarding the causative or disease-enhancing role of these organisms in AIDS versus their role as only one of the many opportunistic infectious agents in this condition.[11]

In support of a causative role of *M. incognitus* in the pathogenesis of AIDS are the fact that *M. incognitus* was first isolated from patients with AIDS, many of whom have antibody to the organism, and data demonstrating that membrane proteins from another mycoplasmal organism, *Acholeplasma laidlawii,* enhance the replication of HIV in vitro.[16] Against such a role is the relatively infrequent identification of the organism in a random population of autopsied AIDS patients[17] and the equal prevalence of colonization with this organism in HIV-positive and HIV-negative patients.[18]

The organism is sensitive in vitro to tetracycline, chloramphenicol, clindamycin, lincomycin, and the quinolones. Sensitivity to the macrolides appears to be very limited.[19]

Animal Mycoplasmas as Human Pathogens

Case reports of human infections caused by mycoplasmas previously thought to infect only animals have recently appeared. One such report describes fatal septicemia caused by *Mycoplasma arginini* in an immunocompromised slaughterhouse worker. This organism is often found in the respiratory tracts of cattle, sheep, and goats.[20]

Genital Mycoplasmas Causing Nongenital Infection

A number of publications indicate that the genital mycoplasmas (*Mycoplasma hominis, Mycoplasma genitalium,* and *Ureaplasma urealyticum*) can cause serious infections involving the respiratory tract, heart, blood stream, central nervous system, sternotomy wounds, and prosthetic valves and joints of infants and adults.[21–31] The urogenital mycoplasma organisms are discussed in detail in Chapter 173.

REFERENCES

1. Barile MF, Hopps HE, Grabowski MW, et al. The identification and sources of mycoplasmas isolated from contaminated cell cultures. Ann N Y Acad Sci. 1973;25:251–264.
2. Elford WJ. Ultrafiltration methods and their application in bacteriological and pathological studies. Br J Exp Pathol. 1929;10:126.
3. Eaton MD, Meiklejohn G, van Herick W, et al. Studies on the etiology of primary atypical pneumonia. II. Properties of the virus isolated and propagated in chick embryos. J Exp Med. 1945;82:317.
4. Madoff S. Introduction to the bacterial L forms. In: Madoff S, ed. The L Forms of Bacteria. New York: Marcel Dekker; 1986:1–20.
5. Rodwell AW, Mitchell A. Nutrition, growth and reproduction. In: Barile MF, Razin S, eds. The Mycoplasmas. v. 1. New York: Academic; 1979:103–139.
6. Taylor-Robinson D. Infections due to species of *Mycoplasma* and *Ureaplasma*: An update. Clin Infect Dis. 1996;23:671–684.
7. Razin S, Freundt EA. The mycoplasmas. In: Krieg NR, Holt JG, eds. Bergey's Manual of Systematic Microbiology. v. 1. Baltimore: Williams & Wilkins; 1984:740–793.
8. Clyde WA Jr. *Mycoplasma pneumoniae* infections of man. In: Tully JG, Whitcomb RF, eds. The Mycoplasmas. v. 2. New York: Academic; 1979: 275–306.
9. Somerson NL, Cole BC. The mycoplasma flora of human and nonhuman primates. In: Tully JG, Whitcomb RF, eds. The Mycoplasmas. v. 2. New York: Academic; 1979:191–216.
10. Lo SC, Dawson MS, Newton PB III, et al. Association of the virus-like infectious agent originally reported in patients with AIDS with acute fatal disease in previously healthy non-AIDS patients. Am J Trop Med Hyg. 1989;41:364.
11. Montagnier L, Blanchard A. Mycoplasmas as cofactors in infection due to the human immunodeficiency virus. Clin Infect Dis. 1993;17(Suppl 1):S309–S315.
12. Wang R Y-H, Shih J W-K, Grandinetti T, et al. High frequency of antibodies to *Mycoplasma penetrans* in HIV-infected patients. Lancet. 1992;340:1312.
13. Hawkins RE, Rickman LS, Vermund SH, et al. Detection of amplified *Mycoplasma fermentans* DNA in blood. J Infect Dis. 1992;165:581.
14. *Mycoplasma incognitus*: A workshop. Am J Trop Med Hyg. 1990;42:399.
15. Lo SC, Dawson M, Wong DM. Identification of *Mycoplasma incognitus* infection in patients with AIDS: An immunohistochemical, in-situ hybridization and ultrastructural study. Am J Trop Med Hyg. 1989;41:601.
16. Chowdhury IH, Munakata T, Koyanagi Y, et al. Mycoplasma can enhance HIV replication in vitro: A possible co-factor responsible for the progression of AIDS. Biochem Biophys Res Commun. 1990;170:1365.
17. Miller-Catchpole R, Shattuck M, Kandalaft P, et al. The incidence and distribution of *Mycoplasma fermentans* (*incognitus* strain) in the Chicago AIDS autopsy series: An immunohistochemical study. Mod Pathol. 1991;4:481.
18. Katseni VL, Gilroy CB, Ryait BK, et al. *Mycoplasma fermentans* in individuals seropositive for HIV-1. Lancet. 1993;341:271.

19. Taylor-Robinson D, Bébéar C. Antibiotic susceptibilities of mycoplasmas and treatment of mycoplasmal infections. J Antimicrob Chemother. 1997;40:622–630.
20. Yechouron A, Lefebvre J, Robson HG. Fatal septicemia due to *Mycoplasma arginini:* A new human zoonosis. Clin Infect Dis. 1992;15:434.
21. Cassell GH, Waites KB, Krouse DT. Perinatal mycoplasmal infections. Clin Perinatol. 1991;18:241.
22. Alonso-Vega C, Wauters N, Vermeylen D, et al. A fatal case of *Mycoplasma hominis* meningoencephalitis in a full-term newborn. J Clin Microbiol. 1997;35:286–287.
23. Cohen JI, Sloss LJ, Kundsin R, et al. Prosthetic valve endocarditis caused by *Mycoplasma hominis.* Am J Med. 1989;86:819.
24. Mohiuddin AA, Coren J, Harbeck RJ, et al. *Ureaplasma urealyticum* chronic osteomyelitis in a patient with hypogammaglobulinemia. J Allergy Clin Immunol. 1991;87:104.
25. Parides GC, Bloom JW, Ampel NM, et al. *Mycoplasma* and *Ureaplasma* in bronchoalveolar lavage fluids from immunocompromised hosts. Diagn Microbiol Infect Dis. 1988;9:55.
26. Smeller H, Wellborne F, Barile MF, et al. Prosthetic joint infection with *Mycoplasma hominis.* J Infect Dis. 1986;153:174.
27. Baseman JB, Dallo SF, Tully JG, et al. Isolation and characterization of *Mycoplasma genitalium* strains from the human respiratory tract. J Clin Microbiol. 1988;26:2266.
28. Cassell GH, Crouse DT, Waites KB, et al. Does *Ureaplasma urealyticum* cause respiratory disease in newborns. Pediatr Infect Dis. 1988;7:535.
29. Couch RB. *Mycoplasma* diseases: Introduction. In: Mandell GL, Douglas RG Jr, Bennett JE, eds. Principles and Practice of Infectious Diseases. New York: Churchill Livingstone; 1990:1445–1446.
30. Sielaff TD, Everett JE, Shumway SJ, et al. *Mycoplasma hominis* infections occurring in cardiovascular surgical patients. Ann Thorac Surg. 1996;61:99–103.
31. Luttrell LM, Kanj SS, Corey GR, et al. *Mycoplasma hominis* septic arthritis: 2 case reports and review. Clin Infect Dis. 1994;19:1067–1070.

Chapter 172

Mycoplasma pneumoniae and Atypical Pneumonia

STEPHEN G. BAUM

The term and concept of atypical pneumonia arose at the onset of the antibiotic era. In the early 1940s, sulfonamides and then penicillins were introduced into clinical practice. At that time, it was recognized that some cases of pneumonia did not respond to these antibiotics and that these were the pneumonias that could not be attributed by Gram stain or culture to a known bacterial cause. The condition was designated *Primary atypical pneumonia* (PAP). The prefix "primary" indicated that no causative agent could be determined.

In the intervening years, with the advent of virology and better techniques for identifying fastidious bacterial and protozoan agents, it has become clear that the atypical pneumonia syndrome can be caused by influenza virus, adenovirus, respiratory syncytial virus, cytomegalovirus, *Chlamydia*, *Legionella*, *Pneumocystis carinii*, *Mycoplasma pneumoniae*, and probably many other agents. Because we now can identify many of the agents, the prefix "primary" should be discarded. In addition, many of these agents do respond to antimicrobial drugs.

Despite the identification of multiple causes, atypical pneumonias share two unifying features. The first is a nonlobar, patchy or interstitial pattern on chest radiography, and the other is the failure to identify a causative organism on Gram stain or culture of sputum as routinely performed. Because the organisms involved are difficult to identify at the time the patient presents to the physician, it is unlikely that the term "atypical pneumonia" will disappear from the infectious diseases or pulmonary lexicon any time soon.

HISTORY

From the time of the description of the atypical pneumonia syndrome in the mid-1940s until the early 1960s, the cause of this syndrome was in question. Bacteria other than the pneumococcus, viruses such as influenza, and other as yet unidentified agents were all implicated at one time or another. However, one organism, *M. pneumoniae*, is probably responsible for more cases of this syndrome than is any other single organism.

In 1944, Eaton and colleagues described an agent that passed through virus filters and caused focal areas of pneumonia when inoculated in several species of rodents.[1] The agent, initially thought to be a virus, could be serially passaged in chick embryos but could not be grown in culture.[2] The relation of this agent to the PAP syndrome was suggested by the fact that human serum from some patients recovering from PAP neutralized the agent.[3] Serum from about 70% of these patients also was found by Finland and colleagues to agglutinate red blood cells when a mixture of the two was exposed to the cold (4°C).[4] This cold agglutination reaction became and has remained the laboratory hallmark of the disease (see "Immunology"). When serum from patients with PAP caused by a known etiologic agent (e.g., influenza virus) was used, cold agglutinins were not demonstrable and there was no neutralization of Eaton's agent.[5] This provided a link between the Eaton agent and a proportion of PAP cases of unknown cause. However, serum from this same group of patients also had antibodies to *Streptococcus* MG. This and other nonspecific antibody formation in these patients served to confuse matters for a time and to detract from the evidence that Eaton agent was a major cause of PAP.

By 1946, the disease could be transmitted to human volunteers by ultrafiltrates from patients, but this transmissibility did not necessarily tie the syndrome to Eaton agent rather than to a virus, because passage of the chick embryo isolate to humans had not been attempted.[5] This link came in 1961 with the evidence that convalescent serum from volunteers inoculated with PAP ultrafiltrate neutralized Eaton's chick embryo "virus."[6] Subsequently, evidence that Eaton agent was a mycoplasma came from Clyde,[7] who grew the agent in tissue culture, Goodburn and Marmion,[8] who described its morphology, and Chanock and coworkers,[9] who were the first, in 1962, to grow the organism on cell-free artificial medium. The ultimate proof of the role of Eaton agent in PAP was the demonstration that the organism isolated in cell-free culture produced the syndrome in volunteers.[10]

Because Eaton agent passed through virologic filters and could be grown only in chick embryos, it was believed throughout most of two decades after its discovery the agent was a virus. In the early 1960s it was established that the organism had many characteristics in common with those that caused pneumonia in cattle, hence the transiently used term *pleuropneumonia-like organism.*[11] These organisms soon were shown to be mycoplasmas[12] of the class Mollicutes, described in Chapter 171.

DESCRIPTION OF THE ORGANISM

M. pneumoniae shares most of the characteristics described for this family of organisms. It is capable of growth on cell-free defined medium, setting it apart from all but one (*Legionella*) of the common cansative organisms of the atypical pneumonia syndrome. *M. pneumoniae*, unlike most of the other human mycoplasmas, grows well aerobically and ferments glucose as its primary energy source, producing acid.[9, 13]

This organism is also relatively unique among human mycoplasmas in being able to reduce the dye tetrazolium from a blue to yellow color, adsorb guinea pig and chick erythrocytes to growing colonies, and lyse red blood cells incorporated into the growth agar by means of the elaboration of hydrogen peroxide. Detection of each of these unique characteristics has been used to establish presumptive identification of this organism in culture.

M. pneumoniae is a short rod (about 10 × 200 nm) and has at one end an organelle that is responsible for attachment of the organism to cell membranes.[14] The major protein of this organelle (P1) has been purified, and it has been suggested that this peptide would serve well as an antigen for a vaccine.[15] This protein may also confer on *M. pneumoniae* its affinity for respiratory epithelium. *M. pneumoniae* is prokaryotic and is bounded by a trilamellar membrane containing sterols. It divides by binary fission with a doubling time of more than 6 hours.[16] This long doubling time makes culturing of *M. pneumoniae* a slow process (5 to 20 days), compared with other bacteria.[13] Colonies of *M. pneumoniae* differ in morphology from those of other mycoplasmas. They have no outer halo and grow in a dense mulberry shape (see Fig. 171–1 in Chapter 171). Because they lack a cell wall, mycoplasmas including *M. pneumoniae* are not affected by β-lactam antibiotics and are not visible on Gram staining.

EPIDEMIOLOGY

Most cases of mycoplasma respiratory infection occur singly or as family outbreaks. In closed populations such as military recruit camps and boarding schools, mycoplasma can cause miniepidemics and may represent from 25 to 75% of pneumonias in such settings.[17] Serologically based epidemiologic studies throughout the world have documented the high incidence of mycoplasma respiratory infection. In the United States, it is estimated that each year at least one case of mycoplasma pneumonia occurs for each 1000 persons, or more than 2 million cases annually. The incidence of mycoplasma non-pneumonic respiratory infection may be 10 to 20 times this high.[18, 19] The highest attack rates are in children 5 to 20 years old, but mycoplasma pneumonia can occur at any age and may cause particularly severe disease in neonates.[20]

A few studies have reported a peak incidence in the fall in temperate climates.[21–23] This is not surprising given the peak age-related incidence and the fact that late summer and fall represent the time of return to schools. Most surveys, however, show little or no seasonal preponderance in sporadic cases. Distribution of the disease is worldwide.[24, 25]

There appears to be an age-related incidence of upper versus lower respiratory tract infection caused by *M. pneumoniae*. Children younger than 3 years of age develop primarily upper respiratory tract infection,[26] whereas those 5 to 20 years old tend to develop bronchitis and pneumonia. In older adults pneumonia is relatively common in infected patients.[27]

TRANSMISSION

M. pneumoniae infection is spread from one patient to another by respiratory droplets produced by coughing. Relatively close association with the index case appears to be required. The disease usually is introduced into families by a young child, and in some studies most of the adults who were infected were the parents of young children.[28, 29]

As opposed to most viral respiratory infections, which are clinically manifest 1 to 3 days after infection, mycoplasma has an incubation period of 2 to 3 weeks.[29] Therefore, a careful history showing several weeks between cases within a family may give an important clue as to mycoplasmal etiology. In experimental situations, the incubation period seemed to be shorter (7 to 10 days) but this may have resulted from the use of large inocula to induce disease.[10]

Organisms can be cultured from the sputum of infected individuals for weeks to months after clinically effective treatment,[30] and the extent of the effect of treatment of an index case on subsequent transmission to family members is unclear.

CLINICAL DISEASE

In view of the very high incidence of mycoplasma pneumonia when studied epidemiologically in large populations, it would appear that specific, confirmed diagnosis of this entity often is not accomplished in individual clinical practice. There are probably three reasons for this. The first is that mycoplasma pneumonia is usually self-limited and rarely fatal. This fact dampens the zeal to establish the cause of infection. Second, mycoplasmas are relatively fastidious and slow growing; therefore culture results, if obtained at all, often return after the patient is well. Finally, there is deficient knowledge of the epidemiology and clinical manifestations of infection, so that the diagnosis often is not considered.

Respiratory Infection

Epidemiologic studies indicate that most *M. pneumoniae* infections lead to clinically apparent disease rather than to subclinical infection. Most of these infections involve only the upper respiratory tract. After a 2- to 3-week incubation period, the disease has an insidious onset composed of fever, malaise, headache, and cough. The latter is the clinical hallmark of *M. pneumoniae* infection (Fig. 172–1). The frequency and severity of cough increase over the next 1 to 2 days and may become debilitating. The gradual onset of symptoms is in contradistinction to the often acute presentation of respiratory infection caused by influenza or adenovirus.

In 5 to 10% of patients, depending somewhat on age, the infection progresses to tracheobronchitis or pneumonia. In these cases, the original manifestations persist and the cough becomes more severe. It is usually relatively nonproductive but may yield white or occasionally blood-flecked sputum. Gram staining of this sputum reveals evidence of inflammatory cells but no predominant bacterial species. With continued cough, the patient may develop parasternal chest soreness due to muscle strain, but true pleuritic pain is unusual. Fever is usually at the level of 101 to 102°F and may be associated with chilly sensations. As opposed to pneumonia caused by *Streptococcus pneumoniae* (pneumococcus), *M. pneumoniae* rarely causes true shaking chills. In comparison to influenza, which can also manifest as an atypical pneumonia syndrome, myalgias and gastrointestinal complaints of nausea and vomiting are unusual. Diarrhea, sometimes a concomitant of adenoviral pneumonia (see Chapter 132), is uncommon in mycoplasmal infection.

On physical examination, the general appearance is a patient who is not terribly ill. In fact, this disease is the paradigm of the term "walking pneumonia." The pharynx may be injected and erythematous, usually without marked cervical adenopathy as seen in group A streptococcal pharyngitis. *M. pneumoniae* is not a common cause of isolated pharyngitis in the pediatric or adult population.[29] Much has been made of the finding of bullous myringitis in this disease. This abnormality was associated with experimentally induced *M. pneumoniae* infection in about 20% of volunteers.[31] However, true bullous myringitis in naturally occurring mycoplasma disease is rare. In a study of a pediatric population, otitis was rarely associated with isolation of mycoplasma and, on the other hand, was often associated with bacterial and viral upper respiratory tract pathogens.[32, 33] The important synthesis of these data is that the absence of myringitis, bullous or otherwise, should not dissuade one from a diagnosis of mycoplasma pneumonia.

Examination of the chest in patients with mycoplasma pneumonia is often unrevealing, even in those patients with severe, productive cough. There may be no auscultative or percussive findings, or only minimal rales may be present. Disparity between physical findings and radiographic evidence of pneumonia in this condition may be the greatest of any of the atypical pneumonia syndromes. Although wheezing can occur in this disease, in one study of asthmatic patients the presence of wheezing had a negative correlation with the isolation of *M. pneumoniae*, compared with viral respiratory pathogens.[34] *M. pneumoniae* also does not seem to be a common pathogen in patients with preexisting chronic obstructive lung disease.[28]

Pleural effusion (usually small) occurs in 5 to 20% of patients with *M. pneumoniae* infection.[35, 36] This low incidence of pleural inflammation is consistent with the rarity of pleuritic pain. If effusion is present, thoracentesis reveals serous fluid that is exudative with minimal inflammatory reaction. The cell differential count in the fluid is variable,[37] and bloody effusions are rare. It is unusual to

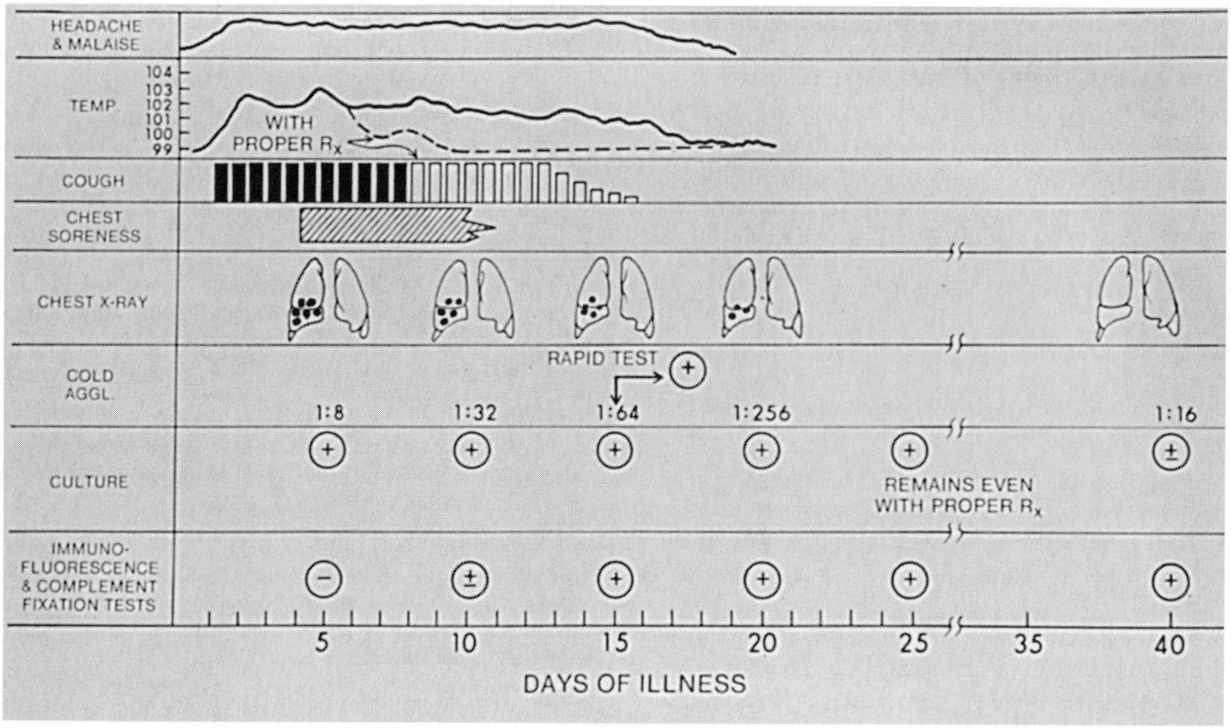

FIGURE 172–1. Major clinical manifestations of mycoplasmal pneumonia. (From Baum SG. Mycoplasmal infections. In: Wyngaarden JB, Smith LH Jr, Bennett JG, eds. Cecil Textbook of Medicine. 19th ed. Philadelphia; WB Saunders; 1992:1615.)

isolate *M. pneumoniae* from effusions when they do occur, but several reports of such isolation exist.[38]

Although pneumonia is usually mild and self-limited, fulminant, severe, and lethal cases have been reported in normal young adults and may be underdiagnosed.[39]

Extrapulmonary Involvement

Abnormalities in almost every organ system have been described as examples of the extrapulmonary manifestations of *M. pneumoniae* infection. The frequency of these extrapulmonary manifestations varies greatly from one report to another and is much less common when viewed as part of a prospective epidemiologic study rather than as the sum of isolated case reports. The lesson from this appears to be that the high prevalence of mycoplasma infection in most populations predisposes to the reporting of many concurrent but perhaps unrelated events as if they were part of the mycoplasmal disease. Several clinical syndromes have been reported with sufficient frequency to provide some support for a causal relationship.

Dermatologic Involvement

A wide variety of transient dermatologic conditions have been reported in conjunction with mycoplasma pneumonia. These include macular, morbilliform, and papulovesicular eruptions as well as erythema nodosum and urticaria.[40, 41] Again, the variety and high incidence of these rashes in the absence of mycoplasma infection makes it difficult to define the relationships, if any, among these occurrences. Further, the role that concurrent antibiotic therapy plays in the development of the exanthems seen during *M. pneumoniae* infection is unknown.

One skin condition that occurs often enough in concert with *M. pneumoniae* infection to provide some basis for relatedness is erythema multiforme major or Stevens-Johnson syndrome. This has been reported in up to 7% of patients with mycoplasma pneumonia.[42–44] Erythema multiforme major consists of erythematous vesicles, plaques, and bullae involving the skin, with particular localization at mucocutaneous junctions. The conjunctivae may also be involved,[45] as may organs of the gastrointestinal and genitourinary tracts and the joints.[42]

These manifestations have been associated in isolated cases with many other infections, including some that can manifest as the atypical pneumonia syndrome. These include legionnaires' pneumonia,[46] adenovirus conjunctivitis,[47] and influenza B infection.[48] However, among possible associations of Stevens-Johnson syndrome with infectious diseases, the association with *M. pneumoniae* infection is by far the most common.[49] This complication tends to occur in the younger patients with mycoplasma pneumonia and has a definite male predominance (2:1 to 4:1) in this disease.

The pathogenesis of this syndrome in any of the diseases in which it occurs is unclear. It has long been supposed that immunity plays a major role,[50, 51] but several reports have noted culture of *M. pneumoniae* from the lesions.[44, 52, 53] The relationship to the level of cold agglutinins in this disease is variable. It has been suggested that development of the Stevens-Johnson syndrome may be the result of augmented sensitivity to antibiotics in the presence of *M. pneumoniae* infection,[54] but some patients develop erythema multiforme major in the absence of prior or concurrent antibiotic therapy. Corticosteroid therapy has been suggested for this complication, but data in support of the usefulness of this therapy are lacking.[55] Most patients clear the lesions in 1 to 2 weeks without scarring unless impetigenization supervenes.

Raynaud's Phenomenon

Although transient reversible vasospasm of the digits on exposure to the cold is not technically a dermatologic syndrome, it is manifest in the skin. This phenomenon occurs in many people, usually women, without any association to infection. It has been reported in patients with acute mycoplasma pneumonia whether or not these patients manifested this syndrome before infection.[41, 56] Although the pathophysiology of this phenomenon in *M. pneumoniae* infection is unclear, it may be related to in vivo action of cold agglutinins (see "Immunology").[57, 58] Other vascular complications reported in *M. pneumoniae* infection include internal carotid artery occlusion and cerebral infarction.[59]

Cardiac Complications

Of all the extrapulmonary manifestations of *M. pneumoniae* infection other than exanthems, cardiac abnormalities are the most commonly reported. Most studies have involved hospitalized patients, so the true incidence of cardiac changes may be underestimated.[60–62] The signs and symptoms suggesting involvement of the heart are arrhythmia, congestive failure, chest pain, and electrocardiographic abnormalities, particularly conduction defects. One report suggests that a loud third heart sound may be the only clue to cardiac involvement.[63] Although cardiac abnormalities have been reported in as many as 10% of cases of *M. pneumoniae* infection, other reports indicate a much lower prevalence. Cardiac abnormalities are more common as the age of the patients studied increases. Cardiac complications prolong illness and have led to death[64] but generally do not appear to appreciably increase mortality. The mechanism of heart damage is unknown, but *M. pneumoniae* was isolated from the blood and pericardial fluid of one patient who died.[65]

Neurologic Complications

Proof of involvement of the central nervous system in mycoplasma pneumonia is somewhat tenuous. Aseptic meningitis and meningoencephalitis,[66, 67] transverse myelitis,[68] brain stem dysfunction,[69] Guillain-Barré syndrome,[70] and peripheral neuropathy have all been reported. The aggregate of these central nervous system manifestations occur no more frequently than 1 per 1000 cases but are more often noted in hospitalized patients.[71] The cerebrospinal fluid findings in these cases are variable, but cellular response is usually minimal, with slightly elevated protein and normal to slightly depressed glucose. Most often, diagnosis of mycoplasma-related central nervous system involvement is made on exclusion of other causes, presence of antecedent or intercurrent respiratory illness, and a rise in antibody titer to *M. pneumoniae* in the serum.[67] Occasionally mycoplasma-specific antibodies have been demonstrated in the cerebrospinal fluid, but these titers have paralleled serum antibody titers.

Neurologic complications are usually reversible when associated with mycoplasma infection, but the mortality of patients with central nervous system involvement is higher than that of others. Although *M. pneumoniae* has been isolated from a few of these patients,[72, 73] immune mechanisms of neural damage have been suggested.[74] Some mycoplasmas elaborate a neurotoxin, but this has not been described for *M. pneumoniae*.[75]

Musculoskeletal Complications

Polyarthralgias are common in mycoplasma pneumonia, but arthritis is rare.[76] Although immune mechanisms have been postulated for this complication, there have been a few reports of isolation of *M. pneumoniae* from joint fluid.[77, 78] When present, arthritis may be monoarticular or migratory. Several of the cases of frank arthritis have been reported in patients with hypogammaglobulinemia.

Renal complications associated with immune complex deposition and high-titer cold agglutinins have been reported (see "Immunology").[79, 80]

Conditions Leading to Increased Susceptibility

Several reports have emphasized the unusually high severity of *M. pneumoniae* infection in patients with sickle cell disease[81] or sickle-related hemoglobinopathies.[82, 83] These patients may develop large pleural effusions and marked respiratory distress. Functional asplenia and its attendant opsinization deficiencies may contribute to overwhelming infection with *M. pneumoniae*, as they do to *S. pneumoniae* infection. It is interesting in this regard that some patients with sickle cell disease and *M. pneumoniae* infection who develop extremely high cold agglutinin titers may experience digital necrosis, as they do with *S. pneumoniae*. One such patient is shown in Figure 172–2, and a hypothesis on pathogenesis is given in the discussion on cold agglutinins in the Immunology section.

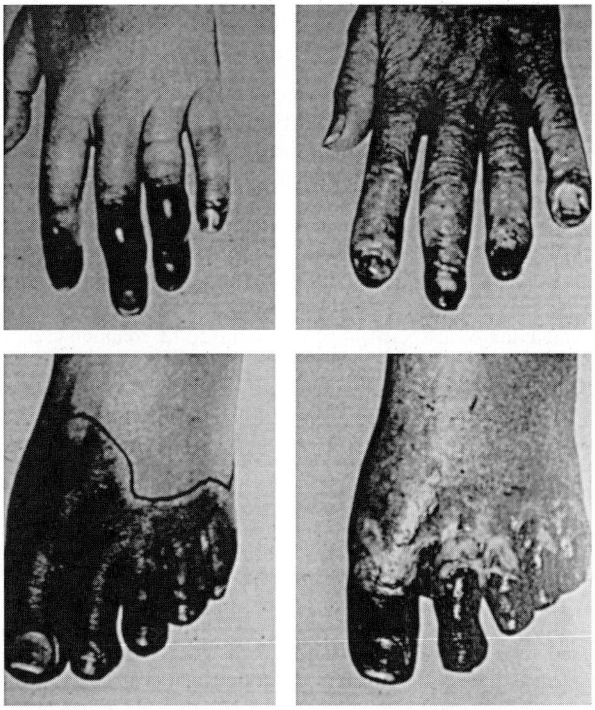

FIGURE 172–2. Digital necrosis in a patient with sickle cell disease and mycoplasmal pneumonia. The patient had a cold agglutinin titer of greater than 1:10,000.

Patients with immune deficiency syndromes have been the subjects of case reports of *M. pneumoniae* infection.[84] Because mycoplasma infections are so common in normal children, the contribution of the immune deficiency is unclear. *M. pneumoniae* does not seem to be a very common opportunistic agent in the acquired immunodeficiency syndrome (AIDS),[84] but another mycoplasma, *Mycoplasma fermentans* (*incognitus* strain) has been identified in these patients[85] (see Chapter 171).

Unusually severe *M. pneumoniae* infection has also been reported in children with Down syndrome.[86] All of these patients survived infection.

IMMUNOLOGY

Mycoplasmas are active in stimulating several components of the immune system. They can act as polyclonal T-cell and B-cell activators[87, 88] and can cause capping of lymphocytes.[89] Macrophages can also be stimulated by some mycoplasmas in vitro.[90] *M. pneumoniae* is capable of inducing several cytokines, including granulocyte-macrophage colony-stimulating factor[91] and interferon.[92] *M. pneumoniae* infection does not seem to induce the cytokine interleukin-2.[93]

In the course of *M. pneumoniae* infection, several classes of antibody are produced. Some of these fulfill the desired role of antibody production in infection, neutralization of the agent,[94] and others appear to be autoantibodies. The latter include agglutinins to lung, brain, cardiolipins, and smooth muscle.[92] The best studied of these autoagglutinins are the cold isohemagglutinins.

In 1943, Finland and colleagues described the presence of cold agglutinins in 50 to 70% of patients with Eaton agent pneumonia.[4, 95, 96] These agglutinins were capable of clumping erythrocytes at 4°C. Agglutination was reversible by warming the serum-erythrocyte mixture to 37°C and, unlike hemagglutination by myxoviruses and paramyxoviruses, was repeatable with the same sample, indicating that receptor-destroying enzyme (neuraminidase) played no role in the dissociation at 37°C.

Cold agglutinins in *M. pneumoniae* infection have been shown to be oligoclonal immunoglobulin M (IgM) antibodies directed against an altered I antigen on the surface of erythrocytes of *M. pneumoniae*–infected patients.[97] The I antigen is one of the blood group antigens, but unlike the A and B isoantigens it seems to be common to almost all mature erythrocytes. Fetal erythrocytes have i antigen instead. Like other IgM antibodies, the mycoplasma-induced cold agglutinins develop early in the disease (7 to 10 days) and therefore are often present by the time the patient seeks medical attention. The titer of these agglutinins peaks at 2 to 3 weeks and persists for 2 to 3 months (see Fig. 172–1).

There are several theories as to the factors triggering formation of cold agglutinins in mycoplasma pneumonia. One is that the organism alters the I antigen so as to make it antigenic to the patient. Hydrogen peroxide elaborated by *M. pneumoniae* could be responsible for this alteration. One study indicates that the I antigen in a sialated state may serve as a receptor for *M. pneumoniae* and that the cold agglutinins are directed at the modified receptor.[98] Other studies indicate that the cold agglutinins are directed at mycoplasma substructures themselves and merely cross-react with the I antigen on red cells.[99] The role in pathogenesis that these antibodies play is unclear. Given their apparent target, they could either contribute to cytolysis and exacerbate infection or interfere with cell-to-cell spread by blocking or disrupting the cell receptor for the mycoplasma.

There is a report of chronic renal failure associated with *M. pneumoniae*–induced cold agglutinins. Fluctuating severity of the renal failure correlated with variations in cold agglutinin titer; respiratory infection associated with complement–fixing antibodies to *M. pneumoniae* preceded the renal failure. There were no immunohistologic analyses done in this case, and the role of cold agglutinins in this patient's renal disease remains speculative.[79, 80] High titers of cold agglutinins also have been associated with hemolysis, presumably as a result of the activation of complement-mediated erythrocyte destruction.[4] The direct Coombs test is positive in many of these patients.[100, 101] Although clinically significant hemolysis is uncommon, subclinical levels of red cell destruction are common.

One syndrome in some patients with mycoplasma pneumonia that could be related to cold agglutinins is Raynaud's phenomenon, described previously. A unifying hypothesis would relate capillary obstruction in extremities exposed to the cold to erythrocyte autoagglutination in the microcirculation of these patients with high-titer cold agglutinins. In support of this hypothesis is the severe vascular damage that occurs in patients with sickle cell disease who contract mycoplasma pneumonia accompanied by high titers of cold agglutinins. The extremities of one such patient, who had a cold agglutinin titer greater than 1:20,000, is shown in Figure 172–2. The hypothetical pathogenesis of vasculopathy in this condition would then extend from reversible in vivo cold agglutination in microvasculature exposed to the cold (Raynaud's), to irreversible vascular damage in patients who have underlying microvascular compromise that is exacerbated and leads to digital necrosis (sickle cell disease).

M. pneumoniae infection leads to the production of complement-fixing antibodies as well. These arise early in the disease (2 to 3 weeks) and persist for 2 to 3 months. Assay of *M. pneumoniae*–specific complement-fixing antibodies has been the standard for retrospective serologic confirmation of infection with this organism.

Clearly, antibody production of both IgG and IgA classes plays a part in protection against the disease.[94] However, second cases of *M. pneumoniae* infection have been reported in apparently immunocompetent individuals.[102] Polymorphonuclear leukocytes and pulmonary macrophages also play a role in containing infection, but they appear to have relative difficulty in clearing the organism, in comparison to the cellular killing of most bacteria.[103]

PATHOLOGY AND PATHOPHYSIOLOGY

Because of two fortunate aspects of mycoplasma pneumonia, namely its low severity and low mortality, there is relatively little information on pathologic findings in this disease, and knowledge rests on relatively few specimens. As stated previously, sickle cell disease, sickle-related hemoglobinopathies, and hypogammaglobulinemia predispose to increased severity and to mortality. Some of the available pathologic data therefore may be influenced by the pathophysiology of these underlying conditions.

When deaths have occurred, they have been in cases of diffuse pneumonia, adult respiratory distress syndrome, thromboembolism, and disseminated intravascular coagulopathy.[39, 104–106]

In a clinicopathologic presentation in which a previously healthy man succumbed to *M. pneumoniae* infection, autopsy revealed diffuse aveolar pneumonia with hyaline membrane formation and multiple pulmonary infarctions. Other evidence of diffuse intravascular coagulopathy included thrombosis and infarction of kidneys, liver, spleen, and brain.[107] Other pathologic findings have included myocarditis[108] and diffuse interstitial fibrosis.[109]

In nonfatal cases in which lung biopsy was performed, the inflammatory process primarily involved the trachea, bronchioles, and peribronchial tissues.[41, 110] The lumen of the respiratory tree was filled with purulent exudate rich in polymorphonuclear leukocytes. The lining of the bronchial and bronchiolar walls showed metaplastic cells, and the walls themselves were infiltrated with monocytic elements, especially plasma cells. There was widening of the peribronchial septae and hyperplasia of type II pneumocytes.

Tracheal organ culture has demonstrated that, on inoculation of *M. pneumoniae*, first ciliary action is stopped, and then loss of cilia and complete desquamation of ciliated epithelial cells into the lumen occur.[111] This sloughing of cells is doubtless responsible for the cough that defines the clinical presentation. Histologic findings in human lung biopsy mirror the findings of ciliated cell damage seen in the animal experiments.[110]

Several characteristics of *M. pneumoniae* probably play a direct role in the respiratory pathogenicity of this organism. The first is the relatively great affinity of *M. pneumoniae* for respiratory epithelial cells. Attachment appears to be between a terminal organelle at one end of the filamentous organism[14] and a sialated glycoprotein (I-FI) on the surface of both respiratory epithelium and erythrocytes,[112–114] which acts as a receptor. The mycoplasmal terminal adhesin protein (P1) has been purified, and antibodies to the protein have been analyzed.[15] *M. pneumoniae* attaches to ciliated epithelial cells at the base of cilia and appears to produce most of its physiologic and cytolytic changes while remaining extracellular. Hydrogen peroxide, which only *M. pneumoniae* of all the human mycoplasmas produces, may be responsible for some in vivo cell damage, as it is for the hemolysis seen when the organisms are grown on blood agar plates.

DIAGNOSIS

Diagnosis is made primarily on clinical recognition of the syndrome. Laboratory findings of a mildly to moderately elevated leukocyte count with few immature forms are entirely nonspecific. Examination of the sputum by Gram staining may be helpful only in the failure to identify large numbers of bacteria in a purulent sputum. Lacking a cell wall, the organism is not definable on Gram staining, and it is too small to be seen by standard light microscopy. Examination of rarely occurring effusions in joints or the pleural space is also unrewarding.

Although a cold agglutination phenomenon is not unique to patients with mycoplasma pneumonia, and although many patients with

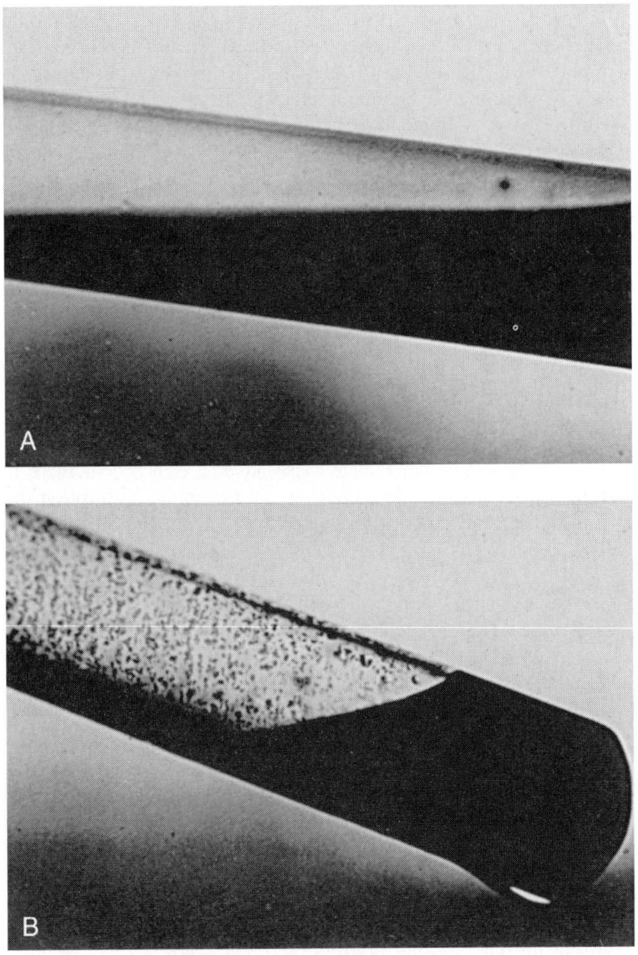

FIGURE 172–3. Bedside cold agglutinin test for confirmation of mycoplasmal pneumonia. *A,* Patient's blood before exposure to the cold. *B,* Patient's blood after 3-minute exposure to 4°C. On rewarming the sample to 37°C, the appearance reverts to that shown in *A.*

mycoplasma pneumonia never develop demonstrable cold agglutinins, this assay has remained the most often used acute laboratory confirmatory test for this disease. Patients with other types of atypical pneumonias may have cold agglutinins. In the diagnostic serology laboratory, cold agglutinins are demonstrated by combining the patient's serum and type O (to avoid A-B incompatibility) erythrocytes. The mixture is incubated at 0°C for several minutes, and the presence or absence of hemagglutination noted. If there is macroscopic red cell clumping, the patient's serum is serially diluted and the test is repeated. The highest dilution causing hemagglutination at 4°C is reported as the cold agglutinin titer. A titer of 1:32 or greater is highly suggestive of infection with *M. pneumoniae*. Other diseases that can give rise to cold agglutinins are mononucleosis caused by Epstein-Barr virus (anti-i),[115] cytomegalovirus (anti-I),[116] some other viral diseases, and lymphoma.

Because the results of this test as performed in a laboratory will not be available for at least a day and in some cases, a week, it is important to know that there is a rapid bedside version of this test that can be performed easily by any health care provider. In this test, 1 ml of the patient's blood is drawn into a tube containing anticoagulant. The type of tube used to collect specimens for prothrombin determination is preferred. Before cooling, examination shows a smooth coating of the tube by red cells, as shown in Figure 172–3A. The blood is cooled to 4°C by placing it on liquid ice or in a standard refrigerator. After 3 to 4 minutes, the tube is examined for the presence of macroscopic agglutination (see Fig. 172–3B). The tube is then rewarmed to 37°C in an incubator, or by exposure to body heat, and reexamined. The agglutination should dissociate at 37°C, and the appearance of the tube again is as shown in Figure 172–3A. This temperature-associated agglutination and dissociation can be repeated many times on the same sample. A positive result in the "bedside" test correlates with a laboratory titer of 1:64 or greater and is therefore less sensitive than the laboratory test. It can be accomplished in minutes, however, and, if positive, it is highly suggestive of mycoplasma-related cold agglutination. The presence of cold agglutinins can also artifactually give rise to macrocytic indices as measured by the Coulter counter method. This is secondary to in vivo clumping of erythrocytes. In this case the red cell distribution width would be high, indicating heterogeneity in measured red cell size.

Laboratory confirmation of *M. pneumoniae* infection has depended on demonstration of cold agglutinins or complement-fixing antibodies. The former, although appearing relatively early in the disease, are both insensitive and nonspecific indicators of *M. pneumoniae* infection. Complement-fixing antibodies, although far more specific, do not arise early enough in infection to be helpful in guiding diagnostic and therapeutic decisions. They are useful primarily in epidemiologic studies or to provide intellectual satisfaction in having made a good clinical diagnosis.

Likewise, culture of *M. pneumoniae* is an elaborate and time-consuming procedure requiring specialized media (see Chapter 171). Mycoplasmas are fastidious in their growth requirements. Because of this and the relative infrequency of requests for culture, most hospital microbiology laboratories are not set up to culture mycoplasmas. If culture is attempted, there are a number of transport media for temporary support of viability. These are similar to virus transport media in that they contain peptide broth, serum albumin, and antibiotics to retard bacterial overgrowth. Culture media contain sources of sterols and preformed nucleic acid precursors. Both liquid and solid media are inoculated. *M. pneumoniae* isolation takes advantage of the fact that this mycoplasma ferments glucose to produce acid, which can be detected by a color change in a dye indicator. In addition, this organism can reduce the dye tetrazolium from blue to yellow color. *M. pneumoniae* on agar produce a "mulberry" colony as opposed a "fried egg" appearance, as shown in Figure 171–1 in Chapter 171. Further identification can be obtained by showing that the colonies hemolyze red cells via hydrogen peroxide production[117] and can hemadsorb chick and guinea pig erythrocytes. Specific direct immunofluorescence of colonies can be used for ultimate identification.[118] Culture requires 1 to 2 weeks for definitive results. Although there are methods using pH and dye indicators that provide presumptive results more rapidly, even these require at least 4 to 5 days (Table 172–1).

Therefore, there has been considerable interest in developing rapid diagnostic tests with high sensitivity and specificity for *M. pneumoniae*. These assays fall into three categories: detection of *M. pneumoniae*–specific immunoglobulins in serum and detection of *M. pneumoniae*–specific antigens or mycoplasmal nucleotide sequences directly in clinical specimens.

The diagnostically most useful *M. pneumoniae*–specific immunoglobulin to detect is IgM, since it is most likely to indicate recent

TABLE 172–1 Identifying Properties of *Mycoplasma pneumoniae*

Slow growth on cell-free media
Both aerobic and anaerobic growth
"Mulberry" rather than "fried egg" colonies
Ferments glucose as major nutritional source, producing acid
Hemadsorption to colonies
Hemolysis by hydrogen peroxide
Affinity for respiratory epithelium
Infection leads to cold agglutinin formation
Resistance to cell wall inhibitors
Inhibited by macrolides, tetracyclines, and quinolones

infection. An enzyme-linked immunoassay has been developed to detect IgM and IgG directed against *M. pneumoniae*.[119] Both immunoglobulins were chosen as targets of the assay because adults with *M. pneumoniae* infection may elaborate only an IgG response. When used in patients with positive assays for complement-fixing antibodies, the enzyme immunoassay had a specificity of more than 99% and a sensitivity of 98%. Specificity was retained but sensitivity dropped to only 46% when IgG alone was the target. Variations on this theme detect IgM antibodies directed at specific *M. pneumoniae* antigens.[120] The tests are simple to perform and have high sensitivity and specificity but are limited in that they do not become positive until 1 to 2 weeks into infection. One study compared three assays designed to detect antimycoplasma IgM: a particle agglutination test, mu-capture enzyme-linked immunosorbent assay, and indirect immunofluorescence.[121] All three assays were about equally sensitive when compared with a standard complement fixation assay, but the particle agglutination assay appeared to give more false-positive results. In that all of these tests are designed to detect IgM antibody, they may all be negative early (less than 7 to 10 days) into infection. Therefore, they do not provide the desired confirmation early enough to guide initial therapy in many cases.

Detection of *M. pneumoniae* antigens directly in sputum specimens has been accomplished with the use of an antigen-capture, indirect enzyme immunoassay.[122] The specificity of the assay was high, the reagents reacting only with *M. pneumoniae* and *Mycoplasma genitalium*. Sensitivity was also relatively high (91%) when the assay was used on sputum and nasopharyngeal aspirates from patients who were shown either by culture or serologically to have *M. pneumoniae* infection.[123]

Detection of *M. pneumoniae*–specific nucleotide sequences directly in clinical material has been accomplished with the use of a commercially available kit, the Gen-Probe Rapid Diagnostic system (Gen Probe, San Diego, Calif.). The test, which can be completed in 2 hours, uses radioiodine-labeled DNA complementary to *M. pneumoniae* ribosomal RNA. When compared in one study with culture as the "gold standard" of proven infection, the nucleotide assay detected 89% of the culture-positive specimens; specificity was also 89%.[124] In a second comparative study, although the probe assay showed excellent sensitivity (95%) and good specificity (85%) compared with culture and serology when sputum was used, sensitivity and specificity on throat washings were considerably less.[125] The manufacturer of the kit recommends that throat swabs be used for the assay.

In a third study,[123] the probe was not as sensitive as indirect enzyme immunoassay when seropositivity rather than culture was used as the benchmark for infection. A comparison of immunologic and molecular biologic diagnostic tests has been published.[126]

TREATMENT

Despite the number and variety of tests for the rapid diagnosis of *M. pneumoniae* infection, most cases are encountered in the ambulatory setting, and institution of antimicrobial therapy remains empiric based on clinical recognition of the syndrome.

Antimicrobial therapy is not necessary for mycoplasmal upper respiratory tract infection, and the mycoplasmal etiology of this syndrome probably most often goes undiagnosed. Pneumonia due to mycoplasma is self-limited and not life-threatening in most cases. However, treatment with effective antimicrobials can markedly shorten the illness and, by reducing cough and the number of organisms per unit volume of sputum, can perhaps reduce the spread of infections in contacts.

As would be predicted by the lack of a cell wall, *M. pneumoniae* is unaffected by treatment with β-lactam antibiotics such as the penicillins and cephalosporins. Aminoglycosides are effective in vitro but have not been evaluated for efficacy in vivo.

The mainstays of treatment for *M. pneumoniae* respiratory tract infection are tetracycline and erythromycin. Use of either of these antimicrobials shortens the duration of illness. The radiographic findings may take a week or longer to resolve, even with appropriate therapy (see Fig. 172–1). In addition, studies have shown that organisms may continue to be culturable from the sputum for several weeks after a complete course of clinically effective treatment.[30] This may be a result of the fact that, although *M. pneumoniae* causes respiratory disease as an extracellular parasite, it has the capacity to reside intracellularly as well. This intracellular residence may make it difficult to eradicate the organism in vivo, as it does in cell cultures. The effect of therapy on extrapulmonary manifestations is unknown.

Although the tetracyclines are very active against *M. pneumoniae*, their use is precluded in young children because of adverse effects of the drug on developing teeth and bones. Erythromycin, on the other hand, is poorly tolerated by many people because of its gastrointestinal side effects. These include nausea, vomiting, abdominal pain, and diarrhea. There is anecdotal information that administration of H_2-blocking drugs can reduce these adverse effects, but there is no information on possible changes in macrolide absorption by concurrent use of these agents. Erythromycin also raises theophylline levels, a consideration in asthmatic patients who may be taking this drug.

Because of the adverse effects of erythromycin and tetracycline, there is considerable interest in the antimycoplasmal efficacy of newer agents. Doxycycline is somewhat better tolerated than tetracycline and can be administered in two daily doses rather than three. In vitro, doxycycline is as effective as tetracycline against *M. pneumoniae*.

Several new classes of antimicrobials have been found to have significant in vitro and in vivo activity against *M. pneumoniae* and other *Mycoplasma* species. These include the fluoroquinolones (ciprofloxacin, ofloxacin, levofloxacin, sparfloxacin, grepafloxacin)[127–129] newer broad-spectrum macrolides (azithromycin, clarithromycin),[130] ketolides (unique macrolide derivatives),[130] and streptogramins (quinupristin-dalfopristin and other synergistic combinations developed to treat resistant gram-positive bacteria).[131]

The macrolides are more active in vitro than the tetracyclines. Sparfloxacin and levofloxacin, the most active of the fluoroquinolones, are also more active than the tetracyclines, but are at least 100 times less active than the macrolides. Nevertheless, the fluoroquinolones have adequate activity for treatment of these infections. The streptogramins are also less active than the macrolides but more active than the tetracyclines.[130, 131] There is a significant cost differential in the use of these drugs. The newer macrolides and quinolones are 50 to 60 times more expensive than the tetracyclines and 6 to 10 times more costly than erythromycin (Table 172–2). No erythromycin-resistant strains of *M. pneumoniae* have been found. Quinolones are relatively contraindicated in children because of their adverse effects on weight-bearing joints in young animals.[128]

TABLE 172–2 Relative Cost for Antimicrobials Having Efficacy against *Mycoplasma pneumoniae**

Antibiotic	Dosage	Cost/D (Units)
	Adults	
Tetracycline	250 mg q6h	1
Erythromycin	250 mg q6h	8
Doxycycline	100 mg q12h	1
Clarithromycin	250 mg q12h	56
Azithromycin	250 mg q24h	52
Ciprofloxacin	250 mg bid	50
Levofloxacin/sparfloxacin	250/200 mg q24h	55/64
	Children	
Erythromycin	250 mg q6h	1
Erythromycin ethyl succinate	10 mg/kg q6h	2

*Cost comparisons are based on pharmacists' acquisition costs from the Red Book, 1997, with thanks to Marc Sloane, M.S., R.Ph.

The recommended therapy for *M. pneumoniae* therefore would be erythromycin, 0.5 g every 6 hours by mouth in adults and 30 to 50 mg/kg/day in divided doses for children weighing less than 25 kg. Children weighing more than 25 kg should receive 1 g/day in divided doses. Tetracycline at comparable doses (0.5 g every 6 hours by mouth) would be appropriate alternative therapy for patients older than 8 years of age. Dosages for other antimicrobials active against *M. pneumoniae* are listed in Table 172–2. The duration of therapy is 10 to 14 days.

PREVENTION

Because of outbreaks of *M. pneumoniae* respiratory infection among military recruits, there was for a time great enthusiasm and activity to produce a vaccine to protect against this organism.[132] The vaccines did induce specific antibody responses, but protection against infection was limited to no more than 50% of vaccine recipients.[133, 134] Live vaccines using attenuated wild-type and temperature-sensitive mutant mycoplasma have proved no more effective.[135, 136]

In one study, volunteers who received vaccine but did not mount an antibody response developed more severe disease when rechallenged with wild-type mycoplasma than did nonvaccinated personnel.[137] Although *M. pneumoniae* continues to be perhaps the leading cause of the atypical pneumonia syndrome in closed populations, the enthusiasm for vaccine development in this disease appears to have waned.

Examination of the effects of prophylactic antibiotic use in family members exposed to mycoplasma has shown a decrease in clinical disease in these patients, but seroconversion was not prevented.[138] A study showed that azithromycin prophylaxis, given as a 500-mg loading dose and 250 mg/day on days 2 through 5, significantly reduced the secondary attack rate of *M. pneumoniae* infection in a long-term care facility.[139]

REFERENCES

1. Eaton MD, Meikeljohn G, van Herick W. Studies on the etiology of primary atypical pneumonia: A filterable agent transmissible to cotton rats, hamsters and chick embryos. J Exp Med. 1944;79:649.
2. Eaton MD, Meikeljohn G, van Herick W, et al. Studies on the etiology of primary atypical pneumonia: II. Properties of the virus isolated and propagated in chick embryos. J Exp Med. 1945;82:317.
3. Eaton MD, van Herick W, Meikeljohn G. Studies on the etiology of primary atypical pneumonia: III. Specific neutralization of the virus by human serum. J Exp Med. 1945;82:329.
4. Finland M, Peterson OL, Allen HE, et al. Cold agglutinins: I. Occurrence of cold isohaemagglutinins in various conditions. J Clin invest. 1945;24:451.
5. Marmion BP. Eaton agent—science and scientific acceptance: A historical commentary. Rev Infect Dis. 1990;12:338.
6. Chanock RM, Mufson MA, Bloom HH, et al. Eaton agent pneumonia. JAMA. 1961;175:213.
7. Clyde WA Jr. Demonstration of Eaton's agent in tissue culture. Proc Soc Exp Biol Med. 1961;107:715.
8. Goodburn GM, Marmion BP. Study of properties of Eaton's primary atypical pneumonia organism. J Gen Microbiol. 1962;29:271.
9. Chanock RM, Hayflick L, Barile MF. Growth on artificial medium of an agent associated with atypical pneumonia and its identification as a PPLO. Proc Natl Acad Sci U S A. 1962;48:41.
10. Chanock RM, Rifkind D, Dravetz HM, et al. Respiratory disease in volunteers infected with Eaton agent: A preliminary report. Proc Natl Acad Sci U S A. 1961;47:887.
11. Marmion BP, Goodburn GM. Effect of an organic gold salt on Eaton's primary atypical pneumonia organism and other observations. Nature. 1961;189:247.
12. Conference on Newer Respiratory Disease Viruses USPHS. Bethesda, Md: National Institutes of Health; 1962:198.
13. Kenny GE. Mycoplasmas. In: Balows A, ed. Manual of Clinical Microbiology. Washington, DC: American Society for Microbiology; 1991:478.
14. Powell DA, Hu PC, Wilson M, et al. Attachment of *Mycoplasma pneumoniae* to respiratory epithelium. Infect Immun. 1976;13:959.
15. Hirschberg L, Holme T, Krook A. Human antibody response to the major adhesin of *Mycoplasma pneumoniae*: Increase in titers against synthetic peptides in patients with pneumonia. APMIS. 1991;99:515.
16. Furness G, Pipes FJ, McMurtrey MJ. Analysis of the life cycle of *Mycoplasma pneumoniae* by synchronized division and by ultraviolet and X irradiations. J Infect Dis. 1968;118:7.
17. Mogabgab WJ. *Mycoplasma pneumoniae* and adenovirus respiratory illness in military and university personnel, 1959–1966. Am Rev Respir Dis. 1968;97:345.
18. Foy HM, Kenny GE, Cooney MK, et al. Long term epidemiology of infections with *Mycoplasma pneumoniae*. J Infect Dis. 1979;139:681.
19. Chanock RM. Mycoplasma infections of man. N Engl J Med. 1965;273:1199.
20. Hers JF, Masurel N. Infection with *Mycoplasma pneumoniae* in civilians in the Netherlands. Ann N Y Acad Sci. 1967;143:447.
21. Foy HM, Kenny GE, McMahan R, et al. *Mycoplasma pneumoniae* pneumonia in an urban area. JAMA. 1970;214:1966.
22. Foy HM, Alexander ER. *Mycoplasma pneumoniae* infections in childhood. Adv Pediatr. 1969;16:301.
23. Denny FW, Clyde WA, Glenzen WP. *Mycoplasma pneumoniae* disease: Clinical spectrum, pathophysiology, epidemiology and control. J Infect Dis. 1971;123:74.
24. Noah ND. *Mycoplasma pneumoniae* infections in the United Kingdom—1967–73. BMJ. 1974;2:544.
25. Toma S. Isolation of *Mycoplasma pneumoniae* from respiratory tract specimens in Ontario. Can Med Assoc J. 1987;137:48.
26. Fernald GW, Collier AM, Clyde WA. Respiratory infections due to *Mycoplasma pneumoniae* in infants and children. Pediatrics. 1975;55:327.
27. McIntosh JC, Gutierrez HH. Mycoplasma infections. In: Smith TF, ed. Immunology and Allergy Clinics of North America: Respiratory Infections. Philadelphia: WB Saunders; 1993:43.
28. Alexander ER, Foy HM, Kenny GE, et al. Pneumonia due to *Mycoplasma pneumoniae*. N Engl J Med. 1966;275:131.
29. Foy HM, Grayston JT, Kenny GE, et al. Epidemiology of *Mycoplasma pneumoniae* infection in families. JAMA. 1966;197:859.
30. Smith CB, Friedewald WT, Chanock RM. Shedding of *Mycoplasma pneumoniae* after tetracycline and erythromycin therapy. N Engl J Med. 1967;276:1172.
31. Ritkind D, Chanock R, Kravetz H, et al. Ear involvement (myringitis) and primary atypical pneumonia following inoculation of volunteers with Eaton agent. Am Rev Respir Dis. 1962;85:479.
32. Klein JO, Teele DW. Isolation of viruses and mycoplasmas from middle ear effusions: A review. Ann Otol Rhinol Laryngol. 1976;85:140.
33. Sobeslavsky O, Syrucek L, Bruckaya M, et al. The etiologic role of *Mycoplasma pneumoniae* in otitis media in children. Pediatrics. 1965;35:652.
34. Nagayama Y, Sakurai N, Yamamota K, et al. Isolation of *Mycoplasma pneumoniae* from children with lower-respiratory-tract infections. J Infect Dis. 1988;157:911.
35. Mansel JK, Rosenow EC III, Smith TF, et al. *Mycoplasma pneumoniae* pneumonia. Chest. 1989;95:639.
36. Fine NL, Smith LR, Sheedy PF. Frequency of pleural effusions in mycoplasma and viral pneumonias. N Engl J Med. 1970;283:790.
37. Tuazon CV, Murray HW. Atypical pneumonias. In: Pennington JE, ed. Respiratory infections: Diagnosis and management. New York: Raven Press; 1989:341.
38. Loo VG, Richardson S, Quinn P. Isolation of *Mycoplasma pneumoniae* from pleural fluid. Diagn Microbiol Infect Dis. 1991;14:443.
39. Chan ED, Welsh CH. Fulminant *Mycoplasma pneumoniae* pneumonia. West J Med. 1995;162:133–142.
40. Cherry JD, Hurwitz ES, Welliver RC. *Mycoplasma pneumoniae* infections and exanthems. J Pediatr. 1975;87:369.
41. Murray HW, Masur H, Senterfit LB, et al. The protean manifestations of *Mycoplasma pneumoniae* in adults. Am J Med. 1975;58:229.
42. Levy M, Shear NH. *Mycoplasma pneumoniae* infections and Stevens-Johnson syndrome. Clin Pediatr (Phila). 1991;30:42.
43. Sanders DY, Johnson HW. Stevens-Johnson syndrome associated with *Mycoplasma pneumoniae* infection. Am J Dis Child. 1971;121:243.
44. Lyell A, Dick HM, Gordon AM, et al. Mycoplasmas and erythema multiforme. Lancet. 1967;2:1116.
45. Arstikaitis MJ. Ocular aftermath of Stevens-Johnson syndrome. Arch Ophthalmol. 1973;90:376.
46. Anderson R, Bergan T, Halvorsen K, et al. Legionnaires' disease combined with erythema multiforme in a 3 year old boy. Acta Pediatr Scand. 1981;70:427.
47. Kierman JP, Schanzlin DJ, Leveille AS. Stevens-Johnson syndrome associated with adenovirus conjunctivitis. Am J Ophthalmol. 1981;92:543.
48. Baine WB, Luby JB, Martin SM. Severe illness with influenza B. Am J Med. 1980;68:181.
49. Tay Y-K, Huff JC, Weston WL. *Mycoplasma pneumoniae* infection is associated with Stevens-Johnson syndrome, not erythema multiforme (von Hebra). J Am Acad Dermatol. 1996;35:757–760.
50. Kazmierowski JA, Wuepper KD. Erythema multiforme: Clinical spectrum and immunopathogenesis. Springer Seminar Immunopathol. 1981;4:45.
51. Goldsmith DP. The erythema syndromes: Erythema multiforme and the Stevens-Johnson syndrome. Pract Pediatr. 1980;3:1.
52. Stutman HR. Stevens-Johnson syndrome and *Mycoplasma pneumoniae*: Evidence for cutaneous infection. J Pediatr. 1987;111:845.
53. Mesegner MA, de Rafael L, Vidal ML. Stevens-Johnson syndrome with isolation of *Mycoplasma pneumoniae* from skin lesions. Eur J Clin Microbiol. 1986;5:167.
54. McCormack JG. *Mycoplasma pneumoniae* and the erythema multiforme-Stevens-Johnson syndrome. J Infect. 1981;3:32.
55. Easterly NB. Corticosteroids for erythema multiforme? Pediatr Dermatol. 1989;6:229.
56. Feizi T, Maclean H. Sommerville RG, et al. Studies on an epidemic of respiratory disease caused by *Mycoplasma pneumoniae*. BMJ. 1967;1:457.
57. Schubothe H. The cold hemagglutinin disease. Semin Hematol. 1966;3:27.

58. Furioli J, Bourdon C, Le Loc'h H. *Mycoplasma pneumoniae* infection: Manifestation in a 3 year old child by Raynaud's phenomenon. Arch Franc Pediatr. 1985;42:313.
59. Visudhiphan P, Chiemchanya S, Sirinavin S. Internal carotid artery occlusion associated with *Mycoplasma pneumoniae* infection. Pediatr Neurol. 1992;8:237.
60. Sands MJ, Satz JE, Soloff LA. Pericarditis and perimyocarditis associated with active *Mycoplasma pneumoniae* infection. Ann Intern Med. 1977;86:544.
61. Ponka A. Carditis associated with *Mycoplasma pneumoniae* infection. Acta Med Scand. 1979;11:1.
62. Karjalainen J, Heikkila J, Nieminen MS, et al. Etiology of mild acute infectious myocarditis. Relation to clinical features. Acta Med Scand. 1983;213:65.
63. Karjalainen J. A loud third heart sound and asymptomatic myocarditis during *Mycoplasma pneumoniae* infection. Eur Heart J. 1990;11:960.
64. Sands MJ Jr, Rosenthal R. Progressive heart failure and death associated with *Mycoplasma pneumoniae*. Chest. 1982;81:763.
65. Naftalin JM, Wellisch G, Kahana Z, et al. *Mycoplasma pneumoniae* septicemia. JAMA. 1974;228:565.
66. Yesnick L. Central nervous system complications of primary atypical pneumonia. Arch Intern Med. 1956;97:93.
67. Lerer RJ, Kalavsky SM. Central nervous system disease associated with *Mycoplasma pneumoniae* infection: Report of five cases and review of the literature. Pediatrics. 1973;52:658.
68. Mills RW, Schoolfield L. Acute transverse myelitis associated with *Mycoplasma pneumoniae* infection: A case report and review of the literature. Pediatr Infect Dis J. 1992;11:228.
69. Ong ELC, Ellis ME, Yuill GM. Neurologic complication of *Mycoplasma pneumoniae* infection. Respir Med. 1989;83:441.
70. Steele JC, Gladstone RM, Thanasophon S, et al. *Mycoplasma pneumoniae* as a determinant of the Guillain-Barre syndrome. Lancet. 1969;2:719.
71. Koskiniemi M. CNS manifestations associated with *Mycoplasma pneumoniae* infections: Summary of cases at the University of Helsinki and review. Clin Infect Dis. 1993;17(Suppl 1):S52–S57.
72. Abramovitz P, Schvartzman P, Harel D, et al. Direct invasion of the central nervous system by *Mycoplasma pneumoniae*: A report of two cases. J Infect Dis. 1987;155:482.
73. Kasahara I, Otsubo Y, Yanase T, et al. Isolation and characterization of *Mycoplasma pneumoniae* from cerebrospinal fluid of a patient with pneumonia and meningoencephalitis. J Infect Dis. 1985;152:823.
74. Biberfeld G. Antibodies to brain and other tissues in cases of *Mycoplasma pneumoniae* infection. Clin Exp Immunol. 1971;8:319.
75. Thomas L, Alen F, Bitensky MW, et al. The neurotoxin of *Mycoplasma neurolyticum*. J Exp Med. 1966;124:1967.
76. Ponka A. Arthritis associated with *Mycoplasma pneumoniae* infection. Scand J Rheumatol. 1979;8:27.
77. Davis CP, Cochran S, Lisse J, et al. Isolation of *Mycoplasma pneumoniae* from synovial fluid samples in a patient with pneumonia and polyarthritis. Arch Intern Med. 1988;148:969.
78. Johnston CLW, Webster ADB, Taylor-Robinson D, et al. Primary late-onset hypogammaglobulinaemia associated with inflammatory polyarthritis and septic arthritis due to *Mycoplasma pneumoniae*. Ann Rheum Dis. 1983;442:108.
79. Vitullo BV, O'Regan S, de Chadarevian JP, et al. *Mycoplasma pneumoniae* associated with acute glomerulonephritis. Nephron. 1978;21:284.
80. Kanayama Y, Shiota K, Kotumi K, et al. *Mycoplasma pneumoniae* pneumonia associated with IgA nephropathy. Scand J Infect Dis. 1982;14:23.
81. Shulman ST, Barlett J, Clyde WA, et al. The unusual severity of mycoplasmal pneumonia in children with sickle-cell disease. N Engl J Med. 1972;287:164.
82. Solanki DL, Berdoff RL. Severe mycoplasma pneumonia with pleural effusions in a patient with sickle cell-hemoglobin C (SC) disease. Am J Med. 1979;66:707.
83. Chusid MJ, Lachman BS, Lazerson J. Severe mycoplasma pneumonia and vesicular eruption in SC hemoglobinopathy. J Pediatr. 1978;93:449.
84. Foy HM. Infections caused by *Mycoplasma pneumoniae* and possible carrier state in different populations of patients. Clin Infect Dis. 1993;17(Suppl 1):S37–S46.
85. Lo SC, Dawson M, Wong DM. Identification of *Mycoplasma incognitus* infection in patients with AIDS: An immunohistochemical, in-situ hybridization and ultrastructural study. Am J Trop Med Hyg. 1989;41:601.
86. Orlieck SL, Walker MS, Kuhls TL. Severe mycoplasma pneumonia in young children with Down syndrome. Clin Pediatr (Phila). 1992;31:409.
87. Biberfeld G, Gronowicz E. *Mycoplasma pneumoniae* is a polyclonal B-cell activator. Nature. 1976;261:238.
88. Naot Y, Tully JG, Ginsburg H. Lymphocyte activation by various mycoplasma strains and species. Infect Immun. 1977;18:310.
89. Stanbridge EJ, Weiss RL. Mycoplasma capping on lymphocytes. Nature. 1978;276:583.
90. Dietz JN, Cole BC. Direct activation of the J774.1 murine macrophage cell line by *Mycoplasma arthritidis*. Infect Immun. 1981;37:811.
91. Mahkoul N, Merchav S, Tatarsky I, et al. Mycoplasma-induced in vitro production of interleukin-2 and colony-stimulating activity. Isr J Med Sci. 1987;23:480.
92. Capobianchi MR, Lorino G, Lun MT, et al. Membrane interactions involved in the induction of interferon-alpha by *Mycoplasma pneumoniae*. Antiviral Res. 1987;8:115.
93. Ruuth E, Praz F. Interactions between mycoplasmas and the immune system. Immunol Rev. 1989;112:133.
94. Brunner H, Greenberg HB, James WD, et al. Antibody to *Mycoplasma pneumoniae* in nasal secretions and sputa of experimentally infected human volunteers. Infect Immun. 1973;8:612.
95. Peterson OL, Ham TH, Finland M. Cold agglutinins (auto-haemagglutinins) in primary atypical pneumonias. Science. 1943;97:167.
96. Turner JC. Development of cold agglutinins in atypical pneumonia. Nature. 1943;151:419.
97. Feizi T, Taylor-Robinson D. Cold agglutinin anti-I and *Mycoplasma pneumoniae*. Immunology. 1967;13:405.
98. Konig AL, Kreft H, Hengge U. Coexisting anti-I and anti-FI/Gd cold agglutinins in infections by *Mycoplasma pneumoniae*. Vox Sang. 1988;55:176.
99. Costea N, Yakulis VJ, Heller P. Inhibition of cold agglutinins (anti-I) by *M. pneumoniae* antigens. Proc Soc Exp Biol Med. 1972;139:476.
100. Feizi T. Cold agglutinins, the direct Coombs' test and serum immunoglobulins in *Mycoplasma pneumoniae* infection. Ann N Y Acad Sci. 1967;143:801.
101. Jacobson LB, Longstreth GF, Edington TS. Clinical and immunologic features of transient cold agglutinin hemolytic anemia. Am J Med. 1973;54:514.
102. Foy HM, Kenny GE, Sefi R, et al. Second attacks of pneumonia due to *Mycoplasma pneumoniae*. J Infect Dis. 1977;135:673.
103. Erb P, Bredt W. Interaction of *Mycoplasma pneumoniae* with alveolar macrophages: Viability of adherent and ingested mycoplasmas. Infect Immun. 1979;25:11.
104. Koletsky RJ, Weinstein AJ. Fulminant mycoplasma pneumonia infection: Report of a fatal case and a review of the literature. Am Rev Respir Dis. 1980;122:491.
105. Nilsson IM, Rausing A, Dennenberg T, et al. Intravascular coagulation and acute renal failure in a child with mycoplasma infection. Acta Med Scand. 1971;189:359.
106. Meyers BR, Hirshman SZ. Fatal infections associated with *Mycoplasma pneumoniae*: Discussion of three cases with necropsy findings. Mt Sinai J Med. 1972;39:258.
107. Scully RE, ed. Case records of the Massachusetts General Hospital: Mycoplasma pneumonia with diffuse alveolar damage and disseminated intravascular coagulation. N Engl J Med. 1992;326:324.
108. Pickens S, Catterall JR. Disseminated intravascular coagulation and myocarditis associated with *Mycoplasma pneumoniae* infection. BMJ. 1978;23:1526.
109. Kaufman JM, Cuvelier CA, Van der Staeten M. Mycoplasma pneumonia with fulminant evolution into diffuse interstitial fibrosis. Thorax. 1980;35:140.
110. Rollin S, Colby T, Clayton F. Open lung biopsy in mycoplasma pneumonia. Arch Pathol Lab Med. 1986;110:34.
111. Hu PC, Collier AM, Baseman JB. Interaction of virulent *Mycoplasma pneumoniae* with hamster tracheal organ cultures. Infect Immun. 1976;14:217.
112. Brunner H, Feldner J, Bredt W. Effect of monoclonal antibodies to the attachment tip on experimental *Mycoplasma pneumoniae* infection of hamsters. Isr J Med Sci. 1984;20:878.
113. Baseman JB, Banai M, Kahane I. Sialic acid residues mediate *Mycoplasma pneumoniae* attachment to human and sheep erythrocytes. Infect Immun. 1982;38:389.
114. Hengge VR, Kirschfink M, Konig AL, et al. Characterization of I/F1 glycoprotein as a receptor for *Mycoplasma pneumoniae*. Infect Immun. 1992;60:79.
115. Rosenfield RE, Schmidt PJ, Calvo RC, et al. Anti-i, a frequent cold agglutinin in infections mononucleosis. Vox Sang. 1965;10:631.
116. Lind K, Spencer ES, Anderson HK. Cold agglutinin production and cytomegalovirus infection. Scand J Infect Dis. 1974;6:109.
117. Clyde WA Jr. Hemolysis in identifying Eaton's pleuropneumonia-like organism. Science. 1963;139:55.
118. Del Giudice RA, Robillard NF, Carski TR. Immunofluorescence identification of mycoplasma on agar by use of incident illumination. J Bacteriol. 1967;93:1205.
119. Uldum SA, Jensen JS, Søndergard-Anderson J, et al. Enzyme immunoassay for detection of immunoglobulin M (IgM) and IgG antibodies to *Mycoplasma pneumoniae*. J Clin Microbiol. 1992;30:1198.
120. Cimolai N, Cheong ACH. IgM anti-PI immunoblotting: A standard for the rapid serologic diagnosis of *Mycoplasma pneumoniae* infection in pediatric care. Chest. 1992;102:477.
121. Barker CE, Sillis M, Wreghitt TG. Evaluation of Serodia, Myco II particle agglutination test for detecting *Mycoplasma pneumoniae* antibody: Comparison with mu-capture ELISA and indirect fluorescence. J Clin Pathol. 1990;43:163.
122. Marmion BP, Williamson J, Worswick DA, et al. Experience with newer techniques for the laboratory detection of *Mycoplasma pneumoniae* infection: Adelaide, 1978–1992. Clin Infect Dis. 1993;17(Suppl 1):S90–S99.
123. Harris R, Marmion BP, Varkanis G, et al. Laboratory diagnosis of *Mycoplasma pneumoniae* infection: 2. Comparison of methods for the direct detection of specific antigen or nucleic acid sequences in respiratory exudates. Epidemiol Infect. 1988;101:685.
124. Dular R, Kajioka R, Kusatiya S. Comparison of Gen-Probe commercial kit and culture technique for the diagnosis of *Mycoplasma pneumoniae* infection. J Clin Microbiol. 1988;26:1068.
125. Kleemola MSR, Karjalainen JE, Raty RKH. Rapid diagnosis of *Mycoplasma pneumoniae* infection: Clinical evaluation of a commercial probe test. J Infect Dis. 1990;162:70.
126. Baum SG. Mycoplasma infection: Immunologic and molecular biologic diagnostic techniques. In: Rose NR, de Macario, EC, Folds JD, et al, eds. Manual of Clinical Laboratory Immunology: Infections caused by bacteria, mycoplasmas, chlamydiae and rickettsiae. Washington, D.C: American Society for Microbiology; 1997:547–557.
127. Rylander M, Hallander HO. In vitro comparison of the activity of doxycycline, tetracycline, erythromycin and a new macrolide, CP 62993, against *Mycoplasma pneumoniae*, *Mycoplasma hominis* and *Ureaplasma urealyticum* Scand J Infect Dis, 1988;53(Suppl):12.
128. Martin SJ, Meyer JM, Chuck SK, et al. Levofloxacin and sparfloxacin: New quinolone antibiotics. Ann Pharmacother. 1998;32:320–336.
129. Ridgway GL, Salman H, Robbins, MJ, et al. The in vitro activity of grepafloxacin

against *Chlamydia* spp., *Mycoplasma* spp., *Ureaplasma urealyticum* and *Legionella* spp. J Antimicrob Chemother. 1997;40(Suppl. A):31–34.
130. Taylor-Robinson, Bébéar C. Antibiotic susceptibilities of mycoplasmas and treatment of mycoplasmal infections. J Antimicrob Chemother. 1997;40:622–630.
131. Izumikawa K, Hirakata Y, Yamaguchi T, et al. In vitro activities of quinupristin-dalfopristin and thestreptogramin RPR 106972 against *Mycoplasma pneumoniae*. Antimicrob Agents Chemother. 1998;42:698–699.
132. Mogabgab WJ. Protective effects of inactive *Mycoplasma pneumoniae* vaccine in military personnel. Am Rev Respir Dis. 1968;97:359.
133. Wenzel RP, Craven RB, Davies JA, et al. Field trial on an inactivated *Mycoplasma pneumoniae* vaccine: I. Vaccine efficacy. J Infect Dis. 1976;134:571.
134. Smith CB, Friedewald WT, Chanock RM. Inactivated *Mycoplasma pneumoniae* vaccine. JAMA. 1967;199:353.
135. Couch RB, Cate TR, Chanock RM. Infection with artificially propagated Eaton agent (*Mycoplasma pneumoniae*). JAMA. 1964;187:442.
136. Greenberg H, Helms CM, Brunner H, et al. Asymptomatic infection of adult volunteers with a temperature sensitive mutant of *Mycoplasma pneumoniae*. Proc Natl Acad Sci U S A. 1974;71:4015.
137. Smith CB, Chanock RM, Friedewald WTK, et al. *Mycoplasma pneumoniae* infections in volunteers. Ann N Y Acad Sci. 1967;143:471.
138. Jensen KE, Senterfit LB, Scully WE, et al. *Mycoplasma pneumoniae* infections in children: An epidemiological appraisal in families treated with oxytetracycline. Am J Epidemiol. 1967;86:419.
139. Klausner JD, Passaro D, Rosenberg J. Enhanced control of an outbreak of *Mycoplasma pneumoniae* pneumonia with azithromycin prophylaxis. J Infect Dis. 1998;177:161–166.

Chapter 173

Ureaplasma urealyticum, Mycoplasma hominis, and *Mycoplasma genitalium*

DAVID TAYLOR-ROBINSON

CHARACTERISTICS, ISOLATION, AND IDENTIFICATION

Of the eight mycoplasma species that have been isolated from the human genital tract (Table 173–1), *Ureaplasma urealyticum* and *Mycoplasma hominis* are found most frequently and *Mycoplasma genitalium* has been increasingly associated with disease. *U. urealyticum* is one of five species in the genus *Ureaplasma*, and *M. hominis* and *M. genitalium* are two of more than 100 species in the genus *Mycoplasma*, within the family Mycoplasmataceae and the class Mollicutes (see Chapter 171). There are now sound reasons based on genome size[1] and other features for separating *U. urealyticum* organisms (referred to as ureaplasmas) into two species. Some of the properties that distinguish these three microorganisms from each other, in addition to those they share with other mycoplasmas that are found less frequently in the genital tract, are presented in Table 173–1.

Detection of mycoplasmas in the genital tract depends usually on culturing specimens on appropriate media and identifying the isolates.[2, 3] The medium most often used, as for other mycoplasmas, comprises a beefheart infusion broth supplemented with fresh yeast extract (10% vol/vol; 25% wt/vol) and horse serum (20% vol/vol). However, the recovery of *M. hominis* may be improved by use of a medium[4] developed originally for the isolation of spiroplasmas and used subsequently for the isolation of *M. genitalium* and other mycoplasmas. Genital mycoplasmas grow well in broth medium under atmospheric conditions, but on agar colonies develop best in an atmosphere of 95% nitrogen and 5% carbon dioxide. The metabolic activity of mycoplasmas is used to detect their growth in broth medium. Clinical material is added to separate vials of broth containing phenol red (0.002%) and 0.1% urea, arginine, or glucose. Ureaplasmas grow best at pH 6.0 or less and possess a urease that breaks down urea to ammonia, thus raising the pH level of the medium so that the color changes from yellow to red. *M. hominis* metabolizes arginine to ammonia; therefore a similar color change is produced in medium initially at pH 7.0. Glucose-fermenting mycoplasmas cause a decrease in the pH value of the medium that initially is set at 7.5 to 7.8. Aliquots of medium from cultures exhibiting these color changes are subcultured onto agar medium, this liquid-to-agar technique providing the most sensitive method for the isolation of both ureaplasmas and *M. hominis*.[2, 3] Culturing of ureaplasmas takes no more than 1 to 2 days, and *M. hominis* requires up to about 1 week, but 1 to 2 months or more may be required to culture *M. genitalium*. Indeed, it is clear that attempts to culture this mycoplasma and *Mycoplasma fermentans* often fail and that they may be detected much more reliably by polymerase chain reaction (PCR) technology.[5–7] The PCR has been used to monitor the growth of *M. genitalium* in cell cultures as an intermediate to isolation in mycoplasmal medium.[8]

Ureaplasmas were originally termed *T strains* or *T mycoplasmas* (T for tiny) because they produce very small colonies ranging from 15 to 60 μm in diameter. Colonies of *M. hominis* and *M. genitalium* are about 200 to 300 μm in diameter and have a characteristic "fried egg" appearance (see Fig. 171–1 in Chapter 171). On blood agar, *M. hominis*, but not ureaplasmas or *M. genitalium*, produces nonhemolytic pinpoint colonies, and it also grows in most routine blood culture media without changing their appearance. A blind subculture onto blood agar can be used in a diagnostic bacteriology laboratory to diagnose blood-stream invasion with *M. hominis*,[9] and the addition of 1% gelatin to blood culture systems containing sodium polyanethol sulfonate (SPS) is helpful because it overcomes the mycoplasmal inhibitory activity of SPS.[10]

Antibacterial agents, such as penicillin and thallous acetate, have often been added to mycoplasmal media to inhibit bacterial growth.

TABLE 173–1 Mycoplasmas Found in the Genital Tract and Some of Their Properties

Mycoplasma	Frequency of Isolation or Detection	Metabolism of	Preferred Atmosphere	pH	Hemadsorption	Susceptibility to: *Thallium*	*Erythromycin*	*Lincomycin*
Ureaplasma urealyticum	Common	Urea	Anaerobic	6.0	Serotype 3 only	Yes	Yes	No
Mycoplasma hominis	Common	Arginine	Aerobic	7.0	No	Yes	No	Yes
Mycoplasma fermentans	Quite common	Glucose and arginine	Anaerobic	7.5	No	No	No	Yes
Mycoplasma genitalium	Quite common*	Glucose	Anaerobic	7.5	Yes	Yes	Yes	Yes
Mycoplasma penetrans	?	Glucose and arginine	Anaerobic	7.5	Yes	?	?	?
Mycoplasma pneumoniae	Very rare	Glucose	Aerobic	7.5	Yes	No	Yes	Yes
Mycoplasma primatum	Rare	Arginine	Anaerobic	7.0	No	No	Yes	Yes
Mycoplasma spermatophilum	?Rare	Arginine	Anaerobic	7.0	No	No	Yes	?

*In disease.

However, it is wise not to use the latter because of its toxicity and because ureaplasmas, *M. genitalium*, and to a lesser extent *M. hominis* are sensitive to it.[2–4]

Serotyping

There are 14 or more serotypes of *U. urealyticum* and at least seven serotypes of *M. hominis* but no indication of phenotypic variants of *M. genitalium*. To date there has not been any convincing suggestion that a particular serotype is associated with a particular disease.

EPIDEMIOLOGY

Colonization of Infants and Children

Infants usually become colonized with genital mycoplasmas during passage through the infected birth canal. Ureaplasmas have been isolated from the genitalia of up to one third of infant girls and *M. hominis* from a smaller proportion[11, 12]; these organisms have been recovered less frequently from the genital tract of infant boys.[12] Mycoplasmas, mainly ureaplasmas, have been isolated from the nose and throat of about 15% of infants of both sexes.[11] The figures mentioned are estimates and vary from one population to another, depending on the proportion of pregnant women who are colonized.

Colonization tends not to persist beyond 2 years of age,[12] but if mycoplasmas do persist, they do so more often in girls. Genital mycoplasmas have seldom been recovered from prepubertal boys, whereas in one study[13] one fifth of prepubertal girls were colonized with ureaplasmas and 6% with *M. hominis*. In sexually abused children, the organisms are found even more frequently,[14] but it would be unwise to suggest that sexual abuse had occurred simply on the basis of their presence.

The occurrence of *M. genitalium* in infants and children has not been studied.

Colonization of Adults

After puberty, colonization with ureaplasmas and *M. hominis* occurs primarily as a result of sexual contact.[15, 16] This may be deduced from the fact that sexually mature people who have no history of sexual contact are infrequently colonized, whereas colonization among those who are sexually experienced increases in relation to the number of sexual partners. These genital mycoplasmas have been isolated more often from black men and women than from white men and women, but the extent to which this difference is caused by differing sexual experiences is not clear. In adults not attending sexually transmitted disease clinics, genital mycoplasmas have been found one third to one half more frequently among those younger than 50 years of age than among older persons, ureaplasmas have been found four times more often than *M. hominis*, and both have been found more often in women than in men.[17] The natural history of *M. genitalium* is less clear. It was discovered originally in the genital tract of men with urethritis[18] and later in the respiratory tract of adults.[19] The results of serologic studies[20] have indicated that it is mainly transmitted sexually. Thus, 5.4% of healthy blood donors had specific antibody to a lipid-associated membrane antigen measured by an enzyme immunoassay, compared with 43% of subjects attending sexually transmitted disease clinics.

Colonization by ureaplasmas and *M. hominis* is also related to socioeconomic status. In Boston, *M. hominis* was isolated from about one half of the clinic patients at a municipal hospital and ureaplasmas from three quarters of them, compared to one fifth and one half, respectively, of the patients visiting private obstetricians and gynecologists in the same area.[21] Whether this apparent socioeconomic difference is a reflection of a difference in sexual experience or whether other factors are involved is unknown. Such factors may involve contraception, menstruation, pregnancy, and menopausal changes and have been discussed elsewhere.[22]

CLINICAL MANIFESTATIONS

Ureaplasmas and *M. hominis* have been associated with various clinical conditions,[3, 22, 23] as summarized in Table 173–2, but are considered a cause of only a few. The role of *M. genitalium* is gradually becoming better defined, as indicated.

Nongonococcal Urethritis

There have been numerous studies concerned with the role of large-colony-forming mycoplasmas in nongonococcal urethritis (NGU).[22] It is clear that most of them (see Table 173–1) cannot be considered as significant causes of NGU because they are isolated so rarely from the genitourinary tract in either healthy or diseased states. *M genitalium* has been associated strongly with acute NGU. In several studies[23] it has been detected by use of PCR technology more frequently, often significantly, in the urethra of men with this disease than in healthy men. Furthermore, antibodies to *M. genitalium* were detected by an enzyme immunoassay more often in the serum of men who were PCR-positive for *M. genitalium* than in the serum of men who were PCR-negative (Taylor-Robinson D, Lo S-C, unpublished data), and *M. genitalium* has produced acute urethritis in nonhuman male primates inoculated intraurethrally.[24] In addition, this mycoplasma was detected by a DNA probe and by PCR in about one quarter of men with persistent or recurrent NGU and may account for some of these cases.[25, 26] Although *M. hominis* may be isolated from up to 30% of patients with acute NGU, the results of numerous studies have failed to implicate it as a cause of the disease.[22, 23] Nevertheless, the fact that some cases of NGU are associated with bacterial vaginosis in sexual partners in whom *M. hominis* flourishes[27] means that it should not be ignored entirely. Several lines of investigation, discussed later, indicate that ureaplasmas are one of the causes of NGU.

Isolation, Antibody, and Antibiotic Studies. In about half of the studies, NGU patients were found to harbor ureaplasmas significantly more often than subjects apparently free from disease, but the recovery of ureaplasmas from healthy persons was difficult to reconcile with pathogenicity. Most studies have been qualitative, and if ureaplasmas are involved in the pathogenic process, it would be reasonable to expect them to be present in larger numbers than if they were behaving only as commensals. A few workers[28–31] have provided quantitative data to support this idea.

Attempts by most workers to detect antibody responses to ureaplasmal infection in NGU have not been very successful,[22] but responses have been detected in about 50% of patients with the use of an enzyme immunoassay.[32]

Some antibiotic studies have been considered helpful in assessing the role of ureaplasmas in NGU. For example, in a placebo-controlled trial of minocycline,[33] there was a significant association between minocycline therapy and the resolution of symptoms and signs in patients from whom only ureaplasmas had been isolated. In another study,[34] the best clinical response (96% cure rate) to short-term minocycline therapy was seen in men who were experiencing their first attack of NGU and who harbored ureaplasmas only. Furthermore about 10% of ureaplasmas are resistant to tetracyclines,[30, 35, 36] and the urethritis of some patients infected by these ureaplasmas is cured only by treatment with antibiotics, such as erythromycin, to which the organisms are susceptible. However, these studies and studies[28, 37] with differential antibiotics that distinguish between *Chlamydia trachomatis* and ureaplasmas and have been supportive of a role for ureaplasmas must be viewed with caution because they were undertaken before *M. genitalium* was discovered.

Animal and Human Inoculation Studies. Some ureaplasma strains, unpassaged in the laboratory, have produced urethritis and an antibody response in chimpanzees inoculated intraurethrally. In addition, the results of human intraurethral inoculation[38, 39] have provided evidence that ureaplasmas have the capacity to induce NGU in men.

TABLE 173-2 Association of *Ureaplasma urealyticum* and *Mycoplasma hominis* with Genitourinary and Reproductive Diseases

	Evidence Suggesting an Association between Indicated Mycoplasma and Disease		Evidence Indicating That Mycoplasma is a Cause of Disease			
Disease	***U. urealyticum***	***M. hominis***	***U. urealyticum***	***M. hominis***	**Reference Number**	**Comments on the Relationship and Proportion of Disease Attributable to Mycoplasmas**
Nongonococcal urethritis (NGU)	+ + +	−	+ + +	−	3, 18, 22, 23, 25, 26, 28–34, 37–39, 85	The proportion of NGU caused by ureaplasmas is unknown.
Urethroprostatitis	+ + +	+	+ +	−	3, 18, 22, 23, 29, 91	Ureaplasmas may cause some acute disease, but there is no evidence that they or *M. hominis* cause chronic disease.
Epididymitis	+ + +	−	+ + +	−	3, 22, 23, 72	One case due to ureaplasmas has been described.
Urinary calculi	+ +	−	+ +	−	3, 23, 73	Experimentally, ureaplasmas cause bladder calculi in male rats, and evidence for a cause of natural human disease is increasing.
Pyelonephritis	+	+ + + +	−	+ + +	3, 23, 40, 41	*M. hominis* causes some cases of acute pyelonephritis and exacerbations.
Reiter's disease	+ +	−	+	−	22, 23, 37, 74	The significance of ureaplasmas should be assessed further.
Abscess of Bartholin's gland	−	+	−	−	22, 23	Doubtful whether *M. hominis* is involved.
Vaginitis, vaginosis, and cervicitis	−	+ + +	−	−	22, 23, 42, 43	*M. hominis* is associated with vaginosis, but a causal relation is unproved.
Pelvic inflammatory disease	+	+ + + +	−	+ +	3, 22, 23, 45–48, 52	*M. hominis* probably causes a small proportion of cases.
Postabortal fever	−	+ + + +	−	+ + +	3, 23	*M. hominis* is responsible for some cases, but the proportion is unknown.
Postpartum fever	+ +	+ + + +	+	+ + +	3, 9, 10, 23, 53, 54	*M. hominis* may be a major cause.
Involuntary infertility	+ +	−	+	−	3, 23, 76, 77, 90	Ureaplasmas are associated with reduced sperm motility and with infertility in women associated with a male factor.
Repeated spontaneous abortion and stillbirth	+ +	+ + +	−	−	3, 18, 23, 70, 78, 79	Maternal and fetal infections associated with spontaneous abortion, but a causal relation is unproved.
Chorioamnionitis	+ +	−	+ +	−	3, 23, 80	Ureaplasmas may be responsible in a few cases.
Low birth weight	+ +	+	−	−	3, 23, 90	An association exists in some studies, but a causal relation is unproved.

Key: + + + +, strong; + + +, good; + +, moderate; +, weak; −, none.

The results of one experiment[39] suggest that these organisms may cause disease the first time they gain access to the urethra, but later insults result in colonization without disease. This may explain the finding of ureaplasmas sometimes in the urethra of healthy men.

Pyelonephritis

M. hominis has been isolated, sometimes in pure culture, from the upper urinary tract of almost 10% of patients with acute pyelonephritis, and antibody to *M. hominis*, measured by an indirect hemagglutination test, has been demonstrated in the serum and urine of some of them. In contrast, recovery has not been achieved from the upper urinary tract of patients with noninfectious urinary diseases, nor has antibody been detected in their urine. Overall, the data[40] suggest that *M. hominis* causes a few cases of acute pyelonephritis or acute exacerbations of chronic pyelonephritis. Ureaplasmas have been recovered very occasionally in the same circumstances and also from aspirates of scarred renal tissue in patients with reflux nephropathy,[41] but their role is not clear.

Vaginitis and Cervicitis

M. hominis exists in the vagina of two thirds or more of women with bacterial vaginosis (BV), compared with about 10% of healthy women.[42,43] Larger numbers of *M. hominis* organisms and higher titers of serum immunoglobulin G antibody to *M. hominis* are also found in women with BV. However, although there is no doubt that *M. hominis* is strongly associated with BV, it is unclear whether the organism contributes significantly to a pathologic process in which so many different bacteria are involved. *U. urealyticum* is less associated with BV than *M. hominis*,[43] and neither microorganism is a cause of cervicitis. *M. genitalium*, unlike *M. hominis*, is not associated with BV. However, it has been detected in the lower genital tract of 7 to 20% of women attending sexually transmitted disease clinics[23] and has been associated with cervicitis.[44]

Pelvic Inflammatory Disease

Like NGU, nongonococcal pelvic inflammatory disease (PID) does not have a single cause. Three types of investigation have been undertaken to determine whether genital mycoplasmas might be involved.

Isolation Studies. *M. hominis* has been prominent in many reports of the isolation of large-colony-forming mycoplasmas from inflamed fallopian tubes, tuboovarian abscesses, and pelvic abscesses or fluid. The most revealing studies of PID, however, have been those of Swedish workers[45] who used laparoscopy to confirm the diagnosis and collect specimens. They isolated *M. hominis* directly from the fallopian tubes of about 10% of women with acute salpingitis, but not from those of women without signs of the disease. Similar observations have been made in the United Kingdom[46] and elsewhere.

Ureaplasmas have been isolated directly from the fallopian tubes of only a small proportion of patients with acute salpingitis, from pelvic fluid, and from a tuboovarian abscess, so that their involvement in PID, if any, is much less than that of *M. hominis*.

Antibody Studies. Swedish workers[47] found antibody to *M. hominis* in about one half of their patients with salpingitis but in only 10% of healthy women. Furthermore, a significant rise or fall in antibody titer occurred during the course of the disease in more than one half of the women who had *M. hominis* in the lower genital tract. Other workers[48] found that patients with gonococcal PID were more likely to respond serologically to *M. hominis* than those without such disease: they suggested that damage caused by the other organisms was a factor in the response and questioned the primary role of *M. hominis*.

Antibody responses to ureaplasmas in patients with PID have been detected less often than responses to *M. hominis*. This is consistent with the impression that ureaplasmas are less important than *M. hominis* in this disease, although the greater difficulty of detecting ureaplasmal antibody responses must not be forgotten. A fourfold or greater rise in the titer of antibody to *M. genitalium* was detected in about one third of women with acute PID who did not have evidence of infection with gonococci, *C. trachomatis* or *M. hominis* in one study.[49] However, in another study,[50] this was not found to be the case.

Organ Culture and Animal Inoculation Studies. In fallopian tube organ cultures, *Neisseria gonorrhoeae* rapidly destroys the epithelium, whereas *M. genitalium* causes far less damage and *M. hominis*, although multiplying, usually produces little more than swelling of some of the cilia. No damage by ureaplasmas of human origin has been detected.[22, 23] This decreasing grade of effect may be a true reflection of the pathogenicity of these microorganisms in vivo, but lack of damage in organ culture does not necessarily mean that the organisms are avirulent. The host immune systems, absent in organ culture, may contribute to pathogenesis, and studies in intact animals may be helpful. It is of interest, therefore, that *M. genitalium* has been shown to cause salpingitis in marmosets, grivet monkeys and baboons[51] and that the introduction of *M. hominis* into grivet monkey oviducts resulted in a self-limiting acute salpingitis and parametritis with an antibody response,[52] whereas ureaplasmas had no effect.

The various data suggest that *M. hominis* has a role in causing some cases of acute PID. However, BV is associated with PID and it is rare to detect *M. hominis* organisms in large numbers other than in BV. Therefore, there must be some question about the role of this mycoplasma as a primary pathogen, although it has been isolated from tubes sometimes apparently in the absence of other BV-associated bacteria. The role of *M. genitalium* in PID will be resolved only when PCR technology is applied to specimens from the upper genital tract.

Postabortal and Postpartum Fever

M. hominis has been isolated from the blood of about 10% of women who have fever after abortion, but not from afebrile women who have abortions or from normal pregnant women. A rise in the titer of *M. hominis* antibody has been detected in about one half of the women who become febrile, but in only a small proportion of those who have abortions and remain afebrile. In addition, *M. hominis* has been isolated from the blood of about 5 to 10% of women with fever after a normal vaginal delivery, sometimes with an antibody response,[9] but seldom from the blood of afebrile women. Therefore, it appears that *M. hominis* induces a small proportion of cases of postabortal and postpartum fever, assuming that it is recovered from the blood in pure culture.[53] In both situations, the patients have a low-grade fever for a day or two after delivery, are not severely ill, and usually recover uneventfully without antibiotic therapy.[9] The role of ureaplasmas is less clear, but they may also be involved.[54]

Hypogammaglobulinemia and Immunosuppression

Some hypogammaglobulinemic patients have a chronic urethrocystitis that seems to be caused by a persistent ureaplasmal and/or *M. hominis* infection, other microorganisms not being isolated.[55] In chronic NGU in one such patient, the very large number of ureaplasmas recovered persistently from the urethra suggested a causal relationship.[56] Easier to establish is the mycoplasmal etiology of arthritis seen in some patients with hypogammaglobulinemia, which should be considered in any such patient who develops an abacterial septic arthritis. Ureaplasmas and *M. hominis*, among other mycoplasmas, have been isolated from synovial fluid of a small proportion of these patients,[57] and chronic osteomyelitis in a hypogammaglobulinemic patient has been attributed to ureaplasmal infection.[58] *M. hominis* has been isolated very occasionally after childbirth in otherwise normal mothers who developed arthritis of sudden onset. The arthritis occurring in hypogammaglobulinemic patients often responds to tetracyclines or other antibiotics to which the ureaplasmas or mycoplasmas are sensitive, that occurring after childbirth seeming particularly responsive, and is a further indication that these microorganisms are a cause of the disease. Occasionally, however, in hypogammaglobulinemic patients the organisms develop antibiotic resistance and persistent infection becomes difficult to eradicate.[59]

Immunosuppression may lead to proliferation of mycoplasmas, and septicemia[60] and peritonitis[61] caused by *M. hominis* have been recorded. Mycoplasmas, particularly *M. fermentans* but not *M. hominis*, can be detected by PCR technology in leukocytes of patients with the acquired immunodeficiency syndrome (AIDS),[7] but because they may be detected also in such cells of uninfected subjects their role in the pathogenesis of AIDS is questionable.

Other Diseases

Neonatal meningitis or brain abscess in which *M. hominis* has been isolated from the cerebrospinal fluid[61–64] or abscess[65, 66] has resulted presumably from infection in utero or from colonization at birth with subsequent infection. The same comment applies to the recovery of ureaplasmas from cerebrospinal fluid,[64] which, overall, is probably a rare event.[67] However, the possibility should be considered in neonatal central nervous system disease when bacteriologic staining and culture of fluid are negative. Apart from fever after abortion or normal childbirth, fever associated with burns and trauma has also been attributed to *M. hominis* infection,[60, 68] as have some wound infections.[69]

Conditions of Rare or Equivocal Mycoplasmal Etiology

M. hominis has also been associated with premature labor.[70] However, because late miscarriage and premature labor have been associated strongly with BV,[71] the latter in early pregnancy being predictive of these events, the involvement of *M. hominis* would seem to be a part of the BV syndrome.

As shown in Table 173–2, there are various other conditions, such as epididymitis, urinary calculi, Reiter's syndrome, infertility, spontaneous abortion, chorioamnionitis, and low birth weight, with which ureaplasmas, in particular, have been associated. In some instances the association is rare, and in others there is insufficient proof or no proof that the organisms are a cause. Ureaplasmas are probably a rare cause of acute nonchlamydial epididymitis, the organisms having been recovered from the epididymis in association with an antibody response.[72] Furthermore, there are studies, which should stimulate further work, on ureaplasmas in urinary calculi,[73] as well as studies on these organisms and *M. genitalium* in Reiter's syndrome or sexually acquired reactive arthritis.[74, 75] Ureaplasmas have also been studied in infertility,[76] particularly among a subgroup of infertile women whose problem is associated with a male factor,[77] abortion,[78, 79] chorioamnionitis,[80] or neonatal respiratory disease,[81, 82] including the respiratory distress syndrome[83] and chronic lung disease.[84] The results of studies on neonatal disease, in particular, point to the importance of ureaplasmas. Worthy of consideration, however, is the notion that in conditions such as abortion, chorioamnionitis, low birth weight, and disease of the newborn, ureaplasmas, as in the case of *M. hominis*, are involved to some extent as part of the BV syndrome and to consider them alone may be misleading.

MANAGEMENT AND TREATMENT

Because culturing for mycoplasmas and other ways of detecting them are not generally available to clinicians, management depends on recognizing clinical syndromes for which mycoplasmas could be responsible and providing therapy that would be adequate to eliminate them.

The weight of accumulated evidence suggests that *C. trachomatis*, *M. genitalium* and *U. urealyticum* cause NGU. However, it is important to emphasize that there is no virtue in testing subjects for ureaplasmas on a routine basis, because the results are difficult for the clinician to interpret and use in patient management. Patients should receive a tetracycline, for example doxycycline, 100 mg twice daily for 7 days. However, about 10% of ureaplasmas are resistant to tetracyclines,[30, 35, 36] and patients with NGU caused by resistant organisms often have no clinical response to the administration of tetracycline.[85] In this circumstance, the patients should be examined for tetracycline-resistant ureaplasmas if laboratory facilities are available. Meanwhile, they should be treated with erythromycin, 0.5 g four times daily for 7 days, because most tetracycline-resistant ureaplasmas are sensitive to this antibiotic, or with one of the newer macrolides or quinolones.[86, 87]

It would be advisable to treat PID with a tetracycline in areas where a substantial proportion of the disease is nongonococcal, because tetracyclines are active against most strains of *M. hominis* as well as *M. genitalium* and *C. trachomatis*, which also causes PID. However, the emergence of tetracycline-resistant strains of *M. hominis*[63, 87, 88] means that other antibiotics, such as clindamycin, may need to be considered.[87] If *M. hominis*–induced fever after abortion or vaginal delivery does not settle rapidly, tetracycline therapy should be instituted keeping tetracycline resistance in mind. Resistance assumes greater importance in other clinical situations, such as arthritis and neonatal disease, where *M. hominis* is considered to be responsible.

Antibiotic treatment for infertility,[89] spontaneous abortion,[78] or low birth weight[90] has been reported. However, for these and other conditions in which genital mycoplasmas have not been proved to be etiologic agents, it is difficult to justify either examination for the organisms or treatment directed against them on a routine basis. Culture of genital specimens from adults with an idiopathic disorder results in the isolation of either ureaplasmas or *M. hominis*, or both, from up to one half of cases. To consider these organisms a cause of the disorder on this basis is not warranted, and to provide routine antibiotic therapy aimed at the mycoplasmas in such instances would seem as unethical as not initiating effective treatment when the cause is understood.

REFERENCES

1. Kakulphimp J, Finch LR, Robertson JA. Genome sizes of mammalian and avian ureaplasmas. Int J Syst Bacteriol. 1991;41:326.
2. Taylor-Robinson D, Furr PM. Recovery and identification of human genital tract mycoplasmas. Isr J Med Sci. 1981;17:648.
3. Taylor-Robinson D. Genital mycoplasma infections. Clin Lab Med. 1989;9:501.
4. Tully JG, Taylor-Robinson D, Rose DL, et al. Evaluation of culture media for the recovery of *Mycoplasma hominis* from the human urogenital tract. Sex Transm Dis. 1983;10:256.
5. Palmer HM, Gilroy CB, Furr PM, et al. Development and evaluation of the polymerase chain reaction to detect *Mycoplasma genitalium*. FEMS Microbiol Lett. 1991;77:199.
6. Palmer HM, Gilroy CB, Claydon EJ, et al. Detection of *Mycoplasma genitalium* in the genitourinary tract of women by the polymerase chain reaction. Int J STD AIDS. 1991;2:261.
7. Katseni VL, Gilroy CB, Ryait BK, et al. *Mycoplasma fermentans* in individuals seropositive and seronegative for HIV-1. Lancet. 1993;341:271.
8. Jensen JS, Hansen HT, Lind K. Isolation of *Mycoplasma genitalium* strains from the male urethra. J Clin Microbiol. 1996;34:286.
9. Wallace RJ Jr, Alpert S, Brown K, et al. Isolation of *Mycoplasma hominis* from blood cultures in patients with postpartum fever. Obstet Gynecol. 1978;51:181.
10. Pratt B. Automated blood culture systems: Detection of *Mycoplasma hominis* in SPS-containing media. Zentralbl Bakteriol. 1990;(Suppl 20):778.
11. Klein JO, Buckland D, Finland M. Colonization of newborn infants by mycoplasmas. N Engl J Med. 1969;280:1025.
12. Foy HM, Kenny GE, Levinsohn EM, et al. Acquisition of mycoplasmata and T-strains during infancy. J Infect Dis. 1970;121:579.
13. Hammerschlag MR, Alpert S, Rosner I, et al. Microbiology of the vagina in children: Normal and potentially pathogenic organisms. Pediatrics. 1978;62:57.
14. Hammerschlag MR, Doraiswamy B, Cox P, et al. Colonization of sexually abused children with genital mycoplasmas. Sex Transm Dis. 1987;14:23.
15. McCormack WM, Lee Y-H, Zinner SH. Sexual experience and urethral colonization with genital mycoplasmas: A study in normal men. Ann Intern Med. 1973;78:696.
16. McCormack WM, Almeida PC, Bailey PE, et al. Sexual activity and vaginal colonization with genital mycoplasmas. JAMA. 1972;221:1375.
17. Furr PM, Taylor-Robinson D. Prevalence and significance of *Mycoplasma hominis* and *Ureaplasma urealyticum* in the urines of a non-venereal disease population. Epidemiol Infect. 1987;98:353.
18. Taylor-Robinson D, Tully JG, Furr PM, et al. Urogenital mycoplasma infections of man: A review with observations on a recently discovered mycoplasma. Isr J Med Sci. 1981;17:524.
19. Baseman JB, Dallo SF, Tully JG, et al. Isolation and characterization of *Mycoplasma genitalium* strains from the human respiratory tract. J Clin Microbiol. 1988;26:2266.
20. Wang RY-H, Grandinetti T, Shih JW-K, et al. *Mycoplasma genitalium* infection and host antibody immune response in patients infected by HIV, patients attending STD clinics and in healthy blood donors. FEMS Immunol Med Microbiol. 1997;19:237.
21. McCormack WM, Rosner B, Lee Y-H. Colonization with genital mycoplasmas in women. Am J Epidemiol. 1973;97:240.
22. Taylor-Robinson D, Csonka GW. Laboratory and clinical aspects of mycoplasmal infections of the human genitourinary tract. In: Harris JRW, ed. Recent Advances in Sexually Transmitted Diseases. London: Churchill Livingstone; 1981:151.
23. Taylor-Robinson D. Infections due to species of *Mycoplasma* and *Ureaplasma*: An update. Clin Infect Dis. 1996;23:671.
24. Tully JG, Taylor-Robinson D, Rose DL, et al. Urogenital challenge of primate species with *Mycoplasma genitalium* and characteristics of infection induced in chimpanzees. J Infect Dis. 1986;153:1046.
25. Taylor-Robinson D, Gilroy CB, Hay PE. The occurrence of *Mycoplasma genitalium* in different populations and its clinical significance. Clin Infect Dis. 1993;17(Suppl 1):566.
26. Hooton TM, Roberts MC, Roberts PL, et al. Prevalence of *Mycoplasma genitalium* determined by DNA probe in men with urethritis. Lancet. 1988;1:266.
27. Keane FEA, Thomas BJ, Whitaker L, et al. An association between non-gonococcal urethritis and bacterial vaginosis and the implications for patients and their sexual partners. Genitourin Med. 1997;73:373.
28. Bowie WR, Wang S-P, Alexander ER, et al. Etiology of nongonococcal urethritis: Evidence for *Chlamydia trachomatis* and *Ureaplasma urealyticum*. J Clin Invest. 1977;59:735.
29. Weidner W, Brunner H, Krause W, et al. Zur Bedeutung von *Ureaplasma urealyticum* bei unspezifischer Prostato-urethritis: Quantitative Untersuchungen am 312 Patienten. Dtsch Med Wochenschr. 1978;103:465.
30. Hawkins DA, Taylor-Robinson D, Evans RT, et al. Unsuccessful treatment of non-gonococcal urethritis with rosoxacin provides information on the aetiology of the disease. Genitourin Med. 1985;61:51.
31. Ahmed-Jushuf IH, Pratt BC, Arya OP. Incidence of *Ureaplasma urealyticum* in endourethral swabs compared with first voided urine from men. Genitourin Med. 1988;64:78.
32. Brown MB, Cassell GH, Taylor-Robinson D, et al. Measurement of antibody to *Ureaplasma urealyticum* by an enzyme-linked immunoassay and detection of antibody responses in patients with nongonococcal urethritis. J Clin Microbiol. 1983;17:288.
33. Prentice MJ, Taylor-Robinson D, Csonka GW. Non-specific urethritis: A placebo-controlled trial of minocycline in conjunction with laboratory investigations. Br J Vener Dis. 1976;52:269.
34. Taylor-Robinson D, Evans RT, Coufalik ED, et al. Effect of short term treatment of non-gonococcal urethritis with minocyline. Genitourin Med. 1986;62:19.
35. Evans RT, Taylor-Robinson D. The incidence of tetracycline-resistant strains of *Ureaplasma urealyticum*. J Antimicrob Chemother. 1978;4:57.
36. Taylor-Robinson D, Furr PM. Clinical antibiotic resistance of *Ureaplasma urealyticum*. Pediatr Infect Dis. 1986;5:S335.
37. Coufalik ED, Taylor-Robinson D, Csonka GW. Treatment of nongonococcal urethritis with rifampicin as a means of defining the role of *Ureaplasma urealyticum*. Br J Vener Dis. 1979;55:36.
38. Taylor-Robinson D, Csonka GW, Prentice MJ. Human intra-urethral inoculation of ureaplasmas. Q J Med. 1977;46:309.
39. Taylor-Robinson D. The history of nongonococcal urethritis. Thomas Parran Award Lecture. Sex Transm Dis. 1996;23:86.
40. Thomsen AC. Mycoplasma infections in the upper urinary tract. Dan Med Bull. 1982;29:309.

41. Birch DF, Fairley KF, Pavillard RE: Unconventional bacteria in urinary tract disease: *Ureaplasma urealyticum*. Kidney Int. 1981;19:58.
42. Hillier S, Holmes KK. Bacterial vaginosis. In: Holmes KK, Mårdh P-A, Sparling PF, et al., eds. Sexually Transmitted Diseases. 2nd ed. New York: McGraw-Hill; 1990:547.
43. Rosenstein IJ, Morgan DJ, Sheehan M, et al. Bacterial vaginosis in pregnancy: Distribution of bacterial species in different gram-stain categories of the vaginal flora. J Med Microbiol. 1996;44:1.
44. Uno M, Deguchi T, Komeda H, et al. *Mycoplasma genitalium* in the cervices of Japanese women. Sex Transm Dis. 1997;24:284.
45. Weström L, Mårdh P-A. Acute salpingitis. Aspects on aetiology, diagnosis, and prognosis. In: Danielsson D, Juhlin L, Mâmrdh P-A, eds. Genital Infections and Their Complications. Stockholm: Almqvist and Wiksell;1975:157.
46. Stacey CM, Munday PE, Taylor-Robinson D, et al. A longitudinal study of pelvic inflammatory disease. Br J Obstet Gynaecol. 1992;99:994.
47. Mårdh P-A, Weström L. Antibodies to *Mycoplasma hominis* in patients with genital infections and in healthy controls. Br J Vener Dis. 1970;46:390.
48. Lind K, Kristensen GB, Bollerup AC, et al. Importance of *Mycoplasma hominis* in acute salpingitis assessed by culture and serological tests. Genitourin Med. 1985;61:185.
49. Møller BR, Taylor-Robinson D, Furr PM. Serological evidence implicating *Mycoplasma genitalium* in pelvic inflammatory disease. Lancet. 1984;1:1102.
50. Lind K, Kristensen GB. Significance of antibodies to *Mycoplasma genitalium* in salpingitis. Eur J Clin Microbiol. 1987;6:205.
51. Taylor-Robinson D, Furr PM, Tully JG, et al. Animol models of *Mycoplasma genitalium* infection. Isr J Med Sci. 1987;23:561.
52. Møller BR, Freundt EA, Black FT, et al. Experimental infection of the genital tract of female grivet monkeys by *Mycoplasma hominis*. Infect Immun. 1978;20:248.
53. Platt R, Lin J-SL, Warren JW, et al. Infection with *Mycoplasma hominis* in postpartum fever. Lancet. 1980;2:1217.
54. Eschenbach DA. *Ureaplasma urealyticum* as a cause of postpartum fever. Pediatr Infect Dis. 1986;5:S258.
55. Webster ADB, Taylor-Robinson D, Furr PM, et al. Chronic cystitis and urethritis associated with ureaplasmal and mycoplasmal infection in primary hypogammaglobulinaemia. Br J Urol. 1982;54:287.
56. Taylor-Robinson D, Furr PM, Webster ADB. *Ureaplasma urealyticum* causing persistent urethritis in a patient with hypogammaglobulinaemia. Genitourin Med. 1985;61:404.
57. Furr PM, Taylor-Robinson D, Webster ADB. Mycoplasmas and ureaplasmas in patients with hypogammaglobulinaemia and their role in arthritis:Microbiological observations over 20 years. Rheum Dis. 1994;53:183.
58. Mohiuddin AA, Corren J, Harbeck RJ, et al. *Ureaplasma urealyticum* chronic osteomyelitis in a patient with hypogammaglobulinemia. J Allergy Clin Immunol. 1991;87:104.
59. Franz A, Webster ADB, Furr PM, et al. Mycoplasmal arthritis in patients with primary immunoglobulin deficiency : Clinical features and outcome in 18 patients. Br J Rheumatol. 1997;36:661.
60. DeGirolami PC, Madoff S. *Mycoplasma hominis* septicemia. J Clin Microbiol. 1982;16:566.
61. Mokhbat JE, Peterson PK, Sabath LD, et al. Peritonitis due to *Mycoplasma hominis* in a renal transplant recipient. J Infect Dis. 1982;146:713.
62. Gewitz M, Dinwiddlle R, Rees L, et al. *Mycoplasma hominis*: A cause of neonatal meningitis. Arch Dis Child. 1979;54:231.
63. Hjelm E, Jonsell G, Linglöv T. et al. Meningitis in a newborn infant caused by *Mycoplasma hominis*. Acta Paediatr Scand. 1980;69:415.
64. Waites KB, Rudd PT, Crouse DT, et al. Chronic *Ureaplasma urealyticum* and *Mycoplasma hominis* infections of central nervous system in preterm infants. Lancet. 1988;1:17.
65. Siber GR, Alpert S, Smith AL, et al. Neonatal central nervous system infection due to *Mycoplasma hominis*. J Pediatr. 1977;90:625.
66. Payan DG, Seigal N, Madoff S. Infection of a brain abscess by *Mycoplasma hominis*. J Clin Microbiol. 1981;14:571.
67. Shaw NJ, Pratt BC, Weindling AM. Ureaplasma and mycoplasma infections of the central nervous system in preterm infants. Lancet. 1989;2:1530.
68. Ti TY, Dan M, Stemke GW, et al. Isolation of *Mycoplasma hominis* from the blood of men with multiple trauma and fever. JAMA. 1982;247:60.
69. Steffenson DO, Dummer JS, Granick MS, et al. Sternotomy infections with *Mycoplasma hominis*. JAMA. 1987;106:204.
70. Lamont RF, Taylor-Robinson D, Wigglesworth JS, et al. The role of mycoplasmas, ureaplasmas and chlamydiae in the genital tract of women presenting in spontaneous early preterm labour. J Med Microbiol. 1987;24:253.
71. Hay PE, Lamont RF, Taylor-Robinson D, et al. Abnormal bacterial colonisation of the genital tract as a marker for subsequent preterm delivery and late miscarriage. BMJ. 1994;308:295.
72. Jalil N, Doble A, Gilchrist C, et al. Infection of the epididymis by *Ureaplasma urealyticum*. Genitourin Med. 1988;64:367.
73. Pettersson S, Brorson JE, Grenabo L, et al. *Ureaplasma urealyticum* in infectious urinary tract stones. Lancet. 1983;1:526.
74. Li F, Bulbul R, Schumacher HR, et al. Molecular detection of bacterial DNA in venereal-associated arthritis. Arthritis Rheum. 1996;39:950.
75. Taylor-Robinson D, Gilroy CB, Horowitz S, et al. *Mycoplasma genitalium* in the joint of two patients with arthritis. Eur J Clin Microbiol Infect Dis. 1994;13:1066.
76. Taylor-Robinson D. Evaluation of the role of *Ureaplasma urealyticum* in infertility. Pediatr Infect Dis. 1986;5:S262.
77. Cassell GH, Younger JB, Brown MB, et al. Microbiologic study of infertile women at the time of diagnostic laparoscopy: Association of *Ureaplasma urealyticum* with a defined subpopulation. N Engl J Med. 1983;308:502.
78. Quinn PA, Shewchuk AB, Shuber J, et al. Efficacy of antibiotic therapy in preventing spontaneous pregnancy loss among couples colonized with genital mycoplasmas. Am J Obstet Gynecol. 1983;145:239.
79. Quinn PA, Shewchuk AB, Shuber J, et al. Serologic evidence of *Ureaplasma urealyticum* infection in women with spontaneous pregnancy loss. Am J Obstet Gynecol. 1983;145:245.
80. Cassell GH, Waites KB, Gibbs RS, et al. Role of *Ureaplasma urealyticum* in amnionitis. Pediatr Infect Dis. 1986;5:S247.
81. Rudd PT, Waites KB, Duffy LB, et al. *Ureaplasma urealyticum* and its possible role in pneumonia during the neonatal period and infancy. Pediatr Infect Dis. 1986;5:S288.
82. Cunningham CK. The role of genital mycoplasmas in neonatal disease. Clin Microbiol Newsl. 1990;12:147.
83. Gallo D, Dupuis KW, Schmidt NJ, et al. Broadly reactive immunofluorescence test for measurement of immunoglobulin M and G antibodies to *Ureaplasma urealyticum* in infant and adult sera. J Clin Microbiol. 1983;17:614.
84. Cassell GH, Waites KB, Crouse DT, et al. Association of *Ureaplasma urealyticum* infection of the lower respiratory tract with chronic lung disease and death in very low birth weight infants. Lancet. 1988;2:240.
85. Stimson JB, Hale J, Bowie WR, et al. Tetracycline-resistant *Ureaplasma urealyticum*: A cause of persistent nongonococcal urethritis. Ann Intern Med. 1981;94:192.
86. Renaudin H, Bébéar C, Robertson JA. In vitro susceptibility of tetracycline-resistant strains of *Ureaplasma urealyticum* to newer macrolides and quinolones, and a streptogramin. Eur J Clin Microbiol Infect Dis. 1991;10:984.
87. Taylor-Robinson D, Bébéar C. Antibiotic susceptibilities of mycoplasmas and treatment of mycoplasmal infections. J Antimicrob Chemother. 1997;40:622.
88. Koutsky LA, Stamm WE, Brunham RC, et al. Persistence of *Mycoplasma hominis* after treatment with different antimicrobials. Sex Transm Dis. 1983;10:374.
89. Toth A, Lesser ML, Brooks C, et al. Subsequent pregnancies among 161 couples treated for T-mycoplasma genital-tract infection. N Engl J Med. 1983;308:505.
90. Kass EH, McCormack WM, Lin J-S, et al. Genital mycoplasmas as a cause of excess premature delivery. Trans Assoc Am Phys. 1981;94:261.
91. Doble A, Thomas BJ, Furr PM, et al. A search for infectious agents in chronic abacterial prostatitis utilising ultrasound guided biopsy. Br J Urol. 1989;64:297.

SECTION E

RICKETTSIOSES AND EHRLICHIOSES

Chapter 174

Introduction to Rickettsioses and Ehrlichioses

ALFRED J. SAAH

The Rickettsiaceae family of microbes is maintained in nature through a cycle involving reservoirs in mammals and arthropod vectors. The public health impact on lives or productivity lost is largely unmeasured, but it is suspected to be quite high worldwide.[1] Humans are incidental hosts and are not useful in propagating the organism in nature. An exception is louse-borne typhus, in which humans are the principal reservoir and the human body louse is the vector, thereby creating a cycle that involves humans alone. However, even louse-borne typhus may also prove to be a zoonotic disease. Data have been reported implicating the flying squirrel as a reservoir of the agent that produces louse-borne typhus,[2, 3] and serologic evidence in humans suggests that louse-borne typhus occurs indigenously in the United States (see Chapter 178).[4–6] The role of fleas in zoonotically transmitting rickettsial organisms, such as *Rickettsia typhi* (murine typhus) and *Rickettsia felis* (a newly recognized typhus-like agent)[7] is an increasing clinical and public health problem. Ehrlichiae are organisms phylogenetically related to rickettsiae, more so, in fact, than *Coxiella* and *Chlamydia,* and their infections share zoonotic or vector-borne features, or both, of other rickettsial infections.[8] Human *Ehrlichia* infections are tick-borne, zoonotic infections in the United States that produce an illness reminiscent of Rocky Mountain spotted fever but with diagnostically helpful laboratory abnormalities and no rash (see Chapter 181).[9]

DESCRIPTION OF THE PATHOGEN

Rickettsiae are fastidious bacterial organisms that are obligate, intracellular parasites. The organisms are small, pleomorphic coccobacilli. Coccal forms usually are 0.3 μm in diameter, whereas bacillary forms measure 0.3 by 1 to 2 μm. The bacterial nature of these organisms is now well established; they multiply by binary fission, contain both RNA and DNA, and have both synthetic and energy-producing enzyme systems. In addition, typhus and spotted fever group rickettsiae contain endotoxins.

With the exception of *Coxiella burnetii* (Q fever), the rickettsiae survive only briefly outside a host (reservoir or vector). *Coxiella burnetii* is a hearty organism that resists desiccation, heat, and sunlight and is transmitted primarily by the airborne route. Based on antigenic similarities and intracellular growth characteristics, the rickettsiae have been broadly divided into spotted fever and typhus groups (Table 174–1).

If isolation of rickettsial organisms is attempted, it should be done only in a reference laboratory or a laboratory skilled in handling rickettsiae. Isolation of *Rickettsia* may become more generally available if techniques become adapted for general laboratory use.[10] If rickettsial isolation is contemplated, it is important to obtain blood before therapy. An anticoagulated blood specimen can be obtained and stored in the refrigerator (4°C) for 24 to 48 hours before shipping and processing or frozen at −70°C if further delay is inevitable.

EPIDEMIOLOGY

The etiologic agents of Rocky Mountain spotted fever (RMSF), murine typhus, scrub typhus, and rickettsialpox (*Rickettsia rickettsii, R. typhi, Orientia tsutsugamushi* [formerly *Rickettsia tsutsugamushi*], and *Rickettsia akari,* respectively) exist in a classically commensal fashion with their insect vectors. Three of these organisms (*R. rickettsii, R. tsutsugamushi,* and *R. akari*) are transmitted transovarially to progeny of their vectors. *Rickettsia prowazekii* (louse-borne typhus) causes the death of its vector (human body louse) in 1 to 3 weeks. The zoonotic reservoirs of the rickettsiae are quite varied but generally are composed of small mammals and livestock (see Table 174–1).

In the United States, RMSF, Q fever, and murine typhus are endemic; rickettsialpox and epidemic typhus may also occur. In addition, recrudescent louse-borne typhus (Brill-Zinsser disease) still occurs—predominantly in immigrants who were living in eastern Europe during World War II.

PATHOLOGIC CHARACTERISTICS

Except for Q fever, the pathogenesis of both spotted fever and typhus group organisms is vasculitis caused by the proliferation of organisms in the endothelial lining of small arteries, veins, and capillaries. Evidence for a rickettsial toxin has been shown in experimental animals, but its relationship to human disease is undefined. The organisms can be seen in histopathologic specimens in the cytoplasm and—in the case of RMSF—in the nuclei of cells as well. The organisms do not stain well with Gram stain but are stained effectively by Giemsa or Gimenez stain. Immunofluorescent and immunohistochemical techniques have helped in the pathologic determination of rickettsial organisms and may be helpful in the early diagnosis of RMSF through skin biopsy specimens.[11–13]

CLINICAL MANIFESTATIONS AND DIAGNOSIS

During the appropriate season—generally spring and summer—the triad of fever, headache, and rash should alert the physician to consider a rickettsial cause. Historic features should be sought such as tick attachment, recent camping, or occupational exposure. Differential diagnoses are included in the chapters that follow.

The diagnosis of a rickettsial illness is most often confirmed by serologic testing. Serologic methods were first used in Poland in 1915 when Weil and Felix found that serum from patients with typhus agglutinated certain strains of *Proteus vulgaris.* Familiarity and the ease of the Weil-Felix reaction has led to its widespread and continued use; the Centers for Disease Control and Prevention in Atlanta, Georgia, have downgraded the Weil-Felix reaction in the diagnosis of RMSF.[14] A case with positive titers by Weil-Felix reaction is considered a probable (formerly confirmed) case of RMSF. More specific tests such as complement fixation, indirect hemagglutination,[15] direct[11, 12] and indirect[16, 17] immunofluorescence tests, and others[18–21] have been developed. However, except for the complement fixation and direct immunofluorescent tests, these procedures are used primarily by reference laboratories.

Serologic evidence of infection occurs no earlier than the second week of illness in any of the rickettsial diseases; therefore, therapy must be instituted on clinical grounds. In RMSF, the direct immunofluorescence test on skin lesions identifies organisms and allows the diagnosis to be made when the rash appears (3 to 5 days). Techniques

TABLE 174-1 Synopsis of Certain Epidemiologic and Clinical Features of Selected Rickettsioses

Disease	Organism	Geographic Area	Arthropods	Vertebrates	Rash Distribution	Eschar
Spotted Fever Group						
Rocky Mountain spotted fever	*R. rickettsii*	Western hemisphere	Ticks	Wild rodents, dogs	Extremities to trunk	No
Boutonneuse	*R. conorii*	Africa, Mediterranean, India	Ticks	Wild rodents, dogs	Trunk, extremities, face	Yes
Queensland tick typhus	*R. australis*	Australia	Ticks	Wild rodents, marsupials	Trunk, extremities, face	Yes
North Asian tick typhus	*R. sibirica*	Siberia, Mongolia	Ticks	Wild rodents	Trunk, extremities, face	Yes
Rickettsialpox	*R. akari*	United States, former Soviet Union, Korea, Africa	Mite	Mouse	Vesicular; trunk, extremities, face	Yes
Typhus Group						
Epidemic typhus	*R. prowazekii*	Highland areas of South America, Africa, Asia, ? United States	Body louse	Humans, flying squirrel	Trunk to extremities	No
Brill-Zinsser disease	*R. prowazekii*	Worldwide based on immigration	None	Humans (recurrence years after primary attack)	Trunk to extremities (may be absent)	No
Murine typhus	*R. typhi*	Worldwide in pockets	Flea	Small rodents	Trunk to extremities	No
Scrub typhus	*Orientia tsutsugamushi*	South Pacific, Asia, Australia	Mite	Wild rodents	Trunk to extremities	Yes
Ehrlichia						
Human monocytic ehrlichiosis	*Ehrlichia chaffeensis* infection	United States, Europe	Ticks	Humans, deer, dogs	None	None
Human granulocytic ehrlichiosis	*Ehrlichia phagocytophila* infection	United States, Europe	Ticks	Humans, dogs, deer, white-footed mouse	None	No
Others						
Q fever	*C. burnetii*	Worldwide	? Ticks	Cattle, sheep, goats, cats (inhalation of organism)	None	No

using the polymerase chain reaction have been shown to diagnose acute infection with *R. prowazekii* and *R. rickettsii.*[22, 23]

DEVELOPMENTS IN THE FIELD

Numerous rickettsial strains have been isolated from ticks in many countries. Some of these strains may be associated with the various clinical types of spotted fever that have been identified in Asia[24] and Africa.[25]

An interesting development involves *R. prowazekii,* its reservoir in the southern flying squirrel, and the serologic evidence that disease (epidemic typhus) in humans is occurring in the United States[2–5] and continues to occur when social conditions are harsh (see Chapter 178).[26]

Another interesting discovery is that at least two *Ehrlichia* species produce naturally acquired infection and disease in humans.[27] The organism is transmitted to humans by ticks and produces an illness similar to RMSF but does not produce a rash (see Chapter 181).

In addition to the well-described abattoir-associated outbreaks of Q fever, parturient cats that are infected with *C. burnetii* have been identified as a reservoir for human disease (see Chapter 177).[27] Another rickettsial infection that may have a connection to cats (and their flea, *Ctenocephalides felis*) is *R. typhi,* which causes murine typhus.[28]

REFERENCES

1. WHO Working Group on Rickettsial Diseases. Rickettsioses: A continuing disease problem. Bull World Health Organ. 1982;60:157–164.
2. Bozeman FM, Masiello SA, Williams MS, et al. Epidemic typhus rickettsiae isolated from flying squirrels. Nature. 1975;255:545–547.
3. Sonenshine DE, Bozeman FM, Williams MS, et al. Epizootiology of epidemic typhus (*Rickettsia prowazekii*) in flying squirrels. Am J Trop Med Hyg. 1978;27:339–349.
4. McDade JE, Shepard CC, Redus MA, et al. Evidence of *Rickettsia prowazekii* infections in the United States. Am J Trop Med Hyg. 1980;29:277–284.
5. Duma RJ, Sonenshine DE, Bozeman FM, et al. Epidemic typhus in the United States associated with flying squirrels. JAMA. 1981;245:2318–2323.
6. Regnery RL, Fu ZY, Spruill CL. Flying squirrel–associated *Rickettsia prowazekii* (epidemic typhus rickettsiae) characterized by a specific DNA fragment produced by restriction endonuclease digestion. J Clin Microbiol. 1986;23:189–191.
7. Higgins JA, Radulovic S, Schriefer ME, Azad AF. *Rickettsia felis:* A new species of pathogenic *Rickettsia* isolated from cat fleas. J Clin Microbiol. 1996;34:671–674.
8. Azad AF, Beard CB. Rickettsial pathogens and their arthropod vectors. Emerg Infect Dis. 1999;4:179–186.
9. Walker DH, Dumler JS. Emergence of the ehrlichioses as human health problems. Emerg Infect Dis. 1996;2:18–29.
10. Marrero M, Raoult D. Centrifugation-shell vial technique for rapid detection of Mediterranean spotted fever rickettsia in blood culture. Am J Trop Med Hyg. 1989;40:197–199.
11. Woodward TE, Pedersen CE, Oster CN, et al. Prompt confirmation of Rocky Mountain spotted fever: Identification of rickettsia in skin tissues. J Infect Dis. 1976;134:297–301.
12. Precop GW, Burchette JL Jr, Howell DN, Sexton DJ. Immunoperoxidase and immunofluorescent staining of *Rickettsia rickettsii* in skin biopsies. A comparative study. Arch Pathol Lab Med. 1997;121:894–899.
13. Walker DH, Feng HM, Ladner S, et al. Immunohistochemical diagnosis of typhus rickettsioses using an anti-lipopolysaccharide monoclonal antibody. Mod Pathol. 1997;10:1038–1042.
14. Centers for Disease Control and Prevention. Case definitions for infectious conditions under public health surveillance. MMWR. 1997;46:28–29.
15. Shirai A, Dietel JW, Osterman JV. Indirect hemagglutination test for human antibody to typhus and spotted fever group rickettsiae. J Clin Microbiol. 1975;2:430–437.
16. Goldwasser RA, Shepard CC. Fluorescent antibody methods in the differentiation of murine and epidemic typhus sera: Specificity changes resulting from previous immunization. J Immunol. 1959;82:373–380.
17. Goldwasser RA, Shepard CC, Jordan ME, et al. The specificity of antibody response in typhus fever. Its alteration during murine typhus infection as a result of previous exposure to epidemic typhus antigen. J Immunol. 1959;83:491–495.
18. Philip RN, Casper EA, Ormsbee RA, et al. Microimmunofluorescence test for the serological study of Rocky Mountain spotted fever and typhus. J Clin Microbiol. 1976;3:51–61.
19. Philip RN, Casper EA, MacCormack JN, et al. A comparison of serologic methods for diagnosis of Rocky Mountain spotted fever. Am J Epidemiol. 1977;105:56–67.

20. Ormsbee R, Peacock M, Philip R, et al. Serologic diagnosis of epidemic typhus fever. Am J Epidemiol. 1977;105:261–271.
21. Kaplan JE, Schonberger LB. The sensitivity of various serologic tests in the diagnosis of Rocky Mountain spotted fever. Am J Trop Med Hyg. 1986;35:840–844.
22. Carl M, Tibbs CW, Dobson ME, et al. Diagnosis of acute typhus infection using the polymerase chain reaction. J Infect Dis. 1990;161:791–793.
23. Sexton DJ, Kanj SS, Wilson K, et al. The use of a polymerase chain reaction as a diagnostic test for Rocky Mountain spotted fever. Am J Trop Med Hyg. 1994;50:59–63.
24. Mahara F. Japanese spotted fever: Report of 31 cases and review of the literature. Emerg Infect Dis. 1997;3:105–111.
25. Xu W, Beati L, Raoult D. Characterization of and application of monoclonal antibodies against *Rickettsia africae,* a newly recognized species of spotted fever group *Rickettsia.* J Clin Microbiol. 1997;35:64–70.
26. Bise G, Coninx R. Epidemic typhus in a prison in Burundi. Trans R Soc Trop Med Hyg. 1997;91:133–134.
27. Langley JM, Marrie TJ, Covert A, et al. Poker players' pneumonia. An urban outbreak of Q fever following exposure to a parturient cat. N Engl J Med. 1988;319:354–356.
28. Dumler JS, Taylor JP, Walker DH. Clinical and laboratory features of murine typhus in south Texas, 1980 through 1987. JAMA. 1991;266:1365–1370.

Chapter 175

Rickettsia rickettsii and Other Spotted Fever Group Rickettsiae (Rocky Mountain Spotted Fever and Other Spotted Fevers)

DAVID H. WALKER
DIDIER RAOULT

The spotted fevers compose a large group of tick- and mite-borne zoonotic infections that are caused by closely related rickettsiae.[1–3] They include Rocky Mountain spotted fever (RMSF), boutonneuse fever, African tick bite fever, North Asian tick typhus, Queensland tick typhus, Flinders Island spotted fever, Japanese spotted fever, and rickettsialpox. Rickettsiae are in many places of the world emerging or reemerging pathogens.[4–8] These diseases have a broad spectrum of severity; the most virulent, RMSF, has a fatality/case ratio of 20% unless treated early and appropriately. Even young and previously healthy people may die of RMSF. In recent years, the wide distribution and potential severity of the other spotted fevers have been recognized, especially in southern Europe, Africa, Australia, China, and Japan. Establishing an early diagnosis remains deceptively difficult.

ROCKY MOUNTAIN SPOTTED FEVER

Pathogen

RMSF was first described in Idaho in the late nineteenth century.[9] Ricketts established the infectious nature of the illness and demonstrated the role of ticks as the vector in western Montana in 1906.[10] Wolbach in 1919 clearly identified the etiologic rickettsiae within endothelial cells.[11]

The etiologic agent, *Rickettsia rickettsii*, belongs to the spotted fever group of rickettsiae, which are genetically related but differ from one another in their surface antigenic proteins.[12] Some presumably nonpathogenic rickettsiae also belong to this group. Spotted fever group (SFG) rickettsiae are obligately intracellular bacteria that reside in the cytosol and less often in the nucleus of their host cells. The rickettsiae are small, measuring approximately 0.3 by 1 μm. They have one of the smallest bacterial genomes, ranging between 1.1 and 1.6 MB.[13] The cell wall has the ultrastructural appearance of a gram-negative bacterium and contains peptidoglycan and lipopolysaccharide. Rickettsiae are difficult to stain with ordinary bacterial stains but are conveniently stained by the Gimenez method or with acridine orange. They have not been cultivated in cell-free medium. Growth requires living host cells such as the yolk sac of embryonated eggs, experimental animals (e.g., guinea pigs), or cell culture (e.g., Vero cells and L cells). Rickettsiae are not a defective or degenerate life form but rather are highly adapted for intracellular survival with effective transport systems and metabolic enzymes.[14] Among the protein antigens of *R. rickettsii*, two surface proteins (outer membrane proteins A [OmpA, 190 kD] and B [OmpB, 135 kD) contain heat-labile epitopes, some of which are species-specific, forming the antigenic basis for serotyping, and others are shared among varied numbers of the members of the group.[15–17] The lipopolysaccharide of SFG rickettsiae contains highly immunogenic antigens that are strongly cross-reactive among all members of the group and cross-react to a lesser extent with *Rickettsia typhi* and *Rickettsia prowazekii*. However, antibodies to lipopolysaccharide do not confer protection against experimental infection of animals.[15] T lymphocytes (particularly CD8 cells) are important effectors of immune clearance of rickettsiae, and interferon-γ and tumor necrosis factor-α activate infected endothelial cells to kill intracellular rickettsiae.[18–22] The OmpA cell wall protein is an important immunogen.[23–25]

Epidemiology

The role of a tick bite in the transmission of RMSF was demonstrated by McCalla and Brereton and reported in 1908[9]; a tick obtained from a patient suffering from RMSF transmitted the disease to two volunteers. The seasonal distribution of RMSF parallels tick activity. The tick is both the vector and the main reservoir.[26] *Dermacentor variabilis*, the American dog tick, is the prevalent vector in the eastern two thirds of the United States and the Far West; *Dermacentor andersoni*, the Rocky Mountain wood tick, in the western states; *Rhipicephalus sanguineus*, in Mexico; and *Amblyomma cajennense*, in Central and South America (see Chapter 287 for illustrations of ticks). Causes of the variation in infection rates among populations of ticks are not clear, although humidity, climatic variations, human activities altering the vegetation and fauna, and the use of insecticides have been suspected to play a role in the fluctuation of the prevalence of human rickettsiosis.

Rickettsia rickettsii is transmitted trans-stadially (stage to stage) and transovarially in ticks, thus maintaining the agent in nature. The likelihood of low-level attrition of the infected ticks due to injury by pathogenic rickettsiae most likely explains the very low prevalence of these rickettsiae in ticks compared with apparently nonpathogenic rickettsiae and implies that horizontal transmission through vertebrate hosts would also be necessary for the maintenance of *R. rickettsii* in nature.[27] In fact, in most mammals rickettsemia is of very short duration and low titer and allows infection of only a small proportion of ticks.[26] Of the three tick stages, larva, nymph, and adult, only the adult *Dermacentor* ticks feed on humans. The prevalence of pathogenic rickettsiae in various populations of ticks is variable. Many rickettsiae of unknown pathogenicity have been isolated and characterized in the United States, including *Rickettsia bellii, Rickettsia montana, Rickettsia rhipicephali*, and *Rickettsia parkeri*.[12, 28] These rickettsiae and the uncultivated *Rickettsia peacockii*[29] may compete for the ecologic niche by an interference mechanism that inhibits the establishment of infection of ticks with *R. rickettsii*.[30]

The tick transmits the disease to humans during a prolonged period of feeding that may last for 1 to 2 weeks. The bite is painless and frequently unnoticed. After the attached tick has fed for 6 to 10 hours, rickettsiae begin to be injected from the salivary glands. An even longer period may be required for reactivation of rickettsial virulence in unfed ticks. Humans may also be infected by exposure to infective tick hemolymph during the removal of ticks from persons or domestic animals, especially when the tick is crushed between the fingers.

Although *R. rickettsii* has rarely been recovered from feral animals, serum antibodies are detected in many of these animals, and the prevalence of antibodies in dogs correlates with the prevalence of human cases in the particular area.

Laboratory-acquired infection transmitted by infectious aerosols or parenteral inoculation of *R. rickettsii* may be prevented by careful technique, biohazard containment hoods, masks, and gloves.[31]

The considerable fluctuation in the annual number of patients with RMSF in the United States (Fig. 175–1) may reflect cyclic changes in the ecology of the tick-rickettsia relationship.[32, 33] The increase in the infection rate that occurred between 1969 and 1977 may have several hypothetic explanations: an increase in the infected tick population or tick contact with humans, an increase in the interest of physicians in the disease, and the development of more sensitive, specific serologic tools. The fall in incidence in 1949 followed the introduction of effective antibiotics, and the increased incidence in the 1970s coincided with a decline in the use of tetracycline as a first-choice antibiotic for many other infections. These correlations imply a substantial occurrence of undiagnosed cases aborted by early treatment.

From the 1870s until 1931, RMSF was recognized as existing only in the western United States. At present, the prevalence of the disease is higher in the South Atlantic states (0.83 per 100,000 inhabitants) and in the west south-central region (0.53 per 100,000) than in the Rocky Mountain states (Fig. 175–2). The local prevalence in highly endemic areas such as North Carolina has been as high 14.59 per 100,000.[34] Moreover, although the incidence of infection may be decreasing in one area, it may be increasing simultaneously in another region. The report of a focus in the South Bronx emphasizes that the ecologic conditions permitting the establishment of RMSF are widely distributed.[35] Most cases are diagnosed during late spring and summer. However, especially in the southern states, a few cases also occur during the winter.[36]

In the southern states, the incidence is highest among children and persons who are known to be exposed more often to ticks than are matched controls.[34] In the western states, owing to transmission by the wood tick *D. andersoni*, a higher proportion of men contract the disease because of occupational factors. The case-fatality rates are significantly higher for nonwhites than for whites, for males than for females, and for patients older than 30 years than for persons younger than 30.[37] The disease also occurs in Central and South America, where it is currently largely unrecognized and possibly misdiagnosed as dengue or other febrile exanthems.[5, 38]

Serosurveys of humans have been conducted to evaluate the prevalence of the disease.[39] The specificity of the assays has been questioned because of cross-reactivity of *R. rickettsii* with other rickettsiae and other bacteria, some of the methods employed, and the selection of minimal significant titers. A recent prospective study of soldiers under conditions of intense tick exposure revealed a high rate of asymptomatic seroconversion.[40] The exact *Rickettsia* species or other antigenic stimulus of the antibody response remains to be determined, but *R. amblyommii* would appear a more likely candidate than *R. rickettsii*.

Pathogenesis

Rickettsiae introduced into the skin apparently spread via lymphatics and small blood vessels to the systemic and pulmonary circulation where, by means of an OmpA and possibly other surface-exposed rickettsial proteins and rickettsial phospholipase, they attach to and induce their phagocytosis by their target cells, the vascular endothelium, to establish numerous disseminated foci of infection.[41–44] After entry by induced phagocytosis, the rickettsiae escape rapidly from the phagosome[45] into the cytosol and less frequently invade the nucleus. Rickettsiae proliferate intracellularly by binary fission and are released from the infected cells via long thin cell projections either extracellularly or into the adjoining cell.[46, 47] The movement of spotted fever rickettsiae in the cytoplasm and into these projections from which they are released is caused by propulsion by the host cell's actin filaments.[48, 49] The consequence of cell-to-cell spread in the body is a focal network of hundreds of contiguous infected endothelial cells corresponding to the lesions (e.g., maculopapular rash). The presence of greater quantities of rickettsiae in damaged

FIGURE 175–1. Rocky Mountain spotted fever rates per year in the United States from 1920 to 1991.

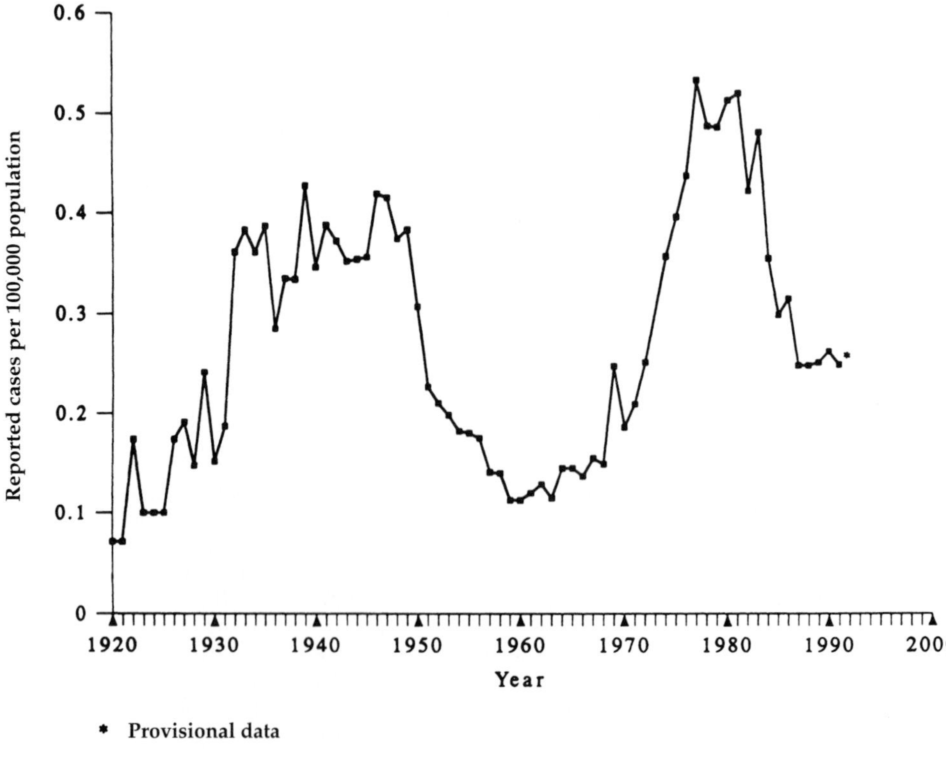

FIGURE 175–2. Reported Rocky Mountain spotted fever cases per 1 million population per year in the United States from 1981 to 1991.

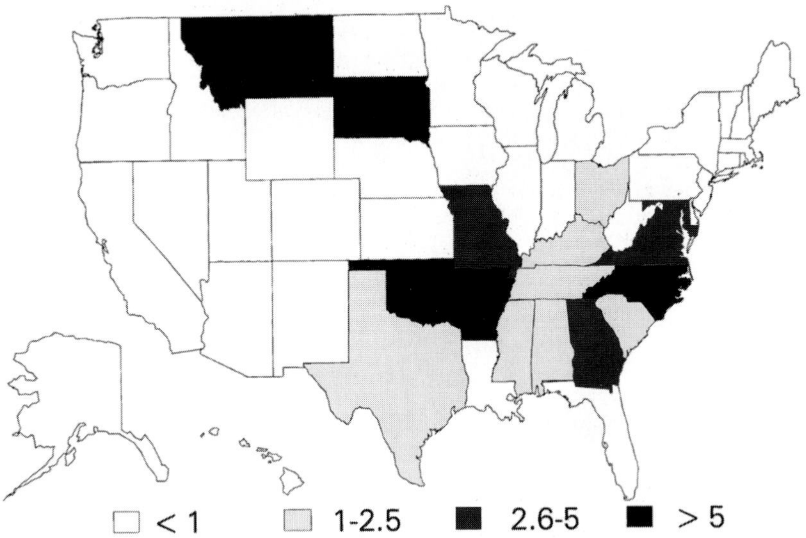

cells supports the concept of direct cell injury.[46] Plaque formation in vitro as well as the pathologic findings indicates that rickettsiae directly injure the infected cells.[50] There are no convincing data to support the activity of endotoxin or exotoxin as a pathogenic mechanism. In vitro studies suggest that rickettsial injury to the host cell may be caused by free radical–induced damage to host cell membranes, rickettsial phospholipase A_2 activity, and protease activity.[51–57] The major pathophysiologic effect of endothelial cell injury is increased vascular permeability, which in turn results in edema, hypovolemia, hypotension, and hypoalbuminemia.[58] Hyponatremia seems to be caused by the secretion of antidiuretic hormone as an appropriate response to hypovolemia.[59] High quantities of rickettsiae infecting the pulmonary microcirculation increase the vascular permeability and cause noncardiogenic pulmonary edema.[60, 61] Vascular injury and the subsequent host lymphohistiocytic response correspond to the distribution of rickettsiae and include interstitial pneumonia, interstitial myocarditis, perivascular glial nodules of the central nervous system, and similar vascular lesions in the skin, gastrointestinal tract, pancreas, liver, skeletal muscles, and kidneys.[41] However, even severe vascular injury rarely leads to clinically significant hemorrhage. Platelets are consumed locally in numerous foci of infection; subsequently, thrombocytopenia is observed in 32 to 52% of patients.[62, 63] Increased adherence of platelets to infected endothelial cells has also been demonstrated in vitro.[64] A procoagulant state occurs, including endothelial injury, release of procoagulant components, activation of the coagulation cascade with thrombin generation, platelet activation, increased antifibrinolytic factors, consumption of natural anticoagulants, activation of the kallikrein-kinin system, and secretion of coagulation-promoting cytokines.[65–72] These findings are supported by results of numerous studies of endothelial cells in culture such as the demonstration that tissue factor is secreted by rickettsia-infected endothelial cells,[73, 74] but true disseminated intravascular coagulation occurs only rarely, and occlusive vascular thrombosis is not the basic pathophysiologic event.

Clinical Manifestations

The incubation period of RMSF ranges from 2 to 14 days, with a median of 7 days.[37] Variation in the incubation time may be related in part to the inoculum size. The disease usually begins with fever, myalgia, and headache, most likely the effects of proinflammatory cytokines (Table 175–1). The temperature is greater than 102°F in 63% of patients during the first 3 days and in 90% later.[62] The variable incidence of reported headache and myalgias in different series may be related to the proportion of young children, who may not complain of pain. Other signs and symptoms are frequently prominent early in the course before the onset of rash. Gastrointestinal involvement with nausea, vomiting, abdominal pain, diarrhea, and abdominal tenderness occurs in substantial portions of patients and may suggest gastroenteritis or an acute surgical abdomen.

The rash, the major diagnostic sign, appears in a small fraction of patients on the first day of the disease and in only 49% during the first 3 days, usually appearing 3 to 5 days after the onset of fever and occurring in 84 to 91%, of patients overall. Rocky Mountain

TABLE 175–1 Symptoms, Signs, and Laboratory Data in Rocky Mountain Spotted Fever, Boutonneuse Fever, and African Tick Bite Fever

Feature	RMSF (%)	BF (%)	ATBF (%)
Fever	99–100	100	100
Headache	79–91	56	
Rash	88–90	97	30
Tache noire	<1	72	100
Multiple eschars	0	0	60
Myalgia	72–83	36	60
Nausea and/or vomiting	56–60		
Abdominal pain	34–52		
Petechial rash	45–49	10	
Conjunctivitis	30	9	
Lymphadenopathy	27		90
Stupor	21–26	10	
Diarrhea	19–20		
Edema	18–20		
Ataxia	5–18		
Meningismus	18	11	
Splenomegaly	14–16	6	
Hepatomegaly	12–15	13	
Jaundice	8–9	2	
Pneumonitis	12–17		
Cough	33	10	
Dyspnea		21	
Coma	9–10		
Seizures	8		
Shock and/or hypotension	7–17		
Decreased hearing	7		
Arrhythmia	7–16		
Myocarditis	5–26	11	
Death	4–8	2.5	
Increased AST level	36–62	39	
Thrombocytopenia	32–52	35	
Anemia	5–24		
Hyponatremia	19–56	25	
Azotemia	12–14	6	

Abbreviations: AST, Aspartate aminotransferase; ATBF, African tick bite fever; BF, boutonneuse fever; RMSF, Rocky Mountain spotted fever.
Data from refs. 62, 63, and 135.

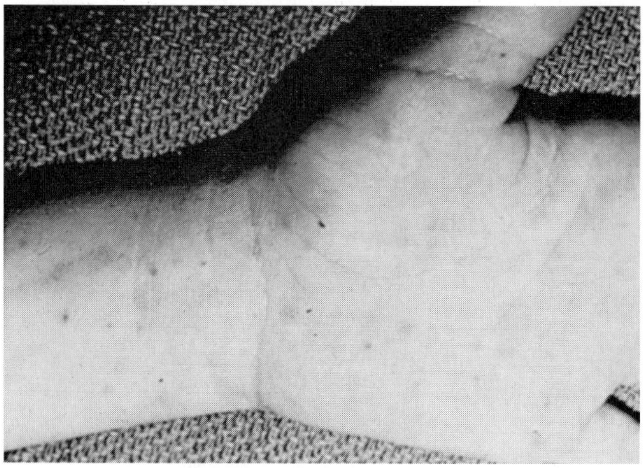

FIGURE 175–3. The wrist and palm manifest the rash of Rocky Mountain spotted fever with central petechiae in some of the maculopapules.

"spotless" fever occurs more often in older patients and in black patients.[62] A delay in diagnosis is at times associated with the absence or late onset of rash. The rash typically begins around the wrists and ankles but may start on the trunk or be diffuse at the onset. Involvement of the palms and soles is considered characteristic yet occurs in only 36 to 82 of patients who have a rash and often appears late in the course (Figs. 175–3 and 175–4). Skin necrosis or gangrene develops in only 4% of patients as a result of rickettsial damage to the microcirculation.[63] Gangrene affects the digits or limbs and occasionally necessitates amputation. A careful examination seldom reveals an eschar at the site of the tick bite in RMSF.[75] Headache is usually quite severe. Focal neurologic deficits, transient deafness, meningismus, and photophobia may suggest meningitis or meningoencephalitis. The cerebrospinal fluid contains increased leukocytes in one third of the patients, with either lymphocytic or polymorphonuclear predominance[63]; the cerebrospinal fluid protein concentration is increased in one third of the patients. However, the glucose concentration is low in the cerebrospinal fluid of only 8% of patients. The electroencephalogram may show diffuse cortical dysfunction. Generally, neurologic involvement portends a bad outcome. Among 37 patients followed for 1 to 8 years after acute RMSF including cases in the preantibiotic era, 21 had residual neurologic abnormalities.[76] These sequelae were headache and other subjective findings, but 12 had electroencephalographic abnormalities. These sequelae

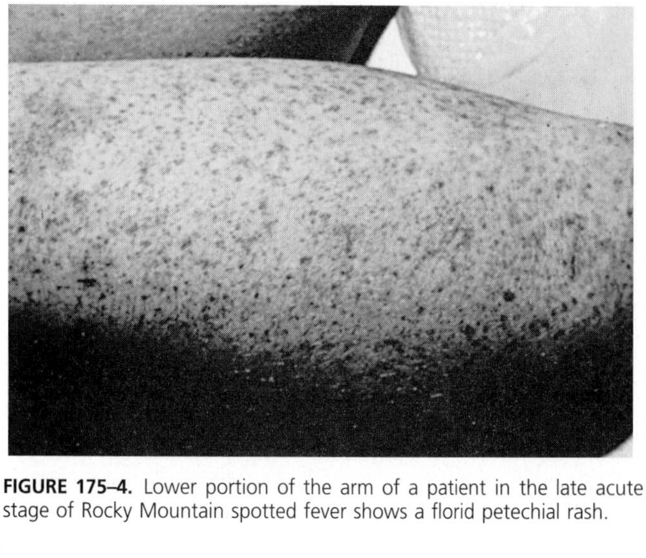

FIGURE 175–4. Lower portion of the arm of a patient in the late acute stage of Rocky Mountain spotted fever shows a florid petechial rash.

occur less often in patients with early antibiotic treatment. On funduscopic examination, retinal vein engorgement, arterial occlusion, flame hemorrhages, and papilledema without increased cerebrospinal fluid pressure have been noted. These changes may reflect retinal vasculitis with increased permeability and focal thrombosis. Renal failure is an important problem in severe RMSF.[77] Prerenal azotemia related to hypovolemia responds to intravenous hydration; however, acute tubular necrosis may require hemodialysis. Pulmonary involvement is suggested by cough and radiologic evidence of changes including alveolar infiltrates, interstitial pneumonia, and pleural effusion.[78] Pulmonary edema with impairment of pulmonary function or adult respiratory distress syndrome may require oxygen therapy and ventilatory assistance. Echocardiographic studies reveal minimal myocardial dysfunction,[79] and normal pulmonary capillary wedge pressure measurements document the noncardiogenic nature of the pulmonary edema.

In classic RMSF, death occurs 8 to 15 days after the onset of symptoms when appropriate therapy is not given in a timely manner. In fulminant RMSF, death occurs within the first 5 days. Several features account for the extreme difficulty in the diagnosis of fulminant RMSF: the course is rapid, the rash develops shortly before death if at all, antibodies to *R. rickettsii* do not have time to develop, and the pathologic lesions even appear different, containing more thrombi and lacking the characteristic lymphohistiocytic component.[80] Fulminant RMSF is more often observed in black males with glucose-6-phosphate dehydrogenase deficiency, apparently owing to an unidentified secondary effect of the usually moderate degree of hemolysis. Other risk factors for a lethal outcome in classic RMSF include older age, male gender, and possibly alcoholism.

Characteristic laboratory data may support the clinical diagnosis of classic RMSF but are relatively nonspecific.[62, 63] The white blood cell count is generally normal, but increased quantities of immature myeloid cells occur frequently. Anemia is observed in 5 to 30%. Thrombocytopenia occurs in the more severe cases, but also in some patients with mild disease. Coagulopathy with prolonged coagulation times and decreased concentrations of fibrinogen and other clotting factors occurs infrequently, as the hemostatic system usually functions effectively to prevent severe bleeding from the vascular lesions and generally does not contribute importantly to the pathologic state. Hyponatremia is observed in half of the patients with RMSF. Increased concentrations of serum lactate dehydrogenase, creatine phosphokinase, and other enzymes are related to diffuse tissue injury including multifocal rhabdomyonecrosis.

The prognosis in RMSF is largely related to the timeliness of initiation of appropriate therapy. The intervals between the onset of disease and the appearance of the rash, clinical diagnosis, and effective antibiotic treatment are significantly longer in patients dying than in patients surviving.[37, 62] In fatal cases, patients more frequently have hepatomegaly, jaundice, stupor, and renal insufficiency and report less often a history of tick exposure.[81] Patients who survive RMSF have solid immunity to *R. rickettsii*. Long-term sequelae are mainly neurologic or due to a loss of limbs.[82–84]

Diagnosis

The diagnosis of RMSF before the onset of the rash is clinical and epidemiologic. The differential diagnosis at the first consultation includes typhoid fever, measles, rubella, respiratory tract infection, gastroenteritis, acute surgical abdomen, enteroviral infection, meningococcemia, disseminated gonococcal infection, secondary syphilis, leptospirosis, immune complex vasculitis, idiopathic thrombocytopenic purpura, thrombotic thrombocytopenic purpura, infectious mononucleosis, drug reaction, and other rickettsial diseases. The laboratory diagnosis of RMSF may be achieved by the isolation of *R. rickettsii* from the blood.[85, 86] Few laboratories undertake isolation of *R. rickettsii* in guinea pigs, embryonated hen's eggs, or cell culture because of the biohazard; however, a centrifugation-enhanced microcell culture system, the shell vial assay used for cytomegalovirus isolation, has been successfully applied to rickettsial isolation.[86] Some hospitals and public health laboratories are able to demonstrate *R. rickettsii* in cutaneous biopsy specimens by immunohistochemical analysis, a timely diagnostic method during the acute phase for patients with a rash.[87–93] Serologic examination, the usual method for confirmation of the diagnosis, is retrospective, serum antibodies becoming detectable during convalescence.[85, 94] Serologic examination does not allow discrimination of the particular causative SFG rickettsia unless cross-absorption with selected antigens is performed.[90] The Weil-Felix test using *Proteus* OX-19 and OX-2 agglutination is not to be relied on. This method lacks sensitivity and specificity. Antibodies to specific rickettsial antigens are detected by indirect immunofluorescence, latex agglutination, and enzyme immunoassay. The diagnostic titer is 1:64 for indirect immunofluorescence and latex agglutination.[85] Indirect immunofluorescence is the most sensitive and specific. Indirect immunofluorescence, latex agglutination, and a dot-enzyme immunoassay have commercially available reagents. Polymerase chain reaction amplification of *R. rickettsii* DNA has not proved to be a sensitive diagnostic method using blood samples except for late in the course, particularly in fatal cases[95, 96]; however, it has been successfully applied to skin biopsied during spotted fever rickettsioses and to ticks.[90] The primers used amplify genes of the 17-kD protein citrate synthase and rickettsial *ompA* and allow the identification of any rickettsia.[97] Early clinical diagnosis remains essential for this life-threatening disease.

Treatment

Since the introduction of chloramphenicol and the tetracyclines, including doxycycline, the lethality of the disease has decreased dramatically, but mortality remains significant at 5%.[81] In vitro and in ovo, *R. rickettsii* is susceptible not only to chloramphenicol and tetracycline, but also to rifampin. Some new quinolone compounds such as ciprofloxacin, pefloxacin, and the macrolide clarithromycin have antirickettsial effects in vitro, but a lack of clinical experience with these agents precludes recommending their use for RMSF.[98, 99] Dogs infected with *R. rickettsii* were effectively treated with enrofloxacin. The organism is resistant to β-lactam antibiotics, aminoglycosides, and trimethoprim-sulfamethoxazole. Erythromycin has a minimal inhibitory concentration of 3 to 8 μg/ml and is not effective.

RMSF responds to treatment with oral tetracycline (25 to 50 mg/kg/day) or chloramphenicol (50 to 75 mg/kg/day) given in four divided doses. Doxycycline, 100 mg every 12 hours, is quite effective. The selected antibiotic is usually administered for 7 days, continuing for 2 days after the patient has become afebrile. A single-day treatment with 200 mg of doxycycline has been proved to be safe and efficient in adults and children with Mediterranean spotted fever but has not been tested and is not recommended in RMSF.[99] Treatment should be given intravenously in patients with nausea and vomiting and in those seriously ill. Doxycycline or another tetracycline is considered the drug of choice, but chloramphenicol is preferred during pregnancy because of the effects of tetracycline on fetal bones and teeth. Although tetracyclines have been avoided in young children because of concerns for staining the teeth, it is recommended that doxycycline be used for suspected RMSF in children of all ages because of the life-threatening nature of RMSF and the unlikelihood that a single course of doxycycline would stain the teeth.[100] Avoiding therapeutic delay is critical for the prognosis.[37, 101] Severely ill patients require intensive supportive care. Fluid maintenance is critical in order to maintain organ perfusion. Because of the increased vascular permeability and the risk of extravasation of fluid into pulmonary alveoli, a Swan-Ganz catheter may be needed to monitor the hemodynamics in some patients. Glucocorticosteroids are sometimes given to severely ill patients, but there has been no documentation of efficacy, and they are not recommended. In experimentally infected dogs treated simultaneously with doxycycline, there were no detrimental effects of prednisolone treatment.[102]

Prevention

Although no vaccine is available currently, the immunodominant surface proteins have been identified, and the genes for the major surface protein antigens (OmpA and OmpB) of *R. rickettsii* and other SFG rickettsiae have been cloned and sequenced.[103–106] Immunization of guinea pigs with OmpA expressed in baculovirus provided protective immunity against a virulent challenge.[24, 25] Further development of an effective vaccine should lead to immunization of high-risk patients in endemic areas.

Currently, the best means of prevention remains the avoidance of contact with ticks by the use of repellents and protective clothing. In the hot weather often associated with the tick season, these techniques are often impractical. Regular checks of the body including scalp, pubic, and axillary hair allow removal of the tick before rickettsial transmission. To remove an attached tick, one may use forceps to detach the intact tick without leaving any mouth parts in the skin. The tick bite wound should be cleansed.

OTHER SPOTTED FEVER GROUP RICKETTSIOSES

Among the eight other SFG rickettsial species known to be pathogenic for humans (*R. conorii, R. sibirica, R. japonica, R. australis, R. honei, R. africae, R. slovaca*, and *R. akari*), the first seven are considered to be transmitted by tick bite. The last, *R. akari*, is discussed in Chapter 176. There are also numerous distinct species and serotypes of SFG rickettsiae (e.g., *R. massiliae, R. helvetica, R. montana, R. rhipicephali, R. parkeri*, and *R. aeschlimannii*) that have been identified only in ticks.[12, 107–109] Although some of these are likely to be nonpathogenic, others may eventually be found to cause human infections, even if only a short nonexanthematous febrile illness or even asymptomatic seroconversion. *Rickettsia conorii* infection has been designated by many geographic names: Marseilles fever, Mediterranean spotted fever, Kenya tick typhus, and Indian tick typhus. *Rickettsia conorii*, a typical SFG rickettsia, has extremely high genetic homology with *R. rickettsii*. However, *R. conorii* exhibits more intraspecies antigenic and genetic diversity than does *R. rickettsii*.[4, 106, 110] There are also cross-reactive protein and lipopolysaccharide antigens, and cross-protection is shared among *R. conorii, R. sibirica*, and *R. rickettsii*.[15–17, 111–113] The conformational antigens on the surface proteins of SFG rickettsiae also contain species- and even strain-specific epitopes, for example, the antigenically different strains of *R. conorii* that cause Israeli spotted fever and Astrakhan fever.[15, 16, 111, 114, 115]

During the 1970s and 1980s, an increased incidence of spotted fever rickettsioses was noticed in many parts of the world, particularly in Spain, France, Italy, Israel, and Australia. Spotted fever rickettsioses have also been described recently in China, Thailand, Japan, Mexico, Australia, and Zimbabwe.[3–8, 116–118] Historically, boutonneuse fever was first described by Conor and Bruch in 1909 in Tunisia, although the *tache noire* ("black spot"), the eschar at the site of the bite, was not described until 1923 by Olmer and Pieri in Marseille. *Rickettsia conorii* has been identified in India, Pakistan, Israel, Russia, Georgia, Ukraine, Ethiopia, Kenya, South Africa, Morocco, and southern Europe. *Rickettsia sibirica* has been documented in Russia, China, Mongolia, and Pakistan. *Rickettsia australis* is limited to eastern Australia, and *R. honei*, the etiologic agent of a newly recognized spotted fever rickettsiosis, has been identified thus far only on Flinders Island, Australia, although it is very closely related to the previously described Thai tick typhus rickettsia, which was isolated from a pool of larval *Ixodes* and *Rhipicephalus* ticks from Thailand.[117, 119–121] The etiologic rickettsia of Japanese spotted fever is another novel species, *R. japonica*; however, the SFG rickettsia of southeastern Asia has yet to be determined. *Rickettsia africae* has been studied principally in Zimbabwe, where there is a high seroprevalence of antibodies to SFG rickettsiae.[122] That infection is likely to be very prevalent in much of sub-Saharan Africa, where the vector ticks, *Amblyomma hebraeum* and *Amblyomma variegatum*, are present.[118, 123] The identification of *R. africae* infections in Guadeloupe, where it apparently conforms to the distribution of *Amblyomma africanum*, and the very close genetic and antigenic relationship of *R. africae* and *R. parkeri* suggest that *R. parkeri* infections should be investigated in the United States.[4, 17, 124] The disease is frequently spotless, but when a rash is observed, it is often vesicular. African tick bite fever is the only tick-transmitted rickettsiosis in which several tache noire inoculation eschars are observed in more than one half of patients.[124–126] *Rickettsia africae* in often observed in patients who have hunted or traveled in the bush in southern Africa. The attack rate in an exposed group can be as high as 30%.[126, 127] Other rickettsioses have been reported recently in Europe, such as infection with *R. slovaca* and with another organism very closely related to *R. sibirica*.[128, 129] The epidemiology of boutonneuse fever and ecology of *R. conorii* are closely related to those of ticks, particularly *Rhipicephalus sanguineus. Rickettsia conorii* is maintained transovarially in ticks and is transmitted to humans by tick bite. The frequent absence of a history of tick bite is likely owing to transmission by the immature larvae and nymphs, which are often not noticed. Cases occur mainly in warm months, with the peak incidence in July, August, and September in many Mediterranean locations. A substantial number of imported cases occur in travelers returning to the United States and northern Europe from Africa and southern Europe. In Russia and northern China, *R. sibirica* has been isolated from humans and ticks. SFG rickettsiae have been isolated from six species of ticks in northern Asia as well as from wild mammals. Transovarial transmission is an important mechanism of survival of *R. sibirica* in nature.

The pathogenic basis for tissue injury in the spotted fevers is well elucidated in the tache noire or eschar at the site of the infective tick bite. Dermal and epidermal necrosis and perivascular edema are the consequences of endothelial injury by *R. conorii*.[130] Necropsies in fatal cases of boutonneuse fever reveal disseminated vascular infection and injury by *R. conorii* including meningoencephalitis and vascular lesions in kidneys, lungs, gastrointestinal tract, liver, pancreas, heart, spleen, and skin.[131, 132] Hepatic biopsy specimens reveal focal hepatocellular necrosis and granuloma-like lesions.[133] Boutonneuse fever is by no means uniformly a benign illness; in France, Israel, and Spain, the death rate among hospitalized patients ranges from 1.4 to 5.6%, similar to that of RMSF.[134, 135] Boutonneuse fever is associated with a procoagulant state,[67, 68, 70] and 9.6% of cases are complicated by deep venous thrombosis late in the course.[136] Plasma levels of tumor necrosis factor rise during infection.[66, 69]

After a mean incubation period of 7 days, fever, myalgias, and headache characterize the onset (see Table 175–1). A careful clinical examination may reveal a tache noire, which facilitates the clinical diagnosis. Severe disease resembling RMSF occurs in patients with underlying conditions such as diabetes mellitus or cardiac insufficiency, alcoholism, old age, and glucose-6-phosphate dehydrogenase deficiency. The disease is milder in children. As with RMSF, the diagnosis may be established by immunohistologic demonstration of *R. conorii* in skin biopsy material to which polymerase chain reaction has also been applied for *R. conorii, R. africae, R. slovaca* (an *R. sibirica*–like organism), and *R. japonica*.[87–93, 128, 130, 131, 137–139] A novel approach that can be used to diagnose boutonneuse fever before the onset of rash is immunofluorescent detection of *R. conorii* in circulating endothelial cells captured by immunomagnetic beads coated with a monoclonal antibody to the human endothelial cell surface.[86, 140] A timely diagnosis can also be established by isolating *R. conorii* in a shell vial cell culture system.[86] During the convalescent phase, production of antibodies to SFG rickettsiae is demonstrated by using microimmunofluorescence, latex agglutination, enzyme immunoassay, Western blot, or complement fixation.[141, 142] Successful treatment is achieved with doxycycline (200 mg/day), tetracycline (25 mg/kg/day), chloramphenicol (2 g/day for 7 to 10 days), or ciprofloxacin (1.5 g/day for 5 to 7 days).[99, 143, 144]

Single-dose treatment with 200 mg of doxycycline has been proposed as well as treatment with josamycin, a macrolide compound, for children and pregnant women.[99]

REFERENCES

1. Roux V, Raoult D. Phylogenetic analysis of the genus *Rickettsia* by 16S rDNA sequencing. Res Microbiol. 1995;146:385–396.
2. Stothard DR, Fuerst PA. Evolutionary analysis of the spotted fever and typhus groups of *Rickettsia* using 16S rRNA gene sequences. Syst Appl Microbiol. 1995;18:52–61.
3. Stenos J, Roux V, Walker D, et al. *Rickettsia honei* sp. nov., the aetiological agent of Flinders Island spotted fever in Australia. Int J Syst Bacteriol. 1998;48:1399–1404.
4. Raoult D, Roux V. Rickettsioses as paradigms of new or emerging infectious diseases. Clin Microbiol Rev. 1997;10:694–719.
5. Zavala-Velazquez JE, Yu X, Walker DH. Unrecognized spotted fever group rickettsiosis masquerading as dengue fever in Mexico. Am J Trop Med Hyg 1996;55:157–159.
6. Sirisanthana T, Pinyopornpanit V, Sirisanthana V, et al. First cases of spotted fever group rickettsiosis in Thailand. Am J Trop Med Hyg. 1994;50:682–686.
7. Cohen MAH, Cheng AFB, Leung NWY. A fatal case of rickettsial spotted fever in Hong Kong—Lion Rock fever. J Hong Kong Med Assoc. 1989;41:185–186.
8. Tseng RY, Ho AK, Li CK, et al. Spotted fever in Hong Kong. Ann Trop Paediatr. 1992; 12: 255–257.
9. Weiss E. History of rickettsiology. In: Walker DH, ed. Biology of Rickettsial Diseases, v. 1. Boca Raton, Fla: CRC; 1988:15–32.
10. Ricketts HT. A micro-organism which apparently has a specific relationship to Rocky Mountain spotted fever. JAMA. 1909;52:379–380.
11. Wolbach SB. Studies on Rocky Mountain spotted fever. J Med Res. 1919;41:2–197.
12. Weiss E, Moulder JW. The rickettsias and chlamydias. In: Kreig NR, Holt JG, eds. Bergey's Manual of Systematic Bacteriology. Baltimore: Williams & Wilkins; 1984:687–739.
13. Roux V, Raoult D. Genotypic identification and phylogenetic analysis of the spotted fever group rickettsiae by pulsed-field gel electrophoresis. J Bacteriol. 1993; 175: 4895–4904.
14. Austin FE, Winkler HH. Relationship of rickettsial physiology and composition to the rickettsia-host cell interactions. In: Walker DH, ed. Biology of Rickettsial Diseases, v. 2. Boca Raton, Fla: CRC Press; 1988:29–49.
15. Li H, Lenz B, Walker DH. Protective monoclonal antibodies recognize heat-labile epitopes on surface proteins of spotted fever group rickettsiae. Infect Immun. 1988;56:2587–2593.
16. Anacker RL, Mann RE, Gonzales C. Reactivity of monoclonal antibodies to *Rickettsia rickettsii* with spotted fever and typhus group rickettsiae. J Clin Microbiol. 1987;25:167–171.
17. Xu WB, Raoult D. Taxonomic relationships among spotted fever group rickettsiae as revealed by antigenic analysis with monoclonal antibodies. J Clin Microbiol. 1998;36:887–896.
18. Manor E, Sarov I. Inhibition of *Rickettsia conorii* growth by recombinant tumor necrosis factor alpha: Enhancement of inhibition by gamma interferon. Infect Immun. 1990;58:1886–1889.
19. Walker DH, Popov VL, Crocquet-Valdes PA, et al. Cytokine-induced, nitric oxide–dependent, intracellular antirickettsial activity of mouse endothelial cells. Lab Invest. 1997;76:129–138.
20. Feng H-M, Popov VL, Walker DH. Depletion of interferon gamma and tumor necrosis factor alpha in mice with *Rickettsia conorii*–infected endothelium: Impairment of rickettsicidal nitric oxide production resulting in fatal, overwhelming rickettsial disease. Infect Immun. 1994; 62: 1952–1960.
21. Walker DH, Popov VL, Welsh CJR, et al. Mechanisms of rickettsial killing within cytokine-stimulated endothelial cells. In: Kazár J, Toman R, eds. Rickettsiae and Rickettsial Diseases. Proceedings of the Vth International Symposium. Bratislava: Slovak Academy of Sciences; 1996:51–56.
22. Feng H-M, Popov VL, Yuoh G, et al. Role of T-lymphocyte subsets in immunity to spotted fever group rickettsiae. J Immunol. 1997;158:5314–5320.
23. McDonald GA, Anacker RL, Garjian K. Cloned gene of *Rickettsia rickettsii* surface antigen: Candidate vaccine for Rocky Mountain spotted fever. Science. 1987; 235: 83–85.
24. Sumner JW, Sims KG, Jones DC, et al. Protection of guinea-pigs from experimental Rocky Mountain spotted fever by immunization with baculovirus-expressed *Rickettsia rickettsii* rOmpA protein. Vaccine. 1995;13:29–35.
25. Vishwanath S, McDonald GA, Watkins NG. A recombinant *Rickettsia conorii* vaccine protects guinea pigs from experimental boutonneuse fever and Rocky Mountain spotted fever. Infect Immun. 1990;58:646–653.
26. Burgdorfer W. Ecological and epidemiological considerations of Rocky Mountain spotted fever and scrub typhus. In: Walker DH, ed. Biology of Rickettsial Diseases, v. 1. Boca Raton, Fla: CRC Press; 1988:33–50.
27. McDade JE, Newhouse VF. Natural history of *Rickettsia rickettsii*. Annu Rev Microbiol. 1986;40:287–309.
28. Philip RN, Casper EA, Anacker RL, et al. *Rickettsia bellii* sp nov: A tick borne rickettsia, widely distributed in the United States, that is distinct from the spotted fever and typhus biogroups. Int J Syst Bacteriol. 1983; 33:94–106.
29. Niebylski ML, Schrumpf ME, Burgdorfer W, et al. *Rickettsia peacockii* sp nov, a new species infecting wood ticks, *Dermacentor andersoni*, in western Montana. Int J Syst Bacteriol. 1997;47:446–452.

30. Burgdorfer W, Hayes SF, Mavros AJ. Nonpathogenic rickettsiae in *Dermacentor andersoni*: A limiting factor for the distribution of *Rickettsia rickettsii*. In: Burgdorfer W, Anacker RL, eds. Rickettsiae and Rickettsial Diseases. New York: Academic Press; 1981:585–594.
31. Johnson JE, Kadull PJ. Rocky Mountain spotted fever acquired in a laboratory. N Engl J Med 1967;227:842–846.
32. Hattwick MAW, O'Brien RJ, Hanson DF. Rocky Mountain spotted fever: Epidemiology of an increasing problem. Ann Intern Med 1976;84:732–739.
33. Centers for Disease Control and Prevention. Rocky Mountain spotted fever and human ehrlichiosis—United States, 1989. MMWR Morb Mortal Wkly Rep. 1990;39:281–284.
34. Wilfert CM, McCormack JN, Kleeman K, et al. Epidemiology of Rocky Mountain spotted fever as determined by active surveillance. J Infect Dis. 1984;150:469–479.
35. Salgo MP, Telzak EE, Currie B, et al. A focus of Rocky Mountain spotted fever within New York City. N Engl J Med. 1988;318:1345–1348.
36. Lange JV, Walker DH, Wester TB. Documented Rocky Mountain spotted fever in wintertime. JAMA. 1982;247:2403–2404.
37. Hattwick MAW, Retailliau H, O'Brien RJ, et al. Fatal Rocky Mountain spotted fever. JAMA. 1979;240:1499–1503.
38. Galvao MAM, Chamone CB, Olson JG, et al. Report of cases of spotted fever disease in Minas Gerais-State-Brazil—1981–1994. In: Kazár J, Toman R, eds. Rickettsiae and Rickettsial Diseases. Proceedings of the Vth International Symposium. Bratislava: Slovak Academy of Sciences; 1996:211–215.
39. Walker DH, Fishbein DB. Epidemiology of rickettsial diseases. Eur J Epidemiol. 1991;7:237–245.
40. Sanchez JL, Candler WH, Fishbein DB, et al. A cluster of tick-borne infections: Association with military training and asymptomatic infections due to *Rickettsia rickettsii*. Trans R Soc Trop Med Hyg. 1992;86:321–325.
41. Walker DH. Pathology and pathogenesis of the vasculotropic rickettsioses. In: Walker DH, ed. Biology of Rickettsial Diseases, v. 1. Boca Raton, Fla: CRC Press; 1988:115–138.
42. Li H, Walker DH. Characterization of rickettsial attachment to host cells by flow cytometry. Infect Immun. 1992;60:2030–2035.
43. Li H, Walker DH. rOmpA is a critical protein for the adhesion of *Rickettsia rickettsii* to host cells. Micro Pathog 1998;24:289–298.
44. Silverman DJ, Santucci LA, Meyers N, et al. Penetration of host cells by *Rickettsia rickettsii* appears to be mediated by a phospholipase of rickettsial origin. Infect Immun. 1992;60:2733–2740.
45. Teysseire N, Boudier JA, Raoult D. *Rickettsia conorii* entry into Vero cells. Infect Immun. 1995;63:366–374.
46. Walker DH, Cain BG. The rickettsial plaque: Evidence for direct cytopathic effect of *Rickettsia rickettsii*. Lab Invest. 1980:43;388–396.
47. Schaechter M, Bozeman FM, Smadel JE. Study on the growth of rickettsiae. II. Morphologic observations of living rickettsiae in tissue culture cells. Virology. 1957;3:160–172.
48. Teysseire N, Chiche-Portiche C, Raoult D. Intracellular movements of *Rickettsia conorii* and *R. typhi* based on actin polymerization. Res Microbiol. 1992;143:821–829.
49. Heinzen RA, Hayes SF, Peacock MG, et al. Directional actin polymerization associated with spotted fever group rickettsia infection of Vero cells. Infect Immun. 1993;61:1926–1935.
50. Walker DH, Firth WT, Edgell CJS. Human endothelial cell culture plaques induced by *Rickettsia rickettsii*. Infect Immun. 1982;37:301–306.
51. Silverman DJ, Santucci LA. Potential for free radical–induced lipid peroxidation as a cause of endothelial cell injury in Rocky Mountain spotted fever. Infect Immun. 1988;56:3110–3115.
52. Silverman DJ, Santucci LA, Sekeyova Z. Heparin protects human endothelial cells infected by *Rickettsia rickettsii*. Infect Immun. 1991;59:4505–4510.
53. Santucci LA, Gutierrez PL, Silverman DJ. *Rickettsia rickettsii* induces superoxide radical and superoxide dismutase in human endothelial cells. Infect Immun. 1992;60:5113–5118.
54. Silverman DJ, Santucci LA. A potential protective role for thiols against cell injury caused by *Rickettsia rickettsii*. Ann N Y Acad Sci. 1990;590:111–117.
55. Devamanohaoran PS, Santucci LA, Hong JE, et al. Infection of human endothelial cells by *Rickettsia rickettsii* causes a significant reduction in the levels of key enzymes involved in protection against oxidative injury. Infect Immun. 1994;62:2619–2621.
56. Walker DH, Firth WT, Ballard JG, et al. Role of phospholipase-associated penetration mechanism in cell injury by *Rickettsia rickettsii*. Infect Immun. 1983;40:840–842.
57. Walker DH, Tidwell RR, Rector TM, et al. Effect of synthetic protease inhibitors of the amidine type on cell injury by *Rickettsia rickettsii*. Antimicrob Agents Chemother. 1984;25:582–585.
58. Harrell GT, Aikawa JK. Pathogenesis of circulatory failure in Rocky Mountain spotted fever. Alteration in the blood volume and the thiocyanate space at various stages of the disease. Arch Intern Med. 1949;83:331–347.
59. Kaplowitz LG, Robertson GL. Hyponatremia in Rocky Mountain spotted fever: Role of antidiuretic hormone. Ann Intern Med. 1983;98:334–335.
60. Walker DH, Crawford CG, Cain BG. Rickettsial infection of the pulmonary microcirculation: The basis for interstitial pneumonitis in Rocky Mountain spotted fever. Hum Pathol. 1980;11:263–272.
61. Lankford HV, Glauser FL. Cardiopulmonary dynamics in a severe case of Rocky Mountain spotted fever. Arch Intern Med. 1980;140:1357–1360.
62. Helmick CG, Bernard KW, D'Angelo LJ. Rocky Mountain spotted fever: Clinical, laboratory, and epidemiological features of 262 cases. J Infect Dis. 1984;150:480–486.
63. Kaplowitz LG, Fischer JJ, Sparling PF. Rocky Mountain spotted fever: A clinical dilemma. In: Remington JB, Swartz HN, eds. Current Clinical Topics in Infectious Diseases, v. 2. New York: McGraw-Hill; 1981:89–108.
64. Silverman DJ. Adherence of platelets to human endothelial cells infected by *Rickettsia rickettsii*. J Infect Dis. 1986;153:694–700.
65. Rao AK, Schapira M, Clements ML, et al. A prospective study of platelets and plasma proteolytic systems during the early stages of Rocky Mountain spotted fever. N Engl J Med. 1988;318:1021–1028.
66. Cillari E, Milano S, D'Agostino P, et al. Depression of CD4 T cell subsets and alteration in cytokine profile in boutonneuse fever. J Infect Dis. 1996;174:1051–1057.
67. Davi G, Giammarresi C, Vigneri S, et al. Demonstration of *Rickettsia conorii*–induced coagulative and platelet activation in vivo in patients with Mediterranean spotted fever. Thromb Haemost. 1995;74:631–634.
68. George F, Brouqui P, Boffa M-C, et al. Demonstration of *Rickettsia-conorii*–induced endothelial injury in vivo by measuring circulating endothelial cells, thrombomodulin, and von Willebrand factor in patients with Mediterranean spotted fever. Blood. 1993;82:2109–2116.
69. Oristrell J, Amengual MJ, Font-Creus B, et al. Plasma levels of tumor necrosis factor-α in patients with Mediterranean spotted fever: Clinical and analytical correlations. Clin Infect Dis. 1994;19:1141–1143.
70. Vicente V, Espana F, Tabernero D, et al. Evidence of activation of the protein C pathway during acute vascular damage induced by Mediterranean spotted fever. Blood. 1991;78:416–422.
71. Vicente V, Estelles A, Moraleda JM, et al. Fibrinolytic changes during acute vascular damage induced by Mediterranean spotted fever. Fibrinolysis. 1993;7:324–329.
72. Yamada T, Harber P, Pettit GW, et al. Activation of the kallikrein-kinin system in Rocky Mountain spotted fever. Ann Intern Med. 1978;88:764–768.
73. Teysseire N, Arnoux D, George F, et al. Von Willebrand factor release and thrombomodulin and tissue factor expression in *Rickettsia conorii*–infected endothelial cells. Infect Immun. 1992;60:4388–4393.
74. Sporn LA, Haidaris PJ, Shi R, Nemerson Y, et al. *Rickettsia rickettsii* infection of cultured human endothelial cells induces tissue factor expression. Blood. 1994;83:1527–1534.
75. Walker DH, Gay RM, Valdes-Dapena M. The occurrence of eschars in Rocky Mountain spotted fever. J Am Acad Dermatol. 1981;4:571–576.
76. Rosenblum MJ, Masland RL, Harrell GT. Residual effects of rickettsial disease on the central nervous system. Arch Intern Med. 1952;90:444–445.
77. Walker DH, Mattern WD. Acute renal failure in Rocky Mountain spotted fever. Arch Intern Med. 1979;139:443–448.
78. Donohue JF. Lower respiratory tract involvement in Rocky Mountain spotted fever. Arch Intern Med. 1980;140:223–227.
79. Feltes TF, Wilcox WD, Feldman WE, et al. M-mode echocardiographic abnormalities in Rocky Mountain spotted fever. South Med J. 1984;787:1130–1132.
80. Walker DH, Hawkins HL, Hudson P. Fulminant Rocky Mountain spotted fever. Its pathologic characteristics associated with glucose-6-phosphate dehydrogenase deficiency. Arch Pathol Lab Med. 1983;107:121–125.
81. Dalton MJ, Clarke MJ, Holman RC, et al. National surveillance for Rocky Mountain spotted fever, 1981–1992: Epidemiologic summary and evaluation of risk factors for fatal outcome. Am J Trop Med Hyg. 1995;52:405–413.
82. Archibald LK, Sexton DJ. Long-term sequelae of Rocky Mountain spotted fever. Clin Infect Dis. 1995;20:1122–1125.
83. Kirkland KB, Marcom PK, Sexton DJ, et al. Rocky Mountain spotted fever complicated by gangrene: Report of six cases and review. Clin Infect Dis. 1993;16:629–634.
84. Hove MGM, Walker DH. Persistence of rickettsiae in the partially viable gangrenous margins of amputated extremities 5 to 7 weeks after onset of Rocky Mountain spotted fever. Arch Pathol Lab Med. 1995;119:429–431.
85. Walker DH, Dumler JS. Rickettsiae: Spotted fever and typhus group. In: Lennette EH, Lennette DA, Lennette ET, eds. Diagnostic Procedures for Viral, Rickettsial, and Chlamydial Infections. Washington, DC: American Public Health Association; 1995:575–582.
86. LaScola B, Raoult D. Diagnosis of Mediterranean spotted fever by cultivation of *Rickettsia conorii* from blood and skin samples using the centrifugation–shell vial technique and by detection of *R. conorii* in circulating endothelial cells: A 6-year follow-up. J Clin Microbiol. 1996;34:2722–2727.
87. Woodward TE, Pedersen CE Jr, Oster CN, et al. Prompt confirmation of Rocky Mountain spotted fever: Identification of rickettsiae in skin tissues. J Infect Dis. 1976;134:297–301.
88. Walker DH, Burday MS, Folds JD. Laboratory diagnosis of Rocky Mountain spotted fever. South Med J. 1980;73:1443–1447.
89. Kaplowitz LG, Lange JV, Fischer JJ, et al. Correlation of rickettsial titers, circulating endotoxin, and clinical features in Rocky Mountain spotted fever. Arch Intern Med. 1983;143:1149–1151.
90. LaScola B, Raoult D. Laboratory diagnosis of rickettsioses: Current approaches to diagnosis of old and new rickettsial diseases. J Clin Microbiol. 1997;35:2715–2727.
91. Dumler JS, Gage WR, Pettis GL, et al. Rapid immunoperoxidase demonstration of *Rickettsia rickettsii* in fixed cutaneous specimens from patients with Rocky Mountain spotted fever. Am J Clin Pathol. 1990;93:410–414.
92. White WL, Patrick JD, Miller LR. Evaluation of immunoperoxidase techniques to detect *Rickettsia rickettsii* in fixed tissue sections. Am J Clin Pathol. 1944;101:747–752.
93. Walker DH, Gile JC, Feng H-M, et al. Diagnosis of spotted fever group rickettsio-

ses by immunohistology with a group-specific anti-lipopolysaccharide monoclonal antibody. Lab Invest. 1994;70:128.
94. Hechemy KE, Michaelson EE, Anacker RL, et al. Evaluation of latex–*Rickettsia rickettsii* test for Rocky Mountain spotted fever in 11 laboratories. J Clin Microbiol. 1983;18:938–946.
95. Tzianabos T, Anderson BE, McDade JE. Detection of *Rickettsia rickettsii* DNA in clinical specimens by using polymerase chain reaction technology. J Clin Microbiol. 1989;27:2866–2868.
96. Sexton DJ, Kanj SS, Wilson K, et al. The use of a polymerase chain reaction as a diagnostic test for Rocky Mountain spotted fever. Am J Trop Med Hyg. 1994;50:59–63.
97. Roux V, Fournier PE, Raoult D. Differentiation of spotted fever group rickettsiae by sequencing and analysis of restriction fragment length polymorphism of PCR amplified DNA of the gene encoding the protein rOmpA. J Clin Microbiol. 1996;34:2058–2065.
98. Rolain JM, Maurin M, Vestris G, et al. In vitro susceptibilities of 27 rickettsiae to 13 antimicrobials. Antimicrob Agent Chemother. 1998;42:1537–1541.
99. Raoult D, Drancourt M. Antimicrobial therapy of rickettsial diseases. Antimicrob Agents Chemother. 1991;35:2457–2462.
100. American Academy of Pediatrics. 1997 Red Book: Report of the Committee on Infectious Diseases, 24th ed. Elk Grove Village, Ill: Author; 1997.
101. Kirkland KB, Wilkinson WE, Sexton DJ. Therapeutic delay and mortality in cases of Rocky Mountain spotted fever. Clin Infect Dis. 1995;20:1118–1121.
102. Breitschwerdt EB, Davidson MG, Hegarty BC, et al. Prednisolone at anti-inflammatory or immunosuppressive dosages in conjunction with doxycycline does not potentiate the severity of *Rickettsia rickettsii* infection in dogs. Antimicrob Agents Chemother. 1997;41:141–147.
103. Anderson BE, McDonald GA, Jones DC, et al. A protective protein antigen of *Rickettsia rickettsii* has tandemly repeated, near-identical sequences. Infect Immun. 1990;58:2760–2769.
104. Gilmore RD Jr, Joste N, McDonald GA. Cloning, expression and sequence analysis of the gene encoding the 120kDa surface-exposed protein of *Rickettsia rickettsii*. Mol Microbiol. 1989;3:1579–1586.
105. Gilmore RD Jr, Cleplak W, Policastro PF, et al. The 120 kilodalton outer membrane protein (rOmp B) of *Rickettsia rickettsii* is encoded by an unusually long open reading frame: Evidence for protein processing from a large precursor. Mol Microbiol. 1991;5:2361–2370.
106. Crocquet-Valdes PA, Weiss K, Walker DH. Sequence analysis of the 190-kDa antigen-encoding gene of *Rickettsia conorii* (Malish 7 strain). Gene. 1994;140:115–119.
107. Beati L, Raoult L. *Rickettsia massiliae* sp nov, a new spotted fever group rickettsia. Int J Syst Bacteriol. 1993;43:839–840.
108. Beati L, Peter O, Burgdorfer W, et al. Confirmation that *Rickettsia helvetica* sp nov is a distinct species of the spotted fever group of rickettsiae. Int J Syst Bacteriol. 1993;43:521–526.
109. Beati L, Meskini M, Thiers B, et al. *Rickettsia aeschlimannii* sp nov, a new spotted fever group rickettsia associated with *Hyalomma marginatum* ticks. Int J Syst Bacteriol. 1997;47:548–554.
110. Walker DH, Liu Q-H, Yu X-J, et al. Antigenic diversity of *Rickettsia conorii*. Am J Trop Med Hyg. 1992;47:78–86.
111. Walker DH, Feng H, Saada JI, Crocquet-Valdes P, et al. Comparative antigenic analysis of spotted fever group rickettsiae from Israel and other closely related organisms. Am J Trop Med Hyg. 1995;52:569–576.
112. Vishwanath S. Antigenic relationships among the rickettsiae of the spotted fever and typhus groups. FEMS Microbiol Lett. 1991;81:341–344.
113. Xu W, Raoult D. Production of monoclonal antibodies against *Rickettsia massiliae* and their use in antigenic and epidemiological studies. J Clin Microbiol. 1997;35:1715–1721.
114. Eremeeva ME, Beati L, Makarova VA, et al. Astrakhan fever rickettsiae: Antigenic and genotypic analysis of isolates obtained from human and *Rhipicephalus pumilio* ticks. Am J Trop Med Hyg. 1994;51:697–706.
115. Yu X-J, Walker DH, Jerrells TR. Polypeptides constituting the antigenic basis for identification of *Rickettsia sibirica* species by the standard serotyping method for spotted fever group rickettsiae. Acta Virol. 1990;34:71–79.
116. Uchida T, Uchiyama T, Kumano K, et al. *Rickettsia japonica* sp nov, the etiological agent of spotted fever group rickettsiosis in Japan. Int J Syst Bacteriol. 1992;42:303–305.
117. Stewart RS. Flinders Island spotted fever: A newly recognized endemic focus of tick typhus in Bass Strait. Med J Aust. 1991;154:94–99.
118. Kelly PJ, Beati L, Mason PR, et al. *Rickettsia africae* sp nov, the etiological agent of African tick bite fever. Int J Syst Bacteriol. 1996;46:611–614.
119. Stenos J, Ross B, Feng H, et al. Protein characterization of Australian spotted fever group rickettsiae and monoclonal antibody typing of *Rickettsia honei*. J Clin Microbiol. 1997;35:261–263.
120. Graves SR, Dwyer BW, McColl D, et al. Flinders Island spotted fever: A newly recognized endemic focus of tick typhus in Bass Strait. Part 2. Serological investigations. Med J Aust. 1991;154:99–104.
121. Robertson RG, Wisseman CL. Tick-borne rickettsiae of the spotted fever group in West Pakistan. Am J Epidemiol. 1973;97:55–64.
122. Kelly PJ, Mason PR, Matthewman LA, et al. Seroepidemiology of spotted fever group rickettsial infections in humans in Zimbabwe. J Trop Med Hyg. 1991;94:304–309.
123. Tissot-Dupont H, Brouqui P, Faugere B, Raoult D. Prevalence of antibodies to *Coxiella burnetii*, *Rickettsia conorii*, and *Rickettsia typhi* in seven African countries. Clin Infect Dis. 1995;21:1126–1133.
124. Parola P, Jourdan J, Raoult D. Tick-borne infection caused by *Rickettsia africae* in the West Indies. N Engl J Med. 1998;338:1391.
125. Brouqui P, Harle JR, Delmont J, et al. African tick-bite fever. An imported spotless rickettsiosis. Arch Intern Med. 1997;157:119–124.
126. Fournier PE, Roux V, Caumes E, et al. An outbreak of *Rickettsia africae* infections among participants of an adventure race from South Africa. Clin Infect Dis. 1998;27:316–323.
127. Smoak BL, McClain B, Brundage JF, et al. An outbreak of spotted fever rickettsiosis in U.S. Army troops deployed to Botswana. Emerg Infect Dis. 1996;12:217–221.
128. Raoult D, Berbis P, Roux V, et al. A new tick-transmitted disease due to *Rickettsia slovaca*. Lancet. 1997;350:112–113.
129. Raoult D, Brouqui P, Roux V. A new spotted-fever-group rickettsiosis. Lancet. 1996;348:412.
130. Walker DH, Occhino C, Tringali GR, et al. Pathogenesis of rickettsial eschars. The tache noire of boutonneuse fever. Hum Pathol. 1988;19:1449–1454.
131. Walker DH, Gear JM. Correlation of the distribution of *Rickettsia conorii*, microscopic lesions, and clinical features in South African tick bite fever. Am J Trop Med Hyg. 1985;34:361–371.
132. Walker DH, Herrero-Herrero JI, Ruiz-Beltran R, et al. The pathology of fatal Mediterranean spotted fever. Am J Clin Pathol. 1987;87:669–672.
133. Walker DH, Staiti A, Mansueto S, et al. Frequent occurrence of hepatic lesions in boutonneuse fever. Acta Trop. 1986;43:175–181.
134. Raoult D, Zuchelli P, Weiller PJ, et al. Incidence, clinical observations and risk factors in the severe form of Mediterranean spotted fever among patients admitted to the hospital in Marseilles 1983–1984. J Infect. 1986;12:111–116.
135. Raoult D, Weiller PJ, Chagnon A, et al. Mediterranean spotted fever: Clinical, laboratory and epidemiological features of 199 cases. Am J Trop Med Hyg. 1986;35:845–850.
136. Vicente V, Alberca I, Ruiz R, et al. Coagulation abnormalities in patients with Mediterranean spotted fever. J Infect Dis. 1986;153:128–131.
137. Williams WJ, Radulovic S, Dasch GA, et al. Identification of *Rickettsia conorii* infection by polymerase chain reaction in a soldier returning from Somalia. Clin Infect Dis. 1994;19:93–99.
138. Furuya Y, Katayama T, Yoshida Y, et al. Specific amplification of *Rickettsia japonica* DNA from clinical specimens by PCR. J Clin Microbiol. 1995;33:487–489.
139. Raoult D, De Micco C, Gallais H, et al. Laboratory diagnosis of Mediterranean spotted fever by immunofluorescent demonstration of *Rickettsia conorii* in cutaneous lesions. J Infect Dis. 1985;150:145–148.
140. Drancourt M, George F, Brouqui P, et al. Diagnosis of Mediterranean spotted fever by indirect immunofluorescence of *Rickettsia conorii* in circulating endothelial cells isolated with monoclonal antibody–coated immunomagnetic beads. J Infect Dis. 1992;166:660–663.
141. Raoult D, Dasch GA. Line blot and Western blot immunoassays for diagnosis of Mediterranean spotted fever. J Clin Microbiol. 1989;27:2073–2079.
142. Teysseire N, Raoult D. Comparison of the Western immunoblot and microimmunofluorescence for diagnosis of Mediterranean spotted fever. J Clin Microbiol. 1992;30:455–460.
143. Raoult D, Gallais H, De Micco C, et al. Ciprofloxacin therapy for Mediterranean spotted fever. Antimicrob Agents Chemother. 1986;30:606–607.
144. Ruiz-Beltran R, Herrero-Herrero JI. Evaluation of ciprofloxacin and doxycycline in the treatment of Mediterranean spotted fever. Eur J Clin Microbiol Infect Dis. 1992;11:427–431.

Chapter 176

Rickettsia akari (Rickettsialpox)

ALFRED J. SAAH

Rickettsialpox is a nonfatal, zoonotic, and febrile disease caused by *Rickettsia akari*. Since the disease was first characterized in 1946,[1] it has been recognized in other urban areas of the United States and in South Africa, Korea, and parts of Russia.

ETIOLOGY

Rickettsia akari is a small, coccobacillary intracellular bacterium. It is best seen in tissue by the Giemsa stain. The organism is in the spotted fever group of rickettsiae and has prominent serologic cross-reactivity with these agents (e.g., *Rickettsia rickettsii*).

EPIDEMIOLOGY

Rickettsialpox is a zoonotic disease. The organism seems to be transmitted among mice *(Mus musculus)* by mouse ectoparasites, and it is transmitted to humans by a mite, *Liponyssoides sanguineus*. This mite is very small and colorless, and its bite is painless.

A reported outbreak from New York[2] reaffirms the importance of continued vigilance for this disease as a marker for excessive proliferation of mice and mites. Adequate control of mice and their ectoparasites prevents disease in humans.

PATHOLOGY AND PATHOGENESIS

After the bite of an infected mite, *R. akari* proliferates locally in the skin. A papule develops and then ulcerates to form the eschar. Seeding of peripheral sites occurs during rickettsemia near the time of onset of clinical symptoms. The rash lesions of rickettsialpox show epidermal infiltration by mononuclear cells. As in other rickettsial diseases, blood vessels are prominently involved and show extravasated erythrocytes and fibrin thrombi.[2–4]

CLINICAL MANIFESTATIONS

The incubation period of rickettsialpox is 9 to 14 days (range, 7 to 21 days). A painless papule that ulcerates and forms the eschar occurs in most cases. The eschar is formed 3 to 7 days before onset; it is approximately 0.5 to 3 cm in diameter. Regional lymphadenopathy is usually present, but it is nontender or minimally so.[5]

The onset of signs and symptoms is sudden. Chills, fever, and headache are most common at onset. Other signs and symptoms that may be present include myalgia, especially backache, and photophobia. Because of the hectic fever, many patients have rigors and profuse sweating.

Within 2 to 3 days after onset (range, hours to 9 days), a generalized papulovesicular rash appears. Lesions usually begin as firm erythematous papules that are 2 to 10 mm in diameter. After the lesions form vesicles, they heal by crusting.

The disease is mild; complications or death is very rare. Untreated illness resolves in 2 to 3 weeks, but residual headache and lassitude may persist for 1 to 2 weeks.

DIAGNOSIS

Routine laboratory tests are nonspecific. Early in the disease, a mild leukopenia can be seen. The Weil-Felix test is negative for all antigens. Complement fixation tests can be used for diagnosis, but the indirect fluorescent antibody test is more sensitive as a rule. Because of the cross-reactivity with other spotted fever group organisms, initial screening of sera can be done by using *R. rickettsii* antigen.

As in other rickettsial diseases, antibiotic treatment blunts and delays the antibody response. Convalescent serum specimens should be obtained 6 to 8 weeks after onset in treated patients if earlier specimens are negative. Direct fluorescent antibody testing using anti–*R. rickettsii* globulin conjugated with fluorescein isothiocyanate is a useful rapid diagnostic test when applied to eschars.[3]

DIFFERENTIAL DIAGNOSIS

Any rickettsial disease that produces an eschar should be considered in the differential diagnoses. These include scrub typhus, Mediterranean spotted fever (boutonneuse fever), Siberian tick typhus, and Queensland tick typhus.

The viral disease that is most like rickettsialpox is chickenpox. Lesions in chickenpox are more vesiculated than in rickettsialpox, which are more papular, with a central vesicle. Other diseases that should be considered include certain enterovirus infections, gonococcemia, and infectious mononucleosis.

TREATMENT AND PREVENTION

Symptoms resolve within 48 hours after antirickettsial therapy is begun. Tetracycline, 15 mg/kg/day in four divided doses, is effective when given for 3 to 5 days. Relapse is very uncommon.

Adequate control of mice and their ectoparasites is effective in preventing infection in humans.[6]

REFERENCES

1. Huebner RJ, Stamps P, Armstrong A. Rickettsialpox—a newly recognized rickettsial disease. 1. Isolation of the etiologic agent. Public Health Rep. 1946;61:1605.
2. Brettman LR, Lewin S, Holzman RS, et al. Rickettsialpox: Report of an outbreak and a contemporary review. Medicine. 1981;60:363–372.
3. Kass EM, Szaniawski WK, Levy H, et al. Rickettsialpox in a New York City hospital. N Engl J Med. 1994;331:1612–1617.
4. Dolgopol VB. Histologic changes in rickettsialpox. Am J Pathol. 1948;24:119.
5. Greenberg M. Rickettsialpox in New York City. Am J Med. 1948;4:866–874.
6. Lackman DB. A review of information on rickettsialpox in the United States. Clin Pediatr (Phila). 1963;2:296–301.

Chapter 177

Coxiella burnetii (Q Fever)

THOMAS J. MARRIE

Q fever is an acute (on occasion chronic) febrile illness that occurs worldwide. The most common animal reservoirs for this zoonosis are cattle, sheep, and goats. These domestic ungulates, when infected, shed the desiccation-resistant organisms in urine, feces, milk, and especially in birth products. The placenta of infected sheep contains up to 10^9 organisms per gram of tissue. Humans are infected by inhalation of contaminated aerosols and after an incubation period of 20 days (range, 14 to 39 days) become ill with severe headache, fever, chills, fatigue, and myalgia. Other signs and symptoms depend upon the organs that are involved. In contrast to other rickettsial infections, rash rarely occurs in acute Q fever. The rash in chronic Q fever (endocarditis) is that of palpable purpura due to an immune complex vasculitis. Other differences between Q fever and the usual rickettsial infections are the aerosol route of infection and the lack of cross-reacting antibodies to *Proteus* X strain (the Weil-Felix reaction).

THE PATHOGEN

Coxiella burnetii, the etiologic agent of Q fever, is a highly pleomorphic coccobacillus with a gram-negative cell wall (Fig. 177–1). It measures 0.3 to 0.7 μm long,[1] but unlike true rickettsiae, it enters the cell by a passive mechanism. Within host cells, it survives within the phagolysosome—the low pH of this environment is necessary for the metabolic functioning of *C. burnetii*. Large and small variants exist, and a spore stage has been described.[2] This spore stage explains the ability of *C. burnetii* to withstand harsh environmental conditions.[3] It survives for 7 to 10 months on wool at 15 to 20°C, for more than 1 month on fresh meat in cold storage, and for more than 40 months in skim milk at room temperature.[4] Although it is destroyed by 2% formaldehyde, the organism has been isolated from infected tissues stored in formaldehyde for up to 4 to 5 months. It has also been isolated from fixed "paraffinized" tissues. Either 1% Lysol or 5% hydrogen peroxide will kill *C. burnetii*.

Coxiella burnetii undergoes "phase" variation.[4, 5] In nature and in laboratory animals it exists in the "phase I" state in which organisms react with late (45 days) convalescent guinea pig sera and

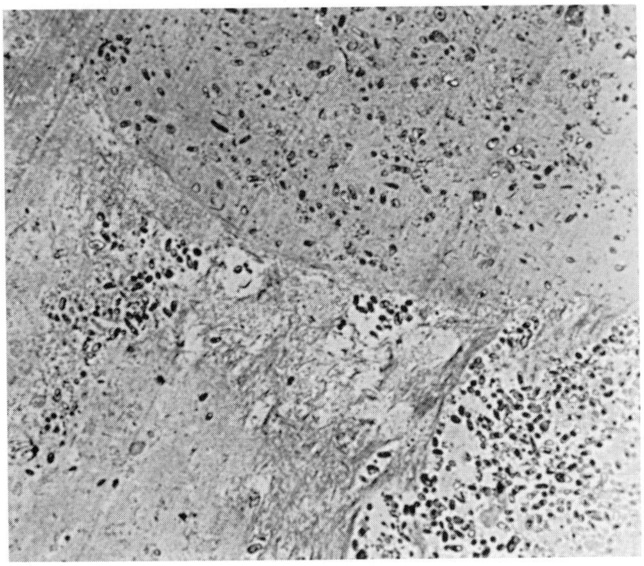

FIGURE 177–1. Transmission electron micrograph of a vegetation from a patient with Q fever endocarditis. Myriad *Coxiella burnetii* cells are evident. The electron-dense material within each cell is DNA. Original magnification, ×46,665.)

only slightly with early (21 days) sera.[4] Repeated passage of phase I virulent organisms in embryonated chicken eggs leads to gradual conversion to phase II avirulent forms. There is no morphologic difference between the two phases, although they differ in the sugar composition of their lipopolysaccharides,[6] in their buoyant density in cesium chloride, and in their affinity for hematoxylin and basic fuchsin dyes. *Coxiella burnetii* lipopolysaccharide is nontoxic to chicken embryos at doses higher than 80 μg per embryo, in contrast to *Salmonella typhimurium* smooth-and-rough type lipopolysaccharide, which is toxic in nanogram amounts.[7]

Plasmids have been found in both phase I and phase II cells.[8] Six different plasmid types varying in length from 36 to 56 kilobases have been identified.[8–11] Initially it was felt that certain plasmids were associated with acute Q fever and others were associated with chronic Q fever.[9] Mallavia and colleagues suggested that there are at least six strains of *C. burnetii*.[12] These are Hamilton, Vacca, Rasche, Biotzere, Corazon, and Dod. Thiel and associates examined 30 *C. burnetii* isolates from diverse geographic regions using pulsed-field gel electrophoresis.[13] They described four different patterns and concluded that the European strains were different from the North American strains.[13] *Coxiella burnetii* is extremely infectious for humans—a single viable organism is enough to cause an infection.[3]

EPIDEMIOLOGY

Humans become infected by inhalation of small-particle aerosols containing *C. burnetii*. The resulting illness has been termed Q fever. In August 1935, Derrick, a medical officer of health in Queensland, Australia, investigated a febrile illness that affected 20 of 800 employees of a Brisbane meat works.[17] He coined the term *Q* (or query) *fever* for this illness, for which he had no diagnosis but suspected was a new disease. Burnet and Freeman showed that the microorganism isolated from the blood and urine of Derrick's patients was a rickettsia.[18] At about the same time Davis and Cox isolated a microorganism from ticks (*Dermacentor andersoni*) collected near Nine Mile Creek, Montana.[19] Later Dyer[20, 21] showed that *Rickettsia burnetii* (Burnet and Freeman's organism) was the same as *Rickettsia diaporica* (Cox's organism)—it is now known as *Coxiella burnetii*.

Coxiella burnetii has been identified in arthropods, fish, birds, rodents, marsupials, and livestock.[1] Worldwide, the most common animal reservoirs are cattle, sheep, and goats.[14] A variety of other animals may be infected by *C. burnetii* including horses, dogs, swine, camels, water buffalo, pigeons, ducks, geese, turkeys, several species of wild birds, squirrels, deer mice, harvest mice, cats, and rabbits. The epidemiology of *C. burnetii* varies from country to country. For example, collared doves have been suspected of carrying *C. burnetii* from Western Europe to Ireland. In Nova Scotia, exposure to infected parturient cats has resulted in several outbreaks of Q fever.[15, 16]

Q fever has been reported from at least 51 countries on five continents.[5] It is usually an occupational disease affecting those with direct contact with infected animals, such as farmers, veterinarians, and abattoir workers.[5] However, indirect contact with infected animals has resulted in outbreaks of Q fever, as in Switzerland, where more than 350 persons who lived along a road over which sheep traveled from mountain pastures developed Q fever.[22] Exposure to contaminated straw, manure, or dust from farm vehicles resulted in Q fever in British residents who lived along a road traveled by these vehicles.[23] Exposure may be even more indirect, as in the case of laundry workers who developed Q fever after handling contaminated laundry.[24] Ingestion of contaminated raw milk,[25] exposure to infected parturient cats,[15] and the skinning of infected wild rabbits are also ways in which Q fever may be acquired. *C. burnetii* has also been isolated from human milk[26] and human placentas.[27] *C. burnetii* is known to undergo reactivation during pregnancy in animals other than humans. It is likely that this happens in humans as well, and Q fever complicating human pregnancy is probably underdiagnosed. Laboratory exposure to *C. burnetii*[28] and transport of infected sheep through hospitals to research laboratories have resulted in large outbreaks of Q fever.[29, 30]

Rarely, Q fever has been transmitted via blood transfusion.[31] Transmission has occurred during an autopsy[32] but has not been documented during clinical care of infected patients. There is one report of apparent human-to-human transmission of Q fever among members of a household.[33]

PATHOGENESIS

The most likely sequence of events in the cycle of transmission of *C. burnetii* to humans is that the organism is maintained in ticks or other arthropods. These ectoparasites infect domestic and other animals including a variety of small mammals by bite or through contamination of the skin by infected feces. Infected domestic ungulates are usually asymptomatic, although abortion or stillbirth may result. The heavily infected placenta contaminates the environment at the time of parturition. Air samples are positive for up to 2 weeks after parturition, and viable organisms are present in the soil for periods of up to 150 days.[34–36] Humans are infected by the inhalation of contaminated aerosols. The microorganisms proliferate in the lung or lungs, and blood stream invasion follows. This results in the onset of systemic symptoms and a variety of clinical manifestations depending on the dose of the microorganism inhaled and likely the characteristics of the infecting strain.[37]

CLINICAL MANIFESTATIONS

Humans are the only animals known to regularly develop illness as a result of *C. burnetii* infection.[38] In one large series of 207 patients, the mortality rate was 2.4%.[39] There are several clinical syndromes.

1. A self-limited febrile illness (2 to 14 days)
2. Pneumonia
3. Endocarditis
4. Hepatitis
5. Osteomyelitis
6. Q fever in the immunocompromised host
7. Q fever in infancy
8. Neurologic manifestations—encephalitis, aseptic meningitis, toxic confusional states, dementia, extrapyramidal disease

Self-limited Febrile Illness

Self-limited febrile illness is probably the most common form of Q fever. In many areas 11 to 12% of individuals have antibodies to *C. burnetii*—most do not recall pneumonia or other severe illness.[40] It is likely that the age at which infection occurs and the dose of the agent determine whether or not Q fever is a mild self-limited febrile illness.[41, 42] There is also a suggestion that some infections may be totally asymptomatic.[43] The proportion of all Q fever infections that represent "asymptomatic" seroconversion is unknown. In the south of Spain, 21% (108/505) of adults who had fever of more than 1 week's and less than 3 weeks' duration had Q fever.[44] There was no radiographic evidence of pneumonia among these individuals.

Pneumonia

There are three presentations of this form of Q fever: atypical pneumonia, rapidly progressive pneumonia, and pneumonia as an incidental finding in a patient with a febrile illness. This last presentation is probably the most common form of Q fever pneumonia.

Atypical pneumonia is a clinical term used to describe pneumonia characterized by a dry nonproductive cough with blood and sputum cultures negative for conventional bacterial pathogens.[45] Cough is a symptom in only 28% of patients with radiographically confirmed Q fever pneumonia. This illness may be of gradual or sudden onset.[46] Fever occurs in all patients. A severe headache is present in about 75% of patients and is a useful clue to the diagnosis. Other symptoms and the frequency with which they occur are fatigue, 98%; chills, 88%; sweats, 84%; myalgia, 68%; nausea, 49%; vomiting, 25%; pleuritic chest pain, 28%; and diarrhea, 21%. On occasion, diarrhea may be a presentation of Q fever.[47]

Physical examination of the chest is often unremarkable. The most common physical finding is inspiratory crackles.[46] Patients with rapidly progressive pneumonia usually have the physical signs of pulmonary consolidation. About 5% of patients have splenomegaly. Fever and severe headache suggest central nervous system infection, and lumbar puncture is often performed. The spinal fluid is usually normal; however, *C. burnetii* has been isolated from the spinal fluid under such circumstances.[48] The rapidly progressive form of Q fever pneumonia mimics legionnaires' disease and the pneumonic form of tularemia, and indeed, all the causes of rapidly progressive pneumonia enter the differential diagnosis.

The radiographic picture of Q fever pneumonia is variable (Fig. 177–2). Nonsegmental and segmental pleural-based opacities are common.[49–51] Multiple rounded opacities are very suggestive of Q fever that follows exposure to infected cat placentas (see Fig. 177–2).[49] Pleural effusion is found in 35% of cases and is usually small but on occasion may be large.[50] Atelectasis, an increase in reticular markings, and hilar adenopathy may occur. In one series, the resolution time ranged from 10 to 70 days, with a mean of 30 days.[50]

C. burnetii pneumonia is rarely fatal, and in such instances there is usually a coexisting condition that contributes to the mortality.[51] Information regarding the histology of this form of pneumonia in humans is limited. Pierce and coworkers found small coccobacilli within alveolar macrophages on transbronchial biopsy in a patient with Q fever.[52] A fatal case of pneumonia in a 43-year-old man was characterized by severe intra-alveolar hemorrhagic and focal necrotizing pneumonia with associated necrotizing bronchitis. Histiocytes, lymphocytes, and plasma cells were in the alveoli. This was felt to be Q fever pneumonia on the basis of organisms seen on a modified Giemsa stain.[53] A resolving, *C. burnetii* pneumonia lesion was characterized by an inflammatory pseudotumor—a lung mass composed of mixtures of macrophages, giant cells, plasma cells, and lymphocytes. The bronchiolar epithelium was focally absent, regenerated, or hyperplastic.[54] The changes that result from the inoculation of the lungs of rhesus monkeys resemble those reported from humans. The resulting consolidation was peribronchial or peribronchiolar.[55] The interstitial infiltrate had more lymphocytes than monocytes (Fig. 177–3).

The white blood cell count is usually normal, but one third of patients have an increased count. A slight elevation (two to three times normal) of the hepatic transaminase levels occurs in almost all patients. The serum bilirubin level is usually normal; however, jaundice may occur. Rarely, the syndrome of inappropriate secretion of antidiuretic hormone occurs.[56]

The treatment of choice for *C. burnetii* pneumonia is tetracycline.[57] Chloramphenicol has been used to treat Q fever.[52] Yeaman and associates performed antibiotic susceptibility testing of *C. burnetii* by using persistently infected L929 fibroblast cells.[58] The most effective agents were quinolones (difloxacin, ciprofloxacin, oxolinic acid) and rifampin. Chloramphenicol, doxycycline, and trimethoprim were somewhat effective, whereas tetracycline, gentamicin, streptomycin, erythromycin, sulfamethoxazole, penicillin G, and polymyxin B were ineffective. Erythromycin is usually the drug of choice for the treatment of atypical pneumonia. Although others have reported an apparent response of *C. burnetii* pneumonia to macrolides,[59–62] we have observed that all of our cases of rapidly progressive pneumonia due to *C. burnetii* have failed to respond to erythromycin therapy despite dosages of up to 4 g/day. The addition of rifampin, 300 mg twice daily orally, resulted in cure.

The diagnosis of Q fever (*C. burnetii*) pneumonia is confirmed serologically since most laboratories do not have the facilities required to isolate *C. burnetii*.[63] The development of primers derived from the *C. burnetii* superoxide dismutase gene has allowed the amplification of *C. burnetii* DNA in clinical specimens using polymerase chain reaction.[64] The microagglutination,[65] complement fixation,[66] and microimmunofluorescence tests[67] as well as the enzyme-linked immunosorbent assay[68] have all been used in the serologic diagnosis of this illness. The complement fixation test is most commonly used. A fourfold rise in titer between acute and convalescent samples is diagnostic of Q fever. To date no cross-reactions have been reported between antibodies to other microorganisms and antibodies to *C. burnetii*.[69] Some authors have advocated using the indirect immunofluorescence test to detect antibodies to immunoglobulin M (IgM), so that a single serum specimen may be used in the diagnosis of acute Q fever.[70] However, IgM antibodies may persist for up to 678 days,[71] and in one study,[72] 3% of 162 patients still had a significant IgM antibody level 1 year after the infection.

C. burnetii is highly infectious, and tissues from patients with Q fever should be processed under biosafety level 3 conditions.

Chronic Q Fever

It is now recognized that chronic Q fever has a variety of manifestations—endocarditis, infection of a vascular prosthesis, infection of aneurysms, osteomyelitis, hepatitis, interstitial pulmonary fibrosis, prolonged fever, and purpuric eruptions.[73]

Endocarditis

Endocarditis is the prime manifestation of "chronic" Q fever.[74–93] Usually, abnormal or prosthetic cardiac valves are affected[92]; however, any part of the vascular tree may become infected,[91] including clot in a left ventricular aneurysm. Such patients have a defective cell-mediated immune response to *C. burnetii*.

The incidence of Q fever endocarditis is increasing, but this may reflect increased recognition of this entity. Turck and colleagues reported 16 cases of chronic Q fever diagnosed between 1968 and 1973; their review of the world's literature yielded 55 cases.[74] Seigman-Igra and associates reported on 408 cases of Q fever from 17 countries in their 1997 review.[93] From 1975 to 1980, 79 cases of Q fever endocarditis were reported to the Public Health Laboratory Service Communicable Disease Surveillance Center in England.[87] Indeed, from 1975 to 1981, *C. burnetii* accounted for 3% of all

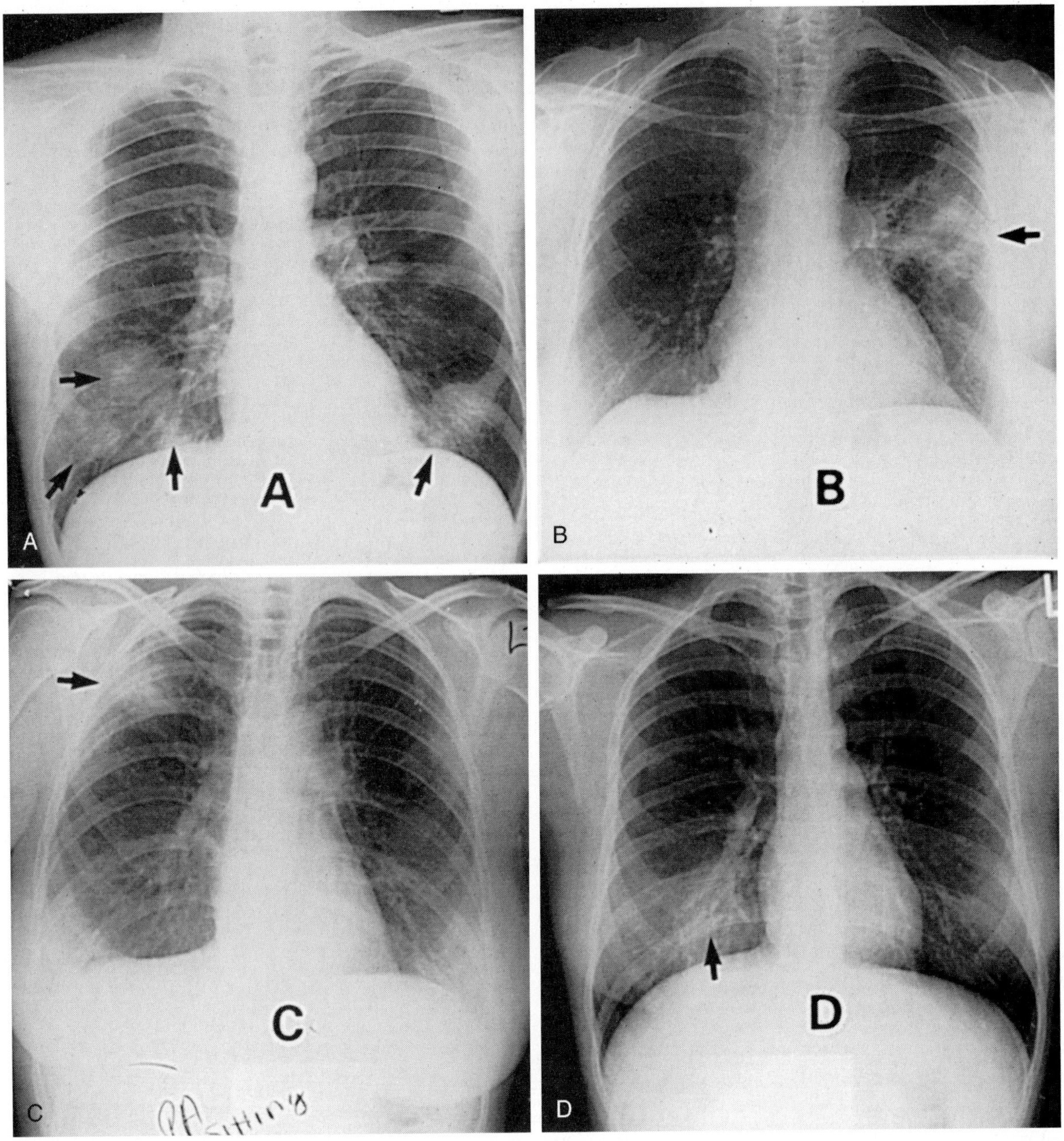

FIGURE 177–2. Radiographic manifestations of Q fever pneumonia. All four patients are members of one family who developed Q fever after exposure to the infected products of feline conception. Their cat gave birth to kittens in their house. *A*, Multiple rounded opacities. *B*, Left upper lobe opacity. *C*, Pleural-based opacity involving the right upper lobe. *D*, Right lower lobe opacity. In an endemic area *A* is characteristic of cat-related Q fever pneumonia, and *C* is suggestive of this diagnosis. However, *B* and *D* are not at all distinctive and could be due to any pulmonary pathogen.

cases of endocarditis reported in England and Wales.[86] The clinical presentation is that of culture-negative endocarditis; however, fever is frequently absent. Q fever endocarditis is rare in children.[90]

Marked clubbing of the fingers and hypergammaglobulinemia are frequently present. Splenomegaly and hepatomegaly are found in slightly more than half the patients. A purpuric rash due to leukocytoclastic vasculitis occurs in about 20%. The erythrocyte sedimentation rate is usually increased; anemia and microscopic hematuria are also found. Arterial emboli complicate the course of one third of the patients.

The vegetations in chronic Q fever differ in both gross and microscopic appearance from those seen in pyogenic bacterial endocarditis. Figures 177–4 and 177–5 show the gross appearance of the vegetations in Q fever endocarditis. Microscopically there is a subacute and chronic inflammatory infiltrate. Many large foamy macrophages are present. Characteristic microorganisms are readily seen with electron microscopy (see Fig. 177–1).

The confirmation of the diagnosis in most instances is serologic. A complement fixation titer of 1:200 or greater to phase I antigen is said to be diagnostic of chronic Q fever, although not all patients in the series of Turck and coworkers had this titer.[74] In acute Q fever, complement fixation antibody titers to phase I antigen do not reach this level.

One study reported high titers of IgA antibodies to phase I antigen in chronic Q fever (endocarditis and granulomatous hepatitis),[94] whereas another found that patients with acute Q fever also produced IgA antibodies to phase I antigen, albeit in low titer.[71] Fournier and collegues used a phase I IgG antibody titer of 1:800 or greater by

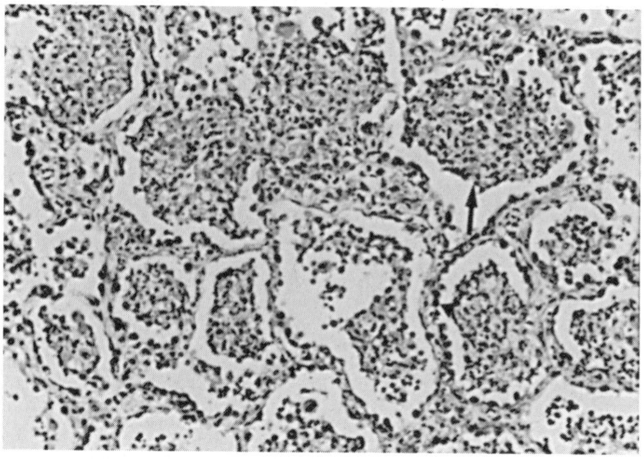

FIGURE 177–3. Photomicrograph of an open lung biopsy specimen from a patient with Q fever pneumonia. The alveolar spaces are filled with an inflammatory exudate consisting of lymphocytes and macrophages *(arrow)*. Note the hyperplasia of the alveolar lining cells *(arrowhead)*. (Magnification, ×500.)

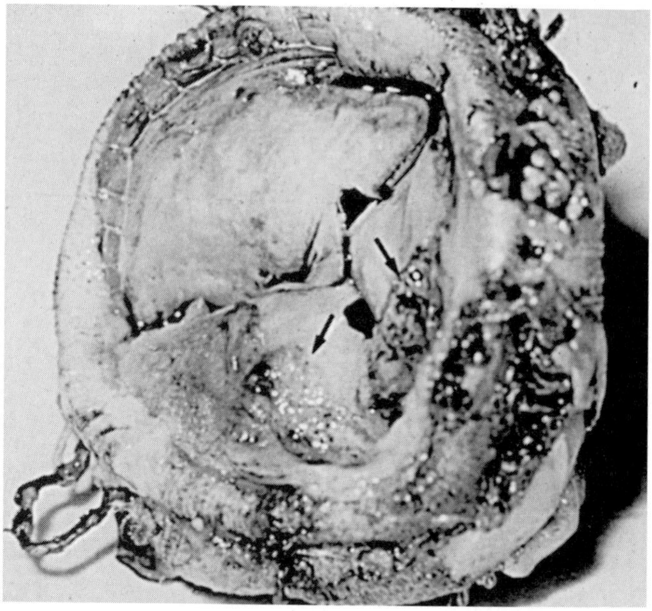

FIGURE 177–5. Bioprosthetic aortic valve from a patient with Q fever endocarditis. Vegetations are indicated by the arrows. (From Raoult D, Raza A, Marrie TJ. Q fever endocarditis and other forms of chronic Q fever. In: Marrie TJ, ed. Q Fever—The Disease. Boca Raton, Fla: CRC Press; 1990: 179–199.)

microimmunofluorescence as diagnostic of Q fever endocarditis.[95] Indeed, they have proposed that this be added as a major criterion to the Duke Endocarditis Service criteria for the diagnosis of infective endocarditis.[96]

Antibody titers fall slowly with treatment. Western immunoblotting of serum samples from patients with chronic Q fever shows that there are IgG antibodies to 12 to 15 antigens of phase I *C. burnetii*, whereas serum from patients with acute Q fever react with 7 to 10 *C. burnetii* antigens.[97] Antibodies to antigens of molecular masses 50, 80, and 160 kD were present only in serum from patients with chronic Q fever.

There is no agreement on the type and duration of antimicrobial therapy for Q fever endocarditis.[71, 72] Some authorities recommend that treatment be continued indefinitely.[71] A consensus is emerging that combination antibiotic therapy is necessary to treat chronic Q fever.[98] We have used doxycycline in combination with ciprofloxacin or rifampin for 2 years to treat this infection. Others have used doxycycline with either pefloxacin or ofloxacin with success.[98] Maurin and coworkers have found that the bactericidal effect of doxycycline was enhanced when alkalinization of the phagolysosome was accomplished with chloroquine or amantadine.[99] Raoult has used doxycycline and hydroxychloroquine to treat patients with Q fever endocarditis with success.[100] Hydroxychloroquine is given in a dose of 200 mg/day, and the dose is adjusted to maintain a serum concentration between 0.8 and 1.2 μg/ml. Antibody titers should be determined every 6 months during therapy and every 3 months for the first 2 years after the cessation of therapy. Successful therapy is accompanied by a falling erythrocyte sedimentation rate, correction

FIGURE 177–4. Mitral valve of a patient with Q fever endocarditis. The nodule *(arrow)* was full of *C. burnetii* organisms within foamy macrophages. (From Raoult D, Raza A, Marrie TJ. Q fever endocarditis and other forms of chronic Q fever. In: Marrie TJ, ed. Q Fever—The Disease. Boca Raton, Fla: CRC Press; 1990: 179–199.)

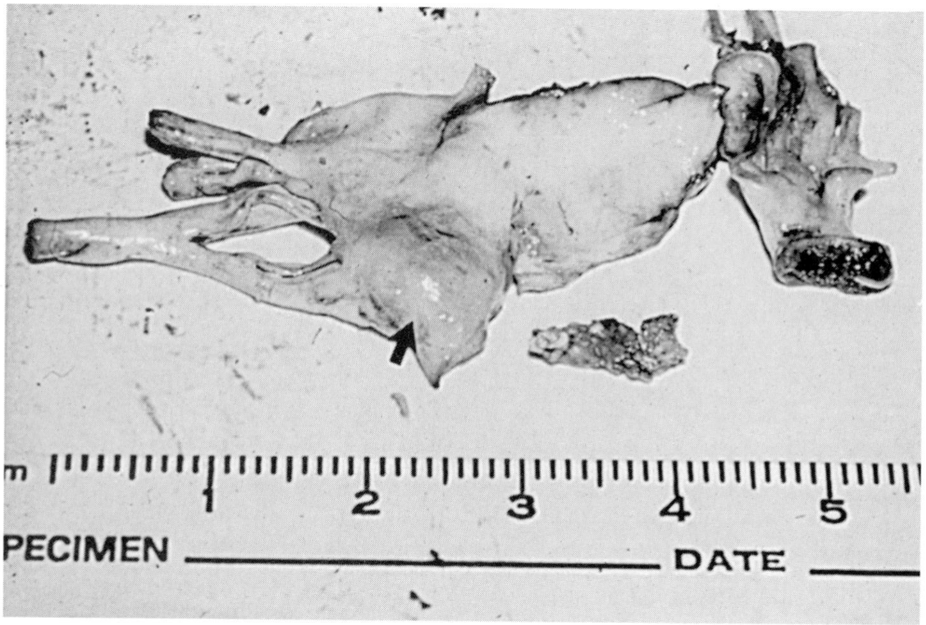

of anemia, and resolution of hyperglobulinemia. Valve replacement is frequently necessary but should be dictated by the patient's hemodynamic status. Patients are considered cured when the IgG phase I antibody titer is less than 1:800 and IgM and IgA antibody titers are less than 1:50 by microimmunofluorescence.[101] The release of interleukin-10 and transforming growth factor-β from unstimulated peripheral blood mononuclear cells is markedly increased in Q fever endocarditis.[102] Interleukin-10 and transforming growth factor-β impair the function of macrophages and monocytes. Interleukin-10 counteracts the shift to a protective helper T cell 1 pattern and also favors the survival of intracellular bacteria.

Hepatitis

Hepatitis is the most common manifestation of *C. burnetii* infection in France.[39] In the United States, 61.9% of all cases of Q fever are manifested as hepatitis. Also, hepatitis is more frequent in sheep- and goat-breeding areas. In Nova Scotia, there have been no cases diagnosed as Q fever hepatitis.

There are three presentations of Q fever hepatitis[103–109]:

1. An infectious hepatitis-like picture
2. Fever of unknown origin with characteristic granulomas on liver biopsy
3. As an incidental finding in a patient with acute Q fever pneumonia

In patients with fever of unknown origin due to Q fever, the typical "doughnut granuloma" is seen on liver biopsy.[105, 106] This is a granuloma with a dense fibrin ring surrounded by a central lipid vacuole. These granulomas are highly suggestive of Q fever but may be seen in Hodgkin's disease and infectious mononucleosis. *Coxiella burnetii* has been isolated from the liver of patients with Q fever hepatitis, but the organism has not been visualized within the hepatic parenchyma.[74] Antibiotic treatment for 2 weeks is probably sufficient. The rare cases of Q fever hepatitis with a serologic profile suggestive of chronic Q fever should be treated for longer than 2 weeks. There are no data on which to base a recommendation for the exact duration of therapy. These patients should be followed with serial antibody titers.

Neurologic Manifestations

Severe headache is the most common manifestation[110–112] and probably represents central nervous system infection, although there is little evidence of serious brain involvement in Q fever.[110] Aseptic meningitis or encephalitis, or both, complicate 0.2 to 1.3% of cases of Q fever. A review of 16 cases of Q fever meningoencephalitis revealed that eight patients had an elevated cerebrospinal fluid white blood cell level, ranging from 18 to 1392 cells/mm^3.[113] In all but one case, mononuclear cells predominated. The protein level was usually increased, and the glucose level was normal.[113] The electroencephalogram was abnormal in five of the six patients in whom this investigation was carried out.

In a study from Plymouth, Reilly and coworkers reported an astoundingly high, 22% incidence of neurologic complications among 103 patients, of whom 46 had acute Q fever, 5 had chronic Q fever, and 52 had past infections.[114] Six of the 45 patients with acute Q fever had residual neurologic impairment—weakness; recurrent meningismus; blurred vision; residual paresthesias; and sensory loss involving the left leg.

The meningoencephalitis of Q fever may be accompanied by seizures and coma.[115]

Behavioral disturbance, cerebellar symptoms and signs, cranial nerve palsies, extrapyramidal disease, and the Miller-Fisher variant of the Guillain-Barré syndrome (areflexia and ophthalmoparesis) have been reported to complicate acute Q fever. Demyelinating polyradiculoneuritis developed in a 71-year-old man 10 weeks after the onset of *C. burnetii* pneumonia.[116]

Q Fever in the Immunocompromised Host

Q fever has been reported infrequently as an infection in the immunocompromised host[117–121]; however; this may be a reflection of infrequent consideration of Q fever in this group of patients. Indeed, when Raoult and coworkers examined serum samples from 500 individuals positive for human immunodeficiency virus, they found that 10.4% of the 500 had IgG antibodies to *C. burnetti* in a titer of 1:25 or greater, compared with 4.1% of 925 apparently healthy blood donors ($p < 0.001$).[121] They also found that over the 3 years from 1987 to 1989, 5 of 68 (7.3%) patients hospitalized with Q fever were positive for human immunodeficiency virus. They estimated that in individuals positive for human immunodeficiency virus, the number of cases of Q fever was 13 times higher and these patients were symptomatic more frequently than the general population.

In a review of all cases of chronic Q fever in France from 1982 to 1990, the investigators noted that 20% of 84 patients were immunocompromised.[73] These were patients with cancer, chronic myeloid leukemia, acquired immunodeficiency syndrome, renal transplantation, corticosteroid therapy, renal dialysis, postpartum state, and chronic alcoholism.

Coxiella burnetii infection resulted in a fatal interstitial pneumonia in an 11-year-old boy with chronic granulomatous disease.[122]

Other Manifestations of Q Fever

Vertebral osteomyelitis is an uncommon manifestation of *C. burnetii* infection.[123] Q fever may also occur in infancy, when it has caused pneumonia, febrile seizures, pyrexia of unknown origin, malaise, and meningeal irritation.[124] Hematologic manifestations include bone marrow necrosis,[125] histiocytic hemophagocytosis,[126] and hemolytic anemia,[127] and on occasion this disease may simulate lymphoma.[128] Other hematologic manifestations include transient hypoplastic anemia,[129] reactive thrombocytosis, rarely thrombocytopenia, and splenic rupture.[130] Optic neuritis[131] and erythema nodosum[132] have also rarely been reported in association with *C. burnetii* infection. In the past, it was thought Kawasaki disease might be a variant of Q fever.[133, 134] Support for this concept has not materialized.

PREVENTION

Vaccination of those at risk for infection (e.g., abattoir workers, veterinarians) should be carried out as soon as a safe vaccine is available.[135, 136] An investigational inactivated vaccine, made from infected egg yolk sacs, has been used to protect laboratory workers handling live *C. burnetii*. Vaccine may be requested under Investigational New Drugs by contacting the Commanding Officer, U.S. Army Medical Research Institute for Infectious Diseases, Fort Detrick, Frederick, MD 21701-5011, U.S.A.

Using only seronegative sheep in research facilities will prevent outbreaks in these institutions. Because of the lack of person-to-person spread, there is no need to isolate patients hospitalized with Q fever.[137] Simple measures, such as the consumption of only pasteurized milk, serve to eliminate cases of Q fever that are transmitted in this manner. In Cyprus, the incidence of *C. burnetii* infection among sheep and goats was reduced by a program in which aborted material was destroyed, affected dams isolated, and the premises disinfected.[138] Control of ectoparasites on cattle, sheep, and goats is also important in the control of Q fever.[138]

REFERENCES

1. Baca OG, Paretsky D. Q fever and *Coxiella burnetii*: A model for host-parasite interaction. Microbiol Rev. 1983;47: 127–149.
2. McCaul TF, Williams JC. Development cycle of *Coxiella burnetii*: Structure and morphogenesis of vegetative and sporogenic differentiations. J Bacteriol. 1981;147:1063–1076.

3. Sawyer LA, Fishbein DB, McDade JE. Q fever: Current concepts. Rev Infect Dis. 1987;9:935–946.
4. Q fever. In: Christie AB. Infectious Diseases, Epidemiology and Clinical Practice. Edinburgh: Churchill Livingstone; 1974:876–891.
5. Leedom JM. Q fever: An update. In: Remmington JS, Schwartz MN, eds. Current Clinical Topics in Infectious Diseases. New York: McGraw-Hill; 1980:304–331.
6. Schramek S, Mayer H. Different sugar compositions of lipopolysaccharides isolated from phase I and pure phase II cells of *Coxiella burnetii*. Infect Immun. 1982;38:53–57.
7. Hackstadt T, Peacock MG, Hitchcock PJ, Cole RL. Lipopolysaccharide variation in *Coxiella burnetii*: Intrastrain heterogeneity in structure and antigenicity. Infect Immun. 1985;48:359–365.
8. Samuel JE, Frazier ME, Mallavia LP. Correlation of plasmid type and disease caused by *Coxiella burnetii*. Infect Immun. 1985;49:775–777.
9. Minnick MF, Heinzen RA, Reschke DK, et al. A plasmid-encoded surface protein found in chronic-disease isolates of *Coxiella burnetii*. Infect Immun. 1991;59:4735–4739.
10. Valkova D, Kazar J. A new plasmid (QPDV) common to *Coxiella burnetii* isolates associated with acute and chronic Q fever. FEMS Microbiol Lett. 1995;125:275–280.
11. Stein A, Raoult D. Phenotypic and genotypic heterogenicity of eight new human *Coxiella burnetii* isolates. Acta Virol. 1992;36:7–12.
12. Mallavia LP, Samuel JE, Frazier ME. The genetics of *Coxiella burnetii*: Etiologic agent of Q fever and chronic endocarditis. In: Williams JC, Thompson HA, eds. Q Fever: The Biology of *Coxiella burnetii*. Boca Raton, Fla: CRC Press;1991:259–284.
13. Thiele D, Willems H, Kopf G, Krauss H. Polymorphism in DNA restriction patterns of *Coxiella burnetii* isolates investigated by pulsed field gel electrophoresis and image analysis. Eur J Epidemiol. 1993;9:419–425.
14. Babudieri B. Q fever: A zoonosis. Adv Vet Sci. 1959;5:81–181.
15. Langley JM, Marrie TJ, Covert A, et al. Poker players pneumonia. An urban outbreak following exposure to a parturient cat. N Engl J Med. 1988;319:354–356.
16. Marrie TJ, Durant H, Williams JC, et al. Exposure to parturient cats is a risk factor for acquisition of Q fever in Maritime Canada. J Infect Dis. 1988;158:101–108.
17. Derrick EH. "Q" fever, new fever entity: Clinical features, diagnosis and laboratory investigation. Med J Aust. 1937;2:281–299.
18. Burnet FM, Freeman M. Experimental studies on the virus of "Q" fever. Med J Aust. 1937;2:299–305.
19. Davis G, Cox HR. A filter-passing infectious agent isolated from ticks: Isolation from *Dermacentor andersoni*, reactions in animals, and filtration experiments. Public Health Rep. 1939;53:2259–2267.
20. Dyer RE. A filter-passing infectious agent isolated from ticks. IV. Human infection. Public Health Rep. 1939;53:2277–2283.
21. Dyer RE. Similarity of Australian Q fever and a disease caused by an infectious agent isolated from ticks in Montana. Public Health Rep. 1939;54:1229–1237.
22. Q fever outbreak—Switzerland. MMWR. 1984;33:355–361.
23. Salmon MM, Howells B, Glencross EJF, et al. Q fever in an urban area. Lancet. 1982;1:1002–1004.
24. Oliphant JW, Gordon DA, Meis A, et al. Q fever in laundry workers presumably transmitted from contaminated clothing. Am J Hyg. 1949;49:76–82.
25. Bell JA, Beck MD, Huebner RJ. Epidemiologic studies of Q fever in southern California. JAMA. 1950;142:868–872.
26. Kumar A, Yadav MP, Kakkar S. Human milk as a source of Q fever infection in breast-fed babies. Indian J Med Res. 1981;73:510–512.
27. Syrucek L, Sobeslavsky O, Gutvirth I. Isolation of *Coxiella burnetii* from human placentas. J Hyg Epidemiol Microbiol Immunol. 1958;2:29–35.
28. Johnson JE II, Kadull PJ. Laboratory acquired Q fever. A report of fifty cases. Am J Med. 1966;41:391–403.
29. Hall CJ, Richmond SJ, Caul EO, et al. Laboratory outbreak of Q fever acquired from sheep. Lancet. 1982;1:1004–1006.
30. Meiklejohn G, Reimer LG, Graves PS, Helmick C. Cryptic epidemic of Q fever in a medical school. J Infect Dis. 1981;144:107–114.
31. Editorial comment on Q fever transmitted by blood transfusion—United States. Can Dis Wkly Rep. 1977;3:210.
32. Harman JB. Q fever in Great Britain; clinical account of eight cases. Lancet. 1949;2:1028–1030.
33. Mann JS, Douglas JG, Inglis JN, Leitch AG. Q fever: Person to person transmission within a family. Thorax. 1986;41:974–975.
34. Welsh HH, Lennette EH, Abinanti FR, Win JF. Air-borne transmission of Q fever: The role of parturition in the generation of infective aerosols. Ann N Y Acad Sci 1958;70:528–540.
35. Lennette EH, Welsh HH. Q fever in California. X. Recovery of *Coxiella burnetii* from the air of premises harbouring infected goats. Am J Hyg. 1951;54:44–49.
36. Welsh HH, Lennette HH, Abinanti FR, et al. Q fever studies XXI. The recovery of *Coxiella burnetii* from the soil and surface water of premises harbouring infected sheep. Am J Hyg. 1959;70:14–20.
37. Baca OG. Pathogenesis of rickettsial infections. Emphasis on Q fever. Eur J Epidemiol. 1991;7:222–228.
38. Stoker MGP, Marmion BP. The spread of Q fever from animals to man. The natural history of a rickettsial disease. Bull WHO. 1955;13:781–806.
39. Dupont HT, Raoult D, Brouqui P, et al. Epidemiologic features and clinical presentation of acute Q fever in hospitalized patients: 323 French cases. Am J Med. 1992;93:427–434.
40. Clark WH, Romker MS, Holmes MA, et al. Q fever in California. VIII. An epidemic of Q fever in a small rural community in northern California. Am J Hyg. 1951;54:25–34.
41. Gonder JC, Kishimoto RA, Kastello MR, et al. Cynomolgus monkey model for experimental Q fever infection. J Infect Dis. 1979;139:191–196.
42. Tigertt WD, Benenson AS, Goscheneur WS. Airborne Q fever. Bacteriol Rev 1961;25:285–293.
43. Luoto L, Casey ML, Pickens EG. Q fever studies in Montana. Detection of asymptomatic infection among residents of infected dairy premises. Am J Epidemiol. 1965;81:356–369.
44. Viciana P, Pachon J, Cuello JA, et al. Fever of indeterminate duration in the community. A seven year study in the south of Spain. Abstract 683. Presented at the 32nd Interscience Conference on Antimicrobial Agents and Chemotherapy, October 11–14, 1992. Am Soc Microbiol, Washington, DC.
45. Cunha BA, Quintiliani R. The atypical pneumonias. A diagnostic and therapeutic approach. Postgrad Med. 1979;66:95–102.
46. Feinstein M, Yesner R, Marks JL. Epidemic of Q fever among troops returning from Italy in the spring of 1945. 1. Clinical aspects of the epidemic at Fort Patrick Henry, Virginia. Am J Hyg. 1946;44:72–87.
47. Lim KCL, Kang JYU. Q fever presenting with gastroenteritis. Med J Aust. 1980;1:327.
48. Robins FC. Q fever in the Mediterranean area: Report of its occurrence in Allied troops. Am J Hyg. 1946;51–71.
49. Gordon JD, MacKeen AD, Marrie TJ, et al. The radiographic features of epidemic and sporadic Q fever pneumonia. J Can Assoc Radiol. 1984;35:293–296.
50. Millar JK. The chest film findings in 'Q' fever—A series of 35 cases. Clin Radiol. 1978;329:371–375.
51. Perin TL. Histopathologic observations in a fatal case of Q fever. Arch Pathol. 1949;47:361–365.
52. Pierce TH, Yucht SC, Gorin AB, et al. Q fever pneumonitis: Diagnosis by transbronchoscopic lung biopsy. West J Med. 1979;130:453–455.
53. Urso FP. The pathologic findings in rickettsial pneumonia. Am J Clin Pathol. 1975;64:335–342.
54. Janigan DT, Marrie TJ. An inflammatory pseudotumor of the lung in Q fever pneumonia. N Engl J Med. 1983;30:86–88.
55. Lille RD, Perrin TL, Armstrong C. An institutional outbreak of pneumonitis. III. Histopathology in man and rhesus monkeys in the pneumonitis due to the virus of "Q: fever." Public Health Rep. 1941;56:1419–1425.
56. Biggs BA, Douglas JG, Grant IWB, et al. Prolonged Q fever associated with inappropriate secretion of anti-diuretic hormone. J Infect. 1984;8:61–63.
57. Turck WPG. Q fever. In: Braude AL, Davis CE, Fierer J, eds. Medical Microbiology and Infectious Diseases. Philadelphia: WB Saunders; 1981:932–937.
58. Yeaman MR, Mitscher LA, Baca OG. In vitro susceptibility of *Coxiella burnetii* for antibiotics, including several quinolones. Antimicrob Agents Chemother. 1987;31:1079–1084.
59. D'Angelo LJ, Hetherington R. Q fever treated with erythromycin. BMJ. 1979;2:305–306.
60. Ellis ME, Dunbar EM. In vivo response of acute Q fever to erythromycin. Thorax. 1982;37:867–868.
61. Kofteridis D, Gikas A, Spiradakis G, et al. Clinical response of Q fever infection to macrolides. Abstract 4.3. Presented at the Fourth International Conference on Macrolides, Azalides, Streptogramins and Ketolides, Barcelona, Spain, January 12–23, 1998:47.
62. Kuzman I, Schonwald S, Culig J, et al. The efficacy of azithromycin in the treatment of Q fever: A retrospective study. Abstract 4.31. Presented at the Fourth International Conference on Macrolides, Azalides, Streptogramins and Ketolides, Barcelona, Spain, January 21–23, 1998:47.
63. Huebner RJ, Jellison WL, Beck MD. Q fever, a review of current knowledge. Ann Intern Med. 1949;30:495–509.
64. Stein A, Raoult D. Detection of *Coxiella burnetii* by DNA amplification using polymerase chain reaction. J Clin Microbiol. 1992;30:2462–2466.
65. Fiset P, Ormsbee RA, Silberman R, et al. A microagglutination technique for detection and measurement of rickettsial antibodies. Acta Virol. 1969;13:60–66.
66. Murphy AM, Field PR. The persistence of complement fixing antibodies to Q fever *(Coxiella burnetii)* after infection. Med J Aust. 1970;1:1148–1150.
67. Field PR, Hunt JG, Murphy AM. Detection and persistence of specific IgM antibody to *Coxiella burnetii* by enzyme-linked immunosorbent assay: A comparison with immuno-fluorescence and complement fixation tests. J Infect Dis. 1983;148:477–487.
68. Peter O, Dupuis G, Burgdorfer W, et al. Evaluation of the complement fixation and indirect immunofluorescence test in the early diagnosis of primary Q fever. Eur J Clin Microbiol. 1985;4:394–396.
69. Peter O, Dupuis G, Peacock MG, et al. Comparison of enzyme-linked immunosorbent assay and complement fixation and indirect antibody tests for detection of *Coxiella burnetii* antibody. J Clin Microbiol. 1987;25:1063–1067.
70. Hunt JG, Field PR, Murphy AM. Immunoglobulin responses to *Coxiella burnetii* (Q fever): Single-serum diagnosis of acute infection using an immunofluorescence technique. Infect Immun. 1983;39:977–981.
71. Worswick D, Marmion BP. Antibody response in acute and chronic Q fever and in subjects vaccinated against Q fever. J Med Microbiol. 1985;119:281–296.
72. Dupuis G, Peter O, Peacock M, et al. Immunoglobulin responses in acute Q fever. J Clin Microbiol. 1985;22:484–487.
73. Brouqui P, Dupont HT, Drancourt M, et al. Chronic Q fever: Ninety-two cases from France; including 27 cases without endocarditis. Arch Intern Med. 1993;153:642–649.
74. Turck WPG, Howitt G, Turnberg LA, et al. Chronic Q fever. Q J Med. 1976;45:193–217.

75. Wilson HG, Neilson GH, Galea EG, et al. Q fever endocarditis in Queensland. Circulation. 1976;53:680–684.
76. Grist NR. Q fever endocarditis. Am Heart J. 1968;75:845–846.
77. Robson AO, Shimin CDGL. Chronic Q fever. 1. Clinical aspects of a patient with endocarditis. BMJ. 1959;2:980–953.
78. Varma MPS, Adgey AAJ, Connolly JH. Chronic Q fever endocarditis. Br Heart J. 1980;43:695–699.
79. Tobin MH, Cahill N, Gearty G, et al. Q fever endocarditis. Am J Med. 1982;72:396–400.
80. Kimbrough RC III, Ormsbee RA, Peacock M, et al. Q fever endocarditis in the United States. Ann Intern Med. 1979;91:400–402.
81. Ross PJ, Jacobson J, Muir JR. Q fever endocarditis of porcine xenograft valves. Am Heart J. 1983;105:151–153.
82. Wiley RF, Matthews MB, Peutherere JF, Marion BP. Chronic cryptic Q fever infection of the heart. Lancet. 1979;2:270–272.
83. Subramanya NI, Wright JS, Khan MAR. Failure of rifampicin and co-trimoxazole in Q fever endocarditis. BMJ. 1982;203;342–343.
84. Marmion BP. Subacute rickettsial endocarditis: An unusual complication of Q fever. J Hyg Epidemiol Microbiol Immunol. 1952;6:79–84.
85. Applefield MM, Bellingsley LN, Tucker JH, Fiset P. Q fever endocarditis: A case occurring in the United States. Am Heart J. 1977;93:669–670.
86. Palmer SR, Young SEJ. Q fever endocarditis in England and Wales, 1975–81. Lancet. 1982;2:1148–1149.
87. Chronic Q fever (Editorial). J Infect. 1984;8:1–4.
88. Haldane EV, Marrie TJ, Faulkner RS, et al. Endocarditis due to Q fever in Nova Scotia: Experience with five patients in 1981–1982. J Infect Dis. 1983; 148:978–985.
89. Raoult D, Etienne J, Massip P, et al. Q fever endocarditis in the south of France. J Infect Dis. 1987;155:570–573.
90. Laufer D, Lew PD, Oberhansli I, et al. Chronic Q fever endocarditis with massive splenomegaly in childhood. J Pediatr. 1986;108:535–539.
91. Raoult D, Piquet PH, Gallais H, et al. *Coxiella burnetii* infection of a vascular prosthesis. N Engl J Med. 1986;315:1358–1359.
92. Tellez A, Sainz C, Echevarria C, et al. Q fever in Spain: Acute and chronic cases, 1981–1985, Rev Infect Dis. 1988;10:198–202.
93. Siegman-Igra Y, Kraufman O, Keysary A, et al. Q fever endocarditis in Israel and a worldwide review. Scand J Infect Dis. 1997;29:41–49.
94. Peacock MG, Philip RN, Williams JC, Faulkner RS. Serological valuation of Q fever in humans: Enhanced phase I titers of immunoglobulins G and A are diagnostic for Q fever endocarditis. Infect Immun 1983;41:1089–1098.
95. Fournier PE, Casalta JP, Habib G, et al. Verification of the diagnostic criteria proposed by the Duke Endocarditis Service to permit improved diagnosis of Q fever endocarditis. Am J Med 1996;100:629–633.
96. Durack DT, Lukes AS, Bright DK. New criteria for diagnosis of infective endocarditis: Utilization of specific echocardiographic findings. Am J Med. 1994;96:200–209.
97. Blondeau JM, Williams JC, Marrie TJ. The immune response to phase I and phase II *Coxiella burnetii* antigens as measured by Western immunoblotting. Ann N Y Acad Sci. 1990;590:187–202.
98. Levy PY, Drancourt M, Etienne J, et al. Comparison of different antibiotic regimens for therapy of 32 cases of Q fever endocarditis. Antimicrob Agents Chemother. 1991;35:533–537.
99. Maurin M, Benoliel AM, Bongrand P, Raoult D. Phagolysomal alkalinization and the bactericidal effect of antibiotics: The *Coxiella burnetii* paradigm. J Infect Dis. 1992;166:1097–1102.
100. Hofmann CER, Heaton JW Jr. Q fever hepatitis. Clinical manifestations and pathological findings. Gastroenterology. 1982;83:474–479.
101. Raoult D, Marrie T. Q fever. Clin Infect Dis. 1995;20:489–496.
102. Capo C, Zaffran Y, Zugun F, et al. Production of interleukin-10 and transforming growth factor β by peripheral blood mononuclear cells in Q fever endocarditis. Infect Immun. 1996;64:4143–4147.
103. Dupont HL, Hornick EV, Levin HA, et al. Q fever hepatitis. Ann Intern Med. 1971;74:198–206.
104. Qizilbash AH. The pathology of Q fever as seen on liver biopsy. Arch Pathol Lab Med. 1983;107:364–367.
105. Travis LB, Travis WD, Li C-Y, et al. Q fever. A clinicopathologic study of five cases. Arch Pathol Lab Med. 1986;110:1017–1020.
106. Weir WRC, Bannister B, Chambers S, et al. Chronic Q fever associated with granulomatous hepatitis. J Infect. 1980;8:56–60.
107. Pellegrin M, Delsol G, Auvergnat JC, et al. Granulomatous hepatitis in Q fever. Hum Pathol. 1980;11:51–57.
108. Voigt JJ, Selsol, Fabre J. Liver and bone marrow granulomas in Q fever. Gastroenterology. 1983;84:887–888.
109. Alkan WJ, Ewenchik Z, Eschar J. Q fever and infectious hepatitis. Am J Med. 1965;38:54–61.
110. Harrell GT. Rickettsial involvement of the central nervous system. Med Clin North Am. 1953;37:395–422.
111. Gomez-Aranda F, Diaz JKP, Acebol MR, et al. Computed tomographic brain scan findings in Q fever encephalitis. Neuroradiology. 1984;26:329–332.
112. Marrie TJ. Pneumonia and meningo-encephalitis due to *Coxiella burnetii*. J Infect. 1985;11:59–61.
113. Marrie TJ, Raoult D. Rickettsial infections of the central nervous system. Semin Neurol. 1992;213–224.
114. Reilly S, Northwood JL, Caul EO. Q fever in Plymouth, 1972–88. A review with particular reference to neurological manifestations. Epidemiol Infect. 1990;105:391–408.
115. Drancourt M, Raoult D, Xeridat B, et al. Q fever meningoencephalitis in five patients. Eur J Epidemiol. 1991;7:134–138.
116. Bonetti B, Monaco S, Ferrari S, et al. Demyelinating polyradiculoneuritis following *Coxiella burnetii* infection (Q fever). Ital J Neurol Sci. 1991;12:415–417.
117. Heard SR, Ronalds CJ, Heath RB. *Coxiella burnetii* infection in immunocompromised patients. J Infect. 1985;11:15–18.
118. Kanfer E, Farraj N, Price C, et al. Q fever following bone-marrow transplantation. Bone Marrow Transplant 1988;3:165–168.
119. Loudon MM, Thompson EN. Severe combined immunoblotting syndrome, tissue transplant, leukemia and Q fever. Arch Dis Child. 1988;63:207–209.
120. Raoult D, Brouqui P, Gastraut JA, Marchou B. Acute and chronic Q fever in patients with cancer. Clin Infect Dis. 1992;14:127–130.
121. Raoult D, Levy P-Y, Dupont HT, et al. Q fever and HIV infection. AIDS. 1993;7:81–86.
122. Meis JFGM, Weemaes CRM, Horrevorts AM, et al. Rapidly fatal Q-fever pneumonia in a patient with chronic granulomatous disease. Infection 1992;20:287–289.
123. Ellis ME, Smith CC, Moffatt MAJ. Chronic or fatal Q-fever infection: A review of 16 patients seen in north-east Scotland (1967–1980). Q J Med. 1983;205:54–66.
124. Richardus JH, Duma AM, Huisman J, et al. Q fever in infancy: A review of 18 cases. Pediatr Infect Dis. 1985;4:369–673.
125. Brada M, Bellingham AJ. Bone marrow necrosis and Q fever. BMJ. 1980;210:1108–1109.
126. Estrov Z, Bruck R, Shtalrid M, et al. Histiocytic hemophagocytosis in Q fever. Arch Pathol Lab Med. 1984;108:7.
127. Cardellach F, Font J, Agusti AGN, et al. Q fever and hemolytic anemia. J Infect Dis. 1983;148:769.
128. Ramos HS, Hodges RE, Meroney WH. Q fever: Report of a case simulating lymphoma. Ann Intern Med. 1957;47:1030–1035.
129. Hitchins R, Cobcroft RG, Hocker G. Transient severe hypoplastic anemia in Q fever. Pathology. 1986;18:254–255.
130. Baumbach A, Brehm B, Sauer W, et al. Spontaneous splenic rupture complicating acute Q fever. Am J Gastroenterol. 1992;87:1651–1653.
131. Schuil J, Richardus JH, Baarsma GS, et al. Q fever as a possible cause of bilateral optic neuritis. Br J Ophthalmol. 1985;69:580–583.
132. Conger I, Mallolas J, Mensa J, et al. Erythema nodosum and Q fever. Arch Dermatol. 1987;123:867.
133. Swaby Ed, Fisher-Hoch S, Lambert HP, et al. Is Kawasaki disease a variant of Q fever? Lancet. 1980;2:146.
134. Weir WRC, Bouchet VA, Mitford E, et al. Kawasaki disease in European adult associated with serological response to *Coxiella burnetii*. Lancet. 1985;2:504.
135. Ascher MS, Berman MA, Ruppaner R. Initial clinical and immunologic evaluation of of a new phase I Q fever vaccine and skin test in humans. J Infect Dis. 1983;148:214–224.
136. Marmion BP, Ormsbee RAD, Kyrkou M, et al. Vaccine prophylaxis of abattoir-associated Q fever. Lancet 1984;2:1411–1411.
137. Grant CG, Ascher Ms, Bernard KW, et al. Q fever and experimental sheep. Infect Control. 1985;6:122–123.
138. Polydorou K. Q fever in Cyprus—recent progress. Br Vet J.

Chapter 178

Rickettsia prowazekii (Epidemic or Louse-Borne Typhus)

ALFRED J. SAAH

Louse-borne typhus is the prototype of the typhus group of rickettsial diseases. The primary illness and its recrudescent form (Brill-Zinsser disease [BZD]) are caused by *Rickettsia prowazekii*. Louse-borne typhus is also known as epidemic typhus, classic typhus, typhus exanthematicus, tarbadillo, fleckfieber, and jail fever.

The primary illness was distinguished from typhoid fever by Gerhard in 1836. In 1910, Brill described an illness that was similar to typhus but was milder and not accompanied by body lice. In 1934, Zinsser postulated its pathogenesis as being recurrent louse-borne typhus; this was subsequently confirmed.

The occurrence of typhus in this century parallels the history of war and famine. An astonishing 30 million cases occurred in the Soviet Union and Eastern Europe during 1918–1922, with an estimated 3 million deaths.

During World War II, typhus struck heavily in concentration camps in Eastern Europe and North Africa. Its reputation as a military medical problem was cleverly used to protect residents of occupied areas from deportation to concentration camps for slave labor. The German army avoided areas of epidemic louse-borne typhus by using the Weil-Felix reaction for diagnosis. Knowing this fact, certain physicians used formalin-killed *Proteus* OX-19 strain organisms as a vaccine to create an artificial "epidemic area" of typhus in Poland. Persons would be unwittingly vaccinated (thinking they were receiving a rejuvenating protein suspension) when they were seen by the physicians with any symptom remotely suggestive of typhus. The scheme worked quite effectively, and much later was made public by Lazowski and Matulewicz.[1]

ETIOLOGY

The etiologic agent is *R. prowazekii*, an obligate intracellular bacterium that is closely related antigenically to the agent that causes murine typhus *(Rickettsia typhi)*. The organism is coccobacillary but has inconstant morphologic characteristics. Reproduction is by binary fission, and diplobacilli are produced that are frequently seen in tissue sections. Special staining, Giemsa or Gimenez, provides good visualization of the organisms in the cytoplasm of cells. If isolation of the organism by animal inoculation is attempted, it should be done by experienced personnel and only in specially designed, full-containment facilities. Storing a blood clot or cells from an anticoagulated specimen from a patient at −70°C will maintain viability of the organism for years. Isolation attempts also can be made from blood clots that have been stored in a refrigerator for no longer than several days.

EPIDEMIOLOGY

Louse-borne typhus is transmitted from person to person by the body louse *(Pediculus humanus corporis)*. The cycle is thought to be initiated by a human case of recrudescent typhus or by a recently introduced case of primary louse-borne typhus. The louse feeds on an infected, rickettsemic person. The organism in the louse infects its alimentary tract, resulting in large numbers of organisms in its feces within about 1 week. Close personal or clothing contact is usually required to transmit lice to others. When the louse takes a blood meal, it defecates. The irritation causes the host to scratch the site, thereby contaminating the bite wound with louse feces. Human infection might also occur by mucous membrane inoculation with contaminated louse feces.

Rickettsia prowazekii and the louse do not coexist harmoniously; the louse dies of its infection (from obstruction of its alimentary tract) in 1 to 3 weeks and does not transmit the organism to its offspring.

Human conditions that foster the proliferation of lice are especially common during winter and during war or natural disasters—wherein clothing is not changed, crowding occurs, and bathing is very infrequent. In rural highlands of Africa and Central and South America, normal conditions favor proliferation of human lice; the resulting disease burden from louse-borne typhus, however, is largely unmeasured,[2] but case-fatality rates are lower now that treatment is more generally available; Ethiopia reported 3.8% for 3759 cases in 1984,[3] and more recently, an epidemic in a Burundi prison produced a crude mortality rate of 2.6% in January 1996.[4]

A reservoir of *R. prowazekii*[5] other than humans apparently exists in the southern flying squirrel *Glaucomys volans*.[6] This squirrel is distributed over the eastern United States from southern Maine to Florida and westward to the center of the United States (Minnesota to eastern Texas). Transmission among these rodents is suspected to be by squirrel lice or fleas, or both.[7]

Fifteen reported human cases of indigenously acquired epidemic typhus have been diagnosed serologically in the eastern United States.[8, 9] Evidence has been presented that implicates the flying squirrel as the probable source of infection,[10] but the mode of transmission is unclear. Confirmation of the cause still requires isolating the organism from humans.

Of the 15 reported patients with epidemic typhus, 14 resided in rural or suburban settings, 12 were white, 3 were black, and 8 were female. The median age for males was 24 years (range, 17 to 35 years) and for females, 44 years (range, 11 to 81 years). Twelve cases had onset during the colder months (November through March). All seven patients in one report[10] and two in the other[6] had direct or indirect contact with flying squirrels; however, such exposure is difficult to interpret without a comparison group. There was no evidence for person-to-person transmission.

PATHOGENESIS AND PATHOLOGIC CHARACTERISTICS

After local proliferation at the site of the louse bite, the organism spreads hematogenously. *Rickettsia prowazekii*, like most rickettsiae, produces a vasculitis by infecting the endothelial cells of capillaries, small arteries, and veins. The process results in fibrin and platelet deposition and then occlusion of the vessel. Perivascular infiltration with lymphocytes, plasma cells, histiocytes, and polymorphonuclear leukocytes occurs with or without frank necrosis of the vessel. The angiitis is most marked in the skin, heart, central nervous system, skeletal muscle, and kidneys.[10, 11] If local thrombosis is extensive, gangrene of skin or distal portions of the extremities, or both, occurs.

CLINICAL MANIFESTATIONS

Signs and Symptoms

After an incubation period of approximately 1 week, an abrupt onset with intense headache, chills, fever, and myalgia is characteristic. There is no eschar. The fever worsens quickly (102 to 104°F) and becomes unremitting, and the patient is soon prostrated by the illness. A rash begins in the axillary folds and upper part of the trunk on about the fifth day of illness and spreads centrifugally. Initially, the rash consists of nonconfluent, pink macules that fade on pressure. Within several days, the rash becomes maculopapular, darker, petechial, and confluent and involves the entire body but spares the face, palms, and soles.

Some manifestations of louse-borne typhus that occur with varying frequency include a nonproductive cough with radiographic evidence of pulmonary infiltrates, deafness,[12] and tinnitus.

Indigenously acquired epidemic typhus is also characterized by abrupt onset and high fever. Overall, however, the illness seems to be milder than classic louse-borne typhus, but life-threatening illness has occurred. When signs and symptoms were known in the 15 reported cases, 9 of 13 patients had headache, 4 of 8 had myalgia, and 8 of 15 had rash. The rash was typical in distribution, but it frequently was evanescent. Signs of central nervous system involvement (other than headache) were found in six patients. The signs ranged from meningismus in one patient, to confusion or delirium in three patients, to coma in two patients. One patient with confusion had cerebrospinal fluid lymphocytic pleocytosis.

Course

In untreated, uncomplicated louse-borne typhus, the fever lyses after 2 weeks of illness; recovery of normal mentation is rapid, but recovery of strength usually requires a prolonged convalescence (2 to 3 months). Overall mortality is quite variable, but it has been reported to be as high as 40% under adverse conditions. Age-specific mortality rates are highest among those older than 60 years. It is a mild illness in children. Specific treatment results in prompt recovery.

Response to antirickettsial agents in indigenously acquired epidemic typhus was reported to have usually occurred within 24 hours, with recovery in most patients after 48 hours. Three of the four patients who did not receive specific therapy recovered in 14 days. The remaining patient developed renal failure, required dialysis, and recovered. The cause of this patient's renal failure, however, is unclear (J. Eastman, personal communication).

Louse-borne typhus in a vaccinated person produces a mild illness that closely mimics murine typhus clinically (see "Diagnosis").

DIAGNOSIS

In the proper setting of cold weather, infrequent bathing and changing of clothes, crowded conditions, and the presence of lice, the clinical symptomatology described previously is compelling evidence for the presence of louse-borne typhus. The progression of rash serves to distinguish the disease from Rocky Mountain spotted fever, which progresses centripetally, beginning on the wrists and ankles.

In the United States, diagnosis requires a high index of suspicion because of the great variability in presenting symptoms. It is important to examine the axillary folds repeatedly for evidence of rash. During the colder months of November through March, if Rocky Mountain spotted fever is suspected from the clinical picture, this should be a clue in considering the diagnosis of epidemic typhus.[13]

The Weil-Felix reaction is the same as in murine typhus; special serologic methods are used to differentiate louse-borne typhus from murine typhus. The polymerase chain reaction may provide a useful alternative to serodiagnosis or rickettsia cultivation.[14]

Nonrickettsial infections that, at some time during their course, may mimic louse-borne typhus include meningococcemia, measles, typhoid fever, bacterial meningitis, secondary syphilis, leptospirosis, relapsing fever, infectious mononucleosis, and rubella.

TREATMENT AND PREVENTION

Treatment

Chloramphenicol and tetracycline both are effective against typhus. The recommended dose for tetracycline is 25 mg/kg of body weight per day in four equally divided oral doses. The dosage for chloramphenicol is 50 mg/kg of body weight per day also in four equally divided oral doses. Oral chloramphenicol is not available in the United States. If the patient is too ill to take drugs orally, an intravenous preparation of chloramphenicol or tetracycline in the dosage described is recommended for use. If renal function is impaired, chloramphenicol or doxycycline (100 mg twice daily) should be used. Therapy should be continued for 2 to 3 days after defervescence.

In louse-borne typhus only, a single dose of doxycycline, 100 mg orally, is curative.[15] Conventional, multidose therapy is recommended for indigenously acquired epidemic typhus and murine typhus.

Treatment before serious complications occur virtually eliminates fatal illness. When antimicrobial therapy begins very early after onset (within 48 hours), an occasional patient will relapse. The recurrent illness responds to a second course of therapy.

Prevention

Control of the human body louse and the conditions that foster its proliferation is the mainstay in preventing louse-borne typhus. A vaccine is also available, but its widespread use is subordinate to delousing the affected population. Delousing should be done with an insecticide shown to be lousicidal for the infecting lice. Usually, dichlorodiphenyltrichloroethane or lindane in powder form is effective. If the lice are not susceptible to these insecticides, then malathion or carbaryl may be used.

Typhus vaccine is prepared from formaldehyde-inactivated *R. prowazekii* grown in embryonated eggs. Typhus vaccination is suggested only for the following special-risk groups[16]: (1) persons such as scientific investigators (e.g., anthropologists, archaeologists, or geologists), oil field and construction workers, missionaries, and some government workers who live in or visit foreign areas where typhus cases actually occur and who will be in close contact with the indigenous population; (2) medical personnel, including nurses and attendants, who provide care for patients in foreign areas in which louse-borne typhus occurs; and (3) laboratory personnel who work with *R. prowazekii*.

No specific action can be recommended to prevent the occurrence of suspected indigenously acquired epidemic typhus.

BRILL-ZINSSER DISEASE

BZD occurs as a recrudescence of previous infection with *R. prowazekii*.[17] It occurs in the United States primarily in immigrants from Eastern Europe whose initial infection was during World War II. Its pathogenesis is unknown, but recurrence is presumed to be precipitated by stress or a waning immune system.

Manifestations and Diagnosis

The illness is similar to louse-borne typhus, but it is usually milder and more closely resembles murine typhus. Serologically, the Weil-Felix reaction is usually negative, but a low titer to OX-19 may be present. The differentiation of primary louse-borne or murine typhus from BZD is made by showing that the antibody produced is immunoglobulin M (murine or primary louse-borne) or immunoglobulin G (BZD).[18]

Treatment and Prevention

Therapy is the same as for primary louse-borne typhus. There is no known method of preventing BZD other than preventing primary infection.

REFERENCES

1. Lazowski ES, Matulewicz S. Serendipitous discovery of artificial positive Weil-Felix reaction used in "private immunological war." ASM News. 1977;43:300–302.
2. Perine PL, Chandler BP, Krause DK, et al. A clinicoepidemiological study of epidemic typhus in Africa. Clin Infect Dis. 1992;14:1149–1158.
3. World Health Organization. Louse-borne typhus. 1983–1984. Weekly Epidemiol Rec. 1984;57:45–46.
4. Bise G, Coninx R. Epidemic typhus in a prison in Burundi. Trans R Soc Trop Med Hyg. 1997;91:133–134.
5. Regnery RL, Fu ZY, Spruill CL. Flying squirrel–associated *Rickettsia prowazekii* (epidemic typhus rickettsiae) characterized by a specific DNA fragment produced by restriction endonuclease digestion. J Clin Microbiol 1986;23:189–191.
6. Bozeman FM, Masiello SA, Williams MS, et al. Epidemic typhus rickettsiae isolated from flying squirrels. Nature. 1975;255:545–547.
7. Sonenshine DE, Bozeman FM, Williams MS, et al. Epizootiology of epidemic typhus *(Rickettsia prowazekii)* in flying squirrels. Am J Trop Med Hyg. 1978;27:339–349.
8. McDade JE, Shephard CC, Redus MA, et al. Evidence of *Rickettsia prowazekii* infections in the United States. Am J Trop Med Hyg. 1980;29:277–284.
9. Duma RJ, Sonenshine DE, Bozeman FM, et al. Epidemic typhus in the United States associated with flying squirrels. JAMA. 1981;245:2318–2323.
10. Wolbach SB, Todd JL, Palfrey FW. The Etiology and Pathology of Typhus. Cambridge, Mass: Harvard University Press; 1922.
11. Committee on Pathology, Division of Medical Sciences, National Research Council. Pathology of epidemic typhus. JAMA. 1953;56:397, 512.
12. Friedmann I, Frohlich A, Wright A. Epidemic typhus fever and hearing loss: A histological study (Hallpike collection of temporal bone sections.) J. Laryngol Otol. 1993;107:275–283.
13. Kaplan JE, McDade JE, Newhouse VF. Suspected Rocky Mountain spotted fever in the winter—epidemic typhus? (Letter). N Engl J Med. 1981;305:1648.
14. Carl M, Tibbs CW, Dobson ME, et al. Diagnosis of acute typhus infection using the polymerase chain reaction. J Infect Dis. 1990;161:791–793.
15. Perine PL, Krause DW, Awoke A, et al. Single-dose doxycycline treatment of louse-borne relapsing fever and epidemic typhus. Lancet. 1974;2:742–744.
16. Centers for Disease Control and Prevention. Typhus vaccine. MMWR Morb Mortal Wkly Rep. 1978;27:189.

17. Green CR, Fishbein D, Gleiberman I. Brill-Zinsser: Still with us (Letter). JAMA. 1990;264:1811–1812.
18. Ormsbee R, Peacock M, Philip R, et al. Serologic diagnosis of epidemic typhus fever. Am J Epidemiol. 1977;105:261–271.

Chapter 179

Rickettsia typhi (Murine Typhus)

J. STEPHEN DUMLER
DAVID H. WALKER

Since 1926, when Maxcy successfully differentiated among typhus fevers and identified murine typhus as a distinct clinical and epidemiologic entity, and 1931, when Dyer isolated a new typhus group rickettsia from rats and fleas, murine typhus has been recognized as a worldwide zoonotic problem.[1] Often underrecognized and believed to be clinically mild, in reality murine typhus may occur in epidemics or with high prevalence in certain geographic regions.[2–6] Illness may be severe, with death occurring in a small proportion of individuals. The identification of a new rickettsial agent of flea-borne typhus and the association of both this agent and the classic murine typhus agent with cat fleas illustrate the changing ecology of this zoonosis and further complicate clinical and laboratory recognition.[7–9]

ETIOLOGY

Long recognized as the etiologic agent of murine typhus, *Rickettsia typhi* is an obligate intracellular bacterium that infects endothelial cells in mammalian hosts and midgut epithelial cells in the flea host. A new rickettsial agent, *Rickettsia felis*, has been recognized to share some antigenic and genetic components with *R. typhi*. This agent has been identified in association with cat fleas[10] and opossums and has been identified in the blood of a patient with flea exposure and suspected murine typhus.[7] Genotypic characterization of the gene for a 17-kD lipoprotein (citrate synthase) and the gene for 16S ribosomal RNA has shown unique sequences for both rickettsiae; in fact, *R. felis* is now recognized to be more closely related to the spotted fever group rickettsiae, *Rickettsia australis*, *Rickettsia akari*, and *Rickettsia helvetica*.[8, 9, 11] *Rickettsia typhi* and *R. felis* share epitopes present on the major protein antigen, the rickettsial outer membrane protein B (rOmpB),[11] a surface array protein similar to that present in other gram-negative bacteria. These organisms are well adapted for intracellular life, and within the host cell, *R. typhi* may accumulate to significant numbers before host cell lysis and further spread of the rickettsiae.

EPIDEMIOLOGY

Murine typhus is found worldwide and is especially prevalent in temperate and subtropical seaboard regions, where the most important rat reservoirs (*Rattus* spp.) and flea vector (*Xenopsylla cheopis*) are found.[1, 12] An important vector in some areas (south Texas and southern California) is the cat flea (*Ctenocephalides felis*), and opossums have been implicated as a reservoir in these areas.[5, 8, 12–14] Thus, residents and visitors to these urban and suburban regions are at risk when flea-bearing animals bring infected fleas into close proximity to humans.

Murine typhus persists at a low level in the United States, where most cases are seen in south Texas and southern California. Yet outbreaks are well documented around the world, especially in regions with inadequate vector and reservoir control.[1, 3, 6, 13–17] In fact, among Khmers displaced into temporary shelters at the Thai-Cambodian border, 70% of patients with unexplained fever had murine typhus, and the calculated attack rate was approximately 172 in 100,000 adult patients during this period.[6] Most patients are adults, although persons of all ages may become ill. Cases are recognized year round, with a peak prevalence from April through June in Texas[5] and during the warm months of summer and early fall elsewhere.[1, 13] It is worthwhile remembering that murine typhus can occur in travelers returning from endemic regions throughout the world.[18–21]

The disease is transmitted after the inoculation of infected flea feces into a pruritic flea bite wound. Since predominantly gut epithelial cells are infected in the flea vector, a reservoir of infected fleas is maintained mostly by horizontal transmission from flea to vertebrate host to uninfected flea.[22] Once infected, the flea maintains the rickettsial infection for the duration of its life. *Rickettsia typhi* may also infect the flea reproductive organs and foregut tissues, which explains the low levels of transovarial (vertical) transmission and direct inoculation via flea bite.[23] *Rickettsia felis*, in contrast, is effectively transmitted transovarially and trans-stadially over generations in the cat flea and may also be transmitted to mammalian hosts in infected flea feces.[12] Fleas are unaffected by gut epithelial cell or disseminated *R. typhi* or *R. felis* infection.[8]

PATHOLOGY AND PATHOGENESIS

There are few accurate descriptions of the histopathology of murine typhus despite the fact that the case-fatality rate ranges between 1 and 4%.[5, 24] Pathologic findings indicate a systemic endothelial infection similar to Rocky Mountain spotted fever.[25, 26] Lymphohistiocytic vasculitis may affect any organ, and in fatal cases interstitial pneumonitis, interstitial nephritis, interstitial myocarditis, meningitis, and portal triaditis may be present. Rickettsiae may be demonstrated in many organs and are especially numerous in foci of vasculitis.[25] This underlying vasculitic lesion and the rickettsia-induced vascular injury account for most or all of the clinicopathologic abnormalities. As vascular injury accumulates, a substantial loss of intravascular volume, albumin, and electrolytes occurs, and leukocytes and platelets are consumed at foci of infection. With multifocal heavy infection and the attendant inflammation, vascular and parenchymal injury may yield localized symptoms, signs, or laboratory findings related to the sites of infection and injury. The induction of hypovolemia insufficiently corrected by normal homeostatic mechanisms further exacerbates compromise of tissue perfusion and may lead to prerenal azotemia. Mild to moderate hepatic injury is a frequent finding in murine typhus and probably results from multifocal infection of hepatic sinusoidal and portal endothelium with "bystander" hepatocyte damage.[5, 27] With extensive rickettsial vascular injury and hypoperfusion secondary to transvascular volume loss, the result may be renal failure, respiratory failure, central nervous system abnormalities, or multiorgan failure.[5]

CLINICAL MANIFESTATIONS

Signs and Symptoms

Usually only a small proportion of patients with murine typhus recall a flea bite or flea exposure, and an incubation period of approximately 1 to 2 weeks may transpire before an abrupt onset of illness.[5, 28] The presentation is often nonspecific, and fever (96%), severe headache (45%), chills (44%), myalgia (33%), and nausea (33%) are the most frequently reported early findings.[5] Rash is noted in only 18% of patients at presentation, and over the course of illness, approximately 50% (range, 2 to 71%) will develop this sign.[5, 28] As the illness progresses, most patients continue with fever and may have nausea (48%), vomiting (40%) and anorexia (35%), or cough (35%).[5] Some studies record the presence of hepatomegaly and splenomegaly in up to 24% and 10% of patients, respectively.[29, 30] Neurologic signs and symptoms have been reported to occur in 1 to 45% of patients and usually include confusion, stupor, seizures, or localized findings such as ataxia.[5, 31, 32]

The absence of rash or lack of petechiae should not dissuade one from a diagnosis of murine typhus. In fact, when rash is identified, it is described as macular or maculopapular in 78%, and petechiae are noted in less than 10%.[5] These lesions are most often distributed on the trunk (88% of cases), but involvement of the extremities (>45%) is not infrequent. The initial rash distribution is equally frequent on the extremities and on the trunk. On occasion, the rash may also be present on the palms and soles.[5]

The clinical course of murine typhus is usually uncomplicated, and childhood murine typhus is often mild, with one series reporting only nighttime fever with normal daytime activities.[33] However, occasional patients develop central nervous system abnormalities, renal insufficiency, hepatic insufficiency, respiratory failure requiring intubation, or hematemesis. Patients are ill enough that 10% require admission to an intensive care facility, and up to 4% of hospitalized patients die from the infection.[5]

Once the diagnosis has been considered and appropriate therapy begun, most patients defervesce rapidly (median 3 days). Findings associated with severe illness include a high leukocyte count; an elevated blood urea nitrogen level, creatinine level, and blood urea nitrogen/creatinine ratio; and low serum calcium, potassium, sodium, and albumin concentrations. Advanced age and a prolonged interval before the administration of specific antirickettsial therapy are also significantly correlated with severity.[5] One report suggests a link between hemolytic disorders such as glucose-6-phosphate dehydrogenase deficiency, hemoglobinopathy, and thalassemia and more severe hepatic involvement including jaundice.[27] A trend toward more severe infection is also noted in patients treated with trimethoprim-sulfamethoxazole.

Laboratory Features

Early mild leukopenia (which coincides with thrombocytopenia) is seen in one fourth to one half of patients during the first 7 days of illness. Subsequently, leukocytosis develops in less than one third.[5] Prothrombin times are occasionally prolonged, but true disseminated intravascular coagulation with hypofibrinogenemia is very infrequently documented. The most frequent laboratory abnormality in murine typhus, a mild to moderate elevation in serum aspartate aminotransferase levels, is present in the vast majority (90 to 92%), and related indices of hepatic and cellular injury (levels of alanine aminotransferase, alkaline phosphatase, lactate dehydrogenase) are often elevated in parallel.[5, 27] The rickettsia-induced vascular damage frequently leads to hypoproteinemia (45%) and hypoalbuminemia (89%) and is probably responsible in large part for the multiple serum electrolyte abnormalities, especially the mild hyponatremia (60%) and hypocalcemia (79%). Even in the presence of symptomatic central nervous system abnormalities, cerebrospinal fluid examination may be normal or reveal pleocytosis and increased protein concentration, resembling the findings in viral or leptospiral meningoencephalitis.[5, 34]

DIAGNOSIS

The early diagnosis of murine typhus is still mainly based on clinical suspicion. Since early and specific antirickettsial therapy is indicated to avoid severe or potentially fatal infections, treatment should not be withheld while awaiting laboratory confirmation. The predominant method of laboratory confirmation is serologic. Since antibodies are infrequently detected during the acute illness, serologic diagnosis is retrospective. The obsolete Weil-Felix agglutination reactions have been proved insensitive, are intrinsically nonspecific, and as such should not be used to establish a definitive diagnosis.[35] Instead, sensitive serologic tests that utilize specific *R. typhi* antigens such as indirect fluorescent antibody, latex agglutination, or solid-phase immunoassay[36] are preferable. With the use of a sensitive and specific test such as indirect fluorescent antibody, diagnostic titers are present in approximately 50% of murine typhus patients within 1 week and in nearly all within 15 days after the onset of illness.[5] Since typhus-group rickettsiae share antigens, serologic evaluation will not distinguish among epidemic typhus, murine typhus, and *R. felis* typhus.[9] In occasional sera, reactions against both typhus and spotted fever groups are observed, creating serodiagnostic difficulties.

Although affording a definitive diagnosis, culture is often considered dangerous and difficult; however, in the age of routine viral isolation and universal precautions, rickettsial isolation must be reconsidered as a valuable adjunct to diagnosis. A shell vial assay for the isolation of spotted fever group rickettsiae has been successfully used to confirm infection during the acute phase of illness. This method could be easily adapted for the isolation of *R. typhi* and the confirmation of murine typhus.[37] For rickettsial isolation from peripheral blood, anticoagulated, sterile specimens should be obtained before antirickettsial therapy and processed immediately. If a delay is unavoidable, specimens should be stored for no longer than 48 hours at 4°C or can be frozen at −70°C until culture is attempted.

Recently described methods for laboratory confirmation of rickettsiosis include the immunohistologic demonstration of *R. typhi* in tissues,[25, 38] polymerase chain reaction amplification of rickettsial nucleic acids in peripheral blood,[39] and immunomagnetic retrieval of circulating endothelial cells coupled with immunocytologic demonstration of intraendothelial cell rickettsiae.[40] The last method might not perform as well for typhus rickettsioses as for spotted fever group rickettsioses because of the lytic destruction of the infected endothelial cell on release of typhus rickettsiae. However, none of these methods have been adequately evaluated for murine typhus, and thus the sensitivities and specificities are unknown.

The reduction in the prevalence of murine typhus has seen a parallel decrease in accurate early diagnosis. Most patients are initially investigated for fever of undetermined origin, and less often patients are investigated for suspected pneumonia, cerebrovascular accident, gastroenteritis, or neoplasms, among other diagnoses.[5, 24] Despite the occasional presence of findings that suggest alternative diagnoses because of isolated organ system involvement, an early clue toward the successful diagnosis of murine typhus is the recognition of the systemic manifestations associated with fever. Other rickettsioses may cause considerable difficulty in the differential diagnosis, and Rocky Mountain spotted fever is the most frequent. Murine typhus and Rocky Mountain spotted fever may be distinguished on the basis of the history, clinical presentation, and serologic tests. Many patients with murine typhus are exposed to flea vectors in urban or suburban regions, and a small proportion (1 to 40%) report a flea bite or exposure, whereas patients with Rocky Mountain spotted fever often acquire illness after rural exposures or documented tick bites and more often develop rash and petechiae. The distribution of rash is of little help in individual cases. The likelihood of monocytotropic or granulocytotropic ehrlichiosis is diminished if leukopenia and thrombocytopenia are minimal or absent, although serum hepatic transaminase levels may be elevated in both murine typhus and the ehrlichioses. Murine typhus, Rocky Mountain spotted fever, and the ehrlichioses occur during warm seasons in which the vector arthropods are most active. In contrast, the louse vector of epidemic typhus is most active and likely to spread its rickettsial agent in cooler seasons when layers of clothing are worn, persons are crowded indoors, and personal hygiene diminishes. Differentiation of the sporadic cases of sylvatic typhus, caused by *Rickettsia prowazekii*, from murine typhus may be exceedingly difficult, but the former illness is suggested when exposure to potential reservoirs (e.g., flying squirrels) is elicited in the history.

The differential diagnosis of murine typhus is quite long because of its usually nonspecific presentation. Aside from the rickettsioses and the ehrlichioses, alternative diagnoses that may need to be considered include meningococcemia, measles, typhoid fever, bacterial and viral meningitis, secondary syphilis, leptospirosis, toxic shock syndrome, and Kawasaki disease.

TREATMENT AND PREVENTION

The preferred agent for treatment of *R. typhi* infection is a tetracycline, such as doxycycline. Recent clinical trials of fluoroquinolones in the treatment of spotted fever group rickettsioses have been performed in Europe; the results of these trials and individual case reports suggest that such drugs including ciprofloxacin, ofloxacin, and pefloxacin may be effective alternatives.[41, 42] In vitro, the fluoroquinolones, sparfloxacin, temofloxacin, and clinafloxacin, as well as the new macrolides, azithromycin and clarithromycin, inhibit rickettsial growth at concentrations achieved routinely in human therapy.[43, 44] *Rickettsia felis* growth is inhibited in vitro and in vivo in a rat model by doxycycline, chloramphenicol, rifampin, and erythromycin.[45] Whether such results may be extrapolated for broad treatment of *R. typhi* or *R. felis* human infections awaits additional studies. The current recommendation for tetracycline is 25 to 50 mg/kg/day in four divided oral doses, and for doxycycline, 100 mg orally twice daily. In severely ill patients, intravenous doxycycline or chloramphenicol is effective, the latter given as 50 to 75 mg/kg/day in four divided doses. Oral chloramphenicol is not currently available in the United States. Corticosteroids are occasionally used for severe central nervous system disease, but no controlled study to evaluate their efficacy has been performed. Infected pregnant patients must be evaluated individually, and either chloramphenicol (early trimester) or doxycycline (late trimester) may be used if necessary. Antimicrobial therapy should be continued until 2 to 3 days after defervescence. After the initiation of therapy, patients become afebrile at a median interval of 3 days. Single-dose doxycycline therapy was effective in nearly 80% of patients in one study[29] but is not routinely advocated since relapse may occur.

Prevention is mainly directed toward the control of flea vectors and potential flea hosts.[8, 13] Since the potential for epidemic spread is associated with foci of infected flea infestations, all suspected cases of murine typhus should be promptly reported to local public health authorities. Although usually considered a mild illness, murine typhus may be fatal or severe if misdiagnosed or inadequately treated. Unfortunately, no vaccine of proven effectiveness exists for murine typhus. Recovery from natural infection confers solid, long-lasting immunity to reinfection.

REFERENCES

1. Azad AF. Epidemiology of murine typhus. Annu Rev Entomol. 1990;35:553–569.
2. Brown AE, Meek SR, Maneechai N, et al. Murine typhus among Khmers at an evacuation site on the Thai-Kampuchean border. Am J Trop Med Hyg. 1989;92:373–378.
3. Al-Awadi AR, Al-Kazemi N, Ezzat G, et al. Murine typhus in Kuwait in 1978. Bull WHO. 1982;60:283–289.
4. Centers for Disease Control and Prevention. Outbreak of murine typhus—Texas. MMWR Morb Mortal Wkly Rep. 1983;32:131–132.
5. Dumler JS, Taylor JP, Walker DH. Clinical and laboratory features of murine typhus in south Texas, 1980 through 1987. JAMA. 1991;266:1365–1370.
6. Duffy PE, Le Buillouzic H, Gass RF, et al. Murine typhus identified as a major cause of febrile illness in a camp for displaced Khmers in Thailand. Am J Trop Med Hyg. 1990;43:520–526.
7. Schriefer ME, Sacci JB Jr, Dumler JS, et al. Identification of a novel rickettsial infection in a patient diagnosed with murine typhus. J Clin Microbiol. 1994;32:949–954.
8. Azad AF, Radulovic S, Higgins JA, et al. Flea-borne rickettsioses: Ecologic considerations. Emerg Infect Dis. 1997;3:319–327.
9. Higgins JA, Radulovic S, Schreifer ME, Azad AF. *Rickettsia felis*: A new species of pathogenic rickettsia isolated from cat fleas. J Clin Microbiol. 1996;34:671–674.
10. Azad AF, Sacci JB, Nelson WM, et al. Genetic characterization and transovarial transmission of a typhus-like rickettsia found in cat fleas. Proc Natl Acad Sci U S A. 1992;89:43–46.
11. Radulovic S, Higgins JA, Jaworski DC, et al. Isolation, cultivation, and partial characterization of the ELB agent associated with cat fleas. Infect Immun. 1995;63:4826–4829.
12. Traub R, Wisseman CL Jr, Farhang-Azad A. The ecology of murine typhus: A critical review. Trop Dis Bull. 1978;75:237–317.
13. Adams JR, Schmidtmann ET, Azad AF. Infection of colonized cat fleas, *Ctenocephalides felis* (Bouché), with a rickettsia-like microorganism. Am J Trop Med Hyg. 1990;43:400–409.
14. Irons JV, Bohls SW, Thurman DC, et al. Probable role of the cat flea, *Ctenocephalides felis*, in the transmission of murine typhus. Am J Trop Med. 1944;24:359–362.
15. Fan MY, Walker DH, Yu SR, et al. Epidemiology and ecology of rickettsial diseases in the People's Republic of China. Rev Infect Dis. 1987;9:823–840.
16. Woodruff PW, Morrill JC, Burans JP, et al. A study of viral and rickettsial exposure and causes of fever in Juba, southern Sudan. Trans R Soc Trop Med Hyg. 1988;82:761–766.
17. Tissot Dupont, H, Brouqui P, Faugere B, Raoult D. Prevalence of antibodies to *Coxiella burnetii, Rickettsia conorii*, and *Rickettsia typhi* in seven African countries. Clin Infect Dis. 1995;21:1126–1133.
18. Abramson MA, Sexton DJ. Diagnosis: Murine typhus *(Rickettsia typhi)*. Clin Infect Dis. 1995;21:991.
19. Hassan ISA, Ong ELC. Fever in the returned traveller. Remember murine typhus! J Infect. 1995;31:173–174.
20. Pether JVS, Jones W, Lloyd G, et al. Fatal murine typhus from Spain. Lancet. 1994;344:897–898.
21. Wilson ME, Brush AD, Meany MC. Murine typhus acquired during short-term urban travel. Am J Med. 1989;87:233–240.
22. Azad AF, Traub R. Transmission of murine typhus rickettsiae by *Xenopsylla cheopis*, with notes on experimental infection and effects of temperature. Am J Trop Med Hyg. 1985;34:555–563.
23. Azad AF, Traub R, Baqar S. Transovarial transmission of murine typhus rickettsiae in *Xenopsylla cheopis* fleas. Science. 1985;227:543–545.
24. Miller ES, Beeson PB. Murine typhus fever. Medicine. 1946;25:1–15.
25. Walker DH, Parks FM, Betz TB, et al. Histopathology and immunohistologic demonstration of the distribution of *Rickettsia typhi* in fatal murine typhus. Am J Clin Pathol. 1989;91:720–724.
26. Binford CH, Ecker HD. Endemic (murine) typhus. Report of autopsy findings in three cases. Am J Clin Pathol. 1947;17:797–806.
27. Silpapojakul K, Mitarnun W, Ovartlarnporn B, et al. Liver involvement in murine typhus. Q J Med. 1996;89:623–629.
28. Betz TG, Rawlings JA, Taylor JP, et al. Endemic typhus in Texas. Texas Med. 1983;79:48–53.
29. Silpapojakul K, Chayakul P, Krisanapan S. Murine typhus in Thailand: Clinical features, diagnosis and treatment. Q J Med. 1993;86:43–47.
30. Tselentis Y, Babalis TL, Chrysanthis D, et al. Clinicoepidemiological study of murine typhus on the Greek island of Evia. Eur J Epidemiol. 1992;8:268–272.
31. Stuart BM, Pullen RL. Endemic (murine) typhus fever: Clinical observations of 180 cases. Ann Intern Med. 1945;23:520–536.
32. Samra Y, Shaked Y, Maier MK. Delayed neurologic display in murine typhus. Report of two cases. Arch Intern Med. 1989;149:949–951.
33. Silpapojakul K, Chupuppakarn S, Yuthasompob S, et al. Scrub and murine typhus in children with obscure fever in the tropics. Pediatr Infect Dis J. 1991;10:200–203.
34. Silpapojakul K, Ukkachoke C, Krisanapan S, Silpapojakul K. Rickettsial meningitis and encephalitis. Arch Intern Med. 1991;151:1753–1757.
35. Hechemy KE, Stevens RW, Sasowski S, et al. Discrepancies in Weil-Felix and microimmunofluorescence test results for Rocky Mountain spotted fever. J Clin Microbiol. 1979;9:292–293.
36. Kelly DJ, Chan CT, Paxton H, et al. Comparative evaluation of a commercial enzyme immunoassay for the detection of human antibody to *Rickettsia typhi*. Clin Diagn Lab Immunol. 1995;2:356–360.
37. Marrero M, Raoult D. Centrifugation–shell vial technique for rapid detection of Mediterranean spotted fever rickettsia in blood culture. Am J Trop Med Hyg. 1989;40:197–199.
38. Walker DH, Feng H-M, Ladner S, et al. Immunohistochemical diagnosis of typhus rickettsioses using an anti-lipopolysaccharide monoclonal antibody. Mod Pathol. 1997;10:1038–1042.
39. Carl M, Tibbs CW, Dobson ME, et al. Diagnosis of acute typhus infection using the polymerase chain reaction. J Infect Dis. 1990;161:791–793.
40. Drancourt M, George F, Brouqui P, et al. Diagnosis of Mediterranean spotted fever by indirect immunofluorescence of *Rickettsia conorii* in circulation endothelial cells isolated with monoclonal antibody–coated immunomagnetic beads. J Infect Dis. 1992;166:660–663.
41. Raoult D, Drancourt M. Antimicrobial therapy of rickettsial diseases. Antimicrob Agents Chemother. 1991;35:2457–2462.
42. Strand Ö, Strömberg A. Case report. Ciprofloxacin treatment of murine typhus. Scand J Infect Dis. 1990;22:503–504.
43. Keren G, Itzhaki A, Oron C, Keysary A. Evaluation of the anti-rickettsial activity of fluoroquinolones. Drugs. 1995;49(Suppl 2):208–210.
44. Kesary A, Itzhaki A, Rubinstein E, et al. The in-vitro anti-rickettsial activity of macrolides. J Antimicrob Chemother. 1996;38:727–731.
45. Radulovic S, Higgins JA, Jaworski DC, Azad AF. In vitro and in vivo antibiotic susceptibilities of ELB rickettsiae. Antimicrob Agents Chemother. 1995;39:2564–2566.

Chapter 180

Orientia tsutsugamushi (Scrub Typhus)

ALFRED J. SAAH

Scrub typhus is an acute, febrile illness of humans that is caused by *Orientia tsutsugamushi*,[1] formerly *Rickettsia tsutsugamushi*; it is transmitted to humans by the bite of larval-stage trombiculid mites (chiggers). Naturally occurring disease in humans occurs only in the Far East, but cases imported to the United States have been recognized.

ETIOLOGY

Orientia tsutsugamushi is an obligate intracellular bacterium that grows free in the cytoplasm of infected cells, that is, has no vacuolar membrane. The organism can best be seen in tissue by using the Giemsa stain. It is rather unusual among rickettsiae because of its large number of serotypes. However, there are three major serotypes (Karp, Gilliam, and Kato) that have sufficient cross-reactivity with antigens from other strains to be useful diagnostically by the indirect microimmunofluorescent test.[2] Research in Japan continues to identify new antigenic types.[3]

EPIDEMIOLOGY

Scrub typhus occurs over a wide area of eastern Asia and the western Pacific region, from Korea to Australia, and from Japan to India and Pakistan. It gets its name from the type of vegetation that harbors the vector, that is, scrub or secondary vegetation in transitional terrain between forest and clearings. The name *scrub* is not altogether accurate because endemic areas are known from sandy beaches to semiarid locations.[4]

Scrub typhus is an important problem for both military personnel and local residents. Civilian disease is endemic in many parts of the Far East. It is found most often in rural inhabitants and is usually occupationally acquired.[5, 6]

Scrub typhus is a zoonotic disease in which humans are accidental hosts. The vector of the organism to humans is the larval stage (chigger) of trombiculid mites (*Leptotrombidium deliense* and others). These mites probably also represent the major reservoir of the organism because of the extraordinarily high rates of transovarial transmission and because most chiggers feed only once, whether on humans or on rodents. Studies have shown that 90 to 100% of individual or pooled offspring from infected female mites are capable of transmitting the organism to white mice.[7] Because of these unique characteristics of the mites and chiggers and because chiggers stay within several meters of where they hatch, highly focal "islands of infection" are created in endemic areas.

PATHOGENESIS AND PATHOLOGIC CHARACTERISTICS

When an infected chigger feeds, it inoculates the host with the etiologic agent of scrub typhus. The infection begins by local multiplication at the site of the bite. This produces a papule that later ulcerates. The ulcer forms a black crust, which is the eschar. Regional lymphadenopathy also occurs at this time and is followed by generalized lymphadenopathy in the next 4 to 5 days. Rickettsemia begins before the onset of symptoms.

CLINICAL MANIFESTATIONS

Signs and Symptoms

Clinical symptoms occur 6 to 18 days (often 10 to 12 days) after the bite of an infected chigger. The onset is usually sudden and is characterized by fever, severe headache, and myalgia. There is usually tender lymphadenopathy in the region of the bite wound or eschar. Temperatures usually rise quickly in the first several days of disease to 104 to 105°F (40 to 40.5°C). Early in the course of illness, the pulse is relatively slow. Other signs and symptoms at this time may include ocular pain, conjunctival injection, nonproductive cough, and apathy. The severity of symptoms varies widely, depending on the susceptibility of the host or the virulence of the infecting strain, or both. After about 5 days of illness, rash occurs on the trunk and spreads to the extremities; it begins as a macular rash and may become papular. It is sometimes evanescent. At this time, there is generalized lymphadenopathy and splenomegaly.

In a small proportion of patients, tremors, delirium, nervousness, slurred speech, deafness, or nuchal rigidity may develop in the second week of illness. In a descriptive study of 25 patients with scrub typhus, mild cerebrospinal fluid pleocytosis was found in about half the cases.[8] White blood cells averaged 16/mm^3 (range zero to 110/mm^3) and were half lymphocytes. The protein level was greater than 50 mg/dl in seven. The nested polymerase chain reaction test was positive in all 25 cerebrospinal fluid specimens.

Eighty-seven American soldiers who became infected in South Vietnam all had fever and headache.[9] Of 74 soldiers, 36 (46%) had an eschar, and only 30 of 87 (34%) had rash. Lymphadenopathy was the most common sign and occurred in 85% (74/84) of patients. A common misdiagnosis in this series was infectious mononucleosis.

In untreated patients, fever subsides after an illness of about 2 weeks. Specific antirickettsial therapy shortens the illness considerably and reduces mortality to essentially nil. Mortality rates have ranged from zero to 30% in untreated patients. Death is usually due to heart failure and circulatory collapse or pneumonia.

Routine laboratory studies are of no diagnostic value. Leukopenia may occur early. Lymphocytosis occurred later in 70% of the 87 American soldiers. Albuminuria was also common. No consistent liver enzyme abnormality was found. Infection with human immunodeficiency virus (median CD4 lymphocyte count of 70/mm^3) did not seem to influence the clinical severity of scrub typhus.[10]

New episodes of disease occur because of the many different serotypes of *O. tsutsugamushi*. Immunity to homologous strains is very good, but immunity to heterologous strains is short-lived.

DIAGNOSIS

The Weil-Felix slide agglutination test is not very sensitive, but it is easy to do in less developed areas of the world. Antibodies to *Proteus* OX-K are found in roughly 50% of patients during the second week of illness. (*Proteus* OX-2 and OX-19 tests are negative.) The test is rather specific but does show cross-reactivity in patients with leptospirosis. The criterion for a positive result is either one determination of a titer of 1:320 or greater, or a fourfold rise in titer starting from 1:50. The indirect microimmunofluorescent test is similar to the Weil-Felix test in sensitivity and specificity. The diagnostic capability of these tests improved markedly when both were considered together in evaluating a Malaysian hospital population.[11] A modification of the fluorescent antibody test, the immunoperoxidase test, has been reported to be simpler to perform than the fluorescent test and yet to yield equivalent results.[12, 13] Treatment in the first several days of illness may blunt or delay the serologic response.

The polymerase chain reaction has been used effectively to diagnose acute infection with *O. tsutsugamushi*.[14]

DIFFERENTIAL DIAGNOSIS

The clinical picture of scrub typhus is nonspecific unless an eschar and regional lymphadenopathy are present in a person who was exposed in an endemic area. Eschars may occur in less than half of cases, but they are very helpful in diagnosis when present. Symptoms are like those of other forms of typhus (severe headache or myalgia). When rash occurs in this setting, the physician should consider a rickettsial infection.

The differential diagnosis includes typhoid fever, brucellosis, leptospirosis, infectious mononucleosis, toxoplasmosis, and flavivirus infection such as dengue.

TREATMENT

Tetracycline and chloramphenicol are both effective in treating scrub typhus; fever dissipates in less than 24 hours in most patients. Tetracycline (25 mg/kg/day in four divided doses) can be used for 3 to 7 days, or chloramphenicol (50 mg/kg/day in four divided doses) can be used. Tetracycline may be more effective in rapidly ameliorating symptoms, and oral chloramphenicol is no longer available in the United States.[15] In Northern Thailand, poorly responsive scrub typhus led to the discovery of naturally occurring resistance to doxycycline and chloramphenicol.[16] Fever cleared in 3 days in 7 patients with susceptible strains but in only 5 of 12 with resistant organisms. The median time to defervescence was 30 hours (range 4 to 58 hours) compared with 80 hours (range 15 to 190 hours), in the drug-susceptible and -resistant groups, respectively. Ciprofloxacin[17] or azithromycin[18] may prove to be effective against human scrub typhus.

Relapse may occur, especially when treatment is begun before the fourth or fifth day of illness. Treatment for up to 2 weeks reduces the likelihood of relapse. Evidence is accumulating that shows single-dose doxycycline therapy to be effective in treating scrub typhus and in preventing relapse. In two studies, a single 200-mg oral dose of doxycycline given at presentation was nearly as effective as 7 days of tetracycline or two doses (days 1 and 7) of doxycycline in preventing relapse.[19, 20] However, the numbers of subjects in these studies are relatively small to have demonstrated equivalent efficacy with reasonable confidence.

PREVENTION

Individuals who are traversing endemic areas should wear protective clothing and use insect repellants to avoid chigger bites.

An effective vaccine for humans has not been developed, mainly owing to the serotypic heterogeneity of the organism.

Studies of chemoprophylaxis using doxycycline (200 mg orally weekly) have been evaluated for intensively exposed troops in the field[21] and in experimental infection.[22] Results are encouraging but preliminary; more work in this area is needed.

REFERENCES

1. Tamura A, Ohashi N, Urakami H, Miyamura S. Classification of *Rickettsia tsutsugamushi* in a new genus, *Orientia* gen nov, as *Orientia tsutsugamushi* comb nov. Int J Syst Bacteriol. 1995;45:589–591.
2. Robinson DM, Brown DW, Gan E, et al. Adaptation of microimmunofluorescent test to the study of human *Rickettsia tsutsugamushi* antibody. Am J Trop Hyg. 1976;25:900–1005.
3. Ohashi N, Tamura A, Sakurai H, et al. Characterization of a new antigenic type, Kuroki, of *Rickettsia tsutsugamushi* isolated from a patient in Japan. J Clin Microbiol. 1990;28:2111–2113.
4. Traub R, Wisseman CL Jr. The ecology of chigger-borne rickettsiosis (scrub typhus). J Med Entomol. 1974;11:237.
5. Olson JG, Bourgeois AL. Changing risk of scrub typhus in relation to socioeconomic development in the Pescadores Islands of Taiwan. Am J Epidemiol. 1979;109: 236–243.
6. Brown GW, Robinson DM, Huxsoll DL, et al. Scrub typhus: A common cause of illness in indigenous populations. Trans R Soc Trop Med Hyg. 1976; 70:444–448.
7. Roberts LW, Robinson DM. Efficiency of transovarial transmission of *Rickettsia tsutsugamushi* in *Leptotrombidium arenicola*. J Med Entomol. 1977;13:493.
8. Pai H, Sohn S, Seong Y, et al. Central nervous system involvement in patients with scrub typhus. Clin Infect Dis. 1997;24:436–440.
9. Berman SJ, Kundin WD. Scrub typhus in South Vietnam, a study of 87 cases. Ann Intern Med. 1973;79:26–30.
10. Kantipong P, Watt G, Jongsakul K, Choenchitra C. Infection with human immunodeficiency virus does not influence the clinical severity of scrub typhus. Clin Infect Dis. 1996;23:1168–1170.
11. Brown GW, Shirai A, Rogers C, et al. Diagnostic criteria for scrub typhus: Probability values for immunofluorescent antibody and *Proteus* OX-K agglutinin titers. Am J Trop Med Hyg. 1983;32:1101.
12. Kelly DJ, Wong PW, Gan E, et al.Comparative evaluation of the serodiagnosis of rickettsial disease. Am J Trop Med Hyg. 1988;38:400–406.
13. Kelly DJ, Wong PW, Gan E, et al. Multi-laboratory evaluation of a scrub typhus diagnostic kit. Am J Trop Med Hyg. 1990;43:301–307.
14. Sugita Y, Nagatani T, Okuda K, et al. Diagnosis of typhus infection with *Rickettsia tsutsugamushi* by polymerase chain reaction. J Med Microbiol. 1992;37:357–360.
15. Sheehy TW, Hazlett D, Turk RE. Scrub typhus, a comparison of chloramphenicol and tetracycline in its treatment. Arch Intern Med. 1973;132:77–80.
16. Watt G, Chouriyagune C, Ruangweerayud R, et al. Scrub typhus infections poorly responsive to antibiotics in northern Thailand. Lancet. 1996;348:86–89.
17. McClain JB, Joshi B, Rice R. Chloramphenicol, gentamicin, and ciprofloxacin against murine scrub typhus. Antimicrob Agents Chemother. 1988;32:285–286.
18. Strickman D, Sheer T, Salata K, et al. In vitro effectiveness of azithromycin against doxycycline-resistant and susceptible strains of *Rickettsia tsutsugamushi*, etiologic agent of scrub typhus. Antimicrob Agents Chemother. 1995;39:2406–2410.
19. Brown GW, Saunders JP, Singh S, et al. Single dose doxycycline therapy for scrub typhus. Trans R Soc Trop Med Hyg. 1978;72:412.
20. Olson JG, Fang RCY, Dennis DT. Risk of relapse associated with doxycycline therapy for scrub typhus. In: Burgdorfer W, Anacker R, eds. Rickettsiae and Rickettsial Diseases. New York: Academic Press; 1981:201.
21. Olson JG, Bourgeois AL, Fang RCY, et al. Prevention of scrub typhus, prophylactic administration of doxycycline in a randomized double blind trial. Am J Trop Med Hyg. 1980;29:989–997.
22. Twartz JC, Shirai A, Selvaraju G, et al. Doxycycline prophylaxis for human scrub typhus. J Infect Dis. 1982;146:811–818.

Chapter 181

Ehrlichia chaffeensis (Human Monocytotropic Ehrlichiosis), *Ehrlichia phagocytophila* (Human Granulocytotropic Ehrlichiosis), and Other Ehrlichiae

DAVID H. WALKER
J. STEPHEN DUMLER

Until 1987, infections by members of the genus *Ehrlichia* were known mainly as veterinary diseases, recognized as causing human illness only in Asia (Table 181–1). Canine ehrlichiosis was first described in 1935 by Donatien and Lestoquard in Algeria. This disease was produced by a rickettsia-like agent transmitted to dogs by the tick *Rhipicephalus sanguineus*. The disease was characterized by fever associated with the presence of clusters of small Giemsa-stained organisms in circulating monocytes. *Ehrlichia* spp. generally have a tick vector and a tropism for either macrophages or granulocytes, in which they grow within cytoplasmic membrane–bound vacuoles. Consequently, *Ehrlichia* was recognized as distinct from other genera of obligate intracellular bacteria of medical importance *(Rickettsia, Coxiella,* and *Chlamydia)*. In 1937, the genus *Ehrlichia* was suggested in honor of the German bacteriologist Paul Ehrlich.[1] Subsequent phylogenetic studies have shown that two other veterinary pathogens, *Anaplasma marginale* (described in 1910) and *Cowdria ruminantium* (described in 1925), are also ehrlichiae. The first human disease demonstrated to have an ehrlichial cause was Sennetsu ehrlichiosis, an infectious mononucleosis–like illness recognized to have occurred only in western Japan and Malaysia.[2]

TABLE 181–1 Ehrlichiae Causing Medical and Veterinary Diseases

Etiologic Agent	Mammalian Host	Major Target Cell	Vector
Ehrlichia chaffeensis	Humans, deer, dogs	Macrophages	Ticks (*Amblyomma americanum* and *Dermacentor variabilis*)
Ehrlichia sennetsu	Humans	Macrophages	Possibly ingestion of raw fish
Ehrlichia phagocytophila group (*Ehrlichia phagocytophila, Ehrlichia equi,* HGE agent)	Humans, white-footed mice, horses, dogs, sheep, cattle, deer, bison	Granulocytes	Ticks (*Ixodes scapularis, Ixodes pacificus, Ixodes ricinus*)
Ehrlichia canis	Dogs, humans	Macrophages	Ticks (*Rhipicephalus sanguineus*)
Ehrlichia ewingii	Dogs, humans	Granulocytes	Ticks (*A. americanum*)
Ehrlichia platys	Dogs	Platelets, macrophages	Unknown
Cowdria ruminantium	Cattle, wild ruminants	Endothelial cells	Tick (*Amblyomma variegatum*)
Anaplasma marginale	Cattle, wild ruminants	Erythrocytes	Ticks (*Boophilus, Rhipicephalus,* and others)
Ehrlichia risticii	Horses	Macrophages, enterocytes, mast cells	Flukes associated with snails
Neorickettsia helminthoeca	Dogs	Macrophages	Ingestion of fluke-infested salmon

Abbreviation: HGE, Human granulocytotropic ehrlichiosis.

The first diagnosed case of human ehrlichiosis in the United States occurred in a 51-year-old man who became ill in April 1986, 12 to 14 days after tick bites in rural Arkansas.[3] His severe course of illness was characterized by fever, hypotension, confusion, acute renal failure requiring hemodialysis, pancytopenia, coagulopathy, cutaneous and gastrointestinal hemorrhages, and hepatocellular injury. The diagnosis of ehrlichial infection was documented by observation of 2- to 5-μm morulae (cytoplasmic vacuoles containing ehrlichial organisms) in 1 to 2% of circulating leukocytes (Fig. 181–1). Electron microscopy demonstrated that the inclusions represented membrane-bound vacuoles containing up to 40 bacteria with a diameter of 0.2 to 0.8 μm and a gram-negative cell wall. Moreover, the patient's serum contained antibodies reactive at a high titer with *Ehrlichia canis*, which is genetically and antigenically closely related to the subsequently identified *Ehrlichia chaffeensis*,[4] the etiologic agent of human monocytotropic ehrlichiosis (HME). In 1994, an *Ehrlichia phagocytophila*–like organism was reported as the causative agent of a distinctly different infection, human granulocytotropic ehrlichiosis (HGE),[5, 6] and in 1999 *Ehrlichia ewingii* was shown to cause human illness.[6a]

ETIOLOGY

Members of the genus *Ehrlichia* are defined not only by their phenotypic characteristics and their host affinities (see Table 181–1), but also by their genetic similarities and differences. Ehrlichiae are small (0.5 μm) gram-negative bacteria. Their clustered inclusion-like appearance in the host cell vacuoles is called a *morula*, from the Latin word for "mulberry."

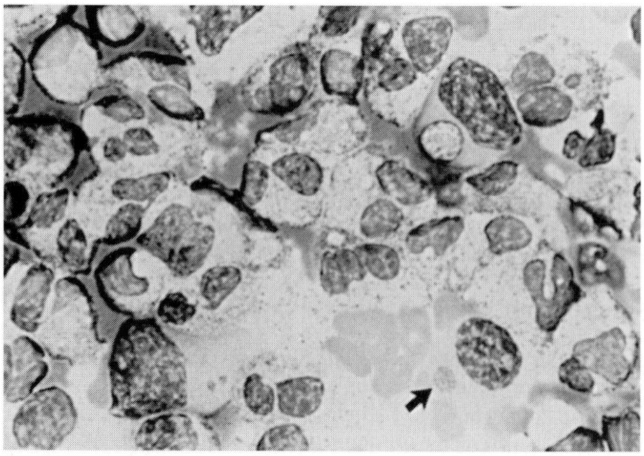

FIGURE 181–1. Peripheral blood smear (buffy coat preparation) showing intracellular inclusions *(arrow)* in mononuclear cells of a patient with human monocytotropic ehrlichiosis. (Leishman stain, × 202.) (From Maeda K, Markowitz N, Hawley RC, et al. Human infection with *Ehrlichia canis*, a leukocytic *Rickettsia*. N Engl J Med. 1987;316:853–856. Copyright © 1987 Massachusetts Medical Society. All rights reserved.)

The taxonomic relationships of *Ehrlichia, Rickettsia, Coxiella*, and *Chlamydia* have been clarified by molecular genetic and metabolic studies. The evolutionary relationships determined by 16S ribosomal DNA comparisons indicate that *Ehrlichia* and *Rickettsia* both evolved from a common ancestor.[4, 7] In contrast, *Coxiella* and *Chlamydia* are phylogenetically unrelated to *Ehrlichia.* Ehrlichiae and chlamydiae superficially resemble one another in that both reside within cytoplasmic vacuoles. Unlike chlamydiae, however, ehrlichiae are able to synthesize adenosine triphosphate (ATP) by the metabolism of glutamine, a metabolic characteristic shared with members of the genus *Rickettsia*.[8] Within the phylogeny of organisms bearing the genus name *Ehrlichia* are three genetic-antigenic clusters that are actually very different from one another. *Ehrlichia chaffeensis* shares many antigens and genetic sequences with the canine pathogens *E. canis* and *E. ewingii*[9]; *Ehrlichia muris*, found in Japanese voles and ticks; and the ruminant pathogen *C. ruminantium*.[4, 9–12] A second cluster includes the human granulocytic *Ehrlichia* that is virtually identical to *E. equi* and *E. phagocytophila* and is closely related genetically to *E. platys* and *A. marginale*.[6] All these organisms are closely related enough to reside in the same genus. However, the third cluster contains *Ehrlichia sennetsu*, which is closely related to *Ehrlichia risticii, Neorickettsia helminthoeca*, and an organism found in Japanese fish flukes, and is so greatly genetically distant that all these organisms belong in a separate genus.[13–15] The taxonomic designations have not yet been settled. Moreover, contemporary methods are both discovering and characterizing ehrlichiae at a greatly accelerating pace.

The cell wall of *E. chaffeensis* differs ultrastructurally from that of *Rickettsia* spp., with thinner outer and inner leaflets reflecting the apparent absence of lipopolysaccharide and lipo-oligosaccharide.[16] Peptidoglycan appears to occupy the periplasmic space.[17] Among the major protein antigens of *E. chaffeensis*, a 58-kD analogue of the GroEL stress protein and other proteins of 44, 55, and 66 kD share antigens and genetic homology with those of many other ehrlichiae.[10, 18] *Ehrlichia canis* and *E. ewingii* also share antigens of the surface-exposed 120-kD protein and a family of proteins of 22 to 30 kD of *E. chaffeensis*.[10, 19, 20] These proteins seem to be characteristic of the *E. chaffeensis* genogroup. A major 42- to 44-kD protein is an immunodominant antigen of the HGE agent–*E. equi*–*E. phagocytophila* complex and an analogue of the major surface protein multigene family of *A. marginale*.[21, 22]

EPIDEMIOLOGY

General

Human ehrlichioses in the United States are tick-borne zoonoses.[5, 23–36] The vast majority of patients give a history of tick exposure during the month before the onset of illness. The seasonality of HME, with a peak incidence in May through July, further suggests a vector-transmitted infection. Exposures are predominantly rural and suburban and involve recreational, peridomestic, occupational, and military activities. More than 80% of patients are male. Documented cases of HME range over 30 states, particularly in the south central and southeastern United States. This region conforms to the distribution of the Lone Star tick, *Amblyomma americanum*, which along with white-tailed deer has been found infected in nature and acquires *E. chaffeensis* from experimentally infected deer and subsequently transmits ehrlichiae to nonimmune deer. On the other hand, HME cases reported in California, Oregon, Washington, Wyoming, Colorado, Europe, and Africa suggest the possibility of additional vectors, including *Dermacentor variabilis*, which has been found to be naturally infected.[23, 37–39]

In a prospective study in Georgia of hospitalized patients with fever of undetermined cause, 11% were demonstrated by seroconversion to have had HME.[32] In Oklahoma, the state with the highest incidence of Rocky Mountain spotted fever, HME is at least as prevalent.

The suspicion that most infections are not diagnosed is supported by a study of soldiers with intense tick exposure in Arkansas.[40] Seroconversion to *E. chaffeensis* occurred in 1.3%, two thirds of whom remained asymptomatic. It has yet to be determined whether *E. chaffeensis* infection can be asymptomatic or whether cross-reactive antibodies might be stimulated by *E. ewingii*, another *Ehrlichia* sp., or another antigenic stimulus. *Ehrlichia canis* has been isolated from the blood of an asymptomatic person in South America.[41]

The epizootiology of canine ehrlichiosis offers insight into the mode of transmission and mechanisms of maintenance of ehrlichiae in nature. The reservoir of *E. canis* is the canine vertebrate host (jackal, coyote, fox, and dog). *Ehrlichia canis* is acquired by *R. sanguineus* feeding as larvae or nymphs on infected canine species. The pathogen is transmitted trans-stadially from larvae to nymphs and from nymphs to adults, but *R. sanguineus* does not transmit *E. canis* transovarially.[42, 43] Consonant with the acquisition of ehrlichiae by feeding on ehrlichemic canines, *E. canis* is observed in the midgut of *R. sanguineus*. The presence of *E. canis* in the salivary glands of *R. sanguineus* confirms the potential for infection during tick feeding. On the other hand, the absence of detectable ehrlichiae in ovaries of *R. sanguineus* emphasizes that transovarial transmission is not the mechanism of maintenance of *E. canis* in nature. Similarly, *A. americanum* is capable of acquiring *E. ewingii* as a nymph during a blood meal from an infected dog, of carrying the infection during molting to the adult stage, and of transmitting the ehrlichiae during feeding upon a susceptible dog.[44] The reservoir of *E. chaffeensis* is apparently deer and possibly also dogs, which are found naturally infected and remain persistently infected after experimental inoculation.[25, 45–48] The discovery of *E. muris* in voles in Japan indicates the possibility of silent rodent reservoirs of ehrlichiae in other parts of the world.[49]

Epidemiology and Epizootiology of Human Granulocytotropic Ehrlichiosis

HGE has a year-round seasonal occurrence, with a bimodal distribution peaking in July and again in November in accordance with the activity of nymphal and adult stages, respectively, of *Ixodes scapularis* ticks in the eastern United States.[35] Although the risk of HGE is associated with outdoor activity, a substantial proportion of cases occur in suburban areas of northeastern and upper midwestern cities.[35, 36] HGE has been diagnosed in 11 different states, but cases are concentrated in southern New England, New York State, northwestern Wisconsin, eastern Minnesota, and northern California. The distribution is identical to that of Lyme disease owing to the shared *Ixodes* spp. tick vectors.

The incidence of HGE is not known; however, active case collection yielded an incidence of 14 to 16 cases per 100,000 population in the upper Midwest between 1990 and 1995, with rates as high as 24 to 58 cases per 100,000 population in certain northwestern Wisconsin counties in 1994–1995.[35] Cross-sectional seroprevalence studies have shown that approximately 15% of the population in northwestern Wisconsin, 1% of Connecticut residents, and 12% of the entire population of Sweden's Koster Islands have antibodies reactive with the *E. phagocytophila* group in the absence of antecedent evidence of HGE.[50–52] The demonstration of proven infection in mildly affected patients who recover spontaneously, even in the absence of specific therapy, suggests that HGE may frequently be subclinical or asymptomatic.[53]

Between 6 and 21% of patients with HGE also have serologic evidence of *Borrelia burgdorferi* or *Babesia microti* infection, both agents also transmitted by *Ixodes* spp. tick bites.[51, 54–56] Concurrent HGE and Lyme disease, documented by isolation of both agents, has been documented.[57] Whether concurrent infection by these agents allows increased severity, prolonged duration of illness, or more frequent and severe sequelae has yet to be determined.

Ehrlichia phagocytophila–group ehrlichiae are transmitted to humans by the bites of nymphal and adult *I. scapularis* in the eastern United States, *Ixodes pacificus* in California, and presumably *Ixodes ricinus* ticks in Europe. Although trans-stadial transmission of the infectious agent occurs, transovarial transmission appears to be inefficient, and thus natural maintenance requires horizontal (tick-mammal-tick) transmission.[28, 58] The major proven reservoir host is the white-footed mouse, *Peromyscus leucopus*; however, other small mammals have been found naturally infected or have serologic evidence of infection, including voles, woodrats, and chipmunks.[28, 59, 60] Current serologic evidence suggests that emergent larval ticks acquire the *E. phagocytophila* group organisms after feeding on small mammals infected earlier in the season by nymphal ticks. White-footed mice develop immunity to *E. phagocytophila* group ehrlichiae after a period of ehrlichemia that may last from several days to weeks.[28, 59, 61] Small mammals are not adversely affected by the infection, and some may become persistently infected.[28, 61] The contribution as reservoir hosts of ruminants, including white-tailed deer *(Odocoileus virginianus)*, which are often persistently infected, requires further investigation.[62]

PATHOGENESIS AND PATHOLOGY

General

After entering the skin by tick bite inoculation and spread presumably via lymphatic and blood vessels, ehrlichiae invade their target cells of the hematopoietic and lymphoreticular systems. Morulae of *E. chaffeensis* have been observed mainly in macrophages and monocytes, less frequently in lymphocytes, and rarely in polymorphonuclear leukocytes.[3, 63–67] Ehrlichial morulae have been identified in peripheral blood, bone marrow, hepatic sinusoids, lymph nodes, splenic cords, sinusoids, periarteriolar lymphoid sheaths, cerebrospinal fluid macrophages, and macrophages within perivascular lymphohistiocytic infiltrates in organs such as the kidney and heart.

The best-studied tissue in HME is bone marrow, largely owing to the frequency of leukopenia, thrombocytopenia, and anemia. Frequent findings include granulomas, myeloid hyperplasia, and megakaryocytosis.[63] Normocellular marrow, pancellular hypoplasia, erythroid hypoplasia, myeloid hyperplasia, erythrophagocytosis, and plasmacytosis occur in smaller proportions of patients with HME. Focal hepatocellular necrosis; hepatic granulomas including ring granulomas; cholestasis; splenic and lymph node necrosis; diffuse mononuclear phagocyte hyperplasia of the spleen, liver, lymph node, and bone marrow; and perivascular lymphohistiocytic infiltrates of various organs including kidney, heart, liver, meninges, brain, and interstitial mononuclear cell pneumonitis have also been observed.[65–67] It is worthy of emphasis that endothelial injury and thrombosis have not been described.

Canine ehrlichiosis during the acute stage has the features of HME and can serve as an animal model.[68, 69] In the acute phase of canine ehrlichiosis, after an incubation period of 7 to 10 days, dogs develop a transient, mild illness characterized by fever, coryza, anorexia, lethargy, weight loss, and pancytopenia. The platelet count is usually less than 100,000/μl; the white blood cell count is 3000 to 7000/μl. The severity of disease depends on the breed of the host dog. Bone marrow hypercellularity is observed at 2 weeks of infection in susceptible dogs and at 4 to 9 weeks in relatively resistant dogs. After a subclinical phase of 2 to 4 months, most susceptible dogs suffer severe chronic disease with bone marrow hypoplasia; disappearance of megakaryocytes; severe pancytopenia; fatal mucosal and cutaneous hemorrhages, particularly epistaxis; fatal secondary infection; dependent edema; weight loss; lymphadenopathy; posterior weakness; and dyspnea.

HME has not been described to have this severe chronic stage. For this reason, the acute phase of canine ehrlichiosis in the relatively resistant breeds of dog may serve as a model of human ehrlichiosis. Resistant animals develop thrombocytopenia, with the lowest platelet counts 14 to 30 days after inoculation, elevated concentration of serum hepatic enzymes on days 21 to 42, decreased serum albumin levels on days 14 to 35, and increased serum immunoglobulin levels after 21 days. They also demonstrate transient lymphadenopathy with lymphoid hyperplasia, splenomegaly, and bone marrow hyperplasia. Perivascular plasma cells, lymphocytes, and macrophages in the kidney, meninges, and other sites may be observed. Pulmonary alveolar septa are thickened by mononuclear cell infiltration. Ehrlichia-infected mononuclear cells adhere to the endothelium of small arteries and capillaries and to other mononuclear cells.

Analysis of the mechanisms of thrombocytopenia in acute canine ehrlichiosis reveals increased platelet destruction with splenic sequestration and consequent accelerated release of platelets from bone marrow when counts are less than 100,000/μl.

Although *E. chaffeensis* has a direct cytopathic effect when grown in cell culture, it would appear likely that the host responses might account for some of the clinical manifestations.[70, 71] In light of the genetic evidence that *E. risticii* and *E. sennetsu* have diverged evolutionarily a substantial distance from the branch leading to *E. chaffeensis*, it would seem wise to exercise caution in the extrapolation of mechanisms established for one group of ehrlichiae to another. Interferon-γ stimulates macrophage killing of *E. chaffeensis* through the sequestration of iron, and opsonization with immune serum enhances the destruction of ehrlichiae by macrophages.[72, 73] *Ehrlichia chaffeensis* appears to circumvent the host defenses by inhibiting the fusion of phagosomes with lysosomes and inhibiting the signal-transduction pathway of interferon-γ antiehrlichial activity.[74, 75] *Ehrlichia risticii* suppresses major histocompatibility complex class II gene product expression on infected, interferon-γ–stimulated macrophages.[76] In contrast, the presence of antigens of *E. risticii* on the surface of infected macrophages provides a potential immune target that could result in harm to ehrlichiae, the host, or both.[77]

Ehrlichia chaffeensis resides in endosomes that accumulate transferrin receptors, presumably as a mechanism for ehrlichial acquisition of iron.[74] Ehrlichial growth is inhibited by a reduction of available iron via deferoxamine treatment, probably because iron is a cofactor in oxidative phosphorylation. In vitro infection of macrophages induces signal transduction mechanisms that associate with upregulation of cytokine genes, suggesting that disease caused by *E. chaffeensis* is partly determined by host immunologic and inflammatory responses.

Human Granulocytotropic Ehrlichiosis

The pathology and pathogenesis of HGE are less well investigated than those of HME. *Ehrlichia phagocytophila*–group ehrlichiae are observed predominantly in neutrophils in the peripheral blood and tissues from infected individuals.[35, 36] In the few published reports, HGE is associated with few specific pathologic findings.[35, 67, 78] The most dramatic findings involve the presence of opportunistic pathogens, especially severe fungal and viral infections. Similar changes are well documented in ruminants with tick-borne fever due to *E. phagocytophila* infection. Experimental tick-borne fever is associated with impairment of T-lymphocyte proliferation to mitogens; decreases in circulating CD4, CD8, and CD5 cells; weak antibody responses to vaccines; and impairment of neutrophil recruitment and phagocytosis.[79] Other pathologic findings observed in humans and animal models include normocellular or hypercellular bone marrow, erythrophagocytosis in mononuclear phagocytic organs, hepatic apoptosis and periportal lymphohistiocytic infiltrates, focal splenic necrosis, and mild interstitial pneumonitis and pulmonary hemorrhage.[67] Vasculitis, endothelial injury, granulomas, and meningeal inflammation have not been described.

Ehrlichia phagocytophila–group ehrlichiae disseminate to bone marrow and spleen after a tick bite. In the bone marrow, progenitors of myeloid and monocytic lineages are infected.[80] The ehrlichiae attach to host cell surface ligands, most likely sialylated mucoproteins, and enter an endosome that avoids lysosomal fusion. Within this vacuole, the ehrlichiae survive and divide. In vitro, *E. phagocytophila*–group ehrlichiae may lead to cytolytic damage by mechanisms that are not yet understood. Approximately 25% and 100% of patients develop specific antibodies detectable at presentation and after 30 days, respectively.[35]

CLINICAL MANIFESTATIONS

Human Monocytotropic Ehrlichiosis

Signs and Symptoms

More than 1500 cases of HME have been diagnosed. The clinical picture in immunocompetent patients is of a mild to severe multisystemic illness, with approximately 40% of patients requiring hospitalization (Table 181–2).[3, 29–34, 65, 66, 80–87] In severely immunocompromised patients, *E. chaffeensis* acts as an opportunistic pathogen and can cause a fatal overwhelming infection.[88–92] The median incubation period is 7 days. Symptoms at the onset of illness include fever, chills, headache, myalgia, and malaise. Later in the course, patients often develop nausea, anorexia, and weight loss. Physical signs are not striking. Less than half of patients have a rash, which is maculopapular and may be petechial. Rash has been observed more

TABLE 181–2 Clinical and Laboratory Abnormalities in Human Monocytotropic and Granulocytotropic Ehrlichioses

Sign, Symptom, or Laboratory Finding	HME Patients with Abnormal Findings (%)	HGE Patients with Abnormal Findings (%)
Fever	97	94–100
Headache	81	61–85
Chills or rigors	67	39–98
Myalgia	68	78–98
Malaise	84	98
Nausea	48	39
Anorexia	66	37
Vomiting	37	34
Diarrhea	25	22
Abdominal pain	22	—
Rash	36	2–11
Cough	26	29
Dyspnea	23	—
Lymphadenopathy	25	—
Confusion	20	17
Leukopenia	60	50–59
Thrombocytopenia	68	59–92
Elevated AST	86	69–91
Elevated ALT	80	61
Elevated urea nitrogen	38	—
Elevated creatinine	29	70

Abbreviations: AST, Aspartate aminotransferase; ALT, alanine aminotransferase; HGE, human monocytotropic ehrlichiosis; HME, human monocytotropic ehrlichiosis.

frequently in children. Adult patients with severe illness are more likely to have cough, diarrhea, and lymphadenopathy, whereas pediatric patients may develop edema of the hands or feet. Severe complications include respiratory insufficiency (18% require mechanical ventilation), renal insufficiency, central nervous system abnormalities, gastrointestinal hemorrhage, and even death.[29, 33, 34, 64–67, 85, 86, 88–93] Cerebrospinal fluid pleocytosis usually contains a predominance of lymphocytes and increased protein concentration. Nearly half of the patients with chest roentgenographic evaluation have infiltrates.

Important laboratory features are mild to moderate leukopenia, thrombocytopenia, and elevations of serum hepatic transminase levels (see Table 181–2).[29, 33, 34] The nadir of leukopenia is usually between 1300 and 4000 cells/μl. Neutropenia or lymphopenia, or both combined, account for the leukopenia. Thrombocytopenia occurs concurrently with leukopenia, with a platelet count usually between 50,000 and 140,000/μl, although occasionally severe (<20,000 platelets/μl).[29]

Course

The clinical course of illness ranges from asymptomatic seroconversion to a fatal outcome. The patients from whom *E. chaffeensis* has been isolated reflect this clinical variation in severity. A 72-year-old man had a near-fatal multisystemic febrile illness with central nervous system involvement, acute renal failure requiring hemodialysis, respiratory failure requiring intubation, and a 4.5-week hospitalization.[64] A 21-year-old soldier was ill for 4 days with fever, headache, pharyngitis, nausea, vomiting, cervical lymphadenopathy, and splenomegaly.[94] He defervesced 24 to 48 hours after the initiation of tetracycline treatment and did not require hospitalization. A substantial portion of the other soldiers in this prospective study developed asymptomatically antibodies reactive with *E. chafeensis*.[40, 94] In individuals infected with human immunodeficiency virus, a virulent form of HME occurs that is often associated with overwhelming infection, a toxic shock– or sepsis-like syndrome, and death.[88, 90, 92] Immune compromise due to corticosteroid therapy or immunosuppression with organ transplantation is also associated with increased severity.[91]

The median duration of hospitalization is about 1 week. Convalescence is often prolonged. Fatalities have occurred in approximately 3% of patients. Many patients treated with doxycycline or tetracycline recover rapidly. On the other hand, most patients receiving no effective antiehrlichial treatment have had uncomplicated complete recovery.

Diagnosis

A diagnosis based on epidemiologic and clinical factors offers the opportunity to administer empirical antiehrlichial treatment. However, the physician's index of suspicion must be high, or an early diagnosis will not be made. Patients presenting with fever, leukopenia, thrombocytopenia, elevated serum transaminase levels, and a history of a recent tick bite in endemic regions from May through July should be considered as possibly having HME. No absolute clinical criteria distinguish HME from Rocky Mountain spotted fever, although patients with ehrlichiosis are less likely to have a rash and more likely to have leukopenia (median white blood cell count, 3500/μl). Although the first recognized case of HME was diagnosed by visualization of ehrlichial morulae in circulating leukocytes, morulae have been observed subsequently in only 7% of patients with HME.

The "gold standard" for etiologic diagnosis of infectious disease, cultivation of the agent, has been achieved in six cases of HME but is a laborious, insensitive approach at the present time.[19, 92, 94, 95] Specialized methods employing unique cell lines may require longer than 1 month of careful cultivation and observation to detect ehrlichiae.

The major diagnostic criterion for human ehrlichiosis is serologic, as determined by indirect immunofluorescence assay with *E. chaffeensis*–infected cells. To be considered positive, the patient's sera must show a fourfold or greater rise or fall in antibody titer during the course of the disease, with a minimal peak titer of 1:80.[29, 96]

Immunofluorescence assays at the Centers for Disease Control and Prevention for 85 patients judged to have a positive result by the criteria described previously showed a peak geometric mean titer of 1280 at 6 weeks after onset.[96] Only 22% of the sera first tested in the first week of illness had a titer of 80 or greater. Among sera from patients first tested in the second week, 68% were diagnostic. All sera tested 4 or more weeks after the onset of illness showed seroconversion. The geometric mean titer decreased between 6 and 12 weeks, and by 17 to 31 weeks the geometric mean titer was less than 80.

Immunohistologic demonstration of ehrlichial morulae provides a timely, specific diagnosis.[63, 65, 66, 97] Unfortunately, a patient sample that is readily available and reliably contains demonstrable organisms has not been identified. Thus, this approach is relatively insensitive. A polymerase chain reaction method employing *E. chaffeensis*–specific primers for amplification and detection of ehrlichial DNA from peripheral blood appears to be the most sensitive technique for a timely laboratory diagnosis.[23, 98]

Differential Diagnosis

Early in the course of the disease, when the patient presents with fever, headache, myalgia, and malaise, the differential diagnosis may include various viral syndromes, Rocky Mountain spotted fever, upper respiratory illness, sepsis, and urinary tract infection. If nausea, vomiting, and anorexia are prominent symptoms, gastroenteritis is often included. If cough is prominent, pneumonia is often considered. Central nervous system signs and symptoms with cerebrospinal fluid pleocytosis suggest viral or bacterial meningoencephalitis. On obtaining a history of recent tick bite, the physician may consider tick-borne febrile illness such as Rocky Mountain spotted fever, relapsing fever, tularemia, Lyme borreliosis, Colorado tick fever, and babesiosis. Other diagnostic considerations include meningococcemia, toxic shock syndrome, leptospirosis, hepatitis, enteroviral infection, influenza, murine typhus, Q fever, typhoid fever, bacterial sepsis, endocarditis, Kawasaki disease, collagen-vascular diseases, and leukemia. A comparison of the ehrlichioses and Rocky Mountain spotted fever is presented in Table 181–3.

Human Granulocytotropic Ehrlichiosis

Signs, Symptoms, and Course

HGE is not a reportable illness in most states; however, approximately 500 cases have been identified in the United States since 1990. Male patients outnumber female patients by 2 to 1, and the median age ranges from 43 to 60 years in different series.[35, 36] After an incubation period of approximately 1 to 2 weeks, HGE presents as a mild to severe illness, with fever, headache, malaise, and myalgias in the majority of patients.[35, 36] Nausea, vomiting, diarrhea, cough, arthralgias, stiff neck, and confusion are present in less than half of patients, and less than 10% have rash. The majority of doxycycline-treated patients are well within 7 days, and if patients are untreated, the median duration of illness is 9 days (range 1 to 60 days).[65] Severe manifestations include respiratory insufficiency, a septic shock–like illness, rhabdomyolysis, and opportunistic infections.[35, 36, 78, 99, 100] Meningoencephalitis and cerebrospinal fluid pleocytosis have not been observed in documented cases of HGE; however, neurologic sequelae may include brachial plexopathy and demyelinating polyneuropathy.[101, 102] At least four patients have died after HGE; three died with severe opportunistic fungal or viral infections.[67]

Laboratory features observed in a substantial portion of cases include leukopenia, thrombocytopenia, mild anemia, and increases in serum hepatic aminotransferase activities within the first 7 days of illness.[35, 36] Neutropenia with a left shift and relative lymphocytosis may occur. Leukocyte, erythrocyte, and platelet counts return to normal by 14 days, but the left shift may persist for longer.[103] Doxycycline therapy reverses the decline in leukocyte and platelet counts and blunts the degree of left shift, usually within 5 to 7 days; anemia responds more slowly.

Diagnosis

Unlike the situation in HME, in which morulae in circulating mononuclear cells are rare, in HGE, between 20 and 80% of patients have had ehrlichial morulae identified in peripheral blood neutrophils (Fig. 181–2).[35, 36] Culture of the HGE agent is promising but usually requires 1 week or more, whereas polymerase chain reaction amplification of HGE agent nucleic acids from blood is 86% sensitive, is highly specific, and may be performed in a timely manner.[104, 105] Serologic diagnosis is most often achieved retrospectively by the detection of antibodies reactive with *Ehrlichia equi, E. phagocytophila*, or the HGE agent in equine neutrophils or in tissue culture cells.[22, 35, 36, 100, 101, 106] By current criteria, a titer of at least 80 is considered significant, but a fourfold rise in titer provides more definitive evidence for infection owing to the fact that 15 to 16% of the population in the upper Midwest and New York State have serologic evidence of prior infection. The role of immunoglobulin M testing, Western immunoblot confirmation, or recombinant antigens for serodiagnosis is not defined.[22, 106]

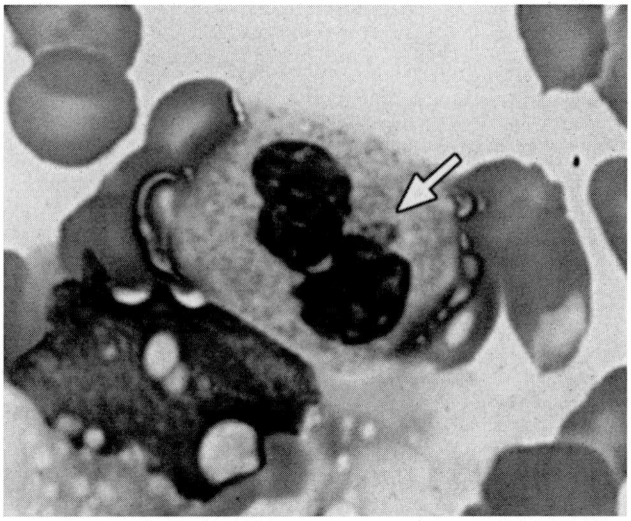

FIGURE 181–2. Peripheral blood smear showing intracellular inclusion within a neutrophil of a patient with human granulocytotropic ehrlichiosis *(arrow)*. (Wright stain, × 1000.)

TREATMENT AND PREVENTION

Tetracycline, 25 mg/kg/day in four equally divided doses, or doxycycline, 100 mg twice daily, has been used successfully. Susceptibility testing of *E. chaffeensis* and the HGE agent in cell culture systems confirms that doxycycline and the rifamycins are ehrlichiacidal and reveals that chloramphenicol is not effective.[107, 108] The clinical effectiveness of rifampin has not yet been evaluated. The fluoroquinolone trovafloxacin has good in vitro efficacy but has not been tested in clinical situations.

Acute canine ehrlichiosis responds promptly to tetracycline treatment, and low-dose tetracycline has been used successfully for prophylaxis against canine ehrlichiosis.[68, 109] Some *Ehrlichia* spp. establish chronic persistent infections and do not stimulate effective protective immunity. For example, dogs cured of acute canine ehrlichiosis are fully susceptible to rechallenge with *E. canis*. These facts suggest that future development of a vaccine may prove difficult.

At present, prevention of human ehrlichiosis must rely on avoidance of exposure to ticks, regular careful search of the body for ticks when exposure occurs, and prompt removal of ticks from the body.

TABLE 181–3 Comparison of Ehrlichioses in the United States with Rocky Mountain Spotted Fever

Similarities
History of tick attachment
Incubation period of about 1 wk between tick bite and onset of symptoms
Peak incidence in late spring and summer
Acute onset with headache, fever, myalgia, and malaise; cough, dyspnea, and vomiting present less commonly
Severe cases may have coagulopathy, azotemia, and encephalopathy
WBC count usually not elevated, platelet count often low, AST (SGOT) may be increased
Diagnosis by acute and convalescent serologic examination
Treatment: A tetracycline (chloramphenicol may not be effective for ehrlichioses)
Differences
RMSF: Rash is present in 90% of patients and is petechial in about half the cases
Ehrlichiosis: Rash is present in less than half of adult patients with HME and rarely in HGE, is maculopapular, and is rarely petechial
Leukopenia and absolute lymphopenia and neutropenia are common in hospitalized patients with HME and neutropenia in HGE but are uncommon in RMSF
Inclusions (morulae) may be seen rarely in monocytes and macrophages of patients with HME, occasionally in neutrophils of patients with HGE, but not with RMSF
Vasculitis, the pathologic hallmark of RMSF, is not observed in ehrlichioses

Abbreviations: AST, Aspartate aminotransferase; HME, human monocytotropic ehrlichiosis; HGE, human granulocytotropic ehrlichiosis; RMSF, Rocky Mountain spotted fever; SGOT, serum glutamate-oxaloacetate transaminase; WBC, white blood cell.

SENNETSU EHRLICHIOSIS

Physicians outside of the Far East are unlikely to see a patient with Sennetsu ehrlichiosis. *Ehrlichia sennetsu* was isolated in 1953 from the blood, bone marrow, and lymph node of a 25-year-old man who had fever, severe headaches, myalgia, anorexia, lymphadenopathy, and an increased quantity of atypical lymphocytes in his peripheral blood.[110] Ehrlichiae isolated in mice were inoculated into human volunteers, who developed a syndrome resembling infectious mononucleosis. Ehrlichiae were recovered from their blood samples.

The average incubation period of 14 days is followed by a sudden onset of chills and a fever that lasts for 2 weeks unless the infection is treated effectively.[2] Patients also complain of headache and myalgia. Postauricular and posterior cervical lymphadenopathy appears 5 to 7 days after onset. Hepatosplenomegaly occurs in one third to one half of patients. Aseptic meningitis is observed only occasionally, and rash, very rarely. Early in the illness, leukopenia occurs; in the late febrile and convalescent phases, absolute lymphocytosis is observed, with 10% or greater atypical lymphocytes. Mild to moderate elevations occur in serum transaminase levels. Laboratory diagnosis can be made by inoculation of mice and by demonstration of specific serum antibody by immunoflourescence assay or complement fixation test. Treatment with one of the tetracycline antimicrobials, such as doxycycline or minocycline, results in defervescence after 1 to 2 days.

REFERENCES

1. Weiss E, Moulder JW. The rickettsias and chlamydias. In: Kreig NR, Holt JG, eds. Bergey's Manual of Systematic Bacteriology. Baltimore: Williams & Wilkins; 1984:1:687–739.
2. Tachibana N. Sennetsu fever: The disease, diagnosis, and treatment. In: Leive L,

ed. Microbiology 1986. Washington, DC: American Society for Microbiology; 1986:205–208.

3. Maeda K, Markowitz N, Hawley RC, et al. Human infection with *Ehrlichia canis*, a leukocytic *Rickettsia*. N Engl J Med. 1987;316:853–856.
4. Anderson BE, Dawson JE, Jones DC, et al. *Ehrlichia chaffeensis*, a new species associated with human ehrlichiosis. J Clin Microbiol. 1991;29:2838–2842.
5. Silpapojakul K, Chayakul P, Krisanapan S. Murine typhus in Thailand: Clinical features, diagnosis and treatment. Queensland J Med. 1993;86:43–47.
6. Chen S-M, Dumler JS, Bakken JS, et al. Identification of a granulocytotropic *Ehrlichia* species as the etiologic agent of human disease. J Clin Microbiol. 1994;32:589–595.

6a. Buller RS, Arens M, Hmiel SP, et al. *Ehrlichia ewingii*, a newly recognized agent of human ehrlichiosis. N Engl J Med. 1999;341:148–155.

7. Weisburg WG. Polyphyletic origin of bacterial parasites. In: Moulder JW, ed. Intracellular Parasitism. Boca Raton, Fla: CRC Press; 1989:2–15.
8. Weiss E, Williams JC, Dasch GA, et al. Energy metabolism of monocytic *Ehrlichia*. Proc Natl Acad Sci U S A. 1989;86:1674–1678.
9. Anderson BE, Greene CE, Jones DC, et al. *Ehrlichia ewingii* sp nov, the etiologic agent of canine granulocytic ehrlichiosis. Int J Syst Bacteriol. 1992;42:299–302.
10. Chen S-M, Dumler JS, Feng H-M, et al. Identification of the antigenic constituents of *Ehrlichia chaffeensis*. Am J Trop Med Hyg. 1993;50:52–58.
11. Wen B, Rikihisa Y, Mott J, et al. *Ehrlichia muris* sp nov, identified on the basis of 16S rRNA base sequences and serological, morphological, and biological characteristics. Int J Syst Bacteriol. 1995;45:250–254.
12. Van Vliet AHM, Jongejan F, van der Zeijst BAM. Phylogenetic position of *Cowdria ruminantium* (Rickettsiales) determined by analysis of amplified 16S ribosomal DNA sequences. Int J Syst Bacteriol. 1992;42:494–498.
13. Wen B, Rikihisa Y, Fuerst PA, et al. Diversity of 16S rRNA genes of new *Ehrlichia* strains isolated from horses with clinical signs of Potomac horse fever. Int J Syst Bacteriol. 1995;45:315–318.
14. Pretzman C, Ralph D, Stothard DR, et al. 16S rRNA gene sequence of *Neorickettsia helminthoeca* and its phylogenetic alignment with members of the genus *Ehrlichia*. Int J Syst Bacteriol. 1995;45:207–211.
15. Wen B, Rikihisa Y, Yamamoto S, et al. Characterization of the SF agent, an *Ehrlichia* sp isolated from the fluke *Stellantchasmus falcatus*, by 16S rRNA base sequence, serological, and morphological analyses. Int J Syst Bacteriol. 1996;46:149–154.
16. Popov VL, Han VC, Chen S-M, et al. Ultrastructural differentiation of the genogroups in the genus *Ehrlichia*. J Med Microbiol. 1998;47:235–251.
17. Rikihisa Y. The tribe Ehrlichieae and ehrlichial diseases. Clin Microbiol Rev. 1991;4:286–308.
18. Sumner JW, Nicholson WL, Massung RF. PCR amplification and comparison of nucleotide sequences from the *groESL* heat shock operon of *Ehrlichia* species. J Clin Microbiol. 1997;35:2087–2092.
19. Chen S-M, Yu X-J, Popov VL, et al. Genetic and antigenic diversity of *Ehrlichia chaffeensis*: Comparative analysis of a novel human strain from Oklahoma and previously isolated strains. J Infect Dis. 1997;175:856–863.
20. Ohashi N, Zhi N, Zhang Y, et al. Immunodominant major outer membrane proteins of *Ehrlichia chaffeensis* are encoded by a polymorphic multigene family. Infect Immun. 1998;66:132–139.
21. Asanovich KM, Bakken JS, Madigan JE, et al. Antigenic diversity of granulocytic *Ehrlichia* isolates from humans in Wisconsin and New York and a horse in California. J Infect Dis. 1997;176:1029–1034.
22. Ijdo JW, Zhang Y, Hodzic E, et al. The early humoral response in human granulocytic ehrlichiosis. J Infect Dis. 1997;176:687–692.
23. Anderson BE, Sumner JW, Dawson JE, et al. Detection of the etiologic agent of human ehrlichiosis by polymerase chain reaction. J Clin Microbiol. 1992;30:775–780.
24. Anderson BE, Sims KG, Olson JG, et al. *Amblyomma americanum*: A potential vector of human ehrlichiosis. Am J Trop Med Hyg. 1993;49:239–244.
25. Ewing SA, Dawson JE, Kocan AA, et al. Experimental transmission of *Ehrlichia chaffeensis* (Rickettsiales: Ehrlichieae) among white-tailed deer by *Amblyomma americanum* (Acari: Ixodidae). J Med Entomol. 1995;32:368–374.
26. Lockhart JM, Davidson WR, Stallknecht DE, et al. Site-specific geographic association between *Amblyomma americanum* (Acari: Ixodidae) infestations and *Ehrlichia chaffeensis*-reactive (Rickettsiales: Ehrlichieae) antibodies in white-tailed deer. *J Med Entomol.* 1996;33:153–158.
27. Lockhart JM, Davidson WR, Dawson JE, et al. Temporal association of *Amblyomma americanum* with the presence of *Ehrlichia chaffeensis* reactive antibodies in white-tailed deer. J Wildl Dis. 1995;31:119–124.
28. Telford III SR, Dawson JE, Katavolos P, et al. Perpetuation of the agent of human granulocytic ehrlichiosis in a deer tick–rodent cycle. Proc Natl Acad Sci U S A. 1996;93:6209–6214.
29. Fishbein DB, Dawson JE, Robinson LE. Human ehrlichiosis in the United States, 1985–1990. Ann Intern Med. 1994;120:736–743.
30. Fishbein DB, Sawyer LA, Holland CJ, et al. Unexplained febrile illnesses after exposure to ticks. JAMA. 1987;257:3100–3104.
31. Harkess JR, Ewing SA, Crutcher JM, et al. Human ehrlichiosis in Oklahoma. J Infect Dis. 1989;159:576–579.
32. Fishbein DB, Kemp A, Dawson JE, et al. Human ehrlichiosis: Prospective active surveillance in febrile hospitalized patients. J Infect Dis. 1989;160:803–809.
33. Eng TR, Harkess JR, Fishbein DB, et al. Epidemiologic, clinical, and laboratory findings of human ehrlichiosis in the United States, 1988. JAMA. 1990;264:2251–2258.
34. Rohrbach BW, Harkess JR, Ewing SA, et al. Epidemiologic and clinical characteristics of persons with serologic evidence of *E. canis* infection. Am J Public Health. 1990;80:442–445.
35. Bakken JS, Krueth J, Wilson-Nordskog C, et al. Clinical and laboratory characteristics of human granulocytic ehrlichiosis. JAMA. 1996;275:199–205.
36. Aguero-Rosenfeld M, Horowitz HW, Wormser GP, et al. Human granulocytic ehrlichiosis (HGE): A series from a single medical center in New York State. Ann Intern Med. 1996;125:904–908.
37. Dawson JE, Warner CK, Standaert S, et al. The interface between research and the diagnosis of an emerging tick-borne disease, human ehrlichiosis due to *Ehrlichia chaffeensis*. Arch Intern Med. 1996;156:137–142.
38. Morais JD, Dawson JE, Green C, et al. First European case of ehrlichiosis. Lancet. 1991;338:633–634.
39. Uhaa IJ, Maclean JD, Greene CR, et al. A case of human ehrlichiosis acquired in Mali: Clinical and laboratory findings. Am J Trop Med Hyg. 1992;46:161–164.
40. Yevich SJ, Sanchez JL, DeFraites RF, et al. Seroepidemiology of infections due to spotted fever group rickettsiae and *Ehrlichia* species in military personnel exposed in areas of the United States where such infections are endemic. J Infect Dis. 1995;171:1266–1273.
41. Perez M, Rikihisa Y, Wen B. *Ehrlichia canis*–like agent isolated from a man in Venezuela: Antigenic and genetic characterization. J Clin Microbiol. 1996;34:2133–2139.
42. Groves MG, Dennis GL, Amyx HL, et al. Transmission of *Ehrlichia canis* to dogs by ticks *(Rhipicephalus sanguineus)*. Am J Vet Res. 1975;36:937–940.
43. Smith RD, Sells DM, Stephenson EH, et al. Development of *Ehrlichia canis*, causative agent of canine ehrlichiosis, in the tick *Rhipicephalus sanguineus* and its differentiation from a symbiotic rickettsia. Am J Vet Res. 1976;37:119–126.
44. Anziani OS, Ewing SA, Barker RW. Experimental transmission of a granulocytic form of the tribe Ehrlichieae by *Dermacentor variabilis* and *Amblyomma americanum* to dogs. Am J Vet Res. 1990;51:929–931.
45. Dawson JE, Stallknecht DE, Howerth EW, et al. Susceptibility of white-tailed deer *(Odocoileus virginianus)* to infection with *Ehrlichia chaffeensis*, the etiologic agent of human ehrlichiosis. J Clin Microbiol. 1994;32:2725–2728.
46. Dawson JE, Ewing SA. Susceptibility of dogs to infection with *Ehrlichia chaffeensis*, causative agent of human ehrlichiosis. Am J Vet Res. 1992;53:1322–1327.
47. Dawson JE, Biggie KL, Warner CK, et al. Polymerase chain reaction evidence of *Ehrlichia chaffeensis*, an etiologic agent of human ehrlichiosis, in dogs from southeast Virginia. Am J Vet Res. 1996;57:1175–1179.
48. Lockhart JM, Davidson WR, Stallknecht DE, et al. Isolation of *Ehrlichia chaffeensis* from wild white-tailed deer *(Odocoileus virginianus)* confirms their role as natural reservoir hosts. J Clin Microbiol. 1997;35:1681–1686.
49. Kawahara M, Suto C, Rikihisa Y, et al. Characterization of ehrlichial organisms isolated from a wild mouse. J Clin Microbiol. 1993;31:89–96.
50. Bakken JS, Goellner P, Van Etter M, et al. Seroprevalence of human granulocytic ehrlichiosis (HGE) among permanent residents of northwestern Wisconsin. Clin Infect Dis 1998;27:1491–1496.
51. Magnarelli LA, Dumler JS, Anderson JF, et al. Coexistence of antibodies to tick-borne pathogens of babesiosis, ehrlichiosis, and Lyme borreliosis in human sera. J Clin Microbiol. 1995;33:2054–3057.
52. Dumler JS, Dotevall L, Gustafson R, et al. A population-based seroepidemiological study of human granulocytic ehrlichiosis (HGE) and Lyme borreliosis on the west coast of Sweden. J Infect Dis. 1997;175:720–722.
53. Petrovec M, Furlan SL, Zupanc TA, et al. Human disease in Europe caused by a granulocytic *Ehrlichia* species. J Clin Microbiol. 1997;35:1556–1559.
54. Pancholi P, Kolbert CP, Mitchell P, et al. *Ixodes dammini* (scapularis) as a potential vector of human granulocytic ehrlichiosis. J Infect Dis. 1995;172:1007–1012.
55. Mitchell PD, Reed KD, Hofkes JM. Immunoserologic evidence of coinfection with *Borrelia burgdorferi, Babesia microti*, and human granulocytic *Ehrlichia* species in residents of Wisconsin and Minnesota. J Clin Microbiol. 1996;34:724–727.
56. Brouqui P, Dumler JS, Lenhard R, et al. Serologic evidence of human granulocytic ehrlichiosis in Europe. Lancet. 1995;346:782–783.
57. Nadelman RB, Horowitz HW, Chen HT, et al. Simultaneous human granulocytic ehrlichiosis and Lyme borreliosis. N Engl J Med. 1997;337:27–30.
58. MacLeod JR, Gordon WS. Studies in tick-borne fever of sheep. I. Transmission by the tick, *Ixodes ricinus*, with a description of the disease produced. Parasitology. 1933;25:273–285.
59. Walls JJ, Greig B, Neitzel DF, Dumler JS. Natural infection of small mammal species in Minnesota with the agent of human granulocytic ehrlichiosis. J Clin Microbiol. 1997;35:853–855.
60. Nicholson WL, Muir S, Sumner JW. Serologic evidence of infection with *Ehrlichia* spp in wild rodents (Muridae: Sigmodontinae) in the United States. J Clin Microbiol. 1998;36:695–700.
61. Hodzic E, Ijdo JWI, Feng S, et al. Granulocytic ehrlichiosis in the laboratory mouse. J Infect Dis. 1998;177:737–745.
62. Belongia EA, Reed KD, Mitchell PD, et al. Prevalence of granulocytic *Ehrlichia* infection among white-tailed deer in Wisconsin. J Clin Microbiol. 1997;35:1465–1468.
63. Dumler JS, Dawson JE, Walker DH. Human ehrlichiosis: Hematopathology and immunohistologic detection of *Ehrlichia chaffeensis*. Hum Pathol. 1993;24:391–396.
64. Dunn BE, Monson TP, Dumler JS, et al. Identification of *Ehrlichia chaffeensis* morulae in cerebrospinal fluid mononuclear cells. J Clin Microbiol. 1992;30:2207–2210.
65. Dumler JS, Brouqui P, Aronson J, et al. Identification of *Ehrlichia* in human tissue. N Engl J Med. 1991;325:1109–1110.

66. Dumler JS, Sutker WL, Walker DH. Persistent infection with *Ehrlichia chaffeensis*. Clin Infect Dis. 1993;17:903–905.
67. Walker DH, Dumler JS. Human monocytic and granulocytic ehrlichioses. Discovery and diagnosis of emerging tick-borne infections and the critical role of the pathologist. Arch Pathol Lab Med. 1997;121:785–791.
68. Buhles WC Jr, Huxsoll DI, Ristic M. Tropical canine pancytopenia: Clinical, hematologic, and serologic response of dogs to *Ehrlichia canis* infection, tetracycline therapy, and challenge inoculation. J Infect Dis. 1974;130:357–367.
69. Reardon MJ, Pierce KR. Acute experimental canine ehrlichiosis. I. Sequential reaction of the hemic and lymphoreticular systems. Vet Pathol. 1981;18:48–61.
70. Lee EH, Rikihisa Y. Absence of tumor necrosis factor alpha, interleukin-6 (IL-6), and granulocyte-macrophage colony-stimulating factor expression but presence of IL-1β, IL-8, and IL-10 expression of human monocytes exposed to viable or killed *Ehrlichia chaffeensis*. Infect Immun. 1996;64:4211–4219.
71. Lee EH, Rikihisa Y. Anti-*Ehrlichia chaffeensis* antibody complexed with *E. chaffeensis* induces potent proinflammatory cytokine mRNA expression in human monocytes through sustained reduction of IκB-α and activation of NF-κB. Infect Immun. 1997;65:2890–2897.
72. Barnewall R, Rikihisa Y. Mechanism of IFN-γ–induced killing of *Ehrlichia chaffeensis* in human monocytes (Abstract). Presented at the 93rd General Meeting of the American Society for Microbiology, Las Vegas, Nevada, 1994.
73. Lewis GE Jr, Hill SL, Ristic M. Effect of canine immune serum on the growth of *Ehrlichia canis* within nonimmune canine macrophages. Am J Vet Res. 1978;39:71–76.
74. Barnewall RE, Rikihisa Y, Lee EH. *Ehrlichia chaffeensis* inclusions are early endosomes which selectivity accumulate transferrin receptor. Infect Immun. 1997;65:1455–1461.
75. Lee EH, Rikihisa Y. Protein kinase A–mediated inhibition of gamma interferon–induced tyrosine phosphorylation of Janus kinases and latent cytoplasmic transcription factors in human monocytes by *Ehrlichia chaffeensis*. Infect Immun. 1998;66:2514–2520.
76. Messick JB, Rikihisa Y. Suppression of Ia antigen expression on gamma interferon treated macrophages infected with *Ehrlichia risticii*. Vet Immunol Immunopathol. 1992;32:225–241.
77. Messick JB, Rikihisa Y. Presence of parasite antigen on the surface of P388D1 cells infected with *Ehrlichia risticii*. Infect Immun. 1992;60:3079–3086.
78. Hardalo CJ, Quagliarello V, Dumler JS. Human granulocytic ehrlichiosis in Connecticut: Report of a fatal case. Clin Infect Dis. 1995;21:910–914.
79. Larsen HJS, Overnes G, Waldeland H, et al. Immunosuppression in sheep experimentally infected with *Ehrlichia phagocytophila*. Res Vet Sci. 1994;56:216–224.
80. Klein MB, Miller JS, Nelson CM, et al. Primary bone marrow progenitors of both granulocytic and monocytic lineages are susceptible to infection with the agent of human granulocytic ehrlichiosis. J Infect Dis. 1997;176:1405–1409.
81. Doran TI, Parmley RT, Logas PC, et al. Infection with *Ehrlichia canis* in a child. J Pediatr. 1989;114:809–812.
82. Harkess JR, Stucky D, Ewing SA. Neurologic abnormalities in a patient with human ehrlichiosis. South Med J. 1990;83:1341–1343.
83. Edwards MS, Jones JE, Leass DL, et al. Childhood infection caused by *Ehrlichia canis* or a closely related organism. Pediatr Infect Dis J. 1988;7:651–654.
84. Barton LL, Foy TM. *Ehrlichia canis* infection in a child. Pediatrics. 1989;4:580–582.
85. Dimmitt DC, Fishbein DB, Dawson JE. Human ehrlichiosis associated with cerebrospinal fluid pleocytosis: A case report. Am J Med. 1989;87:677–678.
86. Moskovitz M, Fadden R, Min T. Human ehrlichiosis: A rickettsial disease associated with severe cholestasis and multisystemic disease. J Clin Gastroenterol. 1991;13:86–90.
87. Schutze GE, Jacobs RF. Human monocytic ehrlichiosis in children. Pediatrics. 1997;100:10–17.
88. Paddock CD, Suchard DP, Grumbach KL, et al. Brief report: Fatal seronegative ehrlichiosis in a patient with HIV infection. N Engl J Med. 1993;329:1164–1167.
89. Fichtenbaum CJ, Peterson LR, Weil GJ. Ehrlichiosis presenting as a life-threatening illness with features of the toxic shock syndrome. Am J Med. 1993;95:351–357.
90. Barenfanger J, Patel PG, Dumler JS, et al. Identifying human ehrlichiosis. Lab Med. 1996;27:372–374.
91. Marty AM, Dumler JS, Imes G, et al. Ehrlichiosis mimicking thrombotic thrombocytopenic purpura. Case report and pathological correlation. Hum Pathol. 1995;26:920–925.
92. Paddock CD, Sumner JW, Shore GM, et al. Isolation and characterization of *Ehrlichia chaffeensis* strains from patients with fatal ehrlichiosis. J Clin Microbiol. 1997;35:2496–2502.
93. Ratnasamy N, Everett ED, Roland WE, et al. Central nervous system manifestations of human ehrlichiosis. Clin Infect Dis. 1996;23:314–319.
94. Dawson JE, Anderson BE, Fishbein DB, et al. Isolation and characterization of an *Ehrlichia* sp from a patient diagnosed with human ehrlichiosis. J Clin Microbiol. 1991;29:2741–2745.
95. Dumler JS, Chen S-M, Asanovich K, et al. Isolation and characterization of a new strain of *Ehrlichia chaffeensis* from a patient with nearly fatal monocytic ehrlichiosis. J Clin Microbiol. 1995;33:1704–1711.
96. Dawson JE, Fishbein DB, Eng TR, et al. Diagnosis of human ehrlichiosis with indirect fluorescent antibody test: Kinetics and specificity. J Infect Dis. 1990;162:91–95.
97. Yu X-J, Brouqui P, Dumler JS, et al. Detection of *Ehrlichia chaffeensis* in human tissue by using a species-specific monoclonal antibody. J Clin Microbiol. 1993;31:3284–3288.
98. Everett ED, Evans KA, Henry RB, et al. Human ehrlichiosis in adults after tick exposure. Diagnosis using polymerase chain reaction. Ann Intern Med. 1994;120:730–735.
99. Wong S, Grady LJ. *Ehrlichia* infection as a cause of severe respiratory distress (Letter). N Engl J Med. 1996;334:273.
100. Shea KW, Calio AJ, Klein NC, et al. *Ehrlichia equi* infection associated with rhabdomyolysis. Clin Infect Dis. 1996;22:605.
101. Horowitz HW, Marks SJ, Weintraub M, et al. Brachial plexopathy associated with human granulocytic ehrlichiosis. Neurology. 1996;46: 1026–1029.
102. Bakken JS, Erlemeyer SA, Kanoff RJ, et al. Demyelinating polyneuropathy associated with human granulocytic ehrlichiosis. Submitted for publication.
103. Bakken JS, Krueth J, Tilden RL, et al. Sequential changes in bloodcounts during the natural course of human granulocytic ehrlichiosis (HGE). Presented at 37th International Conference on Antimicrobial Agents and Chemotherapy, Toronto, Canada, Sept 28–Oct 1, 1997.
104. Goodman JL, Nelson C, Vitale B, et al. Direct cultivation of the causative agent from patients with human granulocytic ehrlichiosis. N Engl J Med. 1996;334:209–215.
105. Edelman DC, Dumler JS. Evaluation of an improved PCR diagnostic assay for human granulocytic ehrlichiosis. Mol Diagn 1996;1:41–49.
106. Ravyn MD, Goodman JL, Kodner CB, et al. Immunodiagnosis of human granulocytic ehrlichiosis by using culture-derived human isolates. J Clin Microbiol. 1998;36:1480–1488.
107. Brouqui P, Raoult D. In vitro antibiotic susceptibility of the newly recognized agent of ehrlichiosis in humans, *Ehrlichia chaffeensis*. Antimicrob Agents Chemother. 1992;36:2799–2803.
108. Klein MB, Nelson CM, Goodman JL. Antibiotic susceptibility of the newly cultivated agent of human granulocytic ehrlichiosis: Promising activity of quinolones and rifamycins. Antimicrob Agents Chemother. 1997;41:76–79.
109. Amyx HL, Huxsoll DI, Zeiler DC, et al. Therapeutic and prophylactic value of tetracycline in dogs infected with the agent of tropical canine pancytopenia. J Am Vet Med Assoc. 1971;159:1428–1432.
110. Misao T, Kobayashi Y. Studies on infectious mononucleosis (glandular fever). I. Isolation of etiologic agent from blood, bone marrow, and lymph node of a patient with infectious mononucleosis by using mice. Kyushu J Med Sci. 1955;6:145–152.

SECTION F

BACTERIAL DISEASES

Chapter 182

Introduction to Bacterial Diseases

HOWARD S. GOLD
BARRY I. EISENSTEIN

Despite great advances in the understanding, diagnosis, and treatment of bacterial infections, the causative pathogens continue to inflict a great deal of human suffering. Tuberculosis alone is estimated to kill nearly 3 million people per year.[1] In 1997, 97% of the 10 million deaths among children younger than 5 years occurred in the developing world, most of them due to infectious diseases combined with malnutrition.[1] Pneumonia, most often caused by *Streptococcus pneumoniae* and *Haemophilus influenzae*, kills nearly 3 million children annually in the developing world.[2] Also in this part of the world, enterotoxigenic *Escherichia coli* and *Shigella* spp. are among the most common pathogens causing diarrhea, a condition that kills nearly 5 million children per year.[3] In contrast, deaths caused by infectious diseases account for only about 1% of deaths in industrialized countries, with the sharp differences in incidence due to sanitation, nutrition, and medical intervention with immunizations and antimicrobial chemotherapy.[1]

In recent years, a number of emerging bacterial infections have become apparent. Defined as diseases whose incidence in humans has increased within the past 2 decades or threatens to increase, they include infections due to organisms previously declining in prevalence that become resurgent and newly identified pathogens.[4, 5] Non-01–type *Vibrio cholerae* has caused several large outbreaks of diarrheal disease in South Asia.[6, 7] *Escherichia coli* O157-H7 is a significant threat as a cause of foodborne diarrheal syndromes ranging from mild to bloody diarrhea and hemolytic uremic syndrome, mediated by the production of a potent toxin.[8, 9] After declining by approximately 5% per year, tuberculosis cases in the United States surged up 14% from 1985 to 1993, coincident with the epidemic of acquired immunodeficiency disease.[10] Epidemic diphtheria reemerged in the states of the former Soviet Union, in large part because of the breakdown of the public health system there, with 125,000 cases and 4000 deaths reported from 1990 to 1995.[11] Group A streptococcal infections seem to be increasingly severe, presumably due to a shift in bacterial virulence.[12] One remarkably favorable trend in bacterial infections in the developed world has been the precipitous decline in invasive *H. influenzae* type B infection due to the development and implementation of a protein-conjugate vaccine, effective in the at-risk pediatric population. In the United States, this has translated into a 95% reduction in the incidence of *H. influenzae* type B invasive disease in children younger than 5 years.[13] *Bartonella henselae* is an example of a newly identified pathogen that has been found to be a causative agent of bacillary angiomatosis in acquired immunodeficiency disease patients and cat-scratch disease in normal hosts.[14]

CLASSIFICATION AND STRUCTURE

Bacteria are prokaryotes; as single-celled organisms that possess neither a nuclear membrane nor other membrane-enclosed organelles, they are distinguished from eukaryotes. Currently accepted taxonomy, based on molecular structures and DNA sequences, has abandoned the eukaryote-prokaryote dichotomy and replaced it with a tripartite division of life on earth, comprising three domains, Bacteria, Archaea, and Eucarya.[15, 16] In addition to the typical bacteria, the domain Bacteria includes rickettsiae, chlamydiae, mycoplasmas, and higher bacteria, that is, actinomycetes, *Nocardia* spp., and mycobacteria.[17] Except for mycoplasmas, bacteria are enclosed in a peptidoglycan-containing cell wall.[18] Archae, formerly designated Archaebacteria, are also prokaryotes. However, beyond that simplistic morphologic distinction, these organisms are as distinct from Bacteria as they are from Eucarya and are not known agents of human disease.[19]

A number of methods are used to classify bacteria, ranging from traditional, simple methods to sophisticated genetic methods. The prototype traditional method is the use of light microscopy to identify the presence and appearance of Gram-stained organisms. With the Gram technique, the initial stains (crystal violet and Gram's iodine) form a complex with bacterial ribonucleotides, imparting a purple color. These complexes are extracted from gram-negative, but not gram-positive, samples by rinsing with alcohol and acetone. The decolorized gram-negative organisms take up the counterstain, safranin, which confers a red color.[20]

Beyond their use in identification, the outer structures of bacteria are critical to bacterial virulence and as a target for antimicrobial drugs. The bacterial cell wall is made up largely of peptidoglycan, a heteropolymer consisting of a sugar backbone and repeating *N*-acetylglucosamine and *N*-acetylmuramic acid molecules. Gram-positive bacteria have a cell wall comprising a thick layer of peptidoglycan surrounding a phospholipid bilayer, the cell membrane. In addition to the lipid component, the cell membrane contains various protein and carbohydrate moieties. The gram-negative cell wall is a thinner layer of peptidoglycan, which surrounds a lipid bilayer cell membrane, and is itself surrounded by an outer cell envelope, a second lipid bilayer containing a relatively high density of protein and lipopolysaccharide.[18, 21] The outermost structure of a number of important human pathogens is a polysaccharide capsule that impairs phagocytosis by host polymorphonuclear leukocytes.

In addition to color, bacteria can be classified by morphology. The cocci are round bacteria and may be arrayed in pairs, chains, or clusters. Bacilli are cylindric or rod shaped, in some cases curved or pleomorphic. Some bacilli are also characterized by the presence of spores. Other morphologies include spiral forms (spirochetes) and branched chains. Last, traditional typing schemes use growth and metabolic properties. Oxygen tolerance is commonly used to classify bacteria into aerobic, facultative, and anaerobic. Among a number of metabolic traits, gram-negative bacilli are divided into those that ferment lactose and those that do not.[22]

Modern methods of classification of bacteria are based on the analysis of genetic material, rather than phenotype. The guanine plus cytosine (G + C) content of bacterial DNA was an early method; more recently, the semiconserved DNA sequences of ribosomal RNA genes have become a preferred analytic target, which has helped redefine the relationships between various bacterial genera.[16] As discussed later, these techniques have also been used to discover previously uncultured organisms and may help to define the relationships between isolates of epidemiologically important bacteria.[23, 24]

GENOMICS AND BACTERIAL GENETICS

A new era in bacteriology began with the publication of the DNA sequence of the complete genome of *H. influenzae* Rd and continued with the public release of genomic sequences of *E. coli, Helicobacter pylori, Mycoplasma pneumoniae, Borrelia burgdorferi*, and *Mycobacterium tuberculosis*, among others.[25, 26] Partial genomic sequences exist for a number of other bacteria, and work continues to complete the full sequences of most major bacterial pathogens.[26] In some instances, more than one strain of an organism is being sequenced by different groups of scientists, allowing comparisons to be made between strains of differing virulence or drug resistance.[27, 28] A number of sequences, completed by private enterprises, are not currently in the public domain, including those of *Staphylococcus aureus, Strep. pneumoniae, Streptococcus pyogenes, Enterococcus faecium* and *Enterococcus faecalis.*[29] The genomes of bacterial pathogens vary in size, ranging from less than 1 to nearly 6 megabases (Mb) (1 Mb is 1 million base pairs of DNA). These genomes contain, on average, 1000 protein-encoding sequences per megabase. It has been suggested that 256 genes is a reasonable approximation of the minimal set of genes required by a bacterium.[30] *Helicobacter pylori* lives in a limited area of the gastric and duodenal mucosa. Given that limited niche, it is not surprising that the *H. pylori* genome is 1.66 Mb, whereas an organism with a more diversified range and metabolism, like *E. coli*, has a larger genome of 4.66 Mb.[31–33] In an attempt to deduce function, sequences from genomic databases can be compared with previously characterized genes. Genes whose protein products use ATP to transport molecules across the cell membrane are the largest family of genes with inferred function in the *E. coli* and *Bacillus subtilis* genomes.[33, 34] A significant proportion of genes in the genomic databases, for example, one third of the *E. coli* and *H. pylori* genomes, do not have known function.[31, 33]

Superficially, the field of bacterial genomics would seem to eclipse older methods of discovering and characterizing bacterial genes; actually, the old and the new are complementary.[26] In addition to the large number of genes sequenced but lacking homology to previously characterized genes (and therefore of unknown function), gene sequences do not typically inform as to the complex ways that gene products interact. Both to characterize genes with unknown function and to analyze and understand sequential signaling, metabolic, and developmental pathways, the more traditional tools of biochemistry and molecular genetics must still be employed. With this augmented information, DNA and derivative protein databases are and will continue to become more robust and powerful. The addition of faster and more intelligent search algorithms then lead to extraordinary predictive approaches "in silico."

Various techniques have been developed to sort through DNA libraries looking for particular subsets of genes.[26] One strategy is to look for genes that are essential to bacterial growth in vitro, the inactivation of which is lethal to cells in culture. Another approach is to select genes that are activated during specific situations, for example, colonization, invasion, and persistence in the mammalian host. One example is in vivo expression technology, or IVET, which was devised to detect genes that are active only during infection of the mammalian host by using the promoters of those genes to drive the expression of various selectable markers.[35, 36] Arbitrarily primed polymerase chain reaction (PCR) of bacterial RNA has been used to compare patterns of gene expression during different conditions.[37] The analysis of pathogens' genomes will be used by researchers to gain understanding of all manner of bacterial functions, including metabolism, reproduction, and virulence. For example, by comparing the full genomes of virulent and avirulent strains of a given species, one might expect to find genes or clusters of genes (potentially arrayed in a "pathogenicity island") that correspond to particular virulence traits.[38]

For biotechnology and pharmaceutical companies, the ultimate aim of these research efforts is to discover new targets for antimicrobial drugs and vaccines. Targets for novel broad-spectrum antimicrobial drugs may include essential proteins that are homologous across a number of bacterial species and distinct from human proteins. For example, at least one pharmaceutical company is searching for drugs to target bacterial transfer RNA synthetases from *Strep. pneumoniae, Strep. pyogenes,* and *Staph. aureus* that have been identified in a proprietary pathogen genome database. New vaccines will target undefined virulence determinants, some of which may be identified by methods like IVET. One theoretical advantage of choosing virulence targets for antimicrobial therapy is the reduced likelihood of preexisting genetic material encoding resistance to that antimicrobial agent, such as may be present in organisms that naturally produce an antibiotic.[39]

In addition to their complement of genomic DNA, many bacteria also contain various mobile genetic elements including plasmids, insertion sequence elements, transposons, and bacteriophages.[39–41] Plasmids are circular DNA molecules ranging in size from a few kilobases (kb) (thousands of bases) to more than 100 kb. They may carry genes that encode antimicrobial drug resistance (in some cases, multiple resistance genes) and virulence factors. Some plasmids are transferable between bacteria, including different species and occasionally between genera. Insertion-sequence elements are short DNA sequences that encode an enzyme needed for the process of transposition, that is, the excision of a piece of DNA from one site in chromosomal or plasmid DNA and reinsertion elsewhere. Insertion-sequence elements also have at their termini small sequences of DNA that are recognized by the enzyme. Some insertion-sequence elements are components of larger elements called *transposons*, which contain genes other than the transposition genes, often antibiotic-resistance genes. Conjugative transposons can mediate their own transfer between bacteria, whereas other transposons require prior integration in a conjugative plasmid to be transferred. Integrons are a type of transposon comprising an integrase gene (which codes for an enzyme required for DNA mobility) along with one or more drug-resistance, virulence, or other genes that are inserted as "cassettes," often under the control of a common promoter.[39, 42] These genes are preceded by a particular short DNA sequence that is recognized by the integrase, allowing a site-specific recombination event to occur between the circularized cassette and the recipient integron, allowing efficient capture of useful genes from disparate bacterial genera. Bacteriophages are viruses that infect bacteria and may transfer bacterial DNA in the process. Virulence in some bacteria (e.g., *V. cholerae*, erythrogenic *Strep. pyogenes,* and *Corynebacterium diphtheriae*) requires the presence of bacteriophages.[43, 44] In sum, the existence of all these mobile elements gives a sense of the remarkable plasticity of the genetic information contained in bacteria, allowing an inexorable exchange of genetic information that may provide selective evolutionary advantage.

As noted previously, molecular techniques make use of the bacterial genetic code for a number of different purposes. The use of PCR with primers complementary to conserved sequences of 16-S ribosomal RNA to amplify intervening variable sequences has allowed the identification of previously uncultured organisms directly from patients' tissue samples.[23] The newly designated species *B. henselae* and *Tropheryma whippelii* are now known to cause bacillary angiomatosis and Whipple's disease, respectively, both previously of questionable bacterial origin. The propagation of an uncultured organism may be aided by understanding which better-characterized organisms are its closest relatives. Various molecular techniques, including PCR and DNA probing, are now common practice in clinical microbiology laboratories, mostly for the identification of organisms, but in some cases for the detection of antibiotic-resistance genes.[45] PCR methods are particularly helpful for the detection of slowly growing or difficult-to-grow organisms, such as *Mycobacteria, Chlamydia,* and *Legionella.*

EPIDEMIOLOGY AND MOLECULAR EPIDEMIOLOGY

An important part of bacteriology is the study of the spread of pathogenic bacteria, their sources, and their modes and frequency of transmission. Epidemiologic studies may begin to determine the relatedness of bacterial isolates with techniques based on phenotype, such as serotyping, biotyping, and antibiotic-resistance patterns, but these methods are increasingly complemented, or even replaced, by molecular techniques.[24, 46] The latter are broadly divided into protein-based and DNA-RNA–based. Nucleic acid–based techniques are diverse. Plasmid profiles have been largely supplanted by techniques that utilize chromosomal DNA, such as restriction-enzyme analysis of chromosomal DNA, restriction-enzyme analysis combined with DNA probing, arbitrarily primed PCR, and the currently accepted gold standard for molecular typing of bacteria in an outbreak setting, pulsed-field gel electrophoresis. Pulsed-field gel electrophoresis entails the extraction of genomic DNA from bacteria preserved in a semisolid matrix (to avoid mechanical damage to the DNA) followed by restriction digestion using an enzyme that cuts the DNA fairly infrequently and finally electrophoresis by a technique that allows clear separation of large fragments of DNA. One weakness of pulsed-field gel electrophoresis is that changes in the restriction pattern may be somewhat random, as they are based on the alteration of a limited number of sites in the DNA recognized by the restriction enzyme. Another DNA-based technique relies on a gene's nucleotide sequence itself, as certain genes would be expected to change over time by accumulating mutations, allowing them to act like a "molecular clock."[24] In an attempt to track the dissemination of resistance genes, researchers have analyzed the arrangement of genes, and in some cases the intergenic DNA in a series of resistance genes, such as has been used to study glycopeptide-resistance determinants in enterococci and various resistance genes arrayed in integrons in gram-negative bacilli.[47, 48] Protein-based techniques are used somewhat less often for typing purposes and include protein electrophoresis and immunoblotting of protein gels.

BACTERIAL ECOLOGY AND VIRULENCE

From Darwinian principles, it can be inferred that the main aim of a bacterium is to become two bacteria. This objective has been the main driver of evolution and adaptation to a variety of environments. Not surprisingly, then, bacteria demonstrate remarkable adaptation to survival in harsh conditions. The mammalian host is one such rigorous environment for bacteria. Environmental stressors may include mechanical factors, the host immune response, and a limited availability of nutrients and other critical molecules, like iron. Bacteria have evolved an array of complex, even elegant, systems, collectively known as *virulence factors,* for surviving and causing infection in the mammalian host.[49] These have functions including adherence to mammalian tissues, colonization, invasion, and metabolic shifts to deal with different nutrient sources and evasion of the host immune response. The expression of virulence genes varies in different hosts, for example, in bacteria that use insect vectors to infect mammalian hosts; this difference, though subtle, is seen even between uropathogenic *E. coli* infecting men and women.[50] Bacteria may interact with the mammalian host to varied degrees as commensals, opportunists, or virulent pathogens, although these relationships may be altered by changes in the dynamic balance between the bacteria and the host, such as loss of the integrity of the epidermis from trauma, the development of neutropenia from cytotoxic cancer chemotherapy, or even the presence of an intercurrent viral infection. The interaction between microbe and host extends to the level of host gene expression. *Pseudomonas aeruginosa* is an important pathogen in the lungs of patients with cystic fibrosis. It has been reported that the *Pseudomonas* lipopolysaccharide upregulates transcription of a host mucin gene, the end result being a host environment that is more hospitable to the pathogen.[51]

A fascinating aspect of the host–microbial pathogen interaction is the pressures these pathogens have placed on human evolution. Genetic mutations that are deleterious when present in a homozygous state have been preserved in humans because they appear to be protective when they are heterozygous. The heterozygous mutation of human hemoglobin that produces sickle cell trait protects against malaria (a protozoan infection), despite producing very morbid disease in the homozygous state. A bacterial parallel has been described: the heterozygous condition for cystic fibrosis seems to be protective against *Salmonella typhi* infection.[52] Researchers studying a gene mutation that provides resistance to infection of macrophages by the human immunodeficiency virus have suggested that this mutation may have been selected in some human populations because it may engender resistance to *Yersinia pestis*, the causative agent of the bubonic plague, or some other infectious agent that targets macrophages.[53]

Various sensing mechanisms allow bacteria to alter their physiology in an adaptive manner. Two-component regulatory systems are one such mechanism, made up of a sensing protein and an effector component that together control gene expression at the transcriptional level.[54, 55] These systems allow bacteria to respond to diverse environmental challenges, such as the induction of glycopeptide resistance by the presence of glycopeptide antibiotics,[55a] or changes in outer membrane porins by alterations in osmolarity. Bacteria alter gene expression in other ways as well. Phase variation is the on-and-off expression of certain bacterial virulence genes. The *E. coli* type 1 fimbria, an important factor for adherence to urinary epithelium, has its expression regulated at the level of transcription by the inversion of a small segment of DNA in different generations of the organism.[56] Other bacterial pathogens (e.g., *Neisseria* species, *B. burgdorferi*, *Salmonella,* and *Strep. pneumoniae*) also use phase variation to alter their physiology to suit various stages of pathogenesis, that is, a particular phase may be adapted for colonization, whereas another may be more effective for tissue invasion.[57, 58] Biofilms, comprising cooperative bacterial communities, are another example of an adaptive physiologic response, used by organisms like *P. aeruginosa* to adhere to implanted medical devices and in the lungs of patients with cystic fibrosis.[59]

Among the numerous stresses faced by bacteria in the mammalian host, a deficiency of available iron is a common theme.[60] In the host, iron is kept in a bound state, leaving little available for use by invading bacteria. The iron-poor environment acts as a defense mechanism for the host while triggering responses from bacteria including the elaboration of siderophores (molecules that bind iron for importation by the microorganism) and the induction of virulence factors.[61] The latter reflects a common theme, that nutrient limitations are important to the induction of virulence. Heat-shock proteins are another bacterial response to environmental stress.[62] They are produced by bacteria (and other organisms) in response to stress, for example, heat or chemical stress, to protect and repair proteins. Their functions include the prevention of unwanted protein interactions and assistance in refolding denatured proteins. Heat-shock proteins and iron-scavenging systems are among the many novel virulence-related targets of experimental vaccine strategies.

Bacterial toxins are virulence factors that often produce significant morbidity and mortality in some bacterial infections. The multitude of bacterial toxins have effects ranging from emesis or diarrhea, or both, caused by preformed enterotoxins in foods and by enteric pathogens, to fever, hypotension, and multiple organ system failure caused by the mediators of toxic shock syndrome. The interaction between the toxin and the host may be complex, although most that have been studied result in some obvious survival and propagation benefits for the pathogen. Bacteria have evolved dedicated mechanisms to export virulence proteins, or in the case of the type III secretory pathways in several gram-negative pathogens, transfer the bacterial product directly into the cytoplasm of eukaryotic cells.[63]

Polysaccharide capsules play a critical role in the virulence of common bacterial pathogens like group A streptococcus, *S. pneumoniae, H. influenzae* type B, and *Neisseria meningitidis*.[64] The phenomenon of capsular type switching has been noted in several bacterial pathogens, including *N. meningitidis* and *S. pneumoniae*.[65, 66] This is a potent mechanism of evading the host immune response and is a concern for vaccine programs.

TREATMENT AND PREVENTION

Through research in bacteriology, we have vastly improved our understanding of bacterial functions and the host-microbe interaction, as well as having a rational basis for therapeutic and preventative strategies for bacterial infections. It is logical to include clindamycin in the antimicrobial therapy of streptococcal toxic shock syndrome complicating severe, invasive group A streptococcus infection (e.g., necrotizing fasciitis) rather than penicillin alone.[67] This approach is supported by several lines of evidence, including the reduced expression of penicillin-binding proteins in streptococci at the high inoculum expected in these infections. Because clindamycin is a protein synthesis inhibitor, it interferes with toxin production and superantigen activity, that is, the ability of streptococcal exotoxins (or other molecules) to stimulate T cells by binding to both the V_β region of the T-cell receptor and the major histocompatibility complex of the antigen-presenting cell.[67, 68] The study of bacterial pathogenesis has added potential new targets for drug therapy and vaccine development. A vaccine against *E. coli* fimbriae with P-antigen–binding specificity has shown efficacy in preventing cystitis in an experimental animal model.[69] A more novel approach has been taken against *S. aureus* infection in experimental animals; using a staphylococcal virulence regulatory protein as a vaccine antigen, researchers were able to show protection against staphylococcal challenge.[70] Two-component signal-transduction systems, noted previously, are a tempting target for antimicrobial drug development because they control so many bacterial functions. A group of compounds with activity against gram-positive organisms has been shown to inhibit these response regulators.[71]

REFERENCES

1. World Health Organization. Executive Summary: The World Health Report 1998—Life in the 21st century—a vision for all. Albany, NY: Boyd Printing; 1998:1–17.
2. Shann F. The management of pneumonia in children in developing countries. Clin Infect Dis. 1995;21(Suppl 3):S218–S225.
3. DuPont HL. Diarrheal disease in the developing world. Infect Dis Clin North Am. 1995;9:313–324.
4. Centers for Disease Control and Prevention. Addressing emerging infectious disease threats: A prevention strategy for the United States. Atlanta: US Department of Health and Human Services; 1994:1–46.
5. Morse SS. Factors in the emergence of infectious diseases. Emerg Infect Dis. 1995;1:7–15.
6. Albert MJ. Epidemiology and molecular biology of *Vibrio cholerae* 0139 Bengal. Indian J Med Res. 1996;104:14–27.
7. Shears P. Cholera. Ann Trop Med Parasitol. 1994;88:109–122.
8. Tarr PI. *Escherichia coli* O157:H7: Clinical, diagnostic, and epidemiological aspects of human infection. Clin Infect Dis. 1995;20:1–8.
9. MacDonald KL, Osterholm MT. The emergence of *Escherichia coli* O157:H7 infection in the United States. The changing epidemiology of foodborne disease. Clin Infect Dis. 1993;269:2264–2266.
10. Raviglione MC, Snider DE Jr, Kochi A. Global epidemiology of tuberculosis: Morbidity and mortality of a worldwide epidemic. JAMA. 1995;273:220–226.
11. Centers for Disease Control and Prevention. Update: Diphtheria epidemic—new independent states of the former Soviet Union, January 1995–March 1996. MMWR Morb Mortal Wkly Rep. 1996;45:693–697.
12. Stevens DL. Invasive group A streptococcus infections. Clin Infect Dis. 1992;14:2–13.
13. Centers for Disease Control and Prevention. Progress toward elimination of *Haemophilus influenzae* type B disease among infants and children—United States, 1987–1995. MMWR Morb Mortal Wkly Rep. 1996;45:901–908.
14. Anderson BE, Neuman MA. *Bartonella* spp. as emerging human pathogens. Clin Microbiol Rev. 1997;10:203–219.
15. Woese CR, Kandler O, Wheelis ML. Towards a natural system of organisms: Proposal for the domains Archaea, Bacteria, and Eucarya. Proc Natl Acad Sci U S A. 1990;87:4576–4579.
16. Pace NR. A molecular view of microbial diversity and the biosphere. Science. 1997;276:734–740.
17. Holt JG. Bergey's Manual of Determinative Bacteriology. 9th ed. Baltimore: Williams & Wilkins; 1994.
18. Schlessinger D, Schaechter M, Eisenstein BI. Biology of infectious agents. In: Schaechter M, Medoff G, Eisenstein BI, eds. Mechanisms of Microbial Disease. 2nd ed. Baltimore: Williams & Wilkins; 1993:27–56.
19. DeLong E. Archaeal means and extremes. Science. 1998;280:542–543.
20. Ryan KJ, Ray CG. Principles of laboratory diagnosis of infectious diseases. In: Ryan KJ, ed. Sherris Medical Microbiology: An Introduction to Infectious Diseases. 3rd ed. Norwalk, Conn: Appleton & Lange; 1994:221–250.
21. Neidhardt FC. Bacterial structures. In: Ryan KJ, ed. Sherris Medical Microbiology: An Introduction to Infectious Diseases. 3rd ed. Norwalk, Conn: Appleton & Lange; 1994:11–24.
22. Baron EJ, Weissfeld AS, Fuselier PA, Brenner DJ. Classification and identification of bacteria. In: Murray PR, Baron EJ, Pfaller MA, et al, eds. Manual of Clinical Microbiology. 6th ed. Washington, DC: American Society for Microbiology; 1995:249–264.
23. Relman DA. The identification of uncultured microbial pathogens. J Infect Dis. 1993;168:1–8.
24. Arbeit RD. Laboratory procedures for the epidemiologic analysis of microorganisms. In: Murray PR, Baron EJ, Pfaller MA, et al, eds. Manual of Clinical Microbiology. 6th ed. Washington, DC: American Society for Microbiology; 1995:190–208.
25. Fleischmann RD, Adams MD, White O, et al. Whole-genome random sequencing and assembly of *Haemophilus influenzae* Rd. Science. 1995;269:496–512.
26. Strauss EJ, Falkow S. Microbial pathogenesis: Genomics and beyond. Science. 1997;276:707–712.
27. Cole ST, Brosch R, Parkhill J, et al. Deciphering the biology of *Mycobacterium tuberculosis* from the complete genome sequence. Nature. 1998;393:537–544.
28. Young DB. Blueprint for the white plague. Nature. 1998;393:515.
29. Marshall E. Is data-hoarding slowing the assault on pathogens? Science. 1997;275:777–780.
30. Mushegian AR, Koonin EV. A minimal gene set for cellular life derived by comparison of complete bacterial genomes. Proc Natl Acad Sci U S A. 1996;93:10,268–10,273.
31. Tomb JF, White O, Kerlavage AR, et al. The complete genome sequence of the gastric pathogen *Helicobacter pylori*. Nature. 1997;388:539–547.
32. Lee A. The *Helicobacter pylori* genome—new insights into pathogenesis and therapeutics. N Engl J Med. 1998;338:832–833.
33. Blattner FR, Plunkett G 3rd, Bloch CA, et al. The complete genome sequence of *Escherichia coli* K-12. Science. 1997;277:1453–1474.
34. Kunst F, Ogasawara N, Moszer I, et al. The complete genome sequence of the gram-positive bacterium *Bacillus subtilis*. Nature. 1997;390:249–256.
35. Mahan MJ, Slauch JM, Mekalanos JJ. Selection of bacterial virulence genes that are specifically induced. Science. 1993;259:686–688.
36. Heithoff DM, Conner CP, Hanna PC, et al. Bacterial infection as assessed by in vivo gene expression. Proc Natl Acad Sci U S A. 1997;94:934–939.
37. Wong KK, McClelland M. Stress-inducible gene of *Salmonella typhimurium* identified by arbitrarily primed PCR of RNA. Proc Natl Acad Sci U S A. 1994;91:639–643.
38. Lee CA. Pathogenicity islands and the evolution of bacterial pathogens. Infect Agents Dis. 1996;5:1–7.
39. Davies J. Inactivation of antibiotics and the dissemination of resistance. Science. 1994;264:375–382.
40. Schaechter M, Eisenstein BI. Genetics of bacteria. In: Schaechter M, Medoff G, Eisenstein BI, eds. Mechanisms of Microbial Disease. 2nd ed. Baltimore: Williams & Wilkins; 1993:57–76.
41. Neidhardt FC. Bacterial genetic determinants. In: Ryan KJ, ed. Sherris Medical Microbiology: An Introduction to Infectious Diseases. 3rd ed. Norwalk, Conn: Appleton & Lange; 1994:45–68.
42. Mazel D, Dychinco B, Webb VA, Davies J. A distinctive class of integron in the *Vibrio cholerae* genome. Science. 1998;280:605–608.
43. Waldor MK, Mekalanos JJ. Lysogenic conversion by a filamentous phage encoding cholera toxin. Science. 1996;272:1910–1914.
44. Cheetham BF, Katz ME. A role for bacteriophages in the evolution and transfer of bacterial virulence determinants. Mol Microbiol. 1995;18:201–208.
45. Podzorski RP, Persing DH. Molecular detection and identification of microorganisms. In: Murray PR, Baron EJ, Pfaller MA, et al, eds. Manual of Clinical Microbiology. 6th ed. Washington, DC: American Society for Microbiology; 1995:130–157.
46. Pfaller MA, Herwaldt LA. The clinical microbiology laboratory and infection control: Emerging pathogens, antimicrobial resistance, and new technology. Clin Infect Dis. 1997;25:858–870.
47. Handwerger S, Skoble J, Discotto LF, Pucci MJ. Heterogeneity of the *vanA* gene cluster in clinical isolates of enterococci from the northeastern United States. Antimicrob Agents Chemother. 1995;39:362–368.
48. Levesque C, Piche L, Larose C, Roy PH. PCR mapping of integrons reveals several novel combinations of resistance genes. Antimicrob Agents Chemother. 1995;39:185–191.
49. Finlay BB, Falkow S. Common themes in microbial pathogenicity revisited. Microbiol Mol Biol Rev. 1997;61:136–169.
50. Ulleryd P, Lincoln K, Scheutz F, Sandberg T. Virulence characteristics of *Escherichia coli* in relation to host response in men with symptomatic urinary tract infection. Clin Infect Dis. 1994;18:579–584.
51. Li JD, Dohrman AF, Gallup M, et al. Transcriptional activation of mucin by *Pseudomonas aeruginosa* lipopolysaccharide in the pathogenesis of cystic fibrosis lung disease. Proc Natl Acad Sci U S A. 1997;94:967–972.
52. Pier GB, Grout M, Zaidi T, et al. *Salmonella typhi* uses CFTR to enter intestinal epithelial cells. Nature. 1998;393:79–82.
53. Stephens JC, Reich DE, Goldstein DB, et al. Dating the origin of the CCR5-32 AIDS-resistance allele by the coalescence of haplotypes. Am J Hum Genet. 1998;62:1507–1515.
54. Hackenbeck R, Stock JB. Analysis of two-component signal transduction systems involved in transcriptional regulation. Methods Enzymol. 1996;273:281–300.
55. Alex LA, Simon MI. Protein histidine kinases and signal transduction in prokaryotes and eukaryotes. Trends Genet. 1994;10:133–138.

55a. Arthur M, Molinas C, Courvalin P. The VanS-VanR two-component regulatory system controls synthesis of depsipeptide peptidoglycan precursors in *Enterococcus faecium* BM4147. J Bacteriol. 1992;174:2582–2591.

56. Abraham JM, Freitag CS, Clements JR, Eisenstein BI. An invertible element of

DNA controls phase variation of type 1 fimbriae of *Escherichia coli*. Proc Natl Acad Sci U S A. 1985;82:5724–5727.
57. Meyer TF, van Putten JP. Genetic mechanisms and biological implications of phase variation in pathogenic neisseriae. Clin Microbiol Rev. 1989;2(Suppl):S139–S145.
58. Weiser JN, Austrian R, Sreenivasan PK, Masure HR. Phase variation in pneumococcal opacity: Relationship between colonial morphology and nasopharyngeal colonization. Infect Immun. 1994;62:2582–2589.
59. Davies DG, Parsek MR, Pearson JP, et al. The involvement of cell-to-cell signals in the development of a bacterial biofilm. Science. 1998;280:295–298.
60. Wooldridge KG, Williams PH. Iron uptake mechanisms of pathogenic bacteria. FEMS Microbiol Rev. 1993;12:325–348.
61. Litwin CM, Calderwood SB. Role of iron in regulation of virulence genes. Clin Microbiol Rev. 1993;6:137–149.
62. Schlesinger MJ. Heat shock proteins. J Biol Chem. 1990;265:1211–1214.
63. Hueck CJ. Type III protein secretion systems in bacterial pathogens of animals and plants. Microbiol Mol Biol Rev. 1998;62:379–433.
64. Wessels MR, Bronze MS. Critical role of the group A streptococcal capsule in pharyngeal colonization and infection in mice. Proc Natl Acad Sci U S A. 1994;91:12,238–12,242.
65. Swartley JS, Marfin AA, Edupuganti S, et al. Capsule switching of *Neisseria meningitidis*. Proc Natl Acad Sci U S A. 1997;94:271–276.
66. Boken DJ, Chartrand SA, Moland ES, Goering RV. Colonization with penicillin-nonsusceptible *Streptococcus pneumoniae* in urban and rural child-care centers. Pediatr Infect Dis J. 1996;15:667–672.
67. Stevens DL. Streptococcal toxic-shock syndrome: Spectrum of disease, pathogenesis, and new concepts in treatment. Emerg Infect Dis. 1995;1:69–78.
68. Sriskandan S, McKee A, Hall L, Cohen J. Comparative effects of clindamycin and ampicillin on superantigenic activity of *Streptococcus pyogenes*. J Antimicrob Chemother. 1997;40:275–277.
69. Langermann S, Palaszynski S, Barnhart M, et al. Prevention of mucosal *Escherichia coli* infection by FimH-adhesin-based systemic vaccination. Science. 1997;275:607–611.
70. Balaban N, Goldkorn T, Nhan RT, et al. Autoinducer of virulence as a target for vaccine and therapy against *Staphylococcus aureus*. Science. 1998;280:438–440.
71. Barrett JF, Goldschmidt RM, Lawrence LE, et al. Antibacterial agents that inhibit two-component signal transduction systems. Proc Natl Acad Sci U S A. 1998;95:5317–5322.

GRAM-POSITIVE COCCI

Chapter 183

Staphylococcus aureus (Including Staphylococcal Toxic Shock)

FRANCIS A. WALDVOGEL

Staphylococci are among the hardiest non–spore-forming bacteria, and they can survive many nonphysiologic environmental conditions. They can be cultured from dried clinical material after several months, are relatively heat resistant, and can tolerate high salt media. Therefore, it is not surprising that despite the availability of potent antimicrobial agents, improved public health conditions, and hospital infection-control measures, *Staphylococcus aureus* has remained a major human pathogen. Indeed, the development of new antibiotic resistance and other epidemiologic conditions have reestablished this microorganism as a major pathogen in human diseases.

The natural history of *S. aureus* infections can be summarized as follows: many neonates and most children and adults will become intermittently colonized by *S. aureus* and harbor the organism either preferentially in their nasopharynx, occasionally on their skin and clothing, more rarely in the vagina (an important prerequisite in toxic shock syndrome [TSS]), or exceptionally in the rectum or perineal area. From these sites, *S. aureus* can contaminate any site on skin or mucous membranes or other subjects by interpersonal transfer, by aerosol, or by direct contact. The mucous membranes and the skin offer a very efficient mechanical barrier against local tissue invasion. If this barrier is breached by trauma or surgery, *S. aureus* may gain access to the underlying tissue and create a characteristic local abscess lesion (Fig. 183–1) that consists of necrotic tissue, fibrin, and a large number of live and dead polymorphonuclear leukocytes (PMNs). Toxin liberation to skin and other organs can cause various types of skin rash and general symptoms, as exemplified by TSS or acute diarrheal disease. At any time, multiplying bacteria can overcome local phagocytic mechanisms and gain access to the lymphatic channels and the blood stream. The ensuing staphylococcal bacteremia is a dreaded complication, and it can lead to metastatic infections (e.g., endocarditis, pneumonia, or osteomyelitis) and to the patient's demise. The many options of *S. aureus* to infect a patient are summarized in Table 183–1.

MICROBIOLOGY

Morphology

The term *Staphylococcus* is derived from the Greek expression *staphyle* (bunch of grapes) and was chosen by a Scottish surgeon, Sir Alexander Ogdson, because of the characteristic microscopic arrangement in clusters.

Microscopically, *S. aureus* is a gram-positive organism characterized by individual cocci with a diameter of 0.5 to 1.7 μm (Fig. 183–2). These cocci occur singly, in pairs, or in short chains and have a strong tendency to form clusters because cell division occurring in

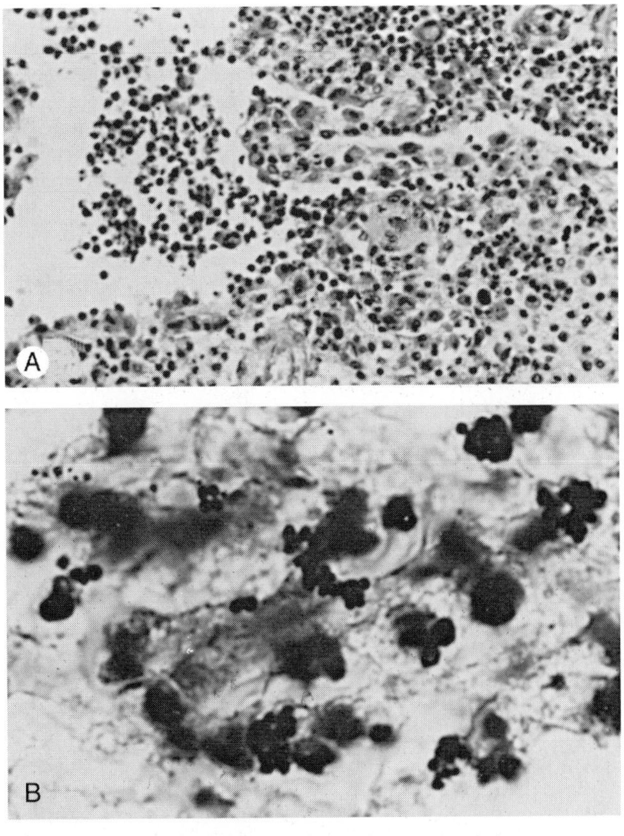

FIGURE 183–1. *A,* Subcutaneous abscess due to *Staphylococcus aureus.* The dense inflammatory infiltrate consists mainly of polymorphonuclear leukocytes (PMN). (H&E, ×400.) *B,* Subcutaneous abscess due to *S. aureus.* Clusters of cocci are surrounded by PMN. (Gram stain, ×1400.)

TABLE 183–1 Clinical Conditions Associated with *Staphylococcus aureus* Contamination/Infection

Carrier state: nasopharynx, skin, vagina, etc.
Direct infection
Skin: folliculitis, carbuncle, impetigo, hidradenitis, cellulitis, wound (surgical and nonsurgical) infection, abscess, etc.
Deep infections, often after trauma, surgery, insertion of foreign material: bursitis, arthritis, osteomyelitis
Blood stream infection secondary to conditions described above
Bacteremia/sepsis
With or without metastatic infection (see below)
With or without vasculitis and coagulopathy
With or without sepsis inflammatory syndrome, multiple organ failure
Metastatic infection: arthritis, osteomyelitis, meningitis, endocarditis, pericarditis, lung abscess, pyomyositis, etc.
Toxin-mediated disease (in association with carrier state or direct infection)
Food poisoning
Scalded skin syndrome
Toxic shock syndrome with multiple organ failure

the three perpendicular planes does not lead to full separation of the daughter cells. Cluster formation is favored by culturing the organism on solid media. These properties, although most often present in laboratory strains, are sometimes missing in clinical specimens and can lead to erroneous diagnoses; thus, dying cells, cells in a stationary phase, or cells ingested by phagocytes occasionally appear as gram-negative on smear; clustering can be very limited in liquid media. The formation of short chains has also been described but never exceeds four to five cocci. Because staphylococcal infections are characterized by abscess formation, most microbiologic specimens of clinical importance should additionally contain a large number of PMNs—except in neutropenic patients.[1]

Macroscopically, *S. aureus* is characterized by rapid growth on blood agar and other nonselective solid media. Individual colonies are sharply defined, smooth, opaque, and convex, with a diameter of 1 to 3 mm within 24 hours; they are β-hemolytic. The classic cream-yellow to golden pigmentation caused by carotenoids may not be readily apparent under certain conditions (e.g., growth under anaerobic conditions or in liquid medium) and may be visible only as a beige hue. Pigment production can be enhanced by further incubation at room temperature and daylight for 24 to 48 hours. Most strains of *S. aureus* produce hemolysis within 24 to 36 hours on horse, sheep, or human blood-agar plates.[2] When encapsulated, the organisms appear as mucoid, sticky colonies. Occasionally, for instance, after aminoglycoside treatment, they may appear as nonpigmented, nonhemolytic small colony variants that revert to normal with hemin and menadione supplementation.

Identification

Within the family Micrococcaceae, the human pathogenic genus *Staphylococcus* can be separated from the nonpathogenic genus *Micrococcus* by various tests, including (1) anaerobic acid production from glucose, (2) sensitivity to 200 μg/ml lysostaphin or to 100 μg furazolidone, and (3) production of acid from glycerol in the presence of 0.4 μg/ml erythromycin, all these tests being positive in the case of staphylococci. Further subclassification into the three main species is of considerable clinical importance (i.e., *S. aureus, Staphylococcus epidermidis,* and *Staphylococcus saprophyticus*). The most important tests performed in a routine laboratory are summarized in Table 183–2. *S. aureus* is finally fully identified by positive reactions in the following tests[2]: (1) catalase, a test that differentiates *S. aureus* from catalase-negative streptococci; (2) coagulase, a test based on the action of either a cell-bound or an extracellular enzyme on thrombin that allows differentiation between *S. aureus* and *S. epidermidis,* the latter being coagulase negative; (3) mannitol fermentation, a test that most often allows differentiation between *S. aureus* (always positive) and *S. epidermidis* (rarely positive), the reaction being based on the anaerobic degradation of mannitol into acid compounds under anaerobic conditions; and (4) the deoxyribonuclease test, in which most *S. aureus* strains give a positive reaction, in contrast to *S. epidermidis,* as demonstrated by the differential solubilization of whole DNA in acid.[3] Finally, novobiocin resistance, tested by disk diffusion with a 5 μg novobiocin disk, allows differentiation of *S. saprophyticus.*

ANTIBIOTIC SUSCEPTIBILITY

Historical Aspects

The interaction between pathogenic organisms and antibiotics is well illustrated by the history of the resistance of *S. aureus* to penicillins.

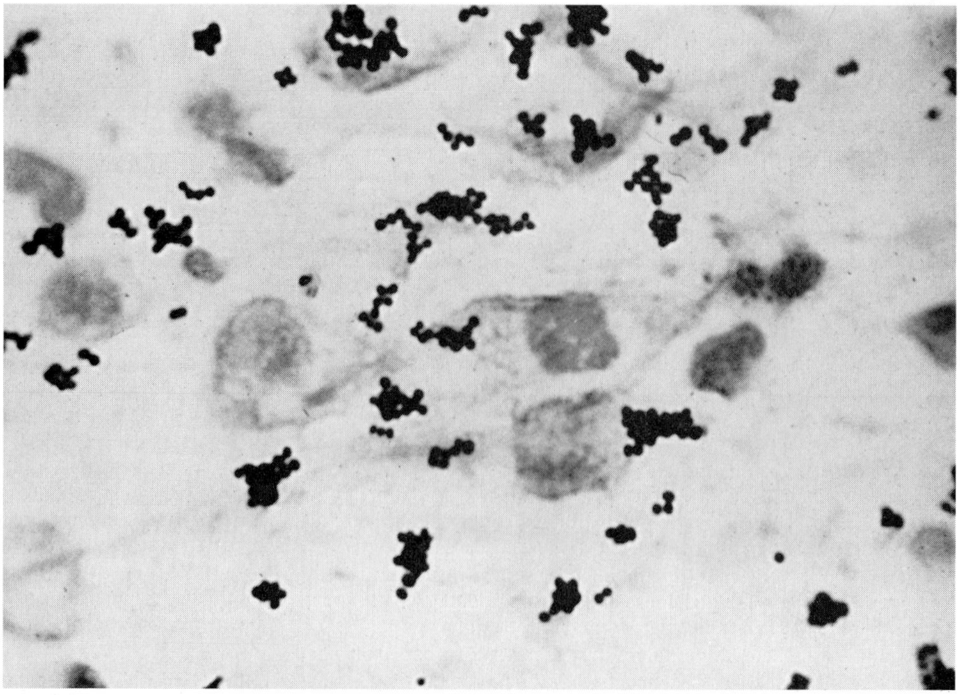

FIGURE 183–2. Expectorated sputum with gram-positive cocci in clumps from a patient with staphylococcal pneumonia.

TABLE 183–2 Major Tests for the Differentiation of Human Staphylococci

Test	*S. aureus*	*S. epidermidis*	*S. saprophyticus*
Coagulase	+	−	−
Acid production by mannitol fermentation	+	−	+ (−)*
DNAse (endonuclease)	+	−	−
Novobiocin resistance	−	−	+†
Anaerobic growth	+	+	(−)‡
Hemolysis	+	− (+)§	−

*Usually positive; occasional negative result.
†Growth in the presence of 1.6 μg/ml novobiocin or less.
‡*Staphylococcus saprophyticus* does not grow under anaerobic conditions or grows only slowly.
§Usually negative; occasional positive result.

Shortly after penicillin G became available, Spink and Ferris reported the isolation of a resistant *S. aureus* strain that produced a β-lactamase (penicillinase) that inactivated the antibiotic.[4] Although initially a sporadic occurrence, this type of resistance rapidly spread to many *S. aureus* isolates and stimulated the development of semisynthetic penicillinase-resistant compounds; methicillin, the isoxazolyl penicillins (oxacillin, cloxacillin, etc.), and nafcillin were produced between 1960 and 1964. They solved the resistance problem only temporarily inasmuch as isolation of methicillin-resistant strains was reported by Barber as early as 1961.[5] These organisms have now emerged as a major therapeutic problem throughout the world, as discussed later.

Sensitivity and Resistance Patterns of *Staphylococcus aureus* to β-Lactam Antibiotics

Sensitivity to Penicillin G. Only a very limited percentage of hospital strains and no more than 20 to 30% of community strains do not produce a β-lactamase and are therefore sensitive to penicillin G. Such strains are also usually sensitive to β-lactamase–stable compounds, although their minimal inhibitory concentration (MIC) and bactericidal concentration (MBC) toward these drugs are usually higher. Thus, in the case of infections with a penicillinase-negative strain, today admittedly an exceptional event, penicillin G remains the drug of choice.

Resistance of *Staphylococcus aureus*. Resistance to β-lactam antibiotics is a major clinical problem. At present, distinction is made between three different types of resistance.[3]

β-Lactamase-Mediated Resistance. In this case, the microorganism produces an extracellular enzyme that inactivates the antibiotic by opening its β-lactam ring before it has caused irreversible changes in the bacterium itself. This mutual time-dependent interaction implies that the presence of a large number of microorganisms will outweigh the effect of the antibiotic and accelerate its destruction. The greatest stability to β-lactamase is observed with methicillin and nafcillin, followed by oxacillin, cloxacillin, and dicloxacillin and obviously ending with penicillin G. Cephalosporins show variable stability, depending on their structure, cephalothin being more resistant than cefazolin to hydrolysis by penicillinase.

S. aureus probably has four different types of β-lactamase, as evidenced by immunologic, isoelectric focusing, and hydrolytic tests. The enzymes are usually inducible and occasionally constitutive. Most often, they are coded for by plasmids, which carry other important genes such as those determining resistance to heavy metals, to erythromycin, and to other antibiotics. A few staphylococcal strains have been reported to harbor chromosomal genes for penicillinase production.

Intrinsic Resistance. Intrinsic resistance, also called methicillin resistance, encompasses all β-lactams, including cephalosporins. It has created over the last decades major therapeutic, management, and epidemiologic problems throughout the world. A 1993 report offers a logical consensus to the diagnosis, management, and prevention of infections caused by methicillin-resistant *S. aureus* (MRSA).[6]

Methicillin resistance is defined as an oxacillin MIC of 4 mg/liter or greater or a methicillin MIC of 16 mg/liter or greater. Several methods are available to detect methicillin resistance, which is improved by supplementing the media with sodium chloride, a low temperature of 30°C, and a high inoculum. Determination in agar dilution should be performed in Mueller-Hinton medium containing 5% sodium chloride and incubated at 37°C for 18 hours or in Mueller-Hinton medium without sodium chloride at 30°C. In liquid media, the MIC is determined in Mueller-Hinton medium containing 2% sodium chloride with an inoculum of 5×10^5 colony-forming units (cfu) per milliliter. When disk diffusion is used, an oxacillin disk charged with 1 μg should be applied to Mueller-Hinton agar containing 5% sodium chloride and incubated at 37°C or without sodium chloride and incubated at 30°C with an inoculum of 10^6 cfu/ml. These methods have been adapted for various automated devices and kits used in the clinical laboratory. Because of difficulty in interpretation with all the methods mentioned earlier, particularly in the presence of heteroresistance, many laboratories use a screening plate containing Mueller-Hinton agar with 6 mg/liter of oxacillin and 4% sodium chloride inoculated with 10^4 cfu per spot and incubated at 37°C for 24 hours. This method has the best correlation with the reference method, detection of the *mecA* gene. The *mecA* gene, which has been cloned and sequenced, can be detected either by DNA probes or by polymerase chain reaction.[7, 8]

Other characteristics of MRSA include penicillinase production and a full armamentarium of pathogenic factors, including coagulase and DNase; catalase seems to be present in enhanced amounts.[9] Numerous in vitro studies have shown MRSA to be fully virulent[10] and to have an intraphagocytic survival potential[11] and a lethality in animal studies[12] similar to that of their sensitive congeners.

Staphylococci normally have at least two essential penicillin-binding proteins (PBPs) bound to the internal cytoplasmic membrane; these PBPs have enzymatic activities and are responsible for cross-linking of the peptidoglycan cell wall. Staphylococci can become resistant to all β-lactams, including β-lactamase inhibitor combinations, and to all cephalosporins and carbapenems by the acquisition of a chromosomal *mecA* gene, which encodes an alternative supplementary target called PBP 2a (or PBP 2′) that has low affinity for β-lactams. This abnormal PBP 2a continues to function when PBP 1, 2, and 3 have been inactivated by β-lactam antibiotics and generates a stable peptidoglycan. Phenotypic expression of the *mecA* gene varies among staphylococci. In some strains, only a minority of cells express resistance, and they are therefore called heteroresistant; in other strains, expression is homogeneous. Expression of the *mecA* gene is regulated by various auxiliary factors, including five *fem* factors (factor essential for resistance to methicillin) and others.[13] The *mecA* gene is located on a large 30- to 40-kilobase DNA element (*mec*) of unknown origin that contains many other genes and is virtually identical in all species of staphylococci. It is flanked by insertion sequence–like elements (IS431 and IS257) that appear to have been acquired by horizontal gene transfer and act as a trap for additional unrelated drug resistance genetic determinants, thereby leading to multiple resistance.[14, 15] Therefore, most of the strains are also resistant to a multitude of antibiotics. Although initially sensitive to the fluoroquinolones, widespread resistance has rapidly developed in MRSA.[16] Vancomycin and teicoplanin remain the drugs of choice, although, as described later, resistance has also developed recently.

The clinical, epidemiologic, and public health problems linked with MRSA are considerable and are discussed later.

Tolerance to the Killing Action of β-Lactam Antibiotics. A tolerant *S. aureus* isolate is defined as a strain exhibiting striking dissociation between the MIC and MBC of the β-lactam antibiotic after testing in a standard dilution test.[5] In practice, most *S. aureus* strains will be nontolerant, that is, will have an MIC/MBC ratio of 1:4, whereas tolerant strains will have MIC/MBC ratios far in excess of 1:32 and ranging up to 1:2000. The phenomenon, when observed in a given strain for one β-lactam antibiotic, is usually reproducible with other β-lactam antibiotics—including the cephalosporins—and sometimes even with vancomycin.[3] The trait tends to disappear in the laboratory on subculture. Based on work performed on other species, it is presently assumed that β-lactam compounds fail to activate autolytic enzymes in tolerant *S. aureus* strains.[17] Tolerance of *S. aureus* was associated, in some studies, with poor clinical response to β-lactam antibiotics in patients with septicemia and endocarditis.[18] These clinical observations have been contradicted by some experimental animal studies that show similar behavior in tolerant and nontolerant strains.[19] Tolerance may nevertheless be of clinical importance in chronic infections associated with foreign material.[20]

***Borderline Oxacillin-Resistant* Staphylococcus aureus.** Resistance to oxacillin is seen in strains harboring the *mecA* gene, as described earlier, and in other strains without the *mecA* gene. The latter resistance is due to hyperproduction of β-lactamase, and such organisms are called borderline oxacillin-resistant *S. aureus.* This hyperproduction of β-lactamase requires high sodium chloride concentrations[21] and does not induce a higher MIC in normal testing conditions.

Sensitivity and Resistance Patterns of *Staphylococcus aureus* to Other Antibiotics

S. aureus possesses a remarkable number of mechanisms for resisting antibacterial action. Thus, depending on the local epidemiologic conditions, 5 to 20% of isolates are resistant to the antibacterial agents commonly used in staphylococcal infections such as erythromycin, lincomycin, and clindamycin. This percentage seems to be lower for fusidic acid, although clinical experience with this drug is limited. Aminoglycoside-resistant strains have been described with increasing frequency. Rifampin, which is remarkably active against *S. aureus,* cannot be used as a single agent because of a high one-step mutation rate of 10^{-7} to 10^{-8} to resistance.[22] Finally, whereas no strain had been described as being fully resistant to vancomycin, glycopeptide resistance has appeared in different parts of the world (see later).

Resistance to fluoroquinolones has been found in methicillin-sensitive[23] and methicillin-resistant strains[15] and is becoming a major epidemiologic problem. Both altered gyrase and energy-dependent efflux mechanisms are implied.[23]

Transfer of Resistance in *Staphylococcus aureus.* Antibiotic resistance in *S. aureus* may be mediated by chromosomes or plasmids. Staphylococci are exchanging genetic material by various mechanisms, including transduction and cell-to-cell contact.[24, 25] Recent evidence is accumulating in favor of transfer of plasmids between *S. aureus* and *S. epidermidis,*[26] a worrisome observation, indeed, if one considers the numerical importance of these saprophytes.

Glycopeptide-resistant *Staphylococcus aureus*

Recently, a new threat has emerged: a first strain of *S. aureus* resistant to glycopeptide (e.g., vancomycin) has been isolated in Japan,[27] followed by various other strains in Japan, the United States, and several other countries. Because their MICs have been shown to be between 2 and 8 μg/ml, they have thus far been named intermediately vancomycin-resistant strains. They usually show heterogenous resistance to vancomycin on population analysis and have higher MICs to teicoplanin. As opposed to vancomycin-resistant enterococci, they do not possess *vanA, vanB,* or *vanC* resistance genes.

Biochemical analysis has shown intermediately vancomycin-resistant *S. aureus* to produce increased amounts of cell wall precursors, express increased amounts of the penicillin-binding protein PBP 2, and have increased transglycosylation activity.[28] *S. aureus* intermediately resistant to vancomycin can be obtained by a stepwise increase in vancomycin concentration. It is presently hypothesized that these *S. aureus* strains "soak up" the antibiotic in their thickened cell walls. They are usually methicillin resistant, but sensitive to the oxazolidinones and to quinupristin/dalfopristin.

The emergence of intermediately vancomycin-resistant *S. aureus* has created considerable concern in the medical community. Perspectives on measures needed for control have been published[29] but are based on incomplete epidemiologic data and encompass very conservative measures of isolation.

Typing Methods of *Staphylococcus aureus* and Methicillin-Resistant *Staphylococcus aureus*

Because MRSA is typically linked to nosocomial infection, precise typing methods to monitor the epidemiology are necessary to distinguish endemic and epidemic strains. Older methods such as resistance phenotype, bacteriophage typing, immunoserology, and serotyping of coagulase have been unsatisfactory. More recently, these methods have been replaced by electrophoretic protein typing, multilocus enzyme electrophoresis, and various genetic techniques, including plasmid analysis, restriction endonuclease analysis of chromosomal DNA, restriction fragment length polymorphisms, ribotyping, nucleotide sequence analysis, and many others. Even if these methods are not necessarily comparable, they have been shown to be very useful for epidemiologic investigations.

EPIDEMIOLOGY

Carriers

Shortly after birth, many neonates are colonized with *S. aureus* by their immediate human surroundings; colonization sites include the umbilical stump, the perineal area, the skin, and sometimes the gastrointestinal tract. *S. aureus* can also contaminate clothing and linen, from which the organism can be shed to further contaminate the atmosphere. Later in life, the major ecologic niches are the anterior nares; up to 25% of children and adults can become carriers. At any given time, the nasal carriage rate in adults is estimated to be about 20 to 40%, depending on seasonal and local epidemiologic factors.[30] Expressed longitudinally, about 20% of the population will be prolonged and 60% will be intermittent carriers of *S. aureus,* whereas 20% will never be colonized.[30] The density of colonization may reach 10^3 to 10^4 organisms, and several strains may be present in the same patient. The incidence of TSS in the female population has led to an evaluation of the vaginal carriage rate in adult premenopausal women; values reported are close to 10%, with an increase in the carriage rate and bacterial counts during menses.[31] Rectal and perineal carriage has also been described.[32]

Some groups of individuals seem to be particularly prone to colonization with *S. aureus.* For example, physicians, nurses, and hospital ward attendants may be nasopharyngeal carriers in a higher percentage of cases (50, 70, and 90%, respectively) than the general population (33%).[33] Diabetic patients receiving insulin injections, patients undergoing chronic hemodialysis or continuous ambulatory peritoneal dialysis, patients with a variety of dermatologic conditions, users of illicit intravenous drugs, and human immunodeficiency virus–positive patients have a higher carriage rate than does the general population.[30, 34–36]

From the anterior nares, carriers transfer the organisms to their skin. Trauma provides a portal of entry for the organism, with subsequent local and possibly generalized infection. It follows that in case of infection, the offending organism is often of endogenous origin, whereas in other cases, it will be transmitted by hospital personnel or a family member.

The carrier state is clinically important because carriers undergoing surgery or sustaining exudative skin conditions will experience more infections than noncarriers will with the infection usually being caused by the same strain that colonized the patient on admission.

Methicillin-Resistant *Staphylococcus aureus*

MRSA strains are usually introduced into an institution by an infected or colonized patient (nasopharynx, tracheostomy site, wound) or by a colonized health care worker. Transfer from one patient to another via the colonized hands of health personnel or the inanimate environment[6] has led to major epidemics in tertiary care hospitals,[37] as well as in chronic care facilities.[38] Risk factors for the acquisition of MRSA include the administration of multiple antibiotics. Colonization of the anterior nares by MRSA carries a significantly greater risk for infection than does colonization by sensitive strains.[39] Thus, epidemiologic surveys and control measures are particularly important regarding MRSA (Table 183–3).

Epidemiologic Control Measures

Careful, repeated, and compulsive hand washing should be a daily routine for hospital personnel and is of utmost importance. In nurseries for the newborn, several strategies have helped prevent infections in infants: cohort nursing, individual care by a limited number of people, cord care, arm and hand washing of the staff with chlorhexidine or an iodophor, and wearing of clean gowns by the staff.

Another means to avoid *S. aureus* transmission has been elimination of the nasal carriage state, which can now be achieved, at least temporarily, either by local or by oral antistaphylococcal treatment.[39, 40] Care has to be taken to use antibacterial compounds to which staphylococci are and remain susceptible. It must be acknowledged that prevention may be of only short duration, recolonization over time being the rule.

Intranasal 2% mupirocin applied twice daily for 5 days appears to be the most effective topical agent for both methicillin-sensitive *S. aureus* and MRSA[41, 42] and eliminates 91% of stable nasal carriers. Follow-up cultures at 6 months and 12 months after treatment showed a nasal carriage rate of 48% and 53%, respectively; these significant results were corroborated by a reduced hand carriage rate.[42] Repeated, rapid development of mupirocin resistance has been observed[41, 43] and recently reviewed in detail.[30]

Rifampin, 600 mg twice daily for 5 days, ciprofloxacin, 750 mg twice daily for 14 days, trimethoprim-sulfoxamethazole, and combinations thereof have all been shown to be substantially effective, with partial recurrence in all cases at a follow-up of 1 month. Oral rifampin has in addition been shown to be effective in reducing shunt infection in dialysis patients.[44]

Guidelines for control of *S. aureus* infection in general and MRSA in particular have been published and are summarized in simplified form in Table 183–3[37] and in other consensus reviews.[6]

TABLE 183–3 Measures to Prevent the Spread of *Staphylococcus aureus* among Hospitalized Patients

Accurate and timely identification of the nosocomial strain (antibiotic sensitivity pattern or genotyping)
Culture surveillance (with microbiologic criteria described above) of patients (and staff on some occasions) in involved areas to define the MRSA reservoir
Establishment of barrier precautions or strict isolation techniques for infected patients
Assignment of employees with dermatitis and positive cultures (same epidemic strain) to nonclinical duties
Reinforcement of hand-washing regulations and disinfection procedures in areas contaminated by the epidemic strain
Identification of MRSA carriers at the time of transfer
Clear notation of the presence of MRSA carriage in the medical and nursing record to take necessary precautions in case of readmission
In case of clear association with particular instrumentation, careful review of sterilization procedures and nursing techniques
Investigation of outbreaks in hospital settings to identify and handle reservoir(s)
Genotyping of epidemic strains at a centralized reference laboratory for epidemiologic research

Abbreviation: MRSA, Methicillin-resistant *Staphylococcus aureus*.
Adapted from Haley RW, Hightower AW, Khabbaz RF, et al. Emergence of methicillin-resistant *Staphylococcus aureus* infections in United States hospitals. Ann Intern Med. 1982;97:297.

MICROBIOLOGIC DETERMINANTS

Important Cell Wall Constituents

The basic component of the cell wall of *S. aureus* that confers shape and stability to the organism and represents 50% of cell wall weight is *peptidoglycan.*[1] It is a polysaccharidic polymer composed of unbranched, β-linked (1 → 4) chains containing alternating subunits of *N*-acetylmuramic acid and *N*-acetylglucosamine. Pentapeptide side chains are linked to the muramic acid residue and are cross-linked by a pentaglycine bridge attached to the L-lysine of one chain and D-alanine on the other chain (Fig. 183–3*A*). The basic polysaccharide polymer is found in many other organisms as well, whereas the pentaglycine cross-linking chain is specific for *S. aureus.*[45] Peptidoglycan has important biologic properties: it elicits the production of interleukin-1 from human monocytes, induces a local Shwartzman reaction, is capable of attracting PMNs, has endotoxin-like activity, activates complement, and elicits the production of opsonic antibodies.[46]

Other important cell wall constituents include a group of phosphate-containing polymers called *teichoic acids,* which contribute about 40% of cell wall weight.[47] Some of these polymers are covalently bound to peptidoglycan and are called cell wall teichoic acids. Others are linked to the lipid of the bacterial cell membrane, hence their name membrane teichoic acids. The backbone of cell wall teichoic acid is an alternating sequence of ribitol-phosphate. Side chains include the single addition of *N*-acetylglucosamine and *N*-acetylgalactosamine[46, 47] (Fig. 183–3*B*). Cell membrane teichoic acids have a very simple backbone made of glycerol-phosphate in repeating units. The side chain on the second carbon atom of the glycerol molecule is an unusual disaccharide, gentobiose, or may exceptionally be alanine (Fig. 183–3*B*). Both teichoic acids are bound covalently to peptidoglycan or to the lipid membrane of the microorganism.

In addition, *S. aureus* covalently incorporates into its outer peptidoglycan layer several proteins, including major adhesins such as fibronectin-binding proteins, clumping factor,[48] and collagen-binding protein.[49] Protein A, which has a molecular weight of 42,000 Da, is present in various amounts in most strains of *S. aureus,* and it is also recovered in the supernatant of actively growing cultures. Although it can activate complement under well-defined conditions, its major interaction with host mechanisms consists of binding to the Fc terminal of all human IgG subclasses except IgG_3.[50]

Finally, many *S. aureus* strains are coated with an external polysaccharide layer meeting the definition of a capsule or a loosely associated slime layer.[51] This polysaccharide can be released during focal infection and be detected in the serum of infected animals.[52] Thus, the many interactions of these surface compounds will determine the overall host response to *S. aureus* infection.

Important Enzymes and Toxins

S. aureus produces and secretes a number of enzymes and toxins that have been variously implicated as possible pathogenic factors.

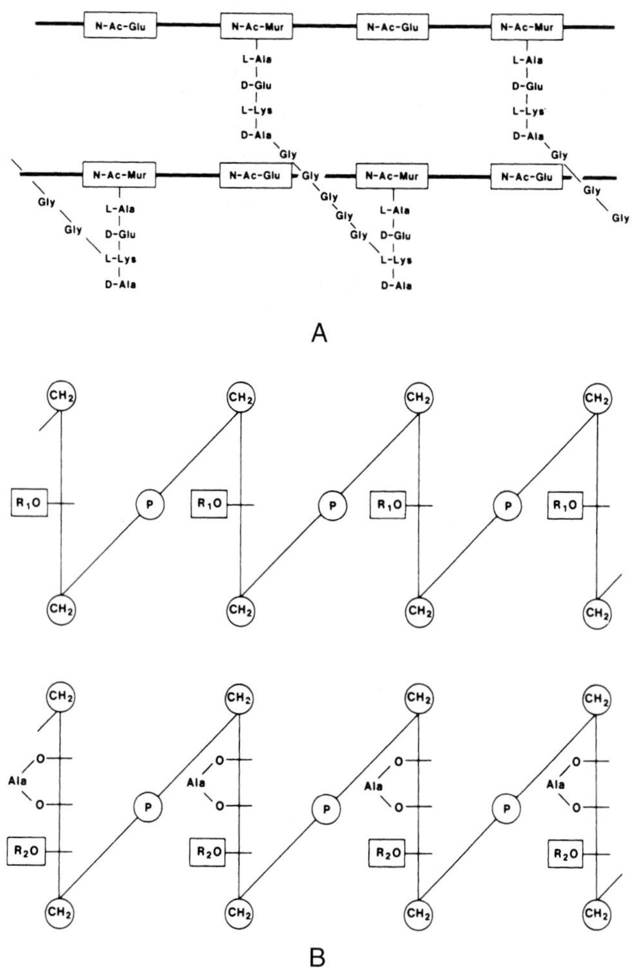

FIGURE 183-3. *A,* Peptidoglycan structure of *Staphylococcus aureus.*[45] The basic polymer is composed of 10 to 12 alternating units of *N*-acetylglucosamine (*N*-Ac-Glu) and *N*-acetylmuramic acid (*N*-Ac-Mur). Side chains are linked to the muramic acid (L-alanine, D-glutamine, L-lysine, D-alanine) and are cross-linked by a pentaglycine bridge (Gly-Gly . | . | .). *B,* The two types of teichoic acids in *S. aureus.*[47] *Above:* glycerol teichoic acid, with a basic structure of glycerol and phosphate. R_1 is gentobiose or alanine. This teichoic acid is bound covalently to the cell membrane (membrane teichoic acid). *Below:* Ribitol teichoic acid, with a basic structure of ribitol and phosphate. R_2 is *N*-acetylglucosamine or *N*-acetylgalactosamine. This teichoic acid is bound covalently to the peptidoglycan (cell wall teichoic acid).

The problem of their pathogenicity is compounded by the fact that purification of many of these enzymes and toxins is technically difficult because of their instability. Therefore, their specific effects are still often disputed.

Enzymes

Catalase. Hydrogen peroxide is produced by all staphylococcal strains and is converted into nontoxic H_2O and O_2 by the action of catalase. Because staphylococcal phagocytic killing is mediated by toxic oxygen radicals produced by PMNs, it has been proposed and shown that catalase production, by counteracting host defense mechanisms, correlates with pathogenicity.[53]

Coagulase. Coagulase is either extracellular or cell bound. It stimulates the conversion of fibrinogen to fibrin by binding to prothrombin with a 1:1 stoichiometry. The complex becomes enzymatically active and initiates fibrin polymerization.[54] The reaction is used to differentiate *S. aureus* from coagulase-negative staphylococci. Isogenic coagulase-producing and non–coagulase-producing strains do not show notable differences in virulence, which casts doubts on the unique and direct role of this enzyme in pathogenesis.

Clumping Factor. *S. aureus* forms clumps when mixed with plasma through an interaction between fibrinogen and a bacterial cell surface compound called clumping factor.[55] This receptor is also responsible for the adherence of *S. aureus* to fibrinogen and fibrin. Genetic evidence and molecular studies have demonstrated that coagulase and clumping factor are distinct entities of *S. aureus.*[56]

Hyaluronidase. Hyaluronidase hydrolyzes hyaluronic acids, a group of acid mucopolysaccharides present in the acellular matrix of connective tissue. Its role in the pathogenicity of *S. aureus* is as yet unsolved.

β-Lactamases. Most β-lactamases are plasmid coded. Their physiologic role in cellular metabolism in the absence of β-lactam antibiotics is unknown. Their role in antibiotic resistance has been reviewed earlier.

Other Enzymes. *S. aureus* produces a nuclease that is tested on a DNA substrate for taxonomic purposes, but in fact it is a phosphodiesterase with both exonuclease and endonuclease activity that cleaves nucleic acids into 3′-phosphomononucleotides. Abscess formation is characterized by the disruption of protein and lipid constituants. Most *S. aureus* strains produce lipolytic enzymes (lipases), and their corresponding genes have been cloned.[57]

Toxins

S. aureus produces a variety of extracellular products that are defined as toxins because they affect host cell function or morphology.[48, 58] Some of them express their detrimental effect by enzymatic action. Others such as enterotoxins and toxic shock toxins, are potent cytokine inducers that act as superantigens and have opened a new field of pathophysiology of infectious diseases (see later).

α-Toxin. Of the five membrane-damaging toxins produced by *S. aureus,* α-toxin is the most extensively studied. Electrophoretically a heterogeneous protein, it acts on a wide variety of eukaryotic cell membranes (e.g., erythrocytes, leukocytes, platelets, fibroblasts, and HeLa cells), but not on bacterial cytoplasmic membranes. Erythrocytes are the most sensitive target cells of the biologic action of *S. aureus,* and they display a species-specific external binding capacity that correlates with their sensitivity to hemolysis. The toxin, when injected subcutaneously, is also dermonecrotic.

β-Toxin. β-Toxin produces its cytotoxic effect by degrading sphingomyelin. It is therefore active on a great variety of cells, including human erythrocytes, leukocytes, and fibroblasts. The effects of β-toxin have been extensively investigated in erythrocytes, where its hemolytic activity depends on the sphingomyelin content or distribution on the membrane surface of erythrocytes.[58]

γ-Toxin. The presence of γ-toxin has now been firmly established by purification from strain 5R, which produces this toxin as its major cytolysin. It lyses erythrocytes from many species, including humans, by unknown mechanisms.[58]

δ-Toxin. This extracellular product is electrophoretically heterogeneous and dissociates into subunits in nonionic detergents. The molecule is strongly surface active, and it disrupts biologic membranes by a detergent-like action. Another interesting property of δ-toxin is its inhibition of water absorption and simultaneous stimulation of cyclic adenosine monophosphate production in the rabbit and guinea pig ileum, which suggests a role in the pathogenesis of acute diarrhea in some staphylococcal infections.[58] Recently, δ-toxin administered at noncytotoxic concentrations was shown to upregulate neutrophil receptor CD3 and monocyte tumor necrosis factor-α production.[59]

Leukocidin. Leukocidin, which consists of two components, apparently exerts an exclusive action on human and rabbit phagocytic cells. A single injection of leukocidin produces deep, reversible granulocytopenia. Its direct membrane-damaging effect can be observed microscopically within 60 minutes. Both components of the toxin act synergistically at the phagocyte membrane level by forming pores, which leads to increased permeability to cations.[58]

Epidermolytic Toxins, Enterotoxins, Toxic Shock Syndrome Toxin, and the Staphylococcal Superantigen Family

Epidermolytic toxins, or exfoliatins, are a group of two serologically and biologically distinct proteins responsible for the major dermatologic findings of scalded skin syndrome. Epidermolytic toxin A is a chromosomal gene product, is thermostable (after 20 minutes at 100°C), and is inactivated by ethylenediametetraacetic acid, whereas epidermolytic toxin B, with the same molecular weight, is of plasmidic origin, is inactivated after incubation at 60°C for 20 minutes, and is stable in ethylenediametetraacetic acid. Although exfoliatin production has been associated with phage group II staphylococci in the United States, toxigenic strains have also been identified among groups I and III. Individual strains, when examined, produce either none, one, or both toxins, and no clear relationship has been found between the phage group and the type of toxin produced.[58]

Exfoliatins produce dramatic changes in the epidermis of neonates that are characterized by extensive scalding (Figs. 183–4 and 183–5). The histologic correlate is the formation of intraepidermal blisters at the granular cell layer. An identical phenomenon can be observed after injection of the toxin into newborn mice[59]; under normal conditions, epidermal cells are cemented together by a matrix of mucopolysaccharides, and individual granular cells are linked to each other by specialized membrane structures called desmosomes. Although initial experiments suggested that injection of exfoliatin at a distant site led to splitting of the desmosome in the stratum granulosum, where it binds to desmoglein I,[60] recent data suggest that epidermolytic toxins are serine proteases and act as superantigens.[61]

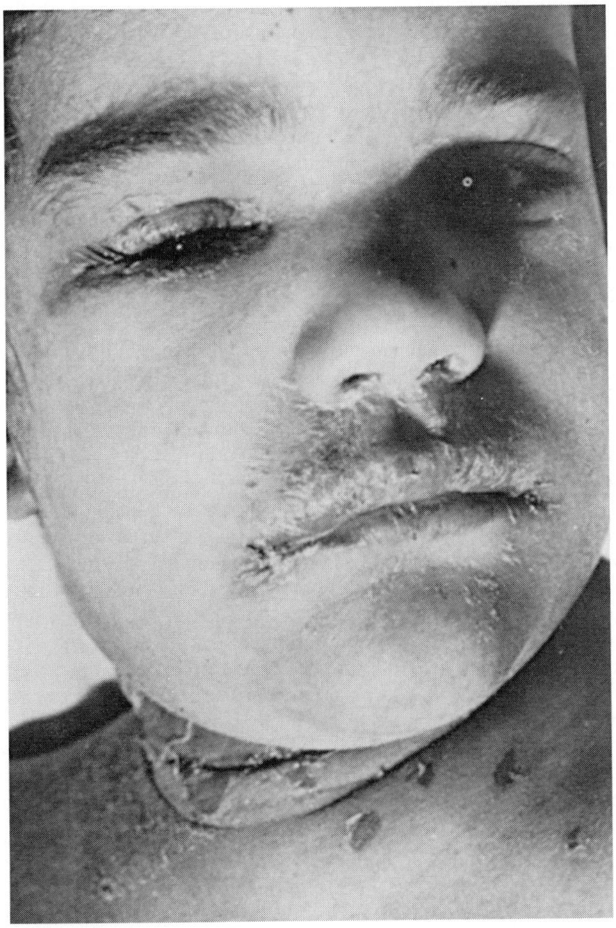

FIGURE 183–4. Child with the staphylococcal scalded skin syndrome (SSSS) due to phage group 2 *Staphylococcus aureus*–producing exfoliative toxin. Note purulent conjunctivitis and the perioral flaky desquamation, whereas newer lesions (probably at the vesicular stage) are just starting to peel on the neck.

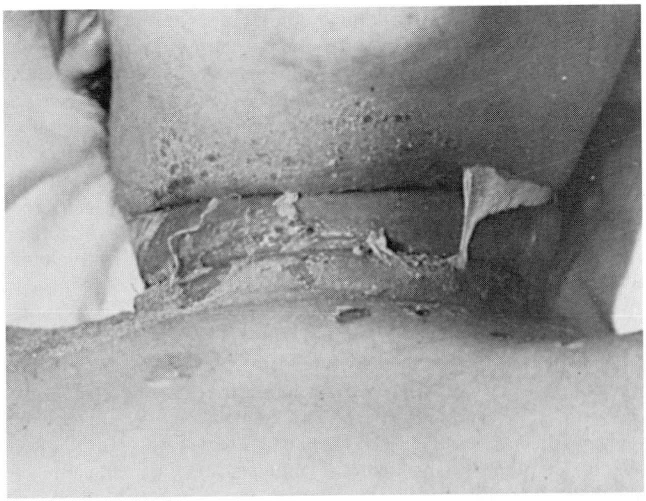

FIGURE 183–5. Same child as in Figure 183–4 showing, at a later stage, an extensive exfoliation of the epidermis due to the toxin-induced cleavage through the stratum granulosum.

The crucial pathogenic role of exfoliatins in the scalded skin syndrome is demonstrated by the fact that specific antibodies are protective and neutralizing in both humans and mice.

Toxic Shock Syndrome Toxin and Enterotoxins. TSS, which is characterized by fever, desquamative skin rash, hypotension, and multisystem involvement, occurs in patients who harbor *S. aureus* strains that elaborate either toxic shock syndrome toxin 1 (TSST-1) or other related enterotoxins.[62–65] This syndrome has also been reported after infections caused by coagulase-negative *Staphylococcus* and *Streptococcus pyogenes*.[66, 67] More details regarding the biology and the mode of action of these toxins are given in later sections.

Enterotoxins. About half of all strains of *S. aureus* isolated produce enterotoxins, and presently five (A to E) serologically distinct types are recognized, with group C being further subdivided into three subtypes. Enterotoxin F is identical to TSST-1. These remarkably heat-stable toxins are major causes of food poisoning and dramatically increase intestinal peristalsis, possibly by sympathetic activation. A central nervous system effect is also suggested by the intensity of vomiting in food poisoning. All these enterotoxins and TSST-1 are 20- to 30-kD polypeptides. Enterotoxins have considerable amino acid homology, mostly at the carboxyl terminus, whereas TSST-1 and the exfoliatins seem to belong to another multigenic family.[68, 69] They all exert their action by stimulating a subset of T lymphocytes and are therefore called bacterial superantigens.[68, 69]

Mechanisms of Action of Staphylococcal Superantigens. TSST-1, enterotoxins, and exfoliative toxins belong to a group of polypeptide products that at a concentration of 10^{-13} to 10^{-14} mol/liter can activate subsets of T lymphocytes to liberate cytokines and thereby lead to major systemic effects such as fever, hypotension, skin lesions, shock, multiorgan failure, and death. They belong to the family of superantigens, which are molecules that share the following characteristics: they bind with high affinity to major histocompatibility complex class II receptors of monocyte-macrophages at sites distinct from the classic antigen-binding groove, as demonstrated by crystallographic methods[70]; this complex is recognized by the variable V_β region of the T-cell receptor of some subsets of T lymphocytes, and superantigen-receptor interaction causes prolific activation or, under certain circumstances, inhibition of T-cell functions, including liberation of interleukin-1, tissue necrosis factor, and interferon-γ.[68, 69] Thus, small foci of superantigen-producing *S. aureus* can lead to dramatic cytokine liberation with systemic effects. Costimulatory signaling pathways are probably also operational.[71]

The interaction of these superantigens from *S. aureus* with monocytes and T lymphocytes is due to a ligand effect of the bacterial product that links the two types of cells at the site of the T-cell receptor. The different types of major histocompatibility complex class II receptors have their own affinities for exotoxins, and the various sequences of the T-cell receptor V_β region possess their own binding constants to the various compounds, which explains the diversity of cytokine responses observed. In the case of food poisoning, it is suggested that the superantigen may bind to mast cells and cause their activation.[72, 73] Endothelial cell activation, either via triggered monocytes or by direct activation, may provide the link between toxin circulation and hallmarks of the syndrome such as rash, edema, and hypotension.[74]

HOST DETERMINANTS

Tissue invasion by *S. aureus* implies a series of interactions of the microorganism with a variety of host structures and mechanisms that can be subdivided into adhesion, invasion, chemotaxis of PMNs, ingestion, and intracellular killing by PMNs.

Adhesion of *Staphylococcus aureus*

Colonization by *S. aureus* requires initial adherence to host cells. Three types of adherence must be considered. Adherence to nasal mucosal cells is mediated by the teichoic acid component of *S. aureus*[31] and by a variety of other cell-associated ligands on S. aureus.[30] It is increased in chronic staphylococcal carriers and after vaccination or infection with influenza A.[75, 76] *S. aureus* binding to mucin may also be critical for colonization of the nasopharyngeal mucosa.[77]

Attachment of *S. aureus* to traumatized or disrupted skin, to foreign surfaces, and to endothelial structures involves interaction with many proteins of the extracellular matrix, the most important ones being fibrinogen,[50] fibronectin,[78] laminin,[79] thrombospondin,[80] vitronectin,[81] elastin,[82] bone sialoprotein,[83] and collagen. The interactions studied in most detail involve fibronectin, fibrinogen, collagen, and elastin, in which the active domains of the host proteins have been characterized and their coating shown to modulate *S. aureus* adherence. *S. aureus* ligands for these host proteins have also been characterized, cloned, and sequenced (fibronectin-binding proteins A and B for fibronectin,[84] clumping factor for fibrinogen,[85] and collagen-binding[86] and elastin-binding protein[87]).

Attachment of *S. aureus* to endothelial cells during septicemia is a complex event, where again the endothelial cell itself, fibronectin, fibrinogen,[88] and possibly laminin play an important role. Postadherent events are of additional importance here, such as phagocytosis of *S. aureus* by endothelial cells—an extension of normal pinocytic activity[89]—and induction of tissue factor procoagulant activity.[90]

Invasion

Invasion of the host after colonization requires penetration of the microorganism through the epithelial or mucosal surface, but little is known regarding the biologic mechanisms subtending penetration.

Chemotaxis

Once *S. aureus* has penetrated through the mucosal or epithelial layer, ingestion and killing by PMNs, as well as by the monocyte-macrophage system, become the major line of defense. Mobilization of phagocytic cells at the site of bacterial growth requires the elaboration of microbial and host-specific signals. Among the former, cell wall–associated and extracellular products of *S. aureus* such as peptidoglycan, teichoic acids, and protein A are certainly involved. The major host signals, however, result from activation of the complement system, all cell wall components identified thus far being able to trigger this reaction by producing C5a among others.[91] Many other mediators of inflammation, reviewed elsewhere, will activate chemotaxis and trigger neutrophil function.

Opsonization

Recognition of *S. aureus* by phagocytes is mediated by their receptors for the Fc fragment of IgG, by their receptors for the activated subunit of the third component of the complement system C3b, and possibly by other complement receptors and coreceptors. This recognition process implies that *S. aureus,* in order to be ingested, has to be coated by C3b, IgG, or both molecules—a process called opsonization. Marked heterogeneity is observed among various *S. aureus* strains regarding their opsonic requirements; a strain such as *S. aureus* Wood 46, for example, is fully opsonized by the presence of complement only, whereas others require predominantly specific IgG.

In serum obtained from healthy *nonimmune* subjects, complement activation via either the classic or alternative pathways provides most of the opsonic activity.[92] However, this normal serum also will contain small amounts of antipeptidoglycan antibodies that result from previous exposure to staphylococci, to other organisms, or possibly to plant components. In contrast, opsonization in hyperimmune subjects occurs predominantly by IgG antibodies, although the peptidoglycan present in *S. aureus* also activates the complement system to some extent, as will the IgG molecules bound to the bacterial surface. This complex sequence of events involving complement is usually overshadowed by the IgG opsonization mechanism of hyperimmune serum.[92]

The peptidoglycan matrix is presently considered to be a major determinant of complement-mediated opsonization. In hyperimmune rabbit serum, a direct opsonic effect of peptidoglycan-specific antibodies can be demonstrated.[93, 94] Because peptidoglycans are ubiquitous in the bacterial world, highly specific antibody activity seems unlikely.[95] Teichoic acids also elicit the production of antibodies, but their role in opsonization is debated and is probably indirect and occurs via activation of the complement cascade. Finally, protein A, a cell wall–associated compound that is also liberated in free form in the surrounding medium, plays a triple antiphagocytic role in the bacteria-cell recognition process by virtue of its binding to the Fc portion of IgG: first, extracellular soluble protein A can react with the Fc terminal of IgG molecules of human serum, thereby producing immune aggregates that consume complement. Second, extracellular protein A can bind to the Fc portion of specific antistaphylococcal antibodies coating the microorganism by their Fab fragment, thereby preventing further interaction of the complex with the Fc receptor of phagocytes. Third, cell-bound protein A binds to the Fc fragment of any IgG molecule in its neighborhood, thereby eliminating nonspecific and specific antibodies.[92]

Intracellular Killing

After being phagocytosed, most intracellular staphylococci are rapidly killed and degraded within the phagocytic vacuole, but prolonged survival of a minority of organisms can be demonstrated by various techniques, which possibly explains the high recurrence rate of some *S. aureus* infections.[96, 97] The major staphylocidal role played by oxygen-dependent bactericidal mechanisms, such as the production of O_2^-, H_2O_2, and other highly reactive radicals, has repeatedly been demonstrated. Oxygen-independent staphylocidal systems include the low pH prevailing in the phagocytic vacuoles, lactoferrin, and granular cationic proteins.

FACTORS PREDISPOSING TO INFECTION

The list of underlying conditions conductive to *S. aureus* infection is extensive and nonspecific. In the following discussion, special emphasis will be given to clinical conditions that particularly predispose to *S. aureus* infection.[96, 97]

Chemotaxis Defects

Impairment of directional movement has been found in a group of patients previously described as having *Job's syndrome,* or recurrent eczema with repeated skin infections and cold abscesses. Many of these patients have very high IgE levels, often exceeding 5000 ng/ml, and decreased chemotactic response of their PMNs.[98] Other conditions with decreased chemotaxis include Chédiak-Higashi syndrome, defined clinically by albinism and recurrent *S. aureus* infections and cytologically by the presence of giant granules in phagocytes and other cells; Wiskott-Aldrich syndrome; and Down syndrome. Examples of acquired chemotactic defects include severe bacterial infection, rheumatoid arthritis, and decompensated acidotic diabetes mellitus.

Opsonization Defects

None of the opsonization defects described thus far specifically predisposes to *S. aureus* infection. Opsonic defects secondary to a variety of congenital and acquired, selective, or combined agammaglobulinemias and caused by several defects in complement levels (particularly C3 and C5) will therefore favor pyogenic infection by a variety of bacterial species, including *S. aureus.*[97, 99]

Staphylocidal Defects of Polymorphonuclear Leukocytes

The major condition in which a staphylocidal defect of phagocytic cells has been clearly identified is chronic granulomatous disease, a group of diseases discussed elsewhere (see Chapter 8). PMNs from patients with chronic granulomatous disease are unable to activate the membrane-bound oxidase system, which results in an almost total absence of superoxide and hydrogen peroxide generation within phagocytic vacuoles. A defect in staphylococcal killing has also been shown in lymphoblastic leukemia, as well as in acute and chronic myelogenous leukemia.[97, 99]

Integration of Predisposing Factors: *Staphylococcus aureus* in Foreign Body Infections

As opposed to congenital defects, acquired phagocytic defects are often due to multiple factors acting in concert, foreign body infections being a case in point.

The role of a foreign body as an important factor favoring infection has been well known by clinicians for years; it is still receiving much attention because of the growing use of intravascular devices and prosthetic material. Many of these infections are due to *S. aureus;* others are due to gram-positive organisms such as coagulase-negative staphylococci. Most foreign body infections occur shortly after surgery and result from local contamination during implantation of the foreign material. Once established, most foreign body infections cannot be eradicated by antibiotics alone, even in the presence of organisms apparently susceptible to the drug used. Once the foreign material is eliminated, infection is easily cured with the same antibiotics, although reimplantation of prosthetic material may be difficult in previously infected sites.[100]

Elek and Conen[101] in classic experiments have shown that a subcutaneous injection of greater than 10^6 cfu of *S. aureus* was easily controlled by host defense mechanisms whereas 3×10^2 cfu of the same organism invariably led to infection in the presence of a suture. Such stitch abscesses were histologically characterized by the presence of myriads of microorganisms and PMNs. Recently, new experimental approaches have suggested at least four mechanisms conducive to foreign body infections or responsible for their persistence. First, various organisms, including most strains of *S. epidermidis* and a few strains of *S. aureus,* have been shown to produce after several hours or days of contact with the foreign body surface an extracellular slime substance[102, 103] essentially composed of a polysaccharide/adhesin[104] or a polysaccharide intercellular adhesin[105] that protects them from the environment.

Second, the resident phagocytic population in the vicinity of an infected implanted foreign body has been shown to be incapable of killing an invading *S. aureus* strain.[106, 107] Third, firm anchoring of *S. aureus* on the fibrinogen, fibronectin, or collagen coating foreign surfaces provides another pathogenic mechanism. The interaction of these pathogenic mechanisms has been reviewed.[108] Fourth, adherence of staphylococci to foreign surfaces modifies their susceptibility to antimicrobial agents within hours: whereas their MICs remain unchanged, a dramatic increase is noted in their MBCs well beyond achievable antibiotic concentrations.

CLINICAL MANIFESTATIONS

The basic anatomic lesion induced by *S. aureus* is a pyogenic exudate or an abscess. In addition, under certain circumstances, exotoxin activation of lymphocytes may dominate the clinical picture (e.g., food poisoning or TSS). Finally, any localized infection—even the most benign-appearing wound infection—can occasionally become the seeding point of a potentially lethal bacteremia, with the subsequent development of metastatic foci. Consequently, the clinical descriptions that follow should not be taken as well-defined entities because they are often intertwined and may have reciprocal effects on each other—provided that septicemic spread has occurred.

Infections of the Skin and Its Appendages

Localized Infections

Skin infections by *S. aureus* are best subdivided into localized pyogenic infections and localized infections with a diffuse skin rash followed by general desquamation.[109] Local pyogenic infections are favored by the staphylococcal carrier state, minor trauma such as friction, maceration, and underlying skin diseases such as eczema and juvenile acne. Most of them are clustered around the hair follicle.

Folliculitis. Folliculitis is the most benign infection and is defined as a pyoderma involving the hair follicle and its immediate surroundings (Fig. 183–6). It is clinically manifested as a series of raised, painful reddish lesions with an indurated basis, each of them being centered on a hair follicle. Folliculitis raises a complex differential diagnosis regarding its etiologies, including other microorganisms (dermatophytes, *Pseudomonas*) and drugs (corticosteroids, actinomycin D, halides). Extensive folliculitis of the bearded area of the face is called *sycosis barbae.* Constitutional symptoms are absent, and folliculitis responds well to local antiseptic measures in most cases.

Furuncles and Carbuncles. Furuncles (boils) represent extension of the infectious process involving the hair follicle. They are defined as a deep-seated infection in and around the hair follicle and are located, by definition, on the hairy areas of the body, with a predilection for the face, neck, axillae, and buttocks. The disease starts as a painful red nodule and rapidly evolves into a hot, very painful, raised, and indurated lesion with a diameter of 1 to 2 cm. Its later evolution is

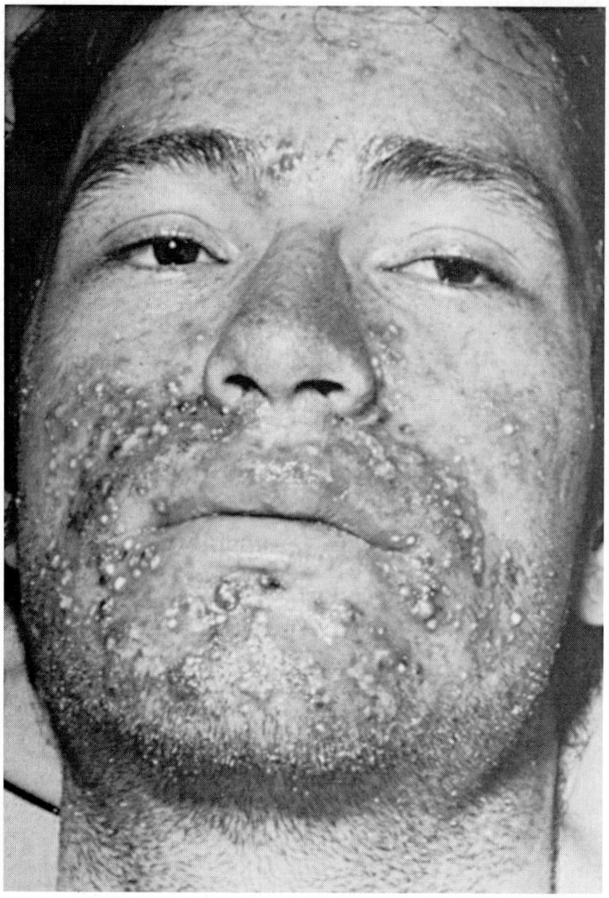

FIGURE 183–6. Folliculitis. Note the pustular eruption with small abscess formation in the hair-bearing areas of the face. General symptoms usually are absent.

characterized by the appearance of a yellowish area in its center. On spontaneous rupture or surgical incision, it liberates a small amount of yellowish, creamy discharge of purulent and necrotic material. Signs of inflammation subside rapidly thereafter, but satellite lesions and new furuncles appearing at distant sites, often secondary to autoinoculation, are frequent. General symptoms are usually absent, although mild fever and malaise are reported in diffuse furunculosis.

Carbuncles are even more serious deep-seated infections of several hair follicles; they result from coalescence and spreading of the infectious process into the depths of inelastic subcutaneous tissue, usually at the base of the neck. Multiple sinus tracts are frequently present (Fig. 183–7). The disease leads to the development of a central necrotic crater, which heals by progressive granulation and by the development of a hard hypertrophic violaceous scar. The development of carbuncles is associated with general symptoms such as fever and malaise. Chills and spiking fevers are more frequent in patients with carbuncles than in those with boils, and they should raise the possibility of an incipient staphylococcal septicemia; if the carbuncle is located around the nares or the upper lip, septic thrombophlebitis of the intracerebral veins should be suspected.

Recurrent furunculosis, characterized by repeated bouts of pyoderma extending over several months or years, is a vexing clinical problem that has not been adequately solved. Young patients with such a disorder, particularly if suppurative lymph nodes coexist, should be investigated for an underlying host defense deficiency, including phagocytic dysfunction and metabolic abnormalities. More important, however, patients and their intimate contacts should be investigated for nasal staphylococcal carriage because most cases are due to recurrent colonization from a family reservoir or are due to autoinoculation.

Impetigo. Impetigo is a very superficial staphylococcal skin infection that affects mostly children, usually on exposed areas of the body (e.g., on the face and the legs) (Fig. 183–8). Although most of these infections are due to *S. aureus,* about 10% are due to *Streptococcus pyogenes;* another 10% will yield both organisms on culture, the two or possibly three diseases being clinically indistinguishable without microbial identification.

The disease usually starts as a red macule that evolves into a vesicle containing cloudy fluid based on an area of erythema. The vesicle rapidly ruptures and leaves a yellowish, thick, wet crust with a diameter often exceeding 1 cm that is surrounded by erythema. Most affected children present with multiple lesions of various duration. The infectious process heals without scarring. General symptoms are absent, but a local inflammatory lymph node reaction is the rule.

The diagnosis can present some problems at the early vesicular stage of the first lesion, and it includes other vesicular eruptions such as herpes simplex and varicella. Gram stain and culture of a lesion will clarify the situation and suggest general antibiotic treatment, which is mandatory to avoid dissemination and recurrence.

Hydradenitis Suppurativa. A recurrent pyogenic infection of the apocrine sweat glands, hydradenitis suppurativa is often due to *S. aureus.* It is manifested as crops of "furuncles" developing in the axillary, perineal, and genital areas. The lesions usually drain spontaneously, with the formation of many sinus tracts and hypertrophic scarring. The differential diagnosis presents no problem when the axillary regions are involved, but it can be difficult if the disease affects the genital areas only, where it may mimic lymphogranuloma venereum.

Local treatment with moist dressings and incision if the lesion becomes fluctuant is usually effective, and administration of an oral antistaphylococcal agent for 7 to 10 days is indicated only if general symptoms are present. Radical excision of hypertrophic scars must sometimes be performed for aesthetic reasons or in case of recurrence.

Mastitis. Of all nursing mothers, various forms of staphylococcal breast infections that encompass the spectrum from a painful erythematous nodule to frank canalicular abscess formation will develop in 1 to 3%, most commonly during the second or third week of the puerperium.[110] General symptoms are absent in the former manifestations but are present in the latter. *S. aureus* is usually isolated from the mother and the infant.

Besides topical treatment, acute mastitis mandates the use of general antibiotic treatment with a β-lactamase–stable penicillin. If abscess formation occurs, incision and drainage will rapidly control the infection. No consensus has been reached on whether nursing should be discontinued.

Wound Infection. Staphylococcal postsurgical infections are characterized by the progressive appearance of edema, erythema, and pain around the surgical incision 2 or more days after surgery, when the signs of acute inflammation caused by the intervention should normally have subsided. Mild constitutional symptoms and fever are frequently present. Removal of one or two stitches and gentle pressure applied on one of the edges of the incision will produce a small amount of cloudy, odorless, and slightly hemorrhagic drainage, which on Gram stain and culture reveals the offending organism.

The specific management of wound infections has to be adapted to each case because many variables need to be evaluated, such as the severity of underlying diseases affecting host defense mechanisms, extension of the infection, severity of the constitutional symptoms, presence of foreign material, and potential contamination of deeper host or prosthetic structures. The most useful approach is a pragmatic one. First, the wound must be explored to determine the depth of

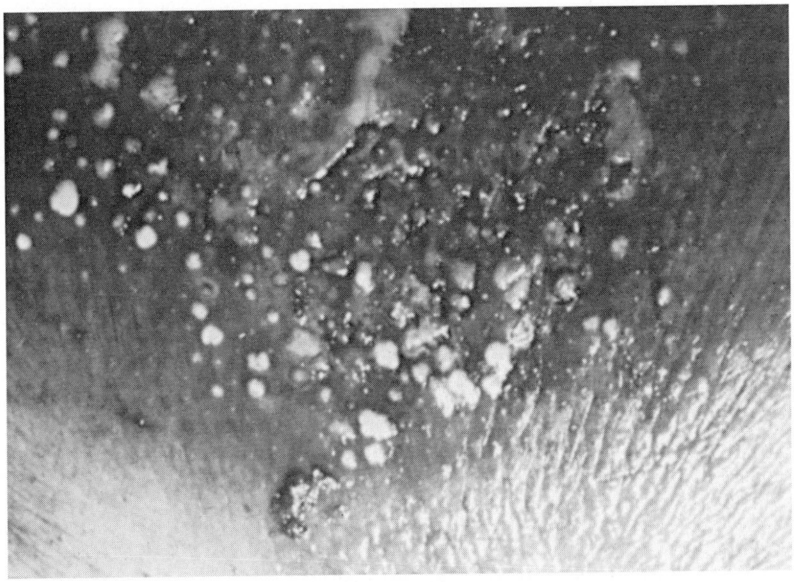

FIGURE 183–7. Carbuncle. Close-up view showing the multiple purulent drainage sites that correspond to the spreading of the infectious process to adjacent follicles.

infection. If deeper structures are not involved, release of the stitches with repeated cleansing of the wound under general antistaphylococcal coverage for 7 to 10 days is usually curative. If the incisional infection is minor and constitutional symptoms are absent, antibiotics are probably dispensable. If the infection involves deeper structures (e.g., bone) or foreign material (e.g., prosthetic devices), effective antibiotics (usually parenteral) should be given for 4 to 6 weeks and be accompanied by local cleansing of the wound, which must be packed open. Even with this optimized therapy, recurrence of infection cannot be prevented in all cases.

Because postsurgical infection has a well-defined date of initiation and many conditions conducive to wound contamination are known, this type of infection lends itself well to preventive measures, which will be discussed later.

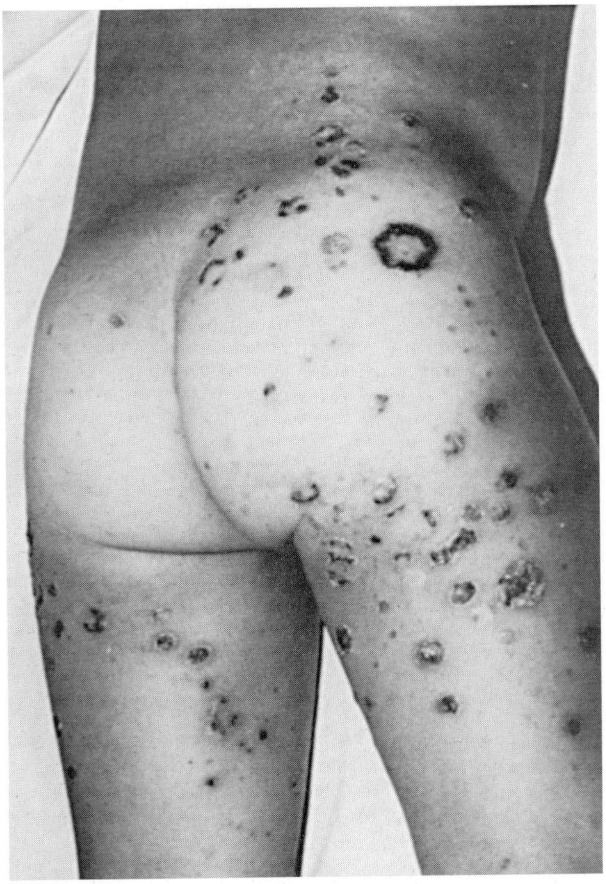

FIGURE 183–8. Impetigo due to *Staphylococcus aureus* in a child. Note the multiple, very superficial lesions, with formation of large vesicopustules and secondary rupture. The same clinical picture can be produced by group A β-hemolytic streptococci.

Spreading Pyodermas. All primary, localized skin infections caused by *S. aureus* are characterized by rapid spread to soft tissues; thus, cellulitis, lymphangitis with lymphadenitis, and even necrotizing fasciitis can be caused by *S. aureus*. These infections are indistinguishable from infections produced by group A streptococci on a clinical basis; the presence of creamy pus, isolated cocci, or clumps of microorganisms on Gram stain should raise the possibility of the presence of *S. aureus* and mandate appropriate antibiotic coverage.

Management of Localized Skin Infections. Local care is of paramount importance in localized *S. aureus* pyoderma. Hair should be gently removed, repeated cleansing with an antiseptic nonirritant solution should alternate with the application of moist dressings, and the infected area should be covered with a sterile dressing. All material used for local care should be considered highly contagious, and hand washing after a dressing change should be reinforced. Surgical incision and drainage are indicated whenever the lesion becomes fluctuant.

The decision whether to use systemic antibiotics in localized *S. aureus* skin infections is controversial and requires common sense. Empirically, local infections are not generally an indication for systemic antibiotics in the absence of fever. Antibiotics are necessary in some cases to avoid further spread of the infection, such as in impetigo, hydradenitis, and diffuse or recurrent furunculosis; a semisynthetic penicillinase-resistant penicillin that is reliably absorbed (e.g., cloxacillin or dicloxacillin) should be given in an oral dose of 30 to 40 mg/kg/day in four equal portions. Erythromycin (15 to 20 mg/kg/day in four equal portions) or clarithromycin or azithromycin can be used in penicillin-allergic patients, and penicillin V (15 to 20 mg/kg/day in four equal doses) is still the drug of choice for the exceptional, well-tested, penicillin G–sensitive organism. The duration of treatment is poorly defined, but it should definitely not exceed 7 to 10 days. The same antibiotics at double the dosage are strongly indicated in the case of pyoderma accompanied by constitutional symptoms, the decision to give them orally or parenterally depending on their severity, the risk of hematogenous spread, and compliance of the patient. The same indication prevails before incision and drainage of a fluctuant lesion, but the duration of treatment can probably be reduced to 3 to 5 days. Finally, "bacteremic" treatment with high doses of a parenteral penicillinase-resistant penicillin such as nafcillin should be instituted if the patient presents with chills, if the infection is severe and involves the face, or if bacteremic spread would have catastrophic consequences, such as in patients with prosthetic heart valves or prosthetic joints.

The problem of MRSA requires special attention besides the control measures defined earlier, the treatment of choice being topical in the absence of constitutional symptoms; otherwise, parenteral vancomycin or teicoplanin has to be considered.

Prevention of *S. aureus* postsurgical wound infection has become, for obvious reasons, the focus of active clinical research. In clean surgery, where *S. aureus* and coagulase-negative staphylococci play the major offending role, a first- or second-generation parenteral cephalosporin is usually indicated. It should be given within 30 minutes of the incision and not exceed 24 hours.[111]

Localized Infections with Diffuse Skin Rash

The two disease entities characterized by skin rash include staphylococcal scalded skin syndrome (SSSS), or Ritter's disease when it occurs in neonates, and TSS.

Staphylococcal Scalded Skin Syndrome. In 1878, Ritter von Rittershain described an exfoliative dermatitis among infants in a foundling home in Prague, Czech Republic. The disease was characterized by the appearance of large bullae and by the separation of extended areas of the epidermis. The disease was subsequently shown to be of staphylococcal etiology and to involve children and, in exceptional cases, adults. Besides being called Ritter's disease, it also became known as the staphylococcal scalded skin syndrome (SSSS). Some confusion occurred in 1956, when Lyell[112] and Lang and Walker[113] independently described a toxic epidermal necrolysis in adults that mimicked SSSS in many ways. This entity, called Lyell's disease, was soon differentiated into two subtypes, one occurring secondary to drug hypersensitivity (barbiturates, sulfonamides, and pyrazolone derivatives) and the other occurring in infants infected with *S. aureus,* which represents what was formerly known as Ritter's disease.

SSSS encompasses a spectrum of clinical features. Bullous impetigo, the most common finding, is a localized skin infection caused by exfoliative toxin–producing staphylococci. It is rarely associated with systemic signs. The bullous lesions contain easily identifiable organisms. Ritter's disease is characterized by general involvement of the skin by exfoliative toxin secondary to a local infection most frequently in the nasopharynx, umbilicus, or urinary tract. Fever, irritability, cutaneous tenderness, and scarlatiniform eruption, often accentuated in the perioral and flexural areas, are hallmarks of the disease. Flaccid blisters and erosions occur within 24 to 48 hours after onset and leave denuded areas. Gentle friction of apparently healthy skin will cause it to wrinkle and slough (Nikolsky's sign). Serous fluid and electrolyte losses can lead to hypovolemia, sepsis syndrome, and death in 1 to 10% of cases.[114] The exfoliated areas will eventually dry with a flaky desquamation lasting 3 to 5 days. After 10 days, recovery is complete in most cases. Hair and nails can shed. Finally, an abortive form of SSSS known as the scarlatiniform variant does not have bullous formation. In all the clinical manifestations, the affected skin does not show the presence of *S. aureus,* which is confined to the primary infectious focus and sometimes invades the blood stream.

The early differential diagnosis of SSSS includes, besides toxic epidermal necrolysis, other bullous lesions and TSS, which occur in a different epidemiologic setting and show specific histologic lesions. In toxic epidermal necrolysis, separation occurs at the dermal-epidermal junction, as opposed to SSSS, where the splitting is observed in the granular layer. Finally, Kawasaki mucocutaneous disorder is characterized by a negative Nikolsky's sign and negative bacterial cultures of the skin lesions.

The great majority of cases of SSSS in the United States occur in children younger than 5 years and is due to phage group II *S. aureus,* with 75% of them belonging to phage type 71,[115] but such an association is less clear in other countries. As demonstrated by Melish and Glasgow,[59] sublethal doses of *S. aureus* isolated from patients with SSSS and injected either subcutaneously or intraperitoneally into neonatal mice simulate the human disease remarkably from a clinical and histologic point of view. Management of SSSS implies eradication of the offending exfoliatin-bearing strain from the focus of infection and usually requires parenteral pennicillinase-resistant β-lactam antibiotics. Supportive skin care and management of fluid and electrolyte losses will lead to prompt recovery in most cases without scarring.

Toxic Shock Syndrome. In 1978, Todd and coworkers described an infectious syndrome in seven children aged 8 to 17 years with the common clinical features of high fever, profound and refractory hypotension, profuse diarrhea, erythroderma, mental confusion, and renal failure.[116] The entity was named toxic shock syndrome and was later considered to be synonymous with staphylococcal scarlet fever, a sporadic disease entity known since 1927.

Menstrual Toxic Shock Syndrome. In January 1980 it suddenly became apparent that this multisystem disease was frequently observed in women, with onset mainly during menstruation.[117] Menstrual TSS reached epidemic proportions in 1980 and 1981 and was probably facilitated by the introduction on the market of new hyperabsorbable tampons.[118] Since their removal from the market and the application of federal regulations, the incidence of the disease has decreased: the proportion in U.S. women 19 to 44 years of age has decreased from 6/100,000 in 1980 to 1/100,000 in 1986 and later. The case-fatality ratio, which was initially high at 5.6%, has now decreased to 3.3%.[119, 120]

Retrospective analysis has shown that from 1970 to 1982, close to 1700 cases were reported to the Centers for Disease Control and Prevention, with 96% involving women and 92% having their onset during menstruation. Another study has shown 98 to 99% of these cases to be associated with tampons.

Nonmenstrual Toxic Shock Syndrome. With the decline in menses-associated TSS, it has become apparent that nonmenstrual TSS was of considerable epidemiologic importance. Some nonmenstrual TSS cases are still associated with vaginal colonization of toxin-secreting strains and occur under conditions such as vaginal infection, use of contraceptive devices, childbirth, abortion, and the postpartum state, where it can be observed from 12 hours to 8 weeks after delivery. Forty percent, however, are associated with usually benign-looking wounds after a great variety of surgical procedures such as herniorrhaphy, mammoplasty, arthroscopy, and surgical wound contamination.[121] The syndrome usually starts 2 days after the procedure, and signs of infection at the site of infection are virtually absent, which implies that great clinical awareness is required to culture an apparently normal wound. Osteomyelitis, other focal infections, and influenza-associated TSS have also been described.[122]

Nonmenstrual TSS has the following characteristics: it occurs at a male-female ratio of 1:3, and it is more often associated with prior antibiotic use, more often acquired in the hospital, and more prone to renal and central nervous system complications.[123] The strains are associated with the production of TSST-1 in only 50% of cases,[124] the non–TSST-1 cases being associated with enterotoxin B and C production again in 50% of residual cases.

Clinical Manifestations. The clinical profile of a patient with menses-associated TSS is a young woman between 15 and 25 years old who is using tampons during her menstrual periods. The disease usually starts abruptly during menses, and the clinical manifestations

TABLE 183–4 Frequency of Signs, Symptoms, and Laboratory Abnormalities in 52 Patients with Toxic Shock Syndrome*

Clinical Sign or Symptom	%	Laboratory Finding	%
Diarrhea	98	Elevated serum creatinine	69
Myalgia	96	Thrombocytopenia†	59
Vomiting	92	Hypocalcemia‡	58
Temperature ≥40°C	87	Azotemia	57
Headache	77	Hyperbilirubinemia	54
Sore throat	75	Elevated hepatic enzymes	50
Conjunctival hyperemia	57	Leukocytosis§	48
Decreased sensorium	40	Abnormal urinary sediment‖	46
Vaginal hyperemia	33	Elevated creatine phosphokinase	41
Vaginal discharge	28	Immature leukocytes ≥50%	36
Rigors	25		

*Rash and shock, being part of the definition, are omitted from the table.
†Platelet count less than 100,000/ml.
‡Serum calcium 7.5 mg/dl or less.
§White blood cell count ≥15,000/mm³ or greater.
‖At least five white blood cells per high-power field, two or more red blood cells per high-power field, or the presence of red blood cells casts.
Reprinted by permission from Davis JP, Chesney PJ, Wand PJ, et al. Toxic-shock syndrome. N Engl J Med. 1980;303:1429.

involve many organ systems, as summarized in Table 183–4.[117] Prominent initial symptoms and signs include intense myalgias, fever, vomiting, and diarrhea. The patient is usually listless and confused but presents without focal neurologic or meningeal signs. Severe hypotension ensues rapidly, with hypovolemic shock secondary to loss of colloids and fluid. An erythematous, deep-red, "sunburn" rash develops within a few hours, accompanied by conjunctival inflammation.[117, 120]

Physical examination discloses, besides the skin rash and hypotension, erythematous mucosal surfaces; vaginal hyperemia is present, and often a vaginal discharge from which *S. aureus* can be recovered is observed. Blood cultures are exceptionally positive, and cerebrospinal fluid cultures are invariably negative.

Some of the important findings observed during the acute phase of TSS are summarized in Table 183–4.[117] Rash and shock, being part of the diagnostic criteria, are omitted from the table. Renal failure is of both the oliguric and nonoliguric type, and it is most often reversible. In case of death (about 3%), main pathologic alterations have included desquamation and ulceration of the vaginal and cervical mucosa, periportal inflammation in the liver, acute tubular necrosis, and the formation of hyaline membranes, which are characteristic of shock lung.[125]

In recent years, more emphasis has been put on the description of nonmenstrual cases. They are often associated with a nonconspicuous infection site, and *S. aureus* is isolated from the wound (41%), trachea, lung, stool, and bone, to name but a few. Seventy-five percent of cases still occur in women. The fatility rate is higher than that in menstrual cases, possibly because of increased difficulty in making the appropriate diagnosis. Recurrence is exceptional.

Criteria for the diagnosis of TSS are presented in Table 183–5. TSS is probable when three or more major criteria are met in the presence of desquamation or more than five are met in its absence.

Although full recovery is the rule, with intense scaling and desquamation of the skin and a predilection for the palms and soles (Fig. 183–9), complications and sequelae have to be expected. Repeated bouts of TSS with fever, myalgia, vomiting, diarrhea, and diffuse rash with desquamation have been described in a number of cases. They usually occurred again during menses and were of decreased intensity. Recurrences were most frequent if tampons were used without a complete previous antibiotic treatment schedule, intermediate if the use of tampons was discontinued in the absence of antibiotic treatment, and lowest if tampons use was discontinued after complete antibiotic treatment. The main sequelae include persistent neuropsychological alterations such as memory loss and lack of concentration, an abnormal electroencephalogram, mild renal failure, late-onset rash, and cyanotic extremities.[126] Increased development of new allergies has been reported.

Finally, a recalcitrant, erythematous desquamating disorder has been described in patients with acquired immunodeficiency syndrome in association with toxin-producing *S. aureus* and could conceivably be observed in other immunocompromised hosts.[127]

Pathogenic Factors Involved in Toxic Shock Syndrome. Arguments in favor of the crucial role played by *S. aureus* in the pathogenesis of TSS are overwhelming and include (1) a vaginal isolation rate of 98% in appropriately cultured menses-associated TSS, as opposed to a carriage rate in various healthy controls of 8 to 10%[31]; (2) isolation of *S. aureus* from other sites in all non–menses-associated cases of TSS[124]; and (3) the low recurrence rate in patients receiving antistaphylococcal antibiotics during the initial episode. TSST-1 has been identified as being highly associated with TSS: approximately 75% of patients' isolates are positive for TSST-1, whereas 25% are positive for other staphylococcal toxins, including enterotoxin B (23%) and C (2%). TSST-1 corresponds to the toxins identified by Bergdoll and colleagues[63] and Schlievert and coworkers,[62] and its mode of action has been discussed previously. It should be underscored that many factors prevailing in the vagina in the presence of hyperabsorbable tampons will favor the production of TSST-1, such as O_2 tension, appropriate CO_2 tension, low Mg concentration, and neutral pH. The exact sequence of events for toxin production in the presence of tampons has not been fully identified yet.[128]

The prevalence of antibodies against TSST-1 is above 90% in the general population but lower in the pediatric population. Practically all patients with menstruation-associated TSS had undetectable antibodies against TSST-1 at onset of the disease. All these data confirm the pivotal role of TSST-1 and other enterotoxins in the development of TSS.

TABLE 183–5 Criteria for the Diagnosis of Toxic Shock Syndrome

Temperature >38.9°C
Systolic blood pressure <90 mmHg
Rash with subsequent desquamation, especially on the palms and soles
Involvement of ≥3 of the following organ systems:
- Gastrointestinal: vomiting, profuse diarrhea
- Muscular: severe myalgias or >5-fold increase in CPK
- Mucous membranes (vagina, conjunctivae, or pharynx): frank hyperemia
- Renal insufficiency: BUN or creatinine at least twice the upper limit of normal with pyuria in the absence of urinary tract infection
- Liver (hepatitis): bilirubin, AST, ALT at least twice the upper limit of normal
- Blood: thrombocytopenia <100,000/mm³
- Central nervous system: disorientation without focal neurologic signs

Negative results of serologic tests for Rocky Mountain spotted fever, leptospirosis, and measles

Abbreviations: ALT, Alanine transaminase; AST, aspartate transaminase; BUN, blood urea nitrogen; CPK, creatinine phosphokinase.

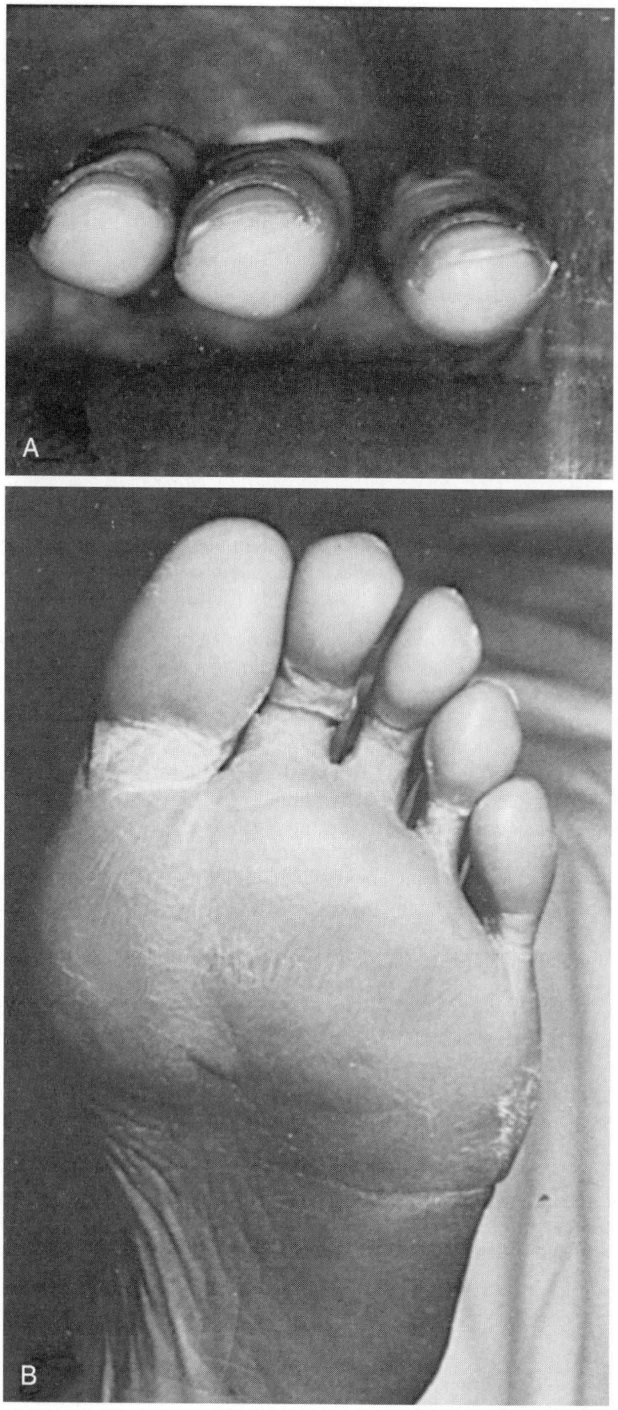

FIGURE 183–9. *A* and *B*, Toxic shock syndrome characterized by late desquamation of skin around fingernails and overlying toes. Unlike the appearance of the scalded skin syndrome, the area under the desquamation is not denuded but still covered by a thin epithelium.

The 1980–1981 epidemic of TSS in the United States and, by extension, the many sporadic cases throughout the world[119, 120] have been statistically linked to the use of hyperabsorbable tampons. Hyperabsorbable tampons, which were introduced in 1977 to the U.S. market, have even further increased this risk[119]; their withdrawal from the market has been paralleled by a decreased prevalence of TSS.

Management and Prevention of Toxic Shock Syndrome. Acute management of a patient with TSS first requires aggressive fluid replacement with saline, colloid, or both. Vaginal examination should be performed immediately thereafter, with removal of any tampon and with vaginal and cervical culturing for *S. aureus*. In variant TSS, cultures of the primary focus should be obtained even if no frank sign of infection is present. A β-lactamase–resistant antistaphylococcal antibiotic such as oxacillin or nafcillin should be administered intravenously at a dosage of 8 to 10 g/day. Exacerbation of the skin rash is sometimes difficult to differentiate from a possible allergic reaction to the β-lactam antibiotic. In the absence of complications such as bacteremic spread or of a primary focus such as osteomyelitis, the treatment period should not exceed 10 to 15 days. Because β-lactam antibiotics have been suspected to increase TSST-1 production and macrolides have been shown in vivo to decrease protein and TSST-1 synthesis, it is commonly suggested that clindamycin be added to the aforementioned regimen, at least for the first days of therapy. Intravenous immune globulins have been used sporadically in very severe cases.

Prevention of recurrence is achieved by parenteral antibiotic treatment of the first episodes as described, education of the patient, and avoidance of tampons. Prevention of first episodes probably requires minimal use of high-absorbancy tampons, education of the population at risk regarding the use of other catamenial products, and better identification of the factors associated with nonmenstrual cases.

Septicemia and Endocarditis

Epidemiologic Aspects; Predisposing Factors. The epidemiology, the clinical spectrum, and the outcome of staphylococcal septicemia have been modified over the years by several factors, including a patient population with an increasing number of underlying diseases and social habits such as the use of recreational intravenous drugs. A careful study performed in Denmark encompassing 2000 cases of bacteremia observed in various hospitals showed that epidemic strains can be replaced by new ones with altered phage susceptibilities and new antibiotic resistance patterns.[129] Before the availability of antibiotics, the clinical manifestations of *S. aureus* bacteremia were remarkably uniform[130]; patients tended to be young, without underlying disease in 70% of cases, and disseminated infection usually led to the establishment of metastatic foci and to death in 82% of cases. More recent studies concentrating on non–intravenous drug abusers have determined the outcome of community-acquired *S. aureus* bacteremia in the era of antibiotics; in a study from South Africa, the overall mortality remained 35% and was associated with acute renal failure, respiratory distress, shock, endocarditis, and platelet counts lower than 100 × 10^9/liter. Twenty-six percent of patients were diabetic.[131] In another study from Brazil, mortality was also 39%, and hospital-acquired bacteremia represented 86% of the episodes, mostly related to intravenous catheter (26%) and respiratory tract (13%) infections.[132] Thus, both community- and hospital-acquired bacteremias are still associated, in spite of adequate antibiotic therapy, with high morbidity and mortality. Additionally, a recent study showed an increase in frequency and that catheter-associated infections represent an important emerging problem.[133]

Clinical Manifestations. In most cases, *S. aureus* bacteremia is the consequence of a local infection that has gained access to the blood stream. Musher and McKenzie have conveniently subdivided these infected foci into extravascular foci (cellulitis, ulcers, burns, osteomyelitis, and pneumonia), intravascular foci (intravenous access devices), and presumed intravascular foci (heroin addiction).[134] In about one third of cases of septicemia, no initial focus of infection could be detected.

In its classic manifestation, the disease starts with chills and sometimes with frank rigors. The patient is often obtunded and complains of joint pain and, more rarely, pleuritic chest pain. In a hospitalized patient, these symptoms associated with the presence of an intravenous catheter will mandate its removal and culture, the drawing of blood for culture, and prompt initiation of antibacterial therapy. In nonhospitalized patients, the disease usually evolves untreated for several days before admission.

Physical examination usually reveals an acutely ill, often listless, febrile, and slightly obtunded patient. Careful examination of the skin can provide major diagnostic clues such as petechiae on the digits and extremities, subconjunctival hemorrhaging, and a full spectrum of larger skin lesions extending from necrotic to necropurulent and hemorrhagic lesions; gangrenous, symmetric involvement of the extremities has also been described (Fig. 183–10), sometimes associated with disseminated coagulopathy. Funduscopic examination will sometimes disclose classic Roth spots and more often small punctiform hemorrhages.

Examination of the heart reveals tachycardia and often additional gallop sounds. Murmurs are difficult to interpret at this stage of the disease; a loud pansystolic murmur may reflect a rapidly developing mitral insufficiency. Tricuspid insufficiency should be suspected if the murmur is accentuated during inspiration and accompanied by a wide jugular pulse. Diastolic murmurs, whether faint or loud, are indicative of aortic valve endocarditis and the development of aortic regurgitation, with diastolic pressure, as opposed to chronic aortic insufficiency, usually being maintained. A pericardial friction rub can be heard occasionally, and it can be replaced by frank signs of pericardial effusion.

The diagnosis of active endocarditis carries an ominous prognosis. The morbidity associated with annular and myocardial abscesses and with central nervous system complications is considerable. Hemodynamic deterioration as a consequence of valve incompetence, myocardial involvement, uncontrolled infection, and repeated embolization warrants surgical intervention. Transthoracic and transesophageal echocardiography are of great help in assessing local anatomic conditions and evaluating the appropriateness of a surgical intervention; these aspects are discussed in detail in Chapter 65.

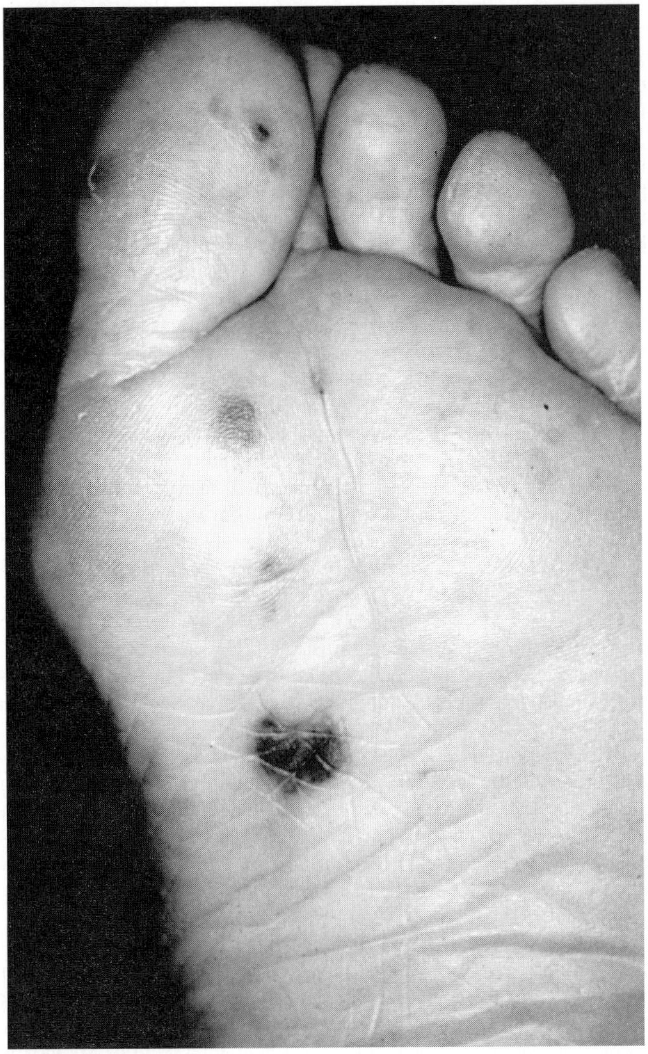

FIGURE 183–10. Janeway lesions in a patient with *Staphylococcus aureus* endocarditis.

Pulmonary examination is of utmost importance, particularly when right-sided endocarditis is suspected. Pleural friction rubs are frequently heard, and a purulent pleural effusion often develops. Pulmonary intraparenchymatous lesions are rarely heard on auscultation and have to be sought by repeated chest radiographs.

The spleen is often slightly enlarged on percussion. Involvement of one or several joints is heralded by the development of exquisite pain and is followed by erythema and local edema. Osteomyelitis is usually manifested as intense pain in a metaphyseal area, with normal overlying skin. Spondylitis can supervene at any stage of the disease, and its initial symptom is usually back pain accompanied by paravertebral spasm. Frank meningeal signs are usually absent, and focal neurologic deficits are an exception, unless embolization from an acute endocarditis is a prominent feature.

Laboratory Investigations. Several blood cultures obtained at timed intervals and cultures of skin lesions, purulent exudate, and urine should be obtained; the latter specimen often shows less than 10^5 bacteria per milliliter on culture.[129] Routine hematologic tests often show mild anemia. The white blood cell count can be either high with a marked shift to the left or low; toxic granulations are often present. Thrombocytopenia is frequently observed and suggests the possibility of disseminated intravascular coagulation—an early, rare, and often fatal complication of *S. aureus* septicemia. Mild renal insufficiency is frequently encountered and reflects either prerenal or intrinsic renal disease; *S. aureus* septicemia can produce either pyelonephritis, multiple cortical abscesses, or focal or diffuse glomerulonephritis.[135–137] The urine can therefore contain white blood cells, granular casts, red blood cells, or red blood cell casts. At present, none of these renal alterations are known to require specific treatment besides antibiotics, and renal biopsy is therefore rarely justified.

The choice of other laboratory investigations will depend on the clinical problems encountered. Electrocardiographic abnormalities suggest myocarditis or pericarditis. Bone scans performed with Tc-phosphonate will help identify a focus of osteomyelitis. Finally, computed tomography (CT) and magnetic resonance imaging (MRI) are of great help in selected cases in which local signs point toward a well-delineated secondary focus of metastatic infection amenable to surgical drainage.

The Clinical Dilemma of Positive Blood Cultures: Septicemia or Endocarditis? Despite recent data suggesting an overall incidence of endocarditis of 10% or less in conjunction with bacteremias, long-term parenteral antibiotic treatment has remained the standard practice in many centers because early studies reported a risk of endocarditis of 60%. Recent observations make it possible in many cases of *S. aureus* septicemia to predict those with and those without endocarditis. These criteria, which are summarized in Table 183–6, should be taken only as evaluation guidelines to allow clinicians to make a probabilistic decision on the management of each individual case and adapt the treatment strategy to the clinical course.

Clinical Patterns. Nolan and Beaty were the first to suggest that patients with staphylococcal bacteremia can be differentiated into two groups.[138] The first group had a recognizable primary site of infection, was older, had significant underlying disorders, and was already hospitalized when bacteremia developed. Secondary foci or endocarditis developed in only 10 and 3% of these patients, respectively. They were treated for less than 2 weeks in most cases and had a relapse rate of less than 2%. In contrast, patients in the second

TABLE 183-6 Criteria Discriminating between *Staphylococcus aureus* Bacteremia with or without Endocarditis

Criteria	Septicemia without Endocarditis	Septicemia with Endocarditis	Comments
Clinical			
Older patients; Presence of underlying diseases; Recognizable primary infection; Hospitalized patients	Probable	Improbable	Primary focus is easily drained/removed
Younger patients; Community-acquired infection (illicit drugs)	Improbable	Most probable	Presence of metastatic foci
Laboratory			
Endocardial vegetations demonstrated by echocardiography	Improbable	Confirmed	Absence of vegetation does not rule out endocarditis
Presence of circulating immune complexes	Improbable	Probable	Negative test does not rule out endocarditis
Presence of antistaphylococcal antibodies (see text)	Improbable	Probable and/or presence of metastatic foci	Predictive value depends on test used
Therapeutic			
Short-term treatment (2–3 wk) effective	Probable	Improbable	Short-term treatment only justified if all clinical and laboratory criteria are fulfilled to rule out endocarditis
Long-term treatment (4–6 wk) necessary	Unlikely	Likely	

group were younger, had no identifiable site of primary infection, and acquired their bacteremia in the community, often by the use of recreational intravenous drugs. In this second group, metastatic foci of infection developed in 95% and endocarditis in 57%. Despite parenteral therapy lasting more than 3 weeks, a sizable number of these patients relapsed. These results have been confirmed by Iannini and Grossley,[139] who successfully treated 29 patients falling into the low-risk group for 15 days without any recurrence. Although these results have been debated,[140, 141] they tend to suggest that some *S. aureus* bacteremias with a well-defined initial focus and rapid clinical response to therapy can be treated for a shorter duration (e.g., 2 to 3 weeks).

Echocardiography. Transthoracic and transesophageal echocardiography of the heart valves can be of help in the positive diagnosis of endocarditis. Negative exploratory findings do not rule out the diagnosis because the technique is not sensitive enough to detect small vegetations and their development probably requires more than 10 days of evolution. The advantages of transesophageal exploration and the general use of echocardiography in the management of acute endocarditis are discussed in Chapter 65.

Immune Complexes. Sustained intravascular infections are associated with the development of rheumatoid factor, cryoglobulins, and circulating immune complexes. It has been suggested that circulating immune complexes can be detected in 50% of patients with *S. aureus* endocarditis, as opposed to patients with septicemia, who have undetectable levels.[142] Although useful in expert hands, these determinations are not infallible and have not received wide recognition, particularly because the antigenic determinants of these circulating immmune complexes are as yet unknown and are not necessarily of staphylococcal origin.

Serology of* Staphylococcus aureus *Infections. Starting with the hypothesis that a metastatic infection or endocarditis caused by *S. aureus* may be a constant immunologic challenge to the host, several investigators have tried to document and correlate its presence with the levels or fluctuation of antistaphylococcal antibodies.[143–148] Whereas antibodies can be demonstrated in almost all cases of endocarditis or bacteremias with metastatic foci, they are also present in a sizable number of uncomplicated septicemias. At present, these tests are still investigational and have not been put into clinical practice as a guide for therapy.

Management of Bacteremia and Endocarditis. The mainstay of treatment is parenteral administration of a potent antistaphylococcal antibiotic, preferably of the β-lactam family. As initial therapy, a semisynthetic intravenous penicillinase-resistant penicillin is recommended, such as nafcillin (1.5 g every 4 hours) or oxacillin (2.0 g every 4 hours). If the microorganism has been shown by adequate laboratory methods to be unable to produce a penicillinase, treatment can be switched to penicillin G at a dosage of 4 million units every 4 hours intravenously.[149]

Whether an aminoglycoside should be combined with a β-lactam antibiotic is a question dealt with in Chapter 65. In brief, whereas aminoglycosides act synergistically with β-lactam antibiotics on most *S. aureus* strains in vitro, they only moderately improve the outcome of experimental endocarditis and do not show any significant effect in clinically documented endocarditis.[149]

In the case of a benign penicillin allergy, several alternatives can be considered, such as cephalosporin at a bacteremic dosage. A better option is vancomycin at a dosage of 1.0 g every 12 hours given as a slow intravenous infusion and with careful monitoring of blood levels in patients with renal impairment. Vancomycin is also the drug of choice in the case of MRSA infection. Teicoplanin (not available in the United States) at high dosages and with monitoring of blood levels has also been shown to be effective. Despite the fact that a sizable number of isolates are associated with the phenomenon of in vitro tolerance, this problem does not seem to warrant special antibiotic strategies.[150]

The second question concerns the duration of therapy. If the criteria previously discussed undoubtedly point toward uncomplicated bacteremia, 2 weeks of treatment will usually suffice, but the patient should be monitored very carefully for possible recurrence.[138, 139] Short-term treatment has also been recommended for right-sided endocarditis[140]; in all other cases (i.e., those with septicemia complicated by metastatic infections or cases of endocarditis), patients should receive a full 4-week course of antibiotic therapy. In the case of endocarditis occurring on prosthetic devices, a 6-week course of an adequately chosen penicillin with an aminoglycoside and possibly rifampin has been recommended as an option (see Chapter 66).

The third question is whether the determination of in vitro minimal bacteriostatic and bactericidal concentrations is of any help in monitoring therapy. It has been recommended that one might select antibiotics that result either individually or, when necessary, in combination in a serum trough level of at least 1:8.[149] This approach has never been put to the test of a formal study and has been largely abandoned.

Finally, various forms of adjuvant therapy and the place of surgery should be briefly discussed. Neither steroid nor anticoagulant administration is indicated. The development of a valvular leak occasionally precipitates acute cardiac failure and may require early surgical valve replacement. Other surgical interventions should be aimed at draining suppurative exudates, such as purulent pericarditis, pleural empyema, or a perinephric abscess. Splenic or renal abscesses, if confirmed by CT scan, are also an indication for surgery, provided that the patient does not defervesce under optimal antibiotic management. If the initial focus of infection is an intravenous access device, it should be removed immediately. If the septicemia originated from a septic thrombophlebitis, strong consideration should be given to ligation and surgical removal of the vein.

Septic Vasculitis. Direct involvement of the venous (septic thrombophlebitis) or the arterial (septic endarteritis) vessel wall is usually due to an intravascular catheter. Catheter-acquired sepsis is discussed in Chapter 292. Septic endarteritis is characterized by pseudoaneurysm formation and peripheral emboli. Excision and 4 to 6 weeks of antibiotic therapy will lead to cure in most cases.[151]

Organ Infection

Because the two major modes of *S. aureus* spread are either by skin colonization and local spread or by hematogenous dissemination, it follows that any organ can occasionally be infected by *S. aureus*, either secondary to local invasion (surgery or trauma) or during disseminated infection (septicemia or endocarditis).

Meningitis

A recent epidemiologic study from Denmark has shown that *S. aureus* may be responsible for 2.4% of cases of community-acquired bacterial meningitis. The mortality was 43%, and the meningitis was associated with comorbidities such as advanced age, cardiovascular diseases, and immune deficiencies. The clinical picture did not differ from that of other bacterial meningitides except that endocarditis was present in 57% of cases.[152]

Pericarditis

Purulent pericarditis results from hematogenous spread as often as from perforating injury to the chest wall (trauma or surgery). An autopsy study has shown that 22% of cases of pericarditis were due to *S. aureus*[153] and that myocardial abscesses, endocarditis, or both were frequent concomitant findings. Aseptic pericardial effusions of various etiologies, including postoperative, postinfarction, and uremic pericarditis, represent predisposing conditions.[154]

The diagnosis of purulent pericarditis is difficult, and antemortem diagnostic rates as low as 20% are still reported. During septicemia or endocarditis, sudden chest pain, a pericardial friction rub, uncontrolled heart failure, or cardiogenic shock even in the absence of cardiac enlargement on chest x-ray films should alert the clinician to perform repeated echocardiograms in search of a pericardial effusion, which often amounts to less than 300 ml. Soon after thoracic surgery, pericarditis may be associated with severe mediastinitis that requires reoperation and drainage, or it may appear a few months later and mimic Dressler's syndrome.

As soon as the diagnosis is suspected, emergency diagnostic measures should be undertaken to confirm the diagnosis; conventional chest x-ray films are superseded by echocardiography and CT scan. Antibiotic therapy has to be instituted immediately as delineated for endocarditis, and diagnostic exploration of the pericardium should be undertaken, which can be accomplished by pericardial aspiration in hematogenous disease but will often require a median sternotomy in cases after open heart surgery.

Pulmonary Infections

S. aureus pneumonia can result from either aspiration or hematogenous spread. In both cases, the pulmonary infection can lead to local complications (e.g., abscesses and pleural empyema).

Inhalation Pneumonia. The disease often strikes a few days after the onset of influenza; the occurrence of a few cases of community-acquired *S. aureus* pneumonia should raise suspicion of an outbreak of an influenza epidemic, whereas within the hospital setting, *S. aureus* pneumonia is usually caused by intubation and aspiration.[155, 156]

No clinical or radiologic features are typical of *S. aureus* inhalation pneumonia. X-ray films can show a continuous spectrum from local consolidation or abscess formation to multiple patchy infiltrates, multiple abscesses of various size and wall thickness, and a miliary pattern of small nodules. Factors that should raise suspicion of a staphylococcal etiology include any of the previously mentioned predisposing factors, poor response to therapy aimed at treating pneumococcal pneumonia, rapid cavitation of a bronchopneumonia, the appearance of multiple areas of pulmonary consolidation (Fig. 183–11), and the development of pleural empyema (10%).[155, 156] Microbiologic confirmation requires either positive blood or empyema cultures or identification of *S. aureus* in a sputum culture. Appropriate therapy implies the intravenous administration of nafcillin or oxacillin, as described for bacteremia, for about 2 weeks and will usually lead to complete clearing of the lung lesions if instituted promptly. The possibility of an infection by MRSA strains should always be considered.

In pediatric patients, staphylococcal pneumonia is a highly febrile illness with nonproductive cough. Chest auscultation may be normal initially, but x-ray films will soon show multiple, thin-walled abscesses, so-called pneumatoceles. The development of air-fluid levels ensues, and pleural empyema can occur at any time. In most cases, blood cultures are negative, and treatment has to be started on an empirical basis. *S. aureus* is also frequently isolated from bronchial secretions in children and young adults with cystic fibrosis. Although it has been suggested that aggressive antistaphylococcal treatment paves the way for superinfection with *Pseudomonas aeruginosa*, current consensus is to treat these patients with a full 2-week course of parenteral β-lactamase–resistant penicillin.

A high incidence of *S. aureus* pneumonia has also been documented in autopsy series of patients with acquired immunodeficiency syndrome; intravenous drug use, coexistent pulmonary Kaposi's sarcoma, or pneumonia secondary to *Pneumocystis carinii* may be contributing factors. The disease may have the classic features of bacterial pneumonia, although multiple cavitary lesions have also been described.[157]

Hematogenous Pneumonias. Hematogenous pneumonias are usually due to the release of infected thrombotic material from the venous system or from infected tricuspid vegetations with subsequent septic infarction. Infection of the venous system is usually suggested by a patient's history or physical examination; many patients are recreational intravenous drug users,[158] others are maintained by chronic hemodialysis and show evidence of an infected access device,[159] and still others have received prolonged intravenous therapy.[160] Physical examination discloses various combinations of localized skin infection, septic phlebitis, right-sided endocarditis, and bilateral pneumonitis. Chest x-ray films usually show multiple discrete, small pulmonary infiltrates; some of them become cavitary within a few days (Fig. 183–12).

Treatment implies administration of a semisynthetic penicillin or vancomycin as delineated for septicemia. Short-term 2-week treatment is probably adequate if clinical response is prompt, no complication supervenes, and left- or right-sided endocarditis can be ruled out with reasonable probability.

Pleural Empyema. *S. aureus* remains one of the common causes of pleural empyema and still accounts for about one third of cases.[161] Acute empyema usually arises by direct extension from *S. aureus* pneumonia or lung abscess. It is also often seen as a complication of thoracic surgery. Direct seeding of the pleural space during septicemia or endocarditis can also occur in rare instances.

Here again, the clinical manifestations are initially overshadowed by the underlying condition (pneumonia, lung abscess, endocarditis, or thoracic surgery). The development of pleural empyema is charac-

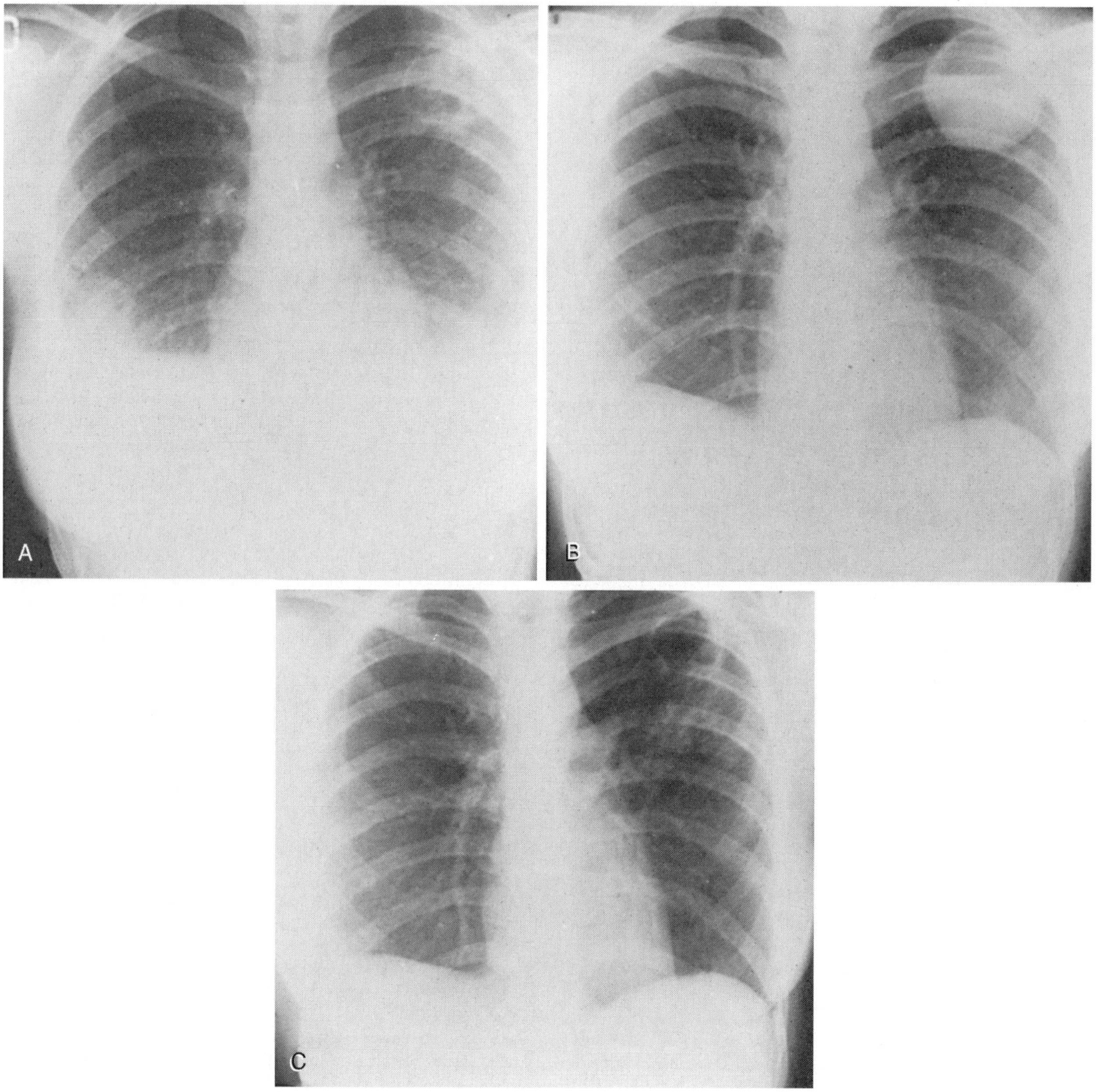

FIGURE 183–11. Radiographs of probably airborne staphylococcal pneumonia in a young girl. *A,* Early abscess formation in the right lower and left upper lobe. *B,* Evolution 2 weeks later, showing fluid accumulation in the left upper lobe abscess. *C,* Another 2 weeks later—progressive clearing of the abscesses after antistaphylococcal treatment.

terized by chest pain and fever, shortness of breath, tachycardia, and signs of pleural effusion. In postsurgical cases, inspection of the wound shows increased signs of inflammation, and cloudy material can sometimes be expressed from the wound. Conventional chest x-ray films, sonography, and CT scan will confirm the diagnosis of pleural effusion and give important information regarding loculation, a feared evolution particularly frequent in *S. aureus* infection. Finally, demonstration of a pleural air-fluid level in the absence of a previous thoracocentesis suggests a bronchopleural fistula, another feared complication of *S. aureus* infection.

The key to the etiologic diagnosis is bacteriologic examination of pleural fluid, which in the case of *S. aureus* empyema can be either cloudy or frankly purulent, but always odorless. Microscopic examination reveals sheets of PMNs and cocci.

Management of empyema implies (1) recognition of its underlying cause, such as a bronchopleural fistula, which requires carefully planned surgery; (2) treatment with antistaphylococcal agents by the intravenous route; and (3) drainage of the empyema. In rare cases, drainage by repeated aspiration is followed by rapid defervescence; in most cases, insertion of a chest tube is necessary and should lead to improvement of the clinical condition in a few days. In more chronic cases not responding to these drainage attempts, surgical drainage by thoracoscopy or thoracotomy is necessary.[162]

Osteomyelitis, Septic Arthritis, Septic Bursitis, and Pyomyositis

Bone and joint infections can occur as complications of *S. aureus* septicemia (hematogenous osteomyelitis), but most of the time they result from an infection secondary to local trauma or injury (osteomyelitis secondary to a contiguous focus of infection).[163]

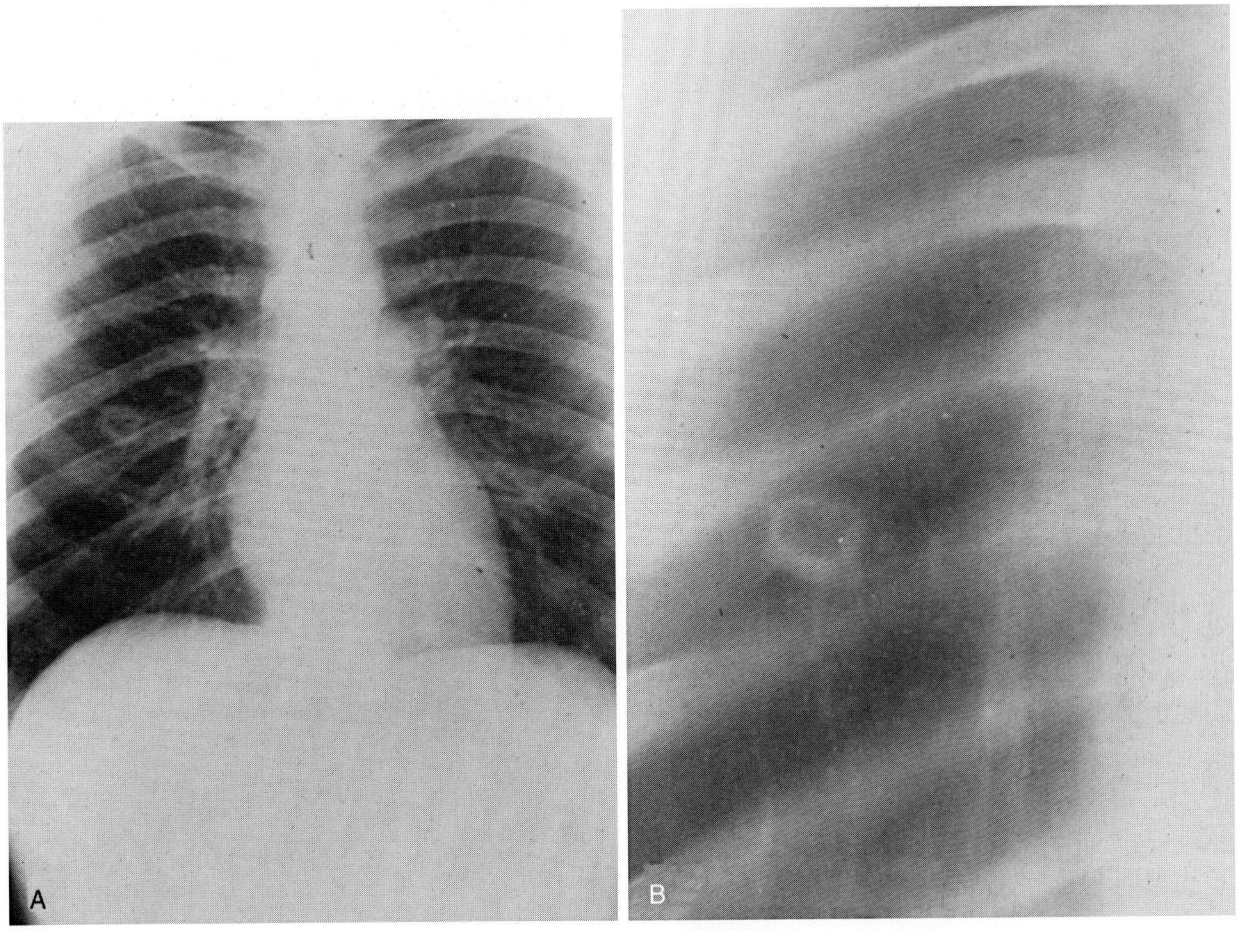

FIGURE 183–12. Radiograph *(A)* and tomogram *(B)* of a septic embolus during right-sided endocarditis in a drug addict.

Osteomyelitis. *Hematogenous osteomyelitis* caused by *S. aureus* is occasionally seen in neonates, where it usually affects the lower extremities as a consequence of an infected umbilical catheter. In children, hematogenous osteomyelitis is characterized by the sudden onset of high fever and pain in the metaphyseal area of a long bone. On physical examination, the overlying skin is normal and the adjacent joints can be freely moved, but pain is barely tolerable when the affected bone is palpated. Laboratory values are usually of little help. The sedimentation rate is high, and a leukocytosis with a left shift is noted. X-ray films of the affected bone are initially normal and usually require 10 to 14 days to show typical changes (i.e., periosteal elevation or a radiolucent and mottled area of bone lysis). In contrast, ^{99m}Tc-phosphonate scanning is of great help in the detection of early bone lesions. Of all the imaging procedures, nuclear magnetic resonance imaging has been shown to have the greatest sensitivity. Although many cases of hematogenous osteomyelitis in this age group are due to *S. aureus,* microbiologic confirmation of the infection remains mandatory. Blood cultures are positive in about 50% of cases. If no positive bacteriologic information is available after 2 to 3 days of evolution and the patient is still febrile, a direct bone biopsy procedure for decompression, culture, and histologic analysis should be performed.[164]

In adults, *S. aureus* bacteremia only rarely leads to osteomyelitis of the long bones, but vertebral osteomyelitis has been increasingly recognized as a frequent complication. In a large survey of 150 cases of vertebral osteomyelitis with an adequate bacteriologic workup, *S. aureus* (and in small part *S. epidermidis*) accounted for 60% of infections.[165] The disease usually starts as a febrile episode with excruciating back pain—most often in the lower thoracic, lumbar, or lumbosacral spine. Percussion over the affected vertebral bodies usually elicits intense pain. Neurologic signs are absent but can supervene at any stage of the disease as the clinical expression of an epidural abscess. Neurologic signs mandate immediate MRI of the spinal canal and neurosurgical decompression if an epidural abscess is present. X-ray films of the spine are of little help at the onset of the disease, but they show narrowing of the intervertebral disk space after 10 to 20 days, with mottling of the two adjacent vertebral plateaus (Fig. 183–13). Anterior bridging occurs within several weeks of evolution under antibiotic therapy. Bone scanning with ^{99m}Tc-phosphonate is helpful in localizing the lesion. Defining the lesion is best done by CT and MRI.[166] Because radiology does not give any clue regarding the offending organism, direct needle aspiration is necessary.

Other rare clinical manifestations of hematogenous *S. aureus* osteomyelitis should be mentioned briefly. A young patient will occasionally seek consultation because of pain on walking without fever, and an x-ray film will show a well-delineated translucent area in the corresponding metaphysis (Fig. 183–14). Biopsy should be performed on such lesions to exclude various types of benign or malignant tumors, but the possibility of Brodie's abscess secondary to *S. aureus* should also be entertained. *S. aureus* osteomyelitis of the sternoclavicular area usually follows septic venous thrombosis of the upper extremity, often caused by an indwelling device.

The prognosis of adequately treated *S. aureus* hematogenous osteomyelitis is good; presently, cure rates are close to 90%. Rest should be prescribed for these patients, particularly in the case of vertebral osteomyelitis. A β-lactamase–resistant semisynthetic penicillin is the drug of choice, and it should be administered intravenously as described in the section on *S. aureus* septicemia. Therapeutic alternatives include vancomycin in allergic patients or if a methicillin-resistant organism has been isolated. Alternatives include a first- or second-generation cephalosporin or clindamycin. Antibiotic treatment should be continued for 4 weeks. Surgery is indicated in case of medullary or periosteal abscess formation, persistence of fever, presence of a sequestrum, or doubts about the offending organism. Vertebral osteomyelitis, because of the risk of paraplegia (10%) from epidural abscess formation, deserves special attention. These patients should have an MRI and be put on a regimen of strict bed rest.[165]

Short-term intravenous antibiotic therapy (i.e., 5 to 9 days of intravenous therapy) followed by 14 to 26 days of oral therapy has been shown to give an immediate cure rate of 95% in children whose infections were well documented bacteriologically and who responded promptly to initial therapy, had no complications, and were compliant.[167] Similar results have been reported for adults,[168] and such treatment is a valid alternative to long-term hospital treatment.

Osteomyelitis secondary to a contiguous focus of infection occurs most of the time as a complication of orthopedic surgery or trauma. In many cases, this form of osteomyelitis does not present major diagnostic problems because inspection of the operative site shows all signs of acute infection, including the early formation of a sinus tract. Isolation of *S. aureus* from the fistulous exudate most often reflects deep-seated infection caused by the same organism. In case of doubt or if multiple organisms have been isolated, culture of a deep bone biopsy specimen is indicated.

Osteomyelitis caused by *S. aureus* presents major diagnostic problems in deep-seated prosthetic infection after total hip or knee replacement. Such patients usually complain of increasing pain on ambulation. Physical examination findings are often normal, and x-ray film changes are compatible with both postsurgical bone remodeling and infection. In some cases, sequential ^{99m}Tc and ^{67}Ga bone scans allow the diagnosis of infection; gallium is concentrated in highly inflammatory lesions. In case of doubt, direct bone aspiration performed under strictly aseptic conditions will provide a solution to this diagnostic dilemma.

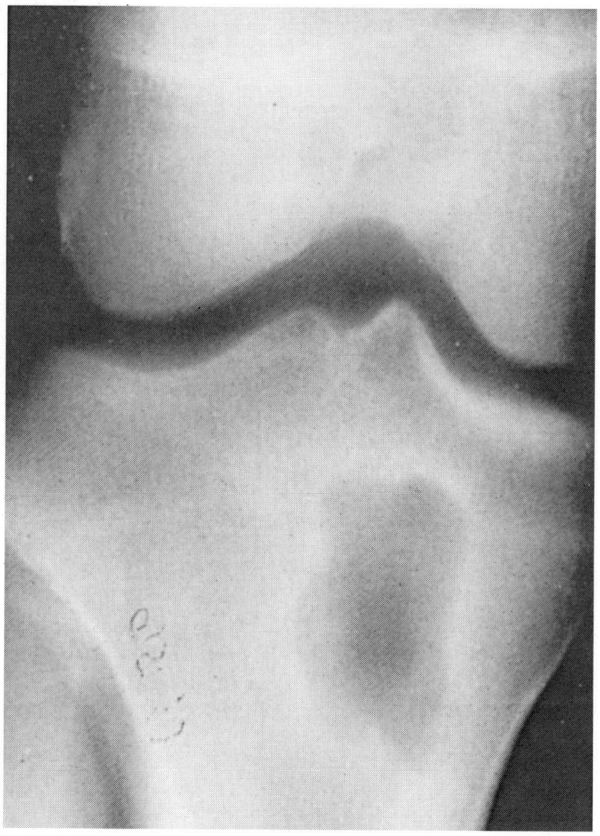

FIGURE 183–14. *Staphylococcus aureus* Brodie's abscess of tibia. Note the radiolucent irregularly shaped area, with no adjacent osteoblastic reaction.

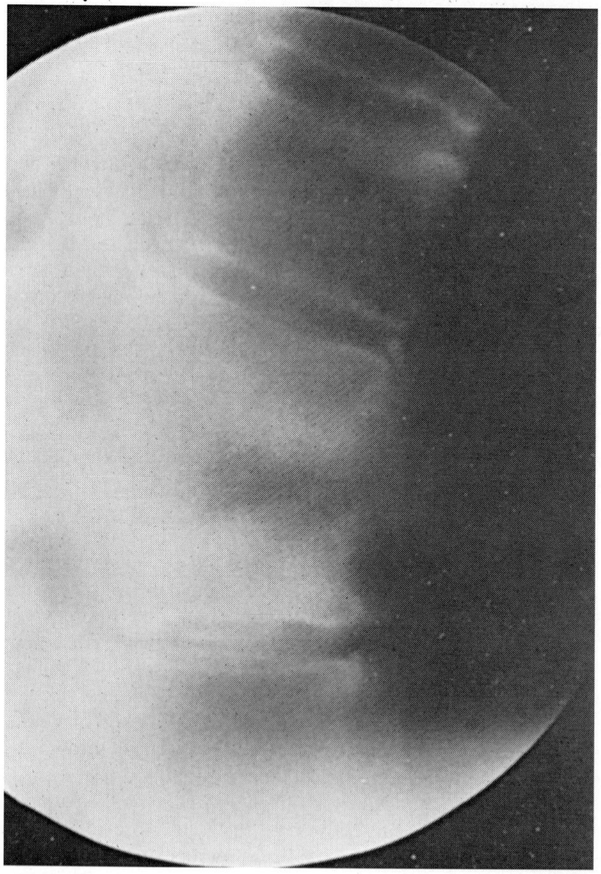

FIGURE 183–13. Tomogram of *Staphylococcus aureus* vertebral osteomyelitis. Note the narrowing of the intervertebral disk, the mottled adjacent cortical bone structures, and the bilateral involvement.

Antibiotic management of *S. aureus* osteomyelitis after surgery follows the recommendations established for hematogenous disease. In contrast with acute hematogenous infection, however, postsurgical or post-traumatic osteomyelitis always requires the collaboration of an orthopedic surgeon. If bone union is stable, orthopedic fixation devices should be kept in place. Removal of the fixation device after consolidation under antibiotic coverage will most often lead to bacteriologic cure. If bone union is unstable, all foreign material, including sequestra, should be removed at the site of infection and replaced, when possible, with an external fixation device. Infected hip or knee prostheses should be removed with excision of the adjacent infected tissue, and a new prosthesis should be inserted as either a one-step or two-step procedure.[169, 170]

Finally, symptomatic improvement can be achieved by oral therapy in patients suffering from chronic *S. aureus* postsurgical osteomyelitis if the use of intravenous antibiotics is contraindicated; long-term oral treatment with cloxacillin, 2 to 4 g/day for many months or years, will decrease the number of flare-ups of the disease.[171] Similarly, excellent results have been obtained in a few cases with a combination of rifampin and a quinolone.[172]

Septic Arthritis. *S. aureus* remains the main etiologic agent of septic arthritis in the prepubertal age group.[173] *S. aureus* septic arthritis also occurs occasionally as a complication of septicemia in adults and in patients with rheumatoid arthritis. Joint destruction occurs in a few days in association with a strong polyclonal B-cell response, as recently documented experimentally.[174] Therefore, a febrile patient with underlying arthritis who complains of acute pain in a single joint should have it aspirated immediately and its fluid examined for bacteriologic growth. Clinical examination shows a hot, swollen, and painful joint that is tender on palpation and mobilization. Susceptible joints in bacteremic *S. aureus* arthritis include, by order of frequency, the knee, hip, elbow, shoulder, and interphalangeal joints. The diagnosis is confirmed by joint aspiration, which yields a cloudy, sometimes purulent exudate that usually contains more than 50,000 granulocytes/mm^3 and gram-positive extracellular cocci on smear.[175]

The prognosis of *S. aureus* hematogenous septic arthritis in children is identical to that of osteomyelitis, that is, good. In adults, hematogenous septic arthritis has the prognosis of the underlying systemic infection (i.e., septicemia or endocarditis). After reconstructive surgery, the foreign material will most often preclude complete bacteriologic cure unless it is removed.[169, 170]

Medical management in all cases of septic arthritis requires the same antibiotic regimen as for hematogenous osteomyelitis. Repeated joint aspiration will alleviate pain, allow bacteriologic monitoring, and probably reduce joint damage. Open joint drainage is generally unnecessary except for hip infections in children, where it seems to prevent necrosis of the femoral head.[176]

Septic Bursitis. Septic bursitis is an acute infection involving the periarticular bursae, and it is most often located in pressure areas such as the olecranon and in the prepatellar area.[177] It is clinically manifested as an acute juxta-articular inflammation. As opposed to osteomyelitis and arthritis, the overlying skin is usually hot, bright red, and edematous, but the underlying joint can be moved freely. The portal of entry is probably local. Ninety percent of cases are due to *S. aureus,* and the bursal fluid usually contains more than 1000 granulocytes/mm^3. The prognosis is good if an antistaphylococcal antibiotic is given for 2 to 3 weeks and if the bursa is aspirated repeatedly. Surgical excision of the bursa, once the inflammation has subsided, is recommended in case of recurrence.

Pyomyositis. Pyomyositis is a purulent infection of skeletal muscles caused by *S. aureus* that is found in tropical climates[178] or among emigrants from tropical countries.[179] The disease starts with fever and muscle pain. The involved muscle is tender, swollen, and woody-hard. A history of blunt trauma to the muscle and an adjacent pyoderma is often elicited.[178] MRI shows inflamed, edematous muscle. The muscle, when aspirated, contains numerous *S. aureus* organisms and PMNs, which are readily seen on aspiration and drainage. Recently, the disease has been observed under nontropical conditions and associated with various comorbid conditions, usually human immunodeficiency virus infection.[180] Surgical incision and antistaphylococcal antibiotics are highly effective.

Staphylococcal Food Poisoning

Acute staphylococcal food poisoning occurs in epidemics. It results from the ingestion of heat-stable enterotoxin B or other enterotoxins, all preformed by a toxigenic strain of *S. aureus* growing in contaminated food.[181] The mechanisms by which the enterotoxin produces intestinal fluid loss and acts as a superantigen have been discussed earlier.

The disease is the second most commonly reported cause of acute food poisoning in the United States. It annually accounts for 20% of outbreaks caused by contaminated food. The epidemiology of staphylococcal food poisoning is characterized by person-to-person transmission. The responsible organism can usually be isolated from a person involved in preparation of the meal. Any food product promoting growth of *S. aureus* has been implicated as the inanimate vector, in particular, custard-filled bakery goods, canned food, processed meat, potato salad, and ice cream. The food has often been only partially cooked and put back into the refrigerator until used and is normal in its appearance, odor, and taste.[181]

Staphylococcal food poisoning starts abruptly as an outbreak with acute salivation, nausea, and vomiting; it is followed by abdominal cramps and diarrhea, which can be hemorrhagic. The disease most often affects all members of a group who have attended a common meal, and it has an incubation period of 2 to 6 hours, depending on the amount of toxin ingested.[182] Physical examination may show dehydration and hypotension commensurate with the fluid loss, but the patient is otherwise normal. In particular, no skin rash is present and the temperature is normal. Although deep prostration may be noted, neurologic findings are normal.

The diagnosis is often missed in individual cases, but it is suggested by community outbreaks of acute vomiting and diarrhea, a short incubation period, and an absence of fever and neurologic findings. Potentially contaminated food should be examined by Gram stain and culture and tested for the presence of enterotoxin B or other enterotoxins because partial cooking may have killed the organism.

The prognosis of staphylococcal food poisoning is good, and symptoms usually disappear in 8 hours. Management implies close monitoring of fluid and electrolyte losses and their replacement. Antibiotics are unnecessary. The disease can be prevented by excluding patients with staphylococcal skin infections from food handling, by rapid refrigeration of partially cooked food to temperatures below 4°C, and by rapid serving when kept at room temperature.

REFERENCES

1. Norse SI. Staphylococci. In: Davis BD, Dulbecco R, Eisen HN, et al, eds. Microbiology. Hagerstown, Md: Harper & Row; 1980:624.
2. Yu PKW, Washington JA II. Identification of aerobic and faculatively anaerobic bacteria. In: Washington JA, ed. Laboratory Procedures in Clinical Microbiology, 2nd ed. New York: Springer-Verlag; 1985:31–250.
3. Sabath LD. Mechanisms of resistance of beta-lactam antibiotics in strains of *Staphylococcus aureus.* Ann Intern Med. 1982;97:339.
4. Spink WW, Ferris V. Quantitative action of penicillin inhibitor from penicillin-resistant strains of staphylococci. Science. 1945;102:221.
5. Barber M. Methicillin-resistant staphylococci. J Clin Pathol. 1961;14:385.
6. Mulligan ME, Murray-Leisure KA, Ribner BS, et al. Methicillin-resistant *Staphylococcus aureus:* A consensus review of the microbiology, pathogenesis, and epidemiology with implications for prevention and management. Am J Med. 1993;94:313.
7. Archer GL, Penell E. Detection of methicillin resistance in staphylococci by using a DNA probe. Antimicrob Agents Chemother. 1990;34:1720–1724.
8. Geha DJ, Uhl JR, Gustaferro CA, et al. Multiplex PCR for identification of methicillin-resistant staphylococci in the clinical laboratory. J Clin Microbiol. 1994;32:1768–1772.
9. Peacock JE, Moorman DR, Wenzel RP, et al. Methicillin-resistant *Staphylococcus aureus:* Microbiologic characteristics, antimicrobial susceptibilities, and assessment of virulence of an epidemic strain. J Infect Dis. 1981;144:575.
10. Kinsman O, Naidoo J, Noble WC. Some effects of plasmids coding for antibiotic resistance on the virulence of *Staphylococcus aureus.* Pathology. 1985;66:325.
11. Vaudaux P, Waldvogel FA. Methicillin-resistant strains of *Staphylococcus aureus:* Relation between expression of resistance and phagocytosis by polymorphonuclear leukocytes. J Infect Dis. 1979;139:547.
12. Peacock JE, Moorman D, Wenzel RP, et al. Methicillin-resistant *S. aureus:* Microbiological characteristics, antimicrobial susceptibility, and assessment of virulence of an epidemiologic strain. J Infect Dis. 1981;144:575.
13. Berger-Bächi B. Expression of resistance to methicillin. Trends Microbiol. 1994;2:389–393.
14. Archer GL, Niemeyer DM. Origin and evolution of DNA associated with resistance to methicillin in staphylococci. Trends Microbiol. 1994;2:343–347.
15. Murakami K, Tomasz A. Involvement of multiple genetic determinants in high-level methicillin resistance in *Staphylococcus aureus.* J Bacteriol. 1989;171:874.
16. Shalit I, Berger SA, Gorea A, et al. Widespread quinolone resistance among methicillin-resistant *S. aureus* isolates in a general hospital. Antimicrob Agents Chemother. 1989;33:593.
17. Tomasz A. From penicillin-binding proteins to the lysis and death of bacteria: A 1979 view. Rev Infect Dis. 1979;1:434.
18. Rajashekaraiah KR, Rice T, Rao VS, et al. Clinical significance of tolerant strains of *Staphylococcus aureus* in patients with endocarditis. Ann Intern Med. 1980;93:796.
19. Goldman PL, Petersdorf RG. Significance of methicillin tolerance in experimental staphylococcal endocarditis. Antimicrob Agents Chemother. 1979;15:802.
20. Chuard C, Lucet JC, Rohner P, et al. Resistance of *Staphylococcus aureus* recovered from infected foreign body in vivo to killing by antimicrobials. J Infect Dis. 1991;163:1369.

21. Sierra-Madero JG, Knapp C, Karaffa C, et al. Role of beta-lactamase and different testing conditions in oxacillin-borderline-susceptible staphylococci. Antimicrob Agents Chemother. 1988;32:1754–1757.
22. Moorman DR, Mandell GL. Characteristics of rifampin-resistant variants obtained from clinical isolates of *Staphylococcus aureus*. Antimicrob Agents Chemother. 1981;20:709.
23. Kaatz GW, Seo SM, Ruble CA. Mechanisms of fluoroquinolone resistance in *Staphylococcus aureus*. J Infect Dis. 1991;163:1080.
24. Udo EE, Love H, Grubb WB. Intra- and interspecies mobilization of non-conjugative plasmids in staphylococci. J Med Microbiol. 1992;37:180.
25. Schaberg DR, Clewell DB, Glatzer L. Conjugative transfer of R-plasmids from *Streptococcus faecalis* to *Staphylococcus aureus*. Antimicrob Agents Chemother. 1982;22:204–207.
26. Cohen MI, Wong ES, Falkow S. Common R-plasmids in *Staphylococcus aureus* and *Staphylococcus epidermidis* during a nosocomial *Staphylococcus aureus* outbreak. Antimicrob Agents Chemother. 1982;21:210–215.
27. Hiramatsu K, Hanaki H, Ino T, et al. Methicillin-resistant *Staphylococcus aureus* clinical strain with reduced vancomycin susceptibility. J Antimicrob Chemother. 1997;40:135.
28. Maranan MC, Moreira B, Boyle-Vavra S, et al. Antimicrobial resistance in staphylococci: Epidemiology, molecular mechanisms and clinical relevance. Infect Dis Clin North Am. 1997;11:813–849.
29. Edmond MB, Wenzel RP, Pasculle AW. Vancomycin-resistant *Staphylococcus aureus:* Perspectives on measures needed for control. Ann Intern Med. 1996;124:329–334.
30. Kluytmans J, Van Belkum A, Verbrugh H. Nasal carriage of *Staphylococcus aureus:* Epidemiology, underlying mechanisms, and associated risks. Clin Microbiol Rev. 1997;10:505–520.
31. Martin RR, Buttram V, Bosch P, et al. Nasal and vaginal *Staphylococcus aureus* in young women: Quantitative studies. Ann Intern Med. 1982;96:951.
32. Rimland D, Roberson B. Gastrointestinal carriage of methicillin-resistant *Staphylococcus aureus*. J Clin Microbiol. 1986;24:137.
33. Godfrey ME, Smith IM. Hospital hazards of staphylococcal sepsis. JAMA. 1958;166:1197.
34. Tuazon CU, Perez A, Kishaba T, et al. *Staphylococcus aureus* among insulin-injecting diabetic patients. An increased carriage rate. JAMA. 1975;231:1272.
35. Kirmani N, Tuazon CU, Murray HW, et al. *Staphylococcus aureus* carriage rate of patients receiving long-term hemodialysis. Arch Intern Med. 1978;138:1657.
36. Tuazon CU, Sheagren JN. Increased rate of carriage of *Staphylococcus aureus* among narcotic addicts. J Infect Dis. 1974;129:725.
37. Haley RW, Hightower AW, Khabbaz RF, et al. Emergence of methicillin-resistant *Staphylococcus aureus* infections in United States hospitals. Ann Intern Med. 1982;97:297.
38. Muder RR, Brennen C, Wagener MM, et al. Methicillin-resistant staphylococcal colonization and infection in a long-term care facility. Ann Intern Med. 1991;114:107.
39. Hill RLR, Duckworth GJ, Casewell MW. Elimination of nasal carriage of methicillin-resistant *Staphylococcus aureus* with mupirocin during a hospital outbreak. J Antimicrob Chemother. 1988;22:377.
40. Kauffman CA, Terpenning MS, Xiaogong HE, et al. Attempts to eradicate methicillin-resistant *Staphylococcus aureus* from a long-term care facility with the use of mupirocin ointment. Am J Med. 1993;94:371.
41. Rode H, Hanslo D, deWet PM, et al. Efficacy of mupirocin in methicillin-resistant *Staphylococcus aureus* burn wound infection. Antimicrob Agents Chemother. 1989;33:1358.
42. Doebbelin BN, Breneman DL, Neu HC, et al. Elimination of *Staphylococcus aureus* nasal carriage in health care workers: Analysis of six clinical trials with calcium mupirocin ointment. Clin Infect Dis. 1993;17:466–474.
43. Hudson LRB. The efficacy of intranasal mupirocin in the prevention of staphylococcal infections: A review of recent experience. J Hosp Infect. 1994;27:81–98.
44. Yu VL, Goetz A, Wagener M, et al. *Staphylococcus aureus* nasal carriage and infections in patients on hemodialysis. Efficacy of antibiotic prophylaxis. N Engl J Med. 1986;2:91–96.
45. Schleifer KH, Kandler O. Peptidoglycan types of bacterial cell walls and their taxonomic implications. Bacteriol Rev. 1972;36:407.
46. Kaplan MH, Tenebaum MJ. *Staphylococcus aureus:* Cellular biology and clinical application. Am J Med. 1982;72:248.
47. Knox KW, Wicken AJ. Immunological properties of teichoic acids. Bacteriol Rev. 1973;37:215.
48. Hawiger J, Timmons S, Strong DD, et al. Identification of a region of human fibrinogen interacting with staphylococcal clumping factor. Biochemistry. 1982;21:1407.
49. Projan SJ, Novick RP. The molecular basis of pathogenicity. In: Crossley KB, Archer GL, eds. The Staphylococci in Human Disease. New York: Churchill Livingstone; 1997:56–81.
50. Forsgren A, Sjogulst J. "Protein A" from *Staphylococcus aureus* I. Pseudo immune reaction with human globulin. J Immunol. 1966;97:822.
51. Wilkinson BJ. Staphylococcal capsules and slime. In: Easmon CSF, ed. Staphylococci and Staphylococcal Disease. New York: Academic; 1983.
52. Arbeit RD, Dunn RM. Expression of capsular polysaccharide during experimental focal infection with *Staphylococcus aureus*. J Infect Dis. 1987;156:947.
53. Mandell GL. Catalase, superoxide dismutase, and virulence of *Staphylococcus aureus*. In vitro and in vivo studies with emphasis on staphylococcal-leukocyte interaction. J Clin Invest. 1975;55:561.
54. Kawabata S, Morita T, Iwanaga S, et al. Enzymatic properties of staphylothrombin, an active molecular complex formed between staphylocoagulase and human prothrombin. J Biochem. 1985;98:1603.
55. Hawiger J, Timmons S, Strong DD, et al. Identification of a region of human fibrinogen interacting with staphylococcal clumping factor. Biochemistry. 1982;21:1407.
56. McDevitt D, Vaudaux P, Foster TJ. Genetic evidence that bound coagulase of *Staphylococcus aureus* is not clumping factor. Infect Immun. 1992;60:1514.
57. Hooper DC. Oral antibiotic therapy. In: Crossley KB, Archer GL, eds. The Staphylococci in Human Disease. New York: Churchill Livingstone; 1997:603–630.
58. Bohach GA, Dinges MM, Mitchell DT, et al. Exotoxins. In: Crossley KB, Archer GB, eds. The *Staphylococci* in Human Disease. New York: Churchill Livingstone; 1997:83–111.
59. Melish ME, Glasgow LA. The staphylococcal scalded skin syndrome: Development of an experimental model. N Engl J Med. 1970;282:1114.
60. Takagi Y, Futamura S, Asada Y. Action site of exfoliative toxin on keratinocytes. J Invest Dermatol. 1990;94:52.
61. Marrack P, Kappler J. The staphylococcal enterotoxins and their relatives. Science. 1990;248:705.
62. Schlievert PM, Shands KN, Dan BB, et al. Identification and characterization of an exotoxin from *Staphylococcus aureus* associated with toxic-shock syndrome. J Infect Dis. 1981;143:509.
63. Bergdoll MS, Crass B, Reiser RF, et al. A new staphylococcal enterotoxin, enterotoxin F, associated with toxic-shock syndrome. *Staphylococcus aureus* isolates. Lancet. 1981;1:1017.
64. Garbe PL, Arka RJ, Reingold AL, et al. *Staphylococcus aureus* isolates from patients with nonmenstrual toxic shock syndrome. JAMA. 1985;253:2538–2542.
65. Parsonnet J, Gillis ZA, Pier GB. Induction of interleukin-1 by strains of *Staphylococcus aureus* from patients with nonmenstrual toxic shock syndrome. J Infect Dis. 1986;154:55–63.
66. Cone LA, Woodward DR, Schlievert PM, et al. Clinical and bacteriologic observations of a toxic shock–like syndrome due to *Streptococcus pyogenes*. N Engl J Med. 1987;317:146–149.
67. Kahler RC, Boyce JM, Bergdoll MS, et al. Case report: Toxic shock syndrome associated with TSST-1 producing coagulase-negative staphylococci. Am J Med Sci. 1986;292:310–312.
68. Marrack P, Kappler J. The staphylococcal enterotoxins and their relatives. Science. 1990;248:705.
69. Johnson HM, Russell JK, Pontzer CH. Staphylococcal enterotoxin superantigens (43321A). Proc Soc Exp Biol Med. 1991;198:765.
70. Kim J, Urban RG, Strominger JL, et al. Toxic shock syndrome toxin-1 complexed with a class II major histocompatibility molecule HLA-DR1. Science. 1994;266:1870–1874.
71. Saha B, Jaklic B, Harlan DM, et al. Toxic shock syndrome toxin-1–induced death is prevented by CTLA4lg. J Immunol. 1996;157:3869–3875.
72. Zumla A. Superantigens, T cells, and microbes. Clin Infect Dis. 1992;15:313.
73. Parsonnet J. Mediators in the pathogenesis of toxic shock syndrome: Overview. Rev Infect Dis. 1989;11(Suppl 1):S263.
74. Krakauer T. Detection of adhesion of superantigen-activated T lymphocytes to human endothelial cells by ELISA. J Immunoassay. 1996;17:1–12.
75. Davison VE, Sanford BA. Factors influencing adherence of *Staphylococcus aureus* to influenza A virus–infected cell cultures. Infect Immunol. 1982;37:946.
76. Fainstein V, Musber DM, Cate TR. Bacterial adherence to pharyngeal cells during viral infection. J Infect Dis. 1980;141:172.
77. Shuter J, Hatcher VB, Lowy FD. *Staphylococcus aureus* binding to human nasal mucin. Infect Immun. 1996;64:310–318.
78. Kuusela P. Fibronectin binds to *Staphylococcus aureus*. Nature. 1978;276:718.
79. Lopes JD, Dos Reis M, Brentani RR. Presence of laminin receptors in *Staphylococcus aureus*. Science. 1985;229:275–277.
80. Hermann M, Suchard SJ, Boxer LA, et al. Thrombospondin binds to *Staphylococcus aureus* and promotes staphylococcal adherence to surfaces. Infect Immun. 1991;59:279.
81. Chhatwal GS, Preissner G, Muller B, et al. Specific binding of the human S protein (vitronectin) to streptococci, *Staphylococcus aureus,* and *Escherichia coli.* Infect Immun. 1987;55:1878–1883.
82. Park PW, Roberts DD, Grosso LE, et al. Binding of elastin to *Staphylococcus aureus*. J Biol Chem. 1991;266:23399–23406.
83. Ryden C, Yacoub AI, Maxe I, et al. Specific binding of bone sialoprotein to *Staphylococcus aureus* isolated from patients with osteomyelitis. Eur J Biochem. 1989;184:331–336.
84. Jonsson K, Signäs C. Muller HP, et al. Two different genes encode fibronectin binding proteins in *Staphylococcus aureus*. The complete nucleotide sequence and characterization of the second gene. Eur J Biochem. 1991;202:1041–1048.
85. McDevitt D, François P, Vaudaux P, et al. Molecular characterization of the clumping factor (fibrinogen receptor) of *Staphylococcus aureus*. Mol Microbiol. 1994;11:237–248.
86. Patti JM, Jonsson H, Guss B, et al. Molecular characterization and expression of a gene encoding *Staphylococcus aureus* collagen adhesin. J Biol Chem. 1992;267:4766–4772.
87. Park PW, Rosenbloom J, Abrams WR, et al. Molecular cloning and expression of the gene for elastin-binding protein (ebpS) in *Staphylococcus aureus*. J Biol Chem. 1996;271:15803–15809.
88. Cheung AL, Krishnan M, Jaffe EA, et al. Fibrinogen acts as a bridging molecule in the adherence of *Staphylococcus aureus* to cultured human endothelial cells. J Clin Invest. 1991;87:2236–2245.

89. Hamill RJ, Vann JM, Proctor RA. Phagocytosis of *Staphylococcus aureus* by cultured bovine aortic endothelial cells: Model for postadherence events in endovascular infections. Infect Immun. 1986;54:833–836.
90. Drake TA, Pang M. *Staphylococcus aureus* induces tissue factor expression in cultured human cardiac valve endothelium. J Infect Dis. 1988;157:749–756.
91. Wilkinson PC. Leukocyte locomotion and chemotaxis: Effects of bacteria and viruses. Rev Infect Dis. 1980;2:293.
92. Verhoef J, Verbrugh HA. Host determinants in staphylococcal disease. In: Creger WP, Coggins CH, Hancock EW, eds. Annual Review of Medicine. Palo Alto, Calif: Annual Reviews; 1981:107–122.
93. Peterson PK, Wilkinson BJ, Kim Y, et al. The key role of peptidoglycan in the opsonization of *Staphylococcus aureus*. J Clin Invest. 1978;61:597.
94. Verbrugh HA, Van Dijk WC, Peters P, et al. Opsonic recognition of staphylococci mediated by cell wall peptidoglycan: Antibody-independent activation of human complement and opsonic activity of peptidoglycan antibodies. J Immunol. 1980;124:1167.
95. Schliefer KH, Kandler O. Peptidoglycan types of bacterial cell walls and their taxonomic implications. Bacteriol Rev. 1972;36:407.
96. Melly MA, Thomison JB, Rogers DB. Fate of staphylococci within human leukocytes. J Exp Med. 1960;112:1121.
97. Quie PG, Hill HR, Davis AT. Defective phagocytosis of staphylococci. Ann N Y Acad Sci. 1974;236:233.
98. Schöpfer K, Douglas SD, Wilkinson BJ. Immunoglobulin E antibodies against *Staphylococcus aureus* cell walls in the sera of patients with hyperimmunoglobulinemia E and recurrent staphylococcal infections. Infect Immunol. 1980;27:563.
99. Clark RA. Disorders of granulocyte chemotaxis. In: Gallin JI, Quio PG, eds. Leukocyte Chemotaxis: Methods, Physiology and Clinical Complication. New York: Raven; 1978:329.
100. Steckelberg JM, Osmon DR. Prosthetic joint infections. In: Bisno AL, Waldvogel FA, eds. Infections associated with indwelling medical devices. 2nd ed. Washington, DC: American Society for Microbiology; 1994:259–290.
101. Elek SD, Conen PE. The virulence of *Staphylococcus pyogenes* for man. A study of the problems of wound infection. Br J Exp Pathol. 1957;38:573.
102. Peters G, Locci R, Pulverer G. Adherence and growth of coagulase-negative staphylococci on surfaces of intravenous catheters. J Infect Dis. 1982;146:479.
103. Christensen GD, Simpson WA, Bisno AL et al. Adherence of slime-producing strains of *Staphylococcus epidermidis* to smooth surfaces. Infect Immun. 1982;37:318–326.
104. Muller E, Takeda S, Shiro H, et al. Occurrence of capsular polysaccharide/adhesin among clinical isolates of coagulase-negative staphylococci. J Infect Dis. 1993;168:1211–1218.
105. Mack D, Fischer W, Krokotsch A, et al. The intercellular adhesin involved in biofilm accumulation of *Staphylococcus epidermidis* is a linear β-1, 6–linked glucosaminoglycan: Purification and structural analysis. J Bacteriol. 1996;178:175–183.
106. Zimmerli W, Waldvogel FA, Vaudaux P, et al. Pathogenesis of foreign body infection: Description and characteristics of an animal model. J Infect Dis. 1982;146:487.
107. Zimmerli W, Lew PD, Waldvogel FA. Pathogenesis of foreign body infection. Evidence for a local granulocyte defect. J Clin Invest. 1984;73:1191–1200.
108. Bisno AL, Waldvogel FA, eds. Infections Associated with Indwelling Medical Devices. 2nd ed. Washington, DC: American Society for Microbiology; 1994:1–398.
109. Swartz MN, Weinberg AN. Infections due to gram-positive bacteria. In: Fitzpatrick TB, Arndt KA, Clark WH, et al, eds. Dermatology in General Medicine. 3rd ed. New York: McGraw-Hill; 1987:2100–2121.
110. Novy MJ. The puerperium. In: Benson RC, ed. Current Obstetric and Gynecologic Diagnosis and Treatment. Los Altos, Calif: Lange; 1980:781.
111. Nichols RL. Prophylaxis for surgical infections. In: Gorbach SL, Bartlett JG, Blacklow NR, eds. Infectious Diseases. 2nd ed. Philadelphia: WB Saunders; 1998:470–480.
112. Lyell A. Toxic epidermal necrolysis: An eruption resembling scalding of the skin. Br J Dermatol. 1956;68:355.
113. Lang R, Walker J. An unusual bullous eruption. S Afr Med J. 1956;30:97.
114. Elias PM, Fritsch P, Epstein EE Jr. Staphylococcal scalded skin syndrome. Arch Dermatol. 1977;113:207.
115. Parker MT, Tomlinson AJH, Williams REO. Impetigo contagiosa. The association of certain types of *Staphylococcus aureus* and *Staphylococcus pyogenes* in superficial skin infections. J Hyg Camb. 1955;53:458.
116. Todd J, Fishaut M. Toxic-shock syndrome associated with phage-group-1 staphylococci. Lancet. 1978;2:1116.
117. Davis JP, Chesney PJ, Wand PJ, et al. Toxic-shock syndrome. N Engl J Med. 1980;303:1429.
118. Kass EH, Parsonnet J. On the pathogenesis of toxic shock syndrome. Rev Infect Dis. 1987;9(Suppl):S482–S489.
119. Osterholm MT, Davis JP, Gibson RW, et al. Tri-state toxic-shock syndrome study. I. Epidemiologic findings. J Infect Dis. 1982;145:431.
120. Davis JP, Osterholm MT, Helms CM, et al. Tri-state toxic-shock syndrome study. II. Clinical and laboratory findings. J Infect Dis. 1982;145:441.
121. Reingold AL, Hargrett N, Dan BB, et al. Nonmenstrual toxic shock syndrome. Anns Intern Med. 1982;96:871.
122. Reingold AL, Hargrett NT, Dan BB, et al. Nonmenstrual toxic shock syndrome. A review of 130 cases. Ann Intern Med. 1982;96:871–874.
123. Kain KC, Schulzer M, Chow AW. Clinical spectrum of nonmenstrual toxic shock syndrome (TSS): Comparison with menstrual TSS by multivariate discriminant analyses. Clin Infect Dis. 1993;16:100.
124. Garbe PL, Arko RJ, Reingold AL, et al. *Staphylococcus aureus* isolates from patients with nonmenstrual toxic shock syndrome. JAMA. 1985;253:2538.
125. Paris AL, Herwaldt LA, Blum D, et al. Pathologic findings in twelve fatal cases of toxic shock syndrome. Ann Intern Med. 1982;96:852.
126. Rosene KA, Copass MK, Kastner LS, et al. Persistent neuropsychological sequelae of toxic shock syndrome. Ann Intern Med. 1982;96:865.
127. Cone LA, Woodard DR, Byrd RG, et al. A recalcitrant erythematous, desquamating disorder associated with toxin-producing staphylococci in patients with AIDS. J Infect Dis. 1992;165:638–643.
128. Schlievert PM. Comparison of cotton and cotton/rayon tampons for effect on production of toxic shock syndrome toxin. J Infect Dis. 1995;172:1112–1114.
129. Jessen Q, Rosendal K, Búlow P, et al. Changing staphylococci and staphylococcal infections. A ten-year study of bacteria and cases of bacteremia. N Engl J Med. 1969;281:627.
130. Skinner D, Keefer CS. Significance of bacteremia caused by *Staphylococcus aureus*. A study of one hundred and twenty two cases and a review of the literature concerned with experimental infection in animals. Arch Intern Med. 1941;68:851.
131. Willcox PA, Rayner BL, Whitelaw DA. Community-acquired *Staphylococcus aureus* bacteremia in patients who do not abuse intravenous drugs. Q J Med. 1998;91:41–47.
132. Conterno LO, Wey SB, Castelo A. Risk factors for mortality in *Staphylococcus aureus* bacteremia. Infect Control Hosp Epidemiol. 1998;19:32–37.
133. Steinberg JP, Clark CC, Hackman BO. Nosocomial and community-acquired *Staphylococcus aureus* bacteremias from 1980 to 1993: Impact of intravascular devices and methicillin resistance. Clin Infect Dis. 1996;23:255–259.
134. Musher DM, McKenzie SO. Infections due to *Staphylococcus aureus*. Medicine (Baltimore). 1977;56:383.
135. Gutman RA, Striker GE, Gillilard BC, et al. The immune complex glomerulonephritis of bacterial endocarditis. Medicine (Baltimore). 1972;51:1.
136. Levy RL, Hong R. The immune nature of subacute bacterial endocarditis (SBE) nephritis. Am J Med. 1973;54:645.
137. Tu WH, Shearn MA, Lee JC. Acute diffuse glomerulonephritis in acute staphylococcal endocarditis. Ann Intern Med. 1969;71:335.
138. Nolan CM, Beaty HN. *Staphylococcus aureus* bacteremia. Current clinical patterns. Am J Med. 1976;60:495.
139. Iannini PB, Grossley K. Therapy of *Staphylococcus aureus* bacteremia associated with a removable focus of infection. Ann Intern Med. 1976;84:558.
140. Di Nubile MJ. Short-course antibiotic therapy for right-sided endocarditis caused by *Staphylococcus aureus* in injection drug users. Ann Intern Med. 1994;121:873–876.
141. Jernigan JA, Farr BM. Short-course therapy of catheter-related *Staphylococcus aureus* bacteremia: A meta-analysis. Ann Intern Med. 1993;119:304–311.
142. Bayer AS, Theofilopoulos AN, Tillman DB, et al. Use of circulating immune complex levels in the serodifferentiation of endocarditic and nonendocarditic septicemias. Am J Med. 1979;66:58.
143. Verbrugh HA, Peters R, Rozenbert-Arska M, et al. Antibodies to cell wall peptidoglycan of *Staphylococcus aureus* in patients with serious staphylococcal infections. J Infect Dis. 1981;144:1.
144. Wheat LJ, Wilkinson BJ, Kohler RB, et al. Antibody response to peptidoglycan during staphylococcal infections. J Infect Dis. 1983;147:16.
145. Wheat LJ, Luft FC, Tabbarah Z, et al. Serologic diagnosis of access device–related staphylococcal bacteremia. Am J Med. 1979;67:603.
146. Tuazon CU, Sheagren JN, Choa MS, et al. *Staphylococcus aureus* bacteremia: Relationship between formation of antibodies to teichoic acid and development of metastatic abscesses. J Infect Dis. 1978;137:57.
147. Wheat LJ, Kohler RB, White A. Solid-phase radioimmunoassay for immunoglobulin G *Staphylococcus aureus* antibody in serious staphylococcal infection. Ann Intern Med. 1978;89:467.
148. Sheagren JN. *Staphylococcus aureus:* The persistent pathogen. N Engl J Med. 1984;310:1437–1442.
149. Sande MA, Scheld WM. Combination antibiotic therapy of bacterial endocarditis. Ann Intern Med. 1980;92:390.
150. Frimodt-Moller N, Espersen F, Rosdahl VT. Antibiotic treatment of *Staphylococcus aureus* endocarditis. A review of 119 cases. Acta Med Scand. 1987;222:175–182.
151. Frazee BW, Flaherty JP. Septic endarteritis of the femoral artery following angioplasty. Rev Infect Dis. 1991;13:620.
152. Lerche A, Rasmussen N, Wandall JH, et al. *Staphylococcus aureus* meningitis: A review of 28 consecutive community-acquired cases. Scand J Infect Dis. 1995;27:569–573.
153. Klacsmann PG, Bulkley BH, Hutchins GM. The changed spectrum of purulent pericarditis. An 86 year autopsy experience in 200 patients. Am J Med. 1977;63:666.
154. Rubin RH, Moellering RC Jr. Clinical, microbiologic and therapeutic aspects of purulent pericarditis. Am J Med. 1975;59:68.
155. Rebhan AW, Edwards HE. Staphylococcal pneumonia: A review of 329 cases. Can Med Assoc J. 1960;82:513.
156. Lindsay MI Jr, Herrmann EC Jr, Morrow GW Jr, et al. Hong Kong influenza: Clinical, microbiologic, and pathologic features in 127 cases. JAMA. 1970;214:1825.
157. Dicpinigaitis PV, Levy DE, Gnass RD, et al. Pneumonia due to *Staphylococcus aureus* in a patient with AIDS: Review of incidence and report of an atypical roentgenographic presentation. South Med J. 1995;88:586–590.

158. Tuazon CU, Cardella TA, Sheagren JN. Staphylococcal endocarditis in drug users. Clinical and microbiologic aspects. Arch Intern Med. 1975;135:1555.
159. Cross AS, Steigbigel RT. Infective endocarditis and access site infections in patients on hemodialysis. Medicine (Baltimore). 1976;55:453.
160. Maki DG, Goldman DA, Rhame FS. Infection control in intravenous therapy. Ann Intern Med. 1973;79:867.
161. Bryant RE, Salmon CJ. Pleural empyema. Clin Infect Dis. 1996;22:747–762.
162. Varkey B, Rose HD, Kutty PK, et al. Empyema thoracis during a ten-year period. Analysis of 72 cases and comparison to a previous study (1952 to 1967). Arch Intern Med. 1981;141:1771.
163. Waldvogel FA, Medoff G, Swartz MN. Osteomyelitis: A review of clinical features, therapeutic considerations and unusual aspects. I. Hematogenous osteomyelitis. II. Osteomyelitis secondary to a contiguous infection and secondary to vascular insufficiency. III. Unusual organisms and unusual locations. N Engl J Med. 1970;282:198, 260, 316.
164. Dich VQ, Nelson JD, Haltalin DC. Osteomyelitis in infants and children: A review of 163 cases. Am J Dis Child. 1975;129:1273.
165. Waldvogel FA, Vasey H. Osteomyelitis: The past decade. N Engl J Med. 1980;303:360.
166. Smith FW, Runge V, Permezel M, et al. Nuclear magnetic resonance (NMR) imaging in the diagnosis of spinal osteomyelitis. Magn Reson Imaging. 1984;2:53.
167. Tetzlaff TR, McCracken GH, Nelson JD. Oral antibiotic therapy for skeletal infections of children. J Pediatr. 1978;92:485.
168. Black J, Hunt TL, Godley PJ, et al. Oral antimicrobial therapy for adults with osteomyelitis or septic arthritis. J Infect Dis. 1987;155:968–972.
169. Schmalzried TP, Amstutz HC, Au MK, et al. Etiology of deep sepsis in total hip arthroplasty. Clin Orthop. 1992;280:200.
170. Ivey FM, Hicks CA, Calhoun JH, et al. Treatment options for infected knee arthroplasties. Rev Infect Dis. 1990;12:468.
171. Bell SM. Further observations on the value of oral penicillins in chronic staphylococcal osteomyelitis. Med J Aust. 1976;2:591.
172. Drancourt M, Stein A, Argenson JN, et al. Oral rifampin plus ofloxacin for treatment of *Staphylococcus*-infected orthopedic implants. Antimicrob Agents Chemother. 1993;37:1214.
173. Goldenberg DL, Cohen AS. Acute infectious arthritis. A review of patients with nongonococcal joint infections (with emphasis on therapy and prognosis). Am J Med. 1976;60:369.
174. Bremell T, Abdelnour A, Tarkowski A. Histopathological and serological progression of experimental *Staphylococcus aureus* arthritis. Infect Immun. 1992;60:2976.
175. Krey PR, Bailen DA. Synovial fluid leukocytosis. A study of extremes. Am J Med. 1979;67:436.
176. Waldvogel FA. Treatment of osteomyelitis and septic arthritis. Bull N Y Acad Med. 1982;58:733.
177. Ho G, Tice AD, Kaplan SR. Septic bursitis in the prepatellar and olecranon bursae. An analysis of 25 cases. Ann Intern Med. 1978;89:21.
178. Brown JD, Wheeler B. Pyomyositis. Report of 18 cases in Hawaii. Arch Intern Med. 1984;144:1749–1751.
179. Levin MJ, Gardner P, Waldvogel FA. Tropical pyomyositis: An unusual infection due to *Staphylococcus aureus*. N Engl J Med. 1971;284:196–198.
180. Patel SR, Olenginski TP, Perruqet JL, et al. Pyomyositis: Clinical features and predisposing conditions. J Rheumatol. 1997;24:1734–1738.
181. Breckinridge JC, Bergdoll MS. Outbreak of foodborne gastroenteritis due to a coagulase-negative enterotoxin-producing staphylococcus. N Engl J Med. 1971;284:541.
182. Effersoe P, Kjerulf K. Clinical aspects of outbreak of staphylococcal food poisoning during air travel. Lancet. 1975;2:595.

Chapter 184

Staphylococcus epidermidis and Other Coagulase-Negative Staphylococci

GORDON L. ARCHER

Staphylococcus epidermidis and other coagulase-negative staphylococci, often previously dismissed as culture contaminants, are assuming greater importance as true pathogens (Table 184–1). Infections caused by these organisms involve indwelling foreign bodies and are increasing as the number of catheters and artificial devices inserted through the skin becomes larger. These infections are characterized by their indolence but may necessitate the removal of the catheter or device. Resistance of infecting isolates to multiple antibiotics may further complicate therapy. The importance of coagulase-negative staphylococci as nosocomial pathogens has prompted more interest in their detailed characterization. A working knowledge of the biology and antimicrobial susceptibility of these organisms may be necessary to distinguish infecting from contaminating isolates and to devise appropriate therapy.

TABLE 184–1 Well-Documented Infections Caused by *Staphylococcus epidermidis* and Other Coagulase-Negative Staphylococci

Urinary tract infections
Hospital acquired (*S. epidermidis*)
Outpatient women (*S. saprophyticus*)
Osteomyelitis
Sternal wound
Hematogenous
Native valve endocarditis
Bacteremia in immunosuppressed patients
Endophthalmitis after ocular surgery
Infections of indwelling foreign devices
Intravenous catheters
Hemodialysis shunts and grafts
Cerebrospinal fluid shunts
Peritoneal dialysis catheters
Pacemaker wires and electrodes
Prosthetic joints
Vascular grafts
Prosthetic cardiac valves
Breast implants
Penile prostheses

MICROBIOLOGY

Identification

All staphylococci are members of the family Micrococcaceae. They are gram-positive cocci that produce catalase and divide in irregular clusters to produce packets of cells. In the clinical microbiology laboratory, staphylococci are differentiated primarily by their capacity to produce or not produce an enzyme (coagulase) that congeals rabbit plasma. Coagulase-positive staphylococci also ferment mannitol, contain an immunoglobin G (IgG)-binding protein (protein A) in their cell walls, and produce a cell-associated protein (clumping factor) that binds fibrinogen, characteristics not shared by most coagulase-negative staphylococci. Agglutination of latex beads coated with IgG, fibrinogen, and capsule-specific antibody is used by clinical microbiology laboratories as an alternative to coagulase testing in differentiating coagulase-positive from negative staphylococci. However, although human coagulase-positive staphylococci compose a fairly uniform species (*Staphylococcus aureus*), human coagulase-negative staphylococci have been subdivided into 32 species, 15 of which are indigenous to humans.[1, 2] The relatedness of all staphylococci at the genus level has been confirmed by their similar DNA content of guanine plus cytosine; their divergence into separate species has been ascertained by the examination of specific DNA sequence homology. Using restrictive criteria for DNA–DNA hybridization studies, groups of staphylococci with less than 50% DNA homology have been designated as separate species. Certain species are more related to one another than others and form species groups. The current species grouping of coagulase-negative staphylococci relevant to humans is shown in Table 184–2.

Kloos and Schleifer devised a scheme by which coagulase-negative staphylococci could be easily differentiated into species by using biochemical characteristics.[3] Biochemical characterization was further simplified by the marketing of miniaturized kits that facilitated the rapid identification of staphylococci.[4] The value of routine speciation of all staphylococci from clinical specimens is unclear, however. Speciation would be of potential clinical value if it could be used for biotyping or if there were clear associations of certain species with specific infections or antibiotic-susceptibility patterns.

TABLE 184-2 Human Coagulase-Negative Staphylococcal Species Groups

*S. epidermidis**	*S. saprophyticus**	*S. simulans*	*S. auricularis*	*S. lugdunensis*	*S. schleiferi*
S. capitis	*S. xylosus*				
S. warneri	*S. cohnii*				
S. haemolyticus					
S. hominis					
S. saccharolyticus†					
S. caprae					
S. pasteuri					

*Species shown to be consistently pathogenic for humans.
†Formerly *Peptococcus saccharolyticus;* strict anaerobe.

S. epidermidis and *Staphylococcus saprophyticus* have been identified as being consistently pathogenic for humans. In addition, some data suggest that of the remaining coagulase-negative staphylococcal species, *S. haemolyticus*, *S. lugdunensis*, and *S. schleiferi* are more likely to cause infections than others.[5–7]

Ecology

Coagulase-negative staphylococci are resident bacteria, indigenous to mammalian hosts, and are natural inhabitants of human skin.[1, 2] *S. epidermidis* is the most prevalent and persistent species on human glabrous skin and mucous membranes, constituting from 65 to 90% of all staphylococci recovered; *Staphylococcus hominis* is the next most frequent species recovered. *Staphylococcus saccharolyticus* (formerly *Peptococcus saccharolyticus*) is the only strictly anaerobic staphylococcus constituting resident skin flora; its prevalence has not yet been evaluated. Other Staphylococcal species are either less frequent members of the resident population (*S. haemolyticus, S. warneri*), found only transiently on skin (*S. xylosus, S. simulans, S. lugdunensis, S. cohnii*), or found only in specific niches (*S. capitis* [head], *S. auricularis* [ear canal], *S. saprophyticus* [genitourinary skin]). The type and location of coagulase-negative species can be altered by antibiotic therapy[8] and the presence on mucous membranes of competing *S. aureus*.[1, 2]

Genetics and Virulence Factors

Plasmid DNA is abundant in all species of coagulase-negative staphylococci,[9] but only a few of the plasma-encoded genes have been identified. Resistances to such antibiotics as penicillin, macrolides, lincosamides, tetracyclines, chloramphenicol, trimethoprim, and aminoglycosides have all been associated with specific plasmids; plasmid-mediated resistance has been confirmed by the transfer of these plasmids to suitable plasmid-free recipients. Of considerable epidemiologic significance is the demonstration that certain aminoglycoside-resistance plasmids found in *S. epidermidis* can be transferred by conjugation to other *S. epidermidis* and to *S. aureus* organisms.[10–12] These conjugative plasmids also encode resistance to penicillin, trimethoprim, mupirocin, and disinfectants (quarternary ammonium compounds) and can mobilize the transfer of plasmids encoding resistance to macrolides, lincosamides, and chloramphenicol. Conjugative resistance transfer may help explain the rapid increase in resistance seen among hospital-associated *S. epidermidis* isolates.[13]

Electron microscopic studies suggest a two-step process in the association of *S. epidermidis* with plastic surfaces.[14] Cells first adhere to the surface and then form multilayered clusters that become embedded in an exopolysaccharide matrix, forming a biofilm. The first, or adherence, phase may involve both polysaccharide factors, such as PS/A,[15] and surface proteins.[16, 17] The second phase, intracellular adhesion, is mediated by a polysaccharide, called PIA[18]; an extracellular protein may also be involved.[19] Biosynthesis of PIA is encoded by a gene cluster designated *ica*. The production of PIA also enables *S. epidermidis* to agglutinate erythrocytes.[20] The role of PS/A, surface proteins, and PIA in the association of *S. epidermidis* with foreign bodies is confirmed by the inability of mutants to form biofilms on plastic surfaces and the abrogation by specific antibody of catheter-related infections in animal models.[15, 17–19] The biofilm that forms on surfaces of intravascular catheters and other foreign devices protects embedded organisms from host phagocytic cells and decreases the ability of some antimicrobial agents to eradicate adherent staphylococcal microcolonies.[21]

S. saprophyticus produces a number of proteins that may be responsible for the organism's propensity to cause urinary tract infections. A protein hemagglutinin may mediate the organism's attachment to uroepithelial cells,[22] surface fibrillar proteins may have a separate role in attachment,[23] and a urease has been implicated in the invasion of the organism into the urinary bladder.[24]

EPIDEMIOLOGY

With the exception of natural valve endocarditis and some infections of peritoneal dialysis catheters, virtually all *S. epidermidis* infections are hospital acquired. In contrast, *S. saprophyticus* infections (urinary tract infections) are all acquired outside the hospital.[25, 26] Hospital-associated *S. epidermidis* isolates are multiply antiobitic-resistant, probably reflecting the selection pressure of widespread antibiotic use in the hospital.[8] Colonization of patients and hospital staff with antibiotic-resistant *S. epidermidis* precedes infection with these organisms. Thus, patients and personnel constitute the hospital reservoir for *S. epidermidis*. The organisms probably gain access to foreign bodies by direct inoculation during the insertion of the device.

Epidemiologic investigations of coagulase-negative staphylococci were hampered in the past by the absence of reliable markers with which to fingerprint isolates. Antibiotic-susceptibility determinations, phage typing, and biotyping all suffer from a lack of sensitivity and specificity,[27] although they may be more helpful when they are used in concert.[28] The molecular analysis of the abundant plasmid DNA in coagulase-negative staphylococci has been used successfully in outbreak investigations[27, 29] and in differentiating infecting from contaminating culture isolates.[30] However, the loss, gain, and rearrangement of plasmid DNA by coagulase-negative staphylococci in their native environment over time diminish the power of this technique for longitudinal studies.[27, 31] Techniques that separate chromosomal DNA into different-size fragments using pulsed field gel electrophoresis or that identify chromosomal DNA fragment polymorphisms using probe hybridization or polymerase chain reaction amplification hold more promise.[32]

ANTIBIOTIC SUSCEPTIBILITY

Coagulase-negative staphylococci from nosocomial infections, particularly *S. epidermidis* and *S. haemolyticus*, are usually resistant to multiple antibiotics, with more than 80% resistant to methicillin.[33] Resistance to methicillin in coagulase-negative staphylococci exhibits the same heterotypic expression, altered by changes in culture or environmental conditions, as do methicillin-resistant *S. aureus*.[34] In addition, DNA probes prepared from the *S. aureus* methicillin-resistance gene (*mecA*) hybridize with chromosomal DNA from methicillin-resistant coagulase-negative staphylococci of many different species.[35]

However, the heterotypy of resistance expression for coagulase-negative staphylococci, particularly *S. epidermidis*, is much greater than that seen for *S. aureus*. This results in a low minimal inhibitory concentration for methicillin or oxacillin, often below the accepted breakpoint for resistance.[36] These isolates with low minimal inhibitory concentration values contain *mecA* and are fully resistant to all β-lactam antibiotics when evaluated in animal models of infection.[37, 38] Because of the difficulty of detecting methicillin resistance in *S. epidermidis*, it has been suggested that oxacillin minimal inhibitory concentration breakpoints for defining resistance be lowered for these organisms.[36] Ultimately, genotyping to identify *mecA* will be the most sensitive and specific resistance-detection method.

In addition to β-lactams, antimicrobials to which more than 50% of *S. epidermidis* and *S. haemolyticus* nosocomial isolates are resistant include erythromycin, clindamycin, chloramphenicol, and tetracycline.[33, 39] Resistance to trimethoprim and gentamicin is high in some hospitals but may be low in others. *Staphylococcus haemolyticus* is the first staphylococcus to demonstrate resistance to vancomycin, but other coagulase-negative stapphylococci, including *S. epidermidis*, have been described that have reduced susceptibility to glycopeptide antibiotics.[39, 40] Like *S. aureus*, virtually all *S. epidermidis* produce β-lactamase.

Antimicrobials to which most coagulase-negative staphylococci are susceptible in vitro include vancomycin, rifampin, and ciprofloxacin. The former two agents are the mainstay of the treatment of deep-seated coagulase-negative staphylococcal foreign body infections (see later), although the development of resistance to rifampin during therapy limits the usefulness of this antibiotic. The efficacy of ciprofloxacin and other fluoroquinolones in the treatment of these infections has yet to be adequately determined, but resistance of colonizing coagulase-negative staphylococci also emerges rapidly in patients receiving ciprofloxacin.[41]

INFECTIONS

Nosocomial Bacteremia

Coagulase-negative staphylococci are the most common cause of nosocomial bacteremia, particularly in areas of the hospital where the use of indwelling vascular catheters is common.[13, 42] However, these organisms are also the most common blood culture contaminants.[43] It is important, therefore, to obtain multiple blood cultures from separate venipuncture or access sites and to use rigorous criteria for defining true bacteremia.

Endocarditis of Native and Prosthetic Valves

Infections of native cardiac valves with coagulase-negative staphylococci are uncommon, accounting for only about 5% of all cases of infective endocarditis.[44] The infection presumably arises as a result of the seeding of damaged cardiac valves and endocardium with the organism after transient bacteremia, in a manner similar to that of infection with viridans streptococci. In fact, the subacute nature of the disease resembles that of infective endocarditis caused by viridans streptococci. However, in one study, 67% of 21 patients with native valve endocarditis had complicated courses (systemic embolization, congestive heart failure, or new conduction abnormalities).[45] As many as one half of the infecting isolates in this study were coagulase-negative staphylococcal species other than *S. epidermidis*.

More than 80% of these isolates were susceptible to penicillinase-resistant semisynthetic penicillins, but most produced inducible β-lactamase and were, therefore, resistant to penicillin G. Some studies report that *S. lugdunensis* may have a particular propensity to cause native valve endocarditis that leads to valve destruction.[46] It may be misidentified as *S. aureus* because it produces clumping factor.

In contrast to the low frequency with which coagulase-negative staphylococci infect native cardiac valves, they are the single most common cause of infections of prosthetic cardiac valves. *Staphylococcus epidermidis* was implicated as the cause of approximately 40% of the cases of prosthetic valve endocarditis at two large medical centers.[47] Furthermore, coagulase-negative staphylococci other than *S. epidermidis* are rarely implicated.[48] More than 80% of patients who develop prosthetic valve endocarditis due to *S. epidermidis* have a complicated infection.[48] That is, there is evidence of prosthetic valve dysfunction or persistent fever during therapy. Complicated prosthetic valve endocarditis results from infection of the valve sewing ring as opposed to infection of the working components or leaflets. Complications arising from infection of the sewing ring are valve dehiscence, dysrhythmia owing to extension of an abscess into the conducting system, or obstruction of the valve orifice owing to overgrowth of vegetative material. Dehiscence and dysrhythmia are more common with aortic prostheses, whereas obstruction is the most common complication of infected mitral prostheses. Fever persists during therapy because the valve-ring abscess is relatively protected from antibiotics. The indolent nature of the infection and the extravascular location of the valve-ring abscesses characteristic of *S. epidermidis* prosthetic valve endocaridtis also result in the absence of such classic endocarditis findings as peripheral emboli and multiple positive blood cultures. Valve dysfunction and fever are often the only findings associated with an infected valve.

Virtually all cases of prosthetic valve endocarditis caused by *S. epidermidis* that occur in the first year after surgery are probably caused by inoculation of organisms at the time of surgery. The usual postsurgical interval of 2 months that differentiates early (surgically acquired) from late (nonsurgically acquired) prosthetic valve endocarditis caused by other organisms is probably not appropriate for *S. epidermidis* infections.[47, 48] This is based on several observations. First, most of the infections that occur in the first year are complicated, involving the sewing ring. Bacteremic seeding of this area after discharge from the hospital would be unlikely. Second, 87% of cases of *S. epidermidis* prosthetic valve endocarditis occurring in the first year after surgery are caused by methicillin-resistant organisms.[48] This multiresistant phenotype is associated with hospital-acquired organisms; patients out of the hospital are colonized with antibiotic-susceptible staphylococci.[8] Third, two patients known to have acquired *S. epidermidis* prosthetic valve endocarditis during an outbreak associated with cardiopulmonary bypass pump contamination had incubation periods of 8 and 13 months before the appearance of symptoms of infection.[29] Thus, patients infected at the time of surgery with *S. epidermidis* can have long latency periods before their disease becomes apparent.

Diagnosis of *S. epidermidis* prosthetic valve endocarditis is based on a high level of suspicion. In a patient with a prosthetic cardiac valve, fever, and even a few blood cultures positive for *S. epidermidis*, every effort should be made to detect valve dysfunction. This should include serial electrocardiograms, two-dimensional echocardiography, and, if necessary, angiography. Multiple blood isolates can also be examined for specific markers in an attempt to differentiate contamination from infection. Repetitive blood isolates with different markers are unlikely to have arisen from a single infected focus.

Therapy of *S. epidermidis* prosthetic valve endocarditis is usually both medical and surgical. The mainstay of antibiotic therapy for methicillin-resistant organisms is vancomycin. However, cure rates have been improved in both animals[36, 49] and humans[48, 50] by the addition of gentamicin, rifampin, or both, to vancomycin. Antibiotics alone are often not adequate for cure, however, and surgical intervention may be crucial. In one series, 30 of 32 patients with complicated *S. epidermidis* prosthetic valve endocarditis who were cured required surgery.[48] Surgical removal of the infected valve should be attempted in any patient with valve dysfunction after stabilization on antibiotics or in any patient who is hemodynamically unstable as a result of a poorly functioning valve. Antibiotics are presumed to be important for sterilizing the perivalvular tissue around an infected prosthesis before implantation of a new valve. The relative roles of antibiotics and surgical débridement in preventing infection of the replacement prosthesis are unknown.

The role that antibiotic prophylaxis plays in preventing *S. epidermidis* prosthetic valve endocarditis is unclear. Antibiotic prophylaxis has been shown to increase the hospital reservoir of resistant organisms.[8] Patients then become infected with *S. epidermidis* resistant to the antibiotics used as prophylaxis.[8] Cephalosporins are the antibiotics most widely used and recommended for prophylaxis although they are ineffective in preventing experimental methicillin-resistant *S. epidermidis* endocarditis when animals are challenged with a high bacterial inoculum.[51] However, cephalosporin prophylaxis may decrease the number of infections with methicillin-sensitive *S. epidermidis*. Prophylaxis with vancomysin during cardiac surgery is currently recommended in institutions that have a high incidence of prosthetic valve endocarditis or sternal wound infections caused by methicillin-resistant coagulase-negative staphylococci.[52]

Intravenous Catheter Infections

S. epidermidis is reported to be the single most common organism infecting intravenous catheters as defined by semiquantitative culture techniques.[53] Studies evaluating central hyperalimentation catheters,[54–56] peripheral intravenous lines,[57, 58] subclavian catheters for plasmapheresis or hemodialysis,[59] Hickman's or Broviac's central lines in infants[60] or cancer patients,[61, 62] and Swan-Ganz catheters[63] have all reported *S. epidermidis* to be the most common infecting organism. From 12 to 37% of all inserted catheters have become infected; *S. epidermidis* accounted for from 50 to 75% of organisms cultured. Along with the increase in catheter-associated infections has been an increase in the incidence of catheter-associated bacteremia due to *S. epidermidis* with a consequent marked increase in the number of cases of nosocomial *S. epidermidis* bacteremia. This increase has resulted in gram-positive bacteria supplanting gram-negative bacteria as the leading cause of hospital-acquired bacteremia.[42]

The reasons for the increase are not entirely clear, but there are various proposed explanations. These explanations include the operative insertion of central lines, resulting in a decrease in contamination with gram-negative bacteria and fungi and an increase in contamination with usual skin bacteria; the decreased use of antibiotics for long-term indwelling catheters, resulting in a decrease in candidal overgrowth; the long period of time that lines stay in place, increasing their chance of contamination with skin bacteria; the increasing resistance of *S. epidermidis* to antibiotics, prolonging the survival of the organisms on the skin of seriously ill patients receiving multiple antibiotics; and the selection of a more catheter-adherent population of colonizing organisms.

The increase in true *S. epidermidis* bacteremias due to the increasing use of long-term indwelling intravenous catheters poses new problems for the clinician faced with positive blood cultures from a patient who does not appear clinically ill. Infected catheters may be present without gross evidence of purulence or erythema, and bacteremia may occur with few symptoms.[57, 62] It seems prudent to regard as significant all percutaneous blood cultures that grow *S. epidermidis* and are obtained from patients who have indwelling catheters. Repeat blood cultures and careful examination of the catheter site would then be warranted. Serious complications, including lung abscesses and death, have been attributed to catheter-related *S. epidermidis* bacteremia.[54]

The use of antimicrobial-impregnated catheters has been shown to decrease the incidence of catheter-related infections significantly, particularly those caused by coagulase-negative staphylococci. Catheters impregnated with minocycline and rifampin are particularly effective in this regard.[63a] However, the impact of the use of these catheters on antimicrobial resistance will have to be monitored carefully.

Therapy for *S. epidermidis* catheter infections would include removal of the catheter, if this is feasible. If the catheter cannot be removed, antibiotic therapy alone has been successful.[64] Antibiotic infusions should be rotated among all the ports of multiport catheters. Vancomycin would be the most logical choice based on the high percentage of isolates from catheter-associated bacteremia that are reported to be methicillin-resistant.

Cerebrospinal Fluid Shunt Infections

S. epidermidis is the most common organism causing infection of cerebrospinal fluid shunts. In one series, 27% of 289 hydrocephalic patients developed shunt infections over a 10-year period; more than 50% of infections were caused by *S. epidermidis*.[65] *S. epidermidis* is also a common cause of infections of ventriculostomy tubes inserted for drainage of cerebrospinal fluid in patients with head trauma and of indwelling cerebrospinal fluid catheters in patients receiving cancer chemotherapy for neoplastic meningitis.[66, 67]

Infections usually occur within 2 weeks of implantation, revision, or manipulation of the shunt. In many cases, usual physical findings of meningitis may be absent, with low-grade temperature, shunt malfunction, or wound infection as the only finding. Cerebrospinal fluid pleocytosis is almost always present but may be modest. Lumbar cerebrospinal fluid may be more normal than ventricular cerebrospinal fluid and is often culture-negative, but both should be obtained to optimize diagnosis. The cerebrospinal fluid glucose level is often only mildly low. A rare complication of prolonged bacteremia associated with ventriculoatrial shunts is glomerulonephritis caused by deposition of immune complexes in the kidney.[68]

Because the infections are hospital acquired, infection with *S. epidermidis* should be assumed to be methicillin-resistant. Therapy usually involves a combination of systemic and intraventricular administration of antibiotics, with vancomycin, rifampin, and gentamicin the drugs of choice.[69–71] Vancomycin and gentamicin can be given intraventricularly. This is the preferred route of administration.[71, 72] Rifampin achieves adequate cerebrospinal fluid concentrations after systemic administration.[70] Patients with methicillin-sensitive *S. epidermidis* infections should receive a semisynthetic, penicillinase-resistant penicillin systemically. Some cerebrospinal fluid shunt infections have been successfully treated without shunt removal,[71, 72] but removal is often required.[73] Although several studies have shown no benefit of using antibiotic prophylaxis during shunt insertion to prevent subsequent infections,[74] a meta-analysis of all available studies concluded that prophylaxis is efficacious.[75]

Peritoneal Dialysis Catheter-Associated Peritonitis

The development of chronic ambulatory peritoneal dialysis as an alternative to hemodialysis for patients with chronic renal failure has been a remarkable breakthrough in the management of these patients. However, as many as 40% of these patients may develop peritonitis during the first year, with the overall incidence ranging from 0.6 to 6.3 episodes per patient-year.[76, 77] The criteria for diagnosis are not uniform among various studies but include some combination of abdominal pain, cloudy fluid, more than 100 white blood cells/mm^3 with the majority polymorphonuclear leukocytes, and a positive culture. Gram stains of peritoneal fluid are usually negative.[78] The organism most frequently isolated from patients with peritonitis is *S. epidermidis*, which is recovered from the peritoneal fluid of from 17 to 50% of patients.[78, 79] However, routine culture of small volumes of fluid may not yield an organism, and more sensitive techniques may be required. These techniques include inoculation and subculture of broth and the filtration or culture of large volumes (more than 100 ml) of peritoneal fluid.[78, 80, 81] Because these techniques detect very small numbers of organisms, there is obviously the possibility that some episodes of *S. epidermidis* peritonitis represent procurement contamination of sterile peritoneal fluid.

Antibiotic therapy of *S. epidermidis* peritonitis in patients on chronic ambulatory peritoneal dialysis is generally successful without catheter removal. Many treatment regimens have been used with approximately equal success. These include semisynthetic penicillinase-resistant penicillins, cephalosporins, sulfamethoxazole-trimethoprim, gentamicin, or vancomycin.[78, 80, 82–84] Parenteral antibiotics alone, parenteral plus oral, oral alone, or intraperitoneal antibiotics have all been effective routes of administration. In contrast to most *S. epidermidis* infections, 75% or more of the isolates recovered from patients with peritonitis are susceptible to methicillin.[79, 85] This probably explains cure rates of 80% or greater with conventional therapy.[78, 83, 84] Infections caused by methicillin-resistant isolates have been successfully treated with weekly injections of vancomycin.[83] Treatment failures require retreatment or catheter removal.

Urinary Tract Infections

Two distinct populations of patients develop urinary tract infections with coagulase-negative staphylococci (Table 184–3). *S. saprophyticus* is a coagulase-negative staphylococcus that is cultured infrequently from the genitourinary mucosa of young women.[26, 86] This organism is readily identified by the clinical microbiology owing to its resistance to a 5-μg novobiocin disk. Novobiocin resistance is rarely found among even multiply resistant coagulase-negative staphylococci of other species that are grown from the urine.[25] *S. saprophyticus* is a true urinary tract pathogen causing both upper and lower urinary tract disease.[87] Symptoms of a urinary tract infection are present in more than 90% of women from whom *S. saprophyticus* is cultured, and pyuria is present in from 70 to 85% of these women; the organism is a culture contaminant only 5% of the time. Conversely, 95% of all coagulase-negative staphylococci cultured from the urine of symptomatic female outpatients are *S. saprophyticus*.[25, 26] Signs, symptoms, and urinalyses of women infected with this organism are indistinguishable from those of women infected with enteric bacteria. It is clearly an organism predominantly infecting young, sexually active women. Almost 70% of women in one study gave a history of sexual intercourse within the 24 hours preceding the onset of symptoms of their urinary tract infection.[26] Studies of female outpatients in Sweden and at the Universities of Florida and Washington found *S. saprophyticus* to be the cause of 32, 30, and 11%, of urinary tract infections, respectively, second only to *Escherichia coli*, the cause of from 65 to 80% of infections.[26, 87, 88] Unlike infections with enteric bacteria, however, there appears to be a seasonal predilection for *S. saprophyticus* urinary tract infections, with the incidence rising in late summer and early fall.[87–89]

TABLE 184–3 Urinary Tract Infections Caused by Coagulase-Negative Staphylococci

Characteristics of Infections	Organism: *S. epidermidis*	*S. saprophyticus*
Age and sex of affected patients	Men and women equal Usually older than 50 yr	Women 95% 16–35 years old
Population at risk	Hospitalized patients with urinary tract complications	Healthy outpatients
Incidence	Uncommon—3.5% or less of all urinary tract infections in hospitalized patients	Common—20% or more of all urinary tract infections in this age group
Presentation	90% asymptomatic	90% symptomatic; indistinguishable from *Escherichia coli* urinary tract infections
Therapy	Often resistant to multiple antibiotics	Responds readily to urinary tract antimicrobials; except nalidixic acid
Outcome	Bacteriuria often persists after therapy	Relapse rare; occasional reinfection

Furthermore, because urine colony counts for *S. saprophyticus* are often lower than those for enteric bacteria (<10^5 cfu/ml) this staphylococcus has been implicated as one cause of the dysuria-pyuria syndrome (acute urethral syndrome or abacteriuric pyuria[90]).

Therapy is usually effective with most urinary tract antimicrobial agents including norfloxacin.[89] However, therapeutic failures have been reported with sulfonamides and nitrofurantoin, and the organism is uniformly resistant to nalidixic acid.[88] Relapse is uncommon, but the infection may recur in 10% or more of patients.

In contrast, other coagulase-negative staphylococci rarely infect the urine. Of non–*S. saprophyticus* coagulase-negative staphylococci cultured from the urine in significant numbers (10^4 cfu/ml), *S. epidermidis* is the predominant species, accounting for 80 to 90% of the isolates.[25] It is cultured almost exclusively from the urine of hospitalized patients with complications of the urinary tract. Half these patients have an indwelling urinary catheter, and nearly all have such complications as recent urinary tract surgery, renal transplantation, neurogenic bladder, stone disease, or obstructive uropathy.[25, 91] Coagulase-negative staphylococci are recovered from less than 5% of all of the urine specimens from hospitalized patients from whom a significant number of bacteria are grown.[91] Furthermore, when it is present in the urine, it is associated with pyuria and a clinically significant urinary tract infection only about 10% of the time.[91, 92] Men and women are equally affected, and most patients are 50 years of age or older. The causative organisms are multiply antibiotic-resistant in at least 50% of the episodes.[25] When treatment is necessary, antibiotic therapy should be tailored to the susceptibility of the organism.

Bacteremia in Immunocompromised Patients

S. epidermidis was not usually considered to be an important pathogen in immunosuppressed patients until reports from two large cancer centers in the United States[62, 93] identified it as the most common cause of bacteremia among patients receiving immunosuppressive therapy in their hospitals. Investigators at the Baltimore Cancer Research Center identified *S. epidermidis* as the single most common cause of bacteremia in their patients between 1977 and 1979.[93] Most patients were neutropenic and heavily colonized with the organism in their rectum. The addition of oral vancomycin to the oral regimen of antibiotics for gut sterilization decreased both gastrointestinal colonization with *S. epidermidis* and bacteremia in these patients. Thus, these investigators considered the gastrointestinal tract to be the source for these *S. epidermidis* bacteremias. In contrast, investigators at the UCLA Center for the Health Sciences felt that infected Hickman or Broviac central intravenous catheters were the source of *S. epidermidis* bacteremias in their patients.[62] Between 1977 and 1980, *S. epidermidis* accounted for 26% of bacteremias in their patients, most of whom were also profoundly neutropenic.

Subsequent studies have more consistently implicated long-term indwelling catheters as the source of bacteremia in patients with hematologic malignancies and bone marrow transplants; the insertion of long-term catheters in these patients has become standard practice. As noted previously (see "Intravenous Catheter Infections"), gram-positive bacteria, particularly *S. epidermidis*, account for 50 to 80% of the organisms causing catheter-related bacteremia in this population.[61, 64, 94–96] Furthermore, *S. epidermidis* bacteremia has been documented to be a prominent source of morbidity and even mortality[97] in immunocompromised patients.

These studies illustrate several important points. First, colonization of the gut and skin with antibiotic-resistant *S. epidermidis* can follow the intensive use of oral and systemic antimicrobials.[8] Bacteremia originating from these sites can result from a compromise in both general and local defense mechanisms in severely immunocompromised patients. Second, *S. epidermidis* can be a lethal pathogen in neutropenic patients and should not be dismissed when it is grown from blood cultures that are appropriately obtained.

Osteomyelitis

Most reports that attempt to implicate *S. epidermidis* as an important cause of chronic osteomyelitis are not convincing. The organism is usually grown from sinus tracts as one of several potential pathogens. However, three infections meet valid criteria that establish *S. epidermidis* as the cause of some infections of bone. These are sternal osteomyelitis resulting from infection of the median sternotomy wound after cardiothoracic surgery,[98–100] infection of bone surrounding a prosthetic joint,[101] and hematogenous osteomyelitis resulting from infections of hemodialysis shunts.[102]

Sternal osteomyelitis is an uncommon but serious complication of cardiothoracic surgery, occurring in from 1 to 4.5% of operations in several series.[98–100] *S. epidermidis* was the cause of 16 to 45% of the infections. Whenever the deep sternal wound becomes infected, osteomyelitis is assumed to be present, and surgical débridement is necessary. However, diagnosis may be difficult with fever, minimal wound erythema, and persistent costochrondral pain as the only symptoms. If these symptoms occur within 30 days of surgery, aggressive diagnostic studies should be undertaken, including computed axial tomography scanning of the chest, needle aspiration of the wound for Gram stain and culture, and, if necessary, exploratory surgery. Advanced infection may require multiple reoperations, delayed secondary closure, and grafting. Complicated infections may have a mortality as high as 75%.[98] For this infection, antibiotics serve only as an adjunct to appropriate surgical debridement.

Osteomyelitis can result from infections of prosthetic joints and is discussed later. Hematogenous osteomyelitis can conceivably result from any bacteremic *S. epidermidis* infection but is surprisingly uncommon given the number of patients with bacteremia caused by this organism.

Infections of Prosthetic Joints (See also Chapter 92)

Although infection rates for implanted hip and knee prostheses are generally 2% or less,[103, 104] such infections are devastating. Infected prostheses usually must be removed, and in only 13 to 20% of patients is reimplantation of a new prosthesis successful.[103] Coagulase-negative staphylococci have been reported to cause from 20 to 40% of these infections. Although they ranked second to *S. aureus* as an etiologic agent in older series,[101, 104] they were the leading cause in a more recent report.[105] In the latter study, 56% of the *S. epidermidis* infections were diagnosed more than a year after surgical implantation of the device and in all but two the organism was felt to be surgically acquired.

The diagnosis is most often suggested by pain in the hip; fever, swelling, joint dislocation, and drainage. These findings are seen in fewer than half of the patients. The erythrocyte sedimentation rate is usually elevated, and radiolucencies may be seen at the bone-cement interface in two thirds of patients. Radionuclide scans, such as indium-111–labeled leukocyte scanning, may be useful in some patients.[105] Definitive diagnosis is made by Gram stain and culture of infected material obtained by needle aspiration, bone biopsy, or at surgery.

Therapy is surgical in all cases with removal of the infected prosthesis and débridement of infected bone; osteomyelitis is invariably present. Long-term antimicrobial therapy directed at the multiresistant infecting organisms is usually required. The disastrous consequences of infection have led to a great deal of attention being paid to its prevention. Laminar flow operating suites, antimicrobial prophylaxis, and antibiotic-impregnated bone cement have all been used with apparent success, but their relative merits are unclear.[106, 107]

Infection of Vascular Grafts

S. aureus and coagulase-negative staphylococci are the most common cause of vascular graft infections. However, although most of the *S. aureus* infections occur in the early postoperative period, coagulase-negative staphylococcal infections are diagnosed months to years after surgery.[108, 109] In one series, *S. epidermidis* caused 18 of 30 (60%) aortofemoral graft infections diagnosed over a 10-year period; the mean interval from surgery to infection was 41 months with a range of 14 to 80 months.[109] Most of the infections are probably acquired at the time of surgery, as suggested by the multiresistant nature of infecting isolates[109] and the frequent perioperative isolation of contaminating *S. epidermidis* from the implanted graft.[110, 111] The incidence of all graft infections is highest in aortofemoral and femoropopliteal grafts in which the surgical incision is made in the groin area; it is lowest in aortoiliac grafts.

Clinical findings suggesting late graft infection with *S. epidermidis* include anastomotic aneurysm and pseudoaneurysm formation, the development of inguinal sinus tracts, and vasculoenteric fistulas with gastrointestinal bleeding. Fever and leukocytosis are often absent.[109]

Surgical replacement of the graft and drainage of local abscesses are always required.[108] Antibiotic therapy is necessary to prevent infection of the replacement graft and should be devised to treat methicillin-resistant bacteria. As with prosthetic cardiac valve infections, vancomycin, rifampin, and gentamicin are most likely to be effective against susceptible organisms. Antibiotic prophylaxis is recommended during initial graft implantation to prevent infection, and a well-designed, controlled clinical trial has documented its efficacy, particularly in abdominal aortic resection and femoral–lower leg bypass surgery.[112]

Pediatric Infections

There has been a dramatic increase in coagulase-negative staphylococcal bacteremia in neonatal intensive care units. The incidence of bacteremia in this area alone has been a major reason for the increase in hospital-wide nosocomial coagulase-negative staphylococcal bacteremia.[13, 42] One longitudinal study conducted over 2.5 years found that 73% of all nosocomial bacteremias in a neonatal intensive care unit were caused by coagulase-negative staphylococci; 22% of all low-birth-weight infants admitted to this unit became bacteremic with these organisms.[113] Bacteremia in neonates is associated with low birth weight, the presence of indwelling peripheral or umbilical catheters, and mechanical ventilation. The administration of intravenous lipid emulsions has also been associated with coagulase-negative staphylococcal bacteremia in neonates.[114] The coagulase-negative staphylococcal isolates from these infants are typically *S. epidermidis* and are resistant to multiple antibiotics[115] but an outbreak of infections caused by multiresistant *S. haemolyticus* in a neonatal intensive care unit has been reported.[7]

An additional intriguing observation has been the association of coagulase-negative staphylococci colonizing the gut of neonates in intensive care units with necrotizing enterocolitis.[116] Whether or not gut colonization with coagulase-negative staphylococci proves to be the cause of necrotizing enterocolitis, it provides another source for the development of bacteremia.

Ocular Infections

S. epidermidis has become the most common cause of endophthalmitis after ocular surgery, especially cataract extraction or lens implantation[117, 119] and is not rare after trauma.[120] This infection has also been reported in intravenous drug abusers.[121] Diagnosis of endophthalmitis is made by physical and ocular examination, often with the aid of echography. The etiologic organism is determined by needle aspiration of the vitreous with Gram's stain and culture of the fluid.[117] Although the prognosis for maintaining sight in the affected eye used to be grim, new aggressive use of antibiotics has improved the outlook markedly.[118] One study reported that visual acuity was preserved in 7 of 10 cases of *S. epidermidis* endophthalmitis by using combined systemic and intravitreal antibiotic administration without vitrectomy.[117] The penicillins, cephalosporins, aminoglycosides, and vancomycin penetrate the vitreous poorly after systemic administration, but all have been injected safely into the vitreous of either rabbits with experimental endophthalmitis or infected patients and shown to produce therapeutic vitreal levels.[117] Rifampin penetrates the vitreous well after systemic administration.

Miscellaneous Infections

Additional foreign bodies that have been associated with infection by *S. epidermidis* include pacemaker wires and power packs,[122] hemodialysis shunts,[102] breast implants,[123] and penile prostheses.[124] As the number of indwelling foreign devices that are implanted increases, the list of foreign bodies associated with *S. epidermidis* infection should also increase. More innovative strategies may have to be devised to prevent these infections in the future.

Although isolated reports of well-documented pneumonias, intra-abdominal abscesses, and wound infections caused by *S. epidermidis* have appeared, most of these infections do not meet strict criteria implicating the organism as a pathogen. The organism is usually isolated in mixed culture with other potential pathogens, is cultured only once or intermittently, and is never reported to have been seen on Gram stain or in pathologic specimens. Because the opportunity for contamination of a culture with *S. epidermidis* is present whenever intact skin is crossed, the interpretation of cultures growing the organism must be cautious. Stricter criteria for infection must be met than with traditional pathogens. However, the growing list of infections in which *S. epidermidis* has been conclusively implicated as the etiologic agent increases the difficulty with culture interpretation. Careful culture collection and Gram stain of infected material are thus more important than ever in these situations.

REFERENCES

1. Kloos W. Taxonomy and systematics of staphylococci indigenous to humans. In: Crossley KB, Archer GL, eds. The Staphylococci in Human Disease. New York: Churchill Livingstone; 1997:113–137.
2. Kloos WE, Bannerman TL. Update on clinical significance of coagulase-negative staphylococci. Clin Microbiol Rev. 1994;7:117–140.
3. Kloos WE, Schleifer KH. Simplified scheme for routine identification of human *Staphylococcus* species. J Clin Microbiol. 1975;1:82–88.
4. Kloos WE, Wolfshohl JF. Identification of *Staphylococcus* species with the API STAPHIDENT system. J Clin Microbiol. 1982;16:509–516.
5. Herchline TE, Ayers LW. Occurrence of *Staphylococcus lugdunensis* in consecutive clinical cultures and relationship of isolation to infection. J Clin Microbiol. 1991;29:419–421.
6. Lambe DW Jr, Ferguson KP, Keplinger JL, et al. Pathogenicity of *Staphylococcus lugdunensis, Staphylococcus schleiferi,* and three other coagulase-negative staphylococci in a mouse model and possible virulence factors. Can J Microbiol. 1990;36:455–463.
7. Low DE, Schmidt BK, Kirpalani HM, et al. An endemic strain of *Staphylococcus haemolyticus* colonizing and causing bacteremia in neonatal intensive care unit patients. Pediatrics. 1992;89:696–700.
8. Archer GL, Armstrong BC. Alteration of Staphylococcal flora in cardiac surgery patients receiving antibiotic prophylaxis. J Infect Dis. 1983;147:642–649.
9. Kloos WE, Orban BS, Walker DD. Plasmid composition of *Staphylococcus* species. Can J Microbiol. 1981;27:271–278.
10. Archer GL, Johnston JL. Self-transmissible plasmids in staphylococci that encode resistance to aminoglycosides. Antimicrob Agents Chemother. 1983;24:70–77.
11. Forbes BA, Schaberg DR. Transfer of resistance plasmids from *Staphylococcus epidermidis* to *Staphylococcus aureus:* Evidence for conjugative exchange of resistance. J Bacteriol. 1983;153:627–634.
12. McDonnell RW, Sweeney HM, Cohen S. Conjugational transfer of gentamicin resistance plasmids intra- and interspecifically in *Staphylococcus aureus and Staphylococcus epidermidis.* Antimicrob Agents Chemother. 1983;23:151–160.
13. Schaberg DR, Culver DH, Gaynes RP. Major trends in the microbial etiology of nosocomial infection. Am J Med. 1991;91(Suppl 3B):72S–75S.
14. Peters G, Locci R, Pulverer G. Microbial colonization of prosthetic devices. II. Scanning electron microscopy of naturally infected intravenous catheters. Zbl Bakt Hyg I Abt Orig B. 1981;172:293–299.
15. Goldmann DA, Pier GB. Pathogenesis of infections related to intravascular catheterization. Clin Microbiol Rev. 1993;6:176–192.
16. Timmermann CP, Fleer A, Besnier JM, et al. Characterization of a proteinaceous adhesin of *Staphylococcus epidermidis* which mediates attachment to polystyrene. Infect Immun. 1991;59:4187–4192.
17. Heilmann C, Hussain M, Peter G, Gotz F. Evidence for autolysin-mediated primary attachment of *Staphylococcus epidermidis* to a polystyrene surface. 1997; Mol Microbiol. 24:1013–1024.
18. Heilmann C, Schweitzer O, Gerke C, et al. Molecular basis of intercellular adhesion in the biofilm-forming *Staphylococcus epidermidis.* Mol Microbiol. 1996;20:1083–1091.
19. Hussain M, Herrmann M, von Eiff C, et al. A 140-kilodalton extracellular protein is essential for the accumulation of *Staphylococcus epidermidis* strains on surfaces. Infect Immun. 1997;65:519–524.
20. Rupp ME, Archer G. Hemagglutination and adherence to plastic by *Staphylococcus epidermidis.* Infect Immun. 1992;60:4322–4327.
21. Peters G, Locci R, Pulverer G. Adherence and growth of coagulase-negative staphylococci on surfaces of intravenous catheters. J Infect Dis. 1982;146:479–482.
22. Gatermann S, Meyer HGW, Wanner G. *Staphylococcus saprophyticus* hemagglutinin is a 160-kilodalton surface protein. Infect Immun. 1992;60:4127–4132.
23. Gatermann S, Kreft B, Marre R, et al. Identification and characterization of a surface-associated protein (Ssp) of *Staphylococcus saprophyticus.* Infect Immun. 1992;60:1055–1060.
24. Gatermann S, John J, Marre R. *Staphylococcus saprophyticus* urease: Characterization and contribution to uropathogenicity in unobstructed urinary tract infection of rats. Infect Immun. 1989;57:110–116.
25. Nicolle LE, Hoban SA, Harding GKM. Characterization of coagulase-negative staphylococci from urinary tract infections. J Clin Microbiol. 1983;17:267–270.
26. Jordan PA, Iravani A, Richard GA, et al. Urinary tract infection caused by *Staphylococcus saprophyticus.* J Infect Dis. 1980;142:510–515.
27. Parisi JT. Coagulase-negative staphylococci and the epidemiologic typing of *Staphylococcus epidermidis.* Microbiol Rev. 1985;49:126–139.
28. Christensen GD, Parisi JT, Bisno AL, et al. Characterization of clinically significant strains of coagulase-negative staphylococci. J Clin Microbiol. 1983;18:258–269.
29. Archer GL, Vishniavsky N, Stiver G. Plasmid pattern analysis of *Staphylococcus epidermidis* isolates from patients with prosthetic valve endocarditis. Infect Immun. 1982;627–632.
30. Archer GL, Karchmer AW, Vishniavsky N, et al. Plasmid pattern analysis for the differentiation of infecting from non-infecting *Staphylococcus epidermidis.* J Infect Dis. 1985;145:913–922.
31. Archer GL, Dietrick DR, Johnston JL. Molecular epidemiology of transmissible gentamicin resistance among coagulase-negative staphylococci in a cardiac surgery unit. J Infect Dis. 1985;151:243–251.
32. Arbeit RD. Laboratory procedures for epidemiologic analysis. In: Crossley KB, Archer GL, eds. The Staphylococci in Human Disease. New York: Churchill Livingstone; 1997:253–286.
33. Archer GL, Climo MW. Antimicrobial susceptibility of coagulase-negative staphylococci. Antimicrob Agents Chemother. 1994;38:2231–2237.
34. Coudron PE, Jones DL, Dalton HP, et al. Evaluation of laboratory tests for detection of methicillin-resistant *Staphylococcus aureus* and *Staphylococcus epidermidis.* J Clin Microbiol. 1986;24:764–769.
35. Archer G, Pennell EA. Detection of methicillin resistance in staphylococci by using a DNA probe. Antimicrob Agents Chemother. 1990;34:1720–1724.
36. McDonald CL, Maher WE, Fass, RJ. Revised interpretation of oxacillin MICs for *Staphylococcus epidermidis* based on *mecA* detection. Antimicrob Agents Chemother. 1995;39:982–984.
37. Vazquez GJ, Archer GL. Antibiotic therapy of experimental *Staphylococcus epidermidis* endocarditis. Antimicrob Agents Chemother. 1980;17:280–285.
38. Berry A, Johnston JL, Archer GL. Imipenem therapy of experimental *Staphylococcus epidermidis* endocarditis. Antimicrob Agents Chemother. 1986;29:748–752.
39. Froggatt JW, Johnston JL, Galetto DW, et al. Antimicrobial resistance in nosocomial isolates of *Staphylococcus haemolyticus.* Antimicrob Agents Chemother. 1989;33:460–466.
40. Sieradzki K, Villari P, Tomasz A. Decreased susceptibilities to teichoplanin and vancomycin among coagulase-negative methicillin-resistant clinical isolates of staphylococci. Antimicrob Agents Chemother. 1998;42:100–107.
41. Kotilainen P, Nikoskelainen J, Huovinen P. Emergence of ciprofloxacin-resistant coagulase-negative staphylococcal skin flora in immunocompromised patients receiving ciprofloxacin. J Infect Dis. 1990;161:41–44.
42. Boyce JM. Epidemiology and prevention of nosomial infections. In: Crossley CB, Archer GL, eds. The Staphylococci in Human Disease. New York: Churchill Livingstone; 1997;309–329.
43. Kirchoff LV, Sheagren JN. Epidemiology and clinical significance of blood cultures positive for coagulase-negative staphylococcus. Infect Control. 1985;6:479–486.
44. Kaye D. Infecting microorganism. In: Kay D, ed. Infective Endocarditis. Baltimore: University Park; 1976:43–54.
45. Caputo GM, Archer G, Calderwood SB, et al. Native valve endocarditis due to coagulase-negative staphylococci: Clinical and microbiologic features. Am J Med. 1987;83:619–625.
46. Vandenesch F, Etienne J, Reverdy ME, et al. Endocarditis due to *Staphylococcus lugdunensis:* Report of 11 cases and review. Clin Infect Dis. 1993;17:871–876.
47. Calderwood SB, Swinski LA, Waternaux CM, et al. Risk factors for the development of prosthetic valve endocarditis. Circulation. 1985;72:31–37.
48. Karchmer AW, Archer GL, Dismukes WE. *Staphylococcus Epidermidis* prosthetic valve endocarditis: Microbiological and clinical observations as guide to therapy. Ann Intern Med. 1983;98:447–455.
49. Kobasa WD, Keye KL, Shapiro T, et al. Therapy for experimental endocarditis due to *Staphylococcus epidermidis.* Rev Infect Dis. 1983; 5:S533–S537.
50. Massanari RM, Donta ST. The efficacy of rifampin as adjunctive therapy in selected cases of staphylococcal endocarditis. Chest. 1978;73:371–375.

51. Archer GL, Vazquez GJ, Johnston JL. Antibiotic prophylaxis of experimental methicillin-resistant *Staphylococcus epidermidis* endocarditis. J Infect Dis. 1980;142:725–731.
52. Antimicrobial prophylaxis in surgery. Med Lett Drugs Ther. 1997;39:97–102.
53. Maki DG, Weise CE, Sarafin HW. A semi-quantitative culture method for identifying intravenous catheter-related infection. N Engl J Med. 1977;296:1305–1309.
54. Christensen GD, Bisno AL, Parisi JT, et al. Nosocomial septicemia due to multiply antibiotic-resistant *Staphylococcus epidermidis.* Ann Intern Med. 1982;96:1–10.
55. Liñares J, Sitges-Serra A, Garau J, et al. Pathogenesis of catheter sepsis: A prospective study with quantitative and semiquantitative cultures of catheter hub and segments. J Clin Microbiol. 1985;21:357–360.
56. Snydman DR, Murray SA, Kornfeld SJ, et al. Total parenteral nutrition-related infections; prospective epidemiologic study using semiquantitative methods. Am J Med. 1982;73:695–699.
57. Moyer MA, Edwards LD, Farley L. Comparative culture methods on 101 intravenous catheters: Routine, semiquantitative, and blood cultures. Arch Intern Med. 1983;143:66–69.
58. Shererty RJ, Falk RJ, Huffman KA, et al. Infections associated with subclavian Udall catheters. Arch Intern Med. 1983;143:52–56.
59. Chessbrough JS, Finch RG, Burden RP. A prospective study of the mechanisms of infection associated with hemodialysis catheters. J Infect Dis. 1986;154:579–589.
60. Raucher HS, Hyatt AC, Barzilai A, et al. Quantitative blood cultures in the evaluation of septicemia in children with Broviac catheters. J Pediatr. 1984;104:29–33.
61. Press OW, Ramsey PG, Larson EB, et al. Hickman catheter infections in patients with malignancies. Medicine. 1984;63:189–200.
62. Winston DJ, Dudnick DV, Chapin M, et al. Coagulase-negative staphylococcal bacteremia in patients receiving immunosuppressive therapy. Arch Intern Med. 1983;143:32–36.
63. Cooper GL, Hopkins CC. Rapid diagnosis of intravacular catheter-associated infection by direct Gram-staining of catheter segments. N Engl J Med. 1985;312:1142–1197.
63a. Darouche RO, Raad II, Heard SO, et al. A comparison of two antimicrobial-impregnated central venous catheters. N Engl J Med. 1999;340:1–8.
64. Read II, Bodey GP. Infectious complications of indwelling vascular catheters. Clin Infect Dis. 1992;15:197–210.
65. Schoenbaum SC, Gardner P, Shillito J. Infections of cerebrospinal fluid shunts: Epidemiology, clinical manifestations, and therapy. J Infect Dis. 1975;131:543–552.
66. Mayhall CG, Archer NH, Lamb A, et al. Ventriculostomy-related infections: A prospective epidemiologic study. N Engl J Med. 1984;310:553–559.
67. Trump DL, Grossman SA, Thompson G, et al. CSF infections complicating the management of neoplastic meningitis: Clinical features and results of therapy. Arch Intern Med. 1982;142:583–586.
68. Dobrin RS, Day NK, Quie PG, et al. The role of complement immunoglobulin, and bacterial antigen in coagulase-negative staphylococcal shunt nephritis. Am J Med. 1975;59:660–673.
69. Gombert ME, Landesman SH, Corrado ML, et al. Vancomycin and rifampin therapy for *Staphylococcus epidermidis* meningitis associated with CSF shunts. Report of three cases. J Neurosurg. 1981;55:633–636.
70. Archer GL, Tenenbaum MJ, Haywood HB III. Rifampin therapy of *Staphylococcus epidermidis:* Use in infections from indwelling foreign devices. JAMA. 1978;240:751–753.
71. Wald SL, McLaurin RL. Cerebrospinal fluid antibiotic levels during treatment of shunt infections. J Neurosurg. 1980;52:41–46.
72. Frame PT, McLaurin RL. Treatment of CSF shunt infections with intrashunt plus oral antibiotic therapy. J Neurosurg. 1984;60:354–360.
73. James HE, Walsh JW, Wilson HD, et al. Prospective randomized study of therapy in cerebrospinal fluid shunt infection. Neurosurgery. 1980;7:459–463.
74. Wang EEL, Prober CG, Hendrick BE, et al. Prophylactic sulfamethoxasole and trimethoprim in ventriculoperitoneal shunt surgery. JAMA. 1984;251:1174–1177.
75. Langbeg JM, LeBlarc JC, Drake J, Milner R. Efficacy of antimicrobial prophylaxis in placement of cerebrospinal fluid shunts: Meta-analysis. Clin Infect. Dis. 1993;17:98–103.
76. Oreopoulos DG, Khanna R, Williams P, et al. Continuous ambulatory peritoneal dialysis—1981. Nephron. 1982;30:293–303.
77. Gokal R. Peritonitis in continuous ambulatory peritoneal dialysis. J Antimicrob Chemother. 1982;9:417–719.
78. Rubin J, Rogers WA, Taylor HM, et al. Peritonitis during continuous ambulatory peritoneal dialysis. Ann Intern Med. 1980;92:7–13.
79. West TE, Walshe JJ, Krol CP, et al. Staphylococcal peritonitis in patients on continuous peritoneal dialysis. J Clin Microbiol. 1986;23:809–812.
80. Knight KR, Polak A, Crump J, et al. Laboratory diagnosis and oral treatment of CAPD peritonitis. Lancet. 1982;3:1301–1304.
81. Dawson MS, Harford AM, Garner BK, et al. Total volume culture technique for the isolation of microorganisms from continuous ambulatory peritoneal dialysis patients with peritonitis. J Clin Microbiol. 1985;22:391–394.
82. DePaepe M, Belpaire F, Bogaert M, et al. Gentamicin for treatment of peritonitis in continuous ambulatory peritoneal dialysis. Lancet. 1981;2:424–425.
83. Krothapalli RK, Senekjian HO, Ayus JC. Efficacy of intravenous vancomycin in the treatment of gram-positive peritonitis in long-term peritoneal dialysis. Am J Med. 1983;75:345–348.
84. Boeschoten EW, Pietra PJGM, Krediet RT, et al. CAPD peritonitis: A prospective randomized trial of oral versus intraperitoneal treatment with cephradine. J Antimicrob Chemother. 1985;16:789–797.
85. Baddour LM, Smalley DL, Kraus AP Jr, et al. Comparison of microbiologic characteristics of pathogenic and saprophytic coagulase-negative staphylococci from patients on continuous ambulatory peritoneal dialysis. Diagn Microbiol Infect Dis. 1986;5:197–205.
86. Rupp ME, Soper D, Archer G. *Staphylococcus saprophyticus* colonization of the female genital tract. J Clin Microbiol. 1992;30:2975–2979.
87. Latham RH, Running K, Stamm WE. Urinary tract infections in young adult women caused by *Staphylococcus saprophyticus*. JAMA. 1983;250:3063–3066.
88. Wallmark G, Arremark I, Telandeer B. *Staphylococcus saprophyticus:* A frequent cause of acute urinary tract infection among female outpatients. J Infect Dis. 1978;138:791–797.
89. The Urinary Tract Infection Study Group. Coordinated multicenter study of norfloxacin versus trimethoprim-sulfamethoxasole treatment of symptomatic urinary tract infections. J Infect Dis. 1987;155:170–177.
90. Stamm WE, Wagner KF, Amsel R, et al. Causes of the acute urethral syndrome in women. N Engl J Med. 1980;303:409–415.
91. Lewis JF, Brake SR, Anderson DJ, et al. Urinary tract infection due to coagulase-negative staphylococcus. Am J Clin Pathol. 1982;77:736–739.
92. Sewell CM, Claridge JE, Young EJ, et al. Clinical significance of coagulase-negative staphylococci. J Clin Microbiol. 1982;16:236–239.
93. Wade JC, Schimpff SC, Newman KA, et al. *Staphylococcus epidermidis:* An increasing cause of infection in patients with granulocytopenia. Ann Intern Med. 1982;97:503–508.
94. Sanz MA, Such M, Rafecas FJ, et al. *Staphylococcus epidermidis* infections in acute myeloblastic leukemia patients fitted with Hickman catheters. Lancet. 1983;2:1191–1192.
95. Lowder JN, Lazarus HM, Herzig RH. Bacteremias and fungemias in oncologic patients with central venous catheters. Arch Intern Med. 1982;142:1456–1459.
96. Pirsch JD, Maki DG. Infectious complications in adults with bone marrow transplantation and T-cell depletion of donor marrow. Ann Intern Med. 1986;104:619–631.
97. Bender JW, Hughes WT. Fatal *Staphylococcus epidermidis* sepsis following bone marrow transplantation. Johns Hopkins Med J. 1980;146:13–15.
98. Grossi EA, Culliford AT, Krieger KH, et al. A survey of 77 major infectious complications of median sternotomy: A review of 7,949 consecutive operative procedures. Ann Thorac Surg. 1985;40:214–223.
99. Bor HB, Rose RM, Modlin JF, et al. Mediastinitis after cardiovascular surgery. Rev Infect Dis. 1983;5:885–897.
100. Miholic J, Hudec M, Domanig E, et al. Risk factors for severe bacterial infections after valve replacement and aortocoronary bypass operations: Analysis of 246 cases by logistic regression. Ann Thorac Surg. 1985;40:224–228.
101. Fitzgerald RH, Nolan DR, Ilstrup DM, et al. Deep wound sepsis following total hip arthroplasty. J Bone Joint Surg Am. 1977;59:847–855.
102. Parker MA, Tuazon C. Cervical osteomyelitis: Infection due to *Staphylococcus epidermidis* in hemodialysis patients. JAMA. 1978;240:50–51.
103. Hunter G, Dandy D. The natural history of the patient with an infected total hip replacement. J Bone Joint Surg [AM]. 1977;59B:293–297.
104. Salvati EA, Robinson RP, Zeno SM, et al. Infection rates after 3175 total hip and total knee replacements performed with and without a horizontal unidirectional filtered air-flow system. J Bone Joint Surg (Am). 1982;64:525–535.
105. Rand JA, Brown ML. The value of indium III–leukocyte scanning in the evaluation of painful or infected total knee arthroplasties. Clin Orthop. 1990;259:179–182.
106. Fitzgerald RH, Bechtol CO, Eftekhar N, et al. Reduction of deep sepsis after total hip arthroplasty. Arch Surg. 1979;114:803–804.
107. Norden CW. A critical review of antibiotic prophylaxis in orthopedic surgery. Rev Infect Dis. 1983;5:928–932.
108. O'Brien T, Collin J. Prosthetic vascular graft infection. Br J Surg. 1992;79:1262–1267.
109. Bandyk DF, Berni GA, Thiele BL, et al. Aorto-femoral graft infection due to *Staphylococcus epidermidis*. Arch Surg. 1984;119:102–108.
110. Wooster DL, Louch RE, Krajden S. Intraoperative bacterial contamination of vascular grafts: A prospective study. Can J Surg. 1985;28:407–409.
111. Bunt TJ. Sources of *Staphylococcus epidermidis* at the inguinal incision during peripheral revascularization. Am Surg. 1986;52:472–473.
112. Kaiser AB, Clayson KR, Mulherin JL, et al. Antibiotic prophylaxis in vascular surgery. Ann Surg. 1978;188:283–289.
113. Anday EK, Talbot GH. Coagulase-negative staphylococcus bacteremia—a rising threat in the newborn infant. Ann Clin Lab Sci. 1985;15:246–251.
114. Freeman J, Goldmann DA, Smith NE, et al. Association of intravenous lipid emulsion and coagulase-negative staphylococcal bacteremia in neonatal intensive care units. N Engl J Med. 1990;323:301–308.
115. Weinstein RA, Kabins SA, Nathan C, et al. Gentamicin-resistant staphylococci as hospital flora: Epiderminology and resistant plasmids. J Infect Dis. 1982;145:374–382.
116. Gruskay JA, Abbasi S, Anday E, et al. *Staphylococcus epidermidis*–associated enterocolitis. J Pediatr. 1986;109:520–524.
117. Diamond JG. Intraocular management of endophthalmitis; a systematic approach. Arch Ophthalmol. 1981;99:96–99.
118. Heaven CJ, Mann PJ, Boase DL. Endophthalmitis following extracapsular cataract surgery: A review of 32 cases. Br J Ophthalmol. 1992;76:419–442.
119. Weber DJ, Hoffman KL, Thoft RA, et al. Endophthalmitis following intraocular lens implantation: Report of 30 cases and review of the literature. Rev Infect Dis. 1986;8:12–20.
120. Fisch A, Salvanet A, Prazuk T, et al. Epidemiology of infective endophthalmitis in France. The French Collaborative Study Group on Endophthalmitis. Lancet. 1991;338:1373–1376.

121. Schlossberg D, Jan AM. Endophthalmitis in intravenous drug abuse. Ann Ophthalmol. 1993;25:77–78.
122. Wohl B, Peters RW, Carliner N, et al. Late unheralded pacemaker pocket infection due to *Staphylococcus epidermidis*: A new clinical entity. PACE. 1982;5:190–195.
123. Burkhardt BR, Fried M, Schnur PL, et al. Capsules, infection, and intraluminal antibiotics. Plast Reconstr Surg. 1981;68:43–49.
124. Kabalin JN, Kessler R. Infectious complications of penile prosthesis surgery. J Urol. 1988;139:953–955.

Chapter 185

Classification of Streptococci

ALAN L. BISNO
IVO VAN DE RIJN

Streptococci are spherical or ovoid bacteria that grow in pairs or chains of varied lengths. Most are facultatively anaerobic, although some are obligate anaerobes. Streptococci are gram-positive, non-spore forming, catalase-negative, and ordinarily nonmotile and have complex but variable nutritional requirements. Taxonomically, these organisms belong to the genus *Streptococcus,* of which there are over 30 identified species.[1] Some of these species are pathogenic for humans, most notably *S. pyogenes* (group A streptococci), *S. agalactiae* (group B streptococci), and *S. pneumoniae* (pneumococci).

No single system of classification suffices to differentiate this heterogeneous group of organisms. Instead, classification depends on a combination of features including patterns of hemolysis observed on blood-agar plates, antigenic composition, growth characteristics, biochemical reactions, and, more recently, genetic analysis. See Chapter 14 for further discussion of laboratory procedures for identifying streptococci.

When streptococci are cultivated on blood-agar plates, notable differences in the surface morphologic characteristics (e.g., colony size, opacity) among individual strains are evident. Moreover, colonies of certain strains are surrounded by clear colorless zones within which the red cells in the medium have been completely lysed (Fig. 185–1). This pattern is designated β-hemolysis and is of considerable importance since it is exhibited by *S. pyogenes* and many of the other streptococci pathogenic for humans. A second group of organisms produces partial hemolysis, or α-hemolysis. Pneumococci are α-hemolytic, as are many of the other streptococcal strains that normally inhabit the upper respiratory and gastrointestinal tract of humans. α-Hemolytic colonies also produce a greenish discoloration in the medium. This greening reaction, which varies with the type of blood in the medium and the duration of incubation, gives rise to the term *viridans streptococci* frequently applied to certain α-hemolytic strains (see Chapter 191). Finally, the term γ-hemolysis has been used to designate strains producing no hemolysis, although the term *nonhemolytic streptococci* is to be preferred.

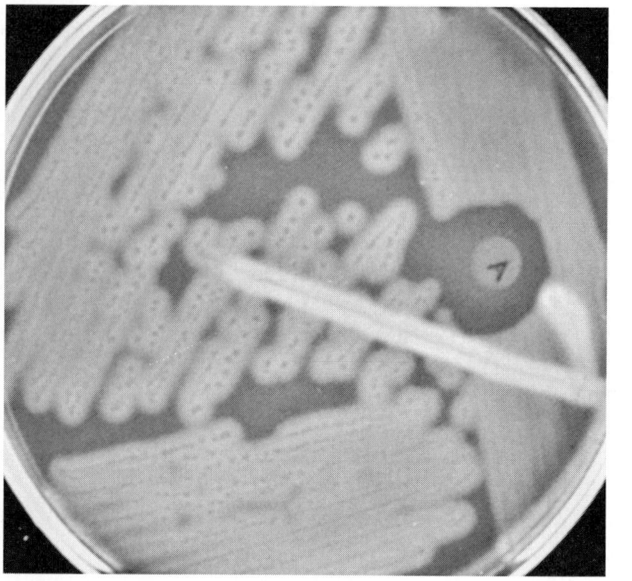

FIGURE 185–1. Group A streptococci growing in pure culture on a sheep blood-agar plate. Individual colonies are surrounded by zones of complete (β) hemolysis. Subsurface hemolysis (agar stab) is due in part to the action of streptolysin O, which is oxygen labile. The zone of inhibition around a low-potency bacitracin disk is a presumptive test for group A organisms.

More precise identification of the β-hemolytic streptococci was accomplished by Lancefield,[2] who succeeded in differentiating these organisms into serogroups by means of antigenic differences in cell wall carbohydrates. Group-specific antigens are readily extracted from streptococcal cell walls and identified by precipitin reactions using specific antisera. To date, serogroups A through H and K through V have been designated. Groups A, B, C, D, and G are those most commonly found in humans (Table 185–1); groups E, L, P, U, and V are isolated from humans rarely if at all. Groups C and G streptococci are discussed in Chapter 191.

Although the Lancefield grouping system was initially devised for the identification of β-hemolytic streptococci, certain α-hemolytic and nonhemolytic strains also contain group-specific antigens. Notable among these are group D streptococci, including the so-called enterococci, most strains of which fail to exhibit β-hemolysis. Certain members of the group D streptococci have been designated as a distinct genus, *Enterococcus.*[3] The enterococci, which are significant causes of human disease, are discussed in detail in Chapter 189.

Streptococci that lack a recognizable group antigen are identified by phenotypic characteristics (fermentation reactions, the production of enzymes) and by DNA hybridization. Using these criteria, the streptococci have been subdivided into various species (Table 185–2). The classification scheme for streptococci is in constant flux due to the advent of new molecular techniques for the speciation of the organisms.[4–6] Furthermore, four species of anaerobic streptococci are

TABLE 185–1 Streptococcal Serogroups Most Frequently Involved in Human Disease*

Serogroup	Group-Specific Cell Wall Antigen	Usual Clinical Features
A	Rhamnose-*N*-acetylglucosamine polysaccharide	Pharyngitis, tonsillitis, otitis media, sinusitis, scarlet fever, erysipelas, cellulitis, impetigo, pneumonia, endometritis, septicemia Delayed nonsuppurative sequelae: acute rheumatic fever, acute glomerulonephritis
B	Rhamnose-glucosamine polysaccharide	Chorioamnionitis, puerperal sepsis, neonatal sepsis and meningitis Bacteremia in nonpregnant adults
C	Rhamnose-*N*-acetylgalactosamine polysaccharide	Upper respiratory infections
D	Glycerol teichoic acid	Genitourinary tract infections, wound infections, endocarditis†
G	Rhamnose-galactosamine polysaccharide	Upper respiratory infections, cellulitis, septicemia, deep-tissue infections

*Further information on speciation and clinical manifestations of serogroups B, C, D, and G is found in Chapters 189, 190, and 191.
†Includes illnesses caused by group D streptococci (*S. bovis, S. equinus*) and *Enterococcus* spp.

TABLE 185-2 Some Other Streptococci Isolated from Humans

Species	Comments
Abiotrophia (S.) adiacens	Endocarditis; oropharynx (nutritionally variant streptococci)
S. anginosus	Purulent infections; oropharynx, skin, and urogenital and intestinal tract
S. bovis	Blood isolate in patients with colon cancer, endocarditis; genital and intestinal tract
S. constellatus	Purulent infections; oropharynx, skin, intestinal tract
S. crista	Oropharynx; new species
Abiotrophia (S.) defectiva	Endocarditis; oropharynx (nutritionally variant streptococci)
S. gordonii	Endocarditis; dental plaque
S. iniae	Cellulitis, bacteremia, endocarditis in fish (tilapia) handlers
S. intermedius	Purulent infections; brain and liver abscesses; oropharynx, skin, intestinal tract
S. mitis	Endocarditis; oropharynx, intestinal tract
S. mutans	Dental caries, endocarditis; dental plaque
S. oralis	Endocarditis; oropharynx, intestinal tract
S. parasanguis	Oropharynx; new species
S. pneumoniae	Pneumonia, otitis media, meningitis; colonizes upper respiratory tract (pneumococcus)
S. salivarius	Rare in infections; colonizes tongue and intestinal tract
S. sanguis	Endocarditis; dental plaque, intestinal tract
S. sobrinus	Dental caries, endocarditis; dental plaque
S. suis	Meningitis
S. vestibularus	New species from oral cavity

recognized in the most recent revision of *Bergey's Manual.* Hemolytic reactions of the organisms are variable. These organisms are at times associated with human infections, particularly infections occurring in necrotic tissues (see also Chapter 238).

REFERENCES

1. Holt JG, Krieg NR, Sneath PHA, et al, eds. Bergey's Manual of Determinative Bacteriology, 9th ed. Baltimore: Williams & Wilkins, 1994:552–558.
2. Lancefield RC. A serological differentiation of human and other groups of hemolytic streptococci. J Exp Med. 1933;57:571–595.
3. Schliefer KH, Kilpper-Balz R. Molecular and chemotaxonomic approaches to the classification of streptococci, enterococci, and lactococci: A review. Syst Appl Microbiol. 1986;10:1–19.
4. Coykendall AL. Classification and identification of the viridans streptococci. Clin Microbiol Rev. 1989;2:315–328.
5. Beighton D, Hardie JM, Whiley RA. A scheme for the identification of viridans streptococci. J Med Microbiol. 1991;35:367–372.
6. Hardie JM, Whiley RA. Classification and overview of the genera *Streptococcus* and *Enterococcus*. Soc Appl Bacteriol Symp Ser. 1997;83:1S–11S.

Chapter 186

Streptococcus pyogenes (Including Streptococcal Toxic Shock Syndrome and Necrotizing Fasciitis)

ALAN L. BISNO
DENNIS L. STEVENS

Streptococcus pyogenes (group A streptococcus) is one of the most important bacterial pathogens of humans. This ubiquitous organism is the most frequent bacterial cause of acute pharyngitis, and it also gives rise to a variety of cutaneous and systemic infections. Its unique place in medical microbiology stems from its propensity to initiate two nonsuppurative sequelae: acute rheumatic fever and poststreptococcal acute glomerulonephritis.

HISTORY

Streptococci were demonstrated in patients with erysipelas and wound infections by Billroth in 1874 and in the blood of a patient with puerperal sepsis by Pasteur in 1879. In 1883, Fehleisen isolated chain-forming organisms in pure culture from erysipelas lesions and then demonstrated that these organisms could induce typical erysipelas in humans. Rosenbach applied the designation *Streptococcus pyogenes* to these organisms in 1884.

Initial progress toward a rational classification of streptococci dates from the description by Schötmuller in 1903 of the blood-agar technique for differentiating hemolytic from nonhemolytic streptococci. In 1919, J. H. Brown[1] made a systematic study of patterns of hemolysis and introduced the terms α-, β-, and γ-hemolysis (see Chapter 185).

Lancefield's classification of β-hemolytic streptococci into distinct serogroups in 1933[2] was a major turning point in our understanding of the epidemiology of streptococcal infections. Most strains pathogenic for humans were found to belong to serogroup A (*S. pyogenes*). Systems of serotyping group A streptococci were developed on the basis of M-protein precipitin reactions (Lancefield) or T-protein agglutination reactions (Griffith). In addition, Lancefield established the critical role of M protein in streptococcal virulence and the type-specific nature of protective immunity to group A streptococcal infection. Studies by Dochez and collaborators and by George and Gladys Dick in the 1920s established the relationship of scarlet fever to hemolytic streptococcal infection. A few years later, Todd's description of the method for titration of anti–streptolysin O (ASO) in serum added still another important tool to the armamentarium available for the study of the immunology and epidemiology of streptococcal disease. Such tools were used by a number of investigators including Coburn, Collis, Rammelkamp, Stollerman, and Wannamaker to establish the relationship of group A streptococcal infection to acute rheumatic fever and acute glomerulonephritis. Much of our knowledge of the detailed epidemiology of streptococcal infections and of acute rheumatic fever derives from the pioneering studies performed at Warren Air Force Base, Wyoming, during the years 1949 to 1951 by Rammelkamp, Wannamaker, and Denny.[3–5]

DESCRIPTION OF THE PATHOGEN

Group A streptococci grow as spheric or ovoid cells 0.6 to 1.0 μm in diameter and occur as pairs or as short to moderate-sized chains in clinical specimens. When growing in broth media enriched with serum or blood, they frequently form long chains, and many strains produce capsules of hyaluronic acid. The organisms are gram-positive, nonmotile, non–spore forming, catalase-negative, and facultatively anaerobic. Group A streptococci are nutritionally fastidious and are usually cultivated in complex media, often supplemented with blood or serum.

When cultured on blood-agar plates, *S. pyogenes* appears as white to gray colonies 1 to 2 mm in diameter surrounded by zones of complete (β) hemolysis. (Strains that fail to produce such hemolysis occur but are rare.) Strains that produce copious amounts of the hyaluronate capsular material appear mucoid, at times resembling a water drop on the plate. Less mucoid strains assume a crinkled, so-called matte appearance. Small opaque colonies of organisms that lack capsules and detectable M protein are termed *glossy.*

A large number of somatic constituents and extracellular products of group A streptococci have been identified. The most important of these are indicated in the following sections.

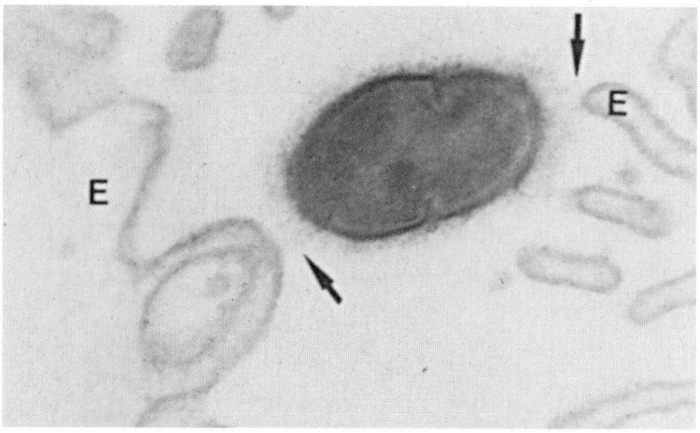

FIGURE 186–1. Electron micrograph of group A streptococcus. Surface fibrils contain type-specific, antiphagocytic epitopes of M protein. Lipoteichoic acid and a fibronectin binding protein facilitate adherence of streptococci to the membrane (*arrows*) of a human oral epithelial cell (E). (×67,500) (From Beachey EH, Ofek I. Epithelial cell binding of group A streptococci by lipoteichoic acid on fimbriae denuded of M protein. J Exp Med. 1976;143:759–771, by copyright permission of the Rockefeller University Press.)

Somatic Constituents

The organism is enveloped in a hyaluronic acid capsule that serves as an accessory virulence factor in retarding phagocytosis by polymorphonuclear leukocytes and macrophages of the host.[6, 7] The cell wall is a complex structure containing many different antigenic substances. The group-specific carbohydrate of group A strains is a dimer of rhamnose and *N*-acetylglucosamine in a ratio of approximately 2:1. The mucopeptide (peptidoglycan) layer provides rigidity to the cell wall; it is composed of polymers of repeating subunits of *N*-acetylglucosamine and *N*-acetylmuramic acid connected by amino acid side chains.

M protein is the major somatic virulence factor of group A streptococci. Strains rich in this protein are resistant to phagocytosis by polymorphonuclear leukocytes, multiply rapidly in fresh human blood, and are capable of initiating disease. Strains that do not express M protein are avirulent.[8] Group A streptococci may be divided into types on the basis of antigenic differences in M-protein molecules, and more recently on the basis of nucleotide differences in the *emm* gene encoding the molecule. More than 90 such types are recognized. Acquired human immunity to streptococcal infection is based on the development of opsonic antibodies directed against the antiphagocytic moiety of M protein. Such immunity is type-specific and quite durable, lasting for many years and perhaps indefinitely. In some instances, cross-protection by antibody to one type against organisms of a heterologous type has been demonstrated.

M protein is a filamentous macromolecule that exists as a stable dimer with an α-helical coiled-coil structure.[9] The molecule, which is anchored to the cell membrane, traverses and penetrates the cell wall. The more proximal portion of the molecule contains epitopes widely conserved among group A streptococci, whereas the more distal portion contains type-specific epitopes.[10] This configuration localizes the type-specific moiety on the tips of fibrils protruding from the cell surface (Fig. 186–1). In the nonimmune host, M protein exerts its antiphagocytic effect by inhibiting activation of the alternate complement pathway on the cell surface.[11, 12] This effect is mediated at least in part by the ability of M protein to bind complement factor H.[13] Fibrinogen also binds to the M protein molecule and is antiphagocytic.[14] The antiphagocytic effect is nullified in the presence of adequate concentrations of type-specific antibody. M proteins analogous to those of group A streptococci are present in many strains of groups C[15] and G[16] streptococci.

Another protein antigen very closely associated with the M protein of group A streptococci is the so-called serum opacity factor (OF). This factor is an α-lipoproteinase that is detected by its ability to opacify horse serum. Strains of 29 of the currently identified M types elaborate this antigen.[17] OF is readily demonstrated in such strains even if they should lose their ability to produce detectable amounts of M protein. OF itself is antigenic and type-specific, that is, its ability to opacify serum can be specifically inhibited by antiserum raised against homologous but not heterologous M types. This substance is of importance for two reasons. First, it is a useful epidemiologic marker that assists in classifying streptococci even when they are not identifiable by M type. Second, type-specific and non–type-specific immune responses to streptococcal M protein are generally weaker after pharyngeal infection with OF-positive than with OF-negative strains.[18]

Many group A streptococcal strains cannot be serotyped by precipitin reactions using anti-M sera, either because they fail to express M protein in adequate amounts or because they belong to undesignated types for which antisera are not available. As mentioned earlier, there is increasing interest in circumventing the cumbersome serotyping technique by sequencing of the gene encoding M protein (*emm*).[19] Non–M-typeable strains may frequently be identified by a subsidiary typing system using slide agglutination reactions and based on antigenic differences in T proteins. Although T protein has proved to be a useful epidemiologic marker, it has no known role in streptococcal virulence.

Two other cell wall constituents, lipoteichoic acid and protein F, play critical roles in the first step in colonization, namely, adherence of *S. pyogenes* to fibronectin on the surface of human epithelial cells.[20–23] A cell-bound peptidase cleaves the C5a component of complement and inhibits neutrophil chemotaxis in vitro and in vivo.[24] An array of multifunctional surface proteins have the ability to bind to host proteins, including immunoglobulin G (IgG) and IgA.[25]

Extracellular Products

During the course of growth in vitro or in vivo, group A streptococci elaborate numerous extracellular products, only a limited number of which have been well characterized. Streptococcal pyrogenic exotoxins, formerly known as erythrogenic toxins, are responsible for the rash of scarlet fever. Experimentally, these substances exhibit a variety of other toxic properties including pyrogenicity, cytotoxicity, and enhancement of susceptibility to the lethal effects of endotoxin. There are currently five recognized streptococcal pyrogenic exotoxins: A, B, and C, mitogenic factor, and streptococcal superantigen. Their pathogenic role is discussed in more detail later.

Two distinct hemolysins are elaborated. Streptolysin O derives its name from its oxygen lability. It is reversibly inhibited by oxygen and irreversibly inhibited by cholesterol. In addition to its effect on erythrocytes, it is toxic to a variety of cells and cell fractions including polymorphonuclear leukocytes, platelets, tissue culture cells, lysosomes, and isolated mammalian and amphibian hearts. Streptolysin O is produced by almost all strains of *S. pyogenes* (as well as many group C and G organisms) and is antigenic. Measurement of ASO antibodies in human sera has proved exceedingly useful as an indicator of recent streptococcal infection.

Streptolysin S is a hemolysin produced by streptococci growing in the presence of serum (hence the *S*) or in the presence of a variety of other substances such as serum albumin, α-lipoprotein, ribonucleic acid, or detergents such as polysorbate/(Tween 80). Streptolysin S is nonantigenic, or at least no antibody to it has been detected that will neutralize its hemolytic activity. Streptolysin S shares with streptolysin O the capacity to damage the membranes of polymorphonuclear leukocytes, platelets, and subcellular organelles. Unlike streptolysin O, it is not inactivated by oxygen, but it is quite thermolabile. Most strains of *S. pyogenes* produce both hemolysins. Hemolysis on the surface of blood-agar plates is due primarily to streptolysin S, whereas streptolysin O exerts its hemolytic effect best in subsurface colonies, in pour plates, or in anaerobic cultures. An occasional strain may produce only one of the two hemolysins. Rarely, strains are encountered that lack both hemolysins.

Several extracellular products may, theoretically, serve to facilitate the liquefaction of pus and the spreading of streptococci through tissue planes. These include (1) four antigenically distinct enzymes that participate in the degradation of deoxyribonucleic acid (DNases A, B, C, and D); (2) hyaluronidase, which enzymatically degrades hyaluronic acid found in the ground substance of connective tissue; and (3) streptokinase, which promotes the dissolution of clots by catalyzing the conversion of plasminogen to plasmin. Antibodies to five of the extracellular products have been used in the serodiagnosis of streptococcal infection. These are ASO, anti–DNase B, antihyaluronidase, antinicotinamide adenine dinucleotidase, and antistreptokinase.

STREPTOCOCCAL PHARNYGITIS

The two most frequent clinical manifestations of streptococcal infection, pharyngitis and pyoderma, differ markedly in their epidemiologic, clinical, and bacteriologic characteristics.[26]

Epidemiology

Streptococcal sore throat is among the most common bacterial infections of childhood. Group A streptococci are responsible for the great majority of such infections, but strains of other serogroups, especially groups C and G,[27] may occasionally be involved. The disease occurs primarily among children 5 to 15 years of age, with the peak incidence occurring during the first few years of school. All age groups are susceptible, however, and severe epidemics are common in military training facilities. There is no sex predilection. The disease is ordinarily spread by direct person-to-person contact, most likely via droplets of saliva or nasal secretions. Crowding such as occurs in schools or barracks favors interpersonal spread of the organism (Fig. 186–2) and may also enhance its virulence by processes of natural selection analogous to those that occur during mouse passage in the laboratory. The effect of crowding in facilitating transmission may account in part for the increased incidence of streptococcal pharyngitis in northern latitudes during the colder months of the year. Explosive food- or waterborne outbreaks are also well documented. Contamination of dust, clothing, blankets, or other fomites does not play a significant role in contagion.

Group A streptococci frequently colonize the throats of asymptomatic persons. Pharyngeal carriage rates among normal schoolchildren vary with the geographic location and season of the year. Carriage rates of 15 to 20% have been noted in several studies. The carriage rate among adults is considerably lower.

Studies of experimentally induced human infections and of transmission within military barracks have shed considerable light on the

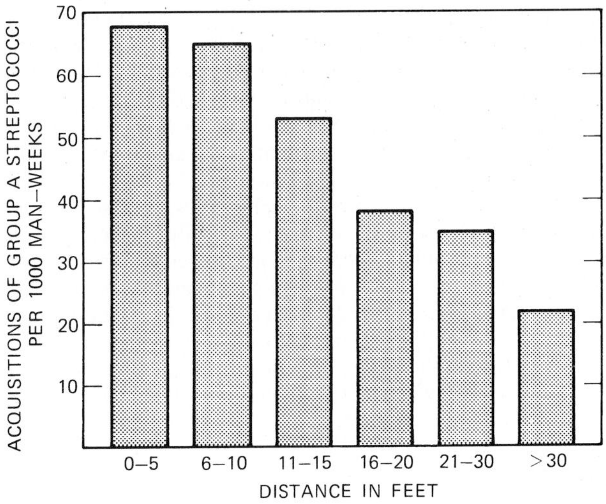

FIGURE 186–2. Transmission of group A streptococci in a military barracks according to bed distance from the nearest carrier. (From Wannamaker LW. The epidemiology of streptococcal infection. In: McCarty M, ed. Streptococcal Infections. New York: Columbia University Press; 1953:157–175.)

variables involved in interpersonal spread. During the acute phase of tonsillopharyngeal infection, M-typeable group A streptococci are frequently present in large numbers in both the nose and the throat. In untreated infections, organisms may persist for many weeks, although the signs and symptoms of illness abate within a few days. During convalescence, the organisms decrease in numbers, and they tend to disappear from the anterior nares sooner than from the throat. In addition, the M-protein content and virulence of persisting organisms gradually decline. The result of these qualitative and quantitative changes is that convalescent carriers are much less likely to transmit the organism to close contacts than are acutely infected persons.

In patients who do not receive effective antibiotic therapy for acute streptococcal pharyngitis, type-specific antibodies are frequently detectable in the serum between 4 and 8 weeks after the infection. These opsonic antibodies protect against subsequent infection with organisms of the same M type, but the person remains susceptible to infection by heterologous types. Prompt and effective antibiotic therapy ablates the type-specific immune response.

Clinical Manifestations

The usual incubation period of streptococcal pharyngitis is 2 to 4 days. The onset of illness is heralded by the rather abrupt onset of sore throat accompanied by malaise, feverishness, and headache. Nausea, vomiting, and abdominal pain are common in children. Prominent physical findings include redness, edema, and lymphoid hyperplasia of the posterior portion of the pharynx; enlarged, hyperemic tonsils studded with grayish-white exudate; enlarged, tender lymph nodes at the angles of the mandibles; and a temperature of 101°F or higher. In the absence of the aforementioned symptoms and signs, simple coryza, hoarseness, cough, or conjunctivitis do not suggest the presence of streptococcal infection. Laboratory findings include a positive throat culture for β-hemolytic streptococci and a total white blood cell count usually exceeding 12,000/mm^3 with increased numbers of polymorphonuclear leukocytes. The level of C-reactive protein is usually elevated.[28]

Not all patients with streptococcal pharyngitis have the full-blown syndrome just described. Endemically occurring infections in open populations manifest a wide spectrum of clinical severity. For example, only about half such patients with sore throats and positive throat cultures have tonsillar or pharyngeal exudates. Patients who have undergone tonsillectomy tend to experience a milder clinical syndrome. In infants, the response to streptococcal infection is much less sharply focalized to the lymphoid tissue of the faucial and posterior pharyngeal area. Rhinorrhea, suppurative complications, low-grade fever, and a more protracted course tend to characterize infections at this age. Exudative pharyngitis in children younger than 3 years rarely has a streptococcal cause.

In the absence of suppurative complications, the disease is self-limited. Fever abates within 3 to 5 days. Virtually all acute signs and symptoms subside within 1 week, although several additional weeks may be required for tonsils and lymph nodes to return to their usual size. Penicillin shortens the period of fever, toxicity, and infectivity.[29–31] Given the rather brief time course of untreated disease, however, such shortening of the clinical syndrome may not be striking unless therapy is initiated within the first 24 hours of illness.

Scarlet Fever

Scarlet fever results from infection with a streptococcal strain that elaborates streptococcal pyrogenic exotoxins (erythrogenic toxins). Although this disease is usually associated with pharyngeal infections, it may follow streptococcal infections at other sites such as wound infections or puerperal sepsis. The clinical syndrome is similar in most respects to that associated with nontoxigenic strains, save for the scarlatinal rash. The latter must be differentiated from those of viral exanthems, drug eruptions, staphylococcal toxic shock syndrome, and Kawasaki disease.

The rash usually appears on the second day of clinical illness as a diffuse red blush with many points of deeper red that blanches on pressure. It is often first noted over the upper part of the chest and then spreads to the remainder of the trunk, neck, and extremities. The palms, soles, and usually the face are spared. Skin folds in the neck, axillae, groin, elbows, and knees appear as lines of deeper red (Pastia's lines). There are scattered petechiae, and the Rumpel-Leede test of capillary fragility is positive. Occlusion of sweat glands imparts a sandpaper texture to the skin, a particularly helpful finding in dark-skinned patients.

The face appears flushed except for marked circumoral pallor. In addition to findings of exudative pharyngitis and tonsillitis, patients display an enanthem characterized by small, red, hemorrhagic spots on the hard and soft palate. The tongue is initially covered with a yellowish white coat through which may be seen the red papillae ("white-strawberry tongue"). Later, the coating disappears and the tongue is beefy red ("red-strawberry tongue"). The skin rash fades over the course of a week and is followed by extensive desquamation lasting for several weeks. A modest eosinophilia may be present early in the course of the illness.

Severe forms of scarlet fever, associated either with local and hematogenous spread of the organism (septic scarlet fever) or with profound toxemia (toxic scarlet fever), are characterized by high fever and marked systemic toxicity. The course may be complicated by arthritis, jaundice, and very rarely, hydrops of the gallbladder. Such severe forms of the disease are quite infrequent in the antibiotic era.

Suppurative Complications

Inflammation in the faucial area induced by acute streptococcal infection may give rise to peritonsillar cellulitis, peritonsillar abscess, or retropharyngeal abscess. The abscesses themselves, however, frequently contain a variety of other oral flora including oral anaerobes, with or without group A streptococci.[32] Direct extension of streptococci into adjacent structures may give rise to acute otitis media or acute sinusitis. Suppurative cervical lymphadenitis and mastoiditis may also occur.

Extension up the cribriform plate of the ethmoid or via the mastoid bone may cause meningitis, brain abscess, or thrombosis of the intracranial venous sinuses. Streptococcal pneumonia, another potential suppurative complication, is discussed later. Finally, bacteremic spread of the streptococci may result in a variety of metastatic foci of infection, such as suppurative arthritis, endocarditis, meningitis, brain abscess, osteomyelitis, or liver abscess. Such complications of streptococcal pharyngitis are extremely rare since the advent of effective chemotherapy.

Nonsuppurative Complications

Nonsuppurative complications of streptococcal pharyngitis, acute rheumatic fever and acute glomerulonephritis, are discussed in Chapter 187. The role of streptococci vis-à-vis other infectious and noninfectious agents in initiating certain other acute inflammatory disorders such as erythema nodosum and anaphylactoid purpura remains unresolved.

Diagnosis

Pharyngitis and tonsillitis may be due to a variety of infectious agents other than *S. pyogenes*.[27] Among these are streptococci of groups C[33, 34] and G.[35–37] *Corynebacterium diphtheriae*, the other major bacterial pathogen associated with exudative pharyngitis, is rare now, and when it occurs in its classic form, it is differentiated by the appearance of the diphtheritic membrane, respiratory embarrassment, severe systemic toxicity, and myocardial and neurologic manifestations. Other bacterial agents such as *Neisseria gonorrhoeae* and perhaps *Neisseria meningitidis* may occasionally cause pharyngitis, as may *Mycoplasma pneumoniae*. Pharyngitis due to oral anaerobes (Vincent's angina) is characterized by a membranous exudate, fetid breath, and oral ulcerations. Fever and constitutional symptoms are not prominent.

Pharyngitis due to *Arcanobacterium* (formerly *Corynebacterium*) *haemolyticum*, although rare, may closely mimic that due to *Strep. pyogenes*.[38, 39] *A. haemolyticum* affects primarily teenagers and young adults, and a high percentage of the patients have exudative pharyngitis and a scarlatiniform rash. The organism is more readily identified on rabbit or human blood agar than on sheep blood agar. Another rare cause of acute pharyngitis is *Yersinia enterocolitica*.[40] Patients infected with this organism may appear quite ill and may or may not have associated enteric symptoms. When *Y. enterocolitica* pharyngitis is associated with disseminated yersiniosis, the mortality may be appreciable. Diagnosis depends on clinical clues because the organism is unlikely to be detected on routine throat cultures and antistreptococcal therapy is unavailing (see Chapter 218).

Acute pharyngitis is more frequently caused by viruses than by bacteria. Infectious mononucleosis and adenovirus infections frequently give rise to exudative pharyngitis and thus may closely mimic streptococcal sore throat. Herpes simplex viruses 1 and 2 and influenza and parainfluenza viruses may simulate streptococcal pharyngitis, as may initially the acute retroviral syndrome in human immunodeficiency virus infection. Even when careful microbiologic techniques are used to detect bacteria, mycoplasma, and viruses, no etiologic agent can be detected in approximately one half of all cases of acute sore throat.[41] A more complete discussion of the differential diagnosis of acute pharyngitis may be found in Chapter 47.

Approximately one quarter to one third of all children complaining of sore throat have a positive throat culture for group A streptococci. Of these, about one half can be demonstrated to have immunologically significant infection, as judged by a significant rise in serum titer of one or more antistreptococcal antibodies. Most of the remainder probably represent asymptomatic carriers, because the average carriage rate among school-aged children in temperate climates during the winter months is approximately 15%. Such asymptomatic carriers are at no risk of developing suppurative and nonsuppurative complications and do not require antibiotic therapy. Thus, on the average, about 15 of every 100 children and adolescents with acute pharyngitis have streptococcal sore throat.

Numerous studies have tested the precision with which physicians may differentiate between streptococcal and nonstreptococcal sore throat by clinical criteria alone. In the presence of a classic scarlatinal rash or during a documented epidemic of streptococcal infections, such differentiation is easy. On the other hand, in the case of endemically occurring infections the problem is much more complex. Certain clinical findings, particularly tonsillopharyngeal exudate and tender, enlarged lymph nodes at the angles of the jaws, have a statistically significant correlation with the presence of positive throat cultures for group A streptococci.[42] Such findings are not diagnostic, however. Although only approximately one half of the patients with immunologically proven streptococcal sore throat have tonsillar exudate, a substantial proportion of cases of exudative pharyngitis have a nonstreptococcal cause. In two separate studies, the presence of a positive throat culture was accurately predicted on clinical grounds alone in 55 and 75% of cases, respectively, whereas a negative throat culture was correctly predicted in 73 and 77% of cases.[43, 44] Thus, even highly experienced clinicians using clinical impressions alone would fail to treat one quarter to one half of the patients with positive throat cultures and would needlessly treat one in four of the large number of persons who are neither infected nor colonized by group A streptococci. It is possible to identify individual patients in whom "strep throat" can be effectively excluded on a combination of epidemiologic (see earlier) and clinical grounds. For example, symptoms of the common cold are not due to *S. pyogenes*. Likewise, the presence of hoarseness and conjunctivitis and the absence of fever or pharyngeal erythema make streptococcal pharyngitis very unlikely. Unless such a determination can be made with a high degree of certainty, however, the diagnosis of streptococcal pharyngitis should be confirmed by a throat culture or rapid antigen-detection test (RADT).

Throat Culture

Throat culture remains the "gold standard" for diagnosing streptococcal pharyngitis. Failure to isolate β-hemolytic streptococci in a carefully obtained and accurately interpreted throat culture rules out the diagnosis of streptococcal sore throat for practical purposes. It is true that approximately 10% of negative throat cultures are weakly positive on reculture. Although the significance of these false-negative cultures cannot be ascertained in a given patient, the phenomenon should not be a cause for undue concern. Most such cultures likely reflect streptococcal carriage rather than acute streptococcal infection. When there is doubt about the validity of a negative culture, it is usually preferable to repeat the culture than to treat empirically with antimicrobial agents.

Although a negative culture eliminates the necessity for therapy, a positive culture does not differentiate between acute infection and asymptomatic carriage. Serum antibody titers do not rise until convalescence and are thus of no help in short-term management. Although the degree of positivity of the throat culture may assist in making this differentiation, it is best to assume that all positive cultures in patients with acute pharyngitis are significant and to treat accordingly, while recognizing that even with the use of the throat culture, some degree of overtreatment is inevitable.

Detailed instructions for obtaining and processing a throat culture have been published by the American Heart Association.[45] Under direct visualization with good illumination, the cotton or Dacron swab should be rubbed over both tonsils, or tonsillar fossae, the oropharynx, and the nasopharynx posterior to the uvula. Care should be taken to avoid the tongue and buccal mucosa. After the sample has been obtained, the swab should be rolled over a portion of the surface of a blood-agar plate, and the inoculated plate should be streaked with a wire loop in a manner that will yield isolated colonies. A stab is made through the agar with the inoculation loop to permit subsurface growth. Alternatively, a cover slip may be placed over the primary inoculum zone. This allows the observation of hemolysis due to the action of streptolysin O, which is oxygen-labile.

Sheep blood agar is preferred because clear-cut patterns of hemolysis are obtained on this medium. Human blood from a blood bank is less desirable because the presence of type-specific antibodies, streptolysin O antibodies, antibiotics, or high concentrations of citrate may inhibit the growth of streptococci or the expression of β-hemolysis. In regard to the isolation of group A streptococci, there is controversy in the literature as to the relative merits of plain sheep blood-agar plates versus plates to which trimethoprim and sulfamethoxazole have been added to suppress competing normal pharyngeal flora. Similar controversy exists as to the optimal atmosphere of incubation: aerobic, aerobic in the presence of 5 to 10% carbon dioxide, or anaerobic. Detailed analyses of these issues have been published elsewhere.[46, 47] If blood-agar plates are not immediately available, the swab may be placed in a dry sterile tube for transportation to the laboratory. After overnight incubation at 35 to 37°C, culture plates from patients with streptococcal pharyngitis show colonies surrounded by clear zones of hemolysis as well as β-hemolysis around the agar stab. Plates that are negative on first reading should be reexamined after an additional 24 hours of incubation. Serologic grouping of β-hemolytic streptococcal isolates may now be readily performed by using commercially available kits. A less expensive and highly serviceable screening procedure, the bacitracin-sensitivity test, may be performed once the organism has been isolated in pure culture. This susceptibility procedure is based on the observation that greater than 95% of all group A streptococcal strains are inhibited by low-potency (0.04 units) bacitracin disks, whereas 80 to 90% of non–group A strains are resistant. Fluorescent antibody techniques provide excellent results and specifically identify group A organisms. No quantitative information is gained as to the degree of positivity of the culture.

Because no group A streptococci resistant to penicillin have yet been described, antibiotic testing is unnecessary if this drug is to be used. The same holds true in general for erythromycin because group A streptococci resistant to this drug are rare in the United States.[48] Rates of erythromycin resistance in excess of 5% have, however, been reported in certain localized areas.[49, 50] Moreover, the prevalence of erythromycin-resistant group A streptococci has been reported to be quite high in portions of Japan,[51] Finland,[52] Australia,[53] Great Britain,[54, 55] and elsewhere. In a number of instances, erythromycin resistance has been correlated with increased erythromycin usage. In areas where resistance to erythromycin is known to be prevalent, antimicrobial-susceptibility testing should be performed if this agent or the newer macrolides are used to treat group A streptococcal infections. Such testing might best be performed by broth or agar dilution in view of questions raised concerning the reliability of disk diffusion methodology.[53, 56]

Rapid Antigen-Detection Tests

RADTs allow detection of the presence of the group A carbohydrate antigen directly from throat swabs. Unlike the throat culture, which requires overnight or longer to yield a definitive result, RADT can be completed in a matter of minutes. By facilitating early diagnosis and therapy, RADT may shorten the duration of illness, decrease the secondary spread of the organism, and allow an earlier return of patients and parents to school and work. Earlier tests based on latex agglutination methodology have been largely replaced by enzyme immunoassays that are easier to interpret and more sensitive. More recently, tests utilizing optical immunoassay and chemiluminescent DNA probes have become available.

Most currently commercially available RADTs are highly specific (95% or greater), so a positive result obviates the need for a throat culture. Unfortunately, the sensitivity of these tests is lower than that of the conventional throat culture, and, therefore, they may be negative in patients in whom conventional culture proves to be positive. Some investigators[57] have found newer tests such as optical immunoassay to have a sensitivity equivalent to that of culture, but others have reached opposite conclusions.[58] For this reason, physicians electing to use RADT should confirm negative test responses with a throat culture.[59]

Therapy

Therapy is directed toward the prevention of acute rheumatic fever and suppurative complications. Data on the preventability of post-streptococcal glomerulonephritis are less clear-cut.[60] The drug of choice in the treatment of streptococcal infection is penicillin, because of its efficacy in the prevention of rheumatic fever, safety, narrow spectrum, and low cost (Table 186–1).[59, 61, 62]

Prevention of acute rheumatic fever is believed to require eradication of the infecting streptococci from the pharynx, an effect that depends on prolonged rather than high-dose penicillin therapy. This objective is accomplished by the administration of a single intramuscular injection of 1.2 million units of penicillin G benzathine. For children weighing 60 pounds or less, the dose is reduced to 600,000 units.[59, 62] Most physicians in the United States elect to administer oral therapy. In this case, penicillin V, in one of the oral regimens listed in Table 186–1, must be continued for a full 10 days. Even compliant patients, however, frequently find it difficult to remember to take the full course of oral therapy once they become asymptomatic. Amoxicillin is often prescribed in preference to penicillin V in children requiring liquid medication because of poor palatability of oral suspensions of penicillin V.

In penicillin-allergic patients, erythromycin is the therapy of choice (see Table 186–1).[59, 62] Although twice-daily dosage appears satisfactory in children, data are limited as to the efficacy of this dosage schedule in adults. The newer macrolides (azithromycin, clarithromycin) appear to be effective, but these agents are more expensive than erythromycin.

A variable percentage of patients, averaging approximately 15%,[63] continue to harbor group A streptococci of the original infecting serotype in their pharynx after the completion of a course of oral penicillin. Such bacteriologic treatment failures are sometimes associated with symptomatic relapse. Treatment failure occurs more frequently when the subject is a streptococcal carrier than it does among acutely infected individuals.[64]

Oral cephalosporins are highly effective in the treatment of streptococcal pharyngitis, and a meta-analysis of 19 studies suggests that streptococcal eradication rates and clinical cure rates attained with these agents are slightly higher than those achieved with penicillin.[63, 65] It has been proposed, but not proved, that this may be due to the presence of β-lactamase–producing bacteria in the throat.[66] Penicillin remains the drug of choice as recommended by expert committees of the American Heart Association,[62] American Academy of Pediatrics,[67] and Infectious Diseases Society of America.[59] First- and second-generation oral cephalosporins are, however, acceptable alternatives. They are also useful in the penicillin-allergic patient whose allergy is not of the immediate type and who cannot tolerate oral erythromycin. The physician should bear in mind the possibility of an increased risk of allergic reactions to cephalosporins when treating penicillin-allergic patients.

There has been considerable interest in abbreviated courses of antimicrobial therapy. When administered for 5 days, azithromycin,[68–70] cefuroxime,[71] cefixime,[72] and cefpodoxine,[73] among others, have been reported to achieve clinical and bacteriologic cure rates equivalent to a 10-day course of oral penicillin V. Further data are required, however, before such courses can be endorsed. In addition, the ecologic effects of utilizing broader-spectrum agents to treat such a common bacterial infection are unclear. This is of special concern in the case of macrolides, whose widespread use has been associated with the development of resistance by group A streptococci.[74] Even when administered for short courses, most of these agents are considerably more expensive than penicillin.

Because tetracycline-resistant group A streptococci are prevalent in many areas, this drug is not recommended. Sulfonamides, which are highly effective in prophylaxis, are ineffective in the eradication of pharyngeal organisms or in the prevention of rheumatic fever when used as therapy for acute pharyngeal infections.

Treatment of group A streptococcal sore throat as long as 9 days after its onset is still effective in the prevention of rheumatic fever.[75] Thus, if the patient is seen early in the course of the illness, the delay in initiation of therapy occasioned by obtaining a positive throat culture is not ordinarily a matter of concern. However, in a minority of patients who are severely ill or toxic at presentation, antimicrobial therapy may be started at the initial visit after a sample has been obtained for throat culture. Such therapy reduces the period of infectivity and, if started early, shortens the duration of the clinical illness.[29–31] If oral therapy is prescribed, the throat culture serves as a guide to the need for completion of a full 10-day course or, alternatively, for recalling the patient for an injection of penicillin G benzathine. As discussed earlier, patients with signs and symptoms of acute pharyngitis and a positive test (properly performed and interpreted) for group A carbohydrate antigen should receive appropriate antimicrobial therapy.

Patients with more severe suppurative infections such as those involving the mastoid or ethmoid may require larger doses of penicillin administered parenterally. When streptococcal upper respiratory infection is complicated by the development of abscesses associated with suppurative cervical adenitis or in the peritonsillar or retropharyngeal soft tissues, incision and drainage are required.

Because the prevention of rheumatic fever appears to require the eradication of the streptococci from the pharynx, treatment failures are of concern. In addition to true treatment failure (i.e., reisolation of the original infecting streptococcal serotype shortly after completion of a full course of antibiotic therapy), causes of post-treatment culture positivity include a failure of compliance with oral medication schedules and reinfection with the same or different streptococcal types in the home or school environment. In everyday practice, it is often impossible to differentiate between these alternatives.

TABLE 186–1 Primary Prevention of Rheumatic Fever (Treatment of Streptococcal Tonsillopharyngitis)*

Agent	Dose	Mode	Duration
Benzathine penicillin G	600,000 U for patients ≤27 kg (60 lb) 1.2 million U for patients >27 kg (60 lb)	Intramuscular	Once
	or		
Penicillin V (phenoxymethylpenicillin)	Children: 250 mg 2–3 times daily Adolescents and adults: 500 mg 2–3 times daily	Oral	10 d
For Individuals Allergic to Penicillin			
Erythromycin			
Estolate	20–40 mg/kg/d 2–4 times daily (maximum 1 g/d)	Oral	10 d
Ethylsuccinate	40 mg/kg/d 2–4 times daily (maximum 1 g/d)	Oral	10 d

*For other acceptable alternatives, see text. The following are not acceptable: sulfonamides, trimethoprim, tetracyclines, and chloramphenicol.
From Dajani A, Taubert K, Ferrieri P, et al. Treatment of acute streptococcal pharyngitis and prevention of rheumatic fever: A statement for health professionals. Committee on Rheumatic Fever, Endocarditis, and Kawasaki Disease of the Council on Cardiovascular Disease in the Young, the American Heart Association. Pediatrics. 1995;96:758–764.

Nevertheless, routine reculture of the throat after a course of antistreptococcal therapy is not advised[59] because the benefit/cost ratio of such cultures continues to decline in parallel with the incidence of acute rheumatic fever in developed countries. Certainly such cultures should be undertaken in high-risk circumstances (e.g., if the patient or a family member has a history of rheumatic fever) or when symptoms compatible with streptococcal infection persist or recur. When an increased incidence of acute rheumatic fever is detected in a community, as happened in a number of U.S. cities during the 1980s, the approach to streptococcal infection must be particularly rigorous, and serious consideration should be given to routine post-treatment cultures. If reculture is undertaken, only a single retreatment course is warranted for patients who still harbor group A streptococci. Retreatment with an oral cephalosporin might be considered, in view of the slightly increased eradication rates observed with these agents.

The presence of persistently but weakly positive throat cultures after repeated courses of antibiotic therapy in an otherwise asymptomatic patient is not a cause for alarm. Such persons are streptococcal carriers[64] who are neither at risk of developing rheumatic fever nor highly likely to spread their infection to others. Their most frequent problem is anxiety produced by multiple medical consultations associated with the streptococcal colonization. If, for medical or psychological reasons, the eradication of chronic streptococcal carriage becomes highly desirable, clindamycin[76] or amoxicillin-clavulanate[77] may be efficacious.[59]

Streptococcal acquisition rates of 25% or greater have been recorded in family contacts. Certainly, family contacts with symptoms of upper respiratory infection should have throat cultures and should be treated appropriately if cultures are positive. Asymptomatic family contacts should also have samples cultured in high-risk circumstances, for example, the presence of a person in the family who has had rheumatic fever or known cases of rheumatic fever or poststreptococcal glomerulonephritis occurring in the general area. In situations of lesser risk, routine cultures from asymptomatic family contacts are not recommended.[59, 62]

There is no firm evidence to suggest that tonsillectomy reduces the incidence of rheumatic fever, either in healthy persons or in persons who have had rheumatic fever and faithfully maintained continuous antibiotic prophylaxis. In certain patients with recurrent bouts of tonsillopharyngitis, however, tonsillectomy may decrease the frequency of incapacitating acute infections.[78] This potential benefit must be balanced against the possibility that tonsillectomized persons may be more likely to experience mild or subclinical infections that go unattended.

STREPTOCOCCAL PYODERMA

Pyoderma is the term used collectively to denote localized purulent streptococcal infections of the skin. For the most part, the term is used synonymously with *streptococcal impetigo* or *impetigo contagiosa* to describe discrete purulent lesions that appear to be primary infections of the skin and are extremely prevalent in many parts of the world.

Epidemiology

Pyoderma occurs most frequently among economically disadvantaged children dwelling in tropical or subtropical climates. It is also prevalent in northern climates during the summer months of the year in certain epidemiologic settings such as the Native American reservations of Minnesota. The peak incidence of pyoderma is in children aged 2 to 5 years, as opposed to streptococcal pharyngitis, which occurs primarily in the 5- to 15-year-old age group. There is no sex predilection, and all races appear to be susceptible. The disease has been intensively studied, for example, among blacks in Mississippi and Alabama, Native Americans in Minnesota, East Indians in Trinidad, and white military personnel in Vietnam.

The prevalence of pyoderma reaches extremely high levels in certain population groups. Among indigent black children attending Project Headstart classes during the summer in rural Mississippi, 40 to 50% were found to have identifiable pyodermal lesions in various stages of evolution. Eighty-five percent of children followed weekly throughout the summer had bacteriologically proven streptococcal impetigo[79]; most of these had multiple lesions. Reports from the United States and Europe have documented outbreaks of streptococcal pyoderma among workers in meat-packing plants, who suffer numerous cutaneous cuts and abrasions.[80]

The prevalence of streptococcal pyoderma is markedly influenced by several factors, the most important of which appear to be climate and the level of hygiene. Studies among Colombian schoolchildren[81] showed the lowest prevalence in Bogotà (8700-foot elevation, cool climate), intermediate prevalence in Medellin (5000-foot elevation, temperate climate), and highest incidence in Apartado (sea level, tropical climate). At each level of elevation, skin lesions were more frequent among persons with poor hygiene than among those with good hygiene. Among Colombian military troops in the field, those conducting operations in humid tropical rain forests experienced a considerably greater incidence of pyoderma than those operating in the dry tropical savanna.

The mode of spread of streptococcal pyoderma is poorly understood. Possible means of transmission include direct contact, environmental contamination, and arthropod vectors such as the *Hippelates* fly, which has been shown to carry group A streptococci on its legs for periods of more than 24 hours.

Meticulous studies performed in children at Red Lake Indian Reservation, Minnesota,[82] have demonstrated that the streptococci responsible for pyoderma initially colonize the unbroken skin, an observation that probably explains the influence of personal hygiene on disease incidence. The development of skin colonization with a given streptococcal type precedes the development of impetiginous lesions due to the same serotype by an average interval of 10 days (Fig. 186–3). The mechanism of production of skin lesions is unproved but is most likely due to intradermal inoculation of surface organisms by abrasions, minor trauma, or insect bites. Lesions of scabies have also been demonstrated to harbor group A streptococci

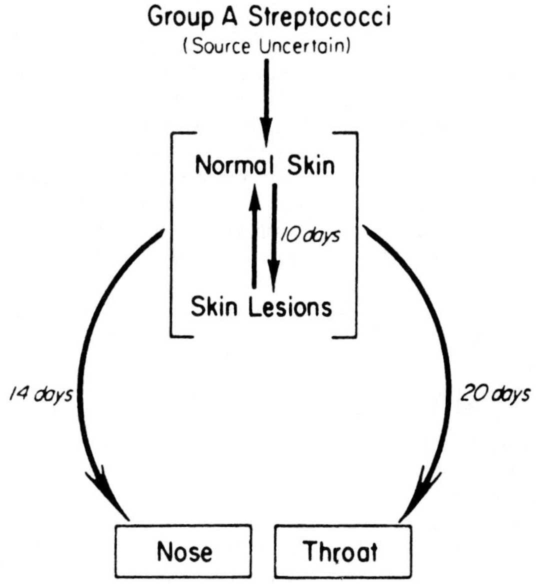

FIGURE 186–3. Representative sequence of the spread of pyoderma strains of group A streptococci among different body sites. (From Ferrieri P, Dajani AS, Wannamaker LW, Chapman SS. Natural history of impetigo. I. Site sequence of acquisition and familial patterns of spread of cutaneous streptococci. J Clin Invest. 1972;51:2851–2862.)

in Trinidad, where epidemics of human scabies and of pyoderma-associated nephritis coexist. Frequently, there is a transfer of the streptococcal strains from the skin or impetigo lesions, or both, to the upper respiratory tract. The interval between colonization of the skin and colonization of the nose or throat, or both, averages 2 to 3 weeks (see Fig. 186–3).

Bacteriology

Streptococci isolated from pyodermal lesions are primarily group A, but occasionally representatives of other serogroups such as C and G are responsible. Group A streptococci that cause impetigo differ in several respects from those usually associated with tonsillitis and pharyngitis. So-called skin strains belong to different M serotypes from the classic "throat strains"; because most have been identified more recently, they tend to constitute the higher-numbered M types. Throat and skin strains can also be differentiated by genetic markers.[83] There is a great multiplicity of M-protein types among the skin strains, and many of these types have never been fully characterized and classified. Therefore, the M typing system is not entirely satisfactory for identifying skin strains. This has led to increased use of the T-aggutination system and, more recently, to genotyping.

The well-known streptococcal M types that frequently give rise to exudative tonsillitis (e.g., types 1, 3, 5, 6, 12, 18, 19, and 24) are rarely found in pyoderma lesions. (This is not necessarily true of more deeply invasive skin and soft tissue infections, as discussed later). On the other hand, as pointed out before, skin strains frequently colonize the throat. In populations in which pyoderma is hyperendemic, streptococcal carriage rates of 10 to 15% are seen during the warmer months, and most of these streptococci belong to "pyoderma" serotypes. For the most part, however, skin strains cause few or no symptoms when lodged in the throat. A relatively small number of serotypes seem capable of regularly initiating both pharyngitis and pyoderma.[84]

Immunology

The ASO response after cutaneous streptococcal infection is weak. There is experimental evidence to suggest that this may be due to local inactivation of streptolysin O by skin lipids. Modest ASO responses are frequently observed when streptococcal pyoderma is accompanied by pharyngeal colonization. In contrast, the immune response to anti–DNase B is brisk; the antihyaluronidase assay is also a useful test in the serodiagnosis of pyoderma.[85, 86]

In uncomplicated pyoderma, type-specific opsonic antibodies are detectable 2 to 3 months after the development of infection. In one study,[87] such antibodies were present in 12% of a small group of patients with pyoderma alone but in more than half of the people who had concomitant pharyngeal carriage. In another study, type-specific antibodies were present in most patients convalescing from pyoderma-associated nephritis due to M-type 55.[88] It is not known whether such antibodies play a role in the prevention of reinfection analogous to that which has been established in pharyngeal infections.

Clinical Manifestations

The lesion begins as a papule that rapidly evolves into a vesicle surrounded by an area of erythema. The vesicular lesions are evanescent and rarely recognized clinically; they give rise to pustules that gradually enlarge and then break down over a period of 4 to 6 days to form characteristic thick crusts (Fig. 186–4). The lesions heal slowly and leave depigmented areas. A deeply ulcerated form of impetigo is known as *ecthyma.*

Streptococcal impetigo occurs on exposed areas of the body, most frequently on the lower extremities. The lesions remain well localized but are frequently multiple. Although regional lymphadenitis may occur, systemic symptoms are not ordinarily present.

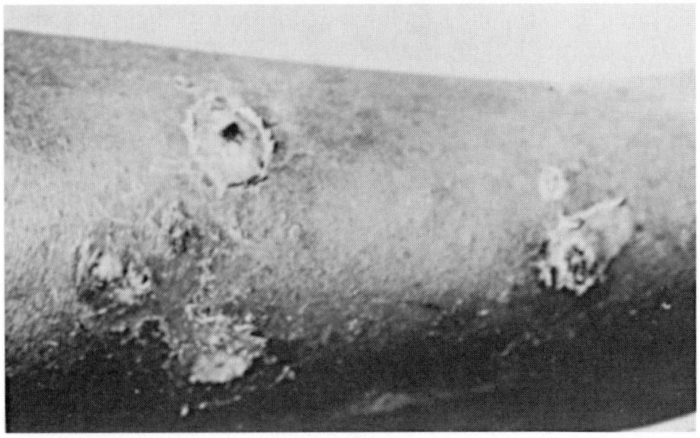

FIGURE 186–4. Multiple pyoderma lesions on the lower extremities of a child in rural Mississippi. (Courtesy of Dr. K. Nelson, Baltimore, Md.)

In the past, the lesions described previously could be rather confidently diagnosed as streptococcal. This was the predominant form of impetigo and could be distinguished from bullous impetigo due to phage group II *Staphylococcus aureus*. Although bullous impetigo remains almost exclusively staphylococcal in cause, the bacteriology of nonbullous impetigo has changed.[89] A number of studies conducted over the past decade have found *S. aureus*, either alone or in combination with *S. pyogenes*, to be the predominant etiologic agent.[90–92] Most such staphylococci are penicillinase producers. Therefore, treatment with penicillin, which in the past had been highly effective in nonbullous impetigo even when both streptococci and staphylococci were isolated from the lesions, now frequently fails.[91]

Therapy and Prevention

A number of oral agents are highly effective in the treatment of pyoderma. These include cloxacillin, cephalexin, cefadroxil, and cefaclor.[92] Erythromycin has long been a mainstay of pyoderma therapy, but its utility is lessened in areas in which erythromycin-resistant strains of *S. aureus* are prevalent. Therapy is usually continued for 10 days. Mupirocin ointment applied topically three times daily to the lesions has achieved cure rates equivalent to those of oral antimicrobial agents,[93, 94] but it is expensive.[95] Adherence to good regimens of personal hygiene, with special attention to frequent scrubbing with soap and water, is the most effective preventive measure currently available.

Complications

Although septicemia accompanies streptococcal impetigo on rare occasions, suppurative complications are on the whole most uncommon. For unexplained reasons, rheumatic fever does not occur after streptococcal pyoderma (see Chapter 187). On the other hand, cutaneous infections with nephritogenic strains of group A streptococci are the major antecedent of poststreptococcal glomerulonephritis in many areas of the world. There are no conclusive data to indicate that treatment of an individual case of pyoderma will prevent the subsequent occurrence of nephritis in these patients. Such therapy is nevertheless important as an epidemiologic measure in eradicating nephritogenic strains from the environment.

INVASIVE STREPTOCOCCAL INFECTIONS OF SKIN AND SOFT TISSUES

In the mid-1980s, outbreaks of acute rheumatic fever began to occur throughout the United States, concomitant with the reappearance of certain streptococcal strains exhibiting characteristics known to be associated with rheumatogenicity (see Chapter 187). Shortly thereafter, invasive streptococcal infections of a frequency and severity not seen in recent decades began to be reported both in the United States and abroad.[96–99] Although strains of a number of group A streptococcal M types has been isolated from invasive infections, there has been a definite and consistent tendency for M types 1 and 3 to be associated with life-threatening infections.[97–101] A high proportion of these cases has occurred in adults, and the portal of entry is frequently the skin or soft tissues. In some instances the infections give rise to shock and multiorgan failure, features that simulate in certain respects the staphylococcal toxic shock syndrome.[102] This entity has thus been named the *streptococcal toxic shock syndrome* (Strep TSS). Clinical features of serious streptococcal skin and soft tissue infections and Strep TSS are summarized later.

Erysipelas

Erysipelas is an acute inflammation of the skin, with marked involvement of cutaneous lymphatic vessels, that is caused by group A streptococci. Occasionally group C strains and rarely group G[103] are responsible. The disease, which occurs primarily in infants and in persons older than 30 years, has become much less common in recent years. Erysipelas often involves the face (Fig. 186–5), and in such cases there is usually a history of preceding streptococcal sore throat, although the exact mode of spread to the skin is unknown. When erysipelas involves the trunk or extremities, it often occurs at the site of a surgical incision or wound.

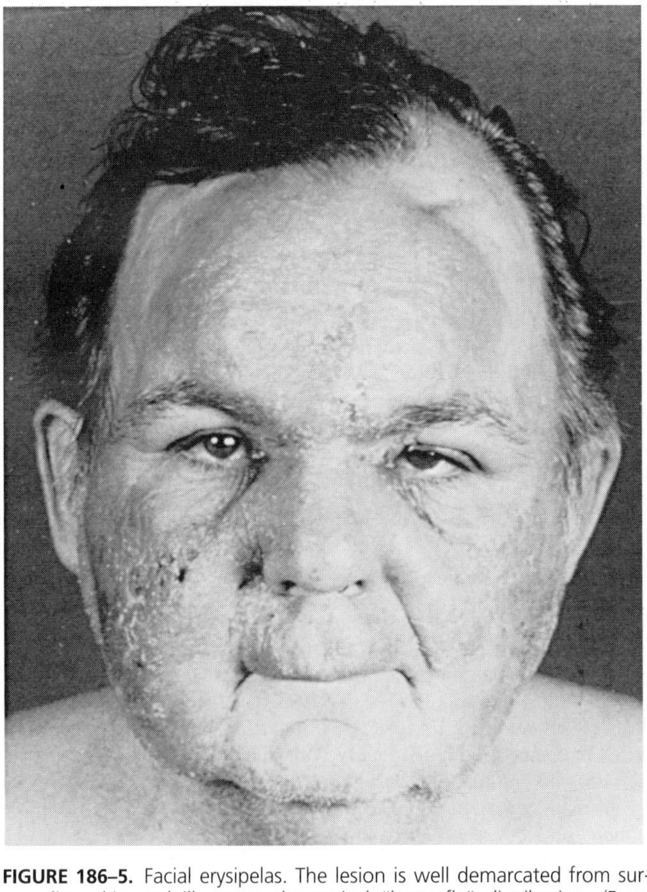

FIGURE 186–5. Facial erysipelas. The lesion is well demarcated from surrounding skin and illustrates the typical "butterfly" distribution. (From Bisno AL. Cutaneous infections: Microbiologic and epidemiologic considerations. Am J Med. 1984;76:172–179. Copyright 1984, with permission from Excerpta Medica, Inc.)

Clinically, the cutaneous inflammation is accompanied by chills, fever, and marked toxicity. The cutaneous lesion begins as a localized area of erythema and swelling and then spreads rapidly with advancing red margins, which are raised and well demarcated from adjacent normal tissue. There is marked edema, often with bleb formation, and in facial erysipelas the eyes are frequently swollen shut. The lesion may demonstrate central resolution while continuing to extend on the periphery. Treatment with penicillin is curative.

Streptococcal Cellulitis

Streptococcal cellulitis, an acute, spreading inflammation of the skin and subcutaneous tissues, results from infection of burns, wounds, or surgical incisions but may also follow mild trauma. Clinical findings include local pain, tenderness, swelling, and erythema. The process may extend rapidly to involve large areas of skin. Systemic manifestations include fever, chills, and malaise, and there may be associated lymphangitis or bacteremia, or both. Cellulitis is differentiated from erysipelas by two physical findings: the lesion is not raised, and the demarcation between involved and uninvolved skin is indistinct. In not all cases, however, is the clinical differentiation between these entities clear-cut.

Two predisposing causes of streptococcal cellulitis deserve special mention. The first is the parenteral injection of illicit drugs.[104–106] These cases are often associated with bacteremia and deep tissue infections such as septic thrombophlebitis, suppurative arthritis, osteomyelitis, and occasionally infective endocarditis. Second, patients who have impaired lymphatic drainage from upper or lower extremities are prone to recurrent episodes of streptococcal cellulitis. Examples include individuals with filariasis and women who have undergone radical mastectomy with axillary node dissection. Recurrent episodes of severe cellulitis have been reported in certain patients who have undergone coronary artery bypass grafts.[107] The lesion invariably occurs in the extremity from which the saphenous vein was removed, and at times it may exhibit features of erysipelas (Fig. 186–6). Patients with tinea pedis of the venectomy limb appear to be particularly at risk.[108–110] As with other forms of cellulitis, pathogenic bacteria are difficult to recover during these episodes. The appearance of the lesions and the response to penicillin therapy suggest, however, a streptococcal cause. The few β-hemolytic streptococci that have been recovered and characterized belong to serogroups other than A.[111]

Perianal cellulitis (or asymptomatic anal infection) occurs most frequently in children, but also in adults. It has been the source of several reported outbreaks of hospital-acquired streptococcal infection.

Cellulitis may be caused by infection with a variety of bacterial pathogens (see Chapter 78), but most cases are due to *S. pyogenes* (or occasionally streptococci of groups C and G[106]) or to *S. aureus*. Although intramuscular or intravenous penicillin is the drug of choice for severe forms of streptococcal cellulitis, it is often impossible to confidently differentiate streptococcal from staphylococcal cellulitis on initial presentation. In this case a semisynthetic, penicillinase-resistant penicillin should be used. In penicillin-allergic patients, a first-generation cephalosporin may be employed if the hypersensitivity is not of the immediate type. Intravenous vancomycin may be used in patients who manifest anaphylactic hypersensitivity to β-lactam antibiotics or if there is reason to suspect infection with methicillin-resistant strains of *S. aureus*. In the absence of positive blood cultures, a specific microbiologic diagnosis may be difficult even in retrospect. Aspirates or biopsies from sites of active cellulitis are helpful when positive on smear or culture, but unfortunately such specimens are usually negative in adult patients.[112–114]

Necrotizing Fasciitis (Streptococcal Gangrene)

General

Necrotizing fasciitis is an infection of the deeper subcutaneous tissues and fascia, characterized by extensive and rapidly spreading

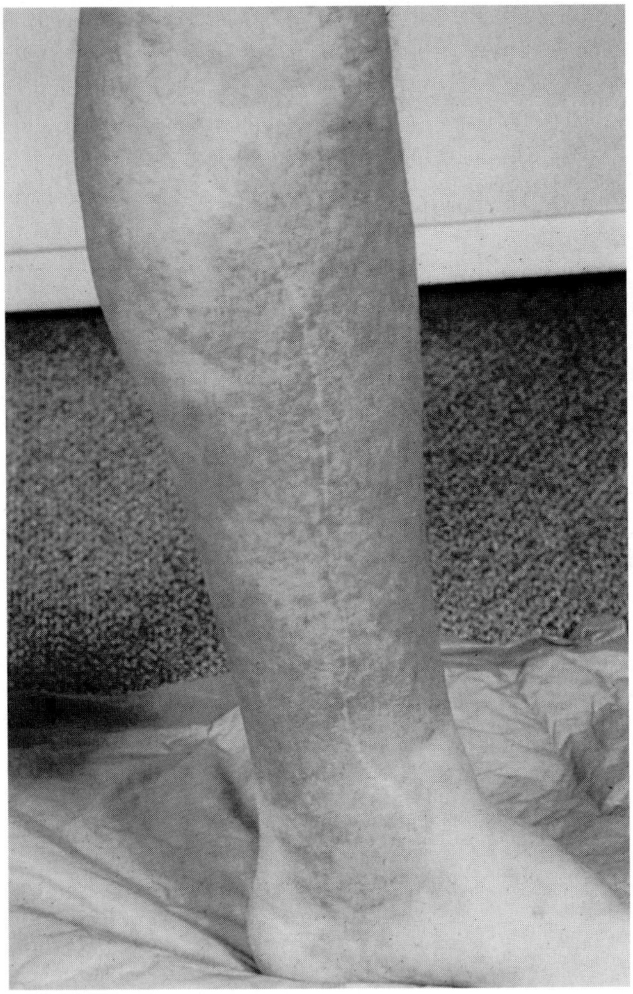

FIGURE 186–6. Erysipelas in saphenous venectomy limb of a patient who had undergone coronary artery bypass grafting.

necrosis and by gangrene of the skin and underlying structures. As detailed in Chapter 78, this entity may arise in several distinct epidemiologic settings, be caused by multiple aerobic and anaerobic microorganisms, and vary in clinical manifestations. The present discussion is limited to necrotizing fasciitis caused by the group A streptococci[115] and described by Meleney in 1924 as hemolytic streptococcal gangrene.[116] Characteristically, streptococcal gangrene begins at a site of trivial or even inapparent trauma or in an operative incision. The initial lesion may appear only as an area of mild erythema but over the next 24 to 72 hours undergoes a rapid evolution. The inflammation becomes more pronounced and extensive, the skin becomes dusky and then purplish, and bullae containing yellow or hemorrhagic fluid appear. Bacteremia is frequently present, and metastatic abscesses may occur. By the fourth to fifth day, frank gangrenous changes are evident in the affected skin,[117] and this is followed by extensive sloughing. The process may march inexorably over large bodily areas unless measures are taken to contain it. The patient with streptococcal gangrene appears perilously ill, with high fever and extreme prostration. Mortality rates are high even with appropriate treatment.[117] Fournier's gangrene, a form of necrotizing fasciitis involving the male genital area, may rarely be due to group A streptococci.

The course of necrotizing fasciitis today appears to be much more fulminant than that described by Meleney. Specifically, ecchymoses and bullae may appear within 2 to 3 days, and associated myonecrosis is more common. In addition, the mortality in 1924 was 20%, whereas mortalities of 20 to 70% have been reported in the current era. This difference is even more remarkable since antibiotics, intravenous fluids, ventilators, and dialysis were not available in 1924.

Diagnosis and Differential Diagnosis

Successful management of necrotizing fasciitis is dependent on early recognition, yet early in their course, patients may present with fever and toxicity at a time when the cutaneous lesion may appear relatively benign. Fever and severe pain are the first manifestations of disease. In those with a defined portal of entry such as a surgical incision, burn, insect bite, or varicella lesion, there is redness of the skin, pain, and swelling. In the 50% of patients who develop necrotizing fasciitis without a defined portal of entry, the infection begins deep to the skin, frequently at the site of a hematoma, muscle strain, or traumatic joint injury. In these, crescendo pain is the most reliable clinical clue. Routine radiographs, computed tomography, and magnetic resonance imaging studies may show localized swelling of the deep structures but characteristically do not show frank abscess formation or gas in the tissue. Unfortunately, these studies serve to delay rather than to facilitate a diagnosis. Necrotizing fasciitis in the absence of a portal of entry mimics deep vein thrombophlebitis, particularly in those with involvement of the lower extremity. Administration of nonsteroidal anti-inflammatory drugs for presumed musculoskeletal pain may further delay diagnosis and may predispose to a worse outcome.[101, 118, 119] The presence of fever and increasingly severe pain, unexplained tachycardia, marked left shift, and elevated creatine phosphokinase levels are all suggestive of necrotizing fasciitis and should prompt surgical inspection of the deep tissues. Gram stains of aspirated fluid reveal chains of gram-positive cocci and few, if any, white blood cells. Similarly, a biopsy with frozen section may aid in the diagnosis of necrotizing fasciitis.

Myositis-Myonecrosis

Most cases of purulent muscle infection occur in the tropics, and *S. aureus* is the predominant etiologic agent. Myositis due to the group A streptococcus has been rare but occurs in many patients with necrotizing fasciitis and Strep TSS. Most of these cases occur following blunt, nonpenetrating trauma or occur spontaneously. Most likely, bacteria are translocated to the deep tissue hematogenously from the throat. Systemic toxicity is common, and a mortality as high as 80% has been reported.[120] Destruction of tissue is poorly understood, but infection and inflammation within the confined muscle compartment space may result in pressures exceeding arterial pressure, necessitating emergent fasciotomy and débridement (Fig. 186–7). There is much overlap in the clinical features of necrotizing fasciitis and myonecrosis,[117, 120] and the differentiation must be made by surgical inspection or biopsy.

Streptococcal Toxic Shock Syndrome

Strep TSS is defined as described in Table 186–2, but simply put, it is any streptococcal infection associated with the sudden onset of shock and organ failure. Such cases were first described in the mid to late 1980s, and reports of Strep TSS have subsequently emanated from North America, Europe, Australia, and Asia.[97, 101, 102, 121–129] Most cases have occurred sporadically with a prevalence of 5 to 10 cases per 100,000 population. The highest incidence of Strep TSS occurred in a small community of Minnesota, where 26 cases per 100,000 population were recorded.[128] In addition, outbreaks of invasive group A streptococcal infections have occurred in closed environments such as nursing homes[130–134] and hospital environments.[135] Secondary cases of Strep TSS are rare, but transmission to family members[135, 136] or health care workers[135, 137] has been well documented by demonstrating identical pulsed-field gel electrophoresis patterns from cross-

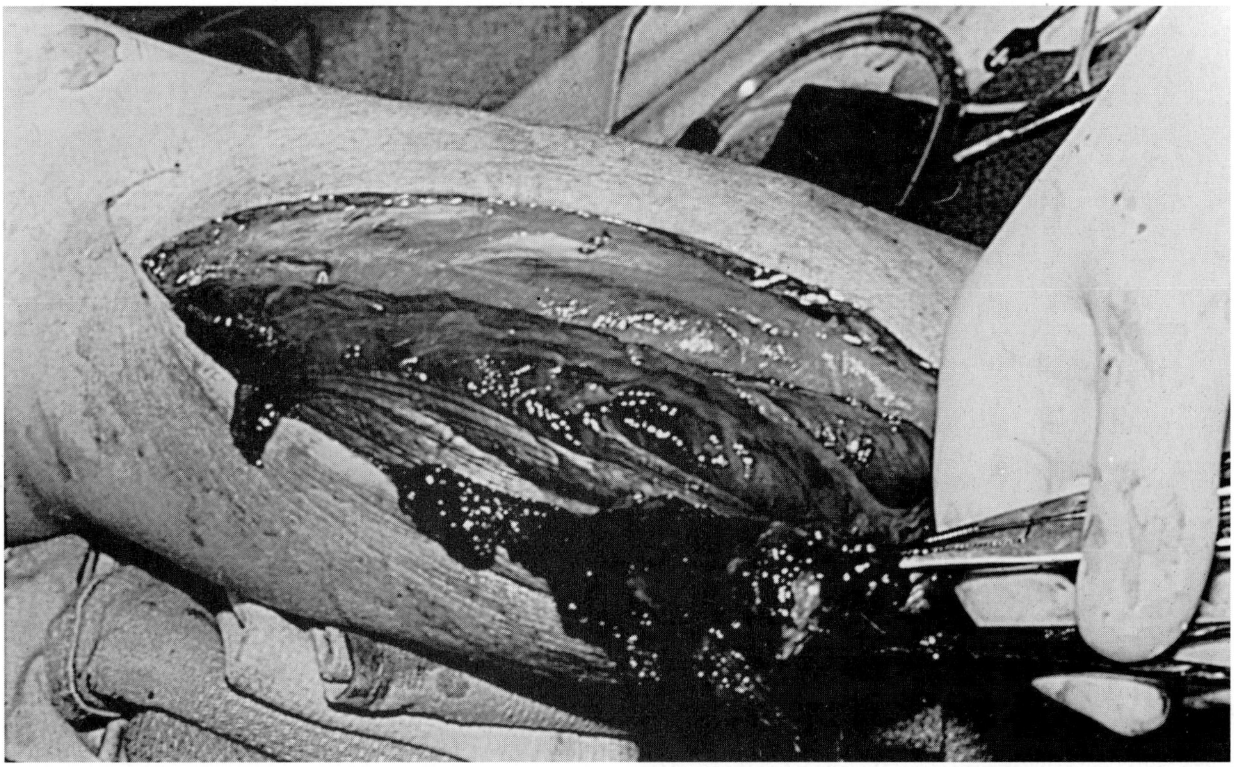

FIGURE 186–7. Surgical exploration of patient with streptococcal toxic shock syndrome with necrotizing fasciitis and myositis that occurred spontaneously with no prior injury to the site. (From Stevens D. Streptococcal toxic shock syndrome. Infect Med. 1992;9:33–39. Copyright © 1992, SCP Communications, Inc.)

infecting strains. Although many of the studies cited previously have described Strep TSS in adults, several reports have documented that this disorder also occurs in children.[122, 127, 128, 138, 139] Thus, persons of all ages are afflicted, and though some have underlying medical conditions such as diabetes and alcoholism,[122, 124, 140–144] many have no predisposing medical condition and are not immunocompromised. This contrasts sharply with reviews of group A streptococcal bacteremia from several decades ago[140–142] that found the disease to occur primarily among the very young and the very old, or in patients suffering from predisposing conditions such as cancer, renal failure, leukemia, severe burns, or iatrogenic immunosuppression.

The portals of entry for streptococci are the pharynx, skin, and vagina in 50% of cases.[101] Surgical procedures such as suction lipectomy, hysterectomy, vaginal delivery, bunionectomy, reduction mammoplasty, hernia repair, bone pinning, and vasectomy have provided portals in such cases (Table 186–3). Rarely, infection occurs secondary to streptococcal pharyngitis.[145–147] Viral infections such as varicella and influenza have provided portals of entry in other cases.[101, 127, 145]

Additional factors that increase the risk of invasive group A streptococcal infection, including bacteremia, Strep TSS, and necrotizing fasciitis, are listed in Table 186–3. Three studies have demonstrated that a high or increasing prevalence of M-1 or M-3 strains among throat isolates may signal an increased incidence of Strep TSS in that community.[127, 128, 143] Nonsteroidal anti-inflammatory agents, taken for muscle strain, trauma, postpartum pain, and so

TABLE 186–2 Proposed Case Definition for Streptococcal Toxic Shock Syndrome*

I. Isolation of group A streptococci (*Streptococcus pyogenes*)
  A. From a normally sterile site (e.g., blood; cerebrospinal, pleural, or peritoneal fluid; tissue biopsy; surgical wound)
  B. From a nonsterile site (e.g., throat, sputum, vagina, superficial skin lesion)
II. Clinical signs of severity
  A. Hypotension: systolic blood pressure ≤90 mmHg in adults or <5th percentile for age in children

and

  B. Two or more of the following signs:
    1. Renal impairment: creatinine level ≥177 μmol/L (≥2 mg/dl) for adults or twice the upper limit of normal for age or greater. In patients with preexisting renal disease, a twofold or greater elevation over the baseline level.
    2. Coagulopathy: platelets ≤100 × 10^9/L (≤100,000/mm^3) or disseminated intravascular coagulation defined by prolonged clotting times, a low fibrinogen level, and the presence of fibrin degradation products.
    3. Liver involvement: alanine aminotransferase (SGOT), aspartate aminotransferase (SGPT), or total bilirubin levels of twice the upper limit of normal for age or greater. In patients with preexisting liver disease, a twofold or greater elevation over the baseline level.
    4. Adult respiratory distress syndrome defined by the acute onset of diffuse pulmonary infiltrates and hypoxemia in the absence of cardiac failure, or evidence of a diffuse capillary leak manifested by the acute onset of generalized edema, or pleural or peritoneal effusions with hypoalbuminemia.
    5. A generalized erythematous macular rash that may desquamate.
    6. Soft tissue necrosis, including necrotizing fasciitis or myositis, or gangrene.

*Illness fulfilling criteria IA and II (A and B) can be defined as a definite case. Illness fulfilling criteria IB and II (A and B) can be defined as a probable case if no other cause of the illness is identified.
From The Working Group on Severe Streptococcal Infections. Defining the group A streptococcal toxic shock syndrome: Rationale and consensus definition. JAMA. 1993;269:390–391.

TABLE 186-3 Factors That Increase Likelihood of Developing Streptococcal Toxic Shock Syndrome

Age (neonates and elderly)
Diabetes
Alcoholism
Surgical procedures
Trauma
Penetrating (insect bites, lacerations, slivers, abrasions, burns)
Nonpenetrating (hematoma, bruise, muscle strain, hemarthrosis)
Varicella
Contact with a patient
High prevalence of invasive strains in the community
Nonsteroidal anti-inflammatory agents*

*Based on limited evidence.

forth, may mask the early signs and symptoms of streptococcal infection or possibly predispose to more severe infection such as necrotizing fasciitis or Strep TSS.[101, 118, 119]

Pathogenesis

Entry of group A streptococci into the deeper tissues and blood stream may occur as a result of a breach of a barrier, or the organism itself may penetrate intact mucous membranes such as the pharyngeal mucosa. Although bacteremia is a very uncommon phenomenon in streptococcal pharyngitis, transient bacteremia must occur in those 50% of patients who develop invasive infections without a portal of entry. In either case, group A streptococci avoid phagocytosis largely due to the antiphagocytic properties of M protein.[8] Adherence of group A streptococci to pharyngeal mucosal cells is prerequisite to colonization or infection and has been related to surface structures such as lipoteichoic acid and fibronectin-binding protein. Penetration or translocation of group A streptococci through respiratory epithelial cells has been demonstrated for M-1 types of group A streptococci. Some suggest that those M-1 strains possessing an invasin (*inv*+) gene penetrate more efficiently.[148] If penetration of mucosal barriers occurs commonly, it does not result in clinically detectable bacteremia in the vast majority of patients since the incidence of invasive infection is very low, that is 1.5 to 7.0 cases per 100,000 population per year. Thus, clearance of group A streptococci must be highly efficient in the vast majority of humans because of either preexisting type-specific immunity or nonspecific clearance mechanisms in the reticuloendothelial system.

Within the deeper tissue and blood stream, the induction of cytokine synthesis plays a critically important role in the production of shock and organ failure. Pyrogenic exotoxins (scarlatina toxins, erythrotoxins) designated A, B, and C (SPEA, SPEB, SPEC) have the ability to cause fever, enhance susceptibility to endotoxin, suppress IgM-antibody synthesis, and act as superantigens. These toxins, like the staphylococcal enterotoxins (A, B, C) and TSS toxin-1, can stimulate T-cell responses through their ability to bind to both the class II major histocompatibility complex of antigen-presenting cells and the V_β region of the T-cell receptor.[149] The net effect is the induction of monocyte cytokines (tumor necrosis factor-α, interleukin-1β, and IL-6) as well as the lymphokines (TNF-β, IL-2, and interferon-γ).[150–153] There is evidence that M-protein fragments may also act as superantigens.[154]

Other streptococcal virulence factors, (i.e., peptidoglycan and lipoteichoic acid) are also capable of inducing proinflammatory cytokines such as TNF-α and IL-1β. SPEB is a potent inducer or releaser of IL-1β from preformed intracellular pools.[155] Streptolysin O also stimulates mononuclear cells to produce TNF-α and IL-1β and in the presence of SPEA has a synergistic effect on IL-1β production.[156] Heat-killed group A streptococci as well as peptidoglycan and lipoteichoic acid are also potent inducers of TNF-α and IL-1β.[157, 158] SPEC and mitogenic factor as well as streptococcal superantigen are also capable of inducing proinflammatory cytokines as well as lymphokines.[159]

Noncytokine mechanisms of shock may also play a role. SPEB, a cysteine protease produced by group A streptococci, has been shown to release bradykinin from high-molecular-weight kininogen.[160] Bradykinin is a potent vasodilator of systemic as well as pulmonary vasculature and could be responsible at least in part for the early hypotension observed in Strep TSS.[160]

Thus there are likely many streptococcal and host factors that contribute to the shock and organ failure characteristic of Strep TSS. That TNF plays a central role is supported by the observations that high levels of TNF are observed in a baboon model of group A streptococcal bacteremia at a point in time when profound hypotension is manifest.[161] In addition, a neutralizing monoclonal antibody against TNF restores normal blood pressure and reduces mortality by 50%.[161]

Clinical Manifestations

Twenty percent of patients have an influenza-like prodrome characterized by fever, chills, myalgias, nausea, vomiting, and diarrhea that precedes hypotension by 24 to 48 hours.[101] Confusion or combativeness, or both, is present in 55% of patients. In patients who have associated necrotizing fasciitis, postpartum infection, peritonitis, or joint space infection, pain that progressively increases in severity is the most common initial symptom and usually precedes any localized evidence of infection.[101] In both children[127] and adults,[101] the soft tissues are the primary site of infection. In the remaining cases, pneumonia, meningitis, endophthalmitis, meningitis, peritonitis, myocarditis, joint infection, and intrauterine infection have been described.[101, 127] Where there is a defined or superficial portal of entry such as a laceration, suspicion of streptococcal infection or frank evidence of infection occurs earlier in the course. Phase 2 of Strep TSS is characterized by tachycardia, tachypnea, persistent fever, and, in patients who subsequently have necrotizing fasciitis or myonecrosis, increasingly severe pain at the site of infection. In others, fever and severe pain are the best early clinical clues.[162] In children, toxicity during varicella or persistence of fever longer than 4 days should also prompt careful evaluation. In many of these situations, diagnosis may be made more difficult due to self-administration of non-steroidal anti-inflammatory drugs. Postpartum patients frequently receive these as well as narcotics as routine management. However, increasing rather than decreasing pain should arouse suspicion of a postpartum complication such as intrauterine infection. In patients with blunt trauma or muscle strain that subsequently develop Strep TSS, the most common mistaken diagnosis is deep vein thrombophlebitis. High fever and excruciating pain, particularly in individuals with no risk factors for deep vein thrombosis, should arouse suspicion of a deep-seated infection.

Phase 3 of Strep TSS is characterized by the previously described symptoms and signs but with the sudden onset of shock and organ failure. Many patients are in florid shock at the time of admission, but in nearly half, hypotension is apparent during the first 4 to 8 hours after admission. Clinical evidence of necrotizing fasciitis is frequently a late finding, and the appearance of purple bullae and dusky-appearing skin is a bad prognostic sign and should prompt emergent surgical exploration (see the section on necrotizing fasciitis). The progression of necrotizing fasciitis from red skin to purple bullae in modern times may take place within a 24-hour period of time, whereas that described by Meleney in 1924 took 7 to 10 days.

The rapidity with which shock and multiorgan failure can progress is impressive, and many patients die within 24 to 48 hours of hospitalization.[101, 128] Laboratory tests are useful because they generally show evidence of renal impairment (creatinine level >2 times normal) even during phase 2, before hypotension is apparent. In addition, creatine phosphokinase levels in serum are markedly elevated in those with necrotizing fasciitis and myonecrosis. The white blood count is usually normal or elevated at admission but with a profound left shift that includes myelocytes and metamyelocytes. Finally, serum albumin and calcium levels are usually low on admission and drop precipitously as a diffuse capillary leak syndrome develops. Thrombocytopenia does not develop until later in the course but is the earliest sign of disseminated coagulopathy.[101]

Management

Prompt and aggressive surgical exploration and débridement of suspected deep-seated streptococcal infection are mandatory. It is as important to establish the cause of the infection as it is to determine the extent of necrosis. Once necrosis is established, extensive débridement is necessary as shock and organ failure continue to progress if devitalized tissue remains. Because of intractable hypotension and diffuse capillary leak, massive amounts of intravenous fluids (10 to 20 liters) per day in an adult may be required. Albumin replacement may be necessary as many patients' serum albumin levels drop to less than 2.0 g/dl.

Prompt antimicrobial therapy with empiric broad-spectrum coverage for septic shock should be instituted initially. Once the streptococcal cause is confirmed, high-dose penicillin and clindamycin should be given. This recommendation is based on the following information: (1) all strains of group A streptococci remain sensitive to penicillin; (2) resistance to erythromycin is currently about 5% in the United States, and there have been reports of resistance to clindamycin, though this is currently very uncommon; (3) clindamycin and erythromycin are more active in experimental models of necrotizing fasciitis and myonecrosis; (4) penicillin-binding proteins are not expressed during the stationary-phase growth of group A streptococci, and thus penicillin is ineffective in severe deep infections where large numbers of bacteria are present; (5) clindamycin suppresses exotoxin and M-protein production by group A streptococci; (6) clindamycin has a much longer half-life; (7) combinations of penicillin and clindamycin have indifferent interaction against group A streptococci in vitro at clinically relevant concentrations of antibiotics (no antagonistic effects were found)[163]; and (8) clindamycin and azithromycin suppress cytokine production by human mononuclear cells.[164, 165]

Pressors such as dopamine are used frequently, though no controlled trials have been performed in Strep TSS. In patients with intractable hypotension, high doses of dopamine, epinephrine, or phenylephrine have been used, but caution should be exercised in those with evidence of disseminated intravascular coagulation and in particular in those with cold, cyanotic digits. Symmetric gangrene involving all 20 digits and toes, the tip of the nose, and the breast areola have been described. In addition, amputations of one, two, three, and even four extremities have been observed (authors' unpublished data).

The rationale for the use of intravenous gamma globulin (IGIV) in the treatment of Strep TSS is based on the data implicating extracellular exotoxins as mediators of shock and organ failure. George and Gladys Dick in 1924 demonstrated that convalescent sera from patients with scarlet fever neutralized scarlatina toxins and that when passively administered, attenuated the course of severe scarlet fever.[166] Just as penicillin was becoming available, anti–scarlatina toxin horse serum became commercially available in the United States, but because of the availability of penicillin and the decline in the severity of scarlet fever, it was never used. Several reports have described the successful use of IGIV in patients with Strep TSS.[167–169] In a comparative observational study, IGIV-treated patients had a significantly better survival than those who did not receive this therapy.[170] The mortality of 67% in the control group was among the highest ever reported, whereas the mortality was 34% in the IGIV group. This mortality is similar to that in some series that did not use IGIV.[101] It is hoped that further, preferably double-blind, studies will resolve this dilemma. It is clear that if IGIV is to be used, it should be given early, and probably more than one dose should be given since batches of IGIV have variable neutralizing activity against streptococcal exotoxins.[159, 171] The rationale for use of IGIV, anticytokine strategies, and other novel therapies is discussed in detail elsewhere.[171a]

There have been no comparative trials describing the efficacy of hyperbaric oxygen treatment in Strep TSS, though some state that such treatment reduces mortality and the need for further débridements.[172] Certainly, use of this modality should not delay or be used in preference to surgical débridement when the latter is indicated.

BACTEREMIA

Group A streptococcal bacteremia has been relatively uncommon in the antibiotic era.[173] Before the mid-1980s, bacteremia occurred predominantly at the extremes of life and was usually community acquired. Occasional cases were seen in young and middle-aged adults associated with surgical wound infections and endometritis.

During the 1990s, however, there has been an increase in the number of reported cases of group A streptococcal bacteremia, reflecting the changing epidemiology and clinical patterns of invasive streptococcal infection as detailed previously. Many of the patients have been previously healthy adults between the ages of 20 and 50 years. There has been an apparent increase in cases associated with parenteral injection of illicit drugs,[104–106, 142] as well as nosocomial outbreaks in nursing homes.[132–134, 174]

Bacteremia in children may emanate from an upper respiratory infection, but it is more commonly associated with cutaneous foci, including burns and varicella. Elderly patients with streptococcal bacteremia present with a variety of chronic illnesses, the relation of which to their bacteremia is often unclear. Diabetes mellitus and peripheral vascular disease do appear, however, to be predisposing factors in older adults, and, as in children, the portal of entry is usually the skin. Malignancy and immunosuppression are risk factors in both age groups.[117, 175] Although group A streptococcal bacteremia may at times be transient and relatively benign,[176] it is more often fulminant. The onset is abrupt, with chills, high fever, and prostration. Rarely, patients may present with acute abdominal pain.[176, 177] Mortality in four series[140, 176–178] ranged from 27 to 38%.

OTHER STREPTOCOCCAL INFECTIONS

Lymphangitis may accompany cellulitis or may occur after clinically minor or inapparent skin infection. Lymphangitis is readily recognized by the presence of red, tender, linear streaks directed toward enlarged, tender regional lymph nodes. It is accompanied by systemic symptoms such as chills, fever, malaise, and headache.

Puerperal sepsis follows abortion or delivery when streptococci colonizing the patient herself or transmitted from medical personnel invade the endometrium and surrounding structures, lymphatics, and blood stream. The resulting endometritis and septicemia may be complicated by pelvic cellulitis, septic pelvic thrombophlebitis, peritonitis, or pelvic abscess. This disease was associated with high mortality in the preantibiotic era. Although endocarditis due to *S. pyogenes* was relatively common in the preantibiotic era, it is now rarely seen.[179, 180] Meningitis due to *S. pyogenes* usually follows upper respiratory infection and is indistinguishable clinically from other forms of acute pyogenic meningeal infection.[181]

Pneumonia due to *S. pyogenes* is frequently associated with preceding viral infections such as influenza, measles, or varicella or with chronic pulmonary disease. Numerous epidemics have been described in military recruit populations.[182] An increased number of cases has been reported over the past few years in association with the resurgence of invasive streptococcal infections. In one third or fewer of the cases, there is a history of preceding streptococcal upper respiratory infection. The onset is typically abrupt, and the disease is characterized by chills, fever, dyspnea, cough productive of blood-streaked sputum, pleuritic chest pain, and in more severe cases, cyanosis. The pulmonary picture is that of bronchopneumonia with consolidation being uncommon. Empyema develops in 30 to 40% of the cases, tends to appear early in the disease, and typically consists of copious amounts of thin serosanguineous fluid. Bacteremia occurs in 10 to 15% of the cases. Complications include mediastinitis, pericarditis, pneumothorax, and bronchiectasis. Mortality is low with penicillin therapy and adequate drainage of empyema, but the clinical course of the disease is often prolonged.

Asymptomatic carriage of group A streptococci in the vagina, anus, scalp, or, rarely, upper respiratory tract has been the source of outbreaks of nosocomial streptococcal infection.[183]

INFECTION CONTROL AND PREVENTION OF SECONDARY CASES OF INVASIVE GROUP A STREPTOCOCCAL INFECTION

Most cases of necrotizing fasciitis and TSS caused by group A streptococcus are community-acquired and sporadic. Yet secondary cases among hospital personnel and health care workers have been described.[135–137, 174] For that reason, it is prudent for the primary physician to evaluate the degree of contact and predisposing factors in the exposed individual (see Table 186–3) and to individualize decisions regarding antimicrobial prophylaxis.[187]

In addition, since 1965, at least 15 posotoperative or postpartum group A streptococcal outbreaks have occurred.[174, 183, 188] Most of the latter cases are attributable to asymptomatic carriage of group A streptococci in health care workers. The most likely site of such carriage is the anus, but vaginal, skin, and pharyngeal carriage have been implicated.[188] When an episode or clusters of cases occur, limited health care worker screening may be undertaken. Guidelines have recently been published by the Centers for Disease Control and Prevention for implementation of these procedures and for treatment of identified health care workers.[188]

REFERENCES

1. Brown JH. The use of blood agar for the study of streptococci. New York: The Rockefeller Institute for Medical Research; 1919.
2. Lancefield RC. A serological differentiation of human and other groups of hemolytic streptococci. J Exp Med. 1933;57:571–595.
3. Rammelkamp CH. Epidemiology of streptococcal infections. Harvey Lect. 1955;51:113–142.
4. Wannamaker LW. The epidemiology of streptococcal infection. In: McCarty M, ed. Streptococcal Infections. New York: Columbia University Press; 1953:157–175.
5. Rammelkamp CH, Denny FW, Wannamaker LW. Studies on the epidemiology of rheumatic fever in the armed services. In: Thomas L, ed. Rheumatic Fever. Minneapolis: University of Minnesota Press; 1952:72–89.
6. Moses AE, Wessels MR, Zalcman K, et al. Relative contributions of hyaluronic acid capsule and M protein to virulence in a mucoid strain of the group A *Streptococcus*. Infect Immun. 1997;65:64–71.
7. Dale JB, Washburn RG, Marques MB, Wessels MR. Hyaluronate capsule and surface M protein in resistance to opsonization of group A streptococci. Infect Immun. 1996;64:1495–1501.
8. Lancefield RC. Current knowledge of type-specific M antigens of group A streptococci. J Immunol. 1962;89:307–313.
9. Phillips GN Jr, Flicker PF, Cohen C, et al. Streptococcal M protein: Alpha-helical coiled-coil structure and arrangement on the cell surface. Proc Natl Acad Sci U S A. 1981;78:4689–4693.
10. Jones KF, Manjula BN, Johnston KH, et al. Location of variable and conserved epitopes among the multiple serotypes of streptococcal M protein. J Exp Med. 1985;161:623–628.
11. Bisno AL. Alternate complement pathway activation by group A streptococci: Role of M-protein. Infect Immun. 1979;26:1172–1176.
12. Peterson PK, Schmeling D, Cleary PP, et al. Inhibition of alternative complement pathway opsonization by group A streptococcal M protein. J Infect Dis. 1979;139:575–585.
13. Horstmann RD, Sievertsen HJ, Knobloch J, Fischetti VA. Antiphagocytic activity of streptococcal M protein: Selective binding of complement control protein factor H. Proc Natl Acad Sci U S A. 1988;85:1657–1661.
14. Whitnack E, Beachey EH. Antiopsonic activity of fibrinogen bound to M protein on the surface of group A streptococci. J Clin Invest. 1982;69:1042–1045.
15. Bisno AL, Collins CM, Turner JC. M proteins of group C streptococci isolated from patients with acute pharyngitis. J Clin Microbiol. 1996;34:2511–2515.
16. Campo RE, Schultz DR, Bisno AL. M-proteins of group G streptococci: Mechanisms of resistance to phagocytosis. J Infect Dis. 1995;171:601–606.
17. Johnson DR, Kaplan EL. A review of the correlation of T-agglutination patterns and M-protein typing and opacity factor production in the identification of group A streptococci. J Med Microbiol. 1993;38:311–315.
18. Widdowson JP, Maxted WR, Notley CM, Pinney AM. The antibody responses in man to infection with different serotypes of group A streptococci. J Med Microbiol. 1974;7:483–496.
19. Beall B, Facklam R, Thompson T. Sequencing *emm*-specific PCR products for routine and accurate typing of group A streptococci. J Clin Microbiol. 1996;34:953–958.
20. Beachey EH, Ofek I. Epithelial cell binding of group A streptococci by lipoteichoic acid on fimbriae denuded of M protein. J Exp Med. 1976;143:759–771.
21. Simpson WA, Courtney HS, Ofek I. Interactions of fibronectin with streptococci: The role of fibronectin as a receptor for *Streptococcus pyogenes*. Rev Infect Dis. 1987;9(Suppl 4):S351–S359
22. Hasty DL, Ofek I, Courtney HS, Doyle RJ. Multiple adhesins of streptococci. Infect Immun. 1992;60:2147–2152.
23. Hanski E, Caparon M. Protein F, a fibronectin-binding protein, is an adhesin of the group A streptococcus *Streptococcus pyogenes*. Proc Natl Acad Sci U S A. 1992;89:6172–6176.
24. O'Connor SP, Cleary PP. In vivo *Streptococcus pyogenes* C5a peptidase activity: Analysis using transposon- and nitrosoguanidine-induced mutants. J Infect Dis. 1987;156:495–504.
25. Boyle MDP. Variation of multifunctional surface binding proteins—A virulence strategy for group A streptococci? J Theor Biol. 1995;173:415–426.
26. Wannamaker LW. Differences between streptococcal infections of the throat and of the skin. N Engl J Med. 1970;282:23–31.
27. Bisno AL. Acute pharyngitis: Etiology and diagnosis. Pediatrics. 1996;97:949–954.
28. Kaplan EL, Wannamaker LW. C-reactive protein in streptococcal pharyngitis. Pediatrics. 1977;60:28–32.
29. Randolph MF, Gerber MA, DeMeo KK, Wright L. Effect of antibiotic therapy on the clinical course of streptococcal pharyngitis. J Pediatr. 1985;106:870–875.
30. Krober MS, Bass JW, Michels GN. Streptococcal pharyngitis: Placebo-controlled double-blind evaluation of clinical response to penicillin therapy. JAMA. 1985;253:1271–1274.
31. Nelson JD. The effect of penicillin therapy on the symptoms and signs of streptococcal pharyngitis. Pediatr Infect Dis J. 1984;3:10–13.
32. Shoemaker M, Lampe RM, Weir MR. Peritonsillitis: Abscess of cellulitis? Pediatr Infect Dis J. 1986;5:435–439.
33. Turner JC, Fox A, Fox K, et al. Role of group C beta-hemolytic streptococci in pharyngitis: Epidemiologic study of clinical features associated with isolation of group C streptococci. J Clin Microbiol. 1993;31:808–811.
34. Meier FA, Centor RM, Graham L Jr, Dalton HP. Clinical and microbiological evidence for endemic pharyngitis among adults due to group C streptococci. Arch Intern Med. 1990;150:825–829.
35. Hill HR, Caldwell GG, Wilson E, et al. Epidemic of pharyngitis due to streptococci of Lancefield group G. Lancet. 1969;2:371–374.
36. McCue JD. Group G streptococcal pharyngitis: Analysis of an outbreak at a college. JAMA. 1982;248:1333–1336.
37. Cimolai N, Elford RW, Bryan L, et al. Do the beta-hemolytic non-group A streptococci cause pharyngitis? Rev Infect Dis. 1988;10:587–601.
38. Miller RA, Brancato F, Holmes KK. *Corynebacterium haemolyticum* as a cause of pharyngitis and scarlatiniform rash in young adults. Ann Intern Med. 1986;105:867–872.
39. Karpathios T, Drakonaki S, Zervoudaki A, et al. *Arcanobacterium haemolyticum* in children with presumed streptococcal pharyngotonsillitis or scarlet fever. J Pediatr. 1992;121:735–737.
40. Tacket CO, Davis BR, Carter GP, et al. *Yersinia enterocolitica* pharyngitis. Ann Intern Med. 1983;99:40–42.
41. Glezen WP, Clyde WAJ, Senior RJ, et al. Group A streptococci, mycoplasmas, and viruses associated with acute pharyngitis. JAMA. 1967;202:455–460.
42. Kaplan EL, Top FH Jr, Dudding BA, Wannamaker LW. Diagnosis of streptococcal pharyngitis: Differentiation of active infection from the carrier state in the symptomatic child. J Infect Dis. 1971;123:490–501.
43. Breese BB, Disney FA. The accuracy of diagnosis of beta-streptococcal infections on clinical grounds. J Pediatr. 1954;44:670–673.
44. Siegel AC, Johnson EE, Stollerman GH. Controlled studies of streptococcal pharyngitis in a pediatric population. I. Factors related to the attack rate of rheumatic fever. N Engl J Med. 1961;265:559–566.
45. Rheumatic Fever Committee AHA. Throat Cultures for Rational Treatment of Sore Throat. New York: American Heart Association; 1972.
46. Kellogg JA, Manzella JP. Detection of group A streptococci in the laboratory or physician's office. JAMA. 1986;255:2638–2642.
47. Kellogg JA. Suitability of throat culture procedures for detection of group A streptococci and as reference standards for evaluation of streptococcal antigen detection kits. J Clin Microbiol. 1990;28:165–169.
48. Coonan KM, Kaplan EL. In vitro susceptibility of recent North American group A streptococcal isolates to eleven oral antibiotics. Pediatr Infect Dis J. 1994;13:630–635.
49. Coonan K, Kaplan EL. Therapeutic implications of erythromycin resistance in group A streptococci. Pediatr Infect Dis J. 1993;12:261–262.
50. Gentry JL, Burns WW. Antibiotic-resistant streptococci. Am J Dis Child. 1980;134:801.
51. Maruyama S, Yoshioka H, Fujita K, et al. Sensitivity of group A streptococci to antibiotics. Am J Dis Child. 1979;133:1143–1145.
52. Seppala H, Nissinen A, Jarvinen H, et al. Resistance to erythromycin in group A streptococci. N Engl J Med. 1992;326:292–297.
53. Stingemore N, Francis GRJ, Toohey M, McGechie DB. The emergence of erythromycin resistance in *Streptococcus pyogenes* in Fremantle, Western Australia. Med J Aust. 1989;150:626–631.
54. Scott RJ, Naidoo J, Lightfoot NF, George RC. A community outbreak of group A

beta haemolytic streptococci with transferable resistance to erythromycin. Epidemiol Infect. 1989;102:85–91.

55. Phillips GD, Parratt D, Orange GV, et al. Erythromycin-resistant *Streptococcus pyogenes*. J Antimicrob Chemother. 1990;25:723–724.
56. Brorson JE, Larsson P. The regression line for erythromycin is not valid for beta-hemolytic streptococci group A. Scand J Infect Dis. 1987;19:243–246.
57. Gerber MA, Tanz RR, Kabat W, et al. Optical immunoassay test for group A β-hemolytic streptococcal pharyngitis: An office-based, multicenter investigation. JAMA. 1997;277:899–903.
58. Schlager TA, Hayden GA, Woods WA, et al. Optical immunoassay for rapid detection of group A beta-hemolytic streptococci. Arch Pediatr Adolesc Med. 1996;150:245–248.
59. Bisno AL, Gerber MA, Gwaltney JM Jr, et al. Diagnosis and management of group A streptococcal pharyngitis: A practice guideline. Clin Infect Dis. 1997;25:574–583.
60. Weinstein L, Le Frock J. Does antimicrobial therapy of streptococcal pharyngitis or pyoderma alter the risk of glomerulonephritis? J Infect Dis. 1971;124:229–231.
61. Shulman ST, Gerber MA, Tanz RR, Markowitz M. Streptococcal pharyngitis: The case for penicillin therapy. Pediatr Infect Dis J. 1994;13:1–7.
62. Dajani A, Taubert K, Ferrieri P, et al. Treatment of acute streptococcal pharyngitis and prevention of rheumatic fever: A statement for health professionals. Committee on Rheumatic Fever, Endocarditis, and Kawasaki Disease of the Council on Cardiovascular Disease in the Young, the American Heart Association. Pediatrics. 1995;96:758–764.
63. Pichichero ME, Margolis PA. A comparison of cephalosporins and penicillins in the treatment of group A beta-hemolytic streptococcal pharyngitis: A meta-analysis supporting the concept of microbial copathogenicity. Pediatr Infect Dis J. 1991;10:275–281.
64. Kaplan EL, Gastanaduy AS, Huwe BB. The role of the carrier in treatment failures after antibiotic therapy for group A streptococci in the upper respiratory tract. J Lab Clin Med. 1981;98:326–335.
65. Pichichero ME. Cephalosporins are superior to penicillin for treatment of streptococcal tonsillopharyngitis: Is the difference worth it? Pediatr Infect Dis J. 1993;12:268–274.
66. Brook I. The role of beta-lactamase-producing bacteria in the persistence of streptococcal tonsillar infection. Rev Infect Dis. 1984;6:601–607.
67. Amercian Academy of Pediatrics. Group A streptococcal infections. In: Peter G, ed. 1997 Red Book: Report of the Committee on Infectious Diseases. 24th ed. Elk Grove Village, Ill: American Academy of Pediatrics; 1997:483–494.
68. Hamill J. Multicentre evaluation of azithromycin and penicillin V in the treatment of acute streptococcal pharyngitis and tonsillitis in children. J Antimicrob Chemother. 1993;31(Suppl E):89–94.
69. Weippl G. Multicentre comparison of azithromycin versus erythromycin in the treatment of paediatric pharyngitis or tonsillitis caused by group A streptococci. J Antimicrob Chemother. 1993;31(Suppl E):95–101.
70. Hooton TM. A comparison of azithromycin and penicillin V for the treatment of streptococcal pharyngitis. Am J Med. 1991;91(Suppl 3A):3A–23A.
71. Aujard Y, Boucot I, Brahimi N, et al. Comparative efficacy and safety of four-day cefuroxime axetil and ten-day penicillin treatment of group A beta-hemolytic streptococcal pharyngitis in children. Pediatr Infect Dis J. 1995;14:295–300.
72. Adam D, Cefixime Study Group, Hostalek U, Troster K. Five-day cefixime therapy for bacterial pharyngitis and/or tonsillitis: Comparison with 10-day penicillin V therapy. Infection. 1995;23:S83–S86.
73. Pichichero ME, Gooch WM, Rodriguez W, et al. Effective short-course treatment of acute group A beta-hemolytic streptococcal tonsillopharyngitis: Ten days of penicillin vs 5 days or 10 days of cefpodoxime therapy in children. Arch Pediatr Adolesc Med. 1994;148:1053–1060.
74. Seppala H, Klaukka T, Vuopio-Varkila J, et al. The effect of changes in the consumption of macrolide antibiotics on erythromycin resistance in group A streptococci in Finland. N Engl J Med. 1997;337:441–446.
75. Catanzaro FJ, Stetson CA, Morris AJ, et al. The role of streptococcus in the pathogenesis of rheumatic fever. Am J Med. 1954;17:749–756.
76. Tanz RR, Poncher JR, Corydon KE, et al. Clindamycin treatment of chronic pharyngeal carriage of group A streptococci. J Pediatr. 1991;119:123–128.
77. Kaplan EL, Johnson DR. Eradication of group A streptococci from the upper respiratory tract by amoxicillin with clavulanate after oral penicillin V treatment failure. J Pediatr. 1988;113:400–403.
78. Paradise JL, Bluestone CD, Bachman RZ, et al. Efficacy of tonsillectomy for recurrent throat infection in severely affected children: Results of parallel randomized and nonrandomized clinical trials. N Engl J Med. 1984;310:674–683.
79. Nelson KE, Bisno AL, Waytz P, et al. The epidemiology and natural history of streptococcal pyoderma. An endemic disease of the rural southern United States. Am J Epidemiol. 1976;103:270–283.
80. Fehrs LJ, Flanagan K, Kline S, et al. Group A beta-hemolytic streptococcal skin infections in a US meat-packing plant. JAMA. 1987;258:3131–3134.
81. Taplin D, Lansdell L, Allen AM, et al. Prevalence of streptococcal pyoderma in relation to climate and hygiene. Lancet. 1973;1:501–503.
82. Ferrieri P, Dajani AS, Wannamaker LW, Chapman SS. Natural history of impetigo. I. Site sequence of acquisition and familial patterns of spread of cutaneous streptococci. J Clin Invest. 1972;51:2851–2862.
83. Fiorentino TR, Beall B, Mshar P, Bessen DE. A genetic-based evaluation of the principal tissue reservoir for group A streptococci isolated from normally sterile sites. J Infect Dis. 1997;176:177–182.
84. Anthony BF, Kaplan EL, Wannamaker LW, Chapman SS. The dynamics of streptococcal infections in a defined population of children: Serotypes associated with skin and respiratory infections. Am J Epidemiol. 1976;104:652–666.
85. Kaplan EL, Anthony BF, Chapman SS, et al. The influence of the site of infection on the immune response to group A streptococci. J Clin Invest. 1970;49:1405–1414.
86. Bisno AL, Nelson KE, Waytz P, Brunt J. Factors influencing serum antibody responses in streptococcal pyoderma. J Lab Clin Med. 1973;81:410–420.
87. Bisno AL, Nelson KE. Type-specific opsonic antibodies in streptococcal pyoderma. Infect Immun. 1974;10:1356–1361.
88. Bergner-Rabinowitz S, Ofek I, Davies MA, Rabinowitz K. Type-specific streptococcal antibodies in pyodermal nephritis. J Infect Dis. 1971;124:488–493.
89. Barnett BO, Frieden IJ. Streptococcal skin diseases in children. Semin Dermatol. 1992;11:3–10.
90. Gonzalez A, Schachner LA, Cleary T, et al. Pyoderma in children. Adv Dermatol. 1989;4:127–142.
91. Demidovich CW, Wittler RR, Ruff ME, et al. Impetigo. Current etiology and comparison of penicillin, erythromycin, and cephalexin therapies. Am J Dis Child. 1990;144:1313–1315.
92. Rasmussen JE. The changing nature of impetigo. Patient Care. 1992;26:233–239.
93. Barton LL, Friedman AD, Sharkey AM, et al. Impetigo contagiosa. III. Comparative efficacy of oral erythromycin and topical mupirocin. Pediatr Dermatol. 1989;6:134–138.
94. Mertz PM, Marshall DA, Eaglstein WH, et al. Topical mupirocin treatment of impetigo is equal to oral erythromycin therapy. Arch Dermatol. 1989;125:1069–1073.
95. Rice TD, Duggan AK, DeAngelis C. Cost-effectiveness of erythromycin versus mupirocin for treatment of impetigo in children. Pediatrics. 1992;89:210–214.
96. Hoge CW, Schwartz B, Talkington DF, et al. The changing epidemiology of invasive group A streptococcal infections and the emergence of streptococcal toxic shock–like syndrome. A retrospective population-based study. JAMA. 1993;269:384–389.
97. Martin PR, Hoiby EA. Streptococcal serogroup A epidemic in Norway 1987–1988. Scand J Infect Dis. 1990;22:421–429.
98. Stromberg A, Romanus V, Burman LG. Outbreak of group A streptococcal bacteremia in Sweden: An epidemiologic and clinical study. J Infect Dis. 1991;164:595–598.
99. Demers B, Simor AE, Vellend H, et al. Severe invasive group A streptococcal infections in Ontario, Canada: 1987–1991. Clin Infect Dis. 1993;16:792–800.
100. Johnson DR, Stevens DL, Kaplan EL. Epidemiologic analysis of group A streptococcal serotypes associated with severe systemic infections, rheumatic fever, or uncomplicated pharyngitis. J Infect Dis. 1992;166:374–382.
101. Stevens DL, Tanner MH, Winship J, et al. Severe group A streptococcal infections associated with a toxic shock–like syndrome and scarlet fever toxin A. N Engl J Med. 1989;321:1–7.
102. Bartter T, Dascal A, Carroll K, Curley FJ. "Toxic strep syndrome." A manifestation of group A streptococcal infection. Arch Intern Med. 1988;148:1421–1424.
103. Shama S, Calandra GB. Atypical erysipelas caused by group G streptococci in a patient with cured Hodgkin's disease. Arch Dermatol. 1982;118:934–936.
104. Lentnek AL, Giger O, O'Rourke E. Group A beta-hemolytic streptococcal bacteremia and intravenous substance abuse: A growing clinical problem? Arch Intern Med. 1990;150:89–93.
105. Barg NL, Kish MA, Kauffman CA, Supena RB. Group A streptococcal bacteremia in intravenous drug abusers. Am J Med. 1985;78:569–574.
106. Craven DE, Rixinger AI, Bisno AL, et al. Bacteremia caused by group G streptococci in parenteral drug abusers: epidemiological and clinical aspects. J Infect Dis. 1986;153:988–992.
107. Baddour LM, Bisno AL. Recurrent cellulitis after saphenous venectomy for coronary bypass surgery. Ann Intern Med. 1982;97:493–496.
108. Semel JD, Goldin H. Association of athlete's foot with cellulitis of the lower extremities: Diagnostic value of bacterial cultures of ipsilateral interdigital space samples. Clin Infect Dis. 1996;23:1162–1164.
109. Greenberg J, DeSanctis RW, Mills RM Jr. Vein-donor-leg cellulitis after coronary artery bypass surgery. Ann Intern Med. 1982;97:565–566.
110. Baddour LM, Bisno AL. Recurrent cellulitis after coronary bypass surgery: Association with superficial fungal infection in saphenous venectomy limbs. JAMA. 1984;251:1049–1052.
111. Baddour LM, Bisno AL. Non-group A beta-hemolytic streptococcal cellulitis: Association with venous and lymphatic compromise. Am J Med. 1985;79:155–159.
112. Hook EWI, Hooton TM, Horton CA, et al. Microbiologic evaluation of cutaneous cellulitis in adults. Arch Intern Med. 1986;146:295–297.
113. Howe PM, Fajardo JE, Orcutt MA. Etiologic diagnosis of cellulitis: Comparison of aspirates obtained from the leading edge and the point of maximal inflammation. Pediatr Infect Dis J. 1987;6:685.
114. Newell PM, Norden CW. Value of needle aspiration in bacteriologic diagnosis of cellulitis in adults. J Clin Microbiol. 1988;26:401–404.
115. Bisno AL, Stevens DL. Streptococcal infections of skin and soft tissues. N Engl J Med. 1996;334:240–244.
116. Meleney FL. Hemolytic streptococcus gangrene. Arch Surg. 1924;9:317–364.
117. Stevens DL. Invasive group A streptococcus infections. Clin Infect Dis. 1991;14:2–13.
118. Stevens DL. Could nonsteroidal antiinflammatory drugs (NSAIDs) enhance the progression of bacterial infections to toxic shock syndrome? Clin Infect Dis. 1995;21:977–980.
119. Barnham M. Nonsteroidal anti-inflammatory drugs: Concurrent or causative drugs in serious infection? Clin Infect Dis. 1997;25:1272–1273.

120. Adams EM, Gudmundsson S, Yocum DE, et al. Streptococcal myositis. Arch Intern Med. 1985;145:1020–1023.
121. Holm SE. Invasive group A streptococcal infections. N Engl J Med. 1996;335:590–591.
122. Wheeler MC, Roe MH, Kaplan EL, et al. Outbreak of group A streptococcus septicemia in children: Clinical, epidemiologic, and microbiological correlates. JAMA. 1991;266:533–537.
123. Gaworzewska ET, Hallas G. Group A streptococcal infections and a toxic shock–like syndrome. N Engl J Med. 1989;321:1546.
124. Schwartz B, Facklam RR, Breiman RF. Changing epidemiology of group A streptococcal infection in the USA. Lancet. 1990;336:1167–1171.
125. Hribalova V. *Streptococcus pyogenes* and the toxic shock syndrome. Ann Intern Med. 1988;108:772.
126. Greenberg RN, Willoughby BG, Kennedy DJ, et al. Hypocalcemia and "toxic" syndrome associated with streptococcal fasciitis. South Med J. 1983;76:916–918.
127. Kiska DL, Thiede B, Caracciolo J, et al. Invasive group A streptococcal infections in North Carolina: Epidemiology, clinical features, and genetic and serotype analysis of causative organisms. J Infect Dis. 1997;176:992–1000.
128. Cockerill FR, MacDonald KL, Thompson RL. An outbreak of invasive group A streptococcal disease associated with high carriage rates of the invasive clone among school-aged children. JAMA. 1997;277:38–43.
129. Davies HD, McGreer A, Schwartz B, et al. Invasive group A streptococcal infections in Ontario, Canada. N Engl J Med. 1996;335:547–554.
130. Auerbach SB, Schwartz B, Facklam RR, et al. Outbreak of invasive group a streptococcal (GAS) disease in a nursing home. Lessons on prevention and control. Arch Intern Med. 1992;152:1017–1022.
131. Hohenboken JJ, Anderson F, Kaplan EL. Invasive group A streptococcal (GAS) serotype M-1 outbreak in a long-term care facility (LTCF) with mortality. In: Abstracts of the 1994 Interscience Conference on Antimicrobial Agents and Chemotherapy, Orlando, Fla.; 1994;J89.
132. Schwartz B, Ussery XT. Group A streptococcal outbreaks in nursing homes. Infect Contrl Hosp Epidemiol. 1992;13:742–747.
133. Harkness GA, Bentley DW, Mottley M, Lee J. *Streptococcus pyogenes* outbreak in a long-term care facility. Am J Infect Control. 1992;20:142–148.
134. Ruben FL, Norden CW, Heisler B, Korica Y. An outbreak of *Streptococcus pyogenes* infections in a nursing home. Ann Intern Med. 1984;101:494–496.
135. DiPersio JR, File TM Jr, Stevens DL, et al. Spread of serious disease-producing M3 clones of group A streptococcus among family members and health care workers. Clin Infect Dis. 1996;22:490–495.
136. Gamba MA, Martinelli M, Schaad HJ. Familial transmission of a serious disease-producing group A streptococcus clone: Case reports and review. Clin Infect Dis. 1997;24:1118–1121.
137. Valenzuela TD, Hooton TM, Kaplan EL, Schlievert P. Transmission of "toxic strep" syndrome from an infected child to a firefighter during CPR. Ann Emerg Med. 1991;20:90–92.
138. Givner LB, Abramson JS, Wasilauskas B. Apparent increase in the incidence of invasive group A beta-hemolytic streptococcal disease in children. J Pediatr. 1991;118:341–346.
139. Brogan TV, Nizet V, Waldhausen JHT, et al. Group A streptococcal necrotizing fasciitis complicating primary varicella: A series of fourteen patients. Pediatr Infect Dis J. 1995;14:588–594.
140. Francis J, Warren RE. *Streptococcus pyogenes* bacteraemia in Cambridge—a review of 67 episodes. Q J Med. 1988;68:603–613.
141. Barnham M. Invasive streptococcal infections in the era before the acquired immune deficiency syndrome: A 10 years' compilation of patients with streptococcal bacteraemia in North Yorkshire. J Infect. 1989;18:231–248.
142. Braunstein H. Characteristics of group A streptococcal bacteremia in patients at the San Bernardino County Medical Center [published erratum appears in Rev Infect Dis. 1991;13:533]. Rev Infect Dis. 1991;13:8–11.
143. Holm SE, Norrby A, Bergholm AM, Norgen M. Aspects of pathogenesis of serious group A streptococcal infections in Sweden, 1988–1989. J Infect Dis. 1992;166:31–37.
144. Stegmayr B, Bjorck S, Holm S, et al. Septic shock induced by group A streptococcal infection: Clinical and therapeutic aspects. Scand J Infect Dis. 1992;24:589–597.
145. Herold AH. Group A beta-hemolytic streptococcal toxic shock from a mild pharyngitis. J Fam Pract. 1990;31:549–551.
146. Bradley JS, Schlievert PM, Peterson BM. Toxic shock–like syndrome, a complication of strep throat. Pediatr Infect Dis J. 1991;10:77–79.
147. Chapnick EK, Gradon JD, Lutwick LI, et al. Streptococcal toxic shock syndrome due to noninvasive pharyngitis. Clin Infect Dis. 1992;14:1074–1077.
148. LaPenta D, Rubens C, Chi E, Cleary PP. Group A streptococci efficiently invade human respiratory epithelial cells. Proc Natl Acad Sci U S A. 1994;91:12,115–12,119.
149. Mollick JA, Rich RR. Characterization of a superantigen from a pathogenic strain of *Streptococcus pyogenes*. Clin Res. 1991;39:213A.
150. Hackett SP, Stevens DL. Superantigens associated with staphylococcal and streptococcal toxic shock syndrome are potent inducers of tumor necrosis factor-beta synthesis. J Infect Dis. 1993;168:232–235.
151. Fast DJ, Schlievert PM, Nelson RD. Toxic shock syndrome–associated staphylococcal and streptococcal pyrogenic toxins are potent inducers of tumor necrosis factor production. Infect Immun. 1989;57:291–294.
152. Norrby-Teglund A, Newton D, Kotb M, et al. Superantigenic properties of the group A streptococcal exotoxin SpeF (MF). Infect Immun. 1994;62:5227–5233.
153. Norrby-Teglund A, Norgren M, Holm SE, et al. Similar cytokine induction profiles of a novel streptococcal exotoxin, MF, and pyrogenic exotoxins A and B. Infect Immun. 1994;62:3731–3738.
154. Kotb M, Ohnishi H, Majumdar G, et al. Temporal relationship of cytokine release by peripheral blood mononuclear cells stimulated by the streptococcal superantigen pep M5. Infect Immun. 1993;61:1194–1201.
155. Kapur V, Majesky MW, Li LL, et al. Cleavage of interleukin 1beta (IL-1beta) precursor to produce active IL-1beta by a conserved extracellular cysteine protease from *Streptococcus pyogenes*. Proc Natl Acad Sci U S A. 1993;90:7676–7680.
156. Hackett SP, Stevens DL. Synthesis of tumor necrosis factor and interleukin-1 by monocytes stimulated with pyrogenic exotoxin A and streptolysin O. J Infect Dis. 1992;165:885.
157. Hackett S, Ferretti J, Stevens D. Cytokine induction by viable group A streptococci: Suppression by streptolysin O. In: Abstracts of the American Society for Microbiology, Las Vegas, Nev; 1994:B249.
158. Muller-Alouf H, Alouf JE, Gerlach D, et al. Comparative study of cytokine release by human peripheral blood mononuclear cells stimulated with *Streptococcus pyogenes* superantigenic erythrogenic toxins, heat-killed streptococci, and lipopolysaccharide. Infect Immun. 1994;62:4915–4921.
159. Norrby-Teglund A, Basma H, Andersson J, et al. Varying titres of neutralizing antibodies to streptococcal superantigens in different preparations of normal polyspecific immunoglobulin G (IVIG): Implications for therapeutic efficacy. Clin Infect Dis. 1998;26:631–638.
160. Herwald H, Collin M, Muller-Esterl W, Bjorck L. Streptococcal cysteine proteinase releases kinins: A novel virulence mechanism. J Exp Med. 1996;184:665–673.
161. Stevens DL, Bryant AE, Hackett SP, et al. Group A streptococcal bacteremia: The role of tumor necrosis factor in shock and organ failure. J Infect Dis. 1996;173:619–626.
162. Stevens DL. Streptococcal toxic-shock syndrome: Spectrum of disease, pathogenesis, and new concepts in treatment. Emerg Infect Dis. 1995;1:69–78.
163. Stevens DL, Madaras-Kelly KJ, Richards DM. In vitro antimicrobial effects of various combinations of penicillin and clindamycin against four strains of *Streptococcus pyogenes*. Antimicrob Agents Chemother. 1998;42:1266–1268.
164. Stevens DL, Bryant AE, Hackett SP. Antibiotic effects on bacterial viability, toxin production and host response. Clin Infect Dis. 1995;20:S154–S157.
165. Stevens DL, Hackett SP, Bryant AE. Suppression of mononuclear cell synthesis of tumor necrosis factor by azithromycin. Abstract 181. In: Abstracts of the Infectious Disease Society of America, San Francisco, Calif; 1997.
166. Dick GF, Dick GH. Therapeutic results with concentrated scarlet fever antitoxin. JAMA. 1925;84:803–805.
167. Lamothe F, D'Amico P, Ghosn P, et al. Clinical usefulness of intravenous human immunoglobulins in invasive group A streptococcal infections: Case report and review. Clin Infect Dis. 1995;21:1469–1470.
168. Barry W, Hudgins L, Donta ST, Pesanti EL. Intravenous immunoglobulin therapy for toxic shock syndrome. JAMA. 1992;267:3315–3316.
169. Stevens DL. Editorial Response: Rationale for the use of intravenous gamma globulin in the treatment of streptococcal toxic shock syndrome. Clin Infect Dis. 1998;26:639–641.
170. Kaul R, McGeer A, Norrby-Teglund A, et al. Intravenous immunoglobulin therapy for streptococcal toxic shock syndrome: A comparative observation study. Clin Infect Dis. 1999;28:800–807.
171. Norrby-Teglund A, Kaul R, Low DE, et al. Evidence for the presence of streptococcal-superantigen–neutralizing antibodies in normal polyspecific immunoglobulin G. Infect Immun. 1996;64:5395–5398.
171a. Norrby-Teglund A, Stevens DL. Novel therapies in streptococcal toxic shock syndrome: Attenuation of virulence factor expression and modulation of the host response. Curr Opin Infect Dis. 1998;11:285–291.
172. Riseman JA, Zamboni WA, Curtis A, et al. Hyperbaric oxygen therapy for necrotizing fasciitis reduces mortality and the need for debridements. Surgery. 1990;108:847–850.
173. Weinstein MP, Reller B, Murphy JR, Lichtenstein KA. The clinical significance of positive blood cultures: A comparative analysis of 500 episodes of bacteremia and fungemia in adults. I. Laboratory and epidemiologic observations. Rev Infect Dis. 1983;5:35–53.
174. Schwartz B, Elliott JA, Butler JC, et al. Clusters of invasive group A streptococcal infections in family, hospital, and nursing home settings. Clin Infect Dis. 1992;15:277–284.
175. Duma RJ, Weinberg AN, Medrek TF, Kunz LJ. Streptococcal infections: A bacteriological and clinical study of streptococcal bacteremia. Medicine. 1969;48:87–127.
176. Dan M, Maximova S, Siegman-Igra Y, et al. Varied presentations of sporadic group A streptococcal bacteremia: Clinical experience and attempt at classification. Rev Infect Dis. 1990;12:537–542.
177. Ispahani P, Donald FE, Aveline AJ. *Streptococcus pyogenes* bacteraemia: An old enemy subdued, but not defeated. J Infect. 1988;16:37–46.
178. Bucher A, Martin PR, Hoiby EA, et al. Spectrum of disease in bacteraemic patients during a *Streptococcus pyogenes* serotype M-1 epidemic in Norway in 1988. Eur J Clin Microbiol Infect Dis. 1992;11:416-4-26.
179. Ramirez CA, Naraqi S, McCulley DJ. Group A beta-hemolytic streptococcus endocarditis. Am Heart J. 1984;108:1383–1386.
180. Baddour LM. Infective endocarditis caused by beta-hemolytic streptococci. The Infectious Diseases Society of America's Emerging Infections Network. Clin Infect Dis. 1998;26:66–71.
181. Murphy DJ Jr. Group A streptococcal meningitis. Pediatrics. 1983;71:1–5.
182. Basiliere JL, Bistrong HW, Spence WF. Streptococcal pneumonia: Recent outbreaks in military recruit populations. Am J Med. 1968;44:580–589.
183. Mastro TD, Farley TA, Elliott JA, et al. An outbreak of surgical wound infections

due to group A *Streptococcus* carried on the scalp. N Engl J Med. 1990;323:968–972.
184. Bisno AL. Cutaneous infections: Microbiologic and epidemiologic considerations. Am J Med. 1984;76:172–179.
185. Stevens D. Streptococcal toxic shock syndrome. Infect Med. 1992;9:33–39.
186. The Working Group on Severe Streptococcal Infections. Defining the group A streptococcal toxic shock syndrome: Rationale and consensus definition. JAMA. 1993;269:390–391.
187. The working group on prevention of invasive group A streptococcal infections. Prevention of invasive group A streptococcal disease among household contacts of case-patients: Is prophylaxis warranted? JAMA. 1998;279:1206–1210.
188. Nosocomial group A streptococcal infections associated with asymptomatic health care workers—Maryland and California, 1997. MMWR Morbid Mortal Wkly Rep. 1999;48:163–166.

Chapter 187

Nonsuppurative Poststreptococcal Sequelae: Rheumatic Fever and Glomerulonephritis

ALAN L. BISNO

RHEUMATIC FEVER

Acute rheumatic fever (ARF) is a disease characterized by nonsuppurative inflammatory lesions involving primarily the heart, joints, subcutaneous tissues, and central nervous system. In its classic form, the disorder is acute, febrile, and largely self-limited. However, damage to heart valves may occur, and such damage may be chronic and progressive and lead to severe cardiac failure, total disability, and, not infrequently, death many years after the acute attack. ARF is extremely variable in its manifestations; it remains, basically, a clinical syndrome for which no specific diagnostic test exists. Insofar as is known, all cases of ARF follow group A streptococcal upper respiratory tract infection, although the exact mechanisms mediating the development of the disease remain speculative. Persons who have suffered an attack of ARF are particularly predisposed to recurrent episodes after subsequent group A streptococcal infections.

History

Guillaume de Baillou (1538–1616), also known as "Ballonius," first used the term *rheumatism* to distinguish acute arthritis from gout as a separate clinical entity. Thomas Sydenham (1624–1689) described chorea but failed to associate this entity with other manifestations of ARF. Raymond Vieussens (1641–1715) published pathologic descriptions of mitral stenosis and aortic insufficiency. It remained, however, for William Charles Wells in 1812 to emphasize the association of rheumatism and carditis and to provide the first clear description of subcutaneous nodules. Jean-Baptiste Bouillard in 1836 and Walter B. Cheadle in 1889 published extensive studies of rheumatic arthritis and carditis that have come to be regarded as classic works in this field and form the basis for modern clinical concepts of ARF. The specific rheumatic lesion in the myocardium was described by Ludwig Aschoff in 1904.

J. K. Fowler pointed out the association of sore throat and rheumatic fever in 1880, and shortly after the dawn of the 20th century, Bela Schick identified ARF as one of the "Nachkrankheiten" of scarlet fever. The introduction of Rebecca Lancefield's grouping system for β-hemolytic streptococci allowed clarification of the epidemiology of the disease by a number of investigators in the United States and the United Kingdom, including Coburn, Collis, Rammelkamp, Wannamaker, Massell, and Stollerman. Finally, the widespread introduction of antibiotic agents after World War II resulted in the development of strategies for the primary and secondary prevention of rheumatic fever.

Etiology and Pathogenesis

ARF is a delayed nonsuppurative sequela of upper respiratory infection due to group A streptococci. Several lines of evidence firmly support this conclusion. There is a close temporal relationship between epidemics of streptococcal sore throat and scarlet fever and epidemics of ARF. Most patients with ARF give a history of preceding pharyngitis. Even in patients without such a clear-cut history, tests of antistreptococcal antibodies nearly always provide evidence of recent streptococcal infection. In prospective studies of primary and recurrent ARF, cases of this disease occur only after an immunologically significant streptococcal infection. Finally, continuous antimicrobial prophylaxis, when successful in preventing intercurrent streptococcal infections, also effectively prevents ARF recurrences in rheumatic persons.

An intriguing and as yet unexplained aspect of the host-parasite relationship is the fact that, insofar as is known, cutaneous streptococcal infections do not initiate ARF. This may indicate a requirement for the pharyngeal site, with its rich endowment of lymphoid tissue, for the initiation of the disease process, or it may result from a lack of rheumatogenicity among the so-called pyoderma strains of group A streptococci.

A substantial body of evidence indicates that group A streptococci do indeed vary in their rheumatogenic potential. Studies of outbreaks of streptococcal pharyngitis reveal that strains of certain M serotypes are strongly and repetitively associated with ARF (Table 187–1),[1] whereas strains of other equally prevalent types fail to initiate the disease or even to reactivate it in exquisitely susceptible hosts.[2] Investigations of endemic ARF cases in Trinidad[3] and Chile[4] indicate that streptococci causing ARF belong to different serotypes than those causing acute glomerulonephritis (AGN) occurring simultaneously in the same population. Pyoderma strains of group A streptococci (see Chapter 186) have never been associated with ARF[5, 6] even when, as frequently happens, they colonize the throat. Moreover, variations in the rheumatogenicity of prevalent group A streptococci likely account for the striking temporal and geographic fluctuations in the incidence of ARF.

Rheumatogenic streptococcal strains exhibit distinct biologic characteristics. Their M-protein molecules share a particular surface-exposed antigenic domain[7] against which ARF patients mount a strong immunoglobulin G (IgG) response.[8] They fail to elaborate α-lipoproteinase (so-called serum opacity factor), and they are frequently heavily encapsulated. The latter feature is manifested by the formation of mucoid colonies on blood-agar plates. Whether such

TABLE 187–1 M Serotypes of Group A Streptococci Associated with Nonsuppurative Sequelae*

ARF	Pharyngitis-Associated AGN	Pyoderma-Associated AGN
1	1	2
3	4	49†
5	12	55†
6	25	57
14		59
18		60
19		61
24		

*This list represents the major serotypes known to be associated with ARF and AGN, but it is not all-inclusive. M typability of streptococcal strains isolated from various geographic areas varies widely.
†M types 49 and 55 have also been reported on occasion to cause pharyngitis-associated AGN.
Abbreviations: AGN, Acute glomerulonephritis; ARF, acute rheumatic fever.

strains express a unique rheumatogenic antigen, however, remains unknown.

It is probable that not all strains of rheumatogenic serotypes are equally dangerous. The propensity of a given strain to elicit ARF may well depend on its phase of virulence, a reflection of quantitative factors such as the production of M protein, hyaluronate, or other less well defined biologic properties. Virulence is likely to be enhanced in epidemiologic settings that favor rapid person-to-person passage.

Although the group A streptococcus is known to be the causative agent of rheumatic fever, the exact mechanism by which this microorganism induces the disease remains unexplained. Suggestions that the disease results from direct tissue invasion by group A streptococci or by cell wall variants of this organism have not been confirmed and are no longer considered tenable. Several theories have been advanced. These include (1) toxic effects of streptococcal products, particularly streptolysins S or O, which are known to be capable of inducing tissue injury; (2) a serum sickness–like reaction mediated by antigen-antibody complexes, perhaps localized to sites of tissue injury; and (3) autoimmune phenomena induced by similarity or identity of certain streptococcal antigens to a wide variety of human tissue antigens.[9]

Although none of these theories have been unequivocally proved or refuted, most attention has been focused on the concept of autoimmunity, or, more precisely, molecular mimicry.[10] Interest in this mechanism has been spurred by the identification of antibodies in the sera of patients with ARF or rheumatic heart disease that react with the human heart in a variety of test systems. These so-called heart-reactive antibodies are also present, albeit in much lower titer, in sera of patients with uncomplicated streptococcal pharyngitis. The presence of bound immunoglobulin and complement in the myocardium of children dying of rheumatic carditis suggests that circulating heart-reactive antibodies may have pathogenetic significance.

Heart-reactive antibodies in ARF sera are directed against several different antigenic specificities in heart tissue, and at least some of these moieties are cross-reactive with group A streptococcal antigens. Indeed, rabbit antisera raised against group A streptococci contain antibodies that bind to the sarcolemma and subsarcolemmal sarcoplasm in cardiac myofibers and skeletal muscle and to smooth muscle of vessel walls and endocardium. These reactions have been studied by immunofluorescence, and whole group A streptococci or fractions thereof have been shown to adsorb the heart-reactive antibodies. Streptococcal antigens cross-reactive with the human heart have been localized to the bacterial cell wall by some investigators[11] and to the cell membrane by others.[12, 13] More recently, improved methods of purification of M protein have been developed, and techniques of molecular biology have been employed in studying the relationship between specific peptides of the M protein and human tissues. Epitopes of streptococcal M proteins have been identified that share antigenic determinants with cardiac myosin,[14, 15] sarcolemmal membrane proteins,[16] synovium, and articular cartilage.[17]

Goldstein and colleagues[18] described a cross-reaction between group A polysaccharide and a structural glycoprotein isolated from human and bovine heart valves. Such a cross-reaction might explain the observation that serum levels of antibodies to group A carbohydrate appear to remain elevated for many years in patients with rheumatic valvulitis (but not in rheumatic patients without valvulitis)[19] and decline remarkably if valve resection is performed.

Chronic remittent nodular lesions were observed in dermal connective tissue after a streptococcal mucopeptide-polysaccharide cell wall complex was injected into experimental animals.[20] Antibodies raised in rabbits against streptococcal hyaluronate cross-react with human hyaluronate.[21] Many children with Sydenham's chorea have circulating antibodies that react both with neurons of the caudate and subthalamic nuclei and with group A streptococcal cell membranes.[22] Taken together, these cross-reactive and toxic phenomena could explain most of the individual manifestations of ARF. On the other hand, it should be emphasized that there is no direct proof that these systems play any role in the pathogenesis of rheumatic fever.

Much of the work reviewed previously, particularly that related to heart-reactive antibodies and group A carbohydrate, is focused on humoral immune responses to streptococci. Indeed, serum antibody responses to streptolysin O, non–type-specific M antigens, and virtually every other streptococcal antigen are on the average more vigorous in patients with ARF than in persons with uncomplicated streptococcal infections. However, it is likely that delayed hypersensitivity responses to streptococcal antigens also play a critical role in the etiology of ARF.[23] Preparations of streptolysin S contain a nonspecific mitogen that is closely related to but separable from the hemolytic activity. Rheumatic persons have a heightened lymphocyte reactivity to streptococcal cell walls and membranes, but the reactivity to membranes is more striking and persists for several years after an acute attack.[24] T lymphocytes from spleens of adult guinea pigs sensitized with streptococcal cells, cell walls, or protoplast membranes are cytotoxic for cultured guinea pig heart cells.[25]

During active rheumatic carditis, both the number of helper (CD4) lymphocytes and the ratio of CD4 to CD8 cells are increased both in heart valves and in peripheral blood.[26, 27] The production of interleukin-1[28] and interleukin-2[28, 29] has been reported to be enhanced. The recognition that both M protein[30] and streptococcal pyrogenic exotoxins[31] function as superantigens suggests a potential mechanism mediating the unrestrained immunologic assault postulated to cause ARF.

A complete elucidation of the pathogenesis of ARF obviously requires not only an understanding of the peculiarities of the etiologic agent but also of the nature of the susceptible host. The fact that even in severe epidemics of exudative pharyngitis, rheumatic fever affects only a small proportion of infected persons, coupled with the known familial aggregation of ARF cases, has long suggested the possibility of a genetic predisposition to rheumatic attacks. Studies of the distribution of class 1 HLA antigens in rheumatic patients versus controls have been inconclusive. A statistically significant association has been reported between certain of the class II HLA antigens (HLA-DR2 in blacks[32] and HLA-DR4 in whites[32, 33]) and rheumatic fever. An intriguing potential link between the genetic constitution of the human host and susceptibility to ARF is the identification of certain alloantigens that are expressed in a higher proportion of circulating B lymphocytes of rheumatic subjects and their family members than of patients with AGN or healthy controls.[34]

Pathologic Findings

Rheumatic fever is characterized pathologically by exudative and proliferative inflammatory lesions of connective tissue, most notably the heart, joints, blood vessels, and subcutaneous tissue. In the early stages of the disease, there is fragmentation of collagen fibers, cellular infiltration that is predominantly lymphocytic, and fibrinoid deposition. This is followed shortly by the appearance of the myocardial Aschoff's nodule. Aschoff's nodule is a perivascular focus of inflammation that consists of an area of central necrosis surrounded by a rosette of large mononuclear and giant multinuclear cells. The nuclei of these cells may have a clear area just within the nuclear membrane ("owl-eyed nucleus") or present a serrated ("caterpillar") appearance depending on their orientation in microscopic cross-section. Such cells are known as *Anichkov's myocytes*, although immunohistochemical studies demonstrate them to be of macrophage-histiocyte origin.[35, 36] Cardiac findings may include pericarditis, myocarditis, or endocarditis, or all of these. Endocarditis involves the left side of the heart in most instances. A thickened and roughened area is frequently seen in the left atrium above the base of the posterior leaflet of the mitral valve (MacCallum's patch). Valvular lesions begin as edema and cellular infiltration of the leaflets and chordae with small verrucae along the line of closure. As healing occurs, the valves may become thickened and deformed, the chordae shortened, and the valve commissures fused, thereby resulting in valvular stenosis or insufficiency.

The joint lesions are characterized by fibrinous exudate over the synovial membrane and serous effusion without joint destruction. Histologic findings include cellular infiltration and fibrinoid degeneration. Subcutaneous nodules resemble Aschoff bodies in many features. They consist of a central zone of fibrinoid necrosis surrounded by histiocytes and fibroblasts; perivascular accumulations of lymphocytes and polymorphonuclear leukocytes are also apparent. Although scattered areas of arteritis and petechial hemorrhages have been found in the brain, their relationship to Sydenham's chorea remains uncertain.

Epidemiology

Acute rheumatic fever is most frequent among children in the 6- to 15-year-old age group. Indeed, its relative rarity in infants and pre–school-aged children has led some observers to question whether repeated "primary" infections might be a prerequisite for the development of this disease. Both initial and recurrent episodes also occur in adults.[37–39] There is no clear-cut sex predilection, although there is a female preponderance in certain clinical manifestations, notably mitral stenosis and Sydenham's chorea when the latter occurs after puberty. In temperate climates rheumatic fever tends to occur less frequently in the summer.

The attack rate of rheumatic fever after untreated streptococcal exudative tonsillitis in military recruit camps has been carefully studied and has been shown to be consistently around 3%.[40] The ARF attack rate is considerably lower after endemically occurring infections among open populations of school-aged children. Siegel and associates[41] studied 519 untreated children with pharyngitis associated with positive throat cultures for group A streptococci. The attack rate of ARF was 0.4%; among those patients with an immunologically significant infection, as judged by a rise in the serum titer of anti–streptolysin O (ASO), the attack rate was 0.9%. In that study, ARF was observed to occur only among the group of 81 patients with exudative pharyngitis, positive throat cultures for group A streptococci, ASO titer rises, and prolonged convalescent streptococcal carriage. In this group, the ARF attack rate, 2.5%, approximated that seen in military recruit camps. These and other data suggest that ARF is *more likely* to occur after more severe forms of streptococcal throat infection, as judged by clinical, bacteriologic, and immunologic criteria. Nevertheless, approximately one third of ARF cases occur after asymptomatic streptococcal infection.

It is difficult for the physician trained in North America to comprehend the magnitude of the problem of ARF in the developing countries of the world. The disease is rampant in the Middle East, the Indian subcontinent, and certain areas of Africa and South America.[42, 43] For example, a World Health Organization survey conducted between 1986 and 1990 estimated the prevalence of rheumatic fever–rheumatic heart disease per 1000 schoolchildren to be 12.6 in Zambia, 10.2 in Sudan, and 7.9 in Bolivia.[42] It has been estimated that there are at least 50,000 episodes of ARF annually in India and more than 1 million patients with rheumatic heart disease.[44] Extremely high rates of ARF and rheumatic heart disease are seen among Aboriginal populations such as those in New Zealand and Australia.[45]

The overall incidence of ARF in the United States cannot be ascertained precisely because of inherent difficulties in diagnosing the disease and because most states no longer maintain operational rheumatic fever registries. There is general agreement, however, that the incidence of ARF and rheumatic heart disease has declined markedly over the course of the 20th century in the United States and western Europe. The rate of decline appears to have been particularly steep during the 1960s and 1970s. Indeed, a survey in Memphis, Tennessee,[46] indicated that during 1977 through 1981, the incidence of ARF among white suburban schoolchildren was only 0.5 per 100,000 per year. Similar rates have been reported from many geographic areas of the United States.[47] Traditionally, ARF in the United States has been largely a disease of lower socioeconomic groups. The incidence has been much higher among blacks than among whites,[46, 48] a fact that appears to relate to basic environmental conditions rather than to any genetic predisposition of the black race for the development of rheumatic fever. The major predisposing environmental condition that has been identified is crowding. The degree of crowding markedly influences the acquisition rate of group A streptococci (see Chapter 186) and hence the risk of development of ARF.[38]

In the mid-1980s, a resurgence of ARF occurred in many communities in the United States.[49] Beginning in early 1985, an epidemic of the disease occurred in Salt Lake City, Utah, and the surrounding intermountain area.[47] By the end of 1992, 274 cases had been admitted to the Primary Children's Medical Center in Salt Lake City.[50] Smaller clusters of ARF, ranging from 15 to 40 cases, were reported during approximately the same time period from Columbus[51] and Akron, Ohio,[52] Pittsburgh, Pennsylvania,[53] Nashville[54] and Memphis, Tennessee,[55] Kansas City, Missouri,[56] Morgantown[57] and Charleston, West Virginia,[58] Dallas, Texas,[59] and New York, New York.[60] Moreover, for the first time in many years, outbreaks occurred in army and navy training camps.[61, 62]

Quite surprisingly, a number of the 1980s civilian outbreaks[47, 51–53, 63] involved children of middle-class white families residing in suburban or rural settings. The group A streptococcal strains most strongly associated epidemiologically with these ARF outbreaks belong to the well-recognized rheumatogenic serotypes (e.g., types 1, 3, 5, 6, and 18).[64] Particularly prominent in this regard were highly mucoid strains of M-18.[64]

Persons who have suffered an initial attack of rheumatic fever have a marked predilection to develop recurrences after subsequent episodes of streptococcal pharyngeal infection. The risk of recurrence after streptococcal infection is highest within the first few years after the initial attack and then declines. It is unclear whether this decline is due to the length of time since the preceding attack or to the increasing age of the patient. Nevertheless, rheumatic patients remain at an increased risk of recurrence well into adult life. Two other factors positively correlated with a risk of rheumatic recurrences after streptococcal infection are the magnitude of the ASO response and the presence of preexisting heart disease. In the classic studies conducted at Irvington House, New York,[65] for example, 56% of streptococcal infections occurring in persons with rheumatic heart disease and accompanied by four-tube or greater ASO titer rises induced ARF recurrences.

Clinical Manifestations

Rheumatic fever manifests itself as a variety of signs and symptoms that may occur singly or in combination. The most important of these, in terms of diagnosis, have been termed the *major manifestations* and include carditis, polyarthritis, chorea, subcutaneous nodules, and erythema marginatum. Certain additional findings that are frequently present in ARF but are nonspecific in nature constitute the so-called *minor manifestations:* fever, arthralgia, heart block, and acute-phase reactants in the blood (C-reactive protein and elevation of the leukocyte count and erythrocyte sedimentation rate).

The latent period between the onset of preceding streptococcal sore throat and the onset of ARF averages 19 days.[66] The range has been difficult to establish precisely but appears to be between 1 and 5 weeks. The average latent period is the same for recurrent attacks as for initial episodes.

The mode of onset is quite variable. If acute polyarthritis is the initial complaint, the disease may have a rather abrupt onset and may be marked by fever and toxicity. On the other hand, when isolated mild carditis is the initial manifestation, the onset of ARF may be insidious or even subclinical.

Most attacks begin with polyarthritis, although occasionally this may be preceded by abdominal pain. Carditis, if it appears, usually does so early in the course of the disease. Overall, arthritis occurs in approximately 75% of first attacks of ARF, carditis in 40 to 50%, chorea in 15%, and subcutaneous nodules and erythema marginatum in less than 10%.[67] These incidences vary with age: carditis occurs most frequently when ARF strikes younger children, whereas the proportion of cases with arthritis increases with the age of the patients.

Carditis is the only manifestation of ARF that has the potential to cause long-term disability or death. Heart involvement in ARF is frequently a pancarditis involving the endocardium, myocardium, and pericardium. Nevertheless, in the absence of high fever or symptoms of acute pericarditis or congestive heart failure, it may be asymptomatic. Carditis almost always manifests itself within the first 3 weeks of an attack of ARF if it is to appear at all. The clinical signs of carditis include the development of organic heart murmur or murmurs not previously present, cardiac enlargement, congestive heart failure, pericardial friction rub, or pericardial effusion.

Severe myocarditis or, perhaps more frequently, severe mitral regurgitation[68, 69] may precipitate intractable heart failure and death in the acute phase of the disease, but fortunately, this occurrence is quite rare. On the other hand, chronic inflammatory changes involving the myocardium and endocardium may lead to the delayed development of chronic rheumatic heart disease (Fig. 187–1). Endocarditis involves the mitral valve more frequently than it does the aortic valve. Characteristic murmurs of acute rheumatic carditis are three: a high-pitched blowing holosystolic apical murmur of mitral regurgitation, a low-pitched apical mid-diastolic flow murmur (Carey-Coombs murmur), and a high-pitched decrescendo diastolic murmur of aortic regurgitation heard at the secondary and primary aortic areas. Murmurs of mitral and aortic stenosis are associated with chronic but not with acute rheumatic valvular disease. Delayed atrioventricular conduction, as manifested by first-degree or even greater degrees of heart block,[70] is a toxic phenomenon associated with ARF but not in itself diagnostic of rheumatic carditis.

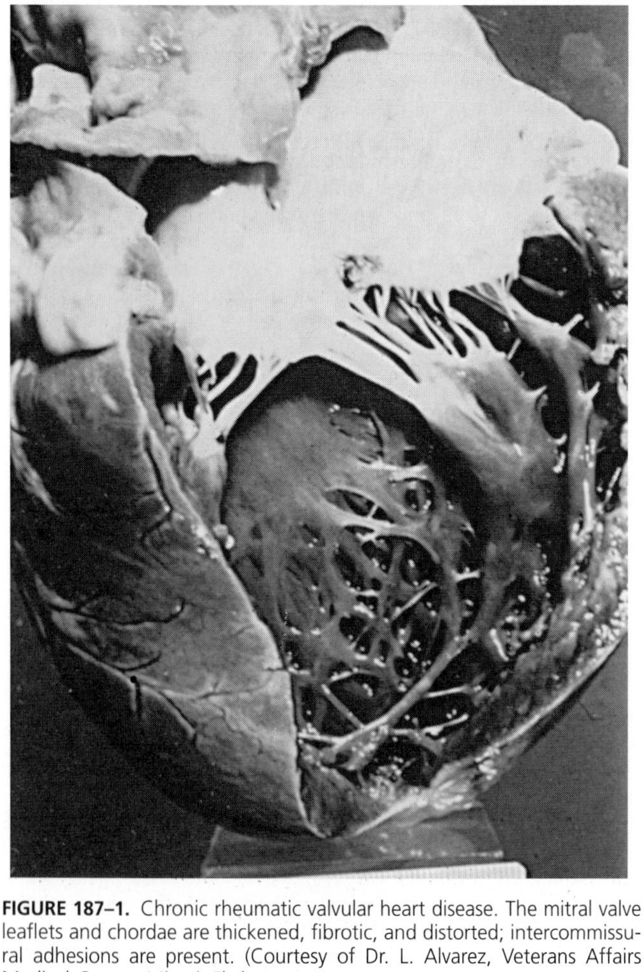

FIGURE 187–1. Chronic rheumatic valvular heart disease. The mitral valve leaflets and chordae are thickened, fibrotic, and distorted; intercommissural adhesions are present. (Courtesy of Dr. L. Alvarez, Veterans Affairs Medical Center, Miami, Fla.)

Joint involvement in ARF ranges from arthralgia without objective findings to frank arthritis characterized by heat, swelling, redness, and exquisite tenderness. There is an inverse relationship between the severity of joint involvement and the risk of development of carditis.[71] The most frequently involved joints are the knees, ankles, elbows, and wrists. The small joints of the hands are less frequently affected, and the spine is only rarely involved. When the course of the illness is not suppressed by anti-inflammatory drugs, multiple joints are usually involved; approximately 50% of the patients develop arthritis in more than six joints. Arthritis in ARF is classically migratory, that is, the inflammation travels from joint to joint. Once a joint becomes involved, inflammation begins to subside within a few days to a week and disappears within 2 to 3 weeks. The evolution of arthritis in individual joints tends to overlap, so multiple joints may be inflamed at the same time. In most instances the entire bout of polyarthritis subsides within 4 weeks, leaving no residual articular damage. One possible exception to this has been claimed by several authors, who report the very rare occurrence of the so-called Jaccoud's form of periarticular fibrosis after rheumatic arthritis.

The existence of a reactive "poststreptococcal arthritis" distinct from ARF has been postulated to occur in certain patients whose arthritis is atypical in the time of onset or duration,[39] is unaccompanied by other major manifestations, and fails to respond promptly to salicylate therapy.[72] The ultimate prognosis of such cases is unknown, but in some instances rheumatic heart disease has ensued.[73] Therefore, it is prudent to consider all cases of poststreptococcal polyarthritis that fulfill the diagnostic criteria of Jones as representing ARF, providing other common causes of polyarthritis have been excluded.[74, 75]

Subcutaneous nodules usually are associated with severe carditis and tend to occur several weeks after its onset. They are firm and painless and vary in size from a few millimeters to 2 cm. Such nodules are usually found over bony surfaces or prominences and over tendons. Common sites are adjacent to elbows, knees, wrists, or ankles and over Achilles tendons, the occiput, or spinous processes of the vertebrae. Their number varies from one to a few dozen. They usually persist for a week or two. Somewhat similar but more persistent lesions are seen in rheumatoid arthritis.

Erythema marginatum is a nonpruritic, nonpainful erythematous eruption usually seen on the trunk or proximal aspects of the extremities. The individual lesions are evanescent, moving over the skin in serpiginous patterns that change before the observer's eyes and are often likened to smoke rings, with a tendency to advance at the margins while clearing in the center. The lesions may be macular or raised and appear to be more a vasomotor phenomenon than a manifestation of cutaneous pathologic changes. Individual lesions may come and go in minutes to hours, but the process may go on intermittently for weeks to months.

Sydenham's chorea ("St. Vitus' dance") is a neurologic disorder characterized by emotional lability, muscular weakness, and rapid, uncoordinated, involuntary purposeless movements. The choreiform movements disappear during sleep and may be partially suppressed by sedation. The nonrhythmic movements are most notable in the face, hands, and feet. Sensation remains intact. Detailed descriptions of the nature of the choreiform movements can be found elsewhere.[76, 77] Individual attacks in hospitalized patients usually last 2 to 4 months.

Chorea may occur in relatively close association with other rheumatic manifestations or in isolated form ("pure chorea"). In cases of pure chorea, laboratory evidence of acute inflammation (C-reactive protein, an elevated erythrocyte sedimentation rate) or recent streptococcal infection (elevated levels of antistreptococcal antibodies) may be lacking. This observation, which led investigators in the past to question the relationship of ARF to pure chorea, is now known to result from the fact that Sydenham's chorea often occurs with a longer latent period than do the other manifestations of ARF. Some patients with pure chorea are found on follow-up to have rheumatic heart disease manifested primarily by mitral stenosis.[78]

Several clinical manifestations of ARF occur with some frequency but are not in themselves specific enough to be considered major manifestations. These include fever, which accompanies almost all ARF attacks at their onset, arthralgia, abdominal pain, and epistaxis. The pulmonary parenchyma in ARF may be involved by a variety of pathologic processes including pulmonary edema, atelectasis, pulmonary embolism, or thromboses. Some observers feel that in addition a specific rheumatic pneumonia may occur in rare instances.[79]

The average duration of an attack, unaltered by anti-inflammatory therapy, is approximately 3 months. Less than 5% of the cases persist for longer than 6 months, justifying the designation "chronic" rheumatic fever. Stollerman[76] lists the criteria for continuing clinical activity as follows: joint symptoms, new organic murmurs, a changing heart size, congestive heart failure in the absence of longstanding valvular disease, subcutaneous nodules, a sleeping pulse rate greater than 100 beats/min, erythema marginatum, chorea, a positive test for C-reactive protein, and a rectal temperature of 100.4°F or higher for 3 or more consecutive days.

Diagnosis

Because ARF can have such diverse manifestations (acute polyarthritis, congestive heart failure, chorea, or combinations of these) and because there is no specific diagnostic test for the disease, the differential diagnostic possibilities in an individual case may be quite broad. Among the diseases that most frequently need to be differentiated are rheumatoid arthritis, juvenile rheumatoid arthritis, systemic lupus erythematosus, serum sickness, sickle cell crisis or cardiopathy, rubella arthritis, septic arthritis (especially gonococcal arthritis in adolescent patients), Lyme disease,[80] infective endocarditis, viral myocarditis, and early stages of Henoch-Schönlein purpura. Less frequent differential diagnostic considerations include gout, sarcoidosis, Hodgkin's disease, and leukemia. Choreiform movements have been described in patients with systemic lupus erythematosus,[81] neoplasms involving the basal ganglia,[82] legionnaires' disease,[83] hypoparathyroidism,[84] antiphospholipid syndrome,[85] Wilson's disease, and Huntington's disease. Chorea is also seen occasionally in women taking oral contraceptives,[86] and during pregnancy (chorea gravidarum).[87]

Arriving at the correct diagnosis is particularly important in ARF, not only in terms of prescribing appropriate therapy for the acute attack and formulating an accurate prognosis but also because of the necessity for prescribing continuous antistreptococcal prophylaxis. To minimize over- and underdiagnosis, the criteria originally formulated by T. Duckett Jones[88] and most recently updated and modified by a committee of the American Heart Association[75] have been generally accepted as the basis for reaching a diagnosis of ARF (Table 187–2). The updated criteria are to be applied most stringently to the diagnosis of an initial ARF attack. Although most patients with recurrences fulfill the criteria, the diagnosis of recurrent ARF may be less apparent. In a patient with established rheumatic heart disease, for example, it may be difficult to confidently diagnose recurrent carditis unless a previously normal valve is affected. The updated criteria therefore allow a presumptive diagnosis of recurrent ARF to be made if clinical findings are suggestive and there is supporting evidence of recent streptococcal infection.

Echocardiograms may at times demonstrate valvular regurgitation in ARF patients who do not have clinical evidence of carditis.[47, 89, 90] The significance of such findings and their relation to the ultimate cardiac prognosis remain to be clarified, and they do not per se establish the diagnosis of acute carditis in the updated Jones criteria.

TABLE 187–2 Guidelines for Diagnosis of Initial Attack of Rheumatic Fever (Jones Criteria, Updated 1992)*

Major manifestations
Carditis
Polyarthritis
Chorea
Erythema marginatum
Subcutaneous nodules
Minor manifestations
Clinical findings
Arthralgia
Fever
Laboratory findings
Elevated acute-phase reactants
Erythrocyte sedimentation rate
C-reactive protein
Prolonged PR interval
Supporting evidence of antecedent group A streptococcal infection
Positive throat culture or rapid streptococcal antigen test
Elevated or rising streptococcal antibody titer

*If supported by evidence of preceding group A streptococcal infection, the presence of two major manifestations or of one major and two minor manifestations indicates a high probability of acute rheumatic fever. Failure to fulfill the Jones criteria should make the diagnosis doubtful except in situations in which rheumatic fever is first discovered after a long latent period from the antecedent infection (e.g., Sydenham's chorea or indolent carditis).

From Dajani AS, Ayoub E, Bierman FZ, et al. Guidelines for the diagnosis of rheumatic fever: Jones criteria, updated 1992. Circulation. 1993;87:302–307.

The criteria are not infallible, particularly when the diagnosis rests on the presence of acute polyarthritis as the sole major criterion with supporting evidence of fever plus an elevated erythrocyte sedimentation rate or a positive test result for C-reactive protein. For this reason, it is important to recognize that evidence of recent streptococcal infection must be obtained to satisfy the revised Jones criteria. Such evidence might include a recent microbiologically documented episode of streptococcal pharyngitis, a positive throat culture for group A streptococci (although here the differentiation of infection from colonization presents a problem), or the demonstration of an elevated serum titer of antistreptococcal antibodies. In most cases, the latter criterion is relied on.

If a serum sample is obtained within 2 months of the onset, approximately 80% of patients with ARF have an ASO titer of greater than 200 Todd units/ml. If a second streptococcal antibody test is performed on the same serum specimen, the proportion of patients with ARF with at least one elevated titer rises to 90%, and if a battery of three tests is performed, this figure exceeds 95%.[91] Although an elevated antistreptococcal antibody titer is certainly not diagnostic of ARF, failure to demonstrate evidence of recent immunologically significant streptococcal infection by a battery of three serologic tests (e.g., ASO, anti–DNase B, antihyaluronidase) makes the diagnosis of ARF very doubtful. An exception to this statement must be made for the patient with pure chorea whose antibody titers may have declined to the normal range due to the long latent period between the antecedent streptococcal infection and the onset of this manifestation. Likewise, the onset of isolated carditis may be difficult to date; if recognition of isolated carditis is delayed, immunologic evidence of recent streptococcal infection may have disappeared.

A simple slide hemagglutination test (Streptozyme, Carter-Wallace, Inc.) has been marketed for the detection of antibodies to streptococcal extracellular antigens.[92] Unfortunately, the exact nature of the antibodies assayed by this test has not been ascertained,[93] and considerable lot-to-lot variability in the standardization of the reagent has been reported.[94] In view of these problems, the test cannot be recommended.

Treatment and Prognosis

The objectives of therapy in ARF are to quiet inflammation, decrease fever and toxicity, and control cardiac failure. The mainstays of

TABLE 187–3 Suggested Schedule of Anti-inflammatory Therapy in Rheumatic Fever

Clinical Severity	Treatment
Arthralgia or mild arthritis; no carditis	Analgesics only, such as codeine or propoxyphene
Moderate or severe arthritis; no carditis, or carditis *with* or *without* cardiomegaly, but without failure	Aspirin, 90–100 mg/kg/d for 2 wk; increased if necessary; 60–70 mg/kg/d for subsequent 6 wk
Carditis with failure, with or without joint manifestations	Prednisone, 40–60 mg/d; increased, if necessary; methyl prednisone sodium succinate IV in fulminating cases; after 2–3 wk, slow withdrawal to be completed in 3 more wk; aspirin to be continued for 1 mo after discontinuation of prednisone

From Stollerman GH. Rheumatic Fever and Streptococcal Infection. New York: Grune & Stratton; 1975.

treatment are salicylates and corticosteroids. Neither of these agents prevents or modifies the development of chronic rheumatic heart disease. A suggested treatment schedule is outlined in Table 187–3. Analgesics without anti-inflammatory properties are recommended for patients with mild disease. This allows complete expression of the clinical manifestations to aid in diagnosis and also avoids post-therapeutic rebounds. Most patients require salicylates. Serum levels of 20 mg/100 ml or more are required to control the inflammatory response. If the high doses of salicylates required cannot be tolerated due to gastric irritation or if symptoms of salicylism develop, a reduction in the aspirin dosage or a change to corticosteroids is necessary. The more potent anti-inflammatory action of corticosteroids should be brought to bear whenever salicylates fail to control the inflammatory process or whenever carditis with congestive heart failure is present. Although the use of nonsteroidal anti-inflammatory agents seems reasonable in patients who cannot tolerate salicylates and who do not require corticosteroids, there is a paucity of data on the use of these agents in ARF. Their role in the management of the disease thus remains to be defined.

Reactivation of clinical or laboratory manifestations of rheumatic inflammation may occur after the cessation of anti-inflammatory therapy. This "rebound" phenomenon is more frequent after therapy with corticosteroids than with aspirin. For this reason, therapy should be tapered rather than discontinued abruptly and aspirin administration should be continued for a month after treatment with adrenal steroids is discontinued.

Heart failure should be treated by using conventional measures. The potential risk of digitalis-induced arrhythmias in the patient with active myocarditis must be kept in mind. Patients with chorea require sedation and a quiet, nonstimulatory environment. Agents such as phenobarbital or diazepam may be employed. In patients with severe and debilitating hyperkinesis, haloperidol has been used. The potential role of plasmapheresis and intravenous immunoglobulin in the rare cases of intractable chorea is under investigation.[95]

ARF patients with positive throat cultures for group A streptococci should receive therapy with one of the regimens listed in Table 186–1, preferably penicillin G benzathine. Such therapy will not alter the course of the disease but is given to minimize the possibility of transmission of a rheumatogenic streptococcal strain.

The only long-term sequela of ARF is rheumatic heart disease. The prognosis in rheumatic patients has been greatly improved by our ability to prevent recurrent attacks with their concomitant threat of additional myocardial and valvular damage. The ultimate prognosis of an individual attack is rather directly related to the severity of cardiac involvement during the acute phase. This was best studied in the United Kingdom–United States Collaborative Study.[96] In that study, only 6% of the patients with no carditis or with only questionable carditis during their attack of ARF were found to have heart murmurs when reexamined 10 years later. Heart disease was present at follow-up in 30% of the patients initially found to have only apical systolic murmurs, in 40% of those with basal diastolic murmurs during the acute phase, and in 68% of those who initially suffered from congestive heart failure, pericarditis, or both. Patients with pure chorea appear to have a relatively high incidence of late development of rheumatic heart disease, even if carditis is not recognized at the time of the initial attack. It may be, however, that the initial findings of carditis are no longer prominent by the time that chorea (which often occurs after a long latent period) becomes apparent.

Prevention

The prevention of ARF in persons without a prior history of this disease depends on an accurate diagnosis and appropriate treatment of the antecedent streptococcal infection. This approach (so-called primary prevention) is outlined in Chapter 186. It is effective[97] but suffers from the limitation that a substantial proportion, probably about one third, of ARF cases follows streptococcal infections that are either entirely subclinical or too mild to bring them to medical attention.

Rheumatic patients are at extremely high risk of developing recurrent ARF after immunologically significant streptococcal upper respiratory infections. These persons require continuous prophylaxis to prevent intercurrent streptococcal infections. The recommended regimen[98] for most patients in the United States and other countries in which ARF incidence is low consists of a single intramuscular injection of 1.2 million units of penicillin G benzathine administered every 4 weeks (Table 187–4). In the most comprehensive study reported to date,[99] children following this regimen experienced a rheumatic fever recurrence rate of only 0.4 per 100 patient-years of observation. In those areas of the world where ARF and rheumatic heart disease remain very highly prevalent, ARF recurrence rates have been found to be even lower when injections of penicillin G benzathine are administered every 3 weeks rather than every 4 weeks.[100] A similar regimen may be appropriate for high-risk individuals such as those with rheumatic heart disease. The possible benefits of the 3-week regimen must be balanced against the potential decrease in patient compliance and increase in associated costs.

Oral sulfadiazine or penicillin V are also acceptable prophylactic agents but are less effective than is penicillin G benzathine (see Table 187–4). The lesser efficacy of oral regimens is due at least in part to the extreme difficulty of enforcing compliance. Patients allergic to penicillin and sulfadiazine may be given erythromycin. Patients requiring protection for many years are often begun on a regimen of penicillin G benzathine, which is changed to oral prophylaxis later in life when the risk of recurrence is deemed to be lower.

The optimal duration of continuous antimicrobial prophylaxis remains controversial. The risk of ARF recurrence is neither continu-

TABLE 187–4 Secondary Prevention of Rheumatic Fever (Prevention of Recurrent Attacks)

Agent	Dose	Mode
Benzathine penicillin G	1.2 million U q 4 wk*	Intramuscular
	or	
Penicillin V	250 mg bid	Oral
	or	
Sulfadiazine	0.5 g once daily for patients ≤27 kg (60 lb) 1.0 g once daily for patients >27 kg (60 lb)	Oral
For Individuals Allergic to Penicillin and Sulfadiazine		
Erythromycin	250 mg bid	Oral

*In high-risk situations, administration every 3 weeks is justified and recommended.
From Dajani A, Taubert K, Ferrieri P, et al. Treatment of acute streptococcal pharyngitis and prevention of rheumatic fever: A statement for health professionals. Committee on Rheumatic Fever, Endocarditis, and Kawasaki Disease of the Council on Cardiovascular Disease in the Young, the American Heart Association. Pediatrics. 1995;96:758–764.

ous nor uniform. It declines with the age of the patient and the number of years since the most recent attack. It is positively correlated with the number of previous attacks and with the presence and severity of preexisting rheumatic heart disease. Thus, the risk of recurrence becomes quite low in older adults without heart disease who are not in intimate contact with school-aged children. In view of these facts, the physician must make the decision about when and whether to discontinue prophylaxis after discussion with the patient and after careful assessment of the patient's risk of acquiring a streptococcal infection, the anticipated recurrence rate per infection, and the likely consequences of such recurrence. In the author's opinion, even when all these factors are favorable, prophylaxis should never be discontinued until the patients have reached their early twenties and at least 5 years have elapsed since the most recent rheumatic attack.[101] Current recommendations of the American Heart Association are set forth in Table 187–5.

In addition to the prevention of recurrences of ARF, patients with residual rheumatic valvular disease must be protected from bacterial endocarditis whenever they undergo dental or surgical procedures that consistently evoke bacteremia or are known to be associated with the development of endocarditis. The antimicrobial regimens suggested for endocarditis prophylaxis are entirely distinct from those required for rheumatic fever prophylaxis. This concept is a frequent source of confusion both to physicians and to dentists. Regimens for the prevention of bacterial endocarditis are discussed in Chapter 67.

Investigative efforts are being directed toward the development of a safe, effective M-protein vaccine for the prevention of streptococcal infection and ARF. Such a vaccine would have to provide protection against the major serotypes associated with ARF and deeply invasive infections. The considerable progress that has been made in recent years in elucidating the molecular biology of group A streptococci may well foreshadow a solution to this problem.[101a]

GLOMERULONEPHRITIS

Poststreptococcal acute glomerulonephritis (AGN) is an acute inflammatory disorder of the renal glomerulus that is characterized pathologically by diffuse proliferative glomerular lesions and clinically by edema, hypertension, hematuria, and proteinuria. The disease is a delayed nonsuppurative sequela of pharyngeal or cutaneous infection with certain "nephritogenic" group A streptococcal strains belonging to a limited number of serotypes.

History

Richard Bright (1789–1858) clearly differentiated cardiac from renal dropsy. He also noted the association between acute diseases, particularly scarlet fever, and AGN.[102] Subsequently, many investigators confirmed the relationship between β-hemolytic streptococcal infections and AGN. Schick[103] in 1907 commented on the similarity of the latent period in serum sickness to that in AGN, thus raising the possibility of an immunologic basis for the latter disease. Rammelkamp and Weaver[104] explained the puzzling variations in the attack rate of AGN after group A streptococcal infection by proposing that only certain serotypes of *Streptococcus pyogenes* were nephritogenic. Detailed prospective studies of the epidemiology, bacteriology, immunology, and natural history of pyoderma-associated nephritis by Wannamaker[105] and associates in Minnesota, Potter and colleagues[106] in south Trinidad, and Dillon and coworkers[107] in Alabama have added greatly to our understanding of this disease.

TABLE 187–5 Duration of Secondary Rheumatic Fever Prophylaxis

Duration	Category
Rheumatic fever with carditis and residual heart disease (persistent valvar disease*)	At least 10 yr since last episode and at least until age 40 yr, sometimes lifelong prophylaxis
Rheumatic fever with carditis but no residual heart disease (no valvar disease*)	10 yr or well into adulthood, whichever is longer
Rheumatic fever without carditis	5 yr or until age 21 yr, whichever is longer

*Clinical or echocardiographic evidence.
From Dajani A, Taubert K, Ferrieri P, et al. Treatment of acute streptococcal pharyngitis and prevention of rheumatic fever: A statement for health professionals. Committee on Rheumatic Fever, Endocarditis, and Kawasaki Disease of the Council on Cardiovascular Disease in the Young, American Heart Association. Pediatrics. 1995;96:758–764.

Etiology and Pathogenesis

Poststreptococcal AGN follows infection with a limited number of group A streptococcal serotypes (see Table 187–1). Type 12 is the most frequent M serotype causing AGN after pharyngitis or tonsillitis, whereas M-49 is the type most frequently related to pyoderma-associated nephritis. Not all streptococcal strains belonging to these serotypes are nephritogenic, however. There are no reliable biologic markers to differentiate nephritogenic from non-nephritogenic streptococci. Poststreptococcal AGN is almost always due to strains of serogroup A. There are, however, well-documented outbreaks due to group C organisms.[108, 109]

The precise mechanism by which streptococcal infection gives rise to AGN has not been delineated. The weight of evidence favors the view that the renal injury is immunologically mediated. Such evidence includes the latent period between infection and the development of AGN; the associated hypocomplementemia; and the fact that immunoglobulins, complement components, and antigens that react with streptococcal antisera are present in the renal glomerulus early in the course of the disease.[110–113] It is possible that antibodies elicited by nephritogenic streptococci react with renal tissues in such a way as to produce glomerular injury. Indeed, antigenic similarities between constituents of the streptococcus and the human kidney have been described.[114–116] On the other hand, the electron microscopic finding of nodular subepithelial "humps" in renal biopsy specimens from patients with AGN suggests that the renal injury may be due to the deposition of preformed complexes consisting of streptococcal antigen and host antibody within the glomerulus. Such subepithelial nodular deposits are a characteristic feature of experimentally induced disease caused by circulating immune complexes. Several groups[117–119] have detected circulating immune complexes in AGN. The possible role of cellular immune mechanisms has been inadequately explored.

The identity of the streptococcal constituent or constituents involved in the pathogenesis of AGN remains unknown. M protein is an obvious candidate because of the close association of nephritogenicity and the M serotype. Indeed, monoclonal antibodies raised against human glomeruli have been found to cross-react with streptococcal M protein.[116] Moreover, in an animal model of nephritis induced by nephritogenic type 12 streptococci, Lindberg and Vosti[120] eluted bound glomerular antibodies and found them to be directed against type 12 M protein but not against other streptococcal and renal antigens. Others, however, have described cross-reactions between fragments of streptococcal cell membrane and human glomerular basement membrane[114] and have produced proliferative glomerular lesions in rhesus monkeys by immunization with streptococcal membrane fragments or by intravenous injection of antibodies to these fragments.[121] Vogt and coworkers[122] have isolated a cationic proteinase from supernatants of nephritogenic streptococci that is present in renal biopsies of patients with AGN. Lange and associates[123] have described an antigen (termed *endostreptosin*) demonstrable in the glomerulus only during the initial phase of AGN that reacts in direct immunofluorescence tests with antibodies present in convalescent sera of AGN patients. An apparently identical antigen, found in a water-soluble fraction of nephritogenic streptococci and most likely derived from streptococcal plasma membrane, has been purified and termed *streptococcal protein preabsorbing antigen*.[124] Another nephritis strain–associated protein, initially identified as an extracellular product of nephritogenic streptococci, has been characterized as a streptokinase.[125] It is not yet clear whether streptococcal protein preabsorbing antigen and nephritis strain–associated protein are identical or distinct proteins. Streptokinase production has been postulated to play a role in the pathogenesis of AGN and, indeed, has been found essential for the development of the disease in a mouse model.[126] However, there is no unique reactivity to group A streptokinase in sera of AGN patients, nor has streptokinase deposition been demonstrated in biopsy specimens obtained early in the disease.[127]

Pathologic Characteristics

In the acute phase of illness, light microscopic examination of renal biopsy specimens demonstrates a marked increase in glomerular intracapillary cellularity due to endothelial and mesangial cell proliferation. These changes involve virtually all the glomeruli, which appear enlarged and bloodless, tending to fill the Bowman space.[128] In addition to this diffuse proliferative endocapillary process, a variable degree of polymorphonuclear leukocytic exudation is observed. Proliferation of parietal and visceral epithelial cells occurs to a modest degree only and is rarely extensive enough to give rise to well-developed crescent formation. Thin sectioning and special strains may reveal discrete deposits on the epithelial side of the basement membrane that correspond to the "humps" visible on electron microscopy. Focal degeneration, interstitial edema, and cellular infiltration also occur in the renal tubules, but these changes are far less prominent than is the glomerulitis. Arterioles are normal or nearly so in most cases of AGN.

Immunofluorescence technique demonstrates considerable variability in the pattern of deposition of immunoglobulin and complement components. Component C3 is virtually always present in the glomeruli, and deposits of IgG are also frequently demonstrable. These substances are present in the form of discrete deposits similar in size and location to the subepithelial humps visualized under the electron microscope,[111, 112] although deposits of C3 may also occur in an interrupted linear pattern along the basement membrane or in the mesangium.[112] Deposits of IgM, C1q, C4, and fibrin are found less commonly. The rather weak and inconsistent deposition of early complement components suggests that activation of the alternate complement pathway may play a role in the immunopathology of AGN.

Epidemiology

The epidemiologic characteristics of AGN largely reflect those of the antecedent group A streptococcal infection, that is, pharyngitis or pyoderma (Table 187–6). Thus, the classic streptococcal sore throat occurs primarily among school-aged children during the cooler months of the year. Pyoderma is largely a disease of children aged 2 to 6 years and occurs, in temperate climates, during the summer and early fall. There are data to suggest that, given a skin infection with a nephritogenic strain, the attack rate of AGN is higher in children 6 years or younger than in older children.[129] The latent period of AGN is variable but averaged 10 days after pharyngeal infection in the studies of Stetson and associates[130]; prospective studies at Red Lake Indian Reservation in Minnesota indicate the usual latent period of pyoderma-associated AGN to be 3 weeks or longer.[129]

Although the attack rate of AGN after throat or skin infection with a nephritogenic strain is substantial (i.e., 10–15%),[123, 129] the disease differs dramatically from acute rheumatic fever in that recurrences are rare. This is due at least in part to the relatively limited number of streptococcal strains that are nephritogenic and presumably also to the acquisition of type-specific protective immunity to the serotype that elicited the initial attack. Moreover, in contrast to rheumatic subjects, there is no evidence that AGN patients are unusually susceptible to recurrent attacks after reinfection with a potentially nephritogenic strain. When second attacks of AGN do occur, they are clinically and histologically indistinguishable from the initial attack.[131] A more commonly recognized phenomenon than recurrent AGN attacks is the propensity for streptococcal infections to precipitate exacerbations of chronic glomerulonephritis.[132] Such exacerbations often occur after a relatively brief latent period of 1 to 4 days. The coexistence of ARF and AGN in the same patient after pharyngeal infection is quite rare, but a few such cases have been reported.[133, 134]

The introduction of a highly nephritogenic strain into a family unit may result in multiple cases. When systematic screening of sibling contacts for hypertension, urinary abnormalities, and serum complement levels has been performed, the incidence of proven and suspected cases of AGN in sibling contacts has been extremely variable,[135–138] with estimates ranging as high as 20%.[139]

TABLE 187-6 Epidemiologic Characteristics of Pharyngitis-Associated and Pyoderma-Associated Acute Glomerulonephritis

Feature	Pharyngitis-Associated AGN	Pyoderma-Associated AGN
Age	Early school age	Preschool age
Sex	Male/female ratio ~2:1	Equally distributed
Season	Winter and spring	Late summer and early fall
Geographic distribution	North and South	Predominantly South
Familial occurrence	Common	Common
Latent period	10 d	3 wk
Attack rate*	10–15%	10–15%
Serologic types	Limited types	Also limited, but different types
Recurrences	Rare	Rare

*After infection with known nephritogenic strain.
Abbreviation: AGN, Acute glomerulonephritis.
Table adapted from data published in Wannamaker LW. Differences between streptococcal infections of the throat and of the skin. N Engl J Med. 1970;282:23–31.

Clinical and Laboratory Features

The typical clinical features of AGN, as seen in children entering the hospital with this disease, include edema, hypertension, and smoky or rusty-colored urine. Patients also exhibit pallor and may complain of lethargy, malaise, weakness, anorexia, headache, and dull back pain. Fever is not prominent.

Facial and periorbital edema are usually present, especially on arising in the morning, but edema also involves dependent areas such as the feet and legs, scrotum, and sacrum. In severe cases, ascites or pleural effusions may occur. Another manifestation of fluid overload is circulatory congestion, which may give rise to dyspnea, orthopnea, rales at the lung bases, distended neck veins, and even frank pulmonary edema. Manifestations of circulatory overload tend to be particularly prominent in the occasional cases of AGN occurring in older adults and, in such persons, may obscure the correct diagnosis if urinary findings are not properly interpreted.

Hypertension occurs in most patients but is usually of modest degree. Hypertensive retinopathy or heart failure does not ordinarily complicate the clinical picture. On the other hand, a small proportion of AGN patients, perhaps 5 to 10%, develop severe hypertension complicated by signs and symptoms of encephalopathy. These range from headache and vomiting to confusion, somnolence, and convulsions.

Although the clinical features enumerated previously are typical of hospitalized patients, many cases of AGN are so mild as to escape detection unless persons at risk are tested prospectively for urinary sediment abnormalities and serum complement levels. Two studies that included renal biopsy data have concluded that in epidemic situations, as many as 50% of cases of AGN may be subclinical.[136, 139] Whatever the exact proportion might be (and chances are this varies considerably in differing epidemiologic settings), it seems clear that subclinical episodes of AGN are by no means rare.

Laboratory findings include a mild normocytic normochromic anemia, elevated erythrocyte sedimentation rate, slight hypoproteinemia, and elevations of the blood urea nitrogen and serum creatinine concentrations. Hypercholesterolemia and hyperlipemia may also be present. Serum levels of total hemolytic complement and C3 complement are markedly reduced in the great majority of patients with clinically apparent AGN. The urine volume may be significantly diminished, and the urine itself is smoky, rusty, or brownish with a high specific gravity and positive test findings for protein and hemoglobin. The total urinary protein excretion is usually less than 3 g/day.[140] Microscopic examination of the urine reveals erythrocytes, leukocytes, and hyaline, granular, and red blood cell casts.

The urinary abnormalities in AGN must be distinguished from the mild hematuria and proteinuria that may be seen during the acute phase of acute streptococcal infection and other febrile illnesses. The relationship, if any, of these early urinary findings to the development of AGN is at present unknown.[141] Finally, diagnostic confusion is almost inevitable in the rare cases in which pronounced clinical manifestations of AGN occur in patients with minimal or no urinary sediment abnormalities.[142]

Diagnosis

The diagnosis of AGN is based on the clinical history, physical findings, and confirmatory evidence of antecedent streptococcal infection. The latter may include a recent history of scarlet fever, isolation of group A streptococci from throat or skin lesions, or demonstration of elevated serum titers of streptococcal antibodies. Even in the absence of bacteriologic isolation of streptococci, the presence of skin lesions morphologically compatible with streptococcal impetigo is highly suggestive.

It is almost always possible to demonstrate an elevated level of streptococcal antibodies in AGN,[92] although in cases with relatively short latent periods, serial bleedings may be necessary. It must be recalled that in pyoderma-associated nephritis, ASO responses are weak and it is frequently necessary to perform serum titrations of anti–DNase B or antihyaluronidase, or both. Although anti-Streptozyme titers rise in pyoderma nephritis, technical problems limit the reliability of the test (see earlier). Finally, if renal biopsy is performed, the demonstration of diffuse proliferative glomerulonephritis with subepithelial electron-dense deposits is a very helpful confirmatory finding.

Poststreptococcal AGN must be differentiated from a variety of other infectious process involving the kidney. It is, for example, often extremely difficult to differentiate an acute exacerbation of chronic glomerulonephritis, such as may be precipitated by a variety of intercurrent infections, from a true attack of AGN. A short latent period of 1 to 4 days suggests that the episode is an exacerbation of preexisting renal disease. Patients with subacute bacterial endocarditis tend to develop high serum levels of circulating immune complexes and may develop either diffuse proliferative or focal glomerulonephritis, both of which may be confused clinically with poststreptococcal nephritis. A variety of other bacterial and protozoan illnesses such as pneumococcal pneumonia, typhoid fever, leptospirosis, syphilis, toxoplasmosis, and *Plasmodium falciparum* malaria have been reported on occasion to be associated with nephritis. Viral infections such as hepatitis B and C, infectious mononucleosis, measles, mumps, and togaviral and enteroviral disease have likewise been implicated as causes of viruria, transient renal dysfunction, or actual glomerulonephritis.[143] In addition to the development of focal and segmental glomerulosclerosis, patients infected with the human immunodeficiency virus may rarely develop an immune complex glomerulonephritis.[144] Other entities that may at times mimic AGN are Henoch-Schönlein disease, systemic lupus erythematosus, polyarteritis nodosa, acute tubular necrosis, focal glomerulonephritis with hematuria, hereditary nephritis, rapidly progressive glomerulonephritis, idiopathic nephrotic syndrome, and malignant hypertension.

Therapy

Because no form of treatment is known to alter the long-term prognosis of AGN, therapy is directed toward management of the acute problems. Attention is directed to what is ordinarily the most immediate problem, namely, circulatory overload. In most cases this is handled adequately by salt and fluid restriction alone, but at times diuretics are required. Digitalis is not indicated because the risk of toxicity is substantial and in most instances myocardial function is intact.[145] Specific antihypertensive therapy is usually unnecessary, but in cases of severe hypertension and hypertensive encephalopathy, potent parenteral agents are required. Patients developing acute pulmonary edema or severe and prolonged oliguria require measures conventionally used in these conditions.

All nonallergic patients should receive penicillin, preferably penicillin G benzathine (see Chapter 186 for dosage schedule), to eradicate the nephritogenic streptococcal strain. Penicillin-allergic patients should receive erythromycin in the doses recommended for the treatment of streptococcal pharyngitis. In addition to urinalysis and serum C3-complement level determination, family contacts should have cultures of throat and skin lesions. Persons with positive cultures for group A streptococci should be treated appropriately. Such treatment is for epidemiologic purposes only and will not modify the course of preexistent AGN or, in all probability, abort the disease in persons who are within the latent period (see later).

With skillful use of the supportive measures outlined previously, deaths during the acute phase of AGN are now rare. Perhaps 1% or fewer of patients develop severe and irreversible renal failure. In the remainder, signs and symptoms often begin to abate within a few days after admission. Serum complement levels return to normal within a month, but microscopic hematuria and cylindruria frequently persist for months despite the patient's general feeling of well-being.

Prevention

Although penicillin treatment of the antecedent streptococcal infection is highly efficacious in preventing acute rheumatic fever, the same does not appear to be the case in AGN. Stetson and coworkers,[130] studying in a controlled fashion an epidemic of pharyngitis-associated (type 12) AGN in a military population, found a small but not statistically significant[146] preventive effect of penicillin. Uncontrolled observations during an epidemic of nephritis in Israel[147] (both throat and skin infections due to M-type 55) documented the occurrence of AGN in a number of subjects who had received prior antibiotic therapy according to a variety of different dosage regimens. Moreover, there was no difference in the clinical severity of AGN between subjects who had and those who had not received antibiotic therapy. Data presently available are not adequate to determine whether penicillin might have a small effect on the primary prevention of AGN, but such effect, at any rate, is not striking.[148]

As indicated previously, penicillin is effective in eradicating nephritogenic strains by treatment of AGN patients and their colonized family contacts. In appropriate high-risk settings during epidemics of AGN, penicillin prophylaxis of selected populations might be considered in a manner somewhat analogous to that used in U.S. military recruit camps for rheumatic fever control. Such prophylaxis is rarely indicated and should be used only after careful consideration of the specific epidemiologic parameters involved.[148a]

Because recurrent episodes of AGN are so rare, continuous antistreptococcal prophylaxis, such as is used in the secondary prevention of rheumatic fever, is unnecessary.

Prognosis

One of the most important issues relating to poststreptococcal glomerulonephritis is the frequency with which patients afflicted with the disease eventually develop chronic glomerulonephritis. In a certain group of AGN patients constituting only a small percentage of its victims, the acute attack is never resolved and the disease enters a subacute phase leading to a virtually complete loss of renal function within 6 months to 2 years. It is the ultimate fate of the remainder of the patients in whom the illness appears clinically to have resolved that remains controversial. Most observers now agree that the long-term prognosis in children is excellent. A 10-year follow-up of 61 patients involved in an epidemic at Red Lake, Minnesota,[149] revealed no cases of chronic glomerulonephritis. Moreover, in a 12- to 17-year follow-up of 534 Trinidadians convalescent from AGN,[150] only 3.5% of the subjects had persistent urine abnormalities, 3.7% were hypertensive, and none had serum creatinine values greater than 1.25 mg/dl. These figures are not in excess of what would be expected in surveys of normal populations. Almost all the Trinidadian patients had been children at the time of their attack of AGN. There was no difference in outcome of sporadic AGN cases as opposed to those associated with epidemics.

These data stand in sharp contrast to the findings of Baldwin,[151] who followed 168 subjects for periods up to 18 years and concluded that "irreversible renal damage has ensued in 50% of these patients, as evidenced by the presence of proteinuria and/or hypertension," although clinical uremia occurred in only 6 patients. Renal biopsy specimens from the subjects in Baldwin's series showed that proliferative changes had decreased, whereas glomerulosclerosis of marked degree was present in more than half of the specimens. Baldwin's study population contained a high proportion of adults, who were generally agreed to have a worse prognosis than do children.[152] Moreover, the results presented have been challenged because of the difficulty of sorting out exacerbations of chronic nephritis from true de novo attacks of AGN in studies of sporadically occurring disease[153] and because of the paucity of published data documenting the poststreptococcal cause of the cases studied.[154]

Based on the bulk of currently available data, it seems likely that more than 90% of the children with AGN make an uneventful recovery and that this disease in the pediatric age group is not an important precursor of chronic glomerulonephritis or hypertension. The prognosis appears more guarded in adult patients,[155] but the proportion who might be left with residual renal function impairment is at present unknown.

REFERENCES

1. Bisno AL. The concept of rheumatogenic and non-rheumatogenic group A streptococci. In: Read SE, Zabriskie JB, eds. Streptococcal Diseases and the Immune Response. New York: Academic Press; 1980:789–803.
2. Kuttner AG, Krumwiede E. Observations on the effect of streptococcal upper respiratory infections on rheumatic children: A three-year study. J Clin Invest. 1941;20:273–287.
3. Potter EV, Svartman M, Mohammed I, et al. Tropical acute rheumatic fever and associated streptococcal infections compared with concurrent acute glomerulonephritis. J Pediatr. 1978;92:325–333.
4. Berrios X, Quesney F, Morales A, et al. Acute rheumatic fever and poststreptococcal glomerulonephritis in an open population: Comparative studies of epidemiology and bacteriology. J Lab Clin Med. 1986;108:535–542.
5. Bisno AL, Pearce IA, Wall HP, et al. Contrasting epidemiology of acute rheumatic fever and acute glomerulonephritis: Nature of the antecedent streptococcal infection. N Engl J Med. 1970;283:561–565.
6. Bisno AL, Pearce IA, Stollerman GH. Streptococcal infections that fail to cause recurrences of rheumatic fever. J Infect Dis. 1977;136:278–285.
7. Bessen DE, Fischetti VA. Differentiation between two biologically distinct classes of group A streptococci by limited substitutions of amino acids within the shared region of M protein–like molecules. J Exp Med. 1990;172:1757–1764.
8. Bessen DE, Veasy LG, Hill HR, et al. Serologic evidence for a class I group A streptococcal infection among rheumatic fever patients. J Infect Dis. 1995;172:1608–1611.
9. Stollerman GH. Rheumatogenic streptococci and autoimmunity. Clin Immunol Immunopathol. 1991;61:131–142.
10. Froude J, Gibofsky A, Buskirk DR, et al. Cross-reactivity between streptococcus and human tissue: A model of molecular mimicry and autoimmunity. Curr Top Microbiol Immunol. 1989;145:5–26.
11. Kaplan MH, Meyeserian M. An immunological cross-reaction between group A streptococcal cells and human heart tissue. Lancet. 1962;1:706–710.
12. Zabriskie JB, Freimer EH. An immunological relationship between group A streptococcus and mammalian muscle. J Exp Med. 1966;124:661–678.
13. Van de Rijn I, Zabriskie JB, McCarty M. Group A streptococcal antigens cross-reactive with myocardium. Purification of heart-reactive antibody and isolation and characterization of the streptococcal antigen. J Exp Med. 1977;146:579–599.
14. Dell A, Antone SM, Gauntt CJ, et al. Autoimmune determinants of rheumatic carditis: Localization of epitopes in human cardiac myosin. Eur Heart J. 1991;12(Suppl D):158–162.
15. Dale JB, Beachey EH. Epitopes of streptococcal M proteins shared with cardiac myosin. J Exp Med. 1985;162:583–591.
16. Dale JB, Beachey EH. Protective antigenic determinant of streptococcal M protein shared with sarcolemmal membrane protein of human heart. J Exp Med. 1982;156:1165–1176.
17. Baird RW, Bronze MS, Kraus W, et al. Epitopes of group A streptococcal M protein shared with antigens of articular cartilage and synovium. J Immunol. 1991;146:3132–3137.
18. Goldstein I, Rebeyrotte P, Parlebas J, Halpern B. Isolation from heart valves of glycopeptides which share immunological properties with *Streptococcus haemolyticus* group A polysaccharides. Nature. 1968;219:866–868.
19. Dudding BA, Ayoub EM. Persistence of streptococcal group A antibody in patients with rheumatic valvular disease. J Exp Med. 1968;128:1081–1098.
20. Schwab JH, Cromartie WJ. Immunological studies on a C polysaccharide complex of group A streptococci having a direct toxic effect on connective tissue. J Exp Med. 1960;111:295–307.
21. Fillit HM, McCarty M, Blake M. Induction of antibodies to hyaluronic acid by immunization of rabbits with encapsulated streptococci. J Exp Med. 1986;164:762–776.
22. Husby G, van de Rijn I, Zabriskie JB, et al. Antibodies reacting with cytoplasm of subthalamic and caudate nuclei neurons in chorea and rheumatic fever. J Exp Med. 1976;144:1094–1110.
23. Zabriskie JB. T-cells and T-cell clones in rheumatic fever valvulitis: Getting to the heart of the matter? Circulation. 1995;92:281–282.
24. Read SE, Fischetti VA, Utermohlen V, et al. Cellular reactivity studies to streptococcal antigens. Migration inhibition studies in patients with streptococcal infections and rheumatic fever. J Clin Invest. 1974;54:439–450.
25. Yang LC, Soprey PR, Wittner MK, Fox EN. Streptococcal-induced cell-mediated-immune destruction of cardiac myofibers in vitro. J Exp Med. 1977;146:344–360.
26. Morris K, Mohan C, Wahi PL, et al. Increase in activated T cells and reduction in suppressor/cytotoxic T cells in acute rheumatic fever and active heart disease: A longitudinal study. J Infect Dis. 1993;167:979–983.
27. Kemeny E, Grieve T, Marcus R, et al. Identification of mononuclear cells and T cell subsets in rheumatic valvulitis. Clin Immunol Immunopathol. 1989;52:225–237.
28. Morris K, Mohan C, Wahi PL, et al. Enhancement of IL-1, IL-2 production and IL-2 receptor generation in patients with acute rheumatic fever and active rheumatic heart disease: A prospective study. Clin Exp Immunol. 1993;91:429–436.
29. Zedan MM, el-Shennawy FA, Abou-Bakr HM, Al-Basousy AM. Interleukin-2 in relation to T cell subpopulations in rheumatic heart disease. Arch Dis Child. 1992;67:1373–1375.
30. Tomai M, Kotb M, Majumdar G, Beachey EH. Superantigenicity of streptococcal M protein. J Exp Med. 1990;172:359–362.
31. Schlievert PM. Role of staphylococcal and streptococcal pyrogenic-toxin superantigens in human disease. Mediguide to Infectious Diseases. 1993;13:1–7.
32. Ayoub EM, Barrett DJ, Maclaren NK, Krischer JP. Association of class II human histocompatibility leukocyte antigens with rheumatic fever. J Clin Invest. 1986;77:2019–2026.
33. Anastasiou-Nana MI, Anderson JL, Carlquist JF, Nanas JN. HLA-DR typing and lymphocyte subset evaluation in rheumatic heart disease: A search for immune response factors. Am Heart J 1986;112:992–997.
34. Khanna AK, Buskirk DR, Williams RC Jr, et al. Presence of a non-HLA B cell antigen in rheumatic fever patients and their families as defined by a monoclonal antibody. J Clin Invest. 1989;83:1710–1716.
35. Chopra P, Wanniang J, Kumar AS. Immunochemical and histochemical profile of Aschoff bodies in rheumatic carditis in excised left atrial appendages: An immunoperoxidase study in fresh and paraffin-embedded tissue. Int J Cardiol. 1992;34:199–207.
36. Husby GH, Arora R, Williams RC, et al. Immunofluorescent studies of florid rheumatic Aschoff lesions. Arthritis Rheum. 1986;29:207–211.
37. Ben-Dov I, Berry E. Acute rheumatic fever in adults over the age of 45 years: An analysis of 23 patients together with a review of the literature. Semin Arthritis Rheum. 1980;10:100–110.
38. Feuer J, Spiera H. Acute rheumatic fever in adults: A resurgence in the Hasidic Jewish community. J Rheumatol. 1997;24:337–340.
39. Deighton C. Beta haemolytic streptococci and reactive arthritis in adults. Ann Rheum Dis. 1993;52:475–482.
40. Rammelkamp CH, Denny FW, Wannamaker LW. Studies on the epidemiology of rheumatic fever in the armed services. In: Thomas L, ed. Rheumatic Fever. Minneapolis: University of Minnesota Press; 1952:72–89.
41. Siegel AC, Johnson EE, Stollerman GH. Controlled studies of streptococcal pharyngitis in a pediatric population. I. Factors related to the attack rate of rheumatic fever. N Engl J Med. 1961;265:559–566.
42. WHO programme for the prevention of rheumatic fever/rheumatic heart disease in 16 developing countries: Report from Phase I(1986–90). Bull World Health Organ. 1992;70:213–218.
43. Eisenberg MJ. Rheumatic heart disease in the developing world: Prevalence, prevention, and control. Eur Heart J. 1993;14:122–128.

44. Vijaykumar M, Narula J, Reddy KS, Kaplan EL. Incidence of rheumatic fever and prevalence of rheumatic fever disease in India. Int J Cardiol. 1994;43:221–228.
45. Carapetis JR, Wolff DR, Currie BJ. Acute rheumatic fever and rheumatic heart disease in the top end of Australia's Northern Territory. Med J Aust. 1996;164:146–149.
46. Land MA, Bisno AL. Acute rheumatic fever: A vanishing disease in suburbia. JAMA. 1983;249:895–898.
47. Veasy LG, Wiedmeier SE, Orsmond GS, et al. Resurgence of acute rheumatic fever in the intermountain area of the United States. N Engl J Med. 1987;316:421–427.
48. Ferguson GW, Shultz JM, Bisno AL. Epidemiology of acute rheumatic fever in a multi-ethnic, multi-racial US urban community: The Miami-Dade experience. J Infect Dis. 1991;164:720–725.
49. Bisno AL. The resurgence of acute rheumatic fever in the United States. Annu Rev Med. 1990;41:319–329.
50. Veasy LG, Tani LY, Hill HR. Persistence of acute rheumatic fever in the intermountain area of the United States. J Pediatr. 1994;124:9–16.
51. Hosier DM, Craenen JM, Teske DW, Wheller JJ. Resurgence of acute rheumatic fever. Am J Dis Child. 1987;141:730–733.
52. Congeni B, Rizzo C, Congeni J, Sreenivasan VV. Outbreak of acute rheumatic fever in northeast Ohio. J Pediatr. 1987;111:176–179.
53. Wald ER, Dashefsky B, Feidt C, et al. Acute rheumatic fever in western Pennsylvania and the tristate area. Pediatrics. 1987;80:371–374.
54. Westlake RM, Graham TP, Edwards KM. An outbreak of acute rheumatic fever in Tennessee. Pediatr Infect Dis J. 1990;9:97–100.
55. Leggiadro RJ, Birnbaum SE, Chase NA, Myers LK. A resurgence of acute rheumatic fever in a mid-South children's hospital. South Med J. 1990;83:1418–1420.
56. Jackson MA, Sotiropoulos SV, Christensen B, et al. Mucoid group A streptococcal disease in Kansas City, MO. Abstract 1024. Pediatr Res. 1988;23(Suppl):372A.
57. Mason R, Fisher M, Kujala G. Acute rheumatic fever in West Virginia: Not just a disease of children. Arch Intern Med. 1991;151:133–136.
58. Eckerd JM, McJunkin JE. Recent increase in incidence of acute rheumatic fever in southern West Virginia. W V Med J. 1989;85:323–325.
59. Burns DL, Ginsburg CM. Recrudescence of acute rheumatic fever in Dallas, Texas. Abstract 496. Pediatr Res. 1987;21:256A.
60. Griffiths SP, Gersony WM. Acute rheumatic fever in New York City (1969 to 1988): A comparative study of two decades. J Pediatr. 1990;116:882–887.
61. Wallace MR, Garst PD, Papadimos TJ, Oldfield EC. The return of acute rheumatic fever in young adults. JAMA. 1989;262:2557–2561.
62. Centers for Disease Control. Acute rheumatic fever among Army trainees—Fort Leonard Wood, Missouri, 1987–1988. MMWR Morb Mortal Wkly Rep. 1988;37:519–522.
63. Zangwill KM, Wald ER, Londino AV Jr. Acute rheumatic fever in western Pennsylvania: A persistent problem into the 1990s. J Pediatr. 1991;118:561–563.
64. Bisno AL. Group A streptococcal infections and acute rheumatic fever. N Engl J Med. 1991;325:783–793.
65. Taranta A, Wood HF, Feinstein AR, et al. Rheumatic fever in children and adolescents. A long-term epidemiologic study of subsequent prophylaxis, streptococcal infections, and clinical sequelae. IV. Relation of the rheumatic fever recurrence rate per streptococcal infection to the titers of streptococcal antibodies. Ann Intern Med. 1964;60(Suppl 5):47–57.
66. Rammelkamp CH Jr, Stolzer BL. The latent period before the onset of acute rheumatic fever. Yale J Biol Med. 1961;34:386–398.
67. Sanyal SK, Thapar MK, Ahmed SH, et al. The initial attack of acute rheumatic fever during childhood in North India; a prospective study of the clinical profile. Circulation. 1974;49:7–12.
68. Marcus RH, Sareli P, Pocock WA, Barlow JB. The spectrum of severe rheumatic mitral valve disease in a developing country: Correlations among clinical presentation, surgical pathologic findings, and hemodynamic sequelae. Ann Intern Med. 1994;120:177–183.
69. Veasy LG, Hill HR. Immunologic and clinical correlations in rheumatic fever and rheumatic heart disease. Pediatr Infect Dis J. 1997;16:400–407.
70. Reddy DV, Chun LT, Yamamoto LG. Acute rheumatic fever with advanced degree AV block. Clin Pediatr. 1989;28:326–328.
71. Feinstein AR, Spagnuolo M. The clinical patterns of acute rheumatic fever: A reappraisal. Medicine. 1962;41:279–305.
72. Arnold MH, Tyndall A. Poststreptococcal reactive arthritis. Ann Rheum Dis. 1989;48:686–688.
73. De Cunto CL, Giannini EH, Fink CW, et al. Prognosis of children with poststreptococcal reactive arthritis. Pediatr Infect Dis J. 1988;7:683–686.
74. Herold BC, Shulman ST. Poststreptococcal arthritis. Pediatr Infect Dis J. 1988;4:681–682.
75. Dajani AS, Ayoub E, Bierman FZ, et al. Guidelines for the diagnosis of rheumatic fever: Jones criteria, updated 1992. Circulation. 1993;87:302–307.
76. Stollerman GH. Rheumatic Fever and Streptococcal Infection. New York: Grune & Stratton; 1975.
77. Taranta A. Rheumatic fever: Clinical aspects. In: Hollander JL, McCarty DJ Jr, eds. Arthritis and Allied Conditions. 8th ed. Philadelphia: Lea & Febiger; 1972:764–820.
78. Bland EF. Chorea as a manifestation of rheumatic fever: A long-term perspective. Trans Am Clin Climatol Assoc. 1961;73:209–213.
79. Burgert SJ, Classen DC, Burke JP, Veasy LG. Rheumatic pneumonia: Reappearance of a previously recognized complication of acute rheumatic fever. Clin Infect Dis. 1995;21:1020–1022.
80. Dlesk A, Balian AA, Sullivan BJ, et al. Diagnostic dilemma for the 1990s: Lyme disease versus rheumatic fever. Wis Med J. 1991;90:632–634.
81. Herd JK, Medhi M, Uzendoski DM, Saldivar VA. Chorea associated with systemic lupus erythematosus: Report of two cases and review of the literature. Pediatrics. 1978;61:308–315.
82. Thompson HG Jr, Carpenter MB. Hemichorea due to metastatic lesion in the subthalamic nucleus. Arch Neurol. 1960;2:83–87.
83. Bamford JM, Hakin RN. Chorea after legionnaire's disease. BMJ (Clin Res Ed). 1982;284:1232–1233.
84. McKinney AS. Idiopathic hypoparathyroidism presenting as chorea. Neurology. 1962;12:485–491.
85. Figueroa F, Berrios X, Gutierrez M, et al. Anticardiolipin antibodies in acute rheumatic fever. J Rheumatol. 1992;19:1175–1180.
86. Riddoch D, Jefferson M, Bickerstaff ER. Chorea and the oral contraceptives. BMJ. 1971;4:217–218.
87. Jonas S, Spagnuolo M, Kloth HH. Chorea gravidarum and streptococcal infection. Obstet Gynecol. 1972;39:77–79.
88. Jones TD. The diagnosis of rheumatic fever. JAMA. 1944;126:481–484.
89. Veasy LG, Dajani AS, Allen HD, Taubert KA. Echocardiography for diagnosis and management of rheumatic fever. JAMA. 1993;269:2084.
90. Minich LL, Tani LY, Pagotto LT, et al. Doppler echocardiography distinguishes between physiologic and pathologic "silent" mitral regurgitation in patients with rheumatic fever. Clin Cardiol. 1997;20:924–926.
91. Stollerman GH, Lewis AJ, Schultz I, Taranta A. Relationship of immune response to group A streptococci to the course of acute, chronic and recurrent rheumatic fever. Am J Med. 1956;20:163–169.
92. Bisno AL, Ofek I. Serologic diagnosis of streptococcus infection. Comparison of a rapid hemagglutination technique with conventional antibody tests. Am J Dis Child. 1974;127:676–681.
93. Bisno AL, Ofek I, Beachey EH. Antigens of group A streptococci involved in passive hemagglutination reactions. Infect Immun. 1976;13:407–412.
94. Kaplan EL, Kunde C. Quantitative evaluation of variation in composition of the Streptozyme agglutination reagent for detection of antibodies to group A streptococcal extracellular antigens. J Clin Microbiol. 1981;14:678–680.
95. Swedo SE. Sydenham's chorea: A model for childhood autoimmune neuropsychiatric disorders. JAMA. 1994;272:1789–1791.
96. United Kingdom and United States Joint Report on Rheumatic Heart Disease. The treatment of acute rheumatic fever in children. A cooperative clinical trial of ACTH, cortisone and aspirin. Circulation. 1955;11:343–377.
97. Gordis L. Effectiveness of comprehensive care programs in preventing rheumatic fever. N Engl J Med. 1973;289:331–335.
98. Dajani A, Taubert K, Ferrieri P, et al. Treatment of acute streptococcal pharyngitis and prevention of rheumatic fever: A statement for health professionals. Committee on Rheumatic Fever, Endocarditis, and Kawasaki Disease of the Council on Cardiovascular Disease in the Young, the American Heart Association. Pediatrics. 1995;96:758–764.
99. Wood HF, Feinstein AR, Taranta A, et al. Rheumatic fever in children and adolescents. A long-term epidemiologic study of subsequent prophylaxis, streptococcal infections, and clinical sequelae. III. Comparative effectiveness of three prophylaxis regimens in preventing streptococcal infections and rheumatic recurrences. Ann Intern Med. 1964;60(Suppl 5):31–46.
100. Lue HC, Wu MH, Wang JK, et al. Three- versus four-week administration of benzathine penicillin G: Effects of incidence of streptococcal infections and recurrences of rheumatic fever. Pediatrics. 1996;97:984–988.
101. Berrios X, del Campo E, Guzman B, Bisno AL. Discontinuing rheumatic fever prophylaxis in selected adolescents and young adults: A prospective study. Ann Intern Med. 1993;118:401–406.
101a. Dale JB. Group A streptococcal vaccines. Infect Dis Clin North Am. 1999;13:227–243.
102. Bright R. Cases and observations, illustrative of renal disease accompanied with the secretion of albuminous urine. Guys Hosp Rep. 1936;1:338–400.
103. Shick B. Die Nachkrankheiten des Scharlach. Jahrb Kinderheilk. 1907;65:132–173.
104. Rammelkamp CH Jr, Weaver RS. Acute glomerulonephritis: The significance of the variations in the incidence of the disease. J Clin Invest. 1953;32:345–358.
105. Wannamaker LW. Differences between streptococcal infections of the throat and of the skin. N Engl J Med. 1970;282:23–31.
106. Potter EV, Ortiz JS, Sharrett R, et al. Changing types of nephritogenic streptococci in Trinidad. J Clin Invest. 1971;50:1197–1205.
107. Dillon HC, Derrick CW, Dillon MS. M-antigens common to pyoderma and acute glomerulonephritis. J Infect Dis. 1974;130:257–267.
108. Duca E, Teodorovici GR, Radu C, et al. A new nephritogenic streptococcus. J Hyg. 1969;67:691–698.
109. Barnham M, Thornton TJ, Lange K. Nephritis caused by *Streptococcus zooepidemicus* (Lancefield group C). Lancet. 1983;1:945–948.
110. Seegal BC, Andres GA, Hsu KC, Zabriskie JB. Studies on the pathogenesis of acute and progressive glomerulonephritis in man by immunofluorescein and immunoferritin technique. Fed Proc. 1965;24:100–108.
111. Michael AF, Drummond KN, Good RA, et al. Acute poststreptococcal glomerulonephritis: Immune deposit disease. J Clin Invest. 1966;45:237–248.
112. Michael AF, Hoyer JR, Westberg NG, Fish AJ. Experimental models for the pathogenesis of acute poststreptococcal glomerulonephritis. In: Wannamaker LW, Masten JM, eds. Streptococci and Streptococcal Disease. New York: Academic Press; 1972:481–500.
113. Zabriskie JB. The role of streptococci in human glomerulonephritis. J Exp Med. 1971;134(Suppl):180S–192S.
114. Lange CF. Chemistry of cross-reactive fragments of streptococcal cell membrane and human glomerular basement membrane. Transplant Proc. 1969;1:959–963.

115. Bisno AL, Wood JW, Lawson J, et al. Antigens in urine of patients with glomerulonephritis and in normal human serum which cross-react with group A streptococci: Identification and partial characterization. J Lab Clin Med. 1978;91:500–513.
116. Goroncy-Bermes P, Dale JB, Beachey EH, Opferkuch W. Monoclonal antibody to human renal glomeruli cross-reacts with streptococcal M protein. Infect Immun. 1987;55:2416–2419.
117. Ooi YM, Vallota EH, West CD. Serum immune complexes in membranoproliferative and other glomerulonephritides. Kidney Int. 1977;11:275–283.
118. Tung KSK, Woodroffe AJ, Ahlin TD, et al. Application of the solid phase C1q and Raji cell radioimmune assays for the detection of circulating immune complexes in glomerulonephritis. J Clin Invest. 1978;62:61–72.
119. Van de Rijn I, Fillit H, Brandeis WE, et al. Serial studies on circulating immune complexes in post-streptococcal sequelae. Clin Exp Immunol. 1978;34:318–325.
120. Lindberg LH, Vosti KL. Elution of glomerular bound antibodies in experimental streptococcal glomerulonephritis. Science. 1969;166:1032–1033.
121. Markowitz AS, Horn D, Aseron C, et al. Streptococcal related glomerulonephritis. 3. Glomerulonephritis in rhesus monkeys immunologically induced both actively and passively with a soluble fraction from nephritogenic streptococcal protoplasmic membranes. J Immunol. 1971;107:504–511.
122. Vogt A, Batsford S, Rodriguez-Iturbe B, Garcia R. Cationic antigens in post-streptococcal nephritis. Clin Nephrol. 1983;20:271–279.
123. Lange K, Ahmed U, Kleinberger H, Treser G. A hitherto unknown streptococcal antigen and its probable relation to acute poststreptococcal glomerulonephritis. Clin Nephrol. 1976;5:207–215.
124. Yoshizawa N, Oshima S, Sagel I, et al. Role of a streptococcal antigen in the pathogenesis of acute poststreptococcal glomerulonephritis. J Immunol. 1992;148:3110–3116.
125. Johnson KH, Zabriskie JB. Purification and partial characterization of the nephritis strain–associated protein from *Streptococcus pyogenes*, group A. J Exp Med. 1986;163:697–712.
126. Nordstrand A, Norgren M, Ferretti JJ, Holm SE. Streptokinase as a mediator of acute post-streptococcal glomerulonephritis in an experimental mouse model. Infect Immun. 1998;66:315–321.
127. Mezzano S, Burgos E, Mahabir R, et al. Failure to detect unique reactivity to streptococcal streptokinase in either the sera or renal biopsy specimens of patients with acute poststreptococcal glomerulonephritis. Clin Nephrol. 1992;38:305–310.
128. Lewy JE, Salinas-Madrigal L, Herdson PB, et al. Clinico-pathologic correlations in acute poststreptococcal glomerulonephritis. A correlation between renal functions, morphologic damage and clinical course of 46 children with acute poststreptococcal glomerulonephritis. Medicine. 1971;50:453–501.
129. Anthony BF, Kaplan EL, Wannamaker LW, et al. Attack rates of acute nephritis after type 49 streptococcal infection of the skin and of the respiratory tract. J Clin Invest. 1969;48:1697–1704.
130. Stetson CA, Rammelkamp CH Jr, Krause RM, et al. Epidemic acute nephritis: Studies on etiology, natural history and prevention. Medicine. 1955;34:431–450.
131. Roy S, Wall HP, Etteldorf JN. Second attacks of acute glomerulonephritis. J Pediatr. 1969;75:758–767.
132. Seegal D, Lyttle JD, Loeb EN, et al. On the exacerbation in chronic glomerulonephritis. J Clin Invest. 1940;19:569–589.
133. Bisno AL. The coexistence of acute rheumatic fever and acute glomerulonephritis. Arthritis Rheum. 1989;32:230–232.
134. Matsell DG, Baldree LA, DiSessa TG, et al. Acute poststreptococcal glomerulonephritis and acute rheumatic fever: Occurrence in the same patient. Child Nephrol Urol. 1990;10:112–114.
135. Poon-King T, Mohammed I, Cox R, et al. Recurrent epidemic nephritis in South Trinidad. N Engl J Med. 1967;277:728–733.
136. Kaplan EL, Anthony BF, Chapman SS, Wannamaker LW. Epidemic acute glomerulonephritis associated with type 49 streptococcal pyoderma. Am J Med. 1970;48:9–27.
137. Derrick CW, Reeves MS, Dillon HC Jr. Complement in overt and asymptomatic nephritis after skin infection. J Clin Invest. 1970;49:1178–1187.
138. Sharrett AR, Poon-King T, Potter EV, et al. Subclinical nephritis in South Trinidad. Am J Epidemiol. 1971;94:231–245.
139. Dodge WF, Spargo BH, Travis LB. Occurrence of acute glomerulonephritis in sibling contacts of children with sporadic acute glomerulonephritis. Pediatrics. 1967;40:1029–1030.
140. Schwartz WB, Kassirer JP. Clinical aspects of acute poststreptococcal glomerulonephritis. In: Strauss MB, Welt LG, eds. Disease of the Kidney. 2nd ed. Boston: Little, Brown; 1971:419–462.
141. Freedman P, Meister HP, Lee HJ, et al. The renal response to streptococcal infection. Medicine. 1970;49:433–463.
142. Berman LB, Vogelsang P. Poststreptococcal glomerulonephritis without proteinuria. N Engl J Med. 1963;268:1275–1277.
143. Smith RD, Aquino J. Viruses and the kidney. Med Clin North Am. 1971;55:89–106.
144. Humphreys MH. Renal complications of HIV infection. In: Sande MA, Volbercling PA, eds. The Medical Management of AIDS. 5th ed. Philadelphia: WB Saunders; 1997:269–272.
145. Balat A, Baysal K, Kocak H. Myocardial functions of children with acute poststreptococcal glomerulonephritis. Clin Nephrol. 1993;39:151–155.
146. Kassirer JP, Schwartz WB. Acute glomerulonephritis. N Engl J Med. 1961;265:686–692.
147. Lasch EE, Frankel V, Vardy PA, et al. Epidemic glomerulonephritis in Israel. J Infect Dis. 1971;124:141–147.
148. Weinstein L, Le Frock J. Does antimicrobial therapy of streptococcal pharyngitis or pyoderma alter the risk of glomerulonephritis? J Infect Dis. 1971;124:229–231.
148a. Johnston F, Carapetis J, Patel M, et al. Evaluating the use of penicillin to control outbreaks of acute poststreptococcal glomerulonephritis. Pediatr Infect Dis J. 1999;18:327–332.
149. Perlman LV, Herdman RC, Kleinman H. Poststreptococcal glomerulonephritis: A ten-year follow-up of an epidemic. JAMA. 1965;194:63–70.
150. Potter EV, Lipschultz SA, Abidh S, et al. Twelve to seventeen-year follow-up of patients with poststreptococcal acute glomerulonephritis in Trinidad. N Engl J Med. 1982;307:725–729.
151. Baldwin DS. Poststreptococcal glomerulonephritis. A progressive disease? Am J Med. 1977;62:1–11.
152. Jennings RB, Earle DP. Post-streptococcal glomerulonephritis: Histopathologic and clinical studies of the acute, subsiding acute and early chronic latent phases. J Clin Invest. 1961;40:1525–1595.
153. Kurtzman NA. Does acute poststreptococcal glomerulonephritis lead to chronic renal disease? N Engl J Med. 1978;298:795–796.
154. Kaplan EL, Vernier RL. Progressive nephritis after strep infection questioned. Am J Med. 1978;64:910–911.
155. Richmond DE, Doak PB. The prognosis of acute post infectious glomerulonephritis in adults: A long-term prospective study. Aust N Z J Med. 1990;20:215–219.

Chapter 188

Streptococcus pneumoniae

DANIEL M. MUSHER

Long recognized as a major cause of pneumonia, meningitis, sinusitis, and otitis media, *Streptococcus pneumoniae* is an important bacterial pathogen in humans; it is a less frequent cause of endocarditis, septic arthritis, and peritonitis and an uncommon cause of a variety of other infectious diseases.

HISTORY

A brief review of the history of *S. pneumoniae* documents the important interrelationship between the study of this microorganism and the history of microbiology.[1–3] In 1881, the organism was identified concurrently in the Old and New Worlds, by Pasteur in France, who named it *Microbe septicèmique du salive,* and by Sternberg in the United States, who called it *Micrococcus pasteuri.* By the late 1880s the term *pneumococcus* was generally used because this bacterium had come to be recognized as the most common cause of lobar pneumonia. The name *Diplococcus* was assigned in 1926 because of its appearance in Gram-stained sputum, and in 1974 the organism was renamed once again, this time as *Streptococcus pneumoniae* because of its morphology during growth in liquid medium.

S. pneumoniae was the first organism to be shown to behave as what is now regarded as a prototypic extracellular bacterial pathogen; in the absence of antibody, this bacterium resists phagocytosis and replicates extracellularly in mammalian tissues. In the early 1890s, Felix and Georg Klemperer showed that immunization with killed pneumococci protected animals against subsequent pneumococcal challenge and, further, that protection could be transferred by infusing serum from immunized mice into naive recipients. Subsequently, serum from persons who had recovered from pneumococcal pneumonia was found to confer the same degree of protection. The basis for this immunity was shown by Neufeld and Rimpau to be the presence of factor(s) in serum that facilitated ingestion by white blood cells (WBCs), a process that these investigators called *opsonization,* which is derived from the Greek word for preparing food. These observations provided the basis for what we now call humoral immunity. Serotypes were also recognized after observing that injection of killed organisms into a rabbit stimulated the production of serum antibody that agglutinated and caused capsular swelling of the immunizing strain, as well as some, but not all other pneumococcal isolates. Early in the 20th century, three serotypes were distinguished and called serotypes 1, 2, and 3; all other pneumococci were called group 4.

In the first decade of the 20th century, Maynard, Lister, Wright, and others began to apply the concepts of humoral immunity to the problem of epidemic lobar pneumonia that each year affected as many as 1 in 10 men who were working in African mines.[1, 4] Inoculation of miners with killed pneumococci caused a substantial reduction in the incidence of pneumonia. In the 1920s, Heidelberger and Avery[5] demonstrated that the antibody that conferred immunity was reactive with surface capsular polysaccharides. Felton[6] prepared the first purified pneumococcal capsular polysaccharides for immunization of human subjects, and a preparation of type 1 polysaccharide was used to abort an epidemic of pneumonia at a state hospital in Worcester, Massachusetts, in 1938.[7] Taken together, these studies supported a novel set of concepts by showing that a specific bacterial polysaccharide antigen could be used to stimulate humoral antibodies that conferred protection against epidemic human infection. Further confirmation was provided during World War II, when MacLeod and coworkers[8] found that vaccinating military recruits with capsular material from four serotypes of *S. pneumoniae* greatly reduced the incidence of pneumonia caused by serotypes in the vaccine, but not by other pneumococcal serotypes.

S. pneumoniae also played a central role in the discovery of DNA. Experiments done by Griffith[9] in the 1920s had shown that intraperitoneal injection of live, unencapsulated (mutant) pneumococci together with heat-killed encapsulated pneumococci into mice led to the emergence of viable, encapsulated bacteria; he called this process *transformation.* This observation remained unexplained until the 1940s, when Avery and coworkers[10] provided conclusive evidence that the capacity to produce capsule was restored to these mutants by transfer of DNA—in other words, that DNA is responsible for transformation and, in fact, is the genetic material that encodes for phenotype.

MICROBIOLOGY

S. pneumoniae is a gram-positive coccus that replicates in chains in liquid medium. The organism is catalase negative, but it generates H_2O_2 via a flavoenzyme system and therefore grows better in the presence of a source of catalase such as red blood cells. Pneumococci produce pneumolysin (formerly called α-hemolysin), which breaks down hemoglobin into a green pigment; as a result, pneumococcal colonies are surrounded by a green zone during growth on blood-agar plates. This property is still termed α-hemolysis, although properly speaking it should not be, because lysis of red blood cells is not responsible. This point becomes readily apparent when one observes the greenish yellow color that appears around colonies of *S. pneumoniae* during growth on chocolate agar, a medium in which all the red blood cells have already been lysed during preparation. Growth of pneumococci is inhibited by ethyl hydrocupreine (optochin), and the organisms are lysed by bile salts. Thus, pneumococci are identified in the microbiology laboratory by four reactions: (1) α-hemolysis of blood agar, (2) catalase negativity, (3) susceptibility to optochin, and (4) solubility in bile salts. The finding of optochin-resistant pneumococci[11] has led to greater reliance on the use of bile solubility for definitive identification. A highly reliable probe that detects rRNA sequences unique to *S. pneumoniae* is also commercially available.

ANATOMY AND PHYSIOLOGY

Nearly every clinical isolate of *S. pneumoniae* contains an external capsule; unencapsulated isolates have mainly been implicated in outbreaks of conjunctivitis.[12] Capsules[13] (Fig. 188–1) are made up of repeating oligosaccharides that are synthesized within the cytoplasm, polymerized, and transported to the bacterial surface by cell membrane transferases. These polysaccharides are covalently bound to peptidoglycan and cell wall (C-) polysaccharide, which explains the difficulty of separating capsular from cell wall polysaccharide. Genetic control of this complex set of events has been elucidated for some serotypes; a cassette of 15 genes that function as a single transcriptional unit is responsible for serogroup 19.[14] Ninety serotypes of *S. pneumoniae* have been identified on the basis of antigenic differences in their capsular polysaccharides. Immunization of rabbits stimulates the appearance of antibodies that cause serotype-specific agglutination and microscopic demonstrability of the capsule, or the quellung reaction, in which antibody renders the capsule refractile and therefore more readily visible. In the American numbering system, serotypes are numbered from 1 to 90 in the order in which they were identified. The more widely accepted Danish numbering system groups serotypes according to antigenic similarities. For example, Danish serogroup 19 includes types 19F, 19A, 19B, and 19C (the letter F indicates the first member of the group to be identified, followed by A, B, C, etc.), which in the American system would be types 19, 57, 58, and 59, respectively. Serotypes that most frequently cause human disease were the earliest to be identified and were the first to be assigned numbers, which explains why the lower-numbered serotypes are generally more likely to be implicated in human infection. Serotyping was clinically relevant in the 1930s, when antisera were administered for therapy, and is of great interest from epidemiologic and public health standpoints today, especially as new vaccines are being developed.

Some DNA sequences that govern capsule formation have been found in all pneumococci studied to date, whereas others are unique to a particular serotype.[15–17] Pneumococci have a remarkable capacity (termed *competence*) to internalize DNA from other pneumococci or from other bacterial species. Because of this property, pneumococci are able to acquire new phenotypic traits, a process called *transformation.* Transformation of capsular types occurs under experimental conditions but, more importantly, also occurs in nature.[18] Careful study of clinical isolates with fingerprinting techniques has shown that pneumococci can acquire a cassette of DNA that encodes the production of a serotypically different capsule—in other words, pneumococci can switch capsules.

As with other streptococci, peptidoglycan and teichoic acid are the principal constituents of the pneumococcal cell wall[19] (see Fig. 188–1). Peptidoglycan consists of long chains of alternating *N*-acetyl-D-glucosamine and *N*-acetylmuramic acid, from which extend chains of four to six amino acids called stem peptides. Stem peptides are cross-linked by pentaglycine bridges, which provides substantial strength to the cell wall. Teichoic acid, a carbohydrate polymer that contains phosphorylcholine, is covalently linked to the peptidoglycan on the outermost surface of the bacterial wall and protrudes into the capsule. This teichoic acid, together with tightly adherent fragments of peptidoglycan makes up C-polysaccharide, a substance that is present in all pneumococci and is otherwise detected only in a few species of viridans streptococci. This region is responsible for the reaction between pneumococci and proteins that appear in the blood stream in certain illnesses (called acute-phase reactants or C-reactive proteins) or that occur in some cases of multiple myeloma. Also expressed on the cell surface are proteins that are thought to play a role in pathogenicity (see later), such as pneumococcal surface protein A, pneumococcal surface adhesin A, choline-binding proteins, and proteins involved in competence. The characteristic three-layered cell membrane consists of lipid and teichoic acid and is called F antigen because of cross-reactivity with Forssman antigens. Other pneumococcal constituents are discussed later under pathogenetic mechanisms.

EPIDEMIOLOGY

As with many other microorganisms, *S. pneumoniae* finds its ecologic niche in colonizing the nasopharynx. On a single occasion,

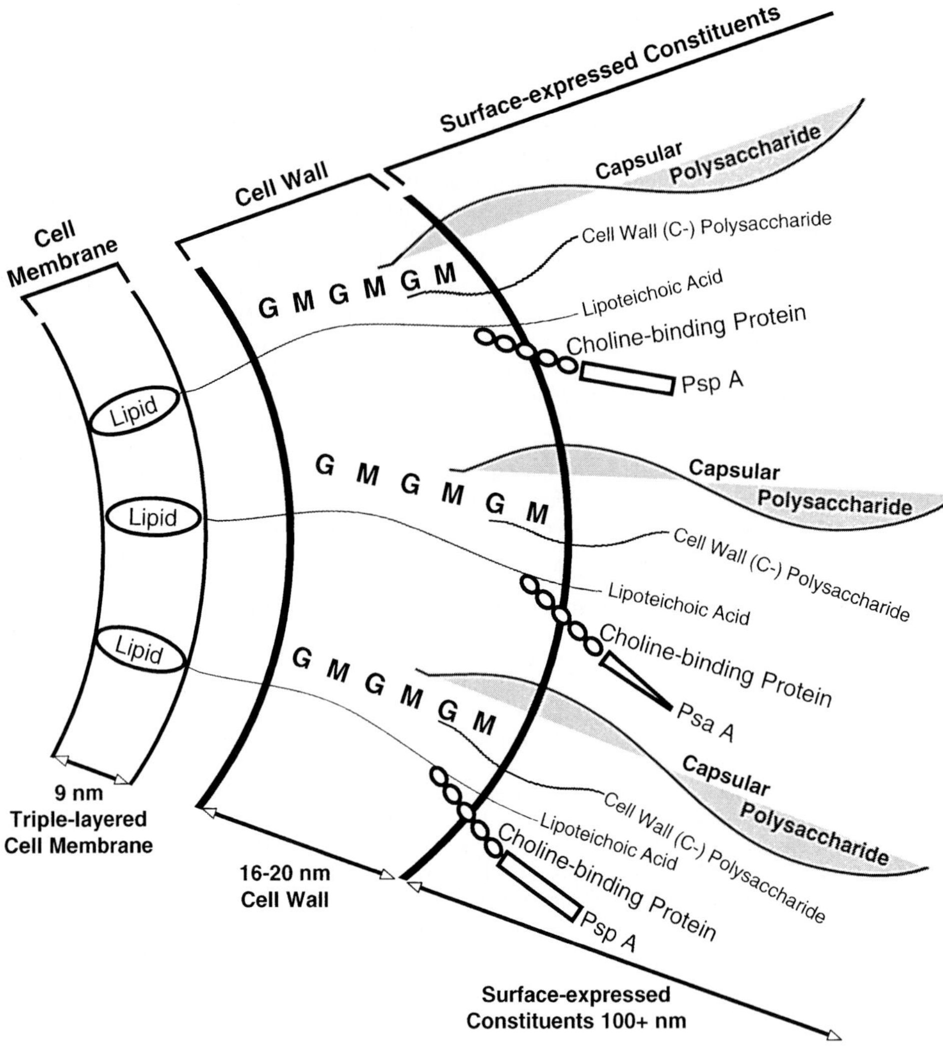

FIGURE 188–1. A representation of the cell membrane, cell wall, and capsule of *Streptococcus pneumoniae.* Within the cell wall, M = *N*-acetylmuramic acid and G = *N*-acetyl-D-glucosamine. The stem peptides and the cross-linked pentaglycine bridges that extend from the long M-G-M-G chains are not shown. Cell wall (C-) polysaccharide consists of teichoic acid with peptidoglycan and phosphorylcholine (not shown). F antigen is the lipid/teichoic acid moiety in the cell membrane that extends into the cell wall.

appropriate culturing yields pneumococci in 5 to 10% of healthy adults and 20 to 40% of healthy children. With repeated attempts at culture, the percentage increases in all age groups, rising to 40 to 60% in toddlers and young children in daycare. For reasons that remain unclear, the rate of colonization is seasonal, with an increase in the midwinter period, although pneumococci can be recovered from healthy children and adults throughout the year, and a huge sample is required to document such seasonality. A careful prospective study in infants[20] showed that the first pneumococcus to colonize an infant is generally acquired at 6 months of age and can be detected for a mean of about 4 months. In adults, an individual serotype persists for shorter periods, usually 2 to 4 weeks,[21] but sometimes much longer.

Population-based studies carried out in different parts of the world (and summarized by Fedson and colleagues[22]) show that the overall rate of invasive pneumococcal disease, defined as the isolation of *S. pneumoniae* from a normally sterile site such as blood, pleural fluid, or cerebrospinal fluid (CSF), is about 15 per 100,000 persons per year. In certain populations, including Native Americans (especially Alaskans)[23] and Australian Aboriginals,[24] the incidence may be increased as much as 10-fold greater, although it is unclear to what extent genetic or environmental factors are responsible. Invasive pneumococcal infection is relatively common in newborns and infants up to 2 years of age and much less so in teenaged children and young adults, again increasing in adults older than 65 years[1, 25, 26] (Fig. 188–2). Data from South Carolina[26] are representative and show the incidence of pneumococcal bacteremia to be 160, 5, and 70 per 100,000 persons, respectively, in infants, young adults, and those 70 years or older. Although the overall incidence of pneumococcal infection in the population is greatly reduced when compared with the preantibiotic era, this relationship to age has not changed. Most cases of bacteremia in adults are due to pneumonia, and probably 3 to 4 cases of nonbacteremic pneumonia occur for every bacteremic one, thus leading to estimates of 25 cases of pneumococcal pneumonia per 100,000 young adults and 280 per 100,000 elderly individuals. Because of lack of ascertainment, the true incidence may be several times greater. By contrast, in the preantibiotic era, about 700 cases of pneumonia occurred per 100,000 young adults.[1] Some reports suggest[27] that the incidence of pneumococcal disease is increasing; confirmation is needed before this finding can be accepted.

The occurrence of infection, for example, otitis media[28, 29] or bacteremia,[30] is related to season, perhaps because of the association with viral respiratory illnesses. A November through April clustering with a clear peak in February was apparent for otitis media in the study of Gray and Dillon.[20] In Houston, Texas (Fig. 188–3), invasive disease in children occurs mainly during September through May, thus coinciding with the school year and sparing the summer months, but with no clear midwinter peak. In contrast, invasive disease in adults clearly reaches a peak in the middle of winter, inversely related to ambient temperature and directly associated with the peak of viral respiratory disease.[30]

Pneumococci are transmitted from one individual to another as a

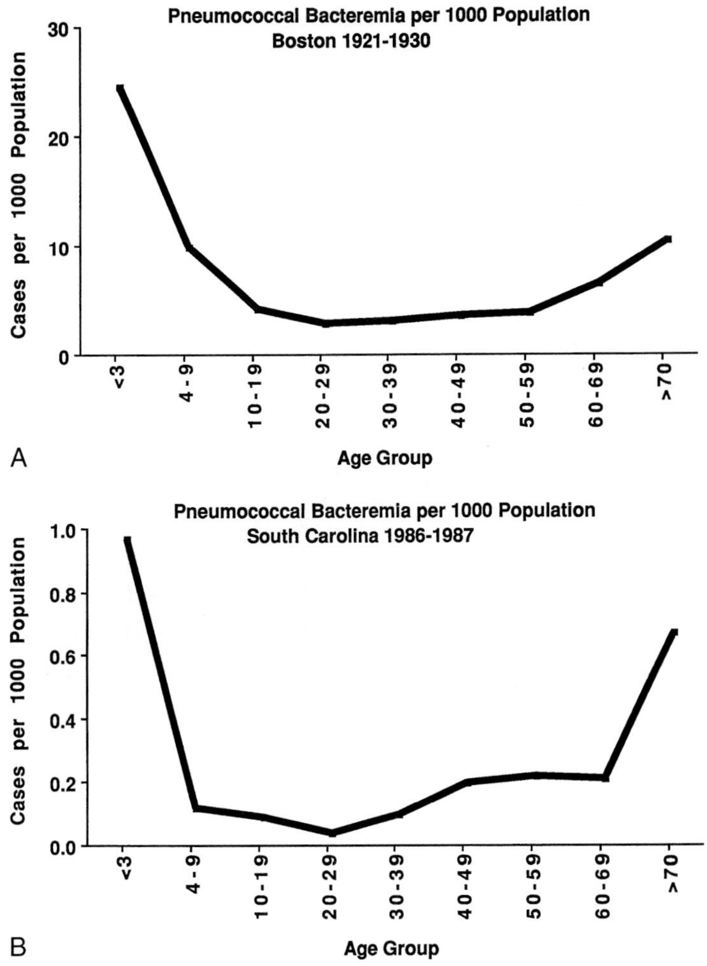

FIGURE 188–2. The relationship between pneumococcal bacteremia and age is shown for two studies, widely separated in time. *A* shows data published in the preantibiotic era. (Adapted from Heffron R. Pneumonia: With Special Reference to Pneumococcus Lobar Pneumonia. Copyright 1939. The Commonwealth Fund. Copyright © 1979 by the President and Fellows of Harvard College. Reprinted by permission of Harvard University Press.) *B,* Includes data from South Carolina obtained in 1986 and 1987.[25] Interestingly, the shape of the curve is remarkably similar, although the vertical axis in the lower curve shows a vastly reduced incidence when compared with that in the upper one. More recent studies continue to confirm these earlier findings.

result of extensive, close contact. Daycare centers are very likely to be places for spread of these organisms in toddlers.[31–33] In adults, close, crowded living conditions such as occur in military camps,[34] prisons,[35] shelters for the homeless,[36] and nursing homes[37] are associated with epidemics, but contact in schools or in the workplace is generally not.

PATHOGENETIC MECHANISMS

To cause disease, pneumococci, like other extracellular bacterial pathogens, must adhere to mammalian cells, replicate in situ, be carried to and replicate in parts of the body that are normally free of them (but perhaps have had a diminution in normal clearance mechanisms), escape phagocytosis, and damage tissue by causing inflammation or producing substances that directly damage cells and, in some cases, invade the blood stream. Many of these reactions are governed by events at a molecular level.[38]

The prevalence of pneumococcal colonization attests to the adaptational success of this organism in adhering to mammalian cells and replicating in situ in the nasopharynx. *S. pneumoniae* attaches to human pharyngeal cells through a variety of mechanisms involving the specific interaction of bacterial surface adhesins (such as pneumococcal surface antigen A and choline-binding proteins) and epithelial cell receptors.[39] Epithelial cell glycoconjugates containing the disaccharide GlcNAcb1-4Gal[40] or asialo-GM_1 glycolipid[41] are possible binding sites. Phase variation of pneumococci may also play a role. Upon culture in vitro, a mixed population of transparent and opaque colonies can be identified. Organisms from transparent colonies have greatly increased quantities of phosphorylcholine, which contributes to their capacity to adhere to mammalian cells,[42] perhaps via the receptor for platelet-activating factor.[43] When an opaque colony is inoculated intranasally into an experimental animal, only those organisms that make transparent colonies persist. In contrast, intraperitoneal inoculation of opaque colonies may be lethal, whereas transparent colonies are less likely to be so; increased capsule production by opaque forms may in part be responsible.

Once colonization has taken place, infection may result if the organisms are carried into cavities from which they are not readily cleared. Under normal circumstances, when organisms find their way into eustachian tubes, sinuses, or bronchi, clearance mechanisms, chiefly ciliary action, lead to their rapid removal. If allergy or coexisting viral infection, for example, has caused edema that obstructs the opening of the eustachian tube into the pharynx or the ostium of a paranasal sinus, clinically recognizable infection may result. Similarly, damage to ciliated bronchial cells or increased production of mucus, whether chronic (from cigarette smoking or occupational exposure) or acute (from influenza or some other viral infection), may prevent the clearance of inhaled or aspirated organisms and lead to infection.

Escape from Phagocytosis

S. pneumoniae causes disease because it is able to escape ingestion and killing by host phagocytic cells. Unlike certain other organisms such as *Streptococcus pyogenes,* which produce a variety of tissue-damaging substances, *S. pneumoniae* produces few toxins and largely causes disease by its capacity to replicate in host tissues and generate an intense inflammatory response. In an immunologically naive host,

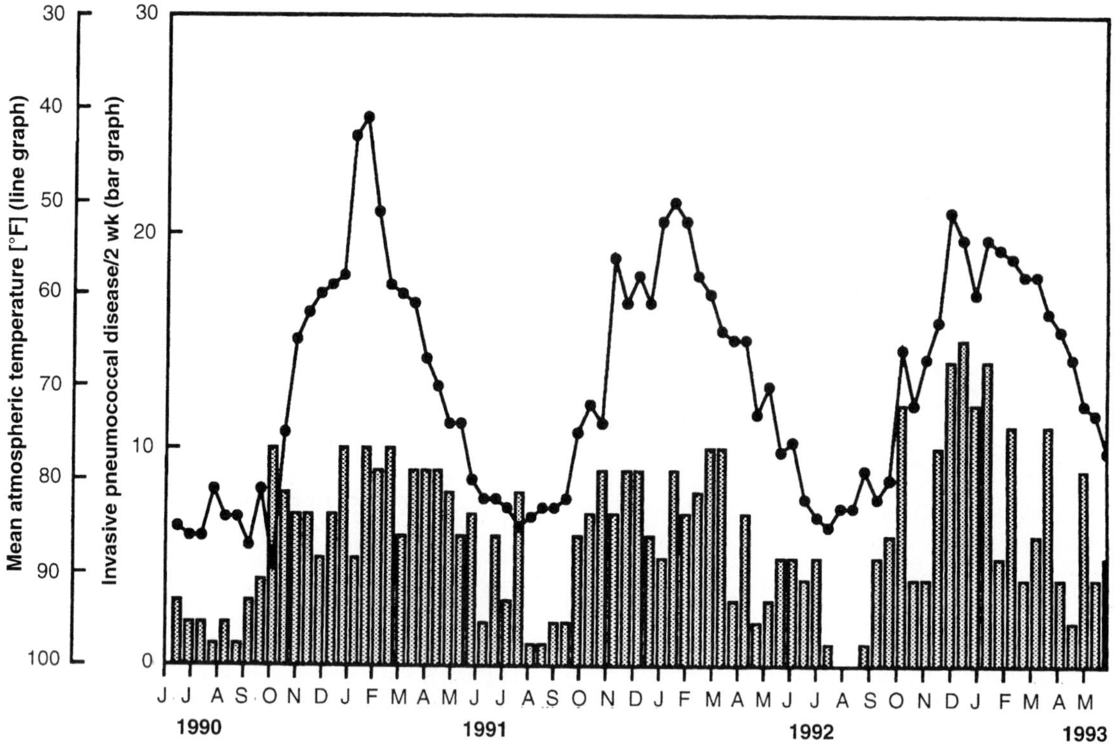

FIGURE 188–3. Each bar shows the number of cases of invasive pneumococcal disease at four tertiary care hospitals (adult and pediatric) in Houston, Texas, during a 2-week period. A fall, winter, and early spring predominance is noted. The line graph[30] is the number of specimens from patients thought to have a viral syndrome, obtained by a consortium of physicians in cooperation with the Influenza Research Center of the Baylor College of Medicine, Houston, Texas.

specifically in the absence of anticapsular antibody, pneumococci are poorly ingested and killed by the host's professional phagocytes, polymorphonuclear leukocytes (PMNs), and macrophages. The capsule plays a central role in preventing phagocytosis. Possible contributing mechanisms include (1) the absence of receptors on phagocytic cells that recognize capsular polysaccharides, (2) the presence of electrochemical forces that repel phagocytic cells, and (3) the masking of antibody to cell wall constituents and C3b that may have fixed to the cell wall but beneath the capsule. Degradation of cell-associated C3b by pneumococcal cell wall constituents probably further contributes to resistance to phagocytosis.[44]

Much of the evidence supporting the overwhelming importance of the capsule as the major determinant of virulence has been summarized earlier in the brief history of pneumococcus. To those concepts should be added that by the use of transposon mutagenesis, interruption of capsule production in *S. pneumoniae* type 3 renders the organism essentially avirulent, with the lethal dose in mice shifted from 2 to 3 colony-forming units to more than 2 to 3×10^7.[45] In addition, a close relationship has been observed between the absolute amount of anticapsular antibody infused into mice and the level of protection against challenge with each of several serotypes of *S. pneumoniae*.[46]

Complement Activation

The cell wall of *S. pneumoniae*, including both teichoic acid and peptidoglycan constituents, stimulates the production of inflammatory cytokines, and activates complement by the alternative pathway.[47, 48] Injection of either of these substances into the subarachnoid space causes an inflammatory reaction that has the characteristics of bacterial meningitis, although the kinetics vary with the substance injected.[48] C-reactive protein may also play an active part.[49] Polysaccharide capsule in addition appears to activate the alternative pathway in vitro,[50, 51] albeit to a somewhat lesser extent. This type of activation is associated with the release of C5a, so even if complement is not fixed on the bacterial surface, thereby leading to opsonophagocytosis, C5a, a potent attractant for PMNs, is released to the surrounding medium. The classic pathway is activated by antibody to cell wall polysaccharides even in the absence of anticapsular antibody.[51] Thus, an intense inflammatory response fueled by vigorous activation of both the alternative and classic complement pathways accompanies pneumococcal infection of an immunologically naive host. The disease process is largely a result of this inflammation and is severe in direct proportion to its intensity.

Other Virulence Factors

Several other constituents, including pneumolysin, surface proteins, and autolysin, contribute to the pathogenesis of pneumococcal disease.[52, 53] Genetically engineered mutants that lack the ability to produce one or more of these substances have generally been shown to have diminished virulence, and immunization with the purified substance has stimulated the production of antibodies that confer protection in experimental animals (Table 188–1). It needs to be emphasized, however, that despite the current interest in these and other protein constituents of *S. pneumoniae*, at the time of this writing (July 1999), no antibody to any of these substances has been shown to be protective in humans.

All serotypes of *S. pneumoniae* produce pneumolysin, a thiol-activated toxin that inserts into the lipid bilayer of cell membranes via its interaction with cholesterol. Pneumolysin is cytotoxic for phagocytic and respiratory epithelial cells and causes inflammation by activating complement and inducing the production of tumor necrosis factor-α and interleukin-1.[54, 55] Injection of pneumolysin into rat lung causes all the histologic findings of pneumonia,[56] and immunization of mice with this substance before infection[57] or chal-

TABLE 188–1 Role of Pneumococcal Constituents as Virulence Factors*

Pneumococcal Constituent	Mechanism	Strength of Evidence as a Virulence Factor: *Antibody Prevents Disease†*	*Mutants Lack Virulence*
Capsular polysaccharide	Prevents phagocytosis, activates complement	4+	4+
Cell wall polysaccharide	Activates complement	0	ND
Pneumolysin	Cytotoxic, activates complement	2+	2–3+
Psp A	Resists phagocytosis	1–2+	1–2+
Psa A	Mediates adherence, ? other	1–2+	1–2+
Autolysin	Bacterial disintegration	1+	2+
Neuraminidase	? Mediates adherence	0–1+	0–1+

*The grading system is subjective and indicates (on a scale of 1+ to 4+) the stringency and importance of the demonstrated effect. For discussion and references, see the text.
†Animal models only except capsular polysaccharides.
Abbreviations: ND, Not done; Psa, pneumococcal surface adhesin; Psp, pneumococcal surface protein.

lenge with genetically engineered pneumococci that do not produce it[58] is associated with a significant reduction in virulence. Different regions of the pneumolysin molecule are responsible for cytotoxic and complement activity properties, and recent studies have used strains with defined point mutations to show that the cytotoxic activity is dominant in causing disease after intraperitoneal but not necessarily after intranasal challenge of mice.[59]

A series of choline-binding proteins may mediate attachment to and penetration of mammalian cells, especially if these cells have been upregulated by prior cytokine exposure.[60] Pneumococcal surface protein A is present on the surface of nearly all pneumococci. Despite some antigenic variability, antibody raised against pneumococcal surface protein A protects experimental animals to a greater or lesser extent against challenge with the same or different strain,[61] and genetically engineered mutants that lack it have reduced virulence for mice.[62] Pneumococcal surface adhesin A, a surface-expressed permease, is universally present in *S. pneumoniae*. This protein shows very little antigenic variability. It may be involved in colonization of the nasopharynx,[53] but it appears to contribute to virulence in other, as yet undetermined ways. Autolysin[58, 63] disrupts the bacterial wall at the site of attachment of stem proteins. In nature, this enzyme contributes to cell wall remodeling. In infection, it probably contributes to disease by releasing peptidoglycan components that more vigorously activate complement, as well as substances (such as pneumolysin) to which the tissues of the infected host might otherwise not be exposed. As with other putative virulence factors, strains that lack autolysin are less virulent in experimental animals, and antibody to autolysin is modestly protective. Pneumococci produce neuraminidase, which may contribute to bacterial adherence and colonization by cleaving sialic acid on mucous membrane surfaces and exposing GlcNAc-Gal, to which *S. pneumoniae* adheres more readily. Immunization of mice with neuraminidase has also provided modest protection against parenteral pneumococcal challenge,[64] perhaps suggesting a role in virulence other than inhibition of colonization. All pneumococci also produce hyaluronidase, but a role in pathogenesis has not been demonstrated.[53] The contribution of phosphorylcholine and transparent phase variation to colonization was mentioned earlier.

IMMUNOLOGICALLY SPECIFIC MECHANISMS OF HOST DEFENSE IN HUMANS

Antibody to Pneumococcal Capsule

Ample evidence shows that in humans, anticapsular antibody is protective against pneumococcal infection, with little or no evidence to date to support a role for antibody to other bacterial constituents: (1) antibody to capsule appears in the blood stream 5 to 8 days after the onset of infection, which is the time that fever spontaneously resolves in the absence of treatment; (2) in the preantibiotic era, administration of serum that contained type-specific antibody was moderately effective in treating pneumococcal pneumonia; and (3) various assays all seem to show greatly increased uptake and killing of pneumococci in vitro in the presence of anticapsular antibody.[1, 65, 66] It is important to note, however, that in the preantibiotic era, some proportion of patients recovered from pneumococcal pneumonia without producing measurable amounts of anticapsular antibody. Furthermore, some adults lack the capacity to make antibody to most pneumococcal capsules,[67] yet live long and healthy lives free of pneumococcal disease. Although IgG antibody as measured by enzyme-linked immunosorbent assay (ELISA) generally predicts protection of experimental animals and opsonophagocytosis activity in vitro, such is not uniformly the case. Some IgG antibody is thought to be relatively less avid for *S. pneumoniae*, which creates a situation with discrepancies between antibody measured by ELISA versus an opsonophagocytosis assay. Thus, when present, anticapsular antibody is regarded as a generally good, but not ideal, surrogate marker of immunity. The converse—namely, that the absence of such antibody indicates a relative degree of susceptibility—is probably true, even though many other factors enter into protection against pneumococcal disease.

Prevalence of Anticapsular Antibody

In the late 1980s, a sensitive and specific ELISA technique was developed that used adsorption to remove cross-reacting antibody to cell wall polysaccharides.[68, 69] This ELISA was used to show that the great majority of 19-year-old military recruits lack antibody to most pneumococcal serotypes.[70] On average, these young adults have type-specific anticapsular IgG to only 15% of commonly infecting serotypes. The rate of reactivity is 33% in working adult men or elderly men. To the extent that immunity is determined by the prevalence of measurable levels of antibody, these data suggest that healthy adults of all ages are susceptible to most serotypes of *S. pneumoniae* that commonly cause infection.

Natural Emergence of Antibody

Antibody to the infecting serotype, as measured in older studies by agglutination in vitro or mouse protection, appears in the serum of adults after pneumonia in about two thirds of cases, with some variability depending on the serotype.[71] In children, the rate of appearance of antibody was even lower[72–74]; these studies need to be repeated with ELISA. The reason or reasons for the failure of detectable levels of antibody to develop after infection remain unclear. The most likely explanation is a genetically mediated incapacity to recognize as foreign the relevant capsular polysaccharide and, therefore, to make antibody to it.[67] Failure to switch to IgG synthesis or to make certain IgG subclasses may also be implicated.[75]

Colonization also leads to antibody formation. Studies of families carried out in the preantibiotic era[76] and of infants and toddlers in the 1970s[20] suggested that the acquisition of antibody also follows colonization. Serotype-specific antibody develops within 30 days in about two thirds of military personnel who become colonized by a pneumococcal strain during an outbreak of pneumococcal pneumonia.[70] Levels of antibody appear to be at least as high as those that follow infection. Thus, colonization with *S. pneumoniae* is an immunizing event, although the cellular and subcellular events responsible for the response are unclear.

Colonization and Immunity

These observations help explain the very low incidence of pneumococcal disease despite the relatively low prevalence of detectable antipneumococcal antibody in the adult population. In the absence of conditions that predispose to infection, antibody to the capsular polysaccharide of a colonizing organism is likely to appear before infection. However, pneumonia is more likely to develop before antibody appears in adults who are likely to aspirate pharyngeal contents or who have diminished mechanisms of lower airway clearance, and otitis media is more likely to precede antibody in children with acute congestion of nasal mucosal membranes secondary to a viral infection. Of course, persons who have a diminished capacity to form antibody remain susceptible as long as they are colonized, which explains the high rate of pneumococcal pneumonia in patients with multiple myeloma, acquired immunodeficiency syndrome, and other such conditions.

The Spleen in Defense of Pneumococcal Infection

The principal organ that clears pneumococci from the blood stream is the spleen.[77, 78] A series of experiments in human subjects have shown that highly opsonized particles are removed from the circulation by the liver but, with decreasing opsonization, the spleen increasingly assumes the role of clearance.[79] The slow passage of blood through the spleen and prolonged contact time with reticuloendothelial cells in the cords of Billroth and the splenic sinuses allow time for the relatively less efficient removal of nonopsonized particles, whereas opsonized ones are taken up well during the more rapid passage through the liver.[80]

Overwhelming pneumococcal infection occurs in children and adults in whom the spleen has been removed or does not function normally. The heralding event in an outbreak of pneumococcal pneumonia in a metropolitan prison[35] was the overwhelmingly rapid, septic death of two prisoners, both of whom had previously undergone splenectomy. Pneumococcal disease progressed so rapidly in these cases that pneumonia was not initially detectable clinically or even with certainty by chest radiographs, although pneumonia was seen at autopsy. The 100-fold increase in the incidence of pneumococcal bacteremia or meningitis in children with sickle cell disease is probably due to splenic dysfunction, although other factors such as complement abnormalities may also contribute.[77, 81]

FACTORS THAT PREDISPOSE TO PNEUMOCOCCAL INFECTION

S. pneumoniae is a prototypic extracellular bacterial pathogen; host defenses against infection rely heavily on humoral factors such as antibody and complement, on the one hand, and phagocytic cells, specifically PMNs, on the other. A representative schema of conditions that have an impact on the immunologic capacity of the host and predispose to pneumococcal infection is shown in Table 188–2 and observed underlying conditions in Table 188–3.

Defective antibody formation, whether congenital or acquired and whatever the cause, has the greatest impact on susceptibility to pneumococcal infection. Bruton's original description of congenital agammaglobulinemia stressed the prominence of *S. pneumoniae* as an infecting agent. Pneumococcus is also a major cause of serious infection in acquired agammaglobulinemia (common variable immunodeficiency)[82] and perhaps in IgG subclass deficiency[83] as well; subtle defects may also be responsible.[75] Homozygous expression of the R131 allele of the FCγII receptor on PMNs, a receptor that binds the Fc of IgG_2 only poorly, or absence of the mannose-binding protein may associate with susceptibility to pneumococcal bacteremia.[83a]

Pneumococcus continues to be the most common bacterial pathogen to infect persons who have multiple myeloma, lymphoma, or chronic lymphocytic leukemia, before chemotherapy and hospitalization tip the balance toward gram-negative infections.[84] Human immunodeficiency virus (HIV) infection causes defects at several points in host defense, but defective antibody production probably predominates in the predisposition to pneumococcal infection. As HIV infection progresses and CD4 lymphocyte counts fall below 500/mm³, the ability to make antibody to pneumococcal capsular polysaccharides

TABLE 188–2 General Schema of Conditions That Predispose to Pneumococcal Infection

Defective antibody formation
Primary
Congenital agammaglobulinemia
Common variable (acquired) hypogammaglobulinemia
Selective IgG subclass deficiency
Secondary
Multiple myeloma
Chronic lymphocytic leukemia
Lymphoma
HIV infection
Defective complement (primary or secondary)
Decreased or absent C1, C2, C3, C4
Insufficient numbers of PMNs
Primary
Cyclic neutropenia
Secondary
Drug-induced neutropenia
Aplastic anemia
Poorly functioning PMNs
Alcoholism
Cirrhosis of the liver
Glucocorticosteroid treatment
Renal insufficiency
? Poorly avid receptors for FCγII (R131 allele)
Defective clearance of pneumococcal bacteremia
Primary
Congenital asplenia, hyposplenia
Secondary
Splenectomy
Sickle cell disease (autosplenectomy)
Multifactorial
Infancy and aging
Glucocorticosteroid treatment
Malnutrition
Cirrhosis of the liver
Renal insufficiency
Diabetes mellitus
Alcoholism
Chronic disease, hospitalization
Fatigue
Stress
Cold exposure
Excess likelihood of exposure
Daycare centers
Military training camps
Prisons
Shelters for the homeless
Prior respiratory infection
Influenza
Other
Inflammatory condition
Cigarette smoking
Asthma
COPD

Abbreviations: COPD, Chronic obstructive pulmonary disease; HIV, human immunodeficiency virus; PMNs, polymorphonuclear leukocytes.

TABLE 188–3 Factors Predisposing Adults to Invasive Pneumococcal Disease*

Predisposing Factor	All Invasive Pneumococcal Infection (Sweden[25])	All Community-Acquired Pneumonia (Pittsburgh[85])	Pneumococcal Bacteremia, Meningitis (Israel[86])	Bacteremic Pneumococcal Pneumonia (Ohio[87])
Alcoholism	32	33	NL	11
Cigarette smoking	40	55	NL	56
Chronic lung disease	17	31	19	28
Congestive heart failure	NL	13	35	16
Diabetes mellitus	6	13	15	18
Malignancy	12	29	NL	26
Kidney disease	1	7	13	4
Liver disease	2	5	6	NL
Autoimmune disease	3	NL	5	NL
Splenectomy	3	3	4	3
Seizure disorder	8	NL	NL	NL
Immunosuppression	NL	36	36	NL
No underlying disease	21	31	22	10

*The finding of low numbers in some studies and much higher ones in others suggests the possibility of incomplete availability of data in the former. In the Swedish study,[25] 20% of patients with meningitis had prior head injury.
Abbreviation: NL, Not listed.

falls off rapidly.[88, 89] The incidence of pneumococcal bacteremia in HIV-infected persons approaches 10 per 1000 per year,[90] a 200-fold increase for an age-related population; if one calculates 3 to 4 nonbacteremic cases of pneumonia for each bacteremic case, 1 in 25 HIV-infected persons may be expected to have pneumococcal pneumonia in a given year.[91] Some authorities recommend that bacteremic pneumonia or unusual pneumococcal infections in young adults[92] trigger a search for HIV infection. The incidence of pneumococcal infection can even be used to estimate the number of HIV-infected persons in a population.[93]

Of the many possible defects in complement, only those factors required to generate C3b are associated with pneumococcal infection. Because pneumococci are not killed by serum, the host response is unaffected by defects in C6, C7, C8, or C9, which results in decreased membrane attack complexes. Deficiencies in C1, C2, and C4, whether congenital or acquired, are expected to be associated with increased susceptibility to pneumococcal infection, although cases documenting the association are reported only rarely.[94]

Neutropenia of whatever cause is associated with *S. pneumoniae* infection, although somewhat surprisingly, leukocyte adhesion deficiency syndrome (Mac-1 deficiency) is generally not.[95] One study[96] has shown that at the time of initial hospitalization for acute leukemia, patients are more likely to have infection caused by more ordinary gram-positive pathogenic bacteria, probably analogous to the pretreatment situation in multiple myeloma.[84] Defective bacterial killing by PMNs as seen in chronic granulomatous disease does not predispose to infection with *S. pneumoniae*; the absence of catalase renders this organism susceptible to the interaction between its endogenous H_2O_2 and myeloperoxidase and the halide present in PMNs.

The susceptibility of aged persons to pneumococcal pneumonia is multifactorial and reflects senescence of the immune system because of diminished production of immunoglobulins, impaired response to tumor necrosis factor and interleukin-1, and a debilitated condition caused by weakening of the gag reflex, malnutrition, and the presence of other diseases. The effect of alcoholism is also multifactorial and involves lifestyle (such as cold exposure and malnutrition), suppression of the gag reflex, and possibly deleterious effects on PMN function, although in most instances these alterations have been difficult to attribute to the effect of alcohol alone.[97, 98] Heffron[1] cites studies that found 30% of patients hospitalized for pneumonia at Johns Hopkins Hospital to have a history of alcoholism and 19% and 29% of those at the Rockefeller Hospital to be heavy and moderate alcohol drinkers, respectively. More recent studies that reflect data in the population at large have found similar results, with about one third of patients being listed as having a history of alcoholism.[25, 85] A disproportionately high number of patients who have pneumococcal infection have diabetes mellitus,[25, 85–87] a condition in which PMN chemotaxis is reduced[99] and phagocytic function is defective,[100] especially if renal insufficiency is present.

Many chronic diseases are associated with pneumococcal pneumonia by virtue of an association with pneumonia of whatever cause, which suggests that the predisposition is a general one rather than being specific for *S. pneumoniae*. Pneumococcal pneumonia follows hospitalization for all causes[101] and is even well documented as a nosocomial infection.[102] Other factors such as cold exposure, stress, and fatigue[1] may predispose to pneumococcal pneumonia by unknown mechanisms.

As mentioned earlier, prior respiratory viral infection, perhaps especially infection caused by influenza virus, appears to play a prominent role in predisposing to pneumococcal infection.[30, 103, 104] Potentially pathogenic bacteria may adhere more readily to nasopharyngeal cells from persons with viral infections[105] and are certainly less well cleared from the airways because of viral-induced damage. Pneumococcal disease is greatly increased in people with altered pulmonary clearance, such as those who have chronic bronchitis, asthma, or chronic obstructive pulmonary disease. It has been surprisingly difficult to identify a study that relates cigarette smoking to susceptibility to pneumonia. Nevertheless, clinical and epidemiologic observations[25, 85] support the general belief that smoking predisposes to pneumococcal infection. It is an interesting sign of the times that Heffron's classic work[1] on the pneumococcus published in 1939 has a section on inhalation of "noxious substances," yet does not mention cigarette smoking.

CLINICAL SYNDROMES

S. pneumoniae causes infection of the middle ear, sinuses, trachea, bronchi, and lungs by direct spread of organisms from the nasopharyngeal site of colonization and causes infection of the central nervous system, heart valves, bones, joints, and peritoneal cavity by hematogenous spread. A schema demonstrating the ways in which these major pathogenetic pathways interrelate is shown in Figure 188–4. Peritoneal infection may rarely occur via extension from the fallopian tubes, and pleural infection may result from direct extension of pneumonia to the visceral pleura or from hematogenous spread of bacteria from pneumonia with seeding of the pleura; in any individual case, the route of spread cannot be determined. Local extension to the central nervous system causes meningitis in patients who have repeated bouts of meningitis because of a dural defect. Bacteremia may occur without an apparent source or focus of infection, in which case it is called primary bacteremia. In a recent population-based study of adults in Israel,[106] pneumonia was present in 71% of cases of pneumococcal bacteremia, meningitis was present in 8%, and

FIGURE 188–4. A schema showing the events that take place between initial response to pneumococci and the eventual development of disease.

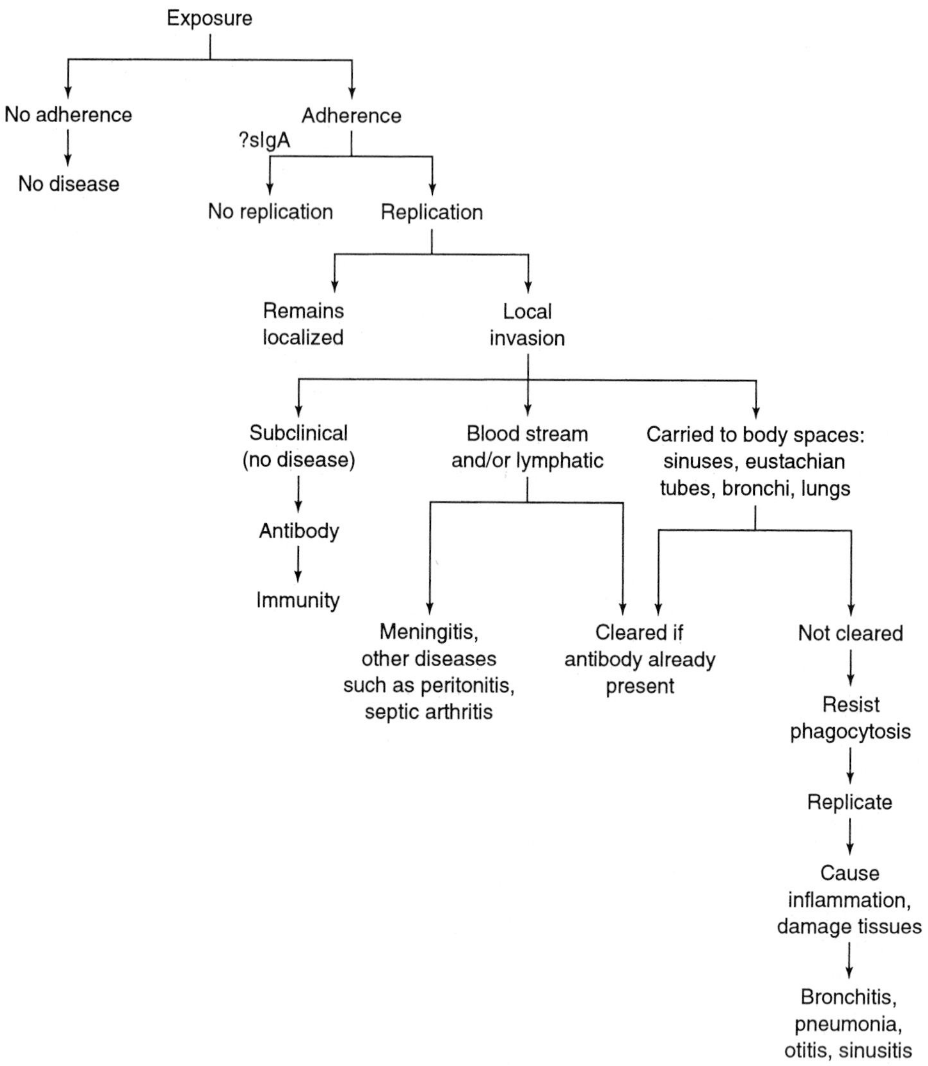

otitis media or sinusitis was found in 4%; bacteremia was primary in 18%. This condition is more common in children than adults; when therapy is withheld, a focus of infection is likely to develop or become apparent.

Otitis Media

Virtually every study of acute otitis media in which material from the middle ear has been cultured has shown *S. pneumoniae* to be the most common isolate or second only to nontypable *Haemophilus influenzae; Moraxella* (*Branhamella*) *catarrhalis* is usually a distant third.[107] In these studies, which are usually carried out in children aged 6 months to 4 years, *S. pneumoniae* is implicated in about 40 to 50% of cases in which an etiologic agent is isolated or in 30 to 40% of all cases. A 1992 report[108] shows the pneumococcus to be most prevalent in otitis media in adults as well. Prior infection by a respiratory virus is thought to play a major contributory role by causing congestion of the opening to the eustachian tube. Prospective longitudinal studies[20, 28, 109] have shown that when infection occurs, in most cases it follows fairly closely after colonization by a new serotype, although, of course, most instances of colonization occur without disease. Perhaps related to more avid adherence to mammalian cells, serotypes 6, 14, 19F, and 23F predominate as both colonizing and infecting organisms; this finding explains why these serotypes are currently under the most intensive study for use in vaccines in young children.

Sinusitis

Acute infection of the sinuses is caused by the same organisms as acute otitis media; thus, *S. pneumoniae* dominates or is second to *H. influenzae*.[110] Important in the pathogenesis of this infection is congestion of the mucosal membranes caused by allergy or viral infection. The resulting obstruction prevents clearance of bacteria. The accumulation of fluid in the paranasal sinus cavities, even during simple colds,[111] provides a medium for bacterial proliferation and subsequent acute sinus infection.

Meningitis

Except during an epidemic of meningococcal infection, *S. pneumoniae* is the most common etiologic agent of bacterial meningitis in adults.[112] In countries that have implemented effective vaccination programs for *H. influenzae* type b, pneumococcus has become the most common sporadic cause of meningitis in infants (although not newborns) and toddlers as well.

The pathogenesis of meningitis may be by direct extension from sinuses or the middle ear or as a result of bacteremia with seeding of the choroid plexus. Favoring the former possibility are the association between acute otitis media or sinusitis and infection of the central nervous system and the well-documented role of *S. pneumoniae* as the most common cause of recurrent bacterial meningitis associated with head trauma, CSF leak, or a break in the integrity of the dura.[16] Favoring the latter is the high association of pneumococcal pneumonia or bacteremia without a known focus with subsequent meningitis. In addition, an autopsy study of the temporal bones of children who died of bacterial meningitis[113] showed no evidence for extension from the middle ear, which supports the concept that even when it follows otitis media, meningitis develops as a result of bacteremia. Hematogenous spread to the choroid plexus was documented in classic original studies and is currently thought to be the pathogenesis in most cases of pneumococcal meningitis. Communication through the cochlear aqueduct between the inner ear and the subarachnoid space[114] may explain deafness in patients with hematogenous bacterial meningitis.

Once pneumococci appear in the subarachnoid space, the capacity to produce inflammation is central to the disease process. As noted earlier, injection of cell wall constituents, principally peptidoglycan and, to a lesser extent, teichoic acid, intracisternally in rabbits causes the CSF abnormalities of bacterial meningitis, presumably through a variety of mediators, including C5a, tumor necrosis factor, interleukin-1, interleukin-6, and other active inflammatory peptides.[115] No distinctive clinical or laboratory features of pneumococcal meningitis enable the physician to suspect *S. pneumoniae* over any other causative agent. Examination of a Gram-stained specimen of CSF should provide the correct diagnosis in nearly all cases,[116] unless some antibiotic has already been administered, in which case the number of bacteria may be greatly decreased. Immunologic detection of pneumococcal capsular material ("bacterial antigen") may be useful in selected cases when patients have received prior antimicrobial therapy.

Pneumonia

Pathogenesis. If potentially protective mechanisms fail to prevent both the access of pneumococci to the alveoli and their subsequent replication, pneumonia results. Bacteria proliferate in alveolar spaces, are carried along the alveolar septa, and activate complement and generate vasoactive substances. Exudative fluid and WBCs accumulate in the septa and alveoli and extend to uninvolved areas through the pores of Kohn. This filling of alveoli with microorganisms and inflammatory exudate defines the presence of pneumonia, and a clinical diagnosis is made when fluid accumulation has been great enough to allow it to be seen radiographically as a nonlucent or "consolidated" area.

Symptoms and Physical Findings. Cough, fatigue, fever, chills, sweats, and shortness of breath are the most frequent symptoms of pneumonia; these are all more prominent in younger than in older patients.[117, 117a] Patients with pneumococcal pneumonia usually appear ill and have a grayish, anxious appearance that differs from that of persons with viral or mycoplasmal pneumonia. The temperature may be elevated to 102°F to 103°F, the pulse to 90 to 110 beats per minute, and the respiratory rate to 20 to 24 per minute. Elderly patients may have only a slight temperature elevation or be afebrile but are more likely to have an increased respiratory rate.[117] The absence of fever in young or middle-aged adults is associated with increased morbidity and mortality, as, especially, is hypothermia.

Physical examination may reveal diminished respiratory excursion (splinting) on the affected side because of pain. Dullness to percussion is present in about half of cases. Crackling sounds are heard on careful auscultation in nearly all cases, but in patients who have chronic lung disease it is often difficult to be certain that such sounds signify the presence of pneumonia. Bronchial or tubular breath sounds may be heard if consolidation is present. Flatness to percussion at the lung base and an inability to detect the expected degree of diaphragmatic motion based on the patient's respiratory excursion suggest the presence of pleural fluid. Unless all the vital signs are normal, which substantially reduces the likelihood of pneumonia, no set of physical findings can reliably replace the chest x ray in diagnosing the presence or absence of pneumonia.[117b] The finding of a heart murmur raises concern about endocarditis, a rare but serious complication. Confusion, obtundation, or especially neck stiffness should lead to consideration of meningitis.

Radiographic Findings. In most cases of pneumococcal pneumonia, chest radiography reveals an area of infiltration involving one or more segments within a single lobe.[118] Lobar consolidation or an air bronchogram is present only in a minority of cases but is more likely to be associated with bacteremia.[87, 118] The frequent presence of underlying chronic lung disease causes a more "moth-eaten," less homogeneous appearance in the involved lung. Rarely, *S. pneumoniae* infection causes a lung abscess.[119] As emphasized earlier, these organisms do not produce highly toxic, tissue-damaging substances. Thus, abscesses do not generally occur, even at a microscopic level, and if an abscess is seen, concurrent anaerobic infection or an anatomic abnormality such as bronchial obstruction, cancer, or pulmonary infarction should be suspected. Although pleural effusion may be found in 40% of patients with pneumococcal pneumonia by careful search, only 10% have sufficient amounts of fluid to aspirate, and in only a minority of these, perhaps 2% of the total, is empyema present.[120]

General Laboratory Findings. Twenty-five percent of patients with pneumococcal pneumonia have a hemoglobin of 10 mg/dl or less. Although the majority have leukocytosis (WBC count >12,000/mm^3), a substantial proportion may have normal WBC counts, at least at the time of admission. A WBC count less than 6000/mm^3 occurs in 5 to 10% of persons hospitalized for pneumococcal pneumonia and indicates a very poor prognosis.[121] Experimental studies have suggested that this situation reflects the accumulation of all available WBCs at the infected site; more often than not, it is seen in the presence of conditions such as ethanol ingestion or malnutrition, which suppress the bone marrow.[122] Serum bilirubin may be increased to 3 to 4 mg/dl; the pathogenesis of this abnormality is multifactorial, with hypoxia, hepatic inflammation, and breakdown of red blood cells in the lung all thought to contribute. Levels of lactate dehydrogenase may be elevated. The likelihood that underlying disease is present must always be considered when evaluating abnormal laboratory findings. Laboratory abnormalities in empyema[120] are reviewed in Chapter 58.

Diagnostic Microbiology. The etiologic role of the pneumococcus in a patient who has pneumonia is strongly suggested by microscopic demonstration of large numbers of PMNs, very few epithelial cells (PMN–epithelial cell ratio, approximately 10 to 20:1), and numerous, slightly elongated gram-positive cocci in pairs and chains in a Gram-stained sputum (Table 188–4). If accepted terminology is strictly followed, a presumptive diagnosis of pneumococcal pneumonia is then made if *S. pneumoniae* is identified by sputum culture and the diagnosis is proved if *S. pneumoniae* is identified by blood culture. The argument that the diagnosis is never certain unless the blood culture is also positive is overly restrictive because most patients with pneumococcal pneumonia do not have detectable bacteremia.

Attempts to make a diagnosis based on an inadequate sputum specimen[123, 124] are largely responsible for studies claiming that microscopic examination and culture of sputum are not reliable. To be reliable, the sputum sample should contain material that on microscopic examination reveals areas with hundreds of WBCs and few epithelial cells at low-power magnification (100×) and at least 10 to 20 WBCs with no epithelial cells under 1000× magnification. At this higher magnification, pneumococci are generally present in large numbers (>25 per field) (Fig. 188–5), although occasionally as few as 1 to 2 may be seen per field. If sufficient numbers of inflammatory cells are not present, relevant material has not been obtained; if many epithelial cells are detected, the finding of bacteria cannot be trusted to reflect what is present in the bronchi or lungs. A good-quality sputum specimen is far more likely to be obtained by a physician, who best understands its central role in establishing an etiologic diagnosis and determining therapy, than by ancillary personnel, who may not.[125, 125a]

TABLE 188-4 Microscopic Examination and Culture of Sputum for Pneumococci

Gram Stain	Sputum Culture	Blood Culture	Comment
+	+	+	Generally regarded as conclusive diagnosis of invasive pneumococcal disease (pneumonia), but does not exclude contribution by another etiology such as influenza virus infection or lung cancer
+	+	−	Good evidence for nonbacteremic pneumococcal pneumonia if a clinical syndrome suggesting pneumonia is present, microscopic examination of Gram-stained sputum is characteristic (see Fig. 188–5), and culture shows strongly predominant growth of pneumococci with no other likely pathogenic bacteria
+ or −	−	+	With symptoms and signs of pneumonia and an infiltrate on the chest radiograph, these findings are generally taken to indicate invasive pneumococcal pneumonia even if organisms are not found in sputum
+	−	−	In the presence of the appropriate clinical syndrome, still remains suggestive of pneumococcal pneumonia because organisms can be missed on culture as a result of sampling error and overgrowth of streptococci from saliva
−	+	−	Less suggestive of pneumococcal disease. Pneumococci can be isolated by culture of sputum from persons who are colonized
−	−	−	Does not support a diagnosis of pneumococcal pneumonia

With a sputum sample of good quality, bacterial culture is expected to support the findings of Gram stain.[126] Concurrence depends greatly on the quality of the specimen, and extra care must be taken to inoculate the plates with sputum rather than saliva. Although colonies of *S. pneumoniae* serotype 3 are highly mucoid and readily recognizable on a blood-agar plate, most pneumococci do not produce distinctively mucoid colonies, and identification in the laboratory depends on distinguishing putative pneumococcal colonies, which may have an umbilicated appearance because of autolysis, from other α-hemolytic streptococci. Failure to detect pneumococci by culture when they are plainly seen on microscopic examination results from the following factors: (1) the most prevalent organisms in saliva are other streptococci; (2) during microscopic examination, the observer focuses on the area of special interest, but the specimen itself may contain an admixture of saliva and sputum, and in that part of the specimen inoculated on the plate viridans streptococci may outnumber pneumococci; and (3) in selecting one or more α-hemolytic colonies for identification, the laboratory technologist may not be able to find the pneumococcus. This circumstance leads to the unfortunate, but all-too-common situation in which the laboratory reports "normal flora" on a specimen that really seemed to show pneumococci.

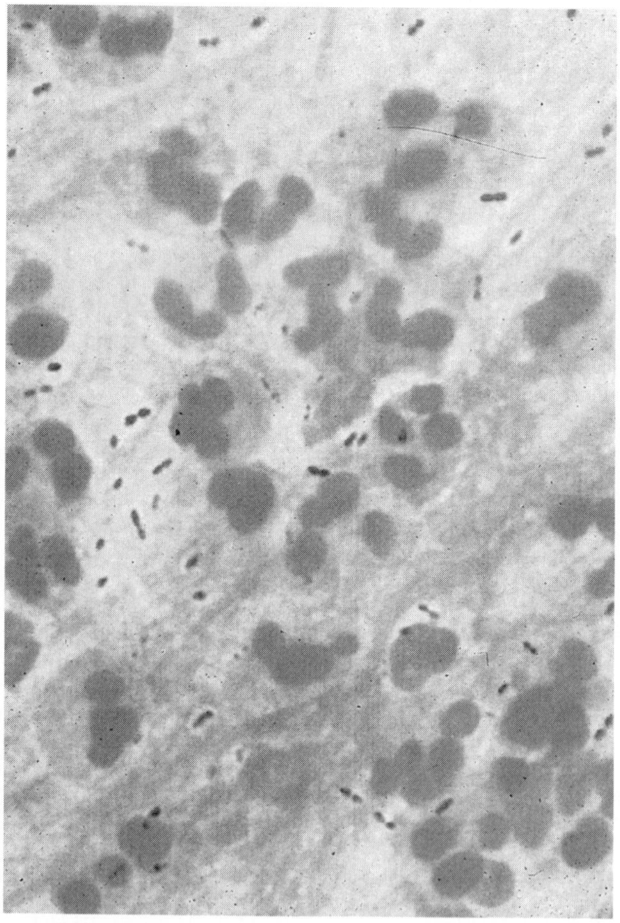

FIGURE 188–5. Gram-stained sputum from a patient with pneumococcal pneumonia at ×1000 magnification showing many polymorphonuclear neutrophils and no epithelial cells with large numbers of slightly elongated, gram-negative cocci in pairs and chains indicative of *Streptococcus pneumoniae*. A clear area surrounding bacteria indicates the capsule.

When a patient who has pneumonia cannot provide an expectorated specimen, the potential problems of empirical therapy should be balanced against the time and trouble that it may take to obtain a specimen, for example, by nasotracheal suction, hydration, or breathing humidified air or hypertonic saline mist.

It is difficult to know the proportion of patients with pneumococcal pneumonia who have positive blood cultures because the denominator is so uncertain; 25% is the number that is given, but it is based on data from the preantibiotic era. Institution of treatment should not be delayed beyond a few hours solely for the purpose of obtaining a good solution.

Other diagnostic techniques focus on the detection of antigen or antibody. In general, if the sputum is not of sufficiently good quality that the Gram stain is positive, other tests, such as coagglutination, antigen detection, or polymerase chain reaction, that look for pneumococci in the sputum will not be helpful because they are confounded by the same problem, namely, the amount of contaminating material relative to the number of pneumococci. Some additional findings, presented in various stages of completeness at the First International Symposium on Pneumococci and Pneumococcal Diseases, Elsinore, Denmark, June 1998, include the following: large amounts of capsular polysaccharide are excreted in the urine and may be detected by latex agglutination in about two thirds of cases or by immunoelectrophoresis in a higher proportion. In children, this test may be falsely positive because of colonization of the nasopharynx. Polymerase chain reaction amplification may be relatively sensitive and quite specific in CSF and less sensitive in blood. Antibody to capsular polysaccharide may be present in immune complexes at the time that adult patients are hospitalized for pneumonia, but tests to detect such antibody have neither the sensitivity nor the specificity to be clinically useful. Diagnosing pneumococcal infection by antibody rises is also problematic because persons who are infected may be the very ones who do not make much antibody and, for reasons that are not understood, infected persons increase their antibody levels to other, noninfecting serotypes as well, at least as detected by ELISA. The U.S. Food and Drug Administration approved a rapid test for urinary pneumococcal C-polysaccharide in August 1999. The manufacturer (Binax, Inc.) reports sensitivity of 86 to 90% in bacteremic pneumococcal pneumonia.

Complications. Empyema, the most common complication of pneumococcal pneumonia in the preantibiotic era, occurred in about 5% of cases and remains the most common today, with an incidence of approximately 2%.[120] As noted earlier, pleural fluid appears in a substantial proportion of cases of pneumonia but is usually reactive. When bacteria reach the pleural space, either hematogenously or as a result of extension of the pneumonia to the visceral pleura with spread via lymphatics, empyema results. The presence of frank pus, a positive Gram stain, or fluid with pH 7.1 or less are all indications for aggressive and complete drainage with repeated needle aspiration or prompt insertion of a chest tube. If no response is seen, thoracotomy is indicated.[127] Persistence of fever, even if "low grade," and leukocytosis after 4 to 5 days of appropriate antibiotic treatment of pneumococcal pneumonia is suggestive of empyema, and this diagnosis is even more likely if the radiograph shows persistence of pleural fluid. One study of medical empyema caused by all organisms found that mortality exceeded 30% in two hospitals where the therapeutic approach was not aggressive versus less than 10% in a third hospital where it was.[128]

Other Syndromes

S. pneumoniae can be implicated in a wide variety of infectious states. Most cases of spontaneous bacterial peritonitis in children[129] and some cases in adults[130, 131] are caused by *S. pneumoniae*. Peritonitis in women may be related to the use of an intrauterine contraceptive device,[132] and pneumococcal infections of the female reproductive organs[133, 134] continue to be described. A case of pneumococcal endocarditis[135] is seen once or twice per decade at a large tertiary care hospital in the United States. A recent study of 14 cases identified in Denmark (population of 5 million) in a 10-year period showed that 3 persons were alcoholic and only 1 had known of prior valvular disease; 8 had pneumonia and 4 had meningitis.

Purulent pericarditis[136] caused by this organism is even more rare, whether it occurs as a separate entity or together with endocarditis. Septic arthritis occurs spontaneously in a natural or prosthetic[137] joint or as a complication of rheumatoid arthritis.[138] Osteomyelitis in adults tends to involve the vertebral bones.[139] Epidural and brain abscesses are rarely described.[140] Soft tissue infections[141, 142] occur, especially in persons who have connective tissue diseases or HIV infection. Finally, the appearance of unusual pneumococcal infections in a young adult might suggest that tests for HIV infection be undertaken.[92]

ANTIBIOTIC SUSCEPTIBILITY

Until the mid-1970s, pneumococci were inhibited or killed by readily achievable levels of all relevant antibiotics, with the possible exception of tetracycline, to which a variable number of strains showed resistance. This remarkable susceptibility of the major bacterial pathogen in otitis, sinusitis, and pneumonia allowed for a somewhat cavalier approach to diagnosis and antibiotic therapy, an approach that may no longer be valid because during the past 2 decades pneumococci have increasingly become more resistant to penicillin and other antibiotics.[143–145]

The susceptibility of *S. pneumoniae* to penicillin is currently defined by the National Committee for Clinical Laboratory Standards as follows. Susceptible isolates are inhibited by 0.06 μg/ml (i.e., minimal inhibitory concentration [MIC] ≤0.06 μg/ml). Isolates with reduced susceptibility (also known as intermediate resistance) are inhibited by 0.1 to 1.0 μg/ml, and resistant isolates are inhibited by 2.0 μg/ml or more. Cutoff points have been selected somewhat arbitrarily, and some tests report MICs at values in between, in which case the MIC is calculated by rounding up to the higher value. A more important problem with these definitions is that from a clinical point of view, the MIC has an entirely different meaning, depending on the infection being treated. A strain with reduced susceptibility (e.g., MIC of 1.0 μg/ml) behaves as a susceptible organism when it causes pneumonia (see "Treatment"), but probably not when it causes otitis and certainly not when it causes meningitis. At the time of this writing, consideration is being given to make the definition of susceptibility depend on the site infected,[146] a concept supported by pharmacokinetic considerations and validated by outcome studies.

Penicillin inhibits the replication of *S. pneumoniae* by binding one or more enzymes needed to make peptidoglycan, including higher-molecular-weight transpeptidases and a lower-molecular-weight carboxypeptidase. The binding is covalent, and a serine ester–linked, enzymatically nonactive penicilloyl complex is formed. The reaction with penicillin is used to recognize these enzymes by two general methods: incubating with radiolabeled penicillin, followed by electrophoresis and autoradiography, or incubating with nonlabeled penicillin, followed by electrophoresis and immunoblotting with anti-penicilloyl antibody. Six such enzymes are identified: 1A, 1B, 2A, 2B, 2X, and 3. In fully susceptible isolates of *S. pneumoniae*, these six enzymes, which are also called penicillin-binding proteins (PBPs), are identifiable after incubation with low concentrations of penicillin. Resistant isolates have PBPs with decreased affinity for penicillin in very approximate proportion to the degree of resistance. Changes in the genes that encode these enzymes, with relatively minor alterations in the amino acids at essential loci,[147] may result in the decreased affinity. Alterations in PBP 2B are more likely to account for low-level resistance, whereas mutations in PBP 2X have been associated with high-level resistance.[148]

Pneumococci have become resistant by acquiring genetic material from other bacteria with which they coexist in close proximity—presumably viridans streptococci in the nasopharynx. In fact, the altered sequence in the gene for PBP 2B in many penicillin-resistant isolates appears to have originated in *Streptococcus mitis*.[149] The unique capacity of *S. pneumoniae* to be transformed is a major determinant of this process. Extensive diversity among isolates[150] or within the transpeptide-encoding region of the pneumococcal genome[148, 151] indicates that many discrete mutational events have occurred, some of which reflect acquisition and others, rearrangement of DNA. Alterations in several PBPs may eventually appear within an individual isolate, and a mosaic array of PBPs results.

In addition to these many separate mutational events, newly resistant strains become prevalent by geographic spread.[152] An example was the arrival in Iceland of a strain that was prevalent in Spain during the 1992 Olympics; this strain rapidly spread throughout that small country.[153] Similarly, European strains have also been implicated as the cause of disease in the United States.[150, 154]

Geographic spread is greatly facilitated by antibiotic pressure. One prominent site for this selection is daycare centers. Point prevalence studies in the United States have shown that at any given time, a remarkably high proportion of children in daycare are receiving antibiotics. These conditions (1) suppress susceptible flora, thereby creating a niche for resistant organisms; (2) spare antibiotic-resistant pneumococci; (3) increase the prevalence of antibiotic-resistant viridans streptococci, thus setting the stage for further transformation of pneumococci to antibiotic resistance; and (4) provide close contact among small children, which allows for the spread of organisms. Other situations characterized by close contact and excessive antibiotic use, such as nursing homes,[37] may also serve as breeding grounds for these organisms.

Resistance to penicillin is certainly notable and easy to track, but this problem is only one part of the picture. Many of the penicillin-resistant strains that were first identified were susceptible to certain third-generation cephalosporins such as cefotaxime or ceftriaxone.

Resistance to these drugs has appeared, also reflecting alterations in PBPs, especially PBP 2X and 1A,[151] such that up to half of penicillin-resistant strains also resist these cephalosporins. Resistance extends far beyond the β-lactam antibiotics. The genetic material that encodes penicillin resistance is contained in DNA sequences that also confer resistance to other commonly used antimicrobials. Thus, pneumococci that are penicillin resistant are usually resistant to several other antibiotics as well, and the best phraseology to describe them is antibiotic resistant.

At present, what proportion of pneumococci exhibit resistance to penicillin and other antibiotics? The best short answer is a substantial proportion and one that appears to be steadily increasing. The longer answer is as follows (Table 188–5). As of June 1998 in the United States, depending on the source of the isolates, 40 to 80% of *S. pneumoniae* isolates from infected persons remain fully susceptible to penicillin. Variations occur from city to city and within segments of the population or even within institutions in a single city, so the actual results vary greatly, depending on the source of the isolates. Two major surveillance programs are currently in place: the SENTRY study tabulates the resistance of lower respiratory isolates at tertiary care hospitals.[145] The rate of penicillin susceptibility at these institutions in the first half of 1997 ranged from 40 to 70% and averaged 50%. The Centers for Disease Control and Prevention is conducting a population-based study that is examining all pneumococcal isolates implicated in invasive disease at 18 sites in the United States; the overall rate of susceptibility was around 75%, but with a similar degree of variation. In these studies, most isolates with reduced penicillin susceptibility were intermediately resistant; the rest were resistant. During the winter of 1997–1998 at the Veterans Affairs Medical Center in Houston, 63% of isolates were fully penicillin susceptible, 24% were intermediately resistant, and 13% were highly resistant; of the highly resistant ones, most were also resistant to cephalosporins. Rates of resistance are substantially higher in most European countries, with notable exceptions such as The Netherlands and Germany, where accepted standards of practice strictly limit antibiotic usage, especially among very young children. A recent study from Iceland suggests that curtailment of antibiotics can lead to a decline in the prevalence of resistance.

Pneumococci that are not resistant to penicillin remain susceptible to nearly all other antibiotics (see Table 188–5). In contrast, some proportion of isolates that exhibit decreased susceptibility to penicillin and a much higher proportion of those that are resistant exhibit resistance to nearly all other commonly used antibiotics. Data presented in Table 188–5 reflect the general situation in the United States as of July 1998 and are highly likely to change.

From this table, the reader can infer that resistance has appeared and seems to be increasing to all antimicrobials except vancomycin. Organisms that resist erythromycin also resist the new macrolides, which will certainly have an impact on empirical therapy for bronchitis, sinusitis, or pneumonia. In the United States at present, most macrolide-resistant isolates bear the so-called M phenotype, an efflux pump abnormality (erythromycin MIC of 1 to 8 μg/ml). This resistance may be overcome by sufficiently high doses of macrolides, and these isolates remain susceptible to clindamycin. In Europe, most macrolide resistance is due to a mutation in *ermB,* which confers high-grade ribosomal resistance to macrolides and also to clindamycin. It is likely that the unavailability of a quinolone for pediatric use has played an important role in sparing this group of antibiotics. Among approved drugs, only vancomycin remains uniformly effective at present.

Of drugs under study, the oxazolidinones[155] and glycopeptides[156] appear to be most promising, with MICs for drug-resistant *S. pneumoniae* being no higher than those for penicillin-susceptible strains. Resistance to streptogramins appears to parallel that of the macrolides, so this class of drugs does not look promising.

TREATMENT

The basic principles of treatment of pneumococcal infection are similar to those for treating other infections: (1) administer an antibiotic that provides a level sufficient to inhibit or kill the infecting organism, (2) continue treatment for a sufficient period, (3) drain infections of closed spaces if necessary, (4) know what response to expect, and (5) be prepared to reevaluate if this response is not observed. These basic principles having been stated, the reader will discover that their application is by no means simple. A few selected factors include the following: (1) for most diseases caused by pneumococcus, when therapy is begun, the etiologic agent is unknown; (2) even if *S. pneumoniae* is presumed to be causative, antibiotic susceptibility is not known when treatment is begun; (3) for most common conditions, the appropriate duration of therapy has not been established by scientific study; (4) in otitis media and sinusitis, the most common infections caused by *S. pneumoniae*, drainage is not usually done; and (5) many physicians do not clearly understand what to expect after treatment has begun.

Otitis Media

In 1998, The Otitis Media Working Group of the Centers for Disease Control and Prevention[107] recommended amoxicillin at twice the

TABLE 188–5 Percentage of *Streptococcus pneumoniae* Strains, Stratified for Penicillin Susceptibility, That Are Susceptible to Various Other Antibiotics, as of July 1, 1999 (Note Disclaimer in Text)

Drug	Penicillin Susceptible	Penicillin Intermediate	Penicillin Resistant
Amoxicillin*†	100	?	?‡
Amoxicillin/clavulanic acid*†	100	?	?
Doxycycline	95	80	65
Erythromycin	96	75	50
Clarithromycin, azithromycin§	95	75	50
Clindamycin	>99	93	80
TMP-SMX	89	65	15
Cefuroxime**	99	60	2
Cefotaxime††	100	95	15
Fluoroquinolones‡‡	98	98	98
Imipenem	100	95	25
Vancomycin	100	100	100

*Some in vitro data and experiments in mice suggest that amoxicillin may be more effective against *S. pneumoniae* than penicillin is alone.
†Pneumonia secondary to intermediately resistant pneumococci responds to usual parenteral doses of penicillin or to amoxicillin. Otitis may not. Meningitis is likely not to respond. Pneumonia caused by resistant strains probably responds to penicillins or third-generation cephalosporins in the usual parenteral doses.
‡Susceptibility depends on the site of infection (see the text).
§Pneumococci resistant to erythromycin are also resistant to these newer macrolides.
**Cefuroxime or cefpodoxime are more active against pneumococci than other oral cephalosporins are.
††Cefotaxime and ceftriaxone are more active against pneumococci than other third-generation cephalosporins are.
‡‡Based on in vitro determination of the minimal inhibitory concentration, the susceptibility to ciprofloxacin is borderline. Newer quinolones, of which levofloxacin, sparfloxacin, and trovafloxacin are examples, are more active at achievable concentrations.
Abbreviation: TMP-SMX, Trimethoprim-sulfamethoxazole.

previously recommended dosage to treat children with otitis media. The group reasoned that (1) *S. pneumoniae* is the most common identifiable cause of this infection and the one associated with the greatest morbidity, (2) penicillin-susceptible and intermediately resistant pneumococci are likely to respond better to this treatment than to any other, and (3) no other oral therapy is likely to be more effective for resistant pneumococci. In a relatively small, but carefully monitored, prospective, randomized comparison of amoxicillin and cefuroxime that included tympanocentesis to monitor etiologic agents and response to therapy, Dagan and associates showed that the bacteriologic response to treatment is closely related to the level of resistance or susceptibility of the infecting bacterium and that amoxicillin provided the best outcome (cited by Dowell and colleagues[107]). When cefuroxime, an oral cephalosporin with good activity against *S. pneumoniae*, was compared with another less active cephalosporin (cefaclor), the failure rate was closely related to the greater MIC for cefaclor and was substantially higher for this latter drug.[146] In the absence of a perforated tympanic membrane, therapy need not be given for more than 5 days.[157]

Patients whose infection does not respond in 24 to 48 hours should be regarded as having infection by a penicillin-resistant pneumococcus or a β-lactamase–producing organism of another genus such as *H. influenzae* or *M. catarrhalis*. In such cases, the Otitis Media Working Group recommends amoxicillin/clavulanate, cefpodoxime orally, or a single parenteral dose of ceftriaxone followed by 3 to 5 days of oral cefpodoxime. This therapy is likely to be effective against *H. influenzae* and *M. catarrhalis*, as well as additional pneumococcal strains. Three to 5 daily doses of ceftriaxone are recommended for more resistant cases. The group considered alternatives, such as azithromycin, but rejected them because of steadily increasing rates of resistance. At present, quinolones have not yet been approved for use in young children.

Under ideal circumstances, a specimen should be obtained (or in the case of failure of therapy, would already have been obtained) from the middle ear, and culturing can help determine the causative organism. If therapy to cover these broader possibilities fails, a drainage problem is likely to be present, and repeat tympanocentesis may be therapeutic, as well as diagnostic. In some communities, this procedure is regarded as essential to correctly diagnose and treat otitis media. In the United States, tympanocentesis is rarely done; perhaps there will be greater need for this procedure in an era of pneumococcal resistance.

Sinusitis

Because the pathogenesis and causative organisms of acute sinusitis are essentially identical to those of otitis media, the same therapeutic considerations apply. Once again, the essential problem of empirical therapy, which is the usual situation in otitis or sinusitis, is twofold: first the physician does not know whether *S. pneumoniae* is present and, second, if it is present, whether it is susceptible or resistant to the selected therapy. Unlike children, for whom quinolones have not been approved, adults can be treated for acute sinusitis with this class of drugs.

Pneumonia

Outpatient Therapy. This section will generally be confined to the selection of therapy for pneumonia caused by *S. pneumoniae* because the broader question of treatment of pneumonia is covered in Chapter 57. Some redundancy is, however, necessary. The Pneumonia Outcomes Research Team[158] showed that (1) in most patients who are treated as outpatients, no attempt is made to establish an etiologic diagnosis; (2) when such attempts are made, *S. pneumoniae* is the predominant agent and accounts for more than half of cases in which a bacterium is cultured and more than one third in which a diagnosis is made (or suspected) by bacteriologic or serologic means; (3) when patients are stratified by risk groups,[159] the mortality reported (without regard to etiology) is negligible in most nonhospitalized patients; and (4) most importantly, although analyzed without regard to etiologic agent, the response appeared to be excellent and was observed irrespective of the therapy chosen. Specifically, treatment with quinolones, macrolides, penicillins or penicillins with β-lactamase inhibitors, trimethoprim-sulfamethoxazole, or doxycycline all seemed to be equally effective. Nevertheless, the study design would not have recognized an association between inappropriate therapy and failure to respond. We have observed individual patients in whom empirical therapy for pneumonia failed and led to hospitalization for serious pneumococcal pneumonia; the uniform theme in these cases has been that an advanced macrolide, doxycycline, or trimethoprim-sulfamethoxazole was given and that a pneumococcus resistant to that antibiotic was responsible. Resistance to trimethoprim-sulfamethoxazole or doxycycline is not overcome by higher doses (see the earlier discussion of erythromycin). We have not observed a similar situation in which a penicillin or cephalosporin was implicated, perhaps because in the usual doses administered to relatively normal hosts, effective levels are achieved in the long term; these agents are not, however, as commonly prescribed for outpatient pneumonia. At present, the use of a quinolone would bypass the resistance problem.

Inpatient Therapy. The importance of the decision to hospitalize or even to directly admit to intensive care cannot be overemphasized (see Chapter 57). Published criteria[127, 160] should be used as guidelines. A decision to hospitalize is not a commitment to long-term hospitalization[127]; in other words, if in doubt, hospitalize, at least for the initiation of therapy. The remainder of this section deals with selection of an antibiotic to treat pneumococcal pneumonia.

The emergence of antibiotic resistance in pneumococci has made the treatment of pneumococcal pneumonia much more difficult than could ever have been imagined 2 decades ago when *S. pneumoniae* was susceptible to nearly all commonly used antibiotics and only the fear of an allergic reaction motivated consideration of another agent. Pneumococcal pneumonia caused by organisms that are susceptible or intermediately resistant to penicillin responds to treatment with penicillin, 1 million units intravenously every 4 hours, or ceftriaxone, 1 g every 24 hours. The principal concern is whether pneumonia caused by resistant organisms responds to such therapy. Retrospective studies[161, 162] have found a similar outcome in patients who were treated with a penicillin or a cephalosporin for pneumococcal pneumonia, without regard to whether the infection was caused by a susceptible or nonsusceptible organism. The number of subjects infected with resistant pneumococci was, however, very small, and no conclusion could be reached. A Centers for Disease Control and Prevention study (Dan Feikin and colleagues, unpublished as of July 1999) found mortality in treated pneumococcal pneumonia to be increased threefold when caused by penicillin-resistant and sevenfold when caused by ceftriaxone-resistant pneumococci, even after adjustment for severity of the underlying illness and previous hospitalization, both of which increase the likelihood that resistant pneumococci will be present. Other studies are in progress. It seems unlikely that we will ultimately be able to count on penicillin or ceftriaxone to cure infection caused by *S. pneumoniae* strains that require 4 to 16 μg/ml or 2 to 8 μg/ml of these drugs, respectively, to inhibit growth.

In summary, at present, levels of cefotaxime or ceftriaxone achievable in the interstitium and alveoli of the lungs suffice to treat pneumonia caused by *S. pneumoniae* strains that are susceptible or intermediately resistant to these drugs and most cases caused by resistant pneumococci. Accordingly, most authorities treat pneumococcal pneumonia, even in critically ill patients, with cefotaxime, 1 g every 6 hours, or ceftriaxone, 1 g every 12 to 24 hours. Many patients have received 2 g ampicillin (together with 1 g sulbactam) every 6 hours or an equivalent therapy for pneumonia caused by *S. pneumoniae* with seemingly good response. Although vancomycin is most likely to provide antibiotic coverage, the impetus to not use this drug is strong because of the fear of emergence of resistant organisms. Some experts favor a quinolone because of more uniform in vitro effectiveness against pneumococci. Vancomycin or a quinolone should be considered for initial treatment of pneumococcal pneumonia in patients who are allergic to β-lactam antibiotics.

Patients who are treated effectively for pneumococcal pneumonia generally have a substantial reduction in fever and feel better within 48 hours. Based on all these considerations, if a patient has responded to treatment with a β-lactam antibiotic, this therapy should probably be continued even if the antibiotic-susceptibility test shows that the causative organism is resistant. If, however, a clear response is not observed and the organism is resistant, therapy should be changed in accordance with susceptibility testing results.

The optimal duration of therapy for pneumococcal pneumonia is uncertain. Pneumococci disappear from sputum within several hours of the first dose of penicillin. A small-scale study in the 1950s showed that a single dose of procaine penicillin, which maintains an effective antimicrobial level for as long as 24 hours, could cure otherwise healthy young adults of pneumococcal pneumonia. Experience obtained early in the antibiotic era showed that 5 to 7 days of therapy sufficed. In the absence of data to prove the benefits of one or another approach, most physicians now treat pneumonia for 10 to 14 days. The inclination to prolong therapy is a two-edged sword because of the risk of emergence of antibiotic-resistant organisms. Three to 5 days of close observation with parenteral therapy for pneumococcal pneumonia and a final few days of oral treatment, in all not exceeding 5 days after the patient has become afebrile (temperature <99°F), may be the best approach. Failure of the patient to defervesce within 2 to 3 days should stimulate a review of the organism's antibiotic susceptibility, as well as a search for a loculated infection such as empyema or perivalvular cardiac abscess.

Meningitis

Pneumococcal meningitis used to be treated with 12 to 24 million units of penicillin every 24 hours or 1 to 2 g ceftriaxone every 12 hours. Either regimen is effective against antibiotic-susceptible *S. pneumoniae* and may be effective against intermediately resistant ones. Penicillin is ineffective against resistant organisms because levels in CSF, even when inflammation is present, are likely to reach only 2 to 10% of serum levels. Accordingly, for the initial treatment of pneumococcal meningitis, vancomycin is given along with a β-lactam antibiotic, the vancomycin because of its more certain antimicrobial efficacy and the β-lactam because it crosses the blood-brain barrier more reliably and the organism may be susceptible.

Some anecdotal reports have claimed a better outcome when rifampin is added to a β-lactam antibiotic in the treatment of pneumococcal meningitis. In experimental animals, the addition of rifampin to ceftriaxone[163] or vancomycin[164] has not produced synergy except in the presence of concomitant glucocorticosteroid administration, which may diminish central nervous system penetration of the antibiotics.[164] A systematic study in vitro has shown indifference or antagonism when rifampin is added to β-lactam drugs.[165] Even though it is still uncertain whether steroids diminish the penetration of vancomycin or third-generation cephalosporins into the central nervous system in humans,[166] some authorities[112] recommend that rifampin be added when steroids are given together with a third-generation cephalosporin. In our view, the data available do not justify the routine addition of rifampin or steroids, although certainly in individual cases such additions may be appropriate when conventional treatment fails. When treating pneumococcal meningitis caused by organisms with reduced susceptibility, repeat spinal taps may be indicated to document abatement of CSF abnormalities.

Miscellaneous

Pneumococcal endocarditis is associated with rapid destruction of heart valves. Initial therapy should probably be with vancomycin and ceftriaxone until the results of minimal bactericidal concentration testing are known. An aminoglycoside may inhibit the bactericidal activity of β-lactam antibiotics[167] and should not be added unless synergy in vitro is documented to occur.

PREVENTION

The subject of vaccination to protect against pneumococcal infection has been reviewed extensively in recent years.[22] As of July 1999, the only pneumococcal vaccine approved for use in the United States contains 25 μg of capsular polysaccharides from each of 23 common infecting serotypes of *S. pneumoniae*. The two formulations, Pneumovax (Merck) and Pnu-Imune (Lederle), are assumed to be equivalent although they have not been compared in published studies.

Antibody Levels Postvaccination

After vaccination, healthy young adults respond with antibody to an average of about three quarters of the antigens.[67] IgG and IgM become detectable within 5 to 7 days after vaccination; in persons with prior exposure, increases in antibody appear according to the same kinetics that would be seen with initial exposure.[70] Although the concept is prevalent that IgM antibody appears first and then production switches to IgG, both classes of antibody appear at the same time in the blood stream, as well as in lymphocytic cultures in vitro.[70, 168] IgG levels then rise to a peak in 4 to 12 weeks, after which they subside gradually and variably over several years; to date, no study has been reported that has used ELISA with adsorption in a sufficient number of subjects to compare results in healthy and ill or aged persons. Protection is thought to persist only as long as antibody is detectable, but it is not known what level of antibody can be used to determine a threshold for immunity.

Genetic factors govern the capacity to make antibody to capsular polysaccharides, and the inheritance is autosomal and dominant.[67] After vaccination, some individuals have high levels of IgG to all capsular polysaccharides, whereas others may fail to respond to most polysaccharides and the IgG levels to the polysaccharide antigens to which they do respond may be very low. Repeated vaccination does not elicit antibody in nonresponders, although IgG to some of the antigens may appear in some subjects after administration of a protein-conjugated vaccine (see later), depending on the protein or the nature of the conjugation.[169] Women may exhibit lower antibody levels than men to some polysaccharides.[170]

A number of disease states suppress responses to vaccine. Antibody responses may be somewhat lower in elderly subjects who have chronic lung or heart disease.[65, 69] Persons who have immunosuppressive conditions that place them at highest risk of pneumococcal infection, such as multiple myeloma, Hodgkin's disease, splenectomy, lymphoma, nephrotic syndrome, renal failure, cirrhosis, sickle cell disease, bone marrow transplantation, and HIV infection,[88, 171] have diminished capacity to make IgG to polysaccharide antigens. Persons with acquired immunodeficiency syndrome may lose responsiveness to some antigens while retaining relatively normal responses to others.[88] Unlike proteins, polysaccharides do not stimulate long-lived lymphocyte lines that respond to a rechallenge with earlier and more vigorous antibody responses. Revaccination years after an initial vaccine leads to antibody levels that are often very close to the original peak, without any anamnestic response.

Protection Postvaccination

Field trials in the first 2 decades of the 20th century showed that vaccination of South African miners with whole, killed organisms was protective.[1] Vaccine efficacy with relatively purified preparations of capsular polysaccharide was also demonstrated in civilians and in members of the armed forces in the 1930s and 1940s[4, 172, 173]; the reduction in pneumococcal disease was thought to be about 60% in these studies. In subgroups in the population who are thought to be at greatest risk of pneumococcal infection, such as elderly persons with underlying diseases, some trials have shown similar efficacy.[174, 175] Others have failed to find a protective effect.[176–178] For example, in a blinded, prospective study carried out under the auspices of the Veterans Administration,[178] 2354 subjects who were at least 55 years old and had one or more underlying diseases for which vaccine is routinely recommended (principally chronic obstructive lung disease, alcoholism, chronic renal insufficiency, and congestive heart failure) were randomized to receive 14-valent pneumococcal vaccine or placebo. During nearly 3 years of follow-up, no difference in the frequency of pneumococcal pneumonia or bronchitis was noted in the two groups. More recently,[179] a placebo-controlled study of pneumococcal vaccine in persons who were discharged from the hospital (a particularly high-risk group) showed a fivefold increase in pneumococcal bacteremia but no difference in what was called pneumococcal pneumonia based on not-well-established serologic techniques.

Two other methods of investigation have been used to show the efficacy of pneumococcal vaccine. Use of an indirect cohort method showed that when organisms causing invasive pneumococcal disease were serotyped, previously vaccinated persons had a significantly lower incidence of infection by vaccine versus nonvaccine serotypes than did controls.[180] Several case-control studies have also shown efficacy.[181–183] In all these studies the efficacy of vaccine was about 60 to 70%, the same efficacy that had been recorded in prospective field trials. In one trial (Table 188–6) the protective effect of pneumococcal vaccine was shown to decline slowly with time; it persisted beyond 5 years in healthy young adults but not in the elderly.[182]

Antibody Efficiency

Recent laboratory investigations have helped explain why vaccine efficacy might be reduced in those who are in greatest need of it. First, although postvaccination IgG levels are similar in very healthy elderly and younger adults, antibody levels in the elderly population at large may be lower. Second, the capacity of IgG to opsonize pneumococci for phagocytosis and to protect experimental animals against pneumococcal challenge is diminished in ill and elderly persons.[184, 185] Thus, antibody levels may be lower or antibody may have lesser capacity to protect those who are in greatest need of vaccine.

Vaccine Recommendations

With data demonstrating its safety, low cost, and efficacy, failure to use pneumococcal vaccine more widely can be regarded as a missed opportunity in public health policy.[186] The Immunization Practices Advisory Committee of the Centers for Disease Control and Prevention[187] recommends pneumococcal vaccine for adults who fall into one of several classifications. In the first category are those who are generally regarded as immunocompetent but who have an increased likelihood of acquiring pneumococcal infection or of having a serious complication of such infection. This category includes, but is not limited to, persons who have chronic pulmonary disease, advanced cardiovascular disease, diabetes mellitus, alcoholism, cirrhosis, chronic renal insufficiency, or CSF leak, as well as all those older than 65 years. In a second category are persons who have an immunocompromised state that is associated with an increased risk of pneumococcal disease or its complications. This category includes any person with splenic dysfunction (especially sickle cell disease) or asplenia, multiple myeloma, lymphoma, Hodgkin's disease, HIV infection, or organ transplantation. Once again, this list should be regarded as exemplary rather than all-inclusive. In addition, pneumococcal vaccine should be considered for ethnic or racial groups that appear to have a particularly high incidence of pneumococcal infection (e.g., certain Native American populations), as well as for persons who are brought together in crowded living conditions such as military recruits and persons in prisons or nursing homes.

With increasing emergence of penicillin-resistant pneumococci, it seems reasonable to give further consideration to liberalizing conditions under which the vaccine is administered. For example, adults older than 60 years could be vaccinated and then revaccinated every 5 to 7 years. Adults older than 75 years could be revaccinated every 3 to 4 years. Persons whose lifestyle places them at risk of acquiring HIV infection could be vaccinated whenever they first have contact with the health care system. If penicillin-resistant pneumococci continue to increase in prevalence, routine immunization of children older than 2 years should also be considered. Such immunization is already recommended for children who have chronic illnesses that predispose to pneumococcal infection.

Protein Conjugate Vaccines

This subject is reviewed in depth elsewhere.[188, 189] Pneumococcal capsular polysaccharides have been covalently conjugated to carrier proteins such as tetanus or diphtheria toxoid, a genetically engineered protein that closely resembles diphtheria toxoid (CRM 197), outer-membrane proteins of *Neisseria meningitidis*, pneumolysin toxoid, and pneumococcal surface protein A. The resulting antigens are recognized as T cell dependent and induce immunologic memory. A series of three injections into infants and young children stimulates reasonably good antibody levels before the age of 18 months. In adults, conjugate vaccine can induce a response in persons who do not make antibody to nonconjugated polysaccharide[169] and may possibly stimulate higher mean levels of IgG in persons who respond normally or in immunocompromised persons. Evidence supporting this last point is not at all clear; two studies[190, 191] have shown no difference in IgG levels after nonconjugated versus conjugated vaccine in older adults, but another study[192] has suggested that if an initial dose of conjugate vaccine is given, a second dose of nonconjugated vaccine stimulates a better response in patients with Hodgkin's disease. At present, conjugate vaccine is not recommended for adults.

TABLE 188–6 Case-Control Study: Protection by Pneumococcal Vaccine*

Age (yr)	Pairs of Subjects	Years since Vaccination <3	3–5	>5
<55	125	93	89	85
55–64	149	88	82	75
65–74	213	80	71	58
75–84	188	67	53	32
≥85	133	46	33	0

*Results of a case-control study[182] that estimated the efficacy of pneumococcal vaccination by matching infected patients with uninfected controls (pairs of subjects) and examining the incidence of prior vaccination in each group. Data are shown as a percentage indicating efficacy as estimated percent protection.

Other Preventive Measures

Prophylactic use of oral penicillin has reduced the likelihood of serious pneumococcal infection in children with sickle cell disease, and this approach has been recommended,[81] but it seems unlikely that such prophylaxis will continue to be of benefit because of the impact of penicillin resistance.

Regular infusion of normal human globulin protects against pneumococcal infection, as has been shown in the case of children with HIV infection[193] and adults with lymphoma.[194] Such patients are unlikely to produce antibody to pneumococcal vaccine. Whether globulin should in fact be infused each month becomes a societal issue because of the high cost. Possible advantages of vaccination with protein constituents of *S. pneumoniae* were discussed in an earlier part of this chapter.

REFERENCES

1. Heffron R. Pneumonia: With Special Reference to Pneumococcus Lobar Pneumonia. A Commonwealth Fund Book. Copyright 1939. The Commonwealth Fund. Reprinted by Harvard University Press: Cambridge; 1979.
2. White B. The Biology of Pneumococcus. The Bacteriologic, Biochemical and Immunological Characters and Activities of *Diplococcus pneumoniae*. Copyright 1938. A Commonwealth Fund Book. Reprinted by Harvard University Press: Cambridge; 1979.
3. Watson DA, Musher DM, Jacobson JW. A brief history of the pneumococcus in biomedical research: A panoply of discovery. Clin Infect Dis. 1993;17:913–924.
4. Musher DM, Watson DA, Dominguez E. Pneumococcal vaccination: Work to date and future prospects. Am J Med Sci. 1990;300:45–52.
5. Heidelberger M, Avery OT. The soluble specific substance of pneumococcus. J Exp Med. 1923;38:73.
6. Felton LD. Studies on the immunizing substances in pneumococci. J Immunol. 1934;27:379–393.
7. Smillie WG, Wornock GH, White HJ. A study of a type I pneumococcus epidemic at the State Hospital at Worcester, Mass. Am J Public Health. 1938;28:293–302.
8. MacLeod CM, Hodges RG, Heidelberger M, Bernhard WG. Prevention of pneumococcal pneumonia by immunization with specific capsular polysaccharides. J Exp Med. 1945;82:445–465.
9. Griffith F. The significance of pneumococcal types. J Hyg. 1928;27:113–159.
10. Avery OT, MacLeod CM, McCarty M. Studies on the chemical nature of the substance inducing transformation of pneumococcal types. J Exp Med. 1944;79:137–157.
11. Munoz R, Fenoll A, Vicioso D, Casal J. Optochin resistant variants of *Streptococcus pneumoniae*. Diagn Microbiol Infect Dis. 1999;13:63–66.
12. Ertugrul N, Rodriguez-Barradas MC, Musher DM, et al. BOX-polymerase chain reaction–based DNA analysis of nonserotypeable *Streptococcus pneumoniae* implicated in outbreaks of conjunctivitis. J Infect Dis. 1997;176:1401–1405.
13. van Dam JEG, Fleer A, Snippe H. Immunogenicity and immunochemistry of *Streptococcus pneumoniae* capsular polysaccharides. Antonie van Leeuwenhoek. 1990;58:1–47.
14. Morona JK, Morona R, Paton JC. Molecular and genetic characterization of the capsule biosynthesis locus of *Streptococcus pneumoniae* type 19B. J Bacteriol. 1997;179:4953–4958.
15. Guildolin A, Morona JK, Morona R, et al. Nucleotide sequence analysis of genes essential for capsular polysaccharide biosynthesis in *Streptococcus pneumoniae* type 19F. Infect Immun. 1994;62:5384–5396.
16. Watson DA, Kapur V, Musher DM, et al. Identification, cloning, and sequencing of DNA essential for encapsulation of *Streptococcus pneumoniae*. Curr Microbiol. 1995;31:251–259.
17. Dillard JP, Caimano M, Kelly T, Yother J. Capsules and cassettes: Genetic organization of the capsule locus of *Streptococcus pneumoniae*. Dev Biol Stand. 1995;85:261–265.
18. Nesin M, Ramirez M, Tomasz A. Capsular transformation of a multidrug-resistant *Streptococcus pneumoniae* in vivo. J Infect Dis. 1998;177:707–713.
19. Sorensen UB. Pneumococcal polysaccharide antigens: Capsules and C-polysaccharide. An immunochemical study. Dan Med Bull, 1995;42:47–53.
20. Gray BM, Dillon HC Jr. Epidemiological studies of *Streptococcus pneumoniae* in infants: Antibody to types 3, 6, 14, and 23 in the first two years of life. J Infect Dis. 1988;158:948–955.
21. Ekdahl K, Ahlinder I, Hansson H, et al. Duration of nasopharyngeal carriage of penicillin-resistance *Streptococcus pneumoniae*: Experiences from the South Swedish pneumococcal intervention project. Clin Infect Dis. 1997;25:1113–1117.
22. Fedson DS, Musher DM, Eskola J. Pneumococcal vaccine. In: Plotkin SA, Orenstein WA, eds. Vaccines. 3rd ed. Philadelphia: WB Saunders; 1998.
23. Davidson M, Parkinson AJ, Bulkow LR, et al. The epidemiology of invasive pneumococcal disease in Alaska, 1986–1990—ethnic differences and opportunities for prevention. J Infect Dis. 1994;170:368–376.
24. Torzillo P, Hanna J, Morey F, et al. Invasive pneumococcal disease in central Australia. Med J Aust. 1995;162:182–186.
25. Burman LA, Norrby R, Trollfors B. Invasive pneumococcal infections: Incidence, predisposing factors, and prognosis. Rev Infect Dis. 1985;7:133–142.
26. Breiman RF, Spika JS, Navarro VJ, et al. Pneumococcal bacteremia in Charleston County, South Carolina: A decade later. Arch Intern Med. 1990;150:1401–1405.
27. Baer M, Vuento R, Vesikari T. Increase in bacteraemic pneumococcal infections in children. Lancet. 1995;345:661.
28. Gray BM, Converse GM III, Dillon HC Jr. Epidemiologic studies of *Streptococcus pneumoniae* in infants: Acquisition, carriage, and infection during the first 24 months of life. J Infect Dis. 1980;142:923–933.
29. Frenck RW Jr, Glezen WP. Respiratory tract infections in children in day care. Semin Pediatr Infect Dis. 1990;1:234–244.
30. Kim P, Musher DM, Glezen WP, et al. Association of invasive pneumococcal disease with season, atmospheric conditions, air pollution, and the isolation of respiratory viruses. Clin Infect Dis. 1996;22:100–106.
31. Henderson FW, Gilligan PH, Wait K, Goff DA. Nasopharyngeal carriage of antibiotic-resistant pneumococci by children in group day care. J Infect Dis. 1988;157:256–263.
32. Rauch AM, O'Ryan M, Van R, Pickering LK. Invasive disease due to multiply resistant *Streptococcus pneumoniae* in a Houston, Texas day care center. Am J Dis Child. 1990;144:923–927.
33. Doyle MG, Morrow AL, Van R, Pickering LK. Intermediate resistance of *Streptococcus pneumoniae* to penicillin in children in day-care centers [published erratum appears in Pediatr Infect Dis J. 1993 Jan;12(1):32]. Pediatr Infect Dis J. 1992;11:831–835.
34. Hodges RG, MacLeod CM. Epidemic pneumococcal pneumonia. Description of the epidemic. Am J Hyg. 1946;44:183–192.
35. Hoge CW, Reichler MR, Dominguez EA, et al. An epidemic of pneumococcal disease in an overcrowded, inadequately ventilated jail. New Engl J Med. 1994;331:643–648.
36. Mercat A, Nguyen J, Dautzenberg B. An outbreak of pneumococcal pneumonia in two men's shelters. Chest. 1991;99:147–151.
37. Nuorti JP, Butler JC, Crutcher JM, et al. An outbreak of multidrug-resistant pneumococcal pneumonia and bacteremia among unvaccinated nursing home residents. N Engl J Med. 1998;338:1861–1868.
38. Watson DA, Musher DM, Verhoef J. Pneumococcal virulence factors and host immune responses to them. Eur J Clin Microbiol Infect Dis. 1995;14:479–490.
39. Cundell DR, Pearce BJ, Sandros J, et al. Peptide permeases from *Streptococcus pneumoniae* affect adherence to eucaryotic cells. Infect Immun. 1995;63:2493–2498.
40. Krivan HC, Roberts DD, Ginsberg V. Many pulmonary pathogenic bacteria bind specifically to the carbohydrate sequence GalNAc B1-4-Gal found in some glycolipids. Proc Natl Acad Sci U S A. 1988;85:6157–6161.
41. Sundberg-Kovamees M, Holme T, Sjorgren A. Interaction of the C-polysaccharide of *Streptococcus pneumoniae* with the receptor asialo-GM_1. Microb Pathog. 1996;21:223–234.
42. Weiser JN, Markiewicz Z, Tuomanen E, Wani JH. Relationship between phase variation in colony morphology, intrastrain variation in cell wall physiology, and nasopharyngeal colonization by *Streptococcus pneumoniae*. Infect Immun. 1996;64:2240–2245.
43. Cundell DR, Gerard NP, Gerard C, et al. *Streptococcus pneumoniae* anchor to activated human cells by the receptor for platelet-activating factor. Nature. 1995;377:435–438.
44. Angel CS, Ruzek M, Hostetter MK. Degradation of C3 by *Streptococcus pneumoniae*. J Infect Dis. 1994;170:600–608.
45. Watson DA, Musher DM. Interruption of capsule expression in *Streptococcus pneumoniae* serotype 3 by insertion of transposon Tn916. Infect Immun. 1990;58:3135–3138.
46. Musher DM, Johnson B Jr, Watson DA. Quantitative relationship between anticapsular antibody measured by enzyme-linked immunosorbent assay or radioimmunoassay and protection of mice against challenge with *Streptococcus pneumoniae* serotype 4. Infect Immun. 1990;58:3871–3876.
47. Winkelstein JA, Tomasz A. Activation of the alternative complement pathway by pneumococcal cell wall teichoic acid. J Immunol. 1978;120:174–178.
48. Tuomanen E, Liu H, Hengstler B, et al. The induction of meningeal inflammation by components of the pneumococcal cell wall. J Infect Dis. 1985;151:859–868.
49. Wolbink GJ, Bossink AWJ, Groeneveld ABJ, et al. Complement activation in patients with sepsis is in part mediated by C-reactive protein. J Infect Dis. 1998;177:81–87.
50. Winkelstein JA, Bocchini JA Jr, Schiffman G. The role of the capsular polysaccharide in the activation of the alternative pathway by the pneumococcus. J Immunol. 1976;116:367–370.
51. Rodriguez-Barradas MC, Das TS, Watson DA, Musher DM. Relative contribution of cell wall and capsular polysaccharides in activating alternative and classical complement pathways by *Streptococcus pneumoniae*. Med Microbiol Lett. 1993;2:427–435.
52. Boulnois GJ. Pneumococcal proteins and the pathogenesis of disease caused by *Streptococcus pneumoniae*. J Gen Microbiol. 1992;138:249–259.
53. Paton JC, Berry AM, Lock R. Molecular analysis of putative pneumococcal virulence proteins. Microb Drug Resist. 1997;3:1–10.
54. Rubins JB, Charboneau D, Paton JC, et al. Dual function of pneumolysin in the early pathogenesis of murine pneumococcal pneumonia. J Clin Invest. 1995;95:142–150.
55. Rubins JB, Janoff EN. Pneumolysin: A multifunctional pneumococcal virulence factor. J Lab Clin Med. 1998;131:21–27.
56. Feldman C, Munro NC, Jeffery PK, et al. Pneumolysin induces the salient histologic features of pneumococcal infection in the rat lung in vitro. Am J Respir Cell Mol Biol. 1991;5:416–423.
57. Alexander JE, Lock R, Peeters CC, et al. Immunization of mice with pneumolysin toxoid confers a significant degree of protection against at least nine serotypes of *Streptococcus pneumoniae*. Infect Immun. 1994;62:5683–5688.

58. Berry AN, Paton JC, Hansman D. Effect of insertional inactivation of the genes encoding pneumolysin and autolysin on the virulence of *Streptococcus pneumoniae* type 3. Microb Pathog. 1992;12:87–93.
59. Berry AM, Alexander JE, Mitchell TJ, et al. Effect of defined point mutations in the pneumolysin gene on the virulence of *Streptococcus pneumoniae*. Infect Immun. 1995;63:1969–1974.
60. Cundell DR, Gerard NP, Gerard C, et al. *Streptococcus pneumoniae* anchor to activated human cells by the receptor for platelet-activating factor. Nature. 1995;377:435–438.
61. McDaniel LS, Sheffield JS, Delucchi P, Briles DE. PspA, a surface protein of *Streptococcus pneumoniae*, is capable of eliciting protection against pneumococci of more than one serotype. Infect Immun. 1991;59:222–228.
62. McDaniel LS, Yother J, Vijayakumar M, et al. Use of insertional activation to facilitate studies of biological properties of pneumococcal surface protein A (PspA). J Exp Med. 1987;165:381–394.
63. Berry AM, Lock RA, Hansman D, Paton JC. Contribution of autolysin to virulence of *Streptococcus pneumoniae.* Infect Immun. 1989;57:2324–2330.
64. Lock R, Hansman D, Paton JC. Comparative efficacy of autolysin and pneumolysin as immunogens protecting mice against infection by *Streptococcus pneumoniae*. Microb Pathog. 1992;12:137–143.
65. Musher DM, Chapman AJ, Goree A, et al. Natural and vaccine-related immunity to *Streptococcus pneumoniae.* J Infect Dis. 1986;154:245–256.
66. Romero-Steiner S, Libutti D, Pais LB, et al. Standardization of an opsonophagocytic assay for the management of functional antibody activity against *Streptococcus pneumoniae* using differentiated HL-60 cells. Clin Diagn Lab Immunol. 1997;4:415–422.
67. Musher DM, Groover JE, Watson DA, et al. Genetic regulation of the capacity to make immunoglobulin G to pneumococcal capsular polysaccharides. J Invest Med. 1997;45:57–68.
68. Siber GR, Priehs C, Madore DV. Standardization of antibody assays for measuring the response to pneumococcal infection and immunization. Pediatr Infect Dis J. 1989;8(Suppl):S84–S91.
69. Musher DM, Luchi M, Watson DA, et al. Pneumococcal polysaccharide vaccine in young adults and older bronchitics: Determination of IgG responses by ELISA and the effect of adsorption of serum with nontype-specific cell wall polysaccharide. J Infect Dis. 1990;161:728–735.
70. Musher DM, Groover JE, Rowland JM, et al. Antibody to capsular polysaccharides of *Streptococcus pneumoniae*: Prevalence, persistence, and response to revaccination. Clin Infect Dis. 1993;17:66–73.
71. Finland M, Winkler AW. Antibody response to infections with type II and with the related type VIII pneumococcus. J Clin Invest. 1934;13:97–107.
72. Finland M, Shuman HI. The type-specific agglutinin response of infants and children with pneumococcal pneumonias. J Immunol. 1942;45:215–223.
73. Sloyer JL Jr, Howie VM, Ploussard JH, et al. Immune response to acute otitis media in children. I. Serotypes isolated and serum and middle ear fluid antibody in pneumococcal otitis media. Infect Immun. 1974;9:1028–1032.
74. Prober CG, Frayha H, Klein M, Schiffman G. Immunologic responses of children to serious infections with *Streptococcus pneumoniae*. J Infect Dis. 1983;148:427–435.
75. Sanders LAM, Rijkers GT, Kuis W, et al. Defective antipneumococcal polysaccharide antibody response in children with recurrent respiratory tract infections. J Allergy Clin Immunol. 1993;91:110–119.
76. Finland M, Tilghman RC. Bacteriological and immunological studies in families with pneumococci infections: The development of type-specific antibodies in healthy contact carriers. J Clin Invest. 1936;15:501–508.
77. Wara DW. Host defense against *Streptococcus pneumoniae*: The role of the spleen. Rev Infect Dis. 1981;3:299–309.
78. Styrt B. Infection associated with asplenia: Risks, mechanisms, and prevention. Am J Med. 1990;88:33N–42N.
79. Jandl JH, Jones AR, Castle WB. The destruction of red cells by antibodies in man. I. Observations on the sequestration and lysis of red cells altered by immune mechanisms. J Clin Invest. 1957;36:1428–1459.
80. Frank MM, Hosea SW, Brown EJ, Hamburger MI. Opsonic requirements for intravascular clearance after splenectomy. N Engl J Med. 1981;304:245–250.
81. Wong WY, Overturf GD, Powars DR. Infection caused by *Streptococcus pneumoniae* in children with sickle cell disease: Epidemiology, immunologic mechanisms, prophylaxis, and vaccination. Clin Infect Dis. 1992;14:1124–1136.
82. Cunningham-Rundles C. Clinical and immunologic analyses of 103 patients with common variable immunodeficiency. J Clin Immunol. 1989;9:22–33.
83. Umetsu DT, Ambrosino DM, Quinti I, et al. Recurrent sinopulmonary infection and impaired antibody response to bacterial capsular polysaccharide antigen in children with selective IgG subclass deficiency. N Engl J Med. 1985;313:1247–1251.
83a. Yee AMF, Phan HM, Zuniga R, et al. The FcγRIIa-R131 allotype increases risk for bacteremic pneumococcal infection. Clin Infect Dis. 1999;29.
84. Savage DG, Lindenbaum J, Garrett TJ. Biphasic pattern of bacterial infection in multiple myeloma. Ann Intern Med. 1982;96:47–50.
85. Fang GD, Fine M, Orloff J, et al. New and emerging etiologies for community-acquired pneumonia with implications for therapy: A prospective multicenter study of 359 cases. Medicine (Baltimore). 1990;69:307–316.
86. Rahav G, Toledano Y, Engelhard D, et al. Invasive pneumococcal infections: A comparison between adults and children. Medicine (Baltimore). 1997;76:295–303.
87. Watanakunakorn C, Bailey TA. Adult bacteremic pneumococcal pneumonia in a community teaching hospital, 1992–1996. A detailed analysis of 108 cases. Arch Intern Med. 1997;157:1965–1971.
88. Rodriguez-Barradas MC, Musher DM, Lahart C, et al. Antibody to capsular polysaccharides of *Streptococcus pneumoniae* after vaccination of human immunodeficiency virus–infected subjects with 23-valent pneumococcal vaccine. J Infect Dis. 1992;165:553–556.
89. Janoff EN, O'Brien J, Thompson P, et al. *Streptococcus pneumoniae* colonization, bacteremia, and immune response among persons with human immunodeficiency virus infection. J Infect Dis. 1993;167:49–56.
90. Musher D, Goree A, Murphy T, et al. Immunity to *Haemophilus influenzae* type b in young adults: Correlation of bactericidal and opsonizing activity of serum with antibody to ribose ribitol phosphate and lipooligosaccharide, before and after vaccination. J Infect Dis. 1986;154:935–943.
91. Redd SC, Rutherford GW III, Sande MA et al. The role of human immunodeficiency virus infection in pneumococcal bacteremia in San Francisco residents. J Infect Dis. 1990;162:1012–1017.
92. Rodriguez MC, Musher DM, Hamill RJ, et al. Unusual manifestations of pneumococcal infection in HIV-infected individuals: The past revisited. Clin Infect Dis. 1992;14:192–199.
93. Schuchat A, Broome CV, Hightower A, et al. Use of surveillance for invasive pneumococcal disease to estimate the size of the immunosuppressed HIV-infected population. JAMA. 1991;265:3275–3279.
94. Figueroa JE, Densen P. Infectious diseases associated with complement deficiencies. Clin Microbiol Rev. 1991;4:359–395.
95. Anderson DC, Schmalstieg FC, Finegold MJ, et al. The severe and moderate phenotypes of heritable Mac-1, LFA-1 deficiency: Their quantitative definition and relation to leukocyte dysfunction and clinical features. J Infect Dis. 1985;152:668–689.
96. Beam TR Jr, Allen JC. Patterns of infection in untreated acute leukemia: Impact of initial hospitalization. South Med J. 1979;72:282–286.
97. Gluckman SJ, Dvorak VC, MacGregor RR. Host defenses during prolonged alcohol consumption in a controlled environment. Arch Intern Med. 1977;137:1539–1543.
98. Young CL, MacGregor RR. Alcohol and host defenses: Infectious consequences. Infect Med. 1989;6:163–175.
99. Mowat AG, Baum J. Chemotaxis of polymorphonuclear leukocytes from patients with diabetes mellitus. N Engl J Med. 1980;142:869–875.
100. Repine JE, Clawson CC, Goetz FC. Bactericidal function of neutrophils from patients with acute bacterial infections and from diabetics. J Infect Dis. 1980;142:869–875.
101. Lipsky BA, Boyko EJ, Inui TS, Koepsell TD. Risk factors for acquiring pneumococcal infections. Arch Intern Med. 1986;146:2179–2185.
102. Chang JL, Mylotte JM. Pneumococcal bacteremia: Updated from an adult hospital with a high rate of nosocomial cases. J Am Geriatr Soc. 1987;35:747–754.
103. Hodges RG, MacLeod CM. Epidemic pneumococcal pneumonia. IV. The relationship of nonbacterial respiratory disease to pneumococcal pneumonia. Am J Hyg. 1946;44:231–243.
104. Jones EE, Alford PL, Reingold AL, et al. Predisposition to invasive pneumococcal illness following parainfluenza type 3 virus infection in chimpanzees. J Am Vet Med Assoc. 1998;185:1351–1353.
105. Fainstein V, Musher DM, Cate TR. Bacterial adherence to pharyngeal cells during viral infection. J Infect Dis. 1980;141:172–176.
106. Raz R, Elhanan G, Shimoni Z, et al. Pneumococcal bacteremia in hospitalized Israeli adults: Epidemiology and resistance to penicillin. Clin Infect Dis. 1997;24:1164–1168.
107. Dowell SF, Butler JC, Giebink GS, et al. Otitis-media—management and surveillance in the era of pneumococcal resistance: A report from the Drug-Resistant *Streptococcus pneumoniae* Therapeutic Working Group. Pediatr Infect Dis J. 1999;18:1–9.
108. Schwartz LE, Brown RB. Purulent otitis media in adults. Arch Intern Med. 1992;152:2301–2304.
109. Faden H, Duffy L, Wasielewski R, et al. Relationship between nasopharyngeal colonization and the development of otitis media in children. J Infect Dis. 1997;175:1440–1445.
110. Gwaltney JMJ, Scheld WM, Sande MA, Sydnor A. The microbial etiology and antimicrobial therapy of adults with acute community-acquired sinusitis: A fifteen-year experience at the University of Virginia and review of other selected studies. J Allergy Clin Immunol. 1992;90:457–462.
111. Gwaltney JMJ, Phillips CD, Miller RD, Riker DK. Computed tomographic study of the common cold. N Engl J Med. 1994;330:25–30.
112. Quagliarello VJ, Scheld WM. Treatment of bacterial meningitis. N Engl J Med. 1997;336:708–716.
112a. Hand WL, Sanford JP. Posttraumatic bacterial meningitis. Ann Intern Med. 1970;72:869–874.
113. Eavey RD, Gao Y, Schuknecht HF, Gonzalez-Pineda M. Otologic features of bacterial meningitis of childhood. J Pediatr. 1985;136:2025–2029.
114. Bhatt SM, Lauretano A, Cabellos C, et al. Progression of hearing loss in experimental pneumococcal meningitis: Correlation with cerebrospinal fluid cytochemistry. J Infect Dis. 1993;167:675–683.
115. Quagliarello V, Scheld WM. Bacterial meningitis: Pathogenesis, pathophysiology, and progress. N Engl J Med. 1992;327:864–872.
116. Dunbar SA, Eason RA, Musher DM, Clarridge JE. Microscopic examination and broth culture of cerebrospinal fluid in the diagnosis of meningitis. J Clin Microbiol. 1998;36:1617–1620.
117. Murphy TF, Fine BC. Bacteremic pneumococcal pneumonia in the elderly. Am J Med Sci. 1984;288:114–118.
117a. Metlay JP, Schulz R, Li Y-H, et al. Influence of age on symptoms at presentation in patients with community-acquired pneumonia. Arch Intern Med. 1997;157:1453–1459.
117b. Metlay JP, Kapoor WN, Fine MJ. Does this patient have community-acquired pneumonia? Diagnosing pneumonia by history and physical examination. JAMA. 1997;278:1440–1445.
118. Ort S, Ryan RL, Barden G, et al. Pneumococcal pneumonia in hospitalized patients. JAMA. 1983;249:214–218.

119. Yangco BG, Deresinski SC. Necrotizing or cavitating pneumonia due to *Streptococcus pneumoniae*: Report of four cases and review of the literature. Medicine (Baltimore). 1980;59:449–457.
120. Light RW, Girard WM, Jenkinson SG, George RB. Parapneumonic effusions. Am J Med. 1980;69:507–512.
121. Hook EW III, Horton CA, Schaberg DR. Failure of intensive care unit support to influence mortality from pneumococcal bacteremia. JAMA. 1983;249:1055–1057.
122. Perlino CA, Rimland D. Alcoholism, leukopenia, and pneumococcal sepsis. Am Rev Respir Dis. 1985;132:757–760.
123. Barrett-Connor E. The nonvalue of sputum culture in the diagnosis of pneumococcal pneumonia. Am Rev Respir Dis. 1971;103:845–848.
124. Perlino CH. Laboratory diagnosis of pneumonia due to *Streptococcus pneumoniae*. J Infect Dis. 1984;150:139–144.
125. Musher DM. Gram stain and culture of sputum to diagnose bacterial pneumonia. J Infect Dis. 1985;152:1096.
125a. Fine MJ, Orloff JJ, Rihs JD, et al. Evaluation of housestaff physicians' preparation and interpretation of sputum gram stains for community-acquired pneumonia. J Gen Intern Med. 1991;6:189–198.
126. Thorsteinsson SB, Musher DM, Fagan T. The diagnostic value of sputum culture in acute pneumonia. JAMA. 1975;233:894–895.
127. Bartlett JG, Breiman RF, Mandell LA, File TM Jr. Community-acquired pneumonia in adults: Guidelines for management. Clin Infect Dis. 1998;26:811–838.
128. Franco M, Musher DM. Thoracic empyema: The impact of management on outcome (Abstract). Am Rev Respir Dis. 1982;124:82.
129. Gorenske MJ, Lebel MH, Nelson JD. Peritonitis in children with nephrotic syndrome. Pediatrics. 1988;81:849–856.
130. Wilcox CM, Dismukes WE. Spontaneous bacterial peritonitis: A review of pathogenesis, diagnosis, and treatment. Medicine (Baltimore). 1987;66:447–456.
131. Shaked Y, Samra Y. Primary pneumococcal peritonitis in patients with cardiac ascites: Report of 2 cases. Cardiology. 1988;75:372–374.
132. Westh H, Skibsted L, Korner B. *Streptococcus pneumoniae* infections of the female genital tract and in the newborn child. Rev Infect Dis. 1990;12:416–422.
133. Robinson EN Jr. Pneumococcal endometritis and neonatal sepsis. Rev Infect Dis. 1990;12:416–422.
134. Rahav G, Ben-David L, Persitz E. Postmenopausal pneumococcal tubo-ovarian abscess. Rev Infect Dis. 1991;13:896–897.
135. Powderly WG, Stanley SL Jr, Medoff G. Pneumococcal endocarditis: Report of a series and review of the literature. Rev Infect Dis. 1986;8:786–791.
136. Case Records of the Massachusetts General Hospital. Weekly clinicopathological exercises. Case 49-1990. A 47-year-old Cape Verdean man with pericardial disease. N Engl J Med. 1990;323:1614–1624.
137. Ryczak M, Sands M, Brown RB, Sklar JH. Pneumococcal arthritis in a prosthetic knee. A case report and review of the literature. Clin Orthop. 1987;224:224–227.
138. Morley PK, Hull RG, Hall MA. Pneumococcal septic arthritis in rheumatoid arthritis. Ann Rheum Dis. 1987;46:482–484.
139. Turner DPJ, Weston VC, Ispahani P. *Streptococcus pneumoniae* spinal infection in Nottingham, United Kingdom: Not a rare event. Clin Infect Dis. 1999;28:873–881.
140. Grigoriadis E, Gold WL. Pyogenic brain abscess caused by *Streptococcus pneumoniae*: Case report and review. Clin Infect Dis. 1997;25:1108–1112.
141. Peters NS, Eykyn SJ, Rudd AG. Pneumococcal cellulitis: A rare manifestation of pneumococcaemia in adults. J Infect. 1989;19:57–59.
142. DiNubile MJ, Albornoz A, Stumacher RJ, et al. Pneumococcal soft-tissue diseases. J Infect Dis. 1991;63:897–900.
143. Appelbaum PC. Antimicrobial resistance in *Streptococcus pneumoniae*: An overview. Clin Infect Dis. 1992;15:77–83.
144. Spika JS, Facklam RR, Plikaytis BD, et al. Antimicrobial resistance of *Streptococcus pneumoniae* in the United States, 1979–1987. J Infect Dis. 1991;163:1273–1278.
145. Doern GV, Pfaller MA, Kugler K, et al. Prevalence of antimicrobial resistance among respiratory tract isolates of *Streptococcus pneumoniae* in North America: 1997 results from the SENTRY antimicrobial surveillance program. Clin Infect Dis. 1998;27:764–770.
146. Dagan R, Abramson O, Leibovitz E, et al. Bacteriologic response to oral cephalosporins: Are established susceptibility breakpoints appropriate in the case of acute otitis media? J Infect Dis. 1997;176:1253–1259.
147. Smith AM, Klugman KP. Alterations in penicillin-binding protein 2B from penicillin-resistant wild-type strains of *Streptococcus pneumoniae*. Antimicrob Agents Chemother. 1995;39:859–867.
148. Smith AM, Klugman KP, Coffey TJ, Spratt BG. Genetic diversity of penicillin-binding protein 2B and 2X genes from *Streptococcus pneumoniae* in South Africa. Antimicrob Agents Chemother. 1993;37:1938–1944.
149. Dowson CG, Coffey TJ, Kell C, Whiley RA. Evolution of penicillin resistance in *Streptococcus pneumoniae*; the role of *Streptococcus mitis* in the formation of a low affinity PBP2B in *S. pneumoniae*. Mol Microbiol. 1993;9:635–643.
150. Versalovic J, Kapur V, Mason EO Jr, et al. Penicillin-resistant *Streptococcus pneumoniae* strains recovered in Houston: Identification and molecular characterization of multiple clones. J Infect Dis. 1993;167:850–856.
151. McDougal LK, Rasheed JK, Biddle JW, Tenover FC. Identification of multiple clones of extended-spectrum cephalosporin-resistant *Streptococcus pneumoniae* isolates in the United States. Antimicrob Agents Chemother. 1995;39:2282–2288.
152. Tomasz A. Antibiotic resistance in *Streptococcus pneumoniae*. Clin Infect Dis. 1997;24(Suppl):S85–S88.
153. Soares S, Kristinsson KG, Musser JM, Tomasz A. Evidence for the introduction of a multiresistant clone of serotype 6B *Streptococcus pneumoniae* from Spain to Iceland in the late 1980s. J Infect Dis. 1993;168:158–163.
154. Munoz R, Musser JM, Crain M, et al. Geographic distribution of penicillin-resistant clones of *Streptococcus pneumoniae*: Characterization by penicillin-binding protein profile, surface protein A typing, and multilocus enzyme analysis. Clin Infect Dis. 1992;15:112–118.
155. Spangler SK, Jacobs MR, Appelbaum PC. Activities of RPR 106972 (a new oral streptogramin), cefditoren (a new oral cephalosporin), two new oxazolidinones (U-100592 and U-100766), and other oral and parenteral agents against 203 penicillin-susceptible and -resistant pneumococci. Antimicrob Agents Chemother. 1996;40:481–484.
156. Fasola E, Spangler SK, Ednie LM, et al. Comparative activities of LY 333328, a new glycopeptide, against penicillin-susceptible and -resistant pneumococci. Antimicrob Agents Chemother. 1996;40:2661–2663.
157. Hendrickse WA, Kusmiesz H, Shelton S, Nelson JD. Five *vs.* ten days of therapy for acute otitis media. Pediatr Infect Dis. 1988;7:14–23.
158. Gleason PP, Kapoor WN, Stone RA, et al. Medical outcomes and antimicrobial costs with the use of the American Thoracic Society guidelines for outpatients with community-acquired pneumonia. JAMA. 1997;278:32–39.
159. Fine MJ, Auble TE, Yealy DM, et al. A prediction rule to identify low-risk patients with community-acquired pneumonia. N Engl J Med. 1997;336:243–250.
160. Niederman MS, Bass JB, Campbell GD. Guidelines for the initial therapy of community-acquired pneumonia: Proceedings of an American Thoracic Society Consensus Conference. Am Rev Respir Dis. 1993;148:1418–1426.
161. Pallares R, Linares J, Vadillo M, et al. Resistance to penicillin and cephalosporin and mortality from severe pneumococcal pneumonia in Barcelona, Spain. N Engl J Med. 1995;333:474–480.
162. Plouffe JF, Breiman RF, Facklam RR. Bacteremia with *Streptococcus pneumoniae*. Implications for therapy and prevention. Franklin County Pneumonia Study Group. JAMA. 1996;275:194–198.
163. Friedland IR, Paris M, Shelton S, McCracken GH. Time-kill studies of antibiotic combinations against penicillin-resistant and -susceptible *Streptococcus pneumoniae*. J Antimicrob Chemother. 1994;34:231–237.
164. Paris MM, Hickey SM, Uscher MI, et al. Effect of dexamethasone on therapy of experimental penicillin- and cephalosporin-resistant pneumococcal meningitis. Antimicrob Agents Chemother. 1994;38:1320–1324.
165. Giron KP, Gross ME, Musher DM, et al. In vitro antimicrobial effect against *Streptococcus pneumoniae* of adding rifampin to penicillin, ceftriaxone or l-ofloxacin. Antimicrob Agents Chemother. 1995;39:2798–2800.
166. Viladrich PF, Gudiol F, Linares J, et al. Evaluation of vancomycin for therapy of adult pneumococcal meningitis. Antimicrob Agents Chemother. 1991;35:2467–2472.
167. Gross ME, Giron KP, Septimus JD, et al. Antimicrobial activities of beta-lactam antibiotics and gentamicin against penicillin-susceptible and penicillin-resistant pneumococci. Antimicrob Agents Chemother. 1995;39:1166–1168.
168. Kehrl JH, Fauci AS. Activation of human B lymphocytes after immunization with pneumococcal polysaccharides. J Clin Invest. 1983;71:1032–1040.
169. Musher DM, Groover JE, Watson DA, et al. IgG responses to protein-conjugated pneumococcal capsular polysaccharides in persons who are genetically incapable of responding to unconjugated polysaccharides. Clin Infect Dis. 1998;27:1487–1490.
170. Sankilampi U, Honkanen PO, Bloigu A, et al. Antibody response to pneumococcal capsular polysaccharide vaccine in the elderly. J Infect Dis. 1996;173:387–393.
171. Janoff EN, Breiman RF, Daley CL, et al. Pneumococcal disease during HIV infection: Epidemiologic, clinical, and immunologic perspectives. Ann Intern Med. 1992;117:314–324.
172. Austrian R, Douglas RM, Schiffman G, et al. Prevention of pneumococcal pneumonia by vaccination. Trans Assoc Am Physicians. 1976;89:184–192.
173. Austrian R. Some observations on the pneumococcus and on the current status of pneumococcal disease and its prevention. Rev Infect Dis. 1981;3(Suppl):S1–S17.
174. Gaillat J, Zmirou D, Mallaret M, et al. Clinical trial of pneumococcal vaccine among institutionalized elderly (French). Rev Epidemiol Sante Publique. 1985;33:437–444.
175. Koivula I, Stén M, Leinonen M, Mäkelä PH. Clinical efficacy of pneumococcal vaccine in the elderly: A randomized, single-blind population-based trial. Am J Med. 1997;103:281–290.
176. Bentley DW. Pneumococcal vaccine in the institutionalized elderly: Review of past and recent studies. Rev Infect Dis. 1981;3(Suppl):S61–S70.
177. Bentley DW, Ha K, Mamot K, et al. Pneumococcal vaccine in the institutionalized elderly: Design of a nonrandomized trial and preliminary results. Rev Infect Dis. 1981;3(Suppl):S71–S81.
178. Simberkoff MS, Cross AP, Al-Ibrahim M, et al. Efficacy of pneumococcal vaccine in high-risk patients. Results of a Veterans Administration Cooperative Study. N Engl J Med. 1986;315:1318–1327.
179. Ortqvist A, Hedlund J, Burman LG, et al. Randomized trial of 23-valent pneumococcal capsular polysaccharide vaccine in prevention of pneumonia in middle-aged and elderly people. Lancet. 1998;351:399–403.
180. Bolan G, Broome CV, Facklam R, et al. Pneumococcal vaccine efficacy in selected populations in the United States. Ann Intern Med. 1986;104:1–6.
181. Sims RV, Steinmann WC, McConville JH, et al. The clinical effectiveness of pneumococcal vaccine in the elderly. Ann Intern Med. 1988;108:653–657.
182. Shapiro ED, Berg AT, Austrian R, et al. The protective efficacy of polyvalent pneumococcal polysaccharide vaccine. N Engl J Med. 1991;325:1453–1460.
183. Farr BM, Johnston BL, Cobb DK, et al. Preventing pneumococcal bacteremia in patients at risk. Results of a matched case-control study. Arch Intern Med. 1995;155:2336–2340.
184. Rubins JB, Puri AK, Loch J, et al. Magnitude, duration, quality and function of pneumococcal vaccine responses in elderly adults. J Infect Dis. 1998;178:431–440.
185. Steiner S, Musher DM, Pais LB, et al. Functional antibody activity against *Streptococcus pneumoniae* in elderly individuals vaccinated with the 23-valent polysaccharide pneumococcal vaccine. Clin Infect Dis. 1999;29:281–288.

186. Fedson DS. Influenza and pneumococcal vaccination in Canada and the United States, 1980–1993: What can the two countries learn from each other? Clin Infect Dis. 1995;20:1371–1376.
187. Centers for Disease Control and Prevention. Prevention of pneumococcal disease: Recommendations of the Advisory Committee on Immunization Practices (ACIP). MMWR Morb Mortal Wkly Rep. 1997;46:1–18.
188. Robbins JG, Schneerson R. Polysaccharide-protein conjugates: A new generation of vaccines. J Infect Dis. 1990;161:821–832.
189. Isaacman DJ, Karasic RB, Reynolds EA, Kost SI. Effect of number of blood cultures and volume of blood on detection of bacteremia in children. J Pediatr. 1996;128:190–195.
190. Powers DC, Anderson EL, Lottenbach K, Mink CM. Reactogenicity and immunogenicity of a protein-conjugated pneumococcal oligosaccharide vaccine in older adults. J Infect Dis. 1996;173:1014–1018.
191. Shelly MA, Jacoby H, Riley GJ, et al. Comparison of pneumococcal polysaccharide and CRM_{197}-conjugated pneumococcal oligosaccharide vaccine in young and elderly adults. Infect Immun. 1997;65:242–247.
192. Chan CY, Molrine DC, George S, et al. Pneumococcal conjugate vaccine primes for antibody responses to polysaccharide pneumococcal vaccine after treatment of Hodgkin's disease. J Infect Dis. 1996;173:256–258.
193. The National Institute of Child Health and Human Development Intravenous Immunoglobulin Study Group. Intravenous immune globulin for the prevention of bacterial infections in children with symptomatic human immunodeficiency virus infection. N Engl J Med. 1991;325:73–80.
194. Weeks JC, Tierney MR, Weinstein MC. Cost effectiveness of prophylactic intravenous immune globulin in chronic lymphocytic leukemia. N Engl J Med. 1991;325:81–86.

Chapter 189

Enterococcus Species, *Streptococcus bovis*, and *Leuconostoc* Species

ROBERT C. MOELLERING, JR.

ENTEROCOCCUS SPECIES

General Clinical Microbiology

Enterococci are gram-positive cocci that occur in singles, pairs, and short chains. As such they are difficult to distinguish morphologically from true streptococci, and until recently they were actually classified as streptococci.[1] In the Lancefield classification scheme, enterococci were included among the group D streptococci, which contained both enterococcal and nonenterococcal species.[2] The nonenterococcal species such as *Streptococcus bovis* and *Streptococcus equinus* remain classified as true streptococci. In the 1980s, however, it was shown that enterococci differ sufficiently from streptococci that they have been classified in their own genus, *Enterococcus,* which contains at least 12 species (Table 189–1).[3, 4] This classification scheme is constantly being modified, and more recent data cast doubt on the validity of including *Enterococcus solitarius* as a major enterococcal species.[5] In addition, a number of other species have recently been proposed, including *E. cecorum, E. columbae, E. saccharolyticus, E. dispar, E. sulfureus, E. seriolicida,* and *E. flavescens.*[5]

Enterococci are facultative anaerobes that are able to grow under rather extreme conditions. Thus they are able to grow in 6.5% NaCl at pH 9.6 and at temperatures ranging from 10°C to 45°C. Many can survive 30 minutes at 60°C, and they grow in the presence of 40% bile salts. They hydrolyze esculin and L-pyrrolidonyl-β-naphthylamide (PYR).[4–6]

TABLE 189–1 Enterococcal Species

E. faecalis	*E. gallinarum*
E. faecium	*E. hirae*
E. durans	*E. mundtii*
E. avium	*E. raffinosus*
E. casseliflavus	*E. solitarius*
E. malodoratus	*E. pseudoavium*

Most clinical isolates of enterococci are *E. faecalis,* which until recently accounted for 80 to 90% of the organisms encountered in the clinical microbiology laboratory.[7] *Enterococcus faecium* accounted for 5 to 10% of isolates. More recent evidence suggests that the prevalence of *E. faecium,* especially multiresistant strains, is increasing in a number of hospital centers. Occasional isolates of *E. durans, E. avium, E. casseliflavus, E. gallinarum, E. raffinosus,* and *E. hirae are encountered clinically.*[7]

Enterococci occur in a remarkable array of environments, because of their ability to grow and survive under harsh conditions. Thus they can be found in soil, food, water, and a wide variety of living animals. The major habitat of these organisms appears to be the gastrointestinal tract of humans and of other animals, where they make up a significant portion of the normal gut flora.[4, 5] Most enterococci isolated from human stools are *E. faecalis,* although *E. faecium* is also commonly found in the gastrointestinal tract of humans.[8] Small numbers of enterococci are occasionally found in oropharyngeal secretions, vaginal secretions, and on the skin, especially in the perineal area.

Pathogenicity and Virulence

Surprisingly little is known about the factors that contribute to the ability of enterococci to cause infections in humans. Studies have documented high mortality rates (42 to 68%) in patients with enterococcal bacteremia, but they have nonetheless failed to establish unequivocally the pathogenicity of the causative organism in this setting.[9] This is because most of the patients in a described series have been severely debilitated, raising the possibility that the enterococcal bacteremia was merely a marker of this state and not the proximate cause of death in these patients. In many cases, enterococci are part of a polymicrobial bacteremia, and their independent contribution to morbidity and mortality is thus hard to assess. Despite these difficulties, several epidemiologic studies have determined an attributed mortality of 31 to 37% in patients with enterococcal bacteremia.[10, 11] What is clear, however, is that enterococci are not as intrinsically virulent as organisms such as *Staphylococcus aureus* and *Streptococcus pyogenes.* Although they are capable of colonizing the oropharynx, enterococci rarely cause lower respiratory tract infections. Even though most enterococci do not have classic virulence factors, the resistance of enterococci to multiple antimicrobial agents allows them to survive and proliferate in patients receiving antimicrobial chemotherapy.[12, 13] This almost certainly accounts for their ability to cause superinfections in patients receiving a number of different broad-spectrum antimicrobial agents. Enterococci are able to adhere to heart valves and renal epithelial cells, properties that undoubtedly contribute to their ability to cause endocarditis and urinary tract infections.[14] The nature of the molecular structures accounting for this is not clear, but there is some evidence that the *aggregation substance* produced in pheromone-responsive strains may contribute to their ability to adhere to renal epithelial cells.[15] Several investigators have suggested that plasmid-mediated hemolysins secreted by some strains of *E. faecalis* may contribute to virulence in animals and humans.[16, 17] However, the ultimate role of hemolysin production in enterococcal pathogenicity in humans remains to be determined. There is little evidence that antibodies play a significant role in defense against enterococcal infections in humans, but this area needs further study before definitive conclusions can be reached. Although enterococci are natural inhabitants of the gastrointestinal tract, they are not known to cause gastroenteritis in humans with the single possible exception of a strain of *E. hirae* (isolated from a patient with diarrhea) that did cause diarrhea in suckling rats.[18]

Enterococci are commonly found in cultures of intra-abdominal and pelvic infections. Despite extensive study, their role in this setting has not been fully defined, but it is clear that a complex set of interactions among various bacteria occur in this setting and that the growth of enterococci is often facilitated by the presence of other organisms or products of other organisms, such as *Bacteroides fragilis*,[18] and it has been suggested that enterococci act synergistically with other bacteria in intra-abdominal sepsis to enhance morbidity or mortality,[19] but the exact role played by enterococci in this setting remains to be fully delineated.[20, 21]

Epidemiology

Because they are part of the normal gut flora of almost all humans, enterococci are capable of causing infections both in and out of the hospital setting, and it was previously thought that most infections due to these organisms were endogenously acquired from the patients' own flora.[22] Most enterococcal infections, however, occur in hospitalized patients or in patients undergoing therapy such as peritoneal or hemodialysis, and the organisms causing such infections often appear to be exogenously acquired. There is clear-cut evidence for the spread of strains of enterococci between patients and even the dissemination of such strains from one institution to another.[23–25] Strains of enterococci causing nosocomial infections have occasionally been found on the hands of medical personnel and have frequently been isolated from environmental sources in hospitals and nursing homes.[25, 26] The importance of these findings is difficult to assess, because the environment may simply have been passively contaminated by stool or urine from infected patients.[25] In fact, studies suggest that with the exception of drug addicted persons, direct cross-infection is rare.[27, 28] Instead, it appears that resistant organisms from patients or hospital personnel first colonized the gastrointestinal tract (or occasionally the skin and groin or other contiguous areas) before causing infections in patients.[29] Moreover, there is evidence that hospital personnel harboring resistant enterococci in their own gastrointestinal tracts may be responsible for colonization of patients under their care.[29] Once colonized with resistant enterococci, patients may carry them in their gastrointestinal tract for months or even years.[30] In addition, devices such as electronic thermometers may also aid in the spread of resistant organisms.[31]

Currently, enterococci rank second or third in frequency as causes of nosocomial infections in the United States.[32] Risk factors for acquiring nosocomial enterococcal infections include gastrointestinal colonization, serious underlying disease, a long hospital stay, prior surgery, renal insufficiency, neutropenia, transplantation (especially liver and bone marrow), the presence of urinary or vascular catheters, and residency in an intensive care unit.[32–35] Prior antibiotic therapy (especially with vancomycin, cephalosporins, or aminoglycosides) is also a major risk factor for the acquisition of resistant enterococci.[22, 26, 33–37] Other antimicrobial agents, including aztreonam, imipenem, and ciprofloxacin, have been associated with nosocomial enterococcal infections.[33, 38, 39] Enterococci have caused a cluster of cases of endocarditis in Cleveland, Ohio, but the source of this infection was not defined, and there have been no subsequent reports of this phenomenon.[40] Enterococcal bacteremia appears to be a surprisingly unusual complication of hematologic malignancy, and when it does occur in this setting, it appears to be a marker of cytotoxic drug damage to the mucosa of the gastrointestinal tract, rather than an invasive infection in the usual sense, and most cases subside spontaneously or rapidly respond to therapy.[41]

Clinical Infections

Urinary Tract Infections

Urinary tract infections are the most common type of clinical disease produced by enterococci, and urine cultures are the most frequent sources of enterococci in the clinical microbiology laboratory.[42] In addition to uncomplicated cystitis or pyelonephritis, or both, enterococci have also been shown to cause prostatitis and perinephric abscess.[4, 43] Most enterococcal urinary tract infections are nosocomial and are associated with urinary catheterization or instrumentation, or both.[44, 45] There is strong evidence to suggest that the prevalence of nosocomial enterococcal urinary tract infections is increasing in a number of hospitals.[32, 44] In contrast, enterococci only rarely cause infections such as uncomplicated cystitis in nonhospitalized women. Bacteremia is a relatively rare complication of enterococcal urinary tract infections.[46]

Bacteremia and Endocarditis

Most cases of enterococcal bacteremia are not associated with endocarditis. Indeed, only about 1 out of 50 cases of enterococcal bacteremia results in endocarditis (R. C. Moellering, Jr., unpublished data). Endocarditis is much more commonly seen in patients whose bacteremia is community acquired than in those with nosocomial enterococcal bacteremia.[47] Nosocomial enterococcal bacteremias are commonly polymicrobial, and in this setting endocarditis appears even less likely.[47] As is true with enterococcal infections in general, nosocomial bacteremias due to these organisms appear to be increasing in a number of institutions.[47, 48] Portals of entry for enterococcal bacteremia include the urinary tract, intra-abdominal (or pelvic) sepsis, wounds (especially thermal burns, decubitus ulcers, or diabetic foot infections), intravenous or intra-arterial catheters, or cholangitis, in roughly that descending order.[42, 47–49] The respiratory tract is an exceedingly rare portal of entry for enterococcal bacteremia.[47] Increasingly, there are reports of "primary enterococcal bacteremia" in patients with severe underlying illness, usually associated with immunosuppression. These bacteremias are usually monomicrobial and come from a presumed gastrointestinal source.[50] Although enterococcal bacteremia can be associated with septic shock or disseminated intravascular coagulation, these complications are rare in pure enterococcal bacteremia, and when they do occur, they are often the result of accompanying gram-negative bacilli in polymicrobial bacteremias.[47] Metastatic infections (other than endocarditis) are rare in enterococcal bacteremia.[51] As noted earlier, the mortality rate in patients with enterococcal bacteremia is high, but this is because enterococcal bacteremia commonly occurs in debilitated patients, and the exact role of the bacteremia in their deaths is often hard to define. Indeed, although enterococcal bacteremias are often transient and self-limited, there is evidence that treatment with appropriate regimens is associated with an improved outcome.[51, 52]

Enterococci account for approximately 5 to 15% of all cases in most series of infective endocarditis.[4, 53] Most are caused by *E. faecalis*, but *E. faecium*, *E. avium*, *E. casseliflavus*, *E. durans*, *E. gallinarum*, and *E. raffinosus* have also been isolated from patients with a presumed diagnosis of endocarditis.[54] Enterococcal endocarditis is increasingly a disease of older patients, with males outnumbering females in most series.[4, 53, 55, 56] Most cases occur in patients with underlying valvular heart disease or prosthetic valves, but *Enterococcus* is capable of causing infections of anatomically normal valves as well.[4, 55] Enterococcal prosthetic valve endocarditis is increasing in prevalence, and in one series the prevalence of enterococcal prosthetic valve endocarditis nearly approximated that of native valve endocarditis.[55] Although studies have suggested an association between enterococcal endocarditis and urinary tract infection or urinary instrumentation in older men and abortion or childbirth in younger female patients, the latter has not been seen in more recent series.[53, 55, 57–59] The gastrointestinal tract often serves as the portal of entry for enterococci, although the association between gastrointestinal malignancy and enterococcal bacteremia is not as strong as that for *S. bovis* bacteremia.[55] Enterococci usually produce left-sided endocarditis with more frequent involvement of the mitral than the aortic valve, even in drug addicted patients.[4, 40, 53, 59] There is a suggestion that patients with aortic valve involvement require surgical intervention more frequently than those with mitral valve endocarditis.[55] Enterococci usually produce a clinical course consistent with subacute bacterial endocarditis; the clinical picture in this setting is unremarkable and basically indistinguishable from that caused by viridans streptococci or *S. bovis*.[4, 53, 59] Acute bacterial endocarditis due to enterococci is seen in some patients, but it is a less frequent presentation.[59] Because the disease process is an indolent one, some patients have symptoms for a prolonged time before seeking medical care. There is a suggestion that the relapse rate is higher in patients who have had symptoms of endocarditis for more than 3 months before treatment.[60] Impaired renal function occurs with relatively high frequency in the course of enterococcal endocarditis, but this is probably related to the fact that most patients with this disease are treated with nephrotoxic agents including aminoglycosides or vancomycin, or both.[55]

Intra-abdominal and Pelvic Infections

Enterococci are frequently found as part of a mixed aerobic and anaerobic flora in intra-abdominal and pelvic infections. Their role in these settings has been questioned, especially because they seem to cause bacteremia less frequently than *Escherichia coli* or *Bacteroides* spp. when present in mixed abdominal or pelvic infections.[21, 61, 62] It has also been noted that treatment with antimicrobial regimens devoid of activity against *Enterococcus* can cure such infections.[61, 63] However, although antimicrobial combinations such as clindamycin or metronidazole plus gentamicin may lack in vitro activity against enterococci, animal studies suggest that these regimens may have in vivo bacteriostatic activity against enterococci and may contribute to the successful therapeutic outcome noted previously.[64] Moreover, perioperative treatment with agents active against enterococci in trauma patients requiring abdominal exploration has been shown to decrease subsequent enterococcal wound infection.[65]

Although the exact role of enterococci in mixed intra-abdominal and pelvic infections remains murky, it is clear that these organisms can cause spontaneous peritonitis in patients with nephrotic syndrome or cirrhosis and can cause peritonitis in patients undergoing chronic ambulatory peritoneal dialysis.[4, 66] "Pure" enterococcal peritonitis is also seen occasionally as a complication of abdominal surgery or trauma. These organisms can also produce abscesses and bacteremia as a complication of endometritis, cesarean section, or acute salpingitis.[49, 67] The presence of enterococci in pure culture in the latter settings is, however, distinctly unusual.

Wound and Tissue Infections

Enterococci by themselves rarely, if ever, cause cellulitis or other deep tissue infections. They are frequently isolated from mixed cultures with gram-negative bacilli and anaerobes in surgical wound infections, decubitus ulcers, and diabetic foot infections, and in these cases, as is true for intra-abdominal and pelvic sepsis, their significance is difficult to assess.[68] On rare occasions, they may cause bacteremia from such a setting, but it is clear that they are not nearly as invasive as organisms such as *S. aureus*.[68] Enterococcal wound colonization and sepsis have been described in burn patients whose wounds were covered with porcine xenografts presumably contaminated with enterococci.[69] Enterococci have also occasionally been found in diabetic and nondiabetic patients with chronic osteomyelitis. In this setting, they are often of doubtful pathogenic significance, and when they are shown to be causes of infection by direct bone biopsy, it is likely that their presence is due to superinfection and does not represent primary enterococcal osteomyelitis. The author has seen a case of enterococcal endophthalmitis in a diabetic patient who had enterococcal bacteremia from a diabetic foot infection several months after undergoing vitrectomy for diabetic retinopathy, again emphasizing that these organisms can be opportunistic pathogens in a variety of settings.

Meningitis

Enterococci rarely, if ever, cause meningitis in normal adults. Most cases of enterococcal meningitis occur in patients with anatomic defects of the central nervous system, prior neurosurgery, or head trauma.[70] Meningitis is a rare complication of high-grade bacteremia in patients with enterococcal endocarditis.[70] Meningitis also occasionally complicates enterococcal bacteremia in patients with severe immunodeficiencies including acquired immunodeficiency syndrome and acute leukemias. It is also seen in neonatal sepsis.[71] Enterococcal meningitis appears to be associated with low cerebrospinal fluid leukocyte counts (usually less than 200/mm^3) in most, but not all, patients.[70, 72]

Respiratory Tract Infections

Respiratory tract infections due to enterococci are exceedingly unusual. Although well-documented cases of enterococcal pneumonia and even lung abscess exist, they usually occur in patients with severe and debilitating diseases.[73, 74] Broad-spectrum antimicrobial therapy (especially with cephalosporins) coupled with enteric feeding in severely debilitated patients has been the setting in which some of the rare cases of enterococcal pneumonia have been described.[73]

Neonatal Sepsis

Enterococci have clearly been documented to cause neonatal sepsis characterized by fever, lethargy, and respiratory difficulty accompanied by bacteremia or meningitis, or both.[71] Although early-onset bacteremia in otherwise normal neonates is characteristic of this disease,[71, 75, 76] several nosocomial outbreaks of bacteremia or meningitis, or both, due to *E. faecium* or *E. faecalis* have been described in premature or low-birth-weight neonates who had nasogastric tubes and intravascular devices.[77, 78] In general, neonates with enterococcal sepsis have responded well to appropriate antimicrobial therapy.[71, 76]

Antimicrobial Susceptibility and Resistance

The most striking attribute of enterococci is the relative and absolute resistance of these organisms to a variety of antimicrobial agents commonly used to treat infections due to gram-positive organisms.[4, 9, 13] Susceptibility of enterococci to certain commonly used antimicrobial agents is shown in Table 189–2. The picture that is provided here is the result of both intrinsic and acquired resistance determinants in enterococci (Table 189–3).[79] Not only are these organisms intrinsically resistant to a large number of antimicrobial agents, but they also show a remarkable ability to acquire new mechanisms of resistance.[13] As a result, susceptibility patterns such as those given in Table 189–2 are subject to considerable temporal and geographic variation. In many hospitals in the United States, for example, there are much higher rates

TABLE 189–2 Antimicrobial Susceptibility of Enterococci

	Enterococcus faecalis		*Enterococcus faecium*	
Antimicrobial	*MIC$_{50}$ (μg/ml)*	*MIC$_{90}$ (μg/ml)*	*MIC$_{50}$ (μg/ml)*	*MIC$_{90}$ (μg/ml)*
Ampicillin	1	1	8	32
Penicillin	2	4	16	64
Piperacillin	2	4	16	64
Imipenem	2	2	16	32
Vancomycin	2	2	1	2
Teicoplanin	0.5	1	0.5	1
Tetracycline	>16	>16	>16	>16
Chloramphenicol	8	>16	4	16
Erythromycin	>256	>256	>256	>256
Ciprofloxacin	1	2	4	16

Abbreviation: MIC, Minimal inhibitory concentration.

TABLE 189-3 Antimicrobial Resistance in Enterococci

Intrinsic resistance
Aminoglycosidic aminocyclitols (low level)
β-Lactams (relatively high MICs)
Lincosamides (low level)
Trimethoprim-sulfamethoxazole (in vivo only)
Acquired resistance
Aminoglycosidic aminocyclitols (high level)
β-Lactams (altered PBPs)
Cell wall–active agents (tolerance)
Fluoroquinolones
Lincosamides (high level)
Macrolides
Penicillin and ampicillin (β-lactamase)
Rifampin
Tetracyclines
Vancomycin

Abbreviations: MIC, Minimal inhibitory concentration; PBP, penicillin-binding protein.

of resistance to ampicillin, penicillin, and vancomycin (especially among *E. faecium*) than depicted in the table. All enterococci, including those from antibiotic-virgin populations, exhibit relative resistance to β-lactam antimicrobial agents, which is due to a diminished affinity of the lower-weight penicillin-binding proteins (especially PBP 5) of *E. faecalis* and *E. faecium* for penicillin, ampicillin, and other β-lactams including the cephalosporins.[80, 81] In general, the cephalosporins (and especially the cephamycins) are less active against enterococci than the penicillins, and none of the presently available cephalosporins have clinically useful activity against enterococci. Although there has been little change in the intrinsic resistance of *E. faecalis* to the penicillins, there has been a striking increase in intrinsic resistance to the penicillins among *E. faecium.* Many isolates of these organisms in the United States and elsewhere are currently relatively and absolutely resistant to penicillin and ampicillin because of further alterations in PBP 5.[82] Intrinsic resistance to the aminoglycosides is due to a decreased ability of these agents to penetrate through the outer cell envelope of enterococci, a phenomenon that can be overcome with the addition of an appropriate cell wall–active agent, resulting in synergistic killing of enterococci.[83] Although enterococci are susceptible to trimethoprim-sulfamethoxazole when tested under the proper conditions in vitro,[4] these organisms are able to use exogenous folinic acid, dihydrofolate, and tetrahydrofolate, and hence in vivo they circumvent the block in folate synthesis produced by trimethoprim-sulfamethoxazole. As a result, trimethoprim-sulfamethoxazole has been shown to fail in the therapy of enterococcal infections in both animal models and patients.[84–86]

In addition to their intrinsic resistance, enterococci have acquired new mechanisms of resistance to a wide variety of antimicrobial agents. Most of these resistance mechanisms are mediated by genes encoded on plasmids or transposons.[4] As subsequently described, enterococci have evolved a number of remarkably efficient methods of transferring resistance genes among themselves, and between themselves and other organisms, and this greatly facilitates their acquisition of new resistance determinants.[87] One important form of acquired resistance that does not appear to be plasmid or transposon mediated is tolerance to cell wall–active agents. Although enterococci from antibiotic-virgin populations exhibit the same relative resistance to the inhibitory effect of penicillins and cephalosporins (manifested by relatively high minimal inhibitory concentrations [MICs]) as strains from populations previously exposed to antimicrobials, enterococci without prior antibiotic exposure are killed (and lysed) by cell wall–active agents.[88] A relatively brief exposure to penicillin or other cell wall–active agents, however, results in the rapid acquisition of *tolerance.*[88] Because of the intrinsic resistance and tolerance of enterococci to antimicrobial agents that inhibit cell wall synthesis, combination therapy with cell wall–active agents plus aminoglycosides is currently the standard treatment for enterococcal infections such as endocarditis and meningitis, which require bactericidal therapy. High-level resistance (MICs > 500 to 2000 μg/ml) to aminoglycosidic aminocyclitol antimicrobial agents can be caused either by ribosomal mutation (for streptomycin only) or by the production of plasmid-mediated aminoglycoside-modifying enzymes.[4, 87, 89] Enterococci with high-level resistance to streptomycin and kanamycin have been relatively common, but high-level resistance to gentamicin has become a clinical problem only since the 1980s.[4, 9, 13] The most prevalent enzyme that mediates high-level gentamicin resistance (a fused 6′-acetytransferase–2′-phosphotransferase) also produces resistance to synergism with all other clinically useful aminoglycosides except streptomycin.[87] Enterococci that contain this gene as well as a 6-adenylyltransferase that modifies streptomycin are resistant to synergy by all combinations of cell wall–active agents and aminoglycosides.[13, 87] Several other gentamicin-phosphorylating enzymes have been described. One, designated APH(2″)-Id, mediates high-level resistance to gentamicin, and the other, APH(2″)-Ic, mediates intermediate levels of resistance that may not be detected by the screening tests currently employed in most clinical microbiology laboratories.[90, 91] Both enzymes eliminate β-lactam–gentamicin synergism. Fortunately, both enzymes are infrequently found at present. All strains of *E. faecium* produce a chromosomally mediated 6′-acetyltransferase that inactivates tobramycin, netilmicin, kanamycin, and sisomicin but that does not produce high-level resistance to these compounds.[92, 93] Thus these agents should not be used, even in combination with cell wall–active agents, against *E. faecium,* because they do not result in enhanced killing of these organisms. *Enterococcus faecalis* and *E. faecium* with high-level resistance to all aminoglycosides are being seen with increased frequency throughout the world, and clinical failures and relapses after therapy in patients with endocarditis due to these organisms are being increasingly encountered.[13, 94] All enterococci from patients with endocarditis or meningitis should be subjected to high-level aminoglycoside testing to determine whether a synergistic aminoglycoside-containing combination should be employed therapeutically. Only time-kill tests for in vitro synergism will reveal the effects of the presence of the rare isolate containing APH(2″)-Ic.

In the late 1980s, vancomycin-resistant enterococci were first described. Initially seen in Europe, these isolates have now begun to have a major impact in the United States as well.[13, 95, 96] A number of phenotypes of vancomycin resistance have been discovered. Strains exhibiting the VanA phenotype show high-level resistance to vancomycin and teicoplanin, and VanB strains exhibit moderate to high-level resistance to vancomycin but remain susceptible to teicoplanin. The genes for both these resistance phenotypes have been cloned and sequenced and have been shown to be transferable.[97–101] Vancomycin resistance of the VanA phenotype is due to the production of a ligase with altered specificity that results in the synthesis of cell wall precursors ending in the depsipeptide D-alanyl-lactate rather than the dipeptide D-alanyl-D-alanine, which is the target for vancomycin.[97] Vancomycin resistance is the result of the inability of vancomycin to bind to the altered depsipeptide, which can nonetheless be cross-linked by enterococcal transpeptidases to form a normal cell wall and thus does not result in a selective disadvantage to the enterococci. Low levels of vancomycin resistance without teicoplanin resistance are also found in *E. gallinarum* (VanC) and *E. casseliflavus.* The genes responsible for this appear to be chromosomally located and are not transferable.[97] A fourth vancomycin-resistance genotype has been described in a strain of *E. faecium* that exhibited moderate levels of resistance to vancomycin and teicoplanin.[102] We have subsequently identified several additional strains from Boston exhibiting the VanD genotype, which is clearly different from the VanA, VanB, and VanC genotypes.[103]

The problem of vancomycin-resistant enterococci (VREs) has risen to alarming proportions since the problem was first reported in 1988. The percentage of nosocomial infections caused by VREs increased more than 20-fold between 1989 and 1993, rising from 0.3 to 7.9%.[104] The trend has continued. The Surveillance Network Database–USA, which obtains data from more than 100 clinical laboratories, found that 52% of 1482 isolates of *E. faecium* collected in 1997 were vancomycin-resistant.[104] Resistance to vancomycin would be less of a concern were not 83% of the 1482 isolates also ampicillin-resistant. The incidence of VREs in that year among *E. faecalis* was only 1.9% of 4364 isolates, illustrating the dramatic difference between these two species. Although hospitals vary, the incidence of VREs in intensive care units now generally exceeds 20% of enterococci, including all species. Factors predisposing to VRE colonization or infection include the percentage of hospital days receiving antimicrobial therapy, the use of intravenous vancomycin, severe underlying disease, immunosuppression, and abdominal surgery.[105] Transmission of VREs within institutions has been indicated by the appearance of predominant strains.[106] Evidence strongly suggests that the vehicle is the hands of medical personnel.[104] Colonization of a patient's gastrointestinal tract appears to precede infection in that patient.

The Centers for Disease Control and Prevention has made a series of recommendations to help control the spread of VREs within hospitals.[105] These include rapid identification of patients who are colonized or infected with VREs and placing them in a separate room or in a room with another VRE patient. All persons entering the room should wear gloves. In addition, those who will have substantial contact with the patient or environmental surfaces in the room should wear a gown. Noncritical items such as stethoscopes, thermometers, and sphygmomanometers should remain in the room. On leaving the room, personnel should remove the gown and gloves, and thorough hand washing should be done. Criteria should be established for allowing isolation to be terminated, such as three negative weekly stool cultures or rectal swabs. Anecdotal reports have suggested that oral bacitracin may help shorten the usual long period of colonization, but success has been modest at best.[107] Terminal cleaning and disinfection of the room should be thorough. Among the other recommendations of the Centers for Disease Control and Prevention were control measures to limit inappropriate vancomycin usage.

A strain of β-lactamase–producing *E. faecium* was initially found in eastern Texas in the early 1980s.[108] Subsequently, β-lactamase–producing strains have been found in a number of other U.S. cities and in Buenos Aires, Argentina.[4] Although the β-lactamase in enterococci is identical to the plasmid-mediated β-lactamase from *S. aureus,* it is produced constitutively in enterococci because the genes that control the inducible production of β-lactamase in *S. aureus* have not been transferred into *Enterococcus* in toto with the β-lactamase genes.[109] β-Lactamase–producing enterococci show a marked inoculum effect and when tested under standard laboratory conditions do not appear to have MICs significantly different from those of non–β-lactamase–producing strains.[4] Accordingly, the clinical laboratory must use a test for β-lactamase production (such as nitrocefin) in order to effectively identify these strains.[4] Interestingly, β-lactamase–producing strains have not become widely disseminated in the United States or elsewhere, and after several initial descriptions of outbreaks of colonization and infection with these organisms, they have not caused further clinical difficulty.[29]

The transfer of resistance genes to and from enterococci can be accomplished by the conjugal exchange of plasmids or transposons.[4, 87] Three separate transfer systems for conjugative transfer have been described in enterococci.[4] The first involves narrow-host-range plasmids that transfer genes at high frequency only among enterococci. This system is due to the response of recipient cells that produce an aggregation substance on exposure to pheromones from the donor cells, resulting in visible clumping between donors and recipients.[110] Broad-host-range plasmids not under pheromone control can be transferred among *Enterococcus* spp. and between these organisms and various species of streptococci, *S. aureus,* lactobacilli, *Bacillus subtilis, Listeria monocytogenes,* and others.[87, 111] Finally, enterococci may exchange conjugative transposons as well.[110] These systems have undoubtedly contributed to the explosive increase in multiple drug resistance among enterococci isolated worldwide.

Therapy

Treatment of enterococcal infections is complicated both by the fact that these organisms often exhibit unusual patterns of susceptibility or resistance and by the fact that it is necessary to use specialized techniques to demonstrate their true susceptibility in the clinical microbiology laboratory. For instance, standard methods of susceptibility testing will not predict resistance to penicillin-aminoglycoside synergism. Instead, the laboratory must test for high-level aminoglycoside resistance or subject the organism to testing against antimicrobial combinations in vitro by methods using time-kill curves.[4, 112] Likewise, standard testing will also fail to demonstrate penicillin or ampicillin resistance in many β-lactamase–producing strains.[4] Finally, susceptibility testing may produce frankly misleading results. The clinician faced with a report suggesting that an organism is only moderately susceptible to penicillin (which is "standard" for these organisms) and susceptible to vancomycin may conclude that vancomycin is better, even though penicillin or ampicillin are the initial agents of choice for most enterococcal infections.

As noted previously, penicillin or ampicillin remain the antibiotics of choice for treating enterococcal infections such as urinary tract infections, peritonitis, and wound infections that do not require bactericidal treatment.[113] Vancomycin (or teicoplanin) is the alternative agent in patients who are allergic to penicillin or for organisms (usually *E. faecium*) with high-level penicillin resistance.[113] Most strains of enterococci (90 to 96% in most centers) remain susceptible to nitrofurantoin, and this agent has been used successfully to treat enterococcal urinary tract infections. Fosfomycin also exhibits good in vitro activity against *E. faecalis* and *E. faecium* and may be useful for urinary tract infections due to these organisms. The fluoroquinolones such as ciprofloxacin and ofloxacin have in vitro activity against enterococci[114] and may be useful for treating some enterococcal urinary tract infections, but their effectiveness for enterococcal infections in general has not been demonstrated convincingly, and increasing resistance in some centers may further decrease their attractiveness for enterococcal infections.[115] Sparfloxacin, levofloxacin, grepafloxacin, and trovafloxacin are more active than ciprofloxacin or ofloxacin against enterococci in vitro, but their activity is diminished against ciprofloxacin-resistant strains, suggesting that their utility for treating infections due to multiresistant enterococci will be limited, at best.[114] Although erythromycin has been used to treat enterococcal infections (with failures documented in occasional cases of endocarditis),[59] most (80 to 90%) enterococci in the United States are now resistant to erythromycin and related macrolides. Tetracycline and chloramphenicol may exhibit in vitro activities against some strains of enterococci, but they are only bacteriostatic against these organisms, and clinical failures of chloramphenicol are documented.[72, 117]

Although it appears that combination therapy is optimal for enterococcal endocarditis and probably for enterococcal meningitis as well,[4, 53, 118] the situation is not as clear-cut in cases of enterococcal bacteremia without endocarditis. Many such cases are transient and self-limited.[51] Nonetheless, there is evidence that appropriate therapy does improve the outcome in uncomplicated enterococcal bacteremia.[52] There is no consensus as to whether combination therapy is required in this setting, and a number of studies have suggested that combination therapy provides no advantage over monotherapy.[51, 119] In the absence of a controlled trial, however, some infectious disease specialists continue to use penicillin or ampicillin plus aminoglycoside therapy, especially when enterococcal bacteremia occurs in critically ill patients.

Combinations of cell wall–active agents (usually penicillin, ampicillin, or vancomycin) with aminoglycosides (usually streptomycin or gentamicin) have been the standard for treatment of enterococcal endocarditis since the first demonstration of penicillin-streptomycin synergy in 1947.[120] Before that, high relapse rates (30 to 60%) were documented in patients with enterococcal endocarditis treated with penicillin alone. Although there has never been a controlled trial of combination versus monotherapy in enterococcal endocarditis, it is generally agreed that combination therapy is necessary for enterococcal endocarditis and meningitis because most enterococci are tolerant to the killing activity of penicillins and glycopeptides.[113, 119, 121, 122] Moreover, relapses are now being demonstrated in patients who have developed enterococcal endocarditis due to organisms with high-level gentamicin resistance and who are treated with penicillin or ampicillin alone.[13] Although penicillin or ampicillin plus streptomycin was originally the regimen of choice for enterococcal endocarditis, it has been shown that penicillin plus gentamicin is equally effective, and this is now generally used for enterococcal endocarditis and enterococcal meningitis.[53, 55, 57–60, 113, 122, 123] Vancomycin is substituted for penicillin or ampicillin in combination with streptomycin or gentamicin in patients who are allergic to penicillin.[113] Dosage recommendations for these regimens are given in Table 189–4. In most cases, 4 weeks of combination therapy appears to be adequate,[53, 55, 60] with the 6-week regimens reserved for patients who have had symptoms for more than 3 months before starting treatment, patients with prosthetic valves, or patients who have relapsed after previous shorter courses of therapy.[53, 60] Similar therapeutic regimens have been used to treat patients with enterococcal meningitis, but there is not a sufficient body of experience with this disease to assess the therapeutic effectiveness or optimal length of treatment. Most patients with enterococcal meningitis seem to respond well to treatment, which is generally given for 2 to 3 weeks.[70]

The emergence of multiply resistant enterococci now greatly complicates the therapeutic choices in some cases. For patients who have endocarditis or meningitis due to enterococci with high-level gentamicin resistance, it is useful to test for high-level streptomycin resistance because some highly gentamicin-resistant strains are synergistically killed by cell wall–active agents plus streptomycin.[13] For endocarditis due to strains with high-level resistance to both streptomycin and gentamicin, no combination will produce synergism. The possible exception would be the strains containing the newly described phosphotransferase mediating high-level resistance to gentamicin without accompanying acetyltransferase activity.[91] Some of these strains are killed synergistically by combinations of cell wall–active agents and amikacin, but others are not, and clinical data to support these in vitro observations are not available. Our current recommendation for the remainder of cases of endocarditis due to enterococci exhibiting high-level resistance to both streptomycin and gentamicin is to treat such patients for long periods (8 to 12 weeks) with intravenous ampicillin (which produces slightly greater killing of enterococci in vitro than penicillin alone) given by continuous infusion. There are not enough data to know how effective such therapy will be, but there are anecdotal examples of success. Nonetheless, this approach should be considered experimental. Surgical excision of infected valves has been required to cure some cases of enterococcal endocarditis caused by organisms with high-level streptomycin and gentamicin resistance.[13, 55, 124] Infections due to *E. faecium* with high-level penicillin resistance (MIC > 16 to 32 μg/ml) should be treated with vancomycin. Many vancomycin-resistant enterococci (especially *E. faecalis*) remain relatively susceptible to penicillin or ampicillin (MICs of O.5 to 2 μg/ml), and these agents can be tried therapeutically for infections caused by such organisms. Infections due to organisms (usually *E. faecium*) with both high-level penicillin resistance and vancomycin resistance are even more of a challenge. The combination of vancomycin plus penicillin or ampicillin has been shown to produce bacteriostatic but not bactericidal synergism against some such organisms in vitro.[124, 125] However, this has not been universally true,[33, 126] and, although combinations of ampicillin plus vancomycin plus gentamicin have demonstrated bactericidal activity against several enterococcal strains in animal models,[127, 128] the clinical effectiveness of such therapy remains to be demonstrated. Despite the fact that vancomycin-resistant enterococci of the VanB phenotype remain susceptible to teicoplanin in vitro, therapy of infections due to such strains with teicoplanin has not been universally successful; in at least one reported case, it has been associated with the emergence of organisms resistant to teicoplanin during therapy.[129] There is now a report of a number of cases of enterococcal endocarditis due to vancomycin-resistant enterococci of the VanB phenotype that were successfully treated with teicoplanin plus a second active antibiotic (usually an aminoglycoside).[130] Combination therapy seems essential in this setting to prevent the emergence of resistance.

β-Lactamase–producing enterococci remain susceptible to vancomycin (and teicoplanin) and to combinations of β-lactams and β-lactamase inhibitors such as ampicillin-sulbactam and amoxicillin-clavulanate. These agents have been shown to be effective in animal models as well.[131] There are no convincing published reports of endocarditis due to β-lactamase–producing organisms, so the clinical effectiveness of these regimens cannot be assessed.

Teicoplanin alone has been used to treat a small number of patients with enterococcal endocarditis (none of which were due to vancomycin-resistant strains) in Europe, and preliminary results show some success in this setting, but there have also been documented failures and relapses.[132, 133] There are reports of in vitro activity of other agents including novobiocin, ciprofloxacin, fosfomycin, and pristinamycin[134] in various combination regimens against enterococci, but none of these have been demonstrated clinically useful. The treatment of infections due to multiply resistant enterococci remains a highly empirical endeavor and requires the backup of a clinical or research laboratory well versed in antimicrobial susceptibility testing.[135]

Several antimicrobial agents under clinical development show some promise for the therapy of infections due to multiply resistant enterococci. These include the streptogramin combination quinupristin-dalfopristin[136]; an oxazolidinone, linezolid[137]; the everninomicin ziracin[138]; and a new semisynthetic glycopeptide, LY333328.[139] All exhibit in vitro activity against multiresistant enterococci. Of these, the most clinical data exist for quinupristin-dalfopristin. This agent is not active against *E. faecalis* but exhibits good (usually bacteriostatic) activity against *E. faecium.* It has been used to treat more than 350 cases of infection due to vancomycin-resistant *E. faecium* with a success rate of approximately 70%.[140]

TABLE 189–4 Antibiotic Therapy of Enterococcal Endocarditis

Antibiotic	Dosage	Route	Duration (wk)
Organism not highly resistant to streptomycin or gentamicin			
Pencillin G	20–30 million U/d	IV	4–6
or			
Ampicillin	12–16 g/d	IV	4–6
plus			
Streptomycin	20 mg/kg/d	IM	4–6
or			
Gentamicin	3–5 mg/kg/d	IM or IV	4–6
Organism highly resistant to streptomycin but not gentamicin			
Penicillin G	20–30 million U/d	IV	4–6
or			
Ampicillin	12–16 g/d	IV	4–6
plus			
Gentamicin	3–5 mg/kg/d	IM or IV	4–6
Patient allergic to penicillin; desensitization not feasible			
Vancomycin	30 mg/kg/d	IV	4–6
plus			
Streptomycin or gentamicin	Use above guidelines in choice of aminoglycoside	IM or IV	4–6
Organism highly resistant to streptomycin and gentamicin			
Ampicillin	12–16 g/d	IV	8–12

STREPTOCOCCUS BOVIS

Streptococcus bovis organisms are gram-positive cocci that may sometimes be misidentified as enterococci or viridans streptococci (especially *Streptococcus salivarius*) unless careful testing is performed in the clinical microbiology laboratory.[141–143] They are classified as group D streptococci on the basis of their reaction with group D–specific antiserum, but this testing is no longer routinely carried out in most clinical laboratories.[142, 145] In addition to their positive reaction with group D antiserum, *S. bovis* share other properties in common with true enterococci including their ability to grow in the presence of 40% bile and to hydrolyze esculin.[142, 145] However, a number of simple tests, including growth in 6.5% salt broth or the pyrrolidonyl arylamidase (PYR) reaction, easily differentiate *S. bovis* from true enterococci.[142, 143, 145] The use of the API Rapid Strep system not only results in accurate identification of *S. bovis* and distinguishes these organisms from viridans streptococci and enterococci, but it also allows identification of *S. bovis* to the biotype level.[143] Several biotypes have been described including *S. bovis* biotype I (also known simply as *S. bovis*) and *S. bovis* biotypes II/1 and II/2 (also known as *S. bovis* variants).[146] This differentiation may be important because bacteremia due to *S. bovis* I shows a much higher correlation with underlying gastrointestinal malignancy and endocarditis (71 and 94%, respectively, in one series) than *S. bovis* II or *S. salivarius*.[143] Although *S. bovis* is occasionally identified in cultures from the urinary tract and in other miscellaneous infections including very rare cases of meningitis or neonatal sepsis,[142, 143, 145] by far the most important clinical infections caused by *S. bovis* are bacteremias and endocarditis.[142, 143, 145–153] The gastrointestinal tract is the usual portal of entry in *S. bovis* bacteremia, although the hepatobiliary tree, the urinary tract, and even dental procedures have been implicated as possible sources.[142, 143, 148, 150] Some or all of the latter cases, however, may represent bacteremias or cases of endocarditis in which *S. salivarius* was misidentified as *S. bovis*.[141, 142, 150] In a high percentage of cases (25 to 50% or more), *S. bovis* bacteremia is associated with endocarditis. The endocarditis produced by these organisms usually runs a subacute course and is clinically indistinguishable from that caused by viridans streptococci with rare peripheral septic complications and excellent response to antimicrobial therapy.[142, 148, 150] *S. bovis* usually, but not always, produces endocarditis in patients with preexisting valvular abnormalities or prosthetic valves.[142]

There is a striking association between *S. bovis* bacteremia and underlying malignancy of the colon.[150–154] Indeed, the prevalence of malignancy exceeds 50% in some series, and all patients with *S. bovis* bacteremia should undergo a careful workup to exclude colonic neoplasms. Although some authors have suggested an association with other gastrointestinal malignancies, the most striking association is with colonic carcinoma.[155] It is not clear if *S. bovis* plays an etiologic role in carcinoma of the colon or is merely a marker for the disease, but several studies have shown a definite increase in stool carriage of *S. bovis* in patients with malignant or premalignant lesions of the colon compared with healthy people, from whom *S. bovis* is rarely isolated in stool cultures.[152, 154]

Unlike enterococci, *S. bovis* is very susceptible to penicillin, with penicillin MICs ranging between 0.01 and 0.12 μg/ml. They are also susceptible to ampicillin, the antipseudomonal penicillins, cephalothin, erythromycin, clindamycin, and vancomycin.[142, 143] Although penicillin-aminoglycoside combinations show synergy against *S. bovis* and have been successfully used to treat infections due to these organisms,[149] it appears that penicillin alone is equally effective when given for 4 weeks to patients with endocarditis.[142, 150] It is likewise the drug of choice for *S. bovis* bacteremia. Vancomycin is a reasonable alternative in penicillin-allergic patients, but the identification of a vancomycin-resistant clinical isolate of *S. bovis* (which contained the *VanB* genome)[144] raises the possibility of more widespread glycopeptide resistance in these organisms in the future and means that it is prudent to confirm vancomycin susceptibility before using this agent therapeutically for *S. bovis* infections.[144]

LEUCONOSTOC SPECIES

Leuconostoc spp. are gram-positive cocci or coccobacilli that grow in pairs and chains and may be morphologically mistaken for streptococci.[157, 158] They are one of several genera of naturally vancomycin-resistant gram-positive organisms that include *Lactobacillus* spp., *Pediococcus* spp., *Erysipelothrix* spp., and some enterococci. *Leuconostoc* are facultative anaerobes that are catalase-negative, are leucine aminopeptidase–positive, and produce gas from glucose.[157] Although several species are known,[159] they are not usually speciated in the clinical microbiology laboratory and are generally identified only as *Leuconostoc* or *Leuconostoc* spp.

Until the 1970s, these organisms were not thought to be pathogenic for humans.[159] They are commonly found on plants and vegetables and less commonly in dairy products and wine.[159, 160] Although they may occasionally be isolated from human stool specimens, there are insufficient data to determine the frequency with which this occurs.[157, 160] Virtually nothing is known about the way in which these organisms colonize or infect humans. Indeed, documented infections due to *Leuconostoc* are rare, in part because it is likely that these organisms are often mistaken or misidentified in the clinical laboratory. Most information on clinical infections due to *Leuconostoc* comes from isolated reports of one or two cases.[160–164] *Leuconostoc* has been isolated from gastrostomy tube sites in the absence of obvious infection.[160, 163] They have been documented to cause isolated bacteremias; intravenous-line sepsis with localized exit site infection or bacteremia, or both; meningitis (including a case of neonatal meningitis); and dental abscess with odontogenic infection of the buccal soft tissues. Many of the documented infections have occurred in severely ill or immunocompromised patients, but a few (including meningitis) have been seen in otherwise healthy persons. Nonetheless, it is clear that *Leuconostoc* is only very rarely pathogenic for humans.

All *Leuconostoc* species are resistant to vancomycin because their pentapeptide cell wall precursors end in a depsipeptide (alanine-lactate) rather than the alanine-alanine dipeptide, which is the binding site for vancomycin in vancomycin-susceptible gram-positive cocci. The ligase for assembling the depsipeptide has not been identified, but it does not appear to be related to the altered ligases responsible for vancomycin resistance in enterococci.[165] These organisms are usually cross-resistant to teicoplanin. Despite their resistance to vancomycin and teicoplanin, *Leuconostoc* remains susceptible to most agents with activity against streptococci.[166–168] Thus, these organisms are generally quite susceptible to penicillin, ampicillin, clindamycin, minocycline, erythromycin, tobramycin, and gentamicin. They are moderately susceptible to imipenem, the cephalosporins, tetracycline, doxycycline, and chloramphenicol. Strains resistant to the sulfonamides, trimethoprim-sulfamethoxazole, fusidic acid, and fosfomycin have been described.[160, 166, 167, 169] From the limited clinical data available it appears that penicillin or ampicillin is the agent of choice for treating documented infections due to *Leuconostoc* spp.

REFERENCES

1. Sherman JM. The streptococci. Bacteriol Rev. 1937;1:3–97.
2. Deibel RH. The group D streptococci. Bacteriol Rev. 1964;28:330–336.
3. Schleifer KH, Kilpper-Balz R. Molecular and chemotaxonomic approaches to the classification of streptococci, enterococci, and lactococci: A review. Syst Appl Microbiol. 1987;10:1–19.
4. Murray BE. The life and times of the enterococcus. Clin Microbiol Rev. 1990;3:46–65.
5. Facklam RR, Sahm DF, Teixeira LM. *Enterococcus. In:* Murray PR, Baron EJ, Pfaller MA, et al., eds. Manual of Clinical Microbiology. 7th ed. Washington, DC: American Society for Microbiology; 1999:297–305.
6. Facklam RR, Collins MD. Identification of *Enterococcus* species isolated from human infections by a conventional test scheme. J Clin Microbiol. 1989;27:731–734.
7. Ruoff KL, de la Maza L, Murtagh MJ, et al. Species identities of enterococci isolated from clinical specimens. J Clin Microbiol. 1990;28:435–437.
8. Mead GC. Streptococci in the intestinal flora of man and other non-ruminant animals. In: Skinner FA, Quesnel LB, eds. Streptococci. London: Academic Press; 1978:345–361.
9. Hoffmann SA, Moellering RC Jr. The enterococcus: "Putting the bug in our ears." Ann Intern Med. 1987;106:757–761.

10. Edmond MB, Ober JF, Weinbaum DL, et al. Vancomycin-resistant *E. faecium* bacteremia: Risk factors for infection. Clin Infect Dis. 1995;20:1126.
11. Edmond MB, Ober JF, Dawson JD, et al. Vancomycin-resistant enterococcal bacteremia: Natural history and attributable mortality. Clin Infect Dis. 1996;23:1234.
12. Moellering RC Jr. Emergence of *Enterococcus* as a significant pathogen. Clin Infect Dis. 1992;14:1173–1178.
13. Moellering RC Jr. The Garrod Lecture: The enterococcus: A classic example of the impact of antimicrobial resistance on therapeutic options. J Antimicrob Chemother. 1991;28:1–12.
14. Guzman CA, Pruzzo C, Lipira G, et al. Role of adherence in pathogenesis of *Enterococcus faecalis* urinary tract infection and endocarditis. Infect Immun. 1989;57:1834–1838.
15. Kreft B, Marre R, Schramm U, et al. Aggregation substance of *Enterococcus faecalis* mediates adhesion to cultured renal tubular cells. Infect Immun. 1992;60:25–30.
16. Ike Y, Hashimoto H, Clewell DB. Hemolysin of *Streptococcus faecalis* subspecies *zymogenes* contributes to virulence in mice. Infect Immun. 1984;45:528–530.
17. Ike Y, Hashimoto H, Clewell DB. High incidence of hemolysin production by *Enterococcus (Streptococcus) faecalis* strains associated with human parenteral infections. J Clin Microbiol. 1987;25:1524–1528.
18. Etheridge ME, Yolken RH, Vonderfecht SL. *Enterococcus hirae* implicated as a cause of diarrhea in suckling rats. J Clin Microbiol. 1988;26:1741–1744.
19. Willey SH, Hindes RG, Eliopoulos GM, et al. Effects of clindamycin and gentamicin and other antimicrobial combinations against enterococci in an experimental model of intra-abdominal abscess. Surg Gynecol Obstet. 1989;169:199–202.
20. Matlow AG, Bohnen JMA, Nohr C, et al. Pathogenicity of enterococci in a rat model of fecal peritonitis. J Infect Dis. 1989;160:142–144.
21. Nichols RL, Muzik AC. Enterococcal infections in surgical patients: The mystery continues. Clin Infect Dis. 1992;15:72–76.
22. Kaye D. Enterococci: Biologic and epidemiologic characteristics and in vitro susceptibility. Arch Intern Med. 1982;142:2006–2009.
23. Murray BE, Singh KV, Markowitz SM, et al. Evidence for clonal spread of a single strain of β-lactamase–producing *Enterococcus faecalis* to six hospitals in five states. J Infect Dis. 1991;163:780–785.
24. Murray BE, Lopardo HA, Rubeglio EA, et al. Intrahospital spread of a single gentamicin-resistant, β-lactamase–producing strain of *Enterococcus faecalis* in Argentina. Antimicrob Agents Chemother. 1992;36:230–232.
25. Zervos MJ, Terpenning MS, Schaberg DR, et al. High-level aminoglycoside-resistant enterococci. Colonization of nursing home and acute care hospital patients. Arch Intern Med. 1987;147:1591–1594.
26. Zervos MJ, Dembinski S, Mikesell T, et al. High-level resistance to gentamicin in *Streptococcus faecalis:* Risk factors and evidence for exogenous acquisition of infection. J Infect Dis. 1986;153:1075–1083.
27. Hall RW, Bayer AS, Mayer WP, et al. Infective endocarditis following human-to-human enterococcal transmission. Arch Intern Med. 1976;136:1173–1174.
28. Hall LMC, Duke B, Urwin G, et al. Epidemiology of *Enterococcus faecalis* urinary tract infection in a teaching hospital in London, United Kingdom. J Clin Microbiol. 1992;30:1953–1957.
29. Rhinehart E, Smith NE, Wennersten C, et al. Rapid dissemination of β-lactamase–producing, aminoglycoside-resistant *Enterococcus faecalis* among patients and staff on an infant-toddler surgical ward. N Engl J Med. 1990;323:1814–1818.
30. Schoonmaker DJ, Bopp LH, Baltch AL, et al. Genetic analysis of multiple vancomycin-resistant *Enterococcus* isolates obtained serially from two long-term-care patients. J Clin Microbiol. 1998;36:2105.
31. Livornese LL Jr, Drus S, Samel C, et al. Hospital-acquired infection with vancomycin-resistant *Enterococcus faecium* transmitted by electronic thermometers. Ann Intern Med. 1992:117:112–116.
32. Schaberg DR, Culver DH, Gaynes RP. Major trends in the microbial etiology of nosocomial infection. Am J Med. 1991;91(Suppl 3B):3B72S–3B75S.
33. Handwerger S, Raucher B, Altarac D, et al. Nosocomial outbreak due to *Enterococcus faecium* highly resistant to vancomycin, penicillin and gentamicin. Clin Infect Dis. 1993;16:750–755.
34. Wells VD, Wong ES, Murray BE, et al. Infections due to beta-lactamase producing, high-level gentamicin-resistant *Enterococcus faecalis.* Ann Intern Med. 1992;116:285–292.
35. Centers for Disease Control and Prevention. Nosocomial enterococci resistant to vancomycin—United States, 1989–1993. MMWR Morb Mortal Wkly Rep. 1993;42:597–599.
36. Moellering RC Jr, Wennersten C, Medrek T, et al. Prevalence of high-level resistance to aminoglycosides in clinical isolates of enterococci. Antimicrob Agents Chemother. 1970;335–340.
37. Moellering RC Jr. Enterococcal infections in patients treated with moxalactam. Rev Infect Dis. 1982;4(Suppl):S708–S711.
38. Zervos MJ, Bacon AE III, Patterson JE, et al. Enterococcal superinfection in patients treated with ciprofloxacin. J Antimicrob Chemother. 1988;21:113–115.
39. Jones RN. Gram-positive superinfections following beta-lactam chemotherapy: The significance of the enterococcus. Infection. 1988;13(Suppl 1):S81–S88.
40. Reiner NE, Gopalakrishna KV, Lerner PI. Enterococcal endocarditis in heroin addicts. JAMA. 1976;235:1861–1863.
41. Venditti M, Tarasi A, Visco Comandini U, et al. Enterococcal septicemia in patients with hematological malignancies. Eur J Clin Microbiol Infect Dis. 1993;12:241–247.
42. Moellering RC Jr. Infections due to group D streptococci. Infect Dis Rev. 1981;6: 1–17.
43. Edelstein H, McCabe RE. Perinephric abscess. Modern diagnosis and treatment in 47 cases. Medicine. 1988;67:118–131.
44. Morrison AJ Jr, Wenzel RP. Nosocomial urinary tract infections due to enterococcus; ten years' experience at a university hospital. Arch Intern Med. 1986;146:1549–1551.
45. Warren JW, Tenney JH, Hoopes JM. A prospective microbiologic study of bacteruria in patients with chronic indwelling uretheral catheters. J Infect Dis. 1982;146:719–723.
46. Krieger JN, Kaiser DL, Wenzel RP. Urinary tract etiology of bloodstream infections in hospitalized patients. J Infect Dis. 1983;148:57–62.
47. Maki DG, Agger WA, Enterococcal bacteremia: Clinical features, the risk of endocarditis, and management. Medicine. 1988;64:248–269.
48. Graninger W, Ragette R. Nosocomial bacteremia due to *Enterococcus faecalis* without endocarditis. Clin Infect Dis. 1992;15:49–57.
49. Shlaes DM, Levy J, Wolinsky E. Enterococcal bacteremia without endocarditis. Arch Intern Med. 1981;141:578–581.
50. Linden PK, Pasculle AW, Manez R, et al. Differences in outcomes for patients with bacteremia due to vancomycin-resistant *Enterococcus faecium* or vancomycin-susceptible *E. faecium.* Clin Infect Dis. 1996;22:663.
51. Gullberg RM, Homann SR, Phair JP. Enterococcal bacteremia: Analysis of 75 episodes. Rev Infect Dis. 1989;11:74–85.
52. Hoge CW, Adams J, Buchanan B, et al. Enterococcal bacteremia: To treat or not to treat, a reappraisal. Rev Infect Dis. 1991;13:600–605.
53. Moellering RC Jr. Treatment of enterococcal endocarditis. In: Sande MA, Kaye D, Root RK, eds. Endocarditis. New York: Churchill Livingstone; 1984:113–133.
54. Facklam RR, Collins MD. Identification of *Enterococcus* species isolated from human infections by a conventional test scheme. J Clin Microbiol. 1989;27:731–734.
55. Rice LB, Calderwood SB, Eliopoulos GM, et al. Enterococcal endocarditis: A comparison of prosthetic and native valve disease. Rev Infect Dis. 1991;13:1–7.
56. Megran DW. Enterococcal endocarditis. Clin Infect Dis. 1992;15:63–71.
57. Koenig MG, Kaye D. Enterococcal endocarditis: Report of nineteen cases with long-term follow-up data. N Engl J Med. 1961;264:257–264.
58. Mandell G, Kaye D, Levison ME, et al. Enterococcal endocarditis. An analysis of 38 patients observed at the New York Hospital–Cornell Medical Center. Arch Intern Med. 1970;125:258–264.
59. Moellering RC Jr, Watson BK, Kunz LJ. Endocarditis due to group D streptococci: Comparison of disease caused by *Streptococcus bovis* with that produced by the enterococci. Am J Med. 1974;57:239–258.
60. Wilson WR, Wilkowske CJ, Wright AJ, et al. Treatment of streptomycin-susceptible and streptomycin-resistant enterococcal endocarditis. Ann Intern Med. 1984;100:816–823.
61. Dougherty SH. Role of enterococcus in intraabdominal sepsis. Am J Surg. 1984;148:308–312.
62. Harding GKM, Buckwold FJ, Ronald AR, et al. Prospective, randomized comparative study of clindamycin, chloramphenicol, and ticarcillin, each in combination with gentamicin, in therapy for intraabdominal and female genital tract sepsis. J Infect Dis. 1980;142:384–393.
63. Bartlett JG, Onderdonk AB, Louis T, et al. A review: Lessons from an animal model of intra-abdominal sepsis. Arch Surg. 1978;113:853–857.
64. Willey SH, Hindes RG, Eliopoulos GM, et al. Effects of clindamycin-gentamicin and other antimicrobial combinations against enterococci in an experimental intraabdominal abscess model. Surg Gynecol Obstet. 1989;169:199–202.
65. Weigelt JA, Easley SM, Thal ER, et al. Abdominal surgical wound infection is lowered with improved perioperative enterococcus and bacteroides therapy. J Trauma. 1993;34:579–585.
66. Weinstein MP, Iannini PB, Stratton CW, et al. Spontaneous bacterial peritonitis: A review of 28 cases with emphasis on improved survival and factors influencing prognosis. Am J Med. 1978;64:592–598.
67. Ledger WJ, Norman M, Gee C, et al. Bacteremia on an obstetric-gynecologic service. Am J Obstet Gynecol. 1975;121:205–212.
68. Horvitz RA, von Graevenitz A. A clinical study of the role of enterococci as sole agents of wound and tissue infection. Yale J Biol Med. 1977;50:391–395.
69. Smith RF, Dayton SL. Colonization of burns by *Streptococcus faecalis* related to contaminated porcine xenografts. Tex Rep Biol Med. 1973;31:47–54.
70. Bayer AS, Seidel JS, Yoshikawa TT, et al. Group D enterococcal meningitis. Clinical and therapeutic considerations with report of three cases and review of the literature. Arch Intern Med. 1976;136:883–886.
71. Buchino JJ, Ciambarella E, Light E. Systemic group D streptococcal infection in newborn infants. Am J Dis Child. 1979;133:270–273.
72. Ryan JJ, Pachner A, Andriole VT, et al. Enterococcal meningitis: Combined vancomycin and rifampin therapy. Am J Med. 1980;68:449–451.
73. Berk SL, Verghese A, Holtsclaw SA, et al. Enterococcal pneumonia. Occurrence in patients receiving broad-spectrum antibiotic regimens and enteral feeding. Am J Med. 1983;74:153–154.
74. Morris JF, Okies JE. Enterococcal lung abscess: Medical and surgical therapy. Chest. 1974;65:688–691.
75. Siegel JD, McCracken GH. Group D streptococcal infections. J Pediatr. 1978;93:542–543.
76. Bavikatte K, Schreiner RL, Lemons JA, et al. Group D streptococcal septicemia in the neonate. Am J Dis Child. 1979;133:493–496.
77. Coudron PE, Mayhall CG, Facklam RR, et al. *Streptococcus faecium* outbreak in a neonatal intensive care unit. J Clin Microbiol. 1984;20:1044–1048.
78. Luginbuhl LM, Rotbart HA, Facklam RR, et al. Neonatal enterococcal sepsis: Case control study and description of an outbreak. Pediatr Infect Dis. 1987;6:1022–1030.

79. Moellering RC Jr, Krogstad DJ. Antibiotic resistance in enterococci. In: Schlessinger D, ed. Microbiology—1979. Washington, DC: American Society for Microbiology; 1979:293–298.
80. Williamson R, Calderwood SB, Moellering RC, et al. Studies on the mechanism of intrinsic resistance to beta-lactam antibiotics in enterococcal group D streptococci. J Gen Microbiol. 1983;129:813–822.
81. Williamson R, LeBouguénec C, Gutmann L, et al. One or two low affinity penicillin-binding proteins may be responsible for the range of susceptibility of *Enterococcus faecium* to benzylpenicillin. J Gen Microbiol. 1985;131:1933–1940.
82. Grayson ML, Eliopoulos GM, Wennersten CB, et al. Increasing resistance to β-lactam antibiotics among clinical isolates of *E. faecium:* A 22-year review at one institution. Antimicrob Agents Chemother. 1991;35:2180–2184.
83. Moellering RC Jr, Weinberg AN. Studies on antibiotic synergism against enterococci. II. Effect of various antibiotics on the uptake of ^{14}C-labelled streptomycin by enterococci. J Clin Invest. 1971;50:2580–2584.
84. Hamilton-Miller JMT. Reversal of activity of trimethoprim against gram-positive cocci by thymidine, thymine, and "folates." J Antimicrob Chemother. 1988;22:35–39.
85. Grayson ML, Thauvin-Eliopoulos C, Eliopoulos GM, et al. Failure of trimethoprim-sulfamethoxazole therapy in experimental enterococcal endocarditis. Antimicrob Agents Chemother. 1991;34:1792–1794.
86. Goodhart GL. In vivo v. in vitro susceptibility of *Enterococcus* to trimethoprim-sulfamethoxazole. JAMA. 1984;252:2748–2749.
87. Leclercq R, Dutka-Malen S, Brisson-Noël A, et al. Resistance of enterococci to aminoglycosides and glycopeptides. Clin Infect Dis. 1992;15:495–501.
88. Zighelboim-Daum S, Moellering RC Jr. Mechanisms and significance of antimicrobial resistance in enterococci. In: Actor P, Daneo-Moore L, Higgins ML, et al, eds. Antibiotic Inhibition of Bacterial Cell Surface Assembly and Function. Washington, DC: American Society for Microbiology; 1988:603–625.
89. Eliopoulos GM, Farber BF, Murray BE, et al. Ribosomal resistance of clinical enterococcal isolates to streptomycin. Antimicrob Agents Chemother. 1984;25:398–399.
90. Chow JW, Zervos MJ, Lerner SA, et al. A novel gentamicin resistance gene in *Enterococcus*. Antimicrob Agents Chemother. 1997;41:511.
91. Tsai SF, Zervos MJ, Clewell DB, et al. A new high-level gentamicin resistance gene, aph(2″)-*Id*, in *Enterococcus* spp. Antimicrob Agents Chemother. 1998;42:1229.
92. Wennersten CB, Moellering RC Jr. Mechanism of resistance to penicillin-aminoglycoside synergism in *Streptococcus faecium.* In: Nelson JD, Grassi C, eds. Current Chemotherapy and Infectious Disease. Proceedings of the 11th International Congress of Chemotherapy and the 19th Interscience Congress on Antimicrobial Agents and Chemotherapy, Boston. Washington, DC: American Society for Microbiology; 1979:710–712.
93. Costa Y, Galimand M, Leclercq R, et al. Characterization of the chromosomal *aac(6′)-Ii* gene specific for *Enterococcus faecium.* Antimicrob Agents Chemother. 1993;37:1896–1903.
94. Eliopoulos GM, Wennersten C, Zighelboim-Daum S, et al. High level resistance to gentamicin in clinical isolates of *Streptococcus (Enterococcus) faecium.* Antimicrob Agents Chemother. 1988;32:1528–1532.
95. Frieden TR, Munsiff SS, Low DE, et al. Emergence of vancomycin-resistant enterococci in New York City. Lancet. 1993;342:76–79.
96. Moellering RC Jr. Vancomycin-resistant enterococci. Clin Infect Dis. 1998;26:1196.
97. Arthur M, Courvalin P. Genetics and mechanisms of glycopeptide resistance in enterococci. Antimicrob Agents Chemother. 1993;37:1563–1571.
98. Williamson R, Al-Obeid S, Shlaes JH, et al. Inducible resistance to vancomycin in *Enterococcus faecium* D 366. J Infect Dis. 1989;159:1095–1104.
99. Handwerger S, Perlman DC, Altarac D, et al. Concomitant high-level vancomycin and penicillin resistance in clinical isolates of enterococci. Clin Infect Dis. 1992;14:655–661.
100. Quintiliani R Jr, Evers S, Courvalin P. The *vanB* gene confers various levels of self-transferable resistance to vancomycin in enterococci. J Infect Dis. 1993;167:1220–1223.
101. Gold HS, Ünal S, Cercenado E, et al. A gene conferring resistance to vancomycin but not teicoplanin in isolates of *Enterococcus faecalis* and *Enterococcus faecium* demonstrates homology with *vanB, vanA,* and *vanC* genes of enterococci. Antimicrob Agents Chemother. 1993;37:1604–1609.
102. Perichon B, Reynolds P, Courvalin P. VanD-type glycopeptide-resistant *E. faecium* BM 4339. Antimicrob Agents Chemother. 1997;41:2016.
103. Ostrowsky B, Clark N, Eliopoulos CT, et al. A cluster of VanD glycopeptide-resistant (GR) *E. faecium:* Molecular characterization and clinical epidemiology. J Infect Dis. 1999. In press.
104. Huycke MM, Sahm DF, Gilmore MS. Multiple-drug resistant enterococci: The nature of the problem and an agenda for the future. Emerg Infect Dis. 1998;4:239–249.
105. Recommendations for preventing the spread of vancomycin resistance. MMWR Morb Mortal Wkly Rep. 1995;44(Sept 22): No. RR12.
106. Murray BE. Diversity among multidrug-resistant enterococci. Emerg Infect Dis. 1998;4:37–47.
107. O'Donovan CA, Fan-Habard P, Tecson-Tumang FT, et al. Enteric eradication of vancomycin-resistant *Enterococcus faecium* with oral bacitracin. Diagn Microbiol Infect Dis. 1994;18:105–109.
108. Murray BE, Mederski-Samoraj B. Transferable β-lactamase: A new mechanism for in vitro penicillin resistance in *Streptococcus faecalis.* J Clin Invest. 1983;72:1168–1171.
109. Zschek KK, Murray BE. Genes involved in the regulation of β-lactamase production in enterococci and staphylococci. Antimicrob Agents Chemother. 1993;37:1966–1970.
110. Clewell DB. Conjugative transposons and the dissemination of antibiotic resistance in streptococci. Am Rev Microbiol. 1986;40:635–659.
111. Schaberg DR, Zervos MJ. Intergenic and interspecies gene exchange in gram-positive cocci. Antimicrob Agents Chemother. 1986;30:817–822.
112. Eliopoulos GM, Moellering RC Jr. Antimicrobial combinations. In: Lorian V, ed. Antibiotics in Laboratory Medicine. Baltimore: Williams & Wilkins; 1991;432:92.
113. The choice of antibiotic agents. Med Lett. 1992;34:49–56.
114. Martinez-Martinez L, Joyanas P, Pascual A, et al. Activity of eight fluoroquinolones against enterococci. Clin Microbiol Infect. 1997;3:497.
115. Schaberg DR, Dillon WI, Terpenning MS, et al. Increasing resistance of enterococci to ciprofloxacin. Antimicrob Agents Chemother. 1992;36:2523–2535.
116. No reference cited.
117. Dougherty SH, Flohr AB, Simmons RL. "Breakthrough" enterococcal septicemia in surgical patients. Arch Surg. 1983;118:232–237.
118. Moellering RC Jr. *Streptococcus faecalis.* In: Magilligan DJ, Quinn EL, eds. Endocarditis. Medical and Surgical Management. New York: Marcel Dekker; 1986:49–56.
119. Watanakunakorn C, Patel R. Comparison of patients with enterococcal bacteremia due to strains with and without high-level resistance to gentamicin. Clin Infect Dis. 1993;17:74–78.
120. Hunter TH. Use of streptomycin in treatment of bacterial endocarditis. Am J Med. 1947;2:436–442.
121. Krogstad DJ, Parquette AR. Defective killing of enterococci: A common property of antimicrobial agents acting on the cell wall. Antimicrob Agents Chemother. 1980;17:965–968.
122. Bisno AL, Dismukes WE, Durack DT, et al. Antimicrobial treatment of infective endocarditis due to viridans streptococci, enterococci and staphylococci. JAMA. 1989;261:1471–1477.
123. Weinstein AJ, Moellering RC Jr. Penicillin and gentamicin therapy for enterococcal infections. JAMA. 1973;223:1030–1032.
124. Herman DJ, Gerding DW. Screening and treatment of infections caused by resistant enterococci. Antimicrob Agents Chemother. 1991;35:215–219.
125. Shlaes DM, Etter L, Gutmann L. Synergistic killing of vancomycin-resistant enterococci of classes A, B, and C by combinations of vancomycin, penicillin and gentamicin. Antimicrob Agents Chemother. 1991;35:776–779.
126. Cercenado E, Eliopoulos GM, Wennersten CB, et al. Absence of synergistic activity between ampicillin and vancomycin against highly vancomycin-resistant enterococci. Antimicrob Agents Chemother. 1922;36:2201–2203.
127. Caron F, Carbon C, Gutmann L. Triple-combination penicillin-vancomycin-gentamicin for experimental endocarditis caused by a moderately penicillin- and highly glycopeptide-resistant isolate of *Enterococcus faecium.* J Infect Dis. 1991;164:888–893.
128. Caron F, Lemeland J-F, Humbert G, et al. Triple combination penicillin-vancomycin-gentamicin for experimental endocarditis caused by a highly penicillin- and glycopeptide-resistant isolate of *Enterococcus faecium.* J Infect Dis. 1993;168:681–686.
129. Hayden MK, Trenholme GM, Schultz JE, et al. In vivo development of teicoplanin resistance in a VanB *Enterococcus faecium* isolate. J Infect Dis. 1993;167:1224–1227.
130. Moellering RC, Harding I, Gibbs M, et al. Compassionate use of teicoplanin in cases of vancomycin hypersensitivity, resistance and failure. Abstract LM-20b. In: Abstracts of the 37th Interscience Conference on Antimicrobial Agents and Chemotherapy (ICAAC). Washington, DC: ASM; 1997:367.
131. Eliopoulos GM, Thauvin-Eliopoulos C, Moellering RC Jr. Contribution of animal models in the search for effective therapy for endocarditis due to enterococci with high-level resistance to gentamicin. Clin Infect Dis. 1992;15:58–62.
132. Presterl E, Graninger W, Georgopoulos A. The efficacy of teicoplanin in the treatment of endocarditis caused by gram-positive bacteria. J Antimicrob Chemother. 1993;31:755–766.
133. Schmitt JL. Efficiency of teicoplanin for enterococcal infections: 63 cases and review. Clin Infect Dis. 1992;15:302–306.
134. Hamilton-Millen JMT. From foreign pharmacopoeias: "New" antibiotics from old? J Antimicrob Chemother. 1991;27:702–705.
135. Eliopoulos GM. Activity of antimicrobials alone and in combination against vancomycin-resistant enterococci. In: Abstracts of 33rd Interscience Conference on Antimicrobial Agents and Chemotherapy (ICAAC), New Orleans, La; 1993:17.
136. Collins LA, Malanoski GJ, Eliopoulos GM, et al. In vitro activity of RP59500 an injectable streptogramin antibiotic, against vancomycin-resistant gram-positive organisms. Antimicrob Agents Chemother. 1993;37:598.
137. Bostic GD, Perri MB, Thal LA, et al. Comparative in vitro and bactericidal activity of oxazolidinone antibiotics against multidrug-resistant enterococci. Diagn Microbiol Infect Dis. 1998;30:109.
138. Cormican MG, Marshall SA, Jones RN. Preliminary interpretive criteria for disk diffusion susceptibility testing of SCH 27899, a compound in the everninomicin class of antimicrobial agents. Diagn Microbiol Infect Dis. 1995;23:157.
139. Van Teil FH, van den Bogaard TE. In vitro susceptibility to LY333328 of vancomycin-resistant enterococci isolated from humans and animals. J Antimicrob Chemother. 1997;40:733.
140. Moellering RC Jr, Cerwinka SL. Early clinical results with quinupristin/dalfopristin for the therapy of bacteremia due to resistant gram-positive bacteria. In: Zinner SH, Young LS, Acar JF, Neu HC, eds. Expanding Indications for the New Macrolides, Azalides, and Streptogramins. New York: Marcel Dekker; 1997:173–176.

141. Ruoff KL, Ferraro MJ, Holden J, et al. Identification of *Streptococcus bovis* and *Streptococcus salivarius* in clinical laboratories. J Clin Microbiol. 1984;20:223–226.
142. Moellering RC Jr, Watson BK, Kunz L. Endocarditis due to group D streptococci. Comparison of disease caused by *Streptococcus bovis* with that caused by the enterococci. Am J Med. 1974;57:239–250.
143. Ruoff KL, Miller SI, Garner CV, et al. Bacteremia with *Streptococcus bovis* and *Streptococcus salivarius:* Clinical correlates of more accurate identification of isolates. J Clin Microbiol. 1989;27:305–308.
144. Poyart C, Pierre C, Quesne G, et al. Emergence of vancomycin resistance from the genus *Streptococcus:* Characterization of a vanB transferable determinant in *Streptococcus bovis.* Antimicrob Agents Chemother. 1997;41:24.
145. Facklam RR. Recognition of group D streptococcal species of human origin by biochemical and physiological tests. Appl Microbiol. 1972;23:1131–1139.
146. Coykendall AL, Gustafson KB. Deoxyribonucleic acid hybridization among strains of *Streptococcus salivarius* and *Streptococcus bovis.* Int J Syst Bacteriol. 1985;35:274–280
147. Raverby WD, Bottone EJ, Keusch GT. Group D streptococcal bacteremia, with emphasis on the incidence an presentation of infections due to *Streptococcus bovis.* N Engl J Med. 1973;289:1400–1403.
148. Hoppes WL, Lerner PI. Nonenterococcal group-D streptococcal endocarditis, caused by *Streptococcus bovis.* Ann Intern Med. 1974;81:588–593.
149. Watanakunakorn C. *Streptococcus bovis* endocarditis. Am J Med. 1974;56:256–260.
150. Murray HW, Roberts RB. *Streptococcus bovis* bacteremia and underlying gastrointestinal disease. Arch Intern Med. 1978;138:1097–1099.
151. Reynolds JG, Silva E, McCormack WM. Association of *Streptococcus bovis* bacteremia with bowel disease. J Clin Microbiol. 1983;17:696–697.
152. Klein RS, Recco RA, Catalano MT, et al. Association of *Streptococcus bovis* with carcinoma of the colon. N Engl J Med. 1977;297:800–802.
153. Klein RS, Catalano MT, Edberg SC, et al. *Streptococcus bovis* septicemia and carcinoma of the colon. Ann Intern Med. 1979;91:560–562.
154. Burns CA, McCaughey M, Lauter CB. The association of *Streptococcus bovis* fecal carriage and colon neoplasia: Possible relationship with polyps and their premalignant potential. Am J Gastroenterol. 1985;80:42–46.
155. Klein RS, Warman SW, Knackmuhs GG, et al. Lack of association of *Streptococcus bovis* with noncolonic gastrointestinal carcinoma. Am J Gastroenterol. 1987;82:540–543.
156. No reference provided.
157. Ruoff KL, *Leuconostoc, Pediococcus, Stomatococcus* and miscellaneous gram-positive cocci that grow aerobically. In: Murray PR, Baron EJ, Pfaller MA, eds. Manual of Clinical Microbiology. 7th ed. Washington, DC: American Society for Microbiology; 1999;306–315.
158. Mackey T, Lejeune V, Janssens M, et al. Identification of vancomycin-resistant lactic bacteria isolated from humans. J Clin Microbiol. 1993;31:2499–2501.
159. Garvie EI. Genus *Leuconostoc.* In: Sneath PHA, Mair NS, Sharpe ME, et al, eds. Bergey's Manual of Systematic Bacteriology, v. 2. Baltimore: Williams & Wilkins; 1986:1071–1075.
160. Ruoff KL, Kuritzkes DR, Wolfson JS, et al. Vancomycin-resistant gram-positive bacteria isolated from human sources. J Clin Microbiol. 1988;26:2064–2068.
161. Buu-Hoi A, Branger C, Acar JF. Vancomycin-resistant streptococci or *Leuconostoc* sp. Antimicrob Agents Chemother. 1985;28:458–460.
162. Coovadia YM, Solwa Z, van den Ende J. Meningitis caused by a vancomycin-resistant *Leuconostoc* sp. J Clin Microbiol. 1987;25:1784–1785.
163. Isenberg HD, Vellozzi EM, Shaprio J, et al. Clinical laboratory challenges in the recognition of *Leuconostoc* spp. J Clin Microbiol. 1988;26:479–483.
164. Wenocur HS, Smith MA, Vellozzi EM, et al. Odontogenic infection secondary to *Leuconostoc* species. J Clin Microbiol. 1988;26:1893–1894.
165. Arthur M, Courvalin P. Genetics and mechanisms of glycopeptide resistance in enterococci. Antimicrob Agents Chemother. 1993;37:1563–1571.
166. De La Maza L, Ruoff KL, Ferraro MJ. In vitro activities of daptomycin and other antimicrobial agents against vancomycin-resistant gram-positive bacteria. Antimicrob Agents Chemother. 1989;33:1383–1384.
167. Swensen JM, Facklam RR, Thornsberry C. Antimicrobial susceptibility of vancomycin-resistant *Leuconostoc, Pediococcus,* and *Lactobacillus* species. Antimicrob Agents Chemother. 1990;34:543–549.
168. Collins LA, Malanoski GJ, Eliopoulos GM, et al. In vitro activity of RP 59500, an injectable streptogramin antibiotic against vancomycin-resistant gram-positive organisms. Antimicrob Agents Chemother. 1993;37:598–601.
169. Martinez-Martinez L, Saavedra JM, Conejo MC. Bacteremia caused by *Leuconostoc* spp. Clin Microbiol Newslett. 1992;14:102–104.

Chapter 190

Streptococcus agalactiae (Group B Streptococcus)

MORVEN S. EDWARDS
CAROL J. BAKER

HISTORICAL PERSPECTIVE

Group B streptococci (*Streptococcus agalactiae*) were first reported as human pathogens in 1935 by Fry, who described three cases of fatal puerperal sepsis.[1] Before Fry, Lancefield and Hare[2] had identified these organisms in vaginal cultures from asymptomatic postpartum women. Human group B streptococcal infection, however, was reported infrequently until the early 1960s, when several authors indicated that disease due to these organisms might be more common than was appreciated previously.[3–5] By the 1970s, group B streptococcus had become the predominant pathogen causing septicemia and meningitis in neonates and infants younger than 3 months. Initially a concern of pediatricians alone, group B streptococcal disease has a presence in the specialties of obstetrics and geriatrics, among others.[6] It is a cause of substantial pregnancy-related morbidity and has emerged as an increasingly common cause of invasive disease in nonpregnant adults.[7] A population-based study reported that one half of patients with invasive group B streptococcal disease were 18 years of age or older, and the disease incidence was highest in nonpregnant adults older than 60 years.[8, 9] Implementation of recommendations for the use of maternal intrapartum chemoprophylaxis has been associated, in some geographic regions, with a significant decrease in the incidence of early-onset disease in neonates.[10]

DESCRIPTION

Classification and Morphologic Characteristics

S. agalactiae is the species designation for streptococci belonging to Lancefield group B. The serologic differentiation of hemolytic streptococci by groups was described in 1933. It is based on the capillary precipitin reaction between the group-specific carbohydrate cell wall antigen with hyperimmune rabbit antisera.[11] Group B streptococci are facultative, gram-positive diplococci that grow on a variety of bacteriologic media. Isolated colonies on sheep blood agar are 3 to 4 mm in diameter and grayish-white. The flat, somewhat mucoid colonies are surrounded by a narrow zone of β-hemolysis that, for some strains, is detectable only on lifting a colony from the agar. Although 1 to 2% of strains are nonhemolytic, rarely are they α-hemolytic. To enhance the accurate detection of even low numbers of group B streptococci from sites such as the genital or gastrointestinal tract, a number of selective broth media have been employed. These usually contain Todd-Hewitt broth with or without sheep red blood cells and antimicrobial agents such as nalidixic acid and gentamicin or colistin.[12]

Identification

Definitive identification of group B streptococci is based on detection of the group B–specific cell wall antigen common to all strains. A number of serologic methods using hyperimmune group B–specific antisera have been developed for the detection of the group B antigen: countercurrent immunoelectrophoresis, enzyme-linked immunosorbent assay, indirect immunofluorescence, staphylococcal coagglutination, and latex agglutination. Latex agglutination is the most widely employed. When the manufacturer's instructions are followed, these products for serogrouping β-hemolytic streptococci (Sero STAT, Scott Laboratories, Inc.; Streptex, Wellcome Research Laboratories, Dartford, England) are comparable to the Lancefield capillary precipitin method.[13]

Nonserologic methods that permit the presumptive identification of group B streptococci include resistance to bacitracin or trimethoprim-sulfamethoxazole, positive sodium hippurate hydrolysis, and the production of an orange pigment during anaerobic growth on certain media. β-Hemolytic streptococci that hydrolyze sodium hippurate belong to either group B or group D; these may be distinguished on the basis of hydrolysis of bile esculin agar. Among group D strains, 99% hydrolyze bile esculin, whereas 99 to 100% of group B strains fail to react.[14] Production of CAMP factor, which is a thermostable extracellular protein that results in synergistic hemolysis on sheep blood agar with the β-lysin of *Staphylococcus aureus*, is observed in 98 to 100% of group B streptococci. A spot CAMP test, available commercially, allows rapid identification of group B streptococci from a single colony of the primary isolation plate.[15] The combination of the CAMP test with bacitracin sensitivity and the bile esculin reaction is adequate for the presumptive differentiation of group B from other serogroups of β-hemolytic streptococci.[16]

Serologic Classification

Lancefield defined two cell wall carbohydrate antigens for group B streptococci, the group B–specific or C substance common to all strains of this serogroup and the type-specific or S substance that allowed classification into the serotypes I, II, and III.[17] Later, Lancefield reported distinct differences in serotype I strains, and in the early 1970s these were designated Ia, Ib, and Ic.[18] These strains possess a capsular polysaccharide antigen, Ia or Ib, and some Ia and all Ib strains also have a surface-protein antigen, now designated C protein, that is found in approximately 60% of type II, and occasional type III and type V strains. The nomenclature of group B streptococci has been revised to designate the capsular polysaccharides as type-specific antigens with surface proteins as additional antigenic markers.[19] Thus, the former type Ic presently is designated type Ia/c, the former type Ib is type Ib/c, and strains designated Ia do not contain C protein. At least two distinct types of C protein, the α- and β-proteins, are defined, and individual strains may contain one or both components. Other proteins, designated R, X, and Rib, are found in some strains, but their biologic significance is not understood. Additional capsular polysaccharide types, IV, V, VI, VII, and VIII (also called JM9), each with unique polysaccharides alone or with protein antigens, have been defined,[20–23] and additional candidates are being evaluated. Antibodies directed against the Ia, Ib, and II polysaccharide antigens, but not against III, were shown by Lancefield to provide passive protection for mice challenged with homologous—but not heterologous—antigen-containing strains.[24] Although mouse virulence for type III strains could not be achieved in the original mouse-protective assay, others subsequently modified this experimental model so that antibody to the type III capsular polysaccharide antigen also protected against challenge with strains containing the homologous but not the heterologous antigens.[25] The α and β C proteins and Rib also can elicit protective antibodies in animals,[26–28] but their role in human infections is not known. Antibodies directed at the group B antigen are not protective.

EPIDEMIOLOGY AND TRANSMISSION

Asymptomatic Colonization

Group B streptococci have been isolated from genital or lower gastrointestinal tract cultures of pregnant and nonpregnant women at rates ranging from 5 to 40%.[29, 30] These variations in the reported prevalence of asymptomatic colonization relate not only to differences in the sites sampled and bacteriologic method for detection of the organism, but also to demographic differences in the populations studied (Table 190–1). When more than one appropriate site such as the lower vagina or the periurethral area and the rectum is sampled and when the selective broth media are utilized, the rate of colonization usually exceeds 20%. Group B streptococci may be associated with asymptomatic bacteriuria during pregnancy,[31] and bacteriuria also is a marker for a high genital inoculum ("heavy colonization"). Heavy vaginal colonization with group B streptococci occurs more frequently among African-American women.[32] Diabetes mellitus also is independently associated with higher rates of group B streptococcal colonization during pregnancy.[33] Significantly lower genital colonization rates have been reported for women who are sexually inexperienced, older than 20 years, or multiparous.[34] Pregnancy itself does not influence the prevalence of colonization with group B streptococcus.

The principal reservoir for group B streptococci may be the lower gastrointestinal tract. Studies documenting a rectal/vaginal isolation ratio exceeding 1 and the rectum as the site most accurately predicting chronicity of carriage support the possibility that genital colonization may reflect contamination from the rectum.[35, 36] Further, group B streptococci have been isolated from the proximal part

TABLE 190–1 Factors Influencing Detection of Group B Streptococcal Colonization

Feature	Effect on Isolation Rate: *Increased*	*Decreased*	*None*
Method employed			
Culture medium	Broth media Antibiotic-containing media	Agar media Nonselective broth media	
Site(s)	Lower vagina and rectum Multiple sites	Cervical os Single site	
Interval	≥2 cultures in 6–8-wk interval	Single sampling time	
Genital carriage in women			
Pregnancy			+
Timing during pregnancy			+
Day of menstrual cycle	First half		
Age	≤20 yr		
Sexual activity	Active	Virgin	
Frequency of sexual intercourse or total number of partners			+
Vaginal discharge			+
Birth control method	Intrauterine device		Oral contraceptives
Parity	Primigravida	>3 pregnancies	
Ethnic origin	African American		
Marital status			+
Socioeconomic group	Lower income		

of the small intestine of adults. The prevalence of oropharyngeal colonization is low (approximately 5%), but this may approach 20% in homosexual men.

Transmission to Neonates

Mucous membrane colonization of newborns results from vertical transmission of the organism from the mother, either in utero by the ascending route or at the time of delivery. The rate of vertical transmission in neonates born to women colonized with group B streptococci at the time of delivery is approximately 50%.[37, 38] Paired isolates from mothers and their neonates usually are of concordant serotypes. A high genital inoculum at delivery, as detected by semiquantitative culture methods, significantly increases the likelihood of vertical transmission.[35, 38, 39] Infants born to heavily colonized women are more likely to develop early-onset (younger than 7 days) disease.[35]

In addition to maternal intrapartum exposure, nosocomial colonization of the neonate may occasionally occur. Nosocomial acquisition is more likely when the maternal population has a high colonization rate and when conditions in the nursery (e.g., crowding, poor hand washing, a prolonged length of stay) promote horizontal transmission. Although high rates have been reported,[40] nosocomial transmission of group B streptococci is negligible in most nurseries. Noya and associates[41] described a cluster of late-onset infections that appeared to result from a single epidemic strain of type Ib/c group B streptococcus. Epidemiologic analysis suggested that infant-to-infant spread via the hands of personnel was the most likely mode of acquisition.[41] A few smaller case clusters have been attributed to nosocomial acquisition of type III strains. Community acquisition of group B streptococci in young infants occurs but infrequently.[42]

Vertical transmission is required for the development of invasive early-onset infection.[37, 38] Factors that increase the incidence of invasive early-onset infection among neonates born to colonized mothers include group B streptococcal bacteriuria; rupture of membranes or delivery at less than 37 weeks of gestation; intrapartum fever (≥38°C) or amnionitis; and rupture of membranes for 18 or more hours before delivery.[43] Studies of maternal features associated with higher attack rates for early-onset neonatal disease have reported African-American origin, an age younger than 20 years, and a history of previous miscarriage.[7, 44] Although some infants who develop late-onset infection acquire the organism from nonmaternal sources,[38] the concordance of serotypes between infant and maternal genital isolates in one half to two thirds of cases suggests that the vertical route of acquisition also is a major determinant of risk for late-onset infections.[45] Additional risk factors for late-onset disease are African-American origin and a gestation of less than 34 weeks.[7]

Incidence and Serotype Distribution of Infection

Since 1970, the reported incidence of early-onset group B streptococcal infection in neonates ranged from 1 to 3 per 1000 live births. A decreasing incidence (less than 1 per 1000 live births) has been documented since 1993 in some geographic areas and is associated with the use of maternal intrapartum chemoprophylaxis.[10] Attack rates for early-onset group B streptococcal disease are inversely related to birth weight and may exceed 20 per 1000 live births among infants with birth weights less than 1000 g.[46] However, approximately 60 to 80% of early-onset infections occur in infants born at gestations of 37 weeks or more.[45–47] The attack rate for late-onset infant infection, which is characterized by the onset of symptoms from 7 days to 3 months of age, is approximately 0.5 to 1.7 per 1000 live births.[45]

Postpartum women are another group of patients in whom group B streptococcal disease is frequently diagnosed. These organisms are estimated to cause 15 to 25% of the cases of peripartum febrile morbidity with or without bacteremia, or an estimated 50,000 cases annually.[48–50] In a study of more than 800 women, intrapartum vaginal colonization with group B streptococci was an independent risk factor for chorioamnionitis, especially with heavy colonization (odds ratio, 3.2).[49] In one population with a known high incidence of carriage, puerperal sepsis due to group B streptococci occurred with an attack rate of 2 per 1000 deliveries.[51] Nonpregnant adults with underlying medical conditions such as diabetes mellitus, chronic liver disease, human immunodeficiency virus infection,[52] malignancy, and stroke also are susceptible to group B streptococcal infections. These nonpregnant adults in a population-based study had an annual incidence of infection of 4.4 cases per 100,000 population and accounted for nearly 50% of all group B streptococcal disease.[8]

In the 1970s and 1980s, type III strains of group B streptococci accounted for one third of early-onset infections, for nearly 90% of late-onset infections, and for most cases of meningitis regardless of the age at the onset of infection.[46] Data from the 1990s indicate a shift in the serotype distribution of invasive isolates from infants and adults.[53, 54] Among neonates with early-onset disease, type Ia predominates and accounts for 35 to 40% of infections, followed by types III (~30%) and V (~15%).[53, 54] Among nonpregnant adults, a population-based surveillance found that types Ia and V were the most prevalent serotypes, each accounting for one third of invasive isolates, with type III strains accounting for another 20% of cases.[55] Types IV, VI through VIII, and nontypable isolates are rarely associated with invasive infection, but in Japan, serotypes VI and VIII are frequently isolated from pregnant women.[56]

PATHOGENESIS

The association between maternal genital tract colonization with group B streptococci at delivery and invasive early-onset infection in neonates is well established.[37, 38] Similarly, there is an increased risk of invasive infection rather than mucosal colonization in neonates when exposure to the organism is *prolonged* by a rupture of membranes for 18 or more hours before delivery or *intensified* by maternal chorioamnionitis or a high genital inoculum.[35, 38, 39, 45] However, these factors do not explain fully the low frequency of invasive infection (estimated at 1 to 2%) among newborns born to colonized mothers.

One explanation for the disparity between the frequency of infant colonization and systemic infection is preterm labor. Heavy maternal colonization with group B streptococcus is associated with an increased risk of delivering a preterm, low-birth-weight infant,[57] and these neonates have a 15-fold increase in risk for early-onset infection when compared with term infants.[38] Ascending infection may be a primary event initiating the rupture of membranes before 37 weeks of gestation.[58] The association of group B streptococcal bacteriuria and rupture of membranes before the onset of labor supports the hypothesis that group B streptococcal infection may predispose to preterm delivery.[59]

Baker and Kasper[60] reported in 1976 that neonates at risk for invasive type III group B streptococcal infection were those with low concentrations of maternal antibodies to the type III capsular antigen; this has been substantiated by others.[61, 62] Since infants born prematurely acquire proportionately lower levels of maternal immunoglobulin G (IgG) than do those born at term, premature infants are less likely to acquire protective levels of type-specific antibodies. Women colonized with type III group B streptococci and delivering healthy neonates have significantly higher concentrations of type III–specific IgG than women whose infants develop early-onset type III disease.[63, 64] A low concentration of maternal antibodies to capsular polysaccharides Ia, Ib, and II at delivery also is a determinant of neonatal susceptibility to infection caused by these serotypes of group B streptococci.[65–67] Antibody to the group B–specific polysaccharide, however, is not protective.[68]

Other host defense factors also contribute to disease susceptibility. For example, the incidence of invasive infection in twins is increased even when corrected for birth weight and gestational age.[69, 70] In addition, classical complement pathway and heat-stable opsonins are required for maximal opsonic activity of strains of the major serotypes.[71–73] The alternative complement pathway participates in opsonophagocytosis of type III strains when specific antibody is present in a sufficient concentration. The opsonophagocytic requirements for type II strains are complex, modulated in part by the C-protein components as well as the type II polysaccharide, and integrity of the classical complement pathway appears essential for effective opsonophagocytosis in vitro.[72, 74] For clinical isolates of type Ia group B streptococcus, opsonization and phagocytosis may proceed by the classical complement pathway in an antibody-independent fashion.[75] Deficient activity by a portion of neonatal sera for clinical isolates of this serotype correlated significantly with low levels of the classic pathway components C1q and C4.[76] Physiologically low levels of complement components or their receptors on phagocytes may provide a partial explanation for age-related susceptibility to group B streptococcal disease. In addition, neutrophil reserves are exhausted rapidly in newborns, so their marrow capacity to infection is limited.[77]

Neutrophil complement and Fc receptors are important in opsonic recognition of group B streptococci. Blockade of complement receptor 3 on neutrophils from adults or neonates inhibits killing of types Ia, III, and V strains of group B streptococci.[73, 78] Blockade of neutrophil Fc receptor III inhibits phagocytosis of type III group B streptococci to an even greater extent.[79] In complement-inactivated serum, Fc receptor II also has a substantial role in mediating ingestion of serotype III strains.[80]

Group B streptococci have been shown in vitro and in experimental models of infection to induce the release of proinflammatory cytokines, including tumor necrosis factor-α, interleukin-1β, interleukin-6, and interleukin-8.[81–84] In animal models, elevated levels of tumor necrosis factor-α have correlated with the severity of disease and with mortality. Purified group-specific polysaccharide and peptidoglycan, rather than serotype-specific capsular polysaccharide, are the bacterial components that induce the inflammatory response.

In addition to host factors, bacterial virulence factors contribute to the host-parasite interaction that determines the outcome between exposure and the development of colonization or invasive group B streptococcal infection. A high quantity of cell-associated sialic acid and its elaboration in supernatant fluid are associated with virulence of type III strains.[85] Transposon mutant strains of type III group B streptococcus have been constructed that are unencapsulated or that express a capsular polysaccharide differing from the wild type in expressing a capsule lacking sialic acid.[86, 87] Each of these changes in capsular expression is associated with a loss of virulence in a neonatal rat model of lethal infection, supporting the critical nature of capsular antigen as a virulence factor.[87] The unique capsular structures of group B streptococci also might enhance the invasiveness of one serotype over another. Type III strains, for example, invade brain microvascular endothelial cells more efficiently than strains from other common serotypes (although the capsule itself does not facilitate invasion).[88] The capsular polysaccharides of types Ia, Ib, II, III, IV, and V each contain glucose, galactose, glucosamine, and sialic acid, but their structural arrangements are distinct. Sialic acid, which constitutes the exclusive terminal residue of the types Ia, Ib, and III—but not type II or V—group B streptococcal capsular polysaccharide, inhibits activation of the alternative pathway of complement.[89] Types VI and VIII lack glucosamine, and type VIII contains rhamnose.[22, 23, 90] A novel insertion sequence in the hyaluronidase gene has been identified predominantly in group B streptococcal strains causing endocarditis.[91] The mechanism by which this genetic alteration and the lack of hyaluronidase increases disease potential is speculative.

CLINICAL MANIFESTATIONS

Neonatal Infections

Early-Onset Infection

As the incidence of neonatal group B streptococcal infections rose during the 1970s, a bimodal distribution of cases by age at the onset of symptoms became apparent. Two distinctive clinical syndromes related to age were described by Franciosi and coworkers[92] (acute and delayed) and by Baker and colleagues[93] (early and late-onset). Early-onset infection, defined as the development of systemic infection during the first 6 days of life, has a mean age of 12 hours at its onset. Maternal obstetric complications are frequent (50 to 60%), and infants born at less than 37 weeks of gestation have significantly higher attack rates than infants born at term. The three major clinical expressions of infection are bacteremia or septicemia, pneumonia, and meningitis, and they occur at frequencies of approximately 60, 30, and 10%, respectively.

The presenting signs of early-onset group B streptococcal infection—lethargy, poor feeding, jaundice, abnormal temperature, grunting respirations, pallor, and hypotension—are indistinguishable from those in neonates with bacterial infections of other causes. Regardless of the focus of infection, respiratory symptoms are observed in the majority. Infants with meningitis have a clinical presentation that initially cannot be distinguished from those without meningeal invasion.[93, 94] Thus, a lumbar puncture is required to identify neonates with meningitis for supportive and specific therapy to be appropriate. One half of the patients with meningitis develop seizures within 24 hours of the onset of meningitis.

Among infants with bacteremia and pneumonia, signs of respiratory distress such as apnea, grunting, tachypnea, and cyanosis, are uniform. Although pulmonary infiltrates on chest radiographs may suggest the diagnosis, at least one half of these infants have a radiographic pattern consistent with and indistinguishable from that of hyaline membrane disease. In most, clinical abnormalities are present at or within a few hours after birth. At postmortem examination, atypical hyaline membranes containing group B streptococci are found in the lungs.[95]

Increased awareness of the disease and improvements in supportive therapy have resulted in decreased mortality among infants with early-onset group B streptococcal infection, and present rates range from 5 to 10%.[6, 96] Mortality rates are inversely proportional to birth weight.

Late-Onset Infection

This syndrome has an onset from 7 days to 3 months of age, with a mean of about 24 days. Maternal obstetric complications are uncommon, and the case-fatality ratio is low.[6, 44, 96] Occult bacteremia or meningitis are common clinical manifestation of late-onset infection, but a variety of focal infections, usually with accompanying bacteremia, also are described. Serotype III strains are isolated from the majority of these patients.[54] The nonspecific initial signs of late-onset disease, such as lethargy, poor feeding, and irritability, generally occur in association with fever (temperature ≥38°C). These infants may present with fulminant infection characterized by rapid progression to a moribund state with septic shock, seizures, and cerebrospinal fluid (CSF) Gram stains with sheets of organisms. An increased risk of death or permanent neurologic sequelae occurs in patients with this fulminant presentation.[97] Additional clinical findings that have been associated with a fatal outcome or permanent neurologic sequelae include neutropenia at admission, prolonged seizures, and high concentrations of type III polysaccharide antigen in admission CSF specimens.[97] Twenty-five to 50% of survivors of group B streptococcal meningitis, whether early- or late-onset, have permanent neurologic sequelae.[94, 97, 98]

Bone and joint infections are the other clinical forms of late-onset group B streptococcal disease that occur relatively frequently.[99] Uncommon foci of infection include cellulitis and adenitis (usually preauricular or submandibular), otitis media, conjunctivitis, pleural empyema, peritonitis, endocarditis, or deep abscesses.[100]

Group B streptococcal osteomyelitis is characterized by an indolent onset in which diminished movement of the involved extremity is the most common symptom. Bone and joint infections are associated with minimal inflammatory changes, and fever is reported in only 20% of patients. Lower extremity involvement is commonly observed in infants with septic arthritis, whereas osteomyelitis has a predilection for involvement of the proximal humerus. However, involvement of the femur, tibia, and flat and small bones has been reported. Most infants have no permanent functional impairment of the involved extremity.

Infection beyond Early Infancy

Infants older than 3 months constitute 10 to 15% of the total with late-onset disease.[96, 101] A number of designations have been suggested for this group, including *late, late-onset* disease; the term *beyond early infancy* is appropriate for patients with group B streptococcal disease who are older than 3 months and younger than 18 years.[102] Many of these infections occur among very low birth weight infants who may still be hospitalized for complications of prematurity; others occur in healthy infants with occult bacteremia.[101] Congenital heart disease and immune deficiency, including human immunodeficiency virus infection, should be considered when group B streptococcal disease is diagnosed beyond early infancy.[102, 103]

Infections in Adults

Invasive group B streptococcal infection causes substantial morbidity and mortality among adults. In one analysis from 1975 to 1984, the composite attack rate for group B streptococcal bacteremia was 0.2 cases per 1000 hospital admissions, and 53% of group B streptococcal blood culture isolates were from adults.[104] In a prospective, population-based assessment of invasive group B streptococcal disease, men and nonpregnant women accounted for 68% (140) of the total adult cases (incidence 4.4 per 100,000 nonpregnant adults per year).[8] Adults with bacteremia unrelated to pregnancy usually are elderly, but ages range from 18 to 99 years.[104–108] The mean age in one report was 62 years, and 57% were male.[8] The incidence increases with age and is higher in African Americans than in whites.[8, 108] The twofold higher rate in black adults compared with whites is particularly high in older African Americans.

One or more conditions predisposing to infection can be identified in most but not all adults with invasive disease (Table 190–2). Diabetes mellitus is the most common underlying medical condition. Neurologic abnormalities associated with infection include dementia, cerebrovascular disease resulting in alterations of mental status, and paraplegia or quadriplegia. Young adults (20 to 40 years of age) with diabetes, cancer, or human immunodeficiency virus infection are at significantly increased risk (28- to 30-fold) for invasive group B streptococcal disease.[8] In a case-control study, cirrhosis, diabetes, stroke, breast cancer, decubitus ulcer, and neurogenic bladder significantly increased the risk for community-acquired group B streptococcal infection. Nosocomial infection was independently associated with the placement of a central venous line, diabetes, congestive heart failure, and a seizure disorder.[109]

TABLE 190–2. Underlying Conditions in 271 Adults with Invasive Group B Streptococcal Infections Unrelated to Pregnancy

Condition	No. of Patients (%)*
Diabetes mellitus	82 (30)
Liver disease and/or history of alcohol abuse	66 (24)
Neurologic impairment	58 (21)
Malignancy	52 (19)
Renal failure	37 (14)
Cardiovascular disease or heart failure	37 (14)
Pulmonary disease	21 (8)
Urologic disease	11 (4)
Peripheral vascular disease	9 (3)
Human immunodeficiency virus infection	7 (3)
Intravenous catheter–related infection	5 (2)
Gastrointestinal disease	5 (2)
Steroid administration	5 (2)
Hypertension	4 (1)
Functional or surgical splenectomy	3 (1)
Other	7 (3)
None	5 (2)

*Some patients had more than one underlying condition.
Data from refs. 8, 104–108.

Mortality is increased in older patients, in those with polymicrobial infection, and in those with diabetes mellitus, liver disease, or malignancy. Case-fatality rates ranging from 8 to 70% have been reported,[104–106, 110, 111] but in more recent years case-fatality rates have ranged from 21 to 34% in nonpregnant adults.[8, 105, 106, 108, 112] Adults currently are more likely to die as a result of group B streptococcal infection than are infants.[7, 100] Shock and alcoholism are associated independently with a significant risk for death.[112] Of the 29 adults with bacteremia described by Opal and associates,[104] only 34% acquired infection in the community. Others have described rates of nosocomial infection from 38 to 70%,[106, 113] but case clustering has not been observed.[104–106, 110, 113] The latter suggests that endogenous respiratory, genitourinary, or gastrointestinal colonization rather than the acquisition of group B streptococci in the hospital is the source of these bacteremias. Approximately one fourth of patients with group B streptococcus isolated from the blood stream have polymicrobial bacteremia. *S. aureus* is a frequently observed second isolate. The age distribution, mortality rate, and proportion of nosocomial cases does not differ among patients with bacteremia caused only by group B streptococcus and those with polymicrobial bacteremia.[109]

Postpartum bacteremia due to group B streptococci increased during the 1970s, an increase that paralleled that reported for neonatal infections. Group B streptococci account for 10 to 20% of blood culture isolates from women admitted to obstetric services.[48, 114] Faro[48] reported an incidence of group B streptococcal–associated endometritis of 1.3 per 1000 deliveries; one third of these patients had concomitant bacteremia. An uncomplicated outcome after appropriate antimicrobial therapy is the rule for these patients, although complications such as meningitis or endocarditis have been described.[49, 110]

Most adult group B streptococcal infections occur in association with one of several clinical expressions of infection.

Primary Bacteremia

When no clear site of active infection can be established, patients in whom group B streptococcus has been isolated from the blood stream are classified as having primary bacteremia. In several reports, primary bacteremia is the single most frequent diagnosis, accounting for 20 to 40% of cases.[104, 107, 111–112] Approximately one half of these patients have a fatal outcome.[111] Among survivors, recurrence of infection may be associated with a focus of infection such as endocarditis or osteomyelitis,[115] or defined ongoing focus.

Infections of the Female Genital Tract

A substantial number of adult infections due to group B streptococcus are associated with pregnancy. The female genital tract is the source of these infections. Group B streptococci alone or as a component of polymicrobial infection are among the most commonly isolated facultative aerobes from women with early postpartum endometritis. A variety of clinical manifestations may occur, but the most common of these are endometritis and wound infection, both associated with cesarean section. Most women with group B streptococcal endometritis develop focal signs and symptoms of infection within 48 hours after delivery. A striking association between abdominal delivery and endometritis has been noted.[51, 116] Minkoff and coworkers[116] found that among patients who delivered abnormally, the 19% who were colonized with group B streptococci had a significantly increased frequency of premature rupture of membranes, postpartum fever, and endometritis when compared with noncolonized women. The clinical findings of endometritis are nonspecific and include fever with or without chills, malaise, moderate uterine tenderness, and normal lochia. In the report by Gibbs and Blanco,[117] the initial lack of symptoms referable to the genital area was followed by the subsequent diagnosis of chorioamnionitis in 19% and endometritis in 81% of patients. The occurrence of life-threatening sequelae of endometritis such as pelvic abscess, septic shock, or septic thrombophlebitis is less than 2%.[118] Another frequent manifestation of morbidity in pregnant women is urinary tract infection. Group B streptococcal peripartum bacteriuria may be asymptomatic or may be diagnosed in association with cystitis or, less frequently, pyelonephritis.[51]

The role of group B streptococcus as an etiologic agent causing vaginitis has not been established. It is regarded as a commensal organism in the vaginal tract and is not considered to elicit a vaginal inflammatory response. There are, however, reports suggesting the pathogenic potential of group B streptococcus in vaginitis and of resolution of the symptoms of vaginitis in association with a short course of antibiotic administration.[119, 120]

Pneumonia

Group B streptococci appear to behave as opportunistic pathogens in patients whose immune function is altered. The specific mechanisms underlying the predilection for this infection have not yet been delineated. However, these patients have in common the apparent inability to limit the spread of the organism from colonizing mucous membrane sites to the blood stream. The most common underlying medical conditions among patients with group B streptococcal pneumonia include diabetes mellitus and neurologic disease. The seven patients described by Verghese and associates[121] were elderly (median age, 78 years), debilitated, and bedridden. All patients were febrile, had leukocytosis, and were hypoxic in room air. Chest radiographs showed bilateral or lobar infiltrates. Infection frequently was polymicrobic, although group B streptococci were the predominant organism. Pleural empyema has been described in association with pneumonia.[122] Fatality rates in patients with pneumonia range from 30 to 85%.

Endocarditis

A major shift in the clinical expression of group B streptococcal endocarditis was documented by Lerner and colleagues.[107] In contrast to the predominance of acute mitral valve endocarditis in pregnant women during the preantibiotic era, cases reported since 1945 have had no sex predilection, have been both acute and subacute in onset, and have occurred in older patients (mean age, approximately 50 years).[107, 123] The mitral valve is most frequently affected (48%); infections involving the aortic (29%), mitral and aortic (10%), and tricuspid valves (5%) have been described. Tricuspid valve involvement is reported usually in intravenous drug abusers.[103] Underlying heart disease is present in more than half of the cases reported since 1962, rheumatic heart disease being the most common diagnosis.[123] Valvular disease, atherosclerotic heart disease, and mitral valve prolapse also may be predisposing conditions.[123, 124] Large friable vegetations are a frequent feature of endocarditis caused by group B streptococcus. These may resemble atrial myxomas, and embolization may occur early in the course.[123] Rapid valve destruction may occur, necessitating early valve replacement in some patients.[125, 126] The mortality rate from group B streptococcal endocarditis is approximately 50%.[107, 110, 123, 127]

Arthritis and Osteomyelitis

Group B streptococcal arthritis generally is monoarticular, most commonly affecting the knee, hip, or shoulder joints, although polyarticular disease with a central pattern has been described.[107] Diabetes mellitus is a common predisposing factor, as are osteoarthritis and joint prostheses. Occasionally, arthritis occurs in the absence of underlying conditions. The most common presenting signs are fever and joint pain. With appropriate antimicrobial therapy, repeated joint aspirations or open drainage and (usually) removal of a prosthesis, if present, complete recovery occurs in one half of the patients. In the remainder, disease is associated with substantial functional sequelae. Osteomyelitis occurs as a consequence of adjacent arthritis, peripheral vascular disease, orthopedic surgery, or adjacent foci of infection such as frontal sinusitis. Hematogenously acquired osteomyelitis is most likely to involve the vertebrae.[128, 129] Osteomyelitis may complicate foot ulcers in adults with long-standing diabetes mellitus.

Skin and Soft Tissue Infections

Skin and soft tissues are the most common sites of focal group B streptococcal infections, accounting for more than one third of infections in some reports.[8, 108, 130] Cellulitis, foot ulcers, abscess, and infection of decubitus ulcers are common manifestations. Cellulitis has occurred in association with foreign bodies, such as breast or penile implants. Less common manifestations of skin and soft tissue infections are pyomyositis, blistering dactylitis, and necrotizing fasciitis.[131, 132] There are no features of these latter infections unique to group B streptococci except that predisposing conditions such as diabetes mellitus generally exist. In one report of 37 patients, the mean age (44 years) of the two thirds who had serious underlying conditions was significantly greater than that of normal hosts (21 years) who often acquired infection in association with minor trauma.[130] Abscess formation was observed in 46% of these infections. Group B streptococcus was the only organism isolated from 71% of patients with an abscess. Appropriate drainage and parenteral antimicrobial therapy effected complete recovery in 89% of these patients.[130]

Meningitis

Meningitis due to group B streptococci has been reported in at least 64 adults, most of whom have had the previously mentioned underlying predisposing conditions.[5, 107, 110, 133–138] The mean age of nonparturient adults is 52 years; almost one half are men. Several have had proven or possible disruption of the anatomic barrier protecting the brain in consequence of surgery for carcinoma or chronic sinusitis. The overall case-fatality rate is 34%. Advanced age and overwhelming illness with presenting features such as coma or septic shock are associated with a poor outcome.[137] Deafness, reported in 7% of the survivors, is the most common neurologic sequela.[133, 137]

Uncommon Manifestations of Infection

Group B streptococci, alone or as a component of mixed infection, have been isolated from a number of patients with keratitis or endophthalmitis. These infections were in eyes with severely damaged surfaces; the outcome was poor, with light perception being lost in one half of the affected eyes.[139, 140]

Group B streptococci are a cause of urinary tract infections in nonobstetric populations, accounting for approximately 2% of positive urine cultures in one prospective evaluation.[141] Such infections are most often community acquired, occurring in middle-aged women. Almost all the patients have an underlying disease, most commonly alterations of urinary flow or stones. Clinical manifestations are referable to the upper or lower urinary tracts in equal numbers. Despite appropriate treatment, the clinical outcome is poor in approximately one fifth of the patients. Treatment failure or relapse is likely due to persistent vaginal or enteric colonization. Group B streptococci also may be a cause of nongonococcal urethritis in men.[142]

Unusual infections caused by group B streptococcus include breast abscess in a nonlactating woman,[143] epiglottic abscess,[144] mycotic aneurysm of the femoral artery,[145] liver abscess,[104, 111] peritonitis,[107, 110, 112] and infection of a pacemaker wire after sigmoidoscopy.[146] Group B streptococcus also has been reported to cause bacteremia after traumatic splenectomy,[147] bacteremia after cardiac catheterization,[148] and fever of unknown origin.[149]

Recurrent Invasive Group B Streptococcal Infection

Approximately 4% of nonpregnant adults surviving an episode of group B streptococcal bacteremia and followed for at least 1 year have a second episode.[115] The mean interval between episodes of bacteremia is 24 weeks, but the interval is shorter (mean 14 weeks) when the recurrent episode is caused by the same strain than when it is caused by another strain (mean 43 weeks between episodes). Several patients in whom primary bacteremia was the diagnosis of the first episode presented with focal infection, such as endocarditis or osteomyelitis, during the second episode.[115] Little is known regarding host factors that predispose adults to developing group B streptococcal infection. Limited data suggest that at least some adults already have relatively high concentrations of antibodies to the infecting serotype when illness occurs.[150] Although a specific antibody may be protective in many cases, the susceptibility of some adult patients to group B streptococcal infection may be due to defects in other aspects of the host defense.

DIAGNOSIS

Isolation of group B streptococcus from blood, CSF, another usually sterile site, or a site of focal suppuration is the only means by which the diagnosis of invasive infection can be documented. Recovery of the organism from mucous membrane sites is of no diagnostic significance. A presumptive diagnosis may be established by detection of group B streptococcal antigen in serum or CSF using methods such as latex agglutination. Antigen tests, however, have poor sensitivity and variable specificity, with the result that they are infrequently useful in establishing a diagnosis. Antigen testing of urine is not recommended.[151]

Intrapartum detection of colonization with group B streptococcus in women presenting for delivery would allow the accurate identification of high-risk patients who might benefit from early chemoprophylaxis or empirical treatment. Reports comparing the results of cultures processed by direct plating of swabs onto nonselective agar with Gram stains of vaginal or cervical swabs from pregnant women found a good sensitivity (90%) but a poor specificity (67%).[152, 153] A method requiring approximately 6 hours for the processing of vaginal swabs detected 40% of colonized patients.[154] Employing a similar technique, Howe and associates[155] reported a sensitivity of 100% and specificity of 92%. In evaluating two enzyme immunoassays and an optical immunoassay, Baker[156] found that none of these tests were sufficiently accurate for routine use in the intrapartum detection of women vaginally colonized with group B streptococcus. For women with heavy colonization, a 100% sensitivity was shown for the optical immunoassay method. Specificity for these assays was high, but there was variability in positive and negative predictive values. A 1997 Food and Drug Administration safety alert specifies that antigen tests are *not* to be used to exclude group B streptococcal colonization in pregnant women.[151] The alert specifies that antenatal screening for colonization requires vaginal *and* rectal cultures processed in selective broth culture media.

Molecular subtyping provides a powerful tool to document the epidemiologic relatedness of group B streptococcal strains.[157, 158] These molecular methods assist in documenting whether recurrent infections are caused by separate or identical strains and in tracking virulent clone families that may be disproportionate causes of invasive disease.[115, 157, 158]

TREATMENT

The antimicrobial regimens recommended for treatment of group B streptococcal infections in infants and adults are summarized in Table 190–3. Group B streptococci remain uniformly susceptible to penicillins in vitro, and penicillin G is the drug of choice once the diagnosis is established.[159] These organisms also are susceptible to ampicillin, vancomycin, teicoplanin, and first-, second- (excluding cefoxitin), and third-generation cephalosporins, although the degree of activity varies.[159–161] Meropenem and imipenem also have good in vitro activity.[159, 162] Ciprofloxacin and rifampin have moderate in vitro activity but have not been evaluated for efficacy.[159, 163] Resistance to erythromycin and clindamycin occurs in 3 to 15% of isolates.[159, 160] Tetracycline resistance has increased to nearly 90%.[159, 164] Group B streptococci are uniformly resistant to nalidixic acid, trimethoprim-sulfamethoxazole, metronidazole, and aminoglycosides.

The initial use of ampicillin and an aminoglycoside for suspected neonatal bacteremia or meningitis due to group B streptococcus is based on their in vitro synergy for these organisms and on the need for broad-spectrum antimicrobial coverage until the diagnosis is established with certainty.[165] Once the diagnosis is established and a clinical response is documented, treatment can be completed with penicillin G alone. The rationale for the high doses of penicillin G recommended for the treatment of group B streptococcal meningitis in infants is twofold: (1) the minimal inhibitory concentration of penicillin G for group B streptococci is fourfold to 10-fold greater (range, 0.01 to 0.4 μg/ml) than that for group A streptococcal strains,[4, 159, 166] and (2) the initial inoculum in the CSF may be 10^7 to 10^8 organisms/ml.[167] Since the inoculum size greatly influences the in vitro susceptibility to penicillin G, these high doses may be required to provide bactericidal activity in vivo. An inoculum effect also has been noted for cefotaxime and imipenem.[168, 169] Penicillin tolerance in vitro has been noted in 4 to 6% of strains, but the clinical importance of this in vitro phenomenon is unknown.[161]

Therapy of 10 days' duration is recommended for the treatment of bacteremia, pneumonia, and pyelonephritis, whereas a 14-day minimal duration is recommended for the treatment of soft tissue infections or meningitis, and a 4-week minimum for the treatment of osteomyelitis, endocarditis, or ventriculitis is recommended. In

TABLE 190–3 Treatment of Group B Streptococcal Infections

Diagnosis	Antibiotic (IV Dose): *Neonate and Infant*	Antibiotic (IV Dose): *Adult*	Alternative Dose for Penicillin-Allergic Adults	Duration
Bacteremia, soft tissue infections	Ampicillin (150 mg/kg/d) plus an aminoglycoside initially, then penicillin G (200,000 U/kg/d)	Penicillin G (10–12 million U/d)	Vancomycin	10 d
Meningitis	Ampicillin (300–400 mg/kg/d) plus gentamicin initially, then penicillin G (500,000 U/kg/d)	Penicillin G (20–30 million U/d)	Vancomycin	14–21 d (minimum)
Osteomyelitis	Penicillin G (200,000 U/kg/d)	Penicillin G (10–20 million U/d)	Vancomycin	3–4 wk
Endocarditis (see Chapter 65)	Penicillin G (400,000 U/kg/d)	Penicillin G (20–30 million U/d) with gentamicin for 2 wk	Vancomycin with an aminoglycoside	4–6 wk

infants, oral therapy is never appropriate. In adults with endocarditis, cardiac surgery early in the course may be necessary due to rapid left-sided valvular destruction.[124] Relapses of infection have occurred in association with both an inadequate dosage and an inadequate duration of therapy. High-dose penicillin therapy does not reliably eliminate mucous membrane infection with group B streptococci, a source that may explain some recurrences.[100, 170]

PREVENTION

Two basic approaches, chemoprophylaxis and immunoprophylaxis, have been suggested to prevent group B streptococcal infections. New insights into the potential feasibility of both approaches have been achieved. Chemoprophylaxis theoretically could be given to pregnant women antenatally or intrapartum, or to neonates at birth. As already discussed (see "Epidemiology and Transmission"), the problem with preventing neonatal infection with antepartum prophylaxis is that oral antimicrobial therapy during pregnancy fails to eradicate group B streptococcal colonization at delivery in nearly 70% of cases.[171] By contrast, successful interruption of vertical transmission by mothers colonized with group B streptococci at delivery has been achieved only through the administration of intravenous ampicillin or penicillin G during labor.[172, 173] This method also is effective in preventing early-onset neonatal disease and reducing postpartum maternal febrile morbidity.[173] Since up to 80% of infants with early-onset sepsis are ill at or within a few hours of birth, prophylaxis of the newborn would be "too late" in most circumstances.

Intrapartum Chemoprophylaxis

In the first prospective, randomized, and controlled trial of maternal chemoprophylaxis to prevent early-onset infection, Boyer and Gotoff[173] detected colonization at 26 to 28 weeks of gestation by the use of lower vaginal and anorectal swabs processed in selective broth medium. Women colonized with group B streptococci who also had an onset of labor at less than 37 weeks of gestation or rupture of membranes for more than 12 hours before delivery received either routine care or intravenous ampicillin (2 g initially, then 1 to 2 g every 4 hours) until delivery. All women with intrapartum fever (>37.5°C) were treated with ampicillin. Of the 79 neonates born to untreated women, five (6.3%) had group B streptococcal sepsis and one died; none of the 85 neonates born to ampicillin-treated women developed sepsis ($p = 0.02$).[173] Another study employed the same approach and noted that 1.8% of infants born to women given ampicillin prophylaxis and 13% of those born to untreated women developed group B streptococcal sepsis ($p = 0.04$).[174] When a cost-effectiveness analysis was applied to the method of selective prophylaxis (based on the detection of colonization and the presence of one or more intrapartum risk factors), efficacy was reported.[175]

To prevent early-onset sepsis, maternal intrapartum chemoprophylaxis ideally should be initiated at least 4 or more hours before delivery and at high doses to achieve a sufficient concentration of penicillin G or ampicillin in the fetal circulation (approximately 15 to 30 minutes after an intravenous dose) and amniotic fluid (estimated at 2 to 4 hours). The earlier that prophylaxis is initiated after the onset of labor or rupture of membranes, the more likely it is it will be effective. Intrapartum chemoprophylaxis has no demonstrated efficacy in the prevention of late-onset infant infection.

The American College of Obstetricians and Gynecologists and the American Academy of Pediatrics each published documents in 1992 concerning intrapartum chemoprophylaxis.[176, 177] Both emphasized the need to reduce maternal and infant morbidity from group B streptococcal infection, but their approach to the selection of women at risk differed, and neither approach was implemented fully. A comprehensive approach now has been endorsed by the American College of Obstetricians and Gynecologists and the American Academy of Pediatrics.[178] The selection of women for chemoprophylaxis is to be determined either by screening cultures of vaginal and rectal sites at 35 to 37 weeks of gestation or by recognizing a factor known to increase the risk for early-onset neonatal infection without screening cultures (Table 190–4). Women with group B streptococcal bacteriuria during the pregnancy and those previously delivering an infant with group B streptococcal infection would always be offered prophylaxis. Risk factors include the onset of labor or membrane rupture earlier than 37 weeks of gestation; intrapartum fever (≥38.0°C); or rupture of membranes for 18 hours or more before delivery. The culture-screening approach is based on group B streptococcal colonization status determined at 35 to 37 weeks of gestation and is estimated to increase the proportion of disease prevented by 30% since carriers without identifiable risk factors would be offered prophylaxis. Pregnant women are willing to perform their own cultures, and the accuracy of culture results from patients' samples correlates well with that of samples collected by nurses.[179, 180]

The maternal intrapartum chemoprophylaxis regimen consists of intravenous penicillin G (5 million units initially; 2.5 million units every 4 hours until delivery). Ampicillin (2 g initially; 1 g every 4 hours until delivery) is an alternative,[178] but penicillin G is preferred because of its narrower spectrum and greater in vitro activity.[159] The recommended antimicrobial for women with serious penicillin allergies is clindamycin (900 mg intravenously every 8 hours until delivery), but because clindamycin-resistant group B streptococci are documented,[159] some experts prefer a first-generation cephalosporin (cefazolin 2 g initially). Efficacy, improved when at least 4 hours (two or more doses) elapses between the initial dose of penicillin and delivery,[181] has been demonstrated only for penicillin G and ampicillin.

Decisions regarding the management of healthy infants born to women receiving chemoprophylaxis depend on the infant's gestational age and the duration or number of doses of prophylaxis before delivery, but all must be observed carefully for at least the first 48 hours of life. Guidelines from the American Academy of Pediatrics provide a detailed algorithm for infant management largely based on expert opinion.[182] Infants at low risk, based on a gestational age of 35 weeks or more and a lack of abnormal signs, whose mothers received at least two doses of penicillin G require neither diagnostic evaluation nor empirical treatment.

Although the current guidelines will not prevent all cases of early-onset disease and are not expected to affect late-onset disease, physicians and patients rank reduction in the risk of infant and maternal infection as the most important priority for a prevention strategy.[183]

Group B Streptococcal Vaccines

Because the risk for invasive group B streptococcal disease in pregnant women and neonates is associated with low concentrations of maternal antibodies to the type-specific capsular polysaccharides of these organisms at delivery,[60] vaccination to prevent these infections has been proposed. Purified capsular polysaccharides from type Ia, II, and III group B streptococci have been evaluated for safety and

TABLE 190–4 Strategies for Maternal Intrapartum Chemoprophylaxis

Universal Antenatal Screening	Selection for Therapy during Labor	Approximate Percentage of Population Targeted	Estimated Proportion of Cases Prevented (%)
Yes	All carriers	20–25	95
No	All at high risk*	15–25	68

*Preterm delivery at less than 37 weeks, preterm rupture of membranes before the onset of labor, rupture of membranes for 18 hours or more before delivery, intrapartum fever (≥38°C) (with or without chorioamnionitis), group B streptococcal bacteriuria during this pregnancy, or previous delivery of an infant with group B streptococcal disease.

immunogenicity in adult volunteers.[184–186] Although the rate of immune response to these vaccines in adults with preexisting type-specific antibodies approaches 100%, that in nonimmune adults ranges from 40 to 85%.[186] Vaccine-induced type III–specific antibodies are predominantly IgG1 and IgG2, cross the placenta efficiently,[187] are protective in animal models of lethal infection,[188] and persist for up to 10 years after immunization.[100] However, because some of these polysaccharides are poorly immunogenic in nonimmune adults, type-specific polysaccharides coupled to tetanus toxoid or other carrier proteins have been developed.[189, 190] The first, composed of type III polysaccharide and tetanus toxoid, was demonstrated to be immunogenic in rabbits and mice, and the antibodies elicited were functional in vitro and protective in vivo.[189] In healthy women, type III group B streptococcal polysaccharide–tetanus toxoid conjugate vaccine is safe and significantly more immunogenic than uncoupled capsular polysaccaride.[191] Additional conjugate vaccines have been developed for capsular types Ia, Ib, II, and V polysaccharides[192–194] and have been found to be safe and immunogenic in nonpregnant adults. Trials now are under way employing a multivalent (Ia, Ib, II, III, V) polysaccharide–tetanus toxoid conjugate vaccine.[195] Another candidate group B streptococcal vaccine employs the β C protein as the protein carrier.[196]

Administration of a multivalent group B streptococcal polysaccharide–tetanus toxoid conjugate vaccine to women during the latter one third of pregnancy theoretically could provide type-specific antibodies in sufficient concentrations to passively protect neonates from early- and late-onset disease. The feasibility of this approach was demonstrated when women were immunized during the last trimester of pregnancy with type III polysaccharide vaccine and their neonates had functionally active IgG antibodies that persisted until the age of 2 months.[187] This approach to prevention, by contrast to maternal intrapartum chemoprophylaxis, offers a method that is simple, cost-effective, and durable and should not promote antimicrobial resistance. Although the immunogenicity of group B streptococcal conjugate vaccines has not been tested among nonpregnant adults at risk for developing systemic group B streptococcal infections because of underlying medical conditions, vaccinating these high-risk patients also may provide protection and should be investigated.

REFERENCES

1. Fry RM. Fatal infections by haemolytic streptococcus group B. Lancet. 1938;1:199–201.
2. Lancefield RC, Hare R. The serological differentiation of pathogenic and nonpathogenic strains of hemolytic streptococci from parturient women. J Exp Med. 1935;61:335–349.
3. Hood M, Janney A, Dameron G. Beta hemolytic streptococcus group B associated with problems of perinatal period. Am J Obstet Gynecol. 1961;82:809–818.
4. Eickhoff TC, Klein JO, Daly AL, et al. Neonatal sepsis and other infections due to group B beta-hemolytic streptococci. N Engl J Med. 1964;271:1221–1228.
5. Butter MNW, DeMoor CE. *Streptococcus agalactiae* as a cause of meningitis in the newborn, and of bacteremia in adults. Antonie van Leeuwenhoek. 1967;33:439–450.
6. Schuchat A. Epidemiology of group B streptococcal disease in the United States: Shifting paradigms. Clin Microbiol Rev. 1998;11:497–532.
7. Zangwill KM, Schuchat A, Wenger JD. Group B streptococcal disease in the United States, 1990: Report from a multistate active surveillance system. MMWR Morb Mortal Wkly Rep. 1992;41(Suppl 6):25–32.
8. Farley MM, Harvey RC, Stull T, et al. A population-based assessment of invasive disease due to group B *Streptococcus* in nonpregnant adults. N Engl J Med. 1993;328:1807–1811.
9. Farley MM. Group B streptococcal infection in older patients. Drugs Aging. 1995;6:293–300.
10. Centers for Disease Control and Prevention. Decreasing incidence of perinatal group B streptococcal disease—United States, 1993–1995. MMWR Morb Mortal Wkly Rep. 1997;46:473–477.
11. Lancefield RC. A serological differentiation of human and other groups of hemolytic streptococci. J Exp Med. 1933;57:571–595.
12. Baker CJ, Clark DJ, Barrett FF. Selective broth medium for isolation of group B streptococci. Appl Microbiol. 1973;26:884–885.
13. Slifkin M, Pouchet-Melvin GR. Evaluation of three commercially available test products for serogrouping beta-hemolytic streptococci. Infect Immun. 1983;11:249–255.
14. Facklam RR, Padula JR, Thacker LG, et al. Presumptive identification of group A, B, and D streptococci. Appl Microbiol. 1974;27:107–113.
15. Ratner HB, Weeks LS, Stratton CW. Evaluation of Spot-CAMP test for identification of group B streptococci. J Clin Microbiol. 1986;24:296–297.
16. Facklam RR, Padula JR, Wortham EC, et al. Presumptive identification of group A, B and D streptococci on agar plate medium. J Clin Microbiol. 1979;9:665–672.
17. Lancefield RC. A serological differentiation of specific types of bovine hemolytic streptococci (group B). J Exp Med. 1934;59:441–458.
18. Wilkinson HW, Eagon RG. Type-specific antigens of group B type Ic streptococci. Infect Immun. 1971;4:596–604.
19. Henrichsen J, Ferrieri P, Jelinkova J, et al. Nomenclature of antigens of group B streptococci. Int J Syst Bacteriol. 1984;34:500.
20. Jelínková J, Motlová J. Worldwide distribution of two new serotypes of group B streptococci: Type IV and provisional type V. J Clin Microbiol. 1985;21:361–362.
21. Wessels MR, DiFabio JL, Benedí V-J, et al. Structural determination and immunochemical characterization of the type V group B *Streptococcus* capsular polysaccharide. J Biol Chem. 1991;266:6714–6719.
22. Von Hunolstein C, D'Ascenzi S, Wagner B, et al. Immunochemistry of capsular type polysaccharide and virulence properties of type VI *Streptococcus agalactiae* (group B streptococci). Infect Immun. 1993;61:1272–1280.
23. Kogan G, Uhrin D, Brisson J-R, et al. Structure and immunochemical characterization of the type VIII group B *Streptococcus* capsular polysaccharide. J Biol Chem. 1996;271:8786–8796.
24. Lancefield RC, McCarty M, Everly WN. Multiple mouse-protective antibodies directed against group B streptococci. Special reference to antibodies effective against protein antigens. J Exp Med. 1975;142:165–179.
25. Baltimore RS, Kasper DL, Vecchitto JS. Mouse protection test for type III strains of group B *Streptococcus*. J Infect Dis. 1979;140:81–88.
26. Stålhammar-Carlemalm M, Stenberg L, Lindahl G. Protein Rib: A novel group B streptococcal cell surface protein that confers protective immunity and is expressed by most strains causing invasive infections. J Exp Med. 1993;177:1593–1603.
27. Michel JL, Madoff LC, Kling DE, et al. Cloned alpha and beta C-protein antigens of group B streptococci elicit protective immunity. Infect Immun. 1991;59:2023–2028.
28. Madoff LC, Michel JL, Gong EW, et al. Protection of neonatal mice from group B streptococcal infection by maternal immunization with beta C protein. Infect Immun. 1992;60:4989.
29. Gordon JS, Sbarra AJ. Incidence, technique of isolation, and treatment of group B streptococci. Am J Obstet Gynecol. 1976;126:1023–1026.
30. Anthony BF, Eisenstadt R, Carter J, et al. Genital and intestinal carriage of group B streptococci during pregnancy. J Infect Dis. 1981;143:761–766.
31. Persson K, Bjerre B, Elfstrom L, et al. A longitudinal study of group B streptococcal carriage during late pregnancy. Scand J Infect Dis. 1987;19:325–329.
32. Newton ER, Butler MC, Shain RN. Sexual behavior and vaginal colonization by group B *Streptococcus* among minority women. Obstet Gynecol. 1996;88:577–582.
33. Ramos E, Gaudier FL, Hearing LR, et al. Group B *Streptococcus* colonization in pregnant diabetic women. Obstet Gynecol. 1997;89:257–260.
34. Baker CJ, Goroff DK, Alpert S, et al. Vaginal colonization with group B *Streptococcus:* A study in college women. J Infect Dis. 1977;135:392–397.
35. Boyer KM, Gadzala CA, Kelly PD, et al. Selective intrapartum chemoprophylaxis of neonatal group B streptococcal early-onset disease. II. Predictive value of prenatal cultures. J Infect Dis. 1983;148:802–809.
36. Dillon HC, Gray E, Pass MA, et al. Anorectal and vaginal carriage of group B streptococci during pregnancy. J Infect Dis. 1982;145:794–799.
37. Baker CJ, Barrett FF. Transmission of group B streptococci among parturient women and their neonates. J Pediatr. 1973;83:919–925.
38. Pass MA, Gray BM, Khare S, et al. Prospective studies of group B streptococcal infections in infants. J Pediatr. 1979;95:437–443.
39. Ancona RJ, Ferrieri P, Williams PP. Maternal factors that enhance the acquisition of group B streptococci by newborn infants. J Med Microbiol. 1980;13:273–280.
40. Paredes A, Wong P, Mason EO Jr, et al. Nosocomial transmission of group B streptococci in a newborn nursery. Pediatrics. 1976;59:679–682.
41. Noya FJD, Rench MA, Metzger TG, et al. Unusual occurrence of an epidemic of type Ib/c group B streptococcal sepsis in a neonatal intensive care unit. J Infect Dis. 1987;155:1135–1144.
42. Gardner SE, Mason EO Jr, Yow MD. Community acquisition of group B *Streptococcus* by infants of colonized mothers. Pediatrics. 1980;66:873–875.
43. Schuchat A, Deaver-Robinson K, Plikaytis BD, et al. Multistate case-control study of maternal risk factors for neonatal group B streptococcal disease. Pediatr Infect Dis J. 1994;13:623–629.
44. Schuchat A, Oxtoby M, Cochi S, et al. Population-based risk factors for neonatal group B streptococcal disease: Results of a cohort study in metropolitan Atlanta. J Infect Dis. 1990;162:672–677.
45. Dillon HC Jr, Khare S, Gray BM. Group B streptococcal carriage and disease. A 6-year prospective study. J Pediatr. 1987;110:31–36.
46. Boyer KM, Gadzala CA, Burd LI, et al. Selective intrapartum chemoprophylaxis of neonatal group B streptococcal early-onset disease. I. Epidemiologic rationale. J Infect Dis. 1983;148:795–801.
47. Pyati SP, Pildes RS, Jacobs NM, et al. Penicillin in infants weighing two kilograms or less with early-onset group B streptococcal disease. N Engl J Med. 1983;308:1383–1389.
48. Faro S. Group B beta-hemolytic streptococci and puerperal infections. Am J Obstet Gynecol. 1981;139:686–689.
49. Yancey MK, Duff P, Clark P, et al. Peripartum infection associated with vaginal group B streptococcal colonization. Obstet Gynecol. 1994;84:816–819.

50. Institute of Medicine, National Academy of Sciences. Committee on Issues and Priorities for New Vaccine Developments. Appendix P: New vaccine development: Establishing priorities. In: Diseases of Importance in the United States, v. 1. Washington, DC: National Academy; 1985:242–439.
51. Pass MA, Gray BM, Dillon HC Jr. Puerperal and perinatal infections with group B streptococci. Am J Obstet Gynecol. 1982;243:147–152.
52. Polsky B, Gold JWM, Whimbey E, et al. Bacterial pneumonia in patients with the acquired immunodeficiency syndrome. Ann Intern Med. 1986;104:38–41.
53. Lin F-YC, Clemens JD, Azimi PH, et al. Capsular polysaccharide types of group B streptococcal isolates from neonates with early-onset systemic infection. J Infect Dis. 1998;177:790–792.
54. Harrison LH, Elliott JA, Dwyer DM, et al. Serotype distribution of invasive group B streptococcal isolates in Maryland: Implications for vaccine formulation. J Infect Dis. 1998;177:998–1002.
55. Blumberg HM, Stephens DS, Modansky M, et al. Invasive group B streptococcal disease: The emergence of serotype V. J Infect Dis. 1996;173:365–373.
56. Lachenauer C, Kasper DL, Shimada J, et al. Serotypes VI and VIII predominate among group B streptococci isolated from pregnant Japanese women. J Infect Dis. 1999;174:1030–1033.
57. Regan JA, Klebanoff MA, Nugent RP, et al. Colonization with group B streptococci in pregnancy and adverse outcome. Am J Obstet Gynecol. 1996;174:1354–1360.
58. Evaldson GR, Malmborg A-S, Nord CE. Premature rupture of the membranes and ascending infection. Br J Obstet Gynecol. 1982;89:793–801.
59. Moller M, Thomsen AC, Borch K, et al. Rupture of fetal membranes and premature delivery associated with group B streptococci in urine of pregnant women. Lancet. 1984;2:69–70.
60. Baker CJ, Kasper DL. Correlation of maternal antibody deficiency with susceptibility to neonatal group B streptococcal infection. N Engl J Med. 1976;294:753–756.
61. Hemming VG, Hall RR, Rhodes PG, et al. Assessment of group B streptococcal opsonins in human and rabbit serum by neutrophil chemiluminescence. J Clin Invest. 1976;58:1379–1387.
62. Stewardson-Krieger PB, Albrandt K, Nevin T, et al. Perinatal immunity to group B β-hemolytic *Streptococcus* type Ia. J Infect Dis. 1977;136:649–654.
63. Baker CJ, Edwards MS, Kasper DL. Role of antibody to native type III polysaccharide of group B *Streptococcus* in infant infection. Pediatrics. 1981;68:544–549.
64. Baker CJ, Kasper DL, Tager IB, et al. Quantitative determination of antibody to capsular polysaccharide in infection with type III strains of group B *Streptococcus*. J Clin Invest. 1977;59:810–818.
65. Boyer KM, Papierniak CK, Gadzala CA, et al. Transplacental passage of antibody to group B *Streptococcus* serotype Ia. J Pediatr. 1984;104:618–620.
66. Gotoff SP, Papierniak CK, Klegerman ME, et al. Quantitation of IgG antibody to the type-specific polysaccharide of group B *Streptococcus* type Ib in pregnant women and infected infants. J Pediatr. 1984;105:628–630.
67. Gray BM, Pritchard DG, Dillon HC Jr. Seroepidemiological studies of group B *Streptococcus* type II. J Infect Dis. 1985;151:1073–1080.
68. Anthony BF, Concepcion NF, Concepcion KF. Human antibody to the group-specific polysaccharide of group B *Streptococcus*. J Infect Dis. 1985;151:221–226.
69. Pass MA, Khare S, Dillon HC. Twin pregnancies: Incidence of group B streptococcal colonization and disease. J Pediatr. 1980;97:635–637.
70. Edwards MS, Jackson CV, Baker CJ. Increased risk of group B streptococcal disease in twins. JAMA. 1981;245:2044–2046.
71. Shigeoka AO, Hall RT, Hemming VG, et al. Role of antibody and complement in opsonization of group B streptococci. Infect Immun. 1978;21:34–40.
72. Baker CJ, Webb BJ, Kasper DL, et al. The role of complement and antibody in opsonophagocytosis of type II group B streptococci. J Infect Dis. 1986;154:47–54.
73. Hall MA, Hickman ME, Baker CJ, et al. Complement and antibody in neutrophil-mediated killing of type V group B *Streptococcus*. J Infect Dis. 1994;170:88–93.
74. Payne NR, Kim Y, Ferrieri P. Effect of differences in antibody and complement requirements on phagocytic uptake and intracellular killing of "c" protein–positive and –negative strains of type II group B streptococci. Infect Immun. 1987;55:1243–1251.
75. Baker CJ, Edwards MS, Webb BJ, et al. Antibody-independent classical pathway-mediated opsonophagocytosis of type Ia, group B *Streptococcus*. J Clin Invest. 1982;63:394–404.
76. Edwards MS, Buffone GJ, Fuselier PA, et al. Deficient classical complement activity in newborn sera. Pediatr Res. 1983;17:685–688.
77. Christensen RD, Hill HR, Rothstein G. Granulocytic stem cell (CFUc) proliferation in experimental group B streptococcal sepsis. Pediatr Res. 1983;17:278–280.
78. Smith CL, Baker CJ, Anderson DC, et al. Role of complement receptors in opsonophagocytosis of group B streptococci by adult and neonatal neutrophils. J Infect Dis. 1990;162:489–495.
79. Yang KD, Bathras JM, Shigeoka AO, et al. Mechanisms of bacterial opsonization by immune globulin intravenous: Correlation of complement consumption with opsonic activity and protective efficacy. J Infect Dis. 1989;159:701–707.
80. Noya FJD, Baker CJ, Edwards MS. Neutrophil Fc receptor participation in phagocytosis of type III group B streptococci. Infect Immun. 1993;61:1415–1420.
81. Vallejo JG, Baker CJ, Edwards MS. Roles of the bacterial cell wall and capsule in induction of tumor necrosis factor alpha by type III group B streptococci. Infect Immun. 1996;64:5042–5046.
82. Gibson RL, Redding GJ, Henderson WR, et al. Group B *Streptococcus* induces tumor necrosis factor in neonatal piglets. Am Rev Respir Dis. 1991;143:598–604.
83. Teti G, Mancuso G, Tomasello F, et al. Production of tumor necrosis factor-α and interleukin-6 in mice infected with group B streptococci. Circ Shock. 1992;38:138–144.
84. Rowen JL, Smith CW, Edwards MS. Group B streptococci elicit leukotriene B_4 and interleukin-8 from human monocytes: Neonates exhibit a diminished response. J Infect Dis. 1995;172:420–426.
85. Takahashi S, Adderson EE, Nagano Y, et al. Identification of a highly encapsulated, genetically related group of invasive type III group B streptococci. J Infect Dis. 1998;177:1116–1119.
86. Rubens CE, Wessels MR, Heggen LM, et al. Transposon mutagenesis of group B streptococcal type III capsular polysaccharide: Correlation of capsule expression with virulence. Proc Natl Acad Sci U S A. 1987;84:7208–7212.
87. Wessels MR, Rubens CE, Benedí V-J, et al. Definition of a bacterial virulence factor: Sialylation of the group B streptococcal capsule. Proc Natl Acad Sci U S A. 1989;86:8983–8987.
88. Nizet V, Kim KS, Stins M, et al. Invasion of brain microvascular endothelial cells by group B streptococci. Infect Immun. 1997;65:5074–5081.
89. Kasper DL, Baker CJ, Edwards MS, et al. The type III group B streptococcal capsular polysaccharide: Structure, immunospecificity, immunogenicity, and relationship to virulence. In: Weinstein L, Fields BN, eds. Seminars in Infectious Disease, v. 4. Bacterial Vaccines. New York: Thieme-Stratton; 1982:275–278.
90. Kogan G, Brisson J-R, Kasper DL, et al. Structural elucidation of the novel type VII group B *Streptococcus* capsular polysaccharide by high resolution NMR spectroscopy. Carbohydr Res. 1995;277:1–9.
91. Granlund M, Öberg L, Sellin M, et al. Identification of a novel insertion element, IS*1548*, in group B streptococci, predominantly in strains causing endocarditis. J Infect Dis. 1998;177:967–976.
92. Franciosi RA, Knostman JD, Zimmerman RA. Group B streptococcal neonatal and infant infections. J Pediatr. 1973;82:707–718.
93. Baker CJ, Barrett FF, Gordon RC, et al. Suppurative meningitis due to streptococci of Lancefield group B: A study of 33 infants. J Pediatr. 1973;82:724–729.
94. Chin KC, Fitzhardinge PM. Sequelae of early-onset group B streptococcal neonatal meningitis. J Pediatr. 1985;106:819–822.
95. Katzenstein A, Davis C, Braude A. Pulmonary changes in neonatal sepsis due to group B β-hemolytic streptococcus: Relation to hyaline membrane disease. J Infect Dis. 1976;133:430–435.
96. Yagupsky P, Menegus MA, Powell KR. The changing spectrum of group B streptococcal disease in infants: An eleven-year experience in a tertiary care hospital. Pediatr Infect Dis J. 1991;10:801–808.
97. Edwards MS, Rench MA, Haffar AAM, et al. Long-term sequelae of group B streptococcal meningitis in infants. J Pediatr. 1985;106:717–722.
98. Wald ER, Bergman I, Taylor HG, et al. Long-term outcome of group B streptococcal meningitis. Pediatrics. 1986;77:217–221.
99. Edwards MS, Baker CJ, Wagner ML, et al. An etiologic shift in infantile osteomyelitis: The emergence of the group B *Streptococcus*. J Pediatr. 1978;93:578–583.
100. Baker CJ, Edwards MS. Group B streptococcal infections. In: Remington JS, Klein JO, eds. Infectious Diseases of the Fetus and Newborn Infant. 4th ed. Philadelphia: WB Saunders; 1995:980–1054.
101. Garcia Pẽna BM, Harper MB, Fleisher GR. Occult bacteremia with group B streptococci in an outpatient setting. Pediatrics. 1998;102:67–72.
102. Hussain SM, Luedtke GS, Baker CJ, et al. Invasive group B streptococcal disease in children beyond early infancy. Pediatr Infect Dis J. 1995;14:278–281.
103. Alsoub H, Najma F, Robida A. Group B streptococcal endocarditis in children beyond the neonatal period. Pediatr Infect Dis J. 1997;16:418–420.
104. Opal SM, Cross A, Palmo M, et al. Group B streptococcal sepsis in adults and infants. Contrasts and comparisons. Arch Intern Med. 1988;148:641–645.
105. Gallagher PG, Watanakunakorn C. Group B streptococcal bacteremia in a community teaching hospital. Am J Med. 1985;78:795–800.
106. Verghese A, Mireault K, Arbeit RD. Group B streptococcal bacteremia in men. Rev Infect Dis. 1986;8:912–917.
107. Lerner PI, Gopalakrishna KV, Wolinsky E, et al. Group B *Streptococcus* (*S. agalactiae*) bacteremia in adults: Analysis of 32 cases and review of the literature. Medicine (Baltimore). 1977;56:457–473.
108. Schwartz B, Schuchat A, Oxtoby MJ, et al. Invasive group B streptococcal disease in adults. A population-based study in metropolitan Atlanta. JAMA. 1991;266:1112–1114.
109. Jackson LA, Hilsdon R, Farley MM, et al. Risk factors for group B streptococcal disease in adults. Ann Intern Med. 1995;123:415–420.
110. Bayer AS, Chow AW, Anthony BF, et al. Serious infections in adults due to group B streptococci. Am J Med. 1976;61:498–503.
111. Colford JM Jr, Mohle-Boetani J, Vosti KL. Group B streptococcal bacteremia in adults: Five years' experience and a review of the literature. Medicine. 1995;74:176–190.
112. Muñoz P, Llancaqueo A, Rodriguez-Créixems M, et al. Group B *Streptococcus* bacteremia in nonpregnant adults. Arch Intern Med. 1997;157:213–216.
113. Roberts FJ. Group A and group B β-hemolytic streptococcal bacteremia. Rev Infect Dis. 1988;10:228–229.
114. Ledger WJ, Norman J, Gee C, et al. Bacteremia on an obstetric-gynecologic service. Am J Obstet Gynecol. 1975;121:205–212.
115. Harrison LH, Ali A, Dwyer DM, et al. Relapsing invasive group B streptococcal infection in adults. Ann Intern Med. 1995;123:421–427.
116. Minkoff HL, Sierra MF, Pringle GF, et al. Vaginal colonization with group B beta-hemolytic streptococcus as a risk factor for post-cesarean section febrile morbidity. Am J Obstet Gynecol. 1982;142:992–995.
117. Gibbs RS, Blanco JD. Streptococcal infections in pregnancy: A study of 48 bacteremias. Am J Obstet Gynecol. 1981;140:405–411.
118. Duff P. Pathophysiology and management of postcesarean endomyometritis. Obstet Gynecol. 1986;67:269–276.

119. Maniatis AN, Palermos J, Kantzanou M, et al. *Streptococcus agalactiae*: A vaginal pathogen? J Med Microbiol. 1996;44:199–202.
120. Boyle D, Smith JR. Group B streptococcal vulvovaginitis. J R Soc Med. 1997;90:298–299.
121. Verghese A, Berk SL, Boelen LJ, et al. Group B streptococcal pneumonia in the elderly. Arch Intern Med. 1982;142:1642–1645.
122. George AL Jr, Savage AM. Fatal group B streptococcal empyema in an adult. South Med J. 1987;80:1436–1438.
123. Gallagher PG, Watanakunakorn C. Group B streptococcal endocarditis: Report of seven cases and review of the literature, 1962–1985. Rev Infect Dis. 1986;8:175–188.
124. Watanakunakorn C, Habte-Gabr E. Group B streptococcal endocarditis of tricuspid valve. Chest. 1991;100:569–571.
125. Pringle SD, McCartney AC, Marshall DAS, et al. Infective endocarditis caused by *Streptococcus agalactiae.* Int J Cardiol. 1989;24:179–183.
126. Scully BE, Spriggs D, Neu HC. *Streptococcus agalactiae* (group B) endocarditis—a description of twelve cases and review of the literature. Infection. 1987;15:169–176.
127. Duma RJ, Weinberg AN, Merdrek RF, et al. Streptococcal infections. A bacteriologic and clinical study of streptococcal bacteremia. Medicine (Baltimore). 1969;48:87–127.
128. Small CB, Slater LN, Lowy FD, et al. Group B streptococcal arthritis in adults. Am J Med. 1984;76:367–375.
129. Pischel KD, Weisman MH, Cone RO. Unique features of group B streptococcal arthritis in adults. Arch Intern Med. 1985;145:97–102.
130. McCarty JM, Haber J. Group B streptococcal soft tissue infections beyond the neonatal period. West J Med. 1987;147:558–560.
131. Riefler J III, Molavi A, Schwartz D, et al. Necrotizing fasciitis in adults due to group B *Streptococcus.* Arch Intern Med. 1988;148:727–729.
132. Sutton GP, Smirz LR, Clark DH, et al. Group B streptococcal necrotizing fasciitis arising from an episiotomy. Obstet Gynecol. 1985;66:733–736.
133. Harburg TD, Leonard HA, Kimbrough RC III, et al. Group B streptococcal meningitis appearing as acute deafness in an adult. Arch Neurol. 1984;41:214–216.
134. Sepkowitz KA, Kasemsri T, Brown AE, et al. Meningitis due to β-hemolytic non-A, non-D streptococci among adults at a cancer hospital: Report of four cases and review. Clin Infect Dis. 1992;14:92–97.
135. Vartian CV, Septimus EJ. Meningitis caused by group B *Streptococcus* in association with cerebrospinal rhinorrhea. Clin Infect Dis. 1992;14:1261–1262.
136. Dunne DW, Quagliarello V. Group B streptococcal meningitis in adults. Medicine. 1993;72:1–10.
137. Domingo P, Barquet N, Alvarez M, et al. Group B streptococcal meningitis in adults: Report of twelve cases and review. Clin Infect Dis. 1997;25:1180–1187.
138. Guerin JM, Leibinger F, Mofredj A, et al. Streptococcus B meningitis in post-partum. J Infect. 1997;34:151–153.
139. Farber BP, Weinbaum DL, Dummer JS. Metastatic bacterial endophthalmitis. Arch Intern Med. 1985;145:62–64.
140. Ormerod LD, Paton BG. Severe group B streptococcal eye infections in adults. J Infect. 1989;18:29–34.
141. Muñoz P, Coque T, Rodriguez Creixems M, et al. Group B *Streptococcus:* A cause of urinary tract infection in nonpregnant adults. Clin Infect Dis. 1992;14:492–496.
142. Lefevre J-C, Lepargneur J-P, Bauriand R, et al. Clinical and microbiologic features of urethritis in men in Toulouse, France. Sex Transm Dis. 1991;18:76–79.
143. Weiss RL, Matsen JM. Group B streptococcal breast abscess. Arch Pathol Lab Med. 1987;111:74–75.
144. Ridgeway NA, Perlman PE, Verghese A. Epiglottic abscess due to group B *Streptococcus.* Ann Otol Rhinol Laryngol. 1984;93:277–278.
145. Burnet NG, Wilkinson RC, Evans DS. Mycotic aneurysm caused by group B *Streptococcus:* A cautionary tale of management problems and a rare organism. Br J Clin Pract. 1990;44:372–374.
146. Baddour LM, Cox JW Jr. Group B streptococcal infection of a pacemaker wire following sigmoidoscopy. Clin Infect Dis. 1992;15:1069.
147. Raz R, Raichman N, Flatau E. Group B streptococcal bacteremia in a normal splenectomized adult. Isr J Med Sci. 1987;23:920–921.
148. Stampfer MJ, Ullman RF, Sacks-Berg A, et al. Group B streptococcal bacteremia after cardiac catheterization. Crit Care Med. 1987;15:625–626.
149. O'Mahony D, Hyland CM. Group B streptococcal infection as a pyrexia of unknown origin. Isr J Med Sci. 1989;158:233.
150. Wessels MR, Kasper DL, Johnson KD, et al. Antibody responses in invasive group B streptococcal infection in adults. J Infect Dis. 1998;178:569–572.
151. Burlington DB. Risks of devices for direct detection of group B streptococcal antigen. FDA Safety Alert, 1997.
152. Feld SM, Harrigan JT. Vaginal gram stain as an immediate detector of group B streptococci in selected obstetric patients. Am J Obstet Gynecol. 1987;156:446–448.
153. Hollis WM, Thomas J, Troyer V. Cervical gram stain for rapid detection of colonization with β-*Streptococcus.* Obstet Gynecol. 1987;69:354–357.
154. Wald ER, Dashefsky B, Green M, et al. Rapid detection of group B streptococci directly from vaginal swabs. J Clin Microbiol. 1987;25:573–574.
155. Howe RS, Voychehovski TH, Uraizee F, et al. Neonatal group B streptococcal disease. N Engl J Med. 1987;316:1163.
156. Baker CJ. Inadequacy of rapid immunoassays for intrapartum detection of group B streptococcal carriers. Obstet Gynecol. 1996;88:51–55.
157. Quentin R, Huet H, Wang F-S, et al. Characterization of *Streptococcus agalactiae* strains by multilocus enzyme genotype and serotype: Identification of multiple virulent clone families that cause invasive neonatal disease. J Clin Microbiol. 1995;33:2576–2581.
158. Blumberg HM, Stephens DS, Licitra C, et al. Molecular epidemiology of group B streptococcal infections: Use of restriction endonuclease analysis of chromosomal DNA and DNA restriction fragment length polymorphisms of ribosomal RNA genes (ribotyping). J Infect Dis. 1992;166:574–579.
159. Fernandez M, Hickman ME, Baker CJ. Antimicrobial susceptibilities of group B streptococci isolated between 1992 and 1996 from patients with bacteremia or meningitis. Antimicrob Agents Chemother. 1998;42:1517–1519.
160. Persson KM-S, Forsgren A. Antimicrobial susceptibility of group B streptococci. Eur J Clin Microbiol. 1986;5:165–167.
161. Kim KS. Antimicrobial susceptibility of GBS. Antibiot Chemother. 1985;35:83–89.
162. Kropp H, Gerckens L, Sundelof JG. Antibacterial activity of imipenem: The first thienamycin antibiotic. Rev Infect Dis. 1985;7(Suppl):389–410.
163. Rolston KVI. Susceptibility of group B and group G streptococci to newer antimicrobial agents. Eur J Clin Microbiol. 1986;5:534–536.
164. Berkowitz K, Regan JA, Greenberg E. Antibiotic resistance patterns of group B streptococci in pregnant women. J Clin Microbiol. 1990;28:5–7.
165. Schauf V, Deveikis A, Riff L, et al. Antibiotic-killing kinetics of group B streptococci. J Pediatr. 1976;89:194–198.
166. Baker CN, Thornsberry C, Facklam RR. Synergism killing kinetics, and antimicrobial susceptibility of group A and B streptococci. Antimicrob Agents Chemother. 1981;19:716–725.
167. Feldman WE. Concentrations of bacteria in cerebrospinal fluid of patients with bacterial meningitis. J Pediatr. 1976;88:549–552.
168. Landesman SH, Corrado ML, Cherubin CE, et al. Activity of moxalactam and cefotaxime alone and in combination with ampicillin or penicillin against group B streptococci. Antimicrob Agents Chemother. 1981;19:794–797.
169. Kropp H, Gerckens L, Sundelof JG. Antibacterial activity of imipenem: The first thienamycin antibiotic. Rev Infect Dis. 1985;7:S389–S410.
170. Paredes A, Wong P, Yow MD. Failure of penicillin to eradicate the carrier state of group B *Streptococcus* in infants. J Pediatr. 1976;89:191–193.
171. Gardner SE, Yow MD, Leeds LJ, et al. Failure of penicillin to eradicate group B streptococcal colonization in the pregnant woman. Am J Obstet Gynecol. 1979;135:1062–1065.
172. Allardice JG, Baskett TF, Seshia MM, et al. Perinatal group B streptococcal colonization and infection. Am J Obstet Gynecol. 1982;142:617–620.
173. Boyer KM, Gotoff SP. Prevention of early-onset neonatal group B streptococcal disease with selective intrapartum chemoprophylaxis. N Engl J Med. 1986;314:1665–1669.
174. Teres FO, Matorras R, Perea AG, et al. Prevention of neonatal group B streptococcal sepsis. Pediatr Infect Dis J. 1987;6:874.
175. Mohle-Boetani JC, Schuchat A, Plikaytis BD, et al. Comparison of prevention strategies for neonatal group B streptococcal (GBS) infection. JAMA. 1993;270: 1442–1448.
176. American College of Obstetricians and Gynecologists. Group B streptococcal infections in pregnancy. ACOG Tech Bull. 1992;170:1–5.
177. Committee on Infectious Diseases and Committee on Fetus and Newborn. Guidelines for prevention of group B streptococcal (GBS) infection by chemoprophylaxis. Pediatrics. 1992;90:775–778.
178. Centers for Disease Control. Prevention of perinatal group B streptococcal disease: A public health perspective. MMWR Morb Mortal Wkly Rep. 1996;45:1–24.
179. Molnar P, Biringer A, McGeer A, et al. Can pregnant women obtain their own specimens for group B *Streptococcus*? A comparison of maternal versus physician screening. Fam Pract. 1997;14:403–406.
180. Mercer BM, Taylor MC, Fricke JL, et al. The accuracy and patient preference for self-collected group B *Streptococcus* cultures. Am J Obstet Gynecol. 1995;173:1325–1328.
181. Pylipow M, Gaddis M, Kinney JS. Selective intrapartum prophylaxis for group B *Streptococcus* colonization: Management and outcome of newborns. Pediatrics. 1994;93:631–635.
182. American Academy of Pediatrics Committee on Infectious Diseases and Committee on Fetus and Newborn. Revised guidelines for prevention of early-onset group B streptococcal (GBS) infection. Pediatrics. 1997;99:489–496.
183. Peralta-Carcelen M, Fargason CA Jr, Coston D, et al. Preferences of pregnant women and physicians for 2 strategies for prevention of early-onset group B streptococcal sepsis in neonates. Arch Pediatr Adolesc Med. 1997;151:712–718.
184. Baker CJ, Edwards MS, Kasper DL. Immunogenicity of polysaccharides from type III, group B *Streptococcus.* J Clin Invest. 1978;61:1107–1110.
185. Eisenstein TK, DeCuenick BJ, Resavy D, et al. Quantitative determination in human sera of vaccine-induced antibody to type-specific polysaccharides of group B streptococci using an enzyme-linked immunosorbent assay. J Infect Dis. 1983;147:847–856.
186. Baker CJ, Kasper DL. Group B streptococcal vaccines. Rev Infect Dis. 1985;4:458–467.
187. Baker CJ, Rench MA, Edwards MS, et al. Immunization of pregnant women with a polysaccharide vaccine. N Engl J Med. 1988;319:1180–1185.
188. Givner LB, Baker CJ. Pooled human IgG hyperimmune for type III group B streptococci: Evaluation against multiple strains in vitro and in experimental disease. J Infect Dis. 1991;163:1141–1145.
189. Wessels MR, Paoletti LC, Kasper DL, et al. Immunogenicity in animals of a polysaccharide-protein conjugate vaccine against type III group B *Streptococcus.* J Clin Invest. 1990;86:1428–1433.
190. Paoletti LC, Kasper DL, Michon F, et al. An oligosaccharide-tetanus toxoid conju-

gate vaccine against type III group B *Streptococcus*. J Biol Chem. 1990;265:18,278–18,283.
191. Kasper DL, Paoletti LC, Wessels MR, et al. Immune response to type III group B streptococcal polysaccharide-tetanus toxoid conjugate vaccine. J Clin Invest. 1996;98:2308–2314.
192. Wessels MR, Paoletti LC, Rodewald AK, et al. Stimulation of protective antibodies against type Ia and Ib group B streptococci by a type Ia polysaccharide–tetanus toxoid conjugate vaccine. Infect Immun. 1993;61:4760–4766.
193. Paoletti LC, Wessels MR, Michon F, et al. Group B *Streptococcus* type II polysaccharide–tetanus toxoid conjugate vaccine. Infect Immun. 1992;60:4009–4014.
194. Wessels MR, Paoletti LC, Pinel J, et al. Immunogenicity and protective activity in animals of a type V group B streptococcal polysaccharide–tetanus toxoid conjugate vaccine. J Infect Dis. 1995;171:879–884.
195. Paoletti LC, Wessels MR, Rodewald AK, et al. Neonatal mouse protection against infection with multiple group B streptococcal (GBS) serotypes by maternal immunization with a tetravalent GBS polysaccharide–tetanus toxoid conjugate vaccine. Infect Immun. 1994;62:3236–3243.
196. Madoff LC, Paoletti LC, Tai JY, et al. Maternal immunization of mice with group B streptococcal type III polysaccharide–beta C protein conjugate elicits protective antibody to multiple serotypes. J Clin Invest. 1994:94;286–292.

Chapter 191

Viridans Streptococci and Groups C and G Streptococci

CAROLINE C. JOHNSON
ALLAN R. TUNKEL

Viridans streptococci and the β-hemolytic streptococci constitute a diverse group of organisms with varying environmental niches and pathogenicity. Although these organisms usually reside as commensals in the respiratory and intestinal tracts of animals and humans, they may also invade sterile body sites, resulting in life-threatening diseases. This chapter reviews infections caused by the viridans streptococci, nutritionally variant (deficient) streptococci (NVS, genus *Abiotrophia*), and β-hemolytic streptococci (other than groups A, B, and D) that are associated with human disease. Although the *Streptococcus milleri* group *(S. anginosus, S. intermedius,* and *S. constellatus)* are viridans streptococci, they are discussed in detail elsewhere (see Chapter 192). *Stomatococcus* and *Pediococcus* are discussed here.

VIRIDANS GROUP STREPTOCOCCI

Microbiology

Viridans streptococci possess the general characteristics common to all streptococci (see Chapter 185). They are facultatively anaerobic, gram-positive cocci that do not produce catalase or coagulase; on blood agar, their colonies rarely produce β-hemolysis. The term *viridans* derives from the Latin word *viridis,* meaning "green." Many species in this group cause partial destruction of erythrocytes with resultant green discoloration on blood agar (α-hemolysis), whereas others have no effect on blood (γ-hemolysis).[1] Although some isolates react with Lancefield grouping antisera, the species do not conform to specific serogroups, and many isolates are entirely nongroupable.[2,3] Viridans streptococci can be distinguished from *Streptococcus pneumoniae,* another species producing α-hemolysis on blood agar, by resistance to optochin and lack of bile solubility. They are distinguished from enterococci by their inability to grow in broth containing 6.5% sodium chloride. One of the nonenterococcal group D streptococci, *Streptococcus bovis,* is often considered to be a member of the viridans group but has a different habitat and clinical significance (see Chapter 189).[4] In practical terms, the viridans group streptococci are what remains after exclusion of pneumococci, enterococci, *Streptococcus pyogenes,* and other biochemically defined, groupable streptococci.

Viridans streptococci are fastidious with respect to their nutritional growth requirements; enriched agars and broths are recommended for optimal recovery from primary cultures.[5] Most strains grow well in conventional blood culture media. On solid agar, viridans streptococci are usually facultatively anaerobic, but some strains are decidedly capnophilic or microaerophilic. The colonies vary in size and appearance depending on the composition of the medium and the atmosphere of incubation.[5] In broth cultures, streptococci appear as spherical or ovoid cells that form chains or pairs. The organisms are nonmotile and non–spore-forming, and they ferment carbohydrates with acid but without gas production.

Species Identification

In the past, the terminology applied to the viridans group of streptococci was confusing and inconsistent. When organisms were recovered in clinical laboratories, species designation often sidestepped identification of the isolate in favor of a generic "nonhemolytic" or "α-hemolytic" descriptive term. In addition, terms such as *Streptococcus mutans* and *Streptococcus sanguis* were used loosely to refer to groups of organisms without clear relationship. In the 1970s, two schemes for identification of viridans streptococci were proposed. Colman and Williams suggested classification of the group into five species: *S. mutans, S. milleri, S. sanguis, S. salivarius,* and *S. mitior,* which they termed "the human oral viridans streptococci."[6] The scheme of Facklam recognized 10 physiologic species: *S. sanguis* I and II, *S. mitis, S. salivarius, S. mutans, S. uberis, S. acidominimus, S. morbillorum,* and two subdivisions of the *S. milleri* group, *S. anginosus-constellatus* and *S. MG-intermedius*.[7] The various species, as defined by these two schemes, were not identical. More recently, a molecular approach has been applied to define the taxonomy of viridans streptococci based on genetic relatedness. These analyses have resulted in emended descriptions of well-recognized species (e.g., *S. mitis, S. sanguis*), the discovery and description of several new species (e.g., *S. gordonii, S. vestibularis*), and the division of the serotypes of the *S. mutans* group into seven distinct species.[8] Expanded batteries of phenotypic tests combined with differences observed between genotypes have permitted laboratories to accurately identify species for correlation with specific clinical syndromes. The relationship between species according to the various classifications is shown in Table 191–1. When reviewing older literature pertaining to the viridans group of streptococci, the extensive changes in taxonomy and nomenclature should be taken into consideration.

Clinically significant species that are currently recognized as belonging to the viridans group of streptococci are *S. anginosus, S. constellatus, S. crista, S. gordonii, S. intermedius, S. mitis,* the *S. mutans* group, *S. oralis, S. parasanguis, S. salivarius, S. sanguis, S. thermophilus,* and *S. vestibularis*.[9] Species can be distinguished phenotypically by their physiologic and biochemical characteristics, in particular their type of hemolysis on blood agar, pattern of acid formation from carbohydrates, ability to hydrolyze esculin and arginine, and production of dextran, levan, alkaline phosphatase, hydrogen peroxide, and acetoin (Table 191–2).[1–18] A simplified scheme, consisting of 14 biochemical tests, has also been proposed.[19] Although rapid, automated systems for species identification of streptococci are commercially available, their performance is variable. With some, the databases have not been updated or expanded to include newer species; others require supplemental procedures to perform accurately. Conventional biochemical tests remain the most reliable method for identification of these organisms in clinical laboratories.[20] A polymerase chain reaction assay based on specific amplification of internal fragments of genes encoding D-alanine:D-alanine ligases has been applied successfully in research laboratories.[21]

S. morbillorum was once considered to be a viridans streptococ-

TABLE 191–1 Species of Viridans Streptococci According to Various Identification Schemes

Colman & Williams*	Facklam†	Current Taxonomic Name‡
S. mitior	*S. mitis*	*S. mitis*
	S. sanguis II	*S. oralis*
S. sanguis	*S. sanguis* I	*S. sanguis*
		S. gordonii
		S. crista
S. salivarius	*S. salivarius*	*S. salivarius*
S. mutans	*S. mutans*	*S. mutans* group§
S. milleri	*S. MG-intermedius*	*S. intermedius*
	S. anginosus-constellatus	*S. constellatus*
		S. anginosus
		S. vestibularis
		S. parasanguis
	S. morbillorum	*Gemella morbillorum*

*Colman G, Williams RED. Taxonomy of some human viridans streptococci. In: Wannamaker LW, Matsen JM, eds. Streptococci and Streptococcal Diseases; Recognition, Understanding, and Management. New York: Academic Press; 1972: 281–299.
†Facklam RR. Physiological differentiation of viridans streptococci. J Clin Microbiol, 1977; 5: 184–201.
‡Data from refs. 4, 10–18.
§Consists of seven species: *S. mutans, S. sorbrinus, S. cricetus, S. ferus, S. macacae, S. downei, S. rattus.*

cus because it failed to produce β-hemolysis on blood agar, lacked distinguishing serogroup antigens, and did not have the biochemical characteristics of enterococci or pneumococci. In Facklam's review, half of the 46 isolates described were associated with serious infections.[7] The organism has recently been reclassified as the second species in the genus *Gemella (G. morbillorum).*[17] Infections associated with this organism are similar to those seen with viridans streptococci, and the principles of treatment are the same.

Although NVS were also once thought to be viridans streptococci, they have been shown to form a genetically unrelated group (*Abiotrophia*; see later discussion).[22, 23]

Epidemiology

Viridans streptococci are an important part of the normal microbial flora of humans and animals. They are indigenous to the upper respiratory tract, the female genital tract, and all regions of the gastrointestinal tract, but are most prevalent in the oral cavity.[1, 5] On average, streptococci represent 28% of the total culturable flora from dental plaque, 29% from gingival crevices, 45% from the tongue, and 46% from saliva.[24] The various species, however, are not distributed uniformly throughout the oral cavity. Studies from the early 1970s showed that strains of *S. salivarius* predominated on the tongue and those of *S. mitis* on the buccal mucosa, whereas *S. mutans* and *S. sanguis* were more often associated with dental structures.[25] Gibbons and van Houte demonstrated that this proportional distribution of viridans streptococcal species was determined by their selective adherence to the various oral tissues.[26] Using the emended descriptions of viridans species, the ecology of strains in the oral cavity and oropharynx can now be described as follows: the buccal mucosa is associated with *S. sanguis* and *S. mitis;* the dorsum of the tongue with *S. mitis* and *S. salivarius;* initial dental plaque with *S. sanguis, S. mitis,* and *S. oralis;* mature supragingival plaque with *S. gordonii;* and subgingival plaque with *S. anginosus.*[27]

In healthy persons, adherence of viridans streptococci may provide "colonization resistance" within the oral cavity to prevent establishment of more pathogenic bacteria. Fibronectin, a complex glycoprotein found on the surface of oral epithelial cells, selectively promotes attachment of *S. salivarius, S. mutans, "S. mitior,"* and other gram-positive cocci.[28] If fibronectin is lost or diminished, as occurs in chronically ill or hospitalized patients, adherence of organisms such as *Pseudomonas aeruginosa* to oral epithelial cells is increased.[29, 30] Because oropharyngeal colonization with enteric gram-negative bacilli often precedes invasion (e.g., development of gram-negative bacillary pneumonia), selective adherence of viridans streptococci in the oral cavity can be viewed as a protective mechanism for the host.[31, 32]

Pathogenicity

Viridans streptococci are considered to be bacteria of low virulence. They are not known to possess endotoxin or secrete exotoxins, and they are fully susceptible to lysis by serum and lysosomal enzymes. Although some species make proteolytic enzymes, these enzymes are not clearly related to the pathogenesis of infection.[33] Therefore, viridans streptococci do not have the traditional virulence factors that characterize more pathogenic bacteria. The exception is the members of the *S. milleri* group, whose propensity for producing localized purulent collections suggests pathogenicity (see Chapter 192).

The pathogenicity of viridans group streptococci is best exemplified by their ability to produce endocarditis. Extracellular dextran plays an important role in adherence and propagation of these organisms on cardiac valves. Clinical observations have noted that after bacteremia caused by dextran-producing streptococci there is a higher incidence of infective endocarditis than when bacteremia is caused by non–dextran-producing streptococci.[34] Investigators have also shown that the amount of dextran produced by a streptococcal strain correlates with its ability to adhere to cardiac valves in vitro and to induce infective endocarditis in experimental animal models.[35, 36] Pretreatment with dextranase abolishes the differences in pathogenicity of various strains. In addition, production of dextran by the pathogen also mediates the response to antimicrobial therapy. Endocarditis caused by dextran-producing strains is more resistant to penicillin treatment and yields larger vegetations than infection caused by dextran-negative strains.[37] Treatment of experimental en-

TABLE 191–2 Biochemical Characteristics for Differentiation of Viridans Streptococci

			Hydrolysis of			Acid Production from						Production of		
Organism	Pattern of Hemolysis	Voges-Proskauer	*Esculin*	*Arginine*	H_2O_2	*Mannitol*	*Sorbitol*	*Lactose*	*Trehalose*	*Inulin*	*Raffinose*	*Alkaline Phosphatase*	*Dextran*	*Levan*
S. mutans	α, β, γ	+	+	–	–	+	+	+	+	+	+	–	+	–
S. mitis	α	–	–	v	+	–	–	+	v	–	v	v	–	–
S. oralis	α	–	–	–	+	–	–	+	v	–	v	+	v	–
S. sanguis	α	–	v	+	+	–	v	+	+	+	v	–	+	–
S. gordonii	α	–	+	+	+	–	–	+	+	+	v	+	+	–
S. crista	α	–	–	v	+	–	–	v	+	–	–	–	v	na
S. salivarius	α	+	+	–	–	–	–	v	v	v	+	v	–	+
S. vestibularis	α	v	+	–	+	–	–	v	v	–	–	v	–	–
S. parasanguis	α	–	v	+	+	–	–	+	v	–	+	+	–	–
G. morbillorum	α, γ	na	–	–	na	–	–	–	–	–	–	na	–	na

Abbreviations and symbols: +, 85% or more of strains positive; –, 85% or more of strains negative; v, variable; na, not available.

docarditis with penicillin and dextranase results in higher rates of valve sterilization than does treatment with penicillin alone.[38] Another bacterial factor that might be related to the pathogenesis of endocarditis is FimA. This surface-associated protein of *S. parasanguis* has been associated with initial colonization of damaged heart tissue in an endocarditis model. Immunization with recombinant FimA resulted in antibody-mediated inhibition of bacterial adherence and protection from endocarditis in an animal model.[39, 40]

Fibronectin, which is secreted by endothelial cells, platelets, and fibroblasts in response to vascular injury, is one possible factor that mediates adherence of streptococci to cardiac valves.[41] It makes up about 4% of the mass of a blood clot and has been found on the surfaces of traumatized rabbit valves.[42] Microorganisms more likely to cause endocarditis bind significantly better to fibronectin in vitro than do non–endocarditis-producing strains.[43] Furthermore, a low-fibronectin-binding mutant of *S. sanguis* was less able to induce endocarditis in an experimental animal model than its high-fibronectin-binding parent strain.[44] Lipoteichoic acid appears to be the fibronectin adhesin on streptococci. Exposure of the organism to subinhibitory concentrations of antibiotics results in loss of surface lipoteichoic acid and a subsequent decrease in ability to produce endocarditis.[45, 46] Once adherent to the surface of the valve, viridans streptococci induce propagation of the infected vegetation by stimulating production of tissue factor from the underlying valvular tissue and by directly triggering further platelet aggregation.[47–49]

In addition to causing infective endocarditis, certain species of viridans streptococci, notably *S. mutans,* have a strong association with development of dental caries. Early experiments noted that caries developed in germ-free animals after they were infected with *S. mutans.* However, colonization of dental surfaces and production of caries occurred only in the presence of dietary sucrose.[50, 51] The organism uses sucrose to synthesize a number of extracellular polysaccharides, including glucans, that serve to bind it to dental enamel and to other bacteria. The high cariogenic potential of *S. mutans* is thought to be related to its dual ability to adhere in large masses on teeth and to produce high concentrations of acid from the fermentation of dietary sugars.[52]

Occasionally, viridans streptococci produce bacteremia and septic shock in neutropenic patients. The mechanism by which this occurs is unclear. However, in vitro studies have shown that clinical isolates of viridans streptococci from shock patients were able to induce tumor necrosis factor-α (TNF-α) in murine macrophages.[53] Production of TNF-α was dose dependent and followed kinetics similar to that produced by an *Escherichia coli* isolate. Similarly, in a study of patients with neutropenia and overwhelming infection, serum levels of TNF-α and interleukin-6 were found to be increased, regardless of whether shock was caused by viridans streptococci or gram-negative bacilli.[54] Therefore, the pathogenesis of viridans streptococcal shock appears to be not unlike that of gram-negative septic shock.

Clinical Manifestations

Endocarditis. In the preantibiotic era, viridans streptococci accounted for approximately 75% of cases of infective endocarditis.[55, 56] In the current era, their relative frequency has declined to 30 to 40%.[57] This change in epidemiology reflects an increase in the number of patients acquiring staphylococcal endocarditis in association with injection drug use or prosthetic valves rather than a decrease in the overall annual incidence of streptococcal endocarditis.[58] Many different species have been reported to cause endocarditis, including *S. mitis, S. sanguis, S. mutans, S. salivarius, S. gordonii,* and *S. oralis.* Because of the changes in taxonomy and the number of isolates previously unspeciated, it is likely that other viridans streptococci have also been associated with infective endocarditis. The clinical manifestations and outcomes associated with the various species causing endocarditis appear to be similar.[59]

Infective endocarditis caused by viridans streptococci occurs most often in patients with underlying valvular heart disease. In the past, rheumatic and congenital heart disease were the major predisposing lesions, accounting for 37 to 76% and 6 to 24% of endocarditis cases, respectively. With the declining incidence of rheumatic fever, mitral valve prolapse (29%) and degenerative valvular lesions (21%) have assumed a more prominent role.[60] Viridans streptococci seem to occur more frequently as the cause of endocarditis in patients known to have heart disease (55%) as opposed to those not previously known to have heart disease (29%).[61] Among cases of infective endocarditis in injection drug users, viridans streptococci account for a small proportion (6%).[62] In patients with prosthetic valves, the incidence of infective endocarditis increases according to the length of time since valve surgery. In early disease (<60 days since valve replacement), only 7% of infections are caused by streptococci; the frequency increases to 30% in patients in whom infection develops 1 year or longer after surgery.[63]

Viridans streptococcal endocarditis has an insidious onset followed by a subacute but progressive course. In most patients symptoms develop within 2 weeks of presumed onset; however, it is often 5 weeks or more from the time of initial symptoms until the diagnosis is established.[64] Fever, the single most common finding in endocarditis, is present in almost all patients except those who have preexisting renal failure, congestive heart failure, or concomitant antibiotic use.[56, 59] Constitutional symptoms such as fatigue, anorexia, weight loss, and malaise often accompany the fever. Cardiac murmurs are detected in more than 90% of patients with streptococcal endocarditis,[65] and splenomegaly is noted in up to half of cases.[66] Manifestations of circulating immune complexes such as Osler's nodes, petechiae, and splinter hemorrhages may also occur (28% of cases).[67]

The critical element for diagnosis of infective endocarditis is the demonstration of continuous bacteremia. With viridans streptococci, the bacteremia is often low grade (1 to 30 colony-forming units per milliliter of blood). In the absence of recent antimicrobial therapy, 96% of first blood cultures and 98% of two blood cultures yield the pathogen.[68] Echocardiography is used as a confirmatory test in patients with blood cultures positive for viridans streptococci; 39 to 72% of patients with endocarditis have vegetations identified on a two-dimensional echocardiogram.[59, 69] Echocardiography can also be used to identify valvular dysfunction, hemodynamic complications, and myocardial abscesses, findings that may indicate the need for surgical intervention. Whether echocardiography provides prognostic information about the risk of systemic emboli is a controversial issue.[70]

Recommended regimens for treatment of streptococcal endocarditis are based largely on clinical observations and studies of antibiotic efficacy in experimental models of endocarditis.[71, 72] In an experimental rabbit model, prolonged penicillin therapy adequately sterilized vegetations, but addition of streptomycin or gentamicin led to more rapid eradication of the pathogen.[73, 74] Penicillin G remains the mainstay of therapy for viridans streptococcal endocarditis. As with other types of infective endocarditis, the antibiotic is administered in high doses for extended periods, usually 4 weeks. If given in combination with an aminoglycoside, the duration of penicillin therapy can be shortened, although the patient is exposed to the additional risk of aminoglycoside toxicity (nephrotoxicity and ototoxicity). Although most clinical experience with two-drug regimens has been with streptomycin plus penicillin, gentamicin is now considered interchangeable with streptomycin in the combination. Because of the ready availability of serum level determinations and the convenience of intravenous administration, gentamicin has become the preferred agent in clinical practice.

Antibiotic regimens that are currently recommended by the American Heart Association are summarized in Table 191–3.[75] For streptococcal strains that are highly susceptible to penicillin (minimal inhibitory concentration [MIC] $\leq$0.1 μg/ml), three regimens are endorsed. All can be expected to achieve very high bacteriologic cure rates. In a review of endocarditis treatment outcomes, Wilson and Geraci found a relapse rate of 0.6% (1/154) for patients receiving 4 weeks

TABLE 191-3 Antimicrobial Therapy for Native Valve Infective Endocarditis due to Viridans and Nutritionally Variant Streptococci (*Abiotrophia*)

Organism (MIC)	Antibiotic	Dosage and Route*	Duration (wk)
Penicillin-susceptible viridans streptococci (≤0.1 μg/ml)	Aqueous crystalline penicillin G	12–18 million U q24h IV, either continuously or in 6 divided doses	4
	Ceftriaxone	2 g once daily IV or IM	4
	Aqueous crystalline penicillin G	12–18 million U q24h IV, either continuously or in 6 divided doses	2
	With gentamicin sulfate†	1 mg/kg IV or IM q8h	2
Relatively resistant viridans streptococci (>0.1 μg/ml and <0.5 μg/ml)	Aqueous crystalline penicillin G	18 million U q24h IV, either continuously or in 6 divided doses	4
	With gentamicin sulfate†	1 mg/kg IV or IM q8h	2
Resistant viridans streptococci (≥0.5 μg/ml) and all nutritionally variant streptococci *(Abiotrophia)*	Aqueous crystalline penicillin G	18–30 million U q24h IV, either continuously or in 6 divided doses	4–6
	With gentamicin sulfate†	1 mg/kg IV or IM q8h	4–6

*Doses should be adjusted according to renal function.

†Dosing should be based on ideal body weight. Peak and trough gentamicin levels of 3 μg/ml and <1 μg/ml, respectively, are desirable. Relative contraindications to the use of gentamicin are age >65 years, renal impairment, or impairment of eighth cranial nerve function.

Abbreviations: IM, Intramuscularly; IV, intravenously; MIC, minimal inhibitory concentration.

Adapted from recommendations of the ad hoc writing group of the Committee on Rheumatic Fever, Endocarditis, and Kawasaki Disease, Council on Cardiovascular Disease in the Young, American Heart Association. Wilson WR, Karchmer AW, Dajani AS, et al. Antimicrobial treatment of adults with infective endocarditis due to streptococci, enterococci, staphylococci, and HACEK microorganisms. JAMA. 1995;274:1706–1713. Copyright 1995, American Medical Association.

of penicillin alone, and 2.0% (6/295) for those treated with a 2-week course of penicillin plus streptomycin.[76] Ceftriaxone shows similar efficacy, with no cases of microbiologic failure or relapse reported in a noncomparative trial (although 10 of the 55 patients ultimately required valve replacement for congestive heart failure or recurrent embolization).[77] Another study compared the efficacy of a daily 2-g dose of ceftriaxone for 4 weeks with that of a regimen of 2 weeks of ceftriaxone followed by 2 weeks of oral amoxicillin (1 g four times daily) and reported relapse in only 1 of 30 patients.[78, 79]

Because relapse is uncommon, selection of a specific antimicrobial regimen should be individualized for each patient. The 2-week regimen is most appropriate for uncomplicated cases of endocarditis occurring in patients at low risk for aminoglycoside toxicity. It is not indicated for patients with extracardiac foci of infection or intracardiac abscess.[75] Longer courses of treatment may also be preferred for patients with protracted illness (symptoms lasting longer than 3 months), aortic insufficiency, moderate to severe congestive heart failure, or a documented relapse.[57] In patients whose infection involves prosthetic valves or other prosthetic material, a 6-week regimen of penicillin is recommended together with gentamicin for at least the first 2 weeks.[75]

Patients with endocarditis caused by viridans streptococci that are resistant to penicillin may be at higher risk of relapse after antimicrobial therapy.[80] For relatively resistant strains (penicillin MIC greater than 0.1 μg/ml but less than 0.5 μg/ml), gentamicin should be given for the first 2 weeks of a 4-week course of penicillin therapy (see Table 191–3). For resistant strains (those requiring 0.5 μg/ml of penicillin or more for inhibition), treatment is the same as for enterococci and consists of penicillin plus gentamicin for a full 4 to 6 weeks. Serum levels of the aminoglycoside should be monitored during therapy to avoid toxicity.

For patients who have immediate-type hypersensitivity to penicillin, 4 weeks of vancomycin is an appropriate alternate regimen. Addition of an aminoglycoside is not required, regardless of whether the isolate is resistant to penicillin. In patients with other types of penicillin allergy (e.g., nonurticarial skin rashes), cefazolin or another first-generation cephalosporin may be administered to treat viridans streptococcal endocarditis caused by isolates that are moderately resistant to penicillin (MICs, 0.1 to 0.5 μg/ml). The cephalosporin may be given alone for 4 weeks or, if there is no contraindication to short-course therapy, given in combination with an aminoglycoside for 2 weeks. Cephalosporins are not indicated in cases where the pathogen is highly resistant to penicillin (MIC ≥0.5 μg/ml).

Bacteremia. Viridans streptococci account for 2.6% of positive blood cultures reported from clinical laboratories. Of these, only 21% are thought to be clinically significant.[81] The remainder have been attributed to contamination despite the fact that viridans streptococci are not typically part of the normal skin flora.[82] In many cases, failure to ascribe clinical significance to these organisms in blood cultures may occur because of their low virulence and the transient nature of the bacteremia.[83] In contrast, prolonged bacteremia has emerged as a genuine problem among patients undergoing cancer chemotherapy. In some centers, viridans streptococci are now a leading cause of bacteremia in febrile, neutropenic patients.[84–86] At the M. D. Anderson Cancer Center in Houston, the incidence of streptococcal bacteremia increased from 1 case per 10,000 admissions in 1972 to 47 per 10,000 in 1989.[87] In another study, viridans streptococci were recovered from the blood in 35 (17.5%) of 200 consecutive recipients of autologous stem cell transplants at a median of 6 days after the procedure.[88]

Viridans streptococcal bacteremia usually occurs in association with aggressive cytoreductive therapy for acute leukemia or allogeneic bone marrow transplantation, especially after high-dose cytosine arabinoside treatment.[89–91] In a study using patients with other gram-positive bacteremias as controls, the risk of streptococcal infection was reported to increase with profound neutropenia, prophylactic administration of trimethoprim-sulfamethoxazole or a fluoroquinolone, and use of antacids or histamine type 2 (H_2) receptor antagonists (e.g., cimetidine).[87] Another risk factor strongly implicated is the presence of mucositis.[85, 90, 92] In one noncomparative study of 32 patients, 78% had oral inflammation or ulceration at the time of their infection.[92] Similarly, Bostrom and Weisdorf reported an association of viridans streptococcal bacteremia with increased radiation dose to the oral cavity,[93] whereas Ringden and colleagues described an association with herpes simplex infection.[94] In the latter report, use of prophylactic acyclovir decreased the frequency of bacteremia after allogeneic bone marrow transplantation. The presence of an indwelling venous catheter poses an additional risk factor for streptococcal bacteremia in neutropenic patients.[85, 86]

Bacteremia with viridans streptococci is more common in children than in adults,[95, 96] typically developing within 15 days of chemotherapy or bone marrow transplantation, at the time of profound neutropenia. In a series of 123 patients, 73% presented with fever alone, whereas 27% also had evidence of organ dysfunction.[95] A fulminant shock syndrome characterized by hypotension, rash, palmar desquamation, and adult respiratory distress syndrome has been described in approximately one fourth of patients.[87, 97] Very few cases of viridans streptococcal bacteremia in immunocompromised patients have been associated with clinically apparent endocarditis.

Despite early initiation of broad-spectrum antibiotics, the mortality rate for viridans streptococcal bacteremia in immunocompromised patients is approximately 6 to 12%.[87, 92, 95] Fatal cases have been characterized by early, fulminant cardiovascular collapse or secondary central nervous system involvement. In most, the isolates were susceptible in vitro to the selected empirical antimicrobial regimen, usually a β-lactam plus an aminoglycoside. Some authorities prefer to add vancomycin to a β-lactam if *S. mitis* bacteremia is known or suspected in a neutropenic patient. Lack of efficacy may have resulted from the poor clinical status of patients at the time of antibiotic initiation.

Use of antimicrobial agents to prevent streptococcal bacteremias is controversial. Some studies have shown potential benefit[97, 98]; others have not.[88] At one cancer institute, the incidence of streptococcal bacteremia decreased from 11.5% in 1989 to 2.5% in 1995 after penicillin was introduced for prophylaxis of neutropenia.[98] Similarly, in a sequential cohort study of 289 bone marrow transplant recipients, both vancomycin and β-lactam prophylaxis were shown to decrease the incidence of gram-positive bacteremia compared with controls (by 40, 27, and 0%, respectively).[99] However, no differences in mortality could be demonstrated. In contrast, Bilgrami and coworkers found that prophylactic use of ampicillin failed to decrease the incidence of viridans streptococcal sepsis in bone marrow transplant recipients.[88] Regardless of efficacy, a consequence of the prophylactic use of β-lactam antibiotics in many of these studies was emergence of resistance. The proportion of penicillin-resistant viridans streptococcal bacteremias increased from 0% in 1989 before any prophylaxis was given to marrow transplant recipients, to 16% in 1991 when quinolones were used for prophylaxis, to 44% when penicillin was added to the quinolones.[98] Fatality rates among neutropenic patients with bacteremia caused by penicillin-resistant viridans streptococci may be higher than for penicillin-susceptible strains.[90, 98, 100] Concerns over hypersensitivity reactions and selection of resistant strains may preclude routine use of penicillin prophylaxis, except in centers with high infection rates.

Meningitis. Despite the frequency with which viridans streptococci cause bacteremia, they are an uncommon cause of meningitis, accounting for approximately 0.3 to 5% of culture-proven cases.[101, 102] Although species designation was often not provided in early literature, more recent reports suggest that *S. salivarius* is most commonly associated with meningitis.[103–108] Cases caused by *S. mitis* and *S. sanguis* have also been described.[3]

The source of infection for most cases of viridans streptococcal meningitis is the patient's endogenous flora. In instances of neonatal meningitis, the infection was presumed to be acquired perinatally from the mother.[106, 109–111] Portals of entry have been various and not always identifiable. In the largest review of viridans streptococcal meningitis (55 cases), ear, nose, or throat pathology was found in 31% of patients, endocarditis in 13%, primary extracranial infection in 13%, and head trauma or neurosurgery in 8%; no portal for entry was identified in 35% of patients.[101] Other predisposing factors include gastrointestinal pathology,[103, 112] gastrointestinal manipulation such as endoscopy with cauterization,[102, 104, 113] trauma,[114] ganglionic thermocoagulation,[102] and severe immunocompromise after chemotherapy.[95, 115] In one series of four cases, iatrogenic viridans streptococcal meningitis was reported to occur after lumbar puncture.[116] Probable cause of the cluster was attributed to nonobservance of infection control measures, especially failure to wear masks during the procedure.

Viridans streptococcal meningitis occurs in patients of all ages, including neonates. Clinical manifestations are typical of acute pyogenic meningitis with evidence of meningeal irritation, neurologic deficits, seizures, and altered sensorium.

When α-hemolytic streptococci other than pneumococci are recovered from cerebrospinal fluid (CSF), they are more likely to be contaminants than true pathogens. In 43 patients from whom various species of α-hemolytic streptococci were isolated on culture of CSF, only eight isolates (19%) were determined to be clinically relevant.[117] The significance of isolation of α-hemolytic streptococci from CSF depends on the clinical setting and CSF laboratory parameters. CSF protein concentrations and white blood cell differential counts are clearly abnormal in patients with true infection, but the CSF glucose may be normal.[112] A positive Gram stain is highly significant but occurs in less than 50% of patients with viridans streptococcal meningitis.[117] Differentiation of these streptococci from *S. pneumoniae* on the basis of a spinal fluid Gram stain is seldom possible.[105]

The finding of positive blood cultures in association with viridans streptococcal meningitis is suggestive of underlying endocarditis. Bacteremia with meningitis in the absence of cardiac involvement has also been described, especially in severely immunocompromised patients.[95] Meningitis is an uncommon complication of viridans streptococcal endocarditis.[118] Among 41 patients with infective endocarditis who also had symptoms suggestive of meningitis or encephalitis, the organism was recovered on CSF culture in only 4 cases.[119]

In the preantibiotic era, viridans streptococcal meningitis was almost uniformly fatal; only nine surviving patients were reported before 1937.[101] After the introduction of antibiotic therapy, mortality rates declined significantly, with most fatalities occurring in patients who were immunocompromised. Although early reports suggested a worse prognosis in infants and children with viridans streptococcal meningitis,[101] this was not substantiated in a later study.[112] Penicillin G in doses of 24 million units per day remains the antibiotic of choice for treatment of viridans streptococcal meningitis. Most clinical isolates have had MICs of 0.1 μg/ml or less and therefore are extremely sensitive. Tolerance to penicillin has been noted in some strains (see later discussion). Meningitis caused by multiple-antibiotic–resistant viridans streptococci has also been described.[115] MICs to penicillin in these strains are 4 μg/ml or greater, similar to those seen with antibiotic-resistant *S. pneumoniae.* Although clinical data are lacking, vancomycin plus a third-generation cephalosporin (either ceftriaxone or cefotaxime) should probably be considered the regimen of choice for treatment of meningitis caused by these strains, pending the results of susceptibility tests. Because of the unpredictable susceptibility patterns of viridans streptococci, in vitro susceptibility testing of all CSF isolates is mandatory.

Pneumonia. Although viridans streptococci are often isolated from respiratory tract specimens, they are rarely ascribed clinical significance. Recovery of these organisms from expectorated sputum is usually attributable to their presence as normal oral flora. However, they may also be cultured from lower respiratory tract specimens obtained by transtracheal aspiration or protected bronchial brush. Here, viridans streptococci occur, in association with other oral organisms (e.g., anaerobes), as part of the aspiration pneumonia syndrome.[120–122] In one study of community-acquired aspiration pneumonia, cultures of transtracheal aspirates yielded streptococci in 9 of 24 patients.[123] In another review, the organism was recovered from 51% of 189 transtracheal aspirations performed on patients with suspected bacterial pneumonia.[124] The relative importance of viridans streptococci in the pathogenesis of these polymicrobial infections is unknown.

Several reports describe isolation of viridans streptococci as sole pathogens in association with lower respiratory tract infections.[125–129] Pratter and Irwin described two patients in whom the diagnosis was ascertained by culture of transtracheal aspirate and pleural fluid.[125] Sarkar and associates reported three cases of acute community-acquired viridans streptococcal pneumonia in which the diagnosis was confirmed by the presence of positive blood cultures.[126] In a series of patients described by Marrie, an association with predisposing host factors was noted. All seven patients with bacteremic community-acquired pneumonia were older (49 to 80 years) and had multiple underlying conditions, such as alcoholism, lung carcinoma, and diabetes mellitus.[130] Viridans streptococcal pneumonia has also been described in three children.[127]

The prognosis for patients with primary viridans streptococcal pneumonia is good. Fatalities are rare in the absence of immunocompromise. Penicillin G has been used successfully as therapy in most cases reported in the literature.

Miscellaneous Infections. Viridans streptococci are associated with a variety of other infections. A pathogenic role in these cases has been confirmed by recovery of the organism in pure culture and often by the concurrent presence of bacteremia. Excluding localized purulent collections associated with the *S. milleri* group (see Chapter 192), viridans strains have been identified in patients with pericarditis,[129] peritonitis,[129] acute bacterial sialadenitis,[131] orofacial odontogenic infections,[132] endophthalmitis (see Chapter 100), and various upper respiratory tract infections (otitis media, sinusitis).[127]

Therapy

In the past, viridans group streptococci were uniformly susceptible to most antimicrobial agents, including β-lactam antibiotics, macrolides, tetracyclines, and aminoglycosides. However, resistance has emerged as a significant problem, especially resistance to penicillin and related β-lactam agents. Among 352 unselected blood culture isolates obtained from across the United States during 1993 and 1994, only 44% were susceptible to penicillin (using the National Committee for Laboratory Standards interpretive criterion of MIC ≤0.125 μg/ml).[133] Resistance seems to occur more frequently in nosocomial blood-stream isolates and in those obtained from immunocompromised patients. In the SCOPE National Surveillance Program, 61% of 98 nosocomial blood-stream isolates were susceptible to penicillin,[134] whereas rates as low as 43% have been reported in neutropenic cancer patients.[100] Resistance in this latter group appears to be selected by the inclusion of antimicrobial prophylaxis with cancer chemotherapy. In contrast, most community isolates of viridans group streptococci appear to be remaining susceptible to penicillin. For example, the susceptibility of endocarditis isolates has not changed appreciably in the last several decades.[135, 136] In a 1986 review, only 2 of 31 viridans streptococcal isolates were reported to be penicillin resistant.[137] Moreover, penicillin prophylaxis given to children with rheumatic fever has not often been complicated by endocarditis due to resistant streptococci,[80] despite increasing numbers of penicillin-resistant strains in the normal flora of the oropharynx.[138, 139]

Some strains of viridans group streptococci exhibit a high level of resistance to penicillin. In a survey of South African blood culture isolates, 9% had penicillin MICs of 4.0 μg/ml or greater.[140] Note that the breakpoint for resistance as defined by National Committee for Laboratory Standards[141] differs from the MIC criterion (≥0.5 μg/ml) used in the American Heart Association guidelines for determining treatment of streptococcal endocarditis (see Table 191–3).[75] Surveys of viridans streptococci from the United States report high-level penicillin resistance in 5 to 13% of blood-stream isolates.[133, 142] Rates reported from other areas of the world approach 50%, depending on the types of patients and specimens studied.[100] Like penicillin-resistant pneumococci, resistant viridans strains are non–β-lactamase-producing and possess altered penicillin-binding proteins.[143] In vitro studies suggest the presence of genes homologous to the pneumococcal PBP 1a and 2b genes in these viridans strains.[144] Transfer of resistance determinants between these gram-positive bacteria has been accomplished in vitro and may be an important means of disseminating resistance in nature.

Species-related differences in penicillin susceptibility have been observed among viridans group streptococci.[135, 145] *S. mitis* appears to be the least sensitive, with only 40% of isolates inhibited by 0.125 μg/ml penicillin or less.[146] *S. sanguis* is the next most resistant, with approximately 74% of strains inhibited by that dosage.

Some strains of viridans streptococci exhibit a phenomenon termed *tolerance,* in which the organism is readily inhibited by low concentrations of penicillin but 32 times that level is required for bactericidal activity. In experimental animal models of endocarditis, tolerant strains are eradicated more slowly from vegetations than nontolerant strains, although this effect may be relevant only when low doses of penicillin are used.[147–149] There are conflicting reports on the incidence of tolerance in viridans streptococci.[150] Tolerance is probably observed in most *S. sanguis* and *S. gordonii* strains, but it occurs in a minority of *S. mitis* strains and rarely, if at all, in *S. salivarius.*[151] No clinical significance has been attached to tolerance in the treatment of infective endocarditis. Relapse after a 4-week course of high-dose parenteral penicillin is rare and has not been associated with tolerance in the pathogen.[76] Addition of an aminoglycoside may enhance bactericidal activity in vitro but is not routinely recommended.[75]

Other β-lactam antibiotics have in vitro activity similar to penicillin against viridans streptococci. Generally, community-acquired endocarditis isolates tend to be highly susceptible. Ceftriaxone inhibited 100% of 20 endocarditis strains at a concentration of 2.0 μg/ml or less, and 16 strains (80%) were susceptible to 0.25 μg/ml or less.[152] In another study, 98% of 49 strains were inhibited by 0.1 μg/ml or less.[77] Among surveys of isolates collected from hospitalized or neutropenic cancer patients, ceftriaxone has been less active, with approximately 15 to 23% of isolates found to be resistant.[134, 142] Most such isolates also have high-level resistance to penicillin (MIC >4 μg/ml) as well as resistance to other antimicrobial agents.[153]

Viridans streptococci are resistant to aminoglycosides when traditional breakpoint concentrations for these agents are applied. However, in vitro studies and experimental models of endocarditis have demonstrated synergistic bactericidal activity for combinations of penicillin and aminoglycosides.[73, 74] In strains with a streptomycin MIC of 1000 μg/ml or greater, synergy is lost for streptomycin but not for gentamicin.[154, 155] The breakpoint for predicting synergy with gentamicin is not clear. Strains with a gentamicin MIC of 16 μg/ml have shown synergy, whereas strains with MICs of 64 and 128 μg/ml have not.[140]

Antibiotics with consistently good in vitro activity against viridans streptococci are chloramphenicol and vancomycin; only rare isolates are resistant to the former, and none to the latter. The fluoroquinolones, ofloxacin, sparfloxacin, and levofloxacin also demonstrate good in vitro activity.[133, 156] However, neutropenic cancer patients who receive prophylaxis with a quinolone often develop breakthrough bacteremia with isolates expressing high-level resistance.[157] Therefore, the role of these agents in therapy is uncertain. Tetracycline, clindamycin, and erythromycin have variable activity, often with 25 to 50% of isolates reported resistant.[153] Most strains of viridans streptococci are resistant to trimethoprim-sulfamethoxazole.[89]

NUTRITIONALLY VARIANT (DEFICIENT) STREPTOCOCCI *(ABIOTROPHIA)*

NVS were first described in 1961 as fastidious gram-positive bacteria that grow as satellite colonies around other bacteria.[158] Originally isolated from patients with endocarditis and otitis media, these organisms were deemed to be mutant subspecies of *S. mitis ("S. mitior")* because of their sugar fermentation and cell wall composition.[58] They also possessed a heat-acid extractable chromophore like that of *S. mitis.*[159] However, despite evidence for similarity between NVS and *S. mitis,* important phenotypic differences were also evident, such as their enzymatic capabilities and patterns of penicillin-binding proteins.[160] On the basis of DNA-DNA hybridization studies, Bouvet and colleagues found that NVS fit the genus description of *Streptococcus* but were taxonomically unrelated to other viridans group organisms. The names *S. adjacens* and *S. defectivus* were proposed as new designations.[22] Subsequently, studies using 16S ribosomal RNA (rRNA) sequence analysis showed that these two species were actually not related to other members of the *Streptococcus* genus. Therefore, in 1995, Kawamura and associates proposed placing them in a new genus *Abiotrophia,* as *A. adiacens* and *A. defectiva.*[23] Both species are resistant to optochin, are susceptible to vancomycin, produce leucine aminopeptidase and arylamidase, lack alkaline phosphatase, and cannot hydrolyze hippurate or arginine. The two species can be differentiated by their patterns of carbohydrate fermentation and production of β-galactosidases. Not all isolates of NVS can be classified as belonging to one of these two species. DNA-DNA hybridization studies among other strains of NVS reveal significant genetic heterogeneity.[161]

NVS are defined by their requirement for pyridoxal or thiol group supplementation for growth. They tend to form satellite colonies around *Staphylococcus aureus* and other microbes, including some Enterobacteriaceae and other streptococci.[162] Colonies of NVS are small, measuring 0.2 to 0.5 mm in diameter, and are either nonhemolytic or α-hemolytic on blood agar. On Gram staining, cells may be pleomorphic and may exhibit variable staining characteristics. There appears to be sufficient pyridoxal in human blood to support growth of NVS in most blood culture media (with the notable exception of unsupplemented tryptic soy broth).[163, 164] For subculture, however, solid media must be supplemented with 0.001% pyridoxal or 0.01% L-cysteine to sustain growth. Alternatively, the subculture plate can be cross-streaked with *S. aureus* to provide these factors and permit growth as satellite colonies. Some studies suggest that blood cultures suspected of harboring NVS should be subcultured within 48 hours, because viability of the organism may decline with continued incubation.[163, 164]

NVS are found as normal flora of the upper respiratory, urogenital, and gastrointestinal tracts of humans. They cause approximately 5% of cases of bacterial endocarditis.[58] Historically, NVS also accounted for most cases of culture-negative endocarditis, but with current laboratory media and techniques, recovery of strains is no longer a significant problem. Endocarditis caused by NVS carries greater morbidity and mortality than endocarditis caused by other streptococci. A comparison between 49 patients with NVS endocarditis and 130 patients with infection caused by other oral species revealed a higher mortality rate (14% versus 5%), more frequent complications of embolization (33% versus 11%) and congestive heart failure (33% versus 18%), and an increased rate of surgical intervention (33% versus 18%).[57] Vegetations visualized by two-dimensional echocardiography are seen in a large proportion of patients (64%).[69] Several reports have indicated that endocarditis caused by NVS carries a higher mortality rate than that reported for viridans streptococci (approximately 15% versus 5%).[58, 165] Similarly, these infections respond poorly to antibiotics; bacteriologic failure and relapse were observed in 41% and 17% of the cases, respectively.[165]

NVS are less susceptible in vitro to penicillin than are most other streptococci. Approximately 33 to 65% of strains are relatively resistant (MICs, 0.2 to 2.0 μg/ml), and some isolates are highly resistant to the antibiotic (MIC >4 μg/ml).[58, 166–169] Depending on the method used, many strains of NVS also exhibit tolerance to penicillin. In a study of 11 strains, tolerance was demonstrated in the presence of pyridoxal, L-cysteine, penicillinase, and a staphylococcal cross-streak in all strains, but in no strains when only pyridoxal and L-cysteine were added to the subculture medium.[170] Aminoglycosides show variable in vitro activity against NVS, with an MIC range of 0.5 to 32 μg/ml.[166, 168] High-level resistance (MIC >500 μg/ml), as seen in enterococci and viridans streptococci, has not been reported in NVS. Synergy between penicillin or vancomycin in combination with an aminoglycoside is observed both in vitro and in experimental animal models of endocarditis for both tolerant and nontolerant strains of NVS.[171–173] One such study suggested that the combination of penicillin with low-dose gentamicin was superior to penicillin combined with low-dose streptomycin.[172] All strains of NVS are susceptible to vancomycin in vitro, and most are also susceptible to clindamycin, chloramphenicol, and erythromycin. The activity of the cephalosporins and tetracycline is variable. In time-kill studies rifampin, which is highly active in vitro, has been observed to produce synergistic bactericidal activity when given in combination with vancomycin.[174]

In vitro antimicrobial susceptibility testing of NVS is beyond the scope of many routine clinical laboratories. Moreover, the results of in vitro susceptibility tests do not correlate well with clinical outcome in patients treated for endocarditis. Even with strains highly susceptible to penicillin, patients may relapse after completing a course of therapy.[171] Because of the difficulties in performing susceptibility tests and correlating the results with clinical outcome, it is recommended that all patients with NVS endocarditis be treated with long-term combination therapy (e.g., penicillin plus gentamicin for 4 to 6 weeks [see Table 191–3]).[75] Even with this regimen, however, the rates of bacteriologic failure and relapse are high.[165]

The precise role of NVS as pathogens in other disease processes is unknown. Because the organisms grow poorly on solid media, they can easily be overlooked if broth cultures are not performed or not subcultured to appropriately supplemented media. Isolation of NVS as a likely pathogen has been reported in patients with pancreatic abscess,[175] otitis media,[158] conjunctivitis,[176] infectious crystalline keratopathy,[177] cirrhosis, and postpartum and postabortal sepsis.[178]

β-HEMOLYTIC STREPTOCOCCI (GROUPS C AND G)

Microbiology

Confusing and conflicting results from taxonomic studies make it impossible to recommend a practical identification scheme that would correlate with genetic descriptions of the non–group A, B, and D β-hemolytic streptococci. For convenience, these streptococci can initially be divided into groups based on colony size.[1] Small or minute colony types (<0.5 mm in diameter) have been placed into the *S. anginosus* group (see Chapter 192). β-Hemolytic streptococci of large colony size (≥0.5 mm in diameter) are almost always groupable with Lancefield antisera using latex agglutination or coagglutination directed against the cell wall carbohydrate of groups A, B, C, or G.[179, 180] Although serologic typing according to cell wall components has classically been used to separate streptococci into species, DNA homology studies have shown that this method is not always valid. Nevertheless, this classification remains useful as an aid to identification of clinical isolates. In many diagnostic microbiology laboratories, bacitracin disk susceptibility is also used as a screening test to separate group A streptococci from other *pyogenes*-like organisms. Studies employing the standard 0.04-unit bacitracin disk have demonstrated that only 6 to 8% of groups C and G β-hemolytic streptococci are susceptible.[181] However, other investigators have found greater variation in the bacitracin susceptibility of these streptococcal strains (see discussion of specific microorganisms).

Large colony-forming β-hemolytic strains not containing group antigens are rarely etiologic agents of human disease. Those possessing group antigens other than A, B, C, and G have been isolated primarily from animals and environmental sources and may be carried as the normal flora of the pharynx, vagina, or skin of wild or domestic animals. Rare infections in humans have been reported to be caused by serogroups E, L, M, N, and O[2, 182–184]; these types are not discussed here. The following sections review in detail the microbiologic and clinical characteristics of groups C and G β-hemolytic streptococci.

Group C Streptococci. Most group C β-hemolytic streptococci produce β-hemolysis on sheep blood agar, although all types of hemolysis have been noted.[185, 186] All group C streptococci are common pathogens in domestic animals, birds, rabbits, and guinea pigs. Although bacitracin resistance characterizes most group C streptococcal isolates, at least one third, and in one study up to 62% of isolates were bacitracin sensitive.[186–189] Therefore, group C streptococci may be misidentified as group A streptococci if sensitivity to bacitracin is used for presumptive identification of group A strains. This indicates the importance of performing Lancefield serologic testing on all bacitracin-sensitive and resistant β-hemolytic streptococci. Identification by antibiotic screening can be improved with the use of a trimethoprim-sulfamethoxazole disk, to which group C organisms are sensitive and group A organisms resistant.[190]

There are four species of group C streptococci; their microbiologic and biochemical characteristics are shown in Table 191–4.[191–193] *Streptococcus dysgalactiae* is uncommon in humans but causes mastitis in cows and suppurative polyarthritis in lambs.[194] It generally produces α-hemolysis or no hemolysis on blood agar, ferments trehalose, and produces a single hemolysin that is not streptolysin O or S.[195]

Streptococcus equisimilis is the most common group C streptococcus to colonize and cause infection in humans. It ferments trehalose but not sorbitol, and it produces streptokinase and streptolysin O but not streptolysin S.[195, 196] The streptokinase used for human thrombolytic therapy is derived from *S. equisimilis.*[197] Because *S. equisimilis* produces streptolysin O, infections caused by this organism may result in elevated antistreptolysin O (ASO) antibody titers, which are classically used to screen patients for antecedent group A β-hemolytic streptococcal infection.[198] *S. equisimilis* has been isolated from the throat, nose, and genital tract of asymptomatic carriers[196, 199, 200] and from the umbilicus of up to two thirds of asymptomatic newborns.[201] Domestic animals (e.g., horses, cattle, pigs, chickens) may also be infected.

Streptococcus zooepidemicus causes significant, often epidemic, infections in domestic animals (horses, cattle, sheep, and pigs). Most cases of human infection can be traced to an animal source.[193] *S. zooepidemicus* has been isolated as the etiologic agent in cases of bovine mastitis, equine respiratory tract infections and infertility, and severe infections in poultry.[194] It ferments sorbitol but not trehalose, produces a novel hemolysin but not streptolysin O or S, does not produce streptokinase, and is not considered part of the normal human flora.[195, 196, 202] Human infection is uncommon and has been associated with consumption of homemade cheese and unpasteurized cow's milk.[203–205] In one study from England, *S. zooepidemicus* represented 1.4% of 214 isolates recovered from a variety of clinical specimens,[206] although it has been suggested that this organism causes a higher proportion of aggressive infections than would be expected from its rare occurrence at superficial sites.

Streptococcus equi is primarily a pathogen of young horses, in which it causes strangles, a serious and highly contagious respiratory disease.[194, 207] It ferments neither trehalose nor sorbitol, produces a soluble hemolysin but not streptolysin O or S, and does not produce streptokinase.

Although large colony–size group C streptococci have traditionally been divided into the four species just described, more recent studies have shown extensive similarities between *S. equi* and *S. zooepidemicus,* suggesting that they represent a single genotype.[208–210] Because of differences in fermentation patterns of lactose and sorbitol, in fructose diphosphate aldolases,[211] and in numerical taxonomic studies,[210] it is recommended that strains previously identified as *S. zooepidemicus* be identified as *S. equi* subsp. *zooepidemicus.*[209] In addition, *S. equisimilis* has been shown to be closely related to *S. dysgalactiae.*[208–210, 212]

Group G Streptococci. β-Hemolytic streptococcal strains carrying the group G antigen were first described by Lancefield and Hare in 1935.[213] The great majority of group G strains demonstrate β-hemolysis when incubated in 5 to 10% carbon dioxide at 35°C for 18 to 48 hours on trypticase soy agar with 5% sheep's blood.[214] One criterion used for separating group A streptococci from other β-hemolytic strains is development of a 10-mm zone of inhibition around a 6-mm disk containing 0.04 units of bacitracin.[214–216] However, with this criterion, 3 to 30% of non–group A β-hemolytic streptococcal strains are also bacitracin-sensitive.[217] Of group G β-hemolytic streptococci, 8 to 67% can be sensitive to bacitracin.[181, 189, 216] These organisms also carry a wide variety of type antigens (i.e., protein T, M types, and polysaccharide), in addition to the Lancefield group G antigen, that are found in other streptococci. Group G β-hemolytic streptococci produce a streptolysin that is antigenically similar to the streptolysin O produced by group A β-hemolytic streptococci.[218] Therefore, patients with group G streptococcal pharyngitis may have a significant increase in serum ASO antibody titers.[219, 220]

Epidemiology

Group C Streptococci. Group C β-hemolytic streptococci have been identified as part of the normal human flora of the nasopharynx,[196] skin,[221] and genital tract[199]; the organism has also been cultured from umbilical specimens in newborns without signs of infection[201] and in routine puerperal vaginal cultures.[222] In addition, many animal species are colonized with group C streptococci; infection in humans has been traced to animal sources. Underlying conditions have been noted in most patients with group C streptococcal infection; in one review of 31 cases, such conditions included cardiopulmonary disease (26%), diabetes mellitus (20%), chronic dermatologic conditions (20%), malignancy (20%), immunosuppression (19%), alcohol abuse (13%), renal or hepatic failure (10%), and injection drug use (6%).[190] In another review of 88 cases of group C streptococcal bacteremia, 73% of the patients had a significant underlying condition (cardiovascular disease in 20%; malignancy in 20%); prior exposure to animals was documented in 24% of cases.[193]

Group G Streptococci. Group G streptococci may be found to colonize the nasopharynx, skin, and genital tract[221]; intestinal colonization has also been reported. Several investigators have noted that up to 65% of patients with group G streptococcal infections have an underlying malignancy.[2, 223, 224] However, a study of 57 cases of group G streptococcal infection in 11 hospitals in northeastern Ohio found that only 21% of patients had an underlying malignancy[224]; 21% were alcohol abusers and 14% had diabetes mellitus. Similar rates were found in two other studies: one found that only 2 of 15 patients with group G streptococcal infection had an underlying malignancy,[225] and in another review of 24 patients with group G streptococcal bacteremia the rate of underlying neoplastic disease was 25%.[226]

Clinical Manifestations

Numerous reports of groups C and G streptococcal suppurative infections of various organ systems have been published.[190, 191, 193, 221, 224, 225, 227, 228] Infection can be endogenous (i.e., from organisms residing on skin or mucous membranes) or exogenous (i.e., from animal

TABLE 191–4 Microbiologic and Biochemical Characteristics of Group C Streptococci*

		Fermentation Pattern			Production of	
Subgroup	**Hemolysis**	***Trehalose***	***Lactose***	***Sorbitol***	***Streptokinase***	***Streptolysin O***
S. dysgalactiae	α or none	+	±	±	−	−
S. equisimilis	β	+	±	−	+	+
S. zooepidemicus	β	−	±	+	−	−
S. equi	β	−	−	−	−	−

*All streptococcal subgroups exhibited large colony size (≥0.5 mm) morphology and were Voges-Proskauer test negative (i.e., did not produce acetoin from glucose in bacterial cultures).
Symbols: +, Ferments consistently or produces streptokinase or streptolysin O; −, does not ferment or does not produce streptokinase or streptolysin O; ±, variable ability to ferment.
Data from refs. 191–193.

sources). Endogenous infection often occurs in hosts predisposed by age (neonate or elderly), alcoholism, injection drug abuse, diabetes mellitus, immunosuppressive therapy with corticosteroids or cytotoxic drugs, or underlying malignancy. Infections are often severe, resembling those caused by groups A and B β-hemolytic streptococci.

Pharyngitis. Non–group A β-hemolytic streptococci have been associated with outbreaks of pharyngitis,[229, 230] although their precise role in the causation of epidemic pharyngitis has not been defined.[231] In one report of children and adolescents with sporadic pharyngitis,[198] 17% of β-hemolytic isolates were non–group A; of these, less than half were groups C and G. The symptoms and signs of pharyngitis caused by group C streptococci are very similar to those caused by group A β-hemolytic streptococci[229] and include fever, mild to moderate sore throat, pharyngeal exudate, and cervical adenopathy. Group C streptococci can cause a severe pharyngitis, followed by bacteremia and metastatic infection.

Several studies comparing group C β-hemolytic streptococcal isolation rates among pharyngitis patients versus controls have reported contradictory results.[231] In five studies, group C streptococci were isolated more frequently from patients than from controls, although the results were statistically significant in only one study.[232] In this study, which used optimal laboratory techniques, the isolation rate of group C streptococci was higher among 1425 adult patients than among 284 controls (6% versus 1.4%; $p = .002$). In five other studies, group C streptococci were isolated from pharyngitis patients as often or more frequently than from controls, although the differences were not statistically significant.[231, 233]

In a carefully done study of 232 college students with pharyngitis,[234] a strong epidemiologic association between group C streptococci and endemic pharyngitis was demonstrated; group C streptococci were isolated significantly more often from patients than from 198 age-matched controls (26% versus 11%; $p < .0001$). Culture-positive patients also had fever, exudative tonsillitis, and anterior cervical adenopathy more often than culture-negative patients, and quantitative colony counts were generally higher among patients compared with controls. The 11% isolation rate among controls suggested that group C streptococci may represent normal oropharyngeal flora. In another study in college students, *S. equisimilis* was isolated more frequently from patients with exudative pharyngitis than from controls (11% versus 2%; $p = .001$).[235] Rapid detection of group C streptococci from throat swabs has been attempted. Compared with culture, the rapid test was poorly sensitive (34.4%) but very specific (99.4%) in detection of group C β-hemolytic streptococci[236]; the sensitivity of the test improved with an increasing quantity of colonies isolated from throat cultures.

Asymptomatic pharyngeal carriage of group G β-hemolytic streptococci occurs in up to 23% of humans.[219] Symptoms and signs in patients with group G streptococcal pharyngitis range from a mild upper respiratory tract infection with coryza to an exudative pharyngitis with fever and lymphadenopathy. As with group C streptococci, the illness is indistinguishable from pharyngitis caused by group A β-hemolytic streptococci. Initial reports that suggested an etiologic role of group G streptococci in pharyngitis consisted of anecdotes, small case clusters, and investigations of predominantly food-borne outbreaks (related to consumption of eggs and chicken salad).[219, 220, 231, 233, 237, 238] Few of these studies were adequately controlled, and the isolation rate of group G streptococci was too low to demonstrate a statistically significant difference between symptomatic and asymptomatic groups. More recently, in an outbreak of pharyngitis among children, throat cultures for group G β-hemolytic streptococci were positive in 56 (25%) of 222 patients; DNA fingerprinting revealed identical strains in 75% of cases.[239] In this outbreak, 67% of isolates were detected within an 8-week period. Patients with group G streptococcal pharyngitis were comparable to those with group A streptococcal pharyngitis with respect to clinical findings, ASO antibody titer response, and clinical response to antimicrobial therapy; however, patients with group G streptococci were significantly older (mean age, 11.5 versus 10.0 years; $p < .05$). In this study, antimicrobial therapy appeared to have a dramatic impact on the clinical course of group G streptococcal pharyngitis, although other investigators have found no evidence that antimicrobial therapy modifies the duration or severity of symptoms.[237]

Complications of Pharyngitis. Poststreptococcal glomerulonephritis has been associated with group C streptococcal pharyngitis.[203, 204] In these reports infection was acquired by consumption of unpasteurized milk from cattle with mastitis; the etiologic agent was *S. zooepidemicus.* No ASO antibody titer response was detected in these outbreaks because *S. zooepidemicus* does not produce streptolysin O. The pathogenesis of poststreptococcal glomerulonephritis from group C streptococcal infection is unclear, although certain group C streptococcal strains recovered from throat cultures were found to possess human antibody receptors that were thought to be virulence factors for these organisms.[240] In addition, endostreptosin, a cytoplasmic polypeptide antigen that plays a role in poststreptococcal glomerulonephritis associated with group A streptococcal infection, was demonstrated in the cytoplasm of infecting group C isolates, and elevated concentrations of anti-endostreptosin antibodies were detected in the patients' sera. Acute glomerulonephritis in association with group G streptococcal infection has also been reported.[241] Type 12 M-protein antigen, identical to the nephritogenic antigen of the group A streptococcus,[242] has been isolated from the group G streptococcus. However, association of group G β-hemolytic streptococci with acute glomerulonephritis is anecdotal; a causal relation is not yet established.[221, 243, 244] Group G streptococcal pharyngitis has also been associated with sterile reactive arthritis.[245] Acute rheumatic fever has not been described in association with either group C or group G streptococcal pharyngitis.

Skin and Soft Tissue Infection. Colonization of human skin with groups C and G streptococci is common, and these organisms have been responsible for various cutaneous and subcutaneous infections including cellulitis, wound infections, pyoderma, erysipelas, impetigo, and cutaneous ulcers.[190, 200, 222, 246, 247] Breeches in skin integrity may provide a portal of entry leading to bacteremia. Group C streptococci have been isolated in patients with cellulitis after vein harvest for coronary artery bypass grafts and in conditions associated with abnormal venous or lymphatic drainage.[248] Accompanying lymphangitis may also be seen.

Group G streptococcal bacteremia often occurs as a complication of skin and soft tissue infections. In one review of 37 patients with group G streptococcal bacteremia,[224] 14 (58%) of 24 patients with an underlying malignancy were thought to have a skin or soft tissue source. Of 13 other patients without a known malignancy, 11 had cellulitis and 2 had cutaneous abscesses. Therefore, a total of 73% of patients from this series became bacteremic from a cutaneous source. This contrasts with other reviews of group G streptococcal infections, in which only 13 to 25% of bacteremic patients had an identified cutaneous focus of infection.[225, 227]

Arthritis. β-Hemolytic streptococci account for 11 to 28% of cases of nongonococcal septic arthritis, with most cases in both children and adults caused by group A streptococci.[249–255] Group C streptococcal arthritis most frequently occurs in joints with preexisting rheumatologic abnormalities.[192, 256, 257] In an extensive literature review of 18 cases of group C streptococcal septic arthritis,[258] underlying conditions, both rheumatic and nonrheumatic, were recognized in 72% of patients. The specific microorganism was identified in nine cases: *S. equisimilis* in six patients and *S. zooepidemicus* in three patients. The skin was the presumed portal of entry in five patients, although in most cases the source of infection was not identified. Almost any joint can be involved, and frequently the arthritis is polyarticular (30% of cases in one review).[192] Infective endocarditis was diagnosed in two patients. Antimicrobial therapy (primarily penicillin G) and surgical drainage were used in most cases. Three of the patients died, all of whom were bacteremic; in two cases death was related to the underlying condition (i.e., congestive heart failure and pneumonia).

Group G streptococci are the second most common of the β-hemolytic streptococci to cause septic arthritis.[259–264] In one review of 57 cases,[265] clinical features were known in 46 patients, including 13 with infected prosthetic joints. Forty-eight percent of those with group G streptococcal septic arthritis of native joints had polyarticular involvement. An extra-articular focus of infection was present in 55% of patients with native joints and 62% of those with prosthetic joints; the major foci were cellulitis and endocarditis. Underlying joint disease was present in 33% of patients with infected native joints. Only four patients had no underlying conditions or joint abnormalities. Antimicrobial therapy included penicillin, penicillin plus an aminoglycoside, and other antimicrobial agents (e.g., cefazolin, vancomycin, erythromycin); length of therapy ranged from 14 to 90 days, with the organism cleared rapidly from the joint in most instances. However, in some patients the clinical course was protracted, and bacteriologic relapse after medical therapy was common. There may be a slow response to antimicrobial therapy despite in vitro susceptibility.[260, 261] Surgical drainage was required in 13 patients, including 5 with prosthetic joints. Patients with infected prosthetic joints have been noted to do well even without joint removal.[265] Coexistent osteomyelitis may be present (see next section), and recurrent sterile joint effusions may also occur.

Osteomyelitis. Isolated reports have described cases of group C streptococcal osteomyelitis.[266–268] A review of the literature described 11 patients with group G streptococcal osteomyelitis,[265] 3 of whom also had septic arthritis. Six of seven patients with group G streptococcal osteomyelitis in this review had underlying conditions (malignancy, alcoholic cirrhosis, osteoarthritis, internal fixation for fractures, and prosthesis). Three patients were treated with antibiotics, and another three patients required antimicrobial therapy plus surgery. Two cases of group G streptococcal vertebral osteomyelitis have also been reported.[269]

Respiratory Tract Infections. The group C streptococcus is an uncommon cause of pneumonia, but it is associated with significant morbidity and mortality, similar to infection caused by the group A streptococcus.[190, 270–275] Development of pneumonia is often preceded by a viral upper respiratory tract infection. In one review of nine cases,[276] the pneumonia was typically lobar and often heralded by fever, chills, dyspnea, and pleuritic chest pain. Bacteremia was documented in 75% of cases. All patients had pleural effusions. Complications included metastatic infection, empyema, and cavitation. All patients received therapy with intravenous penicillin, sometimes in combination with other antimicrobial agents.

Pneumonia caused by the group G streptococcus is rare. In a literature review of eight cases of group G streptococcal pneumonia and empyema,[2, 223, 224, 277, 278] seven occurred in adults with various malignancies. In a more recent series of seven cases,[227] only two patients had an underlying malignancy.

Group C streptococcal sinusitis has also been reported.[279] Common to all cases was age less than 18 years, the presence of central nervous system complications (perhaps secondary to inadequate medical or surgical therapy), and a delay in initiation of adequate therapy. In one review of five cases, three patients were bacteremic and two patients died.[279]

Endocarditis. Infective endocarditis caused by groups C and G streptococci is uncommon, accounting for less than 1% of total cases and 8.4% of cases caused by β-hemolytic streptococci.[190, 224, 225, 227, 280–284] In a review of 4705 cases of infective endocarditis,[285] 166 (3.5%) were caused by β-hemolytic streptococci, 8 were group C, and 14 were group G. The likelihood of infective endocarditis appears to be more common with groups C and G streptococcal bacteremia than with groups A and B, even though the latter more often cause bacteremia.[2, 224]

In a review of 88 cases of group C streptococcal bacteremia,[193] patients with endocarditis (24 cases) usually presented subacutely (mean duration of symptoms, 17.4 days). Major emboli to the central nervous system, eye, limbs, and lungs were observed in 10 cases; one third of the patients died. Response to single-agent β-lactam therapy was poor, leading the authors to favor the use of bactericidal combinations (e.g., penicillin plus gentamicin), although no comparative data were available to make firm recommendations. Four patients required surgical valve replacement for congestive heart failure. In contrast, in another review of group C streptococcal infections in which 20 cases of infective endocarditis were identified,[190] the presentation was typically acute with a propensity for involvement of normal valves, a high mortality rate (approaching 40 to 50%), embolic complications, and a frequent need for valve replacement. More than half of the patients developed cardiac complications, including destruction of the valve leaflets, myocardial abscesses, conduction abnormalities, and severe congestive heart failure. Major systemic emboli to the spleen, kidneys, myocardium, and central nervous system occurred in about half of the patients. In 12 patients for whom there was information on antimicrobial therapy, there were no bacteriologic failures among those treated with penicillin with or without an aminoglycoside. However, patients who received combination therapy required valve replacement less frequently than patients treated with penicillin alone. Combination therapy may be more rapidly bactericidal, although the relation of antimicrobial therapy to surgery cannot be adequately assessed given the small number of patients reviewed.

Group G streptococcal endocarditis tends to occur in older patients with multiple underlying disorders.[225, 227, 286] Both native and prosthetic valves may be affected, and left-sided disease is more common. Infective endocarditis caused by group G streptococci has occurred in patients with normal cardiac valves as well as in those with preexisting congenital or acquired valvular disease. The onset is generally abrupt, with rapid valve destruction and perivalvular infection; metastatic foci are not uncommon. In a review of 40 cases of group G streptococcal endocarditis,[287] the mean age of the patients was 56 years. Underlying conditions included malignancy (six cases), injection drug abuse (three cases), alcohol abuse (four cases), and diabetes mellitus (six cases). The presentation was acute in 26 of 40 patients. The portal of entry was the skin in almost half of the cases. In 17 cases, infective endocarditis complicated underlying valvular heart disease, whereas 16 patients had normal cardiac valves before infection; no details with regard to underlying valvular heart disease were given in the remaining 7 cases. Among the 29 patients in whom complications were reported, 25 had cardiac or embolic complications. The mortality rate was 36%, but it has ranged from 43 to 67% in other studies.[283, 286] There was a trend to improved survival in patients treated with the antimicrobial combination of a β-lactam plus an aminoglycoside for at least 28 days.

Meningitis. Cases of groups C and G streptococcal meningitis have been reported and are often associated with infective endocarditis.[190, 191, 225, 288–291] Infection may occur in healthy patients; one case occurred as a possible equine zoonosis,[289] and one occurred after ingestion of unpasteurized goat's milk.[292] Group C streptococci were also recovered from the CSF in a preterm infant whose mother had received intrapartum antimicrobial therapy for chorioamnionitis.[293] The clinical presentation is typically acute, and the response to antimicrobial therapy slow. In a review of the literature of 18 previous cases (9 in adults) of group C streptococcal meningitis,[294] the case-fatality rate was 55%.

Puerperal Infection. In their original paper, Lancefield and Hare recovered group G streptococci from 5 of 855 antepartum vaginal swabs and from the blood of a patient with puerperal sepsis who was also infected with *S. aureus*.[213] About 5% of asymptomatic women harbor group G β-hemolytic streptococci in their genital tracts. Both group C and group G streptococci have been associated with epidemic and nonepidemic puerperal sepsis and endometritis.[222, 227, 295, 296] When endometritis occurs without bacteremia, it may be relatively mild and associated with few systemic symptoms.

Neonatal Sepsis. Neonatal sepsis caused by group G streptococci occurs in premature or low-birth-weight infants and in the setting of premature rupture of membranes.[297–300] Infection most likely complicates colonization of the birth canal with spread to the child after vaginal delivery. The onset of disease is typically within the first week of life. Infection in the child is also associated with a high incidence of maternal obstetric complications. In a review of neonatal sepsis from one institution over a 5-year period, group G streptococci accounted for 7 of 305 cases.[300] Symptoms and signs included hypothermia, irritability, seizures, apnea, bradycardia, and cardiac arrest. Complications such as progressive respiratory distress, shock, and disseminated intravascular coagulation are invariably fatal.

Bacteremia. Group C streptococci are rarely isolated from blood cultures, accounting for less than 1% of all bacteremias.[2, 228, 301–303] However, in patients with group C streptococcal infections, bacteremia is frequently detected. In one review of 31 cases of group C streptococcal infections,[190] bacteremia was observed in 23 (74%). The bacteremia was polymicrobial in eight patients, with facultative gram-negative bacteria predominating as the second microorganism; *S. aureus* and *Bacteroides fragilis* were also isolated as second organisms in some bacteremic cases. In another review of 88 cases of group C streptococcal bacteremia,[193] 27% of patients had infective endocarditis, 10% had meningitis, 9% had cutaneous infections, and 23% had primary bacteremia; 88% of cases were community-acquired. Many of the patients had underlying illnesses, including cardiovascular disease (20%), malignancy (20%), and immunosuppression (15%); 23 patients (26%) had no underlying diseases. Acute illness with fever, chills, and prostration was most common, except in patients with infective endocarditis, who usually presented subacutely. Mortality rates were high (25%), especially among older patients and those with endocarditis, meningitis, or disseminated infection. In a review of 45 cases of *S. zooepidemicus* septicemia, 27% of patients had underlying cardiovascular disease; the overall mortality rate was 22%.[304] Similar epidemiologic features were observed from a survey of cases of group C streptococcal bacteremia in Israel; morbidity and mortality were high (20 to 30%) in this review, probably reflecting the patients' underlying state as well as the severity of infection.[305]

Group G streptococci account for 8 to 11% of all β-hemolytic streptococcal bacteremias[221]; an underlying malignancy is reported in 21 to 65% of patients.[2, 224–227] Polymicrobial bacteremia is not uncommon, with *S. aureus* the most frequently isolated copathogen. Patients usually have another primary site of infection, such as pneumonia, septic arthritis, ophthalmitis, or meningitis. In a review of 24 cases of group G streptococcal bacteremia over a 29-month period,[226] underlying conditions included alcohol abuse (8 patients), malignancy (6 patients), diabetes mellitus (5 patients), neurologic disease (4 patients), atherosclerotic cardiovascular disease (2 patients), end-stage renal disease (2 patients), and valvular heart disease (2 patients). The rate of underlying malignancy was 25%, compared with rates as high as 65% in other series.[224] The skin was the portal of entry in 79% of cases. Infective endocarditis was uncommon in this series, documented in only one patient. In another review of 56 cases of group G streptococcal bacteremia from 11 hospitals in northeastern Ohio,[227] polymicrobial infection, including bacteremia, was an important feature. The most common copathogen was *S. aureus* (seen in seven of eight cases of polymicrobial bacteremia), probably secondary to the presence of skin and soft tissue infection, the background of surgical procedures and invasive diagnostic maneuvers, and the effects of chemotherapy and underlying malignant disease. Mortality (39% in those with only bacteremia) was usually related to the severity of the underlying disease. In a review from the Mayo Clinic,[224] group G streptococci accounted for 0.3% of all bacteremias and 10.8% of those caused by β-hemolytic streptococci; bacteremia was community-acquired in 70% of cases. Twenty-four of 37 patients had an underlying malignancy, although it was unclear whether this subset of patients was more prone to group G streptococcal colonization. The most frequent portal of entry was the skin (73% of patients), usually in cases with preexisting edema due to chronic venous insufficiency or to previous surgical removal, irradiation, or tumor infiltration of lymph nodes. No portal of entry was found in four patients, although all had malignant disease with severe granulocytopenia related either to the malignancy or to use of immunosuppressive drugs.

Miscellaneous Infections. Several other infections have been reported to be caused by groups C and G β-hemolytic streptococci. These include acute group C streptococcal pericarditis,[306, 307] group C streptococcal pyomyositis in a patient with the acquired immunodeficiency syndrome,[308] Henoch-Schönlein purpura associated with *S. equisimilis* upper respiratory tract infection,[309] and a group G streptococcal spinal epidural abscess.[310] A "toxic shock–like syndrome" associated with both group C and group G streptococci has also been reported,[311–313] although these organisms are not known to secrete any exotoxin. Other documented infections caused by group C streptococci include brain abscess[314] and epiglottitis[315] caused by *S. equisimilis,* cervical lymphadenitis caused by *S. zooepidemicus,*[316] intra-abdominal infections,[190, 196] subdural empyema,[317, 318] infected arteriovenous fistula,[190] and peritonitis in dialysis patients.[190] Group G streptococci have also been reported to cause panophthalmitis,[227] and were found in one case of a polymicrobial brain abscess in a patient infected with the human immunodeficiency virus.[319]

Therapy

Group C Streptococci. The antimicrobial agent of choice for group C β-hemolytic streptococci is penicillin G.[320, 321] Other agents with good in vitro activity include cefazolin, vancomycin, erythromycin, the semisynthetic penicillins, and cefotaxime. However, aside from vancomycin, the clinical experience with antimicrobial agents other than penicillin is not extensive. Strains resistant to erythromycin have been reported[322]; in one study, 95% of isolates manifested resistance due to the presence of the *mefA* or *mefE* drug efflux gene.[323] Tetracycline sensitivity is also variable.[193] A case of pharyngitis caused by penicillin-resistant *S. equisimilis* has been reported, although the mechanism of resistance was not clear.[324] Tolerance has been reported in group C streptococci with minimal bactericidal concentrations ranging from 32- to 512-fold greater than the MIC.[325, 326] The frequency of tolerance is unclear; it was reported in 2 of 25 cases in one series[321] and in 16 of 17 cases in another.[325] A marked synergy for in vitro killing of group C streptococci by penicillin plus gentamicin, independent of penicillin tolerance, has been demonstrated. The addition of gentamicin or rifampin to a β-lactam antibiotic or vancomycin has resulted in bactericidal activity against group C streptococci.[325, 326] Although the clinical relevance of these findings is uncertain, retrospective reviews of group C streptococcal endocarditis noted a trend to better outcome (i.e., fewer patients requiring cardiac valve replacement) in those treated with the combination of penicillin plus gentamicin, compared with penicillin alone,[190] leading the authors to recommend combination therapy in patients with severe infections (endocarditis, meningitis, septic arthritis, or bacteremia in neutropenic hosts) caused by group C streptococci. Tolerance to cephalothin and vancomycin has also been reported for group C streptococci.

Group G Streptococci. Group G streptococci are susceptible in vitro to various antimicrobial agents, including penicillin G, the ureidopenicillins, most cephalosporins, vancomycin, and erythromycin[321]; the most active drugs are penicillin, ampicillin, and cefotaxime.[225] Clindamycin, erythromycin, and chloramphenicol have relatively poor bactericidal activity against group G streptococci.[225] In a study of erythromycin resistance mechanisms in group G streptococci, 94% of resistant isolates had the *ermTR* gene.[323] Combinations of gentamicin with either penicillin, cefotaxime, or vancomycin are synergistic against 80 to 90% of isolates.[327]

Penicillin tolerance is not a major feature of group G streptococci, and it has been demonstrated only in the presence of a high inoculum and stationary growth phase of the organism.[200] When strains were tested at high inocula (10^8 cfu/ml) of stationary-phase cells, there was a marked reduction in killing by penicillin G. This impaired bactericidal effect was not seen either at high inocula of logarithmic-phase organisms or at low inocula of stationary-phase organisms. The paradigm of this high inoculum–stationary phase in vitro situation is infective endocarditis, which may partially explain the relatively poor clinical outcome seen in group G streptococcal endocarditis caused by sensitive organisms. Vancomycin tolerance has also been reported in group G streptococci,[328] although tolerance to this agent may also depend on the growth phase and laboratory media employed.[225] The combinations of gentamicin with a β-lactam and of gentamicin or rifampin with vancomycin are bactericidal against tolerant strains.[326] The clinical significance of tolerance is unclear, because no serious infections caused by tolerant group G streptococci have been described.

STREPTOCOCCUS INIAE

Streptococcus iniae, a pathogen recognized only recently in humans, is a β-hemolytic streptococcus that does not react with any Lancefield grouping sera. The organism was first reported in 1976 as a cause of subcutaneous abscesses in freshwater dolphins.[329] *Streptococcus shiloi,* a cause of meningoencephalitis in trout, is biochemically and genetically identical and is probably synonymous with *S. iniae.*[330]

In the clinical laboratory, *S. iniae* may elude identification. Few commercial laboratory systems include this species in their database. In addition, the organism's β-hemolysis may be inapparent under certain growth conditions. As a result, isolates are often misidentified as viridans group streptococci and discounted as contaminants. In 6 of the 11 patients reported by Weinstein and coworkers, *S. iniae* isolates were initially misidentified as *S. uberis,* a viridans group streptococcus not typically pathogenic in humans.[331]

To date, invasive infections caused by *S. iniae* have been confirmed by the presence of bacteremia. Almost all have had cellulitis of the hand as the presumed primary site of infection. Handling of live or killed fish, especially tilapia, was the suspected exposure source.[331] Patients have responded readily to therapy with a β-lactam antibiotic.

STOMATOCOCCUS AND *PEDIOCOCCUS*

Stomatococcus mucilaginosus is a gram-positive aerobic coccus that can cause oral, cutaneous, and central nervous system infections in impaired hosts as well as intravenous catheter–related sepsis. Most strains are susceptible to third-generation cephalosporins, vancomycin, and carbapenems.[332, 333]

Pediococcus spp. are gram-positive aerobic cocci that have caused nosocomial infections and are often resistant to vancomycin.[334–336]

REFERENCES

1. Baron EJ, Finegold SM. Streptococci and related genera. In: Baron EJ, Finegold SM, eds. Bailey and Scott's Diagnostic Microbiology. 8th ed. St. Louis: CV Mosby; 1986:333–352.
2. Duma RJ, Weinberg AN, Medrek TF, et al. Streptococcal infections: A bacteriologic and clinical study of streptococcal bacteremia. Medicine (Baltimore). 1969;48:87–105.
3. Kilian M, Nyvad B, Mikkelson L. Taxonomic and ecological aspects of some oral streptococci. In: Hamada S, Michalek SM, Kiyono H, et al, eds. Molecular Microbiology and Immunobiology of *Streptococcus mutans.* Amsterdam: Elsevier Science Publishers BV; 1986:391–400.
4. Coykendall AL. Classification and identification of the viridans streptococci. Clin Microbiol Rev. 1989;2:315–328.
5. Facklam RR, Carey RB. *Streptococcus* and related catalase negative gram-positive cocci. In: Balows A, Hausler WJ, Herrmann KL, et al, eds. Manual of Clinical Microbiology. 5th ed. Washington, DC: American Society for Microbiology; 1991:238–257.
6. Colman G, Williams REO. Taxonomy of some human viridans streptococci. In: Wannamaker LW, Matsen JM, eds. Streptococci and Streptococcal Diseases: Recognition, Understanding, and Management. New York: Academic Press; 1972:281–299.
7. Facklam RR. Physiological differentiation of viridans streptococci. J Clin Microbiol. 1977;5:184–201.
8. Koneman EW, Allen SD, Janda WM, et al. The gram-positive cocci: Part II. Streptococci, enterococci, and the "streptococcus-like" bacteria. In: Color Atlas and Textbook of Diagnostic Microbiology. 5th ed. Philadelphia: JB Lippincott; 1997.
9. Bruckner DA, Colonna P. Nomenclature for aerobic and facultative bacteria. Clin Infect Dis. 1997;25:1–10.
10. Handley P, Coykendall A, Beighton D, et al. *Streptococcus crista* sp. nov., a viridans streptococcus with tufted fibrils, isolated from the human oral cavity and throat. Int J Syst Bacteriol. 1991;41:543–547.
11. Kilian M, Mikkelson L, Henrichsen J. Taxonomic study of viridans streptococci: Description of *Streptococcus gordonii* sp. nov. and amended descriptions of *Streptococcus sanguis* (White and Niven 1946), *Streptococcus oralis* (Bridge and Sneath 1982), and *Streptococcus mitis* (Andrews and Horder 1906). Int J Syst Bacteriol. 1989;39:471–484.
12. Whiley RA, Beighton D. Emended descriptions and recognition of *Streptococcus constellatus, Streptococcus intermedius,* and *Streptococcus anginosus* as distinct species. Int J Syst Bacteriol. 1991;41:1–5.
13. Whiley RA, Hardie JM. *Streptococcus vestibularis* sp. nov. from the human oral cavity. Int J Syst Bacteriol. 1988;38:2623–2633.
14. Whiley RA, Fraser HY, Douglas CWI, et al. *Streptococcus parasanguis* sp. nov.: An atypical viridans streptococcus from human clinical specimens. FEMS Microbiol Lett. 1990;68:115–122.
15. Coykendall AL. *Streptococcus sobrinus* nom. rev. and *Streptococcus ferus* nom. rev.: Habitat of these and other mutans streptococci. Int J Syst Bacteriol. 1983;33:883–885.
16. Coykendall AL. Proposal to elevate the subspecies of *Streptococcus mutans* to species status, based on their molecular composition. Int J Syst Bacteriol. 1977;27:26–30.
17. Kilpper-Balz R, Schleifer KH. Transfer of *Streptococcus morbillorum* to the *Gemella* genus, *Gemella morbillorum* comb. nov. Int J Syst Bacteriol. 1988;38:442–443.
18. Schleifer KH, Kilpper-Balz R. Molecular and chemotaxonomic approaches to the classification of streptococci, enterococci, and lactococci: A review. Syst Appl Microbiol. 1987;10:1–19.
19. Beighton D, Hardie JM, Whiley RA. A scheme for the identification of viridans streptococci. J Med Microbiol. 1991;35:367–372.
20. Hinnebusch CJ, Nikolai DM, Bruckner DA. Comparison of API Rapid Strep, Baxter Microscan Rapid Pos ID Panel, BBL Minitek Differential Identification System, IDS RapID STR System, and Vitek GPI to conventional biochemical tests for identification of viridans streptococci. Am J Clin Pathol. 1991;96:459–463.
21. Garnier F, Gerbaud G, Courvalin P, et al. Identification of clinically relevant viridans group streptococci to the species level by PCR. J Clin Microbiol. 1997;35:2337–2341.
22. Bouvet A, Grimont F, Grimont PAD. *Streptococcus defectivus* sp. nov. and *Streptococcus adjacens* sp. nov.: Nutritionally variant streptococci from human clinical specimens. Int J Syst Bacteriol. 1989;39:290–294.
23. Kawamura Y, Hou XG, Sultana F, et al. Transfer of *Streptococcus adjacens* and *Streptococcus defectivus* to *Abiotrophia* gen. nov. as *Abiotrophia adiacens* comb. nov. and *Abiotrophia defectiva* comb. nov., respectively. Int J Syst Bacteriol. 1995;45:798–803.
24. Marsh P, Martin M. Oral Microbiology. 2nd ed. Washington, DC: American Society for Microbiology; 1984.
25. Gibbons RJ, van Houte J. Bacterial adherence in oral microbial ecology. Annu Rev Microbiol 1975;29:19–44.
26. Gibbons RJ, van Houte J. Selective bacterial adherence to oral epithelial surfaces and its role as an ecological determinant. Infect Immun. 1971;3:567–573.
27. Frandsen EVG, Pedrazzoli V, Kilian M. Ecology of viridans streptococci in the oral cavity and pharynx. Oral Microbiol Immunol. 1991;6:129–133.
28. Babu J, Simpson WA, Courtney HS, et al. Interaction of human plasma fibronectin with cariogenic and non-cariogenic oral streptococci. Infect Immun. 1983;41:162–168.
29. Woods DE, Straus DC, Johanson WG Jr, et al. Role of fibronectin in the prevention of adherence of *Pseudomonas aeruginosa* to buccal cells. J Infect Dis. 1981;143:784–790.
30. Woods DE, Straus DC, Johanson WG Jr. Role of salivary protease activity in adherence of gram-negative bacilli to mammalian buccal epithelial cells in vivo. J Clin Invest. 1981;68:1435–1440.
31. Johanson WG Jr, Pierce AK, Sanford JP. Changing pharyngeal flora of hospitalized patients: Emergence of gram-negative bacilli. N Engl J Med. 1969;281:1137–1140.
32. Johanson WG Jr, Pierce AK, Sanford JP, et al. Nosocomial respiratory infections with gram-negative bacilli: The significance of colonization of the respiratory tract. Ann Intern Med. 1972;77:701–706.
33. Straus DC. Protease production by *Streptococcus sanguis* associated with subacute bacterial endocarditis. Infect Immun. 1982;38:1037–1045.
34. Parker MT, Ball LC. Streptococci and aerococci associated with systemic infections in man. J Med Microbiol. 1976;9:275–302.

35. Scheld WM, Valone JA, Sande MA. Bacterial adherence in the pathogenesis of endocarditis. J Clin Invest. 1978;61:1394–1404.
36. Ramirez-Ronda CH. Adherence of glucan-positive and glucan-negative streptococcal strains to normal and damaged heart valves. J Clin Invest. 1978;62:805–814.
37. Pulliam L, Dall L, Inokuchi S, et al. Effects of exopolysaccharide production by viridans streptococci on penicillin therapy of experimental endocarditis. J Infect Dis. 1985;151:153–156.
38. Dall L, Barnes WG, Lane JW, et al. Enzymatic modification of glycocalyx in the treatment of experimental endocarditis due to viridans streptococci. J Infect Dis. 1987;156:736–740.
39. Burnette-Curley D, Wells V, Viscount H, et al. FimA, a major virulence factor associated with *Streptococcus parasanguis* endocarditis. Infect Immun. 1995;63:4669–4674.
40. Viscount HB, Munro CL, Burnette-Curley D, et al. Immunization with FimA protects against *Streptococcus parasanguis* endocarditis in rats. Infect Immun. 1997;65:994–1002.
41. Proctor RA, Mosher DF, Olbrantz PJ. Fibronectin binding to *Staphylococcus aureus*. J Biol Chem. 1982;257:14788–14794.
42. Scheld WM, Keeley JM, Balian G, et al. Microbial adhesion to fibronectin in the pathogenesis of infective endocarditis (Abstract). Clin Res. 1983;31:542A.
43. Scheld WM, Strunk RW, Balian G, et al. Microbial adhesion to fibronectin in vitro correlates with production of endocarditis in rabbits. Proc Soc Exp Biol Med. 1985;180:474–482.
44. Lawrance JH, Baddour LM, Simpson WA. The role of fibronectin binding in the rat model of experimental endocarditis caused by *Streptococcus sanguis*. J Clin Invest. 1990;86:7–13.
45. Lowy FD, Chang DS, Neuhaus EG, et al. Effect of penicillin on the adherence of *Streptococcus sanguis* in vitro and in the rabbit model of endocarditis. J Clin Invest. 1983;71:668–675.
46. Nealon TJ, Beachey EH, Courtney HS, et al. Release of fibronectin-lipoteichoic acid complexes from group A streptococci with penicillin. Infect Immun. 1986;51:529–535.
47. Drake TA, Rodgers GM, Sande MA. Tissue factor is a major stimulus for vegetation formation in enterococcal endocarditis. J Clin Invest. 1984;73:1750–1753.
48. Drake TA, Pang M. Effects of interleukin-1, lipopolysaccharide, and streptococci on procoagulant activity of cultured human cardiac valve endothelial and stromal cells. Infect Immun. 1989;57:507–512.
49. Sullam PM, Valone FH, Mills J. Mechanisms of platelet aggregation by viridans group streptococci. Infect Immun. 1987;55:1743–1750.
50. Hamada S, Slade HD. Biology, immunology, and cariogenicity of *Streptococcus mutans*. Microbiol Rev. 1980;44:331–384.
51. McGhee JR, Michalek SM. Immunobiology of dental caries: Microbial aspects and local immunity. Annu Rev Microbiol. 1981;35:595–638.
52. Gibbon RJ. Microbiol ecology: Adherent interactions which may affect microbial ecology in the mouth. J Dent Res. 1984;63:378–385.
53. Orlicek SL, Branum KC, English BK, et al. Viridans streptococcal isolates from patients with septic shock induce tumor necrosis factor-alpha production from murine macrophages. J Lab Clin Med. 1997;130:515–519.
54. Engel A, Kern P, Kern WV. Levels of cytokines and cytokine inhibitors in the neutropenic patients with α-hemolytic streptococcus shock syndrome. J Infect Dis. 1996;23:785–789.
55. Kaye D, McCormick RC, Hook EW. Bacterial endocarditis: The changing pattern since the introduction of penicillin therapy. Antimicrob Agents Chemother. 1962;1:37–46.
56. Lerner PI, Weinstein L. Infective endocarditis in the antibiotic era. N Engl J Med. 1966;274:323–331.
57. Roberts RB. Streptococcal endocarditis: The viridans and β-hemolytic streptococci. In: Kaye D, ed. Infective Endocarditis. 2nd ed. New York: Raven Press; 1992:191–208.
58. Roberts RB, Kreiger AG, Schiller NI, et al. Viridans streptococcal endocarditis: The role of various species, including pyridoxal-dependent streptococci. Rev Infect Dis. 1979;1:955–965.
59. Sussman JI, Baron EJ, Tenenbaum MJ, et al. Viridans streptococcal endocarditis: Clinical, microbiological, and echocardiographic correlations. J Infect Dis. 1986;154:597–603.
60. McKinsey DS, Ratts TE, Bisno AL. Underlying cardiac lesions in adults with infective endocarditis: The changing spectrum. Am J Med. 1987;82:681–688.
61. Van der Meer JTM, Thompson J, Valkenburg HA, et al. Epidemiology of bacterial endocarditis in the Netherlands: Patient characteristics. Arch Intern Med. 1992;152:1863–1868.
62. Sande MA, Lee BL, Mills J, et al. Endocarditis in intravenous drug users. In: Kaye D, ed. Infective Endocarditis. 2nd ed. New York: Raven Press; 1992:345–360.
63. Douglas JL, Cobbs CG. Prosthetic valve endocarditis. In: Kaye D, ed. Infective Endocarditis. 2nd ed. New York: Raven Press; 1992:375–396.
64. Starkebaum M, Durack D, Beeson P. The "incubation period" of bacterial endocarditis. Yale J Biol Med. 1977;50:49–58.
65. Garvey GJ, Neu HC. Infective endocarditis: An evolving disease. A review of endocarditis at the Columbia Presbyterian Medical Center, 1968–1973. Medicine (Baltimore). 1978;57:105–127.
66. Von Reyn CF, Levy BS, Arbeit RD, et al. Infective endocarditis: An analysis based on strict case definitions. Ann Intern Med. 1981;94:505–518.
67. Bush LM, Johnson CC. Clinical syndrome and diagnosis of endocarditis. In: Donald Kaye, ed. Infective Endocarditis. 2nd ed. Philadelphia: Raven Press; 1992:99–115.
68. Werner AS, Cobbs CG, Kaye D, et al. Studies on the bacteremia of bacterial endocarditis. JAMA. 1967;202:127–131.
69. Steckelberg JM, Murphy JG, Ballard D, et al. Emboli in infective endocarditis: The prognostic value of echocardiography. Ann Intern Med. 1991;114:635–640.
70. Sokil AB. Cardiac imaging in infective endocarditis. In: Kaye D, ed. Infective Endocarditis. 2nd ed. New York: Raven Press; 1992:125–150.
71. Wolfe JC, Johnson WD. Penicillin-sensitive streptococcal endocarditis: In vitro and clinical observations on penicillin-streptomycin therapy. Ann Intern Med. 1974;81:178–181.
72. Tunkel AR, Scheld WM. Experimental models of endocarditis. In: Kaye D, ed. Infective Endocarditis. 2nd ed. New York: Raven Press; 1992:37–56.
73. Sande MA, Irvin RG. Penicillin-aminoglycoside synergy in experimental streptococcal viridans endocarditis. J Infect Dis. 1974;129:572–576.
74. Carrizosa J, Kaye D. Antibiotic concentration in serum, bactericidal activity, and results of therapy of streptococcal endocarditis in rabbits. Antimicrob Agents Chemother. 1977;12:479–483.
75. Wilson WR, Karchmer AW, Dajani AS, et al. Antimicrobial treatment of adults with infective endocarditis due to streptococci, enterococci, staphylococci, and HACEK microorganisms. JAMA. 1995;274:1706–1713.
76. Wilson WR, Geraci JE. Treatment of streptococcal endocarditis. Am J Med. 1985;78(Suppl 6B):128–137.
77. Francioli P, Etienne J, Hoigne R, et al. Treatment of streptococcal endocarditis with a single daily dose of ceftriaxone sodium for 4 weeks: Efficacy and outpatient treatment feasibility. JAMA. 1992;267:264–279.
78. Stamboulian D, Bonvehi P, Arevalo C, et al. Antibiotic management of outpatients with infectious endocarditis due to penicillin-susceptible streptococci. Rev Infect Dis. 1991;13(Suppl 2):S160–S168.
79. Francioli PB. Ceftriaxone and outpatient treatment of infective endocarditis. Infect Dis Clin North Am. 1993;7:97–115.
80. Parillo JE, Borst GC, Mazur MH, et al. Endocarditis due to resistant viridans streptococci during oral penicillin chemoprophylaxis. N Engl J Med. 1979;300:296–300.
81. Swenson FJ, Rubin SJ. Clinical significance of viridans streptococci isolated from blood cultures. J Clin Microbiol. 1982;15:725–727.
82. Roth RR, James WD. Microbial etiology of the skin. Annu Rev Microbiol. 1988;42:441–464.
83. Faden H, Zyndol N. Significance of viridans streptococci in blood cultures from children (Letter). Pediatr Infect Dis J. 1992;11:418.
84. Henslee J, Bostrom B, Weisdorf D, et al. Streptococcal sepsis in bone marrow transplant patients. Lancet. 1984;1:393.
85. Gonzalez-Barca E, Fernandez-Sevilla A, Carratala J, et al. Prospective study of 288 episodes of bacteremia in neutropenic cancer patients in a single institution. Eur J Clin Microbiol Infect Dis. 1996;15:291–296.
86. Weisman SJ, Scoopo FJ, Johnson GM, et al. Septicemia in pediatric oncology patients: The significance of viridans streptococcal infections. J Clin Oncol. 1990;8:453–459.
87. Elting LS, Bodey GP, Keefe BH. Septicemia and shock syndrome due to viridans streptococci: A case-control study of predisposing factors. Clin Infect Dis. 1992;14:1201–1207.
88. Bilgrami S, Feingold JM, Dorsky D, et al. Streptococcus viridans bacteremia following autologous peripheral blood stem cell transplantation. Bone Marrow Transplant 1998;21:591–595.
89. Cohen J, Worsley AM, Goldman JM, et al. Septicaemia caused by viridans streptococci in neutropenic patients with leukaemia. Lancet. 1983;2:1452–1454.
90. Engelhard D, Elishoov H, Or R, et al. Cytosine arabinoside as a major risk factor for *Streptococcus viridans* septicemia following bone marrow transplantation: A 5-year prospective study. Bone Marrow Transplant 1995;16:565–570.
91. Richard P, Amador Del Valle G, Moreau P, et al. Viridans streptococcal bacteraemia in patients with neutropenia. Lancet. 1995;345:1607–1609.
92. Burden AD, Oppenheim BA, Crowther D, et al. Viridans streptococcal bacteremia in patients with haematological and solid malignancies. Eur J Cancer. 1991;27:409–411.
93. Bostrom B, Weisdorf D. Mucositis and α-streptococcal sepsis in bone marrow transplant recipients. Lancet. 1984;1:1120–1121.
94. Ringden O, Heimdahl A, Lonnqvist B, et al. Decreased incidence of viridans streptococcal septicaemia in allogeneic bone marrow transplant recipients after the introduction of acyclovir. Lancet. 1984;1:744.
95. Villablanca JG, Steiner M, Kersey J, et al. The clinical spectrum of infections with viridans streptococci in bone marrow transplant patients. Bone Marrow Transplant. 1990;6:387–393.
96. Mascret B, Maraninchi D, Gastaut JA, et al. Risk factors for streptococcal septicaemia after marrow transplantation. Lancet. 1984;1:1185–1186.
97. Martino R, Manteiga R, Sanchez I, et al. Viridans streptococcal shock syndrome during bone marrow transplantation. Acta Haematol. 1995;94:69–73.
98. Koren P, Krcmery V Jr. Viridans streptococcal bacteremia due to penicillin-resistant and penicillin-sensitive streptococci: Analysis of risk factors and outcome in 60 patients from a single cancer centre before and after penicillin is used for prophylaxis. Scand J Infect Dis. 1997;29:245–249.
99. Arns da Cunha C, Weisdorf D, Shu XO, et al. Early gram-positive bacteremia in BMT recipients: Impact of three different approaches to antimicrobial prophylaxis. Bone Marrow Transplant. 1998;21:173–180.
100. Carratala J, Alcaide F, Fernandez-Sevilla A, et al. Bacteremia due to viridans streptococci that are highly resistant to penicillin: Increase among neutropenic patients with cancer. Clin Infect Dis. 1995;20:1169–1173.

101. Hoyne AL, Herzon H. *Streptococcus viridans* meningitis: A review of the literature and report of nine recoveries. Ann Intern Med. 1950;33:879–902.
102. Enting RH, deGans J, Blankevoort JP, Spanjaard L. Meningitis due to viridans streptococci in adults. J Neurol. 1997;244:435–438.
103. Leiger JF. *Streptococcus salivarius* meningitis and colonic carcinoma. South Med J. 1991;84:1058–1059.
104. Carley NH. *Streptococcus salivarius* bacteremia and meningitis following upper gastrointestinal endoscopy and cauterization for gastric bleeding. Clin Infect Dis. 1992;14:947–948.
105. Lerner PI. Meningitis caused by *Streptococcus* in adults. J Infect Dis. 1975;131:S9–S16.
106. Freedman RM, Baltimore R. Fatal *Streptococcus viridans* septicemia and meningitis: Relationship to fetal scalp electrode monitoring. J Perinatol. 1990;10:272–274.
107. Majka FA, Gysin WM, Zaayer RL. *Streptococcus salivarius* meningitis following lumbar puncture. Nebr State Med J. 1956;41:279–281.
108. Watanakunakorn C, Stahl C. *Streptococcus salivarius* meningitis following myelography (Letter). Infect Control Hosp Epidemiol. 1992;13:454.
109. Heath RE, Rogers JA, Cheldelin LV, et al. *Streptococcus sanguis* sepsis and meningitis: A complication of vacuum extraction. Am J Obstet Gynecol. 1980;138:343–344.
110. Hellwege HH, Ram W, Scherf H, et al. Neonatal meningitis caused by *Streptococcus mitis*. Lancet. 1984;1:743–744.
111. Bignardi GE, Isaacs D. Neonatal meningitis due to *Streptococcus mitis*. Rev Infect Dis. 1989;11:86–88.
112. Koorevaar CT, Scherpenzeel PGN, Neijens HJ, et al. Childhood meningitis caused by enterococci and viridans streptococci. Infection. 1992;20:118–121.
113. Eng RH, Mangia AJ, Smith SM, et al. Meningitis following bacteremia with *Streptococcus sanguis*. N Y State J Med. 1989;98:625–626.
114. Appelbaum E. Meningitis following trauma to the head and face. JAMA. 1960;173:116–120.
115. Goldfarb J, Wormser GP, Glaser JH. Meningitis caused by multiply antibiotic-resistant viridans streptococci. J Pediatr. 1984;105:891–895.
116. Schneeberger PM, Janssen M, Voss A. α-Hemolytic streptococci: A major pathogen of iatrogenic meningitis following lumbar puncture. Infection. 1996;24:29–33.
117. Nachamkin I, Dalton HP. The clinical significance of streptococcal species isolated from cerebrospinal fluid. Am J Clin Pathol. 1983;79:195–199.
118. Smith WF. Meningitis secondary to subacute bacterial endocarditis. N Engl J Med. 1939;220:587.
119. Neal JB, Jackson HW, Appelbaum E. Neurological complications of subacute bacterial endocarditis. N Y State J Med. 1936;36:1819.
120. Gonzalez-CL, Calia FM. Bacteriologic flora of aspiration-induced pulmonary infections. Arch Intern Med. 1975;135:711–714.
121. Brook I, Finegold SM. Bacteriology of aspiration pneumonia in children. Pediatrics. 1980;65:1115–1120.
122. Bartlett JG, Finegold SM. Anaerobic infections of the lung and pleural space. Am Rev Respir Dis. 1974;110:56–77.
123. Lorber B, Swenson RM. Bacteriology of aspiration pneumonia. Ann Intern Med. 1974;81:329–331.
124. Rose H. Viridans streptococcal pneumonia (Letter). JAMA. 1981;245:32.
125. Pratter MR, Irwin RS. Viridans streptococcal pulmonary parenchymal infections. JAMA. 1980;243:2515–2517.
126. Sarkar TK, Murarka RS, Gilardi GL. Primary *Streptococcus viridans* pneumonia. Chest. 1989;96:831–834.
127. Gaudreau C, Delage G. Rousseau D, et al. Bacteremia caused by viridans streptococci in 71 children. Can Med Assoc J. 1981;125:1246–1249.
128. Sattler FR, Ruskin J. Empyema due to *Streptococcus mutans*. Chest. 1977;71:229–231.
129. Catto BA, Jacobs MR, Shlaes DM. *Streptococcus mitis:* A cause of serious infection in adults. Arch Intern Med. 1987;147:885–888.
130. Marrie TJ. Bacteremic community-acquired pneumonia due to viridans group streptococci. Clin Invest Med. 1993;16:38–44.
131. Raad II, Sabbagh MF, Caranasos GJ. Acute bacterial sialadenitis: A study of 29 cases and review. Clin Infect Dis. 1990;12:591–601.
132. Gill Y, Scully C. Orofacial odontogenic infections: Review of microbiology and current treatment. Oral Surg Oral Med Oral Pathol. 1990;70:155–158.
133. Doern GV, Ferraro MJ, Brueggemann AB, et al. Emergence of high rates of antimicrobial resistance among viridans group streptococci in the United States. Antimicrob Agents Chemother. 1996;40:891–894.
134. Pfaller MA, Jones RN, Marshall SA, et al. Nosocomial streptococcal blood stream infections in the SCOPE program: Species occurrence and antimicrobial susceptibility. Diagn Microbiol Infect Dis. 1997;29:259–263.
135. Bourgault AM, Wilson WR, Washington JA II. Antimicrobial susceptibilities of species of viridans streptococci. J Infect Dis. 1979;140:316–321.
136. Roberts RB, Krieger AG, Gross KC. The species of viridans streptococci associated with microbial endocarditis: Incidence and antimicrobial susceptibility. Am Clin Climat Assoc. 1977;89:36–48.
137. Tuazon CU, Gill V, Gill F. Streptococcal endocarditis: Single vs. combination antibiotic therapy and role of various species. Rev Infect Dis. 1986;8:54–60.
138. Spencer WH, Thornsberry C, Moody MD, et al. Rheumatic fever chemoprophylaxis and penicillin-resistant gingival organisms. Ann Intern Med. 1970;73:683–688.
139. Sprunt K, Redman W, Leidy G. Penicillin-resistant α-streptococci in the pharynx of patients given oral penicillin. Pediatrics. 1968;42:957–958.
140. Potgeiter E, Carmichael M, Koornhof HJ, et al. In vitro susceptibility of viridans streptococci isolated from blood cultures. Eur J Clin Microbiol Infect Dis. 1992;11:543–546.
141. National Committee for Clinical Laboratory Standards. Performance standards for antimicrobial susceptibility testing (M7-A2). Villanova, Pa.: NCCLS; 1997.
142. Pfaller MA, Marshall SA, Jones RN. In vitro activity of cefepime and ceftazidime against 197 nosocomial blood stream isolates of streptococci: A multicenter study. Diagn Microbiol Infect Dis. 1997;29:273–276.
143. Farber BF, Eliopoulos GM, Ward JI, et al. Multiple resistant viridans streptococci: Susceptibility to lactam antibiotics and comparison of penicillin-binding protein patterns. Antimicrob Agents Chemother. 1983;24:702–705.
144. Chalkley L, Schuster C, Potgieter E, et al. Relatedness between *Streptococcus pneumoniae* and viridans streptococci: Transfer of penicillin resistance determinants and immunological similarities of penicillin-binding proteins. FEMS Microbiol Lett. 1991;69:35–42.
145. Venditti M, Baiocchi P, Santinin C, et al. Antimicrobial susceptibilities of *Streptococcus* species that cause septicemia in neutropenic patients. Antimicrob Agents Chemother. 1989;33:580–582.
146. Tuohy M, Washington JA. Antimicrobial susceptibility of viridans group streptococci. Diagn Microbiol Infect Dis. 1997;29:277–280.
147. Brennan RD, Durack DT. Therapeutic significance of penicillin tolerance in experimental streptococcal endocarditis. Antimicrob Agents Chemother. 1983;23:273.
148. Pulliman L, Inokuchi S, Hadley KW, et al. Penicillin tolerance of viridans streptococci delays sterilization of vegetations in experimental animals. Clin Res. 1980;28:45A.
149. Lowy FD, Neuhaus EG, Chang DS, et al. Penicillin therapy of experimental endocarditis induced by tolerant *Streptococcus sanguis* and non-tolerant *Streptococcus mitis*. Antimicrob Agents Chemother. 1983;28:607–611.
150. Handwerger S, Tomasz A. Antibiotic tolerance among clinical isolates of bacteria. Rev Infect Dis. 1985;7:368–386.
151. James PA, Young SEJ, White DG. Incidence of penicillin tolerance among blood culture isolates of *Streptococcus sanguis,* 1987–1988. J Clin Pathol. 1991;44:160–163.
152. Etienne J, Vandenesch F, Fauvel JP, et al. Susceptibilities to ceftriaxone of streptococcal strains associated with infective endocarditis. Chemotherapy. 1989;35:355–358.
153. Alcaide F, Carratala J, Linares J, et al. In vitro activities of eight macrolide antibiotics and RP-59500 (quinupristin-dalfopristin) against viridans group streptococci isolated from blood of neutropenic cancer patients. Antimicrob Agents Chemother. 1996;40:2117–2120.
154. Farber BF, Yee Y. High-level aminoglycoside resistance mediated by aminoglycoside-modifying enzymes among viridans streptococci: Implications for the therapy of endocarditis. J Infect Dis. 1987;155:948–953.
155. Enzler MJ, Rouse MS, Henry NK, et al. In vitro and in vivo studies of streptomycin-resistant, penicillin-susceptible streptococci from patients with infective endocarditis. J Infect Dis. 1987;155:954–958.
156. Pfaller MA, Jones RN. Comparative antistreptococcal activity of two newer fluoroquiolones, levofloxacin, and sparfloxacin. Diagn Microbiol Infect Dis. 1997;29:199–201.
157. McWhinney PHM, Patel S, Whiley RA, et al. Activities of potential therapeutic and prophylactic antibiotics against blood culture isolates of viridans group streptococci from neutropenic cancer patients receiving ciprofloxacin. Antimicrob Agents Chemother. 1993;37:2493–2495.
158. Frenkel A, Hirsch W. Spontaneous development of L forms of streptococci requiring secretions of other bacteria or sulphydryl compounds for normal growth. Nature. 1961;191:728–730.
159. Bouvet A, van de Rijn I, McCarty M. Nutritionally variant streptococci from patients with endocarditis: Growth parameters in a semisynthetic medium and demonstration of a chromophore. J Bacteriol. 1981;146:1075–1082.
160. Bouvet A, Villeroy F, Cheng F, et al. Characterization of nutritionally variant streptococci by biochemical tests and penicillin binding proteins. J Clin Microbiol. 1985;22:1030–1034.
161. Stein DS, Libertin CR. Genetic heterogeneity among nutritionally deficient streptococci. Diagn Microbiol Infect Dis. 1992;15:281–285.
162. Ruoff KL. Nutritionally variant streptococci. Clin Microbiol Rev. 1991;4:184–190.
163. Tillotson GS. Evaluation of ten commercial blood culture systems to isolate pyridoxal-dependent streptococcus. J Clin Pathol. 1981;34:930–934.
164. Gross KC, Houghton MP, Roberts RB. Evaluation of blood culture media for isolation of pyridoxal-dependent *Streptococcus mitior (mitis).* J Clin Microbiol. 1981;14:266–272.
165. Stein DS, Nelson KE. Endocarditis due to nutritionally deficient streptococci: Therapeutic dilemma. Rev Infect Dis. 1987;9:908–916.
166. Cooksey RC, Swenson JM. In vitro antimicrobial inhibition patterns of nutritionally variant streptococci. Antimicrob Agents Chemother. 1979;16:514–518.
167. Gephart JF, Washington JA. Antimicrobial susceptibilities of nutritionally variant streptococci. J Infect Dis. 1982;146:536–539.
168. Bosley GS, Facklam RR. Biochemical and antimicrobic testing of "nutritionally variant streptococci." Abstract. Proceedings of the 90th Annual Meeting of the American Society for Microbiology. Washington, DC: American Society for Microbiology; 1990:395.
169. Roberts RB, Wilson WR, Bouvet A, et al. Nutritionally variant streptococcal endocarditis. Abstract. Proceedings of the 22nd Interscience Conference on Antimicrobial Agents and Chemotherapy. Washington, DC: American Society for Microbiology; 1982:130.
170. Holloway Y, Dankert J. Penicillin tolerance in nutritionally variant streptococci. Antimicrob Agents Chemother. 1982;22:1073–1075.

171. Bouvet A, Cremieux AC, Contrepois A, et al. Comparison of penicillin and vancomycin, individually and in combination with gentamicin and amikacin, in the treatment of experimental endocarditis induced by nutritionally variant streptococci. Antimicrob Agents Chemother. 1985;28:607–611.
172. Henry NK, Wilson WR, Roberts RB, et al. Antimicrobial therapy of experimental endocarditis caused by nutritionally variant viridans group streptococci. Antimicrob Agents Chemother. 1986;30:465–467.
173. Carey RB, Brause BD, Roberts RB. Antimicrobial therapy of vitamin B_6-dependent streptococcal endocarditis. Ann Intern Med. 1977;87:150–154.
174. Stein DS, Libertin CR. Time kill curve analysis of vancomycin and rifampin alone and in combination against nine strains of nutritionally deficient streptococci. Diagn Microbiol Infect Dis. 1988;10:139–144.
175. Carey RB, Gross KC, Roberts RB. Vitamin B_6-dependent *Streptococcus mitior (mitis)* isolated from patients with systemic infections. J Infect Dis. 1975;131:722–726.
176. Barrios H, Bump CM. Conjunctivitis caused by a nutritionally variant streptococcus. J Clin Microbiol. 1986;23:379–380.
177. Ormerod LD, Ruoff KL, Meisler DM, et al. Infectious crystalline keratopathy: Role of nutritionally variant streptococci and bacterial factors. Ophthalmology. 1991;98:159–169.
178. McCarthy LR, Bottone EJ. Bacteremia and endocarditis caused by satelliting streptococci. Am J Clin Pathol. 1974;61:585–591.
179. Hahn G, Nyberg I. Identification of streptococcal groups A, B, C, and G by slide co-agglutination of antibody-sensitized protein A-containing staphylococci. J Clin Microbiol. 1976;4:99–101.
180. Facklam RR, Cooksey RC, Wortham EC. Evaluation of commercial latex agglutination reagents for grouping streptococci. J Clin Microbiol. 1979;10:641–646.
181. Pollock HM, Dahlgren BJ. Distribution of streptococcal groups in clinical specimens with evaluation of bacitracin screening. Appl Microbiol. 1974;27:141–143.
182. Foley GE. Further observations on the occurrence of streptococci of groups other than A in human infection. N Engl J Med. 1947;237:809–811.
183. Barnham M, Neilson DJ. Group L β-hemolytic streptococcal infection in meat handlers: Another streptococcal zoonosis. Epidemiol Infect. 1987;9:257–264.
184. Broome CV, Moellering RC Jr, Watson BK. Clinical significance of Lancefield groups L-T streptococci from blood and cerebrospinal fluid. J Infect Dis. 1976;133:382–392.
185. Plummer H. A serological and biochemical study of hemolytic streptococci. J Immunol. 1941;42:91–107.
186. Feingold DS, Stagg NL, Kunz LJ. Extrarespiratory streptococcal infections. N Engl J Med. 1966;275:356–361.
187. Chitwood LA, Jennings MB, Riley HD. Time, cost, and efficacy study of identifying group A streptococci with commercially available reagents. Appl Microbiol. 1969;18:193–197.
188. Damask LJ, Montoya O, Axelrod JL. Rapid slide agglutination test for Lancefield grouping of streptococci. Arch Pathol Lab Med. 1979;103:456–457.
189. Matthieu DE, Wasilauskas BL, Stallings RA. A rapid staphylococcal coagglutination technique to differentiate group A from other streptococcal groups. Am J Clin Pathol. 1979;72:463–465.
190. Salata RA, Lerner PI, Shlaes DM, et al. Infections due to Lancefield group C streptococci. Medicine (Baltimore). 1989;68:225–239.
191. Arditi M, Shulman ST, Davis AT, et al. Group C β-hemolytic streptococcal infections in children: Nine pediatric cases and review. Rev Infect Dis. 1989;11: 34–45.
192. Ortel TL, Kallianos J, Gallis HA. Group C streptococcal arthritis: Case report and review. Rev Infect Dis. 1990;12:829–837.
193. Bradley SF, Gordon JJ, Baumgartner DD, et al. Group C streptococcal bacteremia: Analysis of 88 cases. Rev Infect Dis. 1991;13:270–280.
194. Wilson CD, Salt GFH. Streptococci in animal disease. In: Skinner FA, Quesnel LB, eds. Streptococci. New York: Academic Press; 1978:143–156.
195. Deibel RH, Seeley HW Jr. Streptococcaceae. In: Buchanan RE, Gibbons NE, eds. Bergey's Manual of Determinative Bacteriology. 8th ed. Baltimore: Williams & Wilkins; 1974:490–509.
196. Hare R. The classification of haemolytic streptococci from the nose and throat of normal human beings by means of precipitin and biochemical tests. J Pathol Bacteriol. 1935;41:499–512.
197. Marder VJ. The use of thrombolytic agents: Choice of patients, drug administration, laboratory monitoring. Ann Intern Med. 1979;90:802–808.
198. Schwartz RH, Shulman ST. Group C and group G streptococci: In-office isolation from children and adolescents with pharyngitis. Clin Pediatr. 1986;25:496–502.
199. Christensen KK, Christensen P, Flamholg L, et al. Frequency of streptococci of groups A, B, C, D and G in urethra and cervix swab specimens from patients with suspected gonococcal infection. Acta Pathol Microbiol Scand. 1974;82:470–474.
200. Goldman DA, Breton SJ. Group C streptococcal surgical wound infections transmitted by an anorectal and nasal carrier. Pediatrics. 1978;61:235–237.
201. Drusin LM, Ribble JC, Topf B. Group C streptococcal colonization in a newborn nursery. Am J Dis Child. 1973;125:820–821.
202. Edwards PR. Further studies on the differentiation of human and animal strains of hemolytic streptococci. J Bacteriol. 1933;25:527–536.
203. Duca E, Teodorovici G, Radu C, et al. A new nephritogenic streptococcus. J Hyg. 1969;67:691–698.
204. Barnham M, Thorton TJ, Lange K. Nephritis caused by *Streptococcus zooepidemicus* (Lancefield group C). Lancet. 1983;1:945–948.
205. Centers for Disease Control and Prevention. Group C streptococcal infection associated with eating homemade cheese—New Mexico. MMWR Morb Mortal Wkly Rep. 1983;32:510–516.
206. Barnham M, Kerby J, Chandler RS, et al. Group C streptococci in human infection: A study of 308 isolates with clinical correlations. Epidemiol Infect. 1989;102:379–390.
207. Bryans JT, Moore BO. Group C streptococcal infections of the horse. In: Wannamaker LW, Matsen JM, eds. Streptococci and Streptococcal Diseases: Recognition, Understanding and Management. New York: Academic Press; 1972:327–338.
208. Kilpper-Balz R, Schleifer KH. Nucleic acid hybridization and cell wall composition studies of pyogenic streptococci. FEMS Microbiol Lett. 1984;24:355–364.
209. Farrow JAE, Collins MD. Taxonomic studies on streptococci of serological groups C, G, and L and possibly related taxa. Syst Appl Microbiol. 1984;5:483–493.
210. Feltham RKA. A taxonomic study of the genus *Streptococcus*. In: Parker MT, ed. Pathogenic Streptococci. Surrey, UK: Reedbooks; 1979:247–248.
211. Jones D. Composition and differentiation of the genus *Streptococcus*. In: Skinner FA, Quesnel LB, eds. Streptococci. New York: Academic Press; 1978:1–50.
212. Colman G, Ball LC. Identification of streptococci in a medical laboratory. J Appl Bacteriol. 1984;57:1–14.
213. Lancefield RC, Hare R. The serological differentiation of pathogenic and non-pathogenic strains of hemolytic streptococci from parturient women. J Exp Med. 1935;61:335–349.
214. Coleman DJ, McGhie D, Tebbutt GM. Further studies on the reliability of the bacitracin inhibition test for the presumptive identification of Lancefield group A streptococci. J Clin Pathol. 1977;30:421–426.
215. Maxted WR. The use of bacitracin for identifying group A haemolytic streptococci. J Clin Pathol. 1953;6:224–226.
216. Stoner RA. Bacitracin and coagglutination for grouping of β-hemolytic streptococci. J Clin Microbiol. 1978;7:463–466.
217. Cudney NJC, Albers AC. Group G streptococci: A review of the literature. Am J Med Technol. 1982;48:37–42.
218. Gaunt PN, Seal DV. Group G streptococcal infections. J Infect. 1987;15:5–20.
219. Hill HR, Wilson E, Caldwell GG, et al. Epidemic of pharyngitis due to streptococci of Lancefield group G. Lancet. 1969;2:371–374.
220. Stryker WS, Fraser DW, Facklam RR. Foodborne outbreak of group G streptococcal pharyngitis. Am J Epidemiol. 1982;116:533–540.
221. Rolston KVI. Group G streptococcal infections. Arch Intern Med. 1986;146:857–858.
222. Hutchinson RI. Pathogenicity of group C (Lancefield) hemolytic streptococcus. Br Med J. 1946;2:575–576.
223. Armstrong D, Blevins A, Louria DB, et al. Groups B, C, and G streptococcal infections in a cancer hospital. Ann N Y Acad Sci. 1970;174:511–522.
224. Auckenthaler R, Hermans PE, Washington JA II. Group G streptococcal bacteremia: Clinical study and review of the literature. Rev Infect Dis. 1983;5:196–204.
225. Lam K, Bayer AS. Serious infections due to group G streptococci. Am J Med. 1983;75:561–570.
226. Wasky KL, Kollisch N, Densen P. Group G streptococcal bacteremia: The clinical experience at Boston University Medical Center and a critical review of the literature. Arch Intern Med. 1985;145:58–61.
227. Vartian C, Lerner PI, Shlaes DM, et al. Infections due to Lancefield group G streptococci. Medicine (Baltimore). 1985;64:75–88.
228. Mohr DN, Feist DJ, Washington JA II, et al. Infections due to group C streptococci in man. Am J Med. 1979;66:450–456.
229. Benjamin J, Perriello VA. Pharyngitis due to group C hemolytic streptococci in children. J Pediatr. 1976;89:254–255.
230. Stillerman M, Bernstein S. Streptococcal pharyngitis. Am J Dis Child. 1961;101:476–489.
231. Cimolai N, Elford RW, Bryan L, et al. Do the β-hemolytic non-group A streptococci cause pharyngitis? Rev Infect Dis. 1988;10:587–601.
232. Meier FA, Centor RM, Graham L, et al. Clinical and microbiological evidence for endemic pharyngitis among adults due to group C streptococci. Arch Intern Med. 1990;150:825–829.
233. Hayden GF, Murphy TF, Hendley JO. Non-group A β-hemolytic streptococci in the pharynx: Pathogens or innocent bystanders? Am J Dis Child. 1989;143:794–797.
234. Turner JC, Hayden GF, Kiselica D, et al. Association of group C β-hemolytic streptococci with endemic pharyngitis among college students. JAMA. 1990;264:2644–2647.
235. Turner JC, Hayden FG, Lobo M, et al. Epidemiologic evidence for Lancefield group C beta-hemolytic streptococci as a cause of exudative pharyngitis in college students. J Clin Microbiol. 1997;35:1–4.
236. Hayden GF, Turner JC, Kiselica D, et al. Latex agglutination testing directly from throat swabs for rapid detection of β-hemolytic streptococci from Lancefield serogroup C. J Clin Microbiol. 1992;30:716–718.
237. McCue JD. Group G streptococcal pharyngitis: Analysis of an outbreak at a college. JAMA. 1982;248:1333–1336.
238. Cohen D, Ferne M, Rouach T, et al. Food-borne outbreak of group G streptococcal sore throat in an Israeli military base. Epidemiol Infect. 1987;99:249–255.
239. Gerber MA, Randolph MF, Martin NJ, et al. Community-wide outbreak of group G streptococcal pharyngitis. Pediatrics. 191;87:598–603.
240. Lebrun L, Guibert M, Wallet P, et al. Human Fc(g) receptors for differentiation in throat cultures of group C *"Streptococcus equisimilis"* and group C *"Streptococcus milleri."* J Clin Microbiol. 1988;24:705–707.
241. Gnann JW Jr, Gray BM, Griffin FM Jr, et al. Acute glomerulonephritis following group G streptococcal infection. J Infect Dis. 1987;156:411–412.
242. Maxted WR, Potter EV. The presence of type 12 M-protein antigen in group G streptococci. J Gen Microbiol. 1967;49:119–125.
243. Poon-King T, Mohammed I, Cox R, et al. Recurrent epidemic nephritis in south Trinidad. N Engl J Med. 1967;277:728–733.

244. Reid HF, Bassett DC, Poon-King T, et al. Group G streptococci in healthy schoolchildren and in patients with glomerulonephritis in Trinidad. J Hyg. 1985;94:61–68.
245. Young L, Deighton CM, Chuck AJ, et al. Reactive arthritis and group G streptococcal pharyngitis. Ann Rheum Dis. 1992;51:1268.
246. Portnoy B, Reitler R. Cellulitis due to a haemolytic streptococcus type C. Lancet. 1944;2:597–598.
247. Belcher DW, Afoakwa SN, Osei-Tutu E, et al. Non-group A streptococci in Ghanaian patients with pyoderma. Lancet. 1975;2:1032.
248. Baddour LM, Bisno AL. Non-group A β-hemolytic streptococcal cellulitis: Association with venous and lymphatic compromise. Am J Med. 1985;79:155–159.
249. Goldenberg DL, Cohen AS. Acute infectious arthritis: A review of patients with nongonococcal joint infections (with emphasis on therapy and prognosis). Am J Med. 1976;60:369–377.
250. Manshady BM, Thompson GR, Weiss JJ. Septic arthritis in a general hospital 1966–1977. J Rheumatol. 1980;7:523–530.
251. Ho G, Su EY. Therapy for septic arthritis. JAMA. 1982;247:797–900.
252. Goldenberg DL, Reed JI. Bacterial arthritis. N Engl J Med. 1985;312:764–771.
253. Sharp JT. Lidshy MD, Duffy J, et al. Infectious arthritis. Arch Intern Med. 1979;139:125–130.
254. Barton LL, Dunkle LM, Habib FH. Septic arthritis in childhood: A 13-year review. Am J Dis Child. 1987;141:898–900.
255. Welkon CJ, Long SS, Fisher MC, et al. Pyogenic arthritis in infants and children: A review of 95 cases. Pediatr Infect Dis. 1986;5:669–676.
256. Ike RW. Septic arthritis due to group C streptococcus: Report and review of the literature. J Rheumatol. 1990;17:1230–1236.
257. Sobrino J, Bosch X, Wennberg P, et al. Septic arthritis secondary to group C streptococcus typed as *Streptococcus equisimilis.* J Rheumatol. 1991;18:485–486.
258. Collazos J, Echevarria MJ, Ayarza R, et al. *Streptococcus zooepidemicus* septic arthritis: Case report and review of group C streptococcal arthritis. Clin Infect Dis. 1992;15:744–746.
259. Lin AM, Karaski A, Salit IE, et al. Group G streptococcal arthritis. J Rheumatol. 1982;9:424–427.
260. Fujita NK, Lam K, Bayer AS. Septic arthritis due to group G streptococcus. JAMA. 1982;247:812–813.
261. Nakata MM, Silvers JH, George WL. Group G streptococcal arthritis. Arch Intern Med. 1983;143:1328–1330.
262. Gaunt PN, Seal DV. Group G streptococcal infection of joints and joint prostheses. J Infect. 1986;13:115–123.
263. Rady M, Turner PG, Ross ERS. Group G streptococcal septic arthritis. Br J Clin Pract. 1990;44:287–289.
264. Bronze MS, Whitby S, Schaberg DR. Group G streptococcal arthritis: A case report and review of the literature. Am J Med Sci. 1997;313:239–243.
265. Burkert T, Watanakunakorn C. Group G streptococcus septic arthritis and osteomyelitis: Report and literature review. J Rheumatol. 1991;18:904–907.
266. Asciutto R, Drennan J, Fitzgerald V, et al. Group C streptococcal arthritis and osteomyelitis in an adolescent with a hereditary sensory neuropathy. Pediatr Infect Dis. 1985;4:553–554.
267. Barson WJ. Group C streptococcal osteomyelitis. J Pediatr Orthop. 1986;6:346–348.
268. Asplin CM, Beeching NJ, Slack MPE. Osteomyelitis due to *Streptococcus equisimilis* (group C). Br Med J. 1979;1:89–90.
269. Tobias JH, Lee PYC, Bruckner FE. Group G β-haemolytic streptococcal vertebral osteomyelitis. J Infect. 1992;25:115–116.
270. Stamm AM, Cobbs CG. Group C streptococcal pneumonia: Report of a fatal case and review of the literature. Rev Infect Dis. 1980;2:889–898.
271. Rose HD, Allen JR, Witte G. *Streptococcus zooepidemicus* (group C) pneumonia in a human. J Clin Microbiol. 1980;11:76–78.
272. Noble JT, McGowan K. Group C streptococcal pneumonia in an adolescent. Am J Dis Child. 1983;137:1023.
273. Rivest N, Turgeson PL, Brady JF. Rare case of streptococcal C empyema. Can Med Assoc J. 1985;133:1009–1010.
274. Siefkin AD, Peterson DL, Hansen B. *Streptococcus equisimilis* pneumonia in a compromised host. J Clin Microbiol. 1984;17:386–388.
275. Vartian C. Bacteremic pneumonia due to group C streptococci. Rev Infect Dis. 1991;13:1029–1030.
276. Dolinski SY, Jones PG, Zabransky RJ, et al. Group C streptococcal pleurisy and pneumonia: A fulminant case and review of the literature. Infection. 1990;18:239–241.
277. Ancona RJ, Thompson TR, Ferrieri P. Group G steptococcal pneumonia and sepsis in a newborn infant. J Clin Microbiol. 1979;10:758–759.
278. Vracin W, Gage K, Ortega G, et al. Bacteremic group G streptococcal pneumonia. South Med J. 1982;75:1427.
279. Gallagher PG, Hyer CM III, Crone K, et al. Group C streptococcal sinusitis. Am J Otolaryngol. 1990;11:352–354.
280. Sanders V. Bacterial endocarditis due to group C hemolytic streptococcus. Ann Intern Med. 1963;58:858–861.
281. Lawrence MS, Cobbs CG. Endocarditis due to group C streptococci. South Med J. 1972;65:487–489.
282. Finnegan P, Fitzgerald MXM, Cumming G, et al. Lancefield group C streptococcal endocarditis. Thorax. 1974;29:245–247.
283. Bouza E, Meyer RD, Busch DF. Group G streptococcal endocarditis. J Clin Pathol. 1978;70:108–111.
284. Tuazon CU. Group G streptococcus. Am J Med Sci. 1980;279:121–124.
285. Blair DC, Martin DB. β-Hemolytic streptococcal endocarditis: Predominance of non-group A organisms. Am J Med Sci. 1978;276:269–277.
286. Venezio FR, Gullberg RM, Westenfelder GO, et al. Group G streptococcal endocarditis and bacteremia. Am J Med. 1986;81:29–34.
287. Smyth EG, Pallett AP, Davidson RN. Group G streptococcal endocarditis: Two case reports, a review of the literature and recommendations for treatment. J Infect. 1988;16:169–176.
288. Mohr DN, Feist DJ, Washington JA II, et al. Meningitis due to group C streptococci in an adult. Mayo Clin Proc. 1978;53:529–532.
289. Low DE, Young MR, Harding GKM. Group C streptococcal meningitis in an adult: Probable acquisition from a horse. Arch Intern Med. 1980;140:977–978.
290. Chung SJ. Meningitis caused by *Streptococcus equisimilis* (group C). South Med J. 1982;75:769.
291. Daly MP. Group G streptococcal infection in an elderly patient. South Med J. 1992;85:43–44.
292. Edwards AT, Roulson M, Ironside MJ. A milk-borne outbreak of serious infection due to *Streptococcus zooepidemicus* (Lancefield group C). Epidemiol Infect. 1988;101:43–51.
293. Faix RG, Soskolne EI, Schumacher RE. Group C streptococcal infection in a term newborn infant. J Perinatol. 1997;17:79–82.
294. Mollison LC, Donaldson E. Group C streptococcal meningitis. Med J Aust. 1990;152:319–320.
295. Ramsay AM, Gillespie M. Puerperal infection associated with haemolytic streptococci other than Lancefield's group A. J Obstet Gynecol Br Empire. 1941;48:569–585.
296. Filker RS, Monif GRG. Postpartum septicemia due to group G streptococci. Obstet Gynecol. 1979;53(Suppl):28–30.
297. Baker CJ. Unusual occurrence of neonatal septicemia due to group G streptococcus. Pediatrics. 1974;53:568–569.
298. Krishna Mohan VK, Tilton TC, Raye JR, et al. Fatal group G streptococcal sepsis in a preterm neonate. Am J Dis Child. 1980;134:894–895.
299. Appelbaum PC, Friedman Z, Fairbrother PF, et al. Neonatal sepsis due to group G streptococci. Acta Paediatr Scand. 1980;69:559–562.
300. Dyson AE, Read SE. Group G streptococcal colonization and sepsis in neonates. J Pediatr. 1981;99:944–947.
301. Skogberg K, Simonen H, Renkonen OV, et al. β-Hemolytic group A, B, C and G streptococcal septicemia: A clinical study. Scand J Infect Dis. 1988;20:119–125.
302. Berenguer J, Sampedro I, Cercenado E, et al. Group-C β-hemolytic streptococcal bacteremia. Diagn Microbiol Infect Dis. 1992;15:151–155.
303. Carmeli Y, Ruoff KL. Report of cases of and taxonomic considerations for large-colony-forming Lancefield group C streptococcal bacteremia. J Clin Microbiol. 1995;33:2114–2117.
304. Yuen KY, Seto WH, Choi CH, et al. *Streptococcus zooepidemicus* (Lancefield group C) septicaemia in Hong Kong. J Infect. 1990;21:241–250.
305. Carmeli Y, Schapiro JM, Neeman D, et al. Streptococcal group C bacteremia. Arch Intern Med. 1995;155:1170–1176.
306. Hanson G, Engel PJ. Purulent pericarditis caused by β-hemolytic group C streptococcus: A case report. Arch Intern Med. 1981;141:1351–1353.
307. Marsa RJ, Blomquist IK, Bansal RC, et al. Acute pericarditis due to group C streptococcus: Report of a medically treated case. Am J Med. 1989;86:474–476.
308. Nitta AT, Kuritzkes DR. Pyomyositis due to group C streptococci in a patient with AIDS. Rev Infect Dis. 1991;13:1254–1255.
309. Cimolai N, Macnab A. Schönlein-Henoch purpura and *Streptococcus equisimilis.* Br J Dermatol. 1991;125:403.
310. Klygis LM, Reisberg BE. Spinal epidural abscess caused by group G streptococci. Am J Med. 1991;91:89–90.
311. Keiser P, Campbell W. "Toxic strep syndrome" associated with group C streptococcus. Arch Intern Med. 1992;152:882–883.
312. Natoli S, Fimiani C, Faglieri N, et al. Toxic shock syndrome due to group C streptococci: A case report. Intensive Care Med. 1996;22:985–989.
313. Wagner JG, Schlievert PM, Assimacopoulos AP, et al. Acute group G streptococcal myositis associated with streptococcal toxic shock syndrome: A case report and review. Clin Infect Dis. 1996;23:1159–1161.
314. Dinn JJ. Brain abscess due to *Streptococcus equisimilis* in a maltworker. J Ir Med Assoc. 1971;64:50–51.
315. Schwartz RH, Knerr RJ, Hermansen K, et al. Acute epiglottitis caused by β-hemolytic group C streptococci. Am J Dis Child. 1982;136:558–559.
316. Kohler W, Cederberg A. *Streptococcus zooepidemicus* (group C streptococci) as a cause of human infection. Scand J Infect Dis. 1976;8:217–218.
317. Layton J, McCulley D. Subdural empyema and group C streptococcus. South Med J. 1985;78:64–66.
318. Koenigsberg RA, Roman N, Turtz A, et al. Group C streptococcal leptomeningitis and brain abscess secondary to frontal sinusitis: A case report. J Neuroimaging. 1994;4:239–240.
319. Maniglia RJ, Roth T, Blumber EA. Polymicrobial brain abscess in a patient with human immunodeficiency virus. Clin Infect Dis. 1997;24:449–451.
320. Finland M, Garner C, Wilcox C, et al. Susceptibility of β-hemolytic streptococci to 65 antibacterial agents. Antimicrob Agents Chemother. 1976;9:11–19.
321. Rolston KVI, LeFrock JL, Schell RF. Activity of nine antimicrobial agents against Lancefield group C and group G streptococci. Antimicrob Agents Chemother. 1982;22:930–932.
322. Rotta J. Pyogenic hemolytic streptococci. In: Srveath PH, Sharpe ME, Holt JG, eds. Bergey's Manual of Systemic Bacteriology. 9th ed. Baltimore: Williams & Wilkins; 1986:1047–1054.
323. Kataja J, Seppala H, Skurnik M, et al. Different erythromycin resistance mechanisms in group C and group G streptococci. Antimicrob Agents Chemother. 1998;42:1493–1494.

324. Hutchinson NA, Eltringham IL. Therapeutic failure in group C streptococcal pharyngitis (Letter). Lancet. 1995;346:1367.
325. Portnoy D, Prentis J, Richards GK. Penicillin tolerance of human isolates of group C streptococci. Antimicrob Agents Chemother. 1981;20:235–238.
326. Rolston KVI, Chandraseker PH, LeFrock JL. Antimicrobial tolerance in group C and group G streptococci. J Antimicrob Chemother. 1984;13:389–392.
327. Lam K, Bayer AS. In vitro bactericidal synergy of gentamicin combined with penicillin G, vancomycin, or cefotaxime against group G streptococci. Antimicrob Agents Chemother. 1984;26:260–262.
328. Noble JT, Tyburski MB, Berman M, et al. Antimicrobial tolerance in group G streptococci. Lancet. 1980;2:982.
329. Pier GB, Madin SH. *Streptococcus iniae* sp. nov., a beta-hemolytic streptococcus isolated from an Amazon freshwater dolphin, *Imia geoffrensis.* Int J Syst Bacteriol. 1976;26:545–553.
330. Eldar A, Frelier PF, Assenta L, et al. *Streptococcus shiloi,* the name for an agent causing septicemic infection in fish, is a junior synonym of *Streptococcus iniae.* Int J Syst Bacteriol. 1995;45:840–842.
331. Weinstein MR, Litt M, Kert DA, et al. Invasive infections due to a fish pathogen, *Streptococcus iniae.* N Engl J Med 1997;337:589–594.
332. von Eiff C, Herrmann M, Peters G. Antimicrobial susceptibilities of *Stomatococcus mucilaginosus* and of *Micrococcus* spp. Antimicrob Agents Chemother. 1995;39:268–270.
333. Park MK, et al. Successful treatment of *Stomatococcus mucilaginosus* meningitis with intravenous vancomycin and intravenous ceftriaxone. Clin Infect Dis. 1997;24:278.
334. Sarma PS, Mohanty S. *Pediococcus acidilactici* pneumonitis and bacteremia in a pregnant woman (Letter). J Clin Microbiol. 1998;36:2392–2393.
335. Corocoran Gd, Gibbons N, Mulvihill TE. Septicaemia caused by *Pediococcus pentosaceus:* A new opportunistic pathogen. J Infect Dis. 1991;23:179–182.
336. Mastro TD, Spika JS, Lozano P, et al. Vancomycin-resistant *Pediococcus acidilactici:* Nine cases of bacteremia. J Infect Dis. 1990;1612:956–960.

Chapter 192

Streptococcus intermedius Group

SURESH J. ANTONY
CHARLES W. STRATTON

Streptococcus intermedius, Streptococcus constellatus, and *Streptococcus anginosus* are three distinct species that constitute the "*Streptococcus intermedius* group." This group previously was referred to as the "*Streptococcus milleri* group"[1] or the "*Streptococcus anginosus-milleri* group"[2] or simply as "*Streptococcus anginosus.*"[3] The classification, nomenclature, and identification of members of this group have been confusing in the past. However, genetic and phenotypic studies[4–6] now clearly demonstrate that the *S. intermedius* group consists of at least three distinct species, with the possibility of additional species to be delineated in the future.[7] These species, in part, appear to be associated with a number of different body habitats as well as sites and types of clinical infections.[8]

Clinically, this group has long been characterized by a propensity for invasive pyogenic infections, which readily differentiates them from the other viridans streptococci.[1] Microbiologically, members of this group are recognized by their microaerophilic or anaerobic growth requirements, their formation of minute colonies, and the frequent presence of a characteristic caramel-like odor when cultured on agar plates.[9] This chapter defines the three species currently making up the *S. intermedius* group and discusses their role in clinical infections.

BACTERIOLOGIC CHARACTERISTICS

Members of the *S. intermedius* group share those phenotypic characteristics of the genus *Streptococcus* whose classification in general is based on patterns of hemolysis, Lancefield serologic antigenic reactions (i.e., groupings), growth properties, and biochemical reactions. In contrast to other members of the genus, *S. intermedius* group isolates often require carbon dioxide for growth; because of this, isolates are sometimes mistaken for anaerobic streptococci. Even under microaerophilic-anaerobic growth conditions, the resulting colonies are tiny (<0.5 mm in diameter), only one half to two thirds the diameter of colonies of other streptococci.[10] Some strains of *S. anginosus* isolated from genitourinary sources exhibit a spreading growth on certain types of agar, owing to increased production of extracellular glycocalyx (i.e., capsule).[11] Like other streptococci, these organisms may be β-hemolytic, α-hemolytic, or γ-hemolytic on sheep blood agar.[9, 12, 13] Members of the *S. intermedius* group often exhibit Lancefield antigens A, C, F, or G.[14] Strains containing the group F antigen may cross-react with the other grouping sera. Lancefield groupings therefore are of little value in identifying these organisms, because any one of a number of antigens may be exhibited. In fact, false-positive detection of group A streptococcal antigen has been reported with cross-reacting antigens from *S. intermedius.*[15]

A number of microbiologists have described a characteristic caramel-like odor associated with agar cultures of the *S. intermedius* group.[16] It has been suggested that this odor, when present, may be diagnostic for this group of microorganisms. The caramel-like odor has been shown to be caused by the formation of the metabolite diacetyl, and its presence indeed is of diagnostic value.[17] However, a number of strains that appear to be devoid of an obvious caramel-like odor on agar cultures have been noted to produce the diacetyl metabolite by gas chromatography.

The usefulness of Lancefield groupings and the distinctive caramel-like odor for presumptive identification has been examined in a prospective study of 100 consecutive streptococcal isolates from pus or blood cultures.[18] Lancefield group F alone had a specificity of 100% and a sensitivity of 47%; Lancefield group F accompanied by a caramel-like odor had a specificity of 100% and a sensitivity of only 19.5%. The study reported no significant association between species, Lancefield groupings, site of infection, severity of infection, or pathogenicity.

Gram staining of the members of the *S. intermedius* group reveals spherical or ovoid cells that form chains or pairs in broth culture and that stain gram-positive. It is possible to distinguish members of the *S. intermedius* group from other streptococci using selected biochemical reactions. In addition, the presence of the caramel-like odor can be helpful. The characteristics that allow the presumptive identification of members of the *S. intermedius* group, as adapted from the identification scheme of Whiley and colleagues,[5] are summarized in Table 192–1.

TABLE 192–1 Presumptive Identification of Members of the *Streptococcus intermedius* Group[5]

Growth of minute streptococcal colonies under microaerophilic/anaerobic conditions
- Acid from
  - Inulin −
  - Sorbitol −
  - Salicin +
- Hydrolysis of
  - Hippurate −
  - Esculin +
  - Deoxyribonuclease −
  - Arginine dihydrolysis +
  - Voges-Proskauer test +*
  - Caramel-like odor V

↓

Presumptive *S. intermedius* group

Symbols: +, ≥90% of strains have a positive reaction; −, ≥90% of strains have a negative reaction; V, variable; *, rare exceptions.
Adapted from Whiley RA, Fraser HY, Hardie JM, et al. Phenotypic differentiation of *Streptococcus constellatus, Streptococcus intermedius,* and *Streptococcus anginosus* (the *Streptococcus milleri* group): Association with different body sites and clinical infections. J Clin Microbiol. 1990;28:1497–1501.

TAXONOMY

The diversity of hemolytic and Lancefield groupings and the disagreement regarding taxonomy and speciation of the *S. intermedius* group have contributed to a lack of recognition of these pathogens in many laboratories.[19] Whiley and colleagues[5] noted that almost all *S. intermedius* strains (93%) were not β-hemolytic, whereas 38% of *S. constellatus* and 12% of *S. anginosus* were β-hemolytic. These investigators also found that of those strains of *S. constellatus* and *S. anginosus* that reacted with Lancefield serologic group F antibody, virtually all of the former but almost none of the latter were β-hemolytic.

Laboratories can readily differentiate the three members of the *S. intermedius* group using phenotypic characteristics,[20–22] and it is reasonable to do so.[18, 23] Useful characteristics adapted from the identification scheme of Whiley and colleagues[5] are presented in Fig. 192–1. These characteristics include conventional biochemical tests, which continue to be the recommended method for identification of viridans streptococci, including the *S. intermedius* group.

A number of commercial systems are available for the identification of viridans streptococci. They include API Rapid PosID (Analytab Products, Plainview, NY); Baxter Microscan (West Sacramento, Calif); BBL Minitek Differential System (Becton-Dickinson Microbiology Systems, Cockeysville, Md); Fluo-Card Milleri (KEY Scientific, Round Rock, Tex); IDS RapID STR System (Innovative Diagnostic Systems, Atlanta, Ga); and Vitek GPI (bioMérieux Vitek, Hazelwood, Md). An early comparison of many of these tests with conventional methods revealed that none showed more than 74% agreement.[24] *S. constellatus* and *S. intermedius* were among those isolates most frequently misidentified. However, a more recent comparison with conventional methods for one of these tests (Fluo-Card Milleri) reported a 98% agreement for *S. anginosus* strains, 97% agreement for *S. constellatus* strains, and 88% agreement for *S. intermedius* strains.[25]

Polymerase chain reaction (PCR) assays have now been developed for the identification of clinically relevant viridans group streptococci to the species and group level. One of these assays uses PCR-amplified 23S ribosomal RNA (rRNA) gene sequences followed by species-specific hybridization probes.[26] This molecular genetic approach has already identified several strains suspected of being members of the *S. intermedius* group by biochemical testing as being more closely related to *S. parasanguis*. PCR-amplified partial 16S rRNA gene sequences followed by species-specific hybridization probes have been used in a similar manner to identify a distinct rRNA population sharing 98% sequence homology with *S. constellatus*.[27] Another PCR assay that has been used is based on amplification of specific internal gene fragments encoding D-alanine: D-alanine ligases that are species-specific are ubiquitous in microbial cells possessing peptidoglycans.[28, 29] The availability and use of genetic-based molecular methods for classification of the viridans streptococci promises to place these microorganisms in unequivocal taxonomic positions.

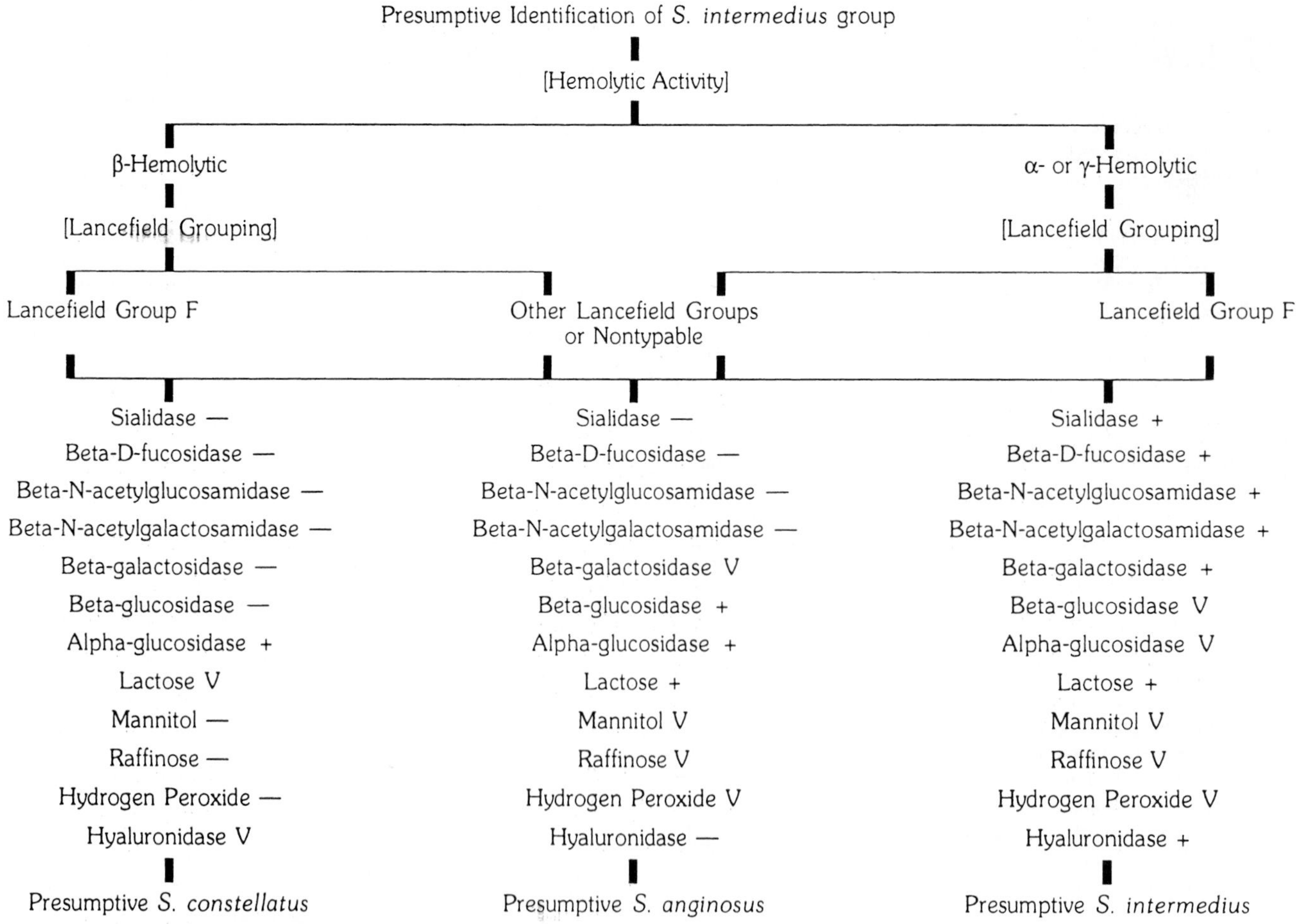

FIGURE 192–1. Phenotypic differentiation of the members of the *Streptococcus intermedius* group. *Abbreviations:* V, Variable; +, at least 90% of strains have a positive reaction; −, at least 90% of strains have a negative reaction. (Adapted from Whiley RA, Fraser HY, Hardie JM, et al. Phenotypic differentiation of *Streptococcus constellatus, Streptococcus intermedius,* and *Streptococcus anginosus* [the *Streptococcus milleri* group]: Association with different body sites and clinical infections. J Clin Microbiol. 1990;28:1497–1501.)

NORMAL HABITAT

Members of the *S. intermedius* group are found in the human oral cavity, where they have been considered harmless commensals.[30] These microorganisms can be isolated from gingival crevices, dental plaque, and dental root canals.[30, 31] They can also be found in the throat and nasopharynx[32]; these latter locations might represent spread from the oral cavity. Not surprisingly, these organisms are also found in the gastrointestinal tract and have been recovered from stool[33] and from the appendix.[34] Within the *S. intermedius* group, *S. intermedius* is most commonly found in dental plaque and *S. anginosus* is most frequently found in the gastrointestinal tract.[8, 23] Spread from the gastrointestinal tract to the vagina with subsequent vaginal colonization is common.[35] *S. anginosus* is the species most often found in the vagina; these isolates are heavily encapsulated.[11] Their presence in the birth canal can result in neonatal infection.[36] Spread from the vagina to the urinary tract appears to occur with these organisms, although infection in these sites is rare.[37]

PATHOGENICITY

The association of the *S. intermedius* group with the tendency to form abscesses has long been recognized.[38] However, the reasons for this pathogenic characteristic are not yet completely understood. Growth characteristics of the *S. intermedius* group appear to be important in their pathogenicity. Members of this group are able to grow well in acidic environments such as those found in abscesses.[39] Part of the explanation also appears to be that mixed infections involving members of the *S. intermedius* group and other microbes (e.g., *Eikenella corrodens* and anaerobes) allow more rapid replication of the streptococci.[40, 41] For example, one study noted that exponential growth for *S. intermedius* and *S. constellatus* in mixed culture with *E. corrodens* occurred within 6 hours after incubation, compared with 25 hours without *E. corrodens*.[40] No growth stimulation *of S. anginosus* was observed. A possible clinical correlate of this in vitro phenomenon has been reported.[42] Another study using a murine model of pneumonia demonstrated a similar synergy between members of the *S. intermedius* group and oral anaerobes.[43] This study found that mortality was higher, abscesses or empyema were more frequently noted on histopathologic examination, and viable bacteria were more numerous in the lungs of mice with mixed infections caused by members of the *S. intermedius* group and oral anaerobes than in the lungs of mice with monomicrobial infection. In vitro studies by these investigators confirmed that anaerobes enhanced the growth of *S. intermedius* group organisms. Finally, the authors pointed out that in 45 cases of acute pneumonia and/or pulmonary abscess and 25 cases of thoracic empyema, the predominant species recovered were anaerobic bacteria and members of the *S. intermedius* group, confirming the clinical importance of this phenomenon in pulmonary infections.

In addition, members of the *S. intermedius* group have been shown to possess intrinsic factors that are likely to be involved in their pathogenesis. Streptococci, including members of the *S. intermedius* group, express a number of different adhesins on their cell surfaces that facilitate adherence to substrates found in their natural environment.[44] Many of these adhesins are cell wall–associated proteins containing repeated sequence blocks of amino acids. Sequences and function of these adhesion proteins among the streptococci have become assorted through gene duplication and horizontal transfer between microbial populations.[45] All members of the *S. intermedius* group are able to bind fibronectin via a cell-surface protein, and some strains are able to bind to platelets-fibrin, fibrin clots, and fibrinogen.[46] This property is thought to be a factor in the ability of these pathogens to cause endocarditis. Fibrinogen binding may, in turn, aid in platelet aggregation, which would also facilitate the development of endocarditis.[47]

These adhesion proteins would explain the success of streptococci in colonizing oral and epithelial surfaces and would allow these pathogens to attach to sites of tissue damage. Attachment to and colonization of sites of tissue damage may precede tissue invasion and immune modulation presaging the development of infection.[48, 49] In an experimental rat endocarditis model in which all three strains of *S. intermedius* were studied, *S. anginosus* strains produced infective vegetations and bacteremia in almost all catheterized rats, *S. constellatus* strains did so less frequently, and *S. intermedius* strains did so only occasionally.[50] Moreover, the vegetations infected with *S. anginosus* strains harbored significantly higher numbers of microorganisms than did those infected by other strains. However, no strong correlation was found between endocardial infectivity and platelet-aggregating capacity of the strains.

Another potential virulence factor is the frequent presence in members of the *S. intermedius* group of a polysaccharide capsule[11] that hinders phagocytosis. The ability to escape phagocytosis would allow these pathogens to replicate after arriving at and adhering to a site of tissue damage.[51, 52] A murine model used to investigate the pathogenicity *of S. constellatus* in pulmonary infections demonstrated that virulent strains are less likely to be phagocytized and killed than avirulent strains, presumably because of capsular variation.[53]

The production of pyrogenic exotoxins by *Streptococcus* species is well known.[54] Despite this known propensity for streptococcal exotoxins, few have been reported for members of the *S. intermedius* group. A unique cytolytic toxin specific for human cells, intermedilysin, was described from a strain of *S. intermedius* isolated from a liver abscess.[55] In particular, intermedilysin was noted to have a potent hemolytic effect on human erythrocytes, suggesting that this or similar exotoxins may be responsible for β-hemolysis on blood agar plates.

In addition, members of the *S. intermedius* group produce a wide variety of hydrolytic enzymes, including hyaluronidase, deoxyribonuclease, and chondroitin sulfatase.[56–59] These enzymes may facilitate the spread of these pathogens through tissues, play a role in microbial nutrition, and assist in liquefaction of pus. One of the most prevalent hydrolytic enzymes is hyaluronidase.[60] Hyaluronidase has been found in pus and shown to be a growth factor.[61, 62] One study used a collection of more than 500 strains of *S. intermedius* to assess the presence of hydrolytic enzymes and found that their presence was related to the clinical significance of the isolates.[22] Ribonuclease activity was equally distributed among all the strains, whereas hyaluronidase activity was linked to *S. intermedius* and *S. constellatus*. Neither enzyme was significantly associated with strains isolated from infections. However, deoxyribonuclease and chondroitin sulfatase activity was also linked to *S. intermedius* and *S. constellatus* and was associated with strains isolated from infections. Chondroitin sulfatase has been shown to be produced by *S. intermedius*.[63] In addition, a novel glycosaminoglycan depolymerase isolated from *S. intermedius* acts on both chondroitin sulphate and hyaluronic acid.[64] Another enzyme that may play a role in pathogenesis is sialidase (neuraminidase), which is produced by *S. intermedius*.[65] Sialidase production by other bacteria such as *Corynebacterium diphtheriae, Streptococcus pneumoniae, Vibrio cholerae,* and *Clostridium perfringens* is considered to be an important feature of their pathogenicity. Sialic acid is known to be a nutrient source for these microorganisms; members of the *S. intermedius* group are able to use sialic acid efficiently as a sole carbon source. Sialidase therefore may be a growth factor and may play an important role in the ability of these microorganisms to proliferate.

A number of other possible virulence factors related to the host immune response have been identified. One of these, a 90-kD protein that suppresses lymphocyte and fibroblast proliferation, was recovered from *S. intermedius*.[66, 67] This protein may have a virulence effect that is mediated by stimulation of suppressor lymphocytes. Leukocyte migration was not affected by this protein. In addition, the absence of receptors for the Fc fragment of human immunoglobulin G has been noted[68] and may be related to virulence.

However, the most important virulence factor for members of the *S. intermedius* group in relation to the host immune response may be superantigens. Superantigens are a diverse collection of molecules that share the ability to activate specific lymphocyte subsets without regard to the antigenic specificity of the T cells and without prior cellular processing.[69] The lymphocyte subsets are stimulated in a manner that is restricted to the variable regions on the β-chain (V_β region) of the T-cell receptor; after stimulation, superantigen-responsive T cells often die through apoptosis.[70] Reports suggest that groups B, C, F, and G streptococci and *S. sanguis* produce pyrogenic toxin superantigens that stimulate T cells to proliferate nonspecifically.[71] This is accomplished by the interaction of these superantigens with class II major histocompatibility complex products on antigen-producing B cells, which are then cross-linked to T cells via the V_β region of the T-cell receptor complex. Because superantigens are potent producers of inflammatory (Th1) cytokines, they may play a central role in determining the severity of invasive streptococcal infections.[72] These superantigens are now thought to produce acute toxic shock syndromes and multisystem illnesses via release of these immune cytokines.[50] Streptococcal erythrogenic exotoxins are known to have superantigen properties,[73] and it is possible that intermedilysin,[55] the recently recognized hemolysin of *S. intermedius,* may act as a superantigen.

That members of *S. intermedius* do have virulence factors, however ill-defined, can be appreciated by the fact that many times these pathogens are the sole isolate from serious infections, including those with abscess formation.[37, 76, 77]

CLINICAL MANIFESTATIONS

Head and Neck Infections

Most of the original isolates first described by Guthof[78] were isolated from dental abscesses. These pathogens continue to be recovered from endodontic and periapical dental abscesses,[79, 80] most often after a dental procedure such as surgery or extraction or after trauma. Although *S. intermedius* group species are often isolated in pure culture, other microorganisms such as *Bacteroides fragilis* may be recovered.[37, 81] Bacteremia may occur with dental abscesses[37] and has been associated with metastatic abscesses.[82] Finally, members of the *S. intermedius* group have been isolated from dental caries and periodontal disease,[9, 31] although their role, if any, in these processes is unclear. The periodontal location would allow transient bacteremias to occur and possibly predispose to metastatic infections.

The presence of members of the *S. intermedius* group in the oral cavity clearly predisposes to oral and maxillofacial infections.[83] Acute pansinusitis with bacteremia caused by members of the *S. intermedius* group has been described.[84] In several series this group represented the most common microorganisms isolated in sinus-induced intracranial sepsis, being recovered from intracranial and orbital empyemas in up to 50% of the cases.[85, 86] Because of the potential for metastatic spread, sinusitis caused by *S. intermedius* group isolates requires aggressive management.[86] Finally, *S. intermedius* group pathogens have been described as causing a fulminant fasciitis of the head and neck that also can be life threatening.[87]

Bacteremia and Endocarditis

Many reports in the adult medical literature have stressed the clinical significance of bacteremia caused by *S. intermedius* group isolates.[1, 9, 23, 37, 83, 87–94] Most of these bacteremic episodes were associated with an identifiable focus of infection—usually a deep-seated abscess in a visceral organ, implicating the gastrointestinal tract as the source. Such bacteremia, therefore, should alert the clinician to initiate an appropriate investigation for the detection of a possible suppurative focus of infection. A number of reports have noted an increase in the rate of viridans streptococcal bacteremia, including isolates from the *S. intermedius* group, in patients with cancer.[95, 96] In one such study, *S. anginosus* was responsible for eight episodes of bacteremia in which the upper respiratory tract was the source of infection.[96] Nosocomial bacteremias caused by streptococci represent an increasingly important problem, particularly among neutropenic cancer patients; the viridans group streptococci, including members of the *S. intermedius* group, account for 50% of the nosocomial blood-stream isolates.[97] Bacteremias by *S. intermedius* group isolates have also been described in neonates[36, 98] and in the pediatric population, including pediatric oncology patients.[99, 100]

Viridans streptococci have been recognized as an increasingly important cause of bacteremia in neutropenic cancer patients undergoing chemotherapy.[95, 96, 100, 101] Viridans streptococci are associated with adult respiratory distress syndrome (ARDS) and a toxic shock–like syndrome in neutropenic patients that is not seen in non-neutropenic patients with viridans streptococci bacteremia. The syndrome observed is clinically similar to the toxic shock syndrome associated with *Staphylococcus aureus* infection and includes a rash with subsequent palmar desquamation, shock, ARDS, and a high mortality rate. Of the *S. intermedius* group, *S. intermedius* and *S. constellatus* have been associated with this syndrome.[102] To date no exotoxins of viridans streptococci have been directly implicated, although streptococcal erythrogenic exotoxins are known to induce cytokines,[75] and *S. intermedius* is known to produce a cytolysin[55, 103] that is an erythrogenic exotoxin. Moreover, cell-free bacterial supernatants derived from viridans streptococci have been shown to induce the production of a number of cytokines from human peripheral blood mononuclear cells.[74] The cytokines included tumor necrosis factor-α, tumor necrosis factor-β, and interleukin-8. Antineoplastic regimens that denude and ulcerate the oral and gastrointestinal mucosa probably predispose to this syndrome. The situation is then complicated by selective overgrowth of microorganisms (e.g., viridans streptococci) that are resistant to trimethoprim-sulfamethoxazole or earlier fluoroquinolones such as ciprofloxacin.[104] This overgrowth is also assisted by an alkaline gastric environment created by antacids or histamine type 2 (H_2) antagonists.[102] Other risk factors include profound neutropenia.

Bacteremia by *S. intermedius* group isolates may be caused by, or may cause, bacterial endocarditis. It is estimated that members of this group represent between 3 and 15% of streptococcal isolates from patients with endocarditis.[1] The propensity for suppuration of these pathogens has resulted in the complication of myocardial abscess or metastatic abscess,[76, 90, 92, 105–107] although these complications do not occur in all patients.[78, 108] The endocarditis most often involves an abnormal heart valve, although the exact attachment mechanism is unknown. *S. intermedius* group strains have been shown to adhere to buccal epithelial cells and also to bind to fibronectin, which may contribute to their pathogenicity in endocarditis.[46–50]

Central Nervous System Infections

S. intermedius group organisms have a strikingly prominent association with brain abscesses and have been isolated in approximately 50 to 80% of these infections.[37, 76, 90, 109–111] These organisms may be isolated in pure culture or mixed with anaerobes. Factors associated with brain abscesses caused by these isolates include congenital heart defects, sinusitis, otitis media, liver disease, and direct trauma. Members of this group have been found to have an affinity for the central nervous system of young mice.[112] Of the three members, *S. intermedius* appears to be the one most commonly isolated from brain abscesses.[9, 113] Although *S. intermedius* can be found in the mouth, it has been suggested that most brain abscesses caused by this pathogen originate from the intestine.[90] On rare occasions, *S. intermedius* group organisms cause meningitis; this often is preceded by trauma or purulent infection at another site.[114, 115] Finally, these bacteria have been isolated from acute spondylodiskitis, spinal epidural abscesses, and subdural empyema.[116–120] Rapid surgical drainage is a critical prognostic factor for effective management of these spinal cord abscesses.

Abdominal Infections

Given that members of the *S. intermedius* group are considered commensal organisms of the intestinal tract, it is not surprising to find these pathogens causing infections within the abdominal cavity. Such infections include liver abscesses,[1, 42, 76, 77, 121–123] peritonitis,[1, 42, 76, 77, 104] pelvic abscesses,[1, 77] subphrenic abscesses,[1, 77] appendicitis,[34, 124] abdominal wound infections,[1] and cholangitis.[1, 76] The use of antimicrobial drugs with minimal or no activity against the *S. intermedius* group for prophylaxis or therapy involving the abdominal cavity has been associated with the development of infections by these organisms clinically[125] and experimentally.[126] Specifically, metronidazole alone or in combination with gentamicin appears to allow these bacteria to become pathogens. Infections caused by members of the *S. intermedius* group can be seen after abdominal surgery, particularly if prophylactic antibiotics do not cover these pathogens. The proclivity for liver abscess and cholangitis must be appreciated. Finally, Whiley and associates[7] reported that *S. anginosus* is the species of the group most frequently recovered from infections in the abdominal cavity.

Thoracic Infections

The presence of *S. intermedius* group organisms in the oropharynx can lead to aspiration pneumonia.[37, 43, 77, 127–131] Pneumonia caused by these pathogens can be complicated by lung abscess or pleural empyema, or both; this is particularly likely to occur with mixed pulmonary infections.[41–43] A retrospective study of lung abscesses and pleural empyemas caused by viridans streptococci revealed that the majority (68%) were caused by members of the *S. intermedius* group.[130] Predisposing factors to *S. intermedius* group pulmonary infections include male gender, previous pneumonia, alcoholism, and cancer.[129] Significant morbidity and mortality (death rates of 15 to 30%) has been associated with these infections. Management of pulmonary infections caused by the *S. intermedius* group must be aggressive.[132] Mediastinitis has also been reported.[133] *S. constellatus* is the species of the group most frequently identified from respiratory tract infections.[8]

Miscellaneous Infections

A number of other infections caused by members of the *S. intermedius* group have been reported. These include osteomyelitis,[37, 77] septic arthritis,[135] and subcutaneous abscess or cellulitis.[14, 37, 77, 118, 134] The latter condition has been described in drug addicts[37, 136] and in patients with chronic hidradenitis suppurativa of the anogenital region.[137] Spontaneous bacterial peritonitis caused by members of the *S. intermedius* group have been reported.[104] Peritonsillar abscesses involving anaerobic microorganisms mixed with *S. intermedius* group members have been described.[88]

ANTIMICROBIAL THERAPY

Early studies reported that most members of the *S. intermedius* group had minimal inhibitory concentrations (MICs) to penicillin G of less than 0.06 μg/ml, with occasional strains resistant to greater than 1.0 μg/ml.[138, 139] However, resistance to penicillin G and other β-lactam agents due to altered penicillin-binding proteins has been reported.[140, 141] In some studies, 29% of viridans streptococci overall, including members of the *S. intermedius* group, were resistant to intermediate concentrations of penicillin G (MICs, 0.25 to 2 μg/ml) and 9% of all strains were resistant to high concentrations of penicillin G (MICs >4 μg/ml).[140] Other studies continue to report penicillin resistance in less than 2% of *S. intermedius* group isolates.[142–145] Nonetheless, the potential for penicillin and cephalosporin resistance clearly exists because of the horizontal transfer of genes among streptococci.[45, 146] When penicillin resistance is seen, it is more common among *S. anginosus* and *S. intermedius* isolates. Although most strains of the *S. intermedius* group are relatively resistant to aminoglycosides, synergy with a β-lactam agent usually can be demonstrated. Therefore, the addition of an aminoglycoside to a β-lactam agent for treatment of endocarditis caused by members of the *S. intermedius* group is a reasonable practice, particularly for strains with intermediate MICs.

Clinically, infections caused by these streptococci have responded well to penicillin G and cephalosporins. Vancomycin and clindamycin have been useful in patients with β-lactam allergies. The recent increase in MICs to penicillin G suggests that initiation of penicillin G combined with gentamicin may be prudent. Alternatively, vancomycin could be used. Of the cephalosporins that are clinically available, cefepime, cefotaxime, and ceftriaxone have been noted to be superior in potency and spectrum for empirical coverage of patients at risk for streptococcal bacteremias.[147, 148] Macrolides, with the possible exception of clindamycin, do not appear to be potent enough for such empirical therapy.[149] Newer agents such as levofloxacin, sparfloxacin, and trovafloxacin and quinupristin-dalfopristin may prove useful; these agents have demonstrated comparable or superior bactericidal activity in comparison to penicillins against *S. intermedius* group and other viridans group streptococci tested.[150–152] Finally, it is important to remember that surgical drainage of abscesses may be needed as adjunctive therapy.

REFERENCES

1. Gossling J. Occurrence and pathogenicity of the *Streptococcus milleri* group. Rev Infect Dis. 1988;10:257–285.
2. Gallis HA. *Streptococcus intermedius* group (*Streptococcus anginosus-milleri* group). In: Mandell GL, Douglas G, Bennett JE, eds. Principles and Practice of Infectious Diseases. New York: Churchill Livingstone; 1990:1572–1574.
3. Coykendall AL, Wesbecher PM, Gustafson KB. *"Streptococcus milleri," Streptococcus constellatus,* and *Streptococcus intermedius* are later synonyms of *Streptococcus anginosus.* Int J Syst Bacteriol. 1987;37:222–228.
4. Whiley RA, Hardie JM. DNA-DNA hybridization studies and phenotypic characteristics of strains within the "*Streptococcus milleri* group." J Gen Microbiol. 1989;135:2623–2633.
5. Whiley RA, Fraser HY, Hardie JM, et al. Phenotypic differentiation of *Streptococcus constellatus, Streptococcus intermedius,* and *Streptococcus anginosus* (the *Streptococcus milleri* group): Association with different body sites and clinical infections. J Clin Microbiol. 1990;28:1497–1501.
6. Whiley RA, Beighton D. Emended descriptions and recognition of *Streptococcus constellatus, Streptococcus intermedius,* and *Streptococcus anginosus* as distinct species. Int J Syst Bacteriol 1991;41:1–5.
7. Whiley RA, Hall LM, Hardie JM, et al. Intra-specific diversity within *Streptococcus anginosus.* Adv Exp Med Biol. 1997;418:367–369.
8. Whiley RA, Beighton D, Winstanley TG, et al. *Streptococcus intermedius, Streptococcus constellatus,* and *Streptococcus anginosus* (the *Streptococcus milleri* group): Association with different body sites and clinical infections. J Clin Microbiol. 1992;30:243–244.
9. Kambal AM. Isolation of *Streptococcus milleri* from clinical specimens. J Infect Dis. 1987;14:217–223.
10. Long PH, Bliss EA. Studies upon minute hemolytic streptococci: I. The isolation and cultural characteristics of minute beta hemolytic streptococci. J Exp Med. 1934;60:619–631.
11. Bergman S, Selig M, Collins MD, et al. *"Streptococcus milleri"* strains displaying a gliding type of motility. Int J Syst Bacteriol. 1995;45:235–239.
12. Ruoff KL, Kunz LJ, Ferraro MJ. Occurrence of *Streptococcus milleri* among beta-hemolytic streptococci isolated from clinical specimens. J Clin Microbiol. 1985;22:149–151.
13. Lawrence J, Yajko DM, Hadley WK. Incidence and characterization of beta-hemolytic *Streptococcus milleri* and differentiation from *S. pyogenes* (group A), *S. equisimilis* (group C), and large-colony group G streptococci. J Clin Microbiol. 1985;22:772–777.
14. Ball LC, Parker MT. The cultural and biochemical characteristics of *Streptococcus milleri* in various body sites. J Clin Pathol. 1979;32:764–768.
15. Rubin LG, Kahn RA, Vellozzi EM, et al. False positive detection of group A *Streptococcus* antigen resulting from cross-reacting *Streptococcus intermedius* (*Streptococcus milleri* group). Pediatr Infect Dis J. 1996;15:715–717.
16. Roberts L, Collignon PL, Garrard A. *Streptococcus anginosus (Streptococcus milleri):* Whose nose knows? Aust Microbiol. 1991;12:433.
17. Chew TA, Smith JMB. Detection of diacetyl (caramel odor) in presumptive identification of the *"Streptococcus milleri"* group. J Clin Microbiol. 1992;30:3028–3029.
18. Brogan O, Malone J, Fox C, et al. Lancefield grouping and smell of caramel for presumptive identification and assessment of pathogenicity in the *Streptococcus milleri* group. J Clin Pathol. 1997;50:332–335.

19. Piscitelli SC, Shwed J, Schreckenberger P, et al. *Streptococcus milleri* group: Renewed interest in an elusive pathogen. Eur J Clin Microbiol Infect Dis. 1992;11:491–498.
20. Gomez-Garces JL, Alos JI, Cogollos R. Bacteriologic characteristics and antimicrobial susceptibility of 70 clinically significant isolates of *Streptococcus milleri* group. Diagn Microbiol Infect Dis. 1994;19:69–73.
21. O'Neill WA, Cook RP. Rapid differentiation *of Streptococcus milleri* from other beta-haemolytic group A, C, and G streptococci by simple screening tests. Br J Biomed Sci. 1994;51:1–4.
22. Jacobs JA, Pietersen HG, Stobberingh EE, et al. *Streptococcus anginosus, Streptococcus constellatus* and *Streptococcus intermedius:* Clinical relevance, hemolytic and serologic characteristics. Am J Clin Pathol. 1995;104:547–553.
23. Jacobs JA, Schouten HC, Stobberingh EE, et al. Viridans streptococci isolated from the bloodstream: Relevance of species identification. Diagn Microbiol Infect Dis. 1995;22:267–273.
24. Hinnebusch CJ, Nikolai DM, Bruckner DA. Comparison of API Rapid Strep, Baxter Microscan Rapid Pos ID panel, BBL Minitek Differential Identification System, IDS RapID STR System and Vitek GPI to conventional biochemical tests for identification of viridans streptococci. Am J Clin Pathol. 1991;96:459–463.
25. Flynn CE, Ruoff KL. Identification of *"Streptococcus milleri"* group isolates to the species level with a commercially available rapid test system. J Clin Microbiol. 1995;33:2704–2706.
26. Sultana F, Kawamura Y, Hou XG, et al. Determination of 23S rRNA sequences from members of the genus *Streptococcus* and characterization of genetically distinct organisms previously identified as members of the *Streptococcus anginosus* group. FEMS Microbiol Lett. 1998;158:223–230.
27. Jacobs JA, Schot CS, Bunschoten AE, et al. Rapid species identification of *"Streptococcus milleri"* strains by line blot hybridization: Identification of a distinct 16S rRNA population closely related to *Streptococcus constellatus.* J Clin Microbiol. 1966;34:1717–1721.
28. Whiley RA, Duke B, Hardie JM, et al. Heterogeneity among 16S–23S rRNA intergenic spacers of species within the "*Streptococcus milleri* group." Microbiology. 1995;141:1461–1467.
29. Garnier F, Gerbaud G, Courvalin P, et al. Identification of clinically relevant viridans group streptococci to the species level by PCR. J Clin Microbiol. 1997;35:2337–2341.
30. Mejare B, Edwardsson S. *Streptococcus milleri* (Guthof): An indigenous organism of the human oral cavity. Arch Oral Biol. 1975;20:757–62.
31. Winkler KC, van Amerongen J. Bacteriologic results from 4,000 root canal cultures. Oral Surg Oral Med Oral Pathol. 1959;12:857–862.
32. Hare R. The classification of haemolytic streptococci from the nose and throat of normal human beings by means of precipitin and biochemical tests. J Pathol Bacteriol. 1935;41:499–512.
33. Unsworth PF. The isolation of streptococci from human faeces. J Hyg Camb. 1980;85:153–164.
34. Pool PM, Wilson G. *Streptococcus milleri* in the appendix. J Clin Pathol. 1977;30:937.
35. Ahmet Z, Warren M, Houang ET. Species identification of members of the *Streptococcus milleri* group isolated from the vagina by ID 32 Strep system and differential characteristics. J Clin Microbiol. 1995;33:1592–1595.
36. Raymond J, Bergeret M, Francoual C, et al. Neonatal infection with *Streptococcus milleri.* Eur J Clin Microbiol. 1995;14:799–801.
37. Shlaes DM, Lerner PI, Wolinsky E, et al. Infection due to Lancefield group F and related streptococci *(S. milleri, S. anginosus).* Medicine (Baltimore). 1981;60:197–207.
38. Andrews FW, Horder TJ. A study of the streptococci pathogenic for man. Lancet. 1906;2:708–713,775–782,852–855.
39. Osawa R, Whiley RA. Effects of different acidulants on growth of "*Streptococcus milleri* group" strains isolated from various sites of the human body. Lett Appl Microbiol. 1995;20:263–267.
40. Young KA, Allaker RP, Hardie JM, et al. Interactions between *Eikenella corrodens* and "*Streptococcus milleri*-group" organisms: Possible mechanisms of pathogenicity in mixed infections. Antonie Van Leeuwenhoek. 1996;69:371–373.
41. Shinzato T, Saito A. A mechanism of pathogenicity of "*Streptococcus milleri* group" in pulmonary infection: Synergy with an anaerobe. J Med Microbiol. 1994;40:118–123.
42. Ouinlivan D, Davis TM, Daly FJ, et al. Hepatic abscess due to *Eikenella corrodens* and *Streptococcus milleri:* Implications for antibiotic therapy. J Infect. 1996;33:47–48.
43. Shinzato T, Saito A. The *Streptococcus milleri* group as a cause of pulmonary infections. Clin Infect Dis. 1995;21(Suppl 3):S238–S243.
44. Jenkinson HF, Lamont RJ. Streptococcal adhesion and colonization. Crit Rev Oral Biol Med. 1997;8:175–200.
45. Dowson CG, Barcus V, King S, et al. Horizontal gene transfer and the evolution of resistance and virulence determinants in *Streptococcus.* Soc Appl Bacteriol Symp Ser. 1997;26:42–51.
46. Wilcox MD, Knox KW. Surface-associated properties of *Streptococcus milleri* group strains and their potential relation to pathogenesis. J Med Microbiol. 1990;31:259–270.
47. Wilcox MD, Oakey HJ, Harty DW, et al. Lancefield group C *Streptococcus milleri* group strains aggregate human platelets. Microb Pathog. 1994;16:451–457.
48. Wilcox MD. Potential pathogenic properties of members of the *"Streptococcus milleri"* group in relation to the production of endocarditis and abscesses. J Med Microbiol. 1995;43:405–410.
49. Kitada K, Inoue M, Kitano M. Infective endocarditis-inducing abilities of *"Streptococcus milleri"* group. Adv Exp Med Biol. 1997;418:161–163.
50. Kitada K, Inoue M, Kitano M. Experimental endocarditis induction and platelet aggregation by *Streptococcus anginosus, Streptococcus constellatus* and *Streptococcus intermedius.* FEMS Immunol Med Microbiol. 1997;19:25–32.
51. Brook I, Walker RI. The role of encapsulation in the pathogenesis of anaerobic gram-positive cocci. Can J Microbiol. 1985;31:176–180.
52. Wessels MR. Biology of streptococcal capsular polysaccharides. Soc Appl Bacteriol Symp Ser. 1997;26:20–31.
53. Toyoda K, Kusano M, Saito A. Pathogenicity of the *Streptococcus milleri* group in pulmonary infections. Kansenshogaku Zasshi. 1995;69:308–315.
54. Bohach GA, Stauffacher CV, Ohlendorf DH, et al. The staphylococcal and streptococcal pyrogenic toxin family. Adv Exp Med Biol. 1996;391:131–154.
55. Nagamune H, Ohnishi C, Katsuura A, et al. Intermedilysin: A cytolytic toxin specific for human cells of a *Streptococcus intermedius* isolated from human liver abscess. Adv Exp Med Biol. 1997;418:773–775.
56. Steffen EK, Hentges DJ. Hydrolytic enzymes of anaerobic bacteria isolated from human infections. J Clin Microbiol. 1981;14:153–156.
57. Marshall R, Kaufman AK. Production of deoxyribonuclease, ribonuclease, coagulase, and hemolysins by anaerobic gram-positive cocci. J Clin Microbiol. 1981;13:787–788.
58. Ruoff KL, Ferraro MJ. Hydrolytic enzymes of *"Streptococcus milleri."* J Clin Microbiol. 1987;25:1645–1647.
59. Wilcox MD, Patrikakis M, Knox KW. Degradative enzymes of oral streptococci. Aust Dent J. 1995;40:121–128.
60. Shain H, Homer KA, Aduse-Opoku J, et al. A conserved region of a hyaluronidase gene from *Streptococcus intermedius.* Adv Exp Med Biol. 1997;418:769–772.
61. Takao A, Nagashima H, Usui H, et al. Hyaluronidase activity in human pus for which *Streptococcus intermedius* was isolated. Mirobiol Immunol. 1997;41:795–798.
62. Homer K, Shain H, Beighton D. The role of hyaluronidase in growth of *Streptococcus intermedius* on hyaluronate. Adv Exp Med Biol. 1997;418:681–683.
63. Shain H, Homer KA, Beighton D. Degradation and utilisation of chondroitin sulphate by *Streptococcus intermedius.* J Med Microbiol. 1996;44:372–380.
64. Shain H, Homer KA, Beighton D. Purification and properties of a novel glycosaminoglycan depolymerase for *Streptococcus intermedius.* J Med Microbiol. 1996;44:381–389.
65. Byers Hl, Homer KA, Beighton D. Sialic acid utilisation by viridans streptococci. Adv Exp Med Biol. 1997;418:713–716.
66. Arala-Chaves MP, Higerd TB, Porto MT, et al. Evidence for the synthesis and release of strongly immunosuppressive noncytotoxic substances by *Streptococcus intermedius.* J Clin Invest. 1979;64:871–883.
67. Arala-Chaves MP, Ribeiro AS, Santarem MMG, et al. Strong mitogenic effect for murine B lymphocytes of an immunosuppressor substance released by *Streptococcus intermedius.* Infect Immun. 1986;54:543–854.
68. Lebrun L, Guibert M, Wallet P, et al. Human Fc(g) receptors for differentiation in throat cultures of group C *"Streptococcus equisimilis"* with group C *"Streptococcus milleri."* J Clin Microbiol. 1986;24:705–707.
69. Proft T, Fraser J. Superantigens: Just like peptides only different. J Exp Med. 1998;187:819–821.
70. Michie CA, Cohen J. The clinical significance of T-cell superantigens. Trends Microbiol. 1998;6:61–65.
71. Rago JV, Schlievert PM. Mechanisms of pathogenesis of staphylococcal and streptococcal superantigens. Curr Topics Microbiol Immunol. 1998;225:81–97.
72. Cavaillon JM, Muller-Alouf H, Alouf JE. Cytokines in streptococcal infections: An opening lecture. Adv Exp Med Biol. 1997;418:869–879.
73. Orlicek SL, Branum KC, English BK, et al. Viridans streptococcal isolates for patients with septic shock induce tumor necrosis factor-alpha production by murine macrophages. J Lab Clin Med. 1997;130:515–519.
74. Soto A, Evans TJ, Cohen J. Proinflammatory cytokine production by human peripheral blood mononuclear cells stimulated with cell-free supernatants of viridans streptococci. Cytokine. 1996;8:300–304.
75. Murr C, Widner B, Gerlach D, et al. Streptococcal erythrogenic toxins induce tryptophan degradation in human peripheral blood mononuclear cells. Int Arch Allergy Immunol. 1997;114:224–228.
76. Murray HW, Gross KC, Masur H, et al. Serious infections caused by *Streptococcus milleri.* Am J Med. 1978;64:759–764.
77. Molina J-M, Leport C, Bure A, et al. Clinical and bacterial features of infections caused by *Streptococcus milleri.* Scand J Infect Dis. 1991;23:659–666.
78. Guthof O. Über pathogene "vergrunen de Streptokokken": Streptokokken-Befunde bei dentogenen Abszessen und Infitraten im Bereich der Mundhöhle. Zentralblatt für Bakteriologie, Parasitenkunde, Infektionskrankheiten. Hygiene. 1956;166:553–564.
79. Wickremesinghe R, Russell C. Viridans streptococci associated with periapical dental abscesses. Infection. 1976;4:196–230.
80. Williams BL, McCann GF, Schoenknecht FD. Bacteriology of dental abscesses of endodontic origin. J Clin Microbiol. 1983;18:770–774.
81. Lewis MAO, MacFarlane TW, McGowan DA. Quantitative bacteriology of acute dentoalveolar abscesses. J Med Microbiol. 1986;21:101–104.
82. Feigenbaum JA, Stein WE. Infections of the cervical disc space after dental extractions. J Neurol Neurosurg Psychiatry. 1974;37:1361–1365.
83. Bancescu G, Lofthus B, Hofstad T, et al. Isolation and characterization of *"Streptococcus milleri"* group stains from oral and maxillofacial infections. Adv Exp Med Biol. 1997;418:165–167.
84. El-Guizaoui AE, Watanakunakorn C. Acute pansinusitis with bacteremia due to a

beta-hemolytic group C streptococcus: *Streptococcus milleri.* South Med J. 1997; 90:1248–1249.
85. Mortimore S, Wormald PJ, Oliver S. Antibiotic choice in acute and complicated sinusitis. J Larygol Otol. 1998:112:264–268.
86. Jones RL, Vioares NS, Chavda SV, et al. Intracranial complications of sinusitis: The need for aggressive management. J Laryngol Otol. 1995;109:1061–1062.
87. Flanagan PG, Mills RG. Fulminant septicemia due to *Streptococcus milleri* infection in a previously healthy adult. Eur J Clin Microbiol Infect Dis. 1994;13:274–278.
88. Duma RJ, Weinberg AN, Medrek TF, et al. Streptococcal infections: A bacteriologic and clinical study of streptococcal infections. Medicine (Baltimore). 1969;48:87–127.
89. Parker MT, Ball LC. Streptococci and aerococci associated with systemic infections in man. J Med Microbiol. 1976;4:196–203.
90. Libertin CR, Hermans PE, Washington JA II. Beta hemolytic group F streptococcal bacteremia: A study and review of the literature. Rev Infect Dis. 1985;7:498–503.
91. Admon D, Ephros MA, Gavish D, et al. Infection with *Streptococcus milleri.* J Infect. 1987;14:55–60.
92. Casariego E, Rodriguez A, Corredoira JC, et al. Prospective study of *Streptococcus milleri* bacteremia. Eur J Clin Microbiol Infect Dis. 1996;15:194–200.
92. Salavert M, Gomez L, Rodgriguez-Carballeira M, et al. Seven-year review of bacteremia caused by *Streptococcus milleri* and other viridans streptococci. Eur J Clin Microbiol Infect Dis. 1996;15:365–371.
94. Sanchez-Porto A, Torres-Tortosa M, Canueto J, et al. Bacteremias due to the *Streptococcus milleri* group: An analysis of 18 episodes. Rev Clin Esp. 1997;197:393–397.
95. Cohen J, Donnelly JP, Worsley AM, et al. Septicemia caused by viridans streptococci in neutropenic patients with leukaemia. Lancet. 1983;2:1452–1454.
96. Awada A, van der Auwera P, Meunier F, et al. Streptococcal and enterococcal bacteremia in patients with cancer. Clin Infect Dis. 1992;15:33–48.
97. Pfaller MA, Jones RN, Marshall SA, et al. Nosocomial streptococcal blood stream infections in the SCOPE Program: Species occurrence and antimicrobial resistance. Diagn Microbiol Infect Dis. 1997;29:259–263.
98. Moomjian AS, Sokal MM, Vijayan S. Pathogenicity of alpha hemolytic streptococci in the neonate. Am J Perinatol. 1984;1:319–321.
99. Hamoudi AC, Hribar MM, Marcon MJ, et al. Clinical relevance of viridans and nonhemolytic streptococci isolated from blood and cerebrospinal fluid in a pediatric population. Am J Clin Pathol. 1990;93:270–272.
100. Weisman SJ, Scoopo FJ, Johnson GM, et al. Septicemia in pediatric oncology patients: The significance of viridans streptococcal infections. J Clin Oncol. 1990;8:453–459.
101. Villablanca JG, Steiner M, Kersey J, et al. The clinical spectrum of infections with viridans streptococci in bone marrow transplant patients. Bone Marrow Transplant. 1990;5:387–393.
102. Elting LS, Bodey GP, Keefe BH. Septicemia and shock syndrome due to viridans streptococci: A case-control study of predisposing factors. Clin Infect Dis. 1992;14:1201–1207.
103. Nagamune H, Ohnishi C, Katsuura A, et al. Intermedilysin: A novel cytotoxin specific for human cells secreted by *Streptococcus intermedius* UNS46. Infect Immun. 1996;64:3093–3100.
104. Barrio J, Castiella A, Lopez P, et al. Spontaneous bacterial peritonitis caused by *Streptococcus milleri* in a cirrhotic patient with selective intestinal decontamination (in Spanish). Gastroenterol Hepatol. 1998;21:27–28.
105. Levandowski RA. *Streptococcus milleri* endocarditis complicated by myocardial abscess. South Med J. 1985;78:892–893.
106. Wallis DE, Venezio FR, Montoya A, et al. *Streptococcus MG-intermedius* endocarditis. South Med J. 1986;79:1313–1314.
107. Hurle A, Nistal JF, Gutierrez JA, et al. Isolated apical intracavitary left ventricular abscess in a normal heart: A rare complication of *Streptococcus milleri* endocarditis. Cardiovasc Surg. 1996;4:61–63.
108. Sussman JI, Baron EJ, Tenenbaum MJ, et al. Viridans streptococcal endocarditis: Clinical, microbiological, and echocardiographic correlations. J Infect Dis. 1986;154:597–603.
109. DeLouvois J, Gortvai P, Hurley R. Bacteriology of abscesses of the central nervous system: A multicentre prospective study. Br Med J. 1977;2:7–11.
110. Chun CK, Johnson JD, Hoffstetter M, et al. Brain abscess: A study of 45 consecutive cases. Medicine (Baltimore). 1986;65:415–431.
111. Mathisen GE, Johnson JP. Brain abscess. Clin Infect Dis. 1997;25:763–781.
112. DeLouvois J, Gortvai P, Hurley R. Affinity of certain streptococci for the central nervous system. J Neurol Neurosurg Psychiatry. 1974;37:1281–1282.
113. DeLouvois J. The bacteriology and chemotherapy of brain abscess. J Antimicrob Chemother. 1978;4:395–413.
114. Koepke JA. Meningitis due to *Streptococcus anginosus* (Lancefield group F). JAMA. 1965;193:739–740.
115. DeLouvois J. Bacteriologic examination of pus from abscess of central nervous systems. J Clin Pathol. 1980;33:66–71.
116. Ghosh K, Duncan R, Kennedy PG. Acute spinal epidural abscess caused by *Streptococcus milleri.* J Infect. 1988;16:303–304.
117. Balsam LB, Shepherd GM, Ruoff KL. *Streptococcus anginosus* spondylodiskitis. Clin Infect Dis. 1997; 24:93–94.
118. Gelfand MS, Bakhtian BJ, Simmons BP. Spinal sepsis due to *Streptococcus milleri:* Two cases and review. Rev Infect Dis. 1991;13:559–563.
119. Lahdou JV, Gilliard C, de Coene BD, et al. *Streptococcus milleri* subacute spinal cord abscess: Apropos of a case. Neurochirurgie. 1996;42:100–104.
120. Faraj A, Krishna M, Mehdian SM. Cauda equina syndrome secondary to lumbar puncture spondylodiscitis caused by *Streptococcus milleri.* Eur Spine J. 1996;5:134–136.
121. Gelfand MS, Hodgkiss T, Simmons BP. Multiple hepatic abscesses caused by *Streptococcus milleri* in association with an intrauterine device. Rev Infect Dis. 1989;11:983–987.
121. Reed TMS, Davidson AI. *Streptococcus milleri* liver abscess. Lancet. 1976;2:648–649.
123. Hatoff D. Perineal Crohn's disease complicated by pyogenic liver abscess during metronidazole therapy. Gastroenterology. 1983;84:194–195.
124. Madden NP, Hart CA. *Streptococcus milleri* in appendicitis in children. J Pediatr Surg. 1985;20:6–7.
125. Tresadern JC, Farrand RJ, Irving MH. *Streptococcus milleri* and surgical sepsis. Ann R Coll Surg Engl. 1983;65:78–79.
126. Onderdonk AB, Cisneros R. Comparison of clindamycin and metronidazole for the treatment of experimental intra-abdominal sepsis produced by *Bacteroides fragilis* and *Streptococcus intermedius.* Curr Ther Res Clin Exp. 1985;38:893–898.
127. Miller SD, Mauff AC, Koornhof HJ. *Streptococcus milleri* causing infection in man. S Afr Med J. 1983;63:684–686.
128. Brook MG, Lucas RE, Pain AK. Clinical features and management of two cases of *Streptococcus milleri* chest infection. Scand J Infect Dis. 1988;20:345–346.
129. Wong CA, Donald F, Macfarlane JT. *Streptococcus milleri* pulmonary disease: A review and clinical description of 25 patients. Thorax. 1995;50:1093–1096.
130. Jerng JS, Hsueh PR, Teng LJ, et al. Empyema thoracis and lung abscesses caused by viridans streptococci. Am J Respir Crit Care Med. 1997;156:1508–1514.
131. Marinella MA, Harrington GD, Standiford TJ. Empyema necessitans due to *Streptococcus milleri.* Clin Infect Dis. 1996;23:203–204.
132. Galea JL, De Souza A, Beggs D, et al. The surgical management of empyema thoraci. J R Coll Surg Edinb. 1997;42:15–18.
133. Shishido H, Watanabe K, Matsumoto K, et al. Primary purulent mediastinitis due to *Streptococcus milleri.* Respiration. 1997;64:313–315.
134. Jackson DS, Welch DF, Pickett DA, et al. Suppurative infections of children caused by non-beta-hemolytic members of the *Streptococcus milleri* group. Pediatr Infect Dis J. 1995;14:80–82.
135. Houston BD, Crouch ME, Finch RG. *Streptococcus MG-intermedius (Streptococcus milleri)* septic arthritis in a patient with rheumatoid arthritis. J Rheumatol. 1980;7:89–92.
136. Müller F, Von Graevenitz A, Ferber T. *Streptococcus milleri* subcutaneous abscesses in drug addicts. Infection. 1987;55:201.
137. Highet AS, Warren RE, Staughton RCD, et al. *Streptococcus milleri* causing treatable infection in perineal hidradenitis suppurativa. Br J Dermatol. 1980;103:375–382.
138. Bourgalt A, Wilson WR, Washington JA. Antimicrobial susceptibilities of species of viridans streptococci. J Infect Dis. 1979;140:316–321.
139. Tillotson GS, Ganguli LA. Antibiotic susceptibilities of clinical strains of *Streptococcus milleri* and related streptococci. J Antimicrob Chemother. 1984;14:557–560.
140. Faber BF, Eliopoulos GM, Ward JI, et al. Multiply resistant viridans streptococci: Susceptibility to β-lactam antibiotics and comparison of penicillin-binding protein patterns. Antimicrob Agents Chemother. 1983;24:702–705.
141. Dorn GV, Ferraro MJ, Brueggemann AB, et al. Emergence of high rates of antimicrobial resistance among viridans group streptococci in the United States. Antimicrob Agents Chemother. 1996;34;891–894.
142. Potgieter E, Carmichael M, Kornhof HJ, et al. In vitro antimicrobial susceptibility of viridans streptococci isolated from blood cultures. Eur J Clin Microbiol Infect Dis. 1992;11:543–546.
143. Bantar C, Fernandez Canigia L, Relloso S, et al. Species belonging to the *"Streptococcus milleri"* group: Antimicrobial susceptibility and comparative prevalence in significant clinical specimens. J Clin Microbiol. 1996;34:2020–2022.
144. Renneberg J, Niemann LL, Gutschik E. Antimicrobial susceptibility of 278 streptococcal blood isolates to seven antimicrobial agents. J Antimicrob Chemother. 1997;39:135–140.
145. Tuohy M, Washington JA. Antimicrobial susceptibility of viridans group streptococci. Diagn Microbiol Infect Dis. 1997;29:277–280.
146. Reichmann P, Konig A, Linares J, et al. A global gene pool for high-level cephalosporin resistance in commensal *Streptococcus* species and *Streptococcus pneumoniae.* J Infect Dis. 1997;176:1001–1012.
147. Pfaller MA, Jones RN. In vitro evaluation of contemporary beta-lactam drugs tested against viridans group and beta-haemolytic streptococci. Diagn Microbiol Infect Dis. 1997;27:151–154.
148. Pfaller MA, Marshall SA, Jones RN. In vitro activity of cefepime and ceftazidime against 197 nosocomial blood stream isolates of streptococci: A multicenter sample. Diagn Microbiol Infect Dis. 1997;29:273–276.
149. Alcaide F, Carratala J, Linares J, et al. In vitro activities of eight macrolide antibiotics and RP-59500 (quinupristin-dalforpristin) against viridans streptococci isolated from blood of neutropenic cancer patients. Antimicrob Agents Chemother. 1996;40:2117–2120.
150. Biedenbach DJ, Jones RN. The comparative antimicrobial activity of levofloxacin tested against 350 clinical isolates of streptococci. Diagn Microbiol Infect Dis. 1996;25:47–51.
151. Pfaller MA, Jones RN. Comparative antistreptococcal activity of two newer fluoroquinolones, levofloxacin and sparfloxacin. Diagn Microbiol Infect Dis. 1997;199–201.
152. Schouten MA, Hoogkamp-Korstanje JA. Comparative in-vitro activities of quinupristin-dalfopristin against gram-positive bloodstream isolates. J Antimicrob Chemother. 1997;40:213–219.

GRAM-POSITIVE BACILLI

Chapter 193

Corynebacterium diphtheriae

ROB ROY MACGREGOR

The name *diphtheria* was coined by Bretonneau from the Greek root for leather, describing the tough pharyngeal membrane that is the hallmark of the disease. The definition of diphtheria as a unique syndrome, the explanation of its pathogenesis, and its subsequent control parallel the development of the fields of pathology, bacteriology, and immunology. During the first half of the 20th century, it was a major worldwide health problem and then yielded to scientifically grounded vigorous public health control measures. Now, since 1990, it has reemerged in epidemic form in the former Soviet Union and other areas in which relaxed immunization practices and social disorganization have allowed its escape from control.

HISTORY

Although clinical descriptions of sore throat, membrane production, and death by suffocation appear in hippocratic writings, epidemics of "throat distemper" are not described until the 16th century.[1] A major epidemic occurred in New England in the early 1700s, killing an estimated 2.5% of the total population and up to one third of all children. Thereafter, similar epidemics were reported at approximately 25-year intervals throughout the 18th and 19th centuries. Diphtheria was not clearly differentiated from other upper respiratory illnesses viewed collectively as "croup" or "distemper" until an epidemic in southern France in 1821, when the clinician-pathologist Pierre Bretonneau first described its unique clinical characteristics.

The first major advance occurred in 1883, when Klebs described chaining cocci and bacilli in microscopic sections of diphtheritic membranes. The following year, working in Koch's laboratory in Berlin, Friedrich Löffler first isolated the diphtheria bacillus in pure culture, aided by a culture medium of his own design that is still used today. He then demonstrated that the organism could reproduce the disease in guinea pigs, thus fulfilling his mentor's postulates for proof that it was the etiologic agent for diphtheria.[2] Using his special culture medium, he demonstrated that healthy individuals could carry the organism asymptomatically in their throats, thus establishing the carrier state as an important phenomenon in the maintenance and spread of the disease. He also noted that the organisms remained in the membrane without invading the tissues of the throat or more distant sites, and theorized that the neurologic and cardiologic manifestations of the disease were caused by a toxic substance elaborated by the organism. In 1888, Roux and Yersin, working at the Pasteur Institute, proved him correct by demonstrating that bacteria-free filtrates of cultures of diphtheria bacilli were able to kill guinea pigs. Two years later, von Behring, also working in Koch's laboratory, demonstrated that antiserum against the toxin was capable of protecting infected animals from death after infection. Then in 1894, after showing that horses were the most efficient animals at producing antitoxin, Roux reported that its administration reduced mortality from diphtheria among foundlings in Paris from 51 to 24%.

In 1913, Schick reported that an individual's local reaction to an injection of toxin into the skin could be used to predict susceptibility to infection (a negative reaction indicated the presence of protective antitoxin antibodies). At the same time, Theobald Smith and von Behring successfully immunized children with a toxin-antitoxin mixture, and in 1923, Ramon, at the Pasteur Institute, found that exposure of toxin to formalin and heat rendered it nontoxic to recipients while retaining the ability to induce an antibody response. The following year, clinical trials showed that injection of this "toxoid" induced a high level of protection among recipients. Problems of antigenic standardization, determining the optimal dosage, the frequency of administration, needs for boosting, and so forth, delayed the widespread use of immunization with toxoid, but between 1930 and 1945 most western countries established programs of childhood immunization. During the 1950s, Freeman, Groman, Barksdale, Pappenheimer, and others demonstrated that toxin production by *Corynebacterium diphtheriae* depended on the presence of a lysogenic β-phage, and during the following decade, the mechanism by which the toxin inhibited protein synthesis was elucidated.[3–5] By the 1980s diphtheria had become a rare occurrence in most countries that had effective immunization programs, but in 1990, a large epidemic of diphtheria began in the former Soviet Union and has extended to eastern Europe and parts of Asia. Analysis of encouraging data from 1997 to 1998 suggests that the reestablishment of vigorous immunization and other public health measures is again controlling this ancient scourge.[6]

PATHOGEN

C. diphtheriae is a nonsporulating, unencapsulated, nonmotile, pleomorphic gram-positive bacillus. Its name is derived from the Greek *korynee*, or "club," referring to its clubbed ends, and *diphthera*, meaning "leather hide," for the characteristic leathery pharyngeal membrane that it provokes. When inoculated on the nutritionally inadequate medium devised by Löffler, consisting of a heat-coagulated mixture of 75% serum and 25% broth, it initially outgrows other throat flora, and so plates should be inspected for growth at 12 to 18 hours. The characteristic metachromatic granules and "Chinese character" palisading morphology that differentiate it from other corynebacteria are displayed more prominently on smears taken from colonies grown on this medium than with direct smears from clinical specimens. Alternatively, selective media containing potassium tellurite inhibit many of the normal throat flora and identify any *C. diphtheriae* present as gray-black colonies containing reduced tellurite. The species is subdivided into three types—gravis, intermedius, and mitis—based on differing colonial morphology on tellurite agar, fermentation reactions, and hemolytic potential. Modern molecular techniques have proved to be more sensitive in more recent outbreaks for tracking different strains: ribotyping—the use of restriction endonucleases to detect polymorphisms of ribosomal RNA genes, pulsed-field gel electrophoresis analysis of genomic DNA, and multilocus enzyme electrophoresis of organism sonicates have shown that an epidemic clone of *C. diphtheriae* emerged in Russia in 1990 and became increasingly common as the epidemic progressed.[7, 8] An international ribotype database has been established at the Pasteur Institute (Prof. P. Grimont) as a project of the WHO International Working Group on Diphtheria. Approximately 45 distinct strains have been identified to date.

Exotoxin production by *C. diphtheriae* depends on the presence of a lysogenic β-phage, which carries the gene encoding for toxin (tox +).[3, 5] In its lysogenic phase, the phage's circular DNA integrates into the host bacterium's genetic material as a prophage, with the result that the host cell now can express the gene necessary for the synthesis of the polypeptide toxin. When induced by stimuli such as ultraviolet light, the phage enters a lytic cycle, destroying the host cell and releasing new β-phage. Strains of *C. diphtheriae* lacking lysogenic phage do not produce toxin, but they can be converted to toxigenicity in the laboratory by infection with the lysogenic tox + phage (*lysogenization*). Evidence has been found that such conversion also occurs in nature.[9] Even though the frequency of carriage of tox + lysogenic *C. diphtheriae* currently is very low in the West, there is an ongoing risk that resident nontoxigenic strains could become lysogenized by the introduction of a β-phage–bearing strain from another part of the world. In addition to the tox+ gene, significant toxin production requires that bacterial growth be slowed by the exhaustion of iron in the environment. Traditionally, toxigenicity of individual *C. diphtheriae* strains has been demonstrated in vivo by lethality in guinea pigs and in vitro by the development of an immunoprecipitin band on antitoxin-impregnated filter paper that has been laid over an agar culture of the organism in question (Elek's test). Polymerase chain reaction probing of suspect organisms for DNA sequences coding for the toxin's A subunit has proved to be sensitive and accurate in rapid identification of tox+ strains.[10]

EPIDEMIOLOGY

Humans are the only known reservoir for *C. diphtheriae*. The primary modes of spread are via airborne respiratory droplets and direct contact with either respiratory secretions or exudate from infected skin lesions. Fomites can play a role in transmission, and epidemics have been caused by contaminated milk. Most respiratory tract disease occurs in the colder months in temperate climates, associated with crowded indoor living conditions and hot, dry air. Asymptomatic respiratory carriage is important in perpetuating both endemic and epidemic diphtheria, and immunization reduces an individual's likelihood of being a carrier. Current reservoirs for disease are obscure. In endemic conditions, 3 to 5% of healthy individuals may harbor the organism in their throats,[11] but in the West, where the disease has become very uncommon, isolation of the organism from healthy individuals has become extremely rare. Skin infection, once thought to be primarily a problem in tropical environments, has caused several epidemics in Europe and North America among alcoholic and other disadvantaged groups.[12, 13] Thus, skin carriage of *C. diphtheriae* can act as a silent reservoir for the organism, and it has been found that person-to-person spread from infected skin sites is more efficient than spread from the respiratory tract.[14, 15]

The incidence and pattern of diphtheria in the western world has changed dramatically in the last 50 to 75 years. From 1921 to 1924, it was the leading cause of death among Canadian children aged 2 to 14 years. Since then, the incidence has decreased steadily (Fig. 193–1) so that now diphtheria is a rare event. For example, 147,991 cases were reported in the United States in 1920 (151 cases/100,000 population), and 5 or fewer since 1980 (<0.002/100,000).[16] From the 1960s to 1990, similar decreases occurred in Europe[17, 18] and, less dramatically, worldwide, although the disease remained endemic in many parts of the Third World (e.g., Brazil, Nigeria, eastern Mediterranean region, the Indian subcontinent, Indonesia, and the Philippines).[19] Moreover, pockets of skin and pharyngeal colonization and disease continue to be identified among Native American groups, destitute inner-city dwellers, substance abusers, and homosexual men, giving rise to concern that outbreaks could occur, particularly among adults in the West, where the proportion of adults with protective antibody levels is as low as 50%.[20]

Beginning in 1990, epidemic diphtheria began in Russia (Fig. 193–2) and swiftly spread to all countries of the newly independent states.[6, 21] In 1995, 50,412 cases were reported in the newly independent states, for a yearly rate of 16.9/100,000. The World Health Organization and the United Nations Children's Fund formulated a strategic plan to control the epidemic, including (1) mass immunization with at least one dose of toxoid to the whole population, (2) early detection and proper management of cases, and (3) early identification and proper management of close contacts. In response, new cases in the Russian Federation fell from 35,652 in 1995 to 13,604 in 1996, and to 4057 in 1997 (2.7/100,000). A defining characteristic of the epidemic has been that half or more of cases have occurred among those 15 years of age or older, suggesting that young people remained relatively well protected by the high rates of infant immunization operative in the 1980s but that older people were vulnerable either because they had not been vaccinated as children or because their protective antibody levels had faded in the absence of subsequent boosting by vaccine or colonization.[20, 22]

When it was common in the West, diphtheria primarily affected children younger than 15 years, but more recent outbreaks have also included unimmunized or poorly immunized adults, particularly urban and rural poor persons. Reports have cited pharyngeal carriage of nontoxigenic strains in homosexual men[23] and invasive disease in

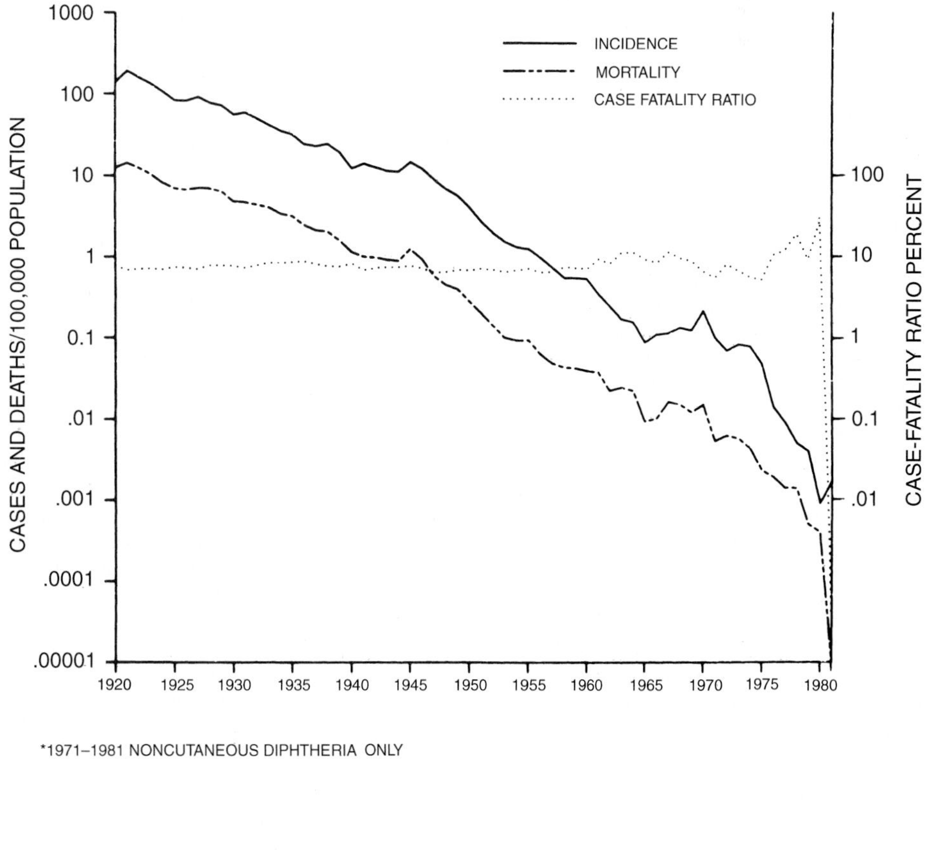

FIGURE 193–1. Annual incidence and mortality rates and case-fatality ratios of diphtheria in the United States, 1920–1981.

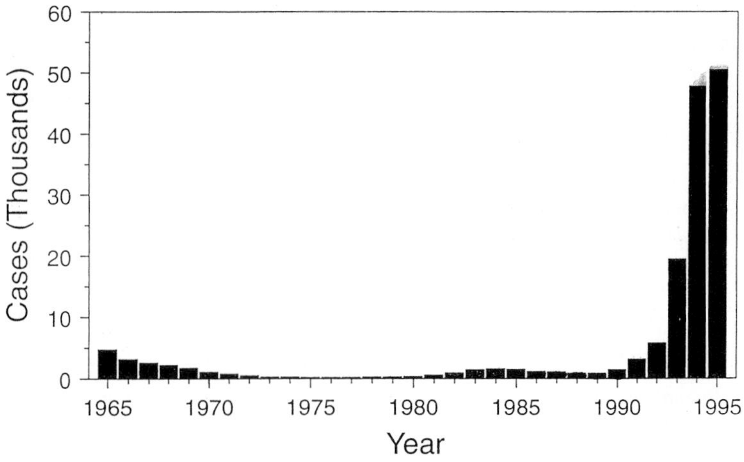

FIGURE 193–2. Number of reported cases of diphtheria in new independent states of the former Soviet Union, 1965–1995. (From Update: Diphtheria epidemic—New Independent States of the former Soviet Union, January 1995–March 1996. MMWR Morb Mortal Wkly Rep. 1996;45:693–697.)

those who use intravenous drugs.[24] Minority racial groups have had attack rates 5 to 20 times higher than those in whites. Cases in the United States have been distributed primarily in the southern and Pacific northwestern states, but sporadic cases have been reported throughout the country.[16, 25] Although immunized individuals can still develop clinical diphtheria, prior immunization reduces the frequency and severity of disease: between 1959 and 1970 in the United States, two thirds of reported cases had received no immunization, 13% had had one to two doses of toxoid, and only 19% reported receiving three or more doses and could be considered fully immunized.[25] Among cases reported since 1980, none were fully immunized.[16] Disease was considered severe in 25% of unimmunized patients but in only 6.3% of those fully immunized. Nineteen percent of unimmunized patients died, compared with 1.3% of those fully immunized; even partial immunization reduced morbidity and mortality by more than 50%. The benefit of prior immunization has also been demonstrated in the Russian epidemic in the 1990s.[26]

The full explanation for the dramatic decrease in diphtheria's incidence in immunized populations is not evident. Immunization with toxoid is generally thought to attenuate only the local and systemic effects of toxin without preventing local colonization with the organism. If so, carriage would be expected to remain high in the population, and epidemics should be an ongoing occurrence among the sizable proportion believed to be inadequately immunized. However, the disease has become rare, and evidence points to an extremely low incidence of the carrier state, despite serologic studies showing what are considered to be subprotective levels of serum antitoxin in 25% of children and 75% of adults tested in three cities in the United States.[27] In 1985, the U.S. preschool immunization rate was only 64.9% for diphtheria-pertussis-tetanus (DPT).[28] Several factors may contribute to our current good fortune: first, although unproved, historical evidence suggests that diphtheria has occurred in cycles that include gaps of 100 years or more.[1] Second, organisms isolated from immunized individuals are less likely to be toxigenic than are those from unimmunized carriers (64 versus 94%).[27] If toxin production confers no advantage to the organism in an immunized host, its metabolic cost would put toxigenic organisms at a selective disadvantage, and so loss of this attribute might be predicted.[4] Third, some experts believe that the local elaboration of toxin, in the absence of antibody, enhances an organism's ability to colonize. Immunization with toxoid could counteract this selective advantage of toxigenic strains. Fourth, some virulence factor or factors other than toxin production may exist. For example, in an outbreak in Sweden, investigators used genetic probes to demonstrate that all clinical cases were caused by a single strain, although several different toxigenic strains were present in the population.[29] To explain the absence of diphtheria in the West and the occurrence of the epidemic in the newly independent states of the former Soviet Union, the following model has been proposed[20–22]: the absence of an effective immunization program allows for high carriage rates of toxigenic strains, and this leads to high rates of infant disease; survivors in such populations are continually immunized by adult colonization with toxigenic strains, which explains low adult disease rates. According to this hypothesis, pediatric immunization programs reduce carriage rates of toxigenic strains because toxin production no longer provides an advantage to the organism, and even nontoxigenic strain carriage falls. As a result, adults lose the opportunity for natural antibody boosting from asymptomatic carriage, and so protective antibody levels wane in the adult population immunized only in childhood. Fortunately, good pediatric immunization programs appear to be sufficient to keep toxigenic strains from circulating and causing adult disease. Ultimately, if pediatric programs lapse, the population then contains *both* vulnerable children and vulnerable adults, a situation promotive of epidemics. Thus, the public health strategy must be to maintain pediatric programs with greater than 90% immunization rates, and to strongly promote periodic adult boosters.

PATHOGENESIS

C. diphtheriae is not a very invasive organism, ordinarily remaining in the superficial layers of the respiratory mucosa and skin lesions, where it can induce a mild inflammatory reaction in the local tissue. The major virulence of *C. diphtheriae* results from the action of its potent exotoxin, which inhibits protein synthesis in mammalian cells but not in bacteria. The 62,000-dalton polypeptide toxin comprises two segments: B, which binds to specific receptors on susceptible cells, and A, the active segment. After proteolytic cleavage of the bound molecule, segment A enters the cell, where it catalyzes inactivation of the transfer RNA translocase, *elongation factor 2,* present in eukaryotic cells but not in bacteria. Loss of this enzyme prevents the interaction of messenger RNA and transfer RNA, stopping further addition of amino acids to developing polypeptide chains (Fig. 193–3).[30] The toxin affects all cells in the body, but the most prominent effects are on the heart (myocarditis), nerves (demyelination), and kidneys (tubular necrosis). Diphtheria toxin is extremely potent: a single molecule can stop protein synthesis in a cell within several hours, and 0.1 μg/kg will kill susceptible animals.

Within the first few days of respiratory tract infection, toxin elaborated locally induces a dense necrotic coagulum composed of fibrin, leukocytes, erythrocytes, dead respiratory epithelial cells, and organisms (Fig. 193–4). Removal of this adherent gray-brown *pseudomembrane* reveals a bleeding edematous submucosa. The membrane can be local (tonsillar, pharyngeal, nasal), or extend widely, forming a cast of the pharynx and tracheobronchial tree. The underlying soft tissue edema and cervical adenitis can be intense, and, particularly in the proportionally smaller airways of children, can

FIGURE 193–3. Action of diphtheria toxin. The toxin-binding (B) portion attaches to the cell membrane, allowing the active (A) portion to dissociate and enter the cell. In the cell, active toxin catalyzes a reaction that ADP-ribosylates and thus inactivates elongation factor 2 (EF2). This factor is essential for ribosomal reactions at the acceptor and donor sites, which transfer triplet code from messenger RNA (mRNA) to amino acid sequences via transfer RNA (tRNA). Inactivation of EF2 stops building of the polypeptide chain.

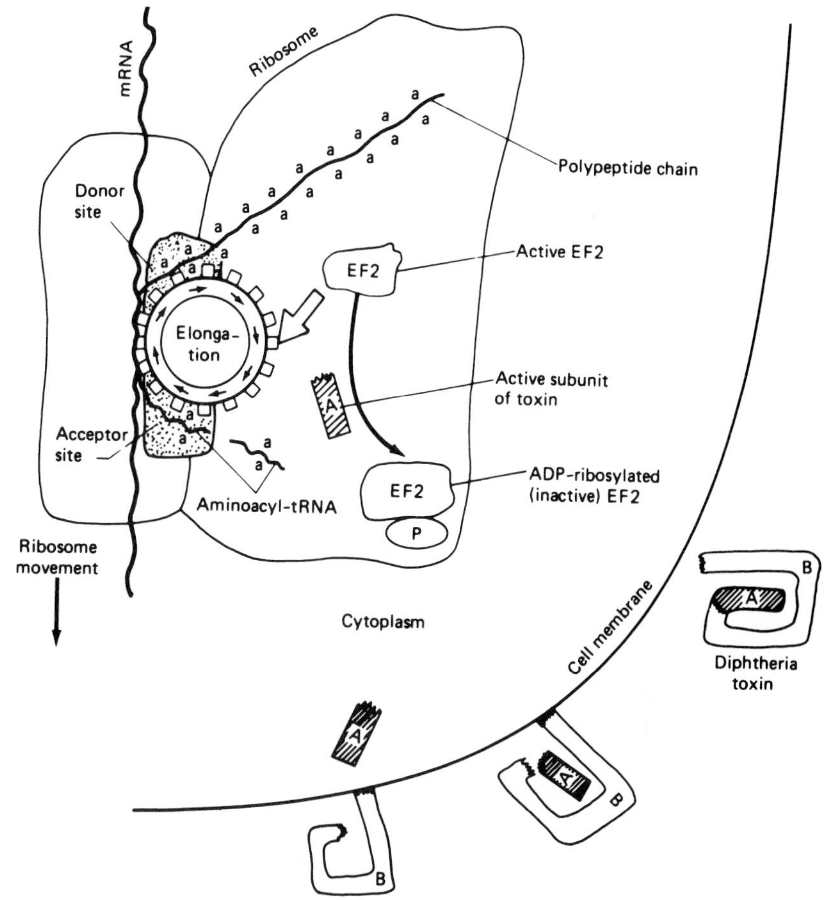

FIGURE 193–4. Diphtheria involving a pharyngeal tonsil. The membrane-tissue junction is clearly marked by intense cellular infiltration. (From Moore RA. A Textbook of Pathology. Philadelphia: WB Saunders. 1944.)

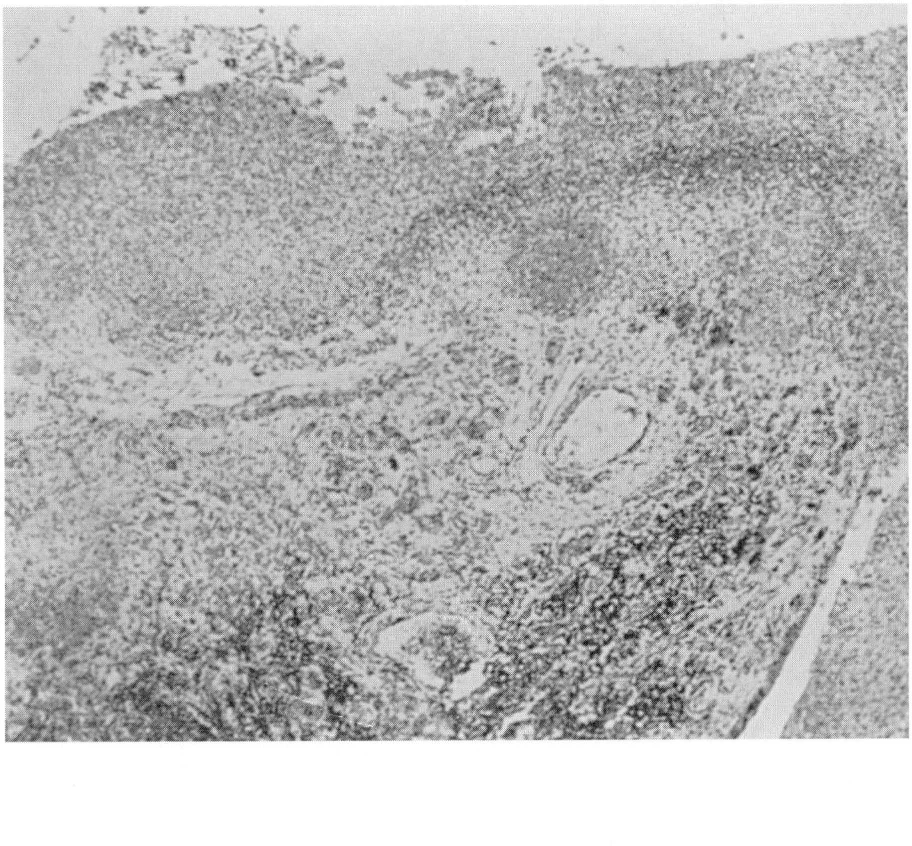

cause respiratory embarrassment and a "bull neck" appearance. In both adults and children, a common cause of death is suffocation after aspiration of the membrane.

CLINICAL MANIFESTATIONS

Symptoms of infection with *C. diphtheriae* occur locally in the respiratory tract and skin secondary to superficial infection of these two organs, and at distant sites secondary to absorption and dissemination of diphtheria toxin. Occasionally, *C. diphtheriae* disseminates from the skin or respiratory tract and causes systemic infections including bacteremia, endocarditis, and arthritis.

Respiratory Tract Diphtheria

Asymptomatic upper respiratory tract carriage of the organism occurs commonly in areas where diphtheria is endemic and is an important reservoir for the maintenance and spread of the organism in a population. However, in the industrial western world, throat colonization has become exceedingly rare except in individuals associated with pockets of infection such as the inner-city (homeless people) and rural poverty areas.

After an incubation period averaging 2 to 4 days, local signs and symptoms of inflammation can develop at various sites within the respiratory tract.

Anterior Nasal

Infection limited to the anterior nares presents with a serosanguineous or seropurulent nasal discharge often associated with a subtle whitish mucosal membrane, particularly on the septum. The discharge can excite an erosive reaction on the external nares and upper lip, but symptoms generally are quite mild, and signs indicating toxin effects are rare.

Faucial

Including the posterior structures of the mouth and the proximal pharynx, this area is the most common site for clinical diphtheria. The onset is usually abrupt, with low-grade fever (rarely >103°F), malaise, sore throat, mild pharyngeal injection, and the development of a membrane typically on one or both tonsils, with extension variously to involve the tonsillar pillars, uvula, soft palate, oropharynx, and nasopharynx (Fig. 193–5). The membrane initially appears white and glossy but evolves into having a dirty-gray color, with patches of green or black necrosis. The extent of the membrane correlates with the severity of symptoms: localized tonsillar disease is often mild, but involvement of the posterior pharynx, soft palate, and periglottic areas is associated with profound malaise, weakness, prostration, cervical adenopathy, and swelling. The latter can distort the normal contour of the submental and cervical area, creating a bull neck appearance and causing respiratory stridor.

Laryngeal and Tracheobronchial

Pharyngeal infection may spread downward into the larynx, or occasionally the disease may begin there. Symptoms then include hoarseness, dyspnea, respiratory stridor, and a brassy cough. Edema and a membrane involving the trachea and bronchi can embarrass respiration further, and a child so afflicted appears anxious and cyanotic, uses accessory muscles of respiration, and demonstrates inspiratory retractions of intercostal, supraclavicular, and substernal tissues. If this state is not relieved promptly by intubation and mechanical removal of membrane, patients become exhausted and die.

Systemic complications are due to diphtheria toxin, which, although toxic to all tissues, has its most striking effects on the heart and nervous system.

Cardiac Toxicity

Subtle evidence of myocarditis can be detected in as many as two thirds of patients, but 10 to 25% develop clinical cardiac dysfunction, with the risk to an individual patient correlating directly with the extent and severity of local disease.[31, 32] Characteristically, the first evidence of cardiac toxicity occurs after 1 to 2 weeks of illness, often when the local oropharyngeal disease is improving. Changes in the electrocardiographic pattern, particularly ST-T wave changes and first-degree heart block, can progress to more severe forms of block, atrioventricular dissociation, and other arrhythmias, which carry an ominous prognosis. Clinically, myocarditis can present acutely with congestive failure and circulatory collapse, or more insidiously with progressive dyspnea, weakness, diminished heart sounds, cardiac dilatation, and gallop rhythm. Because patients without clinical evidence of myocarditis may have significant electric changes, it is important to monitor their cardiograms routinely. Elevations of serum aspartate transaminase concentrations closely parallel the intensity of myocarditis, and so may be used to monitor its course. From a prognostic standpoint, patients with electrocardiographic changes of myocarditis have a mortality rate three to four times higher than those with normal tracings. In particular, atrioventricular and left bundle branch blocks carry a mortality rate of 60 to 90%. Patients with a prolonged PR interval and minor T-wave changes generally do well, and these abnormalities ordinarily resolve with time. Patients with bundle-branch blocks and complete atrioventricular dissociation have a much higher incidence of death, and survivors may be left with permanent conduction defects.[33]

Neurologic Toxicity

This complication is also proportional to the severity of the primary infection: mild disease only occasionally produces neurotoxicity, but up to three fourths of patients with severe disease can develop neuropathy. Within the first few days of disease, local paralysis of the soft palate and posterior pharyngeal wall occurs commonly, manifested by regurgitation of swallowed fluids through the nose. Thereafter, cranial neuropathies causing oculomotor and ciliary paralysis are also common, and dysfunction of facial, pharyngeal, or laryngeal nerves, although rare, can contribute to the risk of aspiration. Peripheral neuritis develops later, from 10 days to 3 months after the onset of disease in the throat.[34] Principally a motor defect, it begins with proximal muscle groups in the extremities and extends distally, particularly affecting the dorsiflexors of the feet. Dysfunction varies from mild weakness with diminished tendon reflexes to total paralysis. Occasionally motor nerves of the trunk, neck, and upper extremity are involved, as are sensory nerves, resulting in a glove-and-stocking neuropathy. Microscopic examination of affected nerves shows degeneration of myelin sheaths and axon cylinders. Although slow, total resolution of all diphtheritic nerve damage is the rule.

Several excellent clinical descriptions of endemic and epidemic diphtheria in the United States indicate that both the frequency of various symptoms and the severity of disease are inversely proportional to the patient's immunization history.[34–38] Roughly one half of these reported cases were categorized as mild, often without a membrane. Mortality rates vary from 3.5 to 12% and have not changed in the last 50 years. Rates are highest in very young and very old patients. Most deaths occur in the first 3 to 4 days, from asphyxia or myocarditis; a fatal outcome is rare in a fully immunized individual. Sore throat (85 to 90%), fever (50 to 85%), and dysphagia (26 to 40%) are the most common symptoms, and membranes and cervical adenopathy are seen in approximately one half of the patients. The experience in Russia in the 1990s has been similar.[26] The frequency

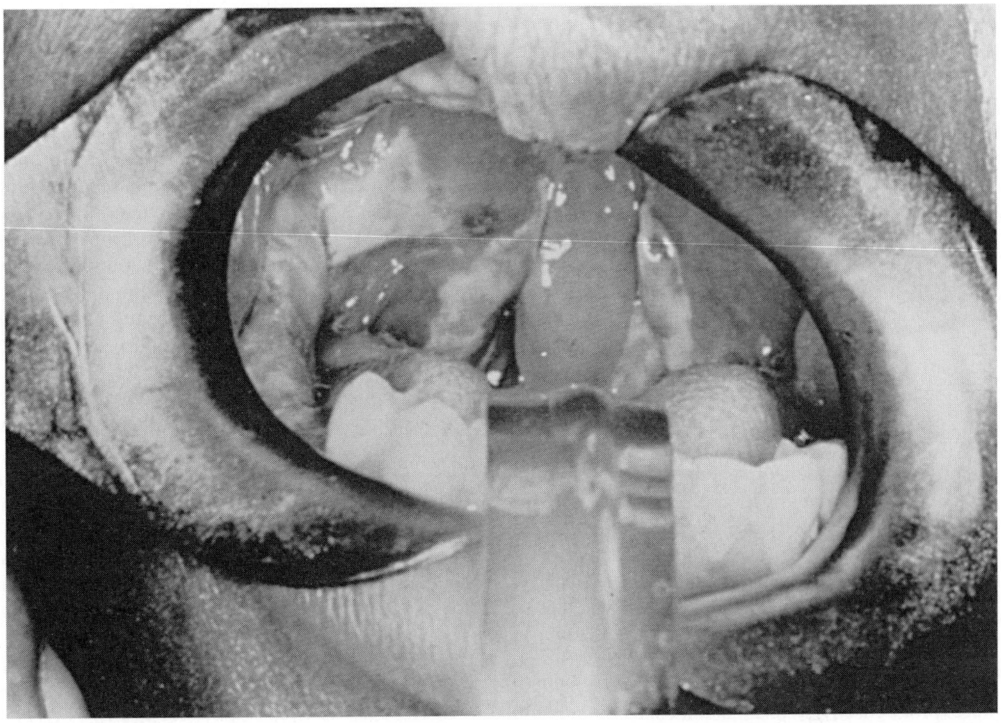

FIGURE 193–5. Pharynx of a 39-year-old woman with bacteriologically confirmed diphtheria. The photograph was taken 4 days after the onset of fever, malaise, and sore throat. Hemorrhage due to removal of the membrane by swabbing appears as a dark area on the left.

of complications such as myocarditis and neuritis is directly related to the time between the onset of symptoms and the administration of antitoxin, and to the extent of membrane formation.

Cutaneous Diphtheria

It has long been recognized that, particularly in the tropics, *C. diphtheriae* can cause clinical skin infections characterized by chronic nonhealing ulcers with a dirty-gray membrane and often associated with *Staphylococcus aureus* and group A streptococci. More recently, the significance of this infection in the United States has been emphasized by several outbreaks among alcoholic homeless men and impoverished groups such as Native Americans.[13–15] The presentation is indolent and nonprogressive and is only rarely associated with signs of intoxication. Nonetheless, these infections can induce high antitoxin levels and thus appear to act as natural immunizing events.[39, 40] They also serve as a reservoir for the organism under conditions of both endemic and epidemic respiratory tract diphtheria: cutaneous sites of *C. diphtheriae* have been shown both to contaminate the inanimate environment and to induce throat infections more efficiently than does pharyngeal colonization, and bacterial shedding from cutaneous infections continues longer than from the respiratory tract.[14, 15, 41] Despite these facts, the clinical significance of isolating the organism from an individual skin lesion is often unclear. Most lesions from which *C. diphtheriae* is isolated are indistinguishable from other chronic dermatologic conditions (eczema, psoriasis, and so forth), and only about 15% fit the classic description of diphtheritic ulcers given previously.[42] Moreover, because *C. diphtheriae* is usually isolated in association with other known skin pathogens, and because the ulcers do not respond to antitoxin therapy, there is debate as to whether or not the isolates are actually causing clinical disease. By 1975, cutaneous diphtheria accounted for 56% of total *C. diphtheriae* isolates reported in the United States, and in 1980, the U.S. Centers for Disease Control and Prevention, in an effort to focus attention on respiratory tract diphtheria, removed nontoxigenic skin isolates from its list of reportable diseases.

Invasive Disease

Endocarditis, mycotic aneurysms, osteomyelitis, and septic arthritis have been described in clusters of drug addicted or alcoholic persons, Australian aborigines, and young adults,[43–46] all caused by nontoxigenic *C. diphtheriae*. Ribotyping has indicated that these outbreaks have been caused by unique epidemic strains, and both skin and throat colonization have been implicated as portals of entry. These illnesses have been characterized by an aggressive course, a high proportion of endocarditis, arterial embolization, metastatic sites of infection (joints, spleen, central nervous system), and high mortality. Why these nontoxigenic strains are so virulent remains a mystery. Coincident with these outbreaks of invasive disease, examples of non–toxin-producing strains causing clinical pharyngitis[47, 48] and even fatal respiratory tract diphtheria[49] have been published since 1990.

Other Sites

On rare occasions, clinical infection with *C. diphtheriae* can be seen in other sites such as the ear, conjunctiva, or vagina.

DIAGNOSIS

The clinical outcome in diphtheria is improved by the prompt initiation of treatment. Therefore, physicians must act on a presumptive diagnosis, based on several clinical clues: (1) mildly painful tonsillitis or pharyngitis, or both, with an associated membrane, especially if the membrane extends to the uvula and soft palate; (2) adenopathy and cervical swelling, especially if associated with membranous pharyngitis and signs of systemic toxicity; (3) hoarseness and stridor; (4) palatal paralysis; (5) serosanguineous nasal discharge with an associated mucosal membrane; and (6) temperature elevation rarely in excess of 103°F. Moderate elevation of white blood cell count and transient proteinuria are common, but nonspecific. In former times when the disease was common, skilled practitioners could often make the diagnosis on examination of methylene blue–stained smears of the membrane or of throat swabs. Currently, rapid diagnosis is sometimes possible with immunofluorescent staining of 4-hour cultures, but definitive identification of *C. diphtheriae* is made on the basis of the colonial morphology, microscopic appearance, and fermentation reactions of isolates from bits of membrane or submembrane swabs cultured on Löffler's or tellurite selective media such as Tindale's agar. Although Tindale's medium has a short shelf life and individual batches may vary in their ability to grow *C. diphtheriae*, it has an advantage in that a black colony with a surrounding gray-brown halo is quite suggestive of the diagnosis. *C. diphtheriae* characteristically shows metachromatic granules when stained with Löffler's stain, but these are best shown when organisms are grown in Löffler's rather than Tindale's medium. The combination of "Chinese characters" as seen on Gram stain, distinctive colonies with halos on Tindale's medium, and the presence of metachromatic granules allows a presumptive identification of *C. diphtheriae*. Final identification requires biochemical tests. Toxin production is normally demonstrated by Elek plate precipitin strips or, in qualified labs, by polymerase chain reaction testing for the toxin A subunit gene.[10] Because routine methods of throat culture do not promote the isolation and identification of *C. diphtheriae*, the laboratory must be alerted to use selective media when the disease is suspected.

The differential diagnosis includes faucial mononucleosis, streptococcal or viral pharyngitis and tonsillitis, Vincent's angina, and acute epiglottitis. The membrane of mononucleosis characteristically remains on the tonsils, rarely loses its creamy-white appearance, and does not cause bleeding when removed. Streptococcal infection usually produces a more intense local pharyngitis, higher fever, and more pronounced dysphagia. Vincent's angina often involves the gums, and Gram stain of the exudate from the necrotic ulcerative pharyngeal lesions shows characteristic fusobacteria and spirochetes. Bacterial epiglottitis from *Haemophilus influenzae* infection often develops more acutely, and indirect laryngoscopy shows a bright red epiglottis without an associated membrane.

TREATMENT

Diphtheria antitoxin, hyperimmune antiserum produced in horses, has been the cornerstone of therapy for diphtheria since it was first shown to reduce mortality from 7 to 2.5% in a controlled trial published in 1898. The antibodies only neutralize toxin before its entry into cells, and so it is critical that diphtheria antitoxin be administered as soon as a presumptive diagnosis has been made. The degree of protection is inversely related to the duration of clinical illness preceding its administration.[35] Although the minimal therapeutic dose has never been determined, traditional (empirical) dosage recommendations assume that the duration of disease and extent of membrane formation roughly indicate the patient's toxin burden. The Committee on Infectious Diseases of the American Academy of Pediatrics recommends 20,000 to 40,000 units of antitoxin for pharyngeal or laryngeal disease of 48 hours' duration; 40,000 to 60,000 units for nasopharyngeal lesions; and 80,000 to 120,000 units for extensive disease of 3 or more days' duration and for anyone with brawny swelling of the neck.[50] It recommends administration by intravenous infusion over 60 minutes to inactivate toxin as rapidly as possible, but other experts suggest intramuscular injection of antitoxin for moderate disease, and combined intramuscular-intravenous administration for severe disease. Repeated injections are of no additional benefit. Because up to 10% of individuals may show some hypersensitivity to horse protein, even very sick patients must be questioned first concerning known allergies and tested with a 1:100 dilution of diphtheria antitoxin applied to the volar aspect of the forearm by scratch or prick. If negative, this is followed with an intracutaneous injection of 0.02 ml of a 1:1000 dilution of antitoxin in saline, with epinephrine available for immediate administration. If an immediate reaction occurs, the patient should be desensitized with progressively higher doses of antiserum. The incidence of serum sickness of approximately 10% is acceptable in light of the pronounced reduction in mortality effected by antitoxin administration. Diphtheria antitoxin is no longer licensed in the United States, but a European-licensed product is available from the National Immunization Program of the Centers for Disease Control and Prevention by calling 404-639-8200.

Antibiotic therapy, by killing the organism, has three benefits: (1) the termination of toxin production; (2) amelioration of the local infection; and (3) prevention of spread of the organism to uninfected contacts. Although several antibiotics, including penicillin, erythromycin, clindamycin, rifampin, and tetracycline, are effective, only penicillin and erythromycin are generally recommended. Intramuscular administration of procaine penicillin G, 25,000 to 50,000 units/kg per day (maximum 1.2 million units), divided into 12-hour intervals is recommended until the patient is able to swallow comfortably, when oral penicillin V (125 to 250 mg qid) or erythromycin estolate or succinate (125 to 500 mg qid) may be substituted for a recommended total treatment period of 14 days. Both drugs are equally effective in resolving the fever and local symptoms, and in the time to the disappearance of the membrane. Because erythromycin is marginally superior to penicillin in eradicating the carrier state, some authorities prefer it for initial treatment, despite a significant incidence of thrombophlebitis when it is given intravenously, and of gastrointestinal symptoms when given orally. Patients should be maintained in strict isolation throughout therapy and, after therapy, should have two consecutive negative cultures at 24-hour intervals to document eradication of the organism.[50] The carrier state has a slow rate of spontaneous resolution (12% after 1 month in one study)[51] and so should be treated to prevent the spread of infection. Erythromycin orally for 7 days is the treatment of choice because of several reports demonstrating its greater efficacy in comparison with penicillin.[37, 38] However, the issue is clouded by a report showing that 21% of cultures taken 2 weeks after the completion of erythromycin treatment were again positive for *C. diphtheriae*.[52] Therefore, it is necessary to obtain cultures at least 2 weeks after the completion of therapy to ensure the eradication of the organism. A single intramuscular dose of benzathine penicillin G (600,000 to 1,200,000 units) is prudent when compliance with oral therapy is uncertain.

Supportive care is also important. Bed rest is recommended during the acute phase of illness, but proof of its benefit once the patient feels able to ambulate is lacking. Early in the disease, respiratory and cardiac complications are the biggest threats: airway obstruction can result from aspiration of dislodged pharyngeal membrane, its direct extension into the larynx, or external compression by enlarged nodes and edema. For this reason, many experts recommend tracheostomy or intubation as an early measure, particularly when the larynx is involved, thereby providing access for mechanical removal of tracheobronchial membranes and avoiding the risk of sudden asphyxia. Vigilance must be maintained to detect the development of primary or secondary bacterial pneumonia. Cardiac complications can be minimized by close electrocardiographic monitoring and the prompt initiation of electric pacing for conduction disturbances, drugs for arrhythmias, or digitalis for heart failure. Physical therapy should preserve a range of motion in paretic extremities while awaiting the return of neurologic function. A study has shown that the treatment of acute diphtheria with prednisone did not reduce the incidence of carditis or neuritis.[53]

The treatment of systemic infection such as endocarditis and arthritis has not been studied systematically, but most reports describe the administration of intravenous penicillin or ampicillin, usually with an aminoglycoside, for 4 to 6 weeks.[46] Mortality rates of 30 to 40% occur with bacteremic disease, and valve replacement is often necessary in cases of endocarditis.[43, 44]

PREVENTION

The major manifestations of diphtheria can be prevented in individual patients by immunization with formalin-inactivated toxin. Therefore, documentation of inadequate levels of antitoxin in a large proportion of the adult population in North America and western Europe has caused great concern that a toxigenic strain introduced into these populations could cause an outbreak of disease similar to that in the former Soviet Union. Serum antitoxin levels can be measured by toxin neutralization tests in rabbit skin, in Vero cell cultures, or by hemagglutination, with roughly equivalent results. Concentrations of 0.1 to 0.01 international units (IU) generally are thought to confer protection. For example, data from one outbreak showed that 90% of clinical cases had antitoxin levels below 0.01 IU/ml, whereas 92% of asymptomatic carriers had titers above 0.1 IU/ml.[54] After immunization, antitoxin levels decline slowly over time so that as many as 50% of individuals older than 60 years have serum titers below 0.01 IU/ml.[20, 55, 56] For this reason, booster doses of toxoid should be administered at 10-year intervals, to maintain antitoxin levels in the protective range.

Recommendations from the Immunization Practices Advisory Committee, published by the Centers for Disease Control and Prevention in 1991,[57] remain current except for the substitution of acellular pertussis vaccine (aP) in DTP (see Chapter 312):

1. For children from 6 weeks to 7 years of age: three intramuscular injections of (DTaP) vaccine should be given at 4- to 8-week intervals, beginning at 6 to 8 weeks of age, followed by a fourth dose 6 to 12 months after the third.

2. For persons 7 years or older: toxoid-adult (Td) vaccine is given twice at a 4- to 8-week interval, with a third dose 6 to 12 months later. Because the risk of pertussis is much less in persons older than 6 years, that component of the vaccine is omitted. Moreover, because persons older than 7 years have a higher incidence of local and systemic reactions to the concentration of diphtheria toxoid in pediatric DPT vaccine (7 to 25 limit flocculation [Lf] units) and because a lower dose of toxoid has been shown to induce protective levels of antitoxin,[58] the Td formulation of vaccine contains a maximal concentration of 2 Lf units of diphtheria toxoid. If the recommended sequence of primary immunizations is interrupted, normal levels of immunity can be achieved simply by administering the remaining doses without a need to restart the series.

3. Booster immunizations: children who have completed their primary immunization before the age of 4 years should receive a booster dose of DPT at the time of school entry. Persons older than 7 years should receive booster immunization with Td at 10-year intervals. As a memory aid, this should be done at decade or mid-decade intervals (e.g., ages 15, 25, 35, or 20, 30, 40). Careful attention to this adult booster strategy is important to ensure population protection in areas with excellent childhood immunization programs. Travelers to areas where diphtheria is still endemic should be particularly careful to be sure their immunization is current. Although the recommended booster dose of 1.5 to 2.0 Lf units increases antitoxin levels to above 0.01 IU in 90 to 100% of previously immunized individuals,[59, 60] some authorities have recommended using 5 Lf units, because antitoxin levels remain above 0.01 IU/ml for a longer period than with 2 Lf units.[59]

Patients should receive toxoid immunization in the convalescent stage of their disease because clinical infection does not always induce adequate levels of antitoxin. Close contacts whose immunization status is incomplete or unclear should promptly receive a dose of toxoid appropriate for their age and complete the proper series of immunizations. In addition, they should receive prophylactic treatment with erythromycin or penicillin, pending the results of pretreatment cultures. Given these preventive measures, the prophylactic use of antitoxin in contacts is considered unwarranted.

REFERENCES

1. English PC. Diphtheria and theories of infectious disease: Centennial appreciation of the critical role of diphtheria in the history of medicine. Pediatrics. 1985;76:1–9.
2. Loeffler F. Untersuchugen über die Bedeutung der Mikroorganismen für die Entstehung der Diphtherie. Mitt Kaiserlichen Gesundheitsamt. 1884;2:421–499.
3. Groman NB. Conversion by corynephages and its role in the natural history of diphtheria. J Hyg (Lond). 1984;93:405–417.
4. Pappenheimer AM. Diphtheria studies on the biology of an infectious disease. Harvey Lect. 1982;76:45–73.
5. Freeman VJ. Studies on the virulence of bacteriophage-infected strains of *Corynebacterium diphtheriae*. J Bacteriol. 1951;61:675–688.
6. Update: Diphtheria epidemic—New Independent States of the former Soviet Union, January 1995–March 1996. MMWR Morb Mortal Wkly Rep. 1996;45:693–697.
7. DeZoysa A, Efstratiou A, George RC, et al: Molecular epidemiology of *C. diphtheriae* from Northwestern Russia and surrounding countries studied by using ribotyping and pulsed-field gel electrophoresis. J Clin Microbiol. 1995;33:1080–1083.
8. Popovic T, Kombarova SY, Reeves MW, et al: Molecular epidemiology of diphtheria in Russia, 1985–1994. J Infect Dis. 1996;174:1064–1072.
9. Pappenheimer AM, Murphy JR. Studies on the molecular epidemiology of diphtheria. Lancet. 1983;2:923–926.
10. Mikhailovich VM, Melnikov VG, Mazurova IK, et al: Application of PCR for detection of toxigenic *Corynebacterium diphtheriae* strains isolated during the Russian diphtheria epidemic, 1990 through 1994. J Clin Microbiol. 1995;33:3061–3063.
11. Kalapothaki V, Sapounas T, Xirouchaki E, et al. Prevalence of diphtheria carriers in a population with disappearing clinical diphtheria. Infection. 1984;12:387–389.
12. Heath CW, Zusman J. An outbreak of diphtheria among skid-row men. N Engl J Med. 1962;267:809–812.
13. Harnisch JP, Tronca E, Nolan CM, et al. Diphtheria among alcoholic urban adults. A decade of experience in Seattle. Ann Intern Med. 1989;111:71–82.
14. Koopman JS, Campbell J. The role of cutaneous diphtheria infections in a diphtheria epidemic. J Infect Dis. 1975;131:239–244.
15. Belsey MA, Sinclair M, Roder MR, et al. *Corynebacterium diphtheriae* skin infections in Alabama and Louisiana. N Engl J Med. 1969;280:135–141.
16. Bisgard KM, Hardy IRB, Popovic T, et al: Respiratory diphtheria in the United States, 1980–1995. Am J Public Health. 1998;88:787–791.
17. Dixon JMS. Diphtheria in North America. J Hyg (Lond). 1984;93:419–432.
18. Kwantes W. Diphtheria in Europe. J Hyg (Lond). 1984;93:433–437.
19. World Health Organization. Expanded Programme on Immunization (EPI) Information System, April 1993. Geneva: World Health Organization; 1993.
20. Galazka AM, Robertson SE: Diphtheria: Changing patterns in the developing world and the industrialized world. Eur J Epidemiol. 1995;11:107–117.
21. Dittmann S: Epidemic diphtheria in the newly independent states of the former USSR—situation and lessons learned. Biologicals. 1997;25:179–186.
22. Hardy IRB, Dittmann S, Sutter RW: Current situation and control strategies for resurgence of diphtheria in newly independent states of the former Soviet Union. Lancet. 1996;347:1739–1744.
23. Wilson APR, Efstratiou A, Weaver E, et al. Unusual non-toxigenic *Corynebacterium diphtheriae* in homosexual men. Lancet. 1992;339:998.
24. Millar OS, Cooper ON, Kakkar VV, et al. Invasive infection with *Corynbacterium diphtheriae* among drug users. Lancet. 1992;339:1359.
25. Brooks GF, Bennett JV, Feldman RA. Diphtheria in the United States, 1959–1970. J Infect Dis. 1974;129:172–178.
26. Rakhmanova AG, Lumio J, Groundstroem K, et al: Diphtheria outbreak in St Petersburg: Clinical characteristics of 1,860 adult patients. Scand J Infect Dis. 1996;28:37–40.
27. Chen RT, Broome CV, Weinstein RA, et al. Diphtheria in the United States, 1971–81. Am J Public Health. 1985;75:1393–1397.
28. Williams BC. Immunization coverage among preschool children: The United States and selected European countries. Pediatrics. 1990;86:1052–1056.
29. Rappuoli R, Perugini M, Falsen E. Molecular epidemiology of the 1984–86 outbreak of diphtheria in Sweden. N Engl J Med. 1988;318:12–14.
30. Pappenheimer AM. The diphtheria bacillus and its toxin: A model system. J Hyg (Lond). 1984;93:397–440.
31. Boyer NH, Weinstein L. Diphtheritic myocarditis. N Engl J Med. 1948;239:913.
32. Morgan BC. Cardiac complications of diphtheria. Pediatrics. 1963;32:549–557.
33. Ledbetter MK, Cannon AB, Costa AF. The electrocardiogram in diphtheritic myocarditis. Am Heart J. 1964;68:599–611.
34. Dobie RA, Tobey DN. Clinical features of diphtheria in the respiratory tract. JAMA. 1979;242:2197–2201.
35. Naiditch MJ, Bower AG. Diphtheria. A study of 1433 cases observed during a ten year period at the Los Angeles County Hospital. Am J Med. 1954;17:229–245.
36. Kallick CA, Brooks GF, Dover AS, et al. A diphtheria outbreak in Chicago. Ill Med J. 1970;137:505–512.
37. Zalma VM, Older JJ, Brooks GF. The Austin, Texas, diphtheria outbreak. JAMA. 1970;211:2125–2129.
38. McCloskey RV, Eller JJ, Green M, et al. The 1970 epidemic of diphtheria in San Antonio. Ann Intern Med. 1971;75:495–503.
39. Bray JP, Burt EG, Potter EV, et al. Epidemic diphtheria and skin infections in Trinidad. J Infect Dis. 1972;126:34–40.
40. Hewlett EL. Selective primary health care: Strategies for control of disease in the developing world. XVIII. Pertussis and diphtheria. Rev Infect Dis. 1985;7:426–433.
41. Belsey MA, LeBlanc DR. Skin infections and the epidemiology of diphtheria: Acquisition and persistence of *C. diphtheriae* infections. Am J Epidemiol. 1975;102:179–184.
42. Jellard CH. Diphtheria infection in Northwest Canada, 1969, 1970, and 1971. J Hyg (Lond). 1972;70:503–510.
43. Lortholary O, Buu-Hoi A, Gutmann L, et al: *Corynebacterium diphtheriae* endocarditis in France. Clin Infect Dis. 1993;17:1072–1074.
44. Tiley SM, Kociuba KR, Heron LG, et al: Infective endocarditis due to nontoxigenic *Corynebacterium diphtheriae*: Report of seven cases and review. Clin Infect Dis. 1993;16:271–275.

45. Gruner E, Opravil M, Altwegg M, et al: Nontoxigenic *Corynebacterium diphtheriae* isolated from intravenous drug users. Clin Infect Dis. 1994;18:94–96.
46. Patey O, Bimet F, Riegel P, et al: Clinical and molecular study of *Corynebacterium diphtheriae* systemic infections in France. J Clin Microbiol. 1997;35:441–445.
47. Wilson APR: The return of *Corynebacterium diphtheriae*: The rise of non-toxigenic strains. J Hosp Infect. 1995;30(Suppl):306–312.
48. Efstratiou A, George RC, Begg NT: Non-toxigenic *Corynebacterium diphtheriae* var *gravis* in England. Lancet. 1993;341:1592–1593.
49. Rakhmanova AG, Lumio J, Groundstroem KWE, et al: Fatal respiratory tract diphtheria apparently caused by nontoxigenic strains of *Corynebacterium diphtheriae*. Eur J Clin Microbiol Infect Dis. 1997;16:816–820.
50. American Academy of Pediatrics, Diphtheria. In: Peter G, ed. 1997 Red Book: Report of the Committee on Infectious Diseases. 24th ed. Elk Grove Village, Ill: American Academy of Pediatrics; 1997:191–195.
51. Kiselev VI. The use of various antibiotic combinations in the control of diphtheria bacilli carrier state. Antibiotiki. 1964;9:361–363.
52. Miller LW, Bickham S, Jones WL, et al. Diphtheria carriers and the effect of erythromycin therapy. Antimicrob Agents Chemother. 1974;6:166–169.
53. Thisyakorn USA, Wongvanich J, Kumpeng V. Failure of corticosteroid therapy to prevent diphtheritic myocarditis or neuritis. Pediatr Infect Dis. 1984;3:126–128.
54. Bjorkholm B, Bottiger M, Christenson B, et al. Antitoxin antibody levels and the outcome of illness during an outbreak of diphtheria among alcoholics. Scand J Infect Dis. 1986;18:235–239.
55. Millian SJ, Cherubin CE, Sherwin R, et al. A serologic survey of tetanus and diphtheria immunity in New York City. Arch Environ Health. 1967;15:776–781.
56. Kjeldsen K, Simonsen O, Heron I. Immunity against diphtheria 25–30 years after primary vaccination in childhood. Lancet. 1985;1:900–902.
57. Centers for Disease Control and Prevention. Diphtheria, tetanus, and pertussis: Recommendations for vaccine use and other preventive measures. MMWR Morb Mortal Wkly Rep. 1991;40:RR10.
58. Myers MG, Beckman CW, Vosdingh RA, et al. Primary immunization with tetanus and diphtheria toxoids. JAMA. 1982;248:2478–2480.
59. Simonsen O, Klaerke M, Klaerke A, et al. Revaccination of adults against diphtheria II: Combined diphtheria and tetanus revaccination with different doses of diphtheria toxoid 20 years after primary vaccination. Acta Pathol Microbiol Immunol Scand C. 1986;94:219–225.
60. Ruben RL, Nagel J, Fireman P. Antitoxin responses in the elderly to tetanus-diphtheria immunization. Am J Epidemiol. 1978;108:145–149.

Chapter 194

Other Corynebacteria and *Rhodococcus*

ARTHUR E. BROWN

In 1896 Lehmann and Neumann proposed that the bacteria morphologically resembling the diphtheria bacillus be incorporated with it into the genus *Corynebacterium.*[1] These nondiphtheria corynebacteria have since been referred to as *diphtheroids* and *coryneforms* and have been considered "colonizers" and contaminants. Barksdale referred to the process of lumping these various organisms together based on morphology as "coryneformity."[2] After decades of confusion about their clinical significance, nondiphtheria corynebacteria have emerged as important pathogens. Noteworthy are the increased numbers of opportunistic infections due to nondiphtheria corynebacteria as the numbers and survival of severely immunocompromised patients increase and the numbers and types of medical devices used in both immunocompromised and immunocompetent patients increase. This is contrasted with the decreasing numbers of reported diphtheria cases from 435 in 1970 to 5 in 1981.[3] Despite the diphtheria epidemic in the former Soviet Union (see Chapter 193), respiratory diphtheria remains rare in the United States in that only 41 cases were reported during the period 1980 to 1995.[4] Because of both increased interest and improved microbiologic techniques, nondiphtheria corynebacteria have been recognized as the cause of a number of human diseases and are less likely to be dismissed as culture contaminants.

By 1982, four reviews of infections in humans had been published.[5–8] A comprehensively updated review by Coyle and Lipsky was published in 1990.[9] The latter reviews,[8, 9] and a report concerning prosthetic valve endocarditis,[10] attempted to determine whether certain species of corynebacteria were associated with specific disease syndromes. Nondiphtheria corynebacteria have been known to cause life-threatening disease. These organisms have caused bacteremia, particularly in association with venous access devices, endocarditis on both prosthetic and native valves, meningitis, neurosurgical shunt infection, brain abscess, peritonitis in association with continuous ambulatory peritoneal dialysis (CAPD), osteomyelitis, septic arthritis, pneumonia, empyema, urinary tract infections, and other serious infections.[5–12] Some species tend to occur with a characteristic clinical syndrome (Table 194–1).

In the tradition of two previously published reviews[8, 9] an excellent comprehensive technical review of the various complex aspects of classification and taxonomy of the corynebacteria has been published[13] as has another two-part review.[14, 15] These authors explore the intricate methodologies of proper identification of corynebacteria and correctly point out the pitfalls of past reports as well as offer suggestions as to how to avoid such problems in the future.

As a result of newer genetic and other techniques that are applied to the characterization and taxonomic classification of the coryneform bacteria, the description of new organisms and the reassignment of "old" organisms to "new" or different genera have occurred.[14] Several new *Corynebacterium* species have been described, and several of the unnamed Centers for Disease Control and Prevention (CDC) coryneform group organisms have been examined, classified, and named. This delineation has been accomplished using several techniques: genetic analyses (e.g., 16-S and 5-S ribosomal RNA sequencing, nucleic acid hybridization), chemotaxonomic methods (mycolic acid detection, peptidoglycan analyses, cellular fatty acid studies, and characterization of electron transport menaquinones), and phenotypic techniques (i.e., conventional assays such as assimilations of carbohydrates and other compounds, and detection of preformed glycosidase or aminopeptidase enzymes).[14, 15]

As a result of the application of these technologies, organisms such as *Corynebacterium* CDC group JK and group D2 are now classified as *Corynebacterium jeikeium* and *Corynebacterium urealyticum,* respectively, whereas organisms such as *Corynebacterium pyogenes, Corynebacterium haemolyticum,* and *Corynebacterium equi* have been moved out of the *Corynebacterium* genus altogether to be named, respectively, *Actinomyces pyogenes, Arcanobacterium haemolyticum,* and *Rhodococcus equi.* A further change is anticipated in the the classification of *A. pyogenes* to *Arcanobacterium pyogenes* because of its cell wall composition and other morphologic, physiologic, and biochemical characteristics, which conform more closely to members of the genus *Arcanobacterium.*[15]

The current classification schema has resulted in the characterization of corynebacteria according to the lipophilic and fermentative features as listed in Table 194–2. True corynebacteria can still be

TABLE 194–1 Manifestations of *Corynebacterium* Infection

Species	Most Common Clinical Presentation
C. ulcerans	Pharyngitis, diphtheria
C. pseudotuberculosis (*C. ovis*)	Suppurative granulomatous lymphadenitis
Arcanobacterium (*Corynebacterium*) *haemolyticum*	Pharyngitis or chronic skin ulcer
C. pseudodiphtheriticum (*C. hofmannii*)	Endocarditis, lower respiratory infection
Rhodococcus equi (*C. equi*)	Necrotizing pneumonia in the immunosuppressed host (AIDS)
C. urealyticum (group D2)	Urinary tract infections; alkaline-encrusted cystitis
C. jeikeium (group JK)	Nosocomial skin colonization leading to wound infection or septicemia

Abbreviation: AIDS, Acquired immunodeficiency syndrome.

TABLE 194–2 Classification of Corynebacteria

Nonlipophilic, Fermentative Corynebacteria
C. ulcerans
C. pseudotuberculosis
C. xerosis
C. striatum
C. minutissimum
C. amycolatum
C. glucuronolyticum
C. argentoratense
C. coyleae
C. imitans
C. matruchotii
Nonlipophilic, Nonfermentive (or Oxidative) Corynebacteria
C. auris
C. pseudodiphtheriticum
C. propinquum
Lipophilic Corynebacteria
C. jeikeium
C. urealyticum
C. afermentans subsp. *lipophilum* (ANF-1)
C. accolens
C. macginleyi
CDC coryneform group G
C. lipophiloflavum

identified by their easily determined phenotypic traits (see "Microbiology").

MICROBIOLOGY

Corynebacteria (from the Greek *koryne,* meaning "club," and *bakterion,* "little rod") are gram-positive, non–acid-fast, catalase-positive, aerobic or facultatively anaerobic, asporogenous rods that are usually nonmotile. The cell wall of some species is weaker at the ends, allowing the organism to assume a club shape. During cell division, the daughter cells can remain attached on one side, forming L's and V's. The arrangement and cuneiform shape of these cells suggests Chinese characters. A wide variety of colonial types are found within the genus. Some are small and α-hemolytic and resemble lactobacilli; some are relatively large and white and resemble yeast colonies. Among the reasons for the difficulty in speciating these organisms are that many require special growth media such as Löffler's or Tinsdale's medium or a tellurite plate, most have highly variable biochemical characteristics often requiring supplemental media for detection, and some grow quite slowly. Because of these difficulties and the confusion regarding the taxonomic status of many species that resemble the genus *Corynebacterium,* these organisms have not always been appreciated as pathogens of human disease.[8, 9, 11–13]

SPECIFIC PATHOGENIC CORYNEBACTERIA

Corynebacterium ulcerans

In 1926 Gilbert and Stewart first isolated and named *Corynebacterium ulcerans* during an investigation of a diphtheria-like illness.[8] Subsequent studies established its pathogenicity and helped to determine the nature of its toxins. Usually a commensal in horses and cattle, *C. ulcerans* causes mastitis in cows and has been isolated from cow's milk. Human infection tends to occur in the summer months among rural populations exposed to domestic livestock, especially cattle. There is no evidence for person-to-person transmission.[48]

Microscopically, the organism is pleomorphic; few metachromatic granules are seen. *C. ulcerans* grows well on Löffler's and Tinsdale's media and tellurite agar. On blood agar the colonies are somewhat larger and more opaque than those of *Corynebacterium diphtheriae* and are generally surrounded by a narrow zone of hemolysis. On Tinsdale's medium the brownish-black colonies with distinct halos cannot be distinguished from *C. diphtheriae* colonies. *C. ulcerans* is urease-positive and nitrate-negative and ferments glucose, maltose, trehalose (slowly), and starch in peptone broth. Liquefaction of gelatin occurs at room temperature.[8, 11] Many strains produce the diphtheria toxin.[16] Independent of diphtheria toxin production, some strains produce the dermonecrotic toxin.

Nearly all human isolates of *C. ulcerans* have been cultured from a respiratory site—primarily the throat in asymptomatic persons. However, an exudative pharyngitis and a diphtheria-like disease do occur, including the pseudomembrane formation and cardiac or neurologic manifestations.[17] Toxigenic *C. ulcerans* can cause a disease that is indistinguishable from diphtheria.[4, 13] In presumed toxigenic cases, diphtheria antitoxin should be administered. A presumed case of pneumonia,[18] an ulcer on the hand of a dairy farmer,[11] and a leg ulcer with cellulitis resulting from a puncture wound[19] have also been reported to be due to *C. ulcerans.* Although the organism is sensitive to most antibacterial agents in vitro, clinical success with erythromycin would suggest that it is the antibiotic of choice.

Corynebacterium pseudotuberculosis (Corynebacterium ovis)

Called the *Preisz-Nocard bacillus* in honor of the researchers who first isolated it in the early 1890s from the necrotic kidney of a sheep,[8] *Corynebacterium pseudotuberculosis* has been the etiologic agent of infections in a variety of other animals including horses, cattle, goats, and deer. The dermonecrotic toxin produced by these organisms was studied by Nicolle and colleagues in 1912 and Hall and Stone in 1916.[8] *C. pseudotuberculosis* is known among veterinarians to produce suppurative lymphadenitis, abscesses, and pneumonia in livestock, but the first report of human infection was not until 1966.[20]

Gram stains of direct smears may not show very many diphtheroid bacilli, and the microscopic morphology of in vitro growth may closely resemble that of streptococci, coccobacilli, or pleomorphic bacilli with metachromatic granules. Pinpoint colonies develop after incubation for 24 hours on sheep or horse blood agar. Biochemical reactions vary considerably. A simple test for phospholipase D readily distinguishes *C. pseudotuberculosis* and *C. ulcerans* from all other *Corynebacterium* spp.[8, 11]

Nearly all strains produce a dermonecrotic toxin, and selected isolates produce a diphtheria toxin.[16] There have not been any clinical cases of diphtheria attributed to infection with *C. pseudotuberculosis.*

Almost all of the 22 reported episodes of human infection with *C. pseudotuberculosis* have been reported from Australia.[21] Except for a veterinary student who developed an eosinophilic pneumonia after exposure in the microbiology laboratory,[22] most others have been cases of suppurative granulomatous lymphadenitis in patients who had contact with animals or who handled offal and hides or drank raw milk.[8, 21, 23–25] All required a prolonged (several weeks) course of erythromycin or tetracycline and surgery for cure. There is preliminary evidence that contaminated fomites may play a role in the transmission of this disease among animals.[26] A preliminary study suggests that vaccination of lambs may provide these animals with immunologic protection.[27]

Corynebacterium xerosis

In 1881, Raymond isolated an organism with the characteristics of *Corynebacterium xerosis* from the conjunctiva of the eye. Although it was initially considered to be a cause of conjunctivitis, most now believe *C. xerosis* to be a commensal that colonizes the conjunctival sac, nasopharynx, and skin.[8]

C. xerosis grows readily on ordinary media and appears on Gram stain as irregularly staining rods. They form small yellow-to-tan colonies and are nonhemolytic. These organisms ferment several carbohydrates, reduce nitrates, and hydrolyze pyrazinamide but do not liquefy gelatin or hydrolyze urea. No toxin production has been reported.[8, 11]

C. xerosis has been described as the cause of both prosthetic valve[28, 29] and native valve endocarditis,[30] bacteremia,[31] pneumonia,[31, 32] septic arthritis,[31] meningitis,[31] intra-abdominal infection,[31, 33, 34] vertebral osteomyelitis,[31] infectious keratitis,[35] mediastinitis,[36] and sternal wound infection[37]—mostly in patients who were immunocompromised or postoperative, or had prosthetic devices. The organism is usually sensitive to the penicillins, cephalosporins, and vancomycin, but multiple resistance has been reported.[32, 36] However, recent reports suggest that misidentification of *Corynebacterium amycolatum* as *C. xerosis* has occurred and that multiresistance is very common among *C. amycolatum* strains, whereas true *C. xerosis* strains are susceptible to nearly all antimicrobial agents tested.[13]

Corynebacterium striatum

Early reports on *Corynebacterium striatum* described the organism as a thick diphtheroid with clear-cut bars (striatum) and large irregular granules. *C. striatum* is part of the normal flora of the anterior nares and skin, particularly the face and upper part of the torso.[9, 11] This organism has been increasingly reported as the etiologic agent of various human infections,[14] including bacteremic[38] and fatal[39] pleuropulmonary infection, catheter-related bacteremia in neutropenic patients with cancer[40, 41] and acquired immunodeficiency syndrome (AIDS),[42] catheter exit-site infection,[41] native valve endocarditis,[43–45] pacemaker-related endocarditis,[46] meningitis,[47] cerebrospinal fluid shunt infections in children,[48] purulent conjunctivitis,[41] and chorioamnionitis,[41] and as possibly contributing to peritonitis[41] and to a pyogenic granuloma of the finger after injury due to a rosebush thorn.[41] Many of these reports involve indwelling prostheses, catheter tips, ventilator tubes, chronic wounds, and the female genital tract with premature rupture of the amniotic membranes—all suggesting the possibility of a mucocutaneous source.[13] *C. striatum* is quite sensitive in vitro to vancomycin and penicillin G; most were susceptible to cephalosporins and carbapenems, and most were resistant to aminoglycosides, fluoroquinolones, trimethoprim-sulfamethoxazole, tetracycline, rifampin, and erythromycin.[49]

Corynebacterium minutissimum

Although erythrasma has been well described since 1859, its causative agent, *Corynebacterium minutissimum,* was first proposed in 1961.[8] However, more recent information[9, 13] has revealed that there is most likely a polymicrobial cause of erythrasma. Erythrasma is a common superficial infection of the skin that is characterized by pruritic, scaling reddish-brown macular patches occurring in intertriginous areas. This dermatologic condition is usually diagnosed by the typical coral red fluorescence of the skin lesions when examined under Wood's lamp. Gram staining and culture of the pulverized stratum corneum yields the organism. On special tissue culture medium containing fetal bovine serum, *C. minutissimum* forms colonies of 1 to 2 mm that show the coral red to orange fluorescence under long-wave ultraviolet light. *Corynebacterium minutissimum* shares many bacteriologic characteristics with *C. xerosis* but may easily be distinguished from the latter by the fact that *C. minutissimum* does not reduce nitrate. *C. minutissimum* produces a porphyrin, hydrolyzes Tween 80, and grows in the presence of hydrogenated castor oil esters.[8, 11, 50]

Although there has been recent concern about the misidentification of *C. amycolatum* as *C. minutissimum,*[13] there have been 10 cases of human infection with *C. minutissimum* other than erythrasma, and a recently reported case of nonfluorescent erythrasma of the vulva deserves mention.[51] There have been four cases of bacteremia caused by *C. minutissimum:* three in patients with hematologic malignancies (chronic myelogenous leukemia,[52] multiple myeloma,[53] and prolymphocytic leukemia[54]) and one in a patient with an infected pseudoaneurysmal fistula who was being hemodialyzed.[54] Two cases of abscesses have been reported: one was severe and recurrent breast abscesses,[50] and the other was a deep abscess after cervical diskectomy.[53] Endocarditis with embolic retinopathy in a patient with mitral valve prolapse,[55] peritonitis complicating peritoneal dialysis,[54] polymicrobial central venous catheter sepsis,[56] and acute pyelonephritis in an infant with marked bilateral hydroureteronephrosis[57] have all been reported. None of these 10 patients had clinical evidence of erythrasma; however, all 10 patients had disruption of the integument. A recent report of clinical isolates of *C. minutissimum* group 1 (propionic acid producing) being multiply resistant to various antibiotics[54] suggests that therapy should be guided by proper identification and antibiotic susceptibility testing.

Corynebacterium amycolatum

Reported in 1988 as a new species of *Corynebacterium* isolated from human skin, *Corynebacterium amycolatum* was so named because it lacks the mycolic acids found in all other corynebacteria. However, 16-S ribosomal-RNA sequence analysis supported its inclusion in the genus. It has become clear from many studies that *C. amycolatum* has probably been variously misidentified by clinical laboratories for many years as *C. minutissimum, C. striatum,* or *C. xerosis.* Therefore, it is likely that some reports on the clinical significance of these other corynebacteria were actually describing abnormalities associated with *C. amycolatum.*[13, 14] Indeed, the three strains of propionic acid–producing *C. minutissimum* described by Van Bosterhaut and colleagues as a cause of opportunistic infection[54] may well be *C. amycolatum.* Two cases of sepsis, one fatal, have been reported to be caused by *C. amycolatum.*[58, 59] Multiple antimicrobial resistance including β-lactams, macrolides, clindamycin, aminoglycosides, quinolones, and rifampin is a hallmark feature of *C. amycolatum.*[13, 14] This feature is helpful to distinguish this species from other more sensitive corynebacteria such as *C. minutissimum* and *C. xerosis* with which it has been confused in the past.[14] The majority of *C. amycolatum* isolates are susceptible to tetracycline, and all isolates tested are susceptible to glycopeptides.[13]

Corynebacterium glucuronolyticum

Corynebacterium glucuronolyticum is a newly defined (1995) nonlipophilic bacterium that has been isolated from male patients with genitourinary tract infections, particularly from the semen of patients with prostatitis or urethritis. This organism may be part of the usual genitourinary tract flora. *C. glucuronolyticum* is usually susceptible to β-lactams, aminoglycosides, rifampin, and vancomycin, but a relatively high proportion are resistant to norfloxacin, ciprofloxacin, clindamycin, erythromycin, and, importantly, tetracycline and doxycycline.[13, 14]

Corynebacterium imitans

Corynebacterium imitans is a new (1997) *Corynebacterium* species that has been recovered from a nasopharyngeal specimen from an unimmunized Romanian boy who had been traveling via the Ukraine to Poland and was suspected of having diphtheria.[60] Seven adults who had contact with either the child or an adult contact person also developed symptoms of pharyngeal diphtheria. However, no diphtherial toxin gene nor its product were detected by polymerase chain reaction assays or by the Elek test.[14]

Other Nonlipophilic *Corynebacterium* Species

Other newly described nonlipophilic *Corynebacterium* species include *Corynebacterium argentoratense,* which has been recovered from throat cultures of patients with tonsillitis, but the role of this bacterium in human disease is not known.[13, 14] *Corynebacterium coyleae* is a newly described species that has been recovered from pleural fluid specimens and blood cultures of patients with fever of unclear cause in the setting of underlying conditions such as AIDS and surgery.[14] *Corynebacteria matruchotii* is notable for its unusual Gram-stain appearance as gram-positive bacilli with "whip handles." It is thought to be an inhabitant of the oral cavity and has only rarely been recovered from the human eye as a cause of infection.[13]

Corynebacterium auris

Corynebacterium auris is another newly (1995) defined *Corynebacterium* species that was isolated from ear specimens of pediatric patients with otitis media. Colonies are nonhemolytic, dry, and slightly adherent to agar and become slightly yellow with time. *C. auris* has only been isolated from patients with ear infections, but clinical microbiological experience with this organism has been relatively limited to date. *C. auris* strains were susceptible in vitro to ciprofloxacin, gentamicin, rifampin, tetracycline, and vancomycin but resistant to penicillin G. Susceptibility to clindamycin and erythromycin was variable.[13, 14]

Corynebacterium pseudodiphtheriticum (Corynebacterium hofmannii)

Corynebacterium pseudodiphtheriticum was most likely first isolated from the throats of humans in 1888 by Von Hoffman. In 1896, Lehmann and Neumann made the detailed description of what was then called *Bacillus pseudodiphtheriticum.* Bergey and coworkers gave the current name of *C. pseudodiphtheriticum* in 1925.[8] This species of *Corynebacterium* does not produce toxins and is considered part of normal pharyngeal flora in humans.

Differing from other corynebacteria, these organisms generally do not demonstrate pleomorphism, and they take the Gram stain well and evenly. The bacterial cells often lie in parallel rows on smear preparations. *Corynebacterium pseudodiphtheriticum* grows well on all media, and the colonial morphology may closely resemble that of *C. diphtheriae.* Although it is inert in carbohydrate fermentation tests, it hydrolyzes urea and reduces nitrates.[8, 11]

Human infection has usually presented as endocarditis, with 18 cases involving both prosthetic and natural valves.[5–8, 10, 61–65] In 1983, *C. pseudodiphtheriticum* was reported as the cause of pneumonia in a man with systemic lupus erythematosus.[66] Since then a case of lung abscess due to *C. pseudodiphtheriticum* has been reported in a patient with AIDS.[67] Necrotizing tracheitis,[68] tracheobronchitis,[69] pneumonia,[70, 71] suppurative lymphadenitis,[72] and an infection of a skin graft donor site[73] all due to *C. pseudodiphtheriticum* in nonimmunocompromised hosts have been reported. In 1994, the isolation of *C. pseudodiphtheriticum* from respiratory specimens of some 30 patients in two separate reports from the United States[74] and Japan[75] suggested that *C. pseudodiphtheriticum* may be emerging as an important pathogen.[14] Most of these infections occurred in patients with underlying diseases or predisposing factors including functional or anatomic abnormalities of the heart; lung and tracheobronchial diseases; endotracheal intubations; and immunosuppressive conditions. Clinicians should also be aware that *C. pseudodiphtheriticum* has been isolated from the exudate of the nasopharynx of patients with suspected diphtheria.[76, 77] Antimicrobial sensitivities may vary; therefore, therapy should be guided by susceptibility testing.

Corynebacterium propinquum

Formerly called CDC coryneform group ANF-3, *Corynebacterium propinquum* is closely related phylogenetically to *C. pseudodiphtheriticum.* However, *C. propinquum* does not produce urease, whereas *C. pseudodiphtheriticum* does. One case of a native valve endocarditis caused by *C. propinquum* has been reported,[78] but this has been questioned by others.[13] All these nonlipophilic isolates have been recovered from human respiratory tract specimens and blood.

Corynebacterium jeikeium (Group JK)

Described in 1976[79] and renamed from *Corynebacterium* CDC group JK,[9] *Corynebacterium jeikeium* has since been reported to cause sepsis primarily in patients with neoplastic diseases with various risk factors: (1) prolonged hospitalization, (2) prolonged neutropenia, (3) treatment with multiple antibiotics, and (4) disruption of the integument.[79–83] Most patients are colonized before infection, and most infections are hospital acquired. *C. jeikeium* appears to exist as part of the skin flora of hospitalized patients (especially males),[84] particularly in the inguinal, axillary, and rectal sites, whereas healthy individuals are generally not colonized with large numbers of these organisms.[82–85] About one third to one half of oncology patients admitted to cancer centers are colonized, and this carriage may persist for weeks to months.[82, 83, 86] *C. jeikeium* can survive in the hospital environment for extended periods of time.[87] Prior broad-spectrum antibiotic therapy in such patients correlates with colonization.[83] Some studies have shown that these organisms are normal flora of the skin that have acquired antibiotic resistance.[88] Outbreaks of infection with *C. jeikeium* have occurred.[89, 90] Recently *C. jeikeium* infections have been recognized in immunocompetent patients,[9] surgical and trauma intensive care patients,[91] and even outpatients.[9] Originally described in American institutions, *C. jeikeium* is now being reported from European hospitals.[9]

There is controversy about the transmission of these organisms. One group has found similar plasmids in isolates from different patients, suggesting that person-to-person transmission of *C. jeikeium* had occurred within the hospital.[92] Other investigators have not been able to demonstrate plasmids.[80, 82, 89] One group indicated that plasmid profiling was not useful and that restriction endonuclease analysis of chromosomal DNA appears to be the appropriate molecular epidemiologic tool for *C. jeikeium.*[93] This same group found marked heterogeneity among the isolates obtained in their study and suggested that patient-to-patient transmission does not occur.[93]

The alternative suggestion is that antibiotic therapy selects out multiresistant *C. jeikeium* strains that are present in low numbers as part of the skin flora.[85, 88] A high prevalence of antibiotic-resistant *C. jeikeium* in many groups of patients has been demonstrated and is long-lasting.[85] Also, there is an inverse relationship between the numbers of antibiotic-susceptible *C. jeikeium* and the highly resistant *C. jeikeium,* which suggests that the niche vacated by the susceptible *C. jeikeium* are then filled by the highly resistant *C. jeikeium.*[85]

Gram-stain morphology of *C. jeikeium* shows gram-positive coccobacillary or coccal forms that may resemble streptococci. The morphology may often be cuneiform. On sheep blood agar, the colonies are slow growing, small, gray to white, glistening, and usually nonhemolytic. Key biochemical reactions that differentiate *C. jeikeium* from other corynebacteria are the inability to produce urease, reduce nitrate, or readily ferment most carbohydrates. No halo is produced on Tinsdale's medium. The antibiogram may well be the most distinguishing feature because most isolates are multiply resistant and are frequently sensitive only to vancomycin.[8, 11, 94] Ultrastructure analysis of these isolates may help in understanding their multidrug-resistance patterns.[95]

Infections have occurred most commonly in neutropenic patients or patients with previous cardiac surgery.[6, 8, 10, 79–83] Most of these infections are related to disruption of the integument and present as bacteremia—often associated with indwelling intravenous catheters. Septicemia with *C. jeikeium* occurs most often in patients with lymphoreticular malignancies, often occurring as a terminal event. Among such neutropenic patients with *C. jeikeium* septicemia, skin and soft tissue manifestations were observed in 25% of cases in one review.[96] Early prosthetic valve endocarditis due to diphtheroids was found to be due to variably sensitive *C. jeikeium.*[10] At least seven previously reported cases of endocarditis attributed to unspecified diphtheroids were subsequently determined to be due to *C. jeikeium.*[94] Recently four cases of *C. jeikeium* endocarditis occurring on native valves have been reported.[97–99] Other infections reported include pneumonitis,[100–102] cavitating pneumonitis,[103] peritonitis in CAPD,[104] meningitis with transverse myelitis in a neutropenic patient,[105] neurosurgical shunt infections,[79, 90, 106–111] wound infections,[106] an infected tibial prosthesis,[112] osteomyelitis after total hip replacement,[113] infectious arthritis after arthroplasty,[114] rash,[100] a liver abscess in a patient with AIDS,[115] an epicardial abscess related to epicardial catheter placement,[116] and various infections in children including venous catheter devices.[117] Therapy is with vancomycin. Removal of the prosthetic device is required if the infection cannot be controlled medically. This is especially so in cases of endocarditis due to *C. jeikeium* when there is left ventricular failure or perivalvular leak. Prevention of sepsis in high-risk patients is best obtained by controlling the skin colonization of resistant *C. jeikeium* by bathing with an antibacterial soap.[118, 119]

Corynebacterium urealyticum (Group D2)

Corynebacterium urealyticum (formerly *Corynebacterium* group D2) is a gram-positive rod described by King in 1972; its culture and biochemical characteristics resemble those of *C. jeikeium.*[120] During a survey for carriage of antibiotic-resistant diphtheroids, investigators at a cancer center found 6 of 52 isolates to be urease-positive and biochemically less active than *C. jeikeium* isolates.[80] These six isolates were subsequently found to be group D2.[11] *C. urealyticum* is slow growing, does not acidify glucose,[9, 11] and is resistant to multiple antibiotics.[120, 121] Like *C. jeikeium, C. urealyticum* is widely distributed on the skin of hospitalized patients (especially women).[84]

C. urealyticum has been isolated from the transtracheal aspirates of an elderly patient with pneumonia[122] and has been the cause of peritonitis,[123] native[124, 125] and prosthetic valve[126] endocarditis, osteomyelitis,[127] wound infection,[128] necrotic scrotal infection in a neutropenic child,[129] and bacteremia.[123, 128, 130] *Corynebacterium urealyticum* is an etiologic agent involved in alkaline-encrusted cystitis, a very severe urinary tract infection that is difficult to treat.[131] Encrusted cystitis is a chronic inflammatory condition of the bladder first described by François in 1914 as a localized ulcerative inflammation with deposits of ammonium magnesium phosphate on the surface and on the walls of the ulcer. This disease has been associated with the implantation of urea-splitting microorganisms (mainly *Proteus* spp.) in a bladder that already harbored some form of inflammatory or neoplastic lesion (vesical ground). The urea-splitting activity of *C. urealyticum* plays an important role in its pathogenicity, which is associated with alkaline urine (pH >8) and struvite (ammonium magnesium phosphate) stones.[132] Risk factors that relate to infection with *C. urealyticum* include immunosuppression, previous urinary tract infections with organisms other than *C. urealyticum,* urologic manipulation, and previous urologic disease that created a vesical ground. Although most reports of *C. urealyticum* urinary tract infection have been from Spain and other parts of Europe,[9] in the United States this organism has been reported to cause a urinary tract infection.[133–136] Because the organism is highly resistant to most antimicrobial agents, vancomycin is recommended until specific antimicrobial sensitivity data are available.[9, 13, 14, 135, 137]

Corynebacterium afermentans Subspecies *lipophilum*

Corynebacterium afermentans subsp. *lipophilum* is the new (1993) name for the CDC coryneform group ANF-1 (ANF = absolute nonfermenter). The original strains were blood-culture isolates, and the three reported clinical cases include a central venous line infection, prosthetic valve endocarditis with perivalvular abscess formation, and brain and liver abscesses.[13, 14] The cases illustrated that such lipophilic corynebacteria may require extended incubation in order to be recovered.[13] Also, the patterns of susceptibility to β-lactam antimicrobials may vary.[13, 14]

Corynebacterium accolens

Remarkable for exhibiting satellitism when grown in the presence of staphylococcal colonies, *Corynebacterium accolens* has been isolated from wound drainage, endocervical specimens, and respiratory sites (sputum and throat swabs). These strains require lipids for optimal growth, so the satellite growth was likely due to fulfillment of the lipid requirement by the action of the staphylococci on the erythrocytes in blood agar.[13, 14] A single case of endocarditis of the native mitral and aortic valves has been reported.[138] *C. accolens* has been reported to be susceptible to penicillin, cephalosporins, erythromycin, clindamycin, tetracycline, and the aminoglycosides.[13, 14]

Group G

CDC coryneform group G organisms have been isolated from vitreous humor specimens, blood, cerebrospinal fluid, skin, and the genitourinary tract.[13, 15] Five cases of human infection with group G organisms have been reported. The first was a male patient who died of endocarditis involving mitral and aortic valve prostheses.[139] The second was a male patient with disseminated intravascular coagulopathy who had large numbers of peripheral blood polymorphonuclear leukocytes each containing as many as 20 bacilli.[140] In these patients, blood cultures did not become positive until after 7 and 10 days of incubation, respectively. A third patient had an 8- × 6-cm mass occupying both outer quadrants of her right breast that appeared suddenly 8 months after a motor vehicle accident with trauma to that area.[141] The fourth was an intravenous drug–abusing patient who had endocarditis caused by *Corynebacterium* group G. In this case the specific microbial diagnosis was delayed because of the slow-growing nature of the organism.[141] The fifth was a patient with systemic lupus erythematosus who had a septic arthritis and endocarditis.[142]

Other Lipophilic *Corynebacterium* Species

Lipophilic *Corynebacterium* spp. that are relatively new include *Corynebacterium macginleyi,* which has been recovered from human ocular specimens,[14] and *Corynebacterium lipophiloflavum,* which has been isolated from a vaginal specimen of a woman with vaginitis.[14] The role of *C. lipophiloflavum* in the pathogenesis of bacterial vaginosis is unclear.[14] *C. lipophiloflavum* produces a biochemical profile similar to that of *C. urealyticum* (except that *C. urealyticum* is rapidly urease-positive and is not pigmented) and *C. lipophiloflavum* is broadly susceptible to many antibiotics, whereas *C. urealyticum* is usually multiply resistant to antimicrobial agents.[14]

Corynebacterium bovis

Although truly a member of the genus *Corynebacterium, Corynebacterium bovis* is now doubted to be a cause of human disease.[9, 13] The source of human infection with *C. bovis* is unclear, because the organism has not been implicated as a human commensal and because there is rarely an antecedent history of animal exposure. Some consider *C. bovis* "an unlikely human pathogen."[9] Others consider *C. bovis* "only an occasional human pathogen" at best, indicating that "it has been questioned if this species, using current criteria for identifying corynebacteria, has indeed ever been recovered from cases of human disease."[13]

"Corynebacterium aquaticum"

Although long considered a *Corynebacterium* species, "*Corynebacterium aquaticum*" has certain properties (e.g., motility and oxidative carbohydrate metabolism) that exclude it from the genus *Corynebacterium.*[15] *C. aquaticum* is a water organism and is closely related to the genus *Aureobacterium.*[13] Although rare cases of human disease including bacteremia, endocarditis, venous access device infection, meningitis, CAPD-associated peritonitis, and urinary tract infection have been described,[13, 15] some of these cases have been questioned as "doubtful from a diagnostic standpoint" as "it remains unclear as to whether the strains were actually '*C. aquaticum*' or *Aureobacterium* spp."[13] A formal proposal for a new name for *C. aquaticum* will likely be published soon.[15]

Actinomyces (Corynebacterium) pyogenes

Actinomyces pyogenes is a well-recognized animal pathogen that was initially described by Lucet in 1893.[8] This organism is both a commensal and a pathogen among domestic animals, causing a variety of suppurative infections in cattle, sheep, goats, and pigs. Human infection, as rarely as it occurs, most likely represents a zoonosis.

Corynebacterium pyogenes has been transferred to the genus *Actinomyces* as *A. pyogenes.* The organism is an aerotolerant anaerobe that is biochemically very similar to *Actinomyces bovis* except that it is hemolytic and actively proteolytic. Gram stains contain both coccal and diphtheroid forms, and on sheep blood agar, *A. pyogenes* produces pinpoint, whitish, β-hemolytic colonies. The hemolytic zone is usually twice the diameter of the colony. *Actinomyces pyogenes* liquefies gelatin, peptonizes litmus milk, and ferments xylose, whereas *Actinomyces haemolyticum* does not. *Actinomyces pyogenes* produces a potent soluble hemolysin.[8, 11]

A few cases of human infection including cutaneous infections complicated by septicemia, acute ulcerative vulvovaginitis, endocarditis, septic arthritis, osteomyelitis, meningitis, pneumonia, and empyema have been reported. However, the specificity of the organism identified in most of these cases could not be distinguished.[7, 8, 11] Some of these cases may have been due to *A. haemolyticum* because of many shared phenotypic characteristics with *A. pyogenes.*[8] A yearly outbreak of leg ulcers among schoolchildren in rural Thailand is attributed to *A. pyogenes.*[143, 144]

Well-documented cases have been reported including bacteremia in a woman with carcinoma of the colon[145] and 11 Danish patients with various infections including abscesses, otitis media, intra-abdominal infections, cystitis, and a bacteremic mastoiditis.[146] *A. pyogenes* is sensitive in vitro to penicillins, cephalosporins, chloramphenicol, tetracycline, aminoglycosides, and ciprofloxacin.

Arcanobacterium (Corynebacterium) haemolyticum

Arcanobacterium haemolyticum was first isolated from infected American soldiers stationed in the South Pacific during World War II. Although this organism closely resembled *A. pyogenes,* the authors felt it was indeed distinct.[8] It has been accepted as a separate species and has now been reclassified in a new genus, *Arcanobacterium,* comprising this single species, *A. haemolyticum.*[147] *Arcanobacterium haemolyticum* is only rarely isolated from animals, and its primary epidemiologic reservoir appears to be human because the organism may be found in the pharynx and on the skin of healthy humans.

The microscopic morphology of cells recovered from Löffler's medium is similar to that of *C. diphtheriae,* but growth on tellurite agar is poor. Colonies on sheep blood agar are small with a narrow band of hemolysis. The organism is distinguished from *A. pyogenes* by its failure to hydrolyze gelatin, peptonize litmus milk, and ferment xylose. A dermonecrotic toxin is produced by some strains of *A. haemolyticum.*[8, 11]

Infections due to *A. haemolyticum* have most commonly included pharyngeal infections[148–153] and chronic skin ulcers. The latter is not unlike the epidemic leg ulcers in Thailand caused by *A. pyogenes.*[144] Less frequent infections include osteomyelitis,[154] meningitis,[154] brain abscess,[154, 155] cavitary pneumonia,[156] septicemia[154, 157–159] (including children with primary Epstein-Barr virus infection[157–159]), and endocarditis.[160] Mixed infections involving soft tissues such as wounds[161] and a tuboovarian abscess[162] have also been reported.

Although evidence supporting the pathogenic role of *A. haemolyticum* in pharyngitis has been strong,[152, 153] this has been challenged.[163, 164] Because of a lack of exclusion of viral and mycoplasmal pathogens, some of the cases have been questioned.[7, 8, 163] However, it is possible that *A. haemolyticum* may act opportunistically or synergistically with other infectious agents such as Epstein-Barr virus. Indeed, the maximal incidence of isolation of *A. haemolyticum* from throat swabs was in the 15- to 18-year-old age group.[165] The presentation may be similar to that of group A streptococcal infection. When it causes an acute pharyngitis or tonsillitis, with lymphadenitis in about 50% of cases, *A. haemolyticum* is associated initially with a scarlatiniform rash in one half of the cases. The rash involves the trunk and proximal aspects of the extremities and usually desquamates as the illness progresses. A few cases of this syndrome have been misdiagnosed as toxic shock syndrome when seen in young, menstruating women.[150] Systemic toxicity such as fever and leukocytosis are usually absent. Recently, a host antibody response to infection with *A. haemolyticum* has been described.[166] *Arcanobacterium haemolyticum* is sensitive to penicillin, erythromycin, azithromycin, ciprofloxacin, vancomycin, clindamycin, chloramphenicol, and doxycycline[13]—any of which may be used for therapy. Susceptibility testing varies among strains to both aminoglycosides and penicillin, and penicillin tolerance has been reported.[167]

RHODOCOCCUS

Rhodococcus spp. are being reported as the cause of various infections with increasing frequency, particularly in immunocompromised patients and those with human immunodeficiency virus (HIV) infection. Among rhodococci, *R. equi* is the most commonly isolated species and should alert the clinician to the possibility of AIDS or other causes of immune suppression. Other species of *Rhodococcus* known to cause human infection are *R. (Gordona) bronchialis, R. (Tsukamurella) aurantiacus, R. luteus, R. erythropolis, R. rhodochrous,* and *R. rubropertinctus.* Two excellent reviews on *R. equi* have been published.[168, 169]

Rhodococcus equi (Corynebacterium equi)

Rhodococcus equi (formerly *C. equi*) has been recognized as an agent of bronchopneumonia in horses since it was first isolated from infected foals in 1923. Since then it has been found to be a pathogen causing sporadic infections in cattle, sheep, swine, and a cat.[8, 168, 170] Its soil habitat has been confirmed.[171] Although *R. equi* is the cause of several important zoonoses, this organism has rarely been isolated from healthy persons. Almost all human infections have occurred in patients who have defects of cell-mediated immunity with or without histories of animal exposure. Infections in both animals and humans are thought to be acquired through the respiratory route.

On Gram stain, the rods vary in length, from cocci to long, curved, clubbed forms. Large, irregular, highly mucoid, pale salmon-pink colonies grow well on ordinary media. *R. equi* is differentiated from other pathogenic corynebacteria by its lack of ability to ferment carbohydrates or liquefy gelatin. Some investigators have found the organism to be acid-fast.[8, 11, 12, 168, 170]

An animal model of disseminated infection has been developed.[172] Because *R. equi* is a facultative intracellular pathogen and survives inside macrophages causing granulomatous inflammation, the result is the eventual destruction of macrophages with purulent granulomas and progression to caseating necrosis. Dissemination from focal sites (usually the lung) to brain, skin, paraspinal tissue, and bone has been described in human infection.[168, 169] Antimicrobial agents that concentrate intracellularly (i.e., erythromycin, rifampin, clindamycin, clarithromycin, azithromycin, and trimethoprim-sulfamethoxazole) might be among the most useful in treatment. In HIV-infected patients particularly, the extracellular as well as the intracellular bacterial load may be high, and initial treatment with a combination of agents with bactericidal action could be followed by maintenance therapy with agents that are intracellularly active.[173]

Of the more than 90 reported cases of human *R. equi* infection, the overwhelming majority involve the lung.[8, 9, 12, 168–170, 173–213] Extrapulmonary infections with *R. equi* include a case of septic arthritis of the knee after a nail puncture and a case of cellulitis, also from a puncture wound[169]; primary subcutaneous abscess of the arm in a heart transplant recipient receiving prednisone and azathioprine who used horse manure in his garden[214]; disseminated subcutaneous abscesses and an intra-abdominal abscess in an adult with chronic lymphocytic leukemia taking prednisone and chlorambucil[215]; endophthalmitis after a penetrating eye injury[216, 217]; thyroid abscess in a patient with AIDS[218]; prostatic abscess[219]; otitis media and mastoiditis in a patient with AIDS[220]; brain abscess[169, 221]; bacteremic inflammatory pelvic mass and psoas abscess in a patient with AIDS[222]; colonic polyps and disseminated infection in a patient with AIDS[223]; osteomyelitis of the femur in a renal transplant recipient,[224] vertebral osteomyelitis in a liver transplant recipient[225]; chronic osteitis of the mandible in a horse breeder[226]; infection in a renal transplant patient with a paraspinal abscess[186]; bacteremia in an AIDS patient with bloody diarrhea and cachexia[222]; infection in two children with cervical lymphadenitis[169, 227]; peritonitis in a patient receiving CAPD[228]; and bacteremia in two adult patients with cancer.[169, 229] Fatal relapsing systemic disease caused by *R. equi* involving the lungs, kidneys, brain, and blood stream was reported in an intravenous drug abuser who was seropositive for HIV.[230] Many patients were receiving corticosteroids. Most were patients with AIDS. All but 10 cases have occurred in patients with diminished T-cell immunity,[169, 179, 186, 216, 217, 226, 227] although one patient was an alcoholic.[179] The clinical presentation may be insidious with fatigue, fever, and nonproductive cough. Chest radiographs often demonstrate cavitary lesions. A single case of spontaneous pneumothorax due to pulmonary *R. equi* infection has been reported in a patient with AIDS.[169] In many instances, an invasive procedure such as bronchoscopy, thoracocentesis, or surgery was required to make the microbiologic diagnosis. Bacteremic pneumonia occurs more frequently in patients with AIDS.[169, 189, 190] In one series, the overall mortality rate was greater among patients who were HIV infected (54.5%) than for non–HIV-infected patients (20%).[190] In another study, four of six HIV-infected patients died, whereas none of the six non–HIV-infected patients died.[169] Necrotizing pneumonia due to *R. equi* closely resembles that of tuberculosis or nocardiosis in that nodules or cavitation of upper lobes, or both, occurs. However, the air-fluid levels seen in *R. equi* lesions are not seen in tuberculosis. Subcutaneous nodular lesions and brain abscess have also been described as in nocardiosis. Furthermore, relapses after short periods of antimicrobial therapy occur. The optimal duration of antimicrobial therapy and the exact role of surgery is uncertain; however, many weeks of antibiotic therapy have been required for cure, and surgical intervention has been applied successfully in many cases. Some authors recommend a minimum of 2 months of therapy because of the frequency of relapses following shorter courses in immunocompromised patients.[169] Antibiotic therapy should be continued until cultures are negative and the condition of the patient is stable. Suppressive therapy should be continued indefinitely in patients with AIDS after resolution of the initial infection.[169] It has been suggested that all regimens should include an agent that penetrates into brain tissue.[169] The organism is sensitive to vancomycin, which is considered to be the drug of choice. Most isolates are also susceptible to erythromycin, rifampin, aminoglycosides, and chloramphenicol, but erythromycin and rifampin are the most active in vitro and, used together, act synergistically.[9, 169] β-Lactam antibiotics should not be used because resistance may easily develop.

Other *Rhodococcus* Species

Infections caused by other species of *Rhodococcus* have largely been associated with procedures involving medical devices. Recently, nosocomially acquired sternal wound infections caused by *R. (Gordona) bronchialis* were described in seven patients after coronary artery bypass surgery.[231] Similarly, central venous catheter sepsis caused by *Rhodococcus (Gordona)* spp. was reported in two patients receiving long-term total parenteral nutrition at home.[232] Meningitis caused by *R. (Tsukamurella) aurantiacus* was described in a man with hairy cell leukemia,[233] as was severe progressive abscesses and necrotizing tenosynovitis in a young woman requiring eventual amputation of the right forearm,[234] and in pulmonary infection.[235] Catheter-related bacteremia caused by *Tsukamurella paurometabolum* was reported in three patients with cancer,[236] as was an unspeciated *Tsukamurella* sp. isolated from catheter blood from a child with acute myelogenous leukemia after an allogenic bone marrow transplant.[237] Chronic endophthalmitis after lens implantation due to *R. luteus* and *R. erythropolis* was also reported.[238] *Rhodococcus erythropolis* was also the cause of peritonitis in a patient on CAPD.[239] *Rhodococcus rhodochrous* has been reported to cause pulmonary disease including bacteremic pneumonia,[240, 241] pericarditis, bone marrow invasion with noncaseating granulomas, various dermatologic lesions,[241] a corneal ulcer,[242] and a ventriculoperitoneal shunt infection.[243] *Rhodococcus rhodochrous* was also isolated from ventricular fluid from a fontanelle puncture in a child with meningoencephalitis.[241] Lung infection caused by *R. rubropertinctus,* clinically resembling tuberculosis, in a 29-year-old Vietnamese woman has also been described.[244] Other unidentified *Rhodococcus* spp. have been found to cause recurrent skin infections,[245] a wrist nodule with axillary adenopathy,[246] meningitis,[247] and septic arthritis and osteomyelitis.[248] Optimal management of these infections is uncertain. Selection of antimicrobial therapy should be based on antimicrobial susceptibility testing and individualized according to clinical response. Surgical resection may be required. Medical devices should be removed.

REFERENCES

1. Lehmann KB, Neumann R. Atlas und Grundriss der Bakteriologie und Lehrbuch der speziellen bacteriologischen Diagnostik. 1st ed. Munich: JF Lehmann; 1896.
2. Barksdale L. The genus *Corynebacterium.* In: Starr MP, Stolp H, Truper HG, et al, eds. The Prokaryotes: A Handbook of Habitats, Isolation, and Identification of Bacteria. Berlin: Springer-Verlag; 1981:1827–1837.
3. Centers for Disease Control and Prevention. Fatal diphtheria—Wisconsin 1982. MMWR. Morb Mortal Wkly Rpt. 1982;31:553–555.
4. Centers for Disease Control and Prevention. Respiratory diphtheria caused by *Corynebacterium ulcerans*—Terre Haute, Indiana, 1996. MMWR Morb Mortal Wkly Rpt. 1997;46:330–332.
5. Kaplan K, Weinstein L. Diphtheroid infections of man. Ann Intern Med. 1969;70:919–929.
6. Johnson WD, Kaye D. Serious infections caused by diphtheroids. Ann N Y Acad Sci. 1970;174:568–578.
7. Washington JA II. Bacteriology, clinical spectrum of disease, and therapeutic aspects in coryneform bacterial infection. In: Remington JS, Swartz MN, eds. Current Clinical Topics in Infectious Diseases. v. 2. New York: McGraw-Hill; 1981:68–88.
8. Lipsky BA, Goldberger AC, Tompkins LS, et al. Infections caused by nondiphtheria corynebacteria. Rev Infect Dis. 1982;4:1220–1235.
9. Coyle MB, Lipsky BA. Coryneform bacteria in infectious diseases: Clinical and laboratory aspects. Clin Microbiol Rev. 1990;3:227–246.
10. Murray BA, Karchmer AW, Moellering RC. Diphtheroid prosthetic valve endocarditis. Am J Med. 1980;69:838–848.
11. Coyle MB, Hollis DG, Groman NB. *Corynebacterium* spp. and other coryneform organisms. In: Lennette EH, Balows A, Hausler WJ Jr, et al, eds. Manual of Clinical Microbiology. Washington, DC: American Society for Microbiology; 1985:193–204.
12. Clarridge JE, Spiegel CA. *Corynebacterium* and miscellaneous irregular gram-positive rods, *Erysipelothrix,* and *Gardnerella.* In: Murray PR, Baron EJ, Pfaller MA, et al, eds. Manual of Clinical Microbiology. Washington, DC: American Society for Microbiology; 1995:357–378.
13. Funke G, von Graevenitz A, Clarridge JE, et al. Clinical microbiology of coryneform bacteria. Clin Microbiol Rev. 1997;10:125–159.
14. Janda WM. *Corynebacterium* species and the coryneform bacteria. Part I: New and emerging species in the genus *Corynebacterium.* Clin Microbiol Newsl. 1998;20:41–52.
15. Janda WM. *Corynebacterium* species and the coryneform bacteria. Part II: Current status of the CDC coryneform groups. Clin Microbiol Newslett. 1998;20:53–66.
16. Wong TP, Groman N. Production of diphtheria toxin by selected isolates of *Corynebacterium ulcerans* and *Corynebacterium pseudotuberculosis.* Infect Immun. 1984;43:1114–1116.

17. Meers PD. A case of classical diphtheria and other infections due to *Corynebacterium ulcerans.* J Infect. 1979;1:139–142.
18. Siegel SM, Haile CA. *Corynebacterium ulcerans* pneumonia. South Med J. 1985;78:1267.
19. Hadfield TL, Monson MH. *Corynebacterium ulcerans* infection. Clin Microbiol Newslett. 1983;5:104–105.
20. Lopez JF, Wong FM, Quesada J. *Corynebacterium pseudotuberculosis:* First case of human infection. Am J Clin Pathol. 1966;46:562–567.
21. Peel MM, Palmer GG, Stacpoole AM, et al. Human lymphadenitis due to *Corynebacterium pseudotuberculosis:* Report of ten cases from Australia and review. Clin Infect Dis. 1996;24:185–191.
22. Keslin MH, McCoy EL, McCusker JJ, et al. *Corynebacterium pseudotuberculosis:* A new cause of infectious and eosinophilic pneumonia. Am J Med. 1979;67:228–231.
23. Goldberger AC, Lipsky BA, Plorde JJ. Suppurative granulomatous lymphadenitis caused by *Corynebacterium ovis (pseudotuberculosis).* Am J Clin Pathol. 1981;76:486–490.
24. Richards M, Hurse A. *Corynebacterium pseudotuberculosis* abscesses in a young butcher. Aust N Z J Med. 1985;15:85–86.
25. House RW, Schousboe M, Allen JP, et al. *Corynebacterium ovis* (pseudo-tuberculosis) lymphadenitis in a sheep farmer: A new occupational disease in New Zealand. N Z Med J. 1986;99:659–662.
26. Augustine JL, Renshaw HW. Survival of *Corynebacterium pseudotuberculosis* in axenic purulent exudate on common barnyard fomites. Am J Vet Res. 1986;47:713–715.
27. LeaMaster BR, Shen DT, Gorham JR, et al. Efficacy of *Corynebacterium pseudotuberculosis* bacterin for the immunologic protection of sheep against development of caseous lymphadenitis. Am J Vet Res. 1987;48:869–872.
28. Geraci JE, Forth RJ, Ellis FH. Postoperative prosthetic valve bacterial endocarditis due to *Corynebacterium xerosis.* Mayo Clin Proc. 1967;42:736–743.
29. Gomez MA, Roncoroni AJ, Smayevski J, et al. Endocarditis due to *Corynebacterium xerosis.* Medicina (Aires). 1989;49:62–64.
30. Malik AS, Johari MR. Pneumonia, pericarditis, and endocarditis in a child with *Corynebacterium xerosis* septicemia. Clin Infect Dis. 1995;20:191–192.
31. Arisoy ES, Demmler GJ, Dimme WM Jr. *Corynebacterium xerosis* ventriculoperitoneal shunt infection in an infant: Report of a case and review of the literature. Pediatr Infect Dis J. 1993;12:536–538.
32. Wallet F, Marquette CH, Courcol RJ. Multiresistant *Corynebacterium xerosis* as a cause of pneumonia in a patient with acute leukemia. Clin Infect Dis. 1994;18:845–846.
33. Vettese TE, Craig CP. Spontaneous bacterial peritonitis due to *Corynebacterium xerosis.* Clin Infect Dis. 1993;17:815.
34. Wood CA. Nosocomial infection of a pancreatic pseudocyst due to *Corynebacterium xerosis.* Clin Infect Dis. 1993;17:934–935.
35. Rubinfeld RS, Cohen EJ, Arentsen JJ, et al. Diphtheroids as ocular pathogens. Am J Ophthalmol. 1989;108:251–254.
36. Lortholary O, Buu-Hoï A, Fagon JY, et al. Mediastinitis due to multiply resistant *Corynebacterium xerosis.* Clin Infect Dis. 1993;16:172.
37. King CT. Sternal wound infection due to *Corynebacterium xerosis.* Clin Infect Dis. 1994;19:1171–1172.
38. Bowstead TT, Santiago SM. Pleuropulmonary infection due to *Corynebacterium striatum.* Br J Dis Chest. 1980;74:198–200.
39. Martínez-Martínez L, Suárez AI, del Carmen Ortega M, et al. Fatal pulmonary infection caused by *Corynebacterium striatum.* Clin Infect Dis. 1994;19:806–807.
40. Dall L, Barnes WG, Hurford D. Septicemia in a granulocytopenic patient caused by *Corynebacterium striatum.* Postgrad Med J. 1989;65:247–248.
41. Watkins DA, Chahine A, Creger RJ, et al. *Corynebacterium striatum:* A diphtheroid with pathogenic potential. Clin Infect Dis. 1993;17:21–25.
42. Tumbarello M, Tacconelli E, Del Forno AD, et al. *Corynebacterium striatum* bacteremia in a patient with AIDS. Clin Infect Dis. 1994;18:1007–1008.
43. Wolde Rufael D, Cohn SE. Native valve endocarditis due to *Corynebacterium striatum:* Case report and review. Clin Infect Dis. 1994;19:1054–1061.
44. Tattevin P, Crémieux AC, Muller-Serieys C, et al. Native valve endocarditis due to *Corynebacterium striatum:* First reported case of medical treatment alone. Clin Infect Dis. 1996;23:1330–1331.
45. Juurlink DN, Borczyk A, Simor AE. Native valve endocarditis due to *Corynebacterium striatum.* Eur J Clin Microbiol Infect Dis. 1996;15:963–965.
46. Melero-Bascones M, Muñoz P, Rodríguez-Créixems M, et al. *Corynebacterium striatum:* an undescribed agent of pacemaker-related endocarditis. Clin Infect Dis. 1996;22:576–577.
47. Weiss K, Labbé AC, Laverdiére M. *Corynebacterium striatum* meningitis: Case report and review of an increasingly important *Corynebacterium* species. Clin Infect Dis. 1996;23:1246–1248.
48. Hoy CM, Kerr K, Livingston JH. Cerebrospinal fluid–shunt infection due to *Corynebacterium striatum.* Clin Infect Dis. 1997;25:1486–1487.
49. Martínez-Martínez L, Pasçaul A, Bernard K, et al. Antimicrobial susceptibility pattern of *Corynebacterium striatum.* Antimicrob Agents Chemother. 1996;40:2671–2672.
50. Berger SA, Gorea A, Stadler J, et al. Recurrent breast abscesses caused by *Corynebacterium minutissimum.* J Clin Microbiol. 1984;20:1219–1220.
51. Mattox TF, Rutgers J, Yoshimori RN, et al. Nonfluorescent erythrasma of the vulva. Obstet Gynecol. 1993;81:862–864.
52. Guarderas J, Karnad A, Alvarez S, et al. *Corynebacterium minutissimum* bacteremia in a patient with chronic myeloid leukemia in blast crisis. Diagn Microbiol Infect Dis. 1986;5:327–330.
53. Golledge CL, Phillips G. *Corynebacterium minutissimum* infection. J Infect. 1991;23:73–76.
54. Van Bosterhaut B, Cuvelier R, Serruys E, et al. Three cases of opportunistic infection caused by propionic acid producing *Corynebacterium minutissimum.* Eur J Clin Microbiol Infect Dis. 1992;11:628–631.
55. Herschorn BJ, Brucker AJ. Embolic retinopathy due to *Corynebacterium minutissimum* endocarditis. Br J Ophthalmol. 1985;69:29–31.
56. Cavendish J, Cole JB, Ohl CA. Polymicrobial central venous catheter sepsis involving a multiantibiotic-resistant strain of *Corynebacterium minutissimum.* Clin Infect Dis. 1994;19:204–205.
57. Craig J, Grigor W, Doyle B. Pyelonephritis caused by *Corynebacterium minutissimum.* Pediatr Infect Dis J. 1994;13:1151–1152.
58. De Miguel-Martinez I, Fernández-Fuertes F, Ramos-Macías A, et al. Sepsis due to multiply resistant *Corynebacterium amycolatum.* Eur J Clin Microbiol Infect Dis. 1996;15:617–618.
59. Berner R, Pelz K, Wilhelm C, et al. Fatal sepsis caused by *Corynebacterium amycolatum* in a premature infant. J Clin Microbiol. 1997;35:1011–1012.
60. Funke G, Efstratiou A, Kuklinska D, et al. *Corynebacterium imitans* sp nov isolated from patients with suspected diphtheria. J Clin Microbiol. 1997;35:1978–1983.
61. Leonard A, Raij L, Shapiro FL. Bacterial endocarditis in regularly dialyzed patients. Kidney Int. 1973;4:407–422.
62. Rubler S, Harvey L, Avitabile A, et al. Mitral valve obstruction in a case of bacterial endocarditis due to *Corynebacterium hofmannii.* N Y State J Med. 1982;82:1590–1594.
63. Lindner PS, Hardy DJ, Murphy TF. Endocarditis due to *Corynebacterium pseudodiphtheriticum.* N Y State J Med. 1986;86:102–104.
64. Morris A, Guild I. Endocarditis due to *Corynebacterium pseudodiphtheriticum:* Five case reports, review, and antibiotic susceptibilities of nine strains. Rev Infect Dis. 1991;13:887–892.
65. Wilson ME, Shapiro DS. Native valve endocarditis due to *Corynebacterium pseudodiphtheriticum.* Clin Infect Dis. 1992;15:1059–1060.
66. Donaghy M, Cohen J. Pulmonary infection with *Corynebacterium hofmannii* complicating systemic lupus erythematosus. J Infect Dis. 1983;147:962.
67. Andavolu RH, Jagadha V, Lue Y, et al. Lung abscess involving *Corynebacterium pseudodiphtheriticum* in a patient with AIDS-related complex. N Y State J Med. 1986;86:594–596.
68. Colt HG, Morris JF, Marston BJ, et al. Necrotizing tracheitis caused by *Corynebacterium pseudodiphtheriticum:* Unique case and review. Rev Infect Dis. 1991;13:73–76.
69. Craig TJ, Maguire FE, Wallace MR. Tracheobronchitis due to *Corynebacterium pseudodiphtheriticum.* South Med J. 1991;84:504–506.
70. Miller RA, Rompalo A, Coyle MB. *Corynebacterium pseudodiphtheriticum* pneumonia in an immunologically intact host. Diagn Microbiol Infect Dis. 1986;4:165–171.
71. Williams EA, Green JD, Salazar S, et al. Pneumonia caused by *Corynebacterium pseudodiphtheriticum.* J Tenn Med Assoc. 1991(May):223–224.
72. LaRocco M, Robinson C, Robinson A. *Corynebacterium pseudodiphtheriticum* associated with suppurative lymphadenitis. Eur J Clin Microbiol. 1987;6:79.
73. Lockwood BM, Wilson J. *Corynebacterium pseudodiphtheriticum* isolation. Clin Microbiol Newslett. 1987;9:5–6.
74. Manzella JP, Kellogg JA, Parsey KS. *Corynebacterium pseudodiphtheriticum:* A respiratory tract pathogen in adults. Clin Infect Dis. 1995;20:37–40.
75. Ahmed K, Kawakami K, Watanabe K, et al. *Corynebacterium pseudodiphtheriticum:* A respiratory tract pathogen. Clin Infect Dis. 1995;20:41–46.
76. Santos MR, Gandhi S, Vogler M, et al. Suspected diphtheria in an Uzbek national: Isolation of *Corynebacterium pseudodiphtheriticum* resulted in a false-positive presumptive diagnosis. Clin Infect Dis. 1996;22:735.
77. Izurieta HS, Strebel PM, Youngblood T, et al. Exudative pharyngitis possibly due to *Corynebacterium pseudodiphtheriticum,* a new challenge in the differential diagnosis of diphtheria. Emerg Infect Dis. 1997;3:65–68.
78. Petit PLC, Bok JW, Thompson J, et al. Native-valve endocarditis due to CDC coryneform group ANF-3: Report of a case and review of corynebacterial endocarditis. Clin Infect Dis. 1994;19:897–901.
79. Hande KR, Witebsky FG, Brown MS, et al. Sepsis with a new species of *Corynebacterium.* Ann Intern Med. 1976;85:423–426.
80. Young VM, Meyers WF, Moody MR, et al. The emergence of coryneform bacteria as a cause of nosocomial infections in compromised hosts. Am J Med. 1981;70:646–650.
81. Pearson TA, Braine HG, Rathbun HK. Corynebacterium sepsis in oncology patients. JAMA. 1977;238:1737–1740.
82. Stamm WE, Tompkins LS, Wagner KF, et al. Infection due to *Corynebacterium* species in marrow transplant patients. Ann Intern Med. 1979;91:167–173.
83. Gill VJ, Manning C, Lamson M, et al. Antibiotic-resistant group JK bacteria in hospitals. J Clin Microbiol. 1981;13:472–477.
84. Soriano F, Rodriguez-Tudela JL, Fernandez-Robas R, et al. Skin colonization by *Corynebacterium* groups D2 and JK in hospitalized patients. J Clin Microbiol. 1988;26:1878–1880.
85. Larson EL, McGinley KJ, Leyden JJ, et al. Skin colonization with antibiotic-resistant (JK group) and antibiotic-sensitive lipophilic diphtheroids in hospitalized and normal adults. J Infect Dis. 1986;153:701–706.
86. Wichmann S, Wirsing von Koenig CH, Becker-Boost E, et al. Group JK corynebacteria in skin flora of healthy persons and patients. Eur J Clin Microbiol. 1985;4:502–504.
87. Telander B, Lerner R, Palmblad J, et al. *Corynebacterium* group JK in a hematolog-

ical ward: Infections, colonization, and environmental contamination. Scand J Infect Dis. 1988;20:55–61.
88. McGinley KJ, Labows JN, Zeckman JM, et al. Pathogenic JK group corynebacteria and their similarity to human cutaneous lipophilic diphtheroids. J Infect Dis. 1985;152:801–806.
89. Quinn JP, Arnow PM, Weil D, et al. Outbreak of JK diphtheroid infections associated with environmental contamination. J Clin Microbiol. 1984;19:668–671.
90. Riebel W, Frantz N, Adelstein D, et al. *Corynebacterium* JK: A cause of nosocomial device–related infection. Rev Infect Dis. 1986;8:42–49.
91. Lepape A, Carry PY, Chomarat M, et al. *Corynebacterium* JK: Surgical infections in non-immunocompromised patients. Intensive Care Med. 1988;15:23–26.
92. Kerry-Williams SM, Noble WC. Plasmids in group JK coryneform bacteria isolated in a single hospital. J Hyg (Lond). 1986;97:255–263.
93. Khabbaz RF, Kaper JB, Moody MR, et al. Molecular epidemiology of group JK *Corynebacterium* on a cancer ward: Lack of evidence for patient-to-patient transmission. J Infect Dis. 1986;154:95–99.
94. Riley PS, Hollis DG, Utter GB, et al. Characterization and identification of 95 diphtheroid (group JK) cultures isolated from clinical specimens. J Clin Microbiol. 1979;9:418–424.
95. Blom J, Heltberg O. The ultrastructure of antibiotic-susceptible and multi-resistant strains of group JK diphtheroid rods isolated from clinical specimens. Acta Pathol Microbiol Immunol Scand. 1986;94:301–308.
96. Dan M, Somer I, Knobel B, et al. Cutaneous manifestations of infection with *Corynebacterium* JK. Rev Infect Dis. 1988;10:1204–1207.
97. Van Bosterhaut B, Surmont I, Vandeven J, et al. *Corynebacterium jeikeium* (group JK diphtheroids) endocarditis: A report of five cases. Diagn Microbiol Infect Dis. 1989;12:265–268.
98. Moffie BG, Veenendaal RA, Thomson J. Native valve endocarditis due to *Corynebacterium* group JK. Neth J Med. 1990;37:236–238.
99. Martinez-Vea A, Costa J, Garcia C, et al. *Corynebacterium* group JK endocarditis in a haemodialysis patient. Nephrol Dial Transplant. 1993;8:177–179.
100. Guarino MJ, Qazi R, Woll JE, et al. Septicemia, rash, and pulmonary infiltrates secondary to *Corynebacterium* group JK infection. Am J Med. 1987;82:132–134.
101. Waters BL. Pathology of culture-proven JK *Corynebacterium* pneumonia: An autopsy case report. Am J Clin Pathol. 1989;91:616–619.
102. Yoshitomi Y, Kohno S, Koga H, et al. Fatal pneumonia caused by *Corynebacterium* group JK after treatment of *Staphylococcus aureus* pneumonia. Intern Med. 1992;31:930–932.
103. McNaughton RD, Villaneuva RR, Donnelly R, et al. Cavitating pneumonia caused by *Corynebacterium* group JK. J Clin Microbiol. 1988;26:2216–2217.
104. Pierard D, Lauwers S, Mouton MC, et al. Group JK *Corynebacterium* peritonitis in a patient undergoing continuous ambulatory peritoneal dialysis. J Clin Microbiol. 1983;18:1011–1014.
105. Johnson A, Hulse P, Oppenheim BA. *Corynebacterium jeikeium* meningitis and transverse myelitis in a neutropenic patient. Eur J Clin Microbiol Infect Dis. 1992;11:473–479.
106. Fisher RA, Rodziewicz G, Selman WR, et al. Liver abscess: Complication of a ventriculoperitoneal shunt. Neurosurgery. 1984;14:480–482.
107. Allen KD, Green HT. Infections due to a "group JK" *Corynebacterium*. J Infect. 1986;13:41–44.
108. Keren G, Geva T, Bogokovsky B, et al. *Corynebacterium* group JK pathogen in cerebrospinal fluid shunt infection: Report of two cases. J Neurosurg. 1988;68:648–650.
109. Morrison VA, Weinshel EL, Luikart SD. *Corynebacterium* JK: A new pathogen in ventriculostomy infections. J Neurooncol. 1991;11:65–69.
110. Greene KA, Clark RJ, Zabramski JM. Ventricular CSF shunt infections associated with *Corynebacterium jeikeium:* Report of three cases and review. Clin Infect Dis. 1993;16:139–141.
111. Knudsen JD, Nielsen CJ, Espersen F. Treatment of shunt-related cerebral ventriculitis due to *Corynebacterium jeikeium* with vancomycin administered intraventricularly. *APMIS* 1994;102:317–320.
112. Claeys G, Vershchraegen G, DeSmet L, et al. *Corynebacterium* JK (Johnson-Kay strain) infection of a Küntscher-nailed tibial fracture. Clin Orthop. 1986;202:227–229.
113. Weller TMA, McLardy-Smith P, Crook DW. *Corynebacterium jeikeium* osteomyelitis following total hip joint replacement. J Infect. 1994;29:113–114.
114. Yildiz S, Yildiz HY, Çetin I, et al. Total knee arthroplasty complicated by *Corynebacterium jeikeium* infection. Scand J Infect Dis. 1995;27:635–636.
115. Turett GS, Fazal BA, Johnston BE, et al. Liver abscess due to *Corynebacterium jeikeium* in a patient with AIDS. Clin Infect Dis. 1993;17:514–515.
116. Gronemeyer PS, Weissfeld AS, Sonnenwirth AC. *Corynebacterium* group JK bacterial infection in a patient with an epicardial pacemaker. Am J Clin Pathol. 1980;74:838–842.
117. Dietrich MC, Watson D, Kumar ML. *Corynebacterium* group JK infections in children. Pediatr Infect Dis J. 1989;8:233–236.
118. Brown AE. Neutropenia, fever, and infection. Am J Med. 1984;76:421–428.
119. Blevins A, Lange M, Sobeck K, et al. Prevention and control of *Corynebacterium* CDC JK bacteremia in cancer patients with prolonged neutropenia. Abstract L 57. In: Proceedings of the 85th Annual Meeting of the American Society for Microbiology, March 3–7, 1985; Las Vegas, Nevada.
120. Santamaria M, Ponte C, Wilhelmi I, et al. Antimicrobial susceptibility of *Corynebacterium* group D2. Antimicrob Agents Chemother. 1985;28:845–846.
121. Roblas RF, Prieto S, Santamaria M, et al. Activity of nine antimicrobial agents against *Corynebacterium* group D2 strains isolated from clinical specimens and skin. Antimicrob Agents Chemother. 1987;31:821–822.
122. Jakobes NF, Perlino CA. "Diphtheroid" pneumonia. South Med J. 1979;72:475–476.
123. Van Bosterhaut B, Claeys G, Gigi J, et al. Isolation of *Corynebacterium* group D2 from clinical specimens. Eur J Clin Microbiol. 1987;6:418–419.
124. Langs JC, de Briel D, Sauvage C, et al. Endocardite à *Corynebacterium* du group D2, à point de départ urinaire. Med Malad Infect. 1988;5:293–295.
125. Ena J, Berenguer J, Pelaez T, et al. Endocarditis caused by *Corynebacterium* groupe D2 (Letter). J Infect. 1991;22:95–96.
126. Notario R, Borda NEG, Gambandé T. Endocarditis en valvula protésica causada por *Corynebacterium urealyticum.* Medicina (B Aires). 1996;56:57–58.
127. Chomarat M, Breton P, Dubost J. Osteomyelitis due to *Corynebacterium* group D2 (Letter). Eur J Clin Microbiol Infect Dis. 1991;10:43.
128. Soriano F, Ponte C, Ruiz P, et al. Non-urinary tract infections caused by multiply antibiotic-resistant *Corynebacterium urealyticum.* Clin Infect Dis. 1993;17:890–891.
129. Saavedra J, Rodríguez JN, Fernández-Jurado A, et al. A necrotic soft-tissue lesion due to *Corynebacterium urealyticum* in a neutropenic child. Clin Infect Dis. 1996;22:851–852.
130. Wood C, Pepe R. Bacteremia in a patient with non-urinary tract infection due to *Corynebacterium urealyticum.* Clin Infect Dis. 1994;19:367–368.
131. Soriano F, Ponte C, Santamaria M, et al. *Corynebacterium* group D2 as a cause of alkaline-encrusted cystitis: Report of four cases and characterization of the organisms. J Clin Microbiol. 1985;21:788–792.
132. Soriano F, Ponte C, Santamaria M, et al. In vitro and in vivo study of stone formation by *Corynebacterium* group D2 *(Corynebacterium urealyticum).* J Clin Microbiol. 1986;23:691–694.
133. Ronci-Koenig TJ, Tan JS, File TM, et al. Infections due to *Corynebacterium* group D2. Arch Intern Med. 1990;150:1965–1966.
134. Ohl CA, Tribble DR. *Corynebacterium* group D2 infection of a complex renal cyst in a debilitated patient (Letter). Clin Infect Dis. 1992;14:1160–1161.
135. Schoch PA, Ferragamo MA, Cunha BA. *Corynebacterium* group D2 pyelonephritis. Urology. 1987;29:66–67.
136. Ryan M, Murray PR. Prevalence of *Corynebacterium urealyticum* in urine specimens collected at a university-affiliated medical center. J Clin Microbiol. 1994;32:1395–1396.
137. Aguado JM, Ponte C, Soriano F. Bacteriuria with a multiply resistant species of *Corynebacterium* (*Corynebacterium* group D2): An unnoticed cause of urinary tract infection. J Infect Dis. 1987;156:144–150.
138. Claeys G, Vanhouteghem H, Riegel P, et al. Endocarditis of native aortic and mitral valves due to *Corynebacterium accolens:* Report of a case and application of phenotypic and genotypic techniques for identification. J Clin Microbiol. 1996;34:1290–1292.
139. Austin GE, Hill EO. Endocarditis due to *Corynebacterium* CDC group G2. J Infect Dis. 1983;147:1106.
140. Lawrence C, Brown ST, Freundlich LF. Peripheral blood smear bacillemia. Am J Med. 1988;85:111–113.
141. Phillips SE, Bracis R. Recognition of *Corynebacterium* group G2 as a cause of infection. Clin Microbiol Newslett. 1991;13:78–80.
142. Quinn AG, Comaish JS, Pedlar SJ. Septic arthritis and endocarditis due to group G-2 coryneform organism. Lancet. 1991;338:62–63.
143. Kotrajaras R, Buddhavudhikrai P, Sukroongreung S, et al. Endemic leg ulcers caused by *Corynebacterium pyogenes* in Thailand. Int J Dermatol. 1982;21:407–409.
144. Kotrajaras R, Tagami H. *Corynebacterium pyogenes:* Its pathogenic mechanism in epidemic leg ulcers in Thailand. Int J Dermatol. 1987;26:45–50.
145. Barnham M. *Actinomyces pyogenes* bacteremia in a patient with carcinoma of the colon. J Infect. 1988;17:231–234.
146. Gahrn-Hansen B, Frederiksen W. Human infections with *Actinomyces pyogenes (Corynebacterium pyogenes).* Diagn Microbiol Infect Dis. 1992;15:349–354.
147. Collins MD, Jones D, Schofield GM. Reclassification of *Corynebacterium haemolyticum* (MacLean, Liebow & Rosenberg) in the genus *Arcanobacterium* gen nov as *Arcanobacterium haemolyticum* nom rev, comb nov. J Gen Microbiol. 1982;128:1279–1281.
148. Green SL, LaPeter KS. Pseudodiphtheritic membranous pharyngitis caused by *Corynebacterium hemolyticum.* JAMA. 1981;245:2330–2331.
149. Kovatch AL, Schuit KE, Michaels RH. *Corynebacterium hemolyticum* peritonsillar abscess mimicking diphtheria. JAMA. 1983;249:1757–1758.
150. Barnham M, Bradwell RA. Acute peritonsillar abscess caused by *Arcanobacterium haemolyticum.* J Laryngol Otol. 1992;106:1000–1001.
151. Tompkins LS. *Corynebacterium hemolyticum.* Clin Microbiol Newslett. 1983; 5:29–30.
152. Miller RA, Brancato F, Holmes KK. *Corynebacterium hemolyticum* as a cause of pharyngitis and scarlatiniform rash in young adults. Ann Intern Med. 1986;105:867–872.
153. Banck G, Nyman M. Tonsillitis and rash associated with *Corynebacterium haemolyticum.* J Infect Dis. 1986;154:1037–1040.
154. Waagner DC. *Arcanobacterium haemolyticum:* Biology of the organism and diseases in man. Pediatr Infect Dis J. 1991;10:933–939.
155. Chhang WH, Ayyagari A, Sharma BS, et al. *Arcanobacterium haemolyticum* brain abscess in a child (a case report). Indian J Pathol Microbiol. 1991;34:145–148.
156. Waller KS, Johnson J, Wood BP. Radiological case of the month. Cavitary pneumonia due to *Arcanobacterium haemolyticum.* Am J Dis Child. 1991;145:209–210.
157. Givner LB, McGehee D, Taber LH, et al. Sinusitis, orbital cellulitis, and polymicrobial bacteremia in a patient with primary Epstein-Barr virus infection. Pediatr Infect Dis. 1984;3:254–256.

158. Givner LB. *Arcanobacterium haemolyticum* sepsis and Epstein-Barr virus infection. Pediatr Infect Dis J. 1992;11:417–418.
159. Goudswaard J, van de Merwe DW, van der Sluys P, et al. *Corynebacterium haemolyticum:* Septicemia in a girl with mononucleosis infection. Scand J Infect Dis. 1988;20:339–340.
160. Alós JI, Barros C, Gómez-Garcés JL. Endocarditis caused by *Arcanobacterium haemolyticum.* Eur J Clin Microbiol Infect Dis. 1995;14:1085–1088.
161. Esteban J, Zapardiel J, Soriano F. Two cases of soft-tissue infection caused by *Arcanobacterium haemolyticum.* Clin Infect Dis. 1994;18;835–836.
162. Batiste-Milton SE, Gander RM, Colvin DD. Tubo-ovarian abscess and peritoneal effusion caused by *Arcanobacterium haemolyticum.* Clin Microbiol Newslett. 1995;17:118–120.
163. Greenman JL. *Corynebacterium hemolyticum* and pharyngitis. Ann Intern Med. 1987;106:633.
164. Robinson BE, Murray DL. *Corynebacterium hemolyticum* and pharyngitis. Ann Intern Med. 1987;106:778–779.
165. Mackenzie A, Fuite LA, Chan FTH, et al. Incidence and pathogenicity of *Arcanobacterium haemolyticum* during a 2-year study in Ottawa. Clin Infect Dis. 1995;21:177–181.
166. Nyman M, Alugupalli KR, Strömberg S, et al. Antibody response to *Arcanobacterium haemolyticum* infection in humans. J Infect Dis. 1997;175:1515–1518.
167. Nyman M, Banck G, Thore M. Penicillin tolerance in *Arcanobacterium haemolyticum.* J Infect Dis. 1990;161:261–265.
168. Prescott JF. *Rhodococcus equi:* An animal and human pathogen. Clin Microbiol Rev. 1991;4:20–34.
169. Verville TD, Huycke MM, Greenfield RA, et al. *Rhodococcus equi* infections of humans. Twelve cases and a review of the literature. Medicine (Baltimore). 1994;73:119–132.
170. Walsh RD, Schoch PE, Cunha BA. *Rhodococcus.* Infect Control Hosp Epidemiol. 1993;14:282–287.
171. Barton MD, Hughes KL. Ecology of *Rhodococcus equi.* Vet Microbiol. 1984;9:65–76.
172. Nordmann P, Kerestedjian JJ, Ronco E. Therapy of *Rhodococcus equi* disseminated infections in nude mice. Antimicrob Agents Chemother. 1992;36:1244–1248.
173. Huffnagle KE, Southern PM. *Rhodococcus equi:* An opportunistic pathogen in a patient with AIDS. Clin Microbiol Newslett. 1992;14:141–142.
174. Van Etta LL, Filice GA, Ferguson RM, et al. *Corynebacterium equi:* A review of 12 cases of human infection. Rev Infect Dis. 1983;5:1012–1018.
175. Sane DC, Durack DT. Infection with *Rhodococcus equi* in AIDS. N Engl J Med. 1986;314:56–57.
176. Samies JH, Hathaway BN, Echols RM, et al. Lung abscess due to *Corynebacterium equi.* Am J Med. 1986;80:685–688.
177. MacGregor JH, Samuelson WM, Sane DC, et al. Opportunistic lung infection caused by *Rhodococcus (Corynebacterium) equi.* Radiology. 1986;160:83–84.
178. Wang HH, Tollerud D, Danar D, et al. Another Whipple-like disease in AIDS (Letter)? N Engl J Med. 1986;314:1577–1578.
179. LeBar WD, Pensler MI. Pleural effusion due to *Rhodococcus equi.* J Infect Dis. 1986;154:919–920.
180. Kunke PJ. Serious infection in an AIDS patient due to *Rhodococcus equi.* Clin Microbiol Newsl. 1987;9:163–164.
181. Sonnet J, Wauters G, Zech F, et al. Opportunistic *Rhodococcus equi* infection in an African AIDS case (1976–1981). Acta Clin Belg. 1987;42:215–216.
182. Weingarten JS, Huang DY, Jackman JD Jr. *Rhodococcus equi* pneumonia—an unusual early manifestation of the acquired immunodeficiency syndrome (AIDS). Chest. 1988;94:195–196.
183. Hillerdal G, Riesenfeldt-Orn I, Pedersen A, et al. Infection with *Rhodococcus equi* in a patient with sarcoidosis treated with corticosteroids. Scand J Infect Dis. 1988;20:673–677.
184. Haglund LA, Trotter JA, Slater LN, et al. Case 9-1989: AIDS and a cavitary pulmonary lesion (Letter). N Engl J Med. 1989;321:395.
185. Allen UD, Niec A, Kerem E, et al. *Rhodococcus equi* pneumonia in a child with leukemia. Pediatr Infect Dis J. 1989;8:656–658.
186. Jones MR, Say PJ, Neale TJ, et al. *Rhodococcus equi:* An emerging opportunistic pathogen? Aust N Z J Med. 1989;19:103–107.
187. Scannell KA, Portoni EJ, Finkle HI, et al. Pulmonary malacoplakia and *Rhodococcus equi* infection in a patient with AIDS. Chest. 1990;97:1000–1001.
188. Egawa T, Hara H, Kawase I, et al. Human pulmonary infection *Corynebacterium equi.* Eur Respir J. 1990;3:240–242.
189. Emmons W, Reichwein B, Winslow DL. *Rhodococcus equi* infection in the patient with AIDS: Literature review and report of a case. Rev Infect Dis. 1991;13:91–96.
190. Harvey RL, Sunstrum JC. *Rhodococcus equi* infection in patients with and without human immunodeficiency virus infection. Rev Infect Dis. 1991;13:139–145.
191. Rouquet RM, Clave D, Massip P, et al. Imipenem/vancomycin for *Rhodococcus equi* pulmonary infection in HIV-positive patient (Letter). Lancet. 1991;337:375.
192. Chavanet P, Bonnotte B, Caillot D, et al. Imipenem/teicoplanin for *Rhodococcus equi* pulmonary infection in an AIDS patient. Lancet. 1991;337:794–795.
193. Doig C, Gill MJ, Church DL. *Rhodococcus equi*—an easily missed opportunistic pathogen. Scand J Infect Dis. 1991;23:1–6.
194. Vestbo J, Lundgren JD, Gaub J, et al. Severe *Rhodococcus equi* pneumonia: Case report and literature review. Eur J Clin Microbiol Infect Dis. 1991;10:762–768.
195. Lasky JA, Pulkingham N, Powers MA, et al. *Rhodococcus equi* causing pulmonary infection: Review of 29 cases. South Med J. 1991;84:1217–1220.
196. Roca V, Vinuelas J, Perez-Cecilia E, et al. Bacteremic pneumonia caused by *Rhodococcus equi* and HIV infection: Report of a new case and review of the literature. Enferm Infecc Microbiol Clin. 1991;9:627–629.
197. Shapiro JM, Romney BM, Weiden MD, et al. *Rhodococcus equi* endobronchial mass with lung abscess in a patient with AIDS. Thorax. 1992;47:62–63.
198. Nordmann P, Chavanet P, Caillon J, et al. Recurrent pneumonia due to rifampicin-resistant *Rhodococcus equi* in a patient infected with HIV (Letter). J Infect. 1992;24:104–107.
199. Gray BM. Case report: *Rhodococcus equi* pneumonia in a patient infected by the human immunodeficiency virus. Am J Med Sci. 1992;303:180–183.
200. Drancourt H, Bonnet E, Gallais H, et al. *Rhodococcus equi* infection in patients with AIDS. J Infect. 1992;24:123–131.
201. Arrieta-Lezama J, Garcia-Arenzana JM, Idigoras-Viedma P, et al. Pulmonary infection caused by *Rhodococcus equi* in a renal transplant recipient. Med Clin (Barc). 1992;99:143–144.
202. Nordmann P, Rouveix E, Guenounou M, et al. Pulmonary abscess due to a rifampin and fluoroquinolone resistant *Rhodococcus equi* strain in an HIV infected patient (Letter). Eur J Clin Microbiol Infect Dis. 1992;11:557–558.
203. Meynard JL, Salord JM, Lesage D, et al. *Rhodococcus equi* pneumonia: First opportunistic manifestation in a patient with HIV-1 (Letter). Ann Med Interne (Paris). 1992;143:216–218.
204. Pailoux G, Dupont B. Lung abscess caused by *Rhodococcus equi* in HIV infection: Two cases (Letter). Presse Med. 1992;21:1086.
205. Ghnassia JP, Gasser B, Fraisse P, et al. *Rhodococcus equi* infection causing pulmonary malacoplakia in a patient with acquired immune deficiency syndrome. Ann Pathol. 1992;12:174–177.
206. Grossman M, Azimi PH. Your diagnosis, please: Which gram-positive rod would you choose? Pediatr Infect Dis J. 1992;11:776, 780.
207. Sasal M, Roig J, Cervantes M, et al. Good response to antibiotic treatment of lung infection due to *Rhodococcus equi* in a patient infected with human immunodeficiency virus (Letter). Clin Infect Dis. 1992;15:747–748.
208. Magnani G, Elia GF, McNeil MM, et al. *Rhodococcus equi* cavitary pneumonia in HIV-infected patients: An unsuspected opportunistic pathogen. J AIDS. 1992;5:1059–1064.
209. Cury JD, Harrington PT, Hosein IK. Successful medical therapy of *Rhodococcus equi* pneumonia in a patient with HIV infection. Chest. 1992;102:1619–1621.
210. Piersantelli N, Casini-Lemmi M, Cavanna E, et al. *Rhodococcus equi* infections in AIDS: Personal cases. Pathologica. 1992;84:517–521.
211. Clotet B, Sirera G, Erice A. *Rhodococcus equi* infection in HIV-infected patients (Letter). J AIDS. 1993;6:429–430.
212. Cecconi L, Mazzuoli G, Busi-Rizzi E, et al. *Rhodococcus equi* pulmonitis in HIV positive: A review of the literature and a case report. Radiol Med (Torino). 1993;85:122–125.
213. Gazquez I, Garcia-Gonzalez M, Pena JM, et al. A pulmonary abscess due to *Rhodococcus equi* in an AIDS patient (Letter). Rev Clin Esp. 1993;192:152.
214. Adal K, Shiner PT, Francis JB. Primary subcutaneous abscess caused by *Rhodococcus equi.* Ann Intern Med. 1995;122:317.
215. Stolk-Engelaar MVM, Dompeling EC, Meis JFGM, et al. Disseminated abscesses caused by *Rhodococcus equi* in a patient with chronic lymphocytic leukemia. Clin Infect Dis. 1995;20:478–479.
216. Ebersole LL, Paturzo JL. Endophthalmitis caused by *Rhodococcus equi* Prescott serotype 4. J Clin Microbiol. 1988;26:1221–1222.
217. Hillman D, Garretson B, Fiscella R. *Rhodococcus equi* endophthalmitis. Arch Ophthalmol. 1989;107:20.
218. Martín-Dávila P, Quereda C, Rodríguez H, et al. Thyroid abscess due to *Rhodococcus equi* in a patient infected with the human immunodeficiency virus. Eur J Clin Microbiol Infect Dis. 1998;17:55–57.
219. Mandarino E, Rachlis A, Towers M, et al. Prostatic abscess due to *Rhodococcus equi* in a patient with acquired immunodeficiency syndrome. Clin Microbiol Newsl. 1994;16:14–16.
220. Lopes Cardoso FL, Stankiewicz Machado E, Souza MJ, et al. *Rhodococcus equi* mastoiditis in a patient with AIDS. Clin Infect Dis. 1996;22:713.
221. Obana WG, Scannell KA, Jacobs R, et al. A case of *Rhodococcus equi* brain abscess. Surg Neurol. 1991;35:321–324.
222. Fierer J, Wolf P, Seed L, et al. Non-pulmonary *Rhodococcus equi* infections in patients with acquired immune deficiency syndrome (AIDS). J Clin Pathol. 1987;40:556–558.
223. Talanin NY, Donabedian H, Kaw M, et al. Colonic polyps and disseminated infection associated with *Rhodococcus equi* in a patient with AIDS. Clin Infect Dis. 1998;26:1241–1242.
224. Novak RM, Polisky EL, Janda WM, et al. Osteomyelitis caused by *Rhodococcus equi* in a renal transplant patient. Infection. 1988;16:186–188.
225. Fischer L, Sterneck M, Albrecht H, et al. Vertebral osteomyelitis due to *Rhodococcus equi* in a liver transplant recipient. Clin Infect Dis. 1998;26:749–752.
226. Bouchou K, Cathébras P, Dumollard JM, et al. Chronic osteitis due to *Rhodococcus equi* in an immunocompetent patient. Clin Infect Dis. 1995;20:718–720.
227. Thomsen VF, Henriques U, Magnusson M. *Corynebacterium equi* Magnusson isolated from a tuberculoid lesion in a child with adenitis coli. Dan Med Bull. 1968;15:135–138.
228. Franklin DB Jr, Yium JJ, Hawkins SS. *Corynebacterium equi* peritonitis in a patient receiving peritoneal dialysis. South Med J. 1989;82:1046–1047.
229. Sladek GG, Frame JN. *Rhodococcus equi* causing bacteremia in an adult with acute leukemia. South Med J. 1993;86:244–246.
230. Sirera G, Romeu J, Clotet B, et al. Relapsing systemic infection due to *Rhodococcus equi* in a drug abuser seropositive for human immunodeficiency virus. Rev Infect Dis. 1991;13:509–510.
231. Richet HM, Craven PC, Brown JM, et al. A cluster of *Rhodococcus (Gordona)*

bronchialis sternal-wound infections after coronary-artery bypass surgery. N Engl J Med. 1991;324:104–109.
232. Buchman AL, McNeil MM, Brown JM, et al. Central venous catheter sepsis caused by an unusual *Gordona (Rhodococcus)* species: Identification with a digoxigenin-labeled rDNA probe. Clin Infect Dis. 1992;15:694–697.
233. Prinz G, Ban E, Fekete S, et al. Meningitis caused by *Gordona (Rhodococcus) aurantiacus.* J Clin Microbiol. 1985;22:472–474.
234. Tsukamura M, Hikosaka K, Nishimura K, et al. Severe progressive subcutaneous abscesses and necrotizing tenosynovitis caused by *Rhodococcus aurantiacus.* J Clin Microbiol. 1988;26:201–205.
235. Tsukamura M, Kawakami K. Lung infection caused by *Gordona aurantiaca (Rhodococcus aurantiacus).* J Clin Microbiol. 1982;16:604–607.
236. Shapiro CL, Haft RF, Gantz NM, et al. *Tsukamurella paurometabolum:* A novel pathogen causing catheter-related bacteremia in patients with cancer. Clin Infect Dis. 1992;14:200–203.
237. Clausen C, Wallis CK. Bacteremia caused by *Tsukamurella* species. Clin Microbiol Newsl. 1994;16:6–8.
238. Von Below H, Wilk CM, Schaal KP, et al. *Rhodococcus luteus* and *Rhodococcus erythropolis* chronic endophthalmitis after lens implantation. Am J Ophthalmol. 1991;112:596–597.
239. Brown E, Hendler E. *Rhodococcus* peritonitis in a patient treated with peritoneal dialysis. Am J Kidney Dis. 1989;14:417–418.
240. Alture-Werber E, O'Hare D, Louria DB. Infections caused by *Mycobacterium rhodochrous* and *scotochromogens.* Am Rev Respir Dis. 1968;97:694–697.
241. Haburchak DR, Jeffrey B, Higbee JW, et al. Infections by *Rhodochrous.* Am J Med. 1978;65:298–302.
242. Gopaul D, Ellis C, Maki A Jr, et al. Isolation of *Rhodococcus rhodochrous* from a chronic corneal ulcer. Diagn Microbiol Infect Dis. 1988;10:185–190.
243. Boughton WH, Atkin JF. Ventricular peritoneal shunt infection caused by a member of the *Rhodochrous* complex. J Clin Microbiol. 1980;11:533–534.
244. Hart DHL, Peel MM, Andrew JH, et al. Lung infection caused by *Rhodococcus.* Aust N Z J Med. 1988;18:790–791.
245. Ellis-Pegler RB, Parr DH, Orchard VA. Recurrent skin infection with *Rhodococcus* in an immunosuppressed patient. J Infect. 1983;6:39–41.
246. Martin T, Hogan DJ, Murphy F, et al. *Rhodococcus* infection of the skin with lymphadenitis in a nonimmunocompromised girl. J Am Acad Dermatol. 1991;24:328–332.
247. DeMarais PL, Kocka FE. Rhodococcus meningitis in an immunocompetent host. Clin Infect Dis. 1995;20:167–169.
248. Broughton RA, Wilson HD, Goodman NL, et al. Septic arthritis and osteomyelitis caused by an organism of the genus *Rhodococcus.* J Clin Microbiol. 1981;13:209–213.

Chapter 195

Listeria monocytogenes

BENNETT LORBER

Listeria monocytogenes is an uncommon cause of illness in the general population. However, in some groups, including neonates, pregnant women, elderly persons, immunosuppressed transplant recipients, and others with impaired cell-mediated immunity, it is an important cause of life-threatening bacteremia and meningoencephalitis.[1, 2] Growing interest in this organism has resulted from foodborne outbreaks and concerns about food safety.

MICROBIOLOGY

L. monocytogenes is a small, facultatively anaerobic, nonsporulating, catalase-positive, oxidase-negative, gram-positive bacillus that grows readily on blood agar, producing incomplete β-hemolysis.[3–5] The bacterium possesses one to five polar flagellae and exhibits a characteristic tumbling motility at 25°C. Optimal growth occurs at 30 to 37°C, but *L. monocytogenes* grows better than other bacteria at refrigerator temperatures (4 to 10°C), and by so-called cold enrichment can be separated from other contaminating bacteria by long incubation in this temperature range. Selective media have been developed to isolate the organism from specimens containing multiple species (food, stool) and appear superior to cold enrichment.[6] When grown on blood-free agar and viewed with light transmitted at a 45-degree angle (Henry's illumination), colonies of *L. monocytogenes* appear blue, whereas other bacterial colonies appear yellowish or orange.

Routine media are effective for isolating *L. monocytogenes* from specimens obtained from normally sterile sites (cerebrospinal fluid [CSF], blood, joint fluid), but media typically used to isolate diarrhea-causing bacteria from stool cultures inhibit listerial growth. *Listeria monocytogenes* grows best at a neutral to slightly alkaline pH and dies at a pH below 5.5.

In clinical specimens, the organisms may be gram-variable and look like diphtheroids, cocci, or diplococci. Laboratory misidentification as diphtheroids, streptococci, or enterococci is not uncommon,[7, 8] and the isolation of a "diphtheroid" from blood or CSF always should alert one to the possibility that the organism is really *L. monocytogenes.*

Of the six species of *Listeria, L. monocytogenes, L. seeligeri, L. welshimeri, L. innocua, L. ivanovii,* and *L. grayi* (Table 195–1), only *L. monocytogenes* is pathogenic for humans. The formerly designated species *L. murrayi* is now considered to be a biotype of *L. grayi.*[9] There are at least 13 serotypes of *L. monocytogenes,* based on cellular O and flagellar H antigens, but almost all disease is due to types 4b, 1/2a, and 1/2b,[1, 10] limiting the value of serotyping for epidemiologic investigations. Phage typing can be accomplished for 60 to 80% of clinical isolates. A number of newer molecular techniques including ribotyping, DNA-macrorestriction analysis, and multilocus enzyme electrophoresis have been employed to separate isolates into distinct groups for epidemiologic purposes.[11–16] Multilocus enzyme electrophoresis can separate *L. monocytogenes* serovars into many unique types and has proved useful in investigating outbreaks.[17]

EPIDEMIOLOGY

L. monocytogenes is an important cause of zoonoses, especially in herd animals. It is widespread in nature, being found commonly in soil, decaying vegetation, and as part of the fecal flora of many mammals.[3, 10] The organism has been isolated from the stool of approximately 5% of healthy adults,[10, 18] with higher rates of recovery reported from household contacts of patients with clinical infection.[19] Many foods are contaminated with *L. monocytogenes,* and recovery rates of 15 to 70% are common from raw vegetables, raw milk, fish, poultry, and meats, including fresh or processed chicken and beef available at supermarkets or delicatessen counters.[4] Ingestion of *L. monocytogenes* must be an exceedingly common occurrence.

Listeriosis is not a reportable disease, but data from two active surveillance studies performed in 1980–1982 and 1986 by the Centers for Disease Control and Prevention (CDC) indicated annual infection rates of 7.4/million population, accounting for approximately 1850 cases/year in the United States with 425 deaths.[17, 20] By 1993, following food industry regulations instituted to minimalize the risk of foodborne listeriosis, the annual incidence had declined to 4.4 cases per million, or 1092 cases with 248 deaths.[21] The highest infection rates are seen in infants younger than 1 month and adults older than 60 years.[20] Pregnant women account for about 30% of all cases and 60% of cases in the 10- to 40-year age group. Almost 70% of nonperinatal infections occur in those with hematologic malignancy, acquired immunodeficiency syndrome (AIDS), or organ transplantation, or those receiving corticosteroid therapy; but seemingly normal persons may develop invasive disease, particularly those older than 60 years.

Subsequent to the 1983 report of a widespread outbreak of foodborne human listerial infection due to contaminated coleslaw,[18] a number of other foodborne outbreaks have been documented with vehicles including milk,[22] soft cheeses,[23, 24] pâté,[25] ready-to-eat pork products,[26] and gravad or cold-smoked trout.[27] Sporadic cases have been traced to contaminated cheese,[28] turkey Frankfurters,[29] and alfalfa tablets.[30] The importance of food as a source for sporadic listeriosis is illustrated by two CDC studies in which 11% of all

TABLE 195–1 Laboratory Differentiation of Species in the Genus *Listeria**

Characteristic	*L. monocytogenes*	*L. grayi*	*L. innocua*	*L. ivanovii* subsp. *ivanovii*	*L. ivanovii* subsp. *londoniensis*	*L. seeligeri*	*L. welshimeri*
β-Hemolysis	+	−	−	+ +†	+ +	+	−
CAMP test reaction							
Staphylococcus aureus	+	−	−	−	−	+	−
Rhodococcus equi	−	−	−	+	+	−	−
Acid production from:							
Mannitol	−	+	−	−	−	−	−
α-Methyl-D-mannoside	+	+	+	−	−	−	+
L-Rhamnose	+	V	V	−	−	−	V
Soluble starch	−	+	−	−	−	ND	ND
D-Xylose	−	−	−	+	+	+	+
Ribose	−	V	−	+	−	−	−
N-Acetyl-β-D-mannosamine				−	+		
Hippurate hydrolysis	+	−	+	+	+	ND	ND
Reduction of nitrate	−	−	−	−	−	ND	ND
Pathogenicity for mice	+	−	−	+	?	−	−
Serotype	1/2a, 1/2b, 1/2c, 3a, 3b, 3c, 4a, 4ab, 4b, 4c, 4d, 4e, 7	S	4ab, US, 6a, 6B	5	5	1/2a, 1/2b, 1/2c, US, 4b, 4d, 6b	1/2b, 4c, 6a, 6b, US

*+, ≥90% of strains are positive; −, ≥90% of strains are negative; + +, usually wide or multiple zones.
†Usually a wide zone or multiple zones.
Abbreviations: ND, Not determined; S, specific; US, undesignated serotype; V, variable.
Adapted from Swaminathan B, Rocourt J, Bille J. *Listeria.* In: Murray PR, Baron EJ, Pfaller MA, et al, eds. Manual of Clinical Microbiology. 6th ed. Washington, DC: ASM; 1995:341–348.

refrigerator food samples were contaminated and 64% of patients had at least one contaminated food, and, in 33% of instances, both the patient and the food isolates had the same multilocus enzyme electrophoresis type (much higher than would be predicted by chance).[31, 32] Delicatessen ready-to-eat meats, especially chicken, had the highest rates of contamination. Patients were more likely than controls to have eaten soft cheeses or delicatessen counter meats, and 32% of sporadic cases could be attributed to these foods.

Although most human listeriosis appears to be foodborne, other modes of transmission occur including from mother to child transplacentally or through an infected birth canal, cross-infection in neonatal nurseries,[33, 34] and one common-source outbreak traced to contaminated mineral oil used for bathing infants.[35] Localized cutaneous infections have occurred in veterinarians and farmers after direct contact with aborted calves and infected poultry.

PATHOGENESIS

Except for vertical transmission from mother to fetus and rare instances of cross-contamination in the delivery suite or newborn nursery,[33, 34] human-to-human infection has not been documented.

Infection most likely begins after ingestion of the organism in a foodborne source. The oral inoculum required to produce clinical infection is unknown; experiments in healthy mammals indicate that 10^9 organisms or more are required.[36] Alkalinization of the stomach by antacids, H_2 blockers, or ulcer surgery may promote infection.[37, 38] The incubation period for invasive illness is not well established, but evidence from a few cases related to specific ingestions points to incubation periods ranging from 11 to 70 days, with a mean of 31 days.[23] In one report, two pregnant women whose only common exposure was attendance at a party developed listerial bacteremia with the same uncommon enzyme type; incubation periods for illness were 19 and 23 days.[39]

Virulent *L. monocytogenes* are probably sufficient to cause disease without promoter organisms, but a 1987 outbreak in Philadelphia that could not be traced to a particular source suggested that intercurrent gastrointestinal infection with another pathogen may enhance invasion in individuals colonized with *L. monocytogenes.*[28] Evidence for this is found in the common history of antecedent gastrointestinal symptoms in patients and household contacts, the long incubation period from ingestion to clinical illness, and two instances in which invasive listeriosis closely followed shigellosis.[40, 41] Listerial meningitis has occurred shortly after colonoscopy.[42]

In the intestine, *L. monocytogenes* crosses the mucosal barrier, perhaps aided by active endocytosis of organisms by endothelial cells.[4] Once in the blood stream, hematogenous dissemination may occur to any site; *L. monocytogenes* has a particular predilection for the central nervous system (CNS) and the placenta.

The intracellular, molecular pathogenesis of listeriosis has been reviewed in detail.[43, 44] Obviously, it is advantageous for an intracellular organism like *L. monocytogenes* to get inside mammalian cells as efficiently as possible. Listeria possess the cell surface protein internalin, an 80-kD member of the family of leucine-rich repeat proteins. Internalin interacts with E-cadherin, a receptor on epithelial cells, resulting in the induction of phagocytosis.[45, 46] Once phagocytosed, listeriolysin O, the major virulence factor, along with phospholipases, enables listeriae to escape from phagosomes and avoid intracellular killing.[47–50] Now free in the cytoplasm, the bacteria can divide (doubling time about 1 hour) and, by inducing host cell actin polymerization, propel themselves to the cell membrane.[51–53] Subsequently, by pushing against the host cell membrane, they form elongated pseudopod-like projections (filopods) that can be ingested by adjacent cells such as macrophages, enterocytes, and hepatocytes. The bacterial oligoproline-containing surface protein Act A is necessary for the induction of actin filament assembly and cell-to-cell spread and, therefore, is a major virulence factor.[43] Thus, through this novel life cycle, *L. monocytogenes* can move from cell to cell without being exposed to antibodies, complement, or neutrophils.

Iron, essential for the life of all microorganisms, appears to be an important virulence factor for *L. monocytogenes. Listeria monocytogenes* siderophores enable it to take iron from transferrin.[4] In vitro, iron enhances organism growth.[54] In animal models of listerial infection, iron overload is associated with enhanced susceptibility to infection, whereas iron depletion results in prolonged survival and iron supplementation in enhanced lethality.[55, 56] The clinical associations of sporadic listerial infection with hemochromatosis[8] and outbreaks with transfusion-induced iron overload in dialysis patients[57] attest to the importance of iron as a virulence factor in humans.

IMMUNITY

Resistance to infection with the intracellular bacterium *L. monocytogenes* is predominantly cell mediated as evidenced by the experiments of Mackaness showing that immunity could be transferred by sensitized lymphocytes but not by serum that contained antibodies.[58, 59] Further evidence is provided by the overwhelming clinical association between listerial infection and conditions of impaired cellular immunity including lymphomas, pregnancy, AIDS, and corticosteroid immunosuppression, particularly, but not exclusively, in transplant recipients.[1, 2, 7, 8, 17, 60–64] Combined treatment with fludarabine and prednisone in patients with chronic lymphocytic leukemia decreased their CD4$^+$ T-lymphocyte counts and increased their incidence of listeriosis; fludarabine alone was not associated with listeriosis.[65] The production of nitric oxide by activated macrophages may play a role in natural immunity to listeriosis independent of T-cell function.[66] The role of humoral immunity is unknown, although both immunoglobulin M (absent in newborns) and classic complement activity (low in newborns) have been shown to be necessary for efficient opsonization of *L. monocytogenes.*[67]

Although listeriosis is 100 to 1000 times more common in patients with AIDS than in an age-matched population,[31, 68–71] it is somewhat surprising that it is not seen more commonly given the ubiquity of the organism.[72–75] A partial explanation may lie in the experimental observation that resistance to listeriosis appears to be mediated by lymphocytes that do not carry CD4 or CD8 markers.[76, 77] Additionally, it is likely that many cases are prevented by routine *Pneumocystis* prophylaxis with trimethoprim-sulfamethoxazole. Most cases have occurred in those with advanced disease, that is, CD4 lymphocyte counts of less than 100/mm^3.

There is no increased frequency of listeriosis in those with deficiencies in neutrophil numbers or function, splenectomy, complement deficiency, or immunoglobulin disorders, the latter not surprising given that *L. monocytogenes* can be passed from cell to cell without being exposed to antibody.

CLINICAL SYNDROMES

The species name derives from the fact that an extract of the *L. monocytogenes* cell membrane has potent monocytosis-producing activity in rabbits,[78, 79] but monocytosis is a very uncommon feature of human infection.

Infection in Pregnancy

During gestation, there is a mild impairment of cell-mediated immunity,[80, 81] and pregnant women are prone to develop listerial bacteremia. Listeriae may proliferate in the placenta in areas that appear to be unreachable by usual defense mechanisms. For unexplained reasons, CNS infection, a commonly recognized form of listeriosis in other groups, is extremely rare during pregnancy in the absence of other risk factors.[1, 17, 20] Bacteremia is manifested clinically as an acute febrile illness, often accompanied by myalagias, arthralgias, headache, and backache. Illness usually occurs in the third trimester, probably related to the major decline in cell-mediated immunity seen at 26 to 30 weeks of gestation.[80] Twenty-two percent of perinatal infections result in stillbirth or neonatal death; premature labor is common.[1] Untreated bacteremia is generally self-limited, although if there is a complicating amnionitis, fever in the mother may persist until the fetus is spontaneously or therapeutically aborted. Early diagnosis and antimicrobial treatment can result in the birth of a healthy infant.[82, 83]

There is no convincing evidence that listeriosis is a cause of habitual abortion in humans.

Neonatal Infection

When in utero infection occurs, it may precipitate spontaneous abortion and the fetus may be stillborn or die within hours of a disseminated form of listerial infection known as *granulomatosis infantiseptica* characterized by widespread microabscesses and granulomas, particularly prevalent in the liver and spleen. In this entity, abundant bacteria are often visible on Gram stain of meconium.[84, 85]

More commonly, neonatal infection manifests like group B streptococcal disease in one of two forms[1]: (1) an early-onset sepsis syndrome usually associated with prematurity and probably acquired in utero, and (2) a late-onset meningitis occurring about 2 weeks postpartum in term babies most likely infected by organisms present in the maternal vagina at parturition, although cases have occurred after cesarean section, and nosocomial transmission has been suggested. In early-onset disease, *L. monocytogenes* can be isolated from the conjunctivae, external ear, nose, throat, meconium, amniotic fluid, placenta, blood, and sometimes CSF; Gram stain of meconium may show gram-positive rods and provide early diagnosis. Highest concentrations of bacteria are found in the neonatal lung and gut, suggesting that infection is acquired in utero by inhalation of infected amniotic fluid rather than via a hematogenous route.[86] Purulent conjunctivitis and a disseminated papular rash rarely have been described in newborns with early-onset disease, but clinical infection is otherwise similar to that due to other bacterial pathogens.

Bacteremia

Bacteremia without an evident focus has been the most common manifestation of listeriosis in compromised hosts; meningitis is second in frequency.[17] Clinical manifestations are similar to those seen in bacteremia with other causes and typically include fever and myalgias; a prodromal illness with diarrhea and nausea may occur. Since immunocompromised patients are more likely than healthy persons to have blood cultured during febrile illnesses, transient bacteremias in healthy persons may go undetected.

Central Nervous System Infection

The organisms that most frequently cause bacterial meningitis *(Streptococcus pneumoniae, Neisseria meningitidis, Haemophilus influenzae)* rarely cause parenchymal brain infections such as cerebritis and brain abscess. In contrast, *L. monocytogenes* has tropism for the brain itself, particularly the brain stem, as well as for the meninges.[2, 8] Many patients with meningitis have altered consciousness, seizures, or movement disorders, or all of these, and truly have a meningoencephalitis.

Meningitis

In an active surveillance study of bacterial meningitis reported by the CDC in 1990, *L. monocytogenes* was the fifth most common cause behind *H. influenzae, S. pneumoniae, N. meningitidis,* and group B streptococcus but had the highest mortality at 22%.[87] In 1995, 5 years after the introduction of *H. influenzae* conjugate vaccines, a survey of bacterial meningitis showed that *H. influenzae* had become less common than *L. monocytogenes,* which accounted for 20% of cases in neonates and 20% in those older than 60 years.[88] Mortality is low (zero to 13%) for adults without serious underlying disease or immunosuppressive treatment.[8, 63, 89]

At a large referral hospital, *L. monocytogenes* was the third most frequent cause of community-acquired bacterial meningitis in adults, accounting for 11% of cases.[90] Worldwide, *L. monocytogenes* is one of the three major causes of neonatal meningitis; is second only to pneumococcus as a cause of bacterial meningitis in adults older than 50 years; and is the most common cause of bacterial meningitis in patients with lymphomas, organ transplant recipients, or those receiving corticosteroid immunosuppression for any reason.[2, 91]

Clinically, meningitis due to *L. monocytogenes* is usually similar to that with more common causes; features particular to listerial meningitis are summarized in Table 195–2.

TABLE 195–2 Clinical Features Particular to Listerial Meningitis Compared with More Common Bacterial Causes

Presentation usually acute but may be subacute and may mimic tuberculous meningitis
Nuchal rigidity less common (not present in 15–20% of adult patients)
Movement disorders (ataxia, tremors, myoclonus) more common (15–20%)
Seizures more common (at least 25%)
Fluctuating mental status common
Blood cultures more likely positive (75%)
Cerebrospinal fluid
Gram stain negative in most (organisms seen in ≈40%)
CSF glucose level not low in most (normal in >60%)
Mononuclear cell predominance present in about one third

Abbreviation: CSF, Cerebrospinal fluid.

Brain Stem Encephalitis (Rhombencephalitis)

An unusual form of listerial encephalitis involves the brain stem[92] and is similar to the unique zoonotic listerial infection known as circling disease of sheep.[93] In contrast to other listerial CNS infections, this illness usually occurs in healthy adults; neonatal cases have not been reported. The typical clinical picture is one of a biphasic illness with a prodrome of fever, headache, nausea, and vomiting lasting about 4 days followed by the abrupt onset of asymmetric cranial nerve deficits, cerebellar signs, and hemiparesis or hemisensory deficits, or both. About 40% of patients develop respiratory failure. Nuchal rigidity is present in about one half, and CSF findings are only mildly abnormal with a positive CSF culture in about 40%. Almost two thirds of patients are bacteremic. Magnetic resonance imaging is superior to computed tomography for demonstrating rhombencephalitis (Fig. 195–1).[92, 93] Mortality is high, and serious sequelae are common in survivors.

Brain Abscess

Macroscopic brain abscesses account for about 10% of CNS listerial infections. Bacteremia is almost always present, and concomitant meningitis with isolation of *L. monocytogenes* from the CSF is found in 25%; both these features are rare in other forms of bacterial brain abscess.[95] About one half of cases occur in known risk groups for listerial infection. Subcortical abscesses located in the thalamus, pons, and medulla are common; these sites are exceedingly rare when abscesses are due to other bacteria. Mortality is high, and survivors usually have serious sequelae.

Endocarditis

Listerial endocarditis accounts for about 7.5% of adult listerial infections,[8] affects the population at risk for viridans streptococcal endocarditis, produces both native valve and prosthetic valve disease, and has a high rate of septic complications and a mortality of 48%.[96, 97] Listerial endocarditis, but not bacteremia per se, may be an indicator of underlying gastrointestinal tract abnormality, including cancer.[55] Cases in the pediatric age group have not been reported.

Localized Infection

Rare reports of focal infections from which *L. monocytogenes* has been isolated include direct inoculation resulting in conjunctivitis,[8] skin infection,[98] and lymphadenitis.[8] Bacteremia can lead to hepatitis and hepatic abscess,[99, 100] cholecystitis,[101] peritonitis,[102–104] splenic abscess,[8] pleuropulmonary infection,[105–107] joint infection,[108] osteomyelitis,[109] pericarditis,[110] myocarditis,[111] arteritis,[112] and endophthalmitis.[8] There is nothing clinically unique about these localized infections; many, but not all, have occurred in those known to be at risk for listeriosis.

Gastroenteritis and Fever

Many patients with listerial bacteremia or CNS infection give a history of antecedent gastrointestinal symptoms including diarrhea, nausea, and vomiting, often accompanied by fever.[8, 28, 37] Large inoc-

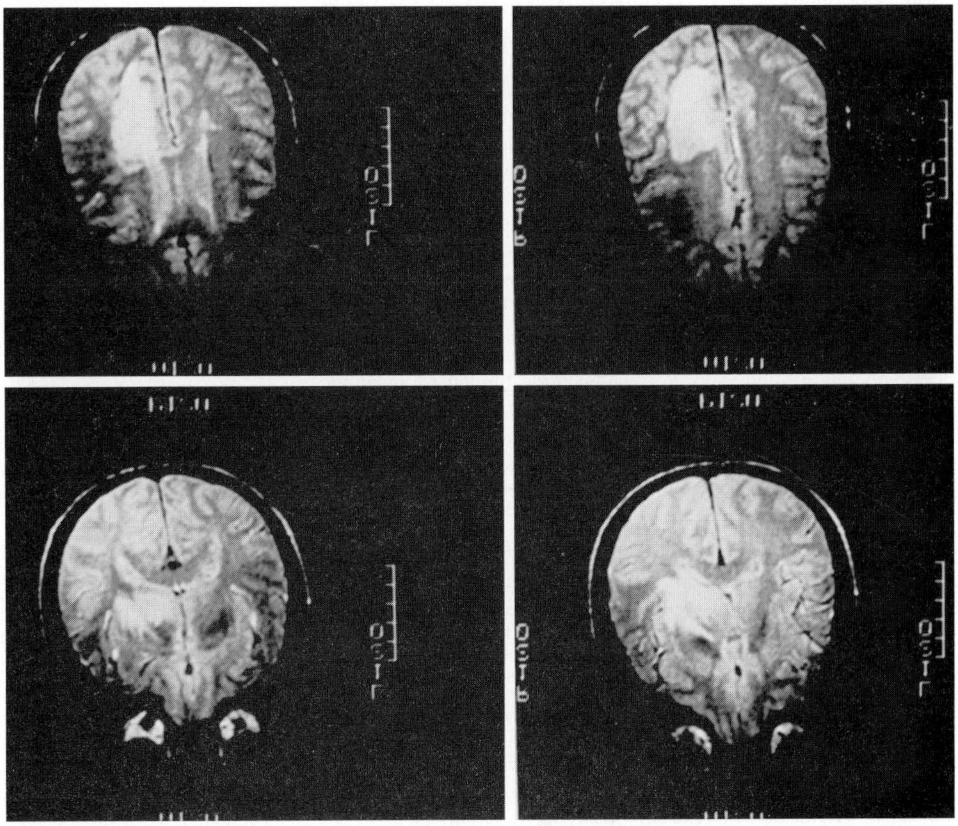

FIGURE 195–1. Magnetic resonance imaging scan of the brain of a patient with chronic lymphocytic leukemia, cerebritis, hemiparesis, *Listeria monocytogenes* in blood cultures, and a negative result on spinal fluid examination. Six weeks of ampicillin and gentamicin resulted in a complete recovery.

ula of orally administered *L. monocytogenes* produce diarrheal disease in primates.[36] Investigation of a point-source foodborne listeriosis outbreak, which resulted in bacteremia in two pregnant women, strongly suggested that ingestion of contaminated food by healthy, nonpregnant individuals produced a self-limited, febrile gastroenteritis.[39]

Convincing evidence that *L. monocytogenes* can cause foodborne noninvasive disease is provided by the report of an outbreak of diarrhea and fever among attendees at a Holstein cow show in Illinois traced to ingestion of contaminated chocolate milk.[113] A high illness attack rate of 75% was seen in the 60 people who consumed the chocolate milk. The most common symptoms were diarrhea (79%), fever (72%), chills (65%), and headache (65%). Also common were myalgias (59%) and abdominal cramps (55%); nausea occurred in 47% and vomiting in 26%. The median incubation period was 20 hours (range 9 to 32), and diarrhea lasted a median of 42 hours with a median of 12 stools during the 24 hours of maximal diarrhea. The contamination level in the milk was exceedingly high, and the median dose of ingested listeriae may have been as high as 2.9×10^{11} CFU/person. The epidemic appeared to be caused by postpasteurization contamination. In this outbreak serologic testing for antibodies to listeriolysin O was shown to be a useful tool for retrospectively identifying infected ill persons. Active surveillance identified three persons with invasive disease (bacteremia, brain abscess) related to ingestion of chocolate milk from the implicated dairy, providing further evidence that many cases of seemingly sporadic invasive disease are, in fact, part of foodborne outbreaks. *Listeria monocytogenes* should be considered as a possible cause of foodborne outbreaks of febrile gastroenteritis when routine stool cultures fail to identify a pathogen.

Complications

Complications of invasive disease including disseminated intravascular coagulation,[114] adult respiratory distress syndrome,[115] and rhabdomyolysis with acute renal failure[116] have been documented. Rare episodes of reinfection have occurred.[117]

DIAGNOSIS

Clinical settings in which listeriosis should be given strong consideration as part of the differential diagnosis are listed in Table 195–3.

Diagnosis requires isolation of *L. monocytogenes* from normally sterile clinical specimens (CSF, blood, joint fluid, and so forth) and identification through standard microbiologic techniques. Antibodies to listeriolysin O have not proved useful for acute diagnosis of invasive disease[118]; nor yet have polymerase chain reaction probes.[119] Serodiagnosis of listeriosis employing measurement of antibodies to listeriolysin O has proved useful for identifying infected individuals with noninvasive disease (asymptomatic infection, gastroenteritis) during foodborne outbreaks.[113] A polypeptide limited to an amino-terminal residue of listeriolysin O, described in 1996,[120] appears to be a more specific antigen for use in serologic tests than those previously employed.[121, 122]

Magnetic resonance imaging is superior to computerized tomography for demonstrating parenchymal brain involvement, especially in the brain stem.[92, 94]

TABLE 195–3 Clinical Settings in Which Listeriosis Should Be Considered Strongly in the Differential Diagnosis

Neonatal sepsis or meningitis
Meningitis or parenchymal brain infection in patients with hematological malignancies, AIDS, organ transplantation, or corticosteroid immunosuppression
Meningitis or parenchymal brain infection in adults older than 50 years
Simultaneous infection of the meninges and brain parenchyma
Subcortical brain abscess
Fever during pregnancy, particularly in the third trimester
Blood, CSF, or other normally sterile specimen reported to have "diphtheroids" on Gram stain or culture
Foodborne outbreak of febrile gastroenteritis when routine cultures fail to identify a pathogen

Abbreviations: AIDS, Acquired immunodeficiency syndrome; CSF, cerebrospinal fluid.

TREATMENT

There have been no controlled trials to establish a drug of choice or the duration of therapy for listerial infection. A comprehensive review of antibiotics for *L. monocytogenes* was published in 1997 by Hof and colleagues.[123] Recommendations regarding therapy are based on data obtained from in vitro susceptibility testing, animal models, and clinical experience with small numbers of patients compared with historical controls and, therefore, are subject to interpretation and individual preferences. In the absence of a positive CSF Gram stain, initial therapy for bacterial meningitis in all adults older than 50 years should include either ampicillin or trimethoprim-sulfamethoxazole, especially if there is no associated pneumonia, otitis, sinusitis, or endocarditis that would point to causes other than *L. monocytogenes.*

Ampicillin is generally considered the preferred agent,[1, 8, 62, 124, 125] although its superiority to penicillin is questionable. The β-lactam antibiotics are often described as being bacteriostatic for listeriae. In fact, they demonstrate delayed in vitro bactericidal activity (48 hours) at levels that are obtainable in the CSF.[126, 127] The same phenomenon has been shown with imipenem and vancomycin.[128] Based on synergy in vitro and in animal models,[129] most authorities suggest adding gentamicin to ampicillin for the treatment of bacteremia in those with severely impaired T-cell function and in all cases of meningitis and endocarditis.[1, 8, 62]

For those intolerant of penicillins, trimethoprim-sulfamethoxazole as a single agent is thought to be the best alternative.[130–132] Although data are limited, this combination is bactericidal for listeriae, and outcomes appear at least comparable to those achieved with ampicillin and gentamicin. In a preliminary study of patients with severe listerial meningoencephalitis, the combination of trimethoprim-sulfamethoxazole plus ampicillin was associated with a much lower failure rate and fewer neurologic sequelae than ampicillin combined with an aminoglycoside.[133]

Chloramphenicol, previously regarded as the agent of choice for penicillin-allergic patients, should not be used to treat listerial infection because of unacceptable failure and relapse rates.[2, 61, 64, 134] No currently available cephalosporin should be used; they have limited activity,[62, 135] and meningitis has developed in patients while receiving cephalosporins.[62, 136] Reports have documented the utility of erythromycin and tetracycline in isolated cases, but these agents are unreliable and should be avoided. Some newer quinolones have good in vitro activity, but clinical experience is lacking.

Vancomycin has been used successfully in a few penicillin-allergic patients,[137, 138] but others have developed listerial meningitis while receiving the drug.[139] Rifampin is quite active in vitro and is known to penetrate into phagocytic cells; however, clinical experience is minimal, and in animal models the addition of rifampin to ampicillin was not more effective than ampicillin alone.[125]

Meningitis doses should be used for all patients, even in the absence of CNS or CSF abnormalities, because of the high affinity of this organism for the CNS. Patients with meningitis should be treated for no less than 3 weeks; bacteremic patients without CSF abnormalities can be treated for 2 weeks.

Patients with rhombencephalitis or brain abscess should be treated for at least 6 weeks and followed with serial magnetic resonance imaging studies (or computed tomography scans). Endocarditis should be treated for 4 to 6 weeks.

Clinically significant antimicrobial resistance has not been encountered, but vigilance is warranted since transfer of resistance from enterococci to *L. monocytogenes* has been documented.[140]

Iron is a virulence factor for *L. monocytogenes* and, clinically,

TABLE 195–4 Dietary Recommendations for Preventing Foodborne Listeriosis

For All Persons

Thoroughly cook raw food from animal sources (e.g., beef, pork, and poultry).
Thoroughly wash raw vegetables before eating.
Keep uncooked meats separate from vegetables, cooked foods, and ready-to-eat foods.
Avoid consumption of raw (unpasteurized) milk or foods made from raw milk.
Wash hands, knives, and cutting boards after handling uncooked foods.

Additional Recommendations for Persons at High Risk (Those Immunocompromised by Illness or Medications, Pregnant Women, and Elderly Persons)

Avoid soft cheeses (e.g., Mexican-style, feta, Brie, Camembert, and blue-veined cheese) (there is no need to avoid hard cheeses, cream cheese, cottage cheese, or yogurt).
Leftover foods or ready-to-eat foods (e.g., hot dogs) should be reheated until steaming hot before eating.
Although the risk for listeriosis associated with foods from delicatessen counters is relatively low, pregnant women and immunosuppressed persons may choose to avoid these foods or to thoroughly reheat cold cuts before eating.

iron-overload states are risk factors for listerial infection. Therefore, in patients with iron deficiency, it seems prudent to withhold iron replacement until treatment for listerial infection is completed. Corticosteroids appear to be important adjunctive agents in treating the most common forms of bacterial meningitis. Their role in the treatment of listerial CNS infections is unknown, but they should probably be avoided since impairment of cellular immunity due to corticosteroid therapy is a major risk factor for the development of listeriosis.

PREVENTION

Recommendations for consumer prevention of listeriosis from a foodborne source were developed by the CDC in 1992[141] and are presented in Table 195–4.

In 1989, following documentation of listeriosis after the ingestion of contaminated turkey franksfurters, the U.S. Department of Agriculture began a surveillance program for *L. monocytogenes* in ready-to-eat processed meats and enforced regulations prohibiting the sale of contaminated meat (so-called zero-tolerance policy).[21] Active surveillance of listeriosis in the United States suggests that industry cleanup efforts combined with the 1992 dietary recommendations for persons at increased risk were effective measures. From 1989 through 1993 there was a 44% reduction in invasive listerial illness and a 48% reduction in deaths.[21]

Second episodes of neonatal listerial infection are virtually unheard of, and intrapartum antibiotics are not recommended for mothers with a history of perinatal listeriosis. There is no vaccine.

Listerial infections are effectively prevented by trimethoprim-sulfamethoxazole given as *Pneumocystis* prophylaxis to organ transplant recipients or individuals with human immunodeficiency virus infection. In areas with a high prevalence of AIDS, the widespread use of trimethoprim-sulfamethoxazole prophylaxis against *Pneumocystis* pneumonia appears to have resulted in a marked decline in nonperinatal listeriosis.[21]

REFERENCES

1. Gellin BG, Broome CV. Listeriosis. JAMA. 1989;261:1313–1320.
2. Lorber B. Listeriosis. Clin Infect Dis. 1997;24:1–11.
3. Gray ML, Killinger AH. *Listeria monocytogenes* and listeric infections. Bacteriol Rev. 1966;30:309–382.
4. Farber JM, Peterkin PI. *Listeria monocytogenes,* a food-borne pathogen. Microbiol Rev. 1991;55:476–511.
5. Swaminathan B, Rocourt J, Bille J. *Listeria.* In: Murray PR, Baron EJ, Pfaller MA, et al, eds. Manual of Clinical Microbiology. 6th ed. Washington, DC: ASM; 1995:341–348.
6. Hayes PS, Graves LM, Ajello GW, et al. Comparison of cold enrichment and US Department of Agriculture methods for isolating *Listeria* monocytogenes from naturally contaminated foods. Appl Environ Microbiol. 1991;57:2109–2113.
7. Buchner LH, Schneierson SS. Clinical and laboratory aspects of *Listeria monocytogenes* infections with a report of ten cases. Am J Med. 1968;45:904–921.
8. Nieman RE, Lorber B. Listeriosis in adults: A changing pattern. Report of eight cases and review of the literature, 1968–1978. Rev Infect Dis. 1980;2:207–227.
9. Boerlin P, Rocourt J, Piffaretti J-C. Taxonomy of the genus *Listeria* by using multilocus enzyme electrophoresis. Int J Syst Bacteriol. 1991;41:59–64.
10. Schuchat A, Swaminathan B, Broome CV. Epidemiology of human listeriosis. Clin Microbiol Rev. 1991;4:169–183.
11. Nocera D, Altwegg M, Lucchine, et al. Characterization of *Listeria* strains from a foodborne listeriosis outbreak by rDNA gene restriction patterns compared to four other typing methods. Eur J Clin Microbiol Infect Dis. 1993;12:162–169.
12. Czajka J, Batt CA. Verification of causal relationships between *Listeria monocytogenes* isolates implicated in food-borne outbreaks of listeriosis by randomly amplified polymorphic DNA patterns. J Clin Microbiol. 1994;32:1280–1287.
13. Bibb WF, Gellin BG, Weaver R, et al. Analysis of clinical and food-borne isolates of *Listeria monocytogenes* in the United States by multilocus enzyme electrophoresis and application of the method to epidemiologic investigations. Appl Environ Microbiol. 1990;56:2133–2141.
14. Graves LM, Swaminathan B, Reeves MW, et al. Comparison of ribotyping and multilocus enzyme electrophoresis for subtyping of *Listeria monocytogenes* isolates. J Clin Microbiol. 1994;32:2936–2943.
15. Brosch R, Chen J, Luchansky JB. Pulsed-field fingerprinting of listeriae: Identification of genomic divisions for *Listeria monocytogenes* and their correlation with serovar. Appl Environ Microbiol. 1994;60:2584–2592.
16. Louie M, Jayaratne P, Luchsinger I, et al. Comparison of ribotyping, arbitrarily primed PCR, and pulsed-field gel electrophoresis for molecular typing of *Listeria monocytogenes.* J Clin Microbiol. 1996;34:15–19.
17. Gellin BG, Broome CV, Bibb WF, et al. The epidemiology of listeriosis in the United States–1986. Am J Epidemiol. 1991;133:392–401.
18. Schlech WF III, Lavigne PM, Bortolussi RA, et al. Epidemic listeriosis—Evidence for transmission by food. N Engl J Med. 1983;308:203–206.
19. Schuchat A, Deaver K, Hayes PS, et al. Gastrointestinal carriage of *Listeria monocytogenes* in household contacts of patients with listeriosis. J Infect Dis. 1993;167:1261–1262.
20. Ciesielski CA, Hightower AW, Parsons SK, et al. Listeriosis in the United States: 1980–1982. Arch Intern Med. 1988;148:1416–1419.
21. Tappero JW, Schuchat A, Deaver KA, et al. Reduction in the incidence of human listeriosis in the United States. Effectiveness of prevention efforts? JAMA. 1995;273:1118–1122.
22. Fleming DW, Cochi SL, MacDonald KL, et al. Pasteurized milk as a vehicle of infection in an outbreak of listeriosis. N Engl J Med. 1985;312:404–407.
23. Linnan MJ, Mascola L, Lou XD, et al. Epidemic listeriosis associated with Mexican-style cheese. N Engl J Med. 1988;319:823–828.
24. Bula CJ, Bille J, Glauser MP. An epidemic of food-borne listeriosis in Western Switzerland: Description of 57 cases involving adults. Clin Infect Dis. 1995; 20:66–72.
25. McLauchin J, Hall SM, Velani SK, et al. Human listeriosis and pâté: A possible association. BMJ. 1991;303:773–775.
26. Goulet V, Rocourt J, Rebiere I, et al. Listeriosis outbreak associated with the consumption of rillettes in France in 1993. J Infect Dis. 1998;177:155–160.
27. Ericsson H, Eklow A, Danielsson-Tham M-L, et al. An outbreak of listeriosis suspected to have been caused by rainbow trout. J Clin Microbiol. 1997;35:2904–2907.
28. Schwartz B, Hexter D, Broome CV, et al. Investigation of an outbreak of listeriosis: New hypotheses for the etiology of epidemic *Listeria monocytogenes* infections. J Infect Dis. 1989;159:680–685.
29. Centers for Disease Control. Listeriosis associated with consumption of turkey franks. MMWR Morb Mortal Wkly Rep. 1989;38:267–268.
30. Farber JM, Carter AO, Varughese PV, et al. Listeriosis traced to consumption of alfalfa tablets and soft cheese. N Engl J Med. 1990;322:338.
31. Schuchat A, Deaver KA, Wenger JD, et al. Role of foods in sporadic listeriosis. 1. Case-control study of dietary risk factors. JAMA. 1992;267:2041–2045.
32. Pinner RW, Schuchat A, Swaminathan B, et al. Role of foods in sporadic listeriosis II. Microbiologic and epidemiologic investigation. JAMA. 1992;267:2046–2050.
33. Farber JM, Peterkin PI, Carter AO, et al. Neonatal listeriosis due to cross-infection confirmed by isoenzyme typing and DNA fingerprinting. J Infect Dis. 1991;163:927–928.
34. McLauchin J, Audurier A, Taylor AG. Aspects of the epidemiology of human *Listeria monocytogenes* infections in Britain 1967–1984; the use of serotyping and phage typing. J Med Microbiol. 1986;22:367–377.
35. Schuchat A, Lizano C, Broome CV, et al. Outbreak of neonatal listeriosis associated with mineral oil. Pediatr Infect Dis. 1991;10:183–189.
36. Farber JM, Daley E, Coates F, et al. Feeding trials of *Listeria monocytogenes* with a nonhuman primate model. J Clin Microbiol. 1991;29:2606–2608.
37. Ho JL, Shands KN, Friedland G, et al. An outbreak of type 4b *Listeria monocytogenes* infection involving patients from eight Boston hospitals. Arch Intern Med. 1986;146:520–524.
38. Schlech WF III, Chase DP, Badley A. A model of food-borne *Listeria monocytogenes* infection in the Sprague-Dawley rat using gastric inoculation: Development and effect of gastric acidity on infective dose. Int J Food Microbiol. 1993;18:15–24.
39. Riedo FX, Pinner RW, Tosca MdeL, et al. A point-source foodborne listeriosis outbreak: Documented incubation period and possible mild illness. J Infect Dis. 1994;170:693–696.

40. Schroter GPJ, Weil R. *Listeria monocytogenes* infection after renal transplantation. Arch Intern Med. 1977;137:1395–1399.
41. Lorber B. Listeriosis following shigellosis. Rev Infect Dis. 1991;13:865–866.
42. Sheehan GJ, Galbraith JCT. Colonoscopy-associated listeriosis: Report of a case. Clin Infect Dis. 1993;17:1061–1062.
43. Southwick FS, Purich DL. Intracellular pathogenesis of listeriosis. N Engl J Med. 1996;334:770–776.
44. Kuhn M, Goebel W. Host cell signaling during *Listeria monocytogenes* infection. Trends Microbiol. 1998;6:11–15.
45. Cossart P, Boquet P, Normark S, et al. Cellular microbiology emerging. Science. 1996;271:315–316.
46. Mengard J, Ohayon H, Gounon P, et al. E-cadherin is the receptor for internalin, a surface protein required for entry of *L. monocytogenes* into epithelial cells. Cell. 1996;84:923–932.
47. McKay DB, Lu CY. Listeriolysin as a virulence factor in *Listeria monocytogenes* infections of neonatal mice and murine decidual tissue. Infect Immun. 1991;59:4286–4290.
48. Barry RA, Bouwer HGA, Portnoy DA, et al. Pathogenicity and immunogenicity of *Listeria monocytogenes* small-plaque mutants defective for intracellular growth and cell-to-cell spread. Infect Immun. 1992;60:1625–1632.
49. Portnoy DA, Chakraborty T, Goebel W, et al. Molecular determinants of *Listeria monocytogenes* pathogenesis. Infect Immun. 1992;60:1263–1267.
50. Freitag NE, Rong L, Portnoy DA. Regulation of the prfA transcriptional activator of *Listeria monocytogenes:* Multiple promoter elements contribute to intracellular growth and cell-to-cell spread. Infect Immun. 1993;61:2537–2544.
51. Tilney LG, Portnoy DA. Actin filaments and the growth, movement and spread of the intracellular bacterial parasite, *Listeria monocytogenes.* J Cell Biol. 1989;109:1597–1608.
52. Dabiri GA, Sanger JM, Portnoy DA, et al. *Listeria monocytogenes* moves rapidly through the host-cell cytoplasm by inducing directional actin assembly. Proc Natl Acad Sci U S A. 1990;87:6068–6072.
53. Sanger JM, Sanger JW, Southwick FS. Host cell actin assembly is necessary and likely to provide the propulsive force for intracellular movement of *Listeria monocytogenes.* Infect Immun. 1992;60:3609–3619.
54. Sword CP. Mechanisms of pathogenesis in *Listeria monocytogenes* infection. I. Influence of iron. J Bacteriol. 1966;92:536–542.
55. Lorber B. Clinical listeriosis—implications for pathogenesis. In: Miller AJ, Smith JL, Somkuti GA, eds. Foodborne Listeriosis. New York: Elsevier; 1990:41–49.
56. Ampel NM, Bejarano GC, Saavedra M Jr. Deferoxamine increases the susceptibility of beta-thalassemic, iron-overloaded mice to infection with *Listeria monocytogenes.* Life Sci. 1992;50:1327–1332.
57. Mossey RT, Sondheimer J. Listeriosis in patients with long-term hemodialysis and transfusional iron overload. Am J Med. 1985;79:379–400.
58. Mackaness GB. Cellular resistance to infection. J Exp Med. 1962;116:381–406.
59. Mackaness GB. Resistance to intracellular infection. J Infect Dis. 1971;123:439–445.
60. Simpson JF, Leddy JP, Harc JD. Listeriosis complicating lymphoma. Report of four cases and interpretive review of pathogenic factors. Am J Med 1967;43:39–49.
61. Stamm AM, Dismukes WE, Simmons BP, et al. Listeriosis in renal transplant recipients: Report of an outbreak and review of 102 cases. Rev Infect Dis. 1982;4:665–682.
62. Cherubin CE, Appleman MD, Heseltine PNR, et al. Epidemiological spectrum and current treatment of listeriosis. Rev Infect Dis. 1991;13:1108–1114.
63. Skoberg K, Syrjanen J, Jahkola M, et al. Clinical presentation and outcome of listeriosis in patients with and without immunosuppressive therapy. Clin Infect Dis. 1992;14:815–821.
64. Chang J, Powles R, Mehta J, et al. Listeriosis in bone marrow transplant recipients: Incidence, clinical features and treatment. Clin Infect Dis. 1995;21:1289–1290.
65. Anaissie E, Kontoyiannis DP, Kantarjian H, et al. Listeriosis in patients with chronic lymphocytic leukemia who were treated with fludarabine and prednisone. Ann Intern Med. 1992;117:466–469.
66. Beckerman KP, Rogers HW, Corbett JA, et al. Release of nitric oxide during the T cell–independent pathway of macrophage activation. J Immunol. 1993;150:888–895.
67. Bortolussi R, Issekutz A, Faulkner G. Opsonization of *Listeria monocytogenes* type 4b by human adult and newborn sera. Infect Immun. 1986;52:493–498.
68. Wenger JD, Schuchat A. Commentary: Listeriosis in the 1990s—progress toward prevention. Infect Dis Clin Pract. 1991;1:298–299.
69. Jurado RL, Farley MM, Pereira E, et al. Increased risk of meningitis and bacteremia due to *Listeria monocytogenes* in patients with human immunodeficiency virus infection. Clin Infect Dis. 1993;17:224–227.
70. Ewert DP, Lieb L, Hayes PS, et al. *Listeria monocytogenes* infection and serotype distribution among HIV-infected persons in Los Angeles County, 1985–92. J Acquir Immune Defic Syndr Hum Retrovirol. 1995;8:461–465.
71. Jensen A, Frederiksen W, Gerner-Smidt P. Risk factors for listeriosis in Denmark, 1989–1990. Scand J Infect Dis. 1994;26:171–178.
72. Mascola L, Lieb L, Chiu J, et al. Listeriosis: An uncommon opportunistic infection in patients with acquired immunodeficiency syndrome. A report of five cases and a review of the literature. Am J Med. 1988;84:162–164.
73. Kales CP, Holzman RS. Listeriosis in patients with HIV infection: Clinical manifestations and response to therapy. J Acquir Immune Defic Syndr. 1990;3:139–143.
74. Berenguer J, Solera J, Diaz MD, et al. Listeriosis in patients infected with human immunodeficiency virus. Rev Infect Dis. 1991;13:115–119.
75. Decker CF, Simon GL, DiGioia RA, et al. *Listeria monocytogenes* infections in patients with AIDS: Report of five cases and review. Rev Infect Dis. 1991;13:413–417.
76. Dunn PL, North RJ. Resolution of primary murine listeriosis and acquired resistance to lethal secondary infection can be mediated predominantly by Thy-1$^+$ CD$^-$ CD8$^-$ cells. J Infect Dis. 1991;164:869–877.
77. Dunn PL, North RJ. Limitations of the adoptive immunity assay for analyzing anti-*Listeria* immunity. J Infect Dis. 1991;164:878–882.
78. Murray EGD, Webb RA, Swann MBR. A disease of rabbits characterized by large mononuclear leukocytosis caused by a hitherto undescribed bacillus *Bacterium monocytogenes* (n sp). J Pathol. 1926;29:407–439.
79. Stanley NF. Studies of *Listeria monocytogenes.* I. Isolation of a monocytosis-producing agent (MPA). Aust J Exp Biol Med Sci. 1949;27:123–131.
80. Weinberg ED. Pregnancy-associated depression of cell-mediated immunity. Rev Infect Dis. 1984;6:814–831.
81. Rich KC, Siegel JN, Jennings C, et al. CD4$^+$ lymphocytes in perinatal human immunodeficiency virus (HIV) infection: Evidence for pregnancy-induced immune depression in uninfected and HIV-infected women. J Infect Dis. 1995;172:1221–1227.
82. Evans JR, Allen AC, Stinson DA, et al. Perinatal listeriosis: Report of an outbreak. Pediatr Infect Dis J. 1985;4:237–241.
83. Kalstone C. Successful antepartum treatment of listeriosis. Am J Obstet Gynecol. 1991;164:57–58.
84. Visintine CM, Oleske JM, Nahmias AJ. *Listeria monocytogenes* infection in infants and children. Am J Dis Child. 1977;131:393–397.
85. Larsson S, Linell F. Correlations between clinical and postmortem findings in listeriosis. Scand J Infect Dis. 1979;11:55–58.
86. Becroft DMO, Farmer K, Seddon RJ, et al. Epidemic listeriosis in the newborn. BMJ. 1971;3:747–751.
87. Wenger JD, Hightower AW, Facklam RR, et al. Bacterial meningitis in the United States, 1986; Report of a multistate surveillance study. J Infect Dis. 1990;162:1316–1623.
88. Schuchat A, Robinson K, Wenger JD, et al. Bacterial meningitis in the United States in 1995. N Engl J Med. 1997;337:970–976.
89. Pigrau C, Almirante B, Pahissa A, et al. Clinical presentation and outcome in cases of Listeriosis. Clin Infect Dis. 1993;17:143–144.
90. Durand ML, Calderwood SB, Weber DJ, et al. Acute bacterial meningitis in adults: A review of 493 episodes. N Engl J Med. 1993;328:21–28.
91. Hooper DC, Pruitt AA, Rubin RH. Central nervous system infection in the chronically immunosuppressed. Medicine. 1982;61:166–188.
92. Armstrong RW, Fung PC. Brainstem encephalitis (rhombencephalitis) due to *Listeria monocytogenes:* Case report and review. Clin Infect Dis. 1993;16:689–702.
93. Gill DA. Circling disease. A meningoencephalitis of sheep in New Zealand. Vet J. 1933;89:258–270.
94. Faidas A, Shepard DL, Lim J, et al. Magnetic resonance imaging in listerial brain stem encephalitis. Clin Infect Dis. 1993;16:186–187.
95. Dee RR, Lorber B. Brain abscess due to *Listeria monocytogenes:* Case report and literature review. Rev Infect Dis. 1986;8:968–977.
96. Carvajal A, Frederiksen W. Fatal endocarditis due to *Listeria monocytogenes.* Rev Infect Dis. 1988;10:616–623.
97. Gallagher PG, Watanakunakorn C. *Listeria monocytogenes* endocarditis: A review of the literature 1950–1986. Scand J Infect Dis. 1988;20:359–368.
98. Cain DB, McCann VL. An unusual case of cutaneous listeriosis. J Clin Microbiol. 1986;23:976–977.
99. Yu VL, Miller WP, Wing EJ, et al. Disseminated listeriosis presenting as acute hepatitis. Case reports and review of hepatic involvement in listeriosis. Am J Med. 1982;73:773–777.
100. Braun TI, Travis D, Dee RR, et al. Liver abscess due to *Listeria monocytogenes:* Case report and review. Clin Infect Dis. 1993;17:267–269.
101. Gordon S, Singer C. *Listeria monocytogenes* cholecystitis. J Infect Dis. 1986;154:918–919.
102. Winslow DL, Steele ML. Listeria bacteremia and peritonitis associated with a peritoneovenous shunt: Successful treatment with sulfamethoxazole and trimethoprim. J Infect Dis. 1984;149:820.
103. Sivalingam JJ, Martin P, Fraimow HS, et al. *Listeria monocytogenes* peritonitis: Case report and literature review. Am J Gastroenterol. 1992;87:1839–1845.
104. Hou C-C, Lee Y-J, Yu K-W, et al. Peritonitis due to *Listeria monocytogenes* in a patient receiving maintenance hemodialysis. Clin Infect Dis. 1998;26:514–516.
105. Mazzulli T, Salit IE. Pleural fluid infection caused by *Listeria monocytogenes:* Case report and review. Rev Infect Dis. 1991;13:564–570.
106. Domingo P, Serra J, Sambeat MA, et al. Pneumonia due to *Listeria monocytogenes.* Clin Infect Dis. 1992;14:787–789.
107. Gradon JD, Chapnick EK, Lutwick LI. Pleuropulmonary listeriosis: Case report and review. Infect Dis Clin Pract. 1992;1:39–42.
108. Ellis LC, Segreti J, Gitelis S, et al. Joint infections due to *Listeria monocytogenes:* Case report and review. Clin Infect Dis. 1995;20:1548–1550.
109. Chirgwin K, Gleich S. *Listeria monocytogenes* osteomyelitis. Arch Intern Med. 1989;149:931–932.
110. Holoshitz J, Schneider M, Yaretzky A, et al. *Listeria monocytogenes* pericarditis in a chronically hemodialyzed patient. Am J Med Sci. 1984;288:34–37.
111. Stamm AM, Smith SH, Kirklin JK, et al. Listerial myocarditis in cardiac transplantation. Rev Infect Dis. 1990;12:820–823.
112. Gauto AR, Cone LA, Woodard DR, et al. Arterial infections due to *Listeria monocytogenes:* Report of four cases and review of world literature. Clin Infect Dis. 1992;14:23–28.

113. Dalton CB, Austin CC, Sobel J, et al. An outbreak of gastroenteritis and fever due to *Listeria monocytogenes* in milk. N Engl J Med. 1997;336:100–105.
114. Plaut M, Gardner P. *Listeria monocytogenes* sepsis with disseminated intravascular coagulation. South Med J. 1972;65:490–492.
115. Boucher M, Yonekura ML, Wallace RJ, et al. Adult respiratory distress syndrome: A rare manifestation of *Listeria monocytogenes* infection in pregnancy. Am J Obstet Gynecol. 1984;149:686–688.
116. Thomas F, Ravaud Y. Rhabdomyolysis and acute renal failure associated with listeria meningitis. J Infect Dis. 1988;158:492–493.
117. Van J-C N, Nguyen L, Guillemam R, et al. Relapse of infection or reinfection by *Listeria monocytogenes* in a patient with heart transplant: Usefulness of pulsed-field gel electrophoresis for diagnosis. Clin Infect Dis. 1994;19:208–209.
118. Chatzipanagiotou S, Hof H. Sera from patients with high titers of antibody to streptolysin O react with listeriolysin. J Clin Microbiol. 1988;26:1066–1067.
119. Greisen K, Loeffelholz M, Purohit A, et al. PCR primers and probes for the 16S rRNA gene of most species of pathogenic bacteria, including bacteria found in cerebrospinal fluid. J Clin Microbiol. 1994;32:335–351.
120. Gholizadeh Y, Poyart C, Jovin M, et al. Serodiagnosis of listeriosis based on detection of antibodies against recombinant truncated forms of listeriolysin O. J Clin Microbiol. 1996;34:1391–1395.
121. Berche P, Reich KA, Bonnichon M, et al. Detection of anti-listeriolysin O for serodiagnosis of human listeriosis. Lancet. 1990;335:624–627.
122. Mater GM, Bibb WF, Helsel L, et al. Immunoaffinity purification, stabilization and comparative characterization of listeriolysin O from *Listeria monocytogenes* serotypes 1/2a and 4b. Res Microbiol. 1992;143:489–498.
123. Hof H, Nichterlein T, Kretschmar M. Management of listeriosis. Clin Microbiol Rev. 1997;10:345–357.
124. Lavetter A, Leedom JM, Mathies AW Jr, et al. Meningitis due to *Listeria monocytogenes*. A review of 25 cases. N Engl J Med. 1971;285:598–603.
125. Scheld WM. Evaluation of rifampin and other antibiotics against *Listeria monocytogenes* in vitro and in vivo. Rev Infect Dis. 1983;5:S593–S599.
126. Winslow DL, Damme J, Dieckman E. Delayed bactericidal activity of β-lactam antibiotics against *Listeria monocytogenes:* Antagonism of chloramphenicol and rifampin. Antimicrob Agents Chemother. 1983;23:555–558.
127. Winslow DL, Bailey EG, Holloway WJ. Effect of newer beta-lactam antibiotics on the bactericidal activity of ampicillin against *Listeria monocytogenes.* Abstract 1056. In: Program and Abstracts of the 24th Interscience Conference on Antimicrobial Agents and Chemotherapy. Washington, DC: American Society for Microbiology; 1984:277.
128. Appleman MD, Cherubin CE, Heseltine PNR, et al. Susceptibility testing of *Listeria monocytogenes:* A reassessment of bactericidal activity as a predictor for clinical outcome. Diagn Microbiol Infect Dis. 1991;14:311–317.
129. Edmiston CE Jr, Gordon RC. Evaluation of gentamicin and penicillin as a synergistic combination in experimental murine listeriosis. Antimicrob Agents Chemother. 1979;16:862–863.
130. Winslow DL, Pankey GA. In vitro activities of trimethoprim and sulfamethoxazole against *Listeria monocytogenes.* Antimicrob Agents Chemother. 1982;22:51–54.
131. Spitzer PG, Hammer SM, Karchmer AW. Treatment of *Listeria monocytogenes* infection with trimethoprim-sulfamethoxazole: Case report and review of the literature. Rev Infect Dis. 1986;8:427–430.
132. Meyer RD, Liu S. Determination of the effect of antimicrobics in combination against *Listeria monocytogenes.* Diagn Microbiol Infect Dis. 1987;6:199–206.
133. Merle-Melet M, Dossou-Gbete L, Meyer P, et al. Is amoxicillin-cotrimoxazole the most appropriate antibiotic regimen for *Listeria* meningoencephalitis? Review of 22 cases and the literature. J Infect. 1996;33:79–85.
134. Cherubin CE, Marr JS, Sierra MF et al. Listeria and gram-negative bacillary meningitis in New York City, 1972–1979. Frequent cases of meningitis in adults. Am J Med. 1981;71:199–209.
135. Espaze EP, Reynaud AE. Antibiotic susceptibilities of *Listeria:* In vitro studies. Infection. 1988;16:S160–S164.
136. Lorber B, Santoro J, Swenson RM. Listeria meningitis during cefazolin therapy. Ann Intern Med. 1975;82:226–229.
137. Blatt SP, Zajac RA. Treatment of listeria bacteremia with vancomycin. Rev Infect Dis. 1991;13:181–182.
138. Bonacorsi S, Doit C, Aujard Y, et al. Successful antepartum treatment of listeriosis with vancomycin plus netilmicin. Clin Infect Dis. 1993;17:139–140.
139. Baldassarre JS, Ingerman MJ, Nansteel J, et al. Development of *Listeria* meningitis during vancomycin therapy: A case report. J Infect Dis. 1991;164:221–222.
140. Charpentier E, Gerbaud G, Jacquet C, et al. Incidence of antibiotic resistance in *Listeria* species. J Infect Dis. 1995;172:277–281.
141. Broome CV. Listeriosis: Can we prevent it? ASM News 1993;59:444–446.

Additional Reading

Ryser ET, Marth EH. Listeria, Listeriosis and Food Safety. New York: Marcel Dekker; 1991.

Chapter 196

Bacillus anthracis (Anthrax)

DANIEL P. LEW

Bacillus anthracis is a gram-positive, spore-forming bacillus that can cause acute infection in both animals and humans. It is primarily a disease of herbivores, which acquire infection after coming into contact with soil-borne spores. In its spore form it can persist in nature for prolonged periods, possibly years. The distribution of anthrax is worldwide.[1]

The disease occurs primarily in three forms: cutaneous, respiratory, and gastrointestinal. The incidence of anthrax has decreased in developed countries, but it remains a considerable health problem in developing countries.

HISTORICAL BACKGROUND

The earliest known description of anthrax is found in the Book of *Genesis,* in which the fifth plague (1491 BC), which appears to have been anthrax, is described as killing the Egyptians' cattle. There are descriptions of anthrax involving both animals and humans in the early literature of Hindus, Greeks, and Romans. In the 17th century, a pandemic referred to as the "black bane" swept through Europe, causing many human and animal deaths. Later, the disease in humans was described as the "malignant pustule."

Several distinguished microbiologists in the 19th century characterized the pathologic basis of the disease and attempted to develop a vaccine because of serious problems with anthrax in the livestock industry.[2] Pasteur developed and field-tested in sheep his attenuated spore vaccine in 1881. In 1939, Sterne reported his development of an animal vaccine that is a spore suspension of an avirulent, nonencapsulated live strain. This is the animal vaccine currently recommended for use.

Outbreaks of occupational cutaneous and respiratory anthrax began to be reported in the mid-1800s in industrial European countries such as England and Germany. Cutaneous anthrax came from handling wool, hair, and hides. Respiratory anthrax came from processes that created an aerosol, such as carding wool (hence the appellation "woolsorter's disease") and handling contaminated sacks of imported dried bones, as occurred in an English bone meal factory. Ninety cases of cutaneous or inhalation anthrax occurred over 24 years in women employed in an Austrian paper factory to tear up rags imported from the Near East. Early in this century, in the United States, the disease occurred in persons who handled materials that had been woven from contaminated animal fibers.

From the beginning of this century the annual number of cases reported in developed countries has steadily decreased. This decrease is the result of use of a cell-free anthrax vaccine in persons employed in high-risk industrial groups, decreased use of imported potentially contaminated animal products, improved hygiene in industry, and improved animal husbandry.

EPIDEMIOLOGY

Anthrax is usually a disease of herbivores and only incidentally infects humans who come into contact with infected animals or their products. Because anthrax remains a problem in developing countries, animal products imported from these areas continue to pose a risk.

Human cases may occur in an industrial or an agricultural environment. Industrial cases result from contact with anthrax spores that contaminate raw materials used in manufacturing processes. In the

United States, occasional epidemics have occurred in industrial settings, probably related to the processing of batches of highly contaminated imported animal fibers, particularly goat hair. These epidemics were primarily of cutaneous anthrax.

One epidemic occurred in Switzerland.[3, 4] Within less than 3 years, 25 workers in one textile factory contracted the disease; 24 cases were of the cutaneous type, and one was inhalation anthrax. The infection was due to goat hair imported from Pakistan. Owing to the rarity of the illness, which contributed to a general lack of experience among medical personnel, recognition of the clinical symptoms was delayed. In addition, repeated attempts failed to identify the pathogenic agent conclusively.

Human cases of anthrax in an agricultural environment result from direct contact with animals that are sick or have died from anthrax. In African wildlife, which cannot easily be vaccinated and in which the other aspects of control are not relevant, the disease remains a major cause of uncontrolled mortality in herbivores.[5]

In Africa there have been multiple epidemics of human disease associated with epizootics of anthrax in cattle. The largest reported agricultural outbreak occurred in Zimbabwe, with more than 10,000 cases reported between 1979 and 1985. Endemic cases continue to occur in the involved area. The majority of patients had cutaneous infections located primarily on the exposed parts of the body; some gastrointestinal cases were also reported. Domestic cattle deaths were noted. A similar large outbreak of human and animal cases of anthrax occurred in Chad, from September to December 1988, infecting more than 50% of donkeys and horses.[6] There were 716 human cases reported, with 88 deaths.

In an epidemiologic study of a human anthrax outbreak in Zimbabwe, the following factors were significantly associated with the disease: skinning and cutting meat of an animal alleged to have shown symptoms of anthrax, eating contaminated meat, and handling contaminated meat in the process of selling it.[7]

Bacillus anthracis Spores Used as a Biologic Warfare Agent

Anthrax has been developed as a biologic warfare agent[8] by Japan, the United Kingdom, the United States, Iraq, and the Soviet Union.

An epidemic of anthrax occurred during April 1979 among people who lived or worked within a distance of 4 km in a narrow zone downwind of a Soviet military microbiology facility in Sverdlovsk (now Ekaterinburg, Russia). In addition, livestock died of anthrax along the extended axis of the epidemic zone out to a distance of 50 km. Later, in 1992, Soviet authorities admitted that the facility had been part of an offensive biologic weapons system and that the epidemic was caused by accidental release of anthrax spores. At least 77 cases and 66 deaths occurred, constituting the largest documented epidemic of inhalation anthrax in history. Main autopsy features included hemorrhagic necrosis of the thoracic lymph nodes in the lymphatic drainage of the lungs and hemorrhagic mediastinitis.[9] More recently, between 1985 and 1991, Iraq developed anthrax for biologic warfare. By the time the Persian Gulf War occurred, Iraq had deployed bombs and missiles laden with biologic agents, which fortunately were not used.

Anthrax spores have several characteristics suitable for a biologic weapon, such as low visibility, high potency, accessibility, and relatively easy delivery, and could be used not only in war but during terrorist activities. A millionth of a gram of anthrax spores constitutes a lethal inhalation dose; a kilogram, depending on meteorologic conditions and means of delivery, has the potential to kill hundreds of thousands of people in a metropolitan area. Concerns have been raised by recent reports from Russia that scientists were able to insert all the *B. anthracis* genes determining the pathogenicity of anthrax into other bacilli, such as *Bacillus cereus*, against which the present available vaccine is ineffective. In addition, the vaccine may not protect against some rare *B. anthracis* strains. It is also possible to produce *B. anthracis* strains that are resistant to antibiotics.

In response to the growing threat of terrorism with chemical and biologic weapons, the United States and several other governments have developed new antiterrorist legislation and concepts of operations of emergency health and medical services response. Because the incubation period of inhalation anthrax may last a few days, the impact of a bioterrorist anthrax exposure could be reduced by early diagnosis; therefore, this disease should be considered in the differential diagnosis for an unusual epidemic.[10]

MICROBIOLOGY

Pus or tissue specimens from patients suspected to have anthrax should be stained by both Gram stain, to reveal gram-positive bacilli (Fig. 196–1*B*), and polychrome methylene blue, to show the polypeptide capsule. Bacilli are usually abundant in the specimen and easy to culture on standard blood or nutrient agar. In heavily contaminated specimens such as stool, it may be necessary to use selective agar or decontamination methods that rely on the resistance of the anthrax spores to heat or ethanol. The colonies are gray-white to white and nonhemolytic. Identification of the isolate depends on the presence of a capsule, lack of motility, catalase positivity, lysis by γ-bacteriophage, penicillin susceptibility, and aerobic endospore production. Commercially available test strips (API Products, Plainview, NY) and fluorescent antibody staining can be used to aid identification. Differentiation of *B. anthracis* from the occasional nonmotile *B. cereus* can be difficult, although *B. cereus* is β-hemolytic and penicillin-resistant. Testing for capsule formation on bicarbonate agar is an additional diagnostic measure. Isolates may need to be sent to a referral laboratory for γ-phage susceptibility testing. Gas chromatographic whole-cell fatty acid analysis has also been used for identification.

MICROBIAL EPIDEMIOLOGY

The ultimate reservoir for *B. anthracis* is the soil; however, the cycle of anthrax bacilli in soil is a complex phenomenon. *B. anthracis* may persist in certain types of soil for years but does not necessarily lead to disease. A vegetative phase is necessary whereby anthrax spores multiply to a sufficient density that grazing animals can become infected. Old descriptions of fields associated with repeated epidemics of anthrax over extensive periods among grazing animals have been reported in Europe. It has been shown that the cycling of the bacteria through herbivores, which then die and release bacteria into the soil and surrounding watercourses, may explain local soil contamination. Seasonal variations in the incidence of the disease may reflect altered patterns of grazing or distribution of spores in the soil.

The precise delineation of the extent of soil contamination would mean that the elimination of *B. anthracis* from positive areas could then become a realistic goal. The recent decontamination of Gruinard Island (off the northwest coast of Scotland), which was deliberately contaminated during World War II, has shown that the organism can be eliminated from a defined area by simple techniques, albeit at considerable cost.[11]

The monitoring and detection of *B. anthracis* in the environment are thus important matters for health authorities. Several direct methods for detecting *B. anthracis* in the soil have been reported. These used selective growth media, but none is totally effective in inhibiting the background flora, particularly *B. cereus, B. subtilis,* and *B. polymyxa,* which differ in very few characteristics. These techniques are of limited sensitivity, but a selective enrichment system for *B. anthracis* has yet to be designed.[12]

During epidemiologic investigations, gram-positive bacilli have been isolated that, on the basis of conventional tests, resemble *B. anthracis* but fail to produce the capsule or to induce anthrax in test animals; such organisms have long been dismissed in clinical and veterinary laboratories as *B. cereus* or simply as unidentified *Bacillus*

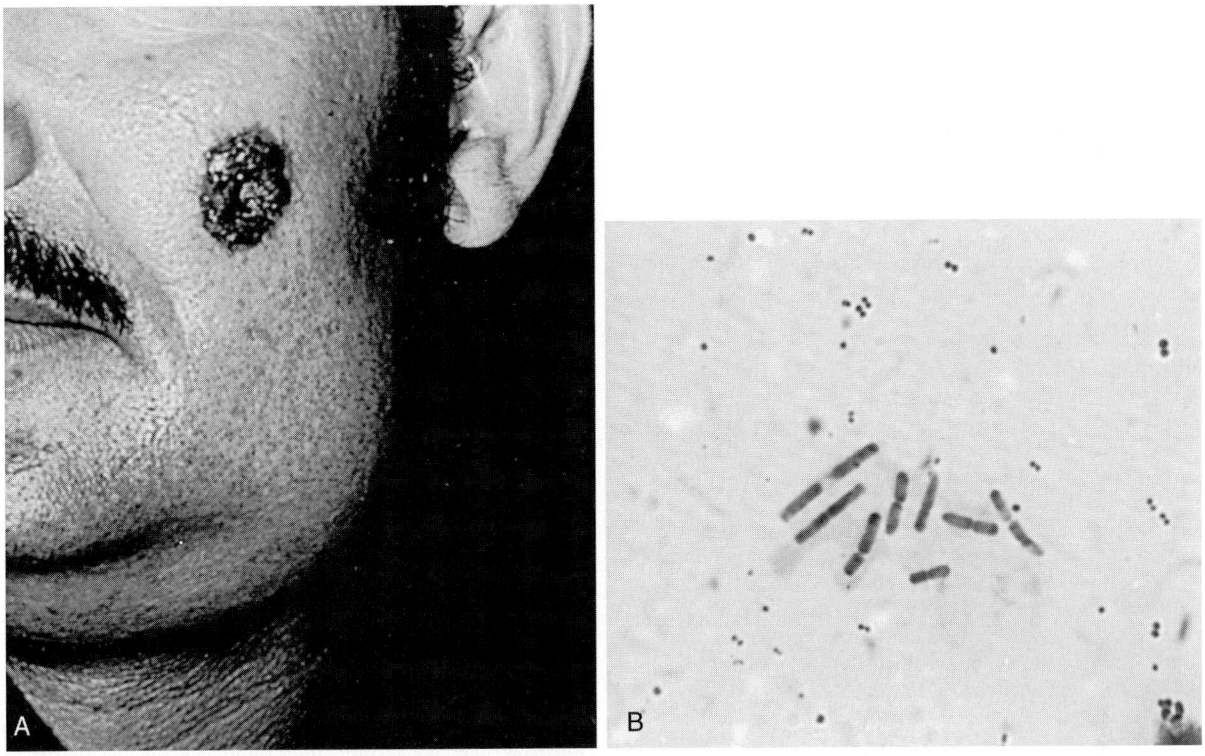

FIGURE 196–1. *A,* A shepherd from Morocco was seen with a painless pruritic facial lesion associated with regional lymphadenopathy. *B,* Gram stain of the vesicular fluid revealed characteristic boxcar-shaped encapsulated bacilli. (Courtesy of Professor Jean-Hilaire Saurat, Chief, Dermatology Clinic, Geneva University Hospital, Geneva, Switzerland.)

spp. and thereupon discarded as inconsequential.[13] The application of newly available DNA probes, polymerase chain reaction techniques,[14] specific toxin antigen detection systems, and monoclonal antibody assays has revealed that a proportion of such strains are *B. anthracis* that lack the plasmid carrying the capsule gene.

PATHOGENESIS

Anthrax toxin, produced by the bacterium *B. anthracis,* is composed of three proteins: protective antigen (PA), edema factor (EF), and lethal factor (LF). PA binds to specific cell surface receptors and, upon proteolytic activation to a 63-kD fragment (PA63), forms a membrane channel that mediates entry of EF and LF into the cell. EF is an adenylate cyclase and together with PA forms a toxin referred to as *edema toxin.* LF and PA together form a toxin referred to as *lethal toxin.* Lethal toxin is the dominant virulence factor produced by *B. anthracis* and is the major cause of death in infected animals. Intravenous injection of lethal toxin into rats causes death in as little as 38 minutes.[15] Production of the toxic factors is regulated by one plasmid and that of the capsular material by a second plasmid.

The effects of anthrax toxin components on human neutrophils have been studied in detail.[16] Phagocytosis of opsonized and radiation-killed *B. anthracis* was not affected by the individual anthrax toxin components. However, a combination of lethal toxin and edema toxin inhibited bacterial phagocytosis and blocked the oxidative burst of polymorphonuclear neutrophils. The two-toxin combination also increased intracellular cyclic AMP levels.

In macrophages, lethal toxin, after internalization via cell surface receptors, induces influx of calcium and inhibition of macromolecular synthesis. Lethal toxin causes apoptosis and necrosis via protein phosphatases,[17] leading to lysis within 2 hours. It has been shown recently that LF is a protease that cleaves the amino terminus of mitogen-activated protein kinase kinases 1 and 2 (MAPKK1 and MAPKK2) and that this cleavage inactivates MAPKK1 and inhibits the MAPK signal transduction pathway.[15]

These studies suggest that two of the protein components of anthrax toxin increase host susceptibility to infection by blocking signal transduction, suppressing polymorphonuclear or macrophage function, and inducing cytotoxic effects.

Experiments performed in animals suggest that spores deposited beneath the skin or in the respiratory or intestinal mucosa germinate, and that the resulting vegetative forms multiply and produce a toxin. The local lesion results from the action of the toxin on the surrounding tissue, which causes tissue necrosis. The toxin or organisms or both may disseminate by the vascular system, causing systemic symptoms and signs of toxicity or bacteremia. Organisms are also often picked up by the lymphatic system, resulting in lymphangitis and lymphadenopathy.

CLINICAL MANIFESTATIONS

Approximately 95% of anthrax cases in developed countries are cutaneous and 5% are respiratory; confirmed epidemic cases of gastrointestinal anthrax have often been reported in Third World countries.

Cutaneous Anthrax

The clinical presentation of cutaneous anthrax is so characteristic that the diagnosis is not often missed by physicians familiar with the disease. Most of the cases occur in exposed skin areas on the arms and hands followed by the face and neck (see Fig. 196–1*A*). The infection begins as a pruritic papule that resembles an insect bite. The papule enlarges and within 1 or 2 days develops into an ulcer surrounded by vesicles. The usual lesion is 1 to 3 cm in diameter and remains round and regular. A characteristic black necrotic central eschar develops later with associated edema. The lesion is most often painless and may first be noticed because of pruritus. After 1 or 2 weeks the lesion dries, and the eschar begins to loosen and shortly thereafter separates, revealing a permanent scar. There may be regional lymphangitis and lymphadenopathy and some systemic symptoms such as fever, malaise, and headache. Antibiotic therapy does not appear to change the natural progression of the lesion itself; however, it will decrease or inhibit development of edema and systemic symptoms. Considerations in the differential diagnosis include conditions such as plague and tularemia due to potential contact with infected animals.

Respiratory Anthrax

An understanding of the pathologic features of respiratory anthrax makes the clinical findings easier to anticipate. Inhaled *B. anthracis* spores do not secrete toxin before germination and cause little inflammatory reaction, so that pneumonia is usually not obvious by symptoms or signs early in the course. The spores germinate into bacilli as they are transported to the hilar and mediastinal nodes, where they cause extraordinary hemorrhagic necrosis and edema of the mediastinum, leading to marked mediastinal widening and substernal pain. As hemorrhagic necrosis extends to the pleura, bloody pleural effusions occur. Findings secondary to effects on the trachea include dry cough and stridor. Extension of edema from the mediastinum into the neck may be visible clinically. Hematogenous spread to the submucosa of the gastrointestinal tract leads to numerous lesions, some of which ulcerate the bowel lumen, causing hematemesis, melena, or both. Sometimes the mesenteric nodes exhibit edema and necrosis. Hematogenous spread to the meninges causes a bloody, purulent meningitis.

Respiratory anthrax shows a biphasic clinical pattern with an initial 1 to 3 days of malaise, low-grade fever, dry cough, and sometimes a subjective feeling of substernal pressure. The second phase is of sudden onset and typically progresses to death from septic shock after 1 or 2 days. Survival is rare, but somewhat slower courses can be observed. This second phase begins with dyspnea at rest, stridor, dry cough, tachypnea, tachycardia, high fever, and profuse diaphoresis, sometimes accompanied by hematemesis or melena. Acute onset of abdominal pain may occur. Patients who survive long enough may exhibit delirium and coma secondary to meningitis. Patients who expire rapidly remain lucid until fatal shock ensues. Physical examination reveals moist, crepitant crackles over the lungs and often evidence of pleural effusion. Radiographs of the chest show widening of the mediastinum and the presence of pleural effusion. Thoracentesis yields grossly bloody fluid, sometimes with *B. anthracis* on smear and culture. Cerebrospinal fluid (CSF) has usually contained anthrax bacilli, but positive blood cultures have been infrequently noted, although it should be recognized that many of the cultures were done by techniques now considered less than ideal. The effect of therapy on symptomatic respiratory anthrax has been marginal, at least in part because early diagnosis is so difficult.[3, 18]

Gastrointestinal Anthrax

During periods of extreme hardship, meat from animals dying of anthrax may be eaten or sold. Persons slaughtering sick animals may develop cutaneous anthrax. Contaminated meat may be made into sausages if meat inspectors are careless or bribed. As recently reported from the Krasnador region of Russia, poorly cooked contaminated meat has been sold by street vendors as skewers of "shashlyk." Ingestion of contaminated meat can cause gastrointestinal anthrax. The incubation period of gastrointestinal anthrax is commonly 3 to 7 days. There are two clinical presentations following ingestion of *B. anthracis*–contaminated food: abdominal and oropharyngeal.

The symptoms of *abdominal* anthrax are initially nonspecific and include nausea, vomiting, anorexia, and fever. Lesions are frequently described in the cecum and adjacent areas of the bowel. Some reports have described lesions in the large bowel, and rarely in the duodenum. With progression of the disease, abdominal pain, hematemesis, and bloody diarrhea develop. With further progression, toxemia develops, with shock, cyanosis, and death. The time from onset of symptoms to death has varied, most frequently ranging from 2 to 5 days. Gastrointestinal anthrax has never been reported in the United States, but such cases are still reported in developing countries.

In the *oropharyngeal* form, edema and tissue necrosis occur in the cervical area.[19, 20] Several reports have described the development of an inflammatory lesion resembling a cutaneous lesion in the oral cavity involving the posterior wall, the hard palate, or the tonsils. The main clinical features are sore throat, dysphagia, fever, lymphadenopathy in the neck, and toxemia. Most affected patients die of toxemia and sepsis.

Meningitis

Meningitis, seen in less than 5% of anthrax cases, may be a complication of any of the three forms of primary anthrax infection.[21]

PATHOLOGIC FINDINGS

Autopsy findings in inhalation anthrax are as described previously. In deaths due to gastrointestinal anthrax, there is typically hemorrhagic enteritis, with congestion, thickening, and edema of the intestinal walls. Mucosal ulcers with necrosis may be seen in the terminal ileum and cecum. The regional lymph nodes are enlarged, edematous, and hemorrhagic, with some necrosis. There may be acute splenitis. Peritonitis with ascitic fluid is often present.

DIAGNOSIS

Of importance in a possible diagnosis of anthrax is a source of exposure to the infectious agent. Only rarely have cases occurred for which the source of infection could not be identified.

Cutaneous anthrax should be suspected when the patient describes a painless, pruritic papule, sometimes surrounded by vesicles, usually on an exposed part of the body. For the detection of anthrax bacilli, sterile swabs should be soaked in the fluid of the vesicles (see Fig. 196–1). Vesicular fluid should reveal *B. anthracis* organisms microscopically and on culture. Anthrax bacilli are easily seen on Gram-stained smears and cultures from vesicular fluid. Considerations in the differential diagnosis include staphylococcal disease, plague, and tularemia.

The initial symptoms of inhalation anthrax are nonspecific and resemble those of an upper respiratory tract infection. Characteristically, with the sudden development of the acute phase there is severe respiratory distress, and radiographic examination of the chest should reveal widening of the mediastinum, a typical occurrence with inhalation anthrax.

In gastrointestinal anthrax, the patient presents with signs and symptoms of gastroenteritis. Organisms may be demonstrable in vomitus and feces from the infected person. Other diagnostic possibilities include diseases that cause moderately severe gastroenteritis, such as shigellosis and yersiniosis. In the cervical form, the signs and symptoms may suggest severe pharyngitis, such as is sometimes seen with streptococcal infections.

In anthrax meningitis and in septicemia, there should be an identifiable primary site of infection.

SEROLOGIC DIAGNOSIS AND THE ANTHRAXIN SKIN TEST

An enzyme-linked immunosorbent assay (ELISA) has been developed that measures antibodies to the lethal and edema toxins. Diagnosis may be confirmed serologically by demonstrating a fourfold change in titer of acute-phase and convalescent-phase serum specimens collected 4 weeks apart, or by a single titer of greater than 1:32. Although extensive serologic studies have not been conducted, antibody titers in some surveys of exposed persons suggest some degree of previous subclinical infection.[22, 23]

A skin test for the diagnosis of human anthrax was evaluated in the former Soviet Union as an alternative to bacteriologic confirmation of human anthrax (which is possible only in 10 to 40% of cases within the first 3 weeks of the disease). Results of the anthraxin skin test, which detects anthrax cell-mediated immunity, were positive in 81% of cases in the first 3 days of the disease and in 97% of cases in the next 2 to 3 weeks. The positivity rate remained 82% in the following 4 or 15 years and was 72% 16 or 31 years after recovery. Thus, the anthraxin skin test appears to be a valuable method for early diagnosis of acute anthrax as well as the only method available for retrospective diagnosis of human anthrax.[24]

CONTROL AND PREVENTION

Early in the 20th century, as an example of preventive intervention, a formaldehyde disinfecting station was built by the British government in Liverpool. Before release for use in manufacture, all "dangerous" imported wool and goat hair was first washed in formaldehyde baths, which successfully reduced contamination of the animal fibers with *B. anthracis.*

In the United States, improvements in industrial hygiene have been of some benefit in reducing the exposure of the worker to infectious materials and aerosols. The most important measures are the use of dust-collecting equipment during the initial processing cycle and the institution of effective environmental clean-up procedures.

The resistance of the spore form of *B. anthracis* to physical and chemical agents is reflected in the persistence of the organism in the inanimate environment. Organisms have been demonstrated to persist for years in factories in which the environment became contaminated during the processing of contaminated imported materials of animal origin. Accordingly, they may serve as the source of infection for people who work in the area. Special efforts are required to decontaminate such environments; one method is to use paraformaldehyde vapor, which is successful in killing *B. anthracis* spores. In the laboratory, surfaces may be decontaminated with either 5% hypochlorite or 5% phenol (carbolic acid); instruments and other equipment may be autoclaved.

Employees should be educated about the disease and the recommendations for working in a contaminated environment and for reducing the risk of developing the disease. Medical consultation services should be available to employees. Adequate clean-up facilities and clothes-changing areas should be available so that workers do not wear contaminated clothes home.

It should be noted that the risk of industrial infection has been reduced significantly as the use of imported animal products has decreased because of changing business conditions, the increased use of synthetic materials, and the use of human vaccine.

Gastrointestinal anthrax can be prevented by forbidding the sale for consumption of meat from sick animals or animals that have died from disease. Depending on the circumstances, it may be important to alert persons who may come in contact with contaminated meat about the disease and about the need to cook all meats thoroughly. Prophylactic penicillin may be used if contaminated food has been ingested.

Animals that graze in areas known as anthrax districts should be vaccinated annually with the animal vaccine. Specimens for microbiologic study should be obtained from all animals suspected of dying from anthrax; blood or tissue smears can be examined microscopically, and cultures can be prepared from these same materials. Necropsy procedures, entailing spillage of contaminated blood with resultant sporulation of organisms, should be avoided. The carcasses of all animals that have died with a confirmed diagnosis of anthrax should be thoroughly burned and the remaining bones and other materials buried deeply.

Control of the disease in humans ultimately depends on control of the disease in animals. Effective animal vaccines are available, and all cases should be reported to state veterinary authorities.

TREATMENT AND CHEMOPROPHYLAXIS

It is estimated that approximately 20% of untreated cases of cutaneous anthrax will result in death, whereas respiratory anthrax is almost always fatal. Deaths are, however, rare after antimicrobial treatment for the cutaneous form.

Intravenous penicillin G is the drug of choice, in a dose of approximately 4 million units every 4 to 6 hours. Lesions become culture-negative in a few hours,[25] but therapy should be continued for 7 to 10 days. Some animal experiments suggest that addition of streptomycin (or gentamicin) may have additional benefit. In the absence of antibiotic susceptibility data, or for the penicillin-allergic patient, ciprofloxacin, 400 mg IV every 8 to 12 hours, or doxycycline, 200 mg IV and then 100 mg IV every 8 to 12 hours, is a satisfactory alternative.

If there is indication that an anthrax outbreak is occurring or that anthrax spores may have been used in biologic warfare, prophylaxis with ciprofloxacin (500 mg by mouth twice a day), or doxycycline (100 mg by mouth twice a day) may be given to potential susceptible nonimmunized persons. The duration of treatment for postexposure prophylaxis is for at least 6 weeks (or 2 weeks after the third vaccine dose when vaccine-induced antibodies are detectable).

Antibiotic therapy ameliorates systemic symptoms, although progression to eschar is not prevented. Excision of the lesion is contraindicated. Topical therapy is not effective. Systemic corticosteroids have been used for patients with extensive or cervical edema and in those with meningitis but indications are not well established. Tracheotomy may be needed when cervical edema compromises the airway.

Dressings with drainage from the lesions should be incinerated, autoclaved, or otherwise disposed of as biohazardous waste. Patients with draining lesions should be placed in "contact isolation." Person-to-person transmission has not been documented, including from patients with inhalation anthrax.

IMMUNIZATION

Both an attenuated live vaccine and a killed vaccine have been developed. In the former Soviet Union the human live anthrax vaccine has undergone mass field trials, which showed good preventive efficacy.[26, 27] However, the only human vaccine in current use in the United States has been produced by the Michigan Biologic Products Institute, but it is now manufactured by BioPort, a new company started for that purpose. The vaccine is a sterile filtrate of cultures from an avirulent nonencapsulated strain that elaborates PA.[28]

This vaccine has protected nonhuman primates from experimental respiratory exposure and was field tested in employees of four different textile mills in the United States. The vaccine had an effectiveness of 92.5%. This vaccine should be used for all persons who may be exposed to contaminated materials or environment. Additionally, anyone who comes into a mill processing *B. anthracis*–contaminated materials should also be vaccinated. Currently, the vaccine is given in a volume of 0.5 ml subcutaneously at 0, 2, and 4 weeks and again at 6, 12, and 18 months followed by an annual booster. Veterinarians and other persons who, because of their occupation, have potential contact with anthrax should also be immunized with the human anthrax vaccine.[29] Postvaccinal cell-mediated immunity may be assessed by the anthraxin skin test or by the presence of specific antibodies. In response to the potential use of anthrax as a biologic warfare agent, the Pentagon decided in 1998 that it would vaccinate every member of the U.S. Armed Forces against anthrax. This amounts to approximately 1.4 million active duty troops and 1 million reservists. Active-duty troops in the Persian Gulf and on the Korean peninsula will be the first to be vaccinated.

Practitioners interested in the anthrax vaccine should contact the Bureau of Disease Control and Laboratory Services, Michigan Department of Public Health, P.O. Box 30035, 3500 N. Logan Street, Lansing, Mich.

The ability to prepare purified components of anthrax toxin by recombinant technology has opened the possibility of new anthrax vaccines.[29] For example, immunization with PA toxoid vaccines or PA-producing live vaccines elicits partial or complete protection against anthrax infection, and these new vaccines deserve careful field testing.

REFERENCES

1. Brachman PS. Bacterial infections of humans—epidemiology and control. In: Evans AS, Brachman PS, eds. Anthrax. 2nd ed. New York: Plenum Press; 1993.
2. Tigertt WD. Anthrax. William Smith Greenfield, M.D., F.R.C.P. Professor Superintendent, The Brown Animal Sanatory Institution (1878–8). Concerning the priority due to him for the production of the first vaccine against anthrax. J Hyg (Camb). 1980;85:415–420.
3. Winter H, Pfisterer RM. Inhalationsanthrax bei einem Textilarbeiter: Ein- nicht-letaler Verlauf. Schweiz Med Wochenschr. 1991;121:832–835.
4. Pfisterer RM. Eine Milzbrandepidemie in der Schweiz. Schweiz Med Wochenschr. 1991;121:813–825.
5. Turnbull PCB, Bell RHV, Sigawa K, et al. Anthrax in wildlife in the Luangwa Valley, Zambia. Vet Rec. 1991;128:399–403.
6. Lamarque D, Haessler C, Champion R, et al. Le charbon au Tchad: Une zoonose encore d'actualité. Med Trop. 1989;49:245–251.
7. Mwenye KS, Siziya S, Peterson D. Factors associated with human anthrax outbreak in the Chikupo and Ngandu villages of Murewa District in Mashonaland East Province, Zimbabwe. Cent Afr J Med. 1996;42:312–315.
8. Christopher GW, Cieslak TJ, Pavlin JA, Eitzen EM Jr. Biological warfare: A historical perspective. JAMA. 1997;278:412–417.
9. Abramova FA, Grinberg LM, Yampolskaya OV, Walker DH. Pathology of inhalational anthrax in 42 cases from the Sverdlosk outbreak of 1979. Proc Natl Acad Sci U S A. 1993;90:2291–2294.
10. Franz DR, Jahrling PB, Friedlander AM, et al. Clinical recognition and management of patients exposed to biological warfare agents. JAMA. 1997;278:399–411.
11. Titball RW, Turnbull PCB, Hutson RA. The monitoring and detection of *Bacillus anthracis* in the environment. J Appl Bacteriol Symposium Suppl. 1991;70:9S–18S.
12. Lawrence D, Heitefuss S, Seifert HSH. Differentiation of *Bacillus anthracis* from *Bacillus cereus* by gas chromatographic whole-cell fatty acid analysis. J Clin Microbiol. 1991;29:1508–1512.
13. Turnbull PCB, Hutson RA, Ward MJ, et al. *Bacillus anthracis* but not always anthrax. J Appl Bacteriol. 1992;72:21–28.
14. Jackson PJ, Hugh-Jones ME, Adair DM, et al. PCR analysis of tissue samples from the 1979 Sverdlovsk anthrax victims: The presence of multiple *Bacillus anthracis* strains in different victims. Proc Natl Acad Sci U S A. 1998;95:1224–1229.
15. Duesbery NS, Webb CP, Leppla SH, et al. Proteolytic inactivation of MAP-kinase-kinase by anthrax lethal factor. Science 1998;280:734–737.
16. O'Brien J, Friedlander A, Dreier T, et al. Effects of anthrax toxin components on human neutrophils. Infect Immun. 1985;47:306–310.
17. Lin CG, Kao YT, Liu WT, et al. Cytotoxic effects of anthrax lethal toxin on macrophage-like cell line j774a.1. Curr Microbiol. 1996;33:224–227.
18. Kaufmann AF, Meltzer MI, Schmid GP. The economic impact of a bioterrorist attack: Are prevention and postattack intervention programs justifiable? Emerg Infect Dis. 1997;3:83–94.
19. Doganay M, Almaç A, Hanagasi R. Primary throat anthrax. A report of six cases. Scand J Infect Dis. 1986;18:415–419.
20. Navacharoen N, Sirisanthana T, Navacharoen W, Ruckphaopunt K. Oropharyngeal anthrax. J Laryngol Otol. 1985;99:1293–1295.
21. Dürst UN, Bartenstein J, Bühlmann H, et al. Anthrax meningitis. Schweiz Med Wochenschr. 1986;116:1222–1228.
22. Harrison LH, Ezzell JW. Evaluation of serologic tests for diagnosis of anthrax after an outbreak of cutaneous anthrax in Paraguay. J Infect Dis. 1989;160:706–710.
23. Turnbull PCB, Doganay M, Lindeque PM, et al. Serology and anthrax in humans, livestock and Etosha National Park wildlife. Epidemiol Infect. 1992;108:299–313.
24. Shlyakhov E, Rubinstein E. Evaluation of the anthraxin skin test for diagnosis of acute and past human anthrax. Eur J Clin Microbiol Infect Dis. 1996;15:242–245.
25. Ronaghy H, Azadeh B, Kohout E. Penicillin therapy of human cutaneous anthrax. Curr Ther Res. 1972;14:721–725.
26. Shlyakhov EN, Rubinstein E. Human live anthrax vaccine in the former USSR. Vaccine. 1994;12:727–730.
27. Shlyakhov E, Rubinstein E, Novikov I. Anthrax post-vaccinal cell-mediated immunity in humans: Kinetics pattern. Vaccine. 1997;15:631–636.
28. Anthrax vaccines. Med Lett Drugs Thera. 1998;40:52–53.
29. Turnbull PCB. Anthrax vaccines: Past, present and future. Vaccine. 1991;9:533–539.

Chapter 197

Other *Bacillus* Species

CARMELITA U. TUAZON

MICROBIOLOGY

Members of the genus *Bacillus* are aerobic or facultatively anaerobic spore-forming rods with round or squared-off ends that can stain as gram-positive or gram-variable and are ubiquitous in nature. *Bacillus subtilis, Bacillus licheniformis,* and *Bacillus megaterium,* like *Bacillus anthracis,* produce a polypeptide capsule under certain conditions. *Bacillus* organisms vary in size, ranging from about 3 by 0.4 μm to 9 by 2 μm, and may appear singly, in a diplobacillary form, or in chains. *Bacillus cereus* and *Bacillus thuringiensis* are motile; their flagellar (H) antigens have been useful for serotyping. Most species grow readily on nutrient agar or peptone media. Single colonies are usually 2 to several millimeters in diameter and may have a finely granular, mealy appearance; others are membranous and wrinkled.[1] In broth, a surface scum may be formed with or without turbidity or a heavy flocculent or membranous deposit. Growth is sometimes improved by glucose, but not by blood or serum. *B. subtilis* grows on minimal media containing glucose, citrate, ammonium phosphate, and the usual mineral salts. *B. cereus* requires the addition of certain amino acids. On carbohydrate media, most members of the genus form acid only, but a few produce gas (e.g., *Bacillus polymyxa, B. licheniformis*). One member of the group, *B. megaterium,* produces a hemolysin similar to that of *Staphylococcus aureus.*

The optimum temperature for growth ranges from 25 to 37°C. In the vegetative form, the bacilli are killed in 1 hour by moist heat at a temperature of 55°C. The spores of *B. subtilis* may withstand boiling for hours.[1]

EPIDEMIOLOGY

Bacillus organisms are usually found in decaying organic matter, dust, soil, vegetables, and water, and some species are part of the normal flora. In the hospital setting, the bacteria present in the environment can readily cause infections in debilitated, immunosuppressed, or traumatized patients. The organism has been implicated as an opportunistic agent in the setting of serious illness associated with prolonged survival. An investigation of an outbreak of *B. cereus* in an intensive care unit setting traced the organism to contaminated ventilator equipment. Sixty-two patients became colonized with the organism including two in whom nonfatal *Bacillus* sepsis developed; one death was due to pneumonia associated with the organism.[2] In another hospital setting, an epidemiologic investigation of two cases of postoperative *B. cereus* meningitis revealed that hospital linen was heavily contaminated with *B. cereus* spores.[3]

Outbreaks of food poisoning caused by *B. cereus* have been reported from Asia, Australia, Europe, and North America. In the United Kingdom and the United States, *B. cereus* accounted for 1 to 3% of reported outbreaks of bacterial food poisoning in the late 1970s and early 1980s. A much higher incidence was reported from the Netherlands and Canada.[4] A variety of sources of *B. cereus* outbreaks have been described including rice, meat loaf, turkey loaf, sprouts, mashed potatoes, beef stew, and apples. The high incidence of *B. cereus* infection in Hungary, when it ranked as the third most common type of food poisoning, has been attributed to the consumption of well-spiced meat dishes.[5] The spices often contained a high number of spores, some of which would survive cooking. Employees of one manufacturing plant reported illnesses traced to hot chocolate sold in vending machines containing *B. cereus* in levels (170,000 colonies/g) capable of causing illness.[6]

In the investigation of outbreaks of food poisoning due to *B. cereus,* the McCoy cell tissue culture system appears to be useful for the rapid identification of enterotoxin-producing *B. cereus* organisms.[7] Phage typing of isolates also assists in such investigations. A correlation of 80 to 100% between phage types of strains isolated from suspected foods and those of strains isolated from stools of symptomatic patients has been observed.[8] A commercially available ELISA can be used for the detection of *Bacillus* diarrheal enterotoxin in a variety of foods and fecal specimens. Proposed criteria for the diagnosis of an outbreak of *B. cereus* diarrhea have been a roughly 10- to 12-hour incubation period, demonstration that the *B. cereus* isolate obtained from the food source produced diarrheal enterotoxin, and detection of enterotoxin in the food or feces, or both.[9]

Other outbreaks of infections due to *Bacillus* organisms include cases of bacteremia related to contamination of dialysis equipment and wound or burn infections as part of a polymicrobial infection.[10, 11]

Strains of *Bacillus alvei* have been isolated from honey bee larvae and honeycombs of bees infected with European foul brood. Few cases of human infections caused by *B. alvei* have been reported.[12]

Epidemiologic studies on the microbiology of street heroin and injection paraphernalia demonstrated *Bacillus* spp. as the predominant isolates from both types of specimens.[13, 14] Serious infections caused by *Bacillus* spp. have been reported among drug abusers. Both contaminated heroin and paraphernalia can be implicated as possible sources of the organism.

PATHOGENESIS

The different species of *Bacillus* produce a variety of extracellular products including antimicrobial substances, enzymes, pigments, and toxins in a few species.[1] Enzymes that can be found on culture include amylase, collagenase, hemolysin, lecithinase, phospholipase, protease, and urease. Production of antimicrobial substances before the onset of sporulation is characteristic of the genus; these substances include bacitracin, gramicidin, polymyxin, and tyrocidine.

Two different types of enterotoxins are produced by *B. cereus* during exponential growth: enterotoxins causing diarrhea and emetic toxin. Detection of emetic toxin in culture medium may be difficult initially because ordinary media do not support its production, but growth on a medium prepared from rice allows its isolation. The toxins causing diarrhea are produced readily on appropriate media, for example, brain-heart infusion broth containing added glucose. At least two diarrheal enterotoxins have been identified; these are called BceT and HBL.[15] The latter is the best characterized and is a potent exotoxin, composed of three proteins that have binding (B) and lytic (L1, L2) activities, respectively. The name derives from *h*emolysin with *B* and *L* proteins, all three of which have been cloned. HBL is cytolytic and dermonecrotic, increases vascular permeability, and leads to fluid accumulation in isolated rabbit ileal loops.[16–18] HBL accounts for about 50% of the retinal toxicity of *B. cereus* culture filtrates in an experimental model.[19] In this model, histologic examination after experimental intraocular injection of HBL showed rapid retinal necrosis and detachment, choroidal edema, detachment and disruption of the retinal pigment epithelium, and rapid infiltration by polymorphonuclear leukocytes.[19] All three components of HBL had to be present in order for retinal toxicity to occur.

Enzymatic activity may contribute to local tissue destruction. *B. cereus* has three different lecithinases; phosphatidylcholine hydrolase is the form most studied and is frequently referred to as phospholipase C. This enzyme may have a secondary role in ocular infections by disrupting host cell membrane phospholipids exposed by the action of other toxins.

CLINICAL MANIFESTATIONS

Despite the widespread distribution of *Bacillus* organisms, they are rarely associated with actual infection and are more frequently isolated as a culture contaminant. Isolation of this organism requires careful clinical evaluation to determine the significance of the finding.

Risk factors that have been associated with serious *Bacillus* infections include intravenous drug abuse, sickle cell disease, foreign bodies including intravascular catheters, immunosuppression from malignancy, neutropenia, corticosteroid therapy, and the acquired immunodeficiency syndrome (AIDS).[20]

Clinical manifestations of infections caused by *Bacillus* spp. include food poisoning, localized infections related to trauma (as in ocular infections), deep-seated soft tissue infections, and systemic infections (e.g., meningitis, endocarditis, osteomyelitis, recurrent bacteremia).[4, 21, 22] Fulminant eye infections are widely recognized complications of non-anthrax *Bacillus* infections. *Bacillus* organisms that have been associated with clinical syndromes are listed in Table 197–1.

Food Poisoning

There are two distinct clinical forms of *B. cereus* food poisoning: emetic and diarrheal.[23] The emetic form, associated with ingestion of contaminated fried rice, has a short incubation period, usually from 1 to 6 hours, and symptoms are predominantly upper gastrointestinal, manifested by vomiting. It mimics staphylococcal food poisoning. In Chinese restaurants, boiled rice is allowed to "dry off" at ambient temperature, after which it may be stored overnight, before it is fried quickly with beaten egg.[5] Such practice results in the survival and proliferation of strains of *B. cereus* originally present in raw rice, which produce spores with the greatest heat resistance. At ambient temperature, the spores germinate in the cooked rice, and there is rapid growth of vegetative bacteria. Levels of *B. cereus* in foods incriminated in the emetic form of food poisoning have ranged from 1.0×10^3 to 5.0×10^{10} colony-forming units (cfu)/g; high numbers are also present in fecal samples from affected persons. The H-1 serotype has been strongly associated with the production of emetic toxin.[24]

The diarrheal form has a longer incubation period that averages between 10 and 12 hours, and manifestations are related to lower gastrointestinal involvement similar to that in *Clostridium perfringens* food poisoning. Symptoms commonly present are abdominal pain, profuse watery diarrhea, tenesmus, and nausea generally lasting

TABLE 197–1 Clinically Significant *Bacillus* Species

Isolate	Clinical Syndrome
Bacillus alvei	Sepsis, meningitis, pneumonia, empyema, bacteremia
Bacillus cereus	Bacteremia, pneumonia, ophthalmitis, osteomyelitis, endocarditis, soft tissue infections; meningoencephalitis, fulminant hepatitis
Bacillus circulans	Meningitis
Bacillus laterosporus	Septicemia
Bacillus licheniformis	Intravascular catheter–acquired sepsis
Bacillus megaterium	Meningitis, bacteremia
Bacillus pumilus	Meningitis, bacteremia
Bacillus sphaericus	Peritonitis, pleuritis, pericarditis, pseudotumor of the lung, meningitis, bacteremia
Bacillus subtilis	Meningitis, otitis, mastoiditis, urinary tract infection, bacteremia, pneumonia, endocarditis, ventriculoatrial shunt infection

no longer than 12 to 24 hours. Such outbreaks are generally related to consumption of contaminated meat or vegetables, and in one particular outbreak, turkey loaf was implicated.[25] The levels of *B. cereus* found in the implicated foods are in most cases in the range of 5×10^5 to 9.5×10^5 cfu/g. The diarrhea is usually characterized by 3 to 10 small bowel movements per day, but in some cases it may be voluminous and require administration of intravenous fluids. In a few patients, symptoms may last for 2 to 10 days.

The diagnosis of *B. cereus* food poisoning should be suspected in patients who present with upper gastrointestinal symptoms of 1 to 6 hours' duration following consumption of fried rice and in those who present with lower intestinal tract illness 6 to 24 hours after a suspect meal. The diagnosis can be confirmed by isolation of 10^5 or more *B. cereus* organisms per gram of the epidemiologically incriminated food. The isolation of *B. cereus* from stools of patients is not sufficient documentation of an outbreak unless negative stool cultures are obtained from a suitable control group.[23] Rates of asymptomatic fecal carriage of *B. cereus* have been reported at between 14 to 43% depending on the population studied. Therefore, proof that a sample of food is responsible for an outbreak requires that the *B. cereus* organisms isolated from both the clinical specimen and the foodstuff be of the same serotype.[4] Serologic typing can be performed for epidemiologic studies, but the antisera are available in only a few centers. No circulating neutralizing antibodies have been detected in symptomatic patients.[25]

Other *Bacillus* spp. have been implicated in food poisoning. *B. subtilis* has been reported in incidents of food poisoning by meat and pastry products and rice dishes containing meat or seafood. Illness due to this organism is characterized by a short incubation period, with a median duration of 2.5 hours, with vomiting as the predominant symptom in most cases. Ten percent of patients report headaches, a flushing sensation, or sweating as an additional symptom. Large numbers of *B. subtilis*—up to 10^7 cfu/g—have been found in the vomitus and acute-phase fecal specimens.[5] *B. licheniformis* has been also reported in food poisoning cases in which cooked meats and vegetables were most commonly implicated.[5] The median period of incubation was about 8 hours, and the predominant symptom was diarrhea with vomiting in about half the cases. In rare cases, *Bacillus pumilus* has also been implicated, mostly involving meat dishes, "scotch eggs," cheese sandwiches, and canned tomato juice. Many strains of *B. thuringiensis* are insect pathogens; therefore, this organism is widely used to control insect pests. *B. thuringiensis* rarely has been implicated in human infections. An outbreak of gastroenteritis in a chronic care facility was attributed to strains of both *B. cereus* and *B. thuringiensis* with very similar cytotoxic properties; the pathogens were differentiated only by staining for toxin crystal formation, as exhibited by the latter organism.[26]

B. cereus food poisoning is self-limited and requires no antimicrobial therapy. Treatment is symptomatic, and some patients may require fluid replacement if they are severely dehydrated. However, a recent case of fulminant liver failure developed after ingestion of a pasta-and-pesto dish contaminated with *B. cereus* toxin. The emetic toxin isolated from *B. cereus* cultures analyzed in rat liver mitochondria was found to be a mitochondrial toxin. Autopsy of the patient's liver revealed diffuse microvesicular steatosis and mid-zonal necrosis that suggested impaired beta oxidation of liver mitochondria due to a mitochondrial toxin.[27]

The main preventive measure for *Bacillus* gastroenteritis is proper food handling. The heat-resistant spores of *B. cereus* survive boiling and germinate when boiled rice is left unrefrigerated.[28] Flash frying or brief rewarming of rice before serving is not adequate to destroy the preformed, heat-stable toxin. The food either should be maintained at a temperature higher than 60°C or, if it is going to be stored, should be cooled rapidly to a temperature below 8 to 10°C to prevent growth or greatly reduce its rate.[5]

Ocular Infections

Bacillus organisms have been recognized as ocular pathogens for many years. Dacryocystitis, conjunctivitis, keratitis, iridocyclitis, panophthalmitis, and orbital abscess caused by *B. subtilis* have been described.[29] Previous reports of *B. subtilis* as a causative agent for ocular infections may have been related to faulty speciation, however. *B. cereus* has been recently recognized as a primary pathogen of ocular infections. In a recent review of post-traumatic *B. cereus* endophthalmitis, *Bacillus* ranked as the second most common pathogen in five of six series.[30] In post-traumatic ophthalmitis caused by *B. cereus,* an intraocular foreign body is often present.[30, 31] Such infections have been observed with metal projectile injuries. Another setting in which *Bacillus* infection occurs is that associated with contamination with soil and dust. Such infection is frequently reported with injuries incurred in rural or farm environments.

The clinical manifestation is characterized by massive destruction of the vitreal and retinal tissue of the eye, with resulting visual compromise, within the first 12 to 48 hours after inoculation. The presence of progressive corneal deterioration and ring abscess formation is a complication of panophthalmitis caused by *B. cereus.*[32] Except for infections caused by *Pseudomonas aeruginosa* and *Proteus* spp., this finding is almost pathognomonic for *B. cereus* infection. The ring abscess is usually observed within 48 hours after periorbital edema, proptosis, and corneal swelling are noted. Often the vitreal infection spreads to the retina. Patients are frequently systemically ill with fever and leukocytosis.

In the setting of drug abuse, patients present with a rapid fulminant endophthalmitis or panophthalmitis that usually results in a complete loss of vision and loss of the eye to enucleation.[14] Initial symptoms include eye pain and decreased vision with chemosis, redness, and proptosis (Fig. 197–1). Although the exact pathogenesis is unclear, there is indirect evidence that the ophthalmitis is secondary to endogenous infection related to contamination of injection paraphernalia and heroin.[13] In one patient, *B. cereus* was isolated from the vitreous aspirate and also from the syringe used by the patient for injecting hydromorphone hydrochloride.[32] In addition to intravenous drugs (e.g., heroin, amphetamine, methylphenidate [Ritalin], cocaine, hydromorphone hydrochloride), panophthalmitis has been reported after the injection of vitamin B in one patient[33] and in another patient after a blood transfusion.[34]

Early diagnosis is important for successful treatment. The clini-

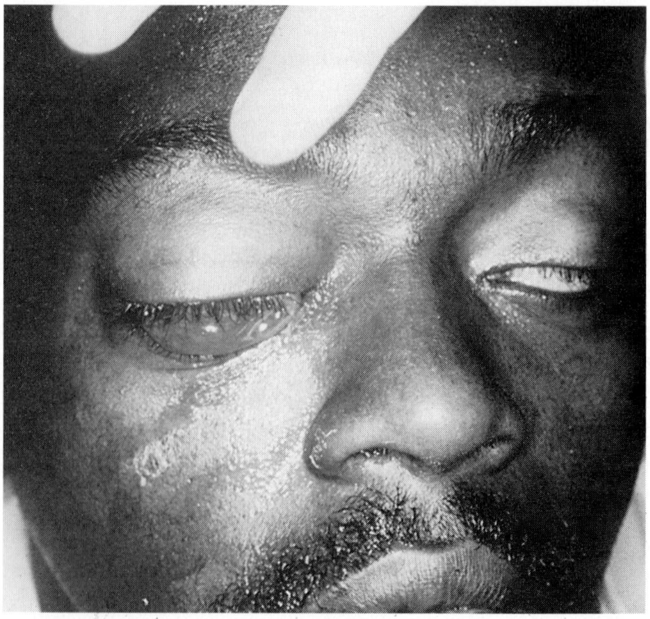

FIGURE 197–1. *Bacillus cereus* endophthalmitis. Note the massive conjunctival edema. (From Shamsuddin D, Tuazon CU, Levy C, et al. *Bacillus cereus* panophthalmitis: Source of the organism. J Infect Dis. 1982;4:97–103. Copyright 1982, The Infectious Diseases Society of America. Published by The University of Chicago Press.)

cian should have a high index of suspicion for *Bacillus* organisms as the pathogen in a patient who presents with ocular infection after trauma or in the setting of drug abuse. With prompt recognition of the infection, appropriate therapy can be instituted before permanent structural changes occur.[31] In patients with post-traumatic *B. cereus* endophthalmitis, aggressive management may be associated with the preservation of anatomic integrity and restoration of useful visual acuity.[35, 36] Adequate samples of ocular fluid should be obtained to ensure complete diagnostic evaluation. Because of serious consequences of panophthalmitis, an aggressive approach with early vitrectomy and vitreal instillation of appropriate antibiotics is indicated.[31] Antibiotics administered systemically, intravitreally, topically, and via periocular routes are used in conjunction with surgical intervention. Aminoglycosides (e.g., gentamicin, tobramycin) have been administered locally and systemically but are inadequate to eradicate the infection. Administration of clindamycin or vancomycin is appropriate before the results of culture because *B. cereus* is the most frequent isolate. The combination of clindamycin, at a dose of 450 μg, and gentamicin, at a dose of 200 to 400 μg, administered intravitreally seems to be favored by ophthalmologists. In addition, 8 μg/ml of gentamicin and 9 μg/ml of clindamycin can be added to the vitrectomy infusion fluid.[37] Imipenem and fluoroquinolones appear active, but more experience is needed in their use.[38] In experimental rabbit models of post-traumatic endophthalmitis caused by *B. cereus,* intravitreal administration of 100 μg of ciprofloxacin prevented the development of disease when given 1 hour and 6 hours after inoculation.[39]

In a swine model of experimental post-traumatic *B. cereus* endophthalmitis, the intravitreal efficacy of ciprofloxacin, vancomycin, and imipenem was evaluated. Vancomycin- and imipenem-treated animals had less inflammation and tissue destruction than noted in control animals. Ciprofloxacin-treated animals showed significantly more intraocular destruction and were indistinguishable from controls.[40]

In the drug abuse setting, both clindamycin and vancomycin have been used for single-agent therapy. Intravitreal dexamethasone (to control the destructive inflammation) and early vitrectomy have recently been recommended for the management of sight-threatening endophthalmitis such as that induced by *B. cereus.* Prognosis is poor, and infection usually results in the loss of the eye, but recent experience indicates that with an aggressive approach, the eye may be salvaged, although with a loss of vision.[31]

Pneumonia

B. cereus is a rare pulmonary pathogen that has been reported to cause pneumonia in the compromised host. A variety of pulmonary presentations have been reported. Cases of necrotizing pneumonitis caused by *B. cereus* have been reported in premature neonates and in patients with acute leukemias and hepatic malignancies.[41, 42] *B. cereus* pneumonia in immunocompetent persons that has a rapidly progressive and fatal course has been reported.[43] Clinical presentation can mimic *B. anthracis*–type infection with a fulminant course, with acute respiratory failure accompanied by overwhelming sepsis. The rapid course and fatal outcome can be attributed to the very potent toxins and enzymes produced by the organism. An immunocompetent patient with pneumonia and empyema associated with a species of *Bacillus* resembling *B. alvei* has been reported.[44] Very rarely, a cavitating pneumonia may be caused by *B. cereus.*[45] A large pseudotumor of the lung caused by *B. sphaericus* has been reported in a patient with chronic asthma on long-term steroid therapy.[46]

The clinical symptoms are indistinguishable from those of other bacterial pneumonias. The outcome is poor and probably related to the nature of the underlying illness. In this setting, early diagnosis is important in preventing death. In immunosuppressed patients, consideration should be given to obtaining adequate specimens by transbronchial bronchoscopy or needle aspiration to facilitate establishing the diagnosis.

Endocarditis

Endocarditis caused by *Bacillus* organisms is rare. In the setting of intravenous drug abuse, endocarditis is a well-recognized complication.[20, 21] As with ocular infections, the heroin and injection paraphernalia remain the most likely sources of the organism. Most cases are related to drug abuse, but endocarditis has been reported in patients with implanted devices such as a prosthetic cardiac valve[47] or ventricular pacemaker. The clinical presentation and course of endocarditis in the drug abuser are similar to those in infection caused by other pathogens, with a predominance of tricuspid valve involvement and a relatively indolent course.

Infiltrates seen on chest x-ray films obtained in patients with *Bacillus* endocarditis have been attributed to extracellular toxin capable of inducing massive thrombi in pulmonary vessels. In tricuspid endocarditis, however, the infiltrates may well represent pulmonary septic emboli.

The diagnosis is made by isolation of *Bacillus* organisms repeatedly from blood cultures plus clinical findings compatible with endocarditis.

Antibiotic therapy with vancomycin or clindamycin has achieved high cure rates in patients with *Bacillus* endocarditis.[20, 21] For infection due to species other than *B. cereus,* a successful outcome has been reported with use of a cephalosporin.[48] The response to antibiotic therapy is excellent, and surgical intervention is usually not required.

Bacteremia and Septicemia

Bacteremia involving *Bacillus* spp. is common, but isolation of the organism from blood cultures does not always indicate infection. In the drug abuser, the spectrum of bloodborne infection can range from transient bacteremia to endocarditis. Again, the drug abuser usually presents with symptoms of fever and positive blood cultures temporally related to heroin injection, findings that implicate heroin injection as the mode of infection. Hemolytic anemia has been reported as a complication of *B. cereus* bacteremia in a drug abuser with hemoglobin SC disease.[49]

Bacillus bacteremia can be a complication among patients with implanted intravascular catheters. Bacteremias due to *B. subtilis, B. licheniformis, B. cereus, B. circulans,* and *B. pumilus* have been reported and have usually required removal of the implanted device to effect cure.[50] Vancomycin therapy through the catheter has been useful to control sepsis but frequently failed to sterilize the catheter.

Cases of *Bacillus* bacteremia in immunocompromised patients have been associated with oral administration of Bactisubtil.[51] Bactisubtil is a parapharmaceutical product that has been used for mild gastrointestinal disturbances to protect the normal flora.

Patients in whom *Bacillus* organisms are present in a single blood culture, particularly those with intravascular catheters, may be asymptomatic. This finding may represent contamination by ubiquitous *Bacillus* spores. However, *Bacillus* bacteremia can also present as a relatively benign illness, as emphasized in a reported AIDS patient.[52] In patients with one positive blood culture and little or no illness, therapy can be withheld pending results of further blood cultures.

Soft Tissue and Musculoskeletal Infections

Serious soft tissue infections caused by *B. cereus* are rare. Only 15 cases have been reported in the English literature in which *B. cereus* was isolated in pure culture and implicated as the causative agent.[53] Most cases occurred in immunocompromised patients with neoplasms without antecedent trauma. Because of the rapid onset of erythema and presence of pustules or vesicles in almost two thirds of the cases, the clinical presentation mimicked that of clostridial myonecrosis. However, most cases secondary to *B. cereus* involved superficial tissues, in contrast to those due to clostridia, wherein necrosis of muscle or fascia is common.[53]

Necrotizing fasciitis caused by *Bacillus* spp. has been reported in a patient with sickle cell disease and in a leukemic patient.[20, 21] In both cases, culture from deep tissue specimens grew pure *Bacillus* colonies. Antibiotic therapy in these cases was not sufficient, and multiple surgical débridement procedures were required; in the patient with leukemia, amputation was necessary.[21] Depending on the species isolated, antibiotic therapy should be tailored accordingly.

Both the acute and chronic forms of osteomyelitis are infrequent presentations of *Bacillus* spp. infection.[20] Acute vertebral osteomyelitis caused by *B. cereus* has been reported in drug abusers; the pathogen is probably introduced via blood stream by injection of contaminated heroin or paraphernalia, or both.[21] Chronic osteomyelitis has usually been related to accidental trauma. Cases of vertebral osteomyelitis caused by *B. cereus* infection have responded well to prolonged intravenous antibiotic therapy. Duration of antibiotic treatment in patients with chronic osteomyelitis due to *B. cereus* can be prolonged.[54] Chronic osteomyelitis, however, is usually difficult to eradicate, requires multiple surgical débridement procedures, and is associated with substantial morbidity.[20]

Clinically significant infections by *Bacillus* spp. in patients who are involved in motor vehicle accidents and sustain injury related to road contact have been reported.[55] *B. cereus* is the major isolate from cultures of wound and bone biopsy specimens from infected sites. Patients require extensive surgical débridement and amputation in some cases, in addition to intravenous vancomycin with or without gentamicin. *B. cereus* has also been recovered from three patients with severe soft tissue infections after close-range gunshot wounds inflicted through clothing.[56] The organism was isolated from traumatic wounds in all three patients, and in one patient, *B. cereus* was also recovered from the blood. Cefuroxime and metronidazole used in the treatment of these patients were not effective. The authors emphasized that antimicrobial coverage should include agents with efficacy against *B. cereus* in the setting of traumatic wounds after gunshot injuries.

Meningitis and Brain Abscess

In an earlier review of *Bacillus* infections that included dissemination, meningitis was not an uncommon presentation.[29] A variety of *Bacillus* spp. were isolated from cerebrospinal fluid in these patients, including *B. subtilis, B. megaterium, B. circulans,* and *B. sphaericus.* Most of the patients developed meningitis after spinal anesthesia. The remaining cases were secondary to other infections such as otitis and mastoiditis, urinary tract infection, and infected subdural hematoma. Ventricular shunts may also become infected by *Bacillus* organisms.[21] Meningitis caused by *Bacillus* spp. has been associated with a high mortality.[29, 57]

Meningitis caused by *B. cereus* is rare and usually occurs in patients with significant predisposing factors. Brain abscess with *B. cereus* has been reported as a postmortem finding in only two patients.[11] The development of multiple brain abscesses and meningitis caused by *B. cereus* shortly after initiation of chemotherapy in a 3-year-old boy with acute lymphocytic leukemia has been reported.[58] Although surgical excision of involved tissue was precluded by the number and location of the multiple abscesses, identification of the organism in brain and abscess material obtained at biopsy was crucial in the management of the patient. The patient responded to intravenous vancomycin and gentamicin given for 5 weeks and, thereafter, vancomycin and rifampin given for an additional 3 weeks. There was complete resolution of the abscesses as visualized on computed tomography scan.[58]

Two rapidly fatal cases of septicemia syndrome in leukemia complicated by meningoencephalitis have been reported.[59, 60] Autopsy revealed necrotizing meningoencephalitis with subarachnoid hemorrhage and necrosis of the liver.

Therapy is with intravenous clindamycin, vancomycin, or penicillin, depending on the *Bacillus* species isolated. Removal of any foreign body, such as a ventricular shunt, is necessary to eradicate the infection.[21]

Miscellaneous Syndromes

Allergic and respiratory symptoms in workers engaged in the manufacture of laundry detergents containing proteolytic enzymes of *B. subtilis* have been reported.[61]

It is not common for *Bacillus* spp. to occur in a mixed infection such as in surgical wounds, infected breast prosthesis, or a necrotic tumor. Most patients with such infections are febrile, and the surgical wound or tumor drainage may be purulent, bloody, or serosanguineous.[11] *Bacillus* organisms are common laboratory contaminants owing to their hardy growth characteristics and have caused various types of pseudoinfections.[62] Sources of *Bacillus* pseudobacteremias have included contaminated broth culture, syringes, alcohol swab used for disinfection of the rubber stoppers of the blood culture bottle, needle in a radiometric blood culture analyzer, and gloves. A pseudoinfection of the lung has resulted from contamination of the automatic suction valve of a fiberoptic bronchoscope. Pseudomeningitis due to *Bacillus* organisms has been traced to intrinsic contamination of commercial culture media.[62]

TREATMENT

Selection of antibiotics for the treatment of serious *Bacillus* infections is based on susceptibility in vitro.[63] Antibiotic susceptibility testing of *Bacillus* spp. indicates that β-lactam antibiotics are rarely effective in vitro against *B. cereus,* the most common isolate in clinically significant infections.[64] Although there is marked variability among species, non–*B. cereus* strains are susceptible to penicillins, semisynthetic penicillins, and cephalosporins. Imipenem, ciprofloxacin, and gentamicin are highly active.[35] Many strains are also susceptible to tetracycline, chloramphenicol, clindamycin, and erythromycin. The minimum bactericidal concentration (MBC) of the latter group of drugs may be greater than the minimum inhibitory concentration, although achievable levels in serum frequently exceed the MBC for these agents.[38] Vancomycin has been found to be bactericidal at or near the same concentration at which it is bacteriostatic.

In vitro susceptibility testing of ocular *B. cereus* isolates has demonstrated that clindamycin, gentamicin, and vancomycin all are relatively effective against *B. cereus* as single agents.[65] A clindamycin-gentamicin combination demonstrated a higher rate of bactericidal synergy than that noted for a vancomycin-gentamicin combination.

In vitro activities against *B. cereus* of newer glycopeptides including ramoplanin and teicoplanin have been determined.[66] Ramoplanin was the most active, with inhibition of all isolates at concentrations of 0.5 μg/ml or less, followed by teicoplanin, which was moderately more active than vancomycin.

Trovafloxacin was more active against *B. cereus* isolates from cancer patients than were ciprofloxacin, levofloxacin, ofloxacin, sparfloxacin, and norfloxacin. The majority of isolates were inhibited by trovafloxacin at 0.12 μg/ml.[67]

As indicated by in vitro data, the drug of choice for serious infections caused by *Bacillus* spp. is vancomycin, because *B. cereus* is the most common isolate.[63] Clinically, both vancomycin and clindamycin have yielded successful outcomes. Whether monotherapy is adequate or combination therapy is better has not been addressed in in vitro models or clinical trials. In patients with *Bacillus* endocarditis, particularly of the mitral or aortic valves, gentamicin, 3 to 5 mg/kg/day, may be indicated in combination with vancomycin 1 g every 12 hours. In bacteremia in parenteral drug abusers, either vancomycin or clindamycin can be used; both have been proved efficacious with successful outcomes. Dosage of clindamycin may vary from 600 to

900 mg, given every 6 to 8 hours, depending on the severity of the illness.

Duration of treatment can vary from 7 to 14 days, depending on the severity of the illness and underlying host defense impairment. Catheter removal is often required for cure of bacteremia in patients with implanted intravascular catheters. Severe wound infection that developed in a patient with bacteremia caused by *B. cereus* was treated successfully with ciprofloxacin, 750 mg every 12 hours for almost 3 months.[68]

Clindamycin or vancomycin may be used for osteomyelitis, and the duration of treatment may be longer, depending on the adequacy of surgical débridement. Treatment for as long as 6 months may be required, depending on healing of wounds and fractures. Either oral clindamycin or ciprofloxacin is an appropriate choice for the extended phase of therapy in bone or soft tissue infections.

In immunocompromised patients in whom gram-positive aerobic rods are isolated from blood cultures, initial coverage with broad-spectrum cephalosporins should be avoided. Vancomycin or clindamycin would be the most appropriate agent for initial antibiotic coverage in patients with suspected *Bacillus* infections who are seriously ill.

REFERENCES

1. Turnbull PCB, Kramer J, Melling J. *Bacillus.* In: Parker MT, Duerden BI. Topley and Wilson's Principles of Bacteriology, Virology and Immunity. London: Edward Arnold; 1990;188–210.
2. Bryce EA, Smith JA, Tweeddale M, et al. Dissemination of *Bacillus cereus* in an intensive care unit. Infect Control Hosp Epidemiol. 1994;14:459–462.
3. Barrie D. Hoffman PN, Wilson JA, Kramer JM. Contamination of hospital linen by *Bacillus cereus.* Epidemiol Infect. 1994;113:297–306.
4. Drobniewski FA. *Bacillus cereus* and related species. Clin Microb Rev. 1993;6:324–338.
5. Lund BM. Foodborne disease due to *Bacillus* and *Clostridium* species. Lancet. 1990;336:982–986.
6. Nelms PK, Larson O, Barnes-Josiah D. Time to *B. cereus* about hot chocolate. Public Health Rep. 1997;112:240–244.
7. Jackson SG. Rapid screening test for enterotoxin-producing *Bacillus cereus.* J Clin Microbiol. 1993;31:972–974.
8. Ahmed R, Sanar-Mistry P, Jackson S, et al. *Bacillus cereus* phage typing as an epidemiological tool in outbreaks of food poisoning. J Clin Microbiol. 1995;33:636–640.
9. Tan A, Heaton S, Farr L, Bates J. The use of *Bacillus* diarrheal enterotoxin (BDE) detection using an ELISA technique in the confirmation of the aetiology of *Bacillus*-mediated diarrhea. J Appl Microbiol. 1997;82:677–682.
10. Curtis JR, Wing AJ, Coleman JC. *Bacillus cereus* bacteraemia—a complication of intermittent hemodialysis. Lancet. 1967;1:136–138.
11. Ihde DC, Armstrong D. Clinical spectrum of infection due to *Bacillus* species. Am J Med. 1973;55:839–845.
12. Reboli AC, Bryan CS, Farrar WE. Bacteremia and infection of a hip prosthesis caused by *Bacillus alvei.* J Clin Microbiol. 1989;27:1395–1396.
13. Tuazon CU, Hill R, Sheagren JN. Microbiologic study of street heroin and injection paraphernalia. J Infect Dis. 1974;129:327–329.
14. Shamsuddin D, Tuazon CU, Levy C, et al. *Bacillus cereus* panophthalmitis: Source of the organism. J Infect Dis. 1982;4:97–103.
15. Jackson NO, Schmieger H, Kayiko M, et al. *Bacillus cereus* may produce two or more diarrheal enterotoxins. FEMS Microbiol Lett. 1997;149:245–248.
16. Granum PE. *Bacillus cereus* and its toxins. Soc Appl Bacteriol Symp Ser. 1994;23:61S–66S.
17. Beecher DJ, Schoeni JL, Wong AC. Enterotoxic activity of hemolysin BL from *Bacillus cereus.* Infect Immun. 1995;63:4423–4428.
18. Beecher DJ, Wong AC. Tripartite hemolysin BL from *Bacillus cereus.* Hemolytic analysis of component interactions and a model for its characteristic paradoxical zone phenomenon. J Biol Chem. 1997;272(1):233–239.
19. Beecher DJ, Pulido JS, Barney NP, Wong AC. Extracellular virulence factors in *Bacillus cereus* endophthalmitis: Methods and implication of involvement of hemolysin BL. Infect Immun. 1995;63:632–639.
20. Sliman R, Rehm S, Shlaes DM. Serious infections caused by *Bacillus* species. Medicine. 1987;66:218–223.
21. Tuazon CU, Murray HW, Levy C, et al. Serious infections from *Bacillus* sp. JAMA. 1979;241:1137–1140.
22. Weber DJ, Rutala WA. *Bacillus* species. Infect Control Hosp Epidemiol. 1988;9:368–374.
23. Terranova W, Blake PA. *Bacillus cereus* food poisoning. N Engl J Med. 1978;298:143–144.
24. Agata N, Ohta M, Mori M. Production of an emetic toxin, cereulide, is associated with a specific class of *Bacillus cereus.* Curr Microbiol. 1996;33:67–69.
25. Gianella RA, Brasile L. A hospital food-borne outbreak of diarrhea caused by *Bacillus cereus:* Clinical, epidemiologic and microbiologic studies. J Infect Dis. 1979;139:366–370.
26. Jackson SG, Goodbrand RB, Ahmed R, Kasatiya S. *Bacillus cereus* and *Bacillus thuringiensis* isolated in a gastroenteritis outbreak investigation. Lett Appl Microbiol. 1995;21:103–105.
27. Mahler H, Pasi A, Kramer JM, et al. Fulminant liver failure in association with the emetic toxin of *Bacillus cereus.* N Engl J Med. 1997;336:1142.
28. Gilbert RJ, Stringer MF, Peace TC. The survival and growth of *Bacillus cereus* in boiled and fried rice in relation to outbreaks of food poisoning. J Hyg (Camb). 1974;73:433–444.
29. Farrar WE. Serious infections due to "non-pathogenic" organisms of the genus *Bacillus:* Review of their status as pathogens. Am J Med. 1963;34:134–141.
30. Davey RT Jr, Tauber WB. Posttraumatic endophthalmitis: The emerging role of *Bacillus cereus* infection. Rev Infect Dis. 1987;9:110–123.
31. O'Day DM, Smith RS, Gregg CR, et al. The problem of *Bacillus* species infection with special emphasis on the virulence of *Bacillus cereus.* Ophthalmology. 1981;88:833–838.
32. Young EJ, Wallace RJ, Ericsson CD, et al. Panophthalmitis due to *Bacillus cereus.* Arch Intern Med. 1980;140:559–560.
33. Bouza E, Grant S, Jordan MC, et al. *Bacillus cereus* endogenous panophthalmitis. Arch Ophthalmol. 1979;97:498–499.
34. Kerkenezov N. Panophthalmitis after a blood transfusion. Br J Ophthalmol. 1953;37:632–636.
35. Foster RE, Martinez JA, Murray TG, et al. Useful visual outcomes after treatment of *Bacillus cereus* endophthalmitis. Ophthalmology. 1996;103:390–397.
36. Barletta JP, Small KW. Successful visual recovery in delayed onset *Bacillus cereus* endophthalmitis. Ophthalmic Surg Lasers. 1996;27:70–72.
37. Hemady R, Zaltas M, Paton B, et al. *Bacillus*-induced endophthalmitis: New series of 10 cases and review of the literature. Br J Ophthalmol. 1990;74:26–29.
38. Weber DJ, Saviteer SM, Rutala WA, et al. In vitro susceptibility of *Bacillus* spp. to selected antimicrobial agents. Antimicrob Agents Chemother. 1988;32:642–645.
39. Alfaro DV, Kim S, Bia F, et al. Experimental *Bacillus cereus* post-traumatic endophthalmitis and treatment with ciprofloxacin. Br J Ophthalmol. 1996;80:755–758.
40. Alfaro DV, Hudson SJ, Offele JJ, et al. Experimental posttraumatic *Bacillus cereus* endophthalmitis in a swine model. Efficacy of intravitreal ciprofloxacin, vancomycin and imipenem. Retina. 1996;16:317–323.
41. Jevon GP, Dunne WM, Hicks MJ, et al. *Bacillus cereus* pneumonia in premature neonates: A report of two cases. Pediatr Infect Dis J. 1993;12:251–253.
42. Bekemeyer WB, Zimmerman GA. Life threatening complications associated with *Bacillus cereus* pneumonia. Am Rev Respir Dis. 1985;131:466–469.
43. Miller JM, Hair JG, Hebert M, et al. Fulminating bacteremia and pneumonia due to *Bacillus cereus.* J. Clin Microbiol. 1997;35:504–507.
44. Coudron PE, Payne JM, Markowitz SM. Pneumonia and empyema infection associated with a *Bacillus* species that resembles *B. alvei.* J Clin Microbiol. 1991;29:1777–1779.
45. Leff A, Jacobs R, Gooding V, et al. *Bacillus cereus* pneumonia. Survival in a patient with cavitary disease treated with gentamicin. Am Rev Respir Dis. 1977;115:151–154.
46. Isaacson P, Jacobs PH, Mackenzie AMR, et al. Pseudotumor of the lung caused by infection with *Bacillus sphaericus.* J Clin Pathol. 1976;29:806–811.
47. Steen MK, Bruno-Murtha LA, Chaux G, et al. *Bacillus cereus* endocarditis: Report of a case and review. Clin Infect Dis. 1992;14:945–946.
48. Reller LB. Endocarditis caused by *Bacillus subtilis.* Am J Clin Pathol. 1973;60:714–718.
49. Rodgers GM, Barrera E Jr, Martin RR. *Bacillus cereus* bacteremia and hemolytic anemia in a patient with hemoglobin SC disease. Arch Intern Med. 1980;140:1103–1104.
50. Blue SR, Singh VR, Saubolle MA. *Bacillus licheniformis* bacteremia: Five cases associated with indwelling central venous catheters. Clin Infect Dis. 1995;20:629–633.
51. Richard V, Van der Auwera P, Smoeck R, et al. Nosocomial bacteremia caused by *Bacillus* species. Eur J Clin Microbiol Infect Dis. 1988;7:783–785.
52. Ball SC, Sepkowitz K. Infection due to *Bacillus cereus* in an injection drug user with AIDS: Bacteremia without morbidity. Clin Infect Dis. 1994;19:216–217.
53. Meredith FT, Fowler VG, Gautier M, et al. *Bacillus cereus* necrotizing cellulitis mimicking clostridial myonecrosis: Case report and review of the literature. Scand Infect Dis. 1997;29:528–529.
54. Schricker ME, Thompson GH, Schreiker JR. Osteomyelities due to *Bacillus cereus* in an adolescent: Case report and review. Clin Infect Dis. 1994;18:863–867.
55. Wong MT, Dolan MJ. Significant infections due to *Bacillus* species following abrasions associated with motor vehicle–related trauma. Clin Infect Dis. 1992;15:855–857.
56. Krause A, Freeman R, Sisson PR, Murphy OM. Infection with *Bacillus cereus* after close-range gunshot injuries. J Trauma. 1996;41:546–548.
57. Allen BT, Wilkinson HA. A case of meningitis and generalized Shwartzman reaction caused by *Bacillus sphaericus.* Johns Hopkins Med J. 1969;125:8–13.
58. Jenson HB, Levy SR, Duncan C, et al. Treatment of multiple brain abscesses caused by *Bacillus cereus.* Pediatr Infect Dis. 1989;8:795–798.
59. Marley EF, Saini NK, Venkatraman C, Orenstein JM. Fatal *Bacillus cereus* meningoencephalitis in an adult with acute myelogenous leukemia. South Med J. 1995;88:969–972.
60. Akiyama N, Mitani K, Tanaka Y, et al. Fulminant septicemic syndrome of *Bacillus cereus* in a leukemic patient. Intern Med. 1997;36:221–226.

61. Flindt MLH. Pulmonary disease due to inhalation of derivatives of *Bacillus subtilis* containing proteolytic enzyme. Lancet. 1969;1:1177.
62. Lettau LA, Benjamin D, Cantrell HF, et al. *Bacillus* species pseudomeningitis. Infect Control Hosp Epidemiol. 1988;9:394–397.
63. Tuazon CU. *Bacillus* (non-*anthracis*) species. In: Merigan T, Barriere S, Yu V, eds. Antimicrobial Chemotherapy and Vaccines. Baltimore: Williams & Wilkins; 1999;41–44.
64. Coonrod JD, Leadley PJ, Eickhoff TC. Antibiotic susceptibility of *Bacillus* species. J Infect Dis. 1971;123:102–105.
65. Gigantelli JW, Torres Gomez J, Osato MS. In vitro susceptibilities of ocular *Bacillus cereus* isolates to clindamycin, gentamicin and vancomycin alone or in combination. Antimicrob Agents Chemother. 1991;35:201–202.
66. Rolston KV, Dholakia N, Ho DH, et al. In vitro activity of ramoplanin (a novel lipoglycopeptide), vancomycin, and teicoplanin against gram-positive clinical isolates from cancer patients. J Antimicrob Chemother. 1996;38:265–269.
67. Rolston KV, Ho DH, LeBlanc B, et al. In vitro activity of trovafloxacin against clinical bacterial isolates from patients with cancer. J Antimicrob Chemother. 1997;39(suppl B):15–22.
68. Kemmerly SA, Pankey GA. Oral ciprofloxacin therapy for *Bacillus cereus* wound infection and bacteremia. Clin Infect Dis. 1993;16:139.

Chapter 198

Erysipelothrix rhusiopathiae

ANNETTE C. REBOLI
W. EDMUND FARRAR

Erysipelothrix rhusiopathiae, formerly known as *Erysipelothrix insidiosa,* is a thin, pleomorphic, nonsporulating, gram-positive rod. First isolated from mice by Robert Koch in 1878 and from swine by Louis Pasteur in 1882, it was established as the etiologic agent of swine erysipelas in 1886 by Löffler and as a human pathogen in 1909 when Rosenbach isolated it from a patient with localized cutaneous lesions.[1, 2] Rosenbach coined the term *erysipeloid* to avoid confusion with *erysipelas,* a superficial cellulitis with prominent lymphatic involvement that is almost always caused by group A streptococci.[2]

MICROBIOLOGY

E. rhusiopathiae is a straight or slightly curved aerobic or facultatively anaerobic bacillary organism; it is 0.2 to 0.4 μm in diameter and 0.8 to 2.5 μm in length. It is gram-positive but may appear gram-negative because it decolorizes readily. Organisms may be arranged singly, in short chains, in pairs in a V configuration, or grouped randomly. Nonbranching filaments that can be longer than 60 μm are sometimes seen. Colonial and microscopic appearance varies with the medium, pH, and temperature of incubation.[1] After growing for 24 hours at 37°C, colonies are small and transparent with a smooth, glistening surface. On blood agar it may be α-hemolytic. *E. rhusiopathiae* is catalase-, oxidase-, indole-, Voges-Proskauer–, and methyl red–negative.[3] Acid without gas is produced from the fermentation of glucose, fructose, lactose, and galactose. Most strains produce hydrogen sulfide, a diagnostically important reaction. On triple sugar iron (TSI) agar slants, hydrogen sulfide causes a blackened butt. *E. rhusiopathiae* is sometimes confused with other gram-positive bacilli, in particular, *Listeria monocytogenes, Actinomyces (Corynebacterium) pyogenes,* and *Arcanobacterium (Corynebacterium) haemolyticum,* but these three species are β-hemolytic on blood agar and do not produce hydrogen sulfide in the butt on TSI agar slants. Furthermore, *L. monocytogenes* is catalase-positive and motile.[4]

EPIDEMIOLOGY

E. rhusiopathiae is found worldwide. It has been reported as a commensal or a pathogen in a wide variety of vertebrate and invertebrate species, but the major reservoir is believed to be domestic swine.[3, 5] It does not appear to cause disease in fish but can persist for long periods of time in the mucoid exterior slime of these animals.[6] It may live long enough in soil to cause infection weeks or months after initial contamination. The greatest commercial impact of *E. rhusiopathiae* infection is due to disease in swine, but infection of turkeys, ducks, and sheep is also important. The organism is communicable from animals to humans by direct cutaneous contact. There have been two reported cases of bacteremia, one with endocarditis, which occurred after ingestion of undercooked pork.[1] The risk of human infection with *Erysipelothrix* is closely related to the opportunity for exposure to the organism; accordingly, most human cases are related to occupational exposure. Although infection with *Erysipelothrix* has been associated with many occupations, persons at greatest risk include fishermen, fish handlers, butchers, slaughterhouse workers, veterinarians, and homemakers.[5, 7, 8] Infection is especially common among persons who handle fish. Of the 329 cases of erysipeloid described by Gilchrist, 323 were associated with injuries from crabs.[9] "Whale finger" is erysipeloid seen in persons who sustain cuts to the fingers and hands while engaged in whaling.[10] Human-to-human transmission of infection has not been reported.

PATHOGENESIS

Abrasions or puncture wounds of the skin probably serve as the portal of entry of *Erysipelothrix* organisms in most cases of infection in humans and in animals. *E. rhusiopathiae* produces a neuraminidase and a hyaluronidase. The activity of these enzymes may correlate with virulence.[11] The neuraminidase may have a role in the pathogenesis of the arteritis and thrombocytopenia seen in an experimental rat model of *Erysipelothrix* infection.[12] The rhomboidal skin lesions seen in swine are the result of thrombotic vasculitis of end-arterioles.[1]

CLINICAL MANIFESTATIONS

Three well-defined clinical categories of human disease have been described: (1) erysipeloid, a localized skin lesion,[13] (2) a diffuse cutaneous eruption with systemic symptoms, and (3) bacteremia, which is often associated with endocarditis.[1]

The localized cutaneous form—the "erysipeloid" of Rosenbach—is a subacute cellulitis and is the most common type of *Erysipelothrix* infection seen in humans. Because the organism is acquired through contact with infected animals or fish, or with products made from them, gaining entrance via cuts or abrasions on the skin, most lesions are on the fingers. Following an incubation period of 2 to 7 days, pain (which is often severe and described as burning, itching, or throbbing) and swelling of the involved digit or part of the hand develop. The lesion is well defined, slightly raised, and violaceous[14] (Fig. 198–1). As it spreads peripherally, the central area fades. Vesiculation may occur. Regional lymphadenopathy and lymphangitis occur in approximately a third of cases.[15] There may be inflammation of an adjacent joint. Systemic symptoms are uncommon. Approximately 10% of the patients have low-grade fever and arthralgias.[15] Clinically, erysipeloid resembles staphylococcal or streptococcal cellulitis, but a history of occupational exposure, lesions on the hands, subacute course, absence of suppuration, lack of pitting edema, violaceous color, and the disproportionate pain should suggest the possibility of erysipeloid.[16] Because organisms are located only in deeper parts of the skin in erysipeloid, aspirates or biopsy specimens should incorporate the entire thickness of the dermis, as well as tissue from the periphery of the lesion, to maximize the chance of recovery of the organism. Erysipeloid usually resolves without treatment within 3 or 4 weeks.

The diffuse cutaneous form, which is rare, occurs when the violaceous cutaneous lesion progresses proximally from the site of

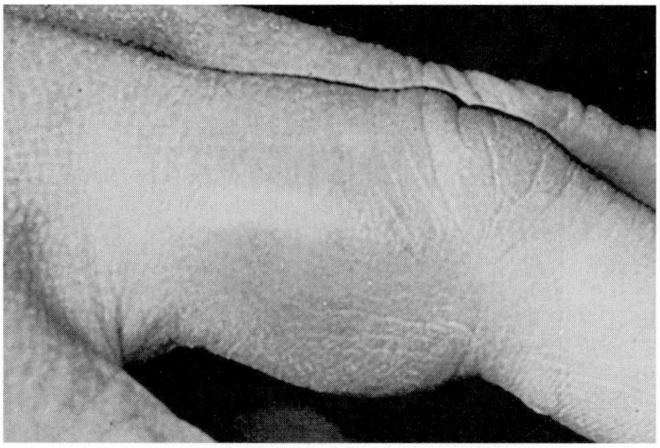

FIGURE 198–1. Lesion of erysipeloid. (From Lambert HP, Farrar WE. Cutaneous manifestations of infection. II: Bacterial infections. In: Lambert HP, Farrar WE, eds. Infectious Diseases Illustrated. London: Gower Medical Publishing; 1982:Section 5.10. By permission of Mosby International Ltd.)

inoculation or appears at remote areas.[1, 14] Lesions may appear urticarial, with the rhomboid pattern characteristic of swine erysipelas.[8] Fever and arthralgias are common. Blood cultures are negative. The course is more protracted than in the localized form, and recurrence is common.

Systemic infection with *E. rhusiopathiae* is unusual. Over 60 cases of bacteremia have been reported, most complicated by endocarditis.[17, 18] All reported cases of endocarditis except two have involved native valves.[19, 20] There was a history of an antecedent or concurrent skin lesion of erysipeloid in 36% of the patients.[18] When clinical features of *E. rhusiopathiae* endocarditis were compared with those of endocarditis caused by other bacteria, there was a higher male-to-female ratio (which probably reflects occupational exposure), a greater propensity for involvement of the aortic valve, and a much higher mortality rate among patients with *E. rhusiopathiae* endocarditis (38% versus 20% in endocarditis due to other organisms).[16] In approximately 60% of patients, *E. rhusiopathiae* endocarditis developed in previously normal heart valves. In patients with bacteremia or endocarditis, or both, routine blood culture techniques are adequate for recovery of the organism.[4] Complications of *Erysipelothrix* endocarditis include congestive heart failure, myocardial abscess, aortic valve perforation, meningitis, and glomerulonephritis. Over one third of the patients required valve replacement.[18]

Bacteremia without endocarditis has been reported with increasing frequency. It has occurred primarily in immunocompromised hosts.[21] Brain abscess, osteomyelitis, and chronic arthritis have also been reported.[1, 14]

Definitive diagnosis of infection with *Erysipelothrix* requires isolation of the organism from a biopsy specimen or blood. There are no reliable serologic tests for the diagnosis of infection in humans.

TREATMENT AND PREVENTION

Susceptibility data for *E. rhusiopathiae* are limited. Most strains are highly susceptible to penicillins, cephalosporins, clindamycin, imipenem, and ciprofloxacin.[22, 23] Penicillin and imipenem are the most active agents in vitro.[22] Susceptibility to chloramphenicol, erythromycin, and tetracycline is variable. Most strains are resistant to vancomycin, sulfonamides, trimethoprim-sulfamethoxazole, novobiocin, teicoplanin, and aminoglycosides. Resistance to vancomycin is important because this agent is often used empirically to treat bacteremia due to gram-positive organisms. Because minimum inhibitory concentrations (MICs) of penicillin range from 0.0025 to 0.06 μg/ml, and minimum bactericidal concentrations (MBCs) have been reported in the range of 0.0025 to 0.75 μg/ml, penicillin G (12 million to 20 million units/day) is the drug of choice for serious infections caused by *E. rhusiopathiae*. Ciprofloxacin has MIC and MBC values similar to those obtained with β-lactam antibiotics.[23] Use of fluoroquinolones may be considered in *Erysipelothrix* infections when β-lactams are contraindicated. In cases of endocarditis, the duration of intravenous antibiotic therapy should be 4 to 6 weeks, although shorter courses (2 weeks of intravenous therapy followed by 2 to 4 weeks of oral therapy) have been successful.[8] Although erysipeloid usually resolves spontaneously, healing is hastened by antibiotic therapy. Oral therapy with amoxicillin or a quinolone can be used.

Prevention of infection for persons in high-risk occupations depends on the use of protective attire such as gloves. Unprotected direct contact with animal body tissues and secretions should be avoided. Live attenuated vaccines are available for veterinary use.[24] Use of vaccination along with other measures such as improved waste disposal has helped to control swine erysipelas.

REFERENCES

1. Grieco M, Sheldon C. *Erysipelothrix rhusiopathiae*. Ann N Y Acad Sci. 1970;174:523–532.
2. Rosenbach FJ. Experimentelle, morphologische und klinische Studie über die krankheitserregenden Mikroorganismen des Schweinerotlauf, des Erysipeloids und der Mäsesepsis. Z Hyg Infektionskr. 1909;63:343–369.
3. Sneath PHA, Abbott JD, Cunliffe AC. The bacteriology of erysipeloid. Br Med J. 1951;2:1063–1066.
4. Reboli AC, Farrar WE. The genus *Erysipelothrix*. In: Balows A, Truper HG, Dworkin M, et al, eds. The Prokaryotes. A Handbook on the Biology of Bacteria: Ecophysiology, Isolation, Identification, Applications. New York: Springer-Verlag; 1992:1629–1642.
5. Woodbine M. *Erysipelothrix rhusiopathiae*. Bacteriol Rev. 1950;14:161–178.
6. Wood RL. *Erysipelothrix* infection. In: Hubbert WT, McCollough WF, Schnurrenburger PR, eds. Diseases Transmitted from Animals to Man. Springfield, Ill: Charles C Thomas; 1975:271–281.
7. Klauder JV. Erysipeloid as an occupational disease. JAMA 1938;111:1345–1348.
8. Reboli AC, Farrar WE. *Erysipelothrix rhusiopathiae:* An occupational pathogen. Clin Microbiol Rev. 1989;2:354–359.
9. Gilchrist TC. Erysipeloid, with a record of 329 cases, of which 323 were caused by crab bites, or lesions produced by crabs. J Cutaneous Dis. 1904;22:507–519.
10. Hillenbrand FKM. Whale finger and seal finger: Their relation to erysipeloid. Lancet. 1953:1:680–681.
11. Krasemann C, Muller HE. The virulence of *Erysipelothrix rhusiopathiae* strains and their neuraminidase production. Zentrabl Bakteriol Mikrobiol Hyg (A). 1975;231:206–213.
12. Nakato H, Shinomiya K, Mikawa H. Possible role of neuraminidase in the pathogenesis of arteritis and thrombocytopenia induced in rats by *Erysipelothrix rhusiopathiae*. Pathol Res Pract. 1986;181:311–319.
13. Klauder JV. *Erysipelothrix rhusiopathiae* infection in swine and in human beings. A comparative study of cutaneous lesions. Arch Dermatol Syph. 1944;50:151–159.
14. Erlich JC. *Erysipelothrix rhusiopathiae* infection in man. Arch Intern Med. 1946;78:565–577.
15. Nelson E. Five hundred cases of erysipeloid. Rocky Mtn Med J. 1955;52:40–42.
16. Robson JM, McDougall R, van der Valk S, et al. *Erysipelothrix rhusiopathiae:* An uncommon but ever present zoonosis. Pathology. 1998;30:391–394.
17. Hill DC, Ghassemian JN. *Erysipelothrix rhusiopathiae* endocarditis. Clinical features of an occupational disease. South Med J. 1997;90:1147–1148.
18. Gorby GL, Peacock JE. *Erysipelothrix rhusiopathiae* endocarditis: Microbiologic, epidemiologic and clinical features of an occupational disease. Rev Infect Dis. 1988;10:317–325.
19. Gransden WR, Eykyn SJ. *Erysipelothrix rhusiopathiae* endocarditis. Rev Infect Dis. 1988;10:1228.
20. Hayek LJ. *Erysipelothrix* endocarditis affecting a porcine heart valve. J Infect. 1993;27:203–204.
21. Ognibene FP, Cunnion RE, Gill V, et al. *Erysipelothrix rhusiopathiae* bacteremia presenting as septic shock. Am J Med. 1985;78:861–864.
22. Takahashi T, Sawada T, Ohmae K, et al. Antibiotic resistance of *Erysipelothrix rhusiopathiae* isolated from pigs with chronic swine erysipelas. Antimicrob Agents Chemother. 1984;25:385–386.
23. Venditti M, Gelfusa V, Tarasi A, et al. Antimicrobial susceptibilities of *Erysipelothrix rhusiopathiae*. Antimicrob Agents Chemother. 1990;34:2038–2040.
24. Takahashi T, Tahagi M, Sawada T. Cross protection in mice and swine immunized with live erysipelas vaccine to challenge exposure with strains of *Erysipelothrix rhusiopathiae* of various serotypes. Am J Vet Res. 1984;45:2115–2118.

GRAM-NEGATIVE COCCI

Chapter 199

Neisseria meningitidis

MICHAEL A. APICELLA

Neisseria meningitidis is still a cause of endemic and epidemic disease in developed[1–3] and developing nations[4–6] despite substantial advances in understanding the pathogenesis,[7] in molecular approaches to epidemiology and diagnosis,[8–11] and in the ability to eradicate the carrier state[12, 13] and to manage systemic infections.[14, 15] Few infections can cause the civil, medical, and social stress that occurs when serious meningococcal disease enters a community. The rapid onset of disease, the fulminant course of some of the infected, and the mortality and morbidity are clearly reasonable causes for the profound dread of this infection. In addition, the problems of rumor and misinformation frequently add substantially to the woes of medical personnel.

Epidemic cerebrospinal fever (meningococcal meningitis) was first described in Geneva by Vieusseaux in 1805.[16] Subsequent reports throughout the 19th century confirmed its episodic, epidemic nature with a propensity for afflicting young children and military recruits assembled in stationary barracks situations.[17] In 1887, Weichselbaum isolated the meningococcus from cerebrospinal fluid (CSF), and the etiologic relationship between this organism and epidemic meningitis was firmly established.[18] Kiefer in 1896[19] and Albrecht and Ghon in 1901[20] found that healthy persons could become carriers of the meningococcus. Serotypes of the meningococcus were first recognized by Dopter in 1909.[21] This finding laid the basis for serum therapy in the treatment of meningococcal infection by Flexner in 1913.[22] Glover was the first to note that carrier rates in military recruit camps rose with periods of crowding, and he believed that they were associated with an increased incidence of cases.[23] In 1928 to 1930[24, 25] and in 1941[26] significant national and worldwide epidemics occurred. In 1937, sulfonamide therapy radically altered the outcome of meningococcal infection and replaced serum in its treatment.[27] Prophylaxis with sulfonamides eradicated the carrier state[28] and provided a simple and safe method for the prevention of epidemics, particularly in the crowded environments of military barracks. With the advent of antibiotic agents, treatment of meningococcal infection became more effective, and mortality declined. Increasing sulfonamide resistance among meningococci was recognized by Schoenback and Phair[29] in 1941 to 1943 but did not become a clinically significant problem until meningococcal epidemics in 1963 in two military bases in California.[30, 31] With the subsequent worldwide emergence of resistant strains and the absence of effective chemoprophylaxis, renewed interest in immunoprevention led to the development of safe and effective vaccines against serogroup A and C meningococcal infection.[32, 33]

Many problems still exist in the understanding, prevention, and treatment of meningococcal infection, including the susceptibilities of certain populations to this infection, its sporadic epidemic nature, the mechanisms responsible for carrier eradication by antibiotics, the reasons for the fulminant nature of the infection, the poor immunogenicity of the group C vaccine in children younger than 2 years, and the inability of humans to develop antibody to the group B polysaccharide vaccine. Until these and many other questions are answered, meningococcal infections will continue to be a scourge among human populations.

ETIOLOGIC AGENT AND MORPHOLOGIC, CULTURAL, AND BIOCHEMICAL CHARACTERISTICS

N. meningitidis is a gram-negative diplococcus (0.6 × 0.8 μm). The adjacent sides are flattened to produce the typical biscuit shape. Because the organism tends to readily undergo autolysis, considerable size and shape variation can be seen in older cultures. The organism produces a polysaccharide capsule, which is the basis of the serogroup typing system. These capsules are not readily visible on Gram stain, but capsules of serogroup A and C strains can be made to undergo the Quellung reaction in the presence of the appropriate serogroup antiserum. Because the organism is considered fastidious in its growth conditions, appropriate media and growth conditions are necessary. These problems in reliable growth may relate as much to nutritional factors as to the presence of substances toxic to the meningococcus in the medium. On solid media, the meningococcus grows as a transparent, nonpigmented, nonhemolytic colony approximately 1 to 5 mm in diameter. Colonies are convex and, if large amounts of polysaccharide are present, will appear mucoid rather than smooth. Optimal growth conditions are achieved in a moist environment at 35°C to 37°C under an atmosphere of 5 to 10% carbon dioxide. The organism will grow well on a number of medium bases, including blood agar base, trypticase soy agar, supplemented chocolate agar, and Mueller-Hinton agar. Semidefined media such as Franz medium also provide the necessary nutrients for excellent growth conditions. Confirmation of the presence of this organism in clinical specimens is dependent on a series of carbohydrate fermentations. The meningococcus will metabolize glucose and maltose to acid without gas formation and fails to metabolize sucrose or lactose. In addition, the organism contains cytochrome oxidase in its cell wall. This enzyme will oxidize the dye tetramethylphenylenediamine from colorless to deep pink. This latter test was initially considered specific for *Neisseria,* but subsequent studies have shown that other genera also exhibit high tetramethylphenylenediamine oxidase activities, including *Pseudomonas, Aeromonas,* and *Moraxella.*

The meningococcus has a rapid autolytic rate. Hebeler and Young have demonstrated the presence of an autolysin, an amidase, that acts on the peptidoglycan layer of the gonococcus.[34, 35] Whether the mechanism of autolysis is similar in the meningococcus is uncertain. The process appears to be enzymatic because autolysis can be stopped by the addition of potassium cyanide or formalin or by heating cultures to 65°C for 30 minutes.

The importance of iron in the survival of microbes has stimulated interest in the mechanisms that *Neisseria* organisms use for iron acquisition. It has been shown that iron-loaded animals are more susceptible to fatal meningococcal infection.[36] The meningococcus does not produce a soluble siderophore but possesses a series of membrane proteins that selectively scavenge iron from hemoglobin, transferrin, and lactoferrin.[37, 38]

Antigenic Structure of the Meningococcus

Capsular Polysaccharides

Shortly after identification of the meningococcus as the etiologic agent in epidemic meningitis and after recognition of healthy nasopharyngeal carriers of the organism, investigations into the application of immunologic methods for the detection and differentiation of meningococci were performed. It became apparent that antigenically diverse meningococci existed, and spurred on by the introduction of serum therapy,[22] English workers identified four antigenically distinct types of meningococci.[39] The relationship between this antigenic polysaccharide[40] and the capsule of the meningococcus was established via the Quellung reaction by Clapp and associates in group A strains.[41] Branham and Carlin, using group C strains, were able to demonstrate that these antigens elicited antibodies that conferred specific protection in mice.[42] Meningococci can now be segregated by seroagglutination into at least 13 serogroups: A, B, C, D[43, 44]; X,

Y, Z[45, 46]; E, W-135[46]; H, I, K[47]; and L.[48] Table 199–1 gives the chemical composition of the capsular polysaccharide of the eight most common capsular serogroups causing human disease. Capsular polysaccharides responsible for the serogrouping specificity of groups A, B, C, X, Y, Z, W-135, and L have been purified. These polysaccharides have been isolated from the broth supernatant of overnight cultures, and a number of effective methods using either detergent precipitation or molecular sieve and ion-exchange chromatography have been used in their separation.[49–51] Group C polysaccharides can be biochemically divided into neuraminidase-sensitive and neuraminidase-resistant polysaccharides.[52, 53]

After the introduction of antibiotics, interest in the development of serogroup-specific antigens for use as vaccines diminished greatly, but Watson and colleagues continued their efforts and identified the specific soluble substance from the group C meningococcus and showed its sialic acid nature.[54] A major impetus that renewed interest in meningococcal immunobiology was the emergence of sulfonamide-resistant meningococci as a clinical problem. This development made antibiotic prophylaxis ineffective, and persistent epidemics of serogroup B and C strains on military recruit reservations during the 1960s prompted reinvestigations into the feasibility of using capsular polysaccharide antigens as vaccine materials.

The immunogenicity of group A and C polysaccharide in humans appears to be a function of their molecular size.[55] In addition, studies have indicated that group C vaccine is stable and immunogenic after up to 4 years of storage. Group B polysaccharide has been purified and described immunochemically,[56–58] but it has proved to be a very poor immunogen in humans. At the present time no effective vaccine preparation exists for this serogroup.[59] With the increasing frequency of clinical cases caused by group Y meningococci, interest in capsular polysaccharide strains from this serogroup has renewed,[60] and studies by Griffiss and coworkers have demonstrated the safety and immunogenicity of group Y and W-135 capsular polysaccharides in humans.[61]

Noncapsular Cell Wall Antigens

The meningococcal outer membrane is similar in structure to that of other gram-negative bacteria. It contains a number of somatic antigens that are important in pathogenesis and immunobiology. The principal antigens that have been studied include lipo-oligosaccharide, which is analogous to the lipopolysaccharide of enteric gram-negative bacilli and the outer membrane proteins. Lipo-oligosaccharide is serologically diverse, and Mandrell and Zollinger have demonstrated at least 12 different serotypes.[62] The chemical structure of the oligosaccharide portion of meningococcal lipo-oligosaccharide from all L types has been studied by Jennings and coworkers.[63, 64] Several of these structures are immunochemically similar to human glycosphingolipid antigens. An association between lipo-oligosaccharide immunotype expression and invasive disease has been found.[65] Ninety-seven percent of isolates from epidemics in England expressed the L3, 7, 9 immunotype. The lipo-oligosaccharide immunotypes of carriers were more heterogeneous. Recent studies have suggested that specific lipo-oligosaccharide epitopes of oligosaccharide may be effective vaccines.[66, 67]

Interest in the meningococcal outer membrane proteins was stimulated by the work of Gold and associates, who showed that a noncapsular typing system could be derived by using bactericidal techniques.[68, 69] Using similar methods, Frasch and Chapman succeeded in identifying 11 distinct serotypes of group B meningococci.[70] Frasch and Gotschlich have shown that the antigens responsible for this serotyping system are protein in nature and reside in the outer membrane as part of a lipoprotein–lipo-oligosaccharide complex. Serogroup B and C meningococci can be subdivided into at least 15 protein serotypes based on antigenically different outer membrane proteins.[71] Studies by Broud and coworkers indicate that endemic meningococcal disease appears to be caused by a broad, heterogeneous distribution of serotypes.[72] This observation is in contrast to epidemics that appear to be caused by a single serotype. Recently, the successful application of molecular techniques has resulted in the cloning of a number of important outer membrane protein antigens of the meningococcus, including the H.8 protein[73] and the class 1 outer membrane protein.[74] Frasch and coworkers[75] suggested revising the classification system for the somatic antigen serotypes of the meningococcus. These investigators have proposed a new schema based on the major class 2 (41,000 kD) and class 3 (38,000 kD) outer membrane proteins and the lipo-oligosaccharides. In their example, a meningococcal strain would be identified by serogroup, protein serotype, and lipo-oligosaccharide serotype. Addition of the class 1 protein (46,000 kD) characteristics could be also used to further define the strain.

Using analysis of multilocus enzyme genotypes, Selander and coworkers have developed a system for defining the clonal distribution of bacterial isolates.[76] Applying this method to studies of the meningococcus, Achtman and colleagues have shown that epidemics caused on a worldwide basis by a strain of serogroup A meningococcus are derived from a single clonotype.[77] Caugant and coworkers have studied 650 meningococcal strains of different capsular serogroups and have shown that over periods of many years the genetic structure of *N. meningitidis* is basically clonal as a result of low rates of recombination of chromosomal genes.[78]

Meningococci have been shown to have pili.[79, 80] Meningococcal pili undergo both phase and antigenic variation. These structures can be maintained under special cultural conditions in vitro, and their role as ligands in attachment to human cells has been studied.[81] Piliated meningococci attach to human nasopharyngeal cells in greater numbers than do meningococci devoid of pili. Trypsin or mechanical shearing causes loss of pili and decreased attachment. Meningococci appear to have wide differences in attachment capability that depend on the site of isolation of the epithelial cell.[82] Unlike gonococci, piliated meningococci form colonies that are indistinguishable from their nonpiliated isogenic forms.[83]

Pathogenesis of Infection

The pathogenesis of *N. meningitidis* begins on the nasopharyngeal surface. The nasopharynx is a mixed epithelial surface containing ciliated secretory and nonciliated nonsecretory cells. The airway epithelial surface is covered with a mucus layer that the organism must penetrate. How penetration occurs is not clearly understood. The meningococcus uses adherence factors to adhere to nonciliated cells on the airway surface. Pili enhance attachment but are not necessary for attachment.[82] They act as long-range attachment organelles. It has been shown that purified pili bind to a 55- to 60-kD doublet band on sodium dodecyl sulfate–polyacrylamide gel electrophoresis of separated human epithelial cell extracts, which may be membrane cofactor protein (or CD46). Membrane cofactor protein is a widely distributed human complement regulatory protein.[84] Attachment of the bacteria to epithelial cells is blocked by polyclonal and monoclonal antibodies directed against membrane

TABLE 199–1 Chemical Composition of Meningococcal Capsular Polysaccharides

Capsular Serogroup Antigen	Chemical Composition of Capsular Polymer
A	Partially O-acetylated 2-acetamido-2-deoxy-D-mannose-6-phosphate
B	(2→8)-Linked *N*-acetylneuraminic acid
C_{1+}	O-acetylated (2→9)-linked *N*-acetylneuraminic acid
C_{1-}	(2→9)-Linked *N*-acetylneuraminic acid
X	2-Acetamido-2-deoxy-D-glucose-4-phosphate
Y	Partially O-acetylated alternating sequence of D-glucose and *N*-acetylneuraminic acid
W-135	Alternating sequence of D-galactose and *N*-acetylneuraminic acid
L	*N*-acetylglucosamine phosphate

cofactor protein, which suggests that this complement regulator is a receptor for piliated *Neisseria*. Recombinant membrane cofactor protein produced in *Escherichia coli* inhibits attachment of the bacteria to target cells. As the organism draws closer to the cell, outer membrane surface proteins such as the class V proteins (Opa and Opc) play a role in attachment and may be important in defining the tissue specificity of the organism.[85]

Only unencapsulated meningococci enter epithelial cells, and capsular biosynthesis has been shown to stop as the meningococcus enters the epithelial cell.[86] Only unencapsulated variants are found to enter epithelial cells.

On contact with epithelial and endothelial cells, the meningococcus initiates cytoskeletal changes within these cell types. It appears that either Opc- or OpaA-mediated adhesion can trigger cortical actin rearrangements.[87, 88] These rearrangements are not triggered by nonadherent meningococcal strains, by heat-killed or chloramphenicol-treated organisms, or by *E. coli* recombinants that adhere to cells via OpaA or Opa1 fusion proteins. These observations suggest that additional neisserial components are involved. Recent studies have indicated that neisserial porin, which can translocate into eukaryotic membranes, might be the factor responsible for actin rearrangement. The bacteria are incorporated into vacuoles and are transported to the basolateral surface of the cell. Factors allowing survival of the organism within the epithelial cell are now being elucidated. So and coworkers have shown that the *Neisseria* type 2 IgA_1 protease cleaves LAMP1 and promotes the survival of bacteria within epithelial cells. Infection of human epithelial cells by *N. meningitidis* and *Neisseria gonorrhoeae* increases the rate of degradation of LAMP1, a major integral membrane glycoprotein of late endosomes and lysosomes.[88a] Nassif and colleagues have suggested that meningococcal *pilC* is upregulated and that pilus-mediated attachment may be important in crossing of the blood-brain barrier.[89]

Human Immunologic Response to Meningococcal Antigens

Goldschneider and associates have demonstrated that the percentage of people with bactericidal activity against *N. meningitidis* in their serum is inversely proportional to the incidence of meningococcal meningitis during the first 12 years of life.[90, 91] At birth, as a result of maternal transfer of antibodies, approximately 50% of infants have bactericidal antibody titers. The prevalence of bactericidal antibody decreases after birth and reaches its nadir between 6 and 24 months of age. Thereafter, a linear increase in antibody occurs until age 12. In early adulthood, the prevalence of bactericidal antibody varies with the serogroup but ranges from 67% for group A to 86% for group B. These same investigators demonstrated the protective nature of bactericidal antibody against homologous serogroups during an epidemic situation. Only 3 of 54 sera from patients contained bactericidal antibody in prebleed specimens against the ultimately infecting serogroup, whereas 444 of 550 prebleed sera from matched control subjects who did not become infected contained homologous bactericidal antibody. Goldschneider and colleagues observed that systemic meningococcal disease developed in 38.5% of persons who lacked bactericidal antibody and acquired the epidemic strain in their nasopharynx in the military recruit environment. Their conclusion was that in the presence of nasopharyngeal colonization with a disease-causing strain, deficiency of circulating antimeningococcal antibodies is firmly associated with the establishment of meningococcemia. It appears that bactericidal antibodies are directed against both the capsular polysaccharide and other cell wall antigens, which may cross-react within the family Neisseriaceae and with other bacterial genera. Goldschneider and associates demonstrated that the meningococcal carrier state is an immunizing process and that production of antibodies to meningococci can be identified within 2 weeks of colonization.[90, 91] Nontypable meningococcal strains, which are seen in carrier studies in children, contain antigens that cross-react with the encapsulated strains, and bactericidal antibody to these strains develops after nasopharyngeal colonization. Goldschneider and coworkers also showed that serogroup-specific antibodies arise during the carrier state.

Studies of Robbins and associates indicate that serologic cross-reactions occur between meningococcal group A polysaccharide and *Bacillus pumilis* and that *E. coli* K1 antigen is immunologically and chemically identical to group B capsular polysaccharide.[92, 93] These unrelated, yet immunologically similar antigens may play a very important role in the development of natural immunity to the meningococcus and ultimately in protection against virulent meningococci. Cross-reactivity has now been clearly demonstrated between neonatal tissue and group B capsular polysaccharide. Monoclonal antibodies specific for this capsule have been used to show that cross-reactivity exists between central nervous system, cardiac, liver, and renal glycoproteins[94] in the infant rat and group B polysaccharide. As the animal matures, the cross-reacting antigens persist in the central nervous system. These studies suggest that the poor immunogenicity of this polysaccharide may be due to the fact that it resembles host antigens.

It should be stressed that although specific antibody is generally protective, this immunity is not absolute. Greenwood and coworkers and Käyhty and associates documented illness in individuals with preexisting antibody titers that are considered protective.[95, 96]

The exact role of local IgA antibody in protection or modulation of the carrier state is unknown. Plaut and colleagues have shown that the meningococcus produces a protease that cleaves the Fc fragment of secretory and serum IgA from the Fab portion of the molecule.[97] Production of this enzyme in *Neisseria* organisms is confined to the pathogenic members, the meningococcus and the gonococcus.[98]

The Meningococcal Carrier State

Carriage of *N. meningitidis* in the nasopharynx in otherwise healthy humans has been recognized since 1896. Like the carrier states seen with cholera, diphtheria, and typhoid, the dichotomy between the presence of these dreaded organisms and absence of the associated disease process seemed a paradox to early investigators. Dopter, before the elucidation of distinct meningococcal serogroups, found organisms in the nasopharynx that had all the characteristics of meningococci but failed to agglutinate with antimeningococcic serum prepared from strains isolated from spinal fluid. He labeled these organisms parameningococci.[21] Considerable confusion arose, but subsequent investigators demonstrated that all four of the known serotypes, including the parameningococci of Dopter, could cause meningitis.

In 1908, Bruns and Hohn noted a close relationship between the carrier rate in a population and the onset, rise, and decline of an epidemic.[99] Glover noted the same association in the British Army military camps of World War I and believed that when the carrier rate exceeded 20%, the community was in danger of an epidemic, usually caused by the predominant carrier serotype.[23]

Transmission of meningococci from carrier to carrier is probably via the respiratory route. The rate of spread of the carrier state through a population has been the subject of a number of studies. During epidemics in military camps, the rate of new carrier acquisition can be very rapid, whereas in nonepidemic situations, both military and civilian, the rate of new carrier acquisition can be considerably slower, and the state of carriage can exist for prolonged periods. Rake demonstrated that carriers fall into three groups—chronic, intermittent, and transient—and that chronic carriers could be constantly affected for up to 2 years.[100] He also demonstrated that such factors as coryza unassociated with concomitant rises in other bacterial flora had no effect on the population of meningococci, whereas streptococcal pharyngitis or any other condition that increases other members of the resident flora of the nasopharynx causes a concomitant decrease in the number of meningococci present. Greenfield and colleagues studied carrier rates in families not exposed to clinically important meningococcal infection during a nonepidemic period. Eighty-eight percent of the strains isolated were groupable, with group B being the most common serogroup isolated.[101] During the 32-month observation period, 18% of the population were carriers at least once. The median duration of carriage was 9.6 months, and in 38% it exceeded 16 months. Adult men had the highest incidence of carriage, from 19 to 39%. The adult male introduced the organism into the household 50% of the time, and when such a pattern occurred, the carrier rate in the children and women in the family increased to levels comparable to those for adult men. The rate of transmission in these circumstances was considered low in comparison to most communicable pathogens, and it was estimated that at this level a susceptible person would have more than a 50% chance of escaping carriage even if continually exposed to household carriers for a 5-year period.

A combination of factors is probably responsible for the transition from nasopharyngeal carriage to invasive disease. Invasive meningococcal disease occurs primarily in persons who are newly infected with the organism.[102] Edwards and coworkers found that 31 of 36 patients had negative nasopharyngeal cultures during the 2 weeks before becoming ill and that 4 of these patients were culture negative the day before the development of disease.[102] The remaining 5 of 36 patients had positive cultures less than 4 days before the onset of illness. Other studies have shown that meningococcal epidemics occur not at times of high pharyngeal carriage but when the rates of acquisition of infection are increasing.[103] Coincident viral infection may affect the acquisition of meningococcal nasopharyngeal carriage. It has been noted that in a study of household contacts, individuals who had a recent history of symptoms of upper respiratory infection had a significantly higher carriage rate than did household members without such symptoms.[104] Moore and coworkers have shown that preceding *Mycoplasma* infection may be a cofactor in meningococcal meningitis in Chad.[105]

The carrier state is an immunizing process. Indirect evidence for this phenomenon is the fact that although military recruits have a high frequency of meningococcal carriage and disease, seasoned veterans have a much lower carriage rate and a disease incidence no different from that of the civilian population. In military recruits, antimeningococcal antibodies have been shown to persist for a minimum of 4 to 6 months after exposure. These antibodies are of the three major immunoglobulin classes and combine with group-specific and cross-reactive antigens.[90, 91] Reller and associates demonstrated the development of bactericidal antibodies to the meningococcus in 38 military recruits who became colonized with nongroupable meningococcal strains. Thirty-nine percent of these men had bactericidal antibody to the homologous strains, and in addition, antibodies directed against groupable strains developed in 7 to 52%.[106] These same investigators found greatly enhanced (10- to 100-fold increase) bactericidal activity to known pathogenic strains of groups A, B, C, and Y after colonization with nongroupable meningococci, which suggests that these organisms may be at least as capable of stimulating cross-reactive antibody as groupable meningococci through either an initial or anamnestic response. A review of the meningococcal carrier state has been provided by Broome.[107]

EPIDEMIOLOGY OF MENINGOCOCCAL DISEASE

Meningococcal disease is still a major worldwide health problem. Feldman estimates that during the period 1939 to 1962, almost 600,000 cases of meningococcal disease developed around the world, more than 100,000 of which were fatal.[108] Recent epidemics in Africa, the countries of the former Soviet Union, and Norway indicate that this infection is a worldwide major public health problem. Children previously and presently account for the greatest percentage of these cases.

The case rate during endemic situations varies widely and has increased in the United States over a 5-year period (1991–1996) from 0.84 to 1.3 per 100,000 population. In 1996, 3437 cases were reported to the Centers for Disease Control and Prevention (CDC).[109] Peltola and coworkers have pointed out that shifts in this age distribution of meningococcal disease in a population can forecast an epidemic situation. Relatively more cases arise in the 5- through 19-year-old group during epidemic than during nonepidemic circumstances.[110, 111] Careful surveillance of age distribution patterns may be valuable in recognizing an epidemic during its inception.

The case-fatality rate varies depending on the prevalence of disease, the nature of the infection, and the socioeconomic conditions of the society in which the infections occur. During endemic situations in industrialized countries, case-fatality rates can be as low as 7% for meningitis and as high as 19% for septicemia without meningeal involvement.[112] During epidemic situations in some Third World countries, mortality for meningitis can vary from 2 to 10% and mortality for septicemia can be as high as 70%.[113, 114] In the United States an 8% case-fatality rate has been reported from major medical centers during endemic periods.[115]

The dramatic effect of antibiotics on the case-fatality rate can be seen by comparing two epidemics. Norton and Gordon described an epidemic in Detroit from 1929 to 1931 that involved 1272 patients. The overall case-fatality rate was 50%, with the highest mortality occurring in infants (84%) and in adults older than 40 years (72%).[24] During an epidemic in Chile in 1940 to 1943,[26] the case rate in the province of Valparaiso during 1942 was 188.1 per 100,000 population. In Santiago at the peak of the same epidemic, the case rate in infants was 838.1 per 100,000 population. The meningococcal serotype responsible for this epidemic was group A. Sulfonamides were used for treatment, and the case-fatality rate was 16%.

It is clear that serogroup A, B, and C strains have different epidemic potential.[116] Serogroup B strains cause epidemics usually in developed nations with attack rates of 50 to 100 cases per 10^5 population. Serogroup C disease occurs in both developed and less developed nations and can have attack rates as high as 500 cases per 10^5 population. Serogroup A epidemics occur in less developed nations and have attack rates usually as high as 500 cases per 10^5 population. In all instances, epidemics occur among the poorest groups, where crowding and lack of sanitation are common.

Areas of the world that have experienced recent epidemic meningococcal disease are Australia, Norway, the Netherlands, China, Egypt, Saudi Arabia, Kenya, and eastern Canada. Epidemics have occurred in schoolchildren in northern Georgia and Los Angeles County. Several reviews about the problems of meningococcal epidemics in Africa have been written.[117, 118] Epidemic meningococcal disease occurs during the dry season in the sub-Sahara regions of Africa with regularity. Because of the poor economic conditions of the countries involved, the inaccessibility of some of the regions, the paucity of the infrastructure, and the lack of funds available to international agencies, little has been done in terms of prevention until these epidemics begin. By that time, thousands of cases with a very high mortality have occurred, primarily in small children. The currently available vaccines have been shown to provide protection for a limited period in young children (between 2 and 4 years old).[119] The development of meningococcal protein-capsular conjugate vaccine may overcome this problem if costs can be kept to a level that these countries can afford.

CLINICAL MANIFESTATIONS

Studies in Boston describing a 20-year experience have shown that *N. meningitidis* is the second most common cause of community-acquired adult bacterial meningitis.[3] The successful use of *Haemophilus influenzae* type B capsular conjugate vaccine has made *N. meningitis* the leading cause of bacterial meningitis in children and young adults in the United States, with an overall mortality rate of 13% for meningitic disease. The clinical manifestations of meningococcal disease can be quite varied and can range from transient fever and bacteremia to fulminant disease with death ensuing within hours of the onset of clinical symptoms. Wolfe and Birbara[120] have described four clinical situations:

1. *Bacteremia without sepsis.* Admission is for an upper respiratory illness or viral exanthem. After recovery and frequently after

discharge without specific antimicrobial therapy, the results of blood cultures are reported as positive for *N. meningitidis*. Sullivan and LaScolea recently reported three children with such occult bacteremia who recovered from meningococcal sepsis spontaneously without antibiotics. The serum level of bacteremia in these children was low, from 22 to 325 organisms per milliliter of blood.[121]

2. *Meningococcemia without meningitis.* In these cases the patient's condition is septic, and signs of leukocytosis, skin rash, generalized malaise, weakness, headache, and hypotension develop on admission or shortly thereafter.

3. *Meningitis with or without meningococcemia.* In these patients, headache, fever, and meningeal signs are present with a cloudy spinal fluid. The state of the sensorium may vary widely from fully alert to completely depressed. Deep tendon and superficial reflexes are present. No pathologic reflexes are seen.

4. *The meningoencephalitic manifestation.* These patients are profoundly obtunded with meningeal signs and septic spinal fluid. The deep tendon and superficial reflexes are altered (either absent or rarely hyperactive). Pathologic reflexes are frequently present.

Variations of these manifestations can occur, and the patient can progress from one to the other during the course of disease.

The wide range of clinical expression requires a high index of suspicion and a careful search for clues of disease, particularly in an endemic situation in which a sporadic case is involved. Carpenter and Petersdorf in 53 such cases of meningococcal meningitis reported that headache, confusion, and stiff neck occurred as symptoms in less than half the patients.[122] In infants and small children, fever and vomiting are often the only complaints, and children are frequently not brought to the hospital until an insidious impairment in consciousness or convulsions occur.

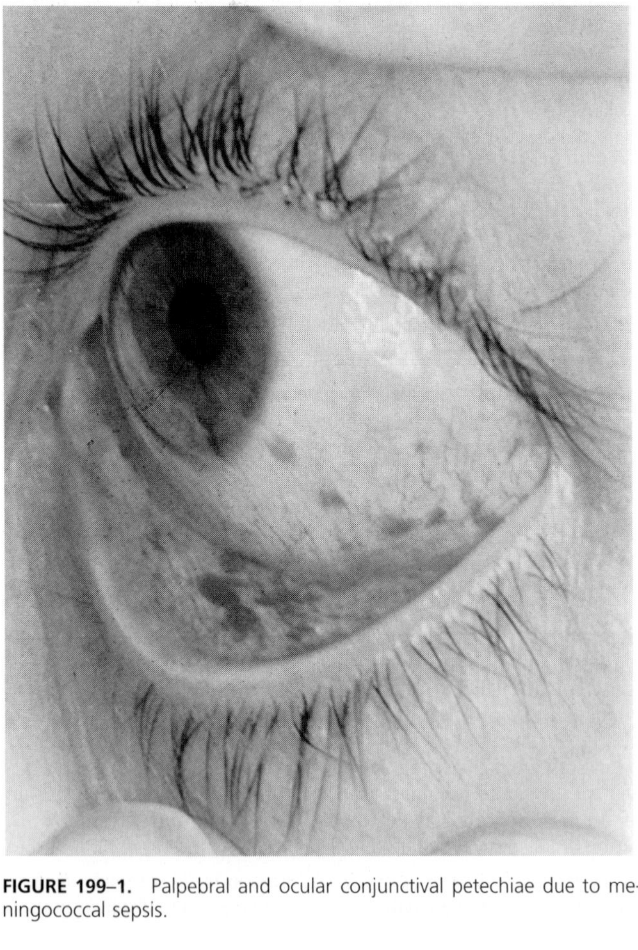

FIGURE 199–1. Palpebral and ocular conjunctival petechiae due to meningococcal sepsis.

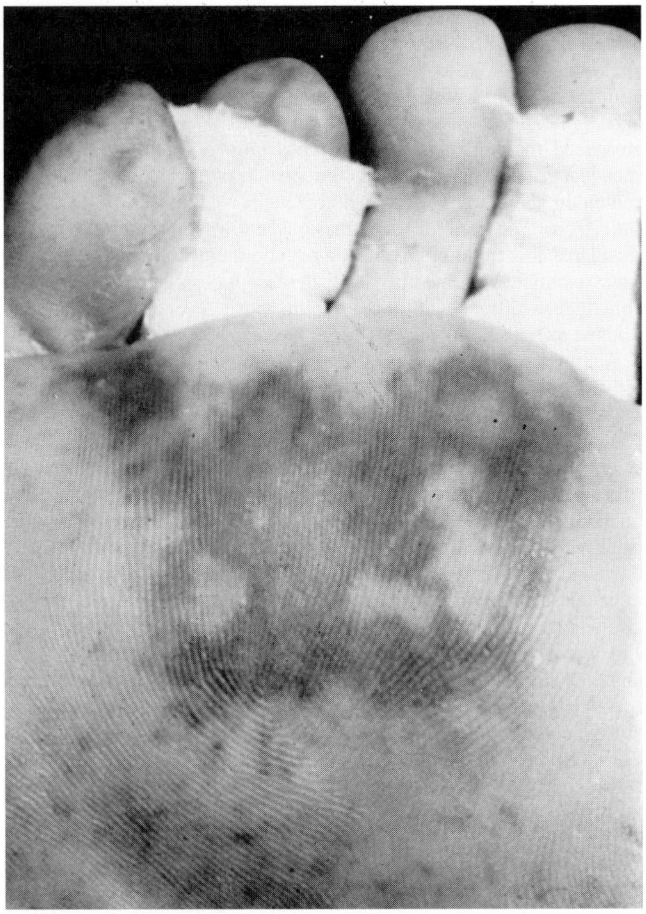

FIGURE 199–2. Subcutaneous ecchymosis on a sole due to meningococcal sepsis.

The signs of meningococcal disease can vary widely. Petechial lesions are a common harbinger of this infection, but occasionally if the patient is not completely undressed when examined or if examination of mucous surfaces such as the palpebral conjunctiva is omitted, important telltale lesions can be missed (Fig. 199–1). The petechial rash is manifested as discrete lesions 1 to 2 mm in diameter most frequently on the trunk and lower portions of the body (Figs. 199–2 and 199–3). These lesions are commonly seen in clusters in areas where pressure may be applied to the skin by elastic in underwear or stockings, thus demonstrating the importance of completely disrobing the patient for an adequate examination. The petechial lesions can coalesce and form larger lesions that appear ecchymotic. These lesions may actually be secondary to subcutaneous hemorrhage, can occasionally be vesicular, and frequently desquamate as the patients recover. The petechiae correlate with the degree of thrombocytopenia and are clinically important as an indicator in the evolution of bleeding complications secondary to the disseminated intravascular coagulopathy (DIC) that ensues.

A number of authors have described another type of rash associated with meningococcal infection.[108, 120] This rash is a maculopapular eruption that can vary somewhat in hue and can be mistaken for a wide variety of viral exanthems, particularly rubella (Fig. 199–4). This eruption is not purpuric or pruritic and is transient; it usually does not last more than 2 days and is frequently gone hours after first observation. Generalized muscle tenderness may also be an important differential sign. Occasionally, the pain from these myalgias is quite intense and causes the patient considerable discomfort.

The neurologic problems seen with meningococcal meningitis are somewhat different from those seen with other forms of purulent meningitis. Evidence of meningeal irritation is common except in the very young and old. Feigin and Dodge showed that focal neurologic signs and seizures were less common in meningococcal meningitis than in pneumococcal meningitis or in meningitis caused by *Haemophilus,* whereas levels of unconsciousness were very similar in the three diseases.[123] This observation correlates with postmortem findings described by Thomas in which focal cerebral involvement in meningococcal meningitis was rare. The cause of death was related to toxins produced by the agent or by cerebral edema and to secondary effects on the vital centers in the midbrain region.[124] Ducker and Simmons supported these clinical findings by observing that doses of meningococcal endotoxin that produced no effect intravenously when introduced into the ventricular system of dogs produced massive hemorrhagic pulmonary edema, subendocardial hemorrhage, hemorrhage and edema of both the mitral and tricuspid valves, visceral congestion, and adrenal hemorrhage.[125] These lesions are similar to those seen outside the central nervous system in soldiers dying of meningococcal meningitis and bacteremia.[126]

Brandtzaeg and coworkers have made major contributions to our understanding of the physiologic effects of lipo-oligosaccharide during sepsis and meningitis caused by *N. meningitidis*.[127–132] These investigators have demonstrated the ability to measure lipo-oligosaccharide in the plasma and CSF of infected patients and have shown a close correlation between plasma lipo-oligosaccharide levels and prognosis. They have demonstrated that compartmentalization of lipo-oligosaccharide production correlates with the clinical findings in meningococcal infection.[129] Lipo-oligosaccharide levels in patients defined as having septicemia were high in plasma (median, 3500 ng) and low in CSF, whereas in patients with meningitis, lipo-oligosaccharide was detectable in the plasma of 3 of 19 patients and in the CSF of 18 of 19 patients with median levels of 2500 ng. Physiologic studies of meningococcal lipo-oligosaccharide in the plasma of infected patients revealed that it has a high sedimentation coefficient. Bacterial outer membrane fragments were found in the plasma of three patients. The plasma of one of these patients contained a bacterium covered with multiple, long membrane protrusions, thus indicating that surplus outer membrane (blebbing) does occur in vivo.[128] Mass spectrometric analysis of the endotoxin from patients with meningococcal sepsis indicated that it was of meningococcal origin rather than arising from the gastrointestinal tract as a result of increased permeability during infection.[132] Sedimentation analysis indicated that the majority of the lipo-oligosaccharide in these patients was not associated with high-density or low-density lipoproteins.

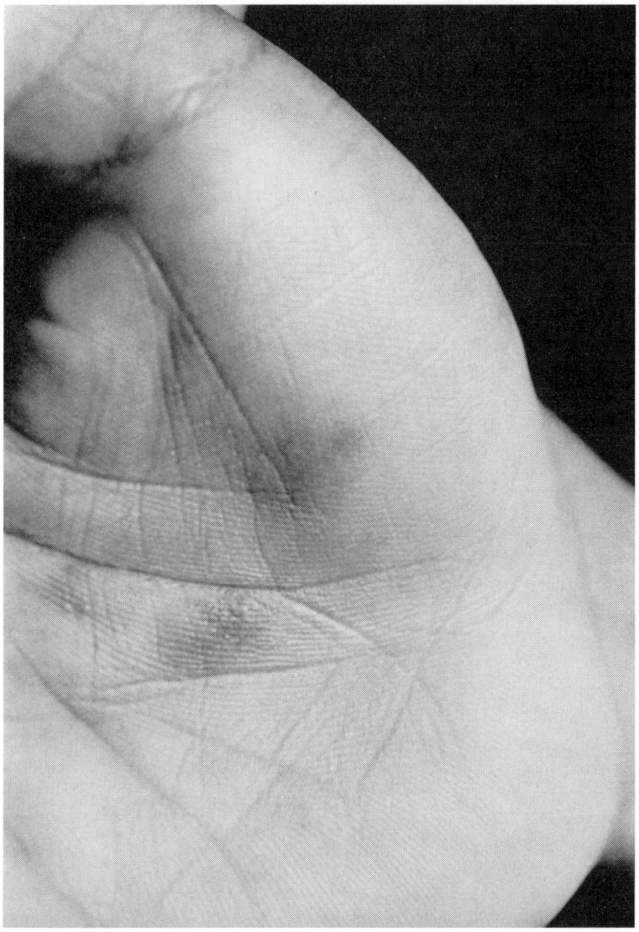

FIGURE 199–3. Embolic lesions on a palm secondary to meningococcal sepsis.

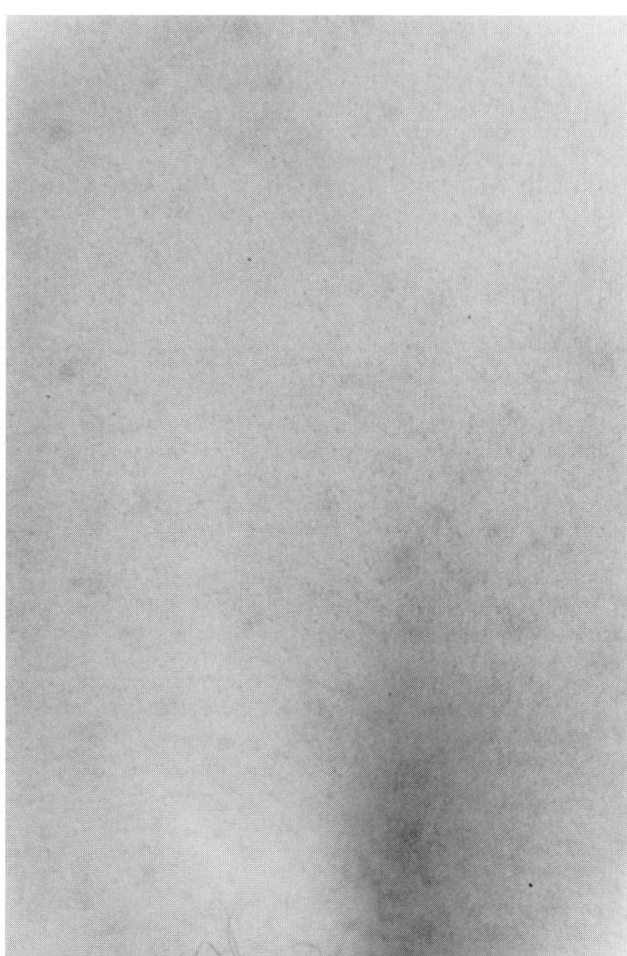

FIGURE 199–4. Rubella-like rash seen early in meningococcal sepsis.

Outer membrane bleb formation by the group A meningococcus was first demonstrated by Cesarini and coworkers.[133] DeVoe and Gilchrist found that strains of meningococcal serogroups A, B, and C released membrane blebs in the log phase of growth but not in the lag phase.[134] The release of lipo-oligosaccharide from the surface of the meningococcus in the form of membrane blebs is now considered to be the principal factor associated with the high endotoxin levels in meningococcal sepsis.

The myocardial problems associated with this infection have been stressed by Levin and Painter and by Kanter and associates.[135, 136] Evidence of myocardial failure as manifested by a gallop rhythm, by congestive heart failure with pulmonary edema, and by high central venous pressure in the face of poor peripheral perfusion has been reported.[135] Treatment of the myocardial failure with cardiac glycosides has resulted in reversing this constellation of problems. Postmortem studies by Hardman[126] and by Gore and Saphir[137] have indicated that myocarditis of varying degrees of severity is present in over half the patients who die of meningococcal disease. More recent studies have also shown myocardial dysfunction in children with acute meningococcemia.[138] Acute meningococcemia was not fatal in children without evidence of myocardial dysfunction. In contrast, three of seven children with evidence of myocardial dysfunction died.

The shock state all too frequently dominates the clinical picture. The patient is poorly responsive, and peripheral vasoconstriction is maximal, with cyanotic, poorly perfused extremities. Arterial blood gas analysis demonstrates evidence of acidosis in the range of pH 7.25 to 7.3, and depending on the degree of shock, anoxia may be manifested by an arterial P_{O_2} below 70 mmHg. Probably the most dramatic consequence of this clinical problem is the presence of DIC. Clinical evidence of its occurrence can be obtained by documenting increasing petechiae within prescribed areas, gastric or gingival bleeding, or oozing at sites of venipuncture or intravenous infusions.

Either concomitant with the initial evaluation of the patient or later in the recovery phase of the illness, a number of unusual complications have been reported, including arthritis, pericarditis, conus medullaris syndrome, and cranial nerve dysfunction, particularly of the sixth, seventh, and eighth cranial nerves.[123, 139–144] The pericarditis can cause massive tamponade. It is of interest that this complication may be unrelated to organism invasion of the pericardium but rather be due to an immunologic reaction or toxin. In the report of Pierce and Cooper, evidence of pericardial involvement occurred after two of the patients were in the recovery phase of their disease.[142] In one of these patients, the first symptoms of pericarditis occurred on the 20th day after the institution of therapy with penicillin. In the other patient, the first symptoms occurred 5 days after therapy began and recurred after pericardiocentesis and prednisone therapy on the 34th hospital day. This patient had a friction rub until the 49th hospital day and was not discharged until almost 3 months after admission. The incidence of this complication, according to Morse and associates, is approximately 19%.[141] All cases of pericarditis seen by these investigators occurred in the convalescent phase of the disease and in disease caused by the group C meningococcus.[141] A recent report described serogroup W-135 in a patient with meningococcal myopericarditis.[142]

Chronic Meningococcemia

Persistent meningococcal bacteremia associated with low-grade fever, rash, and arthritis has been reported.[145–147] The distribution and appearance of the cutaneous lesions are identical to those seen in chronic gonococcemia, for which it is mistaken. Feldman has commented on a patient with chronic meningococcemia who appeared normal in every respect, including the ability to produce antibodies against the capsular polysaccharide of the infecting organism.[108] The frequency of meningococcus in the acute arthritis-dermatitis syndrome appears to be increasing.[146] Rompalo and coworkers compared the isolation of gonococcus and meningococcus from blood or synovial fluid from 1970 to 1972 with isolation of these organisms from 1980 to 1983.[147] The ratio of gonococcal to meningococcal isolates changed from 15 to 1 in 1970 to 1972 to 9 to 5 in 1980 to 1983. These authors believe that systemic meningococcal infection should figure more prominently in the differential diagnosis of the acute arthritis-dermatitis syndrome.

Complement Deficiency and Meningococcemia

The syndrome of chronic meningococcemia must be distinguished from the problem of recurrent episodes of meningococcal meningitis. Studies by Lim and coworkers have demonstrated an absence of the sixth complement component in such a patient.[148] In addition, at least one of the patients with recurrent meningococcal disease studied by Alper and colleagues lacked C3.[149] Studies by Petersen and associates indicated that human deficiency of C8 has been found in some persons with disseminated gonococcal infection and that this complement component is required for serum bactericidal activity against the gonococcus.[150] Ellison and coworkers have evaluated the complement system in 20 patients with first episodes of serious systemic meningococcal infection. Six of 20 had a complement deficiency. Three had deficiencies in a terminal complement protein or proteins, and three had deficiencies of multiple factors associated with underlying disease states.[151] Densen and coworkers have studied a family with properdin deficiency who had a high rate of fatal meningococcal disease.[152] These investigators demonstrated that the bactericidal defect could be corrected by vaccination of this population. Studies by Ross and coworkers suggest that vaccinating individuals deficient in late-complement components may shift the burden of host defense from serum bactericidal activity to phagocytosis.[153] These studies would stress the previously unrecognized importance of the complement system in protection against neisserial infections. The role of complement in meningococcal infection has been reviewed by Densen.[154]

Respiratory Infections with the Meningococcus

Meningococcal pneumonia has been recognized as a clinical syndrome for more than 80 years.[155–158] Because of nasopharyngeal carriage of the meningococcus, establishing the diagnosis by sputum culture alone is hazardous. The incidence of sepsis associated with this type of meningococcal infection appears to be quite low.[156] Therefore, blood cultures may not be of value. Koppes and associates used transtracheal cultures to establish the diagnosis in 68 Air Force recruits with group Y meningococcal pneumonia.[156] In this series, a history of cough, chest pain, chills, and previous upper respiratory infection occurred in over half of the patients. Rales and fever occurred in almost all patients, and evidence of pharyngitis was present in more than 80%. The disease involved more than one lobe in 40%, with the right lower and middle lobes involved most frequently. The prognosis was good, with no deaths occurring in the 68 patients with pneumonia. The association of meningococcal infection with preceding viral respiratory infection has been reported. Young and coworkers investigated an outbreak of meningococcal infection in an aged population, most of whom had serologic evidence of influenza.[159] Goldstein and associates have shown that pulmonary clearance of meningococci is diminished in animals previously exposed to an avirulent encephalomyocarditis virus.[160] In a study of the etiology of community-acquired pneumonia in Finland, *N. meningitidis* was implicated as the etiologic agent in 6 of 162 cases.[161]

Meningococcal upper respiratory tract infection (pharyngitis) associated with contacts of cases and as a prior symptom and sign in cases of serious meningococcal disease has been described by several authors.[162, 163] Suggestions that pharyngeal inflammation is the predecessor to bacteremic dissemination have been made but are unsubstantiated.

Meningococcal Urethritis

Meningococci have been isolated from the urethra and can be the etiologic agent in urethritis.[164, 165] An association between orogenital sex and acquisition of the organism has been suggested.[166] In a population of homosexual males, the organism was isolated from the oropharynx (93% of isolates), rectum (6% of isolates), and urethra (1% of isolates).[166]

LABORATORY DIAGNOSIS OF MENINGOCOCCAL INFECTION

Definitive diagnosis of serious meningococcal infection has as a prerequisite the bacteriologic isolation of *N. meningitidis* from a usually sterile body fluid such as blood, CSF, or synovial, pleural, or pericardial fluid. CSF and blood are the most fruitful sources of positive cultures. In an analysis of 727 cases of meningococcal disease, Hoyne and Brown described the results of 400 blood cultures in which 51.4% were positive for meningococci.[167] Spinal fluid examination of 423 patients from the same series indicated that 94% were positive for gram-negative diplococci by either smear or culture for the meningococci. Carpenter and Petersdorf indicate that 46% of their cases of meningococcal meningitis were positive by CSF culture.[122] In an additional 12% of the cases, the diagnosis was made by smear of the spinal fluid and by the clinical manifestations. Levin and Painter studied 28 patients with culture-proven meningococcal disease, and in 22 of 27 patients tested the spinal fluid was positive, whereas 15 of 28 had positive blood cultures.[135] It is of interest that in 8 of 12 patients considered to have meningococcemia without clinical evidence of meningitis, spinal fluid cultures were positive. Feldman has quantitated the bacterial counts of meningococcal meningitis in CSF and reported a mean of 1.27×10^5 (1.5×10^2 to 6×10^7) organisms per milliliter.[168] The ability to see or to culture meningococci in petechial skin and mucosal lesions varies widely. Hoyne and Brown reported identification in 69.8% of the petechial smears examined.[167] Care should be taken with these specimens because of difficulty in interpretation. Studies of pericardial fluid have failed to demonstrate the organism by smear or culture.[140, 141]

Chemical and cytologic examination of spinal fluid in meningococcal infection can yield variable results. Carpenter and Petersdorf examined the spinal fluid of 58 patients with meningococcal meningitis.[122] The median leukocyte count was approximately 1200 with a range of less than 10 to 65,000/mm^3. Approximately 75% had CSF glucose levels below 40 mg/dl. Unfortunately, spinal fluid–serum glucose ratios were not given. CSF protein levels ranged from 25 to more than 800 mg/dl, with the median value approximately 150 mg/dl. Although not commented on specifically by these authors, the cell type in untreated cases is almost always polymorphonuclear. Partially treated patients may have a pleomorphic spinal fluid.

Studies using counterimmunoelectrophoresis, latex agglutination, and coagglutination have demonstrated the capability of detecting 0.02 to 0.05 μg of meningococcal antigens per milliliter of spinal fluid from infected patients.[168–170] The technique offers rapidity in diagnosis and specificity, provided that organisms containing cross-reacting antigens are not involved (e.g., *E. coli* K1 and group B meningococcus). False-negative results occur commonly. Feigin, as reported by McCracken, could not detect antigen in the blood and CSF of almost half of his patients with meningococcal meningitis.[163] Studies using lactate dehydrogenase or neuraminidase in CSF as indicators of bacterial infection have been reported.[171, 172] It is of interest that the levels of both enzymes are substantially elevated in meningococcal meningitis when compared with pneumococcal, *H. influenzae* type B, or viral central nervous system infections.

Polymerase chain reaction has been used in the diagnosis of meningococcal meningitis by examination of CSF. Ni and coworkers examined 54 CSF samples and controls by polymerase chain reaction in a blinded fashion.[8] The sensitivity and specificity of polymerase chain reaction for the diagnosis of meningococcal meningitis were both 91%. This technique may be particularly useful in confirmation of the diagnosis in situations in which culture has little value because of prior antibiotic administration. As polymerase chain reaction technology improves, it may rival culture as a method of definitive diagnosis of meningococcal infection. It also has the capability of rapidly typing strains, a very useful adjunct in situations that appear to be an evolving epidemic.[173–176]

TREATMENT OF MENINGOCOCCAL INFECTIONS

The introduction of antibiotics has dramatically altered the prognosis of meningococcal disease. Today, the expected mortality under optimal conditions should not exceed 8 to 10%.[112, 120] Random cases frequently fare poorer than those in an epidemic because medical personnel are not alerted to the diagnosis and may overlook the early signs and symptoms. The value of early diagnosis in lowering the mortality is exemplified by the results at Fort Dix, where an intense surveillance program was established between 1968 and 1969 and the mortality was less than 5%.

In addition to the use of antibiotics, the application of supportive care to treat the problems of DIC, shock, heart failure, prolonged mental obtundation, pericarditis, and pneumonia, which complicate this infection, has had a decided impact on prognosis.

Antibiotic Therapy

The era of chemotherapy for meningococcal infection began with a report of Schwentker and associates in 1937 that demonstrated that sulfonamides could be successfully used in the treatment of meningococcal meningitis and meningococcemia.[27] Feldman and coworkers confirmed these observations. A dramatic change occurred in the prognosis of epidemic meningitis.[177] As new antibiotics were introduced through the 1940s and 1950s, reports appeared that documented the efficacy of several agents used alone and in combination. Early studies of penicillin given in relatively low doses (120,000 units/day intramuscularly) indicated that it was not as effective as sulfonamides.[178] Using larger amounts of the drug (360,000 units/day intramuscularly), Kinsman and D'Alonzo demonstrated that treatment results with penicillin were identical to those with sulfonamides.[179] The efficacy of chloramphenicol as a therapeutic agent was demonstrated by McCrumb and coworkers.[180] In 15 patients treated with this drug, all survived, and only 1 patient had a complication secondary to the infection, ophthalmoplegia, which subsequently cleared.

The therapeutic efficacy of first-generation cephalosporins was studied in the 1960s. These agents produced variable results, and their use is now contraindicated in treating meningococcal infection.[181, 182] Third-generation cephalosporins demonstrate excellent in vitro effectiveness against the meningococcus[183] and achieve central nervous system concentrations adequate to treat meningococcal meningeal infection (Table 199–2).

Sulfonamides now have a very limited role in the treatment of meningococcal infection. Studies by Schoenback and Phair[29] and by Love and Finland[187] revealed small populations of sulfonamide-resistant meningococci. In 1963, an epidemic of group B meningococcal infection occurred at Ford Ord, California, in which the infecting strain was resistant to sulfonamides.[35, 188] Since that time, most isolates, primarily serogroups B and C in this country and group A from worldwide locations, have been resistant to sulfadiazine.[189–191]

TABLE 199–2 Treatment and Prevention of Serious Meningococcal Infection

Problem	Treatment
Meningococcal meningitis, meningococcemia, and chronic meningococcemia	Penicillin G, 300,000 U/kg/d IV, up to 24 million U/d. If penicillin allergic, chloramphenicol, 100 mg/kg/d IV, up to 4 g/d.[135] Ceftriaxone, 50 mg/kg/d in children up to 2 g. Adult dose, 2 g/d[184]
Antibiotic chemoprophylaxis for household or intimate contacts	Rifampin: adults, 600 mg q12h for 2 d; children <1 mo, 5 mg/kg q12h for 2 d; children >1 mo, 10 mg/kg for 2 d. Ciprofloxacin: adults, 500 mg, single dose. Ceftriaxone: children <15 yr, 125 mg, single IM dose; adults, 250 mg, single dose[185, 186]
Immunoprophylaxis	Monovalent A, monovalent C, bivalent A-C, or quadrivalent A, C, Y and W-135 vaccine is administered once by volume according to the manufacturer's instructions. The amount of polysaccharide delivered is usually 50 μg. Vaccination should be considered an adjunct to antibiotic chemoprophylaxis for household or intimate contacts of patients with meningococcal disease when appropriate serogroups are causing disease[185]

Penicillin therapy for meningococcal infections is safe and effective. U.S strains remain sensitive to this antibiotic.[185] The drug can be administered intravenously or intramuscularly, but the intrathecal route is contraindicated because of the severe neurotoxicity of penicillin in high concentrations in the central nervous system. A goal of antibiotic therapy for meningitis is to establish concentrations of antibiotics in the spinal fluid that approximate 10 times the minimal inhibitory concentration of the organism for that agent.[192] A dose of 300,000 units/kg/day is recommended, with an upper limit of 24 million units/day as 2 million units every 2 hours.[193] Reports of penicillin-insensitive *N. meningitidis* have come from Great Britain, Spain, and less commonly, the United States.[194, 195] Relative resistance to penicillin is due to a reduced affinity of penicillin-binding proteins 2 and 3.[196] Spinal fluid levels of penicillin averaged 0.8 μg/ml on the first day of therapy. This concentration approximated the minimal inhibitory concentration for penicillin G for the most resistant isolate studied by this group. These strains were also relatively resistant to cefuroxime, but cefotaxime and ceftriaxone appear to be active against these strains in vitro. High-level resistance in β-lactamase–producing strains has also been reported. Although resistant meningococcal strains have been infrequently reported to date, clinicians should be alerted to the possibility of their occurrence in unexplained treatment failures or in cases of slowly resolving, documented meningococcal central nervous system infections. Chloramphenicol is an effective substitute in penicillin-allergic patients and should be administered intravenously in a dose of 100 mg/kg/day up to a maximum of 4 g/day in total dose.[193] Chloramphenicol-resistant strains have been reported but remain rare in the United States (see Chapter 71).[197]

Third-generation cephalosporins, including cefotaxime, ceftriaxone, ceftizoxime, and ceftazidime, have been used successfully in the treatment of pediatric cases of meningococcal meningitis.[15, 184] The second-generation cephalosporin cefuroxime has also been successfully used in meningococcal meningitis.[198] Penetration of second- and third-generation agents into spinal fluid has been studied (Table 199–3).[14] Ceftriaxone, cefotaxime, and ceftazidime achieve levels in CSF several orders of magnitude greater than the susceptibility of the meningococcus to these agents. Special circumstances may occur in which they would be the agents of choice, for example, relatively penicillin-resistant meningococci (care should be taken to choose an active cephalosporin[195, 196]), situations in which skilled medical care is limited and once-daily dosing may be necessary, and drug hypersensitivity reactions that preclude the use of penicillins or chloramphenicol. The duration of antibiotic therapy will vary somewhat with the manifestation of the disease and with the response of the patient. At present, when the meningococcus is sensitive to the agents just mentioned, 10 to 14 days of therapy is usually sufficient.

Studies in England have suggested that administration of parenteral penicillin by practitioners as soon as the diagnosis was suspected led to a significantly more favorable outcome.[206, 207] The doses given in the studies were not provided. Recent studies have confirmed the value of early treatment of invasive meningococcal infection to a favorable outcome.[208] Studies by Barquet and coworkers have shown that receipt of antibiotic therapy before hospital admission was associated with a reduced likelihood of death. In the patient group defined as having acute clinical infection, a single death occurred in 119 patients treated with antibiotics before admission as compared with 15 deaths in 329 similar patients ($p = .04$) who were not given prehospitalization therapy.

TABLE 199–3 Susceptibilities of Meningococci, Kinetics, and Cerebrospinal Fluid Penetration of Selected Second- and Third-Generation Cephalosporins

Cephalosporin	Susceptibility (μg/ml)	CSF Concentration (μg/ml)	CSF Penetration (%)
Cefuroxime	<0.2–1.6	1.1–17.1	11.6–13.7
Ceftriaxone	<0.001	2.1–7.2	1.5–7
Cefotaxime	<0.008	1.2–83 (mean, 6.3)	4–54 (mean, 22.7)
Ceftazidime	0.007–0.5	2.5–30 (mean, 9.8)	14

Data from refs. 199–205.

Supportive Care

Common complications of meningococcal disease are vascular collapse and shock, primarily caused by the effects of meningococcal lipo-oligosaccharide, which is a potent toxin. The cytokine tumor necrosis factor-α (TNF-α) may be a mediator of endotoxic shock because when it is injected into animals, it induces hypotension, metabolic acidosis, and death.[209–212] Studies in animals suggest that treatment or pretreatment with polyclonal[211] or monoclonal[213] antibodies against TNF-α could be beneficial in purpura fulminans. Girardin and coworkers have demonstrated that serum levels of TNF-α, interleukin-1 (IL-1), and interferon-γ correlated with the severity of meningococcemia in children.[214] At the present time, it is not known whether these cytokines play a deleterious or protective role in shock secondary to meningococcal sepsis. Brandtzaeg and coworkers have extensively studied this question during an epidemic in Norway.[127–132, 209] These investigators showed that IL-6 and IL-1 are released into the serum and coexist with TNF-α and lipopolysaccharide in the systemic circulation during the initial phase of meningococcal septic shock. High levels of IL-6 and IL-1 are associated with a fatal outcome, and IL-1 was detected exclusively in patients who had high levels of IL-6, TNF-α, and lipopolysaccharide and a rapid fatal outcome. These investigators also showed that lipopolysaccharide was compartmentalized primarily in the plasma in patients with meningococcemia, whereas patients with meningitis had high levels in CSF and low or undetectable levels in plasma. In other studies, this group has shown that extensive complement activation occurs in fulminant cases of meningococcemia.[130] The results in these studies suggested that the lipopolysaccharide was an important activator of complement in systemic meningococcal disease and that complement-activating products in concert with other mediators may contribute to the multiple organ failure and death occurring in the most severe cases.[130] New therapies are emerging that may have a significant impact on the management of meningococcal sepsis. Preliminary evaluation of the administration of a recombinant protein composed of the N-terminal fragment of human bactericidal/permeability-increasing protein in children with meningococcal sepsis has been encouraging. In a group of children aged 1 to 18 years with a predicted mortality of 30% based on the Glasgow Meningococcal Prognostic Septicemia Score, only 1 of 26 died.[215]

In every case of systemic meningococcal infection, the potential for shock must be always considered. Observation for shock and its therapy[216–219] are best accomplished in an intensive care unit.

The use of steroids, particularly in patients with evidence of purpura fulminans and concomitant adrenal hemorrhage (Waterhouse-Friderichsen syndrome), is still controversial. In the 1950s, several investigators recommended the use of corticosteroid replacement therapy. However, the studies of Belsey and colleagues were inconclusive in demonstrating a beneficial effect of the application of low-dose steroid in meningococcal infection.[220]

As pointed out earlier, the problem of DIC is ominous. Petechiae are frequent accompaniments of meningococcal sepsis. The development of increasing petechial lesions, confluent ecchymoses, persistently bleeding venipuncture sites, and bleeding gums despite adequate antimicrobial therapy and supportive care is indicative of DIC. Heparin treatment of this complication of meningococcal disease is probably not indicated.[221, 222] As many patients can be harmed by the inappropriate treatment of DIC as by DIC itself. To complicate matters, in severe DIC the problem of plasmin activation with fibrinolysis becomes a clinical reality.

Other major life-threatening complications necessitating therapy include adult respiratory distress syndrome, neurologic sequelae ranging from coma to diabetes insipidus, pneumonia that is not necessarily meningococcal but may be secondary to aspiration during the obtunded state, and pericarditis. This last problem can be insidious and can appear in the convalescent stage of disease. Awareness that it can occur will readily lead to its diagnosis and treatment.

The ability to define the outcome of meningococcal sepsis based on a number of indicators has been studied extensively.[223–226] Kornelisse and coworkers have used a set of objective indicators, including the C-reactive protein level, base excess, serum potassium level, and platelet count. This system was predictive of death or survival in 86% of the patients studied.[223]

Chemoprophylaxis of the Meningococcal Carrier

Shortly after the clinical use of sulfonamides for the treatment of serious meningococcal disease, it became apparent that short courses of the sulfadiazine resulted in the disappearance of meningococcal carriage for prolonged periods.[227, 228] As Feldman points out, despite the arguments about the relationship "if there are no carriers, there are no cases," the use of sulfonamides to reduce carrier rates did decrease the number of cases.[108]

Treatment of the meningococcal carrier state with sulfonamides eradicated carriage quickly and for prolonged periods.[229] The length of time was a function of the initial dose of sulfonamides, and with doses as high as 8 g the carrier rate was reduced from approximately 45% to less than 10% at 16 weeks. Cheever demonstrated that after two doses of 3 and 2 g of sulfadiazine the carrier rate dropped from 79 to 0% in 72 hours.[230] On military bases and in closed environments such as boarding schools, institutions, and family units in which cases arose, this form of chemoprophylaxis was effective in disrupting the spread of meningococcal infection.

With the recognition of widespread sulfonamide-resistant meningococci and the failure of sulfadiazine to have an impact on the epidemic at Fort Ord,[30, 31, 188] these agents have been abandoned for meningococcal chemoprophylaxis except in instances in which the meningococcal case strains are known to be sulfa sensitive.

The search for new agents for chemoprophylaxis has been extensive. Penicillin has proved ineffective for several reasons: long-acting mixtures do not eradicate nasopharyngeal carriage, and although massive doses cause people to become noncarriers, the carrier state recurs promptly after discontinuation of use of the drug.[108, 231] Minocycline and rifampin have been shown to eradicate the carrier state rapidly, and this eradication persists for up to 6 to 10 weeks after treatment.[232, 233] Problems occur with both drugs. Minocycline has been shown to cause vertigo, probably secondary to an effect on the vestibular system.[234] Rifampin treatment can result in the emergence of rifampin-resistant meningococci in 10 to 27% of patients treated.[235] In addition, rifampin causes red urine in almost all patients, which can be quite disconcerting unless some forewarning is given. Studies by Pugsley and coworkers have demonstrated in 21 persistent meningococcal nasopharyngeal carriers that ciprofloxacin, 500 mg every 12 hours for 5 days, eradicated the meningococcus from the nasopharynx in 100% of individuals for up to 13 days after the completion of therapy. An untreated comparative control group had a carriage rate of 85% at that time.[236] Gilja and coworkers used a single dose of 400 mg of ofloxacin in a controlled study and showed that it can eradicate nasopharyngeal carriage for up to 33 days in 97% of subjects.[13] A single dose of ceftriaxone (250 mg intramuscularly for adults and 125 mg for children younger than 15 years) has also been shown to eradicate nasopharyngeal carriage for 14 days.[12] The recommended therapy for meningococcal prophylaxis has been expanded to include either rifampin, ciprofloxacin, or ceftriaxone[185] (see Table 199–2).

A number of other agents active against meningococci in vitro have been tested but have failed to provide prophylaxis. These agents include erythromycin, trimethoprim, cephalexin, oxytetracycline, and nalidixic acid. Hoeprich has studied a number of these drugs and speculates that the primary factor determining effectiveness as a meningococcal prophylactic agent is the ability to achieve bactericidal levels in tears and saliva.[237]

The question of who should receive prophylaxis has concerned public health officials since the advent of effective chemoprophylaxis. Initially with sulfonamides, little discrimination between high-risk and low-risk populations was attempted, and the drug was administered very widely to people without the remotest increased risk of disease. Since the clinical emergence of sulfa resistance and the problem in finding agents that are safe and effective, more attention has been paid to the populations at greatest risk who need chemoprophylaxis. During epidemics and in endemic situations in civilian populations, household contacts have been shown to be at increased risk of infection.[24, 26, 115] Analysis by the CDC meningococcal surveillance group showed that the attack rate in this group was 500 to 800 times greater than that determined for the general population studied.[115] Similar high-risk situations exist in closed populations such as in some college dormitories, long-term care hospitals, nursery schools,[238] and military barracks. In the community, chemoprophylaxis is recommended for household contacts, daycare center members, and anyone exposed to the patient's oral secretions, but not school, transportation, or office contacts. Secondary cases usually occur within 10 days of the primary case, but longer intervals have been described. Close surveillance of this group for at least 10 days would ensure prompt treatment of any secondary cases that might arise in the absence of effective chemoprophylaxis. Beginning chemoprophylaxis more than 2 weeks after exposure to the index case would be too late to prevent secondary cases. Hospital personnel are not at increased risk and in general should not receive chemoprophylaxis[239]; however, medical staff who have an intimate exposure such as mouth-to-mouth resuscitation or endotracheal intubation should receive prophylaxis.[108, 240] The index case should also be treated before leaving the hospital if penicillin or ampicillin was used because these antibiotics do not reliably end the carrier state.

Immunoprophylaxis of Meningococcal Infection

Subsequent to the problem of prevention of epidemic meningococcal disease on military recruit bases after the emergence of sulfa-resistant meningococci, an intense effort was directed at the development of a vaccine for prevention of meningococcal infections in this high-risk population. The result was the development of two vaccine preparations derived from the capsular polysaccharide of groups A and C meningococci. Artenstein and coworkers demonstrated the effectiveness of the group C vaccine in studies of U.S. Army recruits.[32] Only 1 case of meningococcal disease occurred among 13,763 vaccinees, whereas 38 bacteriologically proven cases occurred in a control group of 68,072. This vaccine resulted in an 87% reduction in disease, which was statistically significant. Makela and associates showed that administration of group A polysaccharide to Finnish military recruits significantly lowered the incidence of disease caused by this serogroup when compared with an unvaccinated control population.[241] Studies from Finland during a group A epidemic demonstrated the effectiveness of this vaccine in children 3 months to 5 years of age.[31] Studies from Africa by Reingold and colleagues indicate that efficacy in this population 1 year after serogroup A vaccination is less than 30% in children younger than 4 years.[119] The immunologic response of the group C vaccine in children younger than 2 years is poor, and studies from Brazil indicate that group C vaccine is not protective in children younger than 24 months.[242] Studies of the immune response to the A and C vaccine by Gold and coworkers in infants have demonstrated that detectable levels of antibody are generated but that these levels are significantly lower than the levels in older children.[243] In adults, the duration of group C antibody titer persisted for 2 to 4 years after vaccination, and in children studied in Egypt who were vaccinated with group A polysaccharide, protection lasted at least 2 years.[244, 245] The vaccine is safe.[246, 247] Reactions appear to be limited to local erythema at the site of injection in approximately 4% and some increased irritability in young children in about 6% of the vaccine recipients. One instance of immunologic hyporesponsiveness to group C antigen was reported in a population of young adult volunteers who had received group A vaccine contaminated with trace amounts of group C polysaccharide.[248] It is assumed that this hyporesponsiveness represents an example of low-dose tolerance in humans. Commercial vaccine materials are now carefully tested to ensure that such cross-contamination does not occur. Because the meningococcal vaccines are poorly immunogenic in children younger than 2 years and because of the lack of a vaccine to the serogroup B meningococcus, chemoprophylaxis is recommended in lieu of vaccine for the prevention of secondary cases of meningococcal disease in daycare centers.[249]

The use of these vaccines in developing countries in epidemic areas has become increasingly important. Factors such as underlying parasitic infections, the state of nutrition, and age of the vaccine recipient play a role in the response to vaccination.[250]

Current commercial vaccines include a quadrivalent product containing polysaccharides of groups A, C, Y, and W-135.[247] No vaccine is presently available for use in prevention of group B disease. Group B capsular polysaccharide is not sufficiently immunogenic to produce a reliable antibody response in humans to be effective. Several solutions to this problem are being studied, including chemical alteration of capsular B antigen to make it more immunogenic and a search for other cell wall antigens that are capable of eliciting bactericidal antibodies against B meningococci with a minimum of serious side effects.

With the increased frequency of meningococcal disease caused by serogroup C, the CDC has provided recommendations for the evaluation and management of suspected outbreaks. These recommendations include confirmation of the diagnosis, administration of chemoprophylaxis to appropriate contacts, enhancement of surveillance, investigation of linkage between cases, utilization of subtyping of organisms, determination of whether the outbreak is organizational (nursery school, university, etc.) or community based, definition of the population at risk, calculation of the attack rate, and determination of the target group for vaccination.

New vaccines against the meningococcus are under development, as well as methods to enhance the immune response to current vaccines. These advances include vaccines developed to somatic antigens such as detoxified lipo-oligosaccharide and outer membrane proteins and new capsular vaccines consisting of polysaccharide-protein conjugates[251–255] and vaccines developed on the basis of anti-idiotype antibodies.[256, 257]

REFERENCES

1. Patel MS, Merianos A, Hanna JN, et al. Epidemic meningococcal meningitis in central Australia, 1987–1991. Med J Aust. 1993;158:336–340.
2. Scholten RJPM, Bijlmer HA, Poolman JT, et al. Meningococcal disease in the Netherlands, 1985–1990: A steady increase in the incidence since 1982 partially caused by new serotypes and subtypes of *Neisseria meningitidis*. Clin Infect Dis. 1993;16:237–246.
3. Durand ML, Calderwood SB, Weber DJ, et al. Acute bacterial meningitis in adults. N Engl J Med. 1993;328:21–28.
4. Girgis NI, Sippel JE, Kilpatrick ME, et al. Meningitis and encephalitis at the Abbassia fever hospital Cairo, Egypt, from 1966 to 1989. Am J Trop Med Hyg. 1993;48:97–107.
5. Wang JF, Caugant DA, Li X, et al. Clonal and antigenic analysis of serogroup A *Neisseria meningitidis* with particular reference to epidemiological features of epidemic meningitis in the People's Republic of China. Infect Immun. 1992;60:5267–5282.
6. Nejmi S, Belhaj A, Guibourdenche M, et al. Study of ninety strains of serogroup A *Neisseria meningitidis* isolated from cerebrospinal fluid (25) and rhinopharynx (65) in Morocco (December 1989–April 1990). Pathol Biol (Paris). 1992;40:993–998.
7. Stephens DS, Spellman PA, Swartley JS. Effect of the (alpha 2→8)-linked polysialic acid capsule on adherence of *Neisseria meningitidis* to human mucosal cells. J Infect Dis. 1993;167:475–479.
8. Ni H, Knight AI, Cartwright K, et al. Polymerase chain reaction for diagnosis of meningococcal meningitis. Lancet. 1993;340:1432–1434.
9. McLaughlin GL, Howe DK, Biggs D, et al. Amplification of rDNA loci to detect and type *Neisseria meningitidis* and other eubacteria. Mol Cell Probes. 1993;7:7–17.
10. Achtman M, Wang JF. DNA fingerprinting of serogroup A meningococci. Scand J Infect Dis. 1993;25:161–162.
11. Bjorvatn B, Hassen-King M, Greenwood B, et al. DNA fingerprinting in the epidemiology of African serogroup A *Neisseria meningitidis*. Scand J Infect Dis. 1992;24:323–332.
12. Schwartz B. Chemoprophylaxis for bacterial infections: Principles of and application to meningococcal infection. Rev Infect Dis. 1991;13(Suppl 2):S170–S173.
13. Gilja HO, Halstensen A, Digranes A, et al. Single-dose ofloxacin to eradicate tonsillopharyngeal carriage of *Neisseria meningitidis*. Antimicrob Agents Chemother. 1993;37:2024–2026.
14. Cherubin CE, Eng RK, Noorby R, et al. Penetration of newer cephalosporins into spinal fluid. Rev Infect Dis. 1989;11:526–548.
15. Grubbauer HM, Dornbusch HJ, Weippli G, et al. Ceftriaxone monotherapy for bacterial meningitis in children. Chemotherapy. 1990;36:441–447.
16. Vieusseaux M. Memoire sur le maladie qui a regne a Geneve au printemps de 1805. J Med Chir Pharmacol. 1805;11:163.
17. Hedrich AW. The movements of epidemic meningitis, 1915–1930. Public Health Rep. 1931;46:2709.
18. Weichselbaum A. Ueber die Aetiologie der akuten Meningitis cerebrospinalis. Fortschr Med. 1887;5:573.
19. Kiefer F. Zur differential Diagnose des Erregers der epidemischen Cerebrospinalmeningitis und der Gonorrhoea. Berl Klin Wochenschr. 1896;33:628.
20. Albrecht H, Ghon A. Uber die Aetiologie und pathologische Anatomie der Meningitis cerebro spinalis epidemica. Wien Klin Wochenschr. 1901;14:984.
21. Dopter C. Etude de quelques germes isoles du rhino-pharynx, voisans du meningocoque (parameningocoques). C R Soc Biol (Paris). 1909;67:74.
22. Flexner S. The results of the serum treatment in thirteen hundred cases of epidemic meningitis. J Exp Med. 1913;17:553.
23. Glover JA. The cerebrospinal fever epidemic of 1917 at "X" depot. J R Army Med Corps. 1918;30:23.
24. Norton JF, Gordon JE. Meningococcus meningitis in Detroit in 1928–1929. I. Epidemiology. J Prev Med. 1930;4:207.
25. French MR. Epidemiological study of 383 cases of meningococcus meningitis in the city of Milwaukee, 1927–1928 and 1929. Am J Public Health. 1931;21:130.
26. Pizzi M. A severe epidemic of meningococcus meningitis in Chile, 1941 and 1942. Am J Public Health. 1944;34:231–238.
27. Schwentker FF, Gelman S, Long PH. The treatment of meningococcic meningitis with sulfonamide. Preliminary report. JAMA. 1937;108:1407.
28. Kuhns DM, Nelson CT, Feldman HA, et al. The prophylactic value of sulfadiazine in the control of meningococcic meningitis. JAMA 1943;123:335–339.
29. Schoenback EB, Phair JJ. The sensitivity of meningococci to sulfadiazine. Am J Hyg. 1948;47:177–186.
30. Gauld JR, Nitz RE, Hunter DH, et al. Epidemiology of meningococcal meningitis at Fort Ord. Am J Epidemiol. 1965;82:56–72.
31. Bristow MW, Van Peenen PFD, Volk R. Epidemic meningitis in naval recruits. Am J Public Health. 1965;55:1039–1045.
32. Artenstein MS, Gold R, Zimmerly JG, et al. Prevention of meningococcal disease by group C polysaccharide vaccine. N Engl J Med. 1970;282:417–420.
33. Piltola H, Makela PH, Kayhty H, et al. Clinical efficacy of meningococcus group A capsular polysaccharide vaccine in children three months to five years of age. N Engl J Med. 1977;297:686–691.
34. Hebeler BH, Young FE. Mechanism of autolysis of *Neisseria gonorrhoeae*. J Bacteriol. 1976;126:1186–1193.
35. Hebeler BH, Young FE. Autolysis of *Neisseria gonorrhoeae*. J Bacteriol. 1976;122:385–392.
36. Holbein BE. Enhancement of *Neisseria meningitidis* infection in mice by addition of iron bound to transferrin. Infect Immun. 1981;34:120–125.
37. West WF, Sparling PF. The response of *Neisseria gonorrhoeae* to iron limitation: Alterations in expression of membrane proteins without apparent siderophore production. Infect Immun. 1985;47:388–394.
38. Dyer D, West EP, Sparling PF. Effects of seven carrier proteins on the growth of pathogenic *Neisseria* with heme-bound iron. Infect Immun. 1987;55:2171.
39. Gorden MH, Murray EG. Identification of the meningococcus. J R Army Med Corps. 1915;5:411.
40. Scherp HW, Rake GJ. Studies on the meningococcus. VIII. The type I specific substance. J Exp Med. 1935;61:753.
41. Clapp FL, Phillips SW, Stahl HJ. Quantitative use of Neufeld reaction with special reference to titration of type III anti-pneumococcic sera. Proc Soc Exp Biol Med. 1935;33:302.
42. Branham SE, Carlin SA. Comments on a newly recognized group of the meningococcus. Proc Soc Exp Biol Med. 1942;49:141–144.
43. Branham SE. Serological relationship among meningococci. Bacteriol Rev. 1953;17:175–188.
44. Branham SE. Reference strains for the serologic groups of meningococcus (*Neisseria meningitidis*). Int Bull Bacteriol Nomenclature Taxonomy. 1958;8:1–15.
45. Slaterus K. Serological typing of meningococci by means of microprecipitation. Antonie Van Leeuwenhoek. 1961;27:304–315.
46. Evans JR, Artenstein MS, Hunter DH. Prevalence of meningococcal serogroups and a description of new groups. Am J Epidemiol. 1968;87:643–646.
47. Ding S, Ye R, Zhang H. Three new serogroups of *Neisseria meningitidis*. J Biol Stand. 1981;9:305–315.
48. Ashton FE, Ryan A, Diena B, et al. A new serogroup (L) of *Neisseria meningitidis*. J Clin Microbiol. 1983;17:722–727.

49. Gotschlich EC, Liu TY, Artenstein MS. Preparation and immunochemical properties of the group A, group B, and group C meningococcal polysaccharides. J Exp Med. 1969;129:1349–1365.
50. Bundle DR, Jennings JH, Kenny CP. Studies on the group specific polysaccharide of *Neisseria meningitidis* serogroup X and an improved procedure for its isolation. J Biol Chem. 1974;249:4797–4801.
51. Robinson JA, Apicella MA. Isolation and characterization of *Neisseria meningitidis* groups A, C, X and Y polysaccharide antigens. Infect Immun. 1970;1:8–14.
52. Apicella MA. Identification of a subgroup antigen on the *Neisseria meningitidis* group C capsular polysaccharide. J Infect Dis. 1974;129:147–153.
53. Apicella MA. Immunological and biochemical studies of meningococcal C polysaccharide isolated by diethylaminoethyl chromatography. Infect Immun. 1976; 14:106–113.
54. Watson RG, Marinetti GV, Scherp HW. The specific hapten of group C (group II) meningococcus. II. Chemical nature. J Immunol. 1958;81:337–344.
55. Brandt BL, Artenstein MS, Smith CD. Antibody response to meningococcal polysaccharide vaccines. Infect Immun. 1973;8:590–596.
56. Liu TY, Gotschlich EC, Dunne FT, et al. Studies on meningococcal polysaccharides. II. Composition and chemical properties of the group B and group C polysaccharide. J Biol Chem. 1971;246:4703–4712.
57. Bhattacharjee AK, Jennings HJ, Kenny CP, et al. Structural determination of the sialic acid polysaccharide antigens of *Neisseria meningitidis* serogroup B and C with carbon 13 nuclear magnetic resonance. J Biol Chem. 1975;250:1926–1932.
58. Maloney PC, Schneider H, Brandt BL. Production and degrading of serogroup B *Neisseria meningitidis* polysaccharide. Infect Immun. 1972;6:657–661.
59. Wyle FA, Artenstein MS, Brandt BL, et al. Immunologic response of man to group B meningococcal polysaccharide vaccines. J Infect Dis. 1972;126:514–522.
60. Bhattacharjee AK, Jennings JH, Kenny CP. Characterization of 3-deoxy-D-manno-octulosonic acid as a component of the capsular polysaccharide antigen from *Neisseria meningitidis* serogroup 29E. Biochem Biophys Res Commun. 1974;61:489–493.
61. Griffiss JM, Brandt BL, Broud DO. Human immune response to various doses of group Y and W135 meningococcal polysaccharide vaccines. Infect Immun. 1982;37:205–208.
62. Mandrell RE, Zollinger WD. Lipopolysaccharide serotyping of *Neisseria meningitidis* by hemagglutination inhibition. Infect Immun. 1977;16:471–475.
63. Jennings HL, Johnson KG, Kenne L. The structure of the R-type oligosaccharide core obtained from some lipopolysaccharides of *Neisseria meningitidis.* Carbohydr Res. 1983;121:233–241.
64. Gamian A, Beurret M, Michon F, et al. Structure of the L2 lipopolysaccharide core oligosaccharides of *Neisseria meningitidis.* J Biol Chem. 1992;267:922–925.
65. Jones DM, Borrow R, Fox AJ, et al. The lipooligosaccharide immunotype as a virulence determinant in *Neisseria meningitidis.* Microbiol Pathol. 1992;13:219–224.
66. Verheul AFM, Snippe H, Poolman JT. Meningococcal lipopolysaccharides: Virulence factor and potential vaccine component. Microbiol Rev. 1993;57:34–49.
67. Estabrook MM, Baker CJ, Griffiss JM. The immune response of children to meningococcal lipooligosaccharides during disseminated disease is directed primarily against two monoclonal antibody–defined epitopes. J Infect Dis. 1993;167:966–970.
68. Gold R, Wyle FA. New classification of *Neisseria meningitidis* by means of bactericidal reactions. Infect Immun. 1970;1:479–484.
69. Gold R, Winklehake JL, Mars RS, et al. Identification of epidemic strain of group C *Neisseria meningitidis* by bactericidal serotyping. J Infect Dis. 1971;124:593–597.
70. Frasch CE, Chapman SS. Classification of *Neisseria meningitidis* group B into distinct serotypes. III. Application of a new bactericidal-inhibition technique to distribution of serotypes among cases and carriers. J Infect Dis. 1973;127:149–154.
71. Frasch CE, Golschlich EC. Noncapsular surface antigens of *Neisseria meningitidis.* In: Weinstein L, Fields BN, eds. Seminars in Infectious Diseases. New York: Stratton; 1979:304–337.
72. Broud DD, Griffiss JM, Baker CJ. Heterogeneity of serotypes of *Neisseria meningitidis* that cause endemic disease. J Infect Dis. 1979;140:465–470.
73. Kawula TH, Spinola SM, Klapper DG, et al. Localization of a conserved epitope and an azurin-like domain in the H.8 protein of pathogenic *Neisseria.* Mol Microbiol. 1987;1:179–185.
74. Barlow AK, Heckels JE, Clarke IN. Molecular cloning and expression of *Neisseria meningitidis* class 1 outer membrane protein in *Escherichia coli* K-12. Infect Immun. 1987;55:2734–2740.
75. Frasch CE, Zollinger WD, Poolman JT. Proposed schema for identification of serotypes of *Neisseria meningitidis.* In: Schoolnik GK, ed. The Pathogenic Neisseria. Washington, DC: American Society for Microbiology; 1985:519–524.
76. Selander RK, Caugant DA, Ochman H, et al. Methods of multilocus enzyme electrophoresis for bacterial populations genetics and systematics. Appl Environ Microbiol. 1986;132:2855–2861.
77. Olyhoek T, Crowe B, Achtman M. Epidemiological analysis and geographic distribution of *Neisseria meningitidis* group A. In: Schoolnik GK, ed. The Pathogenic Neisseria. Washington, DC: American Society for Microbiology; 1985:530–535.
78. Caugant DA, Mocca IF, Frasch CE, et al. Genetic structure of *Neisseria meningitidis* populations in relation to serogroup, serotype, and outer membrane protein pattern. J Bacteriol. 1987;169:2781–2792.
79. Pinner R, Spellmam P, Stephens DS. Evidence for functionally distinct pili expressed by *Neisseria meningitidis.* Infect Immun. 1991;59:3169–3175.
80. DeVoe IW, Gilchrist JE. Piliation and colonial morphology among laboratory strains of meningococci. J Clin Microbiol. 1978;7:379–384.
81. DeVoe IW, Gilchrist JE. Pili on meningococci from primary culture of nasopharyngeal carriers and cerebrospinal fluid of patients with acute disease. J Exp Med. 1975;141:297–305.
82. Stephens DS, McGee ZA. Attachment of *Neisseria meningitidis* to human mucosal surfaces: Influence of pili and type of receptor cell. J Infect Dis. 1981;143:525–532.
83. McGee ZA, Dourmashkin RR, Gross JG, et al. Relationship of pili to colonial morphology. Infect Immun. 1979;24:194–201.
84. Kallstrom H, Liszewski MK, Atkinson JP, et al. Membrane cofactor protein (MCP or CD46) is a cellular pilus receptor for pathogenic *Neisseria.* Mol Microbiol. 1997;25:639–647.
85. Virji M, Makepeace K, Ferguson DJ, et al. Meningococcal Opa and Opc proteins: Their role in colonization and invasion of human epithelial and endothelial cells. Mol Microbiol. 1993;10:499–510.
86. Hammerschmidt S, Hilse R, van Putten JPM, et al. Modulation of cell surface sialic acid expression in *Neisseria meningitidis* via a transposable genetic element. EMBO J. 1996;15:192–198.
87. Virji M, Makepeace K, Peak IR, et al. Pathogenic mechanisms of pathogenic *Neisseria.* Ann N Y Acad Sci. 1995;797:273–276.
88. Lin L, Ayala P, Larson J, et al. The *Neisseria* type 2 IgA1 protease cleaves LAMP1 and promotes survival of bacteria within epithelial cells. Mol Microbiol. 1997;24:1083–1094.
88a. Lin L, Ayala P, Larson J, et al. The *Neisseria* IgA1 protease cleaves LAMP1 and promotes survival of bacteria within epithelial cells. Mol Microbiol. 1997;24:1083–1094.
89. Nassif X, Marceau M, Pujol C, et al. Type-4 pili and meningococcal adhesiveness. Gene. 1997;192:149–153.
90. Goldschneider I, Gotschlich EC, Artenstein MS. Human immunity to the meningococcus. I. The role of humoral antibody. J Exp Med. 1969;129:1307–1326.
91. Goldschneider I, Gotschlich EC, Artenstein MS. Human immunity to the meningococcus. II. Development of natural immunity. J Exp Med. 1969;129:1327–1328.
92. Robbins JB, Myerowitz RL, Whesnant JK, et al. Enteric bacteria cross-reactive with *Neisseria meningitidis* groups A and C and *Diplococcus pneumoniae* types I and II. Infect Immun. 1972;6:651–656.
93. Grados O, Ewing WH. Antigenic relationship between *Escherichia coli* and *Neisseria meningitidis.* J Infect Dis. 1970;122:100–103.
94. Finne J, Bitter-Suermann D, Goudis C, et al. An IgG monoclonal antibody to group B meningococci cross reacts with developmentally regulated polysialic acid units of glycoproteins in neural and extraneural tissue. J Immunol. 1987;138:4402–4407.
95. Greenwood BM, Greenwood AM, Bradley AK, et al. Factors influencing the susceptibility to meningococcal disease during an epidemic in The Gambia, West Africa. J Infect. 1987;14:167–184.
96. Käyhty H, Jousimies-Somer H, Peltola H, et al. Antibody response to capsular polysaccharides of groups A and C *Neisseria meningitidis* and *Haemophilus influenzae* type b during bacteremic disease. J Infect Dis. 1981;143:32–41.
97. Plaut AG, Gilbert JV, Artenstein MS, et al. *Neisseria gonorrhoeae* and *Neisseria meningitidis*: Extracellular enzyme cleaves human immunoglobulin A. Science. 1975;190:1103–1105.
98. Mulks M, Plaut AG. IgA protease production as a characteristic distinguishing pathogenic from harmless Neisseriaceae. N Engl J Med. 1978;299:973–976.
99. Bruns H, Hohn J. Meningokokken im Nasenrachenram. Klin Jahrb Jena. 1908;28: 285.
100. Rake G. Studies on meningococcus infection. VI. The carrier problem. J Exp Med. 1934;59:553.
101. Greenfield S, Sheede PR, Feldman HA. Meningococcal carriage in a population of "normal" families. J Infect Dis. 1971;123:67–73.
102. Edwards EA, Devine LF, Sengbusch CH, et al. Immunological investigations of meningococcal disease. III. Brevity of group c acquisition prior to disease occurrence. Scand J Infect Dis. 1987;9:105–110.
103. Wenzel RP, Davies JA, Mitzel JR, et al. Nonusefulness of meningococcal carriage rates. Lancet. 1973;2:205.
104. Olcen P, Kellander J, Danielsson D, et al. Epidemiology of *Neisseria meningitidis* prevalence and symptoms from the upper respiratory tract in family members to patients with meningococcal disease. Scand J Infect Dis. 1981;13:105–109.
105. Moore PS, Hierholzer J, DeWitt W, et al. Respiratory viruses and mycoplasma as cofactors for epidemic group A meningococcal meningitis. JAMA. 1990;264:1271–1275.
106. Reller BL, MacGregor RR, Beaty HN. Bactericidal antibody after colonization with *Neisseria meningitidis.* J Infect Dis. 1973;127:56–62.
107. Broome CV. The carrier state: *Neisseria meningitidis.* J Antimicrob Chemother. 1986;18(Suppl A):S25–S34.
108. Feldman HA. Meningococcal infections. Adv Intern Med. 1972;18:117–140.
109. Centers for Disease Control and Prevention. Summary of notifiable diseases, United States. MMWR Morb Mortal Wkly Rep. 1996;45:1–103.
110. Peltola H. Meningococcal disease: Still with us. Rev Infect Dis. 1983;5:71–91.
111. Peltola H, Kataja JM, Makela PH. Shift in the age distribution of meningococcal disease as predictor of an epidemic. Lancet. 1982;2:595–597.
112. Andersen BM. Mortality in meningococcal infections. Scand J Infect Dis. 1978;10:277–282.
113. deMorais JS, Munford RS, Risi JB, et al. Epidemic disease due to serogroup C *Neisseria meningitidis* in Sao Paulo, Brazil. J Infect Dis. 1974;129:568–571.
114. Oberli J, Hoi NT, Caravano R, et al. Etude d'une epidemie de meningococcie au Viet Nam (provinces du Sud). Bull World Health Organ. 1981;59:585–590.
115. The Meningococcal Disease Surveillance Group. Analysis of endemic meningococcal disease by serogroup and evaluation of chemoprophylaxis. J Infect Dis. 1976;134:201.
116. Schwartz B, Moore P, Broome CV. Global epidemiology of meningococcal disease. Clin Rev Microbiol. 1989;2(Suppl):S118–S124.
117. Greenwood BM. The epidemiology of acute bacterial meningitis in tropical Africa.

In: Williams JD, Burnet J, eds. Bacterial Meningitis. New York: Academic Press; 1987:61–92.
118. Tikhomirov E, Santamaria M, Esteves K. Meningococcal disease: Public health burden and control. World Health Stat Q. 1997;50:170–177.
119. Reingold AL, Hightower AW, Bolan GA, et al. Age specific differences in duration of clinical protection after vaccination with meningococcal polysaccharide vaccine. Lancet. 1985;2:114–118.
120. Wolfe RE, Birbara CA. Meningococcal infections at an army training center. Am J Med. 1968;44:243–255.
121. Sullivan TD, LaScolea LJ. *Neisseria meningitidis* bacteremia in children: Quantitation of bacteremia and spontaneous clinical recovery without antibiotic therapy. Pediatrics. 1987;80:63–87.
122. Carpenter RR, Petersdorf RG. The clinical spectrum of bacterial meningitis. Am J Med. 1962;33:262–275.
123. Feigin RD, Dodge PR. Bacterial meningitis: Newer concepts of pathophysiology and neurologic sequelae. Pediatr Clin North Am. 1976;23:541–556.
124. Thomas HM. Meningococcic meningitis and septicemia. Report of an outbreak in the fourth service command during the winter and spring of 1942–1943. JAMA. 1943;123:264–272.
125. Ducker TB, Simmons RL. The pathogenesis of meningitis. Systemic effects of meningococcal endotoxin within the cerebrospinal fluid. Arch Neurol. 1968;18:123–128.
126. Hardman JM. Fatal meningococcal infections: The changing pathologic picture in the '60's. Mil Med. 1968;133:951–964.
127. Brandtzaeg P, Oktedalen O, Kierulf P, et al. Elevated VIP and endotoxin plasma levels in human gram-negative septic shock. Regul Pept. 1989;24:37–44.
128. Brandtzaeg P, Kierulf P, Gaustad P, et al. Plasma endotoxin as a predictor of multiple organ failure and death in systemic meningococcal disease. J Infect Dis. 1989;159:195–204.
129. Brandtzaeg P, Ovsteboo R, Kierulf P. Compartmentalization of lipopolysaccharide production correlates with clinical presentation in meningococcal disease. J Infect Dis. 1992;166:650–652.
130. Brandtzaeg P, Mollnes TE, Kierulf P. Complement activation and endotoxin levels in systemic meningococcal disease. J Infect Dis. 1989;160:58–65.
131. Brandtzaeg P, Sandset PM, Joo GB, et al. The quantitative association of plasma endotoxin, antithrombin, protein C, extrinsic pathway inhibitor and fibrinopeptide A in systemic meningococcal disease. Thromb Res. 1989;55:459–470.
132. Brandtzaeg PK, Bryn P, Kierulf P, et al. Meningococcal endotoxin in lethal septic shock plasma studied by gas chromatography, mass-spectrometry, ultracentrifugation, and electron microscopy. J Clin Invest. 1992;89:816–823.
133. Cesarini JP, Vandekerkove M, Faucon R, et al. Ultrastructure of the wall of *Neisseria meningitidis* (in French). Ann Inst Pasteur. 1967;113:833–841.
134. Devoe IW, Gilchrist JE. Release of endotoxin in the form of cell wall blebs during in vitro growth of *Neisseria meningitidis*. J Exp Med. 1973;138:1156–1167.
135. Levin S, Painter MB. The treatment of acute meningococcal infection in adults. Ann Intern Med. 1966;64:1049–1056.
136. Kanter DM, Mauriello DA, Learner N. Acute meningococcemia with vascular collapse: An analysis of 10 recently treated cases. Am J Med Sci. 1956;232:674–687.
137. Gore I, Saphir Q. Myocarditis, a classification of 1402 cases. Am Heart J. 1947;34:827–831.
138. Boucek MM, Boerth RC, Artman M, et al. Myocardial dysfunction in children with acute meningococcemia. J Pediatr. 1984;105:538–542.
139. Gotschall RA. Conus medullaris syndrome after meningococcal meningitis. N Engl J Med. 1972;286:882–883.
140. Herman RA, Rubin HA. Meningococcal pericarditis without meningitis presenting as tamponade. N Engl J Med. 1974;290:143–144.
141. Morse JR, Oretsky MI, Hudson JA. Pericarditis as a complication of meningococcal meningitis. Ann Intern Med. 1971;74:212–217.
142. Pierce I, Cooper E. Meningococcal pericarditis, clinical features and therapy in five patients. Arch Intern Med. 1972;129:918–922.
143. Maron BJ, Macoul KL, Benaron P. Unusual complications of meningococcal meningitis. Johns Hopkins Med J. 1972;131:64–68.
144. Brasier AR, Macklis JD, Vaughn D, et al. Myopericarditis as an initial presentation of meningococcemia. Unusual manifestations of infection with serotype W135. Am J Med. 1987;82:641–644.
145. Frank ST, Gomez RM. Chronic meningococcemia. Mil Med. 1968;133:918–920.
146. Saslaw S. Chronic meningococcemia: Report of a case. N Engl J Med. 1962;266:605–607.
147. Rompalo AM, Hood EW, Roberts PL, et al. The acute arthritis dermatitis syndrome. The changing importance of *Neisseria gonorrhoeae* and *Neisseria meningitidis*. Arch Intern Med. 1987;147:281–283.
148. Lim D, Gewurz A, Lint TF, et al. Absence of the sixth component of complement in a patient with repeated episodes of meningococcal meningitis. J Pediatr. 1976;89:42.
149. Alper CA, Abramson N, Johnston RB Jr. Increased susceptibility to infection associated with abnormalities of complement-mediated functions and of the third component of complement (C3). N Engl J Med. 1970;282:349–354.
150. Petersen BH, Graham JA, Brooks GF. Human deficiency of the eighth component of complement. The requirement of C8 for serum *Neisseria gonorrhoeae* bactericidal activity. J Clin Invest. 1976;57:283–290.
151. Ellison RT, Kohler PF, Curd JG, et al. Prevalence of congenital or acquired complement deficiency in patients with sporadic meningococcal disease. N Engl J Med. 1983;308:913–916.
152. Densen P, Weiler JM, Griffiss JM, et al. Familial properdin deficiency and fatal bacteremia. Correction of the bactericidal defect by vaccination. N Engl J Med. 1987;316:922–926.
153. Ross SC, Rosenthal PJ, Berberich HM, et al. Killing of *Neisseria meningitidis* by human neutrophils: Implications for normal and complement deficient individuals. J Infect Dis. 1987;155:1266–1275.
154. Densen P. Complement deficiencies and meningococcal disease. Clin Exp Immunol. 1991;86(Suppl 1):S57–S62.
155. Holm MI, Davison WC. Meningococcus pneumonia: I. The occurrence of post-influenzal pneumonia in which *Diplococcus intracellularis meningitidis* was isolated. Bull Johns Hopkins Hosp. 1919;30:324.
156. Koppes GM, Ellenbogen C, Gebhart RJ. Group Y meningococcal disease in United States Air Force recruits. Am J Med. 1977;62:661–666.
157. Putsch RW, Hamilton JD, Wolinsky E. *Neisseria meningitidis*, a respiratory pathogen. J Infect Dis. 1970;121:48–54.
158. Irwin RS, Woelk WK, Coudon WL. Primary meningococcal pneumonia. Ann Intern Med. 1975;82:493–498.
159. Young LS, LaForce FM, Head JJ, et al. A simultaneous outbreak of meningococcal and influenza infections. N Engl J Med. 1972;287:5–9.
160. Goldstein E, Buhlers WC, Akers TC, et al. Murine resistance to inhaled *Neisseria meningitidis* after infection with an encephalomyocarditis virus. Infect Immun. 1972;6:398–402.
161. Kerttula Y, Leinonen M, Koskela M, et al. The etiology of pneumonia, application of bacterial serology and basic laboratory methods. J Infect. 1987;14:21–30.
162. Tobin JL. Complications of meningococcus infection in a series of sixty-three consecutive sporadic cases. Am J Med Sci. 1956;231:241–248.
163. McCracken GH. Rapid identification of specific etiology in meningitis. J Pediatr. 1976;88:706–708.
164. Miller M, Millikin P, Griffin PS, et al. *Neisseria meningitidis* urethritis: A case report. Arch Intern Med. 1979;242:1656–1657.
165. Faur YC, Weisburd MH, Wilson ME. Isolation of *Neisseria meningitidis* from the genitourinary tract and anal canal. J Clin Microbiol. 1975;2:178–182.
166. Salet IE, Frasch CE. Seroepidemiologic aspects of *Neisseria meningitidis* in homosexual men. Can Med Assoc J. 1982;126:38–41.
167. Hoyne AL, Brown RH. 727 Meningococcic cases, an analysis. Ann Intern Med. 1948;28:248–259.
168. Feldman WE. Relation of concentrations of bacteria and bacterial antigen in cerebrospinal fluid to prognosis in patients with bacterial meningitis. N Engl J Med. 1977;296:433–435.
169. Feldman WE. Concentrations of bacteria in cerebrospinal fluid of patients with bacterial meningitis. J Pediatr. 1976;88:549–552.
170. Feigin RD, Stechenberg BW, Chang MJ. Prospective evaluation of treatment of *Hemophilus influenzae* meningitis. J Pediatr. 1976;88:542–548.
171. O'Toole RD, Goode L, Howe C. Neuraminidase activity in bacterial meningitis. J Clin Invest. 1971;50:979–985.
172. Beaty HN. Cerebrospinal fluid lactic dehydrogenase and its isoenzymes in infection of the central nervous system. N Engl J Med. 1968;279:1197–202.
173. Newcombe J, Cartwright K, Palmer WH, et al. PCR of peripheral blood for diagnosis of meningococcal disease. J Clin Microbiol. 1996;34:1637–1640.
174. Borrow R, Claus H, Chaudhry U, et al. siaD PCR ELISA for confirmation and identification of serogroup Y and W135 meningococcal infections. FEMS Microbiol Lett. 1998;159:209–214.
175. Speers DJ, Jelfs J. Typing of *Neisseria meningitidis* by restriction analysis of the amplified *porA* gene. Pathology. 1997;29:201–205.
176. Newcombe J, Dyer S, Blackwell L, et al. PCR–single-stranded conformational polymorphism analysis for non–culture-based subtyping of meningococcal strains in clinical specimens. J. Clin Microbiol. 1997;35:1809–1812.
177. Feldman HA, Sweet LA, Dowling HF. Sulfadiazine therapy of purulent meningitis. War Med. 1942;2:995–1007.
178. Mead M, Harris W, Samper BA, et al. Treatment of meningococcal meningitis with penicillin. N Engl J Med. 1944;231:509–517.
179. Kinsman JM, D'Alonzo CA. Meningococcemia: A description of the clinical picture and a comparison of the efficacy of sulfadiazine and penicillin in the treatment of thirty cases. Ann Intern Med. 1946;24:606–617.
180. McCrumb FR, Hall HE, Meridith AM, et al. Chloramphenicol in the treatment of meningococcal meningitis. Am J Med. 1951;10:696–703.
181. Mangi RJ, Kundargi RS, Quintiliani R, et al. Development of meningitis during cephalothin therapy. Ann Intern Med. 1973;78:347–351.
182. Brown JD, Mathies AW, Ivler D, et al. Variable results of cephalothin therapy for meningococcal meningitis. In: Hobby G, ed. Antimicrobial Agents and Chemotherapy. 1969. Bethesda, Md: American Society for Microbiology; 1970:432.
183. Schribner RK, Wedro BC, Weber AH, et al. Activities of eight new beta-lactam and seven antibiotic combinations against *Neisseria meningitidis*. Antimicrob Agents Chemother. 1982;21:678–680.
184. Neu HC. Cephalosporins in the treatment of meningitis. Drugs. 1987;34(Suppl 2):S135–S153.
185. Centers for Disease Control and Prevention. Control and prevention of meningococcal disease and control and prevention of serogroup C meningococcal diseases: Evaluation and management of suspected outbreaks. MMWR Morb Mortal Wkly Rep. 1997;46(RR-5):1–22.
186. Anonymous. Meningococcal disease prevention and control strategies for practice-based physicians. Committee on Infectious Diseases, American Academy of Pediatrics, Infectious Diseases and Immunization Committee, Canadian Paediatric Society. Pediatrics. 1996;97:404–412.
187. Love BD, Finland M. In vitro susceptibility of meningococcus to 11 antibiotics and sulfadiazine. Am J Med. 1954;228:534–539.

188. Brown JW, Condit PK. Meningococcal infections: Fort Ord and California. Calif Med. 1965;102:171–180.
189. Eickhoff TC, Finland M. Changing susceptibility of meningococci to antimicrobial agents. N Engl J Med. 1965;272:395–398.
190. Feldman HA. Sulfonamide resistant meningococci. Annu Rev Med. 1967;18:495–506.
191. Alexander CE, Sanborn WR, Cherriere G, et al. Sulfadiazine resistant group A *Neisseria meningitidis*. Science. 1968;161:1019.
192. Scheld WM, Sande M. Bactericidal versus bacteriostatic antibiotic therapy of experimental pneumococcal meningitis in rabbits. J Clin Invest. 1983;71:411–419.
193. Berkow R, ed. The Merck Manual of Diagnosis and Therapy. Rahway, NJ: Merck Sharp & Dohme; 1977:1432.
194. Sprott MS, Kearns AM, Field JM. Penicillin insensitive *Neisseria meningitidis* (Letter). Lancet. 1988;1:1167.
195. Mendelman PM, Campos J, Chaffin DO, et al. Relative penicillin G resistance in *Neisseria meningitidis* and reduced affinity of penicillin binding protein 3. Antimicrob Agents Chemother. 1988;32:706–709.
196. Saez-Nieto JA, Lujan R, Berron S, et al. Epidemiology and molecular basis of penicillin-resistant *Neisseria meningitidis* in Spain: A 5-year history (1985–1989). Clin Infect Dis. 1992;14:394–402.
197. Galimand M, Gerbaud G, Guibourdenche M, et al. High level chloramphenicol resistance in *Neisseria meningitidis*. N Engl J Med. 1998;339:868–874.
198. Shaad UB, Krucko J, Pfenninger J. An extended experience with cefuroxime therapy of childhood bacterial meningitis. Pediatr Infect Dis. 1984;3:410–415.
199. Pfenniger J, Schaad UB, Lutschag J, et al. Cefuroxime in bacterial meningitis. Arch Dis Child. 1982;57:539–543.
200. Humbert G, Leroy A, Nair SR, et al. Concentration of cefotaxime and the desacetyl metabolite in serum and CSF of patients with meningitis. J Antimicrob Chemother. 1984;13:487–494.
201. Latif R, Dajani AS. Ceftriaxone diffusion into cerebrospinal fluid of children with meningitis. Antimicrob Agents Chemother. 1983;23:46–48.
202. Modai J, Vittecoq D, Decazes JM, et al. Penetration of ceftazidime into cerebrospinal fluid of patients with bacterial meningitis. Antimicrob Agents Chemother. 1983;24:126–128.
203. Fu KP, Neu H. Antimicrobial activity of ceftizoxime, a beta lactamase–stable cephalosporin. Antimicrob Agents Chemother. 1980;17:583–590.
204. Jones RN, Barry AL, Thornsberry C. Ceftriaxone: A summary of in vitro antibacterial susceptibility tests with 30 μg disks. Diagn Microbiol Infect Dis. 1983;1:295–311.
205. Phillips I, Warren C, Shannon K, et al. Ceftazidime: In vitro antibacterial activity and susceptibility to beta-lactamases compared with that of cefotaxime, moxalactam and other beta-lactam antibiotics. J Antimicrob Chemother. 1981;8(Suppl B):S23–S31.
206. Cartwright K, Reilly S, White D, et al. Early treatment with parenteral penicillin in meningococcal disease. BMJ. 1992;305:143–147.
207. Strang JR, Pugh EJ. Meningococcal infections: Reducing the case fatality rate by giving penicillin before admission to hospital. BMJ. 1992;305:141–143.
208. Barquet N, Domingo P, Cayla JA, et al. Prognostic factors of a bedside predictive model and scoring system. JAMA. 1997;278:491–496.
209. Waage A, Brandtzaeg P, Halstensen A, et al. The complex pattern of cytokines in serum from patients with meningococcal septic shock. J Exp Med. 1989;169:333–338.
210. Beutler B, Milsark IW, Cerami AC. Passive immunization against cachectin/tumor necrosis factor protects mice from the lethal effects of endotoxin. Science. 1985;229:869–871.
211. Beutler B, Cerami A. Cachectin: More than a tumor necrosis factor. N Engl J Med. 1987;316:379–385.
212. Tracey KJ, Beutler B, Lowry SF, et al. Shock and tissue injury induced by recombinant human cachectin. Science. 1986;234:470–474.
213. Tracey KJ, Fong Y, Hesse DG, et al. Anti-cachectin/TNF monoclonal antibodies prevent septic shock during lethal bacteremia. Nature. 1987;330:662–664.
214. Girardin E, Grau GE, Dayr JM, et al. Tumor necrosis factor and interleukin-1 in the serum of children with severe infectious purpura. N Engl J Med. 1988;319:397–400.
215. Girior BP, Quint PA, Barton P, et al. Preliminary evaluation of recombinant amino-terminal fragment of human bactericidal/permeability-increasing protein in children with severe meningococcal sepsis. Lancet. 1997;350:1439–1443.
216. Monsalve F, Rucabado L, Salvador A, et al. Myocardial depression in septic shock caused by meningococcal infection. Crit Care Med. 1984;12:1021–1032.
217. de la Cal MA, Miravalles E, Pascual T, et al. Dose-related hemodynamic and renal effects of dopamine in septic shock. Crit Care Med. 1984;12:22–25.
218. Fisher CJ, Horowilx BZ, Albertson TE. Cardiorespiratory failure in toxic shock syndrome: Effect of dobutamine. Crit Care Med. 1985;13:160–165.
219. Duff P. Pathophysiology and management of septic shock. J Reprod Med. 1980;24:109–117.
220. Belsey MA, Hoffpauir CW, Smith MHD: Dexamethasone in the treatment of acute bacterial meningitis: The effect of study design on the interpretation of results. Pediatrics. 1969;44:503–513.
221. Corrigan JJ Jr, Jordan CM. Heparin therapy in septicemia with disseminated intravascular coagulation. Effect on mortality and on correction of hemostatic defects. N Engl J Med. 1970;283:778–782.
222. Denmark TC, Knight EL. Cardiovascular and coagulation complications of group C meningococcal disease. Arch Intern Med. 1971;127:238.
223. Kornelisse RF, Hazelzet JA, Hop WCJ, et al. Meningococcal septic shock in children: Clinical and laboratory features, outcome, and development of a prognostic score. Clin Infect Dis. 1997;25:640–646.
224. Niklasson P-M, Lundbergh P, Strandell T. Prognostic factors in meningococcal disease. Scand J Infect Dis. 1971;3:17–25.
225. LeClerc F, Chenaud M, Delepoulle F, et al. Prognostic value of C-reactive protein level in severe infectious purpura: A comparison with eight other scores. Crit Care Med. 1991;19:430–432.
226. Pollack MM, Ruttimann UE, Getson PR. Pediatric risk of mortality (PRISM) score. Crit Care Med. 1988;16:1–25.
227. Fairbrother RW. Cerebrospinal meningitis: The use of sulphonamide derivatives in prophylaxis. BMJ. 1940;2:859–862.
228. Gray FC, Gear J. Sulphapyridine, M and B 693 as a prophylactic against cerebrospinal meningitis. S Afr Med J. 1941;15:139.
229. Aycock WL, Mueller JH. Meningococcus carrier rates and meningitis incidence. Bacteriol Rev. 1950;14:115–160.
230. Cheever FS. The control of meningococcal meningitis by mass chemoprophylaxis with sulfadiazine. Am J Med Sci. 1945;209:74–75.
231. Artenstein MS, Lamson TH, Evans JR. Attempted prophylaxis against meningococcal infection using intramuscular penicillin. Mil Med. 1967;132:1009–1011.
232. Guttler RB, Counts GW, Avent CK, et al. Effect of rifampin and minocycline on meningococcal carrier rates. J Infect Dis. 1971;124:199–205.
233. Devine LF, Johnson DP, Rhode SL, et al. Rifampin: Effect of two day treatment on meningococcal carrier state and the relationship of the levels of drug in sera and saliva. Am J Med Sci. 1971;261:79–83.
234. Jacobson JA, Daniel B. Vestibular reactions associated with minocycline. Antimicrob Agents Chemother. 1975;8:453–456.
235. Weidner CE, Dunkel TB, Pettyjohn FS, et al. Effectiveness of rifampin in eradicating the meningococcal carrier state in a relatively closed population: Emergence of resistant strains. J Infect Dis. 1971;124:172–178.
236. Pugsley MP, Dworzack DI, Horowitz EA, et al. Efficacy of ciprofloxacin in treatment of nasopharyngeal carriers of *Neisseria meningitidis*. J Infect Dis. 1987;156:211–213.
237. Hoeprich PD. Prediction of antimeningococcic chemoprophylactic efficacy. J Infect Dis. 1971;123:125–133.
238. DeWals P, Herlozhe L, Borlee-Grimee I, et al. Meningococcal disease in Belgium. Secondary attack rate among household day-care nursery and pre-elementary school contacts. J Infect. 1983;1(Suppl 1):S53–S61.
239. Artenstein MS, Ellis RE. The risk of exposure to a patient with meningococcal meningitis. Mil Med. 1968;133:474–477.
240. Centers for Disease Control and Prevention. Meningococcal infections—United States, 1981. MMWR Morb Mortal Wkly Rep. 1981;30:113–115.
241. Makela PH, Kayhty H, Weekstrom P, et al. Effect of group A meningococcal vaccine in army recruits in Finland. Lancet. 1975;2:883–886.
242. Taunay A de E, Galvao PA, de Morais JS, et al. Disease prevention by meningococcal serogroup C polysaccharide vaccine in pre-school: Results after eleven months in Sao Paulo, Brazil (Abstract). Pediatr Res. 1974;8:429.
243. Gold R, Lepow ML, Goldschneider I, et al. Clinical evaluation of group A and group C meningococcal polysaccharide vaccines in infants. J Clin Invest. 1975;56:1536–1547.
244. Wahdan MH, Rizh F, El-Akkad AM, et al. A controlled field trial of a serogroup A meningococcal polysaccharide vaccine. Bull World Health Organ. 1973;48:667–673.
245. Brandt B, Artenstein MS. Duration of antibody responses after vaccination with group C *Neisseria meningitidis* polysaccharide. J Infect Dis. 1975;131:569.
246. Advisory Committee on Immunization Practices. Meningococcal polysaccharide vaccines. Ann Intern Med. 1976;84:179–180.
247. Lepow ML, Beeler J, Randolph M, et al. Reactogenicity and immunogenicity of a quadrivalent combined meningococcal vaccine in children. J Infect Dis. 1986;154:1033–1036.
248. Artenstein MS, Brandt B. Immunologic hyporesponsiveness in man to group C meningococcal polysaccharide. J Immunol. 1975;115:5–7.
249. Broome CV. Use of bacterial vaccines for prevention of pneumococcal and meningococcal disease in day care settings. Rev Infect Dis. 1986;8:584–588.
250. Greenwood BM, Bradley AK, Blakebrough IS, et al. The immune response to a meningococcal polysaccharide in an African village. Trans R Soc Trop Med Hyg. 1980;74:340–346.
251. Beuvery EC, van Delft RW, Medema F, et al. Immunological evaluation of meningococcal group C polysaccharide–tetanus toxoid conjugate in mice. Infect Immun. 1983;41:609–617.
252. Lieberman JM, Chiu SS, Wong VK, et al. Safety and immunogenicity of a serogroup A/C *Neisseria meningitidis* oligosaccharide-protein conjugate vaccine in young children. A randomized controlled trial. JAMA. 1996;275:1499–1503.
253. Twumasi PA Jr, Kumah S, Leach A, et al. A trial of a group A plus group C meningococcal polysaccharide-protein conjugate vaccine in African infants. J Infect Dis. 1995;171:632–638.
254. Drabick JJ, Tang DB, Moran EE, et al. A randomized, placebo-controlled study of oral cimetidine as an immunopotentiator of parenteral immunization with a group B meningococcal vaccine. Vaccine. 1997;15:1144–1148.
255. Perkins BA, Jonsdottir K, Briem H, et al. Immunogenicity of two efficacious outer membrane protein–based serogroup B meningococcal vaccines among young adults. J Infect Dis. 1998;177:683–691.
256. Westerink MAJ, Campagnari AA, Wirth MA, et al. Development and characterization of an anti-idiotype antibody to the capsular polysaccharide of *Neisseria meningitidis* serogroup C. Infect Immun. 1988;56:1120–1127.
257. Westerink MAJ, Giardina PC, Apicella MA, et al. Peptide mimicry of the meningococcal group C capsular polysaccharide. Proc Natl Acad Sci U S A. 1995;92:4021–4025.

Chapter 200

Neisseria gonorrhoeae

P. FREDERICK SPARLING
H. HUNTER HANDSFIELD

Gonorrhea is a common bacterial infection that is transmitted almost exclusively by sexual contact or perinatally. It primarily affects the mucous membranes of the lower genital tract and less frequently those of the rectum, oropharynx, and conjunctivae. Ascending genital infection in women leads to the predominant complication of acute salpingitis, one of the most common causes of female infertility in the world. Bacteremic infections, neonatal conjunctivitis, and acute epididymitis are additional important consequences.

Gonorrhea is one of the oldest known human illnesses, and references to venereal urethritis can be found in ancient Chinese writings, the Biblical Old Testament (Leviticus), and other works of antiquity. Galen (AD 130) introduced the term *gonorrhea* ("flow of seed"), presumably as a result of confusion of purulent exudate with semen. The causative organism was described by Neisser in 1879 and was first cultivated in 1882 by Leistikow and Löffler. Although untreated infections were known to heal spontaneously over several weeks or months, reinfections were common; however, it is likely that in men a distinction was often not made between recurrent gonorrhea and nongonococcal urethritis. Many therapies were tried, but not until advent of the sulfonamides in the 1930s and penicillin in 1943 was truly effective therapy available. Growth of fundamental knowledge about the organism and the host response to infection was slow for 80 years, but a remarkable surge of new information began in the 1970s, and currently as much is known of the molecular biology of the gonococcus and the pathogenesis of gonorrhea as for any other bacterial pathogen. Gonorrhea has proved difficult to control in most populations and remains a prime example of the influence that social, behavioral, and demographic factors can have on the epidemiology of an infectious disease despite the availability of effective antimicrobial therapy. Nevertheless, the incidence of infection is now declining rapidly in the United States, and gonorrhea has almost disappeared in some industrialized countries.

THE ORGANISM

Description

Neisseria gonorrhoeae is a nonmotile, non–spore-forming, gram-negative coccus that characteristically grows in pairs (diplococci) with adjacent sides flattened. It closely resembles the related pathogen *Neisseria meningitidis,* as well as several species of nonpathogenic *Neisseria.* All *Neisseria* spp. rapidly oxidize dimethylparaphenylene diamine or tetramethylparaphenylene diamine, the basis of the diagnostic oxidase test. Traditionally, gonococci are differentiated from other *Neisseria* by their ability to grow on selective media; to use glucose but not maltose, sucrose, or lactose; and to reduce nitrites; as well as by their inability to grow well at reduced temperature or on simple nutrient agar.[1, 2]

Growth and Cultivation

Gonococci do not tolerate drying, and patient samples should be inoculated immediately onto appropriate agar medium. Ideally, plates should be incubated immediately, but inoculated plates may safely be held in candle extinction jars at room temperature for several hours before incubation. The medium must be relatively fresh and moist. Growth is best for most strains at 35°C to 37°C, and many freshly isolated strains have a relative or absolute requirement for added CO_2 (approximately 5%). All strains are strictly aerobic under usual growth conditions, but the organism grows anaerobically when nitrite is provided as an electron acceptor. Typical colonies appear in 24 to 48 hours, but on most media viability is rapidly lost after 48 hours because of autolysis.[3]

Gonococci are inhibited by many fatty acids, and it is therefore necessary to incorporate starch or other substances that absorb fatty acids into most media. All strains have complex growth requirements, including requirements for several vitamins, amino acids, iron, and other factors. For clinical purposes, a satisfactory medium is chocolate agar enriched with glucose and other defined supplements.[3] Isolation of gonococci from sites that normally contain high concentrations of saprophytic microorganisms (pharynx, rectum, and cervix) may be difficult because of overgrowth of the hardier normal flora. This problem can be largely overcome by use of media containing antimicrobial agents that inhibit most nonpathogenic *Neisseria* and other species but permit growth of most gonococci (as well as meningococci). Chocolate agar that contains vancomycin, colistin, and nystatin (Thayer-Martin medium) has been commonly used for this purpose in the United States.[4] "Modified" Thayer-Martin medium also contains trimethoprim to inhibit *Proteus* spp. and is now used extensively.[3] A translucent selective medium called New York City medium, also widely used, contains vancomycin, colistin, trimethoprim, and either nystatin or amphotericin B.[5]

Selective media fail to support the growth of some gonococci, in part because some strains are relatively sensitive to vancomycin. The prevalence of these strains varies widely, and in some settings the use of vancomycin-containing media may significantly impair the diagnosis of gonorrhea.[3, 6] Material from sites that usually do not harbor indigenous flora (e.g., blood, synovial fluid, cerebrospinal fluid) should be cultured on antibiotic-free medium.

For use in situations that preclude immediate inoculation of growth medium, transport systems using media with self-contained CO_2-generating systems are available. Some non-nutrient transport media (e.g., Amies' modification of Stuart's medium, variations of which are used in many commercial specimen collection kits) can maintain viable gonococci for up to 6 hours before inoculation into growth media.

Surface Structures

The envelope of *N. gonorrhoeae* is similar in basic structure to that of other gram-negative bacteria. As the interface between the gonococcus and host, the cell surface has been intensively studied (Fig. 200–1), and specific surface components have been related to adherence, tissue and cellular penetration, cytotoxicity, and evasion of host defenses both systemically and at the mucosal level.

Pili

Varied colonial forms can be distinguished when *N. gonorrhoeae* is grown on translucent agar.[7] Fresh clinical isolates initially form colony types P^+ and P^{++} (formerly called T1 and T2), and the organisms have numerous pili extending from the cell surface (Fig. 200–2); P^- (formerly T3 and T4) colonies lack pili. Piliated gonococci are better able to attach to human mucosal surfaces[8] and are more virulent in animal and organ culture models[9, 10] and in human inoculation experiments[7] than nonpiliated variants are. Expression of pili is a function of the *pil* gene complex. After 20 to 24 hours of growth, P^- colonies come to predominate. The shift between P^+ or P^{++} and P^- colony types is known as phase variation and is mediated principally by recombination between incomplete (silent) loci that contain slightly variant copies of *pil* DNA and loci with the complete *pil* structural gene *pilE.*[11, 12] Pili traverse the outer membrane of the gonococcus and are composed of repeating protein subunits (pilin) with a molecular weight of 19 ± 2.5 kD.[2, 8] Pilin

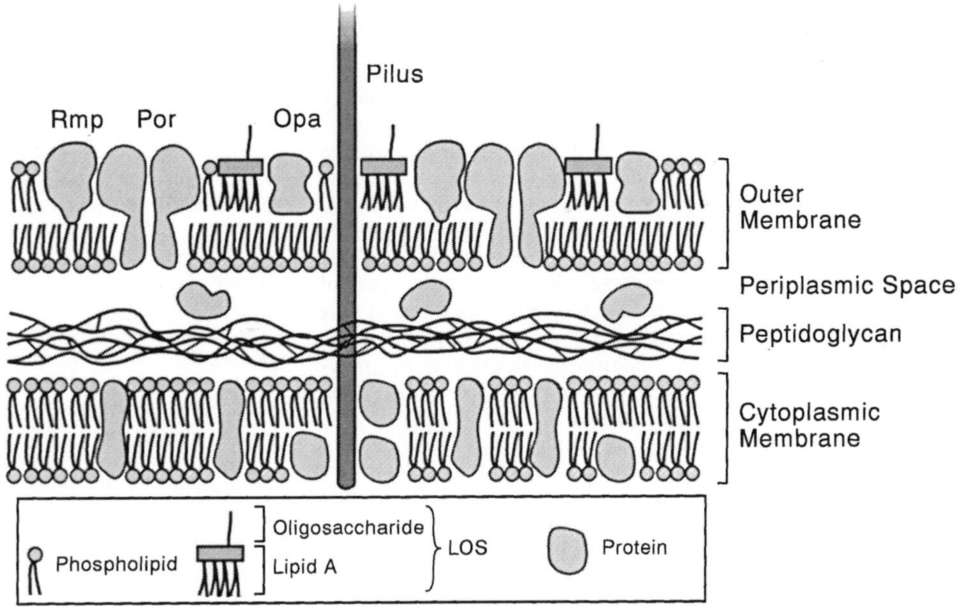

FIGURE 200–1. Schematic representation of the surface structure of *Neisseria gonorrhoeae,* showing the major components that contribute to pathogenicity and antimicrobial resistance. Opa, Por, and Rmp are the designations of the major outer membrane proteins (see text); LOS denotes lipo-oligosaccharide.

has regions of considerable interstrain antigenic similarity, especially near the amino terminus, but areas of extreme antigenic variability are also present.[8, 12] A single strain of *N. gonorrhoeae* is capable of producing pili with differing antigenic composition.[1, 2, 13] These variations have compromised the utility of pilus-based vaccines against gonorrhea, although research continues on the potential of peptides from antigenically conserved regions as the basis for a vaccine.

In addition to mediating attachment, pili contribute to resistance to killing by neutrophils.[14] In the fallopian tube mucosa model (Fig. 200–3), pili facilitate attachment to nonciliated epithelial cells, which initiates a process of entry and transport through these cells into intercellular spaces near the basement membrane or directly into the subepithelial space.[10] Concurrently, nearby ciliated mucosal cells lose their cilia and are sloughed.[10] Recent work has identified CD46 as the pilin receptor.[15] Other factors also mediate attachment, notably, opacity proteins (OPAs), which are discussed in the next section.

Outer Membrane

Like all gram-negative bacteria, the gonococcus possesses a cell envelope composed of three distinct layers: an inner cytoplasmic membrane, a middle peptidoglycan cell wall, and an outer membrane. The outer membrane contains lipo-oligosaccharide (LOS), phospholipid, and a variety of proteins (see Fig. 200–1).

Porin, formerly designated protein I, has a molecular weight of 32 to 36 kD and is closely associated in the membrane with LOS. Porin provides channels that allow aqueous solutes to pass through the otherwise hydrophobic outer membrane and is believed to play an important role in pathogenesis.[16] Porin occurs in two major antigenic classes (PorA and PorB), each of which is composed of many distinct serovars. The serovars are the basis for the most commonly used gonococcal serotyping system.[1, 2, 17] Strains expressing PorA are associated with genotypic resistance of *N. gonorrhoeae* to the bactericidal effect of normal (nonimmune) human serum and, perhaps as a direct result, with an enhanced propensity to cause bacteremia.[1, 2, 17] PorA appears to directly promote invasion of epithelial

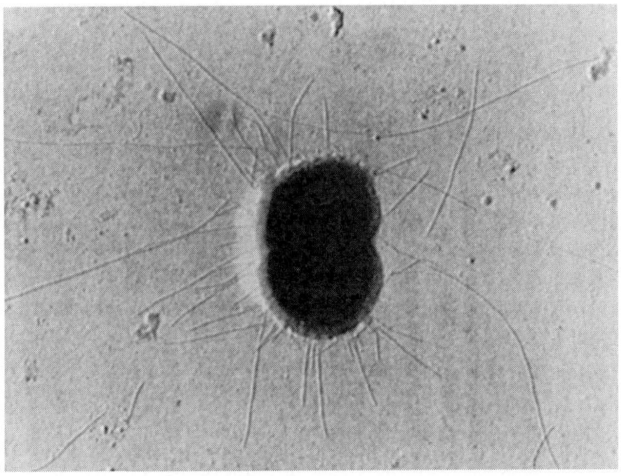

FIGURE 200–2. *Neisseria gonorrhoeae,* with numerous pili extending from the cell surface. (Courtesy of Dr. Gour Biswas, Chapel Hill, NC.)

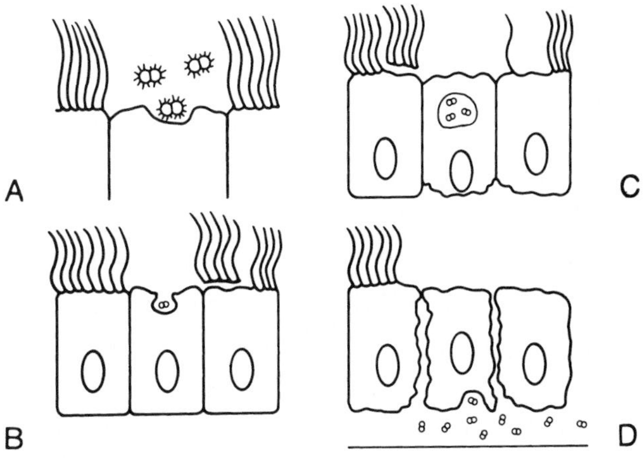

FIGURE 200–3. Schematic representation of the interaction between fallopian tube explant epithelial cells and *Neisseria gonorrhoeae. A,* Attachment of piliated gonococci to surface of nonciliated host cell. *B,* Endocytosis of gonococci; loss of cilia on adjacent cell, mediated by LOS. *C,* Transport of gonococci through epithelial cell in endocytotic vacuole, in which the organism may replicate; progression of LOS-associated cytotoxicity. *D,* Release of organisms into subepithelial space. (From Dallabetta G, Hook EW III. Gonococcal infections. Infect Dis Clin North Am. 1987;1:25–54.)

cells,[18] which also probably helps explain the association between PorA and bacteremia. Porin is the focus of extensive investigation directed toward the development of a gonococcal vaccine.[19]

Opa proteins, formerly called protein II, are outer-membrane proteins with molecular weights of 20 to 28 kD.[1, 2, 20] They are members of a family of proteins, each produced from its own *opa* gene, which may number up to 11 in a single strain.[21] The amino acid sequence of the Opa proteins varies somewhat, primarily because of differences in two hypervariable regions in each protein.[21] When grown on translucent medium, colonies of *N. gonorrhoeae* that lack Opa appear transparent, whereas those with one or more types of Opa are usually opaque.[20] In contrast to porin, expression of Opa varies because of high-frequency variations in *opa* DNA that result in translational frame shifting.[22] An individual strain of *N. gonorrhoeae* can express none or up to 11 Opa variants, but usually not more than 3 at a time.[21, 22]

Opa expression varies considerably during natural infection. For example, most mucosal isolates express Opa and their colonies are opaque, but most cervical isolates during menstruation and isolates from normally sterile sites, such as fallopian tubes, blood, and synovial fluid, form transparent colonies and presumably lack Opa.[20, 23] Many Opa proteins increase adherence between gonococci themselves (thus the opaque colony) and also increase adherence to a variety of eukaryotic cells, including phagocytes.[23, 24] Certain Opa variants appear to promote invasion of epithelial cells.[25] Two classes of Opa receptor on eukaryotic cells have been identified: heparin-related compounds[26] and CD66.[27]

Another important protein is reduction-modifiable protein, formerly known as protein III. This protein has a molecular weight of 30 to 31 kD, is present in all gonococci in close association with porin and LOS, and shows little if any interstrain antigenic variation.[1, 2, 16] Reduction-modifiable protein can stimulate blocking antibodies that reduce serum bactericidal activity against *N. gonorrhoeae,*[28] which may potentiate infection after sexual exposure to an infected partner.[29]

Several other outer-membrane proteins have been identified, including multiple iron-repressible proteins (some of which are shared with *N. meningitidis*). Two of the iron-repressible proteins (85 and 110 kD) constitute a specific receptor for human transferrin,[30] and two others constitute a receptor for human lactoferrin.[31] Recently, an additional two proteins were shown to make up a receptor for hemoglobin.[32] The transferrin receptor was shown to be required for experimental urethral infection in male volunteers.[33] The role of the lactoferrin receptor is unclear inasmuch as half of the isolates are natural mutants of the receptor yet cause infection indistinguishable from that of organisms expressing the receptor.[32] Other proteins are expressed only during anaerobic growth.[34] The ability of *N. gonorrhoeae* to grow anaerobically after removing available oxygen from the microenvironment may contribute to secondary invasion of fallopian tubes by strict anaerobes and thus to the pathogenesis of pelvic inflammatory disease (PID). IgA_1 proteases, present in *N. gonorrhoeae* and *N. meningitidis* but not in nonpathogenic *Neisseria,* are presumed to protect the organism from secretory IgA antibody at mucosal surfaces, but this role has not been proved.[35]

Gonococcal LOS is composed of lipid A and a core oligosaccharide that in contrast to the polysaccharide of most gram-negative bacteria, lacks O-antigenic side chains.[36] Sialylation of LOS core sugars in vitro or in vivo[37] masks epitopes on both LOS and porin and contributes to resistance to bactericidal antibodies.[38] LOS possesses endotoxic activity and contributes to ciliary loss and the death of mucosal cells in the fallopian tube explant model (see Fig. 200–3).[10, 36] LOS core sugars undergo high-frequency phase and antigenic variation in vitro and in vivo,[37, 39] which may contribute to the pathogenesis of infection, including resistance to bacterial anti-LOS antibodies present in normal serum[40] and invasion of epithelial cells.[41]

The peptidoglycan layer of *N. gonorrhoeae* may also contribute to the inflammatory response because gonococcal peptidoglycan fragments are toxic in the fallopian tube explant system and cause complement consumption in vitro.[1, 2, 42] In addition, peptidoglycan fragments have been found in the apparently sterile synovial fluid of patients with gonococcal arthritis-dermatitis syndrome.[43] Gonococci produce a surface polyphosphate that may have capsule-like functions, such as creating a hydrophilic, negatively charged cell surface.[44] However, a carbohydrate capsule analogous to that in *N. meningitidis* or *Streptococcus pneumoniae* is not produced.[1, 2]

Strain Typing

Studies of the pathogenesis and epidemiology of gonorrhea have been greatly enhanced by the development of reproducible methods for typing *N. gonorrhoeae.* Characterization of gonococcal strains is based on two primary methodologies, auxotyping and serotyping. Auxotyping is based on the genetically stable requirements of strains for specific nutrients or cofactors, as defined by isolates' ability to grow on chemically defined media that lack these factors.[45] Examples of the common auxotypes, among over 30 that have been identified, include prototrophic, also known as "zero" or "wild type"; proline requiring; and strains that require arginine, hypoxanthine, and uracil (AHU^-). The most widely used serotyping system is based on porin, which is antigenically classified into two groups, IA and IB.[17] Subdivision of these groups into serovars is in turn based on patterns of coagglutination reactions with panels of monoclonal antibodies that react with various epitopes of Por IA (e.g., serovar IA-4) or IB (e.g., serovar IB-12).[17] In practice, auxotyping and porin serotyping are often used together to provide enhanced discrimination of strains. This system has been instrumental in mapping the geographic and temporal occurrence of gonorrhea in communities, in analyzing patterns of antibiotic resistance, and in studies of disease transmission.[1, 17, 46, 47] Patterns of susceptibility to various antimicrobial agents, antigenic variations in LOS, and the plasmid content of isolates have also been analyzed to distinguish gonococcal strains, but with less success and reproducibility because these characteristics are not genetically stable.[2] Analysis of DNA sequence variations, either by the method of Opa typing[48] or by automated DNA sequencing of particular genes (e.g., *por*), is also playing an important role in strain typing.

Genetics

Plasmids

Many gonococci possess a 24.5-mD conjugative plasmid and can thereby conjugally transfer other non–self-transferable plasmids with high efficiency[49]; chromosomal genes are not mobilized.[50] Many gonococci carry a plasmid (Pc^r) that specifies production of a TEM-1 type of β-lactamase (penicillinase). The two most common Pc^r plasmids have molecular weights of 3.2 and 4.4 mD[50, 51] and are closely related to each other and to similar plasmids found in certain *Haemophilus* spp., including *Haemophilus ducreyi.*[51] In fact, it is suspected that gonococci first acquired Pc^r plasmids from *H. ducreyi.*[51] Pc^r plasmids are commonly mobilized to other gonococci by the conjugative plasmid.[52] Gonococci with plasmid-mediated high-level resistance to tetracycline (minimal inhibitory concentration [MIC] >16 mg/liter) carry the 24.5-mD conjugative plasmid into which the *tetM* transposon has been inserted.[53] The *tetM* determinant also confers tetracycline resistance to a variety of other bacteria, including some *Streptococcus* and *Mycoplasma* spp. and various genital organisms such as *Gardnerella vaginalis* and *Ureaplasma urealyticum.*[53] Because of its location on the conjugative plasmid, high-level tetracycline resistance is readily transferred to other gonococci. The *tetM* determinant functions by encoding a protein that protects ribosomes from the effect of tetracycline. Finally, all gonococci contain a small (2.6 mD) cryptic plasmid of unknown function.[50]

Chromosomal Mutations and Transformation

Chromosomal resistance of *N. gonorrhoeae* to β-lactam antibiotics and the tetracyclines results from interactions between a series of individual mutations, some of which (e.g., the *mtr* and *env* determinants) alter the net accumulation of antimicrobials inside the cell.[50] The *mtr* locus has been shown to be an efflux pump similar to other membrane transporters.[54] The *PenA* locus alters penicillin-binding protein 2 to reduce its affinity for penicillin.[50, 55] For epidemiologic purposes, such strains are classified as resistant only when the MIC is such that clinical failures are common with the maximum practical therapeutic dose (i.e., penicillin G MIC of about 1.0 mg/liter or a tetracycline MIC of about 2.0 mg/liter).[56]

Mutations in biosynthetic pathways are common,[50, 57] presumably reflecting the ready availability in vivo of essential nutrients such as amino acids, purines, and pyrimidines. Nevertheless, *N. gonorrhoeae* is not highly mutable in that it lacks error-prone repair systems and is relatively resistant to external mutagenic stimuli such as ultraviolet light.[58] Instead, gonococci have evolved efficient systems for phase and antigenic variation of surface components (pili, Opa, LOS) that do not depend on such mutagenic pathways.

Gonococci also use transfer of naked DNA between cells (transformation) to promote genetic variability.[50] The piliated variants of virtually all clinical isolates of *N. gonorrhoeae* are highly competent in transformation, but loss of the ability to express pili is always accompanied by a dramatic reduction in transformation competence.[59] Uptake of transforming DNA is limited to homologous (i.e., gonococcal) DNA, which reflects recognition of a unique nucleotide sequence by a surface receptor.[60] No bacteriophages have been found in *N. gonorrhoeae*.

PATHOLOGY

N. gonorrhoeae primarily infects columnar or cuboidal epithelium. The histopathology of gonorrhea is not materially different from that of most mucosal pyogenic infections. Attachment to mucosal epithelium, mediated in part by pili and Opa, is followed within 24 to 48 hours by penetration of the organism between and through epithelial cells to the submucosal tissues.[10] A vigorous response by neutrophils ensues, with sloughing of the epithelium, development of submucosal microabscesses, and exudation of pus. Stained smears usually reveal large numbers of gonococci within a few neutrophils, whereas most cells contain no organisms (Fig. 200–4). The explanation for this phenomenon may involve stimulation or production of cellular receptors for gonococci after initial contact with the first organism, or other alterations of the host cell cytoskeleton[61] might stimulate efficient phagocytosis of additional organisms. In addition, some gonococci may somehow evade killing mechanisms and continue to multiply intracellularly.[62] In untreated infections, neutrophils are gradually replaced by macrophages and lymphocytes. Lymphocytic and mononuclear infiltration persists in tissue for up to several weeks after *N. gonorrhoeae* can no longer be identified histologically or recovered by culture.

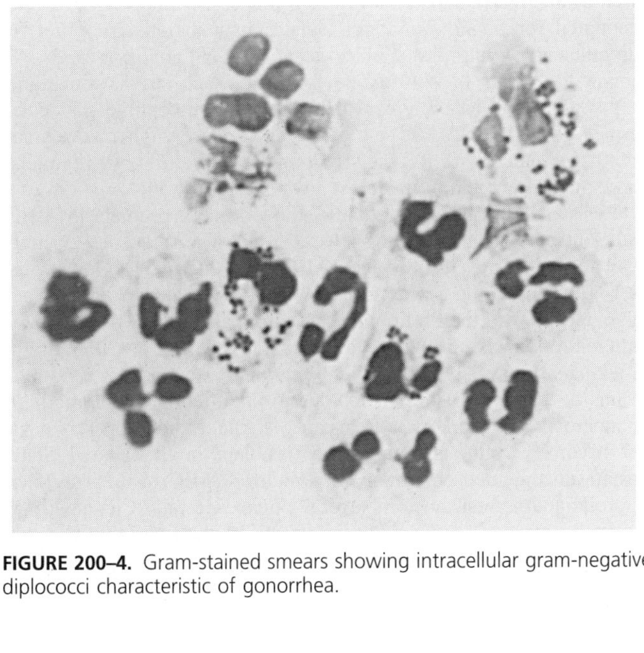

FIGURE 200–4. Gram-stained smears showing intracellular gram-negative diplococci characteristic of gonorrhea.

EPIDEMIOLOGY

Incidence

Only a few countries possess reporting systems that permit accurate estimates of the incidence of gonorrhea. The number of reported cases in the United States (probably about half the true number) rose from approximately 250,000 cases in the early 1960s to a high of 1.01 million cases in 1978. The peak incidence in modern times, 468 cases per 100,000 population, occurred in 1975.[63] The incidence stabilized or slowly declined over most of the next decade and then fell rapidly. By 1995, 149.5 cases per 100,000 were reported, which declined to 124 cases per 100,000 by 1996.[64] The incidence is substantially lower in most European countries, and indigenous gonorrhea has virtually been eliminated in Sweden. The highest incidence of gonorrhea and its complications occurs in developing countries. For example, it has been estimated that in 1987, 10% of all births in Kenya (population of 24 million) were adversely affected by sexually transmitted diseases (STDs), with 50,000 cases of gonococcal ophthalmia neonatorum (4% of all live births).[65] The median prevalence of gonorrhea in unselected populations of pregnant women has been estimated to be 10% in Africa, 5% in Latin America, and 4% in Asia.[65]

In the United States, the highest attack rates occur in 15- to 24-year-old women and men.[63] When adjusted for sexual experience, the highest risk occurs in sexually active 15- to 19-year-old women.[66] More cases are reported in men than women, which reflects a greater ease of diagnosis in men. However, declining cases in homosexually active men[67] and increasingly effective case-finding efforts in women resulted in a decline in the male/female case ratio from 1.5 in 1981 to less than 1.2 in 1995.[63] Although in most jurisdictions cases are not reported according to sexual orientation, in selected locales dramatic declines in cases in homosexually active men were documented during the 1980s. For example, reported cases of gonorrhea among homosexual men attending public STD clinics in Seattle fell from 737 cases in 1982 to 29 cases in 1988,[67] a finding that was replicated in many other settings. However, cases in this population rose again in the early 1990s, thus suggesting behavioral relapse.[67, 68] On the other hand, the rates remained far lower than in the early 1980s.

Table 200–1 shows reported cases and incidence rates of gonorrhea in 1995 according to race and ethnicity. The black/white incidence ratio rose from 12:1 in the early 1980s to 37:1 in 1995.[63] This trend was driven by a substantial rise in the number of cases and incidence rates in blacks, followed by modest declines in blacks and greater declines in whites after 1985. Rates in persons of Hispanic ethnicity and among Native Americans also remained higher than those in whites, whereas the lowest rates were observed in persons of Asian or Pacific Island ancestry. Only a small portion of these differences can be explained by greater attendance of nonwhite populations at public clinics, where case reporting is more complete than in private health facilities.[66] Race and ethnicity are demographic markers of increased risk, not factors that directly denote a high risk for gonorrhea or other STDs. Other factors associated with an increased risk of gonorrhea include lower socioeconomic attainment, lesser education, urban residence, residence in the southeastern part of the United States, and being unmarried.[1, 66] Gonorrhea is associated with illicit drug use in both rural areas and urban centers.[69, 70]

TABLE 200–1 Reported Cases and Incidence Rates of Gonorrhea According to Race/Ethnicity in the United States, 1995

Racial/Ethnic Group	Reported Cases	Cases per 100,000 Population
White, non-Hispanic	50,520	29.1
Black, non-Hispanic	270,867	1086.9
Hispanic	18,394	90.6
Native American	1,722	80.4
Asian/Pacific Islander	1,507	18.9
Total	343,010	147.6

Data from Division of STD/HIV Prevention. Sexually Transmitted Disease Surveillance, 1995. U.S. Department of Health and Human Services. Atlanta: Centers for Disease Control and Prevention; 1996.

Transmission

Aside from perinatal transmission, the overriding risk factor for acquiring gonorrhea is sexual intercourse with an infected partner. The risk of transmission of *N. gonorrhoeae* from an infected woman to the urethra of her male partner is approximately 20% per episode of vaginal intercourse and rises to 60 to 80% after four or more exposures.[71, 72] The risk of male-to-female transmission has been less well studied; it probably approximates 50 to 70% per contact, with little evidence for increased risk with increased number of sexual exposures.[73, 74]

Transmission by rectal intercourse has not been quantified but appears to be relatively efficient. Transmission apparently occurs less readily by fellatio, especially from the oropharynx to the urethra, and transmission in either direction by cunnilingus is believed to be rare.[75] Data are conflicting regarding whether women using anovulatory contraceptives are at increased risk for gonorrhea; if so, the magnitude of the effect appears to be small.[76]

Most cases of gonorrhea are treated within a few weeks. Therefore, high rates of partner change—much higher than the rates experienced by most of the population—are required to maintain a substantial prevalence of infection. Those persons who have unprotected intercourse with new partners with sufficient frequency to sustain the infection are defined as core transmitters.[77, 78] The demographic and social characteristics that directly or indirectly influence the frequency with which new partners are acquired (or the selection by monogamous persons of partners at risk) include young age, low educational and socioeconomic levels, prostitution, illicit drug use, and similar factors.[68, 69, 78] Other determinants of core transmission include poorly understood psychosocial determinants of partner selection, cultural factors that affect the response to early symptoms, real or perceived reduced access to health care, and similar factors. Persons who lack these characteristics often acquire infection by sexual contact with core group members, but transmission is not sustained outside the core group.

Originally developed as a mathematic model,[77, 78] the core transmission hypothesis has been empirically confirmed by several studies,[47, 66, 79, 80] and a central focus of gonorrhea control is to identify the core group and to target members for case finding, treatment, and educational programs. Core groups sustain the transmission of all STDs, although the parameters that define core transmitters are different for each infection. For example, *Chlamydia trachomatis* infections are clinically milder and last longer than most cases of gonorrhea, so lower rates of partner change serve to sustain the prevalence of infection. Thus, chlamydial infections typically affect a broader socioeconomic spectrum of the population than does gonorrhea.[80] Because herpes simplex virus and human papillomavirus persist indefinitely, very low rates of partner change can sustain these infections and the core transmitter group is very large, which partly explains the high, mathematically defined prevalence of these infections in all segments of society.

Gonorrhea and other sexually transmitted infections are usually transmitted by persons with asymptomatic infections or by those who have symptoms that they ignore or discount.[81] The behavioral response to symptoms is presumably determined by education and various demographic and sociocultural factors[66, 78–80]; however, except when persistent sexual activity is driven by economic need or other factors (e.g., drug addiction), most persons with new genital symptoms probably cease sexual activity and seek care. It follows that many transmitters belong to a subset of infected persons who lack or ignore symptoms and do not spontaneously cease sexual activity. This concept underlies the importance of taking active steps to bring the sexual partners of infected persons to treatment.

Antibiotic-Resistant *Neisseria gonorrhoeae*

Penicillinase-producing strains of *N. gonorrhoeae* bearing plasmids with the Pc^r determinant were first documented almost simultaneously in 1975–1976 in the United States, Western Europe, the Philippines, and western Africa.[82] By the early 1980s, penicillinase-producing strains accounted for up to 50% of *N. gonorrhoeae* isolates in some parts of the developing world, but they have never accounted for more than 11% of isolates in the United States. Initially, the predominant Pc^r plasmid in North American gonococci was the 4.4-mD plasmid that was prevalent in Asia and the Philippines, whereas the 3.2-mD plasmid predominated in Europe and Africa.[82] By the mid-1980s, however, both of these plasmid types were common throughout the world,[1, 83, 84] and isolates have been identified with several other plasmid variants.[75] Penicillinase-producing strains of *N. gonorrhoeae* accounted for about 5% of cases of gonorrhea in the United States in 1995,[63] down substantially from the peak of about 11% in 1991.[63] Nevertheless, penicillinase-producing *N. gonorrhoeae* is still a significant problem in the United States and a major problem elsewhere.

Strains of *N. gonorrhoeae* with plasmid-mediated high-level tetracycline resistance were first documented in the United States in 1985 and spread rapidly. In 1995, tetracycline-resistant gonococci caused about 6% of reported gonorrhea cases in the United States.[63] The location of the *tetM* gene on the conjugative plasmid has probably served to enhance the efficiency of transmission of tetracycline resistance among gonococci and thereby rapid dissemination of tetracycline-resistant *N. gonorrhoeae*. These strains are common worldwide.

The prevalence of gonococci with clinically significant chromosomal resistance to the penicillins and tetracyclines also rose steadily in much of the world in the last 25 years. In 1995, non–penicillinase-producing strains of gonococci that had penicillin G MICs of 2.0 mg/liter or greater and tetracycline MICs of 2.0 mg/liter or greater accounted for about 4% of all isolates in a national program for surveillance of antimicrobial resistance in *N. gonorrhoeae*.[63] Although the MICs of ceftriaxone for many such strains are higher (e.g., 0.015 to 0.125 mg/liter) than for fully susceptible gonococci (usually 0.0001 to 0.008 mg/liter), even these higher levels are greatly exceeded with routinely recommended ceftriaxone regimens, and ceftriaxone therapy is almost always effective.[85]

Resistance to fluoroquinolones is now a major problem in Africa and Southeast Asia, including Australia.[86, 87] The frequency of high-level resistance to ciprofloxacin (MIC >1.0 mg/liter, some as high as 16.0 mg/liter) increased from 12% in 1994 to over 70% between 1996 and 1997 in the Philippines.[88] Nearly half of the women treated with ciprofloxacin, 500 mg, failed therapy when the MIC of the infecting strain was greater than 4.0 mg/liter.[88] An outbreak of similar strains in Sydney, Australia, was due to importation by international commercial sex workers.[87] Resistance to fluoroquinolones has not yet become a clinically significant problem in the United States despite documented occurrence of low-level (MIC of 0.25 mg/liter) fluoroquinolone resistance in several cities, especially Cleveland.[89, 90] Resistance is due to the additive effects of multiple chromosomal mutations, particularly in *gyrA* (DNA gyrase) and *parC* (topoisomerase IV).[91] Conceivably, uncontrolled use of oral fluoroquinolones in

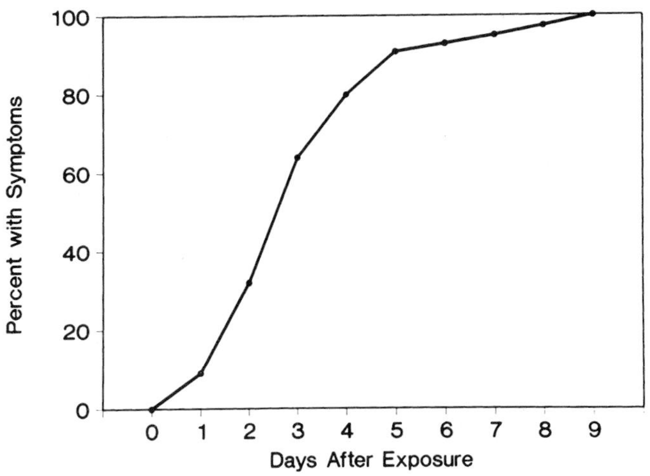

FIGURE 200–5. Incubation period in 44 men with gonococcal urethritis. (Data from Harrison WO, Hooper RR, Weisner PJ, et al. A trial of minocycline given after exposure to prevent gonorrhea. N Engl J Med. 1979;300:1074–1078.)

some parts of the world has selected multistep, additive, phenotypically high-level resistance, which now is in the process of spreading throughout the world.

Gonococci with chromosomal resistance are especially common in homosexually active men,[92] probably because a reservoir of rectal infection is required for propagation of gonorrhea in this population. Fatty acids and bile salts in the rectum create a hostile environment for gonococci and result in selection pressure for *mtr* and other genes that reduce the net entry of antimicrobials and fatty acids through the outer membrane.[93]

CLINICAL MANIFESTATIONS

Genital Infection in Men

Acute urethritis is the predominant manifestation of gonorrhea in men (see Chapter 94). The incubation period is typically 2 to 5 days but ranges from 1 to 10 days or longer (Fig. 200–5).[94] Urethral discharge and dysuria, usually without urinary frequency or urgency, are the major symptoms. The discharge may initially be scant and mucoid, but within a day or two it becomes overtly purulent. These observations have been confirmed in recent well-controlled studies of experimental gonorrhea in humans.[95] When compared with nongonococcal urethritis, the incubation period of gonorrhea is shorter, dysuria is usually more prominent, and the discharge is generally more profuse and more purulent (Fig. 200–6), but exceptions are common.[96] Most cases of untreated gonococcal urethritis resolve spontaneously over several weeks. A small proportion of men with urethral gonorrhea remain asymptomatic and lack signs of urethritis.[81] However, this pattern of disease depends in part on the infecting organism; some Por IA serovars and the AHU and related auxotypes of *N. gonorrhoeae* are more frequently associated with asymptomatic infection in men than are other gonococcal types.[17, 97]

Acute epididymitis is the most common complication of urethral gonorrhea, but it is nonetheless infrequent in industrialized countries and accounts for no more than 10% of cases of epididymitis in young men; most are due to *C. trachomatis* (see Chapter 168).[98] Penile edema without other overt inflammatory signs is occasionally seen in gonococcal or nongonococcal urethritis.[99] Penile lymphangitis, periurethral abscess, acute prostatitis, seminal vesiculitis, and infections of Tyson's and Cowper's glands are now rare complications in industrialized countries. Urethral stricture as a result of gonorrhea is also uncommon; it is likely that some strictures in the preantibiotic era resulted from treatment by urethral irrigation of caustic compounds rather than from the gonorrhea itself.

Uncomplicated Genital Infection in Women

The primary locus of genital infection in women is the endocervix (see Chapter 95). *N. gonorrhoeae* is also frequently recovered from the urethra or rectum and occasionally from the periurethral (Skene's) glands and the ducts of Bartholin's glands, but these organs are rarely the sole infected sites except in women who have undergone hysterectomy. The natural course of gonorrhea is less well understood in women than in men, partly because of the frequency of coinfection with other pathogens such as *C. trachomatis* and *Trichomonas vaginalis*. Symptoms probably develop in most infected

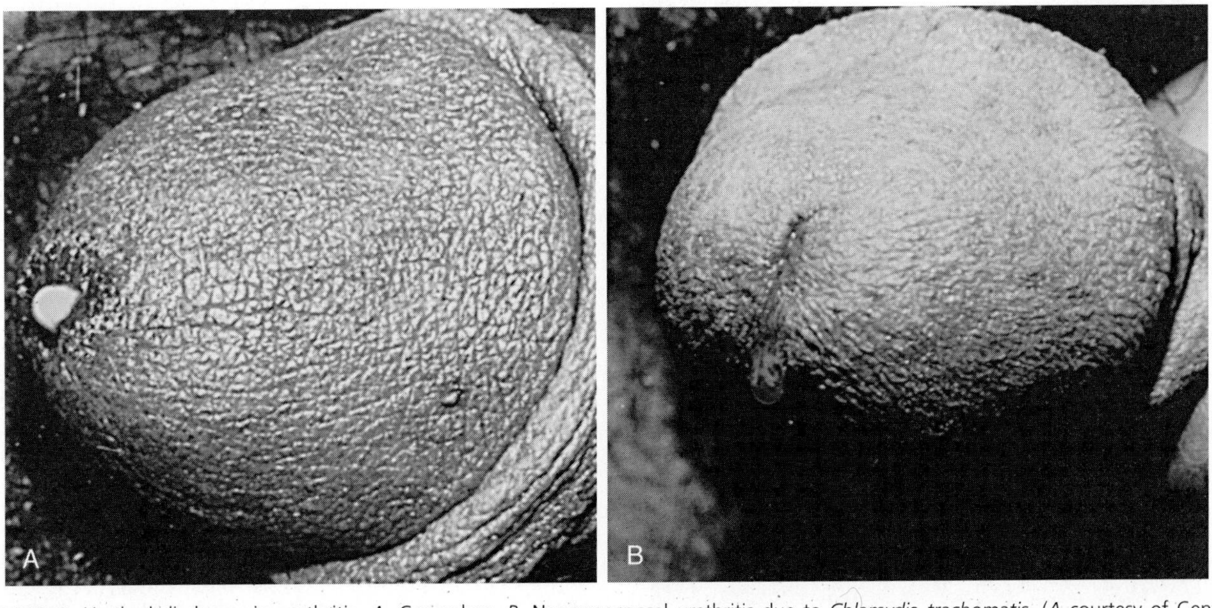

FIGURE 200–6. Urethral discharge in urethritis. *A*, Gonorrhea. *B*, Nongonococcal urethritis due to *Chlamydia trachomatis*. (*A* courtesy of Centers for Disease Control and Prevention, Atlanta, Ga; *B* from Handsfield HH. Gonorrhea. In: Spittell JA Jr, ed. Clinical Medicine. Philadelphia: Harper & Row; 1984:1–17.)

women,[100] but many remain asymptomatic or have only minor symptoms that do not lead to medical care.[101, 102] Thus, women with subclinical infection accumulate in the population, and in settings in which most infections are detected through screening or other case-finding efforts (e.g., family planning clinics), up to 90% of women with gonorrhea may be asymptomatic.[81, 101, 102] As expected, among women in whom gonorrhea is diagnosed in settings that attract symptomatic patients (e.g., hospital emergency departments), most are overtly symptomatic.[100, 101] Women infected with AHU and related auxotypes of *N. gonorrhoeae,* like men, are more likely to have asymptomatic infection and more subtle inflammatory signs than are those infected with other strains.[102]

The incubation period of gonorrhea is more variable and less well defined in women than in men, but most persons who become symptomatic probably do so within 10 days.[100] The dominant symptoms are those of cervicitis and sometimes urethritis and include increased vaginal discharge, dysuria (usually without urgency or frequency), and intermenstrual bleeding.[101, 103] These symptoms may occur in any combination, and they range widely in severity. Abdominal or pelvic pain is usually associated with salpingitis, but it sometimes occurs in infected women, in whom laparoscopy shows normal fallopian tubes. Physical examination may or may not show purulent or mucopurulent cervical exudate (Fig. 200–7) and other signs of mucopurulent cervicitis, such as edema in a zone of cervical ectopy or endocervical bleeding induced by gentle swabbing.[103] However, the specific contribution of *N. gonorrhoeae* to these signs, versus that of other pathogens, remains unclear. Purulent discharge can sometimes be expressed from the urethra or the ducts of Bartholin's glands. Cervical, uterine fundal, or adnexal tenderness is usually associated with ascending infection.[1, 100]

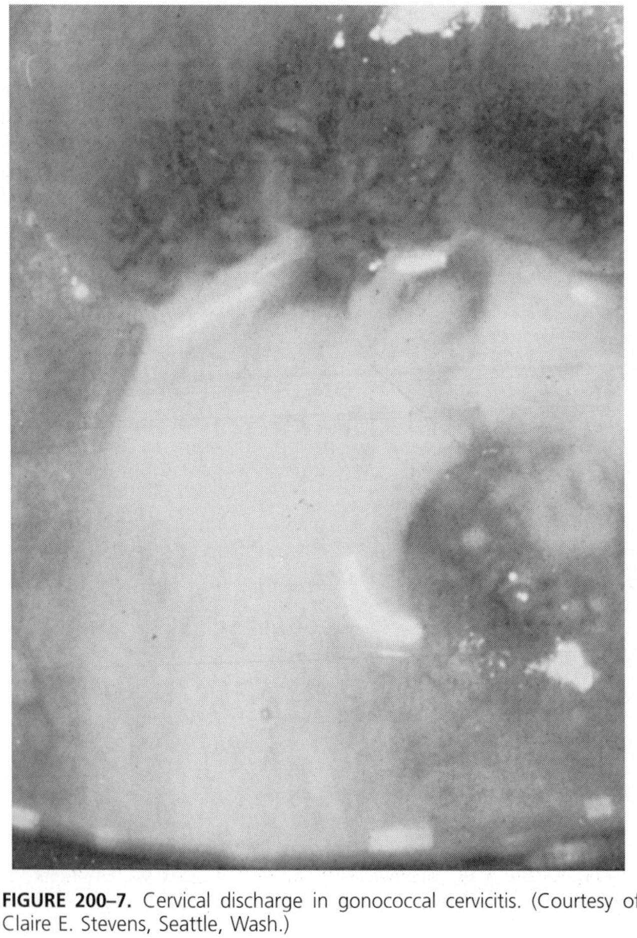

FIGURE 200–7. Cervical discharge in gonococcal cervicitis. (Courtesy of Claire E. Stevens, Seattle, Wash.)

Anorectal Gonorrhea

Up to 40% of women with uncomplicated gonorrhea and a similar proportion of infected homosexual men have positive rectal cultures for *N. gonorrhoeae.* The rectum is the only infected site in about 40% of homosexual men and in 5% or less of women with gonorrhea.[92, 101, 104] Most persons with positive rectal cultures are asymptomatic, but some patients have acute proctitis manifested by anal pruritus, tenesmus, purulent discharge, or rectal bleeding.[105] Anoscopy sometimes reveals mucopurulent exudate and inflammatory changes in the rectal mucosa, but infection with *C. trachomatis,* herpes simplex virus, or other sexually transmitted pathogens can also produce these findings.[105]

Pharyngeal Gonorrhea

The main risk factor for the development of pharyngeal gonococcal infection is orogenital sexual exposure. Acquired more efficiently by fellatio than by cunnilingus,[75] pharyngeal infection can be found in 10 to 20% of heterosexual women with gonorrhea and 10 to 25% of infected homosexual men, but it is present in only 3 to 7% of heterosexual men with gonorrhea.[75, 92, 104] Gonorrhea uncommonly causes overt pharyngitis or cervical lymphadenitis; most pharyngeal infections are asymptomatic.[75]

The importance of documenting pharyngeal infection is debated. Most cases are asymptomatic and resolve spontaneously, transmission from the pharynx to other patients is uncommon, and the pharynx is rarely the only site of infection. Identification of *N. gonorrhoeae* in pharyngeal cultures is more expensive than identification in anogenital cultures. Although some older therapies were less effective in eradicating *N. gonorrhoeae* from the pharynx than other sites, all the currently recommended treatment regimens[106] are effective against pharyngeal gonorrhea. These factors argue against routine attempts at diagnosis. On the other hand, pharyngeal infection is sometimes symptomatic and may occasionally be the source of transmission to sexual partners or systemic dissemination of *N. gonorrhoeae.*[75] Most STD clinics with limited resources do not routinely culture the throats of patients with suspected gonorrhea, unless requested by the patient or if symptoms or signs of pharyngitis are present.

Other Local Manifestations

Ocular infection in adults usually results from autoinoculation of the conjunctiva in a person with genital gonorrhea. Gonococcal conjunctivitis is usually severe, with overt purulent exudate (Fig. 200–8), and corneal ulceration can supervene rapidly in the absence of prompt antibiotic therapy. However, some infections are mild, perhaps related to specific strains of *N. gonorrhoeae.*[107] *N. gonorrhoeae* has been isolated in cases of acute gingivitis, otherwise unexplained oral ulcerations, primary (inoculation) cutaneous infection, and intraoral abscesses.

Pelvic Inflammatory Disease

Ascending genital infection is estimated to occur in 10 to 20% of women with gonorrhea and is manifested by various combinations of endometritis, salpingitis, tuboovarian abscess, pelvic peritonitis, and other local complications.[108, 109] The acute manifestations and long-term sequelae of acute PID are one of the principal reasons to prevent STDs in general and gonorrhea and chlamydial infection in particular.

Although gonococcal, chlamydial, or perhaps other sexually transmitted infections are the proximate cause of 90% or more of cases of acute PID, numerous factors directly contribute to risk.[108–110] Teenage girls are at much higher risk than older women, probably because of both innate susceptibility (perhaps owing to a high prevalence of cervical ectopy) and behavioral factors such as choice of sexual

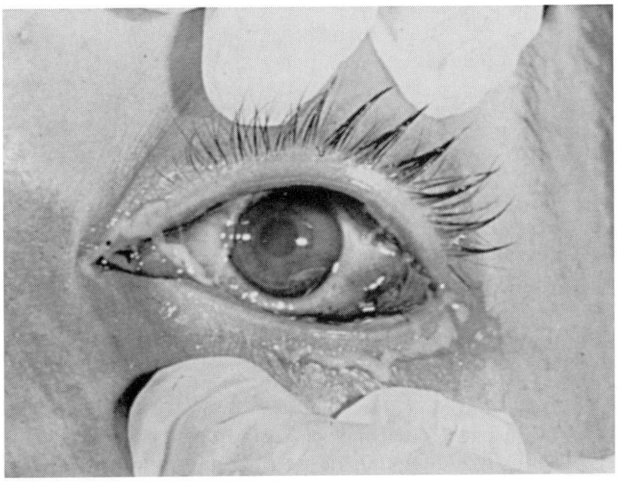

FIGURE 200–8. Acute gonococcal conjunctivitis in an adult. (From Handsfield HH. Gonorrhea. In: Spittell JA Jr, ed. Clinical Medicine. Philadelphia: Harper & Row; 1984:1–17.)

partners. Women using some (perhaps all) intrauterine devices are at increased risk, whereas those using anovulatory hormones have a lower risk of chlamydial (but perhaps not gonococcal) PID.[108–111] Prior PID markedly increases a woman's risk for new episodes, presumably because of altered tubal defense mechanisms. Vaginal douching, whether for perceived infection or as a hygienic measure, is a potent risk factor for PID and ectopic pregnancy.[112–114] Finally, bacterial vaginosis is strongly associated with the occurrence of acute PID and may be a specific risk factor, perhaps because of a marked increase in the vaginal concentration of potentially pathogenic anaerobic bacteria.[115]

The most consistent symptom of PID is low abdominal pain, which is usually bilateral.[108–110] Most women also have symptoms of lower genital tract infection, as described earlier. The onset of gonococcal PID often follows the onset of menses by a few days.[101, 108] Some patients have high fever, chills, nausea, and vomiting, but most patients lack these features.[108–110] The primary finding on physical examination is pelvic adnexal tenderness, usually but not always bilateral. Other common findings are uterine fundal tenderness, pain elicited on moving the cervix, and one or more tender adnexal masses. Abdominal examination usually elicits tenderness over the lower quadrants, and signs of peritoneal inflammation are common in severe cases. Findings of mucopurulent cervicitis or bacterial vaginosis are usually present.

Fever, leukocytosis, and an elevated erythrocyte sedimentation rate or C-reactive protein level are common. However, all these findings are absent in about one third of patients with laparoscopically documented PID.[108–110] In practice, the clinical diagnosis of PID is imprecise; series using laparoscopy have found that the clinical diagnosis of acute PID is both insensitive and nonspecific.[108–110] In general, gonococcal PID causes more overt clinical inflammatory signs than does salpingitis associated only with *C. trachomatis.*

The proportion of PID cases associated with gonorrhea has varied from series to series because of differences in patient selection, varying diagnostic methods, and differing background prevalence rates of gonorrhea and chlamydial infection. In the 1980s, 20 to 40% of cases of PID in most urban areas of the United States were associated with gonorrhea, but regional variation is great; in Sweden, where gonorrhea has been almost eradicated, *N. gonorrhoeae* is a very rare cause of PID. The presence of gonococci in the cervix does not establish that the organism is responsible for upper tract infection and does not exclude coinfection with other organisms. Moreover, because cervical cultures are relatively insensitive, failure to isolate *N. gonorrhoeae, C. trachomatis,* or other pathogens does not exclude their contribution to ascending infection.[108–110] *Mycoplasma hominis* and the facultative and anaerobic bacterial flora of the vagina may also contribute to acute PID, especially in patients with pelvic abscess or otherwise severe infections[108–110] (Fig. 200–9).

Infertility secondary to fallopian tube obstruction is the most common serious sequela of PID and occurs in 15 to 20% of women after a single episode and 50 to 80% with three or more episodes.[109] Infertility may be more common after chlamydial than gonococcal PID, presumably because the more acute inflammatory signs associated with gonorrhea bring women to diagnosis and treatment sooner. A nationwide epidemic of ectopic pregnancies in the United States followed the gonorrhea/chlamydia epidemic of the 1970s and 1980s.[116] Evidence of prior salpingitis can be found in 50 to 80% of women with ectopic pregnancies.[109, 116] Chronic and sometimes disabling pelvic pain occurs in up to 20% of women after PID, but it is often difficult to differentiate recurrent PID from chronic pain caused by adhesions or other poorly understood mechanisms.

Perihepatitis

Acute perihepatitis (Fitz-Hugh–Curtis syndrome) occurs primarily by direct extension of *N. gonorrhoeae* or *C. trachomatis* from the fallopian tube to the liver capsule and overlying peritoneum.[117] Some cases may result from lymphangitic spread or bacteremic dissemination, which perhaps explains rare cases of apparent perihepatitis in men.[117, 118] Perihepatitis results in abdominal pain, hepatic tenderness, and right upper quadrant peritoneal inflammatory signs. Most cases occur with overt PID, but many women lack pelvic symptoms or signs. Perihepatitis should be considered in the differential diagnosis of right upper quadrant pain in young, sexually active women; it is commonly mistaken for acute cholecystitis or viral hepatitis.[117] If laparoscopy is performed, "violin string" adhesions may be seen between the liver capsule and the parietal peritoneum.

Gonorrhea in Pregnancy

Gonorrhea in pregnant women is associated with an increased risk of spontaneous abortion, premature labor, early rupture of fetal membranes, and perinatal infant mortality,[119–121] but it is uncertain whether gonococcal infection is directly responsible for these consequences or is merely a marker for high risk from other pathogenic mechanisms. The clinical manifestations of gonorrhea are unchanged in pregnant women, except that PID and perihepatitis are uncommon after the first trimester, when the products of conception completely obstruct the uterine cavity.[119] One study suggests a higher prevalence of pharyngeal infection in pregnant than nonpregnant women with gonorrhea, perhaps because of an increase in the frequency of fellatio as pregnancy progresses.[122] Reports are conflicting regarding whether

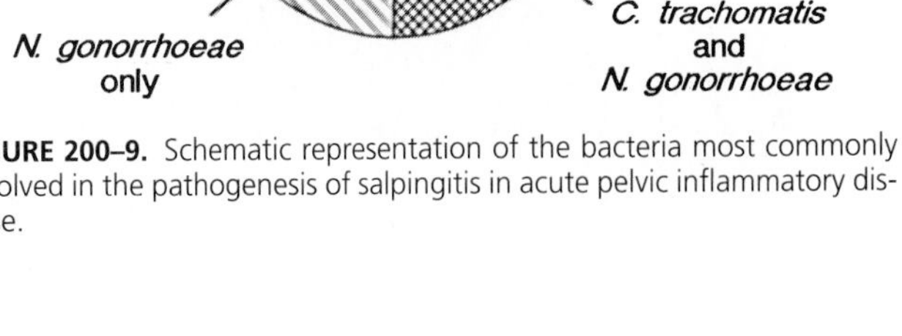

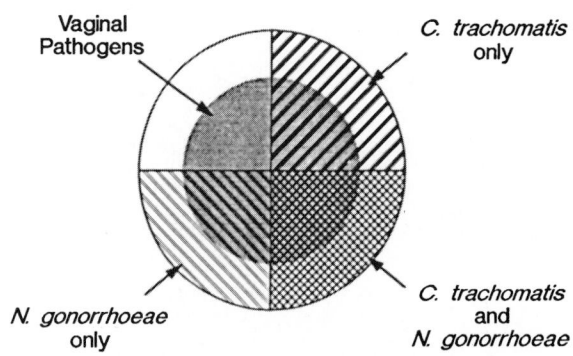

FIGURE 200–9. Schematic representation of the bacteria most commonly involved in the pathogenesis of salpingitis in acute pelvic inflammatory disease.

pregnancy is a risk factor for disseminated gonococcal infection (DGI).[123–126]

Disseminated Gonococcal Infection

DGI results from gonococcal bacteremia and has been said to occur in 0.5 to 3% of infected patients.[123–126] However, this estimate is probably high at present because of a declining prevalence of the strains of *N. gonorrhoeae* most likely to disseminate.[127, 128] Septic arthritis and a characteristic syndrome of polyarthritis and dermatitis are the predominant manifestations, and DGI is a common cause of infective arthritis in young adults.[123–126] *N. gonorrhoeae* was a frequent cause of bacterial endocarditis in the preantibiotic era but is now uncommon.[129, 130] Other rare complications of DGI include meningitis,[131] osteomyelitis,[132] overwhelming sepsis accompanied by the Waterhouse-Friderichsen syndrome,[133] and adult respiratory distress syndrome.[133, 134]

Properties of *N. gonorrhoeae* classically associated with dissemination include resistance to the bactericidal action of nonimmune human serum, the AHU$^-$ auxotype, specific Por IA serovars, and marked susceptibility to penicillin.[17, 127, 128] These characteristics are also associated with asymptomatic gonorrhea. However, other strains can disseminate, and penicillinase-producing strains of *N. gonorrhoeae* and strains with chromosomal antibiotic resistance have caused DGI.[127, 130, 135] An increasing proportion of DGI cases have been associated with other auxotype/serovar classes as the prevalence of Por IA/AHU$^-$ gonococci has declined.[124, 127, 135] One report suggests that this trend has also been associated with an increased proportion of apparent DGI actually caused by *N. meningitidis*.[136]

Complement deficiency predisposes to both gonococcal and meningococcal bacteremia.[137, 138] Up to 13% of patients with DGI have a complement deficiency,[138] and patients with repeated episodes of neisserial bacteremia should be tested, after recovery from acute illness, with an assay for total hemolytic complement activity. Other host factors that may be associated with an enhanced risk of dissemination include female sex, menstruation, and perhaps pharyngeal gonococcal infection and pregnancy.[123–126] In about half of affected women, symptoms of DGI begin within 7 days of the onset of menses.[123–126]

The most common manifestations of DGI constitute the "arthritis-dermatitis syndrome." During the first few days, most patients complain of additive and sometimes migratory polyarthralgias that primarily involve the knees, elbows, and more distal joints; axial skeletal involvement is uncommon. At this stage, physical examination usually shows objective signs of arthritis, tenosynovitis, or other signs of periarticular inflammation in two or more joints.[123–126] Asymmetric involvement of only a few joints helps distinguish DGI from polyarthritis caused by most immune complex deposition syndromes. A characteristic dermatitis (Fig. 200–10) is present in about 75% of patients[123–126] and consists of discrete papules and pustules, often with a hemorrhagic component. Hemorrhagic bullae are occasionally seen, as are overtly necrotic lesions that may mimic ecthyma gangrenosum or the lesions of neutrophilic dermatitis (Sweet's syndrome). The lesions usually number 5 to 40 and occur predominantly on the extremities.[123–126]

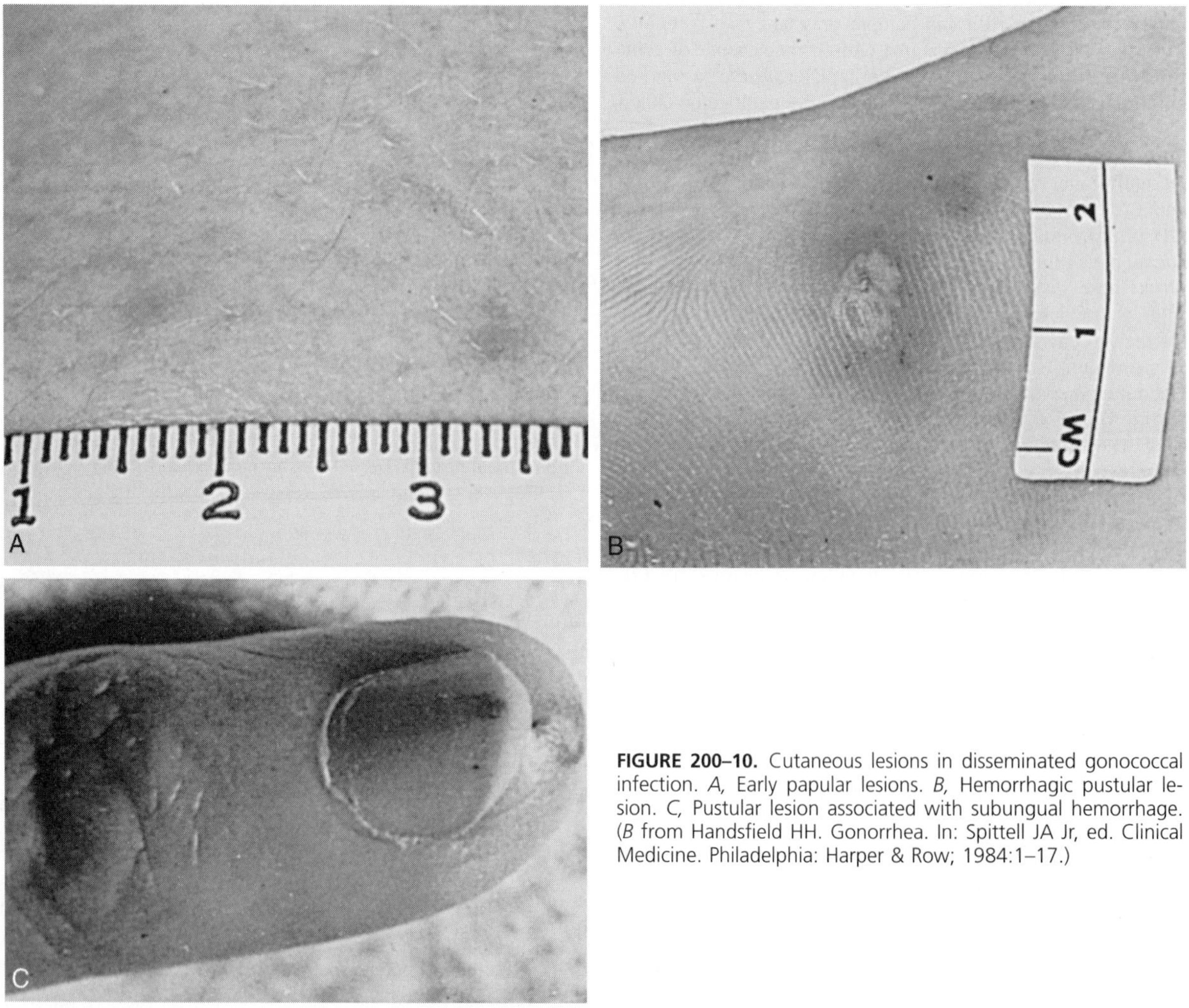

FIGURE 200–10. Cutaneous lesions in disseminated gonococcal infection. *A,* Early papular lesions. *B,* Hemorrhagic pustular lesion. *C,* Pustular lesion associated with subungual hemorrhage. (*B* from Handsfield HH. Gonorrhea. In: Spittell JA Jr, ed. Clinical Medicine. Philadelphia: Harper & Row; 1984:1–17.)

Untreated, arthropathy improves in most joints and the dermatitis usually resolves, but arthritis typically progresses in one or two joints, most commonly the knee, ankle, elbow, or wrist.[123–126] However, any joint may be involved, including those of the hands and feet and the sternoclavicular and temporomandibular joints. At this stage, the clinical picture and synovial fluid findings are those of septic arthritis. Septic gonococcal arthritis develops in some patients without prior polyarthritis or dermatitis.[123–126] In the absence of the characteristic dermatitis or overt genital infection, septic gonococcal arthritis is clinically indistinguishable from other forms of septic arthritis.

DGI results from bacteremic dissemination of *N. gonorrhoeae* to the skin and the joints or periarticular tissue, although immune complexes or other indirect immunologic mechanisms may contribute to some cases.[43, 139] Fever, systemic toxicity, and polymorphonuclear leukocytosis are common, but they are usually mild and are often absent.[123–126] During the polyarthritis-dermatitis stage, gonococci can often be recovered by blood culture, but synovial fluid, if it can be obtained, usually contains fewer than 20,000 leukocytes/mm^3 and is sterile.[123–126] Gonococci can often be seen by immunochemical methods in biopsy specimens of skin lesions, but cultures are generally sterile.[140] In septic gonococcal arthritis, synovial fluid usually contains more than 50,000 leukocytes/mm^3 and culture is often positive, but at this stage blood cultures are usually negative.[123–126]

Overall, only about half of patients with DGI have positive cultures of blood or synovial fluid, but *N. gonorrhoeae* can be recovered from a mucosal site in 80% or more of patients.[123–126] When DGI is suspected, a minimum of three blood cultures should be obtained; synovial fluid, if obtainable, should be cultured; and all potentially infected mucosal sites (urethra or endocervix, rectum, pharynx) should be cultured regardless of symptoms or exposure history, and the sexual partner(s) should be examined and material harvested for culture. Although uncommonly positive, Gram-stained smears and cultures of pustular skin lesions are simple to perform and should be obtained. The diagnosis of DGI is unequivocal if gonococci are recovered from a systemic site (e.g., blood or synovial fluid) and is probable if the organism is isolated from a mucosal site or from the sexual partner of a patient with a typical clinical syndrome that responds to antibiotic therapy.

The differential diagnosis of the gonococcal arthritis-dermatitis syndrome includes meningococcemia,[134] other infective arthritides, and the entire range of inflammatory arthritis.[123–126] Reiter's syndrome and other kinds of reactive arthritis are easily confused with DGI because they are common in sexually active young adults and are associated with urethritis, cervicitis, and skin lesions that sometimes have a pustular component. Usually, careful clinical and microbiologic assessment readily differentiates these disorders, but a trial of antibiotic therapy may be required.[123–126]

Infective endocarditis, which usually affects the aortic valve, is an infrequent but serious manifestation that occurs in an estimated 1 to 2% of patients with DGI.[123, 129] Although often associated with the arthritis-dermatitis syndrome, endocarditis may be the sole manifestation of DGI.[124, 129] The rate of valve destruction and progression of the clinical course tends to be midway between that of acute staphylococcal or pneumococcal endocarditis and subacute endocarditis caused by viridans streptococci; in the preantibiotic era, the median survival was 6 to 8 weeks. However, some cases progress very rapidly.[129, 130]

Neonatal and Pediatric Infections

Infected mothers may transmit *N. gonorrhoeae* to the newborn in utero, during delivery, or in the postpartum period.[141] Gonococcal conjunctivitis of the newborn (ophthalmia neonatorum) is the most common clinically recognized manifestation[141, 142] and was once the most common cause of blindness in the United States; it remains common in some developing countries.[143] Prophylaxis by instillation of a 1% aqueous solution of silver nitrate into the conjunctivae soon after delivery is highly effective, although occasional failures occur.[144] Topical application of erythromycin or tetracycline ointment is probably somewhat less effective.[141, 144] The most important preventive measure is routine screening and treatment of pregnant women for gonorrhea before term.[141, 142]

The diagnosis of gonococcal ophthalmia may be suspected clinically when acute conjunctivitis, usually with overtly purulent exudate, develops within a week (usually 2 to 3 days) of delivery. It is confirmed by identification of gonococci in conjunctival secretions by Gram-stained smear and culture. Systemic illness with septicemia and arthritis can also develop in newborns exposed to gonorrhea,[141] but these conditions are uncommon. *N. gonorrhoeae* can often be recovered from the orogastric aspirates of infants born to infected mothers, but many cases probably reflect transient colonization rather than clinically important infection.[121]

Rectal gonococcal infection is sometimes seen in newborns, but vaginal infection is uncommon, presumably because the neonatal vaginal mucosa is well estrogenized by circulating maternal hormone. However, purulent vaginitis is the primary manifestation of gonorrhea in prepubertal girls after the neonatal period.[145] Otherwise, the clinical manifestations of gonorrhea in children are not materially different from those in adults. After the neonatal period until 1 year of age, most cases in children are probably acquired nonsexually from an infected parent, usually in a setting of poor hygiene.[145] After 1 year of age, most cases are acquired by sexual abuse, most commonly by an older relative or the mother's nonmarital sexual partner.[145, 146] Nonsexual transmission of ocular infection occasionally occurs among young children in tropical settings.

DIAGNOSIS

Laboratory diagnosis of gonorrhea depends on identification of *N. gonorrhoeae* at an infected site. Isolation by culture is the diagnostic standard and should be used whenever practical. For legal purposes, a confirmed culture is the only definitive test. Nonculture diagnostic tests are useful when isolation is impractical because of lack of access to a laboratory with culture capability or difficulties in specimen transport. Detection of antigen in secretions has been performed but is insufficiently sensitive in many situations.[147] Detection of nucleic acids by hybridization or amplification methods is both sensitive and specific, and these methods are now widely used.[147] DNA amplification by polymerase chain reaction or ligase chain reaction (LCR) offers sensitivity and specificity comparable or even superior to those of culture, although clinical experience is not yet great. The great advantages of hybridization- or amplification-based tests for *N. gonorrhoeae* are their sensitivities, which are at least equal to the sensitivity of culture[147]; specificities of at least 99%[147]; and in the case of LCR, their utility with freshly voided urine or self-administered vaginal introital swabs.[148, 149] The convenience of these tests makes screening of females and asymptomatic males much more practical, and urine-based LCR tests are being used more frequently in the diagnosis of gonorrhea in the United States.[150, 151] No clinically useful test for the detection of antibodies has yet been developed.

Culture

A single culture on most selective media has a sensitivity of 95% or more for urethral specimens from men with symptomatic urethritis and 80 to 90% for endocervical infection in women. Results may vary depending on the quality and freshness of the medium and the adequacy of the clinical specimen.[3–5, 152–154] Simultaneous inoculation of selective and nonselective media may provide the highest yield[152, 153] but is impractical in most settings. Although the urethra is commonly infected in women with gonorrhea,[101] culture of urethral specimens does not materially increase the diagnostic yield except in women who lack cervices because of hysterectomy. Rectal and pharyngeal specimens are inoculated onto selective medium only.[3, 75, 105, 152, 154] Specimens from other sites (e.g., Bartholin's gland duct) should be collected when indicated by clinical findings. Normally sterile clinical specimens in which competing bacteria are unlikely to be present (e.g., blood, synovial fluid, cerebrospinal fluid) should be inoculated onto nonselective medium such as enriched chocolate agar. As for blood cultures, the yield from synovial fluid is enhanced by inoculating in broth medium in addition to agar plates,[124] but no published studies have systematically analyzed the detection of *N. gonorrhoeae* in broth cultures with the automated techniques now used by most clinical laboratories.

Male urethral specimens are best obtained by inserting a small swab (e.g., a urethrogenital Calgiswab) 2 to 3 cm into the urethra,[81] although external discharge is adequate if copious. When collection of urethral exudate is impractical, the first 20 to 30 ml of voided urine can be centrifuged and the sediment cultured.[155] The patient's urine may be toxic for some gonococcal strains, so centrifugation and inoculation of growth medium should be done immediately after urine is collected.

Endocervical specimens are collected by first wiping exudate from the exocervix and then placing a swab into the external os and rotating it for several seconds while exercising care to avoid contacting the vaginal mucosa or secretions.[3, 152] Rectal specimens are best obtained by passing a swab 2 to 4 cm into the anal canal; specimens that are heavily contaminated with feces are discarded.[3, 105] In patients with symptomatic proctitis, the sensitivity of stained smears and perhaps of culture is enhanced by performing anoscopy and collecting purulent secretions or swabbing an area of mucosal inflammation under direct visualization.[105] Pharyngeal specimens are obtained by swabbing the posterior of the pharynx, including the tonsillar areas and faucial pillars.[3]

Whenever practical, the swab from any mucosal site should be immediately inoculated onto growth medium at room temperature, which should be promptly placed in an enriched CO_2 environment (e.g., a candle extinction jar) and incubated.[3, 152, 154] However, various non-nutrient transport media (including most commercial transport media) are adequate if the specimen can be transported to the laboratory without refrigeration and inoculated onto growth medium within 6 hours.[3, 152, 154]

The choice of anatomic sites to culture depends on the sites exposed and clinical manifestations. The urethra should usually be cultured in heterosexual men. Endocervical specimens should be collected from women. All symptomatic sites should be tested in homosexually active men; in the absence of symptoms, the highest yield will be achieved by culturing the rectum if the patient has participated in receptive anal intercourse. The yield from urethral culture in the absence of clinical urethritis is low in homosexually active men. A pharyngeal culture should be obtained from both men and women if symptoms of pharyngitis are present or in the case of oral exposure to a person known to have genital gonorrhea. The pharynx is often sampled routinely in homosexually active men, but testing is optional in heterosexual men and women.[75, 92, 104]

Characteristic gonococcal colonies appear on agar medium after 24 to 48 hours of incubation at 35°C to 37°C.[1–3, 13] Documentation of oxidase-positive gram-negative diplococci confirms a *Neisseria* species, and many laboratories report such isolates from genital sites as presumptive *N. gonorrhoeae.* However, up to 5% of such isolates from the genitals and substantially greater proportions of those from the rectum and pharynx are in fact *N. meningitidis.*[75, 102, 156, 157] Therefore, sugar utilization reactions or other methods (hybridization probes) to differentiate these species should be routine for pharyngeal and rectal isolates and are recommended for genital isolates as well.

Testing for β-lactamase production by the chromogenic cephalosporin, acidometric, iodometric, and paper strip methods all give reliable results in a few minutes.[158] Disk diffusion assays are available to screen gonococci for relative or absolute resistance to tetracycline and penicillin. However, the need for routine testing for either β-lactamase or chromosomal resistance is uncertain if currently recommended treatment regimens are used and is cost inefficient in the managed care era. Determination of the MICs of various antibiotics by the agar dilution method is indicated for isolates from patients with disseminated infection.

Gram-Stained Smears

Methylene blue and other dyes have been used successfully to identify gonococci in clinical specimens, but the Gram stain is used almost exclusively in the United States. The Gram stain is considered positive if gram-negative diplococci of typical morphology are observed in association with neutrophils (see Fig. 200–4), negative if no such organisms are seen, and equivocal if typical morphotypes not associated with neutrophils are present or if cell-associated, but morphologically atypical organisms are seen.[3, 152] *N. meningitidis* gives identical findings,[3] but nonpathogenic Neisseriaceae are not usually associated with polymorphonuclear leukocytes. Many apparently gram-negative diplococci are actually bipolar-staining gram-negative bacilli that can readily be differentiated from *Neisseria* spp. by experienced observers.

Table 200–2 shows an approximation of the performance of Gram-stained smears relative to culture when performed by highly trained personnel. For symptomatic urethritis in men, the Gram stain is sufficiently sensitive and specific to make culture confirmation optional[3, 152, 159] if isolating the organism for antimicrobial susceptibility testing is not a priority and medicolegal considerations are not prominent. In theory, the high specificity of the Gram stain in cervical gonorrhea (see Fig. 200–4) would permit reliance on a positive result.[152, 159] However, the performance of the test is often not as good as shown in Table 200–2. The Gram-stained smear should not be used as the sole method to diagnose infection of the rectum, pharynx, or other sites.

Other Diagnostic Methods

Several newer tests have been developed,[152, 160] including enzyme immunoassays for detection of antigen with polyclonal antigonococcal antibodies,[161, 162] fluorescein-conjugated monoclonal antibodies for direct fluorescence microscopy,[163] genetic probes to detect gonococcal DNA,[164, 165] and more recently, DNA amplification tests.[148–151, 166] In recent years, antibody-based tests have been essentially replaced by DNA-based tests. Potential advantages of DNA-based tests over culture include more rapid results, utility when transport problems or other issues preclude the use of culture, increased ease of obtaining a sample (urine), and sensitivity equal to or better than that of culture (Table 200–3). The specificity of the hybridization and amplification (LCR) tests is estimated at 99 and 99.8% respectively.[147] Use of LCR rather than hybridization tests would presumably result in fewer false-positives in low-prevalence populations.[147] Urine or vaginal swab samples are at least equal to cervical or urethral swab samples for detecting *N. gonorrhoeae* by LCR tests in asymptomatic persons.[148, 149] Polymerase chain reaction had not been approved for clinical use in the United States by 1998, but these and other amplification tests will be introduced soon.

TABLE 200–2 Estimated Performance of Gram Stain Relative to Culture for Detection of Genital and Rectal Gonorrhea

Site	Percent Sensitivity	Percent Specificity
Male urethra		
Symptomatic	95–100	95–100
Asymptomatic	50–70	95–100
Endocervix	40–60	95–100
Rectum	40–60	90–95*

*Lower specificity because of an increased prevalence of *Neisseria meningitidis* in the rectum, especially in homosexually active men.[96, 158]

TABLE 200–3 Sensitivity and Specificity of Nucleic Acid Hybridization (PACE 2) and Amplification (LCR) Tests for Gonorrhea

	Culture as Standard				After Discrepant Analysis	
	% Sensitivity		% Specificity		% Specificity	
Site	PACE-2	LCR	PACE-2	LCR	PACE-2	LCR
Endocervix	92.1	96.7	99.7	98.3	99.1	99.7
Male urethra	96.4	98.6	97.9	97.8	98.8	99.9
Urine (women)	—	96.2	—	99.2	—	100.0
Urine (men)	—	98.3	—	99.2	—	100.0

Abbreviation: LCR, Ligase chain reaction.
Modified from Koumans EH, Johnson RE, Knapp JS, et al. Laboratory testing for *Neisseria gonorrhoeae* by recently introduced nonculture tests: A performance review with clinical and public health considerations. Clin Infect Dis. 1998;27:1171–1180.

The major problem with LCR-based tests is cost. The tests are probably best reserved for screening high-risk populations. LCR and related tests have not yet been well studied in low-prevalence populations.[147] Appropriate uses for LCR tests include young sexually active persons, including those in early adolescence; jail and inmate populations; persons exposed to others with gonorrhea; and young sexually active persons in emergency rooms. None of the nonculture tests have been adequately studied for rectal and pharyngeal infection. No practical method currently exists to rapidly identify strains with chromosomal antibiotic resistance when an isolate is not cultured. For these reasons, isolation by culture remains the standard test for the diagnosis of gonorrhea.

TREATMENT

General Principles

Although patterns of antimicrobial susceptibility vary greatly from one geographic area or population to another and fluctuate over time, *N. gonorrhoeae* remains susceptible to a wide variety of antibiotics. Failure to cure a case of gonorrhea has public health implications beyond the interests of the infected patient because of the potential for continued transmission and for rapid emergence of antimicrobial resistance. Therefore, acceptable regimens for the treatment of gonorrhea should have efficacies that approach 100%, and treatments with efficacies less than 95% should never be used.[167]

A variety of factors in addition to antimicrobial susceptibility influence therapeutic decisions for gonococcal infections. These factors include the pharmacokinetic characteristics of the agent, its efficacy in complicated versus uncomplicated infection, differential efficacy at various anatomic sites of infection, toxicity, convenience of administration, and cost. An additional consideration is the potential efficacy of an agent for concurrent infection. Historically, this concern focused on syphilis, which remains an important issue in some settings. However, *C. trachomatis* is by far the most common coexisting pathogen in persons with gonorrhea. Many studies over 2 decades have given remarkably consistent results: 15 to 25% of heterosexual men and 35 to 50% of women with gonorrhea are also infected with *C. trachomatis.*[167, 168] However, anecdotal reports suggest that the prevalence of chlamydial coinfection may be declining in places where effective chlamydia control programs have been implemented. High rates of coinfection have been less well documented in developing countries than in North America and Europe.

Uncomplicated Gonorrhea in Adults

The regimens currently (1998) recommended by the U.S. Public Health Service[106] for the treatment of uncomplicated gonorrhea are summarized in Table 200–4. One of four initial regimens—ceftriaxone, 125 mg intramuscularly, cefixime, 400 mg orally, ciprofloxacin, 500 mg orally, or ofloxacin, 400 mg orally—is recommended as initial therapy for all patients in all areas of the United States. Each of these regimens is effective for infection of the urethra, cervix, rectum, and pharynx.

The 125-mg intramuscular dose of ceftriaxone is fully effective.[85, 169] Ceftriaxone is safe and effective in pregnant women, and it probably aborts incubating syphilis.[170] Its major drawback is the necessity for intramuscular administration. Studies suggested that 250 mg ciprofloxacin orally was as effective as 500 mg orally, but the emergence of less sensitive strains strongly suggests that the higher dose should be used. Even with the higher (500 mg) dose, treatment failure rates are 60% when the infecting gonococcus has an MIC for ciprofloxacin of 1.0 mg/liter or higher.[171] Ciprofloxacin and ofloxacin should be avoided in pregnant women, and because they lack activity against *Treponema pallidum,* these drugs will not abort incubating syphilis. The efficacy of cefixime against incubating syphilis is uncertain.[172] Although cross-reactions between penicillin and the cephalosporins appear to be uncommon in persons treated for gonorrhea and although many clinics routinely use ceftriaxone, cefixime, or other cephalosporins to treat gonorrhea in patients with histories of penicillin allergy, the safest approach in such circumstances would be to use an oral fluoroquinolone.

Single-dose regimens with several other cephalosporins, quinolones, or other antibiotics may be used, but they have no advantages over the four recommended regimens. Spectinomycin, 2.0 g intramuscularly, remains highly effective for genital and rectal gonorrhea in the United States despite the occasional occurrence of spectinomycin-resistant gonococci,[173] but it is ineffective for pharyngeal infection.[174] Its sole remaining indication is the treatment of pregnant women with histories of rapid-onset allergic reactions to penicillin or documented cephalosporin allergy. Spectinomycin does not inhibit *T. pallidum.*[174]

Regardless of the single-dose regimen chosen, the initial treatment should be followed by a regimen active against *C. trachomatis.* In addition to treating chlamydial infection, along with an attendant reduction in the risk of postgonococcal urethritis and salpingitis,[175] giving a second drug may reduce the potential for selection of gonococci with increased antimicrobial resistance. The recommended

TABLE 200–4 Recommended Initial Single-Dose Treatment of Uncomplicated Gonorrhea in Adults

Ceftriaxone, 125 mg IM
or
Cefixime, 400 mg PO
or
Ciprofloxacin, 500 mg PO
or
Ofloxacin, 400 mg PO
plus
Azithromycin, 1.0 g PO in a single dose
or
Doxycycline, 100 mg PO bid for 7 d

Modified from Centers for Disease Control and Prevention. 1998 Guidelines for treatment of sexually transmitted diseases. MMWR Morb Mortal Wkly Rep. 1997;47(Suppl RR-1):S59–S69.

regimens are doxycycline, 100 mg orally twice daily for 7 days, or a single oral dose of azithromycin 1.0 g.[106, 173, 174] The latter is highly effective against genital chlamydial infection.[173] A single dose of 2.0 g azithromycin is effective against both gonorrhea and chlamydial infection, but cost and gastrointestinal intolerance limit its utility.[176] Azithromycin in a single oral dose of 1.0 g is not as effective as other regimens for gonorrhea; failures are not directly correlated with the MIC for azithromycin.[177] Erythromycin, in a divided-dose regimen totaling 2.0 g/day orally, is acceptable as follow-up therapy if neither azithromycin nor a tetracycline can be given.[106, 174]

Pregnant women with uncomplicated gonorrhea should not be treated with quinolones or tetracyclines. Spectinomycin is effective and safe but is less acceptable because of the increased likelihood of pharyngeal gonorrhea during pregnancy.[122] The efficacy of azithromycin in eradicating chlamydial infection has not been determined in pregnant women, and most authorities recommend following ceftriaxone with a 7- to 10-day course of erythromycin.[106, 174]

Retesting to document cure is not recommended by most authorities if one of the recommended treatment regimens is used, unless therapeutic compliance is in question or symptoms persist.[106, 174] However, most patients with gonorrhea continue to have a high risk for STDs, and rescreening for gonorrhea and other infections is recommended 1 to 2 months after treatment. Most patients with gonorrhea that persists after treatment have in fact been reinfected.

Pelvic Inflammatory Disease

Because the specific pathogens responsible for ascending genital infection are not usually known, the recommendations for initial treatment of acute PID are similar regardless of whether the initial lower genital infection is due to *N. gonorrhoeae, C. trachomatis,* or other pathogens.[106, 178–180] Some authorities believe that ideally, all women with PID should be treated initially with parenteral antibiotics, as for almost all other intraperitoneal infections, but practical considerations often preclude this option.

The 1998 treatment guidelines of the U.S. Public Health Service for PID[106] are summarized in Table 200–5. Few studies have directly compared the recommended regimens, and almost all available studies of antibiotic treatment of PID are limited to short-term outcomes. Few data exist on the efficacy of the recommended regimens in preventing infertility, ectopic pregnancy, or chronic pelvic pain. The cefotetan or cefoxitin/doxycycline regimen provides excellent coverage for *C. trachomatis, N. gonorrhoeae,* and most of the facultative and anaerobic organisms that may contribute to PID.[115, 178–180] The clindamycin/gentamicin regimen may have suboptimal activity against *C. trachomatis* but is active against all strains of *N. gonorrhoeae* and a wide spectrum of vaginal bacteria. Some authorities prefer this regimen when chlamydial and gonococcal infection is unlikely or when a mixed facultative and anaerobic flora is probable, as in recurrent PID or when a pelvic abscess is suspected.[178–180] Recent retrospective analysis of treatment outcomes has suggested that ampicillin plus clindamycin plus gentamicin was best when patients had tuboovarian abscess.[181] For all regimens, intravenous therapy is continued for at least 24 hours after definite clinical improvement begins. Oral therapy with doxycycline or clindamycin is then continued to complete 14 days' total treatment.[106] Parenteral treatment either with ampicillin/sulbactam plus doxycycline, with ofloxacin plus metronidazole, or with ciprofloxacin plus doxycycline and metronidazole has been proposed as alternative regimens on the basis of the drugs' in vitro activity and small clinical trials.[178–180] These regimens are listed as secondary options in the U.S. Public Health Service guidelines,[106] but clinical experience is limited.

Two alternative regimens are recommended for the treatment of outpatients with acute PID.[106, 178–180] A regimen using a loading dose of cefoxitin (with probenecid) intramuscularly or ceftriaxone intramuscularly, followed by a 14-day course of doxycycline orally, has been frequently used for outpatient management. For outpatients with severe PID—for example, when hospitalization is indicated but cannot be accomplished—some authorities add metronidazole in a dose of 1.0 to 2.0 g orally daily in divided doses.[178–180]

TABLE 200–5 Recommended Treatment of Acute Pelvic Inflammatory Disease

Hospitalized patients
Regimen A
Cefotetan, 2.0 g IV q12h, or cefoxitin, 2.0 g IV q6h
plus
Doxycycline, 100 mg IV or PO q12h
Continue both drugs IV for 24 h after the patient substantially improves, then continue doxycycline, 100 mg PO bid, to complete 14 d total therapy. Either clindamycin or metronidazole may be added to the oral regimen if tuboovarian abscess is suspected
or
Regimen B
Clindamycin, 900 mg IV q8h
plus
Gentamicin, 2.0 mg/kg IV once, followed by 1.5 mg/kg q8h*
Continue both drugs IV for 24 h after the patient substantially improves, then continue doxycycline, 100 mg PO twice daily, or clindamycin, 450 mg PO 4 times daily, to complete 14 d total therapy. Clindamycin may be preferable when tuboovarian abscess is suspected
Outpatients
Regimen A
Ofloxacin, 400 mg PO bid for 14 d
plus
Metronidazole, 500 mg PO bid for 14 d
or
Regimen B
Single-dose cefoxitin, 2.0 g IM, plus probenecid, 1.0 g PO; or ceftriaxone, 250 mg IM; or other parenteral third-generation cephalosporin (e.g., ceftizoxime or cefotaxime)
plus
Doxycycline, 100 mg PO bid for 14 d

*Single daily dosing may be substituted.
Modified from Centers for Disease Control and Prevention. 1998 Guidelines for treatment of sexually transmitted diseases. MMWR Morb Mortal Wkly Rep. 1997;47(Suppl RR-1):S59–S69.

All fluoroquinolones are active against *N. gonorrhoeae,* and ofloxacin (but not ciprofloxacin) is active against *C. trachomatis*[182]; neither ciprofloxacin nor ofloxacin is highly active against anaerobic bacteria. A regimen consisting of 14 days of treatment with oral ofloxacin plus metronidazole provides comprehensive coverage for all likely pathogens. Several studies have demonstrated good short-term outcomes in women with mild to moderate PID treated with ofloxacin alone,[183, 184] and some investigators believe that most outpatients with acute PID can be safely treated without providing coverage for anaerobic bacteria.[184] However, most authorities agree that it is prudent to routinely add metronidazole (or clindamycin) to improve coverage for anaerobic pathogens.[178–180]

Regardless of the initial treatment, close follow-up is indicated. Clinical progression or failure of the patient to improve within 3 days is an indication to reassess the diagnosis. Laparoscopy may be required both to confirm the diagnosis and to obtain intra-abdominal culture specimens to facilitate selection of improved antimicrobial therapy. If an intrauterine device is present, it should be promptly removed. Other adjunctive treatment measures include bed rest, analgesia as needed, and sexual abstention for 2 to 3 weeks, both for comfort and to prevent reinfection.[106, 178] The sexual partners of women with PID should be evaluated, regardless of the apparent etiology; in most cases, the partners should be routinely treated with regimens effective against both gonorrhea and chlamydial infection.[106, 185]

Acute Epididymitis

Most acute epididymitis in young adults is due to *C. trachomatis,* but *N. gonorrhoeae* accounts for about 10% of cases.[98] Most cases of gonococcal epididymitis can be managed on an outpatient basis with ceftriaxone, 250 mg intramuscularly, plus the usual doxycycline regimen, with the duration of treatment extended to 10 days.[106] It is likely that other single-dose regimens can be substituted for ceftriaxone, but no clinical data are available. An alternative regimen for outpatient management is to treat with ofloxacin (e.g., 400 mg orally twice daily) for 10 days,[182] which provides excellent coverage for *N. gonorrhoeae, C. trachomatis,* and most coliforms and other urinary tract pathogens. Patients with severe acute epididymitis should be hospitalized and managed with parenteral ceftriaxone or an equivalent antibiotic, plus doxycycline if chlamydial infection cannot be excluded,[98] or with ofloxacin. Unlike ofloxacin, ciprofloxacin and most other quinolones are not reliably effective against *C. trachomatis.*[182]

Disseminated Gonococcal Infection

Only anecdotal reports of the treatment of patients with DGI have been reported since the evolution and spread of gonococci with high levels of antibiotic resistance, and all recommendations are empirical. Patients with the gonococcal arthritis-dermatitis syndrome should be treated initially with ceftriaxone, 1.0 g once daily, either intramuscularly or intravenously.[106, 174] If adequate technical and social support is available, some patients without complications may be treated as outpatients.[106] Therapeutically equivalent doses of other third-generation cephalosporins would undoubtedly be effective and are recommended as options, as is treatment with spectinomycin, 2.0 g intramuscularly twice daily.[106] In the absence of septic arthritis or other complications, after clinical improvement begins, treatment may be switched to oral cefixime (400 mg twice daily), ciprofloxacin (500 mg twice daily), or other drugs to complete 7 to 10 days' total therapy.[106] The penicillins or tetracyclines may be used if the infecting organism is documented to be fully susceptible.[186]

Patients with gonococcal endocarditis should receive 4 weeks of parenteral therapy. Treatment should be started with ceftriaxone or an equivalent third-generation cephalosporin,[106, 129] but penicillin may be substituted if antimicrobial susceptibility testing shows the isolate to be susceptible. Meningitis should probably be treated with a 10- to 14-day course of ceftriaxone or an equivalent antibiotic.

Gonorrhea in Children

Because relatively few cases of gonorrhea are seen in children, treatment has not been as well studied as in adults. Uncomplicated infections in neonates and older children should normally be treated with ceftriaxone in a single intramuscular dose of 25 to 50 mg/kg body weight, not to exceed 125 mg.[106, 174] Little is known about the prevalence of chlamydial infection in pediatric patients with gonorrhea. The tetracyclines are contraindicated in young children, and azithromycin and erythromycin have not been well studied in this setting. The usual practice is to perform a test for chlamydial infection and withhold specific treatment unless infection is diagnosed.[145] DGI and gonococcal conjunctivitis in children are treated with 7 to 10 days of ceftriaxone, 25 to 50 mg/kg body weight per day intramuscularly or intravenously, or with an equivalent regimen of another third-generation cephalosporin. Continuous irrigation of the conjunctivae with physiologic saline solution is often used in gonococcal conjunctivitis, but topical antibiotics offer no additional benefit.[144]

Management of Sexual Partners

Management of sexual partners is an integral part of treating patients with gonorrhea and other STDs. Failure to ensure that the partner is examined and treated risks reinfection of the patient and continued spread of the infection to others. In many industrialized countries the local or state health department may assist in the location and notification of the partners of persons with gonorrhea; otherwise, the physician and patient should work together to this end. The partners should be examined and treated with one of the recommended antibiotic regimens, regardless of whether clinical evidence of gonorrhea is found ("epidemiologic" treatment). Diagnostic tests for *N. gonorrhoeae* should always be performed; failure to document infection, if present, usually precludes active case finding in other sexual partners and distorts statistics on the occurrence of gonorrhea. When practical, the sexual partners of patients with gonorrhea or other sexually transmitted infections should be examined and undergo diagnostic tests before treatment. In some circumstances, however, it may be necessary to treat without examination or even personal contact with the partner (e.g., by providing the index case medication to be given to the partner).

PREVENTION AND CONTROL

Condoms, if properly used, provide a high degree of protection from the transmission or acquisition of gonorrhea, chlamydial infection, human immunodeficiency virus (HIV) infection, and other infections transmitted to and from mucosal surfaces. Less protection may be provided against infections transmitted from skin to skin, such as syphilis and genital herpes.[187, 188] It is likely that the female condom would protect against infection, but no data are available and the use-effectiveness ratio of the device is uncertain. Other barrier contraceptive methods (diaphragm, cervical cap) are probably protective, albeit less so than condoms.[187]

Spermicides with nonoxynol 9 have been suggested to modestly reduce the risk of acquiring gonorrhea or chlamydial infection,[189] but they are associated with an enhanced incidence of *Candida* vulvovaginitis.[188] Very frequent use of preparations that contain nonoxynol 9 is associated with mucosal disruption, which might paradoxically enhance the risk of HIV infection in the event of exposure.[190] Therefore, the role of nonoxynol 9 in the prevention of STDs remains uncertain. A recent large controlled trial failed to show benefit of nonoxynol 9 films in the prevention of HIV, gonorrhea, or chlamydia in exposed female commercial sex workers.[191] Other topical microbicides that might be useful in prevention are under development. No evidence has been presented that such time-honored measures as washing, urinating, or douching after exposure materially reduce the risk of infection.

Administration of systemic antibiotics immediately before or soon after sexual exposure can reduce the risk of infection, and mass treatment of populations with a high prevalence of syphilis and other treponematoses has been effective in reducing morbidity. However, these approaches may carry a risk of fostering the spread of resistant gonococci and are not recommended for routine use.

The development of a vaccine to prevent gonorrhea is a high research priority, but an experimental vaccine containing purified gonococcal pili conferred only partial protection against experimental infection with the homologous strain of *N. gonorrhoeae* and no protection from heterologous challenge.[192, 193] Moreover, the extraordinary degree of antigenic variability in pili, Opa, and LOS in the community and during the course of experimental infection[95] presents formidable barriers to developing a gonorrhea vaccine based on these antigens. However, other more antigenically stable proteins, including porin, are under investigation as possible vaccine candidates.[19, 193]

Screening of sexually active persons, especially women, is a mainstay of control of gonorrhea and the other treatable bacterial STDs. Women at risk who are undergoing routine pelvic examination should have specimens collected to test for *N. gonorrhoeae* and *C. trachomatis.* For both infections, however, universal screening of all patients is not cost-effective except in special settings (e.g., STD clinics); in most settings, selective screening of those at highest risk is more practical. Other key elements in gonorrhea control include conducting appropriate diagnostic testing in persons with compatible clinical syndromes, partner notification and treatment, and the use of recommended treatment regimens. Periodic testing of gonococcal isolates for antimicrobial resistance should be pursued in all geographic areas. Reporting of cases is important to monitor the gonorrhea epidemic and to facilitate the targeting of control efforts; the single most potent tool that health officials have to generate resources for disease control is accurate data on local or regional morbidity. Finally, public education and personal counseling, in an effort to induce conservative sexual behavior and the use of barrier contraceptives, is central to the control of gonorrhea and all STDs.

REFERENCES

1. Dallabetta G, Hook EW III. Gonococcal infections. Infect Dis Clin North Am. 1987;1:25–54.
2. Britigan BE, Cohen MS, Sparling PF. Gonococcal infections: A model of molecular pathogenesis. N Engl J Med. 1985;312:1683–1694.
3. Morello JM, Janda WM, Doern GV. *Neisseria* and *Branhamella*. In: Balows A, Hausler WJ, Herrmann KL, et al, eds. Manual of Clinical Microbiology. 5th ed. Washington, DC: American Society for Microbiology; 1991:258–276.
4. Thayer JD, Martin JE Jr. Improved medium selective for the cultivation of *N. gonorrhoeae* and *N. meningitidis*. Public Health Rep. 1966;81:559–562.
5. Faur YC, Weisburd MH, Wilson ME. A new medium for the isolation of pathogenic *Neisseria* (NYC medium): I. Formulations and comparisons with standard media. Health Lab Sci. 1973;10:44–54.
6. Minnett S, Reller LB, Knapp JS. *Neisseria gonorrhoeae* strains inhibited by vancomycin in selective media and correlation with auxotype. J Clin Microbiol. 1981;14:94–99.
7. Kellogg DS Jr, Peacock WL Sr, Deacon WE, et al. *Neisseria gonorrhoeae:* I. Virulence genetically linked to clonal variation. J Bacteriol. 1963;85:1274–1279.
8. Schoolnik GK, Fernandez R, Tai J-Y, et al. Gonococcal pili: Primary structure and receptor binding domain. J Exp Med. 1984;159:1351–1370.
9. Buchanan TM, Chen KCS, Jones RB, et al. Pili and principal outer membrane protein of *Neisseria gonorrhoeae*: Immunochemical, structural, and pathogenic aspects. In: Brooks GF, Gotschlich EC, Holmes KK, et al, eds. Immunobiology of *Neisseria gonorrhoeae*. Washington, DC: American Society for Microbiology; 1978:145–154.
10. McGee ZA, Johnson AP, Taylor-Robinson D. Pathogenic mechanisms of *Neisseria gonorrhoeae:* Observations on damage to human fallopian tubes in organ culture by gonococci of colony type 1 or type 4. J Infect Dis. 1981;143:413–422.
11. Segal E, Billyard E, So M, et al. Role of chromosomal rearrangement in *N. gonorrhoeae* pilus phase variation. Cell. 1985;40:293–300.
12. Forest KT, Bernstein SL, Getzoff ED, So M, et al. Assembly and antigenicity of the *Neisseria gonorrhoeae* pilus mapped with antibodies. Infect Immun. 1996;64:644–652.
13. Heckels JE. Molecular studies on the pathogenesis of gonorrhea. J Med Microbiol. 1984;18:293–307.
14. Ofek I, Beachy EH, Bisno AL. Resistance of *Neisseria gonorrhoeae* to phagocytosis: Relationship to colonial morphology and surface pili. J Infect Dis. 1974;129:310–316.
15. Kallstrom H, Liszewski MK, Atkinson JP, Jonsson AB. Membrane cofactor protein (MCP or CD46) is a cellular pilus receptor for pathogenic *Neisseria*. Mol Microbiol. 1997;25:639–647.
16. Blake MS, Gotschlich EC. Gonococcal membrane proteins: Speculation on their role in pathogenesis. Prog Allergy. 1983;33:298–313.
17. Knapp JS, Tam MR, Nowinski RC, et al. Serological classification of *Neisseria gonorrhoeae* with use of monoclonal antibodies to gonococcal outer membrane protein I. J Infect Dis. 1984;150:44–48.
18. Van Putten JPM. Gonococcal invasion of epithelial cells driven by the P.IA porin. In: Nassif X, Quentin-Millet M-J, Taha M-K, eds. Proceedings of the Eleventh International Pathogenic Neisseria Conference, Nice, France, November 1998. Paris: Éditions E.D.K.; 1998:35.
19. Blake MS, Wetzler LM, Gotschlich EC, et al. Developing a gonococcal protein I vaccine. Adv Exp Med Biol. 1989;251:315–327.
20. Swanson J. Colony opacity and protein II compositions of gonococci. Infect Immun. 1982;37:359–368.
21. Connell TD, Shaffer D, Cannon JG. Characterization of the repertoire of hypervariable regions in the protein II (opa) gene family of *Neisseria gonorrhoeae.* Mol Microbiol. 1990;4:439–449.
22. Stern A, Brown M, Nickel P, et al. Opacity genes in *Neisseria gonorrhoeae:* Control of phase and antigenic variation. Cell. 1986;47:61–71.
23. Fischer SH, Rest RF. Gonococci possessing only certain P.II outer membrane proteins interact with human neutrophils. Infect Immun. 1988;56:1574–1579.
24. Virji M, Heckels JE. The effect of protein II and pili on the interaction of *Neisseria gonorrhoeae* with human polymorphonuclear leucocytes. J Gen Microbiol. 1986;132:503–512.
25. Makino S, van Putten JPM, Meyer TF. Phase variation of the opacity outer membrane protein controls invasion by *Neisseria gonorrhoeae* into human epithelial cells. EMBO J. 1991;10:1307–1315.
26. Van Putten JPM, Duensing TD, Cole RL. Entry of OpaA+ gonococci into Hep-2 cells requires concerted action of glycosaminoglycans, fibronectin and integrin receptors. Mol Microbiol. 1998;29:369–379.
27. Wang J, Gray-Owen SD, Knorre A, et al. Opa binding to cellular CD66 receptors mediates the transcellular traversal of *Neisseria gonorrhoeae* across polarized T84 epithelial cell monolayers. Mol Microbiol 1998;30:657–671.
28. Rice PA, Vayo HE, Tam MR, et al. Immunoglobulin G antibodies directed against protein III block killing of serum-resistant *Neisseria gonorrhoeae* by immune serum. J Exp Med. 1986;164:1735–1748.
29. Plummer FA, Chubb H, Simonsen JN, et al. Antibody to Rmp (outer membrane protein 3) increases susceptibility to gonococcal infection. J Clin Invest. 1993;91:339–343.
30. Cornelissen C, Sparling PF. Iron piracy: Acquisition of transferrin-bound iron by bacterial pathogens. Mol Microbiol. 1994;14:843–850.
31. Biswas GD, Sparling PF. Characterization of *lbpA*, the structural gene for a lactoferrin receptor in *Neisseria gonorrhoeae*. Infect Immun. 1995;63:2958–2967.
32. Chen CJ, Sparling PF, Lewis LA, et al. Identification and purification of a hemoglobin-binding outer membrane protein from *Neisseria gonorrhoeae*. Infect Immun. 1996;64:5008–5014.
33. Cornelissen CN, Kelley M, Hobbs MM, et al. The gonococcal transferrin receptor is required for human infection. Mol Microbiol. 1998;27:611–616.
34. Clark VL, Campbell LA, Palermo DA, et al. Induction and repression of outer membrane proteins by anaerobic growth of *Neisseria gonorrhoeae.* Infect Immun. 1987;55:1359–1364.
35. Mulks MH, Knapp JS. Immunoglobulin A1 protease types of *Neisseria gonorrhoeae* and their relationship to auxotype and serovar. Infect Immun. 1987;55:931–936.
36. Griffiss JM, Schneider H, Mandrell RE, et al. Lipooligosaccharides: The principle glycolipids of the neisserial outer membrane. Rev Infect Dis. 1988; 10(Suppl):S287–S295.
37. Mandrell RE, Lesse AJ, Sugai JV, et al. Phenotypic variation in epitope expression of the *Neisseria gonorrhoeae* lipooligosaccharide. J Exp Med. 1990;171:1649–1664.
38. Elkins C, Carbonetti NH, Varela VA, et al. Antibodies to N-terminal peptides of gonococcal porin are bactericidal when gonococcal lipopolysaccharide is not sialylated. Mol Microbiol. 1992;6:2617–2628.
39. Apicella MA, Shero M, Jarvis GA, et al. Phenotypic variation in epitope expression of the *Neisseria gonorrhoeae* lipooligosaccharide. Infect Immun. 1987;55:1755–1761.
40. Apicella MA, Westerlink MA, Morse SA, et al. Bactericidal antibody response of normal human serum to the lipooligosaccharide of *Neisseria gonorrhoeae.* J Infect Dis. 1986;153:520–526.
41. Van Putten JPM, Robertson BD. Molecular mechanisms and implications for infection of lipopolysaccharide variation in *Neisseria*. Mol Microbiol. 1995;16:847–853.
42. Rosenthal RS, Folkening WT, Miller DR, et al. Resistance of *O*-acetylated gonococcal peptidoglycan to human peptidoglycan-degrading enzymes. Infect Immun. 1983;40:903–911.
43. Fleming TJ, Wallsmith DE, Rosenthal RS. Arthropathic properties of gonococcal peptidoglycan fragments: Implications for the pathogenesis of disseminated gonococcal disease. Infect Immun. 1986;52:600–608.
44. Noegel A, Gotschlich EC. Isolation of a high molecular weight polyphosphate from *Neisseria gonorrhoeae.* J Exp Med. 1983;157:2049–2060.
45. Catlin BW. Nutritional profiles of *Neisseria gonorrhoeae, Neisseria meningitidis,* and *Neisseria lactamica* in chemically defined media and the use of growth requirements for gonococcal typing. J Infect Dis. 1973;128:178–194.
46. Hook EW III, Judson FN, Handsfield HH. Auxotype/serovar diversity and antimicrobial resistance of *Neisseria gonorrhoeae* in two mid-sized American cities. Sex Transm Dis. 1987;14:141–146.
47. Handsfield HH, Rice RJ, Roberts MC, et al. Localized outbreak of penicillinase-producing *Neisseria gonorrhoeae:* Paradigm for introduction and spread of gonorrhea in a community. JAMA. 1989;261:2357–2360.
48. O'Rourke M, Ison CA, Renton AM, et al. Opa-typing: A high-resolution tool for studying the epidemiology of gonorrhoea. Mol Microbiol. 1995;17:865–875.
49. Eisenstein BI, Sox T, Biswas G, et al. Conjugal transfer of the gonococcal penicillinase plasmid. Science. 1977;195:998–1000.
50. Cannon JG, Sparling PF. The genetics of the gonococcus. Annu Rev Microbiol. 1984;38:111–313.
51. Anderson B, Albritton WL, Biddle J, et al. Common b-lactamase–specifying plasmid in *Haemophilus ducreyi* and *Neisseria gonorrhoeae.* Antimicrob Agents Chemother. 1984;25:296–297.
52. Biswas GD, Blackman EY, Sparling, PF. High-frequency conjugal transfer of a gonococcal penicillinase plasmid. J Bacteriol. 1980;143:1318–1324.
53. Morse SA, Johnson SR, Biddle JW, et al. High-level tetracycline resistance in *Neisseria gonorrhoeae* is result of acquisition of streptococcal *tetM* determinant. Antimicrob Agents Chemother. 1986;30:664–670.
54. Shafer WM, Balthazar JT, Hagman KE, et al. Missense mutations that alter the DNA-binding domain of the MtrR protein occur frequently in rectal isolates of *Neisseria gonorrhoeae* that are resistant to faecal lipid. Microbiology. 1995;141:907–911.
55. Spratt BG. Hybrid penicillin-binding proteins in penicillin-resistant strains of *Neisseria gonorrhoeae.* Nature. 1988;332:173–176.
56. Rice RJ, Biddle JW, Jean Louis YA, et al. Chromosomally mediated resistance in *Neisseria gonorrhoeae* in the United States: Results of surveillance and reporting, 1983–1984. J Infect Dis. 1986;153:340–345.
57. Shinners EN, Catlin BW. Arginine and pyrimidine biosynthetic defects in *Neisseria gonorrhoeae* strains isolated from patients. J Bacteriol. 1982;151:295–302.
58. Campbell LA, Yasbin RE. Mutagenesis of *Neisseria gonorrhoeae:* Absence of error-prone repair. J Bacteriol. 1984;160:288–293.
59. Biswas GD, Sox T, Blackman T, et al. Factors affecting genetic transformation of *Neisseria gonorrhoeae.* J Bacteriol. 1977;129:983–992.

60. Elkins C, Thomas CE, Seifert HS, et al. Species-specific uptake of DNA by gonococci is mediated by a 10–base-pair sequence. J Bacteriol. 1991;173:3911–3913.
61. Giardina PC, Williams R, Lubaroff D, et al. *Neisseria gonorrhoeae* induces focal polymerization of actin in primary human urethral epithelium. Infect Immun. 1998;66:3416–3419.
62. Casey SG, Shafer MW, Spitznagel JK. *Neisseria gonorrhoeae* survive intraleukocytic oxygen-independent antimicrobial capacities of anaerobic and aerobic granulocytes in the presence of pyocin lethal for extracellular gonococci. Infect Immun. 1986;52:384–389.
63. Division of STD/HIV Prevention. Sexually Transmitted Disease Surveillance, 1995. U.S. Department of Health and Human Services, Public Health Service. Atlanta: Centers for Disease Control and Prevention; 1996.
64. Fox KK, Whittington WL, Levine WC, et al. Gonorrhea in the United States 1981–1986. Demographic and geographic trends. Sex Transm Dis. 1998;25:386–393.
65. Brunham RC, Embree JE. Sexually transmitted diseases: Current and future dimensions of the problem in the third world. In: Germain A, Holmes KK, Piot P, et al, eds. Reproductive Tract Infections: Global Impact and Priorities for Women's Reproductive Health. New York: Plenum; 1992:35–58.
66. Rice RJ, Roberts PL, Handsfield HH, et al. Sociodemographic distribution of gonorrhea incidence: Implications for prevention and behavioral research. Am J Public Health. 1991;81:1252–1258.
67. Handsfield HH, Schwebke J. Trends in sexually transmitted diseases in homosexually active men in King County, Washington, 1980–1990. Sex Transm Dis. 1990;17:211–215.
68. Evans BG, Catchpole MA, Heptonstall J, et al. Sexually transmitted diseases and HIV-1 infection among homosexual men in England and Wales. BMJ. 1993;306:426–428.
69. Schwarcz SK, Bolan GA, Fullilove M, et al. Crack cocaine and the exchange of sex for money for drugs. Sex Transm Dis. 1992;19:7–13.
70. Alary M, Joly JR, Poulin C. Incidence of four sexually transmitted diseases in a rural community: A prospective study. Am J Epidemiol. 1989;130:547–556.
71. Hooper RR, Reynolds GH, Jones OG, et al. Cohort study of venereal disease: I. The risk of gonorrhea transmission from infected women to men. Am J Epidemiol. 1978;108:136–144.
72. Holmes KK, Johnson DW, Trostle JH. An estimate of the risk of men acquiring gonorrhea by sexual contact with infected females. Am J Epidemiol. 1970;91:170–174.
73. Thin RNT, Williams IA, Nicol CS. Direct and delayed methods of immunofluorescent diagnosis of gonorrhea in women. Br J Vener Dis. 1971;47:27–30.
74. Lin J-S, Donegan SP, Heeren TC, et al. Transmission of *Chlamydia trachomatis* and *Neisseria gonorrhoeae* among men with urethritis and their female sex partners. J Infect Dis. 1988;178:1707–1712.
75. Wiesner PJ, Tronca E, Bonin P, et al. Clinical spectrum of pharyngeal gonococcal infection. N Engl J Med. 1973;288:181–185.
76. McCormack WM, Reynolds GH, Cooperative Study Group. Effect of menstrual cycle and method of contraception on recovery of *Neisseria gonorrhoeae.* JAMA. 1982;247:1292–1294.
77. Yorke JA, Hethcote HW, Nold A. Dynamics and control of the transmission of gonorrhea. Sex Transm Dis. 1978;5:51–56.
78. Anderson RM, May RM. Epidemiological parameters of HIV transmission. Nature. 1988;333:514–519.
79. Rothenberg RB. The geography of gonorrhea: Empirical demonstration of core group transmission. Am J Epidemiol. 1983;117:688–694.
80. Potterat JJ. "Socio-geographic space" and sexually transmissible diseases in the 1990s. Today's Life Sci. 1992; December:16–23.
81. Handsfield HH, Lipman TO, Harnisch JP, et al. Asymptomatic gonorrhea in men: Diagnosis, natural course, prevalence and significance. N Engl J Med. 1973;290:117–123.
82. Perine PL, Morton RS, Piot P, et al. Epidemiology and treatment of penicillinase-producing *Neisseria gonorrhoeae.* Sex Transm Dis. 1979;6(Suppl):S152–S158.
83. Handsfield HH, Sandström EG, Knapp JS, et al. Epidemiology of penicillinase-producing *Neisseria gonorrhoeae* infections: Analysis by auxotyping and serogrouping. N Engl J Med. 1982;306:950–954.
84. Dillon JR, Yeung K-H. b-Lactamase plasmids and chromosomally mediated antibiotic resistance in pathogenic *Neisseria* species. Clin Microbiol Rev. 1989;2:125–133.
85. Handsfield HH, Hook EW III. Ceftriaxone for treatment of uncomplicated gonorrhea: Routine use of a single 125-mg dose in a sexually transmitted disease clinic. Sex Transm Dis. 1987;14:227–230.
86. Van Dyck E, Crabbe F, Nzila N, et al. Increasing resistance of *Neisseria gonorrhoeae* in West and Central Africa. Sex Transm Dis. 1996;24:32–37.
87. Tapsall JW, Limnios EA, Shultz TR. Continuing evolution of the pattern of quinolone resistance in *Neisseria gonorrhoeae* isolated in Sydney, Australia. Sex Transm Dis. 1998;25:415–417.
88. Knapp JS. *Neisseria gonorrhoeae* resistant to ciprofloxacin and ofloxacin. Sex Transm Dis. 1998;25:425–426.
89. Kilmark PH, Knapp JS, Xia M, et al. Intercity spread of gonococci with decreased susceptibility to fluoroquinolones: A unique focus in the United States. J Infect Dis. 1998;177:677–682.
90. Ehret JM, Judson FN. Quinolone-resistant *Neisseria gonorrhoeae*: The beginning of the end? Sex Transm Dis. 1998;25:522–526.
91. Deguchi T, Yasuda M, Nakano M, et al. Quinolone-resistant *Neisseria gonorrhoeae*: Correlation of alterations in the GyrA subunit of DNA gyrase and the ParC subunit of topoisomerase IV with antimicrobial susceptibility profiles. Antimicrob Agents Chemother. 1996;40:1020–1023.
92. Handsfield HH, Knapp JS, Diehr PK, et al. Correlation of auxotype and penicillin susceptibility of *Neisseria gonorrhoeae* with sexual preference and clinical manifestations of gonorrhea. Sex Transm Dis. 1980;7:1–5.
93. Morse SA, Lysko OG, McFarland L, et al. Gonococcal strains from homosexual men have outer membranes with reduced permeability to hydrophobic molecules. Infect Immun. 1982;37:4328.
94. Harrison WO, Hooper RR, Weisner PJ, et al. A trial of minocycline given after exposure to prevent gonorrhea. N Engl J Med. 1979;300:1074–1078.
95. Cohen MS, Cannon JG, Jerse AE, et al. Human experimentation with *Neisseria gonorrhoeae:* Rationale, methods and implications for the biology of infection and vaccine development. J Infect Dis. 1994;169:532–537.
96. Jacobs NF, Kraus SJ. Gonococcal and nongonococcal urethritis in men: Clinical and laboratory differentiation. Ann Intern Med. 1975;82:7–12.
97. Brunham RC, Plummer F, Slaney L, et al. Correlation of auxotype and protein I type with expression of disease due to *Neisseria gonorrhoeae.* J Infect Dis. 1985;152:339–343.
98. Berger RE, Alexander ER, Harnisch JP, et al. Etiology, manifestations and therapy of acute epididymitis: Prospective study of 50 cases. J Urol. 1979;121:750–754.
99. Wright RA, Judson FN. Penile venereal edema. JAMA. 1979;241:157–158.
100. Platt R, Rice PA, McCormack WM. Risk of acquiring gonorrhea and prevalence of abnormal adnexal findings among women recently exposed to gonorrhea. JAMA. 1983;250:3205–3209.
101. McCormack WM, Stumacher RJ, Johnson K, et al. Clinical spectrum of gonococcal infections in women. Lancet. 1977;1:1182–1185.
102. Whittington WL, Rice R, Hale J, et al. Relationship of AHU and PAU gonococcal auxotrophs to cervicitis, pelvic inflammatory disease, and potential for transmission. Abstract 55. Presented at the Tenth International Meeting of the International Society for STD Research, Helsinki, Finland, August 29–September 1, 1993.
103. Brunham RC, Paavonen J, Stevens CE, et al. Mucopurulent cervicitis—the ignored counterpart in women of urethritis in men. N Engl J Med. 1984;311:1–6.
104. Janda WM, Bohnhoff M, Morello JA, et al. Prevalence and site pathogen studies of *Neisseria meningitidis* and *Neisseria gonorrhoeae* in homosexual men. JAMA. 1980;244:2060–2064.
105. Quinn TC, Stamm WE, Goodell SE, et al. The polymicrobial origin of intestinal infections in homosexual men. N Engl J Med. 1983;309:576–582.
106. Centers for Disease Control and Prevention. 1998 Guidelines for treatment of sexually transmitted diseases. MMWR Morb Mortal Wkly Rep. 1997;47(Suppl RR-1):S59–S69.
107. Podgore JK, Holmes KK. Ocular gonococcal infection with little or no inflammatory response. JAMA. 1981;246:242–243.
108. Holmes KK, Eschenbach DA, Knapp JS. Salpingitis: Overview of etiology and epidemiology. Am J Obstet Gynecol. 1980;138:893–900.
109. Weström L. Incidence, prevalence and trends of acute pelvic inflammatory disease and its consequences in industrialized countries. Am J Obstet Gynecol. 1980;138:880–892.
110. Sweet RL. Pelvic inflammatory disease. Hosp Pract. 1993;28(Suppl 2):S25–S30.
111. Wølner-Hanssen P, Eschenbach DA, Paavonen J, et al. Decreased risk of symptomatic pelvic inflammatory disease associated with oral contraceptive use. JAMA. 1990;264:2072–2074.
112. Wølner-Hanssen P, Eschenbach DA, Paavonen J, et al. Association between vaginal douching and acute pelvic inflammatory disease. JAMA. 1990;263:1936–1941.
113. Chow JM, Yonekura ML, Richwald GA, et al. The association between *Chlamydia trachomatis* and ectopic pregnancy: A matched-pair, case-control study. JAMA. 1990;263:3164–3167.
114. Scholes D, Daling JR, Stergachis A, et al. Vaginal douching as a risk factor for acute pelvic inflammatory disease. Obstet Gynecol. 1993;81:601–606.
115. Eschenbach DA. Bacterial vaginosis and anaerobes in obstetric-gynecologic infection. Clin Infect Dis. 1993;16(Suppl 4):S282–S287.
116. Doyle MB, DeCherney AH, Diamond MP. Epidemiology and etiology of ectopic pregnancy. Obstet Gynecol Clin North Am. 1991;18:1–17.
117. Lopez-Zeno JA, Keith LG, Berger GS. The Fitz-Hugh–Curtis syndrome revisited: Changing perspectives after half a century. J Reprod Med. 1985;30:567–582.
118. Davidson AC, Hawkins DA. Pleuritic pain: Fitz-Hugh–Curtis syndrome in a man. BMJ. 1982;284:808.
119. Edwards LE, Barrada MMI, Harmann AA, et al. Gonorrhea in pregnancy. Am J Obstet Gynecol. 1978;132:637–641.
120. Schulz KF, Cates W Jr, O'Mara PR. Pregnancy loss, infant death, and suffering: Legacy of syphilis and gonorrhea in Africa. Genitourin Med. 1987;63:320–325.
121. Handsfield HH, Hodson WA, Holmes KK. Neonatal gonococcal infections: I. Orogastric contamination with *Neisseria gonorrhoeae.* JAMA. 1973;225:697–701.
122. Corman LC, Levison ME, Knight R, et al. The high frequency of pharyngeal gonococcal infection in a prenatal clinic population. JAMA. 1974;230:568–570.
123. Holmes KK, Counts GW, Beaty HN. Disseminated gonococcal infection. Ann Intern Med. 1971;74:979–993.
124. Handsfield HH. Disseminated gonococcal infection. Clin Obstet Gynecol. 1975;18:131–142.
125. O'Brien JA, Goldenberg DL, Rice PA. Disseminated gonococcal infection: A prospective analysis of 49 patients and a review of pathophysiology and immune mechanisms. Medicine (Baltimore). 1983;62:395–406.
126. Kerle KK, Mascola JR, Miller TA. Disseminated gonococcal infection. Am Fam Physician. 1992;45:209–214.
127. Tapsall JW, Phillips EA, Schultz TR, et al. Strain characteristics and antibiotic

susceptibility of isolates of *Neisseria gonorrhoeae* causing disseminated gonococcal infection in Australia. Int J STD AIDS. 1992;3:273–277.
128. Bohnhoff M, Morello JA, Lerner SA. Auxotypes, penicillin susceptibility and serogroups of *Neisseria gonorrhoeae* from disseminated and uncomplicated infections. J Infect Dis. 1986;154:225–230.
129. Jackman JD Jr, Glamann DB. Gonococcal endocarditis: Twenty-five year experience. Am J Med Sci. 1991;301:221–230.
130. Weiss PJ, Kennedy CA, McCann DF, et al. Fulminant endocarditis due to infection with penicillinase-producing *Neisseria gonorrhoeae*. Sex Transm Dis. 1991;19:288–290.
131. Billings FT III, Evans VA, Wittlinger PS, et al. "Primary" gonococcal meningitis. Sex Transm Dis. 1991;18:129–130.
132. Ingram CW, Nichole B, Martinez S, et al. Gonococcal osteomyelitis: Case report and review of the literature. Arch Intern Med. 1991;151:177–179.
133. Walters DG, Goldstein MD. Adult respiratory distress syndrome and gonococcemia. Chest. 1980;77:434–436.
134. Belding ME, Carbone J. Gonococcemia associated with adult respiratory distress syndrome. Rev Infect Dis. 1991;13:1105–1107.
135. Rinaldi RZ, Harrison WO, Fan PT. Penicillin resistant gonococcal arthritis. Ann Intern Med. 1982;97:43–45.
136. Rompalo AM, Hook EW III, Roberts PL, et al. The acute arthritis-dermatitis syndrome: The changing importance of *Neisseria gonorrhoeae* and *Neisseria meningitidis*. Arch Intern Med. 1987;147:281–283.
137. Petersen BH, Lee TJ, Snyderman R, et al. *Neisseria meningitidis* and *Neisseria gonorrhoeae* bacteremia associated with C6, C7, or C8 deficiency. Ann Intern Med. 1979;90:917–920.
138. Ellison RT III, Curd JG, Kohler PF, et al. Underlying complement deficiency in patients with disseminated gonococcal infection. Sex Transm Dis. 1987;14:201–204.
139. Maincourt DH, Orloff S. Gonococcal arthritis-dermatitis syndrome: Study of serum and synovial fluid immune complex levels. Arthritis Rheum. 1982;25:574–578.
140. Tronca E, Handsfield HH, Wiesner PJ, et al. Demonstration of *Neisseria gonorrhoeae* with fluorescent antibody in patients with disseminated gonococcal infection. J Infect Dis. 1974;129:583–586.
141. Alexander ER. Gonorrhea in the newborn. Ann N Y Acad Sci. 1988;549:180–186.
142. Desenclos JC, Garrity D, Scraggs M, et al. Gonococcal infection of the newborn in Florida, 1984–1989. Sex Transm Dis. 1992;19:105–110.
143. Laga M, Naaromara W, Brunham RD, et al. Single-dose therapy of gonococcal ophthalmia neonatorum with ceftriaxone. N Engl J Med. 1986;315:1382–1385.
144. Hammerschlag MR, Cummings C, Roblin PM, et al. Efficacy of neonatal ocular prophylaxis for the prevention of chlamydial and gonococcal conjunctivitis. N Engl J Med. 1989;320:769–772.
145. Rawston SA, Bromberg K, Hammerschlag MR. STD in children: Syphilis and gonorrhea. Genitourin Med. 1993;69:66–75.
146. Ingram DL, White ST, Durfee MF, et al. Sexual contact in children with gonorrhea. Am J Dis Child. 1982;135:994–996.
147. Koumans EH, Johnson RE, Knapp, JS, et al. Laboratory testing for *Neisseria gonorrhoeae* by recently introduced nonculture tests: A performance review with clinical and public health considerations. Clin Infect Dis. 1998;27:1171–1180.
148. Hook EW, Ching SF, Stephens J, et al. Diagnosis of *Neisseria gonorrhoeae* infections in women by using the ligase chain reaction on patient-obtained vaginal swabs. J Clin Microbiol. 1997;35:2129–2132.
149. Stary A, Ching SF, Teodorowicz L, et al. Comparison of ligase chain reaction and culture for detection of *Neisseria gonorrhoeae* in genital and extragenital specimens. J Clin Microbiol. 1997;35:239–242.
150. Xu K, Glanton V, Johnson SR, et al. Detection of *Neisseria gonorrhea* infection by ligase chain reaction testing of urine among adolescent women with and without *Chlamydia trachomatis* infection. Sex Transm Dis. 1998;25:533–538.
151. Oh MK, Smith KR, O'Cain M, et al. Urine-based screening of adolescents in detention to guide treatment for gonococcal and chlamydial infections. Translating research into intervention. Arch Pediatr Adolesc Med. 1998;152:52–56.
152. Ison CA. Laboratory methods in genitourinary medicine: Methods of diagnosing gonorrhea. Genitourin Med. 1990;66:453–459.
153. Bonin P, Tanino TT, Handsfield HH. Isolation of *Neisseria gonorrhoeae* on selective and nonselective media in a sexually transmitted disease clinic. J Clin Microbiol. 1984;19:218–220.
154. Danielsson D, Johanisson G. Culture diagnosis of gonorrhoea: A comparison of the yield with selective and nonselective gonococcal culture media inoculated in the clinic and after transport of specimens. Acta Derm Venereol (Stockh). 1973;53:75–80.
155. Luciano AA, Grubin L. Gonorrhea screening: Comparison of three techniques. JAMA. 1980;243:680–681.
156. Faur YC, Wilson ME, May PS. Isolation of *N. meningitidis* from patients in a gonorrhea screening program: A four-year survey in New York City. Am J Public Health. 1981;71:53–58.
157. Judson FN, Ehret JM, Eickhoff TC. Anogenital infection with *Neisseria meningitidis* in homosexual men. J Infect Dis. 1978;137:458–463.
158. Stratton CW, Cooksey RC. Susceptibility tests: Special tests. In: Balows A, Hausler WJ, Herrmann KL, et al, eds. Manual of Clinical Microbiology. 5th ed. Washington, DC: American Society for Microbiology; 1991:1153–1165.
159. Rothenberg RB, Simon R, Chipperfield E, et al. Efficacy of selected diagnostic tests for sexually transmitted diseases. JAMA. 1976;235:49–51.
160. Dolter J, Bryant L, Janda JM. Evaluation of five rapid systems for the identification of *Neisseria gonorrhoeae*. Diagn Microbiol Infect Dis. 1990;13:265–267.
161. Carballo M, Dillon JR, Lussier M, et al. Evaluation of a urease-based confirmatory enzyme-linked immunosorbent assay for diagnosis of *Neisseria gonorrhoeae*. J Clin Microbiol. 1992;30:2181–2183.
162. Thomason JL, Gelbart SM, Sobeiski VJ, et al. Effectiveness of Gonozyme for detection of gonorrhea in low-risk pregnant and gynecologic populations. Sex Transm Dis. 1989;16:28–31.
163. Nowinski RC, Tam MR, Goldstein LC, et al. Monoclonal antibodies for diagnosis of infectious diseases in humans. Science. 1983;219:637–644.
164. Chapin-Robertson K, Reece EA, Edberg SC. Evaluation of the Gen-Probe PACE II assay for the direct detection of *Neisseria gonorrhoeae* in endocervical specimens. Diagn Microbiol Infect Dis. 1992;15:645–649.
165. Limberger RJ, Biega R, Evancoe A, et al. Evaluation of culture and the Gen-Probe PACE 2 assay for detection of *Neisseria gonorrhoeae* and *Chlamydia trachomatis* in endocervical specimens transported to a state health laboratory. J Clin Microbiol. 1992;30:1162–1166.
166. Ho BS, Feng WG, Bong BK, et al. Polymerase chain reaction for the detection of *Neisseria gonorrhoeae* in clinical samples. J Clin Pathol. 1992;45:439–442.
167. Handsfield HH, McCutchan JA, Corey L, et al. Evaluation of new anti-infective drugs for the treatment of uncomplicated gonorrhea in adults and adolescents. Clin Infect Dis. 1992;15(Suppl 1):S123–S130.
168. Batteiger BE, Jones RB. Chlamydial infections. Infect Dis Clin North Am. 1987;1:55–81.
169. Judson FN. Treatment of uncomplicated gonorrhea with ceftriaxone: A review. Sex Transm Dis. 1986;13:199–202.
170. Hook EW III, Roddy RE, Handsfield HH. Ceftriaxone therapy for incubating and early syphilis. J Infect Dis. 1988;158:881–884.
171. Ng PP, Chan RK, Ling AB. Gonorrhoea treatment failure and ciprofloxacin resistance. Int J STD AIDS. 1998;9:323–325.
172. Handsfield HH, McCormack WM, Hook EW III, et al. A comparison of single-dose cefixime with ceftriaxone as treatment for uncomplicated gonorrhea. N Engl J Med. 1991;325:1337–1341.
173. Martin DH, Mroczkowski TF, Dalu ZA, et al. A controlled trial of a single dose of azithromycin for the treatment of chlamydial urethritis and cervicitis. N Engl J Med. 1992;327:921–925.
174. Moran JS, Zenilman JM. Therapy for gonococcal infections: Options in 1989. Rev Infect Dis. 1990;12(Suppl 6):S656–S664.
175. Stamm WE, Guinan ME, Johnson C, et al. Effect of treatment regimens for *Neisseria gonorrhoeae* on simultaneous infection with *Chlamydia trachomatis*. N Engl J Med. 1984;310:545–549.
176. Handsfield HH, Dalu ZA, Martin DH, et al. Multicenter trial of single-dose azithromycin vs. ceftriaxone in the treatment of uncomplicated gonorrhea. Sex Transm Dis. 1994;21:107–111.
177. Tapsall JW, Shultz TR, Limnios EA, et al. Failure of azithromycin therapy in gonorrhea and discorrelation with laboratory test parameters. Sex Transm Dis. 1998;25:505–508.
178. Peterson HB, Galaid EI, Zenilman JM. Pelvic inflammatory disease: Review of treatment options. Rev Infect Dis. 1990;12(Suppl 6):S656–S664.
179. Walker CK, Kahn JG, Washington AE, et al. Pelvic inflammatory disease: Meta-analysis of antimicrobial regimen efficacy. J Infect Dis. 1993;168:969–978.
180. Eschenbach DA, Faro S. Pelvic inflammatory disease: Key treatment issues and options. JAMA. 1991;266:2605–2611.
181. McNeeley SG, Hendrix SL, Maxxoni MM, et al. Medically sound, cost-effective treatment for pelvic inflammatory disease and tuboovarian abscess. Am J Obstet Gynecol. 1998;178:1272–1278.
182. Oriel JD. Use of quinolones in chlamydial infection. Rev Infect Dis. 1989;11(Suppl 5):S1273–S1276.
183. Wendel GD, Cox SM, Bawdon RE, et al. A randomized trial of ofloxacin versus cefoxitin and doxycycline in the outpatient treatment of acute salpingitis. Am J Obstet Gynecol. 1991;264:1390–1396.
184. Soper DE, Brockwell NJ, Dalton HP. Microbial etiology of urban emergency department acute salpingitis: Treatment with ofloxacin. Am J Obstet Gynecol. 1992;167:653–660.
185. Kamwendo F, Johnsson E, Moi H, et al. Gonorrhea, genital chlamydial infection, and nonspecific urethritis in male partners of women hospitalized and treated for acute pelvic inflammatory disease. Sex Transm Dis. 1993;20:143–146.
186. Handsfield HH, Wiesner PJ, Holmes KK. Treatment of the gonococcal arthritis-dermatitis syndrome. Ann Intern Med. 1976;84:661–667.
187. Stone KM, Grimes DA, Magder LS. Personal protection against sexually transmitted diseases. Am J Obstet Gynecol. 1986;155:180–188.
188. Rosenberg MJ, Davidson AJ, Chen JH, et al. Barrier contraceptives and sexually transmitted diseases in women: A comparison of female-dependent methods and condoms. Am J Public Health. 1992;82:669–674.
189. Niruthisard S, Roddy RE, Chutivongse S. Use of nonoxynol-9 and reduction in rate of gonococcal and chlamydial cervical infections. Lancet. 1992;339:1351–1355.
190. Kreiss J, Ngugi E, Holmes K, et al. Efficacy of nonoxynol-9 contraceptive sponge use in preventing heterosexual acquisition of HIV in Nairobi prostitutes. JAMA. 1992;268:477–482.
191. Roddy, RE, Zekeng L, Ryan KA, et al. A controlled trial of nonoxynol 9 film to reduce male-to-female transmission of sexually transmitted diseases. N Engl J Med 1998;339:504–510.
192. Boslego JW, Tramont EC, Chung RC, et al. Efficacy trial of a parenteral gonococcal pilus vaccine in men. Vaccine. 1991;9:154–612.
193. Tramont RC. Gonococcal vaccines. Clin Microbiol Rev. 1989;2(Suppl):S74–S77.

Chapter 201

Moraxella (Branhamella) catarrhalis and Other Gram-Negative Cocci

TIMOTHY F. MURPHY

Over the past 2 decades, *Moraxella (Branhamella) catarrhalis* has emerged as an important and common human respiratory tract pathogen. Current classification schemes have the family Neisseriaceae composed of five genera: *Neisseria, Moraxella* (including two subgenera *Moraxella* and *Branhamella*), *Kingella, Acinetobacter,* and *Oligella.* The taxonomy and nomenclature of these bacteria are controversial and are the subject of ongoing discussion and debate. The formation of two new families, Moraxellaceae and Branhamaceae, has been proposed by different investigators, and experimental data exist to support both taxonomic groupings.[1–3] The classification of these gram-negative cocci and bacilli will undoubtedly undergo further changes as more is learned about the relationships among them.

In this chapter, *M. catarrhalis* is discussed. In addition, several related bacteria, including *Neisseria* species other than *Neisseria meningitidis* and *Neisseria gonorrhoeae,* other *Moraxella* species, and *Kingella,* which are less common causes of human infection, are considered. *Acinetobacter* is discussed in Chapter 209, and *Oligella* in Chapter 226. *N. meningitidis* and *N. gonorrhoeae* are discussed in Chapters 199 and 200, respectively.

MORAXELLA (BRANHAMELLA) CATARRHALIS

Historical Overview

M. catarrhalis has an interesting and checkered taxonomic history. The bacterium was first described by Ghon and Pfeiffer[4] a century ago and was suspected by Sir William Osler to be the cause of his own terminal pneumonia.[5] After having been initially named *Micrococcus catarrhalis,* the organism's name was subsequently changed to *Neisseria catarrhalis* because of similarities in phenotype and ecologic niche to *Neisseria* organisms. In 1970, it was transferred to the new genus, *Branhamella,* on the basis of fatty acid content and results of DNA hybridization studies compared with other members of the family *Neisseriaceae.*[6] The name *Moraxella (Branhamella) catarrhalis* was subsequently proposed, and this is the most widely accepted name at this time, although controversy regarding nomenclature exists.[7, 8]

For most of this century, *M. catarrhalis* was regarded as an upper respiratory tract commensal. However, since the late 1970s, investigators from many centers have accumulated compelling evidence that *M. catarrhalis* is an important and common respiratory tract pathogen in humans.[8–10]

Microbiology

M. catarrhalis is a gram-negative diplococcus that is indistinguishable from *Neisseria* organisms by Gram staining. Other *Moraxella, Kingella, Acinetobacter,* and *Oligella* organisms are all gram-negative bacilli or coccobacilli. *M. catarrhalis* grows well on blood agar, chocolate agar, and a variety of media. Colonies display the "hockey puck sign" by sliding along the surface of the agar when pushed. *M. catarrhalis* is difficult to distinguish from *Neisseria* organisms on the basis of colony morphology. Because samples from the respiratory tract frequently contain neisseriae, suspicious colonies should be tested for the possibility that they are *M. catarrhalis. M. catarrhalis* produces oxidase, catalase, and DNase. Several kits to speciate *M. catarrhalis* are commercially available.[11]

Epidemiology and Respiratory Tract Colonization

M. catarrhalis has been recovered exclusively from humans. The prevalence of colonization is highly dependent on age. The upper respiratory tract in approximately 1 to 5% of healthy adults is colonized by *M. catarrhalis.*[12, 13] As indicated by results of sputum cultures, adults with chronic lung diseases have a somewhat higher rate of colonization than that seen in healthy adults.[14]

Nasopharyngeal colonization with *M. catarrhalis* is common throughout infancy. Some studies have shown a higher rate of colonization during winter months; this higher rate may be due to the appearance of respiratory viral illnesses during colder months. Substantial regional differences in colonization rates are observed. For example, 66% of infants in a study in Buffalo, New York, were colonized during the first year of life,[15] whereas a similar study in Goteberg, Sweden, showed a colonization rate of approximately half that level.[16] A study in rural aborigines living near Darwin, Australia, revealed that 100% of infants were colonized by *M. catarrhalis* by the age of 3 months.[17] The explanation for the marked differences in rates of colonization is not yet defined. Several factors including living conditions, hygiene, environmental factors (e.g., household smoking), genetic characteristics of the populations, host factors, and others may play a role.

Nasopharyngeal colonization with middle ear pathogens, including *M. catarrhalis,* is associated with otitis media. Early colonization is a risk factor for recurrent otitis media.[15, 18] Otitis-prone children are colonized with *M. catarrhalis* at a higher rate than that seen in healthy children.[15, 17, 19]

In order to study the epidemiology and dynamics of colonization by *M. catarrhalis,* several methods for typing isolates have been employed.[8] The most revealing studies have used restriction enzyme analysis of genomic DNA, pulsed-field gel electrophoresis of genomic DNA, and polymerase chain reaction (PCR) ribotyping. Analysis of isolates recovered prospectively have shown that colonization of the human respiratory tract by *M. catarrhalis* is a dynamic process, with frequent elimination and acquisition of new strains.[14, 15] This active turnover of strains has been demonstrated in both infants and adults with chronic lung disease. Elucidating the immune response that mediates elimination of an isolate from the respiratory tract will be important in identifying potentially protective immune responses to *M. catarrhalis.*

Pathogenesis

M. catarrhalis causes mucosal infections in children and adults. The pathogenesis of infection appears to involve contiguous spread of the bacterium from its colonizing position in the respiratory tract to cause clinical signs of infection. In the case of otitis media, the isolates recovered from the middle ear are present in the nasopharynx, indicating that the middle ear isolate came from the nasopharynx via the eustachian tube.[20] Available data suggest that colonization of the upper respiratory tract with middle ear pathogens including *M. catarrhalis* is a necessary first step in the pathogenesis of otitis media. However, colonization alone is not sufficient to cause disease. An inciting event in a child colonized with a middle ear pathogen is probably necessary for bacteria to move to the middle ear and cause otitis media.

Little is known about the events that lead to the transition of asymptomatic colonization to lower respiratory tract infections in adults with chronic lung disease. An alteration in the host-pathogen relationship probably accounts for the development of infection, but the mechanisms remain to be elucidated.

A reliable animal model that parallels human infection has not yet been developed for *M. catarrhalis* infection. The specificity of *M. catarrhalis* for humans may preclude the development of a useful model to study pathogenesis. The most widely used model is a mouse pulmonary clearance model that measures the rate of clearance of *M. catarrhalis* from the lungs following intratracheal challenge.[21–23] This model does not parallel human infection but has been used as a guide to identify and study potential vaccine antigens.

Surface Antigens

The recognition of *M. catarrhalis* as an important human pathogen has led to substantial progress in the last decade in elucidating the surface antigenic structure of *M. catarrhalis.* Such work is important in understanding mechanisms of pathogenesis, elucidating the human immune response to the bacterium, and guiding vaccine development.

The identification of methods for purifying the outer membrane of *M. catarrhalis* led to the observation that outer membrane protein (OMP) patterns detected by sodium dodecyl sulfate–polyacrylamide gel electrophoresis (SDS-PAGE) showed a high degree of similarity among strains from diverse geographic and clinical sources.[24, 25] Several major OMPs have been identified and characterized, and these are summarized in Table 201–1. The study of OMPs of *M. catarrhalis* is an active area of research. Several of these OMPs are being studied as potential vaccine antigens in an effort to develop a vaccine to prevent infections caused by *M. catarrhalis.*

The outer membrane of *M. catarrhalis* contains lipo-oligosaccharide (LOS). LOS consists of a lipid A core coupled to oligosaccharides. The structure of the LOS resembles that of other nonenteric gram-negative bacteria in that the molecule lacks the long polysaccharide side chains observed in enteric gram-negative bacteria.[26, 27] Three major antigenic types of LOS can be distinguished, accounting for 95% of all strains.[28, 29] The different serotypes are based on differences in terminal sugars in the LOS molecule.[30] As in the case of other gram-negative pathogens, LOS is probably a virulence factor for *M. catarrhalis.*

Most strains of *M. catarrhalis* express pili, and these pili bind to a glycosphingolipid receptor on epithelial cells.[31] Little else is known about the pili of *M. catarrhalis.* As indicated by observations of a variety of other gram-negative pathogens, pili probably play an important role in adherence of *M. catarrhalis* to human epithelial cells.

Clinical Manifestations

Otitis media

Approximately 80% of children experience at least one episode of otitis media by the age of 3 years. A subset of children experiences recurrent otitis media, which is associated with a delay in speech and language development. Careful studies from many centers have defined the etiologic agents of otitis media by culturing middle ear fluid obtained by tympanocentesis. Culture of middle ear fluid is the most reliable method for determining the bacterial cause of otitis media. Figure 201–1 shows a summary of the results of 15 studies from the past decade that employed cultures of middle ear fluids to determine the cause of otitis media.[32–46] Although some differences among findings exist, the results from centers in the United States and Europe are remarkably consistent in showing that *Streptococcus pneumoniae,* nontypeable *Haemophilus influenzae,* and *M. catarrhalis* are the predominant bacterial causes of otitis media. Overall, on the basis of results of middle ear fluid cultures, approximately 15 to 20% of cases of otitis media are caused by *M. catarrhalis.*

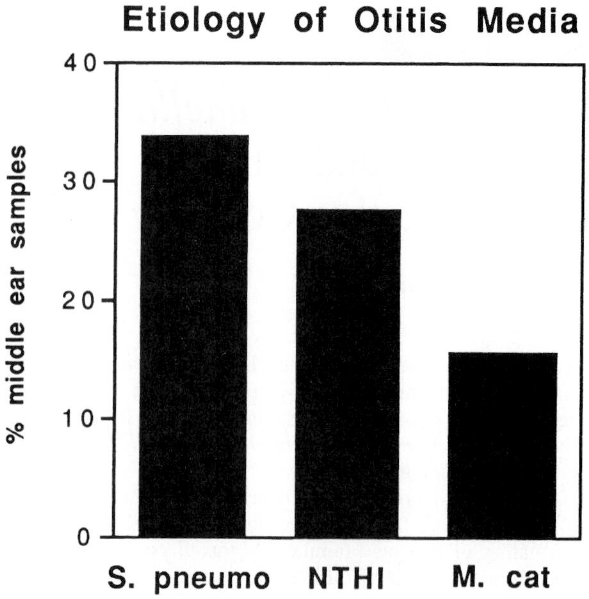

FIGURE 201–1. Results of bacterial culture of middle ear fluids obtained from children with otitis media. Results are averages from 15 studies from 1990 to 1996. *Abbreviations:* M. cat, *Moraxella (Branhamella) catarrhalis;* NTHI, nontypeable *Haemophilus influenzae;* S. pneumo, *Streptococcus pneumoniae.*

More recently, middle ear fluids have been analyzed by using PCR to detect bacterial pathogens.[47–51] PCR is more sensitive than culture in detecting bacterial pathogens in middle ear fluid. Indeed, the presence of bacteria in middle ear fluid is probably more common than is revealed by culture, indicating that culture underestimates the frequency with which *M. catarrhalis* and other pathogens cause otitis media.

Lower Respiratory Tract Infections in Chronic Obstructive Pulmonary Disease

M. catarrhalis causes lower respiratory tract infections in adults, particularly in the setting of chronic obstructive pulmonary disease

TABLE 201–1 Outer Membrane Proteins of *Moraxella catarrhalis*

OMP	Molecular Mass (kD)*	Proposed Function	Other Features	Reference(s)
UspA1†	88 (350–700)	Adhesin	Oligomer with UspA2	23, 133, 134
UspA2†	67 (350–700)	Binds vitronectin	Oligomer with UspA1, may be involved in complement resistance	23, 133, 134
200-kD protein	200	Hemagglutination	Present in many strains	135
CopB	84	Iron uptake	Iron-regulated	136–138
OMP B1	80	Transferrin receptor	Iron-regulated	139–141
OMP CD	45 (60)	Porin	Highly conserved, heat-modifiable	142–144
OMP E	50	Unknown	Highly conserved, heat-modifiable	145, 146

*Molecular mass predicted from gene sequence; values in parentheses indicate apparent molecular mass by SDS-PAGE.
†UspA1 and UspA2 separate in SDS-PAGE as a hetero-oligomer. Also called HMW-OMP.
Abbreviations: OMP, Outer membrane protein; SDS-PAGE, sodium dodecylsulfate–polyacrylamide gel electrophoresis.

(COPD). The recognition of *M. catarrhalis* as a pathogen in this setting was delayed until the past 15 years because *M. catarrhalis* is indistinguishable from commensal neisseriae by Gram stain and difficult to distinguish on the basis of colony morphology. Therefore, unless clinical microbiology laboratories specifically test colonies that appear to be neisseriae, *M. catarrhalis* will be missed as a potential pathogen in sputum.

Several lines of evidence have established that *M. catarrhalis* causes exacerbations of COPD[8–10, 52]:

- Analysis of sputum samples of a subset of patients with exacerbations of COPD demonstrate a predominance of gram-negative diplococci on Gram-stained smears and nearly pure cultures of *M. catarrhalis*.
- Studies employing transtracheal aspiration have revealed pure cultures of *M. catarrhalis* in some patients with exacerbations of COPD.
- Clinical improvement in patients in whom *M. catarrhalis* infection is the presumed cause of exacerbations is observed following administration of antibiotics that are active against *M. catarrhalis*.
- A specific immune response has been observed following exacerbations of COPD associated with *M. catarrhalis* in the sputum.[53]

On the basis of this evidence, *M. catarrhalis* is the second most common bacterial cause of exacerbations of COPD after nontypeable *H. influenzae*. One study estimated that 30% of exacerbations were caused by *M. catarrhalis*.[54]

The clinical manifestations of COPD exacerbations caused by *M. catarrhalis* are similar to those of exacerbations caused by other bacteria such as nontypeable *H. influenzae*. Patients experience increased cough and sputum production, increased sputum purulence, and increased dyspnea compared with baseline symptoms. The single most useful diagnostic test is examination of a Gram-stained sputum sample, which will show intracellular and extracellular gram-negative diplococci as the exclusive or predominant bacterial form (Fig. 201–2).

Pneumonia in the Elderly

Studies from centers in the United States and Europe indicate that *M. catarrhalis* causes a significant proportion of cases of pneumonia in the elderly.[55–57] Because *M. catarrhalis* can colonize the respiratory tract in the absence of clinical infection, it is difficult to state the precise proportion of cases of pneumonia in the elderly caused by *M. catarrhalis*. One prospective study estimated that *M. catarrhalis* caused 10% of community-acquired pneumonia cases in the elderly.[58] Most elderly patients who experience pneumonia due to *M. catarrhalis* have underlying illnesses such as COPD, congestive heart failure, diabetes mellitus, or others. Although *M. catarrhalis* causes illness of significant severity in the elderly, fulminant pneumonia is uncommon.

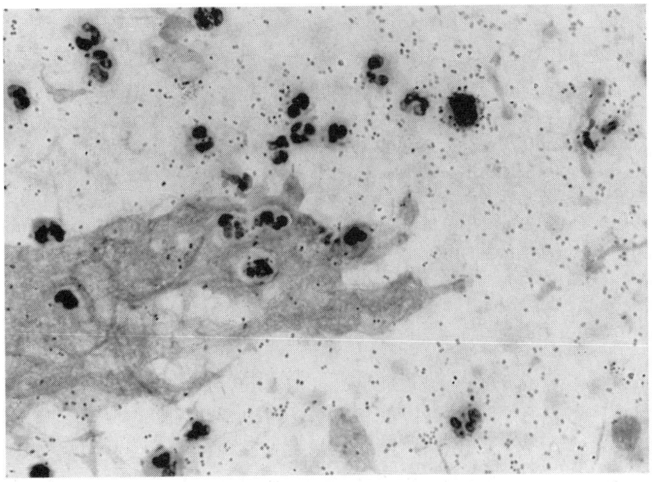

FIGURE 201–2. Photomicrograph (magnification ×1000) of a Gram-stained sputum sample from a patient with chronic bronchitis experiencing an exacerbation caused by *Moraxella catarrhalis.* Note the abundance of leukocytes, the presence of large numbers of gram-negative diplococci as the exclusive bacterial form, and the presence of intracellular bacteria in leukocytes.

Nosocomial Respiratory Tract Infections

Nosocomial lower respiratory tract infections caused by *M. catarrhalis* have been observed since the 1980s.[59–63] Several clusters have occurred in respiratory units. The presence of a susceptible population of adults with underlying cardiopulmonary disease may be important in these apparent outbreaks. Analysis of isolates by various typing methods indicates that some of these clusters involved multiple strains of *M. catarrhalis,* while some were caused by a single strain indicating person-to-person spread of the organism.

Sinusitis

The bacterial cause of sinusitis is determined by culture of specimens obtained by sinus aspiration, a relatively invasive procedure that is not performed routinely. Studies that have used sinus aspiration to determine the cause of sinusitis have shown that *M. catarrhalis* is the third most common cause of sinusitis in adults and children after nontypeable *H. influenzae* and *S. pneumoniae*.[64]

Bacteremia

Recent reports have documented the occurrence of bacteremia due to *M. catarrhalis*.[57, 65–70] Bacteremia is an infrequent manifestation of *M. catarrhalis* infection. The clinical manifestations range in severity from mild to life-threatening. Bacteremia has been reported in people of all ages, from neonates to the elderly. A majority of patients have clinical evidence of respiratory tract infection. Most patients with bacteremia due to *M. catarrhalis* have underlying illnesses such as cardiopulmonary disease, malignancy, or chronic debilitation. A recent review of *M. catarrhalis* bacteremia notes a mortality rate of 21%.[65] The underlying illness is an important determinant of outcome.

Treatment

A rapid increase in the proportion of strains that produce β-lactamase occurred simultaneously in the United States and Europe beginning in the late 1970s.[71] This constitutes one of the most dramatic examples of a rapid increase in antimicrobial resistance by a bacterial species. At present, virtually all strains of *M. catarrhalis* produce β-lactamase. Three different β-lactamases (BRO-1, BRO-2, and BRO-3) have been identified and characterized. The β-lactamase of *M. catarrhalis* is inducible and cell-associated. Because an inoculum-dependent susceptibility to ampicillin has been observed, ampicillin should not be used for β-lactamase–producing strains regardless of the results of susceptibility testing.

Many infections caused by *M. catarrhalis* can be treated with oral antibiotics. The organism is generally susceptible to amoxicillin-clavulanate, trimethoprim-sulfamethoxazole, tetracyclines, extended-spectrum oral cephalosporins (e.g., cefixime, cefpodoxime, cefaclor, loracarbef, cefuroxime), macrolides (e.g., azithromycin, clarithromycin), and fluoroquinolones (e.g., ciprofloxacin, sparfloxacin, trovafloxacin, ofloxacin, grepafloxacin).[72–74] *M. catarrhalis* is also uniformly susceptible to ticarcillin, piperacillin, second- and third-generation cephalosporins, and aminoglycosides. *M. catarrhalis* is resistant to penicillin, ampicillin, vancomycin, clindamycin, and methicillin.

OTHER *NEISSERIA* SPECIES

N. meningitidis and *N. gonorrhoeae* have long been recognized as the "pathogenic *Neisseria.*" Other *Neisseria* species are common

TABLE 201–2 Biochemical and Growth Characteristics of *Neisseria* and *Moraxella catarrhalis*

Species	Production of Acid from										
	Glucose	*Maltose*	*Sucrose*	*Lactose (ONPG)*	*Fructose*	H_2S*	Oxidase	Extra CO_2	Growth at 22°C	Polysaccharide†	Pigment‡
Neisseria gonorrhoeae	+	−	−	−	−	−	+	VI	−	NG	−
Neisseria meningitidis	+	+	−	−	−	−	+	I	−	NG	−
Neisseria lactamica	+	+	−	+	−	+	+	v	v	−	+Y
Neisseria sicca	+	+	+	−	+	+	+	−	+	+	−(slY)
Neisseria subflava	+	+	v	−	v	+	+	−	+	v	+Y
Neisseria mucosa	+	+	+	−	+	+	+	−	+	+	−(slY)
Neisseria flavescens	−	−	−	−	−	+	+	−	+	+	+Y
Neisseria cinerea	−	−	−	−	−		+	−	v	−	G
Neisseria polysaccharea	+	+	−	−	−		+		−	+	−(slY)
Neisseria elongata	−	−	−	−	−		+		+	−	G/slY
Neisseria weaveri	−	−	−	−		+	+		+	−	−(slY)
Moraxella catarrhalis	−	−	+	−	−	+	+	−	v	−	G

*With lead acetate paper.
†Synthesis of polysaccharide from 5% sucrose.
‡On Löffler slant.
Abbreviations and symbols: +, Present; −, absent; G, grayish; H_2S, hydrogen sulfide; I, important for growth; NG, no growth; ONPG, O-nitrophenol-β-D-galactopyranoside; sl, slightly; v, variable; VI, very important for growth; Y, yellow.
From Gröschel DM. *Moraxella catarrhalis* and other gram-negative cocci. In: Mandell GL, Bennett JE, Dolin R, eds. Principles and Practice of Infectious Diseases. 4th ed. New York: Churchill Livingstone; 1995:1926. With permission.

components of the normal flora of the upper respiratory tract of humans. Table 201–2 lists several biochemical and growth characteristics that are used to distinguish other *Neisseria* species from *N. gonorrhoeae, N. meningitidis,* and *M. catarrhalis.* These other *Neisseria* species lack several virulence factors including pili, opacity associated protein, and the H8 antigen, which are expressed by meningococci and gonococci.[75]

Neisseria species such as *Neisseria sicca, Neisseria subflava, Neisseria cinerea, Neisseria lactamica,* and others occasionally cause invasive infections in humans. These infections, documented primarily by individual case reports, include meningitis, endocarditis, bacteremia, ocular infections, pericarditis, empyema, septic arthritis, bursitis, osteomyelitis, and others.[76–83]

Neisseria weaveri (formerly CDC group M5 in the original classification of the Centers for Disease Control and Prevention) is a component of the normal oropharyngeal flora of dogs and is an important cause of infection in dog bite wounds in humans.[84, 85] These infections are occasionally associated with bacteremia.[86]

Many of these infections have been treated successfully with penicillin and ampicillin. However, isolates of *Neisseria* species are showing increased resistance to penicillin in recent years, so susceptibility testing should be performed on isolates that cause invasive infections and the results used to guide antimicrobial therapy.

Neisseria are naturally competent for uptake of DNA. Recent studies have shown that genetic recombination occurs among bacteria that make up the complex flora of the upper respiratory tract. Virulence determinants are exchanged with pathogenic *Neisseria* organisms, genes encoding altered penicillin-binding proteins are passed between species, and extensive interspecies recombination of a variety of genes occurs in vivo.[87–91] These observations have important implications in the role of acquisition of antibiotic resistance and in the evolution of pathogens in the human respiratory tract. Indeed, interspecies transfer of *penA* genes from commensal neisseriae is an important mechanism of acquisition of penicillin resistance of *N. gonorrhoeae* and *N. meningitidis.*[88, 90]

OTHER *MORAXELLA* SPECIES

Bacteria of the genus *Moraxella* are normal commensals of the human upper respiratory tract and are occasionally recovered from the skin and urogenital tract. The taxonomy of *Moraxella* species is a dynamic area of research; accordingly, species classifications are continuing to change as knowledge in the area expands. Genetic transformation and analysis of ribosomal sequences have been particularly useful in elucidating phylogenetic relationships.[3, 92] Species are generally differentiated biochemically. Table 201–3 shows biochemical reactions and growth characteristics that are used to distinguish among several *Moraxella* species.

Moraxella species other than *M. catarrhalis* are unusual pathogens in humans. Several reports have emphasized the role of other *Moraxella* as ocular pathogens. These bacteria cause conjunctivitis, keratitis, and rarely endophthalmitis.[93–97] *M. nonliquefaciens* is most commonly associated with ocular infections. *Moraxella* organisms are susceptible to all conventional topical ocular antibiotics.

Case reports have established *Moraxella* organisms as unusual causes of invasive infections in humans, including endocarditis, bacteremia, septic arthritis, purulent pericarditis, cellulitis, and meningitis.[98–105] Patients who experience meningitis due to *Moraxella* species have a high frequency of inherited and acquired complement deficiencies, and these should be investigated following recovery.[106]

Antimicrobial susceptibility should be performed on isolates recovered from normally sterile sites, but *Moraxella* organisms are generally susceptible to penicillins and cephalosporins.

KINGELLA

History and Microbiology

In 1976, *Moraxella kingae* was transferred to the newly created genus *Kingella.*[107, 108] *Kingella* organisms are short, gram-negative coccoid or medium-sized rods with tapered ends. Four species have been identified: *K. kingae, Kingella indologenes, Kingella denitrificans,* and the newly described *Kingella oralis. Kingella* organisms are recovered from the human respiratory tract and have previously been recognized as rare causes of human disease. However, in the past decade, infections due to *Kingella* have been recognized with surprising frequency in reports from the United States, Europe, and Israel.[99, 109–117]

The recent increase in the recognition of *Kingella* infections may be a result of several factors. Because the bacterium is slow-growing and fastidious, special attention by the microbiology laboratory is often required to isolate the organism. For example, *K. kingae* in joint fluid specimens will often fail to grow when plated directly on solid media but will grow when the joint fluid is inoculated into blood culture bottles.[118] Another factor accounting for the recent increased recognition of *Kingella* as a human pathogen is that the bacterium has probably been misidentified previously as *Moraxella* and other *Neisseria* organisms by many laboratories. Finally, in the

TABLE 201–3 Laboratory Features Useful for Identification of *Moraxella, Oligella, Moraxella*-like Organisms, and *Kingella*

Species	Motility	Oxidase	Catalase	O/F Glucose	Serum Required	Urease	Indole	Nitrate	Phenylalanine	Gelatin	Assimilation of Acetate	Growth on MacConkey's Agar
Moraxella catarrhalis	−	+	+	−	−	−	−	−	−	−	v	v
Moraxella lacunata	−	+	+	−	+	−	−	+	v	v	−	−
Moraxella nonliquefaciens	−	+	+	−	v	−	−	+	−	−	−	−
Moraxella osloensis	−	+	+	−	−	−	−	v	v	−	+	v
Moraxella phenylpyruvica	−	+	+	−	−	+	−	v	+	−	v	v
Moraxella atlantae	−	+	+	−	+	−	−	−	−	−	v	+
Oligella urethralis	−	+	+	−	−	−	−	−	+	−	v	+
Neisseria weaveri (M5)	−	+	+	−	−	−	−	−	+	−	−	−
Neisseria elongata (M6)	−	+	−	−	−	−	−	+	−	−	v	v
*Kingella kingae**	−	+	−	F†	−	−	−	−	−	−		v
Kingella indologenes	−	+	−	F	−	−	+	−	−	−		
Kingella denitrificans	−	+	−	F	−	−	−	+	−	−		−

*Most strains β hemolytic on blood agar.
†May take 3 or more days; some strains require serum supplement.
Abbreviations and symbols: −, Absent; +, present; O/F, oxidation or fermentation; v, variable.
From Gröschel DM. *Moraxella catarrhalis* and other gram-negative cocci. In: Mandell GL, Bennett JE, Dolin R, eds. Principles and Practice of Infectious Diseases. 4th ed. New York: Churchill Livingstone; 1995:1926. With permission.

past, *Kingella* was unfamiliar to most personnel in clinical microbiology laboratories and was probably frequently dismissed as a contaminant.[119]

K. kingae, the most common human pathogen among the *Kingella* species, grows on blood and chocolate agar but fails to grow on MacConkey's agar. The bacterium has a tendency to resist decolorization and may therefore sometimes be mistaken for a gram-positive organism. It is oxidase-positive, produces acid from glucose and maltose, and lacks catalase, urease, and indole. Table 201–3 lists several characteristics that distinguish *Kingella* organisms from related bacteria.

Epidemiology and Respiratory Tract Colonization

K. kingae frequently colonizes the throats of young children.[120] In one prospective study in which cultures were performed every 2 weeks for 11 months, 73% of all children had positive results on at least one throat culture for *K. kingae.*[120] The organism has not been recovered from cultures of the nasopharynx. The highest rate of colonization is observed in children between the ages of 6 months and 4 years, which corresponds to the peak age incidence of invasive disease. Infants below 6 months of age are not colonized. This pattern of colonization parallels that of other respiratory tract pathogens such as *M. catarrhalis* and *S. pneumoniae,* which show low rates of colonization in the neonatal period (presumably owing to the presence of maternal antibodies) followed by higher rates of colonization and infection in infancy and childhood, with a declining incidence of infection in adulthood.

In studies of the microbiology of the human oral cavity, a bacterium that resembled *Eikenella corrodens* was recovered frequently from dental plaque.[121] On the basis of 16S ribosomal sequences, this organism was assigned the new species designation *K. oralis.*[122] *K. oralis* is present in plaque or on the tooth surface in the majority of people with or without periodontal disease.[123] The role of *K. oralis* in periodontal disease is not known at this time.

Clinical Manifestations

K. kingae is the most frequent human pathogen among the *Kingella* species. Approximately 90% of cases of invasive disease caused by *K. kingae* occur in children below the age of 4 years, the majority of cases occurring between the age of 6 months and 2 years. Invasive infections have not been reported in infants younger than 6 months of age. Infection shows a seasonal distribution, with the rate of cases higher in the autumn and winter months.[109, 117] The most common clinical manifestations of *K. kingae* disease are skeletal infections, endocarditis, and bacteremia.

Skeletal Infections

K. kingae has a remarkable propensity to cause infections of the skeletal system in young children. The most common infection is septic arthritis. The disease most frequently affects large, weight-bearing joints, especially the knee and ankle. Results on Gram staining of the joint fluid are usually negative. The diagnosis is made by recovering the organism from culture of joint fluid. Inoculating blood culture bottles with joint fluid substantially enhances the likelihood of recovering the organism as compared with direct inoculation of agar plates.[118] Osteomyelitis caused by *K. kingae* most frequently involves the bones of the lower extremity. The onset is insidious, and the diagnosis is often delayed. Hematogenous invasion of the intervertebral disk by *K. kingae* is observed most commonly in the lumbar intervertebral spaces.[111, 124]

Endocarditis

In contrast to other clinical manifestations of *Kingella* infections, endocarditis can be seen in all age groups, including school-aged children and adults. Endocarditis may involve both native and prosthetic valves.[125–127] Although many affected persons have preexisting valvular disease, *Kingella* can cause endocarditis in normal valves as well. Cases of endocarditis can also be caused by *Kingella denitrificans* and *Kingella indologenes* as well as *K. kingae.*[112, 125, 128] *Kingella* is one of the components of the so-called HACEK group of organisms, which include fastidious bacteria capable of causing endocarditis. The HACEK group consists of *Haemophilus* species (*Haemophilus aphrophilus* and *Haemophilus parainfluenzae*), *Actinobacillus actinomycetemcomitans, Cardiobacterium hominis,* and *E. corrodens,* in addition to *K. kingae.* The difficulty in recovering and identifying *K. kingae* in blood cultures frequently results in a delay in the diagnosis, which may account for the relatively high rate of morbidity seen with *Kingella* endocarditis. Because of the serious nature of *Kingella* endocarditis, all patients with *Kingella* bacteremia should be carefully evaluated for the presence of endocarditis.

Bacteremia

In approximately half of children with *K. kingae* bacteremia a concomitant focal source such as the skeletal system can be identified. In the remainder, the source for the bacteremia is occult.[113–117, 119, 129] The presumed source of the bacteremia is the respiratory tract.

Other Infections

Kingella species have been documented by case reports to cause infections in a variety of sites; pneumonia, epiglottitis, meningitis, abscesses, and ocular infections have been described.[119, 130, 131]

Treatment

The antimicrobial susceptibility of isolates of *Kingella* has not been well studied. *Kingella* organisms appear to be susceptible to a wide variety of penicillins and cephalosporins, although a single isolate of β-lactamase–producing *K. kingae* has been identified.[132] Disease-associated isolates should be tested for antimicrobial susceptibility; if the isolate is susceptible, a penicillin or cephalosporin should be used. Other agents with in vitro activity include aminoglycosides, trimethoprim-sulfamethoxazole, tetracyclines, erythromycin, and ciprofloxacin.

REFERENCES

1. Catlin BW. Branhamaceae fam. nov., a proposed family to accommodate the genera *Branhamella* and *Moraxella*. Intl J System Bacteriol. 1991;41:320–323.
2. Rossau R, Van Landschoot A, Gillis M, De Ley J. Taxonomy of Moraxellaceae fam. nov., a new bacterial family to accommodate the genera *Moraxella, Acinetobacter,* and *Psychrobacter* and related organisms. Int J System Bacteriol. 1991;41:310–319.
3. Enright MC, Carter PE, MacLean IA, McKenzie H. Phylogenetic relationships between some members of the genera *Neisseria, Acinetobacter, Moraxella,* and *Kingella* based on partial 16S ribosomal DNA sequence analysis. Intl J System Bacteriol. 1994;44:387–391.
4. Ghon A, Pfeiffer H. Der *Micrococcus catarrhalis* (R. Pfeiffer) als Krankheitserreger. Z Klin Med. 1902;44:263–281.
5. Berk SL. From *Micrococcus* to *Moraxella*—the reemergence of *Branhamella catarrhalis*. Arch Intern Med. 1990;150:2254–2257.
6. Catlin BW. Transfer of the organism named *Neisseria catarrhalis* to *Branhamella* genus. Int J Syst Bacteriol. 1970;20:155–159.
7. Bovre K. Proposal to divide the genus *Moraxella* into two subgenera, subgenus *Moraxella* and subgenus *Branhamella*. Int J Syst Bacteriol. 1979;29:403–406.
8. Murphy TF. *Branhamella catarrhalis:* Epidemiology, surface antigenic structure, and immune response. Microbiol Rev. 1996;60:267–279.
9. Enright MC, McKenzie H. *Moraxella (Branhamella) catarrhalis*—clinical and molecular aspects of a rediscovered pathogen. J Med Microbiol. 1997;46:360–371.
10. Murphy TF. *Branhamella catarrhalis:* Epidemiological and clinical aspects of a human respiratory tract pathogen. Thorax. 1998;53:124–128.
11. Speeleveld E, Fossepre J-M, Gordts B, Van Landuyt HW. Comparison of three rapid methods, tributyrine, 4-methylumbelliferyl butyrate, and indoxyl acetate, for rapid identification of *Moraxella catarrhalis*. J Clin Microbiol. 1994;32:1362–1363.
12. Ejlertsen T, Thisted E, Ebbesen F, et al. *Branhamella catarrhalis* in children and adults. A study of prevalence, time of colonisation, and association with upper and lower respiratory tract infections. J Infect. 1994;29:23–31.
13. Vaneechoutte M, Verschraegen G, Claeys G, et al. Respiratory tract carrier rates of *Moraxella (Branhamella) catarrhalis* in adults and children and interpretation of the isolation of *M. catarrhalis* from sputum. J Clin Microbiol. 1990;28:2674–2680.
14. Klingman KL, Pye A, Murphy TF, Hill SL. Dynamics of respiratory tract colonization by *Moraxella (Branhamella) catarrhalis* in bronchiectasis. Am J Respir Crit Care Med. 1995;152:1072–1078.
15. Faden H, Harabuchi Y, Hong JJ. Epidemiology of *Moraxella catarrhalis* in children during the first 2 years of life: Relationship to otitis media. J Infect Dis. 1994;169:1312–1317.
16. Aniansson G, Alm B, Andersson B, et al. Nasopharyngeal colonization during the first year of life. J Infect Dis. 1992;165(Suppl 1):S38–S42.
17. Leach AJ, Boswell JB, Asche V, et al. Bacterial colonization of the nasopharynx predicts very early onset and persistence of otitis media in Australian Aboriginal infants. Pediatr Infect Dis J. 1994;13:983–989.
18. Faden H, Duffy L, Wasielewski R, et al. Relationship between nasopharyngeal colonization and the development of otitis media in children. J Infect Dis. 1997;175:1440–1445.
19. Prellner K, Christensen P, Hovelius B, Rosen C. Nasopharyngeal carriage of bacteria in otitis-prone and non–otitis-prone children in day-care centres. Acta Otolaryngol. 1984;98:343–350.
20. Dickinson DP, Loos BG, Dryja DM, Bernstein JM. Restriction fragment mapping of *Branhamella catarrhalis:* A new tool for studying the epidemiology of this middle ear pathogen. J Infect Dis. 1988;158:205–208.
21. Maciver I, Unhanand M, McCracken GH Jr, Hansen EJ. Effect of immunization on pulmonary clearance of *Moraxella catarrhalis* in an animal model. J Infect Dis. 1993;168:469–472.
22. Helminen ME, Maciver I, Latimer JL, et al. A major outer membrane protein of *Moraxella catarrhalis* is a target for antibodies that enhance pulmonary clearance of the pathogen in an animal model. Infect Immun. 1993;61:2003–2010.
23. Chen D, McMichael JC, VanDerMeid KR, et al. Evaluation of purified UspA from *Moraxella catarrhalis* as a vaccine in a murine model after active immunization. Infect Immun. 1996;64:1900–1905.
24. Murphy TF, Loeb MR. Isolation of the outer membrane of *Branhamella catarrhalis*. Microb Pathog. 1989;6:159–174.
25. Bartos LC, Murphy TF. Comparison of the outer membrane proteins of 50 strains of *Branhamella catarrhalis*. J Infect Dis. 1988;158:761–765.
26. Masoud H, Perry MB, Richards JC. Characterization of the lipopolysaccharide of *Moraxella catarrhalis*. Structural analysis of the lipid A from *M. catarrhalis* serotype A lipopolysaccharide. Eur J Biochem. 1994;220:209–216.
27. Fomsgaard JS, Fomsgaard A, Hoiby N, et al. Comparative immunochemistry of lipopolysaccharides from *Branhamella catarrhalis* strains. Infect Immun. 1991;59:3346–3349.
28. Rahman M, Holme T. Antibody response in rabbits to serotype-specific determinants in lipopolysaccharides from *Moraxella catarrhalis*. J Med Microbiol. 1996;44:348–354.
29. Vaneechoutte M, Verschraegen G, Claeys G, Van Den Abeele AM. Serological typing of *Branhamella catarrhalis* strains on the basis of lipopolysaccharide antigens. J Clin Microbiol. 1990;28:182–187.
30. Edebrink P, Jansson P-E, Rahman MM, et al. Structural studies of the O-polysaccharide from the lipopolysaccharide of *Moraxella (Branhamella) catarrhalis* serotype A (strain ATCC 25238). Carbohydrate Res. 1994;257:269–284.
31. Ahmed K, Matsumoto K, Rikimoti N, Nagatake T. Attachment of *Moraxella catarrhalis* to pharyngeal epithelial cells is mediated by a glycosphingolipid receptor. FEMS Microbiol Lett. 1996;135:305–309.
32. Stenfors L-E, Raisanen S. Quantitative analysis of the bacterial findings in otitis media. J Laryngol Otol. 1990;104:749–757.
33. Gan VN, Kusmiesz H, Shelton S, Nelson JD. Comparative evaluation of loracarbef and amoxicillin-clavulanate for acute otitis media. Antimicrob Agents Chemother. 1991;35:967–971.
34. Johnson CE, Carlin SA, Super DM, et al. Cefixime compared with amoxicillin for treatment of acute otitis media. J Pediatr. 1991;119:117–122.
35. Faden H, Bernstein J, Stanievich J, et al. Effect of prior antibiotic treatment on middle ear disease in children. Ann Otol Rhinol Laryngol. 1992;101:87–91.
36. DelBeccaro MA, Mendelman PM, Inglis AF, et al. Bacteriology of acute otitis media: A new perspective. J Pediatr. 1992;120:81–84.
37. Chonmaitree T, Owen MJ, Patel JA, et al. Effect of viral respiratory tract infection on outcome of acute otitis media. J Pediatr. 1992;120:856–862.
38. Owen MJ, Anwar R, Nguyen HK, et al. Efficacy of cefixime in the treatment of acute otitis media in children. Am J Dis Child. 1993;147:81–86.
39. Ruuskanen O, Heikkinen T. Otitis media: Etiology and diagnosis. Pediatr Infect Dis J. 1994;13:S23–S26.
40. Pukander JS, Jero JP, Kaprio EA, Sorri MJ. Clarithromycin vs. amoxicillin suspensions in the treatment of pediatric patients with acute otitis media. Pediatr Infect Dis J. 1993;12:S118–S121.
41. Shurin PA, Rehmus JM, Johnson CE, et al. Bacterial polysaccharide immune globulin for prophylaxis of acute otitis media in high-risk children. J Pediatr. 1993;123:801–810.
42. Aspin MM, Hoberman A, McCarty J, et al. Comparative study of the safety and efficacy of clarithromycin and amoxicillin-clavulanate in the treatment of acute otitis media in children. J Pediatr. 1994;125:135–141.
43. Gehanno P, Berche P, Boucot I, et al. Comparative efficacy and safety of cefprozil and amoxycillin-clavulanate in the treatment of acute otitis media in children. J Antimicrob Chemother. 1994;33:1209–1218.
44. Block SL. Causative pathogens, antibiotic resistance and therapeutic considerations in acute otitis media. Pediatr Infect Dis J. 1997;16:449–456.
45. McCarty J. A multicenter, open label trial of azithromycin for the treatment of children with acute otitis media. Pediatr Infect Dis J. 1996;15:S10–S14.
46. Gooch WM III, Blair E, Puopolo A, et al. Effectiveness of five days of therapy with cefuroxime axetil suspension for treatment of acute otitis media. Pediatr Infect Dis J. 1996;15:157–164.
47. Ueyama T, Kurono Y, Shirabe K, et al. High incidence of *Haemophilus influenzae* in nasopharyngeal secretions and middle ear effusions as detected by PCR. J Clin Microbiol. 1995;33:1835–1838.
48. Virolainen A, Salo P, Jero J, et al. Comparison of PCR assay with bacterial culture for detecting *Streptococcus pneumoniae* in middle ear fluid of children with acute otitis media. J Clin Microbiol. 1994;32:2667–2670.
49. Post JC, Preston RA, Aul JJ, et al. Molecular analysis of bacterial pathogens in otitis media with effusion. JAMA. 1995;273:1598–1604.
50. Post JC, Aul JJ, White GJ, et al. PCR-based detection of bacterial DNA after antimicrobial treatment is indicative of persistent, viable bacteria in the chinchilla model of otitis media. Am J Otolaryngol. 1996;17:106–111.
51. Hendolin PH, Markkanen A, Ylikoski J, Wahlfors JJ. Use of multiplex PCR for simultaneous detection of four bacterial species in middle ear effusions. J Clin Microbiol. 1997;35:2854–2858.
52. Murphy TF, Sethi S. Bacterial infection in chronic obstructive pulmonary disease. Am Rev Respir Dis. 1992;146:1067–1083.
53. Chapman AJ, Musher DM, Jonsson S, et al. Development of bactericidal antibody during *Branhamella catarrhalis* infection. J Infect Dis. 1985;151:878–882.
54. Verghese A, Roberson D, Kalbfleisch JH, Sarubbi F. Randomized comparative study of cefixime versus cephalexin in acute bacterial exacerbations of chronic bronchitis. Antimicrob Agents Chemother. 1990;34:1041–1044.
55. Hager H, Verghese A, Alvarez S, Berk SL. *Branhamella catarrhalis* respiratory infections. Rev Infect Dis. 1987;9:1140–1149.
56. Barreiro B, Esteban L, Prats E, et al. *Branhamella catarrhalis* respiratory infections. Eur Respir J. 1992;5:675–679.
57. Collazos J, de Miguel J, Ayarza R. *Moraxella catarrhalis* bacteremic pneumonia in adults: Two cases and review of the literature. Eur J Clin Microbiol Infect Dis. 1992;11:237–240.
58. Carr B, Walsh JB, Coakley D, et al. Prospective hospital study of community acquired lower respiratory tract infection in the elderly. Respir Med. 1991;85:185–187.

59. McKenzie H, Morgan MG, Jordens JZ, et al. Characterisation of hospital isolates of *Moraxella (Branhamella) catarrhalis* by SDS-PAGE of whole-cell proteins, immunoblotting and restriction-endonuclease analysis. J Med Microbiol. 1992;37:70–76.
60. Morgan MG, McKenzie H, Enright MC, et al. Use of molecular methods to characterize *Moraxella catarrhalis* strains in a suspected outbreak of nosocomial infection. Eur J Clin Microbiol Infect Dis. 1992;11:305–312.
61. Beaulieu D, Scriver S, Bergeron MG, et al. Epidemiological typing of *Moraxella catarrhalis* by using DNA probes. J Clin Microbiol. 1993;31:736–739.
62. Richards SJ, Greening AP, Enright MC, et al. Outbreak of *Moraxella catarrhalis* in a respiratory unit. Thorax. 1993;48:91–92.
63. Kawakami Y, Ueno I, Katsuyama T, et al. Restriction fragment length polymorphism (RFLP) of genomic DNA of *Moraxella (Branhamella) catarrhalis* isolates in a hospital. Microbiol Immunol. 1994;38:891–895.
64. Pentilla M, Savolainen S, Kuikaanniemi H, et al. Bacterial findings in acute maxillary sinusitis—European study. Acta Otolaryngol (Stockh). 1997;(Suppl) 529:S165–S168.
65. Ioannidis JPA, Worthington M, Griffiths JK, Snydman DR. Spectrum and significance of bacteremia due to *Moraxella catarrhalis.* Clin Infect Dis. 1995;21:390–397.
66. Cimolai N, Adderley RJ. *Branhamella catarrhalis* bacteremia in children. Acta Paediatr Scand. 1989;78:465–468.
67. Meyer GA, Shope TR, Waecker NJ Jr, Lanningham FH. *Moraxella (Branhamella) catarrhalis* bacteremia in children. Clin Pediatr. 1995;146–150.
68. Domingo P, Puig M, Pericas R, et al. *Moraxella catarrhalis* bacteraemia in an immunocompetent adult. Scand J Infect Dis. 1995;27:95.
69. Rotta AT, Asmar BI. *Moraxella catarrhalis* bacteremia and preseptal cellulitis. South Med J. 1994;87:541–542.
70. Melendez PR, Johnson RH. Bacteremia and septic arthritis caused by *Moraxella catarrhalis.* Rev Infect Dis. 1991;13:428–429.
71. Nissinen A, Gronroos P, Huovinen P, et al. Development of β-lactamase–mediated resistance to penicillin in middle-ear isolates of *Moraxella catarrhalis* in Finnish children, 1978–1993. Clin Infect Dis. 1995;21:1193–1196.
72. Doern GV, Brueggemann AB, Pierce G, et al. Prevalence of antimicrobial resistance among 723 outpatient clinical isolates of *Moraxella catarrhalis* in the United States in 1994 and 1995: Results of a 30-center national surveillance study. Antimicrob Agents Chemother. 1996;40:2884–2886.
73. Hoogkamp-Korstanje JAA, Dirks-Go SIS, Kabel P, et al. Multicentre in-vitro evaluation of the susceptibility of *Streptococcus pneumoniae, Haemophilus influenzae* and *Moraxella catarrhalis* to ciprofloxacin, clarithromycin, co-amoxiclav and sparfloxacin. J Antimicrob Chemother. 1997;39:411–414.
74. Brueggemann AB, Kugler KC, Doern GV. In vitro activity of BAY 12-8039, a novel 8-methoxyquinolone, compared to activities of six fluoroquinolones against *Streptococcus pneumoniae, Haemophilus influenzae,* and *Moraxella catarrhalis.* Antimicrob Agents Chemother. 1997;41:1594–1597.
75. Aho EL, Murphy GL, Cannon JG. Distribution of specific DNA sequences among pathogenic and commensal *Neisseria* species. Infect Immun. 1987;55:1009–1013.
76. Lopez-Velez R, Fortun J, de Pablo C, Beltran JM. Native-valve endocarditis due to *Neisseria sicca.* Clin Infect Dis. 1994;18:660–661.
77. Domingo P, Coll P, Maroto P, et al. *Neisseria subflava* bacteremia in a neutropenic patient. Arch Intern Med. 1996;156:1762–1765.
78. Amsel BJ, Moulijn AC. Nonfebrile mitral valve endocarditis due to *Neisseria subflava.* Chest. 1996;109:280–282.
79. Kirchgesner V, Plesiat P, Dupont MJ, et al. Meningitis and septicemia due to *Neisseria cinerea.* Clin Infect Dis. 1995;21:1351.
80. Obeid EMH. *Neisseria subflava* causing septic arthritis of the ankle in a child. J Infect. 1993;27:100–101.
81. Heiddal S, Sverrisson JT, Yngvason FE, et al. Native-valve endocarditis due to *Neisseria sicca:* Case report and review. Clin Infect Dis. 1993;16:667–670.
82. Halla JT. Septic olecranon bursitis caused by *Neisseria sicca.* J Rheumatol. 1990;17:1240–1241.
83. Bourbeau P, Holla V, Piemontese S. Ophthalmia neonatorum caused by *Neisseria cinerea.* J Clin Microbiol. 1990;28:1640–1641.
84. Andersen BM, Steigerwalt AG, O'Connor SP, et al. *Neisseria weaveri* sp. nov., formerly CDC group M-5, a gram-negative bacterium associated with dog bite wounds. J Clin Microbiol. 1993;31:2456–2466.
85. Holmes B, Costas M, On SLW, et al. *Neisseria weaveri* sp. nov. (formerly CDC group M-5), from dog bite wounds of humans. Intl J System Bacteriol. 1993;43:687–693.
86. Carlson P, Kontiainen S, Anttila P, Eerola E. Septicemia caused by *Neisseria weaveri.* Clin Infect Dis. 1997;24:739.
87. Lujan R, Zhang Q-Y, Saez-Nieto JA, et al. Penicillin-resistant isolates of *Neisseria lactamica* produce altered forms of penicillin-binding protein 2 that arose by interspecies horizontal gene transfer. Antimicrob Agents Chemother. 1991;35:300–304.
88. Spratt BG, Bowler LD, Zhang Q-Y, et al. Role of interspecies transfer of chromosomal genes in the evolution of penicillin resistance in pathogenic and commensal *Neisseria* species. J Mol Evol. 1992;34:115–125.
89. Frosch M, Meyer TF. Transformation-mediated exchange of virulence determinants by co-cultivation of pathogenic *Neisseria.* FEMS Microbiol Lett. 1992;100:345–350.
90. Bowler LD, Zhang Q-Y, Riou J-Y, Spratt BG. Interspecies recombination between the *penA* genes of *Neisseria meningitidis* and commensal *Neisseria* species during the emergence of penicillin resistance of *N. meningitidis:* Natural events and laboratory simulation. J Bacteriol. 1994;176:333–337.
91. Feil E, Zhou J, Smith JM, Spratt BG. A comparison of the nucleotide sequences of the *adk* and *recA* genes of pathogenic and commensal *Neisseria* species: Evidence for extensive interspecies recombination within *adk.* J Mol Evol. 1996;43:631–640.
92. Juni E, Heym GA, Maurer MJ, Miller ML. Combined genetic transformation and nutritional assay for identification of *Moraxella nonliquefaciens.* J Clin Microbiol. 1987;25:1691–1694.
93. Cobo LM, Coster DJ, Peacock J. *Moraxella* keratitis in a nonalcoholic population. Br J Ophthalmol. 1981;65:683–686.
94. Ebright JR, Lentino JR, Juni E. Endophthalmitis caused by *Moraxella nonliquefaciens.* Am J Clin Pathol. 1982;77:362–363.
95. Kowalski RP, Harwick JC. Incidence of *Moraxella* conjunctival infection. Am J Ophthalmol. 1986;101:437–440.
96. Sherman MD, York M, Irvine AR, et al. Endophthalmitis caused by β-lactamase–positive *Moraxella nonliquefaciens.* Am J Ophthalmol. 1993;115:674–676.
97. Schmidt ME, Smith MA, Levy CS. Endophthalmitis caused by unusual gram-negative bacilli: Three case reports and review. Clin Infect Dis. 1993;17:686–690.
98. Appelbaum A, Giladi A, Borman JB. *Moraxella* purulent pericarditis. J Cardiovasc Surg. 1974;15:479–481.
99. Graham DR, Band JD, Thornsberry C, et al. Infections caused by *Moraxella, Moraxella urethralis, Moraxella*-like groups M-5 and M-6, and *Kingella kingae* in the United States, 1953–1980. Rev Infect Dis. 1990;12:423–431.
100. Johnson DW, Lum G, Nimmo G, Hawley CM. *Moraxella nonliquefaciens* septic arthritis in a patient undergoing hemodialysis. Clin Infect Dis. 1995;21:1039–1040.
101. McCarty DJ, Sienkiewicz PJ. *Moraxella* septic arthritis in an adult. J Rheumatol. 1995;22:578–579.
102. Cox NH, Knowles MA, Porteus ID. Pre-septal cellulitis and facial erysipelas due to *Moraxella* species. Clin Exp Derm. 1994;19:321–323.
103. Buchman AL, Pickett MJ. *Moraxella atlantae* bacteraemia in a patient with systemic lupus erythematosis. J Infect. 1991;23:197–199.
104. Sanyal SK, Wilson N, Twum-Danso K, et al. *Moraxella* endocarditis following balloon angioplasty of aortic coarctation. Am Heart J. 1990;119:1421–1423.
105. Juvin PH, Boulot-Telle M, Triller R, Juvin E. *Moraxella lacunata* infectious arthritis. J Royal Soc Med. 1991;84:629–630.
106. Fijen CAP, Kuijper EJ, Tjia HG, et al. Complement deficiency predisposes for meningitis due to nongroupable meningococci and *Neisseria*-related bacteria. Clin Infect Dis. 1994;18:780–784.
107. Snell JJS, Lapage SP. Transfer of some saccharolytic *Moraxella* species to *Kingella* Henriksen and Bovre 1976, with descriptions of *Kingella indologenes* sp. nov. and *Kingella denitrificans* sp. nov. Int J System Bacteriol. 1976;26:451–458.
108. Odum L, Frederiksen W. Identification and characterization of *Kingella kingae.* Acta Path Microbiol Scand Sect B. 1981;89:311–315.
109. Claesson B, Falsen E, Kjellman B. *Kingella kingae* infections: A review and a presentation of data from 10 Swedish cases. Scand J Infect Dis. 1985;17:233–243.
110. Goutzmanis JJ, Gonis G, Gilbert GL. *Kingella kingae* infection in children: Ten cases and a review of the literature. Pediatr Infect Dis J. 1991;10:677–683.
111. Amir J, Schockelford PG. *Kingella kingae* intervertebral disk infection. J Clin Microbiol. 1991;29:1083–1086.
112. Hassan IJ, Hayek L. Endocarditis caused by *Kingella denitrificans.* J Infect. 1993;27:291–295.
113. Yagupsky P, Dagan R. *Kingella kingae* bacteremia in children. Pediatr Infect Dis J. 1994;13:1148–1149.
114. Birgisson H, Steingrimsson O, Gudnason T. *Kingella kingae* infections in paediatric patients: 5 cases of septic arthritis, osteomyelitis and bacteraemia. Scand J Infect Dis. 1997;29:495–498.
115. Roiz MP, Peralta FG, Arjona R. *Kingella kingae* bacteremia in an immunocompetent adult host. J Clin Microbiol. 1997;35:1916.
116. Krause I, Nimri R. *Kingella kingae* occult bacteremia in a toddler. Pediatr Infect Dis J. 1996;15:557–558.
117. Yagupsky P, Dagan R, Howard CB, et al. Clinical features and epidemiology of invasive *Kingella kingae* infections in southern Israel. Pediatrics. 1993;92:800–804.
118. Yagupsky P, Dagan R, Howard CW, et al. High prevalence of *Kingella kingae* in joint fluid from children with septic arthritis revealed by the BACTEC blood culture system. J Clin Microbiol. 1992;30:1278–1281.
119. Yagupsky P, Dagan R. *Kingella kingae:* An emerging cause of invasive infections in young children. Clin Infect Dis. 1997;24:860–866.
120. Yagupsky P, Dagan R, Prajgrod F, Merires M. Respiratory carriage of *Kingella kingae* among healthy children. Pediatr Infect Dis J. 1995;14:673–678.
121. Chen C-KC, Dunford RG, Reynolds HS, Zambon JJ. *Eikenella corrodens* in the human oral cavity. J Periodontol. 1989;60:611–616.
122. Dewhirst FE, Chen C-KC, Paster BJ, Zambon JJ. Phylogeny of species in the family Neisseriaceae isolated from human dental plaque and description of *Kingella oralis* sp. nov. Int J Syst Bacteriol. 1993;43:490–499.
123. Chen C. Distribution of a newly described species, *Kingella oralis,* in the human oral cavity. Oral Microbiol Immunol. 1996;11:425–427.
124. Woolfrey BF, Lally RT, Faville RJ. Intervertebral diskitis caused by *Kingella kingae.* Am J Clin Pathol. 1986;85:745–749.
125. Wolff AH, Ullman RF, Strampfer MJ, Cunha BA. *Kingella kingae* endocarditis: Report of a case and review of the literature. Heart Lung. 1987;16:579–583.
126. Rabin RL, Wong P, Noonan JA, Plumley DD. *Kingella kingae* endocarditis in a child with a prosthetic aortic valve and bifurcation graft. Am J Dis Child. 1983;137:403–404.
127. Verbruggen A-M, Hauglustaine D, Schildermans F, et al. Infections caused by *Kingella kingae:* Report of four cases and review. J Infect. 1986;13:133–142.

128. Jenny DB, Letendre PW, Iverson G. Endocarditis caused by *Kingella indologenes.* Rev Infect Dis. 1987;9:787–789.
129. Redfield DC, Overturf GD, Ewing N, Powars D. Bacteria, arthritis, and skin lesions due to *Kingella kingae.* Arch Dis Child. 1980;55:411–414.
130. Kennedy CA, Rosen H. *Kingella kingae* bacteremia and adult epiglottitis in a granulocytopenic host. Am J Med. 1988;85:701–702.
131. Mollee T, Kelly P, Tilse M. Isolation of *Kingella kingae* from a corneal ulcer. J Clin Microbiol. 1992;30:2516–2517.
132. Sordillo EM, Rendel M, Sood R, et al. Septicemia due to β-lactamase–positive *Kingella kingae.* Clin Infect Dis. 1993;17:818–819.
133. Aebi C, Maciver I, Latimer JL, et al. A protective epitope of *Moraxella catarrhalis* is encoded by two different genes. Infect Immun. 1997;65:4367–4377.
134. Klingman KL, Murphy TF. Purification and characterization of a high-molecular-weight outer membrane protein of *Moraxella (Branhamella) catarrhalis.* Infect Immun. 1994;62:1150–1155.
135. Fitzgerald M, Mulcahy R, Murphy S, et al. A 200 kDa protein is associated with haemagglutinating isolates of *Moraxella (Branhamella) catarrhalis.* FEMS Immunol Med Microbiol. 1997;18:209–216.
136. Aebi C, Cope LD, Latimer JL, et al. Mapping a protective epitope of the CopB outer membrane protein of *Moraxella catarrhalis.* Infect Immun. 1998;66:540–548.
137. Sethi S, Surface JM, Murphy TF. Antigenic heterogeneity and molecular analysis of CopB of *Branhamella (Moraxella) catarrhalis.* Infect Immun. 1997;65:3666–3671.
138. Aebi C, Stone B, Beucher M, et al. Expression of the CopB outer membrane protein by *Moraxella catarrhalis* is regulated by iron and affects iron acquisition from transferrin and lactoferrin. Infect Immun. 1996;64:2024–2030.
139. Sethi S, Hill SL, Murphy TF. Serum antibodies to outer membrane proteins of *Moraxella (Branhamella) catarrhalis* in patients with bronchiectasis: Identification of OMP B1 as an important antigen. Infect Immun. 1995;63:1516–1520.
140. Campagnari AA, Ducey TF, Rebmann CA. Outer membrane protein B1, an iron-repressible protein conserved in the outer membrane of *Moraxella (Branhamella) catarrhalis,* binds human transferrin. Infect Immun. 1996;64:3920–3924.
141. Mathers KE, Goldblatt D, Aebi C, et al. Characterisation of an outer membrane protein of *Moraxella catarrhalis.* FEMS Immunol Med Microbiol. 1997;19:231–236.
142. Hsiao CB, Sethi S, Murphy TF. Outer membrane protein CD of *Branhamella catarrhalis:* Sequence conservation in strains recovered from the human respiratory tract. Microb Pathog. 1995;19:215–225.
143. Yang Y-P, Myers LE, McGuinness U, et al. The major outer membrane protein, CD, extracted from *Moraxella (Branhamella) catarrhalis* is a potential vaccine antigen that induces bactericidal antibodies. FEMS Immunol Med Microbiol. 1997;17:187–199.
144. Murphy TF, Kirkham C, Lesse AJ. The major heat-modifiable outer membrane protein CD is highly conserved among strains of *Branhamella catarrhalis.* Mol Microbiol. 1993;10:87–98.
145. Bhushan R, Craigie R, Murphy TF. Molecular cloning and characterization of outer membrane protein E of *Moraxella (Branhamella) catarrhalis.* J Bacteriol. 1994;176:6636–6643.
146. Bhushan R, Kirkham C, Sethi S, Murphy TF. Antigenic characterization and analysis of the human immune response to outer membrane protein E of *Branhamella catarrhalis.* Infect Immun. 1997;65:2668–2675.

GRAM-NEGATIVE BACILLI

Chapter 202

Vibrio cholerae

CARLOS SEAS
EDUARDO GOTUZZO

Cholera is a historically feared epidemic diarrheal disease. New epidemics continue to affect different regions of the world and impose significant economic constraint on the already impoverished developing countries. The Latin American extension of the seventh pandemic of cholera at the beginning of 1991, the epidemic of cholera in Zaire in 1994, and the epidemic of cholera caused by *Vibrio cholerae* O139 in 1992 in Asia are recent examples. These epidemics show that it is still not possible to predict when and where a new epidemic of cholera will start, that appropriate therapy may reduce the mortality to values below 1%, and that changes in the etiology of this ancient disease are still taking place.

The term *cholera* has ancient origins and is derived from Greek words meaning a flow of bile.[1, 2] Thomas Sydenham was the first to distinguish cholera the disease from cholera the state of anger.[1] He proposed the term *cholera morbus* for the disease. Because earlier descriptions of the disease confused cholera with other diarrheal diseases, the modern history of cholera began with Sydenham's description in 1817.

The modern era of cholera is characterized by seven pandemics. The first six occurred between 1817 and 1923. These pandemics were most likely caused by *V. cholerae* O1 of the classic biotype and largely originated in Asia, usually the Indian subcontinent, with subsequent extension to Europe and the Americas.[2] Filippo Pacini published his observations on the discovery of a curved bacilli in the stools of victims of cholera in Italy in 1854. He coined the name *Vibrio cholerae.*[3] In 1883 Robert Koch made the same discovery. Transmission of the disease was recognized only after the brilliant work of John Snow during the second pandemic affecting London in 1849, even before knowing the etiology of the disease. He reduced the transmission of cholera by blocking access to contaminated water in one area of London.

The seventh pandemic of cholera differed from the prior six. This pandemic was caused by the biotype El Tor of *V. cholerae* O1, a biotype that had been isolated for the first time in Egypt at the beginning of the century and was associated with sporadic cases until 1961. The pandemic originated in the Celebes Islands, Indonesia, in 1961 instead of the Indian subcontinent. This pandemic has been the longest lasting and has affected more countries and continents than the other six. The last extension of this pandemic in Latin America occurred in 1991, where it caused higher attack rates than seen during the last century but the lowest case-fatality rates.[4, 5] The pandemic is still going on in many countries. Eight countries reported cholera outbreaks to the World Health Organization during 1997. The total number of cases officially reported from 1997 to March 26, 1998, was 120,867, with 89% of these cases being reported from Africa.

Finally, in October 1992, a totally unexpected epidemic of a cholera-like disease was observed in Madras, India, with subsequent cases being reported along the Bay of Bengal.[6] *V. cholerae* of the new serogroup O139 was responsible for this epidemic, the first non-O1 *Vibrio* to do so. The epidemic was widespread in the Asiatic continent, with imported cases reported from developed countries.[7–9] Some regarded this as the eighth cholera pandemic,[10] although the epidemic has remained confined to Bangladesh and India. After 1992, O1 *V. cholerae* was again epidemic in that region.[11]

MICROBIOLOGY

V. cholerae is a curved gram-negative bacillus varying in size from 1 to 3 μm in length by 0.5 to 0.8 μm in diameter that belongs to the family *Vibrionaceae* and shares common characteristics with the family *Enterobacteriaceae.* The bacterium has a single polar flagellum that confers the erratic movement on microscopy. The antigenic structure of *V. cholerae* is similar to that of other members of the family Enterobacteriaceae, with a flagellar H antigen and a somatic O antigen. The former does not distinguish between pathogenic *Vibrio* and other nonpathogenic members of the family, but the O antigen does allow the differentiation. Only *V. cholerae* carrying the somatic antigens O1 and O139 are associated with cholera.

V. cholerae O1 can be classified into three serotypes according to the presence of somatic antigens and into two biotypes according to specific phenotypic characteristics. Serotype Inaba carries the O antigens A and C, serotype Ogawa carries the antigens A and B, and serotype Hikojima carries the three antigens A, B, and C. No evidence of different clinical spectra among these three serotypes of *V.*

cholerae has ever been presented. During epidemics, a shift from one serotype to another may occur.[12] This phenomenon was also reported more recently during the Latin American extension of the seventh pandemic of cholera.[13] The differences between the two biotypes of *V. cholerae* O1 are remarkable. The classic biotype, probably responsible for the first six pandemics of cholera, causes an approximately equal number of symptomatic and asymptomatic cases. In contrast, the El Tor biotype causes more asymptomatic infections, with a ratio between 20 to 100 asymptomatic infections to 1 symptomatic case.[14] The classic biotype is confined to the south of Bangladesh, whereas the El Tor biotype is responsible for the current pandemic.[15] Some evidence suggests that the agents of the last two pandemics of cholera and *V. cholerae* O1 isolated recently from the U.S. Gulf coast originated from nontoxigenic non-O1 strains of *V. cholerae.*[16]

Isolation and Identification

V. cholerae O1 or O139 can easily be observed under darkfield examination. The chaotic movement and the high number of bacteria seen in a stool sample from patients with clinical disease are characteristic of *V. cholerae* infection. The use of specific antisera against the serotype blocks the movement of these vibrios and allows confirmation of the diagnosis. However, under epidemic conditions, the presence of bacteria with a darting movement under darkfield microscopy in a stool sample from patients highly suspected of having cholera is sufficient to make the diagnosis. Rapid diagnosis is desirable, especially in epidemic situations,[17–19] but definitive confirmation still requires isolation of the bacteria in culture. Specific medium is needed to isolate *V. cholerae* from stool. The two media most commonly used are thiosulfate citrate bile salts sucrose agar and tellurite taurocholate gelatin agar. These two media are equally sensitive to isolate either O1 or O139 *V. cholerae.* Enrichment media may be used when the number of bacteria in the stool is small or when environmental samples are evaluated for the presence of *Vibrio.*

PATHOPHYSIOLOGY

V. cholerae O1 and O139 cause clinical disease by secreting an enterotoxin that promotes secretion of fluids and electrolytes by the small intestine. The infectious dose of bacteria varies with the vehicle. When water is the vehicle, more bacteria are needed to cause disease, 10^3 to 10^6, but when the vehicle is food, the amount needed is lower, 10^2 to 10^4.[20] Conditions that reduce gastric acidity, such as the use of antacids or histamine receptor blockers, gastrectomy, or chronic gastritis induced by *Helicobacter pylori,* increase the risk of getting the disease and predispose the patient to more severe clinical forms. Toxin is produced, but *V. cholerae* does not invade the intestinal wall and few neutrophils are found in the stool. The incubation period varies with the infectious dose and gastric acidity and lasts 12 to 72 hours.

Both Robert Koch and John Snow suspected that a toxin was responsible for some of the disease manifestations, but it was not until 1959 that S. N. De and N. K. Dutta and colleagues, working in different laboratories, showed that *V. cholerae* promoted intestinal secretion in animal models.[21, 22] The toxin was finally purified by Finkelstein and LoSpalluto in 1969.[23] The toxin has five B subunits and two A subunits.[24] The B subunits allow binding of the toxin to a specific receptor, a ganglioside (GM_1) located on the surface of the cells lining the mucosa along the intestine of humans and certain suckling mammals. The active, or A, subunit has two components, A1 and A2, linked by a disulfide bond. Activation of the A1 component by adenylate cyclase results in a net increase in cyclic adenosine monophosphate, which blocks the absorption of sodium and chloride by microvilli and promotes the secretion of chloride and water by crypt cells. The result of these events is the production of watery diarrhea with electrolyte concentrations similar to that of plasma, as shown in Table 202–1. A few other toxins have been isolated from pathogenic *V. cholerae,*[25] but their role in genesis of the disease is less clear.

TABLE 202–1 Electrolyte Concentration of Cholera Stools and Common Solutions Used for Treatment

	Electrolyte and Glucose Concentration (mmol/L)				
	Na^+	*Cl^-*	*K^+*	*HCO_3^-*	Glucose
Cholera stool					
Adults	130	100	20	44	
Children	100	90	33	30	
Intravenous solutions					
Ringer's lactate	130	109	4	28*	0
Dhaka	133	98	13	48	0
Normal saline	154	154	0	0	0
Peru polyelectrolyte	90	80	20	30	111
WHO ORS	90	80	20	30†	111

*Ringer's lactate does not contain HCO_3^-; it has lactate instead.
†Bicarbonate is replaced by trisodium citrate, which persists longer than bicarbonate in sachets.
Abbreviation: WHO ORS, World Health Organization oral rehydration solution.

EPIDEMIOLOGY

Cholera has unique epidemiologic features. Perhaps the most intriguing are the predisposition to cause epidemics with pandemic potential and the ability to remain endemic in all affected areas.[26] These two epidemiologic patterns, the epidemic and endemic patterns, are summarized in Table 202–2. Recognizing the different age groups at risk, depending on the epidemiologic pattern, is useful in designing preventive measures.

New insights into the life cycle of *V. cholerae* in recent years has allowed a better understanding of cholera transmission. *V. cholerae* lives in aquatic environments, which are their natural reservoirs.[27] Both O1 and non-O1 strains coexist in these environments, with non-O1 and nontoxigenic O1 strains predominating over toxigenic O1 strains.[28] In its natural environment, *V. cholerae* lives attached to a particular kind of algae or attached to crustacean shells and copepods (zooplankton), as shown in Figure 202–1.[29, 30] When conditions in the environment such as temperature, salinity, and availability of nutrients are suitable, *V. cholerae* multiplies and can survive for years in a free-living cycle without the intervention of humans. Otherwise, when conditions are not suitable for its growth, *V. cholerae* switches from a metabolically active state to a dormant state.[28] In this dormant state *V. cholerae* cannot be cultured from the water on either standard or enrichment media but appears to survive under difficult environmental conditions. Immunofluorescent techniques using monoclonal antibodies have been used to detect dormant *V. cholerae.*[31] Experimentally, the switch from a nonculturable to a culturable state has been attained in the laboratory, as well as in human volunteers.[32] *V. cholerae* may also persist in the environment

TABLE 202–2 Epidemiologic Patterns of Cholera

Epidemiologic Features	Epidemic Pattern	Endemic Pattern
Age at greatest risk	All ages	Children 2–15 yr
Modes of transmission	Single introduction with fecal-oral spread	Multiple modes of introduction: water, food, fecal-oral spread
Reservoir	None	Aquatic reservoir Asymptomatic people
Asymptomatic infections	Less common	More common
Immune status of the population	No preexisting immunity	Preexisting immunity, evidence of infection increases with age
Secondary spread	High	Variable

Modified from Glass RI, Black RE. The epidemiology of cholera. In: Barua D, Greenough WB III, eds. Cholera. New York: Plenum; 1992:129.

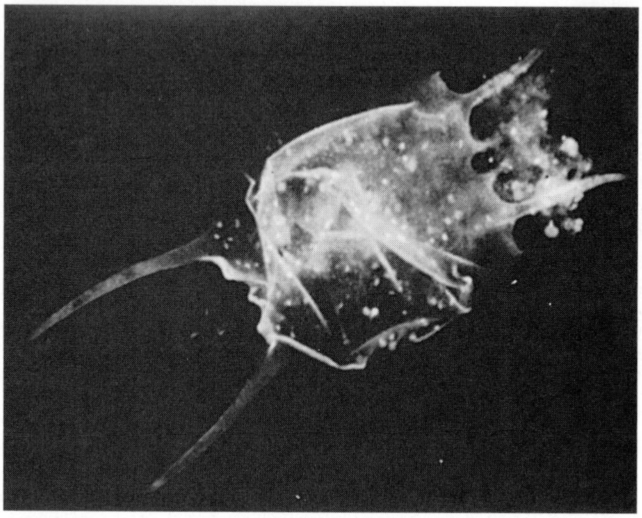

FIGURE 202–1. *Vibrio cholerae* attached to a copepode stained with fluorescent techniques. (Courtesy of Dr. Rita Colwell and Dr. Anwarul Huq, University of Maryland.)

and adopts a rugose form visible on a special agar, Luria agar.[33] These forms are resistant to chlorination and may play a role in persistence of aquatic contamination during epidemics.[34] Humans infected by *V. cholerae* may shed the bacteria for a long time, sometimes for months or years,[35] but their importance as reservoirs is minimal in comparison to the aquatic environment.

From its aquatic environment, *V. cholerae* is introduced to humans through contamination of water sources and contamination of food. The cycle of transmission is closed when infected humans shed the bacteria into the environment and contaminate water sources and food. Once humans are infected, incredibly high attack rates may occur, especially in previously nonexposed populations. Additional evidence of very high household transmission rates exists, as occurred during the last Latin American epidemic or more recently during the epidemic in Zaire in 1994.[36, 37] Transmission via contaminated water and food has been recognized for years.[38–42] During the Latin American epidemic and more recent epidemics in Africa, acquisition of the disease by drinking contaminated water from rivers, ponds, lakes, and even tube well sources has been documented.[42–46] Contamination of municipal water was the main route of transmission of cholera in Trujillo, Peru, during the epidemic in 1991.[47] Drinking unboiled water,[42, 47] introducing hands into containers used to store drinking water,[48, 49] drinking beverages from street vendors,[42, 50] drinking beverages when contaminated ice had been added,[42] and drinking water outside the home were risk factors to acquire cholera.[50] On the other hand, drinking boiled water, acidic beverages, and carbonated water, as well as using narrow-necked vessels for storing water, was protective.[42, 51, 52] *V. cholerae* survives for up to 14 days in some foods, especially when contamination occurs after preparation of the food.[53] Cooking and heating the food eliminate the bacteria. Epidemics of cholera associated with the ingestion of leftover rice,[54] yellow rice in a restaurant,[8] raw fish,[55, 56] cooked crabs,[57] seafood,[58, 59] raw oysters,[60] and fresh vegetables and fruits[47] have been documented.

Transmission of cholera during funerals in Africa has been reported.[61, 62] Risk factors identified included eating at the funeral with a nondisinfected corpse and touching the body.[61] Eating rice at the funeral was the main risk factor for the acquisition of cholera in one study.[62] Person-to-person transmission is less likely to occur because a large inoculum is necessary to transmit disease. Anecdotal reports exist in the literature, however.[63–65] Careful evaluation of these reports shows that other potential risk factors might have been implicated in the transmission. Other vehicles of transmission such as insects and fomites are less likely to be important in epidemic situations.[66]

Seasonality is another typical characteristic of cholera. Epidemics tend to occur during the hot seasons, and countries with more than one hot season per year may also have more than one epidemic, such as seen in Bangladesh.[67] Data from the epidemic of cholera in Peru from 1991 to 1995 also confirm that outbreaks are associated with the warmest months of the year.[68] Some host factors are important in the transmission of cholera. Among them, infection by *H. pylori* and the effect of the O blood group deserve special consideration. Recent data from Bangladesh show that people infected by *H. pylori* are at higher risk of acquiring cholera than are people not infected by *H. pylori*.[69] Additionally, the risk of acquiring severe cholera among people infected by *H. pylori* was higher in patients without previous contact with *V. cholerae,* as measured by the absence of vibriocidal antibodies in the serum.[69] *H. pylori* causes a chronic gastritis that induces hypochlorhydria, which in turn reduces the ability of the stomach to contain the *Vibrio* invasion. The impact of the association of these two infections is particularly interesting because *H. pylori* infection is very common in persons of all ages in developing countries.[70] An unexplained predisposition toward severe disease in persons with the O blood group has been observed in Asia[71] and more recently in Latin America.[72]

Although mainly countries with poor sanitary conditions are affected by cholera, a few developed countries such as the United States, Canada, and Australia have reported indigenous cases. Two different *V. cholerae* O1 strains have been isolated from these regions, and these vibrios differ from the strain responsible for the seventh pandemic.[73–75] Sporadic cases are reported periodically from these areas.

CLINICAL MANIFESTATIONS AND LABORATORY ABNORMALITIES

The hallmark of cholera is the production of watery diarrhea with varying degrees of dehydration ranging from none to severe and life-threatening diarrhea. Patients with mild to moderate dehydration secondary to cholera are difficult to differentiate from those infected by other enteric pathogens such as enterotoxigenic *Escherichia coli* or rotavirus. Patients with severe dehydration from cholera are easy to identify because no other clinical illness produces such severe dehydration in a matter of a few hours as cholera. Onset of the disease is abrupt and characterized by the production of watery diarrhea without strain, tenesmus, or prominent abdominal pain, rapidly followed or sometimes preceded by vomiting. As the diarrhea continues, other symptoms of severe dehydration are present at this time, such as generalized cramps and oliguria. Physical examination will show an alert patient most of the time despite the fact that the pulse is nonpalpable and blood pressure cannot be measured. Fever is observed in less than 5% of cases. Patients look anxious and restless or sometimes obtunded, the eyes are very sunken, mucous membranes are dry, the skin has lost its elasticity and when pinched retracts very slowly, the voice is almost nonaudible, and the intestinal sounds are prominent. Patients in this condition are difficult to confuse with other medical conditions. Figure 202–2 shows a typical patient with severe cholera. Table 202–3 shows the clinical manifestations according to the degree of dehydration as a guide to the proper administration of fluids. Although watery diarrhea is the hallmark of cholera, some patients do not have diarrhea but instead have abdominal distention and ileus, a relatively rare type of cholera called cholera "sicca."[76] Management of these patients is particularly difficult because evaluation of the degree of dehydration is overshadowed by the accumulation of fluid in the intestinal lumen.

Laboratory abnormalities reflect the isotonic dehydration characteristic of cholera. Increases in packed cell volume, serum specific gravity, and total protein are typically seen in patients with moderate to severe dehydration. Although abnormal results of these tests correlate with the degree of dehydration on arrival at a health center, they

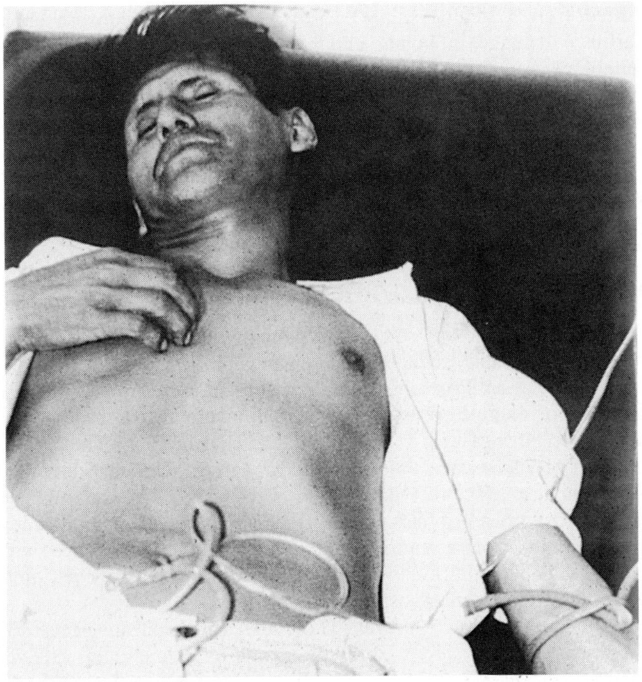

FIGURE 202–2. A Peruvian patient with severe cholera. Sunken eyes and washerwoman's hands are typical of patients with severe dehydration.

are less useful for monitoring rehydration status.[77] Biochemical and acid-base laboratory abnormalities typical of severe dehydration are prerenal azotemia, metabolic acidosis with a high anion gap, normal or low serum potassium levels, and normal or slightly low sodium and chloride levels.[36] The calcium and magnesium content in plasma is also high as a result of hemoconcentration.[78] The white blood cell count is high in patients with severe cholera. Hyperglycemia caused by high concentrations of epinephrine, glucagon, and cortisol stimulated by hypovolemia is more commonly seen than hypoglycemia,[79] but children with hypoglycemia have a higher risk of dying than do nonhypoglycemic children.[80] Acute renal failure is the most severe complication of cholera. Incidence rates of 10.6 cases per 1000 have been reported in Peru during the first months of the epidemic in 1991.[36] Patients with acute renal failure had a history of improper rehydration. All age groups were equally affected, and the mortality rate in this group of patients was extremely high, 18%, particularly in the elderly.[36]

The clinical manifestation of cholera in children is similar to that in adults. However, hypoglycemia, seizures, fever, and mental alteration are more common in children.[81] Cholera in pregnant women carries a bad prognosis and portends more severe clinical illness, especially when the disease is acquired at the end of the pregnancy.[82] Fetal loss occurs in as many as 50% of these pregnancies.[82] Cholera in the elderly also carries a bad prognosis because of more complications, particularly acute renal failure, severe metabolic acidosis, and pulmonary edema.[36] Proper hydration may correct all electrolyte and acid-base abnormalities in elderly patients.[83]

TABLE 202–3 Clinical Findings According to Degree of Dehydration

Finding	Mild Dehydration	Moderate Dehydration	Severe Dehydration
Loss of fluid*	<5%	5–10%	>10%
Mentation	Alert	Restless	Drowsy or comatose
Radial pulse			
rate	Normal	Rapid	Very rapid
intensity	Normal	Weak	Feeble or impalpable
Respiration	Normal	Deep	Deep and rapid
Systolic blood pressure	Normal	Low	Very low or unrecordable
Skin elasticity	Retracts rapidly	Retracts slowly	Retracts very slowly
Eyes	Normal	Sunken	Very sunken
Voice	Normal	Hoarse	Not audible
Urine production	Normal	Scant	Oliguria

*Percentage of body weight.
From Bennish ML. Cholera: Pathophysiology, clinical features, and treatment. In: Wachsmuth IK, Blake PA, Olsvik O, eds. *Vibrio cholerae* and Cholera. Molecular to Global Perspectives. Washington, DC: ASM Press; 1994:229.

TREATMENT

The goal of therapy is to restore the fluid losses caused by diarrhea and vomiting. Although treatment of patients without severe dehydration is easy, treatment of patients with severe dehydration requires experience and proper training. Basic training in how to recognize the degree of dehydration, how to select the proper intravenous solution, and how rapidly to rehydrate the patient is crucial. Recent experience during the epidemic in Zaire where untrained people played a negative role cannot be emphasized more.[37] Guidelines to rehydrate cholera patients have been written and reviewed elsewhere.[84–87] The intravenous route should be restricted to patients with moderate dehydration who do not tolerate the oral route, to those who purge more than 10 to 20 ml/kg/hour, and to patients with severe dehydration. Rehydration should be accomplished in two phases: the rehydration phase and the maintenance phase. The purpose of the rehydration phase is to restore normal hydration status, and it should last no more than 4 hours. Intravenous fluids should be infused at a rate of 50 to 100 ml/kg/hour in severely dehydrated patients. Ringer's lactate solution is the most frequently recommended solution, but other solutions may be used as well, as shown in Table 202–1. Normal saline solution is not recommended because it does not correct the metabolic acidosis. When intravenous access proves difficult, nasogastric tubes or intraosseous catheters can be used,[88] although problems with intravenous access were not common during the recent cholera epidemic in Peru.[68] After finishing the rehydration phase, all signs of dehydration should have abated and the patient should pass urine at a rate of 0.5 ml/kg/hour or greater. Then starts the maintenance phase. During this phase the objective is to maintain normal hydration status by replacing ongoing losses. The oral route is preferred during this phase, and the use of oral rehydration solutions at a rate of 500 to 1000 ml/hour is highly recommended. Oral rehydration therapy uses the principle of common transportation of solutes, electrolytes, and water by the intestine not affected by the cholera toxin. People with diarrhea can undergo successful rehydration with simple solutions containing glucose and electrolytes that may be prepared at home. Evaluation of rehydration status and accurate recording of intake and output volumes are essential. Patients without severe dehydration who tolerate the oral route can be rehydrated with oral rehydration solutions exclusively and discharged promptly from the health center. Practical guidelines have recently been published[87] and are summarized in Table 202–4. Discharging patients from health centers, particularly those with severe dehydration, is a critical issue, especially during epidemics. No significant readmission of patients was observed in Peru during the epidemic in 1991 when the following criteria were used to discharge patients: urine volume higher than 40 ml/hour, diarrhea output below 400 ml/hour, and oral ingestion of rehydration solutions between 600 and 800 ml/hour.[36] Case-fatality rate during epidemics may be reduced to values below 1% even in disaster situations, provided that adequate access to health care centers and proper management of patients can be ensured.[36, 89] Figures as high as 10% have been reported in epidemic settings when patients had no access to health care or received improper treatment.[90] Treatment of cholera caused by O139 *V. cholerae* is the same. No significant differences

TABLE 202–4 Practical Guidelines for the Treatment of Cholera

1. Evaluate the degree of dehydration on arrival
2. Rehydrate the patients in two phases:
   Rehydration phase: lasts 2–4 h
   Maintenance phase: lasts until diarrhea abates
3. Register output and intake volumes in predesigned charts and periodically review the data
4. Use the intravenous route only for
   Severely dehydrated patients during the rehydration phase, in whom an infusion rate of 50–100 ml/kg/h is advised
   Moderately dehydrated patients who do not tolerate the oral route
   High stool purgers (>10 ml/kg/h) during the maintenance phase
5. Use ORS for patients during the maintenance phase at a rate of 800–1000 ml/h, matching ongoing losses with ORS
6. Discharge patients to the treatment center if the following conditions are fulfilled:
   Oral tolerance, ≥1000 ml/h
   Urine volume, ≥40 ml/h
   Stool volume, ≤400 ml/h

Abbreviation: ORS, Oral rehydration solution.
From Seas C, DuPont HL, Valdez LM, et al. Practical guidelines for the treatment of cholera. Drugs. 1996;51:966–973.

in clinical manifestations of the disease caused by these two agents have been found.[91]

Antimicrobial agents play a secondary role in the treatment of cholera. Clinical trials have shown that when patients with severe dehydration are given antibiotics, the duration of diarrhea is decreased and the volume of stool is reduced by nearly half.[92] Early discharge and lessened hydration decrease hospital expense. These benefits are critical in epidemic conditions. Oral tetracycline and doxycycline are the agents of choice in areas of the globe where sensitive strains predominate. A single dose of doxycycline (300 mg) is the preferred regimen.[93] Tetracyclines are not safe in children younger than 7 years, and alternatives such as trimethoprim-sulfamethoxazole, erythromycin, and furazolidone are preferred over tetracyclines. Pregnant women can be treated with erythromycin or furazolidone. Currently recommended regimens are presented in Table 202–5.

In the last 2 decades, selection of an adequate antimicrobial in certain parts of the world has been complicated by the appearance of strains resistant to tetracyclines and other antimicrobial agents.[94–96] New agents have been tested in endemic and epidemic areas, with quinolones being the most effective.[97] Ciprofloxacin has been more extensively studied than other quinolones. Two regimens of ciprofloxacin have shown at least comparable if not better results than other antibiotics in randomized, double-blind clinical trials in patients with severe cholera caused by either O1 or O139 *V. cholerae*: a single dose of 1 g or once-daily regimens of 250 mg for 3 days.[98, 99] However, strains resistant to ciprofloxacin have recently been reported from Calcutta, India.[100] The high cost and concern about cartilage damage in young children are drawbacks to large-scale quinolone use. Chemoprophylaxis of household contacts of cholera cases has been proposed. However, published data do not support this concept.[101] More recently it has been shown that when transmission of the disease is low, as occurs in endemic areas, the utility of chemoprophylaxis is not significant.[102] Prophylaxis with antibiotics might be considered in situations in which the rate of transmission of the disease is high, along with other measures to curtail transmission.

TABLE 202–5 Antimicrobial Regimens for the Treatment of Cholera

Drug	Dose: *Adult*	Dose: *Children*
Tetracycline	500 mg qid for 3 d	50 mg/kg of body weight qid for 3 d
Doxycycline	300 mg as a single dose	Not evaluated
Furazolidone	100 mg qid for 3 d	5 mg/kg per day in 4 divided doses for 3 d or 7 mg/kg as a single dose
Cotrimoxazole	160 mg of trimethoprim/800 mg of sulfamethoxazole bid for 3 d	8 mg of trimethoprim–40 mg of sulfamethoxazole/kg divided in 2 doses for 3 d
Norfloxacin	400 mg bid for 3 d	Not recommended
Ciprofloxacin	250 mg/d for 3 d	Not recommended
	1 g as a single dose	Not recommended

From Seas C, DuPont HL, Valdez LM, et al. Practical guidelines for the treatment of cholera. Drugs. 1996;51:966–973.

PREVENTION AND THE ROLE OF VACCINES

John Snow was the first scientist to show that transmission of cholera may be significantly reduced when uncontaminated water is provided to the population. Providing potable water and ensuring proper management of excreta to avoid contamination of other water sources are important measures to reduce cholera transmission. The limited number of indigenous cases reported from the United States and Australia despite the fact that *Vibrio* is isolated from the environment in these countries provides further evidence that hygiene and sanitation contain cholera transmission. However, the experience with continuing epidemics in developing countries shows that these simple measures are almost impossible to implement.

Alternative ways to prevent cholera transmission are necessary. Water can be made safer to drink by boiling or adding chlorine. Both methods are expensive and difficult to implement under epidemic situations. Exposing water to sunlight has also been considered, but its implementation is again not feasible in developing countries. Education of the population at risk on appropriate hygienic practices is always recommended, but the impact of massive educational campaigns on the reduction of cholera transmission is questionable. Identification of local customs that place people at risk may help in eliminating such practices. Predicting the onset of an epidemic may have a tremendous impact on prevention. Two recent studies conducted in Lima, Peru, showed that identification of *V. cholerae* O1 from municipal sewage and environmental samples preceded the occurrence of human cases by 1 to 3 months.[103, 104] Active surveillance of vibrios in the environment and in populations at risk by the application of uniform case definitions[105] is recommended on the basis of these data. More recently, the possibility of predicting an epidemic by monitoring the movement of plankton by satellite seems attractive, but more data are needed to support this method.[106]

An inability to implement the aforementioned measures to curtail cholera transmission has necessitated a search for vaccines. An ideal vaccine against cholera should elicit a fast and long-lasting immune response with minimal side effects. Additionally, the vaccine should be locally produced, and to increase compliance, a single dose is highly desirable. The disappointing experience with parenteral vaccines and the better knowledge of the immune response to natural infection that has accumulated during recent years clearly show that an oral route for administering the vaccine is preferred. The ideal vaccine is still not available,[107] but significant progress has been made. Two oral vaccines have been studied in epidemic and endemic settings. The oral inactivated vaccine WC-BS (whole cell plus B subunit) has been more extensively evaluated. A large field trial conducted in Matlab-Bangladesh with subsequent follow-up of 3 and 5 years has shown promising results.[108, 109] Two doses 2 weeks apart conferred protection similar to that of three doses. The short-term protective efficacy of this vaccine was very high. Results at 3 and 5 years were less impressive, with only about 50% of vaccines protected. Significant drawbacks were less protection against the El Tor biotype, less protection in children, and less protection in persons with blood group O. People who acquired cholera during the first year of the trial had a lower immune response to the vaccine.[110] Recombinant techniques have been used to produce a B subunit vaccine locally in Vietnam at a significantly reduced cost.[111] Another group of promising oral vaccines are the live-attenuated oral cholera vaccines, especially the third-generation CVD 103–HgR.[112] Although the results of a large field trial in Indonesia are awaited, this vaccine has shown promising results when tested in endemic and epidemic areas in both adults and children.[113–115] Persons with the O blood group antigen seem to have had better protection with the CVD 103–HgR vaccine.[116] New potential vaccine candidates are being tested, including vaccines against El Tor O1 and O139 *V. cholerae*.[117–119] None of the vaccines tested thus far have prevented cholera transmission, and none are recommended for general usage. Clearly, more research on safe, effective vaccines is needed.

Travelers to endemic areas may be considered for vaccination, but the risk is so extremely low[120] that counseling about avoiding risk is more cost-effective. Vaccination of refugee populations could also be considered, but recent epidemics of cholera in Africa have occurred very quickly, with little time for induction of vaccine-induced immunity.[37] Public health measures in refugee camps appear more promising.[121]

REFERENCES

1. Barua D. History of cholera. In: Barua D, Greenough WB, eds. Cholera. New York: Plenum; 1992:1.
2. Pollitzer R. Cholera. Geneva: World Health Organization; 1959.
3. Barua D. Cholera during the last hundred years (1884–1983). In: Takeda Y, ed. *Vibrio cholerae* and Cholera. Tokyo: KTK Scientific; 1988:9.
4. Centers for Disease Control. Cholera—Peru, 1991. MMWR Morb Mortal Wkly Rep. 1991;40:108.
5. Carpenter CJ. The treatment of cholera: Clinical science at the bedside. J Infect Dis. 1992;166:2–14.
6. Cholera Working Group. Large epidemic of cholera-like disease in Bangladesh caused by *Vibrio cholerae* O139 synonym Bengal. Lancet. 1993;342:387–390.
7. Hoge CW, Bodhidatta L, Echeverria P, et al. Epidemiologic study of O1 and O139 in Thailand: At the advancing edge of the eight pandemic. Am J Epidemiol. 1996;143:263.
8. Boyce TG, Mintz DE, Greene KD, et al. *Vibrio cholerae* O139 Bengal infections among tourists to Southeast Asia; an intercontinental foodborne outbreak. J Infect Dis. 1995;172:1401.
9. Cheasty R, Rowe B, Said B, et al. *Vibrio cholerae* serogroup O139 in England and Wales. Lancet. 1993;307:1007.
10. Swerdlow DL, Ries AA. *Vibrio cholerae* non-O1—the eighth pandemic? Lancet. 1993;342:382.
11. Faruque AS, Fuchs GJ, Albert MJ. Changing epidemiology of cholera due to *Vibrio cholerae* O1 and O139 Bengal in Dhaka, Bangladesh. Epidemiol Infect. 1996;116:275.
12. Stroeher UH, Karageogos LE, Morona R, et al. Serotype conversion in *Vibrio cholerae* O1. Proc Natl Acad Sci U S A. 1992;89:2566–2570.
13. Vugia DJ, Rodriguez M, Vargas M, et al. Epidemic cholera in Trujillo, Peru 1992: Utility of a clinical case definition and shift in *Vibrio cholerae* O1 serotype. Am J Trop Med Hyg. 1994;50:566.
14. Mujica O, Seminario L, Tauxe R, et al. Investigación epidemiológica de cólera en el Perú: Lecciones para un continente en riesgo. Rev Med Herediana. 1991;2:121.
15. Siddique AK, Baqui AH, Eusof A, et al. Survival of classic cholera in Bangladesh. Lancet. 1991;337:1125.
16. Karaolis DK, Lan R, Reeves PR. The sixth and seventh cholera pandemics are due to independent clones separately derived from environmental nontoxigenic non-O1 *Vibrio cholerae*. J Bacteriol. 1995;177:3191.
17. Adams LB, Henk MC, Siebeling RJ. Detection of *Vibrio cholerae* with monoclonal antibodies specific for serovar O1 lipopolysaccharide. J Clin Microbiol. 1988;26:1801.
18. Shaffer N, do Santos ES, Andreason PA, et al. Rapid laboratory diagnosis of cholera in the field. Trans R Soc Trop Med Hyg. 1989;83:119.
19. Hasan JAK, Huq A, Tamplin ML, et al. A novel kit for rapid detection of *Vibrio cholerae* O1. J Clin Microbiol. 1994;32:249.
20. Cash RA, Music SI, Libonati JP, et al. Response of man to infection with *Vibrio cholerae*. 1. Clinical, serologic, and bacteriologic responses to a known inoculum. J Infect Dis. 1974;129:45.
21. De SN. Enterotoxicity of bacteria-free culture filtrate of *Vibrio cholerae*. Nature. 1959;183:1533–1534.
22. Dutta NK, Panse MW, Kulkarni DR. Role of cholera toxin in experimental cholera. J Bacteriol. 1959;78:594.
23. Finkelstein RA, LoSpalluto JJ. Pathogenesis of experimental cholera: Preparation and isolation of choleragen and choleragenoid. J Exp Med. 1969;130:185–202.
24. Finkelstein RA. Cholera enterotoxin (choleragen): An historical perspective. In: Barua D, Greenough WB III, eds. Topics in Infectious Diseases: Cholera. New York: Plenum; 1992:155.
25. Kaper JB, Fasano A, Trucksis M. Toxins of *Vibrio cholerae*. In: Wachsmuth IK, Blake PA, Olsvik O, eds. *Vibrio cholerae* and Cholera. Molecular to Global Perspectives. Washington, DC: ASM Press; 1994:145.
26. Glass RI, Black RE. The epidemiology of cholera. In: Barua D, Greenough WB III, eds. Cholera. New York: Plenum; 1992:129.
27. Kaper JB, Morris JG, Levine MM. Cholera. J Clin Microbiol Rev. 1995;8:48–86.
28. Colwell RR, Huq A: Vibrios in the environment: Viable but nonculturable *Vibrio cholerae*. In: Wachsmuth IK, Blake PA, Olsvik O, eds. *Vibrio cholerae* and Cholera. Molecular to Global Perspectives. Washington DC: ASM Press; 1994:117.
29. Huq A, Small EB, West PA, et al. Ecology of *Vibrio cholerae* O1 with special reference to planktonic crustacean copepods. Appl Environ Microbiol. 1983;45:275.
30. Huq A, West PA, Small EB, et al. Influence of water temperature, salinity, and pH on survival and growth of toxigenic *Vibrio cholerae* serovar O1 associated with live copepods in laboratory microcosms. Appl Environ Microbiol. 1983;48:420.
31. Huq A, Colwell RR, Rahman R, et al. Detection of *Vibrio cholerae* O1 in the aquatic environment by fluorescent-monoclonal antibody and culture methods. Appl Environm Microbiol. 1990;56:2370.
32. Colwell RR, Tamplin ML, Brayton PR, et al. Environmental aspects of *Vibrio cholerae* in transmission of cholera. In: Sack RB, Zinnaka Y, eds. Advances in Research on Cholera and Related Diarrheas, v. 7. Tokyo: KTK Scientific; 1990:327.
33. Rice EW, Johnson CJ, Clark RM, et al. Chlorine and survival of rugose *Vibrio cholerae*. Lancet. 1992;340:740.
34. Morris JG, Johnson JA, Rice EW, et al. *Vibrio cholerae* can assume a rugose survival form which resists chlorination, but retains virulence for humans. In: Abstracts of the Twenty-Ninth Joint Conference on Cholera and Related Diarrheal Diseases. Bethesda, Md: National Institutes of Health; 1993:177.
35. Dizon JJ. Cholera carriers. In: Barua D, Burrows W, eds. Cholera. Philadelphia: WB Saunders; 1974:367.
36. Gotuzzo E, Cieza J, Estremadoyro L, et al. Cholera: Lessons from the epidemic in Peru. Med Clin North Am. 1994;8:183.
37. Goma epidemiology group. Public health impact of Rwandan refugee crisis. What happened in Goma, Zaire, in July 1994. Lancet. 1995;345:339–344.
38. Hughes JM, Boyce JM, Levine RJ, et al. Epidemiology of El Tor cholera in rural Bangladesh: Importance of surface water in transmission. Bull World Health Organ. 1982;60:395.
39. Sinclair GS, Mphahlele SM, Duvenhage H, et al. Determination of the mode of transmission of cholera in Lebowa. S Afr Med J. 1982;62:753.
40. Blake PA, Rosenberg ML, Costa JB, et al. Cholera in Portugal, 1974. I. Modes of transmission. Am J Epidemiol. 1977;105:344.
41. Morris JG, West GR, Holck SE, et al. Cholera among refugees in Rangsit, Thailand. J Infect Dis. 1982;145:131.
42. Ries AA, Vugia DJ, Beingolea L, et al. Cholera in Piura, Peru: A modern urban epidemic. J Infect Dis. 1992;166:1429.
43. Tauxe RV, Holmberg SD, Dodin A, et al. Epidemic cholera in Mali: High mortality and multiple routes of transmission in a famine area. Epidemiol Infect. 1988;100:279.
44. Umoh JU, Adesiyun AA, Adekeye JO. Epidemiological features of an outbreak of gastroenteritis/cholera in Katsina, Northern Nigeria. J Hyg. 1983;91:101.
45. Birmingham ME, Lee LA, Ndayimirije N, et al. Epidemic cholera in Burundi: Patterns of transmission in the Great Rift Valley Lake region. Lancet. 1997;349:981.
46. Swerdlow DL, Malenga G, Begkoyian G, et al. Epidemic cholera among refugees in Malawi Africa: Treatment and transmission. Epidemiol Infect. 1997;118:207.
47. Swerdlow DL, Mintz ED, Rodriguez M, et al. Waterborne transmission of epidemic cholera in Trujillo, Peru: Lessons for a continent at risk. Lancet. 1992;340:28.
48. Deb B, Sirkar CBK, Sengupta PG, et al. Studies on interventions to prevent El Tor cholera transmission in urban slums. Bull World Health Organ. 1986;64:127.
49. Deb B, Sirkar CBK, Sengupta PG, et al. Intra-familial transmission of *Vibrio cholerae* biotype El Tor in Calcutta slums. India J Med Res. 1982;76:814.
50. Quick RE, Thompson BL, Zuniga A, et al. Epidemic cholera in rural El Salvador: Risk factors in a region covered by a cholera prevention campaign. Epidemiol Infect. 1995;114:249.
51. Blake PA, Rosenberg ML, Florencia J, et al. Cholera in Portugal, 1974. II. Transmission by bottled mineral water. Am J Epidemiol. 1977;105:344.
52. Deb BC, Sircar BK, Sengupta PG, et al. Studies on intervention to prevent El Tor cholera transmission in urban slums. Bull World Health Organ. 1986;64:127.
53. Kolvin JL, Roberts D. Studies on the growth of *Vibrio cholerae* biotype El Tor and biotype classical in foods. J Hyg. 1982;89:243.
54. Koo D, Aragon A, Moscoso V, et al. Epidemic cholera in Guatemala 1993: Transmission of a newly introduced epidemic strain by street vendors. Epidemiol Infect. 1996;116:121.
55. McIntyre RC, Tira CT, Flood T, et al. Modes of transmission of cholera in a newly infected population on an atoll: Implications for control measures. Lancet. 1979;1:311.
56. Merson MH, Martin WT, Craig JP, et al. Cholera in Guam 1974. Epidemiologic findings and isolation of non-toxigenic strains. Am J Epidemiol. 1977;105:349.
57. Centers for Disease Control: Cholera—New Jersey and Florida. MMWR Morb Mortal Wkly Rep. 1991;40:287.
58. Centers for Disease Control: Importation of cholera from Peru. MMWR Morb Mortal Wkly Rep. 1991;40:287.
59. Centers for Disease Control: Cholera associated with international travel, 1992. MMWR Morb Mortal Wkly Rep. 1992;41:664.
60. Centers for Disease Control: Toxigenic *Vibrio cholerae* O1 infection acquired in Colorado. MMWR Morb Mortal Wkly Rep. 1989;38:19.
61. Gunnlaugsson G, Einarsdottir J, Angulo FJ, et al. Funerals during the 1994 cholera epidemic in Guinea-Bissau, West Africa: The need for disinfection of bodies of persons dying of cholera. Epidemiol Infect. 1998;120:7.
62. St. Louis ME, Porter JD, Helal A, et al. Epidemic cholera in West Africa: The role of food handling and high-risk foods. Am J Epidemiol. 1990;131:719.

63. Mhalu FS, Mtango EDE, Msengi AE. Hospital outbreaks of cholera transmitted through close person-to-person contact. Lancet. 1984;2:82.
64. Cliff JL, Zinkin P, Martelli A. A hospital outbreak of cholera in Maputo, Mozambique. Trans R Soc Trop Med Hyg. 1986;80:473.
65. Mosley WH, Alvero MG, Joseph PR, et al. Studies of cholera El Tor in the Philippines. 4. Transmission of infection among neighborhood and community contacts of cholera patients. Bull World Health Organ. 1965;33:651.
66. Riley LW, Waterman SH, Faruque ASG, et al. Breast-feeding children in the household as a risk factor for cholera in rural Bangladesh: An hypothesis. Trop Geogr Med. 1987;39:9.
67. Glass RI, Becker S, Huq MI, et al. Endemic cholera in rural Bangladesh, 1966–1980. Am J Epidemiol. 1982;116:959.
68. Seas C, Gotuzzo E. Cholera: Overview of epidemiologic, therapeutic, and preventive issues learned from recent epidemics. Int J Infect Dis. 1996;1:37.
69. Clemens J, Albert MJ, Rao M, et al. Impact of infection by *Helicobacter pylori* on the risk and severity of endemic cholera. J Infect Dis. 1995;171:1653.
70. Taylor DN, Blaser MJ. The epidemiology of *Helicobacter pylori* infection. Epidemiol Rev. 1991;13:42.
71. Barua D, Paguio AS: ABO blood group and cholera. Ann Hum Biol. 1977;4:489.
72. Swerdlow DL, Mintz ED, Rodriguez M, et al. Severe life-threatening cholera associated with blood group O in Peru: Implications for the Latin American epidemic. J Infect Dis. 1994;170:468.
73. Rogers RC, Cuffe RG, Cossins YM, et al. The Queensland cholera incident of 1977. 2. The epidemiological investigation. Bull World Health Organ. 1980;58:665.
74. Johnston JM, Martin DL, Perdue J, et al. Cholera on a Gulf Coast oil rig. N Engl J Med. 1983;309:523.
75. Blake PA, Allegra DT, Snyder JD, et al. Cholera—a possible endemic focus in the United States. N Engl J Med. 1980;302:305.
76. Greenough WB III. *Vibrio cholerae* and cholera. In: Mandell GL, Douglas JE, Dolin R, eds. Principles and Practice of Infectious Diseases. 4th ed. New York: Churchill Livingstone; 1995:1934.
77. Chatterjee A, Mahalanabis D, Jalan KN, et al. Plasma specific gravity and haematocrit values as indices of the degree of dehydration in infantile diarrhoea. Indian J Med Res. 1979;70:229.
78. Wang F, Butler T, Rabbani GH, et al. The acidosis of cholera. Contributions of hyperproteinemia, lactic acidemia, and hyperphosphatemia to an increased anion gap. N Engl J Med. 1986;315:1591.
79. Rahaman MM, Majid MA, Monsur KA. Evaluation of two intravenous rehydration solutions in cholera and non-cholera diarrhoea. Bull World Health Organ. 1979;57:977.
80. Bennish ML, Azad AK, Rahman O, et al. Hypoglycemia during diarrhea. Prevalence, pathophysiology and therapy in Asiatic cholera. N Engl J Med. 1990;322:1357.
81. Mahalanabis D, Wallace CK, Kallen RJ, et al. Water and electrolyte losses due to cholera in infants and small children: A recovery balance study. Pediatrics. 1970;45:374.
82. Hirschhorn N, Chowdhury AKMA, Lindenbaum J. Cholera in pregnant women. Lancet. 1969;1:1230.
83. Cieza J, Sovero Y, Estremadoyro L, et al. Electrolyte disturbances in elderly patients with severe diarrhea due to cholera. J Am Soc Nephrol. 1995;6:1463.
84. Guidelines for cholera control. World Health Organization. WHO/CDD/SER/80.4 REV.4, 1992.
85. Mahalanabis D, Molla AM, Sack DA. Clinical management of cholera. In: Barua D, Greenough WB III, eds. Cholera. New York: Plenum; 1992:253.
86. Bennish ML: Cholera: Pathophysiology, clinical features, and treatment. In: Wachsmuth IK, Blake PA, Olsvik O, eds. *Vibrio cholerae* and Cholera. Molecular to Global Perspectives. Washington, DC: ASM Press; 1994:229.
87. Seas C, DuPont HL, Valdez LM, et al. Practical guidelines for the treatment of cholera. Drugs. 1996;51:966–973.
88. Robert M, Flocard F, Adam JC, et al. Emergency intra-osseous rehydration in children during a cholera epidemic. Med Trop. 1995;55:101.
89. Heyman SN, Ginosar Y, Shapiro M, et al. Diarrheal epidemics among Rwandan refugees in 1994. Management and outcome in a field hospital. J Clin Gastroenterol. 1997;25:595.
90. Quick RE, Vargas R, Moreno D, et al. Epidemic cholera in the Amazon: The challenge of preventing death. Am J Trop Med Hyg. 1993;48:597.
91. Dhar U, Bennish ML, Khan WA, et al. Clinical features, antimicrobial susceptibility and toxin production in *Vibrio cholerae* O139 infection: Comparison with *Vibrio cholerae* O1 infection. Trans R Soc Trop Med Hyg. 1996;90:402.
92. Greenough WB III, Gordon RS, Rosenberg IS, et al. Tetracycline in the treatment of cholera. Lancet. 1964;1:355.
93. Alam AN, Alam NH, Ahmed T, et al. Randomized double blind trial of single dose doxycycline for treating cholera in adults. BMJ. 1990;300:1619.
94. O'Grady EM, Lewis J, Pearson NJ. Global surveillance of antibiotic sensitivity of *Vibrio cholerae.* Bull World Health Organ. 1976;54:181.
95. Yamamoto G, Nair GB, Albert MJ, et al. Survey of in-vitro susceptibilities of *Vibrio cholerae* O1 and O139 to antimicrobial agents. Antimicrob Agents Chemother. 1995;39:241.
96. Dubon JM, Palmer CJ, Ager AL, et al. Emergence of multiple drug-resistant *Vibrio cholerae* in San Pedro Sula, Honduras. Lancet. 1997;349:924.
97. Seas C, Gotuzzo E. Recent advances in the treatment and prophylaxis of cholera. Curr Opin Infect Dis. 1996;9:380.
98. Gotuzzo E, Seas C, Echevarría J, et al. Ciprofloxacin for the treatment of cholera: A randomized, double-blind, controlled trial of a single daily dose in Peruvian adults. Clin Infect Dis. 1995;20:1485.
99. Khan WA, Bennish ML, Seas C, et al. Randomized controlled comparison of single-dose ciprofloxacin and doxycycline for cholera caused by *Vibrio cholerae* O1 or O139. Lancet. 1996;348:296.
100. Mukhopadhyay AK, Basu I, Bhattacharya SK, et al. Emergence of fluoroquinolone resistance in strains of *Vibrio cholerae* isolated from hospitalized patients with acute diarrhea in Calcutta, India. Antimicrob Agents Chemother. 1998;42:206.
101. Ghosh S, Sengupta PG, Gupta DN, et al. Chemoprophylaxis studies in cholera: A review of selective works. J Commun Dis. 1992;24:55.
102. Echevarria J, Seas C, Carrillo C, et al. Efficacy and tolerability of ciprofloxacin prophylaxis in adult household contacts of patients with cholera. Clin Infect Dis. 1995;20:1480.
103. Madico G, Checkley W, Gilman RH, et al. Active surveillance for *Vibrio cholerae* O1 and vibriophages in sewage water as a potential tool to predict cholera outbreaks. J Clin Microbiol. 1996;34:2968.
104. Franco AA, Fix AD, Prada A, et al. Cholera in Lima, Peru, correlates with prior isolation of *Vibrio cholerae* from the environment. Am J Epidemiol. 1997;146:1067.
105. Koo D, Traverso H, Libel M, et al. Epidemic cholera in Latin America 1991–1993: Implications of case definitions used for public health surveillance. Bull Pan Am Health Organ. 1996;30:134–143.
106. Colwell RR. Global climate and infectious disease: The cholera paradigm. Science. 1996;274:2025.
107. Finkelstein RA. Why do we not yet have a suitable vaccine against cholera? Adv Exp Med Biol. 1995;37:1633.
108. Clemens JD, Sack DA, Harris JR, et al. Field trial of oral cholera vaccines in Bangladesh: Results from three-year follow-up. Lancet. 1990;335:270.
109. Van Loon FP, Clemens JD, Chakraborty J, et al. Field trial of inactivated oral cholera vaccines in Bangladesh: Results from 5 years of follow-up. Vaccine. 1996;14:162.
110. Clemens J, Rao M, Sack D, et al. Impaired immune response to natural infection as a correlate of vaccine failure in a field trial of killed oral cholera vaccines. Am J Epidemiol. 1995; 142:759.
111. Trach DD, Clemens JD, Ke NT, et al. Field trial of a locally produced killed oral cholera vaccine in Vietnam. Lancet. 1997;349:231.
112. Levine MM, Kaper JB, Herrington D, et al. Safety, immunogenicity, and efficacy of recombinant live oral cholera vaccines, CVD 103 and CVD 103–HgR. Lancet. 1988;2:468.
113. Gotuzzo E, Butron B, Seas C, et al. Safety, immunogenicity, and excretion pattern of single-dose live oral cholera vaccine CVD 103 HgR in Peruvian adults of high and low socio-economic levels. Infect Immun. 1993;61:3994.
114. Migasena S, Pitisuttitham P, Prayurahong B, et al. Preliminary assessment of the safety and immunogenicity of live oral cholera vaccine strain CVD 103–HgR in healthy Thai adults. Infect Immun. 1989;57:3261.
115. Simanjuntak CH, O'Hanley P, Punjabi NH, et al. Safety, immunogenicity, and transmissibility of single-dose live oral cholera vaccine strain CVD 103–HgR in 24- to 59-month-old Indonesian children. J Infect Dis. 1993;168:1169.
116. Lagos R, Avendaño A, Prado V, et al. Attenuated live cholera vaccine strain CVD 103–HgR elicits significantly higher serum vibriocidal antibody titers in persons of blood group O. Infect Immun. 1995;63:707.
117. Coster TS, Kileen KP, Waldor MK, et al. Safety, immunogenicity, and efficacy of live attenuated *Vibrio cholerae* O139 vaccine prototype. Lancet. 1995;345:949.
118. Sack DA, Sack RB, Shimko J, et al. Evaluation of Peru-15, a new live oral vaccine for cholera, in volunteers. J Infect Dis. 1997;176:201.
119. Taylor DN, Tacket CO, Losonsky G, et al. Evaluation of a bivalent (CVD 103–HgR/CVD 111) live oral cholera vaccine in adult volunteers from the United States and Peru. Infect Immun. 1997;65:3852.
120. Snyder JD, Blake PA. Is cholera a problem for US travelers? JAMA. 1982;247:2268.
121. Naficy A, Rao MR, Paquet C, et al. Treatment and vaccination strategies to control cholera in sub-Saharan refugee settings. JAMA. 1998;279:521.

Chapter 203

Other Pathogenic Vibrios

MARGUERITE A. NEILL
CHARLES C. J. CARPENTER

In addition to *Vibrio cholerae* O1 and *Campylobacter fetus* (formerly known as *Vibrio fetus*), three additional major groups of vibrios have been clearly associated with human disease. These include the halophilic *Vibrio parahaemolyticus* and *Vibrio vulnificus,* of which the epidemiologic and clinical features are well delineated; other halophilic vibrios, including *Vibrio alginolyticus, Vibrio fluvi-*

alis, Vibrio hollisae, Vibrio damsela, Vibrio furnissii, Vibrio metschnikovii, Vibrio cincinnatiensis, and *Vibrio carchariae,* which are less common causes of human disease; and the nonhalophilic non-O1 *V. cholerae* and *Vibrio mimicus,* which are worldwide in distribution and have frequently been incriminated in human illness.

In the United States, illnesses caused by the commonly isolated pathogenic vibrios have a marked seasonal peak, with more than 90% of cases occurring between April and October. This presumably reflects seasonal changes in shellfish consumption and recreational water use and the documented increase in numbers of vibrios in both the Chesapeake Bay and the Gulf Coast waters during the warmer months.

VIBRIO PARAHAEMOLYTICUS INFECTIONS

V. parahaemolyticus, a halophilic (salt-requiring) vibrio, has long been recognized as a major cause of acute diarrheal disease in Japan.[1] In the United States, *V. parahaemolyticus* was the most commonly isolated *Vibrio* species during a year-long Gulf Coast surveillance effort,[2] as well as over a 13-year period in Florida.[3] This pathogen was the most common bacterial cause of foodborne disease in Taiwan, accounting for 35% of all outbreaks.[4] *V. parahaemolyticus* is a major pathogen in a number of the less developed countries, in which it has been incriminated in up to 20% of acute diarrheal illnesses. Enteric illness caused by *V. parahaemolyticus* comprises a broad spectrum of clinical manifestations ranging from mild watery diarrhea to a frank dysentery-like syndrome. As suggested by the clinical disease as well as by experimental studies in animals, *V. parahaemolyticus* has the capacities both to produce an enterotoxin and to cause an inflammatory reaction in the small bowel mucosa. The enterotoxin, however, seldom causes major degrees of intestinal fluid loss, and the tissue damage caused by this halophilic vibrio is generally less extensive than that observed in shigellosis.

Epidemiology

Because of lack of specificity of the clinical features of the illness, the epidemiologic history usually provides the most important clue to diagnosis. The halophilic *V. parahaemolyticus* is ubiquitous in coastal waters,[1, 5] although this pathogen typically is not recovered from estuarine waters during winter months in temperate zones. During periods of low temperature or nutrient deprivation, it enters a viable but nonculturable state.[6] Plankton blooms and temperature upshifting in the spring are followed by rapid outgrowth of many *Vibrio* species including *V. parahaemolyticus.* Molluscan shellfish, which are filter feeders, acquire vibrios as part of their normal microflora during the warmer months. Shellfish contamination thus occurs as a consequence of the normal climate-associated changes in vibrio prevalence in coastal waters rather than as a result of sewage contamination of shellfish beds.

Consumption of raw or undercooked shellfish is the most common means of acquiring *V. parahaemolyticus* infection. In the United States, raw oysters are the most common vehicle. Inadequately cooked seafood can harbor small numbers of surviving vibrios, as can food contaminated by seawater on ships. *V. parahaemolyticus* can proliferate rapidly to reach high colony counts in contaminated foods held at ambient temperature for a few hours. This presumably contributes to the high attack rate seen in common-source outbreaks.

Person-to-person transmission has not been documented in the Western Hemisphere[7] or Japan, and secondary cases are rare in areas in which environmental sanitation is less adequate. This observation suggests that the infective dose for normal persons is relatively high.

V. parahaemolyticus has rarely been cultured from asymptomatic people, and no carrier state has been identified. There is no known mammalian reservoir of infection.

Clinical Manifestations

Gastroenteritis is the most common clinical illness associated with *V. parahaemolyticus* infection; wound infections and septicemia may be seen, but much less frequently.[2, 3] Enteric illness commonly begins with the acute onset of explosive watery diarrhea, often accompanied by mild to moderately severe cramping and abdominal pain. In North America and Japan, the onset of illness is generally within 24 hours of ingestion of the contaminated seafood. The diarrhea is accompanied by low-grade fever, mild chills, and headache in less than half of the cases. The fluid loss is rarely severe enough to cause decreased skin turgor or postural hypotension. Deaths due to *V. parahaemolyticus* are rare, usually occurring in very young children, the elderly, or persons with underlying disease.

Laboratory Findings

The diarrheal fluid is characteristically watery, sometimes mucoid, and occasionally bloody (<15%). Fecal leukocytes are often present. *V. parahaemolyticus* is a pleomorphic gram-negative rod that is a facultative anaerobe. It grows poorly on the standard desoxycholate culture plates but is readily identified on the selective thiosulfate citrate bile salts sucrose (TCBS) agar, on which it appears as a distinct opaque green colony. Final identification is made by standard biochemical tests.[1] Enrichment of fecal culture specimens, especially useful for epidemiologic investigation, can be carried out in hypertonic saline containing 3% sodium chloride in 1% peptone broth, pH 7.4,[7] or in taurocholate-tellurite water.[8] Almost all clinical isolates of *V. parahaemolyticus* cause β-hemolysis of human erythrocytes (the Kanagawa reaction), which is due to production of thermostable direct hemolysin (TDH).[9] Environmental isolates of *V. parahaemolyticus* are Kanagawa-negative and lack the *tdh* gene, indicating that TDH is a virulence marker. Of interest, growth in a bile salt–containing environment has been shown to enhance the expression of several virulence traits in *V. parahaemolyticus.*[10]

Differential Diagnosis

Because the halophilic *V. parahaemolyticus* is ubiquitous in coastal waters throughout the temperate and tropical zones of the world, this pathogen must be considered in the differential diagnosis for all acute diarrheal illnesses that follow the ingestion of seafood. There are no clinical features that, in the individual case, reliably distinguish diarrhea caused by *V. parahaemolyticus* from that caused by enterotoxigenic *Escherichia coli* or from milder cases of shigellosis or salmonellosis. Vomiting is characteristically less prominent than in disease caused by staphylococcal enterotoxin, and the cramping abdominal pain is generally less severe than that typical of food poisoning caused by *Clostridium perfringens.*

Treatment

No treatment is required for the majority of patients. The disease is self-limited, and antimicrobial therapy shortens neither the clinical course nor the duration of pathogen excretion. Antiperistaltic agents are of no clear-cut benefit. Occasional patients, usually at the extremes of age, may lose sufficient quantities of fluid to require oral or intravenous electrolyte therapy. In such cases, therapy is guided by the same principles used in the treatment of cholera.

Prevention

Because the illness usually results from the ingestion of raw or inadequately cooked seafood or food that has been rinsed with contaminated seawater, simple means of prevention are available. *V. parahaemolyticus* can remain viable in shrimp or crabmeat for several minutes at temperatures as high as 80°C, and it is especially important in cooking large quantities of such foods to ensure that all portions of the seafood are exposed to cooking temperatures adequate to kill the microorganism. Of only slightly less importance is the necessity of refrigerating cooked seafood if it is not to be ingested immediately after cooking. Shipboard outbreaks can obviously be prevented both by avoiding the use of untreated seawater in galleys and by adequate refrigeration of cooked seafood until it is served.

Prevention of disease due to *V. parahaemolyticus* in Japan remains a problem because of the popularity of uncooked seafood in that nation. Because there is little likelihood of changing the custom of ingesting raw seafood, *V. parahaemolyticus* will probably remain a major cause of acute diarrheal disease in Japan.

Likewise, in delta areas such as Bangladesh in which people have daily contact with contaminated water, there is little likelihood of altering the incidence of *V. parahaemolyticus* infections in the foreseeable future.

Data are not available to determine whether or not protective immunity is conferred by clinical infection. No effective vaccine is currently available.

VIBRIO VULNIFICUS INFECTIONS

Like other potentially pathogenic halophilic vibrios, *V. vulnificus* is part of the normal marine flora and, in the temperate zones, reaches sufficient concentrations to cause clinical illness only in the warmer months of the year. Nearly all oysters harvested in the summer from the Chesapeake Bay contain this pathogen, as do 10% of crabs. This pathogen was the second and third most frequently isolated vibrio in Florida[3] and the Gulf states,[2] respectively. The case-fatality rate of 25% is the highest among infections due to the *Vibrio* species, and *V. vulnificus* is estimated to account for 90% of all seafood-related deaths in the United States. Hippocrates may have provided the first description of a *V. vulnificus* infection in the fifth century BC; he described the rapid progression of a severe foot cellulitis with black blisters in Criton of Thasos, which was fatal in 48 hours.[11]

Clinical Manifestations

V. vulnificus is the most virulent of the noncholera vibrios. It is primarily associated with a severe, distinctive soft tissue infection or septicemia, or both, rather than diarrheal illness.[12, 13] In compromised hosts, especially patients with cirrhosis, *V. vulnificus* has the ability to invade the blood stream without causing gastrointestinal symptoms. The clinical picture is one of abrupt onset of chills and fever, often (in 33% of the cases) followed by hypotension and usually (in 75%) followed by the development of metastatic cutaneous lesions within 36 hours after onset. These begin as erythematous lesions and rapidly evolve to hemorrhagic bullae or vesicles and then to necrotic ulcers. *V. vulnificus* bacteremia has been fatal in over 50% of patients in whom this syndrome has been identified, including all patients in whom hypotension developed.[13] More than 90% of such patients have a history of having consumed raw oysters in the 7 days prior to illness onset; concentrations of *V. vulnificus* of 10^3 colony-forming units (cfu)/g of oyster have produced illness. Although oysters harbor genetically heterogeneous populations of *V. vulnificus,* only one strain type has been recovered from human tissues in invasive infections.[14] Besides cirrhosis, other risk factors for the septicemic form of *V. vulnificus* infection include liver disease, iron overload states such as hemochromatosis, hemolytic anemia, or chronic renal failure, malignancy, human immunodeficiency virus (HIV) infection, and immunosuppressive medications.[3, 15]

In both healthy persons and compromised hosts, *V. vulnificus* causes a rapidly developing, intense cellulitis, necrotizing vasculitis, and ulcer formation and is often associated with bacteremia after contamination of a superficial wound by warm seawater. The cellulitis generally responds to appropriate antimicrobials, but incision and drainage or débridement or both are often necessary.[12] *V. vulnificus* has also rarely been associated with acute, self-limited diarrheal illnesses in persons who were receiving antacid therapy.[16]

The major determinant of virulence in *V. vulnificus* is its polysaccharide capsule, which renders the bacterium resistant to serum killing and which can directly stimulate release of inflammatory cytokines such as tumor necrosis factor-α (TNF-α).[17, 18] Other contributors to pathogenicity include a variety of extracellular proteins and cell wall lipopolysaccharide. Host-derived factors that contribute to the pathogen's virulence include the availability of iron and at least one inflammatory mediator. The predilection of this vibrio to cause disease in patients with iron overload states can be explained by its ability to sequester iron from hemoglobin and 100% saturated (but not 30%, or normally saturated) transferrin. Local bradykinin generation has been shown to enhance *V. vulnificus* bacteremia in mice, and this can be inhibited by a specific antagonist.[19]

Differential Diagnosis

V. vulnificus infection should be suspected in any compromised host (especially with underlying cirrhosis) who develops a septicemic illness associated with necrotizing cutaneous lesions within 1 to 3 days after the ingestion of oysters. Although rare, the clinical syndrome appears to be a distinct one and should suggest this diagnosis.

Similarly, the development of cellulitis in persons occupationally or recreationally exposed to seawater should suggest *V. vulnificus* (especially in the presence of severe, necrotizing cellulitis). Other *Vibrio* species may cause soft tissue infections.

V. vulnificus grows readily on MacConkey agar and the more selective TCBS medium; final identification is made by standard biochemical tests.[8] Because *V. vulnificus* ferments lactose, it can be overlooked in cultures grown on MacConkey agar in a routine diagnostic laboratory unless the technician is advised to look specifically for this microorganism.

Treatment

Soft tissue infections caused by *V. vulnificus* generally respond well to appropriate antibiotics and, when necessary, surgical drainage. Early administration of antibiotics is crucial because the cellulitis can spread very rapidly. Bacteremic *V. vulnificus* infections in compromised hosts respond less well to therapy. *V. vulnificus* is not uniformly susceptible to the aminoglycosides, which are often used in apparently septic patients. A tetracycline is the first-choice agent, with cefotaxime and ciprofloxacin as alternatives. Reported mortality was lowest for bacteremic patients begun on antibiotics within 24 hours of onset of illness but was still unacceptably high at 33%.[13]

Prevention

Although patients with underlying liver disease and other chronic illnesses should be warned of the hazards of eating raw oysters, this has not been accomplished effectively in the United States even when required by law.[20] A capsular polysaccharide conjugate vaccine has been developed, but studies indicate that polyclonal immune globulin, either actively or passively derived, is necessary for cross-protection among capsular types of *V. vulnificus*.[21] At present, thorough cooking of seafood remains the only effective means of prevention.

VIBRIO ALGINOLYTICUS INFECTIONS

V. alginolyticus has been etiologically associated with cellulitis and acute otitis media or externa. These infections have generally occurred after local trauma in otherwise healthy seawater swimmers or fishermen and have responded well to appropriate antibiotics.[22, 23] *V. alginolyticus* occasionally causes life-threatening bacteremia in immunocompromised persons. Isolation is similar to that for *V. vulnificus;* however, *V. alginolyticus* does not ferment lactose.

INFECTIONS DUE TO OTHER HALOPHILIC VIBRIOS

Several other *Vibrio* species have been recognized as causative agents of human disease, and their acquisition is through either ingestion of contaminated seafood or contact of traumatized skin with seawater or brackish water. Surveillance for *Vibrio* infections along the Gulf Coast in the United States has provided a useful perspective on the overall frequency and clinical illnesses associated with these microorganisms.[2, 3] *V. fluvialis* and *V. hollisae* primarily cause diarrhea, whereas *V. damsela* causes wound infections. *Vibrio hollisae* can cause severe cellulitis, mimicking the clinical picture of a *V. vulnificus* infection, but unlike *V. vulnificus,* it grows poorly on the TCBS media typically used for vibrio isolation. *V. furnissii* has been rarely isolated in sporadic cases of diarrhea.[24] *V. metschnikovii* has caused bacteremia,[25] and *V. cincinnatiensis,* bacteremia and meningitis.[26] *Vibrio carchariae* has caused a cellulitis following a shark bite.[27]

INFECTIONS DUE TO NONHALOPHILIC VIBRIOS: NON-O1 *VIBRIO CHOLERAE* AND *VIBRIO MIMICUS*

Vibrios that are biochemically similar to *V. cholerae* but that do not agglutinate in *V. cholerae* O1 or O139 antiserum are taxonomically included in the species *V. cholerae* and are referred to as non-O1 *V. cholerae. V. mimicus* is closely related to non-O1 *V. cholerae* but differs biochemically in being sucrose-negative and Voges-Proskauer–negative. These nonhalophilic vibrios require only trace amounts of sodium chloride for growth in culture medium; this characteristic distinguishes them from the true halophilic vibrios *V. parahaemolyticus, V. vulnificus,* and *V. alginolyticus,* which require larger concentrations of sodium chloride in culture media and have the remarkable ability to grow in 10% sodium chloride.

Clinical Manifestations

Non-O1 *V. cholerae* organisms produce a wide spectrum of diarrheal illness ranging from severe watery diarrhea indistinguishable from cholera to the milder traveler's diarrhea of the type commonly associated with enterotoxigenic *E. coli.* Some clinical isolates of non-O1 *V. cholerae* produce an enterotoxin nearly identical either to cholera toxin of *V. cholerae*[28] or to heat-stable enterotoxin of *E. coli*[29]; other clinical isolates have been nontoxigenic.[30] No clinical features distinguish the severe diarrheal illnesses caused by enterotoxin-producing non-O1 *V. cholerae* from those caused by classic *V. cholerae.*[31] Non-O1 *V. cholerae* strains can rarely cause bacteremia, almost invariably in patients with liver disease.[32]

V. mimicus has caused sporadic outbreaks of acute diarrheal illness in healthy persons who have ingested raw seafood, both along the American Gulf Coast[33] and in Bangladesh.[34] This marine bacterium may rarely cause acute otitis in saltwater swimmers.

Laboratory Findings

With intestinal infections caused by both non-O1 *V. cholerae* and *V. mimicus,* the diarrheal fluid varies from the watery isotonic fluid characteristic of cholera gravis to loose stools in which small numbers of leukocytes and erythrocytes may be seen. The organisms are readily identified on TCBS agar on which *V. cholerae* appears as opaque yellow colonies and *V. mimicus* as green; final speciation is made by biochemical tests and lack of agglutination in O1 antisera.

Treatment

No treatment is required for the large majority of patients with diarrheal disease, and antimicrobials have not been shown to shorten the clinical course.[31] In occasional patients, especially those in the developing world, the intestinal fluid loss is sufficient to require oral or intravenous electrolyte therapy. In this situation, therapy is guided by the same principles used in the treatment of cholera.

Epidemiology

Non-O1 *V. cholerae* organisms are worldwide in distribution and ubiquitous in water sources. Sporadic cases result from the ingestion of very large inocula from contaminated water and, occasionally, food. The burden of clinical disease from these strains has been in the severity of illness in individual patients. They have not been observed to cause sweeping epidemics as have *V. cholerae* O1 and O139, although a few non-O1 strains have caused explosive outbreaks. The molecular basis for this epidemiologic behavioral difference has recently been elucidated.[35] A large (39.5-kb) vibrio pathogenicity island (VPI) has been described in *V. cholerae* and contains gene clusters responsible for cholera toxin acquisition and expression as well as sequences involved in colonization. The group of virulence genes within the VPI is strongly tied to epidemic ability. The VPI is present in epidemic and pandemic *V. cholerae* O1 strains, in Bengal O139, and in two non-O1 *V. cholerae* strains that caused outbreaks. The VPI was absent in sporadic diarrheal and nontoxigenic environmental isolates of non-O1 *V. cholerae.*[35] Horizontal gene transfer of this pathogenicity island may be an initial step for the acquisition of epidemic capability by non-O1 *V. cholerae* strains. Rather than being regarded as a heterogeneous group of lesser consequence, the non-O1 *V. cholerae* organisms are perhaps more properly viewed as strains with the underlying potential to cause epidemic disease if the appropriate complement of virulence genes is acquired.

In every carefully studied major outbreak of cholera, non-O1 vibrios have been isolated from a small proportion of patients (1 to 5%) with illnesses indistinguishable from those caused by *V. cholerae.* Possible explanations for this observation include the loss by certain classic *V. cholerae* strains of the relevant agglutinating surface antigens and the acquisition by non-O1 *V. cholerae* of the gene coding for the production of cholera toxin.

Prevention

Because non-O1 *V. cholerae* organisms exist in a variety of water sources ranging from freshwater rivers to the oceans, purification of water sources and adequate cooking of fish and other seafoods provide the only certain protection against these pathogens.

REFERENCES

1. Zen-Yoji H, Sakai S, Terayama T, et al. Epidemiology, enteropathogenicity, and classification of *Vibrio parahemolyticus.* J Infect Dis. 1965;115:436.
2. Levine WC, Griffin PM, and the Gulf Coast *Vibrio* Working Group. *Vibrio* infections on the Gulf Coast: Results of the first year of regional surveillance. J Infect Dis. 1993;167:479.
3. Hlady WG, Klontz KC. The epidemiology of *Vibrio* infections in Florida, 1981–1993. J Infect Dis. 1996;173:1176.
4. Pan T-M, Wang T-K, Lee C-L, et al. Food-borne disease outbreaks due to bacteria in Taiwan, 1986 to 1995. J Clin Microbiol. 1997;35:1260.
5. Colwell RR. Human pathogens in the aquatic environment. In: Colwell RR, Foster J, eds. Aquatic Microbial Ecology. College Park, Md: University of Maryland Sea Grant Program, 1980:337–344.
6. Jiang X, Chai T-J. Survival of *Vibrio parahaemolyticus* at low temperatures under starvation conditions and subsequent resuscitation of viable, nonculturable cells. Appl Environ Microbiol. 1996;62:1300.
7. Dadisman TA, Nelson R, Molenda JR, et al. *Vibrio parahemolyticus* gastroenteritis in Maryland. I. Clinical and epidemiological aspects. Am J Epidemiol. 1973;96:414.
8. McLaughlin JC. *Vibrio.* In: Murray PR, Baron EJ, Pfaller MA, et al, eds. Manual of Clinical Microbiology. 6th ed. Washington, DC: ASM Press; 1995:465–476.
9. Nishibuchi M, Kaper JB. Thermostable direct hemolysin gene of *Vibrio parahaemolyticus:* A virulence gene acquired by a marine bacterium. Infect Immun. 1995;63:2093.
10. Pace JL, Chai T-J, Rossi HA, et al. Effect of bile on *Vibrio parahaemolyticus.* Appl Environ Microbiol. 1997;63:2372.

11. Baethge BA, West BC. *Vibrio vulnificus:* Did Hippocrates describe a fatal case? Rev Infect Dis. 1988;10:614.
12. Tacket CO, Brenner F, Blake PA. Clinical features and an epidemiologic study of *Vibrio vulnificus* infections. J Infect Dis. 1984;149:558.
13. Klontz KC, Lieb S, Schreiber M, et al. Syndromes of *Vibrio vulnificus* infections: Clinical and epidemiologic features in Florida cases, 1981–1987. Ann Intern Med. 1988;109:318.
14. Jackson JK, Murphree RL, Tamplin ML. Evidence that mortality from *Vibrio vulnificus* infection results from single strains among heterogeneous populations in shellfish. J Clin Microbiol. 1997;35:2098.
15. Johnston JM, Becker SF, McFarland LM. *Vibrio vulnificus:* Man and the sea. JAMA. 1985;253:2850.
16. Johnston JM, Becker SF, McFarland LM. Gastroenteritis in patients with stool isolates of *Vibrio vulnificus.* Am J Med. 1986;80:336.
17. Morris JG. *Vibrio vulnificus*—a new monster of the deep? Ann Intern Med. 1988;109:261.
18. Powell JL, Wright AC, Wasserman SS, et al. Release of tumor necrosis factor alpha in response to *Vibrio vulnificus* capsular polysaccharide in in vivo and in vitro models. Infect Immun. 1997;65:3713.
19. Maruo K, Akaike T, Ono T, et al. Involvement of bradykinin generation in intravascular dissemination of *Vibrio vulnificus* and prevention of invasion by a bradykinin antagonist. Infect Immun. 1998;66:866.
20. Mouzin E, Mascola L, Tormey M, et al. Prevention of *Vibrio vulnificus* infections: Assessment of regulatory educational strategies. JAMA. 1997;278:576.
21. Devi SJN, Hayat U, Powell JL, et al. Preclinical immunoprophylactic and immunotherapeutic efficacy of antisera to capsular polysaccharide–tetanus toxoid conjugate vaccines of *Vibrio vulnificus.* Infect Immun. 1996;64:2220.
22. Schmidt U, Chmel H, Cobbs. *Vibrio alginolyticus* infections in humans. J Clin Microbiol. 1979;10:666.
23. Opal SM, Saxon JR. Intracranial infection by *Vibrio alginolyticus* following injury in salt water. J Clin Microbiol. 1986;23:373.
24. Brenner DJ, Hickman-Brenner FW, Lee JV, et al. *Vibrio furnissii* (formerly aerogenic biogroup of *Vibrio fluvialis*), a new species isolated from human feces and the environment. J Clin Microbiol. 1983;18:816.
25. Jean-Jacques W, Rajashekaraiah KR, Farmer JJ 3rd. *Vibrio metschnikovii* bacteremia in a patient with cholecystitis. J Clin Microbiol. 1981;14:711.
26. Bode RB, Brayton PR, Colwell RR, et al. A new *Vibrio* species, *Vibrio cincinnatiensis,* causing meningitis: Successful treatment in an adult. Ann Intern Med. 1986;104:55.
27. Pavia AT, Bryan JA, Maher KL, et al. *Vibrio carchariae* infection after a shark bite. Ann Intern Med. 1989;111:85.
28. Yamamoto K, Takeda Y, Miwatani T, et al. Evidence that a non-O1 *Vibrio cholerae* produces enterotoxin that is similar but not identical to cholera enterotoxin. Infect Immun. 1983;41:896.
29. Arita M, Takeda T, Honda T, et al. Purification and characterization of *Vibrio cholerae* non-O1 heat-stable enterotoxin. Infect Immun. 1986;52:45.
30. Morris JG Jr, Picardi JL, Lieb S, et al. Isolation of nontoxigenic *Vibrio cholerae* O group 1 from a patient with severe gastrointestinal disease. J Clin Microbiol. 1984;19:296.
31. Morris JG, Wilson R, Davis BR, et al. Non-O group 1 *Vibrio cholerae* gastroenteritis in the United States: Clinical, epidemiologic and laboratory characteristics of sporadic cases. Ann Intern Med. 1982;94:656.
32. Safrin S, Morris JG, Adams M, et al. Non-O1 *Vibrio cholerae* bacteremia. Case report and review. Rev Infect Dis. 1988;10:1012.
33. Shandera WX, Johnston JJ, David BR, et al. Disease from infection with *Vibrio mimicus:* A newly recognized *Vibrio* species. Ann Intern Med. 1983;99:169.
34. Spira WM, Fedorka-Cray PJ: Purification of enterotoxins from *Vibrio mimicus* that appear to be identical to cholera toxin. Infect Immun. 1984;45:679.
35. Karaolis DK, Johnson JA, Bailey CC, et al. A *Vibrio cholerae* pathogenicity island associated with epidemic and pandemic strains. Proc Natl Acad Sci U S A. 1998;95:3134.

Chapter 204

Campylobacter jejuni and Related Species

MARTIN J. BLASER

Campylobacteriosis refers to the group of infections caused by gram-negative bacteria of the genus *Campylobacter.* Among the most common bacterial infections of humans in all parts of the world, campylobacters cause both diarrheal and systemic illnesses. Infection of domesticated animals with campylobacters also is widespread. *Campylobacter* is derived from the Greek *campylos,* meaning "curved," and *baktron,* meaning "rod," and is so named to distinguish this genus from otherwise identically appearing vibrios. Following the recognition of *Campylobacter jejuni* as a major human pathogen, numerous related *Campylobacter, Arcobacter,* and *Helicobacter* species have been identified.

ETIOLOGY

Campylobacter organisms are motile, non–spore-forming, comma-shaped, gram-negative rods.[1] Originally isolated from aborted sheep fetuses in 1909, these and similar organisms were considered subspecies of *Vibrio fetus.* However, because these organisms did not ferment carbohydrates and differed in their guanine plus cytosine (G plus C) DNA content from true members of the genus *Vibrio,* a new genus, *Campylobacter,* was created. Fourteen species have been recognized within the genus; however, in recent years, taxonomic studies have indicated that splitting the genus is more appropriate.[2] The genus *Arcobacter* has been created, which now includes *Arcobacter butzleri* and *Arcobacter skirrowi.*[3] *Helicobacter cinaedi* and *Helicobacter fennelliae* had been named *Campylobacter cinaedi* and *Campylobacter fennelliae* when first discovered.[4] Although transfer to the genus *Helicobacter* is more appropriate on taxonomic grounds, because these two species cause intestinal rather than gastric illnesses, they are discussed in this chapter. *Helicobacter pylori,* previously named *Campylobacter pylori,* is discussed in Chapter 205. It is clear that new members of *Campylobacter* and related genera are being identified with regularity,[5–7] and that many of these will be found to be human pathogens.

Table 204–1 lists the *Campylobacter* and related species most commonly associated with human disease and indicates the differentiating characteristics. Certain species such as *Campylobacter nitrofigilis, Arcobacter cryaerophila,* and *Campylobacter concisus* have not yet been associated with human illness. In contrast, the "nitrate-negative" campylobacters are associated with diarrheal illnesses, but the appropriate nomenclature for the organisms has not been determined. Two types of illnesses are associated with *Campylobacter* spp.: enteric and extraintestinal. For each of these illnesses, one *Campylobacter* species predominates, while other species are less commonly present. The prototype for enteric infection is *C. jejuni;* for extraintestinal infection it is *Campylobacter fetus* (Table 204–2). Because the organisms causing enteric and extraintestinal illnesses are generally the same, they are considered together in the following discussion.

Campylobacters and related organisms grow best in an atmosphere containing 5 to 10% oxygen and are thus considered microaerophilic.[1, 2] Although most of these organisms will not grow under aerobic or anaerobic conditions, *C. jejuni* can grow in candle jars, which permits isolation when the optimal atmosphere cannot be achieved. All campylobacters grow at 37°C; however, *C. jejuni* grows best at 42°C. Because *C. jejuni* is the most common enteric pathogen of humans, many laboratories have used incubation at 42°C for optimal isolation; however, use of this temperature will not permit detection of infections by many of the related species.

Campylobacters multiply more slowly than do the usual bacteria of the enteric flora and therefore cannot be isolated from fecal specimens unless selective techniques are used. The most common isolation methods use blood-based, antibiotic-containing media. Three such media—Skirrow's, Butzler's, and Campy-BAP—or variations of these have been in wide use.[2] The last two media contain cephalothin, which inhibits *C. fetus* and several other *Campylobacter* subspecies, but are best suited for isolating *C. jejuni.* Several enrichment broths have been developed, but because ill humans usually excrete 10^6 to 10^9 *C. jejuni* colony-forming units (cfu)/g of stool, enrichment usually is not necessary. Blood-free media also can be used.[8] Owing to their small size (0.3 to 0.6 μm in diameter) and motility, campylobacters and related organisms pass through 0.45- or 0.65-μm filters that retard the usual enteric flora. Filtration methods

TABLE 204–1 Differential Characteristics of *Campylobacter* and Related Species Most Commonly Associated with Pathogenicity in Humans

Species	Growth			Nitrate Reduction	H_2S Production		Hippurate Hydrolysis	Susceptibility to 30-μg Disk		C-19 Fatty Acid Reduction
	25°C	*37°C*	*42°C*		*On TSI*	*On Lead Acetate Paper*		*Cephalothin*	*Nalidixic Acid*	
Campylobacter jejuni	−	+	+	+	−	+	+*	R	S	+
Campylobacter coli	−	+	+	+	v	+	−	R	S	+
Campylobacter lari	−	+	+	+	−	+	−	R	R	−
Campylobacter fetus subsp. *fetus*	+	+	v	+	−	v	−	S	R	−
Campylobacter hyointestinalis	v	+	v	+	+	+	−	S	R	+
Helicobacter cinaedi	−	+	−	+	−	+	−	S	S	−
Campylobacter upsaliensis†	−	+	+‡	+	−	+	−	S	S	−
Helicobacter fennelliae	−	+	−	−	−	+	−	S	S	−

*About 5 to 10% of *C. jejuni* strains are hippurate-negative.
†Catalase-negative or weak.
‡Occasional isolates fail to grow at 42°C.
Abbreviations and symbols: −, Does not have the characteristic; +, has the characteristic; R, resistant; S, susceptible; TSI, triple sugar iron agar slant; v, variable (some strains show the characteristic).

permit isolation without use of antibiotic-containing media. It is now clear that use of filtration techniques and nonselective rich media such as chocolate agar, with incubation of plates at 37°C, improves stool culture yields of both *C. jejuni* and the "atypical" enteric campylobacters.[9] The development of filtration techniques represents a significant advance over the use of selective media, and such techniques are now recommended for primary isolation of campylobacters from fecal specimens or swabs.

Visible colonies usually appear on the plating media within 24 to 48 hours. Occasionally, growth takes place after 72 to 96 hours of incubation, especially for the "atypical" species. The campylobacters can be distinguished from other microorganisms on the basis of several standard criteria and can be distinguished from one another on the basis of biochemical testing.[2, 10] Organisms from young cultures have a typical vibrioid appearance (Fig. 204–1), but after 48 hours of incubation, organisms appear coccoid. Ability to hydrolyze hippurate distinguishes *C. jejuni* from most other members of the genus, but hippurate-negative *C. jejuni* isolates also occur. State-of-the-art identification to the species level should include polymerase chain reaction (PCR) studies of 16S recombinant RNA or other targets for comparison with known species.[11, 12] Isolation of campylobacters from sites without a normal flora, such as the blood stream, is not difficult, although when this organism is the suspected pathogen, incubation of cultures should be extended to 2 weeks. With radiometric detection systems, turbidity of the medium may not be present, and the increase in released radiolabel may be less than usually specified thresholds, reflecting suboptimal conditions for certain of these organisms.[13] PCR-based techniques have been developed for culture confirmation and for typing of strains.[14–16]

TABLE 204–2 *Campylobacter, Helicobacter,* and *Arcobacter* Species Associated with Different Clinical Manifestations of Infection

Disease Syndrome	
Enteric	*Extraintestinal*
Major pathogen	
Campylobacter jejuni	*Campylobacter fetus*
Minor pathogens	
Campylobacter coli	*Campylobacter jejuni*
Campylobacter lari	*Campylobacter coli*
Campylobacter fetus	*Campylobacter lari*
Helicobacter fennelliae	*Helicobacter fennelliae*
Helicobacter cinaedi	*Helicobacter cinaedi*
Campylobacter upsaliensis	*Campylobacter sputorum*
Arcobacter butzleri	*Campylobacter hyointestinalis*
Arcobacter skirrowi	*Helicobacter rappini*
Arcobacter cryaerophila	

As with other bacteria whose ecologic niche is the gastrointestinal tract of mammals, the serotypic diversity of *C. jejuni* is enormous. More than 90 different serotypes based on somatic (O) antigens and 50 different serotypes based on heat-labile (capsular and flagellar) antigens have been identified[2]; phase variation of flagellar antigens occurs. No group somatic or flagellar antigen has been identified; however, several superficial proteins appear to have broad serotypic specificity, factors that may aid in the development of a broadly specific vaccine.

C. jejuni cannot long withstand drying or freezing temperatures, which are characteristics that limit its transmission.[17] However, *C. jejuni* survives in milk or other foods or in water kept at 4°C for several weeks. Pasteurization effectively destroys the organism, as does chlorine at concentrations in standard use for water disinfection.

EPIDEMIOLOGY

Campylobacteriosis is a worldwide zoonosis. Campylobacters are commonly found as commensals of the gastrointestinal tract in wild or domesticated cattle, sheep, swine, goats, dogs, cats, rodents, and all varieties of fowl.[1, 17] *C. jejuni* has a very varied reservoir, but *Campylobacter coli* and *Campylobacter hyointestinalis* are most commonly isolated from swine, and *Campylobacter upsaliensis* from dogs. *C. fetus* subsp. *fetus* has been isolated from sheep, cattle, poultry, reptiles, and swine.[1] Primary acquisition of *Campylobacter* species by animals often occurs early in life and may lead to morbidity or mortality, but in most colonized animals, a lifelong carrier state develops. The vast reservoir in animals is probably the ultimate source for most enteric *Campylobacter* infections in humans. Meats originating from infected animals frequently become contaminated with intestinal contents during the slaughtering process.[13] In particular, commercially raised poultry is nearly always colonized with *C. jejuni,* slaughterhouse procedures amplify contamination, and chicken and turkey in supermarkets, ready for consumers to take home, frequently is contaminated.[17, 18] Excreta from infected animals may contaminate soil or water. Most infections in humans probably result from consumption of contaminated food and water. Investigations of more than 50 outbreaks indicate that unpasteurized (raw) milk is such a vehicle.[17] Similarly, untreated surface water has been responsible for both endemic and epidemic campylobacteriosis. Backpackers in Wyoming who drank untreated water and developed acute diarrheal illnesses had *Campylobacter* infections three times as commonly as *Giardia* infections.[19] Several large outbreaks have been traced to defects in municipal water systems.[20] Undercooked meats,

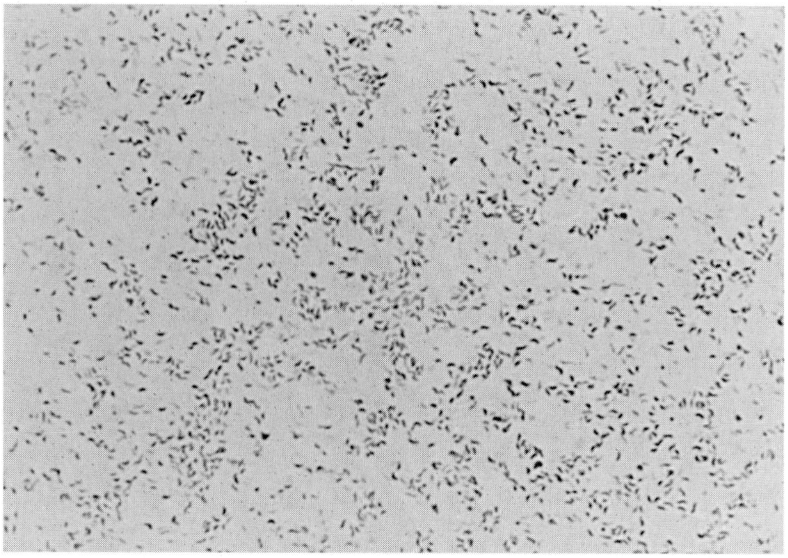

FIGURE 204–1. Fine curved, S-shaped, or spiral, lightly staining gram-negative appearance of *Campylobacter jejuni* in pure culture (×1000).

especially poultry, have been associated with infection.[21] Other vehicles include raw clams, raw or undercooked beef, and unpasteurized cheeses and goat's milk. Nevertheless, consumption of undercooked poultry is estimated to be responsible for 50 to 70% of sporadic *Campylobacter* infections in developed countries. Increases in the isolation of *Campylobacter* spp. reflect both improved recognition and increased consumption of poultry in recent years.

Direct contact with infected animals may result in transmission. Household pets, especially young dogs and cats with diarrhea, have been implicated as vectors for campylobacteriosis.[22] Because healthy dogs, cats, rodents, and birds may excrete campylobacters and related organisms, it is not surprising that human infections associated with these animals also have been reported. Persons with occupational exposure to cattle, sheep, and other farm animals are at increased risk for infection, and laboratory-acquired infections have been reported.

As with other enteric pathogens, fecal-oral person-to-person transmission of *C. jejuni* has been reported. Persons in contact with the excreta of infected persons who are not feces-continent (such as infants) are at risk of infection. Infected school-age children rarely may transmit *Campylobacter* infection. Transmission from infected food handlers who are asymptomatic is at best uncommon. Perinatal transmission from a mother who may not have been symptomatic may be due to exposure in utero, during passage through the birth canal, or during the first days of life.[23] Infection has been associated with blood transfusion from an infected patient.[24] Because of a variety of sexual practices, homosexual men appear to be at increased risk for infection due to *H. cinaedi, H. fennelliae,* and other "atypical" campylobacters.[25] Human immunodeficiency virus (HIV)–infected patients are at substantially increased risk of infection.[26] The standardization of serotyping methods[27] and the development of molecular methods for identification and typing of *C. jejuni* and related organisms[11, 12, 14–16] should improve our understanding of transmission.

C. jejuni infections occur year-round in the United States and other developed countries but with a sharp peak in summer and early fall. *C. fetus* infections show the same seasonal variation, but the peak is less marked. In tropical countries, the seasonal variation of *C. jejuni* infection appears to be influenced by rainfall. Because of incomplete surveillance, the actual incidence of *Campylobacter* infections in the United States is not known. However, laboratory-based studies in the United States and other developed countries indicate that *C. jejuni* is more commonly isolated from fecal specimens obtained from diarrheal patients than either *Salmonella* or *Shigella*.[28] In England, the number of reported *Campylobacter* infections now exceeds those of *Salmonella* and *Shigella* infections combined, and the incidence continues to increase. Based on estimates of the number of *Salmonella* infections, there are probably more than 2 million *Campylobacter* infections annually in the United States. Population-based studies show peak incidence in children under 1 year of age and in persons 15 to 29 years of age[29]; however, cases have been reported in patients of all ages. Males and females appear to be equally affected. The prevalence of infection in healthy people is very low (less than 1%).

The epidemiology of infection in developing countries is markedly different. *C. jejuni* is often isolated from healthy persons and the infection is especially common during the first 5 years of life.[30, 31] During the first 2 years of life, most children have numerous *Campylobacter* infections, but those occurring early in life frequently are symptomatic, whereas later infections are mostly asymptomatic.[31] The source of these frequent infections has not been defined, but preliminary evidence suggests that human-to-human transmission may be more common than in developed countries. The substantial age-related difference in the infection-to-illness ratios in developed and developing countries appears primarily to be due to differences in age- or exposure-related immunity of the populations rather than to differences in the isolates.[32, 33] *C. jejuni* and other campylobacters are important causes for the acute diarrheal illnesses suffered by travelers.[34]

PATHOGENESIS AND PATHOLOGIC CHARACTERISTICS

Not all *Campylobacter* infections produce illness. Although all factors responsible for this phenomenon are not known, two of the most important appear to be the dose of organisms reaching the small intestine and the specific immunity of the host to the pathogen ingested. Among exposed persons who become ill, the incubation period varies from 1 to 7 days, a characteristic that is probably inversely related to the dose ingested. Most infections occur 2 to 4 days after exposure. In one study, volunteers became ill after ingesting as few as 500 organisms, but with a dose of less than 10^4 organisms, illness was infrequent.[40] *C. jejuni,* like *Salmonella typhimurium,* is susceptible to hydrochloric acid.[35] Taken together, these data suggest that the infectious dose for *C. jejuni* is similar to that for *Salmonella*. Vehicles such as milk, fatty foods, and water that favor passage through the gastric acid barrier may permit some infections to occur at relatively low doses. *C. jejuni* multiplies in human bile,[35] a characteristic that aids colonization of the bile-rich upper small intestine early in infection. The sites of tissue injury include the jejunum, ileum, and colon, with similar pathologic features in each. Inspection of affected tissues may reveal a diffuse, bloody, edematous, and exudative enteritis,[36] but pathologic examinations are generally performed on specimens from patients with the most severe cases. Microscopic examination of rectal biopsy specimens has shown a nonspecific colitis with an inflammatory infiltrate of neutrophils, mononuclear cells, and eosinophils in the lamina propria; degeneration, atrophy, loss of mucus, and crypt abscesses in the epithelial glands; and ulceration of the mucosal epithelium.[37, 38] Rectal biopsy samples with these nonspecific features have been interpreted as showing acute ulcerative colitis or Crohn's disease. In other cases, the appearance of the rectal biopsy sample has been similar to that of specimens obtained in *Salmonella* or *Shigella* infections. In a series of 124 patients with *C. jejuni* infection, 18 of the most severely ill patients underwent sigmoidoscopic examination or rectal biopsy; 17 of these procedures showed colonic involvement.[39] Some patients have terminal ileitis as well as colitis. Host factors also are clearly important; in volunteers, a single strain produced a wide spectrum of clinical manifestations.[40]

The presence of bacteremia in some patients and the finding of cellular infiltration in biopsy specimens from patients with *Campylobacter* colitis suggest that tissue invasion may be one pathogenetic mechanism. No animal model closely analogous to human infection has been reported except in primates. Both experimental challenges in monkeys[41] and in vitro studies[42–44] confirm the invasiveness of *C. jejuni. Campylobacter* outer membranes contain lipopolysaccharides (LPSs) with typical endotoxic activity.[45] The structure of the LPS O antigen is highly variable.[27] Many *C. jejuni* O antigens possess sialic acid–containing structures.[46] Their close resemblance to those seen in human gangliosides and their presence in strains isolated from patients who developed the Guillain-Barré syndrome (GBS) suggest a role in the pathogenesis of this disorder.[46]

Extracellular toxins with cytopathic activities have been found, and classic enterotoxins have also been demonstrated, although generally at low concentrations.[47–49] Two strains lacking detectable enterotoxin production and with low-level in vitro cytotoxin production were found to be fully virulent in volunteers.[40] Infected persons do not develop neutralizing antibodies to these toxins, casting further doubt on their in vivo significance. A protein that distends epithelial cells and is cytolethal is expressed by many *C. jejuni* strains, but its role in pathogenesis has not been fully defined.[50] *C. jejuni* may adhere to epithelial cells,[51] which would favor gut colonization. A superficial antigen (PEB1) that appears to be the major adhesin[52] is conserved among *C. jejuni* strains, is a target of the immune response,[53] and may represent a vaccine candidate.[54, 55] Motility is required for infection, and in vivo passage favors flagellated cells.[56]

Patients in developed countries with *Campylobacter* infection excrete the organism in feces for an average of 2 to 3 weeks. By 3 months after infection, convalescent excretion is rare. In developing countries, the period of convalescent excretion is even briefer, probably reflecting high levels of immunity in the population.[32]

Bacteremia sometimes can be detected in patients with *Campylobacter* infections, whether or not they show signs of systemic illness. Most bacteremias reported to the Centers for Disease Control and Prevention (CDC) have been due to *C. fetus* subsp. *fetus,* whereas *C. jejuni* is by far the more common pathogen. One explanation for the apparently greater tendency of *C. fetus* to cause bacteremia is that it is usually resistant, whereas *C. jejuni* is susceptible, to the bactericidal activity present in normal human serum.[57] After oral ingestion and intestinal colonization with or without acute diarrheal disease, *C. fetus* bacteremia may occur.[58]

C. fetus is covered with a surface (S)-layer protein that functions as a capsule.[59, 60] Virtually all human isolates of *C. fetus* possess an S-layer protein that completely disrupts C3b binding to these organisms.[61] Lack of C3b binding explains both serum- and phagocytosis-resistance. In a mouse model, after oral inoculation, strains carrying the S-layer protein develop bacteremia, whereas strains without the S-layer protein do not.[62] *C. fetus* also has the ability to change the major S-layer protein expressed. This results in antigenic variation[63] and is facilitated by recombination among several highly homologous genes encoding full-length proteins.[64] The S-layer protein of *C. fetus* appears to be a major virulence factor explaining its extraintestinal spread (Fig. 204–2).

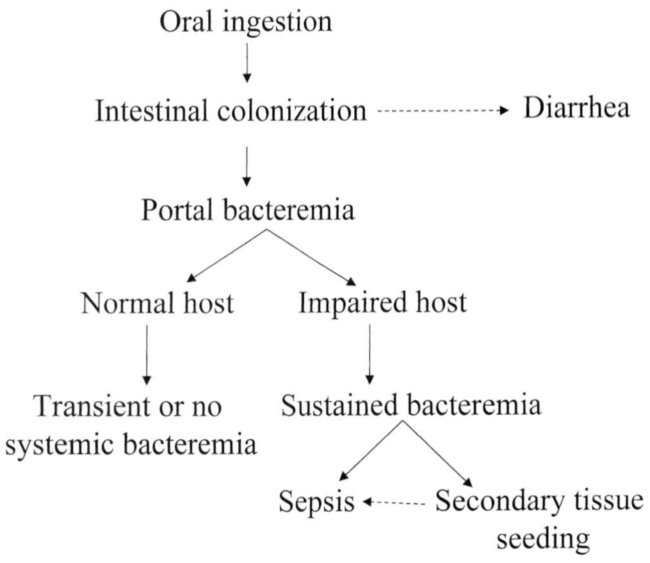

FIGURE 204–2. Pathogenesis of *Campylobacter fetus* infections. (From Blaser MJ. *Campylobacter fetus:* Emerging infection and model system for bacterial pathogenesis at mucosal surfaces. Clin Infect Dis. 1998;27:256–258.)

IMMUNITY

As reported in published studies, volunteers rechallenged with the homologous *C. jejuni* organism developed infection but were protected from illness.[40, 65] In developing countries, where *C. jejuni* infection is hyperendemic, the decreasing case-to-infection ratio with age suggests acquisition of immunity. Patients infected with campylobacters develop specific IgG, IgM, and IgA antibodies in serum[40, 48, 65] and IgA antibodies in intestinal secretions.[65]

In developing countries, specific serum IgA levels rise progressively with age, reflecting recurring exposure to *C. jejuni.* In volunteers, increasing levels of specific serum IgA have been correlated with increasing specific intestinal levels as well.[40, 65] Supporting the notion that humoral immunity is protective against *C. jejuni* infections have been the numerous reports of severe and recurrent *C. jejuni* infection in patients with congenital or acquired hypogammaglobulinemia.[66, 67] In HIV-infected patients as well, failure of *C. jejuni* infection to respond to antimicrobial therapy has been correlated with failure to produce a humoral response to infection.[68] Nevertheless, the markedly increased incidence of *C. jejuni* infection in patients with acquired immunodeficiency syndrome (AIDS)[26] suggests that cell-mediated immunity also is important in preventing and terminating infection.

Despite these exceptions, most patients who become infected with *C. jejuni* were previously healthy and recover rapidly from infection. In contrast, patients with *C. fetus* infections much more frequently have evidence of impaired immunity, including conditions such as chronic alcoholism, liver disease, old age, diabetes mellitus, and malignancies.[69, 70] *C. fetus* infections may produce diarrheal illnesses in healthy people or opportunistic infections in debilitated persons.[58]

CLINICAL MANIFESTATIONS

Campylobacter jejuni Infections

The clinical manifestations of infections due to all of the *Campylobacter* spp. that cause enteric illnesses appear identical; *C. jejuni* infection may be regarded as the prototype.[71] Acute enteritis is the most common presentation of *C. jejuni* infection. Symptoms may last from 1 day to 1 week or longer. Often there is a prodrome with fever, headache, myalgia, and malaise 12 to 24 hours before the onset of intestinal symptoms.[72] In some patients, the constitutional symptoms may coincide with the intestinal phase, or, less often, may follow it. The most common symptoms are diarrhea, malaise, fever, and abdominal pain.[71–74] Diarrhea may range in severity from loose stools to massive watery or grossly bloody stools. In any patient, the entire spectrum of diarrhea may be seen. For most patients, there are 10 or more bowel movements on the worst day of the illness. Abdominal pain is usually cramping in nature and is relieved by defecation; it may be the predominant manifestation of illness. *Campylobacter* enteritis is frequently self-limiting, with a gradual resolution of symptoms over several days; however, illness lasting longer than 1 week occurs in about 10 to 20% of patients seeking medical attention, and relapse may be seen in another 5 to 10% of patients who do not receive treatment.[71–73]

Infection also may be manifested as an acute colitis, with symptoms of fever, abdominal cramps, and bloody diarrhea persisting for 1 week or longer.[37, 74] Fever may be low grade or consist of daily peaks above 40°C. Initially, stools may be watery, but as the illness progresses, they may become frankly bloody; tenesmus is a common symptom. In the severest forms, patients appear very ill, and toxic megacolon has been reported.[75] Because of the propensity of *Campylobacter* infection to affect young adults and the characteristic clinical presentation, it may be readily confused with ulcerative colitis or Crohn's disease.[37, 72] The pathologic findings on rectal biopsy are nonspecific, and the clinical features and radiographic findings also are nondiagnostic. Therefore, the clinician should have a high index of suspicion for *Campylobacter* infection in a patient who presents with this symptom complex. Because of the often fastidious nature of these organisms,[76, 77] a single negative culture does not rule out infection, especially if optimal filtration methods are not used for primary isolation of a pathogen.

Occasionally, acute abdominal pain may be the major or only symptom of infection.[71, 78] Although any quadrant of the abdomen may be affected, patients most often complain of pain in the right lower quadrant. As with *Yersinia enterocolitica* and *Salmonella enteritidis*, *C. jejuni* may cause pseudoappendicitis.[72] In most cases, the removed appendix has shown minimal or no inflammation. Enlarged mesenteric nodes (mesenteric adenitis) and terminal ileitis[34] also may be responsible for symptoms. Diagnosis is often made during the postoperative period, when diarrhea ensues. *Campylobacter* infection occasionally may present solely as a gastrointestinal hemorrhage.[79] Among neonates, *C. jejuni* infection may be manifested as one or more grossly bloody stools and no other symptoms, with findings suggesting intussusception,[80] or with extraintestinal foci.[81] Fever also may be the sole manifestation of *C. jejuni* infection. Temperature elevation may be so severe and persistent that typhoid fever is the initial diagnosis until *C. jejuni* is isolated from stools. Febrile convulsions in young children before the onset of the enteric phase of illness also may occur.[82]

Bacteremia has been noted in less than 1% of patients with *C. jejuni* infection. In part, this low frequency reflects the fact that physicians rarely perceive diarrheal illness as an indication for blood culture, even when fever is present. Nevertheless, bacteremia appears to be more common in infections in persons at the extremes of age.[29, 83] Meningitis and endocarditis are rare manifestations of *C. jejuni* infection. In general, three patterns of extraintestinal *C. jejuni* infection have been noted.[84] First, there may be a transient bacteremia in a normal host with acute *Campylobacter* enteritis. The bacteremia may be discovered several days after blood cultures are obtained, by which time the patient usually has completely recovered. The course is benign, and no specific treatment based on the positive blood culture result is usually indicated. Second, there may be a sustained bacteremia or deep focus of infection in a previously normal host; usually the patient has an acute enteritis as well. The *C. jejuni* isolates are generally relatively or absolutely serum-resistant.[84] Bacteremia usually has its origin in the intestinal tract inflammation and responds to antimicrobial therapy. Third, sustained bacteremia or deep infection may occur in a compromised host; many such patients do not have an acute enteritis. *C. jejuni* isolates usually are serum-sensitive.[84] Antimicrobial therapy, which may need to be prolonged, is required for elimination or suppression of this infection.

C. jejuni may cause septic abortion,[85] but sustained bacteremia in a pregnant patient does not necessarily imply fetal infection or a bad outcome.[84] There have been infrequent reports of *C. jejuni* infections manifesting as acute cholecystitis,[86] pancreatitis,[87, 88] and cystitis.[89, 90] These manifestations probably reflect local extension rather than hematogenous (metastatic) spread of infection. Persons with immunoglobulin deficiencies often develop prolonged, severe, and recurrent *C. jejuni* infections,[66, 67] often with bacteremia and other extraintestinal manifestations such as erysipelas-like skin lesions or osteomyelitis.[91] A reactive arthritis may occur up to several weeks after infection in persons with the HLA-B27 histocompatibility antigens,[92] and prolonged rheumatic symptoms also have been reported. Hepatitis,[93] interstitial nephritis, the hemolytic-uremic syndrome, and IgA nephropathy[94] are other reported complications.

GBS is an uncommon consequence of *C. jejuni* infection (estimated at 1 case per 2000 infections) that usually occurs 2 to 3 weeks after the diarrheal illness.[95, 96] From 20 to 50% of Guillain-Barré cases follow *C. jejuni* infections, reflecting in part the high incidence of these infections.[95–99] A particular *C. jejuni* clone marked by LPS (O) type 19 is overrepresented among persons who develop GBS.[99, 101] O-type 41 also has been implicated, and other sporadic cases may be due to specific *C. jejuni* strains with sialylation of their LPS molecules.[46]

Campylobacter fetus Infections

In contrast to *C. jejuni*, *C. fetus* subsp. *fetus* less frequently causes diarrheal illness. As summarized in Table 204–3, the clinical, laboratory, and epidemiologic characteristics of *C. jejuni* infections differ significantly from those of *C. fetus* subsp. *fetus*, which often produce systemic manifestations. *C. fetus* infections may cause intermittent diarrhea or nonspecific abdominal pain without localizing signs. The diarrheal illness may manifest exactly like *C. jejuni* infection and is more common than was suspected several years ago. Clinical manifestations are similar and sequelae uncommon. Nearly all af-

TABLE 204–3 Biologic and Clinical Characteristics of *Campylobacter jejuni* and *Campylobacter fetus* subsp. *fetus*

Feature	*Campylobacter jejuni*	*Campylobacter fetus* subsp. *fetus*
Epidemiologic characteristics		
Major reservoir	Avian species, food animals	Cattle and sheep
Affected hosts	Normal hosts; all ages affected; often in clusters of cases	Opportunistic agent in debilitated hosts; clustering rare; healthy hosts may be affected
Laboratory characteristics		
Range of growth temperatures	32–42°C	25–37°C*
Usual source of isolation	Feces	Blood stream
Clinical characteristics		
As a cause for diarrheal illness	Common	Uncommon
Clinical manifestations	Acute gastroenteritis, colitis	Systemic illness with bacteremia, meningitis, vascular infections, abscesses; gastroenteritis
Outcome of infection	Usually self-limited	May be fatal in debilitated hosts

*Occasionally grows at 42°C.

fected patients survive the infections when appropriate antibiotic treatment is given and usually do well without antibiotic treatment. *C. fetus* also may cause a prolonged relapsing illness characterized by fever, chills, and myalgias in which a source of infection cannot be demonstrated.[69, 70, 102] Occasionally, secondary seeding to an organ will occur, leading to a more complicated infection[102–105] and sometimes to a fulminant fatal course.

C. fetus infections appear to have a predilection for vascular sites; vascular necrosis occurs in patients with endocarditis and pericarditis due to this organism.[106, 107] Mycotic aneurysms of the abdominal aorta also occur. Thrombophlebitis may be associated with *C. fetus* bacteremia,[108] but whether it is the primary event or a secondary manifestation of the infection is uncertain. Those patients with a bacteremic illness without localization should be carefully evaluated for the presence of septic thrombophlebitis, because when this condition is treated with appropriate antibiotics, the response is good. Infections during pregnancy primarily have been manifested as upper respiratory symptoms, pneumonitis, fever, and bacteremia. However, four of five *C. fetus*–infected second-trimester patients delivered dead infants despite antibiotic therapy. One patient received antibiotic therapy and delivered a normal term infant. All the mothers survived their infection.[109]

Central nervous system (CNS) infections with *C. fetus* occur in neonates and adults. The prognosis is poor for premature infants, but five of six full-term neonates in one series survived infection. Infection is manifested as a meningoencephalitis with a cerebrospinal fluid polymorphonuclear pleocytosis. Subdural effusion may complicate infection. Meningoencephalitis also is the most common CNS manifestation of *C. fetus* infection in adults.[110] Cerebrovascular accidents, subarachnoid hemorrhages, and brain abscesses also occur. The prognosis is better in adults than in neonates, with a survival rate of approximately 67%, although neurologic sequelae are frequent.[102] *C. fetus* has been shown to cause a variety of other types of localized infections, including septic arthritis, spontaneous bacterial peritonitis, salpingitis, lung abscess, empyema, cellulitis, urinary tract infection, vertebral osteomyelitis, and cholecystitis.[102, 111, 112] Although most patients with these illnesses recovered with appropriate antibiotics and drainage procedures, the clinical course was frequently prolonged and relapsing. Antibiotic resistance to fluoroquinolones may develop in immunocompromised patients who receive monotherapy regimens.[113] Nevertheless, in other patients, self-limiting bacteremia without any sequelae has been observed. Hypogammaglobulinemic patients may have persistent bacteremia and local symptoms unless given chronic suppressive therapy with antibiotics.

Infection Due to Other Enteric *Campylobacter* Species

The clinical manifestations of infection due to other enteric campylobacters overlap substantially with those of *C. jejuni* infection.[77, 114, 115] On average, *Campylobacter coli* may produce more mild disease.[32] In one series of homosexual men, *H. cineadi* and *H. fennelliae* infections were more often asymptomatic than were those due to *C. jejuni*.[116] Among immunocompromised patients, especially those with AIDS, bacteremia from the "atypical" campylobacters appears relatively commonly.[117–119] As with *C. fetus, C. upsaliensis* mostly causes diarrheal diseases in previously normal persons,[120] and bacteremia in compromised hosts; most strains of the latter species are serum-resistant.[121] Other extraintestinal manifestations such as breast abscess have been observed.[122] Cellulitis may occur in compromised hosts infected with any of a variety of these "atypical" species.[119] *C. hyointestinalis,* which resembles *C. fetus* in its biochemical characteristics,[123] also may cause bacteremia in compromised hosts. *A. butzleri* may cause abdominal cramps without diarrheal illness.[124] *Helicobacter* (Flexispira) *rappini* has recently been reported to cause bacteremia in compromised hosts.[124a]

C. fetus subsp. *venerealis,* which had never been considered a human pathogen, was reported to have been isolated from stools from two homosexual men in Australia, and from two women with bacterial vaginosis. *C. fetus* subsp. *fetus* has been isolated from two other patients with vaginosis. *Campylobacter sputorum* subsp. *sputorum,* which is indigenous to the human mouth and intestine, has now been isolated from perianal boils and lung abscesses. *C. sputorum* subsp. *bubulus,* a commensal of sheep and cattle, has been isolated from boils and skin abscesses from humans.

DIAGNOSIS

Clinical diagnosis of enteric campylobacteriosis may be established by demonstration of the organisms by direct examination of feces, or by isolation of the organisms. The use of serologic methods for diagnosis is at present a research tool only.

Direct Examination of Feces

Examination of diarrheal fecal specimens by darkfield or phase-contrast microscopy within 2 hours of passage can permit a rapid presumptive diagnosis of *Campylobacter* enteritis if the characteristic darting motility of the *Campylobacter* organism is seen.[74, 125] This test is particularly useful in the acute phase of the illness. Similarly, the presence of vibrio forms in Gram-stained stool specimens is a very specific diagnostic feature, although the sensitivity of this finding is 50 to 75%[126] (Fig. 204–3). Direct microscopy is also of value for detecting red blood cells and neutrophils, which are present in the feces of 75% of patients with *Campylobacter* enteritis.[40, 72] Use of PCR techniques for direct detection of organisms has been successful in research studies but has not yet been applied to the clinical setting.

Bacteriologic Studies

Confirmation of the diagnosis of *C. jejuni* infection is based on a positive result on stool culture or, occasionally, blood culture. Because blood cultures are not often performed in the evaluation of patients presenting with diarrheal symptoms, the frequency of bacteremia is not known. Results with use of radiometric blood culture detection systems may be falsely negative for some *Campylobacter* and related species using standard procedures.[13] Campylobacters cannot be isolated from fecal specimens unless microaerobic incubation conditions and selective techniques that reduce the growth of competing microorganisms are used.[2, 27] *C. fetus* is usually isolated from blood cultures 4 to 14 days after the specimen has been obtained.[70] On occasion, *C. fetus* may be isolated from feces of patients with either diarrheal or systemic infections.[58] If *C. fetus* or another of the atypical species is suspected, incubation at 37°C and use of media without cephalosporins are necessary. The use of filtration techniques will eliminate such difficulties.

THERAPY

Fluid and electrolyte replacement constitutes the cornerstone of treatment of diarrheal illnesses. Patients with *Campylobacter* infections who are severely dehydrated should undergo rapid volume expansion using intravenous solutions of electrolytes in water. For patients with less serious volume depletion, oral rehydration using glucose and electrolyte solutions is indicated. Persons infected with *C. jejuni* who are ill enough to seek medical attention and from whom a fecal culture is obtained represent only a subset of all those infected. Nevertheless, even among these patients, less than half are candidates for specific antimicrobial therapy.[71, 72] Studies in children with dysentery due to *C. jejuni* showed a clear benefit from early treatment with erythromycin.[127] In contrast, other studies in which initiation of treatment was delayed for several days until *C. jejuni* was isolated did not show a therapeutic effect.[128] Therefore, rapid presumptive diagnosis of *Campylobacter* infection by means of direct visualization of the organisms in stool is clinically relevant. On the basis of

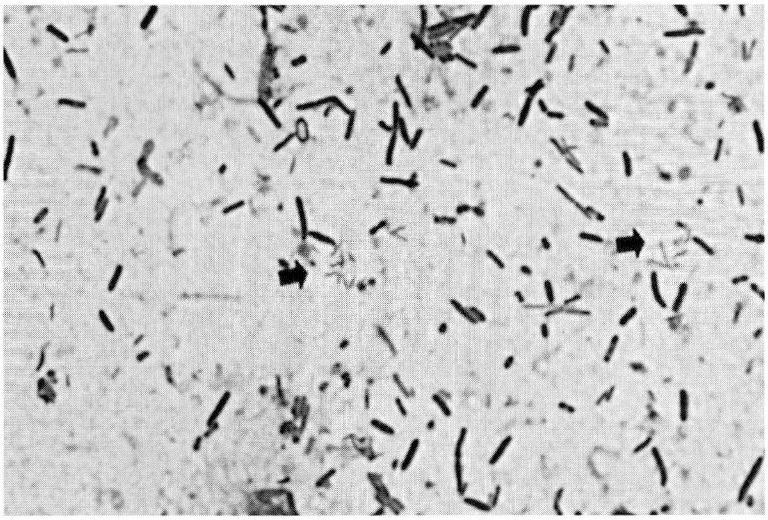

FIGURE 204–3. Gram stain of fecal specimen from a patient with *Campylobacter* enteritis. Arrows point to typical gram-negative fine, small, spiral, and *Vibrio*-like organisms (×1024).

anecdotal reports,[37, 71–73] wide clinical experience, and controlled trials,[127] treatment with antibiotics seems prudent in those patients with high fever, bloody diarrhea, or more than eight stools per day; in patients whose symptoms have not lessened or are worsening at the time the diagnosis is made; or in those in whom symptoms have persisted for more than 1 week.

In vitro, *C. jejuni* is susceptible to a wide variety of antimicrobial agents, including erythromycin, the tetracyclines, the aminoglycosides, chloramphenicol, quinolones, nitrofurans, and clindamycin.[129–133] Because of ease of administration, lack of serious toxicity, and apparent efficacy, erythromycin has been the agent of choice.[74, 134, 135] The recommended dosage for adults is 250 mg PO four times daily for 5 to 7 days; the recommended dosage for children is 30 to 50 mg/kg/day in divided doses for the same period. Therapy with extended-spectrum macrolides such as clarithromycin or azithromycin should be equally effective. An alternative agent is ciprofloxacin, 500 mg PO twice daily for 5 to 7 days, which has activity across a broad spectrum of bacteria causing diarrheal illness as well as against campylobacters. However, owing to the widespread usage of quinolones in both humans and food animals, in many parts of the world including the United States, resistance of *Campylobacter* to these agents is increasing.[136–138] This phenomenon will limit the utility of quinolones for empirical treatment of acute diarrheal illness.[139] Another alternative agent is tetracycline, except in children under 9 years of age; in such patients, clindamycin may be used. Most *C. jejuni* and *C. coli* isolates are not susceptible to most cephalosporins or penicillin, and these agents should not be used. However, amoxicillin or ticarcillin plus clavulanic acid (but not sulbactam or tazobactam) appears to be universally effective.[140] Susceptibility to sulfonamides and metronidazole is variable. Unlike in *Salmonella* infections, treatment with antimicrobial agents does not prolong carriage of *C. jejuni;* on the contrary, erythromycin eliminates carriage within 72 hours in most patients.[128] *H. cinaedi* and those *Campylobacter* strains acquired in developing countries, especially *C. coli,* are more likely to be resistant to erythromycin and tetracycline.[141] In such cases, when treatment is indicated, until susceptibility is known, alternative agents should be used. Use of an antimotility agent appears to prolong duration of symptoms and has been associated with fatalities.[142] The necessity for treating septic or bacteremic episodes with agents other than erythromycin has not been established. For those patients who appear very ill, treatment with gentamicin, imipenem, cefotaxime, or chloramphenicol is indicated, but susceptibility tests should be performed. In hypogammaglobulinemic patients with recurrent *C. jejuni* bacteremias, fresh-frozen plasma concomitant with appropriate antibiotics may eradicate the infection[91]; oral immune globulin therapy may have some value as well for recurrent diarrheal illness.[143] Systemic *C. fetus* infections should be treated parenterally, but erythromycin is not always effective.[144] Occasionally, systemic infections diagnosed only retrospectively by positive results on blood culture resolve after empirical oral therapy. In these cases, follow-up cultures are recommended; and if results are no longer positive, further treatment is not required. When isolates have been susceptible, ampicillin treatment has been associated with good results. Patients with endovascular infections due to *C. fetus* require at least 4 weeks of therapy, and gentamicin is probably the agent of choice. Treatment with ampicillin or third-generation cephalosporins constitutes another alternative. Infections of the CNS should be treated with third-generation cephalosporins, ampicillin, or chloramphenicol for 2 to 3 weeks. Patients with other serious infections should also receive parenteral gentamicin or another aminoglycoside, ampicillin, or chloramphenicol for at least 2 weeks. Because antibodies to *C. fetus* are not usually present in serum from normal persons, intravenous immune globulin is not helpful for this infection in immunodeficient patients.[105] For *C. fetus*–infected patients with diarrheal illness or other less severe infections, treatment need not be as intense or as prolonged.

PROGNOSIS

The vast majority of patients recover fully after *C. jejuni* infections, either spontaneously or after appropriate antimicrobial therapy. The "reactive arthritis," or Reiter's syndrome, occurring in HLA-B27–positive persons closely resembles that seen after *Yersinia, Salmonella,* or *Shigella* infections and should not be considered a specific consequence of *C. jejuni* infection. However, rheumatologic symptoms may persist for several months, or possibly for years in a few affected persons.[145] GBS is an uncommon sequela of *Campylobacter* enteritis, but because of their high prevalence, *Campylobacter* infections are the most important recognized antecedent of this disorder.[95, 96] Occasional deaths after *C. jejuni* infections have been reported in developed countries[142]; in most cases, the victim was an elderly person or a compromised host. However, fatalities in previously healthy young adults may occur, probably as a result of volume depletion. Some of the deaths that occur in Guillain-Barré patients can be attributed to the consequences of *C. jejuni* infection. Because in the developing countries most symptomatic *Campylobacter* infections occur in children under 2 years of age[31] and frequently produce a dysenteric picture, it is reasonable to conclude that *C. jejuni* infection may play a role in the dehydration and malnutrition that often accompany infantile diarrhea in these geographic areas. The outcome of infections due to newly discovered *Campylobacter*-like organisms[5, 124] remains to be determined.

C. fetus infection may be lethal to patients with chronic compensated diseases such as cirrhosis or diabetes mellitus or may hasten the demise of seriously compromised patients. For compromised hosts with systemic *C. fetus* infections, prognosis is most dependent on the rapidity with which appropriate antimicrobial therapy is begun. Previously healthy persons infected with *C. fetus* usually survive the illness without permanent sequelae.

Because *C. jejuni* infections are "accidentally" acquired by humans, and because there is evidence for the natural development of immunity among persons in developing countries, the goal of producing a vaccine is probably achievable.

REFERENCES

1. Smibert RM. Genus *Campylobacter.* In: Krieg NR, Holt HG, eds. Bergey's Manual of Systematic Bacteriology, v 1. Baltimore: Williams & Wilkins; 1984:111–118.
2. Nachamkin I. *Campylobacter, Helicobacter,* and related spiral bacteria. In: Manual of Clinical Microbiology. 6th ed. Washington, DC: American Society for Microbiology; 1996:402–409.
3. Vandamme P, Vancanneyt M, Pot B, et al. Polyphasic taxonomic study of the emended genus *Arcobacter* with *Arcobacter butzleri* comb. nov. and *Arcobacter skirrowi* sp. nov., an aerotolerant bacterium isolated from veterinary specimens. Int J Syst Bacteriol. 1992;42:344–356.
4. Fennell CL, Totten PA, Quinn TC, et al. Characterization of *Campylobacter*-like organisms isolated from homosexual men. J Infect Dis. 1984;149:58–66.
5. Burnens AP, Stanley J, Schaad UB, et al. Novel *Campylobacter*-like organism resembling *Helicobacter fennelliae* isolated from a boy with gastroenteritis and from dogs. J Clin Microbiol. 1993;31:1916–1917.
6. Foley JE, Solnick JV, LaPointe J-M, et al. Identification of a novel enteric *Helicobacter* species in a kitten with severe diarrhea. J Clin Microbiol. 1998;36:908–912.
7. Husman M, Gries C, Jehnichen P, et al. *Helicobacter* sp. strain *Mainz* isolated from an AIDS patient with septic arthritis: Case report and nonradioactive analysis of 16S rRNA sequence. J Clin Microbiol. 1994;32:3037–3039.
8. Bolton GJ, Hutchinson DN, Coates D. Blood-free selective medium for isolation of *Campylobacter jejuni* from feces. J Clin Microbiol. 1984;19:169–171.
9. Steele TW, McDermott JN. Technical note: The use of membrane filters applied directly to the surface of agar plates for the isolation of *Campylobacter jejuni* from feces. Pathology. 1984;16:263–265.
10. Burnens AP, Nicolet J. Three supplementary diagnostic tests for *Campylobacter* species and related organisms. J Clin Microbiol. 1993;31:708–710.
11. van Camp G, Fierens H, Vandamme P, et al. Identification of enteropathogenic *Campylobacter* species by oligonucleotide probes and polymerase chain reaction based on 16S rRNA genes. Syst Appl Microbiol. 1993;16:30–36.
12. Ng L-K, Kingombe CIB, Yan W, et al. Specific detection and confirmation of *Campylobacter jejuni* by DNA hybridization and PCR. Appl Environ Microbiol. 1997;63:4558–4563.
13. Wang WLL, Blaser MJ. Detection of pathogenic *Campylobacter* species in blood culture systems. J Clin Microbiol. 1986;23:709.
14. Giesendorf BAJ, Quint WGV, Henkens MHC, et al. Rapid and sensitive detection of *Campylobacter* spp. in chicken products by using the polymerase chain reaction. Appl Environ Microbiol. 1992;58:3804–3808.
15. Giesendorf BAJ, van Belkum A, Koeken A, et al. Development of species-specific DNA probes for *Campylobacter jejuni, Campylobacter coli,* and *Campylobacter lari* by polymerase chain reaction fingerprinting. J Clin Microbiol. 1993;31:1541–1546.
16. Oyofo BA, Thornton SA, Burr DH, et al. Specific detection of *Campylobacter jejuni* and *Campylobacter coli* by using polymerase chain reaction. J Clin Microbiol. 1992;30:2613–2619.
17. Blaser MJ, Taylor DN, Feldman RA. Epidemiology of *Campylobacter jejuni* infections. Epidemiol Rev. 1983;5:157.
18. Atabay HI, Corry JEL. The prevalence of campylobacters and arcobacters in broiler chickens. J Appl Microbiol. 1997;83:619–626.
19. Taylor DN, McDermott KT, Little JR, et al. *Campylobacter* enteritis associated with drinking untreated water in back-country areas of the Rocky Mountains. Ann Intern Med. 1983;99:38.
20. Mentzing L-O. Waterborne outbreaks of *Campylobacter* enteritis in central Sweden. Lancet. 1981;2:352.
21. Deming MS, Tauxe RV, Blake PA, et al. *Campylobacter* enteritis at a university: Transmission from eating chicken and from cats. Am J Epidemiol. 1987;126:526–534.
22. Skirrow MB. *Campylobacter* enteritis in dogs and cats: A "new" zoonosis. Vet Res Commun. 1981;5:13.
23. Vesikari T, Huttunen L, Maki R. Perinatal *Campylobacter fetus* ss. *jejuni* enteritis. Acta Paediatr Scand. 1981;70:261.
24. Pepersack F, Prigogyne T, Butzler JP, et al. *Campylobacter jejuni* posttransfusional septicemia. Lancet. 1979;2:911.
25. Totten PA, Fennell CL, Tenover FC, et al. *Campylobacter cinaedi* (sp. nov.) and *Campylobacter fennelliae* (sp. nov.): Two new *Campylobacter* species associated with enteric disease in homosexual men. J Infect Dis. 1985;151:131.
26. Sorvillo FJ, Lieb LE, Waterman SH. Incidence of campylobacteriosis among patients with AIDS in Los Angeles County. J Acquir Immune Defic Syndr. 1991;4:598–602.
27. Penner JL. The genus *Campylobacter:* A decade of progress. Clin Microbiol Rev. 1988;1:157–172.
28. Blaser MJ, Wells JF, Feldman RA, et al. *Campylobacter* enteritis in the United States. A multicenter study. Ann Intern Med. 1983;98:360.
29. Tauxe RV. Epidemiology of *Campylobacter jejuni* infections in the United States and other industrialized nations. In: Nachamkin I, Blaser MJ, Tompkins LS, eds. *Campylobacter jejuni.* Current Status and Future Trends. Washington, DC: American Society for Microbiology; 1992;9–19.
30. Glass RI, Stoll BJ, Huq MI, et al. Epidemiologic and clinical features of endemic *Campylobacter jejuni* infection in Bangladesh. J Infect Dis. 1983;148:292.
31. Calva JJ, Ruiz-Pallacios GM, Lopez-Vidal AB, et al. Cohort study of intestinal infection with *Campylobacter* in Mexican children. Lancet. 1988;1:503–506.
32. Taylor DN, Echeverria P, Pitarangsi C, et al. The influence of immunity and strain characteristics on the epidemiology of campylobacteriosis. J Clin Microbiol. 1988;26:863.
33. Taylor DN, Perlman D, Echeverria PD, et al. *Campylobacter* immunity and quantitative excretion rates in Thai children. J Infect Dis. 1993;168:754–758.
34. Speelman P, Struelens MJ, Sanyal SC, et al. Detection of *Campylobacter jejuni* and other potential pathogens in traveler's diarrhea in Bangladesh. Scand J Gastroenterol. 1983;84(18 Suppl):19–23.
35. Blaser MJ, Hardesty HL, Powers B, et al. Survival of *Campylobacter fetus* subsp. *jejuni* in biological milieus. J Clin Microbiol. 1980;11:309.
36. King EO. The laboratory recognition of *Vibrio fetus* and a closely related vibrio isolated from cases of human vibriosis. Ann N Y Acad Sci. 1962;90:700.
37. Lambert ME, Schofield PF, Ironside AG, et al. *Campylobacter* colitis. BMJ. 1979;1:857.
38. Van Spreeuwel JP, Duursma GC, Meijer CJLM, et al. *Campylobacter* colitis: Histologic, immunohistochemical and ultrastructural findings. Gut. 1985;26:945–951.
39. Blaser MJ, Reller LB, Luechtefeld NW, et al. *Campylobacter* enteritis in Denver. West J Med. 1982;136:287.
40. Black RE, Levine MM, Clements ML, et al. Experimental *Campylobacter jejuni* infection in humans. J Infect Dis. 1988;157:472.
41. Russell RG, O'Donnoghue M, Blake DC Jr, et al. Early colonic damage and invasion of *Campylobacter jejuni* in experimentally challenged infant *Macaca mulatta.* J Infect Dis. 1993;168:210–215.
42. Grant CCR, Konkel ME, Cieplak W, et al. Role of flagella in adherence, internalization, and translocation of *Campylobacter jejuni* in nonpolarized and polarized epithelial cell cultures. Infect Immun. 1993;61:1764–1771.
43. Babakhani FK, Joens LA. Primary swine intestinal cells as a model for studying *Campylobacter jejuni* invasiveness. Infect Immun 1993;61:2723–2726.
44. Konkel ME, Hays SF, Joens LA, Cieplak W. Characteristics of the internationalization and intracellular survival of *Campylobacter jejuni* in human epithelial cell cultures. Microb Pathogen 1992;13:357–370.
45. Pérez-Pérez GI, Blaser MJ. Lipopolysaccharide characteristics of pathogenic campylobacters. Infect Immun. 1985;47:353–359.
46. Aspinall GO, Fujimoto S, McDonald AG, et al. Lipopolysaccharides from *Campylobacter jejuni* associated with Guillain-Barré syndrome patients mimic human gangliosides in structure. Infect Immun. 1994;62:2122–2125.
47. Johnson WM, Lior H. Cytotoxic and cytotonic factors produced by *Campylobacter jejuni, Campylobacter coli,* and *Campylobacter laridis.* J Clin Microbiol. 1986;24:275–281.
48. Walker RI, Caldwell MB, Lee EC, et al. Pathophysiology of *Campylobacter* enteritis. Microbiol Rev. 1985;50:81–94.
49. Wassenaar T. Toxin production by *Campylobacter* spp. Rev Clin Microbiol. 1997;10:466–476.
50. Pickett CL, Pesci EC, Cottle DL, et al. Prevalence of cytolethal distending toxin production in *Campylobacter jejuni* and relatedness of *Campylobacter* sp *cdtB* genes. Infect Immun. 1996;64:2070–2078.
51. Fauchere JL, Rosenau A, Veron M, et al. Association with HeLa cells of *Campylobacter jejuni* and *Campylobacter coli* isolated from human feces. Infect Immun. 1986;54:283–287.
52. Kervella M, Pages J-M, Pei Z, et al. Isolation and characterization of two *Campylobacter* glycine-extracted proteins that bind to HeLa cell membranes. Infect Immun. 1993;61:3440–3448.
53. Pei Z, Ellison RT III, Blaser MJ. Identification, purification and characterization of major antigenic proteins of *Campylobacter jejuni.* J Biol Chem. 1991;266:16363–16369.
54. Pei Z, Blaser MJ. PEB1, the major cell-binding factor of *Campylobacter jejuni,* is a homolog of the binding component in gram negative nutrient transport systems. J Biol Chem. 1993;267:18717–18725.
55. Pei Z, Burucoa C, Grignon B, et al. Mutation in the *peb1A* locus of *Campylobacter jejuni* reduces interactions with epithelial cells and intestinal colonization of mice. Infect Immun. 1998;66:938–943.
56. Caldwell MB, Guerry P, Lee EC, et al. Reversible expression of flagella in *Campylobacter jejuni.* Infect Immun. 1985;50:941–943.
57. Blaser MJ, Smith PF, Kohler PA. Susceptibility of *Campylobacter* isolates to the bactericidal activity in human serum. J Infect Dis. 1985;151:227.
58. Blaser MJ. *Campylobacter fetus:* Emerging infection and model system for bacterial pathogenesis at mucosal surfaces. Clin Infect Dis. 1998;27:256–258.
59. Blaser MJ, Smith PF, Hopkins JA, et al. Pathogenesis of *Campylobacter fetus* infections. Serum resistance associated with high molecular weight surface proteins. J Infect Dis. 1987;155:696.

60. Dworkin J, Blaser MJ. Molecular mechanisms of *Campylobacter fetus* surface layer protein expression. Mol Microbiol. 1997;26:433–440.
61. Blaser MJ, Smith PF, Repine JE, et al. Pathogenesis of *Campylobacter fetus* infections. Failure of C3b to bind explains serum and phagocytosis resistance. J Clin Invest. 1988;81:1434–1444.
62. Pei Z, Blaser MJ. Pathogenesis of *Campylobacter fetus* infections. Role of surface array proteins in virulence in a mouse model. J Clin Invest. 1990;85:1036–1043.
63. Wang E, Garcia MM, Blake MS, et al. Shift in S-layer protein expression responsible for antigenic variation in *Campylobacter fetus.* J Bacteriol. 1993;175:4979–4984.
64. Tummuru MKR, Blaser MJ. Rearrangement of *sapA* homologs with conserved and variable regions in *Campylobacter fetus.* Proc Natl Acad Sci U S A. 1993;90:7265–7269.
65. Black RF, Perlman D, Clements ML, et al. Human volunteer studies with *C. jejuni.* In: Nachamkin I, Blaser MJ, Tompkins LS, eds. *Campylobacter fetus.* Current Status and Future Trends. Washington, DC: American Society for Microbiology; 1992;207–215.
66. Johnson RJ, Wang SP, Shelton WR, et al. Persistent *Campylobacter jejuni* infection in an immunocompromised host. Ann Intern Med. 1984;100:832–834.
67. Melamed I, Bujanover Y, Igra YS, et al. *Campylobacter* enteritis in normal and immunodeficient children. Am J Dis Child. 1983;137:752–753.
68. Perlman DM, Ampel NM, Schiffman RB, et al. Persistent *Campylobacter jejuni* infections in patients infected with the human immunodeficiency virus: Association with abnormal serological response to *C. jejuni* and emergence of erythromycin resistance during therapy. Ann Intern Med. 1988;108:540–546.
69. Bokkenheuser V. *Vibrio fetus* infection in man. I. Ten new cases and some epidemiologic observations. Am J Epidemiol. 1970;91:400.
70. Guerrant RL, Lahita RG, Winn EC Jr, et al. Campylobacteriosis in man: Pathogenic mechanisms and review of 91 bloodstream infections. Am J Med. 1978;65:484.
71. Skirrow MB. Campylobacter. Lancet. 1990;336:921–923.
72. Blaser MJ, Berkowitz ID, LaForce FM, et al. *Campylobacter* enteritis; clinical and epidemiologic features. Ann Intern Med. 1979;91:179.
73. Skirrow MB. *Campylobacter* enteritis: A "new" disease. BMJ. 1977;2:9.
74. Karmali MA, Fleming PC. *Campylobacter* enteritis in children. J Pediatr. 1979;94:527.
75. McKinley MJ, Taylor M, Sangree MH. Toxic megacolon with campylobacter colitis. Conn Med. 1980;44:496.
76. Tee W, Anderson BN, Ross BC, et al. Atypical campylobacters associated with gastroenteritis. J Clin Microbiol. 1987;25:1248–1252.
77. Steele TW, Sangster N, Lanser JA. DNA relatedness and biochemical features of *Campylobacter* spp. isolated in Central and South Australia. J Clin Microbiol. 1985;22:71–74.
78. Drake AA, Gilchrist MJR, Washington JA II, et al. Diarrhea due to *Campylobacter fetus* subspecies *jejuni:* A clinical review of 73 cases. Mayo Clin Proc. 1981;56:414.
79. Michalak DM, Perrault J, Gilchrist MJ, et al. *Campylobacter fetus* ss. *jejuni:* A cause of massive lower gastrointestinal hemorrhage. Gastroenterology. 1980;79:742.
80. Anders BJ, Lauer BA, Paisley JW. *Campylobacter* gastroenteritis in neonates. Am J Dis Child. 1981;135:900.
81. Goossens H, Henocque G, Kremp L, et al. Nosocomial outbreak of *Campylobacter jejuni* meningitis in newborn infants. Lancet. 1986;2:146–149.
82. Wright EP, Seager J. Convulsions associated with *Campylobacter* enteritis. BMJ. 1980;281:454.
83. Orlicek SL, Welch DF, Kuhls TL. Septicemia and meningitis caused by *Helicobacter cinaedi* in a neonate. J Clin Microbiol. 1993;31:569–571.
84. Blaser MJ, Perez GP, Smith PF, et al. Extraintestinal *Campylobacter jejuni* and *Campylobacter coli* infections: Host factors and strain characteristics. J Infect Dis. 1986;153:552.
85. Gilbert GL, Davoren RA, Cole ME, et al. Midtrimester abortion associated with septicaemia caused by *Campylobacter jejuni.* Med J Aust. 1981;1:585.
86. Mertens A, DeSmet M. *Campylobacter* cholecystitis. Lancet. 1979;1:1092.
87. Gallagher P, Chadwick P, Jones DM, et al. Acute pancreatitis associated with *Campylobacter* infection. Br J Surg. 1981;68:383.
88. Ezpeleta C, Rojo de Ursua P, Obregon F, et al. Acute pancreatitis associated with *Campylobacter jejuni* bacteremia. Clin Infect Dis. 1992;15:1050.
89. Davies JS, Penfold JB. *Campylobacter* urinary infection. Lancet. 1979;1:1091.
90. Feder HM, Rasoulpour M, Rodriquez AJ. *Campylobacter* urinary tract infection. Value of the urine gram stain. JAMA. 1986;256:2389.
91. Kersten PJSM, Endtz HP, Meis JFGM, et al. Erysipelas-like skin lesions associated with *Campylobacter jejuni* septicemia in patients with hypogammaglobulinemia. Eur J Clin Microbiol Infect Dis. 1992;11:842–847.
92. Kosunen TU, Kauranen O, Martio J, et al. Reactive arthritis after *Campylobacter jejuni* enteritis in patients with HLA-B27. Lancet. 1980;1:1312.
93. Humphrey KS. *Campylobacter* infection and hepatocellular injury. Lancet. 1993;341:49.
94. Carter JE, Cimolai N. IgA nephropathy associated with *Campylobacter jejuni* enteritis. Nephron. 1991;58:101–102.
95. Mishu B, Blaser MJ. The role of *Campylobacter jejuni* infection in the initiation of Guillain-Barré syndrome. Clin Infect Dis. 1993;17:104–108.
96. Rees JH, Soudain SE, Gregory NA, Hughes RAN. *Campylobacter jejuni* infection and Guillain-Barré syndrome. N Engl J Med. 1995;333:1374–1379.
97. Kaldor J, Speed BR. Guillain-Barré syndrome and *Campylobacter jejuni:* A serological study. BMJ. 1984;288:1867–1870.
98. Mishu B, Ilyas AA, Koski CL, et al. Serologic evidence of *Campylobacter jejuni* infection preceding Guillain-Barré syndrome. Ann Intern Med. 1993;118:947–953.
99. Kuroki S, Saida T, Nukina M, et al. *Campylobacter jejuni* strains from patients with Guillain-Barré syndrome belong mostly to Penner serogroup 19 and contain β-*N*-acetylglucosamine residues. Ann Neurol. 1993;33:243–247.
100. Fujimoto S, Allos BM, Misawa N, et al. Restriction fragment length polymorphism analysis and random amplified polymorphic DNA analysis of *Campylobacter jejuni* strains isolated from patients with Guillain-Barré syndrome. J Infect Dis. 1997;176:1105–1108.
101. Allos BM, Lippy FT, Carlsen A, et al. *Campylobacter jejuni* strains from patients with Guillain-Barré syndrome. Emerg Infect Dis. 1998;4:263–268.
102. Franklin B, Ulmer DD. Human infection with *Vibrio fetus.* West J Med. 1974;120:200.
103. Collins HS, Blevins A, Baxter E. Protracted bacteremia and meningitis due to *Vibrio fetus.* Arch Intern Med. 1964;113:361.
104. Park CH, McDonald F, Twohig AM, et al. Septicemia and gastroenteritis due to *Vibrio fetus.* South Med J. 1973;66:531.
105. Neuzil KM, Wang E, Haas D, Blaser MJ. Persistence of *Campylobacter fetus* bacteremia associated with absence of opsonizing antibodies. J Clin Microbiol. 1994;32:1718–1720.
106. Loeb H, Bettag JL, Yantz NK, et al. *Vibrio fetus* endocarditis. Am Heart J. 1966;71:381.
107. Killiam HA, Crowder JG, White AC, et al. Pericarditis due to *Vibrio fetus.* Am J Cardiol. 1966;17:723.
108. Vesely D, MacIntyre S, Ratzan KR. Bilateral deep brachial vein thrombophlebitis due to *Vibrio fetus.* Arch Intern Med. 1975;135:994.
109. Eden AH. Perinatal mortality caused by *Vibrio fetus.* Review and analysis. J Pediatr. 1966;68:297.
110. Gunderson CH, Sack GE. Neurology of *Vibrio fetus.* Neurology (NY). 1971;21:307.
111. Kilo C, Hagemann PO, Maryi J. Septic arthritis and bacteremia due to *Vibrio fetus.* Am J Med. 1965;38:962.
112. Lawrence R, Nibbe AF, Levin S. Lung abscess secondary to *Vibrio fetus* malabsorption syndrome and acquired agammaglobulinemia. Chest. 1971;60:191.
113. Meier PA, Dooley DP, Jorgensen JH, et al. Development of quinolone-resistant *Campylobacter fetus* bacteremia in human immunodeficiency virus-infected patients. J Infect Dis. 1998;177:951–954.
114. Benjamin JS, Leaper S, Owen RJ, et al. Description of *Campylobacter laridis,* a new species comprising the nalidixic acid resistant thermophilic *Campylobacter* (NARTC group). Curr Microbiol. 1983;8:231–238.
115. Simor AE, Wilcox L. Enteritis associated with *Campylobacter laridis.* J Clin Microbiol. 1987;25:10–12.
116. Quinn TC, Goodell SE, Fennell C, et al. Infections with *Campylobacter jejuni* and *Campylobacter*-like organisms in homosexual men. Ann Intern Med. 1984;101:187–192.
117. Kemper CA, Mickelsen P, Morton A, et al. *Helicobacter (Campylobacter) fennelliae*–like organisms as an important but occult cause of bacteremia in a patient with AIDS. J Infect. 1993;26:97–101.
118. Fleisch F, Burnens A, Weber R, Zbinden R. *Helicobacter* species strain *Mainz* isolated from cultures of blood from two patients with AIDS. Clin Infect Dis. 1998;26:526–527.
119. Kiehlbauch JA, Tauxe RV, Baker CN, Wachsmuth IK. *Helicobacter cineadi*–associated bacteremia and cellulitis in immunocompromised patients. Ann Intern Med. 1994;121:90–93.
120. Goosens H, Pot B, Vlaes L, et al. Characterization and description of "*Campylobacter upsaliensis*" isolated from human feces. J Clin Microbiol. 1990;28:1039–1046.
121. Patton CM, Shaffer N, Edmonds P et al. Human disease associated with "*Campylobacter upsaliensis*" (catalase-negative or weakly positive *Campylobacter* species) in the United States. J Clin Microbiol. 1989;27:66–73.
122. Gaudreau C, Lamothe F. *Campylobacter upsaliensis* isolated from a breast abscess. J Clin Microbiol. 1992;30:1354–1356.
123. Edmonds P, Patton CM, Griffin PM, et al. *Campylobacter hyointestinalis* associated with human gastrointestinal disease in the United States. J Clin Microbiol. 1987;25:685–691.
124. Vandamme P, Pugina P, Benzi G, et al. Outbreak of recurrent abdominal cramps associated with *Arcobacter butzleri* in an Italian school. J Clin Microbiol. 1992;30:2335–2337.
124a. Sorlin P, vanDamme P, Nortier J, et al. Recurrent *"Flexispira rappini"* bacteremia in an adult patient undergoing hemodialysis: Case report. J Clin Microbiol. 1999;37:1319–1323.
125. Paisley JW, Mirrett S, Lauer BA, et al. Darkfield microscopy of human feces for the presumptive diagnosis of *Campylobacter* enteritis. J Clin Microbiol. 1982;15:61.
126. Sazie ESM, Titus AE. Rapid diagnosis of *Campylobacter* enteritis. Ann Intern Med. 1982;96:62.
127. Salazar-Lindo E, Sack RB, Chea-Woo E, et al. Early treatment with erythromycin of *Campylobacter jejuni*–associated dysentery in children. J Pediatr. 1986;109:355.
128. Anders BJ, Lauer BA, Paisley JW, et al. Double-blind placebo controlled trial of erythromycin for treatment of *Campylobacter* enteritis. Lancet. 1982;1:131.
129. Vanhoof R, Vanderlinden MP, Dierickx R, et al. Susceptibility of *Campylobacter fetus* subsp. *jejuni* to twenty-nine antimicrobial agents. Antimicrob Agents Chemother. 1978;14:553.
130. Walder M. Susceptibility of *Campylobacter fetus* subsp. *jejuni* to twenty antimicrobial agents. Antimicrob Agents Chemother. 1979;16:37.
131. Vanhoof R, Gordts B, Dierickx R, et al. Bacteriostatic and bactericidal activities

of 24 antimicrobial agents against *Campylobacter fetus* subsp. *jejuni*. Antimicrob Agents Chemother. 1980;18:118.
132. Huang MB, Baker CN, Banerjee S, et al. Accuracy of the E test for determining antimicrobial susceptibilities of staphylococci, enterococci, *Campylobacter jejuni*, and gram-negative bacteria resistant to antimicrobial agents. J Clin Microbiol. 1992;30:3243–3248.
133. Sjögren E, Kaijser B, Werner M. Antimicrobial susceptibilities of *Campylobacter jejuni* and *Campylobacter coli* isolated in Sweden: A 10-year follow-up report. Antimicrob Agents Chemother. 1992;36:2847–2849.
134. Blaser MJ, Reller LB. *Campylobacter* enteritis. N Engl J Med. 1981;305:1444.
135. Skirrow MB, Blaser MJ. *Campylobacter jejuni*. In: Blaser MJ, Smith PD, Ravdin J, et al, eds. Infections of the Gastrointestinal Tract. Philadelphia: Lippincott-Raven; 1995:825–848.
136. Segreti J, Gootz TD, Goodman LJ, et al. High-level quinolone resistance in clinical isolates of *Campylobacter jejuni*. J Infect Dis. 1992;165:667–670.
137. Reina J, Borrell N, Serra A. Emergence of resistance to erythromycin and fluoroquinolone in thermotolerant *Campylobacter* strains isolated from feces 1987–1991. Eur J Clin Microbiol Infect Dis. 1992;11:1163–1166.
138. Smith KE, Besser JM, Hedberg CW, et al. Quinolone-resistant *Campylobacter jejuni* infections in Minnesota, 1992–1998. N Engl J Med. 1999;340:1525–1532.
139. Wistrom J, Jertborn M, Ekwall E, et al. Empiric treatment of acute diarrheal disease with norfloxacin. A randomized, placebo-controlled study. Ann Intern Med. 1992;117:202–208.
140. Lachance N, Gaudreau C, Lamothe F, et al. Susceptibilities of β-lactamase–positive and –negative strains of *Campylobacter coli* to β-lactam agents. Antimicrob Agents Chemother. 1993;37:1174–1176.
141. Taylor DN, Blaser MJ, Echeverria P, et al. Erythromycin-resistant *Campylobacter* infections in Thailand. Antimicrob Agents Chemother. 1987;31:438–442.
142. Smith GS, Blaser MJ. Fatalities associated with *Campylobacter jejuni* infections. JAMA. 1985;253:2873.
143. Hammarström V, Smith CIE, Hammarström L. Oral immunoglobulin treatment in *Campylobacter jejuni* enteritis. Lancet. 1993;341:1036.
144. Francioli P, Herzstein J, Grob J-P, et al. *Campylobacter fetus* subspecies *fetus* bacteremia. Arch Intern Med. 1985;145:289–292.
145. Bremell T, Bjelle A, Svedhem A. Rheumatic symptoms following an attack of campylobacter enteritis: A five year follow up. Ann Rheum Dis. 1991;50:934–948.

Chapter 205

Helicobacter pylori and Related Organisms

MARTIN J. BLASER

Helicobacter pylori (formerly known as *Campylobacter pylori* or *pyloridis*) was first isolated from humans in 1982.[1] This highly motile, curved, gram-negative rod lives within the mucus layer overlying the gastric and occasionally the duodenal or esophageal mucosal epithelium.[2] *H. pylori* is commonly found in the human stomach; essentially all persons colonized with *H. pylori* have a cellular infiltrate in the lamina propria of the gastric antrum and fundus.[3] Of special significance is that *H. pylori* is present in most persons with "idiopathic" peptic ulcer disease. Increasing evidence indicates that the presence of *H. pylori* influences the risk (both positive and negative) of several of the most important upper gastrointestinal inflammatory and neoplastic processes.[4] With the development of effective therapies to eradicate *H. pylori,* physicians are faced with the challenge of determining which patients will benefit from therapy and which may be harmed. This view of the role of *H. pylori* in human disease represents a major departure from the previous decade's assessment of gastroduodenal pathophysiology.

MICROBIOLOGY

H. pylori organisms are small (0.5 to 1.0 μm in width and 2.5 to 4.0 μm in length) curved microaerophilic gram-negative rods.[5,6] Because they closely resemble members of the genus *Campylobacter,* they were initially considered to belong to that genus. However, multiple genotypic and phenotypic characteristics are different from those of campylobacters, and a new genus, *Helicobacter,* has been established.[6] Other newly recognized organisms include *Helicobacter mustelae* in ferrets,[6,7] *Helicobacter felis* in dogs and cats,[7] *Helicobacter muridarum* in mice, *Helicobacter nemestrinae* in nonhuman primates, and *Helicobacter acinonyx* in cheetahs.[8] *Helicobacter heilmannii* is a gastric spirochete of humans and will be considered in a separate section of this chapter. *Helicobacter fennelliae* and *Helicobacter cinaedi* are intestinal organisms causing diarrheal illnesses; because the clinical features of these infections resemble those of *Campylobacter* spp., they are discussed in Chapter 204. Based on the recent and intense interest of microbiologists in gastric bacteria, it is likely that the genus *Helicobacter* will continue to expand. Nevertheless, *H. pylori* is the most important human pathogen and may be considered the prototype for these organisms. *Helicobacter* species (such as *Helicobacter hepaticus, Helicobacter bilis,* and *Helicobacter rappini*) have also been identified in the colon and biliary tract of rodents, and evidence now points to human carriage as well.[8–10] Preliminary evidence suggests that they might colonize the diseased human biliary tract,[11] but whether they participate in the pathophysiologic process is uncertain.[12] They have caused chronic bacteremia and indolent cellulitis in patients with X-linked hypogammaglobulinemia and common variable immunodeficiency.

H. pylori cells are highly motile with a rapid corkscrew motion and have multiple polar sheathed flagella.[6] Although these cells are classically curved or spiral in fresh cultures, spherical (coccoid) forms are present in older cultures. The major biochemical properties of *H. pylori* and several related bacteria are shown in Table 205–1. The outstanding biochemical characteristic of helicobacters is their high production of urease. *H. pylori* urease is a hexadimer consisting of 61- and 28-kD subunits, both of which are essential for activity.[13] Regulation of urease is complex, and at least eight other genes are currently recognized as necessary for full activity.[14,15] All clinical isolates are urease positive, but urease-negative strains have been derived in the laboratory.

The nucleotide sequence of the chromosome from one *H. pylori* strain (26695) has been determined.[16] This feat was a major accomplishment and has opened new avenues for the study of *H. pylori* microbiology. For example, *H. pylori* has few two-component regulatory proteins, but frameshifts are common within open reading frames of certain *H. pylori* enzymes, which suggests that *H. pylori* may use mutation to control phenotype, with the host selecting for the "most fit" organism within a particular environmental niche.

Although *H. pylori* is highly homogeneous in several biochemical characteristics, including oxidase and catalase positivity, wide variation is noted at a genetic level,[17] and such variation can be detected by analysis of profiles after restriction endonuclease digestion,[18] by polymerase chain reaction–based analyses,[19] or by sequencing of variable regions in several genes.[20] Such studies have shown that humans may be simultaneously colonized with more than one strain of *H. pylori.*[21] Plasmids are present in most *H. pylori* isolates; they vary in size and all are cryptic at present.

The most important dichotomy among *H. pylori* strains is the presence of the *cag* pathogenicity island, a 40-kilobase chromosomal region encoding *cagA* and a number of genes related to bacterial secretion.[22–24] Both *cagA*$^+$ and *cagA*$^-$ strains are present in *H. pylori* populations in all parts of the world[25] and in nonhuman primates, which suggests that the acquisition of this region by *H. pylori* is ancient. Both *cag*$^+$ and *cag*$^-$ strains can be present in a single host. The *cag* status of an *H. pylori* strain is relevant to the risk of a number of clinical outcomes (see later). Another heterogeneous locus is *vacA,* the gene that encodes a secreted protein ("vacuolating cytotoxin") that interacts with epithelial cells.[26] Two parts of *vacA* are polymorphic—the *s* region (with alleles s1a, s1b, s1c, and s2) and the *m* region (with alleles m1, m2a, and m2b).[27,28] Although clear geographic differences in the distribution of strains of particular *vacA* genotypes can be found, many such combinations are widely present in the world. Because s1 genotypes are strongly linked to

TABLE 205–1 Biochemical Characteristics of *Helicobacter pylori* and Related Bacteria

Characteristic	*Helicobacter pylori*	*Helicobacter mustelae*	*Helicobacter felis*	*Campylobacter jejuni*
Urease	+	+	+	−
Catalase	+	+	+	+
Oxidase	+	+	+	+
H_2S production	−	−	−	+
Guanosine plus cytosine content	35–38	36	42.5	33–36
Hippurate hydrolysis	−	−	−	+
Nitrate reduction	−	+	+	+
Resistance to nalidixic acid (30-μg disk)	+	−	+	−
Cephalothin (30-μg disk)	−	+	−	+
Growth at 42°C	−	+	+	+
Growth at 37°C	+	+	+	+
Growth at 25°C	−	−	−	−

Data from refs. 6–8.

cag positivity, many of the same clinical associations with *cag* are also present. Other polymorphic loci that relate to the clinical outcome of *H. pylori* colonization have been described, including *iceA*.[29, 30]

EPIDEMIOLOGY

H. pylori has been isolated from persons in all parts of the world[31] (Fig. 205–1). Similar organisms have been isolated from primates, but other animal sources for *H. pylori* have not been identified, nor have reservoirs been found in food, soil, or water. It now appears likely that humans are the major, if not sole reservoir for *H. pylori.* On occasion, transmission occurs from person to person via improperly cleaned endoscopes.[32] *H. pylori* has occasionally been isolated from feces, especially from children.[33] The high prevalence and incidence of colonization among persons in settings where sanitary conditions are suboptimal, including institutions for the mentally retarded, at orphanages, and in developing countries, suggests that fecal-oral transmission occurs.[31, 34] *H. pylori* has been isolated from dental plaque,[21] and DNA products may be detected in saliva by polymerase chain reaction, which raises the possibility of oral-oral transmission as well. However, studies of persons attending clinics for either sexually transmitted diseases or infertility indicate that sexual transmission does not occur very frequently, if at all.[35] The relative contribution of fecal-oral or oral-oral transmission of *H. pylori* is not known. *H. pylori* infection can cluster in families,[36] and the presence of a colonized child is highly associated with large family size and older siblings.

The prevalence of *H. pylori* colonization is chiefly related to age[31, 37] and geographic location. Males and females have essentially equal rates of colonization. In developing countries, by age 10, 70% carry *H. pylori,* and by age 20, carriage is nearly universal. In the United States among non-Hispanic whites, little colonization occurs during childhood, and rates gradually increase during adulthood and reach a prevalence of 50 to 60% among persons older than 60 years.[38, 39] Among blacks and Hispanics, *H. pylori* is acquired earlier in life on average, and a higher prevalence is seen at all ages.[39–41] The annual incidence of infection has ranged from 0.5% among epidemiologists in the United States[42] to 7.4% among persons at an institution for the mentally retarded in Australia.[43] In most populations, *H. pylori* appears to be mainly acquired during childhood.[31, 44] The incidence of *H. pylori* has been progressively declining in the United States and other developed countries,[42, 45] probably as a result of smaller family sizes, decreased crowding, and improved sanitation.[42, 46] Thus, the age-related increase in prevalence reflects both a birth cohort phenomenon (with persons born earlier having higher acquisition rates in childhood) and continuing exposure and low-level new colonization into adulthood. The birth cohort effect predominates. Being an immigrant and of lower socioeconomic status are risk factors for *H. pylori* presence.[39, 47]

PATHOLOGY AND PATHOGENESIS

H. pylori is able to survive and multiply in the gastric environment, which is hostile to the growth of most bacteria.[48] When intraluminal acidity diminishes as a result of gastric atrophy, *H. pylori* is no longer able to colonize, possibly because of competing organisms. Outstanding *H. pylori* characteristics that permit gastric colonization include microaerophilism for survival within the mucus gel; spiral shape and flagella for motility within this viscous layer; and urease activity, which generates ammonium ions that buffer gastric acidity.[49] Studies in gnotobiotic piglets, which can be infected by *H. pylori,* indicate that both motility and urease activity are important determinants of the ability to colonize the stomach.[50] Although most organisms appear to be free living in the mucus layer, smaller numbers appear to be adherent to the mucosal epithelial cells and form "adherence pedestals" resembling those produced by enteropathogenic *Escherichia coli.*[51] Several putative adhesins have been observed.[52, 53]

H. pylori overlies only gastric-type but not intestinal-type epithelial cells. Affected gastric epithelial cells may be in the gastric antrum or fundus[54] or may be ectopic in the duodenum or in the esophagus.[3, 55] In contrast, *H. pylori* does not colonize intestinal epithelium, even when present in the stomach.[3] The gastric tissue underneath *H. pylori* colonization virtually always has a cellular infiltrate. The lamina propria most commonly has an increase in mononuclear cells, including lymphocytes, monocytes, and plasma cells. Neutrophils and, to a lesser extent, eosinophils may be present in the lamina propria and in the epithelium. The epithelial glands usually do not have a regular architecture, and less mucus is found than when *H. pylori* is absent.[3, 56] In children, a follicular lymphoid pattern is common. The evidence is overwhelming that the presence of *H. pylori* induces these changes and is not just a secondary colonizer.

The mechanisms of tissue injury are not clearly established, and both bacterial and host factors may be determinants of outcome. *H. pylori* does not appear to invade tissues, except as an incidental finding. Thus, the lesions are likely to reflect a response to extracellular products or to contact from the organism. Ammonia, produced by urease and by deaminases, is known to be toxic to eukaryotic cells and may potentiate neutrophil-induced mucosal injury.[57] Supernatants from about 50% of *H. pylori* strains contain a protein (*vacA* product) that in vitro produces vacuolation of epithelial cells.[26, 58] Infected persons frequently show antibodies that neutralize this activity, thus indicating that it is produced in vivo.[59] Strains from patients with ulcers more often produce VacA in vitro than do strains from patients with gastritis only.[26, 60] Urease may be shed by *H. pylori* cells, has been observed in affected tissues, and is a chemoattractant and activator of host phagocytic cells.[61, 62]

Bacterial lipopolysaccharide usually has proinflammatory activities, but *H. pylori* lipopolysaccharide has remarkably little.[63] *H.*

FIGURE 205–1. Seroprevalence of *Helicobacter pylori* colonization in populations in developing countries *(A)* and in developed countries *(B)*. *H. pylori* is acquired earlier and is more common at all ages in developing countries than in developed countries. (From Taylor DN, Blaser MJ. The epidemiology of *Helicobacter pylori* infections. Epidemiol Rev. 1991;13:42–59.)

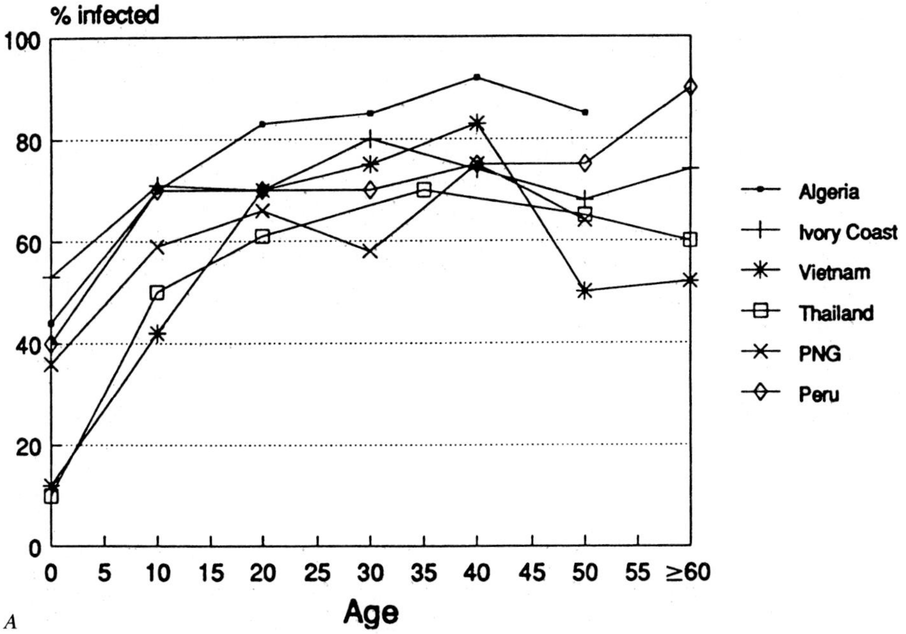

A

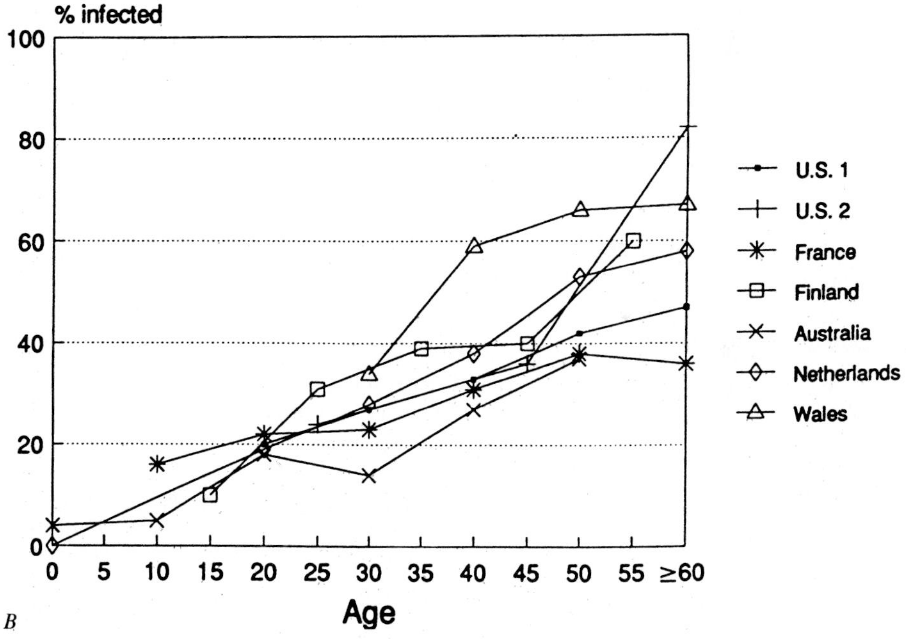

B

pylori lipopolysaccharide may express the Lewis^x, Lewis^y, neither, or both of these antigens.[64] This observation is significant because these antigens are present on gastric epithelial cells and evidence has been presented that the host Lewis phenotype selects for the particular Lewis expression of the *H. pylori* population.[65] The presence of *H. pylori* overlying the gastric mucosa activates epithelial cells to produce proinflammatory cytokines[66] and activates mononuclear and polymorphonuclear cells to produce cytokines, superoxide, tumor necrosis factor-α and other proinflammatory molecules.[62, 67, 68] Because *H. pylori* can persist in the stomach for many decades, these proinflammatory activities must be downregulated to permit this universally stable colonization.[67, 69] About 60% of *H. pylori* strains in the United States possess a gene called *cagA* encoding a highly antigenic protein of 120 to 128 kD[70, 71]; of note is that virtually all patients with duodenal ulceration appear to be colonized by strains possessing *cagA* (and thus the *cag* pathogenicity island).[72] Thus, *cagA,* the first gene described to not be conserved among all *H. pylori* strains, is highly associated with peptic ulcer disease. In the Orient, most *H. pylori* strains are *cagA*$^+$.

Persons colonized with *H. pylori* have different gastric secretory physiology than do those who are not colonized. Colonized persons on average have higher gastrin levels, which are reduced by eradication of the organism.[73, 74] The mechanism for increased gastrin production appears to be related to low gastric somatostatin levels, which may reflect cytokine production in the colonized antrum.[69] Increased gastrin may contribute to the increase in parietal cell mass observed in many patients with duodenal ulceration. In contrast, *H. pylori* products may directly damage parietal cells,[75] which may diminish acid production. That *H. pylori* involves gastric tissues concerned with both acid production (fundus) and its regulation (antrum) may in part be responsible for the multiplicity of potential outcomes of its colonization.[67, 69] Differences among colonized hosts in cell-mediated immunity and cytokine responses to *H. pylori* are other possible determinants of outcome variability.[76]

Similar findings to those observed in humans develop in nonhuman primates colonized with *H. pylori.*[77] Other animal models resembling *H. pylori* colonization in humans have previously been confined to germ-free animals.[50] The inflammation produced occurs only in colonized areas and is limited to the stomach, but the inflammation is predominantly with mononuclear cells. Recently, the development of experimental *H. pylori* infections in conventional rodents has allowed new avenues for exploring host-microbial interactions.[78, 79]

CLINICAL FEATURES OF *HELICOBACTER PYLORI* COLONIZATION

Although *H. pylori* is commonly isolated from the human stomach, colonization is associated with certain types of upper gastrointestinal pathology, appears to protect against other lesions, and is neutral for others (Table 205–2). From a clinical standpoint, the major consequences of *H. pylori* colonization are as follows.

Acute Acquisition

Natural, volunteer, or accidental *H. pylori* infection may cause an acute upper gastrointestinal illness with nausea and upper abdominal pain.[32, 94, 95] Vomiting, burping, and fever may also be present. Symptoms last from 3 to 14 days, with most illnesses persisting less than 1 week. A diagnosis of "food poisoning" may be made in persons seeking medical attention. For many individuals, the acquisition of *H. pylori* is clinically silent. Most data suggesting symptomatic acquisition relate to adults, but worldwide, most acquisition actually occurs in children; the relative proportion of symptomatic and asymptomatic acute acquisition at any age is not known. In the weeks after acquisition, intense gastritis develops; hypochlorhydria ensues and may persist for up to 1 year. One volunteer who ingested *H. pylori* appeared to have had an acute self-limited infection[94]; the frequency of this phenomenon is not known.

Persistent Colonization

It now is clear that after acquisition *H. pylori* persists for years, if not decades in most persons[18, 96] (Fig. 205–2). Tissue and serologic responses to colonization develop in essentially all colonized persons.[37] The acute *H. pylori*–induced upper gastrointestinal symptoms do not return in most persons; most with persistent *H. pylori* colonization are asymptomatic. However, studies of patients with nonulcer dyspepsia indicate that *H. pylori* may be slightly more common in cases than in age-matched controls[97] and that *H. pylori* colonization may be one of the causes of this common but poorly defined and probably heterogeneous group of disorders. Supporting this hypothesis are the results of some studies indicating that some patients with nonulcer dyspepsia who are colonized with *H. pylori* show better responses to antimicrobial therapy than to placebo,[98] an effect not seen in patients with nonulcer dyspepsia but not *H. pylori* infection.[99, 100] However, in other studies, no difference between *H. pylori* treatment and placebo was found.[101] In total, *H. pylori* is unlikely to be responsible for any more than 10% of cases of nonulcer dyspepsia and possibly for far fewer. Even if such an association exists, we do not have any markers that indicate in which patients with nonulcer dyspepsia a real effect occurs. Better definition of nonulcer dyspepsia and ascertainment of both *H. pylori* and host genotypes in individual patients should permit elucidation of the question of whether *H. pylori* persistence is associated with symptoms in particular patients in the absence of ulceration or neoplasia.

TABLE 205–2 Association of *Helicobacter pylori* with Common Pathologic Lesions of the Upper Gastrointestinal Tract

Lesion	Association with *H. pylori*
Chronic diffuse superficial gastritis	Nearly always associated[3, 37]
Type A (pernicious anemia) gastritis	Negative association[80]
NSAID gastropathy	Negative or no association[81]
Acute erosive gastritis (alcohol, aspirin, etc.)	No association[3]
Gastric ulceration	Commonly observed in patients who are not ingesting NSAIDs or aspirin[82, 83]
Duodenal ulceration	Usually associated with "idiopathic" lesions (non–drug induced, non–Zollinger-Ellison syndrome)[82–85]
Gastric adenocarcinoma	Positively associated with (noncardia) cancers of the body and antrum[86–88]
Gastric lymphoma	Strongly associated with MALT-type B-cell lymphomas[89, 90]
Gastroesophageal reflux disease	Presence of *cag*$^+$ strains has protective association[91, 92]
Barrett's esophagus	May colonize distalmost gastric epithelium in patients with gastric colonization.[3] Presence of *cag*$^+$ strains has protective association[92]
Adenocarcinoma of the esophagus	Presence of *cag*$^+$ strains has protective association[93]

Abbreviations: MALT, Mucosa-associated lymphoid tumor; NSAID, nonsteroidal anti-inflammatory drug.

Duodenal Ulceration

More than 90% of patients with duodenal ulceration carry *H. pylori,*[83] a combination that is significantly more common than in age-matched controls.[82] Duodenal ulceration in the absence of aspirin or nonsteroidal anti-inflammatory drug (NSAID) use or the Zollinger-Ellison syndrome is usually associated with *H. pylori* colonization. *H. pylori* may colonize the duodenum but only overlies metaplastic islands of gastric-type epithelium (gastric metaplasia).[3, 85] The occurrence of *H. pylori* colonization and gastric metaplasia is highly associated with active duodenitis, a precursor lesion to ulceration.[102] In an important study, Carrick and colleagues showed that the presence of *H. pylori* in the duodenum versus its absence was associated with a 51-fold increased risk of duodenal ulceration.[85] Prior *H. pylori* colonization is associated with about a threefold to fourfold increased risk of either gastric or duodenal ulceration.[83] In total, a significant body of evidence associating *H. pylori* colonization with "idiopathic" duodenal ulceration has accumulated. A causative role of *H. pylori* in ulcer disease is unproved; none of the experimental human studies have shown progression to ulceration. However, a large number of treatment studies using antimicrobial agents have provided important information about the natural history of ulcer disease. First, the use of antimicrobial agents (in the absence of acid-suppressive therapy) can heal duodenal ulcers at a rate similar to that observed with acid-suppressive therapy alone.[103, 104] Second, after ulcer healing, eradication of *H. pylori* is associated with significantly lower recurrence rates than if the organism remains present.[103, 104] When antimicrobial therapy that eradicates *H. pylori* is added to short-term acid-suppressive treatment, long-term ulcer relapse rates are markedly reduced.[105, 106] Altogether, these findings implicate *H. pylori* as playing a role in ulcer pathogenesis and demonstrate that antimicrobial therapy rather than long-term acid-suppressive therapy is indicated for most patients.[107] However, recent studies have provided evidence that after *H. pylori* eradication, the incidence of reflux esophagitis doubled in comparison to failed eradication.[108] Thus, removal of *H. pylori* from the stomach of patients with duodenal ulceration has both benefits and costs. As evidence becomes available, physicians will need to optimize criteria for treatment to optimize the therapeutic/toxicity ratio.

Gastric Ulceration

A smaller (50 to 80%) proportion of patients with benign gastric ulcers than with duodenal ulceration are colonized by *H. pylori.* The

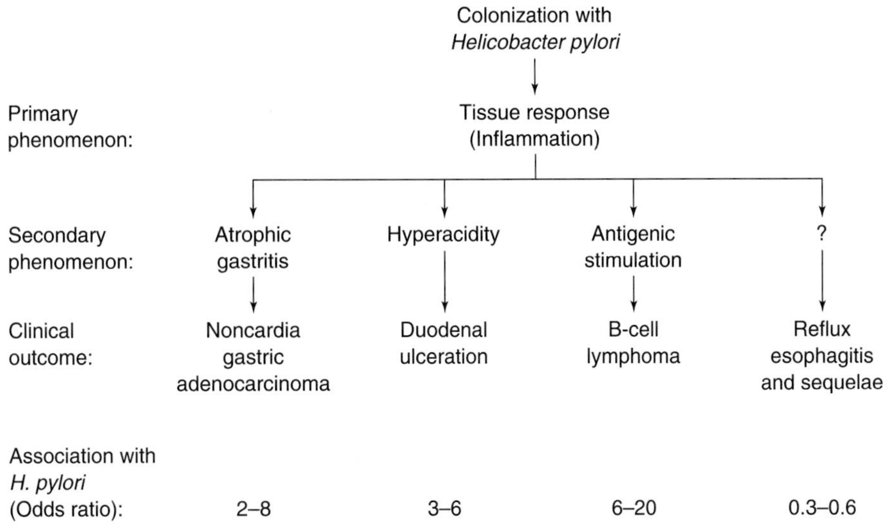

FIGURE 205–2. Association of *Helicobacter pylori* colonization and disease states. After *H. pylori* acquisition, virtually all persons develop persistent colonization that lasts for life. Colonization induces tissue responses termed chronic gastritis. This process affects gastric physiology including glandular structure, acid secretion, and antigen processing. These affect disease risk. Colonization with *H. pylori* increases the risk for certain diseases (duodenal ulcer, gastric ulcer, noncardia gastric adenocarcinoma, and B-cell lymphomas) but appears to decrease the risk for gastroesophageal reflux disease and its complications, including Barrett's esophagus, and adenocarcinoma of the esophagus or gastric cardia.

major reason is that a much higher proportion of gastric ulcers are due to NSAID or aspirin use. When such use is excluded, most of the remaining patients with benign gastric ulcers are colonized with *H. pylori,* which is significantly more common than in age-matched controls.[82] The results of treatment of gastric ulceration with antimicrobial agents parallel the results of treatment of duodenal ulceration.[109]

Gastric Carcinoma

Because *H. pylori* colonization induces a tissue response (termed "chronic gastritis") and because "chronic gastritis" is well known as a risk factor for the development of gastric carcinoma,[110] a role of this organism in carcinogenesis is possible. The decreasing incidence of gastric carcinoma in developed countries is consistent with the later age and decreasing frequency of acquiring *H. pylori* infection as industrialization has proceeded.[111, 112] The epidemiologic characteristics of *H. pylori* colonization, including increasing prevalence at an older age, higher prevalence in blacks, Hispanics, and Asians, association with lower socioeconomic status, and early-life crowding, are all similar to the characteristics associated with gastric cancer.[31] In addition, the development of intestinal metaplasia and atrophic gastritis, two pathologic entities that are risk factors for gastric cancer, is associated with *H. pylori* colonization.[113, 114] Thus, a direct role of this organism in gastric cancer is biologically plausible, and countries with high *H. pylori* prevalence rates have high gastric cancer rates.[115, 116] Prospective studies of gastric cancer conducted in Hawaii, California, and England[86–88] and several retrospective studies each indicate that *H. pylori* is a risk factor for gastric cancer.[117] This association involves adenocarcinoma of the antrum and body of the stomach of both the intestinal and diffuse histologic types.[86–88] Odds ratios range from about 2.7 to 12, and the risk of gastric cancer attributable to *H. pylori* infection is about 60 to 80%.[87, 88, 116] The presumed mechanism for adenocarcinoma involves the chronicity of *H. pylori*–induced tissue responses (inflammation), with progression to atrophic and subsequently metaplastic histology as important pathogenetic steps.[110] However, this process probably requires decades on average, and *H. pylori* colonization is neither necessary nor sufficient for oncogenesis. No positive association has been observed with cancers at the cardia,[86–88] and preliminary data suggest that *H. pylori* carriage may have a positive effect.[93] Further understanding of the role of *H. pylori* in carcinogenesis could lead to reevaluation of the clinical approach to asymptomatic colonization. Definition of additional host and bacterial factors that increase the risk of cancer development (or protection, see later) is an important research priority.

Reflecting the decline in *H. pylori* acquisition in developed countries, the incidence of adenocarcinomas of the gastric antrum and body has fallen. In contrast, the incidence of adenocarcinoma of the gastric cardia (and lower portion of the esophagus) has risen dramatically. This temporal relationship suggests that *H. pylori* loss may play a role in the rise of these cancers, and preliminary evidence supports this hypothesis.[4]

Gastric Lymphoma

Most gastric lymphomas arise from B lymphocytes and are termed mucosa-associated lymphoid tumors (MALToma). *H. pylori* colonization is strongly associated with these tumors,[89, 90] and recent work suggests that eradication of *H. pylori* may lead to improvement in tumor histology.[118] Whether *H. pylori* eradication improves these true malignancies, which are rare in contrast to more benign monoclonal proliferation, is unknown. The pathogenesis of these disorders may involve chronic antigenic stimulation by *H. pylori* and subsequent induction of a polyclonal lymphoid response, a single clone of which proliferates and then undergoes neoplastic transformation.

Esophageal Diseases

Much evidence has accumulated that the incidence of *H. pylori* colonization has been progressively diminishing in developed countries during the 20th century.[112] During this time, three related diseases—gastroesophageal reflux disease (GERD), Barrett's esophagus, and adenocarcinoma of the esophagus—have been rising dramatically. It is generally believed that Barrett's esophagus will develop in a proportion of patients with GERD and that adenocarcinoma will develop in some of these patients. An extremely important question is whether the loss of *H. pylori* from populations in developed countries may in some way predispose to this pathogenetic sequence. Although data are preliminary, *cagA*$^{+}$ *H. pylori* strains appear to have an inverse association with Barrett's esophagus and esophageal adenocarcinomas.[92, 93] Similarly, eradication of *H.*

pylori in patients with duodenal ulceration doubled the rate of GERD development,[108] and patients with GERD are less likely to be colonized with *H. pylori* than are controls.[91] Research is ongoing in this area, but if these observations are confirmed, they will substantially alter clinical approaches to *H. pylori.*

DIAGNOSIS

Ascertainment of *H. pylori* colonization can be made either invasively by endoscopy and biopsy or noninvasively by serologic analysis or the breath test. Properly done, each of these methodologies has diagnostic accuracy exceeding 95%; each has advantages and disadvantages (Table 205–3).

Endoscopy with biopsy involves the most expense and invasion of the patient, but it may be used to yield a great deal of information.[120] Biopsy specimens may be cultured for *H. pylori* on antibiotic-containing media (to diminish overgrowth by any competing flora) such as Skirrow's medium, as well as with a nonselective medium such as chocolate agar.[120] Use of two media increases the yield. Plates should be incubated for 2 to 5 days at 35°C to 37°C in a moist microaerobic atmosphere (with 5% oxygen). Comma- or S-shaped motile organisms with catalase, oxidase, and urease activity may be identified as *H. pylori.*[120] Culture enables a determination of antimicrobial susceptibilities, which may be increasingly important as the indications for treatment broaden. Alternatively, the organisms may be visualized on histologic sections prepared with Gram, silver, Giemsa, or acridine orange stains or by immunofluorescence or immunoperoxidase methods.[120] DNA probe and polymerase chain reaction methodologies have been developed as well, but they have no current clinical justification unless genotyping of strains becomes clinically important.[120] For rapid detection of *H. pylori,* biopsy samples may be incubated at 37°C to examine for preformed urease activity.[121] After incubation for 1 hour, the assay has a sensitivity of about 60% and, by 24 hours, greater than 90%; bacterial overgrowth of the stomach may reduce the test's specificity, especially for longer incubations[120] and in older patients. Endoscopy also permits assessment of structural lesions such as ulcers, masses, and strictures.

High-titer, stable serum IgG responses and, less frequently, IgA responses nearly universally develop in *H. pylori*–colonized persons.[38, 120, 121] Because serology in essence samples the entire stomach whereas biopsy only samples a small region and the inflammatory process may be patchy, serologic analysis may be more sensitive than diagnostic methods involving biopsies.[122] With successful antimicrobial therapy, antibody levels decline, although 3 to 6 months may be required for a noticeable effect; after ineffective therapy, high antibody levels persist.[122, 123] Soon after the initial acquisition of *H. pylori,* IgM seroconversion is noted, but levels return to baseline; with recurrence after inadequate therapy, IgM seroconversion may again be observed.[96] A number of testing services and kits are now commercially available that allow physicians to detect *H. pylori* in individual patients. The serologic assays have generally been standardized for adults, and thus interpretation of results in children requires caution.[124]

The high urease activity of *H. pylori* has also facilitated the development of urease breath tests. Subjects fast and are then given a meal containing ^{13}C- or ^{14}C-urea; over the next hour, their breath is correspondingly examined for $^{13}CO_2$ or $^{14}CO_2$.[125, 126] Results of these assays correlate with numbers of urease-producing *H. pylori* organisms and can be falsely negative after therapy that suppresses but does not eradicate the organism. However, negativity 1 to 3 months after therapy has ceased usually indicates eradication of the organism. Urea breath testing services are also now commercially available.

TREATMENT

Indications

At present, several indications have emerged for considering therapy directed against *H. pylori.* For patients with peptic ulceration who are colonized with *H. pylori,* antimicrobial therapies that eradicate *H. pylori* are associated with substantially lower ulcer recurrence rates than are short-course therapies directed exclusively against gastric acidity.[105, 106] Thus, antimicrobial therapy is now one of the primary therapies for most cases of duodenal ulceration.[107] Gastric ulcers associated with *H. pylori* infection can be treated in the same manner as for duodenal ulceration.[109] In patients with gastric MALTomas, antimicrobial therapy directed against *H. pylori* appears to cause tumor regression in most patients.[118, 119] For most cases of *H. pylori*–associated nonulcer dysplasia, data concerning the efficacy of antimicrobial therapy are not clear cut.[99–101] Treatment is not recommended in asymptomatic persons who are *H. pylori* positive; a possible exception would be a patient with a strong family history of gastric cancer.

Therapies

Virtually all *H. pylori* isolates are susceptible in vitro to a variety of antimicrobial agents, including bismuth salts, amoxicillin, macro-

TABLE 205–3 Modalities for *Helicobacter pylori* Diagnosis

Modality	Advantages	Disadvantages
Endoscopy with biopsy	Permits inspection of pathology, allows detection of ulcers, neoplasms	Invasive, expensive, time consuming
Culture	Permits determination of antimicrobial susceptibilities and pathogenic features of isolates	Not optimally sensitive in most laboratories. Requires several days for results
Histology	Generally more sensitive than culture. Allows direct visualization of organism and extent and nature of tissue involvement	Gastritis may be patchy and biopsy may be performed on wrong area. Insensitivity to detect small numbers of organisms. Requires several days for results
Urease detection	Rapid; most positives seen within 2 h	Increased sensitivity requires longer incubation. May be false positives with bacterial overgrowth
Serology	Noninvasive, rapid, quantitative, inexpensive	No determination of lesions or pathology, no antimicrobial susceptibility. Not rapidly responsive to therapy
Urea breath tests	Relatively noninvasive, relatively rapid, quantitative, rapidly responsive to therapy. Most valuable for assessing response to eradication therapy after 4–8 wk	Involves expensive instrumentation or administration of radioisotopes. More invasive and less convenient than serology. No determination of lesions or pathology, no antimicrobial susceptibility

lides, nitrofurans, tetracyclines, and aminoglycosides.[120, 127, 128] However, in vitro susceptibility is no guarantee of in vivo effectiveness. Primary resistance to imidazoles (such as metronidazole and tinidazole) occurs in 20 to 40% of isolates[128, 129] and is most common in young women, who may have received this agent for gynecologic infections, or in persons from developing countries treated for parasitic infection. However, primary resistance is present in isolates from both men and women in all age groups[130] and is associated with prior exposure to a nitroimidazole, even decades earlier.[131] Primary resistance to macrolides is less common, but increasing.[128]

Several principles of chemotherapy have emerged. First, treatment with a single agent has not yet resulted in apparent eradication of organisms in more than a minority of cases. As a result, all current treatments use combination therapy.[132] Second, certain agents that are effective in vitro may be ineffective in vivo even in combination with other agents. Erythromycin is a good example of this phenomenon.[133] The ineffectiveness of many antibiotics at an acidic pH may be responsible for the lack of activity in vivo. Third, acquired resistance frequently develops after therapy with certain agents but not others. To date, no confirmed resistance to bismuth salts and tetracycline has been reported. In contrast, acquired resistance to quinolones is so frequent that it appears to preclude their use. Secondary resistance to imidazoles occurs in 10 to 30% of cases, even when used in combination with other agents.[134] The development of resistance to macrolides and rifampin has also been reported. Fourth, to determine true eradication of the organism and not just temporary suppression, the patient must be shown to be free of the organism at least 1 month after the cessation of therapy if biopsy or the breath test is used and at least 6 months if serologic examination is used. Better definition of these end points is currently under investigation.

Combination therapy with a bismuth salt and two antibiotics has been widely used. Bismuth salts appear to be particularly useful against slowly growing bacteria.[135] Although bismuth salts vary in their particular minimal inhibitory concentrations toward *H. pylori* and in their pharmacokinetics, the levels achieved in the gastric lumen after oral administration are so high that no difference among the salts is apparent. "Triple therapy" with bismuth salts, metronidazole, and amoxicillin has resulted in eradication rates of 60 to 90%. Tetracycline appears to be at least as beneficial as amoxicillin.[105, 134] Both poor patient compliance[136] and primary and secondary resistance to metronidazole appear to be important factors limiting eradication. The optimal therapeutic regimen has not been defined. One regimen that can be considered is bismuth subsalicylate tablets (available in the United States as Pepto-Bismol), 1 to 2 tablets orally four times daily, tetracycline, 500 mg orally four times daily, and metronidazole, 250 mg orally three times daily for 14 days. In studies of patients with duodenal ulceration, such therapies reduced 1-year recurrence rates from 80% to under 30%.[103–105] For ulcer healing, several excellent regimens have been described in which an acid-suppressing agent is used for 4 to 6 weeks and antimicrobial therapy for the first 10 to 14 days. One standard is ranitidine plus triple therapy[105]; similarly, ranitidine bismuth citrate plus two antibiotics is also highly effective. No evidence has shown any one H_2 antagonist to be superior to the others. Other useful therapies include proton pump inhibitors (PPIs) such as omeprazole or lansoprazole. These agents are directly inhibitory to *H. pylori*[137] and appear to be potent urease inhibitors,[138] in contrast to H_2 receptor antagonists, and are also more effective at inducing pH neutrality, which may permit better antimicrobial efficacy. One week of twice-daily therapy[139] with a PPI plus amoxicillin and clarithromycin or the combination of a PPI, amoxicillin, and metronidazole is also highly effective. Quadruple therapy with a PPI (for 10 days) and bismuth-based triple therapy (for days 4 to 10) appears to be most effective.[140] Physicians must balance the use of these particular regimens with possible adverse consequences, which include medication-induced upper gastrointestinal symptoms and uncommon complications such as antibiotic-associated colitis and candidiasis. Determination of optimal therapy must await head-to-head clinical trials.

In patients in whom *H. pylori* is again isolated after therapy, the organisms are usually identical to the initial isolates, thus indicating that recurrence reflects relapse rather than the acquisition of a new agent. When imidazoles are used and fail, virtually all the recurrent organisms are resistant. After treatment failure, a second course of triple therapy (containing metronidazole) may nevertheless be effective; alternatively, a regimen not including imidazoles may be used.

OTHER GASTRIC HELICOBACTERS

In addition to *H. pylori,* other spiral organisms may occasionally be present in the human stomach. The predominant organisms, originally called "*Gastrospirillum hominis,*" are spirochetal in morphology and are also strongly urease positive.[141–143] Taxonomic study based on rRNA homologies indicates that this organism is a member of the genus *Helicobacter* and the name *H. heilmanii* has been used.[144] *H. heilmanii* is much less commonly observed in the gastric mucosa than *H. pylori* is and occurs in perhaps 1% of persons.[143] Unlike *H. pylori,* this organism has not been cultivated in vitro, which limits studies of its clinical role. However, these 0.5- to 1.0-μm by 4- to 8-μm spirochetes are easily visualized in specimens from colonized persons. Both *H. pylori* and *H. heilmanii* may be present in the same person. In monkeys, these organisms appear to not be pathogens, and their role in humans is uncertain.

REFERENCES

1. Marshall BJ. History of the discovery of *Campylobacter pylori.* In: Blaser MJ, ed. *Campylobacter pylori* in Gastritis and Peptic Ulcer Disease. New York: Igaku Shoin; 1989:7–23.
2. Hazell SL, Lee A, Brady L, et al. *Campylobacter pyloridis* and gastritis: Association with intracellular spaces and adaptation to an environment of mucus as important factors in colonization of the gastric epithelium. J Infect Dis. 1986;153:658–663.
3. Paull G, Yardley JH. Pathology of *pylori*-associated gastric and esophageal lesions. In: Blaser MJ, ed. *Campylobacter pylori* in Gastritis and Peptic Ulcer Disease. New York: Igaku Shoin; 1989:73–98.
4. Blaser MJ. Science, medicine, and the future: *Helicobacter pylori* and gastric diseases. BMJ. 1998;316:1507–1510.
5. Marshall BJ, Warren JR. Unidentified curved bacilli in the stomach of patients with gastritis and peptic ulceration. Lancet. 1984;1:1311–1313.
6. Goodwin CS, Armstrong JA, Chilvers T, et al. Transfer of *Campylobacter pylori* and *Campylobacter mustelae* to *Helicobacter* gen. nov. as *Helicobacter pylori* comb. nov. and *Helicobacter mustelae* comb. nov., respectively. Int J Syst Bacteriol. 1989;39:397–405.
7. Paster BJ, Lee A, Fox JG, et al. Phylogeny of *Helicobacter felis* sp. nov, *Helicobacter mustelae,* and related bacteria. Int J Syst Bacteriol. 1991;41:31–38.
8. Eaton KA, Dewhirst FE, Radin MJ, et al. *Helicobacter acinonyx* sp. nov., isolated from cheetahs with gastritis. Int J Syst Bacteriol. 1993;43:99–106.
9. Fox JG, Dewhirst FE, Tully JG, et al. *Helicobacter hepaticus* sp nov, a microaerophilic bacterium isolated from livers and intestinal mucosal scrapings from mice. J Clin Microbiol. 1994;32:1238–1245.
10. Fox JG, Drolet R, Higgins R, et al. *Helicobacter canis* isolated from a dog liver with multifocal necrotizing hepatitis. J Clin Microbiol. 1996;34:2479–2482.
11. Fox JG, Dewhirst FE, Shen Z, et al. Hepatic *Helicobacter* species identified in bile and gallbladder tissue from Chileans with chronic cholecystitis. Gastroenterology. 1998;114:755–763.
12. Blaser MJ. Helicobacters and biliary tract disease. Gastroenterology. 1998;114:840–842.
13. Dunn BE, Campbell GP, Pérez-Pérez GI, et al. Purification and characterization of *Helicobacter pylori* urease. J Biol Chem. 1990;265:9464–9469.
14. Labigne A, Cussac V, Courcoux P. Shuttle cloning and nucleotide sequences of *Helicobacter pylori* genes responsible for urease activity. J Bacteriol. 1991;173:1920–1931.
15. Cussac V, Ferrero RL, Labigne A. Expression of *Helicobacter pylori* urease genes in *Escherichia coli* grown under nitrogen-limiting conditions. J Bacteriol. 1992;174:2466–2473.
16. Tomb J-F, White O, Kerlavage AR, et al. The complete genome sequence of the gastric pathogen *Helicobacter pylori.* Nature. 1997;388:539–547.
17. Go MF, Kapur V, Graham DY, Musser JM. Population genetic analysis of *Helicobacter pylori* by multilocus enzyme electrophoresis: Extensive allelic diversity and recombinational population structure. J Bacteriol. 1996;178:3934–3938.
18. Langenberg W, Rauws EAJ, Widjojokusumo A, et al. Identification of *Campylo-*

bacter pyloridis isolates by restriction endonuclease DNA analysis. J Clin Microbiol. 1986;24:414–417.
19. Akopyanz N, Bukanov NO, Westblom TU, et al. DNA diversity among clinical isolates of *Helicobacter pylori* detected by PCR-based RAPD fingerprinting. Nucleic Acids Res. 1992;20:5137–5142.
20. Ng EKW, Thompson SA, Pérez-Pérez GI, et al. Difference in amino acid sequence of heat-shock protein A of *H. pylori* in Chinese patients and its correlation to serological responses (Abstract). Gut. 1997;41(Suppl):S64.
21. Shames B, Krajden S, Fuksa M, et al. Evidence for the occurrence of the same strain of *Campylobacter pylori* in the stomach and dental plaque. J Clin Microbiol. 1989;27:2849–2850.
22. Censini S, Lange C, Xiang J, et al. *cag,* a pathogenicity island of *Helicobacter pylori* encodes type I–specific and disease-associated virulence factors. Proc Natl Acad Sci U S A. 1996;93:14648–14653.
23. Akopyanz NS, Clifton SW, Kersulyte D, et al. Analyses of the *cag* pathogenicity island of *Helicobacter pylori.* Mol Microbiol. 1998;28:37–53.
24. Tummuru MKR, Sharma SA, Blaser MJ. *Helicobacter pylori picB,* a homologue of the *Bordetella pertussis* toxin secretion protein, is required for induction of IL-8 in gastric epithelial cells. Mol Microbiol. 1995;18:867–876.
25. Pérez-Pérez GI, Bhat N, Gaensbauer J, et al. Country-specific constancy by age in *cagA*$^{+}$ proportion of *Helicobacter pylori* infections. Int J Cancer. 1997;72:453–456.
26. Cover TL. The vacuolating cytotoxin of *Helicobacter pylori.* Mol Microbiol. 1996;20:241–246.
27. Atherton J, Cao P, Peek RM, et al. Mosaicism in vacuolating cytotoxin alleles of *Helicobacter pylori:* Association of specific *vacA* types with cytotoxin production and peptic ulceration. J Biol Chem. 1995;270:1771–1777.
28. van Doorn L-J, Figueiredo C, Sanna R, et al. Expanding allelic diversity of *Helicobacter pylori vacA.* J Clin Microbiol. 1998;36:2597–2603.
29. Peek RM Jr, Thompson SA, Donahue JP, et al. Adherence to gastric epithelial cells induces expression of a *Helicobacter pylori* gene, *iceA,* that is associated with clinical outcome. Proc Assoc Am Physicians. 1998;110:531–544.
30. van Doorn L-J, Figueirdo C, Samnna R, et al. Clinical relevance of the *cagA, vacA,* and *iceA* status of *Helicobacter pylori.* Gastroenterology. 1998;115:58–66.
31. Taylor DN, Blaser MJ. The epidemiology of *Helicobacter pylori* infections. Epidemiol Rev. 1991;13:42–59.
32. Graham DY, Alpert LC, Smith JL, et al. Iatrogenic *Campylobacter pylori* infection is a cause of epidemic achlorhydria. Am J Gastroenterol. 1988;83:974–980.
33. Thomas JE, Gibson GR, Darboe MK, et al. Isolation of *Helicobacter pylori* from human faeces. Lancet. 1992;340:1194–1195.
34. Pérez-Pérez GI, Bodhidatta L, Wongsrichanalai J, et al. Seroprevalence of *Helicobacter pylori* infections in Thailand. J Infect Dis. 1990;161:1237–1241.
35. Polish LB, Douglas JM, Davidson AJ, et al. Characterization of risk factors for *Helicobacter pylori* infection among men attending an STD clinic: Lack of evidence for sexual transmission. J Clin Microbiol. 1991;29:2139–2143.
36. Drumm B, Pérez-Pérez GI, Blaser MJ, et al. Intrafamilial clustering of *Helicobacter pylori* infection. N Engl J Med. 1990;322:359–363.
37. Dooley CP, Fitzgibbons PL, Cohen H, et al. Prevalence of *Helicobacter pylori* infection and histologic gastritis in asymptomatic persons. N Engl J Med. 1989;321:1562–1566.
38. Pérez-Pérez GI, Dworkin B, Chodos J, et al. *Campylobacter pylori*–specific serum antibodies in humans. Ann Intern Med. 1988;109:11–17.
39. Graham DY, Malaty HM, Evans DG, et al. Epidemiology of *Helicobacter pylori* in an asymptomatic population in the United States: Effect of age, race and socioeconomic status. Gastroenterology. 1991:100:1495–1501.
40. Hopkins RJ, Russell RG, O'Donnoghue M, et al. Seroprevalence of *Helicobacter pylori* in Seventh-Day Adventists and other groups in Maryland. Lack of association with diet. Arch Intern Med. 1990;150:2347–2348.
41. Dehesa M. Dooley CP, Cohen HA, et al. High prevalence of *Helicobacter pylori* in an asymptomatic hispanic population. J Clin Microbiol. 1991;29:1128–1131.
42. Parsonnet J, Blaser MJ, Pérez-Pérez GI, et al. Symptoms and risk factors of *Helicobacter pylori* infection in a cohort of epidemiologists. Gastroenterology. 1992;102:41–46.
43. Lambert JR, Lin SK, Nicholson I, et al. Seroepidemiological study of *Helicobacter pylori* antibodies in institutionalized adults. Rev Esp Enferm Dig. 1990;78(Suppl):S41–S42.
44. Mitchell HM, Li YY, Hu PJ, et al. Epidemiology of *Helicobacter pylori* in southern China: Identification of early childhood as the critical period for acquisition. J Infect Dis. 1992;166:149–153.
45. Banatvala N, Mayo K, Megraud F, et al. The cohort effect and *Helicobacter pylori.* J Infect Dis. 1993;168:219–221.
46. Mendall MA, Googin PM, Molineaux N, et al. Childhood living conditions and *Helicobacter pylori* seropositivity in adult life. Lancet. 1992;339:896.
47. Sitas F, Forman D, Yarnell JWG, et al. *Helicobacter pylori* infection rates in relation to age and social class in a Welsh male population. Gut. 1941;32:25–28.
48. Blaser MJ. *Helicobacter pylori:* Microbiology of a "slow" bacterial infection. Trends Microbiol. 1993;1:255–260.
49. Pérez-Pérez GI, Olivares AZ, Cover TL, et al. Characteristics of *Helicobacter pylori* variants selected for urease deficiency. Infect Immun. 1992;60:3658–3663.
50. Eaton KA, Morgan DR, Krakowka S. *Campylobacter pylori* virulence factors in gnotobiotic piglets. Infect Immun. 1989;57:1119–1125.
51. Smoot DT, Resau JH, Naab T, et al. Adherence of *Helicobacter pylori* to cultured human gastric epithelial cells. Infect Immun. 1993;61:350–355.
52. Evans DG, Evans DJ, Moulds JJ, et al. *N*-acetylneuraminyllactose-binding fibrillar hemagglutinin of *Campylobacter pylori:* A putative colonization factor antigen. Infect Immun. 1988;56:2896–2906.
53. Fauchere JL, Blaser MJ. Adherence of *Helicobacter pylori* cells and superficial components to HeLa cell membranes. Microbiol Pathog. 1990;9:427–439.
54. Morris A, Maher K, Thomsen L, et al. Distribution of *Campylobacter pylori* in the human stomach obtained at postmortem. Scand J Gastroenterol. 1988;23:257–264.
55. Price AB. Histological aspects of *Campylobacter pylori* colonization and infection of gastric and duodenal mucosa. Scand J Gastroenterol. 1988;23:21–24.
56. Gilman RJ, Leon-Barua R, Koch J, et al. Rapid identification of pylori campylobacter in Peruvians with gastritis. Dig Dis Sci. 1986;31:1089–1094.
57. Suzuki M, Miura S, Suematsu M, et al. *Helicobacter pylori*–associated ammonia production enhances neutrophil-dependent gastric mucosal cell injury. Am J Physiol. 1992;263:G719–G725.
58. Leunk RD, Johnson PT, David BC, et al. Cytotoxic activity in broth culture filtrates of *Campylobacter pylori.* J Med Microbiol. 1988;26:93–97.
59. Cover TC, Cao P, Murthy UK, et al. Serum neutralizing antibody response to the vacuolating cytotoxin of *Helicobacter pylori.* J Clin Invest. 1992;90:913–918.
60. Figura N, Guglielmetti P, Rossolini A, et al. Cytotoxin production by *Campylobacter pylori* strains isolated from patients with peptic ulcers and from patients with chronic gastritis only. J Clin Microbiol. 1989;27:225–226.
61. Mai UE, Pérez-Pérez GI, Allen JB, et al. Surface proteins from *Helicobacter pylori* exhibit chemotactic activity for human leukocytes and are present in gastric mucosa. J Exp Med. 1992;175:517–525.
62. Mai UEH. Pérez-Pérez GI, Wahl LM, et al. Soluble surface proteins from *Helicobacter pylori* activate monocytes/macrophages by lipopolysaccharide-independent mechanism. J Clin Invest. 1991;87:894–900.
63. Pérez-Pérez GI, Shepherd VL, Morrow JD, Blaser MJ. Activation of human THP-1 and rat bone marrow–derived macrophages by *Helicobacter pylori* lipopolysaccharide. Infect Immun. 1995;63:1183–1187.
64. Aspinall GO, Monteiro MA, Pang H, et al. Lipopolysaccharide of the *Helicobacter pylori* type strain NCTC 11637 (ATCC 43504): Structure of the O antigen and core oligosaccharide regions. Biochemistry. 1996;35:2489–2497.
65. Wirth HP, Yang M, Peek RM, et al. *Helicobacter pylori* Lewis expression is related to the host Lewis phenotype. Gastroenterology. 1997;113:1091–1098.
66. Sharma SA, Tummuru MKR, Miller GG, Blaser MJ. Interleukin-8 response of gastric epithelial cell lines to *Helicobacter pylori* stimulation in vitro. Infect Immun. 1995;63:1681–1687.
67. Blaser MJ. Ecology of *Helicobacter pylori* in the human stomach. J Clin Invest. 1997;100:759–762.
68. Crabtree JE, Shallcross T, Wyatt JI, et al. Tumour necrosis factor alpha secretion by *Helicobacter pylori* colonized gastric mucosa. Gut. 1991;32:1473–1477.
69. Blaser MJ. Hypotheses on the pathogenesis and natural history of *Helicobacter pylori*–induced inflammation. Gastroenterology. 1992;102:720–727.
70. Covacci A, Censini S, Bugnoli M, et al. Molecular characterization of the 128 kDa immunodominant antigen of *Helicobacter pylori* associated with cytotoxicity and duodenal ulcer. Proc Natl Acad Sci U S A. 1993;90:5791–5795.
71. Tummuru MKR, Cover TL, Blaser MJ. Cloning and expression of a high molecular weight major antigen of *Helicobacter pylori:* Evidence of linkage to cytotoxin production. Infect Immun. 1993;61:1799–1809.
72. Blaser MJ, Crabtree JE. CagA and the outcome of *Helicobacter pylori* infection. Am J Clin Pathol. 1996;106:565–567.
73. Smith JTL, Pounder RF, Nwokolo CU, et al. Inappropriate hypergastrinaemia in asymptomatic healthy subjects with *Helicobacter pylori.* Gut. 1990;31:522–525.
74. McColl KEL, Fullarton GM, Nujumi AM, et al. Lowered gastrin and gastric activity after eradication of *Campylobacter pylori* in duodenal ulcer. Lancet. 1989;2:499–500.
75. Cave DR, Vargas M. Effect of a *Campylobacter pylori* protein on acid secretion by parietal cells. Lancet. 1989;2:187–189.
76. Karttunen R. Blood lymphocyte proliferation, cytokine secretion and appearance of T cells with activation surface markers in cultures with *Helicobacter pylori.* Comparison of the responses of subjects with and without antibodies to *H. pylori.* Clin Exp Immunol. 1991;83:396–400.
77. Hazell SL, Eichberg JW, Lee DR, et al. Selection of the chimpanzee over the baboon as a model for *Helicobacter pylori* infection. Gastroenterology. 1992;103:848–854.
78. Marchetti M, Arico B, Burroni D, et al. Development of a mouse model of *Helicobacter pylori* infection that mimics human disease. Science. 1995;267:1655–1658.
79. Wirth H-P, Beins MH, Yang M, et al. Experimental infection of Mongolian gerbils with wild-type and mutant *Helicobacter pylori* strains. Infect Immun. 1998;66:4856–4866.
80. Fong T-L, Dooley CP, Dehesa M, et al. *Helicobacter pylori* infection in pernicious anemia: A prospective controlled study. Gastroenterology. 1991;100:328–332.
81. Inglehart LW, Edlow DW, Mills L, et al. The presence of *Campylobacter pylori* in nonsteroidal antiinflammatory drug associated gastritis. J Rheumatol. 1989;16:599–603.
82. Blaser MJ, Pérez-Pérez GI, Lindenbaum J, et al. Association of infection due to *Helicobacter pylori* with specific upper gastrointestinal pathology. Rev Infect Dis. 1991;13:(Suppl)S704–S708.
83. Nomura A, Stemmerman GN, Chyou PH, et al. *Helicobacter pylori* infection and the risk for duodenal and gastric ulceration. Ann Intern Med. 1994;120:977–981.
84. Johnston BJ, Reed PI, Ali MH. *Campylobacter*-like organisms in duodenal and antral endoscopic biopsies: Relationship to inflammation. Gut. 1986;27:1132–1137.
85. Carrick J, Lee A, Hazell S, et al. *Campylobacter pylori,* duodenal ulcer and gastric metaplasia: Possible role of functional heterotrophic tissue in ulcerogenesis. Gut. 1989;30:790–797.
86. Forman D, Newell DG, Fullerton F, et al. Association between infection with

Helicobacter pylori and risk of gastric cancer: Evidence from a prospective investigation. BMJ. 1991;302:1302–1305.
87. Nomura A, Stemmerman GN, Chyou P-H, et al. *Helicobacter pylori* infection and gastric carcinoma in a population of Japanese-Americans in Hawaii. N Engl J Med. 1991;325:1132–1136.
88. Parsonnet J, Friedman GD, Vandersteen DP, et al. *Helicobacter pylori* infection and the risk of gastric carcinoma. N Engl J Med. 1991;325:1127–1131.
89. Parsonnet J, Hansen S, Rodriguez L, et al. *Helicobacter pylori* infection and gastric lymphoma. N Engl J Med. 1994;330:1267–1271.
90. Wotherspoon AC, Ortiz Hidalgo C, Falzon MR, et al. *Helicobacter pylori*–associated gastritis and primary B-cell gastric lymphoma. Lancet. 1991;338:1175–1176.
91. Werdmuller BFM, Loffeld RJLF. *Helicobacter pylori* infection has no role in the pathogenesis of reflux esophagitis. Dig Dis Sci. 1997;42:103–105.
92. Vicari JJ, Peek RM, Falk GW, et al. The seroprevalence of *cagA* positive *Helicobacter pylori* strains in the spectrum of gastroesophageal reflux disease. Gastroenterology. 1998;115:50–57.
93. Chow W-H, Blaser MJ, Blot WJ, et al. An inverse relation between *cagA*$^+$ strains of *Helicobacter pylori* infection and risk of esophageal and gastric cardia adenocarcinoma. Cancer Res. 1998;58:588–590.
94. Morris A, Nicholson G. Experimental and accidental *C. pylori* infection of humans. In: Blaser MJ, ed. *Campylobacter pylori* in Gastritis and Peptic Ulcer Disease. New York: Igaku Shoin; 1989:61–72.
95. Ramsey EJ, Carey KV, Peterson WL, et al. Epidemic gastritis with hypochlorhydria. Gastroenterology. 1979;76:1449–1457.
96. Morris AJ, Ali MR. Nicholson GI, et al. Long term follow-up of voluntary ingestion of *Helicobacter pylori.* Ann Intern Med. 1991;114:662–663.
97. Shallcross TM, Rathbone BJ, Heatley RV. *Campylobacter pylori* and non-ulcer dyspepsia. In: Rathbone BJ, Heatley RV, eds. *Campylobacter pylori* and Gastroduodenal Disease. Oxford: Blackwell; 1989:155–166.
98. McColl KEL, Murray LS, El-Omar E, et al. U.K. MRC trial of *H. pylori* eradication therapy for non-ulcer dyspepsia (Abstract). Gastroenterology. 1998;114:222.
99. Rokkas T, Pursey C, Uzoochina F, et al. Non-ulcer dyspepsia and short-term De-Nol therapy: A placebo-controlled trial with particular reference to the role of *Campylobacter pylori.* Gut. 1988;29:1386–1391.
100. Kang JY, Tay HH, Wee A, et al. Effect of colloidal bismuth subcitrate on symptoms and gastric histology in non-ulcer dyspepsia. A double blind placebo controlled study. Gut. 1990;31:476–480.
101. Talley NJ, Janssens J, Lauritsen K, et al. Long-term follow-up of patients with non-ulcer dysepsia after *Helicobacter pylori* eradication. A randomized double-blind placebo-controlled trial (Abstract). Gastroenterology. 1998;114:305.
102. Wyatt JI, Rathbone BJ, Dixon MF, et al. *Campylobacter pyloridis* and acid-induced gastric metaplasia in the pathogenesis of duodenitis. J Clin Pathol. 1987;40:841–848.
103. Coghlan JG, Gilligan D, Humphreys H, et al. *Campylobacter pylori* and recurrence of duodenal ulcers—a 12-month follow-up study. Lancet. 1987;2:1109–1111.
104. Marshall BJ, Goodwin CS, Warren JR, et al. Prospective double-blind trial of duodenal ulcer relapse after eradication of *Campylobacter pylori.* Lancet. 1988;2:1437–1445.
105. Graham DY, Lew GM, Klein PD, et al. Effect of treatment of *Helicobacter pylori* infection on the long-term recurrence of gastric or duodenal ulcer: A randomized, controlled study. Ann Intern Med. 1992;116:705–708.
106. Hentschel E, Brandstatter G, Dragoisics B, et al. Effect of ranitidine and amoxicillin plus metronidazole on the eradication of *Helicobacter pylori* and the recurrence of duodenal ulcer. N Engl J Med. 1993;328:308–312.
107. NIH Consensus Conference. *Helicobacter pylori* in peptic ulcer disease. JAMA. 1994;272:65–69.
108. Labenz J, Blum AL, Bayerdörffer E, et al. Curing *Helicobacter pylori* infection in patients with duodenal ulcer may provoke reflux esophagitis. Gastroenterology. 1997;112:1442–1447.
109. Sung JJ, Chung SC, Ling TK, et al. Antibacterial treatment of gastric ulcers associated with *Helicobacter pylori.* N Engl J Med. 1995;332:139–142.
110. Correa P. Human gastric carcinogenesis: A multistep and multifactorial process—First American Cancer Society Award lecture on cancer epidemiology and prevention. Cancer Res. 1992;52:6735–6740.
111. Blaser MJ, Chyou PH, Nomura A. Age at establishment of *Helicobacter pylori* infection and gastric carcinoma, gastric ulcer, and duodenal ulcer risk. Cancer Res. 1995;55:562–565.
112. Parsonnet J. Incidence of *H. pylori* infection. Aliment Pharmacol Ther. 1995;9(Suppl 2):S45–S51.
113. Craanen ME, Dekker W, Blok P, et al. Intestinal metaplasia and *Helicobacter pylori:* An endoscopic bioptic study of the gastric antrum. Gut. 1992;33:16–20.
114. Kuipers EJ, Uyterlinde AM, Pena AS, et al. Long-term sequelae to *Helicobacter pylori* gastritis. Lancet. 1995;345:1525–1528.
115. Forman D, Sitas F, Newell DG, et al. Geographic association of *Helicobacter pylori* antibody prevalence and gastric cancer mortality in rural China. Int J Cancer. 1990;46:608–611.
116. The Eurogast Study Group. An international association between *Helicobacter pylori* infection and gastric cancer. Lancet. 1993;341:1359–1362.
117. International Agency for Research of Cancer. Monographs on the evaluation of carcinogenic risks to humans. Infection with 26.
118. Neubauer A, Thiede C, Morgner A, et al. Cure of *Helicobacter pylori* infection and duration of remission of low-grade gastric mucosa–associated lymphoid tissue lymphoma. J Natl Cancer Inst. 1997;89:1350–1353.
119. Pinotti G, Zucca E, Roggero E, et al. Clinical features, treatment and outcome in a series of 93 patients with low-grade gastric MALT lymphoma. Leuk Lymphoma. 1997;26:527–537.
120. Dunn BE, Cohen H, Blaser MJ. *Helicobacter pylori.* Clin Microbiol Rev. 1997;10:720–741.
121. Evans DJ Jr. Evans DG, Graham DY, et al. A sensitive and specific serologic test for detection of *Campylobacter pylori* infection. Gastroenterology. 1989;96:1004–1008.
122. Kosunen TU, Seppala K, Sarna S, et al. Diagnostic value of decreased IgG, IgA, and IgM antibody titres after eradication of *Helicobacter pylori.* Lancet. 1992;339:893.
123. Pérez-Pérez GI, Cutler AF, Blaser MJ. Value of serology as a non-invasive method to evaluate the efficacy of treatment in *Helicobacter pylori* infection. Clin Infect Dis. 1997;25:1038–1043.
124. Khanna B, Cutler A, Israel NR, et al. Use caution with serologic testing for *Helicobacter pylori* infection in children. J Infect Dis. 1998;178:460–465.
125. Graham DY, Evans DJ, Alpert LC, et al. *Campylobacter pylori* detected non-invasively by the ^{13}C-urea breath test. Lancet. 1987;1:1174–1177.
126. Marshall BJ, Surveyor I. Carbon-14 urea breath test for the diagnosis of *Campylobacter pyloridis*–associated gastritis. J Nucl Med. 1988;29:11–16.
127. Goodwin CS, Blake P, Blincow E. The minimum inhibitory and bactericidal concentrations of antibiotics and anti-ulcer agents against *Campylobacter pyloridis.* J Antimicrob Chemother. 1986;17:309–314.
128. Megraud F. Resistance of *Helicobacter pylori* to antibiotics. Aliment Pharmacol Ther. 1997;11:43–53.
129. Xia HX, Daw MA, Beattie S, et al. Prevalence of metronidazole-resistant *Helicobacter pylori* in dyspeptic patients. Ir J Med Sci. 1993;162:91–94.
130. Rautelin H, Seppala K, Renkonen OV, et al. Role of metronidazole resistance in therapy of *Helicobacter pylori* infections. Antimicrob Agents Chemother. 1992;36:163–166.
131. European Study Group on Antibiotic Susceptibility of *Helicobacter pylori.* Results of a multicentre European survey in 1991 of metronidazole in *Helicobacter pylori.* Eur J Clin Microbiol Infect Dis. 1992;11:777–781.
132. Pavicic MJ, Namavar F, Verboom T, et al. In vitro susceptibility of *Helicobacter pylori* to several antimicrobial combinations. Antimicrob Agents Chemother. 1993;37:1184–1186.
133. McNulty CAM, Gearty JC, Crump B, et al. *Campylobacter pyloridis* and associated gastritis: Investigator blind, placebo controlled trial of bismuth salicylate and erythromycin ethylsuccinate. BMJ. 1986;293:645–649.
134. Logan RPH, Gummett PA, Misiewicz JJ, et al. One week eradication regimen for *Helicobacter pylori.* Lancet. 1991;338:1249–1252.
135. Millar MR, Pike J. Bactericidal activity of antimicrobial agents against slowly growing *Helicobacter pylori.* Antimicrob Agents Chemother. 1992;36:185–187.
136. Graham DY, Lew GM, Malaty HM, et al. Factors influencing the eradication of *Helicobacter pylori* with triple therapy. Gastroenterology. 1992;102:493–496.
137. Iwahi T, Satoh H, Nakao M, et al. Lansoprazole, a novel benzimidazole proton pump inhibitor, and its related compounds have selective activity against *Helicobacter pylori.* Antimicrob Agents Chemother. 1991;35:490–496.
138. Nagata K, Satoh H, Iwahi T, et al. Potent inhibitory action of the gastric proton pump inhibitor lansoprazole against urease activity of *Helicobacter pylori:* Unique action selective for *H. pylori* cells. Antimicrob Agents Chemother. 1993;37:769–774.
139. Bazzoli F, Zagari RM, Fossi S, et al. Short-term low-dose triple therapy for the eradication of *Helicobacter pylori.* Eur J Gastroenterol Hepatol. 1994;6:773–777.
140. de Boer W, Driessen W, Jansz A, Tytgat G. Effect of acid suppression on efficacy of treatment for *Helicobacter pylori* infection. Lancet 1995;345:817–820.
141. Dent JC, McNulty CAM, Ulff JS, et al. Spiral organisms in the gastric antrum. Lancet. 1987;2:96.
142. McNulty CAM, Dent JC, Curry A, et al. New spiral bacterium in gastric mucosa. J Clin Pathol. 1989;42:585–591.
143. Heilmann KL, Borchard F. Gastritis due to spiral shaped bacteria other than *Helicobacter pylori:* Clinical, histological, and ultrastructural findings. Gut. 1991;32:137–140.
144. Solnick JV, O'Rourke J, Lee A, et al. An uncultured gastric spiral organism is a newly identified *Helicobacter* in humans. J Infect Dis. 1993;168:379–385.

Chapter 206

Enterobacteriaceae

BARRY I. EISENSTEIN
DORI F. ZALEZNIK

Enterobacteriaceae are a large, heterogeneous family of gram-negative bacteria that are both medically and scientifically important. *Escherichia coli*, the most prevalent infecting organism in this family, is one of the prototypic bacteria studied for its genome, genetic characteristics, and virulence properties. A number of genera within the family are major human intestinal pathogens (e.g., *Shigella*, *Salmonella*, *Yersinia*), and several are normal colonizers of the human gastrointestinal tract (e.g., *Escherichia*, *Enterobacter*, *Klebsiella*).[1–4] Enterobacteriaceae often are labeled as "enteric bacteria" because of their predilection for intestinal colonization; however, other gram-negative bacilli that are commonly found in the gastrointestinal tract such as some species of the families Pseudomonaceae and Vironaceae also share this designation. Thus, enteric bacteria and Enterobacteriaceae refer to partially overlapping rather than identical sets of organisms.

Taxonomy schemes employing DNA relatedness have augmented prior phenotype (i.e., biochemical, physiologic, and immunochemical) information.[3] The latest classification by Ewing is presented in Table 206–1.[4] Typical and distinguishing characteristics of this family are that they (1) are non–spore-forming aerobes capable of anaerobic growth (facultative anaerobes), (2) reduce nitrates to nitrites (with some exceptions), (3) do not liquefy alginate, (4) ferment glucose to acid with or without gas, (5) are oxidase-negative, (6) do not have growth enhancement by NaCl, and (7) can be either motile (with peritrichous flagella) or nonmotile.[1–4] Certain close relationships are apparent from the taxonomic scheme such as *Escherichia* and *Shigella*.

Yersinia, *Shigella*, and *Salmonella* are distinctive organisms, which are discussed in separate chapters. This chapter focuses on the important virulence traits and pathogenic features of this family of organisms and specific characteristics of the individual pathogenic genera.

TABLE 206–1 The Tribes and Genera of the Family Enterobacteriaceae That Are Associated with Human Disease

Tribe	Genera
Escherichieae	*Escherichia*
	Shigella
Edwardsielleae	*Edwardsiella*
Salmonelleae	*Salmonella*
Citrobactereae	*Citrobacter*
Klebsielleae	*Klebsiella*
	Enterobacter
	Hafnia
	Serratia
Protease	*Proteus*
	Morganella
	Providencia
Yersinieae	*Yersinia*
Erwinieae	*Erwinia*
Miscellaneous genera (not yet assigned to a tribe)	*Buttiauxella*
	Cedecea
	Ewingella
	Kluyvera
	Tatumella
	Rahnella
	Various "enteric groups" (not yet assigned to a genus)

GENERAL PROPERTIES

Epidemiology

Members of the family Enterobacteriaceae are widely distributed in the soil and on plants and are normal colonizers of the intestinal tracts of humans and animals. Although they are common constituents of normal gastrointestinal flora, it is important to remember that more than 99% of colonic flora is composed of anaerobes, most of which are members of the genus *Bacteroides*. Enterobacteriaceae, although not usually found as a component of normal flora outside of the gastrointestinal tract, are an important cause of infections elsewhere, particularly the genitourinary system. In hospitalized or immunocompromised individuals, especially patients receiving antimicrobial therapy, colonization with gram-negative bacilli, including Enterobacteriaceae, does occur. In these settings infection by these bacteria frequently ensues, often leading to pneumonia, septicemia, meningitis, or abscess formation.

These bacteria account for approximately 80% of significant isolates of gram-negative bacteria in the clinical laboratory.[2] It has been estimated that about one third of the septicemia isolates, two thirds of the bacterial gastroenteritis isolates, and three fourths of the urinary tract isolates are accounted for by the Enterobacteriaceae.[5, 6] Among nosocomial infections, isolates between 1990 and 1992 show for the first time a decrease in the percentage of gram-negative isolates from 52% between 1981 and 1983 to 29% between 1990 and 1992.[7] The previously observed trend toward a marked increase in blood stream isolates of gram-positive bacteria and fungi has continued.[7, 8] Among strains of Enterobacteriaceae recovered in nosocomial infections, there has also been a disturbing trend toward the recovery of more antimicrobial-resistant species: fewer *E. coli*, *Proteus mirabilis*, and *Klebsiella pneumoniae* and more *Enterobacter*.[5, 7]

Because of their important role in hospital outbreaks of infection, it is often necessary to determine whether a given isolate is the same as another recovered from a separate culture site. Such determinations frequently lead to the characterization of the mode of transmission or the point source of transmission, which in turn permits effective control measures. Bacterial spread from one site to another requires growth, DNA duplication, and asexual division. In the absence of major alterations in the genetic content, as with the acquisition of a new plasmid, bacterial offspring are genetically and therefore phenotypically identical to their progenitors. By definition, parent and progeny are "clonal." The evaluation of a number of phenotypic properties, such an antigenic structure and physiologic traits, has been shown to be quite useful in determining clonality and has led to the realization that there are fewer clones extant than would be predicted from all of the theoretic assortments of traits possible. A number of epidemiologic studies have determined that certain clones, identified by unique biochemical signatures, are associated with specific clinical settings (to be discussed later).[9, 11, 12]

As an alternative to phenotypic characterization, investigators have recently turned to genetic analyses to obviate the occasional problems with traits that are variably expressed. Among the simplest has been the use of plasmid analysis to "fingerprint" the isolate, which is useful as long as there has been a minimal amount of selective pressure in the environment, as with antibiotic use, to cause a gain, loss, or change in the plasmid profile.[13–16] Because of this genetic plasticity at the plasmid level, investigators have employed chromosomal analyses for tracking the most stable markers of identity.[17–21] In this regard, the use of restriction fragment length polymorphisms and multilocus enzyme electrophoresis may be most valuable.

Polymerase chain reaction is another useful tool for identifying these pathogens and performing epidemiologic studies. A newer multiplex polymerase chain reaction assay combining primers has been described for detection of different diarrheogenic *E. coli* including enterotoxigenic (ETEC) and enterohemorrhagic (EHEC) strains.[19a, 19b]

Structure

Enterobacteriaceae share with all bacteria numerous structural features such as a rigid cell envelope surrounding a cytoplasmic membrane, a single chromosome consisting of double-stranded DNA and located throughout the cytoplasm (unlike eukaryotes, there is no nucleus), ribosomes that are smaller and less complicated than are eukaryotic ribosomes, and the absence of mitochondria for oxidative metabolism or an endoplasmic reticulum for protein secretion. As gram-negative bacteria, their cell envelope is characterized by a multilamellar structure. The inner (or cytoplasmic) membrane consists of a phospholipid bilayer with interspersed proteins. The next outer layer consists of a thin (relative to gram-positive bacteria) peptidoglycan along with a periplasmic space. The peptidoglycan is an extensively cross-linked polymer that gives the organism its rigid shape. The complex outer membrane consists of another phospholipid bilayer with extensive intercalation of a number of elements, including lipopolysaccharide (LPS), lipoprotein (which is tethered to the peptidoglycan), multimeric porin proteins (whose membrane-spanning pores facilitate transport), and other outer membrane proteins.[24] Among these proteins are complex, outwardly radiating organelles: flagella, used for locomotion that arise from a basal structure located in the inner membrane; fimbriae (or common pili), important as adhesins, as discussed in Chapter 2; and sex pili, present in bacteria that contain conjugative plasmids and used by the bacteria to mediate conjugative transfer of plasmid DNA.

Antigenic Structure of the Bacterial Surface

One of the best-developed and earliest schemes for the classification of bacterial strains by their antigenic profiles is the use of anti-*Salmonella* sera to classify serotypes of *Salmonella*. Serotyping has been used extensively as well for *E. coli*. The major antigenic groups that react with these antisera are conserved in all species of Enterobacteriaceae.[4] The three classes of antigens are (1) the O antigens or somatic antigens, (2) the H or flagellar antigens, and (3) the K or capsular antigens (the VI antigens of some serotypes of *Salmonella* are subtypes of the capsular antigens).

The O antigens consist of the polysaccharide side chains of the envelope LPS found in all gram-negative bacteria.[25–28] Virulent strains of Enterobacteriaceae (i.e., isolates recovered as the causative agents of infection) typically have smooth LPS. This form of LPS consists of the core part of the LPS, which is linked to lipid A, as well as the repeating polysaccharide. Mutant strains can be recovered, typically after sequential laboratory passage, that no longer synthesize the polysaccharide side chains. Because these strains grow as rough-appearing colonies on laboratory agar, the LPS extracted from these strains has, by convention, been called "rough." These strains have lost their O antigens but may in the process unmask R antigens that are more weakly reactive as a consequence of the small degree of residual antigenicity from the remaining LPS. Gram-negative bacteria cannot survive without at least the core LPS. Unlike the other classes of antigens, the O antigens are absolutely heat stable. The classic reaction to demonstrate the presence of these antigens is agglutination with the type-specific antisera. The O antigenic types are widely shared among all the genera of the Enterobacteriaceae, but in some cases cross-reactivity is particularly pronounced.[4, 25] Thus, many of the *E. coli* O serogroups show significant cross-reactivity with members of *Shigella*. Cross-reactivity extends as well to members of *Salmonella*, *Citrobacter*, and *Klebsiella* and is occasionally seen beyond the Enterobacteriaceae.[29, 30] For instance, some *E. coli* O antigens cross react with *Vibrio*, with some human blood groups, and with other cell surface antigens from mammalian tissue.

There is growing recognition that many, if not all, of these O serogroups represent distinct clones of bacteria. This relationship has been best worked out in *E. coli*, in which strains within a given serogroup share numerous other biochemical properties as well. Epidemiologic surveys have demonstrated striking associations between certain O serotypes and clinical infections.[9] Although not conclusively proven, it is now generally felt that the O serogroup may act primarily as a marker for a specific clustering of virulence properties needed for a certain infectious process. Thus, certain serogroups possess adhesive factors that are specifically important in urinary tract infection, whereas other serogroups possess colonization factors and toxins that are necessary for gastroenteritis. One study examined papG alleles of *E. coli* in initial and recurrent urinary tract infection and found predominance of the type III allele as well as association with serogroups O6 and O18.[8a]

H antigens are found on bacterial flagella, which provide many gram-negative bacteria with motility.[4, 31] In contrast to the somatic antigens, H antigens are heat labile and consist of protein. In a flagellate organism, the H antigen is dominant to the O antigen so that the reactivity of the O antigen requires prior denaturation of the H antigen, usually accomplished by heat or treatment with acid or alcohol. The agglutination reactions seen with H antigens are more rapid and dramatic than are the agglutination reactions seen with O antigens.

A particular property of specific anti-H antibody is that it immobilizes flagellate bacteria to which the antibodies are directed. This immunologic reaction is probably important in attenuating the virulence of motile bacteria, particularly in the gastrointestinal and urinary tracts,[32] and was probably responsible for the emergence of flagellar phase variation in *Salmonella*.[33] Phase variation is the property by which a bacterium is capable of alternating the expression of one type of flagellar antigen with an unrelated antigenic type such that the organism can no longer be immobilized by antibody to the first type. Flagellar phase variation is controlled by an invertible element of DNA that turns on and off the expression of one flagellum type[33] and a repressor gene for the unlinked second flagellar type. The use by bacteria of an invertible element of DNA to drive the genetic expression of a surface organelle is also found in *E. coli*, in which a similar type of invertible element controls the on and off expression of type 1 fimbriae.[34, 35]

The last major class of antigens is the K or capsular antigen.[25, 36] K antigens are only partially stable to heat and, although typically composed of polysaccharide-containing capsules, can occasionally be envelope proteins or fimbriae. If the antigen is a capsule, its presence can inhibit the O reaction, which then requires for detection that the capsule be removed or otherwise denatured. Two important examples of K antigens are the VI antigen of *Salmonella typhi*, thought to be important in the virulence of *S. typhi*, and the K1 antigen of *E. coli*, which is associated with neonatal meningitis, bacteremia, and urinary tract infection.[37–41]

Virulence and Virulence Factors

In *E. coli* that are nonpathogenic but still capable of residing successfully in the human gastrointestinal tract, the presence of adhesins is thought to play an important role in allowing the organism to colonize successfully. In that context, however, these factors are not helping to promote any disease, so they cannot be considered virulence factors. Nevertheless, if the same *E. coli* also possessed an enterotoxin, the organism might be now capable of producing gastroenteritis in the human host, which it could not do in the absence of the adhesin. In this new context, the adhesin can be viewed as a conditional or auxiliary virulence factor. In addition to adhesins, the Enterobacteriaceae possess a number of additional auxiliary virulence factors. Flagella permit the organism motility; scavenger molecules and receptors, such as the siderophore system, permit acquisition of limiting nutrients; and capsules block opsonophagocytosis and thereby foil the immunologic machinery of the host.

The primary virulence factors can be further subdivided into those that, by themselves (i.e., in pure isolated form), can replicate at least some part of the illness that the entire organism is capable of producing. The best example of such a factor is a toxin. Nevertheless, most infectious processes are fairly complex, so multiple factors must work together to produce disease. These factors can only play a role in disease production in context of the entire microorganism; although necessary for the disease process, they are insufficient in pure form. Examples of these virulence factors are those involved in the intracellular growth of *Salmonella*[42] or the invasive ability of *Yersinia*.[43]

Primary virulence factors of the type that are necessary but by themselves insufficient for disease production as well as auxiliary virulence factors have been most successfully examined by genetic approaches. In this case, the investigator starts with a virulent microbe, causes a mutation in a single gene that results in loss of the full infective phenotype of the organism, and then characterizes the mutant on the basis of the lost property or properties.[44] A form of "negative cloning" can be used to isolate mutations in specifically chosen genes.[45, 46] The investigator first clones a gene of potential importance in pathogenesis, then mutates this gene in vitro and reintroduces the mutant allele, selecting for a site-specific mutation into the otherwise virulent strain.

What follows is a description of a number of virulence factors (Fig. 206–1) that have been identified in the Enterobacteriaceae along with a discussion, when appropriate, of the approaches used to identify these factors at the molecular level. Mention is confined to factors that are essential for or that potentiate the production of infectious disease, keeping in mind that the primary selective pressure for the evolution of these factors is not in the production of disease but rather in the growth promotion of the organism at the site of its propagation.

Adhesins. Virtually all gram-negative bacteria examined ultrastructurally possess surface organelles known as fimbriae or pili.[47–49] As reviewed in Chapter 2, these organelles are indispensable in promoting the adherence of bacteria to mucosal surfaces, which is an essential first step in the colonization of the host by the organism. A typical bacterium has several hundred of these hairlike organelles radiating in a peritrichous fashion from the surface of the cell in all directions, which effectively doubles the radius of the organism. Each individual fimbria consists of about 1000 subunits of an identical protein arranged in a helix. Among these identical subunits and present on each individual fimbria are a small number of specialized subunits that provide the organelle with its binding specificity.

Fimbriae have been characterized in two different ways, one antigenic and the other functional.[50] Colonization factor antigen (CFA) I and CFA II, defined antigenically, have been found on a number of *E. coli* associated with gastroenteritis. The binding sites on the mucosa to which these fimbriae attach are still unknown, but recent evidence suggests that CFA I binds to a sialoglycoprotein.[51] In contrast, types 1, P, and S fimbriae were initially identified on the basis of their abilities to bind specifically to mannose, digalactose, or sialylgalactoside receptors, respectively. Minor components within types 1,[52, 53] and P fimbriae[54, 55] have been shown to be responsible for their respective binding abilities and have been characterized genetically and biochemically. These lectin-like subunits are located at the tips of the fimbriae,[56] so the vast part of the organelle is mostly a long extension for the actual ligand.

A number of studies have shown the importance of these adhesins in infection. The plasmid-borne CFA class of adhesins is extremely important in many forms of *E. coli*–induced gastroenteritis.[57–61] Epidemiologically, P fimbriae are highly associated with *E. coli* strains that are capable of producing urinary tract infection, particularly pyelonephritis,[62–66] and S fimbriae are associated with *E. coli* strains recovered from neonates with sepsis or meningitis.[67] Mutation studies have shown that the specific loss of P fimbriae abrogates the ability of the *E. coli* strain to cause urinary tract infection in the appropriate animal model. The specific epidemiologic linkage of type 1 fimbriae with disease is less clear-cut. *Escherichia coli* found in sites where

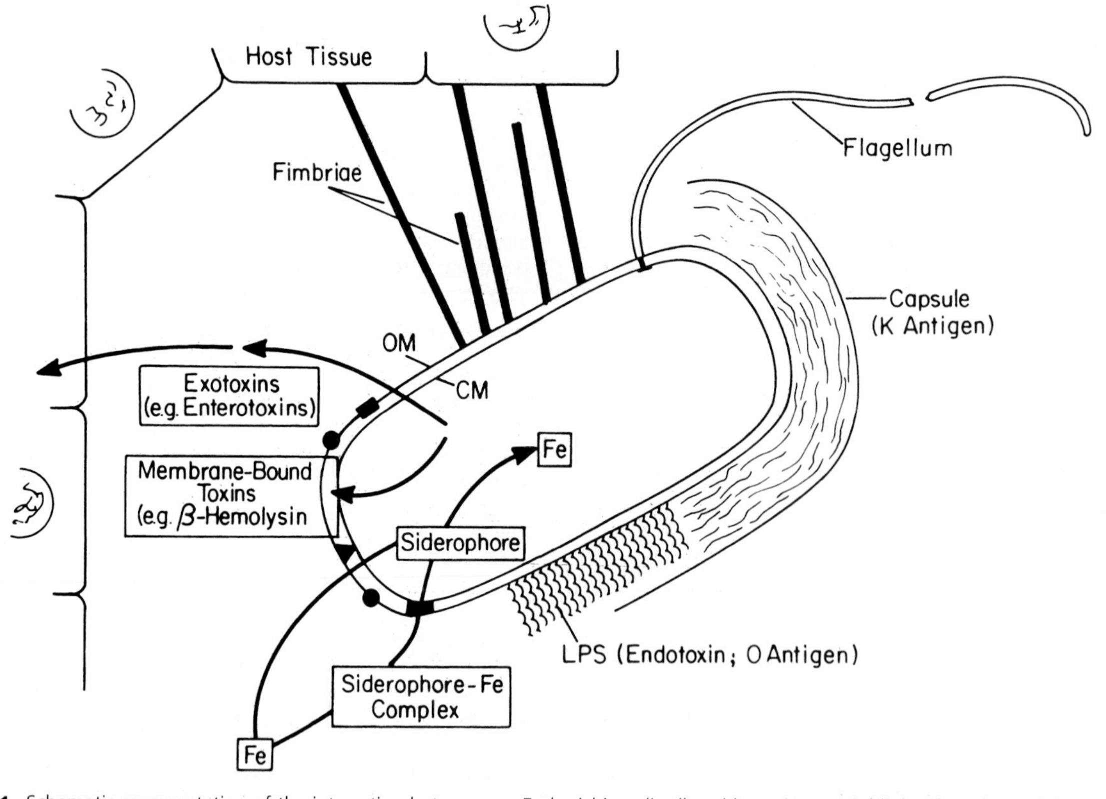

FIGURE 206–1. Schematic representation of the interaction between an *Escherichia coli* cell and host tissue. Highlighted are bacterial structures that are considered important in bacterial pathogenicity. *Abbreviations:* CM, Cytoplasmic membrane; FE, iron; LPS, lipopolysaccharide; OM, outer membrane. (From Eisenstein BI, Jones GW. The spectrum of infectious and pathogenic mechanisms of *Escherichia coli*. Adv Intern Med. 1988; 33:231–252.)

there is no disease, such as the gastrointestinal tract, and *E. coli* recovered from sites of infection, such as the blood stream and the urinary tract, have been shown to possess type 1 fimbriae in equally high proportion.[68] Nevertheless, genetic studies have shown that type 1 fimbriae greatly potentiate the ability of strains of *E. coli* also containing toxin to deliver toxin to susceptible eukaryotic cells.[69] In the same study the type 1 fimbriae were shown to potentiate the ability of the bacteria to extract nutrients by virtue of close adherence from tissue culture cells. In addition, type 1 fimbriae may be involved in effecting bacterial survival and enhanced inflammatory response in the urinary tract.[70] *E. coli* O1:K1:H7 expressing type 1 fimbriae were found to cause more severe disease in children than isolates of the same serotype negative for type 1 fimbriae. Mutation in expression led both to decreased bacterial survival and inflammatory response in a mouse model of urinary tract infection.[70] Thus, type 1 fimbriae are the type of bacterial factor discussed earlier that potentiates growth hardiness of both pathogenic and nonpathogenic organisms in the human environment and potentiates the primary virulence factors (i.e., toxins) of pathogenic organisms.

In enterotoxigenic strains of *E. coli* that cause diarrhea, colonization fimbriae (CFAs) have been proposed in a new typing scheme to be called coli surface antigens and then numbered sequentially. New colonization factors have been identified from strains in various parts of the world and characterized using genetic techniques.[71]

Most bacterial virulence factors that have been studied have been found to be regulated genetically in some way to allow the bacteria to respond flexibly to the environment.[72–74] A well worked out example of such genetic regulation is discussed later in the context of iron acquisition. This type of flexible genetic expression is found with type 1 fimbriae in that individual bacteria can oscillate between expressing and not expressing the organelles. Moreover, an individual organism in either state of fimbriation will shift to the alternative phase at a relatively high frequency of once per hundred to thousand divisions. This process of switching back and forth between fimbriate and afimbriate states is quite similar to the flagellar phase variation first described in *Salmonella*. The pathogenic significance of phase variation of flagella in *Salmonella* probably relates to antigenic evasion, in that motility can be preserved even when significant antibody response has been generated against the first phase of flagella.

The role of phase variation in the pathogenic life cycle of *E. coli* is conjectural but may be connected with the fact that type 1 fimbriae mediate binding of the bacteria not only to mucosal surfaces but also to mannose receptors on phagocytic cells. Based on evidence from an animal model of urinary tract infections in which *P. mirabilis* organisms were inoculated either by the hematogenous or the mucosal route, it has been found that fimbriate organisms are more virulent at the colonization stage of infection, whereas afimbriate bacteria are more virulent in the invasive stage of infection.[75] Given the high rate of phase variation, both fimbriate and afimbriate bacteria are well represented within any given population of *P. mirabilis* or *E. coli*. This population heterogeneity provides survival flexibility under conditions involving rapid changes in the microenvironment, as would occur during an infection. The genetic basis of both fimbrial and flagellar phase variation is the inversion of a small segment of DNA that contains the transcriptional promoter for the respective organelle.[27] Viewed in the broadest context of virulence (i.e., survival of the population in the host), the genetic switch that permits the bacterium to adapt to different environments during an infective process might itself be considered an auxiliary virulence factor.[35]

Toxins. Bacterial toxins, reviewed more extensively in Chapter 1, are the most clear-cut examples of virulence factors. Classic biochemical techniques have been used to purify and characterize these molecules.[76] By definition, toxins in pure form interact in some specific way with the host to produce a response as determined by an alteration in the viability or physiology of the target cell system.[77] Cytotoxins and hemolysins destroy cells, whereas many other toxins cause harm to the whole organism in the absence of individual cell death. Some potent toxins are capable of producing the disease caused by the whole pathogen. For instance, tetanus or botulinum toxin, when injected into animals, reproduces the respective diseases. Likewise, purified endotoxin from gram-negative organisms is capable of reproducing the septic shock picture associated with gram-negative bacteremia. For the most part, however, toxins associated with the Enterobacteriaceae are by themselves insufficient to fully reproduce the infection pathology. Some toxins, in fact, have unknown roles in the process of infection.

An important piece of epidemiologic evidence that hemolysins are important in some diseases caused by *E. coli* is the finding that more than half of *E. coli* organisms isolated in extraintestinal infections possess hemolysin, whereas fewer than 10% of *E. coli* isolated from the gastrointestinal tract possess hemolysin.[78, 79] There seem to be further correlations among virulence factors when one examines the relationship between adhesin production and hemolysin.[67, 80] Thus, most uropathogenic *E. coli* contain both the P fimbriae and hemolysin.[68] Experimental studies demonstrating the importance of hemolysin have shown that laboratory-constructed hemolytic strains and nonhemolytic strains mixed with extracted hemolysin are more virulent in animal model studies compared with strains in which the hemolysin gene has been inactivated.[79, 81, 82] Other epidemiologic studies show that uropathogenic *E. coli* are also resistant to the bactericidal effect of serum.[83]

A number of molecular varieties of *E. coli* cytotoxins have been described.[84] α-Hemolysins are large molecular weight proteins that can be excreted; β-hemolysins remain cell bound.[79] The cytotoxicity of hemolysins is not limited to red blood cells but extends to white blood cells as well and is due to the production of transmembrane pores.[85] There is relative tissue specificity for these toxins; α-hemolysins are more effective cytotoxins of lymphocytes,[86] whereas β-hemolysins are more capable of inhibiting the phagocytosis[87] and chemotaxis[88] of neutrophils. The genetics of hemolysins are probably best worked out for the alpha variety, which are encoded by both plasmid and chromosomal genes.[79, 89] There is little structural homology between the plasmid-encoded and the chromosomally encoded hemolysins, which has led investigators to believe that these hemolysins serve different virulence functions.[90] The regulation of some of these hemolysin genes appears to depend on iron availability.[91] A different class of cytotoxins are those produced by enteropathogenic *E. coli* (EPEC) that are very similar to the cytotoxins of *Shigella dysenteriae*.[92–94] EPEC strains, although consisting of a diversity of serogroups, cause virtually identical gastrointestinal disease (see later discussion). The toxins from these different strains are remarkably similar functionally and are uniformly capable of destroying various tissue culture lines, of causing lethality in mice, and of demonstrating gastrointestinal toxicity in suitable animal models.

Unlike the secreted hemolysins, which can act at a long range and whose targets are widespread, the enterotoxins of ETEC are cell associated, act at short distances, and exhibit more striking tissue specificity.[76, 77] A recent review summarizes the pathogenicity factors of diarrhea-producing *E. coli* strains.[95] There are two major classes of enterotoxins: heat-stable toxin (ST) and heat-labile toxin (LT). The ST is a small molecule that is heavily cross-linked internally with disulfide bonds. It is this cross-linking that provides the stability to heat and enzymatic destruction by proteases (as might be found in the gastrointestinal tract). ST is much more tissue specific than is LT but acts in a similar way in altering the intracellular cyclic nucleotide pools; ST elevates the concentration of cyclic guanine monophosphate (cGMP), which results in altered ion transport and markedly increased fluid excretion by the mucosal cells of the small intestine.[77, 96] LT is a much larger molecule and is virtually identical to the cholera toxin of *Vibrio cholerae*; both display marked serologic cross-reactivity and structural homology.[97] Both are multimeric molecules consisting of a single A polypeptide and a pentameric B polypeptide. The B molecule is the binding part of the toxin, and it binds to a galactoglycoprotein on the mucosal surface of the small intestinal cells, thereby allowing the secondary entry of the A molecule, which is the toxic part of the toxin.[98] Once inside the cell, the A component catalyzes the adenosine diphosphate ribosylation of the guanyl nucleotide-dependent component of adenylate cyclase. The resulting elevated levels of cyclic adenine monophosphate (cAMP) lead to altered electrolyte transport and excessive fluid excretion by the mucosal cells. Tissue cells exhibit an all-or-none susceptibility to LT enterotoxin as a consequence of the tissue binding specificity of the B protomer. Those cells lacking receptors to the B protomer are insensitive to the LT enterotoxin.

Unlike the cytotoxins and enterotoxins whose distribution is restricted to pathogenic strains of the Enterobacteriaceae, endotoxin is ubiquitous in all gram-negative organisms. As discussed earlier, endotoxin consists of the LPS of the outer membrane. Whereas the O antigenic reactivity of the LPS depends on the auxiliary polysaccharide side chains found only in smooth strains, the toxic moiety of LPS resides in the lipid A region found in all strains. Thus, all LPS molecules possess endotoxin function, but only some possess O antigenicity. Antibodies have been raised against the core antigen of LPS, which is conserved in gram-negative bacteria but did not prove to be clinically successful.[99, 100] As discussed in Chapter 63, the septic shock response seen in some patients with gram-negative bacteremia can be ascribed almost entirely to the presence of circulating endotoxin. Purified LPS, when administered to animals, causes fever, leukopenia, thrombocytopenia, disseminated intravascular coagulation, and activation of the complement pathways. Other important effects of endotoxin include the release of vasoactive substances and direct cardiovascular function. Complicating the evaluation of treatment is the complexity of the process[101, 102] and the massive involvement of mediators of inflammation.[103, 104, 106, 107] Some have even challenged the central role of endotoxin.[108, 109] Clearly, though, the inflammatory mediators, including interferons, interleukin-1 and 6 (among others), and tumor necrosis factor can replicate many of the manifestations of the sepsis.[103–105] Interleukin-1 was found to enhance the growth of virulent, but not avirulent, strains of *E. coli*,[110] and was discovered to bind to a specific receptor on the surface of the virulent bacteria. There are counterbalancing host factors, such as the bactericidal/permeability-increasing protein of neutrophils[111] and the trace plasma protein, LPS-binding protein,[112] which might play important roles in containing bacterial proliferation and deleterious inflammatory consequences. LPS-binding protein appears to work closely with soluble CD14 in myeloid cell activation.[113]

Iron Acquisition. The ability to acquire nutrients is an essential attribute of any successful organism. As discussed previously, the life cycle of a pathogenic microorganism brings it into environments with varying degrees of nutritional richness. In the extraintestinal phase of infection by gram-negative bacteria, iron becomes one of the major limiting factors for further growth.[114, 115] This limitation is, in large part, owing to the fact that almost all of the iron in the human body is sequestered in either hemeproteins, such as hemoglobin and myoglobin, or in iron-chelating proteins involved with iron transport, such as transferrin and lactoferrin.[114] It is not surprising, then, that the available concentration of iron significantly influences the virulence of *E. coli*.[116, 117] When injected in conjunction with *E. coli*, iron substantially reduces the dose of bacteria needed for lethality.[118] To get around this enormous limitation of iron availability, bacteria have evolved specialized means to acquire iron that involve a high-affinity iron-capturing system capable of competing with the extremely high affinity systems found in the mammalian tissue. Many bacteria are capable of excreting an iron-chelating compound, or siderophore, that the bacteria can then take up again once an extracellular iron siderophore complex has been formed.[114, 119] In Enterobacteriaceae the catechol enterobactin is the most commonly occurring siderophore. This compound is excreted by the bacteria when it chelates extracellular iron and is returned back into the bacterial cell, where it is then degraded to release the bound iron. *Escherichia coli* strains found specifically in extraintestinal infections have been found to also produce the hydroxymate iron chelator aerobactin, which was initially associated with colicin V plasmids found in many virulent *E. coli* strains.[120, 121] More recently, it has been found that in some K1 strains of *E. coli* the aerobactin genes are chromosomal.[122]

The evidence that siderophores contribute to virulence is best established for aerobactin. Even though the iron-chelating capacity of aerobactin is significantly less than that of enterobactin and transferrin, aerobactin but not enterobactin has been shown to confer a selective advantage for growth in the body.[123–125] Enterobactin, in contrast, is far more antigenic and elicits an antibody response that inhibits enterobactin's iron uptake efficiency.[126] Both the enterobactin and aerobactin systems are tightly regulated genetically such that, under low iron conditions, expression of both siderophore systems is very high.[114, 127]

An alternative way for the bacterium to acquire iron in the blood stream that may not require any siderophore is hemolysis. Because released hemoglobin contains readily available iron, the action of hemolysin in the blood stream may be equally or more important than are the siderophore systems in providing the bacteria with iron. The host, however, has evolved mechanisms to decrease its vulnerability to blood-borne bacteria by markedly increasing its sequestration of iron after the onset of pyrexia.[128] The release by the liver of such acute-phase reactants as transferrin is probably an adaptation to the threat of bacteremia. In addition, transferrin and another iron chelator, lactoferrin, which is found in the specific granules of polymorphonuclear leukocytes, directly damage the outer membranes of gram-negative bacteria.[129]

Capsules. As discussed earlier, the K antigens of *E. coli* consist of either proteinaceous organelles important in the colonization of some bacteria usually not associated with human disease (e.g., porcine and bovine gastroenteritis) or polysaccharide capsules. The capsules act in a purely defensive way to promote bacterial virulence by decreasing the ability of antibodies to bind to bacteria and of white blood cells to phagocytose bacteria. The shieldlike properties depend on two characteristics. First, their polysaccharide composition makes capsules highly hydrophilic, which strongly inhibits phagocytosis by the hydrophobic-surfaced host cells.[130] Second, many capsules are relatively poor immunogens[131] and poor activators of complement.[132] Nevertheless, the antiphagocytic properties of capsules can be overcome by antibodies specifically raised against capsular antigens, a process that has been so successful with pneumococci, meningococci, and *Haemophilus influenzae*. Antibody binding to capsule not only exposes the Fc component of immunoglobulin but also renders the bacterial surface more hydrophobic[130] and allows the activation of the classical pathway of complement.[133]

The best-studied capsule found in *E. coli* is the K1 capsular antigen, which is a polymer of *N*-acetylneuraminic acid. This molecule closely mimics similar compounds found in mammalian tissue and probably is the reason for its poor immunogenicity. In studies with isogenic strains of K1-positive and K1-negative *E. coli*, only the K1-negative mutants were readily killed by complement.[134] Thus, the K1 capsule is unequivocally a virulence factor of the growth-promoting or defensive variety. Although capsules may be the most important component in allowing gram-negative bacteria to invade the blood stream successfully, other components of the bacterial envelope have been shown to contribute to serum resistance. In some strains of *E. coli* that contain the colicin V plasmid, a particular genetic determinant, *iss*, has been shown to encode resistance to the bactericidal action of serum and complement.[136] Other plasmids, including some R plasmids, have also been found to increase the resistance of *E. coli* to serum bactericidal activity.[137] The biochemical basis of non–capsule-mediated serum resistance is not well understood but is believed to be due in some way to the thwarting of the normal deposition of the terminal components of complement.

Plasmids: Drug Resistance and Virulence. Plasmids are self-replicating, nonchromosomal units of DNA that carry their own replication machinery as well as any other genes that might be providing the organism with a phenotype that it would lack if the plasmid were missing. A specialized but extraordinarily important class of plasmids are the R plasmids, which play a predominant role in antimicrobial resistance among gram-negative bacteria.[138] Most of the individual drug resistance determinants found on R plasmids come in a self-contained genetic package called a transposon that possesses not only the gene for the drug resistance but also the self-contained ability to relocate itself as a genetic package to other plasmids and even the chromosome.[139] Although such transposition events are relatively infrequent, plasmids containing multiple transposons can be selected readily by exposing the plasmid-containing bacteria to multiple antimicrobial agents. As a consequence of the enormous use of antimicrobial agents in medicine and in agriculture, most R plasmids have evolved to the point at which they contain multiple transposons and thereby provide a multiple drug resistance phenotype to the bacteria in which they reside.[140–142] As is true with many plasmids, most R plasmids also possess the machinery for conjugal transfer to other strains and species, thereby further spreading drug resistance. Certain conjugation-proficient plasmids, like those of the RK2 class, are capable of promoting the transfer of coresident R plasmids intergenerically at extremely high frequencies.[143]

As has been mentioned in the preceding discussion of individual virulence factors, many, including colonization factors, enterotoxin, and hemolysin, are plasmid borne.[144] Predictably, these virulence factors have been found in plasmids that also contain drug resistance determinants.[145–148] Thus, environmental pressure that selects for further spread of this type of R plasmid, as would be the case with antimicrobial use, is likely to also promulgate the spread of the linked virulence factors. Even in the absence of the drug resistance determinants, plasmids found in certain strains of virulent bacteria have been found to carry multiple virulence factors. For instance, plasmids found in enterotoxigenic strains of *E. coli* have been shown to carry genes both for enterotoxin production and for the colonization factor antigen found to be important in colonization of the human gastrointestinal tract.[57]

Plasmid-Independent Drug Resistance

Although drug resistance, particularly multiple drug resistance, is frequently plasmid borne, it need not be.[149] Certain Enterobacteriaceae, notably *Citrobacter, Enterobacter,* indole-positive *Proteus, Providencia,* and *Serratia,* carry a chromosomal gene that encodes a broad-spectrum β-lactamase, which is usually induced in the presence of some but not all β-lactam antibiotics.[150, 151] Unfortunately, these bacteria can mutate such that these enzymes are produced constitutively, and the bacteria acquire broad resistance to the antimicrobials, sometimes during therapy.[152, 153] A multicenter study in Venezuela examined the susceptibility of 1297 bacterial strains against six broad spectrum agents.[154] Imipenem was active against 97.2% of strains and cefipime 92.8%, compared with ceftazidime 64.7%, and both drugs were active against ceftazidime-resistant strains.[139] Mutations in the chromosome can also have profound effects on drug susceptibilities, with a common theme of altered transport.[155–157] The consequence of the enormous genetic adaptability of bacteria, whether plasmid-dependent or independent, is the continual problem of increasing resistance to useful antimicrobials.[158, 159] This problem can be seen in infected patients,[160] as well as in otherwise healthy, normally colonized individuals.[161]

THE SPECIFIC PATHOGENS

Escherichia coli

Escherichia coli is the best-studied free-living organism.[162] Among clinical isolates these bacteria can be motile or nonmotile, and most ferment lactose. Other biochemical tests frequently used to identify *E. coli* in the clinical microbiology laboratory are as follows: the methyl red reaction is positive, the Voges-Proskauer (VP) test is negative, urease and phenylalanine deaminase activity is absent, H_2S is not produced, citrate cannot be used as the sole carbon source, and the organism will not grow in the presence of potassium cyanide (KCN).[4]

Escherichia coli is the most frequent cause of some of the most common bacterial infections, including urinary tract infections, bacteremia, and bacteria-related traveler's diarrhea. It is also a leading cause of neonatal meningitis and can cause a variety of other clinical infections, including pneumonia.

Strains of *E. coli* normally colonize the large intestine. In a study of the various serogroups and clones recovered from the feces of healthy adults, it was found that strains typically associated with enteropathogenic or enterohemorrhagic disease were not recovered.[163] Also fecal strains in general had fewer virulence-associated factors than what were found in isolates associated with infections of the urinary tract, meninges, and blood stream.[163]

Enteric Infections Due to *Escherichia coli*. *E. coli* was first reported to be an etiologic agent of human infantile diarrhea in the 1920s.[164] In the last decade or so, the organism has been recognized as the major cause of bacterial gastroenteritis associated with traveling abroad.[165–167] Enteric infection caused by *E. coli* can be due to at least five different varieties of bacteria operating through different mechanisms[95]: ETEC strains are an important cause of traveler's diarrhea, EPEC strains are an important cause of childhood diarrhea, enteroinvasive *E. coli* (EIEC) strains cause a disease that is similar to *Shigella*-like dysentery, EHEC strains cause hemorrhagic colitis and have been associated with the hemolytic-uremic syndrome in children, and enteroadherent *E. coli* (EAEC) strains are an important cause of traveler's diarrhea in Mexico and in North Africa. These pathogens share the general properties of demonstrating specific interactions with the intestinal mucosa, of elaborating various toxins, and of possessing plasmid-encoded virulence factors.[95]

Traveler's diarrhea is characterized by symptoms of abdominal cramps and frequent explosive bowel movements as a consequence of the copious outpouring of fluid from the gastrointestinal tract.[168] ETEC disease usually arises in an otherwise healthy individual from an industrialized country visiting tropical or subtropical regions characterized by poor hygienic conditions.[169] ETEC is also an occasional cause of diarrhea in children in the United States.[170, 171] A number of epidemiologic studies have been performed on travelers to Mexico. In one large outbreak of gastroenteritis, 72% of the ill people and 15% of the healthy ones harbored LT-producing ETEC.[168] In that study, the incubation period was 1 to 2 days, the mean duration of the diarrhea was 3 to 4 days, and symptoms tended to be mild. An occasional individual presented with more severe illness including fever, chills, and vomiting. The results of other studies of epidemics due to ST-producing ETEC strains do not differ clinically from the LT-producing strains. Because the organism is passed by the fecal-oral route, contamination most likely occurs through the use of unbottled water and salad vegetables likely to be contaminated with fecal content.

The inoculum of organisms must be high enough to resist the normal defensive barriers of the acid pH of the stomach. Colonization of the small intestine then occurs by virtue of the plasmid-encoded surface fimbriae that enabled the bacteria to adhere to the mucosal surface of the gastrointestinal tract.[57] Typically, the same plasmid encodes the enterotoxin that, as discussed earlier, stimulates massive fluid secretion by the mucosal cells by disrupting intracellular levels of cyclic nucleotides. Human immunity to ETEC gastroenteritis probably depends on the presence of antiadhesive factor antibodies that are secreted into the gastrointestinal lumen and block bacterial adherence and colonization.[58, 172] Because a number of antigenically diverse fimbriae have been identified with ETEC strains, immunity is likely to be type specific.[59] Presumably the lack of gastroenteritis among adult residents of areas associated with traveler's diarrhea is owing to their prior exposure to these colonization antigens and development of the appropriate humoral immunity. One recent approach to this problem is to administer anti-*E. coli* bovine IgG, which prevented diarrhea in adult volunteers but which requires further testing.[61] A number of other organisms produce ETEC-like illness in travelers, including various bacteria (e.g., *Shigella*, *Salmonella*, *Campylobacter*), viruses (e.g., rotavirus, Norwalk agent), and parasites (e.g., *Giardia*, *Entamoeba*).[166, 167] The strains of *V. cholerae* expressing the LT-like cholera toxin that causes classic cholera produce a disease that is initially similar to that produced by ETEC but later becomes a much more severe, life-threatening disease. At the present time it is not clearly understood why *V. cholerae* has the capacity to cause a disease so much more severe than that produced by ETEC, given the marked similarity in the enterotoxins produced by these two bacteria.

Antimicrobial prophylaxis has been effective for traveler's diarrhea, with protection correlated with the lack of acquisition of the pathogenic bacteria in the stool.[173] But because of increasing drug resistance and the possibilities of side effects, many authorities are recommending that travelers avoid antimicrobial prophylaxis and instead use care in their consumption of food and water that may be contaminated. Once disease occurs, antimicrobial agents may be useful in shortening the duration of the disease, but fluid and electrolyte replacement is more important and all that is generally needed.[174] Antimotility drugs may help alleviate the symptoms but might also increase the time during which the pathogenic bacteria remain in the gastrointestinal tract.

The mode of pathogenesis of the non-ETEC varieties of gastroenteritis is less well understood at the cellular and molecular level. EPEC strains are an important cause of childhood diarrhea, particularly in underdeveloped countries.[175] They have been incriminated in institutional outbreaks of diarrhea, particularly in nurseries. Based on O antigen identification, there appear to be a limited number of *E. coli* clones associated with this disease, particularly those of serogroups O608, O25, O26, O111, O119, O125–O128, and O142.[176] These bacteria are capable of disrupting the overlying mucus gel of the host cell.[177] EPEC bacteria have been shown to bind to the membranous cells of Peyer's patches,[178] and "enteroadherence" has been shown to be a mechanism of at least some forms of traveler's diarrhea.[179] Among the classic serotypes of EPEC, the adherence factor is plasmid encoded.[180] Other strains have been shown to produce a Shiga-like toxin. EPEC produces a characteristic lesion in the mucosa with the formation of microcolonies and loss of adjacent microvilli.[181] Several different virulence factors appear to be needed in the pathogenesis of these strains.[182] In addition to a plasmid-associated adherence factor, there is also a chromosomal gene, *eae,* needed for cellular entry.[183] A distinct pilus type has been identified, which might explain the focal adherence pattern.[184]

Whereas the classic strains of EPEC, usually associated with nursery outbreaks and particular serotypes, have been shown to adhere to HEp-2 cells in a focal manner,[185] other types of adherence patterns have been observed in the so-called EAEC strains. (Because of the adherence seen in classic EPEC strains, these are sometimes also referred to as EAEC strains.) A distinguishing feature of the non-EPEC, adherent strains is that they attach to tissue culture cells in an aggregative manner. Therefore, these strains, which are associated with persistent diarrhea in young children, are often referred to as enteroaggressive *E. coli*.[186] A distinct heat-stable, plasmid-encoded enterotoxin has been found in some of these strains.[187]

The enterionvasive *E. coli* (EIEC) are capable of cellular invasion and thus are quite different from the typical *E. coli* pathogen, which limits itself to the mucosal surface.[188] As a consequence of cellular invasion, EIEC strains provoke a significant inflammatory response associated with destruction of the intestinal mucosa. Clinically, these events result in a picture similar to that of bacterial dysentery, with a high incidence of fever and bloody diarrhea that contains inflammatory leukocytes. Fortunately, disease due to EIEC is rare, particularly in the United States. As with ETEC, invasive strains belong to characteristic serogroups, in this case O28, O52, O112, O115, O124, O136, O143, O145, and O147.[189] The ability to invade is genetically encoded by a large plasmid,[190] and the phenotype can be confirmed with the Sereny test (i.e., the ability to evoke conjunctivitis in guinea pigs).

The enterohemorrhagic *E. coli* usually belong to the serotype O157:H7 and were first associated with a multistate outbreak of hemorrhagic colitis in 1982.[191] A case-control study revealed 118 O157 isolates among 30,463 individuals, with 29% occurring in patients older than 50 years; the only risk factor for development of disease was consumption of undercooked ground beef.[192] Unlike classic dysentery, there is no enteroinvasion and inflammation of the mucosa.[193] Typically the patient is afebrile, but in the elderly the disease can be confused with ischemic colitis and can lead to death.[194, 195] These strains have been shown to produce Shiga-like toxins that are cytotoxic for Vero cells.[196, 197] At least one Shiga-like toxin is encoded by a lysogenic toxin-converting bacteriophage.[198] Hemolytic-uremic syndrome has been associated with a number of outbreaks involving these strains.[199–205] Strains of other serotypes have also been associated with the hemolytic-uremic syndrome (see Chapters 85 and 87).[206]

Urinary Tract Infections. Whereas the major site of normal colonization of the Enterobacteriaceae in the body is the gastrointestinal tract, the most common site for infection is the urinary tract. Because the urinary tract is normally sterile, any intrusion of bacteria distally (the urethra) to proximally (the kidney) is abnormal. *Escherichia coli* is the most common cause of urinary tract infection and is capable of causing a wide range of illness, ranging from uncomplicated urethritis to symptomatic cystitis or pyelonephritis to sepsis.[207] The great majority of uncomplicated infections with *E. coli* (i.e., infections that do not lead to pyelonephritis and sepsis) occur in women by virtue of a shortened urethra and the frequent proximate colonization of the periurethral region with coliform bacteria.[208, 209] In contrast, the most important host factor involved in complicated urinary tract infection, whether with *E. coli* or any other bacterium, is the obstruction of normal urinary flow (e.g., prostatic hypertrophy, stones, congenital anomalies) or the presence of a foreign body (e.g., a Foley catheter). Whereas specific virulence factors appear to be necessary for uncomplicated infection,[210] relatively nonpathogenic and opportunistic organisms such as *Pseudomonas*, *Proteus*, or *E. coli* lacking virulence factors[211] are capable of causing disease in the presence of a foreign body[212] or obstruction.

A typical patient with uncomplicated cystitis is a sexually active female who was first colonized in the intestine with a uropathogenic strain of *E. coli*.[213–216] On their subsequent colonization of the periurethral region with the help of specific adherence factors, the organisms are propelled into the bladder during sexual intercourse.[217] Postcoital urination may inhibit the subsequent establishment of colonization by these organisms in the bladder and thereby decrease infection. The adherence factor that has been most closely associated with uropathogenic *E. coli* is the P fimbria (or pili associated with pyelonephritis [PAP] pilus).[62–65] The letter designation is derived from the ability of P fimbriae to bind specifically to the P blood group antigen, which contains the disaccharide β-D-Gal 1-4 α-D-Gal.[218] This antigen is present, not only on red blood cells, but also on uroepithelial cells of approximately 99% of the population. Well-designed epidemiologic studies have shown that uncomplicated *E. coli* infection is virtually never seen in individuals lacking the P antigen.[62]

The typical uropathogenic strain of *E. coli* possesses, in addition to P fimbriae, other factors believed to be necessary for the pathogenesis of urinary tract infection. These factors include hemolysin,[219, 220] colicin V,[221] and resistance to the complement-dependent bactericidal effect of serum.[222] Most urinary tract infections appear to be due to a small number of O types (O4, O6, O75[223]), but these O serogroup strains are also the most prevalent in the gastrointestinal tract.[224] The presence of K antigen is associated with upper urinary tract infections,[225] and antibody to the K antigen has been shown to afford protection against infection in experimental animals.[226] The potential role of hemolysin and resistance to the bactericidal effect of serum on virulence has been discussed previously. It is yet to be shown whether the other characteristics of uropathogenic *E. coli* are truly virulence factors or merely a reflection of clonal distribution of strains capable of causing infection.[227, 228]

The use of DNA probe hybridization revealed that uropathogenic *E. coli* possess the genes encoding type 1 fimbriae as well as those for P fimbriae.[68] In contrast to P fimbriae, type 1 fimbriae do not appear to be specific for uropathogenic strains. Type 1 fimbriae may still potentiate colonization of the bladder, perhaps by aggregating masses of bacteria with the mannose-rich Tamm-Horsfall glycoprotein found in the urine.

Respiratory Infections. In contrast to the gastrointestinal and urinary tract infections, which are characterized by *E. coli* exhibiting specific pathogenic features, infections in the respiratory tract appear to be opportunistic.[229, 230] Thus, normal hosts become infected with virulent *E. coli* in the gastrointestinal and urinary tracts, but abnormal hosts become infected with nonpathogenic gram-negative organisms elsewhere in the body, particularly the lung. No specific virulence factors have yet been found in *E. coli* that are associated with the respiratory tract disease.

Although one portal of entry of *E. coli* into the lung is hematogenous, the vast majority of gram-negative pneumonias are related to microaspiration of upper airway secretions that have been previously colonized with gram-negative organisms.[231, 232] Gastric colonization appears to be an important antecedent event, leading to retrograde pharyngeal spread.[233] Unlike healthy individuals who are infrequently and only transiently colonized by gram-negative organisms, severely ill individuals have an altered physiology that allows such colonization to occur. A key process involves fibronectin, which is a ubiquitous protein that, among other things, coats the mucosa of the respiratory tract and acts as a specific receptor for many gram-positive bacteria.[234] Severe stress to the body from almost any cause is associated with the presence of a fibronectin-degrading protease in the saliva.[235] With destruction of fibronectin, gram-positive bacteria no longer avidly colonize, which leaves an opening in the ecologic niche, and the gram-negative binding receptors underlying the superficial coating of the mucosal tissue become exposed. The result is a markedly enhanced colonization by these gram-negative organisms that, in the context of other inhibitors of normal host response such as foreign bodies in the trachea and a decreased cough reflex, leads to the progression to gram-negative pneumonia.

For these reasons, most cases of *E. coli* pneumonia are nosocomial rather than community acquired. Nevertheless, outpatients with severe underlying disease such as diabetes mellitus, alcoholism, and chronic obstructive pulmonary disease are more disposed to gram-negative pneumonias than is the population of healthy people.[229, 230] The clinical picture is that of a bronchopneumonia involving the lower lobes, with empyema seen in about one third of the patients and bacteremia in another third of the patients. Among the latter, some of the bacteremias precede the pneumonia and are most frequently secondary to another focus such as the kidneys or the gastrointestinal tract. As expected in a condition that affects primarily debilitated hosts, the death rate is 50% or higher. Similar to that of other gram-negative pneumonias, treatment consists of appropriate antibiotics, drainage of any loculated collections of pus, and respiratory support as required.

Neonatal Meningitis. Infants in their first month of life are particularly predisposed to bacterial meningitis,[236] with *E. coli* and the group B streptococci accounting for the vast majority of cases.[237] Unlike in adults who have meningitis due to *E. coli*, in neonates there is a strong association between the presence of the K1 capsular antigen and meningitis and, to a lesser extent, an association with bacteremia.[238, 239]

Epidemiologic studies have shown that pregnancy is associated with an increased rate of colonization with K1 strains and that these strains are the ones that are involved in the subsequent neonatal meningitic cases.[240] The pathogenic mechanisms involved with K1 have not yet been explained, although experiments with neonatal rats show that *E. coli* K1 colonization of the gastrointestinal tract often leads to bacteremia and meningitis.[241] The gastrointestinal tract might be a portal of entry into the blood stream in neonatal humans as well. Fortunately, although such colonization is common, the catastrophic sequelae are rare.

Management of neonatal meningitis requires antibiotic therapy to be directed against *E. coli*, the group B streptococci, and the rare *Listeria monocytogenes* initially. Thus, typical initial therapy should include ampicillin and a third-generation cephalosporin (e.g. ceftriaxone).

Bacteremia and Miscellaneous Infections Due to *Escherichia coli*. Although colonization of mucosal surfaces by *E. coli* is frequent, in the gastrointestinal tract, normal, invasive bacteremia is fortunately fairly uncommon. Most strains of *E. coli* are not invasive, particularly in the setting of a normal host with a normal filtering system in the portal circulation (i.e., the liver and spleen). It is much more common to find bacteremia associated with urinary tract infection, particularly when there is obstruction to urinary flow. Given the source of origin, it is not surprising that phenotypic characteristics associated with uropathogenic *E. coli* are also found in bacteremic *E. coli*.[242, 243] Perhaps not unexpectedly, the trait of resistance to the serum bactericidal effect is particularly frequent in the bacteremia isolates. As mentioned previously, a number of biochemical antigenic factors have been shown to correlate with serum resistance, in particular the K1 antigen.

Perhaps the hallmark of gram-negative bacteremia is the systemic reaction to endotoxin or LPS. LPS, ubiquitous in all gram-negative organisms, may be the most toxic component of most bacteremic isolates of *E. coli* and can lead to the life-threatening responses of shock, disseminated intravascular coagulation, and decomplementation. Some of the problems and controversies in the management of sepsis are discussed earlier (under Toxins); also see Chapter 63.

Escherichia coli, while one of the leading causes of nosocomial bacteremia in the 1970s, in 1990–1992 only accounted for 6.5% of isolates.[7, 244] The primary foci in the hospitalized patient include foreign bodies, in the form of intravenous catheters and endotracheal tubes, and the urogenital, gastrointestinal, and respiratory tracts.[245] Attempts have been made to decrease nosocomial infection originating from the gastrointestinal tract by selective decontamination with oral and nonabsorbable antimicrobials, although this practice is not widespread in the United States.[246] As a consequence either of metastatic spread from bacteremia or of contiguous spread, *E. coli* has been found in a wide variety of miscellaneous infections. Contiguous infection is most often found in the distal extremities of individuals with vascular disease, particularly those with diabetes mellitus. In such cases the organism is part of a polymicrobial mixture that includes anaerobic as well as aerobic bacteria. *E. coli* has also been noted in septic arthritis,[247] endophthalmitis,[248] suppurative thyroiditis,[249] intra-abdominal abscess,[250] spontaneous bacterial peritonitis,[251] liver abscess,[252] brain abscess,[253] endocarditis,[254] osteomyelitis, prostatitis,[255] sinusitis, septic thrombophlebitis, and others. As with any bacterial infection, proper management includes the use of antibiotics on the basis of susceptibility patterns of the organism, the drainage of pus, and surgical débridement when indicated.

TRIBE KLEBSIELLEAE

The four genera *Klebsiella*, *Enterobacter*, *Serratia*, and *Hafnia* belong to the tribe Klebsielleae.[4] Like *E. coli* these organisms are colonizers of the human gastrointestinal tract and are capable of causing a wide variety of clinical syndromes, including urinary tract infection, pneumonia, and bacteremia. Unlike the virulent strains of *E. coli* described previously, however, this group of organisms is rarely associated with disease in the normal host. Nevertheless, they are a major cause of nosocomial and opportunistic infection.[244]

Klebsiella

The genus *Klebsiella* constitutes a group of nonmotile bacteria that have been traditionally speciated into *K. pneumonia*, *K. ozaenae*, and *K. rhinoscleromatis*. This traditional grouping is based on the biochemical reactions of bacteria in the genus. With the introduction of DNA hybridization assays to determine relatedness, the present view is that all these bacteria belong to one species because their DNAs are homologous. But DNA relatedness studies have shown that there is an additional species, *Klebsiella oxytoca*, that is indole positive.[3] Most clinical laboratories still retain the traditional designations because the distinctions are of some value in epidemiologic investigations. Other important characteristics of these bacteria are that they are unencapsulated, lactose fermenting, H_2S- and indole-negative, and capable of growing in KCN and using citrate as a sole carbon source, and they give a positive VP reaction. A notable characteristic of *Klebsiella* is their large appearance by Gram stain. This property as well as the property of forming large mucoid colonies on agar media is due to a prominent polysaccharide capsule. The large capsule has also made K antigen serotyping more important than O antigen serotyping is for *Klebsiella*. More than 70 types of K antigen have been identified, with some of them showing cross-reactivity with capsules of the pneumococcus and *H. influenzae*. Although the capsule is an important virulence factor in preventing phagocytosis and helping to retard leukocyte migration into infected areas, no capsular type has been found to be associated with greater likelihood of infection. Except for endotoxin, no other constant virulence factor has been found in *Klebsiella* that has been characterized in the molecular detail seen with *E. coli*.[256]

Klebsiella pneumoniae is associated with one important primary infection: lobar pneumonia. Even this classic, community-acquired illness can be reviewed as an opportunistic infection, however, given the subset of individuals who develop this disease. *Klebsiella* lobar pneumonia is virtually limited to people with severe enough underlying problems, particularly alcoholism, diabetes mellitus, and chronic obstructive pulmonary disease, that their respiratory host defenses are impaired. As classically described, the disease produces a severe, acute-onset illness characterized by destructive changes in the lung. Because of the necrotic, inflammatory, and hemorrhagic nature of the disease, the sputum is often described as "currant jelly" in quality, and the radiographic appearance is classically that of a swollen infiltrated lobe, which produces the "bowed fissure" radiologic sign. There is a high propensity toward abscess formation, cavitation, empyema, and pleural adhesions. Because of the necrotizing quality of the illness and the debilitated condition of the individuals predisposed to this disease, mortality is high. For this reason, treatment has generally been aggressive in the use of multiple antibiotics; a combination of cephalosporin and an aminoglycoside is preferred at present.

Although the most dramatic presentation of *Klebsiella pneumoniae* is as a lobar pneumonia, most cases are more subtle.[257] Most pulmonary disease comes in the form of either bronchopneumonia or bronchitis and is usually hospital acquired. Capsular types 1, 3, 4, and 5 have been particularly associated with respiratory infection, but even among these strains, the predisposition for nosocomial infection outweighs community-acquired disease. Most isolates are found to be associated not with the respiratory tract but with urinary tract infection. One survey showed *Klebsiella* was the cause of 9% of urinary tract infections and 14% of all primary bacteremias in hospitalized patients, the bacteremic rate second by only a slim margin to *E. coli*.[244] *Klebsiella* has been incriminated in 8% of all nosocomial bacterial infection. The most common foci for such infections are the urinary tract, lower respiratory tract, biliary tract, and surgical wound sites, in that order.[258] Invasive devices found in hospitalized patients, particularly urinary catheters, endotracheal tubes, and intravenous catheters, markedly increase the disposition to any nosocomial infection, particularly gram-negative rods.[259] Like most gram-negative organisms found in the hospital environment, *Klebsiella* is characteristically resistant to multiple antibiotics. Already naturally resistant to ampicillin and carbenicillin, increasing acquisition of R plasmids is providing drug resistance to cephalosporins and aminoglycosides with increased frequency.[260, 261] Intensive care unit outbreaks of *K. pneumoniae* in the so-called extended-spectrum β-lactamase–producing Enterobacteriaceae (ESBLPE) group have been described.[262, 263] The antibiotic treatment of nosocomial *Klebsiella* infections requires susceptibility determinations for optimization. Empirical coverage should be tailored to the drug resistance pattern seen in the local hospital setting.

An uncommon presentation of *K. pneumoniae* is bacterial endophthalmitis, especially in patients with liver abscess and diabetes.[239c]

The other species of *Klebsiella* are less common causes of similar nosocomial infections in hospitalized patients in the United States. *K. ozaenae* and *K. rhinoscleromatis* have been associated with upper respiratory tract infection, predominantly in countries outside the United States. Rhinoscleroma, caused by *K. rhinoscleromatis*, is a chronic granulomatous disease involving the mucosa of the upper respiratory system and leads occasionally to bony invasion and airway obstruction.[265] A characteristic histopathologic feature is the presence in the submucosa of large, foamy, non–lipid-containing histiocytes called Mikulicz cells. In certain endemic areas in Eastern Europe, central Africa, Latin America, and southern Asia, the disease can be quite common,[266] but the disease seems to be generally poorly communicable.[267] An oropharyngeal presentation has been reported in two patients infected with human immunodeficiency virus (HIV).[268] There is a report of a systemic infection.[269] The organism is susceptible to a variety of organisms, including streptomycin, tetracycline, and trimethoprim-sulfamethoxazole, and treatment should be prolonged for 6 to 8 weeks.[270]

The etiologic role of *K. ozaenae* in chronic atrophic rhinitis, called *ozaenia*, is conjectural. The disease is associated with destruction of the mucosa and a fetid mucopurulent discharge. It is unclear whether antibiotic therapy directed against this organism is of any help in alleviating the condition. On the relatively rare occasions when it is found in association with other entities such as pneumonia, it is usually easily treated with a variety of antibiotics, given its high susceptibility. Occasionally the organism is found to be susceptible to ampicillin and carbenicillin, which is in sharp contrast to *K. pneumoniae*.[271]

Enterobacter

The genus *Enterobacter* (formerly *Aerobacter*) consists of *E. aerogenes*; *E. cloacae*; *E. agglomerans* (the Herbicola-Lathyri bacteria and formerly called *Erwinia*); two relatively new species, *E. gergoviae* and *E. sakazakii*[272] (formerly called yellow-pigmented *E. cloacae*); and several species not yet associated with human disease.[4] An outbreak of *Enterobacter hormaechei* infection was described in a neonatal intensive care unit.[273] Until the 1960s, these organisms were lumped into the classification *Klebsiella-Aerobacter*, and little distinction was made between them and *Klebsiella*. Unlike *Klebsiella*, *Enterobacter* organisms are motile and tend to be less heavily encapsulated. They do not produce H_2S on triple sugar iron medium, are indole- and methyl red–negative, give a positive VP result, can grow in the presence of KCN, use citrate as a sole carbon source, and can ferment lactose. Simplified tests for decarboxylation of the diamino acids lysine, arginine, and ornithine differentiate *E. cloacae*, *E. aerogenes*, *E. agglomerans*, and *K. pneumoniae*.[4]

Enterobacter strains are opportunistic pathogens that rarely cause primary human disease. Nevertheless, they are frequent colonizers of hospitalized patients, particularly those treated with antibiotics, and have been associated with burn, wound, respiratory, and urinary tract infections.[244, 274–278] As with most opportunistic, gram-negative infections, patients have been exposed frequently to antibiotics, invasive procedures, and indwelling catheters[279–281]; many are diabetic[282] or neutropenic.[283] These organisms are also found in diabetic ulcers.[284] In contrast to most *Klebsiella*, *Enterobacter* organisms are resistant to first-generation cephalosporins and develop antibiotic resistance readily to second-[285] and third-generation[280] cephalosporins owing to an inducible β-lactamase. From 1995 to 1996, 4725 bacteremic isolates were collected in 50 U.S. medical centers; 230 were *Enterobacter* spp.[286] Thirty-five to 50% of *Enterobacter* and *Citrobacter freundii* strains were resistant to ceftazidime and piperacillin (even combined with tazobactam). Amp C β-lactamase was found to be a particular problem in ceftazidime-resistant strains.[286]

Enterobacter cloacae accounts for most hospital-acquired infections with this genus and, along with *E. agglomerans*, was associated with a major epidemic of intravenous line contamination that involved 378 patients in 25 hospitals.[287, 288] These organisms are capable of horizontal spread in the hospital environment and, like many opportunistic Enterobacteriaceae, can be spread on the hands of hospital personnel who neglect appropriate aseptic technique, especially hand washing, between patients. *Enterobacter taylorae* has been reported as an opportunistic pathogen capable of causing severe nosocomial infection.[289] Unlike most other members of the genus, these isolates were not susceptible to β-lactam antibiotics. An outbreak of *E. aerogenes* resistant to all agents except imipenem and gentamicin was reported from Belgium.[290] Alarmingly, in 2 of 15 patients treated for deep-seated infection with imipenem and gentamicin, imipenem resistance developed.

There is a report of an *E. cloacae* strain isolated from a baby with hemolytic-uremic syndrome producing a Shiga-like toxin differing by only three residues from Shiga-like toxin II from *E. coli*.[291]

Serratia

Like the genus *Enterobacter*, *Serratia* is an opportunist that has been recognized as a human pathogen only since the 1960s. Before that time, under the assumption that the organism was a nonpathogen, the red pigment found in some strains made them attractive as marker organisms to study a number of important questions involving bacterial transmittal. Great controversy arose when it was discovered that the U.S. Army was using these organisms in the 1950s to study population vulnerability to aerosolized bacteria.[292] Although there is no evidence that the aerosolized strain has been specifically involved in subsequent *Serratia* infections, based on the criticism, it is doubtful that any future experiments of this type will ever be acknowledged publicly.

Serratia are motile and ferment lactose slowly, if at all. Most strains do not produce lactose or H_2S on triple sugar iron medium but do have a positive VP reaction, use citrate as a sole carbon source, and grow in the presence of KCN. *Serratia* can be differentiated from other Enterobacteriaceae by the production of an extracellular DNase. There are a large number of named species, but only one, *Serratia marcescens*, has been routinely associated with human disease. There have been rare reports of disease due to *Serratia liquifaciens*, *Serratia rubidaea*, and *Serratia odorifera*[293]; these can be distinguished from *S. marcescens* by decarboxylation and fermentation reactions.

The epidemiology of *Serratia* is somewhat different from other Enterobacteriaceae in that *Serratia* appears to be less likely to colonize the gastrointestinal tract but more likely to colonize the respiratory and urinary tracts of hospitalized adults.[292, 294] In contrast, among neonates the gastrointestinal tract may be an important reservoir for cross-contamination.[295] Like the other opportunistic bacteria related to *Serratia*, hand-to-hand spread by hospital personnel is the most important factor in horizontal transmission.[292]

Among nosocomial infections, *Serratia* has been found to cause approximately 4% of bacteremias and lower respiratory tract infections and 2% of urinary tract, surgical wound, and cutaneous infections.[244] In addition to its importance as a hospital-associated opportunist,[292] it has been specifically associated with infections in heroin addicts.[296, 297] *Serratia* accounted for 14% of addict-associated endocarditis in San Francisco in the early 1970s[296] and has been noted as a cause of osteomyelitis in this population.[297] Most hospital-related cases are associated with the use of intravenous, intraperitoneal, and urinary catheters[298–301] and instrumentation of the urinary and respiratory tracts.[302, 303] *Serratia* organisms, like other members of the Klebsielleae tribe, have also been associated with contaminated intravenous therapy[288] and have been prominent in infections among oncology patients.[304] *Serratia* can cause cellulitis in hemodialysis patients.[305]

In the outpatient setting, *Serratia* is notable for causing septic arthritis among patients receiving intra-articular injections for diagnostic or therapeutic purposes.[306, 307] An epidemic of septic arthritis involving 10 patients was found to be caused by *Serratia* contamination of a benzalkonium chloride antiseptic used to soak cotton balls.[308]

Antibiotic treatment of *Serratia* infections is complicated by the high frequency of multiple drug resistance seen in these bacteria. Nevertheless, many, if not most, strains are susceptible to amikacin,[309, 310] with synergy frequently noted with the addition of an antipseudomonal penicillin.[311] The newer generation of β-lactam antibiotics[312–316] as well as the newer quinolones[317, 318] may be particularly useful for aminoglycoside-resistant strains.

Hafnia

There remains confusion about the relationship between the genus *Hafnia* and the tribe Klebsielleae. At one time *Hafnia* was considered a member of the genus *Enterobacter* and called *Enterobacter hafniae*, but now with the results of DNA relatedness studies and biochemical studies, it is defined as a separate genus with one species, *Hafnia alvei*.[2, 4] It remains a member of tribe Klebsielleae on the basis of the biochemical reactions. The genus is composed of motile bacteria that do not produce indole, hydrolyze urea (with rare exceptions), or liquefy gelatin. The VP reaction is always positive at 22°C and usually so at 37°C. Lysine and ornithine, but rarely arginine, are carboxylated.

Hafnia organisms are not frequently involved with infection; when they are, the infections are typically nosocomial.[319, 320] Antibiotic susceptibilities appear to be similar to those of the *Enterobacter* group, so empirical therapy while awaiting antibiotic susceptibilities should be based on patterns for those organisms within the hospital of isolation.

TRIBE PROTEEAE

Proteeae are motile bacteria that deaminate phenylalanine rapidly. Studies employing DNA relatedness have led investigators to conclude that this tribe consists of at least three genera—*Proteus*, *Morganella*, and *Providencia*—and seven species—*Proteus vulgaris*, *Proteus mirabilis*, *Proteus myxofaciens*, *Morganella morganii* (previously *Proteus morganii*), *Providencia alcalifaciens*, *Providencia stuartii*, and *Providencia rettgeri* (previously *Proteus rettgeri*).[1, 3, 4] The biochemical characteristics of the tribe are that the methyl red reaction is positive, the VP reaction is negative (except for occasional strains of *P. mirabilis*), growth can occur in the presence of KCN, sodium alginate is not used as a sole carbon source, gas production is small, and urea is hydrolyzed rapidly and abundantly by *Proteus*, *Morganella*, and *P. rettgeri* but not by the other *Providencia* spp. Virtually all *P. mirabilis* strains are indole negative, whereas virtually all other strains in the tribe are indole positive. *Proteus* strains are unique in their ability to swarm on moist agar media. This property is a consequence of their extraordinary motility due to hundreds of flagella per cell.[321]

The swarming *Proteus* species are second only to *E. coli* in the percentage of Enterobacteriaceae encountered in clinical laboratories.[2, 244] This high frequency is attributable almost entirely to the propensity of these bacteria to colonize and infect the urinary tract. Several characteristics, one of which is specific for *Proteus*, have been identified that contribute to uropathogenicity. *Proteus*, using the enzyme urease, splits urea into ammonium hydroxide, which raises the urinary pH to levels that promote struvite stone formation.[322–324] These stones act as foreign bodies that obstruct urinary flow and serve as a nidus for persistence of infection, properties that tend to make *Proteus* infections chronic and destructive of renal parenchyma. Urease has also been shown to contribute directly to renal tubular toxicity, in part by alkalizing the urine. *Proteus*, like most other Enterobacteriaceae, possess fimbriae, important for colonization of the uroepithelium,[325–327] and flagella-dependent motility, important for the spread of infection in the urinary tract.[32] Uropathogenic *Proteus* also synthesizes several different hemolysins, which may play a role in virulence.[328–330]

Most *Proteus* infections are due to *P. mirabilis*. Up to 10% of all uncomplicated urinary tract infections are caused by this species, which can also cause wound infections, pneumonia, and septicemia in the debilitated. As with many other opportunistic infections, the reservoir for many drug-resistant *P. mirabilis* infections in the hospital is in the gastrointestinal tracts of the patients who subsequently become infected.[331] Nevertheless, most nosocomial infections caused by members of the tribe Proteeae are due to the indole-positive species rather than to *P. mirabilis*. *P. stuartii* was found to be a common cause of bacteremia in nursing home patients with long-term indwelling catheters.[332, 333] Once established in the hospital setting, the indole-positive Proteeae organisms can cause large outbreaks of nosocomial urinary tract infections.[334, 335]

Antibiotic treatment of this group of bacteria can be difficult. Although *P. mirabilis* used to be relatively susceptible to the commonly used antimicrobial agents, many isolates have become more resistant, although not yet as resistant as the indole-positive species. Because of the high frequency of aminoglycoside resistance among the indole-positive isolates, treatment often requires the use of amikacin,[336] the newer β-lactam antibiotics, or the newer quinolones.

OTHER ENTEROBACTERIACEAE

Citrobacter

There are three recognized species in the genus *Citrobacter*: *C. amalonaticus*, *C. diversus*, and *C. freundii*; all have been associated with human disease. Although this group was formerly classified within the tribe Salmonelleae on the basis of biochemical similarities, the genus is now placed in the separate tribe Citrobactereae.[4] The genus is composed of motile bacteria with positive methyl red reactions, negative VP reactions, growth on Simmons citrate medium (hence its name), and the ability to hydrolyze urea slowly and weakly by most isolates. Production of H_2S is seen only with *C. freundii* bacteria, which may make them mistakenly identified as *Salmonella*. However, in contrast to *Salmonella*, *Citrobacter* usually grows in the presence of KCN. Test results for β-galactosidase with O-nitrophenyl-β-D-galactoside and gas from glucose fermentation are typically positive, whereas tests for DNase, lysine and phenylalanine deamination, and inositol fermentation are negative.[2] Considerable cross-reactivity with the O antigens of other Enterobacteriaceae has been noted.

Although not common, *Citrobacter* has been associated with significant nosocomial infection, particularly involving the urinary and respiratory tracts of debilitated, hospitalized patients.[337, 338] But most isolates recovered represent either secondary infection or colonization without apparent clinical significance. In contrast, *Citrobacter* strains, particularly *C. diversus*, in neonates have been found to be an important cause of both meningitis and brain abscess formation.[340, 341] Epidemiologic investigations of these cases have shown a high colonization rate in associated but uninfected babies.[342, 343] Strains of *C. diversus* recovered from patients with meningitis have been found to be more virulent than are nonmeningitic strains in an animal model and to possess an outer membrane protein not seen in the nonpathologic bacteria.[343] Proof of the molecular association of this protein with disease requires further biochemical and genetic analysis. *Citrobacter* has also been associated with endocarditis[344] and hospital-acquired bacteremias.[345] The latter are often polymicrobial and are accompanied by a high mortality rate, most likely due to the highly debilitated state of the host rather than the intrinsic virulence of the organism.[346]

Treatment requires appropriate antimicrobial susceptibility tests of the infecting organism. Most strains of *C. freundii* and *C. diversus* can be distinguished by their susceptibility patterns; the former are frequently susceptible to carbenicillin but not to cephalothin, whereas the latter are resistant to ampicillin and carbenicillin but sensitive to cephalothin.[338] Most strains are susceptible to the aminoglycoside antibiotics. Eight strains *of C. diversus* were recovered from patients over a 6-month period in an intensive care unit in France; plasmid-mediated extended-spectrum β-lactamases caused resistance to cephalosporins and monobactams. [339]

Edwardsiella

The organisms of the genus *Edwardsiella* are the only members of the tribe Edwardsielleae and make up three species, *E. tarda*, *E. hoshinae*, and *E. ictaluri*. Only *E. tarda* has been associated with human disease. These bacteria are motile and positive for gas from glucose fermentation, H_2S, indole, lysine decarboxylase, and ornithine decarboxylase.[2] The epithet "tarda" is meant to imply biochemical inactivity because the routine reactions not enumerated previously are all negative.[4] Because it does not ferment lactose but does produce H_2S on enteric media, it can be initially misidentified as *Salmonella*.

Edwardsiella rarely causes disease, but when it does it is most often associated with a *Salmonella*-like gastroenteritis.[347] In a survey of thousands of clinical specimens in Panama, there were 50 human isolates of *Edwardsiella*, of which 10 were associated with an intermittent, watery diarrhea that typically lasted several days and was accompanied by vomiting and low-grade fever; 20 isolates were associated with gastrointestinal carriage only.[348] There are case reports of *E. tarda* causing bacteremia,[349] liver abscess,[347, 348] meningitis,[349] and soft tissue infection.[347] Although the organism is susceptible to most commonly used antimicrobial agents,[347] treatment is probably not indicated for uncomplicated gastroenteritis.

Erwinia

The genus *Erwinia* consists of bacteria primarily associated with plants. With the exception of a group known as the Herbicola-Lathyri bacteria, which have been reclassified as *E. agglomerans*, these bacteria are not associated with human disease. Clinically relevant aspects of *E. agglomerans* were discussed earlier under "Tribe Klebsielleae."

Miscellaneous Genera

The Enteric Bacteriology Laboratories of the Centers for Disease Control and Prevention have, for more than 30 years, received cultures of Enterobacteriaceae from clinical laboratories for identification. Many were atypical strains of known genera, but others have been previously unidentified and assigned to new species or new "enteric groups," pending further classification.[350] Over the last decade identification and classification have been greatly augmented with the use of DNA-DNA hybridization, antimicrobial susceptibility patterns, bacteriophage reactivity, and computer-based algorithms. Thus, whereas in 1972 there were only 11 genera and 26 species in the family, by 1985 there were 22 genera, 69 species, and 29 biogroups, or enteric groups.[350] More than 99% of all clinical isolates have already been discussed in this chapter, and 80 to 95% of all isolates recovered in a general hospital setting are *E. coli*, *K. pneumoniae*, or *P. mirabilis*.[350] As of 1985, the bacteria recovered from

TABLE 206-2 Names and Synonyms of Recovered Isolates of Enterobacteriaceae (Excluding *Yersinia, Shigella,* and *Salmonella*)

Current Name	Synonym
Cedecea davisae	Enteric group 15
Cedecea lapagei	*Cedecea* sp. 4
Cedecea neteri	
Cedecea sp. 3	*Levinea amalonatica*
Cedecea sp. 5	
Citrobacter amalonaticus	
Citrobacter diversus	*Citrobacter koseri*
Citrobacter freundii	*Colobactrum freundii*
Edwardsiella tarda	
Enterobacter aerogenes	*Aerobacter aerogenes*
Enterobacter amnigenus	
Enterobacter asburiae	Enteric group 17
	Enterobacter cloacae
	Enterobacter gergoviae
Enterobacter hormaechi	Enteric group 75
Enterobacter sakazakii	
Enterobacter taylorae	Enteric group 19
Escherichia coli	
Escherichia fergusonii	Enteric group 10
Escherichia hermannii	
Escherichia vulneris	
Ewingella americana	
Hafnia alvei	
Klebsiella ornithinolytica	*Klebsiella oxytoca* ornithine positive
Klebsiella oxytoca	
Klebsiella ozaenae	
Klebsiella planticola	
Klebsiella pneumoniae	
Klebsiella rhinoscleromatis	
Kluyvera ascorbata	
Kluyvera cryocrescens	
Leclercia adecarboxylata	*Escherichia adecarboxylata*
Leminorella grimontii	Enteric group 57
Leminorella richardii	
Moellerella wisconsinsis	Enteric group 46
Morganella morganii subsp. *morganii*	*Proteus morganii*
Morganella morganii subsp. *sibonii*	*Proteus morganii*
Pantoea agglomerans	*Enterobacter agglomerans*
Proteus mirabilis	*Proteus vulgaris* indole negative
Proteus penneri	
Proteus vulgaris	*Proteus inconstans*
Providencia alcalifaciens	
Providencia rettgeri	*Proteus rettgeri*
Providencia rustigianii	*Proteus alcalifaciens* biogroup 3
Providencia stuartii	*Proteus inconstans*
	Rahnella aquatilis
	Serratia ficaria
	Serratia fonticola
	Serratia grimesii
Serratia liquefaciens	*Enterobacter liquefaciens*
Serratia marcescens	Centers for Disease Control and Prevention group E9
Serratia odorifera	
Serratia plymuthica	
Serratia proteamaculans subsp. *quinovora*	
Serratia rubidaea	
Tatumella ptyseos	
Trabulsiella guamensis	Enteric group 90
Yokenella regensburgei	*Koserella trabulsii* enteric group 45

Modified from Bruckner DA, Colonna P. Nomenclature for aerobic and facultative bacteria. Clin Infect Dis. 1993;16:598–605. Copyright © 1993, Infectious Diseases Society of America.

humans belonged to the following rare, mostly newly named, genera of Enterobacteriaceae: *Buttiauxella, Cedecea, Ewingella,*[351] *Kluyvera,*[352] *Rhanella,* and *Tatumella.* In addition the enteric groups 17, 41, 45, 57, 58, 59, 60, and 68 have been isolated from clinical specimens. A 1993 review of the nomenclature of these organisms (with synonyms) is summarized in Table 206–2.

REFERENCES

1. Farmer JJ III, Howard BJ, Weissfeld AS. Enterobacteriaceae. In: Howard BJ, Klass J II, Rubin SJ, et al, eds. Clinical and Pathogenic Microbiology. St. Louis: CV Mosby, 1987:289–328.
2. Farmer JJ III, Kelly MT. Enterobacteriaceae. In: Balows A, Hausler WJ Jr, Herrmann KL, et al, eds. Manual of Clinical Microbiology. 5th ed. Washington, DC: American Society for Microbiology; 1991:360–383.
3. Brenner DJ, Family I. Enterobacteriaceae Rahn 1937. In: Krieg NR, Holt JG, eds. Bergey's Manual of Systematic Bacteriology. Baltimore: Williams & Wilkins; 1984:408–516.
4. Ewing WH. Edwards and Ewing's Identification of Enterobacteriaceae. 4th ed. New York: Elsevier Science Publishing; 1986.
5. Schaberg DR. Major trends in the microbial etiology of nosocomial infection. Am J Med. 1991;91(Suppl. 3B):72S–75S.
6. Banerjee SN, Emori G, Culver DH, et al. Secular trends in nosocomial primary bloodstream infections in the United States, 1980–1989. Am J Med. 1991;91(Suppl. 3B):86S–89S.
7. Pittet D, Wenzel RP. Nosocomial bloodstream infections: Secular trends in rates, mortality, and contribution to total hospital deaths. Arch Int Med. 1995;155:1177–1184.
8. Scheckler WE. Temporal trends in septicemia in a community hospital. Am J Med. 1991;91(Suppl 3B):90S–94S.
9. Achtman M, Pluschke G. Clonal analysis of descent and virulence among selected *Escherichia coli.* Annu Rev Microbiol. 1986;40:185–210.
10. Johnson JR, Russo TA, Brown JJ, et al. PapG alleles of *Escherichia coli* strains causing first-episode or recurrent acute cystitis in adult women. J Infect Dis. 1998;177:97–101.
11. Hartl DL, Dykhuizen DE. The population genetics of *Escherichia coli.* Annu Rev Genet. 1984;18:31–68.
12. Whittam TS. Genetic variation and evolutionary processes in natural populations of *Escherichia coli.* In: Neidhardt FC, Curtiss R III, Ingraham JL, et al, eds. *Escherichia coli* and *Salmonella typhimurium*: Cellular and Molecular Biology. 2nd ed. Washington, DC: American Society for Microbiology; 1996:2708–2720.
13. Campbell A. Evolutionary significance of accessory DNA elements in bacteria. Annu Rev Microbiol. 1981;35:55–83.
14. Farrar WE Jr. Molecular analysis of plasmids in epidemiologic investigation. J Infect Dis. 1983;148:1–6.
15. Mercer AA, Morelli G, Huezenroeder M, et al. Conservation of plasmids among *Escherichia coli* of diverse origins. Infect Immun. 1984;46:649–657.
16. Waschsmuth K. Genotypic approaches to the diagnosis of bacterial infections: Plasmid analyses and gene probes. Infect Control. 1985;6:100–109.
17. Thompkins LS, Troup N, Labigne-Roussel A, et al. Cloned, random chromosomal sequences as probes to identify *Salmonella* species. J Infect Dis. 1986;154:156–162.
18. Eisenstein BI. New molecular techniques for microbial epidemiology and the diagnosis of infectious diseases. J Infect Dis. 1990;161:595–602.
19. Pfaller MA. Typing methods for epidemiologic investigation. In: Balows A, Hausler WJ Jr, Herrmann KL, et al, eds. Manual of Clinical Microbiology. 5th ed. Washington, DC: American Society for Microbiology; 1991:171–182.
20. Selander RK, Caugant DA, Ochman H, et al. Methods of multilocus enzyme electrophoresis for bacterial population genetics and systematics. Appl Environ Microbiol. 1986;51:873–884.
21. Woods CR Jr, Versalovic J, Koeuth T, et al. Analysis of relationships among isolates of *Citrobacter diversus* by using DNA fingerprints generated by repetitive sequence-based primers in the polymerase chain reaction (rep-PCR). J Clin Microbiol. 1992;30:2921–2929.
22. Stacy-Phipps S, Mecca JJ, Weiss JB. Multiplex PCR assay and simple preparation method for stool specimens detect enterotoxigenic *Escherichia coli* DNA during the course of infection. J Clin Microbiol. 1995;33:1054–1059.
23. Gannon VP, D'Souza S, Graham T, et al. Use of the flagellar H7 gene as a target in multiplex PCR assays and improved specificity in identification of enterohemorrhagic *Escherichia coli* strains. J Clin Microbiol. 1997;35:656–662.
24. Nikaido H, Vaara M. Outer membrane. In: Neidhardt FC, Ingraham JL, Low KB, et al, eds. *Escherichia coli* and *Salmonella typhimurium*: Cellular and Molecular Biology. Washington, DC: American Society for Microbiology; 1987:7–22.
25. Orskov F, Orskov I, Jann B, et al. Serology, chemistry and genetics of O and K antigens of *E. coli.* Bacteriol Rev. 1977;41:667–710.
26. Luderitz I, Staub AM, Westphal O. Immunochemistry of O and R antigens of *Salmonella* and related Enterobacteriaceae. Bacteriol Rev. 1966;30:192.
27. Hitchcock PJ, Leive L, Makela PH, et al. Lipopolysaccharide nomenclature—past, present, and future. J Bacteriol. 1986;166:699–705.
28. Rick PD. Lipopolysaccharide biosynthesis. In: Neidhardt FC, Ingraham JL, Low KB, et al, eds. *Escherichia coli* and *Salmonella typhimurium*: Cellular and Molecular Biology. Washington, DC: American Society for Microbiology; 1987:648–662.
29. Drach GW, Reed WP, Williams RC. Antigens common to human and bacterial cells. II. *E. coli* 014 and common Enterobacteriaceae antigen blood groups A and B and *E. coli* 086. J Lab Clin Med. 1972;79:38.
30. Springer GF, Horton RE. Blood group isoantibody. Stimulation in man by feeding blood group–active bacteria. J Clin Invest. 1969;48:1280.
31. MacNab RM. Flagella. In: Neidhardt FC, Ingraham JL, Low KB, et al, eds. *Escherichia coli* and *Salmonella typhimurium*: Cellular and Molecular Biology. Washington, DC: American Society for Microbiology; 1987:70–83.
32. Pazin GJ, Braude AI. Immobilizing antibodies in urine. 2. Prevention of ascending spread of *Proteus mirabilis.* Invest Urol. 1974;12:129–133.
33. Simon M, Zeig J, Silverman M, et al. Phase variation: Evolution of a controlling element. Science. 1980;209:1370.
34. Abraham JM, Freitag CS, Clements JR, et al. An invertible element of DNA controls phase variation of type 1 fimbriae of *Escherichia coli.* Proc Natl Acad Sci U S A. 1985;82:5724–5727.

35. Eisenstein BI. Pathogenic mechanisms of *Legionella pneumophila* and *Escherichia coli*. ASM News. 1987;53:621–624.
36. Jann K, Jann B. The K antigens of *Escherichia coli*. Prog Allergy. 1982;33:53–79.
37. Wilfert C. *E. coli* meningitis: K_1 antigen and virulence. Annu Rev Med. 1978;29:129–136.
38. Stevens P, Huang SN-Y, Welch WD, et al. Restricted complement activation by *Escherichia coli* with the K-1 capsular serotype: A possible role in pathogenicity. J Immunol. 1978;121:2174–2180.
39. Kaisjer B, Jodal U, Hanson LA. Studies in antibody response and tolerance to *E. coli* K antigens in immunized rabbits and in children with urinary tract infection. Int Arch Allerg. 1973;44:260–273.
40. Silver RP, Finn CW, Vann WF, et al. Molecular cloning of the K1 capsular polysaccharide genes of *E. coli*. Nature. 1981;289:696–698.
41. Kaisjer B, Larrson P, Olling S, et al. Protection against acute, ascending pyelonephritis caused by *Escherichia coli* in rats, using isolated capsular antigen conjugated to bovine serum albumin. Infect Immun. 1983;39:142.
42. Fields PI, Swanson RV, Haidaris CG, et al. Mutants of *Salmonella typhimurium* that cannot survive within the macrophage are avirulent. Proc Natl Acad Sci U S A. 1986;83:5189–5193.
43. Isberg RR, Falkow S. A single genetic locus encoded by *Yersinia pseudotuberculosis* permits invasion of cultured animal cells by *E. coli* K12. Nature. 1985;317:262–264.
44. Eisenstein BI, Engleberg NC. Applied molecular genetics: New tools for the microbiologist and clinician. J Infect Dis. 1986;153:416–430.
45. Ruvkin GB, Ausubel F. A general method for site-directed mutagenesis in procaryotes. Nature. 1981;289:85–88.
46. Hensel M, Shea JE, Gleeson C, et al. Simultaneous identification of bacterial virulence genes by negative selection. Science. 1995;269:400–403.
47. Jones GW, Isaacson RE. Proteinaceous bacterial adhesins and their receptors. Crit Rev Microbiol. 1983;10:229–260.
48. Klemm P. Fimbrial adhesins of *Escherichia coli*. Rev Infect Dis. 1985;7:321–340.
49. Clegg S, Gerlach GF. Enterobacterial fimbriae. J Bacteriol. 1987;169:937–938.
50. Krogfelt KA. Bacterial adhesion: Genetics, biogenesis, and role in pathogenesis of fimbrial adhesins of *Escherichia coli*. Rev Infect Dis. 1991;13:721–735.
51. Pieroni P, Worobec EA, Paranchych W, et al. Identification of a human erythrocyte receptor for colonization factor antigen I pili expressed by H10407 enterotoxigenic *Escherichia coli*. Infect Immun. 1988;56:1334–1340.
52. Maurer L, Orndorff PE. A new locus, *pilE*, required for the binding of type 1 piliated *Escherichia coli* to erythrocytes. FEMS Microbiol Lett. 1985;30:59–66.
53. Minion FC, Abraham SN, Beachey EJ, et al. The genetic determinant of adhesive function in type 1 fimbriae of *Escherichia coli* is distinct from the gene encoding the fimbrial subunit. J Bacteriol. 1986;165:1033–1036.
54. Lindberg FP, Lund B, Normark S. Gene products specifying adhesion of uropathogenic *Escherichia coli* are minor components of pili. Proc Natl Acad Sci U S A. 1986;83:1891–1895.
55. Uhlin BE, Norgren M, Baba M, et al. Adhesin to human cells by *Escherichia coli* lacking the major subunit of a digalactoside-specific pilus adhesin. Proc Natl Acad Sci U S A. 1985;82:1800–1804.
56. Lindberg F, Lund B, Johansson L, et al. Localization of the receptor-binding protein adhesin at the tip of the bacterial pilus. Nature. 1987;328:84–87.
57. Evans DJ, Silver RP, Evans DJ Jr. Plasmid controlled colonization factor associated with virulence in *E. coli* enterotoxigenic for humans. Infect Immun. 1975;12:656–667.
58. Levine MM, Kaper JB, Black RE, et al. New knowledge on pathogenesis of bacterial enteric infections as applied to vaccine development. Microbiol Rev. 1983;47:510–550.
59. Mooi FR, de Graaf FK. Molecular biology of fimbriae of enterotoxigenic *Escherichia coli*. Curr Top Microbiol Immunol. 1985;118:119.
60. Bernet-Camard MF, Duigon F, Kerneis S, et al. Glucose up-regulates expression of the differentiation-associated brush border binding site for enterotoxigenic *Escherichia coli* colonization factor antigen I in cultured human enterocyte-like cells. Infect Immun. 1997;65:1299–1306.
61. Freedman DJ, Tacket CO, Delchanty A, et al. Milk immunoglobulin with specific activity against purified colonization factor antigens can protect against oral challenge with enterotoxigenic *Escherichia coli*. J Infect Dis. 1998;177:662–667.
62. Lomberg H, Hanson LA, Jacobson B, et al. Correlation of P blood group, vesicoureteral reflux and bacterial attachment in patients with recurrent pyelonephritis. N Engl J Med. 1983;308:1189–1192.
63. Kallenius G, Molby R, Svenson S, et al. Occurrence of P-fimbriated *Escherichia coli* in urinary tract infections. Lancet. 1981;2:1369–1372.
64. Vaisanen V, Elo J, Tallgren L, et al. Mannose-resistant hemagglutination and P antigen recognition are characteristic of *Escherichia coli* causing primary pyelonephritis. Lancet. 1981;2:1366–1369.
65. Svanborg-Eden C, Freter R, Hagberg L, et al. Inhibition of experimental ascending urinary tract infection by an epithelial cell-surface receptor analogue. Nature. 1982;298:560.
66. Gupta R, Gupta S, Ganguly NK. Role of type I fimbriae in the pathogenesis of chronic pyelonephritis in relation to reactive oxygen species. J Med Microbiol. 1997;46:403–406.
67. Korhonen TK, Valtonen MV, Parkkinen J, et al. Serotypes, hemolysin production, and receptor recognition of *Escherichia coli* strains associated with neonatal sepsis and meningitis. Infect Immun. 1985;48:486.
68. O'Hanley P, Low D, Romero I, et al. Gal-Gal binding and hemolysin phenotypes and genotypes associated with uropathogenic *Escherichia coli*. N Engl J Med. 1985;313:414.
69. Zafriri D, Oron Y, Eisenstein BI, et al. Growth advantage and enhanced toxicity of *Escherichia coli* adherent to tissue culture cells due to restricted diffusion of products secreted by the cells. J Clin Invest. 1987;79:1210–1216.
70. Connell I, Agace W, Klemm P, et al. Type 1 fimbrial expression enhances *Escherichia coli* virulence for the urinary tract. Proc Natl Acad Sci U S A. 1996;93:9827–9832.
71. Valvatne H, Sommerfelt H, Gaastra W, et al. Identification and characterization of CS20, a new putative colonization factor of enterotoxigenic *Escherichia coli*. Infect Immun. 1996;64:2635–2642.
72. Miller JF, Mekalanos JJ, Falkow S. Coordinate regulation and sensory transduction in the control of bacterial virulence. Science. 1989;243:916–922.
73. Mekalanos JJ. Environmental signals controlling expression of virulence determinants in bacteria. J Bacteriol. 1992;174:1–7.
74. Kaper JB, McDaniel TK, Jarvis KG, et al. Genetics of virulence of enteropathogenic *E. coli*. Adv Exp Med Biol. 1997;412:279–287.
75. Silverblatt FJ, Ofek I. Influence of pili on the virulence of *Proteus mirabilis* in experimental hematogenous pyelonephritis. J Infect Dis. 1977;138:664–667.
76. Middlebrook J, Dorland RB. Bacterial toxins: Cellular mechanisms of action. Microbiol Rev. 1984;48:199–221.
77. Eidels L, Proia RL, Hart DA. Membrane receptors for bacterial toxins. Microbiol Rev. 1983;47:596–620.
78. Welch RA, Dellinger EP, Minshew B, et al. Haemolysin contributes to virulence of extraintestinal *Escherichia coli* infections. Nature. 1981;294:665–667.
79. Cavalieri SJ, Bohach GA, Snyder IS. *Escherichia coli* alpha-hemolysin: Characteristics and probable role in pathogenicity. Microbiol Rev. 1984;48:326–343.
80. Gadeberg OV, Orskov I. In vitro cytotoxic effect of alpha-hemolytic *Escherichia coli* on human blood granulocytes. Infect Immun. 1984;45:255–260.
81. Waalwijk C, MacLaren DM, de Graaf J. In vivo function of hemolysin in the nephropathogenicity of *Escherichia coli*. Infect Immun. 1983;42:245–249.
82. Waalwijk C, van den Bosch JF, MacLaren DM, et al. Hemolysin plasmid coding for the virulence nephropathogenic *Escherichia coli* strain. Infect Immun. 1982;35:32–37.
83. Hughes C, Hacker J, Roberts A, et al. Hemolysin production as a virulence marker in symptomatic and asymptomatic urinary tract infections caused by *Escherichia coli*. Infect Immun. 1983;39:546–551.
84. Bohach GA, Snyder IS. Chemical and immunological analysis of the complex structure of *Escherichia coli* alpha-hemolysin. J Bacteriol. 1985;164:1071.
85. Bhakdi S, Mackman N, Nicaud JM, et al. *Escherichia coli* hemolysin may damage target cell membranes by generating transmembrane pores. Infect Immun. 1986;52:63–69.
86. Gadeberg OV, Orskov I, Rhodes JM. Cytotoxic effects of an alpha-hemolytic *Escherichia coli* strain on human blood monocytes and granulocytes in vitro. Infect Immun. 1983;41:358–364.
87. Cavalieri SJ, Snyder IS. Effect of *Escherichia coli* alpha-hemolysin on human peripheral leukocyte viability in vitro. Infect Immun. 1982;37:966–974.
88. Pruett TL, Chenoweth DE, Fiegel VD, et al. *Escherichia coli* and human neutrophils: Effect of bacterial supernatant with hemolysin activity upon chemotaxin receptors. Arch Surg. 1985;120:212.
89. Welch RA, Hull R, Falkow S. Molecular cloning and physical characterization of a chromosomal hemolysin from *Escherichia coli*. Infect Immun. 1983;42:178–186.
90. Muller D, Hughes C, Goebel W. Relationship between plasmid and chromosomal hemolysin determinants of *Escherichia coli*. J Bacteriol. 1983;153:846–851.
91. Lebek G, Gruenig HM. Relation between the hemolytic property and iron metabolism in *Escherichia coli*. Infect Immun. 1985;50:682–686.
92. O'Brien AD, LaVeck GD, Thompson MR, et al. Production of *Shigella dysentariae* type 1–like cytotoxin by *Escherichia coli*. J Infect Dis. 1982;146:763–769.
93. O'Brien AD, LaVeck GD. Purification and characterization of a *Shigella dysenteriae* 1–like toxin produced by *Escherichia coli*. Infect Immun. 1983;40:675–683.
94. Strockbine NA, Marques LR, Holmes RK, et al. Characterization of monoclonal antibodies against shiga-like toxin from *Escherichia coli*. Infect Immun. 1985;50:695–700.
95. Nataro JP, Kaper JB. Diarrheagenic *Escherichia coli*. Clin Microbiol Rev. 1998;11:142–201.
96. van Dommelen FS, de Jonge JR. Local changes in fractional saturation of cGMP- and cAMP-receptors in intestinal microvilli in response to cholera toxin and heat-stable *Escherichia coli* toxin. Biochim Biophys Acta. 1986;886:135.
97. Levine MM. *Escherichia coli* that cause diarrhea: Enterotoxigenic, enteropathogenic, enteroinvasive, enterohemorrhagic, and enteroadherent. J Infect Dis. 1987;155:377–389.
98. Holmgren J, Fredman P, Lindblad M, et al. Rabbit intestinal glycoprotein receptor for *Escherichia coli* heat-labile enterotoxin lacking affinity for cholera toxin. Infect Immun. 1982;38:424–433.
99. Quezado ZMN, Natanson C, Alling DW, et al. A controlled trial of human lipid A-reactive monoclonal antibody HA-1A in a canine model of gram-negative septic shock. JAMA 1993;269:2221–2227.
100. Bone RC. The search for the magic bullet to fight sepsis. JAMA. 1993;269:2266–2267.
101. Bone RC. Gram-negative sepsis: A dilemma of modern medicine. Clin Microbiol Rev. 1993;6:57–68.
102. Jack RS, Fan X, Bernheiden M, et al. Lipopolysaccharide-binding protein is required to combat a murine gram-negative bacterial infection. Nature. 1997;389:742–745.
103. Vogels MTE, Van der Meer JWM. Use of immune modulators in nonspecific therapy of bacterial infections. Antimicrob Agents Chemother. 1992;36:1–5.

104. Dinarello CA, Gelfand JA, Wolff SM. Anticytokine strategies in the treatment of the systemic inflammatory response syndrome. JAMA. 1993;269:1829–1835.
105. Ge Y, Ezzell RM, Clark BD, et al. Relationship of tissue and cellular interleukin-1 and lipopolysaccharide after endotoxemia and bacteremia. J Infect Dis. 1997;176:1313–1321.
106. Song S-K, Karl IE, Ackerman JJH, et al. Increased intracellular Ca^{2+}: A critical link in the pathophysiology of sepsis? Proc Natl Acad Sci U S A. 1993;90:3933–3937.
107. Pfeffer K, Matsuyama T, Kundig TM, et al. Mice deficient for the 55 kd tumor necrosis factor receptor are resistant to endotoxic shock, yet succumb to *L. monocytogenes* infection. Cell. 1993;73:457–467.
108. Hurley JC. Reappraisal of the role of endotoxin in the sepsis syndrome. Lancet. 1993;341:1333–1335.
109. Corriveau CC, Danner RL. Endotoxin as a therapeutic target in septic shock. Infect Agents Dis. 1993;2:35–43.
110. Porat R, Clark BD, Wolff SM, et al. Enhancement of growth of virulent strains of *Escherichia coli* by interleukin-1. Science. 1992;254:430–432.
111. Weiss J, Elsbach P, Shu C, et al. Human bactericidal/permeability-increasing protein and a recombinant NH_2-terminal fragment cause killing of serum-resistant gram-negative bacteria in whole blood and inhibit tumor necrosis factor release induced by the bacteria. J Clin Invest. 1992;90:1122–1130.
112. Schumann RR, Leong SR, Flaggs GW, et al. Structure and function of lipopolysaccharide binding protein. Science. 1990;249:1429–1431.
113. Pugin J, Schurer-Maly C-C, Leturcq D, et al. Lipopolysaccharide activation of human endothelial and epithelial cells is mediated by lipopolysaccharide-binding protein and soluble CD14. Proc Natl Acad Sci U S A. 1993;90:2744–2748.
114. Bagg A, Neilands JB. Molecular mechanisms of regulation of siderophore-mediated iron assimilation. Microbiol Rev. 1987;51:509–518.
115. Crosa JH. Signal transduction and transcriptional and posttranscriptional control of iron-regulated genes in bacteria. Microbiol Mol Biol Rev. 1997;61:319–336.
116. Finkelstein RA, Sciortino CV, McIntosh MA. Role of iron in microbe-host interactions. Rev Infect Dis. 1983;5(Suppl):759–777.
117. Litwin CM, Calderwood SB. Role of iron in regulation of virulence genes. Clin Microbiol Rev. 1993;6:137–149.
118. Griffiths E. Iron and the susceptibility to bacterial infections. In: Beers RF, Bassett EG, eds. Nutritional Factors: Modulating Effects on Metabolic Processes. New York: Raven Press; 1981:463–676.
119. Lankford CE. Bacterial assimilation of iron. Crit Rev Microbiol. 1973;2:273–331.
120. Stuart SJ, Greenwood KT, Luke RK. Hydroxamate-mediated transport of iron controlled by ColV plasmids. J Bacteriol. 1980;143:35–42.
121. Williams PH. Novel iron uptake system specified by ColV plasmids: An important component in the virulence of invasive strains of *Escherichia coli*. Infect Immun. 1979;26:925–932.
122. Valvano MA, Silver RP, Crossa JH. Occurrence of chromosome—or plasmid—mediated aerobactin iron transport systems and hemolysin production among clonal groups of human invasive strains of *Escherichia coli* K1. Infect Immun. 1986;52:192–199.
123. Warner PJ, Williams PH, Bindereif A. ColV plasmid-specified aerobactin synthesis by invasive strains of *Escherichia coli*. Infect Immun. 1981;33:540–545.
124. Williams PH, Carbonetti NH. Iron, siderophores, and the pursuit of virulence: Independence of the aerobactin and enterochelin iron uptake systems in *Escherichia coli*. Infect Immun. 1986;51:942–947.
125. Montgomerie JZ, Kalmanson GM, Guze LB. Enterobactin and virulence of *Escherichia coli* in pyelonephritis. J Infect Dis. 1979;140:1013.
126. Moore DG, Yancey RJ, Lankford CE, et al. Bacteriostatic enterochelin-specific immunoglobulin from normal human serum. Infect Immun. 1980;27:418–423.
127. Litwin CM, Calderwood SB. Role of iron in regulation of virulence genes. Clin Microbiol Rev. 1993;6:137–149.
128. Kluger MJ, Rothenburg BA. Fever and reduced iron: Their interaction as a host defense response to bacterial infection. Science. 1979;203:374–376.
129. Ellison RT III, Giehl TJ. Killing of gram-negative bacteria by lactoferrin and lysozyme. J Clin Invest. 1991;88:1080–1091.
130. van Oss CJ. Phagocytosis as a surface phenomenon. Annu Rev. Microbiol. 1978;32:19.
131. Robbins JB, Schneerson R, Egan WB, et al. Virulence properties of bacterial capsular polysaccharides—unanswered questions. In: Smith H, Skehel JH, Turner MJ, eds. The Molecular Basis of Microbial Pathogenicity. Weinheim: Verglag Chemie GmbH; 1980:115–132.
132. Stevens P, Huang SN-Y, Welch WD, et al. Restricted complement activation by *Escherichia coli* with the K1 capsular serotype: A possible role in pathogenicity. J Immunol. 1978;121:2174–2180.
133. Taylor PW. Bactericidal and bacteriolytic activity of serum against gram-negative bacteria. Microbiol Rev. 1983;47:46–83.
134. Cabello FC. Determinants of pathogenicity of *E. coli* K1. In: Timmis KN, Puhler A, eds. Plasmids of Medical, Environmental and Commercial Importance. Amsterdam: North Holland; 1979:155–160.
135. Blattner FR, Plunkett G III, Bloch CA, et al. The complete genome sequence of *Escherichia coli* K-12. Science. 1997;277:1453–1474.
136. Binns MM, Mayden J, Levine RP. Further characterization of complement resistance conferred on *Escherichia coli* by the plasmid genes *traT* of R100 and *iss* of ColV.I-K94. Infect Immun. 1982;35:654–659.
137. Moll A, Manning PA, Timmis KN. Plasmid-determined resistance to serum bactericidal activity: A major outer membrane protein, the *traT* gene product, is responsible for plasmid-specified serum resistance in *Escherichia coli*. Infect Immun. 1980;28:359–367.
138. Davies J, Smith DI. Plasmid-determined resistance to antimicrobial agents. Annu Rev Microbiol. 1978;32:469–518.
139. Cohen S. Transposable genetic elements and plasmid evolution. Nature. 1976;263:731–738.
140. Falkow S. Infectious Multiple Drug Resistance. London: Pion; 1975.
141. Finland M. Emergence of antibiotic resistance in hospitals, 1935–1975. Rev Infect Dis. 1979;1:4–21.
142. O'Brien TF, Acar JF, Medeiros AA, et al. International comparison of prevalence of resistance to antibiotics. JAMA. 1978;239:1518–1523.
143. Guiney DG Jr. Promiscuous transfer of drug resistance in gram-negative bacteria. J Infect Dis. 1984;149:320–329.
144. Elwell LP, Shipley PL. Plasmid-mediated factors associated with virulence of bacteria to animals. Annu Rev Microbiol. 1980;34:465–496.
145. Gowal D, Saxena S, Mago M, et al. Plasmid mediated enterotoxin production and drug resistance amongst *Escherichia coli* from cases of infantile diarrhea. Indian J Pediatr. 1985;52:57–59.
146. Harnet NM, Gules CL. Linkage of genes for heat-stable enterotoxin, drug resistance, K99 antigen, and colicin in bovine and porcine strains of enterotoxigenic *Escherichia coli*. Am J Vet Res. 1985;46:428–433.
147. Murray B, Evans D, Penaranda M, et al. CFA/I-ST plasmids. Comparison of enterotoxigenic *Escherichia coli* (ETEC) of serogroups 025, 063, 078, and 0128 and mobilization from an R factor–containing epidemic (ETEC) isolate. J Bacteriol. 1983;153:566–570.
148. Waalwijk C, Van Den Bosch J, MacLaren D, et al. Hemolysin plasmid coding for the virulence of a nephropathogenic *E. coli* strain. Infect Immun. 1982;35:32–37.
149. Jacoby GA, Archer GL. New mechanisms of bacterial resistance to antimicrobial agents. N Engl J Med. 1991;324:601–612.
150. Bush K. Characterization of beta-lactamases. Antimicrob Agents Chemother. 1989;33:259–263.
151. Sanders CC. β-lactamases of gram-negative bacteria: New challenges for new drugs. Clin Infect Dis. 1992;14:1089–1099.
152. Moellering RC Jr. Meeting the challenges of β-lactamases. J Antimicrob Chemother. 1993;31(Suppl A):1–8.
153. Levy SB. Multidrug resistance—a sign of the times. N Engl J Med. 1998;338:1376-1378.
154. Pfaller MA, Jones RN, Doern GV. Multicenter evaluation of the antimicrobial activity for six broad-spectrum beta-lactams in Venezuela using the E-test method. Diagn Microbiol Infect Dis. 1998;30:45–52.
155. Lomovskaya O, Lewis K. *emr*, an *Escherichia coli* locus for multidrug resistance. Proc Natl Acad Sci U S A. 1992;89:8938–8942.
156. Cohen SP, Hachler H, Levy SB. Genetic and functional analysis of the multiple antibiotic resistance (*mar*) locus in *Escherichia coli*. J Bacteriol. 1993;175:1484–1492.
157. Chopra I. Efflux-based antibiotic resistance mechanisms: The evidence for increasing prevalence. J Antimicrob Chemother. 1992;30:737–739.
158. Neu HC. The crisis in antibiotic resistance. Science. 1992;257:1064–1073.
159. Oethinger M, Conrad S, Kaifel K, et al. Molecular epidemiology of fluoroquinolone-resistant *Escherichia coli* bloodstream isolates from patients admitted to European cancer centers. Antimicrob Agents Chemother. 1996;40:387–392.
160. Cohen ML. Epidemiology of drug resistance: Implications for the post-antimicrobial era. Science. 1992;257:1050–1055.
161. Lester SC, del Pilar M, Wang F, et al. The carriage of *Escherichia coli* resistant to antimicrobial agents by healthy children in Boston, in Caracas, Venezuela, and in Qin Pu, China. N Engl J Med. 1990;323:285–289.
162. Blattner FR, Plunkett G III, Bloch CA, et al. The complete genome sequence of *Escherichia coli* K-12. Science. 1997;277:1453–1474.
163. Siitonen A. *Escherichia coli* in fecal flora of healthy adults: Serotypes, P and type 1C fimbriae, non-P mannose–resistant adhesins, and hemolytic activity. J Infect Dis. 1992;166:1058–1065.
164. Adam A. Biology of colon bacillus dyspepsia and its relation to pathogenesis and to intoxication. Jahrb Kinderberth. 1923;101:295.
165. Ericsson CD, DuPont HL. Traveler's diarrhea: Recent developments. In: Remington JS, Swartz MN, eds. Current Clinical Topics in Infectious Diseases. 6th ed. New York: McGraw-Hill; 1985:66–84.
166. Rubinoff MJ, Field M. Infectious diarrhea. Annu Rev Med. 1991;403–410.
167. Okhuysen PC, Ericsson CD. Travelers' diarrhea: Prevention and treatment. Med Clin North Am. 1992;76:1357–1373.
168. Gorbach SL, Kean BH, Evand DG, et al. Traveler's diarrhea and toxigenic *E. coli*. N Engl J Med. 1975;292:933–936.
169. Steffen R, VanderLinde F, Gyr K, et al. Epidemiology of diarrhea in travelers. JAMA. 1983;249:1176–1180.
170. Sack RB, Hirschorn N, Brownlee I, et al. Enterotoxigenic *E. coli*–associated diarrheal disease in Apache children. N Engl J Med. 1975;292:1041–1045.
171. Ryder RW, Wachsmuter IK, Buston AE, et al. Infantile diarrhea produced by heat stable enterotoxigenic *E. coli*. N Engl J Med. 1976;295:849–853.
172. Tacket CO, Losonsky G, Link H, et al. Protection by milk immunoglobulin concentrate against oral challenge with enterotoxigenic *Escherichia coli*. N Engl J Med. 1988;318:1240–1243.
173. Sack DA, Kaminsky DC, Sack RB, et al. Prophylactic doxycycline for traveler's diarrhea. N Engl J Med. 1978;298:758–763.
174. Ericsson CD, Johnson PC, DuPont HL, et al. Ciprofloxacin or trimethoprim-sulfamethoxazole as initial therapy for traveler's diarrhea. Ann Intern Med. 1987;106:216–220.
175. Ryder RW, Sack DA, Kapikian AZ, et al. Enterotoxigenic *Escherichia coli* and reovirus-like agent in rural Bangladesh. Lancet. 1976;1:659–662.

176. Ewing WH, Tatum HW, Davis BR. The occurrence of *Escherichia coli* serotypes associated with diarrheal disease in the United States. Public Health Lab. 1957;15:118.
177. Ulshen MH, Rollo JR. Pathogenesis of *E. coli* gastroenteritis in man: Another mechanism. N Engl J Med. 1980;302:99–101.
178. Inman LR, Cantey JR. Specific adherence of *Escherichia coli* (strain RDEC-1) to membranous (M) cells of the Peyer's patch in *Escherichia coli* diarrhea in the rabbit. J Clin Invest. 1983;71:1–9.
179. Mathewson JJ, Johnson PC, DuPont HL, et al. A newly recognized cause of travelers' diarrhea: Enteroadherent *Escherichia coli*. J Infect Dis. 1985;151:471–475.
180. Levine MM, Nataro JP, Karch H, et al. The diarrheal response of humans to some classic serotypes of enteropathogenic *Escherichia coli* is dependent on a plasmid encoding an enteroadhesiveness factor. J Infect Dis. 1985;152:550–559.
181. Edelman R, Levine MM. Summary of a workshop on enteropathogenic *Escherichia coli*. J Infect Dis. 1983;147:1108–1118.
182. Fang G. Intestinal *Escherichia coli* infections. Curr Opin Infect Dis. 1993;6:48–53.
183. Francis CL, Jerse AE, Kaper JB, et al. Characterization of interactions of enteropathogenic *Escherichia coli* O157:H6 with mammalian cells in vitro. J Infect Dis. 1991;164:693–703.
184. Giron JA, Ho ASY, Schoolnik GK. An inducible bundle-forming pilus of enteropathogenic *Escherichia coli*. Science. 1991;254:710–713.
185. Echeverria P, Serichantalerg O, Changchawalit S, et al. Tissue culture-adherent *Escherichia coli* in infantile diarrhea. J Infect Dis. 1992;165:141–143.
186. Wanke CA, Schoring JB, Barrett LJ, et al. Potential role of adherence traits of *Escherichia coli* in persistent diarrhea in an urban Brazilian slum. Pediatr Infect Dis J. 1991;10:746–751.
187. Savarino SJ, Fasano A, Watson J, et al. Enteroaggregative *Escherichia coli* heat-stable enterotoxin 1 represents another subfamily of *E. coli* heat-stable toxin. Proc Natl Acad Sci U S A. 1993;90:3093–3098.
188. Harris JR, Wachsmuth IK, David BF, et al. High molecular weight plasmid correlates with *Escherichia coli* invasiveness. Infect Immun. 1982;37:1295–1298.
189. Sakazaki R, Tamura K, Saito M. Enteropathogenic *E. coli* associated with diarrhea in children and adults. Jpn J Med Sci Biol. 1967;20:387.
190. Small PLC, Falkow S. Identification of regions on a 230-kilobase plasmid from enteroinvasive *Escherichia coli* that are required for entry into HEp-2 cells. Infect Immun. 1988;56:225–229.
191. Riley LW, Remis RS, Helgerson SD, et al. Hemorrhagic colitis associated with rare *Escherichia coli* serotype. N Engl J Med. 1983;308:681–685.
192. Slutsker L, Ries AA, Maloney K, et al. A nationwide case-control study of *Escherichia coli* O157:H7 infection in the United States. J Infect Dis. 1998;177:962–966.
193. Riley LW. The epidemiologic, clinical, and microbiologic features of hemorrhagic colitis. Annu Rev Microbiol. 1987;41:383–407.
194. Ryan CA, Tauxe RX, Hosek GW, et al. *Escherichia coli* 0157:H7 diarrhea in a nursing home: Clinical, epidemiologic, and pathologic findings. J Infect Dis. 1986;154:631–638.
195. Tarr PI. Escherichia coli O157:H7 clinical, diagnostic, and epidemiological aspects of human infection. Clin Infect Dis. 1995;20:1–8.
196. Johnson WM, Lior H, Bezanson GS. Cytotoxic *Escherichia coli* 0157:H7 associated with haemorrhagic colitis in Canada. Lancet. 1983;1:76.
197. Padhye VV, Beery JT, Kittell FB, et al. Colonic hemorrhage produced in mice by a unique vero cell cytotoxin from an *Escherichia coli* strain that causes hemorrhagic colitis. J Infect Dis. 1987;155:1249–1253.
198. O'Brien AD, Newland JW, Miller SF, et al. Shiga-like toxin-converting phages from *Escherichia coli* strains that cause hemorrhagic colitis or infantile diarrhea. Science. 1984;226:694–696.
199. Karmali MA, Petric M, Steele BT, et al. Sporadic cases of haemolytic-uremic syndrome associated with faecal cytotoxin and cytotoxin-producing *Escherichia coli* in stools. Lancet. 1983;1:619–620.
200. Karmali MA, Petric M, Lim C, et al. The association between idiopathic hemolytic uremic syndrome and infection by verotoxin-producing *Escherichia coli*. J Infect Dis. 1985;151:775–782.
201. Gransden WR, Damm MAS, Anderson JD, et al. Further evidence associating hemolytic uremic syndrome with infection by Verotoxin-producing *Escherichia coli* 0157:H7. J Infect Dis. 1986;154:522–524.
202. Swerdlow DL, Woodruff BA, Brady RC, et al. A waterborne outbreak in Missouri of *Escherichia coli* O157:H7 associated with bloody diarrhea and death. Ann Intern Med. 1992;117:812–819.
203. Belongia EA, Osterholm MT, Soler JT, et al. Transmission of *Escherichia coli* O157:H7 infection in Minnesota child day-care facilities. JAMA. 1993;269:883–888.
204. Besser RE, Lett SM, Weber JT, et al. An outbreak of diarrhea and hemolytic uremic syndrome from *Escherichia coli* O157:H7 in fresh-pressed apple cider. JAMA. 1993;269:2217–2220.
205. Centers for Disease Control and Prevention. Update: Multistate outbreak of *Escherichia coli* O157:H7 infections from hamburgers—Western United States, 1992–1993. MMWR Morb Mortal Wkly Rep. 1993;42:258–263.
206. Mariani-Kurkdjian P, Denamur E, Milon A, et al. Identification of a clone of *Escherichia coli* O103:H2 as a potential agent of hemolytic-uremic syndrome in France. J Clin Microbiol. 1993;31:296–301.
207. Stamm WE, Turck M. Urinary tract infection. Adv Intern Med. 1983;28:141.
208. Fowler JE Jr, Stamey TA. Studies of introital colonization in women with recurrent urinary tract infections: VII. The role of bacterial adherence. J Urol. 1977;117:472.
209. Schaeffer AJ, Jones JM, Dunn JK. Association of in vitro *Escherichia coli* adherence to vaginal and buccal epithelial cells with susceptibility of women to recurrent urinary-tract infections. N Engl J Med. 1981;304:1062–1066.
210. Johnson JR. Virulence factors in *Escherichia coli* urinary tract infection. Clin Microbiol Rev. 1991;4:80–128.
211. Johnson JR, Roberts P, Stamm WE. P fimbriae and other virulence factors in *Escherichia coli* urosepsis: Association with patients' characteristics. J Infect Dis. 1987;156:225–229.
212. Stamm WE. Catheter-associated urinary tract infections: Epidemiology, pathogenesis, and prevention. Am J Med. 1991;91(Suppl 3B):65S–71S.
213. Stamm WE, McKevitt M, Roberts PL, et al. Natural history of recurrent urinary tract infection in women. Rev Infect Dis. 1991;13:77–84.
214. Brumfitt W. Progress in understanding urinary infections. J Antimicrob Chemother. 1991;27:9–22.
215. Spach DH, Stapleton AE, Stamm WE. Behavioral and genetic factors related to urinary tract infections. Curr Opin Infect Dis. 1993;6:31–35.
216. Andriole VT. Urinary tract infections in the 90s: Pathogenesis and management. Infection. 1992;20(Suppl 4):S251–S256.
217. Buckley RM, McGuckin M, MacGregor RR. Urine bacterial counts following sexual intercourse. N Engl J Med. 1978;298:321.
218. Kallenius G. Structure of carbohydrate part of receptor on human uroepithelial cells for pyelonephritogenic *E. coli*. Lancet. 1981;2:604–606.
219. Minshew BH, Jorgensen J, Counts GW, et al. Association of hemolysin production, hemagglutination of human erythrocytes, and virulence for chicken embryos of extraintestinal *Escherichia coli* isolates. Infect Immun. 1978;20:50–54.
220. Hughes C, Hacker J, Roberts A, et al. Hemolysin production as a virulence marker in symptomatic and asymptomatic urinary tract infections caused by *Escherichia coli*. Infect Immun. 1983;39:546.
221. Davies DL, Falkinere FR, Hardy KG. Colicin V production by clinical isolates of *Escherichia coli*. Infect Immun. 1981;31:574–579.
222. Olling S. Sensitivity of gram negative bacilli to the serum bactericidal activity: A marker of host-parasite relationship in acute and persisting infections. Scand J Infect Dis. 1977;10(Suppl):1–40.
223. Turck M, Petersdorf RG. The epidemiology of nonenteric *E. coli* infections: Prevalence of serological groups. J Clin Invest. 1962;41:1760.
224. Turck M, Ronald AR, Clark H, et al. Studies on the epidemiology of *E. coli* 1960–1968. J Infect Dis. 1969;120:13.
225. Kaijser B. Immunology of *E. coli*: K antigen and its relation to urinary tract infection. J Infect Dis. 1973;127:670.
226. Kaijser B, Ahlstedt S. Protective capacity of antibodies against *E. coli* O and K antigens. Infect Immun. 1977;17:286.
227. Vaisanen-Rhen V, Elo J, Vaisanen E, et al. P-fimbriated clones among uropathogenic *Escherichia coli* strains. Infect Immun. 1984;43:149.
228. Foxman B, Zhang L, Palin K, et al. Bacterial virulence characteristics of *Escherichia coli* isolates from first-time urinary tract infection. J Infect Dis. 1995;171:1514–1521.
229. Verghese A, Berk SL. Bacterial pneumonia in the elderly. Medicine (Baltimore). 1983;62:271–285.
230. Levison ME, Kaye D. Pneumonia caused by gram-negative bacilli: An overview. Rev Infect Dis. 1985;7(Suppl):656–665.
231. Johanson WG Jr, Woods DE, Chaudhuri T. Association of respiratory tract colonization with adherence of gram-negative bacilli to epithelial cells. J Infect Dis. 1979;139:667–673.
232. Johanson WG Jr, Higuchi JH, Chaudhuri TR, et al. Bacterial adherence to epithelial cells in bacillary colonization of the respiratory tract. Am Rev Respir Dis. 1980;121:55.
233. Scheld WM, Mandell GL. Nosocomial pneumonia: Pathogenesis and recent advances in diagnosis and therapy. Rev Infect Dis. 1991;13(Suppl 9):S743–S751.
234. Abraham SN, Beachey EH, Simpson WA. Adherence of *Streptococcus pyogenes*, *Escherichia coli* and *Pseudomonas aeruginosa* to fibronectin-coated and uncoated epithelial cells. Infect Immun. 1983;41:1261.
235. Woods DE, Strauss DC, Johanson WG Jr, et al. Role of salivary protease activity in adherence of gram-negative bacilli to mammalian buccal epithelial cells in vivo. J Clin Invest. 1981;68:1435.
236. Haggerty RJ, Ziai M. Acute bacterial meningitis. Adv Pediatr. 1964;13:129.
237. McCracken GH, Sarff ID. Current status and therapy of neonatal *E. coli* meningitis. Hosp Pract. 1974 Oct:57.
238. Robbins JB, McCracken GH, Gotschlich EC, et al. *Escherichia coli* K1 capsular polysaccharide associated with neonatal meningitis. N Engl J Med. 1974;290:1216–1220.
239. McCracken GH, Sarff ID, Glode MD, et al. Relation between *Escherichia coli* K1 capsular polysaccharide antigen and clinical outcome in neonatal meningitis. Lancet. 1974;2:246–250.
240. Sarff ID, McCracken GH, Schiffer MS, et al. Epidemiology of *Escherichia coli* K1 in healthy and diseased newborns. Lancet. 1975;1:1099–1104.
241. Moxon ER, Glode MP, Sutton A, et al. The infant rat as a model of bacterial meningitis. J Infect Dis. 1977;136(Suppl):186–190.
242. Griffiths E. Candidate virulence markers. In: Sussman M, ed. The Virulence of *Escherichia coli*. London: Academic Press; 1985:193–226.
243. Johnson JR, Russo TA, Scheutz F, et al. Discovery of disseminated J96-like strains of uropathogenic *Escherichia coli* O4:H5 containing genes for both PapG (J96) (class I) and PrsG (J96) (class III) Gal (alph1-4) Gal-binding adhesins. J Infect Dis. 1997;175:983–988.
244. Centers for Disease Control. National nosocomial infection study report. Annual summary 1979, issued March 1982.

245. Gransden WR, Eykyn SJ, Phillips I, et al. Bacteremia due to *Escherichia coli*: A study of 861 episodes. Rev Infect Dis. 1990;12:1008–1018.
246. Cockerill FR III, Muller SR, Anhalt JP, et al. Prevention of infection in critically ill patients by selective decontamination of the digestive tract. Ann Intern Med. 1992;117:545–553.
247. Goldenberg DL, Brandt KD, Catheart ES, et al. Acute arthritis caused by gram-negative bacilli: A clinical characterization. Medicine (Baltimore). 1974;53:197.
248. Faraawi R, Fong IW. *Escherichia coli* emphysematous endophthalmitis and pyelonephritis: Case report and review of the literature. Am J Med. 1988;84:636–639.
249. Saksouk F, Salti I. Acute suppurative thyroiditis caused by *Escherichia coli*. BMJ. 1977;2:23.
250. Altemeier WA. The bacterial flora of acute perforated appendicitis with peritonitis: A bacteriologic study based upon one hundred cases. Ann Surg. 1938;107:517.
251. Conn HO. Spontaneous peritonitis and bacteremia in Laennec's cirrhosis caused by enteric organisms. Ann Intern Med. 1964;60:568.
252. Rubin RH, Swartz MN, Malt R. Hepatic abscess: Changes in clinical bacteriologic and therapeutic aspects. Am J Med. 1974;57:601.
253. Brewer NS, MacCarty CS, Wellman WE. Brain abscess: A review of recent experience. Ann Intern Med. 1975;83:571.
254. Finland M, Barnes MW. Changing etiology of bacterial endocarditis in the antibacterial era. Ann Intern Med. 1970;72:341.
255. Meares EM Jr. Prostatitis. Med Clin North Am. 1991;75:405–424.
256. Highsmith AK, Jarvis WR. *Klebsiella pneumoniae* selected virulence factors that contribute to pathogenicity. Infect Control. 1985;6:75.
257. Carpenter JL. *Klebsiella* pulmonary infections: Occurrence at one medical center and review. Rev Infect Dis. 1990;12:672–682.
258. de la Torre MG, Romero-Vivas J, Martinez-Beltran J, et al. *Klebsiella* bacteremia: An analysis of 100 episodes. Rev Infect Dis. 1985;7:143–150.
259. Montgomerie J. Epidemiology of *Klebsiella* and hospital-associated infections. Rev Infect Dis. 1979;1:736–753.
260. Noriega ER, Leibowitz RE, Richmond AS, et al. Nosocomial infection caused by gentamicin resistant, streptomycin sensitive *Klebsiella*. J Infect Dis. 1975;131(Suppl):45.
261. Rennie RP, Duncan IBR. Emergence of gentamicin resistant *Klebsiella* in a general hospital. Antimicrob Agents Chemother. 1978;11:179.
262. Lucet JC, Chevret S, Decre D, et al. Outbreak of multiply resistant Enterobacteriaceae in an intensive care unit: Epidemiology and risk factors for acquisition. Clin Infect Dis. 1996;22:430–436.
263. Prodinger WM, Fille M, Bauernfeind A, et al. Molecular epidemiology of *Klebsiella pneumoniae* producing SHV-5 beta-lactamase: Parallel outbreaks due to multiple plasmid transfer. J Clin Microbiol. 1996;34:564–568.
264. Chou FF, Kou HK. Endogenous endophthalmitis associated with pyogenic hepatic abscess. J Am Coll Surg. 1996;182:33–36.
265. Reyes E. Rhinoscleroma. Observations based on a study of two hundred cases. Arch Dermatol Syph. 1946;54:531.
266. Muzyka MM, Gubina KM. Problems of the epidemiology of scleroma. J Hyg Epidemiol Microbiol Immunol. 1971;15:233.
267. Krasilnikov AP, Izraitel NA, Krylou A. Focal incidence of scleroma. J Hyg Epidemiol Microbiol Immunol. 1971;15:243.
268. Paul C, Pialoux G, Dupont B, et al. Infection due to *Klebsiella rhinoscleromatis* in two patients infected with human immunodeficiency virus. Clin Infect Dis. 1993;16:441–442.
269. Porto R, Hevia O, Hensley GT, et al. Disseminated *Klebsiella rhinoscleromatis* infection. Arch Pathol Lab Med. 1989;113:1381–1383.
270. Altman G, Ostfeld E, Zohar S, et al. Rhinoscleroma. Isr J Med Sci. 1977;13:62.
271. Berger SA, Polloch AA, Richmond AS. Isolation of *Klebsiella ozaenae* and *Klebsiella rhinoscleromatis* in a general hospital. Am J Clin Pathol. 1971;67:499.
272. Gallagher PG, Ball WS. Cerebral infarctions due to CNS infection with *Enterobacter sakazakii*. Pediatr Radiol. 1991;21:135–136.
273. Wenger PN, Tokars JI, Brennan P, et al. An outbreak of *Enterobacter hormaechei* infection and colonization in an intensive care nursery. Clin Infect Dis. 1997;24:1243–1244.
274. Mayhall CA, Camb AV, Gayle WE, et al. *Enterobacter cloacae* septicemia in a burn unit center: Epidemiology and control of an outbreak. J Infect Dis. 1979;139:166–171.
275. John JR Jr, Sharbough RJ, Bannister ER. *Enterobacter cloacae*: Bacteremia, epidemiology and antibiotic resistance. Rev Infect Dis. 1982;4:13–28.
276. Steinhauer BW, Eickhoff TC, Kislak JW, et al. The *Klebsiella-Enterobacter-Serratia* division: Clinical and epidemiologic characteristics. Ann Intern Med. 1966;65:1180.
277. Flynn DM, Weinstein RA, Nathan C, et al. Patients' endogenous flora as the source of "nosocomial" *Enterobacter* in cardiac surgery. J Infect Dis. 1987;156:363–368.
278. Burchard KW, Barroll DT, Reed M, et al. *Enterobacter* bacteremia in surgical patients. Surgery. 1986;100:857–861.
279. Gallagher PG. *Enterobacter* bacteremia in pediatric patients. Rev Infect Dis. 1990;12:808–812.
280. Chow JW, Fine MJ, Schlaes DM, et al. *Enterobacter* bacteremia: Clinical features and emergence of antibiotic resistance during therapy. Ann Intern Med. 1991;115:585–590.
281. Bodey GP, Elting LS, Rodriguez S. Bacteremia caused by *Enterobacter*: 15 years of experience in a cancer hospital. Rev Infect Dis. 1991;13:550–558.
282. Watanakunakorn C, Weber J. *Enterobacter* bacteremia: A review of 58 episodes. Scand J Infect Dis. 1989;21:1–8.
283. Johnson MP, Ramphal R. Beta-lactam–resistant *Enterobacter* bacteremia in febrile neutropenic patients receiving monotherapy. J Infect Dis. 1990;162:981–983.
284. Louie A, Baltch AL, Smith RP. Gram-negative bacterial surveillance in diabetic patients. Infect Med. 1993;10:33–45.
285. Olson B, Weinstein RA, Nathan C, et al. Broad-spectrum β-lactam resistance in *Enterobacter*: Emergence during treatment and mechanisms of resistance. J Antimicrob Chemother. 1983;11:299–310.
286. Pfaller MA, Jones RN, Marshall SA, et al. Inducible amp C beta-lactamase producing gram-negative bacilli from blood stream infections: Frequency, antimicrobial susceptibility, and molecular epidemiology in a national surveillance program (SCOPE). Diagn Microbiol Infect Dis. 1997;28:211–219.
287. Maki DG, Rhame FS, Mackel DC, et al. Nationwide epidemic of septicemia caused by contaminated intravenous products: Epidemiologic and clinical features. Am J Med. 1976;60:471.
288. Maki DG, Martin WT. Nationwide epidemic of septicemia caused by contaminated infusion products. IV. Growth of microbial pathogens in fluids for intravenous infusion. J Infect Dis. 1975;131:267.
289. Rubinstien EM, Klevjer-Anderson P, Smith CA, et al. *Enterobacter taylorae*, a new opportunistic pathogen: Report of four cases. J Clin Microbiol. 1993;31:249–254.
290. De Gheldre Y, Maes N, Rost F, et al. Molecular epidemiology of an outbreak of multidrug-resistant *Enterobacter aerogenes* infections and in vivo emergence of imipenem resistance. J Clin Microbiol. 1997;35:152–160.
291. Paton AW, Paton JC. *Enterobacter cloacae* producing a Shiga-like toxin II-related cytotoxin associated with a case of hemolytic-uremic syndrome. J Clin Microbiol. 1996;34:463–465.
292. Yu VL. *Serratia marcescens*: Historical perspective and clinical review. N Engl J Med. 1979;300:887–893.
293. Chmel H. *Serratia odorifera* biogroup 1 causing an invasive human infection. J Clin Microbiol. 1988;26:1244–1245.
294. Farmer JJ, Davis BR, Hickman FW, et al. Detection of *Serratia* outbreaks in hospital. Lancet. 1976;2:455–459.
295. Christensen GD, Koranes SB, Reed L, et al. Epidemic *Serratia marcescens* in a neonatal intensive care unit: Importance of the gastrointestinal tract as a reservoir. Infect Control. 1982;3:127–133.
296. Mills J, Drew E. *Serratia marcescens* endocarditis: A regional illness associated with intravenous drug abuse. Ann Intern Med. 1976;84:29.
297. Ashby ME. Serratia osteomyelitis in heroin users. J Bone Joint Surg [Am]. 1976;158:132.
298. Wilfert JN, Barrett FF, Kass EH. Bacteremia due to *Serratia marcescens*. N Engl J Med. 1968;279:286.
299. Stamm WE, Kolff CA, Dones EM, et al. A nursery outbreak caused by *Serratia marcescens*–scalp-vein needles as a portal of entry. J Pediatr. 1976;89:96.
300. Maki DG, Hennekens CG, Phillips CW, et al. Nosocomial urinary tract infection with *Serratia marcescens*: An epidemiologic study. J Infect Dis. 1973;128:579.
301. Schaberg DR, Alford RH, Anderson R, et al. An outbreak of nosocomial infection due to multiply resistant *Serratia marcescens*: Evidence of interhospital spread. J Infect Dis. 1976;134:181–188.
302. Sanders CV, Luby JP, Johanson WG Jr, et al. *Serratia marcescens* infections from inhalation therapy medications: Nosocomial outbreak. Ann Intern Med. 1970;73:15.
303. Webb SF, Vall-Spinosa A. Outbreak of *Serratia marcescens* associated with the flexible fiberbronchoscope. Chest. 1975;68:703.
304. Bodey GP, Rodriguez V, Smith JP. *Serratia* sp. infections in cancer patients. Cancer. 1970;25:199.
305. Bornstein PF, Ditto AM, Noskin GA. *Serratia marcescens* cellulitis in a patient on hemodialysis. Am J Nephrol. 1992;12:374–376.
306. Mayer JW, DeHoratius RJ, Messner RP. *Serratia marcescens*–caused arthritis with negative and positive birefringent crystals. Arch Intern Med. 1976;136:1323.
307. Dorwar BB, Abrutyn E, Schumacher HR. *Serratia* arthritis. JAMA. 1973;225:1642.
308. Nakashima AK, McCarthy A, Martone WJ, et al. Epidemic septic arthritis caused by *Serratia marcescens* and associated with a benzalkonium chloride antiseptic. J Clin Microbiol. 1987;25:1014–1018.
309. Weinstein RJ, Young LS, Hewitt WL. Activity of three aminoglycosides and two penicillins against four species of gram-negative bacilli. Antimicrob Agents Chemother. 1975;7:172.
310. Moellering RC Jr, Wennerstein C, Kunz LJ, et al. Resistance to gentamicin, tobramycin and amikacin among clinical isolates of bacteria. Am J Med. 1977;62:873.
311. Weinstein RJ, Young LS, Hewitt WL. Comparison of methods for assessing in vitro antibiotic synergism against *Pseudomonas* and *Serratia*. J Lab Clin Med. 1975;86:853.
312. Cone LA, Woodard DR. Aztreonam therapy for serious gram-negative bacillary infections. Rev Infect Dis. 1985;7(Suppl):794–802.
313. Cox CE. Aztreonam therapy for complicated urinary tract infections caused by multidrug-resistant bacteria. Rev Infect Dis. 1985;7(Suppl):767–771.
314. Jones RN. Review of the in vitro spectrum of activity of imipenem. Am J Med. 1985;78:22–32.
315. Thomassen MJ, Demko CA, Doershuk CF, et al. *Pseudomonas cepacia*: Decrease in colonization in patients with cystic fibrosis. Am Rev Respir Dis. 1986;134:669–671.
316. Sutherland R, Beale A, Boon RJ, et al. Antibacterial activity of ticarcillin in the presence of clavulanate potassium. Am J Med. 1985;79:13–24.
317. Bassey CM, Baltch AL, Smith RP. Comparative activity of enoxacin, ciprofloxacin, amifloxacin, norfloxacin, and ofloxacin against 177 bacterial isolates. J Antimicrob Chemother. 1986;17:623–628.
318. Wolfson JS, Hooper DC. The fluoroquinolones: Structures, mechanisms of action and resistance, and spectra of activity in vitro. Antimicrob Agents Chemother. 1985;28:581–586.

319. Washington JA III, Birk RJ, Ritts RE. Bacteriologic and epidemiologic characteristics of *Enterobacter hafniae* and *Enterobacter liquefaciens*. J Infect Dis. 1971;124:379.
320. Berger SA, Edberg SC, Klein RS. *Enterobacter hafniae* infection: Report of two cases and review of the literature. Am J Med Sci. 1977;273:101–104.
321. Kotelko K. *Proteus mirabilis*: Taxonomic position, peculiarities of growth, components of the cell envelope. Curr Top Microbiol Immunol. 1986;129:181–215.
322. MacLaren DM. The significance of urease in *Proteus* pyelonephritis: A historical and biochemical study. J Pathol Bacteriol. 1969;97:43–49.
323. Mosher DM, Griffith DP, Yawn D, et al. Role of urease in pyelonephritis resulting from urinary tract infection with *Proteus*. J Infect Dis. 1975;131:177–181.
324. Braude AI, Siemienski J. Role of bacterial urease in experimental pyelonephritis. J Bacteriol. 1960;80:171–179.
325. Silverblatt FJ. Host-parasite interaction in the rat renal pelvis. A possible role for pili in the pathogensis of pyelonephritis. J Exp Med. 1974;140:1696.
326. Wray SK, Hull SI, Cook RG, et al. Identification and characterization of a uropathogenic isolate of *Proteus mirabilis*. Infect Immun. 1986;54:43–49.
327. Mobley HL, Chippendale GR. Hemagglutinin, urease, and hemolysin production by *Proteus mirabilis* from clinical sources. J Infect Dis. 1990;161:525–530.
328. Rozalski A, Kotelko K. Hemolytic activity and invasiveness in strains of *Proteus penneri*. J Clin Microbiol. 1987;25:1094–1096.
329. Peerbooms PG, Verweij AM, MacLaren D. Vero cell invasiveness of *Proteus mirabilis*. Infect Immun. 1984;43:1068–1070.
330. Welch RA. Identification of two different hemolysin determinants in uropathogenic *Proteus* isolates. Infect Immun. 1987;55:2183–2190.
331. Chow AW, Taylor PR, Yoshikawa TT, et al. A nosocomial outbreak of infections due to multiply resistant *Proteus mirabilis*: Role of intestinal colonization as a major reservoir. J Infect Dis. 1979;139:621–627.
332. Gaynes RP, Weinstein R, Chamberlin W, et al. Antibiotic-resistant flora in nursing home patients admitted to the hospital. Arch Intern Med. 1985;145:1804–1807.
333. Warren JW. *Providencia stuartii*: A common cause of antibiotic-resistant bacteria in patients with long-term indwelling catheters. Rev Infect Dis. 1986;8:61–67.
334. Kaslow RA, Lindsey JO, Bisno AL, et al. Nosocomial infection with highly resistant *Proteus rettgeri*. Am J Epidemiol. 1976;104:278.
335. Iannini PB, Eickhoff TC, LaForce FM. Multidrug resistant *P. rettgeri*: An emerging problem. Ann Intern Med. 1976;55:161.
336. Weinstein RA, Nathan C, Gruensfelder R, et al. Endemic aminoglycoside resistance in gram-negative bacilli. J Infect Dis. 1980;141:338–345.
337. Hodges GR, Degener CE, Barnes WG. Clinical significance of *Citrobacter* isolates. Am J Clin Pathol. 1978;70:37–40.
338. Lipsky BA, Hook ER III, Smith A, et al. *Citrobacter* infections in humans: Experience at the Seattle Veterans Administration Medical Center and a review of the literature. Rev Infect Dis. 1980;2:746–760.
339. El Harrif-Heraud Z, Arpin C, Benliman S, et al. Molecular epidemiology of a nosocomial outbreak due to SHV-4-producing strains of *Citrobacter diversus*. J Clin Microbiol. 1997;35:2561–2567.
340. Williams WW, Mariano J, Spurrier M, et al. Nosocomial meningitis due to *Citrobacter diversus* in neonates: New aspects of the epidemiology. J Infect Dis. 1984;150:229–255.
341. Kaplan AM, Itabashi HH, Yoshimori R, et al. Cerebral abscesses complicating neonatal *Citrobacter freundii* meningitis. West J Med. 1977;127:418.
342. Ribeiro CD, Davis P, Jones DM. *Citrobacter kozeri* meningitis in a special care baby unit. J Clin Pathol. 1976;29:1094.
343. Kline MW, Mason EO Jr, Kaplan SL. Characterization of *Citrobacter diversus* strains causing neonatal meningitis. J Infect Dis. 1988;157:101–105.
344. MacCulloch D, Menzies R, Cornere BM. Endocarditis due to *Citrobacter diversus* developing resistance to cephalothin. N Z Med J. 1977;85:182.
345. Shih CC, Chen YC, Chang SC, et al. Bacteremia due to *Citrobacter* species: Significance of primary intraabdominal infection. Clin Infect Dis. 1996;23:543–549.
346. Drelichman V, Band JD. Bacteremias due to *Citrobacter diversus* and *Citrobacter freudii*: Incidence, risk factors, and clinical outcome. Arch Intern Med. 1985;145:1808–1810.
347. Jordan GL, Hadley WK. Human infections with *Edwardsiella tarda*. Ann Intern Med. 1969;70:283.
348. Kourvang M, Vesques MA, Saena R. Edwardsiella in man and animals in Panama. Am J Trop Med Hyg. 1977;26:1183.
349. Sonnenwirth AC, Kallus BA. Meningitis due to *Edwardsiella tarda*. Am J Clin Pathol. 1968;49:92.
350. Farmer JJ, Davis BR, Hickman-Brenner FW, et al. Biochemical identification of new species and biogroups of *Enterobacteriaceae* isolated from clinical specimens. J Clin Microbiol. 1985;21:46–76.
351. Pien FD, Bruce AE. Nosocomial *Ewingella americana* bacteremia in an intensive care unit. Arch Intern Med. 1986;146:111–112.
352. Thaller R, Berlutti F, Thaller MC. A *Kluyvera cryocrescens* strain from gallbladder infection. Eur J Epidemiol. 1988;4:124–126.

Chapter 207

Pseudomonas aeruginosa

MATTHEW POLLACK

MICROBIOLOGY

Pseudomonas aeruginosa is a gram-negative aerobe belonging to the family Pseudomonadaceae. It is rod-shaped, averaging 0.5 to 0.8 by 1.5 to 3.0 μm. It occurs singly, in pairs, or in short chains. It is motile, with polar, monotrichous flagella. It produces diffusible fluorescent pigments, including pyoverdin and a soluble phenazine pigment called pyocyanin; the latter, produced by somewhat more than one half of clinical isolates, appears blue or green at neutral or alkaline pH and is the source of the name *aeruginosa*. Some strains also produce dark red or black pigment (pyorubin and pyomelanin, respectively). *P. aeruginosa* is nutritionally versatile. Organic growth factors are not required, and it can use more than 30 organic compounds for growth. It is an obligate aerobe except in the presence of nitrate. It grows optimally at 37°C and also at 42°C, but not at 4°C. It accomplishes gene transfer by both conjugation and transduction and has guanine + cytosine content in its DNA of approximately 67 mol%.[1]

Identification in the clinical microbiology laboratory is relatively simple because *P. aeruginosa* grows readily in a wide variety of media and the characteristics required for identification are few. It is a gram-negative, straight or slightly curved, motile, nonsporulating rod. It grows aerobically only and does not ferment carbohydrates. It oxidizes sugars such as glucose and xylose, but not maltose. It is indophenol oxidase positive, Simmons citrate positive, and L-arginine dehydrolase positive. It produces gas from nitrate and grows in brain-heart infusion broth at 42°C. It is L-lysine decarboxylase negative and L-ornithine decarboxylase negative and produces no hydrogen sulfide or black butt in Kligler iron agar.

Based on these and other biochemical characteristics, *P. aeruginosa* can be presumptively identified by a number of automated and computer-based gram-negative identification systems. However, these systems cannot always differentiate *P. aeruginosa* from all non-*aeruginosa Pseudomonas* species, which may require differential sugar oxidations, growth at 42°C, and flagella stains. When pyocyanin is present, it is a specific differential characteristic of *P. aeruginosa*. A characteristic sweet, grapelike odor in culture may be an equally specific identifying or confirming quality of *P. aeruginosa*.

EPIDEMIOLOGY

P. aeruginosa is cosmopolitan in its distribution. It is isolated from soil, water, plants, and animals, including humans. It is occasionally pathogenic for plants as well as animals. The minimal nutritional requirements of *Pseudomonas*, as evidenced by its ability to grow in distilled water and its tolerance of a wide variety of physical conditions including temperature, contribute to its ecologic success and ultimately to its role as an effective opportunistic pathogen.

The epidemiology of *P. aeruginosa* reflects its predilection for a moist environment. This is apparent in its natural habitat, where its associations with soil and water are closely related and its identification on plants is a function of humidity. Similarly, human colonization occurs at moist sites such as the perineum, axilla, and ear. Moisture is also a critical factor in hospital reservoirs of *P. aeruginosa*, such as respiratory equipment, clean solutions, medicines, disinfectants, sinks, mops, food mixers, and vegetables. Human *Pseudomonas* disease is also associated with water-related reservoirs outside of hospitals, including swimming pools, whirlpools, hot tubs, and contact lens solutions.

P. aeruginosa is sometimes present as part of the normal microbial flora of humans. The prevalence of colonization in healthy persons outside of or on entry to hospitals is relatively low. Representative site-specific colonization rates are as follows: skin, 0 to 2%; nasal mucosa, 0 to 3.3%; throat, 0 to 6.6%; and stool, 2.6 to 24%.[2] In contrast, hospitalization may lead to greatly increased rates of carriage, particularly on the skin of patients with serious burns, in the lower respiratory tract of patients undergoing mechanical ventilation, in the gastrointestinal tract of patients receiving chemotherapy for neoplastic diseases, or at virtually any site in persons treated with antibiotics. In each instance colonization rates may exceed 50% and colonization often presages invasive infection.[3]

Although colonization by *P. aeruginosa* frequently precedes overt infection, the original source of the organism and the precise mode of transmission are often unclear. Potential reservoirs such as uncooked vegetables, hospital sinks, or even flowers in patients' rooms are suspected sources of endemic *P. aeruginosa* strains. Discrete hospital-acquired outbreaks (epidemics) have been more definitively traced to specific reservoirs such as respiratory equipment, endoscopes, transvenous pacemakers, contaminated antistatic mattresses, antiseptics, orthopedic plaster, operating room suction apparatus, contaminated nursery formula, and physiotherapy and hydrotherapy pools. Patient-to-patient transmission of *Pseudomonas* on the hands of hospital staff or other fomites is often assumed but difficult to prove.[4, 5]

Because of the prevalence of *P. aeruginosa* in the hospital environment, epidemiologic investigation is facilitated by the use of markers that discriminate among strains.[6] Most frequently used but least discriminatory are antibiograms and biochemical properties as determined by Analytical Profile Index (API) profiles. In addition, *P. aeruginosa* can be typed on the basis of pyocin (bacteriocin) production or bacteriophage susceptibility patterns. A more specific typing method is serotyping (or immunotyping) on the basis of immunochemical heterogeneity of outer membrane lipopolysaccharides. Two commonly employed immunotype schemes are the Fisher-Devlin-Gnabasik system, which includes seven types, and the International Antigenic Typing System (IATS), which embraces a total of 20 different types. Type-specific rabbit antisera or monoclonal antibodies may be used in a slide agglutination test to identify different immunotypes. Numerous common-source epidemics have been investigated and reservoirs identified on the basis of immunotyping data. Almost two thirds of such outbreaks, including those occurring outside and within hospitals, have involved IATS serotype ll, which represents only 8% of endemic isolates.[7] Perhaps the most sensitive and specific epidemiologic tools identified to date are DNA probes, which surpass other, conventional typing methods in their discriminatory capacity.[8, 9]

P. aeruginosa is primarily a nosocomial pathogen, and therefore the frequency with which it causes disease can be reliably estimated from annual surveillance data collected by the Centers for Disease Control and Prevention (CDC) National Nosocomial Infections Surveillance (NNIS) system.[10] According to these data, collected between 1990 and 1996, *P. aeruginosa* was the second most common cause of nosocomial pneumonia (17% of isolates), the third most common cause of urinary tract infection (11%), the fourth most common cause of surgical site infection (8%), the seventh most frequently isolated pathogen from the blood stream (3%), and the fifth most common isolate (9%) overall, obtained from all sites.

PATHOGENESIS

The pathogenesis of *P. aeruginosa* infections must be understood in the context of its being an opportunistic pathogen. It rarely causes disease in healthy persons, although it is a common human saprophyte. In most cases the disease process begins with some alteration or circumvention of normal host defenses. This may involve a disruption in the integrity of physical barriers to bacterial invasion, such as the skin or mucous membranes, or circumvention of them, as with intravenous lines, urinary catheters, or endotracheal tubes. In other instances, there is an underlying dysfunction of specific immune mechanisms, as in neutropenia, hypogammaglobulinemia,[11] complement deficiency, iatrogenic immunosuppressive states, or the acquired immunodeficiency syndrome (AIDS). The ecologic resilience of *P. aeruginosa* contributes to its pathogenicity. Its adaptability to a wide variety of physical conditions, minimal nutritional requirements, and relative resistance to antibiotics allow it to survive in large numbers close to its prospective host.

That the pathogenesis of *Pseudomonas* infections is multifactorial is suggested both by the number of potential virulence factors the organism produces and by the broad spectrum of disease it causes. Multiple pathogenic mechanisms must be assumed in such diverse diseases as *Pseudomonas* septicemia in neutropenic patients, chronic lung infections caused by mucoid strains in persons with cystic fibrosis, endocarditis in heroin addicts, dermatitis in hot tub users, malignant external otitis in elderly diabetic patients, and cavitary pneumonia in persons with AIDS.[12]

The pathogenesis of *Pseudomonas* infections appears to be complex in that *P. aeruginosa* is both invasive and toxinogenic, a fact that may help explain the variety of diseases and syndromes with which it is identified. *Pseudomonas* infections may be seen as comprising three distinct stages: (1) bacterial attachment and colonization, (2) local invasion, and (3) dissemination and systemic disease. Each stage has as its prerequisitie the previous one, but the disease process may stop at any stage. Particular virulence factors of *P. aeruginosa* appear to mediate each of these steps in pathogenesis and to be responsible for characteristic syndromes.

There appears to be a clear relation between *Pseudomonas* colonization of the respiratory tract and bacterial adherence to epithelial cells.[13] Protein structures on the surface of the bacterium, called *pili* or *fimbriae*, are at least partly responsible for adherence to respiratory epithelium, and, by analogy, to other epithelial surfaces.[14] Fibronectin ordinarily protects epithelial cells from bacterial attachment, but it apparently is lost as the result of illness or other factors involved in hospitalization. The correlation between in vitro adherence of *Pseudomonas* to buccal epithelial cells and in vivo respiratory tract colonization is particularly pronounced in patients with cystic fibrosis or other forms of chronic lung disease. Sputum from these patients contain high levels of protease, which appears to break down the fibronectin coating of epithelial cells, leading to enhanced bacterial attachment.[15]

Cellular injury may also play a role in the initial attachment of *Pseudomonas* to epithelial cells. For example, *Pseudomonas* adheres to the desquamating trachael epithelial cells of mice infected with influenza virus but not to normal tracheal epithelium.[16] Epithelial injury from endotracheal intubation can produce the same result. This phenomenon of "opportunistic adherence" may represent an important step in the pathogenesis of *Pseudomonas* keratitis[17] and urinary tract infections,[18] as well as those involving the respiratory tract.

It is clear that *Pseudomonas* pili are attachment organelles or "adhesins," because both purified pili and antibodies to these structures block bacterial attachment to epithelial cells. It is likely that specific molecular sequences on these structures act as ligands that react with complementary sequences (receptors) on host cells. Galactose-binding or mannose-binding lectins of *Pseudomonas* may represent such ligands.[19] The mucoid exopolysaccharide of mucoid *Pseudomonas* strains[20] and the pili of nonmucoid strains represent adhesins for tracheal epithelial cells and for tracheobronchial mucin. The receptors for these adhesins appear to contain *N*-acetylneuraminic acid (sialic acid) and, in the case of tracheobronchial mucin, *N*-acetylglucosamine.[21, 22] It has been further proposed that the sialic acid–containing receptor for *Pseudomonas* on tracheal epithelium is a cell surface glycolipid, probably a ganglioside.[23] Recent data suggest that *P. aeruginosa* may express at least two adhesins distinct from pili and mucoid exopolysaccharide that mediate attachment to epithelial cells and mucins.[24, 25] In addition, as indicated later, it is likely that surface-exposed molecules of *Pseudomonas* exoenzyme S serve as adhesins for glycosphingolipids on respiratory cells.[26]

Under certain conditions *P. aeruginosa* produces a polysaccharide capsule, referred to as the glycocalyx[27] or mucoid exopolysaccharide.[28] It consists of mannuronic and guluronic acid in a repeating structure termed *alginate*. Mucoid exopolysaccharide appears to form a matrix around the bacterium, anchoring it to its environment and to its sister cells and protecting it from host immune factors such as the mucociliary mechanism of the respiratory tract, phagocytic cells, antibodies, and complement. This attached, protected, communal mode of growth of mucoid strains of *P. aeruginosa* surrounded by mucoid exopolysaccharide is sometimes referred to as a *biofilm*.[29–31] Biofilm-associated, mucoid strains of *P. aeruginosa* may be less susceptible to antibiotic killing than separately growing (planktonic), nonmucoid strains.[32] Mucoid strains of *P. aeruginosa* are most often isolated from the sputum of patients with cystic fibrosis.[33] Examination of postmortem lung material from patients with cystic fibrosis provides morphologic evidence that *Pseudomonas* forms encapsulated microcolonies in infected alveoli, indicating that formation of the glycocalyx of *Pseudomonas* is an in vivo as well as an in vitro phenomenon.[34] That the mucoid exopolysaccharide of *Pseudomonas* is a pathogenic factor is further suggested by its antiphagocytic properties[35] and by the greater resistance of mucoid *Pseudomonas* strains to opsonization compared with nonmucoid revertants.[36, 37] Moreover, alginate may impair the bactericidal activity of aminoglycoside antibiotics against *P. aeruginosa*.[37, 38] The capacity of mucoid exopolysaccharide to suppress neutrophil and lymphocyte functions[39–41] is dependent in part on its large molecular size and viscosity, factors that apparently contribute to the ability of mucoid *P. aeruginosa* strains to persist in the airways of patients with cystic fibrosis.[41]

A number of factors appear to be involved in the ability of *Pseudomonas* to cause invasive disease. Although cell-associated surface structures protect the organism from host phagocytes, antibodies, and complement, its extracellular enzymes or toxins break down physical barriers to its penetration, further impair host defenses, and render its new milieu more conducive to its physical, nutritional, and reproductive requirements.

Most clinical *P. aeruginosa* isolates produce extracellular proteases. Two of the best characterized, elastase and alkaline protease,[42] are most clearly associated with virulence (i.e., with tissue destruction and bacterial invasion). Both are necrotizing in the skin, lung, and cornea, whereas elastase is capable of producing hemorrhage. Effects attributable to the elastolytic activity of *P. aeruginosa* elastase include intra-alveolar hemorrhage, solubilization of elastin-containing human lung tissue, and degradation of laminin and elastin in vascular tissue. Proteolytic effects of elastase with probable biologic significance for the infected host include cleavage of collagen, immunoglobulin A and G, complement factors, and α_1-proteinase inhibitor.[43, 44] Elastase and alkaline protease also reportedly cause the proteolytic inactivation of human interferon-γ and tumor necrosis factor-α (TNF-α).[45] In addition, alkaline protease appears to mediate potent, plasmin-like anticoagulant activity based on the hydrolysis of fibrin and fibrinogen.[46] Elastase-induced proteolysis of fibronectin and its receptors on human lung fibroblasts may facilitate bacterial adherence to lung tissues.[47] Elastase also appears to cause disruption of human respiratory epithelium, interfering with ciliary function,[48] disturbing the barrier function of respiratory epithelial monolayers,[49] and increasing the permeability of respiratory epithelium to macromolecules by interrupting intercellular tight junctions.[50] Elastase has been implicated in the destructive vascular lesions (ecthyma gangrenosum) associated with septicemic *Pseudomonas* infections and may be responsible for the dissolution of the elastic lamina of blood vessels, which is an important pathologic characteristic of these lesions.[51] Although proteases are not highly cytotoxic, they appear to destroy connections between cells such as the proteoglycan ground substance of the cornea and other supporting structures composed of fibrin and elastin.[52] It has been suggested[53] that *Pseudomonas* proteases make nutrients available to the bacterium through the breakdown of host tissues at local sites of infection, and, in so doing, aid the proliferative and invasive processes.

Another toxic protein widely produced by *P. aeruginosa* from clinical sources is called *cytotoxin*. This 25,000 MW, pore-forming protein,[54] originally called *leukocidin* because of its cytopathic effects on polymorphonuclear leukocytes,[55] appears to be cytotoxic for most eukaryotic cells. It acts primarily on cell membranes, inhibits polymorphonuclear leukocyte function,[56] and produces pulmonary microvascular injury in at least one experimental model.[57] This microvascular lung injury may be related in part to a cytotoxin-induced burst of arachidonic acid–lipoxygenase product formation, which, coupled with direct cell toxicity, may contribute to sepsis-associated lung injury and the development of the acute respiratory distress syndrome (ARDS).[58]

P. aeruginosa produces two hemolysins, one a heat-labile protein called *phospholipase* C[59] and the other a heat-stable rhamnolipid.[60] These two substances appear to act synergistically to break down lipids and lecithin. Like *Pseudomonas* proteases, hemolysins may contribute to tissue invasion through their cytotoxic effects on host tissues. In addition, phospholipase C exerts an important pathologic effect in *Pseudomonas* lower respiratory tract infections through enzymatic degradation of the phosphatidylcholine component of lung surfactant, leading to atelectasis.[61, 62] Moreover, derivatives of phosphatidylcholine induce the production of additional phospholipase C, thereby reinforcing the enzyme's effect. Phospholipase C may also contribute to inflammation associated with *P. aeruginosa* infection through augmentation of arachidonic acid synthesis and release,[62] and interleukin-8 release from human monocytes.[63] Finally, *P. aeruginosa* rhamnolipid (heat-stable hemolysin) may exert an additional pathogenic effect in acute and chronic *Pseudomonas* lower respiratory tract infections by inhibiting the mucociliary transport and ciliary functions of human respiratory epithelium.[64]

Pyocyanin is a blue phenazine pigment secreted by *P. aeruginosa* and found along with its degradation product, l-hydroxyphenazine, in the sputum of patients with cystic fibrosis and bronchiectasis who are chronically colonized with *Pseudomonas*. Pyocyanin impairs the normal function of human nasal cilia,[65] disrupts respiratory epithelium,[65] exerts proinflammatory effects on human phagocytes possibly responsible for neutrophil-mediated tissue damage,[66] and, acting synergistically with the *Pseudomonas* siderophore, ferripyochelin,[67] generates hydroxyl radicals capable of producing endothelial cell damage.[68]

Blood stream invasion and dissemination of *Pseudomonas* from local sites of infection is probably mediated by some of the same cell-associated and extracellular products responsible for more localized disease. In addition to the possible antiphagocytic properties of the mucoid exopolysaccharide and of lipopolysaccharides contained in the outer cell membrane, *Pseudomonas* blood isolates are usually resistant to the direct bactericidal activity of serum.[69] Although *Pseudomonas* is susceptible to so-called natural antibodies, or immunoglobulin M (IgM), optimal bacterial clearance requires specific IgG antibodies, intact classic and alternative complement pathways, and adequate numbers of functioning polymorphonuclear leukocytes.[70, 71] These stringent demands on the host's immune system may be increased by the immunoglobulin-cleaving and complement-inactivating actions of *Pseudomonas* proteases, providing possible mechanisms for the removal of these two important impediments to blood stream invasion.[72]

Although it is not entirely clear how *P. aeruginosa* produces systemic illness, or, in some cases, the death of the infected host, two bacterial products most likely implicated in the systemic toxicity of *Pseudomonas* are its lipopolysaccharide (endotoxin) and exotoxin A.

The lipid A moiety of *Pseudomonas* endotoxin, like that of other bacterial lipopolysaccharides, mediates many of its biologic activities. There is considerable indirect evidence implicating endotoxin in the various clinical syndromes associated with gram-negative septicemia. It is likely that circulating endotoxin plays a role in the causation of fever, hypotension, oliguria, leukopenia or leukocytosis, disseminated intravascular coagulation (DIC), and ARDS. At the cellular and subcellular levels, endotoxin activates the clotting, fibrinolytic, kinin, and complement systems. Endotoxin stimulates the production of arachidonic acid metabolites, including prostaglandins and leukotrienes; it promotes the release of β-endorphins; and it induces the production and release of cytokines such as TNF. All of these factors, TNF in particular,[73, 74] appear to mediate endotoxic (septic) shock.

It has been suggested that, despite comparable structure, *Pseudomonas* lipopolysaccharides are biologically less potent than those of other gram-negative bacteria. It is more likely, however, that these lipopolysaccharides are roughly comparable in their biologic activity.[75] In either case, the biologic assays used to measure the relative potency of various endotoxins bear an uncertain relation to naturally occurring endotoxin-mediated disease processes, and the differences measured tend to be small.

The extracellular enzyme, exotoxin A, is produced by most *P. aeruginosa* clinical isolates.[76] It is a potent inhibitor of mammalian protein synthesis by a mechanism identical to that of diphtheria toxin.[77] Both toxins catalyze the transfer of the adenosine diphosphate–ribose moiety of nicotinamide adenine dinucleotide into covalent linkage with elongation factor 2 (EF 2), itself an enzyme that catalyzes the elongation step in polypeptide assembly; this reaction inactivates EF 2, thereby inhibiting protein biosynthesis. Although the enzymatic activities of *Pseudomonas* exotoxin A and diphtheria toxin are similar, the two toxins have distinct structures and cellular specificities, accounting for their different biologic activities and pathogenic roles. The exotoxin A structural gene has been cloned and expressed in *Escherichia coli*.[78] The toxin is a single polypeptide chain of 613 amino acids, and its three-dimensional structure has been elucidated by x-ray crystallography.[79] Three discrete structural domains have been identified with cell recognition, toxin translocation across cell membranes, and enzymatic activity, respectively.[80, 81]

In contrast to *Pseudomonas* proteases, exotoxin A appears to mediate both local and systemic disease processes.[82, 83] Its necrotizing activity in locally exposed tissues probably contributes to pathologic lesions at primary and metastatic sites of infection as well as bacterial dissemination. Exotoxin A produces dermonecrosis after intradermal injection in guinea pigs[84] and ocular damage resembling that seen in naturally occurring *Pseudomonas* keratitis after topical application on mouse corneas.[85] Experimental corneal infections produced by toxinogenic *P. aeruginosa* strains are more severe than those produced by nontoxinogenic mutants.[86] Similarly, experimental pulmonary infections caused by a toxin-positive parent strain are accompanied by more parenchymal invasion and inflammatory cell infiltration than those caused by toxinless mutants.[87] These experimental observations support a role for exotoxin A in local tissue damage and in bacterial invasion. Finally, data suggest a possible immunosuppressive role for exotoxin A with respect to both human B-lymphocyte[88] and human T-lymphocyte function,[89] which might contribute to bacterial virulence.

In terms of its possible systemic role, purified exotoxin A is highly lethal for animals, including subhuman primates, and produces shock in dogs and rhesus monkeys.[90] Toxin-producing *Pseudomonas* strains have been associated with greater virulence than nontoxinogenic isolates in bacteremic human infections.[91] In addition, it has been shown that patients with high levels of serum antibodies to exotoxin A at the onset of *Pseudomonas* septicemia have a better survival rate than those with low antibody titers.[92] Moreover, exotoxin A–specific monoclonal antibodies reduce mortality in experimental *Pseudomonas* disease.[93] These data suggest not only a lethal role for exotoxin A in septicemic *Pseudomonas* infections but a protective role for toxin-specific antibodies.

Another potentially pathogenic extracellular enzyme produced by most clinical isolates of *P. aeruginosa* is so-called exoenzyme S.[94, 95] Like exotoxin A, this protein is an adenosine diphosphate ribosyltransferase, but unlike exotoxin A, it preferentially ribosylates several low-molecular-weight guanosine triphosphate (GTP)–binding proteins of the *ras* gene superfamily.[26] Purified exoenzyme S is toxic to mice and cytopathic for a variety of tissue culture cell lines.[96] Exoenzyme S–negative *P. aeruginosa* mutants are less virulent than their parent strains in experimental burns[97] and chronic lung infections,[98] apparently on the basis of the enzyme's contribution to bacterial dissemination and lung damage, respectively. In addition, there is some indirect evidence that exoenzyme S contributes to bacterial virulence through impairment of local host defense mechanisms.[26] Exoenzyme S, which is displayed on the bacterial cell surface, also appears to be an important adhesin for glycosphingolipids and buccal cells (i.e., respiratory epithelium), a strong indication that this extracellular protein mediates bacterial attachment as well as toxic and possibly immunosuppressive functions.[99]

CLINICAL MANIFESTATIONS AND TREATMENT

Endocarditis

P. aeruginosa causes infective endocarditis on native heart valves in intravenous (IV) drug users and on prosthetic heart valves.[100] In one study,[101] as much as 58% of addict-associated gram-negative bacterial endocarditis was caused by *P. aeruginosa*, although its occurrence was subject to marked regional variation. Conversely, more than 90% of all reported cases of *P. aeruginosa* endocarditis have occurred in IV drug users. Most of these patients (87%) were young (mean age, 29 years) black men. Although underlying heart disease is relatively uncommon in these patients, some have had previous staphylococcal endocarditis or rheumatic valvular heart disease. The source of the organism is thought to be standing water contaminating drug paraphernalia rather than heroin itself or the addict's skin.[102] In some studies,[103, 104] there was a greater association of *Pseudomonas* endocarditis with IV abuse of pentazocine and tripelennamine ("T's and blues") than with heroin. More frequent use of "T's and blues" in shooting galleries, the absence of boiling before injection, and the selective survival of *P. aeruginosa* in pentazocine and tripelennamine[105] are factors favoring the association of these drugs with *Pseudomonas* infections. An outbreak of serotype O11 *P. aeruginosa* endocarditis was reported among pentazocine and tripelennamine abusers in Chicago between 1977 and 1980,[104] strongly implying a common source for this epidemic strain.

Although the pathogenesis of infective endocarditis remains controversial, it is thought that the organism establishes itself on the endocardium by direct invasion from the blood stream or via neovascular channels resulting from previous subendothelial injury. In the latter case, foreign materials that are mixed with heroin may cause injury leading to fibrosis of the valve leaflets or mural endocardium. Such fibrosis has been observed in the absence of infection on the heart valves of heroin addicts. The high rate of exposure of the tricuspid valve to both trauma and bacteria in IV drug users probably explains the frequency with which this valve is involved in this group of patients. Finally, *P. aeruginosa* appears to have a particularly high affinity for human endocardium, a characteristic it shares with other, more common etiologic agents in endocarditis, including *Staphylococcus aureus* and viridans streptococci.[106]

Endocarditis of the tricuspid valve typically manifests subacutely, whereas that involving the aortic or mitral valves is usually more acute and fulminant. Fever is almost invariably present initially but may subside with treatment despite persistently positive blood cultures. A cardiac murmur is heard in most patients at the time of hospital admission, and subsequently in virtually all. The tricuspid valve is involved in most cases (70% in one large series),[107] but the pulmonic, mitral, and aortic valves, as well as the mural endocardium of either atrium, may also be affected. Biventricular and multiple valve infections are particularly common in *Pseudomonas* endocarditis.[108] Septic pulmonary emboli occur with tricuspid disease and produce cough, purulent sputum, pleuritic chest pain, pulmonary infiltrates (sometimes with abscess), and pleural effusions. Left-sided *Pseudomonas* endocarditis may produce intractable congestive heart failure, large systemic arterial emboli, cardiac valve ring abscesses, and high-grade conduction disturbances.[109]

Brain abscesses, cerebritis, and mycotic aneurysms sometimes occur in *P. aeruginosa* endocarditis; these neurologic complications are particularly common in left-sided disease.[109] Splenomegaly is sometimes accompanied by septic infarcts or abscesses. Skin and soft-tissue manifestations such as Janeway lesions, Osler nodes, and ecthyma gangrenosum are unusual in both right- and left-sided disease.

The diagnosis of *Pseudomonas* endocarditis is made by positive blood cultures in the absence of primary extracardiac sites of infection. Definitive diagnosis is based on culture and histopathologic examination of valvular or endocardial specimens obtained at surgery (or autopsy). In patients with positive blood cultures, an abnormal two-dimensional echocardiogram combined with an abnormal chest radiograph is highly predictive of *Pseudomonas* endocarditis. Tricuspid involvement with vegetations may be documented by echocardiography or cardiac catheterization and cineangiography, the latter demonstrating valvular insufficiency in 50 to 70% of cases. Repeat echocardiograms may demonstrate vegetations when initial studies are negative.

Aggressive antimicrobial therapy and surgery have improved the prognosis in *Pseudomonas* endocarditis.[109, 110] In tricuspid disease, medical therapy should be initiated with high-dose aminoglycoside (e.g., tobramycin, 8 mg/kg per day) plus an extended-spectrum penicillin (e.g., ticarcillin at a dose of 18 g/day). Renal function and aminoglycoside levels must be monitored. If bacteremia persists after 2 weeks of this therapy or after completion of a 6-week course of antibiotics, tricuspid valvulectomy without valve replacement is indicated. At the time of surgery the pulmonic valve should be closely inspected and, if it appears to be involved, it too should be removed without replacement. With medical support after tricuspid valvulectomy most patients are hemodynamically stable, although a small percentage may subsequently develop a substantial impairment of right ventricular function necessitating valve replacement.[111] Patients who are not IV drug users should have the tricuspid valve replaced in a second operation 6 to 8 months after valvulectomy.[107]

In the case of left-sided *Pseudomonas* endocarditis,[109] refractoriness to antibiotic therapy and (to a lesser extent) hemodynamic instability dictate early valve replacement in addition to combination therapy with an aminoglycoside and an extended-spectrum penicillin in the doses indicated previously for right-sided disease. Computed axial tomography of the abdomen should be performed before surgery, and splenectomy should be accomplished before valve replacement if splenic abscesses are present. As in the case of tricuspid involvement, left-sided disease should be treated with antibiotics for at least 6 weeks. Serum aminoglycoside levels and bactericidal activity should be monitored to maintain peak gentamicin or tobramycin levels in the range of 12 to 20 μg/ml and at least 10 times the minimal bactericidal concentration (MBC) of the infecting blood isolate, respectively. The higher dose and peak serum concentrations of gentamicin or tobramycin indicated, compared with those usually recommended for these drugs, have demonstrated efficacy in *Pseudomonas* endocarditis; renal toxicity has generally been mild and reversible.[110]

There is more experience in the treatment of *Pseudomonas* endocarditis with antibiotic combinations that include carbenicillin or ticarcillin than with other extended-spectrum penicillins. Several treatment failures associated with the emergence of resistant, β-lactamase–producing strains have been reported with aminoglycoside-piperacillin combinations.[112, 113] There has also been limited clinical experience with third-generation cephalosporins, with suboptimal clinical responses documented in several cases of left-sided *Pseudomonas* endocarditis treated with the combination of a third-generation cephalosporin and an aminoglycoside.[103] The efficacy of β-lactam antibiotics, as a group, in *Pseudomonas* endocarditis is limited by several theoretical and practical considerations. The β-lactams may exhibit a slow onset of bactericidal activity, lack the so-called postantibiotic effect, and select for or induce resistant β-lactamase–producing strains.[114, 115] These shortcomings may be accentuated by the extremely large numbers of organisms present in the vegetations of *Pseudomonas*-infected heart valves coupled with restricted antibiotic penetration, particularly in left-sided endocarditis.[116] These considerations underlie the need for combination therapy that includes an aminoglycoside, use of the highest possible antibiotic doses consistent with safety, early surgery in the case of left-sided disease, and adequate duration of therapy.

Other antibiotics that may have a role in the treatment of *Pseudomonas* endocarditis include imipenem, ciprofloxacin, and aztreonam, although to date there is limited clinical experience with all of these drugs. Imipenem, used alone or in combination with an aminoglycoside, has demonstrated mixed results in *P. aeruginosa* endovascular infections.[113] Ciprofloxacin has proved efficacious in animal models of *Pseudomonas* endocarditis, particularly against multiple-drug–resistant strains.[117] This quinolone has also been used successfully in the long-term suppression of *P. aeruginosa* prosthetic valve endocarditis.[118] The high bactericidal activity of ciprofloxacin in relation to antibiotic concentrations achievable in vegetations, early onset of action, and postantibiotic effect are probably related to its effectiveness.[114, 117] Finally, although clinical experience is lacking, high-dose aztreonam in combination with amikacin appeared to have a beneficial effect in experimental left-sided *P. aeruginosa* endocarditis.[119]

Poor prognostic indicators in *Pseudomonas* endocarditis include delay in initiation of antibiotic therapy, age older than 30 years, presence of left-sided disease, persistent fever despite therapy for 2 weeks, mural vegetations, systemic embolization, and mixed infections involving both *P. aeruginosa* and *S. aureus*. The success rate in tricuspid *Pseudomonas* endocarditis with medical therapy, and, if necessary, valvulectomy is about 80%. In contrast, the medical cure rate may be as low as 11% for left-sided *Pseudomonas* endocarditis.[103] More recent experience suggests, however, that early valve replacement may achieve both bacteremic and hemodynamic cures in as many as 75% of patients with left-sided disease while substantially improving survival.[103, 109, 120]

Respiratory Infections

Lower respiratory tract infections with *P. aeruginosa* occur almost exclusively in persons with compromised local respiratory or systemic host defense mechanisms. Primary pneumonia occurs in patients with chronic lung disease, congestive heart failure, or both. Exposure to the hospital environment, particularly in an intensive care setting[121]; use of respiratory inhalation equipment; and previous antibiotic therapy increase the likelihood of such infections. *P. aeruginosa* is a common cause of ventilator-associated pneumonia, which is still accompanied by inordinately high morbidity and mortality despite improvements in antibiotic therapy.[122, 123] Occasionally, previously well adults present with life-threatening, primary *Pseudomonas* pneumonia,[124] and severe, community-acquired *Pseudomonas* lower respiratory tract infections may complicate chronic lung disease or other serious underlying ailments.[125] In addition, there is an association between chronic *P. aeruginosa* lung infection and bronchiectasis, with some evidence suggesting that the former plays a role in the development of the latter.[126] Bacteremic *Pseudomonas* pneumonia is seen primarily in patients with malignancies, especially those involving the hematopoietic system, and in patients who are neutropenic as a result of chemotherapy. Finally, chronic *Pseudomonas* lung infections occur in most patients with cystic fibrosis, a genetic disease in which abnormal respiratory secretions impede normal pulmonary toilet.[127, 128] Ineffective bactericidal and bacterial clearance mechanisms may contribute to lower respiratory infections in these patients, especially those caused by *P. aeruginosa*.[129–134]

Primary or nonbacteremic pneumonia[135] results from aspiration of

Pseudomonas from the pharynx and upper respiratory tract, sites that become colonized during the course of hospitalization, serious illness, and previous antibiotic therapy. Despite rigorous cleaning of ventilator equipment and frequent changes of disposable tubing, direct aerosolization of *Pseudomonas* may still occur in patients receiving respirator therapy. Reservoir nebulizers introduce bacteria directly into the lower respiratory tract. Traditional accounts of *Pseudomonas* pneumonia describe a fulminant, usually fatal infection characterized clinically by chills, fever, severe dyspnea, cough productive of copious purulent sputum, cyanosis, apprehension, mental confusion, and severe systemic toxicity. Chest radiographs reveal a diffuse bronchopneumonia, typically bilateral, with distinctive nodular infiltrates, often with small areas of radiolucency. Although this pattern suggests *S. aureus* pneumonia, it is said to be uncommon in other forms of gram-negative pneumonia.[135] Small pleural effusions are common, empyema is rare, and a pattern of lobar consolidation is seen only occasionally. Pathologically, diffuse bronchopneumonia is marked by microabscess formation, necrosis of alveolar septa, and focal hemorrhages. Bacterial invasion of vessel walls and vascular necrosis are not usually seen in this form of pneumonia.

Bacteremic *Pseudomonas* pneumonia[136–138] occurs primarily, although not exclusively, in neutropenic patients after cancer chemotherapy. It is also seen in children and adults with AIDS.[139, 140] The pathogenesis is distinctive in that, although the disease often begins, as does the nonbacteremic form, with the introduction of bacteria by the respiratory route, blood stream invasion produces characteristic pulmonary lesions and sometimes metastatic lesions in other viscera as well. Two types of lung lesions have been described.[141] The first consists of poorly defined, hemorrhagic, nodular areas that are frequently subpleural and sometimes surround a small central area of necrosis. Microscopically, these lesions are consistently located around small and medium-sized pulmonary arteries. Intra-alveolar hemorrhages are seen, alveolar necrosis may be present, and inflammatory cell infiltration is largely absent. The second type of lesion is strikingly different from the hemorrhagic lesions. Grossly, they appear as 2- to 15-mm, firm, yellow-brown or tan, necrotic, umbilicated nodules with a narrow halo of dark red, hemorrhagic parenchyma. Microscopically, some of these lesions are typical abscesses composed of leukocytes and liquefactive necrosis of pulmonary parenchyma. In most cases, however, the lesions demonstrate coagulation necrosis, many bacteria, and necrotic small muscular arteries and veins with bacterial invasion of their walls. These lesions appear to be the pulmonary counterpart of ecthyma gangrenosum lesions seen in the skin of patients with bacteremic *Pseudomonas* infections.

Bacteremic *Pseudomonas* pneumonia is a fulminant disease with death typically occurring 3 to 4 days after the first signs or symptoms of pulmonary or extrapulmonary infection, including those associated with gram-negative sepsis and respiratory failure. Chest radiographs obtained early may show pulmonary vascular congestion, interstitial edema, and areas of pulmonary edema. Central venous pressure and pulmonary capillary wedge pressure are typically normal and rule out congestive heart failure as a cause of this radiographic picture. Chest radiographs obtained 48 to 72 hours after the initial febrile episode disclose a pattern of parenchymal involvement with a mixture of alveolar and interstitial infiltrates. Cavitation often appears after 48 hours, indicating the necrotizing character of the diffuse bronchopneumonia that has developed by this time. The rapid progression of radiographic findings from pulmonary vascular congestion, to pulmonary edema, to necrotizing bronchopneumonia, is said to be typical of bacteremic *Pseudomonas* pneumonia.[138]

The treatment of *Pseudomonas* pneumonia includes antibiotics (see later discussion of the treatment of acute exacerbations of lung infections in cystic fibrosis patients), maintenance of good pulmonary toilet, respiratory assistance if necessary, and other supportive measures dictated by the presence of septic shock or other complications. Because of the life-threatening potential of this disease and variable response to treatment, therapy with at least two antimicrobial agents active against the infecting strain of *P. aeruginosa* is strongly recommended.

The endotracheal or aerosol administration of ceftazidime[142] or tobramycin[143] may complement systemically administered antibiotics by augmenting drug levels in bronchial secretions. In one double-blind study of endotracheal tobramycin in the treatment of patients with gram-negative pneumonia, among whom *P. aeruginosa* was the most common pathogen, the causative organism was eradicated from sputum more frequently in patients who received endotracheal tobramycin in addition to IV antibiotics, compared with those who received IV drugs alone.[143] However, although no adverse effects were attributable to endobronchial tobramycin, no improvement in clinical outcome was documented.[143] Because endotracheal ceftazidime and tobramycin are apparently safe in hospitalized patients with an endotracheal tube or tracheostomy in place, consideration might be given to the administration of one or the other in conjunction with intravenous antibiotics in patients with *Pseudomonas* pneumonia.

Cystic Fibrosis

Lower respiratory tract infection with mucoid strains of *P. aeruginosa* is a function of age in patients with cystic fibrosis, with an incidence ranging from 21% in those younger than 1 year of age to more than 80% in those aged 26 years or older.[144] In one large series, the overall prevalence of *P. aeruginosa* lower respiratory tract colonization among patients of various ages attending a cystic fibrosis clinic was as high as 82%.[145] There has been a significant shift in the age distribution of cystic fibrosis patients, with the proportion of adult patients increasing fourfold between 1969 (8%) and 1990 (33%).[144] This age shift reflects increased longevity among patients with cystic fibrosis lung disease[146] and emphasizes the accompanying need for longer-term management of *Pseudomonas* lower respiratory tract infections in these patients (see Chapter 61).

Although an important pathogenic component of the pulmonary disease in cystic fibrosis ostensibly results from the genetic defect itself,[127, 147] *P. aeruginosa* clearly plays a critical role in the progressive lung lesions and resulting disability observed in most patients with this disease. Although it is not possible, given our present understanding of cystic fibrosis lung disease, to clearly distinguish cause and effect, lower respiratory tract colonization (or infection) with *Pseudomonas* is associated with both acute exacerbations and chronic progression of this disease. In general, more symptomatic patients with more severe and progressive lung disease are more likely to be infected with *Pseudomonas* than those with less serious disease. A direct reflection of this is the greater magnitude of antibody responses to *Pseudomonas*-specific antigens in cystic fibrosis patients with higher Schwachman scores.[148, 149] The striking inflammation observed in patients with cystic fibrosis lung disease, manifested by massive neutrophil infiltration and progressive airway damage, emphasizes the growing recognition that this is an inflammatory airways disease.[150, 151]

Respiratory tract colonization of cystic fibrosis patients by mucoid strains of *P. aeruginosa* correlates with patient age, clinical score, extent of pulmonary disease, severity of radiographic changes, and serum immunoglobulin levels.[150] Although it is unclear whether mucus plugging precedes infection or vice versa, airway obstruction begins as bronchiolitis with plugging caused by inflammatory exudate; once airway obstruction is established, infections follow. Infection produces more mucus plugging, and this leads to chronic suppuration with resulting bronchiectasis, atelectasis, and ultimately fibrosis. Progressive lung involvement leads to pulmonary insufficiency, and resulting hypoxia is associated with altered cardiopulmonary dynamics, pulmonary hypertension, and cor pulmonale.

The clinical manifestations of *Pseudomonas* pulmonary infections in cystic fibrosis[152] vary widely depending on the duration and severity of underlying lung disease and the acuteness of a particular episode or exacerbation. Initially, patients may have frequent upper respiratory tract infections with a lingering cough after each episode.

Other patients may have recurrent bouts of pneumonia with or without a persistent cough between episodes. It is common for some patients to develop lower respiratory tract infection with *Pseudomonas* after previous treatment for persistent staphylococcal colonization or infection. Most patients eventually develop a chronic productive cough of increasing severity, a decrease in appetite, weight loss, and diminished activity, particularly during exacerbations. Other symptoms may include wheezing, tachypnea, and irritability. Low-grade fever often accompanies exacerbations, although high fever is uncommon. Physical signs include evidence of undernutrition, increased anteroposterior diameter, retractions, cyanosis, inspiratory and expiratory wheezing, rhonchi, localized or generalized moist rales, abdominal distention, and clubbing of fingers and toes. A leukocytosis and left shift are usually present during acute exacerbations. Blood gases show varying degrees of hypoxemia with or without hypercarbia. Pulmonary function tests reveal an obstructive defect, and, in the presence of chronic fibrosis, a restrictive defect as well. Chest radiographs demonstrate overaeration, peribronchial thickening, patchy atelectasis caused by mucus plugging of small airways, and patchy pneumonia. In older patients with moderate to more advanced disease, there is severe overaeration, a small heart, depressed diaphragms, and an increased anteroposterior diameter. Extensive peribronchial infiltration with generalized bronchiectasis may be seen; cyst formation and mucus plugging of dilated bronchi are common findings.

Although there is no cure for *Pseudomonas* pulmonary disease in patients with cystic fibrosis, contemporary therapies have significantly improved survival.[144] Early diagnosis of infection and aggressive treatment are critical to the prevention or postponement of irreversible lung damage. It is well established that antibiotics with good in vitro activity against *P. aeruginosa* are effective in the treatment of acute exacerbations of *Pseudomonas* lung infection in patients with cystic fibrosis.[153–157] An aminoglycoside such as gentamicin, tobramycin, or amikacin, combined with an antipseudomonal penicillin such as carbenicillin or ticarcillin, provides effective in vivo activity against *Pseudomonas* respiratory infections in cystic fibrosis. However, the introduction of new antipseudomonal penicillins, extended-spectrum cephalosporins, carbapenems, monobactams, and quinolones has provided additional therapeutic choices, while stimulating new controversies, in the treatment of these infections. Piperacillin,[158] ceftazidime,[159] imipenem,[160] aztreonam,[161] and ciprofloxacin[162] have all been used, alone or in combination with an aminoglycoside, to effectively treat acute exacerbations of chronic *Pseudomonas* pulmonary infections in patients with cystic fibrosis. Imipenem and aztreonam may confer a lower risk of hypersensitivity reactions than other β-lactams in treated cystic fibrosis patients,[163] and aztreonam appears relatively safe in patients who exhibit hypersensitivity to other β-lactams.[164] Finally, the steadily growing experience with fluoroquinolone use in children without evidence of cartilage or joint toxicity[165, 166] has provided further impetus for prescribing fluoroquinolones to young cystic fibrosis patients with lower respiratory tract *Pseudomonas* infections, particularly in the face of previous therapeutic failure or resistance to multiple other antibiotics.[165]

Antibiotic use in cystic fibrosis lung disease is frequently associated with the emergence of resistant strains of *P. aeruginosa*. Imipenem, for example, induces or selects for *P. aeruginosa* respiratory isolates resistant to imipenem, ceftazidime, and piperacillin.[167] Similarly, ciprofloxacin treatment of cystic fibrosis patients leads to the emergence of ciprofloxacin-resistant *P. aeruginosa* strains with altered DNA gyrase and/or outer membrane permeability.[168] Nevertheless, most antimicrobial agents used to treat *P. aeruginosa* lung infections in cystic fibrosis produce good clinical responses despite the appearance and occasional persistence in sputum of resistant strains.

In addition to questions regarding the expanded choice of antimicrobial agents in cystic fibrosis lung infections, controversy also surrounds the use of a single agent (monotherapy) versus antibiotic combinations. Although aminoglycoside-containing combinations have been favored for their synergistic activities and prevention of resistance, single-drug therapy, most notably with piperacillin,[169] ceftazidime,[170, 171] or ciprofloxacin,[172] has also proved efficacious.

Because there is now a wide choice of antimicrobial agents effective against lower respiratory tract *Pseudomonas* infections in patients with cystic fibrosis, the selection of particular drugs depends on local resistance patterns and prescribing practices. All antibiotics are administered in high doses, by the parenteral route, with the exception of oral quinolones.[173] Altered antibiotic pharmocokinetics in cystic fibrosis patients are caused by increased renal tubular secretion, decreased tubular reabsorption, and increased nonrenal clearance.[174] These alterations in antibiotic handling apparently apply to β-lactams as well as aminoglycosides and may necessitate higher than usual antibiotic doses, greater dosing frequency, and, in the case of aminoglycosides, monitoring of serum drug levels and individualization of dosage regimens. Treatment usually is continued until symptomatic improvement occurs, typically 1 to 2 weeks. Improvement in both subjective symptoms and objective measures of pulmonary function can be expected.[153, 155–157] On the other hand, although *Pseudomonas* may temporarily disappear from the sputum of patients after aggressive antibiotic treatment, it may also persist, develop in vitro resistance to the agent or agents employed in treatment, and (almost inevitably) reappear after discontinuation of therapy.[155, 156] Fortunately, clinical improvement is frequently observed despite these less hopeful microbiologic events monitored in the sputum.

The role of antibiotic prophylaxis or chronic suppression of *Pseudomonas* lung infections in cystic fibrosis patients is controversial. True prophylaxis—that is, maintenance of patients on an antibiotic with activity against *P. aeruginosa* before respiratory tract colonization—has not been adequately studied. Likewise, suppressive therapy—that is, maintenance of patients on an antibiotic once colonization has been established to prevent acute exacerbations and arrest chronic progression of *Pseudomonas* lung disease—has been advocated without clear evidence of efficacy. A strategy that shows considerable promise involves regular, intermittent treatment of cystic fibrosis patients with chronic *Pseudomonas* lung infections three to four times each year. This aggressive approach, in which patients are treated expectantly rather than in response to acute exacerbations of their chronic infections, may have contributed to recent improvements in mortality observed among Danish cystic fibrosis patients with *Pseudomonas* pulmonary infections.[175, 176] Facilitating this approach is the availability of quinolone antibiotics, which were administered to adult cystic fibrosis patients in Denmark. Another treatment strategy that has shown some promise in preventing chronic *Pseudomonas* lower respiratory tract colonization is based on the treatment of previously untreated (and not chronically colonized) patients with a combination of oral ciprofloxacin and aerosolized colistin twice daily for 3 weeks whenever *P. aeruginosa* is isolated from routine sputum cultures.[177]

Another promising treatment is the intermittent aerosolization of antibiotics into the respiratory tracts of cystic fibrosis patients with established *Pseudomonas* lung infections.[178] Among the antibiotics tried have been combinations of an aminoglycoside and antipseudomonal penicillin,[179] ceftazidime alone,[180] and a nebulized aminoglycoside accompanied by an oral quinolone.[181] This approach has reportedly succeeded in reducing patients' symptoms, improving pulmonary function, and decreasing the number of required hospitalizations. Supportive data come from a randomized, placebo-controlled crossover study of 28-day treatment with aerosolized tobramycin in chronically colonized but clinically stable patients with cystic fibrosis. This study documented significant improvement in pulmonary function, decreased numbers of *P. aeruginosa* in sputum, no apparent toxicity, and no increase in the emergence of resistant bacteria.[182]

Good pulmonary toilet is a critical adjunct to antibiotic therapy in the treatment of chronic lung infections in cystic fibrosis. Inhalation of hydrating and mucolytic agents, postural drainage, and chest physiotherapy are often useful, and bronchial lavage is sometimes employed, to remove respiratory secretions. Whole-lung lavage can be performed with the use of a Carlens tube or segmental lavage accomplished through a bronchoscope.[183] Although the appropriate use of these procedures is not firmly established, segmental lavage should probably be carried out when obstructive secretions or mucus plugs are thought to hamper effective treatment.

Bilateral lung transplantation and heart-lung transplantation have been employed with moderate success in children and young adults with end-stage cystic fibrosis lung disease associated with chronic *P. aeruginosa* lower respiratory tract infections.[184–188] This generally favorable experience has included mechanically ventilated patients.[186] The potential benefits of such surgery include improved cardiopulmonary function and improved long-term survival. Perioperative morbidity and mortality are substantial, however, and long-term prognosis may be limited by the development of obliterative bronchiolitis.[186]

Bacteremia

P. aeruginosa causes bacteremia primarily in immunocompromised patients. Predisposing conditions include hematologic malignancies, immunoglobulin deficiency states,[189] neutropenia, diabetes mellitus, organ transplantation,[190, 191] severe burns, diffuse dermatitides, and AIDS.[139, 140, 192–194] Other predisposing factors include cancer chemotherapy resulting in neutropenia or ulceration of the respiratory and gastrointestinal tracts, steroid administration, antibiotic therapy, placement of IV lines, urinary tract instrumentation or catheterization, surgery, trauma, and prematurity.

The high prevalence of nosocomial *P. aeruginosa* bacteremia in the 1980s is illustrated by data from a large university teaching hospital, where *P. aeruginosa* bacteremia accounted for 13.6% of all episodes of nosocomial bacteremia and 25.6% of hospital-acquired gram-negative bacteremias, with an overall attack rate of 1.8 episodes per 1000 discharges.[195] *P. aeruginosa* continues to be an occasional cause of bacteremia among granulocytopenic cancer patients despite changing etiologic patterns in this disease.[196] Although most *P. aeruginosa* bacteremias are acquired in hospitals or nursing homes[197] and are associated with some form of immunocompromise including extremes of age, occasional cases of community-acquired disease occur,[197] and rare cases are seen in ostensibly healthy hosts.[195] Mortality remains high despite advances in therapy, ranging from approximately one third to two thirds of cases.[197] Factors associated with an unfavorable outcome include persistent neutropenia; presence of septic shock; inappropriate antibiotic therapy; lung, skin, soft tissue, or unidentified source; renal failure; metastatic foci; rapidly or ultimately fatal underlying disease; and an absolute granulocyte count of less than 100 cells/mm^3.[198] Some studies indicate a higher mortality rate among patients with *Pseudomonas* bacteremia compared with other bacteremias.[199] It is not clear to what extent this high mortality rate reflects the more severe underlying illnesses affecting patients subject to *Pseudomonas* bacteremia and to what extent it is a function of the greater inherent virulence of the organism.[200] The fact that *P. aeruginosa* may cause excess mortality even in patients with less severe underlying diseases[199] underscores its pathogenic potential on reaching the blood stream.

In general, *Pseudomonas* bacteremia is clinically indistinguishable from other forms of gram-negative sepsis.[201–207] Signs and symptoms are variable and depend on primary site of infection and clinical setting. Common primary sites of infection include the respiratory, gastrointestinal, and urinary tracts, skin and soft tissues, and intravascular foci. Fever is almost always present except in very young or premature infants and is usually accompanied by tachycardia and tachypnea. Patients appear toxic and may manifest apprehension, disorientation, or obtundation. Hypotension is common, and refractory shock may develop as a preterminal event. Respiratory failure occurs in the presence of bacteremic *Pseudomonas* pneumonia or in conjunction with ARDS. Azotemia is common, and renal failure may accompany frank shock. Jaundice appears to occur more often than in other forms of gram-negative sepsis.[202, 208] DIC is relatively uncommon.

Skin lesions may be an important distinguishing feature of *Pseudomonas* bacteremia, especially if they represent typical ecthyma gangrenosum.[209–212] These small, round, indurated nodules often begin as vesicles that undergo hemorrhage, necrosis, and ulceration. They are typically surrounded by a rim of erythema and contain little if any pus. Histologically, there is bacterial invasion of small arteries and veins but little inflammatory infiltrate. *P. aeruginosa* can readily be demonstrated in the lesions by Gram stain or culture. Ecthyma lesions usually occur singly or in small numbers on the perineum, buttocks, or extremities or in the axillae, but they may appear anywhere on the body. Ecthyma-like lesions can also be seen on the mucous membranes of the mouth, hard or soft palate, gingiva, or tongue. Although it is present in a relatively small minority of patients with *Pseudomonas* bacteremia and is rarely associated with other bacterial[213] or fungal[214] causes, ecthyma gangrenosum is virtually pathognomonic for *Pseudomonas* infection, especially if microscopic examination reveals typical vascular lesions.

Other types of skin lesions may be seen in conjunction with bacteremic *Pseudomonas* infections.[202] Small, painful vesicles occur in clusters on an erythematous base and contain cloudy, bacteria-laden fluid. Flat, sharply demarcated areas of cellulitis may also occur; they tend to enlarge rapidly, becoming hemorrhagic and necrotic. Diffuse maculopapular eruptions, most concentrated on the trunk, have also been described early in *Pseudomonas* sepsis, and metastatic abscesses of the extremities and fingertips are occasionally seen late in the disease.

Antibiotic therapy of *Pseudomonas* bacteremia is frequently instituted before a specific etiologic diagnosis is made. "Empirical" treatment is usually based on a presumptive diagnosis of sepsis, suggested by nonspecific signs and symptoms and the clinical setting. The necessity for beginning treatment immediately once sepsis is suspected, particularly in neutropenic patients, is widely accepted. The number and choice of antibiotics in this setting are controversial, however. The conventional approach to presumptive therapy in the face of neutropenia or other settings in which *Pseudomonas* is a possible or likely pathogen is to initiate combination treatment with an aminoglycoside and an extended-spectrum antipseudomonal penicillin or cephalosporin. The specific choice of agents should be guided by local antibiotic susceptibility patterns and prescribing practices. If a cephalosporin is used, care should be taken to choose an agent such as ceftazidime, cefepime, or cefoperazone with demonstrated in vitro and in vivo efficacy against *Pseudomonas*. Cefotaxime and ceftriaxone are less satisfactory alternatives in this setting because of their unpredictable activity against *Pseudomonas*.[215]

The use of a single antibiotic (monotherapy) in febrile neutropenic patients is the subject of continuing debate. Ceftazidime was used successfully as initial therapy in one major study,[216] whereas another large study reported superior response rates when ceftazidime was combined with a full rather than a short course of amikacin.[217] The results of another study indicated that imipenem monotherapy may be equivalent or even superior to ceftazidime in neutropenic cancer patients with suspected sepsis, in part because of its greater activity against gram-positive organisms.[218] Yet another study documented similar response rates to double β-lactam therapy (ceftazidime plus piperacillin or cefoperazone plus piperacillin) compared with that achieved with imipenem alone.[219] It should be noted that some clinical studies assessing the effectiveness of various single-agent regimens in febrile neutropenic patients have included relatively few subjects with documented *P. aeruginosa* bacteremia, whereas *Pseudomonas* spp. including *P. aeruginosa* have been disproportionately represented among treatment failures (i.e., relapses and superinfections).[218, 219] Yet, it has been argued that because the incidence of *Pseudomonas* infections has decreased among febrile neutropenic cancer patients, concern about the adequacy of double β-lactam or single-agent therapy of *P. aeruginosa* infection is no longer relevant for many oncology centers.[219] Nevertheless, even those advocating monotherapy in this setting recognize the potential need for modification of the initial antimicrobial treatment when the results of the pretreatment evaluation become available, the patient's condition deteriorates, or fever and neutropenia persist.[216] Therefore, despite the continued controversy regarding monotherapy in febrile neutropenic patients, it is recommended that if *Pseudomonas* sepsis is suspected on the basis of clinical setting or local hospital epidemiology, or if the patient is gravely ill, combination therapy should be instituted with maximum recommended doses of an aminoglycoside and a β-lactam agent with dependable antipseudomonal activity. Moreover, if *Pseudomonas* bacteremia is subsequently documented, a similar combination regimen should be initiated, even if the patient has already responded to single-agent therapy.

According to some studies,[220, 221] immunocompromised patients with documented bacteremia caused by *Pseudomonas* or other gram-negative bacteria have a higher probability of survival when they receive two antibiotics to which their infecting strains are susceptible, particularly when the two drugs act synergistically. It has also been suggested that the utility of antibiotic synergy is particularly important in persistent, profound neutropenia.[222] A prospective study of 200 consecutive patients with *P. aeruginosa* bacteremia,[223] most not neutropenic, documented that patients receiving combination therapy with an antipseudomonal β-lactam agent plus an aminoglycoside experienced improved 10-day survival compared with patients receiving a single agent. The survival benefit of combination therapy was most pronounced among patients with pneumonia, patients with bacteremia of nosocomial origin, and critically ill patients.[223] However, there was no significant correlation in this study between the results of in vitro susceptibility testing and survival, and no significant survival benefit was demonstrated among patients receiving antibiotic combinations that were synergistic in vitro. Yet the preponderance of this and other clinical experience strongly supports the routine use of combination therapy with an antipseudomonal β-lactam agent plus an aminoglycoside in bacteremic *Pseudomonas* disease.[224] For the aminoglycoside component of the combination, serum levels should be closely monitored to maintain the highest possible drug concentrations consistent with safety. The duration of treatment is dictated by the site and severity of the primary infection, the promptness of response, and the presence or persistence of neutropenia. For example, a nonneutropenic patient with *Pseudomonas* urosepsis who defervesces promptly after removal of a Foley catheter and institution of antibiotics may be managed adequately with 7 to 10 days of therapy. In contrast, a neutropenic patient with persistent fever or other signs of sepsis while taking antibiotics may warrant prolonged treatment until the leukocyte count recovers and the fever subsides.

The addition of rifampin to conventional two-drug regimens for *Pseudomonas* bacteremia may favor bacteriologic cure (i.e., prevention of breakthrough or relapsing bacteremia), although the survival benefit, if any, of adding this third antimicrobial agent is as yet unclear.[225]

Because no pathophysiologic mechanisms peculiar to *Pseudomonas*-associated septic shock have been adequately elucidated, no specific therapy other than antibiotics is indicated in this condition. Although controversy may still exist over the role of steroid therapy in septic shock,[226] studies have not confirmed the efficacy of such treatment.[227, 228] Specific immunologic approaches to the treatment of *Pseudomonas* sepsis, such as the passive administration of hyperimmune IV immunoglobulin or *Pseudomonas*-specific monoclonal antibodies, are under investigation but are not available for routine use at the present time.

Central Nervous System Infections

Infection with *P. aeruginosa* causes meningitis and brain abscess. *Pseudomonas* infections of the central nervous system (CNS) result from (1) extension from a contiguous structure such as ear, mastoid, or paranasal sinus; (2) direct inoculation into the subarachnoid space or brain by means of head trauma, surgey, or invasive diagnostic procedures; or (3) bacteremic spread from a distant site of infection such as the urinary tract, lung, or endocardium.[229–232] As in other forms of *Pseudomonas* disease, CNS infections usually occur in the presence of preexisting defects in normal host defenses or other predisposing conditions. The latter include recent neurosurgery; penetrating head trauma; tumors of the head and neck; infections of the ear, mastoid, or paranasal sinuses; lumbar punctures; spinal anesthesia; intraventricular shunts or reservoirs; and cerebrospinal fluid (CSF) leaks. In addition, conditions that predispose patients to *Pseudomonas* bacteremia, such as neutropenia and severe burns, increase the risk of metastatic CNS infection. In a survey of cancer patients with CNS infections,[229] *P. aeruginosa* was the second most common bacterial pathogen isolated in cases of meningitis (after *Listeria monocytogenes*) and the second most frequent cause of brain abscess (*E. coli* was first). To the list of conditions predisposing to the development of *Pseudomonas* CNS infections, AIDS must now be added.[233]

The clinical manifestations of *Pseudomonas* meningitis are like those of other forms of bacterial meningitis and include fever, headache, confusion, and obtundation. The onset of disease may be acute or even fulminant, particularly when it is associated with bacteremia; septic shock and coma may supervene; and early death is common. In nonbacteremic patients, the onset of clinical disease may be more gradual, sometimes in the absence of systemic signs and symptoms. This presentation is particularly common in immunosuppressed patients, in cancer patients, and in those whose meningitis is related to neurosurgery or extension from a contiguous site of chronic infection.[234] *Pseudomonas* meningitis is sometimes characterized by a subacute, relapsing course, probably as a result of release of bacteria from loculated areas of infection. Recurrent or chronic *Pseudomonas* meningitis may be associated with alteration of normal cranial anatomy secondary to trauma, surgery, or malignant disease; indwelling catheters, CSF shunts, or reservoirs; prosthetic materials; active or undrained parameningeal infections; CSF leaks; or AIDS.

The treatment of *P. aeruginosa* meningitis may be complicated by preexisting or emergent antibiotic resistance or by suboptimal antibiotic penetration into the subarachnoid space.[235] Ceftazidime may well be the antimicrobial agent best able to overcome these two limitations. Thus susceptibility of most *P. aeruginosa* strains of ceftazidime, coupled with its ability to cross the blood-brain barrier, usually results in CSF drug levels well in excess of minimal inhibitory concentrations.[236] Although the infrequency of *Pseudomonas* meningitis has precluded large, controlled studies, the efficacy of ceftazidime has been documented by clinical experience.[236–238] Successful treatment of *Pseudomonas* meningitis has been reported with ceftazidime used alone or in combination with an aminoglycoside administered intravenously or intrathecally. Many documented responses to ceftazidime have followed previously unsuccessful treatment with other agents.[218] Although current data suggest that ceftazidime is the antibiotic of choice in *Pseudomonas* meningitis, it is unclear whether it is best used in conjunction with an aminoglycoside. Initial treatment, particularly in desperately ill patients, should probably include both agents administered intravenously at maximal doses consistent with safety. The ability of ceftazidime to enter the CSF in therapeutic concentrations may obviate the need for intrathecal administration of the accompanying aminoglycoside (as previously recommended). However, failure of initial therapy or relapse may necessitate intrathecal therapy,[239] or if there is obstruction of the subarachnoid space or evidence of ventriculitis direct intraventricular aminoglycoside administration via an intraventricular catheter or reservoir may be required.[240, 241] The choice of a particular aminoglycoside should be governed by local susceptibility patterns. Gentamicin, tobramycin, and amikacin have all been administered successfully by both the intrathecal and intraventricular routes; a preservative-free form should be used when available. Extended-spectrum cephalosporins other than ceftazidime are probably contraindicated in *Pseudomonas* meningitis on the basis of variable activity against *Pseudomonas*, poor CSF penetration, or both.[235, 236, 242]

Parenteral ciprofloxacin is another promising antimicrobial agent for use in *Pseudomonas* CNS infections as judged by favorable in vitro susceptibility data, good CSF penetration,[243] and equivalent efficacy compared with ceftazidime and tobramycin in experimental *P. aeruginosa* meningitis in rabbits.[244] However, clinical experience with ciprofloxacin in *Pseudomonas* meningitis is so limited that it should be used only in combination with other agents.

The monobactam antibiotic, aztreonam, has also shown effectiveness when used as the sole agent in the treatment of gram-negative bacterial meningitis, including cases caused by *P. aeruginosa*.[245, 246] However, clinical experience with this antibiotic is limited in *P. aeruginosa* meningitis, and at least one relapse has been documented after cessation of therapy.[245] Yet, the generally favorable record of aztreonam in gram-negative meningitis, good in vitro activity against most *P. aeruginosa* strains, and adequate CSF penetration all suggest that aztreonam may represent at least an effective second-line treatment for *Pseudomonas* meningitis.

The carbapenem agents, meropenem and imipenem, although active against most *P. aeruginosa* strains in vitro, must be used in high doses in meningitis with the attendant risk of CNS toxicity.[247] Moreover, the emergence of imipenem resistance has been documented during treatment for *Pseudomonas* meningitis.[233]

The proper duration of antibiotic therapy for *Pseudomonas* meningitis is dictated by the severity and extent of involvement, degree of disruption of normal anatomy, presence or absence of ventriculitis, and promptness of response to treatment. A minimum of 2 weeks of therapy should ordinarily be expected, and much longer treatment may be necessary to eradicate infection and prevent relapse. Monitoring of lumbar CSF or ventricular fluid by culture, serial cell counts, and determination of antibiotic levels, may help direct therapy and suggest a proper treatment end point. Relapses are common and require retreatment.

Pseudomonas brain abscesses should be surgically drained, if possible, and treated with antibiotics as described previously. Multiple, small (<2 cm), poorly organized, or relatively inaccessible abscesses may be more amenable, at least initially, to medical therapy alone, although subsequent surgery may be necessitated by further abscess enlargement. Excision of an abscess capsule, if it exists, may be required in some cases.[248] Intrathecal or intraventricular aminoglycoside administration is not necessary unless persistent meningitis or ventriculitis is present. Abscesses should be monitored during treatment by serial computed axial tomographic (CT) or magnetic resonance imaging (MRI) scans, and antibiotics should be continued until there is closure or significant diminution in size; 2 to 6 weeks of therapy may be necessary. Failure of an abscess to diminish in size or progression of symptoms may necessitate reaspiration or surgical exploration and drainage. Cure of *Pseudomonas* CNS infections in general may require débridement of necrotic tissue, removal of prosthetic materials, or repair of CSF leaks.

Ear Infections, Including "Malignant" External Otitis

P. aeruginosa is infrequently found in the normal ear but often inhabits the external auditory canal in association with injury, maceration, inflammation, or simply wet or humid conditions. It is the predominant bacterial pathogen in some cases of external otitis[249] (see Chapter 50) and is presumed to play a contributory if not causal role in this usually benign and self-limited disease. External otitis is clearly associated with swimming ("swimmer's ear") and is said to be more frequent in humid, southern climates.[250] Its clinical manifestations include an itchy or painful, discharging ear,[251] with pain worsened by traction on the pinna and a tender edematous canal filled with debris. This infection is successfully treated with local measures, including topical application of antibiotic- and steroid-containing otic solutions,[252] drying agents, and 2% acetic acid to reduce the growth of *Pseudomonas*. Although external otitis is usually cured by these measures, recurrence is common, particularly in frequent swimmers.

Occasionally, *Pseudomonas* infections of the external auditory canal become locally invasive by penetrating the epithelium and invading underlying soft tissues. This process is usually chronic and indolent, but it is also destructive and ultimately life-threatening if not promptly and appropriately treated. Invasive, necrotizing, or, more commonly, "malignant" external otitis is a condition found predominantly in elderly diabetic patients, particularly those with long-standing illness associated with small vessel disease.[250, 253–259] It also occurs occasionally in very young infants with other underlying illnesses,[260–262] and less commonly in apparently normal elderly adults.[263] An unusual case of fatal necrotizing otitis externa associated with *P. aeruginosa* bacteremia was reported in a patient with AIDS.[264] In addition, an association has been demonstrated between aural irrigation with tap water and the development of malignant external otitis in susceptible persons.[265–267]

Tissue invasion by *Pseudomonas* usually begins at the junction between cartilage and bone in the floor of the lateral portion of the external auditory canal, through normal defects in the cartilage called the fissures of Santorini. The invasive process involves soft tissue, cartilage, and ultimately cortical bone and marrow. The necrotizing infection enters the soft tissues of the retromandibular area or parotid space. The infection usually bypasses the tympanic membrane and middle ear, at least early, and enters the mastoid air cells and adjacent temporal bone. Once osteomyelitis of the temporal bone has been established, the infection spreads through the bone at the base of the skull, involving the 7th cranial nerve at the stylomastoid foramen; the 9th, 10th, and 11th cranial nerves at the jugular foramen; and the 12th cranial nerve at the hypoglossal canal. Thrombosis of lateral and sigmoid sinuses may occur, and further spread proceeds in sinuses and along other vascular channels with extension throughout the temporal bone all the way to the petrous apex. Extension can then further proceed across the base of the skull, anterior to the foramen magnum, via the basisphenoid and basiocciput or cavernous sinus to the contralateral petrous apex, and from there may involve contralateral cranial nerves. Frank meningitis and brain abscess are relatively uncommon complications.

Presenting symptoms of malignant external otitis include otalgia and otorrhea. A facial nerve palsy may be present initially, whereas involvement of other cranial nerves usually appears later. Some patients report decreased hearing; the pinna may be tender, and the presence of trismus indicates involvement of the temporomandibular area. Systemic symptoms, including fever and weight loss, occur in a small minority of patients. On physical examination, the external auditory canal is abnormal in almost all patients. It usually appears inflamed, swollen, or erythematous, and a purulent discharge is present. In most cases, granulation tissue is seen in the posteroinferior canal wall or at the junction of the bony and cartilaginous canal. The tympanic membrane is intact in some patients, perforated in others; often it is simply hidden from view by edema, granulation tissue, and debris. Signs of inflammation are often noted in areas outside the ear canal, including the pinna, periauricular and retromandibular areas, and mastoid tip. Local lymphadenopathy and parotid swelling are occasionally present. Bilateral disease is relatively uncommon but does occur.

Leukocytosis is infrequent in malignant external otitis, whereas CSF pleocytosis and protein elevation are occasionally noted. Although it is a nonspecific finding, the erythrocyte sedimentation rate (ESR) appears to be strikingly elevated in most cases, with elevations greater than 100 mm/hour sometimes observed.[266] CT scans document soft tissue and osseous lesions, including fluid in the mastoid air cells, and help define the intracranial and extracranial extent of disease.[268, 269] CT scans are particularly useful for demonstrating soft tissue densities associated with areas of cellulitis involving the base of the skull. The anatomic locations of these densities often correspond to specific cranial nerve deficits.[270] Technetium-99 bone scans are more sensitive than radiographs in demonstrating early bone involvement. MRI may be superior to CT in defining the anatomic extent of disease and delineating soft tissue involvement.[271] Finally, quantitative gallium-67 single photon emission CT appears to be particularly efficacious for assessing the response of malignant external otitis to therapy.[272]

P. aeruginosa is isolated from cultures of the external auditory canal and specimens obtained at the time of surgery in virtually all patients with malignant external otitis. Although other organisms may be isolated in addition, and rare examples have been documented in which malignant external otitis was caused by other organisms,[273] for practical purposes this may be considered a specific *Pseudomonas* disease.

The treatment of malignant external otitis should be aggressive and persistent, commonly involving both surgery and antibiotics.[250, 258] Surgery is aimed at débriding granulation tissue and necrotic material, such as dead bone and cartilage, and draining pus. The nature of the surgery required is determined by sites of involvement and extent of infection. Surgical procedures may include canal débridement, bone or cartilage débridement, mastoidectomy, or facial nerve decompression. Occasionally, a suboccipital approach is used to drain and débride areas of infection in the floor of the skull.[274] In many cases, however, relatively circumscribed surgery may be preferable, in conjunction with aggressive (and effective) antibiotic therapy. Some believe, for example, that facial nerve decompression does not contribute to the recovery of function and should not be routinely performed. Similar opinion holds that the role of surgery in malignant external otitis should generally be limited to local débridement and excision of accessible foci of infection, such as polypectomy or sequestrum removal. This school of thought would reserve more extensive bone resection and drainage of deep-seated cranial abscesses for selected patients whose condition is unresponsive to aggressive medical therapy and more limited surgical débridement.[266]

Conventional antibiotic therapy for malignant external otitis consists of an aminoglycoside in combination with a β-lactam agent with good antipseudomonal activity. This treatment is ordinarily continued for a minimum of 4 weeks in the case of relatively limited disease, and 6 to 8 weeks or longer if extensive disease is present, particularly with cranial nerve involvement. Earlier studies suggested a greater likelihood of recurrent disease when single rather than combined antibiotics were used.[258] For example, a retrospective analysis of patients receiving cefsulodin alone, compared with those receiving conventional therapy (i.e., an aminoglycoside plus antipseudomonal β-lactam), suggested equivalent efficacy only in patients with "moderate" infections.[275]

More recent studies emphasize the changing face of malignant external otitis, with a lower incidence, since 1985, of associated diabetes mellitus, cranial nerve involvement, and treatment failures.[276] With earlier recognition and treatment of malignant external otitis has come a broader spectrum of often less advanced disease and a better overall prognosis.[276, 277] The appropriate treatment of malignant external otitis has changed accordingly,[277] with greater reliance on single-agent therapy with IV ceftazidime[276] or oral ciprofloxacin.[278–280] The duration of monotherapy is typically 6 weeks; after initiation in the hospital, this treatment can often be completed at home. Complicated disease or extensive intracranial involvement may necessitate longer single-agent treatment.[278] Combination therapy of ciprofloxacin plus rifampin and the use of ofloxacin have been advocated, but few data exist.[281, 282]

It is clear that earlier recognition and improved treatment of malignant external otitis have improved outcome. However, patients who present with neurologic deficits have a worse prognosis, commensurate with the extent and severity of their infections. Treatment failures can occur despite optimal therapy, and relapses are observed as long as 4 to 12 months, but usually within 3 months, after termination of antibiotic therapy, necessitating careful long-term follow-up. Disease status may be assessed during treatment and posttreatment periods by monitoring pain, ESR, and soft tissue densities on CT or MRI scans.[268]

Otitis media diagnosed during the first 6 weeks of life is frequently caused by gram-negative bacteria, including *Pseudomonas*, and may manifest atypically.[283] Symptoms include rhinorrhea, irritability, feeding difficulty, cough, and diarrhea. Most patients are afebrile. A routine 10-day course of antibiotic treatment may not result in cure, and *Pseudomonas* is often recovered from the ears in cases of treatment failure, whether or not it was the organism initially isolated. An antipseudomonal antibiotic should therefore be included in the initial treatment of children younger than 6 weeks of age with otitis media, and therapy should be continued for more than 10 days.

P. aeruginosa is the most common bacterial pathogen isolated from the middle and external ear of children and adults with chronic suppurative otitis media. Isolation rates as high as 72% have been reported.[284] Although the microbiology of chronic middle ear infections may be complex, *P. aeruginosa* was identified in 67% of specimens obtained directly from the middle ear of children with chronic suppurative otitis media and was the only organism grown in 31%.[285] Traditionally, tympanomastoid surgery was considered standard management for chronic suppurative otitis media that was unresponsive to topical and oral antimicrobial therapy. More recent evidence suggests, however, that medical management with parenteral antibiotics and daily aural toilet will result in resolution of most chronic suppurative otitis media, without cholesteatoma, in children, thus obviating the need for tympanomastoidectomy in most cases.[286] This finding has been confirmed in studies that used in-hospital, single-agent parenteral therapy with mezlocillin or ceftazidime,[287] outpatient therapy with ceftazidime,[288] or outpatient therapy with oral ciprofloxacin.[289] In each case, approximately 2 to 3 weeks of antibiotic therapy produced good therapeutic responses in most treated patients, and most, but not all, remained free of recurrences during long-term follow-up.[287–289]

P. aeruginosa can cause mastoiditis in association with either malignant external otitis or primary acute otitis media.[290] In either case, patients usually have diabetes mellitus or another underlying disease that adversely affects normal host defenses. In such patients, acute *Pseudomonas* middle ear infections progress to granulomatous mucositis of the mastoid and middle ear, leading to osteomyelitis and bone necrosis. Spontaneous perforation of the tympanic membrane is usual, and seventh cranial nerve palsy is seen in some cases. Treatment consists of local débridement or mastoidectomy and aggressive antibiotic therapy similar to that used in malignant external otitis.

Community-acquired *P. aeruginosa* sinusitis has been reported in nonneutropenic patients with AIDS.[291] Chronic exposure to antibiotics such as trimethoprim-sulfamethoxazole or ciprofloxacin may predispose AIDS patients to such infections by favoring colonization with resistant strains of *P. aeruginosa*. In some instances, AIDS-associated sinusitis may be accompanied by bacteremia. Treatment involves surgical drainage of affected sinuses and administration of appropriate parenteral antibiotics.

Pseudomonas perichondritis of the auricle may follow trauma, burns, ear-piercing procedures that traverse cartilage,[292] acupuncture,[293] or ear surgery.[294] The ear becomes acutely swollen, erythematous, disfigured, and tender as invading bacteria cause a cellulitis as well as inflammation and necrosis of cartilage. Treatment consists of the insertion of drainage tubes and administration of systemic antipseudomonal antibiotics. Excisional procedures are disfiguring and should be avoided if possible.[294]

Eye Infections

P. aeruginosa is a frequent and sometimes devastating pathogen in the human eye. It is one of the most common causes of bacterial keratitis, (see Chapter 99) and is also implicated in endophthalmitis.[295] In addition, it has been reported as the etiologic agent in ophthalmia neonatorum,[296] blepharoconjunctivitis,[297] scleral abscess,[298] and orbital cellulitis.[299]

The pathogenesis of *Pseudomonas* eye infections is a function of the peculiar anatomy and physiology of the eye as well as inherent characteristics of the organism itself. The initial attachment of *Pseudomonas* to the ocular epithelium appears to be mediated by sialic acid (*N*-acetylneuraminic acid)–specific receptors,[300] analogous to those responsible for the organism's attachment to tracheobronchial epithelium. The cornea and the aqueous, and vitreous humors provide a relatively sequestered and avascular milieu that, in the normal state, is relatively devoid of humoral and cellular immune elements. When introduced into this locally immunocompromised environment through trauma or hematogenous spread, *Pseudomonas* is capable of rapid proliferation and production of pathogenic extracellular enzymes, including elastase, alkaline protease, and exotoxin A. The result can be a rapidly progressive and destructive infection leading to loss of the entire eye. Treatment is complicated by the existence of a blood-eye barrier that impedes access of antibiotics to infected intraocular structures.

Pseudomonas infections of the cornea usually begin with some form of trauma, often minor, which causes an interruption in the epithelial surface and allows bacterial invasion of underlying stroma. *Pseudomonas* keratitis appears to be more common in humid environments, such as the southern United States.[301] It is associated with contact lens use,[302] especially that involving extended-wear soft contact lens,[303] but also with other types of extended- and daily-wear disposable lenses.[304, 305] *Pseudomonas* keratitis also has a high incidence in patients with predisposing ocular conditions, particularly those requiring topical steroid therapy, and it has been associated with the use of contaminated ocular medications.[306] Also susceptible to *Pseudomonas* keratitis are patients with serious burns, coma, previous ocular irradiation, previous radial keratotomy,[307] exposure to an intensive care environment,[308, 309] and AIDS.[310, 311] Pediatric intensive care patients may be particularly susceptible to *Pseudomonas* eye infections associated with tracheostomy, endotracheal intubation, and respiratory care, which apparently result in contamination of unprotected eyes by respiratory secretions.[312, 313] *Pseudomonas* keratitis typically begins as a small central ulcer that spreads concentrically, in some cases to involve the entire cornea and parts of the sclera, and internally to involve deeper portions of the stroma, sometimes leading to corneal perforation.

Clinical signs of *Pseudomonas* keratitis may include a rapidly developing, necrotic, grayish stromal infiltrate in the bed of an epithelial injury, surrounding epithelial edema, severe anterior chamber reaction, and abundant mucopurulent discharge tenaciously adherent to the ulcer surface. The time course of *Pseudomonas* keratitis is variable. Classically, it progresses rapidly over 48 hours or less to involve the entire cornea, in some cases leading to perforation. Alternatively, the infection may evolve subacutely over many days. Fever is either absent or low-grade, and other systemic symptoms are unusual. If present, leukocytosis is minimal.

Because a *Pseudomonas* corneal ulcer can lead to the rapid loss of ocular function, it should be approached as a medical emergency. Scrapings are obtained from the floor of the ulcer for Gram stain and culture. The presence of gram-negative rods (or a negative Gram stain necessitates the immediate initiation of combined topical and subconjunctival (or subtenon) therapy with an aminoglycoside antibiotic such as gentamicin or tobramycin. Topical therapy typically consists of an ophthalmic aminoglycoside solution rather than ointment; the optimal concentration of drug in such a preparation is 8 mg/ml or greater (rather than the more dilute 0.3% gentamicin solution commercially available).[314, 315] The solution is applied to the affected eye every 30 to 60 minutes, although continuous lavage has also been advocated.[316] An ophthalmic solution containing a quinolone antibiotic, such as enoxacin, may provide an effective alternative to gentamicin eye drops.[317] Antibiotic-impregnated corneal collagen shields have been evaluated as an alternative drug delivery device in experimental *Pseudomonas* keratitis but may not be as effective as the frequent topical delivery of "fortified" concentrations of an aminoglycoside ophthalmic solution.[318, 319] Topical therapy alone may be sufficient for relatively small, superficial ulcers,[320] but subconjunctival (or subtenon) administration ensures higher aminoglycoside concentrations in the corneal stroma, sclera, and aqueous[321]; the latter may be critical if perforation into the anterior chamber is imminent. Once- or twice- daily subconjunctival injections with 20 mg of gentamicin may be given for the first 3 days of therapy or until negative cultures are obtained. Ceftazidime may be administered alternatively by the same route. There is still some question concerning the bactericidal sufficiency against *P. aeruginosa* of intraocular levels of ciprofloxacin achieved in the uninflamed eye after oral administration,[322–324] making this form of treatment somewhat problematic for the prevention or treatment of anterior chamber involvement or further intraocular spread. Parenteral therapy is usually reserved for documented intraocular spread resulting in endophthalmitis.

Pseudomonas endophthalmitis may result from penetrating injuries, intraocular surgery, posterior perforation of corneal ulcers, or hematogenous spread from other primary sites of infection.[325, 326] It is usually a fulminant disease that threatens permanent loss of vision within days or even hours. This rapid progression serves to clinically differentiate *Pseudomonas* endophthalmitis from that caused by less virulent bacteria, such as *Staphylococcus epidermidis*, α-hemolytic streptococci, or fungi, which are likely to cause more indolent infections. The most common clinical features are pain, conjunctival hyperemia and chemosis, lid edema, decreased visual acuity, hypopyon, or severe anterior uveitis; involvement of the vitreous and panophthalmitis follow.

Early and aggressive therapy of *Pseudomonas* endophthalmitis can sometimes result in the preservation of sight, although *P. aeruginosa* intraocular infections are assoicated with a particularly grave visual outcome.[327, 328] Antibiotic therapy normally consists of an aminoglycoside administered by the parenteral, subconjunctival (or subtenon), topical, and intraocular routes, as well as a parenterally and subconjunctivally administered antipseudomonal penicillin. Parenteral, subconjunctival, and intraocular ceftazidime may represent effective alternative therapy,[329, 330] although clinical experience is limited. Vitrectomy is usually indicated to help clear loculated infection and cellular debris and to facilitate intraocular antibiotic administration, although this surgical approach remains somewhat controversial.[327] The optimal duration of therapy is not well defined, although antibiotics should probably be continued until there has been marked clinical improvement and intraocular and extraocular signs of infection have subsided. Intraocular antibiotic injections may be repeated daily during the first several days of treatment until negative cultures are obtained from the vitreous.

Bone and Joint Infections

Pseudomonas infections of bones and joints result from hematogenous spread from other primary sites or extension from contiguous foci. Blood-borne infections are most commonly seen in IV drug users and in conjunction with urinary tract or pelvic infections. Contiguous infections are usually related to penetrating trauma, surgery, or overlying soft tissue infections. *Pseudomonas* bone and joint infections occur in children, the elderly, the chronically debilitated, and those with underlying diseases or other predisposing factors. *Pseudomonas* osteochondritis occurs after puncture wounds of the foot, particularly, in children; the sternoclavicular and sacroiliac joints, vertebrae, and symphysis pubis are infected in IV drug users; osteomyelitis occurs in conjunction with vascular insufficiency of the lower extremities in patients with diabetes mellitus; diseased large synovial joints are infected in patients with underlying rheumatoid disease; and infections of the long bones occur after open fractures and internal fixation procedures.

Blood-borne *Pseudomonas* appears to have a particular predilection for fibrocartilaginous joints of the axial skeleton. These infections often involve joint space, cartilage, synovium, and contiguous bone, so that it is difficult to determine whether arthritis preceded bone involvement or vice versa. These infections often begin in cartilage within the joint space and progress to invasion of underlying bone. In addtion, the organism may penetrate and damage the epiphyseal plate of growing bone, another cartilaginous structure.

Pseudomonas bone and joint infections are often more indolent than those caused by *S. aureus*, and they tend to be less destructive, or at least less rapidly so. A direct comparison of *P. aeruginosa* and *S. aureus* bone infections in rabbits[331, 332] revealed common pathologic features but differences in severity. Compared with staphylococcal osteomyelitis, that caused by *Pseudomonas* was associated with fewer abscesses, less extensive sequestrum formation, less frequent extraosseus extension, and milder radiographic changes.

Vertebral osteomyelitis caused by *P. aeruginosa* is occasionally associated with complicated urinary tract infections and genitourinary surgery or instrumentation.[201] This disease often occurs in elderly patients and involves the lumbosacral spine primarily; shared venous drainage between pelvis and spine (Batson's plexus) is the presumed route of infection. Reported cases have occurred mainly in IV drug users; most of these patients were young men, and the cervical spine was more commonly involved in these patients (e.g., 27%) than in non–drug users (rarely).[333–335] The duration of symptoms was weeks to months, neck or back pain being the most common symptom. Fever and other systemic symptoms were relatively uncommon. Physical signs included local tenderness and decreased range of motion of the spine. Neurologic deficits were found in approximately 15% of patients and tended to be mild. When present, temperature elevation was usually low-grade. Leukocytosis was variable, and ESR was almost always elevated. *Pseudomonas* occasionally was isolated from the blood. Plain radiographs of the affected spine were sometimes "normal" on admission but rarely remained so during hospitalization. CT scans usually were not positive in the face of normal plain films but were helpful in defining bone and adjacent soft tissue abnormalities when present. These include generalized loss of bone density, a narrowed interspace, destruction of adjacent vertebral end plates, lytic lesions of vertebral bodies, sclerosis, and, particularly late, osteophyte formation. MRI scans, including both axial and sagittal sections, may be the most critical means for assessing changes in interspaces, soft tissue densities, epidural extension, and anatomic extent of involvement. Technetium bone scans are usually positive, even when radiographs are read as normal.

The diagnosis of *Pseudomonas* vertebral osteomyelitis can usually be established by culturing the organism from material obtained by needle biopsy or aspiration. This can sometimes be accomplished under fluoroscopic guidance, but the procedure may have to be repeated. Open biopsy may be necessary to make an etiologic diagnosis in as many as one third of cases. Surgery usually is not required in this disease except when exploration and open biopsy are necessary to establish a diagnosis or decompression is required by a possible epidural or paravertebral abscess (uncommon). Aminoglycoside antibiotics have been employed successfully in vertebral osteomyelitis; when used, they should be administered for at least 4 weeks to reduce the chance of relapse, which is common with shorter courses of treatment. Although there is little evidence of increased therapeutic efficacy of antibiotic combinations, a β-lactam agent with good antipseudomonal activity should probably be used in conjunction with an aminoglycoside. Single-drug therapy with agents such as ceftazidime, imipenem, aztreonam, or ciprofloxacin, although possibly effective, has not been properly evaluated. Longer courses of therapy may be appropriate if extensive disease is present, the ESR remains elevated, or a single antibiotic is used.

Sternoarticular pyarthrosis caused by *Pseudomonas* is another infection found primarily in IV drug users.[336–338] Although the disease is sometimes associated with *Pseudomonas* endocarditis, a primary site of infection usually is not discernible, and the pathogenesis remains obscure. Patients are commonly young men. Joint involvement is usually monoarticular, with the sternoclavicular joint affected more often than sternochondral joints. Major complaints are usually limited to moderate to severe anterior chest discomfort over the affected joint. Painful and restricted movement of the homolateral shoulder is often reported. The duration of symptoms before diagnosis is usually months, although more acute presentations sometimes occur. Most patients are persistently febrile, and physical findings include tenderness, swelling, erythema over the affected joint, and limitation of range of motion of the shoulder on the side of involvement. Leukocytosis is sometimes present, and the ESR is almost always elevated. Arthrocentesis may yield fluid with typical characteristics of pyogenic infection, although smears of the fluid may not reveal bacteria despite subsequent positive culture. Synovial biopsy usually yields the infecting organism, and blood cultures are occasionally positive. Radiographic changes include soft tissue swelling, demineralization of adjacent bone, lytic lesions, and periosteal elevation of the clavicular head, rib, or sternum. Exploratory arthrotomies are usually necessary because contiguous bone involvement is present and requires débridement. In addition, perisynovial or retrosternal abscesses frequently need draining. These infections have been treated effectively with an aminoglycoside administered for at least 6 weeks in combination with an antipseudomonal penicillin. With adequate therapy, full recovery may be expected with minimal functional disability.

Pyogenic infections of the symphysis pubis are associated with prior pelvic surgery and IV drug use and are usually caused by *P. aeruginosa*.[339, 340] These infections may also occur as a late complication of femoral artery cardiac catheterization.[341] The pubic symphysis represents a fibrocartilaginous joint, and, as such, shares with the intervertebral, sternoarticular, and sacroiliac joints a peculiar susceptibility to infection by hematogenously disseminated *Pseudomonas*. Patients with osteomyelitis of the pubis present with hip, groin, thigh, or lower abdominal pain, any of which may be exacerbated by walking. Patients complain of exquisite tenderness over the pubic symphysis and may have fever. The duration of symptoms before medical attention ranges from several days to 2 months. Leukocytosis is variable, and the ESR is elevated. Radiographs of the pelvis may be normal initially but eventually show irregularity of the pubic margins and separation at the symphysis pubis. Osteomyelitis of the pubic rami is invariably present and may be extensive. Bone scans are usually positive. The diagnosis is made by needle aspiration or biopsy of the pubic symphysis and culture. This diagnostic procedure is particularly important to differentiate pyogenic infection from osteitis pubis.[342] The latter is presumably a noninfectious condition that closely mimics osteomyelitis of the pubis and occurs most commonly after pelvic surgery, childbirth, or trauma.

Most patients with *Pseudomonas* osteomyelitis of the pubis can be cured with antibiotics alone and do not require surgical débridement or drainage. Cures have been documented after aminoglycoside administration alone or in combination with an antipseudomonal penicillin. The duration of therapy should be 4 weeks or longer.

P. aeruginosa is the most common pathogen implicated in osteochondritis after puncture wounds of the foot.[343–346] Originally described in children, this entity may also occur in adults.[347] A large majority of children with this infection were wearing tennis shoes at the time of injury,[348] and *P. aeruginosa* has been isolated from the sole of such shoes.[349] As the name implies, *Pseudomonas* osteochondritis reflects the peculiar predilection of the organism for cartilage and involves the small joints and bones of the foot. Typically, a patient experiences early improvement in pain and swelling after a puncture wound of the foot, only to have the symptoms recur or worsen several days later. The average duration of symptoms before diagnosis is more than 1 week, but it may be much longer. Fever and other systemic signs are usually absent. Examination may reveal a superficial area of cellulitis on the plantar surface of the foot overlying the area of involvement, or merely tenderness to deep palpation. Involvement of the proximal phalanges, metatarsals, metatarsophalangeal joints, tarsal bones, and calcaneus have been reported. Radiographic changes may be present at the time of presentation but sometimes develop later; technetium scans are positive. Aspiration of an affected joint may yield a small amount of purulent fluid with bacteria present on Gram stain or culture.

Appropriate treatment of *Pseudomonas* osteochondritis of the foot involves both surgery and antibiotics. Surgical intervention should be prompt and should include débridement of necrotic bone and other devitalized tissue, exploration of the nail tract for foreign material, drainage of intraosseous abscesses, and drainage and irrigation of septic joints.[348] It has been suggested that the parenteral administration of one or two agents with good antipseudomonal activity for as little as 1 week may be sufficient, in conjunction with appropriate surgery, to eradicate most *Pseudomonas* bone and joint infections of the foot.[348] Oral ciprofloxicin therapy (750 mg twice daily for 7 to 14 days) has been employed successfully after surgical débridement.[350] Relapse and long-term sequelae appear to be relatively unusual after combined surgical and short-course antimicrobial therapy. Complicated, poorly responsive, or recrudescent infections should probably be treated longer.

The term *chronic contiguous osteomyelitis*[351] describes a heterogeneous group of infections that result from direct inoculation of bone or direct extension from overlying or adjacent tissue rather than from a hematogenous source. These infections occur in a variety of clinical settings and are often caused by gram-negative bacteria, among which *P. aeruginosa* is one of the most frequently isolated. These infections commonly occur after a compound fracture or as a complication of "clean" surgery required in the management of closed fractures of the long bones. In some cases, these infections are acquired after puncture wounds of the foot (discussed previously) or as a complication of peripheral neuropathy with associated pressure necrosis of skin and soft tissue overlying bone. Contiguous *Pseudomonas* bone infection can also result from extension of infection from ischemic ulcers in patients with peripheral vascular disease. Sternal osteomyelitis after heart surgery represents another category of such infections. The heterogeneity of chronic contiguous osteomyelitis with respect to clinical setting, affected host, relative difficulty of therapy, and prognosis complicates interpretation of the existing therapeutic literature and establishment of general guidelines for treatment. In one large study, for example, oral ciprofloxacin produced very high cure rates in gram-negative infections associated with nail puncture wounds, pressure necrosis secondary to peripheral neuropathy, or postoperative sternal wounds. The same antibiotic was less effective in post-traumatic or postoperative osteomyelitis of the tibia or femur caused by *Pseudomonas* and was least effective in bone infections associated with underlying peripheral atherosclerotic vascular disease and diabetes mellitus.[351]

In light of these difficulties, general, inclusive therapeutic guidelines are difficult to formulate for chronic contiguous *Pseudomonas* osteomyelitis. The immediate goals of antimicrobial therapy are to achieve bactericidal antibiotic levels in blood and bone and to sustain those levels for the prolonged periods required for eradication of chronic infection. The combination of an aminoglycoside and an antipseudomonal penicillin, both used in full therapeutic doses for a minimum of 4 to 6 weeks (longer in complicated cases) may still represent the therapeutic "gold standard." Surgical débridement; excision of necrotic bone, foreign bodies, or sequestra; or removal of prosthetic materials is often a necessary concomitant of therapy. The evaluation of alternative antibiotics for the treatment of *Pseudomonas* bone infections has focused on single-agent and oral therapy. Ceftazidime has been used successfully, at an average dose of 6 g/day, to treat both acute and chronic *Pseudomonas* osteomyelitis.[352–354] Treatment failures have been noted, however, including persistence of infection and relapse, in some cases associated with the emergence of resistance. Imipenem has also been used, with some success, as single-agent therapy in chronic *Pseudomonas* bone infections, but clinical experience with this antibitotic is limited.[354] Aztreonam also appears to be effective in acute and chronic *Pseudomonas* osteomyelitis treated for an average of 40 days.[355] The quinolone antibiotics, ciprofloxacin, ofloxacin, and pefloxacin, have all been evaluated experimentally or clinically for single-agent oral treatment of gram-negative osteomyelitis. These agents achieve sustained concentrations in bone and blood well in excess of bactericidal levels for most strains of *P. aeruginosa*. Both ciprofloxacin and ofloxacin have achieved high rates of cure of chronic *Pseudomonas* osteomyelitis in rabbits.[356, 357] Moreover, ciprofloxacin[351, 358, 359] and pefloxacin[360] have been used successfully as single-agent oral therapy for a variety of acute and chronic *Pseudomonas* bone infections. In one study,[359] oral ciprofloxacin compared favorably with parenteral antibiotics in the treatment of osteomyelitis caused by a variety of gram-positive and gram-negative organisms; among the latter, *P. aeruginosa* was the most common etiologic agent. When *P. aeruginosa* was the sole isolate in this study the oral ciprofloxacin and IV antibiotic regimens appeared to be equally efficacious, but when infections were polymicrobial treatment failures occurred in both treatment groups.[359] Because of the recalcitrance of *Pseudomonas* osteomyelitis, its association with complicating local or systemic host factors, and its polymicrobial etiology, instances of persistence or relapse requiring retreatment are to be expected and do not necessarily signal the inadequacy of a particular antibiotic.

Urinary Tract Infections

P. aeruginosa infections of the urinary tract are frequently hospital acquired and often iatrogenic.[201] They may be related to urinary tract catheterization,[361] instrumentation, or surgery,[362] including renal transplantation.[363, 364] Surveillance data reported to the CDC NNIS system from 1990 to 1996 indicate that *P. aeruginosa* was the third leading cause of hospital-acquired urinary tract infections, accounting for 11% of such infections.[10] *P. aeruginosa* is also a leading cause of urinary tract infections in chronic care facilities,[365] and *Pseudomonas* bacteriuria frequently complicates spinal cord injury.[366] Even when not hospital acquired, *Pseudomonas* urinary tract infections are frequently "complicated" by such factors as obstruction, persistent sites of infection (e.g., chronic prostatitis, stones), previous antibiotic therapy, and recurrent infections. It has been reported that *P. aeruginosa* is the fifth most common cause of recurrent urinary tract infections in schoolchildren and the third most common pathogen when recurrent infections are complicated by obstruction, catheters, or stones.[367] On the other hand, *P. aeruginosa* urinary tract infections are not limited to patients with complicated urinary tract disease but may be seen in outpatient children[368] and women who do not have sites of persistence or stones.[369] In these cases, *Pseudomonas* may transiently colonize the vaginal introitus, which then serves as a reservoir for subsequent infection.

P. aeruginosa appears to be among the most adherent of common urinary pathogens to bladder uroepithelium.[370] It can involve the urinary tract through ascending infection or by bacteremic spread from another primary site. Conversely, the urinary tract represents one of the most frequent sources of *Pseudomonas* bacteremia (approximately 40% of cases in which there was an identifiable single source, in one study.[206] The urinary catheter plays an integral role in the pathogenesis of *Pseudomonas* urinary tract infection in catheterized patients. It probably represents the initial site of bacterial attachment and proliferation in such patients,[371] the focus for protected bacterial "biofilm" formation, and the pathway for bacterial ascent into the urinary bladder.[372]

The clinical manifestations of urinary tract infections caused by *Pseudomonas* are usually indistinguishable from those produced by other bacteria. Rare exceptions occur when ulcerative lesions of the bladder mucosa, ureters, and renal pelvis become necrotic, with sloughing of large pieces of vesical membrane in the urine.[373, 374] Another characteristic, if unusual, form of urinary tract involvement by *Pseudomonas* results from bacterial invasion of small and medium-sized blood vessels in the kidneys of bacteremic patients, producing multiple renal infarcts.[375] These lesions apparently represent one of the visceral equivalents of ecthyma gangrenosum.

The appropriate treatment of *Pseudomonas* urinary tract infections depends on site of involvement, presence or absence of associated sepsis, degree of chronicity, possible sites of persistence (including indwelling Foley catheters), and local patterns of antibiotic susceptibility. Because of these variables and the paucity of conclusive comparative data regarding specific forms of treatment, it is difficult to make general therapeutic recommendations. Nevertheless, several guidelines are possible. All symptomatic *Pseudomonas* urinary tract infections should be treated. Chronic infections in the presence of a site of persistence, including urinary catheters, are best treated, if feasible, by removal or surgical elimination of the site or source of persistence and administration of appropriate antibiotics. When a site of persistence such as a catheter cannot be removed, a reasonable approach may be to treat with an antibiotic only for symptomatic episodes or exacerbations, because eradication of infection is unlikely under these circumstances. An alternative approach in this situation, particularly in the presence of frequent, recurrent symptomatic episodes, is an acute "curative" course of an antibiotic followed by chronic suppression. This approach is hampered by the ineffectiveness against *P. aeruginosa* of many oral agents commonly used to suppress urinary tract infections (e.g., trimethoprim-sulfamethoxazole, nitrofurantoin). Although oral fluoroquinolone antibiotics such as norfloxacin[376] and ciprofloxacin[377–379] have been used to treat acute episodes of complicated or chronic *Pseudomonas* urinary tract infections, there is limited published experience with these agents used as chronic suppressive therapy. Another agent with possible suppressive activity against urinary *Pseudomonas* is a methanamine salt administered with an acidifying agent such as ascorbic acid.

The aminoglycoside antibiotics are probably still the agents of choice for parenteral therapy for most urinary tract infections caused by *P. aeruginosa*. Gentamicin, tobramycin, amikacin, netilmicin, and sisomicin have all been used successfully and are probably equally efficacious. The choice of a specific aminoglycoside should be determined by local susceptibility patterns, availability, and cost. Tobramycin has been advocated in preference to gentamicin in patients with renal dysfunction because of its putatively lower nephrotoxic potential. With the possible exception of bacteremic infections, severe upper tract infections with abscess formation, and infections in neutropenic patients, *Pseudomonas* urinary tract disease can be treated with a single agent. Alternatives to the aminoglycoside antibiotics, particularly in patients with abnormal renal function, are antipseudomonal penicillins, extended-spectrum cephalosporins (especially ceftazidime), imipenem, and aztreonam. The oral quinolone antibiotics, especially ciprofloxacin[377–379] provide a viable alternative to parenteral therapy for *Pseudomonas* urinary tract infections not associated with frank sepsis. Ciprofloxacin is the preferred oral quinolone because of its superior activity against most *P. aeruginosa* isolates and favorable systemic distribution. Ciprofloxacin has been used successfully to treat a variety of complicated *Pseudomonas* urinary tract infections, often in the presence of a urinary catheter or other structural or functional abnormalities.[365] Initial clinical and bacteriologic responses, however, are sometimes followed by relapse associated with ciprofloxacin resistance.[365] It is unclear whether relapse and failure are more likely in complicated *Pseudomonas* urinary tract infection after ciprofloxacin treatment than after parenteral aminoglycoside therapy.[365] One must recognize that relapse is relatively common in complicated infections, even in the face of aggressive therapy. Nonetheless, the emergence of resistant strains after ciprofloxacin treatment of *Pseudomonas* urinary tract infections is a source of significant practical concern.

The suggested duration of parenteral therapy of *Pseudomonas* urinary tract infections is as follows: 3 to 5 days for uncomplicated, nonbacteremic infections limited to the bladder; 7 to 10 days for complicated infections, especially in the presence of an indwelling urinary catheter; at least 10 days for urosepsis; 2 to 3 weeks for documented or strongly suspected pyelonephritis; and possibly longer in the case of intrarenal or perinephric abscess. Most parenteral agents suitable for the treatment of *Pseudomonas* disease achieve high urine concentrations, permitting their use in moderate doses except when the presence of significant renal parenchymal involvement or systemic disease dictates higher doses. Appropriate dosage adjustments should be made for the aminoglycosides in the face of impaired renal function. Optimal dose and duration of oral quinolone treatment of *Pseudomonas* urinary tract infections are largely "empirical." Typically, ciprofloxacin is administered orally at a dose of 500 mg twice each day for 7 to 10 days; a longer duration of therapy may be preferable in complicated cases.

Gastrointestinal Infections

The incidence and potential seriousness of *Pseudomonas* gastrointestinal disease are underestimated because the disease is often clinically inapparent, difficult to separate from that caused by other agents, or simply overshadowed by pathologic events outside of the alimentary canal. *P. aeruginosa* can produce disease in virtually any portion of the gastrointestinal tract, from the oropharynx to the rectum.[373, 380] As in other forms of *Pseudomonas* disease, that involving the gastrointestinal tract occurs primarily in immunocompromised patients. The two most commonly affected groups are young infants[381–387] and patients with hematologic malignancies and neutropenia secondary to chemotherapy.[388–391] As well as being a frequent site of *Pseudomonas* infection, the gastrointestinal tract represents an important portal of entry in *Pseudomonas* septicemia. This is perhaps most striking in cancer patients, who, after exposure to the hospital environment and broad-specturm antibiotics, develop gastrointestinal colonization with *Pseudomonas* and, on receiving granulocytopenia-inducing chemotherapy, become bacteremic from the large reservoir of *Pseudomonas* in their gut.[3] Although local signs of gastrointestinal involvement by *Pseudomonas* are sometimes overt (e.g., in typhlitis or rectal abscess), these infections are more often clinically inapparent and therefore go unrecognized as a primary focus giving rise to bacteremia.

Although *Pseudomonas* has been associated with relatively mild diarrheal disease in children, its clearest implication as an enteric pathogen is in cases of severe, sometimes fatal necrotizing enterocolitis in young infants.[383, 387] A similar disease occurs in neutropenic cancer patients, most commonly with involvement of the distal ileum, cecum, and colon.[388, 390, 391] In both instances, postmortem examination reveals ulcerating lesions beginning in the bowel mucosa and extending into the submucosa.[383, 388] The ulcers are typically hemorrhagic and necrotic and contain many *Pseudomonas* organisms, which can be isolated readily in pure culture. There may be bacterial invasion of blood vessels in the submucosa and extension into the muscularis and serosal layers, sometimes leading to bowel perforation and peritonitis. Although most common in the distal ileum, cecum, and colon, necrotic ulcers may be seen in the oropharynx, esophagus, stomach, and proximal small bowel as well. Bacterial invasion of submucosal blood vessels is occasionally seen in bacteremic patients without demonstrable lesions in the overlying mucosa, probably reflecting its extraintestinal origin. The frequency of vascular involvement and paucity of inflammatory cells characterizing *Pseudomonas*-associated gastrointestinal lesions and ecthyma gangrenosum in the skin underscore their common cause and pathogenesis.

The clinical syndromes associated with *Pseudomonas* gastrointestinal involvement are not necessarily either distinctive or specific for this pathogen. Young infants with necrotizing enterocolitis typically present with irritability, vomiting, diarrhea, and dehydration and may have fever, abdominal distention, and signs of peritonitis. Although *Pseudomonas* is clearly implicated as the primary pathogen in many cases of necrotizing enterocolitis, so too are *E. coli*, *Klebsiella pneumoniae*, and other enteric pathogens. Typhlitis, a disease characteristically seen in leukemia patients, involves localized lesions of the cecum associated with necrosis and gangrene, sometimes resulting in perforation and peritonitis.[390] Although *P. aeruginosa* is the most frequently identified pathogen in this disease, other bacteria have been implicated as well. Anorectal infections represent another localized form of gastrointestinal disease, usually seen in neutropenic cancer patients, in which *P. aeruginosa* is occasionally implicated.[389, 392] Perirectal infections may remain localized or spread into the ischiorectal fossa, the genital area, the supralevator space, the peritoneum, or the retroperitoneum. Although uncommon, the scrotum and penis may become involved, leading to Fournier's gangrene. Anorectal lesions can be accompanied by *Pseudomonas* bacteremia.[392] However, because the lesions may be associated with few signs of local inflammation, they must be suspected and looked for in neutropenic patients with fever; this is particularly true because rectal abscesses can give rise to life-threatening sepsis and must therefore be treated aggressively.

Epidemics of *Pseudomonas*-associated diarrheal disease have been reported in children. The identification of a clear-cut point source in at least one such epidemic subjected to thorough cultural and epidemiologic investigation[382] leaves little doubt as to the primary pathogenic role of *P. aeruginosa*. Clinical manifestations in well-studied epidemics have varied from mild diarrhea to severe diarrhea with dehydration, vascular collapse, and death. A causal role has also been suggested for *P. aeruginosa* in a syndrome that resembles enteric fever. Sometimes called Shanghai fever, this syndrome is associated variably with diarrhea or constipation, skin rash, and fever lasting 1 to 2 weeks.[393, 394] Although *P. aeruginosa* can be isolated from the stools of patients with this syndrome, its pathogenic role is uncertain. Likewise, the demonstration of *P. aeruginosa* in the stools of patients with cholera-like illnesses, and the identification of a putative *Pseudomonas* enterotoxin,[395] do not yet justify the conclusion that *Pseudomonas* is capable of producing toxin-mediated secretory diarrhea.

The treatment of *Pseudomonas* gastrointestinal disease consists of the administration of antibiotics appropriate for the treatment of severe localized or systemic *Pseudomonas* infections and surgery when bowel necrosis, perforation, obstruction, or undrained pus so dictate. Some controversy exists regarding the role of surgery in anorectal infections caused by *Pseudomonas* (or other organisms) in patients with malignant disease and neutropenia. The current trend is toward a greater dependence on aggressive medical management, which appears to be successful by itself in many cases.[392, 396, 397]

Skin and Soft-Tissue Infections

Pseudomonas disease of the skin and mucous membranes can result from primary or metastatic foci of infection. As previously indicated, *Pseudomonas* bacteremia may produce distinctive skin lesions known as ecthyma gangrenosum.[209, 210, 398] The salient features of these lesions are hemorrhage, necrosis, surrounding erythema, and the histologic demonstration of vascular invasion by bacteria.[211, 212] *Pseudomonas* septicemia may also be associated with subcutaneous nodules,[399–401] deep abscesses, cellulitis,[402] vesicular or pustular lesions,[202, 403] bullae,[401] or necrotizing fasciitis.[404–406] Metastatic *Pseudomonas* lesions of the skin and mucous membranes can be extensive as well as destructive, leading to massive necrosis or gangrene involving the head and neck,[407, 408] oropharynx, perineum,[409, 410] or extremities.[411]

Primary *Pseudomonas* skin and soft tissue infections may be either localized or diffuse. Common predisposing factors are a breakdown in the integument resulting from burns, trauma, decubitus ulcers, or dermatitis; high moisture conditions such as those found in the perineal area, under the diapers of infants, on the feet of combat troops in the tropics, in the ears of frequent swimmers, or on the skin of whirlpool users; neutropenia; infancy, particularly associated with prematurity[412]; and AIDS.[413] The pathogenesis and clinical appearance of primary *Pseudomonas* skin lesions are often similar to those of metastatic cutaneous foci associated with bacteremia.[414, 415] Common elements are tissue necrosis and hemorrhage. At the microscopic level, locally invasive primary *Pseudomonas* pyoderma may show the same distinctive vascular lesions characteristic of ecthyma gangrenosum associated with septicemic infections. It is not uncommon, in fact, to see a large area of necrotizing *Pseudomonas* pyoderma arising in the perineal area of a neutropenic patient, probably representing a primary infection,[409] and typical metastatic ecthyma lesions elsewhere on the skin of the same patient.[416] Both lesions demonstrate hemorrhage and necrosis, and both are likely to reveal microscopic vascualr invasion. The original description of ecthyma gangrenosum was actually based on primary rather than metastatic cutaneous sites of *Pseudomonas* infection.[209]

Pseudomonas wound infections and pyoderma arising from secondary infection of areas of dermatitis are often indistinguishable from similar infections caused by other etiologic agents. On occasion, however, these infections may have a characteristic blue-green exudate and fruity odor.[403]

P. aeruginosa has been identified as the causative agent in diffuse, pruritic, erythematous, maculopapular, and vesiculopustular rashes occurring in epidemics associated with the use of contaminated whirlpools, hot tubs, spas, and swimming pools.[2, 417, 418] Thirteen such outbreaks, involving from 2 to 300 persons and embracing a total of 400 cases, were reported to the CDC during the 2-year period, 1989–1990.[419] In addition, at least two nosocomial common-source outbreaks have been documented, one traced to a physiotherapy pool[420] and a second in which the hospital water system was implicated.[421] Most reported cases of *Pseudomonas* dermatitis have occurred as a part of common-source outbreaks associated with IATS serotype 11; other serotypes have also been implicated, however. One well-documented case of *P. aeruginosa* folliculitis was acquired through use of a contaminated loofah sponge.[422]

Pseudomonas-associated skin rashes are most evident in areas covered by bathing suits but can occur more diffusely, sparing only the head and neck. Occasionally associated symptoms include headache, dizziness, earache, sore throat, swollen breasts, sore eyes, sore nose, and abdominal cramps. Fever is uncommon and is of low grade when it does occur. *Pseudomonas* skin rashes are usually self-limited, resolving spontaneously on discontinuation of exposure. However, in several documented instances associated with a single nosocomial outbreak among immunocompromised patients,[421] *Pseudomonas* folliculitis evolved within 24 hours into severe ecthyma gangrenosum. In two other cases, previously healthy children exposed to prolonged bathing developed invasive *Pseudomonas* skin infections marked by subcutaneous nodules or ecthyma gangrenosum requiring parenteral antibiotic therapy.[423] In most self-limited cases, however, no specific therapy is necessary, although acetic acid compresses have been advocated.[417]

Pseudomonas burn wound sepsis is a dreaded complication of extensive thermal injuries.[424] The extraordinarily high mortality rate associated with this disease (78% in one large 25-year survey) does not appear to have been greatly improved by advances in therapy.[425] *Pseudomonas* burn sepsis results from bacterial colonization of the burn site, destruction of the mechanical barrier to tissue invasion, and multiple, systemic immunologic defects related to serious burns. Although a gram-positive flora predominates at burn sites in the immediate postburn period, this is soon replaced by gram-negative bacteria, particularly *P. aeruginosa*. It appears that the hydrotherapy commonly provided to patients with serious burns in a common facility may promote the colonization by multidrug-resistant *P. aeruginosa* of intravenous cutdown sites, wound escharotomies, and skin donor site wounds, leading to invasive wound sepsis, bacteremia, and possibly death.[426] *Pseudomonas* rapidly proliferates in the burn eschar, achieving densities of more than 10^5 bacteria per gram of tissue, followed by invasion of the subeschar space and underlying dermis. Once present in unburned subcutaneous tissue, bacteria spread along fibrous septa, migrate along lymphatics, proliferate in perivascular tissues, and invade blood vessels, resulting in septicemia.

Clinically, *Pseudomonas* burn wound infections are marked by multifocal black, dark brown, or violaceous discoloration of the burn eschar; degeneration of underlying granulation tissue with unexpectedly rapid eschar separation and hemorrhage into subcutaneous tissue; edema and/or hemorrhagic necrosis of previously healthy tissue adjacent to infected burn sites; erythematous nodular lesions in unburned skin; and brown or black neoeschar formation. Systemic manifestations, which may precede bacteremia, include fever or hypothermia, disorientation, obtundation, hypotension, oliguria, ileus, and leukopenia. Metastatic infection may produce ecthyma lesions at sites remote from the infected burn. Pneumonia is common, particularly in the setting of previous inhalation injury.

The appropriate management of *Pseudomonas* burn wound sepsis depends first on early diagnosis based on recognition of local or systemic signs and symptoms.[427] If careful daily burn wound inspection reveals any of the typical wound changes listed, biopsy and quantitative bacterial culture should be undertaken immediately.[424, 428] A 500-mg lenticular-shaped tissue sample should include a portion of burn wound and underlying or adjacent unburned tissue. A bacterial density of more than 10^5 organisms per gram of tissue, or histologic signs such as presence of gram-negative bacilli in unburned tissue, heavy growth of *Pseudomonas* in the subeschar space, vasculitis with perivascular "cuffing," focal hemorrhage, or intense inflammatory reaction at the burn margin indicate burn wound sepsis and the necessity for prompt therapy. An alternative method has been suggested for quantitation of bacteria in burn wounds by means of an absorbent paper disk.[429]

The treatment of *Pseudomonas* burn sepsis includes systemic antibiotic combinations administered in high doses. The choice of agents is governed by local susceptibility patterns that may vary considerably, especially because multiply resistant *P. aeruginosa* strains are often endemic in burn treatment centers.[430] An aminoglycoside to which the infecting strain is sensitive may be combined with a β-lactam antibiotic active against *Pseudomonas*. There is little role for single-agent treatment of *Pseudomonas* burn wound sepsis, because the large populations of bacteria that are present and the problematic antibiotic access to local sites of infection favor the emergence of resistant strains and complicate therapy. Monotherapy with imipenem appears to be specifically contraindicated because of the frequent and rapid development of resistance.[431] In the presence of established burn wound colonization or infection, an absorbable topical agent such as mafenide acetate (Sulfamylon) (silver nitrate and silver sulfadiazine are less well absorbed) should be used to reduce bacterial populations at the burn site. Subeschar injections of antibiotics have also been advocated in focal or multifocal infections that do not extend beneath the investing fascia.[432] In addition, silver sulfadiazine and sodium piperacillin appear to act synergistically against some *Pseudomonas* strains and are active topically in experimental *Pseudomonas* burn sepsis.[433] Surgical removal of infected eschars, débridement of necrotic tissues, or even amputation may be necessary in addition to antibiotic therapy. Hydrotherapy and related wound care in a common facility should probably be avoided in view of the possible increased risk of *Pseudomonas* cross-contamination of burn wounds and skin-graft donor sites and the questionable benefit of this form of therapy.[426] Strict isolation should be maintained in patients with serious burns in order to prevent cross-contamination.

P. aeruginosa has been implicated in unmanageable exacerbations of acne vulgaris[434] and in other forms of folliculitis.[435] In the first instance, the folliculitis was thought to originate from a *Pseudomonas* otitis externa. Treatment of the folliculitis and the external otitis with acetic acid compresses and topical antibiotics, respectively, apparently resulted in prompt cure. In the latter case, a self-limited *Pseudomonas* folliculitis was observed after depilation of the legs, whereas recurrent papular skin rashes, usually associated with hospitalization, are resistant to treatment and can last from 3 months to 3 years.[435]

Noma neonatorum is a relatively uncommon, necrotizing infection of the oral, nasal, or perineal regions in the newborn infant.[412] The disease is usually caused by *P. aeruginosa*, has a predilection for low-birth-weight, ill, or premature infants, and is observed mainly in the non-Western world. The cutaneous lesions are similar or identical to ecthyma gangrenosum and are associated with systemic spread. These infections are usually fulminant and often fatal. Aggressive antibiotic and supportive care are appropriate in the face of a poor prognosis.

Toe web infection, or tropical immersion foot syndrome, is most commonly caused by *P. aeruginosa*.[403, 436] Predisposing conditions include high temperature and humidity, physical stress, tight interdigital spaces, and preexisting tinea pedis infection. The second, third, and fourth toe webs are commonly involved, with marked scaling and maceration, denudation extending onto the plantar surface, a profuse serous or purulent discharge, and, in some cases, greenish discoloration from elaboration of pyocyanin and greenish-white fluorescence under a Wood's light. Treatment consists of appropriate local measures and a systemic antibiotic with activity against *Pseudomonas* and other gram-negative bacteria.[436]

So-called green nail syndrome describes the appearance of greenish discoloration of the nail plate, usually in association with a *Pseudomonas* paronychia, in persons with a history of frequent submersion of their hands.[403] Although bacterial invasion of the nail plate can occur in some cases, the green discoloration usually results simply from diffusion of pyocyanin pigment from an adjacent paronychia. This discoloration may persist for months after resolution of active infection. Treatment consists of local measures including incision and drainage of the associated paronychia. Not to be confused with green nail syndrome is "green foot," described as greenish discoloration of the toenails and sole of an adolescent's foot associated with documented colonization of rubber-soled basketball shoes by a pigmented strain of *P. aeruginosa*.[437]

P. aeruginosa Infections in Patients with Acquired Immunodeficiency Syndrome

P. aeruginosa infections are increasingly associated with AIDS, particularly in its more advanced stages.[139, 438–441] Some of these infections are nosocomial in origin[442] and are related to traditional risk factors for the development of *Pseudomonas* disease, such as neutropenia, indwelling vascular catheters, previous antibiotic therapy, hospitalization, and the breakdown or circumvention of normal anatomic barriers to infection. Many such infections occur in patients with profoundly low $CD4^+$ T-cell counts and a history of opportunistic infections. *P. aeruginosa* infections have been documented, however, in persons who were seropositive for the human immunodeficiency virus (HIV) but previously asymptomatic, including at least one patient whose community-acquired *P. aeruginosa* pneumonia represented his initial AIDS-defining illness.[443]

In contrast to earlier observations, the majority of *P. aeruginosa* infections in AIDS patients are actually community-acquired, although they are sometimes associated with previous antibiotic therapy or hospitalization.

AIDS-associated immunologic factors that predispose patients to *P. aeruginosa* infections have not been specifically identified or ranked in terms of pathogenic significance. It has been speculated, however, that compromised host defense mechanisms such as loss of mucosal integrity, defects in humoral and cellular immunity, and leukocyte abnormalities may render HIV-infected patients more susceptible to serious *P. aeruginosa* infections.[139] Conversely, remission of relapsing *Pseudomonas* broncho-pulmonary infection has been attributed to successful triple antiretroviral therapy.[444]

Bacteremic and nonbacteremic *P. aeruginosa* infections have been reported in patients with AIDS.[441] Bacteremic disease[441] has been associated with infected central venous catheters, lower respiratory tract infections, skin and soft tissue infections, and urinary tract infections. Nonbacteremic infections have been observed most frequently in conjunction with pneumonia, soft tissue sites, and sinusitis.[438] Both types of infection can be life-threatening, and recurrence or relapse is common.

Bronchopulmonary infections account for a large segment of AIDS-related *Pseudomonas* disease in patients with late-stage HIV infection.[12, 445–450] Most are community-acquired, many are chronic or recurrent despite appropriate antibiotic therapy, and a significant number are associated with cavitary lesions.[451] It has been suggested that more fulminant cases of AIDS-related lower respiratory tract infection are associated with hospitalization and other traditional risk factors, whereas more indolent community-acquired *P. aeruginosa* pneumonia is associated with fewer traditional risk factors and a lower acute mortality rate.[447] Regardless, survivors of the initial episode of nonfatal *Pseudomonas* respiratory tract infection are likely to experience relapse and are at risk for death from recurrent disease. This general pattern of recurrent or chronic *Pseudomonas* bronchopulmonary infection has been compared with that observed in patients with cystic fibrosis.[447]

AIDS-associated *P. aeruginosa* lung infections have been reported to produce lobar pneumonia,[448] bronchopneumonia,[447] cavitary lesions,[12, 445] diffuse interstitial involvement,[449] empyema,[139] acute and chronic bronchitis, and bronchiectasis.[446]

Bacteremia caused by *P. aeruginosa* occurs in both children[140, 194, 452] and adults[441] with AIDS. It may be either community or hospital acquired and is associated with primary sites of infection involving lungs, upper respiratory tract, ear, or indwelling vascular catheter.[441] Bacteremic infections can be fulminant, especially in children, and may give rise to signs of sepsis including skin manifestations. Mortality is high, relapse is common, and recurrence or relapse is frequently fatal. Death is not inevitable, however, particularly when the correct diagnosis is established early and appropriate antibiotic therapy is started promptly.[194]

Infections of the paranasal sinuses are common in advanced HIV disease,[453, 454] and these infections are commonly caused by *P. aeruginosa*.[291, 447, 453] *P. aeruginosa* sinus infections are often community acquired, although sometimes they are related to previous hospitalization or antibiotic therapy. These infections may be associated with other respiratory sites and can give rise to blood stream invasion. Multiple sinuses are typically involved, and infections tend to be recurrent or chronic. Treatment consists of administration of antibiotics with antipseudomonal activity and appropriate irrigation or drainage procedures.[454] Repeated courses of treatment or chronic, suppressive therapy may be indicated.

Pseudomonas disease in AIDS patients may be accompanied by any of the following skin manifestations: ecthyma gangrenosum,[455, 456] subcutaneous abscesses or nodules,[413] skin papules, and folliculitis evolving into cellulitis after hot tub exposure. Other AIDS-associated *Pseudomonas* soft tissue and/or bone infections include breast abscess,[457, 458] parapharyngeal abscess,[459] orbital cellulitis,[460] rectovaginal abscess,[461] polymicrobial pyomyositis,[462] and malignant external otitis in the absence of diabetes mellitus.[264, 463, 464]

The treatment of AIDS-related *P. aeruginosa* infections is similar to that of *Pseudomonas* disease in other severely immunocompromised patients. In AIDS-related infections, however, repeated or longer-term therapy may be necessary to control or prevent recurrent or chronic *Pseudomonas* infections such as those involving the paranasal sinuses or lower respiratory tract. Moreover, therapeutic end points are often unclear, and the appropriate duration of treatment may be largely empirical and open-ended.

RECENT TRENDS

Changing Clinical Role. As described previously, *P. aeruginosa* has assumed a prominent clinical role as a major opportunistic pathogen in HIV-infected patients; this role has grown steadily with the AIDS epidemic. The increasing involvement of *P. aeruginosa* in AIDS patients provides further confirmation of its impressive capacity for opportunistic virulence. Meanwhile, there has been a parallel reduction in the incidence of *Pseudomonas* infections in certain other clinical settings, including febrile neutropenia[465] and burn wound sepsis,[427] suggesting a modest basis for optimism regarding the ability of at least some current health care practices to control certain kinds of *Pseudomonas* disease among selected categories of immunocompromised patients. Yet, the dogged persistence of *P. aeruginosa* in still other settings, such as its involvement as a major cause of ventilator-associated pneumonia in intensive care units,[122, 123, 466] tempers broadly optimistic assessments regarding the future of *Pseudomonas* prophylaxis and therapy.

Antibiotic Resistance. *P. aeruginosa* is known for its ability to resist killing by a variety of antibiotics. The commonly observed multidrug resistance of *P. aeruginosa* is based in part on a permeability barrier provided by the bacterial outer membrane[467, 468] and in part on multidrug efflux pumps.[469–473] These mechanisms of intrinsic resistance[474] explain much of the documented cross-resistance of *P. aeruginosa* to unrelated classes of antibiotics[475, 476] and supplement the antibiotic-degrading activities of specific bacterial enzymes, especially β-lactamases.

Multidrug-resistant *P. aeruginosa*, defined on the basis of resistance to antibiotics ordinarily active against *P. aeruginosa* isolates, have increased in frequency.[477, 478] These strains include a substantial number of isolates that are resistant to most or all antipseudomonal agents evaluated.[479, 480]

Newer Antimicrobial Agents. A number of newer antibiotics with antipseudomonal activity have become available.

Cefepime, an extended-spectrum, fourth-generation cephalosporin, is active in vitro against most strains of *P. aeruginosa*, including many multidrug-resistant isolates.[481–483] Cefepime has been used as single-agent therapy for *P. aeruginosa* urinary tract and lower respiratory tract infections and for infections at other sites as well.[481] Yet, clinical experience with cefepime is still limited.

The newer carbapenem antibiotic, meropenem, is more active than imipenem in vitro against many *P. aeruginosa* strains. Morevoer, meropenem is frequently active against isolates that are resistant to imipenem and other antipseudomonal agents.[478, 484–486] Although the results of one clinical study suggested that meropenem monotherapy might be as effective as combination therapy with ceftazidime and amikacin for the empirical treatment of febrile neutropenic patients,[487] including those with *Pseudomonas* infections, more clinical experience is necessary to confirm the efficacy of meropenem employed in conjuction with this and related therapeutic applications.

Two new broad-spectrum fluoroquinolones, levofloxacin[488] and trovafloxacin,[489] are slightly less active against *P. aeruginosa* in vitro compared with ciprofloxacin, although trovafloxacin expresses synergistic activity against many *P. aeruginosa* isolates in combination with other antibiotics.[490] These new quinolones, and perhaps others currently under development, may prove advantageous with respect to such factors as antimicrobial spectrum and pharmacokinetic properties, while providing little ostensible advantage over ciprofloxacin in terms of therapeutic activity against *P. aeruginosa*. More clinical experience may clarify these issues.

REFERENCES

1. Doudoroff M, Palleroni NJ. Part 7: Gram-negative aerobic rods and cocci. Genus I: *Pseudomonas*. In: Buchanan RE, Gibbons NE, eds. Bergey's Manual of Determinative Bacteriology. 8th ed. Baltimore: Williams & Wilkins; 1974:217–243.
2. Morrison AJ, Wenzel RP. Epidemiology of infections due to *Pseudomonas aeruginosa*. Rev Infect Dis. 1984;6(Suppl):S627–S642.
3. Schimpff SC, Moody M, Young VM. Relationship of colonization with *Pseudomonas aeruginosa* to development of *Pseudomonas* bacteremia in cancer patients. In: Hobby GL, ed. Antimicrobial Agents and Chemotherapy—1970. Washington, DC: American Society for Microbiology; 1971:240–244.
4. Widmer AF, Wenzel RP, Trilla A, et al. Outbreak of *Pseudomonas aeruginosa* infections in a surgical intensive care unit: Probable transmission via hands of a health care worker. Clin Infect Dis. 1993;16:372–376.
5. Döring G, Hörz M, Ortelt J, et al. Molecular epidemiology of *Pseudomonas aeruginosa* in an intensive care unit. Epidemiol Infect. 1993;110:427–436.

6. Brokopp CD, Farmer JJ. Typing methods for *Pseudomonas aeruginosa*. In: Doggett RG, eds. *Pseudomonas aeruginosa*: Clinical Manifestations of Infection and Current Therapy. New York: Academic Press; 1979:89–133.
7. Farmer JJ 3rd, Weinstein RA, Zierdt CH, et al. Hospital outbreaks caused by *Pseudomonas aeruginosa*: Importance of serogroup O11. J Clin Microbiol. 1982;16:266–270.
8. Ogle JW, Janda JM, Woods DE, et al. Characterization and use of a DNA probe as an epidemiologic marker for *Pseudomonas aeruginosa*. J Infect Dis. 1987;155:199–126.
9. Blanc DS, Siegrist HH, Sahli R, Francioli P. Ribotyping of *Pseudomonas aeruginosa*: Discriminatory power and usefulness as a tool for epidemiological studies. J Clin Microbiol. 1993;31:71–77.
10. Centers for Disease Control and Prevention. National Nosocomial Infections Surveillance (NNIS) Report, October 1986–April 1996. Am J Infect Control. 1996;24:380–388.
11. Zenone T, Souillet G. X-linked agammaglobulinemia presenting as *Pseudomonas aeruginosa* septicemia. Scand J Infect Dis. 1996;28:417–418.
12. Gallant JE, Ko AH. Cavitary pulmonary lesions in patients infected with human immunodeficiency virus. Clin Infect Dis. 1996;22:671–682.
13. Higuchi JH, Johanson WG Jr. The relationship between adherence of *Pseudomonas aeruginosa* to upper respiratory cells in vitro and susceptibility to colonization in vivo. J Lab Clin Med. 1980;95:698–705.
14. Woods DE, Straus DC, Johanson WG Jr, et al. Role of pili in adherence of *Pseudomonas aeruginosa* to mammalian buccal epithelial cells. Infect Immun. 1980;29:1146–1151.
15. Woods DE, Straus DC, Johanson WG Jr, Bass JA. Role of salivary protease activity in adherence of gram-negative bacilli to mammalian buccal epithelial cells in vivo. J Clin Invest. 1981;68:1435–1440.
16. Ramphal R, Small PM, Shands JW Jr, et al. Adherence of *Pseudomonas aeruginosa* to tracheal cells injured by influenza infection or by endotracheal intubation. Infect Immun. 1980;27:614–619.
17. Ramphal R, McNiece MT, Polack FM. Adherence of *Pseudomonas aeruginosa* to the injured cornea: A step in the pathogenesis of corneal infections. Ann Ophthalmol. 1981;13:421–425.
18. Sobel JD, Vardi Y. Scanning electron microscopy study of *Pseudomonas aeruginosa* in vivo adherence to rat bladder epithelium. J Urol. 1982;128:414–417.
19. Gilboa-Garber N, Mizrahi L. Interaction of the mannose-philic lectins of *Pseudomonas aeruginosa* with luminous species of marine enterobacteria. Microbios. 1979;26:31–36.
20. Ramphal R, Guay C, Pier GB. *Pseudomonas aeruginosa* adhesions for tracheobronchial mucin. Infect Immun. 1987;55:600–603.
21. Ramphal R, Pyle M. Evidence for mucins and sialic acid as receptors for *Pseudomonas aeruginosa* in the lower respiratory tract. Infect Immun. 1983;41:339–344.
22. Vishwanath S, Ramphal R. Tracheobronchial mucin receptor for *Pseudomonas aeruginosa*: Predominance of amino sugars in binding sites. Infect Immun. 1985;48:331–335.
23. Ramphal R, Pyle M. Further characterization of the tracheal receptor for *Pseudomonas aeruginosa*. Eur J Clin Microbiol. 1985;4:160–162.
24. Ramphal R, Carnoy C, Fievre S, et al. *Pseudomonas aeruginosa* recognizes carbohydrate chains containing type 1 (Galβ1-3GlcNAC) or type 2 (Galβ1-4GlcNAC) disaccharide units. Infect Immun. 1991;59:700–704.
25. Simpson DA, Ramphal R, Lory S. Genetic analysis of *Pseudomonas aeruginosa* adherence: Distinct genetic loci control attachment to epithelial cells and mucins. Infect Immun. 1992;60:3771–3779.
26. Coburn J. *Pseudomonas aeruginosa* exoenzyme S. Curr Top Microbiol Immunol. 1992;175:133–143.
27. Costerton JW, Brown MRW, Sturgess JM. The cell envelope. Its role in infection. In: Doggett RG, eds. *Pseudomonas aeruginosa*. New York: Academic Press; 1979:41–62.
28. Pier GB. Terminology relating to extracellular polysaccharides produced by *Pseudomonas aeruginosa* (Letter). J Infect Dis. 1985;152:652.
29. Boyd A, Chakrabarty AM. *Pseudomonas aeruginosa* biofilms: Role of the alginate exopolysaccharide. J Ind Microbiol. 1995. 15:162–168.
30. Kolter R, Losick R. One for all and all for one. Science. 1998;280:226–227.
31. Davies DG, Parsek MR, Pearson JP, et al. The involvement of cell-to-cell signals in the development of a bacterial biofilm. Science. 1998;280:295–298.
32. Anwar H, Strap JL, Chen K, Costerton JW. Dynamic interactions of biofilms of mucoid *Pseudomonas aeruginosa* with tobramycin and piperacillin. Antimicrob Agents Chemother. 1992;36:1208–1214.
33. Doggett RG, Harrison GM, Carter RG Jr. Mucoid *Pseudomonas aeruginosa* in patients with chronic illnesses. Lancet. 1971;1:236–237.
34. Lam J, Chan R, Lam K, Costerton JW. Production of mucoid microcolonies by *Pseudomonas aeruginosa* within infected lungs in cystic fibrosis. Infect Immun. 1980;28:546–556.
35. Schwarzmann S, Boring JR III. Antiphagocytic effect of slime from a mucoid strain of *Pseudomonas aeruginosa*. Infect Immun. 1971;3:762–767.
36. Baltimore RS, Mitchell M. Immunologic investigations of mucoid strains of *Pseudomonas aeruginosa*: Comparison of susceptibility to opsonic antibody in mucoid and non-mucoid strains. J Infect Dis. 1980;141:238–247.
37. Bayer AS, Speert DP, Park S, et al. Functional role of mucoid exopolysaccharide (alginate) in antibiotic-induced and polymorphonuclear leukocyte-mediated killing of *Pseudomonas aeruginosa*. Infect Immun. 1991;59:302–308.
38. Baltimore RS, Cross AS, Dobek AS. The inhibitory effect of sodium alginate on antibiotic activity against mucoid and non-mucoid strains of *Pseudomonas aeruginosa*. J Antimicrob Chemother. 1987;20:815–823.
39. Mai GT, Seow WK, McCormack JG, et al. In vitro immunosuppressive and antiphagocytic properties of the exopolysaccharide of mucoid strains of *Pseudomonas aeruginosa*. Int Arch Allergy Appl Immunol. 1990;92:105–112.
40. Friedl P, König B, König W. Effects of mucoid and non-mucoid *Pseudomonas aeruginosa* isolates from cystic fibrosis patients on inflammatory mediator release from human polymorphonuclear granulocytes and rat mast cells. Immunology. 1992;76:86–94.
41. Mai GT, Seow WK, Pier GB, et al. Suppression of lymphocyte and neutrophil functions by *Pseudomonas aeruginosa* mucoid exopolysaccharide (alginate): Reversal by physicochemical, alginase, and specific monoclonal antibody treatments. Infect Immun. 1993;61:559–564.
42. Morihara K. Production of elastase and proteinase by *Pseudomonas aeruginosa*. J Bacteriol. 1964;88:745–757.
43. Peters JE, Park SJ, Darzins A, et al. Further studies on *Pseudomonas aeruginosa* LaSA: analysis of specificity. Mol Microbiol. 1992;6:1155–1162.
44. Galloway DR. *Pseudomonas aeruginosa* elastase and elastolysis revisited: Recent developments. Mol Microbiol. 1991;5:2315–2321.
45. Parmely M, Gale A, Clabaugh M, et al. Proteolytic inactivation of cytokines by *Pseudomonas aeruginosa*. Infect Immun. 1990;58:3009–3014.
46. Shibuya Y, Yamamoto T, Morimoto T, et al. *Pseudomonas aeruginosa* alkaline proteinase might share a biological function with plasmin. Biochim Biophys Acta. 1991;1077:316–324.
47. Azghani AO, Kondepudi AY, Johnson AR. Interaction of *Pseudomonas aeruginosa* with human lung fibroblasts: Role of bacterial elastase. Am J Respir Cell Mol Biol. 1992;6:652–657.
48. Amitani R, Wilson R, Rutman A, et al. Effects of human neutrophil elastase and *Pseudomonas aeruginosa* proteinases on human respiratory epithelium. Am J Respir Cell Mol Biol. 1991;4:26–32.
49. Azghani AO, Gray LD, Johnson AR. A bacterial protease perturbs the paracellular barrier function of transporting epithelial monolayers in culture. Infect Immun. 1993;61:2681–2686.
50. Azghani AO, Connelly JC, Peterson BT, et al. Effects of *Pseudomonas aeruginosa* elastase on alveolar epithelial permeability in guinea pigs. Infect Immun. 1990;58:433–438.
51. Mull JD, Callahan WS. The role of elastase of *Pseudomonas aeruginosa* in experimental infection. Exp Mol Pathol. 1965;4:567–575.
52. Kreger AS, Gray LD. Purification of *Pseudomonas aeruginosa* protease and microscopic characterization of pseudomonal protease-induced rabbit corneal damage. Infect Immun. 1978;19:630–648.
53. Cicmanec JF, Holder IA. Growth of *Pseudomonas aeruginosa* in normal and burned skin extract: Role of extracellular proteases. Infect Immun. 1979;25:477–483.
54. Lutz F, Xiong G, Jungblut R, et al. Pore-forming cytotoxin of *Pseudomonas aeruginosa*: The molecular effects and aspects of pathogenicity. Antibiot Chemother. 1991;44:54–58.
55. Scharmann W. Cytotoxic effects of leukocidin from *Pseudomonas aeruginosa* on polymorphonuclear leukocytes from cattle. Infect Immun. 1976;13:836–843.
56. Bishop MB, Baltch AL, Hill LA, et al. The effect of *Pseudomonas aeruginosa* cytotoxin and toxin A on human polymorphonuclear leukocytes. J Med Microbiol. 1987;24:315–324.
57. Seeger W, Walmrath D, Neuhof H, Lutz F. Pulmonary microvascular injury induced by *Pseudomonas aeruginosa* cytotoxin in isolated rabbit lungs. Infect Immun. 1986;52:846–852.
58. Grimminger F, Walmrath D, Walter H, et al. Induction of vascular injury by *Pseudomonas aeruginosa* cytotoxin in rabbit lungs is associated with the generation of different leukotrienes and hydroxyeicosatetraenoic acids. J Infect Dis. 1991;163:362–370.
59. Berka RM, Vasil ML. Phospholipase c (heat-labile hemolysin) of *Pseudomonas aeruginosa*: Purification and preliminary characterization. J Bacteriol. 1981;152:239–245.
60. Johnson MK, Boese-Marrazzo D. Production and properties of heat-stable extracellular hemolysin from *Pseudomonas aeruginosa*. Infect Immun. 1980;29:1028–1033.
61. Liu PV. Toxins of *Pseudomonas aeruginosa*. In: Doggett RG, eds. *Pseudomonas aeruginosa*: Clinical Manifestations of Infection and Current Therapy. New York: Academic Press, 1979:63–88.
62. Vasil ML, Graham LM, Ostroff RM, et al. Phospholipase C: Molecular biology and contribution to the pathogenesis of *Pseudomonas aeruginosa*. Antibiot Chemother. 1991;44:34–47.
63. Konig B, Vasil ML, Konig W. Role of haemolytic and non-haemolytic phospholipase c from *Pseudomonas aeruginosa* in interleukin-8 release from human monocytes. J Med Microb. 1997;46:471–478.
64. Read RC, Roberts P, Munro N, et al. Effect of *Pseudomonas aeruginosa* rhammolipids on mucociliary transport and ciliary beating. J Appl Physiol. 1992;72:2271–2277.
65. Kanthakumar K, Taylor G, Tsang KW, et al. Mechanisms of action of *Pseudomonas aeruginosa* pyocyanin on human ciliary beat in vitro. Infect Immun. 1993;61:2848–2853.
66. Ras GJ, Anderson R, Taylor GW, et al. Proinflammatory interactions of pyocyanin and 1-c hydroxyphenazine with human neutrophils in vitro. J Infect Dis. 1990;162:178–185.
67. Coffman TJ, Cox CD, Edeker BL, Britigan BE. Possible role bacterial siderophores in inflammation. Iron bound to the *Pseudomonas* siderophore pyochelin can function as a hydroxyl radical catalyst. J Clin Invest. 1990;86:1030–1037.
68. Britigan BE, Roeder TL, Rasmussen GT, et al. Interaction of the *Pseudomonas*

aeruginosa secretory products pyocyanin and pyochelin generates hydroxyl radical and causes synergistic damage to endothelial cells. Implications for *Pseudomonas* associated tissue injury. J Clin Invest. 1992;90:2186–2196.
69. Young LS. Human immunity to *Pseudomonas aeruginosa*: II. Relationship between heat-stable opsonins and type-specific lipopolysaccharides. J Infect Dis. 1972;126:277–287.
70. Young LS, Armstrong D. Human immunity to *Pseudomonas aeruginosa*: I. In-vitro interaction of bacteria, polymorphonuclear leukocytes, and serum factors. J Infect Dis. 1972;126:257–276.
71. Bjornson AB, Michael JG. Biological activities of rabbit immunoglobulin M and immunoglobulin G antibodies to *Pseudomonas aeruginosa*. Infect Immun. 1970;2:453–461.
72. Tamura Y, Suzuki S, Sawada T. Role of elastase as a virulence factor in experimental *Pseudomonas aeruginosa* infection in mice. Microb Pathog. 1992;12:237–244.
73. Beutler B, Cerami A. The endogenous mediator of endotoxic shock. Clin Res. 1987;35:192–197.
74. Mathison JC, Wolson E, Ulevitch RJ. Participation of tumor necrosis factor in the mediation of gram negative bacterial lipopolysaccharide induced injury in rabbits. J Clin Invest. 1988;81:1925–1937.
75. Pollack M. The virulence of *Pseudomonas aeruginosa*. Rev Infect Dis. 1984;6(Suppl):S617–S626.
76. Pollack M, Taylor NS, Callahan LT. Exotoxin production by clinical isolates of *Pseudomonas aeruginosa*. Infect Immun. 1977;15:776–780.
77. Iglewski BH, Kabat D. NAD-dependent inhibition of protein synthesis by *Pseudomonas aeruginosa* toxin. Proc Natl Acad Sci U S A. 1975;22:2284–2288.
78. Gray GL, Smith DH, Baldridge JS, et al. Cloning, nucleotide sequence and expression in *Escherichia coli* of the exotoxin A structural gene of *Pseudomonas aeruginosa*. Proc Natl Acad Sci U S A. 1984;81:2645–2649.
79. Allured VS, Collier RJ, Carroll SF, McKay DB. Structure of exotoxin A of *Pseudomonas aeruginosa* at 3.0 Ångstrom resolution. Proc Natl Acad Sci U S A. 1986;83:1320–1324.
80. Hwang J, Fitzgerald DJ, Adhya S, Pastan I. Functional domains of *Pseudomonas* exotoxin identified by deletion analysis of the gene expressed in *E. coli*. cell. 1987;48:129–136.
81. Wick MJ, Hamood AN, Iglewski BH. Analysis of the structure-function relationship of *Pseudomonas aeruginosa* exotoxin A. Mol Microbiol. 1990;4:527–535.
82. Pollack M. *Pseudomonas aeruginosa* exotoxin A (Editorial). N Engl J Med. 1980;302:1360–1362.
83. Pollack M. The role of exotoxin A in *Pseudomonas* disease and immunity. Rev Infect Dis. 1983;5(Suppl): S979–S984.
84. Young LS, Pollack M. Immunologic Approaches to the Prophylaxis and Treatment of *Pseudomonas aeruginosa* Infection. Bern: Hans Huber Publishers;1980:119–132.
85. Hazlett LD, Berk RS, Iglewski BH. Microscopic characterization of ocular damage produced by *Pseudomonas aeruginosa* toxin A. Infect Immun. 1981;34:1025–1035.
86. Ohman DE, Burns RP, Iglewski BH. Corneal infections in mice with toxin A and elastase mutants of *Pseudomonas aeruginosa*. J Infect Dis. 1980;142:547–555.
87. Woods DE, Cryz SJ, Friedman RL, Iglewski BH. Contribution of toxin A and elastase to virulence of *Pseudomonas aeruginosa* in chronic lung infections of rats. Infect Immun. 1982;36:1223–1228.
88. Vidal DR, Garrone P, Banchereau J. Immunosuppressive effects of *Pseudomonas aeruginosa* exotoxin A on human B-lymphocytes. Toxicon. 1993;31:27–34.
89. Staugas REM, Harvey DP, Ferrante A, et al. Induction of tumor necrosis factor (TNF) and interleukin-1 (IL-1) by *Pseudomonas aeruginosa* and exotoxin A-induced suppression of lymphoproliferation and TNF, lymphotoxin, gamma interferon, and IL-1 production in human leukocytes. Infect Immun. 1992;60:3162–3168.
90. Pavlovskis OR, Callahan LT, Pollack M. *Pseudomonas aeruginosa* exotoxin. In: Schlessinger D, ed. Microbiology–1975. Washington, DC: American Society for Microbiology; 1975:252–256.
91. Cross AS, Sadoff JC, Iglewski BH, Sokol PA. Evidence for the role of toxin A in the pathogenesis of infection with *Pseudomonas aeruginosa* in humans. J Infect Dis. 1980;142:538–546.
92. Pollack M, Young LS. Protective activity of antibodies to exotoxin A and lipopolysaccharide at the onset of *Pseudomonas aeruginosa* septicemia in man. J Clin Invest. 1979;63:276–286.
93. Kohzuki T, Eguchi Y, Kato M, et al. Protective activity of anti-exotoxin A monoclonal antibody against mice infected with toxin-producing *Pseudomonas aeruginosa*. J Infect Dis. 1993;167:119–125.
94. Iglewski BH, Sadoff JC, Bjorn MJ, Maxwell ES. *Pseudomonas aeruginosa* exoenzyme S: An adenosine diphosphate ribosyltransferease distinct from toxin A. Proc Natl Acad Sci U S A. 1978;75:3211–3215.
95. Frank DW. The exoenzyme S regulon of *Pseudomonas aeruginosa*. Mol Microbiol. 1997;26:621–629.
96. Woods DE, Que JU. Purification of *Pseudomonas aeruginosa* exoenzyme S. Infect Immun. 1987;55:579–586.
97. Nicas TI, Bradley J, Lochner JE, et al. The role of exoenzyme S in infections with *Pseudomonas aeruginosa*. J Infect Dis. 1985;152:716–721.
98. Woods DE, Sokol PA. Use of transposon mutants to assess the role of exoenzyme S in chronic pulmonary disease due to *Pseudomonas aeruginosa*. Eur J Clin Microbiol. 1985;3:163–169.
99. Baker NR, Minor V, Deal C, et al. *Pseudomonas aeruginosa* exoenzyme S is an adhesin. Infect Immun. 1991;59:2859–2863.
100. Fang G, Keys TF, Gentry LO, et al. Prosthetic valve endocarditis resulting from nosocomial bacteremia: A prospective, multicenter study. Ann Intern Med. 1993;119:560–567.
101. Cohen PS, Maguire JH, Weinstein L. Infective endocarditis caused by gram-negative bacteria: A review of the literature, 1945–1977. Prog Cardiovasc Dis. 1980;22:205–242.
102. Rajashekaraiah KR, Rice TW, Kallick CA. Recovery of *Pseudomonas aeruginosa* from syringes of drug addicts with endocarditis. J Infect Dis. 1981;144:482.
103. Wieland M, Lederman MM, Kline-King C, et al. Left-sided endocarditis due to *Pseudomonas aeruginosa*: A report of 10 cases and review of the literature. Medicine (Baltimore). 1986;65:180–189.
104. Shekar R, Rice TW, Zierdt CH, Kallick CA. Outbreak of endocarditis caused by *Pseudomonas aeruginosa* serotype O11 among pentazocine and tripelennamine abusers in Chicago. J Infect Dis. 1985;151:203–208.
105. Botsford KB, Weinstein RA, Nathan CR, Kabins SA. Selective survival in pentazocine and tripelennamine of *Pseudomonas aeruginosa* serotype from drug addicts. J Infect Dis. 1985;151:209–216.
106. Gould K, Ramirez-Ronda CH, Holmes RK, Sanford JP. Adherence of bacteria to heart valves in vitro. J Clin Invest. 1975;56:1364–1370.
107. Reyes MP, Lerner AM. Current problems in the treatment of infective endocarditis due to *Pseudomonas aeruginosa*. Rev Infect Dis. 1983;5:314–321.
108. Levine DP, Crane LR, Zervos MJ. Bacteremia in narcotic addicts and the Detroit Medical Center: II. Infectious endocarditis: A prospective comparative study. Rev Infect Dis. 1986;8:374–396.
109. Komshian SV, Tablan OC, Palutke W, Reyes MP. Characteristics of left-sided endocarditis due to *Pseudomonas aeruginosa* in the Detroit Medical Center. Rev Infect Dis. 1990;12:693–702.
110. Reyes MP, Brown WJ, Lerner AM. Treatment of patients with *Pseudomonas endocarditis* with high dose aminoglycoside and carbenicillin therapy. Medicine (Baltimore). 1978;57:57–67.
111. Arbulu A, Holmes RJ, Asfaw I. Tricuspid valvulectomy without replacement: Twenty years experience. J Thorac Cardiovasc Surg. 1991;102:917–922.
112. Jimenez-Lucho VE, Saravolatz LD, Medeiros AA, Pohlod D. Failure of therapy in *Pseudomonas* endocarditis: Selection of resistant mutants. J Infect Dis. 1986;154:64–68.
113. Fichtenbaum CJ, Smith MJ. Treatment of endocarditis due to *Pseudomonas aeruginosa* with imipenem. Clin Infect Dis. 1992;14:353–354.
114. Ingerman MJ, Pitsakis PG, Rosenberg AF, Levison ME. The importance of pharmacodynamics in determining the dosing interval in therapy for experimental *Pseudomonas* endocarditis in the rat. J Infect Dis. 1986;153:707–714.
115. Bayer AS, Peters J, Parr TR Jr, et al. Role of β-lactamase in in vivo development of ceftazidime resistance in experimental *Pseudomonas aeruginosa* endocarditis. Antimicrob Agents Chemother. 1987;31:253–258.
116. Bayer AS, Crowell DJ, Yih J, et al. Comparative pharmacokinetics and pharmacodynamics of amikacin and ceftazidime in tricuspid and aortic vegetations in experimental *Pseudomonas* endocarditis. J Infect Dis. 1988;158:355–359.
117. Bayer AS, Blomquist IK, Kim KS. Ciprofloxacin in experimental aortic valve endocarditis due to *Pseudomonas aeruginosa*. J Antimicrob Chemother. 1986;17:641–649.
118. Uzun Ö, Akalin HE, Ünal S, et al. Long-term oral ciprofloxacin in treatment of prosthetic valve endocarditis due to *Pseudomonas aeruginosa*. Scand J Infect Dis. 1992;24:797–800.
119. Pefanis A, Giamarellou H, Karayiannakos P, Donta I. Efficacy of ceftazidime and aztreonam alone or in combination with amikacin in experimental left-sided *Pseudomonas aeruginosa* endocarditis. Antimicrob Agents Chemother. 1993;37:308–313.
120. Myerowitz PD, Gardner R, Campbell C, et al. Earlier operation for left-sided *Pseudomonas* endocarditis in drug addicts. J Thorac Cardiovasc Surg. 1979;77:577–581.
121. Silver DR, Cohen IL, Weinberg PF. Recurrent *Pseudomonas aeruginosa* pneumonia in an intensive care unit. Chest. 1992;101:194–198.
122. Brewer SC, Wunderink RG, Jones CB, Leeper KV. Ventilator-associated pneumonia due to *Pseudomonas aeruginosa*. Chest. 1996;109:1019–1029.
123. Rello J, Jubert P, Valles J, et al. Evaluation of outcome for intubated patients with pneumonia due to *Pseudomonas aeruginosa*. Clin Infect Dis. 1996;23:973–978.
124. Henderson A, Kelly W, Wright M. Fulminant primary *Pseudomonas aeruginosa* pneumonia and septicaemia in previously well adults. Intensive Care Med. 1992;18:430–432.
125. Torres A, Serra-Batlles J, Ferrer A, et al. Severe community acquired pneumonia. Epidemiology and prognostic factors. Am Rev Respir Dis. 1991;144:312–318.
126. Nagaki M, Shimura S, Tanno Y, et al. Role of chronic *Pseudomonas aeruginosa* infection in the development of bronchiectasis. Chest. 1992;102:1464–1469.
127. Kubesch P, Dörk T, Wulbrand U, et al. Genetic determinants of airways' colonisation with *Pseudomonas aeruginosa* in cystic fibrosis. Lancet. 1993;341:189–193.
128. Koch C, Høiby N. Pathogenesis of cystic fibrosis. Lancet. 1993;341:1065–1069.
129. Smith JJ, Travis SM, Greenberg EP. Cystic fibrosis airway epithelia fail to kill bacteria because of abnormal airway surface fluid. Cell. 1996;85:229–236.
130. Pier GB, Grout M, Zaidi TS, et al. Role of mutant CFTR in hypersusceptibility of cystic fibrosis patients to lung infections. Science. 1996;271:64–67.
131. Pier GB, Grout M, Zaidi TS, Goldberg JB. How mutant cystic fibrosis transmembrane conductance regulator (CFTR) may contribute to *Pseudomonas aeruginosa* infection in cystic fibrosis. Am J Respir Crit Care Med. 1996;154:S175–S182.
132. Pier GB, Grout M, Zaidi TS. Cystic fibrosis transmembrane conductance regulator is an epithelial cell receptor for clearance of *Pseudomonas aeruginosa* from the lung. Proc Natl Acad Sci U S A. 1997;94:12088–12093.
133. Gosselin D, Stevenson MM, Cowley EA, et al. Impaired ability of Cftr knockout

mice to control lung infection with *Pseudomonas aeruginosa*. Am J Respir Crit Care Med. 1998;157:1253–1262.
134. Cowley EA, Wang C-G, Gosselin D, et al. Mucociliary clearance in cystic fibrosis knockout mice infected with *Pseudomonas aeruginosa*. Eur Respir J. 1997;10:2312–2318.
135. Tillotston JR, Lerner AM. Characteristics of nonbacteremic *Pseudomonas* pneumonia. Ann Intern Med. 1968;68:295–307.
136. Pennington JE, Reynolds HY, Carbone PP. *Pseudomonas* pneumonia: A retrospective study of 36 cases. Am J Med. 1973;55:155–160.
137. Rose HD, Heckman MG, Unger JD. *Pseudomonas aeruginosa* pneumonia in adults. Am Rev Respir Dis. 1973;107:416–422.
138. Iannini PB, Claffey T, Quintiliani R. Bacteremic *Pseudomonas* pneumonia. JAMA. 1974;230:558–561.
139. Kielhofner M, Atmar RL, Hamill RJ, Musher DM. Life-threatening *Pseudomonas aeruginosa* infections in patients with human immunodeficiency virus infection. Clin Infect Dis. 1992;14:403–411.
140. Flores G, Stavola JJ, Noel GJ. Bacteremia due to *Pseudomonas aeruginosa* in children with AIDS. Clin Infect Dis. 1993;16:706–708.
141. Fetzer AE, Werner AS, Hagstrom JWC. Pathologic features of pseudomonal pneumonia. Am Rev Respir Dis. 1967;96:1121–1130.
142. Bressolle F, de la Coussaye J-E, Ayoub R, et al. Endotracheal and aerosol administrations of ceftazidime in patients with nosocomial pneumonia: Pharmacokinetics and absolute bioavailability. Antimicrob Agents Chemother. 1992;36:1404–1411.
143. Brown RB, Kruse JA, Counts GW, et al. Double-blind study of endotracheal tobramycin in the treatment of gram-negative bacterial pneumonia. Antimicrob Agents Chemother. 1990;34:269–272.
144. FitzSimmons SC. The changing epidemiology of cystic fibrosis. J Pediatr. 1993;122:1–9.
145. Kerem E, Corey M, Gold R, Levison H. Pulmonary function and clinical course in patients with cystic fibrosis after pulmonary colonization with *Pseudomonas aeruginosa*. J Pediatr. 1990;116:714–719.
146. Rosenstein BJ, Zeitlin PL. Prognosis in cystic fibrosis. Curr Opin Pulm Med. 1995;1:444–449.
147. Ko YH, Pedersen PL. Frontiers in research in cystic fibrosis: Understanding its molecular and chemical basis and relationship to the pathogenesis of the disease. J Bioenerg Biomembr. 1997;29:417–427.
148. Hoiby N. *Pseudomonas aeruginosa* infection in cystic fibrosis: Diagnostic and prognostic significance of *Pseudomonas aeruginosa* precipitins determined by means of crossed immunoelectrophoresis, a survey. Acta Pathol Mirobiol Scand [C]. 1977;262(Suppl);1–96.
149. Klinger JD, Strauss DC, Hilton CB, Bass JA. Antibodies to proteases and exotoxin A of *Pseudomonas aeruginosa* in patients with cystic fibrosis: Demonstration by radioimmunoassay. J Infect Dis. 1978;138:49–58.
150. Fick RB Jr, Sonoda F, Hornick DB. Emergence and persistence of *Pseudomonas aeruginosa* in the cystic fibrosis airway. Semin Respir Infect. 1992;7:168–178.
151. Fick RB Jr. Pathogenetic mechanisms in cystic fibrosis lung disease: A paradigm for inflammatory airways disease. J Lab Clin Med. 1993;121:632–634.
152. Reynolds HY, Fick RB. *Pseudomonas aeruginosa* pulmonary infections (emphasizing nosocomial pneumonia and respiratory infections in cystic fibrosis). In: Sabath LD, ed. *Pseudomonas aeruginosa*: The Organism, Diseases It Causes, and Their Treatment. Bern: Hans Huber Publishers; 1980:71–88.
153. Wientzen R, Prestidge CB, Kramer RI, et al. Acute pulmonary exacerbations in cystic fibrosis: A double-blind trial of tobramycin and placebo therapy. Am J Dis Child. 1980;134:1134–1138.
154. Beaudry PH, Marks MI, McDougall D, et al. Is anti-*Pseudomonas* therapy warranted in acute respiratory exacerbations in children with cystic fibrosis? J Pediatr. 1980;97:144–147.
155. Møller NE, Høiby N. Antibiotic treatment of chronic *Pseudomonas aeruginosa* infection in cystic fibrosis patients. Scand J Infect Dis. 1981;29(Suppl):87–91.
156. Hyatt AC, Chipps BE, Kumor KM, et al. A double-blind controlled trial of anti-*Pseudomonas* chemotherapy of acute respiratory exacerbations in patients with cystic fibrosis. J Pediatr. 1981;99:307–314.
157. Martin AJ, Smalley CA, George RH, et al. Gentamicin and tobramycin compared in the treatment of mucoid *Pseudomonas* lung infections in cystic fibrosis. Arch Dis Child. 1980;55:604–607.
158. Reed MD, Stern RC, Meyers CM, et al. Therapeutic evaluation of piperacillin for acute pulmonary exacerbations in cystic fibrosis. Pediatr Pulmonol. 1987;3:101–109.
159. Reed MD, Stern RC, O'Brien CA, et al. Randomized double-blind evaluation of ceftazidime dose ranging in hospitalized patients with cystic fibrosis. Antimicrob Agents Chemother. 1987;31:698–702.
160. Strandvik B, Malmborg AS, Bergan T, et al. Imipenem/cilastatin, an alternative treatment of *Pseudomonas* infection in cystic fibrosis. J Antimicrob Chemother. 1988;21:471–480.
161. Bosso JA, Black PG. Controlled trial of aztreonam vs. tobramycin and azlocilliin for acute pulmonary exacerbations of cystic fibrosis. Pediatr Infect Dis J. 1988;7:171–176.
162. Rubio TT, Shapiro C. Ciprofloxacin in the treatment of *Pseudomonas* infection in cystic fibrosis patients. J Antimicrob Chemother. 1986;18(Suppl D):147–152.
163. Koch C, Hjelt K, Pedersen SS, et al. Retrospective clinical study of hypersensitivity reactions to aztreonam and six other beta-lactam antibiotics in cystic fibrosis patients receiving multiple treatment courses. Rev Infect Dis. 1991;13(Suppl 7):S608–S611.
164. Jensen T, Pedersen SS, Høiby N, Koch C. Safety of aztreonam in patients with cystic fibrosis and allergy to beta-lactam antibiotics. Rev Infect Dis. 1991;13(Suppl 7):S594–S597.
165. Douidar SM, Snodgrass WR. Potential role of fluoroquinolones in pediatric infections. Rev Infect Dis. 1989;11:878–889.
166. Schaad UB, Stoupis C, Wedgwood J, et al. Clinical, radiologic and magnetic resonance monitoring for skeletal toxicity in pediatric patients with cystic fibrosis receiving a three-month course of ciprofloxacin. Pediatr Infect Dis J. 1991;10:723–729.
167. Pedersen SS, Pressler T, Jensen T, et al. Combined imipenem/cilastatin and tobramycin therapy of multiresistant *Pseudomonas aeruginosa* in cystic fibrosis. J Antimicrob Chemother. 1987;19:101–107.
168. Diver JM, Schololaardt T, Rabin HR, et al. Persistence mechanisms in *Pseudomonas aeruginosa* from cystic fibrosis patients undergoing ciprofloxacin therapy. Antimicrob Agents Chemother. 1991;35:1538–1546.
169. Jackson MA, Kusmiesz H, Shelton S, et al. Comparison of piperacillin vs. ticarcillin plus tobramycin in the treatment of acute pulmonary exacerbations of cystic fibrosis. Pediatr Infect Dis J. 1986;5:440–443.
170. Gold R, Overmeyer A, Knie B, et al. Controlled trial of ceftazidime vs. ticarcillin and tobramycin in the treatment of acute respiratory exacerbations in patients with cystic fibrosis. Pediatr Infect Dis J. 1985;4:172–177.
171. Bosso JA, Black PG, Matsen JM. Efficacy of aztreonam in pulmonary exacerbations of cystic fibrosis. Pediatr Infect Dis J. 1987;6:393–397.
172. Bayer AS. Clinical utility of new quinolones in treatment of osteomyelitis and lower respiratory tract infections. Eur J Clin Microbiol Infect Dis. 1989;8:1102–1110.
173. Hodson ME, Roberts CM, Butland RJ, et al. Oral ciprofloxacin compared with conventional intravenous treatment for *Pseudomonas aeruginosa* infection in adults with cystic fibrosis. Lancet. 1987;1:235–237.
174. de Groot R, Smith AL. Antibiotic pharmacokinetics in cystic fibrosis: Differences and clinical significance. Clin Pharmacokinet. 1987;13:228–253.
175. Pedersen SS, Jensen T, Høiby N, et al. Management of *Pseudomonas aeruginosa* lung infection in Danish cystic fibrosis patients. Acta Paediatr Scand. 1987;76:955–961.
176. Jensen T, Pedersen SS, Nielsen CH, et al. The efficacy and safety of ciprofloxacin and ofloxacin in chronic *Pseudomonas aeruginosa* infection in cystic fibrosis. J Antimicrob Chemother. 1987;20:585–594.
177. Valerius NH, Koch C, Høiby N. Prevention of chronic *Pseudomonas aeruginosa* colonisation in cystic fibrosis by early treatment. Lancet. 1991;338:725–726.
178. Mukhopadhyay S, Singh M, Cater JI, et al. Nebulised antipseudomonal antibiotic therapy in cystic fibrosis: A meta-analysis of benefits and risks. Thorax. 1996;51:364–368.
179. Hodson ME, Penketh RA, Batten JC. Aerosol carbenicillin and gentamicin treatment of *Pseudomonas aeruginosa* infection in patients with cystic fibrosis. Lancet. 1981;2:1137–1139.
180. Stead RJ, Hodson ME, Batten JC. Inhale ceftazidime compared with gentamicin and carbenicillin in older patients with cystic fibrosis infected with *Pseudomonas aeruginosa*. Br J Dis Chest. 1987;81:272–279.
181. Carswell F. Ward C, Cook DA, Speller DC. A controlled trial of nebulized aminoglycoside and oral flucloxacillin versus placebo in the outpatient management of children with cystic fibrosis. Br J Dis Chest. 1987;81:356–360.
182. Ramsey BW, Dorkin HL, Eisenberg JD, et al. Efficacy of aerosolized tobramycin in patients with cystic fibrosis. N Engl J Med. 1993;328:1740–1746.
183. Ewing CW. Role of the fiberoptic bronchoscope in lung lavage of patients with cystic fibrosis. Chest. 1978;73(Suppl):750–754.
184. Whitehead B, Helms P, Goodwin M, et al. Heart-lung transplantation for cystic fibrosis: 2. Outcome. Arch Dis Child. 1991;66:1022–1026.
185. Ramirez JC, Patterson GA, Winton TL, et al. Bilateral lung transplantation for cystic fibrosis. J Thorac Cardiovasc Surg. 1992;103:287–293.
186. Massard G, Shennib H, Metras D, et al. Double-lung transplantation in mechanically ventilated patients with cystic fibrosis. Ann Thorac Surg. 1993;55:1087–1092.
187. Couetil JPA, Houssin DP, Soubrane O, et al. Combined lung and liver transplantation in patients with cystic fibrosis. A 4 1/2-year experience. J Thorac Cardiovasc Surg. 1995;110:1415–1423.
188. Egan TM, Detterbeck FC, Mill MR, et al. Improved results of lung transplantation for patients with cystic fibrosis. J Thorac Cardiovasc Surg. 1995;109:224–235.
189. Lederman HM, Winkelstein JA. X-linked agammaglobulinemia: An analysis of 96 patients. Medicine (Baltimore) 1985;64:145–156.
190. Korvick JA, Marsh JW, Starzl TE, Yu VL. *Pseudomonas aeruginosa* bacteremia in patients undergoing liver transplantation: An emerging problem. Surgery. 1991;109:62–68.
191. Wagener MM, Yu VL. Bacteremia in transplant recipients: A prospective study of demographics, etiologic agents, risk factors, and outcomes. Am J Infect Control. 1992;20:239–247.
192. Shanson DC. Septicaemia in patients with AIDS. Trans R Soc Trop Med Hyg. 1990:84(Suppl 1):14–16.
193. Nelson MR, Shanson DC, Barter GJ, et al. *Pseudomonas* septicaemia associated with HIV. AIDS. 1991;5:761–763.
194. Roilides E, Butler KM, Husson RN, et al. *Pseudomonas* infections in children with human immunodeficiency virus infection. Pediatr Infect Dis J. 1992;11:547–553.
195. Bisbe J, Gatell JM, Puig J, et al. *Pseudomonas aeruginosa* bacteremia: Univariate and multivariate analyses of factors influencing the prognosis in 133 episodes. Rev Infect Dis. 1988;10:629–635.
196. Ehni WF, Reller LB, Ellison RT III. Bacteremia in granulocytopenic patients in a tertiary-care general hospital. Rev Infect Dis. 1991;13:613–619.

197. Gallagher PG, Watanakunakorn C. *Pseudomonas* bacteremia in a community teaching hospital, 1980–1984. Rev Infect Dis. 1989;11:846–852.
198. Mallolas J, Gatell JM, Miró JM, et al. Epidemiologic characteristics and factors influencing the outcome of *Pseudomonas aeruginosa* bacteremia. Rev Infect Dis. 1990;12:718–719.
199. Kreger BE, Craven DE, Carling PC, McCabe WR. Gram-negative bacteremia: III. Reassessment of etiology, epidemiology and ecology in 612 patients. Am J Med. 1980;68:332–343.
200. Danner RL, Natanson C, Elin RJ, et al. *Pseudomonas aeruginosa* compared with *Escherichia coli* produces less endotoxemia but more cardiovascular dysfunction and mortality in a canine model of septic shock. Chest. 1990;98:1480–1487.
201. Forkner CE. *Pseudomonas aeruginosa* Infections. New York: Grune & Stratton; 1960:6.
202. Forkner CE Jr, Frei E III, Edgcomb JH, Utz JP. *Pseudomonas* septicemia: Observations on twenty-three cases. Am J Med. 1958;25:877–889.
203. Whitecar JP Jr, Luna M, Bodey GP. *Pseudomonas* bacteremia in patients with malignant diseases. Am J Med Sci. 1970;260:216–223.
204. Tapper ML, Armstrong D. Bacteremia due to *Pseudomonas aeruginosa* complicating neoplastic disease. J Infect Dis. 1974;130(Suppl):S14–S23.
205. Flick MR, Cluff LE. *Pseudomonas* bacteremia: Review of 108 cases. Am J Med. 1976;60:501–508.
206. Baltch AL, Griffin PE. *Pseudomonas aeruginosa* bacteremia: A clinical study of 75 patients. Am J Med Sci. 1977;274;119–129.
207. Jackson MA, Wong KY, Lampkin B. *Pseudomonas aeruginosa* septicemia in childhood cancer patients. Pediatr Infect Dis. 1982;1:239–241.
208. Vermillion SE, Gregg JA, Baggenstoss AH, Bartholomew LG. Jaundice associated with bacteremia. Arch Intern Med. 1969;124:611–618.
209. Hitschmann F, Kreibich K. Zur pathogenese des Bacillus pyocyaneus und zur Aetiologie des Ekthyma gangrenosum. Wien Klin Wochenschr. 1897;10:1093–1101.
210. Fraenkel E. Über die Menschenpathogenität des Bacillus pyocyaneus. Z Hyg Infekt. 1912;72:486–522.
211. Dorff GJ, Geimer NF, Rosenthal DR, Rytel MW. *Pseudomonas* septicemia: Illustrated evolution of its skin lesions. Arch Intern Med. 1971;128:591–595.
212. Teplitz C. Pathogenesis of *Pseudomonas* vasculitis and septic lesions. Arch Pathol. 1965;80:297–307.
213. Rajan RK. Spontaneous bacterial peritonitis with ecthyma gangrenosum due to *Escherichia coli*. J Clin Gastroenterol. 1982;4:145–148.
214. Fine JD, Miller JA, Harrist TJ, Haynes HA. Cutaneous lesions in disseminated candidiasis mimicking ecthyma gangrenosum. Am J Med. 1981;70:1133–1135.
215. Pizzo P. Use of third-generation cephalosporins: *Pseudomonas*. Hosp Pract. 1991;26(Suppl 4):18–21; discussion, 48–50.
216. Pizzo PA, Hathorn JW, Hiemenz J, et al. A randomized trial comparing ceftazidime alone with combination antibiotic therapy in cancer patients with fever and neutropenia. N Engl J Med. 1986;315:552–558.
217. EORTC International Antimicrobial Therapy Cooperative Group. Ceftazidime combined with a short or long course of amikacin for empirical therapy of gram-negative bacteremia in cancer patients with granulocytopenia. N Engl J Med. 1987;317:1692–1698.
218. Liang R, Yung R, Chiu E, et al. Ceftazidime versus imipenem-cilastatin as initial monotherapy for febrile neutropenic patients. Antimicrob Agents Chemother. 1990;34:1336–1341.
219. Winston DJ, Ho WG, Bruckner DA, Champlin RE. Beta-lactam antibiotic therapy in febrile granulocytopenic patients: A randomized trial comparing cefoperazone plus piperacillin, ceftazidime plus piperacillin, and imipenem alone. Ann Intern Med. 1991;115:849–859.
220. Klastersky J, Meunier-Carpentier F, Prevost J-M. Significance of antimicrobial synergism for the outcome of gram negative sepsis. Am J Med Sci. 1977;273:157–167.
221. Love LJ, Schimpff SC, Schriffer CA, Wiernik PH. Improved prognosis for granulocytopenic patients with gram-negative bacteremia. Am J Med. 1980;68:643–648.
222. DeJongh CA, Joshi JH, Newman KA, et al. Antibiotic synergism and response in gram-negative bacteremia in granulocytopenic cancer patients. Am J Med. 1986;80(Suppl 5C):96–100.
223. Hilf M, Yu VL, Sharp J, et al. Antibiotic therapy for *Pseudomonas aeruginosa* bacteremia: Outcome correlations in a prospective study of 200 patients. Am J Med. 1989;87:540–546.
224. Korvick JA, Yu VL. Antimicrobial agent therapy for *Pseudomonas aeruginosa*. Antimicrob Agents Chemother. 1991;35:2167–2172.
225. Korvick JA, Peacock JE Jr, Muder RR, et al. Addition of rifampin to combination antibiotic therapy for *Pseudomonas aeruginosa* bacteremia: Prospective trial using the Zelen protocol. Antimicrob Agents Chemother. 1992;36:620–625.
226. Sheagren JN. Septic shock and corticosteroids [editorial]. N Engl J Med. 1981;305:456–458.
227. Bone RC, Fisher CJ Jr, Clemmer TP, et al. A controlled clinical trial of high-dose methylprednisolone in the treatment of severe sepsis and septic shock. N Engl J Med. 1987;317:653–658.
228. Veterans Administration Systemic Sepsis Cooperative Study Group. Effect of high-dose glucocorticoid therapy on mortality in patients with clinical signs of systemic sepsis. N Engl J Med. 1987;317:659–665.
229. Stanley MM. *Bacillus pyocyaneus* infections: A review, report of cases and discussion of newer therapy including streptomycin (concluded). Am J Med. 1947;2:347–367.
230. Chernik NL, Armstrong D, Posner JB. Central nervous system infections in patients with cancer. Medicine (Baltimore). 1973;52:563–581.
231. Wise BL, Mathis JL, Jawetz E. Infections of the central nervous system due to *Pseudomonas aeruginosa*. J Neurosurg. 1969;31:432–434.
232. Bray DA, Calcaterra TC. *Pseudomonas* meningitis complicating head and neck surgery. Laryngoscope. 1976;86:1386–1390.
233. Eng RHK, Lynch AM, Smith SM, et al. Imipenem resistance in a case of AIDS with relapsing *Pseudomonas* meningitis. South Med J. 1990;83:979–980.
234. Berk SL, McCabe WR. Meningitis caused by gram-negative bacilli. Ann Intern Med, 1980;93:253–260.
235. Rahal JJ, Simberkoff MS. Host defense and antimicrobial therapy in gram-negative bacillary meningitis. Ann Intern Med. 1982;96:468–474.
236. Norrby SR. Role of cephalosporins in the treatment of bacterial meningitis in adults: Overview with special emphasis on ceftazidime. Am J Med. 1985;79:56–61.
237. Fong IW, Tomkins KB. Review of *Pseudomonas aeruginosa* meningitis with special emphasis on treatment with ceftazidime. Rev Infect Dis. 1985;7:604–612.
238. Marone P, Concia E, Maserati R, et al. Ceftazidime in the therapy of pseudomonas meningitis. Chemioterapia. 1985;4:289–292.
239. Saha V, Stansfield R, Masterton R, Eden T. The treatment of *Pseudomonas aeruginosa* meningitis: Old regime or newer drugs? Scand J Infect Dis. 1993;25:81–83.
240. Wright DF, Kaiser AB, Bowman CM, et al. The pharmacokinetics and efficacy of an aminoglycoside administered into the cerebral ventricles in neonates: Implications for further evaluation of this route of therapy in meningitis. J Infect Dis. 1981;143:141–147.
241. Swartz MN. Intraventricular use of aminoglycosides in the treatment of gram-negative bacillary meningitis: Conflicting views. J Infect Dis. 1981;143:293–296.
242. Modai J, Wolff M, Lebas J, et al. Moxalactam penetration into cerebrospinal fluid in patients with bacterial meningitis. Antimicrob Agents Chemother. 1982;21:551–553.
243. Norrby SR. 4-Quinolones in the treatment of infections of the central nervous system. Rev Infect Dis. 1988;10(Suppl 1):S253–S255.
244. Hackbarth CJ, Chambers HF, Stella F, et al. Ciprofloxacin in experimental *Pseudomonas aeruginosa* meningitis in rabbits. J Antimicrob Chemother. 1986;18(Suppl D):65–69.
245. Lentnek AL, Williams RR. Aztreonam in the treatment of gram-negative bacterial meningitis. Rev Infect Dis. 1991;13(Suppl 7):S586–S590.
246. Kilpatrick M, Girgis N, Farid Z, Bishay E. Aztreonam for treating meningitis caused by gram-negative rods. Scand J Infect Dis. 1991;23:125–126.
247. Donnelly JP, Horrevorts AM, Sauerwein RW, De Pauw BE. High-dose meropenem in meningitis due to *Pseudomonas aeruginosa* (Letter). Lancet. 1992;339:1117.
248. Gupta SK, Mohanty S, Tandon SC, Asthana S. Brain abscess: With special reference to infection by pseudomonas. Br J Neurosurg. 1990;4:279–286.
249. Feinmesser R, Wiesel YM, Argaman M, Gay I. Otitis externa: Bacteriological survey. ORL J Otorhinolaryngol Relat Spec. 1982;44:121–125.
250. Chandler JR. Malignant external otitis. Laryngoscope. 1968;78:1257–1294.
251. van Asperen IA, de Rover CM, Schijven JF, et al. Risk of otitis externa after swimming in recreational fresh water lakes containing *Pseudomonas aeruginosa*. Br J Med. 1995;311:1407–1410.
252. Jones RN, Milazzo J, Seidlin M. Ofloxacin otic solution for treatment of otitis externa in children and adults. Arch Otolaryngol Head Neck Surg. 1997;123:1193–1200.
253. Dinapoli RP, Thomas JE. Neurologic aspects of malignant external otitis: Report of three cases. Mayo Clin Proc. 1971;46:339–344.
254. Zaky DA, Bentley DW, Lowy K, et al. Malignant external otitis: A severe form of otitis in diabetic patients. Am J Med. 1976;61:298–302.
255. Damiani JM, Damiani KK, Kinney SE. Malignant external otitis with multiple cranial nerve involvement. Am J Otol. 1979;1:115–120.
256. Kohut RI, Lindsay JR. Necrotizing ("malignant") external otitis histopathologic processes. Ann Otol Rhinol Laryngol. 1979;88:714–720.
257. Nadol JB, Jr. Histopathology of *Pseudomonas* osteomyelitis of the temporal bone starting as a malignant external otitis. Am J Otolaryngol. 1980;1:359–371.
258. Doroghazi RM, Nadol JB Jr, Hyslop NE Jr, et al. Invasive external otitis: Report of 21 cases and review of the literature. Am J Med. 1981;71:603–614.
259. Strauss M, Aber RC, Conner GH, Baum S. Malignant external otitis: Long-term (months) antimicrobial therapy. Laryngoscope. 1982;92:397–405.
260. Cóser PL, Stamm AE, Lobo RC, Pinto JA. Malignant external otitis in infants. Laryngoscope. 1980;90:312–316.
261. Sherman P, Black S, Grossman M. Malignant external otitis due to *Pseudomonas aeruginosa* in childhood. Pediatrics. 1980;66:782–783.
262. Nir D, Nir T, Danino J, Joachims HZ. Malignant external otitis in an infant. J Laryngol Otol. 1990;104:488–490.
263. Sutherland GE. Malignant external otitis in a nondiabetic adult. South Med J. 1981;74:516.
264. McElroy EA Jr, Marks GL. Fatal necrotizing otitis externa in a patient with AIDS (Letter). Rev Infect Dis. 1991;13:1246–1247.
265. Ford GR, Courteney-Harris RG. Another hazard of ear syringing: Malignant external otitis. J Laryngol Otol. 1990;104:709–710.
266. Rubin J, Yu VL. Malignant external otitis: Insights into pathogenesis, clinical manifestations, diagnosis, and therapy. Am J Med. 1988;85:391–398.
267. Lindsey D. It's time to stop washing out ears! [letter]. Am J Emerg Med. 1991;9:297.
268. Rubin J, Curtin HD, Yu VL, Kamerer DB. Malignant external otitis: Utility of CT in diagnosis and follow-up. Radiology. 1990;174:391–394.
269. Guy RL, Wylie E, Hickey SA, Tonge KA. Computed tomography in malignant external otitis. Clin Radiol. 1991;43:166–170.

270. Curtin HD, Wolfe P, May M. Malignant external otitis: CT evaluation. Radiology. 1982;145:383–388.
271. Gherini SG, Brackmann DE, Bradley WG. Magnetic resonance imaging and computerized tomography in malignant external otitis. Laryngoscope. 1986;96:542–548.
272. Stokkel MPM, Takes RP, van Eck-Smit BLF, et al. The value of quantitative gallium-67 single-photon emission tomography in the clinical management of malignant external otitis. Eur J Nucl Med. 1997;24:1429–1432.
273. Phillips P, Bryce G, Shepherd J, Mintz D. Invasive external otitis caused by *Aspergillus*. Rev Infect Dis. 1990;12:277–281.
274. Funasaka S, Kumakawa K. Advanced necrotizing external otitis treated by suboccipital craniectomy. Auris Nasus Larynx. 1982;9:9–14.
275. Meyers BR, Mendelson MH, Parisier SC, Hirschman SZ. Malignant external otitis: Comparison of monotherapy vs. combination therapy. Arch Otolaryngol Head Neck Surg. 1987;113:974–978.
276. Johnson MP, Ramphal R. Malignant external otitis: Report on therapy with ceftazidime and review of therapy and prognosis. Rev Infect Dis. 1990;12:173–180.
277. Giamarellou H. Malignant otitis externa: The therapeutic evolution of a lethal infection. J Antimicrob Chemother. 1992;30:745–751.
278. Morrison GAJ, Bailey CM. Relapsing malignant otitis externa successfully treated with ciprofloxacin. J Laryngol Otol. 1988;102:872–876.
279. Sadé J, Lang R, Goshen S, Kitzes-Cohen R. Ciprofloxacin treatment of malignant external otitis. Am J Med. 1989;87(Suppl 5A):138S–141S.
280. Lang R, Goshen S, Kitzes-Cohen R, Sadé J. Successful treatment of malignant external otitis with oral ciprofloxacin: Report of experience with 23 patients. J Infect Dis. 1990;161:537–540.
281. Rubin J, Stoehr G, Yu VL, et al. Efficacy of oral ciprofloxacin plus rifampin for treatment of malignant external otitis. Arch Otolaryngol Head Neck Surg. 1989;115:1063–1069.
282. Levy R, Shpitzer T, Shvero J, Pitlik SD. Oral ofloxacin as treatment of malignant external otitis: A study of 17 cases. Laryngoscope. 1990;100:548–551.
283. Bland RD. Otitis media in the first six weeks of life: Diagnosis, bacteriology, and management. Pediatrics. 1972;49:187–197.
284. Brook I, Finegold SM. Bacteriology of chronic otitis media. JAMA. 1979;241:487–488.
285. Kenna MA, Bluestone CS. Microbiology of chronic suppurative otitis media in children. Pediatr Infect Dis. 1986;5:223–225.
286. Kenna MA, Bluestone CD, Reilly JS, Lusk RP. Medical management of chronic suppurative otitis media without cholesteatoma in children. Laryngoscope. 1986;96:146–151.
287. Fliss DM, Dagan R, Houri Z, Leiberman A. Medical management of chronic suppurative otitis media without cholesteatoma in children. J Pediatr.1990;116:991–996.
288. Dagan R, Fliss DM, Einhorn M, et al. Outpatient management of chronic suppurative otitis media without cholesteatoma in children. Pediatr Infect Dis J.1992;11:542–546.
289. Lang R, Goshen S, Raas-Rothschild A, et al. Oral ciprofloxacin in the management of chronic suppurative otitis media without cholesteatoma in children: Preliminary experience in 21 children. Pediatr Infect Dis J. 1992;11:925–929.
290. Meyerhoff WL, Gates GA, Montalbo PJ. *Pseudomonas* mastoiditis. Laryngoscope. 1977;87:483–492.
291. O'Donnell JG, Sorbello AF, Condoluci DC, Barnish MJ. Sinusitis due to *Pseudomonas aeruginosa* in patient with human immunodeficiency virus infection. Clin Infect Dis. 1993;16:404–406.
292. Cumberworth VL, Hogarth TB. Hazards of ear-piercing procedures which traverse cartilage: A report of *Pseudomonas perichondritis* and review of other complications. Br J Clin Pract. 1990;44:512–513.
293. Warwick-Brown NP, Richards AES. Perichondritis of the ear following acupuncture. J Laryngol Otol. 1986;100:1177–1179.
294. Bassiouny A. Perichondritis of the auricle. Laryngoscope. 1981;91:422–431.
295. Peyman GA, Paque JT, Meisels HI, Bennett TO. Postoperative endophthalmitis: A comparison of methods for treatment and prophylaxis with gentamicin. Ophthalmol Surg. 1975;6:45–55.
296. Armstrong JH, Zacarias F, Rein MF. Ophthalmia neonatorum: A chart review. Pediatrics. 1976;57:884–892.
297. Rosenoff SH, Wolf ML, Chabuer BA. *Pseudomonas* blepharoconjunctivitis: A complication of combination chemotherapy. Arch Ophthalmol. 1974;91:490–491.
298. Berler DK, Alper MG. Scleral abscesses and ectasia caused by *Pseudomonas aeruginosa*. Ann Ophthalmol. 1982;14:665–667.
299. Atkins MC, Harrison GAJ, Lucas GS. *Pseudomonas aeruginosa* orbital cellulitis in four neutropenic patients. J Hosp Infect. 1990;16:343–349.
300. Hazlett LD, Moon M, Berk RS. In vivo identification of sialic acid as the ocular receptor for *Pseudomonas aeruginosa*. Infect Immun. 1986;51:687–689.
301. Liesegang TJ, Forster RK. Spectrum of microbial keratitis in South Florida. Am J Ophthalmol. 1980;90:38–47.
302. Alfonso E, Mandelbaum S, Fox MJ, Forster RK. Ulcerative keratitis associated with contact lens wear. Am J Ophthalmol. 1986;101:429–433.
303. Butrus SI, Klotz SA, Misra RP. The adherence of *Pseudomonas aeruginosa* to soft contact lenses. Ophthalmology. 1987;94:1310–1314.
304. Miller MJ, Wilson LA, Ahearn DG. Adherence of *Pseudomonas aeruginosa* to rigid gas-permeable contact lenses. Arch Ophthalmol. 1991;109:1447–1448.
305. Matthews TD, Frazer DG, Minassian DC, et al. Risks of keratitis and patterns of use with disposable contact lenses. Arch Ophthalmol. 1992;110:1559–1562.
306. Schein OD, Wasson PJ, Boruchoff SA, Kenyon KR. Microbial keratitis associated with contaminated ocular medications. Am J Ophthalmol. 1988;105:361–365.
307. Procope JA. Delayed-onset *Pseudomonas* keratitis after radial keratotomy. J Cataract Refract Surg. 1997;23:1271–1272.
308. Tarr KH, Constable IJ. *Pseudomonas* endophthalmitis associated with scleral necrosis. Br J Ophthalmol. 1980;64:676–679.
309. Parkin B, Turner A, Moore E, Cook S. Bacterial keratitis in the critically ill. Br J Ophthalmol. 1997;81:1060–1063.
310. Nanda M, Pflugfelder SC, Holland S. Fulminant pseudomonal keratitis and scleritis in human immunodeficiency virus-infected patients. Arch Ophthalmol. 1991;109:503–505.
311. Maguen E, Salz JJ, Nesburn AB. *Pseudomonas* corneal ulcer associated with rigid, gas-permeable, daily-wear lenses in a patient infected with human immunodeficiency virus. Am J Ophthalmol. 1992;113:336–337.
312. King S, Devi SP, Mindorff C, et al. Nosocomial *Pseudomonas aeruginosa* conjunctivitis in a pediatric hospital. Infect Control Hosp Epidemiol. 1988;9:77–80.
313. Shah SS, Gallagher PG, Gallagher B. Complications of conjunctivitis caused by *Pseudomonas aeruginosa* in a newborn intensive care unit. Pediatr Infect Dis J. 1998;17:97–102.
314. Leibowitz HM, Kupferman A. Topically administered corticosteroids: Effect on antibiotic-treated bacterial keratitis. Arch Ophthalmol. 1980;98:1287–1290.
315. Davis SD, Sarff LD, Hyndfink RA. Relative efficacy of the topical use of amikacin, gentamicin, and tobramycin in experimental *Pseudomonas* keratitis. Can J Ophthalmol. 1980;15:28–29.
316. Hessburg PC. Treatment of *Pseudomonas* keratitis in humans. Am J Ophthalmol. 1966;61:896–903.
317. Sugar A, Cohen MA, Bein PA, et al. Treatment of experimental *Pseudomonas* corneal ulcers with enoxacin, a quinolone antibiotic. Arch Ophthalmol. 1986;104:1230–1232.
318. Hobden JA, Reidy JJ, O'Callaghan RJ, et al. Quinolones in collagen shields to treat aminoglucoside-resistant *Pseudomonas* keratitis. Invest Ophthalmol Vis Sci. 1990;31:2241–2243.
319. Silbiger J, Stern GA. Evaluation of corneal collagen shields as a drug delivery device for the treatment of experimental *Pseudomonas* keratitis. Ophthalmology. 1992;99:889–892.
320. Leibowitz HM, Ryan WJ Jr, Kupferman A. Route of antibiotic administration in bacterial keratitis. Arch Ophthalmol. 1981;99:1420–1423.
321. Golden B. Subtenon injection of gentamicin for bacterial infections of the eye. J Infect Dis. 1971;124(Suppl):S271–S274.
322. Sweeney G, Fern AI, Lindsay G, Doig MW. Penetration of ciprofloxacin into the aqueous humour of the uninflamed human eye after oral administration. J Antimicrob Chemother. 1990;26:99–105.
323. El Baba FZ, Trousdale MD, Gauderman WJ, et al. Intravitreal penetration of oral ciprofloxacin in humans. Ophthalmology. 1992;99:483–486.
324. Lesk MR, Ammann H, Marcil G, et al. The penetration of oral ciprofloxacin into the aqueous humor, vitreous, and subretinal fluid of humans. Am J Ophthalmol. 1993;115:623–628.
325. Forster RK. Endophthalmitis. In: Duane TD, ed. Clinical Ophthalmology. New York: Harper & Row, 1978:1–20.
326. Ayliffe GAJ, Barry DR, Lowbury EJL, et al. Postoperative infection with *Pseudomonas aeruginosa* in an eye hospital. Lancet. 1966;1:1113–1117.
327. Irvine WD, Flynn HW Jr, Miller D, Pflugfelder SC. Endophthalmitis caused by gram-negative organisms. Arch Ophthalmol. 1992;110:1450–1454.
328. Garg SP, Talwar D, Verma LK. Metastatic endophthalmitis: A reappraisal. Ann Ophthalmol. 1991;23:74–78.
329. Yannis RA, Rissing JP, Buxton TB, Shockley RK. Multistrain comparison of three antimicrobial prophylaxis regimens in experimental postoperative *Pseudomonas* endophthalmitis. Am J Ophthalmol. 1985;100:404–407.
330. Walstad RA, Blika S. Penetration of ceftazidime into the normal rabbit and human eye. Scand J Infect Dis. 1985;44(Suppl):63–67.
331. Norden CW, Keleti E. Experimental osteomyelitis caused by *Pseudomonas aeruginosa*. J Infect Dis. 1980;141:71–75.
332. Norden CW, Myerowitz RL, Keleti E. Experimental osteomyelitis due to *Staphylococcus aureus* or *Pseudomonas aeruginosa*: A radiographic-pathological correlative analysis. Br J Exp Pathol. 1980;61:451–460.
333. Salahuddin NI, Madhavan T, Fisher EJ, et al. *Pseudomonas* osteomyelitis: Radiologic features. Radiology. 1973;109:41–47.
334. Wiesseman GJ, Wood VE, Kroll LL. *Pseudomonas* vertebral osteomyelitis in heroin addicts: Report of five cases. J Bone Joint Surg Am. 1973;55:1416–1424.
335. Sapico FL, Montgomerie JZ. Vertebral osteomyelitis in intravenous drug abusers: Report of three cases and review of the literature. Rev Infect Dis. 1980;2:196–206.
336. Tindel JR, Crowder JG. Septic arthritis due to *Pseudomonas aeruginosa*. JAMA. 1971;218:559–561.
337. Gifford DB, Patzakis M, Ivler D, Swezey RL. Septic arthritis due to *Pseudomonas* in heroin addicts. J Bone Joint Surg Am. 1975;57:631–635.
338. Bayer AS, Chow AW, Louie JS, Guze LB. Sternoclavicular pyarthrosis due to gram-negative bacilli: Report of eight cases. Arch Intern Med. 1977;137:1036–1040.
339. Sequeira W, Jones E, Siegel ME, et al. Pyogenic infections of the pubic symphysis. Ann Intern Med. 1982;96;604–606.
340. del Busto R, Quinn EL, Fisher EJ, Madhaven T. Osteomyelitis of the pubis: Report of seven cases. JAMA. 1982;24:1498–1500.
341. Guthrie R. Osteomyelitis of the symphysis pubis: A complication of cardiac catheterisation. Br J Clin Pract. 1989;43:383–385.
342. Michiels E, Knockaert DC, Vanneste SB. Infectious osteitis pubis. Neth J Med. 1990;36:297–300.

343. Johanson PH. *Pseudomonas* infections of the foot following puncture wounds. JAMA. 1968;204:262–264.
344. Minnefor AB, Olson MI, Carver DH. *Pseudomonas* osteomyelitis following puncture wounds of the foot. Pediatrics. 1971;47:598–601.
345. Green NE, Bruno J III. *Pseudomonas* infections of the foot after puncture wounds. South Med J. 1980;73:146–149.
346. Jacobs RF, Adelman L, Sack CM, Wilson CB. Management of *Pseudomonas* osteochondritis complicating puncture wounds of the foot. Pediatrics. 1982;69:432–435.
347. Siebert WT, Dewan S, Williams TW Jr. Case report: *Pseudomonas* puncture wound osteomyelitis in adults. Am J Med Sci. 1982;283:83–88.
348. Jacobs RF, McCarthy RE, Elser JM. *Pseudomonas* osteochondritis complicating puncture wounds of the foot in children: A 10-year evaluation. J Infect Dis. 1989;160:657–661.
349. Fisher MC, Goldsmith JF, Gilligan PH. Sneakers as a source of *Pseudomonas aeruginosa* in children with osteomyelitis following puncture wounds. J Pediatr. 1985;106:607–609.
350. Raz R, Miron D. Oral ciprofloxacin for treatment of infection following nail puncture wounds of the foot. Clin Infect Dis. 1995;21:194–195.
351. Gilbert DN, Tice AD, Marsh PK, et al. Oral ciprofloxacin therapy for chronic contiguous osteomyelitis caused by aerobic gram-negative bacilli. Am J Med. 1987;82(Suppl 4A):254–258.
352. Gentry LO. Treatment of skin, skin structure, bone, and joint infections with ceftazidime. Am J Med. 1985;79(Suppl 2A):67–74.
353. Bach MC, Cocchetto DM. Ceftazidime as single-agent therapy for gram-negative aerobic bacillary osteomyelitis. Antimicrob Agents Chemother. 1987;31:1605–1608.
354. Gentry LO. Role for newer beta-lactam antibiotics in treatment of osteomyelitis. Am J Med. 1985;78(Suppl 6A):134–139.
355. Conrad DA, Williams RR, Couchman TL, Lentnek AL. Efficacy of aztreonam in the treatment of skeletal infections due to *Pseudomonas aeruginosa*. Rev Infect Dis. 1991;13(Suppl 7):S634–S639.
356. Norden CW, Shinners E. Ciprofloxacin as therapy for experimental osteomyelitis caused by *Pseudomonas aeruginosa*. J Infect Dis. 1985;151:291–294.
357. Norden CW, Niederriter K. Ofloxacin therapy for experimental osteomyelitis caused by *Pseudomonas aeruginosa*. J Infect Dis. 1987;155:823–825.
358. Greenberg RN, Tice AD, Marsh PK, et al. Randomized trial of ciprofloxacin compared with other antimicrobial therapy in the treatment of osteomyelitis. Am J Med. 1987;82(Suppl 4A):266–269.
359. Gentry LO, Rodriguez GG. Oral ciprofloxacin compared with parenteral antibiotics in the treatment of osteomyelitis. Antimicrob Agents Chemother. 1990;34:40–43.
360. Desplaces N, Acar JF. New quinolones in the treatment of joint and bone infections. Rev Infect Dis. 1988;10(Suppl 1):S179–S183.
361. Marrie TJ, Major H, Gurwith M, et al. Prolonged outbreak of nosocomial urinary tract infection with a single strain of *Pseudomonas aeruginosa*. Can Med Assoc J. 1978;119:593–598.
362. Moore B, Forman A. An outbreak of urinary *Pseudomonas aeruginosa* infection acquired during urological operations. Lancet. 1966;2:929–931.
363. Anderson RJ, Schafer LA, Olin DB, Eickhoff TC. Septicemia in renal transplant recipients. Arch Surg. 1973;106:692–694.
364. Krieger JN, Brem AS, Kaplan MR. Urinary tract infection in pediatric renal transplantation. Urology. 1980;15:362–369.
365. Fang G, Brennen C, Wagener M, et al. Use of ciprofloxacin versus use of aminoglycosides for therapy of complicated urinary tract infection: Prospective, randomized clinical and pharmacokinetic study. Antimicrob Agents Chemother. 1991;35:1849–1855.
366. Montgomerie JZ, Guerra DA, Schick DG, et al. *Pseudomonas* urinary tract infection in patients with spinal cord injury. J Am Paraplegia Soc. 1989;12:8–10.
367. Kunin CM. A ten-year study of bacteriuria in school girls: Final report of bacteriologic, urologic and epidemiologic findings. J Infect Dis. 1970;122:382–393.
368. Mocan H, Karaguzel G. Community-acquired *Pseudomonas aeruginosa* urinary tract infection in young children. Pediatr Nephrol. 1997;11:784–788.
369. Stamey TA, ed. Urinary Infections. Baltimore: Williams & Wilkins, 1972:279.
370. Daifuku R, Stamm WE. Bacterial adherence to bladder uroepithelial cells in catheter-associated urinary tract infection. N Engl J Med. 1986;314:1208–1213.
371. Liedberg H, Ekman P, Lundeberg T. *Pseudomonas aeruginosa*: Adherence to and growth on different urinary catheter coatings. Int Urol Nephrol. 1990;22:487–492.
372. Nickel JC, Downey J, Costerton JW. Movement of *Pseudomonas aeruginosa* along catheter surfaces: A mechanism in pathogenesis of catheter-associated infection. Urology. 1992;39:93–98.
373. Stanley MM. *Bacillus pyocyaneus* infections: A review, report of cases and discussion of newer therapy including streptomycin. Am J Med. 1947;2:253–277.
374. Carroll G, Allen HN, Doubly EK. Study of bacillary infections of the urinary tract. JAMA. 1947;135:683–686.
375. Fraenkel E. Weitere Untersuchungen über die Menschenpathogenität des Bacillus pyocyaneus. Z Hyg Infekt. 1917;84:369–423.
376. Corrado ML, Grad C, Sabbaj J. Norfloxacin in the treatment of urinary tract infections in men with and without identifiable urologic complications. Am J Med. 1987;82(Suppl 6B):70–74.
377. Leigh DA, Emmanuel FXS, Petch VJ. Ciprofloxacin therapy in complicated urinary tract infections caused by *Pseudomonas aeruginosa* and other resistant bacteria. J Antimicrob Chemother. 1986;18(Suppl D):117–121.
378. Brown EM, Morris R, Stephenson TP. The efficacy and safety of ciprofloxacin in the treatment of chronic *Pseudomonas aeruginosa* urinary tract infection. J Antimicrob Chemother. 1986;18(Suppl D):123–127.
379. Malinverni R, Glauser MP. Comparative studies of fluoroquinolones in the treatment of urinary tract infections. Rev Infect Dis. 1988;10(Suppl 1):S153–S163.
380. Barker LF. The clinical symptoms, bacteriologic findings and postmortem appearances in cases of infection of human beings with the *Bacillus pyocyaneus*. JAMA. 1897;29:213–216.
381. Epstein JW, Grossman AB. *Bacillus pyocyaneus* in children. Am J Dis Child. 1933;46:132–147.
382. Ensign PR, Hunter CA. An epidemic of diarrhea in the newborn nursery caused by a milk-borne epidemic in the community. J Pediatr. 1946;29:620–628.
383. Schaffer AJ, Oppenheimer EH. *Pseudomonas* (pyocyaneus) infections of the gastrointestinal tract in infants and children. South Med J. 1948;41:460–467.
384. Florman AL, Schifrin N. Observations on a small outbreak of infantile diarrhea associated with *Pseudomonas aeruginosa*. J Pediatr. 1950;36:758–766.
385. Walker SH. Polymyxin B in *Pseudomonas* and *Proteus* enteritis. J Pediatr. 1952;41:176–181.
386. Geppert LJ, Baker HJ, Copple BI, Pulaski EJ. *Pseudomonas* infections in infants and children. J Pediatr. 1952;141:555–561.
387. Stone HH, Kolb LD, Geheber CE. Bacteriologic considerations in perforated necrotizing enterocolitis. South Med J. 1979;72:1540–1544.
388. Amromin GD, Solomon RD. Necrotizing enteropathy: A complication of treated leukemia and lymphoma patients. JAMA. 1962;182:23–29.
389. Schimpff SC, Wiernik PH, Block JB. Rectal abscesses in cancer patients. Lancet. 1972;2:844–847.
390. Sherman NJ, Woolley MM. The ileocecal syndrome in acute childhood leukemia. Arch Surg. 1973;107:39–42.
391. Rodriguez V, Bodey GP, eds. Epidemiology, clinical manifestations, and treatment in cancer patients. Doggett RG, ed. *Pseudomonas aeruginosa*: Clinical Manifestations of Infection and Current Therapy. New York: Academic Press, 1979, 367–407.
392. Angel C, Patrick CC, Lobe T, et al. Management of anorectal-perineal infections caused by *Pseudomonas aeruginosa* in children with malignant diseases. J Pediatr Surg. 1991;26:487–493.
393. Dold H. On pyocyaneus sepsis and intestinal infections in Shanghai due to *Bacillus pyocyaneus*. Chin Med J (Engl). 1918;32:435.
394. Chakravarti DN, Tyagi NN. Pyrexia simulating that of enteric fever caused by *Pseudomonas* pyocyaneus in children. Indian Med Gaz. 1937;72:367–368.
395. Kubota Y, Liu PV. An enterotoxin of *Pseudomonas aeruginosa*. J Infect Dis. 1971;123:97–98.
396. Barnes SG, Sattler FR, Ballard JO. Perirectal infections in acute leukemia: Improved survival after incision and debridement. Ann Intern Med. 1984;100:515–518.
397. Glenn J, Cotton D, Wesley R, et al. Anorectal infections in patients with malignant diseases. Rev Infect Dis. 1988;10:42–52.
398. Greene SL, Wu WP, Muller SA. Ecthyma gangrenosum: Report of clinical, histopathologic, and bacteriologic aspects of eight cases. J Am Acad Dermatol. 1984;11:781–787.
399. Schlossberg D. Multiple erythematous nodules as a manifestation of *Pseudomonas aeruginosa* septicemia. Arch Dermatol. 1980;116:446–447.
400. Bagel J, Grossman ME. Subcutaneous nodules in *Pseudomonas* sepsis. Am J Med. 1986;80:528–529.
401. Fleming MG, Milburn PB, Prose NS. *Pseudomonas* septicemia with nodules and bullae. Pediatr Dermatol. 1987;4:18–20.
402. Roberts R, Tarpay MM, Marks MI, Nitschke R. Erysipelas-like lesions and hyperesthesia as manifestions of *Pseudomonas aeruginosa* sepsis. JAMA. 1982;248:2156–2157.
403. Hall JH, Callaway JL, Tindal JP, Smith JG, Jr. *Pseudomonas aeruginosa* in dermatology. Arch Dermatol. 1968;97:312–324.
404. Duncan BW, Adzick NS, deLorimier AA, et al. Necrotizing fasciitis in two children with acute lymphoblastic leukemia. J Pediatr Surg. 1992;27:668–671.
405. Maqbool M, Ahmad R, Qazi S. Necrotising fasciitis in the head and neck region. Br J Plast Surg. 1992;45:481–483.
406. Murphy JJ, Granger R, Blair GK, et al. Necrotizing fasciitis in childhood. J Pediatr Surg. 1995;30:1131–1134.
407. Koopmann CF, Coulthard SW. Infectious facial and nasal cutaneous necrosis: Evaluation and diagnosis. Laryngoscope. 1982;92:1130–1134.
408. Sevinsky LD, Viecens C, Ballesteros DO. Ecthyma gangrenosum: A cutaneous manifestation of *Pseudomonas aeruginosa* sepsis. J Am Acad Dermatol. 1993;29:106–108.
409. Berg A, Armitage JO, Burns CP. Fournier's gangrene complicating aggressive therapy for hematologic malignancy. Cancer. 1986;57:2291–2294.
410. Boisseau AM, Sarlangue J, Perel Y, et al. Perineal ecthyma gangrenosum in infancy and early childhood: Septicemic and nonsepticemic forms. J Am Acad Dermatol. 1992;27:415–418.
411. Schuster DI. Palatopharyngeal and lower extremity soft tissue loss in an infant secondary to *Pseudomonas* gangrenous cellulitus. Ann Plast Surg. 1981;6:138–141.
412. Lin J-Y, Wang D-W, Peng C-T, et al. Noma neonatorum: An unusual case of noma involving a full-term neonate. Acta paediatr. 1992;81:720–722.
413. Sangeorzan JA, Bradley SF, Kauffman CA. Cutaneous manifestations of *Pseudomonas* infection in the acquired immunodeficiency syndrome. Arch Dermatol. 1990;126:832–833.
414. Huminer D, Siegman-Ingra Y, Morduchowicz G, Pitlik SD. Ecthyma gangrenosum without bacteremia: Report of six cases and review of the literature. Arch Intern Med. 1987;147:299–301.
415. el Baze P, Thyss A, Vinti H, et al. A study of nineteen immunocompromised

patients with extensive skin lesions caused by *Pseudomonas aeruginosa* with and without bacteremia. Acta Derm Venereol (Stockh). 1991;71:411–415.
416. van den Broek PJ, van der Meer JWM, Kunst MW. The pathogenesis of ecthyma gangrenosum. J Infect. 1979;1:263–267.
417. Washburn J, Jacobson JA, Marston E, Thorsen B. *Pseudomonas aeruginosa* rash associated with a whirlpool. JAMA. 1976;235:2205–2207.
418. Thomas P, Moore M, Bell E, et al. *Pseudomonas* dermatitis associated with a swimming pool. JAMA. 1985;253:1156–1159.
419. Herwaldt BL, Craun GF, Stokes SL, Juranek DD. Waterborne-disease outbreaks, 1989–1990. MMWR CDC Surveill Summ. 1991;40:1–21.
420. Schlech WF 3rd, Simonsen N, Sumarah R, Martin RS. Nosocomial outbreak of *Pseudomonas aeruginosa* folliculitis associated with a physiotherapy pool. Can Med Assoc J. 1986;134:909–913.
421. el Baze P, Thyss A, Caldani C, et al. *Pseudomonas aeruginosa* 0-11 folliculitis: Development into ecthyma gangrenosum in immunosuppressed patients. Arch Dermatol. 1985;121:873–876.
422. Bottone EJ, Perez AA II. *Pseudomonas aeruginosa* folliculitis acquired through use of a contaminated loofah sponge: An unrecognized potential public health problem. J Clin Microbiol. 1993;31:480–483.
423. Meislich D, Long SS. Invasive *Pseudomonas* infection in two healthy children following prolonged bathing. Am J Dis Child. 1993;147:18–20.
424. Pruitt BA Jr. Infections of burns and other wounds caused by *Pseudomonas aeruginosa*. In: Sabath LD, eds. *Pseudomonas aeruginosa*: The Organism, Diseases it Causes, and Their Treatment. Bern: Hans Huber Publishers, 1980:55–70.
425. McManus AT, Mason AD Jr, McManus WF, Pruitt BA, Jr. Twenty-five year review of *Pseudomonas aeruginosa* bacteremia in a burn center. Eur J Clin Microbiol. 1985;4:219–223.
426. Tredget EE, Shankowsky HA, Joffe AM, et al. Epidemiology of infections with *Pseudomonas aeruginosa* in burn patients: The role of hydrotherapy. Clin Infect Dis. 1992;15:941–949.
427. Pruitt BA, McManus AT, Kim SH, Goodwin CW. Burn wound infections: Current status. World J Surg. 1998;22:135–145.
428. Pruitt BA Jr, Foley FD. The use of biopsies in burn patient care. Surgery. 1973;73:887–897.
429. Williams HB, Breidenbach WC, Callaghan WB, et al. Are burn wound biopsies obsolete? A comparative study of bacterial quantitation in burn patients using the absorbent disc and biopsy techniques. Ann Plast Surg. 1984;13:388–395.
430. Hansbrough JF, Carroll WB, Zapata-Sirvent RL, et al. Identification and antibiotic susceptibility of bacterial isolates from burned patients. Burns Incl Therm Inj. 1985;11:393–403.
431. Culberston GR, McManus AT, Conarro PA, et al. Clinical trial of imipenem/cilastatin in severely burned and infected patients. Surg Gynecol Obstet. 1987;165:25–28.
432. McManus WF, Goodwin CW Jr, Pruitt BA Jr. Subeschar treatment of burn wound infection. Arch Surg. 1983;118:291–294.
433. Modak S, Fox CL Jr. Synergistic action of silver sulfadiazine and sodium piperacillin on persistent *Pseudomonas aeruginosa* in vitro and in experimental burn wound infections. J Trauma. 1985;25:27–31.
434. Leyden JJ, McGinley KJ, Mills OH. *Pseudomonas aeruginosa* gram-negative folliculitis. Arch Dermatol. 1979;115:1203–1204.
435. Alomar A, Ausina V, Vernis J, de Moragas JM. *Pseudomonas* folliculitis. Cutis. 1982;30:405–409.
436. Eaglstein NF, Marley WM, Marley NF, et al. Gram-negative bacterial toe web infection: Successful treatment with a new third generation cephalosporin. J Am Acad Dermatol. 1983;8:225–228.
437. LeFeber WP, Golitz LE. Green foot. Pediatr Dermatol. 1984;2:38–40.
438. Dropulic LK, Leslie JM, Eldred LJ, et al. Clinical manifestations and risk factors of *Pseudomonas aeruginosa* infection in patients with AIDS. J Infect Dis. 1995;171:930–937.
439. Fichtenbaum CJ, Woeltje KF, Powderly WG. Serious *Pseudomonas aeruginosa* infections in patients infected with human immunodeficiency virus: A case-control study. Clin Infect Dis. 1994;19:417–422.
440. Shepp DH, Tang IT-L, Ramundo MB, Kaplan MH. Serious *Pseudomonas aeruginosa* infection in AIDS. J Acquir Immun Defic Syndr. 1994;7:823–831.
441. Mendelson MH, Gurtman A, Szabo S, et al. *Pseudomonas aeruginosa* bacteremia in patients with AIDS. Clin Infect Dis. 1994;18:866–895.
442. Frank U, Daschner FD, Schulgen G, et al. Incidence and epidemiology of nosocomial infections in patients infected with human immunodeficiency virus. Clin Infect Dis. 1997;25:318–320.
443. Amundson DE, Mancini SA. *Pseudomonas aeruginosa* pneumonia/sepsis as an initial opportunistic infection in an HIV patient. Mil Med. 1996;3:179.
444. Domingo P, Ferre A, Baraldes MA, et al. Remission of relapsing *Pseudomonas aeruginosa* bronchopulmonary infection following antiretroviral therapy. Arch Intern Med. 1998;158:929–930.
445. Schuster MG, Norris AH. Community-acquired *Pseudomonas aeruginosa* pneumonia in patients with HIV infection. AIDS. 1994;8:1437–1441.
446. Verghese A, Al-Samman M, Nabhan D, et al. Bacterial bronchitis and bronchiectasis in human immunodeficiency virus infection. Arch Intern Med. 1994;154:2086–2091.
447. Baron AD, Hollander H. *Pseudomonas aeruginosa* bronchopulmonary infection in late human immunodeficiency virus disease. Am Rev Respir Dis. 1993;148:992–996.
448. Miller RF, Foley NM, Kessel D, Jeffrey AA. Community acquired lobar pneumonia in patients with HIV infection and AIDS. Thorax. 1994;49:367–368.
449. Ali NJ, Kessel D, Miller RF. Bronchopulmonary infection with *Pseudomonas aeruginosa* in patients infected with human immunodeficiency virus. Genitourin Med. 1995;71:73–77.
450. Ainsworth JG, Mitchell D, Harris JRW. Successful prevention of recurrent pneumonia caused by *Pseudomonas aeruginosa* in a patient with AIDS. Intl J STD AIDS. 1995;6:123–124.
451. Furman AC, Jacobs J, Sepkowitz KA. Lung abscess in patients with AIDS. Clin Infect Dis. 1996;22:81–85.
452. Johann-Liang R, Cervia JS, Noel GJ. Characteristics of human immunodeficiency virus-infected children at the time of death: An experience in the 1990s. Pediatr Infect Dis. 1997;16:1145–1150.
453. Godofsky EW, Zinreich J, Armstrong M, et al. Sinusitis in HIV-infected patients: A clinical and radiographic review. Am J Med. 1992;93:163–170.
454. Tami TA. The management of sinusitis in patients infected with the human immunodeficiency virus (HIV). Ear Nose Throat J. 1995;74:360–363.
455. Berger TG, Kaveh S, Becker D, Hoffman J. Cutaneous manifestations of *Pseudomonas* infections in AIDS. J Am Acad Dermatol. 1995;32:279–280.
456. Nelson MR, Barton SE, Langtrey JAA, Gazzard BG. Ecthyma gangrenosum without bacteraemia in an HIV seropositive male. Intl J STD AIDS. 1991;2:295–296.
457. Higgins SP, Stedman YF, Bundred NJ, et al. Periareolar breast abscess due to *Pseudomonas aeruginosa* in an HIV antibody positive male. Genitourin Med. 1994;70:147–148.
458. Roca B, Vilar C, Pérez EV, et al. Breast abscess with lethal septicemia due to *Pseudomonas aeruginosa* in a patient with AIDS. Presse Med. 1996;25:803–804.
459. Sanderson RJ, Anstey ST. Parapharyngeal abscess from *Pseudomonas aeruginosa* infection in an HIV positive patient. J Infect. 1995;31:174.
460. Cano-Parra J, España E, Esteban M, et al. *Pseudomonas* conjunctival ulcer and secondary orbital cellulitis in a patient with AIDS. Br J Ophthalmol. 1994;78:72–73.
461. Sharland M, Peake J, Davies EG. Pseudomonal rectovaginal abscesses in HIV infection. Arch Dis Child. 1995;72:275.
462. Lortholary O, Jehl F. Petitjean O, et al. Polymicrobial pyomyositis and bacteremia in a patient with AIDS. Clin Infect Dis. 1994;19:552–553.
463. Daniels DG, Nelson MR, Barton SE, Gazzard BG. Malignant otitis externa in a patient with AIDS. Intl J STD AIDS. 1992;3:214.
464. Weinroth SE, Schessel D, Tuazon CU. Malignant otitis externa in AIDS patients: Case report and review of the literature. Ear Nose Throat J. 1994;73;772–774, 777–778.
465. Glauser M. Empiric therapy of bacterial infections in patients with severe neutropenia. Diagn Microbiol Infect Dis. 1998;31:467–472.
466. Brun-Buisson C, Sollet JP, Schweich H, et al. Treatment of ventilator-associated pneumonia with piperacillin-tazobactam/amikacin versus ceftazidime/amikacin: A multicenter, randomized controlled trial. Clin Infect Dis. 1998;26:346–354.
467. Chen HY, Yuan M, Livermore DM. Mechanisms of resistance to β-lactam antibiotics amongst *Pseudomonas aeruginosa* isolates collected in the UK in 1993. J Med Microbiol. 1995;43:300–309.
468. Livermore DM. Interplay of impermeability and chromosomal β-lactamase activity in imipenem-resistant *Pseudomonas aeruginosa.* Antimicrob Agents Chemother. 1996;36:2046–2048.
469. Li X-Z, Ma D, Livermore DM, Nikaido H. Role of efflux pump(s) in intrinsic resistance of *Pseudomonas aeruginosa*: Acute efflux as a contributing factor to β-lactam resistance. Antimicrob Agents Chemother. 1994;38:1742–1752.
470. Spikumar R, Kon T, Gotoh N, Poole K. Expression of *Pseudomonas aeruginosa* multidrug efflux pumps MesA-MexB-OprM and MexC-MexD-OprJ in a multidrug-sensitive *Escherichia coli* strain. Antimicrob Agents Chemother. 1998;42:65–71.
471. Li X, Zhang L, Srikumar R, Poole K. β-lactamase inhibitors are substrates for the multidrug efflux pumps of *Pseudomonas aeruginosa.* Antimicrob Agents Chemother. 1998;42:399–403.
472. Nakae T. Multiantibiotic resistance caused by active drug extrusion in *Pseudomonas aeruginosa* and other gram-negative bacteria. Microbiologia. 1997;13:273–284.
473. Kohler T, Michea-Hamzehpour M, Plesiat P, et al. Differential selection of multidrug efflux systems by quinolones in *Pseudomonas aeruginosa.* Antimicrob Agents Chemother. 1997;41:2540–2543.
474. Hancock RE. Resistance mechanisms in *Pseudomonas aeruginosa* and other nonfermentative gram-negative bacteria. Clin Infect Dis. 1998;27(Suppl 1):S93–S99.
475. Masuda N, Ohya S. Cross-resistance to meropenem, cephems, and quinolones in *Pseudomonas aeruginosa.* Antimicrob Agents Chemother. 1992;36:1847–1851.
476. Zhanel GG, Karlowsky JA, Saunders MH, et al. Development of multiple-antibiotic-resistant (Mar) mutants of *Pseudomonas aeruginosa* after serial exposure to fluoroquinolones. Antimicrob Agents Chemother. 1995;39:489–495.
477. Fass RJ, Barnishan J, Solomon MC, Ayers LW. In vitro activities of quinolones, β-lactams, tobramycin, and trimethoprim-sulfamethoxazole against nonfermentative gram-negative bacilli. Antimicrob Agents Chemother. 1996;40:1412-1418.
478. Chen HY, Yuan M, Ibrahim-Elmagboul IB, Livermore DM. National survey of susceptibility to antimicrobials amongst clinical isolates of *Pseudomonas aeruginosa.* J Antimicrob Chemother. 1995;35:521–534.
479. Bert F, Maubec E, Bruneau B, et al. Multi-resistant *Pseudomonas aeruginosa* outbreak associated with contaminated tap water in a neurosurgery intensive care unit. J Hosp Infect. 1998;39:53–62.
480. Sofianou D, Tsakris A, Skoura K, Douboyas J. Extended high-level cross-resistance to antipseudomonal antibiotics amongst *Pseudomonas aeruginosa* isolates in a university hospital. J Antimicrob Chemother. 1997;40:740–742.
481. Holloway WJ, Palmer D. Clinical applications of a new parenteral antibiotic in the treatment of severe bacterial infections. Am J Med. 1996;100(Suppl 6A):52S–59S.
482. Fekete T, Tumah H, Woodwell J, et al. Comparative susceptibilities of *Klebsiella*

species, *Enterobacter* species, and *Pseudomonas aeruginosa* to 11 antimicrobial agents in a tertiary-care university hospital. Am J Med. 1996;100(Suppl 6A):6A–20S.
483. Jones RN, Pfaller MA, Doern GV, et al. Antimicrobial activity and spectrum investigation of eight broad-spectrum β-lactam drugs: A 1997 surveillance trial in 102 medical centers in the United States. Diagn Microbiol Infect Dis. 1998;30:215–228.
484. Edwards JR, Turner PJ, Laboratory data which differentiate meropenem and imipenem. Scand J Infect Dis Suppl. 1995;96:5–10.
485. Pfaller MA, Jones RN. A review of the in vitro activity of meropenem and comparative antimicrobial agents tested against 30,254 aerobic and anaerobic pathogens isolated world wide. Diagn Microbiol Infect Dis. 1997;28:157–163.
486. Edwards JR. Meropenem: A microbiological overview. J Amtimicrob Chemother. 1995;36(Suppl A):1–17.
487. Behre G, Link H, Maschmeyer G, et al. Meropenem monotherapy verus combination therapy with ceftazidime and amikacin for empirical treatment of febrile neutropenic patients. Ann Hematol. 1998;76:73–80.
488. Yamane N, Jones RN, Frei R, et al. Levofloxacin in vitro activity: Results from an international comparative study with ofloxacin and ciprofloxacin. J Chemother. 1994;6:83–91.
489. Haria M, Lamb HM. Trovafloxacin. Drugs. 1997;54:435–445.
490. Visalli MA, Bajaksouzian S, Jacobs MR, Appelbaum PC. Synergistic activity of trovafloxacin with other agents against gram-positive and -negative organisms. Diagn Microbiol Infect Dis. 1998;30:61–64.

Chapter 208

Stenotrophomonas maltophilia and *Burkholderia cepacia*

SHAHE VARTIVARIAN
ELIAS ANAISSIE

Stenotrophomonas maltophilia and *Burkholderia cepacia* have emerged as important causes of morbidity and mortality in hospitalized patients, particularly in intensive care units and cancer centers.[1, 2] These opportunistic pathogens share several significant characteristics: low intrinsic virulence, resistance to many commonly used antimicrobial or disinfectant agents, and an ability to grow in a wide range of microenvironments frequently found in the hospital setting, including water.[3–7]

DESCRIPTION

S. maltophilia, previously named *Pseudomonas*, was transferred to the genus *Xanthomonas (X. maltophilia)* in 1983 and a decade later was reclassified as the single species of the new genus *Stenotrophomonas*.[8] *B. cepacia* was previously known as *Pseudomonas multivorans* and *Pseudomonas kingii* and has now been classified as a new genus, *Burkholderia*.[9]

S. maltophilia and *B. cepacia* are motile, free-living, nonfermentative, gram-negative aerobic bacilli with multitrichous polar flagella. *S. maltophilia* grows readily on most bacteriologic media, typically appearing pale yellow or lavender-green when grown on blood agar. Preliminary identification may be facilitated by its ammonia-like odor. Most clinical isolates are oxidase-negative and use maltose and usually dextrose and xylose.[10] *S. maltophilia* may produce extracellular deoxyribonuclease on selected media, can hydrolyze esculin and orthonitrophenyl-β-D-galactopyranoside, and produces catalase and a strong acid reaction in oxidation-fermentation in maltose medium. Most strains require methionine for growth. *S. maltophilia* can occasionally be mistaken for *B. cepacia*.[11]

The color and shape of *B. cepacia* colonies vary with the individual strain and the culture medium used. Clinical material should be incubated at 37°C for up to 72 hours and then at room temperature for 5 days, preferably in carbon dioxide. Because of the difficulty in isolating this organism, selective media have been developed.[12] However, even cultures using selective media have a low sensitivity. *B. cepacia* may also resemble *Pseudomonas gladioli*; thus, clinical isolates of the latter organism should not be dismissed as contaminants.[13]

VIRULENCE FACTORS AND PATHOGENESIS

S. maltophilia and *B. cepacia* are opportunistic organisms. Potential virulence factors include resistance to most antimicrobial agents,[5, 14–16] adherence to plastic materials,[17–20] and exoenzymes including elastase and gelatinase.[5, 17, 21–24] *B. cepacia* also displays adhesin, a mucin-binding protein[25]; resists nonoxidative neutrophil killing[26]; and produces siderophores, hemolysin, and exopolysaccharide.[22, 23] One epidemic strain of *B. cepacia* was shown to have giant cable pili, which mediate attachment to respiratory mucin.[27] This strain contains a hybrid of two insertion sequences, and a 1.4-kilobase open reading frame, which have been associated with transmissible strains only.[28] Infections by *S. maltophilia* result from any combination of the following events: prolonged hospitalization, especially in intensive care units[4, 18, 29]; administration of broad-spectrum antibiotics[1, 2, 5, 18, 19, 30–33]; malignancy, particularly if associated with immunosuppression[1, 5, 18, 34–39]; a break in the mucocutaneous defense barriers, including instrumentation (intubation or tracheostomy, genitourinary catheterization, peritoneal dialysis, central venous catheterization)[19, 29, 40–42] and foreign body implantation[43–45]; intravenous drug abuse[46]; development of structural abnormalities[1, 18, 19, 47, 48]; and a failure of the host's inflammatory response (such as neutropenia) to eliminate the invading organisms.[1, 18, 34–39] Prolonged hospitalization, administration of any broad-spectrum antibiotic (not only imipenem), catheterization or use of other foreign devices, and trauma predispose to colonization; administration of inactive antibiotics, presence of structural abnormalities such as obstruction and neutropenia facilitate progression from colonization to infection.[1, 4, 5, 18, 19, 32, 40, 49] Conversely, patients with cystic fibrosis,[13, 50] chronic granulomatous disease,[26] and sickle cell hemoglobinopathies[51] appear to be predisposed to infection by *B. cepacia.*

EPIDEMIOLOGY

S. maltophilia and *B. cepacia* are ubiquitous in the environment and can be found in water, soil, plants, animal sources, and decaying organic material.[21, 52–56] In the hospital setting, both pathogens have been recovered from tap and distilled water, nebulizers, water baths, dialysis machines, contaminated disinfectants, solutions and intravenous fluids, catheters, blood gas analyzers, thermometers, ventilator temperature sensors, and intra-aortic balloon pumps.[6, 29, 34, 55–58]

Transmission of nosocomial *S. maltophilia* infection has been associated with contaminated disinfectant solutions,[59] sustained-release ganciclovir implants,[60] or hospital water.[40, 59] A microbial relatedness study revealed that almost a third of the patients' isolates shared the same serotype with those recovered from water-related structures of a cancer center, suggesting that some of the *S. maltophilia* nosocomial infections may have been acquired from the water system.[40] Other outbreaks did not evaluate environmental strains to ascertain whether a single organism from a common source was responsible for some of these infections.[61–63] Techniques to investigate the nosocomial transmission rely on serotyping,[64–66] bacteriocin susceptibility and production,[67] multilocus enzyme electrophoresis,[27, 68, 69] biotyping,[70] ribotyping, pulsed-field gel electrophoresis, and random amplified polymorphic DNA technique.[4, 71–75] Epidemiologic studies of *S. maltophilia* reveal considerable genomic diversity, supporting the view that naturally occurring *S. maltophilia* isolates are selected by antibiotic pressure and that outbreaks of infection are more likely to result from exposure to multiple environmental strains than from cross-infection.[40, 76] However, cross-infections between patients, transmitted in one instance on the hands of health care workers, have been demonstrated.[52, 73, 74] *S. maltophilia* can readily colonize the respiratory and even uncommonly the gastrointestinal tracts of humans.[77, 78]

Transmission of *B. cepacia* to cystic fibrosis patients by close contact with colonized individuals is well documented[71, 72, 79] and may possibly be reduced by segregating patients at risk, a decision that can be psychologically devastating.[35, 80, 81] Environmental transmission (with tremendous clonal diversity) is also established and occurs via exposure to respiratory equipment, disinfectants, and water supplies.[35, 57–59, 77, 78, 81]

CLINICAL MANIFESTATIONS

S. maltophilia and *B. cepacia* cause a wide variety of infections ranging from superficial to deep-seated and disseminated infections. The respiratory system is the most common site of isolation of both pathogens, but the majority of isolates represent colonization rather than infection. Pneumonia may be complicated by bacteremia, septic shock, and multiple organ dysfunction syndrome.[5, 44, 82–84] In *S. maltophilia* pneumonia, the organism reaches the lungs by one of two routes: the respiratory route, likely as a result of aspiration of contaminated oropharyngeal secretions or direct aerosolization (primary pneumonia), and the hematogenous route (secondary pneumonia). We think that even in cases of secondary pneumonia, aspiration may play an important role given the rarity of an extrapulmonary source of infection and the documentation of prior oropharyngeal colonization in some of these patients. Conversely, a local predisposing factor such as tumor is usually present in primary pneumonia. *S. maltophilia* pneumonia is associated with a high mortality, particularly when associated with bacteremia or obstruction. Histologic findings include intra-alveolar hemorrhage with fibrin deposits and dense colonies of *S. maltophilia,* occasional septal necrosis, and minimal or absent inflammatory infiltrates (our observation). The initial chest radiographs commonly demonstrate unilateral lobar or patchy infiltrates, which often progress bilaterally. In other cases, the infiltrates can be bilateral and multinodular and at times associated with *S. maltophilia* sinusitis (our observations). The multinodular nature of infiltrates or the presence of sinopulmonary infection can mimic fungal infections in neutropenic patients. Occasionally, *S. maltophilia* and fungal pneumonias can occur concomitantly in the same patient.

Patients with cystic fibrosis and those with chronic granulomatous disease to a lesser degree are vulnerable to *B. cepacia* pneumonia.[81] Three distinct clinical patterns occur in the setting of cystic fibrosis: (1) chronic asymptomatic carriage; (2) progressive deterioration over months with recurrent fever, weight loss, and repeated hospital admissions; and (3) rapid, at times fatal deterioration in previously mildly affected patients with necrotizing pneumonia and bacteremia.[54, 85, 86] Female gender, severe radiographic changes, and poor pulmonary function are associated with the latter syndrome.[54] Increased mortality has been observed during the first year after colonization with *B. cepacia*. In addition, some patients colonized with *B. cepacia* who are undergoing lung transplantation have been reported to acquire rapidly progressive pneumonia, empyema, and sepsis,[87] leading several centers to avoid lung transplantation in cystic fibrosis patients colonized with this organism. It is important to mention that the studies associating *B. cepacia* with rapid clinical deterioration may have overestimated the strength of this association. The overwhelming majority of cystic fibrosis patients colonized with *B. cepacia* show little change in clinical picture.

A major increase in the incidence of *S. maltophilia* and *B. cepacia* blood stream infections has been observed during the last 2 decades.[34, 40, 44, 88] The clinical spectrum of bacteremia ranges from nearly asymptomatic to fulminant septic shock and is occasionally associated with disseminated intravascular coagulation.[18, 61] The portal of entry in more than half of *S. maltophilia* bacteremic episodes is unknown. The most common identifiable portal of entry is the respiratory tract.[89] The central venous catheter may occasionally lead to bacteremia.[89] Ecthyma gangrenosum is an unusual cutaneous complication of *B. cepacia* and *S. maltophilia* bacteremia.[18, 90]

S. maltophilia infections of skin and soft tissue include localized wound infections and primary or metastatic cellulitis. Localized wound infections result from trauma, surgery, or burns.[18, 91–93] Primary cellulitis may develop around catheter insertion sites (venous or peritoneal dialysis catheters, jejunostomy tubes, and suprapubic catheters) and may result in bacteremia.[18, 44, 94] Metastatic cellulitis following *S. maltophilia* bacteremia can mimic disseminated fungal infections, presenting as nodular skin lesions associated with surrounding and distant cellulitis.[18] The nodular lesions range in size from 0.5 × 1 cm to 5 × 6 cm and are hard, nonfluctuant, tender, and characterized by warmth and a violaceous erythema of the overlying skin.[18] These lesions involve the extremities, scalp, back, and abdomen in decreasing order of frequency.[18, 78, 95] Histologic findings of the nodular lesions include intense inflammatory cell infiltrate, minimal necrosis, and rarely organisms. *B. cepacia* skin and soft tissue infection is more frequently seen in patients with burns[96] and surgical wounds.[97] "Foot rot," a necrotic dermatitis of the foot, has been reported in normal hosts subjected to prolonged immersion in swamp water during military exercise.[98]

The urinary tract is a frequent site of isolation of *S. maltophilia*, often as a colonizer.[1, 40, 93, 95, 99, 100] The majority of these patients have a genitourinary malignancy and a urinary catheter in place. Infected patients can additionally be neutropenic or can have structural abnormalities of the urinary tract, including obstruction, vesicovaginal fistulas, and ileal conduits. Infected patients commonly present with fever and chills and may experience septic shock.[1, 61] The majority of the infections in cancer patients are severe and complicated; however, response to therapy is prompt.[1] Genitourinary tract infection with *B. cepacia* develops after urethral instrumentation, transrectal prostate biopsy, or through exposure to contaminated solutions.[101] *S. maltophilia* has also been recognized as a contaminant of contact lenses and lens care systems and has been reported to cause bacterial keratitis, acute conjunctivitis, infection of scleral buckles, dacryocystitis, and preseptal cellulitis.[102] Risk factors for ocular infections include corneal transplantation, keratoplasty, soft contact lens wear and eyedropper use, herpes simplex virus keratitis, Stevens-Johnson syndrome, and toxic epidermal necrosis.[102, 103]

Other rare infections with *S. maltophilia* and *B. cepacia* include meningitis[20, 104, 105]; endocarditis; pericarditis[106]; oropharyngeal lesions[18]; cholangitis following biliary tract instrumentation[19]; peritonitis in patients undergoing peritoneal dialysis[94, 107–109]; abdominal, periurethral, and scrotal abscesses[104]; and septic arthritis,[41, 110] especially after intravenous drug abuse or trauma.[111] Pseudobacteremia has also been reported.[112–114]

TREATMENT

Therapy for infections with these pathogens is challenging because of their resistance to most antimicrobial agents and the variable antimicrobial susceptibility of different strains.[15, 115–124] In addition, in the case of *S. maltophilia*, guidance by results of susceptibility testing may be misleading because there is often poor correlation within these tests as well as with time kill studies and treatment outcome.[1, 120, 121] Mechanisms of antimicrobial resistance include outer membrane impermeability,[125, 126] constitutive overproduction of β-lactamase and other inactivating enzymes,[73, 118, 125, 127, 128] alterations of antimicrobial target sites,[127] development of bypass pathways around antimicrobial targets or active efflux of antibiotic,[16, 129, 130] and through plasmids.[127, 130] The mechanism of resistance to quinolones is presumably related to decreased permeability as a result of outer membrane protein changes.[14, 131]

Trimethoprim-sulfamethoxazole remains, in the absence of formal therapeutic studies, the drug of choice for treating infections caused by *S. maltophilia.* It is consistently the most active agent in vitro, although development of resistance has been reported.[15, 44, 99, 115, 132] Ticarcillin-clavulanate is active in vitro against *S. maltophilia*, and anecdotal reports suggest that it could be clinically useful.[1, 15, 18, 117] Minocycline has excellent in vitro activity[115]; however, clinical experience with this agent is limited.[133] The role of newer quinolones also needs to be assessed, particularly when agents such as trovafloxacin are used in combination with other antibiotics.[115, 116] About 30% of cancer patients with *S. maltophilia* infections die, with a third of these deaths occurring before initiation of appropriate treatment (our observations). The similarity of some *S. maltophilia* infections to fungal infections may result in delaying therapy. Also, the resistance of this organism to the antibiotics commonly used in the patient population at risk may further delay appropriate treatment. Predictors of poor outcome by univariate analysis include hematologic malignancy, transplantation, immunosuppressive therapy, neutropenia, severity of score of greater than 4,[31] and additionally severe shock or multiorgan failure, disseminated infection, and inappropriate or delayed appropriate therapy.[48] Multivariate analysis has shown that the presence of severe shock at onset of infection and delay in appropriate therapy are the significant predictors of poor outcome.[48] Therefore, we recommend maintaining a high index of suspicion for this infection among patients at risk and initiating empirical use of trimethoprim-sulfamethoxazole and ticarcillin-clavulanate in combination. This recommendation is based on the variable susceptibility of *S. maltophilia* strains, the presence of trimethoprim-sulfamethoxazole–resistant isolates, the lack of cidal activity of trimethoprim-sulfamethoxazole,[115] and the potential for emergence of resistance during therapy.[115, 119] We also recommend the use of these antimicrobials at their highest tolerable dosages (15–20 mg/kg/day of trimethoprim for trimethoprim-sulfamethoxazole and 3.1 g every 4 hours of ticarcillin-clavulanate), because a sizable number of isolates are inhibited at or close to concentrations equivalent to susceptibility breakpoints.[115] A combined surgical-medical treatment can be useful in the setting of infected foci (central venous or peritoneal catheter, Ommaya reservoir) or in the presence of obstruction or structural abnormalities.[1, 19, 20, 48]

Antimicrobial agents that are effective against *B. cepacia* in vitro include trimethoprim-sulfamethoxazole, chloramphenicol, and minocycline. Other potentially active agents include the ureidopenicillins, third-generation cephalosporins, and quinolones.[134] The new carbapenems, in particular meropenem, may offer good activity, although clinical experience is limited.[135] Unfortunately, the activity of antibiotics against strains from patients with cystic fibrosis is greatly diminished, and clearance of these agents is increased in this setting. Thus, serum levels should be monitored to ensure adequate dosing.[136] Whether combination therapy may help to minimize the likelihood of resistance remains to be determined. Because of the poor results with antimicrobial therapy, immunotherapy is being pursued with specific *B. cepacia* antigens.[137] A high severity of illness score, colonization, poor nutritional status, and possibly female gender and older age are associated with an adverse outcome in patients with *B. cepacia* infection.[138]

PREVENTION

Strategies aimed at preventing infection with these multidrug-resistant pathogens include (1) a decrease in the risk of colonization through appropriate antibiotic use; (2) interruption of transmission by strict hand washing and institution of barrier techniques for colonized or infected patients; (3) surveillance among high-risk patients and identification and elimination of potential nosocomial reservoirs such as the water system or contaminated solutions or equipment. Education of health care workers is a cornerstone of such preventive measures.[43, 81, 101, 139–141]

REFERENCES

1. Vartivarian SE, Papadakis KA, Anaissie EJ. *Stenotrophomonas (Xanthomonas) maltophilia* urinary tract infection: A disease that is usually severe and complicated. Arch Intern Med. 1996;156:433–435.
2. Holmes A, Jiang RJ, Sun L, et al. Emergence of epidemic strains of *B. cepacia* involving both cystic fibrosis and non-cystic fibrosis populations. Abstract J32. Proceedings of the 36th Interscience Conference on Antimicrobial Agents and Chemotherapy. Washington, DC: American Society for Microbiology; 1996:224.
3. Talon D, Bailey P, Leprat R, et al. Typing of hospital strains of *Xanthomonas maltophilia* by pulsed-field gel electrophoresis. J Hosp Infect. 1994;27:209–217.
4. Marshall WF, Keating MR, Anhalt JP, Steckelberg JM. *Xanthomonas maltophilia*: An emerging nosocomial pathogen. Mayo Clin Proc. 1989;64:1097–1104.
5. Spencer RC. The emergence of epidemic, multiple-antibiotic-resistant *Stenotrophomonas (Xanthomonas) maltophilia* and *Burkholderia (Pseudomonas) cepacia*. J Hosp Infect. 1995;30(Suppl):453–464.
6. Carson LA, Favero MS, Bond WW, Peterson NJ. Morphological, biochemical, and growth characteristics of *Pseudomonas cepacia* from distilled water. Appl Microbiol. 1973;25:476.
7. Wilcox CM, Waites K, Brookings ES. Use of sterile compared with tap water in gastrointestinal endoscopic procedures. Am J Infect Control. 1996;24:407–410.
8. Palleroni NJ, Bradbury JF. *Stenotrophomonas*, a new bacterial genus for *Xanthomonas maltophilia* (Hugh 1980) Swings et al 1983. Int J Syst Bacteriol. 1993;43:606–609.
9. Yabuuchi E, Kosako Y, Oyaizu H, et al. Proposal of *Burkholderia gen. Nov.* and transfer of seven species of the genus *Pseudomonas* homology group II to the new genus, with the type species *B. cepacia* (Palleroni and Holmes 1981) *comb. Nov.* Microbiol Immunol. 1992;36:1251–1275.
10. Clark WA, Hollis DG, Weaver RE, Riley P. Identification of unusual pathogenic gram negative aerobic and facultative aerobic bacteria. Atlanta, Ga: Centers for Disease Control, 1985.
11. Burdge DR, Noble MA, Campbell ME, et al. *Xanthomonas maltophilia* misidentified as *Pseudomonas cepacia* in cultures of sputum from patients with cystic fibrosis: A diagnostic pitfall with major clinical implications. Clin Infect Dis. 1995;20:445–448.
12. Welch DF, Muszynski MJ, Pai CH, et al. Selective and differential medium for recovery of *Pseudomonas cepacia* from the respiratory tracts of patients with cystic fibrosis. J Clin Microbiol. 1987;25:1730–1734.
13. Simpson IN, Finaly J, Winstanley DJ, et al. Multi-resistant isolates possessing characteristics of both *B. cepacia* and *B. gladioli* from patients with cystic fibrosis. J Antimicrob Chemother. 1994;34:353–361.
14. Lesco-Bornet M, Pierre J, Sarkis-Karam D, et al. Susceptibility of *Xanthomonas maltophilia* to 6 quinolones and study of outer membrane proteins in resistant mutants selected *in vitro*. Antimicrob Agents Chemother. 1992;36:669–671.
15. Smit WJ, Boquest AL, Geddes JE, Tosolini FA. The antibiotic susceptibilities of *Xanthomonas maltophilia* and their relation to clinical management. Pathology. 1994;26:321–324.
16. Parr TRJ, Moore RA, Moore LV, Hancock RE. Role of porins in intrinsic antibiotic resistance of *Pseudomonas cepacia*. Antimicrob Agents Chemother. 1987;31:121–123.
17. Kerr KG, Anson JJ, Patmore R, Smith G. Intravenous line infections. J Hosp Infect. 1994;26:73–75.
18. Vartivarian SE, Papadakis KA, Palacios JA, et al. Mucocutaneous and soft tissue infections caused by *Xanthomonas maltophilia*: A new spectrum. Ann Intern Med. 1994;121:969–973.
19. Papadakis KA, Vartivarian SE, Vassilaki ME, Anaissie EJ: *Stenotrophomonas maltophilia*: An unusual cause of biliary sepsis. Clin Infect Dis. 1995;21:1032–1034.
20. Papadakis KA, Vartivarian SE, Vassilaki ME, Anaissie EJ. *Stenotrophomonas maltophilia* meningitis. Report of two cases and review of the literature. J Neurosurg. 1997;87:106–108.
21. Von Graevenitz A. *Acinetobacter, Alcaligenes, Moraxella*, and other non-fermentive gram-negative bacteria. In: Murray PR, Baron EJ, Pfaller MA, eds. Manual of Clinical Microbiology. 6th ed. Washington DC: American Society for Microbiology; 1995:522.
22. Nelson JW, Butler SL, Kreig D, Govan JR. Virulence factors of *Burkholderia cepacia*. FEMS Immunol Med Microbiol. 1994;8:89–97.
23. Vasil ML, Kreig DP, Kuhns JS, et al. Molecular analysis of hemolytic and phospholipase C activities of *Pseudomonas cepacia*. Infect Immunol. 1990;58:4020–4029.
24. Bottone EJ, Reitano M, Janda JM, et al. *Pseudomonas maltophilia* exoenzymes activity as correlate in the pathogenesis of ecthyma gangrenosum. J Clin Microbiol. 1986;24:995–997.
25. Sajjan US, Corey M, Karmali MA, Forstner JF. Binding of *Pseudomonas cepacia* to human intestinal mucin and respiratory mucin from patients with cystic fibrosis. J Clin Invest. 1992;89:648.
26. Speert DP, Bond M, Woodman RC, Curnutte JT. Infection with *Pseudomonas cepacia* in chronic granulomatous disease. Role of nonoxidative killing by neutrophils in host defense. J Infect Dis. 1994;170:1524–1531.
27. Johnson WM, Tyler SD, Rozee KR. Linkage analysis of geographic and clinical clusters in *Pseudomonas cepacia* infections by multilocus enzyme electrophoresis and ribotyping. J Clin Microbiol. 1994;32:924–930.
28. Mahenthiralingam E, Simpson DA, Speert DP. Identification and characterization of a novel DNA marker associated with epidemic *Burkholderia cepacia* strains recovered from patients with cystic fibrosis. J Clin Microbiol. 1997;35:808–816.
29. Conly JM, Klass L, Larson L. P*seudomonas cepacia* colonization and infection in intensive care units. Can Med Assoc J. 1986;134:363.
30. Elting LS, Khardori N, Bodey GP, Fainstein V. Nosocomial infection caused by *Xanthomonas maltophilia*: A case-control study of predisposing factors. Infect Control Hosp Epidemiol. 1990;11:134–138.
31. Muder RR, Harris AP, Muller S, et al. Bacteremia due to *Stenotrophomonas*

(Xanthomonas) maltophilia: A prospective, multicenter study of 91 episodes. Clin Infect Dis. 1996;22:508–512.
32. Vancouwenberghe CJ, Farver TB, Cohen SH. Risk factors associated with isolation of *Stenotrophomonas (Xanthomonas) maltophilia* in clinical specimens. Infect Control Hosp Epidemiol. 1997;18:316–321.
33. Watanabe K, Aritomi T, Toyoshima H, et al. Pathogenic bacteria isolated from the sputum of the patients with pulmonary emphysema. Kansenshogaku Zasshi. 1995;69:1251–1259.
34. Pegues DA, Carson LA, Anderson RL, et al. Outbreak of *Pseudomonas cepacia* bacteremia in oncology patients. Clin Infect Dis. 1993;16:407.
35. Bosshammer J, Fielder B, Gudowis P, et al. Comparative hygienic surveillance of contamination with pseudomonads in a cystic fibrosis ward over a 4-year period. J Hosp Infect. 1995;31:261–274.
36. Hamill RJ, Houston ED, Georgiou PR, et al. An outbreak of *Burkholderia* (formerly *Pseudomonas*) *cepacia* respiratory tract colonization and infection associated with nebulized albuterol therapy. Ann Intern Med. 1995;122:762–766.
37. Aoun M, Van der Auwera P, Devleeshouwer C, et al. Bacteraemia caused by non-*aeruginosa Pseudomonas* species in a cancer center. J Hosp Infect. 1992;22:307–316.
38. Martino R, Martínez C, Pericas R, et al. Bacteremia due to glucose non-fermenting gram-negative bacilli in patients with hematological neoplasias and solid tumors. Eur J Clin Microbiol Infect Dis. 1996;15:610–615.
39. Krcmery V Jr, Pichna P, Oravcova E, et al. *Stenotrophomonas maltophilia* bacteraemia in cancer patients: Report on 31 cases. J Hosp Infect. 1996;34:75–77.
40. Khardori N, Elting L, Wong E, et al. Nosocomial infections due to *Xanthomonas maltophilia (Pseudomonas maltophilia)* in patients with cancer. Rev Infect Dis. 1990;12:997–1003.
41. Papadakis KA, Vartivarian SE, Vassilaki ME, Anaissie EJ. Septic prepatellar bursitis caused by *Stenotrophomonas maltophilia*. Clin Infect Dis. 1996;22:388–389.
42. Roilides E, Butler KM, Husson RN, et al. *Pseudomonas* infections in children with human immunodeficiency virus infection. Pediatr Infect Dis J. 1992;11:547–553.
43. Villarino ME, Stevens LE, Schable B, Mayers G, et al. Risk factors for epidemic *Xanthomonas maltophilia* infection/colonization in intensive care unit patients. Infect Control Hosp Epidemiol. 1992;13:201–206.
44. Elting LS, Bodey GP. Septicemia due to *Xanthomonas* species and non-*aeruginosa Pseudomonas* species: Increasing incidence of catheter-related infections. Medicine. 1990;69:296–306.
45. Phillips I, Eykyn S, Curtis MA, et al. *Pseudomonas cepacia* (*multivorans*) septicemia in an intensive care unit. Lancet. 1971;1:1050–1051.
46. Noriega ER, Rubinstein E, Simberkoff MS, et al. Subacute and acute endocarditis due to *Pseudomonas cepacia* in heroin addicts. Am J Med. 1975;59:29–36.
47. Papadakis KA, Vartivarian SE, Anaissie EJ, Samonis G. *Xanthomonas maltophilia* bacteremia in cancer patients: An analysis of 44 episodes (Abstract). Clin Infect Dis. 1994;19:588.
48. Vartivarian SE, Papadakis K, Anaissie EJ. Outcome of *Stenotrophomonas (Xanthomonas) maltophilia* infections in cancer patients. Presented at the 37th Interscience Conference on Antimicrobial Agents and Chemotherapy, Toronto, Ontario, Canada, Sept 28–Oct 1, 1997.
49. Carmeli Y, Samore MH. Comparison of treatment with imipenem vs. ceftazidime as a predisposing factor for nosocomial acquisition of *Stenotrophomonas maltophilia*: A historical cohort study. Clin Infect Dis. 1997;24:1131–1134.
50. Goldmann DA, Klinger JD. *Pseudomonas cepacia*: Biology, mechanisms of virulence, epidemiology. J Pediatr. 1986;108:806.
51. Berry MD, Asmar BI. *Pseudomonas cepacia* bacteremia in children with sickle cell hemoglobinopathies. Pediatr Infect Dis J. 1991;10:696–699.
52. Laing FPY, Ramotar K, Read RR, et al. Molecular epidemiology of *Xanthomonas maltophilia* colonization and infection in the hospital environment. J Clin Microbiol. 1995;33:513–518.
53. Gilardi GL. *Pseudomonas cepacia*: Culture and laboratory identification. Lab Management. 1983;21:29–32.
54. Tablan OC, Chorba TL, Schidlow DV, et al. *Pseudomonas cepacia* colonization in patients with cystic fibrosis: Risk factors and clinical outcome. J Pediatr. 1985;107:382–387.
55. Oie S, Kamiya A. Microbial contamination of brushes used for preoperative shaving. J Hosp Infect. 1992;21:103–110.
56. Bassett DC, Stokes KJ, Thomas WR. Wound infection with *Pseudomonas multivorans*. A water-borne contaminant of disinfectant solutions. Lancet. 1970;1:1188–1191.
57. Berthelot P, Grattard F, Mahul P, et al. Ventilator temperature sensor: An unusual source of *Pseudomonas cepacia* in nosocomial infection. J Hosp Infect. 1993;25:33.
58. Hutchinson GR, Parker S, Pryor JA, et al. Home-use nebulizers: A potential primary source of *B. cepacia* and other colistin-resistant, gram negative bacteria in patients with cystic fibrosis. J Clin Microbiol. 1996;34:584–587.
59. Wishart MM, Riley TV. Infection with *Pseudomonas maltophilia* hospital outbreak due to contaminated disinfectant. Med J Aust. 1976;2:710–712.
60. Chen S, Stroh EM, Wald K, Jalkh A. *Xanthomonas maltophilia* endophthalmitis after implantation of sustained-release ganciclovir. Am J Ophthalmol. 1992;114:772–773.
61. Gilardi GL. Infrequently encountered *Pseudomonas* species causing infection in humans. Ann Intern Med. 1972;77:211–215.
62. Yao JD, Conly JM, Krajden M. Molecular typing of *Stenotrophomonas (Xanthomonas) maltophilia* by DNA macrorestriction analysis and random amplified polymorphic DNA analysis. J Clin Microbiol. 1995;33:2195–2198.
63. Fabe C, Rodriguez P, Cony-Makhoul P, et al. Molecular typing by pulsed field gel electrophoresis of *Stenotrophomonas maltophilia* isolated in a department of hematology. Pathol Biol. 1996;44:435–441.
64. Straus DC, Woods DE, Lonon MK, Garner CW. The importance of extracellular antigens in *Pseudomonas cepacia* infections. J Med Microbiol. 1988;26:269–280.
65. Schable B, Rhoden DL, Jarvis WR, Miller JM. Prevalence of serotypes of *Xanthomonas maltophilia* from worldwide sources. Epidemiol Infect. 1992;108:337–341.
66. Schable B, Rhoden DL, Hugh R, et al. Serological classification of *Xanthomonas maltophilia* based on heat stable O antigens. J Clin Microbiol. 1989;27:1011–1014.
67. Govan JR, Harris G. Typing of *Pseudomonas cepacia* by bacteriocin susceptibility and production. J Clin Microbiol. 1985;22:490–494.
68. Karpati F, Jonasson J. Polymerase chain reaction for the detection of *Pseudomonas aeruginosa, Stenotrophomonas maltophilia* and *Burkholderia cepacia* in sputum of patients with cystic fibrosis. Mol Cell Probes. 1996;10:397–403.
69. Schable B, Villarino ME, Favero MS, Miller JM. Application of multilocus enzyme electrophoresis to epidemiologic investigations of *Xanthomonas maltophilia.* Infect Control Hosp Epidemiol. 1991;12:163–167.
70. Richard C, Monetil H, Megraud F, et al. Caracteres phenotypiques de 100 souches de *Pseudomonas cepacia*. Proposition d'un schema de biovars. Am Biol Clin (Paris). 1981;39:9–15.
71. Paul ML, Pegler MAM, Benn RAV. Molecular epidemiology of *B. cepacia* in two Australian cystic fibrosis centres. J Hosp Infect. 1998;38:19–26.
72. Segonds C, Bingen E, Couetdic G, et al. Genotypic analysis of *B. cepacia* isolates from 13 French cystic fibrosis centers. J Clin Microbiol. 1997;35:2055–2060.
73. Bingen EH, Denamur E, Lambert-Zechovsky NY, et al. DNA restriction fragment length polymorphism differentiates crossed from independent infections in nosocomial *Xanthomonas maltophilia* bacteremia. J Clin Microbiol. 1991;29:1348–1350.
74. Davin-Regli A, Bollet C, Auffray JP, et al. Use of random amplified polymorphic DNA for epidemiological typing of *Stenotrophomonas maltophilia.* J Hosp Infect. 1996;32:39–50.
75. Marty N. Epidemiological typing of *Stenotrophomonas maltophilia*. J Hosp Infect. 1997;36:261–266.
76. Gerner-Smidt P, Bruun B, Arpi M, Schmidt J. Diversity of nosocomial *Xanthomonas maltophilia (Stenotrophomonas maltophilia)* as determined by ribotyping. Eur J Clin Microbiol Infect Dis. 1995;14:137–140.
77. Von Graevenitz A, Bucher C. Isolation of *Pseudomonas maltophilia* from human stools with thienamycin. Zbl Bakt Hyg I Abt Orig. 1983;54:403–404.
78. Kerr KG, Corps CM, Hawkey PM. Infections due to *Xanthomonas maltophilia* in patients with hematologic malignancy (Letter). Rev Infect Dis. 1991;13:762.
79. Lipuma JJ, Marks-Austin KA, Holsclaw DS Jr, et al. Inapparent transmission of *Pseudomonas (Burkholderia) cepacia* among patients with cystic fibrosis. Pediatr Infect Dis J. 1994;13:716–719.
80. Thomassen MJ, Demko CA, Doershuk CF, et al. *Pseudomonas cepacia*: Decrease in colonization in patients with cystic fibrosis. Am Rev Respir Dis. 1986;134:669–671.
81. Burdge DR, Nakielna EM, Noble MA. Case-control and vector studies of nosocomial acquisition of *Pseudomonas cepacia* in adult patients with cystic fibrosis. Infect Control Hosp Epidemiol. 1993;14:127–130.
82. Fujita J, Negayama K, Xu G, et al. Nosocomial respiratory infection caused by *Xanthomonas maltophilia* in immunocompromised hosts. Nippon Kyobu Shikkan Gakkai Zasshi. 1994;32:638–643.
83. Sarkar TK, Gilardi G, Aguam AS, et al: Primary *Pseudomonas maltophilia* infection of the lung. Postgrad Med. 1979;65:253–256.
84. Jarvis WR, Olson D, Tablan O, Martone WJ. The epidemiology of nosocomial *Pseudomonas cepacia* infections: Endemic infections. Eur J Epidemiol. 1987;3:233–236.
85. Isles A, Maclusky I, Corey M, et al. *Pseudomonas cepacia* infection in cystic fibrosis: An emerging pathogen. J Pediatr. 1984;14:206–210.
86. Rosenstein BJ, Hall DE. Pneumonia and septicemia due to *Pseudomonas cepacia* in a patient with cystic fibrosis. Johns Hopkins Med J. 1980;147:188–189.
87. Snell GI, De Hoyos A, Kradjen M, et al. *Pseudomonas cepacia* in lung transplant recipients with cystic fibrosis. Chest. 1993;103:466–471.
88. Rutala WA, Weber DJ, Thomann CA, et al. An outbreak of *Pseudomonas cepacia* associated with a contaminated intra-aortic balloon pump. J Thorac Cardiovasc Surg. 1988;96:157–161.
89. Jang TN, Wang PD, Wang LS, et al. *Xanthomonas maltophilia* bacteremia: An analysis of 32 cases. J Formos Med Assoc. 1992;91:1170–1176.
90. Mandell IN, Feiner HD, Price NM, Simberkoff M. *Pseudomonas cepacia* endocarditis and ecthyma gangrenosum. Arch Dermatol. 1977;113:199–202.
91. Baltimore RS, Jenson HB. Puncture wound osteochondritis of the foot caused by *Pseudomonas maltophilia*. Pediatr Infect Dis. 1994;9:143–144.
92. Pedersen MM, Marso E, Pickett MJ. Nonfermentative bacilli associated with man: III. Pathogenicity and antibiotic susceptibility. Am J Clin Pathol. 1970;54:178–192.
93. Holmes B, Lapage SP, Easterling BG. Distribution in clinical material and identification of *Pseudomonas maltophilia*. J Clin Pathol. 1979;32:66–72.
94. Taber TE, Hegeman TF, York SM, et al. Treatment of *Pseudomonas* infections in peritoneal dialysis patients. Perit Dial Int. 1991;11:213–216.
95. Gilardi GL: *Pseudomonas maltophilia* infections in man. Am J Clin Pathol. 1969;51:58–61.
96. Brauner A, Hfiby N, Kjartansson J, et al. *Pseudomonas cepacia* septicemia in patients with burns: Report of two cases. Scand J Infect Dis. 1985;17:63–66.

97. Sobel JD, Hashman N, Reinherz G, et al. Nosocomial *Pseudomonas cepacia* infection associated with chlorhexidine contamination. Am J Med. 1982;73:183–186.
98. Taplin D, Bassett DCJ, Mertz PM. Foot lesions associated with *Pseudomonas cepacia*. Lancet. 1971;2:568–571.
99. Morrison AJ, Hoffman KK, Wenzel RP. Associated mortality and clinical characteristics of nosocomial *Pseudomonas maltophilia* in a university hospital. J Clin Microbiol. 1986;24:52–55.
100. McDonald GR, Pernenkil R. Community-acquired *Xanthomonas maltophilia* pyelonephritis. South Med J. 1993;86:967–968.
101. Keizur JJ, Lavin B, Leidich RB. Iatrogenic urinary tract infection with *Pseudomonas cepacia* after transrectal ultrasound guided biopsy of the prostate. J Urol. 1993;149:523–526.
102. Penland RL, Wilhelmus KR. *Stenotrophomonas maltophilia* ocular infections. Arch Ophthalmol. 1996;114:433–436.
103. Bottone EJ, Madayag RM, Qureshi MN. *Acanthamoeba* keratitis: Synergies between amebic and bacterial cocontaminants in contact lens care systems as a prelude to infection. J Clin Microbiol. 1992;30:2447–2450.
104. Muder RR, Yu VL, Dummer JS, et al. Infections caused by *Pseudomonas maltophilia*: Expanding clinical spectrum. Arch Intern Med. 1987;147:1672–1674.
105. Krcmery V, Havlik J, Vicianova L. Nosocomial meningitis caused by multiply resistant *Pseudomonas cepacia*. Pediatr Infect Dis J. 1987;6:769.
106. Subbannayya K, Ramnarayan K, Shivananda PG, et al. *Pseudomonas maltophilia* endocarditis. Indian J Pathol Microbiol. 1984;27:311–315.
107. Berbari N, Johnson DH, Cunha BA. *Xanthomonas maltophilia* peritonitis in a patient undergoing peritoneal dialysis. Heart Lung. 1993;22:282–283.
108. Szeto CC, Li PK, Leung CB, et al. *Xanthomonas maltophilia* peritonitis in uremic patients receiving continuous ambulatory peritoneal dialysis. Am J Kidney Dis. 1997;29:91–95.
109. Dapena F, Selgas R, Garcia-Perea A, et al. Clinical significance of exit-site infections due to *Xanthomonas maltophilia* in CAPD patients: A comparison with *Pseudomonas* infection. Nephrol Dial Transplant. 1994;9:1774–1777.
110. Sequeira W, Jones E, Siegel ME, et al. Pyogenic infections of the pubic symphysis. Ann Intern Med. 1982;96:604–606.
111. Agger WA, Cogbill TH, Busch H Jr, et al. Wounds caused by corn-harvesting machines: An unusual source of infection due to gram-negative bacilli. Rev Infect Dis. 1986;8:927–931.
112. Semel JD, Trenholme GM, Harris AA, et al. *Pseudomonas maltophilia* pseudosepticemia. Am J Med. 1978;64:403–406.
113. Panlilio AL, Beck-Sague CM, Siegel JD, et al. Infections and pseudoinfections due to povidone-iodine solution contaminated with *Pseudomonas cepacia*. Clin Infect Dis. 1992;14:1078–1083.
114. Henderson DK, Baptist R, Parrillo J, Gill VJ. Indolent epidemic of *Pseudomonas cepacia* bacteremia and pseudobacteremia in an intensive care unit traced to a contaminated blood gas analyzer. Am J Med. 1988;84:75–81.
115. Vartivarian S, Anaissie E, Bodey G, et al. A changing pattern of susceptibility of *Xanthomonas maltophilia* to antimicrobial agents: Implications for therapy. Antimicrob Agents Chemother. 1994;38:624–627.
116. Desjardin JA, Falagas ME, McDermott L, et al. In vitro synergy between trovafloxacin or ciprofloxacin and cefoperazone, ceftazidime, ticarcillin-clavulanic acid, or trimethoprim-sulfamethoxazole against *Stenotrophomonas maltophilia*. Abstract 13:026. In: Program and abstracts of the 8th International Congress on Infectious Diseases, Boston, May 1998.
117. Metchock B, Thornsberry C. Susceptibility of *Xanthomonas (Pseudomonas) maltophilia* to antimicrobial agents: Methodological problems. Antimicrob Newslett. 1989;6:35–40.
118. Neu HC, Saha G, Chin NX. Resistance of *Xanthomonas maltophilia* to antibiotics and the effect of β-lactamase inhibitors. Diagn Microbiol Infect Dis. 1989;12:283–285.
119. Garrison MW, Anderson DE, Campbell DM, et al. *Stenotrophomonas maltophilia*: Emergence of multidrug resistant strains during therapy and in an in vitro pharmacodynamic chamber model. Antimicrob Agents Chemother. 1996;40:2859–2864.
120. Cunha BA, Qadri SM, Ueno Y, et al. Antibacterial activity of trovafloxacin against nosocomial gram-positive and gram-negative isolates. J Antimicrob Chemother. 1997;39(Suppl B):29–34.
121. Hohl P, Frei R, Aubry P. In vitro susceptibility of clinical case isolates of *Xanthomonas maltophilia*. Inconsistent correlation of agar dilution and of disk diffusion test results. Diagn Microbiol Infect Dis. 1991;14:447–450.
122. Gould IM, Milne K. In vitro pharmacodynamic studies of piperacillin/tazobactam with gentamicin and ciprofloxacin. J Antimicrob Chemother. 1997;39:53–61.
123. Fass RJ, Barnishan J, Solomon MC, Ayers LW. In vitro activities of quinolones, β-lactam, tobramycin, and trimethoprim-sulfamethoxazole against nonfermentative gram-negative bacilli. Antimicrob Agents Chemother. 1996;40:1412–1418.
124. Visalli MA, Bajaksouzian S, Jacobs MR, Appelbaum PC. Comparative activity of trovafloxacin, alone and in combination with other agents, against gram-negative nonfermentative rods. Antimicrob Agents Chemother. 1997;41:1475–1481.
125. Cullmann W. Antibiotic susceptibility and outer membrane proteins of clinical *Xanthomonas maltophilia* isolates. Chemotherapy. 1991;37:246–250.
126. Moore RA, Hancock RE. Involvement of outer membrane of *Pseudomonas cepacia* in aminoglycoside and polymixin resistance. Antimicrob Agents Chemother. 1986;30:923–926.
127. Prince A. Antibiotic resistance of *Pseudomonas* species. J Pediatr. 1986;108:830.
128. Cullmann W, Dick W. Heterogeneity of beta-lactamase production in *Pseudomonas maltophilia,* a nosocomial pathogen. Chemotherapy. 1990;36:117–126.
129. Rahmati-Bahram A, Magee JT, Jackson SK. Growth temperature-dependent variation of cell envelope lipids and antibiotic susceptibility in *Stenotrophomonas (Xanthomonas) maltophilia*. J Antimicrob Chemother. 1996;36:317–326.
130. Alonso A, Martinez JL. Multiple antibiotic resistance in *Stenotrophomonas maltophilia*. Antimicrob Agents Chemother. 1997;41:1140–1142.
131. Krcmery V, Langsadl L, Antal M, Seckarova A. Transferable amikacin and cefamandole resistance: *Pseudomonas maltophilia* and *Acinetobacter* strains as possible reservoirs of R plasmids. J Hyg Epidemiol Microbiol Immun. 1985;29:141–146.
132. Munoz JL, Garcia MI, Munoz S, et al. Activity of trimethoprim/sulfamethoxazole plus polymixin B against multiresistant *Stenotrophomonas maltophilia*. Eur J Clin Microbiol Infect Dis. 1996;15:879–882.
133. Fujita J, Yamadori I, Xu G, et al. Clinical features of *Stenotrophomonas maltophilia* pneumonia in immunocompromised patients. Respir Med. 1996;90:35–38.
134. Bhakta DR, Leader I, Jacobson R, et al. Antibacterial properties of investigational, new, and commonly used antibiotics against isolates of *Pseudomonas cepacia* isolates in Michigan. Chemotherapy. 1992;33:319–323.
135. Lewin C, Doherty C, Govan LRW. In vitro activities of meropenem. PD 127391, PD 131628, ceftazidime, chloramphenicol, co-trimoxazole and ciprofloxacin against *Pseudomonas cepacia*. Antimicrob Agents Chemother. 1993;37:123–132.
136. Gold R, Jin E, Levinson H, et al. Ceftazidime alone and in combination in patients with cystic fibrosis; lack of efficacy in treatment of severe respiratory infections caused by *Pseudomonas cepacia*. J Antimicrob Chemother. 1983;12(Suppl):331–336.
137. Burnie JP, Wardi EJ, Williamson P, et al. Defining potential targets for immunotherapy in *Burkholderia cepacia* infection. FEMS Immunol Med Microbiol. 1995;10:157–164.
138. Maningo E, Watanakunakorn C. *Xanthomonas maltophilia* and *Pseudomonas cepacia* in lower respiratory tracts of patients in critical care units. J Infect. 1995;31:89–92.
139. Schoch PE, Cunha BA. *Pseudomonas maltophilia*. Infect Control. 1987;8:169–172.
140. Govan JR. *B. cepacia* in cystic fibrosis. N Engl J Med. 1995;332:819–820.
141. Mathenthiralingam E, Campbell M, Speert DP, et al. *B. cepacia* in cystic fibrosis. N Engl J Med. 1995;332:820–821.

Chapter 209

Acinetobacter Species

DAVID M. ALLEN
BARRY J. HARTMAN

Bacteria that constitute the genus *Acinetobacter* were originally identified in the first decade of the 20th century. However, it was not until the advent of modern infection control that its role as a ubiquitous opportunistic pathogen was appreciated. During the last decade, an improved understanding of the microbiology, taxonomy, and ecology of *Acinetobacter* has emerged. Current issues of clinical relevance include *Acinetobacter* speciation, evolving antimicrobial resistance, and appropriate therapy.

HISTORY AND MICROBIOLOGY

The genus *Acinetobacter* has had a colorful taxonomic history. Before the 1970s, *Acinetobacter* was frequently misidentified owing to an absence of distinguishing features. Subsequent use of transformation and nutritional studies defined the genus *Acinetobacter* and placed it within the family Neisseriaceae.[1]

Historically, rediscoveries of this ubiquitous organism led to the creation of numerous genera with resultant taxonomic chaos. Probably first described in 1908 as *Diplococcus mucosus*, *Acinetobacter* was initially identified by the absence of common characteristics: no color, nonmotile, unable to reduce nitrates, and nonfermenting.[2] The lack of distinctive characteristics was a driving force in the evolving nomenclature of the day: *Micrococcus* (small), *Mima* (mimics), *Achromobacter* (colorless), *Acinetobacter* (motionless), and *anitratus* (nitrate-nonreducing). In the 1930s and 1940s, while attempting to organize *Neisseria*-like organisms morphologically, De Bord proposed a new tribe, Mimeae, to encompass these organisms.[3] Later, Brisou and Prévot proposed the genus *Acinetobacter* to include colorless, nonmotile, saprophytic gram-negative bacilli regardless of oxidase activity.[4] Ultimately, two of the three genera (*Mima* and *Herellea*) in the now-obsolete tribe Mimeae came to be included under the genus *Acinetobacter*. Further refinement emerged when oxidase activity was used to distinguish *Moraxella* (oxidase-positive) from *Acinetobacter* (oxidase-negative).[5]

Although genus clarification was clearly established by 1971,[6] current efforts are directed toward species delineation. When references of bacterial terminology were last updated, standards applied to establish *Acinetobacter* speciation were not universally accepted. References published before the mid-1980s recognized one species, *Acinetobacter calcoaceticus*, with two subspecies (var. *anitratus* and var. *lwoffi*)[5] or two species,[7] *A. calcoaceticus* and *A. lwoffi*. The two subspecies/species were distinguished by the ability of *A. calcoaceticus* var. *anitratus* to produce acid from glucose and the inability of var. *lwoffi* to do so.[5] Efforts to further speciate the genus subsequently included bacteriocin typing,[8] phage typing,[9] characterization of outer membrane proteins,[10–12] serotyping,[13–15] phenotyping,[16, 17] ribotyping,[18] tRNA and genomic fingerprinting,[19, 20] and DNA homology.[21, 22] Serotyping by agglutination has been unsuccessful owing to the difficulties of distinguishing somatic from capsular antibody reactions.[8] As one might anticipate, nucleic acid fingerprinting and DNA homology have been the most reliable methods in recent years. Despite the limitations of the above-mentioned procedures, much progress has been made toward species standardization since 1986.

Based on DNA-DNA hybridization studies, at least 19 different *Acinetobacter* strains (genomic species or "genospecies") have been identified. Seven of the numbered strains have been given species names (Table 209–1).[23] Despite moderate success in applying simple, reproducible phenotypic studies to speciate *Acinetobacter* without resorting to cumbersome hybridization studies, some clusters remain; for example, phenotypically similar genospecies 1, 2, 3, and 13 make up the *A. calcoaceticus–A. baumannii* complex.[24] In routine clinical practice, precise species identification is not necessary and compromises in terminology (e.g., "*A. calcoaceticus–A. baumannii* complex") meet both clinicians' and microbiologists' needs. However, for epidemiologic purposes, additional investigations such as protein electrophoresis or ribotyping may still be required for exact strain identification.[25–27]

TABLE 209–1 Chronologic Nomenclature

1986–Present
Acinetobacter calcoaceticus (genomic species 1)
A. baumannii (genomic species 2)
A. haemolyticus (genomic species 4)
A. junii (genomic species 5)
A. johnsonii (genomic species 7)
A. lwoffi (genomic species 8)
A. radioresistens (genomic species 12)
Acinetobacter species unnamed (≥14 other genomic species)
Before 1986
Acinetobacter calcoaceticus var. *anitratus* (1968)
Achromobacter hemolyticus var. *glucidolytica* (1963)
Achromobacter conjunctivae (1963)
Acinetobacter anitratum (1957)
Moraxella glucidolytica (1956)
Achromobacter anitratum (1954)
Neisseria winogradsky (1952)
B5W (1949)
Bacterium anitratum (1948)
Herellea vaginicola (1942)
Micrococcus calco-aceticus (1911)
?*Diplococcus mucosus* (1908)
Acinetobacter calcoaceticus var. *lwoffi* (1968)
Achromobacter citroalcaligenes (1963)
Achromobacter hemolyticus var. *alcaligenes* (1963)
Alcaligenes metalcaligenes (1963)
Acinetobacter lwoffi (1957)
Acinetobacter polymorpha (1957)
Achromobacter lwoffi (1953)
Moraxella lwoffi (1940)
Mima polymorpha (1939)
Alcaligenes haemolysis (1937)

Acinetobacter are rod shaped during rapid growth and coccobacillary in the stationary phase. They are generally encapsulated, nonmotile (occasionally exhibiting twitching motility), aerobic, gram-negative organisms with a tendency to retain crystal violet and therefore to be incorrectly identified as gram-positive cocci. Versatility in exploiting a variety of carbon and energy sources allows *Acinetobacter* to grow on routine laboratory media and accounts for its prevalence in nature. Colonies are 1 to 2mm, nonpigmented, domed, and mucoid, with smooth to pitted surfaces. Frequent misidentification of *Acinetobacter* as *Neisseria* or *Moraxella* on Gram staining is readily clarified by the negative oxidase reaction of *Acinetobacter*. The inability of *Acinetobacter* spp. to reduce nitrate or to grow anaerobically distinguishes these organisms from Enterobacteriaceae. Additionally, *Acinetobacter* are indole negative and catalase positive. Hemolysis of red blood cells, acidification of glucose, growth at 44°C, and variability in carbon source utilization are a few of the phenotypic characteristics applied to distinguish *Acinetobacter* strains (Table 209–2).

EPIDEMIOLOGY

Acinetobacter differs from other members of the family Neisseriaceae by the simplicity of its growth requirements.[1] The ability to use a variety of carbon sources via diverse metabolic pathways expands its habitat.[28] Related genera (*Moraxella*, *Neisseria*, and *Kingella*) are parasitic in warm-blooded animals, whereas free-living *Acinetobacter* can be found on both animate and inanimate objects. Virtually 100% of soil and water samples yield *Acinetobacter*.[29] *Acinetobacter* has been isolated from pasteurized milk, frozen foods,[29] chilled poultry,[30] foundry[31] and hospital air,[32] vaporizer mist, tapwater faucets,[33] peritoneal dialysate baths,[34] bedside urinals,[35] washcloths,[36] angiography catheters,[37] ventilators,[38] contaminated gloves,[39] duodenoscopes,[40] reused needles,[41] plasma protein fraction,[42] and hospital pillows.[43] Some strains recovered from sink basins have been found to be tolerant of soap.[44] *Acinetobacter* may survive on dry inanimate objects for days, comparable to *Staphylococcus aureus*.[45, 46]

Acinetobacter has been grown from numerous human sources, including sputum, urine, feces, and vaginal secretions.[29] Up to 25% of healthy ambulatory adults exhibit cutaneous colonization,[47] and 7% of adults and infants have transient pharyngeal colonization.[48, 49] It is the most common gram-negative organism persistently carried on the skin of hospital personnel,[50] and it has been found to colonize 45% of inpatient tracheostomy sites.[51]

The prevalence of *Acinetobacter* clinical isolates varies somewhat by country and by specimen site but has generally increased worldwide in the last two decades. Data reported to the Centers for Disease Control and Prevention (CDC) National Nosocomial Infection Surveillance (NNIS) indicated that *Acinetobacter* was the cause 1% of all nosocomial infections and 4% of nosocomial pneumonia in sentinel United States hospitals.[52] The incidence of blood-stream infections had risen to 2% and that of pneumonia to 6% in medical intensive care units (ICUs) as of December 1997 (personal communication to CDC). In Singapore, *Acinetobacter* is the fourth most common gram-negative bacterial isolate, constituting 6.6% of all identified bacteria.[53] In Germany, *Acinetobacter* accounted for 8.1% of positive blood cultures and was the second most common gram-negative bacillus identified from blood in a large reference laboratory in 1990–1991.[54] *Acinetobacter* has been implicated in 9.7% of all nosocomial infections in French reference hospitals.[55]

Risk factors associated with community-acquired *Acinetobacter* infection include alcoholism, cigarette smoking, chronic lung disease, diabetes mellitus, and residence in a tropical developing community.[56] Risk factors specific for nosocomial infection include length of hospital stay, surgery, wounds, previous infection (independent of previous antibiotic use),[57] fecal colonization with *Acinetobacter*,[58, 59] treatment with broad-spectrum antibiotics,[60] parenteral nutrition, in-

TABLE 209-2 Characteristics of the Family Neisseriaceae

Characteristic	*Acinetobacter*	*Neisseria*	*Moraxella*	*Kingella*
Shape	Paired cocci to medium rods	Paired cocci	Paired cocci to short rods	Paired rods
Oxidase	−	+	+	+
Catalase	+	+	+	−
Nitrate reduction	−	+	±	+
Metabolism	Active, varied	Limited, simple	Limited, simple	Limited, simple
Acid from glucose	±	−	−	+

+, present; −, absent.

dwelling central intravenous or urinary catheters,[61] admission to a burn unit or ICU,[62] parenteral nutrition, and mechanical ventilation.[57, 61, 63]

PATHOGENESIS

A limited number of virulence factors reduces this bacterium to the role of an opportunist. Although growth in an acidic pH at lower temperatures may enhance its ability to invade devitalized tissue, no known cytotoxins are produced. Lipopolysaccharide is present in the cell wall, but little is known of its endotoxigenic potential in humans. Additional features that may enhance the survival of *Acinetobacter* include bacteriocin production,[8] presence of a capsule, and prolonged viability under dry conditions.[46] The capsule that surrounds most strains may inhibit phagocytosis and has been speculated to predispose persons with selective complement component deficiencies to infection.[56] In summary, without disruption of normal host defense mechanisms, the role of *Acinetobacter* in human infection remains limited.

CLINICAL MANIFESTATIONS

Acinetobacter spp. can cause suppurative infections in virtually every organ system.[64] Although *Acinetobacter* is acknowledged to be an opportunist in hospitalized patients, community-acquired infections are reported. Interpreting the significance of isolates from clinical specimens is often difficult because of the wide distribution of *Acinetobacter* in nature and its ability to colonize healthy or damaged tissues.[29] Additionally, *Acinetobacter* are often misinterpreted on gram staining to be other gram-negative organisms more commonly associated with particular clinical syndromes (e.g., in cerebrospinal fluid, *Neisseria meningitidis*; in sputum, *Haemophilus influenzae*). The *A. calcoaceticus–A. baumannii* complex makes up 80% of total *Acinetobacter* clinical isolates, whereas nonclinical items (e.g., food) are more likely to harbor non–*A. baumannii* species.[27] However, repeated isolation of non–*A. baumannii* genospecies from appropriate clinical specimens should not be dismissed as contaminant.

Respiratory Tract

The respiratory system is the most common site for *Acinetobacter* infection, because of its transient pharyngeal colonization of healthy persons and a high rate of tracheostomy colonization.[48, 64]

Acinetobacter has been reported to cause community-acquired bronchiolitis and tracheobronchitis in healthy children.[65] Tracheobronchitis can also occur in compromised adults. Pulmonary toilet often eradicates the organism without the use of systemic antibiotics in these latter hosts.

Adult community-acquired *Acinetobacter* pneumonia generally occurs in patients with diminished host defenses (e.g., alcoholism, tobacco use, diabetes mellitus, renal failure, underlying pulmonary disease).[31, 66, 67] Reports from developing tropical regions document a higher local prevalence of community-acquired *Acinetobacter* pneumonia compared with temperate climates.[56, 68] One series from tropical northern Australia found community-acquired *Acinetobacter* pneumonia to account for 10% of all community-acquired bacteremic pneumonias and 21% of gram-negative pneumonias.[56] Mortality in the various series was 40 to 64%. The prevalence of community-acquired *Acinetobacter* pneumonia was speculated to be a consequence of the generally poor health of persons in the communities under study, frequent use of penicillins, or genetic predisposition.

The greatest impact of *Acinetobacter* has been as a causative agent of nosocomial pneumonia, particularly ventilator-associated cases. Predisposing factors for nosocomial *Acinetobacter* pneumonia include endotracheal intubation, tracheostomy, previous antibiotic therapy, ICU residence, recent surgery, and underlying pulmonary disease. Nosocomial spread in the ICU setting has been attributed to ventilator equipment, gloves, colonized nursing and respiratory therapy personnel,[36, 38, 69] and contaminated parenteral nutrition solution.[70] Nosocomial *Acinetobacter* pneumonias are frequently multilobar. Cavitation, pleural effusion, and bronchopleural fistula formation have been observed. Nosocomial pneumonia reports from France found the mortality rate from *Pseudomonas* and *Acinetobacter* spp. to be greater than 70%.[71, 72] Mortality decreases once appropriate antibiotic therapy has been instituted for more than 3 days. Secondary bacteremia and septic shock are associated with a poor prognosis.[64] When attempting to determine the contribution of *Acinetobacter* to the death of critically ill patients it is important to note that either colonization or infection with *A. baumannii* in ICU patients has been independently associated with excess mortality. Therefore, the presence of *Acinetobacter* probably indicates the ICU patient's poor condition as opposed to the virulence of *Acinetobacter*.[57, 63]

Bacteremia

True *Acinetobacter* bacteremia should be distinguished from pseudobacteremia resulting from improper blood culture technique.[33, 47] Rates as high as 8.4% of all bacteremias have been reported to be caused by *Acinetobacter*.[54] *Acinetobacter* bacteremia in neonatal ICU patients has been increasingly reported.[73] Nosocomial *Acinetobacter* bacteremia is frequently associated with respiratory tract infections and use of intravenous catheters; urinary tract, wound, skin, and abdominal infections are less frequent sources.[45, 54, 64] Although descriptions of well-appearing patients with bacteremia are recorded (generally in patients with indwelling catheters),[74] septic shock may be seen in up to 30% of bacteremic patients.[54] The mortality rate from *Acinetobacter* bacteremia has been reported to be 17 to 46% with an inconsistent impact on increasing mortality when associated with polymicrobial bacteremia.[54, 64] *Acinetobacter* bacteremia with species other than *A. baumannii* tends to be less severe.[54]

Genitourinary

Studies isolating *Acinetobacter* from patients with a penicillin-resistant "gonorrhea-like" urethritis led to the erroneous implication of *Acinetobacter* as a cause of this illness.[75, 76] Despite colonization of the lower urinary tract with *Acinetobacter*, it is only rarely invasive. However, cases of cystitis and pyelonephritis have been documented in the setting of an indwelling bladder catheter or nephrolithiasis.[64]

Intracranial Infection

Initially described by Cowan in 1938,[2] *Acinetobacter* meningitis occurs infrequently. Although it is generally found after neurosurgical procedures,[77, 78] there are reports of *Acinetobacter* meningitis occurring in healthy hosts.[79] Meningitis can manifest abruptly or follow a more indolent course. A petechial rash has been noted in up to 30% of patients with *Acinetobacter* meningitis.[65] *Acinetobacter* may be morphologically confused with *N. meningitidis* on Gram stain of spinal fluid. The Waterhouse-Friderichsen syndrome has also been noted in association with *Acinetobacter* meningitis.[80]

Soft Tissue

Acinetobacter can cause cellulitis in association with an indwelling venous catheter. Resolution of catheter-induced cellulitis may occur with catheter removal alone.[81]

Traumatic wounds, burns, and postoperative incisions become colonized by *Acinetobacter* as a result of the organism's ability to thrive on compromised tissue and foreign bodies. During the Vietnam conflict, it was the most common gram-negative bacillus to contaminate traumatic extremity injuries.[82] Serial observations of traumatic wounds in Vietnam revealed *Acinetobacter* to be present early on wounded extremities, with bacteremia occurring 3 to 5 days later. Its soft tissue presence is often one component of a polymicrobial process. Synergistic necrotizing fasciitis in conjunction with *Streptococcus pyogenes* has been described.[64, 82, 83]

Miscellaneous

Acinetobacter infection can occur in any body site. Reported ocular cases include conjunctivitis,[84] endophthalmitis,[85] corneal ulceration due to soft contact lens contamination, and corneal perforation after misdiagnosis and treatment based on a corneal Gram stain.[86, 87] Native and prosthetic valve endocarditis have been described.[88] Osteomyelitis, septic arthritis, and pancreatic and liver abscesses[29] have been reported.

THERAPY

Acinetobacter may colonize the skin, pharynx, gastrointestinal tract, urethra, conjunctiva, and vagina. Interpretation of culture results must take into consideration colonization and potential environmental contamination. Isolation of *Acinetobacter* from colonized patients requires no specific therapy or precaution. In patients who present with localized cellulitis or phlebitis associated with a foreign body (e.g., intravenous cannula or suture), removal of the foreign body with local care is generally sufficient. The same recommendation can be made for urethritis and cystitis associated with an indwelling urinary catheter that can be removed. Tracheobronchitis after endotracheal intubation may resolve with pulmonary toilet alone. Infections involving the eyes and facial structures require systemic and local antibiotic therapy. Patients with more extensive tissue involvement, including wound dehiscence, fasciitis, or abscess formation, require débridement, drainage, and systemic antibiotic therapy. Those with sepsis syndrome, meningitis, endocarditis, osteomyelitis, or bacteremia require intensive systemic antibiotic therapy.

As with other opportunistic gram-negative organisms (e.g., *Stenotrophomonas maltophilia*), increasing antibiotic resistance has hindered therapeutic management. Although there are significant differences in *Acinetobacter* antimicrobial resistance patterns according to species and country of isolation,[89] the overall trend is one of increasing resistance.[90] Documented mechanisms of resistance include aminoglycoside-modifying enzymes, broad-spectrum β-lactamases, quantitative and/or qualitative changes in outer membrane porins, and altered penicillin-binding proteins.[91] Resistance has been tracked to plasmids, transposons, and chromosomes.

In the 1970s, *Acinetobacter* infections were treated with ampicillin, second-generation cephalosporins, minocycline, colistin, carbenicillin, and gentamicin. For several genospecies of *Acinetobacter* these options may no longer exist. Most *A. baumannii* are now resistant to ampicillin, carbenicillin, cefotaxime, and chloramphenicol, with some centers reporting up to 91% of nosocomial *Acinetobacter* resistant to gentamicin.[56] Resistance to tobramycin and amikacin is increasing. Some 4-fluoroquinolones, ceftazidime, trimethoprim-sulfamethoxazole, doxycycline, polymyxin B, and imipenem[90, 92] retain activity against many nosocomial *Acinetobacter*. However, the rapid development of significant quinolone resistance in France and aminoglycoside resistance in Germany are examples of how broad therapeutic generalizations may not accurately consider local resistance patterns. As such, therapy must be individualized with observed antimicrobial resistance principles in mind. Sulbactam has intrinsic bactericidal activity (separate from its inhibition of β-lactamases) against many multidrug–resistant *Acinetobacter* strains.[93] Tazobactam and clavulanic acid activities are less than that of sulbactam, and their clinical relevance is less well documented.[94, 95] Sulbactam's efficacy is borne out in two reports documenting successful treatment of *Acinetobacter* meningitis.[78, 96] Although imipenem remains a reliable agent, outbreaks of imipenem-resistant *Acinetobacter* (up to 12.9% of isolates) are a major concern.[62, 97, 98] In vitro data on more than 200 *A. baumannii* isolates found imipenem to have the lowest minimal inhibitory concentration (MIC), with ampicillin-sulbactam being the most active of the remaining β-lactams.[99] Bactericidal synergy has been demonstrated when carbenicillin and an aminoglycoside are combined, even when moderate aminoglycoside resistance exists.[100] More recently, imipenem with an aminoglycoside and β-lactam/β-lactamase inhibitor with an aminoglycoside were found to be synergistic in vitro against multidrug–resistant nosocomial *A. baumannii* isolates.[101] Additionally, quinolone and amikacin synergy was noted for *A. baumannii* isolates with a low quinolone MIC.[102] Species other than *A. baumannii* tend to exhibit less antimicrobial resistance.

Comparative human clinical trials are not currently available to assess therapy; however, in vitro data correlated with clinical observations does provide some therapeutic guidance. Many mild to moderately severe infections may respond to effective monotherapy. The current approach to treating a serious, deep-seated infection involving *Acinetobacter* should be based on sensitivities of the specific isolate and the use of combination therapy. The clinician using β-lactams should be aware of therapeutic failures and relapses resulting from the emergence of resistance during therapy. The induction of broad-spectrum β-lactamases during cephalosporin therapy has led some to urge avoidance of this class of drugs altogether.[103] Imipenem-cilastatin has been used successfully alone and in combination with a 4-fluoroquinolone,[104] rifampin, or an aminoglycoside.[55] This is supported by in vitro data and clinical observations.[63, 105] Should 4-fluoroquinolones, β-lactams, or sulbactam be used, the addition of an active aminoglycoside may provide a more rapidly bactericidal regimen and/or prevent the development of resistance during therapy.

A hospital outbreak involving multidrug–resistant *Acinetobacter* strains with a similar antibiogram should prompt a review of infection control procedures involving hand washing, patient isolation, ventilator care, and housekeeping. Additionally, a case-control study and a review of local antimicrobial prescribing habits may be in order.

REFERENCES

1. Henriksen SD. *Moraxella, Neisseria, Branhamella,* and *Acinetobacter*. Annu Rev Microbiol. 1976;30:63–83.
2. Cowan ST. Unusual infections following cerebral operations: With a description of *Diplococcus mucosus* (von Lingelsheim). Lancet. 1938;2:1052–1054.
3. De Bord GG. Description of *Mimaeae* Trib. nov. with three genera and three species and two new species of *Neisseria* from conjunctivitis and vaginitis. Iowa State College J Sci. 1942;16:471–480.

4. Brisou J, Prévot A-R. Etudes de systématique bactérienne: Revision des espèces réunies dans le genre Achromobacter. Ann Inst Pasteur. 1954;86:722–728.
5. Juni E. Genus III Acinetobacter Brisou and Prévot 1954, 727[AL]. In: Krieg NR, ed. Bergey's Manual of Systemic Bacteriology. v. 1. Baltimore: Williams & Wilkins, 1984:303–307.
6. Juni E. Interspecies transformation of *Acinetobacter*, genetic evidence for a ubiquitous genus. J Bacteriol. 1972;112:917–931.
7. Skerman VBD, McGowan V, Sneath PHA. Approved lists of bacterial names. Int J Syst Bacteriol. 1980;30:225–420.
8. Andrews HJ. *Acinetobacter* bacteriocin typing. J Hosp Infect. 1986;7:169–175.
9. Santos-Ferreira MO, Vieu JF, Klein B. Phage-types and susceptibility to 26 antibiotics of nosocomial strains of *Acinetobacter* isolated in Portugal. J Intern Med Res. 1984;12:364–368.
10. Alexander M, Ismail F, Jackman PJH, et al. Fingerprinting of *Acinetobacter* strains from clinical sources by numerical analysis of electrophoretic protein patterns. J Med Microbiol. 1984;18:55–64.
11. Dijkshoorn L, Michel MF, Degener JE. Cell envelope protein profiles of *Acinetobacter calcoaceticus* isolated in hospitals. J Med Microbiol. 1987;23:313–319.
12. Mortenson JE, La Rocco MT, Steiner B, et al. Protein fingerprinting for the determinations of relatedness in *Acinetobacter calcoaceticus* subspecies *anitratus* isolated from patients in a surgical intensive care unit. Infect Control. 1987;8:512–515.
13. Carey SG. Serological relationships of *Mimae*, *Moraxella*, *Diplococcus mucosus*, and *Neisseria winogradskyi*. Int Bull Bacteriol Nomencl Taxon. 1961;11:79–86.
14. Das BC, Ayliffe GAJ. Serotyping of *Acinetobacter calcoaceticus*. J Clin Pathol. 1984;37:1388–1391.
15. Traub WH. *Acinetobacter baumannii* serotyping for delineation of outbreaks of nosocomial cross-infection. J Clin Microbiol. 1989;27:2713–2716.
16. Baumann P, Doudoroff M, Stanier RY. A study of the *Moraxella* group: II. Oxidative-negative species (genus *Acinetobacter*). J Bacteriol. 1968;95:1520–1541.
17. Gerner-Smidt P. The epidemiology of *Acinetobacter calcoaceticus*: Biotype and resistance pattern of 328 strains consecutively isolated from clinical specimens. Acta Pathol Microbiol Immunol Scand [B]. 1987;95:5–11.
18. Gerner-Smidt P. Ribotyping of the *Acinetobacter calcoaceticus–Acinetobacter baumannii* complex. J Clin Microbiol. 1992;30:2680–2685.
19. Ehrenstein B, Bernards AT, Dijkshoorn L, et al. *Acinetobacter* species identification by using tRNA spacer fingerprinting. J Clin Microbiol. 1996;34:2414–2420.
20. Dijkshoorn L, Aucken H, Gerner-Smidt P, et al. Comparison of outbreak and nonoutbreak *Acinetobacter baumannii* strains by genotype and phenotypic methods. J Clin Microbiol. 1996;34:1519–1525.
21. Johnson JL, Anderson RS, Ordal EJ. Nucleic acid homologies among oxidase-negative *Moraxella* species. J Bacteriol. 1970;101:568–573.
22. Bouvet PJ, Grimont PAD. Taxonomy of the genus *Acinetobacter* with the recognition of *Acinetobacter baumannii* sp. nov., *Acinetobacter haemolyticus* sp. nov., *Acinetobacter johnsonii* sp. nov., and *Acinetobacter junii* sp. nov. and emended descriptions of *Acinetobacter calcoaceticus* and *Acinetobacter lwoffi*. Int J Syst Bacteriol. 1986;36:228–240.
23. Dijkshoorn L, van der Toorn J. *Acinetobacter* species: Which do we mean? Clin Infect Dis. 1992;15:748–749.
24. Gerner-Smidt P, Tjernberg I, Ursing J. Reliability of phenotypic tests for identification of *Acinetobacter* species. J Clin Microbiol. 1991;29:277–282.
25. Bouvet PJM, Jeanjean S, Vieu J-F, et al. Species biotype, and bacteriophage type determinations compared with cell envelope protein profiles for typing *Acinetobacter* strains. J Clin Microbiol. 1990;28:170–176.
26. Dijkshoorn L, Tjernberg I, Pot B, et al. Numerical analysis of cell envelope protein profiles of *Acinetobacter* strains classified by DNA-DNA hybridization. Syst Appl Microbiol. 1990;13:338–344.
27. Bergogne-Bérézin E, Towner KH. *Acinetobacter* spp. as nosocomial pathogens: Microbiological, clinical, and epidemiological features. Clin Microbiol Rev. 1996;9:148–165.
28. Baumann P. Isolation of *Acinetobacter* from soil and water. J Bacteriol. 1968;96:39–42.
29. Henricksen SD. *Moraxella*, *Acinetobacter* and the Mimeae. Bacteriol Rev. 1973;37:522–561.
30. Thornley MJ. A taxonomic study of *Acinetobacter* and related genera. J Gen Microbiol. 1967;49:211–257.
31. Cordes LG, Brink EW, Checo PJ, et al. A cluster of *Acinetobacter* pneumonia in foundry workers. Ann Intern Med. 1981;95:688–693.
32. Allen KD, Green HT. Hospital outbreak of multi-resistant *Acinetobacter anitratus*: An airborne mode of spread? J Hosp Infect. 1987;9:110–119.
33. Snydman DR, Maloy MF, Brock SM, et al. Pseudobacteremia: False-positive blood cultures from mist tent contamination. Am J Epidemiol. 1977;106:154–159.
34. Abrutyn E, Goodhart GL, Roos K, et al. *Acinetobacter calcoaceticus* outbreak associated with peritoneal dialysis. Am J Epidemiol. 1978;107:328–335.
35. Lowes JA, Smith J, Tabaqchali S, et al. Outbreak of infection in a urological ward. Br Med J. 1982;280:722.
36. Buxton AE, Anderson RL, Werdegar D, et al. Nosocomial respiratory tract infection and colonization with *Acinetobacter calcoaceticus*. Am J Med. 1978;65:507–513.
37. Reyes MP, Ganguly S, Fowler M, et al. Pyrogenic reactions after inadvertent infusion of endotoxin during cardiac catheterizations. Ann Intern Med. 1980;93(Pt I):32–35.
38. Cunha BA, Klimek JJ, Gracewski J, et al. A common source outbreak of *Acinetobacter* pulmonary infections traced to Wright respirometers. Postgrad Med J. 1980;56:169–172.
39. Patterson JE, Vecchio J, Pantelick EL, et al. Association of contaminated gloves with transmission of *Acinetobacter calcoaceticus* var. *anitratus* in an intensive care unit. Am J Med. 1991;91:479–483.
40. Alfa MJ, Sitter DL. In-hospital evaluation of contamination of duodenoscopes: A quantitative assessment of the effect of drying. J Hosp Infect. 1991;19:89–98.
41. Kelkar R, Gordon SM, Giri N, et al. Epidemic iatrogenic *Acinetobacter* spp. meningitis following administration of intrathecal methotrexate. J Hosp Infect. 1989;14:233–243.
42. Harvey K, Schuck S. *Acinetobacter* septicaemia following prolonged intravenous therapy. Med J Aust. 1977;2:121–124.
43. Weernink A, Severin WPJ, Tjernberg I, et al. Pillows, an unexpected source of *Acinetobacter*. J Hosp Infect. 1995;29:189–199.
44. Billing E. Studies on a soap tolerant organism: A new variety of *Bacterium anitratum*. J Gen Microbiol. 1955;13:252–260.
45. Hirai Y. Survival of bacteria under dry conditions; from a viewpoint of nosocomial infection. J Hosp Infect. 1991;19:191–200.
46. Wendt C, Dietze B, Dietz E, et al. Survival of *Acinetobacter baumannii* on dry surfaces. J Clin Microbiol. 1997;35:1394–1397.
47. Al-Khoja MS, Darrell JH. The skin as the source of *Acinetobacter* and *Moraxella* species occurring in blood cultures. J Clin Pathol. 1979;32:497–499.
48. Rosenthal S, Tager IB. Prevalence of gram-negative rods in the normal pharyngeal flora. Ann Intern Med. 1975;83:355–357.
49. Baltimore RS, Duncan RL, Shapiro ED, et al. Epidemiology of pharyngeal colonization of infants with aerobic gram-negative rod bacteria. J Clin Microbiol. 1989;27:91–95.
50. Larson EL. Persistent carriage of gram-negative bacteria on hands. Am J Infect Control. 1981;9:112–119.
51. Rosenthal SL. Sources of *Pseudomonas* and *Acinetobacter* species found in human culture materials. Am J Clin Pathol. 1974;62:807–811.
52. National Nosocomial Infections Surveillance (NNIS) report: Data summary from October 1986–April 1996, issued May 1996. Am J Infect Control. 1996;24:380–388.
53. Department of Pathology, Singapore General Hospital: Annual Report. 1991;66.
54. Seifert H, Strate A, Pulverer G. Nosocomial bacteremia due to *Acinetobacter baumannii*: Clinical features, epidemiology, and predictors of mortality. Medicine (Baltimore). 1995;74:340–349.
55. Bergogne-Bérézin E. The increasing significance of outbreaks of *Acinetobacter* spp.: The need for control and new agents. J Hosp Infect. 1995;30(Suppl):441–452.
56. Anstey NM, Currie BJ, Withnall KM. Community-acquired *Acinetobacter* pneumonia in the northern territory of Australia. Clin Infect Dis. 1992;14:83–91.
57. Lortholary O, Fagon J-Y, Hoi AB, et al. Nosocomial acquisition of multi-resistant *Acinetobacter baumannii*: Risk factors and prognosis. Clin Infect Dis. 1995;20:790–796.
58. Carbella X, Piyol M, Ayats J, et al. Relevance of digestive tract colonization in the epidemiology of nosocomial infections due to multiresistant *Acinetobacter baumannii*. Clin Infect Dis. 1996;23:329–334.
59. Koeleman JGM, Parlevliet GA, Dijkshoorn L, et al. Nosocomial outbreak of multi-resistant *Acinetobacter baumannii* on a surgical ward: Epidemiology and risk factors for acquisition. J Hosp Infect. 1997;37:113–123.
60. Leibovici L, Konisberger H, Pitlik SD, et al. Patients at risk for inappropriate antibiotic treatment of bacteraemia. J Intern Med. 1992;231:371–374.
61. Scerpella EG, Wanger AR, Armitige L, et al. Nosocomial outbreak caused by a multiresistant clone of *Acinetobacter baumannii*: Results of the case-control and molecular epidemiologic investigations. Infect Control Hosp Epidemiol. 1995;16:92–97.
62. Ang SW, Lee ST. Emergence of a multiply-resistant strain of *Acinetobacter* in a burns unit. Ann Acad Med Singapore. 1992;21:660–663.
63. Kaul R, Burt J-A, Cork L, et al. Investigation of a multiyear multiple critical care unit outbreak due to relatively drug-sensitive *Acinetobacter baumannii*: Risk factors and attributable mortality. J Infect Dis. 1996;174:1279–1287.
64. Glew RH, Moellering RC Jr, Kunz LJ. Infections with *Acinetobacter calcoaceticus (Herellea vaginicola)*: Clinical and laboratory studies. Medicine (Baltimore). 1977;56:79–97.
65. O'Connell CJ, Hamilton R. Gram-negative rod infections: II. *Acinetobacter* infections in general hospital. NY State J Med. 1981;81:750–753.
66. Goodhart GL, Abrutyn E, Watson R, et al. Community acquired *Acinetobacter calcoaceticus* var *anitratus* pneumonia. JAMA. 1977;238:1516–1518.
67. Wands JR, Mann RB, Jackson D, et al. Fatal community acquired *Herellea* pneumonia in chronic renal disease: Case report. Am Rev Respir Dis. 1973;108:964–967.
68. Barnes DJ, Naraqi S, Igo JD. Community-acquired *Acinetobacter* pneumonia in adults in Papua New Guinea. Rev Infect Dis. 1988;10:636–639.
69. Stone JW, Das BC. Investigation of an outbreak of infection with *Acinetobacter calcoaceticus* in a special care baby unit. J Hosp Infect. 1985;6:42–48.
70. Ng PC, Harrington RA, Beane CA, et al. An outbreak of *Acinetobacter* septicaemia in a neonatal intensive care unit. J Hosp Infect. 1989;14:363–368.
71. Fagon J-Y, Chastre J, Hance AJ, et al. Nosocomial pneumonia in ventilated patients: A cohort study evaluating *Acinetobacter* mortality and hospital stay. Am J Med. 1993;94:281–288.
72. Fagon J-Y, Chastre J, Domart Y, et al. Mortality due to ventilator-associated pneumonia or colonization with *Pseudomonas* or *Acinetobacter* species: Assessment by quantitative culture of samples obtained by protected specimen brush. Clin Infect Dis. 1996;23:538–542.
73. Regev R, Dolfin T, Zelig T, et al. *Acinetobacter* septicemia: A threat to neonates? Special aspects in a neonatal intensive care unit. Infection. 1993;21:394–396.

74. Robinson RG, Garrison RG, Brown BW. Evaluation of the clinical significance of the genus *Herellea*. Ann Intern Med. 1964;60:19–25.
75. Svihus RH, Lucero EM, Mikolajczyk MT, et al. Gonorrhea-like syndrome caused by penicillin-resistant Mimeae. JAMA. 1961;177:121–124.
76. Kozub WR, Bucolo S, Sami AW, et al. Gonorrhea-like urethritis due to *Mima polymorpha* var. *oxidans*: Patient summary and bacteriological study. Arch Intern Med. 1968;122:514–516.
77. Berk SL, McCabe WR. Meningitis caused by *Acinetobacter calcoaceticus* var *anitratus*: A specific hazard in neurosurgical patients. Arch Neurol. 1981;38:95–98.
78. Allen DM, Wong SY. *Acinetobacter*: A perspective. Singapore Med J. 1990;31:511–514.
79. Olafsson M, Lee YC, Abernethy TJ. *Mima polymorpha* meningitis: Report of a case and review of the literature. N Engl J Med. 1958;258:465–470.
80. Townsend FM, Hersey DF, Wilson FW. *Mima polymorpha* as a causative agent in Waterhouse-Friderichsen syndrome. US Armed Forces Med J. 1954;5:673–679.
81. Gervich DH, Grout CS. An outbreak of nosocomial *Acinetobacter* infections from humidifiers. Am J Infect Control. 1985;13:210–215.
82. Tong MJ. Septic complications of war wounds. JAMA. 1972;219:1044–1047.
83. Amsel MB, Horrilleno E. Synergistic necrotizing fasciitis: A case of polymicrobial infection with *Acinetobacter calcoaceticus*. Curr Surg. 1985;42:370–372.
84. Burns RP, Florey MJ. Conjunctivitis caused by Mimae. Am J Ophthalmol. 1963;56:386–391.
85. Peyman GA, Vastine DW, Diamond JG. Vitrectomy and intraocular gentamicin management of *Herellea* endophthalmitis after incomplete phacoemulsification. Am J Ophthalmol. 1975;80:764–765.
86. Wand M, Olive GM, Mangiaracine AB. Corneal perforation and iris prolapse due to *Mima polymorpha*. Arch Ophthalmol. 1975;93:239–241.
87. Herbet RW. *Herellea* corneal ulcer association with the use of soft contact lenses. Br J Ophthalmol. 1972;56:848–850.
88. Gradon JD, Chapnick EK, Lutwick LI. Infective endocarditis of a native valve due to *Acinetobacter*: Case report and review. Clin Infect Dis. 1992;14:1145–1148.
89. Shaw KJ, Hare RS, Sabateilli FJ, et al. Correlation between aminoglycoside resistance profiles and DNA hybridization of clinical isolates. Antimicrob Agents Chemother. 1991;35:2253–2261.
90. Traub WH, Spohr M. Antimicrobial drug susceptibility of clinical isolates of *Acinetobacter* species (*A. baumannii*, *A. haemolyticus*, genospecies 3 and genospecies 6). Antimicrob Agents Chemother. 1989;33:1617–1619.
91. Amyes SGB, Young H-K. Mechanisms of antibiotic resistance in *Acinetobacter* spp. In: Bergogne-Bérézin E, Joly-Guillou M-L, Towner KJ, eds. *Acinetobacter: Microbiology, Epidemiology, Infections and Management*. New York: CRC Press, 1996;185–223.
92. Seifert H, Baginski R, Schulze A, et al. Antimicrobial susceptibility of *Acinetobacter* species. Antimicrob Agents Chemother. 1993;37:750–753.
93. Urban C, Go E, Mariano N, et al. Effect of sulbactam on infections caused by imipenem-resistant *Acinetobacter calcoaceticus* biotype *anitratus*. J Infect Dis. 1993;167:448–451.
94. Joly-Guillou ML, Decré D, Herrman JL, et al. Bactericidal in-vitro activity of β-lactams and β-lactamase inhibitors, alone or associated, against clinical strains of *Acinetobacter baumannii*: Effect of combination with aminoglycosides. J Antimicrob Chemother. 1995;36:619–629.
95. Amyes SGB. β-lactam resistance and the use of inhibitor combinations. In: Towner KJ, ed. Clinical importance and antibiotic resistance of *Acinetobacter* spp. J Med Microbiol. 1997;46:721–746.
96. Jiménez-Mejías ME, Pachón J, et al. Treatment of multi-drug resistant *Acinetobacter baumannii* meningitis with ampicillin/sulbactam. Clin Infect Dis. 1997;24:932–935.
97. Tankovic J, Legrand P, De Gatines G, et al. Characterization of a hospital outbreak of imipenem-resistant *Acinetobacter baumannii* by phenotypic and genotypic typing methods. J Clin Microbiol. 1994;32:2677–2681.
98. Kuah BG, Kumarasinghe G, Doran J, et al. Antimicrobial susceptibilities of clinical isolates of *Acinetobacter baumannii* from Singapore. Antimicrob Agents Chemother. 1994;38:2502–2503.
99. Visalli MA, Jacobs MR, Moore TD, et al. Activities of β-lactams against *Acinetobacter* genospecies as determined by agar dilution and e-test MIC methods. Antimicrob Agents Chemother. 1997;41:767–770.
100. Ramphal R, Kluge RM. *Acinetobacter calcoaceticus* variety *anitratus*: An increasing nosocomial problem. Am J Med Sci. 1979;277:57–66.
101. Marques MB, Brookings ES, Moser SA, et al. Comparative in vitro antimicrobial susceptibilities of nosocomial isolates of *Acinetobacter baumannii* and synergistic activities of nine antimicrobial combinations. Antimicrob Agents Chemother. 1997;41:881–885.
102. Bajaksouzian S, Visalli MA, Jacobs MR, et al. Activities of levofloxacin, ofloxacin, ciprofloxacin, alone and in combination with amikacin, against acinetobacters as determined by checkerboard and time-kill studies. Antimicrob Agents Chemother. 1997;41:1073–1076.
103. Anstey NM. Use of cefotaxime for treatment of *Acinetobacter* infections (Letter). Clin Infect Dis. 1992;15:374.
104. Ygout J-F, Housset B, Derenne J-P, et al. Hospital-acquired *Acinetobacter baumannii* pneumonitis. Lancet. 1987;1:802.
105. Vila J, Marcos A, Marco F, et al. In vitro antimicrobial production of beta-lactamases, aminoglycoside-modifying enzymes, and chloramphenicol acetyltransferase by and susceptibility of clinical isolates of *Acinetobacter baumannii*. Antimicrob Agents Chemother. 1993;37:138–141.

Chapter 210

Salmonella Species, Including *Salmonella typhi*

SAMUEL I. MILLER
DAVID A. PEGUES

Salmonellae are named for the pathologist Salmon, who first isolated *Salmonella choleraesuis* from porcine intestine.[1] Salmonellae are widely dispersed in nature, including the gastrointestinal tracts of domesticated and wild mammals, reptiles, birds, and insects.[2] They are effective commensals, as well as pathogens that cause a spectrum of diseases in animals. Some *Salmonella* serotypes such as *Salmonella typhi*, *Salmonella paratyphi*, and *Salmonella sendai* are highly adapted to humans and have no other known natural hosts.[3] Other organisms such as *Salmonella typhimurium* have a broad host range and can infect a wide variety of animal hosts.[3] Some salmonellae such as *Salmonella dublin* (cattle)[4] and *Salmonella arizonae* (reptiles)[5, 6] are most adapted to an animal species but occasionally infect humans. The widespread distribution of *Salmonella* in the environment, their increasing prevalence in the global food chain, and their virulence and adaptability result in an enormous medical, public health, and economic impact worldwide.

HISTORY

Before the 19th century, typhus and typhoid fever were confused. Although various clinical distinctions were proposed, none reliably distinguished these syndromes. In 1829 in Paris, P. C. A. Louis separated typhoid from other fevers on the basis of intestinal lymph node and spleen pathology.[7] He also described the clinical phenomena of rose spots, intestinal perforation, and hemorrhage. In the English literature, William Jenner in 1850 settled the question of whether typhus and typhoid were different diseases.[8] He distinguished typhoid by the presence of pathologic evidence of enlargement of Peyer's patches and mesenteric lymph nodes. Jenner also noted that prior attacks of typhoid protected against subsequent attacks, which was not the case for typhus. In 1869 the term *enteric fever* was proposed by Wilson as an alternative to typhoid fever given the anatomic site of infection.[9] Although enteric fever remains a more accurate term, the use of "typhoid fever" persists today.

In 1873 Budd demonstrated that food, water, and fomites could transmit typhoid fever.[10] The typhoid bacillus was isolated by Gaffkey in Germany in 1884 from the spleens of infected patients.[11, 12] In 1896 Pfeiffer and Kalle made the first typhoid vaccine with heat-killed organisms.[13] In the same year, Widal and others demonstrated that convalescent sera from typhoid patients caused the organisms to "stick together in large balls and loose their motility." [14] He coined the term *agglutinin* to describe this observation. The antigenic classification or serotyping of *Salmonella* used today is a result of years of study of antibody interactions with bacterial surface antigens by Kauffman and White during the 1920s to 1940s.[15] In 1948, Theodore Woodward and colleagues announced the successful treatment of Malaysian typhoid with chloramphenicol (Chloromycetin),[16] and the modern age of antimicrobial therapy for typhoid fever began. In 1952 Zinder and Lederberg, using *S. typhimurium,* discovered genetic transduction, the transfer of genetic information from one cell to another by a virus particle, bacteriophage P22.[17] As a result of this initial work, *S. typhimurium* became a model system for genetic study.[18] A byproduct of *S. typhimurium* genetic studies included the development in 1973 of the Ames test, which uses *S. typhimurium* auxotrophic mutants to test the mutagenic activity of chemical compounds.[19] At present, *Salmonella* pathogenesis and immunity are widely studied, with mice and mammalian cells used as models of host-parasite interactions.

CLASSIFICATION AND TAXONOMY

Salmonella is a genus of the family Enterobacteriaceae.[20] Before 1983 the existence of multiple *Salmonella* species was taxonomically accepted. Presently, as a result of experiments indicating a high degree of DNA similarity, all *Salmonella* isolates are classified in a single species, *S. choleraesuis*.[17, 21, 22] The species *S. choleraesuis* can be subclassified into seven subgroups based on DNA similarity and host range. Subgroup I contains almost all the serotypes pathogenic for humans, except for rare human infections with group IIIa and IIIb formally designated *S. arizonae*. Previously, various serotypes and isolates that were formally known as species were classified according to surface antigen structure, biochemical characteristics, and host range. Because these designations are in wide clinical use, it is appropriate, although taxonomically incorrect, to refer to serotypes as species. Therefore, the terminology *S. choleraesuis* or *S. typhi*, which seems to designate these organisms as separate species, is commonly used to distinguish these organisms, although their correct taxonomic names would be *S. choleraesuis* (group I) serotype *choleraesuis* and *S. choleraesuis* (group I) serotype *typhi*.

Members of the seven *Salmonella* subgroups can be serotyped into 1 of more than 2300 serovars according to somatic O, surface Vi, and flagellar H antigens.[23–27] For simplicity, most *Salmonella* serotypes are named for the city in which they were defined, and the serotype is often used as the species designation.[23]

MICROBIOLOGY

Salmonellae are gram-negative, non–spore-forming, facultatively anaerobic bacilli 2 to 3 by 0.4 to 0.6 μm in size. Like other Enterobacteriaceae, they produce acid on glucose fermentation, reduce nitrates, and do not produce cytochrome oxidase.[20, 28] All organisms except *Salmonella gallinarum-pullorum* are motile by peritrichous flagella, and most do not ferment lactose. However, approximately 1% of organisms are able to ferment this sugar and thus may not be detected by clinical laboratories that use MacConkey agar or other semiselective media to identify *Salmonella* based on colorimetric assay for fermentation of lactose. The differential metabolism of sugars can be used to distinguish many *Salmonella* serotypes; *S. typhi* is the only organism that does not produce gas on sugar fermentation.[20]

Freshly passed stool is preferred for the isolation of *Salmonella* and should be plated directly onto agar plates. Low-selective media, such as MacConkey agar and deoxycholate agar, and intermediate-selective media, such as Salmonella-Shigella or Hektoen agar, are widely used to screen for both *Salmonella* and *Shigella* species. Highly *Salmonella*-selective media such as selenite with brilliant green should be reserved for use in stool cultures of suspected carriers and for use during special circumstances such as outbreaks.[29] *Salmonella* enrichment broths, such as tetrathionate broth with brilliant green, can be added to the primary medium to facilitate the recovery of low numbers of organisms.[28] Bismuth sulfite agar, which contains an indicator of hydrogen sulfite production and does not contain lactose, is preferred for the isolation of *S. typhi* and can be used for the detection of the 1% of *Salmonella* strains (including most *Salmonella* serogroup C strains) that ferment lactose.[30] After primary isolation, possible *Salmonella* isolates can be tested in commercial identification systems or inoculated into screening media such as triple sugar iron or lysine-iron agar.[28] Direct detection of *Salmonella* from stool specimens by latex agglutination[31] and polymerase chain reaction–based technology, including detection of virulence genes, is also under development.[32–34]

Isolates with typical biochemical profiles for *Salmonella* should be serogrouped with commercially available polyvalent antisera or sent to a reference or public health laboratory for complete serogrouping. Three kinds of surface antigens determine the organisms' reaction to specific antisera.[28] After treatment with formaldehyde, antibodies to the flagellar or H antigen can be used to agglutinate the organism. After heat, acid, or acetone treatment to abolish the labile flagellar antigen, antibodies to the somatic or polysaccharide O antigen can be used to agglutinate the bacteria. In *S. typhi* and *S. paratyphi* C, the polysaccharide Vi antigen can inhibit O-antigen agglutination because it is so abundant. The Vi antigen is a homopolymer of *N*-acetylgalactosaminouronic acid and is identical to that of the highly related *Citrobacter freundii*.[24–26, 35] Most antigenic variability occurs in the O antigen, which is composed of chains of oligosaccharide attached to a core oligosaccharide linked covalently to lipid A.

Although serotyping of all surface antigens can be used for formal identification, most laboratories perform a few simple agglutination reactions to differentiate specific O antigens into serogroups designated groups A, B, C_1, C_2, D, and E *Salmonella*.[36] Although this grouping is useful in epidemiologic studies and can be used to confirm genus identification, it cannot identify whether the organism is likely to cause enteric fever because considerable cross-reactivity occurs among serogroups. For example, *Salmonella enteritidis*, which typically causes gastroenteritis, and *S. typhi*, which causes enteric fever, are both group D. Similarly, another frequent cause of gastroenteritis, *S. typhimurium*, and some strains of *S. paratyphi*, another cause of enteric fever, are both group B.

Bacteriophage typing can be used to distinguish *Salmonella* within serotypes and may be useful for characterizing outbreak-associated strains.[37–40] Both the lipopolysaccharide content and gene products encoded on virulence plasmids are involved in phage type identity.[41] This method has been most widely used for *S. typhi*. Despite the ability to distinguish *S. typhi* isolates by sensitivity to specific bacteriophages, these organisms appear clonal by multilocus enzyme electrophoresis and DNA hybridization analysis.[42] Thus, the differences in phage typing probably reflect more recent evolutionary events because prophage acquisition is all that is required to alter bacteriophage sensitivity.

Many strains of nontyphoidal *Salmonella*, especially *S. typhimurium*, *S. enteritidis*, and *S. dublin*, contain large 34- to 120-kD plasmids that encode virulence factors.[18, 43] Plasmid profile analysis has been used to characterize *Salmonella* strains associated with common-source outbreaks, as well as sporadic isolates of multidrug-resistant strains.[44–46] More discriminative genotyping techniques, including ribosomal RNA restriction fragment length polymorphism (i.e., ribotyping),[47–50] pulsed-field gel electrophoresis of chromosomal DNA,[51, 52] and analysis of *Salmonella*-specific insertion sequences,[53, 54] have been used in epidemiologic studies to differentiate strains within a given serotype. However, a lack of standardization and time requirements limit the widespread use of these genotyping techniques.

EPIDEMIOLOGY

Salmonella typhi and *Salmonella paratyphi*

S. typhi and *S. paratyphi* colonize only humans, and therefore, disease can be acquired only through close contact with a person who has had typhoid fever or is a chronic carrier. Most often, acquisition of organisms occurs by ingestion of food or water contaminated with human excreta. Usually, waterborne transmission involves the ingestion of fewer microorganisms and, as a result, has a longer incubation period and lower attack rate than foodborne transmission does.[55] Although direct person-to-person transmission is rare, anal-oral transmission of *S. typhi* has been demonstrated.[56] Laboratory accidents have also resulted in typhoid fever transmission to laboratory workers.[57] Occasionally, health care workers can acquire the disease from infected patients as a result of poor hand-washing technique.[58] Sewage workers are not at higher risk of acquiring typhoid, although this concern is only theoretical.[55]

Typhoid fever continues to be a global health problem, with an estimated 12 to 33 million cases occurring worldwide each year.[12] The disease is endemic in many developing countries, particularly the Indian subcontinent, South and Central America, and Africa, with annual incidence rates estimated to be as high as 900 per 100,000 population in Asia.[59] These countries seem to share several characteristics, including rapid population growth, increased urbanization, inadequate human waste treatment, limited water supply, and overburdened health care systems. Recent outbreaks of typhoid fever in Eastern Europe and its newly independent states have followed political and social collapse and ensuing civil war.[60, 61]

In endemic areas the incidence of *S. typhi* infection is highest in children older than 1 year and probably reflects their lack of acquired immunity.[62] When children younger than 1 year acquire typhoid, the disease is often more severe and is associated with a higher rate of complications.[63] In addition, patients with immunosuppression, biliary and urinary tract abnormalities, and reticuloendothelial blockade, such as hemoglobinopathies, malaria, schistosomiasis, bartonellosis, and histoplasmosis, are at increased risk of severe disease.[3, 64–68]

Outbreaks of typhoid fever in developing countries can result in high morbidity and mortality, especially when caused by antimicrobial-resistant strains.[69–73] Antimicrobial resistance in developing countries may be promoted by the widespread use of "over-the-counter" antibiotics, the presence of immigrant workers, and international travel.[74, 75] In the 1970s, epidemic typhoid fever caused by chloramphenicol-resistant strains emerged in Mexico and the Indian subcontinent.[76–78] Since 1989, multidrug-resistant strains of *S. typhi* with H1-type plasmid-encoded resistance to chloramphenicol, ampicillin, and trimethoprim have emerged in the Indian subcontinent, Southeast Asia, and Africa and have been responsible for numerous outbreaks with increased morbidity and mortality.[75] Although these chloramphenicol-resistant and multidrug-resistant strains belong to different Vi phage types, they typically contain a 120-MDa plasmid of the H1 incompatibility type that often also encodes resistance to streptomycin, sulfonamides, and tetracyclines.[52, 75, 77, 78] More recently, chromosomal- and plasmid-encoded resistance to ciprofloxacin has appeared in *S. typhi* isolates from the Indian subcontinent, an area where this antimicrobial has been used to control outbreaks of multidrug-resistant *S. typhi* since 1990.[75, 79]

In the United States, substantial progress has been made in the eradication of *S. typhi.* Since 1966, an average of 400 cases of typhoid fever have been reported each year, for an annual incidence of 0.2 per 100,000 population, compared with 35,994 cases of typhoid fever in 1920.[55, 80] This progress is clearly related to improved food-handling practices and water treatment. Although foodborne outbreaks of typhoid fever are rare today, the potential still exists for outbreaks related to food contamination by a chronic carrier such as "Typhoid Mary" Mallon. Three recent typhoid outbreaks have been reported in Maryland,[81] Skagit County, Washington,[82] and Sullivan County, New York, where 46 confirmed and 24 probable cases of illness occurred among hotel guests and employees at a resort in 1989.[83] The financial costs of typhoid as opposed to nontyphoidal *Salmonella* outbreaks are considerable. Estimates vary from approximately $2500 to $4500 per person for typhoid illness to $645 per person for nontyphoidal salmonellosis.[82]

In the United States, typhoid fever is increasingly associated with international travel, especially to developing countries.[84, 85] Between 1984 and 1994, 72% of the 2445 reported typhoid cases in the United States were associated with recent international travel, including travel to the Indian subcontinent (India, 25%; Pakistan, 8%), Mexico (28%), the Philippines (10%), El Salvador (5%), and Haiti (4%).[84] During this period, antimicrobial resistance increased substantially. Twelve percent of *S. typhi* isolates during 1990 to 1994 were resistant to chloramphenicol, ampicillin, and trimethoprim-sulfamethoxazole compared with 0.6% during 1984 to 1989.

Nontyphoidal Salmonellae

In many countries the incidence of human *Salmonella* infection has increased markedly, although good national or hospital-based surveillance data are lacking in most cases. Based on passive laboratory-based surveillance, an estimated 0.8 to 3.7 million cases of salmonellosis occur annually in the United States,[86] and the incidence rate has doubled in the last 2 decades.[87] In 1996, residents in five U.S. sites underwent population-based active surveillance, and the incidence rate of salmonellosis (16 per 100,000 population) was second only to that of campylobacteriosis among seven potentially foodborne diseases and varied little by geographic region (Fig. 210–1).[88] In 1994, *S. enteritidis* and *S. typhimurium* were the most common serotypes isolated from human sources (Table 210–1). Nontyphoidal salmonellae cause a small but significant proportion of diarrhea in travelers[89] and in young children in developing countries.[90, 91] The incidence of salmonellosis is highest during the rainy season in tropical climates and during May to October in temperate climates, which coincides with the peak in foodborne outbreaks.[92]

In humans, nontyphoidal *Salmonella* infections are most often associated with food products, and such infections are the most frequently identified cause of foodborne disease outbreaks.[92, 93] Foods of animal origin, including meat, poultry, eggs, or dairy products, can become contaminated with *Salmonella.* Eating uncooked or inadequately cooked food—or food cross-contaminated with these products—may lead to human infection. In the developed world, acquisition of nontyphoidal salmonellosis is most often associated with consumption of poultry and eggs,[92–95] but a wide range of vehicles have been implicated in transmission to humans.[5, 92, 93, 96–98]

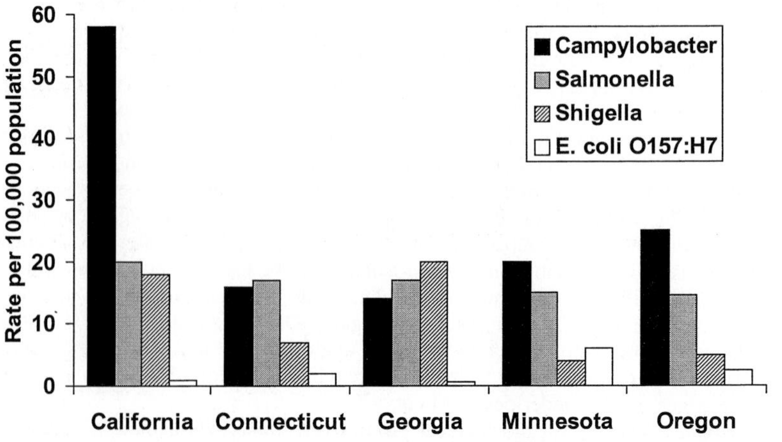

FIGURE 210–1. Incidence rate per 100,000 population of laboratory-confirmed *Campylobacter, Salmonella, Shigella,* and *Escherichia coli* O157:H7 infections by selected sites in the United States. (From Centers for Disease Control and Prevention. Food borne Diseases Active Surveillance Network, 1996. MMWR Morb Mortal Wkly Rep. 1997; 46[12]:258–261.)

TABLE 210–1 The 10 Most Frequently Isolated *Salmonella* Serotypes from Human Sources Reported to the U.S. Centers for Disease Control and Prevention, 1994

Rank	Serotype	Number of Isolates	Percent
1	*S. enteritidis*	10,009	26.1
2	*S. typhimurium*	8,479	22.1
3	*S. heidelberg*	1,855	4.8
4	*S. newport*	1,638	4.3
5	*S. hadar*	1,033	2.7
6	*S. agona*	766	2.0
7	*S. montevideo*	639	1.7
8	*S. oranienburg*	616	1.6
9	*S. muenchen*	562	1.5
10	*S. thompson*	560	1.5
	Other serotypes	12,179	31.7
	Total	38,336	100.0

**Salmonella typhimurium* includes the variant *copenhagen*.

Although foodborne outbreaks predominate, waterborne outbreaks of salmonellosis have also been reported.[99, 100]

Salmonellosis associated with exotic pets is a resurgent public health problem, with an estimated 3 to 5% of all cases of salmonellosis in humans being connected with exposure to exotic pets, especially reptiles.[101] As many as 90% of reptiles may be carriers of *Salmonella*.[102] The recognition of pet turtle–associated salmonellosis led to the banning of pet turtle shipments in several countries, but this measure did not eliminate the problem.[101, 103] Exposure to iguanas has been associated with infection by *Salmonella*, including *Salmonella marina* and *Salmonella chameleon*, especially in infants,[104] and exposure to snakes has been linked to *S. arizonae* infection.[105] Exposure to pet birds, pet rodents, dogs, and cats is also a potential source of salmonellosis.[106, 107]

In the 1980s, *S. enteritidis* associated with shell eggs emerged as the predominant *Salmonella* serotype and *source* of foodborne disease in the United States and some other countries.[94, 95, 108, 109] In the United States the proportion of reported *Salmonella* isolates that were *S. enteritidis* has increased fivefold from 5% in 1974 to 26% in 1994 (Fig. 210–2).[88, 110] During 1985 to 1994, *S. enteritidis* accounted for 582 reported outbreaks, 28,058 cases of illness, 2290 hospitalizations, and 70 deaths.[110] Infection of egg-laying and broiler poultry flocks with *S. enteritidis* is widespread, although the mechanism of transmission from farm to farm is not known. Infection localizes to the ovaries and upper oviduct tissue and is transmitted to the forming egg before shell deposition.[111] An estimated 0.01% to more than 0.1% of shell eggs contain *S. enteritidis*, predominantly phage types 8 and 13a in the United States[95] and phage type 4 in Europe.[108] Outbreaks of *S. enteritidis* infection have been associated with the ingestion of uncooked or lightly cooked eggs (e.g., sunny-side up), egg-containing food products, and inadequately cooked poultry.[95, 112] Although cooking of eggs until all liquid yolk is solidified kills *S. enteritidis*, the use of pasteurized egg products remains the safest alternative for institutions and the general public.

Changes in food consumption and the rapid growth of international trade in agricultural food products have facilitated the dissemination of new *Salmonella* serotypes associated with fresh fruits and vegetables.[87] The surface of fruits and vegetables may be contaminated by human or animal feces. Recent foodborne outbreaks of salmonellosis have been associated with fresh produce including cantaloupe, freshly squeezed orange juice, sliced tomatoes, and alfalfa sprouts.[87, 113]

Manufactured food items pose an enormous potential hazard of foodborne salmonellosis in developed countries because of their centralized production and wide-scale distribution. In 1994 an estimated 224,000 cases of *S. enteritidis* gastroenteritis developed in persons in the United States who ate a nationally distributed ice cream product.[114] The source of the *S. enteritidis* was most likely pasteurized ice cream premix that had been contaminated during transport in tanker trailers that had previously carried nonpasteurized liquid eggs. Other outbreaks associated with manufactured food products include pasteurized milk (United States, *S. typhimurium*),[115] powdered milk products and infant formula (Canada and United States, *Salmonella tennessee*),[116] unpasteurized goat's milk cheese (France, *S. paratyphi*),[117] paprika-powdered potato chips (Germany, multiple serotypes),[118] and a ready-to-eat savory snack.[119]

Antimicrobial resistance among human nontyphoidal *Salmonella* isolates is increasing worldwide and is probably due to the widespread use of antimicrobial agents for the empirical treatment of febrile syndromes[120] and as growth enhancers in animal production.[121, 122] High rates of resistance (>50%) to chloramphenicol, trimethoprim-sulfamethoxazole, and ampicillin have been reported from Africa, Asia, and South America.[123–130] Salmonellae resistant to multiple clinically useful antimicrobial agents are now emerging in developed countries.[131–135] Persons with resistant infection are more likely than those with susceptible infection to have systemic infection, to be hospitalized, and to have been treated with an antimicrobial agent recently.[135] A diversity of transferable resistance plasmids have been identified from multidrug-resistant nontyphoidal *Salmonella* strains[130] and are important in the intergeneric transfer of resistance between enteric bacterial species.[136–138]

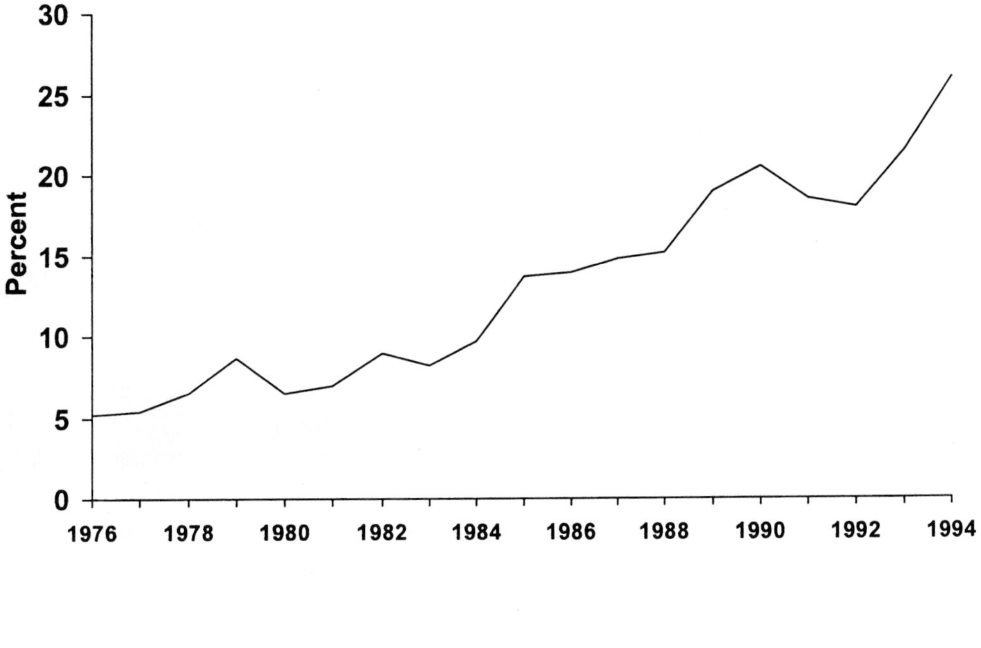

FIGURE 210–2. Percentage of all *Salmonella* isolates that were serotype *enteritidis*, by year, United States, 1976–1994. (From Centers for Disease Control and Prevention. Outbreaks of *Salmonella* serotype *enteritidis* infection associated with consumption of raw shell eggs—United States, 1994–1995. MMWR Morb Mortal Wkly Rep. 1996;45[34]:737–742.)

Of particular concern is the recent emergence of a distinct strain of multidrug-resistant *S. typhimurium* in the United Kingdom, characterized as definitive phage type 104 (DT104), that is resistant to five antimicrobials—ampicillin, chloramphenicol, streptomycin, sulfonamides, and tetracyclines. In the United Kingdom, *S. typhimurium* DT104 is now the second most prevalent strain of *Salmonella* isolated from humans after *S. enteritidis* PT4, and resistance of DT104 strains to trimethoprim and fluoroquinolones is also emerging.[75] In England and Wales, acquisition of DT104 strains has been associated with contact with ill farm animals and with exposure to a variety of meat products.[139, 140] Infection with DT104 may be associated with greater morbidity and mortality than that caused by susceptible *S. typhimurium* strains.[139] In the United States, the prevalence of *S. typhimurium* isolates with the five-drug pattern of resistance increased from less than 1% in 1979–1980 to 34% in 1996, most of which were phage type DT104 with one pulsed-field gel electrophoresis pattern predominating among the DT104 types (Fig. 210–3).[141]

Outbreaks and sporadic cases of nontyphoidal *Salmonella* resistant to third-generation cephalosporins have recently been reported in both developed and developing countries, including Argentina, Turkey, Algeria, and India.[142–147] Resistance to third-generation cephalosporins is conferred by plasmid-encoded, extended-spectrum β-lactamases (cefotaximases), which are transferable.[144–146, 148] Carbapenem-resistant strains have also been reported recently.[149]

Quinolone resistance resulting from mutations of the *gyrA* or *gyrB* DNA gyrase genes is emerging among human and animal *Salmonella* strains.[150–152] In the United States, of 4008 *Salmonella* isolates tested in a national survey conducted between 1994 and 1995, 0.5% were resistant to nalidixic acid and 0.02% were ciprofloxacin resistant.[153] In comparison, in the United Kingdom, the incidence of quinolone resistance increased from 0% in 1993 to 14% in 1996[141, 153]; the incidence was highest among *Salmonella hadar*, *Salmonella virchow*, and *Salmonella newport* isolates.[154] This increase was concurrent with licensing of the fluoroquinolone enrofloxacin for veterinary use in that country in 1993,[155] which raises concern that recent approval of the fluoroquinolone sarafloxacin for use in poultry in the United States may contribute to the emergence of quinolone-resistant *Salmonella* in both humans and food animals.[156]

Although nosocomial salmonellosis is infrequent, such infections have been associated with substantial morbidity and mortality.[58, 157–159] Nosocomial transmission of *Salmonella* from patients to nursing home staff has been associated with handling of soiled linen, noncompliance with barrier precautions, and fecally incontinent residents, but the risk of nosocomial transmission of *Salmonella* from health care workers to patients appears to be low if infection-control measures are carefully observed.[160–162] In contrast, the risk of nosocomial transmission to neonates and infants from chronically or recently infected family members is high.[163] Neonates are at high risk for fecal-oral transmission of *Salmonella* because of their relative gastric achlorhydria and the buffering capacity of ingested breast milk and formula.[164] High-iron infant formula as opposed to breast-feeding may further increase the risk of infant salmonellosis.[165] Outbreaks in daycare centers have also been reported, and control may be difficult because of the need for frequent diaper changing and the higher rate and longer duration of convalescent carriage seen in the preschool age group.[166–168]

The elderly are at increased risk for *Salmonella* bacteremia and extraintestinal infection, possibly because of underlying illness and waning immunity.[67, 169, 170] Residents of nursing homes may be at particular risk for salmonellosis because many of these institutions have only limited infection-control programs.[171–173] From 1975 through 1987, nontyphoidal *Salmonella* infection was the most common etiology of foodborne outbreaks reported from U.S. nursing homes and accounted for 52% of the outbreaks and 81% of outbreak-associated deaths.[172]

PATHOGENESIS

Infectious Dose

Data on the number of *Salmonella* organisms required to cause disease come from volunteer studies and investigations of outbreaks in which numbers of bacteria in contaminated foodstuffs are known. Volunteer studies involving a variety of *Salmonella* serotypes have shown that the attack rate increases with increasing inoculum size and varies with the host specificity of the organism.[174] However, volunteer studies may not be generalizable because few subjects are usually studied, laboratory-passaged bacterial strains may be attenuated in virulence, and higher doses of organisms are probably needed to infect healthy adult volunteers than persons at high risk for salmonellosis. Data from outbreaks of salmonellosis suggest that low inocula (less than 10^3 organisms) may produce nontyphoidal *Salmonella* gastroenteritis and that the ingested dose is an important determinant of the incubation period, symptoms, and disease severity.[174, 175] The most important host factor in lowering the infectious dose appears to be decreased gastric acidity.[176–178]

Gastrointestinal Tract Host-Pathogen Interactions

Ingested salmonellae must transverse the acid barrier of the stomach—the first line of defense against enteric infections.[174, 177]

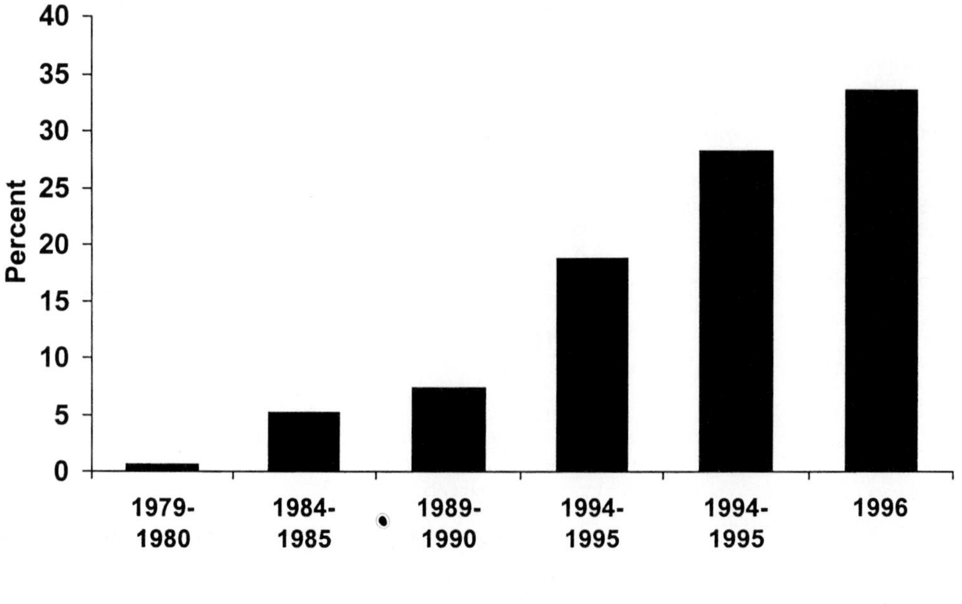

FIGURE 210–3. Prevalence of five-drug resistance (ampicillin, chloramphenicol, streptomycin, sulfonamides, and tetracycline) among *Salmonella typhimurium* isolates identified by national surveys (two for 1994–1995) of antimicrobial drug resistance. United States, 1979–1996. (Adapted from Glynn MK, Bopp C, Dewitt W, et al. Emergence of multidrug-resistant *Salmonella enterica* serotype *typhimurium* DT 104 infections in the United States. N Engl J Med. 1998; 338: 1333–1338. Copyright © 1998 Massachusetts Medical Society. All rights reserved.)

Although salmonellae survive poorly at normal gastric pH (i.e., <1.5), organisms survive well at pH 4.0 or higher and have an adaptive acid-tolerance response that may promote survival at low pH.[179, 180] After leaving the stomach, salmonellae must traverse the mucus layer overlying the epithelium of the small intestine and evade secretory products of the intestine (e.g., antimicrobial defensin peptides secreted by Paneth cells), pancreas, and gallbladder (e.g., bile salts) to result in infection.[181, 182] Secretory IgA and intestinal mucus may also play a role in preventing salmonellae from penetrating to the enterocytes that line the intestinal wall.[183]

After crossing the mucus layer overlying the small intestinal epithelium, salmonellae interact with both the enterocytes and microfold cells (M cells) that overlie the ileal Peyer patches.[184, 185] On contact with M cells, organisms are rapidly internalized and transported into the submucosal lymphoid tissue, where they may enter the systemic circulation. Salmonellae also have the ability to induce nonphagocytic cells, including enterocytes, to internalize them via a process termed bacterial-mediated endocytosis. This process involves the formation of large membrane ruffles around the organisms and cytoskeletal rearrangements similar to those induced by exposure of cells to growth factors.[186–189] Salmonellae are then internalized within membrane-bound vacuoles, through which organisms transcytose from the apical to the basolateral surface in polarized tissue culture cells.[190, 191] Although the efficiency of transcytosis is low in vitro, it may be an important pathway for invasive *Salmonella* to reach deeper tissues in vivo.

After *Salmonella* transcytose the intestinal epithelial barrier, the organisms rapidly interact with macrophages and lymphocytes in Peyer's patches and other lymphoid tissue located in the small intestinal submucosa.[192] Recruitment of additional mononuclear cells and lymphocytes can result in marked enlargement and necrosis of the Peyer patches after several weeks of infection. This process is probably the cause of the abdominal pain that is characteristic of typhoid fever and the pseudoappendicitis that is infrequently associated with nontyphoidal *Salmonella* infection.[3]

Survival within Phagocytes

The ability of salmonellae to survive within macrophages is likely to be essential to typhoid fever pathogenesis and spread of the organisms beyond the bowel to the systemic circulation. In patients with typhoid fever and positive blood cultures, almost all the organisms are contained in the mononuclear cell fraction.[193] Eventually, organisms are taken up by tissue macrophages in the bone marrow, liver, spleen, and Peyer's patches.[3, 194, 195] During the asymptomatic incubation phase of typhoid fever, most organisms are localized intracellularly within macrophages and possibly epithelial cells.[196] Symptoms of typhoid fever occur only when a critical number of organisms have replicated. These symptoms may result from the secretion of cytokines by macrophages in response to bacterial infection.[12, 194] The characteristic enlargement of the liver and spleen is probably related to *S. typhi* survival or replication within reticuloendothelial cells, the pathologic recruitment of mononuclear cells, and the development of a cell-mediated immune response.[3]

The morphology and cell biology of *S. typhimurium* infection of mouse macrophages have been studied. *Salmonella* induces membrane ruffling in macrophages similar to that observed in epithelial cells. Unlike other enteric bacteria such as *Yersinia enterocolitica*, salmonellae enter macrophages by induction of generalized macropinocytosis rather than by receptor-mediated endocytosis, even when they are opsonized with complement.[197] Salmonellae are internalized in 2- to 5-μm membrane-bound vacuoles with a large amount of extracellular fluid (termed macropinosomes); these vacuoles are formed by fusion of the ends of membrane ruffles. After endocytosis, fusion with other macropinosomes can result in the formation of large vacuoles containing *Salmonella* that are termed spacious phagosomes.[197] The *Salmonella*-containing vacuole appears to fuse rapidly with the lysosomal compartment, although the phagosome may have delayed acidification and novel trafficking to the lysosomal compartment.[198–200] Salmonellae have the ability to induce macrophage cell death, and this ability may be another mechanism to survive after phagocytosis and may contribute to the inflammation seen in lymphoid tissue.[201, 202] The ability to induce phagocytosis by macrophages and epithelial cells could also protect *Salmonella* from phagocytosis by neutrophils. Salmonellae are rapidly killed by neutrophils, with less than 10% of an initial inoculum surviving after phagocytosis.[203]

The finding that neutrophils from patients with chronic granulomatous disease are as effective at killing *S. typhimurium* and almost as effective at killing *S. typhi* as normal neutrophils suggests that only oxygen-independent killing mechanisms are required to kill salmonellae within neutrophils.[196] However, resistance to oxygen-dependent killing mechanisms may be more important within macrophages. This concept is supported by the finding that *S. typhimurium recA* and *recBC* mutants, which are characterized by defective recombination and DNA repair, demonstrate attenuated virulence in mice and survive only within macrophages that produce an oxidative burst.[204]

The increase in generalized macropinocytosis demonstrated in the mouse model of typhoid fever may be important clinically in the development of neutropenia in typhoid fever. In a small study of children with typhoid fever and neutropenia, bone marrow examination revealed the presence of histiocytes that had internalized neutrophils, red blood cells, and platelets.[205] In addition, liver biopsy specimens from patients with typhoid show Kupffer cell hyperplasia and erythrophagocytosis.[206] These findings suggest that *Salmonella* stimulation of hemophagocytosis may be an important mechanism in producing anemia, neutropenia, and thrombocytopenia.

Bacterial Factors

Multiple bacterial factors are important in the pathogenesis of salmonellosis. Many of the genes that are important in the virulence of *S. typhimurium* are located on two *Salmonella* "pathogenicity islands" termed SPI1 and SPI2, each consisting of approximately 40 kilobases of DNA located at centrosomes 63 and 30 of the chromosome, respectively.[207, 208] Both these regions encode specialized secretion systems, termed type III systems, and their targets. The targets of this secretion apparatus are translocated to the mammalian cytoplasm on contact with mammalian cells.[209–212] Analogous systems are present in a wide variety of bacterial pathogens and are adapted to alter eukaryotic cell processes, including apoptosis, cytokine production, and cytoskeletal function. As such, these systems may play a role in cell death, inflammation, and alteration of phagocytosis and other essential innate immune responses. SPI1 encodes genes important to the induction of macropinocytosis by epithelial cells and neutrophil transmigration and thus may be important for pathogenic processes at the mucosal surface, including gastroenteritis. Preliminary results suggest that SPI2 is involved in survival within macrophages and systemic pathogenesis. SPI1 and SPI2 are conserved, in part, in a wide variety of pathogenic *Salmonella* serotypes, which suggests that they are important in the pathogenesis of infection with other serotypes in addition to *S. typhimurium*.

Regulatory proteins that control the synthesis of multiple proteins at the level of gene transcription are also essential to *Salmonella* pathogenesis. The best studied example is PhoP/PhoQ, which regulates genes important for survival within macrophages, resistance to cationic antimicrobial proteins and acid pH, and invasion of epithelial cells.[203, 213–216] PhoP/PhoQ-regulated genes encode an acid phosphatase, cation transporters, outer membrane proteins, and genes important to the modification of lipopolysaccharide. These modifications include the addition of palmitate, aminoarabinose, and 2-OH-myristate to lipopolysaccharide.[217, 218] The modifications promote resistance to antimicrobial cationic peptides and alter the ability of lipid A to stimulate tumor necrosis factor-α secretion by macrophages. PhoP/PhoQ mutants of *S. typhi* are avirulent in human volunteers and are promising new live typhoid fever vaccine candidates.[219] Other regulatory genes implicated in pathogenesis include *crp/cya*, which regulates catabolite repression and surface proteins through adenylate cyclase; *ompR/envZ*, the regulators of porin gene transcription; *katF*, an alternative bacterial σ-factor that regulates catalase production[220–222]; and *ssrAB*, which regulates genes in SPI2 that are important for systemic pathogenesis.

The major surface molecules of *Salmonella* appear to be important in pathogenesis. The Vi antigen of *S. typhi* prevents antibody-mediated opsonization, increases resistance to peroxide, and confers resistance to complement activation by the alternative pathway and to complement-mediated lysis.[196] Vi antigen may thus function to inhibit phagocytosis of salmonellae by neutrophils while not interfering with the induction of phagocytosis by more permissive macrophages and epithelial cells. In addition, the lipid A component of lipopolysaccharide is a potent toxin for mammalian cells, and lipopolysaccharide is an essential virulence determinant in *S. typhimurium* infection in mice.[223] Both deep rough (missing the core polysaccharide) and rough mutants (missing the O-polysaccharide side chain) are avirulent.[224] Modification of the O-polysaccharide side chains increases resistance to complement-mediated serum killing and to phagocytosis.[224]

Other bacterial factors, including incompletely characterized cytotoxins,[225] genes that encode the synthesis of essential nutrients, including amino acids and purines,[226] and the virulence plasmids found in many nontyphoidal *Salmonella* serotypes, are also important in *Salmonella* pathogenesis.[69, 227] The virulence plasmids of *S. typhimurium*, *S. dublin*, *S. choleraesuis*, and *S. enteritidis* all contain an 8-kilobase region that appears to confer serum resistance and promote bacteremia in humans.[69]

Pathophysiology of Gastroenteritis

The mechanisms by which nontyphoidal salmonellae cause gastroenteritis remain obscure despite extensive study. Although a number of enterotoxins antigenically similar to cholera toxin and *Escherichia coli* heat-labile toxin have been described in *Salmonella* species, none has ever been purified or fully characterized biochemically.[228, 229] Because of the presence of multiple plasmids in *Salmonella* species, it is possible that the heat-labile toxin, which is carried on a plasmid, is occasionally transferred among *Salmonella* species. However, some of the enterotoxin-producing strains that cause fulminant watery diarrhea in humans produce this toxin activity after plasmid curing.[228]

It seems more likely that the diarrhea is caused by bacterial entry into enterocytes, by the induction of an immune response in the intestine, or by both mechanisms. The entrance of salmonellae into epithelial cells is associated with a number of biochemical alterations, including phosphorylation of the mitogen-associated kinase and activation of leukotriene synthesis through phospholipase A_2; these alterations result in increased vascular permeability and leukocyte chemotaxis.[188, 189] In human intestinal cell lines, *Salmonella* infection has been demonstrated to result in the production of D-*myo*-inositol 1,4,5,6-tetrakisphosphate, and this substance may promote chloride flux and subsequent diarrhea.[230]

Nontyphoidal *Salmonella* gastroenteritis in humans is characterized by massive neutrophil infiltration into both the large and small bowel mucosa, whereas typhoid fever is associated with infiltration of the small bowel mucosa with mononuclear cells.[3] In addition, only *Salmonella* serotypes that cause human gastroenteritis can induce intestinal epithelial cells to secrete interleukin-8, a potent neutrophil chemotactic factor.[231] Interleukin-8 secretion is mediated at least in part through the nuclear factor NFκB and requires an intact SPI1 type III secretion system.[232] Degranulation and release of toxic substances by neutrophils may contribute to inflammation and result in tissue damage and fluid secretion or leakage across the intestinal mucosa via alterations in epithelial cell tight junctions.

Host Factors

The virulence of any microorganism involves a complex interaction between the microorganism and the host's ability to limit infection. In *Salmonella* infection, host specificity is extremely important to disease. For example, *S. typhi* causes potentially lethal typhoid fever in humans but is avirulent in mice.[233] In contrast, *S. typhimurium*, the most common serotype to cause gastroenteritis in humans, causes lethal infection in mice. In inbred mice, susceptibility to *S. typhimurium*, *Mycobacterium*, and *Leishmania* segregates in a dominant mendelian pattern, and a locus (termed *Bcg*, *Lsh*, or *Ity*) identified on mouse chromosome 1 controls susceptibility to these infections through an alteration in macrophage function.[234] A gene designated *Nramp* has been identified within the *Ity* locus[235]; this gene encodes an integral membrane protein with structural similarity to transport proteins and may function in macrophages to transport microbicidal substances into phagosomes.[236, 237]

In humans, the risk of invasive salmonellosis is increased in persons with acquired immunodeficiency syndrome (AIDS), organ transplantation, and lymphoproliferative disease, thus emphasizing the importance of cell-mediated immunity in controlling this intracellular pathogen.[238–244] The importance of interleukin-12 to resistance to *Salmonella* infection was recently demonstrated in that individuals deficient in the interleukin-12 receptor were extremely susceptible to mycobacterial and *Salmonella* infections.[245] This finding demonstrated the importance of cell-mediated immunity to control of intracellular bacterial infections. Because interleukin-12 induces type 1 helper T-cell responses and interferon-γ production, this innate immune pathway is very important in resistance to salmonellosis.

Persons at the extremes of age and those with chronic granulomatous disease or diseases causing phagocytic overload, such as bartonellosis, malaria, schistosomiasis, histoplasmosis, and sickle cell disease, also have an increased incidence of salmonellosis.[65, 66, 68, 246] Susceptibility to salmonellosis can be increased by alterations in the gastrointestinal tract, including decreased gastric acidity,[176, 177] changes in the endogenous flora related to antimicrobial therapy[122] or gastrointestinal surgery,[67, 176] and chronic gastrointestinal diseases such as inflammatory bowel disease and malignancy.[239]

IMMUNITY

Immunity to *S. typhi* requires both cell-mediated and humoral immune responses and is achievable by vaccination.[247] Although most individuals are immune after typhoid infection, reinfection can rarely occur and is often associated with early institution of antimicrobial therapy.[248] Little is known about the immune response to the more than 2000 nontyphoidal *Salmonella* serotypes that infect humans, but the invasive nature of the bacteria and the histology of infection suggest that both cell-mediated and humoral mucosal and systemic immunity is important.

Although both serum and intestinal antibody responses have been documented after typhoid fever or vaccination,[249] little is known about the protective antigens against which an immune response must be generated. Vaccine studies indicate that the Vi polysaccharide antigen should be an important immune target because parenteral immunization with this antigen leads to increased protection in endemic areas.[250] No data exist on whether immunization with this antigen can protect previously unexposed individuals. Chronic carriers of *S. typhi* are immune to active infection and have very high antibody titers to *Salmonella* surface proteins, including the Vi antigen.[251] However, these high titers may reflect chronic exposure to the organism rather than affording protection against clinical disease. By extrapolation from animal studies, it seems likely that antibody to the O polysaccharide of lipopolysaccharide is also important.[252] The importance of an intestinal immune response is suggested by an animal model of infection in which a single monoclonal IgA antibody against O antigen secreted into the intestinal lumen provided measurable protection against *Salmonella* infection.[183]

In addition to antibodies directed against the *Salmonella* surface proteins, lymphocyte proliferation assays have documented that a cell-mediated immune response occurs after *S. typhi* infection.[253] Consistent with this observation are data from live vaccine studies indicating that a cell-mediated immune response against crude typhoid antigen correlates with the development of immunity after vaccination. In addition, cytotoxic $CD4^+$ T lymphocytes can be enhanced by vaccine-induced IgA antibodies.[254]

CLINICAL MANIFESTATIONS

Specific *Salmonella* serotypes most often produce characteristic clinical manifestations that have been given the syndrome designations gastroenteritis, enteric fever, bacteremia and vascular infection, localized infection, and chronic carrier state. Although dividing salmonellosis into these syndromes may be clinically useful, these designations have neither precise pathogenic nor prognostic significance.

Gastroenteritis

Infection with nontyphoidal *Salmonella* most often results in self-limited acute gastroenteritis that is indistinguishable from that caused by many other gastrointestinal bacterial pathogens. Nausea, vomiting, and diarrhea occur within 6 to 48 hours after the ingestion of contaminated food or water.[255] In most cases, stools are loose, of moderate volume, and without blood. In rare cases, stool may be watery and of large volume ("cholera-like") or of small volume associated with tenesmus ("dysentery-like"). Fevers (38°C to 39°C), abdominal cramping, nausea, vomiting, and chills are frequently reported. Headache, myalgias, and other systemic symptoms may also occur. Microscopic examination of stool shows neutrophils and, less frequently, red blood cells. Infrequently, *Salmonella* can cause a syndrome of pseudoappendicitis or mimic the intestinal changes of inflammatory bowel disease.[255, 256]

The diarrhea is usually self-limited, typically lasting for 3 to 7 days.[255] Diarrhea persisting for greater than 10 days should suggest another diagnosis. If fever is present, it usually resolves within 48 to 72 hours. Occasionally, patients require hospitalization because of dehydration. Death occurs rarely; in the United States during the period 1985 to 1991, only 50 (0.4%) of 13,056 outbreak-associated cases of *S. enteritidis* resulted in death.[95] However, case-fatality rates in nursing homes and hospitals were 70 times higher than in other settings.[95, 172]

After resolution of gastroenteritis, the mean duration of carriage of nontyphoidal *Salmonella* in the stool is 4 to 5 weeks and varies by *Salmonella* serotype.[168] Some studies have demonstrated that antimicrobial therapy may increase the duration of carriage.[168, 257] In addition, a higher proportion of neonates have prolonged carriage; in one study, 50% of neonates were still excreting *Salmonella* at 6 months.[258] However, delayed clearance of infection in neonates does not result in permanent carriage because almost all chronic carriers are adults.[168, 258]

Enteric Fever

Human typhoid and paratyphoid fevers are severe systemic illnesses characterized by fever and abdominal symptoms. In the preantibiotic era, approximately 15% of patients with typhoid fever died.[16, 259] More recently, mortality rates of 10 to 30% have been reported in certain Asian and African countries and have been associated with multidrug-resistant strains and delays in antimicrobial therapy, especially when more than 1 week has elapsed from the onset of symptoms.[69–73, 260] In the United States, less than 1% of persons with typhoid fever die.[12, 84, 260]

The syndrome of enteric fever is most often caused by *S. typhi.* A similar but less severe syndrome is caused by *S. paratyphi* A, *S. paratyphi* B (*Salmonella schottmuelleri*), and *S. typhi* C (*Salmonella hirschfeldii*).[194, 259] When enteric fever is caused by *S. typhi,* it is often referred to as typhoid fever, and when caused by *S. paratyphi,* it is referred to as paratyphoid fever. Although enteric fever is classically described as an acute illness with fever and abdominal tenderness, the symptoms are nonspecific and may be insidious in onset. The diagnosis of enteric fever should be strongly considered in the evaluation of travelers who return from tropical and subtropical areas with fever. The differential diagnosis of gradual onset of fever and abdominal pain with hepatosplenomegaly also includes malaria, amebic liver abscess, visceral leishmaniasis, and viral syndromes such as dengue fever.

The incubation period of *S. typhi* ranges from 5 to 21 days depending on the inoculum ingested and the health and immune status of the person. After ingestion of the organism, enterocolitis may develop along with diarrhea lasting several days; these symptoms usually resolve before the onset of fever. Diarrhea is more common in certain geographic areas, in patients with AIDS, and in children younger than 1 year.[63, 261] In one study in Bangladesh the mean duration of diarrhea was approximately 6 days and all patients had fecal leukocytes present.[63] Among patients with diarrhea, stool protein is often increased to a mean value of approximately 9 g/liter. Constipation is present in 10 to 38% of patients.[63] Although fever is a classic sign of typhoid fever, it does not always develop and the pattern of fever is not clinically useful. In addition, only 20 to 40% of patients will initially have abdominal pain; the frequency of other abdominal symptoms varies widely in different clinical series.[259, 262]

Nonspecific symptoms such as chills, diaphoresis, headache, anorexia, cough, weakness, sore throat, dizziness, and muscle pains are frequently present before the onset of fever in typhoid.[263] Neuropsychiatric manifestations, including psychosis and confusion, occur in 5 to 10% of patients with typhoid fever.[259, 264, 265] This so-called typhoid state has been described as "muttering delirium" and "coma vigil."[265] Picking at the bedclothes and at imaginary objects and muscle twitching are characteristic. The pathophysiology of the neuropsychiatric manifestations of typhoid fever is unknown but may be related to cytokine release from *S. typhi*–infected macrophages.[12] Seizures and coma are reported in less than 1% of persons and may represent febrile seizures of childhood. The cerebrospinal fluid is usually normal in patients with typhoid fever. Abnormal cerebrospinal fluid studies or recurrent seizures suggest another diagnosis.

On physical examination, patients with typhoid fever usually appear acutely ill; those who have previously been exposed to *S. typhi* or who seek early medical attention can present with a milder illness. Relative bradycardia is neither a sensitive nor a specific sign of typhoid fever and occurs in less than 50% of patients.[259, 264] Approximately 30% of patients will have rose spots—a faint salmon-colored maculopapular rash on the trunk.[264] Organisms can be cultured from punch biopsies of these lesions, and the pathology is characterized by a perivascular mononuclear cell infiltrate. The rash can be very subtle, especially in highly pigmented individuals, and frequently fades to small macules that appear to be resolving skin hemorrhages. Cervical lymphadenopathy develops in some patients. Rales are infrequently noted in recent series, and chest radiographs are invariably normal.[63, 265] Examination of the abdomen usually reveals pain on deep palpation, and peristalsis is frequently increased. Approximately 50% of patients have hepatosplenomegaly. Pain may localize to the right upper quadrant in the approximately 3% of adults with typhoid fever in whom cholecystitis develops.[259] Pancreatitis has also been described rarely.[266]

Most symptoms resolve by the fourth week of infection without antimicrobial therapy in the approximately 90% of patients who survive. However, weakness, weight loss, and debilitation may persist for months, and 10% of patients will have a relapse.[194, 259, 263] In the preantibiotic era, two thirds of pregnancies complicated by typhoid fever resulted in abortion.[64]

Many of the complications of untreated enteric fever occur in the third or fourth week of infection.[3] Intestinal perforation characterized by recurrent fever, abdominal pain, and intestinal hemorrhage resulting from hyperplasia, ulceration, and necrosis of ileocecal lymphoid tissue develops in as many as 3 to 10% of patients.[12, 63, 83, 260] In such cases, the patient's blood should be recultured and antimicrobial therapy broadened to cover aerobic and anaerobic enteric organisms. Other infectious complications include endocarditis and localized infections such as pericarditis, orchitis, and splenic or liver abscesses.

Hematologic abnormalities associated with typhoid fever include leukopenia and anemia. Leukocytosis can also be seen, most often in children and in the first 10 days of illness. Thrombocytopenia and clotting abnormalities that usually resolve spontaneously develop in some patients. Moderately elevated liver function parameters (i.e., aspartate and alanine aminotransferase, 300 to 500 units/dl) and muscle enzymes are common[267]; liver biopsies demonstrate focal Kupffer cell hyperplasia and mononuclear cell infiltration of the portal space.[206] Rarely, proteinuria and immune complex glomerulonephritis are noted. Creatinine clearance is usually normal, and irreversible loss of renal function has not been reported. Nonspecific ST and T wave electrocardiographic abnormalities are infrequently seen.

Enteric Fever Diagnosis

Definitive diagnosis of enteric fever requires the isolation of *S. typhi* or *S. paratyphi*. Cultures of blood, stool, urine, rose spots, the blood mononuclear cell–platelet fraction, bone marrow, and gastric or intestinal secretions may each be useful in establishing the diagnosis.[268–270] The duodenal string test is especially useful as a noninvasive technique to sample duodenal secretions.[269, 271, 272] A positive culture for *S. typhi* or *S. paratyphi* is obtained in more than 90% of patients if blood, bone marrow, and intestinal secretions are all performed.[270, 273] The sensitivity of blood culture alone is only 50 to 70%,[274] probably because small quantities of *S. typhi* (i.e., <15 organisms/ml) are typically present in the blood of patients with typhoid fever.[193, 275] Oxgall media cultures may increase the sensitivity from blood but not from bone marrow cultures.[12] Because almost all *S. typhi* organisms in blood are associated with the mononuclear cell–platelet fraction, centrifugation of blood and culture of this fraction can reduce the time to isolation of the organism but does not increase the sensitivity.[193]

The sensitivity of bone marrow culture is 90% and, unlike blood culture, is not reduced by up to 5 days of prior antimicrobial therapy.[270, 273, 276] In some patients with negative results on bone marrow cultures, duodenal string cultures have been positive.[273] One study found that in children the combination of blood and duodenal string culture was as sensitive as bone marrow culture.[272] Children also have a higher incidence of positive stool cultures than adults do (60 versus 27%).[12] Therefore, in both adults and children, blood, bone marrow, stool, and duodenal string cultures ideally should all be performed.

A number of serologic tests, including the classic Widal test, have been developed to detect *S. typhi* antigen or antibody.[12, 277–282] None of these tests is sufficiently sensitive, specific, or rapid enough for clinical use. DNA probes for *S. typhi* and other salmonellae have been developed, but these tests are not commercially available and may not be as sensitive as culture.[32, 283]

Bacteremia and Vascular Infection

Classically, *S. choleraesuis* and *S. dublin* produce a syndrome of sustained bacteremia with fever, but any *Salmonella* serotype can cause bacteremia.[255, 284] From 1 to 4% of immunocompetent individuals with *Salmonella* gastroenteritis have positive blood cultures.[67, 168, 284] The proportion is greater for persons at the extremes of age and those who have severe underlying illness or immunosuppression, including persons with AIDS.[66, 68, 238–240, 242, 243, 285–287] Salmonellae have a propensity for infection of vascular sites, and high-grade bacteremia (i.e., greater than 50% of three or more blood cultures positive) suggests endovascular infection.[288] The risk of endovascular infection complicating *Salmonella* bacteremia is estimated to be 25% in persons older than 50 years and is most often associated with seeding of atherosclerotic plaques or aneurysms.[64, 288, 289]

Salmonellosis and Human Immunodeficiency Virus Infection

Persons infected with human immunodeficiency virus (HIV) have an estimated 20- to 100-fold increased risk of salmonellosis when compared with the general population.[242, 290] *Salmonella* is more likely to cause severe invasive disease in persons with AIDS than in immunocompetent persons, including fulminant diarrhea, acute enterocolitis, rectal ulceration, recurrent bacteremia, meningitis, and death despite antimicrobial therapy.[244, 290–294] In several studies of HIV-infected persons in Africa, *Salmonella* species were among the most frequent cause of bacteremia and were associated with a 62 to 80% mortality rate caused primarily by delayed diagnosis and incomplete treatment.[295–297] Focal infections resulting from nontyphoidal *Salmonella* most often occur in severely immunocompromised persons with AIDS (CD4 counts of <100/mm³).[294] In contrast, the severity of *Salmonella* infection in persons with AIDS-related complex or asymptomatic HIV infection is similar to the severity of infection in immunocompetent hosts.

Since 1987, the U.S. Centers for Disease Control and Prevention surveillance definition has included recurrent nontyphoidal *Salmonella* bacteremia in the diagnostic criteria for AIDS.[298] Recurrent infection apparently results from incomplete clearance of the primary infection because of impaired cell-mediated immunity; without maintenance antimicrobial therapy, up to 45% of persons with HIV infection will have recurrent bacteremia.[287] The incidence of recurrent nontyphoidal *Salmonella* bacteremia in persons with HIV has declined in recent years.[244] This decline may be linked to the introduction of zidovudine in 1987 and to the use of trimethoprim-sulfamethoxazole for the prevention of *Pneumocystis* pneumonia.[244, 299] Zidovudine has activity against *Salmonella* in vitro at therapeutic serum concentrations and against *Salmonella*-infected macrophages.[300, 301]

Localized Infections

Localized infections develop in approximately 5 to 10% of persons with *Salmonella* bacteremia, and the signs and symptoms may be delayed.[284, 302] Extraintestinal complications of salmonellosis are summarized in Table 210–2.[300, 302–334]

Long-Term Carrier State

The long-term carrier state is defined as the persistence of salmonellae in stool or urine for periods longer than 1 year. Long-term carriage develops in 0.2 to 0.6% of patients with nontyphoidal salmonellosis[337] and in 1 to 4% of patients with *S. typhi* infection.[64, 259, 263] The frequency of long-term carriage is higher in women and in persons with biliary abnormalities or concurrent bladder infection with *Schistosoma*.[66] Long-term carriage of *S. typhi* and *S. paratyphi* A has been associated with an increased incidence of carcinoma of the gallbladder and other gastrointestinal malignancies.[338, 339] Serologic tests for the Vi antigen can be useful in distinguishing long-term carriage from acute infection inasmuch as long-term carriers will often have a high antibody titer to this antigen.[251]

IMMUNIZATION AGAINST *SALMONELLA TYPHI*

Enteric fever can be prevented by immunization, and three commercially available vaccines are approved for administration to travelers to typhoid-endemic regions. These vaccines have been most exten-

TABLE 210-2 Extraintestinal Infectious Complications of Salmonellosis

Site	Incidence	Risk Factors	Manifestations	Complications	Mortality	Diagnosis	Therapy
Endocarditis[64, 303]	0.2–0.4%	Preexisting valvular heart disease	Valvular vegetation Infected mural thrombus	Valve perforation Relapse (20–25%) Pericarditis	~70%	Blood culture Echocardiography	Early surgery +6 wk P ceph 3 or P amp
Arteritis[288, 289, 304–308, 335]	Rare	Atherosclerosis Prosthetic graft Aortic aneurysm Endocarditis	Prolonged fever Pain—back, chest, or abdomen	Mycotic aneurysm Aneurysm rupture Aortoduodenal fistula Vertebral osteomyelitis	~45%	Blood culture CT or nuclear scan	Early surgical bypass +6 wk P ceph 3 or P amp
Central nervous system[309–315, 336]	0.1–0.9%	Infants (esp. neonates)	Meningitis Ventriculitis Abscess	Seizures Mental retardation Hydrocephalus Brain infarction Relapse	~40–60%	CSF culture CT or MRI scan	≥3 wk P ceph 3, P amp, or carbapenem
Pulmonary[302, 316]	Rare	Lung malignancy Pulmonary disease Sickle cell anemia	Pneumonia	Lung abscess Empyema Bronchopleural fistula	~25–60%	Respiratory tissue culture Chest radiograph	≥2 wk P/PO abx
Bone[317–319]	<1%	Sickle cell anemia Bone disease Immunosuppression	Femur, tibia, humerus Lumbar vertebrae	Relapse Chronic osteomyelitis	Very low	Bone radiograph	≥4 wk P ceph 3 or P amp + surgery for sequestra
Joint—reactive[300, 322–325]	0.6%	HLA-B27	≥3 joints involved (esp. knee, ankle, wrist, sacroiliac)	Prolonged symptoms (mean duration, 5.5 mo)	Negligible	Joint fluid exam and culture	Nonsteroidal anti-inflammatory agent
Joint—septic[320, 321]	0.1–0.2%	Same as bone, joint disease	Knee, hip, shoulder	Joint destruction Osteomyelitis	Very low	Joint fluid exam and culture	Repeated needle aspiration + ≥4 wk P/PO abx
Hepatobiliary[326–328]	Rare	Cholelithiasis Cirrhosis Amebic abscess Echinococcal cyst	Hepatomegaly Cholecystitis Hepatic abscess	Rupture with secondary peritonitis Subphrenic abscess	~10%	Ultrasonography Aspiration	Drainage + ≥2 wk P abx
Splenic[329]	Rare	Sickle cell anemia Splenic cyst Splenic hematoma	Splenomegaly	Left-sided empyema Subphrenic abscess Rupture with secondary peritonitis	<10%	Ultrasonography Aspiration	≥2 wk P abx ± splenectomy
Urinary[240, 330, 331]	0.6%	Urolithiasis Malignancy Renal transplant	Cystitis Pyelonephritis	Renal abscess Interstitial nephritis Relapse	~20%	Urine culture Ultrasonography	Removal of structural abnormality + 1–2 wk P abx + ≥6 wk PO quinolone* or TMP-SMX
Genital[64, 332]	Rare	Pregnancy Renal transplant	Ovarian abscess Testicular abscess Prostatitis Epididymitis	Abscess	Very low	Ultrasonography Aspiration	Drainage of collection + 1–2 wk P abx + ≥6 wk PO quinolone* or TMP-SMX
Soft tissue[333, 334]	<1%	Local trauma Immunosuppression	Pustular dermatitis Subcutaneous abscess Wound infection	Septic thrombophlebitis Endophthalmitis	~15%	Drainage culture	≥2 wk P abx + drainage of collection

*Avoid quinolones in pregnant patients.
Abbreviations: abx, Antibiotic; CSF, cerebrospinal fluid; CT, computed tomography; MRI, magnetic resonance imaging; P amp, parenteral ampicillin; P ceph 3, parenteral third-generation cephalosporin; P/PO, parenteral or oral antimicrobial (e.g., quinolone, ampicillin, trimethoprim-sulfamethoxazole [TMP-SMX], chloramphenicol, or a third-generation cephalosporin).
Adapted from Pegues DA, Miller SI: Non-typhoidal salmonellosis. In: Guerrant RL, Walker DH, Weller PF, eds. Tropical Infectious Disease: Principles, Pathogens, and Practice. Philadelphia: WB Saunders; 1999.

sively evaluated in endemic populations, achieve approximately 50 to 80% efficacy depending on prior exposure, and confer protection that lasts only for several years.[12]

Typhoid vaccine is not required for international travel. However, the Immunization Practices Advisory Committee and the Centers for Disease Control and Prevention recommend that typhoid vaccine be administered to persons traveling to developing countries who have prolonged exposure to contaminated food and drink, particularly those traveling to smaller cities, villages, and destinations off the usual tourist itineraries. In addition, laboratory personnel who work with *S. typhi* and household contacts of known *S. typhi* carriers should be vaccinated.[340, 341] Because vaccine protective efficacy can be overcome by the high inocula common in foodborne exposure—the most frequent exposure among travelers[194, 249, 342]—it is controversial whether all travelers to areas with high rates of typhoid fever should be immunized with the currently available preparations.[343] Immunization is not recommended for persons attending summer camps, persons residing in areas that have experienced floods or other natural disasters, sewer workers, or persons potentially exposed to common-source outbreaks. Immunization is an adjunct and not a substitute for avoiding high-risk foods and beverages or using good laboratory technique. However, with all the currently available vaccines, documented cases of typhoid fever have still occurred in vaccinated travelers.

Since the 19th century, the heat-killed whole-organism *S. typhi* vaccine has been the mainstay of immunization against typhoid fever, and it is currently manufactured by Wyeth-Ayerst. The heat-phenol–inactivated parenteral *S. typhi* vaccine is 51 to 77% more effective than tetanus placebo in endemic populations.[341, 344–347] An acetone-inactivated vaccine provided greater protection (range, 79 to 94%) in endemic populations[344, 348, 349]; the higher efficacy was attributed to the preservation of Vi antigen in this preparation.[343, 345, 347] However, the acetone-inactivated vaccine is associated with more frequent side effects, costs more than the heat-phenol–inactivated vaccine,[342, 350] and in the United States is only available to the military. Both preparations appear to result in equal protection in immunologically naive persons.

Local and systemic adverse reactions occur frequently with the heat-phenol–inactivated vaccine. Side effects include fever (17 to 29%), severe headache (10%), and significant local pain at the site of administration (35 to 60%).[344, 346, 348] More importantly, approximately 25% of individuals missed work or school as a result of vaccination. Reactions occur within hours after administration of the vaccine and can persist for up to 72 hours. In general, reactions are milder with subsequent vaccine doses. Severe reactions to immunization can include anaphylaxis, chest pain, liver damage, neurologic problems, and reactive arthropathy.[351, 352]

The Immunization Practices Advisory Committee recommends a primary immunization series of two doses administered subcutaneously at greater than 4-week intervals and booster doses administered every 3 years.[340] The dose for primary and booster immunization is 0.25 ml administered subcutaneously for children 6 months to 10 years old and 0.5 ml for those older than 10 years.[340] Booster doses for persons 6 months old to adulthood can also be administered at 0.1 ml intradermally.[340]

The live-attenuated oral vaccine Ty21a (Vivotif Berna, Swiss Serum and Vaccine Institute, Bern, Switzerland) has been licensed in the United States since 1989. The molecular basis of attenuation of Ty21a is unknown and is not related to the *galE* mutation present in the vaccine.[353] Its main advantage is that it has a markedly reduced incidence of side effects in comparison to parenteral vaccines.[12, 247, 341] No serious adverse reactions have been observed in large-scale field trials or during postmarketing surveillance in Switzerland.[354–358] After administration of three doses of Ty21a vaccine containing 10^9 organisms on alternate days, the protective efficacy ranged from 43 to 96% in endemic populations.[356, 359]

The current recommendation is that a total of four doses of Ty21a in an enteric-coated capsule be taken 1 hour before a meal every other day. Stored capsules must be refrigerated.[341] Noncompliance with the multidose administration schedule and the requirement for home refrigeration has been reported.[360] A booster series of four capsules is recommended every 5 years, although few data are available on the persistence of antibody titers against *S. typhi*. Evidence for the efficacy of Ty21a in immunologically naive individuals is limited; in some studies in travelers no efficacy was demonstrated.[361, 362] Nevertheless, based on studies in endemic populations, it is likely that Ty21a is as effective as the heat-phenol–inactivated vaccine if compliance is adequate. Because of the possibility of illness associated with administration of a live-attenuated vaccine, Ty21a is not recommended for children younger than 6 years, the immunosuppressed, and those receiving antibiotic therapy.[341] Because it is a live-bacterial vaccine, Ty21a should not be administered to individuals receiving antibiotics, but simultaneous immunoglobulin administration is not a problem. In addition, typhoid vaccination should not be delayed for viral vaccines, and the immune response in volunteers was recently documented to be unaffected by concomitant vaccination with oral polio and yellow fever vaccine. Ty21a is not inhibited in growth in vitro by chloroquine but is by mefloquine. Inhibition of Ty21a by antimalarials is a concern, and it has recently been demonstrated that proguanil inhibited antibody production to *S. typhi* lipopolysaccharide in response to Ty21a administration.

A newly licensed Vi capsular polysaccharide vaccine (ViCPS) is available for parenteral use (Typhim Vi, Pasteur-Merieux). Its main advantages are that the primary vaccination schedule involves a single dose and it has fewer side effects than heat-phenol–inactivated vaccine does. Primary vaccination consists of 25 μg of Vi in 0.5 ml given intramuscularly. Side effects include fever (0 to 1%), headache (1.5 to 3%), and local erythema or induration greater than 1 cm (7%). The manufacturer does not recommend the vaccine for individuals younger than 2 years. Boosters with ViCPS are currently recommended every 2 years. Knowledge of the prolonged efficacy of ViCPS is more limited, but in one study 55% efficacy rates and increased immunologic responses were demonstrated over a 3-year period in South African children living in an area endemic for typhoid fever.[363] The advantages of ViCPS are that fewer doses are required and a lower frequency of side effects is seen than with the heat-killed parenteral vaccine.

In summary, none of the currently available typhoid vaccines has been demonstrated to have sufficient efficacy in travelers to recommend widespread use. Because of the low frequency of side effects, it is reasonable to recommend use of the oral live Ty21a vaccine for travelers spending a prolonged period in a high-risk area despite its limited efficacy and risk of noncompliance. The usefulness of the heat-killed parenteral typhoid vaccine is limited by the high incidence of serious side effects and its failure to protect against high inocula. It is reasonable to consider the use of ViCPS when parenteral vaccination is required or compliance is a concern. Parenteral vaccines are the only options available for persons younger than 6 years or those who are immunosuppressed and prolonged exposure to *S. typhi* is anticipated.[341]

THERAPY FOR SALMONELLOSIS

Typhoid Fever

Chloramphenicol has been the treatment of choice for typhoid fever since its introduction in 1948 and remains the standard against which newer antimicrobials must be compared.[16] Chloramphenicol is inexpensive and highly effective after oral administration, but oral chloramphenicol is no longer available in the United States. Treatment with chloramphenicol (500 mg orally four times daily) reduces typhoid fever mortality from approximately 20 to 1% and the duration of fever from 14 to 28 days to 3 to 5 days.[16, 364] However, chloramphenicol therapy has been associated with the emergence of resistance,[16, 72, 365–367] a high relapse rate (10 to 25%),[194, 364, 368, 369] a high rate of continued and chronic carriage,[194] bone marrow toxicity,[370, 371] and high mortality rates in some recent series from the developing world.[72, 264, 368] If intravenous therapy is required, a different antimicrobial agent should be administered because intravenous chloramphenicol succinate is cleared in the urine before conversion to chloramphenicol, thus resulting in much lower serum concentrations than the equivalent oral dose.[372, 373] Although in vitro studies have not always correlated with in vivo efficacy, chloramphenicol is only bacteriostatic against clinical isolates[374, 375] and against *S. typhi* within cultured human macrophages. In contrast, ceftriaxone, ampicillin, and quinolones are highly bactericidal for intracellular *S. typhi.*[375]

The emergence of plasmid-mediated resistance to chloramphenicol in the 1970s and in outbreaks in Latin America and Asia[363–367, 376, 377] has prompted the use of amoxicillin (1 g orally every 6 hours)[378, 379] and trimethoprim-sulfamethoxazole (one double-strength tablet twice daily)[380, 381] as alternatives for the treatment of typhoid fever. Despite several studies suggesting that ampicillin is inferior to chloramphenicol, these agents are probably equivalent to chloramphenicol when administered orally for treatment of infections caused by susceptible strains and may decrease the relapse rate.[368] Because of the recent emergence of multidrug-resistant strains of *S. typhi*, including resistance to ampicillin and trimethoprim, the efficacy of these drugs has also diminished.[75, 77, 78]

In areas with a high prevalence of multidrug-resistant *Salmonella* infection (e.g., Indian subcontinent, Southeast Asia, and Africa), all patients suspected of having typhoid fever should be treated with a quinolone or third-generation cephalosporin until the results of culture sensitivity studies become available. Parenterally administered third-generation cephalosporins are effective in the treatment of typhoid fever.[310, 382–386] Ceftriaxone (1 to 2 g daily) administered either intravenously or intramuscularly for 10 to 14 days is equivalent to oral or intravenous chloramphenicol administered for the treatment of susceptible *S. typhi* strains.[382, 383, 386] Excellent response rates have been reported with ceftriaxone when administered for 5 to 7 days, but the relapse rate remains incompletely defined.[383] After initial control of typhoid fever symptoms with a parenteral third-generation cephalosporin, many practitioners switch to an oral agent to complete 10 to 14 days of therapy. Oral cefixime (10 to 15 mg/kg orally twice daily) warrants further study for the initial treatment of multidrug-resistant typhoid fever.[387]

Several small studies have reported successful treatment of typhoid fever with aztreonam.[388, 389] However, a prospective clinical trial in children in Malaysia was discontinued because of a high failure rate with aztreonam.[390] First- and second-generation cephalosporins are also clinically ineffective and should not be used to treat typhoid fever or nontyphoidal salmonellosis despite adequate in vitro killing activity.[391–394] In addition, aminoglycosides are clinically ineffective, perhaps because they lack activity against intracellular salmonellae.[395]

Quinolones are highly active against salmonellae in vitro, effectively penetrate macrophages, achieve high concentrations in the bowel and bile lumina, and thus have potential advantages over other antimicrobials in the treatment of typhoid fever.[396, 397] Ciprofloxacin (500 mg orally twice daily for 10 days) remains the drug of choice for the treatment of multidrug-resistant typhoid.[71, 339, 398–400] Other quinolones, including ofloxacin, norfloxacin, fleroxacin, and pefloxacin, have been effective in small clinical trials.[401–403] Short-course therapy with ofloxacin (10 to 15 mg/kg divided twice daily for 2 to 3 days) appears to be simple, safe, and effective in the treatment of uncomplicated multidrug-resistant typhoid fever when the strain is susceptible to nalidixic acid.[404] However, patients infected with relatively quinolone-resistant *S. typhi* strains (resistant to nalidixic acid and a minimal inhibitory ciprofloxacin concentration of 0.125 to 1 mg/dl) who receive short-course quinolone therapy (i.e., <5 days) may not demonstrate clinical recovery and could require repeated or alternative treatment.[404] Therefore, all *S. typhi* isolates should be screened for nalidixic acid resistance and tested against a clinically appropriate quinolone.[404] Patients with nalidixic acid–resistant strains should be treated with higher doses of ciprofloxacin (i.e., 10 mg/kg twice daily for 10 days) or ofloxacin (10 to 15 mg/kg divided twice daily for 7 to 10 days).[404–408]

Currently, it is recommended that quinolones be avoided in children younger than 10 years or pregnant women because of data demonstrating cartilage damage in young animals.[409] The preferred treatment of known or suspected multidrug-resistant typhoid in children is a parenteral third-generation cephalosporin, especially ceftriaxone.[72, 383, 386] However, quinolones have been used to treat multidrug-resistant typhoid in children and pregnant patients without adverse effects.[410–412]

The use of glucocorticosteroids has been advocated for the treatment of severe typhoid fever based on a study in Jakarta that showed a significant reduction in mortality in patients with severe typhoid fever (i.e., associated delirium, obtundation, stupor, coma, or shock) treated with chloramphenicol and dexamethasone as compared with chloramphenicol-treated control patients (case-fatality rate, 10 versus 56%).[63] Although the case-fatality rate in the control group was high and the study has never been repeated, on the basis of this study, dexamethasone, 3 mg/kg intravenously, followed by eight doses of 1 mg/kg every 6 hours, should be considered for the treatment of severe typhoid with altered mental status or shock. Steroid treatment beyond 48 hours may increase the relapse rate.[413]

Nontyphoidal *Salmonella*

Salmonella gastroenteritis is usually a self-limited disease, and therapy should be directed primarily to the replacement of fluid and electrolyte losses.[414] Antimicrobial therapy for uncomplicated nontyphoidal *Salmonella* gastroenteritis, including short-course or single-dose regimens with oral quinolones,[415–420] amoxicillin,[421] or trimethoprim-sulfamethoxazole,[417] does not appear to decrease the duration of symptoms or consistently eliminate stool carriage. In addition, higher rates of bacteriologic relapse have been observed in children and adults who received antimicrobial therapy for *Salmonella* gastroenteritis than in placebo-treated control patients.[419, 421] Therefore, antimicrobials should not be used routinely to treat uncomplicated nontyphoidal *Salmonella* gastroenteritis or to reduce convalescent stool excretion.

Although bacteremia develops in less than 5% of all patients with *Salmonella* gastroenteritis, certain patients are at increased risk for invasive infection and may benefit from preemptive antimicrobial therapy. Antimicrobial therapy should be considered for neonates, persons older than 50 years, and patients with immunosuppression, cardiac valvular or mural abnormalities, or prosthetic vascular grafts. Treatment should consist of an oral or intravenous antimicrobial administered for 48 to 72 hours or until the patient becomes afebrile. Longer treatment may result in a higher rate of chronic carriage and relapse. For susceptible organisms, treatment with an oral quinolone, trimethoprim-sulfamethoxazole, or amoxicillin is adequate. Occasionally, antimicrobial prophylaxis has been required to control institutional outbreaks, especially in long-term care facilities or pediatric wards where compliance with infection-control measures may be difficult.[422, 423]

Although quinolones are not usually recommended in children younger than 10 years,[409] they may have a role in treating severe nontyphoidal salmonellosis in this age group. In one small study, seven children with severe typhoidal or nontyphoidal salmonellosis who failed conventional therapy improved rapidly when treated with oral pefloxacin (12 mg/kg daily for 7 days).[424] In addition, a double-blind placebo-controlled trial from Turkey demonstrated that the administration of intravenous immunoglobulin (500 mg/kg on days 1, 2, 3, and 8) in combination with cefoperazone to preterm neonates with *S. typhimurium* infection reduced the mortality, complications, and duration of antimicrobial therapy in comparison to treatment with cefoperazone alone, a finding that merits further study.[425]

Bacteremia

Because of the increasing prevalence of antimicrobial resistance, empirical therapy for life-threatening bacteremia or focal infection suspected to be caused by nontyphoidal *Salmonella* should include a third-generation cephalosporin and a quinolone until susceptibility patterns are known. It is also important to document whether the bacteremia is high grade (i.e., more than 50% of three or more blood cultures positive) and, if so, to search for endovascular abnormalities by echocardiography or other imaging techniques. Low-grade bacteremia not involving vascular structures should be treated with 7 to 14 days of intravenous antimicrobial therapy. Six weeks of intravenous therapy with a β-lactam antibiotic such as ampicillin or ceftriaxone is recommended to treat documented or suspected endovascular infection. Chloramphenicol should not be used to treat endovascular infection because of high failure rates.[284, 288] In addition, surgical resection of infected aneurysms or other infected endovascular sites is often required.[335, 426] Patients with infected prosthetic vascular grafts that could not be resected have been maintained on suppressive oral therapy for life.[308]

Recurrent *Salmonella* Bacteremia in Persons with Acquired Immunodeficiency Syndrome

In persons with AIDS and a first episode of *Salmonella* bacteremia, 1 to 2 weeks of intravenous antimicrobial therapy followed by 4 weeks of oral quinolone therapy (e.g., ciprofloxacin, 500 to 750 mg twice daily) should be administered in an attempt to eradicate the organism and decrease the risk of recurrent bacteremia.[427] Persons who relapse after 6 weeks of antimicrobial therapy should receive long-term suppressive therapy with a quinolone or trimethoprim-sulfamethoxazole. Quinolones and zidovudine have a synergistic antibacterial effect against *Salmonella*; administration of both drugs may dramatically decrease the risk of recurrent infection.[428, 429] Although data are lacking, because of its efficacy in the prevention of *Pneumocystis carinii* infection, trimethoprim-sulfamethoxazole may be a good choice for long-term suppressive therapy for salmonellosis if the organism is susceptible.[430]

Focal Infections

Treatment recommendations for the management of focal infections are summarized in Table 210–2. Of note, treatment failure with quinolones has been associated with low-dose oral therapy or with administration to patients with undrained abscesses or osteomyelitis, conditions in which antimicrobial penetration may be poor.[405, 406, 431–433]

Long-Term Carrier State

Long-term carriage of nontyphoidal *Salmonella* is managed similar to the management of typhoid carriers. Amoxicillin and trimethoprim-sulfamethoxazole are effective in eradication of long-term carriage, with cure rates of greater than 80% after 6 weeks of therapy.[434, 435] Similar results have been obtained with the use of 4 to 6 weeks of ciprofloxacin or norfloxacin, including the eradication of long-term carriage in a small number of patients with gallstones.[396, 436, 437] The high concentration of amoxicillin and quinolones in bile and the superior intracellular penetration of quinolones are theoretical advantages over trimethoprim-sulfamethoxazole. Cost considerations favor the use of amoxicillin for treating carriage of susceptible organisms. However, antimicrobial agents are infrequently effective in eradicating the carrier state if anatomic abnormalities such as biliary or kidney stones are present. In such cases, surgery combined with antimicrobial therapy is often required for eradication.[337, 438] Long-term suppressive antimicrobial therapy should be considered for patients with persistent carriage in whom no anatomic abnormality can be identified or who relapse after cholecystectomy.

PREVENTION AND CONTROL

Prevention and control of salmonellosis require both an understanding of the complex cycles of transmission and ongoing surveillance to characterize trends in *Salmonella* occurrence and identify outbreaks. Control of foodborne salmonellosis requires coordinated effort on multiple levels, including the farm, food processors, and food handlers, to identify critical control points.[121] Recognition of foodborne outbreaks also requires that clinicians have a high index of suspicion, order the appropriate laboratory test, and promptly report positive culture results to public health departments. In the United States, the recent establishment of a program of active population-based surveillance for foodborne diseases and for antimicrobial resistance among *Salmonella* strains will improve efforts to respond to the problem of foodborne salmonellosis.[88, 156]

Establishment of cooperative international surveillance systems, such as "Salm-Net" in Europe, will facilitate rapid data exchange for the prevention of human salmonellosis associated with widely distributed agricultural and manufactured foods.[439, 440]

Although most cases of *Salmonella* infection occur sporadically, large numbers of persons may potentially become infected when commercial kitchens serve *Salmonella*-contaminated foods that have not been sufficiently cooked or that have been mishandled. Commercial food service establishments can reduce the risk of foodborne *S. enteritidis* illness if they substitute pasteurized eggs for pooled eggs whenever possible and do not serve food containing raw or undercooked eggs. The use of pasteurized eggs for all recipes calling for bulk pooled eggs is recommended for all nursing homes and hospitals.[172]

The most cost-effective approach to the control of salmonellosis in food handlers is attention to good personal hygiene and maintenance of time-temperature standards for food handling. Routine screening of food handlers for carriage of salmonellae after gastroenteritis is common before allowing individuals to return to work. However, there seems to be little justification for this approach inasmuch as few outbreaks are related to specific food handlers, prolonged carriage in food handlers after gastroenteritis is rare, and the number of organisms present is small. Therefore, it is reasonable to allow individuals to return to work after the diarrhea has resolved. Two consecutive negative stool samples should be required only for food handlers whose work involves touching unwrapped foods that are consumed raw or served without further cooking. Routine surveillance of food handlers for asymptomatic stool carriage of *Salmonella* is not recommended.[441]

To limit the risk of nosocomial transmission to patients and health care workers, patients excreting salmonellae should be managed with standard precautions, including the use of barrier precautions when performing patient care or handling soiled articles.[442] Control of *Salmonella* outbreaks in long-term care facilities or neonatal care areas may be difficult because of poor compliance with isolation precautions and the increased susceptibility of these patients.[160] Because *Salmonella* infection in the elderly, immunocompromised, or critically ill can be particularly severe, the Centers for Disease Control and Prevention recommends that staff members who continue to excrete salmonellae after they have returned to work should not care for such high-risk patients until cultures of two consecutive stool specimens collected at least 24 hours apart are negative for this pathogen.[443] However, despite the risk of prolonged carriage, the risk of transmission of *Salmonella* from health care worker to patient appears to be very small. Once the health care worker is clinically recovered and passing formed stool, the risk of transmission appears to be low and individuals should be allowed to return to work if careful hand washing is practiced.

REFERENCES

1. Smith T. The hog-cholera group of bacteria. US Bur Anim Ind Bull. 1894;6:6–40.
2. Committee on *Salmonella,* Division of Biology and Agriculture of the National Research Council. An Evaluation of the *Salmonella* Problem. Washington, DC: National Academy of Sciences; 1969.

3. Rubin RH, Weinstein L. Salmonellosis: Microbiologic, Pathologic, and Clinical Features. New York: Stratton; 1977.
4. Fang FC, Fierer J. Human infection with *Salmonella dublin*. Medicine (Baltimore). 1991;70:198–207.
5. Waterman SH, et al. *Salmonella arizonae* infections in Latinos associated with rattlesnake folk medicine. Am J Public Health. 1990;80:286–289.
6. Bhatt BD, et al. Disseminated *Salmonella arizonae* infection associated with rattlesnake meat ingestions. Am J Gastroenterol. 1989;84:433–435.
7. Louis PCA. Recherches Anatomiques, Pathologiques et Therapeutiques sur la Maladie Connue sous les Noms de Gastroenterite, Fievre Putride, Adymanique, Thiphoide, Comparee avec les Maladies Aigues les Pluis Ordinaires. Paris: J-B Balliere; 1829.
8. Jenner W. On the Identity of Typhoid and Typhus Fevers. London: C & J Adlard; 1850.
9. Wilson JC. A Treatise on the Continued Fevers. New York: Wood; 1881.
10. Budd W. Typhoid Fever: Its Nature, Mode of Spreading, and Prevention. London: Longmans; 1873.
11. Schroeter J. Kryptogamenflora von Schlesien, v. 3. Breslau, Poland: JU Kern; 1885.
12. Edelman R, Levine MM. Summary of an international workshop on typhoid fever. Rev Infect Dis. 1986;8:329–349.
13. Pfeiffer R, Kalle W. Experimentelle untersuchungen zur Frage der Schitzimphung des Menschen gegen thypus abdominalis. Dtsch Med Wochenschr. 1896;22:735.
14. Widal F. Serodiagnostic de la fievre typhoide. Bull Med Hosp Paris. 1896;13:561–566.
15. Kauffman F. The Diagnosis of *Salmonella* Types. Springfield, Ill: Charles C Thomas; 1950.
16. Woodward TE, et al. Preliminary report on the beneficial effect of Chloromycetin in the treatment of typhoid fever. Ann Intern Med. 1948;29:131–134.
17. Zinder ND, Lederberg J. Genetic exchange in *Salmonella*. J Bacteriol. 1952;64:679–699.
18. Sanderson KE, Roth JR. Linkage Map of *Salmonella typhimurium*, Edition VII. Microbiol Rev. 1988;52:485–532.
19. Ames BN, Lee FD, Durston W. An improved bacterial test system for detection and classification of mutagens and carcinogens. Proc Natl Acad Sci U S A. 1973;70:782–786.
20. Farmer JJ. Enterobacteriaceae: Introduction and identification. In: Murray PR, Baron EJ, Pfaller MA, eds. Manual of Clinical Microbiology, 6th ed. Washington, DC: American Society for Microbiology; 1995:438–449.
21. Crosa JH, et al. Molecular relationships among salmonellae. J Bacteriol. 1973;115:307–315.
22. Stoleru L, Le Minor L, Lherithier AM. Polynucleotide sequence divergence among strains of *Salmonella* subgenus IV and closely related organisms. Ann Microbiol. 1976;127:477–486.
23. Popoff MY, Bockemuhl J, Hickman-Brenner FW. Supplement 1995 (no. 39) to the Kauffmann-White scheme. Res Microbiol. 1996;147:765–769.
24. Felix A, Pitt RM. A new antigen of *B. typhosus*. Lancet. 1934;2:186–191.
25. Baker EE, Whiteside RE, Derow MA. The Vi antigen of the Enterobacteriaceae. II. Immunologic and biologic properties. J Immunol. 1959;83:680–686.
26. Daniels EM, et al. Characterization of the *Salmonella paratyphi* C Vi polysaccharide. Infect Immun. 1989;57:3159–3164.
27. World Health Organization, Center for Reference and Research on *Salmonella*. Antigenic formulae of the *Salmonella*. Paris: International *Salmonella* Center, Institute Pasteur; 1980.
28. Gray LD. *Escherichia*, *Salmonella*, *Shigella*, and *Yersinia*. In: Murray PR, Baron EJ, Pfaller MA, eds. Manual of Clinical Microbiology, 6th ed. Washington, DC: American Society for Microbiology; 1995:450–456.
29. Forward KR, Rainnie BJ. Use of selenite enrichment broth for the detection of *Salmonella* from stool: A report of one year experience at a provincial public health laboratory. Diagn Microbiol Infect Dis. 1997;29:215–217.
30. Ruiz J, et al. Comparison of five plating media for isolation of *Salmonella* species from human stools. J Clin Microbiol. 1996;34:686–688.
31. Banffer JRJ, van Zwol-Saaloos JA, Broere LJ. Evaluation of a commercial latex agglutination test for rapid detection of *Salmonella* in fecal samples. Eur J Clin Microbiol Infect Dis. 1993;12:633.
32. Rubin FA. Nucleic acid probes for the identification of *Salmonella*. In: Macario AJL, Macario EC, eds. Gene Probes for Bacteria. New York: Academic; 1990:323.
33. Chiu CH, Ou JT. Rapid identification of *Salmonella* serovars in feces by specific detection of virulence genes, *invA* and *spvC*, by an enrichment broth culture–multiplex PCR combination assay. J Clin Microbiol. 1996;34:2619–2622.
34. Haedicke W, et al. Specific and sensitive two-step polymerase chain reaction assay for the detection of *Salmonella* species. Eur J Clin Microbiol Infect Dis. 1996;15:603–607.
35. Heyns K, Kiessling G. Strukturaufklarung des Vi-antigens aus *Citrobacter freundii (E. coli)* 5396/38. Carbohydr Res. 1967;3:340–352.
36. Gray PW, et al. Cloning of a human neutrophil bactericidal protein. Structural and functional correlations. J Biol Chem. 1989;264:9505–9509.
37. Anderson ES, et al. Bacteriophage typing designations of *Salmonella typhimurium*. J Hyg. 1977;78:297–300.
38. Gershman M. Single phage-typing set for differentiating salmonellae. J Clin Microbiol. 1977;5:302.
39. Threlfall EJ, et al. Interrelationships between strains of *Salmonella enteritidis* belonging to phage types 4, 7, 7a, 8, 13, 13a, 23, 24 and 30. J Appl Bacteriol. 1993;75:43–48.
40. Altekruse S, et al. A comparison of *Salmonella enteritidis* phage types from egg-associated outbreaks and implicated laying flocks. Epidemiol Infect. 1993;110: 17–22.
41. Gulig PA, et al. Molecular analysis of *spv* virulence genes of the *Salmonella* virulence plasmids. Mol Microbiol. 1993;7:825–830.
42. Reeves MW, et al. Clonal nature of *Salmonella typhi* and its genetic relatedness to other *Salmonella* as shown by multilocus enzyme electrophoresis, and proposal of *Salmonella bongori* comb. nov. J Clin Microbiol. 1989;27:313–320.
43. Vatopoulos AC, et al. Molecular epidemiology of ampicillin-resistant clinical isolates of *Salmonella enteritidis*. J Clin Microbiol. 1994;32:1322–1325.
44. O'Brien TF, et al. Molecular epidemiology of antibiotic resistance in *Salmonella* from animals and human beings in the United States. N Engl J Med. 1982;307:1–6.
45. Rodrigue DC, et al. Comparison of plasmid profile, phage types, and antimicrobial resistance patterns of *Salmonella enteritidis* isolates in the United States. J Clin Microbiol. 1992;30:854–857.
46. Threlfall EJ, Hampton MD, Schofield SL, et al. Epidemiological application of differentiating multiresistant *Salmonella typhimurium* DT104 by plasmid profile. Commun Dis Rep CDR Rev. 1996(6):R155–R159.
47. Esteban E, et al. Use of ribotyping for characterization of *Salmonella* serotypes. J Clin Microbiol. 1993;31:233–237.
48. Nastasi A, Mammina C, Villafrate MR. rDNA fingerprinting as a tool in epidemiological analysis of *Salmonella typhi* infections. Epidemiol Infect. 1991;107:565–576.
49. Nastasi A, Mammina C, Villafrate MR. Epidemiology of *Salmonella typhimurium*: Ribosomal DNA analysis of strains from human and animal sources. Epidemiol Infect. 1993;110:553–565.
50. Nastasi A, et al. Epidemiological analysis of strains of *Salmonella enterica* serotype *enteritidis* from foodborne outbreaks occurring in Italy, 1980–1994. J Med Microbiol. 1997;46:377–382.
51. Suzuki Y, et al. Molecular epidemiology of *Salmonella enteritidis*. An outbreak and sporadic cases studied by means of pulsed-field gel electrophoresis. J Infect. 1995;31:211–217.
52. Hampton MD, et al. Molecular fingerprinting of multidrug-resistant *Salmonella enterica* serotype *typhi*. Emerg Infect Dis. 1998;4:317–320.
53. Threlfall EJ, et al. Insertion sequence IS200 fingerprinting of *Salmonella typhi*: An assessment of epidemiological applicability. Epidemiol Infect. 1994;112:253–261.
54. Pelkonen S, et al. Differentiation of *Salmonella* serovar *infantis* isolates from human and animal sources by fingerprinting IS200 and 16S *rrn* loci. J Clin Microbiol. 1994;32:2128–2133.
55. Ryan CA, Hargrett-Bean NT, Blake PA. *Salmonella typhi* infections in the United States, 1975–1984: Increasing role of foreign travel. Rev Infect Dis. 1989;11:1–8.
56. Dritz SK, Braff EH. Sexually transmitted typhoid fever. N Engl J Med. 1977;296:1359.
57. Blaser MJ, et al. *Salmonella typhi:* The laboratory as a reservoir of infection. J Infect Dis. 1980;142:934–938.
58. Weikel CS, Guerrant RL. Nosocomial salmonellosis (Editorial). Infect Control. 1985;6:218–220.
59. Ivanoff B. Typhoid fever: Global situation and WHO recommendations. In: Proceedings of the 2nd Asia-Pacific Symposium on Typhoid Fever and Other Salmonellosis. Bangkok: Infectious Disease Association of Thailand; 1994.
60. Bradaric N, Punda-Polic V, Milas I, et al. Two outbreaks of typhoid fever related to the war in Bosnia and Herzegovina. Eur J Epidemiol. 1996;12:409–412.
61. Centers for Disease Control and Prevention. Epidemic typhoid fever—Dushanbe, Tajikistan, 1997. MMWR Morb Mortal Wkly Rep. 1998;47:752–756.
62. Thikyakorn U, Mansuwan P, Taylor DN. Typhoid and paratyphoid fever in 192 children in Thailand. Am J Dis Child. 1987;141:862–865.
63. Butler T, et al. Patterns of morbidity and mortality in typhoid fever dependent on age and gender: Review of 552 hospitalized patients with diarrhea. Rev Infect Dis. 1991;13:85–90.
64. Cohen JI, Bartlett JA, Corey GR. Extra-intestinal manifestations of *Salmonella* infections. Medicine (Baltimore). 1987;66:349–388.
65. Barrett-Connor E. Bacterial infection and sickle cell anemia: An analysis of 250 infections in 166 patients and a review of the literature. Medicine (Baltimore). 1971;50:97–112.
66. Neves J, Raso P, Marinko PP. Prolonged septicemic salmonellosis intercurrent with *Schistosomiasis mansoni* infection. J Trop Med Hyg. 1971;74:9.
67. Black PH, Kunz KL, Swartz MN. Salmonellosis—a review of some unusual aspects. N Engl J Med. 1960;262:864–870, 921–927.
68. Wheat LJ, et al. Systemic salmonellosis in patients with disseminated histoplasmosis. Case for "macrophage blockade" caused by *Histoplasma capsulatum*. Arch Intern Med. 1987;147:561–564.
69. Goldstein FW, et al. Plasmid-mediated resistance to multiple antibiotics in *Salmonella typhi*. J Infect Dis. 1986;153:261–266.
70. Arand AC, et al. Epidemic multiresistant enteric fever in eastern India. Lancet. 1990;335:352.
71. Sugandhi Rao P, et al. Emergence of multidrug-resistant *Salmonella typhi* in rural southern India. Am J Trop Med Hyg. 1993;48:108–111.
72. Bhutta ZA, Naqvi SH, Razzalf RA, et al. Multidrug-resistant typhoid in children: Presentation and clinical features. Rev Infect Dis. 1991;13:832–836.
73. Vasquez V, Calderon E, Rodriquez R. Chloramphenicol-resistant strains of *Salmonella typhosa*. N Engl J Med. 1972;286:1220.
74. Luby SP, et al. Risk factors for typhoid fever in an endemic setting, Karachi, Pakistan. Epidemiol Infect. 1998;120:129–138.
75. Threlfall EJ, et al. Increase in multiple antibiotic resistance in nontyphoidal salmonellas from humans in England and Wales: A comparison of data for 1994 and 1996. Microb Drug Resist. 1997;3:263–266.
76. Threlfall EJ, Rowe B, Ward LR. Occurrence and treatment of multi-resistant *Salmonella typhi*. Public Health Lab Serv Microbiol Dig. 1991;8:56–59.
77. Vimala KN, Paniker CK. Resistance transfer between *E. coli* and *Salmonella* strains from Kerala. Indian J Med Res. 1972;60:334–338.

78. Anderson ES. The problem and implication of chloramphenicol resistance in the typhoid bacillus. J Hyg. 1975;74:289–299.
79. Anand AC, et al. Epidemic multiresistant enteric fever in eastern India (Letter). Lancet. 1990;335:352.
80. Martin SM, Hardgrett-Bean N, Tauxe RV. An Atlas of *Salmonella* in the United States: Serotype-Specific Surveillance 1968–1986. Atlanta: US Department of Health and Human Services, Public Health Services, Centers for Disease Control; 1987.
81. Lin FYC, Becke JM, Groves C. Restaurant-associated outbreak of typhoid fever in Maryland: Identification of carrier facilitated by measurement of serum Vi antibodies. J Clin Microbiol. 1988;26:1194–1197.
82. Shandera WX, et al. An analysis of economic costs associated with an outbreak of typhoid fever. Am J Public Health. 1985;75:71–73.
83. Birkhead GS, et al. Typhoid fever at a resort hotel in New York: A large outbreak with an unusual vehicle. J Infect Dis. 1993;167:1228–1232.
84. Mermin JH, et al. Typhoid fever in the United States, 1985–1994: Changing risks of international travel and increasing antimicrobial resistance. Arch Intern Med. 1998;158:633–638.
85. Misra S, Diaz PS, Rowley AH. Characteristics of typhoid fever in children and adolescents in a major metropolitan area in the United States. Clin Infect Dis. 1997;24:998–1000.
86. Centers for Disease Control and Prevention. *Salmonella* Surveillance: Annual Tabulation Summary, 1993–1994. Atlanta: US Department of Health and Human Services, Public Health Service; 1995.
87. Altekruse SF, Cohen ML, Swerdlow DL. Emerging foodborne diseases. Emerg Infect Dis. 1997;3:285–293.
88. Centers for Disease Control and Prevention. Foodborne Diseases Active Surveillance Network, 1996. MMWR Morb Mortal Wkly Rep. 1997;46(12):258–261.
89. Gorbach SL, et al. Travelers' diarrhea and toxigenic *Escherichia coli.* N Engl J Med. 1975;292:933–936.
90. Mølbak K, et al. The etiology of early childhood diarrhea: A community study from Guinea-Bissau. J Infect Dis. 1994;169:581–587.
91. Saidi SM, et al. Epidemiological study on infectious diarrheal diseases in children in a coastal rural area of Kenya. Microbiol Immunol. 1997;41:773–778.
92. Bean NH, Goulding JS, Lao C, et al. Surveillance for foodborne-disease outbreaks—United States, 1988–1992. MMWR CDC Surveill Summ. 1996; 45(5):1–66.
93. Todd EC. Epidemiology of foodborne diseases: A worldwide review. World Health Stat Q. 1997;50:30–50.
94. St Louis ME, et al. The emergence of grade A eggs as a major source of *Salmonella enteritidis* infections. New implications for the control of salmonellosis. JAMA. 1988;259:2103–2107.
95. Mishu B, et al. Outbreaks of *Salmonella enteritidis* infections in the United States, 1985–1991. J Infect Dis. 1994;169:547–552.
96. Centers for Disease Control and Prevention. *Salmonella hadar* associated with pet ducklings—Connecticut, Maryland, and Pennsylvania, 1991. MMWR Morb Mortal Wkly Rep. 1992;41(11):185–187.
97. Centers For Disease Control And Prevention. Outbreak of salmonellosis associated with beef jerky—New Mexico, 1995. MMWR Morb Mortal Wkly Rep. 1995;44(42):785–788.
98. Taylor DN, et al. Salmonellosis associated with marijuana: A multistate outbreak traced by plasmid fingerprinting. N Engl J Med. 1982;306:1249–1253.
99. Kramer MH, Herwaldt BC, Craun GF, et al. Surveillance for waterborne-disease outbreaks—United States, 1993–1994. MMWR CDC Surveill Summ. 1996;45:1–33.
100. Angulo FJ, et al. A community waterborne outbreak of salmonellosis and the effectiveness of a boil water order. Am J Public Health. 1997;87:580–584.
101. Woodward DL, Khakhria R, Johnson WM. Human salmonellosis associated with exotic pets. J Clin Microbiol. 1997;35:2786–2790.
102. Chiodini RJ, Sundberg JP. Salmonellosis in reptiles: A review. Am J Epidemiol. 1981;113:494–499.
103. Tauxe RV, et al. Turtle-associated salmonellosis in Puerto Rico. Hazards of the global turtle trade. JAMA. 1985;254:237–239.
104. Mermin J, Hoar B, Angulo FJ. Iguanas and *Salmonella marina* infection in children: A reflection of the increasing incidence of reptile-associated salmonellosis in the United States. Pediatrics. 1997;99:399–402.
105. Sanyal D, Douglas T, Roberts R. *Salmonella* infection acquired from reptilian pets. Arch Dis Child. 1997;77:345–346.
106. Centers for Disease Control and Prevention. *Salmonella* serotype *montevideo* infections associated with chicks—Idaho, Washington, and Oregon, spring 1995 and 1996. MMWR Morb Mortal Wkly Rep. 1997;46(11):237–239.
107. Glaser CA, Angulo FJ, Rooney JA. Animal-associated opportunistic infections among persons infected with the human immunodeficiency virus. Clin Infect Dis. 1994;18:14–24.
108. Rodrigue DC, Tauxe RV, Rowe B. International increase in *Salmonella enteritidis*: A new pandemic? Epidemiol Infect. 1990;105:21–27.
109. Hedberg CW, et al. Role of egg consumption in sporadic *Salmonella-enteritidis* and *Salmonella-typhimurium* infections in Minnesota. J Infect Dis. 1993;167:107–111.
110. Centers for Disease Control and Prevention. Outbreaks of *Salmonella* serotype *enteritidis* infection associated with consumption of raw shell eggs—United States, 1994–1995. MMWR Morb Mortal Wkly Rep. 1996;45(34):737–742.
111. Keller LH, et al. *Salmonella enteritidis* colonization of the reproductive tract and forming and freshly laid eggs of chickens. Infect Immun. 1995;63:2443–2449.
112. Centers for Disease Control and Prevention. Salmonellosis associated with a Thanksgiving dinner—Nevada, 1995. MMWR Morb Mortal Wkly Rep. 1996;45(46): 1016–1017.
113. Mahon BE, et al. An international outbreak of *Salmonella* infections caused by alfalfa sprouts grown from contaminated seeds. J Infect Dis. 1997;175:876–882.
114. Hennessy TW, et al. A national outbreak of *Salmonella enteritidis* infections from ice cream. N Engl J Med. 1996;334:1281–1286.
115. Ryan CA, et al. Massive outbreak of antimicrobial-resistant salmonellosis traced to pasteurized milk. JAMA. 1987;258:3269–3274.
116. Centers for Disease Control and Prevention. *Salmonella* serotype *tennessee* in powdered milk products and infant formula—Canada and United States, 1993. MMWR Morb Mortal Wkly Rep. 1993;42(26):516–517.
117. Desenclos JC, et al. Large outbreak of *Salmonella enterica* serotype *paratyphi* B infection caused by a goats' milk cheese, France, 1993: A case finding and epidemiological study. BMJ. 1996;312:91–94.
118. Lehmacher A, Bockemuhl J, Aleksic S. Nationwide outbreak of human salmonellosis in Germany due to contaminated paprika and paprika-powdered potato chips. Epidemiol Infect. 1995;115:501–511.
119. Killalea D, et al. International epidemiological and microbiological study of outbreak of *Salmonella agona* infection from a ready to eat savory snack—I: England and Wales and the United States. BMJ. 1996;313:1105–1107.
120. Pavia AT, et al. Epidemiologic evidence that prior antimicrobial exposure decreases resistance to infection by antimicrobial-sensitive *Salmonella.* J Infect Dis. 1990;161:255–260.
121. World Health Organization. Control of *Salmonella* infections in animals and prevention of human foodborne *Salmonella* infections. Bull World Health Organ. 1994;72:831.
122. Spika JS, et al. Chloramphenicol-resistant *Salmonella newport* traced through hamburger to dairy farms. A major persisting source of human salmonellosis in California. N Engl J Med. 1987;316:565–570.
123. Zoukh K. [Resistance to antibiotics of salmonellae other than *typhi* and *paratyphi* isolated in Algeria from 1979 to 1985.] Pathol Biol. 1988;36:255–257.
124. Georges-Courbot MC, et al. Cluster of antibiotic-resistant *Salmonella enteritidis* infections in the Central African Republic. J Clin Microbiol. 1990;28:771–773.
125. Mirza NB, Wamola IA. *Salmonella typhimurium* outbreak at Kenyatta National Hospital (1985). East Afr Med J. 1989;66:453–457.
126. Lepage P, Bogaerts J, Van Goethem C, et al. Multiresistant *Salmonella typhimurium* systemic infection in Rwanda. Clinical features and treatment with cefotaxime. J Antimicrob Chemother. 1990;26(Suppl A):53–57.
127. Farhoudi-Moghaddam AA, et al. Antimicrobial drug resistance and resistance factor transfer among clinical isolates of salmonellae in Iran. Scand J Infect Dis. 1990;22:197–203.
128. Chowdhury MN. Antibiotic sensitivity pattern; experience at University Hospital, Riyadh, Saudi Arabia. J Hyg Epidemiol Microbiol Immunol. 1991;35:289–301.
129. Shehabi AA. Extra-intestinal infections with multiply drug-resistant *Salmonella typhimurium* in hospitalized patients in Jordan. Eur J Clin Microbiol Infect Dis. 1995;14:448–451.
130. Kariuki S, et al. Multi-drug resistant non-*typhi* salmonellae in Kenya. J Antimicrob Chemother. 1996;38:425–434.
131. Reina J, Gomez J. Decrease in resistance to ampicillin and co-trimoxazole in *Shigella* species isolated from faeces, 1983–1992 (Letter). J Antimicrob Chemother. 1994;33:1257–1258.
132. Munoz P, et al. Antimicrobial resistance of *Salmonella* isolates in a Spanish hospital. Antimicrob Agents Chemother. 1993;37:1200.
133. Threlfall EJ, Rowe B, Ward LR. A comparison of multiple drug resistance in salmonellas from humans and food animals in England and Wales, 1981 and 1990. Epidemiol Infect. 1993;111:189–197.
134. MacDonald KL, et al. Changes in antimicrobial resistance of *Salmonella* isolated from humans in the United States. JAMA. 1987;258:1496–1499.
135. Lee LA, et al. Increase in antimicrobial-resistant *Salmonella* infections in the United States, 1989–1990. J Infect Dis. 1994;170:128–134.
136. Kariuki S, et al. Antimicrobial susceptibility and presence of extrachromosomal deoxyribonucleic acid in *Salmonella* and *Shigella* isolates from patients with AIDS. East Afr Med J. 1994;71:292–296.
137. Boyd EF, Hartl DL. Recent horizontal transmission of plasmids between natural populations of *Escherichia coli* and *Salmonella enterica.* J Bacteriol. 1997;179:1622–1627.
138. Morosini MI, et al. Characterization of a nosocomial outbreak involving an epidemic plasmid encoding for TEM-27 in *Salmonella enterica* subspecies *enterica* serotype *othmarschen.* J Infect Dis. 1996;174:1015–1020.
139. Wall PG, Morgan D, Lamden K, et al. A case control study of infection with an epidemic strain of multiresistant *Salmonella typhimurium* DT104 in England and Wales. Commun Dis Rep CDR Rev. 1994;4(11):R130–R135.
140. Wall PG, et al. Transmission of multi-resistant strains of *Salmonella typhimurium* from cattle to man. Vet Rec. 1995;136:591–592.
141. Glynn MK, et al. Emergence of multidrug-resistant *Salmonella enterica* serotype *typhimurium* DT104 infections in the United States. N Engl J Med. 1998;338:1333–1338.
142. Bauernfeind A, et al. A new plasmidic cefotaximase from patients infected with *Salmonella typhimurium.* Infection. 1992;20:158–163.
143. Poupart MC, et al. Identification of CTX-2, a novel cefotaximase from a *Salmonella mbandaka* isolate. Antimicrob Agents Chemother. 1991;35:1498–1500.
144. Barguellil F, et al. In vivo acquisition of extended-spectrum beta-lactamase in *Salmonella enteritidis* during antimicrobial therapy. Eur J Clin Microbiol Infect Dis. 1995;14:703–706.
145. Vahaboglu H, et al. Resistance to extended-spectrum cephalosporins, caused by

PER-1 beta-lactamase, in *Salmonella typhimurium* from Istanbul, Turkey. J Med Microbiol. 1995;43:294–299.
146. Bhatia R, et al. Transferable beta lactam resistance against cephalosporins in *Salmonella typhimurium* strains in India. Indian J Med Res. 1994;99:203–205.
147. Wattal C, et al. An outbreak of multidrug resistant *Salmonella typhimurium* in Delhi (India). Indian J Med Res. 1994;100:266–267.
148. Gaillot O, et al. Novel transferable beta-lactam resistance with cephalosporinase characteristics in *Salmonella enteritidis*. J Antimicrob Chemother. 1997;39:85–87.
149. Digranes A, et al. Antibiotic susceptibility of blood culture isolates of Enterobacteriaceae from six Norwegian hospitals 1991–1992. APMIS. 1997;105:854–860.
150. Heisig P. High-level fluoroquinolone resistance in a *Salmonella typhimurium* isolate due to alterations in both *gyrA* and *gyrB* genes. J Antimicrob Chemother. 1993;32:367–377.
151. Reyna F, et al. *Salmonella typhimurium gyrA* mutations associated with fluoroquinolone resistance. Antimicrob Agents Chemother. 1995;39:1621–1623.
152. Griggs DJ, Gensberg K, Piddock LJ. Mutations in *gyrA* gene of quinolone-resistant *Salmonella* serotypes isolated from humans and animals. Antimicrob Agents Chemother. 1996;40:1009–1013.
153. Herikstad H, et al. Emerging quinolone-resistant *Salmonella* in the United States. Emerg Infect Dis. 1997;3:371–372.
154. Frost JA, Kelleher A, Rowe B. Increasing ciprofloxacin resistance in salmonellas in England and Wales 1991–1994. J Antimicrob Chemother. 1996;37:85–91.
155. Threlfall EJ, et al. Increasing spectrum of resistance in multiresistant *Salmonella typhimurium* (Letter). Lancet. 1996;347:1053–1054.
156. Centers for Disease Control and Prevention. Establishment of a national surveillance program for antimicrobial resistance in *Salmonella*. MMWR Morb Mortal Wkly Rep. 1996;45(5):110–111.
157. Maiorini E, et al. Multiply resistant nontyphoidal *Salmonella* gastroenteritis in children. Pediatr Infect Dis J. 1993;12:139–145.
158. Roberts FJ. Nontyphoidal, nonparatyphoidal *Salmonella* septicemia in adults. Eur J Clin Microbiol Infect Dis. 1993;12:205–208.
159. Wall PG, et al. Outbreaks of salmonellosis in hospitals in England and Wales: 1992–1994. J Hosp Infect. 1996;33:181–190.
160. Standaert SM, Hutcheson RH, Schaffner W. Nosocomial transmission of *Salmonella* gastroenteritis to laundry workers in a nursing home. Infect Control Hosp Epidemiol. 1994;15:22–26.
161. Tauxe RV, et al. Salmonellosis in nurses: Lack of transmission to patients. J Infect Dis. 1988;157:370–373.
162. Wall PG, Ryan MJ. Faecal incontinence in hospitals and residential and nursing homes for elderly people (Letter). BMJ. 1996;312:378.
163. Wilson R, et al. Salmonellosis in infants: The importance of intrafamilial transmission. Pediatrics. 1982;69:436–438.
164. Agunod M, et al. Correlative study of hydrochloric acid, pepsin, and intrinsic factor secretion in newborns and infants. Am J Dig Dis. 1969;14:400–414.
165. Haddock RL, Cousens SN, Guzman CC. Infant diet and salmonellosis. Am J Public Health. 1991;81:997–1000.
166. Chorba TL, et al. Control of a non-foodborne outbreak of salmonellosis: Day care in isolation. Am J Public Health. 1987;77:979–981.
167. Evans HS, Maguire H. Outbreaks of infectious intestinal disease in schools and nurseries in England and Wales 1992 to 1994 [published erratum appears in Commun Dis Rep CDR Rev. 1996;16;6(9):R128]. Commun Dis Rep CDR Rev. 1996;6(7):R103–R108.
168. Buchwald DS, Blaser MJ. A review of human salmonellosis: II. Duration of excretion following infection with non-*typhi Salmonella*. Rev Infect Dis. 1984;6:345–356.
169. Blaser MJ, Feldman RA. From the Centers for Disease Control. *Salmonella* bacteremia: Reports to the Centers for Disease Control, 1968–1979. J Infect Dis. 1981;143:743–746.
170. Riley LW, et al. Importance of host factors in human salmonellosis caused by multiresistant strains of *Salmonella*. J Infect Dis. 1984;149:878–883.
171. Taylor JL, et al. Simultaneous outbreak of *Salmonella enteritidis* and *Salmonella schwarzengrund* in a nursing home: Association of *S. enteritidis* with bacteremia and hospitalization (Letter). J Infect Dis. 1993;167:781–782.
172. Levine WC, et al. Foodborne disease outbreaks in nursing homes, 1975 through 1987. JAMA. 1991;266:2105–2109.
173. Smith PW. Consensus conference on nosocomial infections in long-term care facilities. Am J Infect Control. 1987;15(3):97–100.
174. Blaser MJ, Newman LS. A review of human salmonellosis: I. Infective dose. Rev Infect Dis. 1982;4:1096–1106.
175. Mintz ED, et al. Dose-response effects in an outbreak of *Salmonella enteritidis*. Epidemiol Infect. 1994;112:13–23.
176. Waddell WR, Kunz LJ. Association of *Salmonella enteritis* with operation of stomach. N Engl J Med. 1956;255:555–559.
177. Giannella RA, Broitman SA, Zamcheck N. Gastric acid barrier to ingested microorganisms in man: Studies in vivo and in vitro. Gut. 1972;13:251–256.
178. McCullough NB, Eisele CW. Experimental human salmonellosis. IV. Pathogenicity of strains of *Salmonella pullorum* obtained from spray-dried whole egg. J Infect Dis. 1951;89:1540–1545.
179. Gorden J, Small PL. Acid resistance in enteric bacteria. Infect Immun. 1993; 61:364–367.
180. Foster JW, Hall HK. Adaptive acidification tolerance response of *Salmonella typhimurium*. J Bacteriol. 1990;172:771–778.
181. Selsted ME, et al. Enteric defensins: Antibiotic peptide components of intestinal host defense. J Cell Biol. 1992;118:929–936.
182. Lehrer RI, Ganz T, Selsted ME. Defensins: Endogenous antibiotic peptides of animal cells. Cell. 1991;64:229–230.
183. Michetti P, et al. Monoclonal secretory immunoglobulin A protects mice against oral challenge with the invasive pathogen *Salmonella typhimurium*. Infect Immun. 1992;60:1786–1792.
184. Brandtzaeg P. Overview of the mucosal immune system. Curr Top Microbiol Immunol. 1989;146:13–25.
185. Kohbata S, Yokoyama H, Yabuuchi E. Cytopathogenic effect of *Salmonella typhi* GIFU 10007 on M cells of murine ileal Peyer's patches in ligated ileal loops: An ultrastructural study. Microbiol Immunol. 1986;30:1225–1237.
186. Francis CL, Starnbach MN, Falkow S. Morphological and cytoskeletal changes in epithelial cells occur immediately upon interaction with *Salmonella typhimurium* grown under low-oxygen conditions. Mol Microbiol. 1992;6:3077–3087.
187. Finlay BB, Falkow S. Comparison of the invasion strategies used by *Salmonella cholerae-suis, Shigella flexneri* and *Yersinia enterocolitica* to enter cultured animal cells: Endosome acidification is not required for bacterial invasion or intracellular replication. Biochimie. 1988;70:1089–1099.
188. Pace J, Hayman MJ, Galán JE. Signal transduction and invasion of epithelial cells by *S. typhimurium*. Cell. 1993;72:505–514.
189. Galán JE, Pace J, Hayman MJ. Involvement of the epidermal growth factor receptor in the invasion of cultured mammalian cells by *Salmonella typhimurium*. Nature. 1992;357:588–589.
190. Takeuchi A. Electron microscopic studies of experimental *Salmonella* infection I. Penetration into the intestinal epithelium by *Salmonella typhimurium*. Am J Pathol. 1967;50:109–136.
191. Finlay BB, Gumbiner B, Falkow S. Penetration of *Salmonella* through a polarized Madin-Darby canine kidney epithelial cell monolayer. J Cell Biol. 1988;107:221–230.
192. Hackett J, et al. The colonization of Peyer's patches by a strain of *Salmonella typhimurium* cured of the cryptic plasmid. J Infect Dis. 1986;153:1119–1125.
193. Rubin FA, et al. Rapid diagnosis of typhoid fever through identification of *Salmonella typhi* within 18 hours of specimen acquisition by culture of the mononuclear cell–platelet fraction of blood. J Clin Microbiol. 1990;28:825–827.
194. Hornick RB, et al. Typhoid fever: Pathogenesis and immunologic control. N Engl J Med. 1970;283:686–691.
195. Greisman SE, et al. Typhoid fever: A study of pathogenesis and physiologic abnormalities. Trans Am Clin Climatol Assoc. 1961;73:146–161.
196. Looney RJ, Steigbigel RT. Role of the Vi antigen of *Salmonella typhi* in resistance to host defense in vitro. J Lab Clin Med. 1986;108:506–516.
197. Alpuche-Aranda CM, et al. *Salmonella* stimulate macrophage macropinocytosis and persist within spacious phagosomes. J Exp Med. 1994;179:601–608.
198. Alpuche-Aranda CM, et al. *Salmonella typhimurium* activates virulence gene transcription within acidified macrophage phagosomes. Proc Natl Acad Sci U S A. 1992;89:10079–10083.
199. Rathman M, Barker LP, Falkow S. The unique trafficking pattern of *Salmonella typhimurium*–containing phagosomes in murine macrophages is independent of the mechanism of bacterial entry. Infect Immun. 1997;65:1475–1485.
200. Oh Y-K, et al. Rapid and complete fusion of macrophage lysosomes with phagosomes containing *Salmonella typhimurium*. Infect Immun. 1996;64:3877–3883.
201. Chen LM, Kaniga K, Galán JE. *Salmonella* spp. are cytotoxic for cultured macrophages. Mol Microbiol. 1996;21:1101–1115.
202. Monack DM, et al. *Salmonella typhimurium* invasion induces apoptosis in infected macrophages. Proc Natl Acad Sci U S A. 1996;93:9833–9838.
203. Weiss J, et al. Killing of gram-negative bacteria by polymorphonuclear leukocytes: Role of an O_2-independent bactericidal system. J Clin Invest. 1982;69:959–970.
204. Buchmeier NA, et al. Recombination-deficient mutants of *Salmonella typhimurium* are avirulent and sensitive to the oxidative burst of macrophages. Mol Microbiol. 1993;7:933–936.
205. Fame TM, Engelhard D, Riley HD Jr. Hemophagocytosis accompanying typhoid fever. Pediatr Infect Dis. 1986;5:367–369.
206. Calva JJ, Ruiz-Palacios GM. *Salmonella* hepatitis: Detection of salmonella antigens in the liver of patients with typhoid fever (Letter). J Infect Dis. 1986;154:373–374.
207. Mills DM, Bajaj V, Lee CA. A 40 kb chromosomal fragment encoding *Salmonella typhimurium* invasion genes is absent from the corresponding region of the *Escherichia coli* K-12 chromosome. Mol Microbiol. 1995;15:749–759.
208. Shea JE, et al. Identification of a virulence locus encoding a second type III secretion system in *Salmonella typhimurium*. Proc Natl Acad Sci U S A. 1996;93:2593–2597.
209. Collazo CM, Zierler MK, Galán JE. Functional analysis of the *Salmonella typhimurium* invasion genes *invI* and *invJ* and identification of a target of the protein secretion apparatus encoded in the *inv* locus. Mol Microbiol. 1995;15:25–38.
210. Pegues DA, et al. PhoP/PhoQ transcriptional repression of *Salmonella typhimurium* invasion genes: Evidence for a role in protein secretion. Mol Microbiol. 1995;17:169–181.
211. McCormick BA, Miller SI, Carnes D, et al. Transepithelial signaling to neutrophils by salmonellae: A novel virulence mechanism for gastroenteritis. Infect Immun. 1995;63:2302–2309.
212. Hueck CJ, et al. *Salmonella typhimurium*–secreted invasion determinants are homologous to *Shigella* Ipa proteins. Mol Microbiol. 1995;18:479–490.
213. Behlau I, Miller SI. A PhoP-repressed gene promotes *Salmonella typhimurium* invasion of epithelial cells. J Bacteriol. 1993;175:4475–4484.
214. Fields PI, et al. Mutants of *Salmonella typhimurium* that cannot survive within the macrophage are avirulent. Proc Natl Acad Sci U S A. 1986;83:5189–5193.
215. Fields PI, Groisman EA, Heffron F. A *Salmonella* locus that controls resistance to microbicidal proteins from phagocytic cells. Science. 1989;243:1059–1062.

216. Miller SI, Kukral AM, Mekalanos JJ. A two-component regulatory system (*phoP phoQ*) controls *Salmonella typhimurium* virulence. Proc Natl Acad Sci U S A. 1989;86:5054–5058.
217. Gunn JS, Miller SI. PhoP/PhoQ activates transcription of *pmrA/B*, encoding a two-component system involved in *Salmonella typhimurium* antimicrobial peptide resistance. J Bacteriol. 1996;178:6857–6864.
218. Guo L, et al. Regulation of lipid A modifications by *Salmonella typhimurium* virulence genes *phoP-phoQ*. Science. 1997;276:250–253.
219. Hohmann EL, et al. *phoP/phoQ*-deleted *Salmonella typhi* (TY800) is a safe and immunogenic single dose typhoid fever vaccine in volunteers. J Infect Dis. 1996;173:1408–1414.
220. Curtiss RD, Kelly SM. *Salmonella typhimurium* deletion mutants lacking adenylate cyclase and cyclic AMP receptor protein are avirulent and immunogenic. Infect Immun. 1987;55:3035–3043.
221. Dorman CJ, et al. Characterization of porin and ompR mutants of a virulent strain of *Salmonella typhimurium*: ompR mutants are attenuated in vivo. Infect Immun. 1989;57:2136–2140.
222. Fang FC, et al. The alternative sigma factor katF (rpoS) regulates *Salmonella* virulence. Proc Natl Acad Sci U S A. 1992;89:11978–11982.
223. Lindberg AA. Bacterial virulence factors—with particular reference to *Salmonella* bacteria. Scand J Infect Dis Suppl. 1980;24:86–92.
224. Finlay BB, Falkow S. Virulence factors associated with *Salmonella* species. Microbiol Sci. 1988;5:324–328.
225. Reitmeyer JC, Peterson JW, Wilson KJ. *Salmonella* cytotoxin: A component of the bacterial outer membrane. Microb Pathog. 1986;1:503–510.
226. Tacket CO, Hone DM, Curtis R 3d, et al. Comparison of the safety and immunogenicity of Δ*aroC* Δ*aroD* and Δ*cya* Δ*crp Salmonella typhi* strains in adult volunteers. Infect Immun. 1992;60:536–541.
227. Levine MM, et al. Safety, infectivity, immunogenicity, and *in vivo* stability of two attenuated auxotrophic mutant strains of *Salmonella typhi*, 541Ty and 543Ty, as live oral vaccines in humans. J Clin Invest. 1987;79:888–902.
228. Aguero J, et al. Choleriform syndrome and production of labile enterotoxin (CT/LT1)-like antigen by species of *Salmonella infantis* and *Salmonella haardt* isolated from the same patient. Rev Infect Dis. 1991;13:420–423.
229. Peterson NJ. *Salmonella* toxins. In: Dorner F, Drews J, eds. Pharmacology of Bacterial Toxins. New York: Pergamon; 1986:227–234.
230. Eckmann L, Rudolph MT, Ptasznik A, et al. D-myo-Inositol 1,4,5,6,-tetrakisphosphate produced in human intestinal epithelial cells in response to *Salmonella* invasion inhibits phosphoinositide 3-kinase signaling pathways. Proc Natl Acad Sci U S A. 1997;94:14456–14460.
231. McCormick BA, Colgan SP, Delp-Archer C, et al. *Salmonella typhimurium* attachment to human intestinal epithelial monolayers: Transcellular signalling to subepithelial neutrophils. J Cell Biol. 1993;123:895–907.
232. Hobbie S, et al. Involvement of mitogen-activated protein kinase pathways in the nuclear responses and cytokine production induced by *Salmonella typhimurium* in cultured intestinal epithelial cells. J Immunol. 1997;159:5550–5559.
233. O'Brien AD. Innate resistance of mice to *Salmonella typhi* infection. Infect Immun. 1982;38:948–952.
234. Lissner CR, Swanson R, O'Brien A. Genetic control of the innate resistance of mice to *Salmonella typhimurium*: Expression of the *Ity* gene in peritoneal and splenic macrophages isolated *in vitro*. J Immunol. 1983;131:3006–3013.
235. Vidal SM, Malo D, Vogan K. Natural resistance to infection with intracellular parasites: Isolation of a candidate for *bcg* gene. Cell. 1993;73:469–485.
236. Gruenheid S, et al. Natural resistance to infection with intracellular pathogens: The Nramp1 protein is recruited to the membrane of the phagosome. J Exp Med. 1997;185:717–730.
237. Vidal SM, et al. Natural resistance to intracellular infections: *Nramp1* encodes a membrane phosphoglycoprotein absent in macrophages from susceptible ($Nramp1^{D169}$) mouse strains. J Immunol. 1996;157:3559–3568.
238. Han T, Sokal JE, Neter E. Salmonellosis in disseminated malignant diseases. A seven-year review (1959–1965). N Engl J Med. 1967;276:1045–1052.
239. Wolfe MS, et al. Salmonellosis in patients with neoplastic disease. A review of 100 episodes at Memorial Cancer Center over a 13-year period. Arch Intern Med. 1971;128:546–554.
240. Mussche MM, Lameire NH, Ringoir SM. *Salmonella typhimurium* infections in renal transplant patients. Report of five cases. Nephron. 1975;15:143–150.
241. Sperber SJ, Schleupner CJ. Salmonellosis during infection with human immunodeficiency virus. Rev Infect Dis. 1987;9:925–934.
242. Celum CL, et al. Incidence of salmonellosis in patients with AIDS. J Infect Dis. 1987;156:998–1002.
243. Levine WC, et al. Epidemiology of nontyphoidal *Salmonella* bacteremia during the human immunodeficiency virus epidemic. J Infect Dis. 1991;164:81–87.
244. Angulo FJ, Swerdlow DL. Bacterial enteric infections in persons infected with human immunodeficiency virus. Clin Infect Dis. 1995;21(Suppl 1):S84–S93.
245. de Jong R, et al. Severe mycobacterial and *Salmonella* infections in interleukin-12 receptor–deficient patients. Science. 1998;280:1435–1438.
246. Moellering RC Jr, Weinberg AN. Persistent *Salmonella* infection in a female carrier for chronic granulomatous disease. Ann Intern Med. 1970;73:595–601.
247. Levine MM, et al. Progress in vaccines against typhoid fever. Rev Infect Dis. 1989;11(Suppl 3):S552–S567.
248. Marmion DE, Naylor GRE, Stewart IO. Second attacks of typhoid fever. J Hyg. 1953;51:260–267.
249. Forrest BD, et al. The human humoral immune response to *Salmonella typhi* Ty21a. J Infect Dis. 1991;163:336–345.
250. Acharya IL, et al. Prevention of typhoid fever in Nepal with the Vi capsular polysaccharide of *Salmonella typhi*. A preliminary report. N Engl J Med. 1987;317:1101–1104.
251. Lanata CF, et al. Vi serology in detection of chronic *Salmonella typhi* carriers in an endemic area. Lancet. 1983;2:441–443.
252. Blanden RV, Mackaness GB, Collins FM. Mechanisms of acquired resistance in mouse typhoid. J Exp Med. 1966;124:585–600.
253. Murphy JR, et al. Immunity to *Salmonella typhi*: Considerations relevant to measurement of cellular immunity in typhoid-endemic regions. Clin Exp Immunol. 1989;75:228–233.
254. Nencioni L, et al. Cellular immunity against *Salmonella typhi* after live oral vaccine. Adv Exp Med Biol. 1987;216:1669–1675.
255. Saphra I, Winter JW. Clinical manifestations of salmonellosis in man: An evaluation of 7779 human infections identified at the New York *Salmonella* Center. N Engl J Med. 1957;256:1128.
256. Dagash M, et al. Transient radiological and colonoscopic features of inflammatory bowel disease in a patient with severe *Salmonella* gastroenteritis. Am J Gastroenterol. 1997;92:349–351.
257. Aserkoff B, Bennett JV. Effect of antibiotic therapy in acute salmonellosis on the fecal excretion of salmonellae. N Engl J Med. 1969;281:636–640.
258. Szanton VL. Epidemic salmonellosis. Pediatrics. 1957;20:794–808.
259. Stuart BM, Pullen RL. Typhoid: Clinical analysis of three hundred and sixty cases. Arch Intern Med. 1946;78:629–661.
260. Carmeli Y, et al. Typhoid fever in Ethiopian immigrants to Israel and native-born Israelis: A comparative study. Clin Infect Dis. 1993;16:213–215.
261. Gotuzzo E, et al. Association between the acquired immunodeficiency syndrome and infection with *Salmonella typhi* or *Salmonella paratyphi* in an area endemic for typhoid fever. Arch Intern Med. 1991;151:381–382.
262. Hoffman TA, Ruiz CJ, Counts GW. Water-borne typhoid fever in Dade County, FL: Clinical and therapeutic evaluations of 105 bacteremic patients. Am J Med. 1975;59:481.
263. Roland HAK. The complications of typhoid fever. J Trop Med Hyg. 1961;64:143.
264. Hoffman SL, et al. Reduction of mortality in chloramphenicol-treated severe typhoid fever by high-dose dexamethasone. N Engl J Med. 1984;310:82–88.
265. Verghese A. The "typhoid state" revisited. Am J Med. 1985;79:370–372.
266. Hearne SE, Whigham TE, Brady CEI. Pancreatitis and typhoid fever. Am J Med. 1989;86:471–473.
267. El-Newihi HM, Alamy ME, Reynolds TB. *Salmonella* hepatitis: Analysis of 27 cases and comparison with acute viral hepatitis. Hepatology. 1996;24:516–519.
268. Khourieh M, et al. Typhoid fever diagnosed by isolation of *S. typhi* from gastric aspirate. Acta Pediatr Scand. 1989;78:653–655.
269. Avendano A, et al. Duodenal string cultures: Practicality and sensitivity for diagnosing enteric fever in children. J Infect Dis. 1986;153:359–362.
270. Gilman RH, et al. Relative efficacy of blood, urine, rectal swab, bone-marrow and rose-spot cultures for recovery of *Salmonella typhi* in typhoid fever. Lancet. 1975;1:1211–1213.
271. Hoffman SL, et al. Duodenal string-capsule culture compared with bone-marrow, blood, and rectal-swab cultures for diagnosing typhoid and paratyphoid fever. J Infect Dis. 1984;149:157–161.
272. Benavente L, et al. Diagnosis of typhoid fever using a string capsule device. Trans R Soc Trop Med Hyg. 1984;78:564–565.
273. Guerra-Caceres JG, et al. Diagnostic value of bone marrow culture in typhoid fever. Trans R Soc Trop Med Hyg. 1979;73:680–683.
274. Farooqui BJ, et al. Comparative yield of *Salmonella typhi* from blood and bone marrow cultures in patients with fever of unknown origin. J Clin Pathol. 1991;44:258–259.
275. Watson K. Isolation of *Salmonella typhi* from the blood stream. J Lab Clin Med. 1959;47:329–332.
276. Gasem MH, et al. Culture of *Salmonella typhi* and *Salmonella paratyphi* from blood and bone marrow in suspected typhoid fever. Trop Geogr Med. 1995;47:164–167.
277. Isomaki O, Vuento R, Granfors K. Serological diagnosis of *Salmonella* infections by enzyme immunoassay. Lancet. 1989;1:1411–1414.
278. Coovadia YM, et al. Comparison of passive haemagglutination test with Widal agglutination test for serological diagnosis of typhoid fever in an endemic area. J Clin Pathol. 1986;39:680–683.
279. Abraham G, et al. Diagnostic value of the Widal test. Trop Geogr Med. 1981; 33:329–333.
280. Wicks ACB, Cruickshank JG, Musewe N. Observations on the diagnosis of typhoid fever in an endemic area. S Afr Med J. 1974;48:1368–1370.
281. Welch H, Mickle FL. A rapid slide test for the serological diagnosis of typhoid and paratyphoid fevers. Am J Public Health. 1936;26:248–255.
282. Shukla S, Patel B, Chitnis DS. 100 years of Widal test & its reappraisal in an endemic area. Indian J Med Res. 1997;105:53–57.
283. Chaudhry R, et al. Standardisation of polymerase chain reaction for the detection of *Salmonella typhi* in typhoid fever. J Clin Pathol. 1997;50:437–439.
284. Cohen PS, et al. The risk of endothelial infection in adults with *Salmonella* bacteremia. Ann Intern Med. 1978;89:931–932.
285. Barrett-Connor E. Bacterial infection and sickle cell anemia: An analysis of 250 infections in 166 patients and a review of the literature. Medicine (Baltimore). 1971;50:97–112.
286. Moellering RC, Weinberg AN. Persistent *Salmonella* infection in a female carrier for chronic granulomatous disease. Ann Intern Med. 1970;73:595–601.
287. Sperber SJ, Schleupner CJ. Salmonellosis during infection with the human immunodeficiency virus. Rev Infect Dis. 1987;9:925–934.
288. Parsons R, Gregory J, Palmer DL. *Salmonella* infections of the abdominal aorta. Rev Infect Dis. 1983;5:227–231.
289. Gabbi E, Rossi G, Ghidoni I. *Salmonella typhimurium* infection of thoracic aorta aneurysm in immunocompetent subject. Case report and literature review. Infection. 1989;17:306–308.

290. Tocalli L, et al. Salmonellosis diagnosed by the laboratory of the 'L. Sacco' Hospital of Milan (Italy) in patients with HIV disease. Eur J Epidemiol. 1991;7:690–695.
291. Ramos JM, et al. Clinical significance of primary vs. secondary bacteremia due to nontyphoid *Salmonella* in patients without AIDS. Clin Infect Dis. 1994;19:777–783.
292. Gilks CF, Ojoo SA. A practical approach to the clinical problems of the HIV-infected adult in the tropics. Trop Doctor. 1991;21(3):90–97.
293. Gutiérrez A, et al. Recurrent *Salmonella enteritidis* meningitis in a patient with AIDS. Scand J Infect Dis. 1995;27:177–178.
294. Fernández Guerrero ML, et al. Focal infections due to non-*typhi Salmonella* in patients with AIDS: Report of 10 cases and review. Clin Infect Dis. 1997;25:690–697.
295. Vugia DJ, et al. Pathogens and predictors of fatal septicemia associated with human immunodeficiency virus infection in Ivory Coast, West Africa. J Infect Dis. 1993;168:564–570.
296. Gilks CF, et al. Life-threatening bacteraemia in HIV-1 seropositive adults admitted to hospital in Nairobi, Kenya. Lancet. 1990;336:545–549.
297. Archibald LK, et al. Fatal *Mycobacterium tuberculosis* bloodstream infections in febrile hospitalized adults in Dar es Salaam, Tanzania. Clin Infect Dis. 1998;26:290–296.
298. Centers for Disease Control. Revision of the CDC surveillance case definition for acquired immunodeficiency syndrome. Council of State and Territorial Epidemiologists; AIDS Program, Centers for Infectious Diseases. MMWR Morb Mortal Wkly Rep. 1987;36(Suppl 1):S1.
299. Salmon D, et al. Efficacy of zidovudine in preventing relapses of *Salmonella* bacteremia in AIDS. J Infect Dis. 1991;163:415–416.
300. Hermann E, et al. *Salmonella*-reactive synovial fluid T-cell clones in a patient with post-infectious *Salmonella* arthritis. Scand J Rheumatol. 1990;19:350–355.
301. Keith BR, White G, Wilson HR. In vivo efficacy of zidovudine (3′-azido-3′-deoxythimidine) in experimental gram-negative bacterial infections. Antimicrob Agents Chemother. 1989;33:479–483.
302. Aguado JM, et al. [The clinical spectrum of focal infection due to nontyphoid *Salmonella*: 32 years' experience.] Med Clin (Barc). 1994;103:293–298.
303. Alvarez-Elcoro S, Soto-Ramirez L, Metos-Mora M. *Salmonella* bacteremia. Am J Med. 1984;77:61–63.
304. Zak FG, Strauss L, Saphra I. Rupture of diseased large arteries in the course of enterobacterial (*Salmonella*) infection. N Engl J Med. 1958;258:824–828.
305. Morrow C, Safi H, Beall AC Jr. Primary aortoduodenal fistula caused by *Salmonella* aortitis. J Vasc Surg. 1987;6:415–418.
306. Jarrett F, et al. Experience with infected aneurysms of the abdominal aorta. Arch Surg. 1975;110:1281–1286.
307. Mantello MT, Panaccione JL, Moriarty PE, et al. Impending rupture of nonaneurysmal bacterial aortitis: CT diagnosis. J Comput Assist Tomogr. 1990;14:950–953.
308. Donabedian H. Long-term suppression of *Salmonella* aortitis with an oral antibiotic. Arch Intern Med. 1989;149:1452–1453.
309. Wilson K, Feldman R. Reported isolates of *Salmonella* from cerebrospinal fluid in the United States, 1968–1979. J Infect Dis. 1981;143:504–506.
310. Kinsella TR, et al. Treatment of *Salmonella* meningitis and brain abscess with the new cephalosporins: Two case reports and a review of literature. Pediatr Infect Dis J. 1987;6:476–480.
311. Rabinowitz SG, MacLeod NR. *Salmonella* meningitis. A report of three cases and review of the literature. Am J Dis Child. 1972;123:529.
312. Durand ML, et al. Acute bacterial meningitis in adults: A review of 493 episodes. N Engl J Med. 1993;328:21–28.
313. Dunn DW, McAllister J, Craft JC. Brain abscess and empyema caused by *Salmonella*. Pediatr Infect Dis. 1984;4:394–398.
314. Bryan JP, Scheld WM. Therapy of experimental meningitis due to *Salmonella enteritidis*. Antimicrob Agents Chemother. 1992;36:949–954.
315. Huang LT. *Salmonella* meningitis complicated by brain infarctions. Clin Infect Dis. 1996;22:194–195.
316. Aguado JM, et al. Pleuropulmonary infections due to nontyphoidal strains of *Salmonella*. Arch Intern Med. 1990;150:54–56.
317. Diggs LW. Bone and joint lesions in sickle cell disease. Clin Orthop. 1967;52:119–143.
318. Hook BW, et al. *Salmonella* osteomyelitis in patients with sickle cell anemia. N Engl J Med. 1957;257:403–407.
319. Wright J, Thomas P, Serjeant GR. Septicemia caused by *Salmonella* infection: An overlooked complication of sickle cell disease. J Pediatr. 1997;130:394–399.
320. Warren CPW. Arthritis associated with *Salmonella* infection. Ann Rheum Dis. 1970;29:483–487.
321. Stein M, et al. HIV infection and *Salmonella* septic arthritis. Clin Exp Rheumatol. 1993;11:187–189.
322. Hakansson U, et al. HLA-antigen B27 in cases with joint affections in an outbreak of salmonellosis. Scand J Infect Dis. 1976;8:245–248.
323. Maki-Ikola O, et al. *Salmonella*-specific antibodies in reactive arthritis. J Infect Dis. 1991;164:1141–1148.
324. Thomson GT, et al. Post-*Salmonella* reactive arthritis: Late clinical sequelae in a point source cohort. Am J Med. 1995;98:13–21.
325. Leirisalo-Repo M, et al. Long-term prognosis of reactive salmonella arthritis. Ann Rheum Dis. 1997;56:516–520.
326. Marr J, Haff R. Superinfection of an amoebic abscess by *Salmonella enteritidis*. Arch Intern Med. 1971;128:291–294.
327. Matossian RM, Najjar F. Suppurative salmonellosis in human hepatic hydatid cysts. Ann Trop Med Parasitol. 1968;62:143–146.
328. Hirschowitz B. Pyogenic liver abscess. A review with a case report of a solitary abscess caused by *Salmonella enteritidis*. Gastroenterology. 1952;21:291–299.
329. Torres JR, Gottuzo E, Isturiz R, et al. *Salmonella* splenic abscess in the antibiotic era: A Latin American perspective. Clin Infect Dis. 1994;19:871–875.
330. Ramos JM, et al. Clinical spectrum of urinary tract infections due to nontyphoidal *Salmonella* species. Clin Infect Dis. 1996;23:388–390.
331. Ozdemir S, et al. A rare cause of acute tubulointerstitial nephritis: *Salmonella typhimurium* infection (Letter). Nephrol Dial Transplant. 1997;12:1542–1543.
332. Burgmans JP, et al. *Salmonella enteritidis* in an endometriotic ovarian cyst. Eur J Obstet Gynecol Reprod Biol. 1997;72:207–211.
333. Behr MA, McDonald J. *Salmonella* neck abscess in a patient with beta-thalassemia major: Case report and review. Clin Infect Dis. 1996;23:404–405.
334. Carswell W, Magrath IT. Skin ulceration caused by *Salmonella dublin*. BMJ. 1973;1:331–332.
335. Wang JH, et al. Mycotic aneurysm due to non-typhi *Salmonella*: Report of 16 cases. Clin Infect Dis. 1996;23:743–747.
336. Huang LT, Ko SF, Lui CC. *Salmonella* meningitis: Clinical experience of third-generation cephalosporins. Acta Paediatr. 1997;86:1056–1058.
337. Musher DM, Rubenstein AD. Permanent carriers of nontyphosa salmonellae. Arch Intern Med. 1973;132:869–872.
338. Nath G, Singh H, Shukla VK. Chronic typhoid carriage and carcinoma of the gallbladder. Eur J Cancer Prev. 1997;6:557–559.
339. Agalar C, et al. Comparison of two regimens for ciprofloxacin treatment of enteric infections. Eur J Clin Microbiol Infect Dis. 1997;16:803–806.
340. Centers for Disease Control and Prevention. The Yellow Book: Health Information for International Travel 1996–97; Typhoid Fever. Atlanta, Ga: National Center for Infectious Diseases; 1998.
341. Woodruff BA, Pavia AT, Blake PA. A new look at typhoid vaccination. Information for the practicing physician. JAMA. 1991;265:756–759.
342. Murphy JR, et al. Immunogenicity of *Salmonella typhi* Ty21a for young children. Infect Immun. 1991;59:4291–4293.
343. Typhoid vaccination: Weighing the options (Editorial). Lancet. 1992;340:341–342.
344. Yugoslavian Typhoid Commission. A controlled field trial of the effectiveness of acetone-dried and inactivated and heat phenol–inactivated typhoid vaccines in Yugoslavia. Bull World Health Organ. 1964;30:623–630.
345. Hejfec LB. Results of the study of typhoid vaccines in four controlled field trials in the USSR. Bull World Health Organ. 1965;32:1–14.
346. Ashcroft MT, Morrision RJ, Nicholson CC. Controlled field trial in British Guiana school children of heat-killed-phenolized and acetone-killed lyophilized typhoid vaccines. Am J Hyg. 1964;79:196–206.
347. Ashcroft MT, et al. A seven-year field trial of two typhoid vaccines in Guyana. Lancet. 1967;2:1056–1059.
348. Hejfec LB, Salmin LV, Lejtman MZ, et al. A controlled field trial and laboratory study of five typhoid vaccines in the USSR. Bull World Health Organ. 1966;34:321–339.
349. Walter Reed Army Institute of Research. Preparation of dried acetone-inactivated and heat-phenol–inactivated typhoid vaccines. Bull World Health Organ. 1964;30:635–646.
350. Edwards EA, Johnson DP, Pierce WE, et al. Reactions and serologic responses to monovalent acetone-inactivated typhoid vaccine and heat-killed TAB when given by jet injection. Bull World Health Organ. 1974;51:501–505.
351. Wilson GS. The Hazards of Immunization. London: Athlone; 1967.
352. Calin A, Goulding N, Brewerton D. Reactive arthropathy following *Salmonella* vaccination. Arthritis Rheum. 1987;30:1197.
353. Hone DM, et al. A *galA* via (Vi antigen-negative) mutant of *Salmonella typhi* Ty2 retains virulence in humans. Infect Immun. 1988;56:1326–1333.
354. Gilman RH, et al. Evaluation of a UDP-glucose-4-epimeraseless mutant of *Salmonella typhi* as a live oral typhoid vaccine. J Infect Dis. 1977;136:716–723.
355. Wahdan MH, Serie C, Germanier R, et al. A controlled field trial of live oral vaccine Ty21a. Bull World Health Organ. 1980;58:469–474.
356. Wahdan MH, et al. A controlled field trial of live *Salmonella typhi* strain Ty21a oral vaccine against typhoid: Three year results. J Infect Dis. 1982;145:292–295.
357. Black RE, et al. Efficacy of one or two doses of Ty21a *Salmonella typhi* vaccine in enteric-coated capsules in a controlled field trial. Vaccine. 1990;8:81–84.
358. Levine MM, et al. Large-scale field trial of Ty21a live oral typhoid vaccine in enteric-coated capsule formulation. Lancet. 1987;1:1049–1052.
359. Simanjuntak CH, et al. Oral immunisation against typhoid fever in Indonesia with Ty21a vaccine. Lancet. 1991;338:1055–1059.
360. Kaplan DT, Hill DR. Compliance with live oral Ty21a typhoid vaccine. JAMA. 1992;267:1074.
361. Hirschel B, et al. Inefficacy of the commercial live oral Ty21a vaccine in the prevention of typhoid fever. Eur J Clin Microbiol Infect Dis. 1985;4:295–298.
362. Schwartz E, et al. The effect of oral and parenteral typhoid vaccination on the rate of infection with *Salmonella typhi* and *Salmonella paratyphi A* among foreigners in Nepal. Arch Intern Med. 1990;150:349–351.
363. Klugman K, et al. Immunogenicity, efficacy and serological correlate of protection of *Salmonella typhi* Vi capsular polysaccharide vaccine three years after immunization. Vaccine. 1996;14:435–438.
364. El Ramli A. Chloramphenicol in treatment of typhoid fever. Lancet. 1950;1:618.
365. Olarte J, Galindo E. *S. typhi* resistant to chloramphenicol, ampicillin, and other antimicrobial agents: Strains isolated and extensive typhoid fever epidemic in Mexico. Antimicrob Agents Chemother. 1973;4:597–601.
366. Paniker CK, Vimala KN. Transferable chloramphenicol resistance in *Salmonella typhi*. Nature. 1972;239:109–110.

367. Lampe PM, Mansuwan P, Duangmain C. Chloramphenicol-resistant typhoid. Lancet. 1974;1:623–624.
368. Butler T, Rumans L, Arnold K. Response of typhoid-fever caused by chloramphenicol-susceptible and chloramphenicol-resistant strains of *Salmonella typhi* to treatment with trimethoprim-sulfamethoxazole. Rev Infect Dis. 1982;4:551–561.
369. Bouquier Y, Hervonet D, Hilleritean H. Resultats du traitement par la chloromycetine de soixante fievres typhoides. Bull Mem Soc Med Hop Paris. 1949;32:1396.
370. Erselv A. Hematopoietic depression induced by Chloromycetin. Blood. 1953;8:170–174.
371. Wallerstein RO, et al. Statewide study of chloramphenicol therapy and fatal aplastic anemia. JAMA. 1969;208:2045–2050.
372. Glazko AJ, et al. Absorption and excretion of parenteral doses of chloramphenicol sodium succinate (CMS) in comparison with peroral doses of chloramphenicol (CM). Clin Pharmacol Ther. 1977;21:104.
373. Ti TT, et al. Chloramphenicol concentrations in sera of patients with typhoid fever being treated with oral or intravenous preparation. Antimicrob Agents Chemother. 1990;34:1809–1811.
374. Rahal JJJ, Simberkoff MS. Bactericidal and bacteriostatic action of chloramphenicol against meningeal pathogens. Antimicrob Agents Chemother. 1979;16:13–18.
375. Chang HR, Vladoianu IR, Pechere JC. Effects of ampicillin, ceftriaxone, chloramphenicol, pefloxacin and trimethoprim-sulphamethoxazole on *Salmonella typhi* within human monocyte-derived macrophages. J Antimicrob Chemother. 1990;26:689–694.
376. Brown JD, Mo DH, Rhoades ER. Chloramphenicol-resistant *Salmonella typhi* in Saigon. JAMA. 1975;231:162–166.
377. Linh NN, Arnold K. Treatment of typhoid fever and typhoid carriers in Southeast Asia:—viewpoint from South Vietnam (Editorial). Drugs. 1975;9:241–246.
378. Pillay N, Adams EB, North-Coobes D. Comparative trial of amoxycillin and chloramphenicol in treatment of typhoid fever in adults. Lancet. 1975;2:332–334.
379. Scragg JN, Rubidge CJ. Amoxycillin in the treatment of typhoid fever in children. Am Trop Med Hyg. 1975;24:860–865.
380. Herzog C. Chemotherapy of typhoid fever. Infection. 1976;4:166–173.
381. Brodie J, MacQueen IA. Effect of trimethoprim-sulfamethoxazole on typhoid and *Salmonella* carriers. BMJ. 1970;3:318–319.
382. Soe GB, Overturf GD. Treatment of typhoid fever and other systemic salmonelloses with cefotaxime, ceftriaxone, cefoperazone, and other newer cephalosporins. Rev Infect Dis. 1987;9:719.
383. Moosa A, Rubidge CJ. Once daily ceftriaxone vs. chloramphenicol for treatment of typhoid fever in children. Pediatr Infect Dis J. 1989;8:696–699.
384. Pape JW, et al. Typhoid fever: Successful therapy with cefoperazone. J Infect Dis. 1986;153:272–276.
385. Islam A, et al. Randomized treatment of patients with typhoid fever by using ceftriaxone or chloramphenicol. J Infect Dis. 1988;158:742–747.
386. Bhutta ZA. Therapeutic aspects of typhoidal salmonellosis in childhood: The Karachi experience. Ann Trop Paediatr. 1996;16:299–306.
387. Memon IA, Billoo AG, Memon HI. Cefixime: An oral option for the treatment of multidrug-resistant enteric fever in children. South Med J. 1997;90:1204–1207.
388. Tanaka Kido J, Ortega L, Santos JI. Comparative efficacies of aztreonam and chloramphenicol in children with typhoid fever. J Pediatr Infect Dis. 1990;9:44–48.
389. Farid Z, et al. Successful aztreonam treatment of acute typhoid fever after chloramphenicol failure. Scand J Infect Dis. 1990;22:505–506.
390. Choo KE, et al. Aztreonam failure in typhoid fever. Lancet. 1991;337:498.
391. Cherubin CE, et al. Cephalosporin therapy for salmonellosis. Arch Intern Med. 1986;146:2149–2152.
392. Preblud SR, Gill CJ, Campos JM. Bactericidal activities of chloramphenicol and eleven other antibiotics against *Salmonella* spp. Antimicrob Agents Chemother. 1984;3:327–330.
393. Barros F, et al. In vitro antibiotic susceptibility of salmonellae. Antimicrob Agents Chemother. 1977;6:1071–1073.
394. De Carvalho EM, Martinelli R. Cefamandole treatment of *Salmonella* bacteremia. Antimicrob Agents Chemother. 1982;21:334–336.
395. Vaudaux P, Waldvogel FA. Gentamicin antibacterial activity in the presence of human polymorphonuclear leukocytes. Antimicrob Agents Chemother. 1979;16:743–749.
396. Rodriguez-Noriega E, Andrade-Villaneuva J, Amaya-Tapia G. Quinolones in the treatment of *Salmonella* carriers. Rev Infect Dis. 1989;11(Suppl):S1179–S1187.
397. Easmon CSF, Crane JP, Blowers A. Effect of ciprofloxacin on intracellular organisms: In-vitro and in-vivo studies. J Antimicrob Chemother. 1986;18:43–48.
398. Stanley PJ, et al. Open study of ciprofloxacin in enteric fever. J Antimicrob Chemother. 1989;23:789–791.
399. Mandal BK. Treatment of multiresistant typhoid fever (Letter). Lancet. 1990;336:1383.
400. Rowe B, Ward LR, Threlfall EJ. Multidrug-resistant *Salmonella typhi*: A worldwide epidemic. Clin Infect Dis. 1997;24(Suppl 1):S106–S109.
401. Sabbour MS, Osman LM. Experience with ofloxacin in enteric fever. J Chemother. 1990;2:113–115.
402. Sarma PS, Durairaj P. Randomized treatment of patients with typhoid and paratyphoid fevers using norfloxacin or chloramphenicol. Trans R Soc Trop Med Hyg. 1991;85:670–671.
403. Arnold K, Hong CS, Nelwan R, et al. Randomized comparative study of fleroxacin and chloramphenicol in typhoid fever. Am J Med. 1993;94(Suppl 3A):S195–S200.
404. Wain J, et al. Quinolone-resistant *Salmonella typhi* in Viet Nam: Molecular basis of resistance and clinical response to treatment. Clin Infect Dis. 1997;25:1404–1410.
405. Piddock LJ, Whale K, Wise R. Quinolone resistance in *Salmonella*: Clinical experience (Letter). Lancet. 1990;335:1459.
406. Piddock LJ, et al. Ciprofloxacin resistance in clinical isolates of *Salmonella typhimurium* obtained from two patients. Antimicrob Agents Chemother. 1993;37:662–666.
407. Lewin CS. Treatment of multiresistant *Salmonella* infection. Lancet. 1991;337:47.
408. Threlfall EJ, et al. Resistance to ciprofloxacin in pathogenic Enterobacteriaceae in England and Wales in 1996. J Clin Pathol. 1997;50:1027–1028.
409. Christ W, Lehner T, Ulbrich B. Specific toxicologic aspects of the quinolones. Rev Infect Dis. 1988;10(Suppl 1):S141–S146.
410. Cheesbrough JS, et al. Quinolones in children with invasive salmonellosis. Lancet. 1991;338:127.
411. Dawood ST, Uwaydah AK, Hroob A. Treatment of multiresistant *Salmonella typhi* with intravenous ciprofloxacin (Letter). Pediatr Infect Dis. 1991;10:343.
412. Secmeer G, et al. Ofloxacin versus co-trimoxazole in the treatment of typhoid fever in children. Acta Paediatr Jpn. 1997;39:218–221.
413. Cooles P. Adjuvant steroids and relapse of typhoid fever. J Trop Med Hyg. 1986;89:229–231.
414. Richards L, Claeson M, Pierce NF. Management of acute diarrhea in children: Lessons learned. Pediatr Infect Dis J. 1993;12:5.
415. Pichler HET, et al. Clinical efficacy of ciprofloxacin compared with placebo in bacterial diarrhea. Am J Med. 1987;82:329.
416. Noguerado A, et al. Early single dose therapy with ofloxacin for empirical treatment of acute gastroenteritis: A randomised, placebo-controlled, double-blind clinical trial. J Antimicrob Chemother. 1995;36:665–672.
417. Bassily S, et al. Short-course norfloxacin and trimethoprim-sulfamethoxazole treatment of shigellosis and salmonellosis in Egypt. Am J Trop Med Hyg. 1994;51:219–223.
418. Carlstedt G, et al. Norfloxacin treatment of salmonellosis does not shorten the carrier stage. Scand J Infect Dis. 1990;22:553–556.
419. Neill MA, et al. Failure of ciprofloxacin to eradicate convalescent fecal excretion after acute salmonellosis: Experience during an outbreak in health care workers. Ann Intern Med. 1991;114:195–199.
420. Pitkäjärvi T, et al. Norfloxacin and *Salmonella* excretion in acute gastroenteritis—a 6-month follow-up study. Scand J Infect Dis. 1996;28:177–180.
421. Nelson JD, et al. Treatment of *Salmonella* gastroenteritis with ampicillin, amoxicillin or placebo. Pediatrics. 1980;65:1125–1130.
422. Kassis I, et al. The use of prophylactic furazolidone to control a nosocomial epidemic of multiply resistant *Salmonella typhimurium* on pediatric wards. Pediatr Infect Dis J. 1990;9:551–555.
423. Lightfoot NF, Ahmad F, Cowden J. Management of institutional outbreaks of *Salmonella* gastroenteritis. J Antimicrob Chemother. 1990;26:37–46.
424. Gendrel D, et al. Use of pefloxacin after failure of initial antibiotic treatment in children with severe salmonellosis. Eur J Clin Microbiol Infect Dis. 1993;12:209–211.
425. Gokalp AS, et al. Intravenous immunoglobulin in the treatment of *Salmonella typhimurium* infections in preterm neonates. Clin Pediatr (Phila). 1994;33:349–352.
426. Meerkin D, et al. *Salmonella* mycotic aneurysm of the aortic arch: Case report and review. Clin Infect Dis. 1995;21:523–528.
427. Jacobson MA, et al. Ciprofloxacin for *Salmonella* bacteremia in the acquired immunodeficiency syndrome (AIDS). Ann Intern Med. 1989;110:1027–1029.
428. Lewin CS, Allen RA, Amyes SG. Antibacterial activity of fluoroquinolones in combination with zidovudine. J Med Microbiol. 1990;33:127–131.
429. Salmon-Ceron D, et al. [Non-typhic *Salmonella* bacteremias in HIV infections. Clinical and therapeutic data, and course in 68 patients.] Presse Med. 1992;21:847–851.
430. Centers for Disease Control and Prevention. Recommendations for prophylaxis against *Pneumocystis carinii* pneumonia for adults and adolescents infected with human immunodeficiency virus. MMWR Morb Mortal Wkly Rep. 1992;41(RR-4):1–11.
431. Gibb AP, Lewin CS, Garden OJ. Development of quinolone resistance and multiple antibiotic resistance in *Salmonella bovismorbificans* in a pancreatic abscess (Letter). J Antimicrob Chemother. 1991;28:318–321.
432. Workman MR, et al. Emergence of ciprofloxacin resistance during treatment of *Salmonella* osteomyelitis in three patients with sickle cell disease. J Infect. 1996;32:27–32.
433. Pers C, Søgaard P, Pallesen L. Selection of multiple resistance in *Salmonella enteritidis* during treatment with ciprofloxacin. Scand J Infect Dis. 1996;28:529–531.
434. Nolan CM, White PCJ. Treatment of typhoid carrier with amoxicillin. JAMA. 1978;239:2352–2354.
435. Freerksen E, Rosenfield M, Freerksen R, et al. Treatment of chronic *Salmonella* carriers. Chemotherapy. 1977;23:192.
436. Sammalkorpi K, Lahdevirta J, Makela R. Treatment of chronic *Salmonella* carriers with ciprofloxacin. Lancet. 1987;2:164–165.
437. Ferreccio C, et al. Efficacy of ciprofloxacin in the treatment of chronic typhoid carriers. J Infect Dis. 1988;157:1235.
438. Freitag JL. Treatment of chronic typhoid carrier by cholecystectomy. Public Health. 1973;32:869.
439. Fisher IST, et al. 'Salm-Net'-laboratory-based surveillance of human *Salmonella* infections in Europe. PHLS Microbiol Dig. 1994;11:181.
440. Hastings L, et al. Salm-Net facilitates collaborative investigation of an outbreak of *Salmonella tosamanga* infection in Europe. Commun Dis Rep CDR Rev. 1996;6:7:R100–R102.
441. Khuri-Bulos NA, et al. Foodhandler-associated *Salmonella* outbreak in a university hospital despite routine surveillance cultures of kitchen employees. Infect Control Hosp Epidemiol. 1994;15:311–314.

442. Garner JS. Guideline for isolation precautions in hospitals. The Hospital Infection Control Practices Advisory Committee [published erratum appears in Infect Control Hosp Epidemiol. 1996;17:214]. Infect Control Hosp Epidemiol. 1996;17:53–80.
443. Williams WW. Guideline for infection control in hospital personnel. Infect Control. 1983;4(Suppl):326–349.

Chapter 211

Shigella Species (Bacillary Dysentery)

HERBERT L. DUPONT

The term *dysentery* was used by Hippocrates to indicate a condition characterized by frequent passage of stool containing blood and mucus accompanied by straining and painful defecation. It was not until the end of the 19th century, when the causes of amebiasis and bacillary dysentery were determined, that the two great forms of dysentery could be accurately separated. In view of the absence of liver complications, much of the dysentery in the older historical writings is considered to be of bacillary origin (shigellosis). After the causative agents of the two types of dysentery were determined, the different epidemiologic settings were described. In 1859 in Prague, Lambl and then later Osler[1] and Councilman and Lafleur[2] helped verify the pathogenicity of *Entamoeba histolytica*. In 1906, Shiga[3] conclusively demonstrated that a bacterium was present in the stool of many patients with dysentery and that agglutinins could be demonstrated in the serum of the infected patient. At about the same time, Flexner[4] found a similar but serologically different organism in the stools of other patients with dysentery acquired in the Philippines. Rogers[5] stated in 1913 that "epidemic dysentery in asylums, jails, or in long-occupied and unsanitary military camps during the war is nearly certain to be bacillary, while sporadic cases in a warm climate are more frequently amebic."

Medical writings since the beginning of recorded history have dealt with the common problems of dysentery in civilian and military populations; perhaps the greatest historical consideration is the influence that bacillary dysentery has had on military campaigns. Nearly every long campaign and extended siege has produced epidemics of bacillary dysentery, particularly when sanitation and food sources could not be adequately controlled. In many battles described during the Peloponnesian War, the British campaigns in the 18th century, Napoleon's campaigns, the Crimean War, the American Civil War, the Franco-Prussian War, and the Sino-Japanese War, a heavier toll was ascribed to bacillary dysentery than to war-related injuries.[6]

MICROBIOLOGY

Shigella organisms are small gram-negative rods that are members of the family Enterobacteriaceae, tribe Escherichieae, and genus *Shigella*. They are nonmotile and nonencapsulated.

Isolation Techniques

The infecting strain of *Shigella* is generally present in stools in concentrations between 10^3 and 10^9 viable cells per gram of stool, depending on the stage of illness. During the first several days of illness the counts are higher; they drop off to lower levels after several days of clinical disease. During the postconvalescent shedding period, counts fall to 10^2 to 10^3 viable cells per gram of stool. Recovery of the agent microbiologically is not usually difficult in the early stages of disease because of the higher counts present; it is more difficult during later stages of illness because of lower counts of viable bacteria. Careful selection of material and processing on appropriate media give a higher yield of organisms. The sooner after passage that the specimen is processed, the higher the yield. Stools that stand at room temperature for more than 24 hours have a profound drop in the number of viable cells, and recovery is less likely. A rectal swab obtained and seeded immediately at the bedside is an optimal way to perform a stool culture. In performing bacteriologic identification of *Shigella*, a bit of blood or mucus is seeded onto at least two different media. Generally, stool is plated lightly on a medium with only mild inhibiting factors for gram-negative growth, such as MacConkey agar, xylose-lysine-deoxycholate agar, Tergitol-7, or eosin–methylene blue (EMB) agar, whereas a separate specimen is plated heavily on a more inhibitory medium such as *Shigella-Salmonella* medium. The more plates used, the greater the recovery yield. After overnight incubation at 37°C, lactose-negative colonies are transferred to triple sugar iron agar and lysine-iron agar slants and reincubated. Those giving a characteristic reaction (alkaline slant, acid butt, and no gas) are tested biochemically and then serologically identified with *Shigella* grouping and typing antisera.

Group and Type Identification

The approximately 40 serotypes of *Shigella* are divided into four groups depending on serologic similarity and fermentation reactions: group A *(Shigella dysenteriae)*, group B *(Shigella flexneri)*, group C *(Shigella boydii)*, and group D *(Shigella sonnei)*. Commercial antiserum is available for determining group- and type-specific antigenicity. *S. sonnei* accounts for between 60 and 80% of the cases currently reported in the United States.

Invasive *Escherichia coli*

Certain strains of *E. coli* can cause a clinical illness indistinguishable from shigellosis and should be considered as causative agents of bacillary dysentery. Nearly all the *Shigella*-like *E. coli* strains have been shown to possess somatic antigens related to *Shigella* serotypes, further demonstrating the similarity of these two groups of organisms. *E. coli* strains that cause bacillary dysentery have been shown to serologically belong to the following *E. coli* O groups: 28, 29, 112, 115, 124, 136, 143, 144, 147, 152, 164, and 167. Serotyping may ultimately prove to be useful in detecting these strains. A laboratory test for determining the virulence of the bacterial isolate (*Shigella* or invasive *E. coli* strain) is the Sereny test.[7] Keratoconjunctivitis develops after 1 to 7 days in guinea pigs (or rabbits) when an invasive bacterial strain (*E. coli* or *Shigella*) is dropped into the conjunctival sac of the animal (Fig. 211–1). A different form of bacillary dysentery has been shown to be caused by an 0157:H7 strain of *E. coli*.[8] The source of infection has characteristically been contaminated hamburgers obtained at a fast-food chain. Other non-0157:H7 serotypes of *E. coli* have also been implicated as causative agents of the syndrome. Dysentery (bloody diarrhea) develops in affected patients, and colitis can be documented by endoscopy. The illness differs from that associated with invasive *E. coli* in that high fever is not a feature of this so-called hemorrhagic colitis.

PATHOGENESIS

Communicability

Bacillary dysentery is the most communicable of the bacterial diarrheas. Volunteer experiments have demonstrated that shigellosis is unique among bacterial enteropathogens in that fewer than 200 viable cells readily produce the disease in healthy adults.[9] This low dose of organisms probably explains how the illness can be transferred from person to person, why the secondary attack rate is so high when an index case is introduced into a family, and why recurrent bacillary

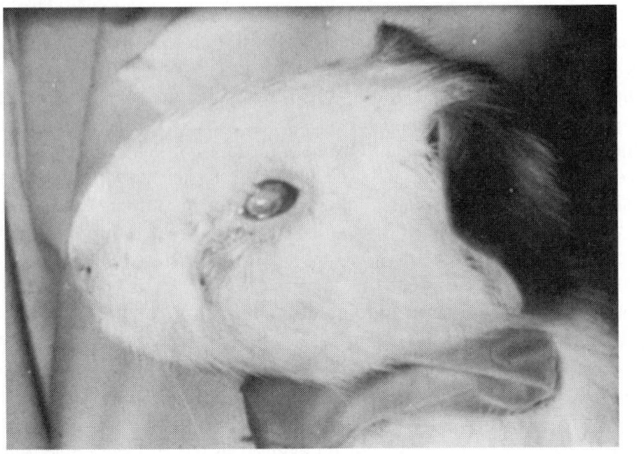

FIGURE 211–1. Guinea pig with keratoconjunctivitis following conjunctival inoculation of invasive *Escherichia coli*. This is a positive Sereny test result.

dysentery is an important problem in institutionalized or crowded populations.

Invasiveness

Virulent *Shigella* and other nontoxigenic invasive *E. coli* strains produce disease after invading the intestinal mucosa,[10] with subsequent multiplication and mucosal destruction. *Shigella* infection is superficial, and only rarely does the organism penetrate beyond the mucosa, which explains the rarity of obtaining positive blood cultures in patients with shigellosis despite the common occurrence of hyperpyrexia and toxemia. Studies designed to characterize the genetics of virulent *Shigella* strains have shown that the property of invasiveness of *Shigella* and *E. coli* is associated with a mixture of soluble bacterial proteins encoded by a 140-MDa plasmid.[11] In some *Shigella* strains a portion of the chromosome also controls invasion of the guinea pig cornea and conjunctiva; it is a locus near the purine E and lactose-galactose regions.[12] Studies using *Shigella–E. coli* hybrids have indicated that the xylose-rhamnose region of the *Shigella* chromosome is also important in determining invasiveness.[13] DNA probes and polymerase chain reaction techniques have been developed to detect *Shigella* and invasive *E. coli*.

Toxigenicity

The Shiga bacillus (*S. dysenteriae* 1) was shown in the early part of the 20th century to produce a neurotoxin that caused paralysis and death in mice and rabbits. It has been suspected since that time that the toxin played an important role in the pathogenesis of clinical illness. Later, an exotoxin in the Shiga bacillus was shown to have enterotoxin activity in the ligated ileal loop model[14] and also to have cytotoxic properties when intestinal mucosa was examined.[15] A possible role for toxin production in the evolution of human shigellosis caused by other organisms was further suggested by showing that an *S. flexneri* strain and an *S. sonnei* strain produce a similar toxin, although in decreased amounts, and that serum obtained from patients recently infected with these two species is able to neutralize the activity of Shiga toxin.[16] Undoubtedly, invasiveness is the primary virulence characteristic of *Shigella* strains, but toxin elaboration probably plays a role in evolution of the local destructive mucosal lesion once the organisms have invaded the colonic mucosa. It is possible that toxin might also help explain the watery small bowel type of diarrhea that is characteristically seen during the first or second day of illness. Shiga toxin production does appear to be the important virulence property of hemorrhagic colitis caused by *E. coli* (0157:H7).[17]

Anatomic Location of Infection

Volunteer studies have helped establish the intestinal localization of bacteria in experimental shigellosis. Within 12 hours after subjects swallow virulent shigellae, the bacteria transiently multiply in the small bowel to concentrations of 10^7 to 10^9 viable cells per milliliter of luminal contents. Abdominal pain, cramping, and fever occur while the bacteria are localized in the small bowel. Within a few days, the infecting strain is no longer detectable in small bowel fluid, the patient's temperature becomes lower, and pain and tenderness become more severe and are generally confined to the lower abdominal quadrants. Urgency, tenesmus, and bloody mucoid stools (dysentery) often occur in the later stages of infection and correlate with a diffuse colonic localization of the bacteria. The density of intramucosal bacteria is greatest at the luminal surface and extends in decreasing concentrations to reach the lamina propria and submucosa. Microabscesses form and coalesce to generate large abscesses that slough and produce mucosal ulcerations. In shigellosis, both humoral and cellular immune mechanisms are stimulated. Cytokine levels (fecal cytokine levels are greater than levels in serum) correlate with disease severity.[18]

EPIDEMIOLOGY

Hippocrates indicated that when a dry winter was followed by a rainy spring, an increase in the number of dysentery cases would follow in the summer. Such an epidemiologic observation has been made by others in more recent years. A tropical environment and poor nutritional standards are associated with an increased prevalence of diarrheal illness in general. However, the relative frequency of specific pathogens appears to be surprisingly similar, irrespective of geographic location. Because of the characteristic clinical picture of bacillary dysentery, it is one of the most accurately diagnosed and reported classes of infectious diarrhea. The greatest frequency of illness is reported in infants and younger preschool children. Disease rates and also complications and severity parallel the degree of malnutrition. Generally, bacillary dysentery is a summertime illness. Flies may be important in the transmission of bacillary dysentery,[19, 20] especially in tropical climates. Dysentery in warm countries is most prevalent when the fly population is at its highest. Bacteriologic surveys of fly populations have been carried out and indicate that flies can occasionally be shown to be positive for *Shigella* bacteria.[19]

Cyclic Patterns of Disease

Since the description of bacteriologic isolation procedures, cyclic epidemics of bacillary dysentery have been described, each lasting 20 to 30 years.[21] In Europe during the first 25 years of the 20th century, dysentery was generally caused by *S. dysenteriae* 1 (the Shiga bacillus), and mortality was higher than subsequently seen when other serotypes became prevalent. Between 1926 and 1938, *S. flexneri* strains became more important than the Shiga bacillus, and currently *S. sonnei* has replaced other agents as the important cause of bacillary dysentery in European countries and the United States. A similar trend has occurred in many parts of the world to the point that *S. sonnei* is the most important cause of dysentery in nearly all developed or industrialized countries. It is of interest that in England from the beginning of the 17th to the middle of the 19th century, similar epidemic cycles of bacillary dysentery were described. The cyclic pattern of serotypes specific for shigellosis suggests that it takes a certain number of years for herd immunity to reach a critical level in a population before one species of *Shigella* will disappear to be replaced by another. It may be that the disease attacks each generation, with the survivors rendered immune, and then must wait for the appearance of nonimmune offspring.[6] Molecular fingerprinting studies have shown that multiple *Shigella* strains typically circulate simultaneously in communities.[22] Occasionally, a single epidemic strain may occur, with sustained propagation between communities in contact.[23]

Incidence of Shigellosis by Geography and Host

Bacillary dysentery in Britain is mainly an acute diarrheal disease in children of school age or younger. In the United States the highest rate of *Shigella* recovery is in those 1 to 4 years of age. A change in the seasonal prevalence of bacillary dysentery has occurred in the United Kingdom, and it now correlates with student enrollment in primary schools. It has been suggested that fecal contamination of lavatory seats in nursery and primary schools occurs from children with diarrhea and that infection is transmitted to the hands of the younger children.[24] Shigellosis has become an important problem in daycare centers for preschool children in the United States. Between 20,000 and 50,000 cases are reported each year in the United Kingdom and approximately 13,000 to 19,000 cases each year in the United States. The actual number of cases is clearly far greater than those reported.

In numerous published studies,[25–27] an etiologic agent has been identified in 10 to 40% of diarrhea cases, depending on geographic location and the severity of illness reported. The major agent identified in these studies was a *Shigella* strain. Bacillary dysentery is primarily a disease of children 6 months to 10 years of age; adults often acquire the illness from their children. Bacillary dysentery does not commonly develop in children younger than 6 months. However, in industrialized countries, *Shigella* strains may (rarely) cause severe illness in newborns,[28] but in developing countries, where breast-feeding is more common, infants are highly resistant to shigellosis,[29] probably because of exclusion from contaminated food or drink, changes in intestinal flora of breast-fed children, or the presence of specific antibody in breast milk. *Campylobacter* has been shown to be an important cause of diarrhea in all regions of the world.

Modes of Spread and Reservoirs in Nature

Most cases of bacillary dysentery are a result of person-to-person transmission. However, in a number of instances, widespread epidemics have occurred in military or civilian populations and among persons on board cruise ships who have ingested contaminated food or water. Water and food appear to be particularly important vectors of *Shigella* transmission in developing countries.[30, 31] Epidemics of waterborne shigellosis generally appear to be due to wells contaminated with fecal material. Felsen[31a] found that dysentery strains could be recovered for up to 6 months from water samples maintained at room temperature. Wells are often located close to cesspools and privies in developing countries where sanitation principles are not followed. In other areas, septic tank discharge may empty into lakes, ponds, or other bodies of water close to intake lines for camp water supplies or adjacent to bathing beaches. Chlorination of water, if appropriately maintained, will remove the threat of such infections. Foodborne transmission of disease is not common when compared with spread by direct contact, but when it occurs, it is associated with large outbreaks. During a 5-year period (1964–1968), the Centers for Disease Control in Atlanta reported 21 foodborne or waterborne outbreaks of shigellosis in the United States,[32] thus indicating the relative rarity of documenting common-source epidemics. An epidemiologic observation has been made that when water sanitation improvements are implemented in a community, the incidence of typhoid fever falls but the prevalence of bacillary dysentery remains unchanged.[31a] In contrast to shigellosis, diseases caused by *Salmonella, Vibrio cholerae*, and *E. coli* appear to be epidemiologically associated in almost all cases with foodborne or waterborne transmission. Such a vehicle of transmission is probably necessary with the latter agents because a larger inoculum is necessary to produce illness.[33]

Hand transmission is likely to be a common means of acquiring infection. At a custodial institution, mentally retarded persons were studied for the prevalence of hand transmission of bacteria.[19] Finger and simultaneous fecal cultures were obtained from 268 institutionalized patients. A *Shigella* strain was isolated from the stool of 39 persons, and the fingers were positive in 4 (10% of those with a positive stool culture). In addition, fecal cultures were found to be negative in an additional 229 patients, whereas a *Shigella* strain was isolated from the hands and fingers of 2 of these patients with negative stool cultures. *E. coli* was recovered from the fingers of 82% of those studied, which demonstrates the common occurrence of fecal organisms on the hands of institutionalized persons. These institutionalized patients had adequate washroom and showering facilities and did not show evidence of decreased personal hygiene.

Secondary cases during outbreaks of shigellosis are common. One study demonstrated that bacillary dysentery develops in 61% of the children younger than 1 year once an index case occurs in a household.[19] The attack rate was approximately 40% for those aged 1 to 4 years and 20% for all ages once an index case was identified. Secondary attack rates are increased in houses having privies and are reduced in families once sanitary toilet facilities are installed. Transmission rates also correlated with poverty and overcrowding. After a bout of shigellosis without antimicrobial therapy, fecal excretion of the infecting strain generally lasts 1 to 4 weeks. Long-term *Shigella* carriage has been well documented in a small percentage of cases and does not appear to correlate with any underlying intestinal dysfunction.[6, 34] In contrast to typhoid and cholera carriers, the organisms in dysentery carriage are confined to a colonic site. In the absence of coexistent parasitic infestation of the intestine, these carriers will generally respond to antimicrobial therapy. Long-term carriers may be important to the epidemiology of foodborne or waterborne illness. The number of organisms excreted by these persons is generally less than that seen in acute dysentery, and thus the disease in such individuals is less communicable than that in active cases.

DIAGNOSIS

History

Bacillary dysentery should be considered in any patient with acute diarrheal illness associated with toxemia and systemic symptoms, particularly when the illness lasts longer than 48 hours, if intrafamily spread occurs with an interval of 1 to 3 days between cases, if fever is present, and if blood or mucus is seen in stools. The occurrence of hyperpyrexia and seizures in infants and children with shigellosis has led some to the conclusion that a neurotoxin is important in the pathogenesis of clinical illness, although there is little to support this notion. In patients able to give a careful history, a descending intestinal tract infection is often described. The first symptoms may be fever and abdominal cramping, followed by voluminous watery stool (these findings correlate with a small bowel site of infection), a decrease in fever, and an increase in the number of stools with smaller volume ("fractional stools"). In a day or two, bloody mucoid stools with fecal urgency and tenesmus may develop. These latter findings reflect a colonic site of infection. It is this evolution in disease symptoms, as the infecting strain descends the intestinal tract, that often leads to a clinical diagnosis of bacillary dysentery and may indicate the need for performing stool culture. Abdominal pain and diarrhea occur in nearly all patients with shigellosis, fever can be documented in approximately one third of cases, and mucus is seen in the stools of half and gross blood in 40% of cases.[35]

Physical Examination

Findings on physical examination are nonspecific and include a variable degree of systemic toxemia, fever (which may be as high as 106°F), abdominal tenderness, especially over the lower abdominal quadrants, and hyperactive bowel sounds. Rectal examination or proctoscopy is generally painful, and an abnormally friable, hyperemic rectal mucosa, increased mucus secretion, and areas of ecchymosis are generally found. Ulcerations of rectal mucosa are seen after several days of illness.

Laboratory Findings

During the acute illness, the infecting strain is present in large enough numbers that stool cultures are generally positive. In the later stages of the disease it may be necessary to culture material directly from the ulceration through a proctoscope or incubate fecal material in enrichment broth before plating. In centers where the service is available, direct fluorescent antibody microscopy may be useful in detecting the organism when present in small numbers,[36] but because of the numerous serotypes potentially responsible for the infection, this procedure does not have widespread application.

The total white blood cell count demonstrates no consistent findings, although leukopenia and brisk leukocytosis are seen on occasion. A "shift to the left" (an increased number of bands in comparison to segmented neutrophils) when a leukocyte differential count is performed in a patient with diarrhea suggests bacillary dysentery. The single most important laboratory test other than stool culture is direct microscopic examination of a stained fecal smear, which will show prevalent polymorphonuclear leukocytes.[37] A wet mount preparation is made by adding stool (mucus if it is present) to an equal amount of methylene blue dye. The preparation is then covered with a coverslip and examined microscopically under the high dry objective. Alternatively, the specimen can be heat-fixed before staining with dilute methylene blue. The specimen can then be examined under oil after drying. This dry preparation can be stored for later review. Numerous sheets of polymorphonuclear leukocytes are normally found in shigellosis and invasive *E. coli* diarrhea (Fig. 211–2). Prevalent leukocytes indicate a colitis in which the colonic mucosa is diffusely involved. The leukocyte test, when positive, indicates a pathologic process, not an etiologic one, and white cells are usually also seen in salmonellosis, *Campylobacter* enteritis, and idiopathic ulcerative colitis.

Serologic evaluation of a patient with bacillary dysentery is not generally helpful in establishing the diagnosis because humoral antibodies do not develop before recovery. Serologic procedures are helpful as an epidemiologic tool in defining the extent of an epidemic in a population known to be infected by a known *Shigella* serotype (especially for the Shiga bacillus). The humoral antibody response correlates with the severity of clinical disease.[35]

TREATMENT AND CLINICAL COURSE

In certain patients with bacillary dysentery (particularly infants and elderly patients), significant dehydration may result from excessive fluid loss through diarrhea and vomiting. The fluid losses can generally be replaced by oral intake because the diarrhea associated with bacillary dysentery is not normally associated with profound fluid and electrolyte depletion. If vomiting or extreme toxemia is a prominent feature of the illness, especially in the very young or the elderly, intravenous fluid replacement may be necessary.

Antibiotics are useful in the management of shigellosis. In illness caused by strains susceptible to these antimicrobials, ampicillin or tetracycline will shorten the period of fecal excretion of the infecting strain and will limit the clinical course of illness.[38] Because the infection is normally self-limited and because antibiotic resistance commonly develops after treatment, some believe that antimicrobial therapy should be reserved for the most severely ill patients.[39] How-

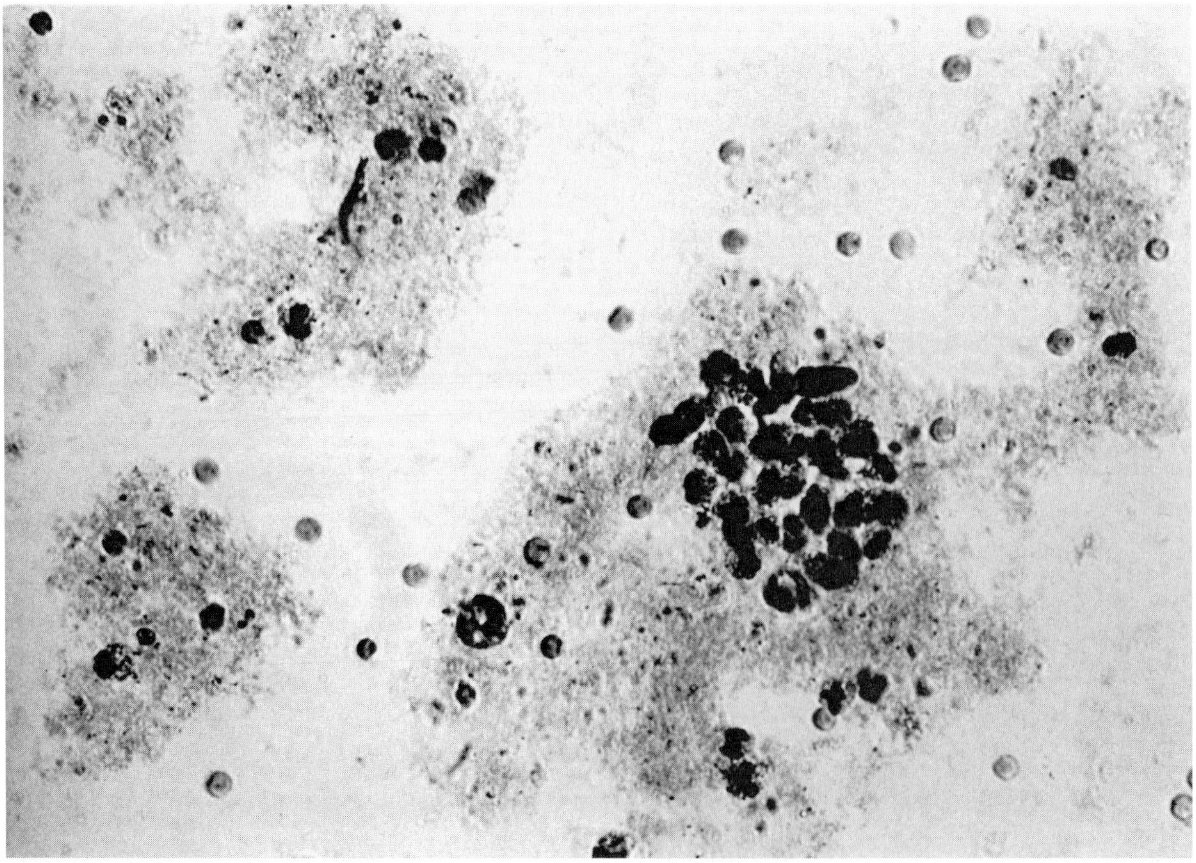

FIGURE 211–2. Methylene blue stain of fecal leukocytes found in colitis. This exudative response may be seen in shigellosis, salmonellosis, *Campylobacter* infection, and colitis due to invasive *Escherichia coli*.

TABLE 211–1 Antimicrobial Therapy for Bacillary Dysentery

First Choice if Strains Are Susceptible		Alternative and for TMP-Resistant Strains*	
Children	*Adults*	*Children (>3 mo)*†	*Adults*
TMP, 10 mg/kg/day, + SMX, 50 mg/kg/day in 2 equal doses q12h PO for 3–5 d	TMP, 160 mg, + SMX, 800 mg q12h PO for 3–5 d	Nalidixic acid, 55 mg/kg/day in 4 equally divided doses PO for 5 d	Ciprofloxacin, 500 mg bid PO for 3–5 d‡ *or* Norfloxacin, 400 mg bid PO for 3–5 d‡ *or* Ofloxacin, 300 mg bid PO for 3–5 d‡

*Strains acquired outside the United States are typically TMP-resistant.
†Ceftriaxone is used in young adults with shigellosis and it can be used in older children as well.
‡For mild to moderately ill subjects, single-dose therapy is adequate.
Abbreviations: SMX, Sulfamethoxazole; TMP, trimethoprim.

ever, because the infection is generally transmitted from person to person and the infected or colonized person represents the major reservoir of infection, for public health reasons each patient with a positive stool culture or with known bacillary dysentery should be treated. The treatment of choice for shigellosis when susceptibility is unknown is trimethoprim-sulfamethoxazole.[40, 41] The dose is indicated in Table 211–1. In certain areas of Southeast Asia, Africa, and South America, trimethoprim resistance commonly occurs in the prevalent strains of *Shigella*.[42] In these areas, for adult patients with shigellosis or when empirical therapy is aimed at both *Shigella* and *Campylobacter*, ciprofloxacin,[43] norfloxacin,[44] or ofloxacin[45] will be effective. For milder forms of illness, single-dose therapy is effective.[46] For children, nalidixic acid can be used in these geographic areas. Alternative drugs in pediatric cases are amdinocillin and for milder cases, furazolidone. Azithromycin has been used successfully for treatment of multidrug-resistant *Shigella* infection in adults.[47]

Intestinal motility patterns may be important in recovery from infection, as well as in preventing mucosal invasion by a bacterial agent. In such cases, diarrhea might be viewed as a protective mechanism, and its inhibition by motility-active drugs may not be wise. Paregoric has occasionally been shown to worsen clinical salmonellosis,[48] and in occasional patients, antidiarrheal drugs such as diphenoxylate (Lomotil) worsen bacillary dysentery and could play a role in the development of toxic dilatation of the colon.[49]

Clinical illness, if left untreated, generally lasts between 1 day and 1 month, with an average of 7 days. Although mortality is unusual in shigellosis except in malnourished children and the elderly, the clinical illness is more striking and more likely to lead to hospitalization than are most other forms of infectious diarrhea. Complications are unusual and generally consist of severe dehydration, febrile seizures, septicemia or pneumonia from coliform organisms (and less commonly the infecting *Shigella* strain), keratoconjunctivitis, and arthritis. A post-*Shigella* Reiter syndrome may develop in patients with HLA-B27 histocompatibility antigen. *S. dysenteriae* (the Shiga bacillus) characteristically produces a more serious form of diarrhea, and the mortality associated with untreated disease during epidemics may be as high as 20%. Bacterial strains that produce Shiga toxin (*S. dysenteriae* 1 and *E. coli* in hemorrhagic colitis) often produce the hemolytic-uremic syndrome as a complication of illness. Now that oral rehydration therapy has reduced the incidence of most cases of dehydration-associated deaths from diarrhea, shigellosis represents the most important form of fatal enteric illness in areas of high endemicity.[50] A rare fulminating form of bacillary dysentery secondary to massive small intestine invasion by the infecting bacteria is seen in children, and death early in infection is common (the "Ikari" syndrome).

CONTROL

Environmental Control

A safe water supply is important for the control of shigellosis and is probably the single most important factor in areas with substandard sanitation facilities.[51] Chlorination is another factor important in decreasing the incidence of all enteric bacterial infections. Of critical importance to the establishment of a safe water supply system is the general level of sanitation in the area and the establishment of an effective sewage disposal system. Insecticides are useful in decreasing the vector population during peak seasons, and a decrease in the incidence of shigellosis, but not salmonellosis, may be seen after their use.[20] At other times of the year it may be helpful to attack breeding places of insects. Garbage collection and disposal of excreta and sewage may also be useful in controlling the vectors. In many areas it is necessary to examine the techniques of home preparation and storage of food. Important features may be improved, such as personal and food hygienic facilities, or refrigeration may be necessary. A major prerequisite in transmission in most cases of bacillary dysentery is the degree of contact and the level of personal hygiene between patients with disease and susceptible persons. Other factors are frequent effective hand washing, voluntary removal of persons with diarrhea from roles as food handlers, and appropriate refrigeration and proper cooking of potentially infected foods. Breast-feeding is an important means of decreasing the incidence of bacillary dysentery in developing countries and in communities with substandard hygienic practices. Also, mothers should be taught how to prepare foods to supplement breast-feeding and to constitute the diet after weaning to improve both sanitation and nutrition. Finally, cases of diarrhea should be adequately diagnosed and isolated, and antimicrobial therapy should be instituted in cases of bacillary dysentery to decrease the reservoir of virulent strains. The degree of symptomatology, personal hygiene, and education about ways that enteric bacteria are spread are important factors that may determine the rate of transmission of the agent, and these factors should influence the decision for antimicrobial therapy.

Immunologic Control

Epidemiologic studies have indicated that a degree of homologous immunity can be demonstrated in those who have recovered from bacillary dysentery.[52–54] These observations have supported the idea that a protective vaccine might be developed. It was shown that killed parenteral vaccines fail to protect animals against experimentally produced shigellosis[55] and to protect humans against naturally occurring illness.[56, 57] Besredka[57] suggested that the immunity against bacillary dysentery conferred by one attack of the disease was due essentially to sensitization of the intestinal mucosa to dysentery bacilli and that the antibodies circulating in serum had a small role or none at all in protection. After more than 80 years, Besredka's concept of intestinal immunity is still held as the primary mode through which immunologic control might be feasible. The nature of the intestinal immune response has not been completely characterized. In natural shigellosis, IgA concentrations in stool increase, as do anti-*Shigella* secretory IgA antibodies directed to homologous lipopolysaccharide.[58] Also, lymphocytes, monocytes, and granulocytes, in the absence of complement but in the presence of antibody, may serve an anti-*Shigella* function through cell-mediated mechanisms.[59] Formal and coworkers worked with both spontaneously derived avirulent *Shigella* mutants and hybrid strains (*Shigella–E. coli*) in monkeys.[60–62] The most significant work in the area of

Shigella vaccine development has been carried out by Mel and colleagues, who used streptomycin-dependent mutant strains of *Shigella* as orally administered immunizing agents in Yugoslavian army soldiers and in children living in areas of hyperendemicity.[63, 64] These workers demonstrated that immunization with a live-attenuated bacterial strain given orally in multiple (at least four) doses would prevent clinical disease but would not alter the carrier status, provided that gastric acidity was first decreased by sodium bicarbonate swallowed just before the vaccine. Serotype-specific protection followed vaccination and lasted for at least 6 months, and the immunizing agent remained protective when combined as a bivalent preparation. Volunteer experiments demonstrated that the protective immunity imparted by oral immunization approximated that after recovery from disease.[9]

In the future, immunologic control may be possible against a limited number of serotypes of shigellae when attack rates are shown to be particularly high. Further research is being directed toward developing an immunizing strain that multiplies in the intestinal tract so that fewer doses may be administered. It may be possible to create such a strain by intergeneric hybridization.[65] Attenuated bacteria can be constructed that are better adapted to host intestinal proliferation and that combine two enteric pathogens in a single vaccine preparation.[66] Also, the importance of exotoxin production by *Shigella* strains must be further studied. It is possible that antitoxin immunity might be important to susceptibility and that a successful immunizing agent should also include a toxoid component.

REFERENCES

1. Osler W. On the amebae coli in dysentery and in dysentery liver abscess. Johns Hopkins Hosp Bull. 1890;1:736.
2. Councilman WT, Lafleur HA. Amebic dysentery. Johns Hopkins Hosp Rep. 1891;2:395.
3. Shiga K. Observations on the epidemiology of dysentery in Japan. Philippine J Sci. 1906;1:485.
4. Flexner S. On the etiology of tropical dysentery. Philadelphia Med J. 1900;6:417.
5. Rogers L. Bacillary dysentery. In: Dysenteries, Their Differentiation and Treatment. London: Oxford University Press; 1913:268.
6. Davison WC. A bacteriological and clinical consideration of bacillary dysentery in adults and children. Medicine (Baltimore). 1922;1:389.
7. Séreny B. Experimental shigella keratoconjunctivitis: A preliminary report. Acta Microbiol Acad Sci Hung. 1955;2:293.
8. Riley LW, Remis RS, Helgerson SD, et al. Hemorrhagic colitis associated with a rare *Escherichia coli* serotype. N Engl J Med. 1983;308:681.
9. DuPont HL, Levine MM, Hornick RB, et al. Inoculum size in shigellosis and implications for expected mode of transmission. J Infect Dis. 1989;159:1126.
10. LaBrec E, Schneider H, Magnani T, et al. Epithelial cell penetration as an essential step in the pathogenesis of bacillary dysentery. J Bacteriol. 1964;88:1503.
11. Hale TL, Oaks V, Formal SB. Identification and antigenic characterization of virulence-associated, plasmid-coded proteins of *Shigella* spp. and enteroinvasive *Escherichia coli*. Infect Immun. 1985;50:620.
12. Formal SB, Gemski P Jr, Baron LS, et al. Chromosomal locus which controls the ability of *Shigella flexneri* to evoke keratoconjunctivitis. Infect Immun. 1971;3:73.
13. Formal SB, LaBrec EH, Kent TH, et al. Abortive intestinal infection with an *Escherichia coli–Shigella flexneri* hybrid strain. J Bacteriol. 1965;89:1374.
14. Keusch GT, Grady GF, Mata LJ, et al. Pathogenesis of shigella diarrhea. I. Enterotoxin production by *Shigella dysenteriae* 1. J Clin Invest. 1972;51:1212.
15. Keusch GT, Grady GF, Takeuchi A, et al. Pathogenesis of shigella diarrhea. II. Enterotoxin-induced acute enteritis in the rabbit ileum. J Infect Dis. 1972;126:92.
16. Keusch GT, Jacewicz M. The pathogenesis of shigella diarrhea. VI. Toxin and antitoxin in *Shigella flexneri* and *Shigella sonnei* infections in humans. J Infect Dis. 1977;135:552.
17. O'Brien AD, Newland JW, Miller RK, et al. Shiga-like toxin–converting phages from *Escherichia coli* strains that cause hemorrhagic colitis or infantile diarrhea. Science. 1984;226:694.
18. Raqib R, Wretlind B, Anderson J, et al. Cytokine secretion in acute shigellosis is correlated to disease activity and directed more to stool than to plasma. J Infect Dis. 1995;171:376.
19. Hardy A, Watt J. Studies of the acute diarrheal diseases. XVIII. Epidemiology. Public Health Rep. 1948;63:363.
20. Watt J, Lindsay D. Diarrheal disease control studies. I. Effect of fly control in a high morbidity area. Public Health Rep. 1948;63:1319.
21. Kostrzewski J, Stypulkowska-Misiurewicz H. Changes in the epidemiology of dysentery in Poland and the situation in Europe. Arch Immunol Ther Exp. 1968;16:429.
22. Ahmed F, Clemens JD, Rao MR, et al. Epidemiology of shigellosis among children exposed to cases of *Shigella* dysentery: A multivariate assessment. Am J Trop Med Hyg. 1997;56:258.
23. Sobel J, Cameron DN, Ismail J, et al. A prolonged outbreak of *Shigella sonnei* infections in traditionally observant Jewish communities in North America caused by a molecularly distinct bacterial subtype. J Infect Dis. 1998;177:1405.
24. Cruickshank R. Diarrheal diseases in the United Kingdom. In: Pemberton J, ed. Epidemiology Reports on Research and Teaching. London: Oxford University Press; 1963:60.
25. Gordon J, Béhar M, Scrimshaw N. Acute diarrheal disease in less developed countries. I. An epidemiological basis for control. In: Control of Gastrointestinal Diseases. Pan-American Health Organization, Technical Discussion, Science Publication 100; 1963:26.
26. Ingram V, Rights F, Khan H, et al. Diarrhea in children of West Pakistan: Occurrence of bacterial and parasitic agents. Am J Trop Med Hyg. 1966;15:743.
27. Ramos-Alvarez M, Olarte J. Diarrheal diseases of children: The occurrence of enteropathogenic viruses and bacteria. Am J Dis Child. 1964;107:218.
28. Haltalin K. Neonatal shigellosis: Report of 16 cases and review of the literature. Am J Dis Child. 1967;114:603.
29. Mata L, Urrutia J, Garcia B, et al. *Shigella* infection in breast-fed Guatemalan Indian neonates. Am J Dis Child. 1969;117:142.
30. Boyce JM, Hughes JM, Alim ARMA, et al. Patterns of *Shigella* infection in families in rural Bangladesh. Am J Trop Med Hyg. 1982;31:1015.
31. Tjoa WS, DuPont HL, Sullivan P, et al. Location of food consumption and travelers' diarrhea. Am J Epidemiol. 1977;106:61.

31a. Felson J. Bacillary Dysentery Colitis and Enteritis. Philadelphia: WB Saunders; 1945.

32. Donadio J, Gangarosa E. Foodborne shigellosis. J Infect Dis. 1969;119:666.
33. DuPont H, Hornick R. Clinical approach to infectious diarrheas. Medicine (Baltimore). 1973;52:265.
34. Levine M, DuPont H, Khodabandelou M, et al. Long-term shigella-carrier state. N Engl J Med. 1973;288:1169.
35. DuPont H, Hornick R, Dawkins A, et al. The response of man to virulent *Shigella flexneri* 2a. J Infect Dis. 1969;119:396.
36. Thomason B, Cowart G, Cherry W. Current status of immunofluorescence techniques for rapid detection of shigellae in fecal specimens. Appl Microbiol. 1965;13:605.
37. Harris J, DuPont H, Hornick R. Fecal leukocytes in diarrheal illness. Ann Intern Med. 1972;76:697.
38. Haltalin K, Nelson J, Ring R II, et al. Double-blind treatment study of shigellosis comparing ampicillin, sulfadiazine and placebo. J Pediatr. 1967;70:970.
39. Weissman J, Gangarosa E, DuPont H, et al. Changing needs in the antimicrobial therapy of shigellosis. J Infect Dis. 1973;127:611.
40. Nelson JD, Kusmiesz H, Jackson LH, et al. Trimethoprim sulfamethoxazole therapy for shigellosis. JAMA. 1976;235:1239.
41. DuPont HL, Reves RR, Galindo E, et al. Treatment of travelers' diarrhea with trimethoprim/sulfamethoxazole and with trimethoprim alone. N Engl J Med. 1982;307:841.
42. Murray BE. Resistance of *Shigella, Salmonella*, and other selected enteric pathogens to antimicrobial agents. Rev Infect Dis. 1986;8(Suppl):S172.
43. Ericsson CD, Johnson PC, DuPont HL, et al. Ciprofloxacin or trimethoprim/sulfamethoxazole as initial therapy for travelers' diarrhea. A placebo-controlled, randomized trial. Ann Intern Med. 1987;106:216.
44. DuPont HL, Corrado ML, Sabbaj J. Use of norfloxacin in the treatment of acute diarrheal disease. Am J Med. 1987;82(Suppl 6B):S79.
45. DuPont HL, Ericsson CD, Mathewson JJ, et al. Five versus three days ofloxacin therapy of traveler's diarrhea: A placebo-controlled study. Antimicrob Agents Chemother. 1992;36:87–91.
46. Bennish ML, Salam MA, Khan WA, et al. Treatment of shigellosis: III. Comparison of one- or two-dose ciprofloxacin with standard 5-day therapy. A randomized, blinded trial. Ann Intern Med. 1992;117:727.
47. Khan WA, Seas C, Dhar U, et al. Treatment of shigellosis: V. Comparison of azithromycin and ciprofloxacin: A double-blind, randomized, controlled trial. Ann Intern Med. 1997;126:697.
48. Sprinz H. Pathogenesis of intestinal infections. Arch Pathol. 1969;87:556.
49. DuPont H, Hornick R. Adverse effects of Lomotil therapy in shigellosis. JAMA. 1973;226:1525.
50. Butler T, Islam M, Azad AK, et al. Causes of death in diarrhoeal diseases after rehydration therapy: An autopsy study of 140 patients in Bangladesh. Bull World Health Organ. 1987;65:317.
51. Nyerges V, Eng N. Plan for the control of gastrointestinal diseases. Environmental sanitation, epidemiology, health education and early diagnosis and treatment. In: Control of Gastrointestinal Diseases. Pan-American Health Organization, Technical Discussion, Science Publication 100; 1963:36.
52. Cruickshank R. Acquired immunity: Bacterial infections. In: Cruickshank R, ed. Modern Trends in Immunology. Washington, DC: Butterworth; 1963:119.
53. DuPont H, Gangarosa E, Reller L, et al. Shigellosis in custodial institutions. Am J Epidemiol. 1970;92:172.
54. Hardy A, Watt J. The acute diarrheal diseases. JAMA. 1944;124:1173.
55. Formal S, Maenza R, Austin S, et al. Failure of parenteral vaccines to protect monkeys against experimental shigellosis. Proc Soc Exp Biol Med. 1967;125:347.
56. Hardy A, DeCapito T, Halbert S. Studies of acute diarrheal diseases. XIX. Immunization in shigellosis. Public Health Rep. 1948;63:685.
57. Besredka A. On the mechanism of dysenteric infection, antidysenteric vaccination per os, and the nature of antidysenteric immunity. Ann Inst Pasteur Paris. 1919;33:301.
58. Winsor DK Jr, Mathewson JJ, DuPont HL. Comparison of serum and fecal antibody responses of patients with naturally acquired *Shigella sonnei* infection. J Infect Dis. 1988;158:1108.
59. Lowell GH, MacDermott RP, Summers PL, et al. Antibody-dependent cell-mediated

antibacterial activity: K lymphocytes, monocytes, and granulocytes are effective against shigella. J Immunol. 1980;125:2778.
60. Formal S, LaBrec E, Palmer A, et al. Protection of monkeys against experimental shigellosis with attenuated vaccines. J Bacteriol. 1965;90:63.
61. Formal S, Kent T, Austin S, et al. Fluorescent-antibody and histological study of vaccinated and control monkeys challenged with *Shigella flexneri*. J Bacteriol. 1966;91:2368.
62. Formal S, Kent T, May H, et al. Protection of monkeys against experimental shigellosis with a living attenuated oral polyvalent dysentery vaccine. J Bacteriol. 1966;92:17.
63. Mel D, Arsic B, Nikolic B, et al. Studies on vaccination against bacillary dysentery. 4. Oral immunization with live monotypic and combined vaccines. Bull World Health Organ. 1968;39:375.
64. Mel D, Gangarosa E, Radovanovic M, et al. Studies on vaccination against bacillary dysentery. 6. Protection of children by oral immunization with streptomycin-dependent *Shigella* strains. Bull World Health Organ. 1971;45:457.
65. DuPont HL, Hornick RB, Snyder MJ, et al. II. Protection induced by oral live vaccine or primary infection. J Infect Dis. 1972;125:12.
66. Baron LS, Kopecko DJ, Formal SB, et al. Introduction of *Shigella flexneri* 2a type and group antigen genes into oral typhoid vaccine strain *Salmonella typhi* Ty21A. Infect Immun. 1987;55:2797.

Chapter 212

Haemophilus influenzae

E. RICHARD MOXON
TIMOTHY F. MURPHY

DESCRIPTION OF THE PATHOGEN

Haemophilus influenzae is a small, nonmotile, non–spore-forming bacterium and a parasite of humans found principally in the upper respiratory tract. First reported by Pfeiffer in 1892, the sensational claim that it was the primary agent of epidemic influenza proved fallacious; nonetheless, it has a wide range of pathogenic potential. Its requirement for growth factors, which can be supplied by erythrocytes, accounts for the generic name *Haemophilus* (blood-loving). In microscopic appearance, it is a small (1×0.3 μm) gram-negative bacterium. Stained organisms obtained from clinical specimens vary microscopically from small coccobacilli to long filaments. This variable morphologic appearance (pleomorphism) and inconsistent uptake of dyes (e.g., safranin) may result in erroneous interpretations of stained smears.

Aerobic growth of *H. influenzae* requires two supplements known as X factor and V factor, although neither refers to a single substance.[1] X factor can be supplied by heat-stable iron-containing pigments that supply protoporphyrins essential for catalases, peroxidases, and cytochromes of the electron transport chain. The requirement for X factor is used to distinguish *H. influenzae* from *Haemophilus parainfluenzae* (requires only V factor); because X factor is not required for anaerobic growth of *H. influenzae,* confusion may arise if *H. influenzae* is grown anaerobically (e.g., after stab inoculation). The heat-labile V factor, a coenzyme, may be supplied by nicotinamide adenine dinucleotide, by nicotinamide adenine dinucleotide phosphate, or by nicotinamide nucleoside. Although present in erythrocytes, V factor must be released from the cell to sustain optimal growth, and thus standard blood agar is an unsatisfactory medium. *H. influenzae* exhibits satellitism around colonies of hemolytic *Staphylococcus aureus* (a source of V factor), and this technique may be used to identify *H. influenzae.* Superior culture results are obtained using media enriched with red blood cells that have been disrupted by heating (e.g., chocolate agar) or by peptide digestion (Fildes medium). Because excessive heat destroys V factor, commercial media must undergo quality control before use. Although it is not a strict requirement, some *H. influenzae* strains grow best in 5 to 10% carbon dioxide. Viability of *H. influenzae* is lost rapidly, so clinical specimens should be inoculated onto appropriate media without delay. A biotyping scheme[2] devised by Kilian (based on indole production, urease, and ornithine decarboxylase activity) may be used to characterize individual isolates. Biotype III includes *Haemophilus aegyptius,* the "Koch-Weeks bacillus."

Colonies of *H. influenzae* are usually granular, transparent (or slightly opaque), circular, and dome-shaped. On chocolate agar, most colonies attain a size of about 0.5 to 0.8 mm during the first 24 hours of growth at 37°C, enlarging to 1.0 to 1.5 mm by 48 hours. Pittman[3] described six antigenically distinct capsular types, designated A to F. Colonies of encapsulated strains are mucoid (iridescent when grown on transparent media and examined using an indirect source of light) and may attain a size of 3 to 4 mm. The production of capsule is of major significance to clinicians because it is an important virulence factor. Strains of *H. influenzae* that lack a polysaccharide capsule are generally referred to as nontypeable because they are nonreactive with typing antisera raised against each of the six capsules. Using the technique of multilocus enzyme electrophoresis to characterize isolates cultured from carriers and cases of disease obtained over several decades and from all continents, the population structure of *H. influenzae* type B has been shown to be clonal.[4] These studies also show that most unencapsulated isolates are not capsule-deficient variants of extant capsule clones; they are genetically distinct and are more heterogeneous in genotype than are clones of capsulate *H. influenzae*.

EPIDEMIOLOGY

H. influenzae is indigenous to humans; no other natural host is known. It is among the bacteria normally found in the pharynx (not the oral cavity) and, to a lesser extent, it also colonizes the mucosae of the conjunctiva and more rarely the genital tract. Surveys have indicated that up to 80% of healthy persons are carriers[5] of nontypeable *H. influenzae.* Before the widespread use of conjugate vaccines, type B strains colonized the nasopharynx of children at a rate of 2 to 4%. The rate of nasopharyngeal colonization by type B strains has decreased substantially with the use of conjugate vaccines to prevent invasive infections caused by *H. influenzae* type B. Table 212–1 summarizes several features of *H. influenzae* carriage.

Spread from one individual to another occurs by airborne droplets or by direct contagion with secretions. Exposure to *H. influenzae* begins after birth so that from infancy onward carriage of one or more strains for periods of days to months is common; these organisms are often not eliminated by antibiotic therapy. Colonization of the respiratory tract is a dynamic process with new strains of nontypeable *H. influenzae* being acquired and cleared from the respiratory tract frequently.[6] Nasopharyngeal colonization by *H. influenzae* in the first year of life is associated with an increased risk of recurrent otitis media compared with children who remain free of

TABLE 212–1 Carriage and Pathogenicity of *Haemophilus influenzae*

Strains	Common Upper Respiratory Tract Carriage Rates (%)	Principal Manifestations of Pathogenicity
Nonencapsulated	30–80	Exacerbations of chronic bronchitis, otitis media, sinusitis, conjunctivitis
Encapsulated, type B	2–4 (prior to widespread use of conjugate vaccines) <1 (in vaccinated populations)	Meningitis, epiglottitis, pneumonia and empyema, septic arthritis, cellulitis, osteomyelitis, pericarditis, bacteremia
Encapsulated types A, C–F	1–2	Rarely incriminated as pathogens

Adapted from Turk DC. Clinical importance of *Haemophilus influenzae*—1981. In: Sell SH, Wright PF, eds. *Haemophilus Influenzae*, Epidemiology, Immunology, and Prevention of Disease. New York: Elsevier; 1982:3–9.

colonization.[7–9] The number of times a child is colonized with *H. influenzae* is directly related to the frequency of otitis media.[10]

Nontypeable *H. influenzae* frequently colonizes the lower respiratory tract in the setting of chronic obstructive pulmonary disease (COPD) and cystic fibrosis. Using selective media improves the recovery rate of *H. influenzae* from the sputum of patients with cystic fibrosis[11]; multiple strains colonize the respiratory tract of these patients simultaneously.[12]

MICROBIAL DETERMINANTS OF COLONIZATION AND VIRULENCE

The first step in pathogenesis is colonization of the upper respiratory tract. The microbial determinants include a variety of adhesins such as fimbriae, outer membrane proteins, and lipopolysaccharide (Table 212–2), each of which has its own specificity for host molecules. In the colonization process, *H. influenzae* is found in association with the mucous layer in locations that are rich in nonciliated epithelial cells and in the intercellular spaces of the respiratory tract epithelia.[13, 14] Nontypeable *H. influenzae* has been found intracellularly in adenoid macrophages.[15, 16] This ability to survive intracellularly may represent an important mechanism that allows the organism to persist in the respiratory tract because of the relatively efficient clearance of bacteria by the mucociliary system. Indeed, in the healthy individual, multiplication of *H. influenzae* occurs constantly, but local defenses such as the mucociliary escalator, innate immune mechanisms, and the acquisition of antibodies act to prevent infection by these bacteria. However, *H. influenzae* possesses a number of virulence factors that, acting in concert and often facilitated by diminished host clearance mechanisms, may sway the balance in favor of contiguous or systemic spread of *H. influenzae* so as to result in disease. Proposed virulence factors include the elaboration of peptidoglycan[17] and lipopolysaccharide,[18] which are inhibitory to cilia and IgA1 proteases[19] that cleave secretory antibodies. Prior virus infections cause loss of ciliated epithelia, and alterations in mucus production occur in response to irritants such as smoke from tobacco or open fires in primitive dwellings. These may act synergistically to produce localized damage and contiguous spread to the eustachian tubes, middle ear, sinuses, and lower respiratory tract. Importantly, *H. influenzae* possesses surface molecules, especially capsular polysaccharides and lipopolysaccharide, that impede complement and antibody-mediated opsonophagocytosis by macrophages and polymorphonuclear cells.

The primacy of type B capsule as a crucial virulence factor in the pathogenesis of invasive disease has been well established by the use of genetic techniques and the exploitation of an infant rat model of bacteremia and meningitis.[20] Following intranasal inoculation, *H. influenzae* B invades the submucosa of the nasopharynx and enters the blood stream within minutes. Meningitis rarely occurs by direct penetration of the central nervous system (e.g., via the cribriform plate) but results from hematogenous spread. The occurrence of meningitis correlates strikingly with the duration and intensity of bacteremia; experimental manipulations that decrease the efficiency of intravascular clearance (e.g., depletion of complement components or splenectomy) increase the incidence of meningitis.[21] In contrast, prior administration of specific serum antibodies or even priming of the immune response with *Escherichia coli* K100 (which has a capsule that is immunologically cross-reactive with polyribosylribitol phosphate [PRP]) decreases the severity of bacteremia and the incidence of meningitis.[22]

The cell envelope of *H. influenzae* also contains lipopolysaccharide, often referred to as lipo-oligosaccharide to distinguish it from the glycolipid of Enterobacteriaceae that possesses distinctive polymerized side chains (O antigens). The oligosaccharide outer core sugars, in concert with capsular polysaccharide, are also important in inhibiting clearance of *H. influenzae* by opsonophagocytosis. These structures exhibit a high degree of interstrain and intrastrain antigenic heterogeneity. The lipopolysaccharide of approximately half of nontypeable strains is sialylated.[23] The lipid A of *H. influenzae* lipo-oligosaccharide demonstrates all the biologic activity typical of endotoxin and is an important factor in mediating tissue damage.[18, 24, 25]

The first step in the pathogenesis of infection by nontypeable *H. influenzae* is colonization of the respiratory tract. Nontypeable strains express several distinct adhesin molecules on the bacterial surface (see Table 212–2), suggesting the importance of adherence in pathogenesis. In contrast to type B strains, which gain access to the blood stream, nontypeable strains cause disease by local invasion of mucosal surfaces. The pathogenesis of otitis media involves direct extension of bacteria from the nasopharynx to the middle ear via the eustachian tube.[26] The lower respiratory tract of adults with COPD is chronically colonized by nontypeable *H. influenzae*. Clinical signs of respiratory tract infection occur when factors yet to be identified upset the host-pathogen relationship.

IMMUNITY

Because of the relative importance of *H. influenzae* B as a cause of meningitis and other systemic infections, careful investigations of the host factors determining susceptibility of humans to strains of this serotype have been made. Fothergill and Wright showed that blood from children aged 3 months to 3 years lacked bactericidal activity against a type B strain, whereas the blood of most neonates, older children, and adults was bactericidal.[27] They proposed that the bactericidal activity of fresh blood was dependent on specific antibodies. Alexander and colleagues observed that when antiserum containing high titers of antibodies to type B capsule was administered as a treatment for *H. influenzae* meningitis, a dramatic increase in the phagocytosis of cerebrospinal fluid (CSF) organisms was observed.[28] They suggested that the polyribosylribitol capsular polysaccharide was intrinsically antiphagocytic and that efficient ingestion by phagocytes was facilitated by opsonization with type-specific antibodies. This hypothesized role for anti-PRP antibodies as a major determinant in mediating protective immunity has been critically investigated, and its essential validity is established.[29, 30] Serum anti-PRP antibodies activate complement-mediated bactericidal[30] and opsonic[31] activity in vitro and mediate protective immunity against

TABLE 212–2 Adhesins of *Haemophilus influenzae*

Adhesin	Molecular Mass	Observation	References
Pili (fimbriae)	20–25 kDa	HifA-hifE gene cluster	131–135
HMW1 and HMW2	120–125 kDa	Homologous with filamentous hemagglutinin of *Bordetella pertussis*	136–142
Hap	155 kDa	Homologous with IgA protease	143, 144
Hsf	~240 kDa	Surface fibrils. Present in type B strains. Homolog of Hia.	145–147
Hia	115 kDa	Hia is absent from strains that express HMW1 HMW2. Present in nontypeable strains	148, 149
OMP P5	~35 kDa	Binds mucin. Also called fimbrin. Homologous with OMP A of *Escherichia coli*	150–152
OMP P2	36–42 kDa	Binds mucin	152
PE binding adhesin	46 kDa	Binds phosphatidyl ethanolamine	153
Lipopolysaccharide	2.5–3.3 kDa	Probable adhesin	154, 155

systemic infections in humans.[32, 33] However, there is an inadequate understanding of the mechanisms determining the age-related, natural acquisition of serum anti-PRP antibodies that occurs in virtually all individuals by age 3 to 4 years.[34] Indeed, some data raise the possibility that these antibodies occur in children who have apparently not been colonized with type B organisms.[35] The antigenic stimulus for these antibodies could be exposure to commensals or ingested food possessing cross-reactive epitopes.[36] In support of this, when human volunteers were fed *E. coli* K100, a normal commensal of the gut that has a capsular polysaccharide immunologically similar to PRP, they responded with increased levels of specific bactericidal and opsonizing antibodies.[37]

At the time of invasive infection, serum anti-PRP antibodies are usually low or absent and, even in convalescence, remain so in very young infants.[38] As a consequence, rare instances of second or third episodes of type B infection have been reported. This failure of the very young to make serum anti-PRP antibodies, even after generalized infection, is not due to immune tolerance but is typical of a natural delay in the immune response of humans to many polysaccharides and other T-cell–independent antigens (i.e., those that do not activate T-helper cells effectively). Calculations of the minimal serum concentrations of anti-PRP antibody associated with protection against *H. influenzae* type B diseases have been estimated to range from 0.04 to 1.00 μg/ml.[39] These estimates must be interpreted cautiously, taking into account the functional variations (e.g., persistence, avidity of binding) of the different subclasses of anti-PRP antibodies. There is much individual variation in levels of anti-PRP antibodies; many adults lack detectable serum anti-PRP antibody but possess substantial serum bactericidal and opsonizing activity against type B organisms that cannot be absorbed out with PRP.[30] Thus, despite the deserved attention and proven importance of anti-PRP antibodies, it has been evident for many years that naturally acquired protective immunity to type B disease is mediated by the eclectic activities of antibodies directed against both capsular and membrane antigens. Natural infection with type B organisms results in antibody responses to lipopolysaccharide and outer membrane proteins, and the protective potential of these antibodies has been shown in experimental infections.

Studies of the genetic basis of susceptibility to type B infection have shown differences in both blood group phenotype (on erythrocytes) and human leukocyte antigen frequencies among individuals with meningitis when compared with those with epiglottitis. Furthermore, age-adjusted serum anti-PRP antibody responses following meningitis were lower than for children with epiglottitis.[40] A low responder phenotype has been directly correlated with absence of the G2m(n) allotype.[41] Interestingly, a low incidence of the G2m(n) phenotype is characteristic of blacks and Hispanics, who, in turn, have higher attack rates compared with whites. Furthermore, the G2m(n) allotype is a heavy chain marker for antibodies of subclass IgG2, the serum concentration of which is predictive of antibody responses to immunization with polysaccharide antigens. A second marker, Km(1) has been associated with lower antibody responses to PRP and other polysaccharide antigens.[42]

An important role for complement components in host defense against *H. influenzae* infections was intimated by the initial studies of Fothergill and Wright, who found that the bactericidal activity of human serum for *H. influenzae* was abolished by heating to 56°C.[27] In vitro, encapsulated and nontypeable *H. influenzae* organisms[43, 44] are able to activate both the classical and alternative pathways.[44] Additional evidence for a biologically significant role for complement components is suggested by the results of experimental infection and by the increased susceptibility to pyogenic infections of patients with specific congenital deficiencies. Individuals with C2 deficiency (two patients), C3b-inactivator deficiency (two patients), and a single individual with homozygous C3 deficiency show an increased susceptibility to *H. influenzae* type B infection[46] (see Chapter 7).

Killing by cellular ingestion or bactericidal action involves the cooperation of serum components (antibody and complement) and either polymorphonuclear leukocytes or cells of the mononuclear phagocytic system. In vitro, polymorphonuclear leukocytes kill *H. influenzae* within minutes when they are incubated in the presence of serum containing type-specific antibodies.[31] However, clearance by cells of the mononuclear phagocytic system is the major factor mediating blood stream clearance. Individuals without spleens have an increased susceptibility to *H. influenzae* B sepsis and meningitis, as do persons with decreased splenic functions (e.g., sickle cell disease).[45] Intensive treatment of individuals with Hodgkin's lymphoma increases susceptibility to *H. influenzae* infections, especially if management includes splenectomy.[46]

The roles of serum and secretory antibodies in host defense against nontypeable *H. influenzae* are complex. A variety of membrane-associated, surface-exposed determinants are immunogenic and potential targets of protective host immune responses. The human immune response to surface antigens of nontypeable strains is intimately involved in the pathogenesis of recurrent infection. For example, outer membrane protein P2, the major porin protein, contains immunodominant, strain-specific determinants on the bacterial surface.[47, 48] Adults with COPD make potentially protective antibodies to strain-specific determinants on P2 following infection.[49] Patients remain susceptible to recurrent infections by other strains. Furthermore, the P2 genes of strains that colonize adults with COPD undergo point mutations in the human respiratory tract.[50–53] The mutations result in amino acid changes in the surface-exposed loops of the P2 molecule. These variants have a selective advantage and are able to evade the host response and cause recurrent or persistent infection. A similar phenomenon has been observed with outer membrane protein P5.[54] The role of local (mucosal) immunity in host defense against *H. influenzae*, whether encapsulated or not, is poorly understood. A possible role for secretory antibodies, which may act by blocking attachment of *H. influenzae* to respiratory tract mucosa, seems reasonable but is speculative.

CLINICAL MANIFESTATIONS OF *HAEMOPHILUS INFLUENZAE* TYPE B

Meningitis

Meningitis is the most serious acute manifestation of systemic infection due to *H. influenzae*. Antecedent symptoms of upper respiratory infection are common. Specific questioning concerning the occurrence of disease in contacts (household, daycare centers) is prudent.[55, 56] None of the clinical features of meningitis due to *H. influenzae* distinguishes it from other forms of purulent meningitis. The peak age incidence varies somewhat among populations depending in part on vaccine use, but this infection primarily affects infants younger than 2 years. Adult cases are infrequent and often have a background of recent or remote head trauma, prior neurosurgery, paranasal sinusitis, otitis, or CSF leak. *H. influenzae* meningitis in neonates is also rare, but such cases can resemble early-onset group B streptococcal infection. The most common signs are fever and altered central nervous system function, but the young child may have few specific signs, and nuchal rigidity is often absent. More obvious manifestations, such as seizures or coma, commonly develop as the disease progresses. The disease may be fulminating in onset, with death occurring in a few hours, usually in a child younger than 1 year. However, the more usual pattern consists of several days of mild illness (e.g., upper respiratory tract infection) followed by an ominous deterioration. Owing to the young age of affected children, subdural effusions are a commonly recognized complication. Clinical suspicion should be greatest when after 2 or 3 days of adequate therapy, there is a tense anterior fontanelle, seizures (particularly if focal), hemiparesis, or neurologic deterioration. In older children, one looks for papilledema and altered mental status.

With appropriate management, the overall mortality rate from *H. influenzae* meningitis is less than 5%, but apparently permanent sequelae occur in many of the survivors.[57]

Epiglottitis

Acute respiratory obstruction caused by a cellulitis of the supraglottic tissues is a potentially lethal disease with a characteristically fulminating onset. Swelling of the epiglottis and aryepiglottic folds with complete obliteration of the vallecular and piriform sinuses is typical. Usually, the patient is a child (aged 2 to 7 years), but occurrence in adults is also well known. The onset is often explosive, initial features being sore throat, fever, and dyspnea progressing rapidly to dysphagia, pooling of oral secretions, and drooling of saliva from the mouth.[58] The child is restless, anxious, and adopts a sitting position, with neck extended and chin protruding to reduce airway obstruction. Abrupt deterioration commonly occurs within a few hours, resulting in death in the absence of adequate treatment. Although these sudden deaths are the result in many instances of airway obstruction, fatal collapse may also result from less well defined mechanisms associated with acute sepsis. In some cases, the course may be less dramatic, with a prodromal illness of sore throat and hoarseness for 24 hours to 7 days preceding the onset of acute symptoms. The characteristic findings are seen above the larynx. The epiglottis is red and swollen and bears a striking resemblance to a bright red cherry obstructing the pharynx at the base of the tongue. This disorder can produce considerable local edema as a result of the loose texture of the submucosa on the lingual aspect of the epiglottis. The trachea appears normal. Examination of the larynx should be performed only in a setting in which an airway can be placed, because this examination, if injudiciously performed, may lead to fatal respiratory obstruction.

Pneumonia and Empyema

The true frequency of primary lung infections due to *H. influenzae* B in children is difficult to determine with accuracy.[59] It is likely that *H. influenzae* B pneumonia occurs more commonly than is recognized. Studies in rural Africa indicate that up to 20% of acute severe lower respiratory tract infection may be caused by type B strains. Typically, the patient is between 4 months and 4 years of age and becomes ill in winter or spring, presenting with a consolidative pneumonia (often with pleural involvement) that is severe enough to require hospitalization. The only clinical feature that tends to distinguish *H. influenzae* pneumonia from bacterial pneumonias due to *S. aureus* or *Streptococcus pneumoniae* is a more insidious onset. The development of severe dyspnea, tachycardia, and evidence of cardiovascular failure suggests pericarditis, an uncommon but important complication. Many have stressed the frequency with which primary pneumonia is accompanied by evidence of infection elsewhere (e.g., meningitis, epiglottitis, otitis).

Cellulitis

Cellulitis is predominantly seen in young children. The clinical features are fever and a raised, warm, tender area of distinctive reddish blue hue, most often located on one cheek or in the periorbital region. The distinctive color, its location, and age of the child should suggest the cause. The soft tissue involvement progresses rapidly over a few hours. Some of these children have, or develop, evidence of other septic foci (e.g., meningitis), because an accompanying bacteremia is extremely common.

Bacteremia without Localized Disease

Children, particularly those 6 to 36 months of age, may acquire bacteremia without evidence of local disease. Although *S. pneumoniae* is the most common cause of this syndrome, *H. influenzae* is the next most common.[60] Typically, fever, anorexia, and lethargy prompt the visit to a physician; the examination is nondiagnostic. This condition is appreciated most often in those with a temperature higher than 102°F (39°C) and an increased peripheral neutrophil count. Children with sickle cell disease or with a previous splenectomy are particularly susceptible. Early diagnosis and therapy are critical because these individuals may worsen rapidly and experience septic shock or a localized purulent focus.

Septic Arthritis

H. influenzae is a common cause of septic arthritis in children younger than 2 years of age. Typically, there is involvement of a single large, weight-bearing joint (without osteomyelitis), displaying decreased mobility, pain on movement, and swelling. Positive cultures of blood and joint fluid are usual. However, the signs and symptoms may be more subtle; for example, septic arthritis is an important cause of prolonged fever and irritability (or prolonged antigenemia) during the treatment of other systemic *H. influenzae* diseases (e.g., meningitis). In this context, culture-negative, antigen-positive joint fluid is common.

Response to systemic antibiotics is dramatic and often curative, but long-term follow-up is important because residual joint dysfunction occurs in a significant percentage of children.

H. influenzae septic arthritis also occurs in adults. A review of 29 adults with *H. influenzae* arthritis found that 14 had multiarticular disease and 15 monoarticular disease, with 6 being in the knee only.[61] Nineteen had extra-articular infection as well, including meningitis, pneumonia, sinusitis, and cellulitis. Twenty-two had predisposing factors such as alcohol abuse, trauma, rheumatoid arthritis, systemic lupus erythematosus, diabetes mellitus, splenectomy, multiple myeloma, lymphoma, or common variable hypogammaglobulinemia.

CLINICAL MANIFESTATIONS OF NONTYPEABLE *HAEMOPHILUS INFLUENZAE*

Otitis Media

Nontypeable *H. influenzae* accounts for about one quarter of all cases of acute bacterial otitis media, and more than 90% of the strains isolated from middle ear fluid are nontypeable.[62–64] Approximately 25 million episodes of otitis media occur annually in the United States.[62] Although such episodes occur at any age, they are most common in children aged 6 months to 5 years. The typical clinical presentation in infants is fever and irritability, whereas older children also complain of ear pain. A prior viral respiratory tract infection is commonly the antecedent of an episode of otitis media. The diagnosis is made by otoscopy. A precise etiologic diagnosis requires tympanocentesis, but this is not performed routinely.

Exacerbations of Chronic Obstructive Pulmonary Disease

It has been recognized for many years that exacerbations of COPD correlate with an increase in the production of purulent sputum from which nontypeable *H. influenzae* is cultured. Such episodes are often precipitated by prior viral infection. Serologic studies and antibiotic trials have established that the most common cause of exacerbations of COPD is nontypeable *H. influenzae*.[65] These infections are characterized by an increase from baseline of productive cough, sputum purulence (change in sputum color), and dyspnea. Fever is usually low grade and infiltrates are not present on chest radiography. A sputum Gram strain often reveals abundant gram-negative coccobacilli.

A current view holds that the progressive damage from chronic lung disease in individuals with conditions such as chronic bronchitis and cystic fibrosis occurs through the heightened and protracted inflammatory response to a variety of bacteria, including nontypeable *H. influenzae*, in individuals whose respiratory tract lacks the appropriate clearance mechanisms.

Community-Acquired Pneumonia

Nontypeable *H. influenzae* is an important cause of pneumonia in adults, particularly in the elderly and those with COPD and acquired immunodeficiency syndrome.[66–69] The clinical features are indistinguishable from those of pneumonia caused by other bacteria and include fever, cough, and purulent sputum, usually of several days' duration. The chest film reveals infiltrates that may be patchy or show lobar distribution. A Gram-stained smear of the sputum shows a predominance of small, gram-negative coccobacilli.

Acute Respiratory Tract Infections in Children in Developing Countries

In many countries in which adverse socioeconomic circumstances are prevalent, acute pneumonia in infants caused by nontypeable *H. influenzae* is a major cause of morbidity and mortality.[70–75] Carefully performed studies in several developing countries have established that nontypeable *H. influenzae* accounts for a significant proportion of pneumonia.[70–74] The importance of acute respiratory tract infections as a major global health problem has deservedly, and perhaps belatedly, resulted in the establishment of major international programs (e.g., through the World Health Organization), with the aim of increasing their recognition, appropriate management, and prevention.

Sinusitis

Studies that have used cultures of direct sinus aspirates have shown that nontypeable *H. influenzae* is a common cause of acute maxillary sinusitis.[76] Patients experience nasal obstruction, purulent nasal discharge, headache, and facial pain. As in the case of otitis media, an invasive procedure (sinus aspiration) is required to establish an etiologic diagnosis.

Neonatal and Maternal Sepsis

Neonatal sepsis due to nontypeable *H. influenzae* has been recognized with increasing frequency since the 1980s.[77–82] The infection is associated with 50% mortality and 90% mortality in premature infants.[78] Many strains that cause neonatal sepsis are biotype 4 and share several genotypic and phenotypic characteristics with one another.[80, 83, 84] Indeed, studies of the genetic relationships of these potentially invasive strains and other nontypeable strains suggest that the invasive biotype 4 strains represent a new species.[85]

These same biotype 4 strains also cause postpartum sepsis associated with endometritis.[86] Nontypeable *H. influenzae* is a well-documented cause of tuboovarian abscess or chronic salpingitis.[87] Diagnosis is established by tubal cultures at laparoscopy or cultures of peritoneal fluid by culdocentesis.

Bacteremia and Invasive Infections

Although the most common clinical manifestations of infections by nontypeable *H. influenzae* are otitis media and nonbacteremic respiratory tract infections in adults, the organism also occasionally causes bacteremia. Population-based studies estimate an incidence of 1.7 cases of invasive disease due to *H. influenzae* per 100,000 adults[88] and, overall, the incidence is highest among the elderly.[89] The majority of adults with bacteremia have underlying conditions such as alcoholism, cardiopulmonary disease, or cancer.[90–91] The respiratory tract is the usual source of infection when bacteremia is present. Bacteremic infections caused by nontypeable *H. influenzae* are associated with significant mortality.

Nontypeable *H. influenzae* is also an unusual cause of a variety of invasive infections that are documented by case reports and small series. Indeed, all the invasive diseases that are commonly caused by type B *H. influenzae* are, on occasion, caused by nontypeable strains as well as types A, C, D, E, and F. These infections include adult epiglottitis, empyema, septic arthritis, cellulitis, osteomyelitis, pericarditis, cholecystitis, intra-abdominal infection, and vascular graft infection.[92–97]

Conjunctivitis

Nontypeable *H. influenzae* is an important cause of purulent conjunctivitis and, in contrast to the sporadic nature of other *Haemophilus* infections, can occur in outbreaks, particularly in daycare centers. Clinical features include conjunctival hyperemia and purulent discharge. Occasionally, nontypeable *H. influenzae* causes severe conjunctivitis that is characterized by copious, purulent discharge, lid edema, chemises, and keratitis.

DIAGNOSIS

A provisional diagnosis of meningitis, epiglottitis, facial cellulitis, or septic arthritis is usually prompted by the history and clinical findings. Confirmation requires microbiologic studies. A positive nasopharyngeal culture for *H. influenzae* is not helpful because of the high carriage rate among healthy persons. Cultures of blood, CSF, and other normally sterile fluids (e.g., from joints or pleural, subdural, or pericardial spaces) are diagnostic and therefore—under the appropriate circumstances—mandatory. Even if antibiotic therapy has been started, the yield is sufficiently great to recommend that they be taken. Cultures of the inflamed epiglottis are generally positive but should be taken only when a functional airway can be guaranteed. Whenever feasible, specimens obtained for culture should also be Gram-stained; in about 70% of cases of meningitis, CSF smears reveal typical organisms. Detection of capsular antigen in serum,[98] CSF, or concentrated urine using immunoelectrophoresis, latex agglutination, or enzyme-linked immunosorbent assay may be diagnostic and can be made in up to 90% of culture-proven cases of meningitis. Despite the widespread distribution of immunologically cross-reactive antigens among bacteria in nature, false-positive reactions are uncommon. Antigen is also often detected in infected pleural, pericardial, or joint fluid and can facilitate diagnosis because it persists after antibiotic therapy. The concentration of PRP in serum or spinal fluid and the duration of antigenemia also provide prognostic information on the clinical outcome and course of the disease.

Because nontypeable *H. influenzae* is a normal commensal of the nasopharynx, diagnosis of both upper and lower respiratory tract infections depends on critical evaluation of sputum samples or the selective use of invasive procedures such as tympanocentesis, transtracheal aspiration, bronchoscopy, or lung aspiration. Although blood cultures are invaluable when positive in individuals with more serious infections, they are insensitive. In view of the difficulty in establishing etiology, the clinician often makes a presumptive clinical diagnosis.

TREATMENT

Without treatment, infection due to *H. influenzae* type B can be rapidly fatal. This is particularly true of meningitis and epiglottitis. Currently, the most favored regimen is the use of certain parenteral third-generation cephalosporins as initial therapy when life-threatening *H. influenzae* infection is known or suspected in children beyond the neonatal period. A cephalosporin that is active against *H. influenzae* and that penetrates well into the CSF is chosen; commonly used agents include cefotaxime and ceftriaxone. For children, cefotaxime is given as 200 mg/kg/day divided into six hourly doses. The pediatric dose of ceftriaxone is 75 to 100 mg/kg divided into 12 hourly doses. Adult doses are ceftriaxone 2 g every 12 hours or cefotaxime 2 g every 4 to 6 hours. Despite their superior in vitro activity against the common meningeal pathogens and greater bactericidal activity in CSF, these cephalosporins do not sterilize CSF cultures more rapidly or improve case-fatality rates when compared with results of older antibiotic regimens.[99, 100] Irrespective of the antibiotic chosen, treatment is continued until the patient is afebrile and without clinical or laboratory signs of infection for 3 to 5 days. The usual duration of therapy is 7 to 10 days. Repeat CSF culture to confirm sterility is ordinarily not indicated. Patients with complications such as endophthalmitis, endocarditis, pericarditis, or osteomyelitis may require 3 to 6 weeks of therapy.

Historically, excellent results were also obtained with ampicillin, but resistant strains were first recognized in the United States in 1973 and are now common. In a study of 1537 isolates recovered between November 1, 1994, and April 30, 1995, 38.9% were ampicillin-resistant and 4.5% were amoxicillin-clavulanate–resistant.[105] β-Lactamase was produced by 36.4%. Of concern were 39 strains that did not produce β-lactamase but had intermediate or complete resistance to ampicillin. Ampicillin should not be used for life-threatening infections due to *H. influenzae* unless susceptibility is ensured. In this case, 200 to 300 mg/kg/day is given intravenously, divided into six hourly doses. Chloramphenicol (75 to 100 mg/kg/day, divided into six hourly doses) can be used in patients who are allergic to penicillin. In the previously cited study, only 0.2% of 1537 isolates were resistant to chloramphenicol. In a few circumscribed regions of Europe, the incidence of resistance has exceeded 50%. Routine susceptibility testing is therefore recommended. Chloramphenicol results in dose-related, reversible toxicity to bone marrow. Although this is rarely a clinical problem, special caution must be taken when treating neonates and persons with liver disease in whom serious toxicity may develop. Although idiosyncratic, irreversible bone marrow aplasia due to chloramphenicol is well described, its occurrence is extremely rare. Oral administration of chloramphenicol is not recommended during the acute stage of meningitis because vomiting, seizures, or other conditions might interrupt drug therapy. Once acute symptoms have subsided, oral treatment with the same dosage regimen is effective. Hospitalization during this period is advisable to ensure compliance. In the United States, oral chloramphenicol is no longer available.

Antibiotic therapy is only one facet of the management of the child with *H. influenzae* infection; critical attention must also be given to supportive therapy. In the management of meningitis, optimal ventilation must be ensured by maintaining an adequate airway. Fluid administration must be judiciously managed so as to obtain adequate perfusion of tissues because hypotension and acidosis may accompany severe infection. Conversely, some degree of cerebral edema and inappropriate secretion of antidiuretic hormone may complicate the course and require fluid restriction. Seizures may complicate *H. influenzae* meningitis and should bring to mind the possibility of electrolyte imbalance or subdural effusion.

Several studies have found that administration of corticosteroids to patients with *H. influenzae* type B meningitis reduces the incidence of neurologic sequelae[101–104] (see Chapter 71 for a review of this subject). The presumed mechanism is the reduction of inflammation that results from release of bacterial cell wall fragments when bacteria are killed by antibiotics. Dexamethasone therapy (0.6 mg/kg/day intravenously in four divided doses for 4 days) has been recommended for children older than 2 months of age.

Many infections due to nontypeable *H. influenzae,* such as otitis media and exacerbations of COPD, can be treated with oral antimicrobial agents. Strains of *H. influenzae* have shown a steady rise in the proportion that produce β-lactamase.[105–107] Approximately 25% of nontypeable strains produce β-lactamase, and projections are that half will acquire β-lactamase by the year 2000.[106] Therefore, ampicillin and amoxicillin should be used only if the susceptibility of the infecting isolate is known. The clinician who manages patients with otitis media and exacerbations of COPD frequently chooses an antimicrobial agent empirically. In this circumstance, the antimicrobial agent should be active against *S. pneumoniae* and *Moraxella catarrhalis* as well as *H. influenzae*.

Oral antimicrobial agents that are active against nontypeable *H. influenzae* include trimethoprim-sulfamethoxazole, erythromycin-sulfisoxazole, amoxicillin–clavulanic acid, fluoroquinolones (e.g., ciprofloxacin, ofloxacin, sparfloxacin, trovafloxacin, grepafloxacin), newer macrolides (e.g., azithromycin, clarithromycin), and various extended spectrum cephalosporins (e.g., cefixime, cefpodoxime, cefaclor, loracarbef, cefuroxime).

Parenteral antibiotic therapy is indicated for more serious infections caused by nontypeable *H. influenzae*. Parenteral antimicrobial agents that are active include newer cephalosporins (e.g., ceftriaxone, cefuroxime, ceftazidime, cefotaxime), ampicillin-sulbactam, fluoroquinolones, and azithromycin.

Individuals with certain immunodeficiencies, especially those with primary deficiency of antibody synthesis, have increased susceptibility to infection, especially with nontypeable *H. influenzae.* These persons benefit from passive infusion of immunoglobulin preparations administered either intramuscularly or intravenously. This form of immunoglobulin replacement undoubtedly decreases the incidence of both systemic infections in these individuals and the number of episodes of both upper and lower respiratory tract infections caused by nontypeable *H. influenzae*.

CHEMOPROPHYLAXIS

In the absence of prior immunization, household contacts younger than 4 years of age have a substantial incidence of disease. In six studies of cases in the month following onset of disease in the index case, the attack rate was 3.8% among children younger than 2 years of age, 1.5% among children 2 to 3 years of age, 0.1% among those 4 to 5 years of age, and 0% among those older than 6 years of age.[108] Rifampin prophylaxis as 20 mg/kg once daily (600 mg maximum) for 4 days has eradicated the carrier state in approximately 95% of carriers and significantly reduced the incidence of secondary cases in household members. Rifampin comes in 150- and 300-mg capsules. The dose can be conveniently given to young children in applesauce. The dose for infants younger than 1 month of age is not established. Some authorities recommend only 10 mg/kg each day. The following recommendations have been made by the American Academy of Pediatrics.[109] Rifampin prophylaxis is recommended for all household members, including adults, when the household contains a contact younger than 48 months of age whose immunization status with the conjugate vaccine is incomplete. A contact is defined as a child who is either a household member or spent 4 or more hours each day with the index case for at least 5 of the 7 days preceding the day the index case was hospitalized. Based on efficacy of the *H. influenzae* type B vaccine, chemoprophylaxis is not recommended when all household contacts younger than 48 months of age have completed their immunization series. Completion is defined as one dose of conjugate vaccine at 15 months of age or older, two doses between 12 and 14 months of age, or a two- to three-dose primary series when the child is younger than 12 months of age with a subsequent booster dose at 12 months of age or later. Implicit in this definition is that in households with a child younger than 12 months of age, who therefore has not received the booster dose, all members should receive rifampin prophylaxis. Children who were immunosuppressed at time of vaccination may not have responded and for this purpose should be considered unvaccinated. If rifampin is to be effective in preventing secondary cases, it must be given within 7 days after the index case is hospitalized. The index case should also be given rifampin if penicillin, ampicillin, or chloramphenicol was used for treatment because these drugs, unlike ceftriaxone and cefotaxime, do not eradicate the carrier state.

The attack rate in daycare centers is less well defined, and authorities disagree about the usefulness of chemoprophylaxis. There is reason to expect that success depends on prompt initiation of rifampin and ensuring that at least 75%, if not all, of the staff and children are treated. A reasonable policy would be that chemoprophylaxis should be instituted when at least two cases of invasive *Haemophilus* type B disease occur within 60 days and the daycare center is composed of unvaccinated or incompletely vaccinated children. Also, when unvaccinated or incompletely vaccinated children younger than 2 years of age were in contact with an index case for at least 25 hours in the week before the index case was hospitalized, rifampin may be warranted.

ACTIVE IMMUNIZATION AGAINST *HAEMOPHILUS INFLUENZAE* TYPE B

A compelling body of evidence supports the case for active immunization against invasive type B infections, largely because of the global problem of meningitis.[110] Mortality from meningitis has been constant at about 5% in developed countries for more than 2 decades and is substantially higher (about 40%) in the developing world.[111] Individuals who survive are susceptible to serious and apparently permanent neurologic sequelae; a recent study found persisting abnormalities in 14% of survivors.[57] A further factor that compromises effective treatment is the increasing prevalence of type B strains that are resistant to antibiotics.[112] The first generation of vaccines against invasive type B diseases consisted of the purified, high-molecular-weight type B polysaccharide (PRP). A trial in 1974 showed that this vaccine was effective in toddlers but did not protect infants younger than about 18 months of age.[113] This led to the development of a second generation of vaccines in which PRP is covalently linked (directly or by a spacer molecule) to a protein. Currently there are several licensed vaccines (Table 212–3), and there have been extensive safety, immunogenicity, and efficacy trials with each of the conjugates.[114] Each has been found to be extremely well tolerated; some short-lived localized redness and swelling may occur in 10 to 15% of infants, more commonly after the first than after subsequent injections.

All conjugates are highly immunogenic in adults and older children. PRP-D has the least immunogenicity in infants, even after three doses. Although it proved highly (>90%) protective in a trial involving Finnish children, it was poorly efficacious in infant Native Alaskans.[115] PRP-D is not licensed for infant use in the United States. It is highly immunogenic when used as a booster in infants 12 to 18 months of age who have already received the primary course of three injections with one of the other conjugates. PRP-OMPC is the only conjugate that produces substantial antibody after the first dose, which is given when the infant is 2 months old. Subsequent doses provide only a modest increase, with the final titer substantially less than that obtained with three doses of HbOC or PRP-T. For this reason, PRP-OMPC is licensed in the United States only as a two-dose series. Use of PRP-OMPC, at least for the first dose, would seem advantageous for populations in which high levels of *H. influenzae* type B disease occur early in life, such as Native Americans or Native Alaskans. PRP-T and HbOC provide little antibody after the injections given when the infant is 2 and 4 months old, but very substantial antibody occurs after the dose at 6 months of age. An initial injection of PRP-OMPC at 2 months of age followed by either PRP-T or PRP-HbOC at 4 to 6 months and again at 12 to 15 months appears theoretically to offer the optimal response.[116] However, in the United Kingdom, no booster dose is given after the primary series, and protection has been sustained in the 6 years following the national introduction of *H. influenzae* type B conjugate vaccine (PRRT).[117] No matter what regimen is chosen for the priming doses given when the child is younger than 12 months of age, titers fall off rapidly unless a booster is given at 12 to 15 months of age. If boosters are given, any one of the Food and Drug Administration–licensed vaccines can be used for this purpose. There are no specific contraindications to initial immunization. Conjugate vaccines are administered at the same time as diphtheria, pertussis, and tetanus and polio immunizations as part of the routine program of childhood immunizations. Conjugates can be mixed with diphtheria, pertussis, and tetanus and, when given by a single injection, result in similar immune responses. In countries where *H. influenzae* type B conjugate vaccines have been incorporated into the routine immunization schedules, there has been a virtual disappearance of invasive type B disease in young children.[118] For example, there has now been more than 5 years of prospective surveillance of the impact of routine immunization of infants (aged 2, 3, and 4 months) in the United Kingdom. Over this period, more than 3.5 million children were immunized. Vaccine effectiveness up to age 5 years is estimated to be 98% (95% confidence interval 97 to 99%). Similar results have been reported from the San Francisco Bay area and Los Angeles County, with a decline of 99% between 1990 and 1996.[119] No compensatory increase in other *H. influenzae* serotypes was observed. A surprising but important finding is that conjugate vaccines appear to reduce colonization of the upper respiratory tract with type B organisms.[120] In addition to the reduction in type B disease in developed countries, the efficacy of conjugate type B vaccines in the developing world has been addressed in a randomized trial in Gambian infants. Vaccine prevented most cases of meningitis and pneumonia and suggested that the introduction of *H. influenzae* type B vaccines into developing countries should substantially reduce childhood mortality due to these diseases.[121]

HAEMOPHILUS INFLUENZAE BIOGROUP AEGYPTIUS

H. influenzae biogroup aegyptius was formerly called *H. aegyptius*. However, recent genetic studies have established that *H. influenzae* and *H. aegyptius* are members of the same species; hence, the organism is now referred to as *H. influenzae* biogroup aegyptius.

H. influenzae biogroup aegyptius has long been known to cause conjunctivitis. In 1984, a fulminant systemic illness was described in a small Brazilian town.[122] Following an episode of purulent conjunctivitis, children experienced high fever, vomiting, and abdominal pain. These symptoms were followed by petechiae, purpura, peripheral necrosis, and vascular collapse. Blood cultures were positive for *H. influenzae* biogroup aegyptius.[122, 123] The mortality was 70%, but subsequent reports have described milder forms of the illness. The illness was called Brazilian purpuric fever and has now been described in several rural Brazilian towns in addition to two cases in Australia.[124, 125] Brazilian purpuric fever has occurred sporadically and as outbreaks. The peak age incidence is 1 to 4 years.

H. influenzae biogroup aegyptius is remarkable in that the organism has acquired the capacity to cause a fulminant, invasive disease in spite of lacking a capsule, which is often associated with invasive

TABLE 212–3 *Haemophilus influenzae* Type B Conjugate Vaccines

Scientific Name	Commercial Name	Carbohydrate	Protein Carrier	Polysaccharide/ Protein Ratio	Recommended Dose Carbohydrate (μg)
PRP-T	Act HIB (Pasteur Merieux Laboratories)	Native PRP	Tetanus toxoid	0.33	10
HbOC	HibTITER (Praxis)	Oligosaccharide	CRM_{197}*	0.40	10
PRP-OMPC	PedvaxHIB (Merck, Sharp & Dohme)	Native PRP	OMPC†	0.05–0.10	15
PRP-D	ProHIBit (Connaught Laboratories)	Sized PRP	Diphtheria toxoid	1.39	25

*Mutant diphtheria toxin protein.
†Outer membrane protein complex derived from *Neisseria meningitidis* serogroup B.

infections. Strains of *H. influenzae* biogroup aegyptius are of a clonal origin. Case clone strains share several characteristics: (1) a 24 mDa plasmid, (2) a typical banding pattern in sodium dodecyl sulfate polyacrylamide gel electrophoresis of whole organism lysates, (3) identical electrophoretic type in multilocus enzyme typing, (4) typical ribosomal DNA restriction patterns, (5) resistance to trimethroprim-sulfamethoxazole, (6) a conserved surface epitope on outer membrane protein P1, and (7) a unique immunoglobulin A1 protease.[126–128] The two Australian strains do not share these features and represent a second clone.[129]

Identifying the virulence factors that give case clone strains the ability to cause invasive disease will be important in understanding Brazilian purpuric fever. From a broader perspective, characterizing the molecular mechanisms that account for the invasive potential in an otherwise noninvasive bacterium (nontypeable *H. influenzae)* is of great interest in understanding the pathogenesis of invasive bacterial infections.

REFERENCES

1. Evans NM, Smith DD, Wicken AJ. Haemin and nicotinamide adenine dinucleotide requirements of *Haemophilus influenzae* and *Haemophilus parainfluenzae.* J Med Microbiol. 1974;7:359–365.
2. Kilian M. A taxonomic study of the genus *Haemophilus* with the proposal of a new species. J Gen Microbiol. 1976;93:9–62.
3. Pittman M. Variation and type specificity in the bacterial species *Haemophilus influenzae.* J Exp Med. 1931;53:471–492.
4. Musser JM, Granoff DM, Pattison PE, et al. A population genetic framework for the study of invasive diseases caused by serotype b strains of *Haemophilus influenzae.* Proc Natl Acad Sci U S A. 1985;82:5078–5082.
5. Moxon ER. The carrier state: *Haemophilus influenzae.* J Antimicrob Chemother. 1986;18(Suppl A):17–24.
6. Samuelson A, Freijd A, Jonasson J, Lindberg AA. Turnover of nonencapsulated *Haemophilus influenzae* in the naospharynges of otitis-prone children. J Clin Microbiol. 1995;33:2027–2031.
7. Smith-Vaughan HC, Leach AJ, Shelby-James TM, et al. Carriage of multiple ribotypes of non-encapsulated *Haemophilus influenzae* in aboriginal infants with otitis media. Epidemiol Infect. 1996;116:177–183.
8. Faden H, Duffy L, Wasielewski R, et al. Relationship between nasopharyngeal colonization and the development of otitis media in children. J Infect Dis. 1997;175:1440–1445.
9. Leach AJ, Boswell JB, Asche V, et al. Bacterial colonization of the nasopharynx predicts very early onset and persistence of otitis media in Australian aboriginal infants. Pediatr Infect Dis J. 1994;13:983–989.
10. Harabuchi Y, Faden H, Yamanaka N, et al. Nasopharyngeal colonization with nontypeable *Haemophilus influenzae* and recurrent otitis media. J Infect Dis. 1994;170:862–866.
11. Smith A, Baker M. Cefsulodin chocolate blood agar: A selective medium for the recovery of *Haemophilus influenzae* from the respiratory secretions of patients with cystic fibrosis. J Med Microbiol. 1997;46:883–885.
12. Moller LVM, Regelink AG, Grasselier H, et al. Multiple *Haemophilus influenzae* strains and strain variants coexist in the respiratory tract of patients with cystic fibrosis. J Infect Dis. 1995;172:1388–1392.
13. Van Schilfgaarde M, van Alphen L, Eijk P, et al. Paracytosis of *Haemophilus influenzae* through cell layers of NCI-H292 lung epithelial cells. Infect Immun. 1995;63:4729–4737.
14. Moller LVM, Timens W, van der Bij W, et al. *Haemophilus influenzae* in lung explants of patients with end-stage pulmonary disease. Am J Respir Crit Care Med. 1998;157:950–956.
15. Forsgren J, Samuelson A, Borelli S, et al. Persistence of nontypeable *Haemophilus influenzae* in adenoid macrophages: A putative colonization mechanism. Acta Otolaryngol. 1996;116:766–773.
16. Forsgren J, Samuelson A, Ahlin A, et al. *Haemophilus influenzae* resides and multiplies intracellularly in human adenoid tissue as demonstrated by in situ hybridization and bacterial viability assay. Infect Immun. 1994;42:673–679.
17. Wilson R, Roberts D, Cole P. Effect of bacterial products on human ciliary function in vitro. Thorax. 1985;40:125–131.
18. Gu X-X, Tsa C-M, Apicella MA, Lim DJ. Quantitation and biological properties of released and cell-bound lipooligosaccharides from nontypeable *Haemophilus influenzae.* Infect Immun. 1995;63:4115–4120.
19. Mulks MH, Kornfield SJ, Plaut AG. Specific proteolysis of human IgA by *Streptococcus pneumoniae* and *Haemophilus influenzae.* J Infect Dis. 1980;141:450–456.
20. Moxon ER, Deich RA, Connelly CJ. Cloning of chromosomal DNA from *Haemophilus influenzae:* Its use for studying the expression of type b capsule and virulence. J Clin Invest. 1984;73:298–306.
21. Moxon ER, Zwahlen A, Rubin LB. Pathogenesis of *Haemophilus influenzae* meningitis: Use of a rat model for studying microbial determinants of virulence. In: Sande M, Smith A, Root R, eds. Bacterial Meningitis. New York: Churchill Livingstone; 1985:23–36.
22. Moxon ER, Anderson P. Meningitis caused by *Haemophilus influenzae* in infant rats: Protective immunity and antibody priming by gastrointestinal colonization with *Escherichia coli.* J Infect Dis. 1979;140:471–478.
23. Mandrell RE, McLaughlin R, Abu Kwaik Y, et al. Lipooligosaccharides (LOS) of some *Haemophilus* species mimic human glycosphingolipids, and some LOS are sialylated. Infect Immun. 1992;60:1322–1328.
24. DeMaria TF, Apicella MA, Nichols WA, Leake ER. Evaluation of the virulence of nontypeable *Haemophilus influenzae* lipooligosaccharide *HtrB* and *rfaD* mutants in the chinchilla model of otitis media. Infect Immun. 1997;65:4431–4435.
25. Syrogiannopoulos GA, Hansen EJ, Erwin AL, et al. *Haemophilus influenzae* type b lipooligosaccharide induces meningeal inflammation. J Infect Dis. 1988;157:237–244.
26. Murphy TF, Bernstein JM, Dryja DD, et al. Outer membrane protein and lipooligosaccharide analysis of paired nasopharyngeal and middle ear isolates in otitis media due to nontypeable *Haemophilus influenzae*: Pathogenetic and epidemiological observations. J Infect Dis. 1987;723–731.
27. Fothergill LD, Wright J. Influenzal meningitis: The relation of age incidence to the bactericidal power of blood against causal organism. J Immunol. 1933;24:273–284.
28. Alexander HE, Ellis C, Leidy G. Treatment of typespecific *Haemophilus influenzae* infections in infancy and childhood. J Pediatr. 1942;20:673–698.
29. Robbins JB, Schneerson R, Argaman M, et al. *Haemophilus influenzae* type b: Disease and immunity in humans. Ann Intern Med. 1973;78:259–269.
30. Anderson P, Johnston R, Smith DH. Human serum activities against *Haemophilus influenzae* type b. J Clin Invest. 1972;51:31–38.
31. Johnston RB, Anderson P, Newman S. Opsonization and phagocytosis of *Haemophilus influenzae* type b. In: Sell SH, Karzon DT, eds. *Haemophilus influenzae.* Nashville, Tenn: Vanderbilt University Press; 1973:99–112.
32. Peltola H, Kayhty H, Virtanen M, et al. Prevention of *Haemophilus influenzae* type b bacteremic infections with the capsular polysaccharide vaccine. N Engl J Med. 1984;310:1561–1566.
33. Eskola J, Peltola H, Takala AK, et al. Efficacy of *Haemophilus influenzae* type b polysaccharide diphtheria toxoid conjugate vaccine in infancy. N Engl J Med. 1987;317:717–722.
34. Anderson P, Smith DH, Ingram DL, et al. Antibody to polyribophosphate of *Haemophilus influenzae* type b in infants and children: Effect of immunization with polyribophosphate. J Infect Dis. 1977;136:S57–S62.
35. Sell SH, Turner DJ, Federspick DF. Natural infections with *Haemophilus influenzae* in childhood. I. Types identified. In: Sell SH, Karzon DL, eds. *Haemophilus influenzae.* Nashville, Tenn: Vanderbilt University Press; 1973:3–11.
36. Bradshaw MW, Schneerson R, Parke JC, et al. Bacterial antigens crossreactive with the capsular polysaccharide of *Haemophilus influenzae* type b. Lancet. 1971;1:1095–1096.
37. Schneerson R, Robbins JB. Induction of serum *Haemophilus influenzae* type b capsular antibodies in adult volunteers fed crossreacting *Escherichia coli* 075.K100:h5. N Engl J Med. 1975;29:1093–1096.
38. Kayhty H, Jousimies Somer H, Peltola H, et al. Antibody response to capsular polysaccharides of groups A and C *Neisseria meningitidis* and *Haemophilus influenzae* type b during bacteremic disease. J Infect Dis. 1981;143:32–41.
39. Kayhty H, Peltola H, Karanko V, et al. The protective level of serum antibodies to the capsular polysaccharide of *Haemophilus influenzae* type b. J Infect Dis. 1983;147:1100.
40. Whisnant JK, Rogentine GN, Gralnick MA, et al. Host factors and antibody response in *Haemophilus influenzae* type b meningitis and epiglottitis. J Infect Dis. 1976;133:448–455.
41. Ambrosino DM, Schiffman G, Gotschlich EC, et al. Correlation between G2m(n) immunoglobulin allotype and human antibody response and susceptibility to polysaccharide encapsulated bacteria. J Clin Invest. 1975;75:1935–1942.
42. Granoff DM, Shackleford PG, Pandey JP, et al. Antibody responses to *Haemophilus influenzae* type b polysaccharide vaccine in relation to the K(m)(1) and G2m(23) immunoglobulin allotypes. J Infect Dis. 1986;154:257–264.
43. Quinn PH, Crosson FJ, Winkelstein JA, et al. Activation of the alternative complement pathway by *Haemophilus influenzae* type b. Infect Immun. 1977;16:400–402.
44. Moxon ER, Winkelstein JA. Interaction of *Haemophilus influenzae* with complement. In: Cabello FC, Pruzzo C, eds. Bacteria, Complement and the Phagocytic Cell. Berlin: Springer Verlag; 1988:177–186.
45. Barrett Connor E. Bacterial infection and sickle cell anemia: An analysis of 250 infections in 166 patients and review of literature. Medicine. 1971;50:97–112.
46. Weitzman SA, Aisenberg AC, Siber GR, et al. Impaired humoral immunity in treated Hodgkin's disease. N Engl J Med. 1977;297:245–248.
47. Haase EM, Campagnari AA, Sarwar J, et al. Strain-specific and immunodominant surface epitopes of the P2 porin protein of nontypeable *Haemophilus influenzae.* Infect Immun. 1991;59:1278–1284.
48. Haase EM, Yi K, Morse GD, Murphy TF. Mapping of bactericidal epitopes on the P2 porin protein of nontypeable *Haemophilus influenzae.* Infect Immun. 1994;62:3712–3722.
49. Yi K, Sethi S, Murphy TF. Human immune response to nontypeable *Haemophilus influenzae* in chronic bronchitis. J Infect Dis. 1997;176:1247–1252.
50. Groeneveld K, van Alphen L, Voorter C, et al. Antigenic drift of *Haemophilus influenzae* in patients with chronic obstructive pulmonary disease. Infect Immun. 1989;57:3038–3044.
51. Van Alphen L, Eijk P, Geelen-van-den-Broek L, Dankert J. Immunochemical characterization of variable epitopes of outer membrane protein P2 of nontypeable *Haemophilus influenzae.* Infect Immun. 1991;59:247–252.
52. Duim B, Vogel L, Puijk W, et al. Fine mapping of outer membrane protein P2

antigenic sites which vary during persistent infection by *Haemophilus influenzae*. Infect Immun. 1996;64:4673–4679.

53. Duim B, van Alphen L, Eijk P, et al. Antigenic drift of non-encapsulated *Haemophilus influenzae* major outer membrane protein P2 in patients with chronic bronchitis is caused by point mutations. Mol Microbiol. 1994;11:1181–1189.
54. Duim B, Bowler LD, Eijk PP, et al. Molecular variation in the major outer membrane protein P5 gene of nonencapsulated *Haemophilus influenzae* during chronic infections. Infect Immun. 1997;65:1351–1356.
55. Glode MP, Daum RA, Goldman DA, et al. *Haemophilus influenzae* type b meningitis: A contagious disease of children. BMJ. 1980;280:899–901.
56. Ward JI, Fraser DW, Baraff LI, et al. *Haemophilus influenzae* meningitis: A national study of secondary spread in household contacts. N Engl J Med. 1979;301:122.
57. Taylor HG, Mills EL, Ciampi A, et al. The sequelae of *Haemophilus influenzae* meningitis in schoolage children. N Engl J Med. 1990;323:1657–1663.
58. Berenberg W, Kevy S. Acute epiglottitis in childhood: A serious emergency readily recognized at the bedside. N Engl J Med. 1958;258:870–874.
59. Ginsburg CM, Howard JB, Nelson JD. Report of 65 cases of *Haemophilus influenzae* pneumonia. Pediatrics. 1979;64:283–286.
60. Marshall R, Teele DW, Klein JO. Unsuspected bacteremia due to *Haemophilus influenzae:* Outcome in children not initially admitted to hospital. J Pediatr. 1979;95:690–695.
61. Borenstein DG, Simon GL. *Haemophilus influenzae* septic arthritis in adults. A report of four cases and a review of the literature. Medicine. 1986;65:191–201.
62. Klein JO. Otitis media. Clin Infect Dis 1994;19:823–833.
63. Block SL. Causative pathogens, antibiotic resistance and therapeutic considerations in acute otitis media. Pediatr Infect Dis J. 1997;16:449–456.
64. Ruuskanen O, Heikkinen T. Otitis media: Etiology and diagnosis. Pediatr Infect Dis J. 1994;13:S23–S26.
65. Murphy TF, Sethi S. Bacterial infection in chronic obstructive pulmonary disease. Am Rev Respir Dis. 1992;146:1067–1083.
66. Bartlett JG, Breiman RF, Mandell LA, File Jr TM. Community-acquired pneuomonia in adults: Guidelines for management. Clin Infect Dis. 1998;26:811–838.
67. Steinhart R, Reingold AL, Taylor F, et al. Invasive *Haemophilus influenzae* infections in men with HIV infection. JAMA. 1992;268:3350–3352.
68. Schlamm HT, Yancovitz SR. *Haemophilus influenzae* pneumonia in young adults with AIDS, ARC, or risk of AIDS. Am J Med. 1989;86:11–14.
69. Polsky B, Gold JWM, Whimbey E, et al. Bacterial pneumonia in patients with acquired immunodeficiency syndrome. Ann Intern Med. 1986;104:38–41.
70. Munson RS Jr, Kabeer MH, Lenoir AA, Granoff DM. Epidemiology and prospects for prevention of disease due to *Haemophilus influenzae* in developing countries. Rev Infect Dis. 1989;11:S588–S597.
71. Lehman D. Epidemiology of acute respiratory tract infections, especially those due to *Haemophilus influenzae*, in Papua New Guinean children. J Infect Dis. 1992;165:S20–S25.
72. Sung RYT, Cheng AFB, Chan RCK, et al. Epidemiology and etiology of pneumonia in children in Hong Kong. Clin Infect Dis. 1993;17:894–896.
73. Weinberg GA, Ghafoor A, Ishaq Z, et al. Clonal analysis of *Hemophilus influenzae* isolated from children from Pakistan with lower respiratory tract infections. J Infect Dis. 1989;160:634–643.
74. Wall RA, Corrah PT, Mabey DCW, Greenwood BM. The etiology of lobar pneumonia in The Gambia. Bull WHO 1986;64:553–558.
75. Klein JO. Role of nontypeable *Haemophilus influenzae* in pediatric respiratory tract infections. Pediatr Infect Dis J. 1997;16:S5–S8.
76. Pentilla M, Savolainen S, Kuikaanniemi H, et al. Bacterial findings in acute maxillary sinusitis—European study. Acta Otolaryngol (Stockh). 1997;s29:165–168.
77. Campognone P, Singer DB. Neonatal sepsis due to nontypable *Haemophilus influenzae*. Am J Dis Child. 1986;140:117–121.
78. Friesen CA, Cho CT. Characteristic features of neonatal sepsis due to *Haemophilus influenzae*. Rev Infect Dis. 1986;8:777–780.
79. Murphy TF, Apicella MA. Nontypable *Haemophilus influenzae*: A review of clinical aspects, surface antigens, and the human response to infection. Rev Infect Dis. 1987;9:1–15.
80. Quentin R, Musser JM, Mellouet M, et al. Typing of urogenital, maternal and neonatal isolates of *Haemophilus influenzae* and *Haemophilus parainfluenzae* in correlation with clinical source of sialation and evidence for a genital specificity of *H. influenzae* biotype IV. J Clin Microbiol. 1998;27:2286–2294.
81. Wallace RJ Jr, Baker CJ, Quinones FJ, et al. Nontypable *Haemophilus influenzae* (biotype 4) as a neonatal, maternal and genital pathogen. Rev Infect Dis. 1983;5:123–135.
82. Webster PB, Maher CF, Farrell DJ. Neonatal infection due to *Haemophilus influenzae* biotype IV. Aust N Z J Med. 1995;35:102–103.
83. Rosenau A, Sizaret PY, Musser JM, et al. Adherence to human cells of a cryptic *Haemophilus* genospecies responsible for genital and neonatal infections. Infect Immun. 1993;61:4112–4118.
84. Murphy TF, Kirkham C, Sikkema DJ. Neonatal, urogenital isolates of biotype 4 nontypeable *Haemophilus influenzae* express a variant P6 outer membrane protein molecule. Infect Immun. 1992;60:2016–2022.
85. Quentin R, Goudeau A, Wallace RJ Jr., et al. Urogenital, maternal and neonatal isolates of *Haemophilus influenzae*: Identification of unusually virulent serologically nontypeable clone families and evidence for a new *Haemophilus* species. J Gen Microbiol. 1990;136:1203–1209.
86. Kragsbjerg P, Nilsson K, Persson L, et al. Deep obstetrical and gynecological infections caused by nontypeable *Haemophilus influenzae*. Scand J Infect Dis. 1993;25:341–346.
87. Wallace RJ, Baker CJ, Quinones FJ, et al. Nontypeable *Haemophilus influenzae* (biotype 4) as a neonatal, maternal and genital pathogen. Rev Infect Dis. 1983;5:123–136.
88. Farley MM, Stephens DS, Brachman PS Jr, et al. Invasive *Haemophilus influenzae* disease in adults. Ann Intern Med. 1992;116:806–812.
89. Najm WI, Cesario TC, Spurgeon L. Bacteremia due to *Haemophilus* infections: A retrospective study with emphasis on the elderly. Clin Infect Dis. 1995;21:213–216.
90. Kostman JR, Sherry BL, Flingner CL, et al. Invasive *Haemophilus influenzae* infections in older children and adults in Seattle. Clin Infect Dis. 1993;17:389–396.
91. McGregor AR, Bell JM, Abdool IM, Collignon PJ. Invasive *Haemophilus influenzae* infection in the Australian Capital Territory region. Med J Aust. 1992;156:569–572.
92. Van Alphen L, Spanjaard L, Dankert J. Non-typable *Haemophilus influenzae* invasive disease. Lancet. 1993;341:1536.
93. Deulogeau F, Nava JM, Bella F, et al. Prospective epidemiological study of invasive *Haemophilus influenzae* disease in adults. Eur J Clin Microbiol Infect Dis. 1994;13:633–638.
94. Verbon A, Husni RN, Gordon SM, et al. Pott's puffy tumor due to *Haemophilus influenzae*: Case report and review. Clin Infect Dis. 1996;23:1305–1307.
95. Falla TJ, Dobson SRM, Crook DWM, et al. Population based study of nontypable *Haemophilus influenzae* invasive disease in children and neonates. Lancet. 1993;341:851–854.
96. Nizet V, Colina KF, Almquist JR, et al. A virulent nonencapsulated *Haemophilus influenzae*. J Infect Dis. 1996;173:180–186.
97. Borenstein DG, Simon GL. *Hemophilus influenzae* septic arthritis in adults. Medicine. 1986;65:191–201.
98. Ward JL, Siber GR, Scheifele DW, et al. Rapid diagnosis of *Haemophilus influenzae* type b infection by latex particle agglutination and counterimmunoelectrophoresis. J Pediatr. 1978;93:37–42.
99. Klein JO, Feigin RD, McCracken GH. Report of the Task Force on Diagnosis and Management of Meningitis. Pediatrics. 1986;78:501–505.
100. Committee on Infectious Diseases. Treatment of bacterial meningitis. Pediatrics. 1988;81:904–907.
101. McCracken GH Jr, Lebal M. Dexamethasone therapy for bacterial meningitis in infants and children. Am J Dis Child. 1989;143:287–289.
102. Leebel MH, Hoyt MJ, Waagner DC, et al. Magnetic resonance imaging and dexamethasone therapy for bacterial meningitis. Am J Dis Child. 1989;143:301–306.
103. Tuomanen E. Partner drugs: A new outlook for bacterial meningitis. Ann Intern Med. 1988;109:690–692.
104. Lebel MH, Freij BJ, Syrogiannopoulos GA, et al. Dexamethasone therapy for bacterial meningitis. Results of two double-blind, placebo-controlled trials. N Engl J Med. 1988;319:964–971.
105. Doern GV, Brueggemann AB, Pierce G, et al. Antibiotic resistance among clinical isolates of *Haemophilus influenzae* in the United States in 1994 and 1995 and detection of β-lactamase–positive strains resistant to amoxicillin-clavulanate: Results of a national multicenter surveillance study. Antimicrob Agents Chemother. 1997;41:292–297.
106. Doern GV. Trends in antimicrobial susceptibility of bacterial pathogens of the respiratory tract. Am J Med. 1995;99:6B-3S–6B-7S.
107. Faden H, Doern G, Wolf J, Blocker M. Antimicrobial susceptibility of nasopharyngeal isolates of potential pathogens recovered from infants before antibiotic therapy: Implications for the management of otitis media. Pediatr Infect Dis J. 1994;13:609–612.
108. Anonymous: Current trends. Prevention of secondary cases of *Haemophilus influenzae* type B disease. MMWR Morb Mortal Wkly Rep. 1982;31:672–674.
109. Peter G, Hall CB, Halsey NA, et al. *Haemophilus influenzae* infections. In: 1997 Red Book: Report of the Committee on Infectious Diseases. 24th ed. Elk Grove Village, Ill: American Academy of Pediatrics; 1997:222, 231.
110. Ward J, Cochi S. *Haemophilus influenzae* vaccines. In: Plotkin SA, Mortimer EA, eds. Vaccines. Philadelphia: WB Saunders; 1988:300–308.
111. Feigin RD, Stechenberg BW, Chang MJ. Prospective evaluation of treatment of *Haemophilus influenzae* meningitis. J Pediatr. 1976;88:542–548.
112. Doern GV, Jergensen JH, Thornsberry C, et al. National collaborative study of the prevalence of antimicrobial resistance among clinical isolates of *Haemophilus influenzae*. Antimicrob Agents Chemother. 1988;32:180–185.
113. Peltola H, Kayhty H, Virtanen M, et al. Prevention of *Haemophilus influenzae* type b bacteremic infections with the capsular polysaccharide vaccine. N Engl J Med. 1984;310:1561–1566.
114. Moxon ER, Rappuoli R. Modern vaccines: *Haemophilus influenzae* infections and whooping cough. Lancet. 1990;335:1324–1329.
115. Ward JI, Margolis H, Lum M, et al. Prevention of *Haemophilus influenzae* in Alaskan Eskimos: Characteristics of a population with an unusual incidence of invasive disease. Lancet. 1981;1:1281–1285.
116. Decker MD, Edwards KM. *Haemophilus influenzae* type b vaccines: History, choice and comparisons. Pediatr Infect Dis J. 1998;17:S113–S116.
117. Booy R, Heath PT, Slack MPE, et al. Vaccine failures after primary immunisation with *Haemophilus influenzae* type-B conjugate vaccine without booster. Lancet. 1997;349:1197–1202.
118. Adams G, Deaver KA, Cochi SL, et al. Decline of childhood *Haemophilus influenzae* type b (Hib) disease in the Hib vaccine era. JAMA. 1993;269:221–226.
119. Anonymous: *Haemophilus influenzae* invasive disease among children aged <5 years—California, 1990–1996. MMWR Morb Mortal Wkly Rep. 1998;47:737–740.
120. Murphy TV, Pastor P, Medley F, et al. Decreased *Haemophilus* colonization in children vaccinated with *Haemophilus influenzae* type b conjugate vaccine. J Pediatr. 1993;122:517–523.

121. Mulholland K, Hilton S, Adegbola R, et al. Randomised trial of *Haemophilus influenzae* type b tetanus protein conjugate vaccine for prevention of pneumonia and meningitis in Gambian infants. Lancet. 1997;349:1191–1197.
122. Brazilian Purpuric Fever Study Group. Brazilian purpuric fever: Epidemic purpura fulminans associated with antecedent purulent conjunctivitis. Lancet. 1987;2:757–761.
123. Brazilian Purpuric Fever Study Group. *Haemophilus aegyptius* bacteremia in Brazilian purpuric fever. Lancet. 1987;2:761–763.
124. Mcintyre P, Wheaton G, Erlich J, Hansman D. Brazilian purpuric fever in central Australia. Lancet. 1987;2:112.
125. Wild BE, Pearman JW, Cambell PB, et al. Brazilian purpuric fever in Western Australia (Letter). Med J Aust. 1989;150:344, 346.
126. Brenner DJ, Mayer LW, Carlone GM, et al. Biochemical, genetic and epidemiologic characterization of *Haemophilus influenzae* biogroup aegyptius (*Haemophilus aegyptius*) strains associated with Brazilian purpuric fever. J Clin Microbiol. 1988;26:1524–1534.
127. Lesse AJ, Gheesling LL, Bittner WE, et al. Stable, conserved outer membrane epitope of strains of *Haemophilus influenzae* biogroup aegyptius associated with Brazilian purpuric fever. Infect Immun. 1992;60:1351–1357.
128. Carlone GM, Gorelkin L, Gheesling LL, et al. Potential virulence factors of *Haemophilus influenzae* biogroup aegyptius in Brazilian purpuric fever. Pediatr Infect Dis J. 1989;8:245–247.
129. Mayer LW, Bibb WF, Birkness KA, et al. Distinguishing clonal characteristics of the Brazilian purpuric fever-producing strain. Pediatr Infect Dis J. 1989;8:241–243.
130. Turk DC. Clinical importance of *Haemophilus influenzae*—1981. In: Sell SH, Wright PF, eds. *Haemophilus Influenzae,* Epidemiology, Immunology and Prevention of Disease. New York: Elsevier; 1982:3–9.
131. van Ham SM, van Alphen L, Mooi FR, van Putten JPM. The fimbrial gene cluster of *Haemophilus influenzae* type b. Mol Microbiol. 1994;13:673–684.
132. Gilsdorf JR, Marrs CF, McCrea KW, Forney LJ. Cloning, expression and sequence analysis of *Haemophilus influenzae* type b strain M43p+ pilin gene. Infect Immun. 1990;58:1065–1072.
133. van Ham SM, van Alphen L, Mooi FR, van Putten JPM. Phase variation of *H. influenzae* fimbriae: Transcriptional control of two divergent genes through a variable combined promoter region. Cell. 1993;73:1187–1196.
134. van Ham SM, van Alphen L, Mooi FR, van Putten JPM. Contribution of the major and minor subunits to fimbriae-mediated adherence of *Haemophilus influenzae* to human epithelial cells and erythrocytes. Infect Immun. 1995;63:4883–4889.
135. Gilsdorf JR, Tucci M, Marrs CF. Role of pili in *Haemophilus influenzae* adherence to, and internalization by, respiratory cells. Pediatr Res. 1996;39:343–348.
136. Barenkamp SJ, Leininger E. Cloning, expression and DNA sequence analysis of the genes encoding nontypeable *Haemophilus influenzae* high-molecular-weight surface-exposed proteins related to filamentous hemagglutinin of *Bordetella pertussis*. Infect Immun. 1992;60:1302–1313.
137. Bakaletz LO, Barenkamp SJ. Localization of high-molecular-weight adhesion proteins of nontypeable *Haemophilus influenzae* by immunoelectron microscopy. Infect Immun. 1993;62:4460–4468.
138. Noel GJ, Barenkamp SJ, St Geme JW III, et al. High-molecular-weight surface-exposed proteins of *Haemophilus influenzae* mediate binding to macrophages. J Infect Dis. 1994;169:425–429.
139. Barenkamp SJ, St Geme JW III. Genes encoding high-molecular-weight adhesion proteins of nontypeable *Haemophilus influenzae* are part of gene clusters. Infect Immun. 1994;62:3320–3328.
140. St Geme JW III, Grass S. Secretion of the *Haemophilus influenzae* HMW1 and HMW2 adhesins involves a periplasmic intermediate and requires the HMWB and HMWC proteins. Mol Microbiol. 1998;27:617–630.
141. Barenkamp SJ. Immunization with high-molecular-weight adhesion proteins of nontypeable *Haemophilus influenzae* modifies experimental otitis media in chinchillas. Infect Immun. 1996;64:1246–1251.
142. Barenkamp SJ, St Geme JW III. Identification of surface-exposed B-cell epitopes on high-molecular-weight adhesion proteins of nontypeable *Haemophilus influenzae*. Infect Immun. 1996;64:3032–3037.
143. St Geme JW III, de la Morena ML, Falkow S. A *Haemophilus influenzae* IgA protease-like protein promotes intimate interaction with human epithelial cells. Mol Microbiol. 1994;14:217–233.
144. Hendrixson DR, de la Morena ML, Stathopoulos C, St Geme JW III. Structural determinants of processing and secretion of the *Haemophilus influenzae* Hap protein. Mol Microbiol. 1997;26:505–518.
145. St Geme JW III. Insights into the mechanism of respiratory tract colonization by nontypeable *Haemophilus influenzae*. Pediatr Infect Dis J. 1997;16:931–935.
146. St Geme JW III, Cutter D. Evidence that surface fibrils expressed by *Haemophilus influenzae* type b promote attachment to human epithelial cells. Mol Microbiol. 1995;15:77–85.
147. St Geme JW III, Cutter D. Influence of pili, fibrils and capsule on in vitro adherence by *Haemophilus influenzae* type b. Mol Microbiol. 1996;21:21–31.
148. Barenkamp SJ, St Geme JW III. Identification of a second family of high-molecular-weight adhesion proteins expressed by nontypeable *Haemophilus influenzae*. Mol Microbiol. 1996;19:1215–1223.
149. St Geme JW III, Kumar VV, Cutter D, Barenkamp SJ. Prevalence and distribution of the *hmw* and *hia* genes and the HMW and Hia adhesins among genetically diverse strains of nontypeable *Haemophilus influenzae*. Infect Immun. 1998;66:364–368.
150. Bakaletz LO, Leake ER, Billy JM, Kaumaya PTP. Relative immunogenicity and efficacy of two synthetic chimeric peptides of fimbrin as vaccinogens against nasopharyngeal colonization by nontypeable *Haemophilus influenzae* in the chinchilla. Vaccine. 1997;15:955–961.
151. Sirakova T, Kolattukudy PE, Murwin D, et al. Role of fimbriae expressed by nontypeable *Haemophilus influenzae* in pathogenesis of and protection against otitis media and relatedness of the fimbrin subunit to outer membrane protein A. Infect Immun. 1994;62:2002–2020.
152. Reddy MS, Murphy TF, Faden HS, Bernstein JM. Middle ear mucin glycoprotein: Purification and interaction with nontypeable *Haemophilus influenzae* and *Moraxella catarrhalis*. Otolaryngol Head Neck Surg. 1997;116:175–189.
153. Busse J, Hartmann E, Lingwood CA. Receptor affinity purification of a lipid-binding adhesin from *Haemophilus influenzae*. J Infect Dis. 1997;175:77–83.
154. Weiser JN. The oligosaccharide of *Haemophilus influenzae*. Microb Pathog. 1992; 13:335–342.
155. Jacquex M. Role of lipo-oligosaccharides and lipopolysaccharides in bacterial adherence. Trends Microbiol. 1996;4:408–410.

Chapter 213

Haemophilus Species (Including Chancroid)

W. LEE HAND

Haemophilus spp. other than *Haemophilus influenzae* have been considered rare causes of human disease. Because of recent interest in these organisms and refinements in their isolation and identification, it is now apparent that they cause infection more commonly than was previously believed. *Haemophilus* spp. that have been well documented to produce human illness include *Haemophilus parainfluenzae*, *Haemophilus aphrophilus*, *Haemophilus paraphrophilus*, *Haemophilus aegyptius* (not clearly differentiated from *H. influenzae*), and *Haemophilus ducreyi*. *Haemophilus haemolyticus* rarely, if ever, causes clinical disease. *Haemophilus segnis* and *Haemophilus parahaemolyticus* are uncommon pathogens.

Most *Haemophilus* species appear to be normal flora of the mouth and upper respiratory tract. Infections caused by these organisms include respiratory tract infection, endocarditis, septicemia, meningitis, brain abscess, and soft tissue infections. *H. ducreyi* is the etiologic agent of chancroid. *H. aegyptius* (the Koch-Weeks bacillus) has long been identified as a cause of acute, contagious conjunctivitis. Bacteremic infection with *H. influenzae* biogroup aegyptius, a unique organism, is the cause of Brazilian purpuric fever.[1, 2] This illness, first recognized in São Paulo state, Brazil, in 1984, is a serious systemic illness of children. The disease is preceded by purulent conjunctivitis, which is followed by fever, development of petechial and then purpuric skin lesions, and shock. Because *H. aegyptius* probably should be classified with *H. influenzae*,[3, 4] this organism (including *H. influenzae* biogroup aegyptius and its infections will not be further considered in this chapter; see Chapter 212).

DESCRIPTION, ISOLATION, AND IDENTIFICATION

Members of the genus *Haemophilus* are small, pleomorphic, gram-negative coccobacilli with fastidious growth requirements.[3] They tend to be slow growing and are strict parasites, needing accessory factors for in vitro growth. Absolute or relative dependence on incubation in carbon dioxide for growth is a characteristic of some species. By definition, these organisms require the presence of X factor (hemin), V factor (nicotinamide adenine dinucleotide), or both for growth in culture. Both of these factors are found in erythrocytes, but lysis of the erythrocytes is required for release of V factor. This is accomplished by heating the cells in the production of chocolate agar. Requirements for X and V factors and the production of hemolysis on various blood sugars are major determinants of separation. Organisms with the "para-" designation require V factor only for growth. The others require X factor or both X and V factors.

There is considerable uncertainty as to the validity of certain *Haemophilus* species designations. Taxonomic studies suggest that *H. ducreyi* is not a member of the genus *Haemophilus*.[3, 5] An extensive study of *Haemophilus* strains by Kilian led him to conclude that *H. parahaemolyticus* and *H. paraprohaemolyticus* do not deserve species status.[4] *H. parahaemolyticus* and *H. paraprohaemolyticus* were assigned to the *H. parainfluenzae* species.

H. aphrophilus was originally described as requiring X factor (hemin) for growth, but there has been controversy as to the growth requirements for this bacterium.[3, 4, 6, 7] *Actinobacillus actinomycetemcomitans*, although classified in another genus, is similar in biochemical tests to *H. aphrophilus* and *H. paraphrophilus*.[3, 8] Growth requirements and some differential characteristics of *Haemophilus* spp. (excluding *H. influenzae*) are listed in Table 213–1.

Initial isolation of *Haemophilus* organisms from specimens other than blood should be on chocolate agar incubated in carbon dioxide. In blood culture, the organisms tend to grow as small colonies along the side walls of the bottle or in the red blood cell mass, leaving the broth clear. One report indicated that an aerobic biphasic blood culture method isolated more of these organisms than did lysis-centrifugation or anaerobic systems.[9] Routine subculture of blood cultures to chocolate agar with subsequent incubation in carbon dioxide is the most reliable means of isolating the organisms under discussion.[10, 11] Because these organisms are difficult to detect and identify, a potential role for molecular techniques (such as identification by 16S ribosomal RNA sequencing) has been suggested.[12]

In the past, recovery of *H. ducreyi* presented special problems. However, enriched chocolate agar containing Isovitalex and vancomycin (3 μg/ml), supplemented GC agar with vancomycin, and supplemented Mueller-Hinton agar with vancomycin are effective for primary isolation of *H. ducreyi* from chancroidal lesions.[3, 13, 14] Culture plates should be incubated in a water-saturated atmosphere with 5% carbon dioxide at a temperature of 33°C.

Haemophilus spp. are members of the normal flora in the upper respiratory tract (oral cavity and pharynx) and perhaps in the genital area.[3, 15, 16] *H. parainfluenzae*, *H. parahaemolyticus*, *H. aphrophilus*, and *H. segnis* are all members of the normal oral and pharyngeal flora in healthy people. *H. aphrophilus* and *H. segnis* are often found in dental plaque or gingival scrapings. *H. ducreyi* is a pathogen in the genital area, but *H. parainfluenzae* has also been isolated from the urethra and vagina.

Clinical infection by *Haemophilus* spp. is the result of local or blood-stream invasion from sites of colonization. However, the pathogenicity of these species (*H. parainfluenzae*, *H. aphrophilus*, and *H. paraphrophilus*) is low compared with that of *H. influenzae*. The pathogenesis of *H. ducreyi* infection is still poorly defined but is receiving considerable attention. Most wild-type organisms express pili.[17, 18] The roles of *H. ducreyi* surface lipooligosaccharide and cytotoxin in producing chancroid lesions are under investigation.[19–24]

TABLE 213–1 Differential Characteristics of *Haemophilus* Species

Organism	Growth Factor Requirement X	Growth Factor Requirement V	CO_2 Dependence	Hemolysis	Catalase
H. aphrophilus	+	−	+	−	−
H. paraphrophilus	−	+	+	−	±
H. parainfluenzae	−	+	−	−	+
H. haemolyticus	+	+	−	+	+
H. parahaemolyticus	−	+	−	+	+
H. ducreyi	+	−	±	±	−

+, present; −, absent.

A soluble cytoxin, produced by most *H. ducreyi* strains, has been characterized and may play a role in production of the ulcerative lesions of chancroid.[22, 23]

CLINICAL SYNDROMES AND MANIFESTATIONS

Haemophilus spp. colonizing the mouth and pharynx may cause local (head or respiratory tract) infection or systemic disease. Present knowledge indicates that *H. parainfluenzae* is the most common pathogen among the *Haemophilus* species. In general, *H. parainfluenzae* infections are clinically similar to those caused by *H. influenzae*. Reported infections caused by this organism include pharyngitis, epiglottitis, otitis media, conjunctivitis, dental abscess, pneumonia, empyema, septicemia, endocarditis, septic arthritis, osteomyelitis, paraspinal abscess, peritonitis, hepatobiliary infection, meningitis, brain abscess, epidural abscess, and urinary tract and genital (prostatic, urethral) infection.[4, 10, 11, 25–41] *H. aphrophilus* has been noted to be a cause of sinusitis, otitis media, pneumonia, empyema, bacteremia, endocarditis, septic arthritis, osteomyelitis, soft tissue abscesses, wound infections, necrotizing fasciitis, meningitis, and brain abscess.[4, 6, 7, 15, 25, 42–45] Cases of laryngitis, epiglottitis, endocarditis, brain abscess, hepatobiliary infection, osteomyelitis, and paronychia due to *H. paraphrophilus*, only recently separated from *H. parainfluenzae* as a distinct species, have been documented.[4, 25, 46–48] Acute appendicitis due to *H. segnis* infection has been reported.[49]

Species of *Haemophilus* (*H. parainfluenzae*, *H. aphrophilus*, and *H. paraphrophilus*) can no longer be considered rare causes of endocarditis.[10, 11, 25, 26, 50–57] *Haemophilus* strains may be the etiologic agents in 5% of cases of infective endocarditis.[25] The reasons for this apparent increase in the frequency of *Haemophilus* endocarditis are uncertain. However, improved ability of clinical microbiology laboratories to isolate and identify these fastidious organisms is probably responsible. It is likely that many of these infections were classified as "culture-negative" endocarditis in the past. *A. actinomycetemcomitans*, which is similar to *H. aphrophilus*, and other small gram-negative rods (*Cardiobacterium hominis, Eikenella corrodens, Kingella kingii*) with fastidious growth requirements may also cause endocarditis.[58–62] These organisms (*Haemophilus* spp. and the other fastidious gram-negative rods) are referred to as the HACEK group.[50] These HACEK organisms probably account for 5 to 10% of native valve endocarditis in patients who are not intravenous drug users.[50, 63]

The clinical setting of *Haemophilus* endocarditis is not distinctive. As might be expected from the knowledge that *Haemophilus* colonizes the oral cavity and pharynx, endocarditis may occur after dental disease, dental procedures, or other oral trauma. In one study, 62% of endocarditis cases caused by HACEK organisms were associated with poor dentition or recent dental work.[64] Several cases of polymicrobial endocarditis due to *H. parainfluenzae* plus viridans streptococci have been reported.[26] Other predisposing factors include respiratory tract infection (sinusitis, pneumonia, and possibly otitis media) and intravenous drug abuse. Occult polymicrobial endocarditis with *H. parainfluenzae* and gram-positive cocci (*Staphylococcus aureus*, streptococci) has been observed in intravenous drug abusers.[56]

The onset of *Haemophilus* endocarditis may be relatively abrupt or indolent.[10, 11, 25, 26, 50–57] A subacute onset, similar to that produced by viridans streptococcal infection, is most common. In a review of 42 cases of *Haemophilus* endocarditis in France, the mean duration of symptoms before diagnosis was 34 days.[57] Underlying valvular heart disease (including mitral valve prolapse), the presence of a prosthetic cardiac valve, and intravenous drug abuse are the usual predisposing factors. Most patients are young to middle-aged adults. Clinically significant arterial embolization (secondary to large valvular vegetations) is common in *Haemophilus* endocarditis, occurring in 50 to 60% of cases, compared with approximately 25% overall in subacute endocarditis. This distinguishing feature of *Haemophilus* endocarditis may result in part from delayed diagnosis caused by the difficulty in isolating and identifying these organisms from blood cultures (especially in earlier reports). The review of French cases reported arterial embolic events in 35.7% of patients.[57] Because *H. paraphrophilus* was rather recently recognized as a distinct species, relatively few cases of endocarditis caused by this organism have been reported.[25, 47, 50, 65] However, some previously reported cases of endocarditis due to *H. parainfluenzae* would now be considered *H. paraphrophilus* infections.

PREVENTION AND TREATMENT

Antibiotic sensitivity studies have often been unsatisfactory because of the difficulty in growing the organism.[66, 67] A new medium, *Haemophilus* test medium (HTM), has been developed for testing *Haemophilus* spp. HTM is available in both agar and broth forms for disk diffusion and broth microdilution susceptibility tests, respectively.[66, 67]

In the United States most tested *Haemophilus* strains have been sensitive to chloramphenicol, aminoglycosides, trimethoprim-sulfamethoxazole, fluoroquinolones, and aztreonam.[10, 11, 26, 42, 63, 68] Previously, all *Haemophilus* spp. and other HACEK organisms were susceptible to ampicillin, but ampicillin resistance, usually associated with β-lactamase production, is being recognized with increasing frequency.[3, 31, 57, 63, 65, 69–71] *Haemophilus* spp. and other HACEK organisms are sensitive to cephalosporins of the third-generation group (e.g., cefotaxime, ceftriaxone, cefoperazone).[63, 66, 68, 69, 72, 73] Ciprofloxacin and other new fluoroquinolone antibiotics have potent activity against *H. influenzae* and other *Haemophilus* spp.[63, 74] In contrast, these bacteria are resistant to clindamycin, vancomycin, and usually methicillin.[7, 10, 26, 30]

The previous therapy for *Haemophilus* endocarditis has been large doses of intravenous ampicillin, often with the addition of an aminoglycoside antibiotic. Ampicillin alone may be adequate if the organism is quite sensitive to the antibiotic.[25, 50] Obviously, therapy should be based on antibiotic sensitivity studies (and assays of β-lactamase production). At the present time, third-generation cephalosporins (ceftriaxone, cefotaxime) are considered the drugs of choice for treatment of endocarditis caused by *Haemophilus* spp. (and other HACEK organisms). Native valve endocarditis should be treated for 4 weeks, and therapy for prosthetic valve infection should be for 6 weeks. The combination of ampicillin plus gentamicin can be considered a therapeutic alternative if the organism is clearly sensitive to ampicillin.[63] Once-daily dosing with ceftriaxone (2 g/day) permits the consideration of outpatient therapy in selected cases.

In the past, a high mortality rate (25 to 50%) was reported for *Haemophilus* endocarditis.[7, 42] However, more recent reports indicate that with appropriate treatment the mortality rate is probably 10 to 15%. In one study, 97% (32) of 33 patients with endocarditis caused by fastidious gram-negative rods of the HACEK group (*Haemophilus* spp., 18 patients; *A. actinomycetemcomitans*, 4; *C. hominis*, 6; *E. corrodens*, 2; *K. kingii*, 2) were successfully treated.[50] The mortality rate related to endocarditis was 4.8% in one review and 4% in another.[57, 64]

Meningitis or other serious infections caused by ampicillin-resistant *Haemophilus* strains should be treated with a third-generation cephalosporin. Less serious infections caused by organisms resistant to penicillin G, ampicillin, and first-generation cephalosporins can be treated with trimethoprim-sulfamethoxazole, a second- or third-generation cephalosporin, or a fluoroquinolone.

CHANCROID

Chancroid (soft chancre) is a sexually transmitted disease caused by *H. ducreyi*.[75, 76] Advances in cultural isolation of the organism and other diagnostic tests have led to improved recognition of chancroid,[13, 14, 77–79] which is a more common cause of ulcerative genital disease than was previously recognized. Evidence linking genital ulcer disease (especially chancroid) to an increase in heterosexual transmission of human immunodeficiency virus (HIV) infection greatly increases the known impact of chancroid.[25, 80, 81] This infection is worldwide in distribution and is typically associated with low socioeconomic status and poor hygienic conditions. Major outbreaks of infection have been reported in Canada and the United States.[82–86] Chancroid is seen most often in nonwhite, uncircumcised men. Only 10% of the reported cases are in women, an observation that might be related to a clinically inapparent carrier state, asymptomatic and overlooked lesions, and/or infected prostitutes with large numbers of contacts.[82–86] The latter situation has been especially important in certain outbreaks, among both military and civilian populations.[76, 82–86]

The incubation period for chancroid (from exposure to clinical disease) varies from 1 day to several weeks, with a median of 5 to 7 days. Lesions are generally confined to the genitalia and perianal areas. Extragenital chancroid (mouth, fingers, or breasts) is rare. Usually the chancroidal lesion begins as a tender papule with surrounding erythema, which soon becomes pustular and then erodes to form an ulcer. These ulcers are typically painful, nonindurated, ragged, undermined, and surrounded with an erythematous halo. The base of the ulcer is composed of granulation tissue, which bleeds easily on manipulation and may be covered with necrotic exudate. Ulcers may be single or multiple, and up to 10 or more separate ulcerations have been reported.[75, 76, 82, 84, 86] Men frequently have single ulcers, whereas women typically have multiple lesions. Individual ulcers vary from 1 to 20 mm in diameter. Adjacent lesions may merge and form confluent giant or serpiginous ulcerations. Superinfection (especially fusospirochetal) of ulcers may occur and may lead to rapid extensive destruction of the external genitalia (phagedenic chancroid). Lesions are most often located on the preputial orifice, internal surface of the prepuce, and frenulum in men and on the fourchette, labia, vestibule, clitoris, cervix, and anus in women.[75, 76, 82, 84] Small abrasions appear to facilitate infection.

Tender regional (inguinal) lymphadenopathy is characteristic of chancroid and occurs in approximately half of the patients. This adenopathy is usually unilateral and painful. If untreated, the process progresses to suppuration with periadenitis (bubo formation) involving the overlying skin. Spontaneous rupture of the abscess and formation of chronic draining sinuses may follow.

The diagnosis of chancroid on clinical grounds, although commonly attempted, is difficult and inaccurate, because genital ulcerative disease caused by syphilis, herpes simplex virus, or even lymphogranuloma venereum may be similar. In addition, these infections may be seen in association with chancroid. Culture of material obtained by swab from the purulent ulcer base or especially by aspiration of a bubo should be performed. As noted previously, isolation of *H. ducreyi* is somewhat complicated but is definitive.[3, 13, 14, 77, 82, 84] Gram stain preparations of exudate material may reveal large numbers of gram-negative coccobacilli, sometimes in "school-of-fish" patterns, but interpretation of these smears is difficult. A positive smear of pus aspirated from a bubo is more reliable for diagnostic purposes. Serologic assays for antibodies against *H. ducreyi* and an immunofluorescence technique to detect organisms in ulcer material have been described.[25, 87, 88] The usefulness of these tests in the diagnosis of chancroid remains to be determined. DNA probes for detection of *H. ducreyi* appear to lack the sensitivity necessary for clinical use. Polymerase chain reaction (PCR) assays for detection of *H. ducreyi* have been evaluated in clinical studies. These assays appear to be sensitive and specific. Multiplex-PCR assays for *H. ducreyi*, *Treponema pallidum*, and herpes simplex virus appear to be more sensitive than standard diagnostic tests for detection of these organisms in genital ulcers.[78, 79] Biopsy of suspected chancroid ulcers is rarely performed except to exclude malignancy, but typical histologic findings have been reported by certain investigators.[76, 89, 90] The cutaneous infiltration of macrophages and $CD4^+$ lymphocytes, consistent with a cell-mediated immune response, could facilitate the transmission of HIV in patients with chancroid.[90, 91]

It is essential to exclude syphilis in every case of suspected chancroid, because the two diseases may be confused and some chancroid patients may have simultaneous primary syphilis.[75, 76] Dark-field examinations of exudate material for *T. pallidum* and serologic tests for syphilis should be performed. If these studies are negative, some recommend three consecutive monthly serologic tests for syphilis. As noted previously, PCR may prove useful in the detection of *T. pallidum* from clinical ulcers.[78, 79]

TREATMENT AND PREVENTION

Oral erythromycin (500 mg four times a day) for at least 7 days is well established as an effective therapy for chancroid in many areas of the world.[92, 93] Azithromycin is even more active than erythromycin against *H. ducreyi* in vitro, and clinical data support its efficacy.[94–97] A single intramuscular dose of ceftriaxone (250 mg) is effective in the treatment of chancroid, but the failure rate is high in men with concurrent HIV infection.[92, 96–98] Some (but not all) studies have shown that patients with both of these infections may respond suboptimally to any antibiotic therapy for chancroid.[81, 92, 99] The trimethoprim-sulfamethoxazole combination was previously useful in the treatment of chancroid. However, resistance of *H. ducreyi* to sulfonamides has been reported worldwide, and many strains are now resistant to trimethoprim.[92, 94, 96, 100] A number of clinical failures with the drug combination have occurred. Single-dose trimethoprim-sulfamethoxazole (640/3200 mg) therapy does not provide satisfactory cure rates.[92, 96, 99]

Many strains of *H. ducreyi* (99% in Thailand) are resistant to tetracycline, which should no longer be used for treatment of chancroid.[100–102] Most *H. ducreyi* strains are resistant to ampicillin and amoxicillin, a resistance that is due to plasmid-mediated β-lactamase production.[92, 94, 102, 103]

Because of the expense and poor patient compliance associated with multiple-dose, multiple-day drug therapies, attempts to identify effective single-dose treatment regimens for chancroid continue. Ceftriaxone in a single dose (already described) is usually adequate therapy, but the drug must be administered intramuscularly, and failures have been reported in patients with HIV coinfection.[24, 92, 96–98] Ciprofloxacin in a single oral dose of 500 mg has had variable success in clinical trials.[24, 99] Failures were not caused by drug resistance. A 3-day regimen of ciprofloxacin (500 mg twice daily) has been more effective in treatment.[104, 105] Other fluoroquinolones require additional evaluation.[92, 94]

Based on current data, several regimens for the treatment of chancroid can be recommended.[106] A 7-day course of erythromycin is effective, but the disadvantages of multidose therapy are obvious. Single-dose ceftriaxone and single-dose azithromycin are recommended regimens. Azithromycin may have the additional advantage of prolonged protection against reinfection.[107] Multidose ciprofloxacin is considered an acceptable alternative regimen.

In addition to antibiotic therapy, needle aspiration of suppurated (fluctuant) nodes should be accomplished through adjacent uninvolved skin to prevent rupture, sinus formation, and scarring.

It is important to identify all sexual partners of infected persons, so that these contacts can be treated with an effective antibiotic regimen.[82–85, 92] Eradication of infection in persons, especially prostitutes, who are sources of multiple cases of infection may be effective in controlling outbreaks of chancroid.[82, 83, 85] Because asymptomatic carriage of *H. ducreyi* can occur, identification and treatment of sexual partners, symptomatic or not, is essential. Soap and water cleansing of the genitalia apparently has no prophylactic value after exposure to chancroid, but a properly used condom theoretically may be helpful. As noted, an additional impetus to the prevention of genital ulcers such as chancroid arises from the observation that these lesions increase the chance of acquiring HIV infection through heterosexual intercourse.[80, 81]

REFERENCES

1. Brazilian Purpuric Fever Study Group. Brazilian purpuric fever: Epidemic purpura fulminans associated with antecedent purulent conjunctivitis. Lancet. 1987;2:757–761.
2. Brazilian Purpuric Fever Study Group. *Haemophilus aegyptius* bacteremia in Brazilian purpuric fever. Lancet. 1987;2:761–763.
3. Kilian M. *Haemophilus*. In: Ballows A, Hausler WJ Jr, Herrmann KL, et al., eds. Manual of Clinical Microbiology. 5th ed. Washington, DC: American Society for Microbiology. 1991;463–470.
4. Kilian M. A taxonomic study of the genus *Haemophilus* with the proposal of a new species. J Gen Microbiol. 1976;93:9–62.
5. Rossau R, Duhamel M, Jannes G, et al. The development of specific rRNA-derived oligonucleotide probes for *Haemophilus ducreyi*, the causative agent of chancroid. J Gen Microbiol. 1991;137:277–285.
6. Page MI, King EO. Infection due to *Actinobacillus actinomycetemcomitans* and *Haemophilus aphrophilus*. N Engl J Med. 1966;275:181–188.
7. Sutter VL, Finegold SM. *Haemophilus aphrophilus* infections: Clinical and bacteriologic studies. Ann NY Acad Sci. 1970;174:468–487.
8. Caugant DA, Selander RK, Olsen I. Differentiation between *Actinobacillus (Haemophilus) actinomycetemcomitans*, *Haemophilus aphrophilus* and *Haemophilus paraphrophilus* by multilocus enzyme electrophoresis. J Gen Microbiol. 1990;136:2135–2141.
9. Cockerill FR III, Hughes JG, Vetter EA, et al. Analysis of 281,797 consecutive blood cultures performed over an eight-year period: Trends in microorganisms isolated and the value of anaerobic culture of blood. Clin Infect Dis. 1997;24:403–418.
10. Dahlgren J, Tally FP, Brothers G, et al. *Haemophilus parainfluenzae* endocarditis. Am J Clin Pathol. 1974;62:607–611.
11. Chunn CJ, Jones SR, McCutchan JA, et al. *Haemophilus parainfluenzae* infective endocarditis. Medicine (Baltimore). 1977;56:99–113.
12. Das I, DeGiovanni JV, Gray J. Endocarditis by *Haemophilus parainfluenzae* identified by 16S ribosomal RNA sequencing. J Clin Pathol. 1997;50:72–74.
13. Hannah P, Greenwood JR. Isolation and rapid identification of *Haemophilus ducreyi*. J Clin Microbiol. 1982;16:861–864.
14. Albritton WL. Biology of *Haemophilus ducreyi*. Microbiol Rev. 1989;53:377–389.
15. Kraut MS, Attebery HR, Finegold SM, et al. Detection of *Haemophilus aphrophilus* in the human oral flora with a selective medium. J Infect Dis. 1972;126:189–192.
16. Kilian M, Heine-Jensen J, Bulow P. *Haemophilus* in the upper respiratory tract of children. Acta Pathol Microbiol Scand [B]. 1972;80:571–578.
17. Spinola SM, Castellazzo A, Shero M, et al. Characterization of pili expressed by *Haemophilus ducreyi*. Microbiol Pathogen. 1990;9:417–426.
18. Castellazzo A, Shero M, Apicella MA, et al. Expression of pili by *Haemophilus ducreyi*. J Infect Dis. 1992;165(Suppl 1):S198–S199.
19. Campagnari AA, Wild LM, Griffiths GE, et al. Role of lipooligosaccharides in experimental dermal lesions caused by *Haemophilus ducreyi*. Infect Immun. 1991;59:2601–2608.
20. Melaugh W, Philips NJ, Campagnari AA, et al. Partial characterization of the major lipooligosaccharide from a strain of *Haemophilus ducreyi*, the causative agent of chancroid, a genital ulcer disease. J Biol Chem. 1992;267:13434–13439.
21. Purven M, Lagergard T. *Haemophilus ducreyi*, a cytotoxin-providing bacterium, Infect Immun. 1992;60:1156–1162.
22. Alfa MJ, DeGagne P, Totten PA. *Haemophilus ducreyi* hemolysin acts as a contact cytotoxin and damages human foreskin fibroblasts in cell culture. Infect Immun. 1996;64:2349–2352.
23. Cope LD, Lumbley S, Latimer JL, et al. A diffusible cytotoxin of *Haemophilus ducreyi*. Proc Natl Acad Sci U S A. 1997;94:4056–4061.
24. Trees D, Morse SA. Chancroid and *Haemophilus ducreyi*. An update. Clin Microbiol Rev. 1995;8:357–375.
25. Geraci JE, Wilkowske CJ, Wilson WR, et al. *Haemophilus* endocarditis: Report of 14 patients. Mayo Clin Proc. 1977;52:209–215.
26. Lyan DJ, Kane JG, Parker RH. *Haemophilus parainfluenzae* and *influenzae* endocarditis: A review of forty cases. Medicine (Baltimore). 1977;56:115–128.
27. Bachman DS. *Haemophilus* meningitis: Comparison of *H. influenzae* and *H. parainfluenzae*. Pediatrics. 1975;55:526–530.
28. Oill PA, Chow AW, Guze LB. Adult bacteremic *Haemophilus parainfluenzae* infections. Arch Intern Med. 1979;139:985–988.
29. Warman ST, Reinitz E, Klein RS. *Haemophilus parainfluenzae* septic arthritis in an adult. JAMA. 1981;246:868–869.
30. Cooney TG, Harwood BR, Meisner DJ. *Haemophilus parainfluenzae* thoracic empyema. Arch Intern Med. 1981;141:940–941.
31. Rhind GB, Gould GA, Ahmad F, et al. *Haemophilus parainfluenzae* and *H. influenzae* respiratory infections: Comparison of clinical features. Br Med J. 1985;291:707–708.
32. Olk DG, Hamill RJ, Proctor RA. *Haemophilus parainfluenzae* vertebral osteomyelitis. Am J Med Sci. 1987;294:114–116.
33. Gallent TE, Malinak LR, Gump DW, et al. *Haemophilus parainfluenzae* peritonitis associated with an intrauterine contraceptive device. Am J Obstet Gynecol. 1977;129:702–703.
34. Blaylock BL, Baber S. Urinary tract infection caused by *Haemophilus parainfluenzae*. Am J Clin Pathol. 1980;71:285–287.
35. Sturm AW. *Haemophilus influenzae* and *Haemophilus parainfluenzae* in nongonococcal urethritis. J Infect Dis. 1986;153:165–167.
36. Clairmont GJ, Zon LI, Groopman JE. *Haemophilus parainfluenzae* prostatitis in a

homosexual man with chronic lymphadenopathy syndrome and HTLV-III infection. Am J Med. 1987;82:175–178.
37. Black CT, Kupferschmid JP, West KW, et al. *Haemophilus parainfluenzae* infections in children, with the report of a unique case. Rev Infect Dis. 1988;10:342–346.
38. O'Bryan TA, Whitener CJ, Katzman M, et al. Hepatobiliary infections caused by *Haemophilus* species. Clin Infect Dis. 1992;15:716–719.
39. Auten GM, Levy CS, Smith MA. *Haemophilus parainfluenzae* as a rare cause of epidural abscess: Case report and review. Rev Infect Dis. 1991;13:609–612.
40. Samuel W, Dryden M, Sampson M, et al. Spinal abscess of *Haemophilus paraphrophilus*: A case report. Spine 1997;22:2763–2765.
41. Bottone EJ, Zhang DY. *Haemophilus parainfluenzae* biliary tract infection: Rationale for an ascending route of infection from the gastrointestinal tract. J Clin Microbiol. 1995;33:3042–3043.
42. Elster SK, Mattes LM, Meyers BR, et al. *Haemophilus aphrophilus* endocarditis: Review of 23 cases. Am J Cardiol. 1975;35:72–79.
43. Bieger RC, Brewer NS, Washington JA II. *Haemophilus aphrophilus*: A microbiologic and clinical review and report of 42 cases. Medicine (Baltimore). 1978;57:345–355.
44. Petty BG, Burrow CR, Robinson RA, et al. *Haemophilus aphrophilus* meningitis followed by vertebral osteomyelitis and suppurative psoas abscess. Am J Med. 1985;78:159–162.
45. Kiddy K, Webberley J. *Haemophilus aphrophilus* as a cause of chronic suppurative pulmonary infection and intraabdominal abscesses. J Infect. 1987;15:161–163.
46. Jones RN, Slepack J, Bigelow J. Ampicillin-resistant *Haemophilus paraphrophilus* laryngo-epiglottitis. J Clin Microbiol. 1976;4:405–407.
47. Bryan JP, Pankey GA. *Haemophilus paraphrophilus* endocarditis. South Med J. 1986;79:480–482.
48. Pajeau AK, Yu PKW, Ebersold MJ, et al. *Haemophilus paraphrophilus* frontal lobe abscess: Case report. Neurosurgery. 1988;23:643–645.
49. Welch WD, Southern PM Jr, Schneider NR. Five cases of *Haemophilus segnis* appendicitis. J Clin Microbiol. 1986;24:851–852.
50. Geraci JE, Wilson WR. Endocarditis due to gram-negative bacteria. Mayo Clin Proc. 1982;57:145–148.
51. Jemsek JG, Greenberg SB, Gentry LO, et al. *Haemophilus parainfluenzae* endocarditis. Am J Med. 1979;66:51–57.
52. Hammond GW, Richardson H, Lian CJ, et al. Two cases of *Haemophilus* endocarditis of prolapsed mitral value: *Haemophilus paraphrophilus* or *parainfluenzae*? Am J Med. 1978;65:537–541.
53. Blair DC, Weiner LB. Prosthetic valve endocarditis due to *Haemophilus parainfluenzae* biotype II. Am J Dis Child, 1979;133:617–618.
54. Julander I, Lindberg AA, Svanbom M. *Haemophilus parainfluenzae*: An uncommon cause of septicemia and endocarditis, Scand J Infect Dis. 1980;12:85–89.
55. Parker SW, Apicella MA, Fuller CM. *Haemophilus* endocarditis: Two patients with complications. Arch Intern Med. 1983;143:48–51.
56. Raucher B, Dobkin J, Mandel L, et al. Occult polymicrobial endocarditis with *Haemophilus parainfluenzae* in intravenous drug abusers. Am J Med. 1989;86:169–172.
57. Darras-Joly C, Lortholary O, Mainardi JL, et al. *Haemophilus* endocarditis: Report of 42 cases in adults and review. Clin Infect Dis. 1997;24:1087–1094.
58. Geraci JE, Wilson WR, Washington JA II. Infective endocarditis caused by *Actinobacillus actinomycetemcomitans*: Report of 4 cases. Mayo Clin Proc. 1980;55:415–419.
59. Kaplan AH, Weber DJ, Oddone EZ, et al. Infection due to *Actinobacillus actinomycetemcomitans*: 15 cases and review. Rev Infect Dis. 1989;11:46–63.
60. Grace CJ, Levitz RE, Katz-Pollak H, et al. *Actinobacillus actinomycetemcomitans* prosthetic valve endocarditis. Rev Infect Dis. 1988;10:922–929.
61. Wormser GP, Bottone EJ. *Cardiobacterium hominis*: Review of microbiologic and clinical features. Rev Infect Dis. 1983;5:680–691.
62. Meyer DJ, Gerding DN. Favorable prognosis of patients with prosthetic valve endocarditis caused by gram-negative bacilli of the HACEK group. Am J Med. 1988;85:104–107.
63. Wilson WR, Karchmer AW, Dajani AS, et al. Antibiotic treatment of adults with infective endocarditis due to streptococci, enterococci, staphylococci, and HACEK organisms. JAMA. 1995;274:1706–1713.
64. Das M, Badley AD, Cockerill FR, et al. Infective endocarditis caused by HACEK organisms. Annu Rev Med. 1997;48:25–33.
65. Coll-Vinent B, Suris X, Lopez-Soto A, et al. *Haemophilus paraphrophilus* endocarditis: Case report and review. Clin Infect Dis. 1995;20:1381–1383.
66. Jorgensen JH, Howell AW, Maher LA. Antimicrobial susceptibility testing of less commonly isolated *Haemophilus* species using *Haemophilus* test medium. J Clin Microbiol. 1990;28:985–988.
67. Doern GV, Jones RN. Antimicrobial susceptibility tests: Fastidious and unusual bacteria. In: Ballows A, Hausler WJ Jr, Herrmann KL, et al., eds. Manual of Clinical Microbiology. 5th ed. Washington, DC: American Society for Microbiology; 1991;1126–1132.
68. Goldberg R, Washington JA II. The taxonomy and antimicrobial susceptibility of *Haemophilus* species in clinical specimens. Am J Clin Pathol. 1978;70:899–904.
69. Jemsek JG, Martin RR, Greenberg SB, et al. Antimicrobial susceptibility testing of *Haemophilus parainfluenzae* by a kinetic killing-curve method. J Infect Dis. 1980;141:310–316.
70. Scheifele DW, Fussell SJ. Frequency of ampicillin-resistant *Haemophilus parainfluenzae* in children. J Infect Dis. 1981;143:495–498.
71. Scheifele DW, Fussell SJ, Roberts MC. Characterization of ampicillin-resistant *Haemophilus parainfluenzae*. Antimicrob Agents Chemother. 1982;21:734–739.
72. Watanakunakorn G, Glotzbecker C. Comparative susceptibility of *Haemophilus* species to cefaclor, cefamandole, and five other cephalosporins and ampicillin, chloramphenicol, and tetracycline. Antimicrob Agents Chemother. 1979;15:836–838.
73. Bulger RR, Washington JA II. Effect of inoculum size and beta-lactamase production on in vitro activity of new cephalosporins against *Haemophilus* species. Antimicrob Agents Chemother. 1980;17:393–396.
74. Wollschlager CM, Raoof S, Khan FA. Controlled, comparative study of ciprofloxacin versus ampicillin in treatment of bacterial respiratory tract infections. Am J Med. 1987;82(Suppl 4A):164–168.
75. Strakosch EA, Kendell HW, Craig RM, et al. Clinical and laboratory investigation of 370 cases of chancroid. J Invest Dermatol. 1945;6:95–107.
76. Gaisin A, Heaton CL. Chancroid: Alias the soft chancre. Int J Dermatol. 1975;14:188–197.
77. Schmid GP, Faur YC, Valu JA, et al. Enhanced recovery of *Haemophilus ducreyi* from clinical specimens by incubation at 33 versus 35°C. J Clin Microbiol. 1995;33:3257–3259.
78. Morse SA, Trees DL, Htun Y, et al. Comparison of clinical diagnosis and standard laboratory and molecular methods for the diagnosis of genital ulcer disease in Lesotho: Association with human immunodeficiency virus infection. J Infect Dis. 1997;175:583–589.
79. Orle KA, Gates CA, Martin DH, et al. Simultaneous PCR detection of *Haemophilus ducreyi*, *Treponema pallidum*, and herpes simplex virus types 1 and 2 from genital ulcers. J Clin Microbiol. 1996;34:49–54.
80. Simonsen JN, Cameron WD, Garinya MN, et al. Human immunodeficiency virus infection among men with sexually transmitted diseases. N Engl J Med. 1988;319:274–278.
81. Jessamine PG, Plummer FA, Achola JON, et al. Human immunodeficiency virus, genital ulcers and the male foreskin: Synergism in HIV-1 transmission. Scand J Infect Dis. 1990;Suppl 69:181–186.
82. Hammond GW, Slutchuk M, Scatiff J, et al. Epidemiologic, clinical, laboratory and therapeutic features of an urban outbreak of chancroid in North America. Rev Infect Dis. 1980;2:867–879.
83. Blackmore CA, Limpakarnjanarat K, Rigau-Perez JG, et al. An outbreak of chancroid in Orange County, California: Descriptive epidemiology and disease-control measures. J Infect Dis. 1985;151:840–844.
84. Ronald AR, Plummer FA. Chancroid and *Haemophilus ducreyi*. Ann Intern Med. 1985;102:805–807.
85. Schmid GP, Sanders LL Jr, Blount JH, et al. Chancroid in the United States: Reestablishment of an old disease. JAMA. 1987;258:3265–3268.
86. Flood JM, Sarafian SK, Bolan GA, et al. Multistrain outbreak of chancroid in San Francisco, 1989–1991. J Infect Dis. 1993;167:1106–1111.
87. Desjardins M, Thompson CE, Filion LG, et al. Standardization of an enzyme immunoassay for human antibody to *Haemophilus ducreyi*. J Clin Microbiol. 1992;30:2019–2024.
88. Alfa MJ, Olson N, Degagne P, et al. Humoral immune response of humans to lipooligosaccharide and outer membrane proteins of *Haemophilus ducreyi*. J Infect Dis. 1993;167:1206–1210.
89. Heyman A, Beeson PB, Sheldon WH. Diagnosis of chancroid. JAMA. 1945;129:935–938.
90. King R, Gough J, Ronald A, et al. An immunohistochemical analysis of naturally occurring chancroid. J Infect Dis. 1996;174:427–430.
91. Spinola SM, Orazi A, Arno JN, et al. *Haemophilus ducreyi* elicits a cutaneous infiltrate of CD4 cells during experimental human infection. J Infect Dis. 1996;173:394–402.
92. Schmid GP. Treatment of chancroid, 1989. Rev Infect Dis. 1990;12(Suppl 6):S580–S589.
93. Dangor Y, Ballard RC, Miller SD, et al. Treatment of chancroid. Antimicrob Agents Chemother. 1990;34:1308–1311.
94. Motley M, Sarafian SK, Knapp JS, et al. Correlation between in vitro antimicrobial susceptibilities and β-lactamase plasmid contents of isolates of *Haemophilus ducreyi* for the United States. Antimicrob Agents Chemother. 1992;36:1639–1643.
95. Slaney L, Chubb H, Ronald A, et al. In-vitro activity of azithromycin, erythromycin, ciprofloxacin and norfloxacin against *Neisseria gonorrhoeae*, *Haemophilus ducreyi*, and *Chlamydia trachomatis*. J Antimicrob Chemother. 1990;25(Suppl A):1–5.
96. Taylor DN, Pitarangsi C, Echeverria P, et al. Comparative study of ceftriaxone and trimethoprim-sulfamethoxazole for the treatment of chancroid in Thailand. J Infect Dis. 1985;152:1002–1006.
97. Martin DH, Sargent SJ, Wendel GD Jr, et al. Comparison of azithromycin and ceftriaxone for the treatment of chancroid. Clin Infect Dis. 1995;21:409–414.
98. Tyndall M, Malisa M, Plummer FA, et al. Ceftriaxone no longer predictably cures chancroid in Kenya. J Infect Dis. 1993;167:469–471.
99. Bogaerts J, Kestens L, Tello WM, et al. Failure of treatment for chancroid in Rwanda is not related to human immunodeficiency virus infection: In vitro resistance of *Haemophilus ducreyi* to trimethoprim-sulfamethoxazole. Clin Infect Dis. 1995;20:924–930.
100. Rutanarugsa A, Vorachit M, Polnikorn N, et al. Drug resistance of *Haemophilus ducreyi*. Southeast Asian J Trop Med Public Health. 1990;21:185–193.
101. Kraus SJ, Kaufman HW, Albritton WL, et al. Chancroid therapy: A review of cases confirmed by culture. Rev Infect Dis. 1982;4(S):S848–S856.
102. Bilgeri YR, Ballard RC, Duncan MO, et al. Antimicrobial susceptibility of 103 strains of *Haemophilus ducreyi* isolated in Johannesburg. Antimicrob Agents Chemother. 1982;22:686–688.
103. Brunton J, Meier M, Ehrman N, et al. Molecular epidemiology of beta-lactamase

specifying plasmids of *Haemophilus ducreyi*. Antimicrob Agents Chemother. 1982;21:857–863.
104. Naamara W, Plummer FA, Greenblatt RM, et al. Treatment of chancroid with ciprofloxacin: A prospective, randomized clinical trial. Am J Med. 1987;82(Suppl 4A):317–320.
105. Bodhidatta L, Taylor DN, Chitwarakorn A, et al. Evaluation of 500- and 1000-mg doses of ciprofloxacin for the treatment of chancroid. Antimicrob Agents Chemother. 1988;32:723–725.
106. Centers for Disease Control and Prevention. Sexually transmitted diseases treatment guidelines. MMWR Morb Mortal Weekly Rep. 1993;42:20–22.
107. Thornton AC, O'Mara EM Jr, Sorensen SJ, et al. Prevention of experimental *Haemophilus ducreyi* infection: A randomized, controlled clinical trial. J Infect Dis. 1998;177:1608–1613.

Chapter 214

Gardnerella vaginalis and *Mobiluncus* Species

CAROL A. SPIEGEL

GARDNERELLA VAGINALIS

History

In 1953 Leopold described a previously unrecognized *Haemophilus*-like organism associated with prostatitis and cervicitis.[1] Two years later, Gardner and Dukes described *Haemophilus vaginalis* as the etiologic agent of bacterial vaginosis (nonspecific vaginitis).[2] Because it required neither hemin (X factor) nor nicotinamide adenine dinucleotide (V factor), and because it sometimes appeared to be gram-positive and formed "Chinese letters," it was removed from the genus *Haemophilus* and renamed *Corynebacterium vaginale*.[3] Its taxonomic position remained unclear until studies performed by Greenwood and Pickett[4] and by Piot and associates[5] showed a lack of genetic relationship between this organism and other morphologically or physiologically similar genera, at which time it was renamed *Gardnerella vaginalis*.[4]

The Pathogen

G. vaginalis[4] is a facultatively anaerobic, oxidase- and catalase-negative, nonsporing, nonencapsulated, nonmotile, pleomorphic, gram-variable rod. (See the excellent review by Catlin.[6]) It is indole, nitrate, and urease negative. Rare obligate anaerobic strains exist. It requires an enriched medium for growth that must include thiamine, riboflavin, niacin, folinic acid, biotin, and two or more purine and pyrimidine bases. It produces a diffuse β-hemolysis on human but not on sheep blood and produces acid from some carbohydrates, including dextrose, maltose, and starch but not raffinose. Acetic acid is the major metabolic end product. Starch and hippurate are hydrolyzed.

Electron microscopic studies have described either a gram-positive[7, 8] or a gram-negative[9] cell wall or a laminated cell wall typical of neither gram-positive nor gram-negative bacteria.[4] The cell wall contains alanine, glutamic acid, glycine, and lysine,[10] and the cell membrane contains predominantly hexadecanoic (16:0), octadecenoic (18:1), and octadecanoic (18:0) acids without hydroxy fatty acids.[11] The amino acid and fatty acid profiles are typical of gram-positive organisms. Endotoxic activity was detected in cell extracts by the *Limulus* amebocyte assay, but lipid A was not present.[4]

G. vaginalis is susceptible to penicillin, clindamycin, and vancomycin and resistant to colistin and nalidixic acid.[12] The organism is relatively resistant to metronidazole and tinidazole but is susceptible to the hydroxy metabolite of metronidazole.[13]

Because of its unusual cell wall, *G. vaginalis* has not been placed in a family, but it is grouped with gram-negative bacteria in the ninth edition of *Bergey's Manual*. A taxonomic study found greater than 92% sequence similarity between *G. vaginalis* and the genus *Bifidobacterium*.[14]

Epidemiology

The natural habitat for *G. vaginalis* is the human vagina, where it has been found in up to 69% of women without signs or symptoms of vaginal infection[15] and 13.5% of girls[16] (see Chapter 95). The organism is found in almost 100% of women with bacterial vaginosis (BV)[15] and in the urethra of a majority of male partners of women with that diagnosis.[17]

Biotyping schemes[18, 19] based on the presence of lipase, hippurate hydrolysis, and β-galactosidase have identified specific biotypes associated with BV. The urethra of men and their partners who had BV were colonized with the same biotype of *G. vaginalis* when the specimens were cultured within 24 hours of each other. The distribution of biotypes was the same in women with and without BV. Treatment, but not a new sexual partner, was associated with acquisition of a new biotype.[19] Restriction endonuclease analysis of isolates from women with BV has indicated that a genetically mixed population is present in the vagina.[20] Several genotypes have been identified with the use of restriction enzymes, but none was specifically associated with BV.[21]

Pathogenesis

The main syndrome with which *G. vaginalis* is associated is BV. Pili have been seen on *G. vaginalis*,[22] and hemagglutinating activity and adherence to McCoy cells[23] have been demonstrated. The capacity of this organism to adhere to vaginal and urinary epithelial cells may play a role in the pathogenesis of BV and urinary tract infections.[23, 24] *G. vaginalis* has been shown to consume ammonia produced in a defined medium by *Prevotella bivia*.[25]

G. vaginalis produces a cytolytic toxin (hemolysin) that forms voltage-dependent cationic channels when incorporated into lipid membranes.[26] Specific vaginal immunoglobulin A response to hemolysin was found in 60% of women with BV and in 9% of those without BV.[27, 28] It has also been identified as a member of the vaginal flora with phospholipase A_2 activity,[29] which initiates labor. This provides one explanation for the observation that BV is associated with premature rupture of membranes.[30]

G. vaginalis is serum resistant,[31] a characteristic that may enable this relatively avirulent organism to survive during blood-stream invasion that occurs at parturition.

Clinical Manifestations

Bacterial Vaginosis. *G. vaginalis* is almost universally present in the vagina of women with BV, where it is found with a mixed anaerobic flora.[32] BV, the most common cause of vaginitis/vaginosis, is associated with an increased vaginal discharge that may have a "fishy" odor, but not with leukorrhea, vulvar burning, or pruritus. This syndrome is best diagnosed by clinical criteria[33] or Gram stain examination of vaginal fluid[34, 35] rather than culture for *G. vaginalis* (see Chapter 95).

Urinary Tract Infection. *G. vaginalis* is a relatively infrequent (<0.5%) urinary tract isolate and may be present with or without pyuria. Because the presence of *G. vaginalis* in midstream urine can represent vaginal contamination, its clinical significance can be difficult to ascertain. However, it has been recovered from suprapubic bladder aspirates from pregnant women,[36] and in association with renal disease[37] and interstitial cystitis.[38]

Bacteremia. *G. vaginalis* causes bacteremia almost exclusively in women and is usually associated with obstetric or gynecologic events,[29, 39] including postpartum endometritis, postpartum fever, chorioamnionitis, septic abortion, and infection after cesarean section. Neonatal infection has also been reported.[40] The frequency of *G. vaginalis* bacteremia may be underestimated because the organism is susceptible to sodium polyanetholesulfonate (SPS),[41] the anticoagulant contained in most blood culture media. Addition of 1.2% gelatin negates the inhibitory effect. *G. vaginalis* bacteremia may have a relatively benign course and may resolve even in the absence of appropriate antimicrobial therapy.[39]

Other Sources. *G. vaginalis* can be recovered from the endometrium and chorioamnion of clinically infected patients in the absence of bacteremia.

Diagnosis, Detection, and Identification

G. vaginalis produces round, opaque, smooth colonies that are pinpoint in size after 24 hours of incubation and 0.5 mm in diameter at 48 hours. Because the colonies are nondescript on chocolate or Columbia CNA agar, a selective or differential medium is used to improve their detection. β-Hemolysis of human blood is a better differential character than starch hydrolysis because the latter is common in members of the vaginal flora. The optimal medium for primary isolation of *G. vaginalis* from a mixed flora is human blood bilayer Tween (HBT).[15] After 24 to 28 hours of incubation in a candle extinction jar, *G. vaginalis* produces colonies with a diffuse zone of β-hemolysis. *G. vaginalis* is also β-hemolytic when grown on this medium anaerobically, but some anaerobic members of the endogenous and BV-associated flora are β-hemolytic as well.

G. vaginalis will grow in commercially available blood culture media that are either SPS-free or supplemented with 1.2% gelatin.[41]

There are several identification schemes available for *G. vaginalis*. Thin, gram-negative or gram-variable short rods that are catalase negative and produce a 1- to 2-mm zone of β-hemolysis with diffuse edges on HBT agar after 48 hours of incubation in CO_2 are *G. vaginalis* 97.5% of the time.[42] This is probably sufficient for identification of vaginal isolates if vaginal cultures are performed.

For more definitive identification of *G. vaginalis*, the presence of β-hemolysis on human but not on sheep blood, negative oxidase and catalase tests, and a positive hippurate test on a small, gram-variable rod are required. These represent the minimum criteria for differentiation of *G. vaginalis* from *Haemophilus aphrophilus* as well as *Corynebacterium*, *Bifidobacterium*, and *Lactobacillus species*.[43] Kits and other methods for identification of *G. vaginalis* have been reviewed.[6]

Therapy and Susceptibility

Ninety percent of strains of *G. vaginalis* are susceptible to penicillin (0.07 mg/liter), ampicillin (0.125 mg/liter), vancomycin (0.5 mg/liter), clindamycin (<0.06 mg/liter), gentamicin (4 mg/liter), and metronidazole (4 mg/liter) and its hydroxy metabolite (1 mg/liter).[12, 13] It is resistant to cephalexin (64 mg/liter), tetracycline (64 mg/liter), nalidixic acid (>128 mg/liter), colistin (>128 mg/liter), sulfadiazine (>128 mg/liter), and quinolones (>4 mg/liter).[12, 44, 45] Although erythromycin is active against *G. vaginalis* (0.06 mg/liter), it cannot be used to treat BV adequately, probably because of inactivation by the acid environment of the vagina.[46]

Oral metronidazole, intravaginal metronidazole gel, or intravaginal clindamycin cream is an accepted choice for treatment of BV.

Prevention

Although *G. vaginalis* biotypes in girls and their mothers have not been compared, horizontal transmission of this organism is possible. Sharing of biotypes by women with BV and their male partners has been shown[18] and implies that sexual transmission from the male to an uncolonized partner is possible. Prevention of BV, however, probably requires control of other members of the vaginosis-associated flora and lactobacilli.

Upper genitourinary tract infection and sepsis in obstetric and gynecologic patients are the most common serious sequelae of vaginal colonization with *G. vaginalis* and, more specifically, with BV. Treatment of BV in the second trimester or before gynecologic procedures is not recommended, because there are insufficient data regarding its effectiveness.

MOBILUNCUS SPECIES

History

Curved rods have been associated with vaginal fluid since before the turn of the 20th century.[47] Curtis[48] was the first to isolate anaerobic curved rods from the vagina and uterine material in a woman with postpartum endometritis. Characteristics of these organisms were reported by Moore[49] and by Durieux and Dublanchet[50] who named them "vibrions succinoproducteurs." Spiegel and Roberts[51] and Hammann and colleagues[52] demonstrated that these organisms represent a previously unrecognized genus.

The Pathogen

Mobiluncus spp. are slowly growing, curved, gram-variable, motile, anaerobic bacteria predominantly found in the human vagina in association with BV. Electron microscopically, their cell wall has a gram-positive appearance.[49, 50] Lipopolysaccharide activity and lipid A are lacking.[51] They are indole, oxidase, H_2S, gelatin, urease, and catalase negative. Succinic, acetic, and lactic acids are produced. An enriched medium is needed for growth, which is stimulated by rabbit or horse serum, maltose, or glycogen. The characteristic corkscrew motility is apparently a result of the presence of multiple flagella. Their attachment site is either subpolar or more centrally located on the concave side of the cell. Fatty acids in the cell wall include myristic (14:0), hexadecenoic (16:1), hexadecanoic (16:0), heptadecanoic (17:0), octadecadienoic (18:2), octadecenoic (18:1), and octadecanoic (18:0) acids. 16:0, 18:2, and 18:1 represent more than 50% of the total fatty acids.[53]

Two species of *Mobiluncus* have been described; *Mobiluncus curtisii* is small (generally 1.5 to 1.7 μm long), gram-variable, and only slightly bent, sometimes giving it a coryneform appearance. *Mobiluncus mulieris* is larger (mean, 2.9 to 3.0 μm), almost invariably gram-negative, and appears crescentic or moonlike. Biochemical tests that have been used to distinguish among the species[51] are less reliable than Gram stain morphology and do not correlate well with antigenic subgroups.[54] The BBL crystal anaerobe identification system correctly identified 5 of 5 *M. curtisii* and 2 of 2 *M. mulieris* specimens.[55]

Epidemiology

Mobiluncus has been detected in the vagina of 6% or fewer of controls[54] and as many as 97% of women with BV.[56] Rectal colonization of healthy women, male partners of women with or without BV, homosexual men, and children has been demonstrated, but pharyngeal colonization has not.[56] Colonization of the male genitourinary tract was found only in male partners of women with vaginal *Mobiluncus*.[56]

Pathogenesis

Adherence of curved rods to vaginal squamous epithelial cells has been observed.[49] Adherence via lateral and polar attachment in situ has been demonstrated and may be caused by a glycocalyx.[57] Pili have not been observed on *Mobiluncus*.[52]

M. mulieris is a better stimulator of oxidative metabolism in polymorphonuclear leukocytes than is *M. curtisii*.[58] This is positively correlated with the observation that *M. curtisii* is the species more commonly associated with extravaginal infections.

Serum antibody to *M. curtisii* was found in 75% of pregnant women, regardless of a clinical history of BV, in 6% of pediatric patients, and in 0% of sexually inexperienced women.[59]

Clinical Manifestations

Mobiluncus spp., like *G. vaginalis*, are frequently found in the vagina of women with BV, where they are found with a mixed anaerobic flora (see earlier discussion and Chapter 95). *Mobiluncus* spp., more commonly *M. curtisii*, are associated with upper genitourinary tract infections including adverse pregnancy outcome. Extragenitourinary tract infections have included nonpuerperal breast abscesses in women and in a man as well as umbilical and mastectomy wounds.[60]

Diagnosis, Detection, Identification

Media used for isolation of *Mobiluncus* spp. and enrichment techniques have been summarized.[60] An enriched medium such as brain-heart infusion or Columbia agar is required. Some media include selective agents to inhibit other BV-associated flora. Isolation of *Mobiluncus* from vaginal fluid is neither necessary nor recommended for the diagnosis of BV. It can be recovered on routine anaerobic media used in clinical laboratories for culture of normally sterile body sites. Small, transparent, moist-appearing colonies may be seen after 2 or 3 days of anaerobic incubation at 35°C.

Therapy and Susceptibility

Ninety percent of strains of *M. curtisii* are susceptible to penicillin (0.062 mg/liter), ampicillin (0.25 mg/liter), cefoxitin (4 mg/liter), clindamycin (0.125 mg/liter), erythromycin (<0.2 mg/liter), imipenem (0.125 mg/liter), and vancomycin (0.5 mg/liter). Ninety percent of strains of *M. mulieris* are susceptible to penicillin (0.015 mg/liter), ampicillin (0.062 mg/liter), cefoxitin (0.4 mg/liter), clindamycin (0.062 mg/liter), erythromycin (≤ 0.2 mg/liter), imipenem (0.062 mg/liter), and vancomycin (0.5 mg/liter). The 90% minimal inhibitory concentration (MIC_{90}) of metronidazole for both species is 256 mg/liter. However, the MIC_{50} for *M. curtisii* is 128 and for *M. mulieris* it is 4 mg/liter.[61] It is not clear whether the hydroxy metabolite of metronidazole is more active than the parent compound.[61, 62] Cycloserine, nalidixic acid, colistin, and tetracycline have reduced or no activity against either species. Because metronidazole is an appropriate therapeutic choice for BV, it is used regardless of whether the organism is isolated.

REFERENCES

1. Leopold S. Heretofore undescribed organism isolated from the genitourinary system. US Armed Forces Med J. 1953;4:263–266.
2. Gardner HL, Dukes CD. *Hemophilus vaginalis* vaginitis: A newly defined specific infection previously classified "nonspecific" vaginitis. Am J Obstet Gynecol. 1955;69:962–976.
3. Zinneman K, Turner GC. The taxonomic position of "*Haemophilus vaginalis*" *(Corynebacterium vaginale)*. J Pathol Bacteriol. 1963;85:213–219.
4. Greenwood JR, Pickett MJ. Transfer of *Haemophilus vaginalis* Gardner and Dukes to a new genus, *Gardnerella: G. vaginalis* (Gardner and Dukes) comb nov. Int J Syst Bacteriol. 1980;30:170–178.
5. Piot P, van Dyck E, Goodfellow M, et al. A taxonomic study of *Gardnerella vaginalis (Haemophilus vaginalis)* Gardner and Dukes 1955. J Gen Microbiol. 1980;119:373–396.
6. Catlin BW. *Gardnerella vaginalis*: Characteristics, clinical considerations, and controversies. Clin Microbiol Rev. 1992;5:213–237.
7. Reyn A, Birch-Anderson A, Lapage SP. An electron microscope study of thin sections of *Haemophilus vaginalis* (Gardner and Dukes) and some possibly related species. Can J Microbiol. 1966;12:1125–1136.
8. Sandhu K, Domingue AG, Chow AW, et al. *Gardnerella vaginalis* has a gram-positive cell-wall ultrastructure and lacks classical cell-wall lipopolysaccharide. J Med Microbiol. 1989;29:229–235.
9. Criswell BS, Marston JH, Stenback WA, et al. *Haemophilus vaginalis* 594, a gram-negative organism? Can J Microbiol. 1971;17:865–869.
10. Harper JJ, Davis GHG. Cell wall analysis of *Gardnerella vaginalis (Haemophilus vaginalis)*. Int J Syst Bacteriol. 1982;32:48–50.
11. Csango PA, Hagen N, Jagars G. Method for isolation of *Gardnerella vaginalis (Haemophilus vaginalis)*: Characterization of isolates by gas chromatography. Acta Pathol Microbiol Immunol Scand Sect B. 1982;90:89–93.
12. McCarthy LR, Mickelsen PA, Smith EG. Antibiotic susceptibility of *Haemophilus vaginalis (Corynebacterium vaginale)* to 21 antibiotics. Antimicrob Agents Chemother. 1979;16:186–189.
13. Bannatyne RM, Jackowski J, Cheung R, et al. Susceptibility of *Gardnerella vaginalis* to metronidazole, its bioactive metabolites, and tinidazole. Am J Clin Pathol. 1986;87:640–641.
14. Van Esbroeck M, Vandamme P, Falsen E, et al. Polyphasic approach to the classification and identification of *Gardnerella vaginalis* and unidentified *Gardnerella vaginalis*–like coryneforms present in bacterial vaginosis. Int J Syst Bacteriol. 1996;46:675–682.
15. Totten PA, Amset R, Hale J, et al. Selective differential human blood bilayer media for isolation of *Gardnerella (Haemophilus) vaginalis*. J Clin Microbiol. 1982;15:141–147.
16. Hammerschlag MR, Alpert S, Rosner I, et al. Microbiology of the vagina in children: Normal and potentially pathogenic organisms. Pediatrics. 1978;62:57–62.
17. Pheifer TA, Forsyth PS, Durfee MA, et al. Nonspecific vaginitis: Role of *Haemophilus vaginalis* and treatment with metronidazole. N Engl J Med. 1978;298:1429–1434.
18. Piot P, van Dyck E, Peeters M, et al. Biotypes of *Gardnerella vaginalis*. J Clin Microbiol. 1984;20:677–679.
19. Briselden AM, Hillier S. Longitudinal study of biotypes of *Gardnerella vaginalis*. J Clin Microbiol. 1990;28:2761–2764.
20. Nath K, Devlin D, Beddoe AM. Heterogeneity in restriction patterns of *Gardnerella vaginalis* isolates from individuals with bacterial vaginosis. Res Microbiol. 1992;143:199–209.
21. Ingianni A, Petruzzelli S, Morandotti G, Pompei R. Genotypic differentiation of *Gardnerella vaginalis* by amplified ribosomal DNA restriction analysis (ARDRA). FEMS Immunol Med Microbiol. 1997;18:61–66.
22. Boustouller YL, Johnson AP, Taylor-Robinson D. Pili on *Gardnerella vaginalis* studied by electron microscopy. J Med Microbiol. 1987;23:327–329.
23. Scott TG, Smyth CJ, Keane CT. In vitro adhesiveness and biotype of *Gardnerella vaginalis* strains in relation to the occurrence of clue cells in vaginal discharges. Genitourin Med. 1987;63:47–53.
24. Johnson AP, Boustouller YL. Extra-vaginal infection caused by *Gardnerella vaginalis*. Epidemiol Infect. 1987;98:131–137.
25. Dybus V, Onderdonk AB. Evidence for a commensal symbiotic relationship between *Gardnerella vaginalis* and *Prevotella bivia* involving ammonia: Potential significance for bacterial vaginosis. J Infect Dis. 1997;175:406–413.
26. Moran O, Zegarra-Moran D, Virginio C, et al. Physical characterization of the pore forming cytolysine from *Gardnerella vaginalis*. FEMS Microbiol Immunol. 1992;5:63–69.
27. Cauci S, Scrimin F, Driussi S, et al. Specific immune response against *Gardnerella vaginalis* hemolysin in patients with bacterial vaginosis. Am J Obstet Gynecol. 1996;175:1601–1605.
28. Cauci AU, Driussi S, Monte R et al. Immunoglobulin A response against *Gardnerella vaginosis* hemolysin and sialidase activity in bacterial vaginosis. Am J Obstet Gynecol. 1998;178:511–515.
29. Bejar R, Curbelo V, Davis C, et al. Premature labor II. Bacterial sources of phospholipase. Obstet Gynecol. 1981; 57:479–482.
30. Gravett MG, Nelson HP, DeRouten T, et al. Independent associations of bacterial vaginosis and *Chlamydia trachomatis* infection with adverse pregnancy outcome. JAMA. 1986;256:1899–1903.
31. Boustouller YL, Johnson AP. Resistance of *Gardnerella vaginalis* to bactericidal activity of human serum. Genitourin Med. 1986;62:380–383.
32. Spiegel CA, Amsel R, Eschenbach D, et al. Anaerobic bacteria in nonspecific vaginitis. N Engl J Med. 1980;303:601–607.
33. Amsel R, Totten PA, Spiegel CA, et al. Nonspecific vaginitis: Diagnostic criteria and microbial and epidemiologic associations. Am J Med. 1983;74:14–22.
34. Spiegel CA, Amsel R, Holmes KK. Diagnosis of bacterial vaginosis by direct Gram stain of vaginal fluid. J Clin Microbiol. 1983;18:170–177.
35. Nugent RP, Krohn MA, Hillier SL. Reliability of diagnosing bacterial vaginosis is improved by a standardized method of Gram stain interpretation. J Clin Microbiol. 1992;29:297–301.
36. McFadyen IR, Eykyn SJ. Suprapubic aspiration of urine in pregnancy. Lancet. 1968;1:1112–1114.
37. McDowall DR, Buchanan JD, Fairley KF, et al. Anaerobic and other fastidious microorganisms in asymptomatic bacteriuria in pregnant women. J Infect Dis. 1981;144:114–122.
38. Wilkins EGL, Payne SR, Pead PJ, et al. Interstitial cystitis and the urethral syndrome: A possible answer. Br J Urol. 1989;64:39–44.
39. Reimer LG, Reller LB. *Gardnerella vaginalis* bacteremia: A review of thirty cases. Obstet Gynecol. 1984;64:170–174.
40. Venkataramani TK, Rathbun HK. *Corynebacterium vaginale (Haemophilus vaginalis)* bacteremia: Clinical study of 29 cases. Johns Hopkins Med J. 1976;139:93–97.
41. Reimer LG, Reller LB. Effect of sodium polyanetholesulfonate and gelatin on the

recovery of *Gardnerella vaginalis* from blood culture media. J Clin Microbiol. 1985;21:686–688.
42. Piot P, van Dyck E, Totten PA, et al. Identification of *Gardnerella (Haemophilus) vaginalis*. J Clin Microbiol. 1982;15:19–24.
43. Greenwood JR, Pickett MJ. Salient features of *Haemophilus vaginalis*. J Clin Microbiol. 1979;9:200–204.
44. Jones BM, Kinghorn GR, Geary I. In vitro susceptibility of *Gardnerella vaginalis* and *Bacteroides* organisms, associated with nonspecific vaginitis, to sulfonamide preparations. Antimicrob Agents Chemother. 1982;21:870–872.
45. Tjiam KH, Wagenvoort JHT, van Klingeren B, et al. In vitro activity of the two new 4-quinolones A56619 and A56620 against *Neisseria gonorrhoeae, Chlamydia trachomatis, Mycoplasma hominis, Ureaplasma urealyticum* and *Gardnerella vaginalis*. Eur J Clin Microbiol. 1986;5:498–501.
46. Durfee MA, Forsyth PS, Hale JA, et al. Ineffectiveness of erythromycin for treatment of *Haemophilus vaginalis*-associated vaginitis: Possible relationship to acidity of vaginal secretions. Antimicrob Agents Chemother. 1979; 16:635–637.
47. Krönig I. Über die Natur der Scheidenheme, speciell über das vorkommen anaërober Schwangerer. Centrabl für Gynakol. 1895;19:409–412.
48. Curtis AH. A motile curved anaerobic bacillus in uterine discharges. J Infect Dis. 1913;12:165–169.
49. Moore B. Observations on a group of anaerobic vaginal vibrios. J Pathol Bacteriol. 1954;67;461–473.
50. Durieux R, Dublanchet A. Les "Vibrions" anaérobies des leucorrhées. I. Technique d'isolement et sensibilité aux antibiotiques. Med Mal Infect. 1980;10:109–115.
51. Spiegel CA, Roberts M. *Mobiluncus* gen. nov., *Mobiluncus curtisii* subspecies *curtisii* sp. nov., *Mobiluncus curtisii* subspecies *holmesii* subsp. nov., and *Mobiluncus mulieris* sp. nov., curved rods from the human vagina. Int J Syst Bacteriol. 1984;34:177–184.
52. Hammann R, Kronibus A, Viebahn A, et al. *Falcivibrio grandis* gen. nov. sp. nov., and *Falcivibrio vaginalis* gen. nov. sp. nov., a new genus and species to accommodate anaerobic motile curved rods formerly described as "Vibrio mulieris" (Prévot 1940), in Breed et al. 1948. Syst Appl Microbiol. 1984;5:81–96.
53. Carlone GM, Thomas ML, Arko RJ, et al. Cell wall characteristics of *Mobiluncus* species. Int J Syst Bacteriol. 1986;36:288–296.
54. Schwebke JR, Lukehart SA, Roberts MC, et al. Identification of two new antigenic subgroups within the genus *Mobiluncus*. J Clin Microbiol. 1991;29:2204–2208.
55. Cavallaro JJ, Wiggs LS, Miller JM. Evaluation of BBL crystal anaerobe identification system. J Clin Microbiol. 1997;35:3186–3191.
56. Holst E. Reservoir of four organisms associated with bacterial vaginosis suggests lack of sexual transmission. J Clin Microbiol. 1990;28:2035–2039.
57. DeBoer JM, Plantema FHF. Ultrastructure of the in situ adherence of *Mobiluncus* to the vaginal epithelial cells. Can J Microbiol. 1988;34:757–766.
58. Moi H, Fredlund H, Tornqvist E, et al. *Mobiluncus* species in bacterial vaginosis: Aspects of pathogenesis. Acta Pathol Microbiol Immunol Scand. 1991;99:1049–1054.
59. Schwebke JR, Morgan SC, Hillier SL. Humoral antibody to *Mobiluncus curtisii*, a potential serological marker for bacterial vaginosis. Clin Diagn Lab Immunol. 1996;3:567–569.
60. Spiegel CA. The genus *Mobiluncus*. In: Balows A, Trüper HG, Dworkin M, et al., eds. Prokaryotes. 2nd ed, Ch. 37a. New York: Springer-Verlag; 1992.
61. Spiegel CA. Susceptibility of *Mobiluncus* species to 23 antimicrobial agents and 15 other compounds. Antimicrob Agents Chemother. 1987;31:249–252.
62. Sprott MS, Ingham HR, Pattman RS, et al. Characteristics of motile curved rods in vaginal secretions. J Med Microbiol. 1983;16:175–182.

Chapter 215

Brucella Species

EDWARD J. YOUNG

Brucellosis is a disease of domestic and wild animals (zoonosis) that is transmittable to humans. The array of nonspecific signs and symptoms of human brucellosis led Simpson to remark, "No disease, not excepting syphilis and tuberculosis, is more protean in its manifestations."[1]

HISTORY

The first accurate description of human brucellosis was reported by Marston, a surgeon serving with the Royal Artillery during the Crimean War.[2] The causative agent remained unknown until 1886, when Bruce isolated *Micrococcus* (later *Brucella*) *melitensis* from the spleens of victims of Malta fever.[3] The Maltese physician Zammit, working with the Mediterranean Fever Commission (1904–1907) identified native goats as the reservoir of the infection, and fresh goat's milk as the vehicle of transmission from animals to humans.[4] In 1895, the Danish veterinarian Bang identified *Bacillus* (later *Brucella*) *abortus* as the cause of contagious abortions in cattle.[5] It was not until the 1920s that the relatedness of the agents of Malta fever and Bang's disease was recognized from the work of American bacteriologist Evans, and the genus was renamed to honor Bruce. The third member of the genus, *Brucella suis*, was isolated from aborted swine by Traum in 1914, and the fourth member, *Brucella canis*, was recovered by Carmichael in 1966 from aborting kennel-bred dogs.[6] Other species, *Brucella ovis* from sheep and *Brucella neotomae* from desert wood rats, were added, but to date they have not been shown to cause human infection. In 1994, British and American workers independently isolated a previously unknown *Brucella* organism from the carcasses of marine mammals and cetaceans on the coast of Scotland[7] and from a captive dolphin in California.[8] These isolates, forming a relatively homogeneous group with distinctive metabolic profiles, dye sensitivities, and phage sensitivities, have tentatively been named *Brucella maris*.[9]

THE PATHOGEN

Brucellae are small, gram-negative coccobacilli that are nonmotile and do not form spores. They grow aerobically, although some species require supplemental carbon dioxide for primary isolation. Any high-quality peptone-based media enriched with blood or serum can serve for in vitro cultivation; however, isolation from clinical specimens can require prolonged (30 days or more) incubation. *Brucella* strains are always catalase-positive, but oxidase and urease activities and the production of H_2S are variable.[10] The major nomen species of *Brucella* and their biovars are differentiated by selective inhibition of growth on media containing dyes, such as thionin and basic fuchsin.[11] A series of brucella-phages can also be used for typing smooth and rough brucellae.[12]

The genus *Brucella* is divided into six (possibly seven) nomen species on the basis of preferred hosts and cultural, metabolic, and antigenic characteristics. However, DNA-DNA hybridization studies have shown a remarkable degree (>95%) of homology between strains, suggesting that it is a monospecific genus with subspecies corresponding to evolutionary lineages adapted to specific hosts.[13] Nevertheless, studies using restriction endonucleases have revealed polymorphism in a number of genes encoding for structural and replicative functions, supporting the differentiation into nomen species.[14, 15]

Phylogenetically, *Brucella* spp. appear to have a common origin with free-living, soil-dwelling organisms. Based on 16S rRNA sequences[16] and analysis of outer membrane proteins,[17] *Brucella* spp. are classified within the α_2-subdivision of the class Proteobacteria. The genome of *Brucella* contains two chromosomes of 2.1 and 1.5 Mb except *B. suis* biovar 3, which has a single chromosome of 3.1 Mb.[18] Native plasmids have not been detected, although transformation has been effected by wide host range plasmids following conjugative transfer or electroporation.[19]

The major cell wall antigen and virulence factor of the brucellae is S-LPS containing the A and M antigens first described by Wilson and Miles. The O side chain is composed of about 100 residues of 4-formamido-4,6-dideoxymannose, which are linked $\alpha_{1,2}$ in A-dominant strains, but with every fifth residue linked $\alpha_{1,3}$ in M-dominant strains.[20] The presence of 4-amino,4,6 dideoxymannose in the LPS is also responsible for the antigenic cross-reactions with certain other gram-negative bacteria, such as *Vibrio cholerae* O1 and *Yersinia enterocolitica* O9. Numerous protein antigens have also been characterized, some of which may be important in inducing protective immunity.

EPIDEMIOLOGY

Brucellosis is a zoonosis, and virtually all infections derive directly or indirectly from exposure to animals.[21] The disease exists worldwide, especially in the Mediterranean basin, the Arabian peninsula, the Indian subcontinent, and in parts of Mexico and Central and South America. *B. abortus* is found principally in cattle, but other species such as buffalo, camels, and yaks can be of local importance. *B. melitensis* occurs primarily in goats and sheep, although camels appear to be an important source in some countries. In recent years, *B. melitensis* infection has been reported in cattle herds in Israel, presumably because of the practice of feeding cows whey from sheep milk. Such atypical infections, occurring in an area where *B. abortus* has been eliminated, only came to light when humans attending the cattle became infected.[22] *B. suis* biovars 1–3 occur in domestic and feral swine and can be a cause of abattoir-associated human disease.[23] In some South American countries, *B. suis* biovar 1 has also become established in cattle, providing another source of human infection.[24] *B. suis* biovar 4 is confined to reindeer and caribou or their predators in the subarctic tundra. *B. canis* is found primarily in kennel-raised dogs; it is the least common cause of human brucellosis, and most infections have been acquired in the laboratory.[25]

In animals, brucellosis is a chronic infection that persists for life. Localization of brucellae within the reproductive organs accounts for the major manifestations: abortion and sterility.[26] Brucellae are shed in large numbers in the milk, urine, and cyetic products of infected animals. Consequently, brucellosis has been an occupational risk for farmers, veterinarians, abattoir workers, and laboratory personnel.[27] Routes of transmission to humans include direct contact with animals or their secretions through cuts and abrasions in the skin, by way of infected aerosols inhaled or inoculated into the conjunctival sac of the eyes, or via the ingestion of unpasteurized dairy products.[28]

Meat products are rarely the source of infection because they are not usually eaten raw and the numbers of organisms in muscle tissue are low.[29] Traditional "delicacies" such as blood[30] and bone marrow[31] have also been implicated as vehicles of transmission in some cultures. Human-to-human transmission is unusual; however, rare cases in which sexual transmission is suspected have been reported,[32] and brucellae have been recovered from banked human spermatozoa.[33] At least one case of presumed intrauterine transmission has recently been reported.[34] Although persons infected with the human immunodeficiency virus are at risk for a number of zoonoses,[35] very few cases of brucellosis have been reported in such patients.[36] In acquired immunodeficiency syndrome patients whose CD4 counts are not severely depressed, the course of brucellosis is not different from the disease in immunocompetent subjects.[37, 38]

Brucellosis is not rare in children as was once believed, especially in areas where *B. melitensis* is enzootic.[39] The manifestations of brucellosis are similar in neonates, children, and adults. It is not uncommon to observe outbreaks of the disease within families, especially when a common food source is involved.[40, 41]

The role of wildlife in the epidemiology of brucellosis remains controversial. Wild hares in Europe are reservoirs for *B. suis* biovar 2 and can sporadically transmit the disease to domestic or feral swine. Many bison in Yellowstone National Park are infected with *B. abortus*, but the risk to cattle sharing common grazing land is speculative.[42]

Although once common in the United States, the eradication or control of bovine brucellosis has reduced the incidence of human infection to less than 0.5 cases per 100,000 population (Fig. 215–1). In states bordering Mexico, such as Texas and California, the epidemiology of brucellosis has changed from a disease associated with exposure to cattle to one linked to ingestion of unpasteurized goat milk products imported from Mexico.[43, 44]

PATHOGENESIS

It is generally considered that *B. melitensis* and *B. suis* are more virulent than *B. abortus* or *B. canis*. Nevertheless, infection with any

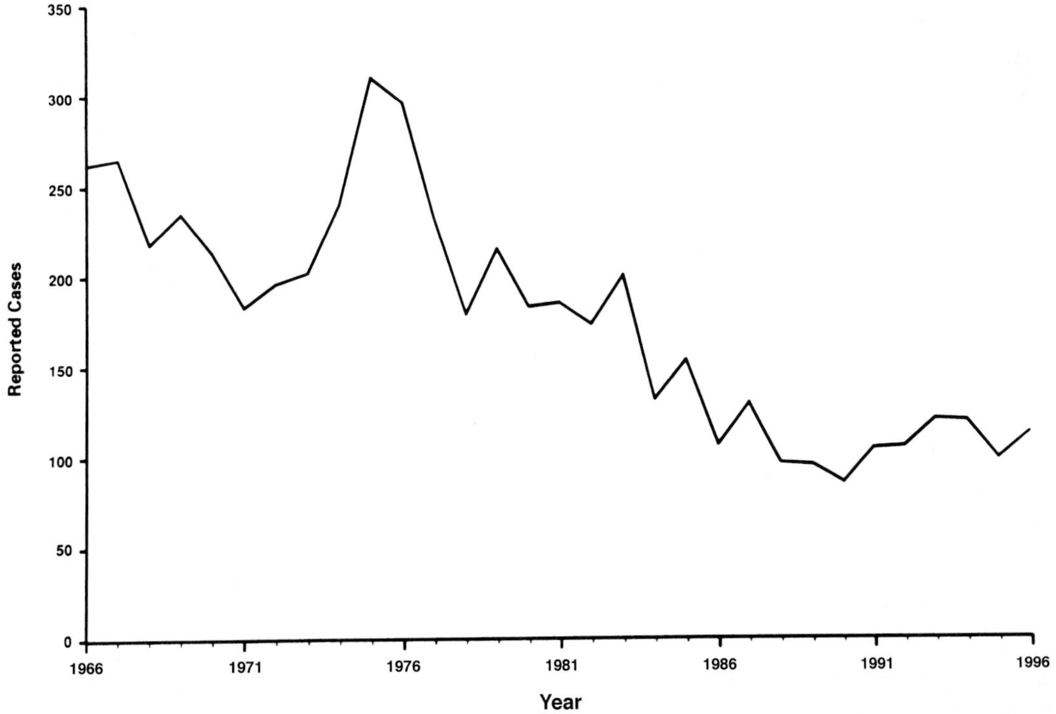

FIGURE 215–1. Cases of human brucellosis reported annually (1966–1996) to the Centers for Disease Control and Prevention. After peaking at more than 300 cases in 1975, the number of brucellosis cases has declined and, for the last 10 years, has remained relatively stable at approximately 100 cases per year. (From Centers for Disease Control and Prevention. Summary of notifiable diseases, United States, 1996. MMWR Morb Mortal Wkly Rep. 1996; 45:26.)

nomen species, including attenuated vaccine strains, can result in serious human illness. The nutritional and immune status of the host, as well as the size of the infectious inoculum and possibly the route of transmission can be determinants of disease. For example, the low pH of gastric juices appears to be more effective in preventing infection with *B. abortus* than with *B. melitensis* when they are administered by the oral route.[45] Consequently, antacids and other drugs that decrease gastric acidity have been implicated in foodborne brucellosis.[46, 47]

Once brucellae gain entry to the body, polymorphonuclear leukocytes are attracted to the site of inoculation by chemotaxis. Normal human serum has limited bactericidal activity against brucellae, but it effectively opsonizes the bacteria for phagocytosis by polymorphonuclear leukocytes.[48] The brucellae are facultative intracellular pathogens that have the capacity to survive and even multiply within phagocytic cells of the host. The mechanisms by which brucellae evade intracellular killing by polymorphonuclear leukocytes is incompletely understood; however, properties of the bacteria appear to enable it to escape detection.[49] Factors believed to contribute to intracellular survival include the production of adenine and guanine monophosphate, which suppresses the myeloperoxide-H_2O_2-halide system,[50] and a Cu-Zn superoxide dismutase, which eliminates reactive oxygen intermediates.[51]

Spink compared brucellosis with typhoid fever in that bacteria enter the lymphatics and replicate within regional lymph nodes. Hematogenous dissemination is then followed by localization of bacteria within organs rich in elements of the reticuloendothelial system, such as liver, spleen, and bone marrow.[52] Reticuloendothelial system localization also explains many of the clinical complications of brucellosis involving these organs. Brucellae ingested by mononuclear phagocytes also survive and replicate initially. Intracellular survival within macrophages is facilitated by the inhibition of phagosome-lysosome fusion by soluble products of brucellae[53] and the production of a number of stress-induced proteins.[54] The eventual elimination of virulent brucellae depends on the activation of macrophages through the development of Th 1–type cell-mediated immunity.[55] Cytokines that appear to contribute to the antibrucella activity of activated macrophages include TNF-α or TNF-γ, or both, as well as IL-1 and IL-12.[56]

The major determinant of virulence and the immunodominant antigen of the brucellae is S-LPS. Nonsmooth strains have reduced virulence and are more susceptible to lysis by normal serum from a variety of potential host species.[57] Naturally rough species (*B. canis* and *B. ovis*) have a greatly restricted host range and a limited capacity to infect other species.[10] Growth of *B. abortus* in placental tissues of cattle is apparently enhanced by the presence of erythritol, which may explain the localization of brucellae in the genital tract of ungulates.[58]

HOST IMMUNITY

Genetic studies in various animals have shown that resistance to intracellular pathogens is polygenic; however, single genes are recognized to have a major effect on immune-mediated resistance.[59] Selected breeding of cattle has yielded evidence for the genetic determination of resistance to bovine brucellosis. Moreover, the data suggest that resistance is reflected in immunoglobulin allotypes and in differences in the ability of macrophages to control the replication of *B. abortus* in vitro.[60]

S-LPS is the major determinant of virulence of the brucellae and dominates the antibody response. Humoral antibodies to S-LPS confer short-term protection as shown by passive transfer experiments using monoclonal and polyclonal antibodies.[61] Antibodies to S-LPS are also used for diagnosis when bacterial isolation is unsuccessful. A variety of serologic tests have been used to measure antibodies to *Brucella*, the earliest of which was the serum agglutination test (SAT) devised by Wright and Smith in 1897.[62] The SAT measures the total quantity of agglutinating antibodies but does not distinguish between immunoglobulin isotypes. Reddin and colleagues modified the SAT by adding 2-mercaptoethanol to differentiate agglutination by IgG antibodies and showed that their presence correlated well with active infection.[63] The combination of SAT and 2-mercaptoethanol test results has been shown to be a useful method to monitor the course of brucellosis and responses to therapy.[64, 65] The application of the enzyme-linked immunosorbent assay has made it possible to measure the immune response in brucellosis more accurately. It was shown that IgM antibodies appear within the first week of infection and are followed by a switch to IgG synthesis after the second week.[66] In time, titers of IgM antibodies decline, and with treatment, titers of IgG antibodies also fall consistent with recovery. A failure of the IgG titer to decline is prognostic of relapse or chronic infection.[67, 68]

Serologic tests employing S-LPS can detect antibodies to the principal nomen species owing to common epitopes; however, infection with *B. canis*, a naturally rough species, requires monospecific antigen.[69] Currently, there is interest in cytoplasmic protein antigens present in both smooth and rough strains that could be used for diagnostic purposes.[70, 71]

CLINICAL MANIFESTATIONS

The symptoms of brucellosis are nonspecific (e.g., fever, sweats, malaise, anorexia, headache, back pain). The onset can be acute or insidious, generally beginning within 2 to 4 weeks after inoculation.[27] An "undulant" fever pattern is observed if patients go untreated for long periods. Some patients complain of malodorous sweat and a peculiar taste in the mouth. Depression is common and is often out of proportion to the severity of other symptoms. In comparison to the plethora of somatic complaints, physical abnormalities may be few. Mild lymphadenopathy is reported in 10 to 20% and splenomegaly or hepatomegaly in 20 to 30% of cases.[72]

Brucellosis is a systemic infection in which any organ or system of the body can be involved. Attempts to categorize the disease into acute, subacute, and chronic, according to the length and severity of symptoms, are purely arbitrary.[73] When involvement of a specific organ predominates, the disease is often referred to as "focal" or localized. However, there is little compelling evidence that such complications necessarily represent a distinct subset of patients. Nevertheless, when the central nervous system or the heart is involved, such cases are more difficult to treat and the outcome can be affected.

A problem in interpreting the literature on brucellosis is differentiating acute and chronic forms of the disease. Because it is necessary to treat patients for prolonged periods, relapses are not uncommon, especially if therapy is discontinued prematurely. Most relapses occur within 3 to 6 months of discontinuing therapy.[74, 75] Relapse is not usually caused by antibiotic resistance because strains of brucellae isolated during relapse have antimicrobial sensitivity patterns identical to the original infecting strains.[76] When the infection persists for more than 12 months, the disease is generally considered "chronic"; however, this definition is also arbitrary.[77] Chronic brucellosis is usually caused by persisting deep foci of infection, such as suppurative lesions in the bone, joints, liver, spleen, or kidneys.[78, 79] In contrast, some patients experience a delayed convalescence after treatment, with persisting nonspecific complaints of ill health, most notably fatigue. Such disease is distinguished from true chronic brucellosis by the absence of objective signs of disease, such as fever. In addition, chronic brucellosis is characterized by persistently high titers of IgG antibodies in the serum,[67, 68] whereas patients with delayed convalescence have absent or only low titers of antibodies.[65] The cause of delayed convalescence is poorly understood, but some authorities believe that it may represent a preexisting psychoneurosis exacerbated by the infection.[80]

Regardless, such patients present a dilemma because their complaints resemble brucellosis, but further antimicrobial therapy is ineffective and they often cling to the belief that they suffer from incurable brucellosis.[81]

COMPLICATIONS

Gastrointestinal Tract

Alimentary tract complications are elicited in up to 70% of patients with brucellosis.[82] Symptoms include anorexia, abdominal pain, nausea, vomiting, diarrhea, or constipation.[83] Pathologic lesions include hyperemia of the intestinal mucosa with inflammation of Peyer's patches.[84] Acute ileitis has been documented radiographically and histologically in patients presenting with colitis caused by *B. melitensis*.[85–87]

Hepatobiliary System

Because the liver is the largest organ of the reticuloendothelial system, it is probably always involved in brucellosis. However, liver function tests are usually only slightly elevated. The spectrum of pathologic findings in *Brucella* hepatitis is varied.[88] Infection with *B. abortus* is characterized by granulomas that are indistinguishable from sarcoidosis.[89] In contrast, infection with *B. melitensis* produces lesions ranging from small, almost insignificant, aggregates of mononuclear cells surrounding foci of necrosis scattered throughout the parenchyma to a diffuse nonspecific inflammation resembling viral hepatitis.[90] Occasionally one finds collections of mononuclear cells forming loose granulomas.[88] Suppurative abscesses of the liver and spleen are more common with infection caused by *B. suis*[91]; however, on occasion, abscesses are caused by *B. melitensis* as well.[92] Hepatic lesions resolve with antimicrobial therapy, and in the absence of other causes (e.g., hepatitis C or alcohol abuse), cirrhosis does not occur despite the severity of the inflammation.[93] *Brucella* is also a rare cause of acute cholecystitis,[94] pancreatitis,[95] and spontaneous bacterial peritonitis.[96]

Skeletal System

Osteoarticular complications are common in brucellosis, having been reported in 20 to 60% of cases.[97] The spectrum of bone and joint lesions includes arthritis, spondylitis, osteomyelitis, tenosynovitis, and bursitis.[98] Sacroiliitis is the most commonly reported complication.[99, 100] Large weight-bearing joints (e.g., hips, knees, ankles) are involved more often than are small joints. Analysis of synovial fluid from brucella joint effusions reveals a predominance of mononuclear cells, and brucellae are recovered in about one half of cases.[73, 100] A reactive postinfectious spondyloarthropathy that may be caused by circulating immune complexes has been described in some patients; however, no association was found with a specific HLA phenotype.[101] Spondylitis predominantly involving the lumbar spine is more common among elderly patients and on rare occasions can be associated with paraspinal abscesses.[102]

Radiographic abnormalities are generally late findings, whereas bone scans may detect inflammation early in the disease.[103] Bone scans are especially useful in differentiating sacroiliitis from hip joint involvement.[98] In cases of spondylitis, the earliest radiographic findings are straightening of the spine and narrowing of the disk space.[104] Computed tomography is especially useful for detecting joint destruction, vertebral osteomyelitis, and paraspinal abscess.[105]

Nervous System

Although depression and mental inattention are common complaints in brucellosis, direct invasion of the central nervous system (CNS) occurs in less than 5% of cases.[106] Nervous system complications include meningitis,[107] encephalitis,[108] myelitis-radiculoneuronitis,[109] brain abscess,[110] epidural abscess,[111] demyelinating syndromes,[112] and meningovascular syndromes.[113] Meningitis (acute or chronic) is the most frequent central nervous system complication, and it can be the presenting finding or it can occur late in the course of the disease. There is little to distinguish it from other causes of meningitis, except that nuchal rigidity occurs in less than 50% of cases.[114] Cerebrospinal fluid analysis reveals a lymphocytic pleocytosis, elevated protein content, and low to normal glucose levels. Gram stains are usually negative and cultures are positive in less than one quarter of the cases; however, the diagnosis is made by finding specific antibodies in the cerebrospinal fluid.[115] Histologic findings include inflammation of the leptomeninges, adhesive arachnoiditis, vasculitis, and leukoencephalitis.[88]

Cardiovascular System

Endocarditis occurs in less than 2% of cases, but it accounts for the majority of brucellosis-related deaths.[116] Before effective therapy, including valve replacement surgery, *Brucella* endocarditis was nearly always fatal.[117] The aortic valve is affected more often than the mitral valve. Both native valve and prosthetic valve infections have been reported.[118] Mycotic aneurysms of the brain, aorta, and other vessels are secondary complications, especially in *B. suis* infections.[119] Rapid techniques to recover brucellae from blood combined with echocardiography have improved the ability to make the diagnosis.[120] Although some patients have been treated with antibiotics alone, combined medical and surgical treatment is usually required for cure.[121] Pericarditis can be a complication of endocarditis, or it can occur as the primary infection.[122]

Respiratory System

Airborne transmission of brucellosis is especially common in abattoirs.[123] Respiratory tract involvement ranges from flulike symptoms with normal chest radiograph results to bronchitis, bronchopneumonia, lung nodules, abscesses, miliary lesions, hilar adenopathy, and pleural effusions.[124–128] Rarely are brucellae identified by stain or culture of expectorated sputum.

Genitourinary Tract

Although brucellae have been recovered from the urine of patients with brucellosis, renal involvement appears to be uncommon. Interstitial nephritis, pyelonephritis, exudative glomerulonephritis, and IgA nephropathy have been reported.[129, 130] Orchitis occurs in up to 20% of men with brucellosis. The testes or epididymis is infiltrated with lymphocytes and plasma cells, and there is atrophy of the seminiferous tubules.[72, 88, 131] In women, rare cases of salpingitis, cervicitis, and pelvic abscess have been reported.

The principal manifestation of brucellosis in animals is spontaneous abortion, and the presence of erythritol in the tissues of susceptible animals is thought to play a role in the localization of brucellae in the genital tract. Brucellosis can also result in human abortions; however, it is unclear whether it is more frequent than with other bacteremic infections.[132, 133]

Hematologic Complications

The hematologic manifestations of brucellosis include anemia, leukopenia, thrombocytopenia, and clotting disorders.[134] Granulomas are found in the bone marrow in up to 75% of cases, but they are small and indistinct.[88] Severe thrombocytopenia with cutaneous purpura has been reported and may be associated with antiplatelet antibodies or hematophagocytic histiocytes in the marrow.[135, 136]

Cutaneous Complications

Cutaneous lesions occur in about 5% of patients with brucellosis. Many transient, nonspecific lesions are described, including rashes, papules, ulcers, erythema nodosum, petechiae, purpura, and vasculitis.[137]

Ocular Complications

A variety of ocular complications have been reported in patients with brucellosis.[138] Uveitis is generally a late manifestation consisting variably of a chronic iridocyclitis, nummular keratitis, multifocal choroiditis, and optic neuritis.[139, 140] *Brucella* uveitis is considered a noninfectious immune response that responds to topical and systemic corticosteroid therapy. Rare cases of endogenous endophthalmitis have been reported in which brucellae have been isolated from vitreous humor.[141]

DIAGNOSIS

The symptoms of brucellosis are nonspecific; therefore, it is important to obtain a detailed history that includes occupation, exposure to animals, travel to enzootic areas, and ingestion of high-risk foods (e.g., unpasteurized dairy products). The white blood cell count is often normal or low and may not suggest an infectious process. Anemia, leukopenia, and thrombocytopenia are common findings.[134] The erythrocyte sedimentation rate is variable and of little diagnostic value.[142] The diagnosis of brucellosis is made with certainty when brucellae are recovered from blood, bone marrow, or other tissues. The rate of isolation from blood ranges from 15 to 70% depending on the methods used and the period of incubation. When brucellosis is suspected, the laboratory should be alerted to maintain cultures for a minimum of 4 weeks. Cultures of bone marrow have a higher yield than blood.[143] Most laboratories now employ rapid isolation techniques (e.g., BACTEC, Dupont Isolator, and so on), which are satisfactory for recovering brucellae.[144] A faster isolation time has been reported for the lysis concentration method.[145] Preliminary studies using the polymerase chain reaction with random or selected primers have been promising, but they require additional evaluation.[146] A presumptive identification of *Brucella* spp. can be made on the basis of morphologic, cultural, and serologic properties; however, confirmation requires oxidative metabolism, phage-typing, or genotyping procedures. The results of rapid bacterial identification systems should be interpreted with caution because some *Brucella* isolates have been misidentified as *Moraxella phenylpyruvica*.[147]

In the absence of bacteriologic confirmation, a presumptive diagnosis can be made on the basis of high or rising titers of specific antibodies.[65] A variety of serologic tests have been applied to brucellosis, of which the SAT is the most widely used. No single titer of *Brucella* antibodies is always "diagnostic"; however, most cases of active infection have titers higher than 1:160. The Rose Bengal test is a rapid screening method; however, positive sera should always be confirmed by SAT. The "febrile agglutinin" tests are insensitive and should not be relied on for diagnosis.[148] False-negative reactions in the SAT can result from a prozone phenomenon, whereas false-positive reactions occasionally result from cross-reactions with antibodies to *Yersinia,* cholera, or tularemia. False-negative and false-positive reactions can be avoided by routinely diluting the serum beyond 1:320. Very rarely, the presence of so-called blocking antibodies yields a negative reaction; however, blocking substances can be identified by the Coombs test or a blocking assay.[149] When agglutination tests are equivocal, the *Brucella* enzyme-linked immunosorbent assay can be definitive.[150]

TREATMENT

Antimicrobial therapy of brucellosis relieves symptoms, shortens the duration of illness, and reduces the incidence of complications, some of which can be life-threatening. A variety of agents have activity against brucellae[151]; however, the results of in vitro susceptibility tests do not always predict clinical efficacy. For example, the β-lactam antibiotics are active in vitro, yet they are often clinically ineffective. It is believed that the intracellular localization of brucellae offers some protection against antimicrobials, and drugs with good intracellular penetration are necessary for a cure.[152]

The tetracyclines are among the most active drugs for treating brucellosis; however, the rate of relapse with single-drug therapy is unacceptably high and combinations of agents are generally recommended. Many studies have shown that the combination of tetracycline (500 mg four times daily by mouth) administered for 6 weeks in combination with streptomycin (1 g/day intramuscularly) for the first 3 weeks is the most effective treatment.[153] Since doxycycline is equally active, can be given less frequently (200 mg/day), and has fewer gastrointestinal side effects, it has become the tetracycline analogue of choice. In 1986, the World Health Organization recommended the use of doxycycline (200 mg/day) in combination with rifampin (600 to 900 mg/day orally), both administered for 6 weeks, as the combination of choice.[154] Subsequent studies comparing doxycycline and rifampin with doxycycline and streptomycin concluded that the latter treatment is more efficacious, especially for patients with complications such as spondylitis.[155, 156] Nevertheless, rifampin has been reported to be effective for treating brucellosis during pregnancy.[157] Further support for the inclusion of an aminoglycoside in the treatment regimen comes from studies suggesting a synergistic effect with other agents in vitro[158] and in clinical use.[150, 159] Although most studies have employed streptomycin as the preferred aminoglycoside, there are compelling reasons to use gentamicin instead. Gentamicin is more active in vitro, less toxic, and can be given as a single daily dose. However, the optimal schedule for gentamicin use has yet to be determined, and studies comparing the two agents are needed.

Although there was initial enthusiasm for trimethoprim-sulfamethoxazole in the treatment of brucellosis, subsequent comparative studies revealed an unacceptably high rate of relapse.[160] Nevertheless, trimethoprim-sulfamethoxazole in combination with an aminoglycoside has been reported to be successful in treating children younger than 8 years of age, a setting in which tetracyclines are contraindicated owing to their potential for staining teeth.[161]

Similarly, the use of quinolone antibiotics has been disappointing despite in vitro activity and good penetration into cells.[162] Consequently, quinolones are best reserved as adjunctive agents.[151, 163]

The treatment of complications of brucellosis such as meningitis and endocarditis pose special problems, and there is no unanimity of opinion regarding the optimal regimen. Nevertheless, most authorities recommend the use of doxycycline in combination with two or more other drugs, with treatment continued for many months depending on the response. Doxycycline crosses the blood-brain barrier better than generic tetracycline, and it has been used successfully with trimethoprim-sulfamethoxazole and rifampin for *Brucella* meningitis[113] and endocarditis.[117] Third-generation cephalosporins also achieve high concentrations in cerebrospinal fluid, but susceptibility of *Brucella* spp. is variable, and in vitro sensitivity should be ensured.[164] Although cases of *Brucella* endocarditis have been cured with antibiotics alone, most cases require a combined medical-surgical approach.[121] Corticosteroids are often recommended for neurobrucellosis; however, in the absence of controlled studies, their efficacy is unproved.[113]

PREVENTION

The prevention of human brucellosis depends on the control and elimination of the disease in domestic animals. In the United States, the state-federal bovine brucellosis eradication program certifies disease-free herds by serologic testing and elimination of reactor cattle.[165] Effective attenuated live bacterial vaccines exist for *B. abortus* (strain 19) and *B. melitensis* (strain Rev-1), but as yet there are no vaccines for *B. suis* or *B. canis*. On rare occasions, accidents with strain 19 and Rev-1 have caused human brucellosis.[166] *B. abortus* strain RB51, a stable rough mutant, has largely replaced strain 19 as the preferred bovine vaccine in the United States. Strain RB51 has the advantage of protecting cattle without inducing an antibody response.[167] In addition, RB51 appears to lack virulence for humans, and despite accidents no proven cases of human RB51 infection are known.[168] As yet, no safe effective vaccine has been developed to immunize humans against brucellosis.[169] The need for such a vaccine becomes evident when one considers the potential use of *Brucella* spp. as agents of biologic warfare.[170]

REFERENCES

1. Simpson WM. Tice's Practice of Medicine. Hagerstown, Md: WF Prior; 1940.
2. Marston JA. Report on fever (Malta). Great Br Army Med Dept Rep. 1861;3:520–521.
3. Bruce D. Notes on the recovery of a microorganism in Malta fever. Practitioner. 1887;39:161.
4. Williams E. The Mediterranean Fever Commission: Its origin and achievements. In: Young EJ, Corbel MJ, eds. Brucellosis: Clinical and Laboratory Aspects. Boca Raton, Fla: CRC Press; 1989:11–23.
5. Bang B. Die Aetiologie des seuchenhaften (infectiosen). Verwerfens z Thiermed Jena. 1897;1:241–278.
6. Carmichael LE. Contagious abortion in Beagles. Hounds Hunting. 1967;64:14–18.
7. Ross HM, Jahans KL, MacMillan AP, et al. *Brucella* species infection in North Sea seal and cetacean populations. Vet Record. 1996;138:647–648.
8. Ewalt DR, Payeur JB, Martin BM, et al. Characteristics of a *Brucella* species from a bottlenose dolphin (*Tursiops truncatus*). J Vet Diagn Invest. 1994;6:448–452.
9. Jahans KL, Foster G, Broughton ES. The characteristics of *Brucella* strains isolated from marine mammals. Vet Microbiol. 1997;57:373–382.
10. Corbel MJ. Microbiology of the genus *Brucella*. In: Young EJ, Corbel MJ, eds. Brucellosis: Clinical and Laboratory Aspects. Boca Raton, Fla: CRC Press; 1989:53–72.
11. Moreira-Jacob M. Studies on methods and techniques for the classification of the bacterial genus *Brucella*. International Symposium on Brucellosis, Tunis, 1968. Symp Series Immunobiol Stand. 1970;12:167–180.
12. Corbel MJ. Brucella-phages: Advances in the development of a reliable phage typing system for smooth and nonsmooth *Brucella* isolates. Ann Inst Pasteur Microbiol. 1987;138:70–73.
13. Michaux-Charachon S, Bourg G, Jumas-Bilak E, et al. Genome structure and phylogeny in the genus *Brucella*. J Bacteriol. 1997;179:3244–3249.
14. Allardet-Servent A, Bourg G, Ramuz M, et al. DNA polymorphism in strains of the genus *Brucella*. J Bacteriol. 1988;170:4603–4607.
15. Ficht TA, Bearden SW, Sowa BA, et al. DNA sequences and expression of the 36-kilodalton outer membrane protein gene of *Brucella abortus*. Infect Immun. 1989;57:3281–3291.
16. Moreno E, Stackebrandt E, Dorsch M, et al. *Brucella abortus* 16s rRNA and lipid A reveal a phylogenetic relationship with members of the alpha-2 subdivision of the class *Proteobacter*. J Bacteriol. 1990;172:3569–3576.
17. Cloeckaert A, Verger J-M, Grayon M, et al. Molecular and immunological characterization of the major outer membrane proteins of *Brucella*. FEMS Microbiol Lett. 1996;145:1–8.
18. Jumas-Bilak E, Michaux-Charachon, Bourg G, et al. Differences in chromosome number and genome rearrangements in the genus *Brucella*. Mol Microbiol. 1998;27:99–106.
19. Rigby CE, Fraser AD. Plasmid transfer and plasmid-mediated genetic exchange in *Brucella abortus*. Can J Vet Res. 1989;53:326–330.
20. Perry MB, Bundle DR. Lipopolysaccharide antigens and carbohydrates of *Brucella*. In: Adams LG, ed. Advances in Brucellosis Research. Austin, Tex: Texas A&M University Press; 1990:76–80.
21. Corbel MJ. Brucellosis: Epidemiology and prevalence worldwide. In: Young EJ, Corbel MJ, eds. Brucellosis: Clinical and Laboratory Aspects. Boca Raton, Fla: CRC Press; 1989:25–40.
22. Shimshony A. Epidemiology of emerging zoonoses in Israel. Emerging Infect Dis. 1997;3:229–238.
23. Buchanan TM, Hendricks SL, Patton CM, et al. Brucellosis in the United States, 1960–1972. An abattoir-associated disease. Part III. Epidemiology and evidence for acquired immunity. Medicine. 1974;53:427–439.
24. Garcia Carrillo C. Animal and human brucellosis in the Americas. Paris: International Office of Epizootics; 1990:287.
25. Rumley RL, Chapman SW. *Brucella canis*: An infectious cause of prolonged fever of undetermined origin. South Med J. 1986;79:626–628.
26. Enright FM. The pathogenesis and pathobiology of *Brucella* infection in domestic animals. In: Nielson K, Duncan JR, eds. Animal Brucellosis. Boca Raton, Fla: CRC Press; 1990:301–320.
27. Young EJ. Human brucellosis. Rev Infect Dis. 1983;5:321–342.
28. Young EJ, Suvannoparrat U. Brucellosis outbreak attributed to ingestion of unpasteurized goat cheese. Arch Intern Med. 1975;135:240–243.
29. Sadler WW. Present evidence on the role of meat in the epidemiology of human brucellosis. Am J Public Health. 1960;50:540–544.
30. Syrjamaki C, Migliazza A, Yarborough JW, et al. *Brucella abortus* endocarditis following ingestion of cow's blood. Nebr Med J. 1984;69:141–143.
31. Chan J, Baxter C, Wenman WM. Brucellosis in an Inuit child probably related to caribou meat consumption. Scand J Infect Dis. 1989;21:337–338.
32. Rubin B, Band JD, Wong P, et al. Person-to-person transmission of *Brucella melitensis*. Lancet. 1991;1:14–15.
33. Vandercam B, Zech F, deCooman S, et al. Isolation of *Brucella melitensis* from human sperm. Eur J Clin Microbiol Infect Dis. 1990;9:303–304.
34. Barnett B. Brucellosis: Congenital transmission in Galveston. Disease Prevention News. Texas Department of Health. 1996;56:1–2.
35. Glaser CA, Angulo FJ, Rooney JA. Animal-associated opportunistic infections among persons infected with the human immunodeficiency virus. Clin Infect Dis. 1994;18:14–24.
36. Moreno S, Espinoza FJ, Podzamczer D, et al. Brucellosis and HIV-infection. Abstract No. 130 Interscience Confererence on Antimicrobial Agents and Chemotherapy. New Orleans, La: 1996;192.
37. Galle C, Struelens M, Liesnard C, et al. *Brucella melitensis* osteitis following craniotomy in a patient with AIDS. Clin Infect Dis. 1997;24:1012.
38. Pedro-Botet J, Coll J, Auguet T, et al. Brucellosis and HIV infection: A casual association? AIDS. 1992;6:1049–1051.
39. Al-Eissa Y, Al-Zamil F, Al-Mugeiren M, et al. Childhood brucellosis: A deceptive infectious disease. Scand J Infect Dis. 1991;23:129–133.
40. Lubani MM, Dudin KI, Sharda DC, et al. Neonatal brucellosis. Eur J Pediatr. 1988;147:520–522.
41. Hines PD, Overturf GD, Hatch D, et al. Brucellosis in a California family. Pediatr Infect Dis J. 1986;5:579–582.
42. Davis DS. Role of wildlife in transmission of brucellosis. In: Adams LG, ed. Advances in Brucellosis Research. College Station, Tex: Texas A&M University Press; 1990:373–385.
43. Taylor JP, Perdue JN. The changing epidemiology of human brucellosis in Texas, 1977–1986. Am J Epidemiol. 1989;130:160–165.
44. Chomel BB, DeBess EE, Mangiamele DM, et al. Changing trends in the epidemiology of human brucellosis in California from 1973 to 1992: A shift toward foodborne transmission. J Infect Dis. 1994;170:1216–1223.
45. Morales-Otero P. Further attempts in experimental infection of man with a bovine strain of *Brucella abortus*. J Infect Dis. 1933;52:54–59.
46. Steffen R. Antacids—a risk factor in travellers' brucellosis? Scand J Infect Dis. 1977;9:311.
47. Arnow PM, Smaron M, Ormiste V. Brucellosis in a group of travellers to Spain. JAMA. 1984;251:505–507.
48. Young EJ, Borchert M, Kretzer FL, et al. Phagocytosis and killing of *Brucella* by human polymorphonuclear leukocytes. J Infect Dis. 1985;151:682–690.
49. Riley LK, Robertson DC. Ingestion and intracellular survival of *Brucella abortus* in human and bovine polymorphonuclear leukocytes. Infect Immun. 1984;46:224–230.
50. Canning PC, Roth JA, Dayoe BL. Release of 5′-guanosine monophosphate and adenine by *Brucella abortus* and their role in the intracellular survival of the bacteria. J Infect Dis. 1986;154:464–470.
51. Bricker BJ, Tabatabai LB, Judge BA, et al. Cloning, expression, and occurrence of the *Brucella* Cu-Zn superoxide dismutase. Infect Immun. 1990;58:2935–2939.
52. Spink WW. The Nature of Brucellosis. Minneapolis, Minn: University of Minnesota Press; 1956.
53. Frenchick PJ, Markham RJF, Cochrane AH. Inhibition of phagosome-lysosome fusion in macrophages by soluble extracts of virulent *Brucella abortus*. Am J Vet Res. 1985;46:332–335.
54. Lin J, Ficht TA. Protein synthesis in *Brucella abortus* induced during macrophage infection. Infect Immun. 1995;63:1409–1414.
55. Corbel MJ. Recent advances in brucellosis. J Med Microbiol. 1997;6:101–103.
56. Jiang X, Baldwin CL. Effect of cytokines on intracellular growth of *Brucella abortus*. Infect Immun. 1993;61:124–134.
57. Nakamuira M, Katsumo M. On the correlation between the virulence of *Brucella abortus* and their growth in sera of several animals. Tohuku J Agric Res. 1974;25:77–81.
58. Keppie J, Williams AE, Witt K, et al. The role of erythritol in the tissue localisation of the *Brucellae*. Br J Exp Pathol. 1965;46:104–110.
59. Skamene E, Schurr E, Gres P. Infection genomics: Nramp1 as a major determinant of natural resistance to intracellular infection. Annu Rev Med. 1998;49:275–287.
60. Templeton JW, Adams LG. Natural resistance to bovine brucellosis. In: Adams LG, ed. Advances in Brucellosis Research. College Station, Tex: Texas A& M University Press; 1990:144–150.
61. Dubray G. Protective antigens in brucellosis. Ann Inst Pasteur Microbiol. 1987;138:84–87.
62. Wright AE, Smith F. On the application of the serum test to the differential diagnosis of typhoid fever and Malta fever. Lancet. 1897;1:656–659.
63. Reddin JL, Anderson RK, Jenness R, et al. Significance of 7S and macroglobulin brucella agglutinins in human brucellosis. N Engl J Med. 1965;272:1263–1268.
64. Buchanan TM, Faber LC. 2-Mercaptoethanol brucella agglutination test: Usefulness for predicting recovery from brucellosis. J Clin Microbiol. 1980;11:691–693.
65. Young EJ. Serologic diagnosis of human brucellosis: Analysis of 214 cases by agglutination tests and review of the literature. Rev Infect Dis. 1991;13:359–372.
66. Ariza J, Pellicer T, Pallares RN, et al. Specific antibody profile in human brucellosis. J Infect Dis. 1992;14:131–140.
67. Pellicer T, Ariza J, Foz A, et al. Specific antibodies detected during relapse of human brucellosis. J Infect Dis. 1988;157:918–924.
68. Gazapo E, Lahoz JG, Subiza JL, et al. Changes in IgM and IgG antibody concentrations in brucellosis over time: Importance for diagnosis and follow-up. J Infect Dis. 1989;159:219–225.
69. Polt SS, Schaefer J. A microagglutination test for human *Brucella canis* antibodies. Am J Clin Pathol. 1982;77:740–744.
70. Goldbaum FA, Leoni J, Wallach JC, et al. Characterization of an 18-kilodalton *Brucella* cytoplasmic protein which appears to be a serologic marker of active

infection of both human and bovine brucellosis. J Clin Microbiol. 1993;31:2141–2145.

71. Rossetti OL, Arese AI, Boschiroli ML, et al. Cloning of *Brucella abortus* gene and characterization of expressed 26-kilodalton periplasmic protein: Potential use for diagnosis. J Clin Microbiol. 1996;34:165–169.
72. Colmenero JD, Reguera JM, Martos F, et al. Complications associated with *Brucella melitensis* infection: A study of 530 cases. Medicine. 1996;75:195–211.
73. Young EJ. Brucellosis: Current epidemiology, diagnosis, and management. Curr Top Infect Dis. 1995;15:115–128.
74. Ariza J, Corredoira J, Pallares R, et al. Characteristics of and risk factors for relapse of brucellosis in humans. Clin Infect Dis. 1995;20:1241–1249.
75. Solera J, Martinez-Alfaro E, Espinoza A, et al. Multivariate model for predicting relapse in human brucellosis. J Infect Dis. 1998;36:85–92.
76. Ariza J, Bosch J, Gudiol F, et al. Relevance of in vitro antimicrobial susceptibility of *Brucella melitensis* to relapse rate in human brucellosis. Antimicrob Agents Chemother. 1986;30:958–960.
77. Spink WW. What is chronic brucellosis? Ann Intern Med. 1951;35:258–274.
78. Martin WJ, Nichols DR, Beahrs OH. Chronic localized brucellosis. Arch Intern Med. 1961;107:143–148.
79. Weed LA, Dahlin DC, Pugh DG, et al. Brucella in tissues removed at surgery. Am J Clin Pathol. 1952;22:10–21.
80. Imboden JB, Canter A, Cluff LE, et al. Brucellosis. III. Psychologic aspects of delayed convalescence. Arch Intern Med. 1959;103:404–414.
81. Cluff LE. Medical aspects of delayed convalescence. Rev Infect Dis. 1991;13(Suppl):138–140.
82. Al Aska AK. Gastrointestinal manifestations of brucellosis in Saudi Arabian patients. Trop Gastroenterol. 1989;10:217–219.
83. Mohamed AES, Ven D, Madkour MM, et al. Alimentary tract presentations of brucellosis. Ann Saudi Med. 1986;6:27–31.
84. Sharp NB. Pathology of undulant fever. Arch Pathol. 1934;18:72–108.
85. Petrella R, Young EJ. Acute brucella ileitis. Am J Gastroenterol. 1988;83:80–82.
86. Stermer E, Levy N, Potasam I, et al. Brucellosis as a cause of severe colitis. Am J Gastroenterol. 1991;86:917–919.
87. Jorens PG, Michielsen PP, Van den Ender EJ, et al. A rare cause of colitis—*Brucella melitensis*. Dis Colon Rectum. 1991;34:194–196.
88. Young EJ. Brucellosis. In: Connor DH, Chandler FW, Manz HJ, et al, eds. Pathology of Infectious Diseases. Stamford, Conn: Appleton & Lange; 1997:447–451.
89. Spink WW, Hoffbauer FW, Walker WW, et al. Histopathology of the liver in human brucellosis. J Lab Clin Med. 1949;34:40–58.
90. Young EJ. *Brucella melitensis* hepatitis: The absence of granulomas. Ann Intern Med. 1979;91:414–415.
91. Spink WW. Host-parasite relationship in human brucellosis with prolonged illness due to suppuration of the liver and spleen. Am J Med Sci. 1964;247:129–136.
92. Vallejo JG, Stevens AM, Dutton RV, et al. Hepatosplenic abscesses due to *Brucella melitensis:* Report of a case involving a child and review of the literature. Clin Infect Dis. 1996;22:485–489.
93. Talley NJ, Eckstein RP, Gattas MR, et al. Acute hepatitis and *Brucella melitensis* infection: Clinicopathological findings. Med J Aust. 1988;148:587–590.
94. Shaheen SEA, El-Taweel AZ, Al-Awadi NZ, et al. Acute calcular cholecystitis associated with *Brucella melitensis*. Am J Gastroenterol. 1989;84:336–337.
95. Odeh M, Oliven A. Acute pancreatitis associated with brucellosis. J Gastroenterol Hepatol. 1995;10:691–692.
96. Demirkan F, Akalin HE, Simsek H, et al. Spontaneous peritonitis due to *Brucella melitensis* in a patient with cirrhosis. Eur J Microbiol Infect Dis. 1993;12:66–67.
97. Rotes-Querol J. Osteo-articular sites of brucellosis. Ann Rheum Dis. 1957;16:63–68.
98. Mousa AR, Muhtaseb SA, Almudallal DS, et al. Osteoarticular complications of brucellosis: A study of 169 cases. Rev Infect Dis. 1987;9:531–543.
99. Gotuzzo E, Alarcon GS, Bocanegra TS, et al. Articular involvement in human brucellosis: A retrospective analysis of 304 cases. Sem Arthritis Rheum. 1982;12:245–255.
100. Khateeb MI, Araj GF, Majeed SA, et al. Brucella arthritis: A study of 96 cases in Kuwait. Ann Rheum Dis. 1990;49:994–998.
101. Alarcon GS, Gotuzzo E, Hinostroza SA, et al. HLA studies in brucellar spondylitis. Clin Rheum. 1985;4:312–314.
102. Mousa AM, Muhtaseb SA, Al-Mudallal DS, et al. Brucellar sternoclavicular arthritis, the forgotten complication. Ann Trop Med Parasitol. 1988;82:275–281.
103. Ariza J, Gudiol F, Valverde J, et al. Brucellar spondylitis: A detailed analysis based on current findings. Rev Infect Dis. 1985;7:656–664.
104. Madkour MM, Sharif HS, Abed MY, et al. Osteoarticular brucellosis: Results of bone scintigraphy in 140 patients. AJR. 1988;150:1101–1105.
105. Bahar RH, Al-Subaili AR, Mousa AM, et al. Brucellosis: Appearance on skeletal imaging. Clin Nucl Med. 1988;13:102–106.
106. Young EJ. Overview of brucellosis. Clin Infect Dis. 1995;21:283–289.
107. Mousa ARM, Koshy TS, Araj GF, et al. Brucella meningitis: Presentation, diagnosis and treatment—a prospective study of ten cases. Q J Med. 1986;60:873–885.
108. Weissenborn K, Wiehler ST, Malin J-P. Meningoenzephalitis durch Brucella-abortus-infektion. Dtsch Med Wochenschr. 1987;112:57–59.
109. Bahemuka M, Shemena AR, Panayiotopoulis CP, et al. Neurologic syndromes of brucellosis. J Neurol Neurosurg Psychiatry. 1988;51:1017–1021.
110. Guvenc H, Kocabay K, Okten A, et al. Brucellosis in a child complicated with multiple brain abscesses. Scand J Infect Dis. 1989;21:333–336.
111. Perez-Calvo J, Mutamala C, Sanjoaquin I, et al. Epidural abscess due to acute *Brucella melitensis* infection. Arch Intern Med. 1994;154:1410.
112. Shakir RA, Al-Din ASN, Araj GF, et al. Clinical categories of neurobrucellosis. Brain. 1987;110:213–223.
113. McLean DR, Russell N, Khan MY. Neurobrucellosis: Clinical and therapeutic features. Clin Infect Dis. 1992;15:582–590.
114. Bouza E, Garcia de la Torre M, Parra F, et al. Brucellar meningitis. Rev Infect Dis. 1987;9:810–822.
115. Sanchez-Sousa A, Torre C, Campello MG, et al. Serological diagnosis of neurobrucellosis. J Clin Pathol. 1990;43:79–81.
116. Al-Harthi SS. The morbidity and mortality patterns of *Brucella* endocarditis. Intern J Cardiol. 1989;25:321–324.
117. Jacobs F, Abramowicz D, Vereerstraeten P, et al. Brucella endocarditis: The role of combined medical and surgical treatment. Rev Infect Dis. 1990;12:740–744.
118. Fernandez-Guerrero ML. Zoonotic endocarditis. Infect Dis Clin North Am. 1993;7:135–152.
119. Fudge TL, Ochsner JL, Ancalmo N, et al. Surgical resection of multiple aortic aneurysms due to *Brucella suis*. Surgery. 1977;81:236–238.
120. Flugelman MY, Galun E, Ben-Chetrit E, et al. Brucellosis in patients with heart disease: When should endocarditis be diagnosed? Cardiology. 1990;77:313–317.
121. Al-Kasab S, Al-Fagih MR, Al-Yousef S, et al. Brucella infective endocarditis: Successful combined medical and surgical therapy. J Thorac Surg. 1988;95:862–870.
122. Gomez-Huelgas R, de Mora M, Parras JJ, et al. *Brucella* and acute pericarditis: Fortuitous or casual association? J Infect Dis. 1986;154:544.
123. Kaufmann AF, Fox MD, Boyce JM, et al. Airborne spread of brucellosis. Ann N Y Acad Sci. 1980;353:105–114.
124. Al-Jam'a AH, Elbashir AM, Al-Faris SS. *Brucella* pneumonia: A case report. Ann Saudi Med. 1993;13:74–77.
125. Patel PJ, Al-Suhaibami H, Al-Aska AK, et al. The chest radiograph in brucellosis. Clin Radiol. 1988;39:39–41.
126. Garcia-Rodriguez JA, Garcia-Sanchez JE, Bellido JLM, et al. Review of pulmonary brucellosis: A case report on brucellar pulmonary edema. Diagn Microbiol Infect Dis. 1989;11:53–60.
127. Rowen JL, Englund JA. Brucellosis presenting with cough. Pediatr Infect Dis J. 1995;14:721–722.
128. Papiris SA, Maniati MA, Haritou A, et al. *Brucella* haemorrhagic pleural effusion. Eur Respir J. 1994;7:1369–1370.
129. Odeh M, Oliven A. Acute brucellosis associated with massive proteinuria. Nephron. 1996;72:688–689.
130. Orte L, Teruel JL, Bellas C, et al. Nefropatia brucelosia: Descripcion de tres casos. Rev Clin Esp. 1979;152:461–464.
131. Ibrahim AIA, Awad R, Shetty SD, et al. Genito-urinary complications of brucellosis. Br J Urol. 1988;61:294–298.
132. Porreco RP, Haverkamp AD. Brucellosis in pregnancy. Obstet Gynecol. 1974;44:597–602.
133. Seoud M, Saade G, Awar G, et al. Brucellosis in pregnancy. J Reprod Med. 1991;36:441–445.
134. Crosby E, Llosa L, Quesada M, et al. Hematologic changes in brucellosis. J Infect Dis. 1984;150:419–424.
135. Janbon M, Bertrand L, Bertrand A, et al. Purpura thrombocytopenique au cours d'une brucellose aigue presence d'anticorps antiplaquettaires. Montpellier Med. 1964;64:73–78.
136. Ulloa V, Rojas J, Gotuzzo E. Purpura trombocitopenica asociada a Brucelosis. Rev Med Hered. 1992;3:87–93.
137. Ariza J, Servitje O, Pallares R, et al. Characteristic cutaneous lesions in patients with brucellosis. Arch Dermatol. 1989;125:380–383.
138. Madkour M. Brucellosis. Boston: Butterworth; 1989:185–188.
139. Walker J, Sharma OP, Rao NA. Brucellosis and uveitis. Am J Ophthalmol. 1992;114:374–375.
140. Elrazak MA. *Brucella* optic neuritis. Arch Intern Med. 1991;151:776–778.
141. Al Faran MF. *Brucella melitensis* endogenous endophthalmitis. Ophthalmologica. 1990;201:19–22.
142. Agnew S, Spink WW. The erythrocyte sedimentation rate in brucellosis. Am J Med Sci. 1949;217:211–215.
143. Gotuzzo E, Carrillo C, Guerra J, et al. An evaluation of diagnostic methods for brucellosis: The value of bone marrow cultures. J Infect Dis. 1986;153:122–125.
144. Yagupsky P, Peled N, Press J, et al. Comparison of BACTEC 9240 peds plus medium and isolator 1.5 microbial tube for detection of *Brucella melitensis* from blood cultures. J Clin Microbiol. 1997;35:1382–1384.
145. Kolman S, Maayan MC, Gotesman G, et al. Comparison of BACTEC and lysis concentration methods for recovering *Brucella* species from clinical specimens. Eur J Clin Microbiol Infect Dis. 1991;10:647–648.
146. Matar FM, Khreissir IA, Abdonoor AM. Rapid laboratory confirmation of human brucellosis by PCR analysis of a target sequence on the 31-kilodalton *Brucella* antigen DNA. J Clin Microbiol. 1996;34:477–478..
147. Barham WB, Church P, Brown JE, et al. Misidentification of *Brucella* species with use of rapid bacterial identification systems. Clin Infect Dis. 1993;17:1068–1069.
148. Zuerlein TJ, Smith PW. The diagnostic utility of the febrile agglutinin tests. JAMA. 1985;254:1211–1214.
149. McCullough NB. Immune response to *Brucella*. In: Rose NR, Friedman H, eds. Manual of Clinical Immunology. Washington, DC: American Society for Microbiology; 1976:304–311.
150. Ariza J. Brucellosis. Curr Opin Infect Dis. 1996;9:126–131.

151. Young EJ. Brucella species. In: Yu V, Merigan TC, Barriere SL, eds. Antimicrobial Therapy and Vaccines. Baltimore: Williams & Wilkins; 1999;71–89.
152. Hall WH. Modern chemotherapy for brucellosis in humans. Rev Infect Dis. 1990;12:1060–1099.
153. Acocella G, Bertrand A, Beytout J, et al. Comparison of three different regimens in the treatment of acute brucellosis: A multinational study. J Antimicrob Agents Chemother. 1989;23:433–439.
154. Joint FAO/WHO Expert Committee on Brucellosis (Sixth Report). Geneva: World Health Organization; 1986.
155. Ariza J, Gudiol F, Pallares R, et al. Treatment of human brucellosis with doxycycline plus rifampin or doxycycline plus streptomycin. Ann Intern Med. 1992;117:25–30.
156. Luzzi GA, Brindle R, Sockett PN, et al. Brucellosis: Imported and laboratory acquired cases, and an overview of treatment trials. Trans R Soc Trop Med Hyg. 1993;87:138–141.
157. Figueroa-Damian R, Rojas-Rodriguez L, Marcano-Tochon ES. Brucellosis in pregnancy: Course and perinatal results. Ginecol Obstet Mex. 1995;63:190–195.
158. Rubinstein E, Lang R, Shasha B, et al. In vitro susceptibility of *Brucella melitensis* to antibiotics. Antimicrob Agents Chemother. 1991;35:1925–1927.
159. Montejo JM, Alberola I, Gonzales-Zarate P, et al. Open, randomized therapeutic trial of six antimicrobial regimens in the treatment of human brucellosis. Clin Infect Dis. 1993;16:671–676.
160. Ariza J, Gudiol F, Pallares R, et al. Comparative trial of co-trimoxazole versus tetracycline-streptomycin in treating human brucellosis. J Infect Dis. 1985;152:1358–1359.
161. Lubani MM, Dudin KI, Sharda DC, et al. A multicenter therapeutic study of 1100 children with brucellosis. Pediatr Infect Dis J. 1989;8:75–78.
162. Lang R, Rubinstein E. Quinolones for the treatment of brucellosis. J Antimicrob Chemother. 1992;29:357–363.
163. Akova M, Uzun D, Akalin HE, et al. Quinolones in treatment of human brucellosis: Comparative trial of ofloxacin-rifampin versus doxycycline-rifampin. Antimicrob Agents Chemother. 1993;37:1831–1834.
164. Lang R, Dagan R, Potasman I, et al. Failure of ceftriaxone in the treatment of acute brucellosis. Clin Infect Dis. 1992;14:506–509.
165. Brown GM. The history of the brucellosis eradication program in the United States. Ann Sclavo. 1977;19:18–34.
166. Spink WW, Thompson H. Human brucellosis caused by *Brucella abortus* strain 19. JAMA. 1953;153:1162–1165.
167. Palmer MV, Cheville NF, Jensen AE. Experimental infection of pregnant cattle with the vaccine candidate *Brucella abortus* strain RB51: Pathologic, bacteriologic, and serologic findings. Vet Pathol. 1996;33:682–691.
168. Anonymous: Human exposure to *Brucella abortus* strain RB51—Kansas, 1997. Centers for Disease Control and Prevention, Atlanta, Ga. MMWR Morb Mortal Wkly Rep. 1998;47:172–175.
169. Corbel MJ. Brucellosis: An overview. Emerging Infect Dis. 1997;3:213–221.
170. Kaufmann AF, Meltzer MI, Schmid GP. The economic impact of bioterrorist attack: Are prevention and postattack intervention programs justifiable? Emerging Infect Dis. 1997;3:83–94.

Chapter 216

Francisella tularensis (Tularemia)

J. THOMAS CROSS, JR.
ROBERT L. PENN

Francisella tularensis is a gram-negative pathogen primarily of animals and occasionally of humans. The disease it causes is now recognized as tularemia in most parts of the world, but it has been called rabbit fever, deer-fly fever, and market men's disease in the United States; wild hare disease (yato-byo) and Ohara's disease in Japan; and water-rat trappers' disease in Russia.[1] Tularemia continues to be responsible for significant morbidity and mortality, despite the availability of numerous antibiotics active against the organism.[2–4]

F. tularensis infections have become a public health issue with rising concerns regarding military or terrorist uses of the organism in biological warfare. *F. tularensis* was incorporated as a weapon in the biological warfare program of the United States during the decades of the 1950s to 1960s.[5] The potential impact of this organism is demonstrated by a report from the Centers for Disease Control and Prevention (CDC): If 100,000 people were exposed to a "tularemic cloud," 82,500 cases (an 82.5% attack rate) with 6188 deaths (6.2% death rate) would be expected. The medical costs of tularemia from this bioterrorist attack would be between $456 million and $561.8 million.[6]

HISTORY

Tularemia has been so intimately linked to investigators in the United States that it has been referred to as an "American disease."[7] However, its history includes important contributions from many other areas of the world, including Japan and the former Soviet Union. Hare-associated illness compatible with tularemia has been known in Japan since 1818, and perhaps the earliest written description of a patient with unmistakable tularemia was provided by Homma-Soken in 1837.[2, 8]

Credit for identifying the organism and recognizing the important clinical syndromes belongs to American workers. While evaluating possible plague outbreaks after the San Francisco earthquake, McCoy[9] described in 1911 a plaguelike illness common in the California ground squirrel, and with Chapin in 1912 he successfully cultured the causative agent.[10, 11] They named it *Bacterium tularense* because this work took place in Tulare County, which "was once covered with extensive marshy beds of the reed tule, a large variety of bulrush."[12] The first human case to have bacteriologic confirmation was an ocular infection reported in 1914 by Vail[13] and by Wherry and Lamb.[14, 15] Wherry and Lamb also found the organism in wild rabbits near the home of another patient with proven conjunctival tularemia.[12, 15] Although the cause was unknown at the time, tularemia was transmitted by biting flies in Utah and was termed deer-fly fever.[16] Dr. Edward Francis, working for the U.S. Public Health Service, established the true cause of deer-fly fever as *B. tularense* (a full decade after the organism was discovered in squirrels), proved the deer fly was the vector, and named the human disease *tularemia* to emphasize the frequent accompanying bacteremia.[17, 18] Francis also contributed to work that improved methods for cultivating *B. tularense* and making a serologic diagnosis, identified tick and other reservoirs for its transmission, clarified the clinical syndromes associated with tularemia, and emphasized the risk to laboratory workers and consumers from infected sources.[12, 19, 20] For this lifetime of achievements, the genus for the organism was renamed *Francisella* in his honor.

In Japan, Ohara had described a rabbit-associated febrile disease, transmitted the illness to his wife by rubbing rabbit hearts over her hand, and recovered an organism from her lymph nodes; Francis later showed that this Japanese organism was identical to *B. tularense*.[19] Tularemia was recognized in Astrakhan, Russia, in 1926, and over the subsequent decades scattered serious outbreaks occurred throughout the country. Scientists in the former Soviet Union also have intensively studied the disease and its causative organism.[8]

DESCRIPTION OF THE PATHOGEN

Francisella are small, aerobic, catalase-positive, pleomorphic, gram-negative coccobacilli. They are more uniformly rod-shaped during logarithmic growth, when they tend to exhibit bipolar staining with Gram or Giemsa methods; this staining pattern accentuates a coccoidal appearance. The cell wall of *Francisella tularensis* is unusually high in fatty acids, and wild strains possess an electron-transparent lipid-rich capsule. Loss of the capsule may lead to loss of virulence, but not viability; however, the capsule is neither toxic nor immunogenic.[21]

Francisella spp. may be categorized on the basis of growth characteristics, biochemical reactions, and virulence properties (Table 216–1). *F. tularensis* biogroup *tularensis*, also referred to as type A, is found predominantly in North America and is the most virulent species. *F. tularensis* biogroup *palearctica*, also referred to as type

TABLE 216–1 Characterization of *Francisella* Species

Features	*F. tularensis* Biogroups			
	Tularensis	*Palearctica*	*Novicida*	*F. philomiragia*
Cysteine growth requirement	+	+	−	−
Growth in broth plus 6% NaCl	−	−	+*	+*
Motility	−	−	−	−
Oxidase	−	−	−	+†
Nitrate reduction	−	−	−	−
Acid from				
Glucose	+*	+*	+*	+*
Glycerol	+	−	+	NA‡
Gelatin hydrolysis	−	−	−	+*
Relative virulence				
Humans	High	Intermediate	Low	Low
Rabbits	High	Low	Low	NA‡

*Variable or delayed.
†Using Kovacs test; negative using cytochrome-oxidase test.
‡NA, not available.
Data from Eigelsbach and McGann,[21] Hollis et al.,[22] and Koneman et al.[28]

B, is found predominantly in Asia and Europe, but also in North America; it is less virulent in humans and of low virulence in rabbits. *F. tularensis* and *Francisella novicida* were previously classified as separate species but are now known to be different strains of the same species[22, 23]; *F. tularensis* biogroup *novicida* is of low virulence.

The taxonomy of *Francisella* has been complicated because biochemical reactions may be variable, weak, or delayed and also in part because of different terms given to organisms isolated in different parts of the world. Synonyms used by investigators in the former Soviet Union have included *F. tularensis nearctica* for *F. tularensis* biogroup *tularensis* and *F. tularensis holarctica* for *F. tularensis* biogroup *palearctica*. Strains isolated in central Asia have been designated *F. tularensis* subsp. *mediaasiatica*, and strains isolated in Japan have been designated *F. tularensis holarctica japonica*.[21, 24] A study of a small number of representative *Francisella* strains found that the traditional biochemical methods for differentiating between biogroups *tularensis* and *palearctica*, testing for fermentation of glycerol and glucose and the presence of citrulline ureidase activity, were imprecise; this was true despite the fact that *palearctica* strains had the expected low virulence for rabbits.[24] The few central Asian and Japanese strains tested also had low virulence in rabbits, but analysis of their 16S rRNA showed them to be genotypically related to *F. tularensis* biogroup *tularensis* and not biogroup *palearctica*.[24]

F. tularensis requires cysteine or cystine (or another sulfhydryl source) for growth, and therefore will not grow on most routine solid media. It may be recovered with the use of glucose cysteine blood agar, thioglycolate broth, chocolate agar suitable for gonococcal growth, modified Thayer-Martin medium, or buffered charcoal-yeast agar.[21, 25] Of concern is the recognition that some strains of *F. tularensis* lack an overt requirement for cysteine or enriched medium for growth, leading the microbiology laboratory to suspect *Haemophilus* species because of the growth of an aerobic, gram-negative coccobacillus. Cellular fatty acid composition analysis can be used to differentiate *Francisella* from other bacteria. Then, agglutination with commercially acquired antiserum can lead to the identification of the specific species.[26] Additionally, clinically significant strains of *Francisella* have been reported that do not show typical fastidious growth characteristics of previous strains.[27]

Visible colonies take 2 to 4 days to appear. Incubation at 35°C is optimal, and growth may be stimulated by an atmosphere of increased CO_2.[28] The recovery of *F. tularensis* from contaminated specimens may be facilitated by the addition of penicillin, cycloheximide, or polymyxin B to the media.[21, 25] Virtually all *F. tularensis* strains are positive for β-lactamase.[29]

Antisera can distinguish between *F. tularensis* biogroups *tularensis* and *novicida* but not between biogroups *tularensis* and *palearctica*; strains within biogroups do not have antigenic differences detectable by antisera. *F. tularensis* produces no known exotoxins. Whole radiation-killed organisms exhibit endotoxin-like activity in rabbits.[2] The lipopolysaccharide (LPS) from the live vaccine strain of *F. tularensis*, however, possesses at least 1000-fold less endotoxin activity than LPS from *Escherichia coli*.[30] Nonetheless, mice immunized with LPS purified from this strain are protected from subsequent intraperitoneal challenge with the vaccine strain.[31] Cowley, and associates[32] demonstrated that the live vaccine strain of *F. tularensis* is capable of phase variation that alters the ability of the organism to induce rat-macrophage nitric oxide (NO) production and, consequently, its growth in the rat macrophage. This phase variation is related to the expression of two forms of LPS: one induces NO production by rat macrophages and the other does not. These two LPS forms differ both antigenically (at the O-antigen level) and functionally (at the lipid A level). This antigenic shift of *F. tularensis* live vaccine strain LPS correlates with the observed change in the organism's ability to induce macrophage NO production and grow in the rat macrophage.

Host immune responses are directed against numerous cell wall antigens, including membrane proteins, LPS, and carbohydrates.[33, 34] Virulence has been associated with the capsule and citrulline ureidase activity. Wild encapsulated strains of *F. tularensis* are resistant to the bactericidal activity of normal serum, but a capsule-deficient mutant is serum sensitive.[33] The contribution of citrulline ureidase to virulence is unclear, and there are pathogenic isolates that do not possess this activity.[24] Virulence studies in mice have shown that the acriflavine agglutination (acf) test can be useful in determining virulence of *F. tularensis*. The acf test–positive (acf^+) variants were exclusively low virulent and the negative (acf^-) variants were either high or low virulent.[35] The acf^- variants had a larger amount of polysaccharide antigens than the acf^+ variants. Fraction 1 and fraction 3 antigens did not correlate with virulence; however, fraction 2 antigen did correlate with virulence in the mouse model.[36]

Francisella philomiragia was previously called *Yersinia philomiragia*. It was reclassified because it shares the unique fatty-acid profile of the *Francisella* and substantial DNA relatedness to this genus, although it has some unique biochemical features (see Table 216–1) and DNA hybridization that distinguish it from *F. tularensis*.[23] *F. philomiragia* is of low virulence for humans and has been isolated from muskrats and water. All strains tested have produced β-lactamase and have been most susceptible to aminoglycosides, cefoxitin, cefotaxime, fluoroquinolones, tetracycline, and chloramphenicol.[37]

An endosymbiotic bacterium found in Rocky Mountain wood ticks, termed *Dermacentor andersoni* symbiont (DAS), has been characterized as belonging to the genus *Francisella* on the basis of 16S ribosomal gene sequence data, the presence of a *Francisella* membrane protein gene, and electron micrography. Although its 16S

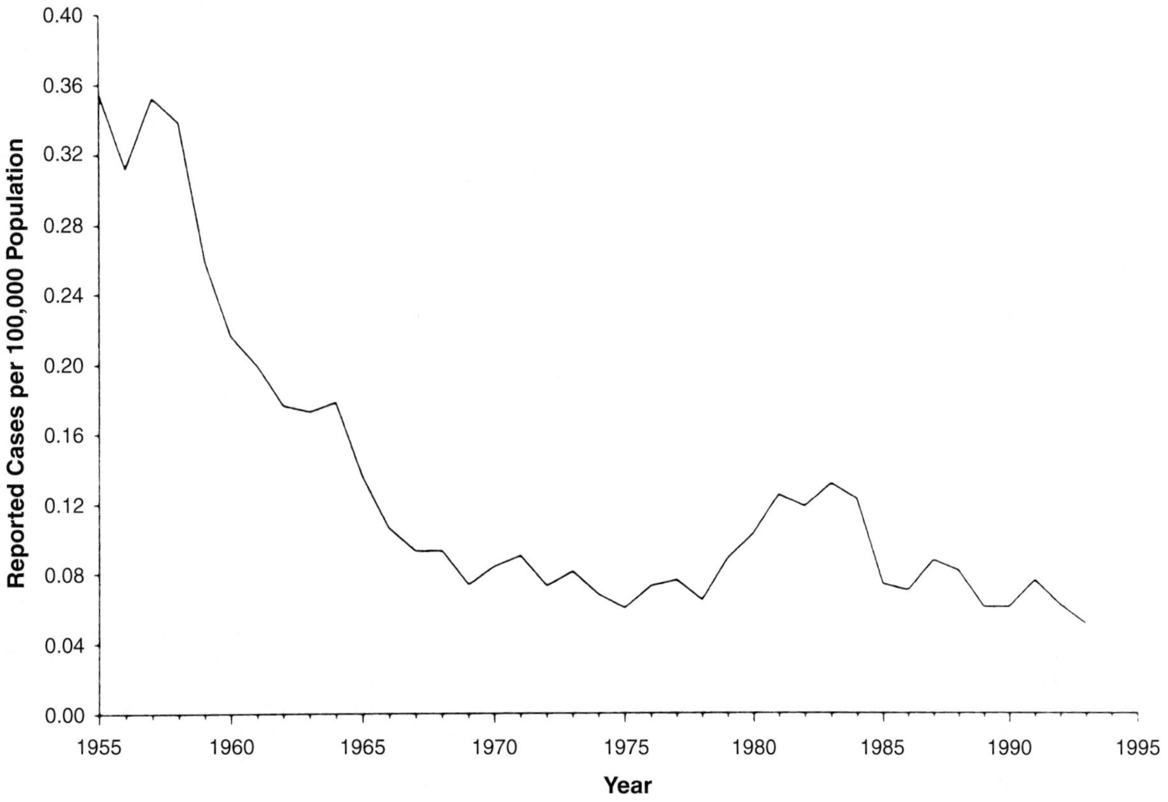

FIGURE 216–1. The incidence of tularemia in the United States from 1955 through 1993. (From Centers for Disease Control and Prevention. Summary of notifiable diseases, United States, 1993. MMWR Morb Mortal Wkly Rep. 1993; 42:61.)

ribosomal sequence was similar to that of *F. tularensis*, the biology of DAS contrasts with that of previously isolated *Francisella* species. The DAS was found to be restricted primarily to the ovarian tissue of female ticks and was not found in male ticks.[38]

EPIDEMIOLOGY

Tularemia is widely distributed, but it is primarily a disease of the Northern Hemisphere and is most common between 30° and 71° north latitude. It has been remarkably absent from the United Kingdom, Africa, South America, and Australia.[2] Tularemia was very common in the United States before World War II. However, its incidence has declined steadily since the 1950s, and it has remained at less than 0.15 cases per 100,000 population since 1965 (Fig. 216–1).[39] In 1994, the last year that tularemia was a nationally reportable disease, the case rate fell to 0.04 per 100,000 population. Nonetheless, two deaths from tularemia were reported in 1995.[40] Arkansas, Missouri, and Oklahoma reported 53% of the total U.S. cases from 1990 through 1994, with South Dakota, Montana, Tennessee, Kansas, Colorado, and Illinois accounting for the next 22% of cases during these years.[40] Contact with state epidemiologists from endemic areas (including Arkansas, Missouri and Oklahoma) has shown that the number of cases reported from 1994 to 1997 has remained at levels seen in the early 1990s. For the years 1994 to 1997, Arkansas (93 cases) and Missouri (76 cases) continued to report large numbers of infections.

Tularemia has become most frequent in June through August and in December, and this trend continues (Fig. 216–2).[40] The summer peak corresponds to a greater number of tick-acquired cases, whereas the smaller peak in late winter reflects an increased number of hunting-associated cases.[41] Males account for up to 75% of cases, perhaps because of greater exposure opportunities.[42] Tularemia can occur at any age (Fig. 216–3). Although 60% of the cases reported in the United States during the early 1990s were in adults aged 30 years and older; 28% were in children between 1 and 14 years of age (see Fig. 216–3).[40] Occupations that have been associated with an increased risk of tularemia are laboratory worker, farmer, veterinarian, sheep worker, hunter or trapper, and cook or meat handler.

F. tularensis is capable of infecting hundreds of different vertebrates and invertebrates, but no more than a dozen mammalian species are important to its ecology in any geographic region.[8] These include lagomorphs, particularly *Sylvilagus* and *Lepus* spp., and ro-

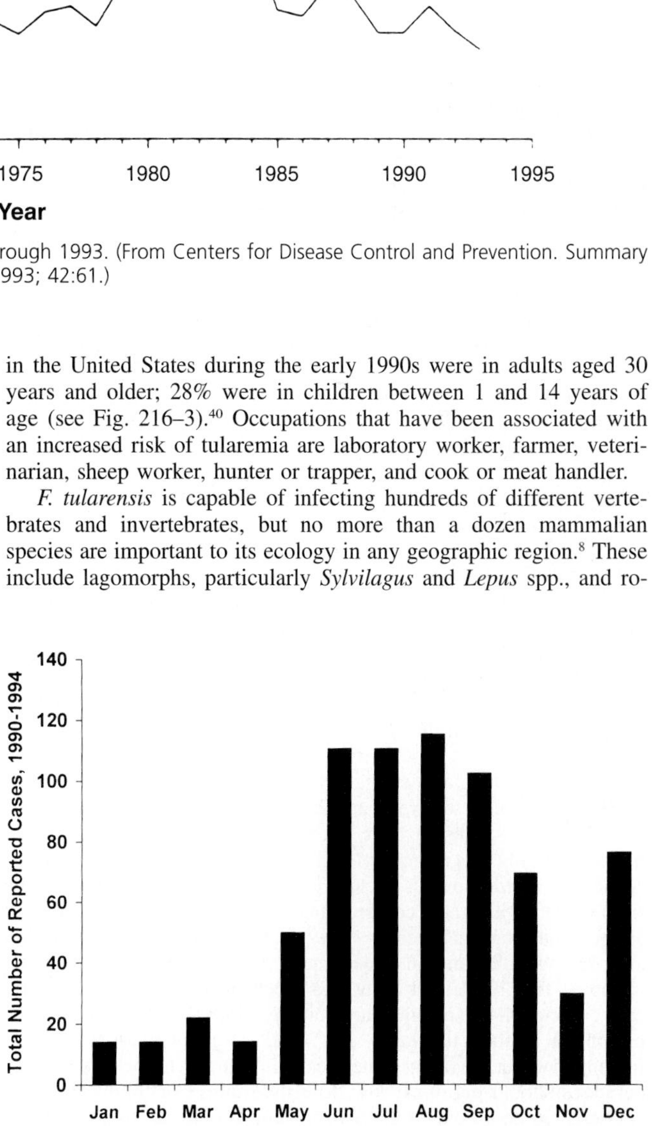

FIGURE 216–2. The total number of tularemia cases reported in each month from 1990 through 1994. (From Centers for Disease Control and Prevention. Summary of notifiable diseases, United States, 1990–1994. MMWR Morb Mortal Wkly Rep, vols. 39–43.)

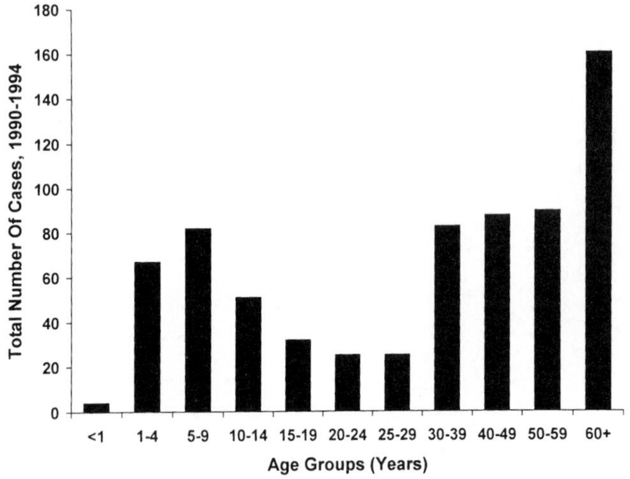

FIGURE 216–3. Ages of tularemia cases reported in the United States form 1990 through 1994. (From Centers for Disease Control and Prevention. Summary of notifiable diseases, United States, 1990–1994. MMWR Morb Mortal Wkly Rep, vols. 39–43.)

dents such as voles, squirrels, muskrat, and beaver in North America; included in the former Soviet Union are voles, hamsters, mice, and hares. Transmission of *F. tularensis* to humans occurs most often through the bite of an insect or contact with contaminated animal products. Other routes of transmission include aerosol droplets, contact with contaminated water or mud, and animal bites. Illness may occur in families or friends because of shared activities and exposures. Nonetheless, human-to-human spread does not occur.

Bloodfeeding arthropods and flies are the most important vectors for tularemia in the United States. Ticks predominate in the central and Rocky Mountain states, whereas biting flies predominate in California, Nevada, and Utah.[25] In contrast, mosquitoes are the most frequent insect vector in Sweden and Finland, and they also are important in the former Soviet Union. At least 13 species of ticks have been found to be naturally infected with *F. tularensis*, and transovarial passage may occur. The dog tick *(Dermacentor variabilis)*, wood tick *(D. andersoni)*, and Lone Star tick *(Amblyomma americanum)* are commonly involved in North America. The organism may be present in tick saliva or feces and may be inoculated either directly or indirectly into the bite wound. Several outbreaks of tickborne tularemia have involved *F. tularensis* biogroup *palearctica* (type B), although this organism is more often linked to water, rodents, and aquatic animals; tick transmission traditionally has been associated with biogroup *tularensis* (type A). Tularemia in children in endemic areas of the United States is now most often associated with tick exposure in the summer.[43]

Animal contact is another important mode of acquiring tularemia. Skinning, dressing, and eating infected animals, including rabbits, muskrats, beavers, squirrels, and birds, have transmitted tularemia, occasionally resulting in large outbreaks in hunters.[41] For example, hamster hunting was responsible for an epidemic in Eastern Europe.[44] Airborne transmission has occurred during these activities, as well as from contact with water, contaminated dust, and hay.[45, 46] Carnivorous animals may transiently carry *F. tularensis* in the mouth or on claws after killing or feeding on infected prey, whether or not they become infected. This is thought to be the mechanism by which domestic cats occasionally transmit tularemia.[47] *F. tularensis* may survive for prolonged periods in water, mud, and animal carcasses even if frozen; however, cooking game meats thoroughly to the proper temperatures should minimize risk from ingestion. Contaminated water continues to be an important environmental source of tularemia.[19, 48]

PATHOGENESIS

F. tularensis is a virulent organism for susceptible species, including the accidental human host. Although the organism is reported to penetrate intact skin, most investigators believe that penetration occurs through sites of inapparent skin disruption.[49] The infectious dose in humans depends on the portal of entry: 10 to 50 organisms when injected intradermally or when inhaled, and 10^8 organisms when ingested. That low numbers of bacteria can cause infection through the skin, mucous membranes, and airways helps to explain in part the extreme risk that *F. tularensis* poses to laboratory workers. In general, *F. tularensis* biogroup *tularensis* causes more severe disease than biogroups *palearctica* and *novicida*. The molecular reasons underlying these differences in virulence are unknown at present.

Over the first 3 to 5 days after cutaneous inoculation, *F. tularensis* multiplies locally and produces a papule; ulceration occurs 2 to 4 days later. Organisms spread from the site of entry to regional lymph nodes and may disseminate via a lymphohematogenous route to involve multiple organs. Bacteremia is probably common in this early phase, although it is only occasionally detected. An elegant description of the pathogenesis is offered by Geyer and colleagues.[50] Infection with *F. tularensis* is characterized by an acute inflammatory response that involves fibrin, neutrophils, macrophages, and T lymphocytes. Neutrophils and macrophages surround earlier inflammatory cells stimulated by the initial inoculum that have become necrotic and degenerated. Eventually lymphocytes, epithelioid cells, and giant cells migrate into the necrotic tissue. This extensive necrosis is noted in both lung tissue and lymph nodes. As the necrotic tissue expands, adjacent veins and arteries may thrombose. The organisms usually are present at the site of the necrotic tissue but are difficult to demonstrate on routine stains. Silver impregnation techniques (Steiner, Dieterle, Warthin-Starry) enhance the visibility of the organisms, which are usually in macrophages and epithelioid cells. Granulomas develop that occasionally may caseate; for this reason, specimens may be mistaken for tuberculosis. These changes can occur in any infected site and have been found at autopsy in lung, liver, spleen, lymph nodes, and bone marrow. Coalescence of necrotic foci may yield abscess formation. *F. tularensis* may remain viable in tissues for prolonged periods.

Humoral immunity, directed against carbohydrate antigens, develops between the second and third week after infection, with the almost simultaneous appearance of immunoglobulin M (IgM), IgG, and IgA agglutinating antibodies.[51] However, antibodies alone are insufficient to protect against virulent *F. tularensis* infection.[33] Opsonizing IgG and IgM antibodies also are produced, with the most efficient opsonization involving both immune serum and complement (C3). Nonetheless, oxygen-dependent neutrophil killing of wild virulent strains is poor; intracellular killing of the attenuated vaccine strain is mediated by hypochlorous acid, but wild strains are resistant to this compound.[33]

Complete recovery from tularemia requires cell-mediated immunity, which is demonstrable about 1 week earlier than antibody responses and is directed against protein antigens.[33] This cell-mediated immunity is α/β T-cell dependent but may involve either $CD4^+$ or $CD8^+$ T cells.[52] Attempts are being made to define the critical molecular determinants that induce protective immunity. *F. tularensis* is a facultative intracellular parasite that is capable of growing within several different cell types, including macrophages, hepatocytes, and endothelial cells.[33] Bacterial survival in rodent macrophages is associated with failure of phagosome-lysosome fusion, phagosome acidification, and utilization of host iron.[53] Interferon-γ and tumor necrosis factor-α (TNF-α) activate macrophages to kill *F. tularensis* through the production of nitric oxide (NO) and other reactive nitrogen products.[54] Several mechanisms are involved in controlling infection before the development of conventional cellular immunity. Initial host defense against tularemia infection requires neutrophils, TNF-α, and interferon-γ (IFN-γ), but these are not sufficient to overcome the infection. For complete resolution, it is necessary that α/β^+ T cells be functional and present after the initial defenses provided by the cytokines and neutrophils.[52] Some of the early responses to primary *F. tularensis* infection in mice are at least in part under genetic control.[55] Specific immunity that is α/β T-cell independent appears in mice within 2 days of intradermal inoculation of the attenuated vaccine strain, requires IFN-γ and TNF-α production, and involves B cells.[56] Expansion of circulating γ/δ T cells has been documented in patients with acute tularemia.[57, 58] Poquet and coworkers[58] showed in 13 tularemia patients that a large increase in Vγ9Vδ2 cells is a characteristic of infection with *F. tularensis*. The observed increase in the levels of Vγ9Vδ2 cells may persist for up to 1 year after infection. The organism's intracellular residence in the liver and other sites may help to protect it from these defenses and permit its early growth. Neutrophils and mononuclear cells accumulate at infected liver foci in mice and lyse hepatocytes harboring *F. tularensis*, thereby releasing organisms from this sequestered environment.[59]

CLINICAL MANIFESTATIONS

The clinical consequences of *F. tularensis* infection depend on the virulence of the particular organism, the portal of entry, the extent of systemic involvement, and the immune status of the host. The result can range from asymptomatic or inconsequential illness to acute sepsis and rapid death. Patients who seek medical attention usually present with at least one of six classic forms of tularemia: ulceroglandular, glandular, oculoglandular, pharyngeal, typhoidal, and pneumonic. This somewhat artificial classification emphasizes only the predominant manifestations commonly encountered, and there is overlap in many patients.

The incubation period averages 3 to 5 days, but ranges from less than 1 to 21 days.[60] Tularemia usually starts abruptly, with the onset of fever, chills, headache, malaise, anorexia, and fatigue. Other prominent symptoms may include cough, myalgias, chest discomfort, vomiting, sore throat, abdominal pain, and diarrhea. A pulse-temperature deficit has been noted in up to 42% of evaluable patients.[2] Fever (usually greater than 101°F) classically lasts for several days, remits for a short interval, and then recurs along with other symptoms.[19] Without treatment fever lasts an average of 32 days, and chronic debility, weight loss, and adenopathy may persist for many months longer.[61] Less virulent strains cause a milder, self-limited illness that may resolve without therapy. Systemic symptoms may abate by the time medical help is sought, so that the clinical picture is dominated by one or more of the six patterns listed; this may lead to confusion as to the correct diagnosis, particularly in the 25 to 50% of patients without an evident source of infection.[2, 61]

Ulceroglandular tularemia has been the presentation in 21 to 87% of cases[62–64]; tick bites and animal contacts are the usually recalled exposures. This is the form that is most quickly recognized as tularemia. The initial specific complaint is often of enlarged and tender localized lymphadenopathy. The inciting skin lesion may appear either before, simultaneously with, or from one to several days after the adenopathy. It starts as a red, painful papule in a region draining into the involved lymph nodes. The papule then undergoes necrosis, leaving a tender ulcer with a raised border (Fig. 216–4). If untreated, the ulcer may take weeks to heal and leave a residual scar. Multiple lesions may occur, particularly in those with animal sources.[2] The location of the ulcer generally reflects the mode of acquisition; animal contacts tend to yield ulcers on the hands and forearms, and tick bites tend to yield ulcers on the trunk, the perineum, the lower extremities, and the head and neck. The distribution of lymphadenopathy also reflects the exposure history, as illustrated in Figure 216–5; overall, cervical and occipital adenopathy is most common in children, and inguinal adenopathy is most common in adults.[43] Skin changes over the involved nodes should suggest underlying suppuration. Some patients have a sporotrichoid presentation with ascending subcutaneous nodules.[19, 65] Lymphangitis is rare unless there is bacterial superinfection of the ulcer.

Glandular tularemia occurs when patients present with tender regional lymphadenopathy but without an evident cutaneous lesion. This form accounts for 3 to 20% of cases in the United States, although 62% of cases in Japan have been of this type.[62, 63] Glandular tularemia represents essentially the same process as ulceroglandular disease, except that a skin lesion either healed before presentation or was minimal or atypical and overlooked. Enlarged lymph nodes may persist for prolonged periods, and in some patients an exposure or prior febrile illness will be forgotten. For this reason, tularemia may not be considered in the initial differential diagnosis of some patients whose primary presentation is lymphadenopathy.[2] In either ulceroglandular or glandular tularemia the lymph nodes may suppurate. When fluctuant, they should be needle-aspirated or surgically drained. The differential diagnosis of ulceroglandular and glandular tularemia includes pyogenic bacterial infections, cat-scratch disease, syphillis, chancroid, lymphogranuloma venereum, tuberculosis, nontuberculous mycobacterial infection, toxoplasmosis, sporotrichosis, rat-bite fever, anthrax, plague, and herpes simplex virus infection.

Oculoglandular tularemia represents only 0 to 5% of cases.[62] In this form, organisms have gained entry through the conjunctiva, either from contaminated fingers or from contaminated splashes and aerosols. Disease is bilateral in less than 12% of patients.[19] Early complaints may include photophobia and excessive lacrimation. Examination shows lid edema and a painful conjunctivitis, with injection, chemosis, and small, yellowish conjunctival ulcers or papules in some patients. Associated tender lymphadenopathy may occur in the preauricular, submandibular, and cervical regions. If the adenopathy is extensive and more prominent than the eye findings, then this syndrome may be mistaken for mumps.[2] Visual loss is rare, but complications include corneal ulceration, dacrocystitis, and nodal suppuration.[61] The differential diagnosis of oculoglandular tularemia includes pyogenic bacterial infections, adenoviral infection, syphilis, cat-scratch disease, and herpes simplex virus infection.

Pharyngeal tularemia, another variant of ulceroglandular disease, is the result of primary invasion through the oropharynx. The source may be contaminated foods or water or contaminated droplets. This form represents 0 to 12% of cases and is being seen with increasing frequency in Japan.[62, 63] Children have been involved more often than adults, and several family members may be affected simultaneously.[2] It must be distinguished from the sore throat that may accompany any of the other major clinical forms of tularemia. In pharyngeal tularemia, the patient's predominant complaint is of severe throat pain. Exudative pharyngitis or tonsillitis is the rule, and one or more ulcers may be seen. A pharyngeal membrane has been described in some patients that is similar to a diphtheritic membrane.[61] Cervical, preparotid, and retropharyngeal nodes may be involved, occasionally with abscess formation.[48, 61] The differential diagnosis includes streptococcal pharyngitis, infectious mononucleosis, adenoviral infection, and diphtheria. Tularemia should be suspected in an endemic area whenever a severe sore throat is unresponsive to penicillin therapy and routine diagnostic tests have been unrewarding.

Typhoidal tularemia refers to a febrile illness caused by *F. tularensis* that is not associated with prominent lymphadenopathy and does not fit into any of the other major forms. From 5 to 30% of cases are typhoidal, and they are the most difficult to diagnose.[62, 63] This form of tularemia may result from any mode of acquisition. Because the portal of entry is usually inapparent clinically, a history of outdoor activities with tick or animal exposure should be sought. Many patients have serious underlying chronic medical disorders and their presentation can be quite dramatic, with acute prostration and rapid death, or a protracted illness.[3, 66, 67] For example, an adolescent boy with human immunodeficiency virus infection was diagnosed with typhoidal tularemia only after blood cultures grew the organism. His only possible exposure was a history of being licked by a diseased fawn with a cleft palate. The patient had a lengthy course with several relapses requiring prolonged antibiotic therapy with gentamicin and tetracycline. He never developed a positive serology, and this was thought to be a consequence of his severe immunocompromise (CD4 count of 0/mm^3).[68] Prominent symptoms of typhoidal tularemia may include any combination of fever with chills, headache, myalgias, sore throat, anorexia, nausea, vomiting, diarrhea, abdominal pain, and cough. Examination may reveal dehydration, hypotension, mild pharyngitis and cervical adenopathy, meningismus,

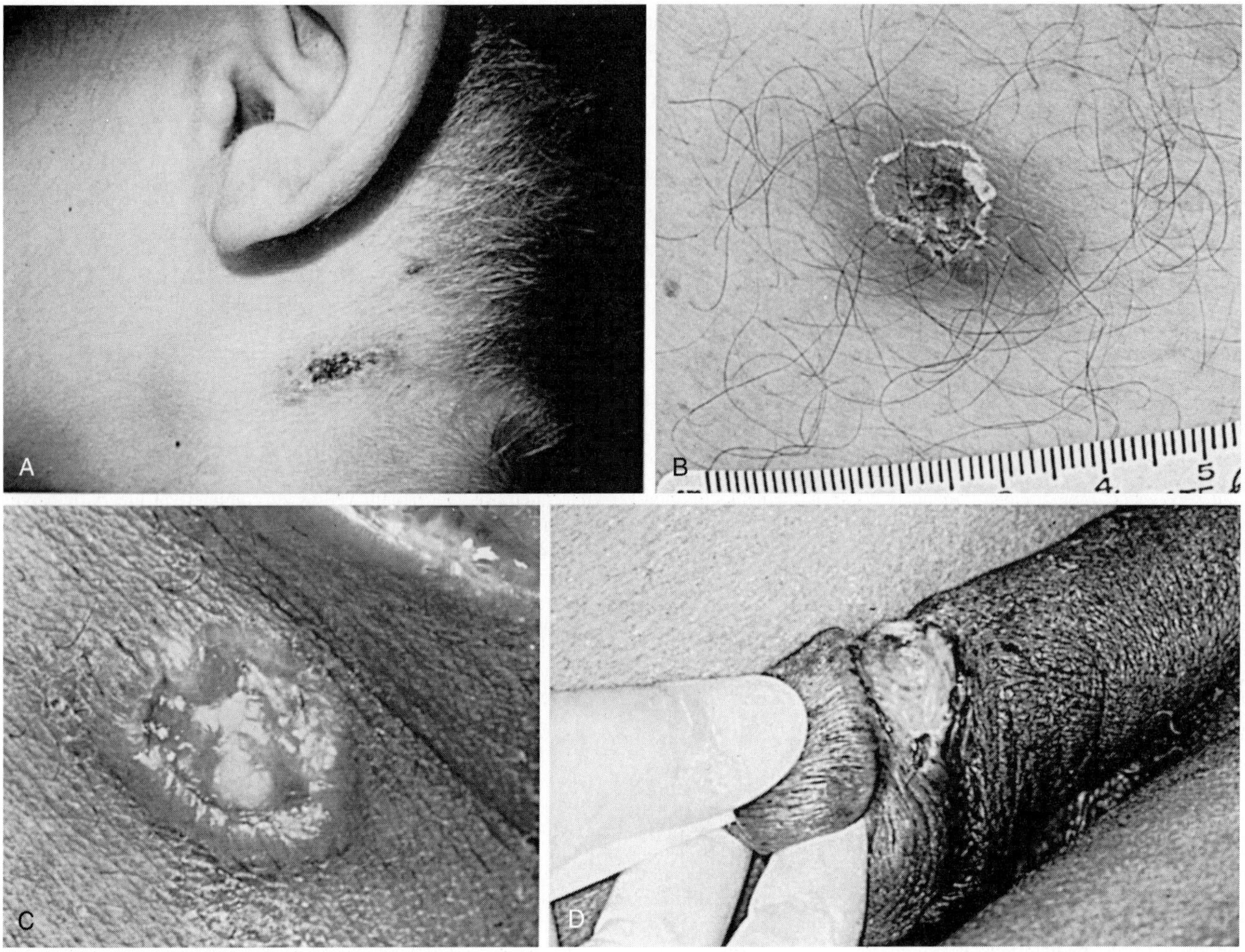

FIGURE 216–4. Examples of primary skin lesions seen in ulceroglandular tularemia, each the result of a tick bite. *A*, Necrotic papule with a large anterior cervical lymph node in a young child. (Courtesy of Dr. Joseph A. Bocchini, Louisiana State University Medical Center, Shreveport, La.) *B*, Papule undergoing central necrosis with desquamation on the thigh of a middle-aged man. *C*, Well-demarcated ulcer, with an inguinal bubo that required surgical drainage. (From Penn RL, Kinasewitz GT. Factors associated with a poor clinical outcome in tularemia. Arch Intern Med. 1987; 147:265–268.) *D*, Penile ulcer that was suspected of being syphilis or another sexually transmitted disease until the history of a recent tick bite was obtained by the infectious diseases consultant. (Courtesy of Dr. John W. King, Louisiana State University Medical Center, Shreveport, La.)

and diffuse abdominal tenderness. Hepatomegaly and splenomegaly are found uncommonly in the acute stages and become more likely the longer the duration of illness. Diarrhea, a major manifestation only in typhoidal tularemia, is loose and watery but only rarely bloody. Children may have more severe intestinal involvement, including focal areas of bowel necrosis.[61] Secondary pleuropulmonary involvement is common in this form, with pulmonary infiltrates or pleural effusions being found in up to 45% of typhoidal cases; it is even more frequent in laboratory-acquired infections. Additional findings in severely ill patients may include hyponatremia, elevated creatine phosphokinase, myoglobinuria, pyuria, renal failure, and positive blood cultures.[2, 3, 66] The differential diagnosis of typhoidal tularemia includes typhoid fever caused by *Salmonella* sp., brucellosis, *Legionella* infection, Q fever, disseminated mycobacterial or fungal infection, rickettsioses, malaria, endocarditis, and any other cause of prolonged fever without localizing signs.

Pneumonic tularemia refers to an illness whose initial presentation is dominated by pulmonary infection. This is found in 7 to 20% of all tularemia cases.[62] It may result from direct inhalation of the organism or from secondary hematogenous spread to the lung. Primary pneumonic tularemia is a risk for certain occupations, including sheep shearers, farmers, and laboratory workers.[46, 69] Cases also have been described as resulting from common exposure in a more casual setting.[45] Although secondary pneumonia may complicate any of the syndromes already discussed, Evans and colleagues[2] found pneumonia to be most frequent in typhoidal (83%) and ulceroglandular (31%) diseases. Scofield and associates[70] reported that patients with pneumonic involvement were more likely to be older, to recall no exposure, to present with typhoidal illness, to have positive cultures, to stay hospitalized longer, and to have a higher mortality rate. From 25 to 30% of patients have radiographic infiltrates without any clinical findings of pneumonia.[2, 7] Common symptoms include fever, cough, no or minimal sputum production, substernal tightness, and pleuritic chest pain. Hemoptysis may occur but is uncommon.[2] Physical examination may be nonspecific or may reveal rales, consolidation, and a friction rub or signs of effusion. Some patients need mechanical ventilation, and adult respiratory distress syndrome may complicate the course of any form of tularemia. Routine examination of sputum does not help to suggest the diagnosis.[2] However, a false-positive direct fluorescent antibody stain for *Legionella* on bronchoscopy specimens has been reported.[71] Infected pleural fluid is exudative, negative on Gram stain, and usually contains more than 1000 leukocytes/mm^3; cells are predominantly lymphocytes, but neutrophilic effusions may occur.[2, 69] Pleural effusions seen with

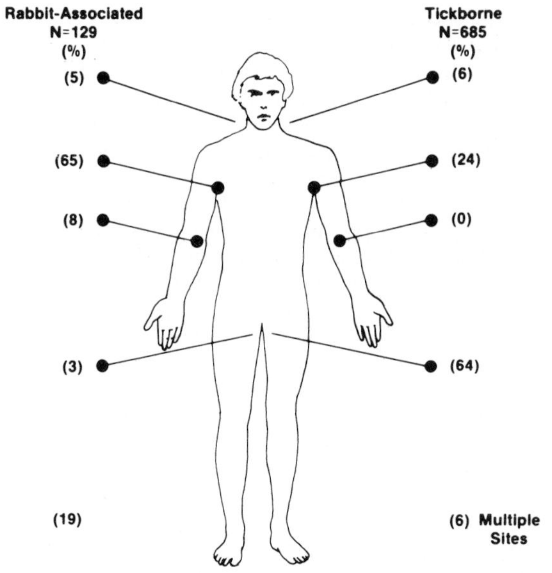

FIGURE 216–5. Distribution of lymphadenopathy in rabbit-associated and tick-borne tularemia.

tularemia frequently mimic those seen with tuberculosis. Similar findings for both include a lymphocyte-rich exudative pleural effusion and a high adenosine deaminase concentration.[72] Granulomas may be found on pleural biopsy and may be confused with tuberculosis.[69] Acute radiographic changes may include subsegmental or lobar infiltrates (Fig. 216–6), hilar adenopathy, pleural effusion, and apical or miliary infiltrates; less common changes include ovoid densities, cavitation, and bronchopleural fistula. Secondary pneumonias are more likely to involve the lower lobes and be bilateral, perhaps because of their hematogenous origin.[70] Healing usually occurs without residual changes, but fibrosis and calcifications may result. Therefore, tularemia may manifest as an enigmatic community-acquired atypical pneumonia that does not respond to routine therapies.[70, 73] The differential diagnosis of pneumonic tularemia includes *Mycoplasma* pneumonia, *Legionella* infection, *Chlamydia pneumoniae* infection, Q fever, psittacosis, tuberculosis, the deep mycoses, and many other causes of atypical or chronic pneumonias.

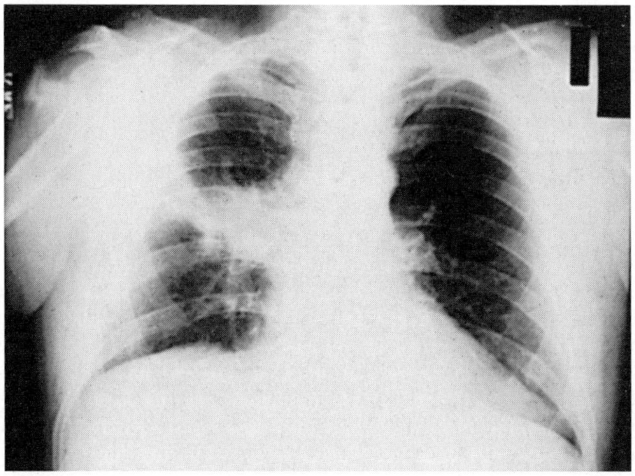

FIGURE 216–6. Chest radiograph of untreated tularemia pneumonia. This patient remained symptomatic for more than 3 months. The diagnosis was established serologically when poorly developed granulomas were found in a transbronchial biopsy, other causes were excluded, and the exposure history was finally obtained. (From Penn RL, Kinasewitz GT. Factors associated with a poor cervical outcome in tularemia. Arch Intern Med. 1987; 147:265–268. Copyright 1987, American Medical Association.)

Secondary skin rashes are an underappreciated part of tularemia and may be found in up to 35% of cases.[74] They usually appear within the first 2 weeks of symptoms, but in a minority are delayed. Rash is more common in women than in men. Cutaneous changes may include diffuse maculopapular and vesiculopapular eruptions, erythema nodosum, erythema multiforme, acneiform lesions, and urticaria. Although any type of secondary rash may be part of any form of tularemia, erythema nodosum has been found to occur most commonly with pneumonic tularemia.[74]

A review of tularemia in Sweden focused on reports of oropharyngeal tularemia, bacteremia, and meningitis. Tularemia was not in the initial differential diagnosis of these infections but was considered only after patients failed to respond to standard therapy for more common causes.[75] This suggests that even in endemic regions tularemia may not be detected or may be diagnosed only after a prolonged delay.

The clinical manifestations of infections caused by *F. tularensis* biogroup *novicida* are less well characterized than for the other biogroups, but are similar to those previously described.[22] *F. philomiragia* has caused pneumonias, sepsis, peritonitis, and meningitis.[37] This organism predominantly infects patients with host defenses impaired by chronic granulomatous disease, near-drowning in salt water or estuaries, or myeloproliferative disorders.[37]

COMPLICATIONS AND OUTCOME

Suppuration of involved lymph nodes is currently the most common complication of tularemia, and this may occur even after specific antibiotic therapy.[43] Patients with severe disease may manifest disseminated intravascular coagulation, renal failure, rhabdomyolysis, jaundice, and hepatitis. Meningitis, encephalitis, pericarditis, peritonitis, osteomyelitis, splenic rupture, and thrombophlebitis have become very rare since antibiotic therapy has become available. The cerebrospinal fluid (CSF) in meningitis almost always shows a mononuclear cell pleocytosis, with a high protein concentration and hypoglycorrhacia.[76]

Tularemia may lead to months of debility in some patients, usually associated with late lymph node suppuration and/or persistent fatigue. Features that are associated with a worse prognosis include increasing age, serious coexisting medical conditions, symptoms of a month or longer before treatment, significant pleuropulmonary disease, typhoidal illness, renal failure, a delay in the diagnosis, and inappropriate antibiotic therapy.[42, 70] Overall death rates in the antibiotic era have been 4% or less, but were as high as 33% before the introduction of streptomycin as treatment.[2, 77]

DIAGNOSIS

The diagnosis of tularemia ultimately rests on clinical suspicion. Results of routine laboratory testing are nonspecific. The leukocyte count and sedimentation rate may be normal or elevated. Thrombocytopenia, hyponatremia, elevated serum transaminases, increased creatine phosphokinase, myoglobinuria, and sterile pyuria are occasionally found.[3] The organism is rarely seen on Gram-stained smears or in tissue biopsies and does not grow in routinely plated cultures. However, *F. tularensis* may be recovered from blood, pleural fluid, lymph nodes, wounds, sputum, and gastric aspirates when processed on supportive media. Because of this and its potential danger to laboratory personnel, they should be notified if tularemia is suspected. Isolations by blood culture using more sensitive radiometric techniques have included *palearctica* strains.[66, 78, 79] The nonradiometric blood culture medium also supports the growth of *F. tularensis*.[80] Methods for rapid diagnosis that show future promise include direct fluorescent antibody staining of smears and tissues, antigen detection in urine, RNA hybridization with a 16S ribosomal probe, and polymerase chain reaction (PCR).[25, 81, 82] Animal inoculation is rarely performed at present, in part because this requires biosafety level 3 facilities; however, biosafety level 2 is sufficient for laboratory handling of clinical materials.[25]

The use of PCR is appealing in that smears and cultures are usually negative, standard microbiologic isolation may be hazardous to laboratory personnel, and serologic diagnosis may take several weeks to confirm. Initial studies done in murine and other animal models showed that PCR was an effective modality for diagnosing infection with *Francisella*.[82–84] Sjostedt and colleagues[85] tested wound swabs from infected patients and found a 73% sensitivity with PCR using a 17-kD lipoprotein *F. tularensis* gene and 50% sensitivity with primers to the 16S rDNA gene. Dolan and associates[86] were able to show that PCR on lymph node aspirates was positive even after antibiotic therapy was initiated. Therefore, PCR may prove useful for diagnosing tularemia in patients already receiving suppressive empiric antibiotic therapy.

Serologic studies are the most common way that the diagnosis of tularemia is confirmed. Antibodies to *F. tularensis* may be demonstrated by tube agglutination, microagglutination, hemagglutination, and enzyme-linked immunosorbent assay (ELISA).[25] Standard tube agglutination titers are usually negative in the first week of illness, are positive in most patients by the end of 2 weeks, and peak after 4 to 5 weeks. The microagglutination assay is up to 100-fold more sensitive than tube agglutination.[25] Both IgM and IgG antibody titers may persist for longer than a decade after infection,[33] limiting the value of a single positive result. A presumptive diagnosis is supported by an acute agglutination titer of 1:160 or more in the face of compatible disease but may also reflect remote infection. Definitive serologic diagnosis requires a fourfold or greater rise in titer between acute and convalescent specimens; serologies may need to be repeated at 7- to 10-day intervals before a rise is demonstrated. Antibodies may cross-react with *Brucella* spp., *Proteus* OX19, and *Yersinia* spp., but titers to *F. tularensis* are almost always higher, and dithiothreitol treatment of the serum eliminates most of these other reactions.[25, 33] False-positive heterophile agglutinins also rarely occur during tularemia.[61, 77] Tests for cell-mediated immunity such as lymphocyte blastogenesis and delayed hypersensitivity skin test reactivity may be positive earlier than serologies, but standardized antigen preparations are not commercially available.[33]

THERAPY

The drug of first choice for the treatment of all forms of tularemia except meningitis is streptomycin, although gentamicin is an acceptable substitute.[87] The minimum dosage of streptomycin that is effective therapy for tularemia is 7.5 to 10 mg/kg intramuscularly every 12 hours for 7 to 14 days. An alternative regimen is 15 mg/kg intramuscularly every 12 hours for the first 3 days, followed by half this dose to complete treatment. In very sick patients, 15 mg/kg every 12 hours may be given throughout a 7- to 10-day course. Doses greater than 2 g/day of streptomycin in adults do not increase efficacy.[60] The pediatric regimens for streptomycin are similar: 30 to 40 mg/kg/day intramuscularly in two divided doses for a total of 7 days; or 40 mg/kg/day intramuscularly in two divided doses for the first 3 days, followed by 20 mg/kg/day intramuscularly in two divided doses for the next 4 days. The first few days of streptomycin rarely may induce a Jarish-Herxheimer–like reaction, with an increase in symptoms and a transient drop of the serum agglutination titer.[2, 61] Gentamicin has proved to be effective therapy.[2, 3] A review of the literature revealed that gentamicin was effective for treatment except that the relapse and failure rates were higher with gentamicin, compared with historical rates for streptomycin.[88] Doxycycline had a much higher relapse rate compared with the aminoglycosides. In pediatric patients, gentamicin was shown to be effective for treatment of tularemia without relapse or failure.[89] Gentamicin is given intravenously at a dose of 3 to 5 mg/kg/day in divided doses for 7 to 14 days, with desired peak serum levels of at least 5.0 μg/ml. The efficacy of single-daily dosing has not been studied. The doses of both streptomycin and gentamicin need to be adjusted for renal insufficiency. Penetration of these drugs into the cerebrospinal fluid is poor and erratic and may be inadequate in tularemic meningitis. Pittman and colleagues[90] reported a central nervous system shunt infection caused by *F. tularensis* that was successfully treated with intrathecal gentamicin. An additional 13 cases of tularemic meningitis in children have been documented.[76] Successful treatment generally included combinations of streptomycin and chloramphenicol. The most recent case was successfully treated with a combination of intravenous gentamicin and oral doxycycline.

Tetracycline and chloramphenicol are bacteriostatic for *F. tularensis*, and this accounts in part for the high rate of relapse after treatment with these agents.[2] Tetracycline should not be used in children younger than 8 years of age, during pregnancy, or during lactation. Tetracycline is most effective in adults when given as 2 g/day in divided oral doses for at least 14 days,[91] a suggested oral regimen in children is 30 mg/kg/day, to a maximum of 2 g/day, in divided doses for the same duration. Doxycycline may also be used and provides the convenience of twice-daily dosing. In general, chloramphenicol should not be chosen to treat tularemia because of its potentially serious toxicity and the availability of more effective alternatives with less dangerous potential side effects. However, chloramphenicol, 50 to 100 mg/kg/day intravenously in divided doses, may be added to streptomycin to treat meningitis. When used in the past for other forms of tularemia, the oral dose of chloramphenicol has been 30 to 50 mg/kg/day in 3 or 4 divided doses for at least 14 days. The oral preparation is no longer available in the United States.

Drugs with well-established clinical efficacy have exhibited achievable minimal inhibitory concentrations (MIC) against *F. tularensis* on in vitro susceptibility tests.[29] Other agents with relatively low MICs include erythromycin, rifampin, cefoxitin, cefotaxime, ceftriaxone, ceftazidime, most aminoglycosides, and several flouroquinolones except cinoxacin.[29, 92] The effectiveness of these drugs in treating tularemia is not fully established. In fact, ceftriaxone has failed in several patients treated as outpatients.[93] Erythromycin has been used successfully in a few patients who were thought to have *Legionella* infections.[71, 94] However, resistance to erythromycin has been described in *F. tularensis* strains from outside of North America.[94] Case reports also suggest that ciprofloxacin,[92, 95] norfloxacin,[92] and imipenem[96] are effective in some patients. A monoclonal antibody to the LPS of *F. tularensis* and serum from vaccinated people are effective passive therapies for murine infection, offering the future hope of immunotherapeutic agents for tularemia.[97, 98] Surgical therapies are limited to drainage of abscessed lymph nodes and chest tube drainage of empyemas.

PREVENTION

Avoiding exposure to the organism is the best prevention of tularemia. Wild animals should not be skinned or dressed using bare hands, or when the animal appeared ill. Gloves, masks, and protective eye covers should be worn when performing such tasks and when disposing of dead animals brought home by household pets. Wild game should be cooked thoroughly before ingestion. Wells or other waters that are contaminated by dead animals should not be used. The most important measure to avoid tick bites in infested areas is wearing clothing that is tight at the wrists and ankles and that covers most of the body. Chemical tick repellants also may be of benefit. Frequent checks should be made for attached ticks so that they may be removed promptly; this must not be done with bare hands, and care should be taken not to crush the tick.

Hospitalized patients with tularemia do not need special isolation because person-to-person spread does not occur, and even in the preantibiotic era secondary cases were not found. Standard universal precautions for contaminated secretions are adequate when handling drainage from wounds or eyes.

Vaccines prepared from killed *F. tularensis* are ineffective, in part because they only induce an antibody response.[33] A live vaccine based on an attenuated strain of *F. tularensis* (LVS), originally obtained from the former Soviet Union, has been developed in the United States.[99] The LVS vaccine is an attenuated, live *F. tularensis* strain that occurs in two colony phenotypes, one of which is immunogenic and has major importance for the induction of protective immunity.[100] A new vaccine lot has been used and has shown to be immunogenic in humans.[101]

Live vaccine strains require constant control of their immunologic properties, because the nonimmunologic phenotype has a tendency to accumulate during storage reducing the efficacy of the vaccine. Additionally, the live vaccine strain of *F. tularensis* cannot provide high immune response in the presence of antimicrobial agents such as doxycycline.[102] This vaccine induces cell-mediated and humoral immunity, is effective in preventing typhoidal disease, and reduces the severity of ulceroglandular disease but does not prevent it.[101, 103] Vaccination may be considered for persons who will be working with *F. tularensis* and for anyone else with repeated occupational exposures. The vaccine, an investigational agent, is available with a monitoring fee through an Investigational New Drug protocol from Headquarters, United States Army Medical Research and Materiel Command, Fort Detrick, Frederick, Maryland 21702-5012, U.S.A.

Antibiotic prophylaxis after potential exposures of unknown risk, such as tick bites, is not recommended. Streptomycin given in the incubation period after experimental inoculation successfully aborts illness, but the bacteriostatic oral drugs do not.[2, 91] Documented exposures from laboratory accidents may be treated preemptively with intramuscular streptomycin. The value of the oral fluoroquinolones for this purpose is unknown. Liposome-encapsulated ciprofloxacin delivered by aerosol inhalation was highly effective in the treatment of respiratory *F. tularensis* infection in mice.[104] The data indicate that this treatment might be effective in humans as postexposure prophylaxis for aerosol exposure to the organism.[104] The efficacies of doxycycline and ciprofloxacin also were examined in the murine model. These antibiotics, given separately 48 hours before challenge and continued through 5 days after challenge, were protective against intraperitoneal infection; however, mice succumbed once the antibiotics were withdrawn. If the antibiotics were extended to 10 days after challenge, relapse was much less likely to occur. When antibiotics were begun 24 hours after exposure instead of prophylactically, there was a 4-fold and 10-fold decrease in efficacy for doxycycline and ciprofloxacin, respectively.[105] The results of these experiments could be useful if *F. tularensis* is continued to be viewed as a possible weapon of biological warfare.

Recovery from tularemia is thought to confer protective immunity for life, although a few recurrent infections have been documented.[103] Most recurrences have been clinically mild ulceroglandular disease, and systemic symptoms have been uncommon. Therefore, previously infected individuals are not candidates for vaccination or preemptive antibiotic therapy after a known exposure.

REFERENCES

1. Jellison WL. Tularemia: Dr. Edward Francis and his first 23 isolates of *Francisella tularensis*. Bull Hist Med. 1972;46:477–485.
2. Evans ME, Gregory DW, Schaffner W, et al. Tularemia: A 30-year experience with 88 cases. Medicine (Baltimore). 1985;64:251–269.
3. Penn RL, Kinasewitz GT. Factors associated with a poor clinical outcome in tularemia. Arch Intern Med. 1987;147:265–268.
4. Sandström G, Sjöstedt A, Tärnvik A. The first International Conference on Tularemia: Umeâ, Sweden, 23–25 August 1995. FEMS Immunol Med Microbiol. 1996;13:170.
5. Franz DR, Jarhling PB, Friendlander AM, et al. Clinical recognition and management of patients exposed to biological warfare agents. JAMA. 1997;278:339–411.
6. Kaufmann AF, Meltzer MI, Schmid GP. The economic impact of a bioterrorist attack: Are prevention and postattack intervention programs justifiable? Emerg Infect Dis. 1997;3:83–94.
7. Martin RE, Bates JH. Atypical pneumonia. Infect Dis Clin North Am. 1991;5:585–601.
8. Hopla CE. The ecology of tularemia. Adv Vet Sci Comp Med. 1974;18:25–53.
9. McCoy GW. A plague-like disease of rodents. Public Health Bull. 1911;43:53–71.
10. McCoy GW, Chapin CW. Bacterium tularense, the cause of a plaguelike disease of rodents. Public Health Bull. 1912;53:17–23.
11. McCoy GW, Chapin CW. Further observations on a plaguelike disease of rodents with a preliminary note on the causative agent *Bacterium tularense*. J Infect Dis. 1912;10:61–72.
12. Francis E. Tularemia. JAMA. 1925;84:1243–1250.
13. Vail DT. *Bacillus tularense* infection of the eye. Opthalmol Rec. 1914;23:487.
14. Wherry WB, Lamb BH. Infection of man with *Bacterium tularense*. J Infect Dis. 1914;15:331–340.
15. Wherry WB, Lamb BH. Discovery of *Bacterium tularense* in wild rabbits, and the danger of its transmission to man. JAMA. 1914;63:2041.
16. Pearse RA. Insect bites. Northwest Medicine. 1911;3:81.
17. Francis E. The occurrence of tularemia in nature as a disease of man. Public Health Rep. 1921;36:1731–1738.
18. Francis E, Mayne B. Experimental transmission of tularemia by flies of the species *Chrysops discalis*. Public Health Rep. 1921;36:1738–1746.
19. Francis E. A summary of the present knowledge of tularemia. Medicine (Baltimore). 928;7:411–432.
20. Sanford JP. Tularemia. JAMA. 1983;250:3225–3226.
21. Eigelsbach HT, McGann VG. Genus *Francisella* Doroféev 1947, 176[AL]. In: Kreig NR, Holt JG, eds. Bergey's Manual of Systematic Bacteriology. Baltimore: Williams & Wilkins, 1984:394–399.
22. Hollis DG, Weaver RE, Steigerwalt AG, et al. *Francisella philomiragia* comb. nov. (formerly *Yersinia philomiragia*) and *Francisella tularensis* biogroup novicida (formerly *Francisella novicida*) associated with human disease. J Clin Microbiol. 1989;27:1601–1608.
23. Forsman M, Sandstrom G, Sjostedt A. Analysis of 16S ribosomal DNA sequences of *Francisella* strains and utilization for determination of the phylogeny of the genus and for identification of strains by PCR. Int J Syst Bacteriol. 1994;44:38–46.
24. Sandström G, Sjöstedt A, Forsman M, et al. Characterization and classification of strains of *Francisella tularensis* isolated in the Central Asian focus of the Soviet Union and in Japan. J Clin Microbiol. 1992;30:172–175.
25. Stewart SJ. *Francisella*. In: Murray PR, Baron EJ, Pfaller MA, et al., eds. Manual of Clinical Microbiology. 6th Edition. Washington, DC: American Society for Microbiology; 1995:545–548.
26. Bernard K, Tessier S, Winstanley J, et al. Early recognition of atypical *Francisella tularensis* strains lacking a cysteine requirement. J Clin Microbiol. 1994;32:551–553.
27. Clarridge JE III, Raich TJ, Sjosted A, et al. Characterization of two unusual clinically significant *Francisella* strains. J Clin Microbiol. 1996;34:1995–2000.
28. Koneman EW, Allen SD, Janda WM, et al. Miscellaneous fastidious gram-negative bacilli. In: Koneman EW, Allen SD, Janda WM, et al. Color Atlas and Textbook of Diagnostic Microbiology. Philadelphia: JB Lippincott, 1992;338–349.
29. Baker CN, Hollis DG, Thornsberry C. Antimicrobial susceptibility testing of *Francisella tularensis* with a modified Mueller-Hinton broth. J Clin Microbiol. 1985;22:212–215.
30. Ancuta P, Pedron T, Girard R, et al. Inability of the *Francisella tularensis* lipopolysaccharide to mimic or to antagonize the induction of cell activation by endotoxins. Infect Immun. 1996;64:2041–2046.
31. Fulop M, Manchee R, Titball R. Role of lipopolysaccharide and a major outer membrane protein from *Francisella tularensis* in the induction of immunity against tularemia. Vaccine. 1995;13:1220–1225.
32. Cowley SC, Myltseva SV, Nano FE. Phase variation in *Francisella tularensis* affecting intracellular growth, lipopolysaccharide antigenicity and nitric oxide production. Mol Microbiol. 1996;20:867–874.
33. Tärnvik A. Nature of protective immunity to *Francisella tularensis*. Rev Infect Dis. 1989;11:440–450.
34. Waag DM, McKee KT Jr., Sandström G, et al. Cell-mediated and humoral immune responses after vaccination of human volunteers with the live vaccine strain of *Francisella tularensis*. Clin Diagn Lab Immunol 1995;2:143–148.
35. Sato T, Fujita H, Ohara Y, et al. Correlation between the virulence of *Francisella tularensis* in experimental mice and its acriflavine reaction. Curr Microbiol. 1992;25:95–97.
36. Fujita H, Sato T, Watanabe Y, et al. Correlation of the polysaccharide antigens of *Francisella tularensis* with virulence in experimental mice. Microbiol Immunol. 1995;39:1007–1009.
37. Wenger JD, Hollis DG, Weaver RE, et al. Infection caused by *Francisella philomiragia* (formerly *Yersinia philomiragia*): A newly recognized human pathogen. Ann Intern Med. 1989;110:888–892.
38. Neibylski ML, Peacock MG, Fischer ER, et al. Characterization of an endosymbiont infecting wood ticks, *Dermacentor andersoni*, as a member of the genus *Francisella*. Appl Environ Microbiol. 1997;63:3933–3940.
39. Centers for Disease Control and Prevention. Summary of notifiable diseases, United States, 1993. MMWR Morb Mortal Wkly Rep. 1993;42:61.
40. Centers for Disease Control and Prevention. Summary of notifiable diseases, United States, 1990–1994. MMWR Morb Mortal Wkly Rep, vols. 39–43.
41. Langley R, Cambell R. Tularemia in North Carolina, 1965–1990. N C Med J 1995;56:314–317.
42. Taylor JP, Istre GR, McChesney TC, et al. Epidemiologic characteristics of human tularemia in the southwest-central states, 1981–1987. Am J Epidemiol. 1991;133:1032–1038.
43. Jacobs RF, Condrey YM, Yamauchi T. Tularemia in adults and children: A changing presentation. Pediatrics. 1985;76:818–822.

44. Münnich D, Lakatos M. Clinical, epidemiological and therapeutical experience with human tularemia. Infection. 1979;7:61–63.
45. Teutsch SM, Martone WJ, Brink EW, et al. Pneumonic tularemia on Martha's Vineyard. N Engl J Med. 1979;301:826–828.
46. Syrjälä H, Kujala P, Myllylä V, et al. Airborne transmission of tularemia in farmers. Scand J Infect Dis. 1985;17:371–375.
47. Cepellan J, Fong IW. Tularemia from a cat bite: Case report and review of feline-associated tularemia. Clin Infect Dis. 1993;16:472–475.
48. Nordahl SHG, Hoel T, Scheel O, et al. Tularemia: A differential diagnosis in oto-rhino-laryngology. J Laryngol Otol. 1993; 107:127–129.
49. Quan SF, McManus AG, von Fintel H. Infectivity of tularemia applied to intact skin and ingested drinking water. Science. 1956;123:942–943.
50. Geyer SJ, Burkey A, Chandler FW. Tularemia. In: Connor DH, ed. Pathology of Infectious Diseases. Stamford, Connecticut, Appleton & Lange, 1997:869–873.
51. Koskela P, Salminen A. Humoral immunity against *Francisella tularensis* after natural infection. J Clin Microbiol. 1985;22:973–979.
52. Yee D, Rhinehart-Jones TR, Elkins KL. Loss of either CD4+ or CD8+ T cells does not affect the magnitude of protective immunity to an intracellular pathogen, *Francisella tularensis* strain LVS. J Immunol. 1996;1957:5042–5048.
53. Fortier AH, Leiby DA, Narayanan RB, et al. Growth of *Francisella tularensis* LVS in macrophages: The acidic intracellular compartment provides essential iron required for growth. Infect Human. 1995;63:1478–1483.
54. Green SJ, Nacy CA, Schreiber RD, et al. Neutralization of gamma interferon and tumor necrosis factor alpha blocks in vivo synthesis of nitrogen oxides from L-arginine and protection against *Francisella tularensis* infection in *Mycobacterium bovis* BCG-treated mice. Infect Immun. 1993;61:689–698.
55. Hernchova L, Kovarova H, Macela A, et al. Early consequences of macrophage-*Francisella tularensis* interaction under the influence of different genetic background in mice. Immunol Lett. 1997;57:75–81.
56. Culkin SJ, Rhinehart-Jones T, Elkins KL. A novel role for B cells in early protective immunity to an intracellular pathogen, *Francisella tularensis* strain LVS. J Immunol. 1997;158:3277–3284.
57. Sumida T, Maeda T, Takahashi H, et al. Predominant expansion of Vγ9/Vδ2 T cells in a tularemia patient. Infect Immun. 1992;60:2554–2558.
58. Poquet Y, Kroca M, Halary F, et al. Expansion of Vγ9Vδ2 T cells is triggered by *Francisella tularensis*-derived phosphoantigens in tularemia but not after tularemia vaccination. Infect Immun. 1998;66:2107–2114.
59. Conlan JW, North RJ. Early pathogenesis of infection in the liver with the facultative intracellular bacteria *Listeria monocytogenes*, *Francisella tularensis*, and *Salmonella typhimurium* involves lysis of infected hepatocytes by leukocytes. Infect Immun. 1992;60:5164–5171.
60. Sanders CV, Hahn R. Analysis of 106 cases of tularemia. J La State Med Soc. 1968;120:391–393.
61. Dienst FT Jr. Tularemia: A perusal of three hundred thirty-nine cases. J La State Med Soc. 1963;115:114–124.
62. Cox SK, Everett ED. Tularemia: An analysis of 25 cases. Mo Med. 1981;78:70–74.
63. Ohara Y, Sato T, Fujita H, et al. Clinical manifestations of tularemia in Japan: Analysis of 1,355 cases observed between 1924 and 1987. Infection. 1991;19:14–17.
64. Foshay L. Tularemia: A summary of certain aspects of the disease including methods for early diagnosis and the results of serum treatment in 600 patients. Medicine (Baltimore). 1940;19:1–83.
65. Kostman JR, DiNubile MJ. Nodular lymphangitis: A distinctive but often unrecognized syndrome. Ann Intern Med 1993;118:883–888.
66. Provenza MJ, Klotz SA, Penn RL. Isolation of *Francisella tularensis* from blood. J Clin Microbiol. 1986;24:453–455.
67. Maranan MC, Schiff D, Johnson DC, et al. Pneumonic tularemia in a patient with chronic granulomatous disease. Clin Infect Dis. 1997;25:630–633.
68. Gries DM, Fairchok MP. Typhoidal tularemia in a human immunodeficiency virus-infected adolescent. Pediatr Infect Dis J. 1996;15:838–840.
69. Schmid GP, Catino D, Suffin SC, et al. Granulomatous pleuritis caused by *Francisella tularensis*: Possible confusion with tuberculous pleuritis. Am Rev Respir Dis. 1983;128:314–316.
70. Scofield RH, Lopez EJ, McNabb SJ. Tularemic pneumonia in Oklahama, 1982–1987. J Okla State Med Assoc. 1992;85:165–170.
71. Roy TM, Fleming D, Anderson WH. Tularemic pneumonia mimicking Legionnaires' disease with false-positive direct fluorescent antibody stains for *Legionella*. South Med J. 1989;82:1429–1431.
72. Petterson T, Nyberg P, Nordström D, et al. Similar pleural fluid findings in pleuropulmonary tularemia and tuberculosis pleurisy. Chest. 1996;109:572–575.
73. Fredricks DN, Remington JS. Tularemia presenting as community-acquired pneumonia: Implications in the era of managed care. Arch Intern Med. 1996;156:2137–2140.
74. Syrjälä H, Karvonen J, Salminen A. Skin manifestations of tularemia: A study of 88 cases in Northern Finland during 16 years (1967–1983). Acta Derm Venerol. 1984;64:513–516.
75. Tarnvik A, Sandstorm G, Sjostedt A. Infrequent manifestations of tularemia in Sweden. Scand J Infect Dis. 1997;29:443–446.
76. Rodgers BL, Duffield RP, Taylor T, et al. Tularemic meningitis. Pediatr Infect Dis J. 1998;17:439–441.
77. Giddens WR, Wilson JW, Dienst FT, et al. Tularemia: An analysis of one hundred forty-seven cases. J La State Med Soc. 1957;109:93–98.
78. Reary BW, Klotz SA. Enhancing recovery of *Francisella tularensis* from blood. Diagn Microbiol Infect Dis. 1988;11:117–119.
79. Hoel T, Scheel O, Nordahl SHG, et al. Water- and airborne *Francisella tularensis* biovar *palearctica* isolated from human blood. Infection. 1991;19:348–350.
80. Brion JP, Recule C, Croizé J et al. Isolation of *Francisella tularensis* from lymph node aspirate inoculated into a non-radiometric blood culture system. Eur J Clin Microbiol Infect Dis. 1996;15:180–181.
81. Forsman M, Kuoppa K, Sjöstedt A, et al. Use of RNA hybridization in the diagnosis of a case of ulceroglandular tularemia. Eur J Clin Microbiol Infect Dis. 1990;9:784–785.
82. Long GW, Oprandy JJ, Narayanan RB, et al. Detection of *Francisella tularensis* in blood by polymerase chain reaction. J Clin Microbiol. 1993;31:152–154.
83. Junhui Z, Ruifu Y, Jianchun L, et al. Detection of *Francisella tularensis* by the polymerase chain reaction. J Med Microbiol. 1996;45:477–482.
84. Fulop M, Leslie D, Titball R. A rapid, highly sensitive method for the detection of *Francisella tularensis* in clinical samples using the polymerase chain reaction. Am J Trop Med Hyg. 1996;54:364–366.
85. Sjostedt A, Erikkson U, Berglund L, Tarnvik A. Detection of *Francisella tularensis* in ulcers of patients with tularemia by PCR. J Clin Microbiol. 1997;35:1045–1048.
86. Dolan SA, Dommaraju CB, DeGuzman GB. Detection of *Francisella tularensis* in clinical specimens by use of polymerase chain reaction. Clin Infect Dis. 1998;26:764–765.
87. The choice of antibacterial drugs. Med Lett Drugs Ther. 1998;40:33–42.
88. Enderlin G, Morales L, Jacobs RF, et al. Streptomycin and alternative agents for the treatment of tularemia: Review of the literature. Clin Infect Dis. 1994;19:42–47.
89. Cross JT, Schutze GE, Jacobs RF. Treatment of tularemia with gentamicin in pediatric patients. Pediatr Infect Dis J. 1995;14:151–152.
90. Pittman T, Williams D, Friedman AD. A shunt infection caused by *Francisella tularensis*. Pediatr Neurosurg. 1996;2:450–451.
91. Sawyer WD, Dangerfield HG, Hogge AL, et al. Antibiotic prophylaxis and therapy of airborne tularemia. Bacteriol Rev. 1966;30:542–548.
92. Syrjälä, Schildt R, Räisäinen S. In vitro susceptibility of *Francisella tularensis* to flouroquinolones and treatment of tularemia with norfloxacin and ciprofloxacin. Eur J Clin Microbiol Infect Dis. 1991;10:68–70.
93. Cross JT, Jacobs RF. Tularemia: Treatment failures with outpatient use of ceftriaxone. Clin Infect Dis. 1993;17:976–980.
94. Harrell RE Jr, Simmons HF. Pleuropulmonary tularemia: Successful treatment with erythromycin. South Med J. 1990;83:1363–1364.
95. Scheel O, Reiersen R, Hoel T. Treatment of tularemia with ciprofloxacin. Eur J Clin Microbiol Infect Dis. 1992;11:447–448.
96. Lee H-C, Horowitz E, Linder W. Treatment of tularemia with imipenem/cilastatin sodium. South Med J. 1991;84:1277–1278.
97. Narayanan RB, Drabick JJ, Williams JC, et al. Immunotherapy of tularemia: Characterization of a monoclonal antibody reactive with *Francisella tularensis*. J Leukocyte Biol. 1993;53:112–116.
98. Drabick JJ, Narayanan RB, Williams JC, et al. Passive protection of mice against lethal *Francisella tularensis* (live tularemia vaccine strain) infection by the sera of human recipients of the live tularemia vaccine. Am J Med Sci. 1994;308:83–87.
99. Waag DM, Galloway A, Sandstrom G, et al. Cell-mediated and humoral immune responses induced by scarification vaccination of human volunteers with a new lot of the live vaccine strain of *Francisella tularensis*. J Clin Microbiol. 1992;30:2256–2264.
100. Sandström G. Review: The tularemia vaccine. J Chem Tech Biotechnol. 1994;59:315–320.
101. Waag DM, Sandström G, England MJ, Williams JC. Immunogenicity of a new lot of *Francisella tularensis* live vaccine strain in human volunteers. FEMS Immunol Med Microbiol. 1996;13:205–209.
102. Kormilitsyna MI, Meshcheryakova IS. The new vaccine strains (or variants) of *Francisella tularensis*. FEMS Immunol Med Microbiol. 1996;13:215–219.
103. Burke DS. Immunization against tularemia: Analysis of the effectiveness of live *Francisella tularensis* vaccine in prevention of laboratory-acquired tularemia. J Infect Dis. 1977;135:55–60.
104. Conley J, Yang H, Wilson T, et al. Aerosol delivery of liposome-encapsulated ciprofloxacin: Aerosol characterization and efficacy against *Francisella tularensis* infection in mice. Antimicrob Agents Chemother. 1997;41:1288–1292.
105. Russell P, Eley SM, Fulop MJ, et al. The efficacy of ciprofloxacin and doxycycline against experimental tularemia. J Antimicrob Chemother. 1998;41:461–465.

Chapter 217

Pasteurella Species

JOHN J. ZURLO

Pasteurella species are gram-negative coccobacilli that inhabit the oral cavity and gastrointestinal tract of many animals and cause various infectious problems including septicemia and pneumonia. In humans infection is most often caused by dog and cat bites resulting in cellulitis, subcutaneous abscesses, and a number of other syndromes. Bacteria belonging to the genus *Pasteurella* were first iso-

TABLE 217–1 Nomenclature for *Pasteurella* Species

Current Name	Synonym
Pasteurella aerogenes	
Pasteurella bettyae	CDC group HB-5
Pasteurella canis	*Pasteurella multocida* biotype 6
Pasteurella dagmatis	*Pasteurella* new species 1 *Pasteurella* "gas"
Pasteurella gallinarum	
Pasteurella haemolytica	
Pasteurella-like	CDC group EF-4
Pasteurella multocida ssp. *gallicida*	*Pasteurella septica*
Pasteurella multocida ssp. *multocida*	
Pasteurella multocida ssp. *septica*	*Pasteurella septica*
Pasteurella pneumotropica	
Pasteurella stomatis	

From Bruckner DA, Colonna P. Nomenclature for aerobic and facultative bacteria. Clin Infect Dis. 1997;25:1–10. Copyright © 1997, Infectious Diseases Society of America.

lated from birds with cholera in 1878; they were characterized 2 years later by Pasteur.[1] In 1886 Hueppe speciated the organism, *Bacterium septicemia haemorrhagica*, as the cause of hemorrhagic septicemia in animals. The first human case of *Pasteurella* infection, a case of puerperal sepsis, was described by Brugnatelli in 1913.[2] The isolation of *Pasteurella multocida* from an infection occurring after a cat bite was first described in 1930.[3] Subsequently, as additional isolates were recovered and characterized, related species were grouped together, first as *Pasteurella septica*, then by the late 1930s as the *P. multocida* group.

DESCRIPTION OF THE PATHOGEN

Species of the genus *Pasteurella* are nonmotile, facultatively anaerobic, gram-negative coccobacilli measuring 1 to 2 μm in length.[4] DNA hybridization studies have determined that they are closely related to *Actinobacillus* species.[5] The majority of strains are fermentative and test indole, catalase, oxidase, and sucrose positive.[4] Many pathogenic isolates are encapsulated. Organisms grow in culture on a variety of commercial media, including sheep blood and chocolate agar media. It has been reported that the oxidase reaction is most reliable when tested on strains grown on chocolate agar.[6] The most common human isolates belong to the *P. multocida* group and appear as smooth, iridescent, blue, and watery mucoid colonies on growth media.[7] Problems with misidentification of *Pasteurella* isolates using commercial test systems have been described.[8, 9] In particular, *Pasteurella* spp. and *Haemophilus* spp. have been confused when the API system (Analytab Products, Plainview, NY) was used.[9]

Table 217–1 lists the most recent classification of the *Pasteurella* species that cause human disease.[10] Holst and associates[11] characterized and speciated 159 strains of *Pasteurella* recovered from clinical specimens from 146 patients over 3 years. The majority of infections were caused by five different species or subspecies: *P. multocida* ssp. *multocida*, *P. multocida* ssp. *septica*, *Pasteurella canis*, *Pasteurella stomatis*, *Pasteurella dagmatis* (Table 217–2).

EPIDEMIOLOGY

Based on case reports and case series of infected patients, *Pasteurella* species, particularly *P. multocida*, appear to have a worldwide distribution.[12] For the majority of *Pasteurella* species, the principal reservoir is in animals. *P. multocida* has been isolated from the upper respiratory tracts of a variety of animals, including dogs, cats, pigs, Norway rats, and buffaloes.[13–16] Dogs and cats have particularly high colonization rates. In most cases, carriage is asymptomatic, although both upper and lower respiratory tract infections and septicemia are well known to occur in animals.[17] Although the reservoirs of some of the non-*multocida Pasteurella* species (*P. canis, P. stomatis, P. dagmatis*,[11] *Pasteurella aerogenes*,[18] and *Pasteurella pneumotropica*[19]) are probably animal, other non-*multocida* species (*Pasteurella ureae* [now *Actinobacillus ureae*][20] and *Pasteurella bettyae*[21]) appear to have nonanimal reservoirs that are not well defined. Respiratory tract colonization by *P. multocida* in humans is well known to occur. In most cases colonized patients have underlying upper or lower respiratory tract diseases including chronic sinusitis and bronchiectasis.[12, 22, 23] Most colonized patients have a history of household or domesticated animal contact.[12, 24, 25]

Broadly speaking human infection with *Pasteurella* species can be divided into three types: infection occurring after animal bites, usually from dogs or cats (see Chapter 311); infection occurring after other animal exposures; and infection with no known animal contact. Infection after animal bites is the most commonly reported clinical setting for the organism.[11, 12, 25–31] In general dog bites are most common, followed by cat bites. Approximately 15 to 20% of dog bite wounds and more than 50% of cat bite wounds become infected.[25, 29] The higher incidence of infection after cat bites probably results from the fact that cat teeth are thinner and more commonly result in puncture wounds, which are known to carry a higher risk of infection. For dog bite infections, *Staphylococcus aureus* and streptococcal species are the most commonly isolated pathogens, with *Pasteurella* species and other organisms next in frequency.[27, 30] For cat bite infections, *Pasteurella* species are the most common pathogens.[30] The difference in incidence of *Pasteurella* infections in dog and cat bites may reflect the higher rate of upper respiratory colonization in cats. Francis and associates, studying bite-related *P. multocida* infections in Oregon between 1962 and 1972, noted that 76% were the result of cat bites and the remaining 24% were from dog bites.[28] *Pasteurella* infections also have been reported after bites from a variety of other animals, including pigs, rats, lions, opossums, and rabbits.[25, 31] In addition to bites, *Pasteurella* infections also have been reported after dog and cat scratches and from the licking of open wounds by these animals.[11, 25]

Pasteurella infections are well known to develop in patients

TABLE 217–2 Clinical Characteristics of 159 Strains of *Pasteurella* Species Isolated from 146 Infected Humans over a 3-Year Period

		Site of Infection			
Species	**N**	***Wound Infections or Abscesses****	***Blood***	***Cerebrospinal Fluid***	***Other***
P. multocida ssp. *multocida*	95	85	5	1	4†
P. multocida ssp. *septica*	21	20		1	
P. canis	28	28			
P. stomatis	10	10‡			
P. dagmatis	5	2§			3‖

*Caused by dog or cat bites or wounds licked by dogs or cats.
†Includes three cases of infection from cut wounds unassociated with any known animal contact.
‡In eight cases of wound infection *P. multocida* ssp. *multocida* was also recovered.
§In cases of wound abscesses, *P. multocida* ssp. *multocida* and *P. canis* were also recovered.
‖One case each of severe cellulitis, groin abscess, throat abscess.
Adapted from Holst E, Rollof J, Larsson L, et al. Characterization and distribution of *Pasteurella* species recovered from infected humans. J Clin Microbiol. 1992;30:2984–2987.

exposed to animals but without a history of bites or scratches. These include skin and soft tissue infections, bone and joint infections, pneumonia, meningitis, endocarditis, and septicemia[25, 32] (see later discussion). Persons at risk for infection from animal exposure include veterinarians, farmers, livestock handlers, pet owners, and food handlers. Although the mode of infection in most reported cases is not clear, most have been presumed to result from inadvertent direct inoculation of organisms or from upper respiratory tract colonization with subsequent dissemination to the target organ or organs.

In a significant proportion of *Pasteurella* cases, no known animal exposure or contact can be identified. Hubbert and associates[32] reviewed in 1970 what was then the world's literature, identified 72 reported cases of *P. multocida* infection unrelated to bites, and described 136 additional cases. In 16% of the reviewed cases and 31% of their additional cases, no animal exposure or contact could be identified.[32] Once again the spectrum of infectious complications was wide, similar to what was described for patients with nonbite animal exposures. Of the non-*multocida Pasteurella* species *P. bettyae* does not appear to have an animal reservoir and has been isolated only from humans. It has been recovered from genital ulcers and may be a cause of genitourinary infections.[33, 34]

PATHOGENESIS

The specific mechanisms of pathogenesis of *Pasteurella* species have been best studied in animals. In these hosts virulent *P. multocida* strains adhere to mucosal epithelial cells in the upper respiratory tract, particularly in the tonsils. In some cases adherence is mediated by fimbriae. In any case, adherence has been best demonstrated among toxigenic strains. The tonsils may be the major site of respiratory colonization by the organism in animals.[35]

Several virulence factors have been described in *Pasteurella* species. Toxin production has been demonstrated in some *Pasteurella* isolates from animals. Specifically, leukotoxin has been isolated from *Pasteurella haemolytica*. Leukotoxin is toxic to ruminant leukocytes and is thought to impair cellular response in lung tissue and to stimulate the inflammatory response.[36] In addition, most virulent *Pasteurella* strains produce polysaccharide capsules. The capsule is antiphagocytic and aids in the resistance to intracellular killing by neutrophils.[37] Finally, binding of transferrin by some pathogenic *Pasteurella* strains has been demonstrated and may be a mechanism used by the bacteria to ensure an iron supply necessary for growth.[38]

The humoral response to *P. multocida* infection has been characterized. Antibodies to both somatic and capsular antigenic determinants develop within 2 weeks after clinical infection. Capsular antibodies are more long-lasting than somatic antibodies.[39] The precise role for such antibodies in host defense in humans is not clear.

CLINICAL MANIFESTATIONS

Most reported *Pasteurella* infections in humans are caused by *P. multocida* and involve skin and soft tissues. Other species have been described much less commonly (see Table 217–2). Beyond skin and soft tissues, other sites of infection are uncommon and have been the subject of individual case reports or small case series.

Skin and Soft Tissue Infections. Infections of skin and soft tissues almost invariably develop after a bite or scratch. Less commonly, infections develop after a dog or cat has licked an open wound. Inflammation, swelling, and tenderness develop at the site of injury, usually within 24 hours from the time of exposure.[25, 26, 28] Regional lymphadenopathy occurs in 30 to 40% of cases.[28] Wound discharge ranging from serosanguineous to frankly purulent has been noted in 21 to 39% of cases; fever develops in approximately 20%.[25, 28] Anatomically, more than 50% of cases of infection from both dog and cat bites occur in the upper extremities, followed by the lower extremities, head, face, and neck; multiple sites of infection are sometimes evident.[28, 31] Abscesses and tenosynovitis are the most frequent complications of *Pasteurella* soft tissue infection, with septic arthritis and osteomyelitis being less common. Bacteremia is rare. Weber and associates[25] noted an overall complication rate of 39% among 23 patients studied.

Bone and Joint Infections. Bone and joint infections with *Pasteurella* species have been reported uncommonly. These infections take three different forms: septic arthritis, osteomyelitis, and combined arthritis and osteomyelitis. Ewing and associates[40] reported two cases each of septic arthritis and osteomyelitis caused by *P. multocida* and reviewed the literature. Among 14 cases of septic arthritis reported and reviewed, 7 (50%) involved dog or cat bites or scratches, 5 (36%) involved animal exposure without recent or known bites or scratches, and in the remaining 2 cases there were no reported animal exposures. The knee was the most common joint involved (11 cases), often in the setting of rheumatoid arthritis, osteoarthritis, or joint prosthesis. Five of the 14 patients were receiving prednisone. Osteomyelitis developed either as the result of direct extension of soft tissue inflammation or by direct inoculation of the periosteum at the time of the bite.[25] Among 13 cases of osteomyelitis reported by this group, 9 (69%) involved animal bites or scratches, 1 (8%) involved animal exposure, and in 3 cases there was no reported exposure. In contrast to septic arthritis, most cases (69%) of osteomyelitis developed in an upper extremity bone, usually the hand or wrist. Also unlike septic arthritis, chronic medical conditions and corticosteroid therapy were not common antecedents. Finally, among seven cases of combined septic arthritis and osteomyelitis, six involved bones and joints of the upper extremities, usually a phalanx and interphalangeal joint infected after a cat bite.[40]

Central Nervous System Infections. Central nervous system infections with *P. multocida* have been reported infrequently. Meningitis is most common; there have been rare cases of focal lesions such as brain abscess and subdural empyema.[25] In general, cases tend to occur in neonates and infants as well as in the elderly. Most patients have a documented animal exposure, usually dog or cat, without a clear invasive injury. The clinical presentation and spinal fluid abnormalities are similar to what is seen in other forms of acute bacterial meningitis, and focal neurologic signs are uncommon.[25, 41]

Septicemia and Endocarditis. Septicemia is another uncommon complication of *Pasteurella* infection. Raffi and associates[42] reported the clinical features of 13 cases of *P. multocida* bacteremia over a 12-year period and reviewed the literature of 82 previously reported cases.[42] Most patients were men (69%), and most had a localized site of infection (pneumonia, meningitis, arthritis, peritonitis). Many had a serious underlying medical condition, with cirrhosis being most common (34% of reported and reviewed cases). Thirty-two percent had associated animal-related trauma.[42] Infective endocarditis has been reported much less frequently than septicemia. Saleh and associates[43] reported a case of *P. gallinarum* infectious endocarditis in an adolescent 10 years after surgery to correct a truncus arteriosus. They found 17 other cases of *Pasteurella* infectious endocarditis in the medical literature caused by many different *Pasteurella* species. In almost half of the cases, no preexisting heart disease was evident. Also, no animal contact was evident in 11 cases.[43]

Respiratory Tract Infections. Respiratory tract infections with *Pasteurella* species involve the upper respiratory tract, causing sinusitis and bronchitis, and the lower respiratory tract, causing both pneumonia and empyema. The respiratory tract is second only to skin and soft tissue in frequency of clinical isolation of *Pasteurella*.[25] Most reported cases are caused by *P. multocida*. As previously discussed, asymptomatic *Pasteurella* colonization of the upper respiratory tract has been reported in patients with underlying respiratory tract disease, including chronic obstructive pulmonary disease and bronchiectasis. Presumably for a subset of this patient group the organism invades and causes disease.[20] There is nothing clinically distinguishing about upper respiratory tract infections. Pneumonia usually occurs in patients with underlying lung disease and is usually lobar with a short prodrome. Cases of multilobar and diffuse pulmonary involvement have been described.[25] *Pasteurella* empyema was the subject of a case report and review of the literature by Nelson and Hammer.[44] Most of the 14 patients were adults with a mean age of 70 years, and most had underlying pulmonary disease, either chronic obstructive pulmonary disease or bronchiectasis. Although respiratory and constitutional complaints were the dominant presenting symptoms, fever was surprisingly uncommon. Pleural fluid was described as purulent in all cases in which a sample was obtained.[44]

Intra-abdominal Infections. Of the few reported cases of *Pasteurella* intra-abdominal infections, spontaneous bacterial peritonitis and appendicitis with or without associated peritonitis have been the most frequent clinical syndromes. Among the reported cases of spontaneous bacterial peritonitis, virtually all have had cirrhosis (usually alcoholic) and preexisting ascites.[45, 46] Raffi and associates reported three cases of *P. multocida* appendiceal peritonitis and identified eight additional well-documented cases of appendicitis in the literature.[47] Accompanying peritonitis was variably present. It was postulated that the source of the organism was most likely from oropharyngeal colonization.[47]

Other *Pasteurella* Infections. Infections of other sites with *Pasteurella* species have been reported rarely and include the genitourinary tract, usually in patients with underlying genitourinary disease such as malignancy.[32] Ocular infections including endophthalmitis also have been reported.[25]

TREATMENT, PREVENTION, AND PROGNOSIS

Several decades of clinical experience with *Pasteurella* and numerous *in vitro* studies indicate that penicillin is the best antimicrobial agent for the treatment of virtually all forms of infection.[12, 25, 28, 48, 49] Minimal inhibitory concentrations (MICs) of various strains of *P. multocida* to penicillin G have ranged from 0.19 to 0.78 μg/ml[49] and from 0.049 to 0.39 μg/ml.[48] Other penicillins with good in vitro activity include penicillin VK, ampicillin, and amoxicillin.[48–50] Antistaphylococcal penicillins including oxacillin, nafcillin, dicloxacillin, and cloxacillin are not as active and are not recommended for treatment of documented *Pasteurella* infections.[48, 49, 51] Amoxicillin-clavulanic acid has excellent in vitro activity.[50] Many cephalosporins demonstrate in vitro activity against *P. multocida*. In general, activity increases with later-generation cephalosporins.[48, 51] Goldstein and associates[51] reported high MICs for cephalexin, cefaclor, and cefadroxil and recommended that they not be used for the treatment of documented infections.[51] The oral cephalosporins, cefuroxime and cefixime, along with parenteral agents including ceftriaxone and cefoperazone, demonstrate excellent in vitro activity and are probably good substitutes for penicillin.[48]

Plasmid-mediated β-lactamase production has been described in *P. multocida* strains isolated from animals. The first β-lactamase–producing *P. multocida* strain isolated from a human source (respiratory tract) was reported in the late 1980s and characterized as an ROB-1 β-lactamase by Rosenau and associates.[52] The isolate was resistant to amoxicillin, ticarcillin, cephalothin, sulfonamides, and tetracyclines. Addition of the β-lactamase inhibitors, clavulanic acid, sulbactam, and tazobactam, reduced the MICs of the isolate by at least 64-fold.[52]

Among non–β-lactam antibiotics, agents with in vitro activity include tetracyclines, fluoroquinolones (ciprofloxacin, enoxacin, ofloxacin, levofloxacin), and chloramphenicol.[49, 50, 51, 53] In comparison with penicillin, limited clinical data on the usefulness of these agents are available. Aminoglycosides have moderate to poor activity in vitro and probably should not be used, particularly given the paucity of clinical experience.[49, 53] Clindamycin and erythromycin consistently demonstrate high MICs in vitro and are not recommended. The newer long-acting macrolides (azithromycin, clarithromycin, roxithromycin, dirithromycin) appear to have better activity but also should not be used, because clinical experience with these agents is limited.[53]

Because animal bite wound infections are frequently polymicrobial and may include *S. aureus*, streptococcal species, and anaerobes in addition to *Pasteurella* species, empirical antibiotic therapy should be directed at such organisms until or unless wound cultures define the specific bacteriology of the infection.[30] Outpatient treatment of documented, uncomplicated *Pasteurella* cellulitis can be undertaken with penicillin VK, amoxicillin, or ampicillin, with close follow-up.[25] Duration of therapy is not well defined, but 10 to 14 days is probably a reasonable time course. Patients with evidence of involvement of deeper structures (e.g., tenosynovitis, arthritis) should be hospitalized and treated parenterally. Drainage and débridement may be necessary for patients who have progressive infection with extensive suppuration.

Treatment of septic arthritis should consist of antimicrobial therapy along with frequent drainage of the involved joints.[40] Most patients recover fully.[40] Similarly, the outcome for osteomyelitis appears to be good, although débridement in addition to antimicrobial therapy is often needed.[40] The outcome of septic arthritis with osteomyelitis is not as good, with residual deformity and loss of function being common.[40] For all bone and joint *Pasteurella* infections, antimicrobial therapy should be continued for 4 to 6 weeks.

Patients with the other end-organ forms of *Pasteurella* infection do poorly overall. High mortality has been reported for most of these conditions. The high mortality rate for meningitis is probably a consequence of the frail nature of its target population, young children and the elderly. Permanent neurologic sequelae among survivors have been uncommon.[25] For patients with bacteremia without endovascular infection, the mortality rate also is high, probably as a result of the infection itself combined with the underlying medical problem, usually alcoholic cirrhosis. For endocarditis, among 17 reported patients, 5 died while 4 required valve replacement.[43] For patients with pneumonia, both morbidity and mortality are high, almost certainly as a result of severe underlying pulmonary disease. Finally, patients with spontaneous bacterial peritonitis have an extremely high mortality rate, whereas those with appendicitis with or without peritonitis generally do well.[46, 47]

Antimicrobial prophylaxis after animal bites has remained a controversial subject. Although a few small trials have been completed, none has been large enough or seen enough patients reach significant end points to unequivocally speak to the efficacy of such therapy. Nonetheless, because the rate of culture positivity of fresh animal bite wounds is high, most experts recommend a short course (3 to 5 days) of oral antimicrobial therapy. Amoxicillin 875 mg with clavulanic acid 125 mg, given twice daily, is a commonly used regimen that has activity against *S. aureus*, streptococci, anaerobes, and *Pasteurella*. Ampicillin, dicloxacillin, first-generation oral cephalosporins, macrolides, tetracyclines, earlier fluoroquinolones, and clindamycin are not recommended (see Chap. 311).

REFERENCES

1. Pasteur L. Sur les maladies virulentes et en particulier sur la maladie appelee vulgairement cholera des poules. CR Acad Sci (Paris). 1880;90:239–248.
2. Brugnatelli E. Puerperal fieber durch einen Bacillus aus der Gruppe, "Hamorrhagische Septikamie" *(Pasteurella)*. Centr Bakteriol Parasitenk I Abt Orig. 1913;70:337–345.
3. Kapel O, Holm J. *Pasteurella* infektion biem menschen nach katzenbiss. Zbl Chir. 1930;57:2906.
4. Holmes B, Pickett MJ, Hollis DG. Unusual gram-negative bacteria, including *Capnocytophaga*, *Eikenella*, *Pasteurella*, and *Streptobacillus*. In: Murray PR, Baron EJ, Pfaller MA, et al, eds. Manual of Clinical Microbiology. Washington, DC: ASM Press; 1995:499–508.
5. Dewhirst FE, Paster BJ, Olsen I, et al. Phylogeny of 54 representative strains of species in the family Pasteurellaceae as determined by comparison of 16S rRNA sequences. J Bacteriol. 1992;174:2002–2013.
6. Grehn M, Muller F. The oxidase reaction of *Pasteurella multocida* strains cultured on Mueller-Hinton medium. J Microbiol Methods. 1989;9:333-336.

7. Heddleston KL, Wessman G. Characteristics of *Pasteurella multocida* of human origin. J Clin Microbiol. 1975;1:377–383.
8. Oberhofer TR. Characteristics and biotypes of *Pasteurella multocida* isolated from humans. J Clin Microbiol. 1981;13:566–571.
9. Hamilton-Miller JM. A possible pitfall in the identification of *Pasteurella* spp. with the API system. J Med Microbiol. 1993;39:78–79.
10. Bruckner DA, Colonna P. Nomenclature for aerobic and facultative bacteria. Clin Infect Dis. 1997;25:1–10.
11. Holst E, Rollof J, Larsson L, et al. Characterization and distribution of *Pasteurella* species recovered from infected humans. J Clin Microbiol. 1992;30:2984–2987.
12. Jones FL, Smull CE. Infections in man due to *Pasteurelia multocida*. Penn Med J. 1973;76:41–44,64.
13. Bailie WE, Stowe EC, Schmitt AM. Aerobic bacterial flora of oral and nasal fluids of canines with reference to bacteria associated with bites. J Clin Microbiol. 1978;7:223–231.
14. Owen CR, Buker EO, Be JF, et al. *Pasteurella multocida* in animal mouths. Rocky Mt Med J. 1968;65:45–46.
15. Schipper GJ. Unusual pathogenicity of *Pasteurella multocida* isolated from the throats of common wild rats. Johns Hopkins Hosp Bull. 1947;81:333.
16. Smith JE. Studies on *Pasteurella septica*: II. Some cultural and biochemical properties of strains from different host species. J Comp Pathol. 1958;68:315.
17. Carter GR. Pasteurellosis: *Pasteurella multocida* and *Pasteurella hemolytica*. Adv Vet Sci. 1967;11:321–379.
18. Ejlertsen T, Gahrn-Hansen B, Sogaard P, et al. *Pasteurella aeragenes* isolated from ulcers or wounds in humans with occupational exposure to pigs: A report of 7 Danish cases. Scand J Infect Dis. 1996;28:567–570.
19. Gadberry JL, Zipper R, Taylor JA, et al. *Pasteurella pneumotropica* isolated from bone and joint infections. J Clin Microbiol. 1984;19:926–927.
20. Starkebaum GA, Plorde JJ. *Pasteurella* pneumonia: Report of a case and review of the literature. J Clin Microbiol. 1977;5:332–335.
21. Moritz F, Martin E, Lemeland JF, et al. Fatal *Pasteurella bettyae* pleuropneumonia in a patient infected with human immunodeficiency virus. Clin Infect Dis. 1996;22:591–592.
22. Bartley EO. *Pasteurella septica* in chronic nasal sinusitis. Lancet. 1960;2:581–582.
23. Cawson RA, Talbot JM. The occurrence of *Pasteurella septica* (syn. *multocida*) in bronchiectasis. J Clin Pathol. 1955;8:49–51.
24. Avril J-L, Donnio P-Y, Pouedras P. Selective medium for *Pasteurella multocida* and its use to detect oropharyngeal carriage in pig breeders. J Clin Microbiol. 1990;28:1438–1440.
25. Weber DJ, Wolfson JS, Swartz MN, et al. *Pasteurella multocida* infections: Report of 34 cases and review of the literature. Medicine (Baltimore). 1984;63:133–154.
26. Arons MS, Fernando L, Polayes IM. *Pasteurella multocida*: The major cause of hand infections following domestic animal bites. J Hand Surg [Am]. 1982;7:47–52.
27. Brook I. Microbiology of human and animal bite wounds in children. Pediatr Infect Dis J. 1987;6:29–32.
28. Francis DP, Holmes MA, Brandon G. *Pasteurella multocida*: Infections after domestic animal bites and scratches. JAMA. 1975;233:42–45.
29. Goldstein EJC. Bite wounds and infection. Clin Infect Dis. 1992;14:633–640.
30. Goldstein EJC, Citron DM, Wield B, et al. Bacteriology of human and animal bite wounds. J Clin Microbiol. 1978;8:667–672.
31. Hubbert WT, Rosen MN. *Pasteurella multocida* infection due to animal bite. Am J Public Health. 1970;60:1103–1108.
32. Hubbert WT, Rosen MN. *Pasteurella multocida* infection in man unrelated to animal bite. Am J Public Health. 1970;60:1109–1117.
33. Baddour LM, Gelfand, Weaver RE, et al. CDC Group HB-5 as a cause of genitourinary infections in adults. J Clin Microbiol. 1989;27:801–805.
34. Bogaerts J, Verhaegen J, Martinez Tello W, et al. Characterization, in vitro susceptibility, and clinical significance of CDC group HB-5 from Rwanda. J Clin Microbiol. 1990;10:2196–2199.
35. Pijoan C, Trigo F. Bacterial adhesion to mucosal surfaces with special reference to *Pasteurella multocida* isolates from atrophic rhinitis. Can J Vet Res. 1990;54:S16–S21.
36. Lo RYC. Molecular characterization of cytotoxins produced by *Haemophilus, Actinobacillus, Pasteurella*. Can J Vet Res. 1990;54:S33–S35.
37. Czuprynski CJ, Sample AK. Interactions of *Haemophilus-Actinobacillus-Pasteurella* bacteria with phagocytic cells. Can J Vet Res. 1990;54:S36–S40.
38. Schryvers AB, Gonzalez GC. Receptors for transferrin in pathogenic bacteria are specific for the host's protein. Can J Microbiol. 1990;36:145–147.
39. Choudat D, Paul G, Legoff C, et al. Specific antibody responses to *Pasteurella multocida*. Scand J Infect Dis. 1987;19:453–457.
40. Ewing R, Fainstein V, Musher DM, et al. Articular and skeletal infections caused by *Pasteurella multocida*. South Med J. 1980;73:1349–1352.
41. Controni G, Jones RS. *Pasteurella* meningitis: A review of the literature. Am J Med Technol. 1967;33:379–386.
42. Raffi F, Barrier J, Baron D, et al. *Pasteurella multocida* bacteremia: Report of thirteen cases over twelve years and review of the literature. Scand J Infect Dis. 1987;19:385–393.
43. Saleh MAF, Al-Madan MS, Erwa HH, et al. First case of human infection caused by *Pasteurella gallinarum* causing infective endocarditis in an adolescent 10 years after surgical correction for truncus arteriosus. Pediatrics. 1995;95:944–948.
44. Nelson SC, Hammer GS. *Pasteurella multocida* empyema: Case report and review of the literature. Am J Med Sci. 1981;281:43–49.
45. Gerding DN, Khan MY, Ewing JW, et al. *Pasteurella multocida* peritonitis in hepatic cirrhosis with ascites. Gastroenterology. 1976;70:413–415.
46. Szpak CA, Woodard BH, White JO, et al. Bacterial peritonitis and bacteremia associated with *Pasteurella multocida*. South Med J. 1980;73:801–803.
47. Raffi F, David A, Mouzard A, et al. *Pasteurella multocida* appendiceal peritonitis: Report of three cases and review of the literature. Pediatr Infect Dis. 1986;5:695–698.
48. Noel GJ, Teele DW. *In vitro* activities of selected new and long-acting cephalosporins against *Pasteurella multocida*. Antimicrob Agents Chemother. 1986;29:344–345.
49. Stevens DL, Higbee JW, Oberhofer TR, et al. Antibiotic susceptibilities of human isolates of *Pasteurella multocida*. Antimicrob Agents Chemother. 1979;16:322–324.
50. Goldstein EJC, Citron DM. Comparative activities of cefuroxime, amoxicillin-clavulanic acid, ciprofloxacin, enoxacin, ofloxacin against aerobic and anaerobic bacteria isolated from bite wounds. Antimicrob Agents Chemother. 1988;32:1143–1148.
51. Goldstein EJC, Citron DM, Richwald GA. Lack of in vitro efficacy of oral forms of certain cephalosporins, erythromycin, and oxacillin against *Pasteurella multocida*. Antimicrob Agents Chemother. 1988;32:213–215.
52. Rosenau A, Labigne A, Escande F, et al. Plasmid-mediated ROB-1 β-lactamase in *Pasteurella multocida* from a human specimen. Antimicrob Agents Chemother. 1991;35:2419–2422.
53. Gaillot O, Guilbert L, Maruejouls C, et al. In-vitro susceptibility to thirteen antibiotics of *Pasteurella* spp. and related bacteria isolated from humans (Letter). J Antimicrob Chemother. 1995;36:878–880.

Chapter 218

Yersinia Species, Including Plague

THOMAS BUTLER

The genus *Yersinia* includes the pathogens *Yersinia pestis*, *Yersinia enterocolitica*, and *Yersinia pseudotuberculosis*. The yersinioses are zoonotic infections that affect predominantly rodents, pigs, and birds; humans are accidental hosts for infection. *Y. pestis* is the cause of plague. The most common clinical form is acute febrile lymphadenitis, called bubonic plague. Less common forms include septicemic, pneumonic, and meningeal plague. Mortality is high in untreated plague, but early antibiotic treatment reduces mortality significantly. *Y. enterocolitica* and sometimes *Y. pseudotuberculosis* produce fever, diarrhea, and abdominal pain that mimics acute appendicitis. Common pathologic lesions are acute enteritis and mesenteric lymphadenitis.

YERSINIA PESTIS

History

Plague is a disease of antiquity that has persisted to modern times. Epidemic bubonic plague was vividly described in biblical and medieval times. This disease was estimated to have killed one fourth of Europe's population in the Middle Ages. The present pandemic of plague began in China in the 1860s and spread to Hong Kong in the 1890s. The genus is called *Yersinia* because Alexandre Yersin (1863–1943) went to Hong Kong in 1894 and successfully isolated the causative organism in pure culture. This pandemic was subsequently spread by rats transported on ships to California and port cities of South America, Africa, and Asia. Urban plague transmitted by rats was brought under control in most affected cities, but the infection was transferred to sylvatic rodents, which allowed it to become entrenched in rural areas of these countries. In the first half of the 20th century, India was severely affected by plague epidemics, with more than 10 million deaths. In the 1960s and 1970s, Vietnam became the leading country for plague; reporting more than 10,000 cases annually.[1] In 1994, India reported 876 cases of pneumonic plague but cultures did not confirm the presence of plague. Before 1970, *Y. pestis* was called by its earlier name, *Pasteurella pestis*.

Description of the Pathogen

Y. pestis is a gram-negative, bipolar-staining bacillus that belongs to the bacterial family Enterobacteriaceae. It grows aerobically on most culture media, including blood agar and MacConkey agar. It does not ferment lactose and forms small colonies on MacConkey agar after 24-hour incubation at 35°C. On triple-sugar-iron agar, *Y. pestis* produces an alkaline slant and acid butt. It is nonmotile and is negative for citrate utilization, urease, and indole.

Like the other yersiniae, the plague bacillus produces V and W antigens, which confer a requirement for calcium to grow at 37°C.[2] This property, mediated by a 45-mD plasmid (70 kilobases), is essential for virulence and plays a role in adapting the organism for intracellular survival and growth. Other important virulence factors include the production of lipopolysaccharide endotoxin, a capsular envelope containing the antiphagocytic principal fraction I antigen, the ability to absorb organic iron into the form of hemin, and the presence of the temperature-dependent enzymes coagulase and fibrinolysin.

Epidemiology

Plague occurs worldwide, with most of the human cases reported from developing countries of Asia and Africa. During 1990–1995, 12,988 cases of plague, with 1009 deaths (8%) were reported to the World Health Organization. The countries that reported more than 100 cases (from greatest to least) were Tanzania, Madagascar, Democratic Republic of Congo, Vietnam, Peru, India, Myanmar, Zimbabwe, Mozambique, Uganda, and China. The emerging threat of plague was shown by unexpected outbreaks in Mozambique, Zimbabwe, Zambia, and Malawi. In the United States, about 10 cases occur each year; most are in the southwestern states of New Mexico, Arizona, Colorado, Utah, and California. Most of these occur during the months of May to October, when people are outdoors and come into contact with rodents and their fleas.

Plague is primarily a zoonotic infection. It is transmitted among the natural animal reservoirs, which are predominantly urban and sylvatic rodents by flea bites or by ingestion of contaminated animal tissues (Fig. 218–1). Throughout the world, the urban and domestic rats *Rattus rattus* and *Rattus norvegicus* are the most important reservoirs of the plague bacillus. The most efficient vector for transmission is the oriental rat flea, *Xenopsylla cheopis*. In sylvatic foci of plague, such as occur in the United States, the important reservoirs are the ground squirrel, rock squirrel, and prairie dog. Humans become accidental hosts in the natural cycle of plague when they are bitten by infected rodent fleas; humans appear to play no role in the maintenance of plague in nature. Only rarely, during epidemics of pneumonic plague, is the infection passed directly from person to person. Humans also rarely develop infection by the direct handling or inhalation of contaminated animal tissues and fluids.

In the United States, males and females have been equally affected. Sixty percent of cases occur in persons younger than 20 years old. Although a majority of cases occur in whites, the attack rate among Native Americans living in endemic areas such as Arizona, New Mexico, and Utah is 10 times the rate among non–Native Americans living in the same states (1.4 cases/100,000 population and 0.1/100,000 population, respectively).[3] Within endemic areas, risk factors associated with acquiring plague include direct contact with rodents or carnivores, the presence of harborage and food sources for wild rodents in the immediate vicinity of the home, and possibly failure to control fleas on pet dogs and cats.[4]

Pathogenesis

When a flea ingests a blood meal from a bacteremic animal infected with *Y. pestis*, the coagulase of the organism causes the blood to clot in the foregut, leading to blockage of the flea's swallowing. *Y. pestis* multiplies in the clotted blood. During attempts to ingest a blood meal, a blocked flea may regurgitate thousands of organisms into a patient's skin. The inoculated bacteria migrate by cutaneous lymphatics to the regional lymph nodes. The flea-borne bacilli possess a small amount of envelope antigen (fraction I) and are readily phagocytized by the host's polymorphonuclear leukocytes and mononuclear phagocytes. *Y. pestis* resists destruction within mononuclear phagocytes and may multiply intracellularly with elaboration of envelope antigen. If lysis of the mononuclear cell occurs, the bacilli released are relatively resistant to further phagocytosis. The involved lymph nodes show polymorphonuclear leukocytes, destruction of normal architecture, hemorrhagic necrosis, and dense concentrations of extracellular plague bacilli. Transient bacteremia is common in bubonic plague, and in the absence of specific therapy purulent, necrotic, and hemorrhagic lesions may develop in many organs. Hypotension, oliguria, altered mental status, and subclinical disseminated intravascular coagulation may be noted and are attributable to endotoxinemia.[5]

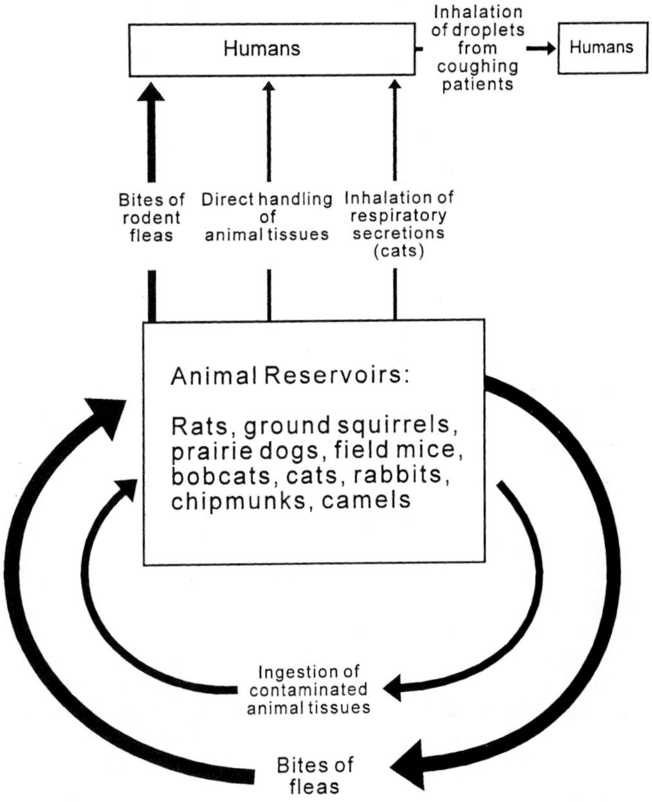

FIGURE 218–1. Transmission of plague. The *wide arrows* indicate common modes of transmission, the *medium arrows* indicate occasional transmission, and the *thin arrows* indicate rare kinds of transmission.

Clinical Manifestations

Bubonic Plague

The most common manifestation of infection is bubonic plague, which presents a distinctive clinical picture (Table 218–1). During an incubation period of 2 to 8 days after the bite of an infected flea, bacteria proliferate in the regional lymph nodes. Patients are typically affected by the sudden onset of fever, chills, weakness, and headache. Usually at the same time, after a few hours, or on the next day, patients notice the bubo, which is signaled by intense pain in one anatomic region of lymph nodes, usually the groin, axilla, or neck. A swelling evolves in this area, which is so tender that the patient typically avoids any motion that would provoke discomfort. For

TABLE 218–1 Plague Syndromes

Syndrome	Features
Bubonic	Fever, painful lymphadenopathy (bubo)
Septicemic	Fever, hypotension without bubo
Pneumonic	Cough, hemoptysis with or without bubo
Cutaneous	Pustule, eschar, carbuncle, or ecthyma gangrenosum usually with bubo
Meningitis	Fever, nuchal rigidity usually with bubo

example, if the bubo is in a femoral area, the patient characteristically flexes, abducts, and externally rotates the hip to relieve pressure on the area and walks with a limp. When the bubo is in an axilla, the patient abducts the shoulder or holds the arm in a splint. When a bubo is cervical in location, the patient tilts the head to the opposite side.

The buboes of patients with plague are oval swellings that vary from 1 to 10 cm in length and elevate the overlying skin, which may appear stretched or erythematous. They may appear either as smooth, uniform, egg-shaped masses or as an irregular cluster of several nodes with intervening and surrounding edema. Palpation typically elicits extreme tenderness. There is warmth of the overlying skin and an underlying firm, nonfluctuant mass. Around the lymph nodes there is usually considerable edema, which can be either gelatinous or pitting in nature. Although infections other than plague can produce acute lymphadenitis, plague is virtually unique for the suddenness of onset of the fever and bubo, the rapid development of intense inflammation in the bubo, and the fulminant clinical course that can

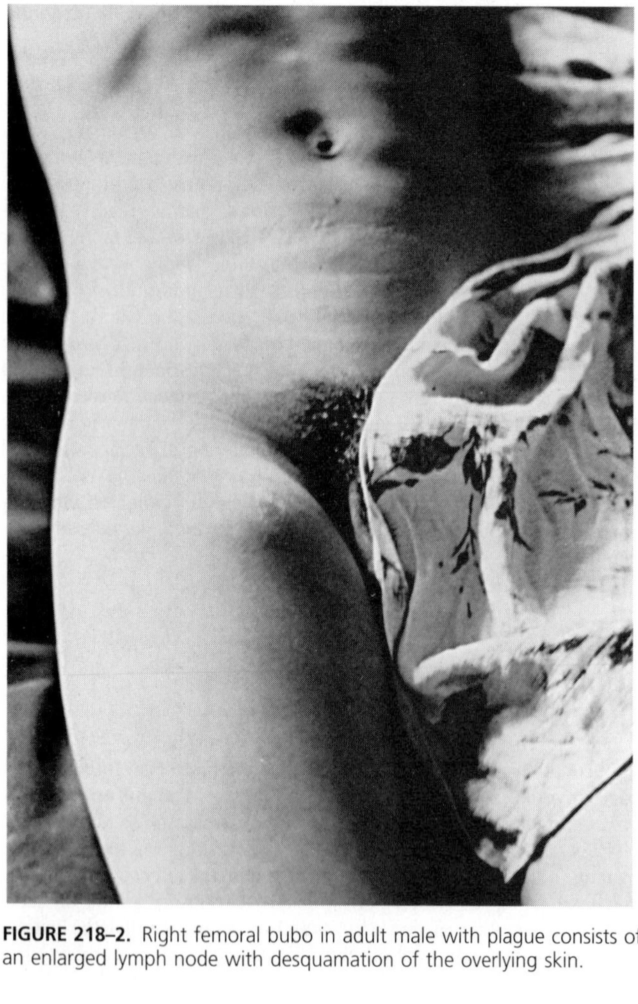

FIGURE 218–2. Right femoral bubo in adult male with plague consists of an enlarged lymph node with desquamation of the overlying skin.

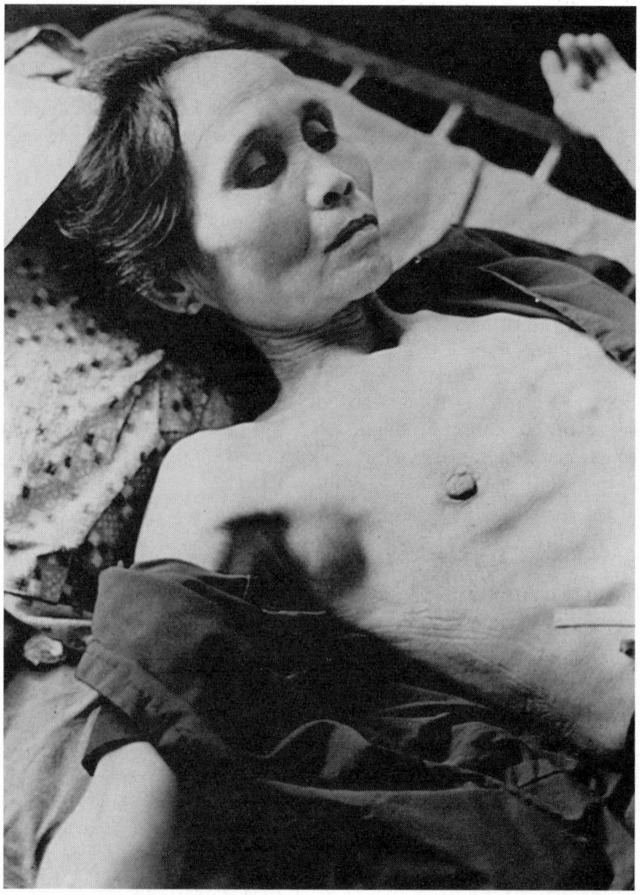

FIGURE 218–3. Right axillary bubo in an adult female who was in septic shock and died the same day.

produce death as quickly as 2 to 4 days after the onset of symptoms. The bubo of plague is also distinctive for the usual absence of a detectable skin lesion in the anatomic region where it is located and for the absence of an ascending lymphangitis near it (Figs. 218–2 and 218–3).

The groin is the most common site of the buboes in plague. In clinical reports that have distinguished femoral from inguinal locations, the femoral site was found to be most common. Other common sites are the axillae and cervical regions. The reason for a given distribution of buboes is presumed to be the distribution of flea bites.

Patients are typically prostrate and lethargic and often exhibit restlessness or agitation. Occasionally, they are delirious with high fever, and seizures are common in children. Temperatures are usually elevated, in the range of 38.5°C to 40.0°C, and pulse rates are increased to 110 to 140 per minute. Blood pressure is characteristically low, in the range of 100/60 mmHg, owing to extreme vasodilation. Lower pressures that are unobtainable may occur if shock ensues. The liver and spleen are often palpable and tender.

The majority of patients with bubonic plague do not have skin lesions; however, about one fourth of the patients in Vietnam did show varied skin findings. Most common were pustules, vesicles, eschars, or papules near the bubo or in the anatomic region of skin that is lymphatically drained by the affected lymph nodes, presumably representing sites of the flea bites (Fig. 218–4). When these lesions are opened, they usually contain leukocytes and plague bacilli. Rarely, these skin lesions progress to extensive cellulitis or abscesses. Ulceration, however, may lead to a larger plague carbuncle.

Another kind of skin lesion in plague is purpura, which is a result of the systemic disease. The purpuric lesions may become necrotic,

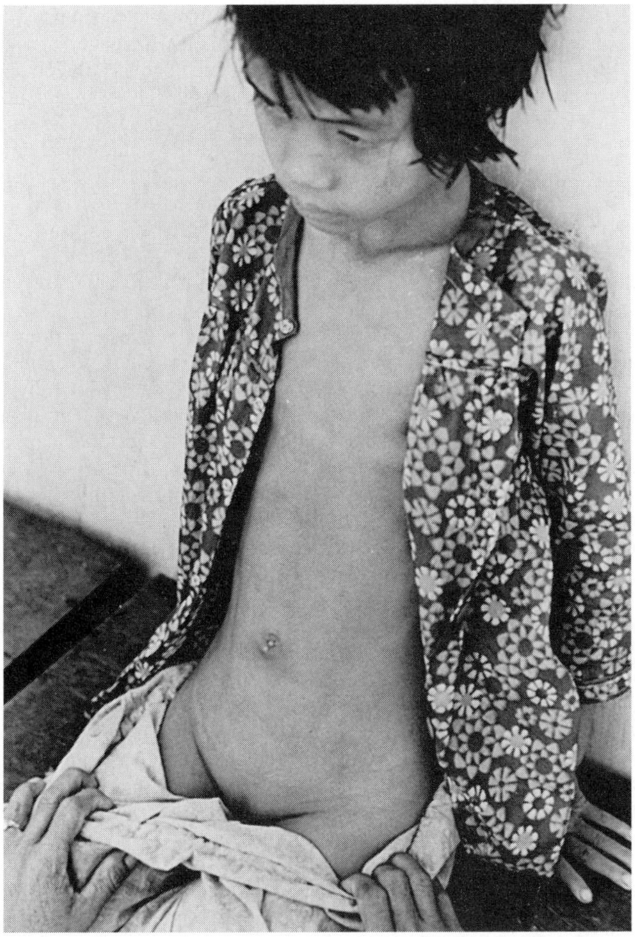

FIGURE 218–4. Pustule on lower rim of umbilicus surrounded by erythema in a young female was the site of the flea bite. She had bilateral enlarged inguinal lymph nodes.

resulting in gangrene of distal extremities, the probable basis of the epithet "Black Death" attributed to plague through the ages. These purpuric lesions contain blood vessels affected by vasculitis and occlusion by fibrin thrombi, resulting in hemorrhage and necrosis.

Septicemic Plague

A distinctive feature of plague, in addition to the bubo, is the propensity of the disease to overwhelm the patient with a massive growth of bacteria in the blood. In the early acute states of bubonic plague, all patients probably have intermittent bacteremia. Single blood cultures obtained at the time of hospital admission in Vietnamese patients were positive in 27% of cases. A hallmark of moribund patients with plague is high-density bacteremia, so that a blood smear revealing characteristic bacilli has been used as a prognostic indicator in this disease (Fig. 218–5). Occasionally in the pathogenesis of plague infection, bacteria are inoculated and proliferate in the body without producing a bubo. Patients may become ill with fever and actually die with bacteremia but without detectable lymphadenitis. This syndrome has been termed *septicemic plague* to denote plague without a bubo. In New Mexico 25% of plague was septicemic in 1980–1984, and the case-fatality rate in these cases (33%) was three times higher than in bubonic plague because of delays in diagnosis and treatment.[6, 7]

Pneumonic Plague

One of the feared complications of bubonic plague is secondary pneumonia. The infection reaches the lungs by hematogenous spread of bacteria from the bubo. In addition to the high mortality rate, plague pneumonia is highly contagious by airborne transmission. It manifests in the setting of fever and lymphadenopathy as cough, chest pain, and often hemoptysis. Radiographically, there is patchy bronchopneumonia, cavities, or confluent consolidation.[8] The sputum is usually purulent and contains plague bacilli.

Primary inhalation pneumonia is rare now but is a potential threat after exposure to a patient with plague who has a cough. Some patients in the United States were exposed to sick domestic cats that had pneumonia or submandibular abscesses.[8] Plague pneumonia is invariably fatal when antibiotic therapy is delayed more than 1 day after the onset of illness.

Other Syndromes

Plague meningitis is a rarer complication and typically occurs more than 1 week after inadequately treated bubonic plague. It results from hematogenous spread from a bubo and carries a high mortality rate compared with that of uncomplicated bubonic plague. There appears to be an association between buboes located in the axilla and the development of meningitis. Less commonly, plague meningitis manifests as a primary infection of the meninges without antecedent lymphadenitis. Plague meningitis is characterized by fever, headache, meningismus, and pleocytosis with a predominance of polymorphonuclear leukocytes. Bacteria are frequently demonstrable with a Gram stain of spinal fluid sediment, and endotoxin has been demonstrated in spinal fluid with the limulus test.

Plague can produce pharyngitis that may resemble acute tonsillitis. The anterior cervical lymph nodes are usually inflamed, and *Y. pestis* may be recovered from a throat culture or by aspiration of a cervical bubo. This is a rare clinical form of plague that is presumed to follow the inhalation or ingestion of plague bacilli.

Plague manifests sometimes with prominent gastrointestinal symptoms of nausea, vomiting, diarrhea, and abdominal pain. These symptoms may precede the bubo; in septicemic plague, they may occur without a bubo and commonly result in diagnostic delay.[9]

Laboratory Findings

The leukocyte count is typically elevated in the range of 10,000 to 20,000 cells/mm^3, with a predominance of immature and mature neutrophils. Severely ill patients tend to have the higher leukocyte counts. Some patients, especially children, may develop myelocytic leukemoid reactions with leukocyte counts as high as 100,000/mm^3. Examination of the leukocytes in the peripheral blood smear typically reveals cytoplasmic vacuolations, toxic granulations, and Döhle bod-

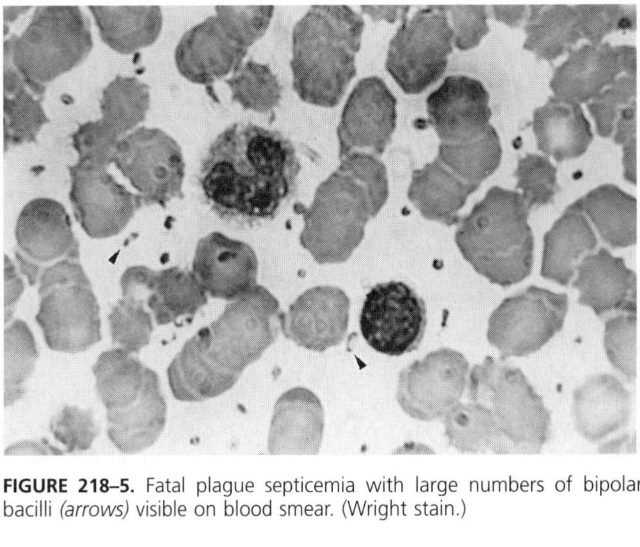

FIGURE 218–5. Fatal plague septicemia with large numbers of bipolar bacilli *(arrows)* visible on blood smear. (Wright stain.)

ies that are characteristic of acute bacterial infections. Blood eosinophils are characteristically diminished or absent in the acute stage of infection but return to normal or increased levels during convalescence. Blood platelets may be normal or low in the early stages of bubonic plague. Although patients with plague rarely develop a generalized bleeding tendency from profound thrombocytopenia, disseminated intravascular coagulation is common in this infection. Fibrinogen-fibrin degradation products in the sera indicative of disseminated intravascular coagulation were detected in elevated titers in most patients tested in Vietnam. Liver function tests, including serum aminotransferases and bilirubin, are frequently abnormally high. Renal function tests may likewise be abnormal in hypotensive patients.

Diagnosis

Plague should be suspected in febrile patients who have been exposed to rodents or other mammals in the known endemic areas of the world. A bacteriologic diagnosis is readily made in most patients by smear and culture of a bubo aspirate. The aspirate is obtained by inserting a 20-gauge needle on a 10-ml syringe containing 1 ml of sterile saline into the bubo and withdrawing it several times until the saline becomes blood-tinged. Because the bubo does not contain liquid pus, it may be necessary to inject some of the saline and immediately reaspirate it. Drops of the aspirate should be placed onto microscopic slides and air-dried for both Gram and Wayson stains. The Gram stain reveals polymorphonuclear leukocytes and gram-negative coccobacilli and bacilli ranging from 1 to 2 μm in length. Wayson stain is prepared by mixing 0.2 g of basic fuchsin (90% dye content) with 0.75 g of methylene blue (90% dye content) in 20 ml of 95% ethyl alcohol. This mixture is then poured slowly into 200 ml of 5% phenol. A smear, after being fixed for 2 minutes in absolute methanol, is stained for 10 to 20 seconds in Wayson stain, washed with water, and dried. *Y. pestis* appears as light blue bacilli with dark blue polar bodies, and the remainder of the slide has a contrasting pink counterstain. Smears of blood, sputum, or spinal fluid can be handled similarly.

The aspirate, blood, and other appropriate fluids should be inoculated onto blood and MacConkey agar plates and into infusion broth. For rapid diagnosis, the direct immunofluorescence test can be applied to smears of fluids or cultures. For definitive identification, cultures can be mailed in double containers to the Centers for Disease Control and Prevention, Vector-borne Infectious Diseases, Fort Collins, CO 80522 (telephone: 970-221-6400). At this same laboratory, a serologic test, the passive hemagglutination test using fraction I of *Y. pestis*, can be performed on acute- or convalescent-phase serum. In patients with negative cultures, a fourfold or greater increase in titer or a single titer of 1:16 or higher is presumptive evidence for plague infection.

Treatment and Prevention

Antibiotics

Untreated plague has an estimated mortality rate of more than 50% and can evolve into a fulminant illness complicated by septic shock. Therefore, the early institution of effective antibiotic therapy is mandatory after appropriate cultures. In 1948, streptomycin was identified as the drug of choice for the treatment of plague when it reduced the mortality rate to less than 5%. No other drug has been demonstrated to be more efficacious or less toxic. Streptomycin should be administered intramuscularly in two divided doses daily, totaling 30 mg/kg of body weight per day for 10 days. Most patients improve rapidly and become afebrile in about 3 days. The 10-day course of streptomycin is recommended to prevent relapses because viable bacteria have been isolated from buboes of patients with plague during convalescence. The risk of vestibular damage and hearing loss due to streptomycin is minimal. This antibiotic should be used cautiously, however, in pregnant women, in older patients who would have trouble adapting to vestibular damage, and in patients with previous hearing difficulty. In such patients, the course of streptomycin can be shortened to 3 days after the disappearance of fever. Renal injury as a result of streptomycin therapy is rare with this regimen; however, renal function should be monitored. If the serum creatinine rises significantly, the dose of streptomycin should be reduced. In mild renal failure, the recommended dose is about 20 mg/kg/day, and in advanced renal failure, it is 8 mg/kg every 3 days. Although gentamicin and tobramycin have not been tested as monotherapy for plague, their in vitro similarities to streptomycin suggest they should be effective.

For patients allergic to streptomycin or in whom an oral drug is strongly preferred, tetracycline is a satisfactory alternative. It is administered orally in a dose of 2 to 4 g/day in four divided doses for 10 days. Tetracycline is contraindicated in children younger than 7 years of age and in pregnant women because it stains developing teeth. It is also contraindicated in renal failure.

For patients with meningitis who require a drug with good penetration into the cerebrospinal fluid and for patients with profound hypotension in whom an intramuscular injection may be poorly absorbed, chloramphenicol should be administered intravenously. This is given as a loading dose of 25 mg/kg of body weight, followed by 60 mg/kg/day in four divided doses. After clinical improvement, chloramphenicol should be continued orally to complete a total course of 10 days. The dosage may be reduced to 30 mg/kg/day to lessen the magnitude of bone marrow suppression, which is reversible after completion of therapy. The irreversible bone marrow aplasia associated with chloramphenicol is so rare (estimated to occur in 1 of 40,000 patients) that its consideration should not deter the use of chloramphenicol in patients who are seriously ill with plague infection.

An isolate from a 16-year-old boy in Madagascar in 1995 was resistant to streptomycin, tetracycline, chloramphenicol, and sulfonamide but was susceptible to trimethoprim-sulfamethoxazole. He recovered after receiving trimethoprim-sulfamethoxazole.[10] Other than this case, antibiotic resistance in human isolates of *Y. pestis* has never been reported, nor has resistance emerged during antibiotic therapy. The antibiotics streptomycin, tetracycline, and chloramphenicol given alone are clinically very effective, and relapses are exceedingly rare. Therefore, there is no rationale for using multiple antibiotics to treat plague. Ciprofloxacin and ofloxacin are active in vitro and in experimental mouse infections but have not been tested in patients.[11, 12]

Supportive Therapy

Most patients are febrile with constitutional symptoms, including nausea and vomiting. Hypotension and dehydration are common. Therefore, intravenous 0.9% saline solution should be given to most patients for the first few days of the illness or until improvement occurs. Patients in shock require additional quantities of fluid with hemodynamic monitoring and the judicious use of epinephrine or dopamine. There is no evidence that corticosteroids are beneficial in plague.

The buboes usually recede without need of local therapy. Occasionally, however, they may enlarge or become fluctuant during the first week of treatment, requiring incision and drainage. The aspirated fluid should be cultured for evidence of superinfection with other bacteria, but this material is usually sterile.

Precautions

All patients with suspected plague should be reported to the Health Department and to the World Health Organization. Patients with uncomplicated infections who are promptly treated present no health hazards to other persons. Those with cough or other signs of pneumonia must be placed in strict respiratory isolation for at least 48 hours after the institution of antibiotic therapy or until the sputum culture is negative. The bubo aspirate and blood must be handled with gloves and with care to avoid aerosolization of these infected fluids. Laboratory workers who process the cultures should be alerted to exercise precautions; however, standard bacteriologic techniques that safeguard against skin contact with and aerosolization of cultures should be adequate.

Prevention

A formalin-killed vaccine, Plague Vaccine U.S.P., was available for travelers to endemic areas and for laboratory workers who handle cultures, but it has been discontinued by its sole manufacturer in the United States. In the absence of vaccination, persons living in endemic areas should provide themselves with as much personal protection against rodents and fleas as possible, including living in ratproof houses, wearing shoes and garments to cover the legs, and applying insecticide dusts to houses.

Reservoir and Vector Control

The control of plague by health departments requires knowledge of the epidemiology of infected animals, vectors, and the contact of humans with these animals in any particular area. In the United States, the Centers for Disease Control and Prevention in Fort Collins, Colorado, has a field team of entomologists, mammalogists, and epidemiologists to investigate cases of plague. A specific approach to each case is chosen and usually consists of using insecticides around homes, trapping animals, and educating people to avoid touching dead rodents or handling sick cats. Urban plague has been successfully controlled in many cities around the world by quarantine, rat control, and the use of insecticides. Sylvatic plague, however, defies definitive control because the wild rodent reservoirs are so widespread and include underground burrows.

YERSINIA ENTEROCOLITICA AND *YERSINIA PSEUDOTUBERCULOSIS*

History

The agents of the nonplague yersinioses were not discovered by Alexandre Yersin, and because they do not cause widespread epidemics with high mortality like plague they have not attracted as much medical attention. In 1975, there were only 84 cases of *Y. enterocolitica* infection reported in the United States and about 6000 cases in the world literature. Subsequently, however, there occurred an increased interest and recognition of this organism as an important cause of diarrhea and the appendicitis-like syndrome. Most of the reported cases were in Scandinavia, other European countries, Canada, and the United States.

Description of the Pathogens

Y. enterocolitica and *Y. pseudotuberculosis* are gram-negative, non–lactose-fermenting, urease-positive bacilli that are motile when grown at 25°C but not at 37°C. Both organisms grow on blood, heart infusion, MacConkey, and SS agars at room temperature and at 37°C, and in buffered saline at 4°C. Colonies are often very small after incubation for 24 hours but are readily apparent at 48 hours. More than 50 serotypes and five biotypes of *Y. enterocolitica* have been described. Most strains from patients belong to serotypes O3, O8, and O9 and to biotypes 2, 3, and 4. Six serotypes (I–VI) and four subtypes of *Y. pseudotuberculosis* have been identified, with O-group I accounting for approximately 80% of human cases.

The virulence of the Yersiniae depends on V and W antigens, which confer dependency on calcium for growth at 37°C. Pathogenic strains are resistant to serum complement, penetrate human epithelial cells (HeLa cells) or guinea pig conjunctivae, are lethal to mice, and demonstrate cytotoxicity. Some of these characteristics are mediated by plasmids with weights of 41 to 82 kD.[13–16] The 70-kilobase plasmid encodes for virulence determinants that include a secreted protein kinase[17] and an outer membrane protein with protein tyrosine phosphatase activity.[18] *Y. enterocolitica* does not produce a siderophore for iron transport and therefore grows better in the presence of other bacteria that produce siderophores and allow the bacteria to transport iron for its growth.[19] Many isolates produce a heat-stable enterotoxin that is similar to the heat-stable enterotoxin produced by *Escherichia coli*.[20] This enterotoxin, which is produced at 22°C but not at 37°C, is probably not important in causing diarrhea during *Yersinia* infection. The organisms produce lipopolysaccharide endotoxin, which has biologic properties similar to that of other gram-negative bacteria.

Epidemiology

Y. enterocolitica is a relatively infrequent cause of diarrhea and abdominal pain in the United States but is more common in northern Europe. Infections have been documented in other parts of the world, including South America, Africa, and Asia, but *Y. enterocolitica* is rarely a cause of tropical diarrhea.[21] Most isolates from Europe are serotypes O3 and O9, whereas most of the isolates from Canada and the United States are serotypes O3 and O8, respectively. Serotype O3 isolates have been recovered from patients in the New York City area,[22] and serious infections caused by serotype O8 have been reported from the Netherlands.[23]

Children and adults of both sexes are susceptible, but children are more often infected than are adults. Transmission of infection occurs by ingestion of contaminated food or water and, less commonly, by direct contact with infected animals or patients (Fig. 218–6). Butchers in Finland are at increased risk of infection.[24] Contaminated blood from blood banks has been a source of *Y. enterocolitica* infection, including blood from autologous donors, resulting in shock and death in 50% of cases.[25]

The natural reservoirs of *Y. enterocolitica* are a variety of animals, including rodents, rabbits, pigs, sheep, cattle, horses, dogs, and cats. Transmission of infection from animals to humans has been suggested through household dogs. In northern European countries, *Y. enterocolitica* is frequently isolated from pigs' tonsils and tongues at slaughterhouses, and ingestion of incompletely cooked pork and contamination of other foods by pork are important in disease transmission.[26] The ability of this organism to grow at 4°C means that refrigerated meats can be good sources of infection. The organism has been isolated from lakes, streams, and drinking water, but only a few cases have been linked to ingestion of water. Epidemics of food-borne disease have occurred in the United States, including one caused by contaminated chocolate milk in New York,[27] one associated with pasteurized milk in Tennessee, one caused by bean sprouts in Pennsylvania, and ones in Atlanta and Baltimore associated with consumption of raw pork intestines (chitterlings) during holiday festivities.[28] Most cases occur in the winter.

Infection caused by *Y. pseudotuberculosis* is the rarest of the yersinioses. It is also a zoonotic infection and has its reservoirs in various rodents, rabbits, deer, farm animals, and birds including turkey, ducks, geese, pigeons, pheasants, and canaries. Although this infection has a worldwide distribution, more cases have been reported from Europe than from other continents. Most patients have been children 5 to 15 years old. Males are affected three times more often than females. Most patients developed their illnesses in the winter. Transmission of their infection is presumed to occur by ingestion of organisms from contact with an infected animal or a

FIGURE 218–6. Transmission routes of *Yersinia enterocolitica*. *Wide arrows* indicate common routes, *medium arrows* indicate occasional routes, and *thin arrows* indicate rare routes.

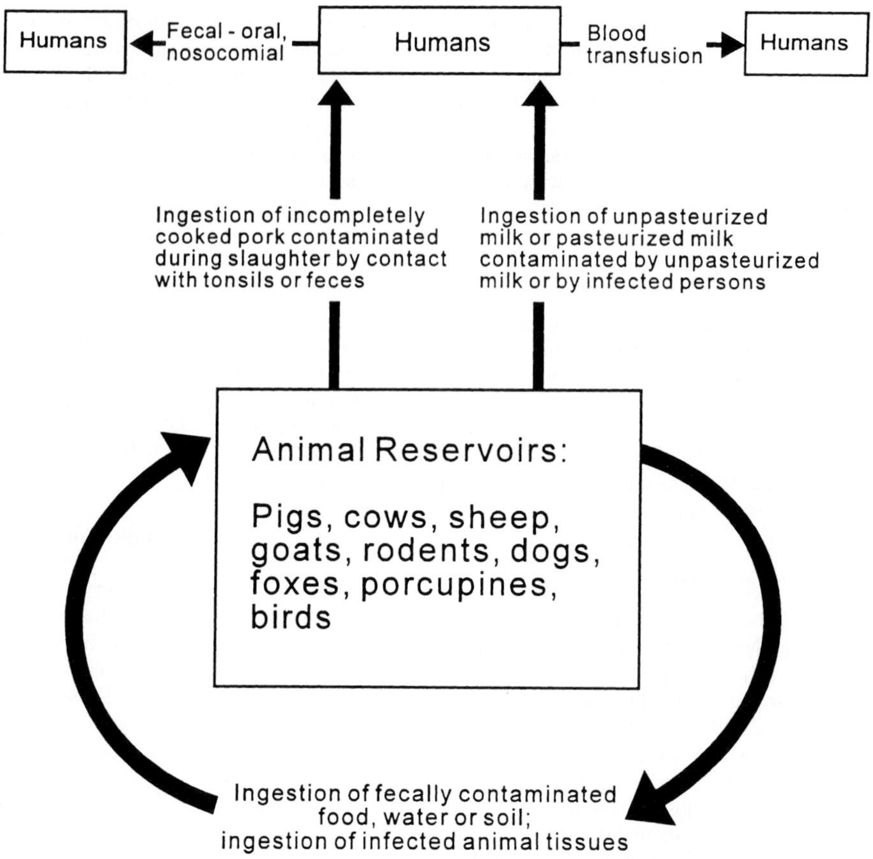

common source of contamination within a family, such as food or water.

Pathogenesis

The alimentary tract is the portal of entry in most cases. An inoculum of 10^9 organisms may be required to cause infection. After an incubation period of 4 to 7 days, this infection causes mucosal ulcerations in the terminal ileum (rarely in the ascending colon), necrotic lesions in Peyer's patches, and enlargement of mesenteric lymph nodes.[29] In most cases, the appendix is histologically normal or shows mild inflammation. If septicemia develops, suppurative lesions may occur in various organ systems (e.g., lung, liver, meninges). A reactive polyarthritis is more common among patients with histocompatibility antigen HLA-B27. Molecular mimicry between HLA-B27 antigen and *Yersinia* antigen has been postulated as a mechanism for reactive arthritis. Superantigenic activity has been found in cultures of *Y. enterocolitica* and could be a mechanism for reactive arthritis.[30]

Clinical Manifestations

Enterocolitis accounts for two thirds of all reported cases and is characterized by fever, diarrhea, and abdominal pain lasting 1 to 3 weeks.[31] In serious cases, rectal bleeding and perforation of the ileum may occur. Fecal excretion of the organism may continue for weeks after symptoms have subsided. Leukocytes and, less commonly, blood or mucus may be present in the stool. Most patients with this syndrome are younger than 5 years of age. Patients with mesenteric adenitis and/or terminal ileitis have fever, right lower quadrant pain, and leukocytosis. This syndrome is most common in older children and adolescents and may be clinically indistinguishable from acute appendicitis.[32]

A reactive polyarthritis, seen in 10 to 30% of adults with *Y. enterocolitica* infection in Scandinavia, begins a few days to a month after onset of acute diarrhea and may involve the knees, ankles, toes, fingers, and wrists. In most cases, two to four joints become inflamed in rapid succession over a period of 2 to 14 days. Symptoms persist for more than 1 month in two thirds of cases and for more than 4 months in one third. After 12 months, most patients are symptomless, but a few have persistent low back pain, including sacroiliitis, which has been specifically related to the presence of HLA-B27.[33] Ankylosing spondylitis rarely occurs. Synovial fluid examination reveals fewer than 25,000 leukocytes/mm^3, with 60 to 95% polymorphonuclear leukocytes. Synovial fluid cultures are usually negative. Reiter's syndrome, with arthritis, urethritis, and conjunctivitis, has also been reported. Like arthritis, this complication is much more likely to develop in persons with the HLA-B27 antigen.[34, 35]

Erythema nodosum occurs in up to 30% of the Scandinavian cases. Skin lesions appear on the patient's legs and trunk 2 to 20 days after onset of fever and abdominal pain and resolve spontaneously within a month in most cases. Women outnumber men by 2 to 1.

Exudative pharyngitis has been documented as part of the spectrum of illnesses caused by *Y. enterocolitica*. In one large outbreak in the United States, 8% of patients presented with acute pharyngitis and fever, without accompanying diarrhea.[36] Cases of pneumonia, empyema, and lung abscess have been reported.[37]

Y. enterocolitica septicemia is less common and is most often reported in patients with diabetes mellitus, severe anemia, hemochromatosis, cirrhosis, or malignancy and in elderly patients. Patients with iron overload, such as patients with thalassemia who receive frequent transfusions, are at risk for septicemia. The treatment of iron-overloaded patients with desferrioxamine has been particularly associated with *Yersinia* sepsis because this iron chelator enhances the growth of the organism and also appears to inhibit polymorphonuclear leukocyte defense against the infection.[19, 38] Septicemic patients may develop hepatic or splenic abscesses, peritonitis, septic arthritis, osteomyelitis, wound infections, or meningitis.[39] Endocarditis and mycotic aneurysms caused by *Y. enterocolitica* have been reported.

By far the most common manifestation of *Y. pseudotuberculosis* infection in humans is mesenteric adenitis, which causes an acute appendicitis-like syndrome with fever and right lower quadrant abdominal pain.[40] At laparotomy, there is usually a normal appendix and enlarged mesenteric lymph nodes that may be accompanied by inflammation of the terminal ileum. The infection is usually self-limited, and patients who have undergone surgery generally begin to improve promptly after laparotomy. Erythema nodosum and polyarthritis have also been described in patients with *Y. pseudotuberculosis* infection. Fewer than 30 cases of *Y. pseudotuberculosis*–induced septicemia have been reported in the world literature.[41] About 50% of septicemic patients have underlying disease such as cirrhosis, hemochromatosis, or diabetes mellitus.

Diagnosis

Stool, mesenteric lymph node, pharyngeal exudate, peritoneal fluid, or blood cultures may yield *Yersinia*, depending on the clinical syndrome. Recovery of organisms from otherwise uncontaminated material such as blood, cerebrospinal fluid, or mesenteric lymph node tissue is not difficult, but isolation of Yersiniae from feces is hampered by their slow growth and by overgrowth of normal fecal flora. Yield of positive stool cultures can be increased by using cold enrichment, alkali treatment, or selective CIN agar, but these methods are not cost-effective in routine diagnosis because usual enteric culturing methods can detect most clinically significant infections.[42]

Serologic tests are useful in diagnosing *Yersinia* infections provided sera are appropriately absorbed. *Y. enterocolitica* and *Y. pseudotuberculosis* cross-react with each other and with other organisms such as *Brucella*, *Vibrio*, and *E. coli*. *Y. pseudotuberculosis* types II and IV cross-react with *Salmonella* groups B and D. Agglutinating antibodies appear soon after onset of illness but generally disappear within 2 to 6 months.

Prevention and Therapy

Public health measures to control *Yersinia* infection should focus on the animal reservoirs in any particular location. The methods of raising and slaughtering pigs can be modified to reduce contamination of meat. For example, workers might prevent contact of meat with the contents of the oral cavity and intestinal tract during slaughter. Meat should not be refrigerated for prolonged periods before consumption.[43] Consumption of uncooked meats, such as chitterlings, should be avoided. In dairies, care must be taken to prevent contamination of milk after pasteurization. In blood banks donors should be asked about recent fever, abdominal pain, and diarrhea and be requested to notify the blood bank if these symptoms develop after donation.[25]

Y. enterocolitica is usually susceptible in vitro to aminoglycosides, chloramphenicol, tetracycline, trimethoprim-sulfamethoxazole, piperacillin, and the third-generation cephalosporins.[44] Isolates usually are resistant to penicillin, and resistance to ampicillin, carbenicillin, and first-generation cephalosporins occurs frequently. The value of antimicrobial therapy in cases of enterocolitis and mesenteric adenitis is unclear, because these infections are usually self-limited. Treatment of enterocolitis with antibiotics shortens the persistence of immunoglobulin G anti-*Yersinia* antibodies to about 3 months. Patients with *Y. enterocolitica*–induced septicemia, which has a mortality rate of 50% despite treatment, should receive antibiotic therapy. The drug of choice has not yet been identified, but gentamicin, 5 mg/kg/day intravenously in divided doses, or chloramphenicol, 50 mg/kg/day orally or intravenously in divided doses, is suggested. Good responses have been reported with trimethoprim-sulfamethoxazole, doxycycline, and ciprofloxacin,[45] whereas failures have occurred with cefuroxime, ceftazidime, and cefoperazone.[44] Laparotomy for suspected appendicitis should be avoided when *Yersinia* infection is a likely diagnosis.

Y. pseudotuberculosis is usually sensitive in vitro to ampicillin, tetracycline, chloramphenicol, cephalosporins, and aminoglycosides. Although antibiotic therapy is probably not warranted in most patients with mesenteric adenitis, patients with septicemia should receive ampicillin, 100 to 200 mg/kg/day intravenously, or streptomycin, 20 to 30 mg/kg/day intramuscularly, or tetracyline, 20 to 30 mg/kg/day orally or intravenously in divided doses. The mortality in *Y. pseudotuberculosis* septicemia is 75% despite antibiotic therapy.

OTHER *YERSINIA* SPECIES

Strains that were formerly considered biochemically atypical isolates of *Y. enterocolitica* have been reclassified as *Yersinia intermedia*, *Yersinia frederiksenii*, and *Yersinia kristensenii*. *Y. intermedia* and *Y. frederiksenii* have seldom been recovered from patients with enterocolitis and have been reported to cause only a small number of soft tissue infections. The pathogenicity of these organisms remains uncertain.

REFERENCES

1. Butler T. Plague and Other *Yersinia* Infections. New York: Plenum; 1983.
2. Ferber DM, Brubaker RR. Plasmids in *Yersinia pestis*. Infect Immun. 1981;31:839–841.
3. Kaufmann AF, Boyce JM, Martone WJ. Trends in human plague in the United States. J Infect Dis. 1980;141:522–524.
4. Mann JM, Martone WJ, Boyce JM, et al. Endemic human plague in New Mexico: Risk factors associated with infection. J Infect Dis. 1979;140:397–401.
5. Butler T. *Yersinia* infections: Centennial of the discovery of the plague bacillus. Clin Infect Dis. 1994;19:655–663.
6. Hull HF, Montes JM, Mann JM. Septicemic plague in New Mexico. J Infect Dis. 1987;155:113–118.
7. Crook LD, Tempest B. Plague: A clinical review of 27 cases. Arch Intern Med. 1992;152:1253–1256.
8. Centers for Disease Control and Prevention. Fatal human plague—Arizona and Colorado, 1996. MMWR Morb Mortal Wkly Rep. 1997;46:617–620.
9. Hull HF, Montes JM, Mann JM. Plague masquerading as gastrointestinal illness. West J Med. 1986;145:485–487.
10. Galimand M, Guiyoule A, Gerbaud G, et al. Multidrug resistance in *Yersinia pestis* mediated by a transferable plasmid. N Engl J Med. 1997;337:677–680.
11. Frean JA, Arntzen L, Capper T, et al. In vitro activities of 14 antibiotics against 100 human isolates of *Yersinia pestis* from a Southern African plague focus. Antimicrob Agents Chemother. 1996;40:2646–2647.
12. Russell P, Eley SM, Bell DL, et al. Doxycycline or ciprofloxacin prophylaxis and therapy against experimental *Yersinia pestis* infection in mice. J Antimicrob Chemother. 1996;37:769–774.
13. Goguen JD, Walker WS, Hatch TP, et al. Plasmid-determined cytotoxicity in *Yersinia pestis* and *Yersinia enterocolitica*. Infect Immun. 1986;51:788–794.
14. Prpic JK, Davey RB, eds. The genus *Yersinia*: Epidemiology, molecular biology and pathogenesis. Basel: Karger, 1987.
15. Cover TL, Aber RC. *Yersinia enterocolitica*. N Engl J Med. 1989;321:16–24.
16. Cornelis G, Laroche Y, Balligand G, et al. *Yersinia enterocolitica*, a primary model for bacterial invasiveness. Rev Infect Dis. 1987;9:64–87.
17. Gaylov EE, Hakansson S, Forsberg A, et al. A secreted protein kinase of *Yersinia pseudotuberculosis* is an indispensable virulence determinant. Nature. 1993;361:730–732.
18. Guan K, Dixon JE. Protein tyrosine phosphatase activity of an essential virulence determinant in *Yersinia*. Science. 1990;249:553–556.
19. Cantinieaux B, Boelaert J, Hariga C, et al: Impaired neutrophil defense against *Yersinia enterocolitica* in patients with iron overload who are undergoing dialysis. J Lab Clin Med. 1988;111:524–528.
20. Boyce JM, Evans DJ, Evans DG, et al. Production of heat-stable, methanol-soluble enterotoxin by *Yersinia enterocolitica*. Infect Immun. 1979;25:532–537.
21. Carniel E, Butler T, Hossain S, et al. Infrequent detection of *Yersinia enterocolitica* in childhood diarrhea in Bangladesh. Am J Trop Med Hyg. 1986;35:370–371.
22. Bottone EJ. Current trends of *Yersinia enterocolitica* isolates in the New York City area. J Clin Microbiol. 1983;17:63–67.
23. Hoogkamp-Korstanje JAA, de Koning J, Samsom JP. Incidence of human infection with *Yersinia enterocolitica* serotypes O3, O8, and O9 and the use of indirect immunofluorescence in diagnosis. J Infect Dis. 1986;153:138–141.
24. Merilahti-Palo R, Lahesmaa R, Granfors K, et al. Risk of *Yersinia* infection among butchers. Scand J Infect Dis. 1991;23:55–61.

25. Centers for Disease Control and Prevention. Red blood cell transfusions contaminated with *Yersinia enterocolitica*—United States, 1991–1996, and initiation of a national study to detect bacteria-associated transfusion reactions. MMWR Morb Mortal Wkly Rep. 1997;46:553–555.
26. Tauxe RV, Vandepitte J, Wauters G, et al. *Yersinia enterocolitica* infections and pork: The missing link. Lancet. 1987;1:1129–1132.
27. Black RE, Jackson RJ, Tsai T, et al. Epidemic *Yersinia enterocolitica* infection due to contaminated chocolate milk. N Engl J Med. 1978;298:76–79.
28. Lee LA, Taylor J, Carter GP, et al. *Yersinia enterocolitica* 0:3: An emerging cause of pediatric gastroenteritis in the United States. J Infect Dis. 1991;163:660–663.
29. Bradford WD, Noce PS, Gutman LT. Pathologic features of enteric infection with *Yersinia enterocolitica*. Arch Pathol. 1974;98:17–22.
30. Stuart PM, Woodward JG. *Yersinia enterocolitica* produces superantigenic activity. J Immunol. 1992;148:225–233.
31. Marks MI, Pai CH, LaFleur L, et al. *Yersinia enterocolitica* gastroenteritis: A prospective study of clinical, bacteriologic, and epidemiologic features. J Pediatr. 1980;96:26–31.
32. Strom H, Johansson C. Appendicitis followed by reactive arthritis in an HLA B27–positive man after infection with *Yersinia enterocolitica*, diagnosed by serotype specific antibodies and antibodies to *Yersinia* outer membrane proteins. Infection. 1997;25:317–319.
33. van der Heijden IM, Res PCM, Wilbrink B, et al. *Yersinia enterocolitica*: A cause of chronic polyarthritis. Clin Infect Dis. 1997;25:831–837.
34. Borg AA, Gray J, Dawes PT. *Yersinia*-related arthritis in the United Kingdom: A report of 12 cases and review of the literature. Q J Med New Ser 84. 1992;304:575–582.
35. Granfors K, Jalkanen S, von Essen R, et al. *Yersinia* antigens in synovial-fluid cells from patients with reactive arthritis. N Engl J Med. 1989;320:216–221.
36. Rose FB, Camp CJ, Antes EJ. Family outbreak of fatal *Yersinia enterocolitica* pharyngitis. Am J Med. 1987;82:636–637.
37. Greene JN, Herndon P, Nadler JP, et al. Case report: *Yersinia enterocolitica* necrotizing pneumonia in an immunocompromised patient. Am J Med Sci. 1993;305:171–173.
38. Chiu HY, Flynn DM, Hoffbrand AV, et al. Infection with *Yersinia enterocolitica* in patients with iron overload. Br Med J. 1986;292:97.
39. Reed RP, Robins-Browne RM, Williams ML. *Yersinia enterocolitica* peritonitis. Clin Infect Dis. 1997;25:1468–1469.
40. Weber J, Finlayson NB, Mark JBD. Mesenteric lymphadenitis and terminal ileitis due to *Yersinia pseudotuberculosis*. N Engl J Med. 1970;283:172–174.
41. Yamashiro KM, Goldman RH, Harris D, et al. *Pasteurella pseudotuberculosis*: Acute sepsis with survival. Arch Intern Med. 1971;128:605–608.
42. Kachoris M, Ruoff KL, Welch K, et al. Routine culture of stool specimens for *Yersinia enterocolitica* is not a cost-effective procedure. J Clin Microbiol. 1988;26:582–583.
43. Christiansen SG. The *Yersinia enterocolitica* situation in Denmark. Contrib Microbiol Immunol. 1987;9:93–97.
44. Gayraud M, Scavizzi MR, Mollaret HH, et al. Antibiotic treatment of *Yersinia enterocolitica* septicemia: A retrospective review of 43 cases. Clin Infect Dis. 1993;17:405–410.
45. Crowe M, Ashford K, Ispahani P. Clinical features and antibiotic treatment of septic arthritis and osteomyelitis due to *Yersinia enterocolitica*: J Med Microbiol. 1996;45:302–309.

Chapter 219

Bordetella Species

ERIK L. HEWLETT

Descriptions of whooping cough date from 1500, but Baillou, the first modern epidemiologist, is credited with providing the "earliest clear account" of the disease in 1640.[1] The name *pertussis*, meaning "violent cough," was first used by Sydenham in 1679.[2] In China the illness is known as "the cough of 100 days," and there are specific terms for this illness in different languages, such as *tos ferina* in Spanish and *coqueluche* in French. The etiologic organism, initially called *Haemophilus pertussis*, was described by Bordet and Gengou in 1906 and subsequently isolated with the use of a medium that bears their names.[3] A detailed history of pertussis is provided in the classic monograph by Lapin.[2]

DESCRIPTION OF THE PATHOGENS

The genus *Bordetella* now consists of seven species—*pertussis, parapertussis, bronchiseptica, avium,* and the recently added *hinzii, holmesii,* and *trematum. B pertussis* and *B. parapertussis* are responsible for the majority of *Bordetella* infections in humans. Most of the other species have been recognized to cause human infection under special circumstances.[4] For example, *B. hinzii* has been isolated from a symptomatic patient with cystic fibrosis,[5, 6] *B. holmesii* has been associated with septicemia,[7, 8] and *B. trematum* has been recovered from wounds and ear infections in humans.[9] *B. bronchiseptica* causes respiratory diseases such as kennel cough in dogs, snuffles in rabbits, pneumonia in koalas, and atrophic rhinitis in swine, but it is also infrequently responsible for a chronic respiratory infection in humans, especially immunocompromised hosts and persons who have contact with animals.[10–12] Evaluation of *B. bronchiseptica* strains isolated from humans has suggested that variants from standard strains may be involved in human disease.[13] *B. avium* is primarily an avian pathogen, causing turkey coryza, but a *B. avium*–like organism has been recovered from a human with chronic otitis.[14, 15]

The bordetellae are minute coccobacillary organisms that appear singly or in pairs. The human pathogens (*B. pertussis* and *B. parapertussis*) are nonmotile. *B. bronchiseptica* and *B. avium* possess peritrichous flagellae that, when expressed, provide motility.[16] Although the newly identified species are still being characterized, several (*B. holmesii* and *B. hinzii*) seem to be most closely related to *B. avium.* The original *Bordetella* species are piliated, aerobic, and oxidize amino acids, but do not ferment carbohydrates. The organisms require nicotinamide (or nicotinic acid) for growth at an optimal temperature of 35°C to 37°C. Although the starch-blood-agar medium originally described by Bordet and Gengou is still used in some places, it is clear that the organisms can grow in totally synthetic medium consisting of buffers, minerals, an amino acid energy source, and growth factors such as nicotinamide.[17] Growth is enchanced by, if not dependent on, additives such as starch or β-methyl cyclodextrin to absorb and neutralize inhibitory compounds.[18, 19] Growth rates and colony sizes differ among the species, with *B. pertussis* requiring 3 to 6 days for the pinpoint colonies to appear in cultures of clinical specimens. *B. parapertussis* grows slightly faster (and grows on sheep blood agar), produces large colonies, is oxidase negative, and in peptone agar or in liquid medium produces a characteristic brownish pigment.[18]

The relatedness of the *Bordetella* spp. has been addressed in several ways. All *Bordetella* possess DNA with a high mol% G+C (guanine+cytosine=66 to 70%).[16] Kloos and coworkers[20] determined by DNA hybridization that *B. pertussis, B. parapertussis,* and *B. bronchiseptica* are not sufficiently diverse to be classified as distinct species. This conclusion was supported by the work of Musser and colleagues,[21] who examined genetic diversity of *Bordetella* spp. by electrophoretic mobility patterns of non–virulence-related enzymes. Arico and associates proposed a phylogenetic tree based on the work of Musser and coworkers[21] and analysis of the pertussis toxin genes from *Bordetella* isolates.[22] They suggested a common ancestral source for the *Bordetella* spp., but with *B. parapertussis* and the 18323 strain of *B. pertussis* (used in vaccine potency testing) being more closely related to *B. bronchiseptica* than to *B. pertussis.* Although apparently closer to *B. avium,* the relatedness of the newly identified species to *B. pertussis* remains to be determined.

Although speciation of clinical isolates is accomplished by phenotypic characterization, serotyping based on detection of heat-labile K agglutinogens has been used to distinguish strains, especially for epidemiologic purposes. However, *Bordetella* organisms have the capacity to change serotypes in vitro or in vivo, thereby limiting the utility of this approach. As a result, more emphasis is being placed on strain classification based on genotype, using techniques such as pulsed-field gel electrophoresis and restriction fragment length polymorphism (RFLP).[23, 24]

B. pertussis produces a number of biologically active substances that are postulated to play a role in disease (reviewed by Hewlett[25]). These include surface components, such as filamentous hemagglutinin (FHA), pertactin (PRN), and fimbriae; toxins such as adenylate cyclase toxin, tracheal cytotoxin, and pertussis toxin; and other products, including tracheal colonization factor and a serum resistance factor. FHA, which derives its name from the ability to agglutinate erythrocytes, is synthesized as a high-molecular-weight protein but processed to a mature form of 220 kD.[26, 27] It appears to be involved in the attachment of *B. pertussis* to ciliated respiratory epithelia and other types of cells, perhaps by its RGD sequence interacting with host integrins.[28–30] (RGD designates the amino acid sequence arginine-glycine-aspartate within a protein.) The structural gene for FHA has been cloned and expressed in *Escherichia coli*, but recombinant FHA has not been tested for use in a component vaccine.[31]

Several of the agglutinogens have been isolated and characterized biochemically. Although the fimbrial nature of agglutinogens 2 and 3/6 suggests a role in attachment to target cells, strains lacking those components do adhere to nonciliated cells and can cause infection.[29, 32] The contribution of these surface proteins to infection remains unresolved, but they are included in several of the acellular pertussis vaccines.[33]

Adenylate cyclase toxin (ACT) is an extracytoplasmic enzyme that is able to interact with and enter mammalian cells.[34, 35] Inside the target cell, it is activated by endogenous calmodulin to catalyze the production of cyclic adenosine monophosphate (cAMP) from adenosine triphosphate. The resulting accumulation of supraphysiologic levels of cAMP may result in impaired leukocyte functions.[34, 36] The toxin, a protein of 1706 amino acids, is a member of the RTX family of bacterial toxins (including *E. coli* hemolysin and *Pasteurella haemolytica* leukotoxin) and is itself hemolytic, responsible for the zone of hemolysis associated with virulent *B. pertussis* on blood agar plates.[37–39] Mutants defective in ACT production are avirulent in suckling mice.[40]

Dermonecrotic toxin (DNT), also known as mouse lethal toxin or heat-labile toxin, was first discovered by Bordet and Gengou when necrotic lesions developed after intradermal injection of *B. pertussis* into suckling mice.[3] The molecule was purified by Nagai and coworkers and was shown to cause vascular smooth muscle contraction by an unknown mechanism, accounting for the resultant ischemic necrosis.[41] Studies indicate a mechanism of action for DNT involving rho protein, similar to the process employed by cytotoxic necrotizing factor of *E. coli*.[42] Nevertheless, no role is attributed to this molecule in the current models of pertussis pathogenesis, based primarily on lack of data.

Tracheal cytotoxin (TCT) is a component of *Bordetella* spp. discovered by virtue of its ability to cause ciliostasis, inhibit DNA synthesis, and ultimately kill tracheal epithelial cells in vitro.[43] The toxin is a tetrapeptide disaccharide derived from bacterial peptidoglycan. Although a TCT-like molecule may be produced by other gram-negative organisms during cell division, it is, under these circumstances, efficiently recovered for recycling and does not accumulate in the medium. Goldman and colleagues demonstrated that *B. pertussis* is deficient in such a reuptake system, accounting for the release of TCT into the growth medium (W. Goldman, unpublished data). The biologic effects of TCT on respiratory epithelial cells involve production of interleukin-1 and nitric oxide.[44–47]

Pertussis toxin (PT) is one of the best known products of *B. pertussis* and is responsible for a number of the biologic activities recognized before its purification.[48, 49] These include induction of lymphocytosis, sensitization to the lethal effects of histamine, enhancement of insulin secretion, and adjuvanticity. PT is a typical A/B toxin for which the binding moeity consists of a hetero pentamer. The active subunit possesses adenosine diphosphate–ribosyl transferase activity with certain members of the G-protein family of signal transduction molecules as the targets. This covalent modification of G proteins inhibits their ability to couple extracellular receptors to intracellular effector pathways, as in inhibition of adenylate cyclase, activation of phospholipase, and opening of ion channels. In addition to PT effects mediated by its enzymatic function, there is a set of events initiated merely by the binding of PT to cell surface receptors. These responses include mitogenicity for lymphocytes and activation of platelets and can be elicited by the B-subunit alone.[50] The PT gene has been cloned and sequenced,[51–53] and the crystal structure of the molecule has been solved.[54] The gene is present in *B. parapertussis* and *B. bronchiseptica* but appears to be silent, because of mutations in the promoter region.[55, 56] Several *B. bronchiseptica* strains isolated from humans have been characterized and found not to produce PT in vitro, even though patients from whom they were isolated possessed anti-PT antibodies.[57] These observations leave open the question of a role for PT in disease caused by non-*pertussis* species.[58]

When compared with that from other gram-negative organisms, *Bordetella* lipopolysaccharide (LPS) has several notable features. It is heterogeneous, with two major forms differing in the phosphate content of the 3-deoxy-2-octulosonic acid portions.[59, 60] Although the unfractionated material possesses the usual effects of LPS (induction of interleukin-1 production, fever, hypotension, and the Schwartzman reaction), the distribution of those activities among the fractions is unusual. Lipid X, but not lipid A, is pyrogenic, and the polysaccharide region is very active as an adjuvant.[61] Furthermore, LPS from *B. pertussis* is more potent in the limulus amoebocyte lysate assay but less potent in pyrogen release from monocytes than LPS from *E. coli*.[62] This means that extrapolation to LPS from other gram-negative organisms for biologic effects and toxicity of *B. pertussis* LPS is not appropriate. In addition, monoclonal antibodies to LPS from *B. pertussis* have protective activity in animals, suggesting that this molecule may actually serve as a protective antigen in the whole cell vaccine.[63]

Roles for these multiple factors in the pathophysiology of pertussis can be considered in the context of a generic sequence of events for an infectious disease: entry and attachment to a specific target tissue, production of local damage, and development of systemic disease, all dependent on an ongoing evasion and disruption of host defense mechanisms.[64] Data from in vitro and in vivo model systems indicate that FHA, pertactin, and possibly PT participate in the attachment of *B. pertussis* to the respiratory epithelium.[26, 28, 32] Ciliostasis and damage to the epithelium by tracheal cytotoxin disturb mucociliary clearance, the first line of defense. The inhibition of phagocyte functions (chemotaxis, phagocytosis, oxidative burst, and bactericidal activity) by ACT represents an acute but reversible disruption of the protection conferred by immune effector cells. PT by covalent modification of proteins, also impairs phagocyte function, but in a more sustained manner.[65] TCT, DNT, and/or adenylate cyclase toxin may contribute to local damage at the respiratory mucosa. At present, PT is the leading candidate to account for systemic manifestations of disease.[66] It clearly produces lymphocytosis in experimental animals infected with *B. pertussis*. Pertussis is not, however, a single-toxin disease like tetanus, diphtheria, and botulism. *B. parapertussis*, although unable to produce PT, can cause clinical disease, which is generally milder but can be of comparable severity to that of *B. pertussis*.[58] PT has been administered intravenously to humans in doses of 0.5 or 1 μg/kg without causing pertussis or any significant adverse effect.[67] It appears, therefore, that in the context of infection with *B. pertussis*, PT can exacerbate the disease process associated with a localized infection of the respiratory tract but is not solely responsible.[25] This issue is particularly important in the context of component pertussis vaccine efficacy (see Prevention).

Although a variety of rodent models, including one that consists of coughing in rats, has been employed to study infection with *B. pertussis*, there is none that fully mimics human disease.[4, 68–70] Intracellular *B. pertussis* organisms have been demonstrated in vitro and in clinical specimens, but the organism is not systemically invasive and does not disseminate beyond the respiratory tract.[71] The significance of intracellular organisms to pathophysiology and transmission is unknown.

The production of virulence factors of *B. pertussis* is regulated in several ways. First, the organisms can undergo a genetic event, originally termed "phase variation" by Leslie and Gardner,[72] that results in loss of most known virulence factors as well as several other undefined outer membrane proteins. Phase variation, which has been shown to occur at a frequency of 1 in 10^4 to 10^6 generations, results from a specific DNA frame shift caused by insertion of a single nucleotide into the bvg (also known as vir) operon.[73] A similar phenomenon, known as *phenotypic modulation*, occurs in response to environmental changes such as temperature or chemical content of the medium and is reversible.[74–78] This adaptive process is mediated by the products of the bvg operon, which are examples of a two-component environmental-sensing system used by many different bacteria.[79] Expression of virulence factors is regulated by the bvg operon so that entry into a host may induce components required for survival and production of disease.[80] There are, in addition, genes repressed by the bvg operon, and expression of these during infection has been observed to be detrimental to the efficiency of infection.[81] There is a fascinating sequence of events that results from bvg activation, first resulting in expression of adherence factors such as FHA and PRN, followed later in time by toxins such as PT and ACT.[78] This sequential onset of expression appears to be explained by molecular events at the promoter level.[82]

EPIDEMIOLOGY

Pertussis continues to be a disease of worldwide importance, with an estimated 40,000,000 cases and 360,000 deaths in 1994.[83] Owing to decreased pertussis vaccine use in several developed nations within the past 15 to 20 years, there have been dramatic increases in the incidence of disease.[84–87] In most populations, the disease is endemic, with regular epidemic cycles superimposed on the background rate, whether at the lower (immunized) rate or at the increased rate occurring after a reduction in vaccine use.[87] The epidemics occur in 3- to 5-year cycles that are attributed to the accumulation of susceptible persons in a population. Although the actual number of organisms required for infection is not known, *B. pertussis* is clearly very contagious. Attack rates among susceptible persons range from 50 to 100%, depending on the nature of exposure.[88] Because the organism is localized to the respiratory tract, it is believed that transmission occurs predominantly by aerosol droplet, with highest attack rates for persons exposed to a coughing patient at a range of 5 feet or less.

Pertussis is novel among childhood infections in that significantly higher attack, morbidity, and mortality rates occur in girls. The reason for this feature is unknown. There are no animal reservoirs, and *B. pertussis* is unable to survive for prolonged periods in the environment. Therefore transmission must occur from infected individual to susceptible host. Although no prolonged carrier state has been identified,[89, 90] asymptomatic culture-positive persons have been detected during outbreaks.[91] These transient "carriers" are unlikely to be a significant source of infection because they are not coughing, but there are no clear data on this question or on the duration of culture positivity.

In the prevaccine era, pertussis was primarily an affliction of children 1 to 5 years of age, at least in part because of passive protection during the first year of life through maternal antibody. For example, in a study from 1937, 60.2% of pertussis patients were 1 to 5 years of age, and only 19.4% younger than 1 year of age.[92] In that setting, with most adults having had pertussis as children and being repeatedly exposed in the population, there was a high level of adult immunity. Whole cell pertussis vaccine has clearly been the major cause of overall reduction in the incidence of disease, yet it has probably also affected a shift in the peak age of disease. In 1982–1983, 53.1% of pertussis cases reported in the United States occurred in children younger than 1 year of age[93]; in 1980–1989, that group had the highest annual incidence of disease (62.8 per 100,000).[94] Because vaccine immunity is of limited duration (generally less than 12 years),[88] fully immunized children are well protected but most adults have little or no residual immunity for passive transfer to infants. Therefore infants who are not yet fully immunized, are at the greatest risk for morbidity and mortality from pertussis and are the least protected. With the limited number of cases in young children, it is clear that adults with atypical, undiagnosed pertussis represent a major source of transmission.[94–96]

Because no booster for pertussis is given beyond the age of 6 years in the United States and elsewhere, virtually all adolescents and adults are susceptible. A number of studies have addressed the incidence of pertussis in these age groups and, in particular, in individuals presenting with cough lasting 1 week or longer. Using primarily serologic techniques for detection of recent exposure to *B. pertussis*, it appears that as many as 20 to 30% of adults with prolonged cough may have pertussis. An outbreak in Vermont illustrates this point, in that the highest number of cases and the highest infection rate were in adolescents ages 10 to 14 years, with a secondary peak in the 40- to 49-year-old age group.[97] Given the level of protection of the pediatric population and the underreporting of pertussis in older groups, it seems likely that the majority of pertussis cases in the United States at the present time occur in adolescents and adults.[98]

CLINICAL MANIFESTATIONS

After an incubation period ranging from less than 1 week to more than 3 weeks, signs and symptoms of the catarrhal phase begin.[2] During the catarrhal phase, the clinical findings, such as rhinorrhea, lacrimation, mild conjunctival injection, malaise, and low-grade fever, are indistinguishable from those of many other upper respiratory tract or systemic infectious diseases. Therefore at the onset of symptoms there is no clue to the diagnosis of pertussis except in the setting of known exposure to an active case. Later during this phase, which can be abbreviated to a few days or last as long as 1 week, a dry, nonproductive cough develops. Evolution of the cough to that which is characteristic of the disease heralds onset of the paroxysmal phase.

Pertussis is generally most severe in infants, but presentation and symptoms may be atypical in that age group, as well as in partially immunized children and previously immunized adolescents and adults.[94–96, 99–101] In those with partial immunity, the catarrhal phase can be shortened or unrecognized, and whoop and leukocytosis can be absent.[95, 101] Prodromal symptoms in adults can include complaints such as pharyngeal discomfort[102–105] and, as a result, correct diagnosis in this age group can be further delayed or missed. The cough paroxysm consists of a series of short expiratory bursts, followed by an inspiratory gasp, which can result in the typical whoop. Not all children with pertussis exhibit the characteristic whoop, and it is relatively uncommon among infants, who may have apneic episodes, and among adults, of whom at most a third report whooping.[106] Paroxysms, which may number more than 30 per 24 hours and be more frequent at night, occur spontaneously or are precipitated by external stimuli such as noises or cold air. They may be sufficiently severe to cause cyanosis and classically end with an episode of vomiting. In adults, paroxysms may be associated with sweating attacks, facial flushing, and even cough syncope. The cough and vomiting may yield thick mucus plugs and watery secretions. Between paroxysms the patient appears relatively well and often sleeps.

During the late catarrhal and early paroxysmal phases, patients may exhibit the typical hematologic feature of the disease, namely leukocytosis with lymphocyte predominance. The total white blood cell count, which may sometimes exceed 50,000 cells/mm^3, consists of a relative lymphocytosis with T and B cells and a less striking increase in neutrophils. A slight hyperinsulinemia and reduced glycemic response to epinephrine have been demonstrated during the disease.[107, 108] Neither was associated with hypoglycemia, but abnormally low blood glucose has been reported in pediatric pertussis patients.[2] These manifestations are less common or less severe in persons who have been immunized previously.

Pulmonary consolidation is seen on chest radiography in more than 20% of hospitalized patients,[109] and pneumonia is present in

25% of reported cases in infants.[94] During the paroxysmal phase, the ability to culture *B. pertussis* diminishes progressively.[110] The convalescent phase begins with a decrease in the intensity of the cough and the frequency of paroxysms. After the patient is no longer coughing, an intercurrent respiratory illness such as a cold, or even transient exposure to a pulmonary irritant, can cause recurrence of the paroxysmal cough. This occurs in the absence of detectable *B. pertussis* organisms and does not represent reinfection. There is no agreement on whether pertussis can cause long-term impairment of pulmonary function.[111, 112]

COMPLICATIONS

The principal complications of pertussis are secondary infections, such as otitis media and pneumonia, and physical sequelae of paroxysmal cough. Pneumonia is a leading cause of death; it can result from aspiration during whooping and vomiting or from impaired clearance mechanisms caused by the actions of various *B. pertussis* components.[64, 113, 114] Presence of these infectious complications is suggested by the onset of fever or a change in the status of the patient between paroxysms.[115]

The increased intrathoracic and intra-abdominal pressures during coughing can result in subconjunctival and scleral hemorrhages, facial and truncal petechiae, epistaxis, hemorrhages in the central nervous system (CNS), subcutaneous emphysema, pneumothorax, umbilical and inguinal hernias, and rectal prolapse. Laceration of the lingual frenulum also occurs with severe cough episodes. With increasing recognition of pertussis in adolescents and adults, there are additional complications that have been identified in these age groups, including urinary incontinence, rib fracture, unilateral hearing loss, herniated disc, and precipitation of angina pectoris.[101–105, 116, 117]

CNS abnormalities occur in patients with pertussis at a relatively high frequency.[118] In children 12 months of age or younger with pertussis in the United States (1980–1989), 69% were hospitalized, convulsions occurred in 3.0%, encephalopathy in 0.9%, and death in 0.6%.[94] Encephalopathy and seizures even occur infrequently in adults with pertussis.[117] The convulsions may be febrile, in conjunction with secondary infection, or afebrile. There are several mechanisms postulated for these CNS sequelae, such as secondary infection with neurotropic viruses, hypoxia, hypoglycemia, and direct effects of pertussis toxin, but the only one documented pathologically is parenchymal hemorrhage in the brain, which has been attributed to venous congestion and increased pressure during cough.[118] At the peak of the paroxysmal phase, frequent vomiting can lead, especially in infants and young children in the developing world, to dehydration and nutritional compromise.

DIAGNOSIS

A variety of methods have been developed for detection of *B. pertussis*, its products, or the immune response to them.[106, 119–121] None, however, is without its limitations in sensitivity, specificity, or practicality. Isolation of *B. pertussis* by culture in the setting of clinical illness is still considered the gold standard but is clearly limited in sensitivity. In addition, the organism can be cultured transiently from asymptomatic contacts who do not develop disease, and therefore isolation by culture is not absolutely specific for the diagnosis of clinical pertussis.[91] The starch-based medium developed by Bordet and Gengou (BG medium) is still in use. Supplemented with methicillin or cephalexin to impair growth of normal flora and used at the bedside immediately after preparation, BG medium is equivalent to any medium available.[18] Other media that have been developed, however, have longer shelf lives and enable recovery of *B. pertussis* from transported specimens.[122, 123] The material to be cultured is obtained by calcium alginate nasopharyngeal swab (cotton inhibits growth of the organism) or by aspiration.[124] The advantage of aspiration is that a specimen of larger volume is obtained and can be used for several diagnostic modalities. The cultured specimen must be examined daily for 5 to 7 days to identify the slow-growing, tiny, hemolytic colonies.

The length of time required for culture prompted development of a direct fluorescein-labeled antibody (FA) to detect *B. pertussis* in nasopharyngeal smears.[18] This method, although widely used, is compromised by interobserver variability.[125] The direct FA method is also used to identify *B. pertussis* colonies from culture. Serologic tests for detection of antibodies in serum are useful epidemiologically, but less so during the acute illness.[119, 126, 127] Because the ability to isolate *B. pertussis* by culture decreases progressively during the disease, the use of a combination of culture and an assay for antipertussis antibodies in serum or nasopharyngeal secretions may provide increased diagnostic sensitivity throughout the course of the illness.[128]

Polymerase chain reaction (PCR) has been applied to pertussis diagnosis in both investigational and routine clinical care settings and has been demonstrated to be both sensitive and specific.[106, 129, 130] The virtue of a PCR-based diagnosis is that the organisms do not have to be viable, as illustrated by the work of Edelman and colleagues.[131] By observing unvaccinated patients with culture-proven pertussis, they found that on the seventh day of erythromycin treatment all cultures were negative but 56% of the samples were still PCR positive.

Several sets of primers have been used for pertussis PCR, including those derived from the ACT gene, the PT gene or its promoter, a region upstream from the porin gene, and insertion sequences, which are present in multiple copies.[132–135] Use of a combination of primers and treatment of the product with restriction enzymes allows for simultaneous detection of, but discrimination between, *B. pertussis* and *B. parapertussis* in the same assay. Although there are significant advantages to the use of PCR for identification of *Bordetella* organisms, it is important that efforts to culture the organism also continue, because strain variation, antibiotic resistance, and other phenotypic and genotypic features in the population will be missed by a single PCR-based detection system.[136]

In light of the limitations of laboratory procedures for pertussis diagnosis, a clinical case definition has been developed to identify persons with the disease. A cough of 2 weeks' duration was found to be a sensitive and specific marker of pertussis in community outbreaks but has been shown to have limitations in efficacy in clinical field trials.[137, 138] The case definition established by a World Health Organization (WHO) panel and used in the clinical trials was 21 or more days of paroxysmal cough with laboratory confirmation or epidemiologic linkage.[139] It is clear in retrospect, however, that this definition resulted in omission from the case roll of culture-positive, symptomatic persons with a shorter duration of cough.[140]

PREVENTION

Before the availability of a vaccine, isolation of infected patients was the only control measure applied to the prevention of pertussis. Because of the nonspecific symptoms early in the clinical course, this approach was effective only in the setting of recognized community outbreaks. Serum from immune persons was thought to be passively protective during the incubation period, but subsequent studies in the 1960s and 1970s found no evidence that pertussis immunoglobulin was efficacious.[141] One report suggested that immunoglobulin might provide some benefit in reducing severity and duration of symptoms, and a preparation of pertussis immune globulin is currently being evaluated on hospitalized patients to test this hypothesis.[142] Antibiotic (erythromycin) prophylaxis is recommended for prevention of disease in contacts of active cases; although not fully efficacious, this has been shown to be a major factor in controlling household transmission and outbreaks[143–146]

Whole Cell Vaccine

Soon after the original isolation of *B. pertussis*, work was begun on preparation of a vaccine. Merthiolate-killed, whole cell vaccines were found to be protective, and in the early 1950s a British Medical Research Council trial documented a correlation between protection in a mouse intracerebral potency test and vaccine protection in children.[147] The vaccine currently recommended by the WHO and used in much of the world is killed, whole cell vaccine combined with diphtheria and tetanus toxoids and aluminum-containing adjuvants (DTP vaccine). Although whole cell vaccine was believed to be more than 80% efficacious, most preparations had never been tested directly in prospective clinical efficacy trials, and calculations of efficacy from a variety of sources ranged from 0 to 100% depending on the vaccine preparation used, the type of study, and the case definition.[87] The phase III trials of acellular vaccines also provided an opportunity for evaluation of several whole cell products, which were found to differ substantially in their efficacies, despite the fact that each passed the standard Kendrick mouse potency test required for lot release. This observation should not be interpreted as an indictment of all whole cell pertussis products but should serve as a warning to heighten awareness of the need for continual assessment of the effectiveness of whole cell vaccines in general use.

A major limitation to whole cell vaccine use has been the associated reactogenicity. When compared with DT, DTP vaccine produces significantly more local and systemic reactions such as pain, swelling, fever, anorexia, fretfulness, and vomiting.[148–150] Encephalopathy and permanent neurologic sequelae, but not infantile spasms or sudden infant death syndrome, have been associated temporally with DTP vaccine administration, but it appears that few if any of these effects are caused by the vaccine.[118, 149–152] Pertussis vaccine development and use was discussed extensively in a review for the American Society of Pediatrics.[153] Considerations of the benefits and risks of whole cell vaccine have repeatedly concluded in favor of its continued use in the general population.[150–154]

At present, whole cell pertussis vaccine is used in adults only under special circumstances for control of hospital outbreaks, but the use of immunization in this setting may well change as more data are acquired about acellular vaccine in adults.[155]

Acellular Vaccine Development

Although efforts were made as early as the 1930s to prepare non–whole cell pertussis vaccines and a product (Eli Lilly's TriSolgen) was available on the market through the mid-1970s, antigen contents of such vaccines were not well characterized, and controlled trials to determine their efficacies were never done.[33] Driven primarily by concerns about the reactogenicity and efficacy of whole cell vaccines, numerous non–whole cell pertussis products have been developed over the past 15 to 20 years. The discoveries by Sato and colleagues that PT was one of two hemagglutinins on the surface of *B. pertussis* and that both PT and FHA can contribute to protection in an animal model of pertussis represented major breakthroughs toward introduction of the acellular vaccine era for pertussis.[156] Clinical interest in acellular vaccines was stimulated by the development and extensive use of such products in Japan during the early 1980s.[33, 156, 157] Because the Japanese products were initially used in children 2 years of age and older, it was deemed necessary for efficacy to be evaluated in infants (beginning at 2 months of age, as in the U.S. immunization schedule) before consideration of licensure in the United States and elsewhere. To address this aspect, pertussis toxoid, alone or in combination with filamentous hemagglutinin, was tested during 1986 and 1987 in Swedish children beginning at 6 months of age.[158] Although both preparations showed protection, they exceeded 70% efficacy only when the case definition included 28 or more days of cough (severe disease) (Table 219–1). No whole cell vaccines were included in that trial, and efficacies of such products remained subject to speculation. The low efficacies of the two acellular vaccines in Sweden precluded their being licensed there or in the United States and led to additional developmental efforts for acellular pertussis vaccines.

The current acellular pertussis vaccines contain one to five components and were tested in at least seven different trials beginning in the early 1990s.[159] All preparations contain PT, inactivated either chemically or genetically. The other components present in at least some vaccines are FHA, pertactin, and types 2 and 3 fimbriae. Other antigens, such as ACT, that have been shown to be protective in animals were not included because of lack of data or unavailability of purified material at the time of acellular product development.

Results from the clinical efficacy trials are showin in Table 219–1 and illustrate the variety of preparations and study designs employed.[140, 160–167] Other differences among the vaccines that may be contributing to differences in efficacy include method of antigen preparation and detoxification, the adjuvant, the preservative, and the DT component.[168] Nevertheless, there are several important observations that can be derived from these results: (1) one- and two-antigen

TABLE 219–1 Results from Efficacy Trials of Acellular and Whole Cell Pertussis Vaccines

Dates	Location	Vaccine*	Source†	Design‡	Efficacy (95% Confidence Interval)	Reference
1986/87	Sweden	PT	Biken	DBPC	54 (26–72)§	138
		PT/FHA	Biken		69 (47–82)	
1994/95	Sweden/Goteborg	PT	AM	DBPC	71 (63–78)‖	157, 158
1994/95	Senegal	PT/FHA	PM	DBPC*	85 (66–93)‖	159
		Whole cell	PM		96 (87–94)	
1993/95	Germany/Munich	PT/FHA	Conn-US	CC	96 (87–99)‖	160
		Whole cell	BE		97 (79–100)	
1994/95	Germany/Mainz	PT/FHA/PRN	SK	PHC	89 (77–95)‖	161
		Whole cell	BE		97 (83–100)	
1994/95	Sweden/Stockholm	PT/FHA	SK	DBPC	59 (51–66)‖	162, 163
		PT/FHA/PRN/FIM(2/3)	Conn-C		85 (81–89)	
		Whole cell	Conn-US		48 (37–58)	
1994/95	Italy	PT/FHA/PRN	SK	DBPC	84 (76–90)‖	138
		PT/FHA/PRN	CB		84 (76–90)	
		Whole cell	Conn-US		36 (14–52)	
1994/95	Germany/Erlangen	PT/FHA/PRN/FIM(2)	WL	DBPC*	86 (62–95)¶	164
		Whole cell	LED		94 (77–99)	

*Vaccine composition—PT, pertussis toxoid; FHA, filamentous hemagglutinin; PRN, pertactin; FIM (2/3), type 2 and 3 fimbriae; FIM(2), type 2 fimbriae only; vaccines contained different quantities of these components.

†Abbreviations for manufacturers: AM, Amvax; PM, Pasteur Mérieux; Conn-US, Connaught US; BE, Behring; SK, SmithKlein; Conn-C, Connaught Canada; CB, Chiron Biocine; WL, Wyeth Lederle.

‡Abbreviations for study designs: DBPC, double blind, prospective control; DBPC* indicates that the study contained an unblinded control group for comparison; PHC, prospective household contact; CC, case control.

§Case definition: culture-confirmed pertussis with any cough.

‖Case definition (WHO): ≥21 days of paroxysmal cough with lab confirmation (culture or serology) or epidemiologic link; modified case definition.

¶Case definition: ≥21 days of cough with paroxysms, whoop, or posttussive vomiting.

vaccines performed less well than preparations with multiple (three to five) antigens; (2) one of four whole cell vaccines was significantly less efficacious than expected and less efficacious than the others, but in general the whole cell vaccines performed as well or better than acellular vaccines. Although the whole cell vaccine with low efficacy had been demonstrated to be less immunogenic in earlier studies,[169] the basis for the reduced efficacy is not clear. In addition to efficacy, the acellular vaccines were associated with significantly lower rates of reactogenicity. On the basis of these data, each of the acellular vaccines tested has been licensed in United States and/or elsewhere. Acellular vaccine is now recommended for all five doses of DPT in children.[170] The same product should be used each time. The duration of protection and the significance of mixing different acellular products in an immunization sequence remain to be determined.

Issues in Vaccine Development

Despite the demonstrated efficacies of most whole cell and acellular vaccines, the mechanisms by which they produce immunity remain unknown. In the early days of studying pertussis immunity, several investigators recognized a correlation between acquisition of pertussis agglutinating antibodies and apparent resistance to infection.[171] It was not clear whether that relation represented a mechanism of protection, a significant marker of immunity, or merely an epiphenomenon. During the first Swedish trials, an effort was made to compare levels of anti-PT and/or anti-FHA antibodies with protection in individual patients, but no meaningful relation was identified, owing in part to the time between collection of serum samples and exposure to the organism. In more recent trials, several groups took a similar approach and conducted retrospective evaluations of the serologic data, using curves of antibody kinetics to determine the level of antibody at the time of exposure. With different data sets, two groups observed that antibodies to pertactin, fimbriae (type 2 or types 2 and 3) and PT were associated with reduced likelihood of pertussis.[172, 173]

Another element of immunity, namely the cell-mediated response, has been implicated as relevant to acquisition and elimination of infection with *B. pertussis*. Several laboratories have demonstrated that animals challenged with *B. pertussis* and patients with pertussis acquire a cell-mediated response to *Bordetella* antigens.[174–180] More recently, however, Mills and colleagues[181] described an animal model in which both the humoral and cellular arms of immunity are involved in the clearance of and resistance to *B. pertussis*. Specimens for evaluation of cellular responses to pertussis antigens were collected in some of the efficacy trials, but analyses comparable to those demonstrating the relation between antibodies and protection are not yet available.

TREATMENT

Supportive Care

Infants with pertussis are at greatest risk of complications with permanent sequelae, and hospitalization should be considered for patients younger than 1 year of age. Appropriate measures for such patients with moderate-to-severe disease include close monitoring of vital signs; quantitation of cough paroxysms and associated vomiting, cyanosis, and apnea; frequent nasotracheal suctioning; and provision of oxygen and parenteral hydration and nutrition.

Specific Therapy

Despite earlier data to the contrary, there is now preliminary evidence that pertussis immune globulin may be useful in reducing the severity of disease, especially in infants and young children who are at high risk of complications or death. An efficacy trial of this material is currently underway. Data from that study may provide an alternative to simple support and antibiotics for early intervention.

In order to be effective against *B. pertussis*, an antibiotic must penetrate the respiratory tract. Although several antibiotics, including erythromycin, tetracycline, trimethoprim-sulfamethoxazole, and chloramphenicol, have been shown to be effective in elimination of *B. pertussis*, erythromycin, especially the estolate ester, appears to be the most reliable, probably because of its higher serum levels and its ability to enter the respiratory tract.[143, 182–185] Contrary to previous dogma, erythromycin does appear to reduce severity and duration of disease, even when it is started during the paroxysmal phase.[184, 185] The recommended dose, 40 to 50 mg/kg/day (maximum 2 g/day) in two doses should be given for a full 14 days to prevent bacteriologic relapse, which may occur as a result of inadequate duration of therapy rather than development of drug resistance by the organism.[145] Trimethoprim-sulfamethoxazole is an alternative that is useful for older patients who cannot tolerate erythromycin, but there is less clinical experience with this preparation. The newer macrolides such as azithromycin and clarithromycin have good in vitro activity against *B. pertussis* and clinical data are becoming available to support their use in this setting.[186] Other antibiotics, such as ampicillin, have activity against *B. pertussis* in vitro but are clinically ineffective and should not be used.

Other therapeutic agents have been evaluated for symptomatic relief during the paroxysmal phase. Corticosteroids (betamethasone, 0.075 mg/kg/day orally, or hydrocortisone succinate, 30 mg/kg/day intramuscularly) may reduce the number, severity, and duration of cough paroxysms, but at present consideration of systemic use of these agents should be limited to infants with life-threatening pertussis.[182, 187] There are anecdotal reports of success with aerosolized corticosteroids in reducing the frequency and severity of paroxysmal cough, but this option has not been evaluated in a controlled manner.[188] Salbutamol, a β-adrenergic agonist, has also been proposed for use in clinical pertussis, but there are conflicting data about its efficacy.[189–191] Standard cough suppressants and antihistamines are not effective, and their administration can be detrimental by inducing cough paroxysms.[182]

REFERENCES

1. Major RH. A History of Medicine. Springfield, Ill: Charles C Thomas; 1954:423.
2. Lapin JH. Whooping Cough. Springfield, Ill: Charles C Thomas; 1943.
3. Bordet J, Gengou O, Le microbe de la coqueluche. Ann Inst Pasteur. 1906;20:731–741.
4. Parton R. New perspectives on *Bordetella* pathogenicity. J Med Microbiol. 1996;44:233–235.
5. Vandamme P, Vancanneyt M, Hoste B, et al. *Bordetella hinzii* sp. nov., isolated from poultry and humans. Int J Syst Bacteriol. 1995;45:37–45.
6. Funke G, Hess T, Vandamme P, Characteristics of *Bordetella hinzii* strains isolated from a cystic fibrosis patient over a 3-year period. J Clin Microbiol. 1996;34:966–969.
7. Tang YW, Hopkins MK, Kolbert CP, et al. *Bordetella holmesii*-like organisms associated with septicemia, endocarditis, and respiratory failure. Clin Infect Dis. 1998;26:389–392.
8. Weyant RS, Hollis DG, Weaver RE, et al. *Bordetella holmesii* sp. nov., a new gram-negative species associated with septicemia. J Clin Microbiol. 1995;33:1–7.
9. Vandamme P, Heyndrickx M, Vancanneyt M, et al. *Bordetella trematum* sp. nov., isolated from wounds and ear infections in humans, and reassessment of *Alcaligenes denitrificans* Ruger and Tan 1983. Int J Syst Bacteriol. 1996;46:849–858.
10. Ghosh HK, Tranter J, *Bordetella bronchicanis (bronchiseptica)* infection in man: Review and a case report. J Clin Pathol. 1979;32:546–548.
11. Byrd LH, Anama L, Gutkin M, et al. *Bordetella bronchiseptica* peritonitis associated with continuous ambulatory peritoneal dialysis. J Clin Microbiol. 1981;14:232–233.
12. Bauwens JE, Spach DH, Schacker TW, et al. *Bordetella bronchiseptica* pneumonia and bacteremia following bone marrow transplantation. J Clin Microbiol. 1992;30:2474–2475.
13. van der Zee A, Groenendijk H, Peeters M, et al. The differentiation of *Bordetella parapertussis* and *Bordetella bronchiseptica* from humans and animals as determined by DNA polymorphism mediated by two different insertion sequence elements suggests their phylogenetic relationship. Int J Syst Bacteriol. 1996;46:640–647.
14. Arp LH, Cheville NF. Tracheal lesions in young turkeys infected with *Bordetella avium*. Am J Vet Res. 1984;45:2196–2200.

15. Vandamme P, Hinz KH, Schemken-Birk EM, et al. Isolation of a *Bordetella avium*-like organism from a human specimen. Eur J Clin Microbiol Infect Dis. 1995;14:451–454.
16. Pittman M. Bordetella. In: Krieg NR, Holt JG, Sneath PHA, et al., eds. Baltimore: Williams & Wilkins, 1994:136.
17. Stainer DW. Growth of *Bordetella pertussis*. In: Wardlaw AC, Parton R, eds. Chichester, England: John Wiley & Sons, 1988:19–37.
18. Gilchrist MJR. Bordetella. In: Hausler WJ Jr, Herrmann KL, Isenberg HD, et al., eds. Manual of Clinical Microbiology. Washington, DC: American Society for Microbiology, 1991:471–477.
19. Imaizumi A, Suzuki Y, Ono S, et al. Heptakis(2,6-*O*-dimethyl)beta-cyclodextrin: A novel growth stimulant for *Bordetella pertussis* phase I. J Clin Microbiol. 1983;17:781–786.
20. Kloos WE, Dobrogosz WJ, Ezzell J. International Symposium on Pertussis: Physiology of *Bordetella pertussis*. Washington, DC: U.S. Government Printing Office, 1979:86–93.
21. Musser JM, Hewlett EL, Peppler MS, et al. Genetic diversity and relationships in populations of *Bordetella* spp. J Bacteriol. 1986;166:230–237.
22. Arico B, Gross R, Smida J, et al. Evolutionary relationships in the genus *Bordetella*. Mol Microbiol. 1987;1:301–308.
23. van der Zee A, Peeters M, van EJ, et al. Dynamics of the population structure of *Bordetella pertussis* as measured by IS1002-associated RFLP: Comparison of pre- and post-vaccination strains and global distribution. Microbiology. 1996;142:3479–3485.
24. Beall B, Cassiday PK, Sanden GN. Analysis of *Bordetella pertussis* isolates from an epidemic by pulsed-field gel electrophoresis. J Clin Microbiol. 1995;33:3083–3086.
25. Hewlett EL. Pertussis: Current concepts of pathogenesis and prevention. Pediatr Infect Dis J. 1997;16:S78–S84.
26. Relman D. Toumanen E, Falkow S, et al. Recognition of a bacterial adhesin by an integrin: Macrophage CR3 (aMb2, CD11b/CD18) binds filamentous hemagglutinin of *Bordetella pertussis*. Cell. 1990;61:1375–1382.
27. Locht C, Bertin P, Menozzi FD, et al. The filamentous haemagglutinin, a multifaceted adhesin produced by virulent *Bordetella* spp. Mol Microbiol. 1993;9:653–660.
28. Urisu A, Cowell JL, Manclark CR. Involvement of the filamentous hemagglutinin in the adherence of *Bordetella pertussis* to human WiDr cultures. In: Manclark CR, Hennessen W, eds. Developments in Biological Standardization: Proceedings of the Fourth International Symposium on Pertussis. Basel: S Karger; 1985:205–214.
29. Leininger E, Kenimer JG, Brennan MJ. Surface protein of *Bordetella pertussis*: Role of adherence. In: Manclark CR, ed. Proceedings of the Sixth International Symposium on Pertussis, Department of Health and Human Services, United States Public Health Service, DHHS Publication No (FDA) 90–1164. Bethesda, Md; 1990:100–105.
30. Relman DA, Domenighini M, Tuomanen E, et al. Filamentous hemagglutinin of *Bordetella pertussis*: Nucleotide sequence and crucial role in adherence. Proc Natl Acad Sci U S A. 1989;86:2637–2641.
31. Guzman CA, Walker MJ, Rohde M, et al. Expression of *Bordetella pertussis* filamentous hemagglutinin in *Escherichia coli* using a two cistron system. Microb Pathog. 1992;12:383–389.
32. Tuomanen E. *Bordetella pertussis* adhesins. In: Wardlaw AC, Parton R, eds. Pathogenesis and Immunity in Pertussis. New York: John Wiley & Sons, 1988:75–94.
33. Hewlett EL, Cherry JD. New and improved vaccines against pertussis. In: Cobon GS, Kaper JB, Woodrow GC, et al., eds. New Generation Vaccines. New York: Marcel Dekker, 1997:387–416.
34. Confer DL, Eaton JW. Phagocyte impotence caused by an invasive bacterial adenylate cyclase. Science. 1982;217:948–950.
35. Hewlett EL, Gray MC. Adenylyl cyclase toxin from *Bordetella pertussis*. In: Aktories K, Just E, eds. Handbook of Experimental Pharmacology; Bacterial Protein Toxins. Heidelburg, Springer-Verlag. In press.
36. Pearson RD, Symes P, Conboy M, et al. Inhibition of monocyte oxidative responses by *Bordetella pertussis* adenylate cyclase toxin. J Immunol. 1987;139:2749–2754.
37. Glaser P, Ladant D, Sezer O, et al. The calmodulin-sensitive adenylate cyclase of *Bordetella pertussis*: Cloning and expression in *Escherichia coli*. Mol Microbiol. 1988;2:19–30.
38. Coote JG, Structural and functional relationships among the RTX toxin determinants of gram-negative bacteria. FEMS Microbiol Rev. 1992;88:137–162.
39. Ehrmann I, Gray M, Gordon VM. Hemolytic activity of adenylate cyclase toxin from *Bordetella pertussis*. FEBS Lett. 1991;278:79–83.
40. Weiss AA, Hewlett EL, Myers GA, et al. Pertussis toxin and extracytoplasmic adenylate cyclase as virulence factors of *Bordetella pertussis*. J Infect Dis. 1984;150:219–222.
41. Nagai M, Endoh M, Burns DL, et al. Heat-labile toxin from *Bordetella parapertussis* induces contraction of smooth muscle cells in culture. Microbiol Immunol. 1992;36:633–636.
42. Lacerda HM, Pullinger GD, Lax AJ, et al. Cytotoxic necrotizing factor 1 from *Escherichia coli* and dermonecrotic toxin from *Bordetella bronchiseptica* induce p21(rho)-dependent tyrosine phosphorylation of focal adhesion kinase and paxillin in Swiss 3T3 cells. J Biol Chem. 1997;272:9587–9596.
43. Goldman WE. Tracheal cytotoxin of *Bordetella pertussis*. In: Wardlaw AC, Parton R, eds. Pathogenesis and Immunity in Pertussis. New York: John Wiley & Sons Ltd, 1988:231–246.
44. Heiss LN, Lancaster JR Jr, Corbett JA, et al. Epithelial autotoxicity of nitric oxide: Role in the respiratory cytopathology of pertussis. Proc Natl Acad Sci U S A. 1994;91:267–270.
45. Luker KE, Collier JL, Kolodziej EW, et al. *Bordetella pertussis* tracheal cytotoxin and other muramyl peptides: Distinct structure-activity relationships for respiratory epithelial cytopathology. Proc Natl Acad Sci U S A. 1993;90:2365–2369.
46. Wilson R, Read R, Thomas M, et al. Effects of *Bordetella pertussis* infection on human respiratory epithelium in vivo and in vitro. Infect Immun. 1991;59:337–345.
47. Flak TA, Goldman WE. Autotoxicity of nitric oxide in airway disease (Review). Am J Respir Crit Care Med. 1996;154:S202–S206.
48. Ui M. Pertussis toxin as a valuable probe for G-protein involvement in signal transduction. In: Moss J, Vaughan M, eds. ADP-ribosylating toxins and G proteins. Washington, DC: American Society for Microbiology, 1990:45–78.
49. Ui M. The multiple biological activities of pertussis toxin. In: Wardlaw AC, Parton R, eds. Pathogenesis and Immunity in Pertussis. New York: John Wiley & Sons, 1988:121–146.
50. Wong WS, Rosoff PM. Pharmacology of pertussis toxin B-oligomer. Can J Physiol Pharmacol. 1996;74:559–564.
51. Locht C, Keith JM. Pertussis toxin gene: Nucleotide sequence and genetic organization. Science. 1986;232:1258–1264.
52. Nicosia A, Perugini M, Franzini C, et al. Cloning and sequencing of the pertussis toxin genes: Operon structure and gene duplication. Proc Natl Acad Sci USA. 1986;83:4631–4635.
53. Nicosia A, Bartoloni A, Perugini M, et al. Expression and immunological properties of the five subunits of pertussis toxin. Infect Immun. 1987;55:963–967.
54. Hazes B, Boodhoo A, Cockle SA, et al. Crystal structure of the pertussis toxin–ATP complex: A molecular sensor. J Mol Biol. 1996;258:661–671.
55. Arico B, Rappuoli R. *Bordetella parapertussis* and *Bordetella bronchiseptica* contain transcriptionally silent pertussis toxin genes. J Bacteriol. 1987;169:2847–2853.
56. Marchitto KS, Smith SG, Locht C, et al. Nucleotide sequence homology to pertussis toxin gene in *Bordetella bronchiseptica* and *Bordetella parapertussis*. Infect Immun. 1987;55:497–501.
57. Stefanelli P, Mastrantonio P, Hausman SZ, et al. Molecular characterization of two *Bordetella bronchiseptica* strains isolated from children with coughs. J Clin Microbiol. 1997;35:1550–1555.
58. Wirsing von Konig CH, Finger H. Role of pertussis toxin in causing symptoms of *Bordetella parapertussis* infection. Eur J Clin Microbiol Infect Dis. 1994;13:455–458.
59. Peppler MS. Two physically and serologically distinct lipopolysaccharide profiles in strains of *Bordetella pertussis* and their phenotype variants. Infect Immun. 1984;43:224–232.
60. Chaby R, Caroff M. Lipopolysaccharides of *Bordetella pertussis* endotoxin. In: Wardlaw AC, Parton R, eds. Pathogenesis and Immunity in Pertussis. New York: John Wiley & Sons, 1988:247.
61. Ayme G, Caroff M, Chaby R, et al. Biological activities of fragments derived from *Bordetella pertussis* endotoxin: Isolation of a nontoxic, Shwartzman-negative lipid A possessing high adjuvant properties. Infect Immun. 1980;27:739–745.
62. Ray A, Redhead K, Selkirk S, et al. Variability in LPS composition, antigenicity and reactogenicity of phase variants of *Bordetella pertussis*. FEMS Microbiol Lett. 1991;63:211–217.
63. Shahin RD, Hamel J, Leef MF, et al. Analysis of protective and nonprotective monoclonal antibodies specific for *Bordetella pertussis* lipooligosaccharide. Infect Immun. 1994;62:722–725.
64. Weiss AA, Hewlett EL. Virulence factors of *Bordetella pertussis*. Ann Rev Microbiol. 1986;40:661–686.
65. Meade BD, Kind PD, Manclark CR. Lymphocytosis-promoting factor of *Bordetella pertussis* alters mononuclear phagocyte circulation and response to inflammation. Infect Immun. 1984;46:733–739.
66. Pittman M, Furman B, Wardlaw A. *Bordetella pertussis*: Respiratory tract infection in the mouse. Pathophysiological response. J Infect Dis. 1980;142:52–66.
67. Toyota T, Kai Y, Kakizaki M, et al. Effects of islet-activating protein (IAP) on blood glucose and plasma insulin in healthy volunteers (phase 1 studies). Tohoku J Exp Med. 1980;130:105–116.
68. Woods DE, Franklin R, Cryz SJJ, et al. Development of a rat model for respiratory infection with *Bordetella pertussis*. Infect Immun. 1989;57:1018–1024.
69. Sato Y, Sato H. Animal models of pertussis. In: Wardlaw AC, Parton R, eds. Pathogenesis and Immunity in Pertussis. New York: John Wiley & Sons, 1988:309–325.
70. Hall E, Parton R, Wardlaw AC. Cough production, leucocytosis and serology of rats infected intrabronchially with *Bordetella pertussis*. J Med Microbiol. 1994;40:205–213.
71. Ewanowich CA, Sherburne RK, Man SFP, et al. *Bordetella parapertussis* invasion of HeLa 229 cells and human respiratory epithelial cells in primary culture. Infect Immun. 1989;57:1240–1247.
72. Leslie PH, Gardner AD. The phases of *Haemophilus pertussis*. J Hyg. 1931;31:423–434.
73. Stibitz S, Aaronson W, Monack D, et al. Phase variation in *Bordetella pertussis* by frameshift mutation in a gene for a novel two-component system. Nature. 1989;338:266–269.
74. Lacey BW. Antigenic modulation of *Bordetella pertussis*. J Hyg. 1960;58:57–93.
75. Miller JF, Mekalanos JJ, Falkow S. Coordinate regulation and sensory transduction in the control of bacterial virulence. Science. 1989;243:916–922.
76. Arico B, Scarlato V, Monack DM, et al. Structural and genetic analysis of the bvg locus in *Bordetella* species. Mol Microbiol. 1991;5:2481–2491.
77. Melton AR, Weiss AA. Environmental regulation of expression of virulence determinants in *Bordetella pertussis*. J Bacteriol. 1989;171:6206–6212.
78. Scarlato V, Arico B, Prugnola A, et al. Sequential activation and environmental regulation of virulence genes in *Bordetella pertussis*. EMBO J. 1991;10:3971–3975.

79. Mekalanos JJ. Environmental signals controlling expression of virulence determinants in bacteria. J Bacteriol. 1992;174:1–7.
80. Merkel TJ, Stibitz S, Keith JM, et al. Contribution of regulation by the bvg locus to respiratory infection of mice by *Bordetella pertussis*. Infect Immun. 1998;66:4367–4373.
81. Martinez de Tejada G, Cotter PA, Heininger U, et al. Neither the Bvg-phase nor the vrg6 locus of *Bordetella pertussis* is required for respiratory infection in mice. Infect Immun. 1998;66:2762–2768.
82. Stibitz S. Mutations affecting the alpha subunit of *Bordetella pertussis* RNA polymerase suppress growth inhibition conferred by short C-terminal deletions of the response regulator BvgA. J Bacteriol. 1998;180:2484–2492.
83. Ivanoff B, Robertson SE. Pertussis: A worldwide problem (Review). Dev Biol Stand. 1997;89:3–13.
84. Kanai K. Japan's experience in pertussis epidemiology and vaccination in the past thirty years. Jpn J Med Sci Biol. 1980;33:107–143.
85. Cherry JD. The epidemiology of pertussis and pertussis immunization in the United Kingdom and the United States: A comparative study. Curr Probl Pediatr. 1984;14:1–78.
86. Romanus V, Jonsell R, Bergquist S-O. Pertussis in Sweden after the cessation of general immunization in 1979. Pediatr Infect Dis J. 1987;6:364–371.
87. Fine PEM, Clarkson JA. Reflections on the efficacy of pertussis vaccines. Rev Infect Dis. 1987;9:866–883.
88. Lambert HJ. Epidemiology of a small pertussis outbreak in Kent County, Michigan. Public Health Rep. 1965;80:365–369.
89. Jenkinson D, Pepper JD. A search for subclinical infection during a small outbreak of whooping cough: Implications for clinical diagnosis. J R Col Gen Prac. 1986;36:547–548.
90. Krantz I, Alestig K, Trollfors B, et al. The carrier state in pertussis. Scand J Infect Dis. 1986;18:121–123.
91. Broome CV, Preblud SR, Bruner B, et al. Epidemiology of pertussis, Atlanta. 1977. J Pediatr. 1981;98:362–367.
92. Luttinger P. The epidemiology of pertussis. Am J Dis Child. 1916;290–315.
93. Anonymous. Pertussis—United States, 1982 and 1983. MMWR Morb Mortal Wkly Rep. 1984;33:573–575.
94. Farizo KM, Cochi SL, Zell ER, et al. Epidemiological features of pertussis in the United States, 1980–1989. Clin Infect Dis. 1992;14:708–719.
95. Herwaldt LA. Pertussis in adults: What physicians need to know. Arch Intern Med. 1991;151:1510–1512.
96. Hewlett EL. Pertussis in adults: Significance for disease transmission and immunisation policy (Editorial). J Med Microbiol. 1992;36:141–142.
97. Anonymous. Pertussis outbreak—Vermont, 1996. MMWR Morb Mortal Wkly Rep. 1997;46:822–826.
98. Cherry JD. Pertussis in adults (Editorial). Ann Intern Med. 1998;128:64–66.
99. Huovila R. Clinical symptoms and complications of whooping cough in children and adults. Acta Paediatr Scand. 1982;298:13–20.
100. Heininger U, Stehr K, Cherry JD. Serious pertussis overlooked in infants. Eur J Pediatr. 1992;151:342–343.
101. Aoyama T, Takeuchi Y, Goto A, et al. Pertussis in adults. Am J Dis Child. 1992;146:163–166.
102. Wright SW, Edwards KM, Decker MD, et al. Pertussis infection in adults with persistent cough. JAMA. 1995;273:1044–1046.
103. Konig CHW, Postels-Multani S, Bock HL, et al. Pertussis in adults: Frequency of transmission after household exposure. Lancet. 1995;346:1326–1329.
104. Schmitt-Grohe S, Cherry JD, Heininger U, et al. Pertussis in German adults. Clin Infect Dis. 1995;21:860–862.
105. Postels-Multani S, Schmitt HJ, Wirsing von Konig CH, et al. Symptoms and complications of pertussis in adults. Infection. 1995;23:139–142.
106. Hewlett EL. Toxins. In: Mandell GL, Bennett JE, Dolin R, eds. Principles and Practice of Infectious Disease. 5th ed. Philadelphia: Churchill Livingstone; 2000.
107. Furman BL. Walker E, Sidey FM, et al. Slight hyperinsulinaemia but no hypoglycaemia in pertussis patients. J Med Microbiol. 1988;25:183–186.
108. Badr-El-Din MK, Aref GH, Mazloum H, et al. The beta-adrenergic receptors in pertussis. J Trop Med Hyg. 1976;79:213–219.
109. Bellamy EA, Johnston IDA, Wilson AG. The chest radiograph in whooping cough. Clin Radiol. 1987;38:39–43.
110. Kwantes W, Joynson DHM, Williams WO. *Bordetella pertussis* isolation in general practice: 1977–79 whooping cough epidemic in West Glamorgan. J Hyg. 1983;90:149–158.
111. Britten N, Wadsworth J. Long term respiratory sequelae of whooping cough in a nationally representative sample. Br Med J. 1986;292:441–444.
112. Howenstine M, Eigen H, Tepper R. Pulmonary function in infants after pertussis. J Pediatr. 1991;118:563–566.
113. Wardlaw AC, Parton R, eds. Pathogenesis and Immunity in Pertussis. Chichester: Wiley & Sons; 1988:1–482.
114. Manclark CR, ed. Proceedings of the Sixth International Symposium on Pertussis. Bethesda Md: United States Public Health Services. 1990.
115. MacLean DW. Adults with pertussis. J R Col Gen Prac. 1982;May:298–300.
116. Shvartzman P, Mader R, Stopler T. Herniated lumbar disc associated with pertussis. J Fam Pract. 1989;28:224–225.
117. Halperin SA, Marrie TJ. Pertussis encephalopathy in an adult: Case report and review. Rev Infect Dis. 1991;13:1043–1047.
118. Hewlett EL. *Bordetella pertussis* and the central nervous system. In: Scheld WM, Whitley RJ, Durack DT, eds. Infections of the Central Nervous System. New York: Raven, 1991:625–635.
119. Onorato IM, Wassilak SGF. Laboratory diagnosis of pertussis: The state of the art. Pediatr Infect Dis J. 1987;6:145–151.
120. Friedman RL. Pertussis: The disease and new diagnostic methods. Clin Microbiol Rev. 1988;1:365–376.
121. Halperin SA, Bortolussi R, Wort AJ. Evaluation of culture, immunofluorescence, and serology for the diagnosis of pertussis. J Clin Microbiol. 1989;27:752–757.
122. Stauffer LR, Brown DR, Sandstrom RE. Cephalexin-supplemented Jones-Kendrick charcoal agar for selective isolation of *Bordetella pertussis*: Comparison with previously described media. J Clin Microbiol. 1983;17:60–62.
123. Aoyama T, Murase Y, Iwata T, et al. Comparison of blood-free medium (cyclodextrin solid medium) with Bordet-Gengou medium for clinical isolation of *Bordetella pertussis*. J Clin Microbiol. 1986;23:1046–1048.
124. Hallander HO, Reizenstein E, Renemar B, et al. Comparison of nasopharyngeal aspirates with swabs for culture of *Bordetella pertussis*. J Clin Microbiol. 1993;31:50–52.
125. Broome CV, Fraser DW, English WJI. Pertussis—Diagnostic methods and surveillance. In: Manclark CR, Hill JC, eds. Third International Symposium on Pertussis. Washington, DC: U.S. Department of Health, Education and Welfare, 1978:19–22.
126. Meade BD, DeForest A, Edwards KM, et al. Description and evaluation of serologic assays used in a multicenter trial of a cellular pertussis vaccines. Pediatrics. 1995;96:570–575.
127. Halperin SA. Interpretation of pertussis serologic tests. Pediatr Infect Dis J. 1991;10:791–792.
128. Goodman YE, Wort AJ, Jackson FL. Enzyme-linked immunosorbent assay for detection of pertussis immunoglobulin A in nasopharyngeal secretions as an indicator of recent infection. J Clin Microbiol. 1981;13:286–292.
129. Meade BD, Bollen A. Recommendations for use of the polymerase chain reaction in the diagnosis of *Bordetella pertussis* infections. J Med Microbiol. 1994;41:51–55.
130. Grimprel E, Begue P, Anjak I, et al. Comparison of polymerase chain reaction, culture, and western immunoblot serology for diagnosis of *Bordetella pertussis* infection. J Clin Microbiol. 1993;31:2745–2750.
131. Edelman K, Nikkari S, Ruuskanen O, et al. Detection of *Bordetella pertussis* by polymerase chain reaction and culture in the nasopharynx of erythromycin-treated infants with pertussis. Pediatr Infect Dis J. 1996;15:54–57.
132. Reizenstein E, Johansson B, Mardin L, et al. Diagnostic evaluation of polymerase chain reaction discriminative for *Bordetella pertussis*, *B. parapertussis*, and *B. bronchiseptica*. Diagn Microbiol Infect Dis. 1993;17:185–191.
133. Birkebaek NH, Heron I, Skjodt K. *Bordetella pertussis* diagnosed by polymerase chain reaction. APMIS. 1994;102:291–294.
134. Douglas E, Coote JG, Parton R, et al. Identification of *Bordetella pertussis* in nasopharyngeal swabs by PCR amplification of a region of the adenylate cyclase gene. J Med Microbiol. 1993;38:140–144.
135. Li Z, Jansen DL, Finn TM, et al. Identification of *Bordetella pertussis* infection by shared-primer PCR. J Clin Microbiol. 1994;32:783–789.
136. Mooi FR, van OH, Heuvelman K, et al. Polymorphism in the *Bordetella pertussis* virulence factors P.69/pertactin and pertussis toxin in the Netherlands: Temporal trends and evidence for vaccine-driven evolution. Infect Immun. 1998;66:670–675.
137. Patriarca PA, Biellik RJ, Sanden G, et al. Sensitivity and specificity of clinical case definitions for pertussis. Am J Public Health. 1988;78:833–836.
138. Blackwelder WC, Storsaeter J, Olin P, et al. Acellular pertussis vaccines: Efficacy and evaluation of clinical case definitions. Am J Dis Child. 1991:145:1285–1289.
139. Anonymous. WHO meeting on case definition of pertussis. Geneva: World Health Organization, 1991;1:4–5.
140. Greco D. Salmaso S, Mastrantonio P, et al. A controlled trial of two acellular vaccines and one whole-cell vaccine against pertussis. N Engl J Med. 1996;334:341–348.
141. Balagtas RC, Nelson KE, Levin S, et al. Treatment of pertussis with pertussis immune globulin. J Pediatr. 1971;79:203–208.
142. Granstrom M, Olinder-Nielsen AM, Holmblad P, et al. Specific immunoglobulin for treatment of whooping cough. Lancet. 1991;338:1230–1233.
143. Steketee RW, Wassilak SGF, Adkins WN Jr, et al. Evidence for a high attack rate and efficacy of erythromycin prophylaxis in a pertussis outbreak in a facility for the developmentally disabled. J Infect Dis. 1988;157:434–440.
144. Sprauer MA, Cochi SL, Zell ER, et al. Prevention of secondary transmission of pertussis in households with early use of erythromycin. Am J Dis Child. 1992;146:177–181.
145. Anonymous. Report of the Committee on Infectious Diseases (Red Book). Elk Grove, IL: American Academy of Pediatrics, 1991:358.
146. Dodhia H, Miller E. Review of the evidence for the use of erythromycin in the management of persons exposed to pertussis. Epidemiol Infect. 1998;120:143–149.
147. Anonymous. Vaccination against whooping cough. Br Med J. 1959;994.
148. Cody CL, Baraff LJ, Cherry JD, et al. Nature and rates of adverse reactions associated with DTP and DT immunizations in infants and children. Pediatrics. 1981;68:650–660.
149. Howson CP, Howe CJ, Fineberg HV, eds. Adverse Effects of Pertussis and Rubella Vaccines. Washington, DC: National Academy Press; 1991:1–367.
150. Hodder SL, Mortimer EA Jr. Epidemiology of pertussis and reactions to pertussis vaccine. Epidemiol Rev. 1992;14:243–267.
151. Peter G, Easton JG, Halsey NA. Committee on Infectious Diseases: The relationship between pertussis vaccine and brain damage: Reassessment. Pediatrics. 1991;397.
152. Golden GS. Pertussis vaccine and injury to the brain. J Pediatr. 1990;116:854–861.
153. Cherry JD, Brunell JD, Golden GS, et al. Report of the task force on pertussis and pertussis immunization—1988. Pediatrics. 1988;81:939–984.
154. Hinman AR, Koplan JP. Pertussis and pertussis vaccine: Reanalysis of benefits, risks, and costs. JAMA. 1984;251:3109–3113.
155. Hewlett EL. Pertussis in adults: Significance for disease transmission and immunisation policy. J Med Microbiol. 1992;36:141–142.

156. Sato Y, Kimura M, Fukumi H. Development of a pertussis component vaccine in Japan. Lancet. 1984;1:122–126.
157. Noble GR, Bernier RH, Esber EC, et al. Acellular and whole-cell pertussis vaccines in Japan: Report of a visit by US scientists. JAMA. 1987;257:1351–1356.
158. Anonymous. Placebo-controlled trial of two acellular pertussis vaccines in Sweden: Protective efficacy and adverse events. Lancet. 1988;1:955–960.
159. Edwards KM, Meade BD, Decker MD, et al. Comparison of 13 acellular pertussis vaccines: Overview and serologic response. Pediatrics. 1995;96:548–557.
160. Trollfors B, Taranger J, Lagergard T, et al. A placebo-controlled trial of a pertussis-toxoid vaccine. N Engl J Med. 1995;333:1045–1050.
161. Taranger J, Trollfors B, Lagergard T, et al. Unchanged efficacy of a pertussis toxoid vaccine throughout the two years after the third vaccination of infants. Pediatr Infect Dis J. 1997;16:180–184.
162. Simondon F, Preziosi MP, Yam A, et al. A randomized double-blind trial comparing a two-component acellular to a whole-cell pertussis vaccine in Senegal. Vaccine. 1997;15:1606–1612.
163. Liese JG, Meschievitz CK, Harzer E, et al. Efficacy of a two-component acellular pertussis vaccine in infants. Pediatr Infect Dis J. 1997;16:1038–1044.
164. Schmitt HJ. von Konig CHW, Neiss A, et al. Efficacy of acellular pertussis vaccine in early childhood after household exposure. JAMA. 1996;275:37–41.
165. Gustafsson L, Hallander HO. Olin P, et al. A controlled trial of a two-component acellular, a five-component acellular, and a whole-cell pertussis vaccine. N Engl J Med. 1996;334:349–355.
166. Olin P, Rasmussen F, Gustafsson L, et al. Randomised controlled trial of two-component, three-component, and five-component acellular pertussis vaccines compared with whole-cell pertussis vaccine. Lancet. 1997;350:1569–1577.
167. Heininger U, Cherry JD, Stehr K, et al. Comparative efficacy of the Lederle/Takeda acellular pertussis component DTP (DTaP) vaccine and Lederle whole-cell component DTP vaccine in German children after household exposure: Pertussis Vaccine Study Group. Pediatrics. 1998;102:546–553.
168. Hewlett EL. Preparation and composition of acellular pertussis vaccines: Consideration of potential effects on vaccine efficacy. Dev Biol Stand. 1997;89:143–151.
169. Edwards KM, Decker MD, Halsey NA, et al. Differences in antibody response to whole-cell pertussis vaccines. Pediatrics. 1991;88:1019–1023.
170. Anonymous. Pertussis vaccination: Use of acellular pertussis vaccines among infants and children: Recommendations of the Advisory Committee on Immunization Practices (ACIP). MMWR Morb Mortal Wkly Rep. RR-7. 1997;46:1–25.
171. Miller JJ Jr, Silverberg RJ, Saito TM, et al. An agglutinative reaction for *Hemophilus pertussis*: I. Persistence of agglutinins after vaccine. J Pediatr. 1943;22:637–651.
172. Storsaeter J, Hallander HO, Gustafsson L, et al. Levels of anti-pertussis antibodies related to protection after household exposure to *Bordetella pertussis*. Vaccine. 1998;16:1907–1914.
173. Cherry JD, Gornbein J, Heininger U, et al. A search for serologic correlates of immunity to *Bordetella pertussis* cough illnesses. Vaccine. 1998;16:1901–1906.
174. De Magistris MT, Romano M, Nuti S, et al. Dissecting human T cell responses against *Bordetella* species. J Exp Med. 1988;168:1351–1362.
175. Mills KHG, Redhead K. Cellular immunity in pertussis. J Med Microbiol. 1993;39:163–164.
176. Petersen JW. Cellular immunity in relation to pertussis vaccination and infection. Dan Med Bull. 1995;42:121–140.
177. Redhead K, Watkins J, Barnard A, et al. Effective immunization against *Bordetella pertussis* respiratory infection in mice is dependent on induction of cell-mediated immunity. Infect Immun. 1993;61:3190–3198.
178. Petersen JW, Ibsen PH, Haslov K, et al. Proliferative responses and gamma interferon and tumor necrosis factor production by lymphocytes isolated from tracheobroncheal lymph nodes and spleen of mice aerosol infected with *Bordetella pertussis*. Infect Immun. 1992;60:4563–4570.
179. Peppoloni S, Nencioni L, Di Tommaso A, et al. Lymphokine secretion and cytotoxic activity of human CD4+ T-cell clones against *Bordetella pertussis*. Infect Immun. 1991;59:3768–3773.
180. Cassone A, Ausiello CM, Urbani F, et al. Cell-mediated and antibody responses to *Bordetella pertussis* antigens in children vaccinated with acellular or whole-cell pertussis vaccines: The Progetto Pertosse-CMI Working Group. Arch Pediatr Adolesc Med. 1997;151:283–289.
181. Mills KHG, Ryan M, Ryan E, et al. A murine model in which protection correlates with pertussis vaccine efficacy in children reveals complementary roles for humoral and cell-mediated immunity in protection against *Bordetella pertussis*. Infect Immun. 1998;66:594–602.
182. Bass JW. Pertussis: Current status of prevention and treatment. Pediatr Infect Dis. 1985;4:614–619.
183. Bergquist S-O, Bernander S, Dahnsjo H, et al. Erythromycin in the treatment of pertussis: A study of bacteriologic and clinical effects. Pediatr Infect Dis J. 1987;6:458–461.
184. Hoppe JE, Haug A. Treatment and prevention of pertussis by antimicrobial agents (part II). Infection. 1988;16:148–152.
185. Hoppe JE. Erythromycin Study Group: Comparison of erythromycin estolate and erythromycin ethylsuccinate for treatment of pertussis. Pediatr Infect Dis J. 1992;11:189–193.
186. Klein JO, Clarithromycin and azithromycin. Pediatr Infect Dis J. 1998;17:516–517.
187. Roberts I, Gavin R, Lennon D. Randomized controlled trial of steroids in pertussis. Pediatr Infect Dis J. 1992;11:982–983.
188. Hewlett EL. Reemerging infections: Recent developments in pertussis. In: Scheld WM, Craig WA, Hughes JM, eds. Emerging Infections 2. Washington, DC: American Society for Microbiology; 1998:145–158.
189. Pavesio D, Ponzone A. Salbutamol and pertussis. Lancet. 1977;1:150–151.
190. Krantz I, Norrby SR, Trollfors B. Salbutamol vs. placebo for treatment of pertussis. Pediatr Infect Dis. 1985;4:638–640.
191. Mertsola J, Viljanen MK, Ruuskanen O. Salbutamol in the treatment of whooping cough. Scand J Infect Dis. 1986;18:593–594.

Chapter 220

Streptobacillus moniliformis (Rat-Bite Fever)

RONALD G. WASHBURN

Rat-bite fever is a rare systemic febrile illness typically transmitted by the bite of a rat or other small rodent. The infection has a worldwide distribution and can be caused by either *Streptobacillus moniliformis* or *Spirillum minus*, bacteria commonly found in the oropharyngeal flora of rodents. Streptobacillary disease accounts for the vast majority of cases of rat-bite fever in the United States,[1] whereas *S. minus* (see Chapter 232) infections occur mainly in Asia. Table 220–1 compares the two different forms of rat-bite fever.

Illness following rat bites has been known in India for over 2000 years,[2] and the characteristic syndrome of rat-bite fever was recorded in the United States as early as 1839.[3] The causative gram-negative bacillus, initially named *Streptothrix muris ratti*, was recovered from an infected individual in 1916.[4] In 1925, a blood culture isolate from a laboratory worker with fever, rash, and arthritis was called *Streptobacillus moniliformis*, based on its morphologic resemblance to a beaded necklace.[5] In 1926, a similar organism, *Haverhillia multiformis*, was grown from the blood of patients during an epidemic illness resembling rat-bite fever in Haverhill, Massachusetts.[6] Both *H. multiformis* and *S. muris ratti* were subsequently shown to be identical to *S. moniliformis*, the causative agent of streptobacillary rat-bite fever.[2]

BACTERIOLOGY

Streptobacillus moniliformis is a pleomorphic, nonmotile, nonsporulating, nonencapsulated gram-negative bacillus measuring 0.3 to 0.7 μm wide by 1 to 5 μm long.[7, 8] Filaments and beadlike chains up to 150 μm long may contain 1- to 3-μm-wide fusiform swellings. The organism is microaerophilic,[7] requiring a partial pressure of CO_2 between 8 and 10% for primary isolation. Trypticase soy agar or broth must be supplemented with 10 to 20% rabbit or horse serum, defibrinated blood, or ascites to support optimal growth. Alterna-

TABLE 220–1 Comparison of Two Different Types of Rat-Bite Fever

	Streptobacillus moniliformis	*Spirillum minus*
Organism	Gram-negative bacillus	Gram-negative coiled rod
Geographic distribution	North America, Europe	Asia
Mode of transmission	Rat bite, ingestion	Rat bite
Clinical syndrome		
Ulceration of initial bite wound	No	Yes
Arthritis	Yes	No
Regional lymphadenopathy	No	Yes
Rash	Yes	Yes
Relapsing fever	Yes	Yes
Diagnosis	Culture, serologic tests	Direct visualization, xenodiagnosis
Therapy	Penicillin G	Penicillin G

tively, media may be supplemented with a papain digest of ox liver.[9] Sodium polyanethol sulfonate, a substance sometimes added to trypticase soy broth or thioglycollate broth to inhibit the antibacterial activity of human blood, impedes growth of *S. moniliformis* in concentrations of at least 0.0125%.[9, 10]

On blood-agar plates, cotton-like colonies, 1 to 2.5 mm in diameter appear after approximately 3 days of incubation at 37°C.[7] In broth media, characteristic flocculent puffballs are seen at the bottom of the broth after 2 to 10 days. Penicillin-resistant L-phase variants may form either spontaneously or in the presence of penicillin both in vivo and in vitro.[11] These L forms impart a slightly turbid appearance to broth media. Sugar fermentation by *S. moniliformis* is variable but often includes galactose, glucose, maltose, and salicin. Fatty acid analysis by gas-liquid chromatography is useful for rapid identification of *S. moniliformis isolates*.[12–15] In addition, sodium dodecyl sulfate–polyacrylamide gel electrophoresis patterns of cellular proteins may be useful for epidemiologic studies of Haverhill fever.[16]

EPIDEMIOLOGY

In the United States, persons who are at risk for percutaneous inoculation with *S. moniliformis* include animal laboratory personnel and individuals (especially children) inhabiting crowded urban dwellings or rural areas infested with wild rats.[1, 17–23] Rat-bite fever is typically transmitted by the bite or scratch of rats, mice, squirrels, or carnivores that prey on those rodents, including cats, dogs, pigs, ferrets, and weasels.[7, 17, 24] One reported case followed the bite of a gerbil.[25] The infection may also be acquired by handling dead rats, with no apparent breach of intact skin.[18, 26] From 50 to 100% of both wild and laboratory rats harbor *S. moniliformis* in their nasopharyngeal flora,[7, 18, 27–29] and they may develop otitis media.[30] Although healthy laboratory mice are generally not colonized with streptobacilli, they do share with rats the susceptibility to epizootic infections characterized by polyarthritis, septicemia, pneumonia, otitis media, and high rates of abortion.[2, 7, 28, 31–33] *Streptobacillus moniliformis* has also been reported to cause pleuritis in a koala,[34] cervical abscesses and pneumonia in guinea pigs,[35] and arthritis in turkeys, with positive cultures from sternal bursa and tendon sheath.

Pathophysiologically, the clinical disease is probably the consequence of failed local cutaneous defenses and bacterial dissemination. The few available published autopsies described focal infiltrations of mononuclear cells.

Oral ingestion of organisms caused several epidemics of Haverhill fever (erythema arthriticum epidemicum), an illness clinically resembling rat-bite fever. Potential sources of such outbreaks include foods such as turkey,[7] or milk or water contaminated with rat excrement.[5, 6, 9, 18, 36, 37] Presumably, once ingested, *S. moniliformis* organisms gain access to the peripheral circulation by penetrating the gastrointestinal mucosa.

CLINICAL MANIFESTATIONS

A brief incubation period usually less than 10 days in duration (range 1 to 22 days) follows the bite of the rat. An abrupt onset of fever, chills, headache, vomiting, and severe migratory arthralgias and myalgias marks the beginning of clinical disease; by that time, the wound itself has usually already healed. Indeed, the diagnosis is often initially obscured by the patient's incognizance of a bite that probably occurred during sleep. Regional lymphadenopathy is minimal or absent, in contrast to *S. minus* infection. The peripheral white blood cell count may range as high as 30,000/mm^3 with a leftward shift.[7] Up to 25% of patients have false-positive serologic tests for syphilis.

Within 2 to 4 days after the onset of fever, a nonpruritic maculopapular, morbilliform, petechial, or pustular[38] rash erupts over the palms, soles, and extremities.[7] Skin lesions may become purpuric or confluent,[7] and they may eventually desquamate.[17] Approximately 50% of patients develop asymmetric polyarthritis or true septic arthritis concurrently with the rash or within a few days thereafter.[19, 39–41] The knees are most commonly involved, followed by the ankles, elbows, wrists, shoulders, and hips.[36, 42, 43] Typically, fever subsides spontaneously after 3 to 5 days without specific antibiotic therapy, and the remaining symptoms gradually resolve within 2 weeks. However, fever may occasionally relapse in an irregular pattern for weeks or months,[11] producing a clinical picture of fever of undetermined origin,[7] or arthritis may persist for as long as 2 years. Haverhill fever differs clinically from percutaneously acquired rat-bite fever chiefly in the heightened severity of vomiting and in the high incidence of pharyngitis.[9, 17]

Reported complications of *S. moniliformis* infection include endocarditis,[7, 18, 36, 41, 44–47] myocarditis,[7, 18, 27] pericarditis,[2, 44] meningitis,[47] pneumonia,[7, 18, 47] amnionitis,[48] and anemia.[2, 27] Abscesses have been observed in virtually all organs, including brain,[49] liver, spleen, kidney,[7] and the female genital tract.[15] In infants and young children, diarrhea and weight loss may be prominent.[18, 22, 47] Mortality of untreated cases ranges as high as 13%,[7, 47] and endocarditis in the preantibiotic era was uniformly lethal. The majority of those intravascular infections involved valves previously damaged by rheumatic valvulitis or calcification.[36]

DIAGNOSIS

In a febrile patient with rash and recent rat exposure, the diagnosis can usually be narrowed to rat-bite fever or leptospirosis. However, the physician caring for a laboratory worker may step into the trap of ascribing a seemingly benign febrile illness to viral infection. Furthermore, without a positive exposure history, the proper diagnosis may be even more elusive, and diagnoses such as meningococcemia, enteric fever, drug reaction, and viral exanthem enter into consideration. When the rash involves the palms and soles, rat-bite fever may mimic Rocky Mountain spotted fever[50] or secondary syphilis. The presence of oligoarticular or migratory polyarthritis heightens concerns about disseminated gonococcal infection, Lyme disease, brucellosis, septic arthritis, infective endocarditis, collagen vascular disease, and acute rheumatic fever.

Direct visualization of pleomorphic bacillary organisms in Giemsa-, Wayson-, or gram-stained smears of blood, joint fluid, and pus may provide an early clue to the diagnosis. However, laboratory diagnosis rests ultimately on culturing *S. moniliformis* using enriched media.[51] Specific agglutinins appear within 10 days after the onset of illness and reach a maximum within 1 to 3 months. An initial titer of 1:80 or greater or a fourfold rise in titer is considered diagnostic. The highest reported titer is 1:5120. Specific agglutinins usually revert to negative within 5 months to 2 years, but low titers may occasionally persist for as long as 7 years. Recently, an enzyme-linked immunosorbent assay has been developed for detection of specific antibody against *S. moniliformis*.[52]

THERAPY AND PREVENTION

Both agents of rat-bite fever, *S. moniliformis* and *S. minus*, are susceptible to penicillin. In the past, procaine penicillin G was given as 600,000 units intramuscularly every 12 hours for 10 to 14 days.[2, 17, 39] Currently, intravenous penicillin G appears more appropriate. The Jarisch-Herxheimer reaction may complicate initial therapy of *S. minus* infections.[7] Oral tetracycline, 500 mg every 6 hours, is preferred for penicillin-allergic patients.[2, 12] Streptomycin, 7.5 mg/kg, can be given intramuscularly every 12 hours, although potential ototoxicity makes this less desirable. Limited experience indicates that erythromycin,[53] chloramphenicol,[14, 50] clindamycin,[18, 27] or ceftriaxone[38] might also be effective.

Most patients respond promptly to therapy. For individuals who appear well after 5 to 7 days, therapy can be completed with an additional week of oral penicillin V or ampicillin, 500 mg every 6 hours. Patients with mild disease can probably be treated orally for the entire course.

Endocarditis is so rare that optimal therapy is uncertain. Probably, 4 weeks of intravenous penicillin, with or without streptomycin, is adequate. A total daily dose of 20 million units has been advocated for patients whose isolates are resistant to 0.1 μg/ml.[45]

After a rodent bite, the wound should be thoroughly cleaned, and tetanus prophylaxis should be administered if warranted by the patient's immunization history. A 3-day course of oral penicillin, 2 g/day, would seem reasonable, although the prophylactic efficacy of penicillin in this setting is unknown, and the patient should be advised to report any subsequent symptoms. Measures to limit the incidence of rat-bite fever include eradication of rats in urban areas, avoidance of nonpasteurized milk and potentially contaminated water, and the use of gloves by laboratory workers when handling rodents.

REFERENCES

1. Anderson LC, Leary SL, Manning PJ. Rat-bite fever in animal research laboratory personnel. Lab Anim Sci. 1983;33:292–294.
2. Roughgarden JW. Antimicrobial therapy of rat-bite fever. Arch Intern Med. 1965;116:39–54.
3. Wilcox W. Violent symptoms from bite of rat. Am J Med Sci. 1839;26:245.
4. Blake FC. Etiology of rat-bite fever. J Exp Med. 1916;23:39.
5. Levaditi C, Nicolau S, Poincloux P. Sur le rôle étiologique de *Streptobacillus moniliformis* (nov spec) dans 1-erythème polymorphe aigu septicemique. C R Acad Sci. 1925;180:1188.
6. Parker F Jr, Hudson NP. The etiology of Haverhill fever (erythema arthriticum epidemicum). Am J Pathol. 1926;2:357–379.
7. Gunning JJ. Rat-bite fevers. In: Hunter GW III, Swartzwelder JC, Clyde DF, eds. Tropical Medicine. 5th ed. Philadelphia: WB Saunders; 1976;246–247.
8. Holmes B, Pickett MJ, Hollis DG. Unusual gram-negative bacteria. In: Murray PR, Baron EJ, Pfaller MA, et al, eds. Manual of Clinical Microbiology. 6th ed. Washington, DC: American Society for Microbiology; 1995;499–508.
9. Shanson DC, Pratt J, Greene P. Comparison of media with and without "panmede" for the isolation of *Streptobacillus moniliformis* from blood cultures and observations on the inhibitory effect of sodium polyanethol sulphonate. J Med Microbiol. 1985;19:181–186.
10. Lambe DW Jr, McPhedran AM, Mertz JA, et al. *Streptobacillus moniliformis* isolated from a case of Haverhill fever: Biochemical characterization and inhibitory effect of sodium polyanethol sulfonate. Am J Clin Pathol. 1973;60:854–860.
11. Dolman CE, Kerr De, Chang H, et al. Two cases of rat-bite fever due to *Streptobacillus moniliformis*. Can J Public Health. 1951;42:228–241.
12. Edwards R, Finch RG. Characterisation and antibiotic susceptibilities of *Streptobacillus moniliformis*. J Med Microbiol. 1986;21:39–42.
13. Rowbotham TJ. Rapid identification of *Streptobacillus moniliformis*. Lancet. 1983;2:567.
14. Rygg M, Brunn CF. Rat bite fever *(Streptobacillus moniliformis)* with septicemia in a child. Scand J Infect Dis. 1992;24:535–540.
15. Pins MR, Holden JM, Yang JM, et al. Isolation of presumptive *Streptobacillus moniliformis* from abscesses associated with the female genital tract. Clin Inf Dis. 1996;22:471–476.
16. Costas M, Owen RJ. Numerical analysis of electrophoretic protein patterns of *Streptobacillus moniliformis* strains from human, murine, and avian infections. J Med Microbiol. 1987;23:303–311.
17. Taber LH, Feigin RD. Spirochetal infections. Pediatr Clin North Am. 1979;26:410–411.
18. McHugh TP, Bartlett RL, Raymond JI. Rat bite fever: Report of a fatal case. Ann Emerg Med. 1985;14:1116–1118.
19. Anderson D, Marrie TJ. Septic arthritis due to *Streptobacillus moniliformis*. Arthritis Rheum. 1987;30:229–230.
20. Cole JS, Stoll RW, Bulger RJ. Rat-bite fever: Report of three cases. Ann Intern Med. 1969;71:979–981.
21. Collins CH. Laboratory-Acquired Infections: History, Incidence, Causes, and Prevention. London: Butterworths; 1983:7–13.
22. Raffin BJ, Freemark M. Streptobacillary rat-bite fever: A pediatric problem. Pediatrics. 1979;64:214–217.
23. Wullenweber M. *Streptobacillus moniliformis*—a zoonotic pathogen. Lab Anim. 1995;29:1–15.
24. Peel MM. Dog-associated bacterial infections in humans: Isolates submitted to an Australian reference laboratory, 1981–1992. Pathology. 1993;25:379–384.
25. Wilkins EGL, Millar JGB, Cockcroft PM, et al. Rat-bite fever in a gerbil breeder. J Infect. 1988;16:177–180.
26. Fordham JN, McKay-Ferguson E, Davies A, Blyth T. Rat bite fever without the bite. Ann Rheum Dis. 1992;51:411–412.
27. Taylor AF, Stephenson TG, Giese HA, et al. Rat-bite fever in a college student—California. MMWR. 1984;33:318–320.
28. Strangeways WI. Rats as carriers of *Streptobacillus moniliformis*. J Pathol. 1933;37:45–51.
29. Koopman JP, van den Brink ME, Vennix PPCA, et al. Isolation of *Streptobacillus moniliformis* from the middle ear of rats. Lab Anim. 1991;25:35–39.
30. Wullenweber M, Jonas C, Kunstyr I. *Streptobacillus moniliformis* isolated from otitis media of conventionally kept laboratory rats. J Exp Anim Sci. 1992;35:49–57.
31. Wullenweber M, Kaspareit-Rittinghausen J, Faroug M. *Streptobacillus moniliformis* epizootic in barrier-maintained C57BL/6J mice and susceptibility to infection of different strains of mice. Lab Anim Sci. 1990;40:608–612.
32. Glastonbury JR, Morton JG, Matthews LM. *Streptobacillus moniliformis* infection in Swiss white mice. J Vet Diagn Invest. 1996;8:202–209.
33. Taylor JD, Stephens CP, Duncan RG, Singleton GR. Polyarthritis in wild mice *(Mus musculus)* caused by *Streptobacillus moniliformis*. Aust Vet J. 1994;71:143–145.
34. Russell EG, Straube EF. Streptobacillary pleuritis in a koala. J Wild Dis. 1979;15:391–394.
35. Kirchner BK, Lake SG, Wightman SR. Isolation of *Streptobacillus moniliformis* from a guinea pig with granulomatous pneumonia. Lab Anim Sci. 1992;42:519–521.
36. McEvoy MB, Noah ND, Pilsworth R. Outbreak of fever caused by *Streptobacillus moniliformis*. Lancet. 1987;2:1361–1363.
37. Place EH, Sutton LE. Infection with *Streptobacillus moniliformis*. Arch Intern Med. 1934;5:659.
38. Cunningham BB, Paller AS, Katz BZ. Rat bite fever in a pet lover. J Am Acad Dermatol. 1998;38:330–332.
39. Mandel DR. Streptobacillary fever: An unusual cause of infectious arthritis. Clev Clin Q. 1985;52:203–205.
40. Rumley RL, Patrone NA, White L. Rat-bite fever as a cause of septic arthritis: A diagnostic dilemma. Ann Rheum Dis. 1987;46:793–795.
41. Rupp ME. *Streptobacillus moniliformis* endocarditis: Case report and review. Clin Infect Dis. 1992;14:769–772.
42. Azimi P. Pets can be dangerous. Pediatr Infect Dis J. 1990;9:670.
43. Holroyd KJ, Reiner AP, Dick JD. *Streptobacillus moniliformis* polyarthritis mimicking rheumatoid arthritis: An urban case of rat bite fever. Am J Med. 1988;85:711–714.
44. Carbeck RB, Murphy JF, Britt EM. Streptobacillary rat-bite fever with massive pericardial effusion. JAMA. 1967;201:703–704.
45. McCormack RC, Kaye D, Hook EW. Endocarditis due to *Streptobacillus moniliformis*: A report of two cases and review of the literature. JAMA. 1967;200:77–79.
46. Simon MW, Wilson D. *Streptobacillus moniliformis* endocarditis: A case report. Clin Pediatr. 1986;25:110–111.
47. Sens MA, Brown EW, Wilson LR, et al. Fatal *Streptobacillus moniliformis* infection in a two month old infant. Am J Clin Pathol. 1989;91:612–616.
48. Faro S, Walker C, Pierson RL. Amnionitis with intact amniotic membranes involving *Streptobacillus moniliformis*. Obstet Gynecol. 1980;55S:9S–11S.
49. Dijkmans BAC, Thomeer RTWM, Vielvoye GJ, et al. Brain abscess due to *Streptobacillus moniliformis* and *Actinobacterium meyerii*. Infection. 1984;12:34–36.
50. Portnoy BL, Satterwhite TK, Dyckman JD. Rat bite fever misdiagnosed as Rocky Mountain spotted fever. South Med J. 1979;72:607–609.
51. Anonymous. Rat-bite fever—New Mexico, 1996. MMWR Morb Mortal Wkly Rep. 1998;47:89–91.
52. Boot R, Bakker RH, Thuis H, et al. An enzyme-linked immunosorbent assay (ELISA) for monitoring rodent colonies for *Streptobacillus moniliformis* antibodies. Lab Anim. 1993;27:350–357.
53. Konstantopoulos K, Skarpas P, Hitjazis F, et al. Rat-bite fever in a Greek child. Scand J Infect Dis. 1992;24:531–533.

Chapter 221

Legionella pneumophila (Legionnaires' Disease)

VICTOR L. YU

HISTORY

In 1976, an outbreak of pneumonia occurred at a hotel at the site of the American Legion Convention in Philadelphia.[1] A total of 182 persons contracted pneumonia, and 34 died. Investigators from the Centers for Disease Control (CDC) isolated a bacterium from autopsy lung specimens that ultimately was named *Legionella pneumophila*. Epidemics of legionnaires' disease were retrospectively identified during an Oddfellows convention at the same Philadelphia hotel in 1974; in a psychiatric hospital in Washington, D.C., in 1965,[2] and in a meat-packing plant in Minnesota in 1957.[3] Serologic

All material in this chapter is in the public domain, with the exception of any borrowed figures or tables.

studies on stored sera revealed antibody seroconversion for *L. pneumophila*.

The clinical syndromes produced by members of the Legionellaceae family are collectively designated as *legionellosis*. *Legionnaires' disease* is pneumonia caused by *L. pneumophila*, and *Pontiac fever* is an acute febrile illness without pneumonia that has been linked serologically to *L. pneumophila* and other *Legionella* species.

DESCRIPTION OF THE PATHOGEN

There are more than 40 species in the Legionellaceae family, with a total of 64 serogroups.[4, 5] *L. pneumophila* is responsible for about 90% of infections caused by members of the Legionellaceae family. *L. pneumophila* contains 15 serogroups, but serogroups 1, 4, and 6 account for most of the strains implicated in human infection. Separation of *L. pneumophila* from other members of the family can be performed by biochemical methods,[6, 7] by fatty acids and ubiquinone analysis,[4, 8–10] by molecular methods,[11, 12] and by serologic methods.[4, 13] Commercially available kits can be used to identify *Legionella* to the species level, based on amplification of DNA coding[14, 15] or an RNA probe.[16]

Morphologic and Physiologic Characteristics

Members of the Legionellaceae family are gram-negative, aerobic, non–spore-forming, unencapsulated bacilli that measure 0.3 to 0.9 μm in width and 2 to 20 μm in length. In tissue and clinical specimens, the organisms are coccobacillary, measuring 1 to 2 μm. Elongated filamentous forms may be seen after growth on some culture media.

The organism can be visualized by Gram stain with some difficulty in clinical specimens (Fig. 221–1); basic fuchsin serves as a better counterstain than safranin. The Gimenez stain is as rapid as the Gram stain and stains the organism more effectively. The silver stains, including the Dieterle and Warthin-Starry stains, allow visualization of *Legionella* in paraffin-fixed tissues.

The organism is nutritionally fastidious and does not grow on standard bacteriologic media. Charcoal yeast extract buffered to pH 6.9 is the primary medium used for isolation of these organisms. L-Cysteine is a critical ingredient in culture, and keto acids and ferric ions together stimulate growth. The active ingredients in yeast extract appear to be purine and pyrimidine derivatives, of which guanine is the most important. The activated charcoal can absorb and detoxify fatty acids and oxygen radicals and prevent the oxidation of cysteine.[17] Addition of α-ketoglutaric acid in charcoal yeast extract promotes the growth of *Legionella,* possibly by stimulating production of oxygen-scavenging enzymes.[18]

L. pneumophila contains catalase, as do all members of the Legionellaceae family; the reaction is weak, however, when compared with those of other catalase-positive bacteria. *L. pneumophila* is asaccharolytic; negative for oxidase, urease, and nitrate; and positive for gelatinase. The organism strongly hydrolyzes hippurate. The organism produces a diffusable melanin-like, brown pigment on media containing tyrosine and a fluorescent yellow-green pigment on agar media when exposed to long-wave ultraviolet light. A single, polar flagellum and multiple fimbriae (pili) are present in most strains on primary isolation.[19, 19a] Other ultrastructural features that are typical of gram-negative bacilli include an inner trilaminar cytoplasmic membrane, a peptidoglycan layer, and an outer trilaminar membrane.[20]

L. pneumophila contains a major outer membrane protein with a molecular weight of 24,000 to 29,000. This protein forms ion-permeable channels in contact with lipid membranes, as is characteristic for porins.[21] The lipopolysaccharide of *L. pneumophila* serogroup 1 is tightly bound to this protein. Antibodies detected by indirect immunofluorescence are directed primarily at the lipopolysaccharide.[22]

The organism produces a number of enzymes and potential toxins that can be detected in culture supernates or in lysates of intact bacteria, including hemolysins, proteases, esterases, phosphatases, aminopeptidases, and endonucleases.[23] The role of these products in pathogenesis and tissue damage is questionable, because many of these products are produced by strains that are avirulent for experimental animals. A major secretory protein, a 38-kD metalloprotease, exhibits hemolytic and cytotoxic properties.[24, 25] However, this protease has not proved to be a required virulence factor for either intracellular growth or cell killing.[24, 26]

EPIDEMIOLOGY

Ecology

The environmental ecology of *L. pneumophila* is particularly pertinent in that legionnaires' disease is one form of pneumonia that theoretically could be prevented with eradication of the organism from its reservoir. The natural habitat for *L. pneumophila* appears to be aquatic bodies, including rivers, lakes, streams, and thermally polluted waters.

L. pneumophila can survive in a wide range of environmental conditions: temperature, 0° to 63°C; pH, 5.0 to 8.5; dissolved oxygen, 0.2 to 15.0 mg/L.[27] The organism can survive for years in water samples stored at 2° to 8°C.

Natural aquatic bodies contain only small numbers of *Legionella.* Because *Legionella* is chlorine-tolerant,[28, 29] the organism survives the water treatment process and passes into the water distribution

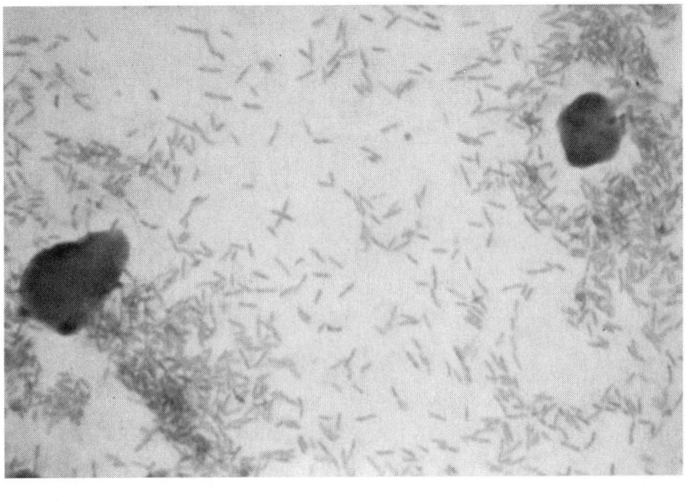

FIGURE 221–1. Gram-negative bacilli on a peripheral blood smear in a patient with acquired immunodeficiency syndrome. Blood culture yielded *Legionella pneumophila.* (From Babe KS, Reinhardt JF. Diagnosis of *Legionella* sepsis by examination of a peripheral blood smear. Clin Infect Dis. 1994;19:1164–1165. Copyright © 1994, Infectious Diseases Society of America.)

system, but again only in small numbers. Subsequent growth and proliferation occur in synthetic habitats (e.g., cooling towers, water distribution systems) that provide favorable water temperatures, physical protection, and nutrients.

The ubiquitous distribution of *L. pneumophila* in constructed aquatic reservoirs is paradoxical considering the difficulties in growth and multiplication under laboratory conditions. It is now well established that the presence of symbiotic microorganisms, including amebas and water bacteria, is necessary for the optimal growth of *L. pneumophila*.[30, 31] *L. pneumophila* can infect and multiply within amebas and ciliated protozoa.[30, 32] When the protozoan host ruptures, large numbers of motile *Legionella* are freed, calling to mind the similar scenario for *Legionella* and human mononuclear cells (see "Pathogenesis"). The intracellular location of the organism may contribute to its survival in otherwise unfavorable environments.

Colonization of water distribution systems by *L. pneumophila* depends on a combination of several factors, including water temperature, sediment accumulation, and commensal microflora.[31] Temperature appears to be a particularly critical parameter.[33–36] The organism is most readily found at the bottom of hot water tanks—a relationship that parallels its propensity for colonization of thermally polluted rivers. In one study, bacteria that populated hot water tanks were more likely to demonstrate a symbiotic relation with *L. pneumophila* than were bacteria populating cold water tanks.[31] *L. pneumophila* is found on the surfaces of sediment accumulating in areas of water systems that are prone to stagnation and even on metallic piping surfaces.[37, 38] Sediment was found to stimulate the growth of commensal microflora in vitro, which in turn stimulated the growth of *L. pneumophila*.[31] Microcolonies of the sessile population of adherent *L. pneumophila* are presumably less sensitive to biocides than a planktonic population would be.

Hot water tanks colonized with *L. pneumophila* were significantly more likely to have lower temperatures (<60°C [140°F]), to have a vertical configuration, to be older, and to have elevated calcium and magnesium concentrations in the water than were noncolonized tanks.[34, 39] Vertical tanks have more diverse temperature strata and thicker sediment accumulation at the bottom of the tank. Cleanliness and regular preventive maintenance measures of the system are not associated with less *Legionella* contamination.[34] Engineering guidelines and building codes that advocate maintenance and cleaning, although well-intentioned, are unlikely to affect *Legionella* colonization.[40]

Sources of Infection

Cooling towers and evaporative condensers transfer heat to ambient air via direct contact with water. The air stream exits from the cooling tower or evaporative condenser in an aerosol form. It has been presumed that contaminated aerosols may disseminate the organism to susceptible persons. Pontiac fever has been linked to aerosols from evaporative condensers, cooling towers, air conditioners, and whirlpools.[41, 42] The importance of cooling towers as a disseminator of legionnaires' disease has been questioned.[43] Most of the original epidemiologic investigations implicating cooling towers antedated the discovery that the organism also existed in potable water distribution systems. It is now known that in many of these outbreaks, cases of legionnaires' disease continued to occur despite disinfection of the cooling towers.

After it was discovered that *L. pneumophila* could colonize water distribution systems,[44, 45] more rigorous investigations established that water distribution systems are the primary reservoir for dissemination of the organism. Using Evan's applications of Koch's postulates, Best[46] and Johnson[47] and their colleagues established a definitive epidemiologic link between contaminated hospital water distribution systems and nosocomial cases of infection; Koch's postulates have not been fulfilled for cooling tower links. Acquisition of community-acquired legionnaires' disease has also been linked to contamination of water supplies in residences,[48, 49] rehabilitation centers,[50, 51] nursing homes,[52–54] and industrial water supplies.[55]

Subtyping of *L. pneumophila* with molecular fingerprinting methods has been useful for epidemiologic investigations. Numerous molecular typing methods have been applied,[56, 57] but restriction enzyme analysis by pulsed-field gel electrophoresis has been the most widely used.[58–60] On the other hand, some studies have suggested that the variability of the *L. pneumophila* genome is limited and that a combination of phenotypic and genotypic methods may be necessary for maximal discrimination.[6, 59, 61–64]

Mode of Transmission

The mode of transmission of *Legionella* to humans is probably multiple; evidence exists for aerosolization, aspiration, and even installation into the lung during respiratory tract manipulation. Investigators from the CDC presented the first evidence to support the aerosolization theory in a report on the hospital outbreak in Memphis.[65] Tracer smoke studies indicated that aerosols from an axillary air conditioning tower could have reached the air intake supplying patient rooms. Possible flaws in this study have been discussed elsewhere.[43]

The strongest evidence for aerosolization with subsequent airborne spread was derived from the 1968 Pontiac fever outbreak in a building in which the central air conditioning unit may have been contaminated by aerosols from an evaporative condensor.[41] *L. pneumophila* was isolated from the lungs of sentinel guinea pigs exposed to the air at the facility.

Because the first environmental isolation of *L. pneumophila* was taken from a showerhead, it was widely assumed that shower aerosols might be a means for dissemination of the organism. However, simulation studies showed that only small numbers of *Legionella* are aerosolized and then only for short distances (inches).[66, 67] Prospective epidemiologic studies have shown that showers are not a risk factor.[68–70]

Respiratory devices filled with tapwater (including nebulizers and humdifiers) can aerosolize the organism[67]; epidemiologic links to nosocomial disease have been suggested in several reports.[71, 72] Rinsing of the chambers of handheld medication nebulizers with tapwater has also been suggested as a source of infection.[73, 74] A community outbreak of legionnaires' disease was linked to an ultrasonic mist machine in a grocery store.[75]

Aspiration of contaminated water is a major mode of infection.[43, 76] Colonization of oropharyngeal flora by *L. pneumophila* is a possibility[77] but has not been consistently documented. Surgical patients undergoing general anesthesia are a well-established risk group.[45, 78, 79] One of the highest incidences of nosocomial legionnaires' disease was in a population of surgical head and neck cancer patients, who have a propensity for aspiration as a sequela of their oral surgery.[47] Nasogastric tubes have been linked to nosocomial legionellosis in several studies; microaspiration of contaminated water was the presumed mode of entry.[54, 69, 80, 81]

Health care personnel may use tapwater to rinse respiratory apparatus and tubing for use in mechanical ventilation machines. Patients with legionnaires' disease were found to have undergone endotracheal tube placement significantly more often or to have had significantly longer duration of intubation than patients with other causes of pneumonia.[70, 82–85] Consumption of water at the implicated hotel during the original 1976 outbreak was significantly associated with acquisition of disease—an association that has been overlooked.[1]

Pneumonia is the presenting clinical syndrome in virtually all cases of legionnaires' disease, suggesting that the primary portal is the respiratory tract. Wound infections have occurred after immersion of the wound in contaminated water.[86, 87] Ingestion of the organism followed by bacteremic dissemination from the gastrointestinal tract is an alternative hypothesis; the organism is now known to be waterborne, and diarrhea is also a prominent symptom of legionnaires' disease. On the other hand, there is little clinical evidence to support this possibility.

Incidence

The incidence of legionnaires' disease depends on the degree of contamination of the aquatic reservoir, the susceptibility of persons exposed to that water, and the intensity of the exposure. However, the discovery of this infection also depends on the availability of specialized laboratory tests and their application to the infected patient. Studies have amply documented the presence of unsuspected legionnaires' disease that surfaced only after routine application of these tests.[70, 83, 85, 88, 89]

Several studies have ranked *L. pneumophila* among the three most common microbial causes of community-acquired pneumonia in patients admitted to the hospital.[90–95] Based on a large study of community-acquired pneumonia in Ohio, CDC investigators suggested that only 3% of sporadic cases of legionnaires' disease are correctly diagnosed.[89] *Legionella* is a rare cause of pneumonia that does not require admission to hospital.[96] On the other hand, it is a common cause of severe pneumonia requiring admission to an intensive care unit,[90, 97–99] often second only to bacteremic pneumococcal pneumonia. The incidence and recognition of nosocomial pneumonia depend on the extent of colonization of the hospital water supply with *Legionella*, the number of immunosuppressed hosts hospitalized, and the availability of culture methods within the hospital.

Cigarette smoking, chronic lung disease, advanced age, and immunosuppression have consistently been implicated as risk factors. Excessive alcohol intake and renal failure have been noted in some studies. Surgery is a major predisposing factor in nosocomial infection, and transplantation recipients are at highest risk.[70, 78, 79, 84, 88, 100, 101]

The spectrum of the disease now extends to children.[102, 103] A few sporadic cases of community-acquired pneumonia in immunocompetent infants have been documented.[104] The most common presentation in the pediatric population is that of a hospital-acquired pneumonia in neonates, immunosuppressed children, and children with underlying pulmonary disease; in hospitals in which epidemiologic investigations were conducted, a link to the hospital water supply was consistently made.[74, 90, 105, 106]

Legionella infection is rare in patients with the acquired immunodeficiency syndrome (AIDS),[92, 107–110] but infections are often progressive, with extrapulmonary manifestations, bacteremia, and lung abscesses.

Pathology

Macroscopic examination of lungs taken from patients with legionnaires' disease typically shows multifocal pneumonia. Histologically, the pneumonia is an acute, fibrinopurulent pneumonitis characterized by acute alveolitis and bronchiolitis. Lesions of longer standing also tend to have a nodular appearance and are composed of a central area containing both cell types, surrounded by an area of predominantly macrophages. Destruction of lung architecture has occasionally been seen in severe cases. Macroscopically visible abscess formation was seen in about 20% of autopsy cases in one series.[111] The presence of fibrin-rich exudate in the alveoli with polymorphonuclear cells and alveolar macrophages is a prominent finding. A striking lysis of the exudate has been described.[111] Interstitial or intra-alveolar edema with membrane formation is occasionally present, although these conditions may reflect the effects of respiratory therapy rather than infection. Patients who survive appear to have few residual lung abnormalities, although pulmonary fibrosis has been described as a sequela.[112]

PATHOGENESIS

Pathogenic microorganisms may enter the lung via aspiration, direct inhalation, or hematogenous dissemination from another focus of infection. Colonization of the oropharynx has not been convincingly demonstrated for *Legionella*,[77] suggesting that subclinical aspiration of contaminated water or direct inhalation is a more likely mode of entry.[76] Symbiosis has also been shown in vitro between oropharyngeal flora and *Legionella*.[113] Once the organisms enter the upper respiratory tract, clearance is effected by cilia on respiratory epithelial cells. This is supported by the consistent epidemiologic association of increased risk of legionnaires' disease with cigarette smoking, chronic pulmonary diseases, and alcoholism—diseases in which mucociliary clearance is impaired. However, *Legionella* can adhere to respiratory epithelial cells via pili. A *Legionella* gene has homology to the type IV pilin genes found in other pathogenic bacteria; mutation of this gene reduces adherence to respiratory tract epithelial cells in vitro.[114] After adherence is accomplished, the organisms enter and replicate within respiratory epithelial cells.[115–117]

After the alveoli are reached, the outcome depends both on the virulent properties of the organism and on the competence of the host in resisting infection. The alveolar macrophage is the critical component in host defense. Alveolar macrophages readily phagocytose *Legionella,* although the process is more avid in the presence of specific opsonizing antibody. After entry into this mononuclear cell, *L. pneumophila* is enclosed within a specialized ribosome-lined phagosome (Fig. 221–2). However, phagosomes containing the organism do not fuse with lysosomes, so that the organism escapes the microbicidal mechanisms of these organelles.[24, 118, 119] Intracellular replication is facilitated by an intracellular multiplication locus[120] and by dot (defect in organelle trafficking) proteins produced by *Legionella*[121]; such replication may be regulated by cellular factors controlled by a gene or gene cluster.[122] The organism then multiplies until the cell ruptures (see Fig. 221–2). The liberated bacteria are phagocytosed by newly recruited cells, and the cycle of ingestion, multiplication, and liberation with cell lysis begins anew.

The next line of defense is provided by polymorphonuclear leukocytes and monocytes, recruited from the blood in proportion to the inoculum of *Legionella*. Phagocytosis by human monocytes is mediated by a three-component phagocytic system consisting of monocyte complement receptors, complement component C3, and the major outer-membrane protein of the surface of *L. pneumophila* (Fig. 221–3).[24] Although blood monocytes can ingest *L. pneumophila* in the absence of specific antibody, its presence as an opsonin improves phagocytosis. The role of polymorphonuclear leukocytes in host defense against *Legionella* is unclear. Neutropenic patients do not have an undue predilection for legionnaires' disease. Although *L. pneumophila* is susceptible to oxygen-dependent microbicidal systems in vitro, *L. pneumophila* resists killing by polymorphonuclear leukocytes. In vitro, *L. pneumophila* is ingested efficiently by neutrophils only in the presence of specific antibody or complement. Unlike monocytes, however, intracellular replication of the organism fails to occur within polymorphonuclear leukocytes.

In vitro studies suggest that humoral immunity plays a secondary role in host defense; for example, antibody does not promote killing of *L. pneumophila* by complement, promotes only modest killing of *L. pneumophila* by phagocytes (polymorphonuclear leukocytes, monocytes, or alveolar macrophages), and does not inhibit intracellular multiplication in monocytes or alveolar macrophages. On the other hand, in patients with legionnaires' disease, type-specific anti-*Legionella* antibody, usually immunoglobulin M (IgM) initially, followed by IgG, is measurable within the first several weeks of infection. Moreover, immunized animals develop a specific antibody response with subsequent resistance to *Legionella* challenge.[123, 124] Serum antibodies appear to activate antibody-dependent cellular cytotoxicity in host cells.[125]

Cell-mediated immunity is the primary host defense against *Legionella,* as for other intracellular pathogens (e.g., *Listeria*, mycobacteria, *Toxoplasma*). Legionnaires' disease is more common and more severe for patients with depressed cell-mediated immunity, including transplant recipients, patients receiving corticosteroids, and AIDS patients. Legionnaires' disease occurs with striking frequency in

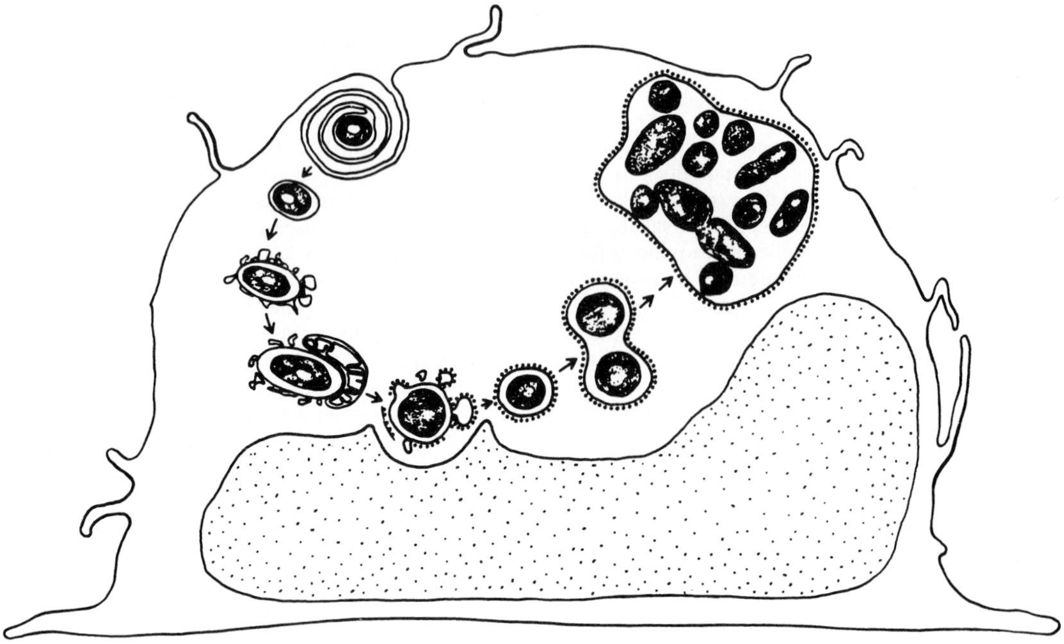

FIGURE 221–2. Replicative cycle of *Legionella pneumophila* within monocytes. *L. pneumophila* is phagocytosed by a process in which a pseudopod coils around the organisms as it is being ingested. A vacuolar phagosome is formed containing the *L. pneumophila;* this phagosome is surrounded by smooth vesicles, then mitochondria, and finally ribosomes. The organism multiplies until the phagosome becomes packed and the cell ruptures, thereby liberating the organisms. (From Horwitz MA. The legionnaires' disease bacterium *[Legionella pneumophila]* inhibits phagosome-lysosome fusion in human monocytes. J Exp Med. 1983;158:2108–2126, by copyright permission of The Rockefeller University Press.)

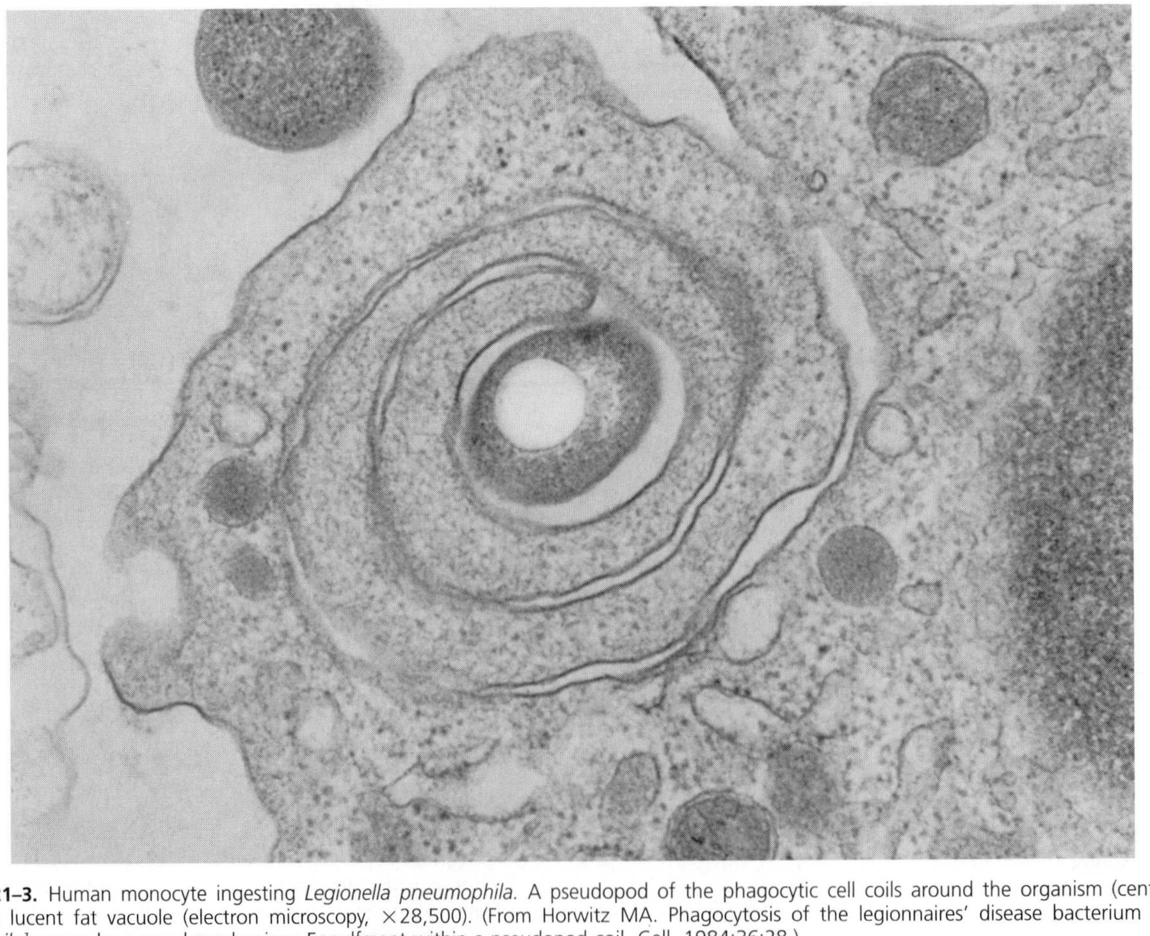

FIGURE 221–3. Human monocyte ingesting *Legionella pneumophila.* A pseudopod of the phagocytic cell coils around the organism (center), which contains a lucent fat vacuole (electron microscopy, ×28,500). (From Horwitz MA. Phagocytosis of the legionnaires' disease bacterium *[Legionella pneumophila]* occurs by a novel mechanism: Engulfment within a pseudopod coil. Cell. 1984;36:28.)

patients with hairy cell leukemia,[126] a malignancy associated with monocyte deficiency and dysfunction.

Cell-mediated immunity is manifested by the appearance of lymphocyte proliferation and cutaneous delayed hypersensitivity to *L. pneumophila* antigens within the first 2 weeks after infection.[124, 125] In infected patients and animals, mononuclear cells respond to *L. pneumophila* antigens with proliferation and with the generation of monocyte-activating cytokines, including interferon-γ (IFN-γ),[125] interleukin-1 (IL-1),[127] and tumor necrosis factor (TNF).[125, 127] Natural killer–like cells triggered by IL-2 have been shown to kill mononuclear cells infected by *L. pneumophila*. TNF-α stimulates resistance of alveolar macrophages and neutrophils to *L. pneumophila* and mediates release of endogenous IL-12 and IFN-γ.[128, 129] IFN-γ–activated monocytes decrease the multiplication rate of *Legionella*, in part by limiting the availability of iron to the organism.

Virulence

Pathogens that are able to survive in the environment for an extended time tend to be relatively virulent.[130] *L. pneumophila* appears to be more virulent than most common bacterial pathogens of community-acquired pneumonia. Patients with legionnaires' disease were significantly more likely to require admission to the intensive care unit than patients with other pneumonias.[90, 98, 99, 131] *L. pneumophila* strains clearly differ in virulence. For example, although multiple strains may colonize water distribution systems, only a few strains are likely to cause disease in patients exposed to the water.[132–136] A surface epitope of *L. pneumophila*, serogroup 1, which is recognized by one particular antibody (Mab-2), may be associated with virulence. *L. pneumophila*, serogroup 6, is more common in nosocomial strains and more likely to be associated with poor outcome. Agar-passaged strains that lose their virulence are more serum-sensitive, unable to multiply in monocytes or inhibit phagosome-lysosome fusion, and less able to kill guinea pigs.[127, 135, 137] Virulence may be enhanced by replication within amebas.[114, 138] Despite numerous laboratory investigations, individual biologic and immunologic factors mediating virulence have not been explicitly defined.[139, 140] Release and movement of heat shock proteins are seen with *Legionella* strains virulent for guinea pigs but not with avirulent strains.[17, 141] A 24-kD protein, called mip (for macrophage infectivity potentiator), appears to be required for expression of virulence in mononuclear phagocytes and guinea pigs.[140]

CLINICAL FEATURES

Legionella infection manifests in two very different forms: Pontiac fever and pneumonia (legionnaires' disease). It is not known why these two different forms occur, but the size of the inoculum, the mode of transmission, and the host factors are probably important.

Pontiac Fever

Pontiac fever is an acute, self-limited, flulike illness without pneumonia.[41, 42, 142, 143] The incubation period is 24 to 48 hours, and the attack rate of those exposed is higher than 90%. The predominant symptoms are malaise, myalgias, fever, chills, and headache. Nonproductive cough, dizziness, and nausea have also been noted. The chest radiograph remains clear. Only symptomatic therapy is required, and complete recovery within 1 week is the rule.

Legionnaires' Disease

Pneumonia is the predominant clinical manifestation of legionnaires' disease. The disease encompasses a broad spectrum of illness, ranging from a mild cough and slight fever to stupor with widespread pulmonary infiltrates and multisystem failure. The incubation period for legionnaires' disease ranges from 2 to 10 days. Early in the illness, patients experience nonspecific symptoms including fever, malaise, myalgia, anorexia, and headache.

The cough is initially mild and only slightly productive. Occasionally, the sputum may be streaked with blood, but gross hemoptysis is rare. Chest pain, either pleuritic or nonpleuritic, can be a prominent feature for some patients; when coupled with hemoptysis, it often suggests an incorrect diagnosis of pulmonary embolus.

Diarrhea is seen in 25 to 50% of cases, with watery rather than bloody stools.[1, 78, 92, 98, 131] Nausea, vomiting, and abdominal pain are seen in about 10 to 20% of cases. Neurologic symptoms range from headache and lethargy to encephalopathy. Change in mental status is the most common neurologic abnormality.[98, 144]

Physical examination typically reveals rales early in the course of the disease and findings of consolidation. Bradycardia relative to temperature elevation has been overemphasized,[145] but it can be seen in elderly patients with advanced pneumonia. Hypotension was seen in 17% of patients with community-acquired pneumonia.[98] Fever is virtually always present; in one series, 19% of patients had temperatures higher than 40.5°C.[145] Shaking chills are more common in patients with advanced stages of pneumonia.

In prospective, comparative studies, clinical manifestations were generally similar for pneumonias caused by *L. pneumophila* and those caused by other organisms.[78, 92] Likewise, laboratory findings including abnormal liver function tests, hypophosphatemia, hematuria, and hematologic abnormalities did not occur more frequently in legionnaires' disease than in pneumonias from other causes. On the other hand, hyponatremia (serum sodium <130 mEq/L) was found to occur significantly more often in legionnaires' disease than in other pneumonias.[78, 92, 145]

Although the clinical presentation is nonspecific, the following clues should raise the possibility of legionnaires' disease in a patient with undiagnosed pneumonia: (1) in the Gram stain of respiratory secretions, neutrophils are present in large numbers, but few, if any, organisms are visualized; (2) hyponatremia (serum sodium <130 mEq/ml) is present; (3) the pneumonia fails to respond to β-lactam (penicillin or cephalosporin) and aminoglycoside antibiotics.

Extrapulmonary involvement has been documented in immunosuppressed patients and can include cellulitis, sinusitis, perirectal abscess, pericarditis, pyelonephritis, peritonitis, pancreatitis, and endocarditis.[146–149] Dissemination apparently occurs by bacteremia. Wound infections have resulted from contamination of the wound by water colonized with *Legionella*.[86, 87]

Hospital-acquired *Legionella* prosthetic valve endocarditis has been described in one hospital.[149] Fever, night sweats, malaise, and symptoms of congestive heart failure were seen. Anemia was a common feature, and its severity correlated with the duration of infection. Unlike endocarditis caused by other organisms, embolic phenomena were not seen presumably because of the small size of the vegetations.

Many miscellaneous findings have been reported, including disseminated intravascular coagulation, thrombocytopenia, glomerulitis, rhabdomyolysis, various rashes, neuropathies, and hepatic failure. These may be nonspecific findings related to the severity of the infection, the type of underlying disease, or perhaps the side effects of drug therapies.

Chest Radiographs

Most patients have abnormal chest radiographic findings on presentation, although in rare nosocomial cases, respiratory symptoms and fever antedate visualization of pulmonary infiltrate.[150] However, almost all patients with legionnaires' disease have radiographic abnormalities by the third day.[151] The initial involvement is usually unilateral, with lower-lobe predominance. The initial infiltrate is typically alveolar and may be segmental-lobar or diffuse and patchy.[42] The initial densities may appear as poorly marginated, rounded opacities, which are often pleural based and may therefore be mistaken for pulmonary infarction. Interstitial infiltrates were described in about

25% of the patients in the 1976 Philadelphia outbreak, although such an appearance has not been prominent in subsequent reports. The initial area of infiltration often progresses to more widespread consolidation over several days.

Pleural effusions are commonplace and may occasionally precede the radiographic appearance of the infiltrate.[42] The effusions are typically modest in amount and rarely complicate patient management, although empyema may occur. Hilar adenopathy and pneumatocele formation have been reported rarely. Cavitation and abscess in the immunosuppressed host receiving corticosteroids is not uncommon.[42, 152] Cavitation may occur up to 14 days after presentation, even after appropriate antibiotic therapy and apparent clinical response. Rupture of a cavity into the pleural space, with formation of empyema or bronchopleural fistula, is a rare complication.

Progression of infiltrates despite appropriate antibiotic therapy is commonplace. The extent of radiographic infiltration does not correlate well with the severity of clinical manifestations or with ultimate outcome. A significant correlation exists between radiographic severity and the presence of *L. pneumophila* in sputum.[153] Presumably, increased numbers of organisms in respiratory secretions reflect more extensive disease as judged radiographically. Radiographic improvement lags behind clinical improvement for several days. The time required for clearing of infiltrate on a chest radiograph ranges from 1 to 4 months.

LABORATORY DIAGNOSIS

Because legionnaires' disease is not specific in its clinical and radiologic presentation, specialized laboratory tests are necessary to establish the diagnosis (Table 221–1). Gram stain of normally sterile sites (transtracheal aspirate, lung biopsy, pleural fluid) can occasionally suggest the diagnosis; the organisms appear as small, pleomorphic, faintly staining, gram-negative rods.

Culture

The definitive method for diagnosis of *Legionella* infection is isolation of the organism from respiratory secretions. Early investigations were hampered by the fact that the causative agent failed to grow on standard bacteriologic media. The standard medium for *Legionella* isolation is buffered charcoal yeast extract (BCYE) agar supplemented with polymyxin, anisomycin, vancomycin, and dyes; the antimicrobial agents prevent the overgrowth of *Legionella* by competing organisms, while the dyes impart a distinctive color to the *Legionella* organisms.[154, 155] The organism grows slowly, requiring 3 to 5 days to produce macroscopically visible colonies. The organisms have a typical ground-glass surface when observed by stereomicroscopy. Clinical isolates exhibit optimal growth between 35°C and 37°C. For maximal sensitivity, simultaneous use of the following three media is recommended: BCYE; BCYE with polymyxin, anisomycin, and cefamandole; and BCYE with polymyxin, anisomycin, vancomycin, and dyes. All of these media are commercially available. For culture plates that are overgrown with other microflora, acid treatment can markedly improve the sensitivity.[156, 157]

TABLE 221–1 Utility of Specialized Laboratory Tests for Diagnosis of Legionnaires' Disease

Test	Sensitivity (%)	Specificity (%)
Sputum culture*	80	100
Direct fluorescent antibody stain of sputum	33–70	96–99
Urinary antigen†	70	100
Antibody serology‡	40–60	96–99

*Use of multiple selective media with dyes.
†Useful only for *L. pneumophila,* serogroup 1.
‡IgG and IgM testing for both acute and convalescent sera. A single titer ≥1:128 in a patient with pneumonia is considered presumptive, and a 4-fold seroconversion is considered definitive.

Legionella can often be isolated from sputum specimens that do not fulfill classic criteria of purulence according to the numbers of squamous epithelial cells and leukocytes.[131, 158] Transtracheal aspiration, although rarely performed, provides an optimal specimen because contamination by oropharyngeal flora is avoided; for these specimens, the sensitivity may approach 90%. The sensitivity of specimens obtained by bronchoscopy is approximately the same as for sputum; bronchoalveolar lavage gives higher yields than bronchial wash specimens. If there is a pleural effusion, thoracentesis should be performed and the fluid should be evaluated by direct fluorescence antibody stain (DFA), culture, and *Legionella* antigen.[159] *Legionella* have also been isolated from pericardial fluid, peritoneal fluid, rectal abscess, and wounds.

Legionella bacteremia can be documented by blind subculture onto BCYE from the radiometric culture bottles in which growth fails to attain the threshold for detection.[145, 158, 160]

Gram Stain

Gram stains can be useful. Fluid or pus from a normally sterile site such as pleural fluid, blood, transtracheal aspirate, or lung can yield small, pleomorphic, faintly staining, gram-negative bacilli[160] (see Fig. 221–1). In sputum, the organisms are poorly visualized and, if visible, cannot be differentiated from *Haemophilus influenzae* or oropharyngeal flora. A useful clinical clue is the presence of numerous leukocytes with few, if any, organisms seen. This pattern is comparable to those seen with other types of "atypical" pneumonia, including mycoplasmal, chlamydial, and viral pneumonia.

Direct Fluorescent Antibody Stain

A major drawback to this rapid diagnostic test is the fact that the sensitivity is less than that of culture, because positive results depend on the presence of large numbers of organisms in the specimen. The DFA is more likely to be positive when multilobar infiltrates are present on chest radiographs.[143] Cross-reactions to non-*Legionella* organisms occur rarely; false-positive DFA tests are usually caused by faulty laboratory technique or contaminated reagents and not by cross-reacting bacteria. Monoclonal antibody reagents are superior to polyclonal reagents in that background staining is improved, and the test is technically easier to perform. On the other hand, the sensitivity is similar, and the monoclonal test is more expensive than the polyclonal test. DFA reagents for the newer species and serogroups are not available commercially.

Antibody Detection by Serology

Indirect fluorescent antibody and enzyme-linked immunosorbent assay (ELISA) have been the most commonly used methodologies. Diagnosis may be made by a fourfold rise in antibody titer. Both acute and convalescent sera are usually required, because an antibody response may take 4 to 12 weeks.[157] Serology is useful in epidemiologic studies but is less helpful to the clinician in making an immediate diagnosis of legionnaires' disease for an individual patient. On the other hand, if the seroprevalence of *L. pneumophila* antibody titers within the community is known to be low, a single elevated titer (1:256) may indicate the presence of acute disease. Twenty-five to 40% of patients have elevated titers in the first week of disease.[23, 157] False-positive results occur rarely as a result of cross-reacting antibody to other gram-negative organisms. The use of IgM and IgG assays provides maximal sensitivity, although IgM antibodies are significantly more likely to be elevated during the disease phase.[157]

Urinary Antigen

A lipopolysaccharide antigen of *Legionella* is detectable in urine.[161] This test is particularly useful because it is often easier to obtain urine than adequate sputum in ill patients and results can be available within hours. The sensitivity is comparable to that of other methodologies (see Table 221–1), and the test can remain positive for months after the episode of pneumonia.[157, 162–164]

The new immunochromatographic assay (NOW) from Binax (South Portland, Me) is easy to perform but is available only for serogroup 1 species; this drawback may be minor, because serogroup 1 accounts for about 80% of *L. pneumophila* infections. The enzyme immunoassay from Biotest (Dreieich, Germany) has the potential to detect other serogroups, but this capability remains to be evaluated.[165]

Polymerase Chain Reaction

Polymerase chain reaction assays have been applied to clinical specimens but have not proved to be more sensitive than culture.[90] PCR has proved to be sensitive in detection of *Legionella* in water samples.[143]

TABLE 221–2 Antibiotic Therapy for *Legionella* Infection

Antimicrobial Agent	Dose* (mg)	Route	Frequency
Azithromycin	500†	PO, IV	q24h
Clarithromycin	500	PO, IV	q12h
Roxithromycin	300	PO	q12h
Erythromycin	1000	IV	q6h
	500	PO	q6h
Levofloxacin	500†	PO, IV	q24h
Ciprofloxacin	400	IV	q8h
	750	PO	q12h
Trovafloxacin	200†	PO, IV	q12h
Doxycycline	100†	PO, IV	q12h
Minocycline	100†	PO, IV	q12h
Tetracycline	500	PO, IV	q6h
Trimethoprim/ sulfamethoxazole	160/800	IV	q8h
	160/800	PO	q12h
Rifampin	300–600	PO, IV	q12h

*Doses are based on clinical experience and not on controlled trials.
†We recommend doubling first dose.

TREATMENT

In vitro susceptibility testing of *Legionella* has not been standardized, but it is now accepted that intracellular models in in vitro or animal studies are more relevant than classic extracellular dilution tests in agar or broth.[166, 167] *Legionella* is an intracellular pathogen, and antibiotics that achieve high intracellular concentration are more likely to be efficacious in humans than those agents with poor intracellular penetration.[167] Intracellular systems using cell culture models confirm that the macrolides, quinolones, rifampin, trimethoprim-sulfamethoxazole, and tetracyclines are effective agents in vivo against *Legionella*. The excellent penetration of the these antibiotics into phagocytic cells is presumably the basis for their clinical superiority over β-lactam and aminoglycoside agents.

Clinical studies of antibiotic efficacy are more compelling if the diagnosis of legionnaires' disease was made by isolation of *Legionella* from culture than by serologic methods; antibiotics that have fulfilled this criterion include azithromycin, ciprofloxacin, levofloxacin, rifampin, trimethoprim-sulfamethoxazole, and tetracycline.[167]

The newer macrolides (especially azithromycin) and quinolones (especially ciprofloxacin, levofloxacin, and trovafloxacin) are the antibiotics of choice for legionnaires' disease. Erythromycin has been supplanted by other macrolides because of its relatively lower activity in vitro and in intracellular models and animal studies. Erythromycin also has a higher frequency of adverse effects, compared with the newer macrolides, including ototoxicity, gastrointestinal symptoms, and thrombophlebitis at the intravenous site. A major drawback of erythromycin in elderly patients with heart and lung disease is the large fluid volume required for administration. Some investigators suggest the combination of a macrolide and rifampin for severe legionnaires' disease.

Although oral antibiotics may be adequate for selected patients, abrupt deterioration can occur in patients with advanced disease who appear stable at the time of diagnosis. Furthermore, because gastrointestinal dysfunction (commonly seen in legionnaires' disease) may compromise absorption of any oral antibiotic, parenteral administration of antibiotics is prudent.

Clinical response, including defervescence and a feeling of well-being, usually occurs within 3 to 5 days. Once a clinical response has been documented, oral therapy can replace parenteral therapy (Table 221–2). Duration of therapy is 10 to 14 days, although longer periods are appropriate for immunosuppressed patients. Relapse has been reported, but a review of most of these reports suggests that they may represent cases of reinfection in patients continually exposed to contaminated water. Delay in administration of appropriate antibiotic therapy adversely affects outcome.[92, 168, 169]

The newer macrolides (e.g., azithromycin, clarithromycin, roxithromycin) may be used for immunocompetent patients hospitalized with community-acquired pneumonia.[170] Quinolone agents have been effective in several anecdotal reports.[84, 150, 167, 171] The addition of a quinolone should be considered for any transplant recipient with nosocomial pneumonia if the organism has not been identified; the macrolides interact pharmacologically with immunosuppressive medications and should be avoided. Successes have been reported for trimethoprim-sulfamethoxazole, clindamycin, and imipenem.[167] With appropriate antibiotic therapy, the mortality rate of legionnaires' disease is low in immunocompetent patients, although in nosocomial infection it may approach 50%, especially if antibiotic therapy is started late.

PREVENTION

Discovery of the environmental reservoir for legionnaires' disease theoretically allows prevention of this pneumonia. Because of the high prevalence of the organism in water distribution systems in hospitals, the CDC and other authorities have advocated culturing of hospital environmental sources only on discovery of cases of legionnaires' disease.[172] On the other hand, studies have shown that nosocomial legionellosis can exist undiagnosed in hospitals lacking specialized laboratory methods for *Legionella*.[70, 83, 88] A clue to the possibility of legionnaire's disease could be the presence of *L. pneumophila* in the hospital water supply.[173–176] Thus, investigators from Pittsburgh have advocated routine environmental culturing in the absence of known cases for facilities that house patients at risk for legionnaires' disease, including hospitals and nursing homes.[176] Routine environmental culturing for *Legionella* should certainly be performed in hospitals in which organ and bone marrow transplantations are performed, given the high risk for legionnaires' disease in these patients.[70, 100, 101, 177] The disease does not appear to be contagious, so isolation precautions are not needed.

Reservoir Disinfection

Cooling towers and evaporative condensers frequently provide a reservoir for *L. pneumophila*. Because controlled experiments have not yet demonstrated aerosol dissemination from cooling towers, rational recommendations concerning biocide treatment have been difficult to formulate. Biocides appear to be ineffective in eradicating *L. pneumophila* from cooling towers and only marginally effective in reducing organism numbers. Complicating this issue is the increasingly uncertain role that cooling towers play in legionnaires' disease.[43]

For treatment of water distribution systems, copper-silver ionization units (LiquiTech, Willowbrook, Ill; Tarn-Pure, Buckinghamshire, United Kingdom) use electrodes to generate metallic ions that disrupt bacterial cell walls, leading to cell lysis and death. These units provide residual protection throughout the water distribution system. *Legionella* are killed rather than suppressed, and controlled studies have shown that this modality is highly effective in eradicating *L. pneumophila*.[40, 178, 179,180]

The "superheat and flush" technique is particularly useful for urgent disinfection during an outbreak.[40, 46, 181] Temperatures of 60°C (140°F) are bactericidal for *L. pneumophila*. The method consists of raising the hot water temperature to between 60°C and 77°C (140°F to 170°F) for several days and then flushing each distal water site with hot water for 30 minutes (flushing for 5 to 10 minutes, as recommended by the CDC,[172] is usually ineffective). The temperature of the water is then maintained at 66°C (150°F). The major drawback of heat eradication is the logistic difficulties involved in flushing distal sites. Scalding of patients and health personnel is a potential hazard.

Ultraviolet light kills *Legionella* by damaging cellular DNA. Systems using ultraviolet light have proved to be effective when disinfection is to be localized, for example to a transplant or an intensive care unit.[40] Because ultraviolet light provides no residual protection, areas distal to the sterilizer must be disinfected with superheat and flush methods after installation. Copper-silver ionization and chlorine are useful adjuncts. Prefiltration is necessary to prevent the accumulation of scale on the ultraviolet light source.

Hyperchlorination is no longer recommended. Breakthrough appearance of *Legionella* is common, because chlorine decomposes at the higher temperature found in hot water systems and *Legionella* are relatively chlorine-tolerant. Major disadvantages of hyperchlorination include expense, corrosion of the plumbing system,[182] production of carcinogenic byproducts,[183] and association with miscarriages in pregnant women.[184]

REFERENCES

1. Fraser DW, Tsai T, Ornstein W, et al. Legionnaires' disease: Description of an epidemic of pneumonia. N Engl J Med. 1977;297:1189–1197.
2. Terranova W, Cohen ML, Fraser DW. Outbreak of legionnaires' disease diagnosed in 1977. Lancet. 1978;2:122–124.
3. Osterholm MT, Chin TD, Osborne DO, et al. A 1957 outbreak of legionnaires' disease associated with a meat packing plant. Am J Epidemiol. 1983;117:60–67.
4. Benson RF, Fields BS. Classification of the genus *Legionella*. Semin Respir Infect. 1998;13:90–99.
5. Helbig JH, Kurtz JB, Pastoris MC, et al. Antigenic lipopolysaccharide components of *Legionella pneumophila* recognized by monoclonal antibodies: Possibilities and limitations for division of the species into serogroups. J Clin Microbiol. 1997;35:2841–2845.
6. Struelens MJ, Maes N, Rost F, et al. Genotypic and phenotypic methods for the investigation of a hospital-acquired *Legionella pneumophila* outbreak and efficacy of control measures. J Infect Dis. 1992;166:22–30.
7. Vesey G, Dennis PJ, Lee J, West A. Further development of simple tests to differentiate the legionella. J Appl Bacteriol. 1988;65:339–345.
8. Lema M, Brown A. Electrophoretic characteristic of soluble protein extracts of *Legionella pneumophila* and other members of the family Legionellaceae. J Clin Microbiol. 1983;17:1132–1140.
9. Ferguson DA, Mayberry WR. Differentiation of *Legionella* species by soluble proteins in polyacrylamide slab gels (Abstract). Microbios. 1987;52:105–114.
10. Verissimo A, Morais PV, Diogo A, et al. Characterization of *Legionella* species by numerical analysis of whole-cell protein electrophoresis. Int J Syst Bacteriol. 1996;46:41–49.
11. Bangsborg JM, Gerner-Smidt P, Colding H, et al. Restriction fragment length polymorphism of rRNA genes for molecular typing of members of the family Legionellaceae. J Clin Microbiol. 1995;33:402–406.
12. Saunders NA, Harrison TG, Haththotuwa A, et al. A method for typing strains of *Legionella pneumophila* serogroup 1 by analysis of restriction fragment length polymorphisms. J Med Microbiol. 1990;31:45–55.
13. Steinmetz I, Rheinheimer CB-SD. Rapid identification of Legionellae by a colony blot assay based on a genus-specific monoclonal antibody. J Clin Microbiol. 1992;30:1016–1018.
14. Kessler HH, Reinthaler FF, Pschaid A, et al. Rapid detection of *Legionella* species in bronchoalveolar lavage fluids with the EnviroAmp Legionella PCR amplification and detection kit. J Clin Microbiol. 1993;31:3325–3328.
15. Matsiota-Bernard P, Pitsouni E, Legakis N, Nauciel C. Evaluation of commercial amplification kit for detection of *Legionella pneumophila* in clinical samples. J Clin Microbiol. 1994;32:1503–1505.
16. Grimot F, Lefevre M, Ageron E, et al. rRNA gene restriction patterns of *Legionella* species: A molecular identification system. Res Microbiol. 1989;140:615–626.
17. Hoffman PS. Bacterial Physiology. In: Thornsberry C, Balows A, Feeley JC, et al., eds. *Legionella*: Proceedings of the 2nd International Symposium. Washington, DC: American Society for Microbiology; 1984:61–67.
18. Pine L, Hoffman PS, Malcolm G, et al. Role of keto acids and reduced oxygen-scavenging enzymes in the growth of *Legionella* species. J Clin Microbiol. 1986;23:33–42.
19. Bosshardt SC, Benson RF, Fields BS. Flagella are a positive predictor for virulence in *Legionella*. Microb Pathog. 1997;23:107–112.
19a. Heuner K, Brard BC, Hacker J. The expression of the flagellum of *Legionella pneumophila* is modulated by different environmental factors. FEMS Microbiol Lett. 1999;175:69–77.
20. Hebert GA, Callaway C, Ewing EP. Comparison of *Legionella pneumophila*, *L. micdadei*, *L. bozemanii*, and *L. dumoffi* by transmission electron microscopy. J Clin Microbiol. 1984;19:116–121.
21. Gabay J, Blake M, Niles W, et al. Purification of *Legionella pneumophila* major outer membrane protein and demonstration that it is a porin. J Bacteriol. 1985;162:85–91.
22. Ciesielski CA, Blaser MJ, Wang WLL. Serogroup specificity of *Legionella pneumophila* is related to lipopolysaccharide characteristics. Infect Immun. 1986;51:397–404.
23. Yu VL. *Legionella pneumophila* (legionnaires' disease). In: Mandell GL, Bennett JE, Dolin R, eds. Principles and Practice of Infectious Diseases. 4th ed. New York:Churchill Livingstone; 1995:2087–2097.
24. Horwitz MA. Toward an understanding of host and bacterial molecules mediating *L. pneumophila* pathogenesis. In: Barbaree JM, Breiman RF, Dufour AP, eds. *Legionella*: Current Status and Emerging Perspectives. Washington, DC: American Society of Microbiology; 1993:55–62.
25. Quinn FD, Keen MG, Tompkins LS. Genetic, immunological, and cytotoxic comparisons of *Legionella* proteolytic activities. Infect Immun. 1989;57:2719–2725.
26. Szeto L, Shuman HA. The *Legionella pneumophila* major secretory protein, a protease, is not required for intracellular growth or cell killing. Infect Immun. 1990;58:2585–2592.
27. Fliermans CB. Philosophical ecology: *Legionella* in historical perspective. In: Thornsberry C, Balows A, Feeley JC, et al., eds. *Legionella:* Proceedings of the 2nd International Symposium. Washington, DC: American Society for Microbiology; 1984.
28. Kuchta JM, States SJ, McNamara AM. Susceptibility of *Legionella pneumophila* to chlorine in tap water. Appl Environ Microbiol. 1983;46:1134–1139.
29. Muraca P, Stout JE, Yu VL. Comparative assessment of chlorine, heat, ozone, and UV light for killing *Legionella pneumophila* within a model plumbing systems. Appl Environ Microbiol. 1987;53:447–453.
30. Fields BS. Legionella and protozoa: Interaction of a pathogen and its natural host. In: Barbaree JM, Breiman RF, Dufour AP, eds. Current Status and Emerging Perspectives of *Legionella*. Washington, DC: American Society for Microbiology; 1993:129–136.
31. Stout JE, Yu VL, Best M. Ecology of *Legionella pneumophila* within water distribution systems. Appl Environ Microbiol. 1985;49:221–228.
32. Rowbotham TJ. Current views on the relationships between amoebae legionellae, and man. Isr J Med Sci. 1986;22:678–689.
33. Groothuis DG, Veenendall HR, Dijkstra HL. Influence of temperature on the number of *Legionella pneumophila* in hot water system. J Appl Bacteriol. 1985;59:529–536.
34. Vickers RM, Yu VL, Hanna SS, et al. Determinants of *Legionella pneumophila* contamination of water distribution systems: 15 hospital prospective study. Infect Control. 1987;8:357–363.
35. Lee TC, Stout JE, Yu VL. Factors predisposing to *L. pneumophila* colonization in residential water systems. Appl Environ Microbiol. 1988;43:59–62.
36. Furuhata K, Takayanogi T, Danno N, et al. Contamination of hot water supply in office buildings by *Legionella pneumophila* and some countermeasures. Jpn J Public Health. 1994;41:1073–1083.
37. Wright JB, Ruseska I, Athar M, et al. *Legionella pneumophila* grows adherent to surfaces in vitro and in situ. Infect Control Hosp Epidemiol. 1989;10:408–415.
38. Rogers J, Doowsett AB, Dennis PJ, et al. Influence of plumbing materials on biofilm formation and growth of *Legionella pneumophila* in potable water systems. Appl Environ Microbiol. 1994;60:1842–1851.
39. Alary M, Joly JR. Factors contributing to the contamination of hospital water distribution systems. J Infect Dis. 1992;165:565–569.
40. Lin YE, Vidic RD, Stout JE, Yu VL. *Legionella* in water distribution systems. J Am Water Works Assoc. 1998;90:112–121.
41. Kaufman AF, McDade J, Patton C, et al. Pontiac fever: Isolation of the etiologic agent (*Legionella pneumophila*) and demonstration of its mode of transmission. Am J Epidemiol. 1981;114:337–347.
42. Vergis EN, Yu VL, Fishman AP, et al., eds. Legionellosis. 3rd ed. New York: McGraw-Hill; 1997.
43. Muder RR, Yu VL, Woo A. Mode of transmission of *Legionella pneumophila*: A critical review. Arch Intern Med. 1986;146:1607–1612.
44. Stout JE, Yu VL, Vickers RM, et al. Ubiquitousness of *Legionella pneumophila* in the water supply of a hospital with endemic legionnaires' disease. N Engl J Med. 1982;36:466–468.
45. Luck PC, Wenchel HM, Helbig JH. Nosocomial pneumonia caused by three genetically different strains of *Legionella pneumophila* and detection of these strains in the hospital water supply. J Clin Microbiol. 1998;36:1160–1163.
46. Best M, Yu VL, Stout J, et al. Legionellaceae in the hospital water supply: Epidemiological link with disease and evaluation of a method of control of

nosocomial legionnaires' disease and Pittsburgh pneumonia. Lancet. 1983;2:307–310.
47. Johnson JT, Yu VL, Best M, et al. Nosocomial legionellosis uncovered in surgical patients with head and neck cancer: Implications for epidemiologic reservoir and mode of transmission. Lancet. 1985;2:298–300.
48. Stout JE, Yu VL, Muraca P, et al. Potable water as the cause of sporadic cases of community-acquired legionnaires' disease. N Engl J Med. 1992;326:151–154.
49. Straus WL, Plouffe JF, File TM, et al. Risk factors for domestic acquisition of legionnaires' disease. Arch Intern Med. 1996;156:1685–1692.
50. Nechwatal R, Ehret W, Klatte OJ, et al. Nosocomial outbreak of legionellosis in a rehabilitation center: Demonstration of potable water as a source. Infection. 1993;21:235–240.
51. Hoebe CJP, Cluitmanans JJM, Wagenvoort JHT. Two fatal cases of nosocomial *Legionella pneumophila* pneumonia associated with a contaminated cold water supply. Eur J Clin Microbiol Infect Dis. 1998;17:740–749.
52. Brennen C, Vickers RM, Yu VL, et al. Discovery of occult pneumonia in a long stay hospital: Results of a prospective serological study. BMJ. 1987;295:306–307.
53. Maesaki S, Kohno S, Kog H, et al. An outbreak of legionnaires' pneumonia in a nursing home. Intern Med. 1992;31:508–512.
54. Loeb M, Simor AE, Mandell L, et al. Two nursing home outbreaks of respiratory infections with *Legionella sainthelensi*. J Am Geriatr Soc. 1999;47:597–552.
55. Muraca PW, Stout JE, Yu VL, et al. Legionnaires' disease in the work environment: Implications for environmental health. Am Ind Hyg Assoc J. 1988;49:584–590.
56. Barbaree JM. Selecting a subtyping technique for use in investigations of legionellosis epidemics. In: Barbaree JM, Brieman RF, Dufour AP, eds. *Legionella*: Current Status and Emerging Perspectives. Washington, DC: American Society for Microbiology; 1993:169–172.
57. Riffard S, Lo Presti F, Vandenesch F, et al. Comparative analysis of infrequent-restriction-site PCR and pulsed-field gel electrophoresis for epidemiological typing of *Legionella pneumophila* serogroup 1 strains. J Clin Microbiol. 1998;36:161–167.
58. Marrie TJ, Johnson W, Tyler S, et al. Potable water and nosocomial legionnaires' disease: Check water from all rooms in which patient has stayed. Epidemiol Infect. 1995;114:267–276.
59. Pruckler JM, Mermel LA, Benson RF. Comparison of *Legionella pneumophila* isolates by arbitrarily primed PCR and pulsed-field gel electrophoresis: Analysis from seven epidemic investigations. J Clin Microbiol. 1995;33:2872–2875.
60. Schoonmaker DJ, Kondracki ST. Investigation of nosocomial legionellosis using restriction enzyme analysis by pulsed field gel electrophoresis. In: Barbaree JM, Breiman RF, Dufour AP, eds. *Legionella*: Current Status and Emerging Perspectives. Washington, DC: American Society for Microbiology; 1993:189–194.
61. Selander RK, McKinney RM, Whittam TS, et al. Genetic structure of populations of *Legionella pneumophila*. J Bacteriol. 1985;163:1021–1037.
62. Drenning S, Stout JE. Analysis of pulsed-field gel electrophoresis (PFGE) patterns of clinical isolates of *Legionella pneumophila* serogroup 1: Similarity breeds contempt (Abstract K-10). Interscience Conference on Antimicrobial Agents and Chemotherapy, American Society of Microbiology, Toronto, September 1997.
63. Georghiou PR, Doggett AM, Kielhofner MA, et al. Molecular fingerprinting of *Legionella* species by repetitive element PCR. J Clin Microbiol. 1994;32:2989–2994.
64. Harrison TG, Saunders NA, Haththotuwa A, et al. Further evidence that genotypically closely related strains of *Legionella pheumophila* can express different serogroup specific antigens. J Med Microbiol. 1992;37:155–161.
65. Dondero TJ Jr, Rendtorff RC, Mallison GF, et al. An outbreak of legionnaires' disease associated with a contaminated air-conditioning cooling tower. N Engl J Med. 1980;302:365–370.
66. Bollin GE, Plouffe JF, Para MF, et al. *Legionella pneumophila* generated by shower heads and hot water faucets. Appl Environ Microbiol. 1986;50:1128–1131.
67. Woo AH, Goetz A, Yu VL. Transmission of *Legionella* by respiratory equipment aerosol generating devices. Chest 1992;102:1586–1590.
68. Shands K, Ho J, Meyer R, et al. Potable water as a source of legionnaires' disease. JAMA. 1985;253:1412–1416.
69. Blatt SP, Parkinson MD, Pace E, et al. Nosocomial legionnaires' disease: Aspiration as a primary mode of transmission. Am J Med. 1993;95:16–22.
70. Kool JL, Fiore AE, Kioski CM, et al. More than ten years of unrecognized nosocomial transmission of legionnaires' disease among transplant patients. Infect Control Hosp Epidemiol. 1998;19:898–904.
71. Arnow P, Chou T, Weil D, et al. Nosocomial legionnaires' disease caused by aerosolized tap water from respiratory devices. J Infect Dis. 1982;146:460–467.
72. Moriaghi A, Castellani Pastoris M, Barral C, et al. Nosocomial legionellosis associated with use of oxygen bubble humidifiers and underwater chest drain. J Hosp Infect. 1987;10:47–50.
73. Mastro TD, Fields BS, Breiman RF, et al. Nosocomial legionnaires' disease and use of medication nebulizers. J Infect Dis. 1991;163:667–671.
74. Brady M. Nosocomial legionnaires' disease in a children's hospital. J Pediatr. 1989;115:46–50.
75. Mahoney FJ, Hoge CW, Farley TA, et al. Community-wide outbreak of legionnaires' disease associated with a grocery store mist machine. J Infect Dis. 1992;165:736–739.
76. Yu VL. Could aspiration be the major mode of transmission for *Legionella*? Am J Med. 1993;95:13–15.
77. Saravolatz L, Pohlod D, Helzer K, et al. *Legionella* infections in renal transplant recipients. In: Thornsberry C, Balows A, Feeley JC, Jakubowski W, eds. *Legionella:* Proceedings of the 2nd International Symposium. Washington, DC: American Society of Microbiology; 1984:231–233.
78. Yu VL, Kroboth FJ, Shonnard J, et al. Legionnaires' disease: New clinical perspective from a prospective pneumonia study. Am J Med. 1982;73:357–361.
79. Roig J, Aguilar X, Ruiz J, et al. Comparative study of *Legionella pneumophila* and other nosocomial-acquired pneumonias. Chest. 1991;99:344–350.
80. Marrie TJ, Haldane D, Macdonald S. Control of endemic nosocomial legionnaires' disease by using sterile potable water for high risk patients. Epidemiol Infect. 1991;107:591–605.
81. Venezia RA, Agresta MD, Hanley EM, et al. Nosocomial legionellosis associated with aspiration of nasogastric feedings diluted in tap water. Infect Control Hosp Epidemiol. 1994;15:529–533.
82. Markowitz L, Tompkins L, Wilkinson H, et al. Transmission of nosocomial legionnaires' disease in heart transplant patients. Program and Abstracts of the 24th Interscience Conference on Antimicrobial Agents and Chemotherapy, American Society of Microbiology, Washington, DC, October 1984.
83. Muder RR, Yu VL, McClure J, Kominos S. Nosocomial legionnaires' disease uncovered in a prospective pneumonia study: Implications for underdiagnosis. JAMA. 1983;249:3184–3188.
84. Seu P, Winston DJ, Olthoft KM, et al. Legionnaires' disease in liver transplant recipients. Infect Dis Clin Pract. 1993;2:109–113.
85. Strebel P, Ramos J, Eidelman I, Tobiansky L. Legionnaires' disease in a Johannesburg teaching hospital: Investigation and control of an outbreak. S Afr Med J. 1988;19:329–333.
86. Brabender W, Hinthorn DR, Asher M. *Legionella pneumophila* wound infection. JAMA. 1983;250:3091–3095.
87. Lowry PW, Blankenship RJ, Gridley W, et al. A cluster of legionella sternal wound infections due to postoperative topical exposure of contaminated tap water. N Engl J Med. 1991;324:109–112.
88. Lepine L, Jernigan DB, Butler JC, et al. A recurrent outbreak of nosocomial Legionnaire's disease detected by urinary antigen testing: Evidence for long-term colonization of a hospital plumbing system. Infect Control Hosp Epidemiol. 1998;19:905–910.
89. Marston BJ, Plouffe JF, File TM, et al. Incidence of community-acquired pneumonia requiring hospitalization: Results of a population based active surveillance study in Ohio. Arch Intern Med. 1997;157:1709–1718.
90. Stout JE, Yu VL. Current concepts: Legionellosis. N Engl J Med. 1997;337:682–687.
91. Vergis EN, Yu VL. Macrolides are ideal for empiric therapy of community-acquired pneumonia in the immunocompromised host. Semin Respir Infect. 1998;12:322–328.
92. Sopena N, Sabria-Leal M, Pedro-Botet ML, et al. Comparative study of the clinical presentation of *Legionella* pneumonia and other community-acquired pneumonias. Chest. 1998;113:1195–1200.
93. Hirani NA, MacFarlane JT. Impact of management guidelines on the outcome of severe community acquired pneumonia. Thorax. 1997;52:17–21.
94. Lieberman D, Porath A, Schlaeffer F, Boldur I. *Legionella* species community-acquired pneumonia: A review of 56 hospitalized adult patients. Chest. 1996;109:1243–1249.
95. Ewig S, Bauer T, Hasper E, et al. Value of routine microbial investigation in community-acquired pneumonia treated in a tertiary care center. Respiration. 1996;63:164–169.
96. Marrie TJ, Peeling RW, Fine MJ, et al. Ambulatory patients with community-acquired pneumonia: The frequency of atypical agents and clinical course. Am J Med. 1996;101:508–515.
97. Rello J, Quintana E, Ausina V, et al. A three year study of severe community-acquired pneumonia with emphasis on outcome. Chest. 1993;103:232–235.
98. Fang GD, Fine M, Orloff J, et al. New and emerging etiologies for community-acquired pneumonia with implications for therapy: A prospective multicenter study of 359 cases. Medicine (Baltimore). 1990;69:307–316.
99. Torres A, Sera-Batilles J, Ferrer A, et al. Severe community acquired pneumonia: Epidemiology and prognostic factors. Am Rev Respir Dis. 1991;144:312–318.
100. Chow J, Yu VL. *Legionella*: A major opportunistic pathogen in transplant recipients. Semin Respir Infect. 1998;13:132–139.
101. Redd SC, Schuster DM, Quan J, et al. Legionellosis cardiac transplant recipients: Results of a nationwide survey. J Infect Dis. 1988;158:651–653.
102. Quaresima T, Castellani Pastoris M. Infezioni da Legionella sp. nel bambino. Riv Ital Pediatr. 1992;18:125–136.
103. Carlson NC, Kuskie MR, Dobyns EL, et al. Legionellosis in children: An expanding spectrum. Infect Dis J. 1990;9:133–137.
104. Famiglietti RF, Bakerman PR, Saubolle MD, Rudinsky M. Cavitary legionellosis in two immunocompetent infants. Pediatrics. 1997;99:899–903.
105. Luck PC, Dinger D, Helbig JH, et al. Analysis of *Legionella neumophila* strains associated with nosocomial pneumonia in a neonatal intensive care unit. Eur J Clin Microbiol Infect Dis. 1994;13:565–571.
106. Green M, Wald ER, Dashefsky B, et al. Field inversion gel electrophoretic analysis of *Legionella pneumophila* strains associated with nosocomial legionellosis in children. J Clin Microbiol. 1996;34:175–176.
107. Chlanger G, Lutwick LI, Kurzman M, et al. Sinusitis caused by *L. pneumophila* in a patient with acquired immune deficiency syndrome. Am J Med. 1984;77:957–960.
108. Marston BJ, Lipman HB, Breiman RF. Surveillance for legionnaires' disease: Risk factors for morbidity and mortality. Arch Intern Med. 1994;154:2417–2422.
109. Morley JN, Crocker Smith L, Baltch AL, Smith RP. Recurrent infection due to *Legionella pneumophila* in a patient with AIDS. Clin Infect Dis. 1994;19:1130–112.
110. Bangsborg JM, Jensen BN, Friis-Moller A, Bruun B. Legionellosis in patients with HIV infection. Infection. 1990;18:342–346.

111. Winn WC, Myerowitz RL. The pathology of the legionella pneumonias. Hum Pathol. 1981;12:401–422.
112. Chastre J, Raghu G, Soler P, et al. Pulmonary fibrosis following pneumonia due to acute legionnaires' disease. Chest. 1987;91:57–62.
113. Stout JE, Best M, Yu VL, Rihs JD. Symbiosis of *Legionella pneumophila* and *Tatlockia micdadei* with human respiratory flora. J Appl Bacteriol. 1986;60:297–299.
114. Stone BJ, Abu KY. Expression of multiple pili by *Legionella pneumophila*: Identification and characterization of a type IV pilin gene and its role in adherence to mammalian and protozoan cells. Infect Immun. 1998;66:1768.
115. Cianciotto NP, Stamos JK, Kamp DW. Infectivity of *Legionella pneumophila* mip mutant for alveolar epithelial cells. Curr Microbiol. 1995;30:247–250.
116. Oldham LJ, Rogers FG. Adhesion, penetration, and intracellular replication of *Legionella pneumophila*: An in vitro model of pathogenesis. J Gen Microbiol. 1985;131:697–706.
117. Mody CH, Paine R, Shahrabadi MS, et al. *Legionella pneumophila* replicates within rat alveolar epithelial cells. J Infect Dis. 1993;167:1138–1145.
118. Horwitz MA. The legionnaires' disease bacterium (*Legionella pneumophila*) inhibits phagosome-lysosome fusion in human monocytes. J Exp Med. 1983;158:2108–2126.
119. Vogel JP, Andrews HL, Wong SK, Isberg RR. Conjugative transfer by the virulence system of *Legionella pneumophila*. Science. 1998;279:873.
120. Miyamoto H, Karuta K, Ogawa M, et al. Spectrum of *Legionella* species whose intracellular multiplication in murine macrophages is genetically controlled by Lgn 1. Infect Immun. 1996;64:1842–1845.
121. Andrews HL, Vogel JP, Isberg RR. Identification of linked *Legionella pneumophila* genes essential for intracellular growth and evasion of the endocytic pathway (Abstract). Infect Immun. 1998;66:950.
122. Yoshido S, Groto Y, Mizuguchi Y, et al. Genetic control of natural resistance in mouse macrophages regulating replication in vitro. Infect Immun. 1991;59:428–423.
123. Rolstad B, Berdal B. Immune defenses against *Legionella pneumophila* in rats. Infect Immun. 1981;32:805–812.
124. Breiman RF, Horwitz MA. Guinea pigs sublethally infected with aerosolized *Legionella pneumophila* develop humoral and cell-mediated immune responses. J Exp Med. 1987;164:799–811.
125. Friedman H, Yamamoto Y, Newton C, Klein T. Immunologic response and pathophysiology of *Legionella* infection. Semin Respir Infect. 1998;13:100–108.
126. Cordonnier C, Farcet JP, Desforges L. Legionnaires' disease and hairy-cell leukemia. Arch Intern Med. 1984;144:2373–2375.
127. Skerrett SJ, Martin TR. Tumor necrosis factor and lipopolysaccharide potentiate gamma interferon-induced resistance of alveolar macrophages to *Legionella pneumophila*. In: Barbaree JM, Brieman RF, Dufour AP, eds. *Legionella*: Current Status and Emerging Perspectives. Washington, DC: American Society of Microbiology; 1993:105–106.
128. Brieland JK, Remick DG, LeGendre ML, et al. In vivo regulation of replicative *Legionella pneumophila* lung infection by endogenous interleukin-12. Infect Immun. 1998;66:65–69.
129. Skerrett SJ, Bagby GJ, Schmidt RA, Nelson S. Antibody-mediated depletion of tumor necrosis factor-alpha impairs pulmonary host defenses to *Legionella pneumophila*. J Infect Dis. 1997;176:1019–1028.
130. Ewald PW. The evolution of virulence. Sci Am. 1993;268:86–93.
131. Falco V, Fernandez de Sevilla T, Alegre J, et al. *Legionella pneumophila*: A cause of several community acquired pneumonias. Chest. 1991;100:1007–1011.
132. Joly JR, McKinney RM, Tobin J, et al. Development of a standardized subtyping scheme for *L. pneumophila*, serogroup 1, using monoclonal antibodies. J Clin Microbiol. 1986;23:768–771.
133. Dournon E, Bibb WF, Rajagopalan P, et al. Monoclonal antibody reactivity as a virulence marker for *Legionella pneumophila* serogroup 1 strains. J Infect Dis. 1988;157:496–501.
134. Stout JE, Joly J, Para M, et al. Comparison of molecular methods for subtyping patients and epidemiologically-linked environmental isolates of *L. pneumophila*. J Infect Dis. 1988;157:486–494.
135. Bollin GE, Plouffe JE, Para MF. Difference in virulence of environmental isolates of *Legionella pneumophila*. J Clin Microbiol. 1985;21:674–677.
136. Plouffe JR, Para MF, Maher WE, et al. Subtypes of *Legionella pneumophila* serogroup 1 associated with different attack rates. Lancet. 1983;2:649–650.
137. Klein TW, Friedman H, Widen R. Relative potency of virulent versus avirulent *Legionella pneumophila* for induction of cell-mediated immunity. Infect Immun. 1984;44:753–759.
138. Cirillo JD, Falkow S, Tompkins LS. *Legionella pneumophila* in *Acanthamoeba castellani* enhances invasion. Infect Immun. 1994;62:3254–3261.
139. Dowling JN, Saha AK, Glew RH. Virulence factors of the family Legionellaceae. Microbiol Rev. 1992;56:32–60.
140. Engleberg CN. Genetic studies of *Legionella* pathogenesis. In: Barbaree JM, Breiman RF, Dufour AP, eds. *Legionella*: Current Status and Emerging Perspectives. Washington, DC: American Society of Microbiology; 1993:63–68.
141. Lema MW, Brown A, Butler CA, Hoffman PS. Heat-shock response in *Legionella pneumophila*. Can J Microbiol. 1988;34:1148–1153.
142. Yabuuchi E, Mori M. An outbreak of Pontiac fever due to *Legionella pneumophila* serogroup 7 in Tokyo. In: Proceedings of the European Working Group on *Legionella* infections. Istanbul: Turkish Microbiological Society; 1995.
143. Miller L, Beebe J, Butler J, et al. Use of polymerase chain reaction in an epidemiologic investigation of Pontiac fever. J Infect Dis. 1993;168:769–772.
144. Johnson JD, Raff M, VanArsdall J. Neurologic manifestations of legionnaires' disease. Medicine (Baltimore). 1984;63:303–310.
145. Kirby BD, Snyder K, Meyer R, Finegold SM. Legionnaires' disease: Report of 65 nosocomially acquired cases and a review of the literature. Medicine (Baltimore). 1980;59:188–205.
146. Shah A, Check F, Baskin S. Legionnaires' disease and acute renal failure: Case report and review. Clin Infect Dis. 1992;14:204–207.
147. Lowry PW, Tompkins LS. Nosocomial legionellosis: A review of pulmonary and extrapulmonary syndromes. Am J Infect Control. 1993;21:21–27.
148. Schlanger G, Lutwick LI, Kurzman M, et al. Sinusitis caused by *L. pneumophila* in a patient with acquired immune deficiency syndrome. Am J Med. 1984;77:957–960.
149. Tompkins LS, Roessler BJ, Redd SC, et al. *Legionella* prosthetic-valve endocarditis. N Engl J Med. 1988;318:530–535.
150. Singh N, Muder RR, Yu VL, Gayowski T. *Legionella* infection in liver transplant recipients: Implications for management. Transplantation. 1993;56:1549–1551.
151. Muder RR, Yu VL, Parry M. Radiology of *Legionella* pneumonia. Semin Respir Infect. 1987;2:242–254.
152. Ebright JR, Tarakji E, Brown WJ, Sunstrum J. Multiple bilateral lung cavities caused by *Legionella pneumophila*: Case report and review. Infect Dis Clin Pract. 1993;2:195–199.
153. Kroboth FJ, Yu VL, Reddy S, Yu AC. Clinicoradiographic correlations with the extent of legionnaires' disease. AJR Am J Roentgenol. 1983;141:263–268.
154. Vickers RM, Stout JE, Yu VL, Rihs JD. Culture methodology for the isolation of *Legionella pneumophila* and other Legionellaceae from clinical and environmental specimens. Semin Respir Infect. 1987;2:274–279.
155. Stout JE. Culture methodology for *Legionella* species. HC Information Resources, Inc. Available at: http://www.hcinfo.com. Accessed August 4, 1999.
156. Vickers RM, Stout JE, Yu VL, Rihs JD. Manual of culture methodology for *Legionella*. Semin Respir Infect. 1987;2:274–279.
157. Vickers RM, Yee YC, Rihs JD, et al. Prospective assessment of sensitivity, quantitation, and timing of urinary antigen, serology, and direct fluorescent antibody for diagnosis of legionnaires' disease (Abstract C17). 93rd Annual Meeting of the American Society of Microbiology, May 1994.
158. Ingram JG, Plouffe J. Danger of sputum purulence screens in culture of *Legionella* species. J Clin Microbiol. 1994;32:209–210.
159. Oliverio MJ, Fisher MA, Vickers RM, et al. Diagnosis of legionnaires' disease by radioimmunoassay of *Legionella* antigen in pleural fluid. J Clin Microbiol. 1991;29:2893–2894.
160. Babe KS, Reinhardt JF. Diagnosis of *Legionella* sepsis by examination of a peripheral blood smear. Clin Infect Dis. 1994;19:1164–1165.
161. Williams A, Lever MS. Characterization of *Legionella pneumophila* antigen in urine of guinea pigs and humans with legionnaires' disease. J Infect. 1995;30:13–16.
162. Kohler RB, Winn WC Jr, Wheat LJ. Onset and duration of urinary antigen excretion in legionnaires' disease. J Clin Microbiol. 1984;20:605–607.
163. Kazandjian D, Chiew R, Gilbert GL. Rapid diagnosis of *Legionella pneumophila* serogroup 1 infection with the Binax enzyme immunoassay urinary antigen test. J Clin Microbiol. 1997;35:954–956.
164. Dominguez JA, Manterola JM, Blavia R, et al. Detection of *Legionella pneumophila* serogroup 1 antigen in nonconcentrated urine and urine concentrated by selective ultrafiltration. J Clin Microbiol. 1996;34:2334–2336.
165. Dominguez JA, Gali N, Pedroso P, et al. Comparison of the Binax *Legionella* urinary antigen enzyme immunoassay (EIA) with the Biotest *Legionella* urine antigen EIA for detection of *Legionella* antigen in both concentrated and nonconcentrated urine samples (Abstract). J Clin Microbiol. 1998;36:2718–2122.
166. Edelstein PH. Antimicrobial chemotherapy for legionnaires' disease: A review. Clin Infect Dis. 1995;21(Suppl 3):S265–S276.
167. Vergis EN, Yu VL. *Legionella* species. In: Yu VL, Merigan TC, Barriere SL, et al, eds. Antimicrobial Therapy and Vaccines. 1st ed. Baltimore: Williams & Wilkins; 1998:257–272.
168. Heath CH, Grove DI, Looke DFM. Delay in appropriate therapy of *Legionella* pneumonia associated with increased mortality. Eur J Clin Microbiol Infect Dis. 1996;15:286–290.
169. El-Ebiary M, Sarmiento X, Torres A, et al. Prognostic factors of severe *Legionella* pneumonia requiring admission to ICU. Am J Respir Crit Care Med. 1997;156:1467–1472.
170. Vergis EN, Yu VL. Macrolides are ideal for empiric therapy of community-acquired pneumonia in the immunocompetent host. Semin Respir Infect. 1997;12:327–328.
171. Williams RR, Stout JE, Yu VL, et al. Levofloxacin is safe and effective in the management of community-acquired pneumonia due to *Legionella* (Abstract). 36th Annual Meeting of the Infectious Disease Society of America, Denver, September 1998.
172. Centers for Disease Control and Prevention. Guidelines for Prevention of Nosocomial Pneumonia. MMWR Morb Mortal Wkly Rep. 1997;46:31–34.
173. Liu WK, Healing DE, Yeomans JT, Ellioit TSJ. Monitoring of hospital water supplies for *Legionella*. J Hosp Infect. 1993;24:1–9.
174. Goetz AM, Stout JE, Jacobs SL, et al. Nosocomial legionnaires' disease discovered in community hospitals following cultures of the water system: Seek and ye shall find. Am J Infect Control. 1998;26:6–11.
175. Modol JM, Pedro-Botet ML, Sabria M, et al. Environmental and clinical legionellosis in hospitals in Catalonia, Spain (Abstract K-490A). 38th Interscience Conference on Antimicrobial Agents and Chemotherapy, American Society of Microbiology, San Diego, Calif.

176. Yu VL. Resolving the controversy on environmental cultures for *Legionella*. Infect Control Hosp Epidemiol. 1998;19:893–897.
177. Patterson WJ, Hay J, Seal DV, McLuckie JD. Colonization of transplant unit water supplies with *Legionella* and protozoa; Precautions required to reduce the risk of legionellosis. J Hosp Infect. 1997;37:7–17.
178. Liu Z, Stout JE, Tedesco L, et al. Controlled evaluation of copper-silver ionization in eradicating *Legionella pneumophila* from a hospital water distribution system. J Infect Dis. 1994;169:919–922.
179. Colville A, Crowley J, Dearden D, et al. Outbreak of legionnaires' disease at a University Hospital, Nottingham: Epidemiology, microbiology, and control. Epidemiol Infect. 1993;10:105–116.
180. Stout JE, Lin YSE, Goetz AM, Muder RR. Controlling *Legionella* in hospital water systems: Experience with the superheat-and-flush method and copper-silver ionization. Infect Control Hosp Epidemiol. 1998;19:911–914.
181. Zacheus OM, Martikainen PJ. Effect of heat flushing on the concentrations of *Legionella pneumophila* and other heterotrophic microbes in hot water systems of apartment buildings. Can J Microbiol. 1996;42:811–818.
182. Grosserode M, Helms C, Pfaller M, et al. Continuous hyperchlorination for control of nosocomial legionnaires' disease: A ten year follow-up of efficacy, environmental effects, and cost. In: Barbaree JM, Breiman RF, Dufour AP, eds. *Legionella*: Current Status and Emerging Perspectives. Washington, DC: American Society for Microbiology; 1993:226–229.
183. Morris RD, Audet AM, Angelillo IF, et al. Chlorination, chlorination by-products, and cancer: A meta-analysis. Am J Public Health. 1993;82:955–963.
184. Swan SH, Waller K, Hopkins B, et al. A prospective study of spontaneous abortion: Relation to amount and source of drinking water consumed in early pregnancy. Epidemiology. 1998;9:126–133.

Chapter 222

Other *Legionella* Species

ROBERT R. MUDER

Since the discovery of *Legionella pneumophila* in 1977, the family Legionellaceae has expanded to include a total of 42 described species, representing 64 serogroups.[1] Like *L. pneumophila*, these other species are found in aquatic environments and soil. The vast majority of human infections are pneumonic, occurring after exposure to an environmental source of *Legionella*.[2] Eighteen species have been documented to cause human infection based on isolation from clinical material, with one additional species demonstrated in tissue by direct fluorescent antibody staining (Table 222–1). Isolates of the other species are limited to water and soil, although several have been implicated in human infection based on seroconversion in the absence of isolation.

TABLE 222–1 *Legionella* Species Other Than *Legionella pneumophila* Causing Human Disease

Species	References
L. micdadei	80, 81
L. bozemanii	9, 54
L. dumoffii	9, 82
L. longbeachae	83
L. wadsworthii	84
L. hackeliae	85
L. maceachernii	86
*L. oakridgensis**	87
L. feeleii	88
L. birminghamensis	58
L. cincinnatiensis	89
L. jordanis	90
L. gormanii	91
L. anisa	92
L. tucsonensis	93
L. sainthelensi	94
L. lansingensis	95
L. parisiensis	96

*Demonstrated by direct fluorescent antibody staining of tissue.

In addition to the described species, there are other organisms that are in all probability members of the genus *Legionella*, based on analysis of 16-S ribosomal RNA sequences.[3] Such phylogenetic analysis suggests that these organisms may represent as many as five distinct *Legionella* species.[4] These organisms, termed *Legionella-like amebal pathogens*, infect freshwater amebae and are found in aquatic environments capable of supporting the growth of *Legionella*. One member of this group, *Legionella*-like amebal pathogen 3, was isolated from a patient with pneumonia by cocultivation of sputum with amebae. *Legionella*-like amebal pathogens grow very poorly or not at all on media supporting the growth of *Legionella*.

In 1977, workers from the University of Pittsburgh and the University of Virginia visualized gram-negative, weakly acid-fast organisms from lung tissue of immunosuppressed patients with acute pneumonitis.[5, 6] Almost all the patients were receiving steroids or cytotoxic chemotherapy; renal transplant recipients were a prominent group. Although organisms could be seen on biopsy and autopsy lung specimens by various stains, they could not be grown on standard bacteriologic culture media. A *Legionella*-like organism was isolated after the clinical specimens were inoculated into guinea pigs and embryonated eggs. Sera from these patients contained high titers of antibodies against this organism, confirming its etiologic role in pneumonia.

This new organism, originally called *Pittsburgh pneumonia agent*, was serologically and genetically distinct from *L. pneumophila*, although it phenotypically resembled *L. pneumophila* in growth requirements and the presence of branched-chain fatty acids in the cell wall. The organism proved to be identical to organisms isolated in 1943 ("TATLOCK") and 1959 ("HEBA") from guinea pigs injected with the blood of two patients with nonpneumonic illnesses.[7, 8] The first documented isolation of *Legionella bozemanii* was in 1959 from the lung tissue of a patient dying of pneumonia after immersion in fresh water.[8, 9]

DESCRIPTION OF THE PATHOGENS

Legionella spp. are gram-negative aerobic bacilli that share a number of common phenotypic features, including growth on buffered charcoal yeast extract agar, a lack of growth on blood agar, catalase activity, and a requirement for cysteine. Tests for urease, nitrate reduction, and fermentative activity are uniformly negative.[10] Although individual species differ in several phenotypic characteristics, such as gelatin liquefaction, hippurate hydrolysis, and oxidase activity, these tests are of limited utility in differentiation. When grown on yeast extract agar, *Legionella* spp. produce a water-soluble, extracellular compound that fluoresces yellow-green on exposure to long-wave ultraviolet light. Several species exhibit a blue-white or red autofluorescence under ultraviolet light. Most species produce β-lactamase; *Legionella micdadei, Legionella maceachernii* and *Legionella feeleii* do not. The cell wall fatty acid profiles and the ubiquinone content are sufficiently distinctive to permit species identification on the basis of gas-liquid chromatography.[11] Differentiation of the common species is most conveniently made in the laboratory by direct fluorescent antibody staining of the isolates. Slide agglutination can also be used for selected isolates.[2, 11] Determination of DNA homology is the definitive method especially for the less common strains. Other biochemical and immunologic methods for species classification of *Legionella* are described in Chapter 221.

Legionella micdadei is unique in that it retains the modified acid-fast stain.[5, 6] *Legionella micdadei* can appear as weakly or partially acid-fast bacilli in clinical specimens. The acid-fast property is not usually present in organisms grown on solid media but may be retained in liquid culture. The modified acid-fast stain substitutes 1% sulfuric acid (a less potent decolorizing agent) for the traditional 3% hydrochloric acid. This characteristic has occasionally led to misidentification of *L. micdadei* infection as mycobacterial infection, with initiation of antituberculous agents.[6, 12, 13]

Based on differences in DNA sequence homology and DNA

guanine and cytosine content, Garrity, Brown, and associates proposed division of the family into three genera, *Legionella (L. pneumophila), Fluoribacter (F. bozemanii, F. gormanii, F. dumoffii)*, and *Tatlockia (T. micdadei, T. maceachernii)*.[14, 15] However, commonly accepted usage includes only the single genus *Legionella.*

EPIDEMIOLOGY

Like *L. pneumophila*, other *Legionella* spp. are widely distributed in aquatic habitats and soil.[16, 17] Several species associated with human disease have been isolated only from clinical specimens. Water distribution systems may be colonized with any of a number of *Legionella* spp. in addition to *L. pneumophila*, including *L. micdadei, L. bozemanii, L. dumoffii, L. anisa*, and *L. feeleii*.[18–23] Recovery of these species is generally less frequent and technically more demanding than is recovery of *L. pneumophila*. Commensal microflora and sediment known to promote proliferation of *L. pneumophila* in water distribution systems do not support the growth of *L. micdadei*.[24] Thus, the growth kinetics of *L. micdadei* may explain its infrequent presence in the water supply, such that only patients with prolonged hospitalization or immunosuppression are susceptible. Like *L. pneumophila*, other species multiply within aquatic protozoa.[25, 26]

Legionella pneumophila causes approximately 85% of reported cases of *Legionella* infection. Of the remainder, 60% are caused by *L. micdadei*, 15% by *L. bozemanii*, 10% by *L. dumoffii*, and 5% by *L. longbeachae*.[2, 27] The other species combined account for the remaining 10%. Interestingly, *L. longbeachae* appears to be a frequent cause of *Legionella* pneumonia in Australia.[28]

Most patients with non-*pneumophila Legionella* infections have been immunocompromised due to corticosteroid therapy, organ transplantation, or malignancy.[2] Patients with *L. micdadei* pneumonia are more likely to be immunosuppressed than those with *L. pneumophila* infection.[29] *Legionella* spp. are frequent opportunistic pathogens in patients undergoing organ transplantation.[5, 13, 30–33] Although most reported cases in transplantation patients are due to *L. pneumophila, L. micdadei* and *L. bozemanii* are next in frequency.[33]

As with *L. pneumophila*, infection with *L. longbeachae* and *L. dumoffii* has occurred in patients with hairy cell leukemia.[34, 35] Human immunodeficiency virus infection is associated with some increased risk of infection due to *L. pneumophila*; cases of *L. bozemanii*,[36] *L. feeleii*,[37] and *L. micdadei*[38] infection occurring in the setting of human immunodeficiency virus infection have also been reported.

There have been clusters of nosocomial pneumonia due to *L. micdadei*,[5, 6, 18, 39, 40] *L. bozemanii*,[19] and *L. dumoffii*.[41] Outbreaks of *L. micdadei* pneumonia have occurred in hospitals with water systems colonized by *L. micdadei*.[18, 39, 40] In two of these,[18, 39] *L. pneumophila* was the predominant species isolated from water, and isolation of *L. micdadei* was relatively infrequent. In one of these facilities, *L. micdadei* infections occurred coincident with epidemic *L. pneumophila* disease[18]; simultaneous infection by both species occurred in several patients. In the other facility, no cases of *L. pneumophila* infection occurred despite widespread water colonization.[39] In both facilities, eradication of *Legionella* from the hospital water system ended the outbreaks.

Clusters of nosocomial *L. bozemanii*[19] and *L. dumoffii*[42] pneumonia have been associated with colonization of hospital water supplies. In the latter instance, *L. dumoffii* was isolated from distilled water used in respiratory therapy equipment and a room humidifier. A cluster of prosthetic valve endocarditis and a cluster of sternal wound infections due to *L. pneumophila* and *L. dumoffii*, singly and in combination, have been reported from a single hospital.[23, 43] Sternal wound infection was the result of contamination of wounds by tap water during bathing.

Two outbreaks of respiratory infection attributed to *L. sainthelensi* occurred in Canadian nursing homes.[44] In one of the facilities, infection was identified by both seroconversion to *L. sainthelensi* and a positive reaction in a polyvalent enzyme-linked immunosorbent assay capable of detecting antigens of multiple *Legionella* spp. *Legionella sainthelensi* was isolated from multiple sites in the facility's potable water system.

In contrast to reports of outbreaks due to *L. pneumophila*, reports of community-based outbreaks of pneumonia due to other *Legionella* spp. are rare. However, cases may be overlooked because cultures for *Legionella* are not obtained in most cases of community-acquired pneumonia, and the urinary antigen test only detects infection with *L. pneumophila* serogroup 1. Investigators in Ohio reported seven culture-confirmed cases of community-acquired *L. bozemanii* pneumonia from a single institution over a 5-year period.[45] In Australia, there have been multiple cases of community-acquired *L. longbeachae* pneumonia associated with exposure to soil.[28, 46, 47] Steele and coworkers isolated *L. longbeachae* from the soil and commercial potting mixes from many of the patients' homes.[46] Potting mixes made in Australia contained the organism, but not mixes made in Europe. Restriction fragment length polymorphism showed that organisms isolated from the patients and soils were closely related.[47]

There are reports of outbreaks of nonpneumonic legionellosis ("Pontiac fever") associated with exposures to contaminated aerosols. One such outbreak involved 317 workers in an automobile plant in which machinery produced aerosols of water-based coolant containing *L. feeleii*.[48] A whirlpool spa contaminated with *L. micdadei* ("Lochgoilhead fever")[49] and a decorative fountain contaminated with *L. anisa*[50] have also been implicated in outbreaks of nonpneumonic disease. An outbreak of Pontiac fever with seroconversion to both *L. pneumophila* and *L. micdadei* occurred in a group of children and adults exposed to a poorly maintained whirlpool spa.[51]

Many reported cases of pneumonia due to *Legionella* spp. are sporadic infections. In such cases, it has generally not been possible to identify an environmental source of the organism. The mode of transmission of the organism from the environment to humans is uncertain except in a limited number of outbreak situations cited previously. There are no reports of outbreaks of pneumonic infection due to nonpneumophila *Legionella* spp. associated with large aerosol-generating devices such as cooling towers. The occurrence of simultaneous infection by *L. pneumophila* and other species[23, 43, 52, 53] suggests that these other species share common modes of transmission with *L. pneumophila*. Reports of pneumonia after immersion in fresh water[8, 54, 55] and aspiration[56] suggest that aspiration is a mechanism of transmission to the patient, as has been documented for *L. pneumophila*. Human-to-human transmission does not occur.

CLINICAL MANIFESTATIONS

The vast majority of human *Legionella* infections present as pneumonia. Clinically and radiographically, pneumonia caused by other *Legionella* spp. resembles that caused by *L. pneumophila*.[2, 29, 39] Fever is present in over 90% of patients, exceeding 103°F (39.4°C) in half. Cough is often nonproductive or minimally productive, although most patients produce some sputum. The majority of patients complain of dyspnea. Sixty percent have some alteration in mental status, ranging from lethargy to obtundation. In immunosuppressed patients, pleuritic chest pain is a frequent complaint,[5, 6] and the presentation may mimic that of pulmonary embolism. Immunosuppressed patients may have fever without any other symptoms of pneumonia despite the presence of radiographic pulmonary infiltrates.[29, 57, 58] Occasionally, *Legionella* infections in these patients present as incidental radiographic abnormalities in the absence of fever.

Documented extrapulmonic infection is rare. Four cases of prosthetic valve endocarditis due to *L. dumoffii* (including one with simultaneous *L. pneumophila* infection) occurred at a single hospital.[43] The patients presented with a chronic syndrome of persistent fever, night sweats, malaise, and weight loss without embolic phenomena. All four patients responded to prolonged therapy with erythromycin and rifampin, although three required valve replacement. Sternal wound infection after cardiac surgery presented as serosanguineous wound drainage in the early postoperative period.[23] Gram stain failed to demonstrate organisms, but cultures yielded *L. dumoffii* and *L. pneumophila*. Cutaneous infection due to *L. micdadei* has occurred after pneumonia, presumably by bacteremic seeding[59] and in the absence of pulmonary infection.[60]

Laboratory data are not distinctive. The majority of patients show a neutrophilic leukocytosis unless receiving cytotoxic agents as immunosuppressive therapy. Elevations of hepatic transaminase or alkaline phosphatase levels are common. Hyponatremia, reportedly more frequent in *L. pneumophila* infection than in other pneumonias, occurs in one third of cases of *L. micdadei* infection.[61]

Radiographic manifestations are similar to those of *L. pneumophila* infection.[62] In nonimmunosuppressed patients, segmental to lobar infiltrates similar to those occurring in other bacterial pneumonias are typical.[63] An expanding pulmonary nodule has been a dramatic finding in some immunosuppressed patients.[5, 57, 64] Cavitation of nodules or infiltrates may occur in immunosuppressed patients (Figs. 222–1 and 222–2).[39, 62] The cavities often enlarge during treatment and clinical improvement and rarely require intervention. Small pleural effusions are common; these usually resolve without drainage, but empyema may occur.

Nonpneumonic disease due to non-*pneumophila* species closely resembles Pontiac fever, the syndrome associated with *L. pneumophila*.[48–50] After a brief incubation period averaging 36 to 48 hours after exposure to a *Legionella*-containing aerosol, patients experience the abrupt onset of a "flulike" syndrome of fever, chills, headache, myalgias, and malaise. Attack rates may exceed 80% among those exposed. Clinical and radiologic evidence of pneumonia are absent; spontaneous recovery after 2 to 7 days is the rule. Diagnosis is made by recognition of the clinical and epidemiologic features, isolation of a *Legionella* spp. from an aerosol generation source, and demonstration of seroconversion to the suspected agent on the part of the patients affected. *Legionella* spp. are generally not detected in clinical material from these patients.

DIAGNOSIS

Isolation of the infecting agent from clinical material (such as sputum or bronchoalveolar lavage fluid) on selective media is the most reliable means of diagnosis. Buffered charcoal yeast extract agar with added antibiotics to suppress commensal flora is available commercially,[65] but these media often have decreased sensitivity for isolation of non-*pneumophila* strains[66]; cefamandole is especially inhibitory. *Legionella* spp. lacking β-lactamase, such as *L. micdadei*, will not grow on buffered charcoal yeast extract formulations containing cephalosporins. Vancomycin, aztreonam, and pimafucin have been successfully used as suppressants of other organisms in selective media.[66] The non-*pneumophila* strains are easily missed in clinical and environmental specimens if dye-containing media are not used. Colonies of *L. micdadei* and *L. maceachernii* are blue on culture media containing bromocresol purple and bromothymol blue dyes, whereas the colonies of other species are yellow-green to apple green[2, 67]; the dyes color the organism, making detection easier.

Direct fluorescent antibody stains for the visualization of *Legionella* spp. in clinical specimens are commercially available for a limited number of species. The sensitivity and specificity of direct fluorescent antibody staining for species other than *L. pneumophila*

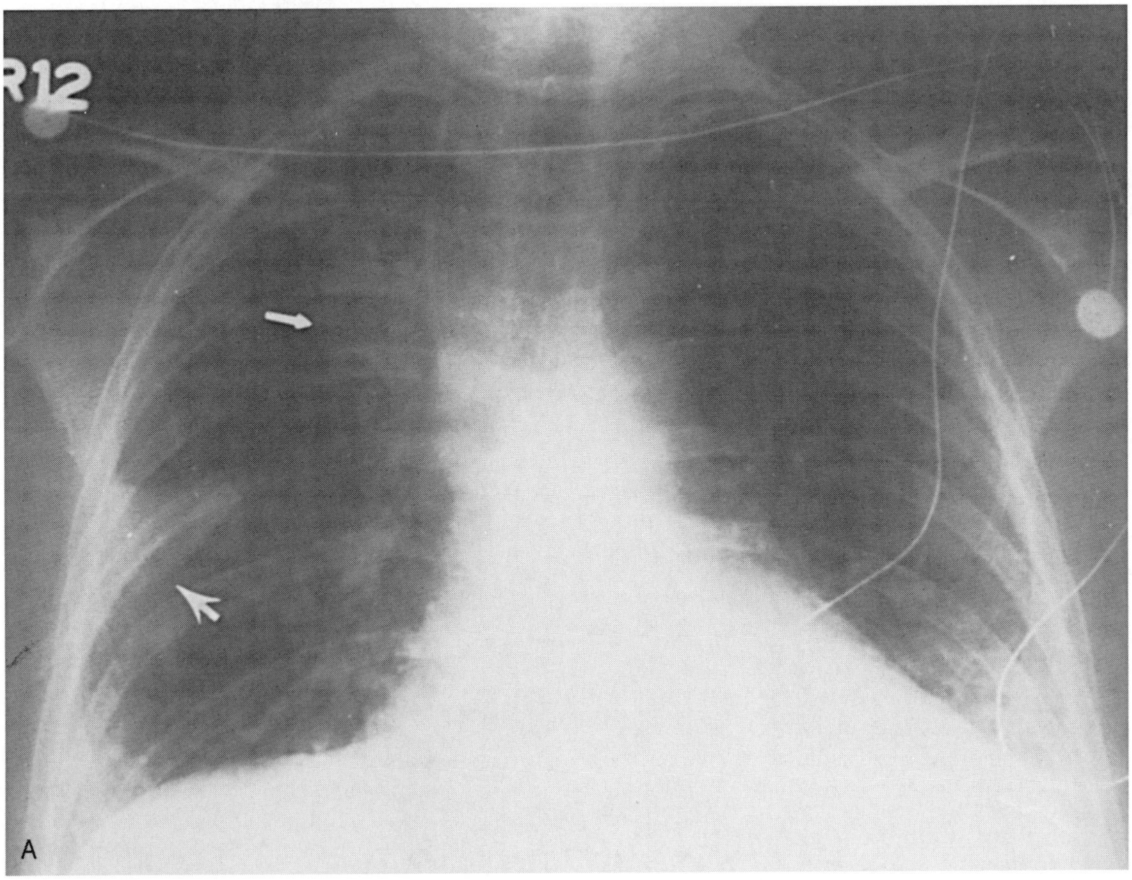

FIGURE 222–1. Nosocomial *Legionella micdadei* in a young woman receiving steroids for systemic lupus erythematosis. On day 3 she experienced abrupt onset of fever, dyspnea, and pleuritic chest pain. *A*, Poorly marginated densities *(small arrow)* and a wedge-shaped density *(large arrow)* were seen on chest films, suggesting pulmonary embolus, although pulmonary angiography was nonconfirmatory. Direct fluorescent antibody stain and culture of sputum yielded *L. micdadei*. Cavitation in the right upper lobe was seen on day 7 and day 10.

Illustration continued on following page

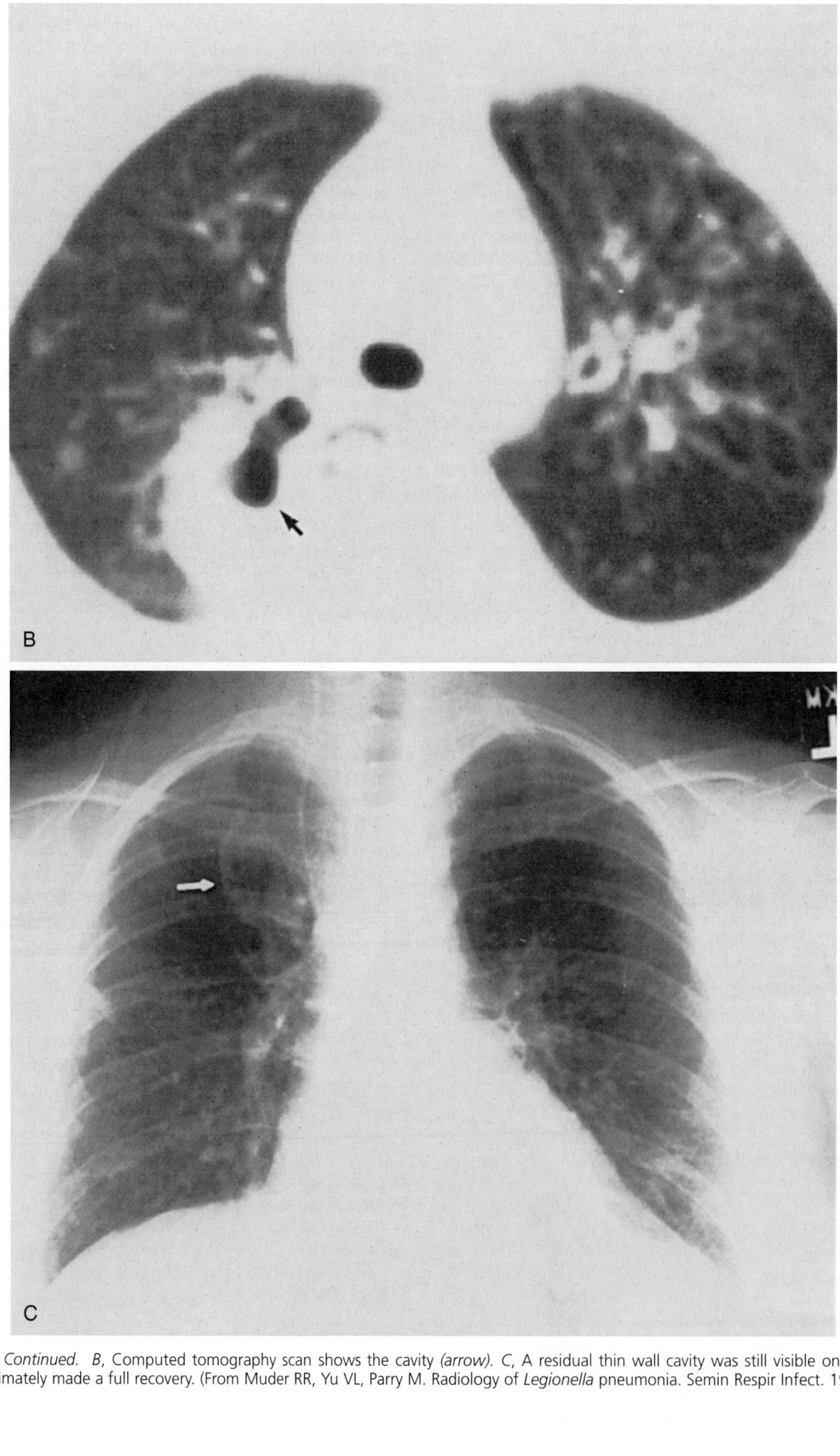

FIGURE 222–1 *Continued.* *B*, Computed tomography scan shows the cavity *(arrow)*. *C*, A residual thin wall cavity was still visible on day 15 *(arrow)*. The patient ultimately made a full recovery. (From Muder RR, Yu VL, Parry M. Radiology of *Legionella* pneumonia. Semin Respir Infect. 1987;2:242–254.)

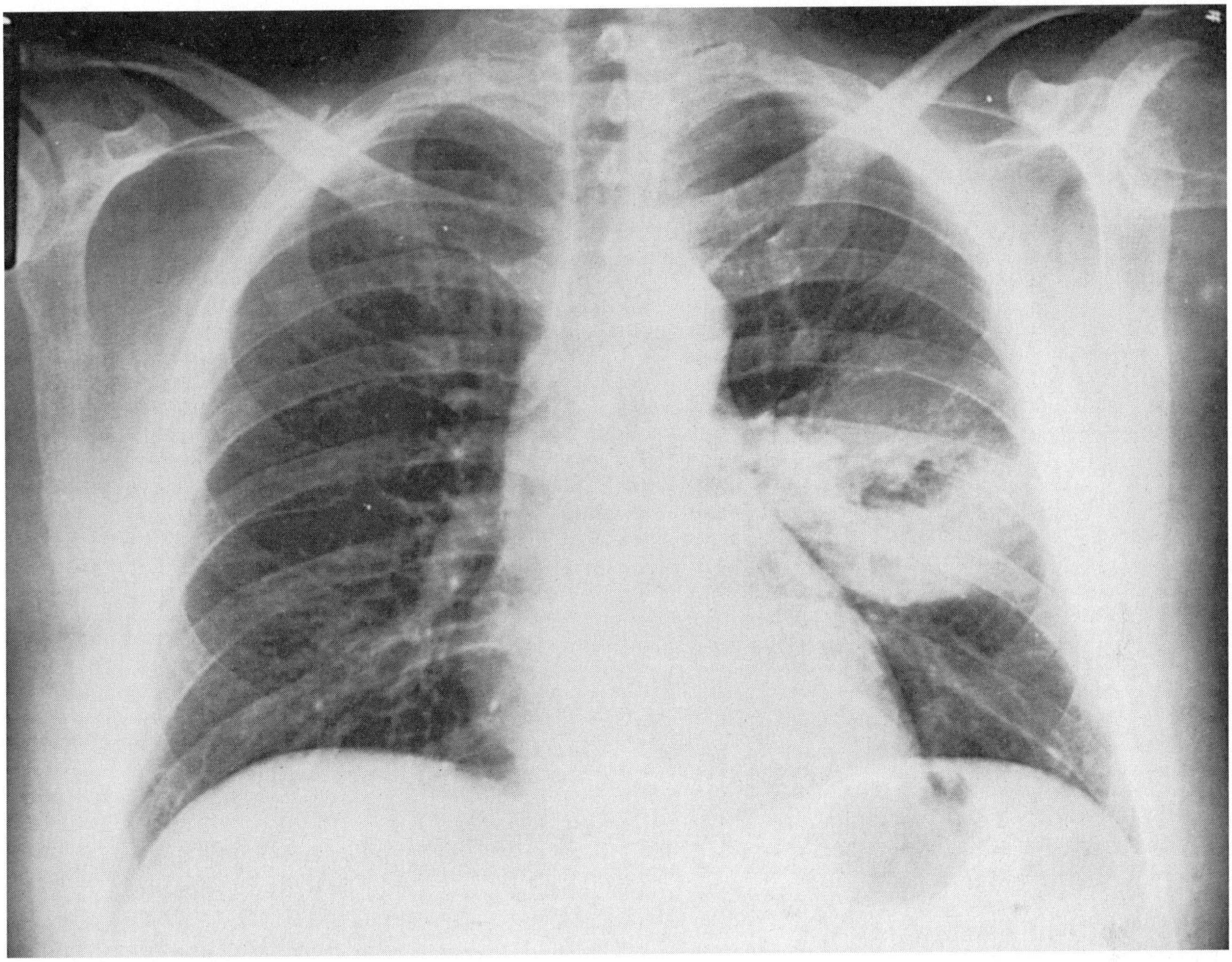

FIGURE 222–2. Nosocomial *Legionella bozemanii* pneumonia in an immunosuppressed patient. Although the patient responded to erythromycin and rifampin, cavitation occurred within the left lower lobe infiltrate. The infiltrate decreased by month 3 and resolved by month 6. (From Muder RR, Yu VL, Parry M. Radiology of *Legionella* pneumonia. Semin Respir Infect. 1987;2:242–254.)

is not precisely known. A *Legionella* DNA probe can detect the presence of multiple *Legionella* spp. but does not differentiate among species. The DNA probe appears to have fewer false-positive reactions than does direct fluorescent antibody staining[68]; it is no longer commercially available. The commercially available test for *Legionella* urinary antigen detects only *L. pneumophila* serogroup 1; it is not useful for other *Legionella* spp. Detection of *Legionella* spp. in clinical specimens by DNA amplification is a promising technique that has been applied in a limited number of cases.[69]

Antibody seroconversion in diagnosing infection due to non-*pneumophila* species is of uncertain specificity. Reports of infection based on seroconversion alone should be viewed with skepticism.

TREATMENT

There are no randomized trials of therapy for *Legionella* infection; the majority of reported clinical experience concerns infection with *L. pneumophila*. In vitro susceptibility data and more limited clinical experience indicate that response to the therapy of infection with other species should be similar. *Legionella* spp. are susceptible in vitro to erythromycin, tetracycline, trimethoprim-sulfamethoxazole, rifampin, and ciprofloxacin.[70, 71]

Erythromycin has been the historical drug of choice based on the observation of a clinical response in the majority of patients.[2, 35, 72] However, there are a number of case reports of erythromycin failure in highly immunocompromised patients.[31, 73–75] Failure of erythromycin may be due to the fact that erythromycin is bacteriostatic rather than bactericidal against intracellular *Legionella*.

The newer macrolide agents are somewhat more active than erythromycin both in vitro and intracellularly against the non-*pneumophila* species.[76–78] They offer a number of other clinical advantages over erythromycin, including better penetration into tissue and alveolar macrophages and improved pharmacokinetics, permitting once-daily dosing. The new quinolones are considerably more active than erythromycin.[78] Based on these factors, the newer macrolides or quinolones (especially ciprofloxacin, levofloxacin, or trovafloxacin) are the therapy of choice for infection due to *Legionella* spp. Patients who are immunocompromised or who are hospitalized with potentially life-threatening infection should receive intravenous therapy with either azithromycin or a fluoroquinolone.[79] Quinolones are preferable when treating transplantation patients receiving cyclosporine or tacrolimus, as macrolides interfere with the metabolism of these antirejection agents.

The optimal duration of therapy with these agents is uncertain. Data from clinical trials of community-acquired pneumonia suggest that in immunocompetent patients, 5 to 10 days of therapy with azithromycin or 10 to 14 days of therapy with a fluoroquinolone constitute adequate therapy.[77] Immunocompromised patients should receive longer courses of therapy (14 to 21 days) in order to prevent relapse. Oral therapy may be used as initial treatment in immunocompetent patients who are not seriously ill. Patients receiving initial parenteral therapy may be switched to oral therapy once a clinical response is apparent.

REFERENCES

1. Benson RF, Fields BS. Classification of the genus *Legionella*. Semin Respir Infect 1998;13:90–99.
2. Fang GD, Yu VL, Vickers RM. Disease due to Legionellaceae (other than *Legionella pneumophila*): Historical, microbiological, clinical and epidemiological review. Medicine. 1989;68:116–139.
3. Birtles RJ, Rowbotham TJ, Raoult D, Harrison TG. Phylogenetic diversity of intra-amoebal legionellae as revealed by 16S rRnA gene sequence comparison. Microbiology. 1996;142:3525–0.
4. Adeleke A, Pruckler J, Benson R, et al. *Legionella*-like amebal pathogens—phylogenetic status and possible role in respiratory diseases. Emerg Infect Dis. 1996;2:225–230.
5. Myerowitz RC, Pasculle AW, Dowling J, et al. Opportunistic lung infection due to "Pittsburgh pneumonia agent." N Engl J Med. 1979;301:953–958.
6. Rogers BH, Donowitz GR, Walker GK, Harding SA, et al. A clinicopathological study of five cases caused by an unidentified acid-fast bacterium. N Engl J Med. 1979;301:959–961.
7. Tatlock H. Studies on a virus from a patient with Fort Bragg fever (pretibial fever). Clin Invest. 1947;26:87–93.
8. Bozeman FM, Humphries JW, Campbell JM. A new group of *Rickettsia*-like agents recovered from guinea pigs. Acta Virol. 1968;12:87–93.
9. Brenner DJ, Steigerwalt A, Gorman GW. *Legionclla bozemanii*, sp nov and *Legionella dumoffi* sp nov: Classification of two additional species of *Legionella* associated with human pneumonia. Curr Microbiol. 1980;4:111–116.
10. Brenner DJ, Steigerwalt AG, Gorman GW, et al. Ten new species of *Legionella*. Int J Syst Bacteriol. 1985;35:50–59.
11. Ruf B, Schurmann D, Morbach Ietal. The incidence of *Legionella* pneumonia: A 1-year prospective study in a large community hospital. Lung. 1989;167:11–22.
12. Hilton E, Freedman RA, Cintron F. Acid-fast bacilli in sputum: A case of *Legionella micdadei* pneumonia. J Clin Microbiol. 1986;24:1102–1103.
13. Schwebke JR, Hackman R, Bowden R. Pneumonia due to *Legionella micdadei* in bone marrow transplant recipients. Rev Infect Dis. 1990;12:824–828.
14. Garrity GM, Brown A, Vickers RM. *Tatlockia* and *Fluoribacter*: Two new genera of organisms resembling *Legionella pneumophila*. Int J Syst Bacteriol. 1980;30:609–614.
15. Fox KF, Brown A. Properties of the genus *Tatlockia*. Differentiation of *Tatlockia (Legionella) maceachernii* and *micdadei* from each other and from other legionellae. Can J Microbiol. 1993;39:486–491.
16. Tison DL, Baross JA, Seidler RJ. *Legionella* in aquatic habitats in the Mount Saint Helens blast zone. Curr Microbiol. 1983;9:345–348.
17. Joly JR, Boissiot M, Duchaine J, Duval M, et al. Ecological distribution of Legionellaceae in the Quebec City area. Can J Microbiol. 1984;30:63–67.
18. Best M, Yu VL, Stout J, et al. Legionellaceae in the hospital water supply—epidemiological link with disease and evaluation of a method of control of nosocomial legionnaires' disease and Pittsburgh pneumonia. Lancet. 1983;2:307–310.
19. Parry MF, Stampleman L, Hutchinson J, et al. Waterborne *Legionella bozemanii* and nosocomial pneumonia in immunosuppressed patients. Ann Intern Med. 1985;103:205–210.
20. Barbaree JM. Selecting a subtyping technique for use in investigations of legionellosis epidemics. In: Barbaree JM, Brieman RF, Dufour AP, eds. *Legionella*: Current Status and Emerging Perspectives. Washington, DC: American Society for Microbiology; 1993:169–172.
21. Bornstein N, Veilly C, Marmet D, et al. Isolation of *Legionella anisa* from a hospital hot water system. Eur J Clin Microbiol. 1985;4:327–330.
22. Palutke WA, Crane LR, Wentworth BB, et al. *Legionella feeleii*–associated pneumonia in humans. N Engl J Med. 1986;86:348–351.
23. Lowry PW, Blankenship RJ, Gridley W, et al. A cluster of legionella sternal wound infections due to postoperative topical exposure of contaminated tap water. N Engl J Med. 1991;324:109–112.
24. Best MG, Stout J, Yu VL, et al. *Tatlockia micdadei* growth kinetics may explain its infrequent isolation from water and the low prevalence of Pittsburgh pneumonia. Appl Environ Microbiol. 1985;49:1521–1522.
25. Wadowsky RM, Wilson TM, Kapp NJ, et al. Multiselection of *Legionella* spp in tap water containing *Hartmanella oerniformis*. Appl Environ Microbiol. 1991;57:1950–1955.
26. Fields BS, Barbaree JM, Sanden GN, Morrill WE. Virulence of *Legionella anisa* strain associated with Pontiac fever: An evaluation using protozoan, cell culture, and guinea pig models. Infect Immun. 1990;58:3139–3142.
27. Reingold A, Thompson B, Brake B, et al. *Legionella* pneumonia in the US: The distribution of serogroups and species causing human illness. J Infect Dis. 1984;149:819–824.
28. Camerson S, Walker C, Roden D, Feldheim J. Epidemiological characteristics of *Legionella* infection in South Australia: Implications for disease control. Aust N Z Med. 1991;21:65–70.
29. Muder RR, Yu VL, Zuravleff JJ. Pneumonia due to the Pittsburgh pneumonia agent: New clinical perspective with a review of the literature. Medicine. 1983;62:120–128.
30. Singh N, Muder RR, Yu VL, Gayowski T. *Legionella* infection in liver transplant recipients: Implications for management. Transplantation. 1993;56:1549–1551.
31. Harrington RD, Woolfrey AE, Bowden R, et al. Legionellosis in a bone marrow transplant center. Clin Infect Dis. 1996;18:361–368.
32. Ernst A, Gordon FD, Hayek J, et al. Lung abscess complication: *Legionella micdadei* pneumonia in an adult liver transplant recipient. Transplantation. 1998;65:130–133.
33. Chow J, Yu VL. *Legionella*: A major opportunistic pathogen in transplant recipients. Semin Respir Infect. 1998;13:132–139.
34. Lang R, Miller I, Manon J, et al. *Legionella longbeachae* in a splenectomized hairy-cell leukemia patient. Infection. 1990;18:31–32.
35. Fang GD, Stout JE, Yu VL, et al. Community-acquired pneumonia caused by *Legionella dumoffii* in a patient with hairy cell leukemia. Infection. 1990;18:383–385.
36. Harris A, Lally M, Albrecht M. *Legionella bozemanii* pneumonia in three patients with AIDS. Clin Infect Dis. 1998;27:97–99.
37. Lo Presti F, Riffard S, Neyret C, et al. First isolation in Europe of *Legionella feeleii* from two cases of pneumonia. Eur J Clin Microbiol Infect Dis. 1998;17:64–66.
38. Johnson KM, Huseby JS. Lung abscess caused by *Legionella micdadei* (see Comments). Chest. 1997;111:252–253.
39. Rudin JE, Wing EJ. A comparative study of *Legionella micdadei* and other nosocomial acquired pneumonia. Chest. 1984;86:875–880.
40. Doebbeling BN, Ishak MA, Wade BH, et al. Nosocomial *Legionella micdadei* pneumonia: 10 years experience and a case-control study. J Hosp Infect. 1989;13:289–298.
41. Brooks RG, Hofflin JM, Jamieson SW, et al. Infectious complications in heart-lung transplant recipients. Am J Med. 1985;79:412–422.
42. Joly JR, Diery P, Gauvrau L, et al. Legionnaires' disease caused by *Legionella dumoffi* in distilled water. Can Med Assoc J. 1986;135:1273–1277.
43. Tompkins LS, Roessler BJ, Redd SC, et al. *Legionella* prosthetic-valve endocarditis. N Engl J Med. 1988;318:530–535.
44. Loeb M, Simor AE, Mandell L, et al. Two nursing home outbreaks of respiratory infections with *Legionella sainthelensi*. J Am Geriatric Soc. 1999;47:547–552.
45. McNally C, Plouffe J. *Legionella bozemanii*—an important etiological agent in community-acquired pneumonia. Abstract 519. Program and Abstracts of the 36th Annual Meeting of the Infectious Diseases Society of America, Denver, Colo, 1998.
46. Steele TW, Moore CY, Sangster N. Distribution of *Legionella longbeachae* serogroup 1 and other legionellae in potting soil in Australia. Appl Environ Microbiol. 1990;56:2984–2988.
47. Lanser JA, Adams M, Doyle R, et al. Genetic relatedness of *Legionella longbeachae* isolates from human and environmental sources in Australia. Appl Environ Microbiol. 1990;56:2784–2790.
48. Herwaldt LA, Gorman GW, McGrath T, et al. A new legionella species: *Legionella feeleii* species nova, causes Pontiac fever in an automobile plant. Ann Intern Med. 1984;100:333–338.
49. Goldberg DJ, Wrench JG, Collier PW, et al. Lochgoilhead fever: Outbreak of non-pneumonic legionellosis due to *Legionella micdadei*. Lancet 1989;1:316–318.
50. Fenstersheib M, Miller M, Diggins C, et al. Outbreak of Pontiac fever due to *Legionella anisa*. Lancet. 1990;336:35–37.
51. Luttichau HR, Vinther C, Uldum A, et al. An outbreak of Pontiac fever among children following use of a whirlpool. Clin Infect Dis. 1998;26:1374–1378.
52. Muder RR, Yu VL, Vickers R, Rihs J, et al. Simultaneous infection with *Legionella pneumophila* and Pittsburgh pneumonia agent—clinical features and epidemiological implications. Am J Med. 1983;74:609–614.
53. Tompkins LS, Trout N, Wood ST, et al. Molecular epidemiology of *Legionella* species by restriction endonuclease and alloenzyme analysis. J Clin Microbiol. 1987;25:1875–1880.
54. Cordes LG, Gorman GW, Wilkinson HW, et al. Atypical *Legionella*-like organisms: Fastidious water-associated bacteria pathogenic for man. Lancet. 1979;2:927–930.
55. Thompson BM, Harris PP, Hicklin MD, Blackman JA, et al. A *Legionella*-like bacterium related to WIGA in a fatal case of pneumonia. Ann Intern Med. 1979;91:673–676.
56. Donegan EA, Deal MM, Melanephy MC, et al. Primary isolation of a new strain of the TATLOCK/Pittsburgh pneumonia agent *(Legionella micdadei)*. West J Med. 1981;134:384–389.
57. Ellis AR, Mayers DL, Martone WJ, Mitchell FL, et al. Rapid expanding pulmonary nodule caused by Pittsburgh pneumonia agent. JAMA. 1981;245:1558–1559.
58. Wilkinson HW, Thacker LW, Benson RF, et al. *Legionella birminghamensis* sp nov isolated from a cardiac transplant recipient. J Clin Microbiol. 1987;25:2120–2122.
59. Ampel NM, Ruben FL, Norden CW. Cutaneous abscess caused by *Legionella micdadei* in an immunosuppressed patient. Ann Intern Med. 1985;102:630–632.
60. Kilborn JA, Manz LA, O'Brien M, et al. Necrotizing cellulitis caused by *Legionella micdadei*. Am J Med. 1992;92:104–106.
61. Fang GD, Yu VL, Vickers RM. Infections caused by the Pittsburgh pneumonia agent. Semin Respir Infect. 1987;2:262–266.
62. Muder RR, Yu VL, Parry M. Radiology of *Legionella* pneumonia. Semin Respir Infect. 1987;2:242–254.
63. Muder RR, Reddy S, Yu VL, Rihs JD, et al. Pneumonia caused by Pittsburgh pneumonia agent: Radiologic manifestations. Radiology. 1984;150:633–637.
64. Pope TL, Armstrong P, Thompson R, et al. Pittsburgh pneumonia agent: Chest film manifestations. Am J Roentgenol. 1982;138:237–241.
65. Vickers RM, Stout JE, Yu VL, Rihs JD. Culture methodology for the isolation of *Legionella pneumophila* and other Legionellaceae from clinical and environmental specimens. Semin Respir Infect. 1987;2:274–279.

66. Lee TC, Vickers RM, Yu VL, Wagener MM. Growth of 28 *Legionella* species on selective culture media: A comparative study. J Clin Microbiol. 1993;31:2761–2768.
67. Vickers RM, Brown A, Garrity GM. Dye-containing buffered charcoal yeast extract medium for the differentiation of members of the family Legionellaceae. J Clin Microbiol. 1981;13:380–382.
68. Finkelstein R, Brown P, Palutke WA, et al. Diagnostic efficacy of a DNA probe in pneumonia caused by *Legionella* species. J Med Microbiol. 1993;38:183–186.
69. Jaulhac B, Reinthaler FF, Pschaid A, et al. Detection of *Legionella* species in bronchoalveolar lavage fluids by DNA amplification. J Clin Microbiol. 1992;30:920–924.
70. Pasculle AW, Dowling JW, Weyent RS, et al. Susceptibility of Pittsburgh pneumonia agent *(Legionella micdadei)* and other newly recognized members of the genus *Legionella* to nineteen antimicrobial agents. Antimicrob Agents Chemother. 1981;20:793–799.
71. Saito A, Koga H, Shigeno H, et al. The antimicrobial activity of ciprofloxacin against *Legionella* species and the treatment of experimental legionella pneumonia in guinea pigs. J Antimicrob Chemother. 1986;18:251–260.
72. Wing EJ, Schafer FJ, Pasculle AW. Successful treatment of *Legionella micdadei* (Pittsburgh pneumonia agent) pneumonia with erythromycin. Am J Med. 1981;21:836–839.
73. Taylor TH, Albrecht MA. *Legionella bozemanii* cavitary pneumonia poorly responsive to erythromycin: Case report and review. Clin Infect Dis. 1995;20:329–334.
74. Koch CA, Robyn JA, Coccia MR. Systemic lupus erythematosis: A risk factor for pneumonia caused by *Legionella micdadei*? Arch Intern Med. 1997;157:2670–2671.
75. Rudin JE, Evans TL, Wing EJ. Failure of erythromycin in treatment of *Legionella micdadei* pneumonia. Am J Med. 1984;76:318–320.
76. Stout JE, Arnold B, Yu VL. Activity of azithromycin, clarithromycin, roxithromycin, dirithromycin, quinupristin/dalfopristin, and erythromycin against *Legionella* species by intracellular susceptibility testing in HL-60 cells. J Antimicrob Chemother. 1999;41:289–291.
77. Vergis EN, Yu VL. *Legionella* species. In: Yu VL, Merigan TC, Barriere SL, et al, eds. Antimicrobial Therapy and Vaccines. 1st ed. Baltimore, Md: Williams & Wilkins; 1998;257–272.
78. Stout JE, Arnold B, Yu VL. Comparative activity of ciprofloxacin, ofloxacin, levofloxacin, and erythromycin against *Legionella* species by broth microdilution and intracellular susceptibility testing in HL-60 cells. Diagn Microbiol Infect Dis. 1998;30:37–43.
79. Stout JE, Yu VL. Current concepts: Legionellosis. N Engl J Med. 1997;337:682–687.
80. Pasculle A, Myerowitz R, Rinaldo C. New bacterial agent of pneumonia isolated from renal transplant recipients. Lancet. 1979;2:58–61.
81. Hebert GA, Steigerwalt AG, Brenner DJ. *Legionella micdadei* species nova: Classification of a third species of *Legionella* associated with human pneumonia. Curr Microbiol. 1980;3:257.
82. Lewallen KS, McKinney RM, Brenner DJ, et al. A newly identified bacterium phenotypically resembling, not genetically distinct from, *Legionella pneumophila*: An isolate in a case of pneumonia. Ann Intern Med. 1979;91:831–834.
83. McKinney RM, Porschen RK, Edelstein PH, et al. *Legionella longbeachae* species nova, another etiologic agent of human pneumonia. Ann Intern Med. 1981;94:739–743.
84. Edelstein PH, Brenner DJ, Moss CW, et al. *Legionella wadsworthii* species nova: A cause of human pneumonia. Ann Intern Med. 1982;97:809–813.
85. Wilkinson HW, Thacker WL, Steigerwalt AG, et al. Second serogroup of *Legionella hackeliae* isolated from a patient with pneumonia. J Clin Microbiol. 1985;22:488–489.
86. Wilkinson HW, Thacker WL, Brenner DJ, Ryan KH. Fatal *Legionella maceachernii* pneumonia. J Clin Microbiol. 1985;22:1055.
87. Tang PW, Toma S, MacMillan LG. *Legionella oakridgenesis*: Laboratory diagnosis of a human infection. J Clin Microbiol. 1985;21:462–463.
88. Thacker WL, Wilkinson HW, Benson RF. Second serogroup of *Legionella feeleii* strains isolated from humans. J Clin Microbiol. 1988;22:1–4.
89. Thacker WL, Benson RF, Staneck JL, et al. *Legionella cincinnatiensis* sp nov isolated from a patient with pneumonia. J Clin Microbiol. 1988;26:418–420.
90. Thacker WL, Wilkinson HW, Benson RF, et al. *Legionella jordanis* isolated from a patient with fatal pneumonia. J Clin Microbiol. 1988;28:1400–1401.
91. Griffith ME, Lindsay DS, Benson RF, et al. First isolation of *Legionella gormanii* from a patient with fatal pneumonia. J Clin Microbiol. 1988;26:380–381.
92. Bornstein N, Mercatello A, Marmet D, et al. Pleural infection caused by *Legionella anisa*. J Clin Microbiol. 1989;27:2100–2101.
93. Thacker WL, Benson RF, Staneck JL, et al. *Legionella tucsonenis* sp nov isolated from a renal transplant recipient. J Clin Microbiol. 1989;27:1831–1834.
94. Benson RF, Thacker WL, Fang FC, et al. *Legionella sainthelensi* serogroup 2 isolated from patients with pneumonia. Res Microbiol. 1990;141:453–463.
95. Thacker WL, Dyke JW, Benson RF, et al. *Legionella lansingensis* sp nov isolated from a patient with pneumonia and underlying chronic lymphocytic leukemia. J Clin Microbiol. 1992;30:2398–2401.
96. Lo Presti F, Riffard S, Vandenesch F, et al. The first clinical isolate of *Legionella parisiensis*. J Clin Microbiol. 1997;35:1706–1709.

Chapter 223

Capnocytophaga

VEE J. GILL

Capnocytophaga is a genus in the family Flavobacteriaceae, within the *Flavobacterium-Cytophaga* ribosomal RNA homology group.[1] These organisms are thin gram-negative bacilli with tapered ends and can be grouped into (1) those species found primarily in the human oral cavity—*C. ochracea, C. gingivalis, C. sputigena, C. haemolytica, C. granulosa*—and (2) those species found in the canine oral cavity, or rarely that of other animals, and associated primarily with dog-bite infections—*C. canimorsus* and *C. cynodegmi. Capnocytophaga* spp. of either human or canine origin cause significant infections in normal as well as in immunocompromised hosts.

TAXONOMY

Capnocytophaga ("eater in carbon dioxide") spp. isolated from the human oral cavity were originally described by Prevot in 1956. The current *Bergey's Manual* describes three species: *C. ochracea, C. gingivalis,* and *C. sputigena.*[2] Older nomenclature for these *Capnocytophaga* spp. has included *Fusobacterium nucleatum* var. *ochraceus* (Prevot), *Ristella ochracea* (Seball), *Bacteroides oralis* var. *elongatus* (Loesche), *Bacteroides ochraceus* (Holdeman and Moore), and Centers for Disease Control and Prevention (CDC) group DF1 (dysgonic fermenter).[2–4] The work of Newman and associates[3] and of Williams and coworkers[4] demonstrated that *B. ochraceus* and CDC group DF1 should be considered synonymous with human oral *Capnocytophaga* spp. Most of the strains examined by Williams and coworkers showed highest DNA homology with *C. ochracea,* although one strain showed homology with *C. gingivalis.* Two new species, *C. haemolytica* and *C. granulosa* have been isolated from supragingival dental plaque of adults but have not yet been significant in human infections.[5]

A previously undescribed gram-negative rod was first isolated in 1976 from blood and spinal fluid of a patient after a dog bite.[6] This organism and similar isolates were later designated by the CDC as group DF2 and were often referred to as the "dog-bite" organism, since most of the isolates were associated with infections following dog bites or exposure to dogs. In 1989, Brenner and colleagues proposed the name *Capnocytophaga canimorsus* (Latin for "dog bite") for this group of organisms.[7] Their investigation also revealed a second group of nine similar organisms, designated as DF2-like, that were biochemically different from DF2 and had been isolated either from dogs or from localized infections following a dog bite. For this latter group of organisms, they proposed the name *Capnocytophaga cynodegmi* (Greek for "dog bite").

MICROBIOLOGIC CHARACTERISTICS

Capnocytophaga organisms are long, thin, gram-negative rods that are typically fusiform. They may be straight or slightly curved, but when stained from older cultures, they show pleomorphism in both size and shape. The optimal temperature for growth is 35°C to 37°C, and blood or chocolate agars generally support growth of these organisms. *Capnocytophaga* organisms are facultatively anaerobic bacteria, but for optimal growth either aerobically or anaerobically, an atmosphere enriched with 5 to 10% CO_2 is required, particularly for initial isolation. When colonies reach sufficient size, generally in 2 to 4 days, they usually show a yellow pigmentation, although both tan and pink colonies have also been described. Colonies are flat, with a shiny but mottled spreading edge that often shows finger-like projections that are due to the gliding motility that is characteristic of the genus. Despite the possession of gliding motility, *Capnocytophaga* flagella are difficult to demonstrate, and traditional motility tests may be negative. Colonies of most species are nonhemolytic, with the exception of *C. cynodegmi,* which may produce β-like hemolysis in rabbit blood agar, and *C. haemolytica* in sheep blood agar. Both the spreading edge and the colony's color are medium-dependent, and thus the appearance of the colony may vary on different media. Additional characteristics that are uniform for the genus include no growth on MacConkey's agar and a lack of indole production.

Although the morphology of the colonies, the morphology on Gram stains, and the optimal growth conditions are similar for both the human oral species and the canine species of *Capnocytophaga, C. canimorsus* is more fastidious than the other species. For example, difficulties have been encountered in subculturing this organism out of blood culture bottles, even when many organisms were seen on smear. Growth of *C. canimorsus* requires enriched agar, such as heart infusion agar with rabbit or sheep blood; in addition, blood culture subcultures should be incubated for at least 5 to 7 days in 5 to 10% CO_2 to obtain visible colonies.

Capnocytophaga spp. can initially be distinguished from other fastidious gram-negative bacilli by their microscopic appearance. The long, delicate, fusiform appearance of *Capnocytophaga* spp. is distinctive and differs from the coccobacillary appearance of *Moraxella, Kingella, Haemophilus,* and *Actinobacillus* spp. and from the straight, narrow, rod forms of *Eikenella* spp. When stained from a blood culture bottle, the fusiform appearance of *Capnocytophaga* spp. may be mistaken for that of the strict anaerobe *F. nucleatum.* Distinguishing between the two is aided by determining whether the organism is a strict anaerobe or microaerophilic. In addition, all *Capnocytophaga* spp. are indole-negative whereas *F. nucleatum* is indole-positive.

Identification of the individual species of *Capnocytophaga* is difficult for most clinical laboratories, because the species are not reliably identified by commercial identification panels, and phenotypic characteristics are not thought to be sufficient for accurate identification of species. The five human oral species are oxidase- and catalase-negative organisms and can therefore be readily differentiated from *C. canimorsus* and *C. cynodegmi,* both of which are oxidase- and catalase-positive. To accurately identify human oral strains requires more than conventional biochemical reactions, and a reference laboratory should be used if the species identification is desired. *Capnocytophaga canimorsus* can be distinguished from *C. cynodegmi* by determining acid production from inulin, melibiose, raffinose, and sucrose, since *C. cynodegmi* is positive for these tests and *C. canimorsus* negative. However, poor growth of the organism may result in false-negative reactions. For reliable carbohydrate testing, supplementation with rabbit serum or rapid fermentation methodology using heavy inocula, or both, is required.[8]

CAPNOCYTOPHAGA OCHRACEA, CAPNOCYTOPHAGA SPUTIGENA, AND *CAPNOCYTOPHAGA GINGIVALIS*: DISEASES AND TREATMENT

Captocytophaga ochracea, C. sputigena, and *C. gingivalis* colonize the subgingival sulcus and other areas within the oral cavity of healthy adults and are thought to play a role in the pathogenesis of localized juvenile periodontitis as well as other forms of periodontal disease.[9] They possess a wide variety of enzymes, including aminopeptidases, acid and alkaline phosphatases, immunoglobulin A (IgA) protease, and trypsin-like enzymes, which may aid in invading periodontal tissues.[2, 10] In addition, extracts and sonicates of *Capnocytophaga* spp. have been shown to inhibit motility and to induce morphologic abnormalities in neutrophils. Resistance to serum bactericidal activity has also been described.[11] The oral cavity is the most common site of origin of disease,[11, 12] although these organisms have also been isolated from the female genital tract and have been associated with intrauterine infections, amnionitis, and neonatal infections in premature infants. Isolates have been obtained from a wide variety of clinical sources, including blood; spinal fluid; nose, throat, sputum, tracheal, and bronchial specimens; pleural fluid; wounds; abscesses; bone; ocular infections; amniotic fluid; and vaginal cultures. Most reports of infections caused by the human oral strains of *Capnocytophaga* do not specify the particular species involved. The few isolates identified to the species level, however, have been called *C. ochracea.*[13, 14]

Sepsis is the most common presentation in immunocompromised patients, particularly in the setting of granulocytopenia and oral mucositis or ulceration.[12, 15] Parenti and Snydman found that of 15 immunocompromised patients infected with *Capnocytophaga* spp., including both children and adults, all had bacteremia.[12] In a review of *Capnocytophaga* sepsis in immunocompromised patients, most patients had either acute myelogenous leukemia or acute lymphocytic leukemia as their underlying illness, followed by solid tumors and a variety of other diseases such as multiple myeloma, systemic lupus erythematosis, and acute myelofibrosis.[11] In a review of patients younger than 18 years and excluding those with solely periodontal infections, Campbell and Edwards found that of 16 immunocompromised children with *Capnocytophaga* spp. infections, all had bacteremia.[13] The majority of these children had either acute lymphocytic leukemia or acute myelogenous leukemia.

In contrast, nonimmunocompromised patients tend to present less frequently with sepsis but instead with a variety of other infections. The role of these *Capnocytophaga* spp. in periodontal infections such as juvenile periodontitis has already been mentioned, but in addition, reported infections include bacteremia, endocarditis, keratitis, conjunctivitis, corneal ulcer, pericardial abscess, mediastinitis, lung and subphrenic abscess, empyema, septic arthritis, cervical and inguinal lymphadenitis, sinusitis, thyroiditis, osteomyelitis, peritonitis, abdominal abscess, wound infection, and peripartum infection. Many infections are polymicrobic, with other oral bacteria isolated concomitantly. In nonimmunocompromised children, as in adults, sepsis is uncommon, but these *Capnocytophaga* spp. have been isolated from kidney, cervical node, conjunctiva, thyroid abscess, bone, joint aspirate, tracheal aspirate, and pleural fluid. The reported infections are diverse, and frequently without known predisposing factors. Three premature neonates with early-onset sepsis have also been described.[13]

In vitro susceptibility testing of these *Capnocytophaga* spp. is hampered by the slow growth and fastidious nature of the organisms. Since the organisms need enriched media to grow, most will not grow in unsupplemented susceptibility test media. As a result of the length of time required to initially grow the organism and then to perform the susceptibility test, antibiotic therapy is most often empirically started before the receipt of in vitro results.

Capnocytophaga ochracea, C. sputigena, and *C. gingivalis* are generally sensitive to clindamycin, erythromycin, tetracycline, chloramphenicol, quinolones, and imipenem, whereas susceptibilities are variable for penicillin, expanded-spectrum cephalosporins, aztreonam, vancomycin, metronidazole, and polymyxin B. These species are usually resistant to trimethoprim and aminoglycosides.[16, 17] Resistance to β-lactam antibiotics, which is due to the production of β-lactamase, has been reported to occur in these organisms. In 1986, Rummens and colleagues showed that 3 of 118 (2.5%) strains produced β-lactamase,[16] whereas in 1992, Roscoe and associates found 6 of 19 (32%) of their strains to be positive using a chromogenic cephalosporin technique.[18] These results suggest that β-lactamase production may be increasing in these species, making penicillin unsuitable as the first-line antibiotic. The use of clindamycin has been suggested as an alternative, since the β-lactamase–producing strains remain susceptible to this agent. Another reasonable choice would be amoxicillin-clavulanate. In a case of bacteremia caused by a β-lactamase–producing strain of *C. ochracea,* the isolate was resistant to ampicillin, carbenicillin, piperacillin, all cephalosporins, aztreonam, gentamicin, tobramycin, colistin, vancomycin, norfloxacin, ciprofloxacin, and trimethoprim-sulfamethoxazole but was susceptible to amoxicillin-clavulanate, rifampin, imipenem, tetracycline, chloramphenicol, erythromycin, and clindamycin. The patient had been empirically started on ceftazidime, piperacillin, and amikacin and remained febrile until the institution of clindamycin.[19] An additional case report of ciprofloxacin resistance in an isolate of *C. sputigena* should add caution to the use of fluoroquinolones for this group of organisms.[20]

Infection with human oral strains of *Capnocytophaga* should be considered in the evaluation of leukemic patients with fever and neutropenia, especially if oral mucositis or ulceration is present. Difficulty in growing these fastidious organisms may delay laboratory isolation and identification. Prognosis is generally good for patients who are appropriately treated, although mortality is higher in immunocompromised patients.

CAPNOCYTOPHAGA CANIMORSUS AND *CAPTOCYTOPHAGA CYNODEGMI*: DISEASES AND TREATMENT

Both *C. canimorsus* and *C. cynodegmi* compose part of the normal oral flora of canines, although occasional infections associated with exposure to other animals (cats and rabbits) have also been described. Among isolates submitted to the CDC for identification, *C. canimorsus* has occurred much more commonly and has caused more serious infections than *C. cynodegmi.* Of the 150 strains of *C. canimorsus* reviewed by the CDC, 88% were from blood, 5% from spinal fluid, 2% from wounds, and 2% from dog mouths, whereas in contrast, the eight *C. cynodegmi* strains were isolated from either dog mouths or localized wound infections caused by dog bites.[7]

Clinical data on 72 *C. canimorsus* strains submitted to the CDC for identification showed that infections occurred predominantly in men (74%), most frequently those in the 50- to 70-year age group. Forty-three percent of the patients had been either bitten or scratched by dogs (or by cats in 2 cases), whereas 10 patients (12%) had reported only exposure to dogs.[7] In a review of 60 cases of *C. canimorsus* sepsis by Kullberg and coworkers, 47% reported a history of dog bite, whereas 27% reported exposure to dogs, without bites or scratches.[15] Thirty-three percent of these patients were asplenic, 22% had a history of alcoholic abuse, and 5% were receiving corticosteroid therapy. Twenty-three patients (38%) had no known underlying condition that might have predisposed them to infection. The interval between bite and hospital admission ranged from 1 to 30 days, with an average of 5.5 days. The case-fatality rate was 28%, including the deaths of 12 of 40 patients who had intact spleens. These characteristics of *C. canimorsus* infection have been substantiated by an additional review of 39 cases of septicemia in Denmark, spanning the years 1982 through 1995.[21]

Capnocytophaga canimorsus can cause a wide spectrum of disease, ranging from mild to fulminant. A more rapid and severe progression occurs particularly in asplenic individuals, alcoholic persons, and patients on corticosteroids. In splenectomized patients, the infection is characterized by shock, disseminated purpuric lesions, and disseminated intravascular coagulation. In addition, renal failure, gangrene of the bite site, and pulmonary infiltrates may occur. In one review, 35% of patients presented with disseminated purpuric lesions and 38% had disseminated intravascular coagulation, often with hypotension and renal insufficiency. Blood cultures became positive after incubation from 1 to 14 days, with a mean of 6 days. In 10 cases, the organism was seen in Gram stains of buffy coats, and of these, 8 were in asplenic patients.[15] Fulminant infection may occur even in healthy people, although these patients generally have a milder course. Cases of meningitis, endocarditis, pneumonia, cellulitis, corneal ulcer, and septic arthritis have been reported.[22] The possibility of *C. canimorsus* infection should be considered early in all infections following a dog bite, but particularly in asplenic patients, in whom the clinical course may be fulminant and the outcome fatal.

Penicillin or amoxicillin/clavulanate recommended when infection with *C. canimorsus* is suspected and can be used for prophylaxis of asplenic patients after a dog bite. Therapy should be initiated promptly, since isolation, identification, and in vitro susceptibility testing of *C. canimorsus* will not be available for days after the cultures are taken, if at all. In vitro susceptibility testing of both these species is difficult to do reliably by any standardized procedure, since there is often slow or insufficient growth. The use of the E test for testing of fastidious organisms may prove to be a method suitable for *Capnocytophaga,* but studies are needed to validate E-test results with dilution procedures for these organisms. In the published studies using either broth or agar dilution techniques, *C. canimorsus* is reported to be susceptible to penicillins, imipenem, erythromycin, vancomycin, clindamycin, third-generation cephalosporins, chloramphenicol, rifampin, doxycycline, and quinolones, but resistant to aztreonam.[17, 23] There is disagreement on results for trimethoprim-sulfamethoxazole and aminoglycosides. Results for aminoglycosides may depend on the method used, with disk diffusion and agar dilution testing more likely to show resistance, and broth dilution to show susceptibility.

REFERENCES

1. Vandamme P, Vancanneyt M, Van Belkum A, et al. Polyphasic analysis of strains of the genus *Capnocytophaga* and Centers for Disease Control group DF-3. Int J System Bacteriol. 1996;46:782–791.
2. Holt SC, Kinder SA. *Capnocytophaga.* In: Staley JT, Bryant MP, Pfenning N, Holt JG, eds. Bergey's Manual of Systematic Bacteriology, v. 3. Baltimore: Williams & Wilkins; 1989:2050–2058.
3. Newman MG, Sutter VL, Pickett MJ, et al. Detection, identification and comparison of *Capnocytophaga, Bacteroides ochraceus,* and DF1. J Clin Microbiol. 1979;10:557–562.
4. Williams BL, Hollis D, Holdeman LV. Synonomy of strains of Centers for Disease Control group DF1 with species of *Capnocytophaga.* J Clin Microbiol. 1979;10:550–556.
5. Yamamoto T, Kajiura S, Hirai Y, Watanabe T. *Capnocytophaga haemolytica* sp nov and *Capnocytophaga granulosa* sp nov, from human dental plaque. Int J Sytem Bacteriol. 1994;44:324–329.
6. Bobo RA, Newton SJ. A previously undescribed gram-negative bacillus causing septicemia and meningitis. Am J Clin Pathol. 1976;65:564–569.
7. Brenner DJ, Hollis DG, Fanning R, et al. *Capnocytophaga canimorsus* sp nov (formerly CDC group DF2), a cause of septicemia following dog bite, and *C. cynodegmi* sp nov, a cause of localized wound infection following dog bite. J Clin Microbiol. 1989;27:231–235.
8. Holmes B, Pickett MJ, Hollis DG. Unusual gram-negative bacteria, including *Capnocytophaga, Eikenella, Bacteroides,* and *Streptobacillus.* In: Murray, ed. Manual of Clinical Microbiology. 6th ed. Washington, DC: American Society for Microbiology; 1995:499–508.
9. Newman MG, Socransky SS, Savitt ED, et al. Studies of the microbiology of periodontosis. J Periodontol. 1976;47:373–379.
10. Soderling E, Makinen PL, Syed S, et al. Biochemical comparison of proteolytic enzymes present in rough and smooth-surfaced *Capnocytophagas* isolated from the subgingival plaque of periodontitis patients. J Periodontol Res. 1991;26:17–23.
11. Bilgrami S, Bergstrom SK, Peterson DE, et al. *Capnocytophaga* bacteremia in a patient with Hodgkin's disease following bone marrow transplantation: Case report and review. Clin Infect Dis. 1992;14:1045–1049.
12. Parenti DM, Snydman DR. *Capnocytophaga* species: Infections in nonimmunocompromised and immunocompromised hosts. J Infect Dis. 1985;151:140–147.
13. Campbell JR, Edwards MS. *Capnocytophaga* species infections in children. Pediatr Infect Dis J. 1991;10:944–948.
14. Schlaes DM, Dul MJ, Lerner PI. *Capnocytophaga* bacteremia in the compromised host. Am J Clin Pathol. 1982;77:359–361.
15. Kullberg JB, Westendorp RGJ, van't Wout JW, et al. Purpura fulminans and symmetrical peripheral gangrene caused by *Capnocytophaga canimorsus* (formerly DF2) septicemia—a complication of dog bite. Medicine. 1991;70:287–292.
16. Rummens JL, Gordts B, van Landuyt HW. In vitro susceptibility of *Capnocytophaga* species to 29 antimicrobial agents. Antimicrob Agents Chemother. 1986;30:739–742.
17. Bremmelgaard A, Pers C, Kristiansen JE, et al. Susceptibility testing of Danish isolates of *Capnocytophaga* and CDC group DF2 bacteria. Acta Pathol Microbiol Immunol Scand. 1989;97:43–48.
18. Roscoe DL, Zemcov SJV, Thornber D, et al. Antimicrobial susceptibilities and β-lactamase characterization of *Capnocytophaga* species. Antimicrob Agents Chemother. 1992;36:2197–2200.
19. Baquero F, Fernandez J, Dronda F, et al. Capnophilic and anaerobic bacteremia in neutropenic patients: An oral source. Rev Infect Dis. 1990;12:S157–S160.
20. Gomez-Garces JL, Alos JI, Sanchez J, Cogollos R. Bacteremia by multidrug-resistant *Capnocytophaga sputigena.* J Clin Microbiol. 1994;32:167–169.

21. Pers C, Gahrn-Hansen B, Frederiksen W. *Capnocytophaga canimorsus* septicemia in Denmark, 1982–1995: Review of 39 cases. Clin Infect Dis. 1996;23:71–75.
22. Vanhonsebrouck AY, Gordts B, Wauters G, et al. Fatal septicemia with *Capnocytophaga* in a compromised host. A case report with review of the literature. Acta Clin Belg. 1991;46:364–370.
23. Verghese A, Hamati F, Berk S, et al. Susceptibility of dysgonic fermenter 2 to antimicrobial agents in vitro. Antimicrob Agents Chemother. 1988;32:78–80.

Chapter 224

Bartonella Species, Including Cat-Scratch Disease

LEONARD N. SLATER
DAVID F. WELCH

BACKGROUND AND CLASSIFICATION

Members of the α_2-subgroup of the Proteobacteria, *Bartonella* spp., are closely related to the genera *Brucella* and *Agrobacterium* on the basis of 16-S ribosomal RNA similarity; members of the family Rickettsiaceae are more distantly related. On the basis of genetic similarity,[1, 2] unification of the genera *Bartonella* and *Rochalimaea* as a single genus and the removal of the family Bartonellaceae from the order Rickettsiales was put forth in 1993[2] and was subsequently accepted.

The genus *Bartonella,* synonymous with *Bartonia*, was described in 1913, and referred to the erythrocyte-adherent organisms originally described by Dr. A. L. Barton in 1909.[3, 4] The type species (and sole member of the genus until 1993) is *Bartonella bacilliformis.* Limited to the Andes mountain regions of South America, *B. bacilliformis* infection had received little attention outside its endemic zone until related bacteria, originally classified in the genus *Rochalimaea*, were found to be pathogens in acquired immunodeficiency syndrome and then in other circumstances.

The former genus *Rochalimaea*, previously grouped with *Bartonella* in the order Rickettsiales, had long contained only two member species, *Rochalimaea vinsonii*, the "Canadian vole agent," and *Rochalimaea quintana* (other synonyms: *Rickettsia quintana*, *Rickettsia pediculi*, *Rickettsia wolhynica*, *Rickettsia weigl*, *Burnetia [Rochalimae] wolhynica*, *Wolhynia quintanae*[5, 6]), the agent of trench fever, a debilitating but self-limited human illness so-named after it affected many military personnel in World War I.[7] Except for sporadic outbreaks, trench fever has all but disappeared from the clinical scene in recent decades. However, *R. quintana* reemerged in the 1990s as a pathogen of considerable interest[8–12] coincident with the discovery of two related species pathogenic to humans, originally named *Rochalimaea henselae* and *Rochalimaea elizabethae*.[13–16]

In 1995, a further merger of a number of species of the genus *Grahamella*, which are intraerythrocytic pathogens of rodents, birds, fish, and other animals, into the genus *Bartonella* took place.[17] An additional species, *Bartonella clarridgeiae*, has been identified, predominantly in cats, sometimes causing coinfection with *Bartonella henselae*,[18–21] and a newly recognized subspecies of *Bartonella vinsonii* has been isolated from dogs, mice, and humans.[22–23b]

A list of presently validated members of the genus *Bartonella,* including the species formerly in the genus *Grahamella* (and not known to be human pathogens), is shown in Table 224–1. New species likely will continue to be added, as exemplified by a report of recovery from various rodent species of isolates phylogenetically distinct from each other and from known species of *Bartonella*[24] and a report characterizing an isolate from the blood of mice, coinfected with *Babesia* or *Borrelia*, that resembles *Bartonella grahamii* and *B. vinsonii* and has been named *B. vinsonii* subspecies *arupensis.*[23a,b] Isolation of more *Bartonella* spp. from additional types of mammals (muskrats and deer as well as voles and mice) has been reported.[25]

EPIDEMIOLOGY OF HUMAN-PATHOGENIC SPECIES

Presumably due to the limited distribution of its sand fly vectors (genus *Lutzomyia* [formerly *Phlebotomus*]), natural transmission of *B. bacilliformis* infections occurs only at altitudes of 1 to 3 km in the Andes Mountains. Even in the modern antibiotic era, focal outbreaks continue. *Bartonella quintana* is globally distributed. Outbreaks of trench fever (also known as Volhynia fever, Meuse fever, His-Werner disease, shinbone fever, shank fever, and quintan or 5-day fever) have been focal and widely separated, often associated with conditions of poor sanitation and personal hygiene that may predispose to exposure to *Pediculus humanus*, the human body louse, *B. quintana*'s only identified vector. No nonhuman vertebrate reservoirs have been identified for *B. bacilliformis* or *B. quintana*.

Bartonella henselae is globally endemic; serologic studies indicate that infection of domestic cats is worldwide, with the prevalence of antibodies being higher in warm, humid climates. Free-ranging and captive wild felids in California also have a substantial prevalence of antibodies reactive with *B. henselae*,[26] although infection with other *Bartonella* spp. could result in cross-reactive antibodies. Rates of bacteremia in cats can vary, even between geographically close locales,[27–30] but generally tend to be higher among feral animals in any particular locale. *Bartonella henselae* bacteremia has been documented in healthy domestic cats that have been specifically associated with bacillary angiomatosis (BA)[27] or typical cat-scratch disease (CSD)[29, 31] in their human contacts.

Transmission of *B. henselae* to humans has been linked to cats by serologic and epidemiologic studies,[32–35] its culture recovery from the lymphadenitis of CSD,[29, 36] and its identification by polymerase chain reaction (PCR)-based DNA identification in further cases of CSD lymphadenitis[37–39] and conjunctival disease,[40] as well as in CSD skin test antigen.[41, 42]

The major arthropod vector of *B. henselae* is the cat flea, *Cteno-*

TABLE 224–1 Species of the Genus *Bartonella*

Names		
Validly Named Species		**Basonym**
Bartonella bacilliformis	Type species	
Bartonella doshiae	New species	
Bartonella elizabethae	New combination	*Rochalimaea elizabethae*
Bartonella grahamii	New species	
Bartonella henselae	New combination	*Rochalimaea henselae*
Bartonella quintana	New combination	*Rochalimaea quintana*
Bartonella taylorii	New species	
Bartonella vinsonii	New combination	*Rochalimaea vinsonii*
Valid Names for Which 16-S rDNA Sequences Are Not Yet Available		**Basonym**
Bartonella clarridgeiae	New species	
Bartonella peromysci	New combination	*Grahamella peromysci*
Bartonella talpae	New combination	*Grahamella talpae*
Bartonella vinsonii subsp. *berkhoffii*	New subspecies	
Bartonella vinsonii subsp. *vinsonii*	New combination	

cephalides felis, as evidenced by epidemiologic associations,[29, 33, 35] identification of *B. henselae* by culture and DNA amplification from such fleas,[27, 29] and transmission of *B. henselae* among cats by such fleas under controlled experimental conditions.[43] Fleas appear to serve primarily as vectors for cat-to-cat transmission; their contribution to human infection is not defined. However, contamination of the claws of cats with flea feces may explain the epidemiologic association between cat scratches and human infection with *B. henselae.*

Bartonella clarridgeiae is also now recognized to be an agent of asymptomatic infection of cats[18, 19, 21] and may be capable of occasional transmission to humans and the uncommon induction of human illness.[20] Less is known about its full geographic distribution (probably similar to that of *B. henselae*[19]) or potential vectors. As there has been only a single isolate of *B. elizabethae*, nothing is known of its epidemiology.

As more are discovered, it becomes evident that most *Bartonella* spp. are primarily infectious agents of nonhuman mammals. It is reasonable to speculate that humans may be incidental hosts in most cases (even though animal hosts of *B. bacilliformis* and *B. quintana* are not yet identified), with transmission to humans occurring via arthropod vectors or direct inoculation.

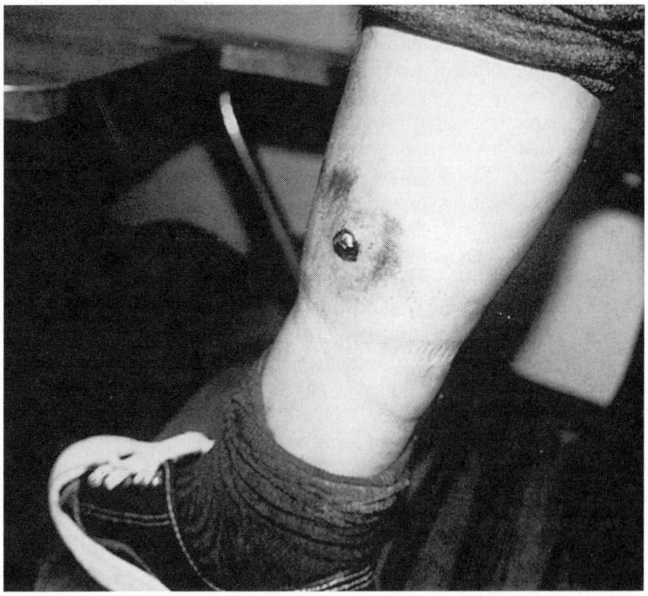

FIGURE 224–2. A single large mulaire lesion of verruga peruana on the leg of an inhabitant of the Peruvian Andes. Such lesions are prone to superficial ulceration, and copious bleeding may occur due to their vascular nature. Ecchymosis of the skin surrounding the lesion is also evident. (Image courtesy of Dr. J. M. Crutcher, Oklahoma State Department of Health.)

CLINICAL MANIFESTATIONS

Oroya Fever and Verruga Peruana: *Bartonella bacilliformis*

The long-suspected link between Oroya fever and verruga peruana was confirmed tragically in 1885 by Daniel Carrión, a medical student who injected himself with blood from a verruga peruana lesion and subsequently died of Oroya fever.[44] The eponym "Carrión's disease" has since denoted the full spectrum of *B. bacilliformis* infection.

Oroya fever, due to primary bacteremia, develops 3 to 12 weeks after inoculation.[45] In its mildest, insidiously developing form, a febrile illness can last less than a week, and may go unrecognized (giving rise to subsequent cutaneous manifestations, which are the first recognized clinical findings[46]). When illness is abrupt in onset, high fever, chills, diaphoresis, headache, and mental status changes are associated with rapidly developing, profound anemia due to bacterial invasion and destruction of erythrocytes.[47–49] Intense myalgias and arthralgias, abdominal pain, lymphadenopathy, thrombocytopenia, and complications such as seizures, delirium, meningoencephalitis, obtundation, dyspnea, hepatic and gastrointestinal dysfunction, and angina can occur during this stage,[50, 51] most believed to be a consequence of the anemia and of microvascular thrombosis, resulting in end-organ ischemia.

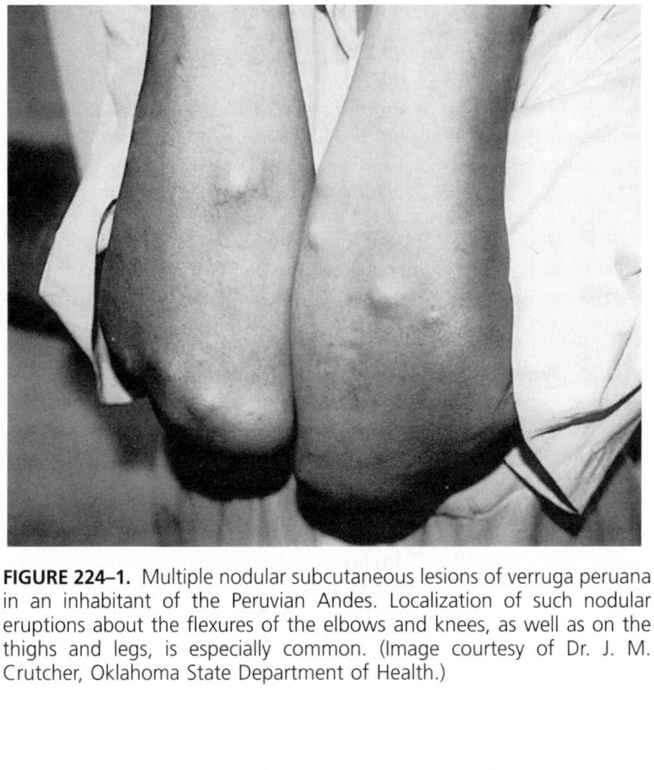

FIGURE 224–1. Multiple nodular subcutaneous lesions of verruga peruana in an inhabitant of the Peruvian Andes. Localization of such nodular eruptions about the flexures of the elbows and knees, as well as on the thighs and legs, is especially common. (Image courtesy of Dr. J. M. Crutcher, Oklahoma State Department of Health.)

Without antimicrobial therapy, fatalities are high.[50] For survivors, convalescence is associated with a decline of fever and disappearance of bacteria on blood smears but also a temporarily increased susceptibility to subsequent (opportunistic) infections such as salmonellosis[51, 52] or toxoplasmosis.[53, 54] Asymptomatic persistent bacteremia with *B. bacilliformis* infection can occur in up to 15% of survivors of acute infection.[55] They may serve as the organism's reservoir.

Verruga peruana lesions usually become evident within weeks to months of the resolution of acute infection if it was not treated with antibiotics. This late-stage manifestation is characterized by crops of skin lesions characterized by an evolution of stages[47]: miliary then nodular (Fig. 224–1) then mulaire (Fig. 224–2), the last of which may ulcerate and bleed; mucosal and internal lesions can also occur. Healing at a particular site, often punctuated by recurrences, usually takes place over several weeks to 3 to 4 months subsequently, and fibrosis of mulaire lesions may occur. The nodules may develop at one site while receding at another. Histologic examination of active lesions demonstrates neovascular proliferation with occasional bacteria evident in interstitial spaces. Bacterial invasion of and replication within endothelial cells (long believed the cause of cytoplasmic inclusions first described by Rocha-Lima) is actually rare.[56]

Bacteremic Illness and Endocarditis: *Bartonella quintana, Bartonella henselae,* Other Species

Deaths due to acute bacteremia with non-*bacilliformis Bartonella* spp., even when persistent, are apparently uncommon. In the era of widespread antibiotic usage, *B. quintana* bacteremic infection outside the context of human immunodeficiency virus (HIV) infection has been identified sporadically, mainly in homeless persons in North America and Europe.[57] Trench fever is characterized by a spectrum of self-limited clinical patterns.[6, 7] Incubation may span 3 to 38 days before the usually sudden onset of chills and fever. In the shortest form, a single bout of fever lasts 4 to 5 days. In the more typical periodic form, there are three to five, and sometimes up to eight, febrile paroxysms, each lasting about 5 days. The continuous form is manifested by 2 to 6 weeks of uninterrupted fever. Afebrile infection is the least common form. The illness may be accompanied by other nonspecific symptoms and signs such as headache, vertigo, retroorbital pain, conjunctival injection, nystagmus, myalgias, arthralgias, hepatosplenomegaly, rash, leukocytosis, and albuminuria.

Bartonella quintana or *B. henselae* bacteremia in HIV-infected persons is often characterized by the insidious development of malaise, body aches, fatigue, weight loss, progressively higher and longer recurring fevers, and sometimes headache. Hepatomegaly may occur, but localizing symptoms or physical findings are often lacking. By way of contrast, *B. henselae* bacteremia in HIV-uninfected persons more often may present with an abrupt onset of fever, which may persist or become relapsing. Localizing symptoms or physical findings remain unusual.[13, 15, 58, 59] Aseptic meningitis concurrent with bacteremia has been documented at least once in an immunocompetent host[59, 60] *Bartonella henselae* bacteremia can evolve into long-term asymptomatic persistence.[59]

Bartonella elizabethae has been isolated only once, as the cause of bacteremia and endocarditis.[16] *Bartonella quintana* and *B. henselae* have been reported increasingly to cause endocarditis, especially of the "blood culture–negative" variety.[9, 11, 61–67] Persons with *B. quintana* endocarditis often have been alcoholic or homeless, or both, whereas persons with *B. henselae* endocarditis more commonly have had cat exposure. Despite the pediatric predominance of CSD, only one case of pediatric *B. henselae* endocarditis has been reported.[67] Most cases have involved valve resection irrespective of antimicrobial use. Diagnoses in blood culture–negative cases were established with serologic tests, DNA amplification from valve tissue, or immunohistochemical tests.

Bartonella vinsonii, generally not considered a human pathogen, has been isolated once causing bacteremia and fever in a rancher from the western United States.[23b] *Bartonella vinsonii* subsp. *berkhoffii* has also been found to be a cause of bacteremia and endocarditis in dogs.[22, 23]

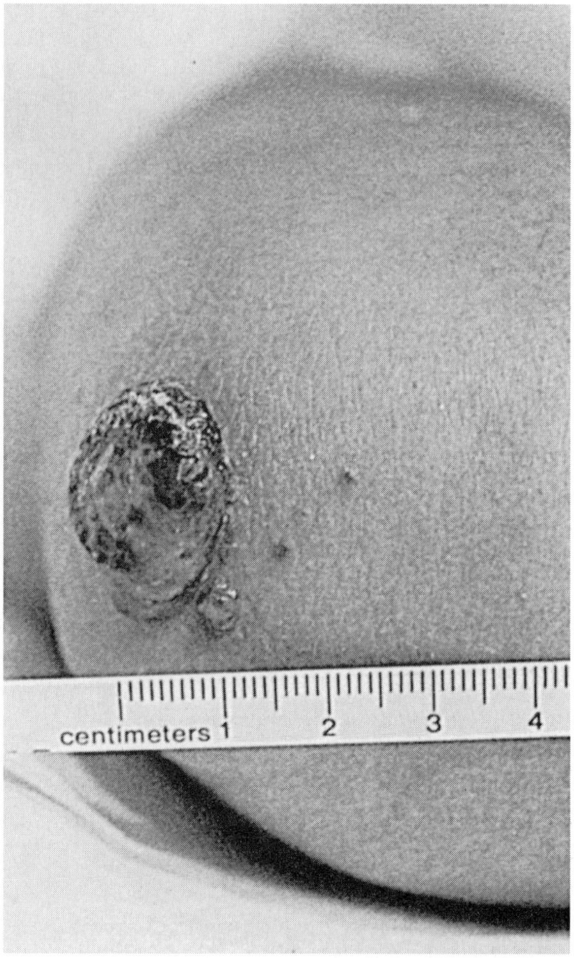

FIGURE 224–3. A crop of cutaneous bacillary angiomatosis lesions on the elbow of a patient with acquired immunodeficiency syndrome. The largest lesion, resembling a mulaire lesion of verruga peruana, was of variegated purple color and had an ulcerated surface that wept serous fluid. It began a month earlier as a small cherry angioma-like lesion, much like the three adjacent smaller lesions that had all since erupted within the preceding week. All lesions involuted with doxycycline therapy.

Bacillary Angiomatosis and Peliosis: *Bartonella quintana* and *Bartonella henselae*

BA (also referred to as *epithelioid angiomatosis* or *bacillary epithelioid angiomatosis*) is a disorder of neovascular proliferation originally described as involving skin and regional lymph nodes of HIV-infected persons.[68–70] It has since been demonstrated to be able to involve a variety of internal organs including liver, spleen, bone, brain, lung, bowel, and uterine cervix,[58, 71–79] and to occur in other immunocompromised[58, 73, 80] as well as immunocompetent hosts.[81, 82] *Bartonella henselae* and *B. quintana* have been inculpated in BA both by direct culture[8, 15, 27, 58, 83] and by PCR amplification from tissue of specific DNA sequences.[27, 33, 80, 82, 84, 85] Either species can cause cutaneous lesions, but subcutaneous and osseous lesions are more often associated with *B. quintana* and hepatosplenic lesions only with *B. henselae*.[85]

Cutaneous BA lesions often arise in crops, but both the temporal pattern of development and the gross morphologic characteristics can vary. They can be remarkably similar to lesions of verruga peruana, but the major clinical differential diagnoses are usually Kaposi's sarcoma[86] and pyogenic granuloma. In gross appearance, BA skin lesions[87] can be subcutaneous or dermal nodules, or single or multiple dome-shaped, skin-colored or red to purple papules, any of which may display ulceration, serous or bloody drainage, and crusting (Figs. 224–3 and 224–4). Lesions can range in diameter from millimeters to centimeters, number from a few to hundreds, be fixed or freely mobile, be associated with enlargement of regional lymph nodes, involve mucosal surfaces or deeper soft tissues, occur in a variety of distributions, and bleed copiously when incised. Visceral lesions can be quite dramatic as well, in both their number and the heterogeneity of the gross appearance (Fig. 224–5). When cutaneous lesions are absent, the diagnosis is often delayed because the features associated with visceral involvement (fever, lymphadenopathy, hepatomegaly, splenomegaly, CD4 lymphopenia, anemia, elevation of levels of serum alkaline phosphatase) are nonspecific.[77]

BA is distinguished from other neovascular tumors histologically.[87, 88] It consists of lobular proliferations of small blood vessels containing plump, cuboidal endothelial cells interspersed with mixed inflammatory cell infiltrates having neutrophil predominance. Endothelial cell atypia, mitoses, and necrosis may be present. Fibrillar- or granular-appearing amphophilic material is often present in interstitial areas when stained by hematoxylin and eosin. Warthin-Starry staining or electron microscopy demonstrates these to be clusters of bacilli.

Bacillary peliosis (BP), originally described as involving the liver and sometimes spleen in HIV-infected persons,[89] has since been identified in other immunosuppressed persons and found to involve lymph nodes as well.[58, 90] Involved organs contain numerous blood-filled cystic structures that can range from microscopic to several millimeters in size. Hematoxylin and eosin–stained tissue reveals partially endothelial cell–lined peliotic spaces often separated from

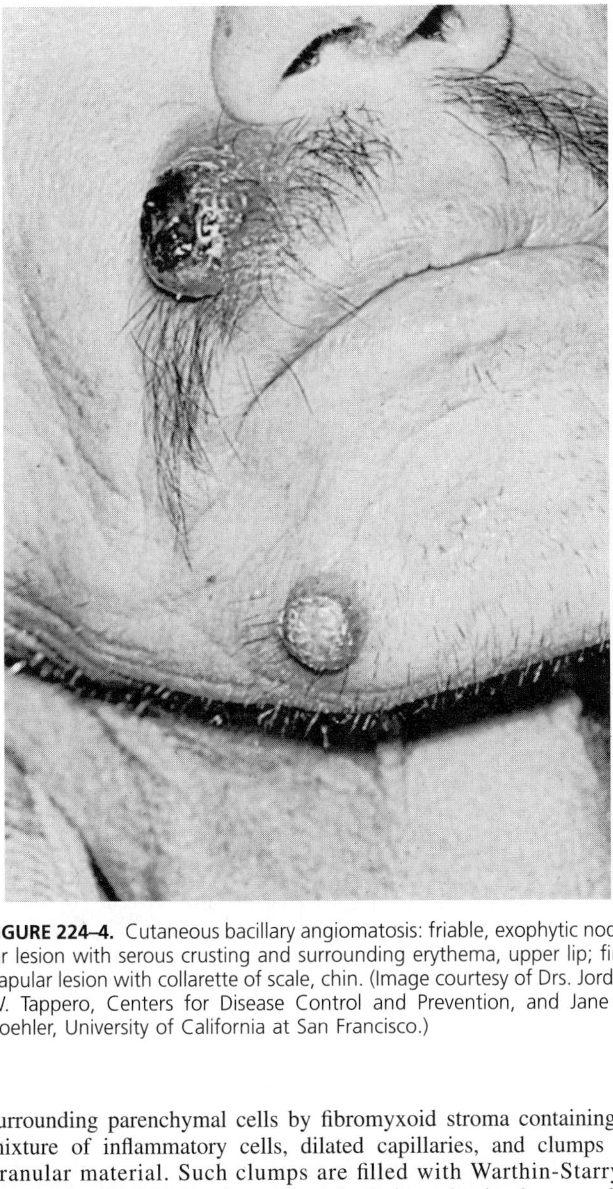

FIGURE 224–4. Cutaneous bacillary angiomatosis: friable, exophytic nodular lesion with serous crusting and surrounding erythema, upper lip; firm papular lesion with collarette of scale, chin. (Image courtesy of Drs. Jordan W. Tappero, Centers for Disease Control and Prevention, and Jane E. Koehler, University of California at San Francisco.)

surrounding parenchymal cells by fibromyxoid stroma containing a mixture of inflammatory cells, dilated capillaries, and clumps of granular material. Such clumps are filled with Warthin-Starry–staining bacilli.[89] Molecular epidemiologic investigation has revealed that only *B. henselae* appears to be culpable in this process.[85]

Inflammatory reactions in immunocompromised hosts due to *B. henselae* infection without associated angiomatosis or peliosis have been reported involving liver, spleen, lymph nodes, heart, lung, and bone marrow.[91, 92] They are characterized by nodular collections of lymphocytes and nonepithelioid histiocytes that may become centrally necrotic, containing aggregates of neutrophils and karyorrhexic debris suggestive of microscopic abscess formation.[91, 92] These may represent a clinical-pathologic link with CSD.[93]

Cat-Scratch Disease: *Bartonella henselae,* Possibly *Afipia felis, Bartonella clarridgeiae*

Among the *Bartonella* spp., CSD has been associated nearly exclusively with *B. henselae*. Evidence indicating its cardinal role includes the serologic responses of persons with CSD[32, 34, 35, 94]; the identification of *B. henselae* in CSD lymphadenitis by culture,[36] PCR-based DNA amplification,[37–39, 95–98] and immunocytochemical analysis[99]; the detection of *B. henselae* in CSD skin test antigens by PCR[41, 42]; and the recovery of *B. henselae* from the blood of healthy cats (which can be persistently bacteremic)[27, 29, 100] and from cat fleas.[27]

The various manifestations that constitute CSD have been recognized over the past hundred years, but "la maladie des griffes de chat" was not defined as a syndrome until 1950.[101] CSD remained an infection in search of an agent for more than 40 years after that. Thus, most cases have been identified by clinical and pathologic criteria, supplemented by reactions to unstandardized skin test antigens in some. It is reasonable to ascribe the majority of CSD to *B. henselae* based on the numerous lines of evidence developed since 1990. Yet it remains likely that occasional "typical" CSD cases can be caused by other agents, such as has been reported with *Afipia felis*[102, 103] and once with *B. clarridgeiae*.[20] (Non-*felis Afipia* spp. have been isolated only from skeletal or pleuropulmonary sites of one patient each and not in the setting of CSD; their roles as pathogens remain speculative.[102])

CSD is the most commonly recognized manifestation of human infection with *Bartonella*. In the United States, estimated CSD cases approach 25,000 annually.[104] Interestingly, veterinary care personnel

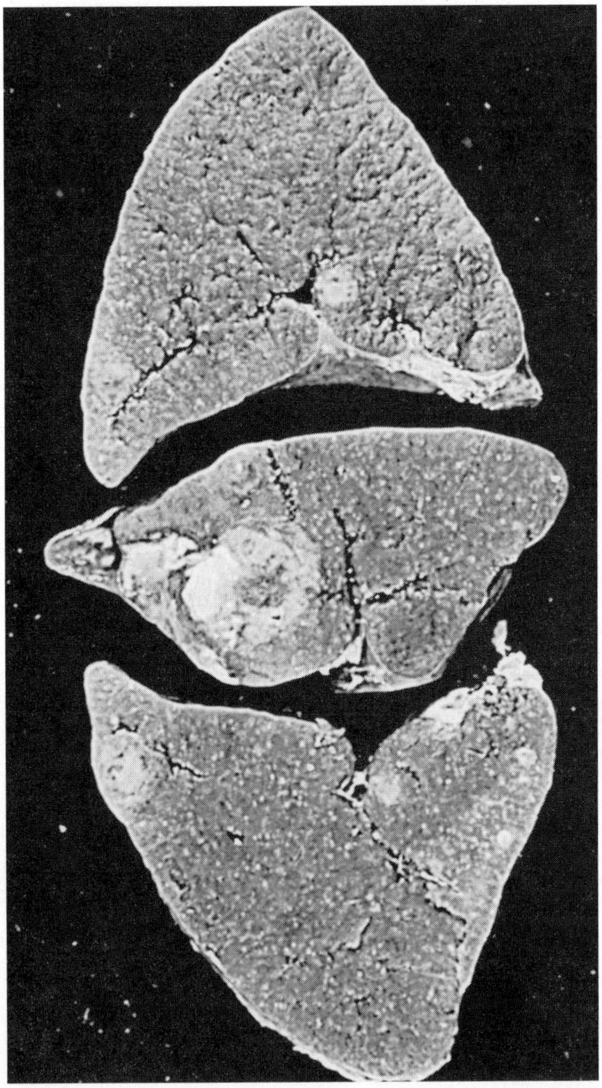

FIGURE 224–5. Cut surfaces of the spleen of a pharmacologically immunosuppressed renal transplant recipient revealed numerous *Bartonella henselae*–induced miliary-appearing nodular lesions ranging in size from millimeters to centimeters, some of the larger of which were necrotic, others containing hemorrhage. Histologic findings included bacillary angiomatosis, bacillary peliosis, and pyogranulomatous changes. (From Slater LN, Welch DF, Min K-Y. *Rochalimaea henselae* causes bacillary angiomatosis and peliosis hepatitis. Arch Intern Med. 1992; 152:602–606. Copyright 1992, American Medical Association.)

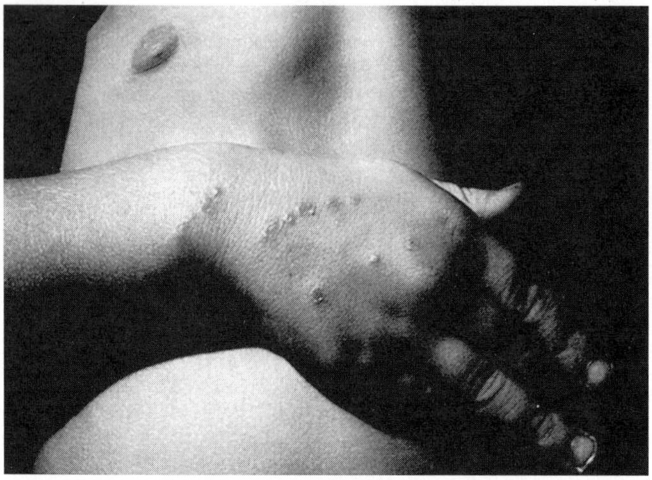

FIGURE 224–6. A child with typical cat-scratch disease demonstrating the original scratch injuries and the primary papule, which soon thereafter developed proximal to the middle finger. (Image courtesy of Dr. V. H. San Joaquin, University of Oklahoma Health Sciences Center.)

do not have evidence of notably higher levels of infection than the general population.[105]

"Typical CSD" represents 88 to 89% of cases overall. A primary cutaneous papule or pustule develops about 3 to 10 days after an animal contact (most commonly a kitten or feral cat) at a site of inoculation (usually a scratch or bite) (Fig. 224–6)[106–108] and may last for 1 to 3 weeks. Regional lymphadenopathy ipsilateral to the inoculation site (mainly head, neck, or upper extremity) that develops in 1 to 7 weeks (Fig. 224–7) is the most prominent and common manifestation (>90% of typical cases) and the one that usually precipitates medical evaluation. Even at the time of such presentation, an inoculation site (scratch, bite, primary papule or pustule) may be detected in over two thirds of patients when actively sought. From 33 to 60% of patients may have low-grade fever lasting several days. One quarter may report malaise or fatigue, and about 10% report headache or sore throat. Transient rash may occur in about 5% of patients. Transient mild leukocytosis, with increased numbers of neutrophils and sometimes eosinophils, and an elevated erythrocyte sedimentation rate may occur.

Nearly half of "typical" CSD patients have single–lymph node involvement; another fifth, multiple-node involvement at one site; and the remaining third, node involvement at multiple sites. Up to one sixth of patients with typical CSD develop lymph node suppuration. Ultrasonography may assist in assessment of the lymph nodes' size and suppuration[29, 109] and may be used to direct needle aspiration of pus (usually done to relieve discomfort). Node enlargement usually persists for 2 to 4 months but may last considerably longer; spontaneous resolution is the rule. The histopathologic appearance of nodes includes a mixture of nonspecific inflammatory reactions including granulomata and stellate necrosis. Bacilli are best demonstrated by Dieterle, Warthin-Starry, or Steiner staining. Hypercalcemia uncommonly may complicate CSD lymphadenopathy due to endogenous overproduction of active vitamin D associated with granuloma formation.[110]

Up to half of the overall 11 to 12% of CSD cases that are atypical represent Parinaud's oculoglandular syndrome, a self-limited granulomatous conjunctivitis and ipsilateral, usually preauricular, lymphadenitis (Fig. 224–8).[111, 112] Various other "atypical" manifestations[113] include self-limited granulomatous hepatitis and/or splenitis, atypical pneumonitis,[114] osteitis,[115] and neurologic syndromes (mainly encephalopathy and neuroretinitis). Most recently, a syndrome of prolonged fever of unknown origin in children has been described.[116]

Due to the insidious and nonspecific nature of the fever and abdominal pain of CSD hepatitis or splenitis, diagnosis may be delayed until a history of cat exposure prompts ultrasonographic or computed tomographic abdominal imaging that usually demonstrates multiple hypodense lesions (Fig. 224–9), and serologic testing.[93, 117–119] Similarly, the nonspecific nature and rarity of many of the other atypical manifestations besides Parinaud's syndrome may result in delay in their accurate diagnosis until a history of cat exposure or suggestive findings on histopathologic examination prompt specific evaluation directed at *B. henselae*.[116]

A dramatic if infrequent manifestation, encephalopathy, was first reported within a few years of the description and naming of CSD.[121–124] Encephalopathy probably occurs in 2 to 4% of all CSD cases recognized, although estimates range as widely as 1 to 7%.[120] Extrapolating

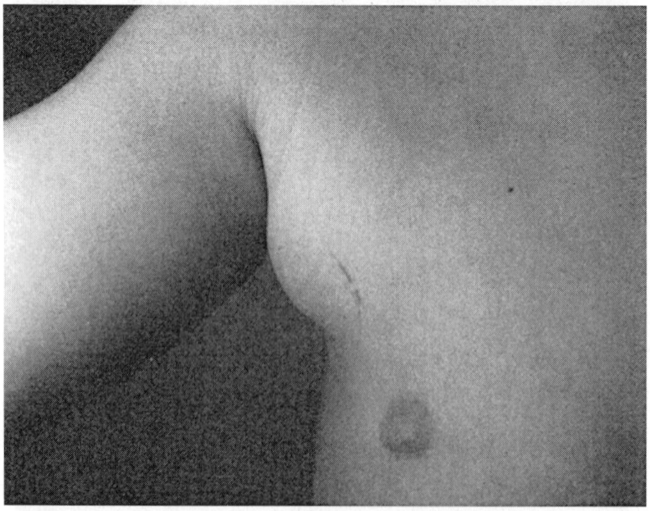

FIGURE 224–7. Right axillary lymphadenopathy followed the scratches and development of a primary papule in this child with typical cat-scratch disease, also illustrated in Figure 224–6. (Image courtesy of Dr. V. H. San Joaquin, University of Oklahoma Health Sciences Center.)

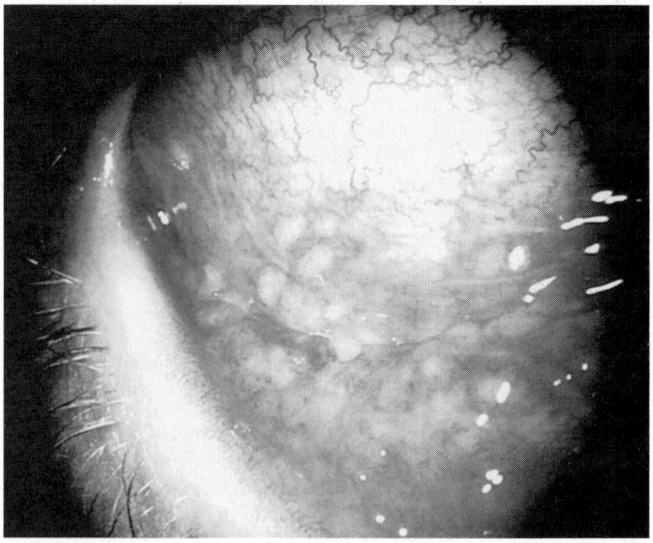

FIGURE 224–8. The granulomatous conjunctivitis of Parinaud's oculoglandular syndrome, illustrated here, is associated with ipsilateral local lymphadenopathy, usually preauricular, and less commonly submandibular.

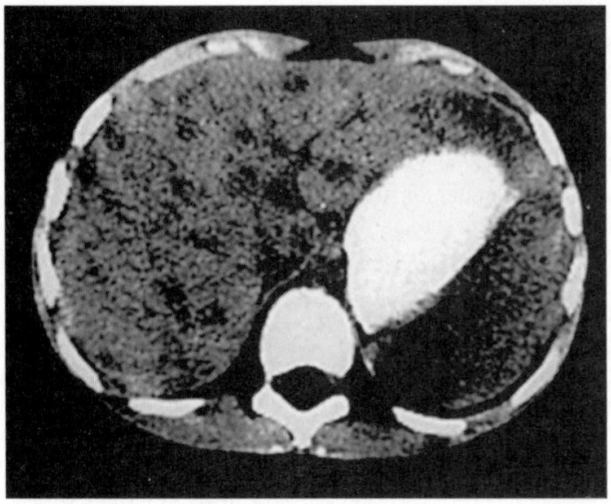

FIGURE 224–9. In this computed tomographic image of a patient with hepatic involvement of cat-scratch disease, the absence of enhancement of the multiple lesions after contrast infusion is consistent with the granulomatous inflammation of this entity. Treated empirically with various antibiotics without improvement before establishment of this diagnosis, the patient subsequently recovered fully with no further antimicrobial therapy. (Image courtesy of Dr. V. H. San Joaquin, University of Oklahoma Health Sciences Center.)

from the estimated U.S. CSD case rate,[104] 500 to 1000 annual CSD encephalopathy cases occur in the United States. Recognition of this phenomenon may increase with the availability of serologic testing and improved blood-culture techniques. It remains predominantly a clinical diagnosis, now subject to laboratory confirmation by techniques described later (predominantly antibody testing). Adolescents and adults may represent a greater proportion of cases of CSD encephalopathy than they do of CSD overall.[125] Although encephalopathy usually follows the development of lymphadenopathy, it has also been reported to precede lymph node involvement or to occur in its absence. Persistent, generalized headache is a common part of the history, but fever is an inconsistent finding. Patients may become very restless, and combativeness is often described. Nearly half of patients can develop seizures that may range from focal to generalized, and from brief and self-limited to status epilepticus. Short-term anticonvulsant therapy may be required, as may supportive therapy in the face of obtundation or coma. Concurrent acute neurologic manifestations may be present transiently, for example, nuchal rigidity, pathologic reflexes, or pupillary dilatation. When they occur, neurologic deficits such as aphasia, cranial nerve palsy, paresis, hemiplegia, and ataxia are also usually self-limited, although the time to resolution may span weeks to months to as long as a year. However, the persistence of intellectual impairment and of seizures has been reported uncommonly.[126–128]

Laboratory studies, such as cerebrospinal fluid (CSF) analysis and culture, generally do not add specific positive diagnostic findings to the clinical picture of CSD encephalopathy but rather serve to exclude other processes. Elevations of CSF protein concentration and leukocytes occur in only about one third of patients (but do not necessarily coincide in the same patients); lymphocytes predominate. Hypoglycorrhachia is rare. CSF cultures have been consistently negative, even since the recognition of the CSD–*B. henselae* association. Studies of the brain with computed tomography or magnetic resonance imaging, or both, are usually normal, but a few cases of persistent structural abnormalities have been reported.[127, 128] Electroencephalography during the acute phase of CSD encephalopathy commonly reveals diffuse slowing, yet another nonspecific feature that resolves with clinical recovery.

Neuroretinitis associated with CSD[60, 125, 129–131] has been confirmed by serologic and culture evidence to be related to *B. henselae*.[60, 132] CSD neuroretinitis, like other CSD manifestations, has been primarily a clinical diagnosis since its first description in 1970,[129] but with the refinement of techniques for culture and nonculture identification of *B. henselae* infection, diagnostic accuracy should improve.

Neuroretinitis manifests as fairly sudden loss of visual acuity, usually unilaterally, sometimes preceded by an influenza-like syndrome or the development of unilateral lymphadenopathy. The most common retinal manifestation is papilledema associated with macular exudates in a star formation (Fig. 224–10), first associated with CSD in 1984.[130] Although this manifestation is characteristic of CSD neuroretinitis, it is not pathognomonic; other types of inflammation also have been reported. Neuroretinitis usually has a favorable spontaneous course. Prospective follow-up of well-documented cases reveals that some have mild residual visual deficits.[60, 133]

Historically, the diagnosis of a case of typical CSD required fulfillment of three of the four following criteria, whereas all four were necessary in an atypical case: (1) a history of an animal (usually cat or dog) contact with the presence of a scratch or primary skin or eye lesion; (2) aspiration of "sterile" pus from the lymph node, or culture and other laboratory testing that excluded other etiologic possibilities; (3) a positive CSD skin test; and (4) a lymph node biopsy revealing abnormality consistent with CSD. Skin test antigen, originally described by Hanger and Rose, is prepared by heating saline-diluted "sterile" pus derived from CSD lymphadenitis to 56°C for 72 hours. It has never been standardized or produced commercially. It is of historic interest because of its confirmatory role in the diagnosis of CSD in the past. However, its potential for the transmission of hepatitis viruses, HIV, and prions is a major contemporary concern, even if its sources are well screened. Its use in the era of other avenues of diagnosis is no longer warranted.

The differential diagnosis of typical CSD includes many causes of (unilateral) lymphadenopathy, among which are typical or atypical mycobacterial infection, tularemia and plague, brucellosis, syphilis, lymphogranuloma venereum, sporotrichosis, histoplasmosis, toxoplasmosis, infectious mononucleosis syndromes, and neoplasms. The diagnosis of CSD can easily be overlooked if the clinician fails to obtain an adequate history, especially in the case of the atypical syndromes, and not uncommonly in the case of adults with the typical syndrome whose clinicians are inexperienced with CSD. With

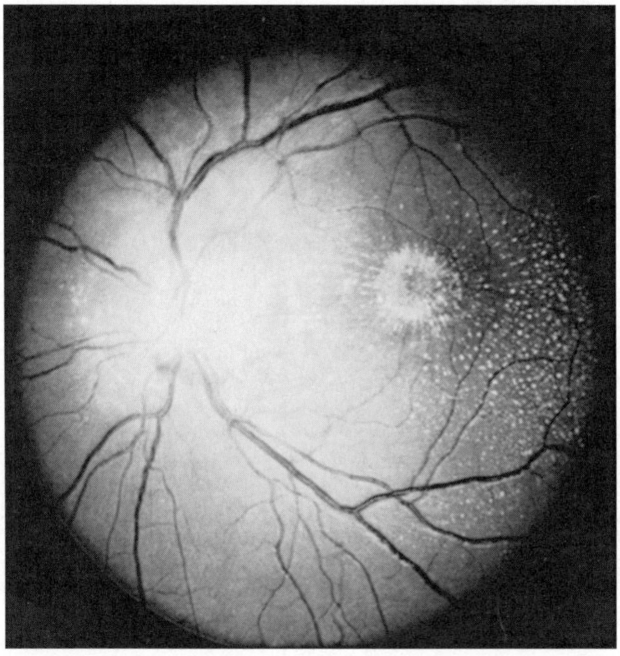

FIGURE 224–10. The most common appearance of the neuroretinitis of cat-scratch disease is papilledema associated with stellate macular exudates.

domestic cats representing the single largest category of companion animals in the United States, the importance of an accurate history regarding animal exposure when a patient with findings consistent with CSD is evaluated cannot be emphasized enough. Fortunately, in most cases, whether typical or atypical, spontaneous resolution occurs.

Human Immunodeficiency Virus–Associated Neurologic Syndromes

Bartonella henselae or *quintana,* or both, have been implicated in a small proportion of cases of HIV-associated brain lesions, meningoencephalitis, encephalopathy, and neuropsychiatric disease[60, 74, 134–137] that cannot be ascribed to other causes.

A case of intracerebral BA has been described.[74] *Bartonella* infection associated with neurologic manifestations complicating HIV infection has been demonstrated by serum and CSF antibodies and CSF DNA amplification,[134] although technical limitations prevented accurate species implication in these cases. A study of autopsy brain tissue reported evidence of *B. henselae* by immunofluorescence staining and by PCR amplification in three acquired immunodeficiency syndrome dementia patients with elevated CSF/serum indices of *B. henselae*–reactive antibody.[136] A nested case-control study has since confirmed an association between the presence of serum anti-*Bartonella* immunoglobulin M (IgM) (implying recent infection) and an increased risk of the development of neuropsychological decline or dementia.[137] At least 4% of new cases of HIV-associated dementia or neuropsychological decline were estimated to result from *Bartonella* infections and therefore to be potentially treatable with antibiotics. Additional case reports have added anecdotal evidence of the utility of antimicrobials in reversing *Bartonella*-associated neuropsychiatric abnormalities in HIV-infected persons.[135]

PATHOGENESIS

In cats, *B. henselae* appears to be a nearly perfectly adapted parasite, capable of causing long-term or cyclic, or both, high-grade bacteremia largely in the absence of illness in its hosts.[27, 31, 43, 138–140] Elucidation of the mechanisms of this host-parasite relationship is in its infancy. Only a small body of fundamental knowledge about the pathogenic mechanisms of *Bartonella* spp. in humans has been developed, primarily focused on interactions with erythrocytes and endothelial cells, the induction of neoangiogenesis, and mechanisms of survival.

Bartonella bacilliformis cells have polar flagellae that confer motility and may participate in adhesion to erythrocytes.[141, 142] Aggregative fimbriae also may play a role in such adhesion.[143] Erythrocyte invasion involves an extracellular deformin protein, the flagellum, and proteins encoded by the invasion-associated locus *(ialAB).*[142, 144–146] Even though *B. henselae* does not bind to human erythrocytes in vitro in a fashion similar to that of *B. bacilliformis*, supernatants of in vitro growth of *B. henselae* contain a protein very similar to the deformin of *B. bacilliformis*. Also in a fashion similar to that of *B. bacilliformis*, *B. henselae* outer membrane proteins bind with a number of erythrocyte ghost membrane proteins.[147]

After entry into erythrocytes, *B. bacilliformis* can replicate within and, occasionally, escape from the endosomal vacuoles.[148] Studies from the high-grade feline bacteremia of *B. henselae* have not yet resolved whether it is truly intra- or extraerythrocytic in cats.[149, 150] In humans, the question remains largely unstudied, although the enhanced efficiency of recovery of these pathogens with lysis-type blood cultures suggests some degree of intracellular localization.

Bartonella bacilliformis has been demonstrated to stimulate endothelial cell proliferation both in vitro and in vivo, likely through a sheddable stimulatory factor.[151–153] Similar in vitro proliferative effects can be induced by *B. henselae* and *B. quintana*. *Bartonella henselae* can also induce endothelial cell migration in vitro. These effects of *B. henselae* are mediated by a factor inactivated by trypsin, therefore likely a protein.[153]

In the process of endothelial cell invasion by *B. bacilliformis*, the host cell appears to be an active participant through the pathogen's induction of rearrangement of the host's cytoskeleton.[154] *Bartonella quintana* has been demonstrated to invade and multiply within endothelial cells in vitro and in vivo and form intracellular blebs in the process.[155] *Bartonella henselae* interaction with the endothelial cell in vitro results in bacterial aggregation on the cell surface and subsequent engulfment and internalization of the bacterial aggregate by a unique structure, the invasome.[156]

Intracellular survival of *Bartonella* spp. may be facilitated by the production of superoxide dismutases[157] and possibly the production of stress-response–processing proteases.[158] Also, *B. henselae* and *B. quintana* produce heat shock proteins of the *groEL* genes, which share signature sequences with genes of other gram-negative bacteria known to invade eukaryotic cells.

LABORATORY DIAGNOSIS

Presumptive diagnosis can be made by direct examination of clinical materials in the context of a *Bartonella*-associated syndrome. Definitive diagnosis of *Bartonella*-associated diseases can be achieved through modified conventional bacteriologic culture methods,[12, 36, 131, 159, 160] coculture with endothelial cells,[8] immunoserologic[32, 94] or immunocytochemical means,[161] or DNA amplification, or all of these.[38, 39, 42, 80] Approaches that are currently practical for the majority of clinical laboratories are direct examination, culture, and serologic tests. Serologic testing is becoming a mainstay of diagnosis, particularly for that part of the clinical spectrum of diseases occupied by CSD and CNS infection.

Direct Examination

Giemsa-stained blood films are commonly used in endemic locales to detect *B. bacilliformis* in patients with Oroya fever. A wide morphologic range is seen in such smears, with the organisms appearing as red-violet rods or rounded forms, occurring singly or in groups and associated with erythrocytes. Bacilli are the most typical form, measuring 0.25 to 0.5 by 1 to 3 μm. The cells are often curved and may show uni- or bipolar enlargement and granules. Rounded organisms measure approximately 0.75 μm in diameter, and a ring-like variety is sometimes abundant.[162] Although appearing adherent to erythrocytes by light microscopy, bacteria also have been observed within erythrocytes when viewed by electron microscopy.[163] The magnitude of human bacteremia associated with *B. henselae* or *B. quintana* does not typically afford direct observation of bacteria in blood smears.

Bartonella spp. are gram-negative, not acid-fast, and stain poorly or not at all in tissue other than by silver-impregnation techniques (e.g., Warthin-Starry, Steiner, Dieterle). *Bartonella henselae* and *B. quintana* are demonstrable by Warthin-Starry staining in BA or BP; *B. henselae* may be silver stained during the early stages of lymphadenopathy in CSD, but typically not during the later granulomatous stage of inflammation. Species-specific direct detection of organisms in tissue by immunocytochemical labeling also has been described,[67, 91, 99, 161] but reagents for such labeling are not widely available.

Specimen Collection and Handling for Culture

The sources from which isolation is attempted most commonly are blood and tissue. The time interval from collection to processing should be minimized. If storage of specimens is necessary, they should be frozen. A controlled study of the effects of blood collection and handling methods has shown that blood specimens from *B. henselae*–infected cats that were collected in either EDTA or Isolator

(Wampole, Cranbury, N.J.) blood-lysis tubes yielded good recovery, and that blood collected in tubes containing EDTA could be plated after 26 days at −65°C with no loss of sensitivity.[164] Whenever possible, specimens should be collected before antimicrobial therapy, especially with the tetracyclines and macrolides. Growth of *B. henselae* is also inhibited by concentrations of sodium polyethylene sulfonate (SPS) that are used in blood-culture media.[165] The precautions of adding agents to neutralize SPS toxicity or using resin-containing media (primarily to lyse erythrocytes) should be taken if blood is cultured in commercial systems. Lytic blood-culture systems (e.g., Isolator) combine the advantage of neutralizing SPS toxicity by hemoglobin freed from erythrocytes with the potential release of intracellular organisms.

Culture

All *Bartonella* spp. can been cultured on cell-free media, unlike members of the order Rickettsiales. Recovery of *Bartonella* spp. is optimized by using freshly prepared rabbit-heart–infusion agar plates.[159] However, various formulations of blood or chocolate agar support their growth, with the best results dependent on the freshness of the media. Approaches used for the recovery of other fastidious pathogens are generally suitable, except that most isolates require more than 7 days of incubation before they can be detected. Therefore, routine bacterial culture protocols rarely allow *Bartonella* spp. to be detected. Protocols designed to yield other slowly growing organisms (e.g., *Histoplasma capsulatum* or *Mycobacterium avium* complex on noninhibitory media) can also result in recovery of *Bartonella* spp. Although cultures are not recommended to diagnose most cases of CSD, isolation of *Bartonella* spp. should be attempted in the settings of (1) fever of unknown origin or neuroretinitis after cat exposure; (2) fever, lymphadenitis, neuroretinitis, or encephalitis of unknown origin in the immunocompromised patient; (3) endocarditis without recovery of typical pathogens; and (4) BA or BP.

Inoculated media should be incubated at 35° to 37°C under conditions of 5 to 10% CO_2 and greater than 40% humidity. (*B. bacilliformis* and possibly some strains of *B. clarridgeiae* spp. have a lower [25° to 30°C] optimal temperature for growth.) The medium should be as freshly prepared as possible. Plates sealed after 24 hours of incubation with plastic film or shrink wrap to preserve the moisture content of the media usually can be incubated up to 30 days without notable deterioration.

Alternative approaches to use of the Isolator for blood cultures include the use of a broth-based culture systems. *Bartonella henselae* has been isolated in the biphasic Septi-Chek system (Roche Diagnostics, Nutley, N.J.) after incubation in excess of 40 days. Evidence of growth, if any, in the broth phase is a pellicle or adherent film on the glass surface. *Bartonella* spp. usually grow best on solid or semisolid media. In broth, *Bartonella* spp. rarely produce turbidity or convert enough oxidizable substrate for CO_2-detection–based systems to indicate growth. However, several isolates have been detected initially using BACTEC and resin-containing media combined with acridine orange staining at the termination of a 7-day incubation period, with recovery subsequently achieved by subculture to solid media.[9, 10, 63] Another CO_2-detection blood-culture system, Bact/Alert, has been reported to yield positive growth algorithms in five cases of *B. henselae* bacteremia. Although Gram stains of the broth and routine 72-hour subcultures proved negative, acridine orange and Warthin-Starry staining demonstrated bacilli, and phase-contrast microscopy of wet mounts revealed bacilli with "rachety motility." Specific immunofluorescent labeling of organisms obtained directly from the broth or subsequently subcultured on semisolid media identified *B. henselae*.[160]

A defined cell-free medium (modified from RPMI 1640) that permits recovery of *Bartonella* spp. from primary clinical specimens has also been described.[131] When supplemented with hemin (250 mg/ml) and peptic digest of blood (8% Fildes reagent), *Brucella* broth has been reported to produce improved growth, but this technique has been applied mainly to propagation rather than primary isolation.[166] Similarly, isolates can be propagated on buffered charcoal yeast extract medium,[13] but this is not recommended for primary isolation.

Bartonella spp. have been isolated from liver, spleen, lymph node, and skin after homogenization either by direct plating of tissue homogenate or aspirate[15, 29, 36, 60, 65] or by cocultivation with various cell lines.[8, 11] *Bartonella henselae* and *B. quintana* grow in endothelial cell cultures as elongated pleomorphic organisms visible in Gimenez-stained preparations 72 hours after inoculation of the cell cultures. The cocultivation method is not practical for most microbiology laboratories, although it may result in recovering occasional isolates missed with cell-free media. In the absence of coculture, more than a month of incubation has often been necessary to yield evident colonies from some tissue specimens.[29, 36] Because selective culture techniques have not been developed, recovery of isolates from specimens such as skin may be more difficult if indigenous or contaminating flora are present.

Identification

Colonies of *Bartonella* spp. are of two morphologic types: (1) irregular, raised, whitish, rough, and dry (variously characterized as "cauliflower" or "molar tooth" or "verrucous") or (2) smaller, circular, tan, and moist, tending to pit and adhere to the agar. Both types are usually present in the same culture. The degree of colonial heterogeneity varies by species and by strain, with *B. henselae* typically displaying a greater proportion of rough colonies than *B. quintana*, which may even appear as uniformly smooth in primary cultures. Repeated subcultures of *B. henselae* tend to have increasing proportions of smooth colonies. Cultures of *B. henselae* on blood agar produce an odor similar to the caramel odor (diacetyl) of *Streptococcus milleri.* Colonies contain small, gram-negative, slightly curved rods resembling *Campylobacter, Helicobacter,* or *Haemophilus*. Cells, especially of *B. henselae,* are very autoadherent, demonstrable when attempting to scrape colonies from agar with a loop. Twitching motility of cells is evident in wet mounts, presumably interrelated to adherence, both features being mediated by fine fimbriae (pili) visible in negatively stained electron microscopic studies. Cells of *B. bacilliformis* and *B. clarridgeiae* possess polar flagella.

The features of incubation more than 7 days before the appearance of colonies, small curved gram-negative bacilli, and negative catalase and oxidase reactions are sufficient for presumptive identification of *B. henselae* or *B. quintana.*[159, 165] Additional methods to confirm the identity of isolates may be employed, or isolates may be referred to a laboratory experienced with *Bartonella* spp. for confirmatory identification. Although the reagents are not widely available, a reliable means to distinguish *B. henselae* from *B. quintana* isolates quickly is immunofluorescence with antisera monospecific for each of these two species.[159, 160, 165, 167] Characterization using conventional tests produces results that identify the *Bartonella* spp. (Table 224–2). (For comparison, the characteristics of *A. felis* are included in this table.)

Commercial identification kits do not contain *Bartonella* spp. in their databases, but the Microscan rapid anaerobe panel distinguishes *Bartonella* spp. from species that are in its database. Using this panel with careful adjustment of inoculum size to a McFarland no. 3 standard, one can also distinguish *Bartonella* spp. on the basis of biotype codes (10077640 = *B. henselae*, 10073640 = *B. quintana*, 10077240 = *B. bacilliformis*).[159] Heavier inocula blur the distinctions. In other systems, the biochemical reactivity of *B. quintana* and *B. henselae* has been enhanced by the addition of hemin to test media.[168]

Determination of the cellular fatty acid composition by gas-liquid chromatography is useful in identifying and distinguishing *Bartonella* spp. from other genera.[13, 159] The Bartonellaceae have relatively simple gas-liquid chromatography profiles consisting mainly of Cl8:l, Cl8:0, and Cl6:0 acids. *Bartonella elizabethae* contains a greater amount of Cl7:0 than the other species. An unusual

TABLE 224–2 Differential Characteristics of Commonly Pathogenic *Bartonella* spp. and *Afipia felis**

Characteristic	*Bartonella bacilliformis*	*Bartonella quintana*	*Bartonella henselae*	*Bartonella elizabethae*	*Bartonella clarridgeiae*	*Afipia felis*
Gram reaction	−	−	−	−	−	−
Catalase	+	−	±	−	−	−
Oxidase	−	±	−	−	−	+
Nitrate reduction	−	−	−	−	−	+
Indole	−	−	−	−	−	−
Urease	−	−	−	−	−	+
Acid from carbohydrates†	−	−	−	−	−	−
Optimal temperature (°C)	25–30	35–37	35–37	35–37	35–37	25–30
Growth in nutrient broth	−	−	−	−	−	+
Hemolysis	−	−	−	−	−	−
Flagella	+	−‡	−‡	−	+	+
Cellular fatty acids constituting >90% of total	$C_{18:\omega 7C}$, $C_{16:0}$, $C_{16:1\omega 7C}$	$C_{18:1\omega 7C}$, $C_{16:0}$, $C_{18:0}$	$C_{18:1\omega 7C}$, $C_{18:0}$, $C_{16:0}$	$C_{18:1\omega 7C}$, $C_{17:0}$, $C_{16:0}$	$C_{18:1\omega 7C}$, $C_{18:0}$, $C_{16:0}$	$C_{18:1\omega 7C}$, $C_{BR19:1}$, $C_{19:0CYC}$

*+, positive reaction; −, negative reaction; ±, negative or weakly positive.
†Glucose, lactose, maltose, mannitol, and sucrose.
‡May demonstrate twitching motility in wet mounts.

branched-chain fatty acid (11-methyloctadec-12-enoic acid) distinguishes *Afipia* spp. from *Bartonella* spp. and other organisms.[102, 169]

Antimicrobial Susceptibility Testing

Clinical correlation studies of susceptibility testing results with *Bartonella* spp. have not been performed to the extent necessary to ensure that meaningful data can be generated. If required, antimicrobial susceptibility testing can be performed by incorporation of antimicrobial agents into either blood or chocolate agar and testing by the agar dilution technique.[13, 170] *Haemophilus* test medium with a broth microdilution technique has also been described, but the Etest (AB Biodisk, Solna, Sweden) may be the most practical means to assess susceptibility.[171] Testing in other types of systems has also been reported.[172–175] Because of the slow growth and fastidious nature of the organisms, some test methods may be inappropriate. Testing of isolates is problematic in any system for those strains displaying the most fastidious growth characteristics.

Generally, *B. henselae* isolates are susceptible in vitro to most antibacterial agents tested, including β-lactams, tetracyclines, macrolides, aminoglycosides, fluoroquinolones, vancomycin, rifampin, chloramphenicol, and co-trimoxazole, but resistant to nalidixic acid. In vitro resistance to penicillin and ampicillin, tetracycline, or vancomycin has been noted. *Bartonella quintana* is similar in its in vitro susceptibility pattern except for resistance to aminoglycosides.

Molecular Methods

PCR-based and DNA hybridization techniques can be used to speciate isolates.[2, 14, 15, 18, 38] Molecular subtyping of strains can also be performed using PCR-based restriction fragment length polymorphisms,[12, 176, 177] repetitive extragenic palindromic PCR,[18, 178] and enterobacterial repetitive intergenic consensus PCR with sodium dodecyl sulfate–polyacrylamide gel electrophoresis.[30] No clear-cut epidemiologic correlations with subtypes have become apparent, although some studies suggest a greater diversity of restriction fragment length polymorphism types in the blood of bacteremic HIV-infected persons than in the CSD lesions of immunocompetent hosts.[176, 179]

Direct detection of *Bartonella* spp. in pus, skin lesions, or tissue also can be effected by amplification of DNA, without the requirement for culture isolation. A gene fragment specific for either citrate synthase or a heat shock protein of *B. henselae* is demonstrable by PCR in the majority of patients with CSD.[39, 96, 98] Amplification of ribosomal RNA gene segments with universal primers followed by direct nucleotide sequence analysis of the amplification product or hybridization with specific probes is another, more sensitive but more laborious, approach.[80, 98, 180]

PCR is becoming widely used and offers potentially high sensitivity. Depending on the method and the source of specimen (freshly aspirated pus, fresh tissue, fixed and paraffin-embedded tissue), the success of identification has ranged from 50 to nearly 100%.[37, 38, 95–98, 181] PCR amplification has also enabled identification of *B. henselae* in CSF and brain tissue of patients with HIV-related neurologic processes in the absence of culture recovery.[134, 136]

Serologic Testing

Enzyme immunoassay (EIA) and radioimmunoprecipitation have been found comparably more sensitive than hemagglutination and immunofluorescence assays in older studies of human antibodies to *B. quintana*.[182] With the EIA, all patients in a small series of acute primary or relapsed trench fever cases were found to have measurable, although often low, levels of anti–*B. quintana* antibodies.[183]

Immunofluorescence assay (IFA)[32, 35, 184–186] and several EIAs[34, 94, 159, 181, 187] have been described for *B. henselae* and *B. quintana.* They have been used most commonly to demonstrate anti-*Bartonella* antibodies in persons with CSD[32, 34, 35, 94, 132, 181, 184, 186, 187] or endocarditis[11, 64–67, 185] and in some patients with HIV-associated aseptic meningitis, encephalopathy, or neuropsychiatric disease.[60, 134, 137] Human antibody responses have often been substantially cross-reactive between *B. quintana* and *B. henselae*,[94, 184] and the reported tests have undergone different degrees of scrutiny and corroboration. Furthermore, in some of these assays, there may be serologic cross-reaction with *Chlamydia* spp. and *Coxiella burnetti*, other potential agents of "culture-negative endocarditis" in humans.[11, 66, 185, 188]

In evaluating patients with the clinical diagnosis of CSD, the IFA and one EIA for antibodies to *B. henselae* and *B. quintana*, both using bacterial whole cell antigens, have been compared with one another, with an EIA for antibodies to *A. felis*, and with findings of cat-scratch antigen skin testing.[94, 184] CSD patients had no higher levels of antibodies to *A. felis* than did control persons, whereas most CSD patients had evidence of elevated anti-*Bartonella* antibodies by IFA and anti-*Bartonella* IgM by EIA compared with controls. Detection of anti-*Bartonella* antibodies was a superior marker of CSD than a reaction to skin test antigen. Even though neither the IFA nor the EIA could discriminate between anti–*B. henselae* and anti–*B. quintana* antibodies, the use of such assays has appropriately supplanted skin testing as a means of confirming a diagnosis of CSD.[29, 109]

Modifications and variations of IFA and EIA assays using whole bacterial cell antigens have generally corroborated that such assays, especially if performed at only one time for a particular subject, appear to be variably and sometimes suboptimally sensitive and specific.[181, 186, 187] Alternative EIA methodology, using partially[67, 159, 189] or highly purified[190] antigen components, ultimately may prove more species-sensitive and -specific. Partially purified antigens used for EIA analysis of patients with CSD (proved using a combination of culture, PCR, skin testing) is highly sensitive (96%) for the detection of anti–*B. henselae* antibodies (IgM or IgG, or both), with considerably less incidence and magnitude of cross-reaction with *B. quintana* and *Chlamydia* spp. than has been reported with other assays.[191]

TREATMENT AND PREVENTION

The standard therapy for acute *B. bacilliformis* infection is oral chloramphenicol in a dose of 2 g/day for at least 1 week. As an alternative, oral doxycycline, other tetracyclines, or ampicillin can be given for a comparable duration. Parenteral therapy can be substituted if oral intake or bowel absorption is impaired.

Unfortunately, in vitro susceptibility of *B. henselae* and *B. quintana* does not necessarily predict the in vivo response to therapy. Indeed, BA or BP can develop and organisms be recovered in the face of therapy with trimethoprim-sulfamethoxazole, β-lactam antibiotics, and fluoroquinolone antibiotics.[85, 192] In contrast, therapy with rifampin, tetracyclines, or macrolides dramatically reduces culture recovery from BA and BP lesions, and macrolide administration appears to protect against BA and BP.[85] The routine use of rifabutin, clarithromycin, and azithromycin for the prevention of *M. avium* complex infections in persons with acquired immunodeficiency syndrome appears to have reduced the incidence of *Bartonella* infections in that population.

The ease of administration, low cost, and observed clinical effectiveness make oral erythromycin or doxycycline the initial agents of choice to treat uncomplicated bacteremia and processes such as BA and BP caused by non-*bacilliformis Bartonella* spp.[85, 192, 193] As long as it is of adequate duration, such therapy appears effective for most manifestations. Exceptions may include bony or parenchymal involvement and endocarditis, for which initial parenteral therapy may be advantageous. In endocarditis, hemodynamic considerations often require valve replacement irrespective of the effect of antimicrobials on bacterial proliferation. For bacteremia, at least 4 weeks of therapy is indicated.[59] Longer-duration treatment (8 to 12 weeks) is appropriate in the HIV-infected patient, if fever or bacteremia is persistent or recurrent in the HIV-uninfected patient,[60] and in the setting of endocarditis. For BA involving only the skin, experienced clinicians recommend 8 to 12 weeks of oral therapy.[192] Relapsing disease has been seen in both immunocompromised and immunocompetent hosts, especially, but not only, if therapy is terminated prematurely. For relapses occurring after adequately long initial treatment, chronic suppressive therapy with doxycycline or erythromycin should be considered.

There have been anecdotal reports of the utility of various agents (rifampin, gentamicin, co-trimoxazole, fluoroquinolones, azithromycin[194–198]) in the treatment of CSD. However, only azithromycin has been demonstrated to accelerate the resolution of typical CSD lymphadenopathy in a placebo-controlled, double-blind study.[109] Although the value of antibiotic therapy of CSD remains debatable in light of the usually benign outcome of most manifestations,[197] azithromycin should be the agent of first choice for treating "typical" CSD lymphadenitis if antimicrobial administration is contemplated. Utility in treatment of "atypical" manifestations of CSD remains undefined.

Although there is no definite evidence of the utility of antibiotic therapy in altering the course of neurologic manifestations of CSD, case reports of neuroretinitis associated with persistent *B. henselae* bacteremia, and of *Bartonella*-associated antibiotic-responsive neuropsychiatric manifestations in the setting of HIV infection, probably support the inclination to treat with antimicrobials. One report has suggested that two-agent therapy for neuroretinitis accelerates resolution in comparison to untreated historic control cases. The agents used in such cases have usually been erythromycin or doxycycline (with or without combined rifampin) or, alternatively, azithromycin, clarithromycin, or ofloxacin.[60, 133, 135]

Prevention of *B. bacilliformis* and *B. quintana* infections is probably best achieved by avoiding the locales or circumstances in which exposure to their arthropod vectors occurs. In contrast, prevention of *B. henselae* (and possibly *B. clarridgeiae*) infection entails avoidance of interactions with cats that might result in scratches, bites, or licks. Feral cats, cats that are allowed outdoors, cats with fleas, and kittens (younger than 12 months) all have a higher chance of being *B. henselae*–infected.[199] Although the role of cat fleas in the transmission of *B. henselae* to humans remains inadequately defined, treatment of pet cats for such infestation may be prudent, especially if human owners or contacts are immunosuppressed. Antibiotic therapy of cats implicated in CSD transmission or otherwise demonstrated to be *B. henselae* or *B. clarridgeiae* infected does not durably eliminate bacteremia[200–202] and is not warranted, except perhaps in the setting of immunosuppressed human contacts. In general, removal of cats from the household of immunocompetent or immunosuppressed humans is unnecessary as long as the contact precautions defined previously are maintained. Although certainly not recommended, direct contact with cat feces or urine does not appear to present a risk for human *B. henselae* infection.

REFERENCES

1. Relman DA, Lepp PW, Sadler KN, Schmidt TM. Phylogenetic relationships among the agent of bacillary angiomatosis, *Bartonella bacilliformis*, and other alpha-proteobacteria. Mol Microbiol. 1992;6:1801–1807.
2. Brenner DJ, O'Connor SP, Winkler HH, Steigerwalt AG. Proposals to unify the genera *Bartonella* and *Rochalimaea*, with descriptions of *Bartonella quintana* comb nov, *Bartonella vinsonii* comb nov, *Bartonella henselae* comb nov, and *Bartonella elizabethae* comb nov, and to remove the family Bartonellaceae from the order Rickettsiales. Int J Syst Bacteriol. 1993;43:777–786.
3. Strong RP, Tyzzer EE, Brues CT, et al. Verruga peruviana, Oroya fever and uta. Preliminary report of the first expedition to South America from the Department of Tropical Medicine of Harvard University. JAMA. 1913;61:1713–1716.
4. Strong RP, Sellards AW. Oroya fever. Second report. JAMA. 1915;64:806–808.
5. Mooser H, Wyer F. Experimental infection of *Macacus rhesus* with *Rickettsia quintana* (trench fever). Proc Soc Exp Biol Med. 1953;83:699–701.
6. Liu W-T. Trench fever: A résumé of literature and a note on some obscure phases of the disease. Chinese Med J (Engl). 1984;97:179–190.
7. McNee JW, Renshaw A. "Trench fever": a relapsing fever occurring with the British forces in France. BMJ. 1916;1:225–234.
8. Koehler JE, Quinn FD, Berger TG, LeBoit PE, Tappero JW. Isolation of *Rochalimaea* species from cutaneous and osseous lesions of bacillary angiomatosis. N Engl J Med. 1992;327:1625–1632.
9. Spach DH, Callis KP, Paauw DS, et al. Endocarditis caused by *Rochalimaea quintana* in a patient infected with human immunodeficiency virus. J Clin Microbiol. 1993;31:692–694.
10. Larson AM, Dougherty MJ, Nowowiejski DJ, et al. Detection of *Bartonella (Rochalimaea) quintana* by routine acridine orange staining of broth blood cultures. J Clin Microbiol. 1994;32:1492–1496.
11. Drancourt M, Mainardi JL, Brouqui P, et al. *Bartonella (Rochalimaea) quintana* endocarditis in three homeless men. N Engl J Med. 1995;332:419–423.
12. Spach DH, Kanter AS, Dougherty MJ, et al. *Bartonella (Rochilmaea) quintana* bacteremia in inner-city patients with chronic alcoholism. N Engl J Med. 1995;332:424–428.
13. Slater LN, Welch DF, Hensel D, Coody DW. A newly recognized fastidious gram-negative pathogen as a cause of fever and bacteremia. N Engl J Med. 1990;323:1587–1593.
14. Regnery RL, Anderson BE, Clarridge JE III, et al. Characterization of a novel *Rochalimaea* species, *R. henselae* sp nov, isolated from blood of a febrile, human immunodeficiency virus-positive patient. J Clin Microbiol 1992;30:265–274.
15. Welch DF, Pickett DA, Slater LN, et al. *Rochalimaea henselae* sp nov, a cause of septicemia, bacillary angiomatosis, and parenchymal bacillary peliosis. J Clin Microbiol. 1992;30:275–280.
16. Daly JS, Worthington MG, Brenner DJ, et al. *Rochalimaea elizabethae* sp nov isolated from a patient with endocarditis. J Clin Microbiol. 1993;31:872–881.
17. Birtles RJ, Harrison TG, Saunders NA, Molyneux DH. Proposals to unify the genera *Grahamella* and *Bartonella,* with descriptions of *Bartonella talpae* comb nov, *Bartonella peromysci* sp nov, *Bartonella taylorii* sp nov, and *Bartonella doshiae* sp nov. Int J Syst Bacteriol. 1995;45:1–8.
18. Clarridge JE III, Raich TJ, Pirwani D, et al. Strategy to detect and identify *Bartonella* species in a routine clinical laboratory yields *Bartonella henselae* from human immunodeficiency virus-infected patient and unique *Bartonella* strain from his cat. J Clin Microbiol. 1995;33:2107–2113.

19. Heller R, Artois M, Xemar V, et al. Prevalence of *Bartonella henselae* and *Bartonella clarridgeiae* in stray cats. J Clin Microbiol. 1997;35:1327–1331.
20. Kordick DL, Hilyard EJ, Hadfield TL, et al. *Bartonella clarridgeiae*, a newly recognized zoonotic pathogen causing inoculation papules, fever and lymphadenopathy (cat scratch disease). J Clin Microbiol. 1997;35:1813–1818.
21. Gurfield AN, Boulouis H-J, Chomel BB, et al. Coinfection with *Bartonella clarridgeiae* and *Bartonella henselae* and with different *Bartonella henselae* strains in domestic cats. J Clin Microbiol. 1997;35:2120–2123.
22. Breitschwerdt EB, Kordick DL, Malarkey DE, et al. Endocaritis in a dog due to infection with a novel *Bartonella* subspecies. J Clin Microbiol. 1995;33:154–160.
23. Kordick DL, Swaminathan B, Greene CE, et al. *Bartonella vinsonii* subsp *berkhoffii* subsp nov, isolated from dogs; *Bartonella vinsonii* subsp *vinsonii*; and emended description of *Bartonella vinsonii*. Int J Syst Bacteriol. 1996;46:704–709.
23a. Hofmeister EK, Kolbert CP, Abdulkarim AS, et al. Cosegregation of a novel *Bartonella* species with *Borrelia burgdorferi* and *Babesia microti* in *Peromyscus leucopus*. J Infect Dis. 1998;177:406–416.
23b. Welch DF, Carroll KC, Hofmeister EK, et al. Isolation of a new subspecies *Bartonella rinsonii* subsp. *arupensis* from a cattle rancher: Identity with isolates found in conjunction with *Borrelia burgdorferi* and *Babesia microti* among naturally infected mice. J Clin Microbiol. 1999;37:2598–2601.
24. Kosoy MY, Regnery RL, Tziamabos T, et al. Distribution, diversity, and host specificity of *Bartonella* in rodents from the southeastern United States. Am J Trop Med Hyg. 1997;57:578–588.
25. Heller R, Kubina M, Delacour G, et al. Isolation of *Bartonella* spp from wildlife in France. Abstract P-21.18 Abstracts of the International Conference on Emerging Infectious Diseases, March 8–11, Atlanta, Ga; 1998:134.
25a. Ellis BA, Regnery RSL, Beati L, et al. Rats of the genus *Rattus* are reservoir hosts for pathogenic *Bartonella* species: An old world origin for a new world disease? J Infect Dis. 1999;180:220–224.
26. Yamamoto K, Chomel B, Lowenstine L, et al. *Bartonella henselae* antibody prevalence in free-ranging and captive wild felids from California. J Wildl Dis. 1998;34:56–63.
27. Koehler JE, Glaser CA, Tappero JW. *Rochalimaea henselae* infection: A new zoonosis with the domestic cat as reservoir. JAMA. 1994;271:531–535.
28. Chomel BB, Abbot RC, Kasten RW, et al. *Bartonella henselae* prevalence in domestic cats in California: Risk factors and association between bacteremia and antibody titers. J Clin Microbiol. 1995;33:2445–2450.
29. Demers DM, Bass JW, Vincent JM, et al. Cat scratch disease in Hawaii: Etiology and seroepidemiology. J Pediatr. 1995;127:23–26.
30. Sander A, Büler C, Pelz K, et al. Detection and identification of two *Bartonella henselae* variants in domestic cats in Germany. J Clin Microbiol. 1997;35:584–587.
31. Kordick DL, Wilson KH, Sexton DJ, et al. Prolonged *Bartonella* bacteremia in cats associated with cat-scratch disease patients. J Clin Microbiol. 1995;33:3245–3251.
32. Regnery RL, Olson JG, Perkins BA, Bibb W. Serologic response to *"Rochalimaea henselae"* antigen in suspected cat-scratch disease. Lancet. 1992;339:1443–1445.
33. Tappero JW, Mohle-Boetani J, Koehler J, et al. The epidemiology of bacillary angiomatosis and bacillary peliosis. JAMA. 1993;269:770–775.
34. Barka NR, Hadfield T, Patnaik M, et al. EIA for detection of *Rochalimaea henselae*–reactive IgG, IgM, and IgA antibodies in patients with suspected cat scratch disease (Letter). J Infect Dis. 1993;167:1503–1504.
35. Zangwill KM, Hamilton DH, Perkins BA, et al. Cat scratch disease in Connecticut. Epidemiology, risk factors, and evaluation of a new diagnostic test. N Engl J Med. 1993;329:8–13.
36. Dolan MJ, Wong MT, Regnery RL, et al. Syndrome of *Rochalimaea henselae* adenitis suggesting cat scratch disease. Ann Intern Med. 1993;118:331–336.
37. Waldvogel K, Regnery RL, Anderson BE, et al. Disseminated cat-scratch disease: Detection of *Rochalimaea henselae* in affected tissue. Eur J Pediatr. 1994;153:23–27.
38. Anderson B, Sims K, Regnery R, et al. Detection of *Rochalimaea henselae* DNA in specimens from cat-scratch disease patients by PCR. J Clin Microbiol. 1994;32:942–948.
39. Goral S, Anderson B, Hager C, Edwards K. Detection of *Rochalimaea henselae* DNA by polymerase chain reaction from suppurative nodes of children with cat-scratch disease. Pediatr Infect Dis J. 1994;13:994–997.
40. Le HH, Palay DA, Anderson B, Steinberg JP. Conjunctival swab to diagnose ocular cat scratch disease. Am J Ophthalmol. 1994;118:249–250.
41. Perkins BA, Swaminathan B, Jackson LA, et al. Case 22-1992. Pathogenesis of cat scratch disease (Letter). N Engl J Med. 1992;327:1599–1600.
42. Anderson B, Kelly C, Threlkel R, Edwards K. Detection of *Rochalimaea henselae* in cat-scratch disease skin test antigens. J Infect Dis. 1993;168:1034–1036.
43. Chomel BB, Kasten RW, Floyd-Hawkins K, et al. Experimental transmission of *Bartonella henselae* by the cat flea. J Clin Microbiol. 1996;34:1952–1956.
44. La verruga peruana y Daniel A Carrion, estudiante de la facultad de medicina, muerto el 5 de octobre de 1885. Lima: Imprenta del Estado; 1886.
45. Ricketts WE. Carrion's disease. A study of the incubation period in thirteen cases. Am J Trop Med. 1947;27:657–659.
46. Amano Y, Rumbea J, Knobloch J, et al. Bartonellosis in Ecuador: Serosurvey and current status of cutaneous verrucous disease. Am J Trop Med Hyg. 1997;57:174–179.
47. Strong RP, Tyzzer EE, Brues CT, et al. Report of the First Expedition to South America, 1913. Cambridge: Harvard University Press; 1915.
48. Ricketts WE. *Bartonella bacilliformis* anemia (Oroya fever). Blood. 1948;3:1025–1049.
49. Reynafarje C, Ramos J. The hemolytic anemia of human bartonellosis. Blood. 1961;17:562–578.
50. Ricketts WE. Clinical manifestations of Carrión's disease. Arch Intern Med. 1949;84:751–781.
51. Magu ĩna C, Gotuzzo E, Carcelén A, et al. Compromiso gastrointestinal bartonellosis o enfermedad de Carrión. Rev Gastroent Peru. 1997;17:31–43.
52. Cuadra M. Salmonellosis complication in human bartonellosis. Tex Rep Biol Med. 1956;14:97–113.
53. Pinkerton H, Weinman D. Toxoplasma infection in man. Arch Pathol. 1940;30:374–392.
54. Garcia-Caceres U, Garcia FU. Bartonellosis. An immunosuppresive disease and the life of Daniel Alcides Carrion. Am J Clin Pathol. 1991;95(Suppl 1):S56–S66.
55. Dooley JR. Bartonellosis. In: Binford CH, Connor DH, eds. Pathology of Tropical and Extraordinary Diseases. Washington, DC: Armed Forces Institute of Pathology; 1976:190–193.
56. Arias-Stella J, Lieberman PH, Erlandson RA, Arias-Stella J Jr. Histology, immunohistochemistry, and ultrastructure of the verruga in Carrion's disease. Am J Surg Pathol. 1986;10:595–610.
57. Jackson LA, Spach DH. Emergence of *Bartonella quintana* infection among homeless persons. Emerg Infect Dis. 1996;2:141–144.
58. Slater LN, Welch DF, Min K-W. *Rochalimaea henselae* causes bacillary angiomatosis and peliosis hepatis. Arch Intern Med. 1992;152:602–606.
59. Lucey D, Dolan MJ, Moss CW, et al. Relapsing illness due to *Rochalimaea henselae* in normal hosts: Implication for therapy and new epidemiologic associations. Clin Infect Dis. 1992;14:683–688.
60. Wong MT, Dolan MJ, Lattuada CP Jr, et al. Neuroretinitis, aseptic meningitis, and lymphadenitis associated with *Bartonella (Rochalimaea) henselae* infection in immunocompetent patients and patients infected with human immunodeficiency virus type 1. Clin Infect Dis. 1995;21:352–360.
61. Hadfield TL, Warren R, Kass M, Levy C. Endocarditis caused by *Rochalimaea henselae*. Hum Pathol. 1993;24:1140–1141.
62. Holmes AH, Greeough TC, Balady GJ, et al. *Bartonella henselae* endocarditis in an immunocompetent adult. Clin Infect Dis. 1995;21:1004–1007.
63. Spach DH, Kanter AS, Daniels NA, et al. *Bartonella (Rochalimaea)* species as a cause of apparent "culture-negative" endocarditis. Clin Infect Dis. 1995;20:1044–1047.
64. Jalava J, Kotilainen P, Nikkari S, et al. Use of polymerase chain reaction and DNA sequencing for detection of *Bartonella quintana* in the aortic valve of a patient with culture-negative infective endocarditis. Clin Infect Dis. 1995;21:891–896.
65. Drancourt M, Birtles R, Chaumentin G, et al. New serotype of *Bartonella henselae* in endocarditis and cat-scratch disease. Lancet. 1996;347:441–443.
66. Raoult D, Fournier P, Drancourt M, et al. Diagnosis of 22 new cases of *Bartonella* endocarditis. Ann Intern Med. 1996;125:646–652.
67. Baorto E, Payne RM, Slater LN, et al. Culture-negative endocarditis due to *Bartonella henselae*. J Pediatr. 1998;132:1052–1054.
68. Stoler MH, Bonfiglio TA, Steigbigel RT, Pereira M. An atypical subcutaneous infection associated with acquired immune deficiency syndrome. Am J Clin Pathol. 1983;80:714–718.
69. Cockerell CJ, Webster GF, Whitlow MA, Friedman-Kien AE. Epithelioid angiomatosis: A distinct vascular disorder in patients with the acquired immunodeficiency syndrome or AIDS-related complex. Lancet. 1987;2:6544–6546.
70. LeBoit PE, Egbert BM, Stoler MH, et al. Epithelioid haemangioma-like vascular proliferation in AIDS: Manifestation of cat scratch disease bacillus infection? Lancet. 1988:960–963.
71. Koehler JE, LeBoit PE, Egbert BM, Berger TG. Cutaneous vascular lesions and disseminated cat-scratch disease in patients with the acquired immunodeficiency syndrome (AIDS) and AIDS-related complex. Ann Intern Med. 1988;109:449–455.
72. Milam MW, Balerdi MJ, Toney JF, et al. Epithelioid angiomatosis secondary to disseminated cat scratch disease involving the bone marrow and skin in a patient with acquired immune deficiency syndrome: A case report. Am J Med. 1990;88:180–183.
73. Kemper CA, Lombard CM, Deresinski SC, Tompkins LS. Visceral bacillary epithelioid angiomatosis: Possible manifestations of disseminated cat scratch disease in the immunocompromised host: A report of two cases. Am J Med. 1990;89:216–222.
74. Spach DH, Panther LA, Thorning DR, et al. Intracerebral bacillary angiomatosis in a patient infected with the human immunodeficiency virus. Ann Intern Med. 1992;116:740–742.
75. Koehler JE, Cederberg L. Intraabdominal mass associated with gastrointestinal hemorrhage: A new manifestation of bacillary angiomatosis. Gastroenterology. 1995;109:2011–2014.
76. Coche E, Beigelman C, Lucidarme O, et al. Thoracic bacillary angiomatosis in a patient with AIDS. Am J Roentgenol. 1995;165:56–58.
77. Mohle-Boetani JC, Koehler JE, Berger TG, et al. Bacillary angiomatosis and bacillary peliosis in patients infected with the human immunodeficiency virus: Clinical characteristics in a case control study. Clin Infect Dis. 1996;22:794–800.
78. Huh YB, Rose S, Schoen RE, et al. Colonic bacillary angiomatosis. Ann Intern Med. 1996;124:735–737.
79. Long SR, Whitfield MJ, Eades C, et al. Bacillary angiomatosis of the cervix and vulva in a patient with AIDS. Obstet Gynecol. 1996;881:709–711.
80. Relman DA, Loutit JS, Schmidt TM, et al. The agent of bacillary angiomatosis: An approach to the identification of uncultured pathogens. N Engl J Med. 1990;323:1573–1580.

81. Cockerell CJ, Bergstresser PR, Myrie-Williams C, Tierno PM. Bacillary epithelioid angiomatosis occurring in an immunocompetent individual. Arch Dermatol. 1990;126:787–790.
82. Tappero JW, Koehler JE, Berger TG, et al. Bacillary angiomatosis and bacillary splenitis in immunocompetent adults. Ann Intern Med. 1993;118:363–365.
83. Cockerell CJ, Tierno PM, Friedman-Kien AE, Kim KS. Clinical, histologic, microbiologic, and biochemical characterization of the causative agent of bacillary (epithelioid) angiomatosis: A rickettsial illness with features of bartonellosis. J Invest Dermatol. 1991;97:812–817.
84. Relman DA, Falkow S, LeBoit PE, et al. The organism causing bacillary angiomatosis, peliosis hepatis, and fever and bacteremia in immunocompromised patients (Letter). N Engl J Med. 1991;324:1514.
85. Koehler JE, Sanchez MA, Garrido CS, et al. Molecular epidemiology of *Bartonella* infections in patients with bacillary angiomatosis-peliosis. N Engl J Med. 1997;337:1876–1883.
86. Tappero JW, Koehler JE. Bacillary angiomatosis or Kaposi's sarcoma? N Eng J Med. 1997;337:1888.
87. Cockerell CJ, LeBoit PE. Bacillary angiomatosis: A newly characterized, pseudoneoplastic, infectious, cutaneous vascular disorder. J Am Acad Dermatol. 1990;22:501–512.
88. LeBoit PE, Berger TG, Egbert BM, et al. Bacillary angiomatosis. The histology and differential diagnosis of a pseudoneoplastic infection in patients with human immunodeficiency virus disease. Am J Surg Pathol. 1989;13:909–920.
89. Perkocha LA, Geaghan SM, Yen TSB, et al. Clinical and pathological features of bacillary peliosis hepatis in association with human immunodeficiency virus infection. N Engl J Med. 1990;323:1581–1586.
90. Leong SS, Cazen RA, Yu GSM, et al. Abdominal visceral peliosis associated with bacillary angiomatosis: Ultrastructural evidence of endothelial cell destruction by bacilli. Arch Pathol Lab Med. 1992;116:866–871.
91. Slater LN, Pitha JV, Herrera L, et al. *Rochalimaea henselae* infection in AIDS causing inflammatory disease without angiomatosis or peliosis: Demonstration by immunocytochemistry and corroboration by DNA amplification. Arch Pathol Lab Med. 1994;118:33–38.
92. Caniza MA, Granger DL, Wilson KH, et al. *Bartonella henselae:* Etiology of pulmonary nodules in a patient with depressed cell-mediated immunity. Clin Infect Dis. 1995;20:1505–1511.
93. Liston TE, Koehler JE. Granulatomous hepatitis and necrotizing splenitis due to *Bartonella henselae* in a patient with cancer: Case report and review of hepatosplenic manifestations of *Bartonella* infection. Clin Infect Dis. 1996;22:951–957.
94. Szelc-Kelly CM, Goral S, Perez-Perez GI, et al. Serologic responses to *Bartonella* and *Afipia* antigens in patients with cat scratch disease. Pediatrics. 1995;96:1137–1142.
95. Dauga C, Mira I, Grimont PAD. Identification of *Bartonella henselae* and B. *quintana* 16S rDNA sequences by branch-, genus-, and species-specific amplification. J Med Microbiol. 1996;45:192–199.
96. Scott MA, McCurley TL, Vnencak-Jones CL, et al. Cat scratch disease. Detection of *Bartonella henselae* DNA in archival biopsies from patients with clinically, serologically and histologically defined disease. Am J Pathol. 1996;149:2161–2167.
97. Mouritsen CL, Litwin CM, Maiese RL, et al. Rapid polymerase chain reaction–based detection of the causative agent of cat scratch disease (*Bartonella henselae*) in formalin-fixed, paraffin-embedded samples. Hum Pathol. 1997;28:820–826.
98. Avidor B, Kletter Y, Abulafa S, et al. Molecular diagnosis of cat scratch disease: A two-step approach. J Clin Microbiol. 1997;35:1924–1930.
99. Min K-W, Reed JA, Welch DF, Slater LN. Morphologically variable bacilli of cat scratch disease are identified by immunocytochemical labeling with antibodies to *Rochalimaea henselae*. Am J Clin Pathol. 1994;101:607–610.
100. Regnery R, Martin M, Olson J. Naturally occurring "*Rochalimaea henselae*" infection in domestic cat (Letter). Lancet. 1992;340:557–558.
101. Debré R, Lamy M, Jammet ML, et al. La maladie des griffes de chat. Semin Ĥop Paris. 1950;26:1895–1904.
102. Brenner DJ, Hollis DG, Moss CW, et al. Proposal of *Afipia* gen nov, with *Afipia felis* sp nov (formerly the cat scratch disease bacillus), *Afipia clevelandensis* sp nov (formerly the Cleveland Clinic Foundation strain), *Afipia broomeae* sp nov, and three unnamed genospecies. J Clin Microbiol. 1991;29:2450–2460.
103. Alkan S, Morgan MB, Sandin RL, et al. Dual role for *Afipia felis* and *Rochalimaea henselae* in cat-scratch disease. (Letter). Lancet. 1995;345:385.
104. Jackson LA, Perkins BA, Wenger JD. Cat scratch disease in the United States: An analysis of three national databases. Am J Public Health. 1993;83:1707–1711.
105. Noah DL, Kramer CM, Verbsky MP, et al. Survey of veterinary professionals and other veterinary conference attendees for antibodies to *Bartonella henselae* and *B. quintana*. J Am Vet Med Assoc. 1997;210:342–344.
106. Carithers HA. Cat-scratch disease. An overview based on a study of 1,200 patients. Am J Dis Child. 1985;139:1124–1133.
107. Moriarty R, Margileth A. Cat scratch disease. Infect Dis Clin North Am. 1987;1:575–590.
108. Margileth AM. Cat scratch disease. Adv Pediatr Infect Dis. 1993;8:1–21.
109. Bass JW, Freitas BD, Sisier CL, et al. Prospective randomized double-blind placebo-controlled evaluation of azithromycin for treatment of cat scratch disease. Pediatr Infect Dis J. 1998;17:447–452.
110. Bosch X. Hypercalcemia due to endogenous overproduction of active vitamin D in identical twins with cat-scratch disease. JAMA. 1998;279:532–534.
111. Parinaud H. Conjontivite infectieuse par les animaux. Ann Ocul. 1889;101:252–253.
112. Cassady JV, Culbertson CS. Cat-scratch disease and Parinaud's oculoglandular syndrome. Arch Ophthalmol. 1953;50:68–74.
113. Margileth AM, Wear DJ, English CK. Systemic cat scratch disease: Report of 23 patients with prolonged or recurrent severe bacterial infection. J Infect Dis. 1987;155:390–402.
114. Abbasi S, Chesney PJ. Pulmonary manifestations of cat scratch disease; a case report and review of the literature. Pediatr Infect Dis J. 1995;14:547–548.
115. Muszynski M, Eppes J, Riley H. Granulomatous osteolytic lesion of the skull associated with cat scratch disease. Pediatr Infect Dis J. 1987;6:199–201.
116. Jacobs RF, Schultze GE. *Bartonella henselae* as a cause of prolonged fever of unknown origin in children. Clin Infect Dis. 1998;26:80–84.
117. Lenoir AA, Storch GA, DeSchryver-Kecskemeti K, et al. Granulomatous hepatitis associated with cat scratch disease. Lancet. 1988;1:1132–1136.
118. Delahoussaye PM, Osborne BM. Cat-scratch disease presenting as abdominal visceral granulomas. J Infect Dis. 1990;161:71–78.
119. Dunn MW, Berkowitz FE, Miller JJ, Snitzer JA. Hepatosplenic cat-scratch disease and abdominal pain. Pediatr Infect Dis J. 1997;16:269–272.
120. Centers for Disease Control and Prevention. Encephalitis associated with cat scratch disease—Broward and Palm Beach Counties, Florida, 1994. MMWR Morb Mortal Wkly Rep. 1994;43:915–916.
121. Stevens H. Cat-scratch fever encephalitis. Am J Dis Child. 1952;84:218–222.
122. Jambor J, Emura E. Benign inoculation lymphoreticulosis (cat scratch disease). Arch Derm Syph. 1953;67:439–442.
123. Thompson TE, Jr, Miller KF. Cat scratch encephalitis. Ann Intern Med. 1953;39:146–151.
124. Weinstein L, Meade RH. Neurological manifestations of cat scratch disease. Am J Med Sci. 1955;229:500–505.
125. Carithers H, Margileth A. Cat scratch disease. Acute encephalopathy and other neurologic manifestations. Am J Dis Child. 1991;145:98–101.
126. Selby G, Walker GL. Cerebral arteritis in cat-scratch disease. Neurology. 1979;29:1413–1418.
127. Revol A, Vighetto A, Jouvet A, et al. Encephalitis in cat scratch disease with persistent dementia. J Neurol Neurosurg Psychiatry. 1992;55:133–135.
128. Hahn J, Sum J, Lee K. Unusual MRI findings after status epilepticus due to cat-scratch disease. Pediatr Neurol. 1994;10:255–258.
129. Sweeney VP, Drance SM. Optic neuritis and compressive neuropathy associated with cat scratch disease. Can Med Assoc J. 1970;103:1380–1381.
130. Dreyer RF, Hopen G, Gass DM, Smith JL. Leber's idiopathic stellate neuroretinitis. Arch Ophthalmol. 1984;102:1140–1145.
131. Wong MT, Thornton DC, Kennedy RC, Dolan MJ. A chemically defined medium that supports primary isolation of *Rochalimaea (Bartonella) henselae* from blood and tissue specimens. J Clin Microbiol. 1995;33:742–744.
132. Golnik KC, Marotto ME, Fanous MM, et al. Ophthalmic manifestations of *Rochalimaea* species. Am J Ophthalmol. 1994;118:145–151.
133. Reed JB, Scales JK, Wong MT, et al. *Bartonella henselae* neuroretinitis in cat scratch disease. Ophthalmology. 1998;105:459–466.
134. Schwartzman WA, Patnaik M, Barka NE, Peter JB. *Rochalimaea* antibodies in HIV-associated neurologic disease. Neurology. 1994;44:1312–1316.
135. Baker J, Ruiz-Rodriguez R, Whitfield M, et al. Bacillary angiomatosis: A treatable cause of acute psychiatric symptoms in human immunodeficiency virus infection. J Clin Psychiatry. 1995;56:161–166.
136. Patnaik M, Schwartzman WA, Peter JB. *Bartonella henselae*: Detection in brain tissue of patients with AIDS-associated neurological disease. Abstract of poster presentation at the 1995 Clinical Research Meeting, San Diego, Cal. J Invest Med. 1995;43(Suppl 2):368A.
137. Schwartzman WA, Patnaik M, Angulo FJ, et al. *Bartonella* (*Rochalimaea*) antibodies, dementia, and cat ownership in human immunodeficiency virus-infected men. Clin Infect Dis. 1995;21:954–959.
138. Abbot R, Chomel B, Kasten R, et al. Experimental and natural infection with *Bartonella henselae* in domestic cats. Comp Immunol Microbiol Infect Dis. 1997;20:41–51.
139. Guptill L, Slater L, Wu C-C, et al. Experimental infection of young specific pathogen-free cats with *Bartonella henselae*. J Infect Dis. 1997;176:206–216.
140. Kordick DL, Breitschwerdt EB. Relapsing bacteremia after blood transmission of *Bartonella henselae* to cats. Am J Vet Res. 1997;58:492–497.
141. Walker TS, Winkler HH. *Bartonella bacilliformis*: Colonial types and erythrocyte adherence. Infect Immun. 1981;31:480–486.
142. Scherer DC, DeBuron-Conners I, Minnick MF. Characterization of *Bartonella bacilliformis* flagella and effect of antiflagellin antibodies on invasion of human erythrocytes. Infect Immun. 1993;61:4962–4971.
143. Minnick MF. Virulence determinants of *Bartonella bacilliformis*. In: Anderson B, Friedman H, Bendinelli M, eds. Rickettsial Infection and Immunity. New York: Plenum; 1997:197–211.
144. Mernaugh G, Ihler GM. Deformation factor: An extracellular protein synthesized by *Bartonella bacilliformis* that deforms erythrocyte membranes. Infect Immun. 1992;60:937–943.
145. Xu Y-H, Lu Z-Y, Ihler GM. Purification of deformin, an extracellular protein synthesized by *Bartonella bacilliformis* which causes deformation of erythrocyte membranes. Biochim Biophys Acta. 1995;1234:173–183.
146. Mitchell SJ, Minnick MF. Characterization of a two-gene locus from *Bartonella bacilliformis* associated with the ability to invade human erythrocytes. Infect Immun. 1995;63:1552–1562.
147. Iwaki-Egawa S, Ihler GM. Comparison of the abilities of proteins from *Bartonella*

bacilliformis and *Bartonella henselae* to deform red cell membranes and to bind to red cell ghost proteins. FEMS Microbiol Lett. 1997;157:207–217.

148. Benson LA, Kar S, McLaughlin G, Ihler GM. Entry of *Bartonella bacilliformis* into erythrocytes. Infect Immun. 1986;54:347–353.
149. Kordick DL, Breitschwerdt E. Intraerythocytic presence of *Bartonella henselae*. J Clin Microbiol. 1995;33:1655–1656.
150. Guptill L, Tobolski J, Wu C-C, et al. Extracellular *Bartonella henselae* in blood of experimentally infected cats. Proceedings of the 77th Annual Meeting of the Conference of Research Workers in Animal Diseases, 1996, p. 1.
151. Garcia FU, Wojta J, Broadley KN, et al. *Bartonella bacilliformis* stimulates endothelial cells in vitro and is angiogenic in vivo. Am J Pathol. 1990;136:1125–1135.
152. Garcia FU, Wojta J, Hoover RL. Interactions between live *Bartonella bacilliformis* and endothelial cells. J Infect Dis. 1992;165:1138–1141.
153. Conley T, Slater L, Hamilton K. *Rochalimaea* spp stimulate endothelial cell proliferation and migration in vitro. J Lab Clin Med. 1994;124:521–528.
154. McGinnis-Hill E, Raji A, Valenzuela MS, et al. Adhesion to and invasion of cultured human cells by *Bartonella bacilliformis*. Infect Immun. 1992;60:4051–4058.
155. Brouqui P, Raoult D. *Bartonella quintana* invades and multiplies within endothelial cells in vitro and in vivo and forms intracellular blebs. Res Microbiol. 1996;147:719–731.
156. Dehio C, Meyer M, Berger J, et al. Interaction of *Bartonella henselae* with endothelial cells results in bacterial aggregation on the cell surface and the subsequent engulfment and internalisation of the bacterial aggregate by a unique structure, the invasome. J Cell Sci. 1997;110:2141–2154.
157. Conley TD, Wack MF, Hamilton KK, Slater LN. Stimulation of angiogenesis and protection from oxidative damage: Two potential mechanisms involved in pathogenesis by *Bartonella henselae* and other *Bartonella* species. In: Anderson B, Friedman H, Bendinelli M, eds. Rickettsial Infection and Immunity. New York: Plenum; 1997:213–232.
158. Mitchell SJ, Minnick MF. A carboxy terminal processing gene is located immediately upstream of the invasion-associated locus from *Bartonella bacilliformis*. Microbiology. 1997;143:1221–1233.
159. Welch DF, Hensel DM, Pickett DA, et al. Bacteremia due to *Rochalimaea henselae* in a child: Practical identification of isolates in the clinical laboratory. J Clin Microbiol. 1993;31:2381–2386.
160. Tierno PM Jr, Inglima K, Parisi MT. Detection of *Bartonella (Rochalimaea) henselae* bacteremia using BacT/Alert blood culture system. Am J Clin Pathol. 1995;104:530–536.
161. Reed J, Brigati DJ, Flynn SD, et al. Immunocytochemical identification of *Rochalimaea henselae* in bacillary (epithelioid) angiomatosis, parenchymal bacillary peliosis, and persistent fever with bacteremia. Am J Surg Pathol. 1992;16:650–657.
162. Peters D, Wigand R. Bartonellaceae. Bacteriol Rev. 1955;19:150–159.
163. Cuadra M, Takano J. The relationship of *Bartonella bacilliformis* to the red blood cell as revealed by electron microscopy. Blood. 1969;33:708–716.
164. Brenner SA, Rooney JA, Manzewitsch P, Regnery RL. Isolation of *Bartonella (Rochilamaea) henselae*: Effects of methods of blood collection and handling. J Clin Microbiol. 1997;35:544–547.
165. Welch DF, Slater LN. *Bartonella*. In: Murray PR, Baron EJ, Pfaller MA, et al., eds. Manual of Clinical Microbiology. 6th ed. Washington, DC: American Society for Microbiology; 1995:690–695.
166. Schwartzman WA, Nesbit CA, Baron EJ. Development and evaluation of a blood-free medium for determining growth curves and optimizing growth of *Rochalimaea henselae*. J Clin Microbiol. 1993;31:1882–1885.
167. Slater LN, Coody DW, Woolridge LK, Welch DF. Murine antibody responses distinguish *Rochalimaea henselae* from *Rochalimaea quintana*. J Clin Microbiol. 1992;30:1722–1727.
168. Drancourt M, Raoult D. Proposed tests for the routine identification of *Rochalimaea* species. Eur J Clin Microbiol Infect Dis. 1993;12:710–713.
169. Moss CW, Holzer G, Wallace PL, Hollis DG. Cellular fatty acid compositions of an unidentified organism and a bacterium associated with cat scratch disease. J Clin Microbiol. 1990;28:1071–1074.
170. Myers WF, Grossman DM, Wisseman CL Jr. Antibiotic susceptibility patterns in *Rochalimaea quintana*, the agent of trench fever. Antimicrob Agents Chemother. 1984;25:690–693.
171. Wolfson C, Branley J, Gottlieb T. The Etest for antimicrobial susceptibility testing of *Bartonella henselae*. J Antimicrob Chemother. 1996;38:963–968.
172. Maurin M, Raoult D. Antimicrobial susceptibility of *Rochalimaea quintana*, *Rochalimaea vinsonii*, and the newly recognised *Rochalimaea henselae*. J Antimicrob Chemother. 1993;32:587–594.
173. Maurin M, Gasquet S, Caroline D, Raoult D. MICs of 28 antibiotic compounds for 14 *Bartonella* (formerly *Rochalimea*) isolates. Antimicrob Agents Chemother. 1995;39:2387–2391.
174. Musso D, Drancourt M, Raoult D. Lack of bactericidal effect of antibiotics except aminoglycosides on *Bartonella (Rochalimaea) henselae*. J Antimicrob Chemother. 1995;36:101–108.
175. Ives TJ, Manzewitsch P, Regnery RL, et al. In vitro susceptibilities of *Bartonella henselae, B. quintana, B. elizabethae, Rickettsia ricketsii, R. conorii, R. akari,* and *R. prowazekii* to macrolide antibiotics as determined by immunofluorescent-antibody analysis of infected vero cell monolayers. Antimicrob Agent Chemother. 1997;44:578–582.
176. Matar GM, Swaminathan B, Hunter SB, et al. Polymerase chain reaction–based restriction fragment length polymorphism analysis of a fragment of the ribosomal operon from *Rochalimaea* species for subtyping. J Clin Microbiol. 1993;31:1730–1734.
177. Roux V, Raoult D. Inter- and intraspecies identification of *Bartonella (Rochalimaea)* species. J Clin Microbiol. 1995;33:1573–1576.
178. Rodriguez-Barradas MC, Hamill RJ, Houston ED, et al. Genomic fingerprints of *Bartonella* species by repetitive element PCR for distinguishing species and isolates. J Clin Microbiol. 1995;33:1089–1093.
179. Bergmans AM, Schellekens JFP, van Embden JDA, Schouls LM. Predominance of two *Bartonella henselae* variants among cat-scratch disease patients in the Netherlands. J Clin Microbiol. 1996;34:254–260.
180. Ritzler M, Altwegg M. Sensitivity and specificity of a commercially available enzyme-linked immunoassay for the detection of polymerase chain reaction amplified DNA. J Microbiol Methods. 1996;27:233–38.
181. Bergmans AMC, Groothedde J-W, Schellekens JFP, et al. Etiology of cat scratch disease: Comparison of polymerase chain reaction detection of *Bartonella* (formerly *Rochalimaea*) and *Afipia felis* DNA with serology and skin tests. J Infect Dis. 1995;171:916–923.
182. Herrmann JE, Hollingdale MR, Collins MF, Vinson JW. Enzyme immunoassay and radioimmunoprecipitation tests for the detection of antibodies to *Rochalimaea (Rickettsia) quintana* (39655). Proc Soc Exp Biol Med. 1977;154:285–288.
183. Hollingdale MR, Herrmann JE, Vinson JW. Enzyme immunoassay of antibody to *Rochalimaea quintana*: Diagnosis of trench fever and serologic cross-reactions among other rickettsiae. J Infect Dis. 1978;137:578–582.
184. Dalton MJ, Robinson LE, Cooper J, et al. Use of *Bartonella* antigens for the serologic diagnosis of cat-scratch disease at a national referral center. Arch Intern Med. 1995;155:1670–1676.
185. La Scola B, Raoult D. Serological cross-reactions between *Bartonella quintana, Bartonella henselae,* and *Coxiella burnettii*. J Clin Microbiol. 1996;34:2270–2274.
186. Dupon M, Savin de Larclause A-M, Brouqui P, et al. Evaluation of serological response to *Bartonella henselae, Bartonella quintana,* and *Afipia felis* antigens in 64 patients with suspected cat-scratch disease. Scand J Infect Dis. 1996;28:361–366.
187. Bergmans AMC, Peeters MF, Schellekens JFP, et al. Pitfalls and fallacies of cat scratch disease serology: Evaluation of *Bartonella henselae*–based indirect fluorescence assay and enzyme-linked immunoassay. J Clin Microbiol. 1997;35:1931–1937.
188. Maurin M, Eb F, Etienne J, Raoult D. Serological cross-reactions between *Bartonella* and *Chlamydia*. J Clin Microbiol. 1997;35:2283–2287.
189. Litwin CM, Martins TB, Hill HR. Immunologic response to *Bartonella henselae* as determined by enzyme immunoassay and Western blot analysis. Am J Clin Pathol. 1997;108:202–209.
190. Anderson B, Lu E, Jones D, Regnery R. Characterization of 17-kilodalton antigen of *Bartonella henselae* reactive with sera from patients with cat scratch disease. J Clin Microbiol. 1995;33:2358–2365.
191. Ephros M, Slater LN, Kletter Y, et al. Enzyme immunoassay for the diagnosis of cat scratch disease. Abstract 245. Presented at the 35th Annual Meeting of the Infectious Diseases Society of America, San Francisco, Cal, September 1997. Clin Infect Dis. 1997;25:401.
192. Koehler JE, Tappero JW. Bacillary angiomatosis and bacillary peliosis in patients infected with human immunodeficiency virus. Clin Infect Dis. 1993;17:612–624.
193. Regnery RL, Childs JE, Koehler JE. Infections associated with *Bartonella* species in persons infected with the human immunodeficiency virus. Clin Infect Dis. 1995;21(Suppl 1):S94–S98.
194. Bogue C, Wise JD, Gray GF, Edwards KM. Antibiotic therapy for cat-scratch disease? JAMA. 1989;262:813–816.
195. Holley HP Jr. Successful treatment of cat-scratch disease with ciprofloxacin. JAMA. 1991;265:1563–1565.
196. Collipp PJ. Cat-scratch disease: Therapy with trimethoprim-sulfamethoxazole. Am J Dis Child. 1992;146:397–399.
197. Margileth AM. Antibiotic therapy for cat-scratch disease: Clinical study of therapeutic outcome in 268 patients and a review of the literature. Pediatr Infect Dis J. 1992;11:474–478.
198. Chia JK, Nakata MM, Lami JL, et al. Azithromycin for the treatment of cat-scratch disease. Clin Infect Dis. 1998;26:193–194.
199. Foley JE, Chomel B, Kikuchi Y, et al. Seroprevalence of *Bartonella henselae* in cattery cats: Association with cattery hygiene and flea infestation. Vet Q. 1998;20:1–5.
200. Greene CE, McDermott M, Jameson PH, et al. *Bartonella henselae* infection in cats: Evaluation during primary infection, treatment, and rechallenge infection. J Clin Microbiol. 1996;34:1682–1685.
201. Regnery RL, Rooney A, Johnson AM, et al. Experimentally induced *Bartonella henselae* infections followed by challenge exposure and antimicrobial therapy in cats. Am J Vet Res. 1996;57:1714–1719.
202. Kordick DL, Papich MG, Breitschwerdt EB. Efficacy of enrofloxacin or doxycycline for treatment of *Bartonella henselae* or *Bartonella clarridgeiae* infection in cats. Antimicrob Agents Chemother. 1997;41:2448–2455.

Chapter 225

Calymmatobacterium granulomatis (Donovanosis, Granuloma Inguinale)

RONALD C. BALLARD

Donovanosis is a chronic, progressive ulcerative disease, usually of the genital region, that is caused by an encapsulated gram-negative bacterium, *Calymmatobacterium granulomatis*. The infection has previously been known by other names including granuloma inguinale tropicum, granuloma pudenda, granuloma venereum, and, most recently, granuloma inguinale. Possible confusion with another sexually transmitted disease, lymphogranuloma venereum, caused by certain invasive serovars of *Chlamydia trachomatis*, has led to the adoption of *donovanosis* as the preferred name for the disease. The first description of the disease has been attributed to McLeod working in India in 1881[1] and the discovery of the causative organism to Donovan in 1905.[2]

BIOLOGY OF THE CAUSATIVE ORGANISM

Calymmatobacterium granulomatis, formerly known as *Donovania granulomatis*, is an encapsulated, pleomorphic gram-negative bacillus measuring 1 to 2 × 0.5 to 0.7 μm that can be found in vacuoles in the cytoplasm of large mononuclear cells.[3] The organisms are frequently described as having bipolar densities that give Donovan bodies the appearance of closed safety pins. The bacteria appear to multiply within these cells and are subsequently released to infect others after the rupture of mature intracytoplasmic vacuoles. Ultrastructurally, the organisms have been described as characteristically gram-negative with a clearly defined capsule with no flagella. However, small surface projections resembling pili or fimbriae have been observed together with electron-dense granules measuring 35 to 45 μm in diameter in the cell periphery. In the past it was thought that these granules provided evidence of bacteriophage infection; however, this remains controversial.[4]

Although culture of the organisms was reported in the early 1940s in chick embryo yolk sacs[5] and later on egg yolk–based media[6] and in defined liquid media, until the late 1990s no pure isolates had been available for study for the previous 50 years. As a result, the organisms have been poorly characterized, although a relationship with *Klebsiella* had previously been suggested owing to common morphologic characteristics. Renewed efforts have been made to isolate *C. granulomatis* from clinical material by using human monocyte cultures[7] and Hep-2 cell monolayers[8] and to further characterize the organisms.

GEOGRAPHIC DISTRIBUTION AND EPIDEMIOLOGY

Donovanosis is a relatively rare disease in the United States, with fewer than 100 cases reported annually, although previously it was encountered more frequently in the southern states. It is recognized as a major cause of genital ulceration in Southeast India, Papua New Guinea, the Caribbean, and parts of South America (particularly Brazil) and has been recorded in Zambia, Zimbabwe, in the KwaZulu-Natal region of South Africa, in Southeast Asia, and among aboriginals in Australia.[3, 9] Cases of donovanosis may be encountered in centers remote from endemic regions as a result of immigration and increased holiday and business travel to these predominantly tropical areas. Although usually assumed to be a sexually transmitted infection, the possibility that the disease may be transmitted nonsexually remains a controversial issue. Goldberg postulated that the causative organism is a commensal of the gastrointestinal tract and that the vagina may become infected by autoinoculation.[10] Extragenital lesions and lesions in young children all indicate alternative modes of spread; however, the age distribution of the disease in endemic areas, the frequent coexistence of other sexually transmitted diseases, and the finding that the genital area is the most frequent anatomic site of donovanosis lesions all indicate that it is primarily a sexually transmitted infection, albeit of low infectivity.

CLINICAL MANIFESTATIONS

The primary lesion of donovanosis begins as a small painless papule or indurated nodule that occurs after an incubation period of between 8 and 80 days. The lesion soon ulcerates to form an exuberant, beefy-red, granulomatous ulcer with rolled edges and with a characteristic satin-like surface that bleeds easily on contact (Fig. 225–1). Multiple lesions may coalesce to form large ulcers, and new lesions may also form as a result of autoinoculation. Characteristically, even large ulcerative lesions are painless unless there is severe secondary infection. The disease spreads subcutaneously and may become progressively more destructive. Spontaneous healing is accompanied by scar formation, which can also produce gross deformities (Fig. 225–2). Lymphedema with consequent elephantiasis of the external genitalia may occur in severe cases as a result of the blockage of the lymphatics by keloid scars. In men, the most common sites of infection are the prepuce, coronal sulcus, and penile shaft. In women, the labia and the fourchette are most commonly involved, but lesions of the vaginal wall and cervix may be an uncommon cause of vaginal bleeding. Donovanosis is frequently diagnosed during pregnancy, and it has been postulated that pregnancy causes exacerbation of the disease.[11] However, this may just be a reflection of the asymptomatic nature of cervical infection and its detection during routine examination during pregnancy. Subcutaneous spread of granulomas into the inguinal region may result in the formation of groin swellings (pseudobubos), which are not a true adenitis.

Rectal lesions have been found to be associated with receptive anal intercourse among male homosexuals,[12] whereas penile lesions are often detected among their sexual partners. Systemic disease is rare but is more common in women with primary lesions of the cervix.[13]

Hematogenous spread of infection to form pelvic granulomas and to involve bones and joints has been documented, together with rare cases of lymphadenitis possibly associated with lymphatic spread.[14] Constitutional symptoms are conspicuously absent except in those

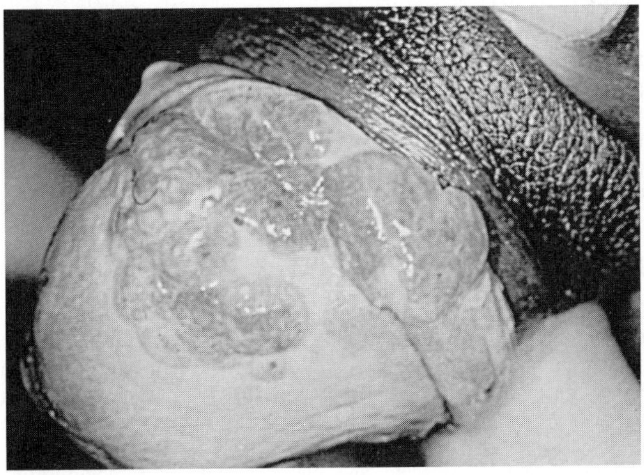

FIGURE 225–1. Early lesion of donovanosis.

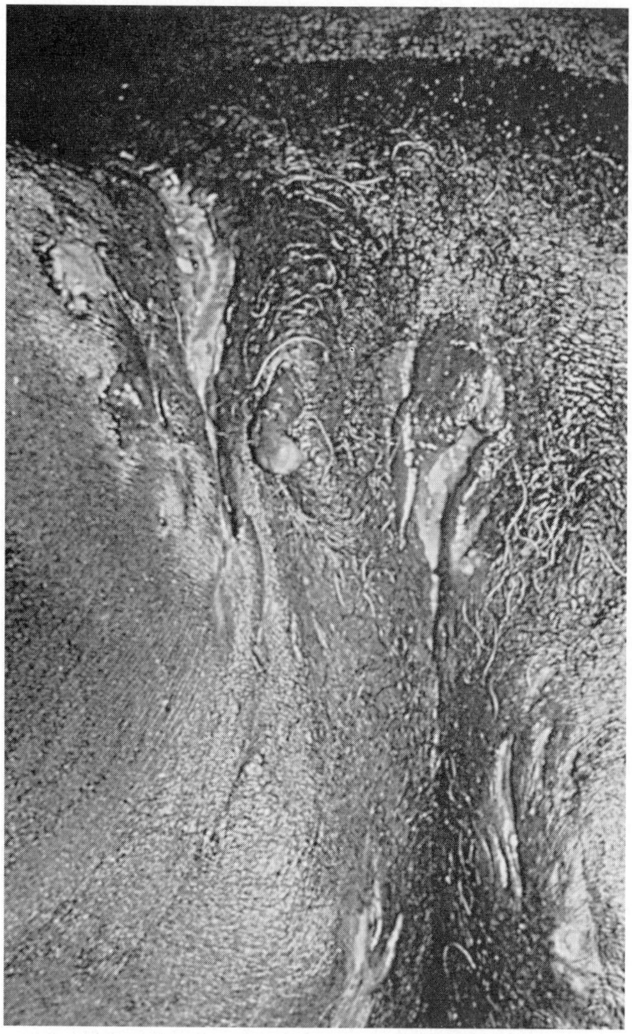

FIGURE 225–2. Late lesions of donovanosis showing extensive scarring and subcutaneous spread.

cases where coinfection with other sexually transmitted diseases has been demonstrated, where secondary bacterial infection is evident, or where extensive spread has occurred. Donovanosis has to be distinguished from other causes of genital ulcer disease, regional lymphadenopathy, and genital elephantiasis. Those lesions most likely to provide diagnostic problems on clinical grounds include cases of "pseudogranulomatous" chancroid, ulcerating genital warts, both primary and secondary syphilis, and squamous carcinoma. Early papers suggested a link between donovanosis and squamous carcinoma of the external genitalia;[15] however, this hypothesis remains unproved, and the possible coexistence of donovanosis and human papillomavirus infection, which has proven oncogenic potential, cannot be ruled out.

DIAGNOSIS

Most cases of donovanosis are diagnosed on the basis of the characteristic clinical manifestations. However, confirmation of the diagnosis can be obtained on the basis of histologic examination of punch biopsy specimens taken from the edges of active lesions, scrapings taken from the edges of lesions, or a crush preparation made from granulation tissue obtained with a thin scalpel. In all cases, active lesions should be selected and cleansed with physiologic saline before sampling.

Although biopsy specimens are mandatory when malignancy has to be excluded, smear or crush preparations are usually adequate for the diagnosis of acute, active disease of short duration.

Ideally, smear preparations for microscopy should be made immediately with fresh, moist tissue and these should be fixed and stained with Giemsa, Leishman, or Wright stain.[3, 16] Although the application of newer, rapid Giemsa techniques can provide an immediate, definitive diagnosis even in resource-poor settings,[17] the standard Giemsa and silver stains are preferred when fixed, embedded tissue specimens are prepared for histologic examination.[3] The demonstration of typical intracellular Donovan bodies in stained smears obtained from lesions (Fig. 225–3) has remained the gold standard for the diagnosis of donovanosis since they were first described by Donovan. Subsequently, Donovan bodies have also been detected in Papanicolaou-stained smears obtained from women with cervical lesions.[18, 19] Earlier, isolation of *C. granulomatis* led to the development of an intradermal skin test and also a complement fixation test for the serologic diagnosis of the disease. Unfortunately, because a source of purified organisms is no longer available, these tests are no longer performed. An indirect immunofluorescence test has been devised that employs tissue sections from proven cases of donovanosis as antigen. This test has proved both sensitive and specific[20] but is unlikely to become routine owing to a lack of suitable clinical material that can be used as antigen. The recent attempts to culture *C. granulomatis* in monocytes[7] and Hep-2 cells,[8] if confirmed to be successful, may prove an appropriate source of antigen for such a serologic test and offer possibilities for testing in vitro activities of antimicrobial agents to provide a more rational basis for treatment of the disease. Isolation of *C. granulomatis* in Hep-2 cell monolayers using techniques similar to those previously used for chlamydial isolation could, for the first time, provide a routine diagnostic test for donovanosis based on culture. Australian workers have demonstrated a high degree of molecular homology between *C. granulomatis* and other *Klebsiella* spp. by sequencing a region of the *pho* E (phosphate porin) gene of *C. granulomatis* from DNA extracted from biopsy material. Although there appears to be a high degree of homology between *C. granulomatis* genes and other *Klebsiella* spp.–specific genes, the same workers found that certain primers targeting genes of the sucrose region of *Klebsiella* did not yield polymerase chain reaction products with DNA derived from *C. granulomatis*. They therefore claim to be able to distinguish between donovanosis-associated organisms and other *Klebsiella* spp. on the basis of two polymerase chain reaction tests, one positive and the other negative.[21] Although these molecular approaches undoubtedly need to be refined, they represent a significant step forward in the diagnosis of the disease and may ultimately provide a viable alternative to culture or microscopy.

TREATMENT

There appears to be no consensus about the ideal treatment for donovanosis because most antibiotics have been evaluated in open trials with few data available from comparative, microbiologically controlled studies. In addition, the optimal duration of treatment for an individual case cannot be stated categorically, because larger lesions appear to require longer periods of therapy. After successful therapy, lesions begin to heal from the edges toward the center.

It is our experience that treatment should be continued until complete epithelialization has taken place, which can take several weeks; otherwise relapse may occur. Tetracycline (500 mg four times daily by mouth) or doxycycline (100 mg twice daily by mouth) has historically been the treatment of choice for the disease, although treatment failures have been recorded.

Trimethroprim-sulfamethoxazole (two tablets twice daily by mouth) has also proved effective, but also with some failures.[3, 9] Erythromycin (500 mg four times daily by mouth) has also been used extensively, especially in pregnancy with considerable success.[3, 11] However, at this dosage, gastrointestinal side effects are common.

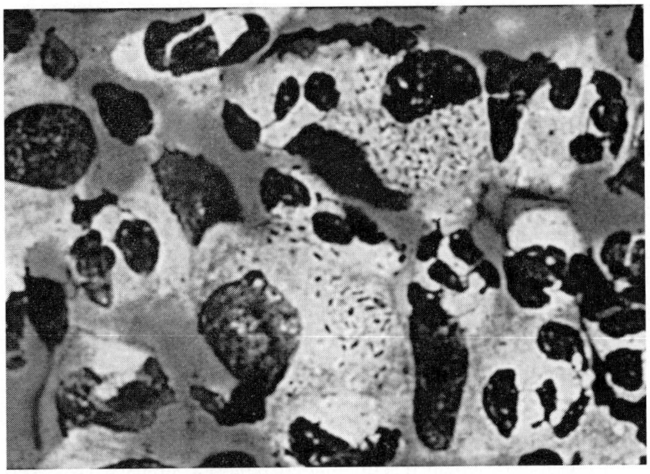

FIGURE 225–3. Scraping from an active lesion of donovanosis showing typical "Donovan" bodies in large mononuclear cells (Giemsa stain).

The antibiotic that shows the most promise in the treatment of donovanosis is azithromycin. Preliminary studies indicate that 1 g taken weekly for 4 weeks is a suitable dosage and duration.[22] It is thought that this antibiotic is particularly appropriate for the treatment of the disease because it concentrates within macrophages, which are the cells infected by *C. granulomatis*, and is released slowly from the tissues, giving it a long tissue half-life. An added advantage of this antibiotic is that it is also active against other sexually transmitted bacteria—notably *Haemophilus ducreyi, Treponema pallidum,* and *C. trachomatis*. Other antibiotics that have proved effective include the quinolones; chloramphenicol and thiamphenicol[3]; ceftriaxone[23]; and the aminoglycosides gentamicin (1 mg/kg twice daily intramuscularly) and streptomycin (1 g twice daily intramuscularly), which are often used to supplement tetracycline therapy in severe cases. In contrast, penicillin appears to be ineffective in the treatment of the disease. Anecdotal evidence suggests that prolonged periods of therapy may be required in those patients with donovanosis who are coinfected with human immunodeficiency virus.

REFERENCES

1. McLeod K. Precis of operations performed in the wards of the first surgeon, Medical College O Hospital (Rio), during the year 1881. Indian Med Gaz. 1882;17:113.
2. Donovan C. Ulcerating granuloma of the pudenda. Indian Med Gaz. 1905;40:414.
3. Richens J. The diagnosis and treatment of donovanosis (granuloma inguinale). Genitourin Med. 1991;67:441.
4. Kuberski T, Papadimitriou JM, Phillips P. Ultrastructure of *Calymmatobacterium granulomatis* in lesions in granuloma inguinale. J Infect Dis. 1980;142:744.
5. Anderson K. The cultivation from granuloma inguinale of a microorganism having the characteristics of Donovan bodies in the yolk sac of chick embryos. Science. 1943;97:560.
6. Dulaney AD, Guo K, Packer H. Donovania granulomatis: Cultivation, antigen preparation, and immunological tests. J Immunol. 1948;59:335.
7. Kharsany ABM, Hoosen AA, Kiepiela P, et al. Culture of *Calymmatobacterium granulomatis* (Letter). Clin Infect Dis. 1996;22:391.
8. Carter J, Hutton S, Sriprakash KS, et al. Culture of the causative organism of donovanosis *(Calymmatobacterium granulomatis)* in Hep-2 cells. J Clin Microbiol. 1997;35:2915.
9. O'Farrell N. Clinico-epidemiological study of donovanosis in Durban, South Africa, Genotourin Med. 1993;69:108.
10. Goldberg J. Studies on granuloma inguinale. VII. Some epidemiological considerations of the disease. Br J Vener Dis. 1964;40:140.
11. O'Farrell N. Donovanosis (granuloma inguinale) in pregnancy. Int J STD AIDS. 1991;2:447.
12. Marmell M. Donovanosis of the anus in the male. An epidemiologic consideration. Br J Vener Dis. 1958;34:565.
13. Bridgen MB, Guard R. Extragenital granuloma inguinale in North Queensland. Med J Aust. 1980;2:565.
14. Freinkel AL. Granuloma inguinale of cervical lymph nodes simulating tuberculosis lymphadenitis: Two case reports and review of published reports. Genitourin Med. 1988;64:339.
15. Alexander LJ, Shields TL. Squamous cell carcinoma of the vulva secondary to granuloma inguinale. Arch Dermatol Syphilol. 1953;67:395.
16. Van Dyck E, Piot P. Laboratory techniques in the investigation of chancroid, lymphogranuloma venereum and donovanosis. Genitourium Med. 1992;68:130.
17. O'Farrell N, Hoosen A, Coetzee K, et al. A rapid stain for the diagnosis of granuloma inguinale. Genitourin Med. 1990;66:200.
18. De Boer AL, de Boer F, van der Merwe JV. Cytologic identification of Donovan bodies in granuloma inguinale. Acta Cytol. 1984;28:126.
19. Leiman G, Markowitz S, Margolius KA. Cytologic detection of cervical granuloma inguinale. Diagn Cytopathol. 1986;2:138.
20. Freinkel AL, Dangor Y, Koomhof HJ, et al. A serological test for granuloma inguinale. Genitourin Med. 1992;68:269.
21. Bastian I, Bowden FJ. Amplification of *Klebsiella*—like sequences from biopsy samples from patients with donovanosis. Clin Infect Dis. 1996;23:1328.
22. Bowden FJ, Mein J, Plunkett C, et al. Pilot study of azithromycin in the treatment of genital donovanosis. Genitourin Med. 1996;72:17.
23. Merianos A, Gilles M, Chuah J. Ceftriaxone in the treatment of chronic donovanosis in central Australia. Genitourin Med. 1994;70:84.

Chapter 226

Other Gram-Negative Bacilli

JAMES P. STEINBERG
CARLOS DEL RIO

A large number of gram-negative aerobic bacilli have been reported to cause human infection. This chapter considers selected gram-negative organisms that have not been described in previous chapters and are of importance in certain clinical or epidemiologic circumstances (nosocomial infection, etc.), are newly described, or present special problems of diagnosis or therapy. Many of these organisms are saprophytic, and their clinical role is uncertain. For some of the bacteria considered here, taxonomy is in a state of flux as classifications based on phenotypic characteristics are replaced by contemporary measures of genetic relationship including 16-S ribosomal-RNA–sequencing studies. Current nomenclature and previous designations are listed in Table 226–1. Unless otherwise specified, the organisms are discussed in their order of appearance in Table 226–1.

The initial suspicion of a particular organism from the group considered here often arises after recovery of a gram-negative bacillus that is not *Pseudomonas aeruginosa* or a member of the Enterobacteriaceae. Identification of some of these organisms is difficult; the automated systems used by many microbiology laboratories cannot identify some of these bacteria and can misidentify others. Consequently, clinical laboratories sometimes use a general description (e.g., *gram-negative nonfermenter*) rather than the genus and species name. The clinical site of infection, as shown in Table 226–2, and the ability of the organism to metabolize carbohydrates by fermentation provide clues that can suggest a particular organism or group of organisms. This information can help select the most effective way to provide definitive identification, because some of these organisms require special procedures for recovery, characterization, or antimicrobial susceptibility testing.[1, 2] The decision to use alternative diagnostic methods is often based on the perceived clinical significance of the isolate, economic considerations, and available expertise. Because species identification is often not pursued, infections caused by some of these uncommon pathogens may go unrecognized.

GLUCOSE FERMENTERS

Actinobacillus

Actinobacillus actinomycetemcomitans, the major pathogen of this genus, is a cause of endocarditis, severe forms of periodontal disease,

The authors acknowledge John E. McGowan, Jr., for his contributions to this chapter in the third and fourth editions of this work.

TABLE 226–1 Current Nomenclature and Previous Names of Gram-Negative Bacteria Discussed in Chapter 226

Current Designation	Previous Names
Glucose Fermenters	
Actinobacillus spp.	
A. actinomycetemcomitans	
A. ureae	*Pasteurella ureae*
Aeromonas	
A. hydrophila	
A. caviae	
A. veronii biovar *sobria*	*Aeromonas sobria*
Cardiobacterium hominis	
Chromobacterium violaceum	
CDC DF-3	
CDC EF-4	
Plesiomonas shigelloides	*Aeromonas shigelloides*
Glucose Nonfermenters (or Weak Fermenters)	
"Achromobacter" groups B and E	
Agrobacterium radiobacter	*Agrobacterium tumefaciens, Agrobacterium* biovar 1, CDC Vd-3
Alcaligenes spp.	
A. faecalis	*Alcaligenes odorans,* CDC VI
A. xylosoxidans subsp. *dendrificans*	*Alcaligenes denitrificans, Alcaligenes denitrificans* subsp. *denitrificans*
A. xylosoxidans subsp. *xylosoxidans*	*Achromobacter xylosoxidans, Achromobacter denitrificans* subsp. *xylosoxidans*
*Bergeyella zoohelcum**	*Weeksella zoohelcum,* CDC IIj
CDC IVc-2	
Chryseobacterium	
C. meningosepticum	*Flavobacterium meningosepticum*
C. indologenes	*Flavobacterium indologenes*
Chryseomonas luteola	*Pseudomonas luteola, Chryseomonas polytrichia,* CDC Ve-1
Eikenella corrodens	*Bacteroides corrodens*
Flavimonas oryzihabitans	*Pseudomonas oryzihabitans, Chromobacterium typhiflavum,* CDC Ve-2
Methylobacterium mesophilicum and *M. extorquens*†	*Pseudomonas mesophilica, Protomonas extorquens, Vibrio extorquens, Protaminobacter rubra,* "the pink phantom"
Ochrobactrum anthropi	CDC Vd, "*Achromobacter*" groups A, C, and D
Oligella spp.	
O. ureolytica	CDC IVe
O. urethralis	*Moraxella urethralis,* CDC M4
Roseomonas spp.	CDC pink coccoid group I through IV
Shewanella putrefaciens	*Pseudomonas putrefaciens,* CDC Ib-1, Ib-2
Sphingobacterium	
S. multivorum	*Flavobacterium multivorum,* CDC IIk-2
S. spiritivorum	*Flavobacterium spiritivorum,* CDC IIk-3
Sphingomonas paucimobilis	*Pseudomonas paucimobilis,* CDC IIk-1
Weeksella virosa	*Flavobacterium genitale,* CDC II-f

*See *Weeksella* in text.
†See *Roseomonas* in text.

and soft tissue infection, the last of these usually in association with *Actinomyces israelii.* Five other species (*Actinobacillus lignieresii, equuli, suis, hominis*, and *ureae*) are rare causes of human disease. The first three are commensals and opportunistic pathogens in animals,[3] whereas the latter two are commensals of the human upper respiratory tract. *A. ureae* was previously known as *Pasteurella ureae*.

Actinobacillus actinomycetemcomitans, formerly *Bacterium actinomycetem comitans*, was first described as a human pathogen in 1912. Initial isolates were recovered only in conjunction with *A. israelii* (hence the species designation), leading to speculation that *A. actinomycetemcomitans* was not itself capable of causing disease. *A. actinomycetemcomitans* is present in at least 30% of actinomycotic lesions.[3] After the introduction of penicillin, it was observed that *A. actinomycetemcomitans* sometimes could be recovered from persistent lesions of actinomycosis after *A. israelii* was eradicated.[4] By the early 1960s, recovery of this organism in pure culture from blood and other normally sterile body fluids was reported widely.[5] The organism also has been isolated in pure culture from patients with meningitis, brain abscess, soft tissue infections, parotitis, septic arthritis, osteomyelitis, urinary tract infection, pneumonia, empyema, and pericarditis.[3, 6–8] Soft tissue infections most commonly involve the cervicofacial area, although they can occur elsewhere including the chest and abdomen. There are reports of *A. actinomycetemcomitans* mimicking actinomycosis (*A. israelii* or mixed infection) and causing pneumonia with chest wall invasion.[8, 9]

Although the organism is part of the endogenous flora of the mouth and can be recovered from about 20% of teenagers and adults, it (along with *Porphyromonas gingivalis*) is one of the major pathogens in adult and juvenile forms of periodontitis.[10] *A. actinomycetemcomitans* is present in the periodontal pockets of over 50% of adults with refractory periodontitis and 90% of patients with localized juvenile periodontitis, a destructive form of periodontitis characterized by loss of the alveolar bone of the molars and incisors.[11] Clonal spread of the organism within families has been demonstrated using polymerase chain reaction–based typing systems.[12] Two virulence factors that appear to be important in the development of periodontal disease are the ability of the organism to invade and multiply inside gingival epithelial cells[13] and the production of a leukotoxin that lyses neutrophils.[14] A bacteriocin (actinobacillin) that inhibits other organisms present in the mouth, endotoxin, chemotaxis- and fibroblast-inhibiting factors, Fc-binding proteins, and collagenases have been described, but their importance is unknown.

Actinobacillus actinomycetemcomitans is one of the HACEK organisms, along with *Haemophilus aphrophilus*, *Haemophilus paraphrophilis*, *Cardiobacterium hominis*, *Eikenella corrodens*, and *Kingella kingae*, which have in common slow growth in culture, the need for incubation in an atmosphere enhanced with CO_2 for recovery in culture, and a predilection for causing endocarditis.[2] The onset of endocarditis is usually insidious, with a mean time to diagnosis of about 3 months. In a comprehensive review of 57 cases of *A. actinomycetemcomitans* endocarditis, 46% had periodontal disease or recent dental work, and 60% had underlying valvular disease, including 25% with prosthetic valves.[3] Fever was present in less than 50%; peripheral manifestations and splenomegaly each occurred in about a third. Therapy was successful in almost 80%, but significant embolization was common (39%), and 23% (13 of 57) required valve replacement. Prosthetic valve endocarditis with *A. actinomycetemcomitans* was usually recognized earlier than native valve endocarditis (42 versus 106 days), which probably was due to a higher index of suspicion. This earlier diagnosis may account for the high cure rate with antibiotics alone and a relative low rate of embolization reported with prosthetic valve infection.[15, 16]

Human disease caused by other species of *Actinobacillus* is rare. *Actinobacillus lignieresii, A. suis*, and *A. equuli* rarely may cause infections after bite wounds from farm animals.[17] These infections can be polymicrobial. One report has described a boar hunter who developed endocarditis caused by an *Actinobacillus* organism that resembled *A. suis* and *A. hominis* biochemically.[18] Of note, the automated system initially misidentified the organism as *Vibrio parahaemolyticus*, and supplemental testing was done after endocarditis was diagnosed and the initial microbiologic identification was questioned. Fatal *A. hominis* bacteremia developed in two patients with severe underlying liver disease.[19] *Actinobacillus ureae* is a rare cause of bacteremia and meningitis. Of 12 reported patients with *A. ureae* meningitis, 8 were post-traumatic and another occurred after neurosurgery.[20, 21] Several patients had underlying chronic illnesses including alcoholism and human immunodeficiency virus (HIV) infection.

Culture isolation of *A. actinomycetemcomitans* is the usual means of diagnosis, and the fastidious, slow-growing nature of the organism makes this difficult. Material obtained from soft tissue lesions should be inoculated on blood and chocolate agar because the organism grows poorly in MacConkey's agar. The cultures must be incubated in an enhanced (5 to 10%) CO_2 atmosphere. By 18 to 24 hours, a few colonies (punctate, nonhemolytic) may be apparent, but the organism grows slowly, and incubation for at least 48 hours is

TABLE 226-2 Classification of Selected Gram-Negative Aerobic Bacilli by Likely Site or Setting of Infection

Organism	Most Likely Sites of Infection							
	Blood Stream	*Device-Associated*	*Intestine*	*Soft Tissue*	*Bite Wound*	*Urine*	*CSF*	*Nosocomial Clusters*
Glucose fermenters								
Actinobacillus	X			X	X		X	
Aeromonas	X		X	X				
Cardiobacterium	X							
Chromobacterium	X			X				
CDC Group DF-3			X					
CDC Group EF-4					X			
Plesiomonas			X					
Glucose nonfermenters (or weak fermenters)								
"*Achromobacter*" groups B and E	X							
Agrobacterium	X	X						
Alcaligenes	X							X
Bergeyella					X			
CDC group Ivc-2	X							
Chryseobacterium	X						X	X
Chryseomonas	X	X						
Eikenella	X			X	X			
Flavimonas	X	X						
Methylobacterium	X	X						
Ochrobactrum	X	X						X
Oligella						X		
Roseomonas	X	X						
Shewanella	X			X				
Sphingobacterium	X							
Sphingomonas	X	X						X
Weeksella						X		

Abbreviation: CDC, Centers for Disease Control and Prevention; CSF, cerebrospinal fluid.

needed. After colonies are seen, the organism continues to grow slowly, sometimes forming a star structure as part of the center of the mature colony. In broth or blood cultures, the organism often grows only in small "granules" adherent to the sides, with the medium remaining clear. In 13 patients with endocarditis, blood cultures required incubation for a mean of 5.6 days (range, 2 to 9 days) before growth was detected.[15] This finding underscores the need to hold blood culture bottles for a prolonged time if endocarditis caused by a fastidious organism is suspected. The appearance of the organism on Gram stain is coccoid to coccobacillary, similar to the appearance of *Haemophilus* spp. *Actinobacillus actinomycetemcomitans* is urease-negative, is indole-negative, reduces nitrate, and usually is oxidase-negative. It is catalase-positive, which helps differentiate it from *H. aphrophilus*. Identification of the other *Actinobacillus* species is problematic. At the genus level, these organisms are biochemically similar to *Pasteurella*. Species identification can be difficult without DNA hybridization studies.[22]

A. actinomycetemcomitans usually is susceptible to cephalosporins (especially third-generation cephalosporins), mezlocillin, rifampin, trimethoprim-sulfamethoxazole, aminoglycosides, ciprofloxacin, tetracycline, azithromycin, and chloramphenicol.[3, 23] In vitro susceptibility to penicillin and ampicillin is variable, but test results do not necessarily correlate with the clinical outcome.[15] In general, treatment of actinomycosis with penicillin and surgical drainage (when necessary) is sufficient, even when mixed infection is present. Vancomycin, erythromycin, and clindamycin have little activity against *A. actinomycetemcomitans*. The organisms display moderate susceptibility to metronidazole, and in vitro synergy between metronidazole and both β-lactams and ciprofloxacin has been reported.[24] Because of strain-to-strain variability, testing of clinical isolates is recommended. Unfortunately, susceptibility testing is sometimes technically difficult because of the slow growth and fastidious nature of the organism. In the past, penicillin or ampicillin combined with an aminoglycoside was the usual treatment for endocarditis due to this organism. Because of the potential for β-lactamase production, reports of failures with penicillin therapy, and difficulties with susceptibility testing, third-generation cephalosporins are now considered the drugs of choice. For endocarditis caused by HACEK organisms, the American Heart Association recommends ceftriaxone 2 g daily for 4 weeks (6 weeks for prosthetic valve endocarditis).[25] Successful treatment of prosthetic valve endocarditis with oral ciprofloxacin has been reported.[26] *A. actinomycetemcomitans* endocarditis has developed after dental procedures despite the prophylactic use of penicillin, erythromycin, or vancomycin. Severe *A. actinomycetemcomitans*–associated periodontitis is usually treated with mechanical débridement in combination with oral tetracycline therapy. Tetracycline failures occur, however, and a report suggests that the combination of metronidazole and amoxicillin is very effective in suppressing subgingival infection.[27] *A. ureae* meningitis has been treated successfully with penicillin and third-generation cephalosporins.[21]

Aeromonas

Aeromonads are ubiquitous inhabitants of fresh and brackish water. They have also been recovered from chlorinated tap water including hospital water supplies. They occasionally cause soft tissue infections and sepsis in immunocompromised hosts and increasingly have been associated with diarrheal disease. *Aeromonas* spp. have been allocated to the family Vibrionaceae, but genetic evidence indicates they should be in their own family, and the family Areomonadaceae has been proposed.[28] Taxonomy of the aeromonads is in transition. In 1984, four species of *Aeromonas (hydrophila, sobria, caviae*, and *salmonicida*) were recognized.[29] These biochemically distinct species (phenospecies) have now been subdivided into DNA hybridization groups (genospecies), and new genospecies have been recognized. The complexity caused by the abundance of new species is compounded by attempts to reconcile genetic relatedness with the established phenospecies. For example, clinical isolates of *A. sobria* reside in the DNA hybridization group of *A. veronii* and should technically be designated *A. veronii* biovar *sobria*. There are currently 14 named species, but only 3, *A. hydrophila, A. caviae,* and *A. veronii* biovar *sobria*, are of major clinical importance.[30]

Aeromonas was first isolated more than 60 years ago, but evidence implicating this genus as a cause of gastrointestinal disease has been amassed only since the early 1980s. Reports from diverse geographic locations have associated *Aeromonas* spp. with diarrheal disease in humans; in some locales they are recovered as commonly as *Shigella* or *Campylobacter*.[31–34] Many laboratories do not routinely culture stool for *Aeromonas*, so the incidence of *Aeromonas*-associated diarrhea may be underestimated. Evidence supporting a causative role in diarrheal disease includes (1) a higher carriage rate in symptomatic compared with asymptomatic individuals; (2) an absence of other enteric pathogens in most symptomatic patients harboring *Aeromonas* spp.; (3) identification of *Aeromonas* enterotoxins[35] (although the absence of an animal model has hampered efforts to directly link toxin production with disease); (4) improvement of diarrhea with antibiotics active against *Aeromonas* spp. and clinical worsening with antibiotics ineffective against the organism; and (5) evidence of a specific secretory immune response coincident with diarrheal disease.[36]

Aeromonas caviae is the predominant isolate from diarrheal stools, but in some geographic areas, *A. hydrophila* and *A. veronii* biovar *sobria* are frequently isolated as well.[31, 33, 37, 38] Other *Aeromonas* species appear to cause asymptomatic carriage only.[30] *Aeromonas*-associated diarrhea usually occurs during the summer, when the concentrations of aeromonads in water are the highest. Most cases are sporadic, but *Aeromonas* is increasingly being recognized as a cause of traveler's diarrhea.[37, 39] Daycare center outbreaks have been reported, although molecular typing did not suggest clonal spread.[40] The clinical manifestations of *Aeromonas*-associated diarrhea are varied. Diarrhea is usually watery and self-limited, but some persons develop fever, abdominal pain, and bloody stools. Fecal leukocytes may be present. Occasionally, diarrhea may be severe or protracted, and hospitalization may be necessary. Chronic colitis following acute *Aeromonas*-associated diarrhea has been reported in adults.[41] Although no controlled trials have validated antimicrobial therapy for *Aeromonas*-associated diarrhea, clinical improvement has occurred with antibiotics active against the organism. Hemolytic uremic syndrome associated with *Aeromonas* enterocolitis occurred in a 23-month-old infant.[42]

Most *Aeromonas* soft tissue infections are caused by *A. hydrophila*. Trauma followed by exposure to fresh water (and not salt water, even though aeromonad density in seawater is similar to that in fresh water[30]) usually, but not invariably, precedes infection. Cellulitis develops within 8 to 48 hours, and systemic signs are common.[43, 44] Suppuration and necrosis around the wound are frequent, and surgical débridement is often necessary. Fasciitis, myonecrosis (occasionally associated with gas formation), and osteomyelitis may develop. In the setting of a rapidly progressive cellulitis after an injury related to water exposure, *Aeromonas* and *Vibrio* spp. infections should be considered in the differential diagnosis. *Aeromonas* soft tissue infections can develop after exposure to soil, in association with crush injuries, and as a complication of burns.[45] *Aeromonas* soft tissue infection is a recognized complication of the use of medicinal leeches in conjunction with reimplantation or flap surgery.[46] *Aeromonas hydrophila* and other *Aeromonas* spp. are normal inhabitants of the foregut of leeches, and enzymes produced by *Aeromonas* assist in the digestion of the blood meal.[47] *Aeromonas* infection has developed in 7 to 20% of patients treated with leeches. Prophylactic antibiotics now have been recommended at the time of leech application.[46, 47] The onset of infection after the application of medicinal leeches ranges from 1 to more than 10 days. Mild wound infection, myonecrosis, and sepsis may ensue.

Aeromonas bacteremia and sepsis are uncommon, but in the largest series reported to date, 59 *Aeromonas* bacteremias occurred in one institution in Taiwan over a 5-year period.[48] This represented 1.6% of all blood isolates at that institution. *Aeromonas hydrophila*, *A. veronii* subtype *sobria*, and *A. caviae* caused 95% of the episodes, with *A. hydrophila* accounting for about two thirds. Most patients were immunocompromised; 38% had chronic liver disease, and 24% had an underlying malignancy. Spontaneous bacterial peritonitis was common in cirrhotic patients with abdominal pain. There was a similar distribution of *Aeromonas* species in a recent study of 53 *Aeromonas* blood isolates collected from 27 medical centers in the United States over a 10-year period.[49] Most patients were immunocompromised, and underlying malignancy was much more common than liver disease in this series. Most patients with *Aeromonas* sepsis do not present with diarrhea. Interestingly, approximately one third of *Aeromonas* becteremias are nosocomial.[48, 50] In some series, the nosocomial cases were not epidemiologically linked and endogenous gut flora was the presumed source.[50] *Aeromonas* has been recovered from hospital water supplies, and clusters of nosocomial *Aeromonas* bacteremia have been described.[51] However, in one study where molecular typing was performed, many different genotypes were found. The mortality rate for *Aeromonas* sepsis is 30 to 50%.[39, 48–50] Two other species, *Aeromonas jandaei* and *A. schubertii*, have rarely been isolated from the blood.[52, 53] A variety of other infections caused by *Aeromonas* spp. have been reported, including intra-abdominal abscess, hepatobiliary infection,[54] spontaneous bacterial peritonitis in patients with cirrhosis,[48] meningitis,[55] endocarditis,[56] suppurative thrombophlebitis, osteomyelitis, urinary tract infection, pneumonia including near-drowning–associated pneumonia,[57] empyema, lung abscess, tonsillitis, and otitis media.

Aeromonas organisms are gram-negative, nonsporulating facultative anaerobic rods that usually are β-hemolytic on blood agar and ferment carbohydrates with acid and gas production. The organisms grow well on MacConkey's agar (some strains are lactose fermenters, and some are not), but growth on thiosulfate citrate bile sucrose medium is variable. Selective techniques are often necessary for the isolation of *Aeromonas* spp. from mixed cultures. The organisms are more difficult to identify in stool cultures because enteric media may be inhibitory for some *Aeromonas* spp. Either blood agar that contains ampicillin (10 or 30 μg/ml) or cefsulodin-irgasan-novobiocin agar can be used as a selective medium.[58] Growth of colonies on plates usually occurs within 24 hours. *Aeromonas* spp. are oxidase-positive, and this test distinguishes these organisms from the oxidase-negative Enterobacteriaceae. *Aeromonas hydrophila* is catalase-positive and motile, converts nitrate to nitrite, and is urease-negative. Identification of *Aeromonas* to the genus level is not difficult; many automated systems (and consequently many clinical laboratories) proceed no further, reporting an *Aeromonas* isolate as "*Aeromonas* species" or "*Aeromonas hydrophila* complex."

Aeromonas hydrophila is sensitive to trimethoprim-sulfamethoxazole, fluoroquinolones, chloramphenicol, and aminoglycosides except streptomycin.[59] The organism is resistant to ampicillin and ticarcillin but often susceptible to aztreonam, carbapenems, and third-generation cephalosporins.[59, 60] Sensitivity to piperacillin, ticarcillin-clavulanate, and tetracyclines is variable. Isolates of *A. veronii* subtype *sobria* are more susceptible to earlier-generation cephalosporins and also are usually susceptible to gentamicin, tobramycin, trimethoprim-sulfamethoxazole, and the fluoroquinolones but vary in their susceptibility to chloramphenicol, tetracycline, ampicillin, carbenicillin, and amikacin.[59] *Aeromonas* spp. harboring a conjugative plasmid that confers multiple antibiotic resistance have been identified.[61] *Aeromonas* spp. produce as many as three β-lactamases including a Bush group 2d penicillinase, a group 1 cephalosporinase, and a metallocarbapenemase.[62] Some isolates exhibit coordinated expression of these β-lactamases both after induction and selection of derepressed mutants. [63] Despite the presence of a carbapenemase, minimal inhibitory concentrations to imipenem typically remain low, although *A. jandaei* and *A. veronii* subtype *veronii* frequently display imipenem resistance.[64] Unlike other known carbapenemases, the *Aeromonas* metallocarbapenemases have narrow substrate profiles and specifically hydrolyze carbapenems.[65]

Cardiobacterium

Cardiobacterium hominis, unlike the other HACEK organisms considered in this chapter, rarely causes disease other than endocarditis.

Cardiobacterium hominis is the only species in the genus. It was originally called group IID and described as a *Pasteurella*-like organism. It is part of the endogenous flora in the nose, mouth, and throat and is present occasionally on other mucous membranes as well as in the gastrointestinal tract.[66]

There are about 50 reported cases of *C. hominis* infection, and all but a few have involved the heart valves. Most patients have had underlying anatomic defects (rheumatic heart disease, ventricular septal defect, congenital bicuspid valve, etc.); prosthetic cardiac valves have been involved in about 10% of reported cases.[67] Many patients with endocarditis have had severe periodontitis or prior dental procedures without antimicrobial prophylaxis. *Cardiobacterium hominis* endocarditis following upper gastrointestinal endoscopy has been reported.[68] A subacute presentation, with an insidious onset (mean of 2 to 5 months before diagnosis) and an absence of fever at the time of diagnosis, is common.[69] Some of the patients have splenomegaly, anemia, and hematuria, consistent with a long period between infection and diagnosis. Large vegetations, and large vessel emboli, are characteristic. Almost all clinical isolates come from blood, although meningitis associated with endocarditis has been described.[70] In one of the very rare cases of infection without endocarditis, a patient with adenocarcinoma of the kidney invading the cecum developed an abdominal abscess and bacteremia; abscess and blood cultures grew *C. hominis* and *Clostridium bifermentans*.[71]

The organism is gram-negative but has a pleomorphic appearance, often has swelling of one or both ends, and may be difficult to decolorize during the Gram stain procedure.[2] Under the microscope, the organisms sometimes form rosettes, but short chains, teardrops, pairs, and clusters are also common. Supplementation of the medium with yeast extract results in a loss of the pleomorphism, and most organisms become sticklike, gram-negative rods with rounded ends.[66] Incubation in high humidity and 3 to 5% CO_2 maximizes recovery of the organism. In such conditions, *C. hominis* grows well on sheep blood agar, chocolate agar, Mueller-Hinton agar, or trypticase soy agar without blood but grows poorly on MacConkey's agar or similar selective media. Colonies of 1 to 2 mm in diameter form on sheep blood agar, usually by 48 to 72 hours after incubation at 37°C under increased CO_2. However, with some systems, incubation for 5 to 7 days before growth can be confirmed is not unusual, and cultures should be held for this period or longer if *C. hominis* is suspected.[66] The colonies produce slight β-hemolysis and develop a rough appearance, with a serpentine pattern of growth from the edge to adjacent colonies.[66] The organism is oxidase-positive, is catalase-negative, and produces indole (although positivity is weak with many strains).[1] Indole production is important for distinguishing *C. hominis* from other HACEK organisms.

Susceptibility tests are difficult to perform because of the organism's slow growth and nutritional requirements. When tested, the organism is usually susceptible to β-lactam drugs, chloramphenicol, and tetracycline. Susceptibility to vancomycin, aminoglycosides, erythromycin, and clindamycin is variable. Penicillin G, with or without the addition of an aminoglycoside, has been the regimen most often employed for therapy. The first β-lactamase–producing clinical isolate was reported in 1994.[72] This isolate was also resistant to cefotaxime and piperacillin but susceptible to β-lactmase inhibitor combinations. Consequently, it is unclear whether the current recommendations to administer third-generation cephalosporins for endocarditis caused by HACEK organisms enhance coverage for *C. hominis*. The role of an aminoglycoside as part of combination therapy is unknown. Although microbiologic cure is usually achieved, complications frequently arise during the course of therapy. Systemic embolization, mycotic aneurysm, or progressive cardiac failure have necessitated replacement of the damaged valve in a number of cases.

Chromobacterium

Chromobacterium violaceum is a rare human pathogen but can cause life-threatening sepsis with metastatic abscesses. The organism is a common soil and water inhabitant in tropical and subtropical areas. More than 20 cases have been reported in the United States, almost all from the Southeast, with 15 occurring in Florida.[73] *C. violaceum* infections have also been reported from Southeast Asia, South America, and Australia.[74, 75] *C. violaceum* is the only species of this genus that causes human disease. Although not considered a normal inhabitant of the human gastrointestinal tract, *C. violaceum* was present in the feces of 3 of 65 children whose stool was cultured at the time of admission to a hospital in Atlanta.[76]

Infection almost always occurs in the summer months and usually follows exposure of nonintact skin to contaminated water (often stagnant) or soil. Two cases followed near-drownings. Symptoms include pain at a local site of infection, fever, nausea, vomiting, abdominal pain, and diarrhea. Local cellulitis, pustules, ulcers with necrotic base, or lymphadenitis commonly precedes evidence of systemic infection. Septic shock develops rapidly, as may pneumonia and visceral abscesses involving the liver, spleen, and lung. This presentation can be confused with septicemic meliodosis, which is more common than *C. violaceum* infection in Southeast Asia, where both diseases are endemic. The mortality rate for reported cases in the United States is approximately 60%. Urinary tract infection, orbital cellulitis, retropharyngeal infection with prevertebral abscess,[77] osteomyelitis, and meningitis[78] have been reported. Infection is more common in patients with chronic granulomatous disease,[79] but cases occur in the apparently normal host. Five of six patients with chronic granulomatous disease survived their infection, a higher survival rate compared with patients without known neutrophil dysfunction. Deficiency of polymorphonuclear leukocyte glucose-6-phosphate dehydrogenase and neutrophil dysfunction also were present in a 3-year-old patient who died with *C. violaceum* sepsis.[80] The pertinent virulence factors are unknown. Preliminary data from the study of only one clinical and one environmental isolate showed greater endotoxin activity and enhanced resistance to phagocytosis in the virulent strain.[81] Diagnosis is made by culture of blood, abscess fluid, or skin exudate.

C. violaceum organisms are long gram-negative bacilli; occasionally, the organisms are slightly curved and can be confused with vibrios. The organisms are facultatively anaerobic, growing readily in 18 to 24 hours on media containing tryptophan, which include common laboratory media such as sheep blood agar, chocolate agar, Mueller-Hinton agar, trypticase soy broth, and MacConkey's agar. Incubation at 37°C usually is effective, although growth is enhanced if incubation occurs at 25°C. Most strains of this organism produce violacein, a pigment insoluble in water (as opposed to the water-soluble pyocyanin of *Pseudomonas* spp.), which imparts a violet-black color to the colonies on solid media, hence the species' name. The color may be lost on subculture or after therapy is begun. The organisms produce hydrogen cyanide, so a faint cyanide smell may be present. The oxidase reaction is usually positive but hard to detect in pigmented strains; sometimes, demonstration of oxidase can be enhanced by incubating the culture anaerobically, which inhibits pigment formation.[75] The organism may or may not produce indole and is usually catalase-positive.

Chromobacterium violaceum isolates are generally susceptible to fluoroquinolones, chloramphenicol, tetracycline, trimethoprim-sulfamethoxazole, and gentamicin.[82] The ureidopenicillins and imipenem are also active, but resistance to cephalosporins is common. Although aztreonam is a natural product of some strains of *C. violaceum*,[83] most clinical isolates are susceptible to this agent. Because of the rarity of infection, the often fulminant course, and the high mortality rate, the optimal antibiotic therapy is unknown. Ciprofloxacin is the most active antibiotic in vitro, but experience with this agent is limited. Most survivors of this infection were treated with chloramphenicol or a penicillin (carboxy or ureidopenicillin) in combination with an aminoglycoside. Relapse has occurred more than 2 weeks after the completion of therapy and apparent cure, presumably due to a residual suppurative focus.[75] Oral trimethoprim-sulfamethoxazole, doxycycline, or ciprofloxacin has been used after intravenous therapy with other antibiotics, with the oral regimen continued for several weeks to a few months to prevent relapse.

Centers for Disease Control and Prevention Group DF-3

DF-3, a fastidious gram-negative coccobacillus, was first associated with human disease in 1988.[84] This organism does not have a genus and species name and is currently designated by the Centers for Disease Control and Prevention (CDC) system of letters referring to growth characteristics. *DF* stands for *dysgonic fermenter*, indicating a fermentative organism that has difficulty growing on routine media. DF-1 and DF-2 now have been classified in the genus *Capnocytophaga* (see Chapter 223). Based on comparative 16-S ribosomal-RNA sequence analysis, DF-3 is not closely related to *Capnocytophaga* spp.[85]

DF-3 has been isolated from diarrheal stools of patients with immune deficiencies including common variable hypogammaglobulinemia, infection with (HIV), diabetes with chronic renal failure, lymphoreticular and other malignancies, and from patients receiving immunosuppressive agents.[84, 86–88] With the use of selective media, DF-3 was isolated from 11 of 690 (1.6%) stools submitted for bacterial culture at the National Cancer Institute.[86] In another prospective study of the role of DF-3 in diarrheal disease, DF-3 was recovered from 2 of 178 specimens (1.1%) submitted for *Clostridium difficile* toxin assay and from 3 of 129 (2.3%) stool specimens from patients with HIV infection. These data suggest that the paucity of reports of recovering DF-3 from stool specimens may not be due to its rarity (as a colonizer or pathogen) but to the inability to recover the organism on conventional media. Antibiotic therapy directed at DF-3 produced a therapeutic response in some of these patients, including 4 of 11 in the first study. Some of the responders had diarrhea of several months' duration with prompt resolution after antibiotic therapy was initiated. In other patients, the clinical significance of DF-3 was unclear; eradication of the organism from the stool was not accompanied by resolution of diarrhea or the diarrhea resolved without specific therapy. DF-3 has also been isolated from the urine of an elderly woman with rectal fissures,[89] from a polymicrobial thigh abscess in a patient with insulin-dependent diabetes,[90] and from the blood of a patient with acute lymphocytic leukemia and prolonged neutropenia.[91]

DF-3 is biochemically similar to DF-1 and can be distinguished from DF-2 by negative catalase and oxidase tests, the production of indole by most strains, and the fermentation of sucrose and xylose. It produces small gray-white colonies with a sweetish odor on blood agar after 1 to 3 days of incubation. DF-3 does not grow on MacConkey's agar or routine enteric media. DF-3 grows on selective *Campylobacter* media when incubated at 37°C, but not 42°C, the routine incubation temperature for *Campylobacter*.[87] Selective media such as cefoperazone–vancomycin–amphotericin B blood agar inhibit normal flora and allow recovery of DF-3 from stool specimens.

Despite a lack of established breakpoints, the Kirby-Bauer disk agar-diffusion method has been used for antimicrobial susceptibility testing. DF-3 appears to be resistant to most β-lactam drugs, ciprofloxacin, metronidazole, vancomycin, and gentamicin. Many strains are susceptible to chloramphenicol, trimethoprim-sulfamethoxazole, clindamycin, and tetracycline. Tetracycline or clindamycin were used in the few reported cases of diarrheal disease that responded promptly to antibiotic administration. Despite a Kirby-Bauer zone size suggesting susceptibility, imipenem failed to clear DF-3 from the blood stream in the one reported bacteremic patient; the bacteremia resolved after therapy with trimethoprim-sulfamethoxazole was initiated.[91]

Centers for Disease Control and Prevention Group EF-4

EF-4, another gram-negative bacillus without genus and species name, is known by its CDC letter and number designation based on growth characteristics. *EF*, or *eugonic fermenter*, refers to an organism that grows well through the fermentation of glucose. Group EF-4 bacteria are normal inhabitants of the oral cavity of dogs. Most human infections follow dog bites, although infections associated with cat bites or scratches occur as well. The organism can be isolated from bite wounds that do not demonstrate signs of inflammation, but cellulitis, abscess formation, and fever may develop. Systemic infection or infection not involving skin or skin structures is extremely rare. Endophthalmitis that is due to *Pasteurella multocida* and EF-4 occurred after a cat scratch in an 8-year-old girl.[92] There is one report of blood stream infection occurring in a patient with hepatic carcinoid who denied being bitten by a dog or cat.[93]

EF-4 bacteria usually appear as short rods on Gram stain, but small coccoid forms or long chains may also be present. The organisms grow well on blood-agar plates, on which colonies usually form within 24 hours, but grow poorly or not at all on MacConkey's and similar agars. The colonies are small, may be slightly yellow-orange, and are smooth; some strains have a "popcorn-like" odor.[2] The organisms are oxidase-positive, are catalase-positive, and reduce nitrate. Biovar EF-4a ferments glucose only and has arginine hydroxylase activity; biovar EF-4b does neither (and is actually a nonfermenter). Initially, EF-4 was thought to resemble the Pasturellaceae family, but recent ribosomal-RNA cistron analysis places EF-4 in the Neisseriaceae family.[94]

Penicillin G, ampicillin, tetracycline, ciprofloxacin, and ofloxacin are all active against EF-4 at concentrations attainable with oral administration.[95] Cephalosporins, particularly first-generation agents, are less active in vitro. Chloramphenicol and aminoglycosides also have activity against EF-4.[93]

Plesiomonas

Plesiomonas shigelloides, a ubiquitous freshwater inhabitant, has been implicated as a cause of acute diarrhea and, rarely, serious extraintestinal disease.[96, 97] The name *Plesiomonas*, from the Greek word for "neighbor," was chosen because the organism was thought to be closely related to *Aeromonas*. It is, in fact, more closely related to *Proteus*,[98] although it is currently classified in the family Vibrionaceae. *P. shigelloides* is the only species in the genus. The organism was originally isolated in 1947 and given the name C27. It has been referred to in the literature as C27, *Pseudomonas shigelloides*, *Aeromonas shigelloides*, or *Vibrio shigelloides*.

P. shigelloides is a water- and soil–associated organism that replicates at temperatures above 8°C. It is found primarily in freshwater or estuary environments within temperate and tropical climates but can exist in seawater during the warm-weather months. Asymptomatic carriage of *P. shigelloides* is very rare among healthy persons. The usual vehicles of transmission of plesiomonads to humans are water, food such as oysters, shrimp, or chicken[96, 97]; and a variety of animals that may be colonized with the organism. The organism has been acquired during foreign travel.[96, 99,100] *P. shigelloides* is associated with gastroenteritis, but the failure to identify an enteropathogenic mechanism, the lack of an animal model, and unsuccessful studies to induce disease in volunteers make it impossible to firmly establish a causal relationship.[101] Potential virulence factors including a β-hemolysin have been identified, but their significance is unknown.[102]

The clinical presentation of *P. shigelloides*–associated diarrhea varies from a mild self-limited illness to mucoid, bloody diarrhea with fecal leukocytes. A predominance of a secretory-type diarrhea has been reported,[97] but other series have found a high percentage with a clinical illness compatible with enteroinvasive disease featuring abdominal pain, fever, bloody diarrhea, and fecal leukocytes.[100] The majority of symptomatic patients have either traveled abroad or been exposed to potentially contaminated water or food. Outbreaks have been reported, particularly from Japan. The role of antibiotics for *Plesiomonas*–associated diarrhea is uncertain. Antimicrobial therapy did not shorten the duration of fever or diarrhea in Thai children with *Plesiomonas*–associated diarrhea.[103] On the other hand, in a small nonrandomized Canadian study in which most patients developed *Plesiomonas*–associated diarrhea after travel abroad, 8 of 9 treated patients were asymptomatic within 2 weeks compared with 6 of 15 controls ($p < 0.05$).[100]

Most descriptions of extraintestinal disease come from individual case reports. These reports include cases of osteomyelitis, septic arthritis, endophthalmitis, spontaneous bacterial peritonitis,[104] pancreatic abscess, cholecystitis, and cellulitis. About 10 cases of neonatal sepsis with meningitis have been described.[105] Bacteremia is rare and usually occurs in immunocompromised hosts,[106] but bacteremia accompanying gastroenteritis has been reported in a healthy 15-year-old girl.[107]

P. shigelloides is a motile, facultatively anaerobic, gram-negative, oxidase-positive bacillus. It is readily isolated from some enteric agars such as MacConkey's agar but does not grow well on thiosulfate citrate bile sucrose medium. Selective techniques may be necessary for isolation of the organism from mixed cultures, such as the use of bile peptone broth or trypticase soy broth with ampicillin.[108] The organism grows well at 35°C and produces visible colonies (nonhemolytic) within 24 hours. The organism does not ferment lactose on most enteric agars.

P. shigelloides is usually susceptible to chloramphenicol, trimethoprim-sulfamethoxazole, quinolones, cephalophorins, and imipenem.[103, 109] Because of β-lactamase production, most isolates are now resistant to penicillins including ureidopenicillins, although the β-lactamase inhibitor combinations appear to be active. Susceptibilities to aminoglycosides and tetracycline are variable.

GLUCOSE NONFERMENTERS (OR WEAK FERMENTERS)

Achromobacter

The genus "*Achromobacter*" remains an enigma. There are no currently recognized species of this genus; thus the name appears in quotes. The name *Achromobacter xylosoxidans* still appears in the clinical literature, but this organism has been renamed *Alcaligenes xylosoxidans* subsp. *xylosoxidans*[110] and is considered with other *Alcaligenes* spp. discussed later. Organisms formerly considered *Achromobacter* groups A, C, and D (and before that CDC groups Vd-1 and Vd-2) are now named *Ochrobactrum anthropi* and also are considered separately. Both genetic and phenotypic studies suggest that two subsets of *Achromobacter*, designated group B and E, are related and represent a single as-yet-unnamed genus and species.[111] These organisms have growth and metabolic characteristics similar to those of strains of *Ochrobactrum anthropi* but differ in flagellar morphology and in that they hydrolyze esculin.[22] Although sometimes considered a contaminant, *Achromobacter* group B has been recovered from the blood of patients with clinical sepsis and endocarditis.[112–114]

Agrobacterium

Organisms of the genus *Agrobacterium* are well-known plant pathogens. Most species contain a large tumor-inducing plasmid, and infection produces neoplastic growth in many plant species. These organisms are present in soil and plants and have a worldwide distribution. Although most clinical isolates appear nonpathogenic, there are about 40 reported cases of human disease caused by *Agrobacterium* spp., primarily *Agrobacterium radiobacter*. The literature contains a few reports of disease caused by another species, *Agrobacterium tumifaciens*. However, *A. tumifaciens* and *A. radiobacter* differ only by the presence or absence of the tumor-inducing plasmid, and there is a proposal to combine the two into a single species that would be named *A. radiobacter*[115]

More than half the reported cases of *A. radiobacter* infection are intravascular catheter-related blood stream infections in compromised hosts, primarily patients with malignancies.[116, 117] Most of these infections were non–hospital acquired. Peritonitis in patients receiving ambulatory peritoneal dialysis is the other common presentation for *A. radiobacter* infection.[118] Urinary tract infections caused by this organism have been in patients with nephrostomy tubes. Thus, the majority of infections involve a device, the removal of which has been necessary in some cases to effect a cure. Other case reports include cellulitis in a patient with multiple myeloma, prosthetic valve endocarditis, and bacteremic pneumonia in a patient with HIV infection.[117] A patient who worked in his garden the evening of cateract surgery developed *A. radiobacter* endophthalmitis 4 days later.[119] This is one of the few cases in which soil contact is mentioned. Thus, the source of the infecting organisms is for the most part unknown. Consistent with this organism's being an opportunistic pathogen of low virulence, all patients have survived.

The organism readily grows on blood agar and MacConkey's media when incubated aerobically. Colony appearance varies for the different species. Flagellar stains show peritrichous distribution. Organisms are oxidase-positive, are catalase-positive, and produce gas from a variety of carbohydrates, including lactose. Rapid hydrolysis of urea and slower hydrolysis of esculin are key features that help to distinguish this organism from *Alcaligenes* spp. and *Pseudomonas* spp., which it otherwise closely resembles. Production of 3-ketolactose is characteristic of the genus but is not universal.

Clinical isolates have been variably susceptible to antibiotics and display variations in susceptibility patterns within classes of antibiotics, so in vitro testing of each isolate is important. For example, most isolates are susceptible to gentamicin but resistant to tobramycin.[116] Many strains are susceptible to third-generation cephalosporins, ciprofloxacin, and trimethoprim-sulfamethoxazole. *A. radiobacter* can produce an inducible cephalosporinase as well as an aminoglycoside acetyltransferase. Monobactams are produced by some soil strains[120]; not surprisingly, clinical isolates are often resistant to aztreonam.

Alcaligenes

Organisms of the *Alcaligenes* genus are another group of nonfermenting gram-negative bacilli found in soil and water. They can also be recovered from the human respiratory tract and gastrointestinal tract in hospitalized patients. Infection results when they are introduced into wounds or colonize those with compromised host defenses. Three clinically relevant species are described: *Alcaligenes xylosoxidans*, which has two subspecies: *xylosoxidans* (the organism formerly known as *Achromobacter xylosoxidans*) and *denitrificans*; *Alcaligenes faecalis* (the former *Alcaligenes odorans*); and *Alcaligenes piechaudii*.[2, 22]

A. xylosoxidans subsp. *xylosoxidans* (sometimes called *Achromobacter xylosoxidans*) is the most clinically important of these organisms. It probably is part of the endogenous flora of the ear and gastrointestinal tract and is a common contaminant of fluids.[121] The organism has been implicated in outbreaks of nosocomial infection associated with contaminated solutions (intravenous fluids, hemodialysis fluid, irrigation fluids, mouthwash, etc.), pressure transducers, incubators and humidifiers, and contaminated soaps and disinfectants.[122–124] Contamination of well water used by the patient was documented in one case of bacteremia.[125]

Clinical illness that is due to *A. xylosoxidans* subsp. *xylosoxidans* has involved isolates from blood, peritoneal and pleural fluids, urine, respiratory secretions, and wound exudates. Bacteremia, often related to intravascular catheters, is the most commonly reported infection.[126] Biliary tract sepsis, meningitis (sometimes with lymphocytic predominance in cerebrospinal fluid), pneumonia (nosocomial and community-acquired), peritonitis, urinary tract infection, osteomyelitis, prosthetic knee infection, and prosthetic valve endocarditis have been reported.[121, 125–128] Patients often have an immunosuppressed state such as cancer[129] and HIV infection,[130] but this is not always the case, especially in nosocomial outbreaks. This organism can colonize the airways of patients with cystic fibrosis and has been associated with exacerbation of respiratory symptoms.[131] Recovery in neonatal infection may result from perinatal transfer from the mother.[132] The organism has been recovered from eye, ear, and pharynx, but its pathogenic potential in these sites is unproved.

Strains of *A. xylosoxidans* subsp. *xylosoxidans* grow well on blood agar and MacConkey's agar plates; they produce flat, spreading and rough colonies and have peritrichous flagellae, features that help distinguish them from pseudomonads. The organisms are oxidase-positive, are catalase-positive, oxidize glucose to produce acid, and (as the species name indicates) oxidize xylose readily.[2] An isolate of *A. xylosoxidans* subsp. *xylosoxidans* can easily be mistaken for a non-*aeruginosa* strain of *Pseudomonas*, but the unusual susceptibility pattern suggests the correct identity.

Usually, strains of *A. xylosoxidans* subsp. *xylosoxidans* are susceptible to trimethoprim-sulfamethoxazole, ureidopenicillins, imipenem, ceftazidime, cefoperazone, and β-lactamase inhibitor combinations.[126] Generally, they are resistant to narrow-spectrum penicillins, other cephalosporins (including cefotaxime and ceftriaxone), aztreonam, and aminoglycosides.[129, 133, 134] Susceptibility to the fluoroquinolones is variable.[129] Hyperproduction of β-lactamases has been implicated in resistance.[135]

A. faecalis can be recovered in a variety of clinical settings. Most isolates of *A. faecalis* from blood or respiratory secretions are related to the contamination of hospital equipment or fluids with the organism, with resulting human colonization or infection. The urine is the other common site of recovery, although it infrequently causes symptomatic urinary tract infection. It also has been recovered from corneal ulcers, ear discharges, wound drainage, and feces.[136, 137] It is rarely recovered in pure culture from any of these sites. By contrast, *A. xylosoxidans* subsp. *denitrificans* has been recovered as a single pathogen from blood, cerebrospinal fluid, and other normally sterile body fluids as well as in mixed culture from sites usually containing normal flora. Few recent publications have addressed the pathogenic role of these organisms. *A. piechaudii* was thought to cause chronic otitis in a diabetic patient; its role as a human pathogen is not well defined.[138]

Identification of *Alcaligenes* spp. is made by recovery of oxidase-positive, catalase-positive, indole-negative, and urease-negative organisms with flat, spreading edges on blood-agar plates. Aerobic incubation is crucial for recovery in culture, and the organisms grow well at 35°C. The organisms also grow on MacConkey's agar. Distinguishing the organisms and confirming identification is made difficult by their lack of reactivity in many biochemical or assimilation tests.[139] *A. faecalis* produces a distinctive sweet odor resembling that of green apples.[2] *A. piechaudii* is distinguished from the other species by its reduction of nitrate and by growth in high concentrations of salt.[2]

Laboratory testing often shows *A. faecalis* strains to be susceptible to trimethoprim-sulfamethoxazole, ureidopenicillins, ticarcillin-clavulanate, carbapenems, and (unlike other *Alcaligenes* spp.) most cephalosporins.[140] Results vary for aztreonam, aminoglycosides, and fluoroquinolones, whereas *A. faecalis* strains are often resistant to amoxicillin, ticarcillin, and gentamicin.[137]

Centers for Disease Control and Prevention Group IVc-2

CDC group IVc-2 is an environmental gram-negative nonfermentative bacillus of low virulence that occasionally causes infections in compromised hosts. Most of the 13 reported human infections are intravascular catheter-related blood stream infections, either nosocomial or community acquired.[141, 142] Peritoneal dialysis–associated peritonitis[143] and tenosynovitis following a cat bite[144] have also been reported. Although infections are quite rare, five of the reported blood stream infections were from one institution, with the cases occurring over a 1-year period.[142] Molecular typing found the isolates to be clonal, but the source of the outbreak was not determined. Intravenous catheter removal was unnecessary in these five patients with nosocomial bacteremia; however, persistent peritonitis necessitated peritoneal catheter removal in one patient with chronic renal failure. Most patients have responded well to antibiotic therapy.

Organisms of CDC group IVc-2 grow well on sheep and horse blood agar as well as on MacConkey's agar at 37°C. Short gram-negative rods, occasionally in chains, are seen on Gram stain. The organisms are motile; have peritrichous flagella; are oxidase-, catalase-, citrate-, and urease-positive; and are negative for nitrate reduction.

Clinical isolates are usually resistant to ampicillin, cephalothin, cefamandole, aminoglycosides, and chloramphenicol and susceptible to third-generation cephalosporins, piperacillin, imipenem, ciprofloxacin, and tetracycline. Results of susceptibility testing to cefoxitin and trimethoprim-sulfamethoxazole are variable.[141, 142]

Chryseobacterium

Many species of the genus *Flavobacterium* have been reclassified into other genera. Two of the species most commonly isolated from clinical specimens, *Flavobacterium meningosepticum* and *Flavobacterium indologenes*, now reside in the genus *Chryseomonas. Flavobacterium odoratum*, a rare clinical isolate, has been placed in a new genus, *Myroides,* and divided into two species, *M. odoratus* and *M. odoratimimus.* These organisms are included for discussion in the group of nonfermenters, although some actually ferment glucose slowly.

Chryseobacterium spp. are inhabitants of soil and water and can be recovered from a variety of foods. They can live in municipal water supplies despite adequate chlorination and have been recovered from the hospital environment, often in conjunction with clusters of clinical isolates. *Chryseobacterium* spp. are organisms of low virulence, and their presence in clinical specimens usually represents colonization and not infection. The exception is *Chryseobacterium meningosepticum*, which is clinically significant in up to half of the adults and in about two thirds of the neonates from whom it is recovered.[145] *Chryseobacterium* spp. produce proteases and gelatinase, which may contribute to virulence; these are responsible for the greenish discoloration around the colonies on blood agar.

C. meningosepticum is a cause of neonatal meningitis, especially in premature infants during the first 2 weeks of life. Clusters of neonatal meningitis have been linked to many sources including contaminated saline solution for flushing eyes, respiratory equipment, and sink drains.[145, 146] Neonatal meningitis is fatal in over half the cases, and severe sequelae are common. Most *C. meningosepticum* infections in adults are hospital acquired and occur in immunocompromised hosts. The respiratory tract is the most common site of infection, and outbreaks have been linked to contaminated ventilator tubing and aerosols.[147, 148] In outbreaks, respiratory tract colonization occurs more often than infection. Bacteremia is the second most common presentation of *C. meningosepticum* infection. In one cluster of blood stream infections related to a contaminated anesthetic, the bacteremia was transient and systemic signs of infection resolved without specific antibiotic therapy, attesting to the low virulence of this organism in adults.[149] *C. meningosepticum* has also caused endocarditis (including prosthetic valve), cellulitis, wound infection, sepsis following extensive burns, abdominal abscess, dialysis-associated peritonitis, and endophthalmitis.[145, 150] Other contaminated sources include contaminated syringes in ice chests, vials, sink traps, tube feedings, flush solutions for arterial catheters, pressure transducers, and antiseptic solutions.[145, 151, 152] Infections including cellulitis, community-acquired respiratory tract infection, and bacteremia have been reported in the absence of underlying diseases.[153–155] *C. indologenes* is a rare cause of human disease. Intravascular catheter-related bacteremia and bacteremia associated with malignancy and neutropenia have been reported.[156] There are few recent reports of *Myroides adoratum* infection, and clinical isolates are rarely considered pathogenic. An exception is a report of necrotizing fasciitis and bacteremia in a patient with underlying cirrhosis.[157]

Chryseobacterium spp. may be long, thin, slightly curved, and occasionally filamentous on Gram stain. *C. indologenes* colonies usually form a dark yellow pigment in culture, whereas *C. meningosepticum* colonies are pale yellow. They grow well and form colonies within 24 hours on blood or chocolate agar and grow at a much slower rate, if at all, on MacConkey's agar.[158] They are not motile and produce positive catalase and oxidase reactions; variable results in other biochemical reactions may in part reflect the methods used for identification. *M. odoratum* produces a fruity odor (like that of *Alcaligenes faecalis*) and grows more readily on MacConkey's agar than most of the other species.[2]

Chryseobacterium spp. are resistant to most antibiotics, and the use of inactive drugs as empirical therapy may contribute to the poor outcome in many infections. In addition, results of susceptibility testing vary when different methods are used; disk diffusion methods especially are unreliable, and broth microdilution should be employed, if possible.[159] *Chryseobacterium* organisms produce β-lactamases and are resistant to most β-lactam drugs, including the carbapenems and aztreonam.[159] They are usually resistant to aminoglycosides, chloramphenicol, and erythromycin. Fluoroquinolones are usually active in vitro, and the newer agents trovafloxacin, sparfloxacin, cinafloxacin, and levofloxacin are somewhat more active than ciprofloxacin.[160] Minocycline was the only agent active against all *C. meningosepticum* strains in two 1997 reports.[145, 159] Doxycycline and trimethoprim-sulfamethoxazole susceptibility was variable. Rifampin is active against most strains and has been used as part of combination therapy to clear persistent infection.[161] Vancomycin, alone or in combination with other agents including rifampin, has been successful in the treatment of meningitis in infants.[162, 163] In some reported cases of meningitis treated successfully with vancomycin, the minimal inhibitory concentrations of vancomycin were 8 to 12 μg/ml.[164] However, in 1997, two groups reported that vancomycin was inactive in vitro (minimal inhibitory concentrations of 16 to >64 μg/ml) and called into question the usefulness of vancomycin against *Chryseobacterium*.[145, 159] Thus, there is no optimal regimen for *C. meningosepticum* meningitis, and therapy should be based on properly performed susceptibility testing. Possible regimens include rifampin in combination with trimethoprim-sulfamethoxazole, vancomycin, a fluoroquinolone, or minocycline.

Chryseomonas

Chryseomonas luteola is another uncommon opportunistic pathogen. It was previously known as CDC group Ve-1, *Pseudomonas luteola*, and *Chryseomonas polytricha*. By 16-S ribosomal-RNA sequencing, *C. luteola* and *Flavimonas oryzihabitans* (see later) share considerable sequence homology with *P. aeruginosa*.[165] *C. luteola* infections are often associated with foreign bodies such as central venous and peritoneal dialysis catheters. Reported infections include bacteremia, peritonitis (associated with appendicitis and colon cancer as well as catheters), osteomylelitis, endocarditis, and meningitis.[166, 167] *Chryseomonas* grows well on MacConkey's and blood-agar media producing yellow-pigmented colonies. It can be distinguished from *F. oryzihabitans*, which also produces yellow colonies, by biochemical features such as esculin hydrolysis and by flagellar morphology. Although *Chryseomonas* is related to the genus *Pseudomonas*, it is oxidase-negative.[158] Clinical isolates are often resistant to first- and second-generation cephalosporins, tetracyclines, ampicillin, and trimethoprim-sulfamethoxazole but are susceptible to third-generation cephalosporins, mezlocillin, imipenem, aminoglycosides, and quinolones.[166]

Eikenella

Eikenella corrodens is a fastidious facultative anaerobic gram-negative bacillus that is part of the normal human oral flora. Henriksen in 1948 identified a gram-negative anaerobic organism that had the peculiar characteristic of creating a depression in the growth medium and referred to this organism as the *corroding bacillus*. In 1958, Eiken described and characterized a gram-negative obligate or facultative anaerobic organism for which he proposed the name *Bacteroides corrodens*. Subsequently, the strictly anaerobic organisms were renamed *Bacteroides corrodens* (and now are called *Bacteroides ureolyticus*), whereas the facultative anaerobes were reclassified in the new genus *Eikenella*.[168]

E. corrodens is present as endogenous flora in the mouth and upper respiratory tract as well as on other mucous surfaces of the body. Although it is recovered most often in as a component of mixed infection,[169] commonly coexisting with streptococci,[170] it has been recovered from sterile sites in pure culture. Characteristic of *Eikenella* infection is an indolent course, generally taking greater than 1 week from the time of injury to clinical manifestation of disease.[171] The most common clinical sources of this organism are human bite wounds,[172] head and neck infections,[173] and respiratory tract infections.[169] The organism is often present in "clenched fist injuries," the most serious of human bite infections,[172] as well as in infections among chronic finger or nail biters.[174, 175] Because of the proximity of bone and joint spaces, these infections may lead to osteomyelitis and septic arthritis. It has also caused infection in insulin-requiring diabetic patients and drug-abusing "skin poppers" who lick their needles.[176] Severe soft tissue infection, with or without underlying osteomyelitis, may be slow to resolve.[177, 178] Suppuration due to *Eikenella* infections is foul-smelling, mimicking an anaerobic process. Gynecologic infections have been reported; some are associated with intrauterine contraceptive devices.[179, 180] *Eikenella* has also been recovered in pure culture from synovial fluid, bone, cerebrospinal fluid, brain, subdural and visceral abscesses, pleuropulmonary infection, orbital cellulitis, and blood.[169, 170, 181, 182] Pulmonary infections, including empyema, pneumonia, and septic emboli in conjunction with internal jugular vein thrombosis (postanginal sepsis), can occur, typically in patients with underlying chronic illnesses or intrathoracic malignancies.[170] *E. corrodens* is another of the so-called HACEK organisms, which, as mentioned, have in common the need for incubation in an atmosphere enhanced with CO_2 for recovery in culture, and a predilection for infecting the heart valves. Endocarditis caused by *E. corrodens* typically has an indolent course, but acute presentations are reported.[168] Endocarditis usually occurs after intravenous drug use or in patients with abnormal heart valves including prosthetic valves.[183]

E. corrodens is a gram-negative, small straight rod that at times can appear pleomorphic or coccobacillary. It grows in either aerobic or anaerobic environments. It is nonmotile and non–spore-forming and does not have a capsule. Cell surface components vary from strain to strain, and these differences may relate to virulence.[184] On blood or chocolate agar, even aided by the presence of 3 to 10% CO_2, the organism grows slowly, and it often requires 2 days or more to recognize the typical pinpoint colonies. Colonies are small and grayish (older colonies may become light yellow), produce a slight greenish discoloration on the blood agar, and elaborate an odor resembling that of bleach (hypochlorite).[2] About half produce the pitting ("corroding") of the agar that is considered characteristic. The organism grows poorly on MacConkey's agar. Strains are oxidase-positive, catalase-negative (a few strains are weakly catalase-positive), urease-negative, and indole-negative and reduce nitrate to nitrite. Lysine and ornithine-decarboxylase activity is present in most strains.

Ampicillin, ureidopenicillins, second- and third-generation cephalosporins, and tetracyclines have been reported effective against *E. corrodens* both in vitro and in producing clinical cure.[95, 185] The organism is susceptible to fluoroquinolones in vitro.[95] However, the organism is uniformly resistant to clindamycin, erythromycin, and metronidazole and often resistant in vitro to aminoglycosides. β-Lactamase production is uncommon at present; some of the β-lactamases produced by *Eikenella* are inhibited by clavulanate and sulbactam.[186]

Flavimonas

Flavimonas oryzihabitans (the species name means "inhabiting rice") is the current name for the organism that at various times past has been called *Chromobacterium typhiflavum*, *Pseudomonas oryzihabitans*, and CDC group Ve-2.[187] It is an infrequent cause of infection with characteristics similar to those of *Pseudomonas* spp. and *Chryseomonas luteola*. *Flavimonas oryzihabitans* is normally found in soil, water, and damp environments such as rice paddies. In the hospital setting, it has been recovered from sink drains and respiratory therapy equipment.[187] Central venous catheter–associated blood stream infection is the most commonly reported infection. In an 8-year study from a major cancer center, 21 of 22 episodes of *F. oryzihabitans* bacteremia were catheter related.[188] In this series, most infections were non–hospital acquired, polymicrobial infections were common, and the majority of bacteremias could be treated without catheter removal. In contrast, in another recent series, all *F. oryzihabitans* bacteremias were hospital acquired and the implicated intravascular devices were removed in the majority of cases.[189] The organism has also been associated with other foreign bodies such as peritoneal dialysis catheters, ventriculostomy tubes, vascular grafts, and prosthetic joints.[166, 190] Soft tissue infections, postoperative wound infections, splenic abscesses, and meningitis have been reported.[167, 191] Although most patients with *F. oryzihabitans* infection are immunocompromised, recovery is the rule.

The organism is an aerobic, oxidase-negative, catalase-positive bacillus. As is true for *Flavobacterium* (and older colonies of *Eikenella*), a yellowish tinge can be seen in colonies grown on MacConkey's agar. *F. oryzihabitans* is distinguished from *Pseudomonas* strains by its polar monotrichous flagella and negative oxidase reaction. The organism is usually susceptible in vitro to ureidopenicillins, third-generation cephalosporins, aztreonam, imipenem, aminoglycosides, fluoroquinolones, and trimethoprim-sulfamethoxazole, with resistance to earlier-generation cephalosporins.[188, 192]

Flavobacterium

The genus *Flavobacterium* consisted of a heterogeneous group of yellow-pigmented bacteria that did not prove to be closely related when subjected to genotypic analysis.[193] Consequently, many *Flavobacterium* species, including the clinically important species, have been reclassified to other genera and are discussed elsewhere. *Flavobacterium meningosepticum*, the most important species, and *Flavobacterium indologenes* are now members of the genus *Chryseobacterium*. *Flavobacterium odoratum*, an uncommon clinical isolate, has been placed in a new genus, *Myroides*, and divided into two species, *M. odoratus* and *M. odoratimimus*. *Flavobacterium multivorum* and *Flavobacterium spiritivorum* now reside in the genus *Sphingobacterium*.

Ochrobactrum

Organisms formerly called CDC group Vd and *Achromobacter* groups A, C, and D are now designated as *Ochrobactrum anthropi* (from the Greek *ochros* meaning "pale yellow").[110] *O. anthropi* is related to *Alcaligenes* spp. and *Agrobacterium radiobacter* and, like these organisms, can be found in the environment. Published reports suggest that infections caused by this organism may be increasing in frequency.[194, 195]

Intravascular catheter–related bacteremia is the most common infection associated with *O. anthropi*.[194, 196] This organism has contaminated biologic products, which have been the source of small outbreaks. Five blood stream infections occurred in organ transplant recipients who received contaminated rabbit antithymocyte globulin.[197] Consistent with this organism's being of low virulence, bacteremia resolved in four of five immunosuppressed patients in this series without antibiotic administration. Three cases of postoperative meningitis in neurosurgical patients were traced to cadaveric pericardial patches possibly contaminated during processing.[198] *O. anthropi* has caused endophthalmitis, both postoperative and secondary to hematogenous spread.[199, 200] Other reported infections include infection of pacemaker leads, pancreatic abscess, necrotizing fasciitis, and osteochondritis following a puncture wound.[195, 201–203] It has also been recovered from bile, urine, wounds, stool, throat, and vagina.[204]

O. anthropi is an oxidase-positive, non–lactose-fermenting gram-negative bacillus that grows readily on MacConkey's agar. The organism oxidizes glucose and xylose, but 72 hours or more of incubation may be required before this is apparent. *O. anthropi* is motile by means of peritrichous flagella, which helps to differentiate it from pseudomonads and *Chryseobacterium*. The organism is similar to *A. xylosoxidans* subsp. *xylosoxidans* in biochemical characteristics, but it can hydrolyze urea and grows poorly on cetrimide agar.[122]

O. anthropi is usually susceptible to trimethoprim-sulfamethoxazole and fluoroquinolones; they are variably susceptible to gentamicin, amikacin, netilmicin, imipenem, and tetracycline and are generally resistant to cephalosporins and penicillins.[196] Failures with imipenem therapy have been reported.

Oligella

The genus *Oligella* was named for the small size of the bacilli on Gram stain and contains two species, *Oligella urethralis* (formerly *Moraxella urethralis* and CDC group M-4) and *Oligella ureolytica* (formerly known as CDC group IVe). *O. urethralis* is a commensal of the genitourinary tract, and most clinical isolates are from the urine, predominantly from men.[22] Although symptomatic infections are rare, bacteremia, septic arthritis mimicking gonococcal arthritis,[205] and peritonitis in two patients receiving chronic ambulatory peritoneal dialysis[206] have been described. *O. ureolytica* is also primarily found in the urine, usually from patients with long-term indwelling urinary catheters or other urinary drainage systems. These patients have a propensity to develop urinary stones that may be related to the organism's ability to hydrolyze urea and alkalinize the urine, leading to precipitation of phosphates. Bacteremia has been reported in a patient with obstructive uropathy.[207] *O. ureolytica* bacteremia has been reported in a patient with acquired immunodeficiency syndrome and infected decubitus ulcers.[208]

Oligella spp., especially *O. urethralis*, resemble *Moraxella* and appear coccobacillary on Gram stain. Most strains will grow on blood or MacConkey's agar but require extended incubation (2 to 4 days) before growth can be detected. The rapidity of the urease reaction (within 5 minutes on a Christensen urea agar slant) is a distinctive feature of *O. ureolytica*. These organisms are oxidase-positive and catalase-positive and reduce NO_3 to NO_2. Contemporary data on antimicrobial susceptibilities are sparse. Strains of *O. urethralis* are usually susceptible to β-lactam antibiotics, but a β-lactamase–producing strain[209] as well as two strains resistant to ciprofloxacin have been reported.[206] In the past, *O. ureolytica* was susceptible to most antibiotics.

Roseomonas and Other "Pink-Pigmented" Gram-Negative Bacilli

The group of organisms previously known as CDC "pink coccoid" groups I through IV have been placed in the new genus *Roseomonas* (*roseus* + *monas*, a rose-colored or pink bacterium).[22, 210] There are currently three named species (*R. gilardii*, *R. cervicalis*, and *R. fauriae*) and three unnamed genospecies. Based on limited number of reports in the literature, *Roseomonas* appears to cause more clinical disease than the related pink-pigmented bacterium *Methylobacterium*.[2, 211] *Methylobacterium* spp., which are so named because of their ability to facultatively utilize methane, have been classified in the past under such names as *Pseudomonas mesophilica*, *Protomonas extorquens*, *Protaminobacter rubra*, "the pink phantom," and *Vibrio extorquens*.[212, 213] The two most clinically relevant species, *M. mesophilicum* and *M. extorquens*, are very similar phenotypically, and some reference laboratories limit identification to the genus level only.[22]

R. gilardii, the most commonly isolated species, is usually recovered in pure culture and, in one retrospective series, appeared to cause clinical illness more often than not.[211] Infections are usually community acquired. Blood stream infection is the most common presentation and may be related to intravascular catheters or secondary to processes at other sites including intra-abdominal abscesses or respiratory tract or urinary tract infections. These infections usually, but not invariably, occur in patients with underlying medical illnesses such as malignancies, acquired immunodeficiency syndrome, chronic renal disease, or diabetes. Device removal may be necessary to clear intravascular catheter–related bacteremia.[214] Peritoneal dialysis–associated peritonitis, vertebral osteomyelitis, septic bursitis, soft tissue infections, and epiglottitis have also been reported.[211, 215, 216] *Methylobacterium* has also caused intravascular catheter–related bacteremia and peritonitis in patients receiving continuous ambulatory peritoneal dialysis and soft tissue infections. A pseudo-outbreak of *Methylobacterium* respiratory tract infections was traced to contaminated tap water in the bronchoscopy suite.[217]

Roseomonas spp. are plump gram-negative rods or coccobacilli. In contrast, *Methylobacterium* spp. do not stain well and can appear gram-variable and also have intracellular vacuoles. Both these organisms can appear weakly oxidase-positive and are catalase-positive and urease-positive. *Roseomonas* can be distinguished from *Methylobacterium* by the inability to oxidize methanol, the inability to assimilate acetamide, and the absence of long-wave ultraviolet light absorption.[210] *Methylobacterium* has been isolated after 1 week of incubation on medium ordinarily used for the isolation of mycobacteria.[213]

Imipenem, aminoglycosides, and tetracycline are the most active antibiotics against *Roseomonas* spp. They are usually resistant to penicillins and cephalosporins with the exception of penicillin β-lactamase inhibitor combinations, which are frequently but not invariably active. *Roseomonas* spp. are often susceptible to fluoroquinolones but resistant to trimethoprim-sulfamethoxazole. *Methylobacterium* grows slowly, and susceptibility testing is not always possible.[212] Many *Methylobacterium* isolates produce a β-lactamase, and the organisms are resistant to penicillins and many cephalosporins. Aminoglycosides, ciprofloxacin, and trimethoprim-sulfamethoxazole are active.

Shewanella

Shewanella (formerly *Pseudomonas*) *putrefaciens* is widely distributed in the environment and has infrequently been implicated as a cause of human disease. *Shewanella* can be recovered from a variety of water sources, natural gas and petroleum reserves, dairy products, meat, and fish. *S. putrefaciens* is genetically heterogeneous, and three distinct biovars have been described. Biovar 1 (CDC group Ib-1) is a major cause of spoilage of refrigerated protein-rich foods. Clinical isolates are usually biovar 2 (CDC group Ib-2), but recent data suggest that most of these isolates should be classified as the genetically distinct species *Shewanella alga*.[218, 219] However, the typing systems currently in use by most clinical microbiology laboratories identify both species as *S. putrefaciens*.[219] Thus, in all likelihood, the use of this species name will continue.

S. putrefaciens is frequently isolated as part of a polymicrobial infection, and its pathogenic role is often unclear. Lower extremity cellulitis in association with chronic ulcers or after burns is one of the more commonly described presentations.[220] *S. putrefaciens* bacteremia, which also is frequently polymicrobial, can accompany soft tissue infection or biliary tract disease or occur in compromised hosts including persons with underlying liver disease or malignancy.[221, 222] Compromised hosts are more likely to have accompanying signs of sepsis and have a poor outcome. Bacteremia and respiratory distress have been described in neonates and premature infants.[221] Less commonly reported infections include peritonitis, pneumonia, empyema, meningitis, osteomyelitis, otitis, urinary tract infection, and endophthalmitis.[220, 222, 223]

On Gram stain, *S. putrefaciens* is a short to long rod and can be filamentous. It is oxidase-positive and is the only nonfermenter that produces hydrogen sulfide on triple sugar iron agar, a key feature that allows easy identification in the laboratory. *Shewanella alba* can be distinguished from *S. putrefaciens* by exhibiting hemolysis on blood agar, growth at 42°C in 6.5% NaCl, and acid production from sucrose, maltose and L-arabinose.[219] *Shewanella* is resistant to penicillin and cefazolin but susceptible to most second- and third-generation cephalosporins and piperacillin.[220] The organisms are also usually susceptible to aminoglycosides, chloramphenicol, and ciprofloxacin but less predictably susceptible to tetracycline and trimethoprim-sulfamethoxazole.[220, 221] A report from South Africa found the majority of isolates resistant to imipenem.[221]

Sphingobacterium

The genus *Sphingobacterium* includes organisms previously classified as *Flavobacterium* species. The organisms that were transferred to this new genus contain large amounts of sphingophospholipid compounds in their cell membranes and have other taxonomic features that distinguish them from flavobacteria.[224] Of the five *Sphingobacterium* species currently named, most isolates from humans are *Sphingobacterium multivorum* (formerly *Flavobacterium multivorum* or CDC group IIk-2) and *Sphingobacterium spiritivorum* (formerly *Flavobacterium spiritivorum* or CDC group IIk-3).

There are reported cases of *S. multivorum* causing peritonitis, septicemia in a dialysis patient, bacteremia in a patient with lymphoma as well as in a patient with diabetes, and respiratory disease in a patient with cystic fibrosis.[225–228] Most cases of *S. multivorum* infection are nosocomial, but the natural habitat of the organism is not well defined. *S. spiritivorum* has been rarely recovered from clinical specimens; urine and blood are the most common sites.[22, 229]

S. multivorum and *S. spiritivorum* grow on blood agar, are oxidase- and catalase-positive, and produce light yellow colonies. They are biochemically similar to *Sphingomonas paucimobilis* (CDC group IIk-1) except that *Sphingobacterium* spp. are nonmotile and are resistant to polymyxin.

Sphingobacterium spp. are intrinsically resistant to many commonly employed antibiotics and can grow in some antiseptics and disinfectants.[226, 230] *S. multivorum* can produce an extended-spectrum β-lactamase and a metallo-β-lactamase conferring resistance to third-generation cephalosporins and carbapenems, respectively.[231] The combination of trimethoprim-sulfamethoxazole and perfloxacin produced cure in a bacteremic patient.[226] A bacteremic patient receiving hemodialysis improved clinically after receiving ampicillin and one dose of tobramycin, despite in vitro testing showing ampicillin resistance.[225]

Sphingomonas

Sphingomonas, a new genus whose name was first proposed in 1990,[232] contains one species that is an occasional human pathogen, *Sphingomonas paucimobilis*. This organism, formerly known as *Pseudomonas paucimobilis* and CDC group IIk-1, is widely distributed in soil and water, including water sources in the hospital environment. It has been implicated in nosocomial outbreaks associated with contaminated water[233] and contaminated ventilator temperature probes.[234]

S. paucimobilis infections typically occur in immunocompromised persons and can be community as well as nosomonially acquired. This is an organism of low virulence, and recovery from infection is the rule, even in debilitated hosts. There are several reports of *S. paucimobilis* intravascular catheter–associated blood stream infection, and catheter removal was necessary in some cases for cure.[235, 236] Blood stream infection has also been reported in hemodialysis patients and after infusion of contaminated autologous bone marrow.[237] Although ventilator-associated pneumonia has been described,[236] airway colonization was much more common than infection in intensive care unit outbreaks.[233, 234] Peritoneal catheter-associated peritonitis, meningitis, ventriculoperitoneal shunt infection, brain abscess, soft tissue infection, wound infection, adenitis, urinary tract infection, and a variety of visceral abscesses have been reported.[236, 238, 239]

S. paucimobilis is strictly aerobic, oxidase-positive, and catalase-positive. Colonies grow on blood agar but not MacConkey's agar, produce a yellow pigment, and can be misidentified as *Flavobacterium* spp. Despite the presence of a single polar flagellum, a low percentage of cells are actively motile, and motility can be difficult to demonstrate in the laboratory (thus the name paucimobilis).[240]

Most isolates are susceptible to trimethoprim-sulfamethoxazole, imipenem, aminoglycosides, tetracyclines, and chloramphenicol.[236, 239] Third-generation cephalosporins are usually active but not predictably so, and resistance to penicillins and first-generation cephalosporins is common. Although fluoroquinolones were active in some reports, many isolates were resistant to ciprofloxacin in one series.[236]

Weeksella and *Bergeyella*

The genus *Weeksella*, when proposed in 1986, contained two species, *W. zoohelcum* (CDC group IIj) and *W. virosa* (CDC group IIf), that differed from most nonfermentative gram-negative bacilli in being susceptible to penicillin. Recently, *W. zoohelcum* has been moved to the new genus *Bergeyella*.[193] *Bergeyella zoohelcum* (from the Greek "animal" + "wound") is part of the normal oral flora of dogs and other animals, and most clinical isolates come from bite wounds.[241, 242] A case report of meningitis following multiple dog bites is the only report of an invasive infection caused by this organism.[243] *W. virosa* has been isolated predominantly from the genital tract and urine of women[244, 245] and is usually not a pathogen. A case of dialysis-associated peritonitis has been reported.[246] Both organisms grow well on blood agar, but most strains do not grow on MacConkey's agar. They are oxidase-positive, catalase-positive, indole-positive, and nonpigmented. In contrast to *W. virosa*, *B. zoohelcum* produces urease. *W. virosa* (from the Latin "slimy") forms coccoid colonies that stick tenaciously to agar surfaces.[244] Both species are susceptible to β-lactam antibiotics including penicillin, chloramphenicol, and fluoroquinolones and are variable in susceptibility to tetracycline and trimethoprim-sulfamethoxazole. *W. virosa* is usually resistant to one or more aminoglycosides. The combination of penicillin susceptibility and aminoglycoside resistance is a clue to the identification of this organism.

New Centers for Disease Control and Prevention Groups

The CDC's Special Bacteriology Reference Laboratory receives unusual isolates from state laboratories and other reference laboratories. Some of these isolates are unnamed and are grouped by growth characteristics. Each of these groups represents one or more species. Although many of the isolates are from sterile sites, clinical information is often limited, and the pathogenic role of these organisms is uncertain. Some of the recently described CDC groups of gram-negative rods or coccobacillary organisms are mentioned as follows.

(1) CDC group NO-1 (NO for nonoxidizer) consists of least 22 strains of fastidious gram-negative bacilli isolated from human wounds, most of which were related to dog or cat bites.[22, 247] These organisms are similar to fastidious *Acinetobacter* strains but have a negative *Acinetobacter* transformation assay, have different cellular fatty acid profiles, and, unlike most *Acinetobacter* organisms, reduce nitrate. They are susceptible to many antimicrobial agents, including β-lactams, aminoglycosides, fluoroquinolones, and tetracycline. (2) CDC Group WO-1 (WO for weak oxidizer) includes 96 oxidase-positive, motile gram-negative rods, most of which were isolated from clinical specimens.[248] One third of the clinical isolates were from blood, and 10% were from cerebrospinal fluid.[248] Signs of sepsis were present in some of the patients, but the clinical significance of this group of organisms remains unclear. (3) CDC group O-3 includes 13 glucose-oxidizing clinical isolates, most of which have been collected since 1991.[249] They are oxidase-positive curved gram-negative rods that do not grow on MacConkey's agar but grow on *Campylobacter*-selective media. One of the isolates was submitted to the CDC having been identified as a *Campylobacter* sp., indicating the potential for misidentification of the O-3 group. The isolates were from a variety of clinical sources including blood, lymph nodes, joint fluid, bone, and lung. They were resistant to most β-lactam antibiotics except imipenem; all were susceptible to aminoglycosides and trimethoprim-sulfamethoxazole but not ciprofloxacin. (4) Fifteen strains of an oxidase-positive gram-negative rod biochemically resembling *Neisseria weaveri* (CDC group M5) are currently designated Gilardi rod group 1 by the CDC.[250] Most of the strains were isolated from human wounds of the extremities or blood cultures. (5) A report from the CDC in 1985 described thermophilic gram-negative bacilli as a source for some human infections.[251] Most of the 31 isolates grew better at 42°C or 50°C than at 35°C. All were oxidase-positive, grew on heart infusion agar plates but not MacConkey's agar, and did not ferment glucose. The thermophiles appeared somewhat heterogeneous and likely represent more than one species. Clinical information was available in 15 cases, including six symptomatic patients from whom the isolates grew in pure culture from normally sterile body sites (cerebrospinal fluid in two cases and blood in four cases including two with endocarditis). All were susceptible to penicillins and cephalosporins.

REFERENCES

1. Holmes B, Pickett MJ, Hollis DG. Unusual gram-negative bacteria, including *Capnocytophaga*, *Eikenella*, *Pasteurella*, and *Streptobacillus*. In: Murray PR, Baron EJ, Pfaller MA, et al, eds. Manual of Clinical Microbiology. 6th ed. Washington, DC: American Society for Microbiology; 1995:499–508.
2. Koneman EW, Allen SD, Janda WM, et al. Color Atlas and Textbook of Diagnostic Microbiology. 5th ed. Philadelphia: JB Lippincott; 1997.
3. Kaplan AH, Weber DJ, Oddone EZ, et al. Infection due to *Actinobacillus actinomycetemcomitans*: 15 cases and review. Rev Infect Dis. 1989;11:46–63.
4. Holm P. Studies on the aetiology of human actinomycosis. II. Do the "other microbes" of actinomycosis possess virulence? Acta Pathol Microbiol Scand. 1951;28:391–406.
5. Page MI, King EO. Infection due to *Actinobacillus actinomycetemcomitans* and *Haemophilus aphrophillus*. N Engl J Med. 1966;275:181–188.
6. Horowitz EA, Pugsley MP, Turbes PG, et al. Pericarditis caused by *Actinobacillus actinomycetemcomitans*. J Infect Dis. 1987;155:152–153.
7. Ellner JJ, Rosenthal MS, Lerner PI, et al. Infective endocarditis caused by slow-growing, fastidious, gram-negative bacteria. Medicine. 1979;58:145-158.
8. Yuan A, Yang PC, Lee LN, et al. *Actinobacillus actinomycetemcomitans* pneumonia with chest wall involvement and rib destruction. Chest. 1992;101:1450–1452.
9. Bowker CM, Connellan SJ, Freeth MG. A case of thoracic *Actinobacillus* infection. Respir Med. 1992;86:53–54.
10. Asikainen S, Chen C, Alaluusua S, et al. Can one acquire periodontal bacteria and periodontitis from a family member? J Am Dent Assoc. 1997;128:1263–1271.
11. Aass AM, Preus HR, Gjermo P. Association between detection of oral *Actinobacillus actinomycetemcomitans* and radiographic bone loss in teenagers. J Periodontol. 1992:63:682–685.
12. Asikainen S, Chen C, Slots J. Likelihood of transmitting *Actinobacillus actinomycetemcomitans* and *Porphyromonas gingivalis* in families with periodontitis. Oral Microbiol Immunol. 1996;11:387–394.
13. Meyer DH, Lippmann JE, Fives-Taylor PM. Invasion of epithelial cells by *Actinobacillus actinomycetemcomitans*: A dynamic, multistep process. Infect Immun. 1996;64:2988–2997.
14. Meyer DH, Fives-Taylor PM. The role of *Actinobacillus actinomycetemcomitans* in the pathogenesis of periodontal disease. Trends Microbiol. 1997;5:224–228.
15. Grace CJ, Levitz RE, Katz Pollak H, et al. *Actinobacillus actinomycetemcomitans* prosthetic valve endocarditis. Rev Infect Dis. 1988;10:922–929.
16. Wilson ME. Prosthetic valve endocarditis and paravalvular abscess caused by *Actinobacillus actinomycetemcomitans*. Rev Infect Dis. 1989;11:665–667.
17. Peel MM, Hornidge KA, Luppino M, et al. *Actinobacillus* spp and related bacteria in infected wounds of humans bitten by horses and sheep. J Clin Microbiol. 1991;29:2535-2538.
18. Arana-Domondon LC, Chen SH, Mann L, et al. Boar hunter's endocarditis. JAMA. 1998;279:198.
19. Wust J, Gubler J, Mannheim W, et al. *Actinobacillus hominis* as a causative agent of septicemia in hepatic failure. Eur J Clin Microbiol Infect Dis. 1991;10:693–694.
20. Kingsland RC, Guss DA. *Actinobacillus ureae* meningitis: Case report and review of the literature. J Emerg Med. 1995;13:623–627.

21. Verhaegen J, Verbraeken H, Cabuy A, et al. *Actinobacillus* (formerly *Pasteurella*) *ureae* meningitis and bacteraemia: Report of a case and review of the literature. J Infect. 1988;17:249–253.
22. Weyant RS, Moss CW, Weaver RE, et al. Identification of Unusual Pathogenic Gram-Negative Aerobic and Facultatively Anaerobic Bacteria. 2nd ed. Baltimore: Williams & Wilkins; 1996.
23. Yogev R, Shulman D, Shulman ST, et al. In vitro activity of antibiotics alone and in combination against *Actinobacillus actinomycetemcomitans*. Antimicrob Agents Chemother. 1986;29:179–181.
24. Pavicic MJ, van Winkelhoff AJ, de Graaff J. In vitro susceptibilities of *Actinobacillus actinomycetemcomitans* to a number of antimicrobial combinations. Antimicrob Agents Chemother. 1992;36:2634–2638.
25. Wilson WR, Karchmer AW, Dajani AS, et al. Antibiotic treatment of adults with infective endocarditis due to streptococci, enterococci, staphylococci, and HACEK microorganisms. JAMA. 1995;274:1706–1713.
26. Babinchak TJ. Oral ciprofloxacin therapy for prosthetic valve endocarditis due to *Actinobacillus actinomycetemcomitans*. Clin Infect Dis. 1995;21:1517–1518.
27. Van Winkelhoff AJ, Tijhof CJ, de Graaff J. Microbiological and clinical results of metronidazole plus amoxicillin therapy in *Actinobacillus actinomycetemcomitans*–associated periodontitis. J. Periodontol. 1992;63:52–57.
28. Colwell RR, MacDonell MT, De Ley J. Proposal to recognize the family *Aeromonadaceae* fam nov. Int J Syst Bacteriol. 1986;36:473–477.
29. Krieg NR, Holt JG, eds. *Bergey's Manual of Systematic Bacteriology*, v. 1. Baltimore: Williams & Wilkins; 1984.
30. Janda JM, Abbott SL. Evolving concepts regarding the genus *Aeromonas*: An expanding panorama of species, disease presentations and unanswered questions. Clin Infect Dis. 1998;27:332–344.
31. Challapalli M, Tess BR, Cunningham DG, et al. *Aeromonas*-associated diarrhea in children. Pediatr Infect Dis J. 1988;7:693–698.
32. Gluskin I, Batash D, Shoseyov D, et al. A 15-year study of the role of *Aeromonas* spp in gastroenteritis in hospitalised children. J Med Microbiol. 1992;37:315–318.
33. Rautelin H, Sivonen A, Kuikka A, et al. Role of *Aeromonas* isolated from feces of Finnish patients. Scand J Infect Dis. 1995;27:207–210.
34. King GE, Werner SB, Kizer KW. Epidemiology of *Aeromonas* infections in California. Clin Infect Dis. 1992;15:449–452.
35. Namdari H, Bottone EJ. Microbiologic and clinical evidence supporting the role of *Aeromonas caviae* as a pediatric enteric pathogen. J Clin Microbiol. 1990;28:837–840.
36. Jiang ZD, Nelson AC, Mathewson JJ, et al. Intestinal secretory immune response to infection with *Aeromonas* species and *Plesiomonas shigelloides* among students from the United States in Mexico. J Infect Dis. 1991;164:979–982.
37. Hanninen ML, Salmi S, Mattila L, et al. Association of *Aeromonas* spp with travellers' diarrhoea in Finland. J Med Microbiol. 1995;42:26–31.
38. Holmberg SD, Schell WL, Fanning GR, et al. *Aeromonas* intestinal infections in the United States. Ann Intern Med. 1986;105:683–689.
39. Jones BL, Wilcox MH. *Aeromonas* infections and their treatment. J Antimicrob Chemother. 1995;35:453–461.
40. De la Morena ML, Van R, Singh K, et al. Diarrhea associated with *Aeromonas* species in children in day care centers. J Infect Dis. 1993;168:215–218.
41. Willoughby JM, Rahman AF, Gregory MM. Chronic colitis after *Aeromonas* infection. Gut. 1989;30:686–690.
42. Bogdanovic R, Cobeljic M, Markovic M, et al. Haemolytic-uraemic syndrome associated with *Aeromonas hydrophila* enterocolitis. Pediatr Nephrol. 1991;5:293–295.
43. Gold WL, Salit IE. *Aeromonas hydrophila* infections of skin and soft tissue: Report of 11 cases and review. Clin Infect Dis. 1993;16:69–74.
44. Semel JD, Trenholme G. *Aeromonas hydrophilia* water-associated traumatic wound infections: A review. J Trauma. 1990;30:324–327.
45. Wakabongo M. Motile *Aeromonas* as agent of infections of the foot. J Am Podiatr Med Asso. 1995;85:505–508.
46. Lineaweaver WC, Hill MK, Buncke GM, et al. *Aeromonas hydrophilia* infections following use of medicinal leeches in replantation and flap surgery. Ann Plast Surg. 1992;29:238–244.
47. Mackay DR, Manders EK, Saggers GC, et al. *Aeromonas* species isolated from medicinal leeches. Ann Plast Surg. 1999;42:275–279.
48. Ko WC, Chuang YC. *Aeromonas bacteremia*: Review of 59 episodes. Clin Infect Dis. 1995;20:1298–1304.
49. Janda JM, Guthertz LS, Kokka RP, et al. *Aeromonas* species in septicemia: Laboratory characteristics and clinical observations. Clin Infect Dis. 1994;19:77–83.
50. Dryden M, Munro R. *Aeromonas* septicemia: Relationship of species and clinical features. Pathology. 1989;21:111–114.
51. Cookson BD, Houang ET, Lee JV. The use of a biotyping system to investigate an unusual clustering of bacteraemias caused by *Aeromonas* species. J Hosp Infect. 1984;5:205–209.
52. Hickman-Brenner FW, Fanning GR, Arduino MJ, et al. *Aeromonas schubertii*, a new mannitol-negative species found in human clinical specimens. J Clin Microbiol. 1988;26:1561–1564.
53. Carnahan A, Fanning GR, Joseph SW. *Aeromonas jandaei* (formerly genospecies DNA group 9 *A. sobria*), a new sucrose-negative species isolated from clinical specimens. J Clin Microbiol. 1991;29:560–564.
54. DeFronzo RA, Murray GF, Maddrey WC. *Aeromonas* septicemia from hepatobiliary disease. Am J Dig Dis. 1973;18:323–331.
55. Parras F, Diaz MD, Reina J, et al. Meningitis due to *Aeromonas* species: Case report and review. Clin Infect Dis. 1993;17:1058–1060.
56. Ong KR, Sordillo E, Frankel E. Unusual case of *Aeromonas hydrophila* endocarditis. J Clin Microbiol. 1991;29:1056–1057.
57. Ender PT, Dolan MJ, Dolan D, et al. Near-drowning–associated *Aeromonas* pneumonia. J Emerg Med. 1996;14:737–741.
58. Janda JM, Abbott SL, Carnahan AM. *Aeromonas* and *Plesiomonas*. In: Murray PR, Baron EJ, Pfaller MA, et al, eds. *Manual of Clinical Microbiology*. Washington, DC: American Society for Microbiology. 1995:477–482.
59. San Joaquin VH, Scribner RK, Pickett DA, et al. Antimicrobial susceptibility of *Aeromonas* species isolated from patients with diarrhea. Antimicrob Agents Chemother. 1986;30:794–795.
60. Motyl MR, McKinley G, Janda JM. In vitro susceptibilities of *Aeromonas hydrophila*, *Aeromonas sobria*, and *Aeromonas caviae* to 22 antimicrobial agents. Antimicrob Agents Chemother. 1985;28:151–153.
61. Chang BJ, Bolton SM. Plasmids and resistance to antimicrobial agents in *Aeromonas sobria* and *Aeromonas hydrophila* clinical isolates. Antimicrob Agents Chemother. 1987;31:1281–1282.
62. Walsh TR, Stunt RA, Nabi JA, et al. Distribution and expression of beta-lactamase genes among *Aeromonas* spp. J Antimicrob Chemother. 1997;40:171–178.
63. Walsh TR, Payne DJ, MacGowan AP, et al. A clinical isolate of *Aeromonas sobria* with three chromosomally mediated inducible beta-lactamases: A cephalosporinase, a penicillinase and a third enzyme, displaying carbapenemase activity. J Antimicrob Chemother. 1995;35:271–279.
64. Overman TL, Janda JM. Antimicrobial susceptibility patterns of *Aeromonas jandaei, A. schubertii, A. trota,* and *A. veronii* biotype *veronii*. J Clin Microbiol. 1999;37:706–708.
65. Rossolini GM, Walsh T, Amicosante G. The *Aeromonas* metallo-beta-lactamases: Genetics, enzymology, and contribution to drug resistance. *Microb Drug Resist*. 1996;2:245–252.
66. Wormser GP, Bottone EJ. *Cardiobacterium hominis*: Review of microbiologic and clinical features. Rev Infect Dis. 1983;5:680–691.
67. Taveras JMd, Campo R, Segal N, et al. Apparent culture-negative endocarditis of the prosthetic valve caused by *Cardiobacterium hominis*. South Med J. 1993;86:1439–1440.
68. Pritchard TM, Foust RT, Cantely JR, et al. Prosthetic valve endocarditis due to *Cardiobacterium hominis* occurring after upper gastrointestinal endoscopy. Am J Med. 1991;90:516–518.
69. Robison WJ, Vitelli AS. Infectious endocarditis caused by *Cardiobacterium hominis*. South Med J. 1985;78:1020–1021.
70. Francioli PB, Roussianos D, Glauser MP. *Cardiobacterium hominis* endocarditis manifesting as bacterial meningitis. Arch Intern Med. 1983;143:1483–1484.
71. Rechtman DJ, Nadler JP. Abdominal abscess due to *Cardiobacterium hominis* and *Clostridium bifermentans*. Rev Infect Dis. 1991;13:418–419.
72. Le Quellec A, Bessis D, Perez C, et al. Endocarditis due to beta-lactamase–producing *Cardiobacterium hominis*. Clin Infect Dis. 1994;19:994–995.
73. Ponte R, Jenkins SG. Fatal *Chromobacterium violaceum* infections associated with exposure to stagnant waters. Pediatr Infect Dis J. 1992;11:583–586.
74. Ti TY, Tan WC, Chong AP, et al. Nonfatal and fatal infections caused by *Chromobacterium violaceum*. Clin Infect Dis. 1993;17:505–507.
75. Kaufman SC, Ceraso D, Schugurensky A. First case report from Argentina of fatal septicemia caused by *Chromobacterium violaceum*. J Clin Microbiol. 1986;23:956–958.
76. Berkowitz FE, Metchock B. Third generation cephalosporin-resistant gram-negative bacilli in the feces of hospitalized children. Pediatr Infect Dis J. 1995;14:97–100.
77. Roberts SA, Morris AJ, McIvor N, et al. *Chromobacterium violaceum* infection of the deep neck tissues in a traveler to Thailand. Clin Infect Dis. 1997;25:334–335.
78. Shetty M, Venkatesh A, Shenoy S, et al. *Chromobacterium violaceum* meningitis—a case report. Indian J Med Sci. 1987;41:275–276.
79. Macher AM, Casale TB, Fauci AS. Chronic granulomatous disease of childhood and *Chromobacterium violaceum* infections in the Southeastern United States. Ann Intern Med. 1982;97:51–55.
80. Mamlok RJ, Mamlok V, Mills GC, et al. Glucose-6-phosphate dehydrogenase deficiency, neutrophil dysfunction and *Chromobacterium violaceum* sepsis. J Pediatr. 1987;111:852–854.
81. Miller DP, Blevins WT, Steele DB, et al. A comparative study of virulent and avirulent strains of *Chromobacterium violaceum*. Can J Microbiol. 1988;34:249–255.
82. Aldridge KE, Valainis GT, Sanders CV. Comparison of the in vitro activity of ciprofloxacin and 24 other antimicrobial agents against clinical strains of *Chromobacteriurn violaceum*. Diagn Microbiol Infect Dis. 1988;10:31–39.
83. Duma RJ. Aztreonam, the first monobactam. Ann Intern Med. 1987;106:766–767.
84. Wagner DK, Wright JJ, Ansher AF, et al. Dysgonic fermenter 3–associated gastrointestinal disease in a patient with common variable hypogammaglobulinemia. Am J Med. 1988;84:315–318.
85. Vandamme P, Vancanneyt M, van Belkum A, et al. Polyphasic analysis of strains of the genus *Capnocytophaga* and Centers for Disease Control group DF-3. Int J Syst Bacteriol. 1996;46:782–791.
86. Gill VJ, Travis LB, Williams DY. Clinical and microbiological observations on CDC group DF-3, a gram-negative coccobacillus. J Clin Microbiol. 1991;29:1589–1592.
87. Heiner AM, DiSario JA, Carroll K, et al. Dysgonic fermenter-3: A bacterium associated with diarrhea in immunocompromised hosts. Am J Gastroenterol. 1992;87:1629–1630.
88. Blum RN, Berry CD, Phillips MG, et al. Clinical illnesses associated with isolation of dysgonic fermenter 3 from stool samples. J Clin Microbiol. 1992;30:396–400.

89. Schonheyder H, Ejlertsen T, Frederiksen W. Isolation of a dysgonic fermenter (DF-3) from urine of a patient. Eur J Clin Microbiol Infect Dis. 1991;10:530–531.
90. Bangsborg JM, Frederiksen W, Bruun B. Dysgonic fermenter 3–associated abscess in a diabetic patient. J Infect. 1990;20:237–240.
91. Aronson NE, Zbick CJ. Dysgonic fermenter 3 bacteremia in a neutropenic patient with acute lymphocytic leukemia. J Clin Microbiol. 1988;26:2213–2215.
92. Vartian CV, Septimus EJ. Endophthalmitis due to *Pasteurella multocida* and CDC EF-4. J Infect Dis. 1989;160:733.
93. Dul MJ, Shlaes DM, Lerner PI. EF-4 bacteremia in a patient with hepatic carcinoid. J Clin Microbiol. 1983;18:1260–1261.
94. Holmes B, Costas M, Wood AC. Numerical analysis of electrophoretic protein patterns of group EF-4 bacteria, predominantly from dog-bite wounds of humans. J Appl Bacteriol. 1990;68:81–91.
95. Goldstein EJ, Citron DM. Comparative activities of cefuroxime, amoxicillin–clavulanic acid, ciprofloxacin, enoxacin, and ofloxacin against aerobic and anaerobic bacteria isolated from bite wounds. Antimicrob Agents Chemother. 1988;32:1143–1148.
96. Holmberg SD, Wachsmuth K, Hickman-Brenner FW, et al. *Plesiomonas* enteric infections in the United States. Ann Intern Med. l986;105:690–694.
97. Brenden RA, Miller MA, Janda JM. Clinical disease spectrum and pathogenic factors associated with *Plesiomonas shigelloides* infections in humans. Rev Infect Dis. 1988;10:303–316.
98. MacDonnell MT, Colwell RR. Phylogeny of the *Vibrionaceae*, and recommendation for two new genera, *Listonella* and *Shewanella*. System Appl Microbiol. 1985;6:171–182.
99. Rautelin H, Sivonen A, Kuikka A, et al. Enteric *Plesiomonas shigelloides* infections in Finnish patients. Scand J Infect Dis. 1995;27:495–498.
100. Kain KC, Kelly MT. Clinical features, epidemiology, and treatment of *Plesiomonas shigelloides* diarrhea. J Clin Microbiol. 1989;27:998–1001.
101. Olsvik O, Wachsmuth K, Kay B, et al. Laboratory observations on *Plesiomonas shigelloides* strains isolated from children with diarrhea in Peru. J Clin Microbiol. 1990;28:886–889.
102. Janda JM, Abbott SL. Expression of hemolytic activity by *Plesiomonas shigelloides*. J Clin Microbiol. 1993;31:1206–1208.
103. Visitsunthorn N, Komolpis P. Antimicrobial therapy in *Plesiomonas shigelloides*–associated diarrhea in Thai children. Southeast Asian J Trop Med Public Health. 1995;26:86–90.
104. Alcaniz JP, de Cuenca Moron B, Gomez Rubio M, et al. Spontaneous bacterial peritonitis due to *Plesiomonas shigelloides*. Am J Gastroenterol. 1995;90:1529–1530.
105. Fujita K, Shirai M, Ishioka T, et al. Neonatal *Plesiomonas shigelloides* septicemia and meningitis: A case and review. Acta Paediatr Jpn. 1994;36:450–452.
106. Clark RB, Westby GR, Spector H, et al. Fatal *Plesiomonas shigelloides* septicaemia in a splenectomised patient. J Infect. 1991;23:89–92.
107. Paul R, Siitonen A, Karkkainen P. *Plesiomonas shigelloides* bacteremia in a healthy girl with mild gastroenteritis. J Clin Microbiol. 1990;28:1445–1446.
108. Rahim Z, Kay BA. Enrichment for *Plesiomonas shigelloides* from stools. J Clin Microbiol. 1988;26:789–790.
109. Kain KC, Kelly MT. Antimicrobial susceptibility of *Plesiomonas shigelloides* from patients with diarrhea. Antimicrob Agents Chemother. 1989;33:1609–1610.
110. Bruckner DA, Colonna P. Nomenclature for aerobic and facultative bacteria. Clin Infect Dis. 1993;16:598–605.
111. Holmes B, Moss CW, Daneshvar MI. Cellular fatty acid compositions of "*Achromobacter* groups B and E." J Clin Microbiol. 1993;31:1007–1008.
112. Jenks PJ, Shaw EJ. Recurrent septicaemia due to "*Achromobacter* group B." J Infect. 1997;34:143–145.
113. Holmes B, Lewis R, Trevett A. Septicaemia due to *Achromobacter* group B: A report of two cases. Med Microbiol Lett. 1992;1:177–184.
114. McKinley KP, Laundy TJ, Masterton RG. *Achromobacter* group B replacement valve endocarditis. J Infect. 1990;20:262–263.
115. Sawada H, Ieki H, Oyaizu H, et al. Proposal for rejection of *Agrobacterium tumefaciens* and revised descriptions for the genus *Agrobacterium* and for *Agrobacterium radiobacter* and *Agrobacterium rhizogenes*. Int J Syst Bacteriol. 1993;43:694–702.
116. Edmond MB, Riddler SA, Baxter CM, et al. *Agrobacterium radiobacter*: A recently recognized opportunistic pathogen. Clin Infect Dis. 1993;16:388–391.
117. Mastroianni A, Coronado O, Nanetti A, et al. *Agrobacterium radiobacter* pneumonia in a patient with HIV infection. Eur J Clin Microbiol Infect Dis. 1996;15:960–963.
118. Hulse M, Johnson S, Ferrieri P. *Agrobacterium* infections in humans: Experience at one hospital and review. Clin Infect Dis. 1993;16:112–117.
119. Miller JM, Novy C, Hiott M. Case of bacterial endophthalmitis caused by an *Agrobacterium radiobacter*–like organism. J Clin Microbiol. 1996;34:3212–3213.
120. Sykes RB, Cimarusti CM, Bonner DP, et al. Monocyclic β-lactam antibiotics produced by bacteria. Nature. 1981;291:489–491.
121. Mandell WF, Garvey GJ, Neu HC. *Achromobacter xylosoxidans* bacteremia. Rev Infect Dis. 1987;9:1001–1005.
122. Cieslak TJ, Robb ML, Drabick CJ, et al. Catheter-associated sepsis caused by *Ochrobactrum anthropi*: Report of a case and review of related nonfermentative bacteria. Clin Infect Dis. 1992;14:902–907.
123. Cieslak TJ, Raszka WV. Catheter-associated sepsis due to *Alcaligenes xylosoxidans* in a child with AIDS. Clin Infect Dis. 1993;16:592–593.
124. Schoch PE, Cunha BA. Nosocomial *Achromobacter xylosoxidans* infections. Infect Control Hosp Epidemiol. 1988;9:84–87.
125. Spear JB, Fuhrer J, Kirby BD. *Achromobacter xylosoxidans* (*Alcaligenes xylosoxidans* subsp *xylosoxidans*) bacteremia associated with a well-water source: Case report and review of the literature. J Clin Microbiol. 1988;26:598–599.
126. Duggan JM, Goldstein SJ, Chenoweth CE, et al. *Achromobacter xylosoxidans* bacteremia: Report of four cases and review of the literature. Clin Infect Dis. 1996;23:569–576.
127. Walsh RD, Klein NC, Cunha BA. *Achromobacter xylosoxidans* osteomyelitis. Clin Infect Dis. 1993;16:176–178.
128. Taylor P, Fischbein L. Prosthetic knee infection due to *Achromobacter xylosoxidans*. J Rheumatol. 1992;19:992–993.
129. Legrand C, Anaissie E. Bacteremia due to *Achromobacter xylosoxidans* in patients with cancer. Clin Infect Dis. 1992;14:479–484.
130. Manfredi R, Nanetti A, Ferri M, et al. Bacteremia and respiratory involvement by *Alcaligenes xylosoxidans* in patients infected with the human immunodeficiency virus. Eur J Clin Microbiol Infect Dis. 1997;16:933–938.
131. Dunne WM Jr, Maisch S. Epidemiological investigation of infections due to *Alcaligenes* species in children and patients with cystic fibrosis: Use of repetitive-element–sequence polymerase chain reaction. Clin Infect Dis. 1995;20:836–841.
132. Hearn YR, Gander RM. *Achromobacter xylosoxidans*. An unusual neonatal pathogen. Am J Clin Pathol. 1991;96:211–214.
133. Mensah K, Philippon A, Richard C, et al. Susceptibility of *Alcaligenes denitrificans* subspecies *xylosoxydans* to beta-lactam antibiotics. Eur J Clin Microbiol Infect Dis. 1990;9:405–409.
134. Cormican MG, Jones RN. Antimicrobial activity of cefotaxime tested against infrequently isolated pathogenic species (unusual pathogens). Diagn Microbiol Infect Dis. 1995;22:43–48.
135. Decre D, Arlet G, Danglot C, et al. A beta-lactamase–overproducing strain of *Alcaligenes denitrificans* subsp *xylosoxidans* isolated from a case of meningitis. J Antimicrob Chemother. 1992;30:769–779.
136. Tayeri T, Kelly LD. *Alcaligenes faecalis* corneal ulcer in a patient with cicatricial pemphigoid. Am J Ophthalmol. 1993;115:255–256.
137. Bizet J, Bizet C. Strains of *Alcaligenes faecalis* from clinical material. J Infect. 1997:35:167–169.
138. Peel MM, Hibberd AJ, King BM, et al. *Alcaligenes piechaudii* from chronic ear discharge. J Clin Microbiol. 1988;26:1580–1581.
139. Pickett MJ, Greenwood JR. Identification of oxidase-positive, glucose-negative motile species of nonfermentative bacilli. J Clin Microbiol. 1986;23:920–923.
140. Bizet C, Tekaia F, Philippon A. In-vitro susceptibility of *Alcaligenes faecalis* compared with those of other *Alcaligenes* spp to antimicrobial agents including seven beta-lactams. J Antimicrob Chemother. 1993;32:907–910.
141. Anderson RR, Warnick P, Schreckenberger. Recurrent CDC group IVc-2 bacteremia in a human with AIDS. J Clin Microbiol. 1997;35:780–782.
142. Moissenet D, Tabone M-D, Girardet J-P, et al. Nosocomial CDC Group IVc-2 bacteremia: Epidemiological investigation by randomly amplified polymorphic DNA analysis. J Clin Microbiol. 1996;34:1264–1266.
143. Zapardiel J, Blum G, Caramelo C, et al. Peritonitis with CDC group IVc-2 bacteria in a patient on continuous ambulatory peritoneal dialysis. Eur J Clin Microbiol Infect Dis. 1991:10:509–511.
144. Musso D, Drancourt M, Bardot J, et al. Human infection due to the CDC Group IVc-2 bacterium: Case report and review. Clin Infect Dis. 1994;18:482–484.
145. Bloch KC, Nadarajah R, Jacobs R. *Chryseobacterium meningosepticum*: An emerging pathogen among immunocompromised adults. Report of 6 cases and literature review. Medicine. 1997;76:30–41.
146. Plotkin SA, McKetrick JC. Nosocomial meningitis of the newborn caused by a *Flavobacterium*. JAMA. 1966;198:194–196.
147. Pokrywka M, Viazanko K, Medvick J, et al. A *Flavobacterium meningosepticum* outbreak among intensive care patients. Am J Infect Control. 1993;21:139–145.
148. Brown RB, Phillips D, Barker MJ, et al. Outbreak of nosocomial *Flavobacterium meningosepticum* respiratory infections associated with use of aerosolized polymixin B. Am J Infect Control. 1989;17:121–125.
149. Olsen H, Frederiksen, Siboni KE. *Flavobacterium meningosepticum*. Lancet. 1965;1:1294–1296.
150. Sheridan RL, Ryan CM, Pasternack MS, et al. Flavobacterial sepsis in massively burned pediatric patients. Clin Infect Dis. 1993;17:185–187.
151. Hekker TA, vanOverhagen W, Schneider AJ. Pressure transducers: An overlooked source of sepsis in the intensive care unit. Intensive Care Med. 1990;16:511–512.
152. Coyle-Gilchrist MM, Crewe P, Roberts G. *Flavobacterium meningosepticum* in the hospital environment. J Clin Pathol. 1976;29:824–826.
153. Bolivar R, Abramovits W. Cutaneous infection caused by *Flavobacterium meningosepticum*. J Infect Dis. 1989;159:150–151.
154. Sundin D, Gold BD, Berkowitz FE, et al. Community-acquired *Flavobacterium meningosepticum* meningitis, pneumonia, and septicemia in a normal infant. Pediatr Infect Dis J. 1991;10:73–76.
155. Ashdown LR, Previtera S. Community acquired *Flavobacterium meningosepticum* pneumonia and septicaemia. Med J Aust. 1992;156:69–70.
156. Hsueh PR, Teng U, Ho SW, et al. Clinical and microbiological characteristics of *Flavobacterium indologenes* infections associated with indwelling devices. J Clin Microbiol. 1996;34:1908–1913.
157. Hsueh PR, Wu JJ, Hsiue TR, et al. Bacteremic necrotizing fasciitis due to *Flavobacterium odoratum*. Clin Infect Dis. 1995;21:1337–1338.
158. Von Graevenitz A. *Acinetobacter*, *Alcaligenes*, *Moraxella*, and other nonfermentative gram-negative bacteria. In: Murray PR, Baron EJ, Pfaller MA, et al, eds. Manual of Clinical Microbiology. 6th ed. Washington, DC: American Society for Microbiology; 1995:520–532.
159. Fraser SL, Jorgensen JH. Reappraisal of the antimicrobial susceptibilities of *Chry-*

seobacterium and *Flavobacterium* species and methods for reliable susceptibility testing. Antimicrob Agents Chemother. 1997;41:2738–2741.

160. Visalli MA, Bajaksouzian S, Jacobs MR, et al. Comparative activity of trovafloxacin, alone and in combination with other agents, against gram-negative nonfermentative rods. Antimicrob Agents Chemother. 1997;41:1475–1481.
161. Hirsh BE, Wong B, Kiehn TE, et al. *Flavobacterium meningosepticum* bacteremia in an adult with acute leukemia. Use of rifampin to clear persistent infection. Diagn Microbiol Infect Dis. 1986;4:65–69.
162. Ratner H. *Flavobacterium meningosepticum*. Infect Control. 1984;5:237–239.
163. Di Pentima MC, Mason EO Jr, Kaplan SL. In vitro antibiotic synergy against *Flavobacterium meningosepticum*: Implications for therapeutic options. Clin Infect Dis. 1998;26:1169–1176.
164. Hawley HB, Gump DW. Vancomycin therapy of bacterial meningitis. Am J Dis Child. 1973;126:261–264.
165. Anzai Y, Kudo Y, Oyaizu H. The phylogeny of the genera *Chryseomonas, Flavimonas*, and *Pseudomonas* supports synonymy of these three genera. Int J Syst Bacteriol. 1997;47:249–251.
166. Rahav G, Simhon A, Mattan Y, et al. Infections with *Chryseomonas luteola* (CDC group Ve-1) and *Flavimonas oryzihabitans* (CDC group Ve-2). Medicine. 1995;74:83–88.
167. Kostman JR, Solomon F, Fekete T. Infections with *Chryseomonas luteola* (CDC group Ve-1) and *flavimonas oryzihabitans* (CDC group Ve-2) in neurosurgical patients. Rev Infect Dis. 1991;13:233–236.
168. Patrick WD, Brown WD, Bowmer MI, et al. Infective endocarditis due to *Eikenella corrodens*: Case report and review of the literature. Can J Infect Dis. 1990;1:139–142.
169. Suwanagool S, Rothkopf MM, Smith SM, et al. Pathogenicity of *Eikenella corrodens* in humans. Arch Intern Med. 1983;143:2265–2268.
170. Joshi N, O'Bryan T, Appelbaum PC. Pleuropulmonary infections caused by *Eikenella corrodens*. Rev Infect Dis. 1991;13:1207–1212.
171. Brooks GF, O'Donoghue JM, Rissing JP. *Eikenella corrodens*: A recently recognized pathogen: Infections in medical-surgical patients and in association with methylphenidate abuse. Medicine. 1974;53:325–342.
172. Goldstein EJC. Bite wounds and infections. Clin Infect Dis. 1992;14:633–640.
173. Tveteras K, Kristensten S, Bach V, et al. *Eikenella corrodens*: A recently recognized pathogen in head and neck infections. J Laryngol Otol. 1987;101:592–594.
174. Newfield RS, Vargas I, Huma Z. *Eikenella corrodens* infections. Case report in two adolescent females with IDDM. Diabetes Care. 1996;19:1011–1013.
175. Sagerman SD, Lourie GM. *Eikenella* osteomyelitis in a chronic nail biter: A case report. Hand Surg Am. 1995;20:71–72.
176. Swisher LA, Roberts JR, Glynn MJ. Needle licker's osteomyelitis. Am J Emerg Med. 1994;12:343–346.
177. Pollner JH, Khan A, Tuazon CU. Severe soft-tissue infection caused by *Eikenella corrodens*. Clin Infect Dis. 1992;15:740–741.
178. Raab MG, Lutz RA, Stauffer ES. *Eikenella corrodens* vertebral osteomyelitis. A case report and literature review. Clin Orthop. 1993:144–147.
179. Jeppson KG, Reimer LG. *Eikenella corrodens* chorioamnionitis. Obstet Gynecol. 1991;78:503–505.
180. Drouet E, De Montclos H, Boude M, et al. *Eikenella corrodens* and intrauterine contraceptive device. Lancet. 1987;2:1089.
181. Hemady R, Zimmerman A, Katzen BW, et al. Orbital cellulitis caused by *Eikenella corrodens*. Am J Ophthalmol. 1992;114:584–588.
182. Stein A, Teysseire N, Capobianco C, et al. *Eikenella corrodens*, a rare cause of pancreatic abscess: Two case reports and review. Clin Infect Dis. 1993;17:273–275.
183. Decker MD, Graham BS, Hunter EB, et al. Endocarditis and infections of intravascular devices due to *Eikenella corrodens*. Am J Med Sci. 1986;292:209–212.
184. Chen C-K, Wilson ME. Outer membrane protein and lipopolysaccharide heterogeneity among *Eikenella corrodens* isolates. J Infect Dis. 1990;162:664–671.
185. Sofianou D, Kolokotronis A. Susceptibility of *Eikenella corrodens* to antimicrobial agents. J Chemother. 1990;2:156–158.
186. Lacroix J-M, Walker C. Characterization of a beta-lactamase found in *Eikenella corrodens*. Antimicrob Agents Chemother. 1991;35:886–891.
187. Chaudhry HJ, Schoch PE, Cunha BA. *Flavimonas oryzihabitans* (CDC Group Ve-2). Infect Control Hosp Epidemiol. 1992;13:485–488.
188. Lucas KG, Kiehn TE, Sobeck KA, et al. Sepsis caused by *Flavimonas oryzihabitans*. Medicine. 1994;73:209–214.
189. Lin RD, Hsueh PR, Chang JC, et al. *Flavimonas oryzihabitans* bacteremia: Clinical features and microbiological characteristics of isolates. Clin Infect Dis. 1997;24:867–873.
190. Hawkins RE, Moriarty RA, Lewis DE, et al. Serious infections involving the CDC group Ve bacteria *Chryseomonas luteola* and *Flavimonas oryzihabitans*. Rev Infect Dis. 1991;13:257–260.
191. Lam S, Isenberg HD, Edwards B, et al. Community-acquired soft-tissue infections caused by *Flavimonas oryzihabitans*. Clin Infect Dis. 1994;18:808–809.
192. Rolston KV, Ho DH, LeBlanc B, et al. In vitro activities of antimicrobial agents against clinical isolates of *Flavimonas oryzihabitans* obtained from patients with cancer. Antimicrob Agents Chemother. 1993;37:2504–2505.
193. Vandamme P, Bernardet J-F, Segers P, et al. New perspectives in the classification of the flavobacteria: Description of *Chryseobacterium* gen nov, *Bergeyella* gen nov and *Empedobacter* nom rev. Int J Syst Bacteriol. 1994;44:827–831.
194. Kern WV, Oethinger M, Kaufhold A, et al. *Ochrobactrum anthropi* bacteremia: Report of four cases and short review. Infection. 1993;21:306–310.
195. Cieslak TJ, Drabick CJ, Robb ML. Pyogenic infections due to *Ochrobactrum anthropi*. Clin Infect Dis. 1996;22:845–847.
196. Gransden WR, Eykyn SJ. Seven cases of bacteremia due to *Ochrobactrum anthropi*. Clin Infect Dis. 1992;15:1068–1069.
197. Ezzedine H, Mourad M, Van Ossel C, et al. An outbreak of *Ochrobactrum anthropi* bacteraemia in five organ transplant patients. J Hosp Infect. 1994;27:35–42.
198. Chang HJ, Christenson JC, Pavia AT, et al. *Ochrobactrum anthropi* meningitis in pediatric pericardial allograft transplant recipients. J Infect Dis. 1996;173:656–660.
199. Braun M, Jonas JB, Schonherr U, et al. *Ochrobactrum anthropi* endophthalmitis after uncomplicated cataract surgery. Am J Ophthalmol. 1996;122:272–273.
200. Berman AJ, Del Priore LV, Fischer CK. Endogenous *Ochrobactrum anthropi* endophthalmitis. Am J Ophthalmol. 1997;123:560–562.
201. Barson WJ, Cromer BA, Marcon MJ. Puncture wound osteochondritis of the foot caused by CDC group Vd. J Clin Microbiol. 1987;25:2014–2016.
202. Brivet F, Guibert M, Kiredjian M, et al. Necrotizing fasciitis, bacteremia, and multiorgan failure caused by *Ochrobactrum anthropi*. Clin Infect Dis. 1993;17:516–518.
203. Earhart KC, Boyce K, Bone WD, et al. *Ochrobactrum anthropi* infection of retained pacemaker leads. Clin Infect Dis. 1997;24:281–282.
204. Alnor D, Frimodt-Moller N, Espersen F, et al. Infections with the unusual human pathogens *Agrobacterium* species and *Ochrobactrum anthropi*. Clin Infect Dis. 1994;18:914–920.
205. Mesnard R, Sire JM, Donnio PY, et al. Septic arthritis due to *Oligella urethralis*. Eur J Clin Microbiol Infect Dis. 1992;11:195–196.
206. Riley UBG, Bignardi G, Goldberg L, et al. Quinolone resistance in *Oligella urethralis*–associated chronic ambulatory peritoneal dialysis. J Infect. 1996;32:155–156.
207. Rockhill RC, Lutwick LI. Group IVe–like gram-negative bacillemia in a patient with obstructive uropathy. J Clin Microbiol. 1978;8:108–109.
208. Manian FA. Bloodstream infection with *Oligella ureolytica, Candida krusei*, and *Bacteroides* species in a patient with AIDS. Clin Infect Dis. 1993;17:290–291.
209. Pugliese A, Pacris B, Schoch PE, et al. *Oligella urethralis* urosepsis. Clin Infect Dis. 1993;17:1069–1070.
210. Rihs JD, Brenner DJ, Weaver RE, et al. *Roseomonas*, a new genus associated with bacteremia and other human infections. J Clin Microbiol. 1993;31:3275–3283.
211. Struthers M, Wong J, Janda JM. An initial appraisal of the clinical significance of *Roseomonas* species associated with human infections. Clin Infect Dis. 1996;23:729–733.
212. Kaye KM, Macone A, Kazanjian PH. Catheter infection caused by *Methylobacterium* in immunocompromised hosts: Report of three cases and review of the literature. Clin Infect Dis. 1992;14:1010–1014.
213. Holton J, Miller R, Furst V, et al. Isolation of *Protomonas extorquens* (the "Red Phantom") from a patient with AIDS. J Infect. 1990;21:87–93.
214. Richardson JD. Failure to clear a *Roseomonas* line infection with antibiotic therapy. Clin Infect Dis. 1997;25:155.
215. Sandoe JA, Malnick H, Loudon KW. A case of peritonitis caused by *Roseomonas gilardii* in a patient undergoing continuous ambulatory peritoneal dialysis. J Clin Microbiol. 1997;35:2150–2152.
216. Nahass RG, Wisneski R, Herman DJ, et al. Vertebral osteomyelitis due to *Roseomonas* species: Case report and review of the evaluation of vertebral osteomyelitis. Clin Infect Dis. 1995;21:1474–1476.
217. Flournoy DJ, Petrone RL, Voth DW. A pseudo-outbreak of *Methylobacterium mesophilica* isolated from patients undergoing bronchoscopy. Eur J Clin Microbiol Infect Dis. 1992;11:240–243.
218. Nozue H, Hayashi T, Hashimoto Y, et al. Isolation and characterization of *Shewanella alga* from human clinical specimens and emendation of the description of *S. alga*. Int J Syst Bacteriol. 1992;42:628–634.
219. Khashe S, Janda JM. Biochemical and pathogenic properties of *Shewanella alga* and *Shewanella putrefaciens*. J Clin Microbiol. 1998;36:783–787.
220. Chen YS, Liu YC, Yen MY, et al. Skin and soft-tissue manifestations of *Shewanella putrefaciens* infection. Clin Infect Dis. 1997;25:225–229.
221. Brink AJ, van Straten A, van Rensburg AJ. *Shewanella (Pseudomonas) putrefaciens* bacteremia. Clin Infect Dis. 1995;20:1327–1332.
222. Kim JH, Cooper RA, Welty-Wolf KE, et al. *Pseudomonas putrefaciens* bacteremia. Rev Infect Dis. 1989;11:97–104.
223. Butt AA, Figueroa J, Martin DH. Ocular infection caused by three unusual marine organisms. Clin Infect Dis. 1997;24:740.
224. Dees SB, Moss CW, Hollis DG, et al. Chemical characterization of *Flavobacterium odoratum, Flavobacterium breve*, and *Flavobacterium*-like groups IIe, IIh, and IIf. J Clin Microbiol. 1986;23:267–273.
225. Potvliege C, Dejaegher–Bauduin C, Hansen W, et al. *Flavobacterium multivorum* septicemia in a hemodialysis patient. J Clin Microbiol. 1984;19:568–569.
226. Freney J, Hansen W, Ploton C, et al. Septicemia caused by *Sphingobacterium multivorum*. J Clin Microbiol. 1987;25:1126–1128.
227. Reina J, Borrell N, Figuerola J. *Sphingobacterium multivorum* isolated from a patient with cystic fibrosis. Eur J Clin Microbiol Infect Dis. 1992;11:81–82.
228. Areekul S, Vongsthongsri U, Mookto T, et al. *Sphingobacterium multivorum* septicemia: A case report. J Med Assoc Thai. 1996;79:395–398.
229. Holmes B, Owen RJ, Hollis DG. *Flavobacterium spiritivorum*, a new species isolated from human clinical specimens. Int J Syst Bacteriol. 1982;32:157–165.
230. Fass RJ, Barnishan J. In vitro susceptibilities of nonfermentative gram-negative bacilli other than *Pseudomonas aeruginosa* to 32 antimicrobial agents. Rev Infect Dis. 1980;2:841–853.
231. Blahova J, Kralikova K, Krcmery V Sr, et al. Hydrolysis of imipenem, meropenem, ceftazidime, and cefepime by multiresistant nosocomial strains of *Sphingobacterium multivorum*. Eur J Clin Microbiol Infect Dis. 1997;16:178–180.
232. Yabuuchi E, Yano I, Oyaizu H, et al. Proposals of *Sphingomonas paucimobilis*

gen nov and comb nov, *Sphingomonas parapaucimobilis* sp nov, *Sphingomonas yanoikuyae* sp nov, *Sphingomonas adhaesiva* sp nov, *Sphingomonas capsulata* comb nov, and two genospecies of the genus *Sphingomonas*. Microbiol Immunol. 1990;34:99–119.
233. Crane LR, Tagle LC, Palutke WA. Outbreak of *Pseudomonas paucimobilis* in an intensive care facility. JAMA. 1981;246:985–987.
234. Lemaitre D, Elaichouni A, Hundhausen M, et al. Tracheal colonization with *Sphingomonas paucimobilis* in mechanically ventilated neonates due to contaminated ventilator temperature probes. J Hosp Infect. 1996;32:199–206.
235. Salazar R, Martino R, Sureda A, et al. Catheter-related bacteremia due to *Pseudomonas paucimobilis* in neutropenic cancer patients: Report of two cases. Clin Infect Dis. 1995;20:1573–1574.
236. Hsueh PR, Teng LJ, Yang PC, et al. Nosocomial infections caused by *Sphingomonas paucimobilis*: Clinical features and microbiological characteristics. Clin Infect Dis. 1998;26:676–681.
237. Lazarus HM, Magalhaes-Silverman M, Fox RM, et al. Contamination during *in vitro* procession of bone marrow for transplantation: Clinical significance. Bone Marrow Transplant. 1991;7:241–246.
238. Boken DJ, Romero JR, Cavalieri SJ. *Sphingomonas paucimobilis* bacteremia: Four cases and review of the literature. Infect Dis Clin Practice. 1988;7:286–291.
239. Reina J, Bassa A, Llompart I, et al. Infections with *Pseudomonas paucimobilis*: Report of four cases and review. Rev Infect Dis. 1991;13:1072–1076.
240. Holmes B, Owen RJ, Evans A, et al. *Pseudomonas paucimobilis*, a new species isolated from human clinical specimens, the hospital environment and other sources. Int J Syst Bacteriol. 1977;27:133–146.
241. Holmes B, Steigerwalt AG, Weaver RE, et al. *Weeksella zoohelcum* sp nov (formerly group IIj), from human clinical specimens. System Appl Microbiol. 1986;8:191–196.
242. Reina J, Borrell N. Leg abscess caused by *Weeksella zoohelcum* following a dog bite. Clin Infect Dis. 1992;14:1162–1163.
243. Bracis R, Seibers K, Julien RM. Meningitis caused by Group IIj following a dog bite. West J Med. 1979;131:438–440.
244. Holmes B, Steigerwalt AG, Weaver RE, et al. *Weeksella virosa* gen nov sp nov (formerly group IIf), found in human clinical specimens. System Appl Microbiol. 1986;8:185–190.
245. Reina J, Gil J, Alomar P. Isolation of *Weeksella virosa* (formerly CDC group IIf) from a vaginal sample. Eur J Clin Microbiol Infect Dis. 1989;8:569–570.
246. Faber MD, delBusto R, Cruz C, et al. Response of *Weeksella virosa* peritonitis to imipenem/cilasatain. Adv Perit Dial. 1991;7:133–134.
247. Hollis DG, Moss CW, Daneshvar MI, et al. Characterization of Centers for Disease Control Group NO-1, a fastidious, nonoxidative, gram-negative organism associated with dog and cat bites. J Clin Microbiol. 1993;31:746–748.
248. Hollis DG, Weaver RE, Moss CW, et al. Chemical and cultural characterization of CDC group WO-1, a weakly oxidative gram-negative group of organisms isolated from clinical sources. J Clin Microbiol. 1992;30:291–295.
249. Daneshvar MI, Hill B, Hollis DG, et al. CDC group O-3: Phenotypic characteristics, fatty acid composition, isoprenoid quinone content, and in vitro antimicrobic susceptibilities of an unusual gram negative bacterium isolated from clinical specimens. J Clin Microbiol. 1998;36:1674–1678.
250. Moss CW, Daneshvar MI, Hollis DG. Biochemical characteristics and fatty acid composition of Gilardi rod group 1 bacteria. J Clin Microbiol. 1993;31:689–691.
251. Rabkin CS, Galaid EI, Hollis DG, et al. Thermophilic bacteria: A new cause of human disease. J Clin Microbiol. 1985;21:553–557.

SPIROCHETES

Chapter 227

Treponema pallidum (Syphilis)

EDMUND C. TRAMONT

Syphilis is a complex systemic illness with protean clinical manifestations caused by the spirochete *Treponema pallidum*. It holds a special place in the history of Western medicine as the "great imitator" or the "great impostor." It is most often transmitted by sexual contact, and, unlike most other infectious diseases, it is rarely diagnosed by isolation and characterization of the causative organism. Instead, less precise methods of diagnosis are used: direct darkfield microscopy, immunofluorescence, immunoperoxidase or silver staining, and epidemiologic, serologic, and clinical findings. Its natural course is clinically divided into the following phases: (1) an incubation period lasting about 3 weeks; (2) a primary stage characterized by a nonpainful skin lesion known as a *chancre* that is usually associated with regional lymphadenopathy and early bacteremia; (3) a florid secondary bacteremic or disseminated stage accompanied by generalized mucocutaneous lesions, lymphadenopathy, and protean clinical findings; (4) a period of subclinical infection (latent syphilis) detected only by reactive serologic tests; and (5) in a small number of patients, a late or tertiary stage characterized by progressive disease involving principally the ascending aorta and/or the central nervous system (CNS) and/or the development of a characteristic granulomatous-like lesion known as a *gumma* that can involve virtually any organ.

ETIOLOGY

The causal agent of syphilis is *T. pallidum* spp. *pallidum,* which belongs to the family Spirochaetaceae. Other members of the genus *Treponema* that can infect humans are *Treponema pallidum* spp. *pertenue* (yaws), *Treponema carateum* (pinta), and *Treponema pallidum* spp. *endemicum* (bejel, nonvenereal, or endemic syphilis). The pathogenic treponemas are closely related morphologically, antigenically, by DNA homology, and by their ability to adhere to mammalian cells. A number of nonpathogenic treponemes have also been isolated from humans, particularly from the oral cavity. Other pathogenic organisms of the family Spirochaetaceae belong to the genera *Borrelia* and *Leptospira*.

The organisms are slender, tightly coiled, unicellular, helical cells 5 to 15 μm long and 0.09 to 0.18 μm wide. The cytoplasm is surrounded by a trilaminar membrane, a peptidoglycan layer, a delicate inner mucopeptide layer known as the *periplast*, an outer lipoprotein membrane containing lipopolysaccharide, and a phospholipid-rich outer membrane containing relatively few surface-exposed proteins.[1, 2] The ends of the cells are tapered, and three fibrils are inserted into each end. The organism moves with a drifting rotary motion and usually has a characteristic flexuose or undulating movement about its center.

Unlike many nonpathogenic treponemas, the virulent treponemes, including *T. pallidum,* cannot be cultivated in vitro.[3] However, they have remained motile in highly enriched and specifically defined media for up to 7 days at 35°C and up to 48 hours at 37°C. Carbon dioxide aids survival. They can be maintained viable in liquid nitrogen, less so at −70°C, and in many mammals. Rabbits are the laboratory animals most commonly used for maintaining virulent organisms.[3]

In contrast to other pathogenic spirochetes, few metabolic or structural immunologic or virulence marker differences among the pathogenic treponemes have been found. However, the complete genome sequence of *T. pallidum* has been determined,[4] and molecular subtyping has been accomplished.[4a]

HISTORY

The historical aspects of syphilis make for fascinating reading, and its impact on folklore appears destined to continue.[5] Few modern clinicians are aware of the extent of syphilis in Western countries through the middle of the 20th century, the persons of notoriety who were infected, or the pervasiveness of this disease in medical practice.[6] For example, syphilis was the leading cause of neurologic and cardiovascular disease among middle-aged persons at the turn of the 20th century. The arguments about the origins of syphilis are still being debated and essentially come down to whether the disease was imported into the Old World from the New World by shipmates of Christopher Columbus or was an established disease that spread throughout Europe as a consequence of urbanization. The two theories have not yet been reconciled,[7] although current DNA characterization techniques could settle the debate.[4]

A pandemic known as the Great Pox (as distinguished from the small pox) ravaged Europe and Asia at the time of the return of Columbus from America and during mass movements of armies and populations in Europe. It cannot be proved with certainty that *T. pallidum* was the cause of this scourge. Nevertheless, the first clear descriptions of this illness, including the sexual mode of transmission, were recorded in the 16th century. As noted in the *Breviary of Helthe*, published in 1547[8]:

In englyshe Morbus Gallicus (syphilis) is named the french pockes, whan that I was yonge they were named the spanyshe pockes the which be of many kyndes of the pockes, some be moyst, some be waterashe, some be drye, and some be skorvie, some be lyke skabbes, some be lyke ring wormes, some be fistuled, some be festered, some be cankarus, some be lyke wennes, some be lyke biles, some be lyke knobbles or burres, and some be ulcerous havyinge a lytle drye skabbe in the middle of the ulcerous skabbe, some hath ache in the jioyntes and no singe of the pockes and yet it may be the pockes. . . . The cause of these impediments or infyrmytes doth come many wayes, it maye come by lyenge in the shetes or bedde there where a pocky person hath the night before lyenin, it maye come with lyenge with a pocky person, it maye come by syttenge on a draught or sege where as a pocky person did lately syt, it may come by drynkynge oft with a pocky person, but specially it is taken when one pocky person doth synne in lechery the one with another.

During this period, syphilis or a disease similar to syphilis was often accompanied by high morbidity and mortality, which attests to the extraordinary virulent nature of the causative organism of that pestilence. It is not known whether the relatively mild nature of present-day syphilis reflects a change in the virulence of the organism, an adaptation of the human host, or the disappearance of a concomitantly occurring but unknown illness. The proponents of the "New World" or "Columbian" theory rest their case on the absence of syphilitic bone lesions in old skeletons despite the fact that the pathologic distinction between old bone lesions of leprosy and those of syphilis is not precise. Modern genetic expansion and characterization techniques should resolve this debate.

One of the difficulties in sorting through older writings is that distinctions among syphilis, gonorrhea, and other venereal diseases did not emerge until the late 19th century. John Hunter's unfortunate self-inoculation with urethral pus containing both *Neisseria gonorrhoeae* and *T. pallidum* only served to prolong misconceptions. However, by the early 20th century, the cause, epidemiology, and clinical manifestations of syphilis were well known, as evidenced by the following anonymous poem, which can be dated from the 1920s:

There was a young man from Back Bay
Who thought syphilis just went away
He believed that a chancre
Was only a canker
That healed in a week and a day.
But now he has "acne vulgaris"—
(Or whatever they call it in Paris);
On his skin it has spread
From his feet to his head,
And his friends want to know where his hair is.
There's more to his terrible plight:
His pupils won't close in the light
His heart is cavorting,
His wife is aborting,
And he squints through his gunbarrel sight.
Arthralgia cuts into his slumber;
His aorta is in need of a plumber;
But now he has tabes,
And sabershinned babies,
While of gummas he has quite a number.
He's been treated in every known way,
But his spirochetes grow day by day;
He's developed paresis,
Has long talks with Jesus,
And thinks he's the Queen of the May.

The nickname "lues" came from the Latin *lues venereum,* which means "disease," "sickness," or "pestilence" and originally was loosely applied to any venereal disease. It became a synonym for syphilis at the turn of the 20th century.

Metchnikoff successfully transferred *T. pallidum* to chimpanzees in 1903. Two years later, the organism was described in the primary lesion and adjacent lymph nodes of syphilitic patients. Soon thereafter, Wassermann described the complement fixation test for diagnosis of syphilis by using fetal calf livers laden with *T. pallidum* and, later, extracts of uninfected beef livers and hearts (the forerunner of the present day nontreponemal tests). With the advent of serologic testing, the prevalence of the disease was determined: between 8% and 14% of adults living in such cities as Paris, Berlin, and New York had positive serologic test results. It was this high prevalence that led to the practice of screening blood donations and hospital admissions,[6] a practice that should be continued today in high-prevalence areas.

During this same period, Ehrlich introduced an arsenic derivative, arsphenamine or salvarsan, as therapy. Mercury and bismuth preparations were added later. Induced-fever therapy (malaria, heat box, hot baths) was thought to be efficacious, and its benefits were known for more than 300 years. Dr. Julius Wagner von Jauregg was awarded the Nobel Prize in 1927 for describing the use of malaria injections to treat "paralytica dementia" (neurosyphilis).[9] But these primarily palliative therapies were quickly forgotten: no other disease was as dramatically affected by the discovery of penicillin as syphilis.

Syphilis continues to have an impact on modern medicine. From 1932 until 1962, 431 black men with syphilis were prospectively followed untreated to better establish the natural history of the disease despite the proven efficacy of penicillin by the late 1940s. The abuse of trust in the medical profession exemplified by this U.S. government–sponsored study was a major impetus for developing a legal basis for the principles of informed consent by patients.[9a]

EPIDEMIOLOGY

Syphilis can be acquired by sexual contact, by passage through the placenta (congenital syphilis), by kissing or other close contact with an active lesion, by transfusion of fresh human blood, or by accidental direct inoculation.[10, 11] The overwhelming majority of cases of syphilis are transmitted by sexual intercourse. A patient is most infectious early in the disease (especially when a chancre, mucous patch, or condyloma latum is present) and gradually becomes less so over time. For all practical purposes, the patient cannot spread syphilis by sexual contact 4 years after acquiring the illness.

Syphilis can be spread by kissing or touching a person who has active lesions on the lips, oral cavity, breasts, or genitals. Conversely, an infected patient may inoculate *T. pallidum* to the area on the body that is kissed. (Wet nurses often spread the disease to infants, especially infants in upper-class European families, for whom the use of a wet nurse was a socially recognized status symbol.)

Congenital syphilis occurs most frequently when the fetus becomes infected in utero, although it is possible for the neonate to acquire the infection while passing through the birth canal.

The acquisition of syphilis through transfused blood or blood products is now very rare because of the low incidence of disease, because of the requirement that all blood donors have a nonreactive nontreponemal blood test (see later discussion) before their blood can be used, and because *T. pallidum* cannot survive longer than 24 to 48 hours under the conditions of blood bank storage.

Accidental direct inoculation can occur by a needlestick or during handling of infected clinical material. Indeed, syphilis of the fingers is most common in medical personnel.

The number of reported new cases of syphilis in the United States has waxed and waned since the 1940s. It reached its peak during World War II, its nadir in the mid-1980s. The incidence then rose dramatically during the late 1980s and early 1990s before falling back to 1960 levels (Fig. 227–1). However, for reasons that remain obscure, the latest epidemic persists in the southeastern United States, from Maryland to Florida to Louisiana. Theoretically, syphilis can be eliminated by aggressive diagnostic, treatment, and follow-up measures.[11a]

A disproportionate number of cases occurred in homosexual men until the mid-1980s, when the incidence of new cases began to decrease coincident with the adoption of safer sex practices by this group in response to the acquired immunodeficiency syndrome (AIDS) epidemic. This was followed, however, by a rapid increase in new cases occurring primarily among heterosexuals, as reflected by the dramatic increase of syphilis cases among women and neonates (congenital syphilis) between 1986 and 1994.[12] This resurgence was primarily caused by the exchange of sex for drugs, especially crack cocaine.[13] Concomitant infection with human immunodeficiency virus (HIV) may also have played a role (see later discussion).

Most cases occur in the most sexually active age group (15 to 30 years). Because some of these persons "incubate" syphilis and have no evidence of active disease, aggressive contact tracing and "epidemiologic treatment" of all recently exposed persons are important aspects of syphilis control. All contacts should be sought and treated unless follow-up examinations can be guaranteed.

PATHOGENESIS

Within hours to days after *T. pallidum* penetrates the intact mucous membrane or gains access through abraded skin, it enters the lymphatics or the blood stream and disseminates throughout the body. This occurs soon after contact, as evidenced by the fact that patients who received blood transfusions from syphilitic donors in the seronegative incubation period have become infected.[10, 11] Virtually any organ in the body can be invaded, especially the CNS.[10, 11, 14] The infectious dose varies from patient to patient, but in rabbits an inoculum containing as few as four spirochetes can establish an infection. The organism divides every 30 to 33 hours. Clinical lesions appear when a concentration is reached of approximately 10^7 organisms per gram of tissue. The incubation period is directly proportional to the size of the inoculum.[15]

Clinically, syphilis can be divided into the following stages: incubating, primary, secondary, latent, and late syphilis. The median incubation period is 3 weeks, but it may vary from 3 to 90 days. Most patients control their infection and do not progress to late disease. The spirochetal and host determinants of the eventual outcome are unknown, although the immune response of the host appears to be critical.[16]

The host develops an intense cellular response and the resulting inflammation is responsible for most of the subsequent clinical manifestations. It has been postulated that, as with other chronic infections, the switch from a predominant Th1 (cellular) response to a Th2 (humoral) response is a critical event in favor of the parasite and development of a chronic infection.[16] It has also been proposed that the paucity of proteins and lipoproteins on the outer membrane of the organism contributes in a substantial manner to the organism's evasion of an effective host response[2, 17, 18] and that antigenic variation results in a subpopulation of spirochetes that are resistant to macrophage phagocytosis.[19]

The primary stage encompasses the development of the primary lesion (chancre), which occurs at the site of inoculation. This lesion does not develop in every case, or it may be so inconspicuous as to go unnoticed. Multiple chancres can occur, especially in persons infected with HIV. Spirochetes are easily demonstrated in the lesions, especially early ones. Chancres usually heal spontaneously in 2 to 8 weeks but may persist for longer periods, especially in immunocompromised hosts (e.g., HIV-infected persons).

The secondary or disseminated stage becomes evident 2 to 12 weeks (mean, 6 weeks) after contact. This generalized condition with parenchymal, constitutional, and mucocutaneous manifestations occurs when the greatest number of treponemes (high antigen load) is present in the body, particularly in the blood stream. Treponemes can also be demonstrated in many other tissues, especially in the skin and lymph nodes. Abnormal laboratory findings or treponemes, or both, can be detected in the CNS, including the aqueous humor of the eye, in up to 40% of these patients.[10, 11, 14] The immune response of the host at this time becomes quite brisk, and an immune-complex glomerulonephritis may occur.[20]

After the secondary stage subsides, the patient enters a latent period during which the diagnosis can be made only by obtaining a positive serologic test response for syphilis. Because relapses of secondary syphilis can occur up to 4 years after contact, this period

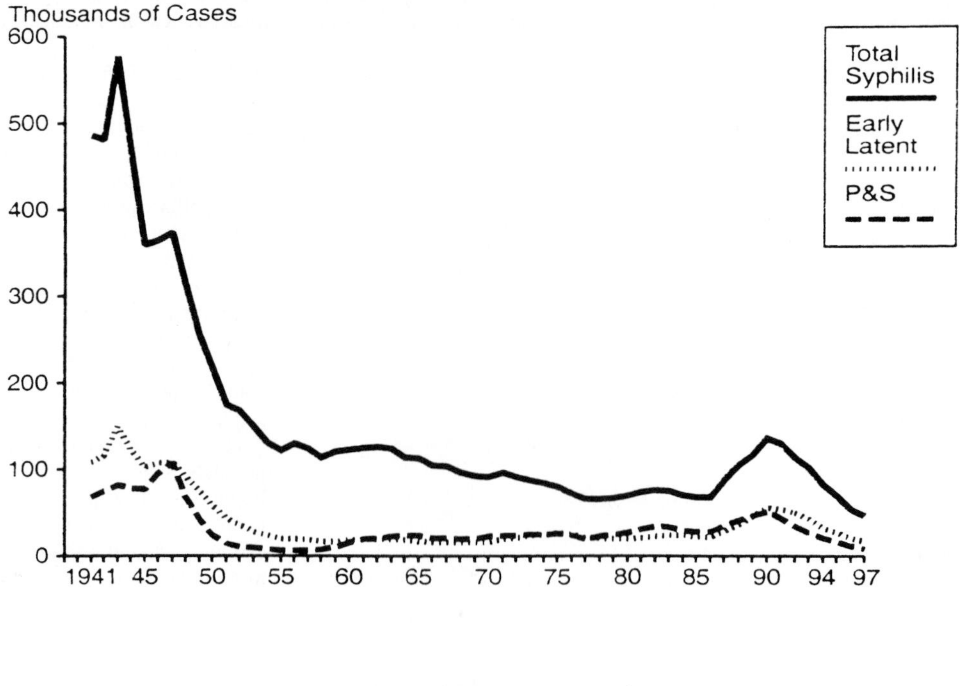

FIGURE 227–1. Syphilis: Reported cases by stage of illness, the United States, 1941–1997. *Abbreviation:* P&S, Primary and secondary.

is divided into *early latent* (relapses possible) and *late latent* (relapses very unlikely) stages. Seventy-five percent of relapses occur within the first year and are a consequence of an immune dysfunction in cellular immunity (e.g., last trimester of pregnancy).

The term *late syphilis* refers to the clinically apparent or inapparent tertiary disease that develops in up to one third of untreated patients. Most of these lesions involve the vaso vasorum of the aorta or the arteries of the CNS, or both; the rest consist principally of gummas, a unique granulomatous lesion with a coagulated or amorphous center and small vessel endarteritis. The skin, liver, bones, and spleen are the most common sites for development of gummas.

PATHOLOGIC CHARACTERISTICS

Obliterative endarteritis consisting of concentric endothelial and fibroblastic proliferative thickening is highly suggestive of syphilis[11] (Fig. 227–2). These pathologic changes are found in all stages of syphilis. In the primary chancre, polymorphonuclear leukocytes and macrophages can often be demonstrated ingesting treponemes. Hyperkeratosis is frequently found in the skin lesions of secondary syphilis and is especially marked in condylomata. Treponemal antigen, immunoglobulin, and complement deposition in the glomeruli typical of immune-complex glomerulonephritis can be demonstrated in patients who develop a nephrotic syndrome.[20] Obliterative endarteritis of the vaso vasorum and small blood vessels is the principal histopathologic finding in cardiovascular syphilis and meningovascular neurosyphilis. Appropriate staining (i.e., direct immunofluorescent, immunoperoxidase, or silver stains) can be used to demonstrate *T. pallidum*.

NATURAL COURSE OF UNTREATED SYPHILIS

The natural course of untreated syphilis was studied in a retrospective fashion in 1404 patients who were diagnosed clinically as having early syphilis (the Oslo study, 1891–1951).[21] There are many shortcomings to this study, the most glaring being the lack of laboratory confirmation of syphilis and the method of patient selection. (The darkfield and Wassermann tests were not available at the time the study was initiated.) However, because a similar study will never be done again, a brief review is warranted.

From 1890 to 1910, Professor Boeck of the University of Oslo, Norway, monitored patients diagnosed as having primary or secondary syphilis. Because he believed that the mercury-containing compounds used at that time were more harmful to the patient than the disease itself, all of his patients were simply observed. Twenty-four percent of these untreated patients developed relapsing secondary lesions within 4 years (leading to the arbitrary designation of early latent, late latent, and late syphilis). Twenty-eight percent eventually developed clinical complications of late syphilis; 10% developed cardiovascular syphilis, but this occurred only in patients who had acquired syphilis after 15 years of age; 6.5% developed symptomatic neurosyphilis; and 16% developed the late benign syphilis or gummas. Many of these patients had one or more "late" complications. Of those who went to autopsy, 35% of the men and 22% of the women had evidence of cardiovascular involvement, especially aortitis. Syphilis was considered the primary cause of death in 15% of the men and 8% of the women.

A prospective study involving 431 black men with seropositive latent syphilis of 3 or more years' duration was undertaken in 1932 (the infamous Tuskeegee study, 1932–1962).[22] This study suggested that hypertension in syphilitic black men 25 to 50 years of age was 17% more common than in similar nonsyphilitic individuals. Cardiovascular complications including hypertension were more common than neurologic complications, and both were increased over control populations. Anatomic evidence of aortitis was found to be 25 to 35% more common in autopsied syphilitic patients, and evidence of CNS syphilis was found in 4% of the patients. Other studies found higher rates of neurosyphilis.[10]

A third large study, involving 382 autopsies of adults, revealed

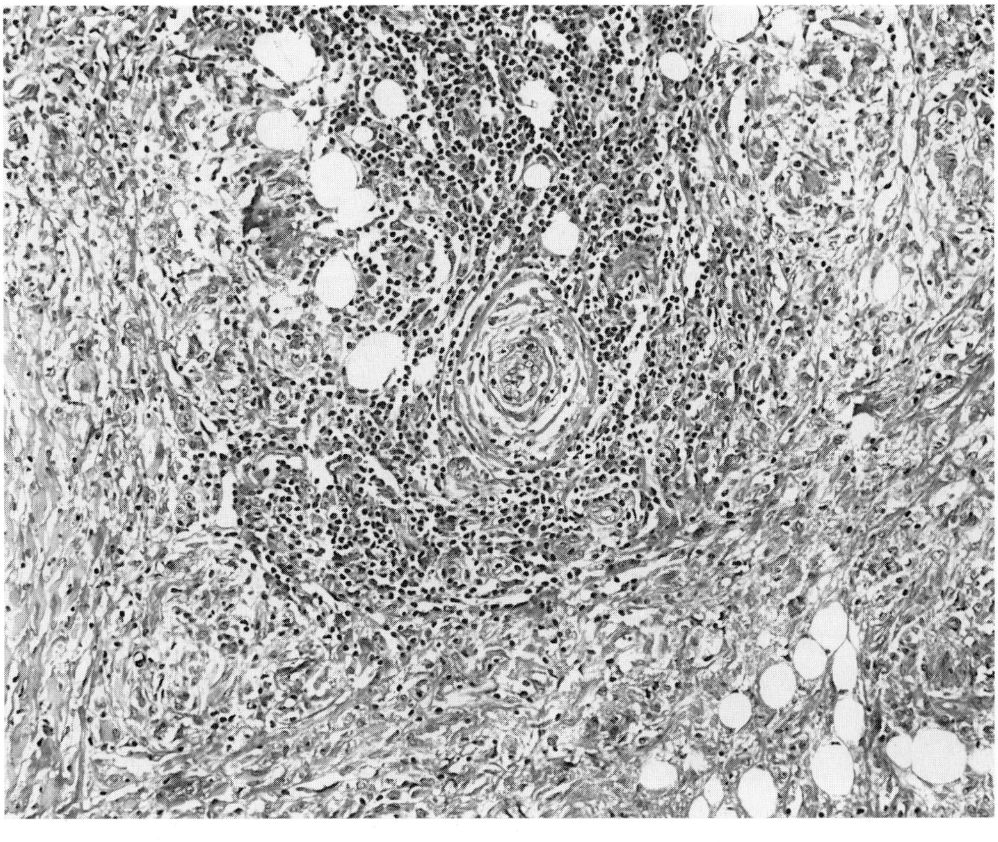

FIGURE 227–2. Characteristic obliterative endarteritis (×150).

similar overall results (the Rosahn study, 1917–1941).[23] Late syphilis was reported in 39%, and about 20% were thought to have died because of these late complications. Late anatomic lesions at autopsy were as follows: cardiovascular, 83%; neurologic, 8%; and gummas, 9%.

These studies documented the variable, waxing and waning course and unpredictable progression to late syphilis. There was an increased overall mortality in syphilitic compared with nonsyphilitic populations. The development of late complications was shown to occur about twice as often in men than in women, and a racial difference was suggested: black patients were more likely to develop cardiovascular syphilis, whereas white patients were more likely to develop neurosyphilis.

CLINICAL MANIFESTATIONS

There was once an adage that "he who knew syphilis knew medicine." Penicillin therapy changed all that, but one of its legacies is the frequency of delayed and erroneous diagnoses that occurs today.[24, 25]

Incubating Syphilis

The median incubation period before clinical manifestations is 21 days (range, 3 to 90 days). An early spirochetemia develops during this phase, which sets the stage for secondary invasion of virtually every bodily organ.

Primary Syphilis

The classic primary chancre begins at the site of inoculation as a single painless papule. It appears after the incubation period, quickly erodes, and becomes indurated (Figs. 227–3 and 227–4). The base is usually smooth; the borders are raised and firm and have a characteristic cartilaginous consistency. Unless secondarily infected, the ulcer has a clean appearance and no exudate. The lesion is painless but slightly tender to touch, and there is little pain or bleeding when the ulcer is scraped as for a darkfield examination. Multiple chancres do occur,[26] especially in persons infected with HIV. Atypical lesions occur in up to 60% of cases, and the absence of a primary skin lesion is also common. The variations in presentation depend on the number of treponemes inoculated, the immune status of the patient, intercurrent antibiotic therapy, and whether the lesion becomes secondarily infected. In human volunteers with no evidence of a previous infection, a small inoculum produces only a papular lesion and a large inoculum produces an ulcerative lesion (chancre) in which treponemes can easily be identified. Persons with a history of previous syphilitic infection fail to develop any lesions or develop only a small, darkfield-negative papule, depending on how long their natural infection went untreated.[15] Therefore, any genital lesion should raise the suspicion of syphilis, and appropriate studies to establish the diagnosis should be undertaken.

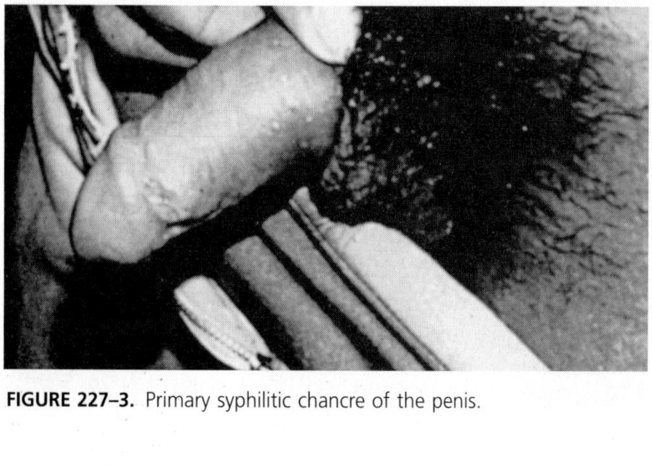

FIGURE 227–3. Primary syphilitic chancre of the penis.

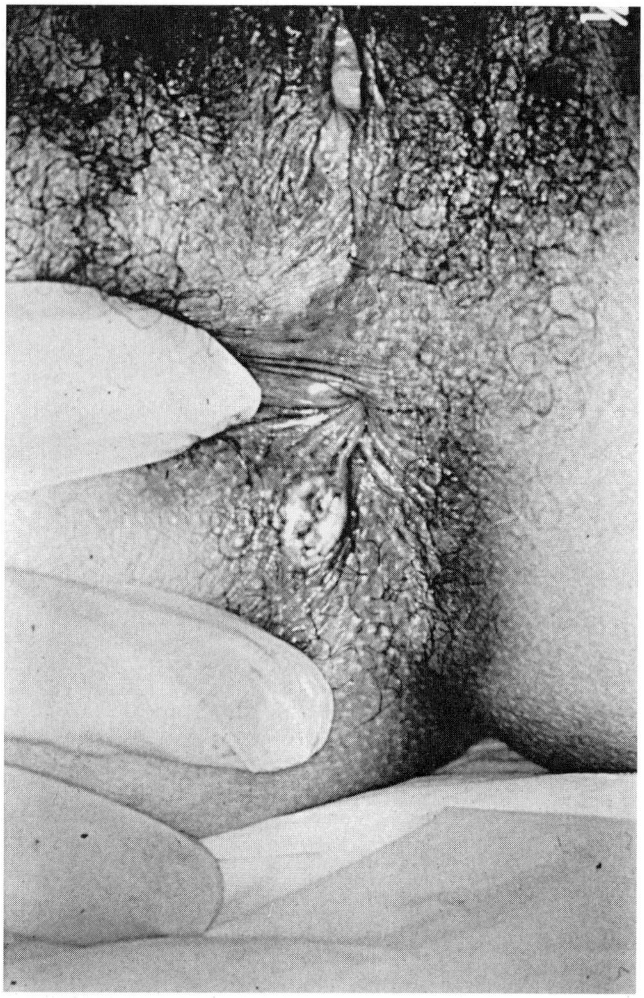

FIGURE 227–4. Primary syphilitic chancre of the perineum.

The chancre is located wherever the inoculation occurred. The external genitalia are most frequently involved. Other common sites include the cervix, mouth, perianal area, and anal canal in the female and the perianal area, anal canal, and mouth in the male homosexual. A secondary infection of the primary lesion is more common with oral and anal lesions. Regional lymphadenopathy consisting of moderately enlarged, firm, nonsuppurative, painless lymph nodes or satellite buboes accompanies the primary lesion.

The chancre heals within 3 to 6 weeks (range, 1 to 12 weeks), leaving either no trace or a thin atrophic scar. The lymphadenopathy usually persists for a longer period. The manifestations of secondary syphilis often develop while the chancre is still present,[10, 11] especially in HIV-infected patients.

Pathologically, the chancre is characterized by an intense infiltration of plasma cells and scattered histiocytes, a concentric endothelial and fibroblastic proliferative thickening of small blood vessels, and, eventually, the omnipresent and almost diagnostic obliterative endarteritis.[11] Spirochetes can be identified by silver, immunofluorescence, or other specific antibody staining methods (see later discussion).

Primary syphilis must be differentiated principally from herpesvirus infections, chancroid, and traumatic suprainfected genital lesions. Primary genital herpes usually begins as a painful erythematous rash that develops into clusters of vesicles accompanied by regional lymphadenopathy and systemic symptoms. It runs a 10- to 14-day course. Recurrent genital herpes is less florid and is characterized by mild to moderately painful vesicles and no adenopathy. A syphilitic rash is never vesicular except in congenital syphilis. Chancroid is characterized by one or more painful, exudative, indurated ulcers associated with tender lymphadenopathy that eventually suppurate if left untreated. The ulcer has overhanging edges and bleeds easily (e.g., when scrapings are collected for a darkfield examination). Early venereal warts, granuloma inguinale, lymphogranuloma venereum, tuberculosis, atypical mycobacterial infections, tularemia, sporotrichosis, anthrax, rat bite fever, or any genital ulcer may resemble early primary syphilis.

Secondary Syphilis

Secondary (disseminated) syphilis is the term used to describe the clinically most florid stage of the infection; it results from multiplication and dissemination of the spirochete and lasts until a sufficient host response develops to exert some immune control over the spirochete. It begins 2 to 8 weeks after the appearance of a chancre, but this period is quite variable. The primary chancre may still be present.[10, 11, 27] At a time when the host's local immune process appears to be bringing the primary lesions under control, the spirochete disseminates widely and achieves its greatest numbers.

The manifestations of secondary syphilis are widespread and protean (Table 227–1). The classic and most commonly recognized lesions involve the skin. Macular, maculopapular, papular, or pustular lesions, and combinations and variations thereof, all occur.[10, 11 27]

TABLE 227–1 The Clinical Manifestations of Secondary Syphilis

Manifestation	Percentage of Cases
Skin	90
Rash	
Macular	
Maculopapular	
Papular	
Pustular	
Condyloma latum	
Generalized lymphadenopathy	
Pruritus	
Mouth and throat	35
Mucous patches	
Erosions	
Ulcer (aphthous)	
Genital lesions	20
Chancre	
Chondyloma latum	
Mucous patch	
Constitutional symptoms	70
Fever of unknown origin	
Malaise	
Pharyngitis, laryngitis	
Anorexia, weight loss	
Arthralgias	
Central nervous system	8–40
Asymptomatic	
Symptomatic	1–2
Headache	
Meningismus	
Meningitis	
Ocular	
Diplopia	
Decreased vision	
Otitic	
Tinnitus	
Vertigo	
Cranial nerve involvement (II–VIII)	
Renal	Unusual
Glomerulonephritis	
Nephrotic syndrome	
Gastrointestinal	Unusual
Hepatitis	Unusual
Intestinal wall invasion	
Arthritis, osteitis, and periostitis	Unusual

Vesicular lesions are conspicuously absent. These lesions usually begin on the trunk and proximal extremities as bilateral, pink to red, discrete macular lesions 3 to 10 mm in diameter. Any surface area of the body can become involved. These lesions usually persist from a few days to 8 weeks and often evolve from macules into red papules (hence, maculopapular); in a few patients, they finally progress into pustular lesions known as *pustular syphilids*. The degree of endarteritis and perivascular mononuclear infiltration progresses in the same manner. All of the different rashes may be present at one time and may become widely distributed to involve the entire body, especially on the palms and soles, locations that strongly suggest the diagnosis (Fig. 227–5). When the hair follicles are involved (follicular syphilids), temporary patchy alopecia[10, 11, 27] or thinning and a loss of eyebrows and beard may develop. Sometimes a superficial scaling occurs (papulosquamous syphilids). In warm, moist intertriginous areas (i.e., perianal area, vulva, scrotum, inner aspects of the thighs, the skin under pendulous breasts, nasolabial folds, cleft of the chin, axillary and antecubital folds, webs of the fingers and toes), the papules enlarge, coalesce, and erode to produce painless, broad, moist, gray-white to erythematous, highly infectious plaques called *condylomata lata*. These highly infectious lesions teeming with spirochetes may also develop on mucous membranes (i.e., lips, mouth, pharynx, tonsils, vulva, vagina, glans penis, inner prepuce cervix, anal canal). These lesions, referred to as *mucous patches*, typically manifest as a silvery gray, superficial erosion with a red periphery (Fig. 227–6). None of these lesions is painful unless it is infected secondarily.

During relapses of secondary syphilis, the skin lesions tend to be less florid, asymmetrically distributed, and more infiltrated, suggesting a more effective host immune response. Condylomata lata, however, are common.

Constitutional symptomatology is also frequently present in secondary syphilis. These manifestations include low-grade fever, malaise, pharyngitis, laryngitis, anorexia, weight loss, arthralgias, and generalized painless lymphadenopathy. Enlargement of the epitrochlear lymph nodes is a unique finding that should always suggest the diagnosis.

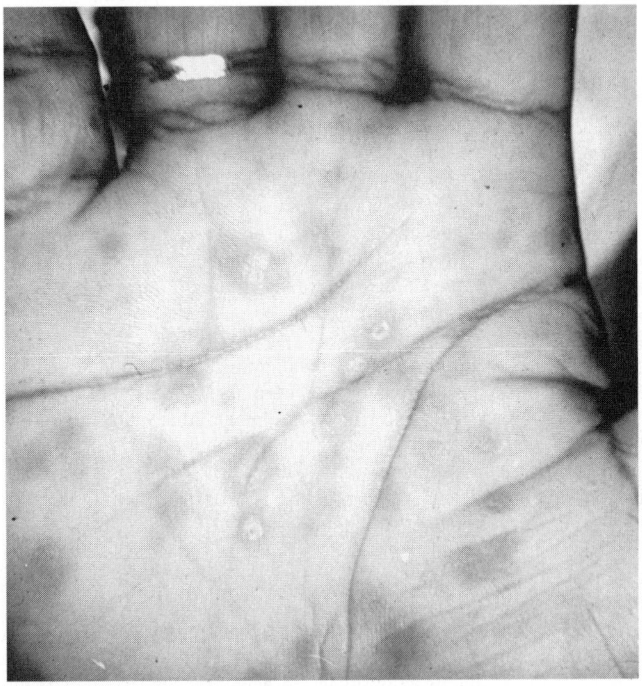

FIGURE 227–5. Palmar lesions of secondary syphilis.

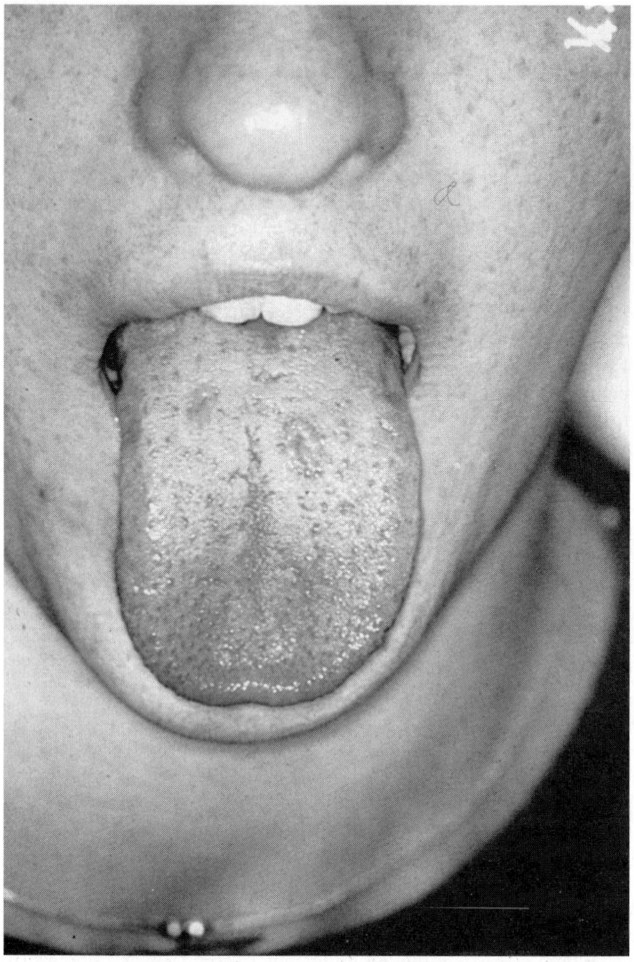

FIGURE 227–6. Mucous patch lesion of secondary syphilis.

The CNS becomes involved in up to 40% of patients[11, 14] as a result of seeding during the inevitable spirochetemia. Headache and meningismus are common, increased cerebrospinal fluid (CSF) protein levels and lymphocyte counts are found in 8 to 40% of the patients,[28] and acute aseptic meningitis occurs in 1 to 2% of the patients. Spirochetes have also been isolated from the CSF of patients with no CSF abnormalities.[14, 28] Individual cranial nerves, especially II through VIII, can be involved.[28] Visual disturbances, hearing loss, tinnitus, and facial weakness are the most common manifestations.

Virtually any organ of the body can be involved. Renal involvement may be in the form of an immune-complex glomerulonephritis (subepithelial electron-dense deposits). Proteinuria is common, an acute nephrotic syndrome may develop, and rarely, hemorrhagic glomerulonephritis occurs.[20]

Syphilitic hepatitis is characterized by a disproportionately high serum alkaline phosphatase level, a normal or moderately elevated serum bilirubin content, and a histologic picture that includes moderate inflammation with polymorphonuclear cells and lymphocytes, some hepatocellular damage, but no cholestasis. It occurs most often in conjunction with syphilitic proctitis and is seen most frequently in persons who engage in anal intercourse.

The gastrointestinal tract may also become extensively infiltrated or ulcerated, or both,[29] and this can be misdiagnosed as a lymphoma or other cancer.[25]

Anterior uveitis, usually mild and asymptomatic, occurs in 5 to 10% of patients with secondary syphilis, especially in HIV-infected persons, and the diagnosis is suggested whenever the uveitis is made worse by steroid treatment.[30]

Synovitis, osteitis, and periosteitis can also occur. These cases are often characterized by nocturnal pain that is increased by heat.[31]

The differential diagnosis of secondary syphilis is extensive, and the appellation "The Great Imitator" is appropriate.

Latent Syphilis

Latent syphilis is by definition that stage of the disease during which a specific treponemal antibody test—fluorescent treponemal antibody absorption (FTA-abs), *T. pallidum* hemagglutination (TPHA), microhemagglutination for *T. pallidum* (MHATP), enzyme-linked immunosorbent assay (ELISA), or *T. pallidum* immobilization (TPI)—is positive but during which there are no clinical manifestations of syphilis, normal cerebrospinal findings, and a normal chest radiograph result. It does not imply a lack of progression of disease. A history compatible with primary or secondary syphilis, exposure to a syphilitic person, or delivery of an infant with congenital syphilis should be sought. Early latent syphilis distinguishes that period of time (first 4 years) during which a relapse may occur and, therefore, the patient is "infectious." Ninety percent of the relapses occur in the first year, and each recurring episode is less florid. Mucocutaneous relapses are the most common.

Late latent syphilis is associated with host resistance to reinfection and to infectious relapse.[15] However, a pregnant woman with late latent syphilis can infect her fetus in utero, and an infection can be transmitted via transfused contaminated blood.

Late Syphilis

Late syphilis (tertiary syphilis) is a slowly progressive, inflammatory disease that can affect any organ in the body to produce clinical illness years after the initial infection. It is generally subdivided into neurosyphilis, cardiovascular syphilis, and gummatous syphilis.

Late Neurosyphilis

Because the CNS may be invaded during the septicemic phase, neurologic manifestations can occur during any phase. Therefore, neurosyphilis must be divided into acute neurosyphilis[28] and late (chronic) neurosyphilis (Fig. 227–7). Late neurosyphilis is usually divided into asymptomatic and symptomatic phases; the latter is further distinguished as meningovascular or parenchymatous neurosyphilis[32] (Table 227–2). Although this classification recognizes the existence of distinctive forms of neurosyphilis, there is almost always overlap with combinations of meningovascular and parenchymatous features. This is not surprising, because neurosyphilis is fundamentally a chronic meningitis involving every portion of the CNS.

The diagnosis of asymptomatic neurosyphilis is given to patients who have no clinical manifestation of neurologic involvement but who have one or more CSF abnormalities: pleocytosis, an elevated protein concentration, a decreased glucose concentration, or a positive nontreponemal or reaginic test (e.g., Venereal Disease Research Laboratory [VDRL], rapid plasma reagin [RPR]). Local CNS production of antibodies to *T. pallidum* is highly suggestive of an active case of neurosyphilis.[33–35] Asymptomatic neurosyphilis is the most common presentation of neurosyphilis.

The incidence of asymptomatic acute neurosyphilis in untreated patients ranges from 8 to 40%.[11, 14, 36–38] How many of these cases progress to symptomatic late neurosyphilis is problematic. With the exception of the presentation of the highly suggestive Argyll Robertson pupil or tabes dorsalis, the symptoms and signs of neurosyphilis are nonspecific (Table 227–3), and there is evidence to suggest that symptomatic neurosyphilis may be present in as many as 4% of patients with normal CSF findings. Because a lumbar puncture is necessary to make the diagnosis of asymptomatic neurosyphilis and because asymptomatic neurosyphilis occurs in at least 40% of patients,[11, 14] a lumbar puncture should be considered as part of the

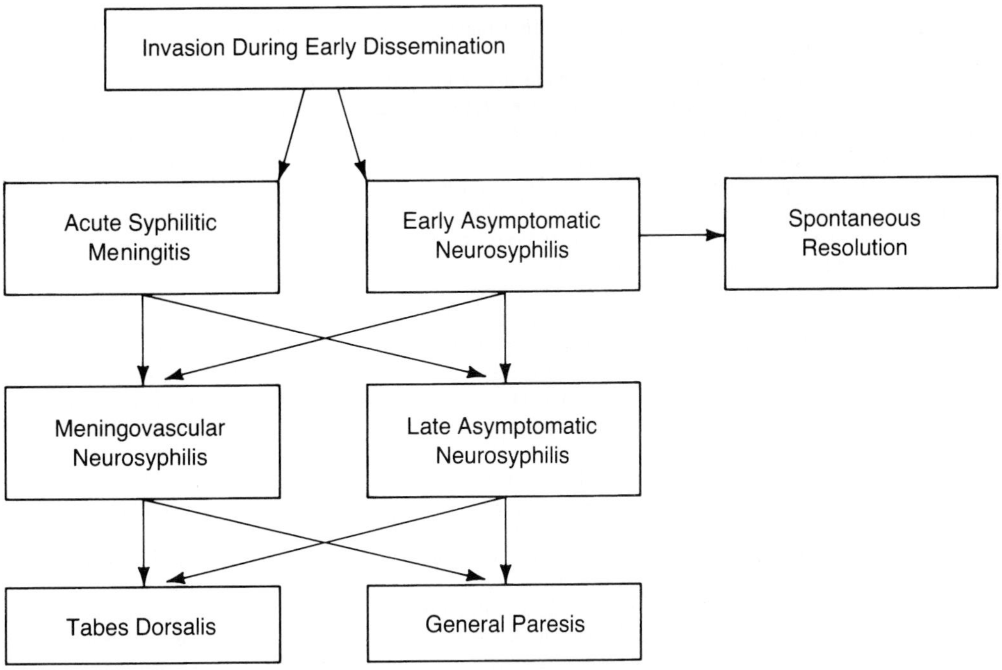

FIGURE 227–7. Chronology of neurosyphilis.

follow-up care for anyone who may not have been adequately treated for neurosyphilis, especially patients treated with benzathine penicillin alone (see later discussion).

Late symptomatic neurosyphilis is divided into two major clinical categories that have been correlated with pathologic findings, namely, meningovascular neurosyphilis and parenchymatous neurosyphilis (see Table 227–3), but a great deal of overlap occurs. (As noted previously, syphilitic meningitis resembling "aseptic" meningitis may occur during the secondary stage.) The term *meningovascular neurosyphilis* refers to the development of typical endarteritis obliterans, which affects the small blood vessels of the meninges, brain, and spinal cord and leads to multiple small areas of infarction. *Parenchymatous neurosyphilis* refers to the actual destruction of nerve cells, principally in the cerebral cortex. The former condition represents an inflammatory process and the latter a degenerative one, but a mixture of the two pathologic processes is always present.

Vascular involvement (meningovascular neurosyphilis) may lead to a wide spectrum of diseases, ranging from focal ischemia and stroke to progressive neurologic deficits, as a result of the gradual destruction of nerve tissue by small-vessel endarteritis. Hemiparesis, aphasia, and either focal or generalized seizures may occur and appear to be more frequent now than in previous reports.[32, 37, 38]

Parenchymatous neurosyphilis includes general paresis (cortical involvement) and tabes dorsalis (spinal cord involvement). It is the result of widespread parenchymal damage and represents a combination of psychiatric manifestations and neurologic findings. Abnormalities correspond to the mnemonic *PARESIS*: *P*ersonality (emotional lability, paranoia); *A*ffect (carelessness in appearance); *R*eflexes (hyperactive); *E*ye (Argyll Robertson pupils); *S*ensorium (illusions, delusions, especially megalomania, hallucinations); *I*ntellect (decreased recent memory, judgment, insight); and *S*peech (slurred). Spinal cord damage involves principally demyelinization of the posterior column, dorsal roots, and dorsal root ganglia, which eventually results in the development of an ataxic, wide-based gait and footslap, paresthesias,

TABLE 227–2 Classification of Neurosyphilis

Manifestation	Percentage of Cases (N = 676)
Syphilitic meningitis as a complication of secondary syphilis	8–40
Asymptomatic	
Symptomatic	1–2
Asymptomatic late neurosyphilis	31
Symptomatic late neurosyphilis	69
Meningovascular	
Cerebromeningeal	6
Diffuse	
Focal	
Cerebrovascular	10
Spinal	3
Parenchymatous	
Tabetic	30
Paretic	12
Taboparetic	3
Ocular	3
Miscellaneous	2

Modified with permission from Merritt HH, Moore M. Acute neurosyphilitic meningitis. Medicine (Baltimore). 1935;14:119.

TABLE 227–3 Clinical Manifestations of Neurosyphilis

- Meningovascular
  - Hemiplegia or hemiparesis
  - Seizures
    - Generalized
    - Focal
  - Aphasia
- Parenchymatous
  - General paresis
    - Changes in personality, affect, sensorium, intellect, insight, and judgment
    - Hyperactive reflexes
    - Speech disturbances (slurring)
    - Pupillary disturbances (Argyll Robertson pupils)
    - Optic atrophy tremors (face, tongue, hands, legs)
  - Tabes dorsalis
    - Shooting or lightning pains
    - Ataxia
    - Pupillary disturbances (Argyll Robertson pupils)
    - Impotence
    - Bladder disturbances
    - Fecal incontinence
    - Peripheral neuropathy
    - Romberg sign
    - Cranial nerve involvement (II–VII)

"shooting" or "lightning" pains (sudden onset, rapid radiation, and disappearance), bladder disturbances, fecal incontinence, impotence, loss of position and vibratory sense, absent ankle and knee jerks, and loss of deep pain and temperature sensation. The Romberg sign (inability to stand with feet together and eyes closed without falling over) is classically present in patients with tabes dorsalis. Trophic degenerative joint disease, known as Charcot's joints, and traumatic ulcers or sores on the lower extremities and feet resulting from the loss of sensation were prominently featured in textbooks of physical diagnosis published before the antibiotic era.

Ocular disturbances are common whenever the CNS is invaded. The Argyll Robertson pupil is a small, irregular pupil that accommodates to near vision but does not react to light or painful stimuli. Optic atrophy occurs over a period of months to years, beginning peripherally and proceeding to the center of the nerve, producing progressive concentric constriction of the visual fields with retention of normal vision. This is referred to as *gunbarrel sight*.

Any inflammatory disease of the eye can be mimicked by syphilitic involvement. Iridocyclitis is the most common abnormal finding; other ocular findings are episcleritis, vitreitis, retinitis, panuveitis, papillitis, and retinal detachment. They may accompany acute syphilitic meningitis or appear as isolated manifestations of secondary syphilis.[28] Uveitis is prone to develop after treatment with corticosteroids.[30] The differential diagnosis of other systemic diseases includes tuberculosis, rheumatoid arthritis, sarcoidosis, toxoplasmosis, histoplasmosis, and ocular *Toxocara canis* infections.

Although any cranial nerve can be affected, those most commonly involved are the seventh and eighth cranial nerves (40%). Involvement results in the gradual development of a loss of facial expression; tremors of the lips, tongue, and facial muscles; and difficulty enunciating multisyllable words (e.g., "Methodist," "Episcopal"). The second, third, and fourth cranial nerves are the next most commonly affected (25%).

Meningovascular syphilis usually occurs 5 to 10 years after the onset of disease, general paresis 15 to 20 years after, and tabes dorsalis 25 to 30 years after.

A distinct form of neurosyphilis is syphilitic otitis (asymmetric deafness, tinnitus). The ear may be involved during any stage of the disease, including congenital syphilis. This may be the only clinically apparent symptom at presentation, and it usually presents diagnostic dilemmas, especially because the CSF parameters are usually normal. In early stages syphilitic otitis is curable[39]; if untreated it causes irreversible damage. A positive treponemal antibody test (e.g., TPHA, FTA-abs) is found in approximately 7% of patients with otherwise unexplained sensorineural hearing loss that is usually unilateral and in 7% of patients with cochleovestibular dysfunction (Meniere's disease), making neurosyphilis a significant cause of these disorders. Congenital otic syphilis is usually bilateral and more severe than otic involvement caused by acquired syphilis. Specialized diagnostic procedures may be required,[40, 41] but any patient with unexplained hearing loss or vestibular disturbances who has a positive treponemal antibody test should be treated for syphilitic otitis.

The conditions from which neurosyphilis must be differentiated are numerous. They include any degenerative neurologic process, disorders that cause chronic inflammation (e.g., tuberculosis; fungal, parasitic, or sarcoid meningitis; tumors; subdural hematoma; Alzheimer's disease; multiple sclerosis; chronic alcoholism), and any disorder that affects the vasculature of the CNS. The axiom that syphilis can mimic any disease is particularly apropos with regard to the CNS.

Given the vagaries of neurosyphilis, the diagnosis can be very difficult to make. In modern medicine, one is loath to label a patient with a specific etiologic infectious diagnosis without isolation of the infecting organism from the patient (by culture, antigen capture, or pathologic demonstration). But because *T. pallidum* cannot be cultured in vitro and isolation in animals is restricted to research laboratories, serologic or antibody tests alone are relied on to diagnose and monitor these patients. However, the demonstration of specific treponemal immunoglobulin G (IgG) and IgM antibody production in the CNS is very helpful,[33–35] and the polymerase chain reaction (PCR) test establishes the presence of the etiologic agent (but not necessarily live or replicating organisms).[41–43]

The aim of treatment has been to develop a rational and safe therapeutic approach so that the patient has a reasonable expectation that the disease will be cured or will not progress to a severe neurologic disability. When considering treatment approaches, several points must be considered. First, a spirochetemia always occurs in patients with syphilis before invasion of the CNS. Therefore, except in patients with immune dysfunction (e.g., HIV infection), the diagnosis of neurosyphilis cannot be made without a positive serum treponemal antibody response (e.g., TPHA, FTA-abs, MHATP). Second, a positive CSF VDRL or CSF RPR test always indicates active neurosyphilis. Third, a positive PCR test in the CSF establishes that CNS invasion has occurred but does not necessarily establish that the infection is active and the spirochetes are replicating.[42] Fourth, any CSF abnormality in the appropriate clinical setting and without an alternative explanation strongly suggests active neurosyphilis. Fifth, local CNS production of antitreponemal antibody is highly suggestive of neurosyphilis. Therefore, any patient with a positive specific serum treponemal antibody test, a positive CSF VDRL, a positive CSF PCR, or evidence of local CNS antibody production with or without otherwise explained neurologic findings warrants therapy or close follow-up for neurosyphilis (see later discussion).

Cardiovascular Syphilis

The underlying pathologic lesion of cardiovascular syphilis is the omnipresent endarteritis obliterans, in this case involving the vaso vasorum of the aorta. This results in a medial necrosis with destruction of elastic tissue and subsequent aortitis with a saccular (or occasionally a fusiform) aneurysm. There is a predilection to involve the ascending aorta, which leads to weakness of the aortic valve ring and distortion of the cups and results in aortic regurgitation and coronary artery stenosis. The transverse segment of the aortic arch is the next most frequently involved area; the aorta below the renal arteries is seldom involved.[10, 11] Symptomatic syphilitic aortitis occurs in approximately 10% of untreated cases, but the pathologic lesions can be demonstrated on postmortem examination in up to 83% of cases of untreated neurosyphilis.[23] A symptomatic syphilitic aortitis should be suspected whenever linear calcifications are noted on chest radiographs of the ascending aorta, a finding seldom seen in arteriosclerotic disease. Syphilitic aneurysms rarely dissect. Neurologic involvement is common in patients with syphilitic aortitis. Other large arteries (e.g., temporal artery) may also be involved. Because of the success of antibiotic treatment, cardiovascular syphilis is now a medical curiosity in the United States.

Late Benign Syphilis (Gumma)

The gumma is a nonspecific, granulomatous-like lesion that occurs in late syphilis[10, 11] but is rarely seen today. These indolent lesions are most commonly found in the skeletal system, skin, and mucocutaneous tissues but can develop in any organ. They may be single or multiple and vary in size from microscopic defects to large, tumor-like masses. They are of clinical importance principally as a cause of local destruction. The cutaneous manifestations range from superficial nodules to deep granulomatous lesions, which may break down to form punched-out ulcers. Involution is followed by the development of a thin, atrophic, noncontractile scar arranged in arciform patterns.[10, 11] Gummatous hepatitis may cause low-grade fever, epigastric pain and tenderness, and eventually cirrhosis (hepar lobatum). Gummas of the bone may result in fractures or joint destruction, whereas those in the upper respiratory tract can lead to perforation of the nasal system or palate. Trauma may predispose to involvement of a specific site. Gummas must be distinguished from other granulomatous lesions (e.g., tuberculosis, sarcoidosis, deep fungal infections) and from neoplasms. The spirochetes in these lesions are difficult to visualize on microscopic examination. A therapeutic trial of penicillin or other effective antibiotics results in a rapid and dramatic response. Gummas were the most common late complication seen in the Oslo study described previously (approximately 15%).

Congenital Syphilis

The incidence of congenital syphilis rose in the United States in the late 1980s and early 1990s, coincident with the rise of syphilis in the heterosexual population. Infection of the fetus in utero can occur at any stage of infection in any untreated or inadequately treated mother but is most likely to occur during the early stages. The risk of fetal infection decreases progressively thereafter. Infection of the fetus before the fourth month of gestation is rare; therefore, early abortion is unlikely to be a result of syphilis. Treatment of the mother during the first 4 months of pregnancy usually ensures that the fetus will not be infected. Depending on the severity of the infection, late abortion, stillbirth, neonatal death, neonatal disease, or latent infection may be seen[10, 11]; these manifestations appear to be caused largely by dysfunction of the maternal-fetal endocrine axis, which results in decreased levels of dehydroepiandrosterone produced by the fetal adrenal glands.[44]

The clinical pattern is variable, but most often there are no abnormal physical findings (Table 227–4).[10, 11, 45] In the perinatal period (infantile form), the most striking lesions affect the mucocutaneous tissues, liver, and bones. The earliest sign of congenital syphilis is usually a rhinitis (snuffles), which is soon followed by a diffuse, maculopapular, desquamative rash with extensive sloughing of the epithelium, particularly on the palms, on the soles, and about the mouth and anus. In contrast to acquired syphilis in the adult, a vesicular rash and bullae may develop. These lesions are teeming with spirochetes and have the characteristic obliterative endarteritis and perivascular mononuclear cuffing on microscopic examination that are found in other syphilitic lesions.

The liver is often heavily infected, with associated splenomegaly, anemia, thrombocytopenia, and jaundice. The generalized spirochetemia may lead to diffuse inflammatory changes of virtually any organ of the body. Neonatal death is usually caused by liver failure, severe pneumonia, or pulmonary hemorrhage. Renal involvement with an immune-complex glomerulonephritis may develop and usually occurs at about the fourth month of life.[20] A generalized osteochondritis and perichondritis may affect the architecture of all bones of the skeletal system, most prominently the nose (saddle nose) and the metaphyses of the lower extremities (anterior bowing or "saber shin"). Neonatal congenital syphilis must be differentiated from other generalized congenital infections such as rubella, cytomegalovirus infection, and toxoplasmosis.

The untreated child who survives the first 6 to 12 months of life enters, with a few notable exceptions, a latent period. The late development of cardiovascular syphilis is rare, but interstitial keratitis is common. Photophobia, pain, circumcorneal inflammation, and superficial and deep vascularization of the cornea may occur any time between the ages of 5 and 30 years. Asymptomatic or symptomatic neurosyphilis is also common in these patients and resembles the disease in adults. Eighth-nerve deafness is particularly common. Necrotizing funisitis, an inflammatory process involving the matrix of the umbilical cord and characterized by perivascular inflammation and obliterative endarteritis, is for all practical purposes pathognomonic of congenital syphilis. This disease should be suspected clinically whenever the umbilical cord is swollen and discolored red, white, and blue to resemble a barber's pole.[46]

Other late characteristic stigmata include recurrent arthropathy and bilateral knee effusions (Clutton's joints); centrally notched, widely spread, peg-shaped upper central incisors (Hutchinson's teeth); frontal bossing; and poorly developed maxillas.[10, 11]

Because at least one third of the mothers who give birth to syphilitic children have had prenatal care and about half have had a nonreactive serologic test during the first trimester of pregnancy, serologic testing is always warranted at the time of delivery, especially in high-risk patients.[10, 45–48] The best means is to combine IgM antibody determination with antigen detection[49] (see later discussion). Because giving penicillin to the neonate is virtually risk-free, all neonates born to syphilitic mothers should be treated, regardless of whether the mother was treated during her pregnancy.

TABLE 227–4 Clinical Signs of Congenital Syphilis

Manifestation	Percentage of Cases
Early	55
Osteochondritis	
Snuffles	40
Rash	40
Anemia	30
Hepatosplenomegaly	20
Jaundice	20
Neurologic signs	20
Lymphadenopathy	5
Mucous patches	5
Late	
Frontal bosses	
Short maxillas	
Saddle nose	
Protruding mandible	
Interstitial keratitis	
Eighth-nerve deafness	
High palatal arch	
Hutchinson's incisors	
Mulberry molars	
Sternoclavicular thickening (Higouménaki's sign)	
Clutton's joints (bilateral painless swelling of knees)	
Saber shins	
Flaring scapulas	

Data from Kampmeier RH. Essentials of Syphilogy. 3rd ed. Philadelphia: JB Lippincott; 1943; and Stokes JH, Beerman H, Ingraham NR. Modern Clinical Syphilogy, Diagnosis, Treatment: Case Study. 3rd ed. Philadelphia: WB Saunders; 1945.

Atypical Presentations of Syphilis

As noted previously, the clinical presentation and course of syphilis are quite varied, and the diagnosis can sometimes elude the clinician even under the best of circumstances. Because some patients may have been treated with antibiotics that are suboptimal (i.e., oral penicillin) or inadequate (spectinomycin) and because of the larger pool of immunocompromised patients and the relative inexperience of today's clinician with syphilitic patients, there is a sense that unusual patterns and atypical presentations have become more common. However, protean manifestations are the hallmark of syphilis. Older clinicians were never surprised by unusual or atypical findings, and today's clinician should not be either.

LABORATORY DIAGNOSIS

Direct Examination for Spirochetes

In primary, secondary, and early congenital syphilis, the darkfield examination or immunofluorescence staining of mucocutaneous lesions is the quickest and most direct laboratory method of establishing the diagnosis.[10, 11] Examination of a serous transudate from moist lesions such as a primary chancre, condyloma latum, or mucous patch is most productive, because these lesions have the largest numbers of treponemes. However, *T. pallidum* can be demonstrated at times from dry skin lesions and from lymph nodes by saline aspiration (the saline must be free of bactericidal additives). For a darkfield examination, the surface of the suspected lesion should be cleaned with saline and gently abraded with dry gauze so as not to produce gross bleeding. The serous exudate can then be squeezed onto a glass slide, covered with a cover slip, and examined with darkfield or phase-contrast microscopy. A drop of nonbactericidal saline may be added if the preparation is too thick. *T. pallidum* has a corkscrew appearance and moves in a spiraling motion with a characteristic 90° undulation about its midpoint (Fig. 227–8). A lesion should be considered nonsyphilitic only after three negative examinations have been made. Specimens from mouth lesions are worthless because *T. pallidum* cannot be distinguished with certainty from nonpathogenic treponemes. A scattering of a few red blood cells indicates that the specimen is adequate. Cleaning of the lesion with a topical antiseptic, soap, or bactericidal saline obscures the diagnosis because dead and nonmotile organisms are difficult to identify. However, if this is inadvertently done, direct or indirect immunofluorescence or immunoperoxidase staining can be used to establish the presence of *T. pallidum*.[50]

Biopsy Specimen

The spirochete can sometimes be demonstrated in biopsy materials. A silver stain is most commonly used, but confusion with elastic tissues can occur. Specific immunofluorescence or immunoperoxidase staining of nonfrozen pathologic specimens is now preferred to silver staining to establish a more precise diagnosis.[50, 51]

Serologic Tests

Confusion surrounds interpretation of the serologic tests for syphilis, principally because two different types of antibodies are measured: the *nonspecific* nontreponemal reaginic antibody and the *specific* antitreponemal antibody. The test for the former is inexpensive, rapid, and convenient for screening large numbers of sera and as an indication of disease activity. Specific antibody tests establish the high likelihood of a treponemal infection, either currently or at sometime in the past (Table 227–5). To establish a diagnosis of syphilis, the two types of serologic tests are most often used in tandem. It should be emphasized that serologic test results for syphilis may be negative in active cases, especially in older patients.[51a]

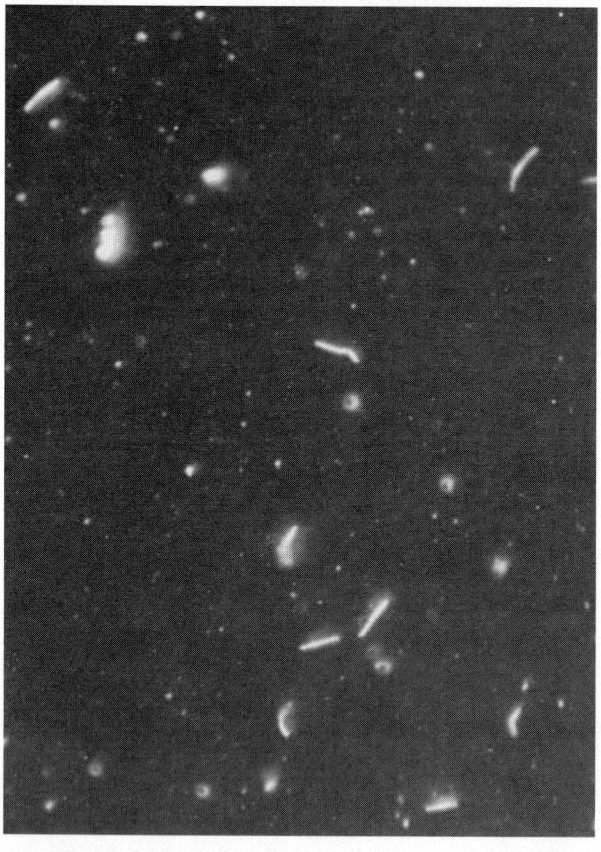

FIGURE 227–8. Darkfield examination. The morphologic characteristics of the spirochetes and the characteristic flexous motion about their centers can be appreciated.

TABLE 227–5 Percentage of Untreated Patients with Positive Responses to Commonly Used Serologic Tests

Type of Test	Early (Primary and Secondary)	Late (Late Latent and Tertiary)
Nontreponemal (reagenic) tests VDRL, RPR, ART TRUST	70–100	60–98
Specific treponemal tests FTA-abs, TPHA, MHA-TP, ELISA	50–85	97–100

The nonspecific nontreponemal tests should revert to negative (nonreactive) when appropriate treatment is given except in unusual circumstances (see text). Specific treponemal tests may also revert to negative if effective treatment is given early.

Nontreponemal Reaginic Tests. Much of the confusion about these tests arises from the term *reagin*. This is the result of an unfortunate quirk in the evolution of medical terminology, because it has nothing to do with the reagin IgE that is involved in allergic reactions. "Syphilis reaginic" antibodies are IgG and IgM directed against a lipoidal antigen resulting from the interaction of host tissues with *T. pallidum* or from *T. pallidum* itself. The earliest cardiolipin antigens used to measure reaginic antibody were crude extracts made from beef livers or beef hearts. False-positive reactions were common. The cardiolipin-cholesterol-lecithin used today is a much purer preparation and gives fewer false-positive reactions. The relationship of these tests with *T. pallidum* infection is fortuitous.

The standard nontreponemal test is the VDRL slide test, in which heated serum (56°C) is tested for its ability to flocculate a suspension of a cardiolipin-cholesterol-lecithin antigen. It is now most often used to monitor a patient's response to therapy. Most laboratories and blood banks have adapted a modification for routine screening for syphilis: the rapid plasma reagin (RPR) card test, the automated reagin test (ART), or the toluidine red unheated test (TRUST).

A prozone phenomenon occurs in about 2% of infected persons, especially in secondary syphilis and pregnancy,[52] and appropriate dilutions should be performed whenever the index of suspicion is high (e.g., patients with another sexually transmitted disease, pregnant women, drug abusers). Nontreponemal antibody tests vary during the course of untreated disease. They reach their highest prevalence and titer during the secondary and early latent stages and decline thereafter, usually to <1:4. At least 25% of untreated persons become VDRL or RPR negative.

One of the more difficult situations to interpret is the patient with a persistently positive VDRL test after apparently adequate therapy ("chronic persistor"). This may be a biologically false reaction, or it may indicate persistent active infection or reinfection, especially when the titer is greater than 1:4. A persistently high-titered RPR or VDRL result is more common in HIV-infected persons because of the polyclonal antibody stimulation, a manifestation of immune dysfunction often seen in these patients, especially in early HIV disease.[53]

The quantitative RPR test should become nonreactive 1 year after successful therapy in primary syphilis and 2 years after successful therapy in secondary syphilis.[54, 55] Most patients with late syphilis should be nonreactive by the fifth year after treatment.[56] The time required for the test to become negative correlates with the interval between contact and institution of therapy and with the severity of illness, especially with the type of skin lesions manifested in the secondary stage (i.e., a patient with a macular rash reverts to a negative titer sooner than does a patient with a papular rash).[57] Therefore, a positive RPR response after 1 year in a patient treated for primary syphilis or after 2 years in a patient treated for secondary syphilis suggests persistent infection, reinfection, or a biologically false-positive reaction. A patient with late syphilis should have a negative response after 5 years.[56] As with all quantitative serologic tests, only a fourfold or greater change in titer is meaningful.

In summary, these tests are inexpensive, reliable, and easy to perform. They have utility for screening sera and in areas of high prevalence (e.g., southeastern United States) should still be used to screen hospital admissions.[58] Also, they have great utility as a gauge for the success of treatment.

Specific Treponemal Tests. The principal specific antitreponemal antibody tests done today are the FTA-abs, TPHA, and MHATP. The FTA-abs is a standard indirect immunofluorescent antibody test that uses *T. pallidum* harvested from rabbit testes as the antigen. The patient's serum is first absorbed with nonpathogenic treponemal antigen (referred to as "sorbent") to remove "natural" cross-reacting antibody that may have been raised against saprophytic treponemes of the oral cavity or genital tract. The test has the disadvantage of being standardized at one serum dilution (1:5), and, as with most immunofluorescence tests, its interpretation can be quite subjective. Therefore, it requires a great attention to detail, is difficult to standardize from one laboratory to the next, and is difficult to quantify. However attempts to make the test more predictive of active disease by testing for IgM antibody have not proved useful.

The TPHA is also used to measure specific treponemal antibody. It has the advantage of being easier to perform than the FTA-abs. It uses a "sorbent" to increase specificity. Although it is as specific as the FTA-abs, it is less sensitive in early disease. For practical purposes, it is interchangeable with the FTA-abs test. The MHATP test is an adaptation of the TPHA that uses a microtiter plate.

These tests would be expensive as screening tests, and if they were applied to a low-risk population, the number of false-positive reactions would increase proportionately. Therefore, their principal use is to verify a positive nontreponemal reaginic test result. Once positive, the patient usually remains positive for life. However, reversion to a nonreactive status may occur in up to 10% of patients, especially in those who are treated early.

The TPI test is rarely used today, but it was the standard against which all specific treponemal tests were compared. It determines the ability of antibody plus complement to immobilize live *T. pallidum* as visualized under a darkfield microscope (i.e., it is a bactericidal test). Because it requires maintenance of replicating *T. pallidum* in rabbits, it is expensive, time-consuming, and difficult to perform. Its utility in today's setting has been questioned. Only a few research laboratories have maintained the capability to perform the TPI test. The elucidation of the antigenic structure of *T. pallidum* should lead to the development of simpler tests, but this depends on the economic impetus to develop such a test.

The comparative reactivities of the most widely used tests are shown in Table 227–5. When the diagnosis of syphilis is being seriously considered in an individual patient, the TPHA, MHA-TP, or FTA-abs test should be done. Once these have become positive and the diagnosis is established, their usefulness is limited. A nontreponemal antibody test is very helpful for monitoring the efficacy of therapy. The failure to become negative suggests a persistent infection, reinfection, or a false-positive test.

Use of the FTA-abs (IgM) test on cord blood to diagnose congenital syphilis has been disappointing, and the best way to monitor these infants is with serial quantitative nontreponemal tests performed over several months. As with all serial serologic determinations, the most credible results are those performed simultaneously on appropriately stored serum samples. The combination of a Western blot for *T. pallidum*–specific IgM and immunofluorescence spirochetal antigen detection on nasopharyngeal and umbilical cord specimens is the most effective means to establish the diagnosis.[49]

Tests for Neurosyphilis. Serologic tests for neurosyphilis have evolved over time. The CSF-VDRL, the oldest test, is insensitive but relatively specific. A positive CSF-VDRL or CSF-RPR result in the appropriate clinical setting establishes the diagnosis of neurosyphilis. A CSF serologic diagnosis based on the production of local antitreponemal antibodies as a discriminator of CNS invasion has improved sensitivity and specificity.[33–35, 59, 60] The most experience has been with the intrathecal *T. pallidum* antibody (ITPA) index and the TPHA index.

The ITPA index is determined as follows:

$$\text{ITPA index} = \frac{\text{TPHA-CSF IgG titer/Total CSF IgG}}{\text{TPHA-serum IgG titer/Total serum IgG}}$$

The total IgG measurements are in milligrams. As long as the albumin serum-to-CSF ratio is greater than 144, indicating an undamaged blood-brain barrier, then a ratio of 3.0 or greater indicates active production of local antitreponemal antibodies.

The TPHA index is determined as follows:

$$\text{TPHA index} = \frac{\text{MHATP-CSF titer}}{\text{CSF albumin} \times 10^3/\text{Serum albumin}}$$

The albumin measurements are in milligrams per deciliter. A TPHA index greater than 100 is indicative of local CNS antibody production.

If the patient is treated early these indices are likely to return to normal, but if the patient is treated late (i.e., after 2 years) they are likely to remain abnormal.[60]

The PCR test for *T. pallidum* in the CSF and IgM immunoblotting are both specific and sensitive, but they are not widely available. Oligoclonal antibodies have also been demonstrated.[60a]

A negative CSF-FTA unabsorbed or negative CSF-TPHA test in essence rules out neurosyphilis in patients with late disease but not in patients with early disease.[14]

The finding of more than five mononuclear cells per cubic millimeter of CSF in the appropriate clinical setting is also suggestive of active neurosyphilis.

False-Positive Serologic Test for Syphilis. The likelihood of false-positive reactions depends on the population being studied. Acute or transient false-positive nontreponemal reaginic test reactions may occur whenever there is a strong immunologic stimulus (e.g., acute bacterial or viral infection, vaccination, early HIV infection).[60] Positive reactions persisting for months occur with parenteral drug abuse; with autoimmune or connective tissue diseases, especially systemic lupus erythematosus; with aging (up to 10% of those older than 70 years of age); and in hypergammaglobulinemic states (Table 227–6). A false-positive nontreponemal reaginic test in this setting tends to be associated with other serum factors frequently associated with

TABLE 227–6 Causes of False-Positive Serologic Test Reactions for Syphilis

Infectious diseases	*Mycoplasma* pneumonia
Lyme disease*	Measles
Leptospirosis	Chickenpox
Relapsing fever	Lymphogranuloma venereum
Ratbite fever (*Spirillum minor*)	Hepatitis
Leprosy	Infectious mononucleosis
Tuberculosis	Early HIV infection
Pneumonococcal pneumonia	Noninfectious diseases
Subacute bacterial endocarditis	Drug addiction
Chancroid	Any connective disease disorder
Scarlet fever	Rheumatoid heart disease
Rickettsial disease	Blood transfusions (multiple)
Malaria	Pregnancy
Trypanosomiasis	"Old age"
Vaccinia (vaccination)	Chronic liver disease

*VDRL (RPR) negative.

autoimmune diseases, such as antinuclear, antithyroid, or antimitochondrial antibodies, rheumatoid factor, and cryoglobulins.

A false-positive nontreponemal reaginic test can usually be verified (and syphilis excluded) by obtaining a negative specific treponemal antibody test (FTA-abs, TPHA, MHA-TP). However, at times the same illnesses that produce a false-positive nontreponemal reaginic test (e.g., systemic lupus erythematosus) also result in a positive or borderline-positive FTA-abs test reaction. Also, the FTA-abs may be positive when the VDRL is negative.[61] This false reaction can often be distinguished by noting a beaded pattern of immunofluorescence on the treponemes, but the only definitive way to make the distinction is to obtain the functional but rarely available TPI test. Other spirochetal illnesses, such as relapsing fever (*Borrelia* spp.), yaws, pinta, leptospirosis, or rat-bite fever *(Spirillum minor),* also yield positive nontreponemal and treponemal tests. Infection with *Borrelia burgdorferi* (Lyme disease) results in a positive FTA-abs test but does not cause a positive nontreponemal reaginic reaction (VDRL or RPR).

In summary, the reaginic antibody tests (RPR, VDRL, ART) are used for screening large numbers of sera, the specific treponemal tests (TPHA, MHA-TP, FTA-abs) for confirming the diagnosis, and the quantitative nontreponemal antibody tests (RPR, VDRL) for assessing the adequacy of therapy.

Isolation of *Treponema pallidum*

Because *T. pallidum* cannot be cultivated on artificial media, inoculation of laboratory animals (higher primates, rabbit testes) is the only means presently available for isolating the organism.[3] The most experience has been with isolation in rabbits. The number of organisms that must be obtained from a human lesion to ensure a positive transfer to the laboratory animals is not known.

The lower portion of the rabbit testis is inoculated with 0.5 to 3.0 ml of the test material. The rabbits should be kept in a cool room (17°C [65°F]). They must be serologically prescreened to exclude concurrent or previous infection with *T. cuniculi*, and they must be fed antibiotic-free chow. The rabbit testes or regional lymph nodes (or both) may be harvested after 3 weeks by mincing and then shaking them in a suitable buffer, usually phosphate-buffered saline, in an atmosphere of 5 to 10% carbon dioxide for 30 minutes. This material can be examined by darkfield or fluorescence antibody examination for treponemes, but if the result is negative, it should be injected into another set of test rabbits through at least two passages. Syphilitic infection in the rabbits should also be verified by serologic testing of the rabbit sera.

There has been limited success maintaining *T. pallidum* in tissue culture.[3]

Congenital Syphilis

The most reliable means to diagnose congenital syphilis is to test the mother at the time of birth. Delayed-onset syphilis (>2 days) is best diagnosed by combining tests for IgM-specific antibodies (ELISA, Relispot, FTA-abs, immunoblotting/Western blot) with antigen detection (darkfield, immunofluorescent staining, PCR). Immunofluorescent staining is superior to darkfield examination. A calcium alginate swab is inserted into the posterior nasopharynx and rolled immediately onto slides for examination.[48, 49] A positive result on any test warrants a diagnosis of congenital syphilis.

TREATMENT

Although the efficacy of penicillin in the treatment of syphilis is well established, there has never been a well-controlled, carefully planned, prospective study to determine the optimal dose or duration of therapy.[62, 63] The following recommendations must be tempered by this knowledge, and it should not be surprising that there are patients who have a persistent infection despite having received "adequate therapy."[14, 64] Nevertheless, the current recommendations, obtained by extrapolation from the pharmacokinetics of penicillin therapy, the effect of the drug on *T. pallidum* in experimental conditions, and the available clinical data, are adequate for the great majority of immunocompetent patients (Table 227–7). For example, it has been shown in experimental infections that *T. pallidum* regenerates if penicillin blood levels are allowed to fall to subinhibitory levels after 18 to 24 hours.[63] Furthermore, it has been found from a variety of clinical and experimental data that a level equivalent to more than 0.03 μg/ml of penicillin is needed to ensure killing of *T. pallidum,* [62] that maintenance of an effective blood level for at least 7 days is necessary to cure early syphilis,[62] and that increasing the dose to more than 0.6 mg/kg over a period of 9 hours does not clear treponemes from primary chancres at an increased rate.[62] Therefore, it can be inferred that the most effective antibiotic treatment would be one that ensures an adequate blood level over a prolonged period (least 2 weeks). For many years it was believed that the most convenient way to achieve this goal was to treat with benzathine penicillin, despite the potential inadequacies of this treatment for neurosyphilis and pregnancy.[14, 64, 65] *T. pallidum* has been isolated from the CSF of patients with only a chancre,[14] reflecting the early spirochetemia that always occurs. Therefore, to reliably cure this readily curable disease, one must adequately treat treponemes in the CNS (neurosyphilis) even in patients with primary or secondary infection. But benzathine penicillin does not reliably achieve treponemicidal levels in the CSF,[66] numerous treatment failures have been recorded,[14, 64–72] and the recommendation that benzathine penicillin be considered the treatment of choice was made despite the fact that retreatment was required in as many as 1 of 33 cases.[73] On the other hand, there is ample clinical experience to suggest that, when an early diagnosis is made, fewer treponemes exist and the likelihood of a complete cure with relatively low doses of penicillin is increased.[62, 63] Therefore, it seems imprudent to totally abandon benzathine penicillin, which at least provides circulating penicillin, albeit at low levels, for 14 days. However, an increasing number of clinicians now treat syphilis with combination or prolonged therapy to substantially increase the likelihood that the most devastating sequela of syphilis (i.e., late neurosyphilis) does not occur. This is especially true when there is evidence to suggest that the host may be immunocompromised, and particularly when the patient is infected with HIV (see later discussion).

Early incubating syphilis is probably aborted when gonorrhea is treated with the currently recommended regimens, spectinomycin excepted.

Because of the high risk of infection, preventive or "epidemiologic" treatment should be given to anyone who has been exposed to infectious syphilis within the preceding 3 months. Serologic studies must be done to establish the diagnosis and to monitor the adequacy of the response to therapy. As noted previously, adequately treated non–HIV-infected patients should have a predictable fall in their nontreponemal reaginic antibody titer. These patients should be considered to have early syphilis.

Pregnant patients should receive penicillin, following dosage schedules appropriate for the stage of syphilis as recommended for nonpregnant patients. If the patient has a well-documented penicillin allergy, the choice is more difficult, because the efficacy of treatment for the fetus in these cases is not well established. Penicillin desensitization is recommended (see Chapter 21).[74] The patient is given gradually increasing doses of oral or intravenous penicillin over a period of 3 to 4 hours, until full tolerance is achieved. Erythromycin was used in the past, but because of well documented unacceptable failure rates it should be used only as a last recourse. Pharmacologic characteristics, studies in rabbit models, and limited studies in humans suggest that ceftriaxone is adequate therapy. However, conflicting clinical experience has been reported in patients who are

TABLE 227–7 Recommended Therapy for Syphilis*

Stage	Patients Not Allergic to Penicillin	Patients Allergic to Penicillin*
Early syphilis (primary, secondary)	Benzathine penicillin G,† 2.4 million units IM weekly for 2 or 3 doses alone or with any of the listed oral regimens Procaine penicillin, 2.4 million units IM daily, *plus* Probenecid, 1.0 g PO qd for 10 d, *or* Doxycycline, 200 mg PO bid for 21 d, *or* Amoxicillin, 3.0 g PO bid, *plus* Probenecid, 1.0 g PO qd for 14 d, *or* Ceftriaxone,§ 250 mg IM qd or IV for 5 d or 1 g IM qd for 14 d	Doxycycline, 200 mg PO bid for 15 d, *or* tetracycline hydrochloride, 500 mg PO qid for 15 d‡
Late syphilis (tertiary), neurosyphilis, or concomitant HIV infections	Aqueous crystalline penicillin G, 2.0–4.0 million units by IV injection q4h for 10 d, *or* Amoxicillin, 3 g, plus 0.5 g probenicid PO bid for 15 d, *or* Doxycycline, 200 mg PO bid for 21 d, *or* Ceftriaxone,¶ 1 g IM or IV for 14 d, *or* Procaine penicillin G, 2.4 million units IM, *plus* Probenecid, 1 g PO daily for 10 d	Chloramphenicol,‖ 2 g IV or 500 mg q6h PO for 30 d
Pregnancy	Same regimen as for nonpregnant patient; only penicillin therapy reliably treats the infant	
Congenital syphilis	Aqueous crystalline penicillin G, 50,000 U/kg IV daily in 2 divided doses for a minimum of 10 d, *or* Procaine penicillin G, 50,000 U/kg IM daily for a minimum of 10 d	

*Therapeutic regimens other than penicillin have not been well studied, especially in patients with syphilis of longer than 1 year's duration; therefore, careful follow up is mandatory. However, by extrapolation from animal studies and limited clinical studies, any penicillin or cephalosporin class of antibiotic should be used at doses that are adequate to treat infection of the central nervous system.
†Many treatment failures with benzathine penicillin have been reported. Therefore, the addition of another drug (e.g., doxycycline, amoxicillin) is prudent. Patients treated with benzathine penicillin must be reevaluated at 6-month intervals for neurosyphilis (see the text).
‡Because of the large number of well-documented treatment failures and corroborating laboratory studies, erythromycin is no longer recommended for the treatment of syphilis.
§Ceftriaxone should be diluted in 1% lidocaine solution (1 g/3.6 ml) for IM injection.
‖Chloramphenicol is theoretically beneficial treatment for neurosyphilis.
¶Treatment failures have been reported.

infected with HIV.[75] Tetracycline, doxycycline, erythromycin estolate, and chloramphenicol are *not* recommended because of potential adverse effects on the mother or fetus, or both. The mother should be monitored closely during and after the pregnancy, and if an increase in a nontreponemal reagin titer or a positive PCR test occurs, she and her infant must be retreated.

The risk of infection for the infant is minimal if the mother has received adequate penicillin treatment during pregnancy. Nevertheless, the child must be examined monthly after delivery and until the nontreponemal reaginic antibody test or PCR becomes negative. Penicillin treatment should never be withheld to "prove the diagnosis," and every neonate born to a syphilitic mother should be treated promptly unless adequate, serologically effective treatment with penicillin can be documented more than 1 month before delivery.[76] There is no evidence that the efficacy of penicillin treatment of syphilis has diminished over 50 years.[62, 63] However, there is evidence that *T. pallidum* can accept resistant plasmids, and the possibility exists that penicillin treatment may become inadequate in the future.

Tetracycline, chloramphenicol, ceftriaxone, and other cephalosporins have all been shown to be effective alternative antibiotics in animal models and in small clinical trials for treatment of early syphilis.

Patients who are also infected with HIV, like any other immunosuppressed group, present special problems (see later discussions). An intact cellular immune system is an important determinant of the severity of syphilitic disease. Therefore, these patients should be considered for treatment as if they had neurosyphilis regardless of their clinical findings, especially when they are in the later stages of their HIV infection.

Late Syphilis, Asymptomatic and Symptomatic Neurosyphilis

Because the CNS is invaded during the spirochetemia in at least 40% of patients[11, 14] and because spirochetemia occurs soon after the infection is contracted, all patients with syphilis should be considered to have neurosyphilis, and therefore a CSF examination should be considered for all. The finding of an elevated mononuclear cell count in the CSF, a positive reactive nontreponemal antibody test (VDRL, RPR), production of local CNS antitreponemal antibody, or a positive PCR test establishes the diagnosis.[34–36, 41–43]

Because benzathine penicillin G seldom produces detectable levels of penicillin in the CSF, this drug cannot be relied on as a treatment of neurosyphilis.[14, 66, 77, 78] To better ensure adequate antibiotic levels in the CNS, 12 to 24 million units of aqueous penicillin G should be given intravenously for 8 to 10 days[64]; alternatively, amoxicillin (3.0 g twice daily) plus probenecid (0.5 to 1.0 g orally) for 14 days,[79, 80] or doxycycline (200 mg orally twice daily) for 21 days,[81] or chloramphenicol (2 g orally daily) for 30 days can be given. Chloramphenicol and cephalothin also reach adequate levels in the aqueous humor of the eye. Procaine benzyl penicillin (1 g intramuscularly) plus probenecid (1 g orally daily) and ceftriaxone (1 g intramuscularly daily) for 14 days has been used successfully, but treatment failures have been documented.[75] Follow-up CSF examinations should be done in every case, every 3 to 6 months for at least 3 years or until serum nontreponemal antibodies disappear, local CNS treponemal antibodies disappear, or CSF oligoclonal bands disappear.

Malignancy of the CNS has been associated with false-positive results on nontreponemal and treponemal tests, but this has almost always been associated with a negative serum TPHA or FTA-abs reaction.

Treatment of Syphilitic Otitis

Although the evidence is not incontrovertible, patients with possible syphilitic hearing loss should be treated.[39, 82] Treatment should be prolonged (6 weeks to 3 months) and, unless contraindicated, should include prednisone, 30 to 60 mg every day or every other day, at least for the first 7 to 8 days.[82] Other antibiotic treatments for neurosyphilis would be an alternative choice to parenteral penicillin.

Persistent Infection

The question of persistent infection despite adequate therapy has been a controversial subject for many years. Although the efficacy of treating *T. pallidum* with penicillin is unquestioned, there are some patients in whom the spirochetes become sequestered in areas where adequate levels of penicillin are not easily achieved, such as the anterior chamber of the eye,[83] the CNS,[14, 64] and the labyrinth of the inner ear.[84] Whether these persistent organisms can cause a clinically evident illness at some later date remains speculative. However, there are a number of reports of unusual neurologic, optic, and otic findings for which there was little or no explanation except a positive serologic test for syphilis. In the past, attempts at isolation of these persistent organisms have met with variable success, and their validity has been questioned. However, there is now little doubt that *T. pallidum* can persist after treatment, particularly in the CNS, and that these organisms can be isolated by inoculation of appropriate human materials into laboratory animals or by PCR.[14, 41, 43] The challenge facing clinicians is to identify and treat these few patients. Anyone with neurologic, optic, or otic abnormalities who has or has had syphilis should be considered for CSF examination, and if there are any abnormalities (see previous discussion) or unexplained neurologic signs or symptoms, the patient should be treated for neurosyphilis.

Follow-up and Retreatment

All patients with early or congenital syphilis should have repeat quantitative nontreponemal tests at 3, 6, and 12 months (see previous discussion). All patients with secondary syphilis or syphilis of more than 1 year's duration should also have a repeat nontreponemal serologic test 24 months after treatment. Examination of the CSF is also warranted in all patients, especially if they were treated with benzathine penicillin. All patients with documented neurosyphilis must be monitored carefully with serologic testing and CSF examinations for at least 5 years unless all abnormal parameters including local CNS production of antibodies normalize.

Retreatment should be considered whenever clinical signs and symptoms of syphilis persist or recur; there is a sustained level or an increase in the titer of a nontreponemal test[55]; a positive RPR reaction persists beyond 12 months in primary syphilis, 24 months in secondary or latent syphilis, or 5 years in late syphilis; or there is a positive PCR test result.

Defining the Adequacy of Treatment

As noted previously, a quantitative decrease in nontreponemal reaginic tests is quite reliable as a measure of the adequacy of treatment. The time required for the tests to become nonreactive depends on the length of time the patient was infected before adequate treatment was instituted, but all patients should be nonreactive, or positive only at a 1:1 dilution, by year 5. Exceptions to this rule occur in persons with a chronic antigenic stimulation or immune dysfunction (e.g. HIV-infected persons).[54–57] Specific treponemal antibody tests can also revert to negative, especially when treatment is instituted early.

Jarisch-Herxheimer Reaction

The Jarisch-Herxheimer reaction is a systemic reaction that occurs 1 to 2 hours after the initial treatment of syphilis with effective antibiotics, especially penicillin. It consists of the abrupt onset of fever, chills, myalgias, headache, tachycardia, hyperventilation, vasodilation with flushing, and mild hypotension. It is particularly common when secondary syphilis is treated (70 to 90%) but can occur in any stage (10 to 25%). It lasts from 12 to 24 hours and has been well correlated with the release from the spirochetes of heat-stable pyrogen.[85] Patients should be warned of the reaction before treatment. Varying degrees of severity occur. The reaction is self-limited and can be treated with aspirin every 4 hours for a period of 24 to 48 hours. Prednisone can also abort the reaction, and one dose of 60 mg should be given as adjunctive therapy to patients with cardiovascular or symptomatic neurosyphilis and to pregnant patients[86] to avoid catastrophic consequences.

Immunity

Magnuson and associates[15] were able to demonstrate in human volunteers that immunity developed to reinfection. This immunity appeared not to be absolute but became more solid the longer the infection remained untreated. Humoral antibodies are only partially protective, because experimental infection in humans and rabbits can be produced when they are present. On the other hand, the granulomatous lesion (gumma), a presumed correlate of cell-mediated immunity, is produced at a time when syphilitic reinfection is resisted. HIV-infected persons who have progressive dysregulation and diminution of their cellular immune status have a propensity to develop more severe disease. Likewise, malnourished patients, who also have a deficit of cellular immune function, are prone to develop more severe syphilitic disease.

T. pallidum has evolved mechanisms to evade host immune defenses and establish a chronic infection.[2, 16] In the rabbit model, testicular injection results in a steady increase in the number of treponemes that plateaus after 10 to 14 days and then rapidly declines over the next 3 to 7 days. Polymorphonuclear cells, T lymphocytes, and macrophages infiltrate the lesion, and complement, antibody, and soluble treponemicidal factors have all been demonstrated. However, sterilizing immunity does not develop. Suggested reasons for this include (1) a waxy, nonimmunogenic coat through which very few protein antigens protrude; (2) residence in nonimmunogenic privileged sites, such as the inner ear, in the eye, or in the CNS; (3) induction of markedly increased levels of prostaglandin E_2; and (4) a subpopulation of spirochetes that are resistant to phagocytosis. In contrast to uninfected rabbits, macrophages from infected rabbits respond to lipopolysaccharide but not to *T. pallidum*. This treponeme-induced macrophage downregulation is primarily caused by decreased production of interleukin-2 secondary to increased levels of prostaglandin E_2.

The likelihood of development of syphilis in a susceptible person who is exposed to a patient with infectious syphilis is about 50%. However, in controlled volunteer experiments, all volunteers without a history of serologic evidence of previous contact with *T. pallidum* developed syphilis. Obviously, the relative importance of variations in sexual and hygienic practices, immune status, inoculum size, and other factors play an important role in the transmissibility of *T. pallidum*. Congenital syphilis does not confer immunity to syphilis.[87]

SYPHILIS IN PERSONS INFECTED WITH THE HUMAN IMMUNODEFICIENCY VIRUS

Concomitant HIV disease and syphilis is common, and the two diseases can affect each other in a number of ways. They may enhance the acquisition and transmission of each other.[88] The natural course of syphilis may be affected, usually resulting in a high antigen load and a more malignant course.[89] The serologic tests for syphilis may be modified, usually resulting in extremely high titers and a failure to decrease in response to adequate treatment[53]; in other cases, a serologic response may fail to develop.[90, 91] Finally, high-dose or prolonged therapy may be required to affect a cure in co-infected persons.[92–102]

There is a strong association between HIV infection and genital ulcer disease, including syphilis. Syphilis in HIV-infected patients often manifests with a more protracted and malignant course,[89, 92–102] greater constitutional symptoms, greater organ involvement, atypical and florid skin rashes, and a significant predisposition to develop neurosyphilis, especially uveitis.[102] However, retrospective studies of patients with syphilis have shown no difference in clinical stage at presentation between those with or without concurrent HIV infection, and the response to treatment is similar. However, the failure of benzathine penicillin to cure co-infected patients has frequently been reported,[92, 102] although the actual failure rate is not known. Given the known failure rate of up to 3% in noninfected persons[73] and the critical role that an intact cellular arm of the immune system plays in clearing the infection,[16] this occurrence should not be surprising. Furthermore, the most conspicuous manifestations of these treatment failures are neurologic or ocular. Therefore, a more vigorous or more prolonged course of antibiotics (sufficient to cure neurosyphilis) is prudent (see Table 227–7).[98] There is also a good possibility that bacteriostatic drugs such as doxycycline may be less effective because of the immune impairment.

HIV-infected patients are more likely to develop aberrant serologic responses.[52, 90, 91] They may have false-positive or increasing reaginic titers despite adequate therapy, especially during the earlier phases of HIV infection, when polyclonal B-cell stimulation is most prevalent. Also, they may fail to develop a response because of an overwhelming antigen load or severe immune dysfunction occurring late in the disease. Finally, as many as 11% of HIV-infected persons have a biologic false-positive serologic test. Therefore, a high index of suspicion and extraordinary means to establish the diagnosis (e.g., special stains of biopsy specimens, PCR tests) may be required.[90, 91]

After treatment, aggressive serologic follow-up is recommended (at 1, 2, 3, 6, 9, and 12 months). Failure of a serologic response should usually lead to retreatment, but clinical judgment must be used when a patient's serologic indications of infection persist.

REFERENCES

1. Hovind-Hougen K. Morphology. In: Shell RF, Muscher DM, eds. Pathogenesis and Immunology of Treponemal Infection. New York: Marcel Dekker; 1983.
2. Blanco DR, Miller JN, Lovett MA. Surface antigens of the syphilis spirochete and their potential as virulence determinants. Emerg Infect Dis. 1997;3:11–20.
3. Jenkin HW, Sandok PL. In vitro cultivation of *Treponema pallidum*. In: Schell RF, Muscher DM, eds. Pathogenesis and Immunology of Treponemal Infection. New York: Marcel Dekker; 1983.
4. Fraser C, Norris S, Weinstock G, et al. Complete genome sequence of *Treponema pallidum,* the syphilis spiochete. Science. 1998;281:375–388.
4a. Pillay A, Liu H, Chen C, et al. Molecular subtyping of *Treponema pallidum* subspecies *pallidum.* Sex Transm Dis. 1998;25:408–414.
5. Hall V, Waisbren BA. Syphilis as a major theme of James Joyce's *Ulysses.* Arch Intern Med. 1980;140:963–965.
6. Parran T. Shadow on the Land: Syphilis. New York: Reynal & Hitchcock; 1937.
7. Baker BJ, Armelagus GJ. The origin and antiquity of syphilis. Curr Anthropol. 1988;29:703–723.
8. Waugh MA. Venereal disease in sixteenth century England. Med Hist. 1973;17:152–161.
9. Austin SC, Stolley PD, Lasky T. The history of malariotherapy for neurosyphilis. JAMA. 1992;268:516–519.
9a. Fairchild AL, Bayer R. Uses and abuses of Tuskegee. Science. 1999;284:219–221.
10. Kampmeier RH. Essentials of Syphilology. 3rd ed. Philadelphia: JB Lippincott; 1943.
11. Stokes JH, Beerman H, Ingraham NR. Modern Clinical Syphilology, Diagnosis, Treatment: Case Study. 3rd ed. Philadelphia: WB Saunders; 1945.
11a. St Louis ME, Wasserheit JN. Elimination of syphilis in the United States. Science. 1998;28:353–354.
12. Ansell DA, Hu T, Straus M, et al. HIV and syphilis seroprevalence among clients with sexually transmitted diseases attending a walk-in clinic at Cook County Hospital. Sex Transm Dis. 1993;21:93–97.
13. Jones DL, Irwin K, Inciardi J, et al. The high-risk sexual practices of crack-smoking sex workers recruited from the streets of three American cities. Sex Transm Dis. 1998;25:187–193.
14. Lukehart S, Hook EW, Baker-Zander SH, et al. Invasion of the central nervous system by *Treponema pallidum*: Implications for diagnosis and therapy. Ann Intern Med. 1988;109:855–862.
15. Magnuson HJ, Thomas EW, Olansky S, et al. Inoculation syphilis in human volunteers. Medicine (Baltimore). 1956;35:33–42.
16. Fitzgerald TJ. The Th_1/Th_2 switch in syphilitic infection: Is it detrimental? Infect Immun. 1992;60:3475–3479.
17. Norgard MV, Riley SB, Richardson JA, et al. Dermal inflammation elicited by synthetic analogs of *Treponema pallidum* and *Borrelia burgdorferi* lipoproteins. Infect Immun. 1995;63:1507–1515.
18. Shevchenko DV, Sellati T, Cox D, et al. Membrane topology and cellular location of the *Treponema pallidum* glycerophosphodiester phosphodiesterase (GlpQ) ortholog. Infect Immun. 1999;67:2266–2276.
19. Lukehart SA, Shaffer JM, BakerZander SA. A subpopulation of *Treponema pallidum* is resistant to phagocytosis: Possible mechanism of persistence. J Infect Dis. 1992;166:1449–1453.
20. O'Regan S, Fong JSC, de Chadarevian JP, et al. Treponemal antigens in congenital and acquired syphilitic nephritis. Ann Intern Med. 1976;85:325–327.
21. Clark EG, Danbolt N. The Oslo study of the natural course of untreated syphilis. Med Clin North Am. 1964;48:613–621.
22. Rockwell DH, Yobs AR, Moore MB. The Tuskeegee study of untreated syphilis: The 30th year of observation. Arch Intern Med. 1964;114:792.
23. Rosahn PD. Autopsy Studies in Syphilis. J Vener Dis 1947;649(Suppl 21).
24. Drusin LM, Topf-Olstein B, Levy-Zombeck E. Epidemiology of infectious syphilis at a tertiary hospital. Arch Intern Med. 1979;135:901–904.
25. Long BW, Johnston JH, Wetzel W, et al. Gastric syphilis: Endoscopic and histiologic features mimicking lymphoma. Am J Gastroenterol. 1995;90:1504–1507.
26. Chapel TA. The variability of syphilitic chancres. Sex Transm Dis. 1978;5:68–72.
27. Chapel TA. The signs and symptoms of secondary syphilis. Sex Transm Dis. 1980;7:161–167.
28. Merritt HH, Moore M. Acute neurosyphilitic meningitis. Medicine (Baltimore). 1935;14:119.
29. Atten MJ, Attar BM, Teopengo E, et al. Gastric syphilis: A disease with multiple manifestations. Am J Gastroenterol. 1994;89:2227–2229.
30. Ross WH, Sutton HF. Acquired syphilitic uveitis. Arch Ophthalmol. 1980;98:496.
31. Hansen K, Hvid-Jacobson H, Lindewald PS, et al. Bone lesions in early syphilis detected by bone scintigraphy. Br J Vener Dis. 1984;60:256–258.
32. Merritt HH, Adams RD, Solomon HC. Neurosyphilis. New York: Oxford University Press; 1946.
33. VanEijk RVW, Wolters EC, Tutuarima JA, et al. Effect of early and late syphilis on central nervous system: Cerebrospinal fluid changes and neurologic deficit. Genitourin Med. 1987;63:77–82.
34. Lugar A, Schmidt BL, Steyer K, et al. Diagnosis of neurosyphilis by examination of the cerebrospinal fluid. Br J Vener Dis. 1981;57:232–237.
35. Muller F, Moskophidis M. Estimation of the local production of antibodies to *Treponema pallidum* in the central nervous system of patients with neurosyphilis. Br J Vener Dis. 1983;59:80–84.
36. Chesney AM, Kemp I. Incidence of *Spirochetea pallida* in cerebrospinal fluid during early stages of syphilis. JAMA. 1924;83:1725–1733.
37. Kelley RE, Bell L, Kelley SE, et al. Syphilis detection in cerebrovascular disease. Stroke. 1989;20:230–234.
38. Hotson JR. Modern neurosyphilis: A partially treated chronic meningitis. West J Med. 1981;135:191–195.
39. Balkany TJ, Dans PE. Reversible sudden deafness in early acquired syphilis. Arch Otolaryngol. 1978;104:60.
40. Wilson WR, Zoller M. Electronystagmography in congenital and acquired syphilis otitis. Ann Otol. 1981;90:21.
41. Sanchez PJ, Wendel GD, Grimprel E, et al. Evaluation of molecular methodologies and rabbit infectivity testing for the diagnosis of congenital syphilis and neonatal central nervous system invasion by *Treponema pallidum.* J Infect Dis. 1993;167:168–177.
42. Tramont EC. Neurosyphilis in patients with human immunodeficiency virus infection. N Engl J Med. 1994;332:1169–1170.
43. Inagaki H, Kawai T, Miyata M, et al. Polymerase chain reaction detection of treponemal DNA in pseudolymphomatous lesions. Hum Pathol. 1996;27:761–765.
44. Parker CR, Wendel GD. The effects of syphilis on endocrine function of the fetoplacental unit. Am J Dis Gynecol. 1988;159:1327–1331.
45. Dorfman DH, Glaser JH. Congenital syphilis presenting in infants after the newborn period. N Engl J Med. 1990;323:1299–1301.
46. Fojaco RM, Hensley GT, Moskowitz L. Congenital syphilis and necrotizing funisitis. JAMA. 1989;261:788–790.
47. Stoll BJ, Lee FK, Larsen S, et al. Clinical and serologic evaluation of neonates for congenital syphilis: A continuing diagnostic dilemma. J Infect Dis. 1993;167:1093–1099.
48. Rawstron SA, Vetrano J, Tannis G, et al. Congenital syphilis: Detection of *Treponema pallidum* in still-borns. Clin Infect Dis. 1997;24:24–27.
49. Bromberg K, Rawstron S, Tannis G. Diagnosis of congenital syphilis by combining *Treponema pallidum specific* IgM detection with immunofluorescent antigen detection for *T. pallidum.* J Infect Dis. 1993;168:238–242.
50. Al-Samarrai HT, Henderson WG. Immunofluorescent staining of *Treponema pallidum* and *Treponema pertenue* in tissues fixed by formalin and embedded in paraffin wax. Br J Vener Dis. 1977;53:1.
51. Beckett JH, Bigbee MA. Immunoperoxidase localization of *Treponema pallidum.* Arch Pathol Lab Med. 1979;103:135.
51a. Muic V, Ljubicic M, Vodopija I. Bayes' theorem-based assessment of VDRL syphilis screening miss rates. Sex Transm Dis. 1999;26:12–15.
52. Berkowitz K, Baxi L, Fox HE. False-negative syphilis screening: The prozone phenomenon, nonimmune hydrops, and diagnosis of syphilis during pregnancy. Am J Obstet Gynecol. 1990;163:975–977.
53. Hutchinson CM, Rompalo AM, Reochart CA, et al. Characteristics of syphilis in patients attending Baltimore STD clinics: Multiple bugle risk sub groups and interactions with HIV infection. Arch Intern Med. 1991;151:511–516.
54. Brown ST, Akbar Z, Larsen SA, et al. Serological response to syphilis treatment. JAMA. 1985;253:1296–1299.
55. Fiumara NJ. Treatment of primary and secondary syphilis: Serological response. JAMA. 1980;243:2500–2503.
56. Fiumara NJ. Serologic responses to treatment of 128 patients with late latent syphilis. Sex Transm Dis. 1979;6:243–246.
57. Fiumara NJ. Reinfection primary, secondary, and latent syphilis. Sex Transm Dis. 1980;7:111–114.
58. Burton AA, Flynn JA, Neumann TM, et al. Routine serologic screening for syphilis in hospitalized patients: High prevalence of unsuspected infection in the elderly. Sex Transm Dis. 1994;21:133–136.
59. Tomberlin MG, Holtom PD, Owens JL, et al. Evaluation of neurosyphilis in human immunodeficiency virus-infected individuals. Clin Infect Dis. 1994;18:288–294.
60. Prange HW, Moskophidis M, Schipper HI, et al. Relationship between neurological features and intrathecal synthesis of IgG antibodies to *Treponema pallidum* in untreated and treated human neurosyphilis. J Neurol. 1983;230:241–252.
60a. Birdsall HH, Baughn RE, Jenkins HA. The diagnostic dilemma of otosyphilis, a new Western Blot Assay. Arch Otolaryngol Head Neck Surg. 1990;116:617–621.

61. Tuffanelli DL, Wuepper KO, Bradford LL. Fluorescent treponemal antibody absorption tests: Studies of false-positive reactions to tests for syphilis. N Engl J Med. 1967;276:258.
62. Idsoe O, Guthe T, Wilcox RR. Penicillin in the treatment of syphilis: The experience of three decades. Bull World Health Organ. 1972;47(Suppl):1.
63. Syphilotherapy, 1976. Sex Transm Dis. 1976;3:98.
64. Tramont EC. Persistence of *Treponema pallidum* following penicillin G therapy. JAMA. 1976;236:2206–2209.
65. Mascola L, Pelosi R, Alexander CE. Inadequate treatment of syphilis in pregnancy. Am J Obstet Gynecol. 1984;150:945–947.
66. Mohr JA, Griffiths W, Jackson R, et al. Neurosyphilis and penicillin levels in cerebrospinal fluid. JAMA. 1976;236:2208.
67. Moskovitz BL, Klimek JJ, Goldman RL, et al. Meningovascular syphilis after "appropriate" treatment of primary syphilis. Arch Intern Med. 1982;142:139–141.
68. Markovitz PM, Bentner KR, Maggio RP, et al. Failure of recommended treatment for secondary syphilis. JAMA. 1986;255:1767–1768.
69. Short DH, Knox JM, Glicksman J. Neurosyphilis: The search for adequate treatment. Arch Dermatol. 1966;93:87–91.
70. Gordon SM, Eaton ME, George R. The response of symptomatic neurosyphilis to high-dose intravenous penicillin G in patients with human immundodeficiency virus infection. N Engl J Med. 1994;331:1469–1473.
71. Savall R, Valls F, Cabre M. Syphilis and HIV infection. Genitourin Med. 1991;67:353–355.
72. Donders GG, Desmyter J, Hoft P, et al. Apparent failure of one injection of benzathine penicillin G for syphilis during pregnancy in human immunodeficiency virus-seronegative African women. Sex Transm Dis. 1997;24:94–101.
73. Schroeter AL, Lucas JB, Price EV, et al. Treatment for early syphilis and reactivity of serologic tests. JAMA. 1972;221:471–476.
74. Wendel GD Jr, Stark BJ, Jamison RB, et al. Penicillin allergy and desensitization in serious infections during pregnancy. N Engl J Med. 1985;312:1229–1232.
75. Dowell ME, Ross PG, Musler DM, et al. Response of latent syphilis or neurosyphilis to ceftriaxone therapy in persons infected with HIV. Am J Med. 1992;481:481–488.
76. McCracken GH, Ginsburg C, Crane DF, et al. Clinical phenomenology of penicillin in newborn infants. J Pediatr. 1973;82:692.
77. Speer ME, Taber LH, Clark DB, et al. Cerebrospinal fluid levels of benzathine penicillin G in the neonate. J Pediatr. 1977;91:996.
78. Giles AJH. Tabes dorsalis progressing to general paresis after 20 years despite routine penicillin therapy. Br J Vener Dis. 1980;56:368.
79. Morrison E, Harrison S, Tramont EC. Oral amoxicillin, an alternative treatment of neurosyphilis. Genitourin Med. 1985;61:359–362.
80. Rolfs RT, Joesorf MR, Hendershot EF, et al. A randomized trial of enhanced therapy for early syphilis in patients with and without human immunodeficiency virus infection. N Engl J Med. 1997;337:307–314.
81. Yim CW, Flynn NM, Fitzgerald FT. Penetration of oral doxycycline into the cerebrospinal fluid of patients with latent or neurosyphilis. Antimicrob Agents Chemother. 1985;28:347–348.
82. Zoller M, Wilson WR, Nodal JB. Treatment of syphilitic hearing loss. Ann Otol. 1979;88:160.
83. Smith JL. Spirochetes in Late Seronegative Syphilis, Penicillin Notwithstanding. Springfield, IL: Charles C Thomas; 1969.
84. Mack LW, Smith JL, Walter ER, et al. Temporal bone treponemes. Arch Otolaryngol. 1969;90:11.
85. Young EJ, Weingarten NM, Baughn RE, et al. Studies on the pathogenesis of the Jarisch-Herxheimer reaction. J Infect Dis. 1982;146:606.
86. Klein VR, Cox SM, Mitchell MD, et al. The Jarisch-Herxheimer reaction complicating syphilotherapy in pregnancy. Obstet Gynecol. 1990;75:375–380.
87. Fiumara NJ. Acquired syphilis in three patients with congenital syphilis. N Engl J Med. 1974;290:1119.
88. Theus SA, Harrich DA, Gaynor R, et al. *Treponema pallidum,* lipoproteins, and synthetic lipoprotein analogues induce human immunodeficiency virus type 1 gene expression in monocytes via NFkB activation. J Infect Dis. 1998;177:941–950.
89. Don P C, Rubinstein R, Christie S. Malignant syphilis (lues maligna) and concurrent infection with HIV. Int J Dermatol. 1995;34:403–407.
90. Hicks CB, Benson PM, Lupton GP, et al. Seronegative secondary syphilis in a patient infected with the human immunodeficiency virus (HIV) with Kaposi sarcoma. Ann Intern Med. 1987;107:492–495.
91. Tikjob G, Russel M, Petersen CS, et al. Seronegative secondary syphilis in a patient with AIDS: Identification of *Treponema pallidum* in biopsy specimen. J Am Acad Dermatol. 1991;24:506–508.
92. Flood JM, Weinstock HS, Guroy ME. Neurosyphilis during the AIDS epidemic, San Francisco, 1985–1992. J Infect Dis. 1998;177:931–940.
93. Holtom PD, Larsen RA, Leal MA. Prevalence of neurosyphilis in immunodeficiency virus infection. J Infect Dis. 1992;165:1020–1025.
94. Kastner RJ, Malone JL, Decker CF. Syphilitic osteitis in a patient with secondary syphilis and concurrent human immunodeficiency virus infection. Clin Infect Dis. 1994;18:250–252.
95. Johns DR, Tierney M, Felsenstein D. Alternation in the natural history of neurosyphilis by concurrent infections with human immunodeficiency virus. N Engl J Med. 1987;316:1569–1572.
96. Horowitz HW, Valsamis MP, Wicher V, et al. Brief report: Cerebral syphilitic gumma confirmed by the polymerase chain reaction in man with human immunodeficiency virus infection. N Engl J Med. 1994;331:1488–1491.
97. Berger JR. Spinal cord syphilis associated with human immunodeficiency virus infection: A treatable myelopathy. Am J Med. 1992;92:101–103.
98. Tramont EC. Syphilis in adults: From Christopher Columbus to Sir Alexander Fleming to AIDS. Clin Infect Dis. 1995;21:1361–1371.
99. Zaidman GW. Neurosyphilis and retrobulbar neuritis in a patient with AIDS. Ann Ophthalmol. 1986;18:260.
100. Kamling RT, Villaobos R, Latina M. Recurrent syphilitic uveitis. N Engl J Med. 1989;320:62.
101. Tomberlin MG, Holton PD, Owens JL, et al. Evaluation of neurosyphilis in human immunodeficiency virus-infected individuals. Clin Infect Dis. 1994;18:288–294.
102. Berry CD, Hooton TM, Collier AC, et al. Neurologic relapse after benzathine penicillin therapy for secondary syphilis in a patient with HIV infection. N Engl J Med. 1987;316:1587–1589.

Chapter 228

Treponema Species (Yaws, Pinta, Bejel)

JEFFREY D. CHULAY

The nonvenereal treponematoses are a group of contagious diseases endemic among rural populations in tropical and subtropical countries. All are caused by bacteria that are transmitted primarily by direct contact among children living in unhygienic conditions. The causative organisms are morphologically identical and antigenically indistinguishable,[1] but differences in clinical manifestations allow the separation of three distinct entities (Table 228–1). Pinta is characterized by skin lesions only; yaws, by skin and bone lesions; and bejel (endemic syphilis), by mucous membrane, skin, and bone lesions. Like venereal syphilis, all three are characterized by self-limited primary and secondary lesions, a latent period without clinically detectable disease, and late lesions that are frequently destructive. Congenital infection is rarely seen, presumably because primary infection usually occurs before the childbearing years. All three diseases result in host serologic responses indistinguishable from one another and from those of venereal syphilis. Some degree of protective immunity mediated by both antibody[2] and immune T cells[3] develops with prolonged infection. In animal models[4, 5] and human challenge studies,[6, 7] this protection extends to heterologous treponemal species. This may explain the increasing incidence of venereal syphilis in some regions where yaws has been reduced to very low levels.[8] Although the transmission of the endemic treponematoses can be diminished by improvements in personal hygiene and general living standards, the introduction of penicillin, to which all these organisms are exquisitely sensitive, has had a dramatic influence on reducing the incidence of these diseases.

DESCRIPTION OF THE PATHOGENS

The genus *Treponema* consists of at least 13 species, among which *Treponema pallidum* (three subspecies) and *Treponema carateum* cause disease in humans.[9] These human pathogens are morphologically indistinguishable and appear as motile tightly coiled helical rods under the dark-field microscope. Their average diameter is 0.13 to 0.15 μm, and their average length is 10 to 13 μm.

Because the treponemes that infect humans cannot be continuously cultivated in vitro, their classification rests on differences in host species susceptibility and in the disease manifestations produced in these hosts. *T. pallidum* subsp. *pallidum*, the most virulent human pathogen, causes venereal syphilis in humans (see Chapter 227) and produces indurated cutaneous and testicular lesions without periorchitis in rabbits. *T. carateum*, the etiologic agent of pinta, is able to infect only humans and chimpanzees. *Treponema pallidum* subsp. *pertenue* causes human yaws and produces periorchitis with nonindurated testicular and cutaneous lesions in rabbits. *T. pallidum* subsp. *endemicum* produces disease in rabbits that is intermediate between that of the syphilis and yaws treponemes. Complicating the classifi-

TABLE 228–1 Differentiation of the Treponematoses

Characteristic	Venereal Syphilis	Yaws	Pinta	Bejel
Causative organism	*Treponema pallidum* subsp. *pallidum*	*Treponema pallidum* subsp. *pertenue*	*Treponema carateum*	*Treponema pallidum* subsp. *endemicum*
Usual mode of transmission	Sexual; congenital	Skin-to-skin	Skin-to-skin	Mouth-to-mouth; via utensils
Geographic distribution	Cosmopolitan	Warm, humid tropics	Warm, arid tropical Americas	Arid subtropical or temperate zones
Usual age of onset	Adolescent–adult	Childhood	Childhood	Childhood
Primary lesions	Genital chancre	Papillomatous skin lesions	Papulosquamous skin lesions	Oral mucous lesions (rarely seen)
Secondary lesions	Maculopapular skin lesions; condylomata lata; mucous patches	Papillomatous skin lesions; periostitis	Dyschromic papulosquamous skin lesions	Mucous patches; split papules; condylomata lata
Late lesions	Aortitis; neurosyphilis; gummas of skin, bone, and viscera	Destructive skin lesions, hyperkeratoses; gummas of bone and skin	Achromic macular skin lesions	Gummas of bone and skin

cation of these organisms is the fact that with serial passage in rabbits or hamsters there may be a change in the pattern of disease produced.[4, 10]

YAWS

History

There is evidence that yaws has probably existed in Africa since prehistoric times, when environmental conditions favored its evolution from pinta.[11] It was introduced into the Western Hemisphere by African slaves in the 16th century. Synonyms of the disease include pian, bouba, and frambesia (from the raspberry-like appearance of papillomatous lesions). Castellani identified *T. pallidum* subsp. *pertenue* in yaws lesions shortly after Schaudinn and Hoffman's discovery of *T. pallidum* subsp. *pallidum* in 1905. The advent of long-acting penicillin therapy made possible the World Health Organization–sponsored mass treatment campaigns that have dramatically reduced the prevalence of this disease.

Epidemiology and Pathogenesis

Yaws occurs among rural populations in warm, humid, tropical areas of Africa, South America, Southeast Asia, and Oceania (Fig. 228–1).

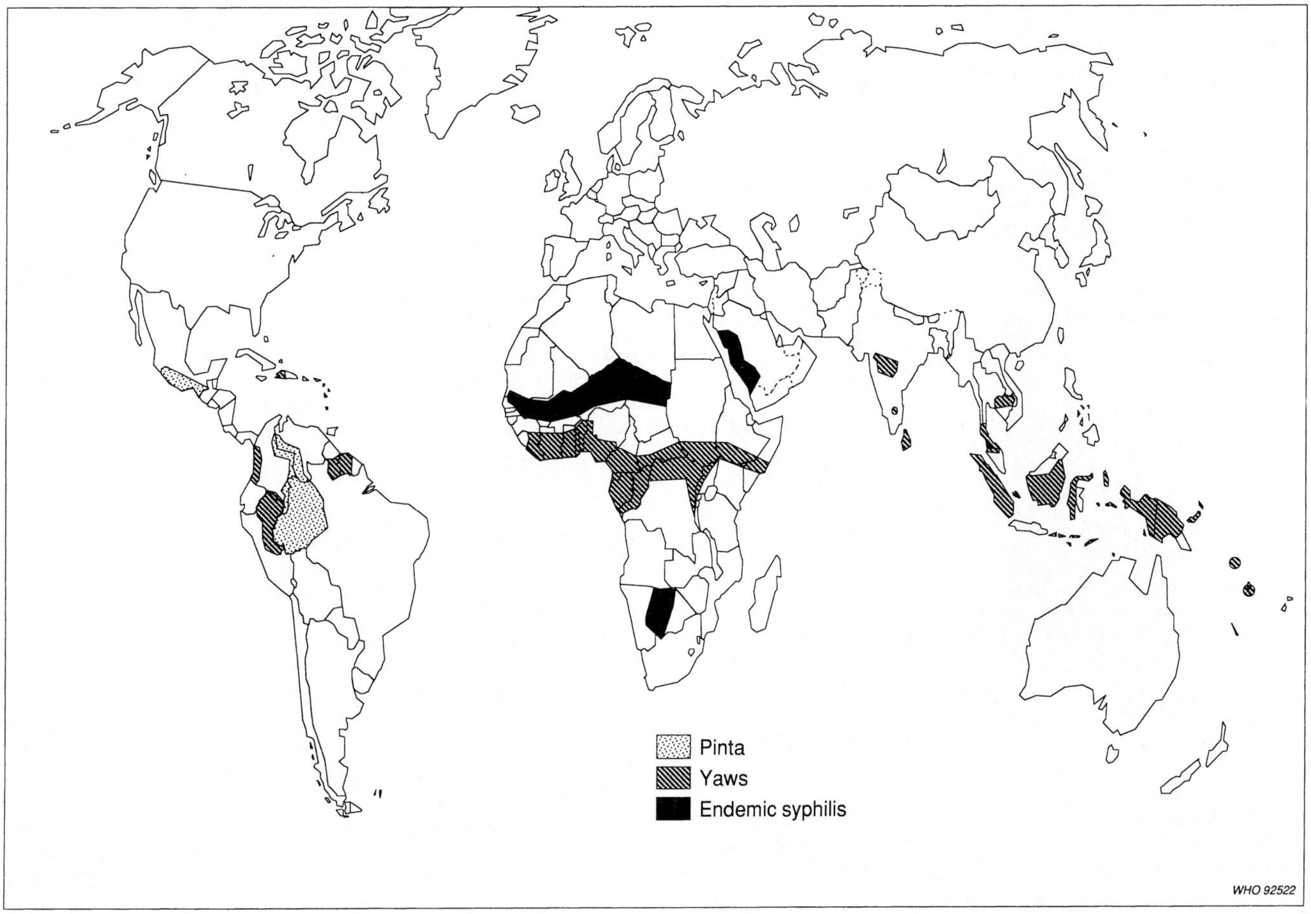

FIGURE 228–1. Geographic distribution of the nonvenereal treponematoses. (From Meheus A, Antal GM. The endemic treponematoses: Not yet eradicated. World Health Organ Stat Q. 1992;45:230.)

The number of persons infected, estimated at 50 to 100 million in the 1950s, was reduced by mass treatment campaigns to fewer than 2 million in the mid-1970s.[12] In the Western Hemisphere, yaws now occurs only sporadically in small regions of Colombia, Guyana, Surinam, and Haiti, with fewer than 500 cases reported annually in the 1980s.[13] However, there has been a resurgence of yaws in West Africa, with thousands of cases occurring each year in Côte d'Ivoire, Togo, Ghana, Benin, and Cameroon. Areas of intensive transmission also continue to occur in parts of Indonesia, Papua New Guinea, and the Solomon Islands.[13]

Transmission occurs when traumatized skin comes in contact with infectious exudate from active yaws lesions. New cases occur more frequently during the rainy season, and primary infection is usually acquired before puberty. Blood stream invasion shortly after the initial infection leads to subsequent involvement of bone, lymph nodes, and distant skin sites. Histopathologic changes in skin lesions consist of granulomatous inflammation indistinguishable from that seen in pinta or syphilis,[14] with endarteritis common in late lesions. Treponemes, numerous in early skin lesions, are rarely found in bone or late skin lesions.

Clinical Manifestations

After an incubation period of 3 to 5 weeks, early lesions usually appear on the extremities, especially the legs. These are characterized by papules that enlarge and become papillomatous with superficial erosion (Fig. 228–2) and then heal spontaneously within 6 months.[15] Weeks to months later, a generalized eruption of similar lesions occurs (Fig. 228–3), although macular and squamous lesions may also be seen. Multiple relapses of these secondary lesions may occur during the first 5 years and are often associated with lymphadenopathy. Osteitis and periostitis can occur during the secondary stage and may involve the fingers (polydactylitis), long bones (saber tibia), or paranasal maxillae (goundou). Early lesions do not ulcerate unless they become secondarily infected. In some areas, yaws appears to have become attenuated, with primary and secondary lesions characterized by dry papillomas and scaling macules.[16]

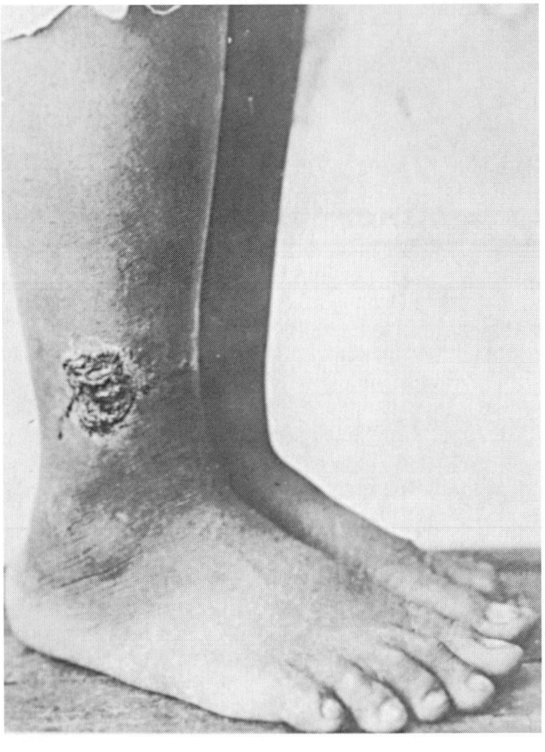

FIGURE 228–2. Primary lesion of yaws (AFIP 39207). (Courtesy of Dr. D. H. Connor, Armed Forces Institute of Pathology, Washington, DC.)

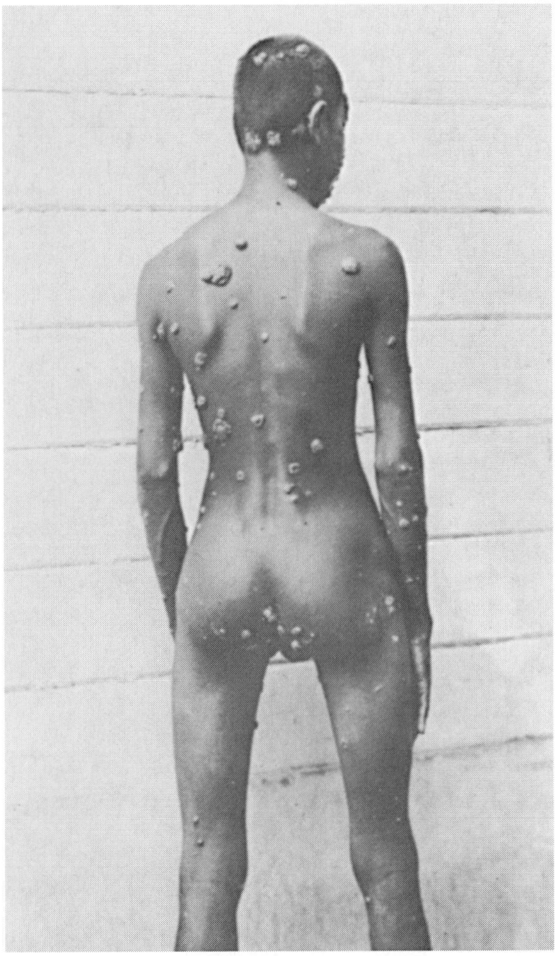

FIGURE 228–3. Disseminated papillomatous nodules in secondary yaws (AFIP 39205). (Courtesy of Dr. D. H. Connor, Armed Forces Institute of Pathology, Washington, DC.)

The late stage of yaws is characterized by cutaneous plaques, nodules and ulcers, hyperkeratoses of the palms and soles, and gummatous lesions involving the skull, sternum, tibia, or other bones. Ulceration of the skin overlying bone lesions is common, and gummatous erosion of nasopharyngeal structures (gangosa) similar to that seen with venereal syphilis occurs occasionally.

Diagnosis

Yaws should be suspected in persons with chronic skin or bone lesions who have resided in tropical areas where transmission of *T. palladum* subsp. *pertenue* occurs (see Fig. 228–1). The diagnosis of yaws can be confirmed by dark-field microscopic examination or fluorescent antibody staining of exudates from cutaneous lesions.[17] In latent yaws, or when treponemes cannot be found, a presumptive diagnosis can be made if cardiolipin (Venereal Disease Research Laboratory, rapid plasma reagin) or treponemal (fluorescent treponemal antibody absorption, microhemagglutination test for *T. pallidum*) antibodies are present (see Chapter 227). Depending on their stage and appearance, the lesions of yaws must be differentiated from pyoderma, tropical ulcer, sickle cell anemia, cutaneous leishmaniasis, blastomycosis, leprosy, and tuberculosis[18] as well as from the other treponematoses.

Prevention and Treatment

Yaws responds rapidly to treatment with a single injection of benzathine penicillin G in doses of 1.2 million units for persons aged 10 years and older and 600,000 units for younger children.[19] Although hyperkeratoses may require several months to heal, early lesions usually heal within 1 to 2 weeks, and relapse is rare. In patients unable to receive penicillin, tetracycline or chloramphenicol at a dose of 25 mg/kg/day for 10 to 14 days has also been effective.[20] As with syphilis, conversion of seroreactivity occurs most often in patients treated in the early stages of disease. Transmission of the disease can be interrupted by treating contacts and latent cases with penicillin at the doses recommended earlier.[19]

PINTA

History

Pinta (Spanish "blemish"), also known as mal de pinto (Spanish "to paint") or carate, is probably the oldest human treponematosis.[11] Although it was recognized as early as 1926 that most patients with pinta had Wassermann's antibodies, it was not until the identification in 1938 of *T. carateum* from pinta lesions that its treponemal cause was firmly established.

Epidemiology and Pathogenesis

Pinta occurs only in remote rural areas of southern Mexico, Central America, and Colombia, most commonly in arid inland regions (see Fig. 228–1). Only a few hundred cases have been reported in each of the past several years, a marked reduction from the estimate of 750,000 made in 1976.[12] Transmission appears to occur only through contact of broken skin with infectious lesions,[7] after which the organisms multiply locally and spread via the blood stream and lymphatics.

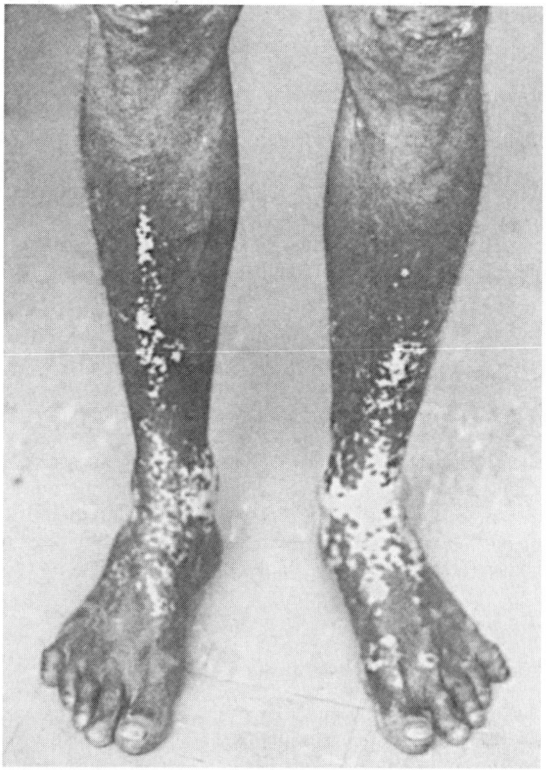

FIGURE 228–5. Achromic lesions of late pinta.

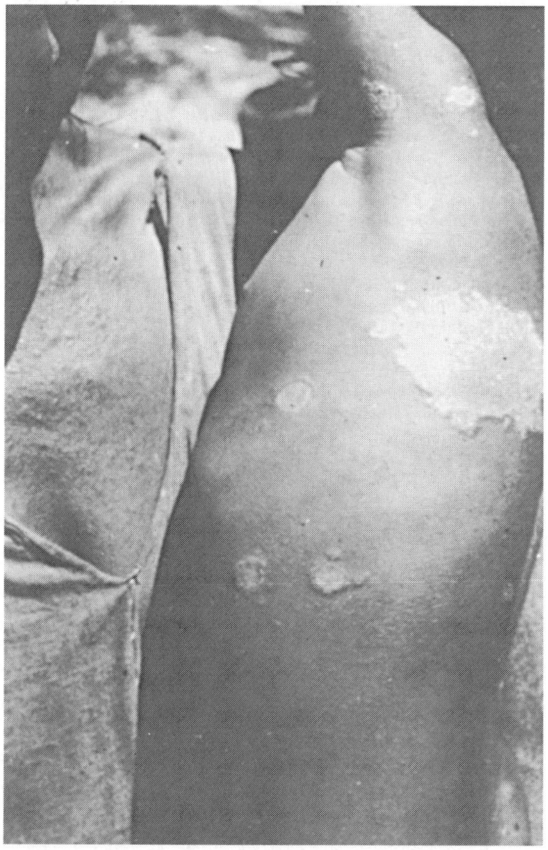

FIGURE 228–4. Large primary and smaller secondary lesions of pinta (AFIP 75-5536-2). (Courtesy of Dr. D. H. Connor, Armed Forces Institute of Pathology, Washington, DC.)

Clinical Manifestations

After an average incubation period of 7 to 21 days,[7] the initial lesions begin as small, erythematous, pruritic papules on the extremities, face, neck, chest, or abdomen.[21] These enlarge, become slightly squamous, and coalesce with surrounding lesions. Primary lesions may persist for several years before healing with residual hypopigmentation. Disseminated lesions (pintids) appear 3 to 12 months after the initial lesions, usually as small scaly papules involving the same sites as the primary lesions (Fig. 228–4). These secondary lesions, and occasionally primary lesions, may develop into dyschromic brown, gray, or blue lesions, especially when located on the face. Pintids may recur up to 10 years into the course of the disease, often in patients with late lesions. The late stage of pinta is characterized by depigmented (achromic) lesions, frequently involving the wrists, elbows, and ankles (Fig. 228–5). Although pinta does not impair general health or affect longevity, the cosmetic disfigurement frequently results in social ostracism.

Diagnosis

Pinta should be suspected in persons with papulosquamous or abnormally pigmented skin lesions who have resided in remote areas of tropical Latin America (see Fig. 228–1). Except for late achromic lesions, treponemes can usually be demonstrated by dark-field microscopy of fluid from the lesions. Serologic tests (Venereal Disease Research Laboratory, fluorescent treponemal antibody absorption) do not become positive until after the appearance of secondary lesions[7] and then usually remain positive for life. Differential diagnosis includes neurodermatitis, tinea versicolor, chloasma, and vitiligo.

Prevention and Treatment

A single 1.2 million–unit dose of long-acting penicillin G is the treatment of choice.[22] The response to treatment varies depending on the stage of disease. Primary and early secondary lesions heal in 4 to 6 months, whereas late secondary lesions require 6 to 12 months to heal. Leukodermic patches remain at the site of dyschromic and hypochromic lesions, and achromic lesions usually show no improvement. Tetracycline or chloramphenicol in doses as for yaws may be used to treat patients allergic to penicillin. Treatment of latent as well as active cases is important to prevent further transmission of the disease.

BEJEL (ENDEMIC SYPHILIS)

History

It has been known for centuries that a syphilis-like disease could be spread by nonvenereal means. Sibbens in Scotland and radesyge in Norway are of historic interest, and dichuchwa in South Africa, njovera in Zimbabwe, skerljevo in Bosnia, and bejel in Syria are local names for more recent examples of this endemic form of syphilis.

Epidemiology and Pathogenesis

Bejel has a focal distribution in Africa and western Asia (see Fig. 228–1). The disease affects primarily children and, like pinta and yaws, occurs only among rural populations with poor standards of living and personal hygiene.[23] In addition to person-to-person spread, transmission is frequently effected via common drinking and eating utensils, with mucosal inoculation felt to be the most common route of infection. The causative organism is *T. pallidum* subsp. *endemicum*.

Clinical Manifestations

The primary lesion is rarely observed, probably because of the small size and oral location of the usual infecting inoculum.[24] Secondary lesions consist of oropharyngeal mucous patches, split papules at the corners of the mouth, condylomata lata, periostitis, and regional lymphadenopathy. Late manifestations, which are clinically apparent more often than are early lesions, include gummatous lesions of the skin, nasopharynx, and bones. Gummas of the breast may be seen in mothers nursing infected infants. Cardiovascular and neurologic lesions are uncommon. As with the other nonvenereal treponematoses, the rarity of congenital disease is probably due to the childhood onset of primary infection in virtually all cases, so blood stream infection does not occur during pregnancy.

Diagnosis

Bejel should be suspected in persons with chronic skin or bone lesions who have lived in endemic areas (see Fig. 228–1). As with the other treponematoses, diagnosis depends on dark-field examination and serologic tests. Because the clinical manifestations and serologic results are often indistinguishable from those of yaws or venereal syphilis, the epidemiologic setting is vital in differentiation among these diseases.

Prevention and Treatment

A single 1.2 million–unit dose of long-acting penicillin G is the treatment of choice for both infected patients and their contacts. The Bosnia experience—where a vigorous mass treatment campaign coupled with the development of efficient health services and concomitant improvements in socioeconomic conditions resulted in the complete interruption of transmission of endemic syphilis[25]—offers hope that with a similar approach the nonvenereal treponematoses may eventually be eradicated elsewhere.

REFERENCES

1. Noordhoek GT, Cockayne A, Schouls LM, et al. A new attempt to distinguish serologically the subspecies of *Treponema pallidum* causing syphilis and yaws. J Clin Microbiol. 1990;28:1600.
2. Azadegan AA, Schell RF, Steiner BM, et al. Effect of immune serum and its immunoglobulin fractions on hamsters challenged with *Treponema pallidum* ssp. *pertenue*. J Infect Dis. 1986;153:1007.
3. Liu H, Steiner BM, Alder JD, et al. Immune T cells sorted by flow cytometry confer protection against infection with *Treponema pallidum* subsp. *pertenue* in hamsters. Infect Immun. 1990;58:1685.
4. Turner TB, Hollander DW. Biology of the Treponematoses. WHO Monograph Series No. 35, Geneva, 1957.
5. Schell RF, Azadegan AA, Nitskansky SG, et al. Acquired resistance of hamsters to challenge with homologous and heterologous virulent treponemes. Infect Immun. 1982;37:617.
6. Turner T. The resistance of yaws and syphilis patients to reinoculation with yaws spirochetes. Am J Hyg. 1936;23:431.
7. Leon Blanco F. Experimental pinta. In: Recent Advances in the Study of Venereal Diseases. A Symposium. Raleigh, NC: Venereal Diseases Education Institute; 1948:275.
8. Willcox RR. Changing patterns of treponemal disease. Br J Vener Dis. 1974;50:169.
9. Smibert RM. Genus *Treponema Schaudinn* 1905, 1728. In: Krieg NR, Holt JG, eds. Bergey's Manual of Systematic Bacteriology. Baltimore: Williams & Wilkins; 1984:49.
10. Treponematosis Research. Report of a WHO Scientific Group, WHO Technical Report Series No. 455, 1970.
11. Hackett CJ. On the origin of the human treponematoses. Bull WHO. 1963;29:7.
12. Hopkins DR. After smallpox eradication: Yaws? Am J Trop Med Hyg. 1976;25:860.
13. Meheus A, Antal GM. The endemic treponematoses: Not yet eradicated. WHO Stat Q. 1992;45:228.
14. Dooley JR, Binford CH. Treponematoses. In: Binford CH, Connor DH, eds. Pathology of Tropical and Extraordinary Diseases, v. 1. Washington, DC: Armed Forces Institute of Pathology; 1976:110.
15. Hackett CJ. An International Nomenclature of Yaws Lesions. WHO Monograph Series No. 36, 1957.
16. Vorst FA. Clinical diagnosis and changing manifestations of treponemal infection. Rev Infect Dis. 1985;7(Suppl 2):327.
17. Perine PL, Nelson JW, Lewis JO, et al. New technologies for use in the surveillance and control of yaws. Rev Infect Dis. 1985;7(Suppl 2):295.
18. Hackett CJ, Loewenthal LJA. Differential Diagnosis of Yaws. WHO Monograph Series No. 45, Geneva, 1960.
19. Treponemial Infections. Report of a WHO Scientific Group, WHO Technical Report Series No. 674, Geneva, 1982.
20. Brown ST. Therapy for nonvenereal treponematoses: Review of the efficacy of penicillin and consideration of alternatives. Rev Infect Dis. 1985;7(Suppl 2):318.
21. Marquez F, Rein CR, Arias O. Mal de pinto in Mexico. Bull WHO. 1955;13:299.
22. Rein CR, Kitchen DK, Marquez F, et al. Repository penicillin therapy of pinta in the Mexican peasant. J Invest Dermatol. 1953;18:137.
23. Csonka G, Pace J. Endemic nonvenereal treponematosis (bejel) in Saudi Arabia. Rev Infect Dis. 1985;7(Suppl 2):260.
24. Grin EI. Epidemiology and Control of Endemic Syphilis. Report on a Mass-treatment Campaign in Bosnia. WHO Monograph Series No. 11, Geneva, 1953.
25. Grin EI, Guthe T. Evaluation of a previous mass campaign against endemic syphilis in Bosnia and Herzogovina. Br J Vener Dis. 1973;49:1.

Chapter 229

Leptospira Species (Leptospirosis)

JORDAN W. TAPPERO
DAVID A. ASHFORD
BRADLEY A. PERKINS

Leptospirosis is a zoonotic disease of worldwide distribution caused by spirochetes of the genus *Leptospira*.[1–3] Leptospires infect a variety of wild and domestic animals that excrete the organism in their urine. Humans, infected through direct contact with infected animals or through exposure to fresh water or soil contaminated by infected animal urine, develop an acute febrile illness that can be followed by a more severe, sometimes fatal illness that may include jaundice and renal failure (Weil's disease), meningitis, myocarditis, hemorrhagic pneumonitis, or hemodynamic collapse.

HISTORY

With the exception of Weil's disease, a well-defined clinical entity described in 1886, leptospirosis was most often misdiagnosed as yellow fever and malaria until its spirochetal cause was discovered by culture in 1914.[4] Confusion with dengue fever, yellow fever, hepatitis, malaria, influenza, and other causes of acute febrile illness persists even today. Between 1914 and 1940, the cause of a number of diseases was discovered to be *Leptospira* spp. These diseases included autumnal fever and seven-day fever in Japan, canefield fever in Australia, swineherd's disease, swamp or mud fever in Europe, and Fort Bragg fever in the United States.[5, 6]

ETIOLOGY

Leptospires are thin, flexible, finely coiled, gram-negative bacteria 0.1 μm in diameter, 6 to 12 μm in length,[7] with a coil amplitude of 0.1 to 0.15 μm (Fig. 229–1*A*).[1] Motility, achieved via paired axial flagella, one at each end, is best visualized by darkfield microscopy. Leptospires are obligately aerobic, slow growing, and require long-chain fatty acids or long-chain alcohols as a primary energy source[1]; the ability to isolate these organisms on artificial media is unique among spirochetes. Their cell walls are surrounded by an outer envelope high in lipopolysaccharide (LPS). The variation in LPS antigens determines the specificity of host immune responses against *Leptospira* spp., and this variation is the basis for the serologic classification scheme that differentiates serologic variants into serovars.

Classification of the genus *Leptospira* has undergone substantial revision. In the traditional classification system based on the serovar, the genus contained two species; the pathogenic species *Leptospira interrogans* with at least 218 serovars, and the saprophytic, free-living, nonpathogenic species *Leptospira biflexa* with a minimum of 60 serovars.[8, 9] Within each species, serovars are organized into serogroups based on shared antigenicity. *L. interrogans* contains 23 serogroups with strains pathogenic for amphibians, reptiles, and mammals including humans. *L. biflexa* contains 28 serogroups with

All material in this chapter is in the public domain, with the exception of any borrowed figures or tables.

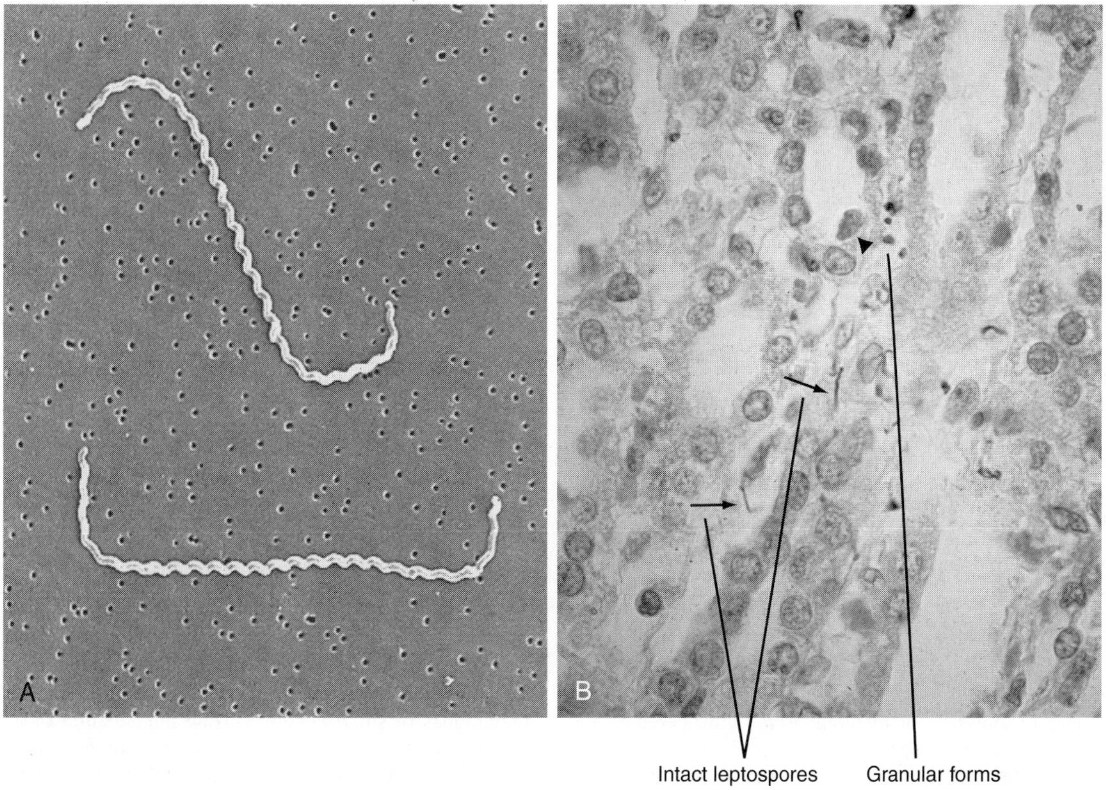

FIGURE 229–1. *A*, Scanning electron micrograph of two *Leptospira* organisms (original magnification, about ×60,000). These spirochetes are right-handed helical with 18 or more coils per cell, and bent or hooked ends. (Courtesy of Robbin S. Weyant, Centers for Disease Control and Prevention.) *B*, Immunostaining of intact leptospires *(arrow)* and granular forms of leptospiral antigens *(arrowhead)* in a kidney of a patient who died of pulmonary hemorrhage. (Original magnification, about ×158, naphthol fast red substrate with hematoxylin counterstain.) (Courtesy of Sherif R. Zaki, Centers for Disease Control and Prevention.)

strains found in fresh water and soils of high moisture and organic matter content that do not cause disease in animals.[8–10]

Studies based on DNA relatedness of leptospires using DNA–DNA hybridization have demonstrated a high degree of genetic heterogeneity within *L. interrogans* and *L. biflexa*. All leptospires are in the family *Leptospiraceae*, which contains three genera: *Leptospira*, *Leptonema* and "*Turneria*" (the genus name *Turneria* is widely used but has not been formally proposed and is therefore shown in quotation marks).[11, 12] The genus *Leptospira* includes (but is not limited to) the pathogenic species *L. interrogans*, *L. sanatarosi*, *L. borgpetersenii*, *L. kirschneri*, *L. noguchii*, *L. inadai*, *L. weilii* and the nonpathogenic species *L. biflexa*, *L. meyeri*, *L. wolbachii*, and *L. alexanderi*.[13, 14] The genera *Leptonema* and "*Turneria*" each contain a single species, *Leptonema illini* and *Turneria parva* (formerly *Leptospira parva*); these species have not been shown to cause human disease, and therefore this chapter focuses on members of the genus *Leptospira*. Neither serogroups nor serovars equate with speciation, as serovars within many serogroups and strains within a given serovar are found in more than one species.

Despite the limitations of the serovar and serogroup designations at the molecular level, these serologic tools are likely to be retained as they are valuable in serologic diagnosis. Both the serovar, serogroup designation and the expanded number of species are useful epidemiologically, as there is a strong association among certain serovars with animal reservoirs, as well as differences in geographic distribution of a number of species. By convention, serovar designations remain italicized and follow the phylogenetically designated genus and species (e.g., *Leptospira interrogans* serovar *icterohaemorrhagiae*).

EPIDEMIOLOGY AND TRANSMISSION

Leptospirosis occurs worldwide. Human infections are endemic in most temperate and tropical climates, having a peak occurrence during or immediately following periods of high precipitation. Reliable incidence data, however, are not available because the clinical presentation is nonspecific and because diagnostic capabilities are usually limited in countries with the greatest burden of disease. In some tropical countries, antibody prevalence rates to local serovars, depicting past or recent infection, exceed 80%. In the United States, the state of Hawaii is disproportionately affected (1974–1978 annual incidence through passive surveillance: United States, 0.05 per 100,000 population; Hawaii, 1.08 per 100,000 population).[15] In 1992, Hawaii reported an annual incidence of roughly 128 per 100,000 population using active surveillance.[16] In 1995, leptospirosis was removed from the United States' list of notifiable diseases, primarily due to the small number of cases detected through passive surveillance.

Leptospirosis is a ubiquitous disease of amphibians, reptiles, and mammals including humans. Wild, domestic, or peridomestic animal infections, such as those occurring in rodents, livestock, and dogs, range from subclinical to symptomatic (e.g., listlessness, anorexia, and abortion). Infected animals may become reservoirs when leptospires persist in immunologically privileged sites, in particular, the renal tubule. Leptospires, excreted in animal urine or tissues of parturition (placenta and amniotic fluid), become established in soil and water, where they can survive for weeks to months. Humans and other animals become infected after contact with this soil or water. Humans and animals can also become infected by direct contact with infected animal tissues and organs. Because humans are rarely chronic carriers,[17, 18] they are considered accidental hosts. Human-to-human transmission of infection is not considered to be an important mode of transmission.

Occupationally acquired leptospirosis can occur among people exposed to animals, animal products, or contaminated soil or water as part of their work. Occupational risk has been established for animal trappers and hunters, dairy farmers, livestock workers, abattoir workers, veterinarians, rice farmers, military personnel, and sewer workers.[1–3, 5] Recreational exposures have been associated with wading, swimming, white-water rafting, canoeing, kayaking, and competitive swimming after indirect exposure to contaminated rivers and lakes.[1, 3, 19–22] Disease is reported more often in men than in women, presumably due to the greater participation of men in these occupational and recreational activities.

Large epidemics of leptospirosis have been documented after investigations of unexplained febrile illness associated with flooding, tropical storms, and hurricanes in the Caribbean and Central and South America.[23–26] Heavy rains resulting from such natural disasters increase human exposure to leptospire-contaminated groundwater and soil and may also facilitate peridomestic rodent infestation resulting in transmission to humans. Walking through streams, creeks, and puddles and observing rodents in food preparation areas were the predominant risk factors associated with disease after these natural disasters. Sporadic and large urban disease outbreaks are also recognized.[27, 28] Leptospirosis may be a common cause of unrecognized febrile illness in both the tropics[29] and large urban centers where pet dogs and rats are likely to play an important role in the peridomestic amplification and transmission of infection.[25, 28]

Establishing an epidemiologic link between the species of *Leptospira* obtained through environmental sampling (e.g., testing water, mud, and animals) and pathogenic serovars of *Leptospira* causing illness in humans in the same environment is difficult.[20] In temperate and tropical climates, both pathogenic and saprophytic species can be found in fresh water, damp soil, vegetation, and mud, particularly during months of high precipitation.[10] Therefore, natural bodies of water frequently contain *Leptospira*. Fortunately, strains representing pathogenic and saprophytic serovars obtained from environmental samples can be distinguished serologically,[7] as well as by a number of molecular techniques.[10, 30–34] Pathogenic *Leptospira* spp. infect a variety of domestic and wild mammals, and it is not uncommon for opossums, skunks, raccoons, and foxes to shed leptospires in their urine 10 to 50% of the time. Nevertheless, because certain serovars have a predilection for particular host species in nature, the identification of the leptospiral serovar causing infection in humans and local epidemiologic knowledge may facilitate identification of potential animal reservoirs of environmental contamination. Serovars *grippotyphosa*, *hardjo*, and *pomona* are frequently associated with cattle, sheep, and goat infecions; serovars *bratislava*, *canicola*, *copenhageni*, *grippotyphosa*, *icterohaemorrhagiae*, *pomona*, *sejroe*, and *tarassovi* with pig infections; serovars *canicola* and *icterohaemorrhagiae* with dog and cat infections; serovar *pomona* with horse infections; and serovars *australis*, *ballum*, *bataviae*, *hardjo*, *grippotyphosa*, *icterohaemorrhagiae*, *javanica*, and *pomona* with rodent infections.[1] *Leptospira* infections are not restricted to mammals; isolation from reptiles and amphibians is well documented.[35] The reasons for these associations between certain serovars and certain species of animals remain incompletely understood.

PATHOGENESIS

Leptospires enter the body through cuts; abraded and softened, waterlogged skin; mucous membranes or conjunctivae; aerosol inhalation of microscopic droplets; and possibly ingestion. On entering the lymphatics and blood stream, leptospires are carried rapidly to organs throughout the body; tissue tropism is not apparent. Invasion into the cerebrospinal fluid (CSF) and aqueous humor of the eye may be facilitated by the burrowing action of paired axial flagella and the release of hyaluronidase.[36] Studies in mice suggest that capillary leakage and hemorrhage result from the disruption of endothelial cell membranes of small vessels via the intercalation of a glycolipoprotein toxin, which displaces host long-chain fatty acids required to maintain vascular cell wall integrity.[37] Regardless of the mechanism, petechial lesions reflect a systemic vasculitis allowing the migration and proliferation of spirochetes into nearly all organs and tissues and accounting for a broad spectrum of clinical illness. Severe vascular injury can ensue, causing, for example, pulmonary hemorrhage, ischemia of the renal cortex leading to tubular-epithelial cell necrosis, and destruction of the hepatic architecture resulting in jaundice and liver cell injury with or without necrosis.[38]

The human humoral immune response is directed at outer envelope LPS side-chain epitopes, the same epitopes used to serotype leptospires. LPS antigens elicit the production of immunoglobulin M (IgM) and later IgG antibodies that specifically bind LPS epitopes of the serovar, or cross-reacting serovar or serovars, causing infection. After opsonization and subsequent phagocytosis in the lung and liver, the spirochetes are cleared from the circulation by the reticuloendothelial system; the rapidity of leptospiral clearance is of prognostic importance. Among survivors, long-lasting immunity is believed to be serovar specific. The duration of detectable IgM and IgG antibody, however, is unknown. Chronic manifestations, such as uveitis, may follow mild or severe illness and can be mediated by antigen-antibody complexes in the apparent absence of organisms.[39]

Virulence factors explaining differences between mild, self-limited infections and more severe infections in humans have yet to be identified. Surface antigens may play some role, as certain serovars are associated with mild illness (*ballum*, *canicola*, *grippotyphosa*, *hardjo*, *hebdomadis*, *hyos*, *pomona*, and *tarassovi*), whereas other serovars, such as members of the serogroup Icterohaemorrhagiae (*australis*, *autumnalis*, *bataviae*, *copenhageni*, *icterohaemorrhagiae*, *lai*, and *pyrogenes*) are associated with more severe disease.[1, 35] Physical factors, such as bent or hooked ends (see Fig. 229–1*A*) and motility, may also play a role as these characteristics are gradually lost after laboratory cultivation, giving rise to less virulent organisms.[1]

CLINICAL MANIFESTATIONS

The severity of *Leptospira* infections ranges from subclinical illness detected by seroconversion among persons with frequent exposure to leptospires to two clinically recognizable syndromes: a self-limited, systemic illness seen in roughly 90% of infections, and a severe, potentially fatal illness accompanied by any combination of renal failure, liver failure, and pneumonitis with hemorrhagic diathesis.[1–3] Both the self-limited and severe forms of illness progress through an acute, septicemic phase that is followed by an immune phase of disease. Although certain serovars are associated with more severe illness, the relationship between phylogenetically classified *Leptospira* spp. and the severity of illness requires further study.

The incubation period is usually 5 to 14 days but ranges from a few days to 30 days or more.[1, 20] The acute, septicemic phase of illness begins abruptly with high, remittent fever (38 to 40°C) and headache (>95%); chills, rigors, and myalgias (>80%); conjunctival suffusion without purulent discharge (30 to 40%); abdominal pain (30%); anorexia, nausea, and vomiting (30 to 60%); diarrhea (15 to 30%); cough and pharyngitis (20%); and a pretibial maculopapular cutaneous eruption (<10%) lasting from 3 to 7 days (Fig. 229–2).[5, 40–42] Conjunctival suffusion and muscle tenderness, most notable in the calf and lumbar areas, are the most distinguishing physical findings; other less common signs include lymphadenopathy, splenomegaly, and hepatomegaly. Routine laboratory tests are nonspecific. Leptospires can be recovered from blood, CSF, and most tissues during the acute phase of illness (Fig. 229–2). Although leptospires may be present in the CSF during the acute phase of illness, meningeal signs are not prominent in this phase. After 5 to 7 days of illness, leptospires may also be recovered from urine. Routine urinalysis reveals mild proteinuria and pyuria with more than five leukocytes per high-power field, with or without hematuria and hyaline or granular casts. With the exception of spontaneous fetal absorption during pregnancy, death is exceedingly rare in the acute phase of illness.[43]

Defervescence heralds the immune phase of illness, which generally lasts from 4 to 30 days (see Fig. 229–2). The production of agglutinating, opsonic IgM antibody accounts for a short-lived, 1- to 3-day abatement of fever and the disappearance of leptospires from the blood and CSF (see Fig. 229–2).[41] Leptospires, however, remain detectable by culture or polymerase chain reaction (PCR) in the kidney, urine, and aqueous humor for several weeks (see Fig. 229–2).[1, 39] Prominent clinical findings include conjunctival suffusion with or without hemorrhage; photophobia; eye pain; muscle tenderness; adenopathy; and hepatosplenomegaly. Circulating antibodies play a likely role in the development of aseptic meningitis; cutaneous, pretibial palpable purpura and plaques; uveitis; iritis; iridocyclitis; and chorioretinitis.[39, 41]

Aseptic meningitis, with or without symptoms, is characteristic of the immune phase of illness, occurring in up to 80% of patients. Symptomatic patients present with an intense, bitemporal and frontal throbbing headache with or without delirium. A lymphocytic pleocytosis occurs with total cell counts generally below 500/mm^3.[5, 41] CSF protein levels are modestly elevated between 50 and 100 mg/ml; the CSF glucose concentration is normal. Rarely, severe neurologic disturbances including coma, hemiplegia, and transverse myelitis occur.[5]

Weil's disease, characterized by impaired hepatic and renal function, is but one form of severe illness that may develop after the acute phase of illness. Patients developing severe disease manifestations may experience the 1- to 3-day improvement in fever and other constitutional symptoms that characteristically follows acute-phase illness, or they may progress rapidly with high fever over 40°C and the onset of liver failure, acute renal failure, hemorrhagic pneumonitis, cardiac arrythmia, or circulatory collapse.[1–4] The clinical manifestations of severe disease and its associated mortality are highly variable and can be attributed in part to differences in the severity of illness caused by different serovars and geographic differences in supportive medical care. Fatality figures for patients developing severe disease have ranged from 5 to 40%.[2, 3–5, 44]

Jaundice typically results from vascular injury to hepatic capillaries in the absence of hepatocellular necrosis. After acute-phase illness, serum bilirubin levels, if elevated, are well below 20 mg/dl, peaking by day 7 in 85% of patients.[3, 5] Hepatosplenomegaly develops in more than 25% of icteric patients. With progression to severe disease caused by more extensive ischemia, conjugated serum bilirubin levels may rise to 80 mg/dl, accompanied by modest elevations in alkaline phosphatase levels.[3] The levels of serum transaminases, alanine aminotransferase and aspartate aminotransferase, rarely exceed 200 U/liter; hypoprothrombinemia is uncommon and uniformly responds to vitamin K administration.[2, 3] Creatine phosphokinase (MM fraction) levels are typically elevated out of proportion to elevations in serum transaminase levels, and this can help to distinguish leptospirosis from other causes of acute hepatitis.[45] Some patients with severe jaundice may have only minimal renal involvement, and death from leptospirosis is rarely caused by hepatic failure in the absence of renal failure.[3] At autopsy, hepatocytes show mild degenerative changes, hypertrophy and hyperplasia of Kupffer cells, erythrophagocytosis, and cholestasis; focal necrosis, when present, is not accompanied by zonal disruption in hepatic architecture.[38, 46]

Acute renal failure is characterized by a rapid onset of uremia and oliguria during the second week of illness, frequently accompanied by jaundice. The blood urea nitrogen level is usually below 100 mg/dl, and the serum creatinine level is usually below 2 to 8 mg/dl during the acute phase of illness, but the levels may exceed 300 and 18 mg/dl, respectively.[2, 3, 5] Thrombocytopenia occurs in the absence of disseminated intravascular coagulation and may accompany progressive renal dysfunction.[47] Renal biopsy reveals acute interstitial nephritis; immune-complex glomerulonephritis may also be present.[48] Concomitant dehydration causing hypovolemia and hypotension compounds renal injury; the development of anuria is a poor prognostic sign. At autopsy, the kidneys are swollen and yellow, with prominent cortical blood vessels.[1, 38] Histologically, a diffuse, mixed tubulointerstitial inflammatory cell infiltrate of lymphocytes, plasma cells, macrophages, and polymorphonuclear leukocytes is accompanied by focal areas of tubular necrosis.[46]

Severe hemorrhagic pneumonitis and acute pulmonary distress

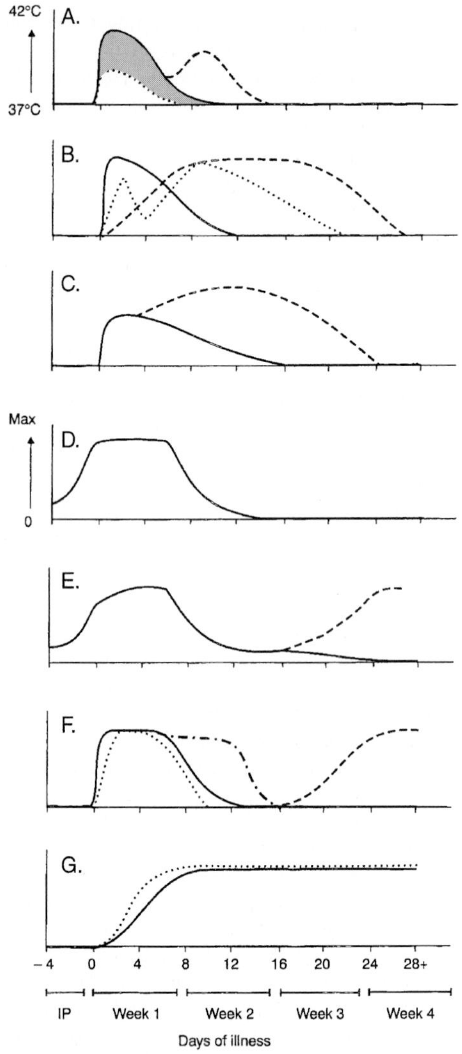

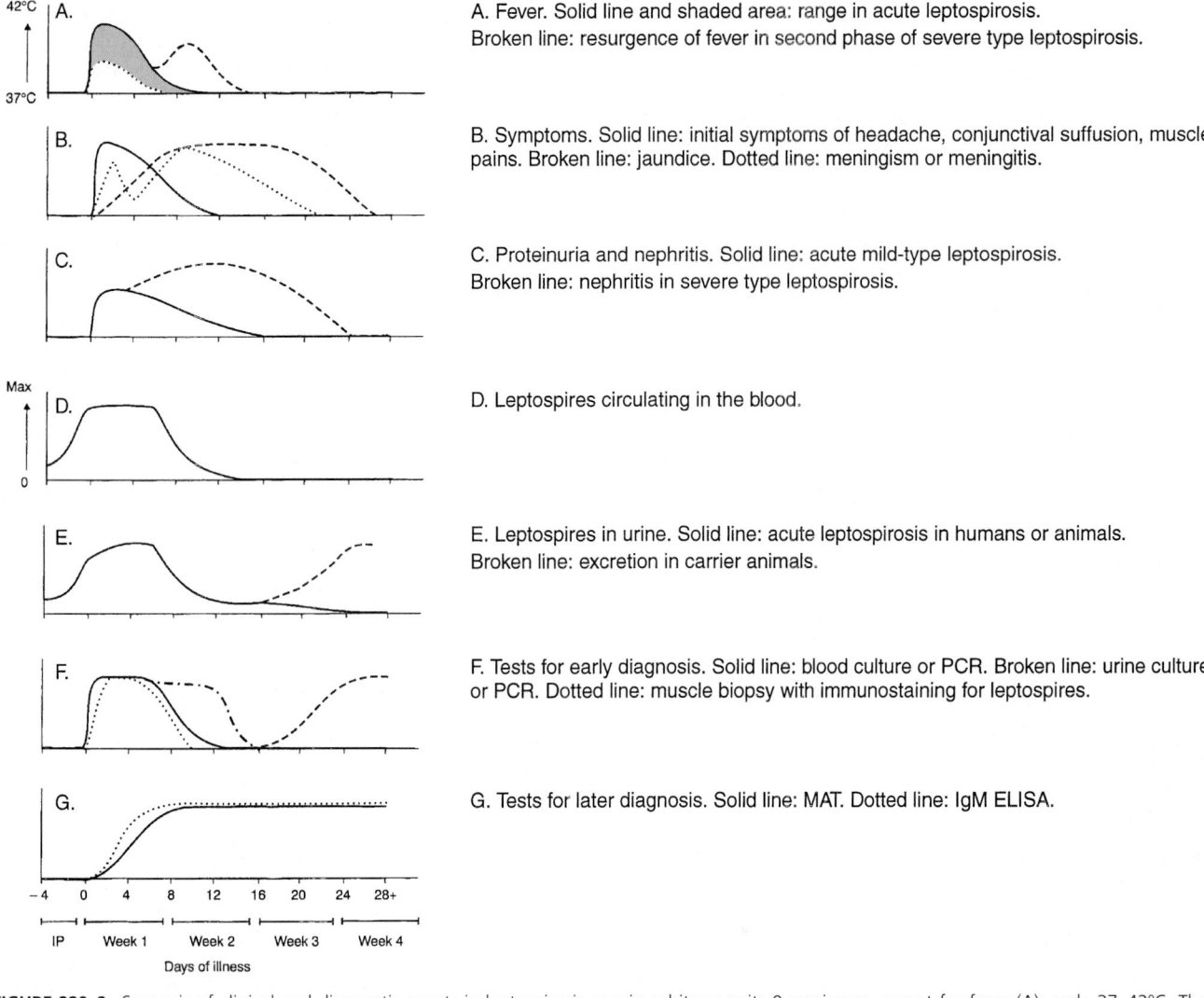

A. Fever. Solid line and shaded area: range in acute leptospirosis. Broken line: resurgence of fever in second phase of severe type leptospirosis.

B. Symptoms. Solid line: initial symptoms of headache, conjunctival suffusion, muscle pains. Broken line: jaundice. Dotted line: meningism or meningitis.

C. Proteinuria and nephritis. Solid line: acute mild-type leptospirosis. Broken line: nephritis in severe type leptospirosis.

D. Leptospires circulating in the blood.

E. Leptospires in urine. Solid line: acute leptospirosis in humans or animals. Broken line: excretion in carrier animals.

F. Tests for early diagnosis. Solid line: blood culture or PCR. Broken line: urine culture or PCR. Dotted line: muscle biopsy with immunostaining for leptospires.

G. Tests for later diagnosis. Solid line: MAT. Dotted line: IgM ELISA.

FIGURE 229–2. Synopsis of clinical and diagnostic events in leptospirosis. *y*-axis: arbitrary units 0-maximum, except for fever (A), scale 37–42°C. The *y*-axis reflects the amount of reaction that might be anticipated, not the frequency of its occurrence. *Abbreviations*: ELISA, Enzyme-linked immunosorbent assay; IP, incubation period; MAT, microscopic agglutination test; PCR, polymerase chain reaction. (Adapted from Faine S. Leptospirosis. In: Hausler WJ Jr, Sussman M, eds. Topley and Wilson's Microbiology and Microbial Infections. 9th ed. London: Arnold; 1988:849–869.)

syndrome can be prominent manifestations of infection and may occur in the absence of hepatic and renal failure.[26, 49] Frank hemoptysis can arise simultaneously with the onset of cough during the acute phase of illness; an auscultatory examination may be normal.[40] With progressive pulmonary involvement, radiographic abnormalities seen most frequently in the lower lobes evolve from small nodular densities ("snowflake-like") to patchy alveolar infiltrates; confluent consolidation is uncommon.[40, 50] Bibasilar rales may be present when radiographic involvement is extensive. At autopsy, the lungs appear grossly congested and demonstrate focal areas of hemorrhage.[46] Histologically, damage to the capillary endothelium leads to congestion with foci of interstitial and intra-alveolar hemorrhage, diffuse alveolar damage, and severe airspace disorganization; inflammatory infiltrates are strikingly absent. Petechial hemorrhage also involves the tracheobronchial tree, diaphragm, and pleura.[40]

Congestive heart failure occurs rarely. However, nonspecific electrocardiographic changes are common.[51] In up to one fifth of patients receiving continuous cardiac monitoring, cardiac arrhythmias may occur, including atrial fibrillation; flutter and tachycardia; and cardiac irritability, including premature ventricular contractions and ventricular tachycardia.[44] Cardiovascular collapse with shock can develop abruptly and in the absence of aggressive supportive care can be fatal. At autopsy, interstitial myocarditis with inflammatory involvement of the conduction system is seen; acute coronary arteritis and aortitis are also common at postmortem examination.[52]

LABORATORY DIAGNOSIS

Isolation of leptospires from human clinical specimens remains the "gold standard" for the diagnosis of leptospirosis. However, isolation can be difficult and can require up to 16 weeks even in experienced laboratories. In addition, the sensitivity of culture for diagnosis is considered to be low. For these reasons, acute-phase serum specimens collected 1 to 2 weeks after the onset of illness and convalescent serum specimens collected 3 to 4 weeks after the onset should always be obtained to facilitate serologic diagnosis. Consultation with a reference laboratory can enhance success with laboratory diagnosis of leptospirosis. In the United States, the World Health Organization Collaborating Center for Reference and Research on Leptospirosis is at the Centers for Disease Control and Prevention (CDC) in Atlanta, Georgia[7]; World Health Organization Collaborating Center reference laboratories are also located in Australia, the United Kingdom, and The Netherlands.

Isolation and Identification

Leptospires can be isolated from blood, CSF, and urine during the first 7 to 10 days of illness, and from urine during the second and third week of illness (see Fig. 229–2). Specimens, collected using aseptic techniques, are inoculated onto a serum-containing semisolid medium, such as Fletcher's, Stuart's, Ellinghausen-McCullough-Johnson-Harris, or PLM-5.[7] All specimens should be inoculated using both selective media, made by the addition of neomycin or 5-fluorouracil, and nonselective media. When inoculation media are not immediately available, blood or CSF specimens can be collected in sterile tubes containing heparin or sodium oxalate for transport to a reference laboratory; citrate solutions are inhibitory and should be avoided. Blood and CSF specimens should be transported under conditions that avoid freezing and excessive heat and inoculated within 1 week of collection. Urine, collected under the most meticulous efforts to reduce contamination, should be inoculated immediately or diluted 1:10 in 1% bovine serum albumin with 5-fluorouracil and transported as rapidly as possible at 5°C to 20°C. Inoculation is performed by adding one to two drops of blood or 0.5 ml of CSF to 5 ml of medium; three to five inoculations per specimen are advised. Inoculation of urine specimens requires serial dilutions with 1:10 sterile buffered saline. Leptospires can also be isolated from either diagnostic or postmortem tissue specimens when processed rapidly; a pea-sized specimen expressed through 5-ml syringe, and diluted in serial dilutions, can be used to inoculate semisolid medium. Inoculated blood, CSF, urine or tissue specimens should be incubated at 20°C to 30°C, checked weekly by darkfield microscopy, and held for up to 4 months before discarding as negative. Upon isolation, organisms recovered using selective media should be transferred to nonselective media. Additional, detailed isolation procedures are described elsewhere.[7, 53]

Animal inoculation methods have proved useful for isolating leptospires from contaminated human specimens, as well as from suspected contaminated water sources such as ponds, streams, and lakes. Several hamsters or young guinea pigs are inoculated intraperitoneally or subcutaneously, and the animals are observed for signs of infection, at which time the animals are sacrificed for blood culture and the microscopic examination of harvested organs.

The final identification of leptospiral isolates to the serovar level is performed by the microscopic agglutination test (MAT), using reference rabbit antisera raised against the type serovars of all recognized serogroups,[7, 53] monoclonal antibodies, or by molecular methods including randomly amplified polymorphic DNA fingerprinting, or PCR–restriction endonuclease analysis.[30, 32] Both serologic and molecular methods require the use of techniques and reagents that are generally limited to reference laboratories.

Indirect Detection Methods

The reference standard serologic test for the detection of leptospiral antibodies is the MAT using live organisms.[7, 53] It is highly sensitive and specific but time-consuming and hazardous to perform. The CDC reference laboratory uses a standard panel of 23 antigens representing 21 serovars and 17 serogroups, supplemented with additional serovars as needed. Serial dilutions of serum in phosphate-buffered saline are added to wells containing live antigen, incubated, and read to the end point defined as the highest dilution that agglutinates 50% or more of leptospires visualized at 100× by darkfield microscopy. A serologically confirmed case of leptospirosis is defined by a fourfold rise in MAT titer to one or more serovars between acute-phase and convalescent serum specimens run in parallel.[7] A titer of at least 1:800 in the presence of compatible symptoms is strong evidence of recent or current infection. Suggestive evidence for recent or current infection includes a single titer of at least 1:200 obtained after the onset of symptoms, or a titer of at least 1:100 on consecutive specimens. Delayed seroconversions are common, with up to 10% of patients failing to seroconvert within 30 days of the clinical onset. Cross-reactive antibodies may be associated with syphilis, relapsing fever, Lyme disease, and legionellosis.[7]

Alternative, more rapid serologic tests including an indirect hemagglutinin assay (IHA) and several recently developed IgM indirect enzyme-linked immunosorbent assays (ELISAs) are available, but these tests lack the ability to provide information about the serogroup or serogroups most likely to be responsible for disease. A commercially available IHA (MRL Diagnostics, Cypress, California) is a Food and Drug Administration–cleared alternative to the MAT for use in the United States.[54] The MRL Diagnostics IHA uses a genus-specific antigen from serovar *andamana*, and in an evaluation conducted in Barbados (West Indies), this assay had a sensitivity, specificity, and positive predictive value of 94% or more when compared with MAT, performance parameters nearly identical to those reported for an IHA evaluated by the CDC in 1975.[55] However, the sensitivity of the MRL Diagnostics IHA may vary substantially geographically; the sensitivity of this IHA was 52% among 63 MAT-confirmed sera obtained from Hawaiian residents (CDC, unpublished data).

New ELISA tests, designed to detect IgM antibodies, offer promising diagnostic utility for the testing of serum samples obtained early in the course of infection. A commercially available IgM ELISA assay (PanBio, Ltd., Brisbane, Australia) evaluated in Australia was reported to have a sensitivity of 100% among 41 patients with MAT- or culture-confirmed leptospirosis, and a specificity of 98 and 93%, respectively, among 59 asymptomatic donors and 233 patients infected with a variety of viral and bacterial pathogens.[56] However, the performance of the PanBio IgM ELISA may vary substantially geographically. This assay was used in 1998 as a rapid screening test during an acute outbreak investigation of leptospirosis in Illinois.[19, 20] Among 30 acute-phase and convalescent serum specimens testing positive by MAT, the sensitivity of the PanBio ELISA was 77% (CDC, unpublished data). Another IgM ELISA test in dipstick format (LEPTO Dipstick, Royal Tropical Institute, The Netherlands) provides an alternative for the testing of sera.[57] Among serum specimens obtained from 284 MAT- or culture-confirmed Dutch leptospirosis patients, the LEPTO Dipstick had a sensitivity of 76%, comparing favorably with a MAT sensitivity of 81%. Testing of 274 Dutch control sera revealed a negative predictive value of 79% by LEPTO dipstick (7% false-positive test rate) compared with a negative predictive value of 99% by MAT (1% false-positive test rate). Further evaluations of dipstick tests are needed, as this technique offers an appropriate screening method for the evaluation of acutely febrile patients residing in developing countries where most cases of leptospirosis occur.

Direct Detection Methods

Darkfield microscopy may provide a presumptive diagnosis of leptospirosis in experienced hands. However, false-negative and false-positive examinations are frequent due to the low concentration of organisms (even after centrifugation) and the presence of fibrin and other filamentous cellular extrusions found in most body fluids.[7]

Immunohistochemical techniques using immunoalkaline phosphatase and/or immunoperoxidase staining methods can readily detect leptospiral antigens and intact leptospires in infected tissue specimens (see Fig. 229–1*B*).[46, 49] This technique has proved both sensitive and specific in recent outbreak investigations[20, 49] and may replace modified silver stains (Dieterle's, Steiner's, Warthin-Starry) in the histologic diagnosis of leptospirosis.

In recent years, PCR methods have been developed for the rapid detection of *Leptospira* DNA in human specimens.[17, 34, 39, 58–60] Specimens in which leptospiral DNA has been detected by PCR include serum, urine, aqueous humor, and CSF (see Fig. 229–2). In two studies conducted among leptospirosis patients, PCR was compared side by side with culture and serologic tests; PCR was more sensitive than culture in patients with serologically confirmed disease in both studies.[58, 59] PCR examination of blood and CSF is most useful in the first 7 to 10 days of illness when leptospiral DNA may be

TABLE 229–1 Agents Recommended for Chemoprophylaxis and Treatment of Leptospirosis

Indication	Drug	Dosage
Chemoprophylaxis	Doxycycline	200 mg once a week
Treatment of mild leptospirosis	Doxycycline	100 mg PO bid
	Ampicillin	500–750 mg q6h
	Amoxicillin	500 mg q6h
Treatment of moderate-to-severe leptospirosis	Penicillin G	1.5 million U IV q6h
	Ampicillin	0.5–1 g IV q6h

From Farr RW. Leptospirosis. Clin Infect Dis. 1995;21:1–8. Copyright © 1995, Infectious Diseases Society of America.

detected before the development of the humoral immune response. PCR examination of urine and aqueous humor may be positive for several weeks in the former, and for several months in the latter.[17, 39] When testing serum, care must be taken to avoid the erythrocyte fraction, which contains PCR inhibitors.

TREATMENT

From the late 1940s through the mid-1960s, a variety of antimicrobial agents were found to be efficacious for leptospirosis using in vitro and experimental animal models.[3] However, placebo-controlled trials comparing penicillin, chloramphenicol, tetracycline, and other antimicrobial agents conducted in the 1950s failed to demonstrate a beneficial effect on the duration or severity of illness with any class of antibiotic, even with the initiation of therapy before the fourth day after the onset of illness.[61–63] Failure of antimicrobial therapy was attributed to the rapid growth and dissemination of leptospires resulting in vascular and end-organ damage within the first few days of the onset of illness, well before antibiotic therapy had been initiated.

Several more recent placebo-controlled trials for leptospirosis, however, have demonstrated clinical efficacy for intravenous penicillin therapy in both severe and late disease,[64, 65] and oral amoxicillin, ampicillin, tetracycline, or doxycycline for mild to moderately severe infections.[66–68] Hence, currently recommended antimicrobial agents and dosages are based on the severity of disease (Table 229–1); mild infections can be treated with oral doxycycline (200 mg/day), and infections requiring hospitalization should be treated with intravenous penicillin (3 million units/day). Even with advanced disease, intravenous penicillin decreases the duration of constitutional symptoms and the persistence of associated laboratory abnormalities and may prevent the development of leptospiruria.[64] Of note, strain variability in susceptibility to penicillins and tetracyclines has been observed,[69–70] although standardized procedures have not been developed for antimicrobial susceptibility testing of leptospires.[7] As with other spirochete infections, a Jarisch-Herxheimer reaction can develop after the initiation of penicillin therapy for leptospirosis.[71] Although these reactions serve as an indicator of therapeutic efficacy, they can be associated with increased morbidity and mortality; patients receiving intravenous penicillin should be monitored for shock-like symptoms.

PREVENTION

Reducing both direct contact with infected animals and indirect contact with animal urine–contaminated fresh water, soil, and mud is the most effective prevention strategy available.[72] Maintaining careful hygienic practices within and around farmyards and abattoirs is encouraged. Flat surfaces should be washed down regularly with sodium hypochlorite (1:4000) or other detergents to kill leptospires.[73] Protective clothing, such as impermeable gloves and high rubber boots for persons with high occupational risk such as sewer workers, is recommended. Although difficult to achieve, rodent pest control after heavy rains in known endemic areas may be useful. The decontamination of large bodies of leptospire-contaminated fresh water is, generally speaking, impractical, although seawater was purported to have been successfully used by German military forces in World War II to decontaminate freshwater canals in Amsterdam.[3]

Immunization of animals with *Leptospira* vaccines can prevent leptospirosis in animals and reduce the transmission of leptospire infections to other animals and humans. *Leptospira* vaccines for livestock and peridomestic animals, such as cattle, pigs, and dogs, have long been available, and their efficacy for preventing acute disease, as well as asymptomatic leptospiruria (carrier state) in these animals is dependent on the quality and quantity of serovar antigens present in the various preparations.[1–3, 73] For example, the canine vaccine in current use in the United States does not include serovar *grippotyphosa*, and dog infections from this serovar have been on the increase in some states, presumably due to increased indirect contact with urine excreted by wild raccoons, as these animals frequently carry this serovar.[46] Although immunization of humans was purportedly successful in preventing leptospirosis infections among mine workers in Poland and Japan, and among rice farmers in Italy and Spain,[35] more recent human vaccine development and use has been hampered by the limited number of serovar antigens they have contained and the likely serovar-specific nature of the immune response they elicit.[74–77]

Chemoprophylaxis offers an alternative prevention strategy for persons with limited exposure to known high-risk areas of endemic disease. After several large outbreaks of leptospirosis among U.S. soldiers training in Panama in 1991 and 1982, a randomized, double-blind placebo-controlled efficacy trial of doxycycline was conducted among two military units deployed on a 3-week jungle training exercise. Oral doxycycline, 200 mg orally, administered once weekly, was shown to be 95% efficacious.[67] Earlier field trials with daily oral penicillin among rice workers suggested some benefit as a chemoprophylactic agent,[78] but postexposure chemoprophylaxis with oral penicillin failed to prevent leptospirosis in a laboratory worker after an accidental needlestick inoculation with a cultivated *Leptospira* strain.[79] Doxycycline chemoprophylaxis may be practical for travelers participating in high-risk water sport activities in known endemic areas, as well as for persons living or working in highly endemic areas after natural disasters resulting in heavy rainfall and flooding.

REFERENCES

1. Faine S. Leptospirosis. In: Hausler WJ Jr, Sussman M, eds. Topley and Wilson's Microbiology and Microbial Infections. 9th ed. London: Arnold; 1998:849–869.
2. Farr RW. Leptospirosis. Clin Infect Dis. 1995;21:1–8.
3. Feigin RD, Anderson DC. Human leptospirosis. Crit Rev Clin Lab Sci. 1975;5:413–467.
4. Inada R, Ido Y, Hoki R, Ito H. The etiology, mode of infection, and specific therapy of Weil's disease (spirochaetosis icterohaemorrhagica). J Exp Med. 1916;23:377–402.
5. Heath CW, Alexander AD, Galton MM. Leptospirosis in the United States: Analysis of 483 cases in man, 1949–1961. N Engl J Med. 1965;273:1–15.
6. Gochenour WS, Smadel JE, Jackson EB, et al. Leptospiral etiology of Fort Bragg fever. Public Health Rep. 1952;67:811–813.
7. Weyant RS, Bragg SL, Kaufmann AF. *Leptospira* and *Leptonema*. In: Murray PR, Baron EJ, Pfaller MA, et al, eds. Manual of Clinical Microbiology. 7th ed. Washington, DC: American Society for Microbiology; 1999:739–745.
8. Kmety E, Dikken H. Classification of the Species *Leptospira interrogans* and History of Its Serovars. Groningen: University of Groningen Press; 1993.
9. Johnson RC, Faine S. Family II. Leptospiraceae. In: Krieg NR, Holt JG, eds. Bergey's Manual of Systematic Bacteriology, v. 1. Baltimore: Williams & Wilkins; 1984:62–67.
10. Henry RA, Johnson RC. Distribution of the genus *Leptospira* in soil and water. Appl Environ Microbiol. 1978;35:492–499.
11. Marshall R. International Committee on Systematic Bacteriology, Subcommittee on the Taxonomy of *Leptospira*, minutes of the meetings, 13 and 15 September 1990, Osaka, Japan. Int J Syst Bacteriol. 1992;42:330–334.
12. Hovind-Hougen K. Leptospiraceae, a new family to include *Leptospira* Noguchi 1917 and *Leptonema* gen nov. Int J Syst Bacteriol. 1979;29:245–251.
13. Yasuda PH, Steigerwalt AG, Sulzer KR, et al. Deoxyribonucleic acid relatedness between serogroups and serovars in the family Leptospiraceae with proposals for seven new *Leptospira* species. Int J Syst Bacteriol. 1987;37:407–415.

14. Brenner DJ, Kaufmann AF, Sulzer KR, et al. Further determination of deoxyribonucleic acid relatedness between serogroups and serovars in the family Leptospiraceae with a proposal for *Leptospira alexanderi* sp nov and four new *Leptospira* genomospecies. Int J Syst Bacteriol. 1999;49:839–858.
15. Martone WJ, Kaufman AF. Leptospirosis in humans in the United States, 1974–1978. J Infect Dis. 1979;140:1020–1022.
16. Sasaki DM, Pang L, Minette HP, et al. Active surveillance and risk factors for leptospirosis in Hawaii. Am J Trop Med Hyg. 1993;48:35–43.
17. Bal AE, Gravekamp C, Hartskeerl RA, et al. Detection of leptospires in urine by PCR for early diagnosis of leptospirosis. J Clin Microbiol. 1994;32:1894–1898.
18. Johnson DW. The Australian experience. Med J Aust. 1950;2:724–731.
19. CDC. Outbreak of acute febrile illness among athletes participating in triathlons—Wisconsin and Illinois, 1998. MMWR Morb Mortal Wkly Rep. 1998;47:585–588. [Erratum, MMWR Morb Mortal Wkly Rep. 1998;47:619.]
20. CDC. Update: Leptospirosis and unexplained acute febrile illness among athletes participating in triathlons—Illinois and Wisconsin, 1998. MMWR Morb Mortal Wkly Rep. 1998;47:673–676.
21. CDC. Outbreak of leptospirosis among white-water rafters—Costa Rica, 1996. MMWR Morb Mortal Wkly Rep. 1997;46:577–579.
22. Jackson LA, Kaufmann AF, Adams WG, et al. Outbreak of leptospirosis associated with swimming. Pediatr Infect Dis. 1993;12:48–54.
23. Sanders EJ, Rigau-Pérez JG, Smits HL, et al. Increase in leptospirosis in dengue-negative patients after a hurricane in Puerto Rico in 1996. Am J Trop Med Hyg. 1999;61:399–404.
24. Trevejo RT, Rigau-Pérez JG, Ashford DA, et al. Epidemic leptospirosis associated with pulmonary hemorrhage—Nicaragua, 1995. J Infect Dis. 1998;178:1457–1463.
25. Perkins BA. Epidemic leptospirosis associated with pulmonary hemorrhage in Nicaragua, other recent outbreaks, and diagnostic testing: Issues and opportunities. In: Scheld WM, Craig WA, Hughes JM, eds. Emerging Infections 2. Washington, DC: American Association for Microbiology; 1998:159–167.
26. CDC. Outbreak of acute febrile illness and pulmonary hemorrhage—Nicaragua, 1995. MMWR Morb Mortal Wkly Rep. 1995;44:841–843.
27. Marotto PCF, Marotto MS, Santos DL, et al. Outcome of leptospirosis in children. Am J Trop Med Hyg. 1997;56:307–310.
28. Vintez JM, Glass GE, Flexner CE, et al. Sporadic urban leptospirosis. Ann Intern Med. 1996;125:794–798.
29. Sanford JP. Leptospirosis—time for a booster. N Engl J Med. 1984;310:524–525.
30. Brown PD, Levett PN. Differentiation of *Leptospira* species and serovars by PCR-restriction endonuclease analysis, arbitrarily primed PCR and low-stringency PCR. J Med Microbiol. 1997;46:173–181.
31. Woo THS, Smythe LD, Symonds ML, et al. Rapid distinction between *Leptospira interrogans* and *Leptospira biflexa* by PCR amplification of 23S ribosomal DNA. FEMS Microbiol Lett. 1997;150:9–18.
32. Ramadass P, Meerarani S, Venkatesha MD, et al. Characterization of leptospiral serovars by randomly amplified polymorphic DNA fingerprinting. Int J Syst Bacteriol. 1997;47:575–576.
33. Zuerner RL, Alt D, Bolin CA. IS1533-based PCR assay for identification of *Leptospira interrogans* sensu lato serovars. J Clin Microbiol. 1995;33:3284–3289.
34. Gravekamp C, Van de Kemp H, Franzen M, et al. Detection of seven species of pathogenic leptospires by PCR using two sets of primers. J Gen Microbiol. 1993;139:1691–1700.
35. Turner LH. Leptospirosis I. Trans R Soc Trop Med Hyg. 1967;61:842–855.
36. Miller NG, Froehling RC, White RJ. Activity of leptospires and their products on L cell monolayers. Am J Vet Res. 1970;31:371–377.
37. Vinh T, Adler B, Faine S. Glycolipoprotein cytotoxin from *Leptospira interrogans* serovar *copenhageni*. J Gen Microbiol. 1986;132:111–123.
38. Arean VM. The pathologic anatomy and pathogenesis of fatal human leptospirosis (Weil's disease). Am J Pathol. 1962;40:393–423.
39. Chu KM, Rathinam R, Namperumalsamy P, Dean D. Identification of *Leptospira* species in the pathogenesis of uveitis and determination of clinical ocular characteristics in South India. J Infect Dis. 1998;177:1314–1321.
40. O'Neil KM, Rickman LS, Lazarus AA. Pulmonary manifestations of leptospirosis. Rev Infect Dis. 1991;13:705–709.
41. Berman SJ, Tsai C-C, Holmes K, et al. Sporadic anicteric leptospirosis in South Vietnam: A study of 150 patients. Ann Intern Med. 1973;79:167–173.
42. Fraser DW, Glosser JW, Francis DP, et al. Leptospirosis caused by serotype *fort-Bragg*: A suburban outbreak. Ann Intern Med. 1973;79:786–789.
43. Shaked Y, Shpilberg O, Samra D, Samra Y. Leptospirosis in pregnancy and its effect on the fetus: Case report and review. Clin Infect Dis. 1993;17:241–243.
44. Edwards CN, Nicholson GD, Hassel TA, et al. Leptospirosis in Barbados: A clinical study. W Indian Med J. 1990;39:27–34.
45. Johnson WD, Silva IC, Rocha H. Serum creatine phosphokinase in leptospirosis. JAMA. 1975;233:981–982.
46. Zaki SR, Spiegel RA. Leptospirosis. In: Nelson AM, Horsburgh CR Jr, eds. Pathology of Emerging Infections 2. Washington, DC: American Society for Microbiology; 1998:73–92.
47. Edwards CN, Nicholson GD, Hassel TA, et al. Thrombocytopenia in leptospirosis: The absence of evidence for disseminated intravascular coagulation. Am J Trop Med Hyg. 1986;35:352–354.
48. Lai KN, Aarons I, Woodroffe AJ, Clarkson AR. Renal lesions in leptospirosis. Aust N Z J Med. 1982;12:276–279.
49. Zaki SR, Shieh W-J. Leptospirosis associated with outbreak of acute febrile illness and pulmonary haemorrhage, Nicaragua, 1995 Letter. Lancet. 1996;347:535–536.
50. Im JG, Yeon KM, Han MC, et al. Leptospirosis of the lung: Radiographic findings in 58 patients. Am J Roentgenol. 1989;152:955–959.
51. Parsons M. Electrocardiographic changes in leptospirosis. BMJ. 1965;2:201–203.
52. De Brito T, Morais CF, Yasuda PH, et al. Cardiovascular involvement in human and experimental leptospirosis: Pathologic findings and immunohistochemical detection of leptospiral antigen. Ann Trop Med Parasitol. 1987;81:207–214.
53. Sulzer CR, Jones WL. Leptospirosis: Methods in laboratory diagnosis (rev ed). HEW Publication (CDC) 80–8275. Washington, DC: US Department of Health, Education, and Welfare; 1978.
54. Levett PN, Whittington CU. Evaluation of the indirect hemagglutination assay for diagnosis of acute leptospirosis. J Clin Microbiol. 1998;36:11–14.
55. Sulzer CR, Glosser JW, Rogers F, et al. Evaluation of an indirect hemagglutination test for the diagnosis of human leptospirosis. J Clin Microbiol. 1975;2:218–221.
56. Winslow WE, Merry DJ, Pirc ML, Devine PL. Evaluation of a commercial enzyme-linked immunosorbent assay for detection of immunoglobulin M antibody in diagnosis of human leptospiral infection. J Clin Microbiol. 1997;35:1938–1942.
57. Gussenhoven GC, van der Hoorn MAWG, Goris MGA, et al. LEPTO dipstick, a dipstick assay for detection of *Leptospira*-specific immunoglobulin M antibodies in human sera. J Clin Microbiol. 1997;35:92–97.
58. Merien F, Baranton G, Perolat P. Comparison of polymerase chain reaction with microagglutination test and culture for diagnosis of leptospirosis. J Infect Dis. 1995;172:281–285.
59. Brown PD, Gravekamp C, Carrington DG, et al. Evaluation of the polymerase chain reaction for early diagnosis of leptospirosis. J Med Microbiol. 1995;43:110–114.
60. Savio ML, Rossi C, Fusi P, et al. Detection and identification of *Leptospira interrogans* serovars by PCR coupled with restriction endonuclease analysis of amplified DNA. J Clin Microbiol. 1994;32:935–941.
61. Liebowitz D, Schwartz H. Leptospiral infection in man treated with terramycin. JAMA. 1951;147:122–135.
62. Fairburn AC, Semple SJG. Chloramphenicol and penicillin in the treatment of leptospirosis among British troops in Malaya. Lancet. 1956;1:13–16.
63. Hall HE, Hightower JA, Rivera RD, et al. Evaluation of antibiotic therapy in human leptospirosis. Ann Intern Med. 1951;35:981–998.
64. Watt G, Padre LP, Tuazon ML, et al. Placebo-controlled trial of intravenous penicillin for severe and late leptospirosis. Lancet. 1988;1:433–435.
65. Kocen RS. Leptospirosis, a comparison of symptomatic and penicillin therapy. BMJ. 1962;1:1181–1183.
66. McClain JBL, Ballou WR, Harrison SM, Steinweg DL. Doxycycline therapy for leptospirosis. Ann Intern Med. 1984;100:696–698.
67. Takafuji ET, Kirkpatrick JW, Miller RN, et al. An efficacy trial of doxycycline chemoprophylaxis against leptospirosis. N Engl J Med. 1984;310:497–500.
68. Münnich D, Lakatos M. Treatment of human leptospira infections with semicillin (ampicillin) or with amoxil (amoxycillin). Chemotherapy. 1976;22:372–380.
69. Broughton ES, Flack LE. The susceptibility of a strain of *Leptospira interrogans* serogroup Icterohaemorrhagiae to amoxicillin, erythromycin, lincomycin, tetracycline, oxytetracycline, and minocycline. Zentralbl Bakteriol Hyg A. 1986;261:425–431.
70. Oie S, Hironaga K, Koshiro A, et al. In vitro susceptibilities of five *Leptospira* strains to 16 antimicrobial agents. Antimicrob Agents Chemother. 1983;24:905–908.
71. Friedland JS, Warrell DA. The Jarisch-Herxheimer reaction in leptospirosis: Possible pathogenesis and review. Rev Infect Dis. 1991;13:207–210.
72. Faine S. Guidelines for the Control of Leptospirosis. Offset publication 67. Geneva: World Health Organization; 1982.
73. Bolin CA, Cassells JA, Zuerner RL, Trueba G. Effect of vaccination with a monovalent *Leptospira interrogans* serovar *hardjo* type hardjo-bovis vaccine on type of hardjo-bovis infection in cattle. Am J Vet Res. 1991;52:1639–1643.
74. Tang YK. A field study on the post-inoculation reaction and immunological effects in vaccinated population immunized with 'Zhejiang type-D' leptospiral vaccine. Chin J Epidemiol (Pei-Ching). 1991;12:335–338.
75. Chen TZ. Development and situation of and techniques for production of leptospirosis vaccine in China. Jpn J Bacteriol. 1985;40:755–762.
76. Shenberg E, Torten M. A new leptospiral vaccine for use in man. I. Development of a vaccine from *Leptospira* grown on chemically defined medium. J Infect Dis. 1973;128:642–646.
77. Torten M, Shenberg E, Gerichter CB, et al. A new leptospiral vaccine for use in man. II. Clinical and serologic evaluation of a field trial of volunteers. J Infect Dis. 1973;128:647–651.
78. Babudieri B. The prevention of leptospirosis infections. Sci Repts 1st Super Sanita. 1962;2:208–221.
79. Broom JC, Norris TStM. Failure of prophylactic oral penicillin to inhibit a human laboratory case of leptospirosis. Lancet. 1957;1:721–722.

Chapter 230

Borrelia Species (Relapsing Fever)

WARREN D. JOHNSON, JR.
LINNIE M. GOLIGHTLY

Relapsing fever is caused by arthropod-borne spirochetes of the genus *Borrelia* and is clinically characterized by recurrent episodes of fever and spirochetemia.[1–4] The human body louse transmits *Borrelia recurrentis*, which causes epidemic relapsing fever, and ticks of the genus *Ornithodoros* transmit the many species of *Borrelia* that cause endemic relapsing fever.

ETIOLOGY

The genus *Borrelia* belongs to the family Treponemataceae, which contains all spirochetal pathogens, including the genera *Treponema* and *Leptospira*.[3] Borreliae are helical, 8 to 30 μm long, and 0.2 to 0.5 μm wide, have 3 to 10 loose spirals, are actively motile, and divide by transverse fission.[1, 5] They are readily stained with aniline or acid dyes, but strains cannot be distinguished by morphologic characteristics. Borreliae have an outer slimelike layer, a cell wall and cytoplasmic membrane, and numerous internal fibrils.[6] They are promptly killed by desiccation and ultraviolet rays but survive and retain their virulence when frozen at −73°C for many months.[1]

Borrelia strains have been cultivated in artificial media with generation times ranging from 18 hours (*Borrelia hermsii*)[7, 8] to 8 to 9 hours (*B. recurrentis*).[9] Rodents (rats, hamsters, guinea pigs) injected with some strains develop latent brain infections.[1] Tick-borne borreliae remain viable in their natural tick vectors for up to 12 years, and this represents the optimal method for maintaining organisms.[5] In mice, *B. hermsii* reversibly changes its major outer surface protein when it is transmitted by the tick to the mammalian host and back to the tick.[10] There is also tick-spirochete specificity, and this has been used to identify *Borrelia* spp.[11, 12]

EPIDEMIOLOGY AND TRANSMISSION

Relapsing fever occurs throughout the world, with the exception of a few areas in the Southwest Pacific.[11, 12] The distribution and occurrence of epidemic relapsing fever is largely determined by socioeconomic and ecologic factors, whereas the distribution of endemic tick-borne disease is governed by the biology of the tick.

Louse-borne relapsing fever is caused only by *B. recurrentis* and is transmitted from person to person by the human body louse (*Pediculus humanus*).[2] After the louse ingests infective human blood, the spirochetes penetrate the midgut and multiply in the hemolymph. Tissues of the louse are not invaded by spirochetes, so disease cannot be transmitted to humans by louse saliva or excrement, or transovarially to the progeny of the louse. Epidemic relapsing fever therefore results from crushing lice, with the release of infective organisms capable of penetrating intact skin or mucous membranes.[12] Lice are infective for their lifetime (10 to 60 days). Humans are the only hosts for this organism. Louse-borne relapsing fever usually occurs in epidemics that are associated with catastrophic events, such as war or famine, that result in overcrowding and dissemination of body lice. The last great epidemic was during World War II in North Africa and Europe and caused an estimated 50,000 deaths.[1, 2] Louse-borne relapsing fever remains endemic in the highlands of Central and East Africa (Ethiopia, Sudan, Somalia, Chad) and in the South American Andes (Bolivia, Peru).[13]

Tick-borne relapsing fever is caused by at least 15 *Borrelia* spp. and is transmitted to humans by soft ticks of the genus *Ornithodoros*. Many rodents and small animals (chipmunks, squirrels, rabbits, rats, mice, owls, lizards) serve as natural reservoirs for these borreliae.[11, 12] Borreliae contained in the blood meal of the tick multiply rapidly and within hours invade all tissues, including salivary glands, excretory organs, and the genital system. Infection of humans occurs when saliva or excrement is released by the tick while feeding. Transovarial passage of borreliae to the tick progeny is an important mechanism for perpetuation of the spirochete, because ticks can survive for up to 15 years without feeding.[12] *Ornithodoros* ticks prefer warm, humid environments and altitudes of 1500 to 6000 feet. They are worldwide in distribution. They inhabit caves, decaying wood, rodent burrows, and animal shelters. Their range of movement is limited (less than 50 yards), but rodents may carry them passively into human dwellings. Their presence may pass unnoticed because they are typically night feeders, lack a painful bite, and complete their blood feeding in 5 to 20 minutes.[12, 13] The intrusion of humans into their environment creates the opportunity for disease transmission. The largest outbreak of tick-borne relapsing fever in the Western Hemisphere was in 62 campers residing in log cabins (Arizona, 1973).[14] The magnitude of this outbreak may have been related to concurrent epizootic plague that killed many of the natural rodent hosts of the tick.[12]

PATHOPHYSIOLOGY

Borreliae are present in blood during the febrile illness, disappearing before afebrile periods and returning to the blood stream during the subsequent febrile episodes. Spirochetemia in louse-borne disease may reach 100,000 organisms/mm^3 of blood.[2] Borreliae are sequestered in internal organs during the afebrile periods and reemerge antigenically modified.[15] This cyclic process of antigenic variation followed by specific antibody production is responsible for the relapsing course of this disease. With successive relapses, borreliae revert to antigenic types similar to those present in earlier relapses. The ultimate termination of clinical disease has been attributed primarily to the development of specific borreliacidal antibody rather than to the activity of phagocytic cells.[1, 16]

At autopsy, hepatitis and hepatic necrosis, miliary splenic abscesses, central nervous system lesions (hemorrhages, perivascular infiltrates, degenerative lesions), myocarditis, and hemorrhagic, gastrointestinal, and renal lesions have been described.[2, 3, 17]

CLINICAL MANIFESTATIONS

The clinical manifestations of louse-borne and tick-borne relapsing fever are quite similar.[1–4] The variations that occur may be related to differences in spirochete strains, inoculating dose, host immunity, and general condition of the patients. The clinical features of relapsing fever are summarized in Table 230–1.

The incubation period of both forms of relapsing fever may be difficult to establish, because louse exposure is often long-term, and the tick bite may not be recognized. Generally, louse-borne disease has a longer incubation period, longer febrile periods and afebrile intervals, and fewer relapses than tick-borne disease. Characteristically, both types of relapsing fever have an acute onset of high fever with rigors, severe headache, myalgias, arthralgias, lethargy, photophobia, and cough. Prodromal symptoms are rare. Initial physical findings often include conjunctival suffusion, petechiae, and diffuse abdominal tenderness with hepatomegaly and splenomegaly. Less common findings include nuchal rigidity, pulmonary rales and rhonchi, lymphadenopathy, and jaundice. During the course of the illness the fever is remittent and accompanied by tachycardia and tachypnea. Hemorrhage is common but rarely severe (petechiae, epistaxis, hemoptysis, hematuria, hematemesis). Iritis and iridocycli-

TABLE 230–1 Summary of Clinical Features of Relapsing Fever

Manifestation	Mean Value or Incidence	
	Louse-Borne Disease	Tick-Borne Disease
Case-fatality rate (%)	4–40	2–5
Incubation period (d)	8 (4–18)*	7 (4–18)*
Duration of first febrile attack (d)	5.5	3
Duration of afebrile interval (d)	9	7
Duration of relapses (d)	2	2–3
Number of relapses	1–2 (1–5)*	3 (0–13)*
Maximal temperature (°F)	101–102	105
Splenomegaly (%)	77	41
Hepatomegaly (%)	66	17
Jaundice (%)	36	7
Rash (%)	8	28
Respiratory symptoms (%)	34 (cough)	16
Central nervous system involvement (%)	30	9

*Range.
From Southern PM Jr, Sanford JP. Relapsing fever: A clinical and microbiological review. Medicine. 1969;48:129–149.

tis may result in permanent impairment of vision. Pneumonia, bronchitis, and otitis media may occur. A truncal skin rash of 1 to 2 days' duration is common at the end of the primary febrile episode.[3] The rash can be petechial, macular, or papular. Neurologic findings are reported in up to 30% of patients and include coma, cranial nerve palsies, hemiplegia, meningitis, and seizures.[3, 17] Myocarditis with associated arrhythmias, cerebral hemorrhage, and hepatic failure are the most common causes of death.

The primary febrile episode characteristically terminates abruptly in 3 to 6 days. This crisis may be associated with fatal hypotension and shock. After 7 to 10 days, fever and symptoms suddenly recur. The duration and the intensity of the symptoms progressively decrease with each relapse. Louse-borne relapsing fever is usually associated with a single relapse, whereas multiple relapses are the rule in tick-borne disease. Relapsing fever during pregnancy is associated with increased maternal and infant morbidity and mortality.[18–20]

DIAGNOSIS

The definitive diagnosis of relapsing fever is established by the demonstration of borreliae in the peripheral blood of febrile patients (Fig. 230–1). Spirochetes are found in 70% of cases when wet blood smears are examined by darkfield microscopy or in Giemsa- or Wright-stained thick and thin smears.[3, 21] Organisms are rarely found during afebrile periods. The diagnostic yield can be increased by the examination of acridine orange–stained smears by fluorescence microscopy.[22]

Agglutinating, complement-fixing, borreliacidal, and immobilizing antibodies are detectable in serum. However, these tests are not generally available and, if performed, are of limited diagnostic value owing to antigenic variation of strains and the complexity of the relapse phenomenon.[16, 21] *Proteus* OXK agglutinin titers are elevated in relapsing fever, with the highest titers being found in patients with louse-borne disease (1:80 or greater). Antibodies to OX-19 and OX-2 are rare. The serologic tests for syphilis are positive in 5 to 10% of patients. Serologic tests for Lyme disease may be positive.[23] Leukocytosis (to 25,000 cells/mm^3) and an increased erythrocyte sedimentation rate (to 110 mm/hour) are common. The cerebrospinal fluid pressure is usually elevated in patients with central nervous system involvement and is associated with a pleocytosis (15 to 2200 cells/mm^3) and with an elevated protein concentration (to 160 mg/100 ml).[3] The spinal fluid glucose level is normal. Spirochetes have been detected in cerebrospinal fluid by smear or by animal inoculation in up to 12% of the patients with central nervous system signs.

An early clinical diagnosis of louse-borne relapsing fever is not difficult during epidemics unless there is coexisting epidemic typhus, a disease also transmitted by the body louse. During the initial febrile episode of an isolated case of relapsing fever, the differential diagnosis can include malaria, typhoid fever, hepatitis, leptospirosis, rat-bite fever, Colorado tick fever, and dengue.[24] Epidemiologic considerations, the occurrence of relapses, and the demonstration of spirochetemia will exclude these diagnoses. The diagnosis of tick-borne relapsing fever may be complicated in regions where Lyme disease is endemic owing to the similar neurologic manifestations of the diseases and cross-reactive serologic assays.[23, 25]

TREATMENT AND PREVENTION

Relapsing fever has been treated successfully with tetracycline, chloramphenicol, penicillin, and erythromycin.[26–29] Tetracycline, in a single oral dose (0.5 g), is the preferred therapy in louse-borne relapsing fever except in pregnant women and children younger than 8 years (teeth and bone staining).[29] Erythromycin, 0.5 g in a single oral dose, is an equally effective alternative therapy.[28] Tick-borne relapsing fever is often treated with either tetracycline or erythromycin, 0.5 g every 6 hours for 5 to 10 days, because of the higher rate of treatment failures and relapses in these patients.[3, 26, 27] Meningitis or encephalitis should be treated with parenteral antibiotics, such as penicillin G, cefotaxime, or ceftriaxone, for 14 days or more.[17] The mortality of treated relapsing fever is less than 5%.[3] Untreated epidemic louse-borne disease has a mortality of up to 40%.[1, 2]

Antibiotic treatment typically induces a Jarisch-Herxheimer reaction with severe rigors, leukopenia, an increase in temperature, and a decrease in blood pressure. The onset of the reaction occurs within 2 hours of initiating therapy and coincides with clearing of the spirochetemia. The reaction appears to be an exaggeration of the crisis observed in untreated patients and is most severe in louse-borne disease treated with penicillin. A significant percentage of patients with tick-borne relapsing fever, however, also develop the reaction. Because the reaction may be life-threatening, it has been recommended that patients be kept under observation for approximately 2 hours after the initiation of treatment.[23] Spirochetal endotoxemia with activation of kinins and fibrinolytic and complement factors may have a major role in both the acute illness and the

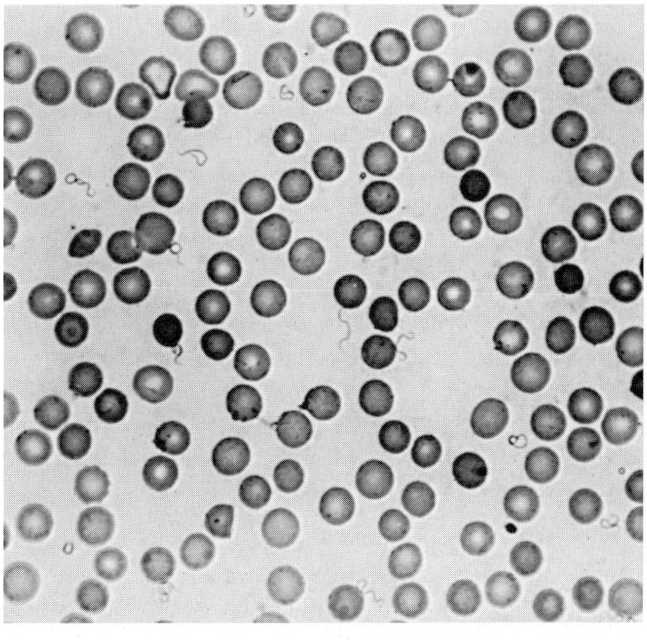

FIGURE 230–1. Peripheral blood smear stained with Wright stain. The *Borrelia* spirochetes can be seen readily. (Original magnification, ×1000.) (Courtesy of Dr. Thomas Butler, Lubbock, Tex.)

development of this reaction.[30] The Jarisch-Herxheimer reaction is associated with transient elevations of levels of plasma tumor necrosis factor, interleukin-6, and interleukin-8 concentrations.[31] It is prevented by prior administration of antibodies against tumor necrosis factor-α.[32–34] The prior administration of hydrocortisone is ineffective.[26, 29]

Prevention of relapsing fever requires avoidance or elimination of the arthropod vectors. The varied habitats and the vast geographic areas populated by *Ornithodoros* ticks make their eradication impossible. Insecticides can be used in dwellings and surrounding areas, and insect repellents applied to clothing and persons may further decrease exposure opportunities. Prevention of louse-borne disease is accomplished by good personal hygiene and, if necessary, delousing procedures. DDT-resistant louse strains have developed since World War II, and other insecticides may be required, for example, dimethyl dithiophosphate (malathion).[26]

REFERENCES

1. Felsenfeld O. *Borrelia*: Strains, Vectors, Human and Animal Borreliosis. St Louis: Warren H Green; 1971:180.
2. Bryceson ADM, Parry EHO, Perine PL, et al. Louseborne relapsing fever. A clinical and laboratory study of 62 cases in Ethiopia and a reconsideration of the literature. Q J Med. 1970;39:129–170.
3. Southern PM Jr, Sanford JP. Relapsing fever: A clinical and microbiological review. Medicine. 1969;48:129–149.
4. Barbour AG, Hayes SF. Biology of *Borrelia* species. Microbiol Rev. 1986;50:381–400.
5. Felsenfeld O. Borreliae, human relapsing fever, and parasite vector host relationships. Bacteriol Rev. 1965;29:46.
6. Hovind-Hougen K. *Treponema* and *Borrelia* morphology. In: Johnson RC, ed. The Biology of Parasitic Spirochetes. New York: Academic Press; 1976:7.
7. Kelly RT. Cultivation and physiology of relapsing fever borreliae. In: Johnson RC, ed. The Biology of Parasitic Spirochetes. New York: Academic Press; 1976:87.
8. Kelly R. Cultivation of *Borrelia hermsii*. Science. 1971;173:443–444.
9. Cutler SJ, Fekade D, Hussein K, et al. Successful in-vitro cultivation of *Borrelia recurrentis*. Lancet. 1994;343:242.
10. Schwan TG, Hinnebusch BJ. Bloodstream- versus tick-associated variants of a relapsing fever bacterium. Science. 1998;280:1938.
11. Burgdorfer W. The enlarging spectrum of tickborne spirochetoses: R R Parker Memorial Address. Rev Infect Dis. 1986;8:932–940.
12. Burgdorfer W. The epidemiology of relapsing fevers. In: Johnson RC, ed. The Biology of Parasitic Spirochetes. New York: Academic Press; 1976:191.
13. Felsenfeld O. The problem of relapsing fever in the Americas. Indiana Med. 1973;42:7.
14. Centers for Disease Control and Prevention. Relapsing fever. MMWR Morb Mortal Wkly Rep. 1973;22:242–246.
15. Barbour AG. Antigenic variation of a relapsing fever *Borrelia* species. Ann Rev Microbiol. 1990;44:155–171.
16. Felsenfeld O. Immunity in relapsing fever. In: Johnson RC, ed. The Biology of Parasitic Spirochetes. New York: Academic Press; 1976:351–358.
17. Cadavid D, Barbour AG. Neuroborreliosis during relapsing fever: Review of the clinical manifestations, pathology, and treatment of infections in human and experimental animals. Clin Infect Dis. 1998;26:151.
18. Jongen VHWM, van Roosmalen J, Tiems J, et al. Tick-borne relapsing fever and pregnancey outcome in rural Tanzania. Acta Obstet Gynecol Scand. 1997;76:834.
19. Dupont HT, La Scola B, Williams R, Raoult D. A focus of tick-borne relapsing fever in southern Zaire. Clin Infect Dis. 1997;25:139.
20. Borgnolo G, Hailu B, Ciancarelli A, et al. Louse-borne relapsing fever: A clinical and an epidemiological study of 389 patients in Asella Hospital, Ethiopia. Trop Geogr Med. 1993;45:66.
21. Burgdorfer W. The diagnosis of relapsing fever. In: Johnson RC, ed. The Biology of Parasitic Spirochetes. New York: Academic Press; 1976:225.
22. Sciotto CG, Lauer BA, White WL, et al. Detection of *Borrelia* in acridine orange–stained blood smears by fluorescence microscopy. Arch Pathol Lab Med. 1983;107:384–386.
23. Dworkin MS, Anderson DE Jr, Schwan TG, et al. Tick-borne relapsing fever in the northwestern United States and southwestern Canada. Clin Infect Dis. 1998;26:122.
24. Le CT. Tickborne relapsing fever in children. Pediatrics. 1980;66:963–966.
25. Rawlings JA. An overview of tick-borne relapsing fever with emphasis on outbreaks in Texas. Tex Med. 1995;91:56.
26. Sanford JP. Relapsing fever-treatment and control. In: Johnson RC, ed. The Biology of Parasitic Spirochetes. New York: Academic Press; 1976:389–394.
27. Horton JM, Blaser MJ. The spectrum of relapsing fever in the Rocky Mountains. Arch Intern Med. 1985;145:871–875.
28. Perine PL, Teklu B. Antibiotic treatment of louseborne relapsing fever in Ethiopia: A report of 377 cases. Am J Trop Med Hyg. 1983;32:1096–1100.
29. Butler T. Relapsing fever: New lessons about antibiotic action. Ann Intern Med. 1985;102:397.
30. Galloway RE, Levin J, Butler T, et al. Activation of protein mediators of inflammation and evidence for endotoxemia in *Borrelia recurrentis* infection. Am J Med. 1977;63:933–938.
31. Negussie Y, Remick DG, DeForge LE, et al. Detection of plasma tumor necrosis factor, interleukins 6 and 8 during the Jarisch-Herxheimer reaction of relapsing fever. J Exp Med. 1992;175:1207–1212.
32. Fekade D, Knox K, Hussein K, et al. Prevention of Jarisch-Herxheimer reactions by treatment with antibodies against tumor necrosis factor α. N Engl J Med. 1996;335:311.
33. Beutler B, Munford RS. Tumor necrosis factor and the Jarisch-Herxheimer reaction. N Engl J Med. 1996;335:347.
34. Coxon RE, Fekade D, Knox K, et al. The effect of antibody against TNF α on cytokine response in Jarisch-Herxheimer reactions of louse-borne relapsing fever. Q J Med. 1997;90:213.

Chapter 231

Borrelia burgdorferi (Lyme Disease, Lyme Borreliosis)

ALLEN C. STEERE

Lyme disease or Lyme borreliosis, which is caused by the tick-borne spirochete *Borrelia burgdorferi*, occurs in temperate regions of North America, Europe, and Asia.[1] It is now the most common vector-borne disease in the United States.[2] The illness usually begins in summer (stage 1) with a characteristic expanding skin lesion, called *erythema migrans* (EM), that occurs at the site of the tick bite.[3, 4] Within several days to weeks (stage 2), the spirochete may spread to many other sites, particularly to other skin sites,[3] the nervous system,[5] the heart,[6] or the joints.[7] After months to years (stage 3), sometimes following long periods of latent infection, the spirochete may cause persistent disease, most commonly affecting the joints,[7] nervous system,[8–11] or skin.[12] Serologic testing is the most practical laboratory aid in diagnosis.[13, 14] All stages of the disorder are usually curable by appropriate antibiotic therapy.[1, 15]

Lyme disease was recognized as a separate entity in 1975 because of close geographic clustering of affected children in Lyme, Connecticut, who were thought to have juvenile rheumatoid arthritis.[16] However, parts of the illness were recognized previously in Europe and were given different names, including erythema chronicum migrans,[17] Bannwarth's syndrome,[18] or acrodermatitis chronica atrophicans.[12] Although there are regional variations, the basic outlines of the disease are similar worldwide.

CAUSATIVE ORGANISM

Like all spirochetes, the *Borrelia* spp. have a protoplasmic cylinder that is surrounded first by a cytoplasmic membrane, then by the periplasm, which contains the flagella, and finally by an outer membrane that is only loosely associated with the underlying structures (Fig. 231–1).[19] The *Borrelia* spp. are longer and more loosely coiled than the other spirochetes. Of the *Borrelia* spp., *B. burgdorferi* is the longest (20 to 30 μm) and narrowest (0.2 to 0.3 μm), and it has fewer flagella (7 to 11).[20] The unusual feature of *B. burgdorferi* is that its chromosome and some of its plasmids are linear DNA molecules.[21]

The complete genome of a prototypic *B. burgdorferi* strain (B31) was recently sequenced.[22] The total genome was small (approximately 1.5 megabases); it included a linear chromosome of 950 kilobases along with 9 circular and 12 linear plasmids, which made up 40% of the genome. The organism had a minimal number of proteins with biosynthetic activity, and apparently it depends on the host for much of its nutritional requirements. The remarkable aspect

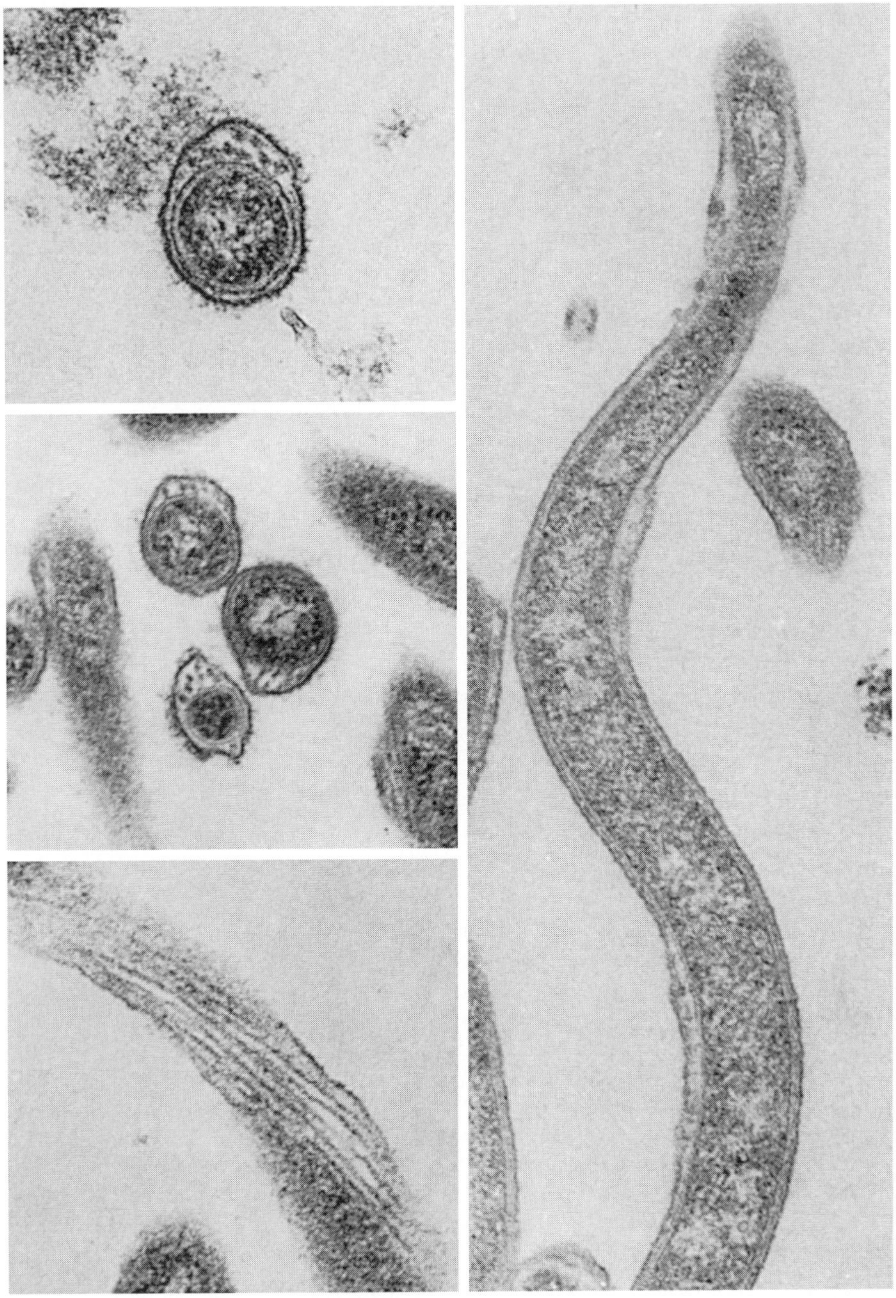

FIGURE 231–1. Electron micrographs of *Borrelia burgdorferi.* The spirochetes have a transverse diameter of about 0.2 μm and 7 to 11 flagella, which are shown *(left panel)* in cross-section in the upper and middle pictures and in tangential section in the lower picture. In longitudinal section *(right panel),* the organism has an apparent slime layer, an outer membrane, flagellae, a cell wall, and cytoplasmic constituents; its length is 11 to 39 μm. (40,000, except upper left [60,000]). (From Steere AC, Grodzicki RL, Kornblatt AN, et al. The spirochetal etiology of Lyme disease. N Engl J Med. 1983;308:733.)

of the *B. burgdorferi* genome was the large number of sequences for predicted and known lipoproteins. Some of these proteins are differentially expressed and presumably help the spirochete to adapt and survive in markedly different arthropod and mammalian environments.

Known lipoprotiens include outer-surface proteins (Osp) A through F.[23–30] Two major outer-surface proteins, OspA and OspB, are encoded by the same 50 kilobase linear plasmid and share 56% sequence homology.[23] Along with lipoprotein 6.6 (Lp6.6), these proteins are expressed primarily in the arthropod phase of the enzootic cycle.[24, 25] OspA has an antiparallel β strand topology with a middle nonglobular region connecting globular N- and C-terminal domains.[26] During tick feeding, as the spirochete migrates from the midgut to the salivary gland, OspC, which is encoded by a 26 kb circular plasmid,[27] is upregulated.[28] OspE and OspF are immunogenic in some patients.[30]

A number of proteins have been identified that are differentially expressed by the spirochete during early infection,[31–38] including decorin-binding proteins A and B (DbpA and DbpB)[31] and a 47 kD fibronectin-binding protein.[32] During this phase of the infection, another surface exposed lipoprotein, called VlsE, has been reported to undergo extensive antigenic variation.[33] However, this variation does not depend on an intact immune system. Additional spirochetal proteins include a 39-kD *Borrelia* membrane protein A (BmpA),[39] the 41-kD flagellar antigen,[40] 60- and 73-kD heat shock proteins,[41, 42] a 66-kD integral outer-membrane protein that may function as a porin,[43] and a 93-kD antigen that is a part of the protoplasmic cylinder.[44]

B. burgdorferi grows best at 33°C in a complex liquid medium called Barbour-Stoenner-Kelly medium[45] and less well on various solid media.[46] It has been cultured readily from EM skin lesions,[47] but culture from other sites has been difficult.

Three pathogenic groups of the *B. burgdorferi sensu lato* complex have now been identified.[48–51] To date, all North American strains have belonged to the first group, *B. burgdorferi sensu stricto.*[48] All three groups have been found in Europe, but most isolates there have been group 2 (*Borrelia garinii*) and 3 (*Borrelia afzelii*) strains.[48, 49] Only the latter two groups have been found in Asia. These differences may well account for regional variations in the clinical picture of Lyme borreliosis. Several apparently nonpathogenic *Borrelia* groups have been described, including *B. andersoni, B. bissetti, B. japonica, B. lusitaniae,* and *B. valaisiana.*[52]

VECTOR OF TRANSMISSION AND ANIMAL HOSTS

The vectors of Lyme borreliosis are several closely related ixodid ticks that are part of the *Ixodes ricinus* complex.[53–56] In the northeastern and midwestern United States, *Ixodes scapularis* (also called *Ixodes dammini*) is the vector, and *Ixodes pacificus* is the vector in the West. In Europe, *Ixodes ricinus* is the primary vector, and in Asia it is *Ixodes persulcatus.*[57–59] In field studies in Connecticut and New York, the spirochetal pathogen has been found in 10 to 50% of nymphal and adult *I. scapularis.*[60, 61] Although *B. burgdorferi* has been demonstrated in mosquitoes and deer flies,[62] only ticks of the *I. ricinus* complex seem to be important in the transmission of the spirochete to humans.

The peak questing periods for adult *I. scapularis* are spring and fall; for nymphs, May through July; and for larvae, August and September.[63] The nymphal stage is primarily responsible for transmission of the disease. In studies of experimental transmission in rodents, tick attachment for 24 hours or more was necessary before transmission of the spirochete occurred.[64]

In the northeastern and mid-Atlantic states, immature *I. scapularis* (larvae and nymphs) feed primarily on rodents, particularly on white-footed mice *(Peromyscus leucopus),*[65] and adults usually feed on larger mammals, especially deer *(Odocoileus virginianus).*[66] Infection with *B. burgdorferi* in these areas is maintained by horizontal transmission of the organism from infected nymphal *I. scapularis* to *P. leucopus* to larval *I. scapularis,* which then molt to infected nymphs to complete the cycle.[67] Deer, which are not involved in the life cycle of the spirochete, are quite important for the life cycle of *I. scapularis,* and deer are abundant in the areas of New England where Lyme disease is endemic.[66]

The vector ecology of *B. burgdorferi* is different on the West Coast. This is because the nymphal stage of *I. pacificus* prefers to feed on lizards rather than rodents, and lizards are not susceptible to infection with *B. burgdorferi.*[68] There, the spirochete is maintained in nature in a horizontal cycle between the dusky-footed woodrat *Neotoma fuscipes* and *Ixodes neotomae*, a tick that does not feed on humans.[69] Only the relatively few larval and nymphal *I. pacificus* ticks that feed on infected woodrats rather than lizards are responsible for transmitting the spirochete to humans when they molt to the next stage. Accordingly, the infection rate of *I. pacificus* ticks is only 1 to 3%, and the number of cases on the West Coast is much less than that on the East Coast.

The tick has been found on and cultured from many other wild and domestic animals,[70–72] including birds,[73] which may be responsible for the spread of the tick over wide areas. Although zoonotic infection with *B. burgdorferi* is widespread within endemic foci, illness is not known to develop in wild animals.[70–73] In contrast, clinical Lyme disease does occur in domestic animals, including dogs,[74] horses,[75] and cattle.[76]

EPIDEMIOLOGY

According to data from the Centers for Disease Control and Prevention, Lyme disease is now the most common vector-borne infection in the United States.[2] Since surveillance was begun in 1982, more than 100,000 cases have been reported, and during the 1990s, more than 10,000 new cases have been noted each summer.[2] Although cases have been reported in 48 states, to date the complete life cycle of *B. burgdorferi* has been documented only in 19 states. The disorder occurs primarily in three distinct foci: in the Northeast from Massachusetts to Maryland, in the Midwest in Wisconsin and Minnesota, and in the West in California and Oregon.[56] Lyme borreliosis also occurs in temperate regions of the Northern Hemisphere in Europe,[57] Scandinavia,[58] the former Soviet Union,[59] China,[77] and Japan.[78]

In the United States, the infection is spreading and has caused focal epidemics, particularly in the northeastern United States.[79–81] From 1985 to 1989, the number of counties in New York State with documented *I. scapularis* ticks increased from 4 to 22, and the number of counties endemic for Lyme disease increased from 4 to 8.[82] During the subsequent 10 years, *I. scapularis* ticks have spread to 54 of the 58 counties in the state (personal communication: Drs. Dennis White and Dale Morse, New York State Health Department). In the United States, the majority of affected individuals have had symptoms of the illness,[79–81] whereas in Europe, the majority have been asymptomatic. Of 346 people who were studied in the highly endemic area of Liso, Sweden, 41 (12%) had symptoms of the illness and 89 (26%) had evidence of subclinical infection.[83] In a serosurvey of 950 Swiss orienteers, 26% had detectable IgG antibodies to *B. burgdorferi,* but only 2 to 3% had a past history of definite or probable Lyme borreliosis.[84]

The ages of patients range from 2 to 88 years (median, 28 years), and the sex ratio is nearly 1:1.[3] Age-adjusted attack rates show a bimodal distribution, with the greatest risk of acquiring the illness in children and middle-aged adults. In the northeastern and midwestern U.S., the onset of the illness is generally between May 1 and October 30; most onsets occur in June and July.[3, 53]

PATHOGENESIS

To maintain its complex enzootic cycle, *B. burgdorferi* must adapt to two markedly different environments, the tick and the mammalian host. For example, in the midgut of the tick, the spirochete expresses OspA and OspB.[24] When the blood meal is taken, OspC is upregulated as the organism traverses to the tick salivary gland and to the mammalian host.[28] Later, during mammalian infection, other proteins are presumably expressed that are essential for disease pathogenesis.[85]

After injection of *B. burgdorferi* by the tick and an incubation period of 3 to 32 days, the spirochete usually first multiplies locally in the skin at the site of the tick bite. Several days later, the organism begins to spread in the skin, and within days to weeks, it may disseminate to many sites. Early in the illness, the spirochete has been recovered from EM skin lesions, blood, and cerebrospinal fluid,[47, 86–88] and it has been seen in small numbers in specimens of myocardium, retina, muscle, bone, spleen, liver, meninges, and brain.[89] In a rat model, permeability changes in the blood-brain barrier occur within 12 hours after inoculation of the spirochete, and the organism may be cultured from cerebrospinal fluid within 24 hours.[90]

Bacterial spread within the host is probably facilitated by the spirochete's ability to bind human plasminogen and urokinase-type plasminogen activator to its surface.[91, 92] Plasmin, the activated form of plasminogen, is a potent protease that could promote tissue invasion. *B. burgdorferi* may adhere to many different types of mammalian cells, and to date, two binding mechanisms have been identified. First, the spirochete attaches to several members of the integrin family of receptors, including the platelet-specific integrin receptor[93] and the vitronectin and fibronectin receptors.[94] A second pathway for cell attachment is mediated by host cell sugars, particularly glycosaminoglycans.[95] *B. burgdorferi* seems to cross a cell monolayer at intracellular junctions, although it can penetrate through the cytoplasm of a cell.[96] In in vitro systems, intracellular localization of a few *B. burgdorferi* has been demonstrated within human endothelial cells,[97] macrophages,[98] and fibroblasts,[99] but it is not yet clear if the spirochete can survive intracellularly in vivo. Dendritic cells isolated from the dermis readily engulf *B. burgdorferi* in vitro, preferentially by coiling phagocytosis.[100] Such spirochetes would be localized in the cytosol, suggesting presentation by MHC class I molecules, whereas intravesicular spirochetal antigens would be presented by MHC class II molecules.

Initially, the immune response in Lyme disease seems to be suppressed,[101] which may be an important mechanism in allowing the spirochete to disseminate. Within days to weeks, peripheral blood mononuclear cells begin to have heightened responsiveness to *B. burgdorferi* antigens and mitogens.[101–104] In vitro, the organism is a potent inducer of proinflammatory cytokines, including tumor necrosis factor-α[105] and interleukin-1β (IL-1β)[106] from peripheral blood mononuclear cells. *B. burgdorferi*–specific CD8$^+$ T cells, as well as CD4$^+$ T cells, probably play an important role in the control of the infection.[107] T helper (Th) cells from patients with Lyme arthritis or neuroborreliosis produce preferentially the proinflammatory cytokine, interferon-γ (IFN-γ).[108, 109] A novel population of Th cells secreting both IFN-γ and IL-10 has been described, induced by IL-12 secretion.[110]

The antibody response to *B. burgdorferi* develops slowly. The specific IgM response peaks between the third and the sixth week of infection[86] and often is associated with polyclonal activation of B cells, including elevated total serum IgM levels,[111] circulating immune complexes,[112] and cryoglobulins.[111] Membrane lipoproteins, including OspA, are mitogenic for B cells.[113] The specific IgG response develops gradually over months to an increasing array of spirochetal polypeptides[14, 114, 115] and nonprotein antigens.[116] Immune antibodies are required for the immune-mediated killing of spirochetes by the classical complement pathway.[117] Histologically, all affected tissues show an infiltration of lymphocytes and plasma cells.[89] Some degree of vascular damage, including mild vasculitis or hypervascular occlusion, may be seen in multiple sites, suggesting that the spirochete may have been in or around blood vessels.

Despite an active immune response, *B. burgdorferi* may survive for years in untreated patients in certain niches within the joints, nervous system, or skin; it is not yet known how it is able to sequester itself in these sites.

ANIMAL MODEL

Animal models of Lyme disease have been developed in mice,[118, 119] hamsters,[120] dogs,[121] and nonhuman primates.[122] Particularly important has been the murine model of Lyme disease in inbred C3H/HeJ mice, which develop acute arthritis and carditis 2 to 4 weeks after inoculation with *B. burgdorferi*; they do not develop EM or neurologic abnormalities.[118] Macrophages are the primary infiltrating cell in cardiac lesions, and cellular immunity is critical for the control of carditis.[123] In contrast, polymorphonuclear leukocytes and then lymphocytes are the prominent infiltrating cells in synovial tissue, and antibody is crucial for the resolution of arthritis.[124] Despite the resolution of acute lesions, spirochetes persist throughout the life of this inbred mouse strain, primarily in the skin. Recurrent waves of spirochetemia from that site may lead to recurrent attacks of arthritis. However, this murine strain does not develop the equivalent of human, chronic Lyme arthritis.

Comparison of infection in different inbred murine strains has shown the importance of genetic susceptibility, spirochetal burden, and the early immune response in the variability of subsequent arthritis. C3H/HeJ mice, which carry $H\text{-}2^k$ alleles, develop severe arthritis when infected with *B. burgdorferi*, whereas BALB/c mice, which carry $H\text{-}2^d$ alleles, develop only mild arthritis.[125] C3H/HeJ mice have a greater burden of spirochetes in their joints than BALB/c mice.[126] As an explanation for these findings, C3H/HeJ mice produce IFN-γ (Th1 response) when infected with the spirochete.[125] Although *B. burgdorferi*–infected BALB/c mice initially produce large amounts of IFN-γ, they switch to interleukin-4 (IL-4) production (Th2 response).[127] CD8$^+$ T cells are the main source of IFN-γ in both strains.[128] In this way, BALB/c mice seem to reduce the numbers of spirochetes initially and dampen the inflammatory response of the subsequent arthritis.

As with neurosyphilis, only human and nonhuman primates are known to be susceptible to neuroborreliosis. In one report, peripheral neuropathy was observed in all five rhesus monkeys that were infected with *B. burgdorferi*.[122] On postmortem examination, nerve lesions were observed, including nerve sheath fibrosis and focal demyelinization.

CLINICAL CHARACTERISTICS

As with other spirochetal infections, human Lyme borreliosis generally occurs in stages, with remissions and exacerbations and different clinical manifestations at each stage. Early infection consists of stage 1 (localized EM), followed within days or weeks by stage 2 (disseminated infection). Late infection, or stage 3 (persistent infection), usually begins months to years after the disease onset, sometimes following long periods of latent infection.[1] In an individual patient, however, the infection is highly variable, ranging from brief involvement in only one system to chronic, multisystem involvement of the skin, nerves, and joints for a period of years.

Early Infection: Stage 1 (Localized Infection)

EM, which occurs at the site of the tick bite, usually begins as a red macule or papule (Fig. 231–2*A* and Table 231–1).[3, 4] Of 314 patients in one study, 31% recalled a tick bite at the skin site where EM developed 3 to 32 days later.[3] As the area of redness around the center expands (final median diameter, 15 cm; range, 3 to 68 cm), most lesions continue to have bright red outer borders (usually flat, but occasionally raised) and partial central clearing. The centers of early lesions sometimes become intensely erythematous and indurated, vesicular, or necrotic. In some instances, migrating lesions remain an even intense red, several red rings are found within the outside one, or the central area turns blue before it clears. Although the lesion can be located anywhere, the thigh, groin, and axilla are particularly common sites. If EM is on the head, only a linear streak might be seen to emerge from the hairline. The lesion is hot to touch but often not painful. Perhaps as many as 25% of patients do not exhibit this characteristic skin manifestation.

Early Infection: Stage 2 (Disseminated Infection)

Within several days after the onset of the initial EM skin lesion, patients in the United States may develop multiple annular secondary lesions (see Fig. 231–2*B* and Table 231–1).[3, 4] Although their appearance is similar to that of the initial lesions, they are generally smaller, migrate less, and lack indurated centers; they are not associated with previous tick bites. Individual lesions sometimes appear and fade at different times, and their borders sometimes merge. During this period, some patients develop malar rash, conjunctivitis, or, rarely, diffuse urticaria. EM and secondary lesions usually fade within 3 to 4 weeks (range, 1 day to 14 months).

EM is often accompanied by malaise and fatigue, headache, fever and chills, generalized achiness, and regional lymphadenopathy.[3, 4] In addition, patients sometimes have evidence of meningeal irritation,

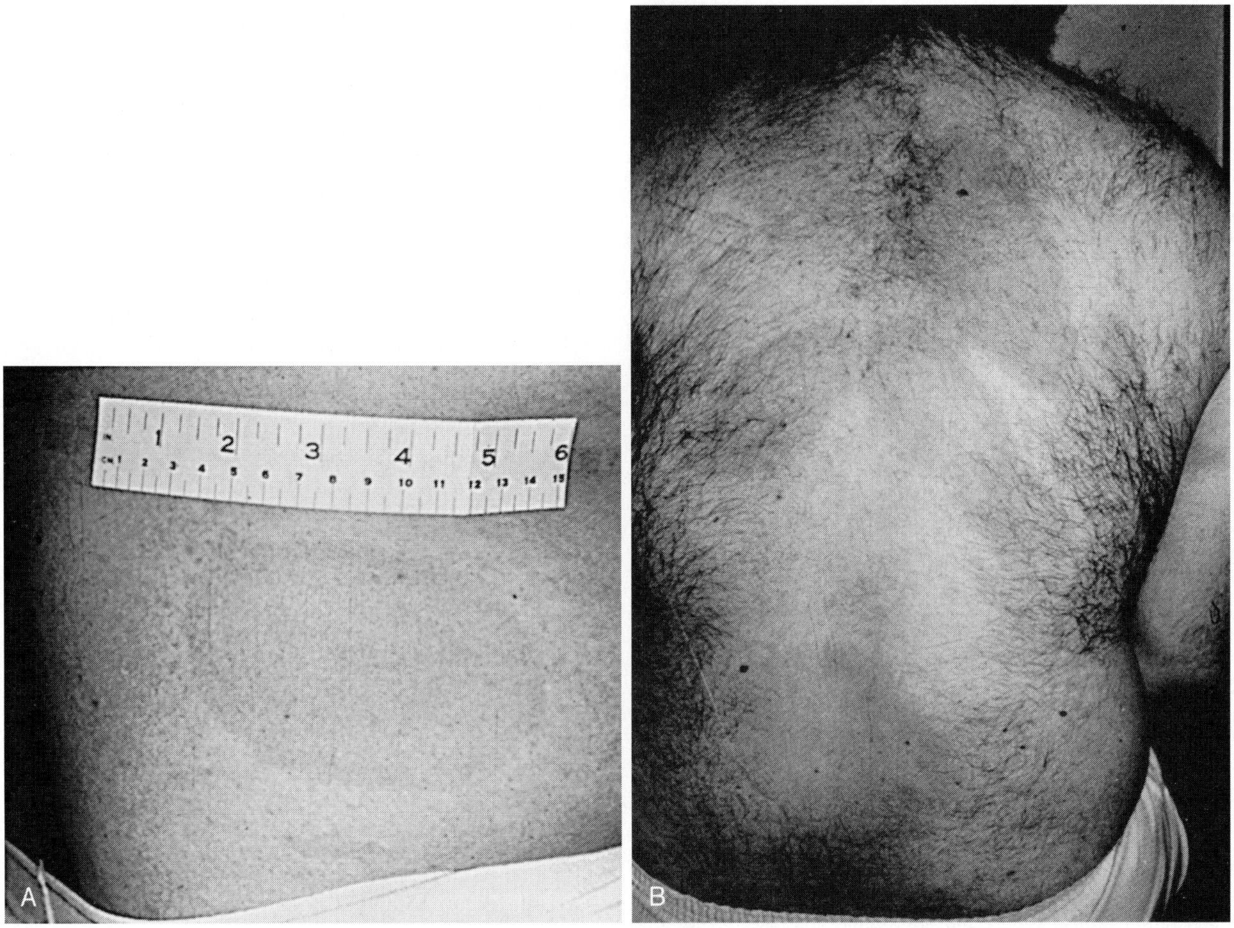

FIGURE 231–2. *A,* An early erythema migrans skin lesion is seen 4 days after detection. *B,* Four days after the onset of the initial skin lesion, secondary lesions have appeared, and several of their borders have merged. (From Steere AC, Bartenhagen NH, Cratt JE, et al. The early clinical manifestations of Lyme disease. Ann Intern Med. 1983;99:76.)

mild encephalopathy, migratory musculoskeletal pain, hepatitis, generalized lymphadenopathy or splenomegaly, sore throat, nonproductive cough, or testicular swelling. Except for fatigue and lethargy, which are often constant, the early signs and symptoms are typically intermittent and changing. For example, a patient might experience predominantly headache and a stiff neck for several days. After a few days of improvement, musculoskeletal pain might begin. Associated symptoms may occur several days before EM and, conversely, may last for months (particularly fatigue and lethargy) after the skin lesions have disappeared.

Symptoms suggestive of meningeal irritation may occur at the beginning of the illness when EM is present.[3, 4] Individuals with such symptoms often have episodic attacks of excruciating headache and neck pain, stiffness, or pressure, typically lasting for hours. During the first days of illness, such symptoms are not associated with a spinal fluid pleocytosis or objective neurologic deficit. After several weeks to months, however, about 15% of untreated patients in the United States develop frank neurologic abnormalities, including meningitis, encephalitis, cranial neuritis (including bilateral facial palsy), motor and sensory radiculoneuritis, mononeuritis multiplex, or myelitis—alone or in various combinations.[5] The usual pattern consists of fluctuating symptoms of meningitis with superimposed cranial (particularly facial palsy) or peripheral radiculoneuropathy. On examination, such patients usually have neck stiffness only on extreme flexion; Kernig's and Brudzinski's signs are not present. Facial palsy, or Bell's palsy, frequently occurs alone, and it may be the presenting manifestation of the disease.[129] In Europe, the most common manifestation is Bannwarth's syndrome, which includes neuritic pain, lymphocytic pleocytosis without headache, and sometimes cranial neuritis.[18] This syndrome has also been called tick-borne meningopolyneuritis (Garin-Bujadoux-Bannwarth syndrome),[130] lymphocytic meningoradiculitis, or chronic lymphocytic meningitis.

In patients with meningitis, cerebrospinal fluid (CSF) typically has a lymphocytic pleocytosis of about 100 cells/mm^3, often with an elevated protein but a normal glucose level.[5] Mononuclear cells responsive to *B. burgdorferi* are concentrated there[131]; specific IgG, IgM, or IgA antibody to the spirochete is produced intrathecally,[132, 133] and *B. burgdorferi*–specific oligoclonal bands may be present.[134] Antibodies to the flagellar antigen of *B. burgdorferi* have been shown to bind to a component of normal human axons identified as chaperonin-HSP60.[135] However, it is not known whether autoreactivity causes tissue damage or is a secondary epiphenomenon. Electrophysiologic studies of affected extremities suggest primarily axonal nerve involvement.[10, 11] Histologically, the lesions show axonal nerve injury with perivascular infiltration of lymphocytes and plasmocytes around epineural blood vessels.[136] Several cases of pseudotumor cerebri have been reported in children,[136] a syndrome characterized by increased intracranial pressure not caused by a space-occupying lesion. Stage 2 neurologic abnormalities usually last for weeks or months, but they may recur or become chronic.

Within several weeks after the onset of illness, about 5% of untreated patients develop cardiac involvement.[6] The most common abnormality is fluctuating degrees of atrioventricular block (first-degree, Wenckebach, or complete heart block).[6, 137] However, some patients have evidence of more diffuse cardiac involvement, including electrocardiographic changes or a gallium scan[138] compatible with acute myopericarditis, radionuclide evidence of mild left ventricular dysfunction, or, rarely, cardiomegaly. No patients have had heart

TABLE 231–1 Manifestations of Lyme Disease by Stage*

	Early Infection		Late Infection
System†	*Localized Stage 1*	*Disseminated Stage 2*	*Persistent Stage 3*
Skin	Erythema migrans (EM)	Secondary annular lesions Malar rash Diffuse erythema or urticaria Evanescent lesions Lymphocytoma	Acrodermatitis chronica atrophicans Localized scleroderma-like lesions
Musculoskeletal		Migratory pain in joints, tendons, bursae, muscle, bone Brief arthritis attacks Myositis‡ Osteomyelitis‡ Panniculitis‡	Prolonged arthritis attacks Chronic arthritis Peripheral enthesopathy Periostitis or joint subluxations below acrodermatitis
Neurologic		Meningitis Cranial neuritis, Bell's palsy Motor or sensory radiculoneuritis Subtle encephalitis Mononeuritis multiplex Pseudotumor cerebri Myelitis‡ Cerebellar ataxia‡	Chronic encephalomyelitis Spastic parapareses Ataxic gait Subtle mental disorders Chronic axonal polyradiculopathy
Lymphatic	Regional lymphadenopathy	Regional or generalized lymphadenopathy Splenomegaly	
Heart		Atrioventricular nodal block Myopericarditis Pancarditis	
Eyes		Conjunctivitis Iritis‡ Choroiditis‡ Retinal hemorrhage or detachment‡ Panophthalmitis‡	Keratitis
Liver		Mild or recurrent hepatitis	
Respiratory		Nonexudative sore throat Nonproductive cough Adult respiratory distress syndrome‡	
Kidney		Microscopic hematuria or proteinuria	
Genitourinary		Orchitis‡	
Constitutional symptoms	Minor	Severe malaise and fatigue	Fatigue

*The staging system provides a guideline for the expected timing of the different manifestations of the illness, but this may vary in an individual case.
†The systems are listed from the most to the least commonly affected.
‡Because the inclusion of these manifestations is based on one or a few cases, they should be considered possible but not proven manifestations of Lyme disease.
From Steere AC. Lyme disease. N Engl J Med. 1989; 321:586. Copyright © 1989 Massachusetts Medical Society. All rights reserved.

murmurs. The duration of cardiac involvement is usually brief (3 days to 6 weeks); complete heart block rarely persists for more than 1 week, and the insertion of a permanent pacemaker is unnecessary. One patient is known to have died of cardiac involvement of Lyme disease.[139] At autopsy, that patient had a lymphoplasmacellular infiltrate in the epicardium, myocardium, and endocardium, and a few spirochetes were seen in the myocardium. Spirochetes have also been demonstrated in the myocardium in vivo by endomyocardial biopsy.[140] One patient has been reported with chronic cardiomyopathy that was due to infection with *B. burgdorferi.*[141]

During this stage, musculoskeletal pain is common. The typical pattern is one of migratory pain in joints, tendons, bursae, muscle, or bones, often without joint swelling. The pain tends to affect only one or two sites at a time and usually lasts a few hours to several days in a given location. In addition, a few patients have been described with osteomyelitis,[142] myositis,[143] panniculitis,[144] or eosinophilic fasciitis.[145] Conjunctivitis is the most common eye abnormality in Lyme disease,[3] but deeper tissues in the eye may be affected as well. There are case reports of iritis followed by panophthalmitis,[146] choroiditis with exudative retinal detachments,[147] or interstitial keratitis,[148] similar to that seen in syphilis. About 20% of patients have evidence of mild hepatitis early in the illness.[3] Finally, a patient was reported with cough, fever, generalized maculopapular rash, myositis, and markedly abnormal liver function test findings.[149] She died of adult respiratory distress syndrome, which was believed to be secondary to Lyme disease.

Late Infection: Stage 3 (Persistent Infection)

Months after the onset of the illness, within the context of strong cellular and humoral immune responses to *B. burgdorferi*, about 60% of patients begin to experience intermittent attacks of joint swelling and pain, primarily in large joints, especially the knee, usually one or two joints at a time (see Table 231–1).[7] Affected knees are commonly more swollen than painful and are often hot but rarely red. Baker cysts may form and rupture early. However, both large and small joints may be affected. Attacks of arthritis generally last from a few weeks to months separated by periods of complete remission. Joint fluid white blood cell counts range from 500 to 110,000 cells/mm^3, most of which, in patients with high white blood cell counts, are polymorphonuclear leukocytes. Although the spirochete has been cultured from the joint fluid of only two patients with Lyme arthritis,[1] *B. burgdorferi* DNA may be detected by polymerase chain reaction (PCR) in the synovial tissue or joint fluid of most patients.[150, 151] *B. burgdorferi*–specific T cells, reactive with multiple spirochetal polypeptides, are concentrated in joint fluid.[102, 152] These T cells secrete primarily the proinflammatory Th1 cytokine IFN-γ,[109] and a Th1 response is dominant in synovium,[153] a pattern that leads to a delayed hypersensitivity response. The synovial lesion, which is similar to that seen in other forms of chronic inflammatory arthritis, shows synovial cell hyperplasia, vascular proliferation, and a heavy infiltration of mononuclear cells[154, 155]—a histologic picture that is suggestive of a delayed hypersensitivity immune response.

The total number of patients who continue to have recurrent attacks of arthritis decreases by about 10 to 20% each year.[7] However, attacks of knee swelling sometimes become longer during the second or third year of illness. It is usually during this period that a small percentage of untreated patients develop chronic arthritis, defined as 1 year or more of continuous joint inflammation.[7] The beginning of prolonged episodes of arthritis is often associated with the development of a marked IgG antibody response to OspA and OspB of the spirochete.[114]

Although most patients with either acute or chronic arthritis respond to antibiotic treatment, a small percentage have persistent joint inflammation for months or even several years after therapy. In these patients, *B. burgdorferi* DNA can usually not be detected in synovial tissue or joint fluid after antibiotic treatment,[150] suggesting that joint inflammation may continue in some patients after the eradication of the spirochete from the joint with antibiotic therapy. This outcome is associated with certain immunogenetic and immune markers,[156] including HLA-DRB1*0401 alleles and cellular immunity with dominant epitopes of OspA. The dominant epitope of OspA in the context of 0401 alleles was shown to have significant homology with human lymphocyte function–associated antigen (hLFA-1).[157] Moreover, hLFA-1 induced Th reactivity in 9 of 11 patients tested with treatment-resistant Lyme arthritis, but it did not induce Th reactivity in those with other forms of chronic inflammatory arthritis. Molecular mimicry between this dominant OspA epitope and hLFA-1 would provide an explanation for an ongoing T-cell response in genetically susceptible human subjects, resulting in persistent joint inflammation after the apparent eradication of the spirochete from the joint with antibiotic therapy.

From months to years after disease onset, sometimes following long periods of latent infection, patients may develop chronic neurologic manifestations of the disorder.[8–11] The most common form of chronic central nervous system involvement is a subacute encephalopathy affecting memory, mood, or sleep, sometimes with subtle language disturbance.[8, 9, 158] Patients with these symptoms often have CSF abnormalities, including increased CSF protein levels or evidence of intrathecal antibody production to *B. burgdorferi*, or both; frequently memory impairment can be demonstrated on neuropsychological tests,[8, 9, 159] and single photon emission computed tomography (SPECT) scanning of the brain often shows decreased perfusion of frontal cortical and subcortical structures.[160] In addition, patients may have peripheral sensory symptoms, either distal paresthesias or spinal or radicular pain.[10, 11] Even though sensory symptoms are often localized, electrophysiologic testing frequently shows a diffuse axonal polyneuropathy affecting both proximal and distal nerve segments.[10] Borrelial encephalomyelitis, which has been described primarily in Europe, is a severe neurologic disorder characterized by spastic parapareses, ataxia, cognitive impairment, bladder dysfunction, and cranial neuropathy, particularly of the seventh or eighth cranial nerve, accompanied by intrathecal antibody production of IgG antibody to *B. burgdorferi*.[161]

Acrodermatitis chronica atrophicans, which sometimes follows years after EM, has been observed primarily in Europe in association with *B. afzelii* infection.[49] Acrodermatitis chronica atrophicans begins with red violaceous lesions that become sclerotic or atrophic.[12] These lesions, which may be the presenting manifestation of the disease, may last for many years, and *B. burgdorferi* has been cultured from such lesions as much as 10 years after their onset.[162] Histologically, the rete ridges of the epidermis are typically lost, and a mononuclear cell infiltrate and telangiectasia are manifest throughout the underlying dermis.[163] Sclerotic lesions may resemble localized scleroderma.[164]

CONGENITAL INFECTION

In the mid-1980s, the transplacental transmission of *B. burgdorferi* was reported in two infants whose mothers had Lyme borreliosis during the first trimester of pregnancy.[165, 166] Both infants died during the first week of life. In both, spirochetes were seen in various fetal tissues stained with the Dieterle silver stain, but cultures and serologic testing were not done. In a retrospective review of 19 cases of Lyme disease during pregnancy, 5 were associated with adverse fetal outcomes.[167] Because all of the outcomes differed, they could not be linked conclusively to maternal Lyme disease. In subsequent prospective studies, no cases of congenital infection have been linked to the Lyme disease spirochete.[168] In a study of pregnant white-footed mice *(P. leucopus),* all of whom were infected with *B. burgdorferi*, there was an absence of transplacental transmission of the spirochete to their offspring.[169] Although it is possible that *B. burgdorferi* may cause an adverse fetal outcome in humans, it has not been documented conclusively.

COINFECTION

I. scapularis ticks transmit not only *B. burgdorferi*, the Lyme disease agent, but also other infectious agents, including *Babesia microti* and the agent of human granulocytic ehrlichiosis. Each of these pathogens may cause flulike symptoms during summer, and coinfection with these tick-borne agents may lead to more severe initial illness.[170] Of 240 patients diagnosed with Lyme disease in Connecticut, 26 (11%) were coinfected with babesiosis.[170] At a Westchester County site in New York, 5.5% of nymphal *I. scapularis* ticks were coinfected with *B. burgdorferi* and the human granulocytic ehrlichiosis agent.[171] Serologic diagnosis may be confounded by the fact that ehrlichial infection may cause a false-positive IgM Western blot for Lyme disease.[172] Although both babesiosis and ehrlichiosis may produce acute infection, in the case of babesiosis primarily in splenectomized individuals and in the case of ehrlichiosis more often in older individuals, these agents are not known to cause chronic infection, as with untreated *B. burgdorferi* infection. In Europe and Asia, *I. ricinus* and *I. persulcatus* ticks, the vectors of *B. burgdorferi sensu lato*, also transmit tick-borne encephalitis virus.

LABORATORY DIAGNOSIS

The diagnosis of Lyme disease is based primarily on the presence of a characteristic clinical picture, exposure in an endemic area, and an elevated antibody response to *B. burgdorferi*. Culture of the spirochete from patient specimens permits a definitive diagnosis, but with few exceptions, this procedure has yielded positive results only in patients with EM skin lesions.[47] Similarly, it is often difficult to find spirochetes in histologic sections. Although serologic testing in Lyme disease can be performed with a high degree of sensitivity and specificity,[13, 14] false-negative and false-positive results and interlaboratory differences in results have been a considerable problem.[173] Guidelines for the laboratory evaluation of Lyme disease have been published.[174]

Serodiagnosis early in the infection is insensitive because the specific immune response in Lyme disease develops slowly. Only 30 to 40% of patients with EM are seropositive in acute phase sera, and 60 to 70% are positive by convalescence 2 to 4 weeks later.[13, 14, 175] In patients in the northeastern United States, the early responses are most commonly directed against the 23-kD OspC protein and the 41-kD flagellar antigen of the spirochete,[14, 175] whereas in those in the midwest, the 39-kD protein seems to elicit the most common early response.[13] In patients with active infection, the antibody response continues to expand during the following months to other spirochetal polypeptides, including those at 18, 28, 30, 39, 45, 66, and 93 kD.[14, 176–178] The culmination of the antibody response is the development of IgG reactivity with the 31-kD OspA and the 34-kD OspB proteins of the spirochete, from 5 months to 7 years after the onset of disease.[114] After the first 4 to 6 weeks of infection, 90% or more of patients have an elevated IgG response to the spirochete. After antibiotic treatment, antibody titers fall slowly, but most patients who had later manifestations of the illness remain seropositive for years. In addition, from 10 to 20% of patients in the United States[81, 82] and the majority of affected individuals in Europe[83, 84] have asymptomatic infection with *B. burgdorferi*. If patients with past infection or asymptomatic infection have symptoms caused by another illness, they may be wrongly attributed to Lyme disease.

For serologic testing in Lyme disease, the Centers for Disease Control and Prevention recommends a two-test approach in which samples are first tested by enzyme-linked immunosorbent assay (ELISA) and those with equivocal or positive results are tested by Western blotting (Fig. 231–3).[179, 180] During the first month of infection, both IgM and IgG responses to the spirochete should be determined, preferably in both acute and convalescent serum samples. After that time, the great majority of patients have a positive IgG response, and a single test is usually sufficient. In persons with illness persisting longer than 1 month, a positive IgM test alone is likely to be a false-positive result. According to the current criteria adopted by the Centers for Disease Control and Prevention, an IgM Western blot is considered positive if two of the following three bands are present: 23, 39, and 41 kD; however, a combination of the 23- and the 41-kD bands may still be a false-positive result. An IgG blot is considered positive if 5 of the following 10 bands are present: 18, 23, 28, 30, 39, 41, 45, 58, 66, and 93 kD (Fig. 231–4).

In patients with neuroborreliosis, comparison of the antibody response to *B. burgdorferi* in CSF and serum by antibody-capture immunoassay is a helpful diagnostic test.[132, 133] With this method, a CSF to serum ratio of specific antibody of greater than 1 is suggestive of intrathecal antibody production. In a small subset of patients with an attenuated form of late Lyme disease who are incompletely treated with antibiotics during the first several weeks of infection, the humoral immune response to *B. burgdorferi* may be aborted, but a cellular immune response to the spirochete may usually be demonstrated in these patients by the T-cell proliferative assay.[103, 181]

Because culture of *B. burgdorferi* has been a low-yield procedure and because serologic tests do not distinguish active from inactive infection, it has been hoped that PCR might have a role in the diagnosis of active Lyme disease that would be equivalent to culture in common bacterial infections. Primer-probe sets encoding flagellin, OspA, or unassigned portions of the spirochetal chromosome have been used to amplify spirochetal DNA in blood,[182] CSF,[183–185] urine,[183, 184] skin,[186, 187] and synovial fluid samples.[150, 151] In one study, *B. burgdorferi* DNA was detected in synovial fluid samples in 75 of 88 patients (85%) and in none of 64 control patients.[150] However, the sensitivity of PCR determinations in CSF in patients with neuroborreliosis has been much lower.[184, 185] There seems to be little, if any, role for PCR in the detection of *B. burgdorferi* DNA from blood or urine samples.

The most common nonspecific laboratory abnormalities, particularly early in the illness, are a high erythrocyte sedimentation rate, an elevated serum IgM level, or an increased serum glutamic-oxaloacetic transaminase (SGOT) level.[3] Most patients with elevated SGOT levels also have increased levels of serum glutamic-pyruvic transaminase and lactate dehydrogenase. The enzyme levels generally return to normal within several weeks. Patients may be mildly anemic early in the illness and occasionally have elevated white blood cell counts with shifts to the left in the differential count. A few patients have had microscopic hematuria, sometimes with mild proteinuria (dipstick); values for creatinine and blood urea nitrogen have been normal. Throughout the illness, C3 and C4 levels are generally normal or elevated.[112] Tests for rheumatoid factor or antinuclear antibodies are usually negative.

DIFFERENTIAL DIAGNOSIS

The most common problem has been in distinguishing Lyme arthritis, encephalopathy, or polyneuropathy from chronic fatigue syndrome or fibromyalgia.[188–191] This problem is compounded by the fact that a small percentage of patients develop fibromyalgia in association with or soon after Lyme disease,[189, 192] suggesting that *B. burgdorferi*

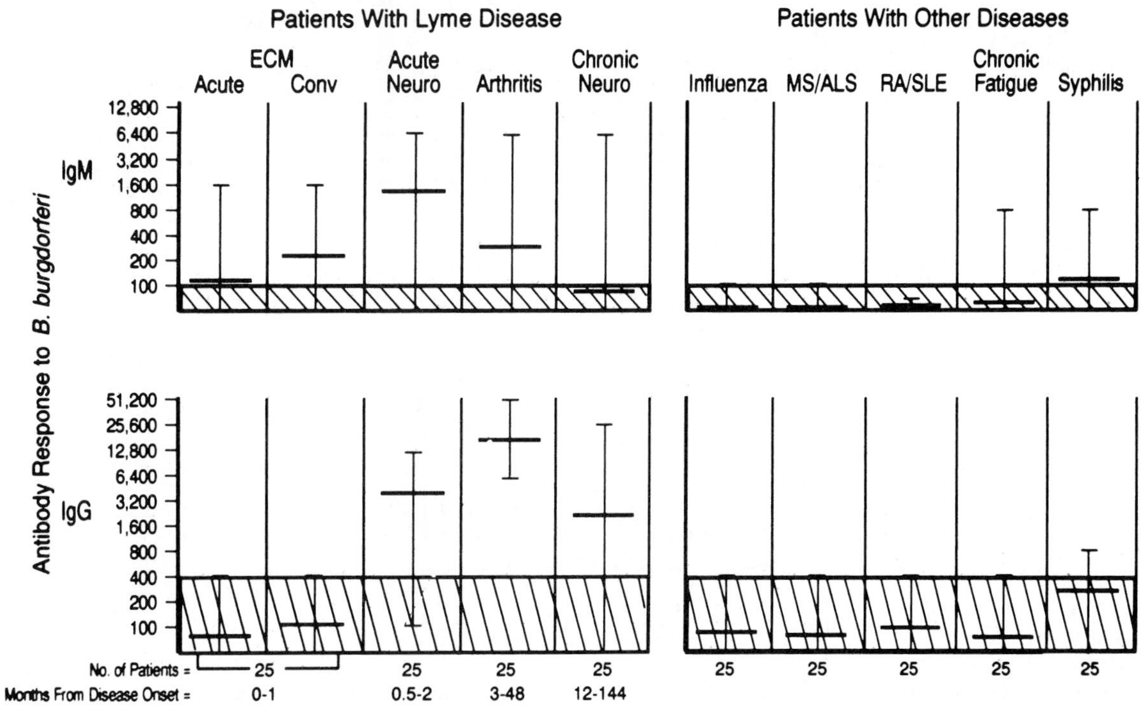

FIGURE 231–3. Antibody titers to *Borrelia burgdorferi* by enzyme-linked immunosorbent assay (ELISA) in patients with various manifestations of Lyme disease and in control subjects. Horizontal bars = mean; vertical bars = range; hatched bars = normal range. Normal range was derived from sera from 50 healthy control subjects. *Abbreviations:* ALS, Amyotrophic lateral sclerosis; Con V, convalescent phase; EM, erythema migrans; acute neuro, meningitis; chronic neuro, encephalopathy or polyneuropathy; MS, multiple sclerosis; RA, rheumatoid arthritis; SLE, systemic lupus erythematosus. (From Dressler F, Whalen JA, Reinhardt BN, et al. Western blotting in the serodiagnosis of Lyme disease. J Infect Dis. 1993;167:392.)

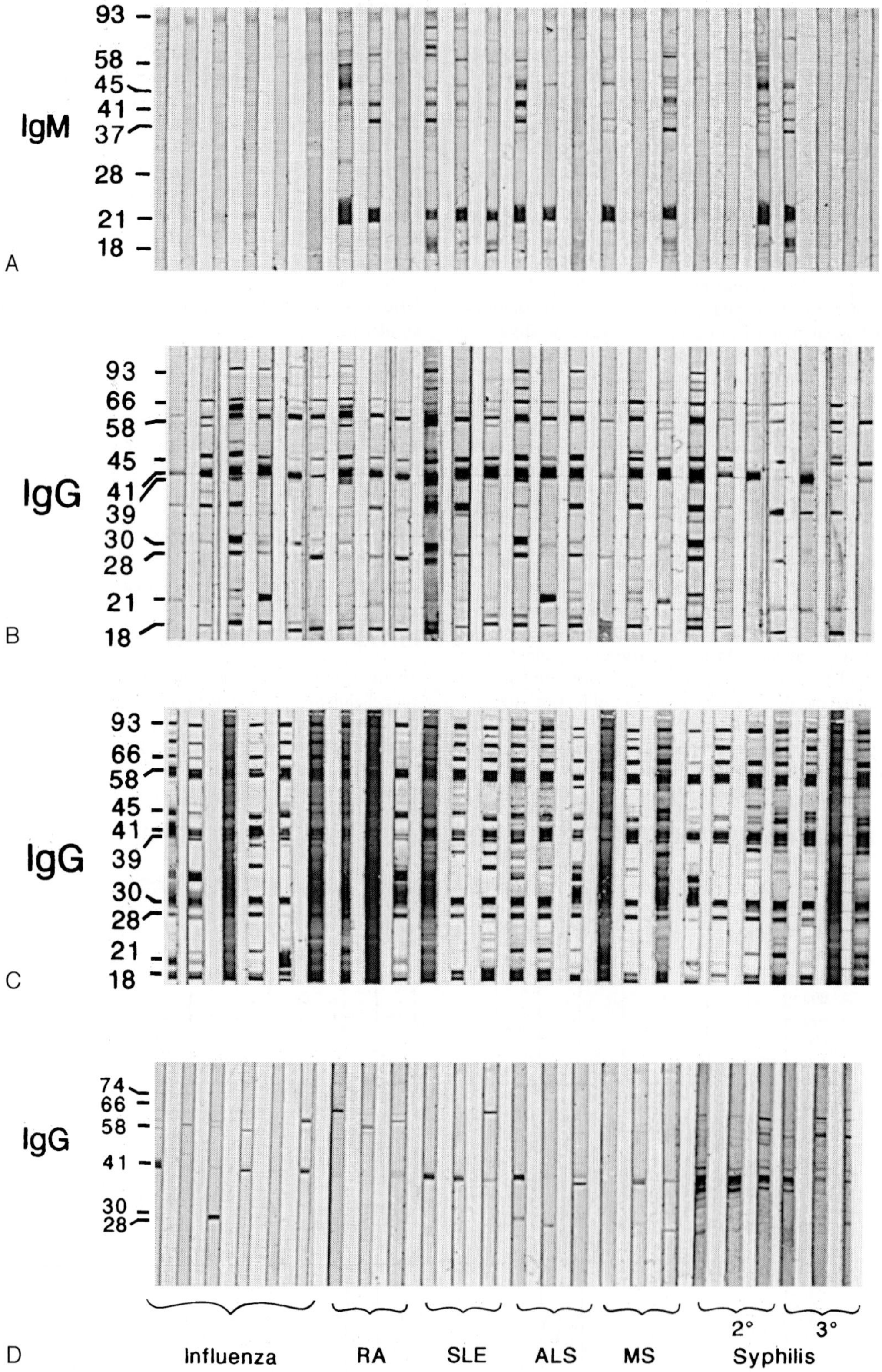

FIGURE 231–4. Western blots of *A,* acutephase sera from 25 patients with erythema migrans, *B,* 25 patients with Lyme meningitis or facial palsy. *C,* 25 patients with Lyme arthritis, and *D,* 24 representative patients (controls) who had influenza vaccinations, rheumatoid arthritis (RA), systemic lupus erythematosus (SLE), amyotrophic lateral sclerosis (ALS), multiple sclerosis (MS), or secondary or tertiary syphilis. Molecular masses (kD) are at left. (From Dressler F, Whalen JA, Reinhardt BN, et al. Western Blotting in the serodiagnosis of Lyme disease. J Infect Dis. 1993; 167:392.)

is one of the infectious agents that may trigger this chronic pain syndrome. Compared with Lyme disease, chronic fatigue syndrome or fibromyalgia tends to produce more generalized and disabling symptoms. They include marked fatigue, severe headache, diffuse musculoskeletal pain, multiple symmetric tender points in characteristic locations, pain and stiffness in many joints, diffuse dysesthesias, difficulty with concentration, or sleep disturbance. Patients with these conditions lack evidence of joint inflammation; they have normal neurologic test results; and they usually have a greater degree of anxiety and depression.[159]

TREATMENT

The various manifestations of Lyme disease can usually be treated with oral antibiotic therapy, except for objective neurologic abnormalities, which seem to require intravenous therapy (Table 231–2). For early Lyme disease, doxycycline, 100 mg twice a day, or amoxicillin, 500 mg four times daily, is recommended,[193, 194] but doxycycline should not be given to children or to pregnant women. An advantage of the doxycycline regimen is that it is effective for the treatment of ehrlichiosis as well as Lyme disease. Cefuroxime axetil, 500 mg twice a day, is an effective alternative.[195] Erythromycin, 250 mg four times daily,[196] and its cogeners, such as azithromycin,[197] are less effective clinically, but they are alternatives in patients who are allergic to the other medications. In children, amoxicillin is effective (20 mg/kg/day); in cases of penicillin allergy, cefuroxime axetil or erythromycin can be given. For patients with infection localized to the skin or in those with early disseminated infection, courses of 20 to 30 days are recommended. In a large multicenter trial, doxycycline, 100 mg twice a day for 3 weeks, and ceftriaxone, 2 g per day for 2 weeks, were equally effective in the treatment of acute disseminated infection.[198] Approximately 15% of patients with early disseminated infection experience a Jarisch-Herxheimer–like reaction during the first 24 hours of therapy.[196] In vitro, *B. burgdorferi* is sensitive to tetracycline, penicillin, erythromycin, and their cogeners and to third-generation cephalosporins, but it is resistant to rifampin, ciprofloxacin, and the aminoglycoside antibiotics.[199–202]

Lyme arthritis may usually be treated successfully with either oral or intravenous antibiotic therapy. In most cases, 30-day courses of oral doxycycline or amoxicillin[203] or 2- to 4-week courses of intravenous ceftriaxone are adequate.[204] In a decision analysis, oral therapy was preferable initially because it is easier to administer; it has fewer side effects, and it is considerably less expensive.[205] Its disadvantage, both for early disease and for arthritis, is that a small percentage of patients may still develop neuroborreliosis. Moreover, despite treatment with either oral or intravenous therapy, a subset of patients, primarily those with certain HLA-DR4 alleles and reactivity to OspA, may have persistent joint inflammation for months or even several years after antibiotic therapy.[203] If patients have persistent arthritis after 2 months of oral therapy or 1 month of intravenous therapy, I treat such patients with anti-inflammatory agents. If this approach fails, arthroscopic synovectomy may be successful.[206]

For objective neurologic abnormalities, with the possible exception of facial palsy alone, parenteral antibiotic therapy seems to be necessary. Intravenous ceftriaxone, 2 g/day for 2 to 4 weeks, is most commonly used for this purpose,[5, 8, 204] but intravenous cefotaxime, 2 g three times a day,[207] or intravenous penicillin G, 5 million units four times a day, may also be effective.[208] In patients with high-degree atrioventricular block or a PR interval of greater than 0.3 seconds, intravenous ceftriaxone or intravenous penicillin for at least part of the course and cardiac monitoring are recommended. In patients with complete heart block or congestive heart failure, corticosteroids may be of benefit if the patient does not improve on antimicrobial therapy alone within 24 hours. Because complete heart block rarely persists, insertion of a permanent pacemaker is not necessary.

Although it has not been studied systematically, patients with asymptomatic infection are often given a course of oral antibiotics. Because the risk of maternal-fetal transmission seems to be very low, standard therapy for the stage and manifestation of the illness

TABLE 231–2 Treatment Regimens for Lyme Disease*

Early infection (local or disseminated)	
Adults	Doxycycline, 100 mg orally 2 times/d for 20–30 d Amoxicillin, 500 mg orally 3 times/d for 20–30 d Alternatives in case of doxycycline or amoxicillin allergy: Cefuroxime axetil, 500 mg orally twice daily for 20–30 d Erythromycin, 250 mg orally 4 times/d for 20–30 d
Children (age 8 or younger)	Amoxicillin, 250 mg orally 3 times/d or 20 mg/kg/d in divided doses for 20–30 d Alternatives in case of penicillin allergy: Cefuroxime axetil, 125 mg orally twice daily for 20–30 d Erythromycin, 250 mg orally 3 times/d or 30 mg/kg/d in divided doses for 20–30 d
Arthritis (intermittent or chronic)	Doxycycline, 100 mg orally 2 times/d for 30–60 d Amoxicillin, 500 mg orally 4 times/d for 30–60 d *or* Ceftriaxone, 2 g IV once a day for 14–30 d Penicillin G, 20 million U IV in 4 divided doses daily for 14–30 d
Neurologic abnormalities (early or late)	Ceftriaxone, 2 g IV once/d for 14–30 d Penicillin G, 20 million U IV in 4 divided doses daily for 14–30 d Alternative in case of ceftriaxone or penicillin allergy: Doxycycline, 100 mg orally 3 times/d for 14–30 d†
Facial palsy alone	Oral regimens may be adequate
Cardiac abnormalities	
First-degree AV block (P-R interval >0.3 sec)	Oral regimens, as for early infection
High-degree AV block	Ceftriaxone, 2 gm IV once/d for 14–30 d‡ Penicillin G, 20 million U IV in 4 divided doses daily for 30 d‡

*Treatment failures have occurred with any of the regimens given, and a second course of therapy may be necessary.
†In my experience, this regimen is ineffective for the treatment of late neurologic abnormalities of Lyme disease.
‡Once the patient has stabilized, the course may be completed with oral therapy.
Abbreviations: AV, Atrioventricular.

may be sufficient for pregnant patients. Reinfection may occur in patients who are treated with antibiotics early in the illness,[209] but I have not observed reinfection in a patient with the expanded immune response associated with late infection.

The outcome of treatment with these antibiotic regimens is generally excellent, particularly in those with early Lyme disease.[210] In rare cases, treatment failure may occur, and one additional course of antibiotic therapy may be necessary. However, objective evidence of relapse is rare. Some patients have subjective symptoms after Lyme disease, including fatigue, arthralgia, myalgia, headache, or cognitive difficulties. This clinical picture, which has been referred to as post-Lyme syndrome, chronic Lyme disease, or chronic Lyme disease syndrome, is similar to that of chronic fatigue syndrome or fibromyalgia. These syndromes seem not to respond to antibiotic therapy.[189, 192] However, the most common reason for apparent lack of response to antibiotic therapy in Lyme disease is misdiagnosis.[188–191]

PREVENTION

The risk of tick bites in high-risk areas can be reduced by simple measures, particularly by wearing long trousers tucked into socks and by checking for ticks after exposure in wooded areas. Immature *I. scapularis* usually stay within a few inches of the ground; they often transfer to the lower extremities of the host and attach to moist parts of the body, such as the groin or axillae. In small children, they may also be found on the head and neck, which are unusual sites for tick attachment in adults. Insecticides containing DEET (*N,N*-diethylmetatoluamide) or permethrin effectively deter ticks,[211] but permethrin can be applied only on clothing, and DEET may cause serious side effects when excessive amounts are applied directly to the skin.[212]

Should patients with tick bites receive prophylactic antibiotic therapy? In a double-blind, placebo-controlled trial in the Lyme, Connecticut, region, the risk of Lyme disease in placebo-treated subjects with recognized tick bites was only 1.2%,[213] perhaps because 24 to 48 hours of tick attachment is often required for transmission of the spirochete.[64] Based on a meta-analysis of all relevant studies, the risk of infection with *B. burgdorferi* after a recognized tick bite was so low that the authors concluded that even in an area in which Lyme disease is endemic, prophylactic antimicrobial treatment is not indicated.[214] Despite this recommendation, a study of clinical practice in Maryland showed that most physicians treat patients with tick bites with needless antibiotic therapy and do unnecessary, costly serologic testing.[215] However, if follow-up is difficult or if the patient is quite anxious, it may still be preferable to treat. Amoxicillin or doxycycline therapy for 10 days will probably prevent the occurrence of Lyme disease.

Environmental control of ticks over widespread areas is difficult. In one study, eradication of deer on a small island greatly reduced the number of deer ticks during a 5-year period.[216] Aerial application of carbaryl during the fall has also been reported to be successful at reducing the number of ticks through the following spring.[217] Of three commercially available insecticides evaluated in a suburban residential area, chlorpyrifos and cyfluthrin formulations were more effective than carbaryl, and a single well-timed spring application was sufficient to reduce the number of nymphal ticks for an entire season.[218] Another method involves the distribution of permethrin-treated cotton balls, intended as rodent nesting material, around individual residences during the summer and fall. Although this method reduces the number of ticks on white-footed mice,[219, 220] it may not be sufficient to reduce the risk of tick exposure in humans.[220]

VACCINE DEVELOPMENT

Because the risk of Lyme disease in endemic areas is great and because personal protection and environmental control measures may be impractical, development of a safe and effective vaccine for Lyme disease has been a high priority. Using an experimental animal model of Lyme disease, mice vaccinated with recombinant OspA were protected from infection with *B. burgdorferi,* primarily by antibody-mediated killing of the spirochete within the tick before disease transmission.[221, 222]

In a phase III efficacy and safety trial of nearly 11,000 subjects,[223] three injections of an OspA vaccine with adjuvant prevented most definite cases of Lyme disease and had an acceptable reactogenicity profile. In year 1, following two injections, 22 subjects in the vaccine group and 43 in the placebo group had definite Lyme disease; therefore, vaccine efficacy was 49%. In year 2, after the third injection, 16 vaccine recipients and 66 placebo recipients had definite Lyme disease; vaccine efficacy was 76%. Among subjects with asymptomatic infection, vaccine efficacy was 83% in year 1 and 100% in year 2. Injection of the vaccine was associated with mild-to-moderate local or systemic reactions lasting a median duration of 3 days. Because the mechanism of action of this vaccine is thought to be antibody-mediated killing of the spirochete in the tick, OspA antibody titers are likely to be the determining factor in vaccine efficacy. It will be critical to learn how long protection lasts after three injections and how often additional booster injections may be necessary. This vaccine is now commercially available.

Immunization with other spirochetal proteins, including OspC[224] and decorin-binding protein A,[225] may also induce protective immunity. Vaccination with these proteins is being researched.

REFERENCES

1. Steere AC. Lyme disease. N Engl J Med. 1989;321:586.
2. Centers for Disease Control and Prevention. Lyme disease—United States. MMWR Morb Mortal Wkly Rep. 1995;45:481.
3. Steere AC, Bartenhagen NH, Craft JE, et al. The early clinical manifestations of Lyme disease. Ann Intern Med. 1983;99:76.
4. Nadelman RB, Nowakowski J, Forseter G, et al. The clinical spectrum of early Lyme borreliosis in patients with culture-confirmed erythema migrans. Am J Med. 1996;100:502.
5. Pachner AR, Steere AC. The triad of neurologic manifestations of Lyme disease: Meningitis, cranial neuritis, and radiculoneuritis. Neurology. 1985;35:47.
6. Steere AC, Batsford WP, Weinberg M, et al. Lyme carditis: Cardiac abnormalities of Lyme disease. Ann Intern Med. 1980;93:8.
7. Steere AC, Schoen RT, Taylor E. The clinical evolution of Lyme arthritis. Ann Intern Med. 1987;107:725.
8. Logigian EL, Kaplan RF, Steere AC. Chronic neurologic manifestations of Lyme disease. N Engl J Med. 1990;323:1438.
9. Halperin JJ, Luft BJ, Anand AK, et al. Lyme neuroborreliosis: Central nervous system manifestations. Neurology. 1989;39:753.
10. Logigian EL, Steere AC. Clinical and electrophysiological findings in chronic neuropathy of Lyme disease. Neurology. 1992;42:303.
11. Halperin JJ, Little BW, Coyle PK, et al. Lyme disease: Cause of treatable peripheral neuropathy. Neurology. 1987;37:1700.
12. Asbrink E, Brehmer-Andersson E, Hovmark A. Acrodermatitis chronica atrophicans—a spirochetosis: Clinical and histopathologic picture based on 32 patients; course and relationship to erythema chronicum migrans Afzelius. Am J Dermatopathol. 1986;8:209.
13. Engstrom SM, Shoop E, Johnson RC. Immunoblot interpretation criteria for serodiagnosis of early Lyme disease. J Clin Microbiol. 1995;33:419.
14. Dressler F, Whalen JA, Reinhardt BN, et al. Western blotting in the serodiagnosis of Lyme disease. J Infect Dis. 1993;167:392.
15. Rahn DW, Malawista SE. Lyme disease: Recommendations for diagnosis and treatment. Ann Intern Med. 1991;114:472.
16. Steere AC, Malawista SE, Snydman DR, et al. Lyme arthritis: An epidemic of oligoarticular arthritis in children and adults in three Connecticut communities. Arthritis Rheum. 1977;20:7.
17. Afzelius A. Report to Verhandlungen der dermatologischen Gesellschaft zu Stockholm on December 16, 1909. Arch Dermatol Syph. 1910;101:405.
18. Bannwarth A. Chronische lymphocytare Meningitis, entzundliche Polyneuritis und "Rheumatismus." Arch Psychiatr Nervenkr. 1941;113:284.
19. Barbour AG, Hayes SF. Biology of *Borrelia* species. Microbiol Rev. 1986;50:381.
20. Hovind-Hougen K, Asbrink E, Stiernstedt G, et al. Ultrastructural differences among spirochetes isolated from patients with Lyme disease and related disorders, and from *Ixodes ricinus.* Zentralbl Bakteriol Hyg. 1986;263:103.
21. Saint Girons IGO, Davidson BE. Molecular biology of the *Borrelia* bacteria with linear replicons. Microbiology. 1994;140:1803.
22. Fraser CM, Casjens S, Huang WM, et al. Genomic sequence of a Lyme disease spirochete, *Borrelia burgdorferi.* Nature. 1997;390:580.
23. Bergstrom S, Bundoc VG, Barbour AG. Molecular analysis of linear plasmid

encoded major surface proteins, OspA and OspB, of the Lyme disease spirochaete *Borrelia burgdorferi*. Molecular Microbiol. 1989;3:479.
24. Montgomery RR, Malawista SE, Feen KJM, Bockenstedt LK. Direct demonstration of antigenic substitution of *Borrelia burgdorferi* ex vivo: Exploration of the paradox of the early immune response to outer surface proteins A and C in Lyme disease. J Exp Med. 1996;183:261.
25. Lahdenne P, Porcella SF, Hagman KE, et al. Molecular characterization of a 6.6-kilodalton *Borrelia burgdorferi* outer membrane-associated lipoprotein (lp6.6) which appears to be downregulated during mammalian infection. Infect Immun. 1997;65:412.
26. Li H, Dunn JJ, Luft BJ, Lawson CL. Crystal structure of Lyme disease antigen outer surface protein A complexed with a Fab. Proc Natl Acad Sci U S A. 1997;94:3584.
27. Marconi RT, Samuels DS, Garon CF. Transcriptional analyses and mapping of the *ospC* gene in Lyme disease spirochetes. J Bacteriol. 1993;175:926.
28. Schwan TG, Piesman J, Golde WT, et al. Induction of an outer surface protein on *Borrelia burgdorferi* during tick feeding. Proc Natl Acad Sci U S A. 1995;92:2909.
29. Marconi RT, Samuels DS, Landry RK, Garon CF. Analysis of the distribution and molecular heterogeneity of the *ospD* gene among the Lyme disease spirochetes: Evidence for lateral gene exchange. J Bacteriol. 1994;176:4572.
30. Lam TT, Nguyen TPK, Montgomery R, et al. Outer surface proteins E and F of *Borrelia burgdorferi,* the agent of Lyme disease. Infect Immun. 1994;62:290.
31. Feng S, Hodzic E, Stevenson B, Barthold SW. Humoral immunity to *Borrelia burgdorferi* N40 decorin binding proteins during infection of laboratory mice. Infect Immun. 1998;66:2827.
32. Probert WS, Johnson BJB. Identification of a 47 kDa fibronectin-binding protein expressed by *Borrelia burgdorferi* isolate B31. Mol Microbiol. 1998;30:1003.
33. Zhang J-R, Hardham JM, Barbour AG, Norris SJ. Antigenic variation in Lyme disease Borreliae by promiscuous recombination of VMP-like sequence cassettes. Cell. 1997;39:275.
34. Champion CI, Blanco DR, Skare JT, et al. A 9.0-kilobase-pair circular plasmid of *Borrelia burgdorferi* encodes an exported protein: Evidence for expression only during infection. Infect Immun. 1994:62:2653.
35. Fikrig E, Barthold SW, Sun W, et al. *Borrelia burgdorferi* P35 and P37 proteins, expressed in vivo, elicit protective immunity. Immunity. 1997;6:531.
36. Suk K, Das S, Sun W, et al. *Borrelia burgdorferi* genes selectively expressed in the infected host. Proc Natl Acad Sci U S A. 1995;92:4269.
37. Akins DR, Porcella SF, Popova TG, et al. Evidence for *in vivo* but not *in vitro* expression of a *Borrelia burgdorferi* outer surface protein F (OspF) homolog. Mol Microbiol. 1995;18:507.
38. Wallich R, Brenner C, Kramer MD, Simon MM. Molecular cloning and immunological characterization of a novel linear-plasmid-encoded gene, *pG*, of *Borrelia burgdorferi* expressed only in vivo. Infect Immun. 1995;63:3327.
39. Simpson WJ, Schrumpf ME, Schwan TG. Reactivity of human Lyme borreliosis sera with a 39-kilodalton antigen specific to *Borrelia burgdorferi*. J Clin Microbiol. 1990;28:1329.
40. Coleman JL, Benach JL. Identification and characterization of an endoflagellar antigen of *Borrelia burgdorferi*. J Clin Invest. 1989;84:322.
41. Hansen K, Bangsborg JM, Fjordvang H, et al. Immunochemical characterization of and isolation of the gene for a *Borrelia burgdorferi* immunodominant 60-kilodalton antigen common to a wide range of bacteria. Infect Immun. 1988;56:2047.
42. Anzola J, Luft BJ, Gorgone G, et al. *Borrelia burgdorferi* HSP70 homolog: Characterization of an immunoreactive stress protein. Infect Immun. 1992;60:3704.
43. Skare JT, Mirzabekov TA, Shang ES, et al. The Om66 (p66) protein is a *Borrelia burgdorferi* porin. Infect Immun. 1997;65:3654.
44. Luft BJ, Mudri S, Jiang W, et al. The 93-kilodalton protein of *Borrelia burgdorferi:* An immunodominant protoplasmic cylinder antigen. Infect Immun. 1992;60:4309.
45. Barbour AG. Isolation and cultivation of Lyme disease spirochetes. Yale J Biol Med. 1984;57:521.
46. Preac-Mursic V, Wilske B, Reinhardt S. Culture of *Borrelia burgdorferi* on six solid media. Eur J Clin Microbiol Infect Dis. 1991;10:1076.
47. Berger BW, Johnson RC, Kodner C, et al. Cultivation of *Borrelia burgdorferi* from erythema migrans lesions and perilesional skin. J Clin Microbiol. 1992;30:359.
48. Baranton G, Postic D, Saint Girons I, et al. Delineation of *Borrelia burgdorferi* sensu stricto, *Borrelia garinii* sp. nov., and group VS461 associated with Lyme borreliosis. Int J Syst Bacteriol. 1992;42:378.
49. Canica MM, Nato F, du Merle L, et al. Monoclonal antibodies for identification of *Borrelia burgdorferi* sp. nov. associated with late cutaneous manifestations of Lyme borreliosis. Scand J Infect Dis. 1993;25:441.
50. Boerlin P, Peter O, Bretz AG, et al. Population genetic analysis of *Borrelia burgdorferi* isolates by multilocus enzyme electrophoresis. Infect Immun. 1992;60:1677.
51. Marconi RT, Garon CF. Development of polymerase chain reaction primer sets for diagnosis of Lyme disease and for species-specific identification of Lyme disease isolates by 16S rRNA signature nucleotide analysis. J Clin Microbiol. 1992;30:2830.
52. Postic D, Ras NM, Lane RS, et al. Expanded diversity among California borrelia isolates and description of *Borrelia bissetti* sp. nov. (formerly Borrelia group DN 127). J Clin Microbiol. 1998;36:3497.
53. Steere AC, Broderick TE, Malawista SE. Erythema chronicum migrans and Lyme arthritis: Epidemiologic evidence for a tick vector. Am J Epidemiol. 1978;108:312.
54. Wallis RC, Brown SE, Kloter KO, et al. Erythema chronicum migrans and Lyme arthritis: Field study of ticks. Am J Epidemiol. 1978;108:322.
55. Burgdorfer W, Kierans JE. Ticks and Lyme disease in the United States. Ann Intern Med. 1983;99:121.
56. Steere AC, Malawista SE. Cases of Lyme disease in the United States: Locations correlated with distribution of *Ixodes dammini*. Ann Intern Med. 1989;91:730.
57. Schmid GP. The global distribution of Lyme disease. Rev Infect Dis. 1985;7:41.
58. Berglund J, Eitrem R, Ornstein K, et al. An epidemiologic study of Lyme disease in southern Sweden. N Engl J Med. 1995;333:1319.
59. Korenberg EI, Kryuchechnikov VN, Kovalevsky YV. Advances in investigations of Lyme borreliosis in the territory of former USSR. Eur J Epidemiol. 1993;9:86.
60. Magnarelli LA, Anderson JF, Apperson CS, et al. Spirochetes in ticks and antibodies to *Borrelia burgdorferi* in white-tailed deer from Connecticut, New York State, and North Carolina. J Wildl Dis. 1976;22:178.
61. Bosler EM, Coleman JL, Benach JL, et al. Natural distribution of the *Ixodes dammini* spirochetes. Science. 1983;220:321.
62. Magnarelli LA, Anderson JF. Ticks and biting insects infected with the etiologic agent of Lyme disease, *Borrelia burgdorferi*. J Clin Microbiol. 1988;26:1482.
63. Wilson ML, Spielman A. Seasonal activity of immature *Ixodes dammini* (Acari: Ixodidae). J Med Entomol. 1985;22:408.
64. Piesman J, Mather TN, Sinsky RJ. Duration of tick attachment and *Borrelia burgdorferi* transmission. J Clin Microbiol. 1987;25:557.
65. Levine JF, Wilson ML, Spielman A. Mice as reservoirs of the Lyme disease spirochete. Am J Trop Med Hyg. 1985;34:355.
66. Wilson ML, Adler GH, Spielman A. Correlation between abundance of deer and that of the deer tick, *Ixodes dammini* (Acari: Ixodidae). Ann Entomol Soc Am. 1985;78:172.
67. Matuschka FR, Spielman A. The emergence of Lyme disease in changing environment in North America and central Europe. Exp Appl Acarol. 1986;2:337.
68. Manweiler SA, Lane RS, Tempelis CH. The western fence lizard *Sceloporus occidentalis*: Evidence of field exposure to *Borrelia burgdorferi* in relation to infestation by *Ixodes pacificus* (Acari: *Ixodidae*). Am J Trop Med Hyg. 1992;47:328.
69. Brown RN, Lane RS. Lyme disease in California: A novel enzootic transmission cycle of *Borrelia burgdorferi*. Science. 1992;256:1439.
70. Anderson JF, Magnarelli LA, Burgdorfer W, et al. Spirochetes in *Ixodes dammini* and mammals from Connecticut. Am J Trop Med Hyg. 1983;32:818.
71. Magnarelli LA, Anderson JF, Burgdorfer W, et al. Parisitism by *Ixodes dammini* (Acari: Ixodidae) and antibodies to spirochetes in mammals at Lyme disease foci in Connecticut, USA. J Med Entomol. 1984;21:52.
72. Anderson JF, Johnson RC, Magnarelli LA, et al. Identification of endemic foci of Lyme disease: Isolation of *Borrelia burgdorferi* from feral rodents and ticks *(Dermacentor variabilis)*. J Clin Microbiol. 1985;22:36.
73. Anderson JF, Johnson RC, Magnarelli LA, et al. Involvement of birds in the epidemiology of the Lyme disease agent *Borrelia burgdorferi*. Infect Immun. 1986;51:394.
74. Kornblatt AN, Urband PH, Steere AC. Arthritis caused by *Borrelia burgdorferi* in dogs. J Am Vet Med Assoc. 1985;186:960.
75. Marcus LC, Patterson MM, Gilfillan RE, et al. Antibodies to *Borrelia burgdorferi* in New England horses: Serologic survey. Am J Vet Res. 1985;46:2570.
76. Burgess EC. *Borrelia burgdorferi* infection in Wisconsin horses and cows. Ann N Y Acad Sci. 1988;539:235.
77. Ai C, Hu R, Hyland KE, et al. Epidemiological and aetiological evidence for transmission of Lyme disease by adult *Ixodes persulcatus* in an endemic area in China. Int J Epidemiol. 1990;19:1061.
78. Kawabata M, Baba S, Iguchi K, et al. Lyme disease in Japan and its possible incriminated tick vector, *Ixodes persulcatus.* J Infect Dis. 1987;156:854.
79. Lastavica CC, Wilson ML, Berardi VP, et al. Rapid emergence of a focal epidemic of Lyme disease in coastal Massachusetts. N Engl J Med. 1989;320:133.
80. Steere AC, Taylor E, Wilson ML, et al. Longitudinal assessment of the clinical and epidemiologic features of Lyme disease in a defined population. J Infect Dis. 1986;154:295.
81. Hanrahan JP, Benach JL, Coleman JL, et al. Incidence and cumulative frequency of endemic Lyme disease in a community. J Infect Dis. 1984;150:489.
82. White DJ, Chang HG, Benach JL, et al. The geographic spread and temporal increase of the Lyme disease epidemic. JAMA. 1991;266:1230.
83. Gustafson R, Svenungsson B, Forsgren M, et al. Two-year survey of the incidence of Lyme borreliosis and tick-borne encephalitis in a high-risk population in Sweden. Eur J Clin Microbiol Infect Dis. 1992;11:894.
84. Fahrer H, van der Linden S, Sauvain MJ, et al. The prevalence and incidence of clinical and asymptomatic Lyme borreliosis in a population at risk. J Infect Dis. 1991;163:305.
85. Akin DR, Bourell KW, Caimaro MJ, et al. A new animal model for studying Lyme disease spirochetes in a mammalian host-adapted state. J Clin Invest. 1998;101:2240.
86. Steere AC, Grodzicki RL, Kornblatt AN, et al. The spirochetal etiology of Lyme disease. N Engl J Med. 1983;308:733.
87. Nadelman RB, Pavia CS, Magnarelli LA, et al. Isolation of *Borrelia burgdorferi* from the blood of seven patients with Lyme disease. Am J Med. 1990;88:21.
88. Karlsson M, Hovind-Hougen K, Svenungsson B, Stiernstedt G. Cultivation and characterization of spirochetes from cerebrospinal fluid of patients with Lyme borreliosis. J Clin Microbiol. 1990;28:473.
89. Duray PH, Steere AC. Clinical pathologic correlations of Lyme disease by stage. Ann N Y Acad Sci. 1988;539:65.
90. Garcia-Monco JC, Villar BF, Alen JC, et al. *Borrelia burgdorferi* in the central nervous system: Experimental and clinical evidence for early invasion. J Infect Dis. 1990;161:1187.

91. Klempner MS, Noring R, Epstein MP, et al. Binding of human plasminogen and urokinase-type plasminogen activator to the Lyme disease spirochete, *Borrelia burgdorgferi*. J Infect Dis. 1995;171:1258.
92. Coleman JL, Gebbia JA, Piesman J, et al. Plasminogen is required for efficient dissemination of *B. burgdorferi* in ticks and for enhancement of spirochetemia in mice. Cell. 1997;89:1111.
93. Coburn J, Leong JM, Erban JK. Integrin αIIbβ3 mediates binding of *Borrelia burgdorferi* to human platelets. Proc Nat Acad Sci U S A. 1993;90:7059.
94. Coburn J, Magoun L, Bodary SC, Leong JM. Integrins $\alpha_v\beta_3$ and $\alpha_5\beta_1$ mediate attachment of Lyme disease spirochetes to human cells. Infect Immun. 1998;66:1946.
95. Leong JL, Morrissey PE, Ortega-Barria E, et al. Hemagglutination and proteoglycan binding by the Lyme disease spirochete, *Borrelia burgdorferi*. Infect Immun. 1995;63:874.
96. Comstock LE, Thomas DD. Characterization of *Borrelia burgdorferi* invasion of cultured endothelial cells. Microb Pathog. 1991;10:137.
97. Ma Y, Sturrock A, Weis J. Intracellular localization of *Borrelia burgdorferi* within human endothelial cells. Infect Immun. 1991;59:671.
98. Montgomery RR, Nathanson MH, Malawista SE. The fate of *Borrelia burgdorferi*, the agent for Lyme disease, in mouse macrophages. Destruction, survival, recovery. J Immunol. 1993;150:909.
99. Georgilis K, Peacocke M, Klempner MS. Fibroblasts protect the Lyme disease spirochete, *Borrelia burgdorferi*, from ceftriaxone in vitro. J Infect Dis. 1992;166:440.
100. Filgueira L, Nestle FO, Rittig M, et al. Human dendritic cells phagocytose and process *Borrelia burgdorferi*. J Immunol. 1996;157:2998.
101. Moffat CM, Sigal LH, Steere AC, et al. Cellular immune findings in Lyme disease: Correlation with serum IgM and disease activity. Am J Med. 1984;77:625.
102. Sigal LH, Steere AC, Freeman DH, et al. Proliferative responses of mononuclear cells in Lyme disease: Reactivity to *Borrelia burgdorferi* antigens is greater in joint fluid than in blood. Arthritis Rheum. 1986;29:761.
103. Dattwyler RJ, Volkman DJ, Luft BJ, et al. Seronegative Lyme disease: dissociation of the specific T- and B-lymphocyte responses to *Borrelia burgdorferi*. N Engl J Med. 1988;319:1441.
104. Krause A, Brade V, Schoerner C, et al. T cell proliferation induced by *Borrelia burgdorferi* in patients with Lyme borreliosis. Arthritis Rheum. 1991;34:393.
105. Defosse DL, Johnson RC. In vitro and in vivo induction of tumor necrosis factor alpha by *Borrelia burgdorferi*. Infect Immun. 1992;60:1109.
106. Miller LC, Isa S, Vannier E, et al. Live *Borrelia burgdorferi* preferentially activate IL-1β gene expression and protein synthesis over the interleukin1 receptor antagonist. J Clin Invest. 1992;90:906.
107. Busch DH, Jassoy C, Brinkmann U, et al. Detection *of Borrelia burgdorferi*--specific CD8+ cytotoxic T cells in patients with Lyme arthritis. J Immunol. 1996;157:3534.
108. Oksi J, Savolainen J, Pene J, et al. Decreased interleukin-4 and increased gamma interferon production by peripheral blood mononuclear cells of patients with Lyme borreliosis. Infect Immun. 1996;64:3620.
109. Gross DM, Steere AC, Huber BT. Dominant T helper 1 response is antigen specific and localized to synovial fluid in patients with Lyme arthritis. J Immunol. 1998;160:1022.
110. Pohl-Koppe A, Balashov KE, Steere AC, et al. Identification of a T cell subset capable of both IFN-γ and IL-10 secretion in patients with chronic *Borrelia burgdorferi* infection. J Immunol. 1998;160:1804.
111. Steere AC, Hardin JA, Ruddy S, et al. Lyme arthritis: Correlation of serum and cryoglobulin IgM with activity and serum IgG with remission. Arthritis Rheum. 1979;22:471.
112. Hardin JA, Steere AC, Malawista SE. Immune complexes and the evolution of Lyme arthritis: Dissemination and localization of abnormal Clq binding activity. N Engl J Med. 1979;301:1358.
113. Ma Y, Weis JJ. *Borrelia burgdorferi* outer surface lipoproteins OspA and OspB possess B cell mitogenic and cytokine stimulatory properties. Infect Immun. 1993;61:3843.
114. Kalish RA, Leong JM, Steere AC. Association of treatment resistant chronic Lyme arthritis with HLA-DR4 and antibody reactivity to OspA and OspB of *Borrelia burgdorferi*. Infect Immun. 1993;61:2774.
115. Akin E, McHugh GL, Flavell RA, et al. The immunoglobulin (IgG) antibody response to OspA and OspB correlates with severe and prolonged arthritis and the IgG response to P35 with mild and brief arthritis. Infect Immun. 1999;67:173.
116. Wheeler CM, Garcia-Monco JC, Benach JL, et al. Nonprotein antigens of *Borrelia burgdorferi*. J Infect Dis. 1993;167:665.
117. Kochi SK, Johnson RC. Role of immunoglobulin G in killing of *Borrelia burgdorferi* in the classical complement pathway. Infect Immun. 1988;56:314.
118. Barthold SW, DeSouza MS, Janotka JL, et al. Chronic Lyme borreliosis in the laboratory mouse. Am J Pathol. 1993;143:959.
119. Schaible UE, Gay S, Museteanu C, et al. Lyme borreliosis in the severe combined immunodeficiency (scid) mouse manifests predominantly in the joints, heart, and liver. Am J Pathol. 1990;137:811.
120. Lim LCL, England DM, DuChateau BK, et al. Development of destructive arthritis in vaccinated hamsters challenged with *Borrelia burgdorferi*. Infect Immun. 1994;62:2825.
121. Appel MJ, Allan S, Jacobson RH, et al. Experimental Lyme disease in dogs produces arthritis and persistent infection. J Infect Dis. 1993;167:651.
122. Philipp MT, Aydintug MK, Bohm RP Jr, et al. Early and early disseminated phases of Lyme disease in the Rhesus monkey: A model for infections in humans. Infect Immun. 1993;61:3047.
123. Ruderman EM, Kerr JS, Telford SR III, et al. Early murine Lyme carditis has a macrophage predominance and is independent of major histocompatibility complex class II-CD4+ T cell interactions. J Infect Dis. 1995;171:362.
124. Barthold SW, DeSouza M, Feng S. Serum-mediated resolution of Lyme arthritis in mice. Lab Invest. 1996;74:57.
125. Keane-Myers A, Nickell SP. T cell subset-dependent modulation of immunity to *Borrelia burgdorferi* in mice. J Immunol. 1995;154:1770.
126. Yang L, Weis JH, Eichwald E, et al. Heritable susceptibility to severe *Borrelia burgdorferi*--induced arthritis is dominant and is associated with persistence of large numbers of spirochetes in tissues. Infect Immun. 1994;62:492.
127. Kang I, Barthold SW, Persing DH, Bockenstedt LK. T-helper-cell cytokines in the early evolution of murine Lyme arthritis. Infect Immun. 1997;65:3107.
128. Dong Z, Edlestein M, Glickstein LJ. CD8+ T cells are activated during the early Th1 and Th2 immune responses in the murine Lyme disease model. Infect Immun. 1997;65:5334.
129. Clark JR, Carlson RD, Sasaki CT, et al. Facial paralysis in Lyme disease. Laryngoscope. 1985;95:1341.
130. Horstrup P, Ackermann R. Durch zecken ubertragene Meningopolyneuritis (Garin-Bujadoux, Bannwarth). Fortschr Neurol Psychiatr. 1973;41:583.
131. Pachner AR, Steere AC, Sigal LH, et al. Antigen-specific proliferation of CFS lymphocytes in Lyme disease. Neurology. 1985;35:1642.
132. Steere AC, Berardi VP, Weeks KE, et al. Evaluation of the intrathecal antibody response to *Borrelia burgdorferi* as a diagnostic test for Lyme neuroborreliosis. J Infect Dis. 1990;161:1203.
133. Hansen K, Lebech AM. Lyme neuroborreliosis: A new sensitive diagnostic assay for intrathecal synthesis of *Borrelia burgdorferi*--specific immunoglobulin G, A, and M. Ann Neurol. 1991;30:197.
134. Hansen K, Cruz M, Link H. Oligoclonal *Borrelia burgdorferi*--specific IgG antibodies in cerebrospinal fluid in Lyme neuroborreliosis. J Infect Dis. 1990;161:1194.
135. Dai Z, Lackland H, Stein S, et al. Molecular mimicry in Lyme disease: Monoclonal antibody H9724 to *B. burgdorferi* flagellin specifically detects chaperonin-HSP60. Biochim Biophys Acta. 1993;1181:97.
136. Vallat JM, Leboutet MJ, Loubet A, et al. Tick bite neuropathy: An analysis of nerve biopsies from seven cases. Neurology. 1984;34:180.
136a. Kan L, Sood SK, Maytal J. Pseudotumor cerebri in Lyme disease: a case report and literature review. Pediatr Neurol. 1998;18:439.
137. McAlister HF, Klementowicz PT, Andrews C, et al. Lyme carditis: An important cause of reversible heart block. Ann Intern Med. 1989;110:339.
138. Alpert LI, Welch P, Fisher N. Gallium-positive Lyme disease myocarditis. Clin Nucl Med. 1985;10:617.
139. Marcus LC, Steere AC, Duray PH, et al. Fatal pancarditis in a patient with coexistent Lyme disease and babesiosis: Demonstration of spirochetes in the heart. Ann Intern Med. 1985;103:374.
140. Reznick JW, Braunstein DB, Walsch RL, et al. Lyme carditis. Electrophysiologic and histologic study. Am J Med. 1986;81:923.
141. Stanek G, Klein J, Bittner R, et al. Isolation of *Borrelia burgdorferi* from the myocardium of a patient with longstanding cardiomyopathy. N Engl J Med. 1990;322:249.
142. Oksi J, Mertsola J, Reunanen M, et al. Subacute multiple-site osteomyelitis caused by *Borrelia burgdorferi*. Clin Infect Dis. 1994;19:891.
143. Reimers CD, DeKoning J, Neubert U, et al. *Borrelia burgdorferi* myositis: Report of eight patients. J Neurol. 1993;240:278.
144. Kramer N, Rickert RR, Brodkin RH, et al. Septal panniculitis as a manifestation of Lyme disease. Am J Med. 1986;81:149.
145. Granter SR, Barnhill RL, Hewins ME, Duray PH. Identification of *Borrelia burgdorferi* in diffuse fasciitis with peripheral eosinophilia: Borrelial fasciitis. JAMA. 1994;272:1283.
146. Steere AC, Duray PH, Kauffmann DJH, et al. Unilateral blindness caused by infection with the Lyme disease spirochete, *Borrelia burgdorferi*. Ann Intern Med. 1985;103:382.
147. Bodine SR, Marino J, Camisa TJ, et al. Multifocal choroiditis with evidence of Lyme disease. Ann Ophthalmol. 1992;24:169.
148. Kornmehl EW, Lesser RL, Jaros P, et al. Bilateral keratitis in Lyme disease. Ophthalmology. 1989;96:1194.
149. Kirsch M, Ruben FL, Steere AC, et al. Fatal adult respiratory distress syndrome in a patient with Lyme disease. JAMA. 1988;259:2737.
150. Nocton JJ, Dressler F, Rutledge BJ, et al. Detection of *Borrelia burgdorferi* DNA by polymerase chain reaction in synovial fluid in Lyme arthritis. N Engl J Med. 1994;330:229.
151. Bradley JF, Johnson RC, Goodman JL. The persistence of spirochetal nucleic acids in active Lyme arthritis. Ann Intern Med. 1994;120:487.
152. Yoshinari NH, Reinhardt BN, Steere AC. T cell responses to polypeptide fractions of *Borrelia burgdorferi* in patients with Lyme arthritis. Arthritis Rheum. 1991;34:707.
153. Yin Z, Braun J, Neure L, et al. T cell cytokine pattern in the joints of patients with Lyme arthritis and its regulation by cytokines and anticytokines. Arthritis Rheum. 1997;40:69.
154. Johnston YE, Duray PH, Steere AC, et al. Lyme arthritis: Spirochetes found in synovial microangiopathic lesions. Am J Pathol. 1985;118:26.
155. Steere AC, Duray PH, Butcher EC. Spirochetal antigens and lymphoid cell surface markers in Lyme synovitis: Comparison with rheumatoid synovium and tonsillar lymphoid tissue. Arthritis Rheum. 1988;31:487.
156. Steere AC, Dwyer E, Winchester R. Association of chronic Lyme arthritis with HLA-DR4 and HLA-DR2 alleles. N Engl J Med. 1990;281:703.

157. Gross DM, Forsthuber T, Tary-Lehman M, et al. Identification of LFA-1 as a candidate autoantigen in treatment-resistant Lyme arthritis. Science. 1998;281:703.
158. Bloom BJ, Wyckoff PM, Meissner HC, Steere AC. Neurocognitive abnormalities in children following classic manifestations of Lyme disease. Pediatr Infect Dis J. 1998;17:189.
159. Kaplan RF, Meadows ME, Vincent LC, et al. Memory impairment and depression in patients with Lyme encephalopathy: Comparison with fibromyalgia and nonpsychotically depressed patients. Neurology. 1992;42:1263.
160. Logigian EL, Johnson KA, Kijewski MF, et al. Reversible cerebral hypoperfusion in Lyme encephalopathy. Neurology. 1997;49:1661.
161. Ackermann R, Rehse-Kupper B, Gollmer E, et al. Chronic neurologic manifestations of erythema migrans borreliosis. Ann N Y Acad Sci. 1988;539:16.
162. Asbrink E, Hovmark A. Successful cultivation of spirochetes from skin lesions of patients with erythema chronica migrans afzelius and acrodermatitis chronica atrophicans. Acta Pathol Microbiol Immunol Scand. 1985;93:161.
163. DeKoning J, Tazelaar DJ, Hoogkamp-Korstanje JA, Elema JD. Acrodermatitis chronica atrophicans: A light and electron microscopic study. J Cutan Pathol. 1995;22:23.
164. Aberer E, Klade H, Hobisch G. A clinical, histological, and immunohistochemical comparison of acrodermatitis chronica atrophicans and morphea. Am J Dermatopathol. 1991;13:334.
165. Schlesinger PA, Duray PH, Burke BA, et al. Maternal-fetal transmission of the Lyme disease spirochete, *Borrelia burgdorferi*. Ann Intern Med. 1985;103:67.
166. Weber K, Bratzke HJ, Neubert U, et al. *Borrelia burgdorferi* in a newborn despite oral penicillin for Lyme borreliosis during pregnancy. Pediatr Infect Dis J. 1988;7:286.
167. Markowitz LE, Steere AC, Benach JL, et al. Lyme disease in pregnancy. JAMA. 1986;256:3394.
168. Williams CL, Stobino B, Weinstein A, et al. Maternal Lyme disease and congenital malformations: A cord blood serosurvey in endemic and control areas. Paediatr Perinat Epidemiol. 1995;9:320.
169. Mather TN, Telford SR III, Adler GH. Absence of transplacental transmission of Lyme disease spirochetes from reservoir mice *(Peromyscus leucopus)* to their offspring. J Infect Dis. 1991;164:564.
170. Krause PJ, Telford SR III, Spielman A, et al. Concurrent Lyme disease and babesiosis: Evidence for increased severity and duration of illness. JAMA. 1996;275:1657.
171. Schwartz I, Fish D, Daniels TJ. Prevalence of the rickettsial agent of human granulocytic ehrlichiosis in ticks from a hyperendemic focus of Lyme disease. N Engl J Med. 1997;337:49.
172. Wormser GP, Horowitz HW, Nowakowski J, et al. Positive Lyme disease serology in patients with clinical and laboratory evidence of human granulocytic ehrlichiosis. Am J Clin Pathol. 1997;107:142.
173. Bakken LL, Case KL, Callister SM, et al. Performance of 45 laboratories participating in a proficiency testing program for Lyme disease serology. JAMA. 1992;268:891.
174. Tugwell P, Dennis DT, Weinstein A, et al. Laboratory evaluation in the diagnosis of Lyme disease. Ann Intern Med. 1997;127:1109.
175. Aguero-Rosenfeld ME, Nowakowski J, Bittker S, et al. Evolution of the serologic response to *Borrelia burgdorferi* in treated patients with culture-confirmed erythema migrans. J Clin Microbiol. 1996;34:9.
176. Zoller L, Burkard S, Schafer H. Validity of Western immunoblot band patterns in the serodiagnosis of Lyme borreliosis. J Clin Microbiol. 1991;29:174.
177. Ma B, Christen C, Leung D, Vigo-Pelfrey C. Serodiagnosis of Lyme borreliosis by Western immunoblot: Reactivity of various significant antibodies against *Borrelia burgdorferi*. J Clin Microbiol. 1992;30:370.
178. Kowal K, Weinstein A. Western blot band intensity analysis. Application to the diagnosis of Lyme arthritis. Arthritis Rheum. 1994;37:1206.
179. Centers for Disease Control. Proceedings of the Second National Conference on Serologic Diagnosis of Lyme Disease. Washington, DC: Association of State and Territorial Public Health Laboratory Directors; 1994:111.
180. Centers for Disease Control. Recommendations for test performance and interpretation from the Second International Conference on serologic diagnosis of Lyme disease. MMWR Morb Mortal Wkly Rep. 1995;44:1.
181. Dressler F, Yoshinari NH, Steere AC. The T cell proliferative assay in the diagnosis of Lyme disease. Ann Intern Med. 1991;115:533.
182. Guy EC, Stanek G. Detection of *Borrelia burgdorferi* in patients with Lyme disease by the polymerase chain reaction. J Clin Pathol. 1991;44:610.
183. Priem S, Rittig MG, Kamradt T, et al. An optimized PCR leads to rapid and highly sensitive detection of *Borrelia burgdorferi* in patients with Lyme borreliosis. J Clin Microbiol. 1997;35:685.
184. Lebech AM, Hansen K. Detection of *Borrelia burgdorferi* DNA in urine samples and cerebrospinal fluid samples from patients with early and late Lyme neuroborreliosis by polymerase chain reaction. J Clin Microbiol. 1992;30:1646.
185. Nocton JJ, Bloom BJ, Rutledge BJ, et al. Detection of *Borrelia burgdorferi* DNA by polymerase chain reaction in cerebrospinal fluid in patients with Lyme neuroborreliosis. J Infect Dis. 1996;174:623.
186. Melchers W, Meis J, Rosa P, et al. Amplification of *Borrelia burgdorferi* DNA in skin biopsies from patients with Lyme disease. J Clin Microbiol. 1991;29:2401.
187. Schwartz I, Wormser GP, Schwartz JJ, et al. Diagnosis of early Lyme disease by polymerase chain reaction amplification and culture of skin biopsies from erythema migrans lesions. J Clin Microbiol. 1992;30:3082.
188. Steere AC, Taylor E, McHugh GL, et al. The overdiagnosis of Lyme disease. JAMA. 1993;269:1812.
189. Sigal LH. Summary of the first 100 patients seen at a Lyme disease referral center. Am J Med. 1990;88:577.
190. Reid MC, Schoen RT, Evans J, et al. The consequences of overdiagnosis and overtreatment of Lyme disease: An observational study. Ann Intern Med. 1998;128:354.
191. Sigal LH, Patella SJ. Lyme arthritis as the incorrect diagnosis in pediatric and adolescent fibromyalgia. Pediatrics. 1992;90:523.
192. Dinerman H, Steere AC. Lyme disease associated with fibromyalgia. Ann Intern Med. 1992;117:281.
193. Dattwyler RJ, Volkman DJ, Conaty SM, et al. Amoxycillin plus probenecid versus doxycycline for treatment of erythema migrans borreliosis. Lancet. 1990;336:1404.
194. Massarotti EM, Luger SW, Rahn DW, et al. Treatment of early Lyme disease. Am J Med. 1992;92:396.
195. Nadelman RB, Luger SW, Frank E, et al. Comparison of cefuroxime axetil and doxycycline in the treatment of early Lyme disease. Ann Intern Med. 1992;117:273.
196. Steere AC, Hutchinson GJ, Rahn DW, et al. Treatment of the early manifestations of Lyme disease. Ann Intern Med. 1983;99:22.
197. Luft BJ, Dattwyler RJ, Johnson RC, et al. Azithromycin compared with amoxicillin in the treatment of erythema migrans: A double-blind, randomized, controlled trial. Ann Intern Med. 1996;124:785.
198. Dattwyler RJ, Luft BJ, Kunkel MJ, et al. Ceftriaxone compared with doxycycline for the treatment of acute disseminated Lyme disease. N Engl J Med. 1997;337:289.
199. Johnson RC, Kodner C, Russell M. In vitro and in vivo susceptibility of the Lyme disease spirochete, *Borrelia burgdorferi*, to four antimicrobial agents. Antimicrob Agents Chemother. 1987;31:164.
200. Preac-Mursic V, Wilske B, Schierz G, et al. Comparative antimicrobial activity of the new macrolides against *Borrelia burgdorferi*. Eur J Clin Microbiol Infect Dis. 1989;8:651.
201. Agger WA, Callister SM, Jobe DA. In vitro susceptibilities of *Borrelia burgdorferi* to five oral cephalosporins and ceftriaxone. Antimicrob Agents Chemother. 1992;36:1788.
202. Dever LL, Jorgensen JH, Barbour AG. In vitro antimicrobial susceptibility testing of *Borrelia burgdorferi:* A microdilution MIC method and timekill studies. J Clin Microbiol. 1992;30:2692.
203. Steere AC, Levin R, Molloy P, et al. Treatment of Lyme arthritis. Arthritis Rheum. 1994;37:878.
204. Dattwyler RJ, Halperin JJ, Volkman DJ, Luft BJ. Treatment of late Lyme borreliosis—randomized comparison of ceftriaxone and penicillin. Lancet. 1988;1:1191.
205. Eckman MH, Steere AC, Kalish RA, Pauker SG. Cost effectiveness of oral as compared with intravenous antibiotic therapy for patients with early Lyme disease or Lyme arthritis. N Engl J Med. 1997;337:357.
206. Schoen RT, Aversa JM, Rahn DW, et al. Treatment of refractory chronic Lyme arthritis with arthroscopic synovectomy. Arthritis Rheum. 1991;34:1056.
207. Pfister HW, Preac-Mursic V, Wilske B, et al. Randomized comparison of ceftriaxone and cefotaxime in Lyme neuroborreliosis. J Infect Dis. 1991;163:311.
208. Steere AC, Pachner AR, Malawsita SE. Neurologic abnormalities of Lyme disease: Successful treatment with high-dose intravenous penicillin. Ann Intern Med. 1983;99:767.
209. Pfister HW, Neubert V, Wilske B, et al. Reinfection with *Borrelia burgdorferi*. Lancet. 1986;11:984.
210. Gerber MA, Shapiro ED, Burke GS, et al. Lyme disease in children in southeastern Connecticut. N Engl J Med. 1996;335:1270.
211. Schreck CE, Snoddy EL, Spielman A. Pressurized sprays of permethrin or DEET on military clothing for personal protection against *Ixodes dammini* (Acari: Ixodidae). J Med Entomol. 1986;23:396.
212. Oransky S, Roseman B, Fish D, et al. Seizures temporarily associated with the use of DEET insect repellent—New York and Connecticut. MMWR Morb Mortal Wkly Rep. 1989;38:678.
213. Shapiro ED, Gerber MA, Holabird NB, et al. A controlled trial of antimicrobial prophylaxis for Lyme disease after deer-tick bites. N Engl J Med. 1992;327:1769.
214. Warshafsky S, Nowakowski J, Nadelman RB, et al. Efficacy of antibiotic prophylaxis for prevention of Lyme disease: A meta-analysis. J Gen Intern Med. 1996;11:329.
215. Fix AD, Strickland GT, Grant J. Tick bites and Lyme disease in an endemic setting. JAMA. 1998;297:206.
216. Wilson ML, Telford SR III, Piesman J, et al. Reduced abundance of immature *Ixodes dammini* (Acari: Ixodidae) following elimination of deer. J Med Entomol. 1988;25:224.
217. Schulze TL, Taylor GC, Vasvary LM, et al. Effectiveness of an aerial application of carbaryl in controlling *Ixodes dammini* (Acari: *Ixodidae*) adults in a high use recreational area in New Jersey. J Med Entomol. 1992;29:544.
218. Curran KL, Fish D, Piesman J. Reduction of nymphal *Ixodes dammini* (Acari: Ixodidae) in a residential suburban landscape by area application of insecticides. J Med Entomol. 1993;30:107.
219. Mather TN, Riberio JMC, Spielman A. Lyme disease and babesiosis: Acaricide focused on potentially infected ticks. Am J Trop Med Hyg. 1986;36:609.
220. Stafford KC III. Effectiveness of host-targeted permethrin in the control of *Ixodes dammini* (Acari: Ixodidae). J Med Entomol. 1991;28:611.
221. Fikrig E, Barthold SW, Kantor FS, Flavell RA. Protection of mice against the Lyme disease agent by immunizing with recombinant OspA. Science. 1990; 250:553.
222. Fikrig E, Telford SR III, Barthold SW, et al. Elimination of *Borrelia burgdorferi* from vector ticks feeding on OspA-immunized mice. Proc Natl Acad Sci U S A. 1992;89:5418.

223. Steere AC, Sikand V, Meurice F, et al. Vaccination against Lyme disease using recombinant *Borrelia burgdorferi* outer-surface lipoprotein A with adjuvant. N Engl J Med. 1998;339:209.
224. Preac-Mursic V, Wilske B, Patsouris E, et al. Active immunization with pC protein of *Borrelia burgdorferi* protects gerbils against *B. burgdorferi* infection. Infection. 1992;20:342.
225. Hanson MS, Cassatt DR, Guo BP, et al. Active and passive immunity against *Borrelia burgdorferi* decorin binding protein A (DbpA) protects against infection. Infect Immun. 1998;66:2143.

Chapter 232

Spirillum minus (Rat-Bite Fever)

RONALD G. WASHBURN

Spirillum minus is one of the two etiologic agents of rat-bite fever. The other causative bacterium, *Streptobacillus moniliformis,* is discussed in Chapter 220. *Spirillum minus* causes a significant portion of the cases of rat-bite fever in Asia but rarely produces infection in the United States.[1, 2] In Japan, the infection is called *sodoku* (*so*: rat; *doku*: poison).

The causative organism was discovered by Carter during the 19th century.[3] In the early years of the 20th century, specimens from patients with *sodoku* were shown to contain spirochetes capable of infecting guinea pigs. Those bacteria were initially called *Spirocheta morsus muris* or *Sporozoa muris.*[4] The organism was renamed *Spirillum minus* in 1924.[5]

BACTERIOLOGY

Spirillum minus is a short, thick, gram-negative, tightly coiled spiral rod measuring 0.2 to 0.5 μm $\times$ 3 to 5 μm.[6, 7] The organism has two to six regular helical turns.[7] Terminal polytrichous flagella confer darting motility, which can be demonstrated with darkfield examination. The flagella can be stained with silver impregnation methods (e.g., Fontana-Tribondeau). *Spirillum minus* cannot be cultured on artificial media.

EPIDEMIOLOGY, PATHOGENESIS, AND PATHOLOGY

The epidemiology of *S. minus* infections is similar to that of streptobacillary rat-bite fever, with the exception that oral ingestion has not been shown to cause spirillary disease. The major route of transmission is through rat bites. Approximately 25% of tested rats are positive for *S. minus* in conjunctival and nasopharyngeal secretions, pulmonary lesions, and blood.[6, 8] Human-to-human transmission has not been documented.

Relapses of spirillary rat-bite fever have been postulated to be due to seeding of blood and distant foci during periodic reactivation of the primary bite lesion.[6] The available recorded autopsies show granulomatous inflammation at the original site of inoculation, with epithelial necrosis and mononuclear infiltration of the dermis. Regional lymph nodes are hyperplastic.[6] Deep tissue specimens from distant areas of skin rash contain dilated blood vessels and round cell infiltrates. Liver, spleen, renal tubules, myocardium, and meninges may be hemorrhagic, with areas of necrosis in liver and kidney.

CLINICAL MANIFESTATIONS

The initial bite wound heals promptly but then becomes painful, swollen, and purple approximately 1 to 4 weeks later; it is associated with regional lymphangitis and lymphadenitis.[6] This local inflammatory lesion ushers in a systemic illness characterized by fever, chills, headache, and malaise. In contrast with streptobacillary rat-bite fever, arthritis and myalgias are rare in *Spirillum minus* infection. Leukocytosis with peripheral white blood cell counts in the range of 10,000 to 20,000/mm^3 may be observed, and up to 50% of patients have false-positive syphilis serologies.[6, 7] Next, the bite wound commonly progresses to chancre-like ulceration and induration with eschar formation. During the first week of fever, a blotchy violaceous or reddish-brown macular rash erupts over the extremities, face, scalp, and trunk, and then fades during subsequent afebrile intervals. Occasionally, the rash may be urticarial.[9]

Without specific antibiotic therapy, fevers lasting 3 to 4 days recur at regular intervals between afebrile periods of 3 to 9 days. Spontaneous cure usually occurs within 1 to 2 months, but in selected instances fevers have relapsed for years.[9]

The most serious complication of untreated spirillary rat-bite fever is endocarditis. Most of these rare intravascular infections have been observed in patients with preexisting valvular disease, but one reported case occurred on a normal aortic valve.[10] The spectrum of reported complications also includes myocarditis, pleural effusions, hepatitis, splenomegaly, meningitis, epididymitis, conjunctivitis, and anemia.[4, 6, 9, 11] Overall mortality of untreated *S. minus* infections in the pre-antibiotic era was 6 to 10%.

DIAGNOSIS

In the absence of a history of rat bite or typical clinical features, other diagnoses that might enter into the differential diagnosis of relapsing fever would include *Borrelia,* malaria, and lymphoma. Because *S. minus* cannot be grown on synthetic media, initial diagnosis relies on direct visualization of characteristic spirochetes in blood, exudate, or lymph node tissue using Giemsa stain, Wright stain, or darkfield microscopy. Organisms can also be recovered from mice or guinea pigs 1 to 3 weeks after intraperitoneal inoculation,[4, 9, 12] with the precaution that the animals must be prescreened to rule out the presence of preexisting spirochete infections. No specific serologic test is available for *S. minus* infection.

TREATMENT

The usual treatment is penicillin for 10 to 14 days. Further details are given in Chapter 220.

REFERENCES

1. Anderson LC, Leary SL, Manning PJ. Ratbite fever in animal research laboratory personnel. Lab Anim Sci. 1983;33:292–294.
2. Cole JS, Stoll RW, Bulger RJ. Ratbite fever: Report of three cases. Ann Intern Med. 1969;71:979–981.
3. Hiatt JR, Hiatt N. The forgotten first career of Doctor Henry Van Dyke Carter. J Am Coll Surg. 1995;181:464–486.
4. Roughgarden JW. Antimicrobial therapy of ratbite fever. Arch Intern Med. 1965;116:39–54.
5. Robertson A. Causal organism of ratbite fever in man. Ann Trop Med. 1924;18:157.
6. Gunning JJ. Ratbite fevers. In: Hunter GW III, Swartzwelder JC, Clyde DF, eds. Tropical Medicine. 5th ed. Philadelphia: WB Saunders; 1976:245–246.
7. Baron EJ, Weissfeld AS, Fuselier PA, et al. Classification and identification of bacteria. In: Murray PR, Baron EJ, Pfaller MA, et al, eds. Manual of Clinical Microbiology, 6th ed. Washington, DC: American Society for Microbiology; 1995:249–264.
8. McHugh TP, Bartlett RL, Raymond JI. Rat bite fever: Report of a fatal case. Ann Emerg Med. 1985;14:1116–1118.
9. Taber LH, Feigin RD. Spirochetal infections. Pediatr Clin North Am. 1979;26:410–411.
10. McIntosh CS, Vickers PJ, Isaacs AJ. Spirillum endocarditis. Postgrad Med J. 1975;51:645–648.
11. Raffin BJ, Freemark M. Streptobacillary ratbite fever: A pediatric problem. Pediatrics. 1979;64:214–217.
12. Dow GR, Rankin RJ, Saunders BW. Ratbite fever. N Z Med J. 1992;105:133.

ANAEROBIC BACTERIA

Chapter 233

Anaerobic Bacteria: General Concepts

SYDNEY M. FINEGOLD

Anaerobic bacteria are important because they dominate the indigenous flora, they are commonly found in infection, and some of these infections are serious and have a high mortality rate. It is relatively easy to overlook anaerobic infections because special precautions are needed for appropriate collection and transport of specimens. Furthermore, particularly in this period of cost containment, some clinical laboratories fail to fully identify or even to grow many anaerobes. Growth and identification of anaerobic bacteria are often slow processes. Although both clinicians and microbiologists are much better informed about anaerobic infections than was true 2 or 3 decades ago, such infections are undoubtedly still the most commonly overlooked of bacterial infections.

In addition to the aforementioned problems, treatment of anaerobic infections may be difficult. Failure to provide antibacterial coverage against the anaerobes in a mixed aerobic-anaerobic infection may lead to an inadequate response, which may be attributed to another factor such as the possibility of an undrained abscess. Resistance of anaerobic bacteria to antibacterial agents is increasing, and a number of antimicrobials have poor or no activity against anaerobes. Surgical management, particularly drainage and débridement, is an important aspect of treatment of most anaerobic infections.

WHAT IS AN ANAEROBE?

For practical, operational purposes, an anaerobe may be defined as a bacterium that fails to grow on the surface of solid media in 10% CO_2 in air (18% oxygen). Facultative bacteria can grow in both the presence and absence of air. Bacteria are considered to be microaerophilic if they grow poorly or not at all aerobically but grow distinctly better under 10% CO_2 in air or anaerobically; ideally, the definition should include demonstration of better growth under reduced oxygen tension than is true for obligate anaerobes. Loesche[1] classified anaerobes as strict (not capable of growth on an agar surface in the presence of greater than 0.5% oxygen) or moderate (tolerant of oxygen levels of 2 to 8%). Strict anaerobes included some *Treponema* spp., *Selenomonas*, and *Clostridium haemolyticum*. In the moderate group were *Bacteroides fragilis*, what was then called *Bacteroides melaninogenicus* (now *Prevotella melaninogenica* or a closely related form), *Bacteroides* (now *Prevotella*) oralis, and *Fusobacterium nucleatum*, all important clinical pathogens. Differences from strain to strain can be detected; for example Rosebury[2] found one strain of *B. melaninogenicus* that grew well in the presence of 0.1% oxygen but not at 1% and another that grew at 2% but not at 4% oxygen.

The relative importance of the oxygen concentration, superoxide radical concentration, peroxides, and oxidation-reduction potential is difficult to determine because various experiments, most of which do not come close to duplicating clinical conditions, seem to show one or another as being most important. Most anaerobes do not possess catalase, but clinically significant anaerobes often possess superoxide dismutase and general, but not universal, correlation is found between the amount of this enzyme and the degree of aerotolerance of the organism.[3, 4] Fresh clinical isolates, with a maximum of two transfers since isolation, were quite oxygen sensitive. Certain strains of *Peptostreptococcus, Bacteroides* other than *B. fragilis*, and non–spore-forming gram-positive bacilli failed to grow in greater than 0.4% oxygen.[5] Certain anaerobes such as *Clostridium tertium* routinely grow well aerobically.[6]

HISTORICAL ASPECTS

Although clinical and bacteriologic studies of anaerobic infections go back 1 century, earlier studies described certain infections or toxemias now known to be related to anaerobes. Hippocrates gave a good clinical description of tetanus in the fourth century BC. In the fourth century AD, Xenophon described evidence of acute necrotizing ulcerative gingivitis in Greek soldiers. Von Langenbeck described the clinical manifestations of actinomycosis in 1845.

The first evidence that microorganisms might live under anaerobic conditions was that of Antonie van Leeuwenhoek, who noted that some of his "animalcules" were able to live and move about in the absence of air. The phenomenon of anaerobiosis was more clearly described by Louis Pasteur in 1861 when he discovered that *Vibrion butyrique (Clostridium butyricum)* lost its motility in a wet preparation under the microscope when it approached the edge of the preparation where it was exposed to the air. Pasteur used the name "anaérobies," which was the origin of our word "anaerobes."[7]

The first study of a patient with an anaerobic infection (rather than toxin-related disease such as tetanus or botulism) was published by Levy in Germany in 1891.[8] In this postpartum infection a parametrial mass extended to produce a "gas abscess" in the upper part of the thigh. The foul-smelling pus from this patient yielded a chaining gram-positive anaerobic rod plus a small number of *Streptococcus pyogenes*; it was possible to keep the anaerobic organism alive for only a short period. Veillon, in Paris in 1893,[9] was able to recover and maintain an anaerobic coccus from each of four patients with various infections. One of these isolates was in pure culture and the other three were found in combination with *S. pyogenes*; the foul odor of the pus was shown to be due to the anaerobe alone. In 1897, Veillon and Zuber[10] published a classic paper describing a large number of diverse types of anaerobes recovered from 25 cases of gangrenous or fetid suppuration, including brain abscess, pulmonary gangrene, appendicitis, pelvic abscess, and purulent arthritis. This landmark paper set the tone for subsequent clinical practice and for further investigations.

Subsequent studies further advanced our knowledge and facilitated working with the fastidious anaerobes. Anaerobic jars were introduced in 1916 by McIntosh and Fildes.[11] The more recent introduction of cold catalysts and commercial packets that generate hydrogen and carbon dioxide after the addition of water greatly facilitated work in the average hospital clinical laboratory. The importance of working only with pure cultures of organisms is a major principle of bacteriology, but anaerobic bacteria may be particularly difficult to isolate in pure culture, primarily because of very special growth requirements often supplied by coinfecting organisms. Thus, especially in the early history of anaerobic bacteriology, a significant problem was that new taxa were being described inappropriately because cultures were contaminated with other organisms and different biochemical reactions were produced.[12]

From 1926 to 1981 (a span of 55 years), Prévot[7] published an extensive number of monographs on anaerobic bacteriology and large texts with emphasis on bacteriology and taxonomy, but he also provided clinical information with his colleagues Weinberg and Nativelle. Additional influential works were Meleney's *Treatise on Surgical Infections* published in 1948,[13] *Microorganisms Indigenous to Man* published by Rosebury in 1962,[14] *Infections Humaines à Bactéries Anaérobies Non-Toxigènes* published by Beerens and Tahon-Castel in 1965,[15] and *Clostridia of Wound Infection* published by Willis in 1969.[16]

In the 1940s and 1950s, potent antibacterial compounds (penicillin G, tetracyclines, and chloramphenicol) became available for the treatment of anaerobic infections. In the 1960s and 1970s, several new antimicrobials with good activity against anaerobic bacteria also became available. Not only were these drugs extremely useful in the management of anaerobic infections, but their availability permitted firm establishment of the major role of anaerobic bacteria in various clinically significant infections, particularly intra-abdominal, female genital tract, and pleuropulmonary infection. This development provided a huge stimulus for both clinical studies and careful anaerobic bacteriology.

TAXONOMY

The taxonomy of the anaerobes has been very confusing, but recent changes and some excellent recent summaries have been very helpful.[6, 17–19] The widespread use of genetic studies for characterization of anaerobic bacteria has recently established these changes on much firmer ground than when phenotypic characteristics and more crude genetic analyses were used. Differentiation between similar organisms may have important implications regarding the type and severity of infections produced and antimicrobial susceptibility patterns.[20, 21] Table 233–1 is a relatively detailed breakdown of the current anaerobic taxa and their differentiation. Table 233–2 summarizes the recent taxonomic changes among anaerobic bacteria. The most important anaerobes encountered clinically are listed in Table 233–3. For those not heavily involved with the anaerobes, it is comforting to note that five organisms or groups of organisms, taken together, account for approximately two thirds of the anaerobes recovered from clinically significant infections involving anaerobes (Table 233–4).

PRESENCE AS NORMAL FLORA

Two major monographs detail the indigenous flora of the human body,[14, 22] and Hentges has provided a brief but excellent overview of this topic.[23] Table 233–5 is a succinct summary of the various anaerobes found as indigenous flora at different sites in the body.

It is interesting to note that anaerobes are prevalent in certain areas of the body exposed to air—the skin, nose, mouth, and throat. Two principal explanations have been presented for this prevalence: oxygen consumption by aerobic and facultative flora also present at these sites and protection from air in microhabitats with low oxidation-reduction potential, such as the gingival crevice, tonsillar crypts, and hair follicles.

The indigenous microflora may be profoundly modified by pathophysiologic states and by exposure to antimicrobial agents and other drugs. Normally, the stomach has a sparse flora. Patients with peptic ulcer and bleeding or obstruction and patients with gastric carcinoma may have significant increases in the numbers and types of organisms present in the stomach, and the flora may even resemble that of the colon.[24] In patients with major bowel resection after superior mesenteric artery occlusion, the bowel flora may have a preponderance of gram-positive anaerobes.[25] Marked overgrowth of anaerobes is noted in the bypassed segment of patients undergoing ileal bypass for obesity[26] and in other settings leading to bowel stasis, such as small bowel diverticula and other causes of the blind loop syndrome.[27] Antimicrobial agents that achieve high levels in the gut may lead to

TABLE 233–1 Differentiation of Genera of Anaerobes

- Gram-negative bacilli
  - Nonmotile or peritrichous flagella
    - Produce butyric acid without isoacids
      - *Fusobacterium*
    - Produce major lactic acid
      - *Leptotrichia*
    - Produce acetic acid, reduce sulfate
      - *Desulfomonas*
    - Not as above
      - *Anaerorhabdus*
      - *Bacteroides*
      - *Bilophila*
      - *Megamonas*
      - *Porphyromonas*
      - *Prevotella*
      - *Sutterella*
  - Motile, not peritrichous flagella
    - Fermentative
      - Produce butyric acid
        - *Butyrivibrio*
      - Produce succinic acid
        - Spiral-shaped cells, single polar flagellum
          - *Succinivibrio*
        - Spiral-shaped cells, bipolar tufts of flagella
          - *Anaerobiospirillum*
        - Ovoid cells
          - *Succinimonas**
      - Produce propionic and acetic acids
        - Single polar flagellum
          - *Anaerovibrio**
        - Tufts of flagella on concave side
          - *Selenomonas*
        - Flagella in a spiral path along cell body
          - *Centipeda*
      - Produce acetic acid, twitching motility
        - *Mobiluncus*
    - Nonfermentative
      - Produce succinic acid from fumarate
        - *Wolinella, Campylobacter*
      - Produce acetic acid, reduce sulfate
        - *Desulfovibrio*
- Gram-negative cocci
  - Produce propionic and acetic acids
    - *Veillonella*
  - Produce butyric and acetic acids
    - *Acidaminococcus*
  - Produce isobutyric, butyric, isovaleric, valeric, and caproic acids
    - *Megasphaera*
- Gram-positive cocci
  - Require a fermentable carbohydrate
    - Produce butyric (plus other acids)
      - *Coprococcus*
    - No butyric produced
      - *Ruminococcus*
  - Do not require a fermentable carbohydrate
    - Lactic acid sole major product
      - *Streptococcus*
      - *Gemella*
    - Not as above
      - *Peptostreptococcus*
      - *Peptococcus*
- Gram-positive spore-forming bacilli
  - *Clostridium*
- Gram-positive non–spore-forming bacilli
  - Produce propionic and acetic acids as major end products
    - *Propionibacterium*
  - No propionic acid produced
    - Produce acetic and lactic acids (A ≥ L)
      - *Bifidobacterium*
    - Produce lactic acid as sole major end product
      - *Lactobacillus*
    - Produce moderate acetic acid plus one of the following:
      - Major succinic and lactic acids
      - Major succinic acid
        - *Actinomyces*
    - Other: butyric with or without others, acetic, or no major acids
      - *Eubacterium*

*No known human isolates.

Modified from Summanen P, Baron EJ, Citron DM, et al. Wadsworth Anaerobic Bacteriology Manual. 5th ed. Belmont, Calif: Star; 1993:1. Reprinted with permission of Star Publishing Company, Belmont, CA.

TABLE 233-2 Recent Taxonomic Changes among Anaerobic Bacteria

Pigmented and Nonpigmented *Prevotella* Species

Current Nomenclature	*Previous Nomenclature/Synonym*
Pigmented species	
P. corporis	
P. denticola	
P. intermedia	
P. loescheii	
P. melaninogenica	
P. nigrescens	New species
P. tannerae	New species
P. pallens	PINLOs
Nonpigmented species	
*P. bivia**	
P. buccae	
P. buccalis	
*P. disiens**	
P. heparinolytica†	
P. oralis	
P. oris	
P. oulorum	
P. veroralis	
P. zoogleoformans†	
P. enoeca	New species
P. dentalis	*Mitsuokella dentalis* *Hallella seregens*

*May fluoresce yellowish red under ultraviolet light; older cultures appear light tan on media containing lysed blood.
†Will be moved to the genus *Bacteroides*.
Abbreviation: PINLOs, *Prevotella intermedia/nigrescens*–like organisms.

***Porphyromonas* Species Isolated from Humans and Animals**

Current Nomenclature	*Previous Nomenclature/Synonym*
Human isolates	
P. asaccharolytica	
P. endodontalis	
P. gingivalis	
P. catoniae	*Oribaculum catoniae*
Animal isolates	
P. cangingivalis	New species
P. canoris	New species
P. cansulci	New species
P. circumdentaria	
P. crevioricanis	New species
P. gingivalis (catalase positive)	
P. gingivicanis	New species
P. levii	*Bacteroides levii*
P. macacae	*Bacteroides macacae* *Porphyromonas salivosa*
P. levii–like organisms	
P. endodontalis–like organisms	

New or Reclassified *Fusobacterium* Species

Current Nomenclature	*Previous Nomenclature/Synonym*
F. alocis	New species
F. necrophorum subspecies *funduliforme*	*F. necrophorum* biovar B (lipase and hemagglutinin negative)
F. necrophorum subspecies *necrophorum*	*F. necrophorum* biovar A (lipase and hemagglutinin positive)
F. nucleatum subspecies *animalis*	New subspecies
F. nucleatum subspecies *fusiforme*	New subspecies
F. nucleatum subspecies *nucleatum*	New subspecies
F. nucleatum subspecies *polymorphum*	New subspecies
F. nucleatum subspecies *vincentii*	New subspecies
F. periodonticum	New species
F. varium	*F. necrophorum* biovar C, *F. pseudonecrophorum*
F. ulcerans	New species

New Genera and Species after Reclassification of *Bacteroides*

Current Nomenclature	*Previous Nomenclature/Synonym*
Anaerorhabdus furcosus	*B. furcosus*
*Catonella morbi**	New species
*Dialister pneumosintes**	*B. pneumosintes*
Dichelobacter nodosus	*B. nodosus*
Fibrobacter succinogenes	*B. succinogenes*
*Johnsonella ignava**	New species
Megamonas hypermegas	*B. hypermegas*
*Mitsuokella multiacida**	*B. multiacidus*
Rikenella microfusus	*B. microfusus*
Ruminobacter amylophilus	*B. amylophilus*
Sebaldella termitidis	*B. termitidis*
*Tissierella praeacuta**	*B. praeacutus*
Capnocytophaga ochracea†	*B. ochraceus*
Capnocytophaga granulosa†	New species
Capnocytophaga haemolytica†	New species
Leptotrichia buccalis†	
Leptotrichia sanguinegens†	New species

*Belongs to the *Clostridium* subphylum of gram-positive bacteria.
†Not true anaerobes.

New or Reclassified *Campylobacter, Bilophila,* and *Sutterella* Species

Current Nomenclature	*Previous Nomenclature/Synonym*
C. rectus	*Wolinella recta*
C. curvus	*Wolinella curva*
C. showae	New species
C. gracilis	*Bacteroides gracilis*
Bilophila wadsworthia	New genus and species
Sutterella wadsworthensis	New genus and species (partly *Campylobacter* [*B.*] *gracilis*)

New Species of *Peptostreptococcus*

Current Nomenclature	*Previous Nomenclature/Synonym*
P. hydrogenalis	New species
P. lacrimalis	New species
P. lactolyticus	New species
P. vaginalis	New species

Gram-Positive, Non–Spore-Forming Rods

Current Nomenclature	*Previous Nomenclature/Synonym*
Actinomyces georgiae	*Actinomyces* DO8
Actinomyces gerencseriae	*A. israeli* serotype II
Actinomyces naeslundii/Actinomyces viscosus	*A. viscosus, A. naeslundii*
Actinomyces neuii	CDC coryneform group 1
Actinomyces neuii subspecies *neuii*	New species and subspecies
Actinomyces neuii subspecies *anitratus*	New species and subspecies
Actinomyces radingae	CDC coryneform group E; APL1
Actinomyces turicensis	CDC coryneform group E; APL10
Arcanobacterium bernardiae	CDC coryneform group 2, *Actinomyces bernardiae*
Atopobium minutum	New genus and species
Atopobium parvulum	New genus and species
Atopobium rimae	New genus and species
Bifidobacterium inopinatum	New species*
Bifidobacterium denticolens	New species*
Eubacterium brachy	New species
Eubacterium exiguum	New species
Eubacterium infirmum	New species
Eubacterium minutum	New species
Eubacterium nodatum	
Eubacterium saphenum	
Eubacterium tardum	New species
Eubacterium yurii subspecies *yurii*	New species and subspecies
E. yurii subspecies *margaretiae*	New species and subspecies
E. yurii subspecies *schtitka*	New species and subspecies
Lactobacillus paraplantarum	New species
Lactobacillus uli	New species
Pseudoramibacter	New genus
Pseudoramibacter alactolyticus	*Eubacterium alactolyticum*
Propionibacterium propionicus	*Arachnia propionica*

*Formerly part of *Bifidobacterium dentium*.
Abbreviations: APL, *Actinomyces pyogenes*–like; CDC, Centers for Disease Control and Prevention.
Modified from Jousimies-Somer H. Recently described clinically important anaerobic bacteria: Taxonomic aspects and update. Clin Infect Dis. 1997;25(Suppl 2):S78–S87.

TABLE 233-3 Major Anaerobes Encountered Clinically

Gram-negative bacilli
- *Bacteroides fragilis* group
  - Especially *B. fragilis, B. thetaiotaomicron, B. distasonis, B. ovatus, B. vulgatus*
- Other *Bacteroides*
  - *B. gracilis*
  - *B. ureolyticus*
- *Porphyromonas* spp.
  - Especially *P. asaccharolytica*
- Pigmented *Prevotella* spp. (*P. corporis, P. denticola, P. intermedia, P. loescheii, P. melaninogenica, P. nigrescens*)
- Other *Prevotella* spp.
  - *P. oris*
  - *P. buccae*
  - *P. oralis* group
  - *P. bivia*
  - *P. disiens*
- *Fusobacterium* spp.
  - *F. nucleatum*
  - *F. necrophorum*
  - *F. mortiferum*
  - *F. varium*
- *Bilophila wadsworthia*
- *Sutterella wadsworthensis*

Gram-positive cocci
- *Peptostreptococcus*
  - Especially *P. anaerobius, P. intermedius,* * *P. micros, P. magnus, P. asaccharolyticus, P. prevotii*
- Microaerophilic streptococci*

Gram-positive spore-forming bacilli
- *Clostridium perfringens*
- *C. ramosum*
- *C. septicum*
- *C. novyi*
- *C. histolyticum*
- *C. sporogenes*
- *C. sordellii*
- *C. bifermentans*
- *C. clostridioforme*
- *C. fallax*
- *C. difficile*
- *C. innocuum*
- *C. botulinum*
- *C. tetani*

Gram-positive non–spore-forming bacilli
- *Actinomyces (israelii, meyerii, naeslundii, odontolyticus, viscosus, neuii, radingae, turicensis)*
- *Propionibacterium propionicum*
- *Propionibacterium acnes*
- *Bifidobacterium dentium*

*Not true anaerobes.

major alterations in bowel flora as a result of elimination of susceptible organisms and replacement by resistant ones.[28] H_2 blockers and even antacids may lead to significant increases in the flora of the stomach for variable periods after each dose. The flora at various sites in the body may also vary with age, loss of teeth, menstrual cycle, and pregnancy.

More studies of indigenous flora are needed, particularly with the recent changes in taxonomy. In a number of cases, organisms have been inferred to be part of a particular flora, such as oral flora, by virtue of their presence in infection related to that site. Studies of normal flora typically detect only the numerically dominant elements unless good selective or differential media are available for the retrieval of organisms present in small numbers. These latter organisms may be very important in infection or in other ways, despite not dominating the flora.

On the skin, the dominant anaerobic organisms belong to the genus *Propionibacterium. Propionibacterium acnes* is most prevalent, but *Propionibacterium granulosum* and *Propionibacterium avidum* are also seen with some frequency. *P. acnes* and *P. granulosum* are also found in the hair follicles and sebaceous glands. They are detected in adults in greatest numbers in skin with a high sebum content (e.g., the scalp, forehead, and sides of the nose). Unlike the other two species, *P. avidum* is rarely found in the lipid-rich areas of the skin, but rather in moist areas (e.g., the axilla and the anterior of the nose). Strains of *Peptostreptococcus* are also found with some frequency on the skin. Other anaerobes do not appear to be resident skin flora but may be seen as a function of contamination of the skin from orifices such as the anus. This factor may be important in certain types of infections. Gas gangrene (clostridial myonecrosis), for example, is a rare but dreaded complication of hip surgery. The organisms involved in this infection have their origin in the colonic flora. Various non–spore-forming bacteria that can be important in infected decubitus ulcers and infected ulcers of the feet in diabetics or others with impaired circulation can similarly have their origin in the bowel flora.

The flora of the nose is similar to that of the skin, with *P. acnes* dominating. Anaerobes commonly isolated from the oropharynx include anaerobic cocci, *Bacteroides, Prevotella, Porphyromonas*, and *Fusobacterium.*

In the oral cavity, anaerobes are found in the tonsillar crypts, in the crypts of the tongue, in plaque forming on the surfaces of the teeth, and in the gingival crevices. Areas with low oxidation-reduction potentials have the greatest colonization of anaerobes. In periodontal pockets this value can vary from -47.8 to -300 mV. The clean enamel surface of the teeth has an oxidation-reduction potential of 200 mV, but the potential drops to -141 mV after 7 days of plaque development. Dental plaque is a deposit of bacteria embedded in an adhesive matrix made up of salivary glycoproteins and extracellular bacterial polymers. Counts of anaerobes in saliva and elsewhere in the oral cavity reach 10^7 to 10^8/ml. Anaerobic organisms encountered in the human oral cavity include *Bacteroides, Prevotella, Porphyromonas, Campylobacter, Fusobacterium, Bilophila, Leptotrichia, Selenomonas, Wolinella, Actinomyces, Bifidobacterium, Eubacterium, Lactobacillus, Propionibacterium, Peptostreptococcus, Streptococcus, Veillonella*, and *Treponema.*

Normally, counts of anaerobes and other bacteria in the stomach and the upper part of the small bowel are quite low (10 to 1000/ml). The organisms are derived primarily from swallowed oral flora. Counts may reach 10^5/ml for 2 to 3 hours after meals. In the terminal ileum, counts of bacteria vary from 10^4 to 10^6/ml, and the flora is rather diverse and resembles colonic flora. In the colon, the bacterial population is the greatest of any inhabited region of the human body. Bacterial counts can exceed 10^{11} organisms per gram of dry weight of colonic contents. Anaerobes outnumber nonanaerobes by a ratio of about 1000:1. Members of the *B. fragilis* group dominate; the two most frequently encountered species are *Bacteroides vulgatus* and *Bacteroides thetaiotaomicron*, but *Bacteroides distasonis, B. fragilis*, and *Bacteroides ovatus* are also quite common. Various non–spore-forming gram-positive rods, *Peptostreptococcus* spp., and *Clostridium* spp. are also found in high counts. In all, dozens of genera and perhaps 300 to 400 different species inhabit the lower bowel.[29, 30]

Various anaerobes, including *Bacteroides, Fusobacterium, Peptostreptococcus, Eubacterium*, and *Clostridium*, can be found in the urethral flora in counts of 10^2 to 10^4/ml. In normal vaginal flora, lactobacilli predominate, but various anaerobic cocci, *Bacteroides, Prevotella*, and clostridia are also commonly found. Other anaerobes isolated from normal vaginal flora include *Porphyromonas, Fusobacterium, Bilophila, Actinomyces, Bifidobacterium, Eubacterium*, and *Propionibacterium.*

P. acnes is found as normal conjunctival flora.

TABLE 233-4 Anaerobes Most Commonly Encountered in Infection*

- *Bacteroides fragilis* group (especially *B. fragilis*)
- *Prevotella* and *Porphyromonas*
- *Fusobacterium nucleatum*
- *Peptostreptococcus*
- *Clostridium perfringens, Clostridium ramosum*

*These five groups together account for about two thirds of anaerobes from clinically significant infections involving anaerobes.

TABLE 233-5 Incidence of Various Anaerobes as Indigenous Flora in Humans

	Gram-Positive							Gram-Negative			
	Clostridium	***Actinomyces***	***Bifidobacterium***	***Eubacterium***	***Lactobacillus****	***Propionibacterium***	**Cocci**	***Bacteroides fragilis* Group**	***Fusobacterium***	**Other Gram-Negative Rods**	**Cocci**
Skin	0	0	0	+/−	0	2	1	0	0	0	0
Upper respiratory tract†	0	1	0	+/−	0	1	1	0	1	2	1
Mouth	+/−	1	1	1	1	+/−	2	0	2	2	2
Intestine	2	+/−	2	2	1–2	+/−	2	2	1	2	1
External genitalia	0	0	0	U	0	U	1	+/−	+/−	1	0
Urethra	+/−	0	0	U	+/−	0	+/−	+/−	+/−	1	U
Vagina	+/−	+/−	+/−	+/−	2	+/−	2	+/−	+/−	1	+/−
Endocervix	+/−	0	0	+/−	1	+/−	2	+/−	+/−	1	+/−

*Includes anaerobic, microaerophilic, and facultative strains.
†Includes nasal passages, nasopharynx, oropharynx, and tonsils.
Abbreviations: U, Unknown; 0, not found or rare; +/−, irregular; 1, usually present; 2, usually present in large numbers.
From Summanen P, Baron EJ, Citron DM, et al. Wadsworth Anaerobic Bacteriology Manual. 5th ed. Belmont, Calif: Star; 1993:1. Reprinted with permission of Star Publishing Company, Belmont, CA.

ROLE IN NORMAL HOST PHYSIOLOGY

One of the most important functions of the indigenous flora is to prevent colonization and infection by pathogenic organisms from outside sources. The flora provides a nonspecific stimulus to the host's immune system from birth. Germ-free animals have marked deficiencies in lymphoid and reticuloendothelial tissues, immunoglobulins, and components of complement. The indigenous flora also directly interferes with potential invading pathogens—a process called bacterial interference or colonization resistance. Mechanisms of such interference include bacteriocin production, elaboration of toxic metabolic end products, production of adverse environmental conditions such as low pH, depletion of nutrients, and interference with mucosal association by pathogens. *Propionibacterium* spp. hydrolyze triglycerides and thereby produce free fatty acids that are inhibitory to *S. pyogenes* and *Staphylococcus aureus*.[23] In the intestinal tract, volatile fatty acids (metabolic end products of anaerobes primarily) inhibit the multiplication of nonindigenous organisms at the pH levels of intestinal contents.[23] The indigenous flora also interferes with adherence of nonindigenous organisms to mucosal surfaces. Hydrogen peroxide, produced by some strains of a number of different species of *Lactobacillus*, is bactericidal to *Gardnerella vaginalis* and *Prevotella bivia* in vitro, and the presence of most of the organisms encountered in the vaginal secretions of women with bacterial vaginosis is inversely related to vaginal colonization by H_2O_2-producing lactobacilli.[31] This point is of major importance because bacterial vaginosis plays an important role in the development of chorioamnionitis, postpartum endometritis, vaginal cuff cellulitis after hysterectomy, postabortal pelvic inflammatory disease, and upper genital tract infections such as amniotic fluid infection and chorioamnion infection associated with premature delivery.[32] It might also be that maintenance of the normal H_2O_2-producing *Lactobacillus* flora would protect against urinary tract infection.[33]

In my opinion, we have not yet learned to control colonization resistance effectively (despite efforts at "selective decontamination") to prevent infection or superinfection after the use of antimicrobial prophylaxis or therapy; this approach, however, is a logical and important one that we must strive to master.

Our indigenous flora also contributes to our well-being in other ways. In the intestinal tract, for example, vitamin K production by intestinal bacteria may be important to the host. Both *Escherichia coli* and *B. fragilis* can synthesize vitamin K, but *B. fragilis* may be more important because it greatly outnumbers *E. coli*.[34] Bile acids are essential in fat absorption, bile formation, and regulation of cholesterol metabolism. Deconjugation of bile acids may be carried out by *B. fragilis*, various *Fusobacterium* spp., *Bifidobacterium* and other gram-positive anaerobic bacilli, and *Enterococcus faecalis*.[35, 36] Dehydroxylation of bile acids is carried out by various gram-positive anaerobic bacilli and, to a limited extent, by some strains of *B. fragilis, Veillonella*, and some aerobes.[36] Intestinal anaerobes can also effect other changes in bile acids and can biotransform bile pigments, cholesterol, and other steroid compounds.[22, 33] As nitrogen sources, intestinal bacteria use ammonia (derived from urea diffusing into the gut from the blood), small intestinal secretions, mucopolysaccharides, and sloughed epithelial cells; to derive energy, they metabolize undigested dietary carbohydrates (including plant cell walls), host-derived epithelial cells, and glycoproteins.[22]

Intestinal anaerobes can also modify various drugs and food additives.[22, 37] Several anaerobes and other intestinal bacteria can metabolize sulfasalazine.[38] Certain strains of *Eubacterium lentum* reduce digoxin to an inactive compound, so some patients with this organism in their bowel flora require increased dosage.[39] Therapy with erythromycin or tetracycline in such patients almost doubles digoxin serum levels.[40]

ROLE IN PATHOPHYSIOLOGIC STATES

Sources of contamination of the small bowel with increased numbers of bacteria include gastrocolic or enterocolic fistula, surgically created blind loops, diverticula, disease or therapy leading to decreased gastric acidity, disease causing impaired motility or stricture, an infected biliary tract draining into the duodenum, and IgA deficiency with lymphonodular hyperplasia of the small bowel.[41] Other factors include total starvation, alcoholism, diabetic neuropathy, intestinal scleroderma, and ileal bypass for obesity. Manifestations of malabsorption—diarrhea, steatorrhea, vitamin B_{12} deficiency, protein malnutrition, and impaired absorption of sugars—may be seen.

Ileal bypass surgery may lead to bypass enteropathy (diarrhea, proctocryptitis, pneumatosis cystoides intestinalis) and to extraenteric manifestations such as hepatic damage, arthritis, renal damage, and skin lesions.[42]

D-Lactic acidosis may be seen in patients with short-bowel syndrome or sometimes after ileal bypass. As noted earlier, such patients may have a predominance of gram-positive non–spore-forming anaerobic rods *(Bifidobacterium, Lactobacillus*, and *Eubacterium)* in their fecal flora.[25] Excessive levels of D-lactic acid may accumulate in such individuals under certain circumstances; this compound cannot be metabolized by humans. These patients may manifest confusion, loud and slurred speech, decreased coordination, ataxia, weakness, dizziness, lethargy, stupor, asterixis, and hostile behavior; the mechanism for these disturbances is unknown, but it is probably not due to the acidosis or D-lactic acid per se. Some patients have had coma and some have been committed to psychiatric institutions.

An association among diet, bowel flora, and the incidence of colon and breast cancer may well be possible, but no one to date has found a specific association with particular elements of the colonic bacterial flora or particular metabolic activities of such organisms that would affect the incidence of these malignancies. However, dietary flavonoid glycosides are anticarcinogenic, and these compounds can be destroyed in the colon by C-ring cleavage mediated by *Clostridium orbiscindens*.[43]

EPIDEMIOLOGY

Virtually all anaerobic infections arise from the indigenous flora of the body. A few, however, may be of exogenous origin, such as certain clostridial infections. In this category are a minority of cases of gas gangrene after trauma. Most cases of clostridial myonecrosis secondary to war wounds are actually of endogenous origin and relate to reduced hygiene under battle conditions. Similarly, clostridial myonecrosis secondary to surgery is traceable to the patient's own bowel flora.

Other exogenous infections, including nosocomial infection, can occur through the gastrointestinal tract and can involve intoxication as well as infection. These infections include *Clostridium difficile*–associated disease (principally pseudomembranous colitis related to antimicrobial or antineoplastic drugs),[44–46] type A *Clostridium perfringens* food poisoning and antibiotic-associated diarrhea, type C *C. perfringens*–induced enteritis necroticans, infant botulism, and perhaps some cases of adult botulism. *C. difficile* colitis can clearly be a nosocomial problem arising from contamination of the hospital environment and hands of personnel.

Wound botulism is another example of exogenous infection. Tetanus is a prime example of an anaerobic intoxication, the microbial agent of which *(Clostridium tetani)* is principally transmitted via an exogenous source. Transmission of anaerobic infection from animals to humans occurs on occasion, principally by means of a bite. Human bites also commonly involve anaerobes, and transfer by sexual transmission may occasionally occur (e.g., granuloma inguinale, genital ulcers infected with anaerobes).

Long-term use of intrauterine contraceptive devices increases the number of anaerobes in the cervical flora and may predispose to local disease (e.g., actinomycosis) as well as to bacterial vaginosis and pelvic inflammatory disease.[47]

PATHOLOGY AND PATHOPHYSIOLOGY OF ANAEROBIC INFECTIONS

Anaerobic infections are characterized by suppuration, frank abscess formation, and tissue destruction. The tissue destruction may be extensive and gangrenous. Gas may also be noted in tissues, and septic thrombophlebitis may occur.

In the case of *C. difficile*–associated colitis, the pathology varies from nonspecific colitis, with varying severity of inflammation, edema, and sometimes hemorrhage and necrosis, to frank pseudomembranous colitis; early disease may be found only in the right colon and may appear as 1- to 2-mm round, yellowish spots surrounded by erythema, with mildly granular mucosa.[48] Later, the yellowish plaques vary in size from a few millimeters to 2 cm. When they become larger, they become confluent and the shaggy yellowish pseudomembrane of necrotic mucosa develops.[49] Rarely, toxic megacolon may occur. Histologically, the characteristic picture is that of an early intercryptal "summit lesion" (destruction of surface epithelium and replacement by fibrin and acute inflammatory cells), then disruption and destruction of crypts, and eventually an inflammatory slough resting on the muscularis mucosae. Acute inflammatory cells are seen.

TABLE 233–6 Important Factors in the Pathogenesis of Anaerobic Infection

Primary source of anaerobes is normal flora
Break in anatomic barrier—surgery, trauma, disease
Host defense mechanisms
Antibody
Complement system
Polymorphonuclear leukocytes
Cell-mediated immune responses (T cells)
Lowering of oxidation-reduction potential
Size of bacterial inoculum
Synergy with other organisms
Virulence features of organisms
Adherence
Invasion
Toxins, enzymes
Surface constituents

TABLE 233–7 Conditions Predisposing to Anaerobic Infection

General	Decreased redox potential
Diabetes mellitus	Obstruction and stasis
Corticosteroids	Tissue anoxia
Neutropenia	Tissue destruction
Hypogammaglobulinemia	Aerobic infection
Malignancy	Foreign body
Immunosuppression	Calcium salts
Cytotoxic drugs	Burns
Splenectomy	Vascular insufficiency
Collagen vascular diseases	

Actinomycosis also presents some unique pathologic features. Draining sinuses occur much more frequently than in other types of anaerobic infection. When the lung is involved, the process has a significant tendency to extend to the pleural space and the chest wall itself. Pathologically, granuloma formation and suppuration may occur, and fibrosis is commonly seen. The characteristic "sulfur granules" are actually colonies of organisms. Histologically, sulfur granules may be noted to be made up of gram-positive branching filamentous forms of *Actinomyces* with a fringe or rosette of eosinophilic clublike structures that represent the host's reaction to the organism.

Important features of the pathogenesis of anaerobic infection are summarized in Table 233–6. The two key opposing factors that determine the outcome are the inoculum size plus the virulence of the infecting organisms (and their synergy) and host defense mechanisms. Certain characteristics of the host, such as breaks in anatomic (especially mucosal) barriers and the presence of factors lowering the oxidation-reduction potential, also play an important role pathogenetically. Table 233–7 lists conditions that decrease the redox potential and other general conditions that predispose to anaerobic infection, and Table 233–8 lists specific clinical situations that predispose to such infection. Certain associations between underlying host diseases and anaerobic infections are noted in Table 233–9.

The three major virulence factors in anaerobes are the ability to adhere to or invade epithelial surfaces; the production of toxins, enzymes, or other factors that play a pathogenic role; and the presence of surface constituents such as capsular polysaccharide or lipopolysaccharide.

The ability to adhere to epithelial cells is vital to the establishment of colonization or infection. Both *B. melaninogenicus* (*P. melaninogenica* or a closely related form) and *F. nucleatum* are known to

TABLE 233–8 Specific Clinical Situations Predisposing to Anaerobic Infection

Malignancy
Colon, uterus, lung
Leukemia
Surgery on oral or gastrointestinal tract or female pelvic area
Oral, gastrointestinal, genital tract disease or trauma
Human and animal bites
Aspiration
Therapy with aminoglycosides, trimethoprim-sulfamethoxazole, earlier quinolones
Acatalasemia[50–52]

TABLE 233–9 Specific Associations Between Underlying Diseases and Infections Involving Anaerobic Bacteria

Diabetes mellitus—cholecystitis, osteomyelitis
Colon cancer—*Clostridium septicum, Clostridium perfringens* infection
Neutropenia—colitis, *C. septicum, C. perfringens, Clostridium tertium* infection
Down syndrome—severe periodontal disease
AIDS—severe periodontal disease
Acatalasemia—oral gangrene[50–52]

Abbreviation: AIDS, Acquired immunodeficiency syndrome.

adhere to the crevicular epithelium in the oral cavity, and the former shows an ability to attach to certain gram-positive organisms in vitro. *Porphyromonas gingivalis*, thought to be an important organism in human periodontal disease, possesses fimbriae that facilitate attachment. Binding and degrading of human fibrinogen by *P. gingivalis* may mediate colonization with this organism in the gingival crevice. The three different types of structures shown to be responsible for the adherence of *B. fragilis* to epithelium are the capsule, negative-staining structures consistent with pili, and lectin-like adhesins. Enzymes believed to be important for invasion by anaerobes include phospholipase A, collagenase, and hyaluronidase.

Numerous toxins, enzymes, and other substances play a role in bacterial virulence. The importance of superoxide dismutase in permitting anaerobic bacteria to survive exposure to oxygen has been discussed. *C. perfringens* serves as a model for toxin production among anaerobes. Its major toxin is α-toxin, a phospholipase C. This enzyme hydrolyzes lecithin and sphingomyelin in the cell membranes of a number of cell types, including red blood cells, platelets, endothelial cells, and muscle cells. This toxin and two others produced by *C. perfringens* affect capillary permeability. *C. perfringens* also produces a collagenase. Other toxins and enzymes produced by anaerobes include hydrolytic enzymes, elastase, chondroitin sulfatase, fibrinolysin, gelatinase, lipase, lecithinase, immunoglobulin proteases, fibrinolysin, neuraminidase, DNase, RNase, phosphatase, heparinase, leukocidin, other leukotoxic substances such as volatile fatty acids, hemolysins, hemagglutinins, lysophospholipase, proteinases, other proteases, other sulfatases, sialidase, various enterotoxins, lipopolysaccharide, tetanus neurotoxin, tetanolysin, and botulinal toxin.

Anaerobes produce certain growth factors that may offer a selective advantage or facilitate synergy with other organisms. Included are menadione, hemin, succinate, amino acids, peptides, and steroids.

Surface constituents include capsules and lipopolysaccharide or endotoxin. The capsular polysaccharide of *B. fragilis*, free of other components of the bacterial cell, is capable of inducing abscess formation mediated by a T-cell–dependent immune mechanism.[53] Capsules also inhibit macrophage migration and are antiphagocytic.

Host defense mechanisms are important in protection from anaerobic infection. Certain gram-negative anaerobic bacilli are killed directly by serum complement. Random migration of polymorphonuclear leukocytes does not differ significantly under aerobic and anaerobic conditions. However, anaerobes attract polymorphonuclear leukocytes by activation of complement and by direct mechanisms. Also, it is likely that anaerobes are susceptible to killing by macrophages. In the polymorphonuclear leukocyte, both oxidative and nonoxidative mechanisms contribute to killing of anaerobes.

Acquired immunity involves both humoral and cell-mediated immune mechanisms. Circulating antibody and complement protect against bacteremia associated with experimental intra-abdominal infection, and T lymphocytes contribute to resistance against abscess formation.

Anaerobes can exert adverse effects on humoral and cellular host defense mechanisms. Some anaerobes bind or deplete opsonins, which prevents binding of opsonins to nonanaerobes and thereby prevents the phagocytosis of nonanaerobes. *Capnocytophaga* has caused a reversible acquired neutrophil chemotactic defect. Under certain conditions in vitro, anaerobes may directly depress the function of polymorphonuclear leukocytes, macrophages, and lymphocytes. Short-chain fatty acids generated by *Bacteroides* and other gram-negative anaerobic rods, at low extracellular pH, inhibit the killing activity of neutrophils.[54] Also, interaction between *B. fragilis* and peritoneal macrophages induces procoagulant activity; fibrin deposition at the site of infection appears to impair bacterial clearance.[54]

INFECTIONS PRODUCED BY ANAEROBES

All types of bacterial infection may involve anaerobes. Table 233–10 lists infections in which anaerobes are commonly involved and also infections in which anaerobes are seldom important. Tetanus and botulism are important intoxications caused by anaerobes. Table 233–11 is a summary of a number of studies on the incidence of anaerobes in various infections.

The *B. fragilis* group is the most commonly encountered and among the most resistant of all the anaerobes to antimicrobial agents. This group accounts for about one quarter of all anaerobic bacteria recovered from clinical specimens. Although *B. fragilis* is the most commonly encountered species, other species such as *B. thetaiotaomicron* are seen with some frequency and are more resistant to antimicrobials. The pigmented *Prevotella* and *Porphyromonas* spp. are seldom found in pure culture because of their special nutritional needs; however, *Prevotella* spp. appear to be especially important in infection. *Sutterella wadsworthensis* is more virulent than the related organisms *Bacteroides ureolyticus* and *Campylobacter gracilis* and

TABLE 233–10 Role of Anaerobes in Infection

Infections in which anaerobes are commonly involved
Brain abscess
Subdural empyema
Endophthalmitis, panophthalmitis
Periodontal disease
Root canal infection
Odontogenic infections
Chronic sinusitis
Chronic otitis media, mastoiditis
Peritonsillar abscess
Neck space infections
Aspiration pneumonia
Lung abscess
Pleural empyema
Pyogenic liver abscess
Peritonitis
Intra-abdominal abscess
Appendicitis
Postoperative wound infection after bowel or female genital tract surgery
Endometritis
Salpingitis
Tuboovarian abscess
Human and animal bite infections
Infected foot ulcers, especially in diabetics
Decubitus ulcers
Anaerobic cellulitis
Clostridial myonecrosis
Synergistic nonclostridial anaerobic myonecrosis
Anaerobic streptococcal myonecrosis
Necrotizing fasciitis
Chronic osteomyelitis
Actinomycosis
Clostridium difficile–associated colitis
Infections in which anaerobes seldom play a role
Meningitis
Acute sinusitis
Acute otitis media
Pharyngitis
Bronchitis
Acute cholecystitis
Spontaneous peritonitis
Pyelonephritis
Cystitis
Acute osteomyelitis

TABLE 233–11 Infections Commonly Involving Anaerobes

Infection	Percentage of All Cultures Yielding Anaerobes	Proportion of Cultures Positive for Anaerobes that Yield Only Anaerobes
Bacteremia[55, 56]	10	4/5
Bacteremia secondary to tooth extraction[57]	84	21/25
Ocular infections[58]	38	10/43
Corneal ulcers[59]	7	9/11
Central nervous system		
Brain abscess[60]	89	1/2–2/3
Subdural empyema[61]	29 (84 cases)	
Epidural abscess[61]	39 (41 cases)	
Head and neck		
Chronic sinusitis[62]	52	4/5*
Acute sinusitis[63]	7	
Chronic otitis media[64–66]	56	1/10
	59	11/115
	33	0
Cholesteatoma[67]	92	1/11
Neck space infections[68]	100	3/4
Wound infection after head and neck surgery[69]	95	0
Peritonsillar abscess[70, 71]	94	6/32
	76	6/28
Dental, oral, facial		
Orofacial, of dental origin[72]	94	4/10
Root canal infection[73,74]	100	18/55
	95	13/18
Periapical granuloma[75]	86	12/14
Periapical abscess[76]	94	16/30
Periodontal abscess[77]	100	0/9
Dental abscess, endodontic origin[78]	100	8/12
Thoracic		
Aspiration pneumonia[79–81]	93	1/2†
	62	1/3
	100	1/3
Lung abscess[15, 82]	93	1/2–2/3
	85	3/4
Bronchiectasis[83–85]	56	0/5
	27	
	17 (18 cases)	3/3
Empyema (nonsurgical)[86]	76	29/63
Abdominal		
Intra-abdominal infection (general)[87–89]	86‡	1/10‡
	90	1/3
	81	1/3
	94	1/7
Appendicitis with peritonitis[90]	92	8/71
Liver abscess[91]	52	1/3
Other intra-abdominal infection (postsurgery)[92]	93	1/6
Wound infection after bowel surgery[93]	60 (33 cases)	5/20
Biliary tract[94, 95]	45	0
	41	2/117
Obstetric-gynecologic		
Miscellaneous types[96–98]	100	1/3
	74	1/3
	72	
Pelvic abscess[99]	88	1/2
Vulvovaginal abscess[100]	75	1/4
Vaginal cuff abscess[101]	98	1/30
Septic abortion, sepsis[102–104]	69	18/20
	67	
	63	
Pelvic inflammatory disease[105, 106]	25	1/14
	48	1/7
Soft tissue and miscellaneous		
Nonclostridial crepitant cellulitis[107]	75	1/12
Pilonidal abscess[108]	88 (41 cases)	
Bite wound infections		
Dog bites[109]	30–41	
Human bites[109]	50–56§	
Diabetic foot ulcers[110]	95	1/20
Infected diabetic gangrene (deep tissue culture)[111]	85	1/11
Soft tissue abscesses[112]	60	1/4
Cutaneous abscesses[113]	62	1/5
Decubitus ulcers with bacteremia[114]	63	10/12
Osteomyelitis[115]	40	1/10
Gas gangrene (clostridial myonecrosis)[116]	100	
Breast abscess, nonpuerperal[117–119]	53	5/8
	83	18/34
	79	5/41
Perirectal abscess[108]	77 (74 cases)	

*Twenty-three of 28 cultures (82%) yielding heavy growth of one or more organisms had only anaerobes present.
†Aspiration pneumonia occurring in the community rather than in the hospital involves anaerobes to the exclusion of aerobic or facultative forms two thirds of the time.
‡Unpublished data.
§Includes clenched fist injuries.
Modified from Summanen P, Baron EJ, Citron DM, et al. Wadsworth Anaerobic Bacteriology Manual. 5th ed. Belmont, Calif: Star; 1993:1. Reprinted with permission of Star Publishing Company, Belmont, CA.

is resistant to a number of antimicrobial agents. *Sutterella* shows significant resistance to metronidazole, cefotetan, and clindamycin.[21] Ten to 20 percent of strains are resistant to ceftizoxime, piperacillin, piperacillin/tazobactam, and trovafloxacin. *Fusobacterium necrophorum* is clearly the most virulent of the non–spore-forming anaerobes. It is seen much less frequently now than before the availability of antimicrobial agents. Despite its susceptibility to many antimicrobial agents, however, *F. necrophorum* often produces overwhelming sepsis and metastatic infections. *F. nucleatum* is the most commonly encountered of the fusobacteria and exhibits significant virulence. A relatively newly described gram-negative anaerobic rod, *Bilophila wadsworthia*, is found in approximately one half of patients with gangrenous or perforated appendicitis. This virulent organism, like the *B. gracilis* group, is fastidious and may take a week to grow. It is bile resistant like the *B. fragilis* group. It has been found in other infections such as liver abscess, pericarditis, empyema, bacteremia, purulent arthritis, and soft tissue infection.[120, 121] Almost all strains produce β-lactamase, although this enzyme may be hard to demonstrate. *Peptostreptococcus magnus* seems to be particularly pathogenic among the anaerobic cocci.[122]

Among the clostridia, *C. perfringens* is the most commonly isolated and is extremely virulent. *Clostridium ramosum*, although much less virulent, is seen with about the same frequency as *C. perfringens* and is much more resistant to antimicrobial agents. *Clostridium septicum* and *C. tertium* are of particular importance because of their association with malignancy of the bowel, particularly the cecal area, and with neutropenic enterocolitis. *Actinomyces, Propionibacterium propionicus, P. acnes, Eubacterium nodatum*, and *Bifidobacterium dentium (eriksonii)* are the best-documented pathogens among the gram-positive non–spore-forming bacilli.

Central Nervous System Infection

Focal pyogenic infections such as brain abscess and subdural empyema commonly involve anaerobic bacteria; anaerobes are less commonly seen in epidural abscess and are seldom involved in meningitis. The precise location of these focal infections is an important determinant of the clinical picture.

The most common predisposing condition for brain abscess is an adjacent infection such as sinusitis, otitis media, or mastoiditis, all usually chronic in nature, and the infection extends to the brain directly or by local vascular routes. Infections of the ear and mastoid are most likely to extend to the temporal lobe or less commonly to the cerebellum. Sinusitis usually leads to frontal lobe abscess. Less common precursors of brain abscess are oral and dental infection via direct extension or bacteremia. Anaerobic pulmonary or pleural infection may lead to brain abscess by hematogenous seeding, as may congenital heart disease with a right-to-left shunt. Uncommonly, bacteremia from other sources or from endocarditis may lead to anaerobic infection of the brain. Except for those associated with congenital heart disease, brain abscesses that are metastatic from distant sites tend to be multiple. I have seen two patients in the past several years with at least 10 discrete brain abscesses each.

Brain abscess begins with localized inflammation or cerebritis. In the absence of appropriate therapy, this condition progresses to liquefaction of brain tissue, frank abscess formation, and ultimately, fibrous encapsulation.

The anaerobes most commonly encountered in brain abscess include *Bacteroides, Prevotella, Fusobacterium, Peptostreptococcus*, and less commonly, clostridia and *Actinomyces*. *B. fragilis* or other members of the *B. fragilis* group are seen relatively often. Aside from the anaerobes, various streptococci, including microaerophilic and viridans group streptococci, and other nonanaerobes are present less commonly.

Clinically, brain abscess is primarily manifested as a space-occupying lesion with severe headache, altered mental status, nausea and vomiting, and seizures at times. Only about half the patients will manifest fever. Findings particularly helpful in suggesting a mass lesion are papilledema, focal neurologic deficits, and seizures. Lumbar puncture is contraindicated until a mass lesion is excluded; with brain abscess, spinal fluid examination is not likely to be helpful in any case. Also usually found are a moderate increase in pressure, 25 to 300 cells/mm^3, elevated protein levels, and a normal glucose content. Computed tomographic scan of the head is very useful for establishing the diagnosis and characteristically shows an area of low density surrounded by a contrast-enhanced ring; other imaging studies, particularly magnetic resonance imaging, may be useful as well (Chapter 74).

Standard therapy in the past has been surgical excision or drainage plus antimicrobial therapy. However, many brain abscesses, particularly if diagnosed at the stage of cerebritis, will respond to medical therapy alone. The first-line drugs are metronidazole, penicillins, and chloramphenicol, but the choice of drug may vary with the specific etiology and susceptibility patterns of isolates.

Mortality associated with brain abscess has dropped distinctly with the introduction of computed tomography and metronidazole as one of the mainstays of therapy.

Subdural empyema and epidural abscess are similar to brain abscess in many respects but tend to progress rapidly and are often neurosurgical emergencies.

Head and Neck Infection

These infections (chronic otitis media, chronic mastoiditis, chronic sinusitis, peritonsillar abscess, all deep neck space infections, and odontogenic infections) commonly involve anaerobes and, on occasion, may be life threatening. Anaerobes are also frequently involved in wound infection after surgery for malignancies in the head and neck area, depending on the prophylactic antimicrobial agents used.

Anaerobes are found in at least 30 to 50% of cases of chronic otitis media. Cholesteatoma material and infected mastoid tissue obtained surgically yield anaerobes in 90% of cases. The bacteriology is representative of the indigenous flora of the upper airways, but the *B. fragilis* group is encountered more frequently (5 to 20%) than would be anticipated. In addition to the anaerobes, one may find streptococci, *Staphylococcus aureus, Pseudomonas aeruginosa*, and coliforms. Major complications include extension to the central nervous system and septic thrombophlebitis of the lateral venous sinus or the jugular vein.

Anaerobes are recoverable from appropriate specimens from over two thirds of cases of chronic sinusitis. Among the anaerobes recovered from such cases are the *B. fragilis* group, other *Bacteroides, Prevotella, Porphyromonas, Fusobacterium*, and *Peptostreptococcus*. In addition to the anaerobes, various streptococci, *S. aureus*, and *Haemophilus influenzae* may be present.

Culture of peritonsillar abscess yields anaerobes in most cases. The specific organisms recovered again reflect the usual indigenous flora of the area, but *F. necrophorum* is a particularly important organism in this setting, especially in the presence of a tonsillar pseudomembrane with a foul odor or complications such as bacteremia and metastatic abscesses to the lung, liver, joints, and so forth.

Deep neck space infections are potentially life threatening. Of greatest concern are airway compromise, vascular involvement, and extension to vital structures. The most common precursors of these infections are oral, dental, and pharyngeal infections. Retropharyngeal and associated prevertebral space infections are characterized by dysphagia, hoarseness, bulging of the posterior of the pharynx, and sometimes neck rigidity. Lateral pharyngeal (or parapharyngeal) space infection leads to dysphagia, bulging of the lateral pharyngeal wall, trismus, and at times, external swelling at the angle of the jaw. This infection is of great concern because of its proximity to the carotid artery and internal jugular vein. Submandibular space infection has been termed Ludwig's angina and is usually seen as a rapidly spreading cellulitis of this space. Clinical features include dysphagia, bulging of the floor of the mouth with elevation of the tongue, trismus, anterior neck cellulitis, drooling, change in voice, and dyspnea.

Odontogenic infections almost invariably involve anaerobic bacteria. The clinical manifestations of oral and dental infections vary with the specific anatomic structures involved. Infection may originate in dental tissue or in surrounding soft tissue. Root canal infection progresses to form periapical abscess and may involve the surrounding alveolar bone extensively if not treated early. Untreated odontogenic infections extend to the face or the deep neck compartments. Infection around the maxillary teeth may extend to the periorbital tissue and even the orbit. Complications of odontogenic infection include mediastinitis and intracranial infection.

Pleuropulmonary Infection

The most important background factors for this type of infection are aspiration of oropharyngeal or gastric contents and gingivitis or periodontal disease. Pleuropulmonary disease represents a continuum from uncomplicated pneumonitis in the earliest stages to solitary lung abscess or necrotizing pneumonia with multiple small excavations each less than 2 cm in diameter, with or without complicating empyema. Distinctive features, in terms of the distribution of lesions, are a predilection for dependent pulmonary segments, especially the posterior segments of the upper lobes and the superior segments of the lower lobes, and a tendency for the process to be pleural based with pyramidal-shaped lesions in which the apices point toward the hilum of the lung. Again, the infecting flora is derived from the indigenous flora of the upper airways and includes various *Bacteroides*, including the *B. fragilis* group in about 5% of cases, *Prevotella, Fusobacterium* (especially *F. nucleatum*), *Peptostreptococcus*, and less commonly, non–spore-forming gram-positive bacilli and clostridia. Nonanaerobes include viridans group streptococci and nosocomial pathogens such as *S. aureus*, various Enterobacteriaceae, and *Pseudomonas*. A variety of other organisms may be involved in immunosuppressed patients.

Other clues that an anaerobic process may be involved in addition to the presence of predisposing conditions and the unique distribution of lesions include a subacute or chronic course in two thirds of patients, foul-smelling discharge, and a unique appearance of bacteria on Gram stain of respiratory tract secretions.

Expectorated sputum cannot be used for culture because normal flora from the upper airways includes the same organisms that cause anaerobic pleuropulmonary infections. For a culture to be meaningful, specimens should have relatively little or no contamination with this indigenous flora. Useful specimens that have been collected properly and cultured quantitatively include bronchoalveolar lavage fluid, material obtained bronchoscopically via a bronchial brush protected in a double-lumen plugged catheter, percutaneous transtracheal aspirates, and empyema fluid obtained by thoracentesis.

Therapy involves appropriate antimicrobial agents (see later) and proper drainage of the pleural space if empyema is present.

Bacteremia

In various studies in the past, the incidence of anaerobes in bacteremia was often as high as 10 to 15%.[124, 125] More recently,[126] the incidence has been distinctly lower, often 5% or less; this lower incidence may reflect the widespread use of antimicrobial agents with activity against anaerobes for prophylaxis and early treatment of anaerobic or mixed infections. Two thirds to three fourths of clinically significant anaerobic bacteremias are caused by gram-negative anaerobic rods, primarily the *B. fragilis* group. Next most common are strains of *Peptostreptococcus* (about 10% of isolates) and clostridia (about 5 to 10% of isolates). Anaerobes are often present in polymicrobial bacteremias. As blood culture techniques improve, more relatively obscure anaerobes are found in bacteremia, including organisms such as *Leptotrichia, Selenomonas*, and *Anaerobiospirillum*. Anaerobic bacteremia is typically secondary to a focal primary infection. The predominance of *B. fragilis* group isolates in bacteremia points to bowel flora as the source and, to a much lesser extent, the female genital tract flora. A review of 855 episodes of bacteremia[125] found that the portal of entry was the gastrointestinal tract in 52%, the female genital tract in 20%, and the lower respiratory tract, the head and neck area, skin, and soft tissue sites in about 5% each.

Clinical features of anaerobic bacteremia are for the most part not distinctive and include fever, chills, leukocytosis, and on occasion, anemia, shock, and disseminated intravascular coagulation. Features believed to be more indicative of anaerobic bacteremia, such as suppurative thrombophlebitis, metastatic infection, hyperbilirubinemia, and a high mortality rate, have not been seen that frequently in the antibiotic era.

Intra-abdominal Infection

Anaerobic bacteria account for well over 99% of the normal colonic flora and, accordingly, are frequently seen in intra-abdominal infection. In a study of 71 patients with gangrenous and perforated appendicitis,[90] an average of 11.6 organisms was recovered per specimen, 8.5 of which were anaerobes and 3.1 nonanaerobes. The predominant aerobic and facultative bacteria recovered were *E. coli* in 75% of specimens and various streptococci, including viridans group streptococci and enterococci in one third of specimens or less. The predominant anaerobes, in order, were *B. fragilis* (73%), *B. thetaiotaomicron* (70%), *Peptostreptococcus micros* (57%), and *B. wadsworthia* (47%). Other anaerobes recovered from at least one third of patients were *Bacteroides splanchnicus, Prevotella intermedia, Lactobacillus* spp., *B. ovatus, B. vulgatus, Fusobacterium* spp., and *Eubacterium* spp. Clostridia, less commonly encountered, can produce devastating disease and must be taken into consideration, particularly in view of the fact that two commonly used antimicrobial agents have less than optimum activity against these organisms. One third of clostridia other than *C. perfringens* are resistant to cefoxitin, and 20 to 30% of many species of clostridia other than *C. perfringens* are resistant to clindamycin. The principal clostridia involved in gas gangrene related to carcinoma of the bowel are *C. perfringens, C. septicum*, and *C. tertium*.[127, 128] As noted earlier, intra-abdominal infections are the principal portal of entry for anaerobic bacteremia.

The association of anaerobic abdominal infection and carcinoma of the bowel is significant. This type of infection may be the first manifestation of the malignancy. Vascular, obstructive, inflammatory, and other bowel lesions may also be a source of anaerobic infection.

In biliary tract infection, the principal pathogens are *E. coli, Klebsiella*, and enterococci. In 1% of such infections, however, *C. perfringens* may be encountered and may produce overwhelming disease. In complicated biliary tract infections such as those in the older age group and those in patients with common bile duct obstruction, carcinoma, and repeated biliary tract surgery or manipulation, *B. fragilis* may also be encountered.

Female Genital Tract Infection

The usual infecting anaerobic organisms encountered in female genital tract infection are *Peptostreptococcus, Prevotella* (especially *P. bivia* and *Prevotella disiens* and the pigmenters), *Porphyromonas*, clostridia (including *C. perfringens*), and *Actinomyces* and *E. nodatum*, the latter two particularly in patients with intrauterine contraceptive devices. The *B. fragilis* group is less commonly encountered than some of the others, but when present, it is associated with a higher incidence of abscess and a poorer prognosis. Nonanaerobes encountered include various streptococci (including groups A and B and viridans streptococci), *E. coli, Klebsiella*, gonococci, and *Chlamydia* in sexually active females, and *Mycoplasma hominis* in postpartum infections. As noted earlier, bacterial vaginosis is associated with radically altered vaginal flora and predisposes to a large variety of female genital tract infections. Anaerobes can participate in virtually every type of gynecologic or obstetric infection, which can range from minor to life threatening in severity. Infections of the female genital tract commonly involving anaerobes include bacterial vaginosis, abscess of the perineal soft tissues or glands, endometritis, salpingitis, tuboovarian abscess, pelvic peritonitis and abscess, septic abortion, postoperative gynecologic infection, intrauterine device–associated infection,[129] and pyometra. Clinical findings associated with anaerobic infection in this setting include a foul-smelling discharge, gas in tissues, abscess formation, and pelvic thrombophlebitis.

Soft Tissue Infections

In a large number of soft tissue infections, anaerobes may play an important role. Among these are superficial infections of the skin and skin structures such as cellulitis, infected cutaneous ulcers, infected sebaceous or inclusion cysts, hidradenitis suppurativa, pyoderma, paronychia, and tropical ulcer. Infections involving subcutaneous tissue, with or without skin involvement, include cutaneous and subcutaneous abscesses, infected diabetic (vascular or trophic) ulcers, infected decubitus ulcers, bite wound infections,[130] anaerobic cellulitis and gas abscess, bacterial synergistic gangrene, infected visceral sinus tracts, noma (cancrum oris), infected pilonidal sinus or cyst, Meleney's ulcer, and burn wound infections.

Infections primarily involving fascia are necrotizing fasciitis, Fournier's gangrene, and clostridial fasciitis. The final category is that involving muscle primarily; included here are clostridial myonecrosis (gas gangrene), anaerobic streptococcal myositis, synergistic nonclostridial anaerobic myonecrosis (synergistic necrotizing cellulitis), infected vascular gangrene, and anaerobic muscle abscess. The most serious of all soft tissue infections are those that involve the deeper tissues (i.e., fascia and muscle). These latter infections, except for anaerobic streptococcal myositis, infected vascular gangrene, and anaerobic muscle abscess, are potentially life threatening and require early involvement of a competent surgeon in addition to optimal antimicrobial therapy. These most serious infections are almost always associated with significant pain and toxemia, and often a sense of impending doom on the part of the patient is present. Infected decubitus ulcers are typically relatively benign but are not uncommonly complicated by anaerobic bacteremia, which leads to a poorer prognosis.

The bacteriology of soft tissue infections varies according to the specific type of infection, but gram-negative anaerobic rods (the *B. fragilis* group, other *Bacteroides, Prevotella*, and *Fusobacterium*), anaerobic gram-positive cocci, non–spore-forming anaerobic gram-positive rods, and clostridia are the principal anaerobes encountered. Group A and viridans group streptococci (including the "*Streptococcus milleri*" group), enterococci, staphylococci, and gram-negative facultative or aerobic rods may also be present. In the case of bite wound infections, *Eikenella corrodens* is an important pathogen in human bites, and *Pasteurella multocida* and related forms are important in animal bites.

The importance of early, vigorous surgical management of serious, deep-seated soft tissue infections has been stressed. Débridement and drainage are also important considerations in the management of less severe soft tissue infections. Revascularization, when needed and possible, may be extremely helpful. Hyperbaric oxygen has not been established as an important aspect of therapy in my opinion, but it may be useful in clostridial myonecrosis in delineating the extent of infection and the optimum site for amputation.

Osteomyelitis

Osteomyelitis involves anaerobic bacteria much more frequently than is generally appreciated. The clinical findings of anaerobic osteomyelitis often resemble those of aerobic osteomyelitis. Features indicative of anaerobic involvement include a foul odor of the exudate, association with an indolent foot ulcer in the presence of vascular insufficiency, association with decubitus ulcers, involvement of the skull or facial bones, and the presence of unique morphology suggestive of anaerobes on Gram stain.

Approximately two thirds to three fourths of cases of anaerobic osteomyelitis involve the lower extremity or pelvis. Long bones may be infected via hematogenous seeding, during surgical placement of a foreign body, or by superinfection of a fracture site previously involved with aerobic osteomyelitis. Osteomyelitis of the feet is usually associated with diabetes mellitus, severe trauma, or other causes of vascular insufficiency. Anaerobic osteomyelitis of the facial and skull bones is usually secondary to chronic suppurative infections such as otitis media, sinusitis, or mastoiditis. Anaerobic osteomyelitis of the jaw may develop at a site where a fracture or surgery has led to disruption of the mucous membranes of the oral cavity.

In terms of the bacteriology of anaerobic osteomyelitis, peptostreptococci account for about 50% of anaerobic isolates and gram-negative anaerobic rods for 20 to 30%.

Antimicrobial Agent–Associated Pseudomembranous Colitis

The primary cause of this entity is *C. difficile,* but *S. aureus* still accounts for rare cases, as do several other species of *Clostridium* (see also Chapter 84). Nonspecific colitis associated with antimicrobial agents may also involve *C. difficile,* but less commonly. Diarrhea without colitis is not often related to *C. difficile.*

Diarrhea is a nearly universal symptom; on occasion it is severe or protracted, and mucus or gross blood may be seen. Other findings may include abdominal pain and tenderness, fever, dehydration, electrolyte imbalance, and protein-losing enteropathy. Rare complications include toxic megacolon and perforation.

Several toxins are produced by *C. difficile,* but the enterotoxin and the cytotoxin are the principal ones. Suppression of elements of the normal flora by the inducing antimicrobial agent is thought to be the major factor that predisposes to the disease. The disease usually begins during antimicrobial therapy, but it may occur as late as 6 to 8 weeks after discontinuation of use of the offending drug.

Most cases are diagnosed by various tests that detect the toxins of *C. difficile,* but it should be appreciated that both the organism and its toxins may be present in stool specimens, even in high count and high titer, in the absence of any evidence of disease. The only definitive way to diagnose the disease is to detect the characteristic yellowish plaques or pseudomembrane by endoscopy; however, it is not always feasible to perform endoscopy.

As noted previously, this disease may be acquired nosocomially, and a number of outbreaks have been described. Several typing systems have been used effectively in investigating such outbreaks.

A number of cases will respond to simply discontinuing use of the offending antimicrobial or antineoplastic agent, if feasible. In terms of therapy, the agents that are used most often are oral vancomycin and oral metronidazole. Metronidazole is a great deal less expensive and is comparable in effectiveness. When the patient cannot take oral medication, intravenous metronidazole is preferable to intravenous vancomycin because it is more likely to yield effective levels in the bowel lumen. About 25 to 30% of patients will experience relapses regardless of the therapy used, and sometimes multiple relapses occur. In difficult cases of relapse, administration of a yeast, *Saccharomyces boulardii,* has been advocated by some. Supportive care, particularly in terms of fluid and electrolyte balance, is important in management.

CLUES TO ANAEROBIC INFECTION

Clues useful for the clinician and microbiologist to suspect anaerobic infection are noted in Table 233–12. The definitive clue is a foul or

TABLE 233–12 Clues to Anaerobic Infection

Foul odor of lesion or discharge
Location of infection in proximity to a mucosal surface
Classical clinical picture of anaerobic infection such as gas gangrene, actinomycosis, lung abscess, etc.
Infections secondary to human or animal bites
Gas in tissues or discharges
Tissue necrosis, gangrene, abscess formation
Septic thrombophlebitis
Infection associated with malignancy (especially colon, uterus, lung)
Previous therapy with aminoglycoside antibiotics (such as neomycin, gentamicin, and amikacin), trimethoprim-sulfamethoxazole, most older quinolones, monobactams, cephalosporins with poor activity vs anaerobes (e.g., ceftazidime)
Black discoloration of blood-containing exudates; these exudates may fluoresce red under ultraviolet light (pigmented *Prevotella* or *Porphyromonas* infections)
Presence of "sulfur granules" in discharge material (actinomycosis)
Unique morphology on Gram stain
No growth on routine culture—"sterile pus"
Failure to grow aerobically; organisms seen on Gram stain of original exudate
Growth in anaerobic zone of fluid media or agar deeps
Growth anaerobically on media containing 75–100 μg/ml of kanamycin, neomycin, or paromomycin (or medium also containing vancomycin in the case of gram-negative anaerobic bacilli)
Characteristic colonies on agar plates anaerobically (e.g., *Fusobacterium nucleatum* and *Clostridium perfringens*)
Young colonies of pigmented anaerobic gram-negative rods may fluoresce red under ultraviolet light (blood-agar plate)

putrid odor of tissue or discharge material; no other type of infection in humans leads to such an odor. However, certain anaerobes do not produce the end products responsible for these odors, and sometimes in deep-seated infections these odors cannot be appreciated, so the absence of odor does not rule out anaerobic infection. Although many of the other clues are nonspecific, they may still be suggestive, particularly if two or three (e.g., gas, abscess formation) are present together, as is commonly the case.

ANAEROBIC INFECTIONS AS CLUES TO OTHER PROBLEMS IN PATIENTS

Under certain circumstances, an anaerobic infection may provide an important and early clue to an unsuspected underlying problem that may still be amenable to correction. Lung abscess in an edentulous patient is strong presumptive evidence of an underlying bronchogenic malignancy. *Capnocytophaga* sepsis may relate to an underlying leukemia. *E. lentum* infection of a joint may indicate a lesion in the colon, although an incidental bacteremia may have been responsible for seeding the joint. Septicemia with *C. septicum* or other clostridia[127, 128] or spontaneous myonecrosis of the abdominal wall indicates the likelihood of a malignant or other process in the cecum or elsewhere in the colon. Brain abscess may relate to an underlying dental problem such as a periapical abscess.

UNDERLYING CLINICAL CONDITIONS AS CLUES TO THE NATURE OF AN ANAEROBIC INFECTION

Conversely, an underlying condition can provide a clue to the type of anaerobic infection that might be present. A patient with leukemia undergoing chemotherapy who manifests oral mucosal lesions and a clinical picture of sepsis should be suspected of having bacteremia with *Capnocytophaga* or another oral organism such as *Leptotrichia buccalis*. Patients with neutropenia, fever, vomiting, diarrhea, and nondescript abdominal pain may have neutropenic colitis, often accompanied by bacteremia,[127] in which *C. septicum, C. tertium,* or *C. perfringens* may be key pathogens along with gram-negative facultative rods.[128] Women with intrauterine contraceptive devices in place in whom pelvic infection develops may have actinomycosis or a similar infection involving another anaerobic gram-positive non–spore-forming bacillus, *E. nodatum*.[129] Patients with pneumonia involving a dependent pulmonary segment, particularly if they have had recent anesthesia or some condition predisposing to aspiration or periodontal disease, probably have aspiration pneumonia; this condition almost always involves anaerobes. Patients with infected decubitus ulcers and sepsis[114] without another explanation commonly have bacteremia caused by *B. fragilis* group organisms, with the decubitus ulcer serving as the portal of entry. Anaerobes that are important in infections associated with inserted prosthetic devices include primarily *Propionibacterium* spp. and *P. magnus*; however, nonanaerobes are more common in this setting. Patients with bite-related infections typically have oral anaerobes and streptococci in the infecting flora, as well as *E. corrodens* in the case of human bites and *Pasteurella* spp. in the case of animal bites.[130]

DIAGNOSTIC CONSIDERATIONS

Certain anaerobic infections are diagnosed clinically, and culture is not helpful and could even be misleading. Examples are tetanus, botulism, and gas gangrene. In other cases, anaerobes are certain to be part of the infecting flora, but documenting their presence and even identifying specific anaerobes may not be important clinically. This situation would certainly be true for minor skin and soft tissue infections. The bacteriology of appendicitis and its complications is well established, and it is of no particular value in management of an individual patient to perform detailed cultures, except perhaps in the rare case with serious complications such as generalized peritonitis and bacteremia. In general, cultures are indicated primarily in cases of serious infection, in lesser infections in patients who have significant underlying illness or are at the extremes of age, in infection requiring prolonged therapy (e.g., osteomyelitis), and in infection that has failed to respond to empirical therapy. Even in these cases it is not always necessary or desirable to perform detailed anaerobic cultures; it may be sufficient to rule out (or rule in) the presence of virulent, antimicrobial-resistant organisms such as the *B. fragilis* group.

Timing of cultures and reporting of results become important issues here as well. Initial therapy must almost always be given empirically and is based on the nature of the clinical infection, on the usual bacteriology of such infection, on the potential modification of infecting flora by prior antimicrobial therapy or prophylaxis and by pathophysiologic factors, and on information obtained from Gram stain. It may still be very useful to obtain bacteriologic data even after the patient has been treated for 2 days or longer. With the recognition that it may take many days or even weeks to get definitive bacteriologic data, it is incumbent on the laboratory to provide interim reports to the clinician in the case of a seriously ill patient. Nothing can be better for the patient, the physician, and the laboratory than direct, personal interaction between the microbiologist and the physician.

Specimen Collection and Transport

Good anaerobic bacteriology starts with proper collection of the specimen. Sites normally inhabited by a rich indigenous flora, such as the intestinal tract or vagina, should not be sampled for anaerobes except under special circumstances and in special ways (e.g., quantitative study of upper small bowel flora in the blind loop syndrome). Avoidance of contamination from sites to be sampled is of major concern. Lower respiratory tract specimens and endometrial samples are especially difficult to obtain without contaminating the sample with indigenous flora. Double-lumen catheter bronchial brushings and bronchoalveolar lavage fluid, both cultured quantitatively, and pleural fluid represent good specimens for the former, and an endometrial suction curette biopsy suffices for the latter site. Instructions for collection of specimens applicable to different body sites and types of infections are presented in Table 233–13.[6, 131]

Ulcers should be carefully débrided and proper samples collected from the base or progressive edge where bacteria actively multiply,

TABLE 233-13 Specimen Collection for Anaerobic Bacteriology*

Site of Infectious Process	Appropriate Specimen	Collection Method
Head and neck	Aspirate	Percutaneous needle aspiration
	Tissue biopsy	Surgically obtained
Periodontal	Gingival pocket debris	Sterile paper points into anaerobic transport broth
	Aspirate	Scaler or needle aspiration
Pulmonary	Lung aspirate	Percutaneous needle aspiration of lung
	Tissue biopsy	Surgically obtained tissue biopsy
	Deep bronchial secretions	Bronchoalveolar lavage, transtracheal aspirate, or protected bronchial brush
	Pleural fluid	Thoracentesis
Joint	Joint fluid	Percutaneous needle aspiration
Abdominal	Peritoneal fluid	Percutaneous needle aspiration
	Abscess contents	Aspirate obtained at surgery or under computed tomography or ultrasound guidance (avoiding contamination with bowel contents)
	Bile	Bile obtained at surgery or from T tube
	Tissue biopsy	Surgically obtained
Female genital tract	Peritoneal fluid	Culdocentesis
	Endometrial material	Endometrial suction, protected collector
	Tissue biopsy (others)	Surgically obtained
Bone	Biopsy	Curettage material or scrapings obtained surgically
	Aspirate	Aspirate of bone via uninvolved skin surface
Other soft tissue	Tissue biopsy	Surgically obtained
	Aspirate	Percutaneous needle aspiration
	Tissue	Curettage material
Urine	Bladder urine	Suprapubic aspirate

*Aspirates should be collected after decontamination of the intact skin surface with alcohol, followed by povidone-iodine.
Modified from Summanen P, Baron EJ, Citron DM, et al. Wadsworth Anaerobic Bacteriology Manual. 5th ed. Belmont, Calif: Star; 1993:1. Reprinted with permission of Star Publishing Company, Belmont, CA.

not from unremoved crust or surface pus, which is often contaminated by other bacteria that do not reflect the true infecting flora.

Pus, when present, is best aspirated into a syringe through a needle and injected into an anaerobic (oxygen-free) transport vial containing an oxidation-reduction indicator. Syringes used for aspiration should not be used as transporters because of the potential danger of needlestick injuries and because oxygen diffuses through plastic syringes. Anaerobic vials are commercially available from several manufacturers. Pieces of infected tissue obtained by excision or biopsy are always preferable to pus, which in turn is preferable to a specimen obtained by a swab. Tissue samples are best transported in loosely capped containers sealed in anaerobic gas-impermeable bags. Swabs may dry and may carry too small a volume of sample to be cultured quantitatively or on certain media.

Conditions and the time of transport should be such that the viability or relative proportions of bacteria present in the specimen are not affected. Rapid delivery always ensures the most reliable culture results. Room temperature is best for the transport of specimens; oxygen diffuses better at lower temperatures.

Direct Examination of Samples

The gross appearance (purulence, necrotic tissue) and odor of the specimen can give the laboratory valuable clues to the presence of anaerobes. These features and the information obtained from Gram-stained smears should be incorporated in the preliminary report and sent or phoned to the clinician in a timely manner. A fetid or putrid odor from volatile short-chain fatty acids and amines is *always* associated with the presence of anaerobes in the sample. Because anaerobic bacteriology is so time consuming, several interim reports are desirable. For example, at 24 hours the report can give Gram-stain results (these can be done immediately if circumstances warrant) and preliminary information on the aerobic/facultative flora. At 48 hours, more definite information on the nonanaerobes can be given, along with preliminary information on the anaerobes.

Gram-stained smears should be prepared from all specimens accepted for anaerobic culture. The morphotypes and relative quantities of both the host and bacterial cells present in the preparation will provide information on specimen quality and may give clues to the presence of particular bacterial species and suggest the need for special selective media. Furthermore, Gram-stain information also provides quality control for specimen transport and isolation efficiency. If specimens for anaerobic culture must be sent to distant centers, it is always advisable to make a smear at the patient's bedside and send it, properly packed, along with the specimen so that the relative proportions of organisms present at the time of collection will be reflected. If appropriate, darkfield or phase-contrast microscopy can further help in recognizing the presence of motile organisms, spores, and morphotypes (spirochetes) not cultivable on ordinary media.

Immunofluorescence staining of specimens may be helpful for the detection of special organisms such as *Actinomyces* spp. and *P. propionicus* (formerly *Arachnia propionica*), but the reagents are not widely available. This method, if used for detection of the *B. fragilis* group and pigmented gram-negative rods, suffers from cross-reactions as well as false-positive and false-negative results. More specific and sensitive commercial reagents are needed.

Direct gas chromatographic analysis of specimens other than blood cultures does not add relevant information to what is obtainable from Gram-stained smears.

Primary Inoculation

Specimens submitted for anaerobic culture should be processed without delay. Exact clinical information, such as the type of infection, underlying diseases/conditions, and antimicrobial therapy, should be sent along with the specimen. This information, combined with the clues obtained from direct macroscopic and microscopic examination, is essential to guide the microbiologist in choosing a proper set of media for primary plating. If fresh media are not available, prereduced primary plating media are recommended. Smaller laboratories may have difficulty maintaining a large set of selective media. However, they should tailor the most effective sets for their needs to different categories of specimens according to the patient population served and procedures performed.

A nonselective, enriched agar medium supplemented by blood, vitamin K_1, and hemin, such as *Brucella* agar, Centers for Disease Control and Prevention (CDC) anaerobe agar, brain-heart infusion agar, trypticase soy agar, fastidious anaerobe agar, or Schaedler agar, must always be inoculated in parallel with selective media. The basic composition of each nonselective medium differs in its ability to support the growth of certain groups of anaerobes. *Brucella* base has been found superior to trypticase soy (CDC base agar) and Schaedler base for isolation of gram-negative bacilli, but CDC base supports the growth of anaerobic gram-positive cocci better. Brain-heart infusion base was found superior to trypticase soy in isolation efficiency of *Eubacterium* spp. but worse for pigmented gram-negative rods from subgingival and other samples. In academic centers performing large-scale anaerobic bacteriology, it would be ideal to use two different basic media to maximize isolation efficiency.

The use of selective media along with nonselective media will increase the yield and save time in terms of recognition and isolation of colonies. By inoculating specimens onto a nonselective agar plus a single selective medium, kanamycin-vancomycin laked blood agar (KVLB), the yield of anaerobes increased from 77 to 94%. *Bacteroides* bile-esculin agar, which effectively inhibits most other anaerobes and aerobes but allows the growth of *B. fragilis* group organisms and *B. wadsworthia* (the latter forms pinpoint to small colonies with black centers after 2 to 3 days or more of incubation), has been found useful in the primary isolation of anaerobes. Other useful selective media include KVLB, which allows the growth and rapid pigmentation of most *Prevotella* spp. If used for the isolation of *Porphyromonas* spp., the concentration of vancomycin must be decreased to 2 μg/ml or lower instead of the 7.5 μg/ml of the original formulation. Phenylethylalcohol agar is an excellent medium for the exclusion of swarming *Proteus* spp. and other aerobic gram-negative rods and is therefore useful for the inoculation of specimens such as those from decubitus ulcers and foot ulcers. Fastidious anaerobe agar with added neomycin and vancomycin is an excellent selective medium for fusobacteria. If clostridia are specifically sought, egg-yolk–neomycin agar is a useful selective medium. After inoculation, the media should be placed in an anaerobic environment as soon as possible.

Alternatives to Conventional Identification Methods

Conventional methods for detailed identification of anaerobic bacteria often involve the use of labor-intensive and time-consuming procedures such as the inoculation of pure cultures to prereduced anaerobically sterilized biochemicals for the demonstration of carbohydrate fermentation and other biochemical activities and the determination of short-chain fatty acid profiles of metabolic end products by gas-liquid chromatography. Because these methods are dependent on active bacterial growth and therefore have long incubation periods, they are prone to aeration and contamination. Many laboratories are not able to maintain the vast selection of biochemicals needed. Therefore, more rapid and simple alternatives have been eagerly sought.

First-generation alternatives to conventional prereduced anaerobically sterilized tests include micromethods such as API 20A and Minitek. Both of these methods perform best with fast-growing anaerobes such as members of the *B. fragilis* group or *C. perfringens*. Problems are unavoidable, however, when slow-growing or less saccharolytic species are tested. Kits that rapidly detect preformed enzymes are commercially available and are very useful for anaerobic bacteriology. These systems detect mainly glycosidases and aminopeptidases and some other enzymes by means of chromogenic substrates. A heavy inoculum with a short incubation period (4 hours in air) minimizes contamination and gives rapid results. Overall performance of these systems has varied from moderate to good; 60 to 90% of the isolates are identified to the species level. The performance is affected by the source and the nature of the isolates; it can be improved by supplementing with simple methods mentioned previously.

A recent approach to identify anaerobes rapidly that is also useful for many other organisms is based on the determination of cellular, rather than metabolic fatty acids by gas chromatography with a capillary column. A large library of listed organisms is available. Cellular fatty acids are more conserved (more stable) than those of metabolic end products and are useful, in some cases, for taxonomic studies. The equipment and software are expensive, but subsequent costs are low.

Nucleic acid probes are not yet standardized and are not commercially available for clinically important anaerobes. However, a number of oral microbiology laboratories and commercial concerns have developed sets of probes designed for the identification of indicator bacteria of periodontal disease. The probes are most useful for rapid identification of colonies directly from primary plates or from pure cultures. Because the vast majority of anaerobic infections arise from our indigenous flora, polymerase chain reaction would not ordinarily be useful, except for normally sterile body fluids or tissues.

TABLE 233-14 β-Lactamase–Producing Anaerobes*

Bacteroides fragilis group	*Porphyromonas* spp. (animal strains primarily)
B. coagulans	*Fusobacterium nucleatum*
B. splanchnicus	*F. mortiferum/varium*
Pigmented *Prevotella*	*Megamonas hypermegas*
P. oralis	*Mitsuokella multiacida*
P. bivia	*Clostridium ramosum*
P. disiens	*C. clostridioforme*
P. buccae	*C. butyricum*
P. oris	*Bilophila wadsworthia*

*Some strains of these species produce β-lactamases.
From Summanen P, Baron EJ, Citron DM, et al. Wadsworth Anaerobic Bacteriology Manual. 5th ed. Belmont, Calif: Star; 1993:1. Reprinted with permission of Star Publishing Company, Belmont, CA.

WHICH IS THE REAL PATHOGEN?

Interpretation of results of a mixed culture containing multiple isolates is difficult. Rough quantitation of cultures, together with Gram-stain results (provided that the specimen was properly taken and transported), is helpful because bacteria present in pure culture, in large numbers, or on repeat cultures are most probably of major importance. The nature of the bacteria can also give clues to their importance in the infectious process. Organisms of the *B. fragilis* group, especially *B. fragilis* and *B. thetaiotaomicron, S. wadsworthensis,* and *B. wadsworthia,* are more virulent and resistant to antimicrobial drugs than many other anaerobes are. Some disease-bacterium associations are well known: *C. perfringens* and myonecrosis, *F. necrophorum* and postanginal sepsis syndrome (Lemierre's disease), *Actinomyces* spp. and chronic draining sinuses, and *Porphyromonas endodontalis* and root canal infection, for example. Frequent, close consultation between the clinician and the microbiologist is essential for proper interpretation of culture results.

SUSCEPTIBILITY TESTING

Susceptibility testing of anaerobes is useful for determining the activity of new drugs, for monitoring resistance patterns in individual institutions and regions, and for management of individual patients. For patient management, tests are usually done on isolates from serious infections, on anaerobes isolated in pure culture or from normally sterile body fluids, on known virulent organisms, on isolates from infections requiring prolonged therapy (e.g., endocarditis, osteomyelitis), and on isolates from infections not responding to empirical therapy. Because susceptibility patterns cannot always be predicted reliably and resistance of anaerobes to antimicrobial agents is clearly increasing, many clinicians and laboratories test most isolates of anaerobes that are judged to be significant pathogens.

Methods

The methods recommended by the National Committee for Clinical Laboratory Standards (NCCLS) include agar dilution testing, micro-

TABLE 233–15 Susceptibility of Anaerobes to Antimicrobial Agents

Percent Susceptible*	*Bacteroides fragilis*	Other *B. fragilis* Group†	Other *Bacteroides*	*Prevotella*	*Porphyromonas*	*Sutterella wadsworthensis*
>95	Ampicillin + sulbactam Piperacillin + tazobactam Ticarcillin + clavulanate Cefoperazone + sulbactam Imipenem Chloramphenicol Clinafloxacin Metronidazole Trovafloxacin	Ampicillin + sulbactam Cefoperazone + sulbactam Piperacillin + tazobactam Ticarcillin + clavulanate Imipenem Chloramphenicol Clinafloxacin Metronidazole Minocycline Trovafloxacin	Ampicillin + sulbactam Piperacillin Ticarcillin + clavulanate Cefoperazone Cefoperazone + sulbactam Cefotaxime Cefoxitin Imipenem Chloramphenicol Clinafloxacin Clindamycin Trovafloxacin	Amoxicillin + clavulanate Ceftizoxime Imipenem Chloramphenicol Clinafloxacin Clindamycin Metronidazole Trovafloxacin	Amoxicillin + clavulanate Ceftizoxime Imipenem Chloramphenicol Clinafloxacin Metronidazole Minocycline Trovafloxacin	Ampicillin + sulbactam Amoxicillin + clavulanate Ticarcillin + clavulanate Cefoxitin Ceftriaxone Chloramphenicol Ciprofloxacin Imipenem Meropenem
85–95	Cefotetan Cefoxitin Ceftizoxime Piperacillin Clindamycin Minocycline	Piperacillin Ceftizoxime	Cefotetan Ceftazidime Ceftizoxime Ceftriaxone Minocycline		Ciprofloxacin Clindamycin	Piperacillin Piperacillin + tazobactam Trovafloxacin
70–84	Moxalactam	Cefoxitin Clindamycin	Penicillin G Moxalactam	Minocycline		Ceftizoxime Metronidazole
50–69	Cefoperazone Cefotaxime Ceftazidime Ceftriaxone	Cefoperazone Cefotetan Moxalactam	Ciprofloxacin Tetracycline	Ciprofloxacin Tetracycline	Tetracycline	Cefotetan Clindamycin
<50	Penicillin G Ciprofloxacin Tetracycline	Penicillin G Cefotaxime Ceftazidime Ceftriaxone				

Table continued on following page

TABLE 233–15 Susceptibility of Anaerobes to Antimicrobial Agents *Continued*

Percent Susceptible	*Fusobacterium nucleatum*	*Fusobacterium mortiferum/ varium*	Other *Fusobacterium*	*Bilophila wadsworthia*	*Pepto-streptococcus*	*Clostridium difficile*‡	*Clostridium ramosum*	*Clostridium perfringens*	Other *Clostridium*	NSF-GPR
>95	Amoxicillin + clavulanate Ceftizoxime Imipenem Chloramphenicol Clinafloxacin Clindamycin Metronidazole Minocycline Tetracycline Trovafloxacin	Imipenem Chloramphenicol Clinafloxacin Metronidazole Minocycline Trovafloxacin	Ampicillin + sulbactam Ceftizoxime Penicillin G Piperacillin Piperacillin + tazobactam Imipenem Chloramphenicol Clinafloxacin Clindamycin Minocycline Trovafloxacin	Amoxicillin + clavulanate Ampicillin + sulbactam Piperacillin Ticarcillin Cefoxitin Ceftizoxime Imipenem Chloramphenicol Ciprofloxacin Clindamycin Metronidazole Minocycline Tetracycline Trovafloxacin	Ampicillin + sulbactam Penicillin G Piperacillin Ticarcillin + clavulanate Cefoperazone Cefoperazone + sulbactam Cefotetan Ceftazidime Ceftriaxone Imipenem Chloramphenicol Ciprofloxacin Clinafloxacin Metronidazole Moxalactam Trovafloxacin	Amoxicillin + clavulanate Ampicillin + sulbactam Ticarcillin + clavulanate Ampicillin Ticarcillin Cefotetan Imipenem Clinafloxacin Metronidazole Trovafloxacin	Amoxicillin + clavulanate Piperacillin + tazobactam Ticarcillin + clavulanate Ceftizoxime Imipenem Chloramphenicol Clinafloxacin Metronidazole	Ampicillin + sulbactam Amoxicillin + clavulanate Piperacillin + tazobactam Ticarcillin + clavulanate Ampicillin Piperacillin Ticarcillin Cefotetan Cefoxitin Ceftizoxime Imipenem Chloramphenicol Ciprofloxacin Clinafloxacin Clindamycin Metronidazole Trovafloxacin	Ampicillin Ampicillin + sulbactam Amoxicillin Carbenicillin Penicillin G Piperacillin Ticarcillin Imipenem Chloramphenicol Clinafloxacin Minocycline Trovafloxacin	Ampicillin + sulbactam Amoxicillin + clavulanate Penicillin G Piperacillin Ticarcillin + clavulanate Ceftizoxime Cefotaxime Imipenem Chloramphenicol Clindamycin Clinafloxacin Minocycline Trovafloxacin
85–95		Amoxicillin + clavulanate	Ticarcillin + clavulanate Cefoperazone Cefoperazone + sulbactam Cefotaxime Cefotetan Cefoxitin Ceftriaxone		Clindamycin Minocycline	Chloramphenicol	Ampicillin + sulbactam Ampicillin Piperacillin Trovafloxacin		Moxalactam	Cefoperazone + sulbactam Cefotetan Cefoxitin
70–84	Ciprofloxacin	Clindamycin Tetracycline	Ceftazidime Moxalactam				Cefoxitin Clindamycin	Minocycline	Clindamycin Tetracycline	Cefoperazone Moxalactam Tetracycline
50–69		Ciprofloxacin			Tetracycline	Clindamycin Minocycline Tetracycline	Minocycline Tetracycline	Tetracycline	Cefoperazone Cefotaxime Cefoxitin Ceftizoxime Ceftriaxone	Ciprofloxacin Metronidazole
<50		Ceftizoxime		Amoxicillin Ampicillin Penicillin G		Cefoxitin Ceftizoxime Ciprofloxacin	Ciprofloxacin		Ceftazidime Ciprofloxacin	

NOTE: Data from Wadsworth Anaerobic Bacteriology Laboratory. Drugs not listed have not been tested. The order of listing of drugs within percent susceptible categories is not significant.
*According to the National Committee for Clinical Laboratory Standards–approved breakpoints (M11-A4), using the intermediate category as susceptible.
†Excluding *B. fragilis*.
‡Breakpoint is used only as a reference point. *C. difficile* is primarily of interest in relation to antimicrobial-induced pseudomembranous colitis. These data must be interpreted in the context of the level of drug achieved in the colon and the effect of the agent on indigenous colonic flora.
Abbreviation: NSF-GPR, Non–spore-forming gram-positive rod.
Modified from Finegold SM, Wexler HM. Present studies of therapy for anaerobic infections. Clin Infect Dis. 1996;23 (Suppl 1); S9–S14.

broth dilution, and macrobroth dilution.[132] Other options include the E-test and the spiral gradient end point system.

With certain antimicrobial agents such as most β-lactam agents, clindamycin, and chloramphenicol, the minimal inhibitory concentrations (MICs) of a large percentage of strains appear to cluster near the breakpoint (see later). MICs of 50 to 60% of all anaerobes fall within one twofold dilution of the breakpoint for many β-lactam agents, and 38% fall within one twofold dilution of the breakpoint for clindamycin. An even higher percentage (approximately 70%) of *B. fragilis* group isolate MICs fall within one twofold dilution of the breakpoint (46% for clindamycin). Systems that form a continuous concentration gradient rather than the twofold dilution steps of the agar dilution system minimize the uncertainty caused by this clustering. Another approach that has helped is the introduction of "intermediate" end points, as well as "susceptible" and "resistant."[132]

Difficulties in End Point Determination

The exact method that different technologists use to read the plates is important. Technologists using a dark background tend to ignore the haze and read the MIC as the "marked change from the growth control." Reading against a light background seems to enhance the appearance of the haze and make consistent determination of a marked change more difficult. The use of a viable dye, tetrazolium chloride, may aid in reading susceptibility results, and the results of MIC determinations using tetrazolium chloride correlate with viability counts from agar dilution plates. Rewording the definition of end point to emphasize the "marked change from the growth control" (as has been done in the latest NCCLS document[132]) has led to more consistent results.

Mechanisms of Resistance to Antimicrobial Agents

The mechanisms by which anaerobic bacteria become resistant to β-lactam antibiotics are similar to those described in aerobes and include the production of β-lactamases (Table 233–14), changes in penicillin-binding proteins, and changes in outer membrane permeability to β-lactams. Chloramphenicol inactivation may occur by reduction of chloramphenicol by nitroreductase or by a constitutively produced acetyltransferase. Metronidazole resistance in anaerobes is mediated by a decrease in nitroreduction of the compound to the active agent, and plasmid-mediated transfer of metronidazole resistance has been described. Efflux mechanisms are also important with certain drugs. Multiple mechanisms may exist in a single strain. These mechanisms are discussed more thoroughly in a review.[133]

Clinical Correlation

Expecting exact correlation of laboratory results with clinical outcome is not realistic. Infections involving anaerobes are typically polymicrobial; it is often not necessary to eradicate all the organisms to effect a cure. Appropriate surgical manipulations, the patient's general health status, and the microenvironment at the site of the infection will have a significant impact on the outcome, regardless of whether a particular isolate is susceptible to the antimicrobial regimen. Nevertheless, accurate information regarding the efficacy of a certain agent in inhibiting or killing the organism will certainly give the clinician useful information for choice of a therapeutic agent. A consensus group of infectious disease clinicians concluded that in the most serious infections involving anaerobes, susceptibility test results correlate with the clinical response.[134] The current antibiograms available for a clinically relevant group of anaerobic organisms at the Wadsworth Veterans Affairs Hospital is presented in Table 233–15.

TABLE 233–16 Prevention of Anaerobic Infections

Principles
Avoid conditions that reduce the redox potential of tissues
Prevent the introduction of anaerobes (usually from normal flora) into wounds, body cavities, etc.
Protect against toxin (e.g., tetanus)
Prevent metastatic spread (e.g., lung to brain)
Avoiding reduced redox potential in tissues
Débridement and cleansing of wounds
Removal of foreign bodies
Elimination of dead space
Reestablishment of good circulation
Good surgical technique
Avoid devitalizing tissue
Maintain good blood supply
Avoid creating dead space
Provide meticulous hemostasis
Use delayed primary closure when indicated
Preventing introduction of anaerobes
Cleansing (showering, irrigation)
Germicides (iodophors, benzalkonium, peroxide)
Antimicrobial agents (topical, "bowel preparation," systemic)
Preventing aspiration of oropharyngeal or gastric contents
Isolation of surgical field
Avoiding prolonged labor
Gentle technique for endoscopy, etc.
Avoiding intravenous catheters in inguinal area

THERAPY

Because anaerobic bacteria produce significant tissue destruction and are likely to produce abscesses, surgical management is commonly required for débridement of necrotic tissue and for drainage of the collections of pus. Surgery may also be necessary for elimination of dead space, maintenance of an airway, and so forth. At times, particularly with intra-abdominal abscesses, it is feasible to perform drainage percutaneously under the guidance of ultrasound or computed tomography.

Antimicrobial therapy is the other major approach to the management of anaerobic infection. One must take into account not only in vitro susceptibility patterns of the anaerobes but also other factors such as the need for bactericidal activity, penetration of certain areas such as the central nervous system, spectrum of activity against any nonanaerobes that may be present, toxicity, impact on normal flora, and cost. Because of the difficulty in achieving good drug levels in abscesses and in poorly perfused or necrotic tissue, the highest recommended dosages of the various agents should be used, along with proper surgical management. Accordingly, it is appropriate to choose the "intermediate" end points of susceptibility tests as the breakpoints. Antimicrobial therapy should be given for prolonged periods because relapse is otherwise common in anaerobic infections.

In the case of septic thrombophlebitis, in addition to any surgery that might be required, anticoagulation could be useful. However, anticoagulant therapy does pose some potential risk to the patient in that small bits of infected clot may embolize. Exchange transfusion has been recommended in postabortion or other septicemia caused by *C. perfringens* when significant intravascular hemolysis is present. General supportive measures are essential in patients who are quite ill with anaerobic infections. These measures include blood transfusion, maintenance of fluid and electrolyte balance, adequate immobilization of the infected injured part, treatment of shock, relief of pain, and management of renal failure. The use of antitoxins may be important if toxin is a key factor in the pathogenesis, as in tetanus and botulism.

PROPHYLAXIS

The principles of prophylaxis (and therapy) are (1) controlling the environment so that anaerobic bacteria find it difficult or impossible to proliferate, (2) checking the spread of anaerobic bacteria into healthy tissue, and (3) neutralizing toxins produced by anaerobes.

Antimicrobial agents are an important factor in limiting the spread of anaerobes into healthy tissue. Toxin neutralization is achieved primarily with specific antitoxin, a process applicable to tetanus and botulism. Preventive measures are outlined in Table 233–16.

REFERENCES

1. Loesche WJ. Oxygen sensitivity of various anaerobic bacteria. Appl Microbiol. 1969;18:723–727.
2. Rosebury T. Glove-box Procedures for Cultivation of Spirochetes and Other Fastidious Anaerobes. With Preliminary Data on Isolation, Cultivation, and Maintenance of Oral Spirochetes and on Limiting Oxygen Concentrations for Surface Growth of These and Other Anaerobic Bacteria. Washington, DC: U.S. Public Health Service; 1966.
3. Tally FP, Jacobus NV, Goldin BR, et al. Superoxide dismutase in anaerobic bacteria (Abstract). Clin Res. 1975;23:418.
4. Tally FP, Stewart PR, Sutter VL, et al. Oxygen tolerance of fresh clinical anaerobic bacteria. J Clin Microbiol. 1975;1:161–164.
5. Tally FP, Jacobus NV, Sullivan N, et al. Superoxide dismutase activity in anaerobic bacteria (Abstract). Clin Res. 1975;23:108.
6. Summanen P, Baron EJ, Citron DM, et al. Wadsworth Anaerobic Bacteriology Manual. 5th ed. Belmont, Calif: Star; 1993:1.
7. Finegold SM. A century of anaerobes: A look backward and a call to arms. Clin Infect Dis. 1993;16(Suppl 4):S453–S457.
8. Levy E. Ueber einen Fall von Gasabscess (VI). Dtsch Z Chir. 1891;32:248–251.
9. Veillon A. Sur un microcoque anaérobie trouvé dans des suppurations fetides. C R Soc Biol (Paris). 1893;45:807–809.
10. Veillon A, Zuber A. Sur quelques microbes strictement anaérobies et leur role dans la pathologie humaine. C R Soc Biol (Paris). 1897;49:253.
11. McIntosh J, Fildes P. A new apparatus for the isolation and cultivation of anaerobic microorganisms. Lancet. 1916;1:768–770.
12. Robertson M. Notes upon certain anaerobes isolated from wounds. J Pathol Bacteriol. 1916;20:327–349.
13. Meleney FL. Treatise on Surgical Infections. London, New York: Oxford University Press; 1948.
14. Rosebury T. Microorganisms Indigenous to Man. New York: McGraw-Hill; 1962.
15. Beerens H, Tahon-Castel M. Infections Humaines à Bactéries Anaérobies Non-Toxigènes. Brussels: Presses Académique Européenes; 1965:1.
16. Willis AT. Clostridia of Wound Infection. London: Butterworths; 1969:1.
17. Summanen P. Microbiology terminology update: Clinically significant anaerobic gram-positive and gram-negative bacteria (excluding spirochetes). (Summary of current nomenclature, taxonomy, and classification of various microbial agents.) Clin Infect Dis. 1993;16:606–609.
18. Shah HN, Gharbia SE. Ecophysiology and taxonomy of *Bacteroides* and related taxa. Clin Infect Dis. 1993;16(Suppl 4):S160–S167.
19. Jousimies-Somer H. Recently described clinically important anaerobic bacteria: Taxonomic aspects and update. Clin Infect Dis. 1997;25(Suppl 2):S78–S87.
20. Wexler HM, Reeves D, Summanen PH, et al. *Sutterella wadsworthensis* gen. nov., sp. nov. for bile-resistant microaerophilic *Campylobacter gracilis*–like isolates. Int J Syst Bacteriol. 1996;46:252–258.
21. Molitoris E, Wexler HM, Finegold SM. Sources and antimicrobial susceptibilities of *Campylobacter gracilis* and *Sutterella wadsworthensis*. Clin Infect Dis. 1997;25(Suppl 2):S264–S265.
22. Hentges DJ, ed. Human Intestinal Microflora in Health and Disease. New York: Academic Press; 1983.
23. Hentges DJ. The anaerobic microflora of the human body. Clin Infect Dis. 1993;16(Suppl 4):S175–S180.
24. Nichols RL, Smith JW. Intragastric microbial colonization in common disease states of the stomach and duodenum. Ann Surg. 1975;182:557–561.
25. Stolberg L, Rolfe R, Gitlin N, et al. D-Lactic acidosis due to abnormal gut flora: Diagnosis and treatment of two cases. N Engl J Med. 1982;306:1344–1348.
26. Corrodi P, Wideman PA, Sutter VL, et al. Bacterial flora of the small bowel before and after bypass procedure for morbid obesity. J Infect Dis. 1978;137:1–6.
27. Polter DE, Boyle JD, Miller LG, et al. Anaerobic bacteria as cause of the blind loop syndrome. A case with observations on response to antibacterial agents. Gastroenterology. 1968;54:1148–1154.
28. Finegold SM, Mathisen GE, George WL. Changes in human intestinal flora related to the administration of antimicrobial agents. In: Hentges DJ, ed. Human Intestinal Microflora in Health and Disease. New York: Academic Press; 1983:355–446.
29. Finegold SM, Sutter VL, Mathisen GE. Normal indigenous intestinal flora. In: Hentges DJ, ed. Human Intestinal Microflora in Health and Disease. New York: Academic Press; 1983:3–31.
30. Holdeman LV, Good IJ, Moore WE. Human fecal flora: Variation in bacterial composition within individuals and a possible effect of emotional stress. Appl Environ Microbiol. 1976;31:359–375.
31. Hillier SL, Krohn MA, Rabe LK, et al. The normal vaginal flora, H_2O_2-producing lactobacilli, and bacterial vaginosis in pregnant women. Clin Infect Dis. 1993;16(Suppl 4):S273–S281.
32. Eschenbach DA. Bacterial vaginosis and anaerobes in obstetric-gynecologic infection. Clin Infect Dis. 1993;16(Suppl 4):S282–S287.
33. Bokkenheuser V. The friendly anaerobes. Clin Infect Dis. 1993;16(Suppl 4):S427–S434.
34. Gibbons RJ, Engle LP. Vitamin K compounds in bacteria that are obligate anaerobes (Abstract). Science. 1964;146:1307–1309.
35. Shimada K, Bricknell KS, Finegold SM. Deconjugation of bile acids by intestinal bacteria: Review of literature and additional studies. J Infect Dis. 1969;119:73–81.
36. Hill MJ, Drasar BS. Degradation of bile salts by human intestinal bacteria. Gut. 1968;9:22–27.
37. Soleim HA, Scheline RR. Metabolism of xenobiotics by strains of intestinal bacteria. Acta Pharmacol Toxicol (Copenhagen). 1972;31:471.
38. Peppercorn MA, Goldman P. The role of intestinal bacteria in the metabolism of salicylazosulfapyridine. J Pharmacol Exp Ther. 1972;181:555–562.
39. Mathan VI, Wiederman J, Dobkin JF, et al. Geographic differences in digoxin inactivation, a metabolic activity of the human anaerobic gut flora. Gut. 1989;30:971–977.
40. Lindenbaum J, Rund DG, Butler VP Jr, et al. Inactivation of digoxin by the gut flora: Reversal by antibiotic therapy. N Engl J Med. 1981;305:789–794.
41. Finegold SM. The significance of the intestinal microflora. Del Med J. 1970;42:341–345, 350.
42. Drenick EJ, Finegold SM, Stanley TM, et al. Bacterial complications of intestinal bypass. In: Bray GA, ed. Recent Advances in Obesity Research II: Procedings of the 2nd International Congress on Obesity. New York: Newman; 1977:407–414.
43. Winter J, Popoff MR, Grimont P, et al. *Clostridium orbiscindens* sp. nov., a human intestinal bacterium capable of cleaving the flavonoid C-ring. Int J Syst Bacteriol. 1991;41:355–357.
44. McFarland LV, Elmer GW, Stamm WE, et al. Correlation of immunoblot type, enterotoxin production, and cytotoxin production with clinical manifestations of *Clostridium difficile* infection in a cohort of hospitalized patients. Infect Immun. 1991;59:2456–2462.
45. Wilson KH. The microecology of *Clostridium difficile*. Clin Infect Dis. 1993;16(Suppl 4):S214–S218.
46. McFarland LV, Mulligan ME, Kwok RY, et al. Nosocomial acquisition of *Clostridium difficile* infection. N Engl J Med. 1989;320:204–210.
47. Haukkamaa M, Stranden P, Jousimies-Somer H, et al. Bacterial flora of the cervix in women using different methods of contraception. Am J Obstet Gynecol. 1986;154:520–524.
48. Gebhard RL, Gerding DN, Olson MM, et al. Clinical and endoscopic findings in patients early in the course of *Clostridium difficile*–associated pseudomembranous colitis. Am J Med. 1985;78:45–48.
49. Borriello SP, ed. Antibiotic Associated Diarrhoea and Colitis. Boston: Martinus Nijhoff; 1984:1.
50. Eaton JW. Acatalasemia. In: Scriver CR, Beaudet AL, Sly WS, et al, eds. The Metabolic Basis of Inherited Disease, v. 2. 6th ed. New York: McGraw-Hill; 1989:1551–1561.
51. Nishimura ET, Hamilton HB, Kobara TY, et al. Carrier state in human acatalasemia. Science. 1959;130:333–334.
52. Takahara S. Progressive oral gangrene probably due to lack of catalase in the blood (acatalasaemia). Lancet. 1952;2:1101–1104.
53. Tzianabos AO, Kasper DL, Onderdonk AB. Structure and function of *Bacteroides fragilis* capsular polysaccharides: Relationship to induction and prevention of abscesses. Clin Infect Dis. 1995;20(Suppl 2):S132–S140.
54. Rotstein OD. Interactions between leukocytes and anaerobic bacteria in polymicrobial surgical infections. Clin Infect Dis. 1993;16(Suppl 4):S190–S194.
55. Felner JM, Dowell VR Jr. "*Bacteroides*" bacteremia. Am J Med. 1971;50:787–796.
56. Washington JA II. Conventional approaches to blood culture. In: Washington JA II, ed. The Detection of Septicemia. Boca Raton, Fla: CRC Press; 1978:41–48.
57. Crawford JJ, Sconyers JR, Moriarty JD. Bacteremia after tooth extraction studied with the aid of pre-reduced anaerobically sterilized culture media. Appl Microbiol. 1974;27:927.
58. Jones DB, Robinson NM. Anaerobic ocular infections. Trans Am Acad Ophthalmol Otolaryngol. 1977;83:309–331.
59. Perry LD, Brinser JH, Kolodner H. Anaerobic corneal ulcers. Ophthalmology. 1982;89:636–642.
60. Heineman HS, Braude AI. Anaerobic infection of the brain. Am J Med. 1963;35:682–697.
61. Swartz MN. Central nervous infections. In: Finegold SM, George WL, eds. Anaerobic Infections in Humans. San Diego: Academic Press; 1989:156–212.
62. Frederick J, Braude AI. Anaerobic infection of the paranasal sinuses. N Engl J Med. 1974;290:135–137.
63. Hamory BH, Sande MA, Sydnor A Jr, et al. Etiology and antimicrobial therapy of acute maxillary sinusitis. J Infect Dis. 1979;139:197–202.
64. Brook I, Finegold SM. Bacteriology of chronic otitis media. JAMA. 1979;241:487–488.
65. Ayyagari A, Pancholi VK, Pandhi SC, et al. Anaerobic bacteria in chronic suppurative otitis media. Indian J Med Res. 1981;73:860–864.
66. Jokipii AMM, Karma P, Ojala K, et al. Anaerobic bacteria in chronic otitis media. Arch Otolaryngol. 1977;103:278–280.
67. Iino Y, Hoshino E, Tomioka S, et al. Organic acids and anaerobic microorganisms in the contents of the cholesteatoma sac. Ann Otol Rhinol Laryngol. 1983;92:91–96.
68. Bartlett JG, Gorbach SL. Anaerobic infections of the head and neck. Otolaryngol Clin North Am. 1976;9:655–678.
69. Becker GD, Parell GJ, Busch DF, et al. Anaerobic and aerobic bacteriology in head and neck cancer surgery. Arch Otolaryngol. 1978;104:591–594.
70. Brook I, Frazier EH, Thompson DH. Aerobic and anaerobic microbiology of peritonsillar abscess. Laryngoscope. 1991;101:289–292.

71. Flödstrom A, Hallander HO. Microbiological aspects of peritonsillar abscesses. Scand J Infect Dis. 1976;8:157–160.
72. Chow AW, Roser SM, Brady FA. Orofacial odontogenic infections. Ann Intern Med. 1978;88:392–402.
73. Goodman AD. Isolation of anaerobic bacteria from the root canal systems of necrotic teeth by use of a transport solution. Oral Surg. 1977;43:766–770.
74. Sundqvist G. Bacteriological Studies of Necrotic Dental Pulps. University of Umea, Sweden: Umea University Odontological Dissertations; 1976:1.
75. Iwu C, MacFarlane TW, MacKenzie D, et al. The microbiology of periapical granulomas. Oral Surg Oral Med Oral Pathol. 1990;69:502–505.
76. Brook I, Frazier EH, Gher ME. Aerobic and anaerobic microbiology of periapical abscess. Oral Microbiol Immunol. 1991;6:123–125.
77. Newman MG, Sims TN: The predominant cultivable microbiota of the periodontal abscess. J Periodontol. 1979;50:350–354.
78. Brook I, Grimm S, Kielich RB. Bacteriology of acute periapical abscess in children. J Endod. 1981;7:378–380.
79. Bartlett JG, Gorbach SL, Finegold SM. The bacteriology of aspiration pneumonia. Am J Med. 1974;56:202–207.
80. Lorber B, Swenson RM. Bacteriology of aspiration pneumonia. A prospective study of community and hospital acquired cases. Ann Intern Med. 1974;81:329–331.
81. Cesar L, Gonzalez C, Calia FM. Bacteriologic flora of aspiration-induced pulmonary infections. Arch Intern Med. 1975;135:711–714.
82. Bartlett JG, Gorbach SL, Tally FP, et al. Bacteriology and treatment of primary lung abscess. Am Rev Respir Dis. 1974;109:510–518.
83. Greey PH. The bacteriology of bronchiectasis. An analysis based on nine cases in which lobectomy was done. J Infect Dis. 1932;50:203–212.
84. Schreiner A. Anaerobic pulmonary infections. Scand J Infect Dis Suppl. 1979;19:77–79.
85. Bjerkestrand G, Digranes A, Schreiner A. Bacteriological findings in transtracheal aspirates from patients with chronic bronchitis and bronchiectasis: A preliminary report. Scand J Respir Dis. 1975;56:201–207.
86. Bartlett JG, Gorbach SL, Thadepalli H, et al. The bacteriology of empyema. Lancet. 1974;1:338–340.
87. Moore WEC, Cato EP, Holdeman LV. Review. Anaerobic bacteria of the gastrointestinal flora and their occurrence in clinical infections. J Infect Dis. 1969;119:641–649.
88. Swenson RM, Lorber B, Michaelson TC, et al. The bacteriology of intra-abdominal infections. Arch Surg. 1974;109:398–399.
89. Gorbach SL. Management of anaerobic infections: Intra-abdominal sepsis. Ann Intern Med. 1975;83:377–379.
90. Bennion RS, Thompson JE, Baron EJ, et al. Gangrenous and perforated appendicitis with peritonitis—treatment and bacteriology. Clin Ther. 1990;12:31–44.
91. Sabbaj J, Sutter VL, Finegold SM. Anaerobic pyogenic liver abscess. Ann Intern Med. 1972;77:629–638.
92. Gorbach SL, Thadepalli H, Norsen J. Anaerobic microorganisms in intraabdominal infections. In: Balows A, DeHaan RM, Dowell VR Jr, et al, eds. Anaerobic Bacteria: Role in Disease. Springfield, Ill: Charles C Thomas; 1974:399–407.
93. Peach S, Hayek L. The isolation of anaerobic bacteria from wound swabs. J Clin Pathol. 1974;27:578–582.
94. Shimada K, Inamatsu T, Yamashiro M. Anaerobic bacteria in biliary disease in elderly patients. J Infect Dis. 1977;135:850–854.
95. England DM, Rosenblatt JE. Anaerobes in human biliary tracts. J Clin Microbiol. 1977;6:494–498.
96. Thadepalli H, Gorbach SL, Keith L. Anaerobic infections of the female genital tract: Bacteriologic and therapeutic aspects. Am J Obstet Gynecol. 1973;117:1034–1040.
97. Swenson RM, Michaelson TC, Daly MJ, et al. Anaerobic bacterial infections of the female genital tract. Obstet Gynecol. 1973;42:538–541.
98. Ledger WJ, Gee CL, Pollin R, et al. The use of pre-reduced media and a portable jar for the collection of anaerobic organisms from clinical sites of infection. Am J Obstet Gynecol. 1976;125:677–681.
99. Altemeier WA. The anaerobic streptococci in tubo-ovarian abscess. Am J Obstet Gynecol. 1940;39:1038–1042.
100. Parker RT, Jones CP. Anaerobic pelvic infections and developments in hyperbaric oxygen therapy. Am J Obstet Gynecol. 1966;96:645–659.
101. Hall WL, Sobel AI, Jones CP, et al. Anaerobic postoperative pelvic infections. Obstet Gynecol. 1967;30:1–7.
102. Chow AW, Marshall JR, Guze LB. A double-blind comparison of clindamycin with penicillin plus chloramphenicol in treatment of septic abortion. J Infect Dis. 1977;135(Suppl):S35–S39.
103. Rotheram EB Jr, Schick SF. Nonclostridial anaerobic bacteria in septic abortion. Am J Med. 1969;46:80–89.
104. Smith JW, Southern PM Jr, Lehmann JD. Bacteremia in septic abortion: Complications and treatment. Obstet Gynecol. 1970;35:704–708.
105. Chow AW, Malkasian KL, Marshall JR, et al. The bacteriology of acute pelvic inflammatory disease. Am J Obstet Gynecol. 1975;122:876–879.
106. Eschenbach DA, Buchanan TM, Pollock HM, et al. Polymicrobial etiology of acute pelvic inflammatory disease. N Engl J Med. 1975;293:166–171.
107. MacLennan JD. The histotoxic clostridial infections of man. Bacteriol Rev. 1962;26:177–276.
108. Whitehead SM, Leach RD, Eykyn SJ, et al. The aetiology of perirectal sepsis. Br J Surg. 1982;69:166–168.
109. Goldstein EJC. Bite infections. In: Finegold SM, George WL, eds. Anaerobic Infections in Humans. San Diego: Academic Press; 1989:455–465.
110. Louie TJ, Bartlett JG, Tally FP, et al. Aerobic and anaerobic bacteria in diabetic foot ulcers. Ann Intern Med. 1976;85:461–463.
111. Sapico FL, Canawati HN, Witte JL, et al. Quantitative aerobic and anaerobic bacteriology of infected diabetic feet. J Clin Microbiol. 1980;12:413–420.
112. Husain M, Rajashekariah K, Menda K, et al. Anaerobic microbiology of soft tissue abscess (Abstract). Presented at the Fifteenth Interscience Conference of Antimicrobial Agents and Chemotherapy, 1975:56.
113. Meislin HW, Lerner SA, Graves MH, et al. Cutaneous abscesses. Anaerobic and aerobic bacteriology and outpatient management. Ann Intern Med. 1977;87:145–149.
114. Chow AW, Galpin JE, Guze LB. Clindamycin for treatment of sepsis caused by decubitus ulcers. J Infect Dis. 1977;135(Suppl):S65–S68.
115. Lewis RP, Sutter VL, Finegold SM. Bone infections involving anaerobic bacteria. Medicine (Baltimore). 1978;57:279–305.
116. Altemeier WA, Fullen WD. Prevention and treatment of gas gangrene. JAMA. 1971;217:806–813.
117. Leach RD, Eykyn SJ, Phillips I, et al. Anaerobic subareolar breast abscess. Lancet. 1979;1:35–37.
118. Brook I. Microbiology of non-puerperal breast abscesses. J Infect Dis. 1988;157:377–379.
119. Edmiston CE Jr, Walker AP, Krepel CJ, et al. The nonpuerperal breast infection: Aerobic and anaerobic microbial recovery from acute and chronic disease. J Infect Dis. 1990;162:695–699.
120. Finegold S, Summanen P, Gerardo SH, et al. Clinical importance of *Bilophila wadsworthia.* Eur J Clin Microbiol Infect Dis. 1992;11:1058–1063.
121. Kasten MJ, Rosenblatt JE, Gustafson DR. *Bilophila wadsworthia* bacteremia in two patients with hepatic abscess. J Clin Microbiol. 1992;30:2502–2503.
122. Bourgault A-M, Rosenblatt JE, Fitzgerald RH. *Peptococcus magnus*: A significant human pathogen. Ann Intern Med. 1980;93:244–248.
123. Wilson WR, Martin WJ, Wilkowske CJ, et al. Anaerobic bacteremia. Mayo Clin Proc. 1972;47:639–646.
124. Finegold SM. Anaerobic Bacteria in Human Disease. New York: Academic Press; 1977:1.
125. Dorsher CW, Rosenblatt JE, Wilson WR, et al. Anaerobic bacteremia: Decreasing rate over a 15-year period. Rev Infect Dis. 1991;13:633–636.
126. de Virgilio C, Klein S, Chang L, et al. Clostridial bacteremia: Implications for the surgeon. Am Surg. 1991;57:388–393.
127. King BM, Ranck BA, Daugherty FD, et al. *Clostridium tertium* septicemia. N Engl J Med. 1963;269:467–469.
128. Alpern RJ, Dowell VR Jr. *Clostridium septicum* infections and malignancy. JAMA. 1969;209:385–388.
129. Hill GB. *Eubacterium nodatum* mimics *Actinomyces* in intrauterine device–associated infections and other settings within the female genital tract. Obstet Gynecol. 1992;79:534–538.
130. Goldstein EJC, Richwald GA. Human and animal bite wounds. Am Fam Physician 1987;36:101–109.
131. Finegold SM, Baron EJ, Wexler H. A Clinical Guide to Anaerobic Infections. Belmont, Calif: Star; 1992.
132. Hecht DW, NCCLS Working Group on Susceptibility Testing of Anaerobic Bacteria. Methods for Antimicrobial Susceptibility Testing of Anaerobic Bacteria. 4th ed. Approved Standard. NCCLS Document M11-A4, v. 13. no. 26. Wayne, Pa: 1997.
133. Wexler HM. Susceptibility testing of anaerobic bacteria: Myth, magic, or method? Clin Microbiol Rev. 1991;4:470–484.
134. Rosenblatt JE, Brook I. Clinical relevance of susceptibility testing of anaerobic bacteria. Clin Infect Dis. 1993;16(Suppl 4):S446–S448.

Chapter 234

Clostridium tetani (Tetanus)

THOMAS P. BLECK

HISTORY

Tetanus was well known to the ancients; descriptions by Egyptian and Greek physicians survive to the present. They recognized the frequent relationship between injuries and the subsequent development of fatal spasms. Gowers provided the quintessential description of tetanus in 1888: "Tetanus is a disease of the nervous system characterized by persistent tonic spasm, with violent brief exacerbations. The spasm almost always commences in the muscles of the neck and jaw, causing closure of the jaws (trismus, lockjaw), and involves the muscles of the trunk more than those of the limbs. It is always acute in onset, and a very large proportion of those affected die."[1]

Nicolaier isolated a strychnine-like toxin from anaerobic soil bacteria in 1884[2]; 6 years later, Behring and Kitasato described active immunization with tetanus toxoid.[3] This latter discovery should have reduced tetanus to a historical curiosity, but we still fail to fulfill this promise.

EPIDEMIOLOGY

The global incidence of tetanus is thought to be about 1 million cases annually, or about 18 per 100,000 population. The U.S. Centers for Disease Control and Prevention receive reports of about 70 domestic cases per year; this represents underreporting of about 60%.[4] Data through 1990 are summarized in Figure 234–1. The majority of reported cases are in patients older than 60 years of age[5]; this is one of several indicators that waning immunity is an important risk factor.[6] This may be a particularly serious problem in older women.[7, 8] Changes in patterns of immigration may increase the number of nonimmunized or inadequately immunized patients presenting for care in developed countries.[9] Injection drug abuse places patients at risk for tetanus,[10] as do other potentially unsterile practices that allow inoculation of spores.[11]

In developing countries, mortality rates are as high as 28 per 100,000; in North America the rate is less than 0.1 per 100,000.

Neonatal tetanus accounts for about half of the tetanus deaths in developing nations. In a study of neonatal mortality in Bangladesh, 112 of 330 deaths were attributed to tetanus.[12] In up to one third of neonatal tetanus cases, the mother had previously had an afflicted child, highlighting failure to immunize as a major cause of tetanus.[13] Immunization programs clearly decrease neonatal tetanus deaths,[14] and some recent evidence suggests progress in prevention.[15] Neonatal tetanus still occurs rarely in developed countries, usually in persons who avoid standard practices of immunization and obstetric care.[16]

Acute injuries account for about 70% of U.S. cases, evenly divided between punctures and lacerations.[17] Other identifiable conditions are noted in 23%, leaving about 7% of cases without an apparent source. Other studies cite rates of cryptogenic tetanus as high as 23%.

CHARACTERISTICS OF *CLOSTRIDIUM TETANI*

Clostridium tetani is an obligately anaerobic bacillus that is gram-positive in fresh cultures but that may have variable staining in older cultures or tissue samples.[18] During growth, the bacilli possess abundant flagellae and are sluggishly motile. Two toxins, *tetanospasmin* (commonly called "tetanus toxin") and *tetanolysin,* are produced during this phase. Tetanospasmin is encoded on a plasmid, which is present in all toxigenic strains.[19] Tetanolysin is of uncertain importance in the pathogenesis of tetanus. Mature organisms lose their flagellae and develop a terminal spore, coming to resemble a squash racquet (Fig. 234–2).[20] The spores are extremely stable in the environment, retaining the ability to germinate and cause disease indefinitely. They withstand exposure to ethanol, phenol, or formalin but can be rendered noninfectious by iodine, glutaraldehyde, hydrogen peroxide, or autoclaving at 121°C and 103 kPa (15 psi) for 15 minutes. Growth in culture is optimal at 37°C under strictly anaerobic conditions, but culture results are of no diagnostic value. Antibiotic sensitivity is discussed in a later section.

PATHOGENESIS

The clostridial toxins that produce tetanus and botulism are similar in structure and function despite the almost diametrically opposed clinical manifestations of the diseases. These toxins are zinc-dependent matrix metalloproteinases, a category encompassing a diverse group of enzymes ranging from normal human cellular constituents necessary for cellular remodeling,[21] through determinants of neoplastic cell function,[22] to exotoxins of other microorganisms such as *Bacteroides fragilis.*[23] Tetanospasmin is synthesized as a single 151-kD chain that is cleaved extracellularly by a bacterial protease into a 100-kD heavy chain and a 50-kD light chain (fragment A), which

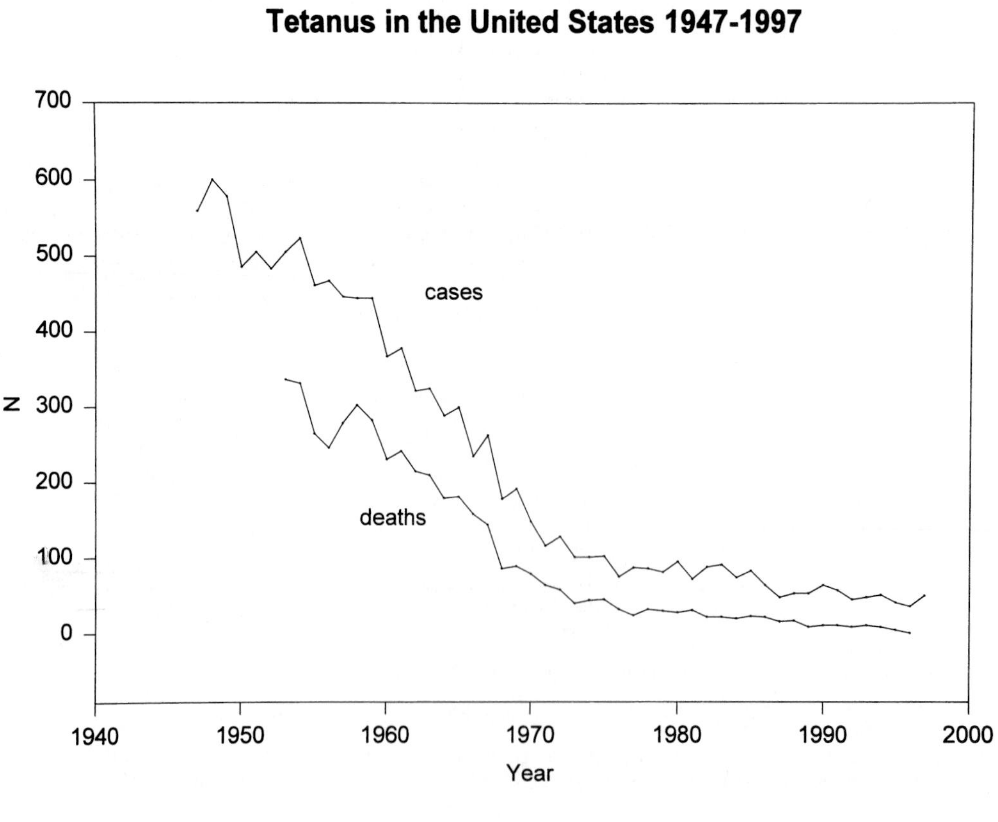

FIGURE 234–1. Cases of and deaths due to tetanus in the United States; reported rates per 100,000 population. (Data from Centers for Disease Control and Prevention, Atlanta, GA.)

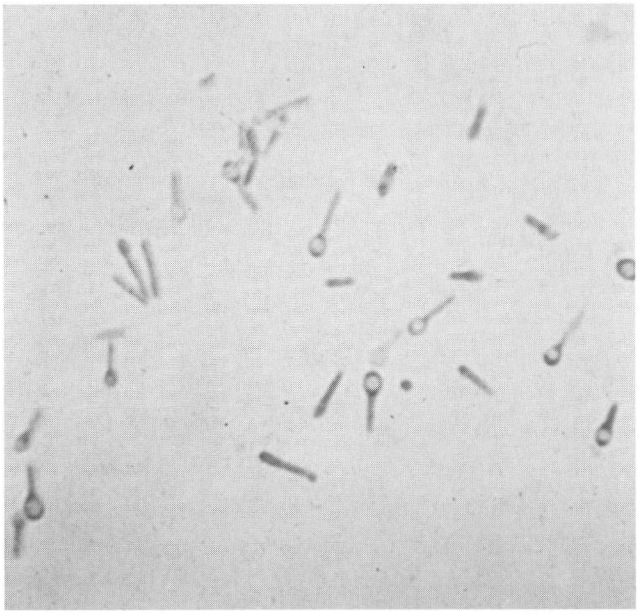

FIGURE 234–2. Gram stain of a culture of *Clostridium tetani.* (From Bleck TP, Brauner JS. Tetanus. In: Scheld WM, Whitley RJ, Durack DT, eds. Infections of the Central Nervous System. 2nd ed. Philadelphia: Lippincott-Raven; 1997:629–653.)

remain connected by a disulfide bridge.[24] The heavy chain can be further divided into fragments B and C by pepsin. The heavy chain appears to mediate binding to cell surface receptors and transport proteins, whereas the light chain produces the presynaptic inhibition of transmitter release, which produces clinical tetanus. The nature of the receptor to which tetanospasmin binds, previously thought to be a ganglioside, remains debated.[25] The toxin enters the nervous system primarily via the presynaptic terminals of lower motor neurons, where it can produce local failure of neuromuscular transmission. It then exploits the retrograde axonal transport system and is carried to the cell bodies of these neurons in the brain stem and spinal cord, where it expresses its major pathogenic action.[26]

Once the toxin enters the central nervous system, it diffuses to the terminals of inhibitory cells, including both local glycinergic interneurons and descending γ-aminobutyric acid–secreting (GABAergic) neurons from the brain stem. The toxin degrades synaptobrevin, a protein required for docking of neurotransmitter vesicles with their release site on the presynaptic membrane.[27] By preventing transmitter release from these cells, tetanospasmin leaves the motor neurons without inhibition. This produces muscular rigidity by raising the resting firing rate of motor neurons and also generates spasms by failing to limit reflex responses to afferent stimuli. Excitatory transmitter release in the spinal cord can also be impaired, but the toxin appears to have greater affinity for the inhibitory systems. The autonomic nervous system is affected as well; this is predominantly manifested as a hypersympathetic state induced by failure to inhibit adrenal release of catecholamines.

Toxin binding appears to be an irreversible event. At the neuromuscular junction, recovery depends on sprouting a new axon terminal; this is probably the case at other affected synapses as well.

CLINICAL MANIFESTATIONS

Tetanus is classically divided into four clinical types: generalized, localized, cephalic, and neonatal. These are valuable diagnostic and prognostic distinctions, but they reflect host factors and the site of inoculation rather than differences in toxin action. Terms describing the initial stages of tetanus include incubation period (time from inoculation to the first symptom) and period of onset (time from the first symptom to the first generalized spasm). The shorter these periods, the worse the prognosis.[28] Various rating scales are available.[29] Certain portals of entry (e.g., compound fractures) are associated with poorer prognoses. Tetanus may be particularly severe in narcotic addicts, for unknown reasons.[30]

Generalized tetanus is the most commonly recognized form; it often begins with trismus (masseter rigidity, known as "lockjaw") and a risus sardonicus (increased tone in the orbicularis oris). Figure 234–3 illustrates these findings. Abdominal rigidity may also be present. The generalized spasm resembles decorticate posturing and consists of opisthotonic posturing with flexion of the arms and extension of the legs (Fig. 234–4). The patient does not lose consciousness and experiences severe pain during each spasm. The spasms often are triggered by sensory stimuli. During the spasm, the upper airway can be obstructed, or the diaphragm may participate in the general muscular contraction. Either compromises respiration, and even the first such spasm may be fatal. In the modern era of intensive care, however, the respiratory problems are easily managed, and autonomic dysfunction, usually occurring after several days of symptoms, has emerged as the leading cause of death.[31]

The illness can progress for about 2 weeks, reflecting the time required to complete the transport of toxin that is already intraaxonal when antitoxin treatment is given. The severity of illness may be decreased by partial immunity.[32] Recovery takes an additional

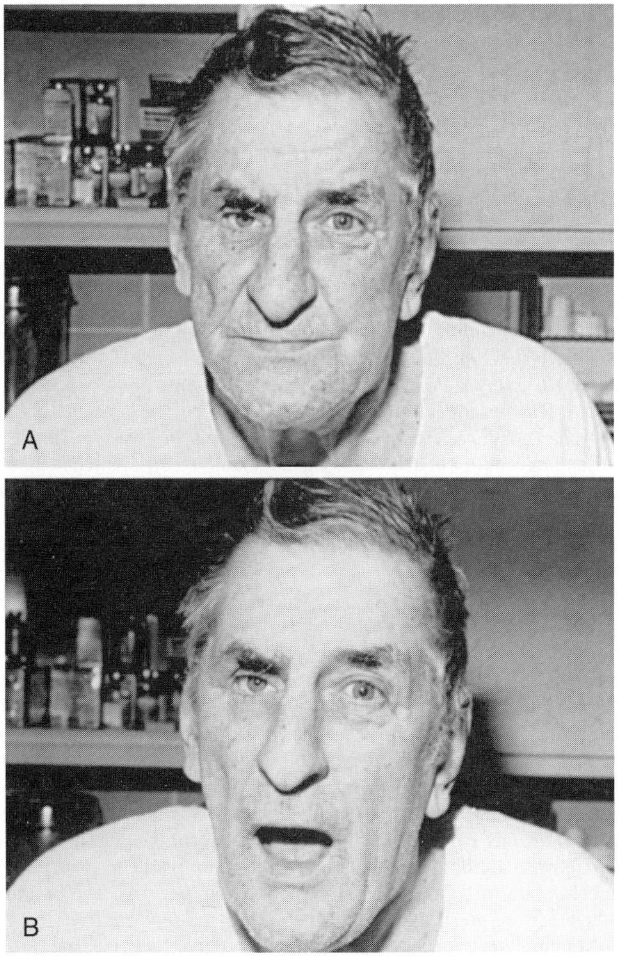

FIGURE 234–3. *A,* Risus sardonicus. Note the straightened upper lip at rest. *B,* Trismus. The patient is opening his mouth as fully as possible. (From Bleck TP, Brauner JS. Tetanus. In: Scheld WM, Whitley RJ, Durack DT, eds. Infections of the Central Nervous System. 2nd ed. Philadelphia: Lippincott-Raven; 1997:629–653.)

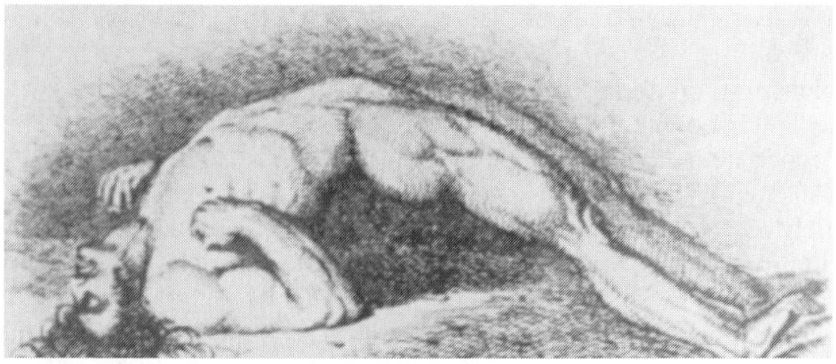

FIGURE 234–4. Opisthotonus. (From Bell C. Essays on the Anatomy and Physiology of Expression. 2nd ed. London: J Murray; 1824.)

month and is complete unless complications supervene. Lower motor neuron dysfunction may not be apparent until spasms remit, and recovery from this deficit in neuromuscular transmission may take additional weeks.[33] Recurrent tetanus may occur if the patient does not receive active immunization, because the amount of toxin produced is inadequate to induce immunity.[34]

Localized tetanus involves rigidity of the muscles associated with the site of spore inoculation. This may be mild and persistent and often resolves spontaneously. Lower motor neuron dysfunction (weakness and diminished muscle tone) is often present in the most involved muscle. This chronic form of the disease probably reflects partial immunity to tetanospasmin.[35] However, localized tetanus is more commonly a prodrome of generalized tetanus, which occurs when enough toxin gains access to the central nervous system.

Cephalic tetanus is a special form of localized disease affecting the cranial nerve musculature (Fig. 234–5). Although earlier reports linked cephalic tetanus to a poor prognosis, more recent studies have revealed many milder cases. A lower motor neuron lesion, frequently producing facial nerve weakness, is often apparent.[36] Extraocular muscle involvement is occasionally noted.

Neonatal tetanus (Fig. 234–6) follows infection of the umbilical stump, most commonly as a result of a failure of aseptic technique in mothers who are inadequately immunized.[37] Cultural practices may also contribute.[38] The condition usually manifests with generalized weakness and failure to nurse; rigidity and spasms occur later. The mortality rate exceeds 90%, and developmental delays are common among survivors.[39] Poor prognostic factors include age younger than 10 days, symptoms for fewer than 5 days before presentation to hospital, and the presence of risus sardonicus or fever.[40] Apnea is the leading cause of death among neonatal tetanus patients in the first week of life, and sepsis in the second week.[41] Bacterial infection of the umbilical stump leads to sepsis in almost half of babies with neonatal tetanus; this contributes to the substantial rate of mortality despite treatment.[42]

DIAGNOSIS

Tetanus is diagnosed by clinical observation and has a limited differential diagnosis. Laboratory testing cannot confirm or exclude the condition, and it is primarily useful for excluding intoxications that can mimic tetanus. Electromyographic studies are occasionally useful in questionable cases. Such testing becomes more important when no portal of entry is apparent. Antitetanus antibodies are undetectable in most tetanus patients, but many reports document the disease in patients with antibody levels above the commonly cited "protective" concentration of 0.01 IU/L.[43] Rare patients apparently develop antibodies that are not protective.[44]

Attempts to culture *C. tetani* from wounds are not useful in diagnosis, since (1) even carefully performed anaerobic cultures are frequently negative; (2) a positive culture does not indicate whether the organism contains the toxin-producing plasmid; and (3) a positive culture may be present without disease in patients with adequate immunity.[45]

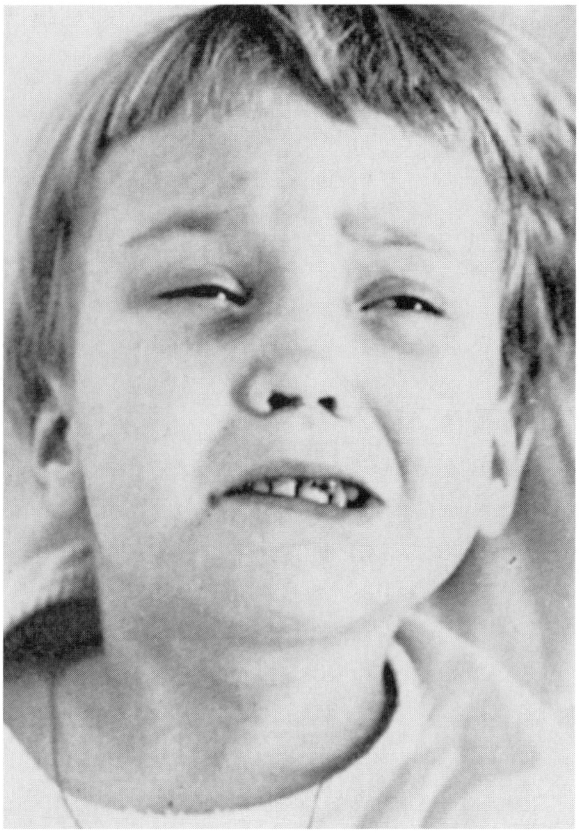

FIGURE 234–5. Cephalic tetanus. Right facial paresis is present in addition to the grimace. (From Veronesi R, Focaccia R. The clinical picture. In: Veronesi R, ed. Tetanus: Important New Concepts. Amsterdam: Excerpta Medica; 1981:183–206.)

Strychnine poisoning, in which glycine is antagonized, is the only condition that truly mimics tetanus; toxicologic studies of serum and urine should be performed when tetanus is suspected, and tetanus should be considered even if strychnine poisoning appears likely. Because the initial treatments of tetanus and strychnine intoxication are similar, therapy is instituted before the assay results are available. Dystonic reactions to neuroleptic drugs or other central dopamine antagonists may be confused with the neck stiffness of tetanus, but the posture of patients with dystonic reactions almost always involves lateral head turning, which is rare in tetanus. Treatment with anticholinergic agents (benztropine or diphenhydramine) is rapidly effective against dystonic reactions. Dental infections can produce

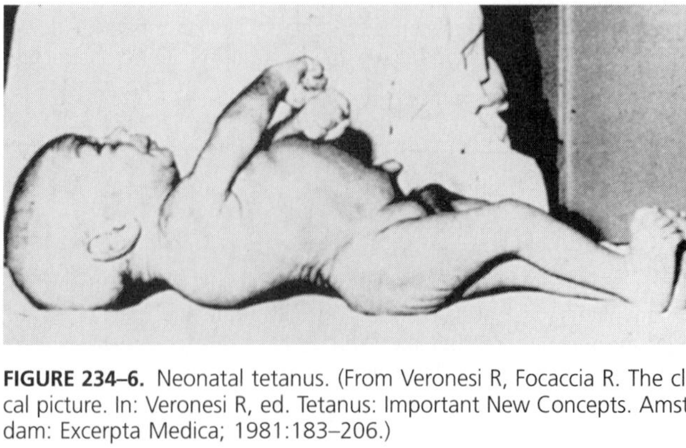

FIGURE 234–6. Neonatal tetanus. (From Veronesi R, Focaccia R. The clinical picture. In: Veronesi R, ed. Tetanus: Important New Concepts. Amsterdam: Excerpta Medica; 1981:183–206.)

trismus, and should be sought, but they do not cause the other manifestations of tetanus.

TREATMENT

The patient with tetanus requires simultaneous attention to several concerns. Attention to the airway and to ventilation is paramount at the time of presentation, but the other aspects of care, especially passive immunization, must be pursued as soon as the respiratory system is secure. Table 234–1 presents a suggested management protocol.

TABLE 234–1 Suggested Management Protocol for Generalized Tetanus

I. Diagnosis and stabilization: first hour after presentation
   A. Assess airway and ventilation. If necessary, perform endotracheal intubation using benzodiazepine sedation and neuromuscular blockade (e.g., vecuronium 0.1 mg/kg).
   B. Obtain samples for antitoxin level, strychnine and dopamine antagonist assays, electrolytes, blood urea nitrogen, creatinine, creatine kinase, and urinary myoglobin determination.
   C. Determine the portal of entry, incubation period, period of onset, and immunization history.
   D. Administer benztropine (1–2 mg, intravenously) or diphenhydramine (50 mg, intravenously) to rule out a dystonic reaction to a dopamine blocking agent.
   E. Administer a benzodiazepine intravenously (diazepam in 5-mg increments, or lorazepam in 2-mg increments) to control spasm and decrease rigidity. Initially, employ a dose that is adequate to produce sedation and minimize reflex spasms. If this dose compromises the airway or ventilation, intubate using a short-acting neuromuscular blocking agent. Transfer the patient to a quiet, darkened area of the intensive care unit.
II. Early management phase: first 24 hours
   A. Administer human tetanus immunoglobulin (HTIG), 500 IU, intramuscularly; as an alternative, consider intravenous pooled immune globulin (see text).
   B. At a different site, administer adsorbed tetanus toxoid such as tetanus-diphtheria vaccine (0.5 ml) or diphtheria-pertussis-tetanus vaccine (0.5 ml), as appropriate for age, intramuscularly. Adsorbed tetanus toxoid without diphtheria toxoid is available for patients with a history of reaction to diphtheria toxoid; otherwise, the correct combination for the patient's age should be employed.
   C. Begin metronidazole 500 mg, intravenously, every 6 h for 7–10 d.
   D. Perform a tracheostomy after placement of an endotracheal tube and under neuromuscular blockade if spasms produce any degree of airway compromise.
   E. Débride any wounds as indicated for their own management.
   F. Place a soft, small-bore nasal feeding tube or a central venous hyperalimentation catheter, and begin feeding. Patients receiving total parental nutrition should also be given parenteral H_2 blockade or other gastric protection.
   G. Administer benzodiazepines as required to control spasms and produce sedation. If adequate control is not achieved, institute long-term neuromuscular blockade (e.g., vecuronium 6 to 8 mg/h); continue benzodiazepines for sedation with intermittent electroencephalographic monitoring to ensure somnolence. Neuromuscular junction blockade should be discontinued daily to assess the patient's physical examination and to decrease the possibility of excessive accumulation of the blocking agent.
III. Intermediate management phase: next 2–3 wk
   A. Treat sympathetic hyperactivity with labetalol (0.25–1.0 mg/min as needed for blood pressure control) or morphine (0.5–1.0 mg/kg/h by continuous infusion; see text for other recommendations). Consider epidural blockade with a local anesthetic. Avoid diuretics for blood pressure control, because volume depletion worsens autonomic instability.
   B. If hypotension is present, initiate saline resuscitation. Place a pulmonary artery catheter and an arterial line and administer fluids, dopamine, or norepinephrine as indicated.
   C. Sustained bradycardia usually requires a pacemaker. Atropine or isoproterenol may be useful during pacemaker placement.
   D. Begin prophylactic heparin.
   E. Use a flotation bed, if possible, to prevent skin breakdown and peroneal nerve palsies. Otherwise, ensure frequent turning and employ antirotation boots.
   F. Maintain benzodiazepines until neuromuscular blockade, if employed, has been terminated and the severity of spasms has diminished substantially. Then taper the benzodiazepine dose over 14–21 d.
   G. Begin rehabilitation planning.
IV. Convalescent stage: 2–6 weeks
   A. After spasms are no longer present, begin physical therapy. Many patients require supportive psychotherapy.
   B. Before discharge, administer another dose of tetanus-diphtheria vaccine or diphtheria-pertussis-tetanus vaccine.
   C. Schedule a third dose of toxoid to be given 4 weeks after the second.

Adapted from Bleck TP, Brauner JS. Tetanus. In: Scheld WM, Whitley RJ, Durack DT, eds. Infections of the Central Nervous System. 2nd ed. Philadelphia: Lippincott-Raven; 1997:629–653.

Tetanic spasms sometimes demand that the airway be secured before other lines of therapy are possible. An orotracheal tube can be passed under sedation and neuromuscular junction blockade; a feeding tube should be placed at the same time. Because the endotracheal tube can stimulate spasms, an early tracheostomy may be beneficial.[46]

Benzodiazepines have emerged as the mainstay of symptomatic therapy for tetanus.[47] These drugs are $GABA_A$ agonists and thereby indirectly antagonize the effects of the toxin. They do not restore glycinergic inhibition. The patient should be kept free of spasms and may benefit from the amnestic effects of the drugs. Diazepam has been studied most intensively, but lorazepam or midazolam seems equally effective. Tetanus patients have unusually high tolerance for the sedating effect of these agents and commonly remain alert at doses normally expected to produce anesthesia.[48]

The intravenous formulations of both diazepam and lorazepam contain propylene glycol; at the doses required to control generalized tetanus, this vehicle may produce lactic acidosis.[49] Nasogastric delivery of these agents is often possible, but some tetanus patients develop gastrointestinal motility disorders and do not absorb drugs well. Intravenous midazolam (5 to 15 mg/hour or more) is effective and does not contain propylene glycol, but it must be given as a continuous infusion because of its brief half-life.[50] Propofol infusion is also effective[51] but very expensive, and the amount necessary to control symptoms may exceed the patient's tolerance of the lipid vehicle. After the symptoms of tetanus subside, these agents must be tapered over at least 2 weeks to prevent withdrawal effects. Intrathecal baclofen is also effective in controlling tetanus but has no clear advantage over benzodiazepines. Neuroleptic agents and barbiturates, previously used for tetanus, are inferior for this indication and should not be used. Magnesium infusion may emerge as a useful therapeutic technique in generalized tetanus.[52]

Rarely, tetanus cannot be adequately controlled with benzodiazepines alone; neuromuscular junction blockade is then indicated, with the caveat that sedation is still required for psychological reasons. All of the available drugs have side effects, including the potential for prolonged effects after the drug is discontinued. Vecuronium (by continuous infusion) or pancuronium (by intermittent injection) is an adequate choice. These agents should be stopped at least once daily to assess the patient's progress and to observe for possible complications. Electroencephalographic monitoring is a useful adjunct for this purpose.[53]

In tetanus patients, the portal of entry is still apparent at presentation. If the wound itself requires surgical attention, this may be performed after spasms are controlled. However, the course of tetanus is not affected by wound débridement.

Passive immunization with human tetanus immune globulin (HTIG) shortens the course of tetanus and may lessen its severity. A dose of 500 IU appears to be as effective as larger doses.[54] There is no apparent advantage to intrathecal HTIG administration.[55] Intrathecal HTIG has also been shown to be ineffective in neonatal tetanus.[56] Pooled intravenous immune globulin has been proposed as an alternative to HTIG.[57] Active immunization must also be initiated.

The role of antimicrobial therapy in tetanus remains debated. The in vitro susceptibilities of *C. tetani* include metronidazole, penicillins, cephalosporins, imipenem, macrolides, and tetracycline. A study comparing oral metronidazole with intramuscular penicillin showed a better survival rate, shorter hospitalization, and less progression of disease in the metronidazole group.[58] This may reflect a true advantage of metronidazole over penicillin, but it more likely corresponds to a negative effect of penicillin, a known GABA antagonist. Topical antibiotic application to the umbilical stump appears to reduce the risk of neonatal tetanus.[8]

Autonomic dysfunction generally reflects excessive catecholamine release and may respond to combined α- and β-adrenergic blockade with intravenous labetalol.[59] β-blockade alone is rarely employed, because the resulting unopposed α-effect can produce severe hypertension. If β-blockade is chosen, the short-acting agent esmolol should be employed.[60] Other approaches to hypertension include morphine infusion,[61] magnesium sulfate infusion,[62] and epidural blockade of the renal nerves.[63] Hypotension is less common; if present, it may require norepinephrine infusion. Myocardial dysfunction is also common[64] and may represent a further reflection of catecholamine excess.[65]

Nutritional support should be started as soon as the patient is stable. The volume of enteral feeding needed to meet the exceptionally high caloric and protein requirements of these patients may exceed the capacity of the gastrointestinal system.

The mortality rate in mild and moderate tetanus is presently about 6%; for severe tetanus, it may reach as high as 60%, even in expert centers.[66] Among adults, age has very little effect on mortality, with octogenarians and nonagenarians faring as well as middle-aged patients.[67] Tetanus survivors often have serious psychological problems related to the disease and its treatment that persist after recovery and may require psychotherapy.[68]

PROPHYLAXIS

Tetanus is preventable in almost all patients, leading to its description as the "inexcusable disease."[69] A series of three monthly intramuscular injections of alum-adsorbed tetanus toxoid provides almost complete immunity for at least 5 years. Patients younger than 7 years of age should receive combined diphtheria-tetanus-pertussis vaccine, and other patients should receive combined diphtheria-tetanus vaccine. Routine booster injections are indicated every 10 years; more frequent administration may increase the risk of a reaction. The Advisory Committee on Immunization Practices in the United States recommends visits at age 11 or 12 years and age 50 years for health care providers to review vaccination histories and administer any needed vaccine.[70] Toxoid vaccination remains the standard; DNA-based vaccination is less efficacious.[71]

Some patients with humoral immune deficiencies may not respond adequately to toxoid injection[72]; such patients should receive passive immunization for tetanus-prone injuries regardless of the period since the last booster injection. Approximately half of patients lose tetanus immunity after chemotherapy for leukemia or lymphoma.[73] Patients who have undergone bone marrow or stem cell transplantation require revaccination after the procedure[74]; two doses (given at 12 and 24 months after transplant) are probably sufficient.[75] Most young patients with human immunodeficiency virus (HIV) infection appear to retain antitetanus antibody production if their primary immunization series was completed before HIV infection was acquired[76]; however, only a minority respond adequately to booster immunization.[77] Vitamin A deficiency interferes with the response to tetanus toxoid.[78]

Although a full series of maternal immunizations is ideal, even one or two doses of tetanus toxoid confers substantial protection against neonatal tetanus.[79] Tetanus occurred in babies of women immunized with toxoid that later was shown to be devoid of potency; this disconcerting report underscores the need for quality control in toxoid production.[5] Application of topical antimicrobial agents to the umbilical cord stump markedly decreases the incidence of neonatal tetanus when maternal immunization is insufficient.[80]

Although any wound may be inoculated with tetanus spores, some types of injury are more frequently associated with tetanus (tetanus prone). These include wounds that are contaminated with dirt, saliva, or feces; puncture wounds, including unsterile injections; missile injuries; burns; frostbite; avulsions; and crush injuries. Patients with these wounds who have not received adequate active immunization in the past 5 years, or in whom immunodeficiency is suspected, should receive passive immunization with HTIG (250 to 500 IU, intramuscularly) in addition to active immunization.[81]

Mild reactions to tetanus toxoid (e.g., local tenderness, edema, low grade fever) are common. More severe reactions are rare; some are actually caused by hypersensitivity to the preservative thiomersal.[82] Although there have been reports suggesting a connection of tetanus immunization with the Guillain-Barré syndrome, a careful epidemiologic analysis did not confirm such an association.[83]

REFERENCES

1. Gowers WR. A Manual of Diseases of the nervous system. Philadelphia: Blackiston, 1888.
2. Nicolaier A. Üeber infectiösen tetanus. Dtsch Med Wochenschr. 1884;10:842–844.
3. Behring E, Kitasato S. Üeber das zustandekommen der diphtherie-immunität und der tetanus-immunität bei thieren. Dtsch Med Wochenschr. 1890;16:1113–1114.
4. Sutter RW, Cochi SL, Brink EW, Sirotkin BI. Assessment of vital statistics and surveillance data for monitoring tetanus mortality, United States, 1979–1984. Am J Epidemiol. 1990;131:132–142.
5. Gergen PJ, McQuillan GM, Kiely M, et al. Å population-based serologic survey of immunity to tetanus in the United States. N Engl J Med. 1995;332:761–766.
6. Richardson JP, Knight AL. The prevention of tetanus in the elderly. Arch Intern Med. 1991;151:1712–1717.
7. Horton E, Singer C, Kozarsky P, et al. Status of immunity to tetanus, measles, mumps, rubella, and polio among U.S. travelers. Ann Intern Med. 1991;115:32–33.
8. Böttiger M, Gustavsson O, Svensson Å. Immunity to tetanus, diphtheria and poliomyelitis in the adult population of Sweden in 1991. Int J Epidemiol. 1998;27:916–925.
9. Henderson SO, Mody T, Groth DE, et al. The presentation of tetanus in an emergency department. J Emerg Med. 1998;16:705–708.
10. Talan DA, Moran GJ. Tetanus among injecting-drug users—California, 1997. Ann Emerg Med. 1998;32:385–386.
11. O'Malley CD, Smith N, Braun R, Prevots DR. Tetanus associated with body piercing. Clin Infect Dis. 1998;27:1343–1344.
12. Hlady WG, Bennett JV, Samadi AR, et al. Neonatal tetanus in rural Bangladesh: Risk factors and toxoid efficacy. Am J Public Health. 1992;82:1365–1369.
13. Traverso HP, Kamil S, Rahim H, et al. A reassessment of risk factors for neonatal tetanus. Bull World Health Organ. 1991;69:573–579.
14. Bjerregaard P, Steinglass R, Mutie DM, et al. Neonatal tetanus mortality in coastal Kenya: A community survey. Int J Epidemiol. 1993;22:163–169.
15. Hodges M, Williams RA. Registered infant and under-five deaths in Freetown, Sierra Leone from 1987–1991 and a comparison with 1969–1979. West Afr J Med. 1998;17:95–98.
16. Neonatal tetanus—Montana, 1998. MMWR Morb Mortal Wkly Rep. 1998;47:928–930.
17. Bleck TP. Tetanus: Dealing with the continuing clinical challenge. J Crit Illness. 1987;2:41–52.
18. Cato EP, George WL, Finegold SM. Genus *Clostridium praemozski* 1880, 23[AL]. In: Smeath PHA, Mair NS, Sharpe ME, Holt JG, eds. Bergey's Manual of Systematic Bacteriology, v. 2. Baltimore: Williams & Wilkins, 1986:1141–1200.
19. Eisel U, Jarausch W, Goretzki K, et al. Tetanus toxin: Primary structure, expression in *E. coli,* and homology with botulinum toxins. EMBO J. 1986;5:2495–2502.
20. Hoeniger JFM, Tauschel HD. Sequence of structural changes in cultures of *Clostridium tetani* grown on a solid medium. J Med Microbiol. 1974;7:425–432.
21. Geisler S, Lichtinghagen R, Boker KH, Veh RW. Differential distribution of five members of the matrix metalloproteinase family and one inhibitor (TIMP-1) in human liver and skin. Cell Tissue Res. 1997;289:173–183.
22. Rooprai HK, Van Meter T, Rucklidge GJ, et al. Comparative analysis of matrix metalloproteinases by immunocytochemistry, immunohistochemistry and zymography in human primary brain tumours. Int J Oncol. 1998;13:1153–1157.
23. Wu S, Lim KC, Huang J, et al. *Bacteroides fragilis* enterotoxin cleaves the zonula adherens protein, E-cadherin. Proc Natl Acad Sci U S A. 1998;95:14979–14984.
24. Matsuda M. The structure of tetanus toxin. In: Simpson LL, ed. Botulinum Neurotoxin and Tetanus Toxin. San Diego: Academic Press; 1989:69–92.
25. Middlebrook JL. Cell surface receptors for protein toxins. In: Simpson LL, ed. Botulinum Neurotoxin and Tetanus Toxin. San Diego: Academic Press; 1989:95–119.
26. Bleck TP, Brauner JS. Tetanus. In: Scheld WM, Whitley RJ, Durack DT, eds. Infections of the Central Nervous System, ed 2. New York: Raven Press; 1997:629–653.
27. Cornille F, Martin L, Lenoir C, et al. Cooperative exosite-dependent cleavage of synaptobrevin by tetanus toxin light chain. J Biol Chem. 1997;272:3459–3464.
28. Veronesi R, Focaccia R. The clinical picture. In: Veronesi R, ed. Tetanus: Important New Concepts. Amsterdam: Excerpta Medica: 1981:183–206.
29. Habermann E. Tetanus. In: Vinken PJ, Bruyn GW, eds. Handbook of Clinical Neurology, vol. 33. Amsterdam: North-Holland; 1978:491–547.
30. Cherubin CE. Clinical severity of tetanus in narcotic addicts in New York City. Arch Intern Med. 1968:121:156–158.
31. Edmondson RS, Flowers MWW. Intensive care in tetanus: Management, complications, and mortality in 100 patients. BMJ. 1979;1401–1404.
32. Luisto M, Iivanainen M. Tetanus of immunized children. Dev Med Child Neurol. 1993;35:351–355.
33. Bleck TP, Calderelli DD. Vocal cord paralysis complicating tetanus. Neurology. 1983;33(suppl 2):140.
34. Spenney J, Lamb RN, Cobbs CG. Recurrent tetanus. South Med J. 1971;64:859.
35. Risk WS, Bosch EP, Kimura J, et al. Chronic tetanus: Clinical report and histochemistry of muscle. Muscle Nerve. 1981;4:363–366.
36. Mayo J, Berciano J. Cephalic tetanus presenting with Bell's palsy. J Neurol Neurosurg Psychiatry. 1985;48:290.

37. Schofield FD, Tucker VM, Westbrook GR. Neonatal tetanus in New Guinea: Effect of active immunization in pregnancy. BMJ. 1961:2:785–789.
38. Traverso HP, Bennett JV, Kahn AJ, et al. Ghee application to the umbilical cord: A risk factor for neonatal tetanus. Lancet. 1989;486–488.
39. Anlar B, Yalaz K, Dizmen R. Long-term prognosis after neonatal tetanus. Dev Med Child Neurol. 1989;31:76–80.
40. Gürses N, Aydin M. Factors affecting prognosis of neonatal tetanus. Scand J Infect Dis. 1993;25:353–355.
41. Kurtoglu S, Caksen H, Ozturk A, et al. A review of 207 newborn with tetanus. JPMA J Pak Med Assoc. 1998;48:93–98.
42. Egri-Okwaji MT, Iroha EO, Kesah CN, Odugbemi TO. Bacteria causing septicaemia in neonates with tetanus. West Afr J Med. 1998;17:136–139.
43. Goulon M, Girard O, Grosbius S, et al. Les corps antitétaniques. Presse Med. 1972;1:3049–3050.
44. Crone NE, Reder AT. Severe tetanus in immunized patients with high anti-tetanus titers. Neurology. 1992;42:761–764.
45. Bleck TP. Clinical aspects of tetanus. In: Simpson LL, ed. Botulinum Neurotoxin and Tetanus Toxin. New York: Academic Press, 1989;379–398.
46. Mukherjee DK. Tetanus and tracheostomy. Ann Otol. 1977;86:67–72.
47. Vassa T, Yajnik VH, Joshi KR, et al. Comparative clinical trial of diazepam with other conventional drugs in tetanus. Postgrad Med J. 1874;50:755–758.
48. Bleck TP. Tetanus. Disease-A-Month. 1991;37:547–603.
49. Kapoor W, Carey P, Karpf M. Induction of lactic acidosis with intravenous diazepam in a patient with tetanus. Arch Intern Med. 1981;141:944–945.
50. Orko R, Rosenberg PH, Himberg JJ. Intravenous infusion of midazolam, propofol and vecuronium in a patient with severe tetanus. Acta Anaesthesiol Scand. 1988;32:590–592.
51. Borgeat A, Dessibourg C, Rochani M, Suter PM. Sedation by propofol in tetanus: Is it a muscular relaxant? Intensive Care Med. 1991;17:427–429.
52. Attygalle D, Rodrigo N. Magnesium sulphate for control of spasms in severe tetanus. Can we avoid sedation and artificial ventilation? Anaesthesia. 1997;52:956–962.
53. Luisto M, Seppäläinen A-M. Electroencephalography in tetanus. Acta Neurol Scand. 1989;80:157–161.
54. Blake PA, Feldman RA, Buchanan TM, et al. Serologic therapy of tetanus in the United States. JAMA. 1976;236:42–44.
55. Abrutyn E, Berlin JA. Intrathecal therapy in tetanus: A meta-analysis. JAMA. 1991;266:2262–2267.
56. Begue RE, Lindo-Soriano I. Failure of intrathecal antitoxin in the treatment of neonatal tetanus. J Infect Dis. 1991;164:619–620.
57. Lee DC, Lederman HM. Anti-tetanus toxoid antibodies in intravenous gamma globulin: An alternative to tetanus immune globulin. J Infect Dis. 1992;166:642–645.
58. Ahmadsyah I, Salim A. Treatment of tetanus: An open study to compare the efficacy of procaine penicillin and metronidazole. BMJ. 1985;291:648–650.
59. Domenghetti GM, Savary S, Striker H. Hyperadrenergic syndrome in severe tetanus responsive to labetalol. BMJ. 1984;288:1483–1484.
60. King WW, Cave DR. Use of esmolol to control autonomic instability of tetanus. Am J Med. 1991;91:425–428.
61. Rocke DA, Wasley AG, Pather M, et al. Morphine in tetanus: The management of sympathetic nervous system overactivity. S Afr Med J. 1986;70:666–668.
62. Lipman J, James MFM, Erskine J, et al. Autonomic dysfunction in severe tetanus: Magnesium sulfate as an adjunct to deep sedation. Crit Care Med. 1987;15:987–988.
63. Southorn PA, Blaise GA. Treatment of tetanus-induced autonomic dysfunction with continuous epidural blockade. Crit Care Med. 1986:14:251–252.
64. Udwadia FE, Sunavala JD, Jain MC, et al. Haemodynamic studies during the management of severe tetanus. Quart J Med. 1992;83:449–460.
65. Tseuda K, Oliver PB, Richter RW. Cardiovascular manifestations of tetanus. Anesthesiology. 1974;40:588–592.
66. Nolla-Salas M, Garcés-Brusés J. Severity of tetanus in patients older than 80 years: Comparative study with younger patients. Clin Infect Dis. 1993;16:591–592.
67. Jolliet P, Magnenat JL, Kobel T, Chevrolet JC. Aggressive intensive care treatment of very elderly patients with tetanus is justified. Chest. 1990;97:702–705.
68. Edwards RA, James B. Tetanus and psychiatry: Unexpected bedfellows. Med J Aust. 1979;1:483–484.
69. Edsall G. The inexcusable disease. JAMA. 1876;235:62–63.
70. Bardenheier B, Prevots DR, Khetsuriani N, Wharton M. Tetanus surveillance—United States, 1995–1997. MMWR Morb Mortal Wkly Rep. 1998;47:1–13.
71. Saikh KU, Sesno J, Brandler P, Ulrich RG. Are DNA-based vaccines useful for protection against secreted bacterial toxins? Tetanus toxin test case. Vaccine. 1998;16:1029–1038.
72. Webster ADB, Latif AAA, Brenner MK, Bird D. Evaluation of test immunization in the assessment of antibody deficiency syndromes. BMJ. 1984;288:1864–1866.
73. Hamarstrom V, Pauksen K, Svensson H, et al. Tetanus immunity in patients with hematological malignancies. Support Care Cancer. 1998;6:469–472.
74. Hammarström V, Pauksen K, Simmonsson B, et al. Tetanus immunity in autologous bone marrow and blood stem cell transplant recipients. Bone Marrow Transplant. 1998;22:67–71.
75. Vance E, George S, Guinan EC, et al. Comparison of multiple immunization schedules for *Haemophilus influenzae* type b-conjugate and tetanus toxoid vaccines following bone marrow transplantation. Bone Marrow Transplant. 1998;22:735–741.
76. Kurtzhals JAL, Kjeldsen K, Heron I, Skinhøj P. Immunity against diphtheria and tetanus in human immunodeficiency virus-infected Danish men born 1950–1959. APMIS. 1992;100:803–808.
77. Talesnik E, Vial PA, Labarca J, et al. Time course of antibody response to tetanus toxoid and pneumococcal capsular polysaccharides in patients infected with HIV. J Acquir Immune Defic Syndr Hum Retrovirol. 1998;19:471–477.
78. Semba RD, Muhilal, Scott AL, et al. Depressed immune response to tetanus in children with vitamin A deficiency. J Nutr. 1992;122:101–107.
79. Koenig MA, Roy NC, McElrath T, et al. Duration of protective immunity conferred by maternal tetanus toxoid immunization: Further evidence from Matlab, Bangladesh. Am J Public Health. 1998;88:903–907.
80. Parashar UD, Bennett JV, Boring JR, Hlady WG. Topical antimicrobials applied to the umbilical cord stump: A new intervention against neonatal tetanus. Int J Epidemiol. 1998;27:904–908.
81. Brand DA, Acampora D, Gottlieb AD, et al. Adequacy of antitetanus prophylaxis in six hospital emergency rooms. N Engl J Med. 1983;309:636–639.
82. Jacobs RL, Lowe RS, Lanier BQ. Adverse reactions to tetanus toxoid. JAMA. 1982;247:40–42.
83. Tuttle J, Chen RT, Rantala H, et al. The risk of Guillain-Barré syndrome after tetanus-toxoid–containing vaccines in adults and children in the United States. Am J Public Health. 1997;87:2045–2048.

Chapter 235

Clostridium botulinum (Botulism)

THOMAS P. BLECK

Botulism and tetanus result from intoxication with the protein neurotoxins elaborated by two related species of clostridia. The toxins are very similar in structure and function, but differ dramatically in their clinical effects because they target different cells in the nervous system. Botulinum neurotoxins predominantly affect the peripheral neuromuscular junction and autonomic synapses, and its effects are primarily manifested as weakness. In contrast, although tetanus toxin can affect the same systems, its effects reflect tropism for inhibitory cells of the central nervous system and are primarily manifested as rigidity and spasm. Both conditions have potentially high fatality rates, and both are preventable through education and public health measures. The cost of care per botulism patient in Canada and the United States was estimated to be $340,000 in 1989.[1]

Clostridium botulinum produces most cases of botulism, with a few other clostridial strains accounting for the remainder. Botulinum toxins are designated types A through G based on antigenic differences.[2] Types A, B, E, and F produce human disease, whereas types C and D are almost exclusively confined to animals.[3] Type G toxin has not been associated with naturally acquired disease. The clinical forms of botulism include *foodborne botulism, infant botulism, wound botulism,* and *botulism of undetermined etiology.* In the past decade, botulinum A toxin has achieved prominence as a therapeutic modality in conditions resulting from excessive muscle activity such as torticollis.

HISTORY OF BOTULISM

The term *botulism* derives from the Latin word *botulus,* or sausage. Outbreaks of poisoning related to sausages and other prepared foods occurred in Europe in the 19th century. Justinus Kerner, a district health officer in southern Germany, recognized the connection between sausage and the paralytic illnesses of 230 patients in 1820 and made sausage poisoning a reportable disease.[4] At about the same time, physicians in Russia recognized a disease with similar symptoms that they termed *fish poisoning.*[5] In 1897, van Ermengen published the first description of *C. botulinum* and showed that the organism elaborated a toxin that could induce weakness in animals.[6] This substance was subsequently shown to be type A toxin; type B was discovered in 1904.[7] Wound botulism was described in 1943[8] and infant botulism in 1976.[9] The occurrence of sporadic cases without an apparent etiology, many related to gastrointestinal colonization, was first reported in 1986.[10] Type A toxin was isolated and purified in 1946.[11]

EPIDEMIOLOGY

In the United States, type A botulism is found most commonly in the west and type B is more common in the east. This distribution mirrors that of the spore type found in those regions.[12] Type E is frequently associated with fish products.[13] Type F has a less defined geographic distribution. Wound botulism may be caused by either type A or type B organisms; infant botulism occurs with type A, B, or F. The infant form is often attributed to honey ingestion,[14] but other sources have emerged as feeding honey to infants has been discouraged.[15] Two infants without other exposure are believed to have contracted botulism via soil contamination.[16] Rare cases of infant botulism have been associated with *Clostridium baratii*[17] or *Clostridium butyricum.*[18] Adult botulism of unknown etiology usually involves type A toxin, but types B and F have also been implicated.[19] One adult case of type F botulism was caused by *C. baratii.*[20]

Foodborne botulism is most frequently recognized in outbreaks, whereas the other forms are sporadic. Although commercially canned foods were commonly the source of toxin in the early part of the 20th century, home-canned vegetables, fruits, and fish products are now the most common sources. In some cultures, such as among Alaskan natives, preferred food preparation practices involving fish fermentation commonly lead to botulism.[21] In China, homemade fermented beans are the leading cause.[22] Commercial foods and restaurants are still occasional sources.[23–25] Consumption of peyote for religious reasons has resulted in botulism.[26] The pH of the implicated products is usually greater than 4.6.[27]

One hundred twenty-four outbreaks of foodborne botulism were reported to the Centers for Disease Control and Prevention (CDC) between 1976 and 1984.[18] The mean number of cases in an outbreak was 2.7, and single cases or small outbreaks were usually related to home-prepared foods. Large outbreaks were associated with restaurants and accounted for over 40% of cases. Since 1973, the median number of reported cases per type is infant, 71; foodborne, 24; and wound, 3.[28] Before the advent of critical care, the case-fatality rate exceeded 60%; in the early 1970s, it was 23.1%.[29] The case-fatality rate for the period 1976 to 1984 was 7.5%. For patients older than 60 years, however, the fatality rate was 30%. The first (or only) patient in an outbreak has a 25% risk of death, whereas subsequent cases, in whom botulism is generally diagnosed and treated more quickly, carry only a 4% risk.[30]

CHARACTERISTICS OF *CLOSTRIDIUM BOTULINUM*

C. botulinum is a large, usually gram-positive, strictly anaerobic bacillus that forms a subterminal spore.[31] The species is divided into four physiologic groups. Group I organisms are proteolytic in culture and can produce toxin types A, B, or F. Group II organisms are nonproteolytic and can produce toxin types B, E, or F. Group III organisms produce toxin types C or D, whereas group IV produces type G. A single strain almost always produces only one toxin type. Group II organisms grow optimally between 25°C and 30°C, whereas the other groups grow best between 30°C and 37°C. Although each strain of the organism typically contains several plasmids, only type G toxin is encoded on one (c.f., *Clostridium tetani,* in which the toxin is encoded on a plasmid).[32]

C. botulinum spores are found throughout the world in soil samples and marine sediment.[33] These spores are able to tolerate 100°C at 1 atm for several hours; because boiling renders solutions more anaerobic, it may actually favor the growth of *C. botulinum.*[34] Proper preparation of food in a pressure cooker will kill spores.

PATHOGENESIS

In foodborne botulism, toxin is ingested with the food in which it was produced. It is absorbed primarily in the duodenum and jejunum and passes into the blood stream, by which it reaches peripheral cholinergic synapses (including the neuromuscular junction). In cases of wound botulism, spores are introduced into a wound, where they germinate and produce toxin. Wound botulism is increasingly associated with the intramuscular or subcutaneous injection of black tar heroin.[35] Infant botulism and probably adult botulism of unknown etiology follow the ingestion of spores. Achlorhydria and antibiotic use may predispose to gastrointestinal colonization with *C. botulinum.* The clinical manifestations of botulism depend on the type of toxin produced rather than the site of its production.

Botulinum toxin is synthesized as a single polypeptide chain of low potency; its molecular weight varies from 150 to 165 kD, depending on the toxin type. Botulinum toxins are zinc-dependent metalloproteinases,[36] as is tetanospasmin. It is then nicked by a bacterial protease to produce two chains, with the light chain constituting approximately one third of the total mass. As with tetanospasmin, the chains remain connected by a disulfide bond. The nicked toxin type A becomes, on a molecular weight basis, the most potent toxin found in nature. In contrast to the spores, the toxin is heat labile. Different toxin types may undergo different postsynthetic processing.[37]

Once present at the synapse, the toxin prevents the release of acetylcholine, apparently via a three-stage process.[38] The heavy chain of the toxin mediates binding to presynaptic receptors. The nature of these receptors is uncertain; different toxin types bind to different receptors, with type B receptors outnumbering type A receptors by a factor of 4.[39] The toxin enters the cell by receptor-mediated endocytosis.[40] Once inside the neuron, the toxin types differ in the mechanisms by which they inhibit acetylcholine release.[41] The release of synaptic vesicles by an action potential is initiated by an abrupt rise in the intracellular free Ca^{2+} concentration mediated by voltage-dependent calcium channels[42] (Fig. 235–1). This increase in free calcium triggers an interaction between synaptotagmin (in the vesicle membrane) and syntaxin (on the presynaptic cell membrane) that clamps the vesicle to the presynaptic membrane. Synaptobrevin (also referred to as vesicle-associated membrane protein[43]) also binds to syntaxin and appears to dock the vesicle to the membrane at the proper location for fusion. Different isoforms of synaptobrevin are found within neurons; a protein termed cellubrevin performs a similar function in non-neuronal secretory cells.[44] Synaptophysin, the third major component of this mechanism, probably forms the fusion pore that allows release of the vesicle contents into the synaptic cleft.[45]

Clostridial neurotoxins inhibit vesicle release by cleaving peptide bonds in these proteins.[46] Each toxin has a specific locus of activity. Tetanospasmin, along with botulinum neurotoxins B, D, F, and G, cleaves synaptobrevin.[47, 48] Tetanospasmin and botulinum neurotoxin B appear to share the same cleavage site on synaptobrevin.[49] In contrast, botulinum toxins A[50] and E act on a 25-kD synaptosomal-associated protein,[51] and botulinum toxin C1 affects syntaxin. The toxins only affect free proteins; once proteins have complexed to cause transmitter release, they are not subject to attack.[52] Synaptobrevin and synaptotagmin cleavage also occurs normally as an effect of an endogenous protease and are probably involved in organelle recycling.[53] The endogenous protease does not appear homologous to the clostridial toxins. However, the result is that stimulation of the presynaptic cell (e.g., the alpha motor neuron) fails to produce transmitter release, thus producing paralysis in the motor system or autonomic dysfunction when parasympathetic nerve terminals or autonomic ganglia are involved.

Once damaged, the synapse is apparently rendered permanently useless. Recovery of function requires sprouting of the presynaptic axon and subsequent formation of a new synapse.

Botulinum toxin is transported within nerves in a manner analogous to tetanospasmin and can thereby gain access to the central nervous system. However, symptomatic central nervous system involvement is rare.[54]

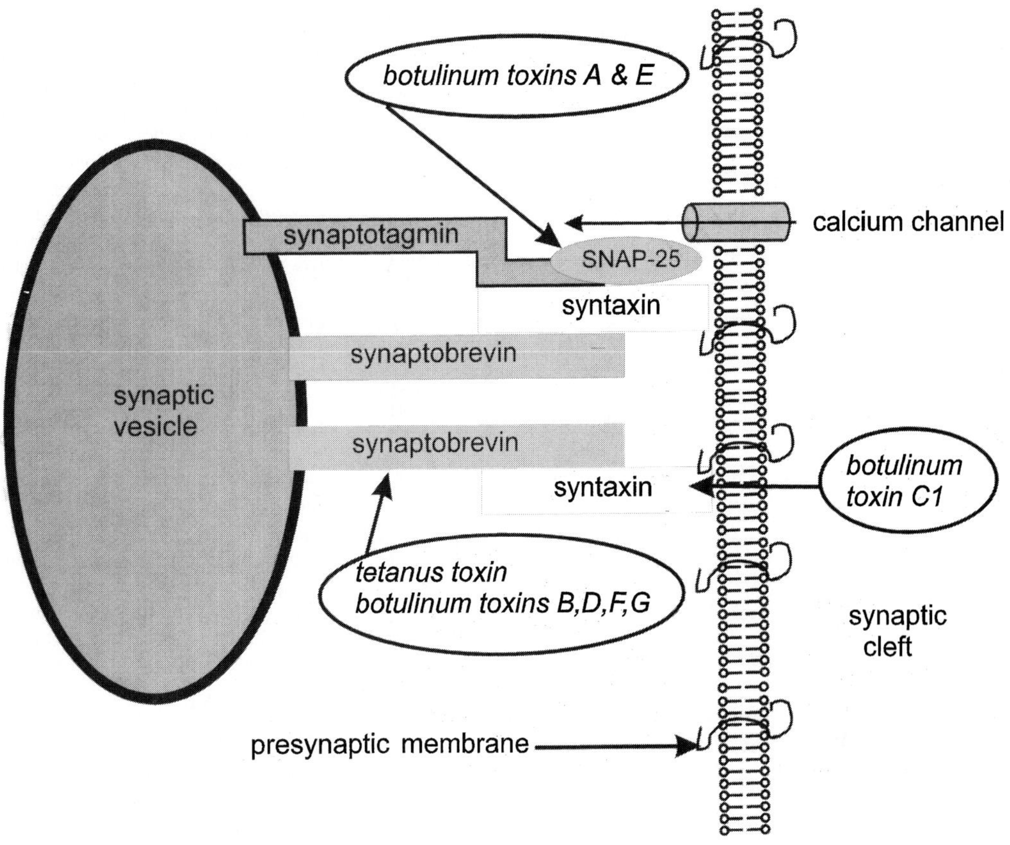

FIGURE 235–1. Components of the transmitter release mechanism. (From Bleck TP, Brauner JS. Tetanus. In: Scheld WM, Whitley RJ, Durack DT, eds. Infections of the Central Nervous System. 2nd ed. Philadelphia: Lippincott-Raven; 1997:629–653.)

CLINICAL MANIFESTATIONS

The classic picture of botulism is that of a patient in whom acute, bilateral cranial neuropathies develop in association with symmetric descending weakness. The CDC suggests attention to the following cardinal features: (1) fever is absent (unless a complicating infection occurs), (2) the neurologic manifestations are symmetric, (3) the patient remains responsive, (4) the heart rate is normal or slow in the absence of hypotension, and (5) sensory deficits do not occur (except for blurred vision).[20] The first two features were important for the exclusion of poliomyelitis; rare exceptions have been noted to most of these generalizations.

Foodborne botulism usually develops between 12 and 36 hours after toxin ingestion. The patient initially complains of nausea and a dry mouth, and diarrhea may occur at this stage. Evidence of cranial nerve dysfunction most commonly starts with the eyes; parasympathetic involvement causes blurred vision from pupillary dilation, or nerves III, IV, or VI may be involved.[55] Pupillary reactions may remain abnormal for months after motor recovery.[56] Nystagmus is occasionally noted, usually in type A disease. Lower cranial nerve dysfunction is manifested as dysphagia, dysarthria, and hypoglossal weakness. Weakness then spreads to the upper extremities, the trunk, and the lower extremities. Respiratory dysfunction may result from either upper airway obstruction (the weakened glottis tending to close during attempted inspiration) or diaphragmatic weakness. Patients requiring mechanical ventilation respectively require mean periods of 58 days (type A) and 26 days (type B) for ventilatory weaning.[57] Recovery may not begin for up to 100 days.[58] Autonomic problems may include gastrointestinal dysfunction, alterations in the resting heart rate, loss of responsiveness to hypotension or postural change, hypothermia, or urinary retention.[59]

Hughes and colleagues have summarized published reports to analyze differences in the clinical findings of intoxication with different toxin types[27] (see Table 235–1). Type A is significantly more commonly associated with dysarthria, blurred vision, dyspnea, diarrhea, sore throat, dizziness, ptosis, ophthalmoplegia, facial paresis, and upper extremely weakness. Types B and E appear to produce more autonomic dysfunction. None of these differences is diagnostic of the toxin type, however. It is important to note that the pupils are either dilated or unreactive in less than 50% of patients; although these signs are very useful when present, their absence in no way diminishes the likelihood of botulism.

Patients with infant botulism present with constipation, which may be followed by feeding difficulties, hypotonia, increased drooling, and a weak cry.[60] Upper airway obstruction may be the initial sign[61] and is the major indication for intubation.[62] In severe cases, the condition progresses to include cranial neuropathies and respiratory weakness, with ventilatory failure occurring in about 50% of patients with diagnosed botulism. The condition progresses for 1 to 2 weeks and then stabilizes for another 2 to 3 weeks before recovery starts.[25] Relapses of infant botulism may occur.[63]

Wound botulism lacks the prodromal gastrointestinal disorder of the foodborne form, but it is otherwise similar in signs and symptoms. Fever, if present, reflects wound infection rather than botulism. The wound itself may rarely appear to be healing well while neurologic manifestations are occurring. Conversely, *C. botulinum* infection may produce abscesses[64]; botulism has also been associated with *C. botulinum* sinusitis after cocaine inhalation.[65] The reported incubation period varies from 4 to 14 days.

Dysphagia and other symptoms of neuromuscular impairment have been reported rarely after the therapeutic use of botulinum A toxin.[66]

DIAGNOSIS

A history appropriate to the type of botulism suspected is the most important diagnostic test. If others are already affected, the condition is easily recognized. However, because the toxin may not be evenly

TABLE 235-1 Symptoms and Signs in Patients with the Common Types of Human Botulism

Sequelae	Type A (%)	Type B (%)	Type E (%)
Neurologic symptoms			
Dysphagia	96	97	82
Dry mouth	83	100	93
Diplopia	90	92	39
Dysarthria	100	69	50
Upper extremity weakness	86	64	NA
Lower extremity weakness	76	64	NA
Blurred vision	100	42	91
Dyspnea	91	34	88
Paresthesias	20	12	NA
Gastrointestinal symptoms			
Constipation	73	73	52
Nausea	73	57	84
Vomiting	70	50	96
Abdominal cramps	33	46	NA
Diarrhea	35	8	39
Miscellaneous symptoms			
Fatigue	92	69	84
Sore throat	75	39	38
Dizziness	86	30	63
Neurologic findings			
Ptosis	96	55	46
Diminished gag reflex	81	54	NA
Ophthalmoparesis	87	46	NA
Facial paresis	84	48	NA
Tongue weakness	91	31	66
Pupils fixed or dilated	33	56	75
Nystagmus	44	4	NA
Upper extremity weakness	91	62	NA
Lower extremity weakness	82	59	NA
Ataxia	24	13	NA
DTRs diminished or absent	54	29	NA
DTRs hyperactive	12	0	NA
Initial mental status			
Alert	88	93	27
Lethargic	4	4	73
Obtunded	8	4	0

Abbreviations: DTRs, Deep tendon reflexes; NA, not available.
Data from refs. 13, 27, and 34.

distributed in foodstuffs, the absence of other patients does not eliminate the diagnosis.

Botulism has a limited differential diagnosis. Myasthenia gravis and the Eaton-Lambert myasthenic syndrome each share some of the characteristics of botulism, but the former conditions are rarely fulminant and lack autonomic features. An edrophonium test may be considered, but an improvement in strength is not pathognomonic of myasthenia gravis and has been reported in botulism.[67] Tick paralysis is excluded by careful physical examination because the *Dermacentor* tick will still be attached. Classic acute inflammatory polyneuropathy (Guillain-Barré syndrome) frequently begins with sensory complaints, rapidly produces areflexia, rarely begins with cranial nerve dysfunction, and does not alter pupillary reactivity. Patients with botulism do not become areflexic until the affected muscle group is completely paralyzed. The Miller-Fisher variant of acute inflammatory polyneuropathy is characterized by oculomotor dysfunction and may produce other cranial neuropathies, but it includes a prominent ataxia that is lacking in botulism. Patients with polio are febrile on initial examination and have asymmetric weakness. Magnesium intoxication may mimic botulism.[68] Rarely, botulism may be confused with diphtheria, organophosphate poisoning, or brain stem infarction.[69]

Laboratory evaluation includes anaerobic cultures and toxin assays of serum, stool, and the implicated food if available. Confirmation and toxin typing are obtained in almost 75% of cases.[70] In early cases the diagnosis is more likely to be made by the toxin assay, whereas those studied later in the disease course are more likely to have a positive culture than a positive toxin assay.[71] Specimens should be obtained and sent in consultation with the appropriate epidemiologic officials (in the United States, the state epidemiologist and the CDC). The most sensitive test for toxin remains the mouse bioassay.[72] Serum from patients with acute inflammatory polyneuropathy can produce paralysis in mice, however, so the test is not completely specific.[73] Alternatively, the toxin may be detected by gel hydrolysis or enzyme-linked immunosorbent assay. Toxin excretion may continue up to 1 month after the onset of illness, and stool cultures may remain positive for a similar period.

Electrophysiologic studies reveal normal nerve conduction velocities; the amplitude of compound muscle action potentials is reduced in 85% of cases, although not all motor units may demonstrate this abnormality.[74] Repetitive nerve stimulation at high rates (20 Hz or greater, as compared with the 4-Hz rate used in the diagnosis of myasthenia gravis) may reveal a small increment in the motor response (Fig. 235–2). This test is very uncomfortable and should not be requested unless botulism or the Eaton-Lambert myasthenic syndrome is a serious consideration. Botulism can be distinguished electrophysiologically from the Eaton-Lambert syndrome.[75] In infant botulism, the increments may be very dramatic. In questionable cases, single-fiber electromyographic studies may be useful. Currently, the sensitivity of electrodiagnostic techniques is being debated in cases of infant botulism.[76] The therapeutic use of botulinum A toxin for dystonic disorders can produce electrophysiologic evidence of toxin dissemination to distant sites.[77]

TREATMENT

The importance of supportive therapy for botulism is underlined by the progressive improvement in mortality rates with advances in critical care, especially ventilatory support. The decision to intubate should be based on (1) bedside assessment of upper airway competency and (2) changes in vital capacity (in general, an appropriately performed vital capacity measurement below 12 ml/kg is frequently an indication for intubation). One should not wait for the P_{CO_2} to rise or the oxygen saturation to fall before intubating the patient. In contrast to tetanus, the autonomic dysfunction of botulism is rarely life threatening, and patients who receive appropriate airway and ventilator management should recover unless complications supervene. Patients intubated with high-volume, low-pressure endotracheal tubes should not automatically undergo tracheostomy, regardless of the duration of intubation, unless required for mechanical reasons.[78] A detailed account of the critical care management of botulism patients is beyond the scope of this text; Tacket and Rogawski have presented a useful approach.[34]

If contaminated food may still reside in the gastrointestinal tract, purgatives may be useful unless ileus has occurred.

Antitoxin therapy is usually carried out with a trivalent (types A, B, and E) equine serum; in the United States it is obtained from state health departments or the CDC (404-639-2206 workdays, 404-639-2888 other times). Its use is supported by inferential studies[30]; controlled clinical trials are lacking. Reported hypersensitivity rates vary between 9 and 20%.[79] Skin testing is performed before administering the antitoxin, and a regimen for desensitization is included in the package. The standard antitoxin dose is one vial intravenously and one vial intramuscularly; although the package insert recommends repeating the dose in 4 hours in severe or progressive cases, repeat dosing is not necessary.[80] Human botulinum immune globulin is not currently available outside clinical trials in infant botulism[81] (contact the Infant Botulism Prevention Program, California State Department of Health Services, 510-540-2646).

Patients with wound botulism should also undergo débridement, even if the wound appears to be healing well. Anaerobic cultures should be obtained at the time of surgery. The value of local instillation of antitoxin is unknown. The role of antibiotic treatment is untested, but penicillin G, 10 to 20 million units daily, is frequently recommended. Metronidazole may be an effective alternative. Aminoglycosides and tetracyclines, which can impair neuron calcium entry, worsen infant botulism.[82] Lysis of *C. botulinum* in the gut by

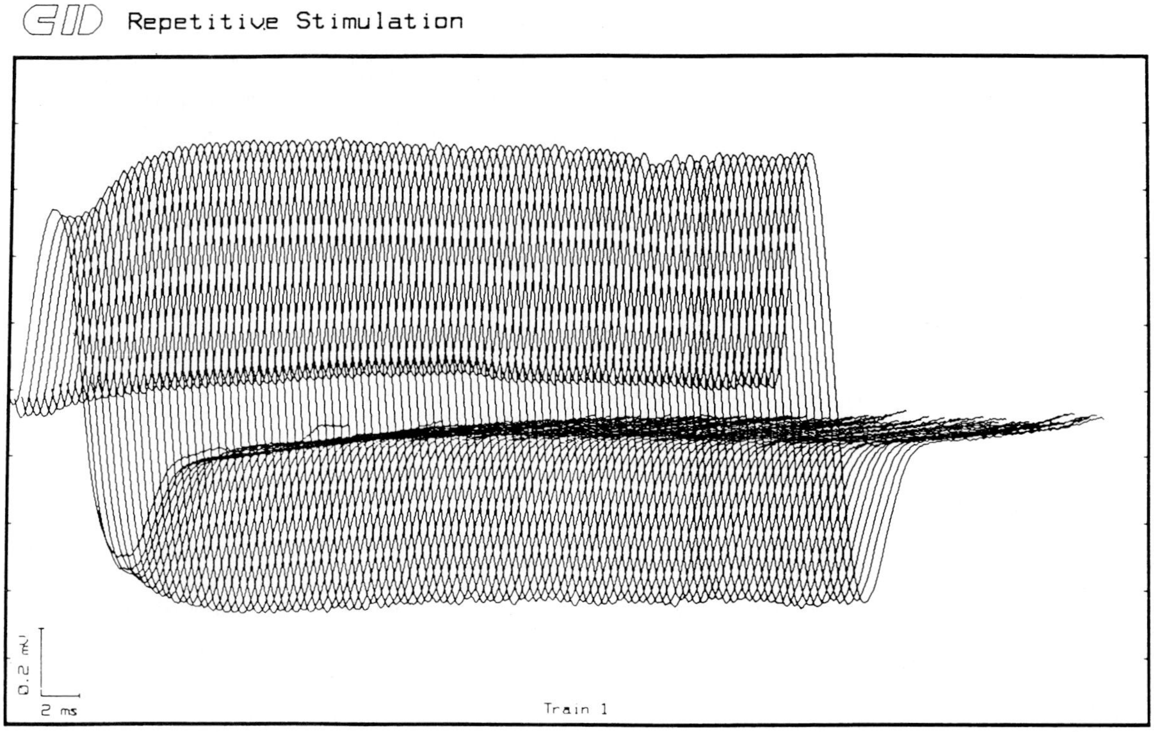

FIGURE 235–2. Repetitive nerve stimulation in infant botulism. Note the increment in response amplitude during the initial stimulations. (Courtesy of Vern Juel, MD, Department of Neurology and Laboratory of Electromyography, University of Virginia.)

antibiotics may also increase the toxin available in infant botulism.[80] This effect has not been reported in adult cases but should be considered when the gastrointestinal tract is a likely portal of entry for the infection.

Agents that may improve acetylcholine release at the neuromuscular junction have been tried in botulism without success. Guanidine has received the most attention,[83] and other drugs are under study.

Although the greatest improvement in muscle strength occurs in the first 3 months of recovery from botulism, patients still show improvement in strength and endurance for up to 1 year after disease onset.[84] Recovery from botulism may also be followed by persistent psychological dysfunction, which may require mental health intervention.[85]

PREVENTION

The most important aspect of botulism prevention is proper food handling and preparation. It is impractical or undesirable to treat many foods in a manner to eliminate *C. botulinum* spores; hence, methods for the control of botulism focus on the inhibition of bacterial growth and toxin production.[80] Because the toxin is heat labile, terminal boiling or similarly intense heating of contaminated food will inactivate it. Food containers that appear to bulge may contain gas produced by *C. botulinum* and should not be opened. Other foods that appear to be spoiled should not be tasted.

Immunity to botulinum toxin does not develop even with severe disease, and repeated occurrence has been reported.[86] An experimental vaccine is available for laboratory workers. A recombinant vaccine expressing the type A binding domain[87] or vaccination with the carboxy-terminal fragment[88] promises to make vaccination less expensive and painful.

REFERENCES

1. Todd ECD. Costs of acute bacterial foodborne disease in Canada and the United States. Int J Food Microbiol. 1989;9:313–326.
2. Hatheway CL. Bacterial sources of clostridial neurotoxins. In: Simpson LL, ed. Botulinum Neurotoxin and Tetanus Toxin. San Diego, Calif: Academic, 1989:4–25.
3. Oguma K, Yokota K, Hayashi S, et al. Infant botulism due to *Clostridium botulinum* type C toxin. Lancet. 1990;336:1449–1450.
4. Kerner J. Neue Beobachtungen über die in Würtemburg so haüfig vorfallen Vergiftung durch den Genuss gerauchter Würst. Tubingen, 1820. Quoted in Damon SR. Food Infections and Food Intoxications. Baltimore: Williams & Wilkins; 1928:67.
5. Young JH. Botulism and the ripe olive scare of 1919–1920. Bull History Med. 1976;50:372–391.
6. van Ermengen E. Ueber einen neuen anaëroben Bacillus und seine Beziehungen zum Botulismus. Z Hyg Infektionskrankh. 1897;26:1–56.
7. Landman G. Ueber die Ursache der Darmstadter Bohnen Vergiftung. Hyg Rundsch. 1904;14:449–452.
8. Davis JB, Mattman LH, Wiley M. *Clostridium botulinum* in a fatal wound infection. JAMA. 1951;146:646–648.
9. Midura TF, Arnon SS. Infant botulism: Identification of *Clostridium botulinum* and its toxin in faeces. Lancet. 1976;2:934–936.
10. Chia JK, Clark JB, Ryan CA, Pollack M. Botulism in an adult associated with foodborne intestinal infection with *Clostridium botulinum.* N Engl J Med. 1986;315:239–241.
11. Lamanna C, McElroy OE, Eklund HW. The purification and crystallization of *Clostridium botulinum* type A toxin. Science. 1946;103:613–614.
12. Smith LDS. The occurrence of *Clostridium botulinum* and *Clostridium tetani* in the soil of the United States. Health Lab Sci. 1978;15:74–80.
13. Weber JT, Hibbs RG, Darwish A, et al. A massive outbreak of type E botulism associated with traditional salted fish in Cairo. J Infect Dis. 1993;167:451–454.
14. Midura TF, Snowden S, Wood RM, et al. Isolation of *Clostridium botulinum* from honey. J Clin Microbiol. 1979;9:282–283.
15. Spika JS, Shaffer N, Hargrett-Bean N, et al. Infant botulism in the United States: An epidemiologic study of cases occurring outside of California. Am J Public Health. 1983;73:1385–1388.
16. Hurst DL, Marsh WW. Early severe infantile botulism. J Pediatr. 1993;122:909–911.
17. Gimenez JA, Gimenez MA, DasGupta BR. Characterization of the neurotoxin isolated from a *Clostridium baratii* strain implicated in infant botulism. Infect Immun. 1992;60:518–522.
18. Suen JC, Hatheway CL, Steigerwalt AG, et al. Genetic confirmation of the identities of neurotoxigenic *Clostridium baratii* and *Clostridium butyricum* implicated as agents of human botulism. J Clin Microbiol. 1988;26:2191–2192.
19. MacDonald KL, Cohen ML, Blake PA. The changing epidemiology of adult botulism in the United States. Am J Epidemiol. 1986;124:794–799.
20. McCroskey LM, Hatheway CL, Woodruff BA, et al. Type F botulism due to neurotoxigenic *Clostridium baratii* from an unknown source in an adult. J Clin Microbiol. 1991;29:2618–2620.
21. Shaffer N, Wainwright RB, Middaugh JP, Tauxe RV. Botulism among Alaska

Natives. The role of changing food preparation and consumption practices. West J Med. 1990;153:390–393.
22. Gao QY, Huang YF, Wu JG, et al. A review of botulism in China. Biomed Environ Sci. 1990;3:326–336.
23. Centers for Disease Control. Botulism and commercial pot pie—California. MMWR Morb Mortal Wkly Rep. 1983;32:39–40, 45.
24. Pourshafie MR, Saifie M, Shafiee A, et al. An outbreak of food-borne botulism associated with contaminated locally made cheese in Iran. Scand J Infect Dis. 1998;30:92–94.
25. Angulo FJ, Getz J, Taylor JP, et al. A large outbreak of botulism: The hazardous baked potato. J Infect Dis. 1998;178:172–177.
26. Hashimoto H, Clyde VJ, Parko KL. Botulism from peyote. N Engl J Med. 1998;339:203–204.
27. Hughes JM, Hatheway CL, Ostroff SM. Botulism. In Scheld WM, Whitley RJ, Durack DT, eds. Infections of the Central Nervous System. 2nd ed. Philadelphia: Lippincott-Raven; 1997:615–628.
28. Shapiro RL, Hatheway C, Swerdlow DL. Botulism in the United States: A clinical and epidemiologic review. Ann Intern Med. 1998;129:221–228.
29. Centers for Disease Control. Botulism in the United States, 1899–1973. Handbook for Epidemiologists, Clinicians, and Laboratory Workers. Atlanta: Department of Health, Education and Welfare, 1974.
30. Tacket CO, Shandera WX, Mann JM, et al. Equine antitoxin use and other factors that predict outcome in type A foodborne botulism. Am J Med. 1984;76:794–798.
31. Cato EP, George WL, Finegold SM. Genus *Clostridium praemozski* 1880, 23[AL]. In: Smeath PHA, Mair NS, Sharpe ME, Holt JG, eds. Bergey's Manual of Systematic Bacteriology, v. 2. Baltimore: Williams & Wilkins; 1986:1141–1200.
32. Eklund MW, Poysky FT, Habig WH. Bacteriophages and plasmids in *Clostridium botulinum* and *Clostridium tetani* and their relationship to the production of toxin. In: Simpson LL, ed. Botulinum Neurotoxin and Tetanus Toxin. San Diego, Calif: Academic; 1989:25–51.
33. Hauschild AHW. *Clostridium botulinum.* In: Doyle MP, ed. Foodborne Bacterial Pathogens. New York: Marcel Dekker; 1989:112–189.
34. Tacket CO, Rogawski MA. Botulism. In: Simpson LL, ed. Botulinum Neurotoxin and Tetanus Toxin. San Diego, Calif: Academic Press; 1989:351–378.
35. Passaro DJ, Werner SB, McGee J, et al. Wound botulism associated with black tar heroin among injecting drug users. JAMA. 1998;279:859–863.
36. Fu FN, Lomneth RB, Cai S, Singh BR. Role of zinc in the structure and toxic activity of botulinum neurotoxin. Biochemistry. 1998;37:5267–5278.
37. Critchley EMR, Mitchell JD. Human botulism. Br J Hosp Med. 1992;43:290–292.
38. Simpson LL. Kinetic studies on the interaction between botulinum toxin type A and the cholinergic neuromuscular junction. J Pharmacol Exp Ther. 1980;212:16–21.
39. Black JD, Dolly JO. Interaction of ^{125}I-labeled botulinum neurotoxins with nerve terminals. I. Ultrastructural autoradiographic localization and quantitation of distinct membrane acceptors for types A and B on motor nerves. J Cell Biol. 1986;103:521–534.
40. Black JD, Dolly JO. Interaction of ^{125}I-labeled botulinum neurotoxins with nerve terminals. II. Autoradiographic evidence for its uptake into motor nerves by receptor-mediated endocytosis. J Cell Biol. 1986;103:535–544.
41. Simpson LL. Peripheral actions of the botulinum toxins. In: Simpson LL, ed. Botulinum Neurotoxin and Tetanus Toxin. San Diego, Calif: Academic Press, 1989:153–178.
42. Bleck TP, Brauner JS. Tetanus. In: Scheld WM, Whitley RJ, Durack DT, eds. Infections of the central nervous system. 2nd ed. New York: Raven; Press, 1997:629–653.
43. Trimble WS, Cowan D, Scheller RH. VAMP-1: A synaptic vesicle associated integral membrane protein. Proc Natl Acad Sci U S A. 1988;85:4538–4542.
44. McMahon HT, Ushkaryov YA, Edelmann L, et al. Cellubrevin is a ubiquitous tetanus-toxin substrate homologous to a putative synaptic vesicle fusion protein. Nature. 1993;364:346–349.
45. Buckley KM, Floor E, Kelly RB. Cloning and sequence analysis of cDNA encoding p38, a major synaptic vesicle protein. J Cell Biol. 1987;105:2447–2456.
46. Blasi J, Binz T, Yamasaki S, et al. Inhibition of neurotransmitter release by clostridial neurotoxins correlates with specific proteolysis of synaptosomal proteins. J Physiol Paris. 1994:88:235–241.
47. Schiavo G, Benfenati F, Poulain B, et al. Tetanus and botulinum-B neurotoxins block neurotransmitter release by proteolytic cleavage of synaptobrevin. Nature. 1992;359:832–835.
48. Nowakowski JL, Courtney BC, Bing QA, Adler M. Production of an expression system for a synaptobrevin fragment to monitor cleavage by botulinum neurotoxin B. J Protein Chem. 1998;17:453–462.
49. Foran P, Shone CC, Dolly JO. Differences in the protease activities of tetanus and botulinum B toxins revealed by the cleavage of vesicle-associated membrane protein and various sized fragments. Biochemistry. 1994;33:15365–15374.
50. Lacy DB, Tepp W, Cohen AC, et al. Crystal structure of botulinum neurotoxin type A and implications for toxicity. Nat Struct Biol. 1998;5:898–902.
51. Sciavo G, Santussi A, Dasgupta BR, et al. Botulinum neurotoxins serotypes A and E cleave SNAP-25 at distinct COOH-terminal peptide bonds. FEBS Lett. 1993;335:99–103.
52. Hayashi T, McMahon H, Yamasaki S, et al. Synaptic vesicle membrane fusion complex: Action of clostridial neurotoxins on assembly. EMBO J. 1994;13:5051–5061.
53. Hausinger A, Volknandt W, Zimmerman H. Calcium-dependent endogenous proteolysis of the vesicle proteins synaptobrevin and synaptotagmin. Neuroreport. 1995;6:637–641.
54. Jones S, Huma Z, Haugh C, et al. Central nervous system involvement in infantile botulism. Lancet 1990;335:228.
55. Terranova W, Palumbo JN, Berman JG. Ocular findings in botulism type B. JAMA. 1979;241:475–477.
56. Friedman DI, Fortanasce VN, Sadun AA. Tonic pupils as a result of botulism. Am J Ophthalmol. 1990;109:236–237.
57. Hughes JM, Blumenthal JR, Merson MH, et al. Clinical features of types A and B foodborne botulism. Ann Intern Med. 1981;95:442–445.
58. Colerbatch JG, Wolff AH, Gilbert RJ, et al. Slow recovery from severe foodborne botulism. Lancet. 1989;2:1216–1217.
59. Vita G, Girlanda P, Puglisi RM, et al. Cardiovascular-reflex testing and single-fiber electromyography in botulism. A longitudinal study. Arch Neurol. 1987;44:202–206.
60. Cornblath DR, Sladky JT, Summer AJ. Clinical electrophysiology of infantile botulism. Muscle Nerve. 1983;6:448–452.
61. Oken A, Barnes S, Rock P, Maxwell L. Upper airway obstruction and infant botulism. Anesth Analg. 1992;75:136–138.
62. Schreiner MS, Field E, Ruddy R. Infant botulism: A review of 12 years experience at the Children's Hospital of Philadelphia. Pediatrics. 1991;87:159–165.
63. Glauser TA, Maquire HC, Sladky JT. Relapse of infant botulism. Ann Neurol. 1990;28:187–189.
64. Elston HR, Wang M, Loo LK. Arm abscesses caused by *Clostridium botulinum.* J Clin Microbiol. 1991;29:2678–2679.
65. Kudrow DB, Henry DA, Haake DA, et al. Botulism associated with *Clostridium botulinum* sinusitis after intranasal cocaine abuse. Ann Intern Med. 1988;109:984–985.
66. Comella CL, Tanner CM, DeFoor-Hill L, Smith C. Dysphagia after botulinum toxin injections for spasmodic torticollis: Clinical and radiologic findings. Neurology. 1992;42:1307–1310.
67. Edell TA, Sullivan CP, Osborn KM, et al. Wound botulism associated with a positive Tensilon test. West J Med. 1983;139:218–219.
68. Cherington M. Botulism. Semin Neurol. 1990;10:27–31.
69. Dunbar EM. Botulism. J Infect. 1990;20:1–3.
70. Dowell VR, McCroskey LM, Hatheway CL, et al. Coproexamination for botulinal toxin and *Clostridium botulinum.* A new procedure for laboratory diagnosis of botulism. JAMA. 1977;238:1829–1832.
71. Woodruff BA, Griffin PM, McCroskey LM, et al. Clinical and laboratory comparison of botulism from toxin type A, B, and E in the United States, 1975–1988. J Infect Dis. 1992;166:1281–1286.
72. Notermans S, Nagel J. Assays for botulinum and tetanus toxins. In Simpson LL, ed. Botulinum neurotoxin and tetanus toxin. San Diego, Calif: Academic; 1989:319–331.
73. Notermans SHW, Wokke JHJ, van den Berg LH. Botulism and Guillain-Barré syndrome. Lancet. 1992;340:303.
74. Cherington M. Electrophysiologic methods as an aid in diagnosis of botulism. A review. Muscle Nerve. 1982;6:528–529.
75. Gutmann L, Pratt L. Pathophysiologic aspects of human botulism. Arch Neurol. 1976;33:175–179.
76. Graf W, Hays RM, Astley SJ, Mendelman PM. Electrodiagnosis reliability in the diagnosis of infant botulism. J Pediatr. 1992;120:747–749.
77. Buchman AS, Comella CL, Stebbins GT, et al. Quantitative electromyographic analysis of changes in muscle activity following botulinum toxin therapy for cervical dystonia. Clin Neuropharmacol. 1993;16:205–210.
78. Barrett DH. Endemic food-borne botulism: Clinical experience, 1973–1986. Alaska Med. 1991;33:101–108.
79. Black RE, Gunn RA. Hypersensitivity reactions associated with botulinal antitoxin. Am J Med. 1980;69:567–570.
80. Centers for Disease Control and Prevention. Botulism in the United States 1899–1996. Handbook for Epidemiologists, Clinicians, and Laboratory Workers (Draft). Atlanta: Centers for Disease Control and Prevention; 1998.
81. Frankovich TL, Arnon SS. Clinical trial of botulism immune globulin for infant botulism. West J Med. 1991;154:103.
82. Wilson R, Morris JG, Snyder JD, Feldman RA. Clinical characteristics of infant botulism in the United States: A study of the non-California cases. Pediatr Infect Dis. 1982;1:148–150.
83. Kaplan JE, Davis LE, Narayan V, et al. Botulism, type A, and treatment with guanidine. Ann Neurol. 1979;6:69–71.
84. Wilcox PG, Morrison NJ, Pardy RL. Recovery of the ventilatory and upper airway muscles and exercise performance after type A botulism. Chest. 1990;98:620–626.
85. Cohen FL, Hardin SB, Nehring SB, et al. Physical and psychosocial health status 3 years after catastrophic illness—botulism. Issues Mental Health Nurs. 1988;9:387–398.
86. Beller M, Middaugh JP. Repeated type E botulism in an Alaskan Eskimo. N Engl J Med. 1990;322:855.
87. Byrne MP, Smith TJ, Montgomery VA, Smith LA. Purification, potency, and efficacy of the botulinum neurotoxin type A binding domain from *Pichia pastoris* as a recombinant vaccine candidate. Infect Immun. 1998;66:4817–4822.
88. Oshima M, Hayakari M, Middlebrook JL, Atassi MZ. Immune recognition of botulinum neurotoxin type A: Regions recognized by T cells and antibodies against the protective H(C) fragment (residues 855–1296) of the toxin. Mol Immunol. 1997;34:1031–1040.

Chapter 236

Gas Gangrene and Other *Clostridium*-Associated Diseases

BENNETT LORBER

The genus *Clostridium* includes all anaerobic, gram-positive spore-forming bacilli. Species can be readily isolated from soil and the intestinal tract of humans and many animals. Some produce potent exotoxins that are responsible for clinically distinctive syndromes.

MICROBIOLOGY

Almost 90 species of *Clostridium* are recognized.[1] Fewer than 20 of these species are associated with clinical illness in humans.[2] Cell wall structure, as seen by electron microscopy, indicates that clostridia are gram-positive bacteria. Many strains, however, appear gram-negative or gram-variable. Loss of gram-positive appearance occurs most frequently in direct stains of clinical material, in cultures after incubation for extended periods, and in species showing terminal spores. These straight or slightly curved rods may vary in length and width, and the ends may be rounded, blunt, or tapered. Cells may occur singly, in pairs, or in short or long chains. Clostridial species vary in oxygen tolerance, motility, nutritional requirements, and limiting or optimal temperatures for growth. Some organisms such as *Clostridium histolyticum* and *Clostridium tertium* are relatively aerotolerant and may actually replicate, but not sporulate, with aerobic incubation. Other species such as *Clostridium novyi* and *Clostridium haemolyticum* are strict anaerobes and will not replicate when oxygen concentrations exceed 0.05%. Aerotolerant clostridia may be confused with *Bacillus* spp. Distinction is usually made easily by showing that *Bacillus* spp. produce catalase and fail to produce spores when grown anaerobically whereas clostridia infrequently produce catalase and rarely produce spores when grown aerobically.

Endospores are oval or spherical and usually distend the cell. Some strains such as *Clostridium perfringens,* the most common clinical isolate, and *Clostridium ramosum* do not readily form spores. Most clostridia, however, will sporulate at incubation temperatures below those required for optimal growth, usually 30°C. Spore formation is optimally stimulated by heating starch-broth cultures to 70°C to 80°C for 10 minutes (heat shock) or by ethanol shock using an equal volume of 95% ethanol for 45 minutes with subsequent demonstration of survival by incubation at conventional temperatures. Speciation is largely based on morphology; location of spores as central, terminal, or subterminal; biochemical reactions; and gas-liquid chromatography to distinguish products of fermentation (Table 236–1).

The production of lecithinase (α-toxin, phospholipase C) may be demonstrated by growth on agar plates containing egg yolk. When α-toxin is present, a zone of opaque precipitate surrounds colonial growth and is due to lysis of the lecithin in the medium. The reaction may be inhibited by the addition of polyvalent gas gangrene antitoxin to the medium (Nagler reaction). The Nagler reaction cannot be used to identify *C. perfringens* definitively, but *C. perfringens* is clearly the most common lecithinase-producing *Clostridium* species found in clinical specimens. Egg-yolk agar may also be used to demonstrate lipase production. Lipase-producing organisms such as *Clostridium botulinum, Clostridium sporogenes,* and *C. novyi* type A break down free fats in the egg yolk to liberate free fatty acids, which appear as an oily, iridescent sheen. Other characteristics commonly used to distinguish species include the ability to ferment various carbohydrates, hydrolyze gelatin, and digest the casein in milk.[1, 3] Microbiology laboratories should be able to speciate *C. perfringens* because of its importance in clinical medicine, frequency of recovery, and ease of identification. *Clostridium septicum* should also be identifiable because its growth from blood or untraumatized tissue often indicates underlying bowel pathology. The need to speciate other clostridia is controversial.

Clostridia are ubiquitous and found in soil, decaying vegetation, marine sediment, and the intestinal tract of humans, other vertebrates, and insects. They are also commonly recovered from infected sites but usually as a component of a polymicrobial flora, which makes their role in pathogenesis difficult to establish. The most characeristic and well-documented clostridial diseases are the histotoxic syndromes, in which specific clostridial toxins appear to be responsible for the pathophysiology of the disease process (Table 236–2). Diagnosis in these cases requires recovery of the putative agent or demonstration of the implicated toxin.

Industrially, clostridia are used to produce acids and alcohols and serve as markers for adequate sterilization of canned foods and medical equipment.

Clostridium perfringens

First described by Veillon and Zuber[4] in 1898, *C. perfringens* (formerly *Clostridium welchii*) is the most frequent clinical isolate of *Clostridium.* It may be found in various clinical sources and is responsible for three distinctive histotoxic clostridial syndromes (see Table 236–2). Its major habitats are soil and the intestines of humans and animals. Virtually every soil sample ever examined, with the exception of the sands of the Sahara, has been shown to contain *C. perfringens.*[5, 6] This organism has also been found in stool specimens from virtually every vertebrate animal investigated, including pets, wild and domesticated herd animals, carnivores, rodents, birds, marine mammals, and humans.[5–8] Studies of fecal flora by Finegold and colleagues showed that *C. perfringens* was recovered from 28 of 40 adult subjects in mean concentrations of approximately 10^9/g.[8]

C. perfringens is nonmotile and generally has a distinctive "boxcar" appearance on Gram stain of clinical material or subcultures. The oval, central spores are rarely seen in clinical specimens or in

TABLE 236–1 Differential Features of Clinically Important Clostridia

Species	Lecithinase*	Spores	Motility	β-Hemolysis	Ferment Lactose	Ferment Glucose	H_2S	Urease	Indole	Nitrate Reduction
C. perfringens	+	C	0	+	+	+	+	0	0	+
C. septicum	0	ST	+	+	+	+	+	0	0	+
C. novyi	+	ST	+	+	0	+	+	0	0	+
C. sordellii	+	C	+	+	0	+	+	+	+	+
C. histolyticum	0	ST	+	+	0	0	+	0	0	0
C. difficile	0	ST	+	0	0	+	0	0	0	0
C. tetani	0	T	+	+	0	0	0	0	+	0
C. botulinum	0	ST	+	+	0	+	+	0	0	0

*Determined by Nagler reaction.
Abbreviations: C, Central; ST, subterminal; T, terminal.

TABLE 236–2 Histotoxic Clostridial Syndromes

Clinical Illness	Organism	Toxin	Mouse LD_{50} (ng)*
Soft tissue infection			
Gas gangrene	*C. perfringens*	α-Toxin (others)	50
Enteric diseases			
Food poisoning	*C. perfringens* type A	Enterotoxin	1400
Enteritis necroticans	*C. perfringens* type C	β-Toxin	8
Antibiotic-associated colitis	*C. difficile*	Toxin A	26 (ip)
Neutropenic enterocolitis	*C. septicum* (others)	Unknown, β-toxin?	
Neurologic syndromes			
Tetanus	*C. tetani*	Tetanospasmin	0.015 (ip)
Botulism	*C. botulinum*	Botulinal toxins A–G	0.00625 (type A, ip)

*Lethal dose for 50% of animals (LD_{50}) after intravenous challenge unless otherwise noted.
Abbreviation: ip, Intraperitoneal.

cultures grown in the usual laboratory media.[9] All types produce lecithinase (α-toxin), which can be demonstrated with the Nagler reaction. *C. perfringens,* one of the easiest of all obligate anaerobes to grow, replicates rapidly under anaerobic conditions with a generation time as short as 8 minutes at 43°C to 45°C. The organism is relatively aerotolerant and shows "stormy fermentation" in milk. On blood agar, the colonies are typically surrounded by a "double zone of hemolysis": an inner zone of complete hemolysis that is due to θ-toxin and a larger outer zone of incomplete hemolysis that is due to α-toxin. Virtually all large series indicate that *C. perfringens* is the most common clinical isolate among clostridia, including blood cultures and cultures from infected sites such as intra-abdominal sepsis, genital tract infections, and soft tissue infections.[10–12]

With regard to the genus *Clostridium,* the term *toxin* refers to biologically active proteins that are antigenic and capable of neutralization by specific antisera. Many are lethal to animals.[2] Among the 12 toxins produced by *C. perfringens* are 4 major lethal toxins that are used to divide the species into five serologic types classified A to E. Additional virulence factors include enterotoxin, neuraminidase (sialidase), non–α-δ-θ-hemolysins, and the organism's vigorous metabolic activity.[2, 10] Only type A strains are found in the microflora of both soil and the intestine. Because these strains are found in the soil as vegetative cells, it is assumed that soil is a natural habitat. When types B to E are added to soil, they are gradually eliminated over a period of months, thus indicating an inability to compete with the native type A strains.[11]

INFECTIONS

Clostridial species may be recovered from a wide variety of commonly encountered infections, usually as a component of a polymicrobial flora. In most instances, no distinctive features are noted, and the role of *Clostridium* spp. in the pathogenesis of infection is problematic. The common denominator of these infections is that they are endogenous and reflect the normal habitat of clostridia on the skin and mucous membranes of the host. Unique features of clostridial infection that characterize a minority of cases are the production of gas at the infected site and histotoxic clostridial syndromes that reflect the activity of specific toxins; rarely, massive intravascular hemolysis may be seen.[12, 13] Most *Clostridium* spp. produce large amounts of volatile fatty acids in vitro. Production of hydrogen and nitrogen gas in vivo presumably accounts for the finding in some patients of gas at the infected site that may be detected by palpation, radiograph, or scans. Examples include crepitant cellulitis, emphysematous cholecystitis, and emphysematous cystitis. In each instance, other pathogens have also been implicated as causes of these conditions. At least 30 clostridial species have been isolated from infected sites; *C. perfringens,* the dominant species, accounts for about 20 to 30% of all isolates. The histotoxic clostridial syndromes (see Table 236–2) are discussed later and elsewhere in this text (see Chapters 84, 234, and 235).

Bacteremia

The frequency of anaerobic bacteremia appears to be declining.[14–16] *Clostridium* spp., second only to *Bacteroides* spp. as clinically significant anaerobic isolates, account for less than 3% of all blood cultures, but the higher rates seen in cancer hospitals reflect the importance of underlying intestinal carcinoma and leukemia.[17] *C. perfringens* is the most common isolate, followed by *C. septicum.*[17, 18] Clostridial endocarditis is rare but has been reported to occur on native valves as well as vascular prostheses.[19] In many instances, no obvious association can be found between the underlying illness and clostridial bacteremia, and one has the impression that the bacteremia often represents either contamination, presumably from the skin, or transient bacteremia of no clinical consequence. As many as 50% of clostridial isolates are judged to be contaminants. An early study noting the paradox of bacteremia with a potentially lethal pathogen producing no obvious clinical consequence was reported by Ramsay.[20] He observed 28 women with clostridial bacteremia associated with septic abortion, all of whom had a benign, self-limited course despite the lack of any specific antibiotic treatment. Similar observations were noted in 1975 by Gorbach and Thadepalli, who reviewed their experience with positive blood culture of 65 strains of clostridia from 49 patients seen at Cook County Hospital.[21] The authors found that clostridial bacteremia was usually unrelated to the clinical syndrome and occurred in such settings as pulmonary tuberculosis, aspiration pneumonia, and meningococcemia. Their interpretation was that the organism was either a contaminant or simply caused transient bacteremia of no clinical importance. Other investigators have made similar observations,[20, 22] but some more recent studies have suggested a much higher percentage of clinically significant isolates.[19, 23] In some clinical settings such as intra-abdominal and soft tissue infections, decubitus ulcers, or gynecologic infections, clostridial isolates from the blood may be associated with the microbial flora of the infected site without the devastating consequences of clostridial toxins. A clear-cut clinical relevance is found in a minority of conditions, such as infections associated with gas production, clostridial myonecrosis (gas gangrene), and *C. septicum* bacteremia in association with colon carcinoma or leukemia. An underlying bowel source is found in most clinically significant bacteremias.[23, 24] The dominant clostridial species isolated from blood culture, regardless of clinical significance, is *C. perfringens,* which accounts for 25 to 50%.[19, 21, 25] Polymicrobial bacteremia reflecting an intestinal source is seen in about one third, with other isolates usually being *Bacteroides* spp. and Enterobacteriaceae.[18, 19, 23]

C. septicum bacteremia appears to be a unique syndrome associated with specific underlying diseases and a devastating clinical course.[26–28] Toxins produced in vivo by this organism include lecithinase, deoxyribonuclease, hyaluronidase, and a hemolysin. *C. septicum* is a relatively rare cause of gas gangrene and has been infrequently encountered in positive blood cultures for clostridia; at the Mayo Clinic during a 15-month review period, it accounted for only 3 of 360 cultures.[25] When *C. septicum* bacteremia occurs, 70 to 80%

of cases are associated with malignancies, most frequently leukemia in relapse or colon carcinoma. In some instances, isolation of *C. septicum* from blood culture preceded the identification of malignancy; the finding of *C. septicum* bacteremia mandates imaging of the lower intestine to rule out a carcinoma.[26, 27, 29, 30] An association is also seen with cyclic neutropenia, but not other forms of congenital severe neutropenia and neutropenia secondary to leukemia and cytotoxic drugs.[25, 31–33] As many as 25% of patients with *C. septicum* bacteremia will have myonecrosis at metastatic sites,[25, 27, 28, 34] and others may have unusual manifestations, including meningitis,[35] osteomyelitis,[36] septic arthritis,[37] panophthalmitis,[38] facial cellulitis,[39] splenic abscess,[40] and endocarditis.[41] *C. septicum* is a less common isolate in normal flora studies than *C. perfringens* is; it is recovered in stool in only about 2% of cases, although carriage rates in the appendix are reported at 10 to 63%.[42]

C. tertium is second to *C. septicum* as a cause of bacteremia in the setting of neutropenic enterocolitis.[43] Clostridial bacteremia has been reported in association with acquired immunodeficiency syndrome,[23] and *Clostridium sordellii,* a rare cause of bacteremia, has produced fatal infection after liver biopsy in a liver transplant recipient.[44]

Intra-abdominal Infections

Clostridia are constant inhabitants of the intestine and are commonly encountered in endogenous infections involving bowel flora, including secondary peritonitis, intra-abdominal abscess, and wound infections after intestinal surgery. Isolation rates from intra-abdominal infections range from approximately 10 to 50% when appropriate anaerobic culture techniques are used[45–50]; in polymicrobial infections, many isolates are species other than *C. perfringens.*[49] The great majority of these infections are polymicrobial, and the pathogenic significance of the clostridial isolates is unknown. Exceptions are the association of colon carcinoma with *C. septicum* bacteremia, as reviewed in the previous section, along with emphysematous cholecystitis and neutropenic enterocolitis (see earlier).

Biliary Tract Infections

Clostridia have been isolated from 10 to 20% of all diseased gallbladders at surgery.[51–53] Usually, the organism can be visualized by Gram stain of bile obtained at surgery. Cholecystitis involving clostridial species is similar to that caused by other organisms with two exceptions. First, clostridia in bile are the presumed source for gas gangrene of the abdominal wall, a rare but catastrophic complication of biliary tract surgery. The second exception is emphysematous cholecystitis, in which radiographs show gas in the gallbladder lumen, pericholecystic tissue, or biliary ducts.[54–56] Clostridia, particularly *C. perfringens,* are implicated in more than 50% of cases. At surgery the gallbladder is usually tense, gas is present under pressure in the lumen, the mucosa is gangrenous and often separated from the muscularis, pericholecystic abscess formation is common, and the gallbladder luminal contents are putrid and purulent. This severe form of biliary tract infection is most frequent in patients with diabetes and in men. The finding of gas in the biliary tract on radiography or computed tomography is a clear indication for early surgical intervention and antimicrobial treatment directed against clostridia, along with other enteric bacteria.

Female Genital Tract Infections

Clostridia are isolated from 4 to 20% of women with genital tract infections not involving sexually transmitted pathogens.[57–60] The most frequent conditions are tuboovarian and pelvic abscesses. These organisms have been recovered as part of normal vaginal flora in approximately 5 to 10% of women, and when present, the mean concentration was 10^8/ml of vaginal secretion.[61, 62] In the postabortion period, the isolation frequency has been reported to be 19 to 29%.[63] Consequently, cultures or stains of specimens that are subject to contamination with vaginal flora, as well as most clostridia isolated from deep infected sites or even blood, cannot be meaningfully interpreted. As reviewed earlier, Ramsay considered clostridia "benign saprophytes" in blood cultures of women with septic abortion.[20] Similar observations have been noted by others.[21, 64–66] A notable exception in which clostridia clearly play a major pathogenic role is uterine gas gangrene, now a rare complication that was previously seen in the setting of septic abortion. Rarely, uterine gas gangrene has followed vaginal delivery or cesarean section or has complicated a uterine tumor or amniocentesis.[67, 68] *C. sordellii* has been reported as a cause of uterine gas gangrene and as a possible agent of a toxic shock–like syndrome.[69] Debate continues about the role of hysterectomy in the management of clostridial uterine infection.[64, 66, 67]

Pleuropulmonary Infections

Clostridia have been recovered from 8 to 10% of anaerobic pulmonary infections, with *C. perfringens* accounting for half of the isolates.[70] These organisms have been reported primarily in empyema fluid but also from transtracheal aspirates.[70] In many cases the clostridia are part of a polymicrobial flora.[21, 71] In fewer than 20 English literature reports, clostridia have been recovered as the only isolates; the species is usually *C. perfringens.*[72–77] Aspiration of oropharyngeal flora has been considered to be the likely pathophysiologic mechanism in some cases, although clostridia are uncommonly isolated from typical aspiration pneumonia cases and never in pure culture.[78, 79] Occasional cases have occurred after penetrating chest injury or thoracotomy for lung resection,[80, 81] and several patients have had antecedent thoracentesis or pleural biopsy, thus suggesting an iatrogenic cause.[74] Less often, a hematogenous source has been suggested by cases complicating pulmonary infarction.[77] The clinical features of these infections are similar to those involving other anaerobic bacteria, although an occasional case is characterized by extensive gas production in the pleural space[72, 73] or extensive necrosis of tissue and a rapidly progressive course.[72, 75] Patients may be afebrile when first examined and without cough; pleuritic pain and pleural effusion are common. The mortality rate is similar to that for pleuropulmonary infections involving other anaerobic bacteria.[70]

Central Nervous System Infections

Intracranial infections involving *Clostridium* spp. are rare.[82–88] The great majority are manifested as cerebral abscess, with or without meningitis. Most cases involve penetrating trauma, such as lawn dart injuries[88]; additional cases are associated with infections of the middle ear. A characteristic feature is rapid evolution of symptoms after the traumatic event, often within 24 to 48 hours. Radiographs or computed tomographic scans typically show focal collections of gas. Although these cases are occasionally reported as "gas gangrene of the brain," the tendency for spread and systemic toxicity as seen with myonecrosis is minimal.

Soft Tissue Infections

Clostridia may play a role in various infections of the skin, subcutaneous tissue, and muscle. Such infections include (1) common soft tissue infections, in which clostridia are often a component of polymicrobial flora; (2) crepitant cellulitis; (3) suppurative myositis; and (4) clostridial myonecrosis (gas gangrene).

Included in the first category are a heterogeneous group of commonly encountered polymicrobial infections such as wound infections after abdominal surgery, perirectal cellulitis, perirectal abscesses, diabetic foot ulcers, decubitus ulcers, infections associated with vascular insufficiency, and stump infections after amputation. The pathogenic role of clostridia in these polymicrobial infections is unclear; clinically, they are similar to infections in which clostridia are not isolated. Numerous clostridial species may be involved, but the predominant isolates are *C. perfringens* and *C. ramosum.* The accompanying organisms are those that are commonly encountered in intra-abdominal infections, and the presumed source is the colonic flora. Monomicrobial osteomyelitis secondary to traumatic inoculation of soft tissue has been reported rarely.[89]

Crepitant cellulitis is characterized by clinically detectable gas formation in the soft tissue.[90–93] These infections usually occur after trauma, the incubation period from the time of wounding to clinical evaluation is usually 3 days or longer, and systemic toxicity is generally minimal. Findings at the infected site include crepitance on palpation resulting from gas formation, which is usually far more abundant than that seen in myonecrosis. Pain is minimal, the site shows edema with little skin discoloration, and a thin, dark discharge is present, often with a characteristic foul odor, that on Gram stain shows neutrophils and typical bacteria. Clostridia, particularly *C. perfringens,* are the most common cause, although other bacteria such as Enterobacteriaceae and *Staphylococcus aureus* may be implicated.[94] Rarely, patients have a more fulminant course, with rapid spread through fascial planes and evidence of clostridial toxemia.

Suppurative myositis that is due to clostridia is similar to tropical pyomyositis caused by *S. aureus.* It is seen most often in misusers of parenteral drugs and usually involves the thigh or forearm and not necessarily the area of trauma or drug injection.[21] In distinction from gas gangrene, which also involves muscle, clostridial myositis is characterized by a suppurative collection without myonecrosis and lack of the severe systemic complications associated with gas gangrene. These infections generally respond well to drainage and antimicrobials. Operative findings may include abscess formation, localized myositis, and dissecting fasciitis.[21]

Clostridial Myonecrosis (Gas Gangrene)

Few infections are as critical as clostridial myonecrosis (gas gangrene), a rare, rapidly progressive, and devastating infection characterized by muscle necrosis and systemic toxicity caused by potent clostridial exotoxins.

History. In 1892, Welch and Nuttall characterized a gram-positive, gas-producing, anaerobic bacillus that reproduced rapidly in blood vessels postmortem.[95] Four years later, Welch and Flexner associated this organism with a variety of clinical syndromes, including gas gangrene.[96] The organism was known as *Bacillus aerogenes capsulatus,* later as *Bacillus perfringens,* still later as *C. welchii,* and now as *C. perfringens.* The history of the clinical entity, gas gangrene, is largely the history of wars of the 20th century.[97] Although scattered reports go back to antiquity, before World War I the disease was curiously rare, even in times of conflict, including the American Civil War. During World War I, the clostridial infections gas gangrene and tetanus were both common and due to severe trauma, gross soil contamination, and delayed surgical intervention.

The incidence of gas gangrene complicating battlefield trauma in World War I was 5% and dropped to 0.3 to 0.7% in World War II, 0.2% in the Korean War, and 0.0002% during the war in Vietnam.[90, 98–101] These declining rates reflect improving management of battlefield trauma with prompt wound cleansing and débridement and, in Vietnam, rapid transport of casualties to sites of high-quality trauma surgery.

Pathogens. *C. perfringens* is the major causative species and accounts for approximately 80% of cases with positive cultures. Other clostridial causative species include *C. septicum, C. novyi, C. sordellii, C. histolyticum, Clostridium fallax,* and *Clostridium bifermentans.* During World War I, *C. septicum* was second only to *C. perfringens* in causing gas gangrene, and it ranked third in World War II.[90] Some patients have more than one species of clostridia at the infected site, as well as other species of bacteria at the infected site. Implicated clostridial species produce at least 12 exotoxins, including 7 that are lethal when injected intraperitoneally into mice (Table 236–3). In gas gangrene, the most important toxins are thought to be phospholipase C (α-toxin), which has a molecular weight of about 43,000 Da and is responsible for splitting lecithin, the major phospholipid in eukaryotic cell membranes, to phosphoryl choline and diacylglycerol, and a thiol-activated hemolysin (θ-toxin or perfringolysin O).[2, 10] The role of other extracellular enzymes such as collagenase (κ-toxin), hyaluronidase (μ-toxin), DNase (ν-toxin), and neuraminidase (sialidase) is unclear. Since 1988 the structural genes for α-toxin *(plc)* and θ-toxin *(pfoA)* have been cloned and mapped. Expression of these genes in *Escherichia coli* has permitted the production of pure toxin products allowing for the elucidation of structure-function relationships. Intravenous administration of α-toxin in experimental animals results in massive hemolysis, platelet destruction, capillary damage, and death.

Using recombinant α-toxin and θ-toxin in rabbits, Asmuth, Stevens, and colleagues demonstrated that α-toxin is the major lethal factor in *C. perfringens* infections and induces cardiovascular collapse by direct inhibition of myocardial contractility; hypotension resulting from θ-toxin is not associated with direct cardiotoxicity and is probably due to induction of endogenous mediators.[102, 103]

Immunocompetent survivors of *C. septicum* myonecrosis, but not bacteremia alone, form antibodies to α-toxin.[104]

Epidemiology. Gas gangrene usually complicates wounds associated with trauma or surgery. Routine cultures from traumatic open wounds indicate that 20 to 80% percent are contaminated by clostridia, although gas gangrene remains rare. MacLennan reported that in the Western Desert Campaign of World War II, 20 to 30% of all battlefield wounds were contaminated by clostridia, but gas gangrene developed in only 0.32% of these wounds.[98] A review of 187,936 major open wounds of violence by Altemeier and Furste found the incidence of gas gangrene to be 1.7%.[99] Interestingly, no difference was seen between the bacteriology of wounds in which gas gangrene later developed and those in which it did not. These observations emphasize the importance of local wound conditions in the pathogen-

TABLE 236–3 *Clostridium perfringens* Toxins

Toxin	Biologic Activity*	Strain Type
Major lethal		
α	Lethal, lecithinase, necrotizing, hemolytic	A–E
β	Lethal, necrotizing, transmural necrosis with small bowel inoculation; trypsin labile	B, C
ϵ	Lethal; permease, trypsin activatable	B, D
ι	Lethal, dermonecrotic, binary, ADP ribosylating, trypsin activatable	E
Minor		
δ	Hemolysin, lethal	B, C
θ	Hemolysin (O_2 labile), cytolysin, lethal	A–E
κ	Collagenase, gelatinase, necrotizing, lethal	A–E
λ	Protease	B, D, E
μ	Hyaluronidase	A–E
ν	Deoxyribonuclease, leukocidin, hemolytic, necrotizing, lethal	A–E
Neuraminidase	*N*-acetylneuraminic acid, glycohydrolase	A–E
Other		
Enterotoxin	Enterotoxic, cytotoxic	A, C, D (B, E not tested)

*Lethality tested in mice with intravenous or intraperitoneal injection.
Abbreviation: ADP, Adenosine diphosphate.

esis of infection. Factors that promote the replication of vegetative forms and elaboration of toxins in the setting of hypoxic tissue include the presence of foreign bodies, vascular insufficiency, and concurrent infection with other microbes. The minimum dose of bacteria required to produce gas gangrene in guinea pigs was reduced by 10^3 by injection into devitalized tissue and reduced by 10^6 by contamination of muscle with sterile dirt.[105]

In the civilian population, approximately half of gas gangrene cases follow trauma, and most others occur postoperatively. The most frequent traumatic injuries are vehicular or agricultural accidents with open fractures, followed by crush injuries, industrial accidents, and gunshot wounds.[101] In the surgical setting, the most frequent antecedent procedures are intestinal surgery, especially colon resection and biliary tract surgery. Occasional cases of gas gangrene are associated with vascular insufficiency in the lower extremities occurring in association with vascular gangrene, diabetic foot ulcers, and decubitus ulcers, or they are seen as a complication of burns or amputation. Other cases have occurred after intramuscular or even subcutaneous injection of epinephrine.[106] Uterine gas gangrene usually occurs in the setting of a septic, usually criminal abortion and less commonly with other gynecologic procedures or after delivery.[67–69] Spontaneous or nontraumatic gas gangrene is a rare form of the infection without any associated traumatic or surgical wounding. Recent data suggest that most cases of spontaneous gas gangrene are due to *C. septicum.*[28]

Unlike typical cases of gas gangrene, which follow trauma, in most of those caused by *C. septicum,* no obvious external portal of entry can be found. In this more recently recognized syndrome, often referred to as nontraumatic or spontaneous gas gangrene, the presumed source is the colon.[27, 28] Typical symptoms include a sudden onset of fever, abdominal pain, vomiting, and diarrhea, and rapid progression to shock is common. The patient may initially appear to have appendicitis, but the fulminant course is clearly atypical. Intravascular hemolysis is rarely encountered. Up to 25% of patients have myonecrosis at metastatic sites,[25, 27, 34] and nearly all patients have evidence of altered integrity of the bowel mucosa that is due to leukemic infiltrates, tumor, or "neutropenic enterocolitis."

The source of the organism has been controversial. Clostridia are ubiquitous and found in soil and air samples, including operating room air, dust, food, and clothing.[107, 108] Concentrations vary, but fertile soil typically contains 10^8/g. The highest concentrations are in the intestinal tract; intestinal strains are also believed to be more virulent, and an endogenous source is suspected even in cases associated with gross soil contamination. Person-to-person transmission is rare,[92] although occasional "outbreaks" have been reported.[108] Altemeier and Furste showed that *C. perfringens* strains recovered from an infected wound were 10^3 to 10^6 times more virulent in guinea pigs than were soil strains.[105]

Clinical Manifestations. Gas gangrene is a fulminant infection with prominent findings at the infection site and severe systemic toxicity.[90, 98, 101, 109–113] Typical clinical settings are (1) traumatic injury or a penetrating wound, usually of an extremity; (2) surgery, primarily of the intestine or biliary tract; (3) septic criminal abortion or delivery; (4) soft tissue lesions associated with vascular insufficiency or burns; and (5) underlying colorectal or pelvic cancer or neutropenia complicating leukemia or cytotoxic therapy.

The usual incubation period from the time of injury to the onset of symptoms is 1 to 4 days (range, 6 hours to 3 weeks). The earliest symptom noted by the patient is the sudden onset of unrelenting and severe pain at the site of the wound; less commonly, the sensation is described as heaviness or pressure. Initial physical examination of the site may be normal, and a sudden onset of severe pain in the proper clinical setting, even in the absence of local findings, should alert the practitioner to the possibility of gas gangrene. The disease process progresses rapidly, and within minutes to hours, localized tense edema, pallor, and tenderness are seen. Gas may be noted in the soft tissues by palpation, radiographs, or scans, but crepitance is a late finding and should not be considered a sine qua non; it is neither a sensitive nor specific feature. The skin initially appears pale and then progresses to a magenta or bronze discoloration, often followed by the appearance of hemorrhagic bullae and gross subcutaneous emphysema (Fig. 236–1). As the lesion progresses, a thin, dirty brown, serosanguineous discharge may be present along with a characteristic offensive odor described as sweetish or "mousey" and different from the putrid odor of other more common anaerobic infections. Gram stain of the discharge often shows a large number of typical gram-positive or gram-variable rods with sparse or no white blood cells (see Fig. 236–1). When *C. perfringens* is involved, the organism shows the typical boxcar appearance without spores. The absence of white cells locally is ascribed to the lecithinase, θ-toxin, or other toxins that lyse neutrophils. Stevens and colleagues examined bulla fluid from a patient with nontraumatic gas gangrene caused by *C. septicum* and demonstrated the typical finding of numerous gram-positive bacilli with an absence of neutrophils.[28] Using standard assays, they were unable to demonstrate α-toxin or θ-toxin in the blister fluid; however, they were able to show, in vitro, that minute amounts of fluid had adverse effects on neutrophil viability, morphology, and function, including chemotaxis and phagocytosis.

In a mouse model of gas gangrene, Stevens and associates used isogenic, toxin-deficient mutants of *C. perfringens* and toxin-neutralizing monoclonal antibodies to show that both α-toxin and θ-toxin attenuate the inflammatory response by impeding directed migration of neutrophils and destroying neutrophils at the site of infection. Furthermore, toxins induce dysregulation of neutrophil–endothelial cell adhesion, thereby contributing to vascular leukostasis, impaired tissue perfusion, and the rapid invasion of viable tissue.[114]

Profound systemic findings accompany these changes at the wound site, including diaphoresis, tachycardia disproportionate to temperature, and extreme anxiety on the part of the patient, who often remains exceedingly alert until the very terminal stages. Fever may be deceptively low or absent in the early stages. Late complications include intravascular hemolysis, hemoglobinuria, hypotension, renal failure, and metabolic acidosis. Terminally, coma develops and the patient's entire body may become swollen and crepitant with a typical magenta or bronze color.

Diagnosis. Early diagnosis is critical. The diagnosis of gas gangrene is based on the clinical findings, demonstration of myonecrosis at surgery, and supporting microbiologic data. Early clinical clues to this infection include the recognized settings of infection, severe pain disproportionate to the physical findings, and systemic toxicity with tachycardia. Typical findings at the site of injury include tense edema, discoloration, and hemorrhagic bullae; evidence of gas in soft tissue; Gram stains of exudate showing typical rods with sparse or absent white blood cells; the typical discharge with an offensive odor; and computed tomography or magnetic resonance imaging showing muscle compartment involvement with gas in the muscle and fascial planes.

Bacteriologic studies support the diagnosis when clostridia are seen in the Gram stain of exudate and when the species implicated in gas gangrene (primarily *C. perfringens*) are recovered in cultured exudate or blood. Only 10 to 15% of patients with clostridial myonecrosis will have documented bacteremia.

In the differential diagnosis, the major considerations are other severe soft tissue infections, among which are crepitant cellulitis, streptococcal fasciitis, necrotizing fasciitis resulting from a mixed aerobic-anaerobic infection, and synergistic necrotizing cellulitis. Ultimately, gas gangrene is a surgical diagnosis made when involved muscle is visualized. Affected muscle has a pale or darkened "cooked" appearance and fails to contract when incised or electrically stimulated; the cut surface does not bleed. The extent of myonecrosis is often greater than the skin changes indicate.

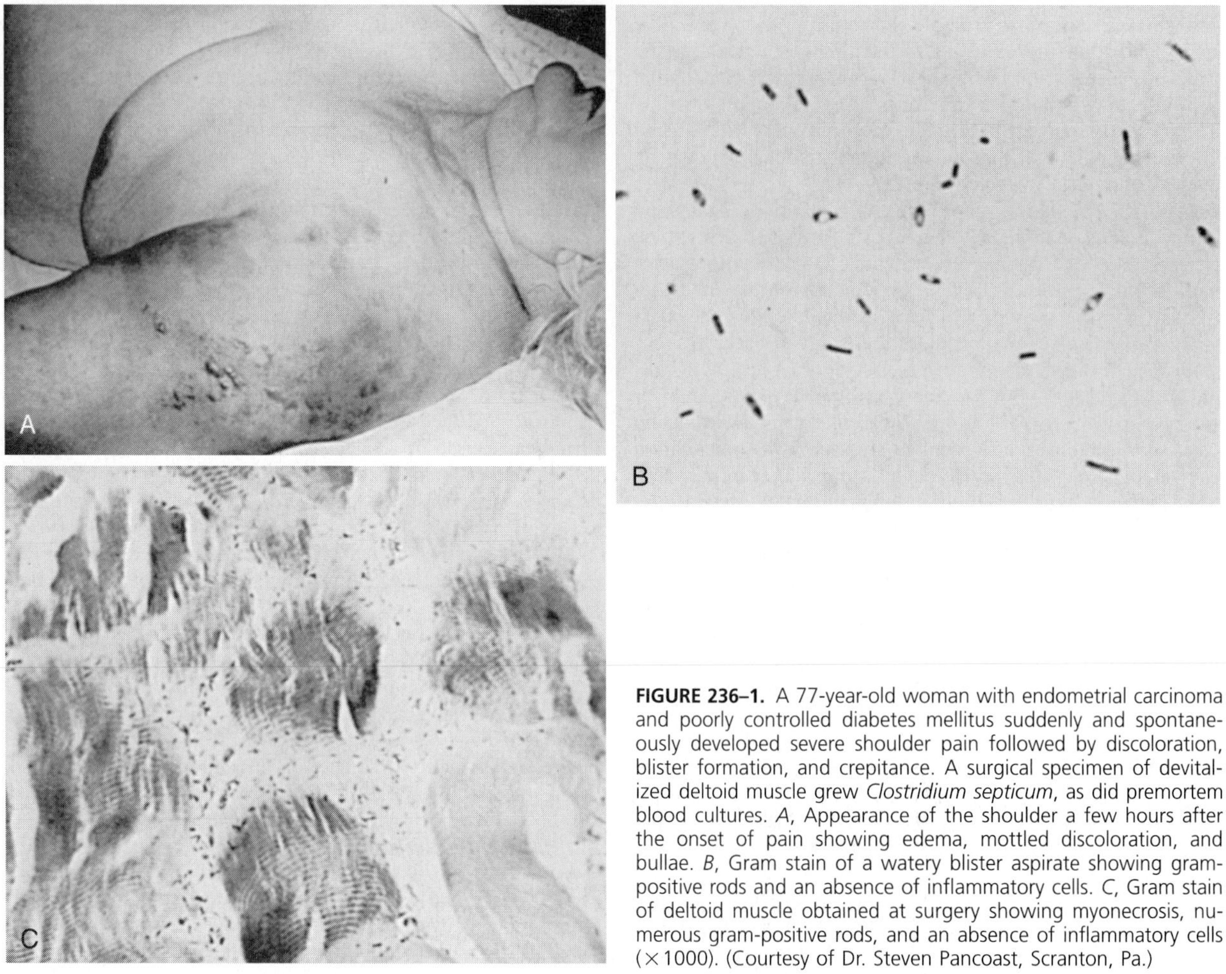

FIGURE 236–1. A 77-year-old woman with endometrial carcinoma and poorly controlled diabetes mellitus suddenly and spontaneously developed severe shoulder pain followed by discoloration, blister formation, and crepitance. A surgical specimen of devitalized deltoid muscle grew *Clostridium septicum*, as did premortem blood cultures. *A*, Appearance of the shoulder a few hours after the onset of pain showing edema, mottled discoloration, and bullae. *B*, Gram stain of a watery blister aspirate showing gram-positive rods and an absence of inflammatory cells. *C*, Gram stain of deltoid muscle obtained at surgery showing myonecrosis, numerous gram-positive rods, and an absence of inflammatory cells (×1000). (Courtesy of Dr. Steven Pancoast, Scranton, Pa.)

Therapy. Current treatment practice has been derived from many retrospective human studies and a number of animal model experiments (Fig. 236–2). The most important component of treatment is prompt and extensive surgical débridement, with wide excision of involved muscle when the abdominal wall is involved, aggressive débridement or amputation of an involved extremity, and hysterectomy in most cases of uterine gas gangrene. All necrotic muscle must be débrided, which often requires daily reoperation. Some authors argue that antecedent hyperbaric oxygen therapy (see later) facilitates surgery by clearly demarcating viable tissue and permitting less radical tissue excision.[113, 115] Patients with evidence of a compartment syndrome should have prompt fasciotomy without delay for hyperbaric oxygen, even if it is immediately at hand.[110]

Demello and colleagues used a dog model of gas gangrene to evaluate the roles of antibiotics, surgery, and hyperbaric oxygen in varied combinations.[115] These studies showed that only antibiotics consistently enhanced survival and that without antibiotics, regardless of alternative treatment, no dogs survived. Treatment of human infection solely with surgery and hyperbaric oxygen in the antibiotic era has been reported,[116] but the weight of evidence is that early antimicrobial therapy is essential for an optimal outcome.

Penicillin G in dosages of 10 to 24 million units daily is generally considered to be the drug of choice for patients with gas gangrene.[110, 117] Recent data indicate increasing resistance of *C. perfringens* and more profound resistance in other species.[118, 119] Nevertheless, most authorities continue to regard penicillin as the preferred agent because most strains are still susceptible at easily obtained drug levels.[120] Alternatives for patients who have contraindications to penicillin or when resistance is a concern include chloramphenicol, metronidazole, and imipenem. In vitro, these drugs are active against virtually all strains of clostridia, but extensive clinical experience is lacking. Other agents with good in vitro activity are erythromycin, rifampin, clindamycin, and tetracycline.[118, 119, 121] Cefoxitin is less active against clostridia than are most other cephalosporins and should be avoided. Gas gangrene has been reported to develop during and in spite of surgical prophylaxis with cephalothin.[122]

Concerns about the efficacy of penicillin G arise not only from in vitro susceptibility data showing increasing resistance but also from experimental animal studies. Studying gas gangrene in guinea pigs, Altemeier and coworkers showed that tetracycline and chloramphenicol were superior to penicillin.[99, 123] More recently, Stevens and associates evaluated antimicrobials in a mouse model of gas gangrene in which infection was produced with a strain of *C. perfringens* that was susceptible to all tested antibiotics and survival was the end point. Penicillin-treated animals fared no better than untreated controls, but improved outcomes were achieved with clindamycin, metronidazole, rifampin, and tetracycline.[124] This group also found that protein synthesis inhibitors were better inhibitors of toxin synthesis than were cell wall–active agents and that the combination of penicillin plus clindamycin had considerably better efficacy than penicillin did alone.[125, 126] The impact that such studies should have on antibiotic recommendations is not obvious. However, in view of these observations and the severity of clostridial myonecrosis, it would seem prudent to consider substitution of another agent such as clindamycin, metronidazole, or imipenem or the combination of such an agent with penicillin as initial therapy. If Gram stain of exudate

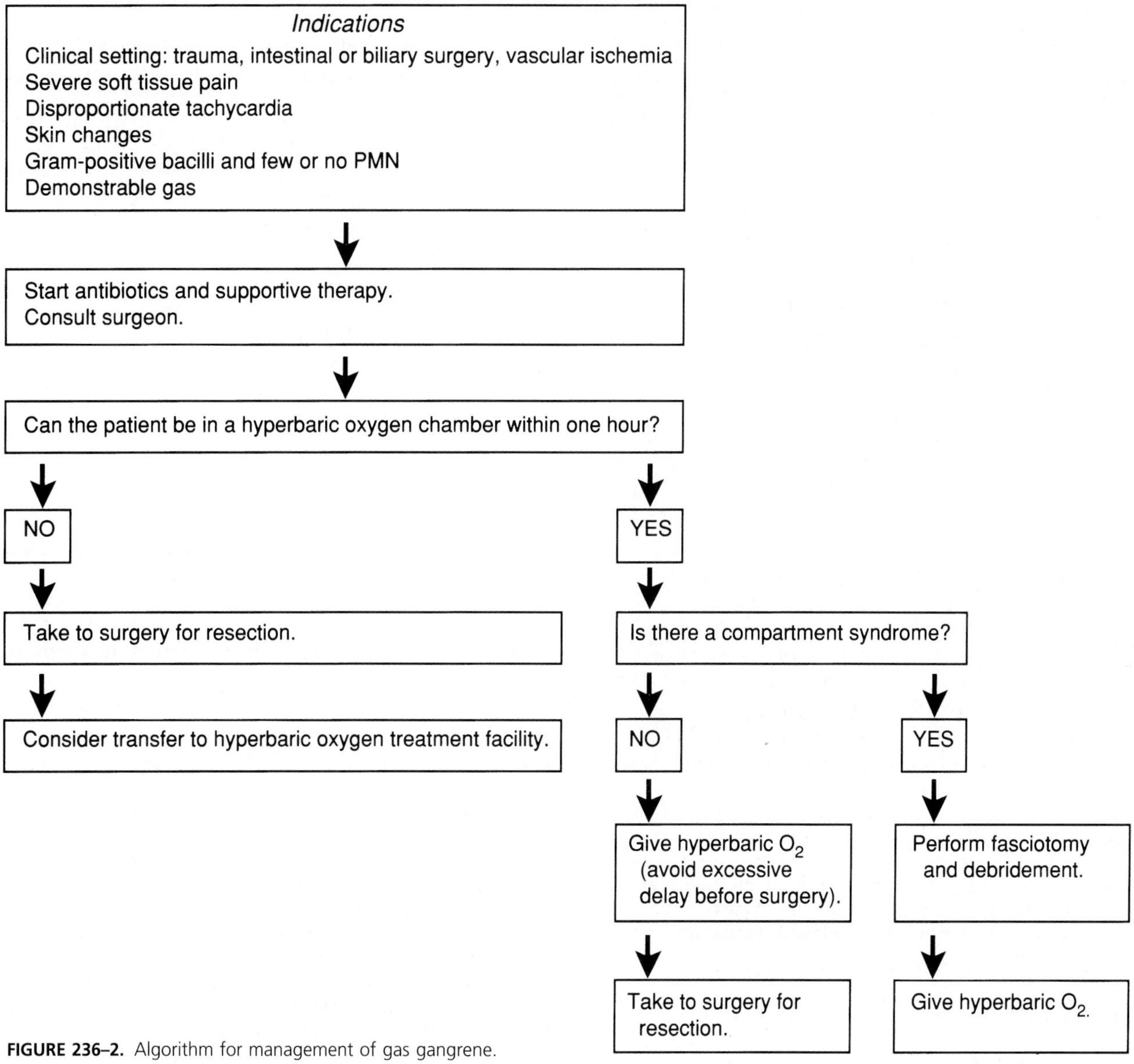

FIGURE 236–2. Algorithm for management of gas gangrene.

demonstrates polymicrobial infection, other antibiotics should be added accordingly.

Antitoxin for gas gangrene was introduced in 1918 and was later commercially developed and used widely in World War II.[127] Later studies of this horse serum prepared against the toxins of five clostridial species known to cause gas gangrene showed a lack of efficacy and a high frequency of allergic reaction.[109, 115, 127] Antitoxin is no longer available commercially.

Hyperbaric oxygen treatment for gas gangrene has been used for over 30 years, but consensus has still not been reached on its value. Adequately controlled trials do not exist, and many reports include patients who did not have confirmed myonecrosis. The debate about efficacy continues, with passionate voices on both sides.[100–112, 115, 116, 128–130] The rationale for the use of hyperbaric oxygen includes the observations that raising local tissue oxygen concentrations arrests clostridial replication and α-toxin production and that hyperbaric oxygen treatment of experimental animals reduces mortality.[113, 115, 131] Using a murine model of clostridial myonecrosis, Stevens and colleagues showed an additive beneficial effect of hyperbaric oxygen combined with metronidazole or penicillin in animals challenged with a large inoculum of *C. perfringens*. In this model, clindamycin was superior to both penicillin and metronidazole, and its efficacy was not enhanced further by adjunctive treatment with hyperbaric oxygen.[132] The weight of clinical evidence indicates that hyperbaric oxygen therapy reduces morbidity and mortality when combined with surgery and antibiotics; however, efficacy is generally determined by comparison to historical controls, and some argue that institutions with hyperbaric chambers are referral centers more likely to provide aggressive surgery and medical support and, therefore, more likely to obtain good results. In uterine myonecrosis, hyperbaric oxygen has been less efficacious, and most authorities do not advocate its use.

Controversy continues about the timing of hyperbaric oxygen treatment and surgery. If fasciotomy is indicated, it should not be delayed for hyperbaric oxygen therapy. Use of hyperbaric oxygen before surgery has the potential benefit of (1) more clearly demarcating involved muscle and thus enabling the surgeon to define the extent of resection necessary and spare some viable tissue and (2) potentially halting toxin production. The standard treatment regimen includes five "dives" of 3 atm of pressure within the first 48 hours.[130, 133] Ideally, the first treatment would be given before surgery,

TABLE 236-4 Enteric Diseases That Are Due to Histotoxic Clostridia

Feature	*Clostridium perfringens* Food Poisoning	Enteritis Necroticans	*C. difficile* Colitis	Neutropenic Enterocolitis
Pathogen	*C. perfringens* type A	*C. perfringens* type C	*C. difficile*	*C. septicum* (*C. tertium, C. perfringens,* others)
Toxin	Enterotoxin (cytotoxin)	β-Toxin	Toxin A	Unknown; β-toxin?
MW (daltons)	35,000	48,000	440,000	?
Trypsin sensitivity	No	Yes	Yes	?
Mouse LD_{50} (ng)	1400	8	26	?
Rabbit ileal loop	Fluid flux, epithelial damage	Segmental transmural necrosis	Mucosal hemorrhage, fluid flux	?
Distribution	Worldwide	Papua New Guinea; other Third World countries	Worldwide	Worldwide
Carrier rate (stool)	90–95% for *C. perfringens;* up to 30% for enterotoxin-producing strains	20–70% in endemic areas	3% in healthy adults	2% for *C. septicum* (10–63% in appendix)
Diagnosis	Serology, enterotoxin assay of stools, quantitative culture of food source and stools	Serology, fluorescence-labeled antibody to demonstrate organism	Tissue culture assay for toxin B	Blood cultures
Clinical findings	Diarrhea, abdominal cramps, minimal systemic toxicity	Bloody diarrhea, vomiting, abdominal pain	Diarrhea, fever	Bacteremia, abdominal pain, vomiting, diarrhea, shock
Pathology	Small bowel epithelial damage, polymorphonuclear infiltrate	Small bowel segmental transmural necrosis	Colitis ± pseudomembranes	Colitis (usually cecal) with hemorrhagic necrosis
Treatment	None (self-limited)	Penicillin ± surgery	Metronidazole or vancomycin orally	Penicillin ± surgery
Mortality	Extremely rare	15–45% (serious cases)	10–20% (serious cases; untreated)	50–75%

Abbreviations: LD_{50}, Lethal dose for 50%; MW, molecular weight.

but surgery should not be delayed if a chamber is not immediately at hand or available at a referral center within a 1-hour time frame.

Prognosis. Before the availability of penicillin, mortality rates reported for gas gangrene encountered in the world wars were 27 to 31%.[90] In the antibiotic era, mortality rates are generally around 20 to 25%, but many patients are left severely crippled or disfigured by the necessary surgery.[129] Poor prognostic findings include leukopenia, intravascular hemolysis, renal failure, advanced age, involvement of the abdominal wall, "spontaneous gas gangrene," and underlying colorectal cancer or leukemia and *C. septicum* infection.[26] Without treatment, mortality approaches 100% within 48 hours of the onset of symptoms.[116] Prompt treatment is essential, and treatment delay is associated with increased mortality.

Enteric Infections

Four histotoxic clostridial syndromes that involve the gastrointestinal tract are recognized: *C. perfringens* food poisoning, enteritis necroticans, *Clostridium difficile*–induced diarrhea or colitis, and neutropenic enterocolitis (Table 236–4). In all but neutropenic enterocolitis, the responsible toxin has been defined, and when that toxin is used, the disease has been reproduced in experimental animals. In neutropenic enterocolitis, in which *C. septicum* is the usual, but not exclusive pathogen, the responsible toxin is not known, although β-toxin is an attractive candidate because of similarities to enteritis necroticans. These conditions show considerable variation in pathophysiologic mechanisms, risk factors, clinical features, and treatment (see Table 236–4). *C. difficile* colitis is discussed elsewhere in this text (see Chapter 84). Neonatal necrotizing enterocolitis has been associated with clostridial species, particularly *Clostridium butyricum* and *C. perfringens,* but the role of these bacteria in its pathogenesis remains unclear.[134]

Enteritis Necroticans

Enteritis necroticans is a necrotizing infection of the small intestine caused by the β-toxin of *C. perfringens* type C. An important enteric disease of sheep, calves, and piglets in veterinary medicine, its human equivalent appears to occur only in the presence of a unique combination of societal and nutritional factors in which protein malnutrition, pig feasts, sweet potatoes, and nematodes all play contributing roles.

History. After the end of World War II, hundreds of cases of enteritis necroticans occurred in malnourished individuals in northwestern Germany, where the disease was named Darmbrand.[135] Workers at that time suspected *C. perfringens* type F (later reclassified as type C) on the basis of its recovery in stool from afflicted patients and the production of a similar disease by injecting broth cultures of the organism into the small intestine of experimental animals.[136] Subsequent work demonstrated that the pathologic lesion could be attributed to an exotoxin. Renewed interest in the disease occurred in the 1960s, when enteritis necroticans, known locally as "pig-bel," was found to be endemic in the highlands of Papua New Guinea.[137] Most of the important studies have been conducted in Papua New Guinea by Lawrence, Murrell, Walker, and their associates.[138–142]

Pathogen. *C. perfringens* type C is widely distributed in soil and has been found in the stools of many asymptomatic humans, as well as animals; carrier rates are reportedly 20 to 70% in endemic areas.[139] Exposure to the etiologic organism is therefore common, and other factors must be invoked in the pathophysiology of the disease. Especially important is the β-toxin, a protein exotoxin of about 48,000 Da that is extremely sensitive to proteolytic enzymes.[143]

Epidemiology. Enteritis necroticans is endemic in the highlands of Papua New Guinea, where surveys in 1964 showed a prevalence of 50 cases per 10,000 population with a mortality rate of 14 per 100,000.[139, 142] At the time it was the most common cause of acute abdomen in surgical practice and the most common cause of death in children older than 12 months in the region; over 86% of adults in the area had circulating antibody to the β-toxin. Sporadic outbreaks have been reported from Southeast Asia, the South Pacific, Africa, China, and Western countries. It is thought that the disease is more frequent than generally appreciated, especially in areas with widespread malnutrition. This contention is supported by a report of 30 cases in a Khmer refugee camp at the Thai-Kampuchean border in 1985.[144]

The high prevalence of the disease in Papua New Guinea is attributed to unique cultural habits. Although all people are presumably exposed, it is postulated that the inoculum is especially high during pig feasts, in which cooking is usually inadequate to eliminate clostridial spores or inactivate preformed toxin; the sudden protein intake is thought to encourage the growth of *C. perfringens* and toxin production. The organism appears to adhere to the small bowel, probably through specific pili, and produce β-toxin, which is protected from normal proteolytic enzyme destruction by several contributing factors, including (1) protein malnutrition, which results in depletion of protease enzymes; (2) the dietary staple of sweet potato *(Ipomoea batalas),* which contains heat-stable inhibitors of trypsin; and (3) a high incidence of colonization (70 to 80%) with *Ascaris lumbricoides,* which secretes trypsin inhibitors. Trigger meals with peanuts and meats other than pork are reported. The high prevalence of the disease in children appears to reflect immunologic naiveté. Experimental support for the proposed mechanism is based on studies showing that inocula of broth cultures or culture filtrates produce typical segmental, transmural necrosis, which can be prevented by combining the filtrate with pancreatin (which destroys β-toxin) or by challenge to animals immunized with β-toxoid vaccine.[140]

Clinical and Pathologic Features. Enteritis necroticans is a segmental disease of the small intestine chiefly involving the jejunum and rarely the ileum; the colon is never involved. The pathologic spectrum of disease ranges from small necrotic patches with normal intervening mucosa to full-thickness necrosis involving large segments.[145, 146] With advanced lesions the bowel wall becomes thin and subject to perforation. Microscopic studies show mucosal infarction with edema, hemorrhage, and a transmural neutrophilic infiltrate.

The usual initial symptoms are severe upper abdominal pain, distention, vomiting, passage of bloody stool, and later, signs of small bowel obstruction.[138, 139, 141, 142] The incubation period after ingestion of the high-protein meal is usually about 1 to 4 days but varies from hours to a week.

Considerable variation is noted in the spectrum of clinical features, which range from mild diarrhea mimicking common forms of gastroenteritis to acute enteritis, intestinal obstruction, and a fulminant course with death in 24 hours.

Diagnosis. In the endemic area, the diagnosis is usually made by clinical observations, sometimes supported by typical pathologic changes in the small bowel noted at surgery or autopsy. Fluorescent-stained antibody to the clostridial capsular antigen has been used to identify the causative agent in stool or bowel contents.[142] Cultures are difficult to interpret because of the relatively high carrier rates in asymptomatic persons and the frequent overgrowth of *C. perfringens* type A in stool cultures.[147]

Treatment. The preferred antibiotics are penicillin G, metronidazole, or chloramphenicol. Indications for surgical intervention include persistent toxicity, persistent intestinal obstruction, suspected perforation, and severe recurrent bleeding. Approximately 50% of patients with serious disease require surgery, which generally consists of resecting 50 to 200 cm of jejunum. Excluding patients with mild disease, the mortality rate is reported at 15 to 45%. Administration of antiserum has no role. A very promising development has been prevention of the disease by using a β-toxoid vaccine prepared from culture filtrates of *C. perfringens* type C.[148] In 1980, after a successful controlled trial of this toxoid demonstrated protection for over 2 years, the Papua New Guinea health services initiated an immunization program with pig-bel vaccine (Wellcome, Beckenham, United Kingdom) for children at 2, 4, and 6 months of age.[149, 150] Within 2 years, hospital admissions that were due to enteritis necroticans dropped to less than one fifth of prevaccination levels.

Neutropenic Enterocolitis

Neutropenic enterocolitis (typhlitis) is seen with congenital neutropenia, leukemia, or neutropenia resulting from cytotoxic chemotherapy.[151, 152] It characteristically involves the cecum but may extend throughout the bowel. *C. septicum* is the usual cause, and the major risk factor is neutropenia, but antecedent mucosal damage may be important inasmuch as some patients have severe mucositis. Common initial findings are fever, abdominal pain, and diarrhea, which is watery and occasionally bloody. Abdominal distention, tenderness often localizing to the right lower quadrant, and decreased bowel sounds are found. At autopsy or laparotomy, the cecum and adjacent bowel show edema, hemorrhage, and necrosis, with typical organisms invading the bowel wall. Physicians should consider clostridial infection in any patient with known gastrointestinal or pelvic malignancy or neutropenia in whom abdominal pain, tenderness, and fever develop because early institution of antibiotics will salvage up to one half of patients.[153] The role of surgery is controversial.[151, 152, 154, 155] Some cases respond to bowel rest and antibiotics; in others, extensive surgery is sometimes necessary to débride gangrenous lesions of the bowel. In addition to *C. septicum,* other clostridia that are less commonly implicated in neutropenic enterocolitis include *C. perfringens, C. sporogenes, Clostridium sphenoides, C. sordellii, Clostridium paraperfringens,* and *C. tertium.*[18, 156–160] *C. tertium,* a rare cause of bacteremia overall, is the second most frequent blood culture isolate in this setting but is clinically distinctive in that it causes a milder illness than *C. septicum* does and has a favorable prognosis with antibiotic treatment. Fecal carriage of *C. tertium* in the setting of neutropenia may be increased when compared with healthy people and may be related to selection by previously administered antibiotics.[43]

Clostridum perfringens *Food Poisoning*

Enterotoxin-producing strains of *C. perfringens* type A cause a mild and common form of food poisoning that is found worldwide.[161, 162] Less commonly, they produce sporadic diarrhea that may or may not be associated with antibiotic use.[163, 164]

Pathogen. *C. perfringens* type A is responsible for nearly all cases of *C. perfringens* food poisoning. Some authors prefer to refer to the responsible toxin as a cytotoxin because it produces cellular damage in order to distinguish it from true enterotoxin, which produces no such cell toxicity.[165] Some investigators believe that the enterotoxin is a structural, but not essential component of the spore coat; others claim that high levels are produced in the cytoplasm after activation of the enterotoxin gene *(cpe)* by transcriptional factors that also control sporulation genes.[10] Methods of detecting toxigenic potential include techniques for enhancing sporulation. The most frequently used method is the "DS" medium described by Duncan and Strong.[166] Yasukawa and colleagues studied sonicates from 7-hour broth cultures in DS media with an agar gel double-immunodiffusion assay to detect enterotoxin.[167] They detected enterotoxin production by 51 of 66 strains from foodborne disease cases as compared with 1 of 117 strains recovered from the stools of healthy controls. Later work showed that heat treatment before incubation in DS medium enhanced toxin production and that reversed passive hemagglutination appeared more sensitive for toxin detection. Using this technique, Uemura showed that 11 of 35 (31%) healthy persons harbored toxigenic strains.[168]

The enterotoxin is a polypeptide of 320 amino acids, has a molecular weight of about 35,000 Da, and is susceptible to pronase, but not trypsin, chymotrypsin, or papain.[2, 10] Biologic activities of the heat-labile toxin include fluid accumulation in the rabbit ileal loop 90 minutes after challenge, induction of vomiting in cynomolgus monkeys with orogastric challenge, lethality after an intravenous challenge to mice with a median lethal dose of 80 μg, and cytotoxicity to Vero cells.[2, 169–172] In the small bowel, the enterotoxin binds to a brush-border membrane receptor and then induces a calcium ion–dependent breakdown in permeability that results in the loss of low-molecular-weight metabolites and ions.[10, 169, 171, 173] This loss alters intracellular metabolic function, including macromolecular synthesis, and is associated with morphologic damage and eventual cell lysis.

Bowness and associates demonstrated that *C. perfringens* enterotoxin acts as a superantigen and, in the absence of antigen processing, significantly stimulates human lymphocytes.[174] Thus, the pathogenesis of *C. perfringens* food poisoning may involve a massive release of inflammatory mediators through superantigen reacting with a large proportion of T lymphocytes.

Epidemiology. *C. perfringens* food poisoning follows the ingestion of food containing at least 10^8 enterotoxin-producing organisms and is virtually always associated with food that was inadequately stored. The most frequent vehicles are animal protein foods such as cooked meat, poultry, stews, meat pies, and gravies that have become grossly contaminated during long periods of slow cooling after cooking and storage at ambient temperature.[175] On occasion, vegetable protein sources such as beans have been the vehicle for *C. perfringens* food poisoning.[176] The spores survive cooking, the heat-activated spores germinate as the food cools, and optimal growth in meat is achieved at 43°C to 47°C with a generation time of 10 to 12 minutes. Most outbreaks have been associated with commercially prepared food in restaurants and institutions; home outbreaks are uncommon, in contrast to those caused by *S. aureus* and *Salmonella* spp. To prevent disease, cooked meat should be refrigerated if not served immediately to prevent the growth of vegetative cells; rewarmed meats should be heated to an internal temperature of greater than 75°C before serving.

C. perfringens is a relatively common cause of foodborne outbreaks. Data from the Centers for Disease Control and Prevention indicate that *C. perfringens* accounts for approximately 3 to 10% of such outbreaks in the United States, with an average of 24 victims per outbreak.[162, 164, 175] About 25 outbreaks are reported annually. It is likely that many outbreaks go undetected as a result of the relatively mild clinical symptoms and the specialized laboratory techniques required to confirm *C. perfringens* as the cause. Recent studies have expanded the epidemiologic spectrum of *C. perfringens*–induced diarrheal disease, and the organism has been implicated in sporadic cases of diarrhea, antibiotic-associated diarrhea, and diarrhea in chronic care facilities.[163, 164, 177] The diarrhea in these alternative forms lasts longer, with an average duration of 11 days.[163]

Clinical Features. Most cases occur in the setting of a common-source outbreak, with meat being the most frequent vehicle.[175, 178] Sporadic cases are presumably common as well but are unlikely to be investigated. In outbreaks, the attack rate in exposed persons averages 50 to 60%. One of the largest outbreaks was seen after a banquet in New York City attended by 1800 people, over 900 of whom later had symptomatic disease.[179] The incubation period after exposure is brief, usually 7 to 15 hours with a range of 6 to 24 hours. The usual symptoms are watery diarrhea in over 90% and abdominal cramps in about 80%.[175, 180] Less frequent symptoms are nausea (25%), vomiting (9%), and fever (24%). Nearly all patients have spontaneous resolution of symptoms within 6 to 24 hours; fatalities are extremely rare.

Diagnosis. *C. perfringens* food poisoning is suspect in any outbreak of diarrhea occurring 7 to 15 hours after ingestion of a common food source. Suggested diagnostic criteria include (1) detection of 10^5 *C. perfringens* colony-forming units per gram in the suspected food source and (2) stools obtained within 48 hours of symptoms that show 10^6 *C. perfringens* spores per gram.[181] However, mean fecal spore counts of this magnitude may be seen in patients without symptoms.[181] A more preferred method is direct analysis of stool for enterotoxin, which can be achieved by using a reverse passive latex agglutination assay,[182, 183] enzyme-linked immunoassay,[184] or a tissue culture assay using Vero cells with neutralizing antibody to inhibit cytopathic effects.[161]

Several molecular epidemiologic techniques have been used to show identity of patient isolates with food sources, including phage typing, bacteriocin typing, plasmid profiles, and DNA probes.[10]

PREVENTION AND TREATMENT

Clostridial species are involved in a very heterogeneous group of human infections. Specific treatment recommendations have been discussed earlier in the context of unique clinical syndromes. Some general principles are reviewed here.

Because the histotoxic clostridial syndromes (see Table 236–2) are due to antigenic protein exotoxins, active or passive immunization is a possibility. Tetanus toxoid vaccine is universally recommended, and β-toxoid vaccine has been used with great success to prevent enteritis necroticans in Papua New Guinea. Tetanus immune globulin is recommended for patients with tetanus and botulinum antitoxin for adults with botulism. Horse serum antitoxin was once available for use in gas gangrene, but efficacy was not established, toxicity was significant, and the antisera is no longer commercially available. A *C. sordellii* antitoxin reacts with *C. difficile* toxins and, in vitro, neutralizes both toxin A and toxin B. It has never been tested for potential clinical efficacy. Thus, although potentially useful in principle, immunotherapy plays a small role in the treatment of histotoxic clostridial syndromes.

Traumatic wounds should be irrigated copiously and meticulously débrided of all dirt, foreign bodies, and devitalized tissue. Appropriate antimicrobial prophylaxis should be given for surgery of the intestine and biliary tract, for limb surgery associated with vascular insufficiency, and for contaminated trauma. Intramuscular epinephrine should not be given in the buttock.

Surgical intervention depends on the specific infection. Most clostridial infections are polymicrobial, and physicians should follow the standard guidelines for surgery that would apply if clostridia were not present. Some clostridial infections may require aggressive surgical intervention in terms of timing or the extent of resection. Included in this group are emphysematous cholecystitis, neutropenic enterocolitis, enteritis necroticans, wounds associated with tetanus, some cases of crepitant cellulitis, and all cases of gas gangrene.

Penicillin G is generally considered the drug of choice for clostridial infections. Exceptions are *C. difficile*–induced diarrheal disease, for which oral metronidazole or vancomycin is effective, and botulism and *C. perfringens* food poisoning, for which antibiotics are not indicated. Alternative agents that are highly active in vitro against most clostridial strains are chloramphenicol, imipenem, metronidazole, clindamycin, most expanded-spectrum cephalosporins, and combinations of a β-lactam and β-lactamase inhibitor.[118–121, 185] Extended-spectrum penicillins, including ampicillin, and the antipseudomonal penicillins are also very active. Despite their in vitro activity, the clinical efficacy of cephalosporins and clindamycin is uncertain. Gas gangrene has developed in some patients while receiving cephalothin,[122] and the published clinical experience with cephalosporins is limited. Clindamycin is relatively inactive in vitro against some species other than *C. perfringens,* but this drug has shown excellent in vivo activity in an animal model of gas gangrene.[124] *C. sordellii* displays susceptibilities similar to those of *C. perfringens,* and the same is true for *C. septicum,* although resistance to clindamycin and extended-spectrum penicillins has occasionally been reported.[27, 28, 44, 121] *C. tertium* is resistant to the newer cephalosporins.[43]

Concern can be raised about the continued recommendation of penicillin G as the drug of choice for clostridial infections. Some studies have shown increasing resistance of clostridia to penicillin, although nearly all strains of *C. perfringens* remain susceptible to levels easily achieved with parenteral doses. β-Lactamase production has been noted with *C. butyricum, Clostridium clostridiiforme,* and *C. ramosum,* and decreased affinity for penicillin-binding proteins has been demonstrated for some strains of *C. perfringens.* Plasmid-mediated transferable resistance to tetracycline-chloramphenicol and clindamycin-erythromycin has been observed with *C. perfringens*. Additionally, penicillin is ineffective in animal models of gas gangrene in which metronidazole, clindamycin, rifampin, and tetracycline are effective.[99, 123, 124] Most authorities continue to recommend penicillin as the preferred agent for clostridial infections, but because of concerns raised by in vitro data and animal studies, alternative drugs should be considered.

REFERENCES

1. Cato EP, George WL, Finegold SM. Genus *Clostridium* Prazmowski 1880. In: Sneath PHA, Mair NS, Sharpe ME, et al, eds. Bergey's Manual of Systematic Bacteriology. v. 2. Baltimore: Williams & Wilkins; 1986:1141–1200.
2. Hatheway CL. Toxigenic clostridia. Clin Microbiol Rev. 1990;3:66–98.
3. Willis AT. Anaerobic Bacteriology: Clinical and Laboratory Practice. 3rd ed. London: Butterworth; 1977:68–172.
4. Veillon A, Zuber A. Recherches sur quelques microbes strictement anaerobies et leur role en pathologic. Arch Med Exp Anat Pathol. 1898;10:517–545.
5. Smith LDS. The Pathogenic Anaerobic Bacteria. 2nd ed. Springfield, Ill: Charles C Thomas; 1975:115–324.
6. Smith LDS, Gardner VM. Vegetative cells of *Clostridium perfringens* in soil. J Bacteriol. 1949;58:407–408.
7. Beerens H, Delcourte F. Caractere differential entre *Clostridium perfringens* fecal et tellurique. Ann Inst Pasteur. 1958;95:739–740.
8. Finegold SM, Attebery HR, Sutter VL. Effect of diet on human fecal flora: Comparison of Japanese and American diets. Am J Clin Nutr. 1974;27:1456–1469.
9. Kuberski TT. Intraleukocytic spore formation and leukocytic vacuolization during *Clostridium perfringens* septicemia. Am J Clin Pathol. 1977;68:794–796.
10. Rood JI, Cole ST. Molecular genetics and pathogenesis of *Clostridium perfringens*. Microbiol Rev. 1991;55:621–648.
11. Stringer MF, Watson GN, Gilbert RJ, et al. Fecal carriage of *Clostridium perfringens*. J Hyg. 1985;95:277–288.
12. Gutiérrez A, Florencio R, Ezpeleta C, et al. Fatal intravascular hemolysis in a patient with *Clostridium perfringens* septicemia. Clin Infect Dis. 1995;20:1064–1065.
13. Meyerhoff A, Renzi RM, Wehbe T, et al. Fatal clostridial sepsis in a previously healthy woman. Clin Infect Dis. 1995;20:1066–1067.
14. Dorsher CW, Rosenblatt JE, Wilson WR, et al. Anaerobic bacteremia: Decreasing rate over a 15 year period. Rev Infect Dis. 1991;13:633–636.
15. Grandsen WR, Eykyn SJ, Phillips I. Anaerobic bacteremia: Declining rate over a 15-year period. Rev Infect Dis. 1991;13:1255–1256.
16. Lombardi DP, Engleberg NC. Anaerobic bacteremia: Incidence, patient characteristics, and clinical significance. Am J Med. 1992;92:53–60.
17. Bodey GP, Rodriquez S, Fainstein V, et al. Clostridial bacteremia in cancer patients. A 12-year experience. Cancer. 1991;67:1928–1942.
18. Ingram CW, Cooper JN. Clostridial bloodstream infections. South Med J. 1989;82:29–31.
19. Mendes CM, Oplostil CP, dos Santos TJL, et al. *Clostridium perfringens* as a cause of endocarditis in a patient with a vascular prosthesis. Clin Infect Dis. 1996;22:866–867.
20. Ramsay AM. The significance of *Clostridium welchii* in the cervical swab and blood-stream in postpartum and postabortium sepsis. J Obstet Gynaecol. 1949;56:247–248.
21. Gorbach SL, Thadepalli H. Isolation of *Clostridium* in human infections: Evaluation of 114 cases. J Infect Dis. 1975;131(Suppl):S81–S85.
22. Alpern RJ, Dowell VR Jr. Nonhistotoxic clostridial bacteremia. Am J Clin Pathol. 1971;55:717–722.
23. Myers G, Ngoi SS, Cennerazzo W, et al. Clostridial septicemia in an urban hospital. Surg Gynecol Obstet. 1992;174:291–296.
24. Miguélez M, Aguado JM. Recurrent episodes of spontaneous clostridial myonecrosis related to colorectal carcinoma. Clin Infect Dis. 1996;22:582–583.
25. Martin WJ. Isolation and identification of anaerobic bacteria in the clinical laboratory. A 2-year experience. Mayo Clin Proc. 1974;49:300–308.
26. Larson CM, Bubrick MP, Jacobs DM, et al. Malignancy, mortality and medicosurgical management of *Clostridium septicum* infection. Surgery. 1995;118:592–598.
27. Kornbluth AA, Danzig JB, Bernstein LH. *Clostridium septicum* infection and associated malignancy. Medicine (Baltimore). 1989;68:30–37.
28. Stevens PL, Musher DM, Watson DA, et al. Spontaneous, nontraumatic gangrene due to *Clostridium septicum*. Rev Infect Dis. 1990;12:286–296.
29. Case Records of the Massachusetts General Hospital (case 5–1993). N Engl J Med. 1993;328:340–346.
30. Panwalker AP. Unusual infections associated with colorectal cancer. Rev Infect Dis. 1988;10:347–364.
31. Rifkin GD. Neutropenic enterocolitis and *Clostridium septicum* infection in patients with agranulocytosis. Arch Intern Med. 1980;140:834–835.
32. Hopkins DG, Kushner JP. Clostridial species in pathogenesis of necrotizing enterocolitis in patients with neutropenia. Am J Hematol. 1983;14:289–295.
33. Bar-Joseph G, Halberthal M, Sweed Y, et al. *Clostridium septicum* infection in children with cyclic neutropenia. J Pediatr. 1997;131:317–319.
34. Tikko SK, Distenfield A, Davidson M. *Clostridium septicum* septicemia with identical metastatic myonecrosis in a granulocytopenic patient. Am J Med. 1985;79:256–258.
35. Gorse GJ, Slater LM, Sobol E, et al. CNS infection and bacteremia due to *Clostridium septicum*. Arch Neurol. 1984;41:882–884.
36. Neimkin RJ, Jupiter JB. Metastatic nontraumatic *Clostridium septicum* osteomyelitis. J Hand Surg [Am]. 1985;10:281–284.
37. Macy NJ, Lieber L, Habermann ET. Arthritis caused by *Clostridium septicum*. J Bone Joint Surg Am. 1986;68:465–466.
38. Insier MS, Karcioglu ZA, Naugle T. *Clostridium septicum* panophthalmitis with systemic complications. Br J Ophthalmol. 1985;69:774–777.
39. Moses AE, Hardan I, Simhon A, et al. *Clostridium septicum* bacteremia and diffuse spreading cellulitis of the head and neck in a leukemic patient. Rev Infect Dis. 1991;13:525–527.
40. Kinnaird DW, Melo JC, KcKeown JM. Splenic abscess due to *Clostridium septicum* in a patient with multiple myeloma. South Med J. 1987;80:1318–1320.
41. Cohen CA, Almeder LM, Israni A, et al. *Clostridium septicum* endocarditis complicated by aortic-ring abscess and aortitis. Clin Infect Dis. 1998;26:495–496.
42. George WL, Finegold SM. Clostridia in the human gastrointestinal flora. In: Boriello SP, ed. Clostridia in Gastrointestinal Disease. Boca Raton, Fla: CRC; 1985:1–37.
43. Speirs G, Warren RE, Rampling A. *Clostridium tertium* septicemia in patients with neutropenia. J Infect Dis. 1988;158:1336–1340.
44. Mory F, Lozniewski A, Guirlet MN, et al. Severe sepsis caused by *Clostridium sordellii* following liver biopsy in a liver transplant recipient. Clin Infect Dis. 1995;21:1522–1523.
45. Moore WEC, Cato EP, Holdeman LV. Anaerobic bacteria of the gastrointestinal flora and their occurrence in clinical infections. J Infect Dis. 1969;119:641–649.
46. Gorbach SL, Thadepalli H, Norsen J. Anaerobic microorganisms in intraabdominal infections. In: Balows A, DeHann RM, Dowell VR Jr, et al, eds. Anaerobic Bacteria Role in Disease. Springfield, Ill: Charles C Thomas; 1974:399–407
47. Stone HH, Kolb LD, Geheber CE. Incidence and significance of intraperitoneal anaerobic bacteria. Ann Surg. 1975;181:705–714.
48. Lorber B, Swenson RM. The bacteriology of intra-abdominal infections. Surg Clin North Am. 1975;55:1349–1354.
49. Stone HH, Strom PR, Fabian TC, et al. Third-generation cephalosporins for polymicrobial surgical sepsis. Arch Surg. 1983;118:193–200.
50. Dunn DL, Simmons RL. The role of anaerobic bacteria in intraabdominal infections. Rev Infect Dis. 1984;6(Suppl):S139–S147.
51. Lykkegaard Nielsen M, Justesen T. Anaerobic and aerobic bacteriological studies in biliary tract disease. Scand J Gastroenterol. 1976;11:437–446.
52. England DM, Rosenblatt JE. Anaerobes in human biliary tracts. J Clin Microbiol. 1977;6:494–498.
53. Shimada K, Inamatsu T, Yamashiro M. Anaerobic bacteria in biliary disease in elderly patients. J Infect Dis. 1977;135:850–854.
54. Edinburgh A, Geffen A. Acute emphysematous cholecystitis. A case report and review of the world literature. Am J Surg. 1958;96:66–75.
55. Sarmiento RV. Emphysematous cholecystitis: Report of four cases and review of the literature. Arch Surg. 1966;93:1009–1014.
56. Mentzer RM Jr, Golden GT, Chandler JG, et al. A comparative appraisal of emphysematous cholecystitis. Am J Surg. 1975;129:10–15.
57. Thadepalli H, Gorbach SL, Keith L. Anaerobic infections of the female genital tract: Bacteriologic and therapeutic aspects. Am J Obstet Gynecol. 1973;117:1034–1040.
58. Sweet RL. Anaerobic infections of the female genital tract. Am J Obstet Gynecol. 1975;122:891–901.
59. Ledger WJ, Norman M, Gee C, et al. Bacteremia on an obstetric-gynecologic service. Am J Obstet Gynecol. 1975;121:205–212.
60. DiZerega GS, Yonekura ML, Keegan K, et al. Bacteremia in post-cesarean section endomyometritis: Differential response to therapy. Obstet Gynecol. 1980;55:587–590.
61. Ohm JJ, Galask RP. The effect of antibiotic prophylaxis on patients undergoing vaginal operations. Am J Obstet Gynecol. 1975;123:597–604.
62. Bartlett JG, Onderdonk AB, Drude E, et al. Quantitative bacteriology of the vaginal flora. J Infect Dis. 1977;136:271–277.
63. Holtz F, Mauch EW. Gas gangrene of the uterus. Survival following hysterectomy. Obstet Gynecol. 1962;19:545–548.
64. Decker WH, Hall W. Treatment of abortions infected with *Clostridium welchii*. Am J Obstet Gynecol. 1966;95:394–399.
65. Smith LP, McLean APH, Maughan GB. *Clostridium welchii* septicotoxemia. A review and report of 3 cases. Am J Obstet Gynecol. 1971;110:135.
66. Pritchard JA, Whalley PJ. Abortion complicated by *Clostridium perfringens* infection. Am J Obstet Gynecol. 1971;111:484–492.
67. Dylewski J, Wiesenfeld H, Latour A. Postpartum uterine infection with *Clostridium perfringens*. J Infect Dis. 1989;11:470–473.
68. Hovar Y, Hornstein E, Pollack RN, et al. Sepsis due to *Clostridium perfringens* after second-trimester amniocentesis. Clin Infect Dis. 1995;21:235–236.
69. Soper DE. Clostridial myonecrosis arising from an episiotomy. Obstet Gynecol. 1986;68(Suppl):S26–S28.
70. Bartlett JG. Anaerobic bacterial infections of the lung. Chest. 1988;91:901–909.
71. Finland M, Barnes MW. Changing ecology of acute bacterial empyema: Occurrence and mortality at Boston City Hospital during 12 selected years from 1935 to 1972. J Infect Dis. 1978;137:274–291.

72. Sweeting J, Rosenberg L. Primary clostridial pneumonia. Ann Intern Med. 1959;51:805–810.
73. Goldberg NM, Rifkind D. Clostridial empyema. Arch Intern Med. 1965;115:421–425.
74. Bayer AS, Nelson SC, Galpin JE, et al. Necrotizing pneumonia and empyema due to *Clostridium perfringens*: Report of case and review of the literature. Am J Med. 1975;59:851–856.
75. Bekemeyer WB Jr. Clostridial infections of the lungs and pleura. South Med J. 1986;79:1393–1397.
76. Corbett CE, Wall BM, Cohen M. Case report: Empyema with hydropneumothorax and bacteremia caused by *Clostridium sporogenes*. Am J Med. 1996;312:242–245.
77. Bashir Y, Benson MK. Necrotizing pneumonia and empyema due to *Clostridium perfringens* complicating pulmonary embolus. Thorax. 1990;45:72–73.
78. Lorber B, Swenson RM. Bacteriology of aspiration pneumonia. A prospective study of community- and hospital-acquired cases. Ann Intern Med. 1974;81:329–331.
79. Bartlett JG, Gorbach SL, Finegold S. The bacteriology of aspiration pneumonia. Am J Med. 1974;56:202–207.
80. Elliot TR, Henry H. Infection of hemothorax by anaerobic gas producing bacilli. BMJ. 1917;1:413–418.
81. Lynch JF, Strieder J. Hemothorax complicated by infection with *Clostridium welchii*. N Engl J Med. 1942;226:685.
82. Cairns H, Calvert CA, Daniel P, et al. Complications of head wounds with special reference to infection. Br J Surg. 1947;1(Suppl):S198–S243.
83. Colwell FG, Sullivan J, Shuman HH, et al. Acute purulent meningitis due to *Clostridium perfringens*. N Engl J Med. 1960;262:618–619.
84. Russell JA, Taylor JC. Circumscribed gas gangrene abscess of the brain. Case report together with an account of the literature. Br J Surg. 1963;50:434.
85. Keogh AJ. Clostridial brain abscess and hyperbaric oxygen. Postgrad Med J. 1973;49:64–66.
86. Klein MA, Kelly JD, Jacobs IG. Diffuse pneumocephalus from *Clostridium perfringens* meningitis: CT findings. Am J Neuroradiol. 1989;10:447.
87. Domingo Z. Clostridial brain abscesses. Br J Neurosurg. 1994;8:691–694.
88. Lew JF, Wiedermann BL, Sneed J, et al. Aerotolerant *Clostridium tertium* brain abscess following a lawn dart injury. J Clin Microbiol. 1990;28:2127–2129.
89. Spitzer RD, Ratzan KR. Chronic osteomyelitis due to *Clostridium clostridiiforme*. South Med J. 1991;84:671–672.
90. MacLennan JD. Anaerobic infections of war wounds in the Middle East. Lancet. 1943;2:94–98.
91. Qvist G. Anaerobic cellulitis and gas gangrene. BMJ. 1941;2:217.
92. Wilson TS. The significance of *C. welchii* infections and their relationship to gas gangrene. Can J Surg. 1960;4:35.
93. Filler RM, Griscom NT, Pappas A. Post-traumatic crepitation falsely suggesting gas gangrene. N Engl J Med. 1969;278:758–761.
94. VanBeek A, Zook E, Yaw P, et al. Nonclostridial gas-forming infections. A collective review and report of seven cases. Arch Surg. 1974;108:552–527.
95. Welch WH, Nuttall GHF. A gas-producing bacillus capable of rapid development in the blood-vessels after death. Bull Johns Hopkins Hosp. 1892;3:81–91.
96. Welch WH, Flexner S. Observations concerning the *Bacillus aerogenes capsulatus*. J Exp Med. 1896;1:5–45.
97. Willis AT. History. In: Finegold SM, George L, eds. Anaerobic Infections in Humans. New York: Academic; 1989:1–22.
98. MacLennan JD. The histotoxic clostridial infections of man. Bacteriol Rev. 1962;26:177–276.
99. Altemeier WA, Furste WL. Gas gangrene. Surg Gynecol Obstet. 1947;84:507–523.
100. Simeone F. Clostridial myositis. In: Symposium on Military Medicine in the Far East Command. Surg Circ Lett Med Section. 1951;Sept(Suppl).
101. Brown PW, Kinman PB. Gas gangrene in a metropolitan community. J Bone Joint Surg Am. 1974;56:1445.
102. Asmuth DM, Olson RD, Hackett SP, et al. Effects of *Clostridium perfringens* recombinant and crude phospholipuse C and θ-toxin on rabbit hemodynamic parameters. J Infect Dis. 1995;172:1317–1323.
103. Stevens DL, Bryant AE. Pathogenesis of *Clostridium perfringens* infection: Mechanisms and mediators of shock. Clin Infect Dis. 1997;25(Suppl 2):S160–S162.
104. Johnson S, Driks MR, Tweten RK, et al. Clinical course of seven survivors of *Clostridium septicum* infection and their immunologic responses to α-toxin. Clin Infect Dis. 1994;19:761–764.
105. Altemeier WA, Furste WL. Studies in virulence of *Clostridium welchii*. Surgery. 1949;25:12.
106. Hallagan LF, Scott JL, Horowitz BC, et al. Clostridial myonecrosis resulting from subcutaneous epinephrine suspension injection. Ann Emerg Med. 1992;21:434–436.
107. Lowbury EJL, Lilly HA. The sources of hospital infection of wounds with *Clostridium welchii*. J Hyg. 1958;56:169–182.
108. Eickhoff TC. An outbreak of surgical wound infections due to *Clostridium perfringens*. Surg Gynecol Obstet. 1962;114:102–108.
109. Altemeier WA, Fullen WD. Prevention and treatment of gas gangrene. JAMA. 1971;217:806–813.
110. Weinstein L, Barza M. Gas gangrene. N Engl J Med. 1973;289:1129–1131.
111. Caplan ES, Kluge RM. Gas gangrene: Review of 34 cases. Arch Intern Med. 1976;136:788–791.
112. Heimbach RD. Gas gangrene: Review and update. HBO Rev. 1980;1:41.
113. Cline KA, Turnbull TL. Clostridial myonecrosis. Ann Emerg Med. 1985;14:459–466.
114. Stevens DL, Tweten RK, Awad MM, et al. Clostridial gas gangrene: Evidence that α and θ toxins differentially modulate the immune response and induce tissue necrosis. J Infect Dis. 1997;176:189–195.
115. Demello FJ, Maglin JJ, Hitchcock CR. Comparative study of experimental *Clostridium perfringens* infection in dogs treated with antibiotics, surgery and hyperbaric oxygen. Surgery. 1973;73:936–941.
116. Roding B, Groeneveld PHA, Boerema I. Ten years of experience in the treatment of gas gangrene with hyperbaric oxygen. Surg Gynecol Obstet. 1972;134:579–585.
117. Darke SG, King AM, Slack WK. Gas gangrene and related infection: Classification. Clinical features and etiology, management and mortality. A report of 88 cases. Br J Surg. 1977;64:104–112.
118. Marrie TJ, Haldane EV, Swantee CA, et al. Susceptibility of anaerobic bacteria to nine antimicrobial agents and demonstration of decreased susceptibility of *Clostridium perfringens* to penicillin. Antimicrob Agents Chemother. 1981;19:51–55.
119. Alexander CJ, Citron DM, Brazier JS, et al. Identification and antimicrobial resistance patterns of clinical isolates of *Clostridium clostridiiforme, Clostridium innocuum,* and *Clostridium ramosum* compared with those of clinical isolates of *Clostridium perfringens*. J Clin Microbiol. 1995;33:3209–3215.
120. Musial CE, Rosenblatt JE. Antimicrobial susceptibilities of anaerobic bacteria isolated at the Mayo Clinic during 1982 through 1987: Comparison with results from 1977 through 1981. Mayo Clin Proc. 1989;64:392–399.
121. Brazier JS, Levett PN, Stannard AL, et al. Antibiotic susceptibility of clinical isolates of *clostridia*. J Antimicrob Chemother. 1985;15:181–185.
122. Mohr JA, Griffiths W, Holm R, et al. Clostridial myonecrosis (gas gangrene) during cephalosporin prophylaxis. JAMA. 1978;239:847–849.
123. Altemeier WA, McMurrin JA, Alt AP. Chloromycetin and aureomycin in experimental gas gangrene. Surgery. 1950;28:621–631.
124. Stevens DL, Maier KA, Laine BM, et al. Comparison of clindamycin, rifampin, tetracycline, metronidazole, and penicillin for efficacy in prevention of experimental gas gangrene due to *Clostridium perfringens*. J Infect Dis. 1987;155:220–228.
125. Stevens DL, Maier KA, Mitten JE. Effect of antibiotics on toxin production and viability of *Clostridium perfringens*. Antimicrob Agents Chemother. 1987;31:213–218.
126. Stevens DL, Laine BM, Mitten JE. Comparison of single and combination antimicrobial agents for prevention of experimental gas gangrene caused by *Clostridium perfringens*. Antimicrob Agents Chemother. 1987;31:312–316.
127. Langley FH, Winkelstein LB. Gas gangrene: A study of 96 cases treated in an evacuation hospital. JAMA. 1945;128:783–792.
128. Slack WK, Hanson GC, Chew HER. Hyperbaric oxygen in the treatment of gas gangrene and clostridial infection. A report of 40 patients treated in a single-person hyperbaric oxygen chamber. Br J Surg. 1969;56:505–510.
129. Hart GB, Lamb RC, Strauss MB. Gas gangrene: I. A collective review II. A 15-year experience with hyperbaric oxygen. J Trauma. 1983;23:991–1000.
130. Trivedi DR, Raut VV. Role of hyperbaric oxygen therapy in the rapid control of gas gangrene infection and its toxaemia. J Postgrad Med. 1990;36:13–15.
131. Hill GB, Osterhout S. Experimental effects of hyperbaric oxygen on selected clostridial species. I. In-vitro studies. J Infect Dis. 1972;125:17–25.
132. Stevens DL, Bryant AE, Adams K, et al. Evaluation of therapy with hyperbaric oxygen for experimental infection with *Clostridium perfringens*. Clin Infect Dis. 1993;17:231–237; 2 editorial responses: Thom S. Editorial response: A role for hyperbaric oxygen in clostridial myonecrosis. p 238; and Heimbach D. Editorial response: Use of hyperbaric oxygen. pp 239–240.
133. Brummelkamp WH, Boerema I, Hoogendyk L. Treatment of clostridial infections with hyperbaric oxygen drenching: A report on 26 cases. Lancet. 1963;1:235–238.
134. Kliegman RM. The role of clostridia in the pathogenesis of neonatal necrotizing enterocolitis. In: Borrielo SP, ed. Clostridia in Gastrointestinal Disease. Boca Raton, Fla: CRC; 1985:67–92.
135. Zeissler J, Rassfeld-Sternberg L. Enteritis necroticans due to *Clostridium welchii* type F. BMJ. 1949;1:267–269.
136. Field HI, Goodwin RFW. The experimental reproduction of enterotoxaemia in piglets. J Hyg. 1959;57:81–91.
137. Murrell TGC. Enteritis necroticans. In: Finegold SM, George WL, eds. Anaerobic Infections in Humans. New York: Academic; 1989;639–659.
138. Murrell TGC, Roth L. Necrotizing jejunitis: A newly discovered disease in the highlands of New Guinea. Med J Aust. 1963;1:61–69.
139. Lawrence G, Murrell TGC, Walker PD, eds. Symposium on pig-bel. Papua New Guinea Med J. 1979;22:1–108.
140. Lawrence G, Cooke R. Experimental pigbel: The production and pathology of necrotizing enteritis due to *Clostridium welchii* type C in the guinea pig. Br J Exp Pathol. 1980;61:261–271.
141. Murrell TGC. Pig-bel in Papua New Guinea: An ancient disease rediscovered? Int J Epidemiol. 1983;12:211–214.
142. Davis M. A review of pig-bel (necrotizing enteritis) in Papua New Guinea 1961–1984. Papua New Guinea Med J. 1985;2:75–82.
143. Akama K, Otani S, Kameyama S. Purification of B-toxin of *Clostridium perfringens* type C. Jpn J Med Sci Biol. 1969;21:423–426.
144. Karanth S, Coninx R, Dickson C, et al. Enteritis necroticans (pig-bel) on Thai/Kampuchean border? Lancet. 1986;1:1437.
145. Cooke R. The pathology of pigbel. Papua New Guinea Med J. 1979;22:35–38.
146. Walker PD, Murrell TGC, Nagy LK. Scanning electron microscopy of the jejunum in enteritis necroticans. J Med Microbiol. 1980;13:445–450.
147. Hain E. On the occurrence of *C. welchii* type F in normal stools. BMJ. 1949;1:271.
148. Lawrence G, Shann F, Freestone DS, et al. Prevention of necrotizing enteritis in Papua New Guinea by active immunization. Lancet. 1979;1:227–230.

149. Lawrence GW, Lehmann D, Anian G, et al. Impact of active immunization against enteritis necroticans in Papua New Guinea. Lancet. 1990;336:1165–1167.
150. Murrell TGC, Walker PD. The pigbel story of Papua New Guinea. Trans R Soc Trop Med Hyg. 1991;85:119–122.
151. Alt B, Glass NR, Sollinger H. Neutropenic enterocolitis in adults. Review of the literature and assessment of surgical intervention. Am J Surg. 1985;149:405–408.
152. Mower WJ, Hawkins JA, Nelson EW. Neutropenic enterocolitis in adults with acute leukemia. Arch Surg. 1986;121:571–573.
153. Koransky JR, Stargel MD, Dowell VR. *Clostridium septicum* bacteremia. Its clinical significance. Am J Med. 1979;66:63–66.
154. Moir CR, Scudamore CH, Benny WB. Typhlitis: Selective surgical management. Am J Surg. 1986;151:563–566.
155. Shamberger RC, Weinstein HJ, Delorey MJ, et al. The medical and surgical management of typhlitis in children with acute nonlymphocytic (myelogenous) leukemia. Cancer. 1986;57:603–609.
156. Felitti VJ. Primary invasion by *Clostridium sphenoides* in a patient with periodic neutropenia. Calif Med. 1973;113:76–78.
157. Gruter H. Gas gangrene following antibiotic-associated enterocolitis in hereditary neutropenia. Arch Anat Cytol Pathol. 1985;33:23–25.
158. Thaler M, Gill V, Pizzo PA. Emergence of *Clostridium tertium* as a pathogen in neutropenic patients. Am J Med. 1986;81:596–600.
159. Newbold KM, Lord MG, Baglin TP. Role of clostridial organisms in neutropenic enterocolitis. J Clin Pathol. 1987;40:471.
160. Yates P, MacGowan AP, Potter M, et al. Clostridia and neutropenic enterocolitis. Lancet. 1988;1:185.
161. Meer RR, Songer JG, Park DL. Human disease associated with *Clostridium perfringens* enterotoxin. Rev Environ Contam Toxicol. 1997;150:75–94.
162. Aucott JN. Food poisoning. In: Blaser M, Smith PD, Rardin JI, et al, eds. Infections of the Gastrointestinal Tract. New York: Raven; 1995:237–250.
163. Larson HE, Borriello SP. Infectious diarrhea due to *Clostridium perfringens.* J Infect Dis. 1988;157:390–391.
164. Borriello SP. Clostridial diseases of the gut. Clin Infect Dis. 1995;(Suppl 2):S242–S250.
165. Sears CL, Guerrant RL, Kaper JB. Enteric bacterial toxins. In: Blaser MJ, Smith PD, Rardin JI, et al, eds. Infections of the Gastrointestinal Tract. New York: Raven; 1995;617–634.
166. Duncan DL, Strong SH. Improved medium for sporulation of *Clostridium perfringens.* Appl Microbiol. 1968;16:82–89.
167. Yasukawa A, Okada Y, Kitase T, et al. Distribution of enterotoxin producing strains of *Clostridium perfringens* type A in human beings, food and soils. J Food Hyg Soc Jpn. 1975;16:313–317.
168. Uemura T. Incidence of enterotoxigenic *Clostridium perfringens* in healthy humans in relation to the enhancement of enterotoxin production by heat treatment. J Appl Bacteriol. 1978;44:411–419.
169. McDonel JL, McClane BA. Binding versus biologic activity of *Clostridium perfringens* enterotoxin in Vero cells. Biochem Biophys Res Commun. 1979;87:497–504.
170. Niilo L. Measurement of biological activities of purified and crude enterotoxin of *Clostridium perfringens.* Infect Immun. 1975;12:440–442.
171. McDonel JL. Binding of *Clostridium perfringens* (125I) enterotoxin in rabbit intestinal cells. Biochemistry. 1980;19:4801–4807.
172. Tollesang H, Skjelkvale R, Berg T. Quantitation of binding and subcellular distribution of *Clostridium perfringens* enterotoxin in rat liver cells. Infect Immun. 1982;37:486–491.
173. McClane BA, McDonel JL. The effects of *Clostridium perfringens* enterotoxin on morphology viability and macromolecular synthesis in Vero cells. J Cell Physiol. 1979;99:191–199.
174. Bowness P, Moss PA, Tranter H, et al. *Clostridium perfringens* enterotoxin is a superantigen reactive with human T cell receptors. V beta 6.9 and V beta 22. J Exp Med. 1992;176:893–896.
175. Shandera WX, Tacket CO, Blake PA. Food poisoning due to *Clostridium perfringens* in the United States. J Infect Dis. 1983;147:167–170.
176. Roach RL, Sienko DG. *Clostridium perfringens* outbreak associated with minestrone soup. Am J Epidemiol. 1992;136:1288–1291.
177. Jackson SG, Yip-Chuck DA, Clark JB, et al. Diagnostic importance of *Clostridium perfringens* enterotoxin analysis in recurring enteritis among elderly, chronic care psychiatric patients. J Clin Microbiol. 1986;23:748–751.
178. Collee JG, Knowlden JA, Hobbs BC. Studies on the growth, sporulation and carriage of *Clostridium welchii* with special reference to food poisoning strains. J Appl Bacteriol. 1961;24:326.
179. Finegold SM. *Clostridium perfringens* food poisoning. In: Anaerobic Bacteria in Human Disease. New York: Academic; 1977:511–512.
180. Skjelkvale R, Uemura T. Experimental diarrhoea in human volunteers following oral administration of *Clostridium perfringens* enterotoxin. J Appl Bacteriol. 1977;43:281–286.
181. Birkhead G, Vogt RL, Heun EM, et al. Characterization of an outbreak of *Clostridium perfringens* food poisoning by quantitative fecal culture and fecal enterotoxin measurement. J Clin Microbiol. 1988;26:471–474.
182. McClane BA, Snyder JT. Development and preliminary evaluation of a slide latex agglutination assay for determination of *Clostridium perfringens* type A enterotoxin. J Immunol Methods. 1987;100:131–136.
183. Harmon SM, Jautter DA. Evaluation of reversed passive latex agglutination test kit for *Clostridium perfringens.* J Food Prot. 1986;49:523–525.
184. McClane BA, Strouse RJ. Rapid detection of *Clostridium perfringens* type A enterotoxin by enzyme-linked immunosorbent assay. J Clin Microbiol. 1984;19:112–115.
185. Finegold SM, George WL, Mulligan ME. Anaerobic infections. Dis Mon. 1985;31:10–77.

ADDITIONAL READING

Rood JI, McClane BA, Songer JG, et al, eds. The Clostridia: Molecular Biology and Pathogenesis. San Diego: Academic; 1997.

Chapter 237

Bacteroides, Prevotella, Porphyromonas, and *Fusobacterium* Species (and Other Medically Important Anaerobic Gram-Negative Bacilli)

BENNETT LORBER

The anaerobic gram-negative bacilli that make up the genus *Bacteroides* are among the most important constituents of the normal human flora and are plentiful in the oral cavity, the gastrointestinal tract, and the vagina. From these endogenous sources a wide variety of human infections may occur, many of which (1) are polymicrobial and involve multiple anaerobic species, as well as facultative organisms, and (2) have a tendency for abscess formation. Among the common infections caused by these bacteria are periodontal disease, postaspiration pleuropulmonary infection, genital tract infections in women, and intra-abdominal abscesses. *Bacteroides fragilis* is the most important species, and its putative presence has implications for antimicrobial selection.

MICROBIOLOGY

In 1988 Shah and Collins[1] proposed that some *Bacteroides* spp. be reclassified into a new genus, *Porphyromonas*, and in 1990 these authors[2] proposed that others be redesignated as the novel genus *Prevotella* (Table 237–1). More than 20 genera of anaerobic gram-negative bacilli are recognized,[3, 4] but human infection is largely restricted to 4 of these, namely, *Bacteroides, Prevotella, Porphyromonas*, and *Fusobacterium.* Unlike clostridial species, none of these anaerobic bacteria form spores. These bacteria are identified presumptively (Table 237–2) on the basis of colonial morphology, Gram-stain characteristics, pigment production, fluorescence with long-wave ultraviolet light, susceptibility to special-strength antibiotic disks, and biochemical tests.[3] Definitive identification requires multiple biochemical tests that are tedious to perform and, because of expense, not feasible for most clinical laboratories. Because of its clinical importance and relative antimicrobial resistance, identification of *B. fragilis* is essential.

The *B. fragilis* group can be distinguished from other species of anaerobic gram-negative bacilli by growth in 20% bile and resistance to special-strength kanamycin, vancomycin, and colistin antibiotic

TABLE 237-1 Clinically Important Anaerobic Gram-Negative Bacilli

Current Name	Previous Name (*Bacteroides*)
Bacteroides fragilis group	
B. fragilis	
B. thetaiotaomicron	
B. vulgatus	
B. distasonis	
B. ovatus	
B. uniformis	
B. caccae	*B. fragilis* group "3452A"
Bacteroides spp., other	
B. ureolyticus	
B. forsythus	*B. corrodens*
Prevotella	
P. bivia	*B. bivius*
P. buccae	*B. buccae*
	B. ruminicola
	B. capillus
P. denticola	*B. denticola*
P. disiens	*B. disiens*
P. intermedia	*B. intermedius*
	B. melaningogenicus subsp. *intermedius*
P. melaninogenica	*B. melaninogenicus* subsp. *melaninogenicus*
P. oralis	*B. oralis*
P. oris	*B. oris*
	B. ruminicola
Porphyromonas	
P. asaccharolytica	*B. asaccharolyticus*
	B. melinogenicus subsp. *asaccharolyticus*
P. endodontalis	*B. endodontalis*
P. gingivalis	*B. gingivalis*
Fusobacterium	
F. necrophorum	
F. nucleatum	
Bilophila wadsworthia	
Campylobacter gracilis	*B. gracilis*

disks. *B. fragilis* forms 1- to 3-mm nonhemolytic, glistening colonies on blood agar and is aerotolerant. On Gram stain, *B. fragilis* usually appears as a pale gram-negative bacillus but may appear pleomorphic (coccobacillary) and may be gram-variable with irregular or bipolar staining.

The pigmenting anaerobic gram-negative bacilli are made up of saccharolytic and asaccharolytic species of the genera *Prevotella* and *Porphyromonas*, respectively. These organisms form brown to black colonies after about a week when grown on rabbit laked blood agar; under ultraviolet light, young unpigmented colonies exhibit brick red fluorescence. On Gram stain they appear as small, pale-staining, coccobacillary gram-negative rods.

Fusobacterium organisms are long, thin, gram-negative rods with pointed ends, often arranged end to end in pairs. *Bilophila wadsworthia* is a recently described slow-growing, asaccharolytic, nonmotile bacillus that is strongly catalase positive and derives its name from its resistance to 20% ox bile.

The commercial development and widespread clinical use of anaerobic culture environments, such as anaerobic chambers, jars, or pouches, has led in the last 30 years to an appreciation of the major role that these anaerobic gram-negative bacilli play in human infection.

NORMAL FLORA

Anaerobes are the predominant constituents of the normal human bacterial flora, and anaerobic gram-negative bacilli, particularly *Bacteroides* and *Prevotella* spp., are numerically the most prevalent organisms. These bacteria are not prominent skin flora but are abundant on all mucosal surfaces and reach their largest concentrations in the tonsillar crypts, the crypts of the tongue, dental plaque, and the gingival crevices in the oral cavity; the colon in the gastrointestinal tract; and the vagina.

Colonization of the oral cavity begins at or shortly after birth, with specific bacterial adherence being an important determinant of the microecology.[5, 6] Anaerobes become prominent in childhood in association with the eruption of teeth and the anaerobic environment created by the establishment of gingival crevices (redox potential as low as −350 mV).[7] *Prevotella melaninogenica* is found in the gingival crevices of 18 to 40% of 5-year-olds and virtually 100% of teenagers. *Porphyromonal gingivalis* is found in 37% of subjects, with similar frequencies at all ages, and may be acquired in the first days of life.[8] Colonization concordance is found in families, which suggests that *P. gingivalis* is transmitted by contact within the home.[9] Other important oral anaerobes include *Fusobacterium nucleatum, Fusobacterium necrophorum, Prevotella oralis, Prevotella disiens, Prevotella oris, Prevotella buccae*, and *Bacteroides forsythus*. In dental plaque and gingival sulci, concentrations of bacteria may reach 10^{12}/ml, which approximates the physical limits of space.[10] The microecology in the mouth is complex, and many bacteria are dependent on other species for survival; for example, *P. melaninogenica* requires vitamin K produced by other species, and oral spirochetes are dependent on metabolites produced by *Fusobacterium* spp.[11]

The largest concentration of bacteria in the human body is found in the colon, where more than 400 genera may coexist. Anaerobes outnumber aerobes 1000:1, reach numbers of 10^{11}/g of fecal material,[12] and are usually found in intimate association with the mucosa and mucous sheath.[13] The infant alimentary tract, sterile at birth, is rapidly colonized by aerobic bacteria and later by anaerobes, with the fecal flora resembling that of an adult by the end of the second year of life.[14] The small bowel contains fewer anaerobes (10^2 to 10^4/g) and an equal number of aerobes, but if intestinal motility is interrupted by obstruction or if a diverticulum or surgical blind loop is present, the flora changes to resemble that of the colon.[15] Numerically, the major colonic organisms are *Bacteroides* spp., with *Bacteroides vulgatus* and *Bacteroides thetaiotaomicron* being the most common. *B. fragilis*, the most important anaerobic in clinical infection, is present in virtually all humans but accounts for only 0.5% of the flora. The intestinal anaerobic flora carries out a variety of metabolic activities[11] and may be important in protecting the host from colonization with potential pathogens ("colonization resistance").[16]

The adult vaginal flora, which contains bacterial concentrations of 10^5 to 10^8/ml, is dominated by anaerobes, of which the gram-positive lactobacilli are most plentiful, but as many as 20% of women have no detectable anaerobes or very low concentrations.[17, 18] *B. fragilis* is found in only 2 to 4% of subjects, and the most commonly found anaerobic gram-negative bacilli are *P. melanino-*

TABLE 237-2 Characteristics of Anaerobic Gram-Negative Rods

Genus and Species	Growth in 20% Bile	Kanamycin, 1000 μg	Vancomycin, 5 μg	Colistin, 10 μg	Catalase	Indole	Lipase	Pigment	Brick Red Fluorescence
Bacteroides fragilis group	Yes	Resistant	Resistant	Resistant	Variable	Variable	Negative	No	No
Prevotella	No	Resistant	Resistant	Variable	Negative usually	Variable	Variable	Yes	Usually
Porphyromonas	No	Resistant	Sensitive	Resistant	Negative usually	Positive	Variable	Yes	Usually
Fusobacterium	Variable	Sensitive	Resistant	Sensitive	Negative	Variable	Variable	No	No
Bilophila	Yes	Sensitive	Resistant	Sensitive	Positive	Negative	Negative	No	No

genica, *Prevotella bivia*, and *P. disiens*, which are present in one quarter to one third of women. Anaerobes predominate in the normal vaginal flora of prepubertal girls in numbers higher than those found in premenopausal adults,[19] and gram-negative anaerobes are less prevalent in postmenopausal women than in women of reproductive age.[20] The flora of the vagina is dynamic and less stable than that of the gastrointestinal tract and may vary with the menstrual cycle, pregnancy, postmenopausal state, gynecologic surgery, and antimicrobial therapy.

PATHOGENESIS

Synergy

Infections involving anaerobic bacteria characteristically contain multiple anaerobes and often facultative organisms as well. Considerable evidence points to true synergy between unrelated bacterial species in the pathogenesis of these infections. In 1930, Smith[21] isolated multiple bacterial types from patients with purulent gingivitis and used these organisms singly and in combinations in an animal model of lung abscess. He demonstrated that multiple agents together might produce an infection that could not be produced with the individual components used singly. Anaerobic bacilli in combination with facultative bacteria induce the formation of intra-abdominal abscesses more readily than either component does alone,[22] and mixtures containing *Bacteroides* spp. enhance the growth of some facultative bacteria.[23] In an animal model of oral mucosal infection, the virulence of the pathogen *P. melaninogenica* was enhanced by an avirulent diphtheroid that provided necessary vitamin K.[24]

It is postulated that by lowering the oxidation-reduction potential in the microenvironment, facultative organisms may promote more favorable conditions for anaerobic growth and that the anaerobic component in mixed infection may facilitate the growth of facultative bacteria through inhibition of phagocytes.[25] *B. fragilis* produces detectable levels of β-lactamase in abscess fluid that may protect normally susceptible components of mixed infections from the actions of antimicrobials.[26]

Virulence

The importance of virulence factors (Table 237–3) in the pathogenesis of infections caused by anaerobic gram-negative bacilli is indicated by the fact that *B. fragilis* and *Fusobacterium* spp. are isolated from clinical infections with a frequency disproportionate to their prevalence in the normal gastrointestinal and oral flora.

TABLE 237–3 Virulence Factors of Anaerobic Gram-Negative Bacilli

Factor	Comment
Capsular polysaccharide	Found in *Bacteroides fragilis* and *Prevotella melaninogenica,* inhibits opsonophagocytosis, promotes abscess formation, promotes adherence to epithelial cells
Pili and fimbriae	Found in the *B. fragilis* group and *Porphyromonas gingivalis,* promotes adherence to epithelial cells and mucus
Endotoxin	*Fusobacterium* spp. have a biologically active form; *Bacteroides* lipopolysaccharide lacks lipid A and is biologically impotent
Succinic acid	Produced by many species, inhibits phagocytosis and intracellular killing of the producer and others in its milieu
Enzymes Hyaluronidase, hemolysin, peroxidase, collagenase, phospholipase, protease, fibrinolysin, heparinase, neuraminidase	Produced by many species, contribute to tissue damage and/or promote invasion and spread
Superoxide dismutase	Produced by many clinically important anaerobes, defends against oxygen radicals and enhances aerotolerance

Kasper demonstrated that *B. fragilis* has an immunologically distinct capsule composed of two polysaccharides,[27, 28] and subsequent studies have indicated the important role of the capsule as a virulence factor.[29] A similar capsule is found in *P. melaninogenica.* The capsule seems to promote abscess formation, possibly by inhibiting opsonophagocytosis,[30, 31] and is capable of inducing experimental abscess formation even in the absence of viable bacteria.[32]

The adherence of *B. fragilis* and *Bacteroides ovatus* to intestinal epithelium and mucus is promoted by pili; the adherence of piliated and encapsulated strains is five times that of nonpiliated and nonencapsulated or encapsulated-only counterparts.[33] Similar surface structures have been identified as important attachment factors in *P. gingivalis*.

Lipopolysaccharide endotoxin is formed by *Fusobacterium* and *Bacteroides* spp., but although this virulence factor contributes to abscess formation, the lipopolysaccharide formed by *Bacteroides* does not contain lipid A and is less biologically active than conventional endotoxin.[34]

B. fragilis, like many other anaerobes, produces the short-chain fatty acid succinic acid, which inhibits phagocytosis.[35] Through this product, as well as others, anaerobic bacteria may protect coinfecting facultative organisms from the action of phagocytic cells.[36]

A variety of enzymes produced by *Bacteroides* spp. may contribute to tissue damage or enable these pathogens to escape host defenses.[34, 37, 38] Among these enzymes are hyaluronidase, collagenase, neuraminidase, heparinase, and fibrinolysin. *P. melaninogenica* and *Prevotella intermedia* produce a phospholipase A that may disrupt the integrity of epithelial cells.[39] *P. gingivalis*, in addition to having hemagglutination properties, specifically degrades human fibrinogen and possesses a potent collagenase.[40] Many clinically important anaerobes, including *B. fragilis*, have some degree of oxygen tolerance, presumably through production of the important enzyme superoxide dismutase.[41]

Toxins that are so important in disease caused by *Clostridium* spp. do not contribute significantly to the pathogenesis of infection caused by anaerobic gram-negative rods.

Immunity and Resistance

The role of humoral immunity in *Bacteroides* infection is unclear. Pathogenic anaerobic gram-negative bacilli activate complement[42] and induce B-cell activation and the production of antibody.[43, 44] Both the alternative and classic pathways of the complement system contribute to opsonization. The alternative complement pathway is important for effective in vitro opsonization of *B. fragilis* and *B. thetaiotaomicron*[45] and is activated in the absence of antibody. Pooled human immunoglobulin has been shown to facilitate in vitro killing of *B. thetaiotaomicron* and *B. fragilis*. Antibody to capsular polysaccharide enhances killing primarily by the classic complement pathway.[46] Specific hyperimmune globulin to *B. fragilis* capsular polysaccharide does not seem to play a protective role in experimental intra-abdominal abscesses but did facilitate clearance of *B. fragilis* bacteremia.[47]

Cell-mediated immunity surprisingly appears to be more important with regard to *B. fragilis*–induced abscesses than is humoral immunity, as demonstrated in an animal model.[28, 47, 48] Immunization of rats with *B. fragilis* capsular polysaccharide protected against *B. fragilis*–induced abscesses. However, passive transfer of immunoglobulin from immunized animals did not protect naive animals, whereas transfer of splenic cells and fractionated T cells was protective.

Neutrophils are prominent in exudates associated with clinical infection caused by anaerobic gram-negative bacilli and are abundant in abscesses caused by these bacteria. These organisms induce neutrophil chemotaxis, phagocytosis, and chemiluminescence,[25] and phagocytic leukocytes are active against anaerobic bacteria[49] and kill *Bacteroides* spp. under anaerobic conditions.

In spite of the considerable laboratory evidence for roles of host complement, antibody, cellular immunity, and phagocytes in protecting against anaerobic gram-negative bacillary infection, few clinical observations support the relative importance of these defense mechanisms. In an intriguing clinical observation, Fisher and colleagues[50] described *B. fragilis* as the most common cause of postoperative bacteremia in children who had elective appendectomy at the time of renal transplantation; profound lymphopenia was a risk factor for infection. Generally speaking, however, patients with complement or antibody deficiencies, as well as those with impaired cellular immunity or neutropenia, rarely acquire infections with *Bacteroides* or *Prevotella* spp. unless the underlying illness is associated with a more obvious predisposition to infection such as colon carcinoma with perforation.

INFECTIONS

Central Nervous System Infections

Meningitis. Anaerobic bacterial meningitis is so rare that most laboratories do not culture cerebrospinal fluid anaerobically. Durand and associates[51] reviewed 493 episodes of bacterial meningitis in adults seen over a 27-year period and found anaerobes involved in only 3 instances; the species were not identified. When anaerobic meningitis has been described, *B. fragilis* has been the most frequently cited etiologic agent. Feder[52] reviewed nine cases of *B. fragilis* meningitis reported from 1963 to 1985, seven of which occurred in premature infants and neonates. Underlying conditions included necrotizing enterocolitis, bowel perforation, chronic otitis media (the two cases seen after the neonatal period), and a cerebrospinal fluid shunt infection.

Brain Abscess. In contrast to their rare association with meningitis, anaerobes are frequently implicated as causative agents in brain abscess,[53–56] which is not surprising given that the predisposing condition in 20 to 40% of brain abscess cases is chronic sinusitis or chronic otitis media, conditions commonly caused by anaerobes. *Prevotella* spp., *Bacteroides* spp., and *Fusobacterium* spp. are all commonly isolated, often in mixed culture and often in association with other anaerobes and streptococcal species, including *Streptococcus intermedius*.

Anaerobic gram-negative bacilli have also been reported to cause subdural empyema, cranial epidural abscess, and less commonly, spinal epidural abscess and lateral sinus thrombophlebitis.[56]

Infections of the Oral Cavity and Upper Respiratory Tract

Many infections of the oral cavity and adjacent structures involve anaerobic bacteria. The pattern of bacteria found tends to be similar for most of these infections. The predominant pathogens include peptostreptococci and anaerobic gram-negative bacilli, particularly *P. melaninogenica, P. oralis, P. oris, P. buccae, P. disiens, F. nucleatum, F. necrophorum, Porphyromonas asaccharolytica*, and *Bacteroides ureolyticus*. Most infections involve multiple anaerobes and in many instances facultative organisms as well, including *Eikenella* and *Capnocytophaga*. *B. fragilis* is not part of the oral flora, and reports indicating the presence of *B. fragilis* in infections of the oral cavity and upper respiratory tract probably represent misidentification in many instances.

Odontogenic Infections. Virtually all clinically important dental infections, including endodontic infection[57] and periapical abscess,[58] involve anaerobes. From these sites, infection may spread to a number of potential spaces bounded by muscles and fascia; some of these infections can be quite severe and even life threatening.[59] One such process is Ludwig's angina, a cellulitis of the sublingual and submandibular spaces that can progress to elevation of the floor of the mouth with the tongue forced posteriorly, thereby resulting in strangulation. Surgical decompression is the mainstay of treatment. Another serious complication of perimandibular infection is Lemierre's syndrome, or postanginal septicemia, a suppurative infection of the lateral pharyngeal space associated with *F. necrophorum* bacteremia and septic jugular vein thrombophlebitis that can lead to septic embolization to the lung with metastatic abscess formation.[60]

Odontogenic orofacial infections caused by anaerobic gram-negative bacilli are associated with more severe clinical illness than are such infections caused by other bacterial species; especially severe are those involving *F. nucleatum*.[61]

Periodontal disease, including pyorrhea and gingivitis, is extremely common and a major contributor to tooth loss as infection progresses from spongy, easily bleeding gums to abscess formation around teeth and bone destruction.[62, 63] *P. melaninogenica, P. intermedia, P. gingivalis*, and *B. forsythus* are thought to be important pathogens in this setting.[64, 65] An uncommon, but severe and distinctive form of gingivitis is Vincent's angina, or "trench mouth," also known as acute necrotizing ulcerative gingivitis.[66] In this infection, an acute destructive and ulcerative gingivitis causes a putrid breath odor and severe pain; fever may be present. Imputed etiologies include oral fusospirochetes along with the usual mouth anaerobes. Antibiotic treatment should be directed at anaerobes.

Pharyngitis. Anaerobic bacteria do not play an important role in acute pharyngitis, but they are important pathogens when peritonsillar abscess, also known as quinsy, occurs.[67] *P. melaninogenica* is commonly isolated along with other mouth anaerobes, facultative flora, and group A streptococci.

Sinusitis. Although rarely found in acute sinusitis, anaerobes are the predominant pathogens found in chronic sinusitis (of more than 3 months' duration). Using surgically obtained specimens from 83 patients with chronic paranasal sinusitis, Frederick and Braude[68] found that 31% had only anaerobes, 23% had only aerobes, 20% had mixed flora, and 25% had sterile specimens. In a study of 40 children with chronic sinus infection, Brook[69] found anaerobes in all children with positive cultures. Predominant anaerobic isolates in chronic sinusitis include *Peptostreptococcus* spp., *Prevotella* spp., *Bacteroides* spp. (non-*fragilis* group), and *Fusobacterium* spp.[68–70] The common isolation of these bacteria from intracranial suppurative infection complicating chronic sinusitis supports their important role in chronic sinus infection.

Otitis. Oral cavity anaerobes are found very uncommonly in acute otitis media but are isolated from 15 to 50% of cultures obtained from patients with chronic otitis media.[71, 72] In cases complicated by mastoiditis or cholesteatoma, the frequency of anaerobes isolated from surgical specimens rises to 65 to 95%.[73, 74]

Parotitis. Suppurative infection of the parotid salivary gland is usually due to *Staphylococcus aureus*, but recent reports indicate a pathogenic role for anaerobes, including *P. melaninogenica* and *Peptostreptococcus* spp.[75] A Gram stain of pus expressed from the salivary duct may provide an immediate clue to the etiology.

Pleuropulmonary Infections

Pleuropulmonary infections, including community-acquired aspiration pneumonia, necrotizing pneumonia, lung abscess, and empyema, are among the most common and important clinical infections in which anaerobic gram-negative bacilli play a role.[76–80] These infections are thought to follow aspiration of oropharyngeal flora, and many patients have obvious periodontal disease, the likely reservoir for the infecting bacteria. The clinical picture is similar to pyogenic lung infection of any etiology, although the tempo of the illness is typically slower. In advanced disease with cavitation, empyema, or both, as many as one half to two thirds of patients will have putrid sputum or pleural fluid, but in early infection this important clinical clue to the anaerobic etiology is often absent.[81] Gram stain of empyema fluid demonstrating a mixed flora with morphologies consistent with *Prevotella* and *Fusobacterium* spp. will often provide prompt diagnosis.

The bacteriology of these infections is similar to that found in odontogenic infections: most are polymicrobial and usually contain three to four anaerobic species and often, but not always, a facultative organism such as a viridans streptococcus. *P. melaninogenica, P. intermedia, F. nucleatum*, and *B. ureolyticus* are among the most commonly isolated bacterial species. Many of these infections are probably truly synergistic.[18] *B. fragilis* is virtually never found in the oropharyngeal flora, and earlier studies of the bacteriology of anerobic pleuropulmonary infection citing a *B. fragilis* isolation rate of approximately 15% probably represent misidentification of penicillin-resistant organisms such as *P. buccae* and *P. disiens*.

Concern about increasing antimicrobial resistance among mouth anaerobic species has caused most authorities to substitute new regimens for penicillin, the long-standing drug of choice in this setting (see later).

Intra-abdominal Infections

Bacteroides spp., particularly *B. fragilis*, are the organisms most frequently recovered from intra-abdominal abscesses (intraperitoneal and visceral), as well as from peritonitis occurring after a breach of the integrity of the intestinal mucosa, whether it be from a surgeon's scalpel, a ruptured appendix, or a perforating cancer of the colon. The fact that *B. fragilis* makes up a small part of the fecal inoculum (0.5% of the colonic microflora) but is the dominant anaerobe isolated from clinical infection attests to the virulence of this organism. The pathogenic role played by *B. fragilis* in the formation of abdominal abscesses has been suggested by the study of animal models.[47, 82]

Generally, intra-abdominal infections are mixed and polymicrobial and contain an average of five organisms, three anaerobic and two facultative (often coliforms), with anaerobes being present in 80 to 90% of infections and *Bacteroides* spp. in roughly two thirds of these.[83–85] Exceptions to these generalizations include "spontaneous" peritonitis, pancreatic abscesses or infected pancreatic pseudocysts, and acute cholecystitis, which are often due to a single coliform or streptococcal species; another exception is peritonitis complicating peritoneal dialysis, which is often due to a single staphylococcal or coliform organism. *Bacteroides* spp. are important pathogens in liver abscess, the most common of visceral abdominal infections.[86] This finding is not surprising given that the most common ways in which infecting bacteria are introduced into the hepatic parenchyma are from the intestinal flora via the biliary tract or the portal venous system.

Although *B. fragilis* is the predominant isolate from intra-abdominal infections, other members of the *B. fragilis* group, including *B. thetaiotaomicron, Bacteroides distasonis*, and *B. vulgatus*, are commonly recovered, as is *P. melaninogenica.*

Bilophila wadsworthia was described in 1989 as a novel genus of a bile-tolerant gram-negative anaerobe that was isolated from appendicitis specimens and human feces.[87] Occasionally it has been found in the vagina and in saliva.[88] Although it is found in the stool in mean counts of only 10^5 to 10^6/g (total bacterial counts, $\sim 10^{12}$/g), it is the third most common anaerobe isolated from infections in the setting of gangrenous or perforated appendices, and its presence can be demonstrated in nearly one half of such cases.[89, 90] It has occasionally been reported in other infections, including hepatic abscess, cholecystitis, and soft tissue infections, usually as part of a polymicrobial flora, but it has been reported to cause bacteremia.[91] Another bile-tolerant, asaccharolytic, anaerobic, gram-negative rod, *Sutterella wadsworthensis*, has recently been described and is most frequently found in association with appendicitis, peritonitis, and intra-abdominal abscesses.[92–94]

Diarrhea. In three case-controlled studies, enterotoxin-producing strains of *B. fragilis* have been implicated as the cause of self-limited, watery diarrhea. Disease appears limited to children 1 to 5 years old, and 5 to 20% of cases of diarrhea in this age range are thought to be due to this etiology.[95–97] The toxin is an extracellular, heat-labile metalloprotease with a mass of about 20 kD that possesses both secretory and cytotoxic effects. As with other enteric pathogens, carriage of enterotoxigenic *B. fragilis* may be clinically silent and has been reported in 6.5% of healthy persons. It may be transmitted through contaminated water.

Genital Tract Infections in Women. Anaerobic gram-negative bacilli figure prominently in the normal vaginal flora and are important pathogens in most genital tract infections in women, excluding those resulting from sexually transmitted organisms. A wide variety of infections can involve anaerobes, including Bartholin's cyst abscess, pelvic inflammatory disease, tuboovarian abscess, endometritis, amnionitis, and wound infections complicating obstetric procedures or gynecologic surgery.[98–100]

These infections are characteristically polymicrobial and involve anaerobes, particularly anaerobic gram-negative rods and peptostreptococci, along with aerobes, including possibly *Gardnerella vaginalis, Escherichia coli* (coliforms less common than in intra-abdominal infections), and group B streptococci. In a study of salpingitis,[101] Sweet demonstrated that patients typically had mixed anaerobic infection in the fallopian tubes even when the sexually transmitted pathogens *Neisseria gonorrhoeae* and *Chlamydia trachomatis* were isolated from the endocervix.

P. bivia and *P. disiens* are important pathogens in genital tract infections of women, and earlier reports indicating a high isolation rate for *B. fragilis* probably represent organism misidentification in many instances.[102]

An extremely common infection involving anaerobic gram-negative bacilli is bacterial vaginosis, which is characterized by a foul-smelling discharge, increased concentration of succinic acid and an elevated pH in vaginal fluid, loss of the normally predominant lactobacilli, a marked quantitative increase in *Prevotella* spp., and response to metronidazole or topical clindamycin.[103] Other bacteria commonly found are *G. vaginalis* and the curved, anaerobic gram-positive rod *Mobiluncus*. Bacterial vaginosis is associated with an increased risk of pelvic inflammatory disease,[104] and heavy anaerobic colonization of the vagina is associated with an increased risk of intra-amnionotic infection, as well as preterm delivery[105, 106] (see also Chapter 95).

Bacteremia. *B. fragilis* is one of the most common organisms isolated from blood cultures, and it is the dominant isolate (70%) in cases of anaerobic bacteremia.[80, 107–111] Additional common isolates are other members of the *B. fragilis* group, particularly *B. thetaiotaomicron*, and *Fusobacterium* spp. Unlike anaerobic gram-positive cocci and rods, which often represent contaminants when found in blood cultures, isolation of anaerobic gram-negative bacilli from blood is virtually always associated with clinical infection.[109] The significance of *Bacteroides* bacteremia is indicated by an associated mortality of 15 to 30%, with a 60% mortality reported in cases when therapy was not directed at these organisms.[112] In one controlled study, *B. fragilis* group bacteremia resulted in 16 days of additional hospitalization and an attributable mortality of 19%.[113]

The source of bacteremia caused by anaerobic gram-negative bacilli is found to be intra-abdominal infections in one half to two thirds of cases (particularly when associated with abscesses, malignancy, surgery, and intestinal obstruction or perforation); female genital tract infections in about 8 to 25%; soft tissue infections, including decubitus ulcers, in about 5 to 10%; and the oropharynx and lower respiratory tract in about 5% each.[80, 110, 114] *Fusobacterium* bacteremia is usually associated with oropharyngeal and lung infection, and *P. disiens* or *P. bivia* bacteremia generally correlates with obstetric and gynecologic sources of infection. When *B. fragilis* is isolated from the blood of a febrile patient without obvious localizing signs or symptoms, an intra-abdominal source should be investigated.

The clinical picture of *Bacteroides* bacteremia is similar to that produced by anaerobic gram-negative bacilli, with the exception that the "gram-negative sepsis syndrome," shock, and disseminated intravascular coagulation appear to be less common in anaerobic bacteremia, perhaps related to the absence of lipid A from *B. fragilis* endotoxin.[34]

A decline in the frequency of anaerobic gram-negative rod bacteremia has been reported in the last 2 decades.[111, 115, 116] This decline may be due to improved surgical prophylaxis, newer imaging techniques permitting earlier diagnosis and drainage of abscesses, and heightened awareness of the role of anaerobes in infection with specific antimicrobial treatment directed at these organisms. Noting this decline, some authorities have suggested abandoning routine anaerobic blood cultures.[117] In some recent reports, anaerobes have accounted for about 4% of all bacteremias without demonstrable decline. Because of attributable morbidity and mortality, along with increasing antibiotic resistance and the fact that anaerobic blood cultures enhance the isolation of *Streptococcus pneumoniae*, other streptococci, enterococci, and *Listeria monocytogenes*, routine anaerobic blood cultures remain warranted.[118]

Endocarditis

Anaerobic bacteria are uncommon causes of infective endocarditis, with incidences reported to range from 1 to 16% of total cases. Anaerobic streptococci and *B. fragilis* are the most frequent causes,[119] with *B. fragilis* being the etiologic agent in approximately one third of cases. A polymicrobial etiology is more commonly found in anaerobic endocarditis than in cases caused by facultative bacteria, with more than one organism isolated from 14 to 24% of the former; in polymicrobial cases, *P. melaninogenica* is often found in combination with anaerobic or facultative streptococcal species.[119, 120] *Fusobacterium* spp., particularly *F. necrophorum*, are second only to *B. fragilis* as the etiology of endocarditis caused by anaerobic gram-negative bacilli. The valve distribution and subacute clinical course in most instances of anaerobic endocarditis is similar to that caused by viridans streptococci, but underlying heart disease is less common, being present in 43 to 64% of patients. *B. fragilis* endocarditis is associated with the formation of large vegetations,[80] with systemic embolization reported in 60 to 70% of cases.[119, 120] It has been suggested that the high frequency of thromboembolic complications in *B. fragilis* endocarditis may be related to the heparinase that it produces. Mortality in cases caused by anaerobic gram-negative bacilli is higher than in those caused by anaerobic gram-positive cocci, with a rate of 46% reported for cases caused by *B. fragilis. F. necrophorum* can cause acute endocarditis with rapid valve destruction and a 75% mortality.[120] Pericarditis secondary to anaerobes is rare.[121]

Skin and Soft Tissue Infections

Anaerobic gram-negative bacilli do not contribute significantly to the normal skin flora, but these bacteria are important pathogens when the skin and underlying soft tissue are damaged by trauma or vascular insufficiency and contaminated with fecal or upper airway flora. Examples of infections commonly involving *Bacteroides* and *Prevotella* spp. are wound infections after intestinal or gynecologic surgery, dog and human bite infections,[127] infected pilonidal cysts,[123] necrotizing fasciitis,[124] and infections complicating decubitus and diabetic ulcers.

B. fragilis is the most common species found in the mixed flora colonizing both diabetic[125] and decubitus ulcers.[126] When these ulcers lead to cellulitis, osteomyelitis, bacteremia, or a combination of these conditions, *B. fragilis* is commonly recovered from clinical specimens.[114, 127, 128]

Cutaneous abscesses below the waist have often been found to be caused by colonic flora anaerobes, including *B. fragilis* and *P. melaninogenica*.[129] Breast abscesses, although usually caused by *S. aureus*, may result from anaerobic gram-negative bacilli, particularly in nonpuerperal women; *P. bivia, B. ureolyticus*, and *P. asaccharolytica* have been common isolates and are often present with anaerobic cocci.[130]

Bone and Joint Infections

Osteomyelitis. Hematogenous anaerobic osteomyelitis is very rare, but anaerobes play a prominent role in osteomyelitis of the long bones after trauma and fracture; osteomyelitis associated with vascular insufficiency; osteomyelitis of the skull bones complicating odontogenic infection, chronic sinusitis, or chronic otitis; osteomyelitis contiguous to deep diabetic or decubitus ulcers; and osteomyelitis complicating human bites or clenched-fist injuries.[131–134] Anaerobic osteomyelitis of the pubis has been described in women after pelvic surgery. *B. fragilis*, the most common isolate, is found in about one third of cases in which anaerobes are found; *P. melaninogenica, F. necleatum*, and *Porphyromonas* spp. are common pathogens in osteomyelitis of the facial bones and in human bite wounds. Purulent drainage has a foul odor in 48% of cases.[134] A rare form of hematogenous osteomyelitis is that seen complicating Gaucher's disease, and interestingly, most of these cases have been due to anaerobic gram-negative bacilli.[135]

Septic Arthritis. Infectious arthritis caused by anaerobic bacteria is rare, but infection has occurred secondary to hematogenous spread, including cases complicating rheumatoid arthritis.[136] A number of prosthetic joint infections have been reported,[132] the presumption being that the infecting agents were introduced at the time of surgery. Brook and Frazier[134] reported 65 cases seen at a military hospital over a 10-year period. The hip and knee were most commonly affected. Unlike other anaerobic infections, including osteomyelitis, polymicrobial infection was uncommon. One anaerobe was typically found per infection, and facultative organisms were coinfecting agents in only 11% of cases. Anaerobic gram-positive cocci were the most commonly isolated pathogens and were often associated with prosthetic device infections. *B. fragilis* group organisms were isolated in nine instances, five in association with distant-site infection; *Fusobacterium* spp. were implicated in five cases, three of which had concomitant oropharyngeal infection. The mean symptom duration before diagnosis was 4.5 days, fever was present in 80%, blood cultures were negative in all cases when obtained, and purulent joint fluid had a foul odor 37% of the time.

TREATMENT

Surgical Treatment

Drainage of abscesses and débridement of necrotic tissue continue to be mainstays of the treatment of anaerobic infections. For localized, accessible abscesses, particularly in the abdomen, it is now possible in many instances to achieve adequate drainage through the use of percutaneous catheters placed under radiographic guidance.[137, 138] An attempt at percutaneous drainage is a reasonable first step, with open drainage reserved if the abscess is inaccessible, if drainage is incomplete, or if the clinical response is inadequate. Although surgical drainage is generally a critical determinant in the treatment of abscesses, there are exceptions involving anaerobic gram-negative bacilli that have been successfully managed with antimicrobial therapy alone. Brain, liver, and tuboovarian abscesses have been managed with antimicrobials after diagnostic aspiration or with empirical antimicrobials without diagnostic aspiration.[139–141] Lung abscesses rarely require drainage.

Hyperbaric Oxygen

In certain infections involving anaerobic gram-negative bacilli, including necrotizing fasciitis and osteomyelitis, hyperbaric oxygen has been used as adjunctive therapy to débridement and antimicrobials.[142,143] In animal experiments, hyperbaric oxygen has been reported to improve survival in mixed aerobic and anaerobic infection[144] and to improve sinus tract healing and bone stabilization in a model of mandibular osteomyelitis.[145] However, despite occasional testimonials and some experimental data to support its use, no controlled trials have studied the efficacy of hyperbaric oxygen, and its value in the treatment of infections involving anaerobic gram-negative bacilli remains to be proved.

Antibiotic Therapy

The selection of antimicrobials to treat infections imputed or proved to be due to *B. fragilis* and other anaerobic gram-negative bacilli is largely empirical. This approach is necessary because most of the infections involving these bacteria are polymicrobial and require considerable laboratory time to separate and identify all species, in addition to the fact that most laboratories cannot reliably perform susceptibility testing for anaerobic bacteria. The choice of antimicrobials is generally based on (1) studies of the activity of new agents, (2) ongoing studies that monitor national susceptibility patterns to determine changes in susceptibility to commonly used agents, and (3) studies of clinical efficacy. In vitro susceptibility testing is advisable for anaerobic isolates recovered from patients with certain infections, including brain abscess, endocarditis, prosthetic device infections, and refractory bacteremia.

For a long time penicillin was considered the drug of choice for anaerobic infections above the diaphragm because penicillin resistance was largely confined to *B. fragilis*, a pathogen usually restricted to infections found below the diaphragm. Oropharyngeal anaerobes, particularly *P. melaninogenica*, have shown increasing resistance to penicillin as a result of β-lactamase production, and these organisms have been associated with penicillin treatment failure in tonsillitis and orofacial infection.[146]

Most *Fusobacterium* spp. remain susceptible to penicillin,[147] but treatment failure because of β-lactamase production has been reported.[148] *Campylobacter gracilis*, a newly recognized pathogen found in serious head and neck infections, is also often penicillin resistant.[149] Although some odontogenic and pulmonary infections will still respond to penicillin, it should not be used as initial therapy for serious infections, involving mouth anaerobes. Such infections include Ludwig's angina, peritonsillar abscess, necrotizing anaerobic pneumonia, anaerobic empyema, and human bite infections, as well as infections after clenched-fist injuries.

Antimicrobial susceptibilities for the *B. fragilis* group are shown in Table 237–4. The antibiotics that are most predictably active against anaerobic gram-negative bacilli, including the *B. fragilis* group, are metronidazole, chloramphenicol, clindamycin, imipenem, cefoxitin, and combinations of a β-lactam plus a β-lactamase inhibitor, examples being amoxicillin-clavulanate, ampicillin-sulbactam, and ticarcillin-clavulanate.[3,150–154] Cefotetan and cefmetazole have activity similar to that of cefoxitin, although these agents tend to be less active against the non-*fragilis* species.[157,158] *B. fragilis* has shown increasing resistance in recent years to some of the antimicrobials commonly used to treat infections with this organism, including cefoxitin, clindamycin, and the anti-*Pseudomonas* pencillins.[150,153,159] Drugs having poor activity against anaerobic gram-negative bacilli include aminoglycosides, trimethoprim-sulfamethoxazole, and most third-generation cephalosporins, quinolones, and monobactams. One quinolone, trovafloxacin, is highly active against all anaerobic gram-negative rods and has demonstrated efficacy in an animal model of mixed-flora intra-abdominal infection.[155,159]

In the treatment of cerebral abscess, metronidazole has proved to be a useful drug because of its activity and good penetration into the brain.[160] Because metronidazole has poor activity against anaerobic gram-positive cocci and no activity against commonly found aerobes such as *S. intermedius*, it is generally combined with penicillin, ampicillin, or a third-generation cephalosporin.[139]

Common bacterial isolates from human bite infections and infected clenched-fist injuries include *Prevotella* spp., which may be penicillin resistant, *Eikenella corrodens*, which is clindamycin and metronidazole resistant, and often staphylococci.[122] Therefore, appropriate therapies would include two-drug regimens such as clindamycin and penicillin, clindamycin and a fluorinated quinolone, or

TABLE 237–4 Antimicrobial Activity against Anaerobic Gram-Negative Bacilli

Antibiotic	% Susceptible at Breakpoint				
	Bacteroides fragilis	*B. fragilis* Group*	*Porphyromonas* and *Prevotella*	*Fusobacterium*	*Bilophila*
Amoxicillin-clavulanate	>95	>95	>95	>95	>95
Ampicillin-sulbactam	>95	>95	>95	>95	>95
Cefotaxime	50–70	<50	>95	85–95	70–85
Cefotetan	85–95	50–70	85–95	85–95	70–85
Cefoxitin	85–95	70–85	>95	85–95	>95
Ceftizoxime	70–85	70–85	>95	>95	<50
Ciprofloxacin	<50	<50	50–85	50–85	>95
Chloramphenicol	>95	>95	>95	>95	>95
Clindamycin	85–85	70–85	>95	>95	85–95
Imipenem	>95	>95	>95	>95	>95
Levofloxacin	50–85	<50	75–85	50–85	>95
Metronidazole	>95	>95	>95	>95	>95
Ofloxacin	<50	<50	50–85	50–85	>95
Penicillin	<50	<50	70–85	>95	<50
Piperacillin	70–85	70–85	>95	>95	>95
Piperacillin-tazobactam	>95	>95	>95	>95	>95
Ticarcillin-clavulanate	>95	>95	>95	>95	>95
Trovafloxacin	>95	>95	>95	>95	>95

*Includes *B. distasonis, B. ovatus, B. thetaiotaomicron,* and *B. vulgatus.*
Data from refs. 3 and 150–156.

a β-lactam and a β-lactamase combination such as amoxicillin-clavulanate.

In pulmonary infections caused by anaerobic mouth flora, commonly used regimens are clindamycin alone, which was superior to penicillin in two randomized studies of the treatment of lung abscess,[161, 162] and the combination of penicillin with metronidazole.[78] Metronidazole should not be used alone because of its lack of activity against the frequently present streptococcal species and its poor efficacy as monotherapy in clinical trials.[163]

Intra-abdominal infections characteristically involve *B. fragilis*, other anaerobes, and coliforms. Typical treatment regimens include two drugs, one for the anaerobes (clindamycin, metronidazole, cefoxitin) and a second for the coliforms (aminoglycoside, third-generation cephalosporin, quinolone, monobactam). Newer agents having activity against both components, including imipenem and ticarcillin-clavulanate, have been used as monotherapy. Many comparative trials have shown that as long as the regimen is active against coliforms and anaerobes, including *B. fragilis*, efficacy is similar.[164–168] Almost all strains of *B. wadsworthia*, an important pathogen in appendicitis, produce β-lactamase; they are susceptible to agents active against *B. fragilis*.

Genital tract infections in women are typically mixed and involve coliforms, streptococcal species, and anaerobes. Although *B. fragilis* is not as frequent a pathogen as it is in intra-abdominal infections, it is present in a significant number of patients. *P. bivia* is a common anaerobe recovered in genital tract infections of women and has susceptibilities similar to those of *B. fragilis*.[169] Therefore, therapeutic options for these infections are like those used in the treatment of abdominal infections.[169–171]

Guidelines for treatment of skin and soft tissue infections involving mixed aerobic-anaerobic flora are like those for intra-abdominal infections.

Antimicrobial resistance in *Bacteroides* and *Prevotella* spp. has a direct impact on the choice of agents used to treat infections thought to involve anaerobic bacteria. A number of resistance mechanisms have been defined[172]; among these mechanisms, the production of β-lactamase is currently considered to be of greatest clinical importance. Resistance to metronidazole and clindamycin occurs through other unique mechanisms, and disturbingly, resistance to multiple antibiotic classes has been seen in a single organism. Because susceptibility testing of anaerobic bacteria is problematic[173] and not routinely available, physicians must continue to monitor susceptibility data provided through reference centers to be aware of changing patterns of antimicrobial activity and to ensure optimal treatment of their patients.

REFERENCES

1. Shah HN, Collins MD. Proposal for reclassification of *Bacteroides asaccharolyticus, Bacteroides gingivalis* and *Bacteroides endodontalis* in a new genus, *Porphyromonas*. Int J Syst Bacteriol, 1988;38:128–131.
2. Shah HN, Collins MD. *Prevotella*, a new genus to include *Bacteroides melaninogenicus* and related species formerly classified in the genus *Bacteroides*. Int J Syst Bacteriol. 1990;40:205–208.
3. Jousimies-Somer HR, Summanen PH, Finegold SM. *Bacteroides, Prophyromonas, Prevotella, Fusobacterium*, and other gram-negative bacteria. In: Murray PR, Baron EJ, Pfaller MA, et al, eds. Manual of Clinical Microbiology. 6th ed. Washington, DC: American Society for Microbiology; 1995:603–620.
4. Jousimies-Somer H. Recently described clinically important anaerobic bacteria: Taxonomic aspects and update. Clin Infect Dis. 1997:25(Suppl 2):S78–S87.
5. Gibbons RJ, van Houte J. Bacterial adherence in oral microbial ecology. Annu Rev Microbiol. 1975;29:19–44.
6. Long SS, Swenson RM. Determinants of the developing oral flora in normal newborns. Appl Environ Microbiol. 1976;32:494–497.
7. Socransky SS, Manganiello SD. The oral microbiota of man from birth to senility. J Periodontol. 1971;42:485–496.
8. McClellan DL, Griffen AL, Leys EJ. Age and prevalence of *Porphyromonas gingivalis* in children. J Clin Microbiol. 1996;34:2017–2019.
9. Tuite-McDonnell M, Griffen AL, Moeschberger ML, et al. Concordance of *Porphyromonas gingivalis* colonization in families. J Clin Microbiol. 1997;35:455–461.
10. Sutter VL. Anaerobes as normal oral flora. Rev Infect Dis. 1984;6(Suppl):S62–S66.
11. Hentges DJ. The anaerobic microflora of the human body. Clin Infect Dis. 1993;16(Suppl):S175–S180.
12. Moore WEC, Holdeman LV. Human fecal flora: The normal flora of 20 Japanese-Hawaiians. Appl Microbiol. 1974;27:961–979.
13. Croucher SC, Houston AP, Bayliss CE, et al. Bacterial populations associated with different regions of the colon wall. Appl Environ Microbiol. 1983;45:1025–1033.
14. Stark PL, Lee A. The microbial ecology of the large bowel of breast-fed and formula-fed infants during the first year of life. J Med Microbiol. 1982;15:189–203.
15. Gorbach SL. Intestinal microflora. Gastroenterology. 1971;60:1110–1129.
16. van der Waaij D, Berghuis de Vries JM, Lekkerkerk van der Wees JEC. Colonization resistance of the digestive tract in conventional and antibiotic treated mice. J Hyg. 1971;69:405–411.
17. Sautter RL, Brown WJ. Sequential vaginal cultures from normal young women. J Clin Microbiol. 1980;11:479–484.
18. Barlett JG, Polk BF. Bacterial flora of the vagina: Quantitative study. Rev Infect Dis. 1984;(Suppl):S67–S72.
19. Hill GB, St Claire KK, Gutman LT. Anaerobes predominate among the vaginal microflora of prebubertal girls. Clin Infect Dis. 1995;20(Suppl 2):S269–S270.
20. Hillier SL, Lau RJ. Vaginal microflora in postmenopausal women who have not received estrogen replacement therapy. Clin Infect Dis. 1997;25(Suppl 2):S123–S126.
21. Smith DT. Fusospirochetal disease of the lungs produced with cultures from Vincent's angina. J Infect Dis. 1930;46:303–310.
22. Onderdonk AB, Bartlett JG, Louie T, et al. Microbial synergy in experimental intra-abdominal abscess. Infect Immun. 1976;13:22–26.
23. Brook I. Enhancement of growth of aerobic and facultative bacteria in mixed infections with *Bacteroides* species. Infect Immun. 1985;50:929–931.
24. MacDonald JB, Socransky SJ, Gibbons RJ. Aspects of the pathogenesis of mixed anaerobic infections of mucous membranes. J Dent Res. 1963;42:529–544.
25. Styrt B, Gorbach SL. Recent developments in the understanding of the pathogenesis and treatment of anaerobic infections. N Engl J Med. 1989;321:240–246.
26. Brook I. Presence of beta-lactamase–producing bacteria and beta-lactamase activity in abscesses. Am J Clin Pathol. 1986;86:97–101.
27. Kasper DL. The polysaccharide capsule of *Bacteroides fragilis* subspecies *fragilis*: Immunochemical and morphologic definition. J Infect Dis. 1976;133:79–87.
28. Tzianabos AO, Kasper DL, Onderdonk AB. Structure and function of *Bacteroides fragilis* capsular polysaccharides: Relationship to induction and prevention of abscesses. Clin Infect Dis. 1995;20(Suppl 2):S132–S140.
29. Onderdonk AB, Kasper DL, Cisneros RL, et al. The capsular polysaccharide of *Bacteroides fragilis* as a virulence factor: Comparison of the pathogenic potential of encapsulated and unencapsulated strains. J Infect Dis. 1977;136:82–89.
30. Zaleznik DF, Kasper DL. The role of anaerobic bacteria in abscess formation. Annu Rev Med. 1982;33:217–229.
31. Simon GL, Klempner MJ, Kasper DL, et al. Alterations in opsonophagocytic killing by neutrophils of *Bacteroides fragilis* associated with animal and laboratory passage: Effect of capsular polysaccharide. J Infect Dis. 1982;145:72–77.
32. Kasper DL, Onderdonk AB, Polk BF, et al. Surface antigens as virulence factors in infection with *Bacteroides fragilis*. Rev Infect Dis. 1979;1:278–290.
33. Brook I, Myhal ML. Adherence of *Bacteroides fragilis* group species. Infect Immun. 1991;59:742–744.
34. Hofstad T. Pathogenicity of anaerobic gram-negative rods: Possible mechanisms. Rev Infect Dis. 1984;6:189–199.
35. Rotstein OD, Masmith PE, Grinstein S. The *Bacteroides* by-product succinic acid inhibits neutrophil respiratory burst by reducing intracellular pH. Infect Immun. 1987;55:864–870.
36. Rotstein OD. Interactions between leukocytes and anaerobic bacteria in polymicrobial surgical infections. Clin Infect Dis. 1993;16(Suppl):S190–S194.
37. Duerden BI. Virulence factors in anaerobes. Clin Infect Dis. 1994;18(Suppl):S253–S259.
38. Botta GA, Araese A, Minisini R, et al. Role of structural and extracellular virulence factors in gram-negative anaerobic bacteria. Clin Infect Dis. 1994;18(Suppl):S260–S264.
39. Bulkacz J, Schuster GS, Singh B, et al. Phospholipase A activity of extracellular products from *Bacteroides melaninogenicus* on epithelium tissue cultures. J Periodont Res. 1985;20:146–153.
40. Grenier D, Mayrand D. Selected characteristics of pathogenic and non-pathogenic strains of *Bacteroides gingivalis*. J Clin Microbiol. 1987;25:738–740.
41. Tally FP, Goldin BR, Jabobus NV, et al. Superoxide dismutase in anaerobic bacteria of clinical significance. Infect Immun. 1977;16:20–25.
42. Bjornson AB. Role of complement in host resistance against members of the Bacteroidaceae. Rev Infect Dis. 1984;6(Suppl):S34–S39.
43. Mangan DF, Lopatin DE. Polyclonal activation of human peripheral blood B lymphocytes by *Fusobacterium nucleatum*. Infect Immun. 1983;40:1104–1110.
44. Sonnenwirth AC. Antibody response to anaerobic bacteria. Rev Infect Dis. 1979;1:337–341.
45. Bjornson AB, Magnafichi PI, Schrieber RD, et al. Opsonization of *Bacteroides* by the alternative complement pathway reconstructed from isolated plasma proteins. J Exp Med. 1987;164:777–798.
46. Zalenik DF, Farmer T, Kasper DL. Antibody mediated killing of *Bacteroides fragilis* is strain specific and proceeds via the classical complement pathway (Abstract). Clin Res. 1988;36:583.

47. Onderdonk AB, Markham RB, Zaleznik DF, et al. Evidence for T cell–dependent immunity to *Bacteroides fragilis* in an intraabdominal abscess model. J Clin Invest. 1982;69:9–16.
48. Zaleznik DF, Finberg RW, Shapiro ME, et al. A soluble suppressor T cell factor protects against experimental intraabdominal abscesses. J Clin Invest. 1985;75:1023–1027.
49. Klempner MS. Interactions of polymorphonuclear leukocytes with anaerobic bacteria. Rev Infect Dis. 1984;6(Suppl):S40–S44.
50. Fisher ML, Baluarte HJ, Long SS. Bacteremia due to *Bacteroides fragilis* after elective appendectomy in renal transplant recipients. J Infect Dis. 1981;143:635–638.
51. Durand ML, Calderwood SB, Weber DJ, et al. Acute bacterial meningitis in adults. A review of 493 episodes. N Engl J Med. 1993;328:21–28.
52. Feder HM Jr. *Bacteroides fragilis* meningitis. Rev Infect Dis. 1987;9:783–786.
53. deLouvois J, Gortvai P, Hurley R. Bacteriology of abscesses of central nervous system: A multicentre prospective study. BMJ. 1977;2:981–984.
54. Brook I. Bacteriology of intracranial abscess in children. J Neurosurg. 1981;54:484–488.
55. Chun CH, Johnson JD, Hufstetter M, et al. Brain abscess. A study of 45 consecutive cases. Medicine (Baltimore). 1986;65:415–431.
56. Swartz MN. Central nervous system infections. In: Finegold SM, George WL, eds. Anaerobic Infections in Humans. New York: Academic; 1989;155–212.
57. Zavistoski J, Dzink JA, Onderdonk AB, et al. Quantitative bacteriology of endodontic infections. Oral Surg Oral Med Oral Pathol. 1980;49:171–174.
58. Dymock D, Weightman AJ, Scully C, et al. Molecular analysis of microflora associated with dentoalveolar abscesses. J Clin Microbiol. 1996;34:537–542.
59. Chow AW. Life-threatening infections of the head and neck. Clin Infect Dis. 1992;14:991–1004.
60. Sinave CP, Hardy GJ, Fardy PW. The Lemierre syndrome: Suppurative thrombophlebitis of the internal jugular vein secondary to oropharyngeal infection. Medicine (Baltimore). 1989;68:85–94.
61. Heimdahl A, von Konow L, Satoh T, et al. Clinical appearance of orofacial infections of odontogenic origin in relation to microbiological findings. J Clin Microbiol. 1985;22:299–302.
62. Newman MG. Anaerobic oral and dental infection. Rev Infect Dis. 1984;6(Suppl):S107–S114.
63. Tanner A, Stillman N. Oral and dental infections with anaerobic bacteria: Clinical features, predominant pathogens, and treatment. Clin Infect Dis. 1993;16(Suppl):S304–S309.
64. Moore WEC. Microbiology of periodontal disease. J Periodontal Res. 1987;22:335–341.
65. Gersdorf H, Meissner A, Pelz K, et al. Identification of *Bacteroides forsythus* in subgingival plaque from patients with advanced periodontitis. J Clin Microbiol. 1993;31:941–946.
66. Loesche WJ, Syed SA, Laughon BE, et al. The bacteriology of acute necrotizing ulcerative gingivitis. J Periodontol. 1982;53:223–230.
67. Brook I, Frazier EH, Thompson DH. Aerobic and anaerobic microbiology of peritonsillar abscess. Laryngoscope. 1991;101:289–292.
68. Frederick J, Braude AI. Anaerobic infection of the paranasal sinuses. N Engl J Med. 1974;290:135–137.
69. Brook I. Bacteriologic features of chronic sinusitis in children. JAMA. 1981;246:967–969.
70. Nord CE. The role of anaerobic bacteria in recurrent episodes of sinusitis and tonsillitis. Clin Infect Dis. 1995;20:1512–1524.
71. Brook I, Finegold SM. Bacteriology of chronic otitis media. JAMA. 1979;241:487–488.
72. Brook I. Aerobic and anaerobic bacteriology of chronic mastoiditis in children. Am J Dis Child. 1981;135:478–479.
74. Brook I. Aerobic and anaerobic bacteriology of cholesteatoma. Laryngoscope. 1981;91:250–253.
75. Brook I, Frazier EH, Thompson DH. Aerobic and anaerobic microbiology of acute suppurative parotitis. Laryngoscope. 1991;101:170–172.
76. Lorber B, Swenson RM. Bacteriology of aspiration pneumonia. A prospective study of community- and hospital-acquired cases. Ann Intern Med. 1974;81:329–331.
77. Bartlett JG, Finegold SM. Anaerobic infections of the lung and pleural space. Am Rev Respir Dis. 1974;110:56–77.
78. Bartlett JG. Anaerobic bacteria infections of the lung and pleural space. Clin Infect Dis. 1993;16(Suppl):S248–S255.
79. Civen R, Jousimies-Somer H, Marina M, et al. A retrospective review of cases of anaerobic empyema and update of bacteriology. Clin Infect Dis. 1995;20(Suppl 1):S224–S229.
80. Finegold SM, George WL, Mulligan ME. Anaerobic infections. Part I. Dis Mon. 1985;31:1–77.
81. Bartlett JG. Anaerobic bacterial pneumonitis. Am Rev Respir Dis. 1979;119:19–23.
82. Weinstein WM, Onderdonk AB, Bartlett JG, et al. Antimicrobial therapy of experimental intraabdominal sepsis. J Infect Dis. 1975;132:282–286.
83. Lorber B, Swenson RM. The bacteriology of intra-abdominal infections. Surg Clin North Am. 1975;55:1349–1354.
84. Gorbach SL. Intraabdominal infections. Clin Infect Dis. 1993;17:961–967.
85. McClean KL, Shechan GJ, Harding GKM. Intraabdominal infection: A review. Clin Infect Dis. 1994;19:100–116.
86. Rubin RH, Swartz MN, Malt R. Hepatic abscess: Changes in clinical, bacteriologic and therapeutic aspects. Am J Med. 1974;57:601–610.
87. Baron EJ, Summanen P, Downes J, et al. *Bilophila wadsworthia*, gen. nov. and sp. nov., a unique gram-negative anaerobic rod recovered from appendicitis specimens and human faeces. J Gen Microbiol. 1989;135:3405–3411.
88. Baron EJ, Corren M, Henderson G, et al. *Bilophila wadsworthia* isolates from clinical specimens. J Clin Microbiol. 1992;30:1882–1884.
89. Bennion RS, Baron EJ, Thompson JE Jr, et al. The bacteriology of gangrenous and perforated appendicitis—revisited. Ann Surg. 1990;211:165–171.
90. Baron EJ, Bennion R, Thompson J, et al. A microbiologic comparison between acute and advanced appendicitis. Clin Infect Dis. 1992;14:227–231.
91. Summanen PH, Jousimies-Somer H, Manley S, et al. *Bilophila wadsworthia* isolates from clinical specimens. Clin Infect Dis. 1995;20(Suppl 2):S210–S211.
92. Wexler HM, Reeves D, Summanen PH, et al. *Sutterella wadsworthensis* gen. nov., sp. nov. for bile-resistant microaerophilic *Campylobacter gracilis*–like clinical isolates. Int J Syst Bacteriol. 1996;46:252–258.
93. Molitoris E, Wexler HM, Finegold SM. Sources and antimicrobial susceptibilities of *Campylobacter gracilis* and *Sutterella wadsworthensis*. Clin Infect Dis. 1997;25(Suppl 2):S264–S265.
94. Finegold SM, Jousimies-Somer H. Recently described clinically important anaerobic bacteria: Medical aspects. Clin Infect Dis. 1997;25(Suppl 2):S88–S93.
95. Sears CL, Myers LL, Lazenby A, et al. Enterotoxigenic *Bacteroides fragilis*. Clin Infect Dis. 1995;20(Suppl 2):S142–S148.
96. Mundy LM, Sears CL. Detection of toxin production by *Bacteroides fragilis*: Assay development and screening of extraintestinal clinical isolates. Clin Infect Dis. 1996;23:269–276.
97. Pantosti A, Malpeli M, Wilks M, et al. Detection of enterotoxigenic *Bacteriodes fragilis* by PCR. J Clin Microbiol. 1997;35:2482–2486.
98. Swenson RM, Michaelson TC, Daly MJ, et al. Anaerobic bacterial infections of the female genital tract. Obstet Gynecol. 1973;42:538–541.
99. Eschenbach DA. Bacterial vaginosis and anaerobes in obstetric-gynecologic infections. Clin Infect Dis. 1993;16(Suppl):S282–S287.
100. Eschenbach DA, Buchanan TM, Pollock HM, et al. Polymicrobial etiology of acute pelvic inflammatory disease. N Engl J Med. 1975;293:166–171.
101. Sweet RL. Pelvic inflammatory disease. Sex Transm Dis. 1986;13:192–198.
102. Snydman PR, Tally FP, Knoppel R, et al. *Bacteroides bivius* and *Bacteroides disiens* in obstetrical patients: Clinical findings and antimicrobial susceptibilities. J Antimicrob Chemother. 1980;6:519–525.
103. Spiegel CA. Bacterial vaginosis. Clin Microbiol Rev. 1991;4:485–502.
104. Sweet RL. Role of bacterial vaginosis in pelvic inflammatory disease. Clin Infect Dis. 1995;20(Suppl 2):S271–S275.
105. Krohn MA, Hillier SL, Lee ML, et al. Vaginal *Bacteroides* species are associated with an increased rate of preterm delivery among women in preterm labor. J Infect Dis. 1991;164:88–93.
106. Krohn MA, Hillier SL, Nugent RP, et al. The genital flora of women with intraamnionotic infection. J Infect Dis. 1995;171:1475–1480.
107. Felner JM, Dowell VR Jr. "*Bacteroides*" bacteremia. Am J Med. 1971:50:787–796.
108. Wilson WR, Martin WM, Wilkowski CJ, et al. Anaerobic bacteremia. Mayo Clin Proc. 1972;47:639–646.
109. Weinstein MP, Reller LB, Murphy JR, et al. The clinical significance of positive blood cultures: A comprehensive analysis of 500 episodes of bacteremia and fungemia in adults. I. Laboratory and epidemiologic observations. Rev Infect Dis. 1983;5:35–53.
110. Brook I. Anaerobic bacterial bacteremia: 12-year experience in two military hospitals. J Infect Dis. 1989;160:1071–1075.
111. Lombardi DP, Engleberg NC. Anaerobic bacteremia: Incidence, patient characteristics, and clinical significance. Am J Med. 1992;92:53–60.
112. Chow AW, Guze LB. Bacteriodaceae bacteremia: Clinical experience with 112 patients. Medicine (Baltimore). 1974;53:93–123.
113. Redondo MC, Arbo MDJ, Grindlinger J, et al. Attributable mortality of bacteremia associated with the *Bacteroides fragilis* group. Clin Infect Dis. 1995;20:1492–1496.
114. Galpin JE, Chow AW, Bayer AS, et al. Sepsis associated with decubitus ulcers. Am J Med. 1976;61:346–350.
115. Dorsher CW, Rosenblatt JE, Wilson WR, et al. Anaerobic bacteremia: Decreasing rate over a 15 year period. Rev Infect Dis. 1991;13:633–636.
116. Weinstein MP, Towns ML, Quartey SM, et al. The clinical significance of positive blood cultures in the 1990s: A prospective comprehensive evaluation of the microbiology, epidemiology, and outcome of bacteremia and fungemia in adults. Clin Infect Dis. 1997;24:584–602.
117. Morris AJ, Wilson ML, Mirrett S, et al. Rationale for selective use of anaerobic blood cultures. J Clin Microbiol. 1993;31:2110–2113.
118. Cockerill FR, Hughes JG, Vetter EA, et al. Analysis of 281,797 consecutive blood cultures performed over an eight-year period: Trends in microorganisms isolated and the value of anaerobic culture of blood. Clin Infect Dis. 1997;24:403–418.
119. Felner JM, Dowell VR Jr. Anaerobic bacterial endocarditis. N Engl J Med. 1970;282:1188–1192.
120. Nastro LJ, Finegold SM. Endocarditis due to anaerobic gram-negative bacilli. Am J Med. 1973;54:482–496.
121. Skeist DJ, Steiner D, Werner M, et al. Anaerobic pericarditis: Case report and review. Clin Infect Dis. 1994;19:435–440.
122. Goldstein EJC, Citron DM, Finegold JM. Role of anaerobic bacteria in bite-wound infections. Rev Infect Dis. 1984;6(Suppl):S177–S183.
123. Pearson HE, Smiley DF. *Bacteroides* in pilonidal sinuses. Am J Surg. 1968;115:336.
124. Brook I, Frazier EH. Clinical and microbiological features of necrotizing fasciitis. J Clin Microbiol. 1995;33:2382–2387.

125. Louie TJ, Bartlett JG, Tally FP, et al. Aerobic and anaerobic bacteria in diabetic foot ulcers. Ann Intern Med. 1976;85:461–463.
126. Brook I. Anaerobic and aerobic bacteriology of decubitus ulcers in children. Am Surg. 1980;46:624–626.
127. Bryan CS, Dew CE, Reynolds KL. Bacteremia associated with decubitus ulcers. Arch Intern Med. 1983;143:2093.
128. Gerding D. Foot infections in diabetic patients; The role of anaerobes. Clin Infect Dis. 1995;20(Suppl 2):S283–S288.
129. Meislin HW, Lerner SA, Graves MH, et al. Cutaneous abscesses. Anaerobic and aerobic bacteriology and outpatient management. Ann Intern Med. 1977;87:145–149.
130. Edmiston CE, Walker AP, Krepel CJ, et al. The nonpuerperal breast infection: Aerobic and anaerobic microbial recovery from acute and chronic disease. J Infect Dis. 1990;162:695–699.
131. Raff MJ, Melo JC. Anaerobic osteomyelitis. Medicine (Baltimore). 1978;57:83–103.
132. Nakata MN, Lewis RP. Anaerobic bacteria in bone and joint infections. Rev Infect Dis. 1984;6(Suppl):S165–S170.
133. Gardiner W. Complicated frontal sinusitis: Valuation and management. Otolaryngology. 1986;95:333–343.
134. Brook I, Frazier EH. Anaerobic osteomyelitis and arthritis in a military hospital: A 10-year experience. Am J Med. 1993;94:21–28.
135. Finkelstein R, Nachum Z, Reissman P, et al. Anaerobic osteomyelitis in patients with Gaucher's disease. Clin Infect Dis. 1992;15:771–773.
136. Rosenkranz P, Lederman MM, Gopabkrishna KV, et al. Septic arthritis caused by *Bacteriodes fragilis*. Rev Infect Dis. 1990;12:20–30.
137. Olak J, Christou NV, Stein LA, et al. Operative vs. percutaneous drainage of intra-abdominal abscesses: Comparison of morbidity and mortality. Arch Surg. 1986;121:141–146.
138. Mueller PR, van Sonnenberg E. Interventional radiology in the chest and abdomen. N Engl J Med. 1990;322:1364–1374.
139. Boom WH, Tuazon CU. Successful treatment of multiple brain abscesses with antibiotics alone. Rev Infect Dis. 1985;7:189–199.
140. Herbert DA, Fogel DA, Rothman J, et al. Pyogenic liver abscesses: Successful non-surgical therapy. Lancet. 1992;1:134–136.
141. Landers DV, Sweet RL. Current trends in the diagnosis and treatment of tubo-ovarian abscess. Am J Obstet Gynecol. 1985;151:1098–1110.
142. Gozal D, Ziser A, Shupak A, et al. Necrotizing fasciitis. Arch Surg. 1986;121:233–235.
143. Mainous EG, Boyne PJ, Hart GB. Hyperbaric oxygen treatment of mandibular osteomyelitis: Report of three cases. J Am Dent Assoc. 1973;87:1426–1430.
144. Thom SR, Lauermann MW, Hart G-B. Intermittent hyperbaric oxygen therapy for reduction of mortality in experimental polymicrobial sepsis. J Infect Dis. 1986;154:504–510.
145. Triplett RG, Brahham GB, Gilmore JD, et al. Experimental mandibular osteomyelitis: Therapeutic trials with hyperbaric oxygen. J Oral Maxillofac Surg. 1982;40:640–646.
146. Heimdahl A, von Konow L, Nord CE. Isolation of β-lactamase–producing *Bacteroides* strains associated with clinical failures with penicillin treatment of human orofacial infections. Arch Oral Biol. 1980;25:689–692.
147. Brook I, Yocum P, Foote PA Jr. Changes in the core tonsillar bacteriology of recurrent tonsillitis: 1977–1993. Clin Infect Dis. 1995;21:171–176.
148. Goldstein EJC, Summanen PH, Citron DM, et al. Fatal sepsis due to a β-lactamase–producing strain of *Fusobacterium nucleatum* subspecies *polymorphum*. Clin Infect Dis. 1995;20:798–800.
149. Johnson CC, Reinhardt JF, Edelstein MAC, et al. *Bacteroides gracilis*, an important anaerobic bacterial pathogen . J Clin Microbiol. 1985;22:799–802.
150. Musial CE, Rosenblatt JE. Antimicrobial susceptibilities of anaerobic bacteria isolated at the Mayo Clinic during 1982 through 1987: Comparison with results from 1977 through 1981. Mayo Clin Proc. 1989;64:392–399.
151. Cuchural GJ Jr, Tally FP, Jacobus NV, et al. Comparative activities of newer β-lactam agents against members of the *Bacteroides fragilis* group. Antimicrob Agents Chemother. 1990;34:479–480.
152. Appelbaum P, Spangler S, Jacobs MR. Susceptibilities of 394 *Bacteroides fragilis*, non–*B. fragilis* group *Bacteroides* species, and *Fusobacterium* species to newer antimicrobial agents. Antimicrob Agents Chemother. 1991;35:1214–1218.
153. Cuchural GJ Jr, Tally FB, Jacobus NV, et al. Susceptibility of the *Bacteroides fragilis* group in the United States: Analysis by site of isolation. Antimicrob Agents Chemother. 1988;32:717–722.
154. Snydman DR, McDermott L, Cuchural GJ Jr, et al. Analysis of trends in antimicrobial resistance patterns among clinical isolates of *Bacteroides fragilis* group species from 1990 to 1994. Clin Infect Dis. 1996;23(Suppl 1):S54–S65.
155. Wexler HM, Molitoris E, Molitoris D, et al. In vitro activities of trovafloxacin against 557 strains of anaerobic bacteria. Antimicrob Agents Chemother. 1996;40:2232–2235.
156. Citron DM, Appleman MD. Comparative in vitro activities of trovafloxacin (CP-99,219) against 221 aerobic and 217 anaerobic bacteria isolated from patients with intra-abdominal infections. Antimicrob Agents Chemother. 1997;41:2312–2316.
157. Cornick NA, Jacobus NV, Gorbach SL. Activity of cefmetazole against anaerobic bacteria. Antimicrob Agents Chemother. 1987;31:2010–2012.
158. Wexler HM, Finegold SM. In vitro activity of cefotetan compared with that of other antimicrobial agents against anaerobic bacteria. Antimicrob Agents Chemother. 1988;32:601–604.
159. Thadepalli H, Reddy U, Chuah SK, et al. In vivo efficacy of trovafloxacin (CP-99,217), a new quinolone, in experimental intra-abdominal abscesses caused by *Bacteroides fragilis* and *Escherichia coli*. Antimicrob Agents Chemother. 1997;41:583–586.
160. Ingham HR, Selkon JB, Roxby CM. Bacteriological study of otogenic cerebral abscesses: Chemotherapeutic role of metronidazole. BMJ. 1977;2:991–993.
161. Levison ME, Mangura CT, Lorber B, et al. Clindamycin compared with penicillin for the treatment of anaerobic lung abscess. Ann Intern Med. 1983;98:466–471.
162. Gudiol F, Manresa F, Pallares R, et al. Clindamycin vs penicillin for anaerobic lung infections. High rate of penicillin failures associated with penicillin-resistant *Bacteroides melaninogenicus*. Arch Intern Med. 1990;150:2525–2529.
163. Sanders CV, Hanna BJ, Lewis AC. Metronidazole in the treatment of anaerobic infections. Am Rev Respir Dis. 1979;120:337–343.
164. Harding GKM, Buckwold FJ, Ronald AR, et al. Prospective, randomized comparative study of clindamycin, chloramphenicol, and ticarcillin, each in combination with gentamicin, in therapy for intra-abdominal and female genital tract sepsis. J Infect Dis. 1980;142:384–393.
165. Smith JA, Skidmore AG, Forward AD, et al. Prospective, randomized, double-blind comparison of metronidazole and tobramycin with clindamycin and tobramycin in the treatment of intra-abdominal sepsis. Ann Surg. 1980;192:213–220.
166. Polk HC Jr, Fink MP, Laverdiere M, et al. Prospective randomized study of surgically treated intra-abdominal infection. Am Surg. 1993;59:598–605.
167. Tally FP, Gorbach SL. Therapy of mixed anaerobic-aerobic infections: Lessons from studies of intra-abdominal sepsis. Am J Med. 1985;78:145–153.
168. Solomkin JS, Dellinger EP, Christou NV, et al. Results of a multicenter trial comparing imipenem/cilastatin to tobramycin/clindamycin for intra-abdominal infections. Ann Surg. 1990;212:581–591.
169. Hill GB, Ayers OM. Antimicrobial susceptibilities of anaerobic bacteria isolated from female genital tract infections. Antimicrob Agents Chemother. 1985;27:324–331.
170. Landers DV, Sweet RL. Tubo-ovarian abscess: Contemporary approach to management. Rev Infect Dis. 1983;5:876–884.
171. Pastorek JG II, Sanders CV Jr. Antibiotic therapy for post cesarean endomyometritis. Rev Infect Dis. 1991;13(Suppl):S752–S757.
172. Rasmossen BA, Bush K, Tally FP. Antimicrobial resistance in anaerobes. Clin Infect Dis. 1997;24(Suppl 1):S110–S120.
173. Wexler HM. Susceptibility testing of anaerobic bacteria—the state of the art. Clin Infect Dis. 1993;16(Suppl):S328–S333.

Chapter 238

Anaerobic Cocci

ELLEN M. MASCINI
JAN VERHOEF

Anaerobic cocci are found as commensal flora of all skin and mucosal surfaces and are, after the gram-negative bacilli, the second most common group of anaerobes encountered in human infection. The most clinically important anaerobic cocci are included in the genera *Peptostreptococcus, Streptococcus, Gemella*, and *Veillonella*. Often they are recovered mixed with other bacteria, which always makes it difficult to define their exact role in the cause of the infection. Other genera are seldom cutured from relevant clinical specimens.[1] The microaerophilic gram-positive cocci *Streptococcus anginosus, Streptococcus constellatus*, and *Streptococcus intermedius*, as well as *Gemella morbillorum*, which are often isolated in primary anaerobic culture but adapt to microaerophilic growth on successive subculture,[1, 2] are discussed in Chapters 191 and 192.

TAXONOMY AND MICROBIOLOGY

In 1977 Watt and Jack defined anaerobic cocci as cocci that grow well under satisfactory conditions of anaerobiosis and do not grow on suitable solid media in 10% carbon dioxide in air even after incubation for 7 days at 37°C.[2] Until recently, classification and definition of these organisms were always extremely difficult because the earlier attempts at identification had included cocci that were likely to be microaerophilic. The genus *Peptostreptococcus* consists of obligatory anaerobic gram-positive cocci that neither require fermentable carbohydrate for growth nor produce lactic acid as their sole major metabolic end product.[3–5] Cell size was the method usually recommended to distinguish two of the most important species, *Peptostreptococcus magnus* and *Peptostreptococcus micros*.[6] Most gram-positive anaerobic cocci use proteins and amino acids as their major energy source and are not amenable to identification methods based on carbohydrate fermentation reactions.[4] In the past, inadequate taxonomy yielded misleading descriptions of the mean pathogenicity and biochemistry of gram-positive anaerobic cocci "species," which were in fact mixed groups. The difficulties in identification and a poor predictive value of identification discouraged clinical microbiologists for a long time, but this circle has been broken: the introduction of nucleic acid techniques (guanosine plus cytosine content, 16S RNA sequencing, DNA homology) in the 1980s has revolutionized the taxonomy of these bacteria.[7, 8] Most species formerly classified as *Peptococcus* have been transferred to the genus *Peptostreptococcus*.[1, 4, 5, 8, 9] The notorious exception is *Peptococcus niger*, the former type species of the genus, and another species, *Peptococcus saccharolyticus*, which has been reclassified as *Staphylococcus saccharolyticus* (aerotolerant on subculture). In fact, *P. niger* phylogenetically clusters within the Actinomycetales and will probably be renamed accordingly.[1, 4, 7] *Streptococcus pleomorphus, Streptococcus parvulus*, and *Streptococcus hansenii* have been transferred to other genera.[1, 7] Besides genetic analysis, preformed enzyme profiles based on tests for the presence of saccharolytic and proteolytic enzymes provide a simple method for identification in clinical surveys.[3, 4, 6, 8] Unlike the true anaerobic cocci, microaerophilic streptococci are resistant to metronidazole; this characteristic is useful for differentiation of species and is an important factor to be taken into account in predicting therapeutic antimicrobial coverage.[1, 2] The major features that differentiate these microaerophilic cocci from *Peptostreptococcus* species are their strong saccharolytic nature and their production of lactic acid as the sole major end product.[1] Together, these developments now allow routine laboratory identification of gram-positive anaerobic cocci to groups with defined and distinct clinical properties, thus giving predictive value to the identification of gram-positive anaerobic cocci.

Currently, the genus *Peptostreptococcus* consists of 10 species of human origin (*Peptostreptococcus anaerobius, Peptostreptococcus asaccharolyticus, Peptostreptococcus hydrogenalis, Peptostreptococcus lacrimalis, Peptostreptococcus lactolyticus, P. magnus, P. micros, Peptostreptococcus prevotii, Peptostreptococcus tetradius*, and *Peptostreptococcus vaginalis*).[10] *P. magnus* and *P. micros* are generally accepted as being homogeneous taxa, whereas the heterogeneity of the two species *P. asaccharolyticus* and *P. prevotii* is beyond dispute. *P. anaerobius* is only distantly related to other species in the genus and clusters with some members of the genus *Clostridium*.[3, 7, 8, 10] The peptidoglycan types and DNA-rRNA hybridization data suggest that *Peptostreptococcus* is not a well-defined genus but contains some very heterogeneous species with differences marked enough to designate new genera[3, 4, 7, 8, 10] (Fig. 238–1). *Veillonella* is a small, nonmotile, nonfermentative, obligatory anaerobic gram-negative coccus that fluoresces red under ultraviolet light and reduces nitrate.[3, 11] Several species have been described, of which *Veillonella parvula* appears to be the most common in specimens from humans.[3, 9]

NORMAL FLORA

Peptostreptococcus species are part of the normal flora of the mouth, upper respiratory tract, intestinal tract, vagina, and skin.[8, 12, 13] *V. parvula* is universally present in the upper airways and normally inhabits the mouth, gastrointestinal tract, and vagina in humans.[3, 11–16] It has been suggested that their production of volatile fatty acids may be important in inhibiting the growth of enteropathogens in vivo.[16]

CLINICAL ISOLATES

Clinically important obligatory anaerobic cocci include *Peptostreptococcus* and *Veillonella*.[3, 5, 17] Additional anaerobic cocci, including *Coprococcus, Peptococcus, Ruminococcus, Sarcina*, and *S. saccharolyticus*, are rarely isolated from clinical specimens.[5, 9] Most anaerobic cocci express their pathogenicity via synergistic interaction with other (facultative) anaerobic organisms. Very little is known of the pathogenesis of infections caused by anaerobic cocci. Studies of virulence factors might clarify the pathogenic potential of different species of anaerobic cocci.

Peptostreptococcus Species

Peptostreptococci, the second most common group of anaerobes, consistently account for 20 to 40% of all anaerobes isolated from

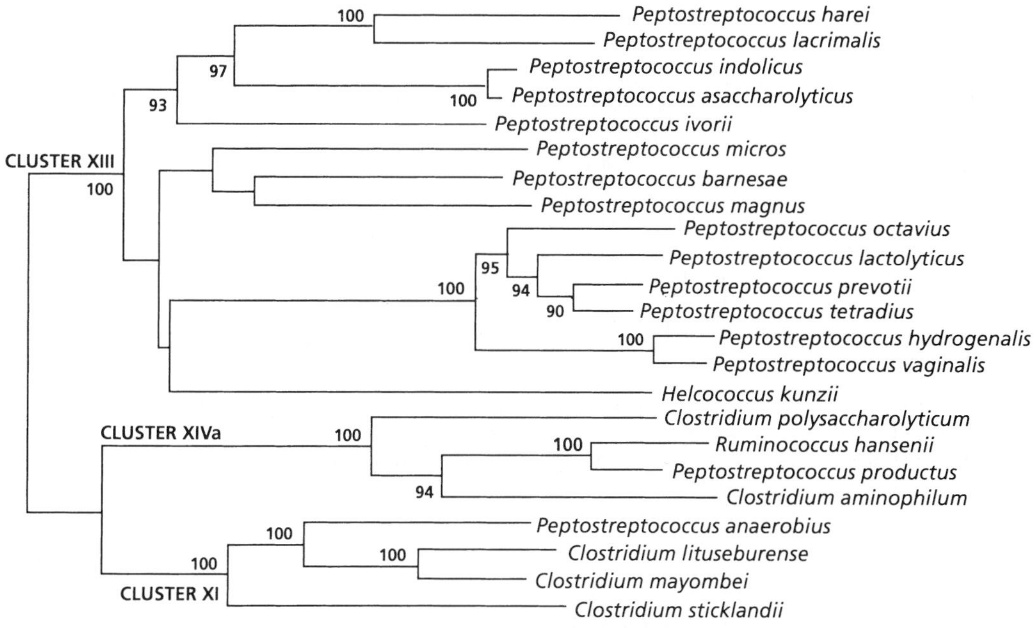

FIGURE 238–1. Phylogenetic tree constructed by the neighbor-joining method, showing the position of *Peptostreptococcus* species within *Clostridium* rRNA clusters XI, XIII, and XIVa. Significant bootstrap values (90% and higher), expressed as a percentage of 500 replications, are indicated at the branching points. (Adapted from Murdoch DA. Gram-positive anaerobic cocci. Clin Microbiol Rev. 1998;11:81–120.)

clinical sources and are involved in a wide variety of clinically significant infections.[3, 6, 8, 9, 12, 17] *P. magnus, P. micros, P. asaccharolyticus*, and *P. anaerobius* are the most important clinical isolates. Their contribution to anaerobic clinical isolates was reported to amount to 27%.[6, 8] *Peptostreptococcus* spp. are among the most important causative microbes in abscesses, (e.g., brain abscesses), especially in association with chronic otitis media, mastoiditis, chronic sinusitis, and pleuropulmonary infections.[8, 12, 18] *Peptostreptococcus* species *(P. micros, P. magnus*, and *P. anaerobius)* have been recognized as common causative microbes in anaerobic pleuropulmonary disease, usually in mixed culture.[8, 12, 19, 20] *Peptostreptococcus* species recovered from blood were associated with all sources, but especially with oropharyngeal, pulmonary, and female genital tract sources.[3, 8, 21, 22] They appear to cause significant morbidity much less often than gram-negative anaerobes do, particularly *Bacteroides* species. Predisposing factors to peptostreptococcal bacteremia include malignancy,[21, 22] recent gastrointestinal, obstetric, or gynecologic surgery, ulceration of the extremities, dental extraction, and immunosuppression.[3, 22] *Peptostreptococcus* species are among the most common organisms in anaerobic osteomyelitis and arthritis at all sites, including bites and cranial infections.[12, 23] When mixed with other aerobes and anaerobes, they may be involved in severe, soft tissue infections such as cellulitis, streptococcal myonecrosis, necrotizing fasciitis, and Fournier's gangrene.[6, 8, 12, 24]

Different species are associated with different sites, as shown in Figure 238–2.[3, 6, 8, 12] *P. magnus* stands out as the most pathogenic species of anaerobic cocci; it is the most frequently isolated species and by far the most common species isolated in pure culture. It is associated with abscesses arising from sebaceous cysts and superficial wound infections, and it is isolated in 15 to 20% of diabetic foot infections.[3, 6, 8] In addition, *P. magnus* is recognized as a significant cause of septic arthritis, usually in the presence of joint prostheses, nonpuerperal breast infections, and puerperal sepsis.[3, 6, 23] Case reports of fatal endocarditis, paravalvular abscess around a bioprosthetic aortic valve, purulent pericarditis, and mediastinitis have very rarely been documented.[6, 8] The pathogenic potential of other species is very poorly understood, mainly because of problems with identification, but also because most isolates come from mixed cultures, often from superficial sites where they could be part of the normal commensal flora. *P. micros* was usually isolated from soft tissue abscesses, never from the skin, and with a characteristic mixed flora consisting of the *Streptococcus milleri* group and anaerobic gram-negative rods. It might be the predominant anaerobic coccus in oral pathology because it is associated with endodontic abscesses, dental implant infections, progressive periodontitis, and peritonsillar abscesses.[6, 8, 12] Sporadically, it has also been implicated in vertebral and mastoid ethmoid osteomyelitis, nonpuerperal mastitis, bacteremia, and diabetic foot infections.[6, 23] *P. anaerobius* is associated with polymicrobial, soft tissue, and dental abscesses; however, most isolates are from intra-abdominal sepsis or the female genitourinary tract in association with fecal flora.[3, 6] *P. asaccharolyticus* is cultured from a wide variety of sites, typically mixed with both aerobes and anaerobes, and frequently from abscesses not associated with any particular site or infection.[6, 10] *P. vaginalis* is usually cultured from superficial sites, often from postoperative wound infections with *Staphylococcus aureus*.

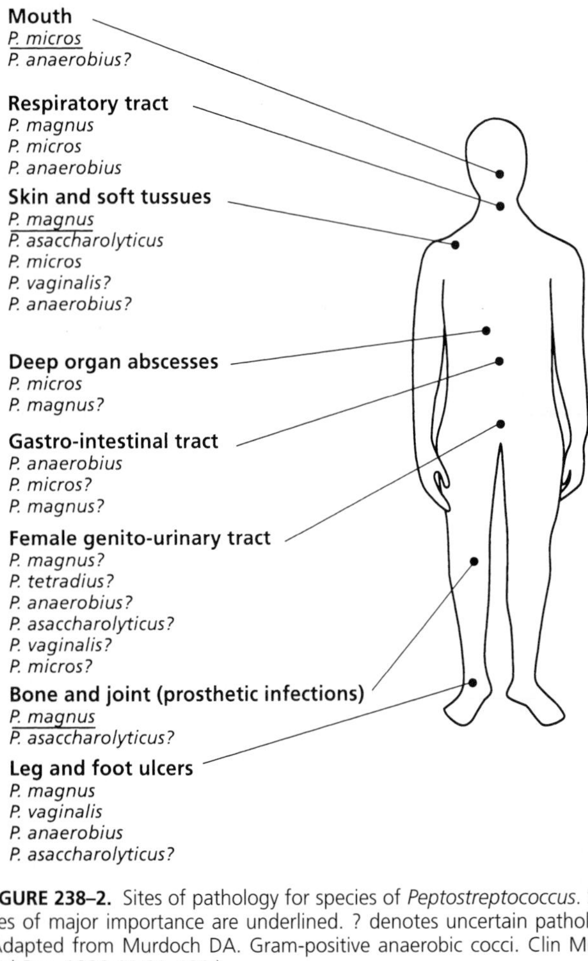

FIGURE 238–2. Sites of pathology for species of *Peptostreptococcus*. Species of major importance are underlined. ? denotes uncertain pathology. (Adapted from Murdoch DA. Gram-positive anaerobic cocci. Clin Microbiol Rev. 1998;11:81–120.)

Veillonella

Veillonella species were recovered in less than 0.5 to 4% of clinical specimens cultured for anaerobic bacteria.[3, 9, 12, 15, 17] *V. parvula* appears to be the most common species in human specimens.[9, 11] When isolated from clinical specimens, it is often regarded as a contaminant or a commensal.[11, 14] However, it has been isolated in pure culture from various sites and implicated as a pathogen in the sinuses, lungs, liver, central nervous system, heart, and bone.[11, 12] The most frequently reported infection caused by *V. parvula* is osteomyelitis.[11, 23] Occasionally, *V. parvula* has been recovered from blood in association with osteomyelitis, malignancy, low-birth-weight neonates, and gastrointestinal endoscopy.[11, 15, 21, 22] *Veillonella* species have been reported as a cause of endocarditis, pleuropulmonary infections, chronic sinusitis, abscesses, burn site infections, meningitis, and myositis.[11, 15, 25, 26] *V. parvula* is usually isolated as part of a polymicrobial process,[15] which combined with the fact that *V. parvula* is a normal inhabitant of the mouth, upper airways, gastrointestinal tract, and vagina, has made elucidation of its pathogenetic role difficult. In patients with underlying disease or immune suppression, *V. parvula* should be considered a pathogen.

TREATMENT

Successful treatment is often the result of a combination of surgical management involving débridement of necrotic tissue, removal of foreign bodies, drainage, and improvement in circulation with the administration of antimicrobial agents. Because anaerobic cocci are generally recovered mixed with aerobic or other anaerobic organisms, selection of proper therapy becomes more complicated. The appropriate antibiotics should have efficacy against all target organisms. It may be difficult to achieve reliable culture because of problems in obtaining appropriate specimens. Another problem is the lack of consensus about the best method for routine sensitivity testing of anaerobic cocci or, indeed, of any anaerobes.[27, 28] Moreover, because both procedures are time consuming, empirical treatment of many patients is necessary until culture results become available. Gram-positive anaerobic cocci and *V. parvula* typically respond well to therapy with a penicillin or clindamycin, but occasional isolates may, however, show resistance to these agents.[3, 9, 15, 19, 21, 25, 28, 29] Metronidazole is effective against obligate anaerobic cocci and has superior penetration into pus.[8] Tetracyclines and macrolides have variable activity against gram-positive anaerobic cocci, but the newer quinolones show promise.[3, 8, 28, 29] *Veillonella* species are generally resistant to vancomycin and tetracycline and have only intermediate susceptibility to erythromycin.[11, 15] Other antimicrobial agents to which the anaerobic cocci are usually susceptible in vitro include cephalosporins, imipenem, metronidazole, and chloramphenicol.[3, 9, 11, 15, 19, 28, 29] Drugs that have virtually no activity are aminoglycosides, aztreonam, and trimethoprim-sulfamethoxazole.[20]

REFERENCES

1. Jousimies-Sommer H. Recently described clinically important anaerobic bacteria: Taxonomic aspects and update. Clin Infect Dis. 1997;25(Suppl 2):S78–S87.
2. Watt B, Jack EP. What are anaerobic cocci? J Med Microbiol. 1977;10:461–468.
3. Wren MWD. Anaerobic cocci of clinical importance. Br J Biomed Sci. 1996;53:294–301.
4. Murdoch DA, Magee JT. A numerical taxonomic study of the gram-positive anaerobic cocci. J Med Microbiol. 1995;45:148–155.
5. Summanen S. Recent taxonomic changes for anaerobic gram-positive and selected gram-negative organisms. Clin Infect Dis. 1993;16(Suppl 4):S168–S174.
6. Murdoch DA, Mitchelmore IJ, Tabaqchali S. The clinical importance of gram-positive anaerobic cocci isolated at St Bartholomew's Hospital, London, in 1987. J Med Microbiol. 1994;41:36–44.
7. Collins MD, Lawson PA, Willems A, et al. The phylogeny of the genus *Clostridium*: Proposal of five new genera and eleven new species combinations. Int J Syst Bacteriol. 1994;44:812–826.
8. Murdoch DA. Gram-positive anaerobic cocci. Clin Microbiol Rev. 1998;11:81–120.
9. Koneman EW, Allen SE, Janda WM, et al. The anaerobic bacteria. In: Color Atlas and Textbook of Diagnostic Microbiology. 5th ed. Philadelphia: JB Lippincott; 1997:709–784.
10. Pelz K, Mutters R. Taxonomic update and clinical significance of species within the genus *Peptostreptococcus*. Clin Infect Dis. 1997;25(Suppl 2):S94–S97.
11. Fisher RG, Denison MR. *Veillonella parvula* bacteremia without an underlying source. J Clin Microbiol. 1996;34:3235–3236.
12. Finegold SM. Anaerobic Bacteria in Human Disease. New York: Academic; 1977.
13. Evaldson G, Heimdahl A, Kager L, et al. The normal human anaerobic microflora. Scand J Infect Dis Suppl. 1982;35:9–15.
14. Bartlett JG. Bacteriologic diagnosis in anaerobic pleuropulmonary infections. Clin Infect Dis. 1993;16(Suppl 4):S443–S445.
15. Brook I. *Veillonella* infections in children. J Clin Microbiol. 1996;34:1283–1285.
16. Hinton A, Hume ME. Inhibition of *Listeria monocytogenes* growth by *Veillonella* cultured on tartrate medium. Clin Infect Dis. 1997;25(Suppl 2):S120.
17. Bernard K, Cooper C, Johnson W. Prevalence of anaerobes referred to the Canadian National Reference Centre from 1984 to 1996. Clin Infect Dis. 1997;25(Suppl 2):S241–S243.
18. Brook I. Brain abscess in children: Microbiology and management. J Child Neurol. 1995;10:283–288.
19. Marina M, Strong CA, Civen R, et al. Bacteriology of anaerobic pleuropulmonary infections: Preliminary report. Clin Infect Dis. 1993;16(Suppl 4):S256–S262.
20. Bartlett JG. Anaerobic infections of the lung and pleural space. Clin Infect Dis. 1993;16(Suppl 4):S248–S255.
21. Fainstein V, Elting LS, Bodey GP. Bacteremia caused by non-sporulating anaerobes in cancer patients. Medicine (Baltimore). 1989;68:151–162.
22. Brook I. Anaerobic bacterial bacteremia: 12-year experience in two military hospitals. J Infect Dis. 1989;160:1071–1075.
23. Brook I, Frazier E. Anaerobic osteomyelitis and arthritis in a military hospital: A 10-year experience. Am J Med. 1993;94:21–28.
24. Gorbach SL. IDCP guidelines: Necrotizing skin and soft tissue infections. Part II: Myositis, Meleney's gangrene, pyomyositis, necrotizing cellulitis, and Fournier's gangrene. Infect Dis Clin Pract. 1997;5:463–471.
25. Beumont MG, Duncan J, Mitchell SD, et al. *Veillonella* myositis in an immunocompromised patient. Clin Infect Dis. 1995;21:678–679.
26. Borowski AD, Stein SM, Tulipan NB, et al. Meningitis caused by mixed anaerobic species complicating tethered cord syndrome. Clin Infect Dis. 1995;21:706–707.
27. Rosenblatt JE, Brook I. Clinical relevance of susceptibility testing of anaerobic bacteria. Clin Infect Dis. 1993;16(Suppl):S446–S448.
28. Duerden BI. Role of the reference laboratory in susceptibility testing of anaerobes and a survey of isolates referred from laboratories in England and Wales during 1993–1994. Clin Infect Dis. 1995;20(Suppl 2):S180–S186.
29. Cullman W, Frei R, Krech T. Antibacterial activity of oral antibiotics against anaerobic bacteria. Chemotherapy. 1993;39:169–174.

Chapter 239

Anaerobic Gram-Positive Nonsporulating Bacilli

ELLEN M. MASCINI
JAN VERHOEF

Gram-positive, anaerobic, non–spore-forming rods include species of *Actinomyces, Atopobium, Bifidobacterium, Eubacterium, Lactobacillus, Mobiluncus, Propionibacterium,* and *Pseudoramibacter.* These bacilli share a preference for anaerobic growth conditions, although some of them can be cultured in the presence of 5 to 10% CO_2 as well. *Actinomyces* and *Propionibacterium propionicum* cause actinomycosis and are discussed elsewhere. Other species of *Propionibacterium* will be discussed here. *Propionibacterium, Eubacterium, Bifidobacterium,* and *Lactobacillus* are the most frequently isolated species, apart from those that cause actinomycosis. Their contribution to anaerobic isolates amounts to about 20 to 40%, *Propionibacterium* spp. being the most common isolates.[1–5]

TAXONOMY AND MICROBIOLOGY

In routine microbiologic laboratories, gram-positive, nonsporulating bacilli are differentiated to the genus level phenotypically according to their metabolic end products and their morphology. *Propionibacterium* spp., occasionally branching, irregularly or regularly shaped rods, produce propionic and acetic acids as major end products. They are distinguished from *Bifidobacterium, Lactobacillus,* and *Eubacterium* spp. by a positive catalase reaction.[1] *Bifidobacterium* appears as very irregular rods with bifid and branching forms that produce acetic and lactic acid. Short to long and slender rods with chain formation are observed in *Lactobacillus,* which produces lactic acid as its sole major end product. Eubacteria, nonmotile obligatory anaerobic rods that may form endospores, are distinguished from other genera mainly on the basis of negative metabolic characteristics.[1, 6–8] In addition to this marked phenotypic heterogeneity, it is recognized that the eubacteria are not phylogenetically homogeneous either, with species dispersed among many of the different groups of the *Clostridium* genus.[6, 7] The slow and minimal growth of many strains of gram-positive, nonsporulating rods on the media commonly used in clinical microbiology suggests that these isolates are often missed. Also, the time and effort required to isolate and identify all anaerobic bacteria from mixed infections involving numerous species means that in many instances, even no attempt to isolate these bacteria is made. Even if isolated, anaerobic gram-positive rods have often presented problems with identification, which has led clinical laboratories to report nonclostridial isolates only by Gram stain or to give very presumptive identifications.[9]

Currently, taxonomic assessments are based on nucleic acid analyses (e.g. guanosine plus cytosine content, DNA homology, and RNA sequencing).[6–8] On the basis of 16S rRNA sequence analysis, a major reorganization is under way, especially among the very heterogenous organisms classified within the genus *Eubacterium*; new genera such as *Atopobium* and *Pseudoramibacter* have been introduced.[6, 7] *Atopobium* was created to include one new species *(Atopobium rimae)* and two renamed *Lactobacillus* species, *Atopobium minutum* and *Atopobium parvulum. Atopobium* is phylogenetically located among the Actinomycetales. The clinical significance of these oral organisms is poorly understood.[6, 10] *Pseudoramibacter* is a strictly anaerobic, nonmotile bacillus that occurs in pairs resembling flying birds, clumps, or Chinese characters.[7] *Mobiluncus* was tentatively assigned to the family Bacteroidaceae, which includes phenotypically similar organisms. However, electron microscopic studies show a structurally gram-positive cell wall and lipopolysaccharide was absent. Cells are curved with tapered ends, are motile by multiple subpolar flagella, and appear gram-variable or gram-negative.[1, 8] A phylogenetic relationship between *Mobiluncus* and *Actinomyces* was revealed by 16S rRNA sequencing.

NORMAL FLORA

Most bacilli discussed in this chapter are widely distributed and ubiquitous in humans and form part of the indigenous flora of the skin and mucosal layers. Bowel mucosa is inhabited by *Bifidobacterium, Lactobacillus, Eubacterium,* and *Propionibacterium,* which thus contribute to host defense of the enteric ecosystem.[5, 11] It has been suggested that the host defense mechanism attributed to bifidobacteria and lactobacilli is related to the fermentative production of acetic and lactic acid, hydrogen peroxide, and antimicrobial substances.[12] Several studies have indicated a protective effect of lactobacilli and bifidobacteria against potential pathogens in the gastrointestinal tract.[12, 13] Lactobacilli are recognized in the oral cavity and the vagina.[5, 11] Bifidobacteria are the second most numerous group of microorganisms in the gastrointestinal tract, especially in breast-fed infants.[1, 5, 11] Furthermore, *Propionibacterium acnes* and other *Propionibacterium* spp. are part of the normal flora of the skin, nasopharynx, oral cavity, and genitourinary tract.[1, 5]

CLINICAL ISOLATES

The rarity of disease caused by *Bifidobacterium, Eubacterium,* and *Lactobacillus* spp. may be secondary to the low pathogenicity of these bacteria, as well as the difficulty in culturing these organisms. The fastidious nature and often prolonged generation time have implicated these germs as a possible cause of culture-negative infections (endocarditis, sepsis, abscesses).[14, 15]

Propionibacterium

As inhabitants of the skin, propionibacteria are common contaminants of cultures of blood and body fluids. They have traditionally been considered nonpathogenic for humans, but several well-documented cases of infection can be found in association with implanted prostheses or central nervous system shunts.[4, 5, 16] *Propionibacterium* spp. have been identified as causes of brain abscess, subdural empyema, parotid and dental infections, endocarditis, conjunctivitis associated with a contact lens, pulmonary infections, and peritonitis.[5, 16, 17] Significant infections by *Propionibacterium* species have been documented in association with isolates from blood, lymph glands, abscesses, wounds, cysts, and sinuses.[16] In addition to the inflammatory process in acne lesions, *P. acnes* has been identified as a frequently recovered cause of anaerobic arthritis in association with prosthetic joints, vascular disease, and peripheral neuropathy.[5, 16, 18] In addition, isolation of these microorganisms from patients with osteomyelitis has been reported.[18] Because propionibacteria are capable of inducing significant infections, especially in some high-risk patients, efforts should be made to obtain specimens free of contamination by the normal flora of the mucous membranes and skin, where *Propionibacterium* species reside. Determination of the clinical significance of each isolate must be made with caution because such determination influences the need to direct therapy against that isolate.

Bifidobacterium, Eubacterium, and *Lactobacillus*

These organisms have been found most commonly in infections associated with predisposing or underlying conditions such as previous surgery, malignancy, immunodeficiency, diabetes mellitus, dental extraction, broad-spectrum antibiotics, and the presence of a foreign body.[2, 4, 5, 14, 16, 19, 20] Many (30 to 44%) of these isolates were reported to cause significant infection.[19] Most infections from which these species are recovered are polymicrobial and yield a mixture of aerobic and anaerobic bacteria.[2] Although *Bifidobacterium, Eubacterium,* and *Lactobacillus* spp. are infrequently associated with infections (each <5% of anaerobic isolates), they do occasionally cause serious illness.[2–4, 19] Mortality associated with infection caused by anaerobic, nonsporulating, gram-positive rods was reported to be very low.[4]

Lactobacillus

Unrelated to particular species, lactobacilli have infrequently been reported as a cause of serious infections in either immunocompetent or immunocompromised hosts. Subacute endocarditis, the most commonly reported severe clinical infection, is characterized by a high mortality rate of 23 to 27%.[15, 21, 22] Typically, it occurs in patients with preexisting structural heart disease and often with some form of recent dental infection or manipulation.[5, 15, 21–23] Relapses were observed in 24 to 39%, especially in patients treated with a single antibiotic. Embolization is a common complication observed in about 40% of patients, and occasionally cardiac surgery is required.[15, 21, 22] In addition published cases have reported involvement of *Lactobacillus* in pleuropulmonary infections, (intra-abdominal) abscesses, meningitis, conjunctivitis, dental caries, and endometritis.[2, 5, 17, 19, 21, 24] *Lactobacillus* septicemia, a rare condition usually seen in patients with severe underlying illnesses, may develop subsequent to a documented infection with the same organisms related to the urogenital or gastrointestinal tract.[2, 14, 21, 23, 25] The fact that *Lactobacillus* is not part of the skin flora supports true infection. The actual mortality rate associated with *Lactobacillus* sepsis was reported to be low; some patients have survived without therapy or with therapy that would be unlikely to be active against these pathogens.[14, 15, 19] Additionally, low virulence of the organism is suggested by the infrequent association of lactobacilli with bacteremic infections in spite of the ubiquitous presence of these organisms in the gastrointestinal tract and their widespread consumption in fermented milk products.[14, 15, 19, 23]

Bifidobacterium

Because bifidobacteria are usually recovered together with other commensals, little is known of their pathogenic potential. Blood stream infections by bifidobacteria are rarely diagnosed, usually along with other flora, in patients with complications associated with childbirth, gastrointestinal disorders, malignancies, or systemic lupus erythematosus.[19–21, 25] Involvement of *Bifidobacterium* species has occasionally been reported in chronic otitis media, pleuropulmonary infections, cholesteatoma, peritonitis, abscesses in the head and neck, meningitis, and paronychia.[2, 17, 19]

Eubacterium

Eubacteria have been recognized as pathogens in infections of the female genital tract associated with intrauterine devices[9] and in chronic periodontal disease.[8] The endogenous mouth flora, particularly in the presence of oral infection, can serve as a reservoir of opportunistic species that can infect sites in the head, neck, and lung, so numerous sites of infections by eubacteria may not be unexpected.[9] *Eubacterium* spp. have been recovered from pleuropulmonary infections, (brain) abscesses, osteomyelitis of the skull, peritonitis, wound infections, genitourinary sites, decubitus ulcers, and bites.[2, 5, 9, 17, 19] Occasionally, *Eubacterium* spp. have been reported as a cause of clinically significant bacteremia in patients with malignancies, gastrointestinal or obstetric disorders, and endocarditis.[2, 4, 5, 20, 25]

Pseudoramibacter alactolyticus

The description of this organism is based on that of *Eubacterium alactolyticus.* These organisms are isolated from dental calculus and the gingival crevices of patients with periodontal disease, from root canals, and from patients with various infections, including purulent pleurisy, cellulitis, postoperative wounds, and abscesses of the brain, lung, intestinal tract, and mouth.[7, 26]

Mobiluncus

Mobiluncus has been isolated from vaginal samples of women with nonspecific vaginitis (or bacterial vaginosis), but an etiologic role has not been established.[1, 8, 27, 28] Incidentally, *Mobiluncus* species were recovered from blood after a gynecologic infection and from anaerobic breast abscesses.[28]

TREATMENT

Eradication of organisms from deep-seated sites of infection may be difficult. Surgical intervention such as drainage of abscesses and removal of foreign bodies is commonly required in the treatment of infections with anaerobic gram-positive nonsporulating bacilli. Prolonged antimicrobial therapy is the other major approach in the elimination of anaerobic bacteria. The frequently polymicrobial nature of these infections should be taken into account when antibiotics are prescribed. In addition, antimicrobial susceptibility patterns of anaerobic bacteria in vitro are available only after a considerable number of days, so therapy often has to be started empirically. Unfortunately, consensus has not been reached about performance of susceptibility patterns because no specific method has proved to be satisfactorily reliable.[29] Thus, determination of susceptibility is not routinely performed in most diagnostic microbiologic laboratories, except for isolates obtained from blood or otherwise normally sterile material.

Anaerobic gram-positive nonsporulating bacilli are generally susceptible to most antibiotics used for the treatment of anaerobic infections, including penicillins, carbapenems, and clindamycin.[1, 2, 5, 16, 17, 25, 28, 30–32] Most eubacteria are susceptible to metronidazole, whereas *Lactobacillus, Propionibacterium,* and other facultatively anaerobic microorganisms regularly show resistance to nitroimidazoles.[1, 5, 16, 30] Erythromycin, tetracycline, and cephalosporins showed variable activity.[2, 30–32] Lactobacilli appear to be uniformly resistant to vancomycin and variably resistant to the cephalosporins and quinolones.[14, 22, 26] Synergistic therapy with a penicillin and an aminoglycoside appeared to provide optimal medical treatment of *Lactobacillus* endocarditis and should possibly be considered for other deep-seated infections.[14, 15, 22, 30] Neither vancomycin nor cephalosporins, both often used as alternatives to penicillins in the treatment of gram-positive bacterial infections, should be prescribed for the treatment of *Lactobacillus* endocarditis.[22] Poor response to antimicrobial therapy in *Lactobacillus* endocarditis may lead to relapse of infection and a need for valve replacement.

REFERENCES

1. Koneman EW, Allen SE, Janda WM, et al. The anaerobic bacteria. In: Color Atlas and Textbook of Diagnostic Microbiology. 5th ed. Philadelphia: JB Lippincott; 1997:709–784.
2. Brook I. Isolation of non-sporing anaerobic rods from infections in children. J Med Microbiol. 1996;45:21–26.
3. Bernard K, Cooper C, Johnson W. Prevalence of anaerobes referred to the Canadian National Reference Centre from 1984 to 1996. Clin Infect Dis. 1997;25(Suppl 2):S241–S243.
4. Brook I. Anaerobic bacterial bacteremia: 12-year experience in two military hospitals. J Infect Dis. 1989;160:1071–1075.
5. Finegold SM. Anaerobic Bacteria in Human Disease. New York: Academic; 1977.
6. Jousimies-Sommer H. Recently described clinically important anaerobic bacteria: Taxonomic aspects and update. Clin Infect Dis. 1997;25(Suppl 2):S78–S87.
7. Willems A, Collins MD. Phylogenetic relationships of the genera *Acetobacterium* and *Eubacterium* sensu stricto and reclassification of *Eubacterium alactolyticum* as *Pseudoramibacter alactolyticus* gen. nov., comb. nov. Int J Syst Bacteriol. 1996;46:1083–1087.
8. Summanen P. Recent taxonomic changes for anaerobic gram-positive and selected gram-negative organisms. Clin Infect Dis. 1993;16(Suppl 4):S168–S174.
9. Hill GB, Ayers OM, Kohan AP. Characteristics and sites of infection of *Eubacterium nodatum, Eubacterium timidum, Eubacterium brachy,* and other asaccharolytic eubacteria. J Clin Microbiol. 1987;25:1540–1545.
10. Collins MD, Wallbanks S. Comparative sequence analyses of the 16S rRNA genes of *Lactobacillus minutus, Lactobacillus rimae* and *Streptococcus parvulus*: Proposal for the creation of a new genus *Atopobium.* FEMS Microbiol Lett. 1992;95:235–240.
11. Evaldson G, Heimdahl A, Kager L, et al. The normal human anaerobic microflora. Scand J Infect Dis Suppl. 1982;35:9–15.
12. Lidbeck A, Nord CE. Lactobacilli and the normal human anaerobic microflora. Clin Infect Dis. 1993;16(Suppl):S181–S187.
13. Gibson GR, Wang X. Regulatory effects of bifidobacteria on the growth of other colonic bacteria. J Appl Bacteriol. 1994;77:412–420.
14. Antony SJ, Stratton CW, Dummer JS. *Lactobacillus* bacteremia: Description of the clinical course in adult patients without endocarditis. Clin Infect Dis. 1996;23:773–778.
15. Sussman JI, Baron EJ, Goldberg SM, et al. Clinical manifestations and therapy of *Lactobacillus* endocarditis: Report of a case and review of the literature. Rev Infect Dis. 1986;8:771–776.
16. Brook I, Frazier EH. Infections caused by *Propionibacterium* species. Rev Infect Dis. 1991;13:819–822.
17. Marina M, Strong CA, Civen R, et al. Bacteriology of anaerobic pleuropulmonary infections: Preliminary report. Clin Infect Dis. 1993;16(Suppl 4):S256–S262.
18. Brook I, Frazier E. Anaerobic osteomyelitis and arthritis in a military hospital: A 10-year experience. Am J Med. 1993;94:21–28.
19. Brook I, Frazier EH. Significant recovery of nonsporulating anaerobic rods from clinical specimens. Clin Infect Dis. 1993;16:476–480.
20. Fainstein V, Elting LS, Bodey GP. Bacteremia caused by non-sporulating anaerobes in cancer patients. Medicine (Baltimore). 1989;68:151–162.
21. Gasser F. Safety of lactic acid bacteria and their occurrence in human clinical infections. Bull Inst Pasteur. 1994;92:45–67.
22. Griffiths JK, Daly DS, Dodge RA. Two cases of endocarditis due to *Lactobacillus* species: Antimicrobial susceptibility, review, and discussion of therapy. Clin Infect Dis. 1992;15:250–255.
23. Saxelin M, Chuang NH, Chassy B, et al. Lactobacilli and bacteremia in southern Finland, 1989–1992. Clin Infect Dis. 1996;22:564–566.
24. van Houte J. Role of micro-organisms in caries etiology. J Dent Res. 1994;73:672–681.
25. Bourne KA, Beebe JL, Lue YA, et al. Bacteremia due to *Bifidobacterium, Eubacterium* or *Lactobacillus*; twenty-one cases and review of the literature. Yale J Biol Med. 1978;51:505–512.
26. Finegold SM, Jousimies-Somer H. Recently described clinically important anaerobic bacteria: Medical aspects. Clin Infect Dis. 1997;25(Suppl 2):S88–S93.
27. Wathne B, Holst E, Hovelius B, et al. Erythromycin versus metronidazole in the treatment of bacterial vaginosis. Acta Obstet Gynecol Scand. 1993;72:470–474.
28. Mayer J, Hegewald S, Sartor VE, et al. Extragenital infection due to *Mobiluncus mulieris*; case report and review. Diagn Microbiol Infect Dis. 1994;20:163–165.
29. Rosenblatt JE, Brook I. Clinical relevance of susceptibility testing of anaerobic bacteria. Clin Infect Dis. 1993;16(Suppl):S446–S448.
30. Bayer AS, Chow AW, Conception N, et al. Susceptibility of 40 lactobacilli to 6 antimicrobial agents with broad gram-positive anaerobic spectra. Antimicrob Agents Chemother. 1978;14:720–722.
31. Cullman W, Frei R, Krech T. Antibacterial activity of oral antibiotics against anaerobic bacteria. Chemotherapy. 1993;39:169–174.
32. Spiegel CA. Susceptibility of *Mobiluncus* species to 23 antimicrobial agents and 15 other compounds. Antimicrob Agents Chemother. 1987;31:249–252.

MYCOBACTERIAL DISEASES

Chapter 240

Mycobacterium tuberculosis

DAVID W. HAAS

The term *tuberculosis* describes a broad range of clinical illnesses caused by *Mycobacterium tuberculosis* (or less commonly *Mycobacterium bovis*). It is the most frequent cause of death worldwide due to a single infectious agent, and in 1993 the World Health Organization declared tuberculosis a global public health emergency. Tuberculosis can affect virtually every organ, most importantly the lungs, and is typically associated with granuloma formation.

HISTORY

There is evidence of spinal tuberculosis in neolithic, pre-Columbian, and early Egyptian remains. However, tuberculosis did not become a major problem until the Industrial Revolution, when crowded living conditions favored its spread. In the 17th and 18th centuries, tuberculosis caused one fourth of all adult deaths in Europe. Before antimicrobial agents became available, the cornerstone of treatment was rest in the open air in specialized sanatoria. Sanatorium regimens probably benefitted cases diagnosed before cavitation but had little impact on cavitary disease. When it became clear that cavitation was the pivotal event in progressive pulmonary tuberculosis, most special therapies focused on cavity closure.

The modern era of tuberculosis began in 1946 with demonstration of the efficacy of streptomycin (STM). In 1952, the much more effective drug isoniazid (INH) became available, making tuberculosis curable in the great majority of patients, and in 1970 rifampin (RMP) came to be recognized as at least equal to INH. The availability of drugs led to new treatment principles. With drug coverage it became possible to resect tuberculous tissue successfully, but with drug treatment resection was rarely necessary. Bed rest and collapse therapy added nothing to chemotherapy; treated patients rapidly became noninfectious; and specialized sanatoria ultimately disappeared. The duration of chemotherapy progressively decreased from approximately 2 years before the availability of RMP, to 9 months with INH and RMP given together, and to 6 months using multidrug therapy including INH, RMP, and pyrazinamide (PZA). With INH it also became practical to treat asymptomatic people thought to harbor tubercle bacilli based on positive tuberculin tests.

In the United States, reported cases of tuberculosis had declined nearly every year since accurate statistics became available. However, in 1985 case rates began increasing for the first time in more than 20 years, largely because of infections in individuals coinfected with human immunodeficiency virus (HIV) and transmission of infection from them to others. Unfortunately, tuberculosis control programs in some large cities were not equipped to manage this emerging problem. The often interrelated factors of illicit drug use, homelessness, and HIV infection predispose to reactivation of remote tuberculosis, to the acquisition and at times epidemic spread of new disease, and, because of irregular adherence to drug therapy, to the development and spread of drug-resistant strains. Epidemics of multidrug-resistant (MDR) tuberculosis emerged in these populations and spread to HIV-negative persons, including health care workers. Treatment programs were often unsuccessful because of drug resistance and patient nonadherence. Since 1992, tuberculosis case rates in the United States have again declined and in 1997 reached the lowest in recorded history.[1] This is a tribute to the success of intensified diagnostic, treatment, and prevention efforts and to the control of HIV-induced immunosuppression by newer antiretroviral agents.[2] In response to the resurgence in tuberculosis, the search for new chemotherapeutic agents has resumed. Adequate funding for tuberculosis control and research programs must be maintained if recent favorable epidemiologic trends are to continue.

MICROBIOLOGY

The term *tubercle bacillus* designates two species of the family Mycobacteriaceae, order Actinomycetales: *M. tuberculosis* and *M. bovis.* They differ from many other mycobacterial species that share the staining characteristic referred to as *acid fastness.* Three other species—*Mycobacterium ulcerans; Mycobacterium microti,* a pathogen for rodents; and *Mycobacterium africanum,* an organism thought to be intermediate between *M. tuberculosis* and *M. bovis* and a rare cause of human tuberculosis in Africa—are closely related and are the other members of the *M. tuberculosis* complex. Disease due to *M. bovis* is relatively rare, and the terms *tubercle bacillus* and *M. tuberculosis* are, practically speaking, synonymous.

Humans are the only reservoir for *M. tuberculosis.* It is an aerobic, non–spore-forming, nonmotile bacillus with a high cell wall content of high molecular weight lipids. Growth is slow, the generation time being 15 to 20 hours, compared with much less than 1 hour for most common bacterial pathogens, and visible growth takes from 3 to 6 weeks on solid media. The organism tends to grow in parallel groups, producing the colonial characteristic of serpentine cording.

Through the first half of this century, mycobacteria were speciated by pathogenicity in guinea pigs. When effective drugs became available and the importance of drug resistance was appreciated, more precise mycobacteriology became necessary. Early on, it was noted that INH-resistant strains were less avid for neutral red dyes, did not produce catalase, and were somewhat less pathogenic for guinea pigs. This led to recognition of mycobacteria that had colonial characteristics different from *M. tuberculosis,* lacked pathogenicity for guinea pigs, and were resistant to INH and produced catalase. Ernest Runyon classified these "anonymous" mycobacteria based on colonial characteristics into four groups (photochromogens, scotochromogens, nonchromogens, and rapid growers). Precise speciation has now replaced the Runyon classification system (see Chapters 242 and 243). They all differ from *M. tuberculosis* in being free-living with no significant person-to-person spread.

The term *acid-fast bacilli* is practically synonymous with mycobacteria, although some other organisms, notably *Nocardia,* are variably acid fast. In the Ziehl-Neelsen stain, a fixed smear covered with carbol-fuchsin is heated, rinsed, decolorized with acid-alcohol, and counterstained with methylene blue. The Kinyoun stain is modified to make heating unnecessary. The organisms appear as slightly bent, beaded rods 2 to 4 μm long and 0.2 to 5 μm wide. In sputum they often lie parallel, or two organisms adhere at one end to form a V. An estimated 10,000 organisms/ml of sputum are required for smear positivity, and a single organism on an entire slide is highly suspicious. Most laboratories now use a fluorochrome stain with phenolic auramine or auramine-rhodamine, a slightly modified acid-alcohol decolorization step, and potassium permanganate counterstaining. The fluorescent mycobacteria can be easily seen with a $\times 20$ or $\times 40$ low-magnification objective. Any biologic fluid or material can be examined directly, although thin fluids are best examined after sedimentation by centrifugation. When sputum digestion and concentration are carried out for culture, a smear of the concentrate is productive. Positive smears from concentrated gastric aspiration material are usually due to *M. tuberculosis.* On Gram staining of sputum, *M. tuberculosis* is either weakly gram-positive or appears as colorless rods or "ghosts."

Culture methods use either solid or liquid media. Samples of sputum or tissue require initial liquefaction-decontamination, most commonly using *N*-acetyl-L-cysteine as a mucolytic in 1% sodium hydroxide solution. This kills other organisms, whereas mycobacteria are relatively protected by their fatty acid-rich cell walls. The sample is then neutralized, centrifuged, and the sediment inoculated onto media. Uncontaminated fluids or normally sterile tissues should not be decontaminated, as some loss of mycobacterial viability occurs. Solid culture media are of two general types: agar-based (e.g., Middlebrook 7H11) and egg-based (e.g., Löwenstein-Jensen). Most contain antibacterials that are slightly inhibitory for tubercle bacilli as well. Noninhibitory media, on which growth is more rapid, are available. Growth is more rapid in 5 to 10% carbon dioxide.

The BACTEC radiometric system for culturing mycobacteria is widely used (Johnston Laboratories, Towson, Md). This liquid culture system generally detects metabolism within 9 to 16 days, depending on the number of organisms in the specimen. Inclusion of *p*-nitro-acetyl-amino-hydroxy-propiophenone in a parallel incubation inhibits *M. tuberculosis* complex (including *M. bovis* and *M. africanum)* but not mycobacteria other than tuberculosis, providing rapid preliminary identification.[3] Prior decontamination is required for sputum and other specimens likely to be contaminated with bacteria, yeasts, or molds. A mixture of antibacterial and antifungal antibiotics is added to the BACTEC bottle to inhibit contaminants. Sterile specimens such as blood and cerebrospinal, peritoneal, and pleural fluids may be directly inoculated into BACTEC bottles.

The lysis-centrifugation method detects intracellular pathogens in peripheral blood. Whole blood is directly inoculated into a tube containing a chemical that lyses blood cells, the specimen is centrifuged, and the pellet is used for stain and culture (Isolator system, Wampole Laboratories, Cranbury, NJ). Although useful for diagnosing both fungal and mycobacterial blood stream infection in patients with acquired immunodeficiency syndrome (AIDS), it offers no advantage over the BACTEC system for culturing mycobacteria from blood.

M. tuberculosis can be differentiated from other mycobacteria with a few simple tests. *M. tuberculosis* grows slowly, lacks pigment, produces niacin, reduces nitrates, produces heat-sensitive catalase (inactivated by heating to 68°C at pH 7.0) in small quantity, and is usually sensitive to INH. INH-resistant strains do not produce catalase. *M. bovis* is usually niacin-negative and does not reduce nitrates. The other mycobacteria are generally niacin-negative, do not reduce nitrates, produce heat-stable catalase in large amounts, and are highly resistant to INH. Stained smears prepared from BACTEC bottles demonstrate serpentine "cording," a reasonably sensitive and specific marker for *M. tuberculosis,* whereas mycobacteria other than tuberculosis orient randomly.[4]

Alternative methods may be used to speciate mycobacteria in culture. Nucleic acid hybridization methods using highly specific DNA probes can specifically identify *M. tuberculosis* and some other mycobacterial species (GenProbe, San Diego, Calif). This requires several hours to complete and is most suitable for organisms in pure culture. When the burden of organisms is high, direct testing of clinical specimens with DNA probes may be positive. Speciation of bacilli in pure culture may also be rapidly performed using computer-assisted gas-liquid chromatography.

Drug susceptibility testing of tubercle bacilli is necessary to guide therapy. Many laboratories now provide this routinely, with the BACTEC system being as reliable as more traditional solid media methods.[3, 5] One method compares growth of appropriately diluted inocula on drug-containing media to growth on drug-free media and may be reported as the percentage resistant. For most drugs, resistance is significant when growth on drug-containing media exceeds 1% of control; 6 to 10% resistance or more indicates that the drug will add nothing to multiple-drug therapy. Concentration-based susceptibility breakpoints may also be used.[6] Unique culture conditions must be applied to PZA susceptibility testing because it is active only at acid pH.

Rapid nucleic acid amplification techniques such as polymerase chain reaction (PCR) allow direct identification of *M. tuberculosis* in clinical specimens. Such methods can detect fewer than 10 organisms in clinical specimens, compared with the 10,000 necessary for smear positivity. PCR does not distinguish live from killed bacteria so that patients receiving therapy may remain PCR-positive for a time despite mycobacterial sterilization. The U.S. Food and Drug Administration has approved at least two methods, which include the Amplified *M. tuberculosis* Direct Test (GenProbe, San Diego, Calif), which targets ribosomal RNA, and the AMPLICOR *M. tuberculosis* Test (Roche Molecular Systems, Branchburg, NJ), which targets DNA. For smear-positive cases, sensitivity and specificity of nucleic acid amplification exceeds 95%, and specificity for smear-negative cases is also extremely high. However, sensitivity for smear-negative cases has varied from 40 to 77%.[7] In one international study using various amplification methods, 20 blinded sputum samples containing 0, 100, or 1000 *M. bovis* BCG cells (with only one copy of the target IS*6110* gene) were sent to laboratories in 18 different countries. Only 5 (16%) of 30 laboratories correctly identified the presence or absence of mycobacterial DNA in all 20 samples, and 17 (57%) reported false-positive results.[8]

It is the opinion of most experts that nucleic acid amplification tests may complement, but should not yet replace, more traditional methods.[9] Direct amplification tests are generally not necessary when clinical suspicion for tuberculosis is high and acid-fast smears are positive, nor when clinical suspicion is low and acid-fast smears are negative. In addition, when smear and direct amplification tests are both positive, the diagnosis of tuberculosis is almost certain, and when both tests are negative, cultures will almost always remain negative. However, considerable clinical judgment is necessary when acid-fast smear and nucleic acid amplification results are discordant.[10] The suggested utility of such tests is provided in Table 240–1. It should be emphasized that *M. tuberculosis* nucleic acid amplification tests are currently unnecessary in many, if not most, clinical situations and do not replace sound clinical judgment.

Reliable methods for rapid determination of *M. tuberculosis* drug

TABLE 240–1 Potential Utility of Direct Nucleic Acid Amplification Testing

Test								
Acid-fast smear	+	+	+	+	–	–	–	–
Clinical suspicion for tuberculosis	Int	Int	Low	Low	High	High	Int	Int
Nucleic acid amplification result	+	–	+	–	+	–	+	–
Clinical action								
Begin antituberculous therapy	Yes	?	Yes	No	Yes	?	Yes	?
Further diagnostic tests	No	Yes	No	Yes	No	Yes	No	Yes
Begin contact investigation	Yes	?	Yes	No	Yes	Yes	Yes	?

Abbreviations: ?, divided opinion; Int, intermediate; –, negative; +, positive.
Adapted from Barnes PF. Rapid diagnostic tests for tuberculosis—progress but no gold standard. Am J Respir Crit Care Med. 1997;155:1497–1498 *and* the ATS Workshop. Rapid diagnostic tests for tuberculosis—what is the appropriate use? Am J Respir Crit Care Med. 1997;155:1804–1814. © American Lung Association.

susceptibility are urgently needed. Both *genotypic* and *phenotypic* methods are being pursued. Extensive studies by numerous investigators have identified chromosomal mutations associated with drug resistance. For RMP, mutations of the β-subunit of RNA polymerase, *rpoB*, are the major determinants. INH resistance is more complex and is encoded by multiple genes: the catalase-peroxidase gene *katG*, the *inhA* gene involved in fatty acid biosynthesis, the *ahpC* gene, the *oxyR* gene, and a β-ketoacyl carrier protein synthetase gene *kasA*.[11] Mutations associated with resistance to PZA, EMB, STM, and fluoroquinolones have also been identified.[12] This information has allowed the development of molecular methods to identify resistance mutations, including DNA sequencing; heteroduplex, solid-phase hybridization; and PCR single-strand conformation polymorphism analyses. In general, genotypic assays are highly specific but are of variable sensitivity.[12–16] They may become widely available for clinical use if this issue can be resolved. Two novel and elegant phenotypic susceptibility assays have also been described, neither of which is yet clinically available. They use mycobacteriophages to detect metabolically active mycobacteria grown in the presence of antituberculous agents and have the advantage that no knowledge of the genetic basis of resistance is needed.[12, 17, 18]

For epidemiologic studies, molecular "DNA fingerprinting" based on restriction fragment length polymorphisms had become the gold standard for identifying individual strains of *M. tuberculosis*. In one standardized method, DNA fragments produced by the restriction endonuclease *pvu*II are electrophoretically separated and visualized using a probe to a repetitive DNA sequence, insertion sequence (IS)*6110*.[19] Because numerous copies of IS*6110* are present in the chromosome and at highly variable locations, isolates with identical restriction fragment length polymorphisms patterns represent the same strain, making epidemiologic analyses possible. *M. bovis* contains a single copy of IS*6110*.

Clinical strains of *M. tuberculosis* may vary in their virulence and transmissibility, although the mechanisms are not known. A particularly successful strain caused a recent outbreak in a small rural community in the southeastern United States.[20] Skin test positivity was documented in 72% of persons exposed to an active case (three- to fourfold greater than expected for such an outbreak), and some persons developed active disease despite only brief, casual exposure. This strain also grew extremely rapidly in a mouse model of tuberculosis. This organism is of historic interest, as it is one of two selected for complete genomic sequence determination, which may ultimately reveal important determinants of *M. tuberculosis* virulence and transmissibility.[21]

EPIDEMIOLOGY

General Considerations

M. tuberculosis infects one third of the world's population and in 1996 caused more than 6 million cases of tuberculosis worldwide. Tuberculosis is the leading cause of death worldwide due to any single infectious agent.[22] The two factors essential for its rapid spread are crowded living conditions and a population with little native resistance. In the 19th century, tuberculosis caused more than 30% of all adult deaths in Europe, eliminating those with the least native resistance. A downward trend had been established before the turn of the century. Epidemiologists once believed the disease would eventually disappear, based on the assumptions that 10% of infections result in active disease and half of diseased persons acquire pulmonary cavities (i.e., become contagious). Thus, each cavitary case would have to infect 20 persons to maintain case rates.[23] In Holland before World War II, one infectious case produced only 13 new infections,[23] and since the turn of the century and before drug treatment, the annual decrement in mortality and morbidity was 4 to 6% in developed countries. This rate approximately doubled after chemotherapy became widespread. The prechemotherapy trend was probably due to progressively higher natural residual resistance in those who survived infection and to living conditions less conducive to airborne spread. Epidemics appeared much later in previously unexposed populations such as Native Americans, Eskimos, and remote tribes in the Amazonian rain forest.[24]

Recent Morbidity and Mortality Trends

In the United States the steady decline in tuberculosis morbidity reached a nadir in 1984, but from 1985 to 1992 an estimated 64,000 "excess" cases of active tuberculosis were reported, which peaked at 10.5 reported cases/100,000 population.[1, 25] Factors responsible for this increase included urban homelessness, intravenous drug abuse, growing neglect of tuberculosis control programs, and most notably the AIDS epidemic. After 1992, reported cases declined, reaching 7.4 cases/100,000 population in 1997, the lowest in recorded history (Fig. 240–1).[1] Although declines occurred in all age groups, there

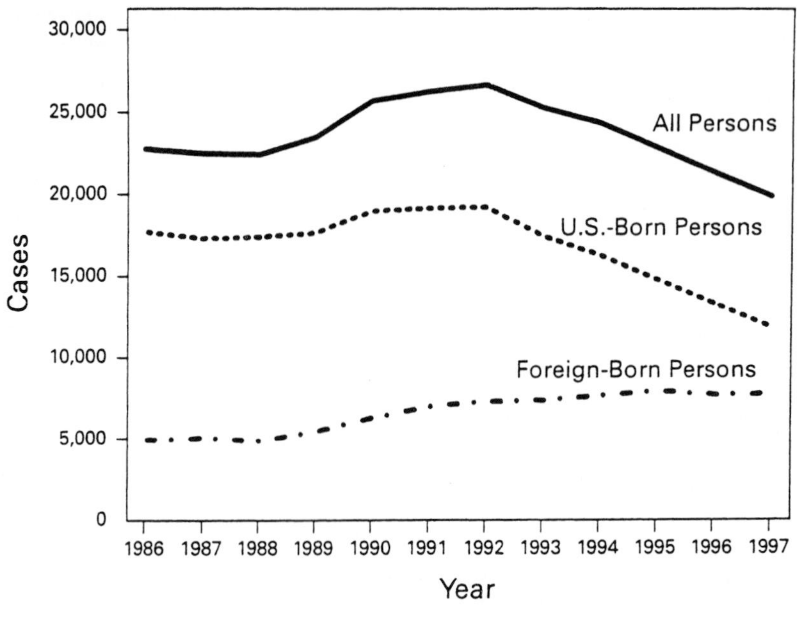

FIGURE 240–1. Number of reported cases of tuberculosis in the United States by country of birth, 1986–1997. (From Centers for Disease Control and Prevention. Tuberculosis morbidity—United States, 1997. MMWR Morb Mortal Wkly Rep. 1998;47:253–257.)

TABLE 240–2 Reported Tuberculosis Cases and Rates in Immigrants to the United States According to Place of Birth: 1986–1994.

World Region of Origin	Number of Cases	Crude Rate (per 100,000 Person-Years)
United States	160,839	7.8
Asia		
Phillipines	7342	89.2
Vietnam	5818	120.0
Korea	2897	57.0
Mainland China	2689	56.4
Other	6038	37.7
Latin America		
Mexico	13,902	36.2
Haiti	2650	133.0
Other	7935	22.8
Sub-Saharan Africa	1426	58.5
Middle East	1459	20.4
Formerly socialist Europe	1328	11.9
Established market economies*	1903	5.4
Total foreign-born cases	55,387	32.6

*Excluding the United States.
Adapted from Zuber PLF, McKenna MT, Binken NJ, et al. Long-term risk of tuberculosis among foreign-born persons in the United States. JAMA. 1997;278:304–307.

has been a steady increase in tuberculosis among foreign-born persons, who now account for 39% of all reported cases in the United States.[1] This reflects increased immigration from high-prevalence countries. In one half of all immigrants, the duration of United States residence was less than 5 years at the time tuberculosis was diagnosed, suggesting that infection was acquired abroad; the risk declines with duration of residency, indicating that most infections were acquired before immigration.[26] The likelihood of developing tuberculosis after immigrating varies by country of origin, with persons from established market economies and Eastern Europe being at lowest risk (Table 240–2).[27]

Tuberculosis has also become concentrated in certain medically underserved populations—the urban poor, alcoholics, intravenous drug users, the homeless, migrant farm workers, and prison inmates, often occurring in contact-based microepidemics. In 1990, the annual new-case rate was 5 to 10 times higher in African Americans, Hispanics, Asian Pacific Islanders, and Native Americans than in whites; two thirds of all cases occurred in racial and ethnic minorities.[28] The age distribution of tuberculosis reflects the degree of ongoing transmission in a given population. Disease in the elderly is generally due to reactivation of infection acquired in the remote past, whereas tuberculosis in young children indicates ongoing active transmission in the community. In this regard, 80% of childhood cases were diagnosed in racial and ethnic minorities. Tuberculosis is frequent in geographic regions and demographic groups where AIDS is most prevalent, notably urban blacks and Hispanics between 25 and 45 years of age.[28] Persons with active tuberculosis are more frequently HIV-positive than is the general population. In 1997, approximately 750,000 persons in the United States were living with HIV,[29] and the percentage of tuberculosis patients 25 to 44 years of age in the United State who were reported to be coinfected with HIV ranged from 0% in North and South Dakota to 48% in Florida (based on fragmentary reporting data).[1] Among populations with a high prevalence of tuberculin positivity, waning immunity due to HIV infection results in enormous tuberculosis case rates. For example, development of AIDS in Haitians, in whom tuberculin conversion in childhood is almost universal, has resulted in active tuberculosis in 60%.[29] Since 1993, the Centers for Disease Control and Prevention (CDC) AIDS surveillance case definition has included any form of active tuberculosis in an HIV-positive person with fewer than 200 CD4 cells/mm^3.[31]

Despite a predominantly urban epidemiology, large tuberculosis outbreaks have also affected small communities.[20, 32] One well-characterized outbreak began in a coastal Maine village (population

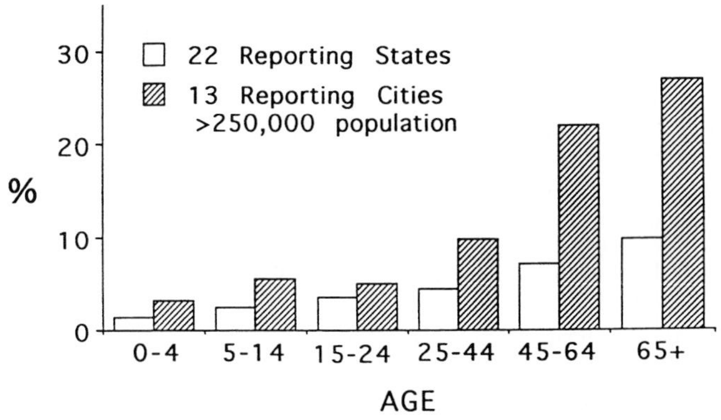

FIGURE 240–2. Percentage of positive tuberculin reactors by age, selected areas, United States, 1979. (From Centers for Disease Control and Prevention. Tuberculosis Control Division. Tuberculosis in the United States, 1979. Atlanta: Centers for Disease Control and Prevention; 1981:4–31.)

10,200) in 1988.[32] Tuberculosis had not been reported in this town in the previous 3 years. However, a shipyard worker with cavitary tuberculosis was the source of 21 subsequent active cases and 697 new tuberculous infections. In retrospect, the source patient had repeatedly sought medical attention for cough, sore throat, and hoarseness during 8 months before tuberculosis was diagnosed and treated. This report highlights the need for vigilance among all segments of the population, not just those known to have high tuberculosis case rates.

Figure 240–2 presents tuberculin positivity by age group in the United States in 1979.[33] These figures are probably representative of other Western developed countries. The estimated annual risk of new tuberculous infection among white men in the United States is currently 0.03%. Estimates for other segments of the population are pending.[34] Immigrants for the most part retain the tuberculin positivity and tuberculosis rates of the country of origin (see Table 240–2).[27] Other groups, such as intravenous drug users, patients with end-stage renal disease, residents of institutions for the homeless, and, to a lesser degree, nursing home residents, demonstrate morbidity rates greatly in excess of the general population (Table 240–3).[30, 35–41]

On a global scale, tuberculosis has a devastating impact in developing nations,[22] with 13 countries accounting for nearly 75% of all cases (Table 240–4).[22] In 1993, the World Health Organization declared tuberculosis a global public health emergency and intensified major initiatives to address the problem. Central to this strategy is universal implementation of directly observed therapy (DOT). However, the challenges are daunting. More persons died of tuberculosis in 1995 than in any year in previous history, and an estimated 50

TABLE 240–3 Incidence of Active Tuberculosis in Certain Groups

Group	Incidence per 100,000	Reference
Hostel residents in Glasgow	1946	35
Hostel residents in Boston	317	36
Nursing home residents, tuberculin-positive on admission	2400	37
Nursing home residents, tuberculin-converters	5900	37
Tuberculin-positive Indochinese refugees		38
All ages, both sexes	926	
Older than 65 yr, both sexes	7160	
Males older than 65 yr	14,180	
Dialysis patients, San Francisco	5800	39
East Indian dialysis patients, London	25,000	40
AIDS patients, New York, 1986	7000 (approx.)	41
Haitian AIDS patients, 1984	60,000	30

TABLE 240–4 Estimated Tuberculosis Case Rates among Countries That Account for Nearly Three Fourths of Cases Worldwide: 1996

Country	Cases	Rate per 100,000 Population
India	2,058,600	237
China	1,038,200	90
Indonesia	436,500	226
Phillipines	270,300	411
Bangladesh	265,000	227
Pakistan	210,700	179
Brazil	161,800	104
Democratic Republic of Congo	146,200	386
Russia	145,500	99
Thailand	101,700	179
Ethiopia	85,300	169
Mexico	56,200	62

Adapted from World Health Organization. Report on the Tuberculosis epidemic, 1997. Geneva, Switzerland.

million persons are infected with drug-resistant strains. Profound poverty, civil war, and refugee migration all impede success, but financial support from the World Bank is helping. Some countries have made considerable progress in recent years. Most remarkable is China, where DOT has been expanded since 1990 to cover 12 provinces and more than 500,000,000 persons. There is hope that India will be successful, especially since historically, many fundamental principles of DOT were first developed there. However, in Pakistan it is estimated that fewer than one fourth of tuberculosis cases are ever diagnosed, and only one in seven physicians knows how to prescribe effective treatment. In Moscow, tuberculosis death rates nearly doubled from 1991 to 1994. In Thailand, where one half of patients in some areas do not complete effective treatment and antituberculous agents are available without a prescription, it is not surprising that there were an estimated 3000 MDR cases in 1996.[22]

At least 30 million persons worldwide are now living with HIV. The potential for continued interaction between AIDS and tuberculosis is therefore immense. In some developing countries where most persons harbor tubercle bacilli before adulthood, the prevalence of HIV infection becomes the only determinant of coinfection. The situation is currently worst in Africa, where in 1990 half of the estimated 5 million HIV-infected persons between the ages of 15 and 49 years were also infected with *M. tuberculosis*, accounting for 78% of persons in the world dually infected with HIV and tuberculosis. In 1995, annual death rates due to tuberculosis in sub-Saharan Africa were greater than 100/100,000 population.[22] Many other regions are also being profoundly affected by the coepidemics of tuberculosis and AIDS. In Brazil, an estimated 200,000 persons are coinfected with HIV and *M. tuberculosis*, particularly in the cities of Rio de Janeiro and São Paulo, and in Thailand tuberculosis is now the most common opportunistic infection in AIDS patients.[22]

Mode of Spread

Although now rare, *M. bovis* infection from ingestion of contaminated milk was once commonplace. Skin inoculation of *M. tuberculosis* from contamination of an abrasion occurs in pathologists and laboratory personnel (prosector's wart), and venereal transmission has been recorded. However, almost all infections are due to inhalation of droplet nuclei—infectious particles aerosolized by coughing, sneezing, or talking—which dry while airborne, remain suspended for long periods, and reach the terminal air passages. Although the source is pulmonary in the vast majority of cases, aerosolization of organisms during irrigation of cutaneous lesions or at autopsy has caused spread to health care workers.[42, 43] A cough can produce 3000 infectious droplet nuclei, talking for 5 minutes an equal number, and sneezing many more than that.[44] Accordingly, the air in a room occupied by a person with pulmonary tuberculosis may remain infectious even after his or her absence. Although in theory one droplet nucleus may be sufficient to establish infection, prolonged exposure and multiple aerosol inocula are usually required, and brief contact carries little risk. Infection does not generally occur out of doors. However, *M. tuberculosis* strains may vary widely in their transmissibility, and a recent outbreak in Kentucky included persons infected despite brief casual contact with the index case.[20] Large drops of respiratory secretions and fomites are unimportant in transmission, and special housekeeping measures for dishes and bed clothes are unnecessary.

Risk of Infection

The most important determinants of infection of tuberculin-negative persons are closeness of contact and infectiousness of the source. Cases with positive smears are highly infectious; those positive only on culture are much less so. The degree of sputum positivity and pattern of coughing are important. Compared with measles, one case of which will infect 80% of susceptible casual contacts, tuberculosis is only moderately infectious in most circumstances.

Tuberculosis morbidity in a population is determined both by the risk of infection and of acquiring active disease once infected. In Holland in the 1970s, 50% of 0- to 14-year-old household contacts of smear-positive cases became tuberculin-positive but only 5% did so when the contact case was culture-positive but smear-negative.[23] In the United States, approximately 27% of household contacts of smear-positive cases become infected, although rates as high as 80% occur in closed environments.[45]

In the pre-AIDS era, cavity formation was almost always necessary for contagiousness. However, patients with AIDS and pulmonary tuberculosis may be highly contagious in the absence of cavitation and even with normal chest roentgenograms, although not inherently more infectious than HIV-negative patients with sputum smear-positive pulmonary tuberculosis.[46–49] In one large study from Kinshasa, Democratic Republic of Congo, household contacts of HIV-positive patients with pulmonary tuberculosis were no more likely to become infected with *M. tuberculosis* than were household contacts of HIV-negative tuberculosis patients.[46]

Influence of Chemotherapy on Spread of Infection

Patients receiving appropriate chemotherapy promptly become noninfectious as cough subsides and the concentration of organisms in sputum decreases. There is abundant, albeit indirect, evidence that this occurs within 2 weeks in patients with drug-sensitive tuberculosis.[49] Thus, case finding and treatment is the most effective method of tuberculosis control.

In reaction to outbreaks of MDR tuberculosis, the CDC in 1994 established very stringent criteria for removing patients from respiratory isolation, including three consecutive negative sputum smears on different days, which was a marked change from previous practice.[51] Although a recent report from a New York City hospital noted that one half of their patients with pulmonary tuberculosis did not achieve three consecutive negative smears until after 3 weeks of treatment (especially those with cavitary disease or numerous bacilli on initial smear),[52] the occurrence of new infections is virtually eliminated soon after initiating effective chemotherapy, and many smear-positive sputa in treated patients are culture-negative.[53] It has been appropriately argued that the CDC guidelines requiring three negative smears for removal from isolation represent "an exaggerated response to some unusual circumstances" that are quite uncommon today, and strict adherence will increase the cost of care immensely and unnecessarily. Rather, the focus should be rapid screening for drug resistance in smear-positive cases.[50]

Risk of Progression from Infection to Active Disease

In general, approximately 3 to 4% of infected individuals acquire active tuberculosis during the first year after tuberculin conversion, and a total of 5 to 15% do so thereafter. These estimates are based on heavy exposures during disease-prone periods of life. Persons infected with small inocula or during disease-resistant periods probably have a much smaller risk,[44] whereas the risk of progression in immunocompromised persons is greater. In one study of 12,876 unvaccinated adolescents, 10.4% of those who converted their tuberculin tests acquire clinical tuberculosis, 54% of these within 1 year and 78% within 2 years.[23] The three periods of life during which infection is most likely to produce disease are infancy, ages 15 to 25 years, and old age. (The effect of age on disease progression is discussed in "Pulmonary Tuberculosis.")

The likelihood of active disease developing varies with the intensity and duration of exposure. Persons with intense exposures are most at risk not only for infection but also for disease.[45] The degree of tuberculin positivity has some predictive value. Malnutrition, alcoholism, homelessness, incarceration, renal failure, and immunosuppression all favor progression of infection to active disease, but by far the strongest risk factor is AIDS (see Table 240–3). Among tuberculin-positive HIV-positive intravenous drug users in one methadone clinic population, 8%/year acquired active tuberculosis.[54] It seems likely that active tuberculosis may ultimately develop in all persons with AIDS who are tuberculin-positive unless prophylactic therapy is given, another fatal complication of AIDS supervenes, or HIV-induced immunosuppression is reversed with antiretroviral therapy. During outbreaks in hospitals or hospices, as many as 40% of patients with AIDS exposed to an active case have contracted active tuberculosis, often within 2 months.[55]

Host genetic factors also influence disease expression, although study results have been mixed. Reports from India have shown that HLA-DR2 is associated with increased risk of progression to advanced pulmonary disease,[56] that the DRB1*1501 allele correlates with advanced disease and treatment failure, and that DRB1*1502 correlates with decreased risk.[57] A recent study from Gambia, West Africa, examined polymorphisms of a gene called *NRAMP1* (a homologue of the natural-resistance-associated macrophage protein 1 gene of mice, also known as *Bcg, Lsh/Ity,* and *Nramp1*) in HIV-negative adults with smear-positive tuberculosis. Three *NRAMP1* alleles were much more frequent among the 410 tuberculosis patients than among 417 ethnically matched controls.[58] It is yet not known whether the protein product of *NRAMP1* plays a direct role in either protection against establishment of initial infection or disease progression.

Institutional Spread of Tuberculosis

Hospitals. Tuberculosis has long been a recognized risk to health care workers. However, with declining disease rates and rising confidence in chemotherapy, hospital tuberculosis control programs atrophied. Occasional microepidemics of nosocomial tuberculosis in intensive care units were reported, but generally little attention was paid to the problem. However, beginning in the 1980s, numerous explosive outbreaks of tuberculosis occurred among AIDS patients on specialized wards and hospices in the United States and Europe. Numerous such nosocomial epidemics have now been described.[55, 59–62] In the first reported outbreak on an HIV ward, the index patient had fever, cough, a normal chest roentgenogram, and negative acid-fast smears but a positive sputum culture for *M. tuberculosis.*[59] Thirty-nine percent of other AIDS patients on the same ward acquired active tuberculosis within 60 days. Major factors contributing to these outbreaks have included (1) delays in diagnosis, especially in AIDS patients with noncavitary pulmonary disease; (2) inadequate negative-pressure ventilation in patient rooms; (3) use of aerosol-generating procedures such as bronchoscopy, sputum induction, and aerosolized pentamidine treatments; (4) rapid progression to active, infectious tuberculosis in a large percentage of AIDS patients secondarily exposed; and (5) in the case of MDR tuberculosis, prolonged infectivity despite antituberculous chemotherapy.[63] Health care workers are also at risk. Patients with AIDS and tuberculosis may be highly infectious in the absence of cavitation and even when the chest roentgenogram is normal.[59, 60]

Phage typing and antibiotic susceptibility patterns as ways of tracing spread of individual strains of *M. tuberculosis* from patient to patient have largely been replaced by DNA fingerprinting by restriction fragment length polymorphisms analysis.[19] This method has confirmed the nosocomial spread of tuberculosis among AIDS patients and to HIV-negative health care workers,[55] demonstrated that AIDS patients treated for one strain of *M. tuberculosis* may be reinfected with a different strain,[64] and has confirmed cross-contamination of cultures in the laboratory.

Shelters for the Homeless. Poor nutrition, intravenous drug use, alcoholism, and crowding increase the risk for both endogenous reactivation of remote infection and acquisition of new (exogenous) infection in homeless shelter clients.[36] A study from New York City demonstrated that HIV infection was also a major factor in homeless shelter tuberculosis. Of 169 men seen at one shelter between 1986 and 1989, 62% were HIV-positive and 26% also had active tuberculosis. Conversely, 90% of those with active tuberculosis were HIV-positive.[65] The extraordinary frequency of HIV positivity and tuberculosis in homeless men prompted aggressive public health measures, which included identifying active cases and administering effective therapy under supervision. Rates of tuberculosis have since declined. The number of active, culture-positive tuberculosis cases diagnosed in New York City during the month of April decreased from 466 in 1991 to 332 in 1994.[66, 67]

Correctional Facilities. In the New York State prison system, the incidence of tuberculosis increased sevenfold from 1976 to 1986, reaching 105.5 cases/100,000. High-risk populations—including young black and Hispanic men, intravenous drug users, and HIV-infected persons—are overrepresented in prison populations.[68] Although most prison cases are due to reactivation of old infections, outbreaks of MDR tuberculosis have shown that transmission of new (exogenous) infection occurs as well. Although difficult for obvious reasons, preventive and curative services in correctional facilities have been identified as high public health priorities. Crowding may be the strongest risk factor for transmission in prisons, but this may be offset by effective chemoprophylaxis.[68] Transmission in prisons and jails may also serve as a reservoir for spread to the community, especially to inner city populations.

Outbreaks of Multidrug-Resistant Tuberculosis. Since the early 1990s, there have been numerous well-documented hospital outbreaks of MDR tuberculosis. Most cases of MDR tuberculosis have been from New York City and Miami. By DNA fingerprinting it has been shown that nearly one fourth of all MDR isolates in the United States between 1990 and 1993, and isolated from patients in 41 different hospitals, had the same DNA fingerprint, designated strain "W."[70] However, outbreaks in suburban areas underscore the potential for MDR tuberculosis to spread much more widely. Fortunately, more recent trends in the United States have also been associated with declines in MDR tuberculosis cases, and from 1991 to 1994, there was a 52% decrease in the number of patients with MDR tuberculosis in New York City.[66]

Controlling Nosocomial Spread. Spread of tuberculosis in the health care setting has raised justifiable concern. Tuberculin conversion rates as high as 50% among health care workers on HIV wards have been reported.[60] Delays in diagnosis are critical both for outcome and infectiousness for others.[63] The HIV status of patients may not be known on admission, tuberculosis is often not an early consideration, an appropriate number of sputum specimens for examination (three) is often not submitted, and sputum acid-fast stains may be negative. Further, the clinical picture of extrapulmonary or disseminated tuberculosis may be confusing. Accordingly, tuberculosis must be considered in any HIV-positive patient with subacute or chronic pulmonary symptoms or symptoms compatible with extrapulmonary tuberculosis. Rapid culture methods including the BACTEC system and the lysis centrifugation technique applied to blood, liver, and bone marrow biopsy specimens, needle aspiration of peripheral nodes, determination of adenine deaminase in body fluids, and PCR methods may expedite diagnosis.[7, 10, 63]

Hospitalized HIV-positive patients with respiratory symptoms should be admitted to negative-pressure isolation rooms (so that air flows from the corridor into the room and is safely exhausted to the outside) with six air changes per hour. Procedures that stimulate coughing such as sputum induction, bronchoscopy, and aerosolized pentamidine treatment should be carried out in negative-pressure rooms or special booths. The use of particulate respirator masks further reduces risk and is recommended by the CDC. Ultraviolet radiation of the air—either pulled by a fan through a radiation chamber or with the ultraviolet beam directed into the uppermost parts of the room so as to avoid direct radiation of personnel—is also advised by knowledgeable experts. The CDC has published guidelines for control of transmission of tuberculosis in health care settings.[51]

IMMUNOLOGY

Tuberculosis is the prototype of infections that require a cellular immune response for their control[71] (see Chapter 9). Although abundant antibodies are also produced during infection, these play no apparent role in host defense mechanisms. In the first few weeks after exposure, the host has almost no immune defense against infection by *M. tuberculosis.* Small inhaled inocula multiply freely in alveolar spaces or within alveolar macrophages. The bacteriostatic influence of alveolar macrophages on intracellular bacilli at this stage is probably minimal. Unrestrained replication proceeds for weeks, both in the initial focus and in lymphohematogenous metastatic foci, until the development of tissue hypersensitivity and cellular immunity supervene. Tissue hypersensitivity is florid in comparison to other intracellular infections, perhaps because of the adjuvant activity of mycobacterial lipids.

All persons have a native population of lymphocytes, mostly $CD4^+$ cells bearing $\alpha\beta$ T-cell receptors, capable of recognizing mycobacterial antigens that have been processed and presented by macrophages in a major histocompatibility class II context. When the lymphocyte encounters antigen in this manner it is activated (transformed) and proliferates, producing a clone of similarly reactive lymphocytes. T cells, in turn, produce many distinct secretory proteins (lymphokines), which attract, retain, and activate macrophages at the site of antigen. Activated macrophages accumulate high concentrations of lytic enzymes and reactive metabolites that greatly increase their mycobactericidal competence, but if released into surrounding tissues they may cause tissue necrosis. Activated macrophages also secrete a number of regulatory factors (tumor necrosis factor-α, platelet-derived growth factor, transforming growth factor-β, and fibroblast growth factor), which in concert with lymphocyte secretory proteins (interferon-γ, migration-inhibitory factor) determine the character of the pathologic and clinical response. Epithelioid cells, characteristic of the tuberculous granuloma, are highly stimulated macrophages. The Langhans giant cell consists of fused macrophages oriented around tuberculosis antigen with the multiple nuclei in a peripheral position, representing the most successful type of host tissue response. CD4 T cells are able to lyse mononuclear phagocytes infected with *M. tuberculosis* directly. In addition, there is a subset of T cells that expresses the $\gamma\delta$ form of the T-cell receptor that expands in response to mycobacterial antigens. Although their exact function is unknown, they appear to play a role in host defense against tuberculosis.[71]

When the population of activated lymphocytes reaches a certain size, cutaneous delayed reactivity to tuberculin, or tissue hypersensitivity, becomes manifest. The speed with which this occurs varies, but generally develops within 3 to 9 weeks after infection. At the same time, enhanced macrophage microbicidal activity, or cellular immunity, appears. It is a matter of dispute whether cellular immunity, which connotes resistance to infection, and tissue hypersensitivity, which describes altered cellular reactivity (granuloma formation, tissue necrosis), are end points of the same sequence of immunologic and chemical events or are parallel and closely associated phenomena that depend on different antigens or lymphocyte populations, or both.

The pathologic features of tuberculosis are the result of the degree of hypersensitivity and the local concentration of antigen. When the antigen load is small and tissue hypersensitivity is high, organization of lymphocytes, macrophages, Langhans giant cells, fibroblasts, and capillaries results in granuloma formation. Foci characterized by the resulting hard tubercles are termed *proliferative* or *productive* and constitute a successful tissue reaction with containment of infection, healing with eventual fibrosis, encapsulation, and scar formation. When both antigen load and degree of hypersensitivity are high, epithelioid cells and giant cells are sparse or entirely lacking; lymphocytes, macrophages, and granulocytes are present in a less organized fashion; and tissue necrosis may be present, a type of tissue reaction that has been called *exudative.* In the absence of necrosis, exudative lesions may heal completely, but more frequently some degree of tissue necrosis persists. Necrosis in tuberculosis tends to be incomplete, resulting in solid or semisolid acellular and amorphous material referred to as *caseous* because of its cheesy consistency. The chemical environment and oxygen tension in solid caseous material tends to inhibit microbial multiplication. However, caseous necrosis is inherently unstable, especially in the lungs, where it tends to liquefy and discharge through the bronchial tree, producing a tuberculous cavity and providing conditions in which bacterial populations reach titers 5 to 6 logs greater than in noncavitary lesions. Infectious material sloughed from a cavity results in new exudative foci in other parts of the lung (bronchogenic spread). A cross section of a pulmonary cavity demonstrates all these pathologic reactions, from the least to the most successful in terms of containment of infection. The central cavity, which contains myriad bacilli, is surrounded by a layer of caseous material with fewer organisms, a more peripheral layer of macrophages and lymphocytes with little organization and still fewer organisms, an area that is even more peripheral with epithelioid cells and giant cells in which the bacterial content is quite low, and most peripherally, a bacillus-free layer of encapsulating fibrosis.

When the degree of hypersensitivity is very low, the tissue reaction may be nonspecific, consisting of a few polymorphonuclear leukocytes and mononuclear cells with huge numbers of tubercle bacilli, a condition termed *nonreactive tuberculosis.*[72] The immunologic spectrum from florid hypersensitivity to little or no specific tissue reaction is similar to that seen in leprosy and is recapitulated in HIV-infected persons as the $CD4^+$ count decreases.

The sustained immunity to new infection that follows natural infection is most likely due to persistence of viable tubercle bacilli in the tissues with in vivo boosting. In tuberculin-positive persons, endogenous foci may reactivate repeatedly, and active CD4 surveillance is necessary to maintain quiescence.[73] However, reactivation disease may arise from these sites of boosting. In murine models of protective immunity to tuberculosis, CD4 cells are more important than CD8 and $\gamma\delta$ T cells, and the cytokines interferon-γ and tumor necrosis factor-α are essential. However, activation of human monocytes with tumor necrosis factor-α, not interferon-γ, most effectively inhibits intracellular replication of *M. tuberculosis*. Conversely, transforming growth factor-β has an opposite influence, favoring bacterial survival and multiplication.[74] In humans, an effective response to *M. tuberculosis* tends to follow a Th1 CD4 pattern with preferential expression of interferon-γ, interleukin (IL)-2, and IL-12 by mononuclear cells.

When macrophages from patients with established tuberculosis encounter *M. tuberculosis,* they produce cytokines that modulate the activity to CD4 cells. These CD4 cells are essential for optimal macrophage bactericidal activity. Costimulatory cytokines elaborated by macrophages (IL-1, tumor necrosis factor-α, and IL-6) activate

CD4 cells and induce inteferon-γ production. However, macrophages also produce cytokines (TGF-β and IL-10) that depress interferon-γ production, inhibit blastogenesis, and block the activity of IL-12. Mycobacterial antigens have a unique ability to promote expression of inhibitory cytokines, and it has been suggested that the suppression of CD4 cell responses contributes to immunosuppression, deactivation of macrophage effector function, and disease progression in tuberculosis.[73]

The antigens of *M. tuberculosis* necessary for protective immunity are not known, and there are currently no validated human surrogate markers for protective immunity. Two antigens of *M. tuberculosis,* ESAT-6 and the 30-kD (or 85B) antigen, are leading candidates.[73]

A gene designated *Bcg* (also known as *Nramp1* and *Lsh/Ity*) is important for immunity to some intracellular pathogens in inbred mice. This gene encodes the natural resistance–associated macrophage protein 1 and is expressed only in reticuloendothelial cells.[75] Specific alleles of *Bcg* in mice confer resistance to the early stages of infection by *M. bovis* (BCG), *Mycobacterium avium* complex, and other intracellular pathogens, although its role for *M. tuberculosis* is less clear. However, an epidemiologic study from West Africa suggests that a homologue of *Bcg* may play an important role in human immunity to tuberculosis.[58] (See "Risk of Progression from Infection to Active Disease.")

TUBERCULIN TEST

Koch's tuberculin (old tuberculin) was an extract of a boiled culture of tubercle bacilli. In 1934, Siebert made a simple protein precipitate (purified protein derivative [PPD]) of old tuberculin, which became the preferred reagent in most areas. In 1941, a large single lot was adopted as the biologic standard (PPD-S) to which other preparations are now standardized. A 5-tuberculin unit (TU) dose of PPD is equivalent to 0.0001 mg of PPD-S protein in 0.1 ml of solution. It is slightly stronger than first-strength (1:10,000) old tuberculin. The 250-TU dose is roughly bioequivalent to second-strength (1:100) old tuberculin.[76]

Dosage

The sensitivity and specificity of the 5-TU dose were derived in populations in which the incidence of tuberculosis was accurately known. A 5-TU dose of tuberculin clearly separated groups with 100% infection, such as sanatorium patients, from groups with a very low incidence of tuberculosis, such as infants from noninfectious environments. In the former, tuberculin reactions peaked at 16 to 17 mm; in the latter 0- to 5-mm reactions were elicited.

Technical Aspects

Although multiple puncture techniques (Heaf and Tine tests) are preferred in Britain, quantitative tuberculin testing is best performed by intracutaneous injection of 5 TU of PPD in 0.1 ml of solution, usually on the volar aspect of the forearm, using a short, beveled 26- or 27-gauge needle (Mantoux test). Precise injection producing a raised, blanched wheal is necessary. Deeper injections may be washed out by vascular flow, resulting in false-negative results. The loss of potency that occurs when PPD adsorbs to glass surfaces is prevented by the addition of the detergent polysorbate 80 (Tween 80). Tween-stabilized tuberculin in solution is light-sensitive and must be refrigerated. The reaction is usually read in 48 to 72 hours, although it can be accurately read up to a week later. A positive test is generally defined as greater than 10 mm of induration, not erythema, in response to 5 TU, and can be measured by viewing the reaction tangentially against a light background. An alternative is to use a medium-point ballpoint pen to draw a line starting 1 to 2 cm away from the skin reaction and moving toward its center. The pen is lifted when resistance is felt, the procedure repeated from the opposite direction, and the distance between opposing lines measured.

Interpretation

Ninety percent of persons with 10 mm of induration and virtually all with greater than 15 mm of induration to 5 TU are infected with *M. tuberculosis.* Lesser induration, or reactions requiring 250 TU to be elicited, are frequently cross-reactions due to infection with other mycobacterial species. However, even 5- to 10-mm reactions are suspicious for tuberculous infection in geographic areas substantially free of other mycobacteria, such as the northeastern United States, and among persons with a high likelihood of tuberculosis, such as contacts of active cases (although this latter point is debated).[77, 78] Reactions of 5 to 10 mm may also be due to Calmette-Guérin bacillus (BCG) vaccination. However, unless the vaccination was very recent, tuberculin reactions of greater than 10 mm should not be attributed to BCG.

Booster Effect. Although tuberculin cannot sensitize an uninfected person, it can restimulate remote hypersensitivity that has deteriorated. This booster effect (a positive tuberculin test after a negative one) develops within several days after a first injection and may be persistent. This causes interpretative problems, because a negative test result followed by a positive test result approximately 10 weeks later may be a product of either a recent infection or a booster effect. This problem is circumvented by retesting nonreactors 1 week later. If the second test result is positive, this indicates boosting rather than recent tuberculin conversion. Tuberculin positivity only after boosting is more common in older persons, in persons infected with nontuberculous mycobacteria, and in BCG vaccinees. Persons with a booster response are at low risk and can be managed as nonreactors.

False-Positive and False-Negative Reactions. False-positive reactions represent nontuberculous mycobacterial infection. False-negative reactions, although uncommon in otherwise healthy patients with tuberculosis, occur in at least 20% of all persons with known active tuberculosis. In one study, 25% of 200 patients with active tuberculosis were nonreactive to 5 TU, and 10% were also nonreactive to 250 TU.[79] Both false-positive and false-negative reactions to 250 TU limit the usefulness of this dose.[76] (The 1 TU dose is occasionally used in very young children.) Most false-negative test results in patients with tuberculosis are attributed to general illness and become positive 2 to 3 weeks after effective treatment is initiated. Protein malnutrition diminishes all cutaneous delayed hypersensitivity reactions. Sarcoidosis may cause false-negative tuberculin test results, although most sarcoidosis patients with tuberculosis are tuberculin-positive. Intercurrent viral infections, reticuloendothelial disease, and corticosteroid therapy may cause false-negative tuberculin reactions. Control antigens (e.g., mumps, *Candida*, tetanus toxoid) are commonly applied to detect cutaneous anergy. However, attempts to correlate negative tuberculin tests with generalized anergy have not been illuminating, and such "anergy testing" provides little practical information (see "Tuberculin Testing and Human Immunodeficiency Virus Infection"). Intraobserver reliability in reading reactivity may vary by as much as 3 mm, causing some classification uncertainty if induration is close to the cutoff value.[80]

Variant ("Delayed") Tuberculin Reactivity. An unusual form of tuberculin response (so-called delayed reactivity) has been described among Indochinese immigrants. This involves induration of less than 10 mm at 48 to 72 hours, which increases to greater than 10 mm when the skin test is read again at 6 days. In a study of Vietnamese immigrants in North Carolina, 32 (26%) of 121 demonstrated delayed reactivity, 65% of whom boosted to a positive test 10 to 12 weeks later.[81] The authors concluded that Indochinese persons should have tuberculin tests read at 24 to 72 hours and again at 6 days, that delayed tuberculin responses should be considered true positives, and that those demonstrating less than 10 mm induration at 48- to 72-hour and 6-day readings should be booster-tested at 1 to 2 weeks.

Loss of Tuberculin Reactivity. Earlier in the 20th century, lifelong tuberculin positivity was maintained by frequent re-exposure to tubercle bacilli or to continued active disease. However, a positive tuberculin test will revert to negative unless restimulated by new aerosol inocula or persisting infection. In one tuberculin survey, 8.1% of positive reactors reverted to true negative when retested 1 year later (Table 240–5).[82] Persons with a history of a positive skin test result can be safely retested. Two negative tests a week apart (to exclude boosting) indicate true negativity and resumed susceptibility to new infection.

Tuberculin Testing and Human Immunodeficiency Virus Infection. During HIV infection, tuberculin reactivity decreases as the CD4 cell count falls. One study of patients with active tuberculosis demonstrated 10 mm or greater of induration to 5 TU in only 60% of persons with HIV infection and in 35% of those with AIDS.[83] Induration of 5 mm in persons with HIV infection is sufficient to warrant chemoprophylaxis (see farther on)[84]; it has even been suggested that a 2-mm induration be considered positive in this setting. Testing simultaneously for cutaneous anergy with ubiquitous antigens such as mumps, tetanus toxoid, and *Candida* was once advocated by the CDC.[84] However, the usefulness of anergy testing suffers from lack of standardization and reproducibility, by variable risk of tuberculosis among anergic persons, because cutaneous anergy does not predict *M. tuberculosis* infection, and because responsiveness to control antigens but not PPD does not exclude tuberculous infection. Two studies failed to demonstrate that 6 months of INH preventive therapy administered to anergic HIV-positive persons significantly reduced tuberculosis rates.[85, 86] Based on these considerations, routine anergy testing is no longer recommended for HIV-positive persons at risk for tuberculosis (see "Chemoprophylaxis").[87]

PATHOGENESIS

Airborne droplet nuclei containing tubercle bacilli reach the terminal air spaces where multiplication begins. The initial focus is usually subpleural and in the midlung zone (the lower parts of the upper lobes and the upper parts of the lower and middle lobes) where greater airflow favors deposition of bacilli. (Very rarely, nonpulmonary initial foci will involve abraded skin, the intestine, the oropharynx, or the genitalia, all associated with foci in regional lymph nodes.)

The initial pulmonary focus is typically single, although multiple foci are present in about one fourth of cases. The bacteria are ingested by alveolar macrophages, which may be able to eliminate small numbers of bacilli. However, bacterial multiplication tends to be mostly unimpeded, destroying the macrophage. Blood-borne lymphocytes and monocytes are attracted to this focus, the latter differentiating into macrophages, which ingest bacilli released from degenerating cells, and pneumonitis slowly develops. Infected macrophages are carried by lymphatics to regional (hilar, mediastinal, and sometimes supraclavicular or retroperitoneal) lymph nodes, but in the nonimmune host may spread hematogenously throughout the body. During this occult preallergic lymphohematogenous dissemination, some tissues favor retention and bacillary multiplication. These include the lymph nodes, kidneys, epiphyses of the long bones, vertebral bodies, and juxtaependymal meningeal areas adjacent to the subarachnoid space, but most importantly, the apical posterior areas of the lungs. Before the development of hypersensitivity (tuberculin reactivity), microbial growth is uninhibited, both in the initial focus and metastatic foci, providing a nidus for subsequent progressive disease in the lung apices and in extrapulmonary sites, either promptly or after a variable period of latency.

TABLE 240–5 Annual Tuberculin Conversion Rates (Positive to Negative) According to Age Groups, Victoria County, Canada, 1959–1962

Age Groups	Positive Reactors Retested after 1 Year	Number of Reversions to Negative	Reversion Rate (%)
0–19	99	22	22.2
20–39	200	16	8.0
40–59	525	25	4.8
60 and older	377	34	9.0
TOTAL	1201	97	8.1

From Grzybowski S, Allen, EA. The challenge of tuberculosis in decline: A study based on the epidemiology of tuberculosis in Ontario, Canada. Am Rev Respir Dis. 1964;90:707–720. © American Lung Association.

Evolution of the Primary Infection

Tuberculin positivity appears 3 to 8 weeks after infection and marks the development of cellular immunity and tissue hypersensitivity. In most instances, the infection is controlled, with the only evidence of infection being a positive skin test result. In a minority of cases, antigen concentration in the primary complex, consisting of the initial pulmonary focus (the Gohn focus) and the draining regional nodes, will have reached sufficient size that the development of hypersensitivity results in necrosis and roentgenographically visible calcification, producing the Ranke complex (parenchymal and mediastinal calcific foci). Much less commonly, pulmonary apical and subapical metastatic foci contain sufficient bacilli that necrosis ensues with the onset of hypersensitivity, producing tiny calcific deposits (Simon foci) in which viable bacilli may persist.

The onset of tuberculin hypersensitivity may be associated with erythema nodosum or phlyctenular keratoconjunctivitis (a severe unilateral inflammation of the eye), although these manifestations are unusual in the United States. The primary complex may progress. In children, large hilar or mediastinal lymph nodes may produce bronchial collapse with distal atelectasis or may erode into a bronchus and spread infection distally. Also, typically in children but also in nonwhite races with less constitutional resistance to tuberculosis, those infected in advanced age,[37] and AIDS patients,[88] the primary focus may become an area of advancing pneumonia, the so-called progressive primary, which may cavitate and spread via the bronchi. Again, typically in the very young, preallergic lymphohematogenous dissemination may progress directly to hyperacute miliary tuberculosis as a result of caseous material directly reaching the blood stream, either from the primary complex or from a caseating metastatic focus in the wall of a pulmonary vein (Weigart focus). Hematogenous dissemination in the very young is often followed within weeks by tuberculous meningitis. In adolescents and young adults, the subpleural primary focus may rupture, delivering bacilli and antigen into the pleural space to produce serofibrinous pleurisy with effusion. Overwhelmingly, the most important consequence of preallergic lymphohematogenous dissemination is seeding of the apical posterior areas of the lung, where disease may progress without interruption or after a latent period of months or years, resulting in pulmonary tuberculosis of the adult or reactivation type (endogenous reinfection).

Primary (Childhood) and Reinfection (Adult) Tuberculosis

The traditional terms *primary* or *childhood* and *reinfection* or *adult pulmonary tuberculosis* followed roentgenographic observations early in the 20th century when initial (primary) infection in childhood was thought to be universal.[89] Children's roentgenograms characteristically demonstrated large mediastinal or hilar lymph nodes with inconspicuous pneumonitis in the lower or middle lung field, whereas in adolescents and adults, apical or subapical infiltrates, often with cavitation and no hilar adenopathy, were the rule. These clinical and roentgenographic differences are due to age-related immunologic factors. Although many primary infections in adolescents and adults resemble primary infection in childhood, in others in this age group, an apical posterior metastatic pulmonary focus progresses within weeks to "adult"-type pulmonary disease, whereas the initial focus in the lower lung field and hilar nodes involutes undetected.

Chronic Pulmonary Tuberculosis

Apical Localization. In adults, apical localization of pulmonary tuberculosis has often been attributed to the hyperoxic environment of the apices and the aerobic nature of the tubercle bacillus. A more plausible theory attributes it to deficient lymphatic flow at the lung apices, especially the posterior apices, where the pumping effect of respiratory motion is minimal. Deficient lymph traffic would favor retention of bacillary antigen and, when hypersensitivity ensues, tissue necrosis. Apical posterior localization with a tendency to cavitation and progression is characteristic of pulmonary tuberculosis in adolescents and adults. In contrast, infection contracted in the elderly often causes nondescript lower lobe pneumonia similar to progressive primary infection of childhood.[37]

Endogenous versus Exogenous Reinfection. Resistance to exogenous reinfection in the previously infected host is generally so great that new inocula are destroyed before significant multiplication occurs, with nearly all cases of active tuberculosis in such patients reflecting reactivation of latent foci.[89] Although probably true in developed countries where the level of contagion is low, when contagion is high exogenous reinfection is the rule.[23, 90] Airflow in the apical posterior areas of the lung is low, but when inhaled droplet nuclei reach that location, as is more likely with high levels of contagion, bacillary multiplication will be favored by the same local factors that enhance multiplication of blood-borne organisms. Support for this comes from a study from India that showed that disease in household contacts of active cases was most common in the middle-aged and elderly who were certain to have been previously infected.[91] A microepidemic in a shelter for homeless men demonstrated that a single strain of *M. tuberculosis* caused infection among men known to have been previously infected.[36] Repeated inhalational exposures to tubercle bacilli maintain high degrees of tissue hypersensitivity and cellular immunity, making superinfection more difficult; but when the airborne inoculum is large, or in immunocompromised hosts, superinfection may occur.

Influence of Age on Tuberculous Infection

Many of the best clinical descriptions of tuberculosis come from the preantimicrobial era, when infection occurred early in life and cellular immunity was maintained by frequent exposure to tubercle bacilli. However, in industrialized countries, infection more often occurs later in life, and cellular immunity may wane in the absence of restimulation. Accordingly, clinical patterns have changed. At one time, most patients were adolescents and young adults with apical cavitary disease. In developed countries, the incidence of tuberculosis (cases/100,000) is now greatest in older persons in whom hypersensitivity is less marked and in whom the clinical manifestations may be different and more subtle. Hypersensitivity and cellular immunity likely become less vigorous with age (see "Epidemiology").

Infection in Infancy and Childhood. Infection in infants often results in disease, with local progression and dissemination (miliary-meningeal disease). The younger the patient, the greater is the risk of progressive disease until the age of 5 years. From age 5 until puberty is a time of relative resistance to progressive disease, although not to infection. When disease occurs, it is usually the childhood type of pulmonary tuberculosis. Involvement of lymph nodes, bones, and, less commonly, other progressive extrapulmonary foci may develop, but tuberculosis confined to the lung in this age group usually heals spontaneously. The short-term prognosis in these cases is good even if untreated, but there is a high frequency of relapse with chronic cavitary tuberculosis when the more disease-prone periods of adolescence and young adulthood arrive.[92]

Infection in Adolescence and Young Adulthood. Clinical disease developing after infection in adolescence or young adulthood may resemble childhood infection (lower lung field pneumonitis, hilar adenitis) but with less parenchymal and hilar calcification (Fig. 240–3). This is particularly the case in dark-skinned races and in immunocompromised patients, including those with AIDS.[88] Rarely the roentgenographic picture may be mixed, with features of childhood disease subsiding while chronic upper lobe (adult) disease progresses. However, disease in this age group frequently first appears as chronic upper lobe tuberculosis with no clinical features of childhood disease. The tendency toward apical cavitation soon after the initial infection appears soon after puberty and is marked in young adults.[92] Because most young people in industrialized countries are tuberculin-negative (see Fig. 240–2), most pulmonary tuberculosis in adolescents and young adults is due to recent initial infections rather than to late progression of childhood infections.

Infection in Midadulthood. Infection acquired during the middle years has a much better immediate and probably long-term prognosis than infection acquired in the teens and early twenties, presumably because of a reduced tendency to tissue necrosis.[92, 93] One study demonstrated progression from infection (tuberculin conversion) to cavitary tuberculosis in 23% of patients infected from 15 to 19 years of age, 13% infected from 20 to 24 years of age, 4% infection from 25 to 29 years of age, and only 2% of those infected after 30 years of age. Progression occurred in 3 months in many and within 1 year in most. (Elderly individuals were not included in the study.)[94]

Infection in Old Age. The incidence of tuberculosis is highest in the elderly. Infections acquired years earlier can progress as age compromises immunity, producing typical apical-posterior disease. Studies of tuberculosis in nursing homes, however, have demon-

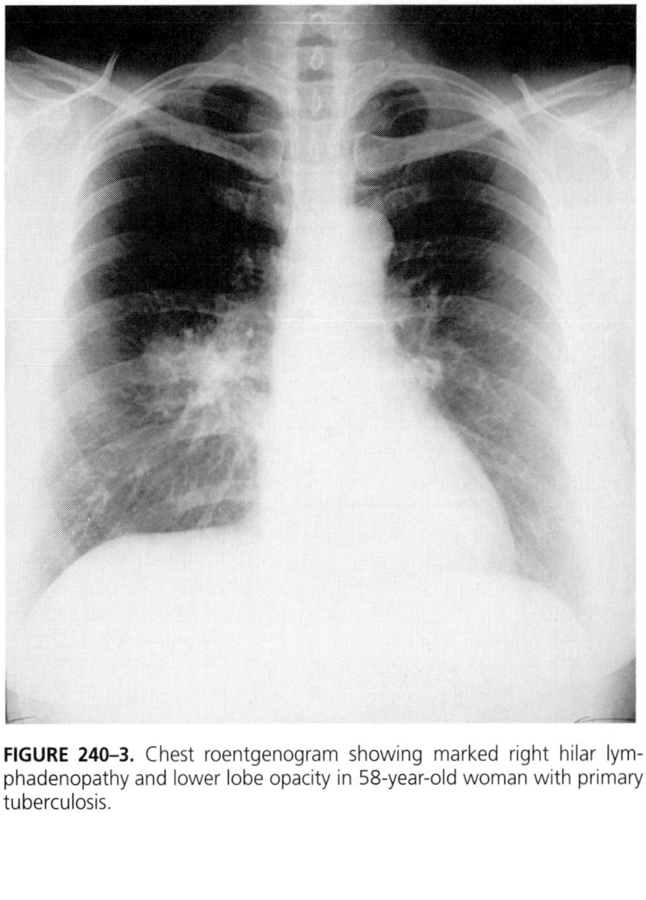

FIGURE 240–3. Chest roentgenogram showing marked right hilar lymphadenopathy and lower lobe opacity in 58-year-old woman with primary tuberculosis.

strated that elderly patients are often tuberculin-negative (70 to 80%), either because they had never been infected or because ancient infections had been completely cleared, with a loss of tissue hypersensitivity. Such tuberculin-negative persons are susceptible to new infection, and if this occurs, they acquire active disease with a frequency similar to that of adolescents. This is typically a nondescript, poorly resolving pneumonitis in the lower or middle lobes, or anterior segments of the upper lobes, sometimes with pleural effusion and resembling primary infection in children except for much less hilar-mediastinal lymphadenopathy.[37] Even with prompt diagnosis and treatment, death from tuberculosis appears to be more frequent after age 65.

Late Hematogenous Tuberculosis

Chronic tuberculosis is probably always associated with recurrent abortive episodes of hematogenous spread. However, when aging or other factors compromise cellular immunity, such episodes may become progressively frequent, producing the subtle and often fatal syndrome of late hematogenous or progressive generalized tuberculosis.

Intercurrent Events

General stress, poor health, and malnutrition favor progression of infection. During pregnancy, the time of special risk is probably the early postpartum period. Therapy with corticosteroids or other immunosuppressive agents compromises host defenses, as do hematopoietic-reticuloendothelial diseases, particularly malignancies. Development of tuberculosis in patients with myeloproliferative disorders may cause confusion because disseminated tuberculosis can cause aplastic anemia, thrombocytopenia, leukopenia, and leukemoid reactions that may mimic leukemia. However, most patients with tuberculosis and hematologic findings suggesting leukemia will have both diseases. The postgastrectomy state, jejunal-ileal bypass surgery, and end-stage renal disease are all risk factors (see "Chemoprophylaxis"). Viral illnesses, particularly in children, may predispose to progression of infection. Destructive local pulmonary processes such as lung abscess, carcinoma, cavitary histoplasmosis, and pulmonary resection occasionally are followed by activation of previously quiescent pulmonary foci. The development of bone and joint tuberculosis after physical injury, tuberculous peritonitis after tubal insufflation, progressive hematogenous tuberculosis after curettage of a tuberculous endometrium, and late generalized hematogenous tuberculosis after major trauma all illustrate that the balance between host and infection can be altered by both systemic factors and local physical disturbance.

Tuberculosis in Acquired Immunodeficiency Syndrome. The earliest descriptions of tuberculosis in AIDS emphasized the very great risk of reactivation of remote infection as a result of progressively compromised cellular immunity. In studies in Haitians, all of whom were likely infected with *M. tuberculosis* in childhood, AIDS was associated with development of active tuberculosis in 60%.[30] Subsequent studies of HIV-positive and tuberculin-positive methadone clinic patients in New York City showed that active tuberculosis developed in 8% yearly.[54] This and other studies suggest that nearly all tuberculin-positive patients with HIV infection eventually develop active tuberculosis unless either HIV or the tuberculous infection, or both, are effectively treated, or another fatal complication of AIDS occurs.

As discussed in "Epidemiology," HIV-infected patients are predisposed not only to reactivation of remote infection but also to rapid progression of recently acquired infection.[55, 59] It is also probable that AIDS increases susceptibility to acquisition of new infection, although this has not been rigorously established.

Management of tuberculosis in AIDS may be complicated by concomitant intravenous drug use and homelessness. The difficulty in isolating and completing treatment in such patients is the underlying reason for recent outbreaks of MDR tuberculosis in this population. It is of interest that long before (and independent of) the AIDS epidemic, illicit intravenous drug use was shown to favor an increased incidence of extrapulmonary disease.[95]

PULMONARY TUBERCULOSIS

Primary Tuberculosis in Childhood

The initial focus of pulmonary tuberculosis occurs most frequently in the midlung zones but may develop anywhere. At the time of tuberculin conversion, fever and lassitude and rarely erythema nodosum or phlyctenar keratoconjunctivitis may be present briefly. Clinical manifestations of the initial infection depend on the age of the patient. It is most often symptomatic in childhood because of an age-related tendency to extensive regional lymphadenitis. This may compress central bronchi, causing a brassy cough or atelectasis of a segment or lobe, or may rupture into a bronchus, seeding infection distally, causing pneumonia. In the very young, there is a tendency to progressive lymphohematogenous dissemination with miliary meningeal disease. Uncommonly, again more in infants, local progression of the initial pneumonia results in progressive primary disease, which may cavitate and spread via the bronchial tree or the blood stream. However, most infections during the relatively disease-resistant period of childhood (ages 4 to 15 years) are nonprogressive over the short term; healing by involution, encapsulation, and frequently calcification does not seem to be accelerated by chemotherapy.[92] Progression, if any, usually occurs in extrapulmonary metastatic foci or with the development of apical posterior pulmonary tuberculosis when the patient reaches puberty and young adulthood. Treatment of asymptomatic childhood infection is usually with INH alone for a year except when drug resistance seems likely. The recommended dose is larger (10 to 15 mg/kg) than the adult dose, the risk of INH toxicity being negligible in the young. Symptoms of bronchial compression often respond to brief corticosteroid treatment (predni-

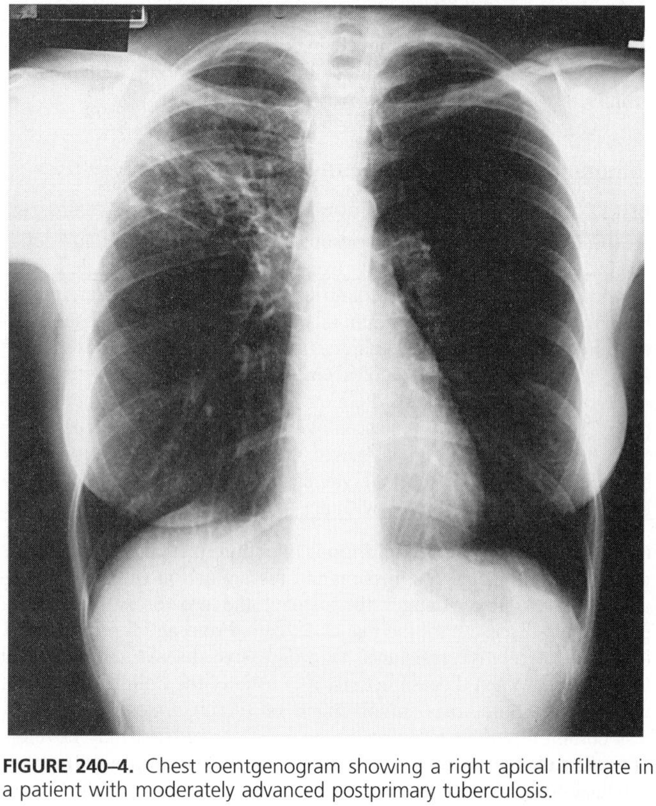

FIGURE 240–4. Chest roentgenogram showing a right apical infiltrate in a patient with moderately advanced postprimary tuberculosis.

sone, 20 to 40 mg/day). Progressive disease with caseation should be treated with a multidrug regimen.

Pulmonary Tuberculosis in Adolescents and Adults

Primary Tuberculosis after Childhood. Primary infection in adolescents and adults (1) may occur without symptoms and signs, (2) may produce a typical primary complex, or (3) may result in typical chronic pulmonary tuberculosis without a demonstrable primary complex. Any pneumonic infiltrate, especially if rounded, associated with a hilar or mediastinal node, or in an unusual location, particularly anterior to the tracheal plane, may represent primary infection. These lesions may undergo caseation, liquefaction, and bronchogenic spread just as with classic chronic pulmonary tuberculosis.

Postprimary (Adult-type) Pulmonary Tuberculosis. Postprimary pulmonary tuberculosis in adults is usually asymmetric and characterized by caseation, cavity formation, and fibrosis. It begins as a patch of pneumonitis in the subapical posterior aspect of an upper lobe, usually just below the clavicle or first rib (Fig. 240–4). A less frequent location is the apex of the lower lobe, where it may be obscured by the heart and hilum on chest roentgenogram. The inflammatory response in the sensitized host produces a fibrin-rich alveolar exudate containing a mixture of inflammatory cells. Serial roentgenograms may demonstrate waxing and waning and sometimes complete regression. If the process accelerates, however, an area of caseous necrosis surrounded by epithelioid cells, granulation tissue, and eventually fibrosis develops. This may arrest by inspissation of the caseous area, fibrous encapsulation, and healing. Caseation, however, tends to liquefy and drain into the bronchial tree, spreading bacillary contents by coughing. The cavity is prevented from collapsing by the fibrous capsule and the inelasticity of the surrounding lung. For unclear reasons, the pulmonary cavity favors bacillary multiplication to enormous titers, 5 to 6 logs greater than in noncavitary lesions.[96] The progressive nature of pulmonary tuberculosis in the sensitized host is due to (1) the tendency of apical caseous foci to liquefy, (2) the enormous concentrations of organisms in the resulting pulmonary cavities, and (3) spread of this bacilli-rich material through the bronchial tree. Progression from minimal infiltrate to far-advanced cavitary disease can occur within a few months (Fig. 240–5).

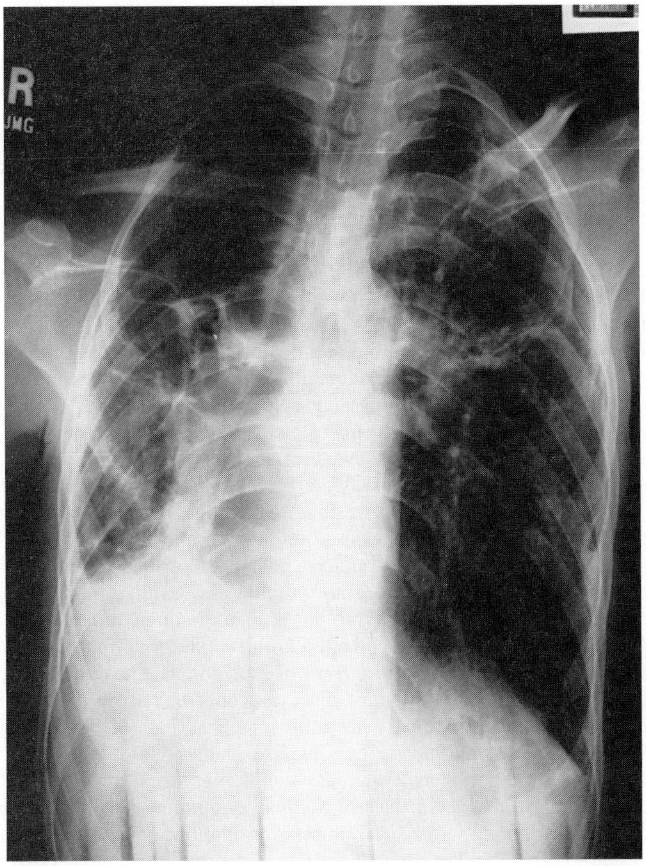

FIGURE 240–5. Chest roentgenogram showing far-advanced bilateral apical cavitary pulmonary tuberculosis in a 32-year-old woman from Ethiopia.

Coughing aerosolizes infectious cavity secretions that may distribute widely throughout the lung (bronchogenic spread). New foci eventually develop, which, in turn, may undergo caseation, fibrosis, and healing or slough, resulting in new cavities. The segment or lobe containing the initial cavity is typically involved first with scattered patchy disease, but the contralateral apex is often secondarily involved with progressive disease. Bronchogenic spread may establish foci of infection in the lower lobe and anterior portions of the upper lobe, producing a polymorphous mottling on chest roentgenogram, but these are usually nonprogressive and heal with fibrosis. Although hematogenous spread from an established pulmonary focus can occur, it is usually limited by hypersensitivity-induced thrombosis. Regional lymphadenitis and calcification are not features of chronic pulmonary tuberculosis in adults.

The highly infectious secretions from a cavity always cause some degree of endobronchial inflammation and ulceration, which may be extensive. Ulcerative tuberculous laryngitis is an extension of this process, as is local disease throughout the upper airways, mouth, middle ear, and gastrointestinal tract.

Mechanisms of healing are the same whether spontaneous or under the influence of chemotherapy. Without drug therapy, solid caseous foci surrounded by contracting fibrous tissue occasionally arrest. However, viable bacilli almost always persist in such lesions, which can later reactivate. Before drug therapy, open healing of persisting cavities never occurred, although some large, thick-walled cavities in shrunken fibrotic lobes could persist for years with minimal symptoms while remaining highly infectious (chronic fibroid tuberculosis). With drug therapy, open healing of cavities is typical when sputum conversion has been prompt, sometimes with complete re-epithelialization. Their major risk is superinfection with organisms such as *Aspergillus* or nontuberculous mycobacteria.

Lower Lobe and Endobronchial Tuberculosis. These terms are not appropriate for chronic pulmonary tuberculosis of the ordinary kind that happens to involve the apex of the lower lobes. In adults, *lower lung field tuberculosis* describes three different but often associated processes: progressive lower lobe pneumonia in recently infected older individuals; endobronchial tuberculosis, often with parenchymal consolidation-collapse; and tuberculosis complicating AIDS. These processes do not suggest tuberculosis roentgenographically and in the former two have a low bacterial content.

Progressive Lower Lobe Disease in Older Persons. Tuberculous infection in an older tuberculin-negative individual frequently causes a nonspecific, nonresolving pneumonitis in the lower or middle lobes or anterior segments of the upper lobes, similar to primary infection in childhood, except with much less hilar and mediastinal adenopathy.[45] Tuberculosis should be considered in any slowly or nonresolving pneumonitis in an older patient.

Endobronchial Tuberculosis. In the past, superficial endobronchial lesions due to infectious secretions were common, sometimes spreading to the larynx and beyond or causing obstructive atelectasis with collapse. These superficial lesions respond quickly to chemotherapy. Now endobronchial disease is most frequently caused by rupture of an adjacent node into the bronchial tree or less frequently to direct spread from parenchymal tuberculosis.[97] The chest roentgenogram typically reveals collapse-consolidation but may be normal in as many as 20% of cases. Sputum smear results are usually negative, but the bronchial wash result is frequently positive.[97]

The usual bronchoscopic findings are mucosal edema, ulceration, and narrowing, but in 30% of cases, bulky granulation tissue may resemble bronchogenic carcinoma. Endobronchial involvement is usual in lower lung field tuberculosis,[98] and endobronchial ulcers occasionally produce positive sputum smears with normal chest roentgenograms. Large parenchymal cavities may be present, associated with an air-fluid level at times due to intermittent obstruction and poor drainage. Bronchial perforation by tuberculous nodes with endobronchial mass formation and lower lobe consolidation has been observed during AIDS.

Calcified nodes can erode into the bronchial tree and cause hemoptysis, expectoration of calcific material (lithoptysis), or spread of previously quiescent bacilli. The atelectatic pneumonitis, with or without new active disease, which may result is most frequently seen in the anterior segment of the upper lobe and medial segment of the middle lobe.

Tuberculomas. Asymptomatic rounded lesions may develop as the parenchymal residua of the initial infection or as an upper lobe caseous lesion encapsulates (Fig. 240–6). These are ordinarily static, but larger ones may cavitate to produce new spread of disease. In some persons, excessive fibrosis occurs with small caseous or granulomatous residua becoming surrounded by concentric layers of fibrous tissue, at times with central or concentric calcification resembling histoplasmomas. Most such lesions are stable and important only in being confused with cancer.

Pulmonary Tuberculosis in Acquired Immunodeficiency Syndrome. Tuberculosis as first described in Haitians with advanced AIDS was characterized by middle or lower lung field location, absence of cavitation, a greatly increased incidence of extrapulmonary disease, and usually a negative tuberculin test result.[99] Although it was certain on epidemiologic grounds that this represented recrudescence of earlier infection, it resembled childhood tuberculosis clinically except for a negative tuberculin test result and less prominent hilar and mediastinal lymphadenopathy. A later study of tuberculosis in a much less ill population in clients of tuberculosis clinics unaware of their HIV infection found a clinical picture no different from ordinary reactivation tuberculosis in HIV-negative patients, with apical, often cavitary, disease and tuberculin positivity being the rule.[100] The clinical picture of tuberculosis during HIV infection is determined by the degree of immunocompromise (Table 240–6).[88]

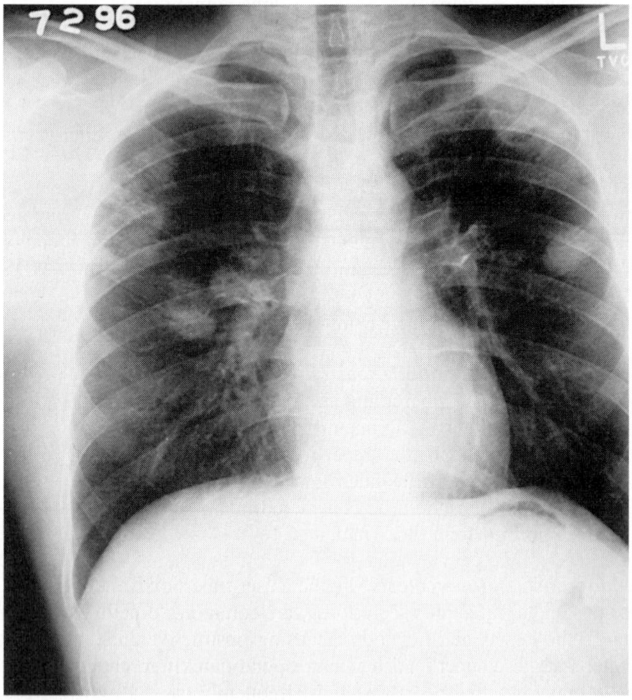

FIGURE 240–6. Chest roentgenogram demonstrating multiple bilateral pulmonary tuberculomas in an asymptomatic 35-year-old man from Poland.

TABLE 240–6 Clinical Manifestations of Active Tuberculosis in Early versus Late Human Immunodeficiency Virus Infection*

	Early	Late
Tuberculin test	Usually positive	Usually negative
Adenopathy	Unusual	Common
Pulmonary distribution	Upper lobe	Lower and middle lobe
Cavitation	Often present	Typically absent
Extrapulmonary disease	10–15% of cases	50% of cases

*For practical purposes, early and late may be defined as CD^{4+} cell counts >300 cells/mm³ and <200 cells/mm³, respectively.

Adapted from Murray JF. Cursed duet: HIV infection and tuberculosis. Respiration. 1990;57:210–220. Reproduced with permission of S. Karger AG, Basel.

HIV-positive persons may also acquire new infection from others in their environment, a risk that was first observed in HIV wards and domiciles. The clinical picture in these patients was diffuse rapidly progressive noncavitary disease that was often fatal. In some instances, the infecting person had a normal chest roentgenogram and a negative sputum stain at the time infection of others took place.[55, 59]

It is important to consider tuberculosis in HIV-positive individuals with respiratory failure in the intensive care unit. Patients may have adult respiratory distress or sepsis syndrome with multiple organ system failure. The diagnosis can be made readily by stain and culture if appropriate samples are submitted to the laboratory.

Symptoms. Early pulmonary tuberculosis is asymptomatic, usually discovered by chance on a chest roentgenogram. As the bacillary population grows, however, nonspecific constitutional symptoms such as anorexia, fatigue, weight loss, chilly sensations, afternoon fever, and night sweats may ensue. These late manifestations are gradual in onset, surprisingly well tolerated, and often not even recognized by the patient. Local symptoms also indicate advanced disease. A productive cough is usually present. Coughing to clear cavitary secretions is usually mild and well tolerated but may become bothersome when bronchial involvement is extensive. The mucopurulent sputum is nonspecific, and both cough and sputum may be ignored by patients with chronic bronchitis. Hemoptysis due to caseous sloughing or endobronchial erosion is usually minor but connotes advanced disease. Sudden massive hemoptysis due to erosion of a pulmonary artery by an advancing cavity (Rasmussen's aneurysm) was an occasional terminal event in the predrug era but is now seldom seen. In inactive disease, brisk hemoptysis may be due to *Aspergillus* superinfection of residual cavities (aspergilloma). Chest pain is usually due to extension of inflammation to the parietal pleura. Pleural involvement adjacent to an established cavity tends to cause visceral-parietal pleural symphysis without effusion (dry pleurisy). Serofibrinous pleurisy with effusion is often an early postprimary event but may complicate chronic pulmonary tuberculosis. Rarely, chest pain leads to discovery of tuberculous empyema. Some patients do not seek help until disease occurs in tissues bathed in highly infectious pulmonary secretions such as painful pharyngeal ulcers; indolent and nonhealing ulcers of the mouth or tongue; hoarseness and dysphagia that are due to laryngeal involvement; tuberculous otitis media; gastrointestinal symptoms that are due to enteric ulceration, perforation, or mass formation; or anal pain that is due to tuberculous perirectal abscess and fistula formation. Lower lobe tuberculosis due to bronchial lymph node perforation may be associated with lithoptysis (stone spitting) and characteristically produces symptoms of severe endobronchial disease with serious cough and often hemoptysis.

Physical Examination. Physical findings are not specific, in general underestimating the extent of the illness, and may be absent in spite of extensive disease. Dullness with decreased fremitus may indicate pleural thickening or fluid. Rales may be appreciated only when the patient breathes in after a short cough (post-tussive rales) and may persist long after healing owing to permanent distortion of small airways. With large lesions, signs of consolidation with open bronchi (whispered pectoriloquy, tubular breath sounds) can be heard. Distant hollow breath sounds heard over cavities are called *amphoric*, like the sound made by blowing across the mouth of a jar (amphora).

Roentgenologic Findings. The chest roentgenogram is central to diagnosis, determination of the extent and character of disease, and evaluation of the response to therapy. Certain patterns are highly suggestive, although not diagnostic, of tuberculosis. A patchy or nodular infiltrate in the apical or subapical posterior areas of the upper lobes or the superior segment of a lower lobe is highly suspicious for early chronic tuberculosis, especially if bilateral or associated with cavity formation (see Fig. 240–4). Cavities may be more apparent by computed tomography (CT) or magnetic resonance imaging. Cavitation in the apical segment of the lower lobe may be obscured by the heart shadow and, in the lateral view, by the dorsal spine. Air-fluid levels are uncommon in upper lobe tuberculosis (less than 10%) but occur more frequently in lower lobe cavities.[76] Fresh bronchogenic spread from recent spillage of infectious cavity contents appears as multiple, discrete, soft, fluffy infiltrates, or a confluent infiltrate adjacent to a cavity, or in the middle or lower lung field on the same or opposite side. These latter types of spread are seldom progressive and heal by rounding up into more discrete lesions with regular borders.

Both chronicity and histopathologic features can be estimated based on the chest roentgenogram. Productive lesions (granulomatous) tend to be small, nodular, and sharply defined indicating few organisms and a good host response. Exudative lesions (pneumonic) tend to have soft, indistinct borders and are more unstable. Fibrotic scars have sharp margins and tend to contract. Caseation causes increased density. Healing exudative lesions first become smaller and less dense and then, as scarring develops, become more sharply defined. Lower lobe tuberculosis is nonspecific roentgenographically. Other patterns include poorly resolving pneumonia, atelectasis, mass lesions, and large cavities with air-fluid levels; initial misdiagnosis is the rule. Pneumonia associated with hilar adenopathy should always suggest primary tuberculosis, regardless of the lung fields involved and patient age.

Other Laboratory Findings. Normocytic, normochromic anemia, hypoalbuminemia, and hypergammaglobulinemia are characteristic of advanced disease. The white blood cell count is usually normal but may be between 10,000 and 15,000 cells/mm^3. Many HIV-negative patients with active tuberculosis have CD4 cell counts much lower than 500 cells/liter, which return toward normal with treatment.[101] Monocytosis is seen in less than 10% of cases. Hematuria or pyuria should suggest coexisting renal tuberculosis. Hyponatremia with features of inappropriate secretion of antidiuretic hormone is characteristic of tuberculous meningitis but also occurs with isolated pulmonary involvement. Hyponatremia should also suggest associated Addison's disease. Hypercalcemia is also seen during pulmonary tuberculosis, usually in the first weeks of therapy.

Diagnosis. A strong presumptive diagnosis can often be made based on the roentgenographic pattern. A positive sputum smear, usual in extensive disease, is almost conclusive in the proper setting. However, an intercurrent cancer or lung abscess, particularly in the apices, may erode a quiescent focus and cause brief shedding of tubercle bacilli without causing active disease. The best diagnostic sputum specimen is an early morning sample. Three daily collections suffice for almost all cases. Aspiration of gastric contents, obtained early in the morning to sample sputum swallowed during sleep, is an alternative when sputum is not produced. Sputum induction by heated saline aerosols is also an effective substitute in ambulatory patients. Although pulmonary tuberculosis in AIDS patients is often noncavitary, both sensitivity and specificity of sputum acid-fast stains are comparable to those in HIV-negative patients.[101] In addition, positive sputum smears are much more likely to indicate *M. tuberculosis* than *M. avium* complex, even in areas where both diseases are common.[102] A negative tuberculin reaction does not exclude tuberculosis even when the dose is 250 TU.[79, 103] In AIDS patients, tuberculin negativity is the rule.[88] Granuloma formation on histologic examination, even with acid-fast bacilli, is still only strong presumptive evidence, since similar findings may be produced by mycobacteria other than tuberculosis. Definitive diagnosis requires culture and speciation.

Fiberoptic Bronchoscopy. Diagnostic fiberoptic bronchoscopy with transbronchial biopsy and bronchial washings is an efficient way to obtain diagnostic materials when sputum does not suffice. In most cases of other than miliary disease, however, it is culture of washings rather than acid-fast staining or histologic features that provides the diagnosis, and most cases diagnosed by bronchoscopy are later found to have been positive using specimens obtained less invasively. Bronchoscopy specimens cultured by radiometric methods more frequently grow saprophytic nontuberculous mycobacteria than tuberculosis.[3] In AIDS patients with pulmonary tuberculosis but negative smears, bronchoscopy yields a rapid diagnosis (based on smears and histologic features) in only one third of cases.[103–106] Thus, a negative acid-fast stain at bronchoscopy does not exclude tuberculosis, although such cases are certainly less contagious.

Tuberculosis Diagnosed at Autopsy. From 1985 through 1988, 5.1% of all reported tuberculosis cases in the United States were diagnosed at death.[107] Usually, the patient is old, has underlying diseases, and very frequently is tuberculin-negative. Both nonresolving pulmonary processes and extrapulmonary tuberculosis, particularly chronic miliary and meningeal disease, are represented in this group. The usual reason for failure to diagnose tuberculosis in this setting is failure to look for it.

Tuberculosis and Cancer. It has been estimated that 1 to 5% of tuberculosis patients also have cancer, most being male smokers. It is possible that cancer can arise in tuberculous scars, and it is certain that cancer can erode old quiescent tuberculous foci, causing active disease. However, in many patients the diseases will be anatomically remote. No one cancer cell type predominates.

When tuberculosis and cancer occur together, diagnosis of the latter is often difficult but should be kept in mind in older smoking men with tuberculosis, and sputum cytologic studies should be performed. There are certain roentgenographic findings that suggest concomitant cancer, such as progression of one area while the remainder of the lesion is regressing, a large (>3 cm) mass lesion admixed with infiltrative disease, the presence of hilar nodes in adult chronic pulmonary tuberculosis, and postobstructive atelectasis.[108]

TREATMENT OF TUBERCULOSIS

Before effective drugs were available, 50% of patients with active pulmonary tuberculosis died within 2 years, and only 25% were cured.[23] With the advent of chemotherapy, successful treatment became a reasonable goal in all adults. In practice, failures occur because of drug resistance or an inappropriate regimen but most importantly because of nonadherence, which is often carefully concealed by the patient as health returns and motivation declines. Resistance to antituberculous agents can be either *primary*, that is, present before initiating therapy, or *secondary*, indicating emergence of resistance in the setting of inadequately prescribed or taken therapy.

Primary Resistance

During the 1970s, primary resistance to at least one drug was observed in less than 3% of cases in the United States. In 1997, approximately 8% of *M. tuberculosis* isolates in the United States were resistant to at least INH, and 1.3% were resistant to at least INH and RMP.[1] Resistance rates are not uniform across the United States. Fortunately, worrisome resistance trends in New York City and other areas have reversed in response to vigorous efforts by physicians and public health personnel.[65]

Secondary Resistance

Historical clues that suggest drug resistance include prior antituberculous chemotherapy or prophylaxis, infection acquired in regions where resistance is prevalent (including Asia, Latin America, and Africa), and contact with a drug-resistant case. One study from southern California recorded resistance in 71% of patients with tuberculosis who had been previously treated and had cavitary disease.[109] Homelessness, illicit drug use, and AIDS all favor acquisition or development of drug-resistant infections. More than 60% of tuberculosis cases among residents of a Boston shelter for homeless persons were resistant to at least one drug,[36] and a study performed between 1982 and 1987 in one Manhattan hospital confirmed the correlation between homelessness and drug-resistant tuberculosis. Resistance was present in 8% of patients with homes, 21% of those without homes, and in 42% of homeless blacks.[110] Adherence to treatment is unlikely in persons facing the more pressing problems of homelessness. Resistance to at least one drug was present in 33% of *M. tuberculosis* isolates during 1 month in 1991 in New York City and to both INH and RMP in a remarkable 19%.[111] By 1994, these numbers had declined to 24 and 13%, respectively.[65] Fluoroquinolone resistance was also noted.[112]

Effect of Resistance to Different Drugs on Response to Chemotherapy

Surprisingly, studies of four-drug, 6-month chemotherapy demonstrated that initial INH or STM resistance did not compromise outcome, but results were very poor (>50% lack of conversion or relapse) when initial RMP resistance was present. Six or 9-month therapy is contraindicated in RMP-resistant cases.[113]

Antituberculous Drugs

See Chapter 34 for dosage and pharmacology.

Isoniazid. INH is the cornerstone of therapy and should be included in all regimens unless a high degree of INH resistance exists and the regimen includes RMP. (The increased hepatotoxicity of INH and RMP given together likely outweighs any advantage of continuing INH in the face of INH resistance.)

Rifampin. RMP is the second major antituberculous agent. The most important complication of RMP is hepatitis. This occurs four times more frequently in regimens containing both INH and RMP than in those containing INH alone.[114] Although biochemical evidence of hepatic toxicity may occur promptly after administration of INH alone, clinical hepatitis rarely occurs in the first month.[115] In contrast, fulminant hepatitis complicating INH and RMP may occur within the first 2 weeks of therapy. This appears to be due to accelerated production of a hepatotoxic product of INH oxidation by RMP, a hypothesis supported by the observation that phenobarbital and phenytoin, also inducers of the microsomal P-450 system, have been associated with fulminant hepatic failure in persons receiving INH and RMP.[114] INH hepatotoxicity is rare in children, but as many as 25% of children taking INH and RMP together acquire jaundice. This may not be the same phenomenon as in adults.

Of special concern is that RMP, by inducing hepatic P-450 cytochrome oxidases, leads to suboptimal HIV-1 protease inhibitor levels, inadequate control of viral replication, and emergence of drug-resistant virus. In this setting, RMP may be replaced by rifabutin, which has comparable antituberculous activity but is a weaker enzyme inducer.[116] This is often preferable to discontinuing the protease inhibitor. Monitoring protease inhibitor blood levels may also be justified. Rifampin-resistant tuberculosis has occurred in AIDS patients receiving rifabutin chemoprophylaxis for *M. avium* complex infection.[117]

Pyrazinamide. PZA is an essential component of 6-month regimens. Early studies of PZA using high doses recorded such serious hepatotoxicity that it was largely abandoned. However, at currently recommended doses and durations, PZA does not add to the hepatotoxicity of INH and RMP.[118] It is thought to be ineffective in preventing emergence of resistance to companion drugs, and its benefit effect is limited to the first 2 months in regimens containing both INH and RMP. Side effects include hyperuricemia, mild nongouty polyarthralgias that respond to nonsteroidal anti-inflammatory agents, and gout. *M. bovis* is uniformly resistant to PZA.[119]

Ethambutol. EMB is a component of most regimens. It is given at a daily dosage of 15 mg/kg. When multidrug resistance is highly likely, 25 mg/kg daily may be warranted but is associated with an increased risk of ocular toxicity.

Streptomycin. STM, the first major antituberculous drug, was promptly replaced by INH as the cornerstone of therapy.

Fluoroquinolones. Although experience with these agents is not extensive, their in vitro activity and favorable clinical results suggest that some fluoroquinolones are as effective as traditional first-line agents.[120] However, fluoroquinolones should not be used as first-line therapy but rather reserved for treatment of MDR cases as part of a well-designed multidrug regimen. Of fluoroquinolones currently approved by the U.S. Food and Drug Administration, levofloxacin has a favorable activity profile against *M. tuberculosis*.

Second-Line Agents. Second-line agents are less efficacious or more toxic, or both, than first-line drugs. They include ethionamide, prothionamide, cycloserine, kanamycin, capreomycin, thiacetazone, para-aminosalicylic acid, and other agents discussed in Chapter 34.

Selecting a Drug Regimen

Before RMP was available, excellent results in drug-sensitive infections were obtained with INH plus either para-aminosalicylic acid (PAS) or EMB given for 18 to 24 months, "reinforced" in extensive disease by STM for the first 6 to 12 weeks. Relapse rates were unacceptably high with shorter courses. However, demonstration that RMP was equal to INH in efficacy led to studies of shorter treatment regimens. In definitive studies, drug-sensitive infections responded as effectively to 9 months of INH and RMP as to 18- to 24-month regimens not containing RMP.[121, 122] It was subsequently demonstrated that 6-month regimens based on an initial 2-month intensive "bactericidal phase" of INH, RMP, PZA, and either STM or EMB, and a "continuation phase" of INH and RMP for 4 more months performed as well.[123] It was also established that "continuation phase" drugs could be administered twice or thrice weekly, facilitating directly observed therapy. Next it was shown that neither STM nor EMB improved results over a three-drug regimen (INH, RMP, and PZA) during the first 2 months of intensive therapy when the isolate was fully susceptible.[123] This 6-month three-drug regimen is perfectly acceptable for drug-sensitive infections. However, given concerns about resistance, EMB is almost always included until susceptibility testing results are known. Regimens lacking RMP are used very infrequently in Western nations.

Standard Nine-Month Regimens Based on Isoniazid and Rifampin. The combination of INH (300 mg) plus RMP (600 mg) daily by mouth on an empty stomach for 9 months is highly effective for almost all forms of drug-sensitive tuberculosis, both pulmonary and extrapulmonary.[124] Most authorities, however, advise addition of PZA (25 mg/kg) plus either STM (1 g) or EMB (15 or 25 mg/kg) initially pending sensitivity results, especially when primary drug resistance is suspected.

An intermittent 9-month regimen consisting largely of twice-weekly doses of INH and RMP is an acceptable alternative.[125] INH and RMP are administered daily, as described for 1 to 2 months, and twice weekly thereafter with the same dose of RMP but a larger (900 mg) dose of INH. This is not advised in cases with any likelihood of antimicrobial resistance.

Six-Month Regimens. The CDC has endorsed several regimens for the initial treatment of tuberculosis.[126] The degree to which INH resistance compromises the efficacy of a three-drug (INH, RMP, and PZA) regimen is not known, whereas it appears to make little difference with four-drug regimens (INH, RMP, PZA, and either EMB or STM).[113] Considering the current incidence of drug resistance, and the safety of EMB when given under proper supervision, there is little to be lost and potentially much to be gained by routinely using such a four-drug regimen in the initial 2 months of treatment. Results of all 6-month regimens in patients with initial resistance to RMP are poor, and such cases probably require 18- to 24-month courses, as was the case before RMP was available.[113]

When hepatitis occurs in patients receiving both INH and RMP, both drugs should be discontinued until hepatic transaminase levels normalize. INH may then be cautiously reintroduced in graduated doses while monitoring serum transaminase levels, and a more prolonged (18- to 24-month) regimen based on INH, and at least one companion drug other than RMP can be continued. Similarly, when patients in whom drug-related hepatitis develops with INH and RMP have demonstrated microbial resistance to INH but not RMP, RMP can usually be gradually reintroduced and a more prolonged (18- to 24-month) regimen based on RMP and preferably two new companion drugs other than INH continued. In the uncommon situation when both INH and RMP must be reintroduced, this can be carried out sequentially with close supervision in many patients.[114]

Directly Observed Therapy in Nonadherent Patients. The failure of conventional treatment programs to cure persons who do not adhere to therapy, together with the fact that most of a 6-month regimen can be given on a less than daily basis, has led to regimens in which the total number of doses is small and DOT is practical. Several acceptable regimens have been endorsed by the CDC.[126] One well-studied regimen is presented in Table 240–7.[127] EMB may be substituted for STM without loss of efficacy. Importantly, DOT is cost effective, especially when considering the cost of caring for MDR cases. Since all doses are observed, compliance is assured, and the likelihood of emergence of resistance minimized. The ability of mandatory DOT to control drug resistance in a community is well established.[66, 128] In some cases, recalcitrant patients must be detained for completion of therapy. It has been recommended that all patients with organisms resistant to either INH or RMP and all patients receiving less than daily therapy receive DOT.[125]

TABLE 240–7 A 62-Dose, Four-Drug Regimen for Tuberculosis in Adults

First 2 wk (once-daily dose for 14 consecutive days)	
INH	300 mg
RMP	600 mg
PZA	1.5 g if ≤50 kg body weight, 2.0 g if 51–74 kg, 2.5 g if ≥75 kg
STM	750 mg if ≤50 kg body weight, 1.0 g if >50 kg
Wk 3–8 (twice weekly)	
INH	15 mg/kg
RMP	600 mg
PZA	3.0 g if ≤50 kg body weight, 3.5 g if 51–74 kg, 4.0 g if ≥75 kg
STM	1.0 g if ≤50 kg body weight, 1.25 g if 51–74 kg, 1.5 g if ≥75 kg
Wk 9–26 (twice weekly)	
INH	15 mg/kg body weight
RMP	600 mg

Abbreviations: INH, Isoniazid; PZA, pyrazinamide; RMP, rifampin; STM, streptomycin.
From Cohn DL, Catlin BJ, Peterson KL, et al. A 62-dose, 6-month therapy for pulmonary and extrapulmonary tuberculosis: A twice-weekly, directly observed, and cost-effective regimen. Ann Intern Med. 1990;112:407–415.

Regimens of Less than Six Months for Minimal Disease. Extent of disease can be quantified by the mycobacterial content of sputum, with smear- and culture-positive representing most severe disease, smear-negative and culture-positive representing intermediate disease, and smear- and culture-negative representing the least amount of disease. Good results have been obtained with as little as 2 to 4 months of four-drug therapy in patients with less than extensive tuberculosis.[129] Although these abbreviated courses are not recommended, the fact that even short periods of intense therapy cure many patients further supports the use of DOT because it avoids irregular drug taking and has some chance of cure even when terminated prematurely. (The good results with 3 months of therapy in smear- and culture-negative cases also suggests a role for multiple-drug chemoprophylaxis when exposure to resistant organisms is suspected.)

Combination Tablets. Fixed-dose preparations containing either 300 mg of INH and 600 mg of RMP (Rifamate), or INH, RMP, and PZA (Rifater) are available. These prevent the patient from omitting one of the drugs at the risk of inducing resistance to the others.

Regimens Based on Isoniazid and Ethambutol. For drug-sensitive infections, the only advantage of shorter regimens is improved compliance. Because RMP increases the risk of hepatotoxicity when given with INH, this needs to be justified when treating drug-sensitive disease of limited extent in highly compliant patients. Treatment with 18 to 24 months of INH plus EMB is a low-cost, effective alternative to shorter regimens for all forms of drug-sensitive tuberculosis, often with daily STM (1 g) added in more advanced or symptomatic cases during the first 2 months. This may be the preferred regimen (1) for patients with less than extensive disease whose compliance is certain and for whom supervision consists of no more than monthly clinic visits, (2) for patients who are likely to be noncompliant but who absolutely cannot receive supervised therapy (this should be exceptionally rare), and (3) for patients with severe liver disease.

Treatment of Multidrug-Resistant Tuberculosis. When initiating treatment for tuberculosis that is resistant to both INH and RMP, extensive susceptibility testing should be performed and expert advice sought. If a suboptimal regimen is prescribed, resistance to additional drugs may emerge and the opportunity for success lost. In a discouraging study from Denver, only one half of 171 HIV-negative patients with MDR tuberculosis ever converted sputum cultures to negative despite prolonged administration of carefully selected regimens (not including fluoroquinolones).[130] In contrast, a more recent report from New York City noted remission in virtually all evaluable HIV-negative patients treated for MDR tuberculosis using fluoroquinolone-based regimens.[120] Therapy was administered for a median of 18 months. For tuberculosis that is INH- and RMP-resistant but fluoroquinolone-susceptible, a fluoroquinolone should always be administered along with other drugs to which the organism is susceptible. Levofloxacin may be preferred, although there is experience with ciprofloxacin. Companion drugs may include aminoglycosides (STM, kanamycin, or amikacin) or capreomycin, ethionamide, and cycloserine.[6, 120, 124, 126] To prevent the emergence of resistant strains, fluoroquinolones should be reserved for known drug-resistant cases but not be a routine part of initial therapy for tuberculosis.[112]

Course of Treatment and Duration of Observation

The diagnosis of tuberculosis is usually relatively well established before therapy is initiated. In smear-negative cases, five or six sputum samples and, if available, specimens obtained at bronchoscopy should be submitted before beginning treatment. In severely ill patients with presumed tuberculosis, treatment should be initiated immediately; a few days of antituberculous treatment will not interfere with bacteriologic diagnosis. If treatment is initiated before a microbiologic diagnosis is established, the response to treatment often confirms the diagnosis. Periodic chest roentgenograms are helpful, although monthly films are not necessary. Beginning 1 month after initiation of therapy, an early morning sputum specimen culture should be obtained for culture to monitor conversion or, if sputum positivity persists, to detect the emergence of drug resistance. It may be more practical to obtain several sputum specimens for culture at 2, 4, and 6 months of therapy. Sputum cultures should convert to negative within 2 months with regimens containing both INH and RMP and not much longer with INH plus EMB.[53] In a minority of patients, smears remain positive after cultures revert to negative. Sporadic positive smears for long periods presumably represent inactive bacilli released from caseous foci. When cultures remain positive beyond 4 months, emerging drug resistance is a major concern. This almost never occurs when both INH and RMP are reliably taken as initial therapy for drug-sensitive tuberculosis and suggests initial drug resistance or noncompliance, or both. Sensitivity testing should be performed and consideration given to adding at least two new drugs to which the organism was sensitive at the outset of treatment, at least until sensitivities are known. Addition of only one drug risks rapid resistance to the added drug.

Patients receiving INH should be instructed about symptoms of hepatitis and, when possible, hepatic transaminase levels monitored every 1 to 2 months. This is more important in patients receiving both INH and RMP. Patients receiving EMB should be regularly questioned regarding visual symptoms and their visual acuity measured (Snellen chart). Testing of red-green color discrimination is desirable when the 25 mg/kg dosage is given. Patients receiving STM should be examined for balance and high-frequency hearing loss if they are older than 50 years of age.

Relapse after adequate treatment of drug-sensitive infections is very infrequent. Prolonged follow-up of appropriately treated patients is not necessary except in the case of unusually extensive disease, slow bacteriologic response to treatment, suspicion of poor compliance, or high-risk patients with intercurrent diseases. Although observation may be discontinued on completion of a 6- or 9-month regimen containing both INH and RMP, continued observation for 2 years is preferred when practical.

Retreatment. Clinical judgment based on experience is critical in retreatment cases, and susceptibility testing to all potentially useful drugs is required.[124] Some generalizations concerning retreatment can be made. (1) A relapse after prompt sputum conversion indicates that drugs were stopped too soon. When drugs are taken reliably but stopped prematurely, the infection usually remains susceptible and will respond again to the initial regimen. (2) If relapse occurs with organisms resistant to INH when initial treatment was with INH and EMB or INH, EMB, and STM, retreatment with RMP plus two other drugs to which the organism is susceptible for at least 24 months is highly effective. A 9-month regimen that uses RMP, STM, PZA, and EMB for 2 months, followed by RMP and EMB for 7 months has performed well in infections resistant to INH but sensitive to RMP and EMB.[131] (3) If compliance has been irregular, resistant organisms will probably be present. (4) When drug resistance is suspected, a two- or three-drug combination including at least one "new" strong drug (INH, RMP, STM, EMB at 25 mg/kg, levofloxacin, or PZA) and a "new" weak drug (ethionamide, PAS, or cycloserine) may be added to drugs previously given pending susceptibility results. (5) Capreomycin or amikacin can replace STM. Kanamycin is less effective and more toxic and is used as a last resort. (6) In infections multiply resistant to INH, RMP, STM, EMB, levofloxacin, and PZA, three or four weak drugs (ethionamide, cycloserine, PAS, and capreomycin) may be used together with high-dose INH (15 mg/kg), because INH may retain some suppressive effect even when in vitro resistance is demonstrated.

Other Forms of Treatment. Bed rest does not influence outcome when effective chemotherapy is given. In treatment failures resistant to all drugs, strict bed rest with continued INH may salvage some otherwise hopeless cases and may also be beneficial during retreatment of cases resistant to all but the weakest drugs. Resection still has a role in the salvage of patients in whom treatment fails and who have localized, resectable disease, and resistance to all but the weakest drugs.

Corticosteroids. In severely debilitated patients or those with marked constitutional symptoms, adjunctive prednisone (20 to 30 mg daily and slowly tapered) will effect prompt symptomatic improvement, abolish fever, and reverse serious anemia, and hypoalbuminemia. When life-threatening hypoxemia complicates extensive pulmonary inflammation, higher doses (60 to 80 mg daily) may improve oxygenation. Disseminated drug-sensitive tuberculosis associated with high fever and clinical deterioration in AIDS patients may respond to corticosteroids.

Treatment of Tuberculosis in Human Immunodeficiency Virus–Infected Patients. A report from the CDC provides excellent advice in this complicated and rapidly changing arena.[131] The document may be viewed on the CDC web site—http://www.cdc.gov/epo/mmwr/mmwr_rr.html. Updates appear periodically and should be consulted because new antiretroviral agents and new interactions are being discovered. Special attention to drug interactions is required for patients who have tuberculosis and whose HIV infection should be treated with highly active antiretroviral therapy. The rifamycins interact extensively with both protease inhibitors and non-nucleoside reverse transcriptase inhibitors. Among the rifamycins, RMP has the most interactions, rifabutin the least, and rifapentine an intermediate amount. RMP is contraindicated in patients receiving either a protease inhibitor (saquinavir, ritonavir, indinavir, nelfinavir or amprenavir) or a non-nucleoside reverse transcript inhibitor (nevirapine, delavirdine, and efavirenz). Rifabutin should not be used with ritonavir, hard gel saquinavir (Invirase), or delavirdine. Ritonavir increases rifabutin concentrations by 35-fold and causes rifabutin toxicity, such as arthalgia, uveitis, skin discoloration, and leukopenia. Rifabutin decreases serum concentrations of delavirdine and several protease inhibitors, the decrease being most serious for the hard gel saquinavir because of its low bioavailability. Some authorities recommend that patients receiving rifabutin should have the dose of nelfinavir increased from 750 mg three times a day to 1000 mg three times a day and indinavir increased from 800 mg every 8 hours to 1200 mg every 8 hours. The effect of rifabutin on amprenavir metabolism appears to be insufficient to warrant dose adjustment. The dose of rifabutin should be lowered from 300 mg daily to 150 mg daily in patients receiving indinavir, nelfinavir or amprenavir in order to avoid rifabutin toxicity. In contrast, patients taking efavirenz, the rifabutin dose given daily or twice weekly should be increased from 300 mg to 450 mg. Despite this impressive list of interactions, it is not recommended that treatment of tuberculosis be delayed or that highly active antiretroviral therapy be avoided. Because antimycobacterial drugs other than the rifamycins do not have substantial interactions, an alternative regimen with INH, STM, PZA, and EMB can be considered. For adults, one regimen is that STM can be given as 1 g intramuscularly daily for the first 8 weeks, along with INH 300 mg, PZA 2 g, and EMB 1600 mg daily. For the remainder of the 9- to 12-month treatment, the duration depending on response, the patient is given STM 1.5 g intramuscularly, INH 900 mg, and PZA 3.5 g two times per week. The inconvenience and ototoxicity of STM has made this regimen unpopular. Regimens recommended by the CDC are given in Table 240–8.[132]

Other complications of treating tuberculosis in HIV-infected patients include the higher incidence of drug resistance and the paradoxical worsening that may be seen when patients are begun on

TABLE 240-8 Treatment Regimens for Human Immunodeficiency Virus–Related Tuberculosis

Induction Phase		Continuation Phase			
Drugs	*Interval and Duration*	*Drugs*	*Interval and Duration*	**Considerations for Human Immunodeficiency Virus Therapy**	**Comments**
Six-month RFB-based therapy (may be prolonged* to 9 mo)					
INH RFB PZA† EMB†	Daily for 2 mo (8 wk)	INH RFB	Daily or 2 times/wk for 4 mo (18 wk)	RFB should not be used concurrently with ritonavir, hard-gel saquinavir (Invirase), or delavirdine.	If the patient also is taking indinavir, nelfinavir, or amprenavir, the daily dose of RFB is decreased from 300 mg to 150 mg. The twice-weekly dose of RFB (300 mg) remains unchanged if the patient is taking these protease inhibitors.
	Or		*Or*	A 20–25% increase in the dose of protease inhibitors or NNRTIs may be necessary.	
INH RFB PZA† EMB†	Daily for 2 wk, then 2 times/wk for 6 wk	INH RFB	2 times/wk for 4 mo (18 wk)	The patient should be monitored carefully for RFB toxicity (arthralgia, uveitis, leukopenia) if RFB is used concurrently with protease inhibitors or NNRTIs. Evidence of decreased response to antiretroviral therapy should be assessed with HIV RNA levels. No contraindication exists for the use of RFB with NRTIs.	If the patient also is taking efavirenz, the daily or twice weekly dose of RFB is increased from 300 mg to 450 mg. Three-times-a-week RFB in combination with antiretroviral therapy has not been studied.
Nine-month RFB-based therapy (may be prolonged* to 12 mo)					
INH STM PZA EMB	Daily for 2 mo (8 wk)	INH STM PZA	2–3 times/wk for 7 mo (30 wk)	Can be used concurrently with antiretroviral regimens that include protease inhibitors, NRTIs, and NNRTIs.	STM is contraindicated during pregnancy.
	Or		*Or*		
INH STM PZA EMB	Daily for 2 wk, then 2–3 times/wk for 6 wk	INH STM PZA	2–3 times/wk for 7 mo (30 wk)		Every effort should be made to continue STM for the total duration of treatment. When STM is not used for the recommended 9 mo, EMB should be added and the treatment duration prolonged from 9 mo (38 wk) to 12 mo (52 wk).
Six-month RMP-based therapy (may be prolonged* to 9 mo)					
INH RMP PZA‡ EMB‡ (or STM)	Daily for 2 mo (8 wk)	INH RMP	Daily or 2–3 times/week for 4 mo (18 wk)	Protease inhibitors or NNRTIs should not be administered concurrently with RMP. NRTIs can be administered concurrently with RMP.	STM is contraindicated during pregnancy.
	Or		*Or*		
INH RMP PZA‡ EMB‡ (or STM)	Daily for 2 wk, then 2–3 times/wk for 6 wk	INH RMP	2–3 times/wk for 4 mo (18 wk)	If appropriate, patients should be assessed every 3 mo to evaluate the decision to initiate antiretroviral therapy.	
	Or		*Or*	A 2-week "P-450 induction washout" period may be necessary between the last dose of RMP and the first dose of protease inhibitors or NNRTIs.	
INH RMP PZA EMB (or STM)	3 times/wk for 2 mo (8 wk)	INH RMP PZA EMB (or STM)	3 times/wk for 4 mo (18 wk)		

*Duration should be prolonged if the response to therapy is delayed. Criteria for delayed response should be assessed after 2 mo and include (1) lack of culture conversion to negative or (2) lack or resolution of signs or symptoms of tuberculosis.
†Continue PZA and EMB for the total induction phase (8 wk).
‡Continue PZA for the total induction phase (8 wk). EMB can be stopped after test results indicate *M. tuberculosis* susceptibility to INH and RMP.
Abbreviations: EMB, Ethambutol; HIV, human immunodeficiency virus; INH, isoniazid; NNRTI, non-nucleoside reverse transcriptase inhibitor; NRTI, nucleoside reverse transcriptase inhibitor; PZA, pyrazinamide; RFB, rifabutin; RMP, rifampin; STM, streptomycin.
From Anonymous. Prevention and treatment of tuberculosis among patients infected with human immunodeficiency virus: Principles of therapy and revised recommendations. MMWR Morb Mortal Wkly Rep. 1998;47:1–58.

highly active antiretroviral therapy. HIV-infected patients with tuberculosis who were born in the United States who have not previously been treated for tuberculosis have an incidence of INH resistance of 11.3% and RMP resistance of 8.9%, both figures being nearly double the incidence in the HIV-negative population.[132] A paradoxical worsening of the signs and symptoms of tuberculosis may occur when patients are treated effectively for their tuberculosis and are begun on effective antiretroviral therapy. High fever, swollen lymph glands, and increased pulmonary infiltrates may appear. The patients usually do not appear toxic despite the new symptoms. In the absence of bacteriologic signs of failure, treatment should not be modified.

If the patient does not require a protease inhibitor or non-nucleoside reverse transcriptase inhibitor, RMP and INH-containing regimens are very effective in patients with susceptible strains.[133] However, a study from the Democratic Republic of Congo reported an increased relapse rate after "standard" (although admittedly less effective) therapy with INH, thiacetazone, and STM, contrasted with similarly treated HIV-negative patients.[134] Patients with AIDS who relapsed after treatment with organisms remaining sensitive to the prescribed drugs have also been reported. It is important to follow response to treatment carefully and prolong therapy if the response is slow or suboptimal.[123] Treatment should be continued for at least 6 months beyond sputum culture conversion. Patients with HIV-related enteropathy may not respond to chemotherapy because of inadequate absorption of oral agents, and in rare cases pharmacokinetic monitoring may be necessary.[135] The optimal regimen for MDR tuberculosis in AIDS patients is uncertain. One group has reported that fever beyond 7 to 14 days of antituberculous therapy in an HIV-positive patient suggests drug resistance and the need to add at least two drugs.[136]

Other Special Treatment Circumstances

Childhood. Pulmonary tuberculosis in childhood should be treated with INH (10 mg/kg, up to 300 mg daily) and RMP (15 mg/kg, up to 600 mg daily) for 1 year. STM (20 mg/kg) or EMB (15 mg/kg) may be added if extensive disease is present, but the inability to monitor visual acuity limits the use of EMB in very young children.[124] PZA is recommended in tuberculous meningitis.

Pregnancy. Treatment should not be deferred during pregnancy. For drug-sensitive tuberculosis, INH plus EMB is the regimen of choice. RMP is also safe and may be used in advanced disease or when a 9-month regimen is desirable. STM should not be used during pregnancy because of eighth nerve toxicity in the fetus. Although PZA is routinely recommended by international organizations, use in the United States has not been recommended because of inadequate teratogenicity data.[124] Since INH chemoprophylaxis may be associated with a very slightly increased risk of fatal maternal hepatitis, added caution with respect to INH-induced hepatotoxicity is indicated.

Uremia and End-Stage Renal Disease. Dosages of INH and RMP need not be adjusted for renal failure but should be administered after dialysis, and pyridoxine supplementation should be routine. In anephric patients, EMB should be used at 8 to 10 mg/kg. PZA should probably be used at 15 to 20 mg/kg. STM should be used only in very unusual circumstances, and its blood level closely monitored. Biochemical monitoring of hepatotoxicity during renal failure may be complicated by abnormally low transaminase levels in uremia.

Liver Disease. The selection and dosage of antituberculous agents do not need to be modified in most patients with alcoholism or liver disease, although an 18- to 24-month course of INH and EMB with or without STM may be preferred for patients with severe liver disease and drug-sensitive infections (see "Regimens Based on Isoniazid and Ethambutol"). Preexisting liver disease may complicate the detection of drug-related hepatotoxicity; accordingly, clinical and biochemical supervision should be assiduous.

Patients Receiving Immunosuppressive Drugs. Tuberculosis that develops during immunosuppressive treatment of another disease should be treated with the same regimens used to treat immunocompetent hosts. Immunosuppressive therapy need not be discontinued.

Chemoprophylaxis

Soon after INH became available, it became widely used in the United States to treat not only persons with active disease or recent infection but also persons who have had positive tuberculin test results. This enthusiasm has never been shared in most of Europe.[77] Arguments for and against chemoprophylaxis hinge on estimates of relative risks of tuberculosis and INH-induced hepatotoxicity. Those who support a more conservative approach argue that analyses favoring chemoprophylaxis have lumped together disparate patient populations with different risks for both disease and toxicity.[137] The value of chemoprophylaxis in recent tuberculin converters, especially when young, is well established. There is less agreement, however, concerning positive tuberculin tests of unknown duration. As discussed earlier, long-term tuberculin positivity results either from reexposures to *M. tuberculosis* or, more commonly in the United States, from low-grade or intermittent activity of a chronic focus of tuberculosis. Because INH is effective principally against rapidly metabolizing bacilli, it is unclear whether it is the best prophylactic regimen for old infection, or whether multiple drugs including some with "sterilizing" activity might be preferred.[138] However, pending definitive studies, INH remains the chemoprophylactic agent of choice. Recommendations from the CDC are summarized in Table 240–9.[77]

It deserves emphasis that for nonimmunocompromised health care workers, the appropriate cutoff for tuberculin reactivity after exposure has been debated. In contrast to CDC recommendations, Stead argued from personal experience that in this situation new tuberculous infection warranting preventive therapy is almost always associated with induration of at least 15 mm to 5-TU of PPD at 8 weeks after exposure and that the risk of INH hepatotoxicity outweighs the benefit for most lesser reactions (see "Treatment of Contacts of Active Cases" and Fig. 240–7).[78]

Drug Regimens. One year of INH, 300 mg daily, has long been recommended for chemoprophylaxis. However, 6 months of INH may provide a more favorable benefit:risk ratio in most cases. Twelve months are recommended in HIV-infected persons.[124] When necessary, supervised intermittent chemoprophylaxis with INH, 900 mg twice weekly, can be used. Pyridoxine supplementation, 10 to 25 mg daily, is recommended for persons older than 65 years of age; pregnant women; persons with diabetes mellitus, chronic renal failure, or alcoholism; persons undergoing treatment with anticonvulsants; and persons who are malnourished.

Optimal chemoprophylaxis when drug resistance is likely is not known. In at least one instance in which the source case was INH-resistant, RMP chemoprophylaxis failed, with RMP-resistant tuberculosis developing in the recipient.[139] When the likelihood of drug resistance is substantial, there is much to recommend treating as if drug-resistant active infection were present, using a 6-month regimen (INH/RMP/STM/PZA or INH/RMP/EMB/PZA for 2 months and INH/RMP for 4 months).

Risk of Isoniazid Hepatotoxicity during Chemoprophylaxis. A Public Health Service survey found the incidence of probable hepatitis per 1000 persons to be 0 for those younger than age 20, 3 for ages 20 to 34, 12 for ages 35 to 49, 23 for ages 50 to 64, and 8 for age older than 64.[115] The incidence in daily drinkers of alcohol was also

TABLE 240–9 Criteria for Prescribing Preventive Therapy for Persons with Positive Tuberculin Reactions, by Category and Age Group

Category	Age Group: *Less than 35 Yr*	Age Group: *35 Yr and Older*
With risk factor*	Treat at all ages if reaction to 5 TU (PPD) ≥10 mm (or ≥5 mm and patient is recent contact, HIV infected, or has roentgenographic evidence of old TB)	
No risk factor, high-incidence group†	Treat if PPD ≥10 mm	Do not treat
No risk factor, low-incidence group	Treat if PPD ≥15 mm‡	Do not treat

*Risk factors: HIV infection, known recent exposure, recent skin test conversion, abnormal chest roentgenogram, intravenous drug abuse, certain medical risk factors.
†High-incidence groups: immigrants from high-incidence areas, medically underserved populations, residents of long-term care facilities.
‡Lower or higher cutoff points may be used, depending on the prevalence of *M. tuberculosis* infection and nonspecific cross-reactivity in the population.
Abbreviations: HIV, Human immunodeficiency virus; PPD, purified protein derivative; TB, tuberculosis; TU, tuberculin unit.
From Centers for Disease Control and Prevention. The use of preventive therapy for tuberculous infection in the United States: Recommendations of the Advisory Committee for the Elimination of Tuberculosis. MMWR Morb Mortal Wkly Rep. 1990;39:9–12.

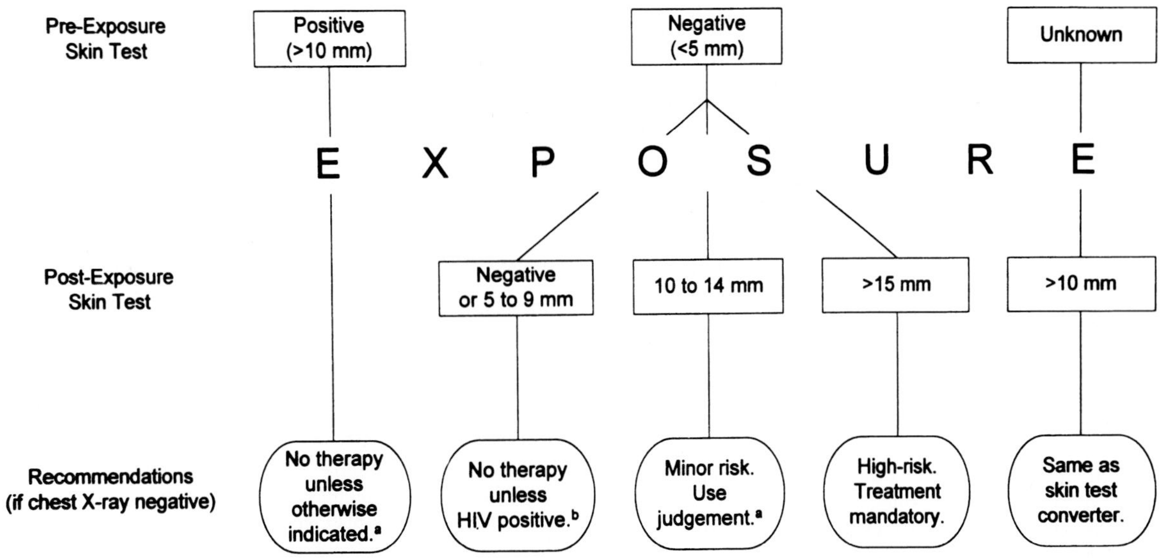

FIGURE 240–7. Proposed strategy for managing health care workers following inadvertent exposure to an active case of tuberculosis.
[a]For persons younger than 35 years, preventive therapy should be considered regardless of exposure.
[b]If the person has been very heavily exposed isoniazid should be started. This can be discontinued if the skin test result is still negative. (From Stead WW. Management of health care workers after inadvertent exposure to tuberculosis: A guide for the use of preventive therapy. Ann Intern Med. 1995;122:906–912.)

high (26.5/1000). The number in the elderly was probably falsely low because of a small sample size. A much larger experience recorded hepatitis in 4.6% of patients older than 65.[140] A large European study reported a hepatitis incidence of 520/100,000; the figure was 280/100,000 for those younger than 35 years, and 770/100,000 for those older than 54 years.[141] Most hepatitis develops within the first 3 months, and the risk of death, once clinical hepatitis develops, is approximately 9%.[115] Biochemical monitoring will likely prevent some deaths, because there is a subclinical phase of at least several weeks. Byrd and colleagues recorded elevated serum transaminase levels in 18.3% of patients taking INH but no deaths in a biochemically monitored population. Many patients with severe biochemical hepatitis would not have been detected by monitoring symptoms only.[142]

Snider and Caras analyzed 177 cases of fatal hepatitis from various sources,[143] and estimated a case rate of 14/100,000 of those starting, and 23/100,000 of those completing therapy. Sixty-nine percent were female, and clustering around pregnancy suggested that chemoprophylaxis should be avoided at this time. Although INH toxicity has been regarded as very rare in young persons, 9% of fatalities were in persons younger than age 20. Israel and coworkers reported three cases of rapidly fatal hepatitis occurring 3 to 6 months into therapy given for indications that in retrospect were questionable.[137]

Assumptions underlying the usual recommendations for chemoprophylaxis often group together populations with widely disparate likelihoods of acquiring active tuberculosis. Although the benefits of chemoprophylaxis in many circumstances are well established, these fatalities, together with the fact that INH is given five times more frequently for chemoprophylaxis than for treatment in the United States, indicate that the decision to prescribe chemoprophylaxis is not trivial.[137]

Treatment of Contacts of Active Cases. The U.S. Public Health Service contact study showed that chemoprophylaxis decreased the incidence of subsequent tuberculosis among contacts of active cases from 1550 to 610 cases/100,000, a 61% reduction over 10 years.[144] In those who were tuberculin-negative when first surveyed, the figures (per 100,000) were 510 without and 150 with chemoprophylaxis, a 59% reduction. Estimates of the risk to contacts in some smaller studies are much higher. One year of INH therapy is only 60 to 80% effective in preventing disease, with failures most often due to nonadherence. INH prophylaxis may also fail in drug-resistant infections. It seems unlikely that prophylactic INH monotherapy taken reliably by contacts results in subsequent INH resistance.

Chemoprophylaxis is indicated for most persons later found to be tuberculin-positive after contact with an active case. The advantage is clearest in the young, in whom the risk of INH toxicity is least and the likelihood of recent infection greatest. Tuberculin-positive young adults who are close contacts of active cases should also be treated, but in persons older than 50 years of age, it is reasonable to observe rather than treat in view of the greater risk of INH toxicity and the greater possibility that tuberculin reactions represent remote infections. The case for treating tuberculin-negative contacts of active cases is less secure. Most authorities would advise treatment in those younger than age 5, with repeated tuberculin testing after 3 months. If skin test conversion occurs, a 12-month course can be completed. If the skin test result is negative and the source case is no longer infectious, INH can be discontinued. In older tuberculin-negative contacts, the skin test should be repeated in 2 to 3 months and treatment given only if the test result becomes positive.

To address the risk to health care workers inadvertently exposed to tuberculosis, Stead reviewed 33 previously investigated hospital and nursing home outbreaks.[78] In this setting, on discovering that exposures have occurred, a list of all exposed personnel and their skin test results before exposure should be assembled. Nonreactors should be retested 8 weeks after the exposure to allow time for skin test conversion. However, if exposure is particularly heavy, or in HIV-positive health care workers, preventive therapy should be started even before retesting. Chemoprophylaxis can later be discontinued in HIV-negative persons if they remain tuberculin-negative. Based on extensive experience, Stead favored a tuberculin conversion of greater than or equal to 15 mm, rather than greater than or equal to 10 mm as recommended by the CDC,[77] as a definite indication for preventive therapy after exposure. General guidelines for managing health care workers inadvertently exposed to tuberculosis are presented in Figure 240–7 (see "Chemoprophylaxis").[78]

Treatment of Quiescent, Previously Untreated Pulmonary Tuberculosis. Tuberculin-positive patients with fibrotic upper lobe lesions and patients who had active tuberculosis before drugs were available relapse sufficiently frequently that a year of INH prophylaxis is advised. Representative studies demonstrated relapse rates (per 100,000) of 2450 over 5 years in controls compared with 350 with treatment[145]; 1940 over 7 years in controls compared with 560 with treatment[146]; and 1430 over 5 years in controls compared with 360 with treatment.[141] The longer the lesion has been stable, the less is the risk of relapse. In the major European study, the relapse rate in untreated patients (1450 over 5 years) was about 450 in the first year but fell to one third of that by the fifth year, far less than their risk of INH hepatotoxicity.[141] It was concluded that 6 months of INH prophylaxis might be preferred. Conversely, a Canadian study questioned whether INH alone is sufficient if these cases represent low-grade active disease.[145] Of 1017 patients treated for 1 year with INH alone, three relapsed, two with drug-resistant infections, whereas none relapsed when treated with INH and PAS. The declining risk of aquiring active disease over time, and the greater effectiveness of combined drug treatment in the Canadian study, suggest that chemoprophylaxis of presumably quiescent lesions only benefits cases that are low-grade active infections, for which single-drug therapy may not be appropriate. Some have suggested multiple-drug therapy (INH/RMP/STM/PZA or INH/RMP/PZA) for 3 months and then stopping if cultures are negative and the roentgenogram is stable. This has the advantage of being sufficient treatment for sputum- and culture-negative active tuberculosis and includes drugs (RMP and PZA) that kill slowly metabolizing organisms.

Treatment of the Tuberculin Converter. The first 2 years after tuberculin conversion is the period of greatest risk for development of active disease. Most authorities recommend chemoprophylaxis for any person known to have converted within 2 years, regardless of age. Reactions that require boosting to be elicited are not recent conversions and do not require treatment.

Treatment of Positive Tuberculin Reactions of Uncertain Duration. All infections in children may be presumed to be recent. In developed countries, this is also the case in adolescents and young adults (see Fig. 240–2). Based on a calculation of the relative risk of tuberculosis versus hepatitis, the CDC has recommended that tuberculin-positive persons younger than age 35 with no contraindications and no special epidemiologic risks should receive chemoprophylaxis. As indicated in Table 240–9, the size of the reaction meriting treatment in this group has been increased to a 15-mm induration, although others have argued that the upper age limit for chemoprophylaxis in this situation should be as low as 20 years of age.[147]

Chemoprophylaxis in Persons with Human Immunodeficiency Virus Infection. Tuberculin-positive, HIV-positive intravenous drug users acquire active tuberculosis at approximately 8%/year and chemoprophylaxis with INH effectively prevents this.[54] Studies in the same population have also showed that the risk of active tuberculosis developing in HIV-positive persons with cutaneous anergy (to tuberculin and a panel of skin-test antigens) was almost as great.[148] As indicated in Table 240–9, the CDC recommends that a tuberculin reaction of 5 mm be considered an indication for chemoprophylaxis in persons with known or suspected HIV infection. Some have suggested that 2 mm induration may be more appropriate. There is general agreement that, when indicated, INH chemoprophylaxis should be prescribed to HIV-positive persons for 1 year.[124]

Considerable effort has been devoted to determining whether testing for skin test anergy to "control" antigens might be helpful in this situation. The CDC in 1991 recommended that HIV-infected persons who are anergic and members of populations with at least a 10% incidence of tuberculosis should receive chemoprophylaxis.[84] However, anergy testing in this situation offers no practical advantage, and its utility has since been refuted by two studies.[85, 86] Therefore, since 1997 the CDC stopped recommending routine anergy testing for HIV-positive persons at risk for tuberculosis (see "Tuberculin Testing and Human Immunodeficiency Virus Infection").[87]

HIV-infected patients who need chemoprophylaxis but are not receiving protease inhibitors or non-nucleoside reverse transcriptase inhibitors can be given daily therapy with RMP, 600 mg, and PZA, 2.0 g, (adult doses) for 2 months. Efficacy appears comparable to that obtained with 9 months of INH, 300 mg daily.[131, 149] It is possible that rifabutin may be used with pyrazinamide for 2 months provided that the patient is not taking ritonavir, delavirdine, or hard gel saquinavir, but rifabutin toxicity and decreased antiretroviral effect are possible consequences. The advantages of the 2-month regimens are better likelihood of compliance and an overall cost-saving.[149]

Tuberculin-Positive Persons with Additional Risk Factors. Chemoprophylaxis is advised for tuberculin-positive individuals from groups with a known high incidence of tuberculosis, including immigrants from developing countries, intravenous drug users, the homeless, prisoners, and residents of long-term care facilities.[77] An argument has been made for chemoprophylaxis in tuberculin-positive patients after gastrectomy and jejunoileal bypass surgery for obesity. There is a greatly increased incidence of tuberculosis in patients undergoing chronic renal dialysis[39] and in renal transplant patients. The regular occurrence of pyridoxine deficiency in uremia complicates the situation. Preventive therapy has been recommended in tuberculin-positive patients with silicosis, but relapse after preventive therapy has been observed. Chemoprophylaxis has also been recommended for tuberculin-positive patients with myeloproliferative disorders and hematologic malignancies, especially when corticosteroids are given, but with no real documentation of risks or benefits. Prolonged treatment with high doses of corticosteroids undoubtedly predisposes to activation of latent tuberculosis.

The Nursing Home Problem. A major analysis by Stead and colleagues showed that 3.8% of men and 2.3% of women who were tuberculin-positive on admission to nursing homes acquired active disease and that this could be decreased 10-fold with chemoprophylaxis.[140] However, because of the high incidence of INH toxicity and drug intolerance, the authors did not recommend chemoprophylaxis in this group. Chemoprophylaxis was clearly beneficial in patients who tuberculin-convert after admission, with 11.6% of men and 7.6% of women acquiring active disease without chemoprophylaxis but only 0.2% with chemoprophylaxis.

Vaccination

BCG, a live attenuated vaccine derived from a strain of *M. bovis,* is used in young children throughout much of the world. Most evidence indicates that BCG vaccination of children results in a 60 to 80% decrease in the incidence of tuberculosis.[150] Its use is reasonable in high prevalence situations, greater than those that now exist in the United States and most industrialized nations. It should be administered only to tuberculin-negative persons. Although BCG vaccine does not prevent infection, it usually prevents progression to clinical disease, and it is highly effective in preventing disseminated disease in young children. Infants and children in the United States for whom vaccination is recommended include those at unavoidable risk for exposure to tuberculosis, especially MDR tuberculosis, and for whom other methods of control and prevention are not effective.[124] Vaccination may also be reasonable for certain groups residing in high prevalence areas, such as some military and foreign service personnel. The risk of disseminated BCG infection after vaccination in infants born to HIV-positive mothers is small. BCG should not be given to persons known to be infected with HIV. Prior BCG vaccination does not alter guidelines for tuberculin skin test interpretation.

The effect of BCG vaccination on tuberculin reactivity depends on the age at vaccination and interval before skin testing. In a study in Montreal, children vaccinated once with BCG before the age of 1 year had a 7.9% prevalence of positive tuberculin skin tests 10 to 25 years later, comparable to those who never received BCG.[151] Prevalence of positive tuberculin skin tests was 18% among those vaccinated between 1 and 5 years of age and 25.4% among those vaccinated after age 5. Although tuberculin reactivity wanes after infant

BCG vaccination, later skin testing can cause a booster effect, a potential source of confusion.

Intravesicular BCG, used to treat bladder cancer, is a rare cause of miliary granuloma in the liver or lung, psoas abscess, or osteomyelitis.[152–154] This mycobacteriosis responds to treatment with INH and RMP. Developing a more effective vaccine for tuberculosis is a high priority.[155]

EXTRAPULMONARY TUBERCULOSIS

Extrapulmonary tuberculosis can be divided into three groups based on pathogenesis. The first comprises superficial mucosal foci due to the spread of infectious pulmonary secretions via the respiratory and gastrointestinal tracts. Such lesions were once almost inevitable complications of extensive cavitary pulmonary disease but are now rare. The second group comprises foci established by contiguous spread, such as from a subpleural focus into the pleural space. The third group comprises foci established by lymphohematogenous dissemination, either at the time of primary infection or, less commonly, from established chronic pulmonary or extrapulmonary foci. Progression of foci established by lymphohematogenous dissemination implies some degree of compromised immunity.

Acquired Immunodeficiency Syndrome and Extrapulmonary Tuberculosis

Before 1985, cases of pulmonary tuberculosis decreased each year, whereas the number of extrapulmonary cases remained stable at about 4000/year. The percentage of cases due to extrapulmonary disease subsequently increased, largely due to coinfection with HIV, and in 1991, 21% of extrapulmonary cases in the United States were associated with AIDS.[156, 157] Unlike non-AIDS patients, concomitant pulmonary and extrapulmonary disease was very common in AIDS patients with tuberculosis. Cases of HIV-associated pulmonary and extrapulmonary tuberculosis have declined in the United States since 1992.[1] There are certain distinguishing features of AIDS-associated extrapulmonary tuberculosis. The frequency of disseminated disease (more than one focus or progressive hematogenous disease) is high, 38% in one series,[157] and rapidly progressive forms with diffuse pulmonary infiltrates, acute respiratory failure, and disseminated intravascular coagulation have been observed. Tuberculosis pleuritis, when it occurs, is often bilateral and part of a disseminated process. Visceral lymphadenopathy, both mediastinal and abdominal, is frequent, and a contrast-enhanced CT scan showing nodes with central low attenuation suggests the diagnosis. Abscesses of the liver, pancreas, prostate, spleen, chest, abdominal wall, and other soft tissues have also been described.

General Comments on Treatment of Extrapulmonary Tuberculosis

Extrapulmonary foci usually respond to treatment more rapidly than does cavitary pulmonary tuberculosis. Therapy with three-drug regimens (INH, PZA, and RMP) for 6 months, with PZA stopped after 2 months, is advised in most cases caused by drug-sensitive organisms, the exception being children who have miliary tuberculosis, bone and joint involvement, or tuberculous meningitis. In these cases, at least 12 months of therapy is recommended.[124] Extrapulmonary disease at sites that carry special risk to the patient, such as the central nervous system, the spine, and possibly the pericardium, should be treated with maximal chemotherapy. Other foci of drug-sensitive extrapulmonary tuberculosis respond well to INH and RMP for 9 months or INH and EMB for 18 months.

Miliary Tuberculosis

The term *miliary tuberculosis,* first used to describe the resemblance of the pathologic lesions to millet seeds, now describes any progressive disseminated hematogenous tuberculosis. Miliary tuberculosis can be roughly divided into three groups: (1) acute miliary tuberculosis associated with a brisk and histologically typical tissue reaction; (2) cryptic miliary tuberculosis, a more prolonged illness with subtle clinical findings and an attenuated histologic response; and (3) nonreactive tuberculosis characterized by huge numbers of organisms, little organized tissue response, and often, a septic or typhoidal clinical picture.[72]

Usual (Acute) Miliary Tuberculosis. In the prechemotherapy era, miliary tuberculosis occurred either soon after primary infection in children or young adults or as a terminal event in untreated chronic organ tuberculosis. In children, the illness is acute or subacute, with high intermittent fevers, night sweats, and occasional rigors. Pleural effusion, peritonitis, or meningitis occur in as many as two thirds of persons. The illness in young adults is usually more chronic and initially less severe. However, miliary tuberculosis is now more frequently observed in older individuals, often with underlying illnesses or conditions that may confuse diagnosis.

Four large series in the chemotherapy era[158–161] have emphasized the frequency of miliary tuberculosis in minority racial groups, and the importance of underlying conditions such as alcoholism, cirrhosis, neoplasm, pregnancy, rheumatologic disease, and treatment with immunosuppressive agents (Table 240–10). There is usually no prior history of tuberculosis, and the onset is often subtle. Generalized symptoms of fever, anorexia, weakness, and weight loss are nonspecific. Headache, when present, may indicate meningitis; abdominal pain may be due to peritonitis; and pleural pain may result from pleuritis. Physical findings are likewise usually nonspecific, but a careful search for cutaneous eruptions, sinus tracts, scrotal masses, and lymphadenopathy may yield a prompt biopsy diagnosis. A miliary infiltrate on chest roentgenogram is the most helpful finding and the usual reason miliary tuberculosis is suspected (Fig. 240–8). Unfortunately, many patients, particularly the elderly, succumb to miliary tuberculosis before the chest roentgenogram becomes abnormal.[162] The white blood cell count is usually normal, and anemia is the rule. Hyponatremia with the laboratory features of inappropriate

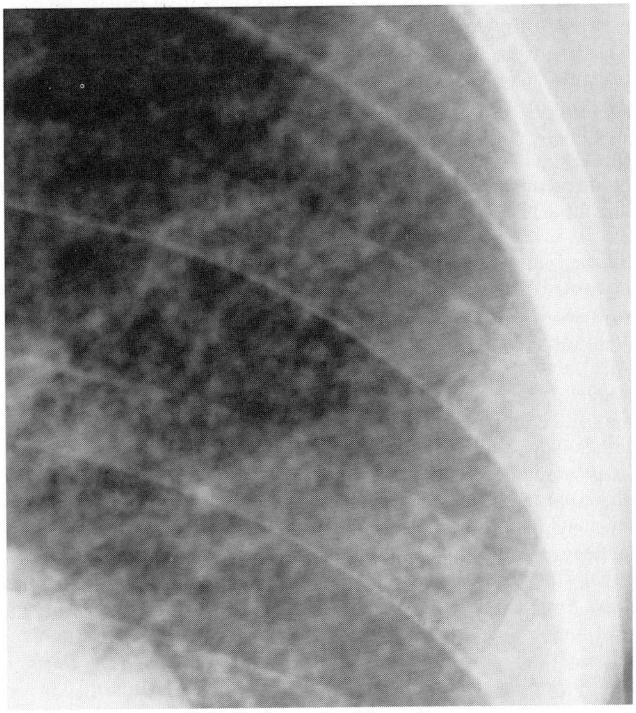

FIGURE 240–8. Detail of a chest roentgenogram (left midlung zone) showing countless 0.5 to 1.0 mm nodules typical of miliary tuberculosis.

TABLE 240-10 Miliary Tuberculosis

	Reference			
	158	159	160	161
Number of cases	69	68	109	38%*
Mean age	51	50	—	60%*
Minority race	85%	87%	94%	79%*
Predisposing factors	15%	31%	42%	66%*
Weeks of symptoms	2–16	3–24	1–52	—
Meningitis	17%	19%	22%	—
Tuberculin positive	61%	84%	43%	28%*
Miliary roentgenogram	93%	97%	—	91%*
Other foci of tuberculosis	32%	23%	—	—
Positive sputum smear	—	39%	33% (21/64)	36% (12/33)
Marrow diagnostic†	—	20%	41% (9/22)	9% (2/22)
Transbronchial biopsy diagnostic‡	—	—	76% (39/51)	62% (5/8)

*This percentage includes interstitial and diffuse alveolar patterns.
†Marrow diagnostic if caseating granuloma or acid-fast bacilli are seen.
‡Transbronchial biopsy diagnostic if any granuloma or acid-fast bacilli are seen.

secretion of antidiuretic hormone is frequent, particularly with meningitis.[159] Addison's disease should be considered as a cause of hyponatremia, especially if corticosteroid treatment is anticipated. Elevations of alkaline phosphatase and transaminases are common, and hypoxemia, hypocapnia, and impairment of pulmonary diffusion capacity can be demonstrated. Cultures of sputum, gastric contents, urine, and cerebrospinal fluid (CSF) are positive in some combination in most cases, but smears of sputum and pulmonary secretions alone are positive in less than one third of cases. Immediate diagnosis often results from examination of tissue (lymph nodes, scrotal masses when present, liver biopsy, or bone marrow specimens). Mycobacterial blood cultures may also be positive. Transbronchial biopsy, however, is the best way to obtain tissue and should be performed promptly when the diagnosis is suspected.[163] The finding of caseating granulomas or acid-fast bacilli is virtually diagnostic, but even noncaseating granulomas should prompt therapy. Rapid diagnosis is mandatory. However, treatment should be initiated immediately based on strong clinical suspicion, as mortality from miliary tuberculosis is most often due to delays in treatment. Therapy with at least INH, RMP, and PZA is advised, especially if meningitis is present. Response may be prompt or may take several weeks. Fulminant miliary tuberculosis may be associated with severe refractory hypoxemia (adult respiratory distress syndrome) and disseminated intravascular coagulation. In such cases, adjunctive corticosteroids (60 to 80 mg of prednisone daily) are indicated. Some also advise corticosteroids in debilitated patients with a poor initial response to therapy.

Cryptic Miliary Tuberculosis and Late Generalized (Chronic Hematogenous) Tuberculosis. Chronic organ tuberculosis is probably always associated with intermittent, nonprogressive seeding of the blood stream. In some individuals, however, especially as age or other factors compromise immunity, this becomes continuous and produces progressive hematogenous tuberculosis long after the primary infection.[164] The term *cryptic miliary tuberculosis* usually describes older patients with miliary tuberculosis in whom the diagnosis is obscure because of normal chest roentgenograms, negative tuberculin test results, and often confounding underlying illnesses to which symptoms are mistakenly attributed[165]; this term has also been applied to miliary tuberculosis diagnosed at autopsy.[162]

The foci responsible for late generalized tuberculosis are often clinically silent, for example, renal, genitourinary, osseous, or visceral lymph nodes.[164] Chronic pulmonary foci are at times involved but are rarely the only source. More than one seeding focus is usually present, suggesting a change in immune status that favors simultaneous reactivation. The clinical picture is frequently fever of unknown origin, often with a normal chest roentgenogram and a negative tuberculin test result. Fever may be absent and in one series, diagnosis was made antemortem in only 15% of cases.[164] Late generalized tuberculosis may be associated with major hematologic abnormalities (see farther on).

Nonreactive Tuberculosis. The histologic appearance in this rare form of disseminated hematogenous tuberculosis shows nonspecific necrosis containing disintegrating polymorphonuclear leukocytes and enormous numbers of tubercle bacilli.[72] In the typical case, granulomas and epithelioid cells are lacking, although intermediate cases have areas more typical for tuberculosis. The gross pathologic findings are soft abscesses from minute to 1 cm, which always involve the liver and spleen, usually the marrow, commonly the lungs and kidneys, but never the meninges. The clinical picture may be overwhelming sepsis, with splenomegaly and often an inconspicuous diffuse mottling on the chest roentgenogram. Major hematologic abnormalities are common (see farther on).

Miliary Tuberculosis and Hematologic Abnormalities. Some patients with late generalized tuberculosis and most with nonreactive tuberculosis have serious hematologic abnormalities, including leukopenia, thrombocytopenia, anemia, leukemoid reactions, myelofibrosis, and polycythemia.[166] Leukemoid reactions may suggest acute leukemia, although most patients in whom hematogenous tuberculosis coexists with the clinical picture of leukemia have both diseases. Disseminated tuberculosis should be considered when pancytopenia is associated with fever and weight loss or as a cause of other obscure hematologic disorders.

Primary Hepatic Tuberculosis. Rarely, miliary tuberculosis may mimic cholangitis with fever, liver function test abnormalities suggestive of obstructive disease, and little evidence of hepatocellular disease. Diagnosis is made by liver biopsy.

Miliary Tuberculosis in Acquired Immunodeficiency Syndrome. In AIDS patients, 10% with tuberculosis and 38% with extrapulmonary tuberculosis have miliary disease.[104, 157] Major constitutional symptoms and hectic fevers are characteristic. The chest roentgenogram is abnormal in 80% and may include typical miliary mottling. Only 10% are tuberculin-positive.[104] The sputum smear is positive in only 25%,[157] but cultures of many materials will be positive, including blood in 50 to 60%. Biopsies during life show typical tuberculous histologic appearance but with more stainable organisms than in non-HIV miliary tuberculosis. In fatal cases, in contrast, the histologic picture is often nonreactive tuberculosis.[104]

Miliary tuberculosis in HIV-infected persons may also cause the acute respiratory distress syndrome or tuberculous papular skin lesions. Smears of respiratory secretions are positive in 80%.

Abscesses of various soft tissue and visceral organs have been described in patients with AIDS and tuberculosis, usually with other evidence of disseminated disease. Locations include the liver, spleen, pancreas, psoas muscle without spinal involvement, mediastinum, neck, chest wall, abdominal wall, and prostate.[104, 157, 167] Diagnosis is usually made by CT or ultrasonography and confirmed by needle or catheter aspiration. Clinical response to chemotherapy and drainage is usually good. An abscess may appear or reappear during therapy and respond to repeated aspiration.

Central Nervous System Tuberculosis

Tuberculous Meningitis. This condition is usually caused by rupture of a subependymal tubercle into the subarachnoid space rather than direct hematogenous seeding. Meningitis complicating miliary disease usually develops several weeks into the illness. In childhood, meningitis is an early postprimary event, and three fourths of these persons have a concurrently active primary complex, pleural effusion, or miliary tuberculosis. Subependymal foci may remain quiescent indefinitely before rupturing. This may follow head trauma or be associated with general depression of host immunity as a result of alcoholism or other factors.

Pathologic Features. Meningeal involvement is most pronounced at the base of the brain. In long-standing cases, a gelatinous mass may extend from the pons to the optic nerves, being most prominent adjacent to the optic chiasm. In more chronic cases, fibrous tissue may encase cranial nerves. Vasculitis of local arteries and veins may lead to aneurysm, thrombosis, and focal hemorrhagic infarction. Perforating vessels to the basal ganglia and pons are most often involved, producing movement disorders or lacunar infarcts; involvement of branches of the middle cerebral artery may cause hemiparesis.

Clinical Findings. The usual illness begins with a prodrome of malaise, intermittent headache, and low-grade fever, followed within 2 to 3 weeks by protracted headache, vomiting, confusion, meningismus, and focal neurologic signs. The clinical spectrum is broad, ranging from chronic headache or subtle mental status changes to sudden, severe meningitis progressing to coma. Fever may be absent, and the peripheral white blood cell count is usually normal. Mild anemia is usual, and hyponatremia due to inappropriate antidiuretic hormone secretion is common. Evidence of concomitant extrameningeal tuberculosis is present in roughly three fourths of cases,[168] with miliary shadowing on the chest roentgenogram being most suggestive. In many cases, however, there is no clinical or historical clues to suggest tuberculosis.

The cornerstone of diagnosis is examination of the CSF. The cell count generally ranges from 0 to 1500/mm^3; the protein is usually moderately elevated; and the CSF glucose, said to be characteristically low, was greater than 45 mg/100 ml in 83% of cases in one large series.[168] A lymphocytic predominance is usual, although one quarter of cases demonstrate a polymorphonuclear pleocytosis, usually early in the course. Identifying bacilli often requires examination of large volumes of fluid from repeated lumbar punctures. In one study, stains of sediment revealed acid-fast bacilli in 37% of cases on initial examination, but 90% when fluids from four large-volume lumbar punctures were examined.[168] Initial atypical findings such as a polymorphonuclear pleocytosis, normal glucose, or even entirely normal CSF indices evolve to more typical mononuclear cell predominance with hypoglycorrhachia over time. PCR for *M. tuberculosis* may be very helpful in this setting, although false-negative results have been reported.[169, 170] In patients with meningitis, CT or magnetic resonance imaging may reveal rounded lesions presumed to be tuberculomas, basilar arachnoiditis, cerebral infarction, and hydrocephalus (Fig. 240–9).

Prognosis is influenced by age, duration of symptoms, and neurologic deficits. Mortality is greatest in patients younger than age 5 (20%), older than age 50 (60%), or in whom illness has been present for more than 2 months (80%).[168] Clinical staging is based on neurologic status: stage 1 = rational, no focal neurologic signs or hydrocephalus; stage 2 = confusion or focal neurologic deficits; stage 3 = stuporous or dense paraplegia or hemiplegia. Patients who are stage 1 at the start of treatment are likely to recover, but approximately half of stage 3 patients die or recover with severe residual neurologic defects.[168] HIV infection does not appear to alter the clinical and laboratory manifestations or the prognosis of tuberculous meningitis, except that central nervous system mass lesions are more likely.[171]

Treatment. In the presence of meningeal inflammation, both INH and PZA reach concentrations in the CSF equaling those in blood. RMP penetrates the blood-brain barrier less well but still adequately. All three drugs should be used. Increased dosage of INH, 10 mg/kg and somewhat higher in children, may be preferred until improvement has been established. Otherwise, the dosages are as for pulmonary tuberculosis.

Most authorities recommend adjunctive corticosteroids in stage 2 and stage 3 patients, beginning prednisone at 60 to 80 mg daily. This may be gradually reduced after 1 to 2 weeks and discontinued by 4 to 6 weeks, as guided by symptoms. Symptoms and CSF abnormalities may rebound transiently as steroids are tapered. Ventricular shunting may be beneficial if symptomatic hydrocephalus supervenes.[141]

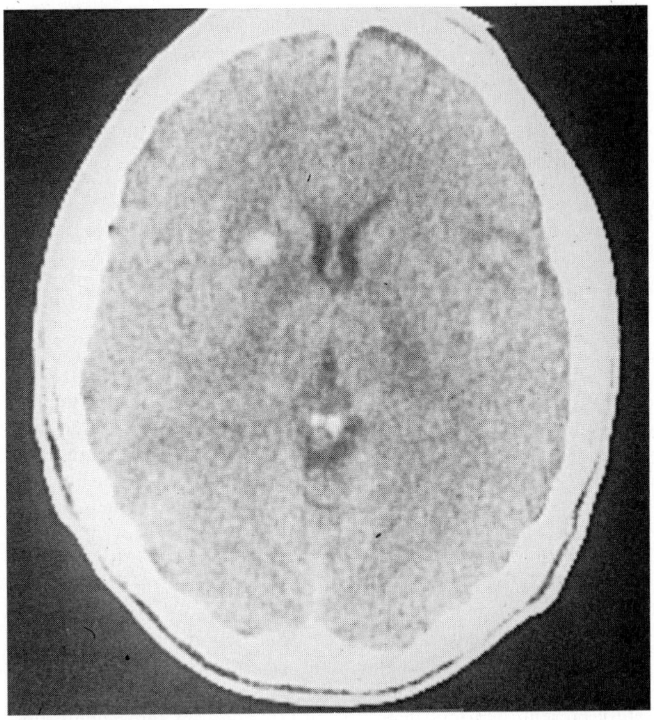

FIGURE 240–9. Multiple cerebral cortical densities on computed tomography of a patient with tuberculous meningitis.

Tuberculomas. Intracranial tuberculomas are space-occupying lesions that may manifest with seizures. They are most frequently multiple but can be single, appearing on imaging studies as avascular masses with surrounding edema. When diagnosis is secure, chemotherapy should be attempted before resorting to surgery. Corticosteroids reduce edema and decrease symptoms, and chemotherapy prevents spread of infection in cases diagnosed at operation. In India, where tuberculomas are frequent, biopsy confirmation followed by medical therapy without resection is the preferred management.

Tuberculous Spinal Meningitis. Infrequently, tuberculosis causes spinal meningitis with or without intracranial involvement. In advanced cases, the cord may be completely encased in a gelatinous exudate. An intramedullary tuberculoma or an extradural granulomatous mass can cause symptoms without meningeal involvement. Nerve root or cord compression causes pain, bladder or rectal sphincter weakness, hypesthesia, anesthesia, paresthesias in the distribution of a nerve root, or paralysis. Subarachnoid block may cause CSF protein concentrations to be extremely high, with or without cells.

Tuberculous Pleurisy (Serofibrinous Pleurisy with Effusion)

Early Postprimary Pleurisy with Effusion. When infection occurs early in life, tuberculous pleurisy with effusion follows the primary infection within weeks or months. The pathogenesis is rupture of a large subpleural component of the primary infection and delivery of infectious, antigenic material into the pleural space, with inflammation and seeding of foci over the visceral and parietal pleura. In the past, this affected mostly adolescents and young adults, and rarely older adults. Immediate prognosis was excellent, with resolution of the effusion within several months in as many as 90% of cases. However, studies of soldiers during World War II (before chemotherapy) demonstrated that 65% relapsed with chronic organ tuberculosis within 5 years.[172] Early postprimary serofibrinous pleurisy with effusion identifies quantitatively large primary infections with a relatively poor long-term prognosis.

Pleurisy with Effusion Complicating Chronic Pulmonary Tuberculosis. In contrast to early studies,[172] an increasing proportion of pleurisy with effusion since the early 1980s occurs in older individuals with chronic pulmonary tuberculosis, often with complicating illnesses such as cirrhosis or congestive heart failure to which the effusion is mistakenly attributed. In one study, one half of pleurisy cases occurred in the setting of established chronic pulmonary tuberculosis.[173]

Pleurisy with Effusion Complicating Miliary Tuberculosis. Pleural effusions occur in 10 to 30% of cases of miliary tuberculosis.[158, 160] These may be associated with other progressive extrapulmonary foci and involvement of other serous membranes. Cases with coexistent pleural (at times bilateral), peritoneal, and pericardial tuberculosis have been referred to as *tuberculous polyserositis.*

Clinical Features and Diagnosis. The clinical presentation may be low grade and subtle or abrupt and severe, easily confused with acute bacterial pneumonia. Cough and pleuritic chest pain are usual, and fever may be high. The effusion is usually less than massive and almost always unilateral except when associated with miliary tuberculosis. The pleural fluid typically contains 500 to 2500 white blood cells/mm^3, with more than 90% lymphocytes in two thirds of cases. However, 38% of cases in one series had predominantly polymorphonuclear leukocytes, and 15% had more than 90% polymorphonuclear leukocytes on the first tap.[174] Repeated taps demonstrate a shift to lymphocytic predominance. Mesothelial cells, characteristic of neoplastic effusions, are sparse or absent, eosinophils are rarely present, and less than 10% of effusions are serosanguineous. The pleural fluid protein usually exceeds 2.5 g/dl; glucose is usually moderately low compared with serum values but rarely less than 20 mg/dl; the pH is almost always 7.3 or lower and may be as low as 7.0. In the usual case of early postprimary pleurisy with effusion, the acid-fast stain of the fluid sediment is seldom positive, the culture is positive in 25 to 30%, pleural needle biopsy yields granulomas in 75%, and culture of a needle biopsy specimen may be positive even in the 25% of cases with nonspecific pleuritis on histologic examination. Cases complicating chronic pulmonary tuberculosis more often have positive pleural acid-fast smears (50%) and positive cultures (60%) but are less likely (25%) to demonstrate granulomas on pleural biopsy. Repeat pleural biopsy may be necessary to establish the diagnosis, and a small open pleural biopsy or pleuroscopy is diagnostic in virtually all cases. Smears of sputum or gastric fluid are rarely positive in early postprimary cases, and cultures are positive in 25 to 33%. In contrast, sputum smear is positive in 50% and the culture is positive in 60% of "reactivation" cases.[173] Tuberculosis is often not considered as the cause of a pleural effusion in an older person with complicating illnesses such as cirrhosis or congestive heart failure.[174] When pleural effusion complicates miliary tuberculosis, findings associated with the latter condition usually dominate the clinical picture. Elevated levels of adenosine deaminase in pleural fluid may be highly specific for tuberculosis, although this assay is not routinely available in the United States.

Treatment. Early postprimary pleural effusions spontaneously resolve in 2 to 4 months. Chemotherapy does not hasten resolution but prevents active disease elsewhere in the body, which will otherwise occur in two thirds of cases. Therapy is as described for pulmonary tuberculosis. Multiple thoracenteses are not necessary once the diagnosis is established and treatment initiated. A small minority heal with pleural fibrosis. Corticosteroid therapy hastens symptomatic improvement and fluid resorption, but no long-term benefit has been shown.

Tuberculous Empyema and Bronchopleural Fistula

Tuberculous empyema occurs when a major cavity ruptures into the pleural space. This often catastrophic illness is usually associated with bronchopleural fistula formation and frank pus. Before antituberculous drugs were available, tuberculous empyema was almost always rapidly fatal. It virtually never occurs in patients being treated with chemotherapy.

Late Complications of Collapse Therapy

Before the advent of potent antituberculous drugs, cavitary pulmonary tuberculosis was treated by collapse of the affected lung. Repeated instillation of air into the pleural space sometimes led to chronic, often calcified pleural shadows that could increase in size and cause pain, bronchopleural fistulas, and empyemas (both tuberculous and nontuberculous) many years later. CT may reveal collections of fluid under a thickened, calcified pleura. The response to prolonged antibiotic therapy, both antituberculous and routine, should be assessed before undertaking surgery in such cases. A conservative approach may be successful in almost half of cases, an important observation considering the technical difficulty of surgery.

Tuberculous Pericarditis

Tuberculous pericarditis is most often caused by extension from a contiguous focus of infection, usually mediastinal or hilar nodes, but also the lung, spine, or sternum. Less commonly, it occurs during miliary tuberculosis. It may develop during the course of otherwise effective drug therapy, probably because the response of caseous lymph nodes to chemotherapy is not always predictable. Tuberculous pericarditis in patients with AIDS is uncommon in the United States, but in a series from Africa, 32 of 37 cases of effusive pericarditis were tuberculous, and 30 were in HIV-positive patients.[175]

Clinical Features and Diagnosis. The onset may be abrupt, resembling acute idiopathic pericarditis or insidious, resembling congestive heart failure. Symptoms of infection or cardiovascular compromise may be present. Individual cases may present with chronic constrictive pericarditis and may be mistaken for cirrhosis with ascites. As many as 39% also have a pleural effusion, providing a convenient source for diagnostic fluid and tissue.[176, 177] Echocardiography demonstrates effusion when present and may reveal multiple loculations suggestive of tuberculosis.

Pericarditis with effusion is usually quickly diagnosed based on physical findings and radiologic examination, but establishing that it is tuberculous in nature is often difficult. The tuberculin test result may be negative and evidence of extrapericardial tuberculosis lacking. In areas of high endemicity, a presumptive diagnosis is often correctly made.[176, 177] In the United States, however, many cases are initially misdiagnosed as idiopathic, uremic, or rheumatoid pericarditis.[178]

Pericardiocentesis (ideally performed in a cardiac catheterization laboratory) is indicated for hemodynamic compromise. However, because pericardiocentesis carries risk, and because 90% of acute pericarditis in the United States is idiopathic (presumed viral) and subsides spontaneously in 2 to 3 weeks, some authorities advise against early pericardiocentesis. If improvement has not occurred by that time, a subxyphoid pericardial window can be performed. This provides both fluid and tissue for diagnosis, although in some cases the biopsy demonstrates only nonspecific inflammation.[176, 177] Tuberculous pericardial fluid demonstrates many of the characteristics of tuberculous pleural fluid, with acid-fast smears being rarely positive and cultures being positive in approximately 50% of cases. The usefulness of adenosine deaminase determinations on pericardial fluid is not certain, but PCR for *M. tuberculosis* may be useful.

Treatment. Antibiotic treatment is the same as for pulmonary tuberculosis. In a large study from South Africa, treatment with corticosteroids (60 mg/day for 4 weeks, 30 mg/day for 4 weeks, and 15 mg/day for 2 weeks) decreased mortality from 11% in controls to 4% in treated cases. Pericardiectomies were also less frequently necessary in patients given corticosteroids (30% in controls versus 11% in steroid-treated patients). Surgical drainage via a subxyphoid pericardial window at the outset did not decrease either mortality or the eventual need for pericardiectomy, although it provided diagnostic tissue and obviated the need for recurrent pericardiocenteses. However, 2% surgical mortality was associated with the procedure.[176]

When hemodynamic compromise persists for 6 to 8 weeks, pericardiectomy is usually indicated, and this should probably be performed earlier rather than later. Approximately two thirds of patients, however, do well without surgery.

Skeletal Tuberculosis

Pott's Disease (Tuberculous Spondylitis). One third of cases of skeletal tuberculosis involve the spine, as a result of past hematogenous foci, contiguous disease, or lymphatic spread from pleural disease. The earliest focus is the anterior superior or inferior angle of the vertebral body. This usually spreads to the intervertebral disk and adjacent vertebra, producing the classic roentgenographic picture of anterior wedging of two adjacent vertebral bodies with destruction of the intervening disk and the physical finding of a tender spine prominence or gibbus. The lower thoracic spine is involved most frequently, the lumbar next, and the cervical and sacral least (Fig. 240–10).

In endemic countries, Pott's disease usually occurs in older children and young adults, but in developed countries it has become a disease of older persons.[179] Evidence of other foci of tuberculosis and systemic symptoms are often absent, early complaints may be simply back pain or stiffness with an initially normal roentgenogram, and diagnosis may be delayed until signs of advanced disease such as paralysis, deformity, or sinus formation develop. Bacilli are sparse, and smear and culture of pus or tissue are positive in only one half of cases. Histologic studies reveal granulomas with or without caseation in three fourths of cases.

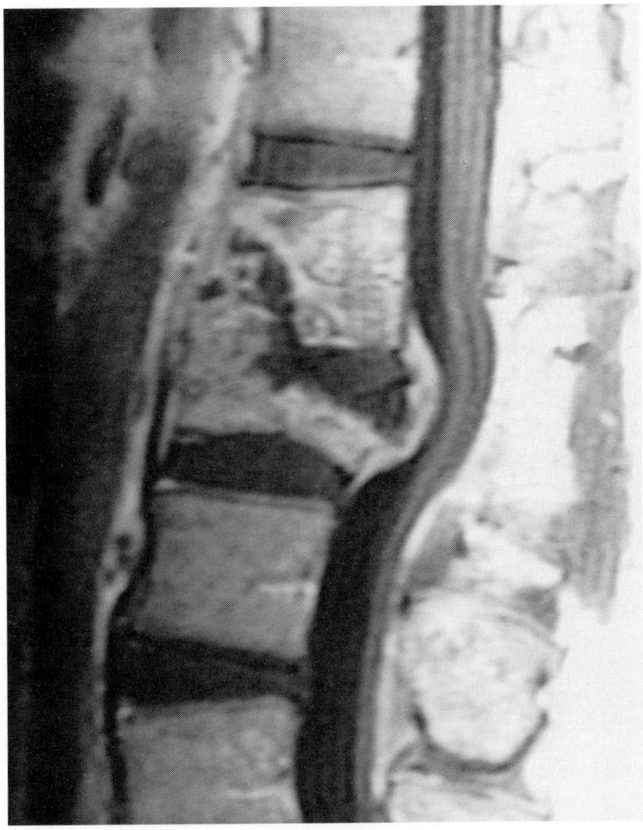

FIGURE 240–10. Magnetic resonance imaging study showing extensive destruction of L1 and L2 vertebral bodies and the intervening disk with posterior extension in a Pakistani man with Pott's disease.

Abscess and Sinus Formation. Paraspinal cold abscesses develop in 50% or more, in some appearing after treatment has been initiated, and in some cases visible only by CT or magnetic resonance imaging. The pus, confined by tight ligamentous investments, can dissect along tissue planes for long distances to present as a mass or a draining sinus in the supraclavicular space, above the posterior iliac crest in the Petit triangle, the groin, the buttock, or even the popliteal fossa. Perforation into the bowel producing a gas-filled psoas abscess has been reported. The abscess can spread infection to distant vertebral bodies, sometimes without affecting the intervening vertebrae.

Pott's Paraplegia. In approximately half of cases, weakness or paralysis of the lower extremities is present or develops after treatment has begun. Some authorities believe this is due to arachnoiditis and vasculitis.[179] Less frequently, it will be due to compression of the cord by an inflammatory mass or rarely pressure in the abscess producing ischemic changes in the subjacent cord. Inflammatory thrombosis of the anterior spinal artery can occur, and sudden cord compression may result from marked spinal instability.

Treatment. In adults, recommended antimicrobial therapy is as described for pulmonary disease. In infants and children, treatment for at least 12 months may be warranted.[124] Major studies from Africa demonstrated a favorable response in 90% of cases without neurologic involvement treated with chemotherapy, modified bed rest until pain abated, and early ambulation, without orthopedic surgery.[180] Even with paraplegia, 40% of this young population did well with conservative management. In another series of older patients, 3 of 26 were treated with laminectomy, 2 without improvement, 12 of 15 cases with abscess required single or multiple needle aspirations, and 3 were drained surgically because of progression on therapy.[179] The authors emphasized that laminectomy should not be undertaken without demonstration of anatomic cord compression and suggested steroid therapy for paraplegia due to arachnoiditis. Advanced neurologic defects and severe instability of the spine may require more aggressive surgery.

Peripheral Osteoarticular Tuberculosis. Older reports described peripheral tuberculous arthritis as a chronic, slowly progressive monoarthritis in 90% of cases,[181] often without systemic symptoms or extraskeletal tuberculosis, and most frequently in the hip or knee. A history of trauma was common, followed weeks or months later by indolent progressive inflammation. More recent reports suggest a shift to an older population with a different clinical picture, including more systemic symptoms, multiple joint involvement, and periarticular abscess formation.[182] In one series, most patients older than 60 years had shoulder involvement.[183] Tenosynovitis of the hand, arthritis of the wrist, and carpal tunnel syndrome can be caused by tuberculosis. Clinical confusion occurs when tuberculosis superinfects joints previously involved with gouty or other arthritides.

The earliest manifestation of tuberculous arthritis is pain, which may precede signs of inflammation and roentgenographic changes by weeks or months. Roentgenograms initially may show soft tissue swelling but later demonstrate osteopenia, periarticular bony destruction, periosteal thickening, and eventually destruction of cartilage and bone. Cold abscesses and draining sinuses often develop in chronic cases.

In the absence of coexistent extra-articular tuberculosis, diagnosis almost always requires biopsy. Histologic features compatible with tuberculosis warrants chemotherapy, although other chronic infections (fungi, nontuberculous mycobacteria) can cause identical clinical and histologic pictures. For early cases, prolonged chemotherapy results in complete resolution. Surgery is necessary only when serious joint instability requires fusion, and then only after chemotherapy has failed.

Tuberculous osteomyelitis can affect any bone, including the ribs, skull, phalanx, pelvis, and long bones.[184] Other causes of osteomyelitis of the rib are rare, and tuberculosis is the most common infectious cause of single or multiple osteomyelitic rib lesions. Tuberculous osteomyelitis outside the vertebral body presents as a cold abscess, with swelling and only modest erythema or pain.

Genitourinary Tuberculosis

Renal Tuberculosis. Asymptomatic renal cortical foci may occur during all forms of tuberculosis. An autopsy study of pulmonary tuberculosis revealed unsuspected renal foci in 73% of cases, usually bilateral; 25% of miliary cases have positive urine cultures.[185] Cortical foci tend to be stable unless they penetrate to the medulla, where local factors favor accelerated infection. Most patients have evidence of concomitant extragenitourinary disease, usually pulmonary and most frequently inactive. In normal hosts, the interval between infection and active renal disease is usually years and sometimes decades. Local symptoms predominate, and advanced tissue destruction may occur long before the diagnosis is made. This is mostly a disease of middle-aged adults.

The clinical features in two large series of cases are presented in Table 240–11.[186, 187] Although sterile pyuria is typical of renal tuberculosis, positive cultures for routine bacterial pathogens may lead to misdiagnosis, sometimes for years. The intravenous pyelogram is usually abnormal. Early findings are nonspecific, but later changes may be more suggestive, including papillary necrosis, ureteral strictures, "pipe stem" changes, "corkscrewing," "beading," hydronephrosis, gross parenchymal cavitation, and autonephrectomy. Focal calcification is particularly suggestive. The clinical disease is usually unilateral, although microscopic changes are probably always bilateral. Culture of three morning urine specimens for mycobacteria establishes the diagnosis in 80 to 90% of cases. When a renal abnormality is present but urine cultures are negative, cytologic studies and culture of material obtained by fine-needle biopsy may be diagnostic.

Chemotherapy with drug regimens containing INH and RMP as for pulmonary tuberculosis are recommended. Ureteral cicatrization and obstruction may occur during healing, and the urologic literature recommends frequent pyelograms during therapy, corticosteroid therapy if obstruction develops, and ureteral reimplantation if the obstruction does not resolve.[188] However, obstruction did not develop among 102 treated cases reported by Christensen.[187] Surgery has rarely been required in most recent series.

Hypertension is not a feature of renal tuberculosis, and renal function is usually preserved. However, a rare condition called *tuberculous interstitial nephritis* may cause renal failure.[189] It is characterized by interstitial granulomas and normal-sized kidneys, usually in the presence of active extrarenal tuberculosis. Acid-fast bacilli have been seen but not cultured from renal biopsy specimens, and renal dysfunction responds to corticosteroid therapy but not antituberculous chemotherapy alone. It is unclear that tuberculous interstitial nephritis is actually caused by tuberculous infection.

TABLE 240–11 Clinical Features of Genitourinary Tuberculosis in Two Series of Patients

Clinical Features	Reference 186	187
Number of patients	102	78
Primarily genitourinary symptoms	61%	71%
Back and flank pain	27%	10%
Dysuria, frequency	31%	34%
Constitutional symptoms	33%	14%
Abnormal urine, no symptoms	5%	20%
Abnormal urine analysis	66%	93%
Abnormal intravenous pyelogram	68%	93%
Tuberculin-positive	88%	95%
Abnormal chest roentgenogram	75%	66%
Active pulmonary tuberculosis	38%	7%
Other old or active extrapulmonary disease	5%	20%
Urine culture positive	80%	90%
For tuberculosis		
For routine pathogens	45%	12%
Epididymitis, orchitis	19%	17%
Chronic prostatitis	6%	6%

Male Genital Tuberculosis. Eighty percent of male genital tuberculosis is associated with coexistent renal disease, and most advanced renal tuberculosis is associated with some male genital focus.[190] Spread of infection from renal foci involves the prostate, seminal vesicles, epididymis, and testis in that order. The usual clinical finding is a scrotal mass that may be tender or associated with a draining sinus. Oligospermia is common and may not improve with treatment. Stones may form with treatment of prostatic tuberculosis. Genital foci not associated with renal disease can be established by lymphohematogenous spread and usually present as a painful testicular or scrotal mass. Diagnosis may be suggested by the presence of epididymal or prostatic calcification, although the latter also occurs with nontuberculous chronic prostatitis. The diagnosis is usually established by surgery, and response to chemotherapy is excellent.

Genitourinary Tuberculosis in Acquired Immunodeficiency Syndrome. In a study of 79 HIV-positive patients with tuberculosis, 77% had positive urine cultures, usually as an incidental finding. Only two had male genital involvement, none had symptoms of renal disease, and in only 4% was the genitourinary tract the only apparent site of tuberculosis.[157]

Female Genital Tuberculosis. Female genital tuberculosis begins with a hematogenous focus in the endosalpinx, from which it may spread to the endometrium (50%), ovaries (30%), cervix (10%), and vagina (1%).[191] In the cervix, a granulomatous ulcerating mass may resemble carcinoma. Common complaints are infertility or local symptoms consisting of menstrual disorders and abdominal pain. The clinical picture may suggest pelvic inflammatory disease that is unresponsive to therapy. Systemic symptoms are uncommon, and evidence of old tuberculosis need not be present. Pregnancies that occur in the presence of pelvic tuberculosis are often ectopic. Although cultures of menstrual blood or endometrial scrapings may be positive, the diagnosis is usually made by examination of tissue removed at operation. Response to chemotherapy is excellent, and surgery is needed only for residual large tuboovarian abscesses.

Gastrointestinal Tuberculosis

Before effective chemotherapy was available, 70% of patients with advanced pulmonary disease acquired gastrointestinal tuberculosis from swallowing infectious secretions, and usually developed diarrhea and abdominal pain. Although most cases at present are likely due to swallowed respiratory secretions, roentgenographic evidence of pulmonary tuberculosis is found in fewer than 25% of cases, the diagnosis being discovered unexpectedly by surgery or endoscopy.[192]

Any location from mouth to anus can be involved. Nonhealing ulcers of the tongue or oropharynx and nonhealing sockets after tooth extraction may be due to tuberculosis. Esophageal disease is most frequently caused by an adjacent caseous node, which leads to stricture with obstruction or tracheoesophageal fistula formation, and rarely fatal hematemesis from an aortoesophageal fistula. Stomach involvement may be ulcerative or hyperplastic and may cause gastric outlet obstruction. Isolated duodenal disease can produce symptoms of peptic ulcer or obstruction. Small bowel involvement may lead to perforation, obstruction, enteroenteric and enterocutaneous fistulas, massive hemorrhage, and severe malabsorption. Small bowel lesions are frequently multiple. The ileocecal area is the most typical site of enteric tuberculosis, producing pain, anorexia, diarrhea, obstruction, hemorrhage that may be severe, and often a palpable mass. Clinical, roentgenographic, endoscopic, and even operative findings may suggest carcinoma. A successful diagnosis is usually made by colonoscopy. In a study of 50 cases, ileocecal involvement, with or without involvement of other areas was found in 35 cases; isolated segmental colonic disease was found in 13 cases; and pancolitis was initially misdiagnosed as ulcerative colitis in 2 cases. Evidence of pulmonary tuberculosis was present in only 18 cases.[193] The clinical manifestations of anal tuberculosis are rare and include ulcers, perianal warty growths, and fistulas. The response of gastrointestinal tuberculosis to chemotherapy is excellent. Once the diagnosis is established, surgery should be deferred if possible until the results of chemotherapy have been assessed.

Pancreatic tuberculosis may manifest as an abscess or as a mass involving local nodes and resembling carcinoma. The biliary tract may be obstructed by tuberculous nodes, and tuberculous ascending cholangitis has been described. Tuberculosis is a frequent cause of granulomatous hepatitis. This is usually asymptomatic but may be associated with an elevated alkaline phosphatase level that is out of proportion to bilirubin levels with normal transaminase levels. Very rarely, tuberculous granulomatous hepatitis causes jaundice without evidence of extrahepatic tuberculosis. This is called *primary tuberculosis of the liver. Focal hepatic tuberculosis* describes single or multiple tuberculous abscesses. These appear to occur most frequently in racial groups with little natural immunity to tuberculosis and in children.[194]

Gastrointestinal Tuberculosis in Acquired Immunodeficiency Syndrome. Bowel involvement is not a common feature of extrapulmonary tuberculosis in AIDS patients. One series reported bowel fistulas in less than 4% of such cases,[157] another reported CT evidence of gastrointestinal abnormalities in 4 of 23 cases,[195] and a third study noted positive stool cultures for *M. tuberculosis* in 4 of 10 cases.[196] Tuberculous visceral abscesses, including hepatic, splenic, and pancreatic, may occur in AIDS patients. Pain and fever are usually present. Diagnosis is often made by CT or ultrasonographically guided drainage procedures. Chemotherapy alone has not been effective in all cases.[167]

Tuberculous Peritonitis

Tuberculous peritonitis results either from spread of adjacent tuberculous disease such as an abdominal lymph node, intestinal focus, or fallopian tube, or during miliary tuberculosis. In a summary of 11 series, evidence of associated pleuropulmonary tuberculosis was present in 25 to 83% of cases and the tuberculin test was positive in 30 to 100% of cases.[197] Pleural effusion is the most frequent associated finding, but evidence of tuberculosis in other sites is often present. AIDS patients do not have an increased frequency of peritonitis.[157]

The clinical picture has been divided into *plastic* and *serous* types. The less common plastic type is characterized by tender abdominal masses and a "doughy abdomen." Serous effusions present as ascites with or without signs of peritonitis. Symptoms of fever, abdominal pain, and weight loss are common.[197] The onset may be insidious, and cases diagnosed at routine hernia repair have been described. However, acute presentations resembling bacterial peritonitis also occur. In the past, diagnosis was often made at surgery for a mass or an acute abdomen. Tuberculous peritonitis often goes undiagnosed in patients with concomitant cirrhosis with ascites.[198] Of 20 patients with both conditions, the diagnosis of tuberculous peritonitis was suspected antemortem in only 11. Tuberculous peritonitis has been reported in peritoneal dialysis patients with the clinical picture of bacterial peritonitis unresponsive to routine antibiotics.[199]

The peritoneal fluid is exudative, usually containing 500 to 2000 cells. Lymphocytes typically predominate, although in some cases polymorphonuclear leukocytes are more abundant early in the process. Acid-fast smear of peritoneal fluid is seldom positive, and culture is positive in only 25% of cases. Measurement of adenosine deaminase activity in ascitic fluid has been reported to have a high degree of sensitivity (86%) and specificity (100%).[200] Analysis of peritoneal fluid by PCR may also yield a specific diagnosis. However, in the absence of other foci of tuberculosis, peritoneal tissue must often be obtained to make the diagnosis. Histologic examination of peritoneal biopsy specimens obtained by a Cope needle were positive in 64% of cases and by peritoneoscopy in 85% in one series.[201] However, fatal hemorrhages after both Cope needle biopsy and peritoneoscopy have been recorded.[197]

Treatment is the same as for pulmonary tuberculosis. There is some evidence that adjunctive corticosteroids decrease the likelihood of late intestinal obstruction,[201] but pending definitive studies, the routine use of adjunctive corticosteroids cannot be recommended.[202]

Tuberculous Lymphadenitis (Scrofula)

Peripheral Nodes. Lymphadenitis is the most frequent form of extrapulmonary tuberculosis. In HIV-negative persons, it is usually unilateral and cervical in location.[203] The most common site is along the upper border of the sternocleidomastoid muscle where it presents as a painless, red, firm mass. It is seen most frequently in young adult females of minority races, although it can affect any age or race. Children often have an ongoing primary infection, but in other age groups evidence of extranodal tuberculosis and systemic symptoms are usually absent. Lymphadenopathy outside the cervical and supraclavicular area indicates more serious tuberculosis, usually with systemic symptoms. The tuberculin test result is almost always positive. Fine-needle aspiration demonstrates cytologic evidence of granuloma, but smears or cultures are usually negative.[204] Biopsy with culture is often required for diagnosis, because nodes with a nonspecific histologic appearance have been positive for *M. tuberculosis* on culture, and material with typical histologic features may be due to other mycobacteria or fungi. Complete excision of involved nodes with no drain left in place is recommended to diminish the possibility of postoperative fistula formation. Chemotherapy with a 6-month regimen of INH and RMP, with PZA during the first 2 months is effective. Untoward events such as node enlargement with pain, suppuration, sinus formation, and appearance of new nodes occur in 25 to 30% of cases, both during and after chemotherapy and do not indicate failure of drug treatment. These likely represent reactions to retained tuberculous antigens rather than uncontrolled infection, they usually subside spontaneously, and short courses of corticosteroids may be beneficial when the problem persists.[205]

Conversely, in individuals with AIDS, peripheral tuberculous lymphadenitis is almost always multifocal and associated with major systemic symptoms such as fever, weight loss, and evidence of tuberculosis in the lungs (parenchyma, nodes, or pleura) or elsewhere (Fig. 240–11).[205] In one series from New York City, tuberculosis caused 57% of generalized lymphadenopathy in HIV-positive intravenous drug users.[206] In contrast to non–HIV-infected persons, material removed by fine-needle aspiration is positive on acid-fast stain in the great majority of cases—as frequently as it is by culture. However, both cytologic and histologic findings are less specific than in non–HIV-infected persons.[207]

Mediastinal Tuberculous Lymphadenopathy. Mediastinal adenopathy during primary infection is often visible roentgenologically, especially in children. In minority races, mediastinal adenopathy due to tuberculosis may also be seen in young adults, and cases in very old persons have been reported.[208] Associated systemic symptoms may or may not be present, causing confusion with other mediastinal masses such as histoplasmosis, lymphoma, and carcinoma. The finding of low-density areas in the nodes on CT suggests tuberculosis, but diagnosis usually requires mediastinoscopy. In HIV-infected persons with tuberculosis, in contrast, mediastinal lymphadenopathy is frequent. Multiple nodes are usually involved, coalescing into large mediastinal masses with low-density centers, peripheral contrast enhancement, and no calcification.[209, 210]

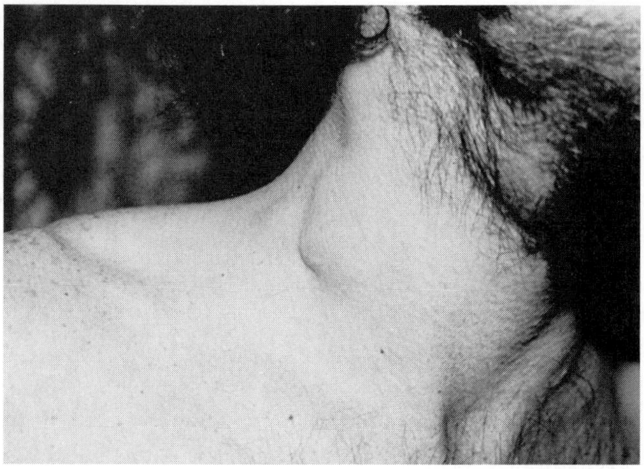

FIGURE 240–11. Cervical lymphadenitis due to *Mycobacterium tuberculosis* in a patient with acquired immunodeficiency syndrome.

Fibrosing Mediastinitis. Tuberculosis can cause fibrosing mediastinitis, although less commonly than histoplasmosis. Patients present with dyspnea on exertion due to compression of pulmonary veins and arteries or, less commonly, superior vena cava syndrome. Hilar adenopathy or active pulmonary disease is rarely found. A perfusion lung scan helps define the extent of pulmonary vascular compression, but thoracotomy is required for diagnosis. Mediastinoscopy is either contraindicated because of superior vena cava syndrome or unsuccessful because of fibrosis.

Mesenteric Tuberculous Lymphadenitis. In HIV-negative persons, isolated symptomatic mesenteric lymphadenitis without bowel disease or peritonitis is rare. It may cause abdominal pain, fever, a palpable mass, or symptoms of partial small bowel obstruction. In AIDS patients with tuberculosis, abdominal lymphadenopathy is common and may be massive.[210, 211] Involvement is more often intra-abdominal than retroperitoneal, and occasionally obstruction of the biliary tract, ureters, or bowel is observed. As with thoracic disease, the nodes often are low density or have low-density centers and peripheral enhancement. Other abnormalities on CT may include abscesses in the liver, spleen, pancreas, or kidney, local ileal thickening, extraluminal bowel gas indicating fistula formation, and ascites.

Cutaneous Tuberculosis

In the past, a number of cutaneous conditions were associated with tuberculosis elsewhere in the body, although *M. tuberculosis* could not be identified in the lesions. These have been considered allergic reactions to the infection and termed *tuberculids.* They include erythema induratum of Bazin, papulonecrotic tuberculids, and others. This association has been questioned, and some have attributed tuberculids to other processes such as sarcoidosis.[212] *M. tuberculosis* DNA has been detected in erythema induratum skin lesions by PCR.[213] Erythema nodosum has been attributed to primary tuberculosis, although organisms cannot be cultured from the lesions.

The pathogenesis of cutaneous involvement in tuberculosis is varied. Skin involvement may result from exogenous inoculation (which in the previously nonsensitized host is associated with regional lymphadenitis), spread from an adjacent focus to the overlying skin (as from lymphadenitis, osteomyelitis, or epididymitis), and hematogenous spread from a distant focus or as a part of the generalized hematogenous dissemination. This last is seen in patients with AIDS and tuberculous bacteremia.[214] The clinical picture of all cutaneous mycobacterial infections including tuberculosis is highly variable, and any unexplained skin lesion, especially if it has nodular or ulcerative components, may be due to tuberculosis, particularly in AIDS patients.

Tuberculous Laryngitis

In the prechemotherapy era, laryngeal tuberculosis occurred in more than a third of patients dying of pulmonary tuberculosis, often associated with painful ulcers of the epiglottis, pharynx, tonsils, and mouth, as well as middle ear involvement. Laryngeal disease was highly infectious and often caused terminal widespread bronchogenic dissemination throughout the lungs. At present, however, more than one half of laryngeal tuberculosis cases are due to hematogenous seeding. Such cases are still highly contagious. Lesions vary from erythema to ulceration and exophytic masses resembling carcinoma.[215] Symptoms include cough, wheezing, hemoptysis, dysphagia, odynophagia, and otalgia.

Tuberculous Otitis

Tuberculous otitis media is rare and frequently misdiagnosed. Half of the cases have no other evidence of present or past tuberculosis. The classic clinical picture is painless otorrhea with multiple tympanic perforations, exuberant granulation tissue, early severe hearing loss, and mastoid bone necrosis. The diagnosis has been missed for years by excellent otolaryngologists, even when tissue was available. Tuberculous otitis may be complicated by facial nerve paralysis. Response to drug therapy is excellent, and surgery is usually not required.[216]

Miscellaneous Conditions

Tuberculosis of the aorta with or without aneurysm formation can be caused by spread from contiguous diseased nodes, pericarditis, spondylitis, paravertebral abscesses, or empyema. Extensive hematogenous dissemination or aortic rupture may occur. Tuberculosis produces various ocular syndromes, including choroidal tubercles, uveitis, iritis, and episcleritis. Tuberculosis may also involve the breast, producing abscesses, sclerosing lesions resembling carcinoma, and multiple nodules. Destructive nasal lesions resembling Wegener's granulomatosis both clinically and histologically have been caused by tuberculosis.[217] Tuberculosis of the adrenal glands may cause adrenal enlargement with or without calcification, as may histoplasmosis, but granulomatous adrenal tuberculosis may cause Addison's disease without either calcification or adrenal enlargement.[218]

REFERENCES

1. Centers for Disease Control and Prevention. Tuberculosis morbidity—United States, 1997. MMWR Morb Mortal Wkly Rep. 1998;47:253–257.
2. Palella FJ, Delaney KM, Moorman AC, et al. Declining morbidity and mortality among patients with advanced human immunodeficiency virus infection. N Engl J Med. 1998;338:853–860.
3. Russell MD, Torrington KG, Tenholder MF. A ten-year experience with fiberoptic bronchoscopy for mycobacterial isolation: Impact of the BACTEC system. Am Rev Respir Dis. 1986;133:1069–1071.
4. Yagupsky PV, Kaminski DA, Palmer KM, et al. Cord formation in BACTEC 7H12 medium for rapid, presumptive identification of *Mycobacterium tuberculosis* complex. J Clin Microbiol. 1990;28:1451–1453.
5. Masters RN. Mycobacteriology. In: Isenberg HD, ed. Clinical Microbiology Procedures Handbook. Washington, DC: American Society of Clinical Microbiology; 1992.
6. Iseman MD. Treatment of multidrug-resistant tuberculosis. N Engl J Med. 1993;329:784–791.
7. Barnes PF. Rapid diagnostic tests for tuberculosis—progress but no gold standard. Am J Respir Crit Care Med. 1997;155:1497–1498.
8. Noordhoek GT, vanEmbden JDA, Kolk AHJ. Reliability of nucleic acid amplification for detection of *Mycobacterium tuberculosis*: An international collaborative quality control study among 30 laboratories. J Clin Microbiol. 1996;34:2522–2525.
9. Centers for Disease Control and Prevention. Nucleic acid amplification tests for tuberculosis. MMWR Morb Mortal Wkly Rep. 1996;45:951.

10. ATS Workshop. Rapid diagnostic tests for tuberculosis—what is the appropriate use? Am J Respir Crit Care Med. 1997;155:1804–1814.
11. Khisimuzi M, Slayden RA, Zhu Y, et al. Inhibition of a *Mycobacterium tuberculosis* β-ketoacyl ACP synthetase by isoniazid. Science. 1998;280:1607–1616
12. Drobniewski FA, Wilson SM. The rapid diagnosis of isoniazid and rifampicin resistance in *Mycobacterium tuberculosis*—a molecular story. J Med Microbiol. 1998;47:189–196.
13. Telenti A, Honoré N, Bernasconi C, et al. Genotypic assessment of isoniazid and rifampin resistance in *Mycobacterium tuberculosis*—a blinded study at reference laboratory level. J Clin Microbiol. 1997;35:719–723.
14. Williams DL, Spring L, Gillis TP, et al. Evaluation of a polymerase chain reaction–based universal heteroduplex generator assay for direct detection of rifampin susceptibility of *Mycobacterium tuberculosis* from sputum specimens. Clin Infect Dis. 1998;26:446–450.
15. Kim B-J, Kim S-Y, Park B-H, et al. Mutations in the *rpoB* gene of *Mycobacterium tuberculosis* that interfere with PCR-single-strand conformation polymorphism analysis for rifampin susceptibility testing. J Clin Microbiol. 1997;35:492–494.
16. Nachamkin I, Kang C, Weinstein MP. Detection of resistance to isoniazid, rifampin, and streptomycin in clinical isolates of *Mycobacterium tuberculosis* by molecular methods. Clin Infect Dis. 1997;24:894–900.
17. Jacobs WR, Barletta RG, Udani R, et al. Rapid assessment of drug susceptibilities of *Mycobacterium tuberculosis* by means of luciferase reporter phages. Science. 1993;260:819–822.
18. Wilson SM, Al-Suwaidi Z, McNerney R, et al. Evaluation of a new rapid bacteriophage-based method for drug susceptibility testing of *Mycobacterium tuberculosis*. Nature Med. 1997;3:465–468.
19. van Embden JD, Cave MD, Crawford JT, et al. Strain identification of *Mycobacterium tuberculosis* by DNA fingerprinting: Recommendations for a standardized methodology. J Clin Microbiol. 1993;31:406–409.
20. Valway SE, Sanchez MPC, Shinnick TK, et al. An outbreak involving extensive transmission of a virulent strain of *Mycobacterium tuberculosis*. N Engl J Med. 1998;338:633–639.
21. Bloom BR, Small PM. The evolving relationship between humans and *Mycobacterium tuberculosis*. N Engl J Med. 1998;338:677–678.
22. World Health Organization Report on the Tuberculosis Epidemic, 1997. Geneva, Switzerland.
23. Styblo K. Recent advances in epidemiological research in tuberculosis. Adv Tuberc Res. 1980;20:1–63.
24. Sousa AO, Salem JI, Lee FK, et al. An epidemic of tuberculosis with a high rate of tuberculin anergy among a population previously unexposed to tuberculosis, the Yanomami Indians of the Brazilian Amazon. Proc Natl Acad Sci U S A. 1997;94:13227–13232.
25. American Thoracic Society. Control of tuberculosis in the United States. Am Rev Respir Dis. 1992;146:1623–1633.
26. Binkin NJ, Zuber PLF, Wells CD, et al. Overseas screening for tuberculosis in immigrants and refugees to the United States: Current status. Clin Infect Dis. 1996;23:1226–1232.
27. Zuber PLF, McKenna MT, Binkin NJ, et al. Long-term risk of tuberculosis among foreign-born persons in the United States. JAMA. 1997;278:304–307.
28. Jereb JA, Kelly GD, Dooley SW, et al. Tuberculosis morbidity in the United States: Final data, 1990. MMWR Morb Mortal Wkly Rep. 1991;40:23–27.
29. Barnes PF, Bloch AB, Davidson PT, et al. Tuberculosis in patients with human immunodeficiency virus infection. N Engl J Med. 1991;100:191–200.
30. Pitchenik AE, Cole C, Russell BW, et al. Tuberculosis, atypical mycobacteriosis, and the acquired immunodeficiency syndrome among Haitian and Non-Haitian patients in South Florida. Ann Intern Med. 1984;101:641–645.
31. Centers for Disease Control and Prevention. 1993 Revised certification system for HIV infection and expanded surveillance case definition for AIDS among adolescents and adults. MMWR Morb Mortal Wkly Rep. 1992;41:1–19.
32. Mishu Allos B, Gensheimer KF, Bloch AB, et al. Management of an outbreak of tuberculosis in a small community. Ann Intern Med. 1996;125:114–117.
33. Centers for Disease Control and Prevention. Tuberculosis Control Division. Tuberculosis in the United States, 1979. Atlanta: Centers for Disease Control; 1981:4–31.
34. Daniel TM, Debanne SM. Estimation of the annual risk of tuberculous infection for white men in the United States. J Infect Dis. 1997;175:1535–1537.
35. Patel KR. Pulmonary tuberculosis in residents of lodging houses, night shelters and common hostels in Glasgow: A 5-year prospective study. Br J Dis Chest. 1985;79:60–66.
36. Nardell E, McInnis B, Thomas B, et al. Exogenous reinfection with tuberculosis in a shelter for the homeless. N Engl J Med. 1986;315:1570–1575.
37. Stead WW, Lofgren JP, Warren E, et al. Tuberculosis as an endemic and nosocomial infection among the elderly in nursing homes. N Engl J Med. 1985;312:1483–1487.
38. Centers for Disease Control, and Prevention. Special report: Tuberculosis among Indochinese refugees. In: Tuberculosis in the United States. Atlanta: Centers for Disease Control; 1981:40.
39. Andrew OT, Schoenfeld PY, Hopewell PC, et al. Tuberculosis in patients with end-stage renal disease. Am J Med. 1980;68:59–65.
40. Cuss FM, Carmichael DJ, Linington A, et al. Tuberculosis in renal failure: A high incidence in patients born in the third world. Clin Nephrol. 1986;25:129–133.
41. Louie E, Rice LB, Holzm RS. Tuberculosis in non-Haitian patients with acquired immunodeficiency syndrome. Chest. 1986;90:542–545.
42. Frampton MW. An outbreak of tuberculosis among hospital personnel caring for a patient with a skin ulcer. Ann Intern Med. 1992;117:312–313.
43. Templeton GL, Illing LA, Young L, et al. The risk for transmission of *Mycobacterium tuberculosis* at the bedside and during autopsy. Ann Intern Med. 1995;122:922–925.
44. Bates JH, Stead WW. The history of tuberculosis as a global epidemic. Med Clin North Am. 1993;77:1205–1217.
45. Stead WW. Tuberculosis among elderly persons: An outbreak in a nursing home. Ann Intern Med. 1981;94:606–610.
46. Klausner JD, Ryder RW, Baende E, et al. *Mycobacterium tuberculosis* in household contacts of human immunodeficiency virus type 1–seropositive patients with active pulmonary tuberculosis in Kinshasa, Zaire. J Infect Dis. 1993;168:106–111.
47. Elliot AM, Hayes RJ, Halwiindi B, et al. The impact of HIV on infectiousness of pulmonary tuberculosis: A community in Zambia. AIDS. 1993;7:981–987.
48. Nunn P, Mungai M, Nyamwaya J, et al. The effect of human immunodeficiency virus type-1 on the infectiousness of tuberculosis. Tuber Lung Dis. 1994;75:25–32.
49. Cauthen GM, Dooley SW, Onorato IM, et al. Transmission of *Mycobacterium tuberculosis* from tuberculosis patients with HIV infection or AIDS. Am J Epidemiol. 1996;144:69–77.
50. Iseman MD. An unholy trinity—three negative sputum smears and release from tuberculosis isolation. Clin Infect Dis. 1997;25:671–672.
51. Centers for Disease Control and Prevention. Guidelines for preventing the transmission of *Mycobacterium tuberculosis* in health-care facilities, 1994. MMWR Morb Mortal Wkly Rep. 1994;43:1–132.
52. Telzak EE, Fazal BE, Pollard CL, et al. Factors influencing time to sputum conversion among patients with smear-positive pulmonary tuberculosis. Clin Infect Dis. 1997;25:666–670.
53. Kim TC, Blackman RS, Heatwole KM, et al. Acid fast bacilli in sputum smears of patients with pulmonary tuberculosis: Prevalence and significance of negative smears pretreatment and positive smears post-treatment. Am Rev Respir Dis. 1984;129:264–268.
54. Selwyn PA, Hartel D, Lewis VA, et al. A prospective study of the risk of tuberculosis among intravenous drug users with human immunodeficiency virus infection. N Engl J Med. 1989;320:545–555.
55. Daley CL, Small PM, Schecter GF. An outbreak of tuberculosis with accelerated progression among persons infected with the human immunodeficiency virus. N Engl J Med. 1992;36:231–235.
56. Brahmajothi V, Pitchappan RM, Kakkanaiah VM, et al. Association of pulmonary tuberculosis and HLA in South India. Tubercle. 1991;72:123–132.
57. Rajalingham R, Mehra NK. Molecular analysis of HLA-DR2 subtypes and DR51 group haplotypes in mycobacterial infectious disease response to chemotherapy. Abstract 4862. Presented at the Ninth International Congress of Immunology, San Francisco, Federation of American Societies for Experimental Biology, 1995:819.
58. Bellamy R, Ruwende C, Corrah T, et al. Variations in the *NRAMP1* gene and susceptibility to tuberculosis in West Africans. N Engl J Med. 1998;338:640–644.
59. Di Perri G, Danzi MC, DeChecchi G. Nosocomial epidemic of active tuberculosis among HIV-infected patients. Lancet. 1989;2:1502–1504.
60. Pearson ML, Jereb JA, Frieden TR. Nosocomial transmission of multidrug-resistant *Mycobacterium tuberculosis:* A risk to patients and healthcare workers. Ann Intern Med. 1992;117:191–196.
61. Fischl MA, Uttamchandani RB, Daikos GL, et al. An outbreak of tuberculosis caused by multiple-drug resistant tubercle bacilli among patients with HIV infection. Ann Intern Med. 1992;11:177–183.
62. Edlin BR, Tokars JI, Grieco MH, et al. An outbreak of multidrug-resistant tuberculosis among hospitalized patients with the acquired immunodeficiency syndrome. N Engl J Med. 1992;326:1514–1521.
63. Kramer F, Modilevsky T, Waliany AR, et al. Delayed diagnosis of tuberculosis in patients with human immunodeficiency virus infection. Am J Med. 1990;89:451–456.
64. Small PM, Shafer RW, Hopewell PC. Exogenous reinfection with multidrug-resistant *Mycobacterium tuberculosis* in patients with advanced HIV infection. N Engl J Med. 1993;328:1137–1144.
65. Torres R, Mani S, Altholz J, et al. Human immunodeficiency virus infection among homeless men in a New York City shelter. Arch Intern Med. 1990;150:2030–2036.
66. Fujiwara PI, Cook SV, Rutherford CM, et al. A continuing survey of drug-resistant tuberculosis, New York City, April 1994. Arch Intern Med. 1997;157:531–536.
67. Pablos-Mendez A, Knirsch CA, Barr RG, et al. Nonadherence in tuberculosis: Predictors and consequences in New York City. Am J Med. 1997;102:164–170.
68. Braun MM, Truman BI, Maguire B. Increasing incidence of tuberculosis in a prison inmate population: Association with HIV infection. JAMA. 1989;261:393–397.
69. MacIntyre DR, Kendig N, Kummer L, et al. Impact of tuberculosis control measures and crowding on the incidence of tuberculous infection in Maryland prisons. Clin Infect Dis. 1997;24:1060–1067.
70. Frieden TR, Sherman LF, Maw KL, et al. A multi-institutional outbreak of highly drug-resistant tuberculosis: Epidemiology and clinical outcomes. JAMA. 1996;275:452–457.
71. Orme IM, Andersen P, Boom WH. T cell response to *Mycobacterium tuberculosis*. J Infect Dis. 1993;167:1481–1497.
72. O'Brien JR. Nonreactive tuberculosis. J Clin Pathol. 1954;7:216–225.
73. Ellner JJ. The immune response in human tuberculosis: Implications for tuberculosis control. J Infect Dis. 1997;176:1351–1359.
74. Hirsch CS, Hussain R, Toossii Z, et al. Cross-stimulatory role for transforming growth factor β in tuberculosis: Suppression of antigen driven interferon γ production. Proc Natl Acad Sci U S A. 1996;93:3193–3198.
75. Vidal SM, Malo D, Vogan K, et al. Natural resistance to infection with intracellular parasites: Isolation of a candidate for Bcg. Cell. 1993;73:469.
76. Snider DE, Jr. The tuberculin skin test. Am Rev Respir Dis. 1982;125:108–118.
77. Centers for Disease Control and Prevention. The use of preventive therapy for

tuberculous infection in the United States: Recommendations of the Advisory Committee for the Elimination of Tuberculosis. MMWR Morb Mortal Wkly Rep. 1990;39:9–12.
78. Stead WW. Management of health care workers after inadvertent exposure to tuberculosis: A guide for the use of preventive therapy. Ann Intern Med. 1995;122:906–912.
79. Nash DR, Douglass JE. Anergy in active pulmonary tuberculosis: A comparison between positive and negative reactors and an evaluation of 5 TU and 250 TU skin test doses. Chest. 1980;77:32–37.
80. Pouchot J, Grasland A, Collet C, et al. Reliability of tuberculin skin test measurement. Ann Intern Med. 1997;126:210–214.
81. Robertson JM, Burtt DS, Edmonds KL, et al. Delayed tuberculin reactivity in persons of Indochinese origin: Implications for preventive therapy. Ann Intern Med. 1996;124:779–784.
82. Grzybowski S, Allen EA. The challenge of tuberculosis in decline: A study based on the epidemiology of tuberculosis in Ontario, Canada. Am Rev Respir Dis. 1964;90:707–720.
83. Johnson MP, Coberly JS, Clermont HC, et al. Tuberculin skin test reactivity among adults infected with human immunodeficiency virus. J Infect Dis. 1992;166:194–198.
84. Centers for Disease Control and Prevention. Purified protein derivative (PPD) tuberculin anergy and HIV infection: Guidelines for anergy testing and management of anergic persons at risk of tuberculosis. MMWR Morb Mortal Wkly Rep. 1991;40::27–33.
85. Gordin FM, Matts J, Miller C, et al. A controlled trial of isoniazid in persons with anergy and human immunodeficiency virus infection who are at high risk for tuberculosis. N Engl J Med. 1997;337:315–320.
86. Whalen CC, Johnson JL, Okwera A, et al. A trial of three regimens to prevent tuberculosis in Ugandan adults infected with the human immunodeficiency virus. N Engl J Med. 1997;337:801–808.
87. Centers for Disease Control and Prevention. Anergy skin testing and preventive therapy for HIV-infected persons: Revised guidelines. MMWR Morb Mortal Wkly Rep. 1997;46:1–10.
88. Murray JF. Cursed duet: HIV infection and tuberculosis. Respiration. 1990;57:210–220.
89. Stead WW. Pathogenesis of a first episode of chronic pulmonary tuberculosis in man: Recrudescence of residuals of the primary infection or exogenous reinfection? Am Rev Respir Dis. 1967;95:729–745.
90. Romeyn JA. Exogenous reinfection in tuberculosis. Am Rev Respir Dis. 1970;101:923–927.
91. Kumar RA, Saran M, Verma BL, et al. Pulmonary tuberculosis among contacts of patients with tuberculosis in an urban Indian population. J Epidemiol Community Health. 1984;38:253–258.
92. Dahl RH. First appearance of pulmonary cavity after primary infection with relation to time and age. Acta Tuberc Scand. 1952;27:140–149.
93. Stead WW, Kerby Gr, Schlueter DP, et al. The clinical spectrum of primary tuberculosis in adults: Confusion with reinfection in the pathogenesis of chronic tuberculosis. Ann Intern Med. 1968;68:731–745.
94. Gedde-Dahl T. Tuberculous infection in the light of tuberculin matriculation. Am J Hyg. 1952;56:139–214.
95. Reichman LB, Felton CP, Edsall JR. Drug dependence, a possible new risk factor for tuberculosis disease. Arch Intern Med. 1979;139:337–339.
96. Canetti G. Present aspects of bacterial resistance in tuberculosis. Am Rev Respir Dis. 1965;92:687–703.
97. Lee JH, Park SS, Lee DH, et al. Endobronchial tuberculosis: Clinical and bronchoscopic features in 121 cases. Chest. 1992;102:990–994.
98. Chang S, Lee P, Perug P. Lower lung field tuberculosis. Chest. 1987;91:230–232.
99. Pitchenik AE, Rubinson HA. The radiographic appearance of tuberculosis in patients with the acquired immune deficiency syndrome (AIDS) and pre-AIDS. Am Rev Respir Dis. 1985;131:393–396.
100. Theuer P, Hopewell PC, Elias D, et al. Human immunodeficiency virus infection in tuberculosis patients. J Infect Dis. 1990;162:8–12.
101. Jones BE, Oo MM, Taikwel EK, et al. CD4 cell counts in human immunodeficiency virus–negative patients with tuberculosis. Clin Infect Dis. 1997;24:988–991.
102. Yajko DM, Nassos PS, Sanders CA, et al. High predictive value of the acid-fast smear for *Mycobacterium tuberculosis* despite the high prevalence of *Mycobacterium avium* complex in respiratory specimens. Clin Infect Dis. 1994;19:334–336.
103. Menzies R, Vissandjee B, Rocher I, et al. The booster effect in two-step tuberculin testing among adults in Montreal. Ann Intern Med. 1994;120:190–198.
104. Salzman SH, Schindel ML, Aranda CP, et al. The role of bronchoscopy in the diagnosis of pulmonary tuberculosis in patients at risk for HIV infection. Chest. 1992;102:143–146.
105. Miro AM, Gibilara E, Powell S, et al. The role of fiberoptic bronchoscopy for diagnosis of pulmonary tuberculosis in patients at risk for AIDS. Chest. 1992;101:1211–1214.
106. Kennedy DJ, Lewis WP, Barnes PF. Yield of bronchoscopy for the diagnosis of tuberculosis in patients with human immunodeficiency virus infection. Chest. 1992;102:1040–1044.
107. Reider HL, Kelly GD, Bloch AB, et al. Tuberculosis diagnosed at death in the United States. Chest. 1991;100:678–681.
108. Mok CK, Nandi P, Ong GB. Coexistent bronchogenic carcinoma and active pulmonary tuberculosis. J Thorac Cardiovasc Surg. 1978;76:469–472.
109. Ben-Dov I, Mason G. Drug-resistant tuberculosis in a southern California hospital: Trends from 1969 to 1984. Am Rev Respir Dis. 1987;135:1307–1310.
110. Pablos-Mendez A, Raviglione MC, Battan R, et al. Drug resistant tuberculosis among the homeless in New York City. N Y State J Med. 1990;90:351–355.
111. Frieden TR, Sterling T, Pablos-Mendez A, et al. The emergence of drug resistant tuberculosis in New York City. N Engl J Med. 1993;328:521–526.
112. Sullivan EA, Kreiswirth BN, Palumbo L, et al. Emergence of fluoroquinolone-resistant tuberculosis in New York City. Lancet. 1995;345:1148–1150.
113. Mitchison DA, Nunn AJ. Influence of initial drug resistance on the response to short-course chemotherapy of pulmonary tuberculosis. Am Rev Respir Dis. 1986;133:423–430.
114. Steele MA, Burk RF, DesPrez RM. Toxic hepatitis with isoniazid and rifampin: A metaanalysis. Chest. 1991;99:465–471.
115. Kopanoff DE, Snider DE Jr, Caras GJ. Isoniazid-related hepatitis: A U.S. Public Health Service cooperative surveillance study. Am Rev Respir Dis. 1978;117:991–1001.
116. Centers for Disease Control and Prevention. Clinical update: Impact of HIV protease inhibitors on the treatment of HIV-infected tuberculosis patients with rifampin. MMWR Morb Mortal Wkly Rep. 1996;45:921–925.
117. Bishai WR, Graham NMH, Harrington S, et al. Rifampin-resistant tuberculosis in a patient receiving rifabutin prophylaxis. N Engl J Med. 1996;334:1573–1576.
118. Steele MA, DesPrez RM. The role of pyrazinamide in tuberculosis chemotherapy. Chest. 1988;94:842–844.
119. Dankner WM, Waecker NJ, Essey MA, et al. *Mycobacterium bovis* infections in San Diego: A clinicoepidemiologic study of 73 patients and a historical review of a forgotten pathogen. Medicine. 1993;72:11–37.
120. Telzak EE, Sepkowitz K, Alpert P, et al. Multidrug-resistant tuberculosis in patients without HIV infection. N Engl J Med. 1995;333:907–911.
121. Perez-Stable EJ, Hopewell PC. Current tuberculosis treatment regimens: Choosing the right one for your patient. Clin Chest Med. 1989;10:323–339.
122. Davidson PT, Le HQ. Drug treatment of tuberculosis—1992. Drugs. 1992;43:651–673.
123. Snider DE Jr, Zierski M, Graczyk J, et al. Short-course tuberculosis chemotherapy studies conducted in Poland during the past decade. Eur J Respir Dis. 1986;68:12–18.
124. Treatment of tuberculosis and tuberculous infection in adults and children. Am J Respir Crit Care Med. 1994;149:1359–1374.
125. Dutt AK, Moers D, Stead WW. Short-course chemotherapy for tuberculosis with mainly twice-weekly isoniazid and rifampin: Community physicians' seven-year experience with mainly outpatients. Am J Med. 1984;77:233–242.
126. Centers for Disease Control and Prevention. Initial therapy for tuberculosis in the era of multidrug resistance: Recommendations of the Advisory Council for the Elimination of Tuberculosis. JAMA. 1993;270:694–698.
127. Cohn DL, Catlin BJ, Peterson KL, et al. A 62-dose, 6-month therapy for pulmonary and extrapulmonary tuberculosis: A twice-weekly, directly observed, and cost-effective regimen. Ann Intern Med. 1990;112:407–415.
128. Weis SE, Slocum PC, Blais FX, et al. The effect of directly observed therapy on the rates of drug resistance and relapse in tuberculosis. N Engl J Med. 1994;330:1179–1184.
129. Hong Kong Chest Service Tuberculosis Research Center, Madras, British Medical Research Council. A controlled trial of 3-month, 4-month, and 6-month regimens of chemotherapy for sputum smear-negative pulmonary tuberculosis: Results at 5 years. Am Rev Respir Dis. 1989;139:871–876.
130. Goble M, Iseman MD, Madsen LA. Treatment of 171 patients with pulmonary tuberculosis resistant to isoniazid and rifampin. N Engl J Med. 1993;328:527–532.
131. Babu Swai O, Aluoch JA, Githui WA. Controlled clinical trial of a regimen of two durations for the treatment of isoniazid resistant pulmonary tuberculosis. Tubercle. 1988;69:5–14.
132. Anonymous. Prevention and treatment of tuberculosis among patients infected with human immunodeficiency virus: Principles of therapy and revised recommendations. MMWR Morb Mortal Wkly Rep. 1998;47:1–58.
133. Small PM, Schecter GF, Goodman PC, et al. Treatment of tuberculosis in patients with advanced human immunodeficiency virus infection. N Engl J Med. 1991;324:289–294.
134. Haas DW, Des Prez RM. Tuberculosis and acquired immunodeficiency syndrome: A historical perspective on recent developments. Am J Med. 1994;96:439–450.
135. Berning SE, Huitt DA, Iseman MD, Peloquin CA. Malabsorption of antituberculous medications by a patient with AIDS. N Engl J Med. 1992;327:1817–1818.
136. Busillo CP, Lessnau KD, Sanjana V. Multidrug resistant *Mycobacterium tuberculosis* in patients with human immunodeficiency virus infection. Chest. 1992;102:797–801.
137. Israel HL, Gottlieb JE, Maddrey WC. Perspective: Preventive isoniazid therapy and the liver. Chest. 1992;101:1298–1301.
138. Porter JDH, McAdam KPWJ. Tuberculosis in Africa in the AIDS era: The role of chemoprophylaxis. Trans R Soc Trop Med Hyg. 1992;86:467–469.
139. Livengood JR, Sigler TG, Foster LR, et al. Isoniazid-resistant tuberculosis: A community outbreak and report of a rifampicin prophylaxis failure. JAMA. 1985;253:2847–2849.
140. Stead WW, To T, Harrison RW, et al. Benefit-risk considerations in preventive treatment of tuberculosis in elderly persons. Ann Intern Med. 1987;107:843–845.
141. International Union Against Tuberculosis. Efficacy of various durations of isoniazid preventive therapy for tuberculosis: Five years of follow-up in the IUAT trial. Bull World Health Organ. 1982;60:555–564.
142. Byrd RB, Horn BR, Griggs GA, et al. Isoniazid chemoprophylaxis: Association with detection and incidence of liver toxicity. Arch Intern Med. 1970;137:1130–1133.

143. Snider DE Jr, Caras GJ. Isoniazid-associated hepatitis deaths: A review of available information. Am Rev Respir Dis. 1992;145:494–497.
144. Ferebee SH. Controlled chemoprophylaxis trials in tuberculosis: A general review. Bibl Tuberc Med Thorac. 1970;26:28–106.
145. Grzybowski S, Ashley MJ, McKinnon NE, et al. In Canada: A trial of chemoprophylaxis in inactive tuberculosis. CMAJ. 1969;101:81–86.
146. Falk A, Fuchs GF. Prophylaxis with isoniazid in inactive tuberculosis: A Veterans Administration cooperative study. Chest. 1978;73:44–48.
147. Taylor WC, Aronson MD, Delbanco TL. Should young adults with a positive tuberculin test take isoniazid? Ann Intern Med. 1981;94:808–813.
148. Selwyn PA, Sckell BM, Alcabes P, et al. High risk of active tuberculosis in HIV-infected drug users with cutaneous anergy. JAMA. 1992;268:504–507.
149. Rose DN. Short course prophylaxis against tuberculosis in HIV-infected patients. Ann Intern Med. 1998;129:779–786.
150. Luelmo F. BCG vaccination. Am Rev Respir Dis. 1982;125:70–72.
151. Menzies R, Vissandjee B. Effect of bacille Calmette-Guérin vaccination on tuberculin reactivity. Am Rev Respir Dis. 1992;145:621–624.
152. Hakim S, Heaney JA, Heinz T, et al. Psoas abscess following intravesical bacillus Calmette-Guérin for bladder cancer: A case report. J Urol. 1993;150:188–189.
153. McParland C, Cotton DJ, Gowda KS, et al. Miliary *Mycobacterium bovis* induced by intravesical bacille Calmette-Guérin immunotherapy. Am Rev Respir Dis. 1992;146:1330–1333.
154. Lamm DL, Stogdill VD, Stogdill BJ, et al. Complications of bacillus Calmette-Guérin immunotherapy in 1278 patients with bladder cancer. J Urol. 1986;135:272–274.
155. Glassroth J. Vaccines for tuberculosis: The glass remains half empty. Ann Intern Med. 1997;127:403–404.
156. Reider HL, Snider DE, Cauthen GM. Extrapulmonary tuberculosis in the United States. Am Rev Respir Dis. 1990;141:347–351.
157. Shafer RW, Kim DS, Weiss JP, et al. Extrapulmonary tuberculosis in patients with human immunodeficiency virus infection. Medicine. 1991;70:384–397.
158. Biehl JP. Miliary tuberculosis: A review of sixty-eight adult patients admitted to a municipal general hospital. Am Rev Tuberc. 1958;77:605–622.
159. Munt PW. Miliary tuberculosis in the chemotherapy era: With a clinical review in 69 American adults. Medicine. 1972;51:139–155.
160. Maartens G, Willcox PA, Benatar SR. Miliary tuberculosis: Rapid diagnosis, hematologic abnormalities, and outcome in 109 treated adults. Am J Med. 1990;89:291–296.
161. Kim JH, Langston AA, Gallis HA. Miliary tuberculosis: Epidemiology, clinical manifestations, diagnosis, and outcome. Rev Infect Dis. 1990;12:583–590.
162. Yu YL, Chow WH, Humphries MJ, et al. Cryptic miliary tuberculosis. Q J Med. 1986;59:421–428.
163. Willcox PA, Potgieter PD, Bateman ED, et al. Rapid diagnosis of sputum negative miliary tuberculosis using the flexible fiberoptic bronchoscope. Thorax. 1986;41:681–684.
164. Slavin RE, Walsh TJ, Pollock AD. Late generalized tuberculosis: A clinical pathologic analysis and comparison of 100 cases in the pre-antibiotic and antibiotic eras. Medicine. 1980;59:351–366.
165. Proudfoot AT, Akhar AJ, Douglas AC, et al. Miliary tuberculosis in adults. BMJ. 1969;2:273–276.
166. Cameron SJ. Tuberculosis and the blood: A special relationship. Tubercle. 1974;55:55–72.
167. Lupatkin H, Brau N, Flomenberg P, et al. Tuberculous abscesses in patients with AIDS. Clin Infect Dis. 1992;14:1040–1044.
168. Kennedy DH, Fallon RJ. Tuberculous meningitis. JAMA. 1979;241:264–268.
169. Haas DW. Current and future applications of polymerase chain reaction for *Mycobacterium tuberculosis*. Mayo Clin Proc. 1996;71:311–313.
170. Taylor GR, Dannecker GE, Hoppe JE, et al. Negative polymerase chain reaction in a child with tuberculous meningoencephalitis. Infection. 1997;25:256–257.
171. Dube MP, Holtom PD, Larsen RA. Tuberculous meningitis in patients with and without human immunodeficiency virus infection. Am J Med. 1992;93:520–524.
172. Roper WH, Waring JJ. Primary serofibrinous pleural effusion in military personnel. Am Rev Tuberc. 1955;71:616–634.
173. Antoniskis D, Amin K, Barnes PF. Pleuritis as a manifestation of reactivation tuberculosis. Am J Med. 1990;89:447–450.
174. Epstein DM, Kline LR, Albelda SM, et al. Tuberculous pleural effusions. Chest. 1987;91:106–109.
175. Taelman H, Kagame A, Batungwanayo J, et al. Pericardial effusion and HIV infection. Lancet. 1990;335:924.
176. Strang JIG, Gibson DG, Mitchison DA, et al. Controlled clinical trial of complete open surgical drainage and of prednisolone in treatment of tuberculous pericardial effusion in Transkei. Lancet. 1988;2:759–763.
177. Strang JIG, Gibson DG, Nunn AJ, et al. Controlled trial of prednisolone as adjuvant in treatment of tuberculous constrictive pericarditis in Transkei. Lancet. 1987;23:1418–1422.
178. Agner RC, Gallis HA. Pericarditis differential diagnostic considerations. Arch Intern Med. 1979;139:407–412.
179. Janssens JP, De Haller R. Spinal tuberculosis in a developed country: A review of 26 cases with special emphasis on abscesses and neurologic complications. Clin Orthop. 1990;257:67–75.
180. Griffiths DL. Tuberculosis of the spine: A review. Adv Tuberc Res. 1980;20:92–110.
181. Davidson PT, Horowitz I. Skeletal tuberculosis: A review with patient presentations and discussion. Am J Med. 1970;48:77–84.
182. LiZares LF, Valcarcel A, Del Castillo JM, et al. Tuberculous arthritis with multiple joint involvement. J Rheumatol. 1991;18:635–636.
183. Garrido G, Gomez-Reino JJ, Fernandez-Dapica P, et al. A review of peripheral tuberculous arthritis. Semin Arthritis Rheum. 1988;18:142–149.
184. Muradali D, Gold WL, Vellend H, et al. Multifocal osteoarticular tuberculosis: Report of four cases and review of management. Clin Infect Dis. 1993;17:204–209.
185. Bentz RR, Dimcheff DG, Nemiroff MJ, et al. The incidence of urine cultures positive for *Mycobacterium tuberculosis* in a general tuberculosis patient population. Am Rev Respir Dis. 1975;111:647–650.
186. Simon HB, Weinstein AJ, Pasternak MS, et al. Genitourinary tuberculosis: Clinical features in a general hospital population. Am J Med. 1977;63:410–420.
187. Christensen WI. Genitourinary tuberculosis: Review of 102 cases. Medicine. 1974;53:377–390.
188. Gow JG. Genitourinary tuberculosis: A study of the disease in one unit over a period of 24 years. Ann R Coll Surg Engl. 1971;49:50–70.
189. Morgan SH, Eastwood JB, Baker LRI. Tuberculous interstitial nephritis: The tip of an iceberg? Tubercle. 1990;71:5–6.
190. Gorse GJ, Belshe RB. Male genital tuberculosis: A review of the literature with instructive case reports. Rev Infect Dis. 1985;7:511–524.
191. Carter JR. Unusual presentations of genital tract tuberculosis. Int J Gynecol Obstet. 1990;33:171–176.
192. Jakubowski A, Elwood RK, Enarson DA. Clinical features of abdominal tuberculosis. J Infect Dis. 1988;158:687–692.
193. Shah S, Thomas V, Mathan M, et al. Colonoscopic study of 50 patients with colonic tuberculosis. Gut. 1992;33:347–351.
194. Kielhofner MA, Hamill RJ. Focal hepatic tuberculosis in a patient with acquired immunodeficiency syndrome. South Med J. 1991;84:401–404.
195. Hulnick DH, Megibow AJ, Naidich DP, et al. Abdominal tuberculosis: CT evaluation. Radiology. 1985;157:199–204.
196. Modilevsky T, Sattler FR, Barnes PF. Mycobacterial disease in patients with human immunodeficiency virus infection. Arch Intern Med. 1989;149:2201–2205.
197. Bastani B, Shariatzadeh MR, Dehdashti F. Tuberculous peritonitis: Report of 30 cases and review of the literature. Q J Med. 1985;56:549–557.
198. Burack WR, Hollister RM. Tuberculous peritonitis. Ann Intern Med. 1960;28:510–523.
199. Cheng IKP, Chan PCK, Chan MK. Tuberculous peritonitis complicating long-term peritoneal dialysis. Am J Nephrol. 1989;9:155–161.
200. Fernandez-Rodriguez CM, Perez-Arguelles BS, Ledo L, et al. Ascites adenosine deaminase activity is decreased in tuberculous ascites with low protein content. Am J Gastroenterol. 1991;86:1500–1503.
201. Singh MM, Bhargava AN, Jain KP. Tuberculous peritonitis: An evaluation of pathogenetic mechanisms, diagnostic procedures and therapeutic measures. N Engl J Med. 1969;281:1091–1094.
202. Haas DW. Are adjunctive corticosteroids indicated during tuberculous peritonitis? Clin Infect Dis. 1998;27:57–58.
203. Summers GD, McNicol MW. Tuberculosis of superficial lymph nodes. Br J Dis Chest. 1980;74:369–373.
204. Dandapat MC, Mishra BM., Dash SP, et al. Peripheral lymph node tuberculosis: A review of 80 cases. Br J Surg. 1990;77:911–912.
205. Campbell IA. The treatment of superficial tuberculous lymphadenitis. Tubercle. 1990;71:1–3.
206. Hewlett D Jr, Duncanson FP, Jagadha V, et al. Lymphadenopathy in an inner city population consisting principally of intravenous drug abusers with suspected acquired immunodeficiency syndrome. Am Rev Respir Dis. 1988;137:1275–1279.
207. Shriner KA, Mathisen GE, Goetz MB. Comparison of mycobacterial lymphadenitis among persons infected with human immunodeficiency virus and seronegative controls. Clin Infect Dis. 1992;15:601–605.
208. Van den Brande P, Vijgen J, Demedts M. Isolated intrathoracic tuberculous lymphadenopathy. Eur Respir J. 1991;4:758–760.
209. Pastores SM, Naidich DP, Arnada CP, et al. Intrathoracic adenopathy associated with pulmonary tuberculosis in patients with human immunodeficiency virus infection. Chest. 1993;103:1433–1437.
210. Perich J, Ayuso MC, Vilana R, et al. Disseminated lymphatic tuberculosis in acquired immunodeficiency syndrome: Computed tomography findings. Can Assoc Radiol J. 1990;41:353–357.
211. Radin DR. Intraabdominal *Mycobacterium tuberculosis* vs *Mycobacterium avium-intracellulare* infections in patients with AIDS: Distinction based on CT findings. AJR Am J Roentgenol. 1991;156:487–491.
212. Beyt BE, Jr, Ortbals DW, Santa Cruz DJ, et al. Cutaneous mycobacteriosis: Analysis of 34 cases with a new classification of the disease. Medicine. 1981;60:95–109.
213. Yen A, Rady PL, Cortes-Franco R, et al. Detection of *Mycobacterium tuberculosis* in erythema induratum of Bazin using polymerase chain reaction. Arch Dermatol. 1997;133:532–533.
214. Rohatgi PK, Palazzolo JV, Saini NB. Acute miliary tuberculosis of the skin in acquired immunodeficiency syndrome. J Am Acad Dermatol. 1992;26:356–359.
215. Lindell MM Jr, Jing BS, Wallace S. Laryngeal tuberculosis. AJR Am J Roentgenol. 1977;129:677–680.
216. Lee PY, Drysdale AJ. Tuberculous otitis media. A difficult diagnosis. J Laryngol Otol. 1993;107:339.
217. Harrison NK, Knight RK. Tuberculosis of the nasopharynx misdiagnosed as Wegener's granulomatosis. Thorax. 1986;41:219–220.
218. Kelestimur F, Ozbakir O, Saglam A. Acute adrenocortical failure due to tuberculosis. J Endocrinol Invest. 1993;16:281–284.

Chapter 241

Mycobacterium leprae (Leprosy, Hansen's Disease)

ROBERT H. GELBER
THOMAS H. REA

More than other infectious diseases, leprosy, or Hansen's disease, has historically been especially feared and has resulted in the most social stigma. In many cultures, certain of its relevant physical deformities are commonly recognized by lay people and mark individuals for isolation. In the Bible, leprosy patients were judged "unclean" and placed "outside the camp." In medieval Spain, sufferers were declared legally dead and their worldly goods dispersed, and in Norway into the 20th century, cowbells were placed around the necks of leprosy patients to warn others of their coming. In Asian societies, leprosy patients are commonly abandoned by families and communities, and Mohammed advised his followers to flee lepers as one would a lion. Until recently, the medical establishment isolated patients in leprosaria as the only perceived means of disease control because no effective chemotherapy was available until the 1940s. Babies born to diseased mothers were often separated from them at birth.

Now, patients who are fortunate enough to have early diagnosis and institution of effective chemotherapy can potentially avoid leprosy's peripheral neuropathy and consequent deformity and disability. Irrespective of physical sequelae, patients often suffer from the psychosocial aspects of leprosy. Loss of social status inherent in the inability to perform a normal job and rejection by family and friends compounds the misfortune. In working with affected persons, understanding, reassurance, and patient and community education and counseling are as important to the outcome as the use of standard medical treatments.

The burden that leprosy places on society is increased by the location of most cases in underdeveloped areas of the world, where health resources are few. Drug cost, shortage of health workers, and the need to monitor compliance have encouraged trials that use intermittent therapy and the shortest possible courses of therapy. Clinical response is slow, and freedom from relapse requires 7 to 10 years to assess.

Since the early 1980s, there has been a change in our fundamental understanding of leprosy and the potential for disease control. Previously, it was recognized that the severe lepromatous form of leprosy was by several orders of magnitude the most bacilliferous of human diseases and was associated with a cellular immune anergic state; patients were treated with antimicrobials indefinitely, primarily dapsone monotherapy. We now have come to understand that even in untreated patients, only about 1% of *Mycobacterium leprae* is viable and that, at least in some patients, the anergy is reversible with treatment[1, 2]; furthermore, with the development of newer antimicrobial agents, particularly rifampin, which is bactericidal for *M. leprae,* several regimens of combination antimicrobial therapy, and in particular one recommended by the World Health Organization (WHO MDT),[3] which incorporates certain once-monthly treatments, have been applied to patients for durations of 6 months to no more than 2 years. Early responses suggest those shorter course treatments are effective, but many patients treated by WHO MDT had previously received monotherapy dapsone, which is curative for 80% of even the most severe cases. Unfortunately, 7 years or even longer follow-up after discontinuation of therapy in previously untreated highly bacilliferous patients is necessary to detect relapse in rifampin-treated patients,[4] and in the one study of WHO MDT with careful prolonged follow-up of such duration, relapse rates of 20 to 40%, depending on the initial bacterial load, were found.[5] Nonetheless, with the advent of WHO MDT, proclamations of control of Hansen's disease as a public health problem in the near future and even disease eradication have resulted.[6] However, the worldwide incidence of new cases has yet to decline, and most current leprosy patients reside in areas with ineffective medical infrastructures for the delivery of effective therapy. It should be remembered that with the advent of effective short-course chemotherapy for pulmonary tuberculosis, a similar optimism concerning worldwide control of tuberculosis emerged in the 1970s, that optimism being shattered in the past decade by an increased incidence of tuberculosis in the United States and elsewhere.

EPIDEMIOLOGY

Worldwide, there are an estimated 6 million persons with leprosy, 3 million of whom are still untreated. Leprosy is endemic in Asia, Africa, Latin America, and the Pacific; Africa has the highest disease prevalence, and Asia has the greatest number of cases. Except as imported cases, leprosy is virtually absent from Canada, northern and western Europe, and the United States. In the United States, there are about 7000 patients, mostly immigrants from Mexico, Southeast Asia, the Philippines, and the Caribbean, and there is an annual incidence of 100 to 200 newly diagnosed patients.

Leprosy is associated with poverty, rural residence, and at times in North America, armadillo contact,[7] but not acquired immunodeficiency syndrome. Distribution of leprosy within endemic countries is very nonhomogeneous, and even adjacent villages may have striking differences in disease prevalence. Likely genetic factors play a role in disease expression, as HLA-DR-3 has been associated with tuberculoid disease,[8] HLA-MTI with lepromatous leprosy,[9] and a concordance between disease prevalence and type has been demonstrated in monozygotic twins but not in dizygotic twins.[10] Residence in an endemic country imposes a greater risk of disease than that posed to household contacts in nonendemic locales.[11] The disproportion of the polar forms of leprosy varies widely in different populations: In India and Africa, 90% of patients are tuberculoid, and in Southeast Asia 50% are lepromatous and 50% tuberculoid, whereas in Mexico 90% are lepromatous. It is entirely unclear whether these differences are a result of hereditary predisposition, prior mycobacterial contact and consequent immunity, or even route of transmission.

The mode of transmission of leprosy remains uncertain. The most commonly held view is that it is spread from human to human, primarily as a nasal droplet infection. The number of bacilli in a sneeze from a patient with untreated lepromatous leprosy is similar in magnitude to the number of bacilli in a cough from patients with untreated pulmonary tuberculosis,[12] and immunosuppressed mice placed in an aerosol of *M. leprae* become diseased.[13] It has been postulated that the primary site of inoculation is the nose, with subsequent hematogenous dissemination to the subcutaneous tissue and nerves. Evidence to support this postulate is that polymerase chain reaction has been used to detect *M. leprae* DNA in nasal swabs from asymptomatic persons in endemic areas.[14–16] Skin-to-skin contact, formerly thought to be an important mechanism of leprosy transmission, is not likely the general route, because organisms are not found histologically in the epidermis or most superficial layers of the dermis. Certainly, however, trauma, secondary infection, and certain lepromatous reactions may result in exfoliation of the epidermis, thereby allowing for a direct route of egress of organisms. Currently mounting evidence from several sources suggests that leprosy may be transmitted by soil: (1) The *M. leprae*–specific phenolic glycolipid 1 (PGL-1) has been found in soil[17, 18]; (2) leprosy is primarily a rural and not an urban disease; and (3) direct dermal inoculation, such as occurs in tattoo parlors, has been associated with disease transmission.[19] Leprosy decreased in several nations coincident with industrialization, but in many endemic countries, wearing of shoes in rural villages is uncommon. Also, insect vectors may play a role in disease transmission. Bed bugs and mosquitoes in the areas of leprosaria commonly harbor *M. leprae,*[20] and *M. leprae* can be transmitted to mice by affected mosquitoes.[21] In Louisiana and Texas, 15% of wild armadillos are infected with *M. leprae.*[22] Although this zoonosis is not present in leprosy-endemic countries, contact with armadillos in these states and perhaps in Mexico may result in disease.

The incubation period for leprosy is uniquely long among bacterial diseases, a minimum of 2 to 3 years, averaging 5 to 7 years, and can be as long as 40 years or more. The incubation period can be inferred from two principal sources: the youngest diagnosed children and the occasional individual from a nonendemic country who resides for a time in an endemic locale and returns home, enabling the time of infection to be pinpointed. The long incubation period is a function of at least two factors: *M. leprae* multiplies very slowly (doubling every 14 days in mice), and the number of bacilli harbored by a lepromatous patient on initial diagnosis is far greater than that of any other human bacterial disease—10^{15}. Although leprosy may affect persons of all ages, the peak age of onset is in young adults; children rarely acquire lepromatous leprosy.

It is noteworthy that there are far more infected persons with antibody to PGL-1 and lepromin (whole, killed *M. leprae*) skin-test positivity than persons who contract the disease. It is estimated that fully 90% of persons are naturally immune. The disseminated, lepromatous form of leprosy is twice as common in men as in women. Hormonal influence on immune responsiveness and hence growth of mycobacteria has been demonstrated for *Mycobacterium smegmatis* in mice.[23]

MICROBIOLOGIC CHARACTERISTICS OF *MYCOBACTERIUM LEPRAE*

M. leprae is an acid-fast bacillus (AFB) best visualized in tissue sections and homogenates by a modified Fite stain. It is 1 to 8 μm long, 0.3 to 0.5 μm wide, and cannot be distinguished morphologically from other mycobacteria. Gram-variable *M. leprae* is more akin to gram-positive than gram-negative bacteria. Unique properties of *M. leprae* include (1) loss of acid-fastness by pyridine extraction,[24] (2) presence of dopa oxidase activity,[25] and (3) multiplication in the mouse footpad with a doubling time of about 12 to 14 days.[26] Although *M. leprae* has not been grown in cell-free media or tissue culture, its maintenance of metabolism in short-term cultures has allowed for analysis of its antimicrobial sensitivity.[27–29] Viable *M. leprae* stain brightly and uniformly, whereas dead bacilli stain irregularly. This characteristic has allowed for a useful field assessment of *M. leprae* viability in both dermal skin smears and tissue sections, termed the *morphologic index,* the percentage of solidly staining bacilli. In addition, the *bacteriologic index*, a logarithmic measurement of the numbers of AFB in the dermis, also has utility in the field evaluation of patients and the efficacy of chemotherapy. *M. leprae* grows best in mice and in humans at temperatures lower than 37°C and hence has predilection for the cooler areas of the body, grows luxuriously in cold-blooded armadillos, and only in distal parts of rodents.

M. leprae is an obligate intracellular parasite that may remain viable outside the body for several days. Recent molecular biologic analysis of *M. leprae* has suggested that its genome is considerably smaller than that of other bacteria, including *M. tuberculosis,*[30] implying the absence of critical enzymatic pathways that necessitate reliance on host parasitism. Humans and the nine-banded armadillo[31] (found to date only in Texas and Louisiana) are its only known hosts in nature; certain armadillos are capable of acquiring disseminated infection resembling human lepromatous leprosy after experimental inoculation. Although several species of subhuman primates (including chimpanzees and mangabey, rhesus, and African green monkeys) have rarely been found to have disseminated *M. leprae* infection and may be experimentally infected,[32] natural infection in those species may be a consequence of contact with diseased humans. The local self-limited experimental infection of the mouse footpad, wherein $5 \times 10^3 - 1 \times 10^4$ *M. leprae* multiply to about 10^6, has provided a means to evaluate the activity of antimicrobials against *M. leprae,*[33] dissect protective immunity,[34] and evaluate potential candidate vaccines.[35] Furthermore, evidence for soil residence of *M. leprae* is now accumulating.

M. leprae in tissue section has a dense, largely lipid outer capsule outside the cell wall, which is rich in an *M. leprae*–specific phenolic glycolipid, termed *phenolic glycolipid 1* (PGL-1).[36] This outer capsule has been implicated as a scavenger of free radicals,[37] allowing for intracellular survival and limiting antimicrobial penetration. The PGL-1 itself has served as the antigen for a serologic test for leprosy.[38] It and a complex glycoprotein of *M. leprae,* lipoarabinomannan, have also been implicated as causing immunologic unresponsiveness of both lymphocytes[39, 40] and macrophages[41] in the anergic, highly bacilliferous, lepromatous form of leprosy. In fact, it has been found that vaccination of mice with subfractions of *M. leprae* largely devoid of resident lipids and carbohydrates provided protective immunity at lower quantities of mycobacteria and for a longer duration as compared with whole killed *M. leprae.*[42, 43]

Immunology

Leprosy expressions or types, such as the high-resistance tuberculoid and the low-resistance lepromatous forms, in contrast to leprosy susceptibility, have associations with the major histocompatibility locus, as demonstrated by nonrandom haplotype inheritance in affected persons,[44, 45] and a high frequency of HLA DR-2 in tuberculoid patients.[46] No specific mechanism has been identified to explain these divergent outcomes. Thus, the origins of lepromin unresponsiveness, a surrogate for the lepromatous outcome, remain a central problem in the immunology of leprosy.

The lepromin skin test and its in vitro correlate, the *M. leprae*–stimulated lymphocyte transformation test are positive in all TT patients, most (85%) BT patients, and most unaffected adults in leprosy endemic or nonendemic locales, but are negative in untreated BB, BL, and LL.[47–49] The terminology used here represents the spectrum between tuberculoid and lepromatous leprosy, as follows: TT—tuberculoid tuberculoid, BT—borderline tuberculoid, BB—borderline borderline, BL—borderline lepromatous and LL—lepromatous lepromatous leprosy. Thus, lepromin skin tests have no diagnostic value but may be useful in classification. In our experience, the unresponsiveness is specific for antigens of *M. leprae,*[50] such patients having normal recall responses and not being at risk for opportunistic infections. Conversion from negative to positive responses both in vitro and in vivo may be seen in reversal reactions, after reduction in bacillary load occurring in association with prolonged chemotherapy,[1, 2] or in vitro in some lepromatous patients with the addition of interleukin (IL)-12 and anti–IL-10 to the mononuclear suspension.[51] This suggests that, at least in part, the anergy of the lepromatous leprosy is a result of the disease, not strictly its cause.

Immunophenotyping of T cells has demonstrated a 2:1 predominance of the $CD\text{-}4^+$ over the $CD\text{-}8^+$ subset of T cells in TT and BT tissues, the $CD\text{-}8^+$ cells also being mostly $CD\text{-}28^+$, that is, the cytotoxic phenotype. In contrast, in LL tissues there is a 2:1 predominance of the $CD\text{-}8^+$ over the $CD\text{-}4^+$ subset, and the former are mostly $CD\text{-}28^-$, that is, the suppressor phenotype.[52]

TT and BT tissues are rich in the mRNAs coding for the proinflammatory Th1 family of cytokines, IL-2, interferon (INF-γ), and IL-12, but IL-4, IL-5, and IL-10 mRNAs are scarce. In contrast, LL tissues show a type Th2 cytokine profile—that is to say, they are rich in the mRNAs coding for IL-4, IL-5, and IL-10 but poor in IL-2, INF-γ, and IL-12. The prospect that cytokines mediate the tissue response is supported by the injection of INF-γ or IL-2 into lepromatous lesions, which results in decreased numbers of AFB and the conversion of the tissue response toward a tuberculoid pattern.[53, 54]

Although the presence of data to the contrary does not permit the complete exculpation of macrophages,[53, 54] the preponderance of evidence indicates that macrophages have no intrinsic defect that explains leprosy expression (i.e., tuberculoid or lepromatous) or lepromin unresponsiveness.[55] For example, HLA-DR–matched lepromatous macrocytes can present antigen to tuberculoid lymphocytes.[56]

Also, peripheral blood monocytes from leprosy patients are functionally normal in their response to INF and microbicidal potential.[55] Furthermore, peripheral blood-adherent cells from treated tuberculoid and lepromatous patients elaborate cytokines similarly when challenged with *M. leprae* or its components.[51] However, *M. leprae* or some of its constituents, once internalized and established, do modify the behavior of macrophages, thus altering the lesional environment to the extent that the behavior of newly recruited monocytes may be affected.[55] The human NRAMP1g (natural resistance–associated macrophage protein 1), whose murine homologue confers genetic resistance to *M. lepraemurium* infection, has been linked to leprosy susceptibility in a number of, but not all, populations.[57–59]

Antibodies directed against a number of *M. leprae* epitopes, both *M. leprae*–specific and cross reactive with other mycobacterial species, are found in the sera of more than 95% of lepromatous and about 50% of tuberculoid patients,[60] thus excluding a protective role for these antibodies. In endemic areas, up to 45% of household contacts and 9% of normal noncontacts have such antibodies,[38, 60] making them putatively subclinically infected individuals, which makes serologic testing of little value in diagnosis but useful in epidemiologic studies. Anti–*M. leprae* dimeric IgA in nasal mucosa may be an important host-resistance factor.[61]

Probably as a consequence of polyclonal T-cell activation, lepromatous patients are hypergammagobulinemic and also have a wide variety of autoantibodies, producing false-positive serologic test results for syphilis, rheumatoid arthritis, lupus erythematosus, and others that may result in diagnostic confusion but are of little clinical importance.

Antibody responses are directed against a number of *M. leprae* constituents, including PGL-1 lipoarabinomannan as well as the specific and cross-reacting epitopes of the heat shock proteins (HSP).[60] Concerning cellular immunity, PGL-1 elicits a suppressive response,[62] but the cell wall–associated HSP are strong promoters of Th1 cytokines.[63] Lipoarabinomannan has a nonspecific inhibitory effect on antigen- or mitogen-induced lymphocyte processes and suppresses the macrophage response to INF-γ, but it elicits an antigen-specific Th1 cytokine response when presented to a small subset of T cells.[64]

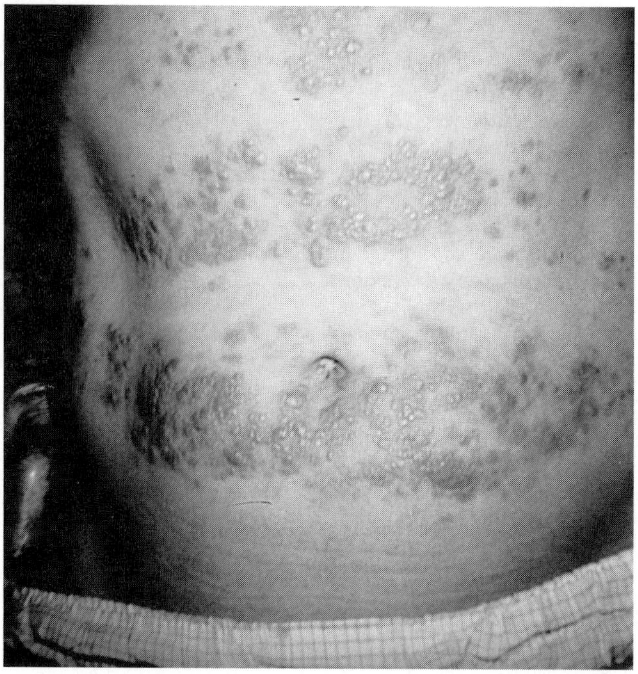

FIGURE 241–1. Lepromatous leprosy characterized by extensive papule formation over abdomen. Minimal or no sensory loss is present in the affected areas.

CLINICAL MANIFESTATIONS

Clinical Spectrum of Leprosy

Leprosy is a disease with a well-defined clinical, histologic, and immunologic spectrum.[65] The form of leprosy is important in predicting disease complications, reaction states likely to be encountered, and intensity and duration of required chemotherapy. Clinical manifestations of leprosy are largely confined to the skin, upper respiratory system, eyes, testes, and peripheral nerves. Most of the serious sequelae are a result of *M. leprae's* having unique tropism for peripheral nerves. Small nerve fibers are most commonly functionally impaired, resulting in loss of fine touch, pain, and hot and cold sensation; position and vibration sense are generally maintained. Both major nerve trunks and microscopic dermal nerves may be affected in leprosy patients, the most common nerve trunk impairment being the ulnar nerve at the elbow, leading to clawing of the fourth and fifth fingers, loss of dorsal interosseous musculature, and loss of sensation of the hand in the ulnar distribution. Nerve damage appears to result from either bacterial multiplication within Schwann cells or granulomatous damage to the perineurium. Loss of protective sensation in the feet may result in troublesome, recurrent plantar ulceration, generally at the metatarsal heads. Leprosy results in peripheral nerve enlargement, which is pathognomonic for this disorder and for two rare hereditary peripheral neuropathies, Marie-Charcot-Tooth disease and Dejerine-Sottas disease.

On one pole of the leprosy spectrum is the patient with lepromatous leprosy. These patients have symmetric skin nodules, plaques, and a thickened dermis (Fig. 241–1). Because *M. leprae* grows best at low temperatures, the cool areas of the body, such as the ear lobes, are commonly affected and the feet are scaly and ichthyotic. The warmer areas—the scalp, axilla, groin, and midline of the back—are generally spared. In patients who are almost exclusively from Mexico and the Caribbean, there is a type of lepromatous leprosy without visible skin lesions but only diffuse dermal infiltration, termed *diffuse lepromatosis.* Lepromatous leprosy patients may have loss of eyebrows, especially the lateral portions, and at times eyelashes and body hair. In untreated lepromatous leprosy, organisms can be detected in sputum, and a high-level afebrile continuous bacteremia is frequently found, which may be so profuse that organisms are found in stained smears of peripheral blood "buffy" coats.[66]

In lepromatous patients, the upper respiratory system, particularly the nasal mucosa, are infiltrated with organisms, leading to chronic nasal congestion and epistaxis. In the preantibiotic era and occasionally even today, this process may extend to the nasal cartilage, leading to septal collapse and a "saddle nose" deformity. Peripheral neuropathy in lepromatous patients, when present, is often generalized and symmetric and frequently is associated with acral distal anesthesia of the hands and feet.

Tuberculoid leprosy represents the other pole of the leprosy spectrum. Patients with tuberculoid leprosy have one or a few hypopigmented anesthetic plaques with distinct, often elevated and erythematous borders. Skin lesions are often dry, scaly, and anhydrotic. Lesions may vary in size from a few to many centimeters in diameter. At times, lesions may not manifest hypoesthesia. Large and pathologic asymmetric peripheral nerve trunk involvement, often spatially associated with skin lesions, is found in tuberculoid leprosy. At times, patients may have large and functionally impaired nerve trunks (generally only one) without skin lesions, termed *neural leprosy,* as the sole manifestation of tuberculoid leprosy. Tuberculoid leprosy, unlike lepromatous leprosy, does not result in upper respiratory signs and symptoms. At times, tuberculoid leprosy heals spontaneously.

The majority of leprosy patients have manifestations intermediate between the two polar forms of leprosy, a condition termed *borderline leprosy*, which does not heal spontaneously. Depending on whether these manifestations are closer to the tuberculoid pole or lepromatous pole, they are classified *borderline lepromatous* (*BL*) or *borderline tuberculoid* (*BT*) (Fig. 241–2).

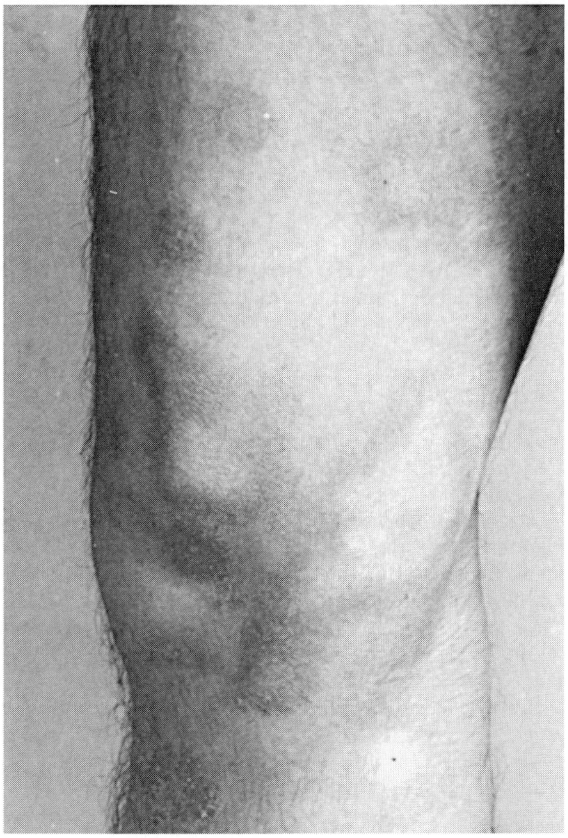

FIGURE 241–2. Borderline (BL) leprosy showing macular lesions with moderately well-defined borders and hypopigmented centers. There is sensory impairment in the affected areas.

Histologic Features

Skin biopsies from leprosy patients should be stained with both hematoxylin and eosin stain and an acid-fast stain (always with a known positive control), preferably Fite,[67] because *M. leprae* may be entirely decolorized when stained by Ziehl-Neelsen. Also, at times, silver stains alone reveal the presence of *M. leprae.* In lepromatous patients, nodules or plaques are the preferred sites for biopsies, but normal-appearing skin also will be pathologic. In tuberculoid patients, biopsies should be performed on lesions and preferably the rims of lesions, because clinically uninvolved skin will not prove diagnostic. Neural leprosy presents a diagnostic quandary, insofar as nerve biopsy itself may result in loss of sensory or motor function, or both. However, when the clinical picture is sufficiently unclear, nerve biopsy may be required and is reasonably safe if only lateral neural fascicles, preferably of a purely sensory nerve, such as the radial cutaneous nerve at the wrist, are removed.

Skin biopsies in lepromatous leprosy reveal numerous AFB, sometimes in clumps termed *globi*. Although causing clinically important changes in a limited number of organs, bacilli are widely disseminated, sparing only the lungs and central nervous system. On hematoxylin and eosin stain, lepromatous skin biopsies are noteworthy for the prevalence of numerous, highly vacuolated cells of macrophage lineage termed *foam cells* (Virchow cells) and few lymphocytes. Foam cells are laden with AFB and stain highly positive with stains for fat owing largely to the high lipid composition of *M. leprae* and particularly its outer capsule. In lepromatous leprosy, there are granulomatous changes in the liver, spleen, bone marrow, and lymph nodes. Granulomatous architecture replaces the T-cell–laden paracortical areas of the lymph nodes, often with associated hyperplasia of the largely B-cell–containing germinal centers.[68]

In tuberculoid leprosy, AFB are rarely found at skin biopsy. The dermal, and not infrequently epidermal, granulomas are composed of epithelioid cells, lymphocytes, and Langhans giant cells, often in proximity to dermal appendages, especially dermal nerves. Actual granulomatous invasion and destruction of dermal nerves, occasionally with caseous necrosis, are pathognomonic for tuberculoid leprosy. In the various forms of borderline leprosy, tissue responses consist of incremental changes between the tuberculoid and lepromatous extremes, involving primarily the differentiation of macrophages, the number and distribution of lymphocytes, and the number of bacilli. Unlike pure tuberculoid leprosy, in BT leprosy the epidermis is only focally infiltrated by lymphocytes. BL, as opposed to pure lepromatous leprosy, demonstrates many more lymphocytes and fewer AFB.

DIAGNOSIS AND DIFFERENTIAL DIAGNOSIS

To the experienced leprosy clinician, the presenting clinical and histologic picture in most cases of leprosy, particularly BL and LL disease, is reasonably straightforward. A firm diagnosis of leprosy requires the presence of a characteristic peripheral nerve abnormality (including peripheral nerve enlargement) or the demonstration of AFB. In atypical cases of TT/BT leprosy, in which AFB usually are not found, we require two of the following three criteria for a diagnosis: a clinically compatible skin lesion, dermal granuloma on biopsy, and hypoesthesia within the lesion (with the caveat that acute and chronic inflammation of any cause may result in some hypoesthesia). If the patient has no history of residence in an endemic area, a diagnosis of leprosy should be regarded with skepticism. When there is diagnostic uncertainty, we would rather treat someone who does not have leprosy than not treat someone who does have the disease.

To those inexperienced with the disease and in certain atypical cases, the differential diagnosis may include lupus vulgaris, sarcoidosis, dermal leishmaniasis, lymphoma, syphilis, yaws, granuloma annulare, various disorders causing hypopigmentation, and so on. It is important to recognize in lepromatous leprosy that sputum smears will commonly demonstrate AFB that will not grow in culture. Sarcoidosis may result in peripheral nerve dysfunction and granulomatous involvement surrounding dermal nerves with involvement of the perineurium but not actual dermal nerve invasion or destruction.

LEPRA TYPE-1 REACTIONS (DOWNGRADING AND REVERSAL REACTIONS)

An abrupt increase in inflammation within previously quiescent skin lesions, as well as new skin lesions, neuritis, and low-grade fever, may develop in borderline leprosy patients (BT to BL) before therapy (downgrading reaction) or after the initiation of therapy (reversal reaction). If neuritis is not treated promptly and vigorously, irreversible nerve damage and consequent deformity and muscular dysfunction may result. Edema in the granuloma is the most common microscopic characteristic, but the diagnosis is primarily clinical.

Reversal reactions are associated with histologic shifts toward the tuberculoid end of the spectrum, and downgrading is associated with shifts toward the lepromatous end. Lesions have a Th1 cytokine profile and demonstrate increased numbers of $CD4^+$ helper cells and increased levels of INF-γ, and IL-2. In addition, type 1 reactions have an abundance of T cells bearing gamma/delta receptors, perhaps part of an early immune response to mycobacteria. This latter pattern is shared with Mitsuda-positive skin test results and does not occur spontaneously otherwise in leprosy.[69]

LEPRA TYPE-2 REACTION (ERYTHEMA NODOSUM LEPROSUM)

Erythema nodosum leprosum (ENL) is a syndrome affecting nearly half of BL and LL leprosy patients, 90% of the time occurring after the initiation of antimicrobial therapy and generally within the first 2 years of treatment. Clinical manifestations include, in order of frequency, painful nodules, generally on the extensor surfaces of extremities, which may pustulate and ulcerate and may appear as recurrent crops; neuritis (most frequently the ulnar nerve); fever; malaise; anorexia; leucocytosis; anemia; uveitis; lymphadenitis; orchitis; and glomerulonephritis. The severity of ENL varies greatly as does the frequency with which crops of lesions occur. The syndrome in any given patient may be trivial or may be severe and unremittent, producing extensive morbidity. Episodes of ENL may occur over a period of 5 years or even longer. Lepromatous leprosy patients should be forewarned of signs and symptoms of ENL, lest their appearance result in loss of confidence with antimicrobial therapy and noncompliance. Microscopically ENL is a panniculitis with a variable vasculitis, primarily thought to be secondary to immune complex deposition. The inflammatory infiltrate preferentially involves the deeper dermis or subcutaneous tissue with increased numbers of lymphocytes and the presence of neutrophils.

ENL tissues have a Th2 cytokine profile, as well as high levels of IL-6 and IL-8, consistent with an immune complex–mediated pathogenesis.[70] However, this attractive hypothesis is confounded by several observations, including the HLA-DR framework antigen on epidermal keratinocytes[71] (a marker for delayed-type hypersensitivity response) and, as compared with LL tissues, increased numbers of cells staining for IL-2[72] and an increased number of cells synthesizing INF-γ.[73]

LUCIO'S REACTION AND NERVE ABSCESSES

Patients with diffuse lepromatosis may experience recurrent crops of sharply marginated hemorrhagic infarcts with serrated borders, which appear similar to other cutaneous septic infarcts. The infarcts often progress to form slowly healing ulcers, particularly on the legs. Microscopically, the lesions show an ischemic necrosis of the epidermis and upper dermis with endothelial proliferation and thrombus formation in the larger vessels of the deep dermis. Heavy parasitization of endothelial cells by AFB both in normal and abnormal vessels is a characteristic finding. In our experience, new lesions cease with the administration of rifampin, suggesting a strict requirement for viable bacilli. When generalized, Lucio's reaction is frequently fatal, usually a result of secondary bacterial infection and sepsis. Immune complex mediation is likely.[74]

Also, leprosy patients, particularly BT or neural leprosy patients, may acquire nerve abscesses requiring urgent surgical decompression and drainage. Microscopically, these are similar to rheumatoid or rheumatic nodules.[75]

DEFORMITY

The most commonly involved motor nerve trunk in leprosy is the ulnar nerve at the elbow, perhaps owing to its superficial, cool site and the stretch imposed by elbow extension. Damage of the ulnar nerve leads to clawing of the fourth and fifth fingers and loss of dorsal interosseous musculature. Median nerve dysfunction is less common and results in inability to oppose the thumb and grasp and hold objects. Radial nerve dysfunction is unusual in leprosy but, when present, results in wrist drop. Peroneal nerve dysfunction results in foot drop. Loss of distal parts of digits in leprosy is due to insensitivity, trauma, secondary infection, and an osteoporotic (lytic) bony process of lepromatous leprosy itself. Plantar ulceration, particularly under the metatarsal heads, is a major cause of disability in leprosy. Ulcers are often recurrent, may become infected secondarily, and result in adjacent osteomyelitis. Plantar ulcerations are treated most effectively by avoiding weight-bearing activities, which may be effected by a total-contact walking cast, bed rest, crutches, or a healing boot; instituting therapy for secondary infection; and, after the ulcerations are healed, wearing specially molded shoes and assiduous shaving of the subsequent thick calluses, which themselves cause recurrence.

Nasal collapse, although not as common in the postantibiotic era, still affects some patients. Nasal reconstruction surgery can largely ameliorate the cosmetic defect, making the appearance of affected patients once again socially acceptable.

AMYLOIDOSIS

Secondary amyloidosis is currently an uncommon consequence of long-untreated lepromatous leprosy and ENL. Although liver dysfunction may result, the major organ found functionally impaired is the kidney, leading at times to renal failure and the requirement for dialysis.

EYE INVOLVEMENT

In lepromatous leprosy, the anterior chamber of the eye is invaded by *M. leprae,* and ENL may be associated with uveitis. These may result in glaucoma and cataract formation. Eye involvement in leprosy is also a consequence of corneal insensitivity (associated with small lepromas), resulting in "beaded" corneal nerves, which leads to trauma (trichiasis), secondary infection, and scarring. Also, such consequences may result from muscle paralysis secondary to disease of the trigeminal branch of the facial nerve and resultant lagophthalmos. Some of the eye complications may be forestalled by the use of artificial tears during the day and ophthalmic ointment at night. Removal of eyelashes that scratch the cornea and corrective surgery for lagophthalmos are frequently required. In addition, lepromatous leprosy is associated with loss of eyebrows and eyelashes, the lack of which is an important cosmetic embarrassment.

TESTICULAR DYSFUNCTION

In lepromatous leprosy, bacilli invade the testes; furthermore, the testes may be involved in ENL. Testicular dysfunction occurs in 85% of LL men (25% of BL men) and in severity ranges from mild elevation of serum follicle-stimulating hormone (FSH) and/or luteinizing hormone to high follicle-stimulating hormone and luteinizing hormone elevations and low sperm counts and testosterone levels, resulting in infertility or impotence, or both.[76] For such patients, testosterone replacement may prove beneficial.

THERAPY

Immunotherapy

Because untreated lepromatous leprosy is associated with anergy to *M. leprae* itself, various approaches to immunotherapy have been tried. These include experimental vaccination of lepromatous leprosy patients with killed nonpathogenic mycobacteria[77–79] and local injection of IL-2 and INF-γ. Although all have resulted in at least partial reversal of anergy and more rapid clearance of dead *M. leprae,* it is not clear whether these modalities add to the efficacy of conventional antimicrobial therapy.

Antimicrobial Therapy

Because of the relative lack of acute symptoms in leprosy and the long durations of therapy required, compliance rates frequently have been found to be low. The antimicrobial therapy of lepromatous leprosy, owing to its enormous bacterial burden and associated immune defect, generally requires more extensive treatment than does tuberculoid leprosy. In fact, in the preantibiotic era, tuberculoid leprosy was frequently found to heal spontaneously. Two problems compound the effective treatment of lepromatous leprosy: the documented emergence of drug resistance (particularly to dapsone) and the frequent presence of viable, drug-sensitive *M. leprae* ("persisters"), which can be found in the tissues of lepromatous patients despite long periods of effective chemotherapy.

Between 1943 and 1970, sulfone monotherapy, particularly dapsone, was the only treatment employed to treat all forms of leprosy. Lepromatous infiltration resolved with this treatment , and the dermis generally became negative for AFB by slit skin smears in 3 to 6 years. Sulfone monotherapy was found to be remarkably effective, with only 10% of lepromatous leprosy patients relapsing with dapsone resistance,[80] and when patients were treated for approximately 20 years and therapy was discontinued, only 1% had relapsed annually after 9 years' follow-up.[81] Several other series, however, demonstrated that both secondary and even primary dapsone resistance created a much larger problem.[82] Almost all primary dapsone resistance has been documented only to levels much less than those obtained therapeutically, and in California in a large series, even this occurred only 1% of the time.[83] However, many authorities have concluded that the prevalence and implications of primary dapsone resistance are such that it cannot be relied on as generally effective. Furthermore, with the demonstration that other drugs were active against *M. leprae* and, unlike dapsone, bactericidal, multidrug therapy has become the universally recommended treatment for lepromatous leprosy.

Several studies have demonstrated that patients treated for many years with dapsone alone or several years with rifampin additionally still harbor viable *M. leprae*.[84, 85] At issue is with what frequency these "persisters" result in clinical relapse if treatment is discontinued. The World Health Organization (WHO) in 1982, with some revision in 1988,[3] recommended a multidrug therapy regimen for lepromatous leprosy and advocated, rather than conventional lifelong therapy, that treatment be discontinued after as little as 2 years in lepromatous leprosy patients. This therapy has reduced the number of leprosy patients under treatment worldwide by more than half. In tallies of leprosy cases by the WHO, a patient no longer being treated is not considered to have leprosy, irrespective of deformity or subsequent reactional states. However, the worldwide incidence of new disease has not been affected, remaining at 600,000 annually, and the period of follow-up after discontinuation of therapy has not been sufficiently long to ensure that cure rates are acceptable. This is because although relapses after dapsone monotherapy of lepromatous leprosy begin as soon as therapy is discontinued, with regimens including rifampin, such as advocated by the WHO, relapses begin only several years subsequently.[4, 5]

Agents to Treat Leprosy

Established agents used to treat leprosy include dapsone (50 to 100 mg daily), clofazimine (50 to 100 mg daily or 100 mg three times weekly), and rifampin (600 mg daily or monthly), rifampin being the most bactericidal drug of all in the therapy of leprosy.[33, 85] Also, ethionamide and prothionamide (250 to 500 mg daily), as well as certain aminoglycosides (streptomycin, kanamycin, amikacin, but not gentamicin and tobramycin) have been used to some extent.[86] Unfortunately, the requirement of aminoglycosides for intramuscular administration and the long-term therapy required for leprosy make them impractical for most developing countries where leprosy is endemic.

In the past several years, antimicrobials from three classes of antibiotics, each of which appears more bactericidal than dapsone and clofazimine, have been found promising for the treatment of leprosy. Minocycline is consistently bactericidal for *M. leprae* in mice,[87, 88] and in a clinical trial in lepromatous leprosy, 100 mg daily resulted in very rapid and consistent clinical improvement as well as rapid clearance of viable *M. leprae* from the dermis.[89–91] Minocycline has the advantage over the other newer agents of proven safety on chronic administration. Clarithromycin appears bactericidal for *M. leprae* in mice[29, 92, 93] and effective in clinical trials.[90, 94] A number of fluoroquinolones appear bactericidal for *M. leprae* in mice.[95–97] Pefloxacin[98, 99] and ofloxacin[99] appear to be bactericidal in lepromatous leprosy patients. Toxicity of the fluoroquinolones and clarithromycin on long-term administration has not yet been evaluated. These new agents not only offer alternatives to the few standard drugs now available to treat leprosy but, because of their potency, also offer the potential that shorter course regimens might prove effective.

Regimens to Treat Leprosy

To simplify field work, the WHO[3] classified leprosy as paucibacillary and multibacillary, each with its own treatment regimen. Initially, paucibacillary leprosy included only patients with a BI of 0 to 1+, whereas multibacillary patients had a BI of 2+ or more. More recently, in the belief that microscopy in many developing countries was cumbersome and unreliable, the requirement for it has now been omitted, paucibacillary being defined as no more than five skin lesions and no nerve damage.

For paucibacillary leprosy, the WHO[3] advocates dapsone, 100 mg daily, and rifampin, 600 mg once monthly, for 6 months. In a multicenter clinical trial single-day therapy (rifampin 600 mg, ofloxacin 400 mg, and minocycline 100 mg [called *ROM*]) for paucibacillary leprosy was found equally effective as standard WHO MDT.[100] Patients included in the study were those who had only one skin lesion, negative skin smears, no prior treatment for leprosy, no evidence of peripheral nerve trunk involvement, and no known human immunodeficiency virus (HIV) infection and who were not pregnant. The WHO Expert Committee has endorsed this controversial regimen, which is most applicable to developing and isolated areas of the world.[101] However, serious reservations about such therapy have been expressed,[102] and trials in paucibacillary leprosy are notoriously difficult to interpret, as objective measures, such as loss of viable bacilli, are not possible. Also, after short-course therapy, both reactions and relapse are not uncommon and are often difficult to distinguish from one another. We treat tuberculoid (paucibacillary) leprosy with dapsone, 100 mg daily, for 5 years because of the lack of clinically significant primary dapsone resistance[83] and to obviate the problems just raised.

The WHO[3] treats multibacillary leprosy with daily dapsone (100 mg) and clofazimine (50 mg) and monthly-supervised rifampin (600 mg) and clofazimine (300 mg). The WHO[3] recommended that treatment be maintained for a minimum of 2 years or until skin-smear negativity occurs (generally 5 years) and then be discontinued. More recently, and without prior clinical trial, the WHO[101] has shortened this duration of therapy to 1 year, which has caused some controversy.[103, 104] With a regularly successful outcome, we[105] treat lepromatous leprosy with daily dapsone (100 mg) and daily rifampin (600 mg) for the first 3 years or so, maintaining dapsone lifelong. This is owing to (1) the late relapse rate of 20 to 40% found in previously untreated highly bacilliferous patients, who are given 2 years of WHO MDT[5]; (2) the lack of clinically significant primary dapsone resistance[83]; and (3) clofazimine's being cosmetically unacceptable to many light-skinned persons.

Response to Therapy

Lepromatous infiltration resolves with effective chemotherapy, and nodules and plaques flatten. Clinical improvement, however, may be slow, often taking a few months to become apparent and a few years to be complete. At times, peripheral neuropathy may also improve, but this is not generally the case, depending largely on whether dysfunction is a result of bacterial invasion and inflammation or whether neuronal degeneration has already occurred.

In lepromatous leprosy, the percentage of well-stained organisms in a skin biopsy or smear of tissue juice expressed from a skin slit can be enumerated and this is called the *morphologic index*. The morphologic index falls to zero with even dapsone monotherapy in 2 to 3 months. With more bactericidal drugs, such as rifampin, this occurs in only a few weeks. Clinical studies have also injected mouse foot pads with biopsy tissue from patients during study, using inocula with different numbers of organisms. The mice are killed 12 months later, and the number of organisms in the foot pad tissue are enumerated. The presence and proportion of viable organisms can be counted and used to compare regimens.[106] Independent of the degree of bactericidal activity of the regimen used, the bacteriologic index falls slowly, about 1 unit/year, and 93% of patients are skin-smear negative within 6 years.[107]

With effective therapy, tuberculoid skin lesions may resolve somewhat, disappear entirely, or show little to no apparent change; this last result does not indicate that treatment failure has occurred. Anesthesia or hypoesthesia of affected skin is frequently permanent. The appearance of new tuberculoid lesions or clinical activity of old lesions, especially when associated with signs of inflammation, may occur after discontinuation of therapy. The appearance of new and especially uninflamed lesions suggests treatment failure, whereas the appearance of inflammation within previously affected skin lesions suggests that a late reversal reaction is occurring. However, because of the frequent lack of demonstrable bacilli in tuberculoid lesions, the distinction between microbiologic relapse and late reversal reactions is frequently difficult.

Therapy of Reactions

Lepra type-1 reactions can be treated effectively with corticosteroids only. We generally initiate therapy with prednisone, 40 to 60 mg daily. Because relapses commonly occur if steroids are discontinued rapidly, steroids at reduced doses as signs and symptoms allow must be maintained for at least 2 to 3 months. Because of the requirement that steroids be maintained for long durations with their known serious complications, strict indications are neuritis, lesions that threaten to ulcerate, and lesions that appear on cosmetically important places such as the face.

Lepra type-2 reactions (ENL) can also be treated effectively with corticosteroids, and short durations are often sufficient. If ENL is recurrent, thalidomide in a nightly dose of 100 to 300 mg is the treatment of choice. In the United States, thalidomide is commercially available for use in leprosy treatment, but use is tightly regulated. The mechanism of action of thalidomide for ENL is not fully understood but may be a result of its action to reduce IgM synthesis,[108] retard polymorphonuclear leukocyte migration,[109] and reduce tumor necrosis factor levels.[110] Other than resultant birth defects when administered to pregnant women in the first trimester and peripheral neuropathy (only rarely seen in leprosy), thalidomide is nontoxic, its only common side effects being tranquilization, to which tolerance develops quickly, as well as mild leukopenia and constipation.

Neither thalidomide nor corticosteroid therapy has proved effective therapy for Lucio's reaction. In severe cases, exchange transfusion may be effective. In general, however, the principles of good wound care and appropriate antibiotics for sepsis are recommended.

PROPHYLAXIS

Dapsone prophylaxis of household contacts of leprosy patients to a limited extent reduces the subsequent prevalence of the development of tuberculoid leprosy but only forestalls the onset of lepromatous leprosy and is not generally recommended.[111]

Calmette-Guérin bacillus vaccination trials for leprosy have proved moderately effective (80%[112]) to ineffective.[113, 114] It has been found that vaccination with heat-killed *M. leprae* in addition to Calmette-Guérin bacillus does not further vaccine efficacy.[115] It has been demonstrated in mice that subunits of *M. leprae,* largely devoid of immunosuppressive fats and carbohydrates and mostly proteinaceous, are more effective than whole, killed *M. leprae* as vaccines,[42, 43] suggesting that more effective vaccines for leprosy and perhaps tuberculosis are possible.

REFERENCES

1. Esquenazi DA, Sampaio EP, Moreira AL, et al. Effect of treatment on immune responsiveness in lepromatous leprosy patients. Lepr Rev. 1990;61:251–257.
2. Cree IA, Smith WCS, Rees RJW, et al. The influence of antimycobacterial chemotherapy on delayed hypersensitivity skin-test reactions in leprosy patients. Lepr Rev. 1988;59:145–151.
3. WHO Expert Committee on Leprosy, 1988. Sixth Report, Technical Report Series No. 768, World Health Organization, Geneva, Switzerland.
4. Grosset J-H, Guelpa-Lauras CC, Bobin P, et al. Study of 39 documented relapses of multibacillary leprosy after treatment with rifampin. Int J Lepr. 1989;57:507–614.
5. Marchoux Chemotherapy Study Group (prepared by Jamet P, Ji B). Relapses in multibacillary leprosy patients after stopping treatment with rifampin-containing combined regimens. Int J Lepr. 1992;60:525–535.
6. Noordeen SK. A look at world leprosy. Lepr Rev. 1991;62:72–86.
7. Thomas DA, Mines JS, Thomas DC, et al. Armadillo exposure among Mexican-born patients with lepromatous leprosy. J Infect Dis. 1987;156:990–992.
8. van Eden W, De Vries RRP, D'Amaro J, et al. HLA-DR associated genetic control the type of leprosy in a population from Surinam. Hum Immunol. 1982;4:343.
9. van Eden W, Gonzalez NM, De Vries RR, et al. HLA-linked control of predisposition to lepromatous leprosy. J Infect Dis. 1985;151:9.
10. Chakravartti MR, Vogel F. A twin study on leprosy. Stuttgart: Georg Thieme; 1973.
11. Leiker DL. Epidemiology of leprosy in the Netherlands. Quad Coop Sani. 1980;1:60–64.
12. Davey TF, Rees RJW. The nasal discharge in leprosy: Clinical and bacteriological aspects. Lepr Rev. 1974;45:121–134.
13. Rees RJW, McDougall AC. Airborne infection with *Mycobacterium leprae* in mice. Int J Lepr. 1976;44:99–103.
14. Kazda J, Ganapati R, Revankar C, et al. Isolation of environment-derived *Mycobacterium leprae* from soil in Bombay. Lepr Rev. 1986;57:201–208.
15. Narayanan E, Manja KS, Bedi BMS, et al. Arthropod feeding experiments in lepromatous leprosy. Lepr Rev. 1977;43:188–193.
16. Narayanan E, Sreevatsa, Kirchheimer WF, et al. Transfer of leprosy bacilli from patients to mouse footpads by *Aedes aegypti.* Lepr India. 1977;49:181–189.
17. Blake LA, West BC, Lary CH, et al. Environmental nonhuman sources of leprosy. Rev Infect Dis. 1987;9:562–577.
18. Truman RW, Franzblau SG, Job CK. The nine-banded armadillo, *Dasypus novemcinctus,* as an animal model to study the transmission of leprosy (Abstract No. U-23). In: Abstracts of the Annual Meeting of the American Society for Microbiology: 86th Annual Meeting. Washington, DC: American Society for Microbiology; 1986:123.
19. Porrit RJ, Olsen RE. Two simultaneous cases of leprosy developing in tattoos (Extended abstract). Int J Lepr. 1948;16:514–520.
20. Narayanan E, Manja KS, Bedi BMS, et al. Arthropod feeding experiments in lepromatous leprosy. Lepr Rev. 1977;43:188–193.
21. Narayanan E, Sreevatsa, Kirchheimer WF, et al. Transfer of leprosy bacilli from patients to mouse footpads by *Aedes aegypti.* Lepr India. 1977;49:181–189.
22. Smith JH, Folse DS, Lang EG, et al. Leprosy in wild armadillos (*Dasypus novemcinctus*) of the Texas Gulf Coast: Epidemiology and mycobacteriology. J Reticuloendothel Soc. 1983;34:75–88.
23. Yamamoto Y, Saito H, Setoqawa T, et al. Sex differences in host resistance to *Mycobacterium marinum* infection in mice. Infect Immun. 1991;59:4089–4096.
24. Fisher CA, Barksdale L. Cytochemical reactions of human leprosy bacilli and mycobacteria: Ultrastructural implications. J Bacteriol. 1973;113:389.
25. Prabhakaran K, Kirchheimer WF, Harris EB. Oxidation of phenolic compounds by *Mycobacterium leprae* and inhibition of phenolase by substrate analogues and copper chelators. J Bacteriol. 1968;95:2051.
26. Shepard CC. The experimental disease that follows the injection of human leprosy bacilli into footpads of mice. J Exp Med. 1960;112:445–454.
27. Franzblau SG. Oxidation of palmitic acid by *Mycobacterium leprae* in an axenic medium. J Clin Microbiol. 1988;26:18–21.
28. Franzblau SG. Drug susceptibility testing of *Mycobacterium leprae* in the BACTEC 460 system. Antimicrob Agents Chemother. 1989;33:2115–2117.
29. Franzblau SG, Hastings RC. In vitro and in vivo activities of macrolides against *Mycobacterium leprae.* Antimicrob Agents Chemother. 1988;32:1758–1762.
30. Cole ST. The genome of *Mycobacterium leprae.* Int J Lepr. 1994;62:122–125.
31. Walsh GP, Storrs EE, Meyers W, et al. Naturally acquired leprosy-like disease in the nine-banded armadillo (*Dasypus novemcinctus*): Recent epizootiologic findings. J Reticuloendothel Soc. 1989;22:363–367.
32. Wolf RH, Gormus BJ, Martin LN, et al. Experimental leprosy in three species of monkeys. Science. 1985;227:229–230.
33. Shepard CC. A survey of the drugs with activity against *M. leprae* in mice. Int J Lepr. 1971;39:340–348.
34. Welch TM, Gelber RH, Murray LP, et al. Viability of *Mycobacterium leprae* after multiplication in mice. Infect Immun. 1980;30:325.
35. Shepard CC, van Landingham RM, Walker LL, et al. Comparison of the immunogenicity of vaccines prepared from viable *Mycobacterium bovis* BCG, heat killed *Mycobacterium leprae,* and a mixture of the two for normal and *Mycobacterium leprae*-tolerant mice. Infect Immun. 1983;40:1096–1103.
36. Hunter SW, Fujiwara T, Brennan PJ. Structure and antigenicity of the major specific glycolipid antigen of *Mycobacterium leprae.* J Biol Chem. 1982;257:15072–15078.
37. Klebanoff SJ, Shepard CC. Toxic effect of the peroxidase-hydrogen peroxide-halide antimicrobial system on *Mycobacterium leprae.* Infect Immun. 1984;44:534–536.
38. Cho SN, Fujiwara T, Gelber RH, et al. Use of an artificial antigen containing the 3,6-di-O-methyl-beta-D-glycopyranosyl epitope for the serodiagnosis of leprosy. J Infect Dis. 1984;150:311–322.
39. Mehra V, Brennan PJ, Rada E, et al. Lymphocyte suppression in leprosy induced by unique *Mycobacterium leprae* glycolipid. Nature (London). 1984;308:194–196.

40. Kaplan G, Gandhi RR, Weinstein DE, et al. *Mycobacterium leprae* antigen–induced suppression of T cell proliferation in vitro. J Immunol. 1987;138:3028–3034.
41. Sibley LD, Hunter SW, Brennan PJ, et al. Mycobacterial lipoarabinomannan inhibits gamma interferon–mediated activation of macrophages. Infect Immun. 1983;56:1232–1236.
42. Gelber RH, Brennan PJ, Hunter SW, et al. Effective vaccination of mice against leprosy bacilli with subunits of *Mycobacterium leprae*. Infect Immun. 1990;58:711–718.
43. Gelber RH, Murray L, Siu P, et al. Vaccination of mice with a soluble protein fraction of *Mycobacterium leprae* provides consistent and long-term protection against *M. leprae* infection. Infect Immun. 1992;60:1840–1844.
44. Xu K, de Vries RRP, van Leeuwen A, et al. HLA-linked control of predisposition to lepromatous leprosy. Int J Lepr. 1985;53:56–63.
45. De Vries RRP, Lai-A-Fat RFM, Nijenhuis LE, et al. HLA-linked control of host responses to *Mycobacterium leprae*. Lancet. 1976;2:1328–1330.
46. Rees RJW. The significance of the lepromin reaction in man. Prog Allerg. 1964;8:258–264.
47. Rotberg A, Bechelli IM, Keil H. The Mitsuda reaction in a non-leprous area. Int J Lepr. 1950;18:209–220.
48. Doull JA, Guinto RS, Mabalay MC. The origin of natural reactivity to lepromin. Int J Lepr. 1959;27:31–42.
49. Myrvang B, Godal T, Ridley DS, et al. Immune responsiveness to *Mycobacterium leprae* and other mycobacterial antigens throughout the clinical and histopathological spectrum of leprosy. Clin Exp Immunol. 1973;14:541.
50. Rea TH, Quismorio FP, Harding B, et al. Immunologic responses in patients with lepromatous leprosy. Arch Dermatol. 1976;112:791–800.
51. Sieling PA, Wang XH, Gately MK, et al. IL-12 regulates T helper type 1 cytokine responses in human infectious disease. J Immunol. 1994;153:3639.
52. Modlin RL, Rea TH. Immunology of leprosy granulomas. Springer Semin Immunopathol. 1998;10:359–374.
53. Nathan CF, Kaplan G, Levis WR, et al. Local and systemic effects of intradermal recombinant interferon-gamma in patients with lepromatous leprosy. N Engl J Med. 1986;315:6–15.
54. Kaplan G, Kiessling R, Teklemariam S, et al. The reconstitution of cell-mediated immunity in the cutaneous lesions of lepromatous leprosy by recombinant interleukin 2. J Exp Med. 1989;169:893–907.
55. Krahenbuhl JL. Role of the macrophages in resistance to leprosy. In: Hastings RC, ed. Leprosy. New York: Churchill Livingstone; 1994:137.
56. Kikuchi I, Ozawa T, Hirayama K, Sasazuki T. An HLA-linked gene controls susceptibility to lepromatous leprosy through T-cell regulation. Lepr Rev. 1986;57(Suppl 2):139–142.
57. Abel L, Sanchez FO, Oberti J, et al. Susceptibility to leprosy is linked to the human NRAMP1 gene. J Infect Dis. 1998;177:133–145.
58. Blackwell JM. Genetics of host resistance and susceptibility to intra-macrophage pathogens: A study of multiple families of tuberculosis, leprosy, and leishmaniasis in north-eastern Brazil. Int J Parasitol. 1998;98:21–28.
59. Rober M, Levee G, Chanteau S, et al. No evidence for linkage between leprosy susceptibility and the human natural rsistance–associated macrophage protein 1 (NRAMP1) gene in French Polynesia. Int J Lepr. 1997;65:197–202.
60. Buchanan TM: Serology of leprosy. In: Hastings RC, ed. Leprosy. New York: Churchill Livingstone; 1994:157.
61. Cree IA, Smith WC. Leprosy transmission and mucosal immunity: Towards eradication. Lepr Rev. 1998;69:112–121.
62. Modlin RL, Kato H, Mehra V, et al. Genetically restricted suppressor T-cell clones derived from lepromatous leprosy lesions. Nature. 1986;323:459–461.
63. Mehra V, Bloom BR, Bajardi AC, et al. A major T-cell antigen of *Mycobacterium leprae* is a 10-kD heat-shock cognate protein. J Exp Med. 1992:175:275–284.
64. Sieling PA, Chatterjee D, Porcelli SA, et al. CD1-restricted T-cell recognition of microbial lipoglycan antigens. Science. 1995;269:227–230.
65. Ridley DS, Jopling WH. Classification of leprosy according to immunity. Int J Lepr. 1966;31:255.
66. Drutz DJ, Chen TSN, Lu WH. The continuous bacteremia of lepromatous leprosy. N Engl J Med. 1972;287:159–164.
67. Ridley DS, Job CK. The pathology of leprosy. In: Hastings RC, ed. Leprosy. New York: Churchill Livingstone; 1985:129.
68. Turk JL, Waters MFR. Immunological significance of changes in lymph nodes across the leprosy spectrum. Clin Exp Immunol. 1971;8:363–376.
69. Modlin RL, Pirmez C, Hofman FM, et al. Lymphocytes bearing antigen-specific gamma/delta T-cell receptors in human infectious disease lesions. Nature. 1989;339:544–548.
70. Yamamura M, Wang X-H, Ohmen JD, et al. Cytokine patterns of immunologically mediated tissue damage. J Immunol. 1992;149:1470–1475.
71. Rea TH, Shen J-Y, Modlin RL. Epidermal keratinocyte 1a expression. Langerhans cell hyperplasia and lymphocytic infiltration in skin lesions of leprosy. Clin Exp Immunol. 1986;65:253–259.
72. Modlin RL, Hofman FM, Horowitz DA, et al. *In situ* identification of cells in human leprosy granulomas with monoclonal antibodies to interleukin 2 and its receptor. J Immunol. 1984;132:3085–3090.
73. Cooper CL, Mueller C, Sinchaisri T-A, et al. Analysis of naturally occurring delayed-type hypersensitivity reactions in leprosy by *in situ* hybridization. J Exp Med. 1989;169:1565–1581.
74. Quismorio FP, Rea TH, Chandor S, et al. Lucio phenomenon: An immune complex deposition syndrome in lepromatous leprosy. Clin Immunol Immunopathol. 1978;9:187–193.
75. Chandi SM, Chacko CJG, Fritschi EP, Job CK. Segmental necrotizing granulomatous neuritis of leprosy. Int J Lepr. 1980;48:41–47.
76. Rea TH. A comparative study of testicular involvement in lepromatous and borderline lepromatous leprosy. Int J Lepr. 1988;56:383–388.
77. Zaheer SA, Mukherjee R, Ramkumar B, et al. Combined multidrug and *Mycobacterium w* vaccine therapy in patients with multibacillary leprosy. J Infect Dis. 1993;167:401–410.
78. Deo MG, Bapat CV, Bhalerao V, et al. Anti-leprosy potentials of the ICRC vaccine: A study in patients and healthy volunteers. Int J Lepr. 1983;51:540–549.
79. Stanford JL, Torres P, Terencio de las Aguas J. Immunoterapia en pacientes de lepra lepromatosa de Fontilles. Fontilles Rev Leprol. 1985;15:309–312.
80. Pearson JMH, Rees RJW, Waters MFR. Sulfphone resistance in leprosy: A review of one hundred proven clinical cases. Lancet. 1975;2:69–72.
81. Waters MFR, Rees RJW, Laing ABG, et al. The rate of relapse in lepromatous leprosy following completion of twenty years of supervised sulfone therapy. Lepr Rev. 1986;57:101–109.
82. Baohong J. Drug resistance in leprosy: A review. Lepr Rev. 1985;56:265.
83. Gelber RH, Rea TH, Murray LP, et al. Primary dapsone-resistant Hansen's disease in California: Experience with over 100 *Mycobacterium leprae* isolates. Arch Dermatol. 1990;126:1584–1586.
84. Waters MFR, Rees RJW, McDougall AC, et al. Ten years of dapsone in lepromatous leprosy: Clinical, bacteriological and histological assessment and finding of viable leprosy bacilli. Lepr Rev. 1974;45:288–298.
85. Waters MF, Rees RJ, Pearson JM, et al. Rifampicin for lepromatous leprosy: Nine years' experience. BMJ. 1978;1:133–136.
86. Gelber RH, Henika PR, Gibson JB. The bactericidal activity of various aminoglycoside antibiotics against *Mycobacterium leprae* in mice. Lepr Rev. 1984;55:341–347.
87. Gelber RH. Activity of minocycline in *Mycobacterium leprae*–infected mice. J Infect Dis. 1987;156:236–239.
88. Ji B, Perani EG, Grosset JH. Effectiveness of clarithromycin and minocycline alone or in combination against experimental *Mycobacterium leprae* infection in mice. Antimicrob Agents Chemother. 1991;35:579–581.
89. Gelber RH, Fukuda K, Byrd S, et al. A clinical trial of minocycline in lepromatous leprosy. BMJ. 1992;304:91–92.
90. Ji B, Jamet P, Perani EG, et al. Powerful bactericidal activities of clarithromycin and minocycline against *Mycobacterium leprae* in lepromatous leprosy. J Infect Dis. 1993;168:188–190.
91. Fajardo TT, Villahermosa LG, dela Cruz EG, et al. Minocycline in lepromatous leprosy. Int J Lepr. 1995;63:8–17.
92. Gelber RH, Siu P, Tsang M, et al. Activities of various macrolide antibiotics against *Mycobacterium leprae* infection in mice. Antimicrob Agents Chemother. 1991;35:760–763.
93. Ji B, Perani EG, Grosset JH. Effectiveness of clarithromycin and minocycline alone and in combination against experimental *Mycobacterium leprae* infection in mice. Antimicrob Agents Chemother. 1991;35:579–581.
94. Chan GP, Garcia-Ignacio BY, Chavez VE, et al. Clinical trial of clarithromycin for lepromatous leprosy. Antimicrob Agents Chemother. 1994;38:515–517.
95. Guelpa-Lauras C-C, Perani EG, Giroir AM, et al. Activities of pefloxacin and ciprofloxacin against *Mycobacterium leprae* in the mouse. Int J Lepr. 1987;55:70–77.
96. Grosset JH, Ji B, Guelpa-Lauras CC, et al. Activity of ofloxacin against *Mycobacterium leprae* in the mouse. Int J Lepr. 1988;56:259–264.
97. Gelber RH, Iranmanesh A, Murray L, et al. Activities of various quinolone antibiotics against *Mycobacterium leprae* in infected mice. Antimicrob Agents Chemother. 1992;36:2554–2557.
98. N'Deli L, Guelpa-Lauras C-C, Perani EG, et al. Effectiveness of pefloxacin in the treatment of lepromatous leprosy. Int J Lepr. 1990;58:12–18.
99. Grosset JH, Ji B, Guelpa-Lauras CC, et al. Clinical trial of pefloxacin and ofloxacin in the treatment of lepromatous leprosy. Int J Lepr. 1990;58:281–295.
100. Single-Lesion Multicentre Trial Group. Efficacy of single-dose multidrug therapy for the treatment of single-lesion paucibacillary leprosy. Lepr Rev. 1997;68:341–349.
101. WHO Expert Committee on Leprosy. World Health Organ Tech Rep Ser. 1998; 874:1–43.
102. Katoch VM. Is there a microbiological rationale for single-dose treatment of leprosy. Lepr Rev. 1998;69:2–5.
103. Ji B. Why multidrug therapy for multibacillary leprosy can be shortened to 12 months. Lepr Rev. 1998;69:106–109.
104. Waters MFR. Is it safe to shorten multidrug therapy for lepromatous (LL and BL) leprosy to 12 months? Lepr Rev. 1998;69:110–111.
105. Gelber RH. Our experience with another multidrug therapy regimen for leprosy. Int J Lepr. 1998;66:9A–10A.
106. Gelber RH. Chemotherapy of lepromatous leprosy: Recent developments and prospects for the future. Eur J Clin Microbiol Infect Dis. 1994;942–952.
107. Wade HW. The examination of skin lesions for bacilli. Int J Lepr. 1963;31:242.
108. Shannon EJ, Miranda RO, Morales MJ, et al. Inhibition of de novo IgM antibody synthesis by thalidomide as a relevant mechanism of action in leprosy. Scand J Immunol. 1981;13:553–562.
109. Barnhill RL, Doll NJ, Millikan LE, et al. Studies on the anti-inflammatory properties of thalidomide: Effects on polymorphonuclear leukocytes and monocytes. J Am Acad Dermatol. 1984;11:814–819.
110. Sampaio EP, Sarno EN, Galilly R, et al. Thalidomide selectively inhibits tumor necrosis factor alpha production by stimulated human monocytes. J Exp Med. 1991;173:699–703.

111. Lechat MF. Control programs in leprosy. In: Hastings RC, ed. Leprosy. New York: Churchill Livingstone; 1985:255.
112. Stanley SJ, Howland C, Stone MM, et al. BCG vaccination of children against leprosy in Uganda: Final results. J Hyg. 1981;87:233–248.
113. Irwin KT, Sundaresan T, Gyi MM, et al. BCG vaccination of children against leprosy: Fourteen-year findings of the trial in Burma. Bull World Health Organ. 1985;63:1069–1078.
114. Noordeen SK. Vaccination against leprosy: Recent advances and practical applications. Lepr Rev. 1985;56:703–710.
115. Convit J, Sampson C, Zuniga M, et al. Immunoprophylactic trial with combined *Mycobacterium leprae*/BCG vaccine against leprosy: Preliminary results. Lancet. 1992;339:446–450.

Chapter 242

Mycobacterium avium Complex

DIANE V. HAVLIR
JERROLD J. ELLNER

Mycobacterium avium causes a tuberculosis-like infection in chickens, pigeons, and other birds. The Battey bacillus (now called *Mycobacterium intracellulare*) was a frequent isolate from the sputum of patients at a tuberculosis sanitarium in Battey, Georgia. In 1907, Koch and Rabinowitsch described disseminated infection with mycobacteria other than *Mycobacterium tuberculosis*.[1] Nontuberculous mycobacteria also were found to cause pulmonary disease, usually in the form of an indolent cavitating pneumonitis complicating the course of severe preexisting lung disease.[2] The most common nontuberculous organisms responsible for pulmonary and disseminated disease are members of the *M. avium* complex (MAC), which includes both *M. avium* and *M. intracellulare*.[3]

The prevalence of disease caused by MAC increased notably in association with the acquired immunodeficiency syndrome (AIDS) epidemic.[4] Before the availability of potent antiretroviral therapy for human immunodeficiency virus (HIV) infection, disseminated infection with MAC was the most frequent bacterial complication of AIDS, occurring in as many as 43% of patients.[5] Advances in HIV chemotherapy and the use of MAC prophylaxis have resulted in a profound reduction of disseminated MAC disease in AIDS patients. Pulmonary disease caused by MAC remains a significant problem in non-AIDS patients with underlying lung disease, and the affliction of women without previous lung disease has been increasingly recognized. Improved MAC treatment regimens have dramatically improved the outcome of disease in both AIDS and non-AIDS patients.

EPIDEMIOLOGY

MAC is ubiquitous in the environment and has been isolated from a variety of sources around the world, including soil, natural water, municipal water systems, food, house dust, and domestic and wild animals.[3–7] Although MAC is an important disease in poultry and swine, and organisms excreted in feces from infected animals persist in the soil for prolonged periods, serologic and molecular epidemiologic studies do not support the hypothesis of animals as an important reservoir in human infections.[8–10] There is no evidence for person-to-person transmission of MAC.

Environmental isolates are thought to be the source of most human infections, although most of these differ from clinical isolates in regard to optimal growth conditions, antimicrobial susceptibility, and plasmid content.[11, 12] The identification of aerosolized *M. intracellulare* over Atlantic coast waters with a plasmid content similar to that of clinical isolates in patients with pulmonary disease suggests that inhalation of aerosolized organisms is a source of infection.[13]

MAC can be cultured in a substantial number of AIDS patients from sputum or stool before the diagnosis of disseminated disease is made, suggesting that infection is acquired through ingestion or inhalation.[14] However, the principal exposure or source of infecting organisms in AIDS patients with disseminated MAC disease is not known. In one study, only decreased $CD4^+$ T-lymphocyte counts and ingestion of hard cheese increased the risk for development of MAC.[15] The failure to culture MAC from cheese questions the validity of this association. In another study, which used molecular typing to compare patient isolates with those obtained from the home environment, only in a few cases were soil (but not water or food) isolates identical to the disease isolate.[16] MAC is readily identified in municipal and institutional water systems, reflecting the tolerance of MAC to heat and modern chlorination treatments.[17, 18] Hospital water systems appeared to be the source of infection in five AIDS patients with MAC.[19]

The distribution of serovars of MAC in isolates from patients with AIDS or disseminated disease differs from that of serovars in non-AIDS patients or in the environment. More than 90% of MAC isolates from AIDS patients are of serovars 1, 4, or 8[16, 20, 21]; these are *M. avium*. There is some variation within the United States, with serovar 4 being the most common serovar in New York and San Francisco, and serovar 8 the most common in Los Angeles.[22] In non-AIDS patients without disseminated disease, isolates are evenly split between *M. avium* and *M. intracellulare*.[22, 23]

The most important risk factor for acquisition of pulmonary MAC identified in early clinical investigations was the presence of underlying lung disease. Chronic obstructive pulmonary disease, chronic bronchitis, bronchiectasis, recurrent aspiration, pneumoconiosis, healed or active tuberculosis, pulmonary mycosis, and malignancy were observed at a high prevalence in patients with pulmonary disease.[3, 24, 25] Patients who had undergone gastrectomy also were at higher risk to develop disease.[25, 26] Because patients with cystic fibrosis now survive into third and fourth decades of life, they represent another risk group for MAC pulmonary disease.[27]

It has been found that a substantial number of pulmonary MAC cases (24 to 46%) occur in patients without any underlying lung condition or identifiable immunodeficiency.[28] In contrast to earlier reports, in which males made up more than 90% of the patients, females predominated in this group.[28] In one report, there was a striking number of women with lingular or middle lobe disease.[29] Iseman reported a high prevalence of pectus excavatum, thoracic scoliosis, and mitral valve prolapse among women with pulmonary MAC disease and speculated that an underlying connective tissue disorder increased the susceptibility of these patients to respiratory pathogens such as MAC.[29] One study failed to find genetic mutations in the interferon-γ receptor (IFN-γR1) or in natural resistance–associated macrophage protein (NRAMP1) in women with MAC pulmonary disease.[30]

Historically, the risk for pulmonary MAC was greatest in persons living in the southeastern United States. Skin testing conducted between 1950 and 1962 documented greater reactivity to Battey bacillus (purified protein derivative, PPD-B) in this area, and surveillance of state laboratories in the 1970s suggested MAC disease was concentrated in, but not limited to, this area.[31, 32] Because MAC is not a reportable disease, the incidence in the United States is not known.

Among HIV-infected patients, studies have shown variable regional differences in the incidence of MAC bacteremia in the United States.[33, 34] One study conducted in North America suggested that patients living in Canada and the northern United States had a lower risk for development of MAC bacteremia, compared with those living in the southern United States.[35] Lower frequencies of disseminated MAC disease, compared with rates in the United States, have been reported from some European countries, although these types of comparisons are also limited by differing patient populations and approaches to diagnosis.[36]

In systematic surveys of African patients, MAC was either not isolated or infrequently isolated from the blood of patients with advanced AIDS.[37–39] This observation cannot be explained by absence of MAC in the environment in these areas. MAC has been isolated from water and soil, including serotypes found in AIDS patients.[40] Moreover, in patients tested with tuberculin and an *M. avium* serovar 2 sensitin, *M. avium*–dominant skin test reactivity in Kenya was 12%, identical to that found in Boston and New Hampshire.[41] Colonization of the gastrointestinal tract in AIDS patients has also been observed with one study reporting recovery of MAC from the stool in 12% of AIDS patients in the Democratic Republic of Congo. No gastrointestinal disease was identified on biopsies obtained from colonized patients.[42] Some investigators have speculated that the low rates of disseminated disease in Africa are a result of the fact that few patients survive long with CD4 cell counts less than 100/mm^3, because of competing morbidities. Others have speculated that acquired mycobacterial immunity provides protection against MAC and is greater in developing countries, where tuberculosis rates are high, and in countries that use bacille Calmette-Guérin (BCG) vaccination.[43] Epidemiologic data from the United States, Sweden, and Africa support this latter hypothesis. A history of tuberculosis was associated with a reduced risk for MAC in one study in the United States, and low rates of MAC have been reported in countries such as Sweden, where many people received childhood vaccination with BCG.[44, 45]

The CD4 cell count is a powerful predictor of disseminated MAC in AIDS patients, and for this reason it is used as a criterion to determine when MAC prophylaxis is indicated. In a natural history study of HIV-infected patients in Texas, the incidence of MAC bacteremia in a cohort of patients with CD4 cell counts less than 200/mm^3 cultured monthly was 43% at 2 years; rates were highest in those patients with the lowest CD4 cell counts (39% at 1 year for CD4 cell counts less than 10/mm^3).[46] Only 3% of patients with cell counts higher than 100/mm^3 had developed bacteremia at 1-year follow-up. More recent studies recognized that the level of plasma HIV RNA also predicts the risk for MAC, independent of the CD4 cell count. Rates of MAC in patients with less than 75 CD4 cells per milliliter increased three-fold in patients with more than 100,000 copies of HIV RNA per milliliter of plasma, compared with patients with less than 100,000 copies per milliliter.[47]

Other factors associated with the development of disseminated MAC in AIDS patients include anemia, time since onset of AIDS-defining condition, previous opportunistic infections, and interruption of antiretroviral therapy.[48] There appears to be no difference in incidence of risk in adults based on gender or mode of acquisition of HIV.[34] Disseminated MAC is the most common cause of disseminated nontuberculous mycobacterial infection in children. It appears to be more common in pediatric patients with HIV infection associated with hemophilia (12.9%) or with transfusion (13.8%) than in those with perinatally acquired HIV infection (4.6%).[49] Median CD4 cell counts for children with MAC are similar to those seen in the adult population.[49–51]

Early in the HIV epidemic, disseminated MAC was a very common disease in patients with AIDS; autopsy studies identified the disease in up to 50% of patients.[52, 53] After prophylaxis for *Pneumocystis carinii* pneumonia (PCP) became standard practice, disseminated MAC became almost as common as PCP as an AIDS-defining opportunistic infection.[54] Subsequently, the use of rifabutin prophylaxis produced a discernible reduction in the incidence of MAC in a Baltimore cohort.[55] Most recently, new cases of disseminated MAC in the United States have been significantly reduced, a result attributable to use of potent antiretroviral therapy that increases CD4 cells and reduces HIV RNA levels. In one study spanning the introduction of these therapies in clinical practice, rates of MAC disease decreased from 21.9 to 3.7 cases per 100 persons in the years between 1994 and 1997.[56]

THE PATHOGEN

Classification and Microbiology

The MAC consists of *M. avium, M. intracellulare,* and some strains not yet definitively classified. *Mycobacterium scrofulaceum,* which includes three serovars, is often included within the MAC, although this classification is controversial.[57] The MAC organisms are in Runyan group III (nonphotochromogens), grow slowly at 36°C (10 to 21 days on routine medium), and produce characteristic thin-translucent or domed-opaque smooth colonies and rough variants. Some strains may produce a yellow pigment that increases with light exposure.

Typing of MAC by several methods has been useful for taxonomic classification and epidemiologic studies. Serologic typing based on reactivity with the glycopeptidolipids (GPLs) in the cell wall reveals 28 serovars.[58] DNA probes indicate that types 1 through 6, 8 through 11, and 21 are *M. avium* and types 7, 12 through 20, and 25 are *M. intracellulare.*[58] Molecular typing has been accomplished by characterization of restriction fragment length after digestion of MAC DNA with endonucleases and by multilocus enzyme electrophoresis.[10, 59–63] Genetic heterogeneity is present within MAC serovars by these techniques, providing a more sensitive epidemiologic tool. Unique restriction patterns are present in persons infected with MAC, except in the few cases of water-associated outbreaks. Twenty percent of AIDS patients exhibit polyclonal infection with two or more distinct isolates.[61]

Pathogenesis

Most cases of disseminated MAC probably arise from recent acquisition of the organism through inhalation or ingestion of MAC in patients with profound immunodeficiency.[4, 14, 41, 64] In vitro, MAC can bind and invade intestinal mucosal cell lines.[65] A number of receptor-ligand structures have been identified that enable MAC entry into host cells. MAC gains entry to monocytes by opsonic or complement-mediated pathways via complement receptor type 3 (CR3), mannose, transferrin, or an integrin receptor.[66–69] *M. avium* and other virulent mycobacteria are distinguished by a C2a-mediated entry pathway that enables C3b opsonization of *M. avium* and macrophage uptake.[70] This may be particularly relevant in an opsonin-poor environment such as the lung. A 68-kD protein on the surface of MAC plays a role in attachment to the integrin receptor and upregulates CR3 expression.[71] In vitro, intracellular growth is associated with preferential uptake via transferrin and β_1-integrin receptor.[72] HIV tat and HIV gp-120 (via release of prostaglandin E_2) also enhance uptake of MAC into monocytes in vitro.[73, 74]

The frequent occurrence of a few serovars of *M. avium* as a cause of disseminated disease in patients with AIDS and their content of plasmids suggest that these strains are more virulent.[75, 76] In fact, they were found to be more virulent in the beige mouse model.[77] Studies have indicated that transfection of a plasmid into a nonplasmid-containing strain of *M. avium* is associated with increased intracellular replication.[77a] Colonial morphotype is a key determinant of intracellular growth. Flat, transparent colonies are more pathogenic in animal models[78] and demonstrate increased replication intracellularly.[79, 80]

The GPLs are responsible for the colonial morphology of *M. avium.* In mice that are chronically infected with *M. avium,* organisms within phagosomes are surrounded by a multilamellar electron translucent zone that resembles GPLs structurally and constitutes a barrier to intracellular killing.[81, 82] During in vitro culture, a morphotype switch may occur from transparent to opaque colonies, with a corresponding decrease in virulence. Because rough mutants also may be virulent, factors other than GPLs must affect intracellular survival.

Inhibition of phagosome-lysozyme fusion is a key virulence factor for intracellular survival of MAC, although access to plasmalemma contents is not entirely restricted.[83–86] Localization of *M. avium* in less acidic vacuoles that exhibit a decreased proton adenosine triphosphatase is critical to intracellular survival of *M. avium.*[87, 88] This property protects the organism from host enzymes, potentially inhibits antigen presentation, and limits antimicrobial activity of antimicrobials (e.g., clarithromycin) that require an acidic environment.[89, 90]

It is becoming increasingly clear that the nature of the host cytokine response after ingestion of *M. avium* is an important determinant of the capacity for intracellular replication and that certain MAC strains alter this environment to their advantage, as discussed later. Epidermal growth factor, which is abundant in areas of tissue necrosis, may also enhance MAC replication.[91]

In AIDS patients, HIV and MAC appear to produce reciprocal enhancement of replication. Patients developing MAC showed increased plasma HIV RNA levels at the onset of MAC bacteremia, compared with a control group who did not develop bacteremia.[92] Activation of cells latently infected with HIV and a cytokine-mediated increase in available cells for new HIV infection are two possible explanations for this observation. One study evaluating lymph node biopsies from AIDS patients with disseminated MAC demonstrated upregulation of HIV replication in macrophages.[93] In vitro, infection of monocytes with HIV enhanced the intracellular replication of *M. avium* when cultures were continued for 14 days,[94, 95] an effect that was not apparent with shorter culture periods.[96] HIV-1 gp120 protein also promotes intracellular replication of *M. avium* through a CD4-dependent mechanism.[97]

Host Immunity

The frequent occurrence of disseminated infection with *M. avium* at CD4 cell counts lower than 100/mm^3 provides clear evidence for a role of CD4 cells in protective immunity. In vitro T-cell proliferative responses to *M. avium* are diminished or absent in patients with AIDS who develop MAC.[98, 99] There is evidence from experimental murine models that natural killer cells[100] play a role in host defense against *M. avium,* and in vitro evidence indicates that interleukin (IL)-2–activated killer cells also do so.[101, 102] A reduction in antigen-responsive CD4 memory cells may inhibit the effector phase of cytotoxic CD4 cells.[98]

Serum factors may also play a role in host defense against MAC.[103] Apotransferrin is an inhibitory serum factor that in patients without HIV infection decreases intracellular replication of MAC.[104] The addition of iron and triglycerides is associated with accelerated MAC growth in vitro.[105] High triglyceride levels and alterations in iron metabolism are known to occur in advanced AIDS patients and may favor MAC replication.

Cytokines have bidirectional effects on the growth of *M. avium.* Both IL-1α and IL-6 enhance extracellular growth of the organism,[106, 107] as does IL-13 (H Shiratsuchi, unpublished data, 1997). *M. avium* expresses receptors that bind IL-6.[107, 108] IL-6 also promotes intracellular growth of *M. avium,* apparently by downregulating membrane receptors for tumor necrosis factor (TNF)-α.[108]

IFN-γ plays a critical role in the host immune response to MAC. A familial genetic deletion in the gene encoding the IFN-γ receptor was the underlying defect in children with the rare clinical entity of disseminated MAC in the absence of HIV infection.[109] IL-12 is also important to host response; it enhances lymphocyte proliferative responses and cytotoxic activity and upregulates production of IFN-γ.[110–112] In non-AIDS patients with disseminated MAC, reduced IL-12 production was associated with impaired production of IFN-γ and inability to control MAC infection.[110] Another study in mice indicated that IL-12 in combination with antimicrobial agents provided dramatic synergism in clearing *M. avium* from blood and tissues.[113]

TNF-α with or without IL-2, and granulocyte-macrophage colony-stimulating factor (GM-CSF) with or without IL-2, demonstrate macrophage activating factor (MAF) activity against *M. avium.*[102, 114, 115] Pentoxifylline, a nonspecific cytokine inhibitor, greatly enhances MAC replication in vitro.[116] The first cytokine described, migration inhibitory factor (MIF), has dramatic MAF activity.[117] IL-7 may also have an inhibitory effect mediated through a TNF-α pathway.[118] In vitro, IL-10 had no detectable effect on macrophage killing of MAC.[119]

The balance between growth-enhancing and growth-inhibiting cytokines may modulate the intracellular growth potential of *M. avium.* Ingestion of *M. avium* by human monocytes induces expression of GM-CSF, TNF-α, IL-6, and transforming growth factor (TGF)-β.[65, 102] Downstream effects of these cytokines are likely to have an important influence. For example, TGF-β production is associated with diminished response to IFN-γ.[120] The colonial morphotypes differ in their ability to induce cytokine production. Smooth-domed exceed smooth-transparent forms in the induction of IL-1 and TNF-α,[121–123] apparently because of greater translational efficiency.[122] Because TNF-α possesses MAF activity, its differential induction may bear on virulence.

The study of HIV-1–infected persons has not yielded a clear understanding of the basis for the predisposition to disseminated *M. avium* infection. Johnson and colleagues found normal ingestion and intracellular growth inhibition of *M. avium* in monocytes from AIDS patients and a normal response to IFN-γ.[124] Studies further indicated that monocytes from AIDS patients show comparable induction of TNF-α, decreased expression and altered compartmentalization of IL-1, and increased expression of the growth-promoting cytokine IL-6.[125] Qualitative and quantitative defects in CD4 and cytotoxic lymphocyte responses, local fluxes of growth-enhancing and growth-inhibiting cytokines, and metabolic perturbations influencing MAC growth are likely contributing factors. The extent to which immune reconstitution produced by potent therapy against HIV influences susceptibility to MAC may provide clues to the necessary components of host defense. Also, the potential effectiveness and mechanism of action of immunotherapy for the treatment of *M. avium* (e.g., IL-12) may clarify the critical effector mechanisms against MAC.

DIAGNOSIS

The diagnosis of disease caused by MAC requires isolation of the organism and compatible clinical and pathologic features. Colonization can occur in both normal and immunocompromised hosts and must be distinguished from true disease because of the therapeutic implications.[14, 126]

In contrast to the more virulent *M. tuberculosis,* identification of MAC in an isolated sputum culture does not constitute definite evidence of disease. MAC can colonize healthy persons and has a propensity for colonizing patients with underlying pulmonary disease. However, it has been recognized through the application of computed tomography (CT) that many patients previously considered to be only "colonized" with MAC in fact have invasive lung disease that can be confirmed by bronchial biopsy.[127] High-resolution CT can reveal multifocal bronchiectasis or multiple small nodules that are characteristic of pulmonary MAC disease, and bronchoscopy (and biopsy) can increase the yield of sputum cultures. These tests are recommended, in addition to at least three sputum evaluations, for patients in whom MAC is suspected but the diagnosis is not clear.[128, 129]

Diagnostic criteria for pulmonary MAC have been published based on clinical reports from the literature and expert opinion.[126] For patients with radiographic evidence of disease, a positive sputum culture with at least 2+ growth on culture and at least one acid-fast smear (2+ or greater), or a positive culture and multiple positive smears, is considered diagnostic. Additional diagnostic criteria include two positive cultures and one smear within a 1-year period or three positive cultures within 1 year. Patients with positive cultures for MAC from a pulmonary biopsy, or typical histologic features of MAC disease on biopsy, and at least a positive sputum culture meet diagnostic criteria for pulmonary MAC disease. The unpredictable nature of disease progression in patients with pulmonary MAC disease, the potential adverse consequences of delayed diagnosis, and the availability of efficacious therapy all argue for an aggressive diagnostic approach to this disease.

Current methodology used for digestion and decontamination of sputum for the isolation of *M. tuberculosis* is also suitable for MAC. Kinyoun, Ziehl-Neelsen, and fluorescent stains are effective in identifying MAC. However, the microscopic appearances of *M.*

tuberculosis and MAC are indistinguishable, and culture confirmation is always required. Löwenstein-Jensen and Middlebrook 7H10 or 7H11 are the media most commonly used for isolation of MAC.

Biochemical tests assist in identification of the organism after sufficient growth is obtained on culture; specific DNA probes are used for rapid identification of *M. avium* and *M. intracellulare.* Serotyping and molecular typing in general are for research purposes only, but the latter may be useful in excluding laboratory contamination. Direct amplification testing from the sputum, which is available for *M. tuberculosis,* is not available for *M. avium.* Patients can be coinfected with both *M. tuberculosis* and *M. avium,* and therefore it is important to examine cultures for both organisms.

Dual tuberculin and *M. avium* skin testing has been studied as a tool to distinguish these two diseases, which often exhibit indistinguishable clinical presentations.[130, 131] Although this approach may have use as an adjunctive diagnostic tool, anergy, geographic variability in disease prevalence, and the controversy regarding criteria for "anergy" are limitations of this approach. Rapid identification of *M. avium* in clinical specimens using polymerase chain amplification of sequences specific to *M. avium* is under active investigation and will probably improve the accuracy and speed of diagnosis.[132–134]

Blood cultures are highly sensitive for the detection of disseminated MAC in AIDS patients. A single blood culture has a high diagnostic yield (90 to 95% sensitive); subsequent cultures provide marginal improvement in detection and should be used only in undiagnosed cases when symptoms are suggestive of MAC.[135, 136] A variety of culture systems are available[136–138]; liquid media are superior to conventional culture on Löwenstein-Jensen agar slants. In the Bactec radiometric system, blood from the patient is inoculated into 12B or 13A culture media containing a radiolabeled substrate that is metabolized in the presence of mycobacteria to carbon dioxide and detected by radiorespirometric methods. In AIDS patients, a growth signal usually can be detected within 8 to 14 days, although specimens with low colony counts may require up to 4 weeks. Once sufficient growth is achieved, the diagnosis of MAC can be made in a few hours with the use of DNA probes that hybridize specifically with the RNA of the organism. Probes for both *M. avium* and *M. intracellulare* are commercially available and detect more than 95% of isolates with biochemical characteristics of MAC.[139, 140] In lysis centrifugation techniques, the mononuclear cells containing phagocytosed bacteria are lysed, and the supernatant is plated out on solid media, on which colony-forming counts may be enumerated. Concentrating blood using the lysis-centrifugation system before placing the sediment in the Bactec 12B medium is not recommended because the lysis-centrifugation mixture introduces inhibitors into the Bactec system.[141] Quantitation has been used in clinical trials to assess therapeutic response, but the utility of this labor-intensive methodology in clinical care has not been established. Kinyoun- or auramine-stained buffy coat blood smears may reveal the presence of mycobacteria in cases with a high number of circulating organisms[142]; however, culture confirmation is always necessary to make the diagnosis.

The diagnosis of disseminated infection can also be made by identification of MAC from a sterile site. Most cases of MAC can be diagnosed more readily and with less morbidity with noninvasive testing (blood cultures).[143–145] However, in rare cases, bone marrow and liver biopsies may be useful.[146] In AIDS patients with a focal lymphadenitis syndrome, blood cultures are often negative and a lymph node biopsy is required for diagnosis.

The physical examination may provide clues for the diagnosis of MAC in AIDS patients, but there are no pathognomonic findings. The differential diagnosis of the typical symptoms associated with disseminated MAC infection in a patient with advanced HIV disease is extensive and includes tuberculosis, *Mycobacterium genevense* infection, fungal diseases, lymphoproliferative disorders, enteric bacteremias, cytomegalovirus, and AIDS wasting syndrome. Patients often appear weak and debilitated, but when disseminated MAC is detected early some patients may not have fever and may not appear acutely or chronically ill. Transient mycobacteremia has been reported, although most such patients eventually developed sustained detectable levels of the organism if left untreated.[147]

Gastrointestinal and respiratory colonization occur in patients with advanced AIDS and presage the development of disseminated disease in 48 to 70%. However, only 21 to 33% of patients with disseminated MAC have positive stool or sputum cultures before bacteremia.[14, 148] Therefore, routine screening of these sites is not clinically useful.

CLINICAL MANIFESTATIONS

Non–Acquired Immunodeficiency Syndrome Patients

The symptoms associated with pulmonary MAC disease are nonspecific and similar in patients with and without underlying pulmonary conditions (Table 242–1).[25, 28, 149–151] The clinical manifestations may be subtle and unobtrusive, and delays in diagnosis occur when complaints are attributed to underlying lung disease or bronchitis. In one series, cough was present for a mean of 26 weeks before a diagnosis was made.[28]

Most patients have a productive cough; hemoptysis occurs in less than 25% of patients. Fever and weight loss occur in about one third of patients. The typical patient does not appear acutely ill, and the features of chronic disease (e.g., anemia, hypoalbuminemia) often are absent.[28]

The radiographic appearances of pulmonary MAC fall into three overlapping categories. The classic radiographic picture mimics reactivation tuberculosis with cavitation (Fig. 242–1), although there are several caveats. MAC cavities tend to be smaller and with thinner walls than those produced by *M. tuberculosis.*[149] Spread is more apt to be contiguous than bronchogenic, and basal disease, effusions, and mediastinal adenopathy are exceptional.[3] Patchy, nodular infiltrates without cavities in an upper-lobe distribution represent a second radiographic presentation. Many of these patients have evidence of bronchiectasis detectable on CT scanning.[129, 152, 153] A subset of these patients, typically elderly women, have lingular or middle-lobe infiltrates as the most common radiographic presentation (Fig. 242–2).[29] The absence of cavitary disease has been attributed in these patients to diagnosis at a less advanced stage. Finally, isolated pulmonary nodules represent an important part of the spectrum of disease.[152, 154] In some institutions, MAC has surpassed *M. tuberculosis* as the most common mycobacterial cause of solitary pulmonary lesions sampled by biopsy.[154]

The clinical course of pulmonary MAC disease is highly variable, although progression of the disease is slow and indolent in most patients. Some patients have radiographic patterns that are stable for as long as 9 years.[28] In one retrospective series, 46% of patients were alive 5 year after diagnosis with active or quiescent disease.[25] Patients whose disease is detected at a later stage, with more extensive parenchymal involvement, appear to progress more rapidly.[26, 28] Without treatment, patients can die of respiratory failure even in the absence of underlying pulmonary disease. In contrast, patients with

TABLE 242–1 Signs and Symptoms of Pulmonary *Mycobacterium avium* Complex Disease

Symptom	Percentage of Patients	Range
Cough	84	78–89
Sputum production	79	49–97
Weight loss	39	14–58
Fever	24	14–51
Hemoptysis	21	8–35
Radiographic findings		
Localized disease	26	23–28
Diffuse disease	74	72–76
Cavitation	55	24–87

Data from refs. 28, 149–151, and 290.

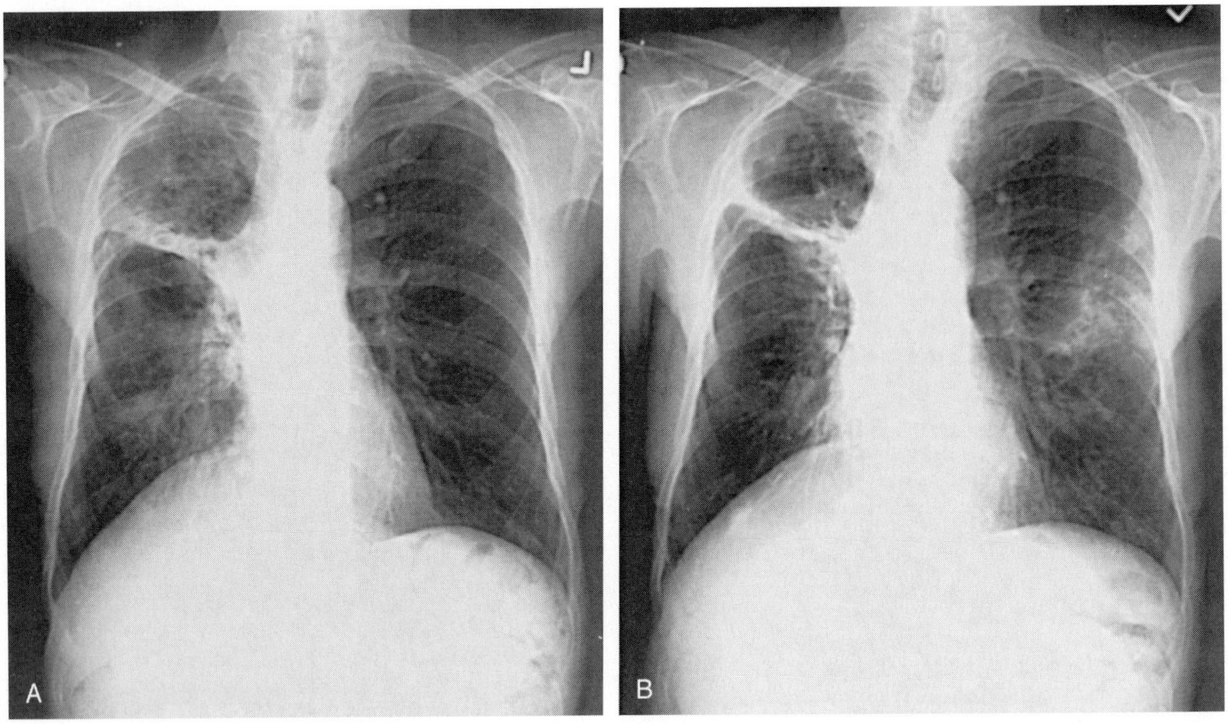

FIGURE 242–1. *A,* Chest radiograph of middle-aged man with pulmonary *Mycobacterium avium* complex (MAC). Right upper lobe cavitation and peritracheal adenopathy are present. *B,* Progression of MAC to involvement in left midlung field. (Courtesy of Dr. Richard J. Blinkhorn, Cleveland, Ohio.)

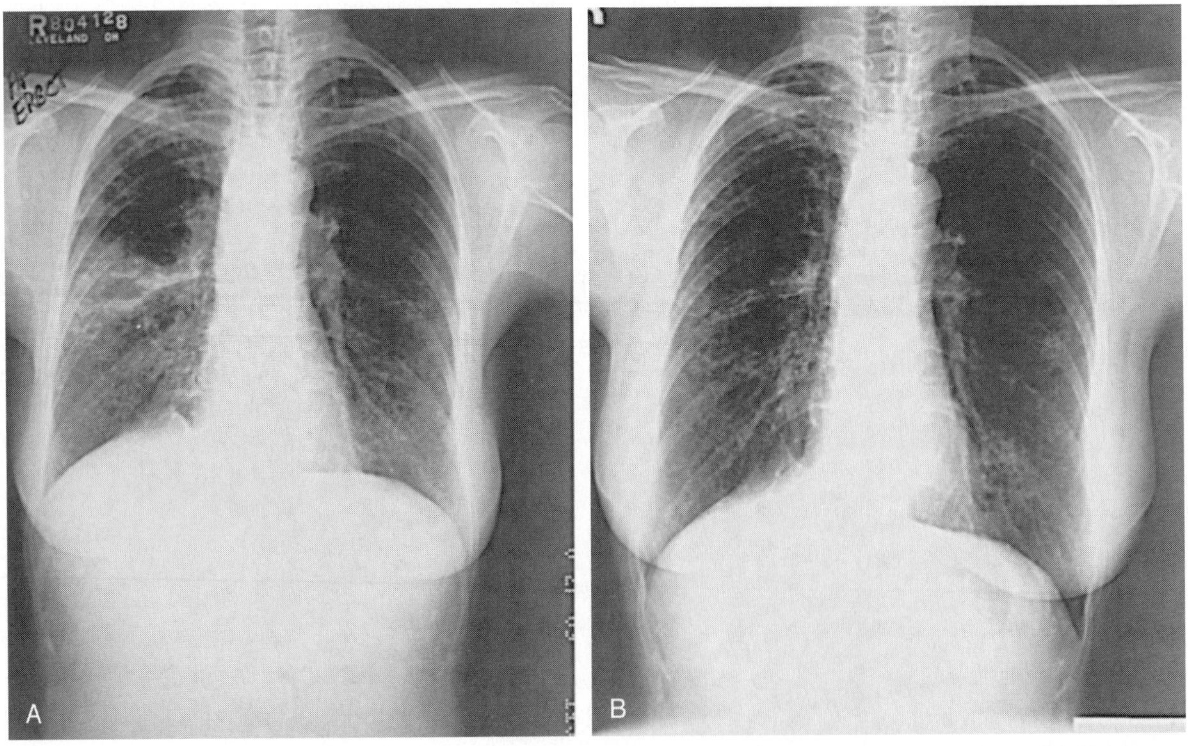

FIGURE 242–2. *A,* A middle-aged woman diagnosed with pulmonary *Mycobacterium avium* complex with a history of underlying bronchiectasis. The chest radiograph shows a cavity in the right midlung field with air-fluid level and right upper and left lower lobe infiltrates. *B,* After 2 years of chemotherapy, the chest radiograph shows dramatic improvement in cavitary lesions and infiltrates. (Courtesy of Dr. Richard J. Blinkhorn, Cleveland, Ohio.)

limited disease or nodules that are surgically resected have an excellent prognosis and can be cured with little morbidity.[25, 155]

Superficial lymphadenitis is the most common manifestation of MAC in children. Ingestion of mycobacteria is the usual portal of entry; this unique manifestation of MAC is seen almost exclusively in children between the ages of 2 and 5 years.[156–159] Rare cases have been reported in adults.[3, 159] MAC has now surpassed *M. scrofulaceum* as the most common cause of cervical adenitis in developed countries.[156, 157, 160] *M. tuberculosis* can produce an identical clinical picture and remains the most common cause of cervical adenitis in areas where tuberculosis is endemic.

The disease usually manifests as unilateral, nontender, enlarged lymph nodes involving the submandibular, preauricular, parotid, and postauricular chains, although involvement of other superficial nodes (e.g., inguinal, femoral, epitrochlear, axillary) has been reported.[156, 157, 161] Because this is a localized disease, constitutional symptoms are rarely exhibited; the tuberculin skin test is variably reactive. The differential diagnosis includes *M. tuberculosis,* cat-scratch disease, infectious mononucleosis, mumps, abscess, stone or tumor in the parotid gland, bronchial cleft cyst, and malignancy.[3, 161] Both the diagnosis and the treatment of this syndrome are accomplished by surgical excision; incision and drainage can, however, result in fistula formation with chronic drainage.[160, 162–164] Some authors recommend needle aspiration in those cases in which the nodes overlie the facial nerve because of the risk of drainage to the nerve and its branches during excision.[165] In these cases, medical therapy with a macrolide-containing regimen may be appropriate.[156, 166] Rare cases of intrathoracic infection with MAC have been reported in children; outcome has been favorable with surgical or medical treatment.[167]

Disseminated MAC infection occurs rarely in the non-AIDS population. Horsburgh reviewed 13 cases from National Jewish Hospital and an additional 24 cases from the literature.[168] Ten patients were younger than 10 years old; seven of these were younger than 3 years. Only half of the patients were known to be compromised hosts; previous treatment with adrenocorticosteroids was the most common cause of underlying immunodeficiency. As in the AIDS population, *M. avium* strains were much more common than *M. intracellulare* and the predominant symptoms were fever, weight loss, and weakness. Twenty-seven percent of patients had pulmonary symptoms, but only 14% had gastrointestinal symptoms. Localized pain attributed to bony lesions was also reported. Involvement of the reticuloendothelial organs (lymph node, bone marrow, liver, and spleen) was common. Transplantation patients undergoing prolonged immunosuppressive courses also are at increased risk for disseminated disease.[169] Disseminated disease in the pediatric population was reviewed by Stone and associates[170]; most striking was the mortality rate of 82%.

Cutaneous disease caused by MAC may be either primary or a manifestation of disseminated infection. A wide spectrum of lesions has been reported, including ulcers, abscesses, plaques resembling lepromatous leprosy, ecthyma, deep-seated inflammatory nodules, panniculitis, and draining sinuses.[171–174] MAC should be considered in the differential diagnosis of unexplained skin lesions that develop in an immunosuppressed patient, even when AIDS is not the primary illness. MAC may rarely cause a variety of other clinical syndromes, including granulomatous renal disease,[175, 176] prostatitis,[177] peritonitis,[178] corneal ulceration,[179] mastoiditis,[180, 181] mastitis,[182] osteomyelitis,[183, 184] endocarditis,[185] septic arthritis,[186, 187] and synovitis.[188, 189]

Patients with Acquired Immunodeficiency Syndrome

Fever, drenching night sweats, and weight loss are the hallmarks of disseminated disease in AIDS patients.[190–193] Diarrhea, malaise, and anorexia are frequently present (Table 242–2). When patients with disseminated MAC were compared to controls with CD4 cell counts less than 100/mm^3, fever, anemia, weight loss, diarrhea, and increased alkaline phosphatase levels were associated with MAC.[194] One study demonstrated that weight loss, fever, and elevation in the serum lactate dehydrogenase concentration preceded MAC bacteremia by 3, 2, and 1 months, respectively.[195] Widespread involvement of the reticuloendothelial system is common and results in hepatomegaly, splenomegaly, and lymphadenopathy.[196] Anemia may be profound, necessitating frequent transfusions.[197] Disseminated MAC occurs as a late opportunistic infection in HIV-related disease. In most series the median time from the onset of AIDS-defining conditions (1987 Centers for Disease Control criteria) to disseminated MAC was 8 to 9.3 months.[52, 194]

TABLE 242–2 Signs and Symptoms of Disseminated *Mycobacterium avium* Complex in Acquired Immunodeficiency Syndrome Patients

Symptom	Percentage of Patients	Range
Fever	93	56–100
Night sweats	87	86–87
Anorexia	74	66–81
Weight loss	60	50–69
Hepatomegaly	42	14–69
Diarrhea	40	0–63
Splenomegaly	32	11–53
Abdominal pain	28	5–41

Data from refs. 53, 219, 248, and 251.

The earliest studies of disseminated infection emphasized high circulating levels of MAC (10^4 CFU/ml), widespread organ involvement, and an extraordinary tissue burden of organisms (10^6/g)[198] (Fig. 242–3). One study suggested that the extent of organ disease is a function of survival and that only half of patients have visible organ involvement at the time of diagnosis.[199] Culture and histologic evidence of infection has been reported in the heart, lungs, eye, brain, skin, thyroid, tongue, adrenals, stomach, pancreas, skeletal system, and peripheral nerves.[52, 200, 201] Characteristic foamy histiocytes filled with massive numbers of mycobacteria are thought to be pathognomonic for disseminated MAC; however, there is a broad spectrum of pathologic findings.[202, 203] Granulomas are rare; necrotizing acute and chronic inflammation with foamy histiocytes was the predominant pattern in a review of the pathology.[204]

The gastrointestinal tract is frequently involved in disseminated disease; pathologic lesions may resemble those of Whipple's disease, with malabsorption and infiltration of the mucosal folds and foamy histiocytes[205, 206] (Fig. 242–4). Colonic, duodenal, and ileal involvement are well described[207, 208]; the rectum can also be involved.[209]

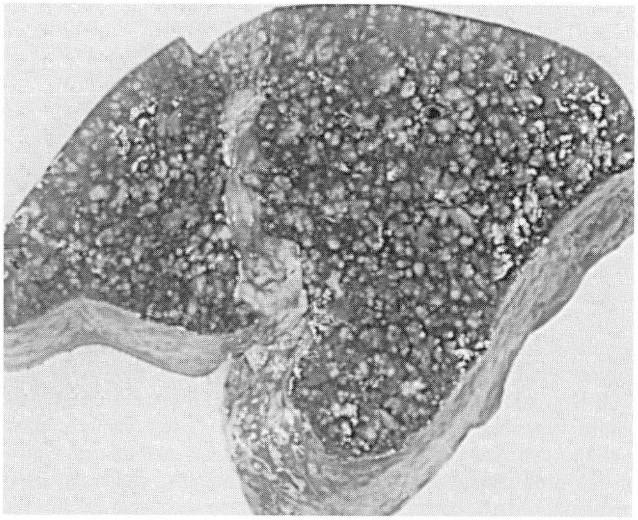

FIGURE 242–3. Gross pathology of spleen removed at autopsy from patients with acquired immunodeficiency syndrome with disseminated *Mycobacterium avium* complex showing widespread granulomatous disease. (Courtesy of Dr. Marjorie Graf, Galveston, Tex.)

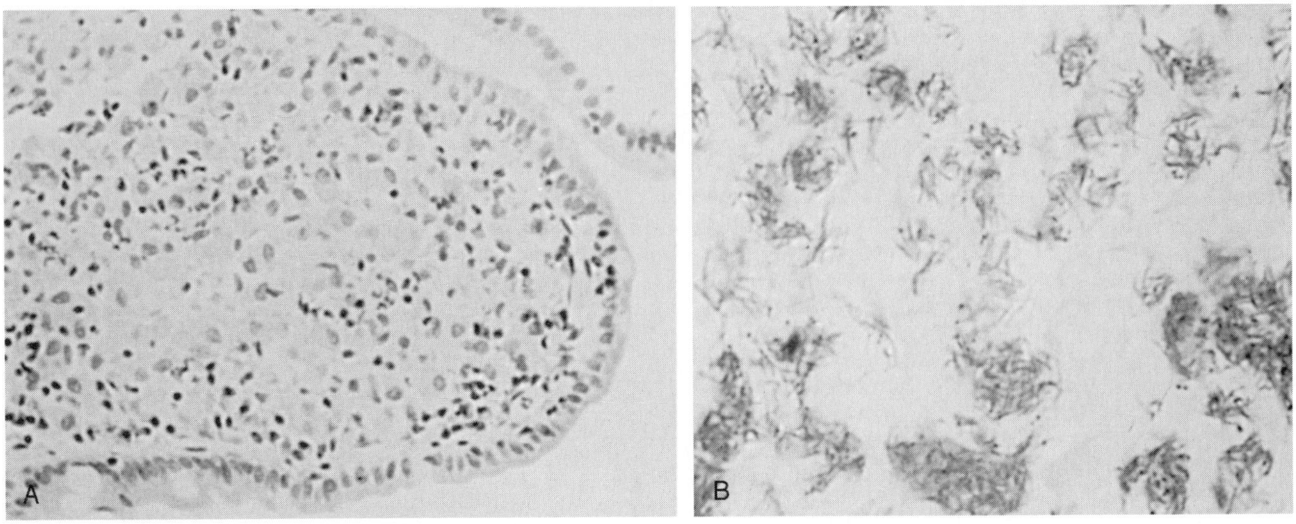

FIGURE 242–4. *A,* Small bowel biopsy in patients with acquired immunodeficiency syndrome with Whipple's-like presentation. Villi are blunted and infiltrated with foamy histiocytes (H&E). *B,* The AFB stain shows the histiocytes to be loaded with organisms.

Nausea, vomiting, watery diarrhea, and abdominal pain commonly are seen with gastrointestinal involvement. Abdominal pain can be severe; it has been suggested that extensive intra-abdominal lymphadenopathy is responsible. Gastrointestinal obstruction and gastrointestinal bleeding (caused by bulky intra-abdominal adenopathy or extensive ileal disease) also have been reported.[207, 210–212] Elevations of the serum alkaline phosphatase concentration are common and reflect liver involvement.

In contrast to non-AIDS patients, the lung is an unusual site of disease in AIDS. MAC may be isolated from the sputum, but in most cases it is a colonizer, other putative pulmonary pathogens are present, and therapy for MAC is not necessary.[213] MAC pulmonary disease occurs in approximately 3% of patients with bacteremia but can also manifest in patients without disseminated infection who have more than 100 CD4 cells/mm^3.[214, 215] Manifestations of pulmonary MAC disease in these cases include diffuse interstitial infiltrates, nodular lesions, endobronchial lesions, and adenopathy.[214–218] Distinguishing MAC from *M. tuberculosis* is not possible on clinical grounds in patients with advanced HIV infection. Although pleural disease and lymphadenopathy are more common in tuberculosis,[219] the overlap in symptoms is such that only cultural confirmation can definitively distinguish the two. Other unusual manifestations of MAC disease in the AIDS population include cutaneous disease,[220–222] arthritis,[223–225] sinusitis,[226] orchitis,[227] peritonitis,[228] chylous ascites,[229] appendicitis,[230, 231] endophthalmitis,[232] choroiditis,[233] pancreatitis,[234] pericarditis,[235, 236] and meningitis.[237]

A new clinical syndrome of focal adenitis MAC has been recognized in AIDS patients. After the initiation of potent antiretroviral therapy, patients develop intra-abdominal, intrathoracic, or peripheral lymphadenopathy. Systemic symptoms of fever, abdominal pain, and malaise may be present, and blood cultures may be negative for MAC.[238] This syndrome has also been observed in patients with chronic MAC who initiate potent antiretroviral therapy and presumably restore immune response to MAC.

If left untreated, the course of disseminated disease is progressive clinical deterioration, although the pace varies even among patients with the same CD4 cell counts. Median survival time after diagnosis in untreated patients ranges from 2 to 7 months; higher levels of circulating MAC bacteremia are associated with shorter survival times.[14, 194, 239–241] In two case-control studies in which patients were matched for CD4 cell counts and antiretroviral therapy, patients with disseminated MAC had a median survival time 3 to 7 months shorter than that of controls.[240, 242] Despite the widespread organ involvement and high levels of circulating bacteria, *M. avium* is considered to be the direct cause of death in few cases.

Treatment

Treatment of disseminated MAC disease has been markedly altered as a result of the potent antimycobacterial agents clarithromycin and azithromycin. These drugs are exquisitely active against MAC, concentrate intracellularly into macrophages, and achieve excellent tissue penetration.[243, 244] They are relatively well tolerated and require only once-daily or twice-daily dosing. Before the availability of these drugs, treatment regimens for disseminated MAC were palliative, rarely sterilized blood cultures, were complex to administer, and were associated with intolerable side effects.[245–248] When clarithromycin and azithromycin were first used for the treatment of disseminated MAC disease in AIDS patients, the clinical and microbiologic effects were striking. Fevers and abdominal pain resolved, patient weights increased, and MAC was cleared from the blood.[249–251]

The superiority of these drugs in the treatment of MAC was confirmed in clinical trials. Bacteremia was reduced by 2.7 log 10 CFU/ml of plasma with clarithromycin, compared with reductions of 1.4 to 1.5 log 10 CFU/ml reported with combination therapies.[247–249] In one clinical trial that directly compared a clarithromycin-containing regimen with a standard multidrug regimen of rifampin, ethambutol, clofazimine, and ciprofloxacin, patients receiving clarithromycin had greater improvement in clinical status, faster clearance of MAC from the blood, and prolonged survival time.[252] Based on these and other clinical studies in patients with MAC bacteremia or pulmonary disease, clarithromycin (or azithromycin) has emerged as the essential component of an effective MAC treatment regimen.

Currently recommended MAC treatment regimens contain at least two drugs, because monotherapy with either clarithromycin or azithromycin is associated with the emergence of drug-resistant organisms within weeks to months after treatment initiation[249] (Table 242–3). Resistance has been documented both in AIDS patients undergoing treatment for disseminated disease and in non-AIDS patients treated for pulmonary MAC disease. In AIDS patients, resistant organisms appear fastest in patients with the highest levels of bacteremia.[249] Molecular fingerprinting studies suggest that resistant organisms represent a minority population that arises from the initial infecting strain under selective drug pressure.[253, 254] Resistant organisms contain a mutation within domain V of the 23S rRNA

TABLE 242-3 Treatment Recommendations for *Mycobacterium avium* Complex

Clinical Syndrome	Treatment
Cervical adenitis	Surgical resection
Pulmonary disease	
Nodule	Surgical resection
Infiltrate/invasive disease	Clarithromycin (500 mg twice daily) or azithromycin (500 mg daily), plus ethambutol (15 mg/kg daily) and rifabutin (300 mg daily). Streptomycin (1 g 3–5 d/wk for 6–12 wk) may be added initially for cavitary disease.
Disseminated disease	Clarithromycin (500 mg twice daily) (preferred) or azithromycin (500 mg daily) plus ethambutol (15 mg/kg daily), with or without rifabutin, 300 mg, daily
Salvage therapy*	Continue clarithromycin or azithromycin, add rifabutin and amikacin (7.5–15 mg/kg daily) and/or sparfloxacin, ofloxacin, levofloxacin. Interferon-γ (subcutaneous or inhaled) has proved useful in some cases.
Prophylaxis (HIV disease)	Azithromycin (1200 mg once weekly) or clarithromycin (500 mg twice daily). Rifabutin (300 mg daily) can be used as an alternative but is less effective and has drug interactions with HIV protease inhibitors.

*Patients who are clinically or microbiologically failing a first-line treatment regimen and who have developed macrolide resistance.

gene, the binding site of the macrolides,[253, 255, 256] and are resistant to both clarithromycin and azithromycin.[257]

In vitro testing of susceptibility to macrolides is useful because of the correlation between this measure and clinical response. Patients undergoing treatment with a macrolide regimen who demonstrate microbiologic and clinical relapse harbor macrolide-resistant organisms.[249, 253] Minimal inhibitory concentrations (MIC) tested at pH 6.8 to 6.9 with clarithromycin increase from 2.0 μg/ml or less in drug-susceptible organisms to 32 μg/ml or more in drug-resistant organisms.[258] In vitro susceptibility testing for azithromycin reveals MIC of 128 μg/ml or less in sensitive isolates and 256 μg/ml or more in resistant isolates.[259, 260] For drugs other than the macrolides, susceptibility testing has not proved to be a useful clinical tool.[261, 262]

Uncertainty persists regarding the optimal drugs that should accompany a macrolide to enhance durability of the microbiologic and clinical response. The addition of antimycobacterial agents to a macrolide regimen delays or prevents the development of resistance but does not enhance initial clearance rates of MAC.[263] The choice of a second and third agent should be guided by results of clinical trials and not by in vitro susceptibility testing to these agents, because there is no discernible relation between in vitro testing and clinical outcome for any MAC agents apart from the macrolides. Ethambutol is recommended as a second drug because it is generally well tolerated, has proven efficacy as monotherapy in AIDS patients with MAC bacteremia, and, most importantly, reduced relapse of bacteremia by over 50% in AIDS patients with MAC bacteremia receiving a clarithromycin-containing regimen.[263, 264]

Rifabutin has well established activity in the prophylaxis and treatment of MAC and may be beneficial as a third agent in a multidrug regimen.[259, 260, 264–265] Rifabutin can produce some unusual side effects, including uveitis, arthralgias, and orange discoloration of the skin,[266, 267] and the toxicity of rifabutin is enhanced by drugs such as clarithromycin and fluconazole, which inhibit the metabolism of rifabutin.[252, 268, 269] Patients with low body mass appear to be particularly susceptible to this toxicity and should receive no more than 300 mg daily of rifabutin.[270] Rifabutin also lowers clarithromycin levels through hepatic enzyme induction, although the clinical significance of these observations is unclear.[271]

Clofazimine was widely used in the past for the treatment of MAC, but it is no longer recommended. Clinical studies demonstrated no antimicrobial activity when this drug was administered as monotherapy, and in one randomized study patients receiving clarithromycin plus clofazimine had a worse outcome than those not receiving clofazimine.[272, 273]

Other drugs, such as quinolones (ciprofloxacin, sparfloxacin, levofloxacin, ofloxacin), cycloserine, and ethionamide, have been used in relatively effective MAC multidrug treatment regimens, but the antimicrobial activity of each of these drugs is unknown. In view of their low potency and high toxicity, drugs such as ethionamide and cycloserine should be considered in salvage regimens only. Aminoglycosides such as amikacin and streptomycin are active and reduce the incidence of resistance in macrolide-containing regimens in animal models of MAC; they have been used in successful treatment regimens, and have been favored by pulmonologists for the treatment of MAC pulmonary disease.[126, 274] However, one randomized clinical trial of disseminated MAC in AIDS patients failed to show a beneficial effect of amikacin.[275] The potential risks and benefits of this therapy should be weighed carefully, particularly in view of toxicity observed with long-term administration.

Some patients receiving multidrug macrolide-containing regimens who initially respond to therapy develop recrudescence of bacteremia or relapse of pulmonary disease. Intolerance to medications, malabsorption, and insufficient antimicrobial activity to inhibit an overwhelming organism burden are all possible contributing factors to this clinical scenario.[276] In patients who adhere to therapy, resistance to clarithromycin and azithromycin is usually present. For these patients, most experts advocate continuation of a macrolide, because mixed populations of macrolide-susceptible and macrolide-resistant organisms may be present.[276a] The addition of two new agents in this setting is optimal. Because of the limited number of drugs that have proved active against MAC, it is often difficult to implement a salvage regimen within these guidelines that does not present significant risks of microbiologic failure and drug toxicity. For this reason, all efforts should be made to ensure that patients tolerate, adhere to, and respond to the initial treatment regimen.

There are limited data on the efficacy of adjunctive immune therapy in patients in whom MAC chemotherapy is failing either clinically or microbiologically. In patients without AIDS but with a familial predisposition to disseminated mycobacterial disease, subcutaneous IFN-γ was associated with clinical and microbiologic improvement.[277] Aerosolized IFN-γ has been used to treat refractory MAC pulmonary disease.[278] Anecdotal improvement in AIDS patients treated with subcutaneous IFN-γ has also been reported.[279] Kemper and colleagues reported that GM-CSF augmented in vitro macrophage responses to MAC, although a microbiologic response was not detected.[280] Steroids have also been advocated as adjunctive therapy in AIDS patients with disseminated MAC in whom treatment is failing.[281–283] Corticosteroids should be considered only in two settings. For patients who are highly symptomatic and have failed or are intolerant to all antimycobacterial agents, steroids can be administered as a palliative measure. However, before corticosteroids are considered, a thorough investigation to exclude previously unrecognized coexisting pathology should be pursued,[283] adjunctive immune therapy such as IFN-γ should be considered, and, in AIDS patients, antiretroviral therapy should be optimized. A temporary course of corticosteroids may be required to reduce inflammation in AIDS patients initiating potent antiretroviral therapy who develop lymphadenitis compromising a critical anatomic structure.

Pulmonary Disease in Patients without Acquired Immunodeficiency Syndrome

The outlook for MAC pulmonary disease has improved dramatically with the use of macrolide-containing regimens. In the past, observation of some patients with MAC pulmonary disease was advocated, because in patients with few or no symptoms the toxicity of the recommended multidrug regimens exceeded the expected clinical benefits. Although this probably is still true for asymptomatic patients with a limited life expectancy, pulmonary MAC has an unpredictable clinical course and advanced disease is more difficult to treat; therefore therapy with a macrolide-containing regimen should be considered for most patients.[126]

Comparative studies have not been conducted in patients with MAC pulmonary disease, but the best reported results have been achieved with a regimen containing clarithromycin, ethambutol, rifampin, or rifabutin and 2 to 4 months of streptomycin.[284] Sputum conversion rates of 91% were reported with this regimen, and 83% of patients exhibited negative sputum cultures by 6 months. Favorable results have also been reported with azithromycin, although it is difficult to compare the results of these trials because monotherapy was prescribed initially in some patients.[285, 286] The relative contribution of each of the components in these multidrug regimens is unknown, and patients must be carefully monitored for drug toxicity and skillfully managed to ensure adherence to a macrolide and at least one additional agent.

In elderly patients and patients with low body mass who are receiving macrolides, ototoxicity and gastrointestinal toxicity are common side effects, and doses may need to be reduced.[287] In general, higher doses of ethambutol have been used in patients treated for MAC pulmonary disease (25 mg/kg for the first 2 months, then 15 mg/kg) than in those with AIDS and disseminated disease (800 mg daily), although the necessity of the higher dose is unproven. Rifabutin is preferred to rifampin because of the established efficacy of rifabutin in the prevention and treatment of MAC in AIDS patients. A rifabutin daily dose of no more than 300 mg should be prescribed, because higher doses are associated with extremely high rates of toxicity.[288] Most experts recommend the addition of streptomycin to a treatment regimen only in the case of patients with extensive cavitary disease.[126] Patients receiving streptomycin must be monitored for side effects including renal dysfunction, ototoxicity, and vestibular dysfunction. Patients receiving treatment for MAC pulmonary disease should have monthly evaluations of sputum cultures to document sterilization of the sputum and to monitor for bacteriologic relapse. Isolates obtained after sterilization of cultures or after 6 months of therapy should be evaluated for macrolide resistance. The duration of treatment with macrolide-containing regimens is not known, but clinical experience suggests that patients treated for 1 year after conversion of sputum cultures have extremely low relapse rates for at least 18 months after termination of therapy. Symptomatic patients should exhibit clinical improvement within 3 to 6 months after initiation of therapy.

Surgical excision is curative in patients with an isolated MAC pulmonary nodule. The role of surgical intervention as adjunctive therapy in all other cases of MAC pulmonary disease, now that more effective antimicrobial regimens are available, is less clear. Patients who are intolerant to medical therapy or in whom such therapy is failing who have disease localized to one lung may benefit from resectional surgery.[289, 290] Patients must be carefully selected as surgical candidates; thoracotomy and resectional surgeries are associated with significant morbidity and mortality, particularly in the presence of underlying chronic pulmonary disease.

Disseminated *Mycobacterium avium* Complex in Patients with Acquired Immunodeficiency Syndrome

Multiple clinical trials have documented the beneficial effects of macrolide-containing multidrug regimens for the treatment of disseminated MAC in AIDS patients. In patients who are able to tolerate therapy, clinical symptoms of MAC resolve within the first few weeks after initiation of therapy, quality of life is improved, and survival is prolonged. MAC becomes undetectable in the blood of most patients within 3 months after initiation of treatment. Autopsy studies suggest that reduction of levels of MAC in the blood is associated with reduction in levels of MAC in the tissues, although reservoirs in tissues such as the bone marrow may remain.[199, 291, 292]

Treatment regimens should include at least clarithromycin and ethambutol, and addition of a third agent should be considered.[293] Although clearance of bacteremia is faster in patients receiving a 2000-mg compared with a 1000-mg daily dose of clarithromycin, toxicity is greater with the higher dose, rifabutin toxicity is augmented in patients receiving both drugs, and in one study mortality was inexplicably higher in patients receiving the higher dose.[294] Azithromycin can be used in place of clarithromycin, but the efficacy and durability of azithromycin multidrug regimens in disseminated MAC disease in AIDS patients are less well documented.[294a]

Rifabutin can be used in the initial treatment regimen in AIDS patients, and may be beneficial in improving microbiologic response and reducing the risk for developing macrolide resistance.[265a] One large, randomized trial of patients found that survival was greater in patients receiving clarithromycin and ethambutol plus rifabutin than in those not receiving rifabutin.[265b] There is an important caveat in using rifabutin to treat patients with disseminated MAC. Complex drug interactions exist between rifabutin and HIV protease and non-nucleoside reverse transcriptase inhibitors. The HIV protease inhibitor ritonavir inhibits rifabutin metabolism, increasing drug exposure by seven-fold and increasing drug toxicity.[295] Indinavir and nelfinavir also increase rifabutin levels. Of greater concern in using these drugs together is that hepatic enzyme induction by rifabutin reduces levels of indinavir, nelfinavir, nevirapine, and delavirdine, necessitating dosing adjustments or avoidance of certain drug combinations.[296, 297, 298]

Patients with previous exposure to macrolides and those who develop MAC while receiving clarithromycin or azithromycin for MAC prophylaxis should have their initial isolate tested for macrolide susceptibility. There have been cases reported in adults of a clarithromycin-resistant MAC culture in patients who have not previously received macrolide therapy.[299] Patients with a resistant isolate should be treated initially with a three- to four-drug macrolide-containing regimen. All patients receiving MAC therapy should be monitored monthly for clinical response to therapy and drug toxicities. Blood cultures can document clearing of bacteremia and may be useful in determining whether recrudescence of clinical symptoms is caused by MAC or by another opportunistic infection. Patients with recrudescent bacteremia should have isolates tested for macrolide susceptibility. Salvage regimens for patients with macrolide-resistant disease are limited. Antiretroviral therapy should be optimized in all patients and may produce immunologic changes that enhance host control of MAC.

Until recently, AIDS patients with MAC bacteremia were committed to lifelong therapy. The profound increases in CD4 cell counts observed in patients responding to potent antiretroviral therapy challenges this therapeutic dictum. The localized MAC inflammatory syndromes observed in patients in whom potent antiretroviral therapy was initiated suggest that some immune responses to MAC are reconstituted. Anecdotal reports of AIDS patients with a history of MAC bacteremia and increases in CD4 cell count to more than 100 cells/mm^3, who were receiving antiretroviral therapy and discontinued MAC therapy without resurgence of bacteremia or clinical symptoms, suggest that MAC therapy may not need to be continued indefinitely.[300, 301] Clinical studies are ongoing to systematically assess the outcome of this therapeutic strategy.

PROPHYLAXIS

Prophylaxis for MAC, with either azithromycin (1200 mg once weekly) or clarithromycin (500 mg twice daily) is now recommended for all AIDS patients with CD4 cell counts lower than 50 cells/mm^3.[298] The rationale for this recommendation is based on the high incidence of MAC bacteremia in this population, the increased morbidity and mortality associated with disseminated MAC, and the efficacy of the available prophylactic agents.[259, 260, 302–307] In a randomized, placebo-controlled trial, MAC bacteremia was reduced by 69% in patients receiving clarithromycin compared with placebo, and survival was prolonged.[303] In a similar trial of patients receiving azithromycin, 1200 mg once weekly, MAC bacteremia was reduced by 66%.[260] Clarithromycin and azithromycin have also been shown to be superior to rifabutin for MAC prophylaxis.[259, 307] Rifabutin should be considered an alternative agent to the macrolides for prophylaxis when a macrolide is contraindicated. Rifabutin prophylaxis reduces the risk of MAC bacteremia by half, is associated with increased survival, and is not associated with resistance.[308] The combination of rifabutin and azithromycin was superior to azithromycin alone in one study, but cost, toxicity, and potential drug interactions argue against the routine use of this intensive regimen for MAC prophylaxis.[259] Clarithromycin and azithromycin also provide increased protection against bacterial infections and PCP, and clarithromycin and rifabutin may protect against cryptosporidiosis.[259, 303, 309, 310]

Macrolide resistance has been identified in up to 16% of patients failing azithromycin prophylaxis and in 29 to 58% of patients failing clarithromycin prophylaxis. An animal model of MAC suggests that the development of resistance may also be less with azithromycin compared with clarithromycin, but direct comparative clinical trials in humans have not been conducted.[311] Nevertheless, the overall efficacy of either clarithromycin or azithromycin is high, and the risk in a patient receiving azithromycin prophylaxis for development of MAC with a resistant isolate is less than 1%. Therefore, the possible selection of macrolide-resistant organisms, although a concern, should not discourage the use of MAC prophylaxis.

Before initiating prophylaxis, patients should have a blood culture obtained to exclude MAC bacteremia. The possibility of active tuberculosis should be thoroughly excluded. Routine screening of blood cultures is not recommended after prophylaxis is initiated. Lifelong MAC prophylaxis may not be necessary for HIV-infected patients who respond to potent antiretroviral therapy with increases in CD4 cell counts above 100 cells/mm^3. Epidemiologic data suggest that the risk for MAC is extremely low in patients with fewer than 50 CD4 cells/mm^3 who experience rises in cell counts above 100 cells/mm^3.[312] In addition, observational data demonstrate that rates of MAC are significantly reduced in patients receiving potent antiretroviral therapy, independent of the use of MAC prophylaxis.[56]

REFERENCES

1. Koch M, Rabinowitsch I. Die Tuberculose der Vogel und Ihre Beziehungen zur Sangertiertuberculose. Virchows Arch Pathol Anat. 1907;190:246.
2. Chapman JS. The Atypical Mycobacteria and Human Mycobacteriosis, v. 16. New York: Plenum Medical; 1977.
3. Wolinsky E. Nontuberculous mycobacteria and associated diseases. Am Rev Respir Dis. 1979;119:107–159.
4. Inderlied CB, Kemper CA, Bermudez LE. The *Mycobacterium avium* complex. Clin Microbiol Rev. 1993;6:266–310.
5. Benson CA. Disseminated *Mycobacterium avium* complex infection: Implications of recent clinical trials on prophylaxis and treatment. AIDS Clin Rev. 1997–98; 271–287.
6. Wolinsky E, Rynearson TK. Mycobacteria in soil and their relation to disease-associated strains. Am Rev Respir Dis. 1968;97:1032–1037.
7. Falkinham JO 3rd. Epidemiology of infection by nontuberculous mycobacteria. Clin Microbiol Rev. 1996;9:177–215.
8. Meissner G, Anz W. Sources of *Mycobacterium avium* complex infection resulting in human diseases. Am Rev Respir Dis. 1977;116:1057–1064.
9. Ahrens P, Giese SB, Klausen J, Inglis NF. Two markers, IS901-IS902 and p40, identified by PCR and by using monoclonal antibodies in *Mycobacterium avium* strains. J Clin Microbiol. 1995;33:1049–1053.
10. Guerrero C, Bernasconi C, Burki D, et al. A novel insertion element from *Mycobacterium avium,* IS1245, is a specific target for analysis of strain relatedness. J Clin Microbiol. 1995;33:304–307.
11. Jensen AG, Bennedsen J, Rosdahl VT. Plasmid profiles of *Mycobacterium avium/intracellulare* isolated from patients with AIDS or cervical lymphadenitis and from environmental samples. Scand J Infect Dis. 1989;21:645–649.
12. Meissner PS, Falkinham JO. Plasmid DNA profiles as epidemiological markers for clinical and environmental isolates of *Mycobacterium avium, Mycobacterium intracellulare,* and *Mycobacterium scrofulaceum.* J Infect Dis. 1986;153:325–331.
13. Parker BC, Ford MA, Gruft H, Falkinham JO. Epidemiology of infection by nontuberculous mycobacteria: IV. Preferential aerosolization of *Mycobacterium intracellulare* from natural waters. Am Rev Respir Dis. 1983;128:652–656.
14. Chin DP, Hopewell PC, Yajko DM, et al. *Mycobacterium avium* complex in the respiratory or gastrointestinal tract and the risk of *M. avium* complex bacteremia in patients with human immunodeficiency virus infection. J Infect Dis. 1994;169:289–295.
15. Horsburgh CR Jr, Chin DP, Yajko DM, et al. Environmental risk factors for acquisition of *Mycobacterium avium* complex in persons with human immunodeficiency virus infection. J Infect Dis. 1994;170:362–367.
16. Yajko DM, Chin DP, Gonzalez PC, et al. *Mycobacterium avium* complex in water, food, and soil samples collected from the environment of HIV-infected individuals. J Acquir Immun Defic Syndr Hum Retrovirol. 1995;9:176–182.
17. du Moulin GC, Stottmeier KD, Pelletier PA, et al. Concentration of *Mycobacterium avium* by hospital hot water systems. JAMA. 1988;260:1599–1601.
18. Montecalvo MA, Forester G, Tsang AY, et al. Colonisation of potable water with *Mycobacterium avium* complex in homes of HIV-infected patients. Lancet. 1994;343:1639.
19. von Reyn CF, Maslow JN, Barber TW, et al. Persistent colonization of potable water as a source of *Mycobacterium avium* infection in AIDS. Lancet. 1994;343:1137–1141.
20. Tsang AY, Denner JC, Brennan PJ, McClatchy JK. Clinical and epidemiological importance of typing of *Mycobacterium avium* complex isolates. J Clin Microbiol. 1992;30:479–484.
21. Drake TA, Herron RMJ, Hindler JA, et al. DNA probe reactivity of *Mycobacterium avium* complex isolates from patients without AIDS. Diagn Microbiol Infect Dis. 1988;11:125–128.
22. Yakrus MA, Good RC. Geographic distribution, frequency, and specimen source of *Mycobacterium avium* complex serotypes isolated from patients with acquired immunodeficiency syndrome. J Clin Microbiol. 1990;28:926–929.
23. Horsburgh CRJ, Cohn DL, Roberts RB, et al. *Mycobacterium avium-M. intracellulare* isolates from patients with or without acquired immunodeficiency syndrome. Antimicrob Agents Chemother. 1986;30:955–957.
24. Corpe RF. Clinical aspects, medical and surgical, in the management of Battey-type pulmonary disease. Dis Chest. 1964;45:380–382.
25. Yeager HJ, Raleigh JW. Pulmonary disease due to *Mycobacterium intracellulare.* Am Rev Respir Dis. 1973;108:547–552.
26. Rosenzweig DY. Pulmonary mycobacterial infections due to *Mycobacterium intracellulare-avium* complex: Clinical features and course in 100 consecutive cases. Chest. 1979;75:115–119.
27. Kilby JM, Gilligan PH, Yankaskas JR, et al. Nontuberculous mycobacteria in adult patients with cystic fibrosis. Chest. 1992;102:70–75.
28. Prince DS, Peterson DD, Steiner RM, et al. Infection with *Mycobacterium avium* complex in patients without predisposing conditions. N Engl J Med. 1989;321:863–868.
29. Reich JM, Johnson RE. *Mycobacterium avium* complex pulmonary disease presenting as an isolated lingular or middle lobe pattern: The Lady Windermere syndrome. Chest. 1992;101(6):1605–1609.
30. Huang JH, Oefner PJ, Adi V, et al. Analyses of the NRAMP1 and IFN-gammaR1 genes in women with *Mycobacterium avium-intracellulare* pulmonary disease. Am J Respir Crit Care Med. 1998;157:377–381.
31. Edwards LB, Acquaviva FA, Livesay VT, et al. An atlas of sensitivity to tuberculin, PPD-B, and histoplasmin in the United States. Am Rev Respir Dis. 1969;99:1–18.
32. Good RC, Snider DEJ. Isolation of nontuberculous mycobacteria in the United States, 1980. J Infect Dis. 1982;146:829–833.
33. Hoover DR, Graham NM, Bacellar H, et al. An epidemiologic analysis of *Mycobacterium avium* complex disease in homosexual men infected with human immunodeficiency virus type 1. Clin Infect Dis. 1995;20:1250–1258.
34. Horsburgh CRJ, Selik RM. The epidemiology of disseminated nontuberculous mycobacterial infection in the acquired immunodeficiency syndrome (AIDS). Am Rev Respir Dis. 1989;139:4–7.
35. Horsburgh CR Jr, Schoenfelder JR, Gordin FM, et al. Geographic and seasonal variation in *Mycobacterium avium* bacteremia among North American patients with AIDS. Am J Med Sci. 1997;313:341–345.
36. Low N, Pfluger D, Egger M. Disseminated *Mycobacterium avium* complex disease in the Swiss HIV Cohort Study: Increasing incidence, unchanged prognosis. AIDS. 1997;11:1165–1171.
37. Morrissey AB, Aisu TO, Falkinham JO, et al. Absence of *Mycobacterium avium* complex disease in patients with AIDS in Uganda. J Acquir Immune Defic Syndr Hum Retrovirol. 1992;5:477–478.
38. Okello DO, Sewankambo N, Goodgame R, et al. Absence of bacteremia with *Mycobacterium avium-intracellulare* in Ugandan patients with AIDS. J Infect Dis. 1990;162:208–210.
39. Gilks CF, Brindle RJ, Mwachari C, et al. Disseminated *Mycobacterium avium* infection among HIV-infected patients in Kenya. J Acquir Immune Defic Syndr Hum Retrovirol. 1995;8:195–198.
40. von Reyn CF, Waddell RD, Eaton T, et al. Isolation of *Mycobacterium avium* complex from water in the United States, Finland, Zaire, and Kenya. J Clin Microbiol. 1993;31:3227–3230.
41. von Reyn CF, Barber TW, Arbeit RD, et al. Evidence of previous infection with *Mycobacterium avium-Mycobacterium intracellulare* among healthy subjects: An international study of dominant mycobacterial skin test reactions. J Infect Dis. 1993;168:1553–1558.
42. Colebunders R, Nembunzu M, Portaels F, et al. Isolation of mycobacteria from stools and intestinal biopsies from HIV seropositive and HIV seronegative patients with and without diarrhea in Kinshasa, Zaire. Ann Soc Belg Med Trop. 1990;70:303–309.
43. Grange JM. Is the incidence of AIDS-associated *Mycobacterium avium-intracellulare* disease affected by previous exposure to BCG, *M. tuberculosis* or environmental mycobacteria? Tuber Lung Dis. 1994;75:234–236.

44. Horsburgh CR Jr, Hanson DL, Jones JL, Thompson SE 3rd. Protection from *Mycobacterium avium* complex disease in human immunodeficiency virus-infected persons with a history of tuberculosis. J Infect Dis. 1996;174:1212–1217.
45. Kallenius G, Hoffner SE, Svenson SB. Does vaccination with bacille Calmette-Guérin protect against AIDS? Rev Infect Dis. 1989;11:349–351.
46. Nightingale SD, Byrd LT, Southern PM, et al. Incidence of *Mycobacterium avium-intracellulare* complex bacteremia in human immunodeficiency virus-positive patients. J Infect Dis. 1992;165:1082–1085.
47. Williams PL, Currier JS, Swindells S. Joint effects of HIV-1 RNA levels and CD4 lymphocyte cells on the risk of specific opportunistic infections. AIDS. 1999;13:1035–1044.
48. Chaisson RE, Moore RD, Richman DD, et al. Incidence and natural history of *Mycobacterium avium* complex infections in patients with advanced human immunodeficiency virus disease treated with zidovudine. The Zidovudine Epidemiology Study Group. Am Rev Respir Dis. 1992;146:285–289.
49. Horsburgh CRJ, Caldwell MB, Simonds RJ. Epidemiology of disseminated nontuberculous mycobacterial disease in children with acquired immunodeficiency syndrome. Pediatr Infect Dis J. 1993;12:219–222.
50. Rutstein RM, Cobbs P, McGowan KL, et al. *Mycobacterium avium-intracellulare* complex infection in HIV-infected children. AIDS. 1993;7:507–512.
51. Hoyt L, Oleske J, Holland B, Connor E. Nontuberculous mycobacteria in children with acquired immunodeficiency syndrome. Pediatr Infect Dis J. 1992;11:354–360.
52. Hawkins CC, Gold JW, Whimbey E, et al. *Mycobacterium avium* complex infections in patients with the acquired immunodeficiency syndrome. Ann Intern Med. 1986;105:184–188.
53. Wallace JM, Hannah JB. *Mycobacterium avium* complex infection in patients with the acquired immunodeficiency syndrome: A clinicopathologic study. Chest. 1988;93:926–932.
54. Hoover DR, Saah AJ, Bacellar H, et al. Clinical manifestations of AIDS in the era of *Pneumocystis* prophylaxis. Multicenter AIDS Cohort Study. N Engl J Med. 1993;329:1922–1926.
55. Moore RD, Chaisson RE. Natural history of opportunistic disease in an HIV-infected urban clinical cohort. Ann Intern Med. 1996;124:633–642.
56. Palella FJ Jr, Delaney KM, Moorman AC, et al. Declining morbidity and mortality among Patients with advanced human immunodeficiency virus infection. HIV Outpatient Study investigators. N Engl J Med. 1998;338:853–860.
57. Wayne LG, Sramek HA. Agents of newly recognized or infrequently encountered mycobacterial diseases. Clin Microbiol Rev. 1992;5:1–25.
58. Denner JC, Tsang AY, Chatterjee D, Brennan PJ. Comprehensive approach to identification of serovars of *Mycobacterium avium* complex. J Clin Microbiol. 1992;30:473–478.
59. Arbeit RD, Slutsky A, Barber TW, et al. Genetic diversity among strains of *Mycobacterium avium* causing monoclonal and polyclonal bacteremia in patients with AIDS. J Infect Dis. 1993;167:1384–1390.
60. Roiz MP, Palenque E, Guerrero C, Garcia MJ. Use of restriction fragment length polymorphism as a genetic marker for typing *Mycobacterium avium* strains. J Clin Microbiol. 1995;33:1389–1391.
61. Slutsky AM, Arbeit RD, Barber TW, et al. Polyclonal infections due to *Mycobacterium avium* complex in patients with AIDS detected by pulsed-field gel electrophoresis of sequential clinical isolates. J Clin Microbiol. 1994;32:1773–1778.
62. Mazurek GH, Hartman S, Zhang Y, et al. Large DNA restriction fragment polymorphism in the *Mycobacterium avium-Mycobacterium intracellulare* complex: A potential epidemiologic tool. J Clin Microbiol. 1993;31:390–394.
63. Yakrus MA, Reeves MW, Hunter SB. Characterization of isolates of *Mycobacterium avium* serotypes 4 and 8 from patients with AIDS by multilocus enzyme electrophoresis. J Clin Microbiol. 1992;30:1474–1478.
64. Mazurek GH, Chin DP, Hartman S, et al. Genetic similarity among *Mycobacterium avium* isolates from blood, stool, and sputum of persons with AIDS. J Infect Dis. 1997;176:976–983.
65. Bermudez LE, Young LS. Factors affecting invasion of HT-29 and HEP-2 epithelial cells by organisms of the *Mycobacterium avium* complex. Infect Immunol 1994;62:2021–2026.
66. Bermudez LE, Young LS, Enkel H. Interaction of *Mycobacterium avium* complex with human macrophages: Roles of membrane receptors and serum proteins. Infect Immun. 1991;59:1697–1702.
67. Rao SP, Gehlsen KR, Catanzaro A. Identification of a beta 1 integrin on *Mycobacterium avium-Mycobacterium intracellulare.* Infect Immun. 1992;60:3652–3657.
68. Rao SP, Ogata K, Morris SL, Catanzaro A. Identification of a 68 kd surface antigen of *Mycobacterium avium* that binds to human macrophages. J Lab Clin Med. 1994;123:526–535.
69. Roecklein JA, Swartz RP, Yeager H Jr. Nonopsonic uptake of *Mycobacterium avium* complex by human monocytes and alveolar macrophages. J Lab Clin Med. 1992;119:772–781.
70. Schorey JS, Carroll MC, Brown EJ. A macrophage invasion mechanism of pathogenic mycobacteria. Science. 1997;277:1091–1093.
71. Hayashi T, Rao SP, Catanzaro A. Binding of the 68-kilodalton protein of *Mycobacterium avium* to alpha(v)beta3 on human monocyte-derived macrophages enhances complement receptor type 3 expression. Infect Immun. 1997;65:1211–1216.
72. Bermudez LE, Parker A, Goodman JR. Growth within macrophages increases the efficiency of *Mycobacterium avium* in invading other macrophages by a complement receptor-independent pathway. Infect Immun. 1997;65:1916–1925.
73. Denis M. Tat protein from HIV-1 binds to *Mycobacterium avium* via a bacterial integrin: Effects on extracellular and intracellular growth. J Immunol. 1994;153:2072–2081.
74. Denis M, Ghadirian E. *Mycobacterium avium* infection in HIV-1-infected subjects increases monokine secretion and is associated with enhanced viral load and diminished immune response to viral antigens. Clin Exp Immunol. 1994;97:76–82.
75. Crawford JT, Bates JH. Analysis of plasmids in *Mycobacterium avium-intracellulare* isolates from persons with acquired immunodeficiency syndrome. Am Rev Respir Dis. 1986;134:659–661.
76. Pethel ML, Falkinham JO III. Plasmid-influenced changes in *Mycobacterium avium* catalase activity. Infect Immun. 1989;57:1714–1718.
77. Gangadharam PR, Perumal VK, Crawford JT, Bates JH. Association of plasmids and virulence of *Mycobacterium avium* complex. Am Rev Respir Dis. 1988;137:212–214.
77a. Beggs ML, Crawford JT, Eisenach KD. Isolation and sequencing of the replication region of *Mycobacterium avium* plasmid pLR7. J Bacteriol. 1995;177(17):4836–4840.
78. Schaefer WB, Davis CL, Cohn ML. Pathogenicity of transparent, opaque, and rough variants of *Mycobacterium avium* in chickens and mice. Am Rev Respir Dis. 1970;102:499–506.
79. Meylan PR, Richman DD, Kornbluth RS. Characterization and growth in human macrophages of *Mycobacterium avium* complex strains isolated from the blood of patients with acquired immunodeficiency syndrome. Infect Immun. 1990;58:2564–2568.
80. Shiratsuchi H, Johnson JL, Toba H, Ellner JJ. Strain- and donor-related differences in the interaction of *Mycobacterium avium* with human monocytes and its modulation by interferon-gamma. J Infect Dis. 1990;162:932–938.
81. Rulong S, Aguas AP, da Silva PP, Silva MT. Intramacrophagic *Mycobacterium avium* bacilli are coated by a multiple lamellar structure: Freeze fracture analysis of infected mouse liver. Infect Immun. 1991;59:3895–3902.
82. Reddy VM, Luna-Herrera J, Gangadharam PR. Pathobiological significance of colony morphology in *Mycobacterium avium* complex. Microb Pathog. 1996;21:97–109.
83. Crowle AJ, Dahl R, Ross E, May MH. Evidence that vesicles containing living, virulent *Mycobacterium tuberculosis* or *Mycobacterium avium* in cultured human macrophages are not acidic. Infect Immun. 1991;59:1823–1831.
84. Frehel C, de Chastellier C, Lang T, Rastogi N. Evidence for inhibition of fusion of lysosomal and prelysosomal compartments with phagosomes in macrophages infected with pathogenic *Mycobacterium avium.* Infect Immun. 1986;52:252–262.
85. Russell DG, Dant J, Sturgill-Koszycki S. *Mycobacterium avium-* and *Mycobacterium tuberculosis*-containing vacuoles are dynamic, fusion-competent vesicles that are accessible to glycosphingolipids from the host cell plasmalemma. J Immunol. 1996;156:4764–4773.
86. Oh YK, Straubinger RM. Intracellular fate of *Mycobacterium avium:* Use of dual-label spectrofluorometry to investigate the influence of bacterial viability and opsonization on phagosomal pH and phagosome-lysosome interaction. Infect Immun. 1996;64:319–325.
87. Sturgill-Koszycki S, Schlesinger PH, Chakraborty P, et al. Lack of acidification in *Mycobacterium* phagosomes produced by exclusion of the vesicular proton-ATPase. Science. 1994;263:678–681.
88. Xu S, Cooper A, Sturgill-Koszycki S, et al. Intracellular trafficking in *Mycobacterium tuberculosis* and *Mycobacterium avium*-infected macrophages. J Immunol. 1994;153:2568–2578.
89. Holsti MA, Allen PM. Processing and presentation of an antigen of *Mycobacterium avium* require access to an acidified compartment with active proteases. Infect Immun. 1996;64:4091–4098.
90. Fréhel C, Offredo C, de Chastellier C. The phagosomal environment protects virulent *Mycobacterium avium* from killing and destruction by clarithromycin. Infect Immun. 1997;65:2792–2802.
91. Bermudez LE, Petrofsky M, Shelton K. Epidermal growth factor-binding protein in *Mycobacterium avium* and *Mycobacterium tuberculosis:* A possible role in the mechanism of infection. Infect Immun. 1996;64:2917–2922.
92. Havlir DV, Haubrich R, Hwang J, et al. Human immunodeficiency virus replication in AIDS patients with *Mycobacterium avium* complex bacteremia: A case control study. California Collaborative Treatment Group. J Infect Dis. 1998;177:595–599.
93. Orenstein JM, Fox C, Wahl SM. Macrophages as a source of HIV during opportunistic infections. Science. 1997;276:1857–1861.
94. Kallenius G, Koivula T, Rydgard KJ, et al. Human immunodeficiency virus type 1 enhances intracellular growth of *Mycobacterium avium* in human macrophages. Infect Immun. 1992;60:2453–2458.
95. Ghassemi M, Andersen BR, Reddy VM, et al. Human immunodeficiency virus and *Mycobacterium avium* complex coinfection of monocytoid cells results in reciprocal enhancement of multiplication. J Infect Dis. 1995;171:68–73.
96. Meylan PR, Munis JR, Richman DD, Kornbluth RS. Concurrent human immunodeficiency virus and mycobacterial infection of macrophages in vitro does not reveal any reciprocal effect. J Infect Dis. 1992;165:80–86.
97. Shiratsuchi H, Johnson JL, Toossi Z, Ellner JJ. Modulation of the effector function of human monocytes for *Mycobacterium avium* by human immunodeficiency virus-1 envelope glycoprotein gp120. J Clin Invest. 1994;93:885–891.
98. Ravn P, Pedersen BK. *Mycobacterium avium* and purified protein derivative-specific cytotoxicity mediated by CD4+ lymphocytes from healthy HIV-seropositive and -seronegative individuals. J Acquir Immune Defic Syndr Hum Retrovirol. 1996;12:433–441.
99. Murray HW, Scavuzzo DA, Chaparas SD, Roberts RB. T lymphocyte responses to mycobacterial antigen in AIDS patients with disseminated *Mycobacterium avium-Mycobacterium intracellulare* infection. Chest. 1988;93:922–925.
100. Harshan KV, Gangadharam PR. In vivo depletion of natural killer cell activity leads to enhanced multiplication of *Mycobacterium avium* complex in mice. Infect Immun. 1991;59:2818–2821.
101. Bermudez LE, Young LS. Natural killer cell-dependent mycobacteriostatic and mycobactericidal activity in human macrophages. J Immunol. 1991;146:265–270.
102. Blanchard DK, Michelini-Norris MB, Pearson CA, et al. Production of granulocyte-

macrophage colony-stimulating factor (GM-CSF) by monocytes and large granular lymphocytes stimulated with *Mycobacterium avium-M. intracellulare:* Activation of bactericidal activity by GM-CSF. Infect Immun. 1991;59:2396–2402.

103. Crowle AJ, Cohn DL, Poche P. Defects in sera from acquired immunodeficiency syndrome (AIDS) patients and from non-AIDS patients with *Mycobacterium avium* infection which decrease macrophage resistance to *M. avium.* Infect Immun. 1989;57:1445–1451.
104. Douvas GS, May MH, Ross E, Crowle AJ. Characterization of inhibition of *Mycobacterium avium* replication in macrophages by normal human serum. Infect Immun. 1992;60:345–352.
105. Douvas GS, May MH, Pearson JR, et al. Hypertriglyceridemic serum, very low density lipoprotein, and iron enhance *Mycobacterium avium* replication in human macrophages. J Infect Dis. 1994;170:1248–1255.
106. Shiratsuchi H, Johnson JL, Ellner JJ. Bidirectional effects of cytokines on the growth of *Mycobacterium avium* within human monocytes. J Immunol. 1991;146:3165–3170.
107. Denis M, Gregg EO. Recombinant tumour necrosis factor-alpha decreases whereas recombinant interleukin-6 increases growth of a virulent strain of *Mycobacterium avium* in human macrophages. Immunology. 1990;71:139–141.
108. Bermudez LE, Wu M, Petrofsky M, Young LS. Interleukin-6 antagonizes tumor necrosis factor-mediated mycobacteriostatic and mycobactericidal activities in macrophages. Infect Immun. 1992;60:4245–4252.
109. Newport MJ, Huxley CM, Huston S, et al. A mutation in the interferon-gamma–receptor gene and susceptibility to mycobacterial infection. N Engl J Med. 1996;335:1941–1949.
110. Frucht DM, Holland SM. Defective monocyte costimulation for IFN-gamma production in familial disseminated *Mycobacterium avium* complex infection: Abnormal IL-12 regulation. J Immunol. 1996;157:411–416.
111. Newman GW, Guarnaccia JR, Vance EA 3rd, Interleukin-12 enhances antigen-specific proliferation of peripheral blood mononuclear cells from HIV-positive and negative donors in response to *Mycobacterium avium.* AIDS. 1994;8:1413–1419.
112. Bermudez LE, Wu M, Young LS. Interleukin-12–stimulated natural killer cells can activate human macrophages to inhibit growth of *Mycobacterium avium.* Infect Immun. 1995;63:4099–4104.
113. Doherty TM, Sher A. IL-12 promotes drug-induced clearance of *Mycobacterium avium* infection in mice. J Immunol. 1998;160:5428–5435.
114. Newman GW, Gan HX, McCarthy PLJ, Remold HG. Survival of human macrophages infected with *Mycobacterium avium intracellulare* correlates with increased production of tumor necrosis factor-alpha and IL-6. J Immunol. 1991;147:3942–3948.
115. Bermudez LE, Young LS. Tumor necrosis factor, alone or in combination with IL-2, but not IFN-gamma, is associated with macrophage killing of *Mycobacterium avium* complex. J Immunol. 1988;140:3006–3013.
116. Sathe SS, Tsigler D, Sarai A, Kumar P. Pentoxifylline impairs macrophage defense against *Mycobacterium avium* complex. J Infect Dis. 1995;172:863–866.
117. Orme IM, Furney SK, Skinner PS, et al. Inhibition of growth of *Mycobacterium avium* in murine and human mononuclear phagocytes by migration inhibitory factor. Infect Immun. 1993;61:338–342.
118. Tantawichien T, Young LS, Bermudez LE. Interleukin-7 induces anti-*Mycobacterium avium* activity in human monocyte-derived macrophages. J Infect Dis. 1996;174:574–582.
119. Shiratsuchi H, Hamilton B, Toossi Z, Ellner JJ. Evidence against a role for interleukin-10 in the regulation of growth of *Mycobacterium avium* in human monocytes. J Infect Dis. 1996;173:410–417.
120. Bermudez LE. Production of transforming growth factor-beta by *Mycobacterium avium*–infected human macrophages is associated with unresponsiveness to IFN-gamma. J Immunol. 1993;150:1838–1845.
121. Michelini-Norris MB, Blanchard DK, Pearson CA, Djeu JY. Differential release of interleukin (IL)-1 alpha, IL-1 beta, and IL-6 from normal human monocytes stimulated with a virulent and an avirulent isogenic variant of *Mycobacterium avium-intracellulare* complex. J Infect Dis. 1992;165:702–709.
122. Shiratsuchi H, Toossi Z, Mettler MA, Ellner JJ. Colonial morphotype as a determinant of cytokine expression by human monocytes infected with *Mycobacterium avium.* J Immunol. 1993;150:2945–2954.
123. Fattorini L, Xiao Y, Li B, et al. Induction of IL-1 beta, IL-6, TNF-alpha, GM-CSF and G-CSF in human macrophages by smooth transparent and smooth opaque colonial variants of *Mycobacterium avium.* J Med Microbiol. 1994;40:129–133.
124. Johnson JL, Shiratsuchi H, Toba H, Ellner JJ. Preservation of monocyte effector functions against *Mycobacterium avium-M. intracellulare* in patients with AIDS. Infect Immun. 1991;59:3639–3645.
125. Johnson JL, Shiratsuchi H, Toossi Z, Ellner JJ. Altered IL-1 expression and compartmentalization in monocytes from patients with AIDS stimulated with *Mycobacterium avium* complex. J Clin Immunol. 1997;17:387–395.
126. Society AT. Diagnosis and treatment of disease caused by nontuberculous mycobacteria. Am J Respir Crit Care Med. 1997;156:S1–S25.
127. Tanaka E, Amitani R, Niimi A, et al. Yield of computed tomography and bronchoscopy for the diagnosis of *Mycobacterium avium* complex pulmonary disease. Am J Respir Crit Care Med. 1997;155:2041–2046.
128. Moore EH. Atypical mycobacterial infection in the lung: CT appearance. Radiology. 1993;187:777–782.
129. Swensen SJ, Hartman TE, Williams DE. Computed tomographic diagnosis of *Mycobacterium avium-intracellulare* complex in patients with bronchiectasis. Chest. 1994;105:49–52.
130. Pinto-Powell R, Olivier KN, Marsh BJ, et al. Skin testing with *Mycobacterium avium* sensitin to identify infection with *M. avium* complex in patients with cystic fibrosis. Clin Infect Dis. 1996;22:560–562.
131. von Reyn CF, Williams DE, Horsburgh CR Jr, et al. Dual skin testing with *Mycobacterium avium* sensitin and purified protein derivative to discriminate pulmonary disease due to *M. avium* complex from pulmonary disease due to *Mycobacterium tuberculosis.* J Infect Dis. 1998;177:730–736.
132. Iralu JV, Sritharan VK, Pieciak WS, et al. Diagnosis of *Mycobacterium avium* bacteremia by polymerase chain reaction. J Clin Microbiol. 1993;31:1811–1814.
133. Emler S, Böttger EC, Broers B, et al. Growth-deficient mycobacteria in patients with AIDS: Diagnosis by analysis of DNA amplified from blood or tissue. Clin Infect Dis. 1995;20:772–775.
134. Kulski JK, Khinsoe C, Pryce T, Christiansen K. Use of a multiplex PCR to detect and identify *Mycobacterium avium* and *M. intracellulare* in blood culture fluids of AIDS patients. J Clin Microbiol. 1995;33:668–674.
135. Stone BL, Cohn DL, Kane SM, et al. Utility of paired blood cultures and smears in diagnosis of disseminated *Mycobacterium avium* complex infections in AIDS patients. J Clin Microbiol. 1994;32:841–842.
136. Havlir D, Kemper CA, Deresinski SC. Reproducibility of lysis-centrifugation cultures for quantification of *Mycobacterium avium* complex bacteremia. J Clin Microbiol. 1993;31:1794–1798.
137. Sewell DL, Rashad AL, Rourke WJJ, et al. Comparison of the Septi-Chek AFB and BACTEC systems and conventional culture for recovery of mycobacteria. J Clin Microbiol. 1993;31:2689–2691.
138. Agy MB, Wallis CK, Plorde JJ, et al. Evaluation of four mycobacterial blood culture media: BACTEC 13A, Isolator/BACTEC 12B, Isolator/Middlebrook agar, and a biphasic medium. Diagn Microbiol Infect Dis. 1989;12:303–308.
139. Ellner PD, Kiehn TE, Cammarata R, Hosmer M. Rapid detection and identification of pathogenic mycobacteria by combining radiometric and nucleic acid probe methods. J Clin Microbiol. 1988;26:1349–1352.
140. Kiehn TE, Edwards FF. Rapid identification using a specific DNA probe of *Mycobacterium avium* complex from patients with acquired immunodeficiency syndrome. J Clin Microbiol. 1987;25:1551–1552.
141. Wasilauskas B, Morrell R Jr. Inhibitory effect of the Isolator blood culture system on growth of *Mycobacterium avium-M. intracellulare* in BACTEC 12B bottles. J Clin Microbiol. 1994;32:654–657.
142. Nussbaum JM, Dealist C, Lewis W, Heseltine PN. Rapid diagnosis by buffy coat smear of disseminated *Mycobacterium avium* complex infection in patients with acquired immunodeficiency syndrome. J Clin Microbiol. 1990;28:631–632.
143. Kilby JM, Marques MB, Jaye DL, et al. The yield of bone marrow biopsy and culture compared with blood culture in the evaluation of HIV-infected patients for mycobacterial and fungal infections. Am J Med. 1998;104:123–128.
144. Roger PM, Mondain V, Saint Paul MC, et al. Liver biopsy is not useful in the diagnosis of mycobacterial infections in patients who are infected with human immunodeficiency virus. Clin Infect Dis. 1996;23:1302–1304.
145. Benito N, Núñez A, de Górgolas M, et al. Bone marrow biopsy in the diagnosis of fever of unknown origin in patients with acquired immunodeficiency syndrome. Arch Intern Med. 1997;157:1577–1580.
146. Cavicchi M, Pialoux G, Carnot F, et al. Value of liver biopsy for the rapid diagnosis of infection in human immunodeficiency virus-infected patients who have unexplained fever and elevated serum levels of alkaline phosphatase or gamma-glutamyl transferase. Clin Infect Dis. 1995;20:606–610.
147. Kemper CA, Havlir D, Bartok AE, et al. Transient bacteremia due to *Mycobacterium avium* complex in patients with AIDS. J Infect Dis. 1994;170:488–493.
148. Havlik JA Jr, Metchock B, Thompson SE III, et al. A prospective evaluation of *Mycobacterium avium* complex colonization of the respiratory and gastrointestinal tracts of persons with human immunodeficiency virus infection. J Infect Dis. 1994;168:1045–1048.
149. Christensen EE, Dietz GW, Ahn CH, et al. Initial roentgenographic manifestations of pulmonary *Mycobacterium tuberculosis, M. kansasii,* and *M. intracellulare* infections. Chest. 1981;80:132–136.
150. Contreras MA, Cheung OT, Sanders DE, Goldstein RS. Pulmonary infection with nontuberculous mycobacteria. Am Rev Respir Dis. 1988;137:149–152.
151. Engbaek HC, Vergmann B, Bentzon MW. Lung disease caused by *Mycobacterium avium/Mycobacterium intracellulare:* An analysis of Danish patients during the period 1962–1976. Eur J Respir Dis. 1981;62:72–83.
152. Hartman TE, Swensen SJ, Williams DE. *Mycobacterium avium-intracellulare* complex: Evaluation with CT. Radiology. 1993;187:23–26.
153. Kubo K; Yamazaki Y, et al. *Mycobacterium avium-intracellulare* pulmonary infection in patients without known predisposing lung disease. Lung. 1998;176(6):381–391.
154. Gribetz AR, Damsker B, Bottone EJ, et al. Solitary pulmonary nodules due to nontuberculous mycobacterial infection. Am J Med. 1981;70:39–43.
155. Teirstein AS, Damsker B, Kirschner PA, et al. Pulmonary infection with *Mycobacterium avium-intracellulare:* Diagnosis, clinical patterns, treatment. Mt Sinai J Med. 1990;57:209–215.
156. Wolinsky E. Mycobacterial lymphadenitis in children: A prospective study of 105 nontuberculous cases with long-term follow-up. Clin Infect Dis. 1995;20:954–963.
157. Lincoln EM, Gilbert LA. Disease in children due to mycobacteria other than *Mycobacterium tuberculosis.* Am Rev Respir Dis. 1972;105:683–714.
158. Hsu KH. Atypical mycobacterial infections in children. Rev Infect Dis. 1981;3:1075–1085.
159. Lai KK, Stottmeier KD, Sherman IH, McCabe WR. Mycobacterial cervical lymphadenopathy: Relation of etiologic agents to age. JAMA. 1984;251:1286–1288.
160. Schaad UB, Votteler TP, McCracken GHJ, Nelson JD. Management of atypical mycobacterial lymphadenitis in childhood: A review based on 380 cases. J Pediatr. 1979;95:356–360.
161. Margileth AM, Chandra R, Altman RP. Chronic lymphadenopathy due to mycobacterial infection: Clinical features, diagnosis, histopathology, and management. Am J Dis Child. 1984;138:917–922.

162. Schuit KE, Powell DA. Mycobacterial lymphadenitis in childhood. Am J Dis Child. 1978;132:675–677.
163. Harris BH, Webb HW, Wilkinson AHJ, Santelices AA. Mycobacterial lymphadenitis. J Pediatr Surg. 1982;17:589–590.
164. Taha AM, Davidson PT, Bailey WC. Surgical treatment of atypical mycobacterial lymphadenitis in children. Pediatr Infect Dis J. 1985;4:664–667.
165. Alessi DP, Dudley JP. Atypical mycobacteria-induced cervical adenitis: Treatment by needle aspiration. Arch Otolaryngol Head Neck Surg. 1988;114:664–666.
166. Green PA, von Reyn CF, Smith RPJ. *Mycobacterium avium* complex parotid lymphadenitis: Successful therapy with clarithromycin and ethambutol. Pediatr Infect Dis J. 1993;12:615–617.
167. Fergie JE, Milligan TW, Henderson BM, Stafford WW. Intrathoracic *Mycobacterium avium* complex infection in immunocompetent children: Case report and review. Clin Infect Dis. 1997;24:250–253.
168. Horsburgh CRJ, Mason UG, Farhi DC, Iseman MD. Disseminated infection with *Mycobacterium avium-intracellulare:* A report of 13 cases and a review of the literature. Medicine (Baltimore). 1985;64:36–48.
169. Novick RJ, Moreno-Cabral CE, Stinson EB, et al. Nontuberculous mycobacterial infections in heart transplant recipients: A seventeen-year experience. J Heart Lung Transplant. 1990;9:357–363.
170. Stone AB, Schelonka RL, Drehner DM, et al. Disseminated *Mycobacterium avium* complex in non-human immunodeficiency virus-infected pediatric patients. Pediatr Infect Dis J. 1992;11:960–964.
171. Sanderson TL, Moskowitz L, Hensley GT, et al. Disseminated *Mycobacterium avium-intracellulare* infection appearing as a panniculitis. Arch Pathol Lab Med. 1982;106:112–114.
172. Cox SK, Strausbaugh LJ. Chronic cutaneous infection caused by *Mycobacterium intracellulare.* Arch Dermatol. 1981;117:794–796.
173. Ichiki Y, Hirose M, Akiyama T, et al. Skin infection caused by *Mycobacterium avium.* Br J Dermatol. 1997;136:260–263.
174. Kullavanijaya P, Sirimachan S, Surarak S. Primary cutaneous infection with *Mycobacterium avium intracellulare* complex resembling lupus vulgaris. Br J Dermatol. 1997;136:264–266.
175. Pergament M, Gonzalez R, Fraley EE. Atypical mycobacteriosis of the urinary tract: A case report of extensive disease caused by the Battey bacillus. JAMA. 1974;229:816–817.
176. Newman H. Renal disease associated with atypical mycobacteria: Battey type. Case report. J Urol. 1970;103:403–405.
177. Mikolich DJ, Mates SM. Granulomatous prostatitis due to *Mycobacterium avium* complex. Clin Infect Dis. 1992;14:589–591.
178. Pulliam JP, Vernon DD, Alexander SR, et al. Nontuberculous mycobacterial peritonitis associated with continuous ambulatory peritoneal dialysis. Am J Kidney Dis. 1983;2:610–614.
179. Knapp A, Stern GA, Hood CI. *Mycobacterium avium-intracellulare* corneal ulcer. Cornea. 1987;6:175–180.
180. Wardrop PA, Pillsbury HC. *Mycobacterium avium* acute mastoiditis. Arch Otolaryngol Head Neck Surg. 1984;110:686–687.
181. Kinsella JP, Grossman M, Black S. Otomastoiditis caused by *Mycobacterium avium-intracellulare.* Pediatr Infect Dis J. 1986;5:704–706.
182. Lee D, Goldstein EJ, Zarem HA. Localized *Mycobacterium avium-intracellulare* mastitis in an immunocompetent woman with silicone breast implants. Plast Reconstr Surg. 1995;95:142–144.
183. Weiner BK, Love TW, Fraser RD. *Mycobacterium avium intracellulare:* Vertebral osteomyelitis. J Spinal Disord. 1998;11:89–91.
184. Kourtis AP, Ibegbu CC, Snitzer JA, Nesheim SR. Recurrent multifocal osteomyelitis due to *Mycobacterium avium* complex. Clin Infect Dis. 1996;23:1194–1195.
185. Landymore RW, Murphy DA, Marrie TJ, Johnston BL. *Mycobacterium avium-intracellulare* endocarditis causing rupture: Replacement and repair with aortic homograft. Can J Cardiol. 1992;8:729–732.
186. Hoffman GS, Myers RL, Stark FR, Thoen CO. Septic arthritis associated with *Mycobacterium avium:* A case report and literature review. J Rheumatol. 1978;5:199–209.
187. Jones AR, Bartlett J, McCormack JG. *Mycobacterium avium* complex (MAC) osteomyelitis and septic arthritis in an immunocompetent host. J Infect. 1995;30:59–62.
188. Sutker WL, Lankford LL, Tompsett R. Granulomatous synovitis: The role of atypical mycobacteria. Rev Infect Dis. 1979;1:729–735.
189. Hellinger WC, Smilack JD, Greider JL Jr, et al. Localized soft-tissue infections with *Mycobacterium avium/Mycobacterium intracellulare* complex in immunocompetent patients: Granulomatous tenosynovitis of the hand or wrist. Clin Infect Dis. 1995;21:65–69.
190. Horsburgh CRJ. *Mycobacterium avium* complex infection in the acquired immunodeficiency syndrome. N Engl J Med. 1991;324:1332–1338.
191. Macher AM, Kovacs JA, Gill V, et al. Bacteremia due to *Mycobacterium avium-intracellulare* in the acquired immunodeficiency syndrome. Ann Intern Med. 1983;99:782–785.
192. Zakowski P, Fligiel S, Berlin GW, Johnson LJ. Disseminated *Mycobacterium avium-intracellulare* infection in homosexual men dying of acquired immunodeficiency. JAMA. 1982;248:2980–2982.
193. Greene JB, Sidhu GS, Lewin S, et al. *Mycobacterium avium-intracellulare:* A cause of disseminated life-threatening infection in homosexuals and drug abusers. Ann Intern Med. 1982;97:539–546.
194. Horsburgh CRJ, Havlik JA, Ellis DA, et al. Survival of patients with acquired immune deficiency syndrome and disseminated *Mycobacterium avium* complex infection with and without antimycobacterial chemotherapy. Am Rev Respir Dis. 1991;144:557–559.
195. Gordin FM, Cohn DL, Sullam PM, et al. Early manifestations of disseminated *Mycobacterium avium* complex disease: A prospective evaluation. J Infect Dis. 1997;176:126–132.
196. Radin DR. Intraabdominal *Mycobacterium tuberculosis* vs *Mycobacterium avium-intracellulare* infections in patients with AIDS: Distinction based on CT findings. AJR Am J Roentgenol. 1991;156:487–491.
197. Gascon P, Sathe SS, Rameshwar P. Impaired erythropoiesis in the acquired immunodeficiency syndrome with disseminated *Mycobacterium avium* complex. Am J Med. 1993;94:41–48.
198. Wong B, Edwards FF, Kiehn TE, et al. Continuous high-grade *Mycobacterium avium-intracellulare* bacteremia in patients with the acquired immune deficiency syndrome. Am J Med. 1985;78:35–40.
199. Torriani FJ, McCutchan JA, Bozzette SA, et al. Autopsy findings in AIDS patients with *Mycobacterium avium* complex bacteremia. J Infect Dis. 1994;170:1601–1605.
200. Wallace RJ Jr. *Mycobacterium avium* complex lung disease and women: Now an equal opportunity disease. Chest. 1994;105:6–7.
201. Sohn CC, Schroff RW, Kliewer KE, et al. Disseminated *Mycobacterium avium-intracellulare* infection in homosexual men with acquired cell-mediated immunodeficiency: A histologic and immunologic study of two cases. Am J Clin Pathol. 1983;79:247–252.
202. Klatt EC, Jensen DF, Meyer PR. Pathology of *Mycobacterium avium-intracellulare* infection in acquired immunodeficiency syndrome. Hum Pathol. 1987;18:709–714.
203. Solis OG, Belmonte AH, Ramaswamy G, Tchertkoff V. Pseudogaucher cells in *Mycobacterium avium intracellulare* infections in acquired immune deficiency syndrome (AIDS). Am J Clin Pathol. 1986;85:233–235.
204. Farhi DC, Mason UG, Horsburgh CRJ. Pathologic findings in disseminated *Mycobacterium avium-intracellulare* infection: A report of 11 cases. Am J Clin Pathol. 1986;85:67–72.
205. Roth RI, Owen RL, Keren DF, Volberding PA. Intestinal infection with *Mycobacterium avium* in acquired immune deficiency syndrome (AIDS): Histological and clinical comparison with Whipple's disease. Dig Dis Sci. 1985;30:497–504.
206. Gillin JS, Urmacher C, West R, Shike M. Disseminated *Mycobacterium avium-intracellulare* infection in acquired immunodeficiency syndrome mimicking Whipple's disease. Gastroenterology. 1983;85:1187–1191.
207. Schneebaum CW, Novick DM, Chabon AB, et al. Terminal ileitis associated with *Mycobacterium avium-intracellulare* infection in a homosexual man with acquired immune deficiency syndrome. Gastroenterology. 1987;92:1127–1132.
208. Wolke A, Meyers S, Adelsberg BR, et al. *Mycobacterium avium-intracellulare*–associated colitis in a patient with the acquired immunodeficiency syndrome. J Clin Gastroenterol. 1984;6:225–229.
209. Gray JR, Rabeneck L. Atypical mycobacterial infection of the gastrointestinal tract in AIDS patients. Am J Gastroenterol. 1989;84:1521–1524.
210. Cappell MS, Hassan T, Rosenthal S, Mascarenhas M. Gastrointestinal obstruction due to *Mycobacterium avium intracellulare* associated with the acquired immunodeficiency syndrome. Am J Gastroenterol. 1992;87:1823–1827.
211. Cappell MS, Geller AJ. The high mortality of gastrointestinal bleeding in HIV-seropositive patients: A multivariate analysis of risk factors and warning signs of mortality in 50 consecutive patients. Am J Gastroenterol. 1992;87:815–824.
212. Cappell MS, Gupta A. Gastrointestinal hemorrhage due to gastrointestinal *Mycobacterium avium-intracellulare* or esophageal candidiasis in patients with the acquired immunodeficiency syndrome. Am J Gastroenterol. 1992;87:224–229.
213. Tenholder MF, Moser RJ, Tellis CJ. Mycobacteria other than tuberculosis: Pulmonary involvement in patients with acquired immunodeficiency syndrome. Arch Intern Med. 1988;148:953–955.
214. Kalayjian RC, Toossi Z, Tomashefski JF Jr, et al. Pulmonary disease due to infection by *Mycobacterium avium* complex in patients with AIDS. Clin Infect Dis. 1995;20:1186–1194.
215. Hocqueloux L, Lesprit P, Herrmann JL, et al. Pulmonary *Mycobacterium avium* complex disease without dissemination in HIV-infected patients. Chest. 1998;113:542–548.
216. Packer SJ, Cesario T, Williams JHJ. *Mycobacterium avium* complex infection presenting as endobronchial lesions in immunosuppressed patients. Ann Intern Med. 1988;109:389–393.
217. Marinelli DL, Albelda SM, Williams TM, et al. Nontuberculous mycobacterial infection in AIDS: Clinical, pathologic, and radiographic features. Radiology. 1986;160:77–82.
218. Mehle ME, Adamo JP, Mehta AC, et al. Endobronchial *Mycobacterium avium-intracellulare* infection in a patient with AIDS. Chest. 1989;96:199–201.
219. Modilevsky T, Sattler FR, Barnes PF. Mycobacterial disease in patients with human immunodeficiency virus infection. Arch Intern Med. 1989;149:2201–2205.
220. Clark JA, Margolis DM. A cutaneous lesion in a patient with AIDS: An unusual presentation of infection due to *Mycobacterium avium* complex. Clin Infect Dis. 1993;16:555–557.
221. Barbaro DJ, Orcutt VL, Coldiron BM. *Mycobacterium avium-Mycobacterium intracellulare* infection limited to the skin and lymph nodes in patients with AIDS. Rev Infect Dis. 1989;11:625–628.
222. Inwald D, Nelson M, Cramp M, et al. Cutaneous manifestations of mycobacterial infection in patients with AIDS. Br J Dermatol. 1994;130:111–114.
223. Vinetz JM, Rickman LS. Chronic arthritis due to *Mycobacterium avium* complex infection in a patient with the acquired immunodeficiency syndrome. Arthritis Rheum. 1991;34:1339–1340.
224. Disla E, Reddy A, Cuppari G, Mullen M. Primary *Mycobacterium avium* complex septic arthritis in a patient with AIDS. Clin Infect Dis. 1995;20:1432–1434.
225. Sheppard DC, Sullam PM. Primary septic arthritis and osteomyelitis due to *Mycobacterium avium* complex in a patient with AIDS. Clin Infect Dis. 1997;25:925–926.

226. Sussman SJ. Sinusitis caused by *Mycobacterium avium-intracellulare* in a patient with human immunodeficiency virus. Pediatr Infect Dis J. 1995;14:726–727.
227. De Paepe ME, Guerrieri C, Waxman M. Opportunistic infections of the testis in the acquired immunodeficiency syndrome. Mt Sinai J Med. 1990;57:25–29.
228. Fernandez-Miranda C, Medina J, Palenque E, et al. Peritonitis with *Mycobacterium avium* in a patient with hepatic cirrhosis. Am J Gastroenterol. 1993;88:615.
229. Rollhauser C, Borum M. Case report: A rare case of chylous ascites from *Mycobacterium avium intracellulare* in a patient with AIDS. Review of the literature. Dig Dis Sci. 1996;41:2499–2501.
230. Livingston RA, Siberry GK, Paidas CN, Eiden JJ. Appendicitis due to *Mycobacterium avium* complex in an adolescent infected with the human immunodeficiency virus. Clin Infect Dis. 1995;20:1579–1580.
231. Domingo P, Ris J, Lopez-Contreras J, et al. Appendicitis due to *Mycobacterium avium* complex in a patient with AIDS. Arch Intern Med. 1996;156:1114.
232. Cohen JI, Saragas SJ. Endophthalmitis due to *Mycobacterium avium* in a patient with AIDS. Ann Ophthalmol. 1990;22:47–51.
233. Whitcup SM, Fenton RM, Pluda JM, et al. *Pneumocystis carinii* and *Mycobacterium avium-intracellulare* infection of the choroid. Retina. 1992;12:331–335.
234. Cappell MS, Javeed M. Pancreatic abscess due to mycobacterial infection associated with the acquired immunodeficiency syndrome. J Clin Gastroenterol. 1990;12:423–429.
235. Choo PW, Donahue JG, Manson JE, Platt R. The epidemiology of varicella and its complications. J Infect Dis. 1995;172:706–712.
236. Woods GL, Goldsmith JC. Fatal pericarditis due to *Mycobacterium avium-intracellulare* in acquired immunodeficiency syndrome. Chest. 1989;95:1355–1357.
237. Flor A, Capdevila JA, Martin N, et al. Nontuberculous mycobacterial meningitis: Report of two cases and review. Clin Infect Dis. 1996;23:1266–1273.
238. Race EM, Adelson-Mitty J, Kriegel GR, et al. Focal mycobacterial lymphadenitis following initiation of protease-inhibitor therapy in patients with advanced HIV-1 disease. Lancet. 1998;351:252–255.
239. Kerlikowske KM, Katz MH, Chan AK, Perez-Stable EJ. Antimycobacterial therapy for disseminated *Mycobacterium avium* complex infection in patients with acquired immunodeficiency syndrome. Arch Intern Med. 1992;152:813–817.
240. Horsburgh CR Jr, Metchock B, Gordon SM, et al. Predictors of survival in patients with AIDS and disseminated *Mycobacterium avium* complex disease. J Infect Dis. 1994;170:573–577.
241. Ives DV, Davis RB, Currier JS. Impact of clarithromycin and azithromycin on patterns of treatment and survival among AIDS patients with disseminated *Mycobacterium avium* complex. AIDS. 1995;9:261–266.
242. Chin DP, Reingold AL, Stone EN, et al. The impact of *Mycobacterium avium* complex bacteremia and its treatment on survival of AIDS patients: A prospective study. J Infect Dis. 1994;170:578–584.
243. Lode H, Borner K, Koeppe P, Schaberg T. Azithromycin: Review of key chemical, pharmacokinetic and microbiological features. J Antimicrob Chemother. 1996;37(Suppl C):1–8.
244. Rapp RP, McCraney SA, Goodman NL, Shaddick DJ. New macrolide antibiotics: Usefulness in infections caused by mycobacteria other than *Mycobacterium tuberculosis*. Ann Pharmacother. 1994;28:1255–1263.
245. Hoy J, Mijch A, Sandland M, et al. Quadruple-drug therapy for *Mycobacterium avium-intracellulare* bacteremia in AIDS patients. J Infect Dis. 1990;161:801–805.
246. Agins BD, Berman DS, Spicehandler D, et al. Effect of combined therapy with ansamycin, clofazimine, ethambutol, and isoniazid for *Mycobacterium avium* infection in patients with AIDS. J Infect Dis. 1989;159:784–787.
247. Chiu J, Nussbaum J, Bozzette S, et al. Treatment of disseminated *Mycobacterium avium* complex infection in AIDS with amikacin, ethambutol, rifampin, and ciprofloxacin. California Collaborative Treatment Group. Ann Intern Med. 1990;113:358–361.
248. Kemper CA, Meng TC, Nussbaum J, et al. Treatment of *Mycobacterium avium* complex bacteremia in AIDS with a four-drug oral regimen: Rifampin, ethambutol, clofazimine, and ciprofloxacin. Ann Intern Med. 1992;116:466–472.
249. Chaisson RE, Benson CA, Dube MP, et al. Clarithromycin therapy for bacteremic *Mycobacterium avium* complex disease: A randomized, double-blind, dose-ranging study in patients with AIDS. AIDS Clinical Trials Group Protocol 157 Study Team. Ann Intern Med. 1994;121:905–911.
250. Dautzenberg B, Truffot C, Legris S, et al. Activity of clarithromycin against *Mycobacterium avium* infection in patients with the acquired immune deficiency syndrome: A controlled clinical trial. Am Rev Respir Dis. 1991;144:564–569.
251. Young LS, Wiviott L, Wu M, et al. Azithromycin for treatment of *Mycobacterium avium-intracellulare* complex infection in patients with AIDS. Lancet. 1991;338:1107–1109.
252. Shafran SD, Singer J, Zarowny DP, et al. A comparison of two regimens for the treatment of *Mycobacterium avium* complex bacteremia in AIDS: Rifabutin, ethambutol, and clarithromycin versus rifampin, ethambutol, clofazimine, and ciprofloxacin. Canadian HIV Trials Network Protocol 010 Study Group. N Engl J Med. 1996;335:377–383.
253. Meier A, Heifets L, Wallace RJ Jr, et al. Molecular mechanisms of clarithromycin resistance in *Mycobacterium avium:* Observation of multiple 23S rDNA mutations in a clonal population. J Infect Dis. 1996;174:354–360.
254. Picardeau M, Varnerot A, Lecompte T, et al. Use of different molecular typing techniques for bacteriological follow-up in a clinical trial with AIDS patients with *Mycobacterium avium* bacteremia. J Clin Microbiol. 1997;35:2503–2510.
255. Nash KA, Inderlied CB. Genetic basis of macrolide resistance in *Mycobacterium avium* isolated from patients with disseminated disease. Antimicrob Agents Chemother. 1995;39:2625–2630.
256. Meier A, Kirschner P, Springer B, et al. Identification of mutations in 23S rRNA gene of clarithromycin-resistant *Mycobacterium intracellulare.* Antimicrob Agents Chemother. 1994;38:381–384.
257. Heifets L, Mor N, Vanderkolk J. *Mycobacterium avium* strains resistant to clarithromycin and azithromycin. Antimicrob Agents Chemother. 1993;37:2364–2370.
258. Heifets L. Susceptibility testing of *Mycobacterium avium* complex isolates. Antimicrob Agents Chemother. 1996;40:1759–1767.
259. Havlir DV, Dube MP, Sattler FR, et al. Prophylaxis against disseminated *Mycobacterium avium* complex with weekly azithromycin, daily rifabutin, or both. N Engl J Med. 1996;335:392–398.
260. Oldfield ECI, Fessel WJ, Dunne MW, et al. Once weekly azithromycin therapy for prevention of *Mycobacterium avium* complex infection in patients with AIDS: A randomized, double-blind, placebo-controlled multicenter trial. Clin Infect Dis. 1997;26:611–619.
261. Sison JP, Yao Y, Kemper CA, et al. Treatment of *Mycobacterium avium* complex infection: Do the results of in vitro susceptibility tests predict therapeutic outcome in humans? J Infect Dis. 1996;173:677–683.
262. Shafran SD, Talbot JA, Chomyc S, et al. Does in vitro susceptibility to rifabutin and ethambutol predict the response to treatment of *Mycobacterium avium* complex bacteremia with rifabutin, ethambutol, and clarithromycin? Canadian HIV Trials Network Protocol 010 Study Group. Clin Infect Dis. 1998;6:1401–1405.
263. Dube MP, Sattler FR, Torriani FJ, et al. A randomized evaluation of ethambutol for prevention of relapse and drug resistance during treatment of *Mycobacterium avium* complex bacteremia with clarithromycin-based combination therapy. J Infect Dis. 1997;176:1225–1232.
264. May T, Brel F, Beuscart C, et al. Comparison of combination therapy regimens for treatment of human immunodeficiency virus-infected patients with disseminated bacteremia due to *Mycobacterium avium.* ANRS Trial 033 Curavium Group: Agence Nationale de Recherche sur le Sida. Clin Infect Dis. 1997;25:621–629.
265. Sullam PM, Gordin FM, Wynne BA. Efficacy of rifabutin in the treatment of disseminated infection due to *Mycobacterium avium* complex. The Rifabutin Treatment Group. Clin Infect Dis. 1994;19:84–88.
265a. Gordin FM, Sullam PM, Shafran SD, et al. A randomized, placebo-controlled study of rifabutin added to a regimen of clarithromycin and ethambutol for treatment of disseminated infection with *Mycobacterium avium* complex. Clin Infect Dis. 1999;28:1080–1085.
265b. Benson C, Williams P, Currier J, et al. An open, prospective randomized study comparing efficacy and safety of clarithromycin (C) plus ethambutol (E), rifabutin (R), or both for treatment (Rx) of MAC disease in patients with AIDS (Abstract). In: Sixth Conference on Retroviruses and Opportunistic Infections, Chicago, 1999:249.
266. Siegal FP, Eilbott D, Burger H, et al. Dose-limiting toxicity of rifabutin in AIDS-related complex: Syndrome of arthralgia/arthritis. AIDS. 1990;4:433–441.
267. Saran BR, Maguire AM, Nichols C, et al. Hypopyon uveitis in patients with acquired immunodeficiency syndrome treated for systemic *Mycobacterium avium* complex infection with rifabutin. Arch Ophthalmol. 1994;112:1159–1165.
268. Narang PK, Trapnell CB, Schoenfelder JR, et al. Fluconazole and enhanced effect of rifabutin prophylaxis. N Engl J Med. 1994;330:1316–1317.
269. Trapnell CB, Narang PK, Li R, Lavelle JP. Increased plasma rifabutin levels with concomitant fluconazole therapy in HIV-infected patients. Ann Intern Med. 1996;124:573–576.
270. Shafran SD, Singer J, Zarowny DP, et al. Determinants of rifabutin-associated uveitis in patients treated with rifabutin, clarithromycin, and ethambutol for *Mycobacterium avium* complex bacteremia: A multivariate analysis. Canadian HIV Trials Network Protocol 010 Study Group. J Infect Dis. 1998;177:252–255.
271. Wallace RJ Jr, Brown BA, Griffith DE, et al. Reduced serum levels of clarithromycin in patients treated with multidrug regimens including rifampin or rifabutin for *Mycobacterium avium-M. intracellulare* infection. J Infect Dis. 1995;171:747–750.
272. Kemper CA, Havlir D, Haghighat D, et al. The microbiologic effect of individual antimycobacterial agents, clofazamine, ethambutol, or rifampin, on *Mycobacterium avium* complex bacteremia in patients with AIDS. J Infect Dis. 1994;170:157–164.
273. Chaisson RE, Keiser P, Pierce M, et al. Clarithromycin and ethambutol with or without clofazimine for the treatment of bacteremic *Mycobacterium avium* complex disease in patients with HIV infection. AIDS. 1997;11:311–317.
274. Horsburgh CRJ, Mason UG, Heifets LB, et al. Response to therapy of pulmonary *Mycobacterium avium-intracellulare* infection correlates with results of in vitro susceptibility testing. Am Rev Respir Dis. 1987;135:418–421.
275. A phase II/III trial of antimicrobial therapy with or without amikacin in the treatment of disseminated *Mycobacterium avium* infection in HIV-infected individuals. AIDS Clinical Trials Group Protocol 135 Study Team. AIDS. 1998;12 (18):2439–2446.
276. Gordon SM, Horsburgh CR Jr, Peloquin CA, et al. Low serum levels of oral antimycobacterial agents in patients with disseminated *Mycobacterium avium* complex disease. J Infect Dis. 1993;168:1559–1562.
276a. Dube MP, Torriani FJ, See D, et al. Successful short-term suppression of clarithromycin-resistant *Mycobacterium avium* complex bacteremia in AIDS. California Collaborative Treatment Group. Clin Infect Dis. 1999;28(1):136–138.
277. Holland SM, Eisenstein EM, Kuhns DB, et al. Treatment of refractory disseminated nontuberculous mycobacterial infection with interferon gamma: A preliminary report. N Engl J Med. 1994;330:1348–1355.
278. Chatte G, Panteix G, Perrin-Fayolle M, Pacheco Y. Aerosolized interferon gamma for *Mycobacterium avium* complex lung disease. Am J Respir Crit Care Med. 1995;152:1094–1096.
279. Squires KE, Murphy WF, Madoff LC, Murray HW. Interferon-gamma and *Mycobacterium avium intracellulare* infection. J Infect Dis. 1989;159:599–600.
280. Kemper CA, Bermudez LE, Deresinski SC. Immunomodulatory treatment of *Mycobacterium avium* complex bacteremia in patients with AIDS by use of recombinant granulocyte-macrophage colony-stimulating factor. J Infect Dis. 1998;177:914–920.
281. Wormser GP, Horowitz H, Dworkin B. Low-dose dexamethasone as adjunctive

therapy for disseminated *Mycobacterium avium* complex infections in AIDS patients. Antimicrob Agents Chemother. 1994;38:2215–2217.
282. Dorman SE, Heller HM, Basgoz NO, Sax PE. Adjunctive corticosteroid therapy for patients whose treatment for disseminated *Mycobacterium avium* complex infection has failed. Clin Infect Dis. 1998;26:682–686.
283. Goetz MB. Editorial response: Are corticosteroids useful adjunctive agents in the treatment of disseminated *Mycobacterium avium* complex infection associated with human immunodeficiency virus infection? Clin Infect Dis. 1998;26:687–688.
284. Dautzenberg B, Piperno D, Diot P, et al. Clarithromycin in the treatment of *Mycobacterium avium* lung infections in patients without AIDS. Clarithromycin Study Group of France. Chest. 1995;107:1035–1040.
285. Griffith DE, Brown BA, Girard WM, et al. Azithromycin activity against *Mycobacterium avium* complex lung disease in patients who were not infected with human immunodeficiency virus. Clin Infect Dis. 1996;23:983–989.
286. Wallace RJ Jr, Brown BA, Griffith DE, et al. Initial clarithromycin monotherapy for *Mycobacterium avium-intracellulare* complex lung disease. Am J Respir Crit Care Med. 1994;149:1335–1341.
287. Brown BA, Griffith DE, Girard W, et al. Relationship of adverse events to serum drug levels in patients receiving high-dose azithromycin for mycobacterial lung disease. Clin Infect Dis. 1997;24:958–964.
288. Griffith DE, Brown BA, Girard WM, Wallace RJ Jr. Adverse events associated with high-dose rifabutin in macrolide-containing regimens for the treatment of *Mycobacterium avium* complex lung disease. Clin Infect Dis. 1995;21:594–598.
289. Nelson KG, Griffith DE, Brown BA, Wallace RJ Jr. Results of operation in *Mycobacterium avium-intracellulare* lung disease. Ann Thorac Surg. 1998:66 (2):325–330.
290. Moran JF, Alexander LG, Staub EW, et al. Long-term results of pulmonary resection for atypical mycobacterial disease. Ann Thorac Surg. 1983;35:597–604.
291. Wiley EL, Perry A, Nightingale SD, Lawrence J. Detection of *Mycobacterium avium-intracellulare* complex in bone marrow specimens of patients with acquired immunodeficiency syndrome. Am J Clin Pathol. 1994;101:446–451.
292. Hafner R, Inderlied CB, Peterson DM, et al. Correlation of quantitative bone marrow and blood cultures in AIDS patients with disseminated *Mycobacterium avium* complex infection. J Infect Dis. 1999;180:438–447.
293. Masur H. Recommendations on prophylaxis and therapy for disseminated *Mycobacterium avium* complex disease in patients infected with the human immunodeficiency virus. Public Health Service Task Force on Prophylaxis and Therapy for *Mycobacterium avium* Complex. N Engl J Med. 1993;329:898–904.
294. Cohn D, Fisher EJ, Peng GT, et al. A prospective randomized trial of four three-drug regimens in the treatment of disseminated *Mycobacterium avium* complex disease in AIDS patients: Excess mortality associated with high-dose clarithromycin. Clin Infect Dis. 1999;29:125–133.
294a. Ward TT, Rimland D, Kauffman C, et al. Randomized, open-label trial of azithromycin plus ethambutol vs. clarithromycin plus ethambutol as therapy for *Mycobacterium avium* complex bacteremia in patients with human immunodeficiency virus infection. Veterans Affairs HIV Research Consortium. Clin Infect Dis. 1998;27 (5):1278–1285.
295. Sun E, Heath-Chiozzi M, Cameron DW, et al. Concurrent ritonavir and rifabutin increases risk of rifabutin-associated adverse events (Abstract). In: 11th International Conference on AIDS, Vancouver, B.C., 1996:18.
296. Thestrup-Pedersen K, Indinavir (MK 639) drug interaction studies (Abstract). In: 11th International Conference on AIDS, Vancouver, B.C., 1996:18–19.
297. Cox SR, Herman BD, Batts DH, et al. Delavirdine (D) and rifabutin (R); pharmacokinetic (PK) evaluation in HIV-1 patients with concentration-targeting of delavirdine (Abstract). In: 5th Conference on Retroviruses and Opportunistic Infections, Chicago, 1998:144.
298. Centers for Disease Control and Prevention. 1999 USPHS/IDSA guidelines for the prevention of opportunistic infections in persons infected with human immunodeficiency virus. MMWR Morb Mortal Wkly Rep. 1999;48:1–59.
299. Aberg JA, Yajko DM, Jacobson MA. Eradication of AIDS-related disseminated *Mycobacterium avium* complex infection after 12 months of antimycobacterial therapy combined with highly active antiretroviral therapy. J Infect Dis. 1998;178(5):1446–1449.
300. Aberg JA, Yajko DM, Jacobson MA. Eradication of disseminated *Mycobacterium avium* complex (DMAC) in four patients after twelve months anti-mycobacterial therapy and response to highly active antiretroviral therapy (HAART) (Abstract). In: 5th Conference on Retroviruses and Opportunistic Infections, Chicago, 1998.
301. Hadad DJ, Lewi DS, Pignatari AC, et al. Resolution of *Mycobacterium avium* complex bacteremia following highly active antiretroviral therapy. Clin Infect Dis. 1998;26:758–759.
302. Moore RD, Chaisson RE. Survival analysis of two controlled trials of rifabutin prophylaxis against *Mycobacterium avium* complex in AIDS. AIDS. 1995;9:1337–1342.
303. Pierce M, Crampton S, Henry D, et al. A randomized trial of clarithromycin as prophylaxis against disseminated *Mycobacterium avium* complex infection in patients with advanced acquired immunodeficiency syndrome. N Engl J Med. 1996;335:384–391.
304. Kravcik S, Toye BW, Fyke K, et al. Impact of *Mycobacterium avium* complex prophylaxis on the incidence of mycobacterial infections and transfusion-requiring anemia in an HIV-positive population. J Acquir Immune Defic Syndr Hum Retrovirol 1996;13:27–32.
305. Freedberg KA, Scharfstein JA, Seage GR 3rd, et al. The cost-effectiveness of preventing AIDS-related opportunistic infections. JAMA. 1998;279:130–136.
306. Freedberg KA, Cohen CJ, Barber TW. Prophylaxis for disseminated *Mycobacterium avium* complex (MAC) infection in patients with AIDS: A cost-effectiveness analysis. J Acquir Immune Defic Syndr Hum Retrovirol. 1997;15:275–282.
307. Benson CA, Cohn DL, Williams P, Team at ACS. A phase III prospective, randomized, double-blind study of the safety and efficacy of clarithromycin vs. rifabutin vs. clarithromycin plus rifabutin for prevention of *Mycobacterium avium* complex disease in HIV+ patients with CD4 counts less than or equal to 100 cells/mL (Abstract). In: The 3rd Conference on Retroviruses and Opportunistic Infections, Washington, DC, 1996.
308. Nightingale SD, Cameron DW, Gordin FM, et al. Two controlled trials of rifabutin prophylaxis against *Mycobacterium avium* complex infection in AIDS. N Engl J Med. 1993;329:828–833.
309. Holmberg SD, Moorman AC, Von Bargen JC, et al. Possible effectiveness of clarithromycin and rifabutin for cryptosporidiosis chemoprophylaxis in HIV disease. HIV Outpatient Study (HOPS) Investigators. JAMA. 1998;279:384–386.
310. Jablonowski H, Fätkenheuer G, Youle M, et al. Ancillary benefits of *Mycobacterium avium-intracellulare* complex prophylaxis with clarithromycin in HIV-infected patients. Drugs. 1997;54(Suppl 2):16–22; discussion, 8–9.
311. Bermudez LE, Petrofsky M, Kolonoski P, Young LS. Emergence of *Mycobacterium avium* populations resistant to macrolides during experimental chemotherapy. Antimicrob Agents Chemother. 1998;42:180–183.
312. Dworkin M, Hanson D, Jones J, et al. The risk of *Pneumocystis carinii* pneumonia (PCP) and disseminated non-tuberculous mycobacteriosis (dMb) after an antiretroviral therapy (ART) associated increase in the CDR^+ T-lymphocyte count (Abstract). In: Sixth Conference on Retroviruses and Opportunistic Infections, Alexandria, Va, 1999:LB7.

Chapter 243

Infections Due to Nontuberculous Mycobacteria

BARBARA A. BROWN
RICHARD J. WALLACE, JR.

The increase in the incidence of *Mycobacterium tuberculosis* has evoked a resurgence of interest in disease caused by nontuberculous mycobacteria (NTM). This group of mycobacteria is composed of species other than *M. tuberculosis, Mycobacterium africanum, Mycobacterium bovis*, and *Mycobacterium leprae*. Previous names for this group of organisms include "atypical mycobacteria" or "mycobacteria other than *M. tuberculosis*."[1–3] Currently, approximately 50 species of NTM are considered to be potential sources of disease. NTM have been categorized into different groups based on characteristic colony morphology, growth rate, and pigmentation (the Runyon system of classification). This system has become less useful as we focus on more rapid molecular systems of diagnostics. Growth rates have, however, remained a practical means for grouping species within the laboratory and are thus listed here.

Rapidly Growing Mycobacteria. This group of organisms includes nonpigmented and pigmented species that produce mature growth on agar plates within 7 days. Nonpigmented pathogenic species are mostly grouped within the *Mycobacterium fortuitum* complex. This complex includes the *M. fortuitum* group (*M. fortuitum, Mycobacterium peregrinum*, and *M. fortuitum* third biovariant complex)[4, 5] and the *Mycobacterium chelonei/abscessus* group, which consists of *M. chelonae* (formerly *M. chelonae* subspecies *chelonae), M. abscessus* (formerly *M. chelonae* subspecies *abscessus*), and *Mycobacterium mucogenicum* (formerly *M. chelonae*–like organism).[4, 6–8] *Mycobacterium smegmatis* may be either pigmented or nonpigmented.[9] Pigmented, rapidly growing species are difficult to identify by traditional laboratory methods and are not usually clinically significant. Rapidly growing pigmented species occasionally isolated in clinical disease include *Mycobacterium phlei, Mycobacterium aurum, Mycobacterium flavescens, Mycobacterium neoaurum, Mycobacterium vaccae*, and the thermophilic species *Mycobacterium thermoresistible*.[3]

Slowly Growing Mycobacteria. This group includes species of mycobacteria that require more than 7 days of incubation for mature growth; some may require nutritional supplementation of routine mycobacterial media.[2, 10, 11] The most common, clinically important species found in this group include the *Mycobacterium avium* com-

TABLE 243–1 Major Clinical Syndromes Associated with Nontuberculous Mycobacterial Infections

Syndrome	Relatively Common Causes	Less Frequent Causes
Chronic bronchopulmonary disease (usually adults)	*M. avium* complex (*M. intracellulare* and *M. avium*), *M. kansasii, M. abscessus*	*M. xenopi, M. malmoense, M. szulgai, M. smegmatis, M. scrofulaceum, M. celatum, M. simiae*
Cervical or other local lymphadenitis (especially children)	*M. avium* complex	*M. scrofulaceum, M. malmoense* (northern Europe), *M. abscessus, M. fortuitum*
Skin and soft tissue disease	*M. fortuitum, M. chelonae, M. abscessus, M. marinum*	*M. kansasii, M. haemophilum, M. smegmatis, M. ulcerans* (Australia, tropical countries only)
Skeletal (bone, joint, tendon) infection	*M. marinum, M. avium* complex, *M. kansasii, M. fortuitum* group, *M. abscessus, M. chelonae*	*M. haemophilum, M. scrofulaceum, M. smegmatis, M. terrae/nonchromogenicum* complex
Disseminated infection		
HIV-seropositive host	*M. avium, M. kansasii*	*M. haemophilum, M. genavense, M. xenopi, M. marinum, M. simiae, M. intracellulare, M. scrofulaceum, M. fortuitum*
HIV-seronegative host	*M. abscessus, M. chelonae*	*M. marinum, M. kansasii, M. haemophilum*
Catheter-related infections	*M. fortuitum, M. abscessus, M. chelonae*	*M. mucogenicum*

Abbreviation: HIV, Human immunodeficiency virus.

plex (*M. avium* and *Mycobacterium intracellulare*), *Mycobacterium kansasii, Mycobacterium xenopi, Mycobacterium simiae, Mycobacterium szulgai, Mycobacterium scrofulaceum, Mycobacterium malmoense, Mycobacterium terrae/Mycobacterium nonchromogenicum* complex, *Mycobacterium haemophilum*, and *Mycobacterium genavense*.[2] These organisms grow best at 35°C to 37°C, with the exception of *M. haemophilum*, which has a preference for lower temperatures (28°C to 30°C), and *M. xenopi*, which grows well at 42°C. Newer, more rarely isolated slowly growing species, including *Mycobacterium celatum, Mycobacterium interjectum, Mycobacterium confluentis, Mycobacterium triplex, Mycobacterium lentiflavum, Mycobacterium branderi, Mycobacterium conspicuum, Mycobacterium cookii*, and *Mycobacterium asiaticum*, are also classified in this group of NTM.

Intermediately Growing Mycobacteria. This group includes *Mycobacterium marinum* and *Mycobacterium gordonae*. These organisms are usually pigmented and require 7 to 10 days of incubation for mature growth. *M. marinum* has an optimal growth temperature of 30°C, whereas *M. gordonae* prefers 35°C.[12, 13]

NTM are ubiquitous in the environment (including soil, water, animals, and birds), although some species such as *M. haemophilum* and *Mycobacterium ulcerans* have yet to be recovered from such sources. Although an association with an environmental source may be present, a direct link is often difficult to prove except for nosocomial disease, and no evidence of person-to-person spread has been reported.[2, 3, 14] NTM produce six major clinical disease syndromes (Table 243–1), which are covered in the following sections.

PULMONARY DISEASE

Chronic pulmonary disease in a human immunodeficiency virus (HIV)-negative host is the most common localized clinical disease caused by NTM.[2, 3, 15] In the United States, *M. avium* complex, followed by *M. kansasii*, is the most frequently recognized pathogen.[2] In Canada, some parts of the United Kingdom, and Europe,[2, 16] *M. xenopi* ranks second after *M. avium* complex, whereas *M. malmoense* is second in Scandinavia and northern Europe.[17] In southeast England, *M. xenopi* and *M. kansasii* (known to be present in local water supplies) are both more common than *M. avium* complex.[18] In the United States, the third most common cause of NTM pulmonary disease is *M. abscessus*, which produces 80% of pulmonary infections caused by rapidly growing mycobacteria.[19] Other NTM that less commonly cause pulmonary disease include *M. fortuitum, M. smegmatis*,[9] *M. szulgai*,[20] *M. simiae*,[21, 22] *M. celatum, M. asiaticum*, and *M. gordonae*.[2, 3, 23] Two major disease settings are recognized for *M. avium* complex in an HIV-negative host (Table 243–2). Upper lobe cavitary disease that mimics tuberculosis develops in patients with a history of heavy tobacco abuse and often alcohol abuse (usually middle-aged males). The second disease setting is nonsmoking elderly patients, usually female, with no apparent underlying disease. These patients have multiple nodular midlung infiltrates, usually involving the right middle lobe and lingula. By chest computed tomography, these patients have nodular infiltrates with associated cylindric bronchiectasis. These patients can have multiple strains of *M. avium* complex or multiple species of NTM (usually *M. avium* complex and *M. abscessus*). Other less frequently encountered clinical settings include patients with advanced HIV disease, who are at risk for pulmonary disease and disseminated NTM disease; patients with preexisting lung problems (usually with associated bronchiectasis) such as post-tuberculous bronchiectasis or cystic fibrosis; and patients with achalasia. The clinical setting for other NTM species is less well established, but they probably occur in one or both of the same two major groups of patients. Pulmonary NTM disease does not usually develop in children, except for those with cystic fibrosis.[2, 24]

TABLE 243–2 Clinical Settings for Nontuberculous Mycobacterial Lung Disease

Radiographic Disease	Setting	Usual Pathogen* (Rare Pathogen)
Upper lobe cavitary	Male smokers, often abusing alcohol, usually early 50s	*M. avium* complex, *M. kansasii*
RML, lingular nodular bronchiectasis	Female nonsmokers, usually older than 60 yr	*M. avium* complex, *M. abscessus (M. kansasii)*
Localized alveolar, cavitary disease	Prior granulomatous disease (usually tuberculosis) with bronchiectasis	*M. abscessus, M. avium* complex
Not well established	Adolescents with cystic fibrosis	*M. avium* complex, *M. abscessus*
Reticulonodular or alveolar lower lobe disease	Achalasia, chronic vomiting secondary to GI disease, exogenous lipoid pneumonia (mineral oil aspiration, etc.)	*M. fortuitum* (*M. abscessus, M. avium* complex, *M. smegmatis*)
Reticulonodular disease	HIV-positive hosts, ? prior bronchiectasis secondary to PCP, etc.	*M. avium* complex

*Too little information is available for selected pathogens such as *M. xenopi, M. simiae, M. malmoense, M. szulgai, M. celatum*, and *M. asiaticum*
Abbreviations: GI, Gastrointestinal; HIV, human immunodeficiency virus; PCP, *Pneumocystis carinii* pneumonia; RML, right middle lobe.

TABLE 243–3 American Thoracic Society Diagnostic Criteria for Nontuberculous Mycobacterial Lung Disease

In symptomatic patients with reticulonodular or cavitary disease or a high-resolution computed tomography scan revealing multifocal bronchiectasis and/or small nodules:

1. Two positive sputum/bronchial wash cultures within 12 mo if one or both specimens is AFB smear positive; *or*
2. Three positive sputum/bronchial wash cultures within 12 mo if none of the specimens is AFB smear positive; *or*
3. In patients unable to produce sputum, one positive bronchial wash culture with a ≥2+ + AFB smear and/or growth on solid media; *or*
4. In the absence of diagnostic sputum/bronchial wash evaluations, a transbronchial or lung biopsy yielding NTM or a biopsy showing mycobacterial histopathologic features (granulomatous inflammation and/or AFB) and one or more respiratory cultures positive for NTM even in low numbers.

*Applies to human immunodeficiency virus–negative patients and has not been studied for most NTM other than *M. avium* complex.

Abbreviations: AFB, Acid-fast bacillus; NTM, nontuberculous mycobacteria.

From Wallace RJ Jr, Cook JL, Glassroth J, et al. Diagnosis and treatment of disease caused by nontuberculous mycobacteria. American Thoracic Society Statement. Am J Respir Crit Care Med. 1997;156(Suppl):S1–S25.

Because the signs and symptoms of NTM lung disease are often variable and nonspecific, disease with NTM is difficult to diagnose without multiple positive respiratory cultures.[2] Patients often present with chronic cough, sputum production, and fatigue. Less frequently, complaints of malaise, dyspnea, fever, hemoptysis, and weight loss may also be present. Clinical studies should include microbiologic cultures for acid-fast bacilli and routine chest radiographs. High-resolution chest computed tomography is helpful in patients suspected of having nodular bronchiectasis. Recovery of NTM from a single sputum sample is not proof of NTM disease, especially when the acid-fast bacillus smear is negative and NTM are present in low numbers. The American Thoracic Society recently issued a revised statement[2] that included four suggested diagnostic criteria to determine lung disease caused by NTM and specifically by *M. avium* complex (Table 243–3). For NTM disease due to organisms other than *M. avium* complex, these criteria may need to be adjusted because too few data are available to evaluate these criteria. At least three respiratory samples should be evaluated and other lung disease excluded.[2]

Treatment of lung disease caused by *M. avium* complex has been addressed in this same document by the American Thoracic Society[2] (Table 243–4). Recommended treatment of HIV-negative patients consists of multiple drugs, including clarithromycin or azithromycin, rifampin or rifabutin, and ethambutol, to be given until patients are culture negative for 1 year. In some complicated or far-advanced cases, additional agents such as streptomycin or amikacin may be indicated.[2, 25, 26] Success rates for these regimens are probably 60 to 90%, with drug intolerance the major reason for treatment failure.[25, 26] Lower daily doses of clarithromycin (500 or 750 mg daily) or an intermittent regimen (Monday-Wednesday-Friday) may be required in elderly patients weighing 50 kg or less. Fever and chills are not uncommon with rifabutin, as is lowering of the white blood cell count to 3000 to 4000 cells/mm^3.[2] Few data are available on the efficacy of other agents such as ethionamide, the newer quinolones such as sparfloxacin, and clofazimine in treatment of pulmonary *M. avium* complex.[2] More details are included in the chapter on the *M. avium* complex. An effective treatment regimen for clarithromycin-resistant *M. avium* complex has not been established or recommended.

Treatment of lung disease caused by *M. kansasii* has traditionally been less difficult than that for *M. avium* complex since the introduction of rifampin.[27] A regimen of daily rifampin, 600 mg, isoniazid, 300 mg, and ethambutol, 15 mg/kg, has been widely accepted in the United States and is currently recommended by the American Thoracic Society[2] (see Table 243–3). In the United Kingdom, isoniazid is omitted from the regimen.[28] In HIV-positive patients who need to receive a protease inhibitor, rifampin can be replaced by rifabutin, 150 mg daily, if the patient is receiving indinavir, nelfinavir, soft-gel saquinavir (Fortovase), or amprenavir. Rifabutin causes less reduction in the blood level of protease inhibitor than rifampin does. If the patient is taking ritonavir, hard-gel saquinavir (Invirase), or

TABLE 243–4 Frequently Used Treatment Regimens for Common Nontuberculous Mycobacterial Pathogens

Species	Disease*	Drug	Daily Adult Doses†	Duration
M. avium complex	Pulmonary	Clarithromycin *plus*	500 mg bid	Until culture negative for 12 mo
		Ethambutol *plus*	15 mg/kg	
		Rifampin *or*	600 mg	
		Rifabutin	150–300 mg	
	Disseminated, HIV positive	Clarithromycin *plus*	500 mg bid	For life (?)
		Ethambutol *plus*	15 mg/kg	
		? Rifabutin	300 mg	
	Lymphadenitis, children	Surgical excision		
		? Clarithromycin *plus*		
		? Rifabutin *or*		
		Ethambutol		
M. kansasii	Pulmonary			
	USA	Isoniazid *plus*	300 mg	18 mo, culture negative at least 12 mo
		Rifampin *plus*	600 mg	
		Ethambutol	15 mg/kg	
	UK	Rifampin *plus*	600 mg	9–12 mo
		Ethambutol	15 mg/kg	
	Disseminated	Same as pulmonary		
	HIV positive	Same as pulmonary (USA) but replace rifampin with rifabutin *or* clarithromycin	150 mg 500 mg bid	Same as pulmonary (USA)
M. abscessus	Pulmonary	Amikacin IV *plus* cefoxitin IV	15 mg/kg (see text) 12 g/d	2 wk (designed to improve, not cure)
		Clarithromycin	500 mg bid	6 mo
	Cutaneous localized	Clarithromycin	500 mg bid	6 mo
	Disseminated or extensive cutaneous	Same 3 drugs as above		
M. marinum	Cutaneous	Clarithromycin *or*	500 mg bid	3 mo minimum for all regimens
		Minocycline *or*	100 mg bid	
		Rifampin *plus*	600 mg	
		Ethambutol	15 mg/kg	

*Human immunodeficiency virus (HIV)-negative host unless otherwise stated.

†Drugs by mouth unless otherwise stated.

delavirdine (a non-nucleoside reverse transcriptase inhibitor), the reduction in blood level is so substantial that neither rifampin nor rifabutin can be used and clarithromycin, 500 mg twice daily, is recommended.[2, 29] Patients should be treated for at least 18 months with at least 12 months of culture negativity.[2] For patients resistant or intolerant to rifampin, clarithromycin is a reasonable, but unproven alternative agent. Untreated strains of *M. kansasii* are susceptible to low concentrations of rifampin, rifabutin, ethambutol, ethionamide, streptomycin, sulfonamides, clarithromycin, and the newer quinolones, although information is limited on the clinical utility of these latter three agents.[2, 30–32] Acquired mutational resistance of rifampin to *M. kansasii* can occur, but this organism is readily treated with multidrug regimens.[30, 32]

Treatment of *M. abscessus* lung disease with drugs has generally been unsuccessful.[2] Courses of therapy with clarithromycin and several weeks of high-dose cefoxitin (12 g/day in three or four divided doses) and low-dose amikacin (peaks at 20 μg/ml on twice-daily dosing) produce good clinical improvement but do not result in microbiologic cure. Treatment of lung disease caused by other slowly growing mycobacteria such as *M. simiae, M. szulgai, M. xenopi*, and *M. malmoense* has not been established.[2, 17, 20, 22, 33] Drug combinations similar to what is used with *M. avium* complex, such as clarithromycin, ethambutol, rifabutin, and perhaps an aminoglycoside with 12 months of negative cultures, seem reasonable at the present time.[17, 20, 22, 33]

LYMPHADENITIS

Localized lymphadenitis is the most common NTM disease in children, with a peak incidence between 1 and 5 years of age.[34–37] NTM-affected lymph nodes are usually in the anterior cervical chain and are unilateral and painless. The nodes may enlarge rapidly with the formation of fistulas to the skin, and prolonged drainage may occur.[37] Occasionally, other nodes outside the head and neck such as the mediastinal lymph nodes may be involved.[35] A definitive diagnosis of NTM lymphadenitis is made by recovery of the etiologic organism from lymph node cultures. The tuberculin skin test is often weakly positive (5 to 10 mm), but it may be more than 10 mm.[35] Efforts to develop a useful *M. avium* complex skin test have thus far been unsuccessful.[38] Routine biopsy or incision and drainage should be avoided because these procedures often result in the formation of fistulas and chronic drainage.[37] Fine-needle aspiration with cytology and culture has been used increasingly with apparently few associated problems.[2]

Treatment of NTM cervical lymphadenitis is still evolving. The potential role of chemotherapy without surgery or as a supplement to surgery in complicated or recurrent disease is being considered with increasing frequency. Clarithromycin combined with ethambutol or rifabutin is the usual suggested regimen (see Table 243–3). However, the established treatment of routine NTM cervical lymphadenitis remains surgical excision without chemotherapy.

Since the early 1980s, 80% of cases of culture-positive NTM lymphadenitis in children in the United States have been caused by *M. avium* complex.[34] The remainder of the cases in Australia and the United States are caused by *M. scrofulaceum*, and only about 10% of the cases have been caused by *M. tuberculosis*.[34, 35, 37] In parts of northern Europe, including Scandinavia and the United Kingdom, *M. malmoense* has become the second most common pathogen after *M. avium* complex.[18, 39–41] Rarely, other species are recovered, including rapidly growing mycobacteria, *M. kansasii*, and *M. haemophilum*.[18, 41, 42] This last species has a special growth requirement for hemin or iron and may present some diagnostic difficulties if iron- or hemin-supplemented media and lower temperatures (incubation at 28°C to 30°C) are not used.[2, 10, 43] A surprising number of specimens are acid-fast bacillus smear positive and culture negative, so a presumptive diagnosis is often based on typical caseating granulomas and a negative culture for *M. tuberculosis* in the common clinical setting.

LOCALIZED CUTANEOUS AND SOFT TISSUE INFECTIONS

Although all species of NTM have been incriminated in cutaneous NTM disease,[2, 3] *M. marinum* and the rapidly growing mycobacteria most often cause localized skin infections. *M. marinum* causes an infection historically recognized as "swimming pool" or "fish tank granuloma."[1, 3, 44] This common name is derived from the epidemiologic niche of the organism. Most infections occur 2 to 3 weeks after contact with contaminated water from one of these sources. The lesions are most often small violet papules on the hands and arms that may progress to shallow crusty ulcerations and scar formation. Lesions are usually singular. However, multiple ascending lesions resembling sporotrichosis ("sporotrichoid disease") can occasionally occur.[2, 44] Most patients are clinically healthy with a previous local hand injury that becomes infected while cleaning a fish tank, or patients may sustain scratches or puncture wounds from saltwater fish, shrimp, fins, and so forth contaminated with *M. marinum*. Diagnosis is made from culture and histologic examination of biopsy material, along with a compatible history of exposure.[2, 44] No treatment of choice is recognized for *M. marinum* (see Table 243–3). Treatments have traditionally been a two-drug combination of rifampin plus ethambutol or monotherapy with doxycycline, minocycline, clarithromycin, or trimethoprim-sulfamethoxazole given for a minimum of 3 months.[12, 45, 46] Clarithromycin has been used increasingly because of good clinical efficacy and minimal side effects, although published experience is limited.[2]

The rapidly growing species *M. abscessus, M. fortuitum*, and *M. chelonae* are probably the most common NTM involved in cases of community-acquired infections of skin and soft tissue.[47] Localized traumatic injury, such as puncture wounds from stepping on a nail, and open lacerations or fractures are the usual scenarios. Occasionally, these infections may involve slowly growing species, including *M. avium* complex, *M. kansasii*, and *M. terrae/M. nonchromogenicum* complex.[3]

Sporadic cases of nosocomial skin and soft tissue disease have also been described. These cases include infections of long-term intravenous or peritoneal catheters, postinjection abscesses, surgical wound infections such as after cardiac bypass surgery, and augmentation mammaplasty.[3, 14, 47, 48] In ophthalmology, rapidly growing species may cause keratitis and corneal ulceration after surgery, as well as infection after local accidental trauma.[1] Clustered outbreaks or pseudo-outbreaks of mycobacterial skin, soft tissue, or bone infections have been described and usually result from contaminated fluids such as ice made from tap water, water, injectable medicines, and topical skin solutions/markers.[14, 49, 50] Most of the outbreaks have involved the rapidly growing species *M. fortuitum* and *M. abscessus*. The reservoir for these outbreaks has generally been municipal or distilled (hospital) water supplies.[14, 49, 50] These and other species such as *M. avium* complex and *M. xenopi* are incredibly hardy, can endure temperatures of 45°C and above (*M. avium* complex and *M. xenopi*), and may resist the activity of commonly used disinfectants.[3, 14, 51]

Diagnosis of all types of skin and soft tissue infections is made by culture of specific NTM from drainage material or tissue biopsy. Treatment may include amikacin, cefoxitin, ciprofloxacin, clarithromycin, doxycycline, sulfonamides, and imipenem for the *M. fortuitum* group, whereas only amikacin, cefoxitin, imipenem, and clarithromycin or only amikacin, imipenem, tobramycin, and clarithromycin have activity against *M. abscessus* and *M. chelonae*, respectively.[6] Clarithromycin is generally the drug of choice for localized disease caused by *M. chelonae* and *M. abscessus*.[2, 6] The duration of therapy is usually 4 to 6 months. Antituberculous agents have no efficacy against any of the rapidly growing mycobacteria other than ethambutol for *M. smegmatis*. Treatment of slowly growing species is similar to that for chronic lung disease, except that the duration of therapy may only be 6 to 12 months.[2]

Two unusual species causing skin and soft tissue infections in select situations are *M. ulcerans* and *M. haemophilum*. *M. ulcerans* is not endemic in the United States, but it is endemic in areas of Australia and tropical locations of the world, where it is commonly known as the "Buruli ulcer."[52] This infection progresses from an itchy nodule most often on the extremities to a necrotic lesion that may result in severe deformity. Treatment success is common in early disease with excisional surgery, rifampin, sulfonamides, and clofazimine, but for advanced ulcerative disease, therapeutic response has generally been poor.[53] Surgical débridement and skin grafting then become the usual therapeutic measures of choice.[1, 3, 53] Recent studies suggest that clarithromycin is highly active in vitro.[53]

The second unusual species, *M. haemophilum*, causes cutaneous infections (primarily of the extremities) in immunosuppressed patients, especially in the setting of organ transplantation, long-term high-dose steroid use, or HIV.[10, 54, 55] A recent review by Saubolle and coworkers cited more than 50 cases of *M. haemophilum*, with almost 80% of them involving skin and soft tissue infections.[43] Careful attention to culture technique is essential because this species requires heme or iron to grow in culture. Therapy for this species usually includes clarithromycin and rifampin or rifabutin.[10, 42, 55]

INFECTION OF TENDON SHEATHS, BONES, BURSAE, AND JOINTS

Both rapidly growing and slowly growing species of NTM have been implicated in chronic granulomatous infections involving tendon sheaths, bursae, bones, and joints after direct inoculation of the pathogen through accidental trauma, surgical incisions, puncture wounds, or injections.[3, 6, 47, 48] Most patients have no underlying immune suppression, but high risk for some pathogens such as *M. chelonae* and *M. haemophilum* is seen in patients who are immunosuppressed. *M. avium* complex and *M. marinum* have been described as causing tenosynovitis of the hand,[3, 46] although the rapidly growing mycobacteria,[47] *M. kansasii*, and *M. terrae* complex (especially *M. nonchromogenicum*)[56–58] have also been associated with a chronic type of disease.[3, 23] Osteomyelitis of the sternum caused by *M. fortuitum* and *M. abscessus* has also been found in clustered outbreaks and sporadic cases after cardiac surgery.[48, 59–61] Additionally, *M. haemophilum* has a tendency to involve bones and joints, usually with concurrent draining skin lesions and bacteremia.[1, 10, 43, 55]

Management of mycobacterial rheumatologic infections often requires surgical débridement for both diagnosis and therapy, especially for the closed spaces of the hand and the wrist and for patients with infected bones such as fractured long bones or the sternum after cardiac surgery. Drug therapy for the specific pathogen is also essential.

DISSEMINATED DISEASE

In the setting of advanced HIV infection, most disseminated NTM disease is due to *M. avium*. However, other NTM, including *M. kansasii, M. genavense, M. intracellulare, M. haemophilum, M. simiae, M. celatum, M. malmoense, M. marinum*, and rapidly growing mycobacteria, have also been cited.[11, 13, 43, 62–66]

In the absence of HIV infection, cases of disseminated *M. avium* complex are rare.[67] Disseminated infection by other NTM species in non-AIDS patients such as organ transplant recipients or patients receiving chronic steroids has occurred in all age groups, almost exclusively in immunosuppressed patients.[2, 6, 68, 69]

The most commonly reported physical findings in disseminated *M. avium* infection include fever, weight loss, skin lesions, and enlargement of organs of the reticuloendothelial system. Although anemia often occurs with a hematocrit of less than 25% and one third of patients with disseminated *M. avium* infection have elevated alkaline phosphatase levels, laboratory studies and chest radiographs are not usually conclusive in establishing the diagnosis of disseminated NTM disease. The usual method of diagnosis is mycobacterial blood cultures in patients with AIDS. The diagnosis of disseminated *M. avium* is rare in HIV-infected patients with greater than 100 $CD4^+$ lymphocytes.[70, 71]

Disseminated *M. kansasii* is the second most frequent cause of disseminated NTM disease.[3, 66] Pulmonary and cutaneous manifestations have occurred[66, 69] in patients with chronic lymphocytic leukemia, after organ transplantation, and in those infected by HIV. One study reported five patients with disseminated *M. kansasii* infection, including three patients with pulmonary and extrapulmonary involvement and two patients with exclusive extrapulmonary involvement. All patients had CD4 lymphocyte counts less than 200 cells/μl. The most common clinical manifestation was pulmonary disease with thin-walled cavitary lesions.[66]

Treatment of disseminated *M. avium* in patients with AIDS involves a multidrug regimen including clarithromycin (500 mg twice daily) and ethambutol at 15 mg/kg/day[2, 72] (see Table 243–4). One recent study suggests that rifabutin, 300 mg daily, does not add to bacteriologic response or survival but does protect against the development of clarithromycin resistance.[73] Rifabutin is also problematic if concomitantly administered with protease inhibitors. Rifampin and, to a lesser degree, rifabutin enhance the hepatic metabolism of protease inhibitors, which may result in subtherapeutic levels of these agents (saquinavir, ritonavir, and indinavir) and may promote the emergence of resistant HIV strains.[29] Clofazimine and the quinolones have been used, but neither seems to be effective and clofazimine has been associated with an increased mortality.[74] For other NTM disseminated disease, evaluation of the importance of a rifamycin has been suggested.

The incidence of disseminated *M. avium* infection can be reduced by the use of prophylactic antimicrobials. Rifabutin, 300 mg daily,[71] clarithromycin, 500 mg twice daily,[75] and azithromycin, 1200 mg weekly either alone or in combination with rifabutin,[76] have all been shown in controlled trials to be effective as prophylactic agents for the prevention of *M. avium* disseminated disease and are recommended in patients with fewer than 75 $CD4^+$ cells, even when levels improve with HIV therapy.

Treatment of disseminated disease caused by NTM other than *M. avium* is with regimens similar to those used for pulmonary disease (see Table 243–4).

CATHETER-RELATED INFECTIONS

Currently, catheter-related infections are the most common nosocomial NTM infections encountered.[3, 14] They are seen most often with long-term central intravenous catheters, but they may also occur with peritoneal or shunt catheters. The usual pathogens are rapidly growing mycobacteria (see Table 243–1). These infections may be manifested as fever, local catheter site drainage, or bacteremia or occasionally as lung infiltrates or granulomatous hepatitis. The usual treatment is catheter removal combined with appropriate antibiotics for 6 to 12 weeks.[3, 14]

LABORATORY ASPECTS

Culture. The methods used for staining and culture of *M. tuberculosis* generally work well for the NTM. Middlebrook 7H10 or 7H11 agar, BACTEC broth, and the newer rapid broth systems all support growth of the common NTM.[2] Cultures of skin and soft tissue need to be plated at 28°C to 30°C, as well as 35°C, because some species such as *M. marinum, M. chelonae*, and *M. haemophilum* grow only at low temperatures on primary isolation. *M. genavense* (BACTEC broth for 6 to 8 weeks)[77] and *M. haemophilum* (iron or heme in the media)[2, 10] require special growth requirements.

Identification. As a consequence of the demand for more rapid diagnosis of *M. tuberculosis*,[2, 78] identification of NTM increasingly focuses on the use of rapid diagnostic systems: high-performance liquid chromatography, which assesses the patterns of long-chain fatty acids (mycolic acids) found in different NTM species[79]; genetic methods such as polymerase chain reaction–restriction fragment length polymorphism analysis of a 439–base pair fragment of the 65-kD heat shock protein gene[80, 81]; and genetic probes. Commercial genetic probes for mycobacterial RNA are currently available for the identification of *M. tuberculosis* complex, *M. avium, M. intracellulare, M. gordonae*, and *M. kansasii*.[2] For some of the newer species such as *M. celatum*,[81] *M. genavense*,[11] *M. cookii*, and *M. triplex*, high-performance liquid chromatography, 16S ribosomal DNA sequencing, or both are important or essential to make a species identification. Traditional biochemical testing to determine carbohydrate utilization and other standard mycobacterial tests such as arylsulfatase, nitrate reduction, and iron uptake provide alternative, although slower methods for identification of both slowly growing and rapidly growing NTM.[2, 4]

Strain Comparison. For epidemiologic studies, standard biochemical and susceptibility testing have been useful in initial strain comparison for most outbreaks involving NTM. Molecular methods such as Southern hybridization with repetitive elements, arbitrarily primed polymerase chain reaction, and pulsed-field gel electrophoresis ("DNA fingerprinting") of NTM are now the standard for definitive strain comparison of NTM outbreaks.[14, 82, 83]

Susceptibility Testing. ***Rapidly Growing Mycobacteria.*** The three accepted methods of susceptibility testing of rapidly growing mycobacteria include agar disk elution, broth microdilution,[84] and most recently, the E-test gradient minimal inhibitory concentration. Standardization of the methods is pending further studies by the National Committee for Clinical Laboratory Standards (NCCLS). The antimicrobials used are selected bacterial agents because antituberculous drugs are not effective against these species. Current minimal recommendations for testing the rapidly growing mycobacteria include clarithromycin (used as a class drug for the new macrolides), amikacin, cefoxitin, imipenem, tobramycin, doxycycline, ciprofloxacin, and a sulfonamide.[2, 85, 86]

Slowly Growing Nontuberculous Mycobacteria. The proportion method in agar, broth microdilution, E-test, and in some cases, BACTEC radiometric detection have been used for determining minimal inhibitory concentrations of the slowly growing NTM.[2, 84] None of these methods has been standardized by the NCCLS, but they are currently being evaluated, which means that definitions of "susceptible" and "resistant" vary from laboratory to laboratory. Standard first-line antituberculous agents (ethambutol, rifampin, isoniazid) are commonly tested along with other agents, including clarithromycin, rifabutin, streptomycin, amikacin, quinolones, and a sulfonamide. Susceptibility testing to pyrazinamide is not recommended because it has no efficacy against NTM. Currently, susceptibility testing is recommended for *M. kansasii* (rifampin only), *M. avium* complex (clarithromycin only), and less commonly encountered slowly growing species such as *M. xenopi* (all of the aforementioned drugs).[2]

Isolates of *M. avium* complex should be tested only for clarithromycin susceptibility because no correlation has been shown between susceptibility results and outcome except for clarithromycin. The American Thoracic Society recently asserted that susceptibility testing to agents other than clarithromycin is not indicated for strains of *M. avium* complex.[2]

REFERENCES

1. Hirschel B. Infections due to nontuberculous mycobacteria. In: Fauci AS, Braunwald E, Isselbacher KJ, et al, eds. Harrison's Principles of Internal Medicine. 14th ed. New York: McGraw-Hill; 1998:1019–1022.
2. Wallace RJ Jr, Cook JL, Glassroth J, et al. Diagnosis and treatment of disease caused by nontuberculous mycobacteria. American Thoracic Society Statement. Am J Respir Crit Care Med. 1997;156(Suppl):S1–S25.
3. Wolinsky E. State of the art: Nontuberculous mycobacteria and associated diseases. Am Rev Respir Dis. 1979;119:107–159.
4. Silcox VA, Good RC, Floyd MM. Identification of clinically significant *Mycobacterium fortuitum* complex isolates. J Clin Microbiol. 1981;14:686–691.
5. Wallace RJ Jr, Brown BA, Silcox VA, et al. Clinical disease, drug susceptibility, and biochemical patterns of the unnamed third biovariant complex of *Mycobacterium fortuitum*. J Infect Dis. 1991;163:598–603.
6. Wallace RJ Jr, Brown BA, Onyi GO. Skin, soft tissue, and bone infections due to *Mycobacterium chelonae chelonae*: Importance of prior corticosteroid therapy, frequency of disseminated infections, and resistance to oral antimicrobials other than clarithromycin. J Infect Dis. 1992;166:405–412.
7. Band JD, Ward JI, Fraser DW, et al. Peritonitis due to a *Mycobacterium chelonei*–like organism associated with intermittent chronic peritoneal dialysis. J Infect Dis. 1982;145:9–17.
8. Wallace RJ Jr, Silcox VA, Tsukamura M, et al. Clinical significance, biochemical features, and susceptibility patterns of sporadic isolates of the *Mycobacterium chelonae*-like organism. J Clin Microbiol. 1993;31:3231–3239.
9. Wallace RJ Jr, Nash DR, Tsukamura M, et al. Human disease due to *Mycobacterium smegmatis*. J Infect Dis. 1988;158:52–59.
10. Kiehn TE, White M. *Mycobacterium haemophilum*: An emerging pathogen. Eur J Clin Microbiol Infect Dis. 1994;13:925–931.
11. Böttger EC: *Mycobacterium genavense*: An emerging pathogen. Eur J Clin Microbiol Infect Dis. 1994;13:932–936.
12. Edelstein H. *Mycobacterium marinum* skin infections. Arch Intern Med. 1994;154:1359–1364.
13. Weinberger M, Berg SL, Feuerstein IM, et al. Disseminated infection with *Mycobacterium gordonae*: Report of a case and critical review of the literature. Clin Infect Dis. 1992;14:1229–1239.
14. Fraser V, Wallace RJ Jr. Nontuberculous mycobacteria. In: Mayhall CG, ed. Hospital Epidemiology and Infection Control. Baltimore: Williams & Wilkins; 1996:1224–1237.
15. Hobby GL, Redmond WB, Runyon EH, et al. A study on pulmonary disease associated with mycobacteria other than *Mycobacterium tuberculosis*: Identification and characterization of the mycobacteria. Am Rev Respir Dis. 1967;95:954–971.
16. Thomas P, Liu F, Weiser W. Characteristics of *Mycobacterium xenopi* disease. Bull Int Union Tuberc Lung Dis. 1988;63(3):12–13.
17. Henriques B, Hoffner SE, Petrini B, et al. Infection with *Mycobacterium malmoense* in Sweden: Report of 221 cases. Clin Infect Dis. 1994;18:596–600.
18. Yates MD, Pozniak A, Uttley AHC, et al. Isolation of environmental mycobacteria from clinical specimens in South-East England: 1973–1993. Int J Tuberc Lung Dis. 1997;1:75–80.
19. Griffith DE, Girard WM, Wallace RJ Jr. Clinical features of pulmonary disease caused by rapidly growing mycobacteria: An analysis of 154 patients. Am Rev Respir Dis. 1993;147:1271–1278.
20. Maloney JM, Gregg CR, Stephens DS, et al. Infections caused by *Mycobacterium szulgai* in humans. Rev Infect Dis. 1987;9:1120–1126.
21. Bell RC, Higuchi JH, Donova WN, et al. *Mycobacterium simiae*: Clinical features and follow-up of twenty-four patients. Am Rev Respir Dis. 1983;127:35–38.
22. Valero G, Peters J, Jorgensen JH, et al. Clinical isolates of *Mycobacterium simiae* in San Antonio, Texas. Am J Respir Crit Care Med. 1995;152:1555–1557.
23. Falkinham JO. Epidemiology of infection by nontuberculous mycobacteria. Clin Microbiol Rev. 1996;9:177–215.
24. Lincoln EM, Gilbert LA. Disease in children due to mycobacteria other than *Mycobacterium tuberculosis*. Am Rev Respir Dis. 1972;105:683–714.
25. Dautzenberg B, Piperno D, Diot P, et al. Clarithromycin in the treatment of *Mycobacterium avium* lung infections in patients without AIDS. Chest. 1995;4:1035–1040.
26. Wallace RJ Jr, Brown BA, Griffith DE, et al. Clarithromycin regimens for pulmonary *Mycobacterium avium* complex—the first 50 patients. Am J Respir Crit Care Med. 1996;153:1766–1772.
27. Pezzia W, Raleigh JW, Bailey MC, et al. Treatment of pulmonary disease due to *Mycobacterium kansasii*: Recent experience with rifampin. Rev Infect Dis. 1981;3:1035–1039.
28. Jenkins PA, Banks J, Campbell IA, et al. *Mycobacterium kansasii* pulmonary infection: A prospective study of the results of nine months of treatment with rifampicin and ethambutol. Thorax. 1994;49:442–445.
29. Centers for Disease Control and Prevention. Impact of HIV protease inhibitors on the treatment of HIV-infected tuberculosis patients with rifampin. MMWR Morb Mortal Wkly Rep. 1996;45:921–925.
30. Ahn CH, Wallace RJ Jr, Steele LC, et al. Sulfonamide-containing regimens for disease caused by rifampin-resistant *Mycobacterium kansasii*. Am Rev Respir Dis. 1987;135:10–16.
31. Gay JD, DeYoung DR, Roberts GD. In vitro activities of norfloxacin and ciprofloxacin against *Mycobacterium tuberculosis, M. avium* complex, *M. chelonei, M. fortuitum*, and *M. kansasii*. Antimicrob Agents Chemother. 1984;26:94–96.
32. Wallace RJ Jr, Dunbar D, Brown BA, et al. Rifampin-resistant *Mycobacterium kansasii*. Clin Infect Dis. 1994;18:736–743.
33. Dautzenberg B, Papillon F, Lepitre M, et al. *Mycobacterium xenopi* infections treated with clarithromycin-containing regimens. Abstract 1125. Presented at the Thirty-third Interscience Conference on Antimicrobial Agents and Chemotherapy, New Orleans, 1993.
34. Lai KK, Stottmeier KD, Sherman IH, et al. Mycobacterial cervical lymphadenopathy. JAMA. 1984;251:1286–1288.
35. Wolinsky E: Mycobacterial lymphadenitis in children: A prospective study of 105 nontuberculous cases with long-term follow-up. Clin Infect Dis. 1995;20:954–963.
36. Margileth AM, Chandra R, Altman P. Chronic lymphadenopathy due to mycobacterial infection. Am J Dis Child. 1984;138:917–922.

37. Schaad UB, Votteler TP, McCracken GH, et al. Management of atypical mycobacterial lymphadenitis in childhood: A review based on 380 cases. J Pediatr. 1979;95:356–360.
38. Huebner RE, Schein MF, Cauthen GM, et al. Usefulness of skin testing with mycobacterial antigens in children with cervical lymphadenopathy. Pediatr Infect Dis J. 1992;11:450–456.
39. Zaugg M, Salfinger M, Opravil M, et al. Extrapulmonary and disseminated infections due to *Mycobacterium malmoense*: Case report and review. Clin Infect Dis. 1993;16:540–549.
40. Buchholz UT, McNeil MM, Keyes LE, et al. *Mycobacterium malmoense* infections in the United States, January 1993 through June, 1995. Clin Infect Dis. 1998;27(Suppl):S51–S58.
41. Grange JM, Yates MD, Pozniak A. Bacteriologically confirmed non-tuberculous mycobacterial lymphadenitis in southeast England: A recent increase in the number of cases. Arch Dis Child. 1995;72:516–517.
42. Armstrong KL, James RW, Dawson DJ, et al. *Mycobacterium haemophilum* causing perihilar or cervical lymphadenitis in healthy children. J Pediatr. 1992;121:202–205.
43. Saubolle MA, Kiehn TE, White MH, et al. *Mycobacterium haemophilum*: Microbiology and expanding clinical and geographic spectra of disease in humans. Clin Microbiol Rev. 1996;9:435–447.
44. Collins CH, Grange JM, Noble WC, et al. *Mycobacterium marinum* infections in man. J Hyg Camb. 1985;94:135–149.
45. Black MM, Eykyn S. The successful treatment of tropical fish tank granuloma *(Mycobacterium marinum)* infections with co-trimoxazole. Br J Dermatol. 1977;97:689–692.
46. Donta ST, Smith PW, Levitz RE, et al. Therapy of *Mycobacterium marinum* infections. Arch Intern Med. 1986;146:902–904.
47. Wallace RJ Jr, Swenson JM, Silcox VA, et al. Spectrum of disease due to rapidly growing mycobacteria. Rev Infect Dis. 1983;5:657–679.
48. Wallace RJ Jr, Musser JM, Hull SI, et al. Diversity and sources of rapidly growing mycobacteria associated with infections following cardiac surgery. J Infect Dis. 1989;159:708–716.
49. Maloney S, Welbel S, Daves B, et al. *Mycobacterium abscessus* pseudoinfection traced to an automated endoscope washer: Utility of epidemiologic and laboratory investigation. J Infect Dis. 1994;169:1166–1169.
50. Safranek TJ, Jarvis WR, Carson LA, et al. *Mycobacterium chelonae* wound infections after plastic surgery employing contaminated gentian violet skin-marking solution. N Engl J Med. 1987;317:197–201.
51. Gross WN, Hawkins JE, Murphy DB. Origin and significance of *Mycobacterium xenopi* in clinical specimens. Bull Int Union Tuberc Lung Dis. 1976;51:267–269.
52. Marston BJ, Diallo MO, Horsburgh CR Jr, et al. Emergence of Buruli ulcer in the Daloa region of Cote d'lvoire. Am J Trop Med Hyg. 1995;52:219–224.
53. Portaels F, Traore H, De Ridder K, et al. In vitro susceptibility of *Mycobacterium ulcerans* to clarithromycin. Antimicrob Agents Chemother. 1998;42:2070–2073.
54. McBride ME, Rudolph AH, Tschen JA, et al. Diagnostic and therapeutic considerations for cutaneous *Mycobacterium haemophilum* infections. Arch Dermatol. 1991;127:276–277.
55. Plemmons RM, McAllister CK, Garces MC, et al. Osteomyelitis due to *Mycobacterium haemophilum* in a cardiac transplant patient: Case report and analysis of interactions among clarithromycin, rifampin, and cyclosporine. Clin Infect Dis. 1997;24:995–997.
56. Edwards MS, Huber TW, Baker CJ. *Mycobacterium terrae* synovitis and osteomyelitis. Am Rev Respir Dis. 1978;117:161–163.
57. May DC, Kutz JE, Howell RS, et al. *Mycobacterium terrae* tenosynovitis: Chronic infection in a previously healthy individual. South Med J. 1987;76:1445–1447.
58. Ridderhof JC, Wallace RJ Jr, Kilburn JO, et al. Chronic tenosynovitis of the hand due to *Mycobacterium nonchromogenicum*: Use of high-performance liquid chromatography for identification of isolates. Rev Infect Dis. 1991;13:857–864.
59. Hoffman PC, Fraser DW, Robiesek F, et al. Two outbreaks of sternal wound infections due to organisms of the *Mycobacterium fortuitum* complex. J Infect Dis. 1981;143:533–542.
60. Kuritsky JN, Bullen MG, Broome CV, et al. Sternal wound infections and endocarditis due to organisms of the *Mycobacterium fortuitum* complex. Ann Intern Med. 1983;98:938–939.
61. Szabó I, Sárközi L. *Mycobacterium chelonei* endemy after heart surgery with fatal consequences. Am Rev Respir Dis. 1980;121:607.
62. Bennett C, Vardiman J, Golomb H. Disseminated atypical mycobacterial infection in patients with hairy cell leukemia. Am J Med. 1986;80:891–896.
63. Horsburgh CR: *Mycobacterium avium* complex infection in the acquired immunodeficiency syndrome. N Engl J Med. 1991;324:1332–1338.
64. Huminer D, Dux S, Samra Z, et al. *Mycobacterium simiae* infection in Israeli patients with AIDS. Clin Infect Dis. 1993;17:508–509.
65. Jemni L, Hmouda H, Letaief A. Disseminated infection due to *Mycobacterium malmoense* in a patient infected with human immunodeficiency virus. Clin Infect Dis. 1994;19:203–204.
66. Lillo M, Orengo S, Cernoch P, et al. Pulmonary and disseminated infection due to *Mycobacterium kansasii*: A decade of experience. Rev Infect Dis. 1990;2:760–767.
67. Horsburgh CR Jr, Mason UG, Farhi DC, et al. Disseminated infection with *Mycobacterium avium-intracellulare*. Medicine (Baltimore). 1985;64:36–48.
68. Akiyama H, Maruyama T, Uetake T, et al. Systemic infection due to atypical mycobacteria in patients with chronic myelogenous leukemia. Rev Infect Dis. 1991;13:815–818.
69. Patel R, Roberts GD, Keating MR, et al. Infections due to nontuberculous mycobacteria in kidney, heart, and liver transplant recipients. Clin Infect Dis. 1994;19:263–273.
70. Nightingale SD, Byrd LT, Southern PM, et al. Incidence of *Mycobacterium avium-intracellulare* complex in human immunodeficiency virus–positive patients. J Infect Dis. 1992;165:1082–1085.
71. Nightingale SD, Cameron DW, Gordin FM, et al. Two controlled trials of rifabutin prophylaxis against *Mycobacterium avium* complex infection in AIDS. N Engl J Med. 1993;329:828–833.
72. Shafran SD, Singer J, Zarowny DP, et al. A comparison of two regimens for the treatment of *Mycobacterium avium* complex bacteremia in AIDS: Rifabutin, ethambutol, and clarithromycin versus rifampin, ethambutol, clofazimine, and ciprofloxacin. N Engl J Med. 1996;335:377–383.
73. Gordin FM, Sullam PM, Shafran SD, et al. A randomized, placebo-controlled study of rifabutin added to a regimen of clarithromycin and ethambutol for treatment of disseminated infection with Mycobacterium avium complex. Clin Infect Dis. 1999;28:1080–1085.
74. Chaisson RE, Keiser P, Pierce M, et al. Clarithromycin and ethambutol with or without clofazimine for the treatment of bacteremic *Mycobacterium avium* complex disease in patients with HIV infection. AIDS. 1997;11:311–317.
75. Pierce M, Crampton S, Henry D, et al. A randomized trial of clarithromycin as prophylaxis against disseminated *Mycobacterium avium* complex infection in patients with advanced acquired immunodeficiency syndrome. N Engl J Med. 1996;335:384–391.
76. Havlir DV, Dubé MP, Sattler FR, et al. Prophylaxis against disseminated *Mycobacterium avium* complex with weekly azithromycin, daily rifabutin, or both. N Engl J Med. 1996;335:392–398.
77. Coyle MB, Carlson LDC, Wallis CK, et al. Laboratory aspects of "*Mycobacterium genavense,*" a proposed species isolated from AIDS patients. J Clin Microbiol. 1992;30:3206–3212.
78. Tenover FC, Crawford JT, Huebner RE, et al. The resurgence of tuberculosis: Is your laboratory ready? J Clin Microbiol. 1993;31:767–770.
79. Butler WR, Cage G, Desmond E, et al. Standardized Method for the HPLC Identification of Mycobacteria. Atlanta: Centers for Disease Control and Prevention; 1996.
80. Steingrube VA, Gibson JL, Brown BA, et al. PCR amplification and restriction endonuclease analysis of a 65-kilodalton heat shock protein gene sequence for taxonomic separation of rapidly growing mycobacteria. J Clin Microbiol. 1995;33:149–153.
81. Telenti A, Marchesi F, Balz M, et al. Rapid identification of mycobacteria to the species level by polymerase chain reaction and restriction enzyme analysis. J Clin Microbiol. 1993;31:175–178.
82. Mazurek GH, Hartman S, Zhang Y-S, et al. Large DNA restriction fragment polymorphism in the *Mycobacterium avium–M. intracellulare* complex: A potential epidemiologic tool. J Clin Microbiol. 1993;31:390–394.
83. Wallace RJ Jr, Zhang Y, Brown BA, et al. DNA large restriction fragment patterns of sporadic and epidemic nosocomial strains of *Mycobacterium chelonae* and *Mycobacterium abscessus*. J Clin Microbiol. 1993;31:2697–2701.
84. Hawkins JE, Wallace RJ Jr, Brown BA. Antibacterial susceptibility tests: Mycobacteria. In: Balows A, ed. Manual of Clinical Microbiology. 5th ed. American Society for Microbiology; 1991:1138–1152.
85. Brown BA, Wallace RJ Jr, Onyi GO, et al. Activities of four macrolides, including clarithromycin, against *Mycobacterium fortuitum, Mycobacterium chelonae*, and *M. chelonae*–like organisms. Antimicrob Agents Chemother. 1992;36:180–184.
86. Swenson JM, Wallace RJ Jr, Silcox VA, et al. Antimicrobial susceptibility of five subgroups of *Mycobacterium fortuitum* and *Mycobacterium chelonae*. Antimicrob Agents Chemother. 1985;28:807–811.

HIGHER BACTERIAL DISEASES

Chapter 244

Nocardia Species

TANIA C. SORRELL
JONATHAN R. IREDELL
DAVID H. MITCHELL

Nocardia is a genus of aerobic actinomycetes responsible for localized or disseminated infections in animals and humans. The genus is named after Edmond Nocard, who in 1888 described the isolation of an aerobic actinomycete from cattle with bovine farcy. The first human case of nocardiosis was reported by Eppinger in 1890. Cases of human disease have increased substantially in the last 2 decades in association with an increasing population of immunocompromised hosts and improved methods for detection and identification of *Nocardia* spp. in the clinical laboratory.

CLASSIFICATION

The aerobic actinomycetes are a large and diverse group of gram-positive bacteria[1, 2] that appear on microscopy as branching, filamentous cells (Fig. 244–1). Members of the group are often only distantly related phylogenetically. A subgroup, the "aerobic nocardiform actinomycetes," is the most important cause of human infection and includes *Mycobacterium, Corynebacterium, Nocardia, Rhodococcus, Gordona,* and *Tsukamurella.* All members of this group have cell walls containing mesodiaminopimelic acid, arabinose, galactose (type IV cell wall),[1] and mycolic acids of various chain lengths. The latter are responsible for varying acid fastness on appropriate staining. In addition, *Nocardia* spp. are characterized by an ability to grow in media containing lysozyme, produce urease, and form aerial hyphae.[1]

Traditional laboratory methods for identification of *Nocardia* spp.,[3] which are based on simple biochemical reactions and hydrolysis tests, are limited in their ability to differentiate these organisms. In particular, isolates belonging to the *Nocardia asteroides* complex, the most common species associated with disseminated infection, cannot be differentiated in the routine laboratory. At least 12 species within the genus *Nocardia* have been defined by the use of expanded biochemical and susceptibility tests,[4] chromatographic analysis of cell wall components,[5] and in particular, the application of molecular techniques, including ribotyping[6] and DNA amplification followed by restriction endonuclease analysis.[7] Of these, *N. asteroides* sensu strictu, *Nocardia farcinica, Nocardia nova* (included in the *N. asteroides* complex), *Nocardia brasiliensis, Nocardia otitidiscaviarum,* and *Nocardia transvalensis* are the most important causes of human infection.[8] Some strains previously assigned to the species *N. brasiliensis* have been assigned to a new species, *Nocardia pseudobrasiliensis,* based on mycolic acid patterns, decomposition of adenine, nitrate reduction, and antimicrobial susceptibilities.[9]

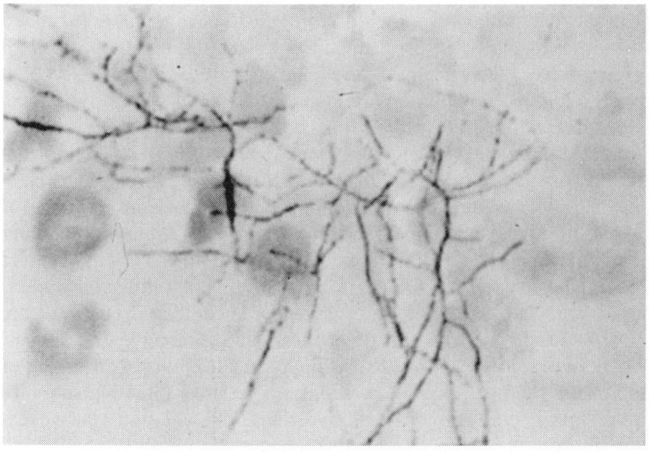

FIGURE 244–1. Photomicrograph of direct Gram-stained smear from a *Nocardia* lung abscess (oil immersion).

ECOLOGY AND EPIDEMIOLOGY

Nocardia spp. are ubiquitous environmental saprophytes, living in soil, organic matter, and water.[2, 10] Human infection usually arises from direct inoculation of skin or soft tissues or by inhalation. Mycetoma secondary to *N. brasiliensis* is the most common *Nocardia* infection reported from tropical regions, particularly Central America. Worldwide, respiratory and disseminated infections are most often due to members of the *N. asteroides* complex.[2, 8]

Nocardia spp. are well recognized causes of infection in animals, with bovine mastitis being the most common.[2] Animal-to-human or human-to-human transmission has not been reported. Clusters of invasive nocardiosis have been described in patients in oncology and transplant units, presumed to be associated with inhalation of contaminated dust.[2, 11, 12] Concurrent transmission via the hands of staff or contaminated fomites appeared likely in one of these outbreaks.[11] Hospital construction work may have been a risk factor in separate clusters of postsurgical wound infections caused by *Nocardia* spp.[12, 13] Pulsed-field gel electrophoresis[13] and random amplification of polymorphic DNA (fingerprinting)[14] have been successfully used for confirming clusters and defining common sources.

PATHOLOGY AND PATHOGENESIS

Sections of tissues infected with *Nocardia* spp. usually demonstrate an acute pyogenic inflammatory reaction. Branching, beaded, filamentous bacteria, similar to those seen in smears taken from cultures, may be demonstrated within the abscesses on Gram staining. "Sulfur granules" (bacterial macrocolonies) similar to those seen in actinomycosis may be found in nocardial mycetomas. *Nocardia* spp. will usually stain acid fast in tissue sections if a method such as that of Fite-Faraco is used, whereas *Actinomyces* spp. and other anaerobic actinomycetes do not.[15]

The interaction between the host and parasitizing nocardiae has been comprehensively reviewed.[16] Disease manifestations of nocardiosis are determined principally by the portal of entry, tissue tropism, growth rates in vivo, ability to survive phagocyte attack, the nature of the host immune reaction, and characteristics of the infecting strain. Protective immune responses are primarily T cell mediated, and nocardiosis is more problematic in patients with impaired cell-mediated immunity. *Nocardia* spp. elicit little in the way of an effective humoral response.[17, 18]

In murine models of infection, virulent nocardiae are cleared from the blood within a few hours of intravenous inoculation and localize in a number of organs (lung, brain, kidneys, liver, spleen). The outcome of infection is largely determined by the ability of a given strain to resist the initial neutrophil leukocyte response and subsequent attack by activated macrophages.[16] Early neutrophil mobilization, although often inadequate in itself to abort infection, appears to retard the process until lymphocyte-mediated cytotoxicity and activated macrophages effect a definitive response.[16, 18–20]

Specific Virulence Determinants

The nocardial envelope is structurally similar to that of other actinomycetes. Fifteen to 25% of the cell wall mass in rapidly growing organisms (nearly twice that in the stationary phase) is composed of peptidoglycan.[21, 22] Differences in cell wall ultrastructure and chemical composition are evident during the logarithmic and stationary phases of growth and may contribute to intrastrain differences in toxicity to host cells, as well as virulence in animal models.[16, 22] Mycolic acid polymers such as trehalose-6,6′-dimycolate ("cord factor") are members of a group of biologically active cell wall glycolipids found in many actinomycetes, including *Nocardia* spp.,[21, 23, 24] and are virulence associated.[25–28] They are toxic in vitro and, in animal models,[26, 29] insert themselves into phospholipid bilayers in vitro and contribute to inhibition of phagosome-lysosome fusion and acidification in macrophages.[25] Variation in the cell wall composition of virulent *N. asteroides*, including the relative saturation and the chain length of mycolates, exhibits some concordance with virulence and toxicity in vitro and in vivo.[27, 28, 30] However, even though the immunostimulant activity of the actinomycete cell wall is well described, the immunologic response to cord factor itself is complex and varies in vitro with the mode of antigen presentation (for review, see Goren[24]). Thus, the nocardial cell wall composition influences and is in turn influenced by the immune response, particularly that of phagocytes. Cell wall–deficient forms (L-forms) of *Nocardia* spp. have been isolated from serious human and animal infections[31–33] and have been shown to fulfill Koch's postulates in animals models.[16] Interstrain[34] and intrastrain[16, 22] variation is also observed: L-forms appear more likely to arise from less virulent strains[18] and in the setting of normal host immunity.[32] L-forms can be induced and maintained in macrophages in vitro,[33] which may help explain occasional late relapse of nocardial infections.[16, 35]

Nocardia spp. contain no cell wall lipopolysaccharide, exopolysaccharide capsule, or surface fimbriae. However, strain-dependent specific adhesins and invasion properties influence the outcome of infection in animal models.[36, 37] Virulent strains of *N. asteroides* are relatively resistant to neutrophil-mediated killing,[38] and organisms in the logarithmic growth phase are more toxic to macrophages.[39] They inhibit phagosome-lysosome fusion more successfully in vitro[40] and give rise to L-forms, which can be isolated from within macrophages many days later.[41, 42] The ability to use macrophage lysosomal acid phosphatase as a sole carbon source may be significant in vivo,[43, 44] but inhibition of macrophage phagosome acidification and resistance to the oxidative burst of polymorphonuclear leukocytes and macrophages are probably more important. Nonspecific interactions with neutrophils may contribute to the indolence of nocardiosis in the context of reduced cell-mediated immunity.[8] Patients with specific defects in the phagocyte oxidative burst, for example, chronic granulomatous disease,[8] are more vulnerable to this infection. Highly pathogenic *Mycobacterium tuberculosis* and *N. asteroides* secrete superoxide dismutase into growth media, whereas nonpathogenic *Mycobacterium* and *Nocardia* spp. do not.[45–47] Antibodies to surface-presented superoxide dismutase halved the survival of a virulent strain of *N. asteroides* (but not a less virulent strain) in the presence of activated neutrophils in vitro, with added catalase having a protective effect for the less virulent strain.[47] Specific toxins, including hemolysins, have been identified but are not thought to be widespread or important virulence factors.[48, 49]

Ciliated epithelia appear to be relatively resistant to invasion by *Nocardia* spp., although a range of susceptible lung- and airway-associated cell types has been observed in rat models of infection.[37] Seeding of the central nervous system (CNS) may follow hematogenous spread from any focus, and tropism for cerebral tissue is evident experimentally. Electron microscopic studies of infected macrophage and astrocytoma-derived or astrocytoma-related cell lines suggest that the penetration competence of invasive *N. asteroides* is localized to the bacterial apex.[48] Neuroinvasiveness varies significantly between strains. Certain strains of *N. asteroides* are more competent for cytochalasin B–resistant penetration into macrophages,[49] thus implying a mechanism of entry independent of ordinary phagocytosis. Specific lectins have been shown to determine site specificity in the murine brain,[48] and a characteristic extrapyramidal movement disorder has been observed in infected animals.[50] However, *Nocardia* spp. have never been shown to play an etiologic role in human Parkinson's disease.[51]

CLINICAL MANIFESTATIONS

Members of the *N. asteroides* complex are responsible for about 80% of noncutaneous invasive disease and for most systemic and CNS disease.[16] *N. farcinica* is an important[52] and generally more antibiotic-resistant member of this complex. *N. brasiliensis* is the most often reported cause of cutaneous and lymphocutaneous disease, but it may also cause systemic and, occasionally, CNS infection. Noncutaneous disease is the most frequent manifestation of nocardiosis caused by the less common pathogens *N. transvalensis*[53] and *N. otitidiscavarium*,[16] although both may cause severe cutaneous infection.[54] Superficial nocardiosis after minor skin trauma is not necessarily associated with compromised cell-mediated immunity, but it may progress to disseminated disease in that setting.[54]

Immunocompromise is a well-established risk factor for nocardiosis. *Nocardia* spp. may therefore be considered opportunistic pathogens that cause serious and disseminated disease in settings such as organ transplantation and lymphoreticular neoplasia,[16, 54–57] with the relative risk of progressive disease reflecting the level of immunosuppression.[54, 58] A compilation of over a thousand randomly selected cases from the literature showed that more than 60% of all cases of nocardiosis reported are associated with preexisting immune compromise ranging from alcoholism and diabetes to organ transplantation and acquired immunodeficiency syndrome (AIDS).[16] Such was also the case in more than one third of *N. farcinica* infections.[52] Persons with chronic pulmonary disorders, notably, pulmonary alveolar proteinosis, and almost any condition requiring long-term corticosteroid usage are also at risk. Although cases of nocardiosis have been described in patients with AIDS, the overall incidence is low and not fully explained by the use of sulfonamide prophylaxis against *Pneumocystis carinii* pneumonia.[2, 59, 60]

Ubiquitous in soil, all of the nocardiae can establish superficial infection after relatively trivial inoculation injuries, which may vary from insect and animal bites to puncture wounds and contaminated abrasions. *N. brasiliensis* is the most common cause of progressive cutaneous and lymphocutaneous (sporotrichoid) disease, whereas *N. asteroides* more commonly causes self-limited skin infection.[8, 16] Because the initial response to *Nocardia* is pyogenic, self-limited skin lesions may be disregarded or treated as staphylococcal in origin. Severe and invasive systemic disease is almost certainly overrepresented in the literature,[16] and the extent to which mycetoma is relatively underreported and nocardial infection underdiagnosed overall is unknown. Mycetoma is a chronically progressive, destructive disease occurring days to months after inoculation and is typically located in a distal position on the limbs. Eumycetoma (of fungal etiology) and actinomycetoma (caused by actinomycetes) are equally prominent in the literature, the epidemiology varying with the geographic location.[61] Overall, *Streptomyces* spp. and *Actinomadura* appear to be of equal or greater importance than *Nocardia* spp. among causative agents of actinomycetoma. Suppurative granulomas, progressive fibrosis and necrosis, sinus formation with destruction of adjacent structures, and macroscopically visible infective granules are regular features of nocardial mycetoma.[61] Inoculation injury occasionally results in infection of the cornea.

Pulmonary disease is the predominant clinical finding (more than 40% of reported cases), with almost 90% of such cases caused by members of the *N. asteroides* complex.[16] Pulmonary nocardiosis is usually suppurative, but granulomatous or mixed responses may occur. Clinical manifestations of established infection include endobronchial inflammatory masses,[62, 63] pneumonia, lung abscess, and cavitary disease with contiguous extension to surface and deep structures, including effusion and empyema.[8, 55] Radiologic manifestations include irregular nodules (usually cavitating when large), reticulonodular or diffuse pneumonic infiltrates, and pleural effusions (Fig. 244–2). Progressive fibrotic disease may develop after inadequate therapy, and diagnosis is often difficult.[64, 65] Pulmonary nocardiosis may be a fatal complication of advanced human immunodeficiency virus (HIV) infection, often occurring as alveolar infiltrates rather than cavitary disease.[66] It occurs most commonly in severely immunocompromised patients (CD4 cell count, $<200/mm^3$,[67–69] in whom nonspecific radiologic findings oblige a search for a definitive diagnosis.[66, 70] Relentless progression has been described.[60, 71, 72] Nocardiosis should always be considered in the differential diagnosis of indolent pulmonary disease, particularly in the setting of cellular immune compromise, along with other actinomycetes (e.g., *Mycobacterium, Actinomyces* spp.) and eumycetes (e.g., *Cryptococcus neoformans, Aspergillus* spp.). Clues to a nocardial etiology include spread to contiguous structures, especially with soft tissue swelling or external fistulas, and to the CNS. Secondary cerebral localization and silent destructive infection are sufficiently common that cerebral imaging, preferably magnetic resonance imaging, should be performed in all cases of pulmonary and disseminated nocardiosis. Invasive diagnostic procedures should be considered early in an immunocompromised host because disease may follow a rapidly progressive course in patients with severe immunodeficiency and coincident pathology with similar clinical characteristics (e.g., aspergillosis, tuberculosis, malignancy) is well documented.[55]

CNS involvement was recognized in over 44% of all cases of systemic nocardiosis in one large survey.[16] Up to a quarter of reported nocardial disease other than mycetoma involves the CNS, with nearly half of these cases exclusively involving the CNS.[16, 56, 73, 74] Insidious manifestations are often mistaken for neoplasia because of the paucity of clinical and laboratory signs of bacterial inflammation, and silent invasion and persistence make diagnosis and management more difficult.[8, 16] Clinical manifestations of CNS nocardiosis usually result from local effects of granulomas or abscesses in the brain and, less commonly, the spinal cord or meninges[5, 6, 8, 73, 74] (Fig. 244–3). Disease frequently progresses over months to years and causes a broad range of neurologic deficits, including chronic behavioral and psychiatric disturbances; these deficits reflect localization in the cerebral cortices, basal ganglia, and midbrain.[16, 50] Tissue diagnosis of a cerebral mass in the setting of proven pulmonary nocardiosis is not always necessary.[8] However, cerebral biopsy should be considered early in an immunocompromised patient because of the higher incidence of serious coexisting pathology and a more aggressive course than that traditionally ascribed to cerebral nocardiosis.[16] Disseminated infection is characterized by widespread abscess formation. The most commonly reported sites include the CNS and eyes (particularly the retina), skin and subcutaneous tissues, kidneys, joints, bone, and heart.[8, 16, 66, 73, 74]

Colonization

Occasional instances of transient colonization of sputum and skin by *Nocardia* spp. have been reported and appear to indicate aerosol contamination or soil-derived contamination. Colonization of the sputum is typically found in patients with underlying pulmonary pathology who are not receiving steroid therapy, and such colonization requires no specific therapy. Significant isolates of *Nocardia* should be visible on Gram stain, produce a pure or predominant growth in culture, and be repeatedly isolated from clinical specimens.[74] However, the extent to which spontaneously resolving or subclinical pulmonary infection occurs in the population is ill defined, and at least one leading authority warns against dismissing positive sputum cultures as harmless.[16]

LABORATORY DIAGNOSIS

The microbiology laboratory should always be informed when nocardiosis is suspected inasmuch as the diagnosis may be missed by routine laboratory methods. Respiratory secretions, skin biopsies, or aspirates from deep collections are the most common specimens from which *Nocardia* spp. are isolated. Direct smears from such specimens typically show gram-positive, beaded, branching filaments that are usually acid fast. Bacteremia as demonstrated by positive blood cultures is reported in a minority of patients with nocardiosis.[75] *Nocardia* spp. will grow on most nonselective media used routinely for culture of bacteria, fungi, and mycobacteria. However, in specimens containing mixed flora (e.g., respiratory secretions), nocardial colonies are easily obscured by those of more rapidly growing bacteria, and the yield is increased by the use of selective media

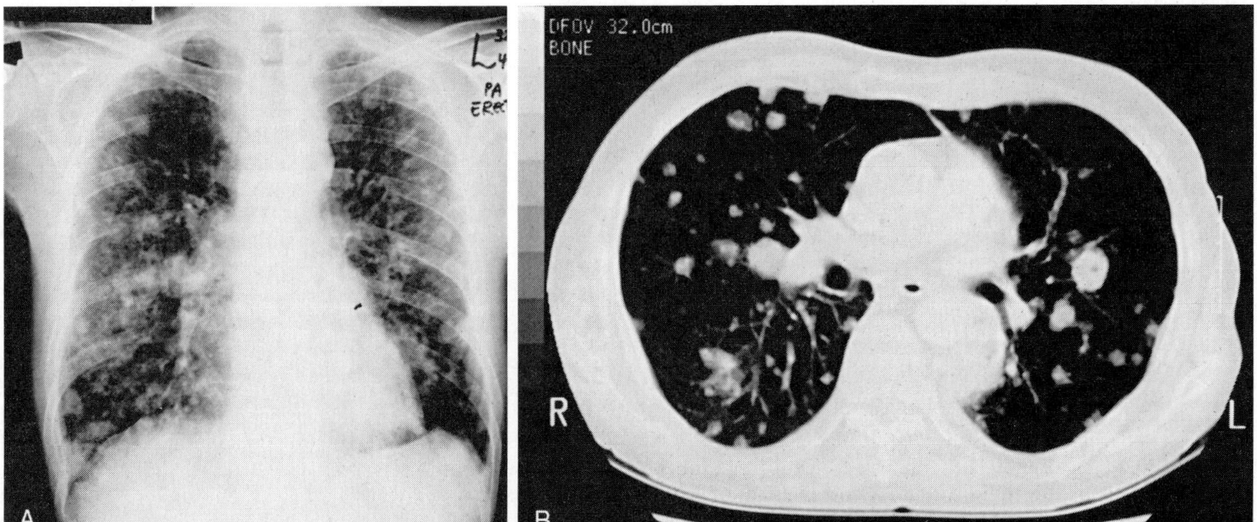

FIGURE 244–2. Chest radiograph *(A)* and computed tomography scan *(B)* from a heavily immunosuppressed patient with systemic lupus erythematosus, demonstrating multiple pulmonary abscesses due to *Nocardia farcinica*.

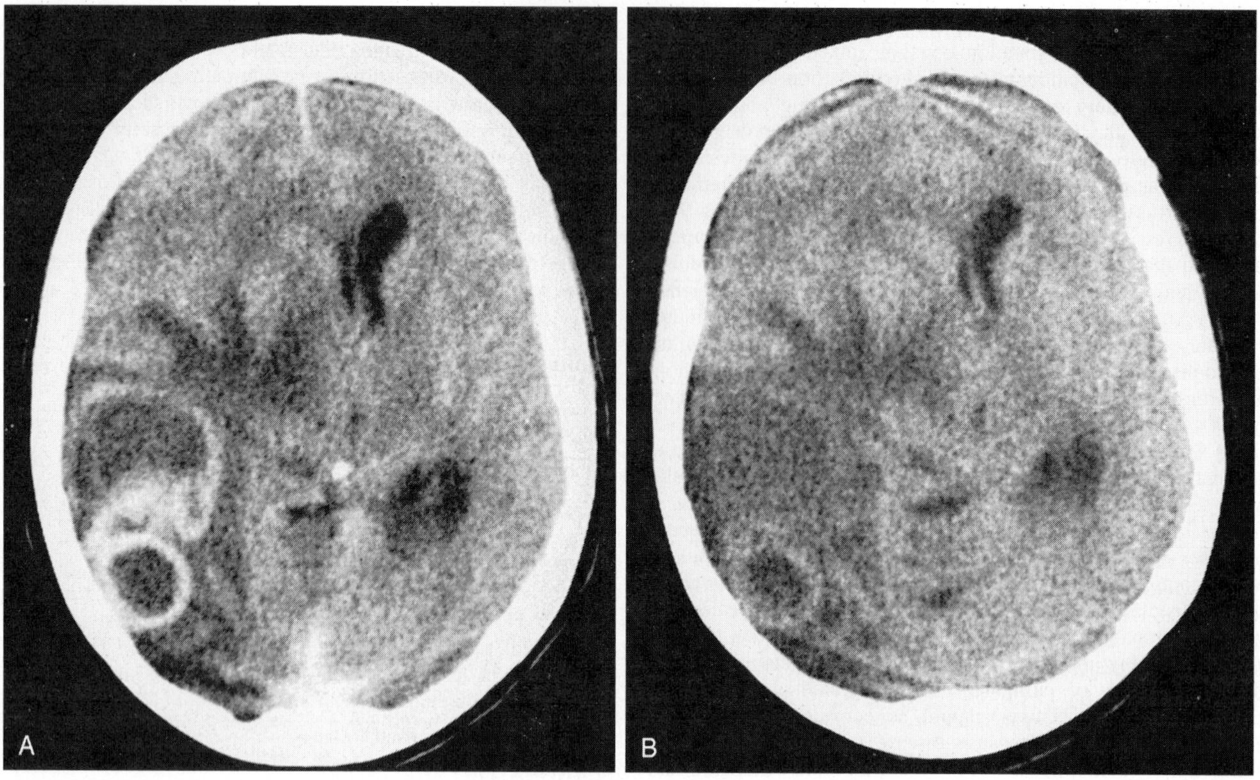

FIGURE 244–3. Cerebral computed tomography scan with *(A)* and without *(B)* intravenous contrast, demonstrating single enhancing lesion in a lymphoma patient. Biopsy revealed an abscess due to *Nocardia asteroides*.

such as Thayer-Martin agar with antibiotics[76] or paraffin agar.[77] Decontamination methods used for mycobacterial culture are too harsh for *Nocardia* spp. and may substantially reduce the number of viable organisms present in the specimen.[78] The traditional selective method of paraffin baiting[79] is probably inferior to the use of selective media.[76] Buffered charcoal-yeast extract medium, which is commonly used for selective growth of *Legionella* spp., may also be useful for isolation of *Nocardia* spp. from respiratory specimens.[80]

Growth of *Nocardia* spp. may take from 48 hours to several weeks, but typical colonies are usually seen after 3 to 5 days. *Nocardia* spp. appear as either buff or pigmented waxy cerebriform colonies or as chalky white if aerial hyphae are produced.[1] Most isolates are acid fast by a method such as the modified Kinyoun technique, but this characteristic may vary with the strain and culture media used.

Isolates identified presumptively as *Nocardia* spp. can be assigned to traditional groupings based on the hydrolysis of casein, tyrosine, xanthine, hypoxanthine, and testosterone.[3] These methods are relatively expensive, slow, and limited by their inability to differentiate members of the *N. asteroides* complex. Expanded biochemical tests and patterns of resistance to antibiotics can be used to differentiate *N. farcinica*[4, 81] and *N. nova*[4, 82] from *N. asteroides* sensu strictu. Although resistance to third-generation cephalosporins is considered characteristic of *N. farcinica*,[81] such resistance if variable and should not be used as the sole criterion for differentiating this species from *N. asteroides* sensu strictu.[4]

Commercially available identification systems, including Microscan RAI/HNID panels[83] and the ID32C Yeast Identification System,[84] may provide more rapid methods for differentiating *Nocardia* spp. Analysis of cell wall mycolic acid profiles by high-performance liquid chromatography can be used to aid speciation of *Nocardia*,[5] although lack of availability and apparent variability in profiles produced by different culture conditions have limited the use of this technique.[1] Molecular techniques, including gene probes,[85] ribotyping,[6] and restriction endonuclease analysis after polymerase chain reaction,[7, 86] have been used to differentiate among the *Nocardia* and to characterize new species. These techniques may become the methods of choice in the future. Immunodominant antigens of *Nocardia* spp. have been described and serologic tests developed, but at present these tests remain experimental.[1, 87]

MANAGEMENT

Clinical experience has shown that successful therapy requires the use of antimicrobial drug(s) in combination with appropriate surgical drainage or débridement. Optimal antimicrobial regimens have not been established by controlled clinical trial. Initial selection of a therapeutic regimen should take into account the site and severity of infection, host immune status, potential drug interactions/toxicity, and the species of *Nocardia*. Antimicrobial susceptibility testing is recommended as a guide to therapy in some circumstances (see later), but such testing may be misleading because of the lack of an internationally accepted, validated reference method and the paucity of studies correlating laboratory data with clinical outcome. Indeed, discrepancies between in vitro data and clinical outcome are well documented. Techniques such as agar dilution, broth microdilution, and disk diffusion, which identify inhibitory rather than bactericidal end points, have furnished consistent susceptibility profiles, provided that variations in results secondary to the effect of inoculum size, homogeneity, media composition, and incubation time have been eliminated.[88] Tentative breakpoints and interpretive criteria have been proposed.[1, 88] The E-test and the BACTEC radiometric method have recently been shown to correlate with broth microdilution[89, 90] and should ultimately prove useful in the clinical laboratory. At present, it is appropriate that susceptibility test results be confirmed by a reference laboratory. Indications for testing include patients in whom *Nocardia* spp. are isolated from areas of deep-seated or disseminated infection, patients with a lack of response to initial therapy or who relapse after therapy, patients in whom therapeutic alternatives to sulfonamides are being considered, and those from whom relatively resistant *Nocardia* spp. such as *N. farcinica*[56, 81, 91] and *N. otitidiscaviarum*[14, 92, 93] have been isolated. Susceptibility profiles of *Nocardia* species are summarized in Table 244–1. A notable, but unexplained discrepancy can be seen in the data on susceptibility of *N. asteroides* to sulfonamides in a study from continental Europe when compared with American and British data (Table 244–1).

Sulfonamides, which have been the mainstay of therapy since their introduction in the 1940s, have resulted in substantial improvement in outcome. They are the treatment of choice for nocardiosis caused by *N. brasiliensis*,[102, 103] *N. asteroides* complex, and *N. transvalensis*.[8, 53] Although sulfonamides are less effective in vitro against *N. otitidiscaviarum*,[14, 92, 93] they have been curative in cases of cutaneous infection.[97] Trimethoprim-sulfamethoxazole (TMP-SMX) is the formulation currently preferred by most clinicians despite the absence of conclusive clinical data supporting increased efficacy of the combination in comparison to sulfadiazine and sulfisoxazole and in spite of the increased myelotoxicity of the combination, especially in patients receiving myelosuppressive therapy.[102] TMP-SMX (available in a fixed ratio of 1:5) has potential pharmacokinetic and antibacterial advantages. In vitro, synergistic activity has been demonstrated against a majority of isolates,[102, 104] with optimal drug ratios for demonstration of synergy varying between 1:10 to 1:5 or less in different studies.[104–106] The usual ratio of these drugs in serum and cerebrospinal fluid is 1:20.[104] Relative levels in tissues and pus, including cerebral nocardial abscesses, approximate 1:7 or less.[102, 107] Therapeutic responses to the combination have been reported despite high minimal inhibitory concentrations of TMP in comparison to achievable serum levels and evidence of antagonism between TMP and SMX in vitro.[108]

In adults with normal renal function and localized disease, the recommended dose of TMP-SMX is 5 to 10 mg/kg TMP and 25 to 50 mg/kg SMX in two to four divided doses, depending on the extent of disease.[102] In patients with primary cutaneous infection, including sporotrichoid nocardiosis, TMP-SMX at 5 mg/kg/day (TMP component) is sufficient in combination with appropriate surgical débridement.[102] Higher initial doses (15 mg/kg TMP and 75 mg/kg SMX) intravenously or by mouth are frequently used in patients with cerebral abscesses, patients with severe, extensive, or disseminated infection, and patients with AIDS.[71, 104] Doses can generally be reduced and therapy changed from intravenous to oral after 3 to 6 weeks, depending on clinical response. Cure of cerebral nocardiosis has been noted with lower doses of TMP-SMX, approximately 10 mg/kg/day of the TMP component[108, 109] or less.[107] Immunocompromised patients do not necessarily need higher doses of TMP-SMX; for example, 5 mg/kg/day (TMP component) in two doses has been successful in the treatment of pulmonary infection in renal transplant patients.[58] However, in severely ill or immunosuppressed patients, two or more drugs, which may include sulfonamides, are frequently prescribed despite the lack of clinical data.[104, 110] It has been recommended that a serum sulfonamide level determined 2 hours after an oral dose at steady state is useful to confirm that gastrointestinal tract absorption is adequate and that recommended therapeutic levels of sulfonamide (100 to 150 mg/liter) have been achieved.[2] In practice, measurement of serum drug levels may be of value in selected patients, such as those in whom absorption from the gastrointestinal tract is uncertain, those at risk for dose-related toxicity in whom high drug doses are indicated, and those with poor therapeutic response.

Sulfadiazine and sulfisoxazole demonstrate equal efficacy in the treatment of nocardiosis and, based on accumulated clinical experience, were the antimicrobial agents of choice for many years. Sulfadiazine may cause oliguria, azotemia, and crystalluria in patients who fail to maintain a high fluid intake and can be prevented by alkalinizing the urine. Sulfisoxazole is less likely to cause oliguria. Trisulfapyrimidine combinations should be as effective and less toxic.[8] In adults with normal renal function, dose schedules of 6 to 12 g/day in four to six oral doses after a loading dose of 4 g should lead to a therapeutic serum level of 100 to 150 mg/liter 2 hours postdose.[8] Although doses of 3 to 6 g/day are effective in most cases of pulmonary and systemic disease,[74] higher doses have been favored in immunosuppressed patients with AIDS[70] and after cardiac transplantation.[111]

Alternative antimicrobial agents should be considered in patients with infections caused by *N. otitidiscaviarum*, which demonstrates inconsistent susceptibility to sulfonamides (see Table 244–1), those failing sulfonamide therapy, and those intolerant of sulfonamide-containing regimens because of hypersensitivity, gastrointestinal toxicity, or myelotoxicity. Sulfonamide intolerance occurs in up to 55% of patients with AIDS.[71, 112] Desensitization is an option for continuation of TMP-SMX in patients with hypersensitivity reactions and has been used successfully in patients with AIDS.[113] Renal transplantation is associated with an increased risk of myelotoxicity in patients receiving azathioprine[114] and with reversible nephrotoxicity in patients receiving cyclosporine.[115] Anecdotal data indicate that immunocompromised patients with severe, progressive nocardial infection may respond to primary therapy with non–sulfonamide-containing regimens.[110]

The choice of alternative therapeutic drugs has necessarily been

TABLE 244–1 Antimicrobial Susceptibility of *Nocardia asteroides* (% Isolates Susceptible)

Antibiotic	*N. asteroides* Complex	*N. asteroides* Sensu Strictu	*N. farcinica*	*N. nova*	*N. brasiliensis*	*N. transvalensis*	*N. otitidiscaviarum*
Sulfamethoxazole	91–100	(8)* 96–199	(<20) 89–100	89–97	99–100	90	V
Trimethoprim-sulfamethoxazole	91–100	(8)* 100	(0)*	N/A	100	88	V
Ampicillin	18–40	40–93	0–5	100	14	10	NR
Amoxacillin-clavulanate	41–58	53–67	47–71	3–6	65–97	30	R
Cefotaxime	79–82	94–100	0–7	87–100	75–100	50	R
Ceftriaxone	79–82	94–100	0–73	100	88–100	50	NR
Imipenem	71–100	77–98	64–87	100	20–30	90	R
Amikacin	78–95	100	100	100	100	82†	S
Doxycycline	NR	48–88	0–14	19–94	NR	NR	NR
Minocycline	94–100	78–94	20–96	89–100	75–90	54	S
Ciprofloxacin	29–50	38–98	68–88	0	12–30	60	R
Erythromycin	22–35	23–93	0–3	100	40	50	NR
Dapsone	NA	92	86	94	NR	NR	NR

*Discrepant results from a continental European study.
†Amikacin susceptibility of the small number of isolates tested has varied; resistance to amikacin has been suggested by one group as a criterion for phenotypic characterization of *N. transvalensis*.[94]
Abbreviations: N/A, Not available; NR, not reported; R, resistant; S, sensitive; V, variable sensitivity.
Composite data from refs. 4, 14, 53, 56, 81, 82, 88, 91–93, and 95–100. Interpretation of sensitivity is based on National Committee for Clinical Laboratory Standards breakpoints for bacteria that grow aerobically.[101] Data for *N. transvalensis* are based on one study of 11 isolates,[53] and data for *N. otitidiscaviarum* on three studies involving 6 to 27 isolates.[14, 92, 93]

based on in vitro susceptibility data and efficacy in animal models, especially short-term murine models of cerebral and pulmonary nocardiosis.[116, 117] Assessment of these regimens in human nocardiosis is complicated by the paucity of case reports, the fact that multiple antimicrobial drugs have often been used either in combination or sequentially,[118] and the variable and chronic course of nocardiosis. Clinical experience with amikacin and imipenem, which appear to be the most active agents in vitro and in animal models, has been encouraging.[8, 118] Although amikacin is potentially nephrotoxic and ototoxic, twice-daily dose regimens make it a desirable drug for use in home intravenous therapy programs. In one study, cure was effected in seven of eight patients given amikacin in combination with agents found to demonstrate synergy in vitro.[119] In vitro, amikacin exhibits excellent activity against all species of *Nocardia*, with the possible exception of *N. transvalensis* (see Table 244–1). Imipenem is highly active in vitro except against *N. brasiliensis*, although more than 10% of isolates of *N. farcinica, N. transvalensis*, and in one study, *N. asteroides* sensu strictu were resistant (see Table 244–1). Synergy between TMP-SMX and amikacin has been demonstrated in vitro; with imipenem, the effect is predominantly additive.[120] In the short-term murine models of cerebral and pulmonary nocardiosis, imipenem and amikacin were significantly more effective than TMP-SMX.[116, 117] The effect of imipenem was not enhanced by TMP-SMX despite demonstration of synergy in vitro.[121] The apparent inferior efficacy of TMP-SMX may be model dependent.[122] Amikacin has been used successfully, usually in combination with other agents, including sulfonamides, in patients with nocardiosis involving several different body sites and in immunocompromised patients.[118, 123] An initial parenteral regimen of imipenem and amikacin (10 to 15 mg/kg/day in two divided doses) has been recommended as primary therapy in pulmonary nocardiosis[124] and in very ill patients,[8] although clinical data supporting this approach are meager. Meropenem is a theoretically attractive alternative to imipenem in patients with cerebral nocardiosis because it has a similar pharmacokinetic profile, good cerebrospinal fluid penetration, and activity against *Nocardia* species and is associated with a lower incidence of seizures.[94, 125] No reports on the use of meropenem in nocardiosis have been published.

Third-generation cephalosporins have the advantages of excellent cerebrospinal fluid penetration and low toxicity. Those with long serum half-lives are suitable for use in ambulatory intravenous therapy programs. In several case reports the efficacy of ceftriaxone-containing regimens in the treatment of nocardiosis has been documented.[118] Ceftriaxone, cefotaxime (see Table 244–1), and cefuroxime[8] exhibit significant in vitro activity against *Nocardia* spp. with the exception of *N. farcinica, N. transvalensis,* and *N. otitidiscaviarum*. Synergy between cefotaxime and imipenem has been noted against susceptible strains of *Nocardia* in vitro, although not in the murine model of cerebral nocardiosis.[121] Cefuroxime and amikacin also exhibit synergistic activity in vitro.[119]

Oral alternatives to sulfonamides include minocycline (100 to 200 mg twice daily), which may be effective when used alone, in combination with other drugs, or as sequential therapy.[65, 71, 126–132] A genetically distinct, minocycline-resistant subset of *N. brasiliensis* that causes invasive infection has been assigned to a new species, *N. pseudobrasiliensis*.[9, 99] Amoxicillin-clavulanate has been effective in individual patients when used as sequential therapy or in combination with other agents[71, 130, 133] and may be especially useful in the treatment of cutaneous infections caused by *N. brasiliensis*, a consistent β-lactamase producer.[134] Mutation in the β-lactamase gene of *N. brasiliensis* has resulted in relapse during therapy with amoxicillin-clavulanate.[135] In continental Europe, amoxicillin-clavulanate or imipenem combined with amikacin has been recommended, especially for infections by *N. farcinica*.[110] The use of amoxicillin-clavulanate should be guided by in vitro sensitivity data because susceptibility is variable and species dependent (see Table 244–1), demonstration of β-lactamase production is not necessarily predictive of resistance to β-lactam drugs, and species such as *N. nova* may be sensitive to ampicillin but not to amoxicillin-clavulanic acid.[82] In vitro susceptibility data should also guide the choice of alternative agents for which few clinical data are available, such as doxycycline, erythromycin, clarithromycin, ampicillin, dapsone, and fluoroquinolone drugs, some of which have been used in combination.[136–140]

The place of surgery in the management of nocardiosis depends on the site and extent of infection. In extraneural disease, indications for aspiration, drainage, or excision of abscesses are similar to those for other chronic bacterial infections. Therapeutic aspiration is generally inadequate in patients with thick-walled multiloculated abscesses, which contain little free-flowing pus, including patients with mycetomas.[141] In patients with brain abscesses, surgery should be performed when the abscesses are accessible and relatively large, the patient's condition deteriorates or lesions progress within 2 weeks of therapy, or no reduction in abscess size is seen within a month.[142] Decompression of lesions can be accomplished by stereotactic aspiration, although cure in many cases is effected only after craniotomy and total excision.[109, 142] Small abscesses can be cured by prolonged antimicrobial therapy. Because abscesses may progress in the face of appropriate therapy, all patients must be monitored frequently with cranial computed tomography or other imaging modalities.[122, 142]

Duration of Therapy and Prognosis

Clinical improvement is generally evident within 3 to 5 days[122] or, at the most, 7 to 10 days[2] after the initiation of therapy. Parenteral therapy can usually be safely changed to an oral regimen and high doses of TMP-SMX reduced after 3 to 6 weeks, depending on clinical response. Patients with extensive nocardiosis, patients with necrotic foci not amenable to surgery, or those who respond slowly may benefit from prolongation of parenteral and, subsequently, oral therapy.[8] Lack of response to initial therapy may be due to primary drug resistance, inadequate penetration of drug into sites of infection (dependent on the dose, bioavailability of oral drugs, abscess location and pathology, and patient compliance), the presence of a sequestered abscess requiring surgical drainage, and in an immunocompromised host, overwhelming nocardial infection or a coexisting or secondary opportunistic infection. In patients receiving immunosuppressive medication, therapy should generally be continued during treatment of nocardiosis to contain the underlying disease or to prevent transplant rejection. Reduction or cessation of immunosuppressive drugs may be required in patients whose *Nocardia* infection is uncontrolled and progressive despite adequate serum levels of appropriate antimicrobial drugs.

Recommendations on the duration of therapy are necessarily empirical and based primarily on reports of relapse after sulfonamide therapy of different durations.[70, 102, 104, 109, 143] In rare case reports, cure of extrapulmonary abscesses has followed short-course parenteral therapy (7 to 8 weeks) with amikacin and surgical drainage[52, 144] or with amikacin plus ceftriaxone, as in a case of cerebral nocardiosis.[145] One- to 3-month courses of therapy are curative in patients with primary cutaneous infection, including sporotrichoid nocardiosis and superficial ulcers.[74, 102] Prolonged therapy is required in patients with mycetoma.[141] Nonimmunosuppressed patients with pulmonary or systemic nocardiosis (excluding CNS involvement) should be treated for at least 6 months, and those with CNS involvement, for 12 months. These patients should be monitored for at least a year after completion of therapy to detect late relapses.[109, 143] In non–HIV-infected, immunosuppressed patients, therapy should be continued for 12 months or longer, depending on intercurrent increases in immunosuppression, for example, for episodes of graft rejection. For patients who must be maintained with steroid or cytotoxic therapy, consideration should be given to indefinite low-dose prophylaxis after completion of the primary course of therapy.[104] The appropriate maintenance regimen has not been defined, but daily low-dose therapy seems appropriate because TMP-SMX administered twice or three times weekly did not prevent the development of nocardiosis after bone marrow transplantation.[123, 146] In patients with AIDS, early institution of a prolonged course of antinocardial therapy is essential because treatment of patients with late manifestations or whose *Nocardia* infection has relapsed has usually been unsuccessful.[70] In this group, low-dose maintenance therapy should be continued for life.

Primary prophylaxis directed specifically against nocardial infection is not generally necessary in patients who are immunosuppressed post-transplantation because of the low incidence of nocardiosis, especially since the introduction of cyclosporine.[130] The daily use of TMP-SMX as prophylaxis against alternative infections may prevent some cases of nocardiosis, as has been observed after renal transplantation,[147] although the overall impact of such therapy is reduced by the late occurrence of cases of nocardiosis after transplantation.[130] TMP-SMX prophylaxis has not been of proven benefit in the prevention of nocardiosis in patients with AIDS inasmuch as the overall incidence based on autopsy series is low,[2, 60] although it is notable that when nocardiosis has been reported in this group, most patients had not been receiving sulfonamide prophylaxis against other pathogens.[59, 71]

The clinical outcome of therapy for nocardiosis is dependent on the site and extent of disease and underlying host factors. Cure rates of almost 100% are found in patients with skin/soft tissue involvement, as compared with 90% in pleuropulmonary disease, 63% in disseminated infection, and 50% in brain abscess.[104] Mortality in patients with brain abscesses diagnosed antemortem approximates 31%, but it is higher (41%) in patients with multiple abscesses and in immunocompromised patients (55%).[142] In an early, large series of patients with nocardiosis, mortality was significantly increased in patients with Cushing's disease and those receiving corticosteroids or antineoplastic drugs, but it was not related to the severity of the underlying disease.[148] Although immunosuppressive therapy increases the risk of pulmonary and disseminated nocardiosis in recipients of organ transplants, it is not clear to what extent maintenance of immunosuppressive therapy during treatment of nocardiosis interferes with outcome. In fact, most patients can be cured with appropriate antimicrobial therapy even if immunosuppressive drugs are continued, provided that the diagnosis is made early and appropriate full-dose therapy is continued for an adequate period.[111, 130, 146] On the other hand, delay in diagnosis and early cessation of therapy are poor prognostic factors that in patients with AIDS have been associated with failure of subsequent therapy.[70]

In summary, the choice and dose of antimicrobial drugs and the duration of therapy depend on the site(s) and extent of infection, underlying host factors, the species of *Nocardia*, and the clinical response to initial management. Sulfonamide therapy remains the treatment of choice in patients with nocardiosis. The use of additional drugs in severely ill patients, for example, amikacin, imipenem, or ceftriaxone, may improve the prognosis, especially in an immunocompromised host. Alternative regimens are required in patients unable to tolerate or who fail therapy with sulfonamides and often in those infected by *N. otitidiscaviarum*. As primary therapy, parenteral combinations containing imipenem, amikacin, a third-generation cephalosporin, or any combination of these drugs should be considered experimental until further data are available. New macrolides, quinolone drugs, and dapsone-like drugs offer promise for the future.

REFERENCES

1. Beaman BL, Saubolle MA, Wallace RJ: *Nocardia, Rhodococcus, Streptomyces, Oerskovia*, and other aerobic actinomycetes of medical importance. In: Murray PR, Baron EJ, Pfaller MA, et al, eds. Manual of Clinical Microbiology. 6th ed. Washington, DC: ASM; 1995:379–399.
2. McNeil MM, Brown JM: The medically important aerobic actinomycetes: Epidemiology and microbiology. Clin Microbiol Rev. 1994;7:357–417.
3. Mishra SK, Gordon RE, Barnett DA: Identification of nocardiae and streptomycetes of medical importance. J Clin Microbiol. 1980;11:728–736.
4. Workman MR, Philpott-Howard J, Yates M, et al: Identification and antibiotic susceptibility of *Nocardia farcinica* and *N. nova* in the UK. J Med Microbiol. 1998;47:85–90.
5. Butler WR, Kilburn JO, Kubica GP: High-performance liquid chromatography analysis of mycolic acids as an aide in laboratory identification of *Rhodococcus* and *Nocardia* species. J Clin Microbiol. 1987;25:2126–2131.
6. Laurent F, Carlotti A, Boiron P, et al. Ribotyping: A tool for taxonomy and identification of the *Nocardia asteroides* complex species. J Clin Microbiol. 1996;34:1079–1082.
7. Steingrube VA, Brown BA, Gibson JL, et al. DNA amplification and restriction endonuclease analysis for differentiation of 12 species and taxa of *Nocardia*, including recognition of four new taxa within the *Nocardia asteroides* complex. J Clin Microbiol. 1995;33:3096–3101.
8. Lerner PI: Nocardiosis. Clin Infect Dis. 1996;22:891–905.
9. Ruimy R, Riegle P, Carlotti A, et al. *Nocardia pseudobrasiliensis* sp. nov. A new species of *Nocardia* which groups bacterial strains previously identified as *Nocardia brasiliensis* and associated with invasive diseases. Int J Syst Bacteriol. 1996;46:259–264.
10. Pier AC, Fichtner RE. Distribution of serotypes of *Nocardia asteroides* from animal, human and environmental sources. J Clin Microbiol. 1981;13:548–553.
11. Houang ET, Lovett IS, Thompson FD, et al. *Nocardia asteroides* infection—a transmissible disease. J Hosp Infect. 1980;1:31–40.
12. Sahathevan M, Harvey FA, Forbes G, et al. Epidemiology, bacteriology and control of an outbreak of *Nocardia asteroides* infection on a liver unit. J Hosp Infect. 1991;18(Suppl A):473–480.
13. Blumel J, Blumel E, Yassin AF, et al. Typing of *Nocardia farcinica* by pulsed-field electrophoresis reveals an endemic strain as source of hospital infections. J Clin Microbiol. 1998;36:118–122.
14. Provost F, Laurent F, Camacho Uzcategui LR, et al. Molecular study of persistence of *Nocardia asteroides* and *Nocardia otitidis-caviarum* strains in patients with long-term nocardiosis. J Clin Microbiol. 1997;35:1157–1160.
15. Robby SJ, Vickery AL. Tinctorial and morphologic properties distinguishing actinomycosis and nocardiosis. N Engl J Med. 1970;282:593–596.
16. Beaman L, Beaman BL. *Nocardia* species: Host-parasite relationships. Clin Microbiol Rev. 1994;7:213–264.
17. Beaman BL, Gershwin ME, Ahmed A, et al. Response of CBA/N × DBA2/F1 mice to *Nocardia asteroides*. Infect Immun. 1982;35:111–116.
18. Deem RL, Doughty FA, Beaman BL. Immunologically specific direct T lymphocyte–mediated killing of *Nocardia asteroides*. J Immunol. 1983;130:2401–2406.
19. Beaman BL, Goldstein E, Gershwin ME, et al. Lung response of congenitally athymic (nude), heterozygous, and Swiss Webster mice to aerogenic and intranasal infection by *Nocardia asteroides*. Infect Immun. 1978;22:867–877.
20. Deem RL, Beaman BL, Gershwin ME. Adoptive transfer of immunity to *Nocardia asteroides* in nude mice. Infect Immun. 1982;38:914–920.
21. Beaman BL. Structural and biochemical alterations of *Nocardia asteroides* cell walls during its growth cycle. J Bacteriol. 1975;123:1235–1253.
22. Beaman BL, Moring SE. Relationship among cell wall composition, stage of growth, and virulence of *Nocardia asteroides* GUH-2. Infect Immun. 1988;56:557–563.
23. Beaman BL, Serrano JA, Serrano AA. Comparative ultrastructure within the *Nocardia*. Zentralbl Bakteriol Mikrobiol Hyg. 1977;1(Suppl 6):201–220.
24. Goren MB. Mycobacterial fatty acid esters of sugars and sulfosugars. In: Kates M, ed. Glycolipids, Phospholipids, and Sulfoglycolipids, v. 6. Lipid Research. New York: Plenum; 1990:363–461.
25. Spargo BJ, Crowe LM, Ioneda T, et al. Cord factor (trehalose 6,6′-dimycolate) inhibits fusion between phospholipid vesicles. Proc Natl Acad Sci U S A. 1991;88:737–740.
26. Tamplin ML, McClung NM. Quantitative studies of the relationship between trehalose lipids and virulence of *Nocardia asteroides* isolates. In: Ortiz-Ortiz L, Bojalil LF, Yakeloff V, eds. Biological, Biochemical and Biomedical Aspects of Actinomycetes. Orlando, Fla: Academic; 1984:251–258.
27. Beaman BL. An ultrastructural analysis of *Nocardia* during experimental infection in mice. Infect Immun. 1993;8:828–840.
28. Beaman BL. Possible mechanisms of nocardial pathogenesis. In: Goodfellow M, Brownell GH, Serrano JA, eds. Biology of the Nocardiae. London: Academy, 1976:386–417.
29. Silva CL, Tinciani I, Brandao-Filho SL, et al. Mouse cachexia induced by trehalose dimycolate from *Nocardia asteroides*. J Gen Microbiol. 1988;134:1629–1633.
30. Baylot D, Berthier S, Lucht F, et al. Cerebral nocardiosis cured by repeated stereotaxic punctures and antibiotic therapy. Presse Med. 1991;20:744–746.
31. Beaman BL. Nocardiosis: Role of the cell wall deficient state of *Nocardia*. In: Domingue GJ, ed. Cell Wall Defective Bacteria: Basic Principles and Clinical Significance. Reading, Mass: Addison-Wesley; 1990:231–255.
32. Beaman BL, Scates SM. Role of L-forms of *Nocardia caviae* in the development of chronic mycetomas in normal and immunodeficient murine models. Infect Immun. 1981;33:893–907.
33. Buchanan AM, Beaman BL, Pedersen NC, et al. *Nocardia asteroides* recovery from a dog with steroid- and antibiotic-unresponsive idiopathic polyarthritis. J Clin Microbiol. 1983;18:702–708.
34. Bourgeois L, Beaman BL. In vitro sphaeroplast and L-form induction within the pathogenic nocardiae. J Bacteriol. 1976;127:584–594.
35. Beaman BL. In vitro response of rabbit alveolar macrophages to infection with *Nocardia asteroides*. Infect Immun. 1977;15:925–937.
36. Beaman BL. The cell wall as a determinant of pathogenicity in *Nocardia*: The role of L-forms in pathogenesis. In: Ortiz-Ortiz L, Bojalil LF, Yakeloff V, eds. Biological, Biochemical and Biomedical Aspects of Actinomycetes. Orlando, Fla: Academic; 1984:89–105.
37. Beaman BL. Differential binding of *Nocardia asteroides* in the murine lung and

brain suggest multiple ligands on the nocardial surface. Infect Immun. 1996;64:4859–4862.
38. Filice GA, Beaman BL, Krick JA, et al. Effects of human neutrophils and monocytes on *Nocardia asteroides*: Failure of killing despite occurrence of the oxidative metabolic burst. J Infect Dis. 1980;142:432–438.
39. Beaman BL. Structural and biochemical alterations of *Nocardia asteroides* cell walls during its growth cycle. J Bacteriol. 1975;123:1235–1253.
40. Davis-Scibienski C, Beaman BL. Interaction of *Nocardia asteroides* with rabbit alveolar macrophages: Association of virulence, viability, ultrastructural damage, and phagosome-lysosome fusion. Infect Immun. 1980;28:610–619.
41. Beaman BL, Smathers M. Interaction of *Nocardia asteroides* with cultured rabbit alveolar macrophages. Infect Immun. 1976;13:1126–1131.
42. Bourgeois L, Beaman BL. Probable L-forms of *Nocardia asteroides* induced in cultured mouse peritoneal macrophages. Infect Immun. 1974;9:576–590.
43. Black CM, Beaman BL, Donovan RM, et al. Effect of virulent and less virulent strains of *Nocardia asteroides* on acid-phosphatase activity in alveolar and peritoneal macrophages maintained in vitro. J Infect Dis. 1983;148:117–124.
44. Black CM, Beaman BL, Donovan RM, et al. Intracellular acid phosphatase content and the ability of different macrophage populations to kill *Nocardia asteroides*. Infect Immun. 1985;47:375–383.
45. Beaman BL, Scates SM, Moring SE, et al. Purification and properties of a unique superoxide dismutase from *Nocardia asteroides*. J Biol Chem. 1983;258:91–96.
46. Kusunose E, Ichihara K, Noda Y, et al. Superoxide dismutase from *Mycobacterium tuberculosis*. J Biochem. 1976;80:1343–1352.
47. Beaman L, Beaman BL. Monoclonal antibodies demonstrate that superoxide dismutase contributes to protection of *Nocardia asteroides* within the intact host. Infect Immun. 1990;58:3122–3128.
48. Beaman BL, Ogata SA. Ultrastructural analysis of attachment to and penetration of capillaries in the murine pons, mid-brain, thalamus, and hypothalamus by *Nocardia asteroides*. Infect Immun. 1993;61:955–965.
49. Beaman L, Beaman BL. Differences in the interactions of *Nocardia asteroides* with macrophage, endothelial and astrocytoma cell lines. Infect Immun. 1994;62:1787–1798.
50. Kohbata S, Beaman BL. L-Dopa responsive movement disorder caused by *Nocardia asteroides* localized in the brains of mice. Infect Immun. 1991;59:181–191.
51. Hubble JP, Cao T, Kjelstrom JA, et al. *Nocardia* species as an aetiologic agent in Parkinson's disease: Serological testing in a case-control study. J Clin Microbiol. 1995;33:2768–2769.
52. Schiff TA, McNeil MM, Brown JM. Cutaneous *Nocardia farcinica* infection in an immunocompromised patient: Case report and review. Clin Infect Dis. 1993;16:756–760.
53. McNeil MM, Brown JM, Georghiou PR, et al. Infections due to *Nocardia transvalensis*: Clinical spectrum and antimicrobial therapy. Clin Infect Dis. 1992;15:453–463.
54. Forbes GM, Harvey FAH, Philpott-Howard J, et al. Nocardiosis in liver transplantation: Variation in presentation, diagnosis and therapy. J Infect. 1990;20:11–19.
55. Farina C, Boiron P, Goglio A, et al. Human nocardiosis in northern Italy from 1982 to 1992. Northern Italy Collaborative Group on Nocardiosis. Scand J Infect Dis. 1995;27:23–27.
56. Boiron P, Provost F, Chevrier G, et al. Review of nocardial infections in France 1987 to 1990. Eur J Clin Microbiol Infect Dis. 1992;11:709–714.
57. Exmelin L, Malbruny B, Vergnaud M, et al. Molecular study of nosocomial nocardiosis outbreak involving heart transplant recipients. J Clin Microbiol. 1996;34:1014–1016.
58. Wilson JP, Turner HR, Kirchner KA, et al. Nocardial infections in renal transplant recipients. Medicine (Baltimore). 1989;68:38–57.
59. Kim J, Minamoto GY, Grieco MH. Nocardial infection as a complication of AIDS: Report of six cases and review. Rev Infect Dis. 1991;13:624–629.
60. Niedt GW, Schinella RA. Acquired immunodeficiency syndrome. Arch Pathol Lab Med. 1985;109:727–734.
61. Mahgoub ES. Agents of mycetoma. In Mandell GL, Bennett JE, Dolin R, eds. Mandell, Douglas and Bennett's Principles and Practice of Infectious Diseases, v. 2. 4th ed. New York: Churchill Livingstone; 1995:2327–2330.
62. Casty FE, Wencel M. Endobronchial nocardiosis. Eur Respir J. 1994;7:1903–1905.
63. Pickles RW, Malcolm JA, Sutherland DC. Endobronchial nocardiosis in a patient with AIDS. Med J Aust. 1994;161:498–499.
64. Balikian JP, Herman PG, Kopit S. Pulmonary nocardiosis. Radiology. 1978;126:145–169.
65. Curry WA. Human nocardiosis: A clinical review with selected case reports. Arch Intern Med. 1980;140:818–826.
66. Kramer MR, Uttamchandani RB. The radiographic appearance of pulmonary nocardiosis associated with AIDS. Chest. 1990;98:382–385.
67. Neu HC, Silva M, Hazen E, et al. Necrotizing nocardial pneumonitis. Ann Intern Med. 1967;66:274–284.
68. Krick JA, Stinson EB, Remington JS. *Nocardia* infection in heart transplant patients. Ann Intern Med. 1975;82:18–26.
69. Javaly K, Horowitz HW, Wormser GP. Nocardiosis in patients with human immunodeficiency virus infection: Report of two cases and review of the literature. Medicine (Baltimore). 1992;71:128–138.
70. Gallant JE, Ko AH. Cavitary pulmonary lesions in patients infected with human immunodeficiency virus. Clin Infect Dis. 1996;22:671–682.
71. Lucas SB, Hounnou A, Peacock C, et al. Nocardiosis in HIV-positive patients: An autopsy study in West Africa. Tuber Lung Dis. 1994;75:301–307.
72. Uttamchandani RB, Daikos GL, Reyes RR, et al. Nocardiosis in 30 patients with advanced human immunodeficiency virus infection: Clinical features and outcome. Clin Infect Dis. 1994;18:348–353.
73. Schaal KP, Lee HJ. Actinomycete infections in humans—a review. Gene. 1992;115:201–211.
74. Georghiou PR, Blacklock ZM. Infection with *Nocardia* species in Queensland: A review of 102 clinical isolates. Med J Aust. 1992;156:692–697.
75. Arabi Y, Fairfax MR, Szuba MJ, et al. Adrenal insufficiency, recurrent bacteremia and disseminated abscesses caused by *Nocardia asteroides* in a patient with acquired immunodeficiency syndrome. Diagn Microbiol Infect Dis. 1996;24:47–51.
76. Ashdown LR. An improved screening technique for isolation of *Nocardia* species from sputum specimens. Pathology. 1990;22:157–161.
77. Shawar RM, Moore DG, La Rocco MT. Cultivation of *Nocardia* spp. on chemically defined media for selective recovery of isolates from clinical specimens. J Clin Microbiol. 1990;28:508–512.
78. Murray PR, Heeren RA, Niles AC. Effect of decontamination procedures on recovery of *Nocardia* spp. J Clin Microbiol. 1987;25:2010–2011.
79. Singh M, Sandha RS, Randhawa HS. Comparison of paraffin baiting and conventional culture techniques for isolation of *Nocardia asteroides* from sputum. J Clin Microbiol. 1987;25:176–177.
80. Vickers RM, Rihs JD, Yu VL. Clinical demonstration of isolation of *Nocardia asteroides* on buffered charcoal-yeast-extract media. J Clin Microbiol. 1992;30:227–228.
81. Wallace RJ, Tsukamura M, Brown BA, et al. Cefotaxime resistant *Nocardia asteroides* strains are isolates of the controversial species *Nocardia farcinica*. J Clin Microbiol. 1990;28:2726–2732.
82. Wallace RJ, Brown BA, Tsukamura M, et al. Clinical and laboratory features of *Nocardia nova*. J Clin Microbiol. 1991;29:2407–2411.
83. Biehle JR, Cavalieri SJ, Felland T, et al. Novel method for rapid identification of *Nocardia* species by detection of preformed enzymes. J Clin Microbiol. 1996;34:103–107.
84. Muir DB, Pritchard RC. Use of the BioMerieux ID 32C Yeast Identification System for identification of aerobic actinomycetes of medical importance. J Clin Microbiol. 1997;35:3240–3243.
85. McNeil MM, Ray S, Kozarsky PE, et al. *Nocardia farcinica* pneumonia in a previously healthy woman: Species characterization with use of a digoxigenin-labelled cDNA probe. Clin Infect Dis. 1997;25:933–934.
86. Wilson RW, Steingrube VA, Brown BA, et al. Clinical application of PCR–restriction enzyme pattern analysis for rapid identification of aerobic actinomycete isolates. J Clin Microbiol. 1998;36:148–152.
87. Kjelstrom JA, Beaman BL: Development of a serological panel for the recognition of nocardial infections in a murine model. Diagn Microbiol Infect Dis. 1993;16:291–301.
88. Saubolle MA: In vitro susceptibility testing of clinical isolates of *Nocardia*. Clin Microbiol Newslett. 1993;15:169–172.
89. Biehle JR, Cavalieri SJ, Saubolle MA, et al. Comparative evaluation of the E test for susceptibility testing of *Nocardia* species. Diagn Microbiol Infect Dis. 1994;19:101–110.
90. Ambaye A, Kohner PC, Wollan PC, et al. Comparison of agar dilution, broth microdilution, disk diffusion, E-test and BACTEC radiometric methods for antimicrobial susceptibility testing of clinical isolates of the *Nocardia asteroides* complex. J Clin Microbiol. 1997;35:847–852.
91. McNeil MM, Brown JM, Hutwagner LC, et al. Evaluation of therapy for *Nocardia asteroides* complex infections. Infect Dis Clin Pract. 1995;4:287–292.
92. Berkey P, Moore D, Rolston K. In vitro susceptibilities of *Nocardia* species to newer antimicrobial agents. Antimicrob Agents Chemother. 1988;32:1078–1079.
93. Boiron P, Provost F. In-vitro susceptibility testing of *Nocardia* spp. and its taxonomic implication. J Antimicrob Chemother. 1988;22:623–629.
94. Wilson RW, Steingrube VA, Brown BA, et al. Recognition of a *Nocardia transvalensis* complex by resistance to aminoglycosides, including amikacin, and PCR–restriction fragment length polymorphism analysis. J Clin Microbiol. 1997;35:2235–2242.
95. Yazawa K, Mikami Y, Ohashi S, et al. In-vitro activity of new carbapenem antibiotics: Comparative studies with meropenem, L-627 and imipenem against pathogenic *Nocardia* spp. J Antimicrob Chemother. 1992;29:169–172.
96. Khardori N, Shawar R, Gupta R, et al. In vitro antimicrobial susceptibilities of *Nocardia* species. Antimicrob Agents Chemother. 1993;37:882–884.
97. Clark NM, Braun DK, Pasternak A, et al. Primary cutaneous *Nocardia otitidiscaviarum* infection: Case report and review. Clin Infect Dis. 1995;20:1266–1270.
98. Gombert ME. Susceptibility of *Nocardia asteroides* to various antibiotics, including newer beta-lactams, trimethoprim-sulfamethoxazole, amikacin and *N*-formimidoyl thienamycin. Antimicrob Agents Chemother. 1982;21:1011–1012.
99. Wallace RJ Jr, Steele LC, Sumter G, et al. Antimicrobial susceptibility patterns of *Nocardia asteroides*. Antimicrob Agents Chemother. 1988;32:1776–1779.
100. Wallace RJ Jr, Brown BA, Blacklock Z, et al. New *Nocardia* taxon among isolates of *Nocardia brasiliensis* associated with invasive disease. J Clin Microbiol. 1995;33:1528–1533.
101. National Committee for Clinical Laboratory Standards. Methods for dilution. In: NCCLS Antimicrobial Susceptibility Tests for Bacteria that Grow Aerobically. 4th ed. Wayne, Pa, NCCLS; 1997.
102. Wallace RJ Jr, Septimus EJ, Williams TW Jr, et al. Use of trimethoprim-sulfamethoxazole for treatment of infections due to *Nocardia*. Rev Infect Dis. 1982;4:315–325.
103. Smego RA Jr, Gallis HA. The clinical spectrum of *Nocardia brasiliensis* infection in the United States. Rev Infect Dis. 1984;6:164–180.

104. Smego RA Jr, Moeller MB, Gallis HA. Trimethoprim-sulfamethoxazole therapy for *Nocardia* infections. Arch Intern Med. 1983;143:711–718.
105. Beaumont RJ. Trimethoprim as a possible therapy for nocardiosis and melioidosis. Med J Aust. 1971;21:1123–1127.
106. Bennett JE, Jennings AE. Factors influencing susceptibility of *Nocardia* species to trimethoprim-sulfamethoxazole. Antimicrob Agents Chemother. 1978;13:624–627.
107. Maderazo EG, Quintiliani R. Treatment of nocardial infection with trimethoprim and sulfamethoxazole. Am J Med. 1974;57:671–675.
108. Smith PW, Steinkraus GE, Henricks BW, et al. CNS nocardiosis. Response to sulfamethoxazole-trimethoprim. Arch Neurol. 1980;37:729–730.
109. Byrne E, Brophy BP, Perrett LV. *Nocardia* cerebral abscess: New concepts in diagnosis, management, and prognosis. J Neurol Neurosurg Psychiatry 1979;42:1038–1045.
110. Beaman BL, Boiron P, Beaman L, et al. *Nocardia* and nocardiosis. J Med Vet Mycol. 1992;30(Suppl 1):S317–S331.
111. Simpson GL, Stinson EB, Egger MJ, et al. Nocardial infections in the immunocompromised host: A detailed study in a defined population. Rev Infect Dis. 1981;3:492–507.
112. Gordin FM, Simon GL, Wofsy CB. Adverse reactions to trimethoprim-sulfamethoxazole in patients with the acquired immunodeficiency syndrome. Ann Intern Med 1984;100:495–499.
113. Maclean S, Iwamoto GK, Richerson HB, et al. Trimethoprim-sulfamethoxazole desensitization in the acquired immunodeficiency syndrome (Letter). Ann Intern Med. 1987;106:335.
114. Bradley PP, Warden GD, Maxwell JG, et al. Neutropenia and thrombocytopenia in renal allograft recipients treated with trimethoprim-sulfamethoxazole. Ann Intern Med. 1980;93:560–562.
115. Sands M, Brown RB. Interactions of cyclosporine with antimicrobial agents. Rev Infect Dis. 1989;11:691–697.
116. Gombert ME, Aulicino TM, duBouchet L, et al. Therapy of experimental cerebral nocardiosis with imipenem, trimethoprim-sulfamethoxazole, and minocycline. Antimicrob Agents Chemother. 1986;30:270–273.
117. Gombert M, Berkowitz L, Aulicino T, et al. Therapy of pulmonary nocardiosis in immunocompromised mice. Antimicrob Agents Chemother. 1990;34:1766–1768.
118. Threlkeld SC, Hooper DC. Update on management of patients with *Nocardia* infection. Curr Clin Top Infect Dis. 1997;17:1–23.
119. Goldstein FW, Hautefort B, Acar JF. Amikacin containing regimens for treatment of nocardiosis in immunocompromised patients. Eur J Clin Microbiol Infect Dis. 1987;6:198–200.
120. Gombert ME, Aulicino TM. Synergism of imipenem and amikacin in combination with other antibiotics against *Nocardia asteroides*. Antimicrob Agents Chemother. 1983;24:810–811.
121. Gombert ME, duBouchet L, Aulicino TM, et al. Antimicrobial synergism in the therapy of experimental cerebral nocardiosis. J Antimicrob Chemother. 1989;23:39–43.
122. Filice GA, Simpson GL. Management of *Nocardia* infections. Curr Clin Top Infect Dis. 1984;5:49–64.
123. Choucino C, Goodman SA, Greer JP, et al. Nocardial infections in bone marrow transplant recipients. Clin Infect Dis. 1996;23:1012–1019.
124. Menendez R, Cordero PJ, Santos M, et al. Pulmonary infection with *Nocardia* species: A report of 10 cases and review. Eur Respir J. 1997;10:1542–1546.
125. Wiseman LR, Wagstaff AJ, Brogden RN, et al. Meropenem. A review of its antibacterial activity, pharmacokinetic properties and clinical efficacy. Drugs. 1995;50:73–101.
126. Bach MC, Monaco AP, Finland M. Pulmonary nocardiosis. Therapy with minocycline and with erythromycin plus ampicillin. JAMA. 1973;224:1378–1381.
127. Ochiae T, Ameniya H, Watanabe K, et al. Successful treatment of *Nocardia asteroides* infection with minocycline in kidney transplant recipients. Jpn J Surg. 1978;8:138–144.
128. Wren MV, Savage AM, Alford RD. Apparent cure of intracranial *Nocardia asteroides* infection by minocycline. Arch Intern Med. 1979;139:249–250.
129. Bross JE, Gordon G. Nocardial meningitis: Case reports and review. Rev Infect Dis. 1991;13:160–165.
130. Arduino RC, Johnson PC, Miranda AG. Nocardiosis in renal transplant recipients undergoing immunosuppression with cyclosporine. Clin Infect Dis. 1993;16:505–512.
131. Norden CW, Ruben FL, Selker R. Nonsurgical treatment of cerebral nocardiosis. Arch Neurol. 1983;40:594–595.
132. Hall WA, Martinez AJ, Dummer JS, et al. Nocardial brain abscess: Diagnostic and therapeutic use of stereotactic aspiration. Surg Neurol. 1987;28:114–118.
133. Wortman PD. Treatment of a *Nocardia brasiliensis* mycetoma with sulfamethoxazole and trimethroprim, amikacin and amoxicillin and clavulanate. Arch Dermatol. 1993;129:564–567.
134. Wallace RJ, Nash DR, Johnson WK, et al. β-lactam resistance in *Nocardia brasiliensis* is mediated by β-lactamase and reversed in the presence of clavulanic acid. J Infect Dis. 1987;156:959–966.
135. Steingrube VA, Wallace RJ Jr, Brown BA, et al. Acquired resistance of *Nocardia brasiliensis* to clavulanic acid related to a change in beta-lactamase following therapy with amoxicillin–clavulanic acid. Antimicrob Agents Chemother. 1991;35:254–258.
136. Hadley MN, Spetzler RF, Martin NA, et al. Middle cerebral artery aneurysm due to *Nocardia asteroides*: Case report of aneurysm excision and extracranial-intracranial bypass. Neurosurgery. 1988;22:923–928.
137. Bath PMW, Pettingale KW, Wade J. Treatment of multiple subcutaneous *Nocardia asteroides* abscesses with ciprofloxacin and doxycycline. Postgrad Med J. 1989;65:190–191.
138. Yew W, Wong P, Kwan S, et al. Two cases of *Nocardia asteroides* sternotomy infection treated with ofloxacin and a review of other active antimicrobial agents. J Infect. 1991;23:297–302.
139. Thaler F, Gotainer B, Teodori G, et al. Mediastinitis due to *Nocardia asteroides* after cardiac transplantation. Intensive Care Med. 1992;18:127–128.
140. Tokumoto JIN, Jacobs RA. Case report: *Nocardia* osteomyelitis. Am J Med Sci. 1994;307:428–433.
141. Lopes CF. Trimethoprim-sulfamethoxazole in the treatment of actinomycotic mycetoma by *Nocardia brasiliensis*. Folha Med 1996;73:89–92.
142. Mamelak AN, Obana WG, Flaherty JF, et al. Nocardial brain abscess: Treatment and factors influencing outcome. Neurosurgery. 1994;35:622–631.
143. Geiseler PJ, Andersen BR. Results of therapy in systemic nocardiosis. Am J Med Sci. 1979;278:188–194.
144. Meier B, Metzger U, Müller F, et al. Successful treatment of a pancreatic *Nocardia asteroides* abscess with amikacin and surgical drainage. J Clin Microbiol. 1986;29:150–151.
145. Garlando F, Bodmer T, Lee C, et al. Successful treatment of disseminated nocardiosis complicated by cerebral abscess with ceftriaxone and amikacin: Case report. Clin Infect Dis. 1992;15:1039–1040.
146. van Burik JA, Hackman RC, Nadeem SQ, et al. Nocardiosis after bone marrow transplantation: A retrospective study. Clin Infect Dis. 1997;24:1154–1160.
147. Peterson PK, Ferguson R, Fryd DS, et al. Infectious diseases in hospitalized renal transplant recipients: A prospective study of a complex and evolving problem. Medicine (Baltimore). 1982;61:360–372.
148. Presant CA, Wiernik PH, Serpick AA. Factors affecting survival in nocardiosis. Am Rev Respir Dis. 1973;108:1444–1448.

Chapter 245

Agents of Actinomycosis

THOMAS A. RUSSO

Actinomycosis is an indolent, slowly progressive infection caused by anaerobic or microaerophilic bacteria that normally colonize the mouth, colon, and vagina. Virtually any site in the body can be affected. When the organisms invade tissue, they form tiny but visible clumps called grains. Although grains are a defining characteristic of actinomycosis, grains are also found in mycetoma (Chapter 252) and botryomycosis, a chronic bacterial infection to be discussed later. Lesions of actinomycosis are purulent foci surrounded by dense fibrosis. Classic features include extension to contiguous structures by crossing natural anatomic boundaries and the formation of fistulas and sinus tracts. This infection is commonly confused with a neoplasm. Although actinomycosis was common in the preantibiotic era, today its incidence is diminished, and as a result, so is its timely consideration and recognition.[1] It has been called "the most misdiagnosed disease," and there is "no disease which is so often missed by experienced clinicians." [2] The clinical manifestations of this disease are myriad, and it remains a diagnostic challenge. An awareness of the full spectrum of disease manifestations will expedite diagnosis and treatment and minimize the unnecessary surgical interventions and morbidity and mortality that all too often occur with actinomycosis.

ETIOLOGIC AGENTS

Actinomycosis is most commonly caused by the gram-positive, higher bacterium *Actinomyces israelii*. *Actinomyces naeslundii*,[3–5] *Actinomyces odontolyticus*,[6–9] *Actinomyces viscosus*,[10, 11] *Actinomyces meyeri*,[12] and *Propionibacterium propionicum* (formerly *Arachnia propionica*)[13–15] are established but less common causes of disease.

Recent advances in microbiologic taxonomy have resulted in an increasing number of bacterial species isolated from human clinical specimens being classified as *Actinomyces*. Although their role in disease has not always been defined, *Actinomyces europaeus* (abscess),[16] *Arcanobacterium (Actinomyces) pyogenes* (blood, abscess, wound, endocarditis, otitis),[17, 18] *Arcanobacterium (Actinomyces) bernardiae* (urine, blood, abscess),[19, 20] *Actinomyces neuii* (abscess, urine, blood),[21] *Actinomyces radingae, Actinomyces graevenitzii, and Actinomyces turicensis*[22] appear to be infrequent and often opportunistic human pathogens. However, the nature of infections described to date do not clearly establish these agents as causes of the typical syndrome of actinomycosis. Although *Eubacterium* species have been reported to cause pelvic disease in association with intrauterine contraceptive devices (IUCDs), as well as "lumpy jaw," [23, 24] additional reports would be desirable to confirm this genus as an agent of actinomycosis.

Despite some conflicting reports,[11, 25, 26] the bulk of evidence supports the concept that most, if not all, actinomycotic infections are polymicrobial in nature.[1, 27–29] Although monomicrobic infections undoubtedly occur, inadequate bacteriologic evaluation or diagnoses made on clinical or pathologic grounds will result in a failure to identify concomitant bacterial species. *Actinobacillus actinomycetemcomitans, Eikenella corrodens, Fusobacterium, Bacteroides, Capnocytophaga, Staphylococcus, Streptococcus,* and Enterobacteriaceae have been commonly isolated in various combinations depending on the site of the infection. The contribution of these additional isolates to the pathogenesis of actinomycosis is difficult to assess; however, it seems reasonable to consider them as being potential copathogens when designing therapeutic regimens.

EPIDEMIOLOGY

In 1890, Bostroem reported culturing an aerobic organism responsible for actinomycosis from grain, grasses, and soil, which resulted in the misconception that actinomycosis is an exogenous infection and that chewing grass or straw or having an occupation such as farming was a risk factor. This myth, although long in dying, has been dispelled. The agents of actinomycosis have been clearly established as members of the endogenous flora of mucous membranes. Although it is infrequently isolated from children younger than 3 years, *A. israelii* is always found in the oral cavity when appropriate anaerobic methodology is used.[25, 29] It is also often cultured from the gastrointestinal tract, bronchi, and female genital tract.[30] *A. israelii* has never been cultured from nature, and no person-to-person transmission has ever been documented.[31]

Infection may occur in individuals of all ages. The peak incidence of actinomycosis is reported to be in the mid-decades, with cases in individuals younger than 10 and older than 60 years being less frequent.[32] Nearly all series have reported males to be infected more frequently than females at an approximately 3:1 ratio.[1, 26, 29, 32–35] Plausible but unproven explanations for this discordance include poorer dental hygiene and increased oral trauma in males.[32, 36]

Studies on the occurrence of actinomycosis estimated a yearly incidence of 1:100,000 in the Netherlands and Germany in the 1960s and 1:300,000 in the Cleveland area during the 1970s, which makes this disease uncommon but not rare.[29, 32] Its frequency has undoubtedly diminished since the preantibiotic era, when this disease was not only common but more malignant in nature. Improved dental hygiene and early antimicrobial treatment of infections before the development of a characteristic actinomycotic syndrome are probable contributing factors. However, individuals or populations that do not have access to dental or medical care are undoubtedly at higher risk than the population at large in this country. Furthermore, many unrecognized cases, especially in the oral-cervicofacial area, probably occur and are successfully treated empirically.

PATHOGENESIS AND PATHOLOGY

A pivotal step in the pathogenesis of actinomycosis is disruption of the mucosal barrier. Oral and cervicofacial disease is frequently associated with dental procedures, trauma, and oral surgery. Likewise, pulmonary infections often arise in the setting of possible aspiration, and abdominal infection is usually preceded by conditions that result in loss of mucosal integrity such as gastrointestinal surgery, diverticulitis, appendicitis, or foreign bodies such as fish bones.[1, 32, 33] Recognition of factors that enable bacterial entry into deep tissues, however, may be absent.[26] The lack of such a history should not prevent consideration of this disease when the clinical circumstance is appropriate.

Other bacterial species concomitantly present have been designated "companion microbes." They may serve as copathogens by aiding in the inhibition of host defenses or by reducing oxygen tension. The difficulty in establishing an animal model of infection with *Actinomyces* alone and enhancement of infection by coinoculation of *E. corrodens* supports the concept that additional organisms are important for the initiation of infection.[37] Furthermore, coaggregation of *Actinomyces* and *Streptococcus* spp. occurs and results in increased resistance to phagocytosis and killing.[38]

An acute inflammatory phase manifested by a painful, cellulitic reaction is occasionally observed with oral-cervicofacial disease or with soft tissue infection elsewhere in the body. The chronic phase of this disease is more often seen.[26, 39] Classic disease is characterized by a densely fibrotic lesion that undergoes slow, contiguous spread and ignores tissue planes. However, no studies have addressed the factor (bacterial and/or host?) responsible for the unique pathogenesis of this disease. Lesions usually appear as either single or multiple indurated swellings. As the lesion matures, it becomes soft and fluctuant and suppurates centrally. The fibrous walls of the mass have been described as "wooden" and, in the absence of suppuration, have frequently been confused with neoplasms. This extensive fibrosis, which is one of the hallmarks of actinomycosis, may be minimal, especially in pulmonary and central nervous system lesions. Given time, sinus tracts will often extend from the abscess to either the skin or the adjacent organs or bone, depending on the location of the lesion. Sinus tracts can close spontaneously and then re-form. Overlying skin may assume a red to bluish hue. Hematogenous dissemination can occur from these local sites and occasionally be fulminant, although in the antibiotic era this clinical syndrome has become rare.[40]

Microscopically, lesions have an outer zone of granulation consisting of collagen fibers and fibroblasts. A central purulent loculation contains neutrophils surrounding the sulfur granules present. Granules are conglomerations of organisms and are virtually diagnostic of this disease. One to six granules may be present per loculation, and they range from microscopic to macroscopic in size (see "Diagnosis"). As many as 50 loculations may be present per lesion, and these loculations are separated by granulation tissue or foamy macrophages and may undergo coalescence. Lymphocytes and plasma cells are usually present, and eosinophils were seen in 15% of abscesses. Multinucleated giant cells were occasionally seen, primarily in pulmonary lesions, but they have also been described in disease elsewhere.[26] Suppuration is a constant feature of active disease but may not be present in all areas of the lesion.

The association of pelvic actinomycosis with IUCDs suggests that at least this foreign body in this setting contributes to pathogenesis. Associations with actinomycosis and foreign material elsewhere are less strong. Several reports describe periapical actinomycosis in conjunction with root fillings,[41] mandibular osteomyelitis associated with wire used in the treatment of a fracture,[33, 42] and infection of the tongue in the presence of a foreign body.[43] *Actinomyces* infection of prosthetic joints through presumed hematogenous spread is rare but has been reported.[44–46]

Cases of actinomycosis have been described in the setting of steroid use,[47] acute lymphocytic leukemia during chemotherapy,[48] lung and renal transplantation,[9, 49] and human immunodeficiency virus infection.[50–57] Ulcerative mucosal lesions (herpes simplex virus, cytomegalovirus, chemotherapy) and abnormalities in host defenses probably facilitated the development of actinomycosis in these cases;

however, it remains unclear which arm or arms of the host defense are critical in preventing or controlling this infection and the degree to which (if at all) the incidence of infection is increased in these settings.

CLINICAL MANIFESTATIONS

Oral-Cervicofacial Disease

Actinomycosis most commonly occurs and is best recognized in the oral-cervicofacial location. Its frequency varies in different series and ranges from a low of 11%[39] to a high of 97.7%[29] with a mean of 55%.[32] Oral-cervicofacial disease probably accounts for even a greater majority because it is underrepresented in autopsy and referral center series.

Oral-cervicofacial disease can be manifested as a soft tissue swelling, an abscess, or a mass lesion.[32, 33, 58] The diagnosis of actinomycosis not only should be considered in the classic setting of a painless mass at the angle of the jaw[47] (Fig. 245–1) but also should be included in the differential diagnosis of any mass lesion in the head and neck region. When lesions appear to be solid, neoplasm is the usual diagnostic consideration.[59] Soft tissue infections of the head and neck may also be manifested as chronic, recurring abscesses. The common scenario of temporary improvement with a short course of empirical antibiotic therapy, followed by relapse, should always arouse suspicion of actinomycosis, regardless of the location.[34] The disease spreads to adjacent structures without regard for normal tissue planes. Lymphatic spread and associated lymphadenopathy are uncommon. Extension to any contiguous structure may occur, including the carotid artery, cranium, cervical spine, trachea, or thorax.[60–62] Pain, fever, and leukocytosis are variably present.[32, 33]

Periapical actinomycosis probably occurs far more frequently than is recognized.[63] Appropriate dental intervention and antibiotic therapy usually result in cure before more extensive disease develops.

The most common location for diagnosed actinomycosis is the perimandibular region. Periapical infection or trauma is often, but not always, the inciting event. The classic lesion located at the angle of the jaw is the most frequent location (submandibular), but the cheek, submental space, retromandibular space, and temporomandibular joint may be affected.[64–69] As noted, a hallmark of this disease is the potential for unrestricted contiguous extension. Spread to the skin may result in sinus tract formation, which can spontaneously close and open elsewhere. The overlying skin often acquires a bluish or purplish red hue. Involvement of the muscles of mastication frequently occurs and results in trismus.[1, 59] Associated mandibular periostitis or osteomyelitis may also be present but is surprisingly infrequent. A lytic lesion, rarefaction with sclerosis, or sclerosis alone may be seen, and this last pattern may be confused with tumor.[70, 71]

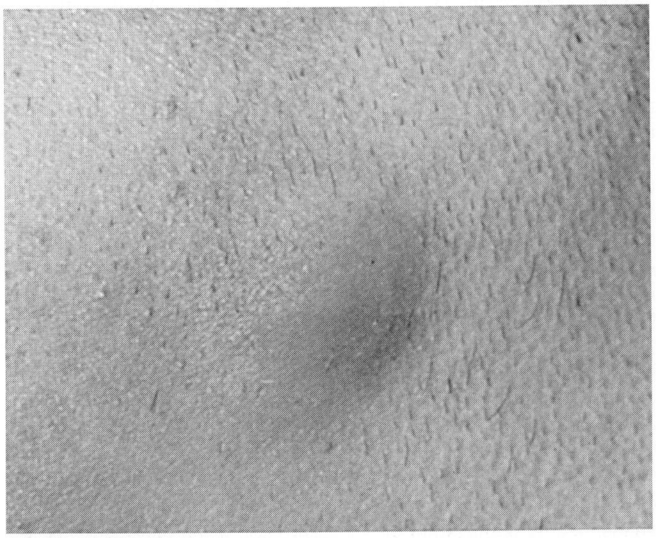

FIGURE 245–1. Submandibular actinomycotic abscess.

Maxillary disease, including osteomyelitis, occurs less frequently.[72] Associated soft tissue lesions[8] and maxillary sinus and cutaneous fistulas can occur. Maxillary and ethmoid sinusitis may be manifested as isolated disease or can be concomitant with infection of the maxilla.[73] The hard palate may also be involved and may appear as a mass lesion.[1]

Isolated lesions can also occur in the tongue,[74] vallecula,[75] nasal septum,[51] soft tissues of the head and neck,[32, 76] salivary glands,[77, 78] patent thyroglossal duct,[79] thyroid,[80] branchial cleft cyst,[81] and hypopharynx and larynx.[82] Although *Actinomyces* is frequently isolated and sulfur granules are occasionally identified in tonsillar tissue, the absence of a pathologic tissue reaction suggests that this finding represents colonization and that *Actinomyces* does not cause tonsillitis.[83]

Infection of the external ear and temporal bone may occur from the spread of facial disease. Actinomycosis is also an uncommon but important cause of primary otitis media inasmuch as untreated cases may result in fatal extension into the mastoid and then the central nervous system. It is characterized by numerous episodes of otitis media that transiently respond to conventional short-course therapy and by resistance to myringotomy. Diagnosis can be made by pathologic and microbiologic examination of infected material from the middle ear, which may appear to be a cholesteatoma.[84]

Actinomycosis can cause lacrimal canaliculitis and postoperative endophthalmitis after intraocular lens implantation.[15, 85, 86] Rarely, secondary extension into the orbit from infected maxillary or ethmoid sinuses can occur.[33]

Thoracic Disease

Thoracic involvement accounts for approximately 15% of cases of actinomycosis.[87] Aspiration of organisms from the oropharynx is the usual source of infection. Direct extension may occur from disease in either the head and neck or abdominal cavity; however, such secondary spread has become increasingly uncommon since the advent of efficacious antimicrobial therapy.[35, 87]

The most common clinical picture is an indolent, slowly progressive process that involves some combination of the pulmonary parenchyma and pleural space. Chest pain, fever, weight loss, and, less commonly, hemoptysis are prominent symptoms, and a cough, when present, is variably productive.[35, 88] No radiographic manifestations are specific, and any lobe may be involved. The usual appearance is either a mass lesion or pneumonitis with or without pleural involvement[89] (Fig. 245–2). The presence of an air bronchogram within a mass lesion (the open bronchus sign) should suggest the possibility of a non-neoplastic process such as actinomycosis.[90] Pleural thickening, effusion, or empyema is present in more than 50% of cases of thoracic actinomycosis. Rarely, actinomycosis may be seen as an isolated effusion.[91] The spontaneous drainage of an empyema through the chest wall should raise suspicion of this disease.[92] Cavitary disease may develop and is more readily detected by computed tomography (CT) scans because multiple small cavities are more common than large ones.[93] Hilar adenopathy may be present.[94] Pulmonary disease that extends across fissures or pleura, involves the mediastinum, or has contiguous bony disease should suggest actinomycosis and may be more readily appreciated by CT.[90, 93] Extension to the chest wall with the development of a soft tissue mass, a draining sinus, or both is a telltale sign when present. In the absence of this classic scenario, however, thoracic actinomycosis is almost never suspected. It is mistaken for either malignant disease,[95] with the diagnosis made by the pathologist postresection, or an empyema or pneumonitis secondary to more usual causes. Tuberculosis, nocardiosis, histoplasmosis, blastomycosis, cryptococcosis, mixed anaero-

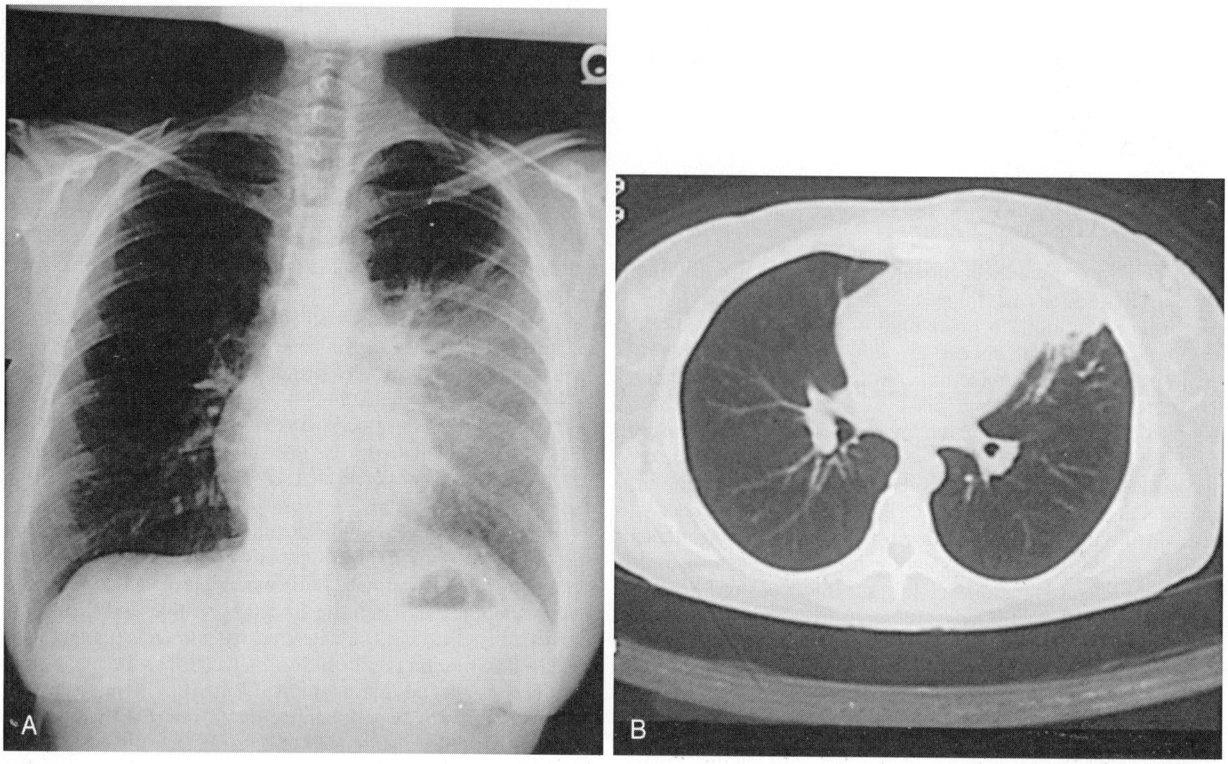

FIGURE 245–2. Chest radiograph *(A)* and computed tomography scan *(B)* showing a left lingular actinomycotic pneumonia extending to the anterior chest wall.

bic infection, bronchogenic carcinoma, lymphoma, mesothelioma, and pulmonary infarction are among the entities confused with pulmonary actinomycosis.

Mediastinal actinomycosis is an uncommon event. The structures within the anterior or posterior mediastinum and the heart can be involved alone or in combination, so a diverse array of clinical findings are possible. Infection usually results from contiguous spread from the thorax but can arise from perforation of the esophagus, from chest trauma, or from extension of head and neck or abdominal disease. Involvement of cardiac structures is noted in most mediastinal infections reported. Pericarditis is most common and may be initially asymptomatic or hemodynamically insignificant, but if it is allowed to progress, cardiac tamponade and constrictive or adhesive pericarditis will develop.[96] Less frequently, myocardial or endocardial infection occurs, either via extension from the pericardium or by initial hematogenous seeding of the endocardium.[97] Anterior mediastinal involvement may be manifested as an isolated mass or, rarely, as superior vena cava syndrome.[98, 99] Concomitant anterior chest wall infection is common, but associated sternal disease is rare.[87] Posterior mediastinal involvement may result in paraspinous muscle and soft tissue disease, esophageal fistula or encasement, vertebral body infection, or any combination of these conditions. Because of the slow progression of the disease, both vertebral body destruction and new bone formation occur and result in a mottled, saw-toothed or honeycombed appearance of bone on radiographs. The transverse processes and, with disease progression, the pedicles and spinous processes are similarly involved as the bodies, in contrast to their usual sparing in tuberculosis. The corresponding posterior ends of ribs are generally involved, and a typical wavy periostitis may be present, but unlike in tuberculosis, vertebral body collapse and disk space narrowing are not usually seen.[90] Extension to the epidural space with spinal cord compression may occur.[100] Primary esophageal disease in the setting of acquired immunodeficiency syndrome has also been described.[52, 101]

Other less common manifestations of thoracic actinomycosis include multiple pulmonary nodules,[102] miliary disease,[90, 103] and endobronchial lesions.[104] Primary breast disease either is manifested as persistent or recurring abscess(es) or it mimics malignancy.[105]

Abdominal Disease

The proportion of reported cases involving the abdomen averages 20%, with a range of 0 to 63%.[32–34] Any disease or event that allows the agents of actinomycosis to breach the gastrointestinal mucosa has the potential to be complicated by this infection. Most abdominal infections are due to this mechanism, although the inciting conditions are not always apparent. However, it is important to note that ascension of IUCD-associated actinomycosis from the female genital tract has become an increasingly recognized source of abdominal disease. Hematogenous dissemination and extension from the thorax are other portals of entry. As a consequence of the flow of peritoneal fluid or direct extension of primary disease, virtually any abdominal organ, region, or space can be involved either alone or in combination, regardless of the initial site of infection. Abdominal actinomycosis is perhaps the greatest diagnostic challenge. This infection is rarely considered before establishment of the diagnosis by the clinical laboratory or pathologist. Months to years usually pass from the time of the inciting event to clinical recognition of this indolent disease.[26] Associated symptoms are generally nonspecific, with fever, weight loss, change in bowel habits, abdominal pain, or sensation of a mass being most common. Abdominal actinomycosis is usually manifested as either an abscess or a firm to hard mass lesion that is often fixed to the underlying tissue and mistaken for tumor. Sinus tracts with drainage from either the abdominal wall or perianal region may develop[106, 107] (Fig. 245–3). CT findings usually demonstrate a mass lesion with focal areas of decreased attenuation or a thick-walled cystic mass, both of which frequently enhance with contrast. Lesions often appear invasive and suggestive of tumor, but associated lymphadenopathy is uncommon.[108, 109]

Appendicitis, especially with perforation, is the most common

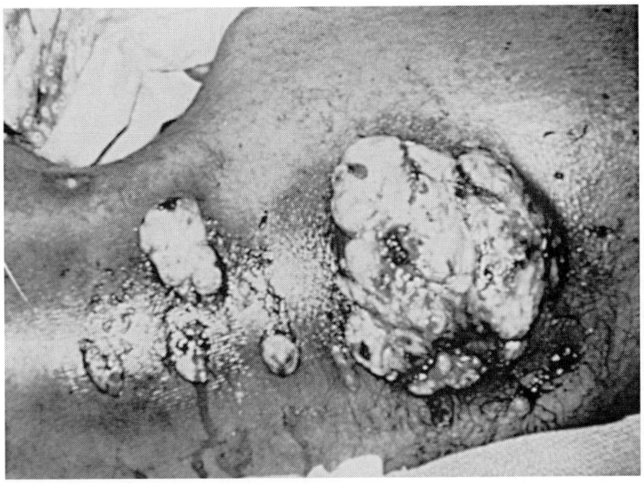

FIGURE 245–3. Multiple draining sinuses of the right flank secondary to intra-abdominal actinomycosis associated with appendicitis.

predisposing event and is associated with 65% of cases of abdominal actinomycosis.[110] As a result, the right iliac fossa is the most frequent primary site of abdominal disease, and right-sided abdominal infection is more common than left abdominal infection. It is also one of the potential inciting events for tuboovarian infection. Diverticulitis or foreign body perforation of the transverse or sigmoid colon tends to be associated with left-sided disease and accounts for 7.3% of cases, a surprisingly low percentage in view of the incidence of diverticulitis. The loss of gastric mucosal integrity from peptic ulcer disease or gastrectomy often results in subdiaphragmatic infection and is associated with 4.4% of cases. Isolated gastric disease has also been described.[111] Additional associations include antecedent bowel surgery, typhoid fever, amebic dysentery, mucosal damage due to ingestion of chicken or fish bones, trauma, and hemorrhagic pancreatitis.[33, 112] Interestingly, actinomycosis rarely develops as a consequence of Crohn's disease or ulcerative colitis.

Perirectal or perianal disease may result from extension of pelvic infection or, less commonly, from more distant disease. Primary disease occurs with either local mucosal damage or anal crypt infection. The most common finding is single or multiple perianal abscesses, sinus or fistula tract formation, or both. Infiltrating masses may develop in the buttock, posterior of the thigh, scrotum, or inguinal region.[113, 114] Disease recurring over months to years and wounds that fail to heal after drainage or fistulotomy are clues that should suggest actinomycosis, particularly in the absence of documented inflammatory bowel disease. Strictures of the rectum can also occur and cause an alteration in bowel habits that mimics primary bowel or metastatic prostatic or pelvic tumors.[115] This form of the disease is most often due to extension of pelvic disease.

Hepatic infection was present in 5% of cases of actinomycosis[26] and 19 of 122 cases of abdominal disease.[112] Spread to the liver occurs via extension from a contiguous abdominal focus or hematogenously from more distant but established abdominal or extra-abdominal foci. Hepatic involvement is common in disseminated actinomycosis. The entity of primary or isolated disease presumably occurs via hematogenous seeding from cryptic foci. Single or multiple abscesses or lesions suggesting neoplasia are the usual findings. Generally, a more indolent course is observed than that occurring with the more usual causes of pyogenic hepatic abscess, but "companion organisms" may contribute to a more acute manifestation.[116] Symptoms and laboratory findings often point to the right upper quadrant, but liver function test findings may be normal. The imaging modalities and percutaneous diagnostic techniques available at present have allowed for the diagnosis of an increasing number of cases without surgery. Uncommon findings or sequelae of hepatic actinomycosis include cholangitis, portal vein occlusion/thrombosis, cholestasis, and extension into the thorax.[117–119]

All levels of the urogenital tract can be infected by the agents of actinomycosis. Renal involvement can occur either as a result of hematogenous dissemination from a cryptic or defined focus or via direct extension within the pelvis, peritoneum, or thorax. The disease is usually manifested as pyelonephritis, a renal carbuncle, perinephric abscess, or tumor. Tuberculosis, neoplasm, or more usual bacterial agents are generally considered to be the causative agents.[120, 121] Hematuria and pyuria are often present, and *Actinomyces* can be successfully detected in the urine if appropriate stains and anaerobic cultures are performed.[122] Renal arteriography usually demonstrates a normal or diminished pattern of vascularization. Ureteric obstruction is most commonly a sequela of contiguous spread from abdominal disease, especially pelvic infection, and may lead to hydronephrosis and renal failure. Because the incidence of pelvic disease appears to be increasing, the pelvis is the most likely site for urinary tract involvement at present.[123] Infiltration, compression or encasement of the bladder, a pubic mass, or vesicocolic, ileovesicular, vesicouterine, or vesicocutaneous fistulas are usually a consequence of secondary involvement from pelvic infection[122, 124, 125] or occasionally from extension from the rectum.[126] Prostatic, testicular, and urachal involvement may also occur.[127, 128]

Actinomycosis of the gallbladder manifested as cholecystitis or a suspected neoplasm can occur but is exceedingly rare,[129] as is pancreatic involvement.[130] "Primary" actinomycosis of the omentum, abdominal wall, and retroperitoneum has been reported, but most of these cases are probably due to secondary spread from a cryptic or obscured abdominal source.[131] Isolated peritonitis associated with peritoneal dialysis[132] has also been reported.

Pelvic Disease

Actinomycotic involvement of the pelvis may occur as a consequence of an intra-abdominal inciting event such as appendicitis or rectal disease. However, the most common portal of entry is ascension from the uterus in association with the presence of any type of IUCD. This clinical syndrome was first described in conjunction with a "modern" IUCD by Henderson in 1973,[133] although cases had been previously described that were associated with pessaries, an endocervical contraceptive device, and a retained hairpin used for an abortion.[134, 135] Since that time, an increasing number of cases have been reported in the literature. Data from the Public Health Laboratory Service of England and Wales suggest that the incidence of pelvic actinomycosis is increasing and represents a growing proportion of cases of actinomycosis overall, although increased recognition may be playing a role.[123] On average, an IUCD has been in place for 8 years in pelvic actinomycosis–associated cases. Disease rarely develops when an IUCD has been in place for less than 1 year, and risk of infection probably increases with time.[136, 137] Pelvic actinomycosis has occurred months after removal of the IUCD, so a history of prior use is important when this disease is a diagnostic consideration.[138] Although the precise risk of IUCD-associated actinomycosis has not been quantified, it would appear to be small.

Findings are typically indolent, with fever, weight loss, abdominal pain, and abnormal vaginal bleeding or discharge being common symptoms. The earliest form of pelvic actinomycosis associated with IUCD use may be an endometritis. A pelvic mass or unilateral or bilateral tuboovarian abscesses represent the next stage of disease progression (Fig. 245–4).[137] Unfortunately, diagnosis is often delayed. A "frozen pelvis" mimicking malignancy or endometriosis is commonly present by the time of recognition. Disease frequently involves the ureters, bladder, or both and results in hydroureter and hydronephrosis. Rectal involvement is also common. Extension to the abdominal wall may lead to sinus tract development, and entrapment of small or large bowel may cause a fistula or bowel obstruction. Occasionally, the ovaries and fallopian tubes are spared and disease is evident only in contiguous organs. Rarely, acute peritonitis, dis-

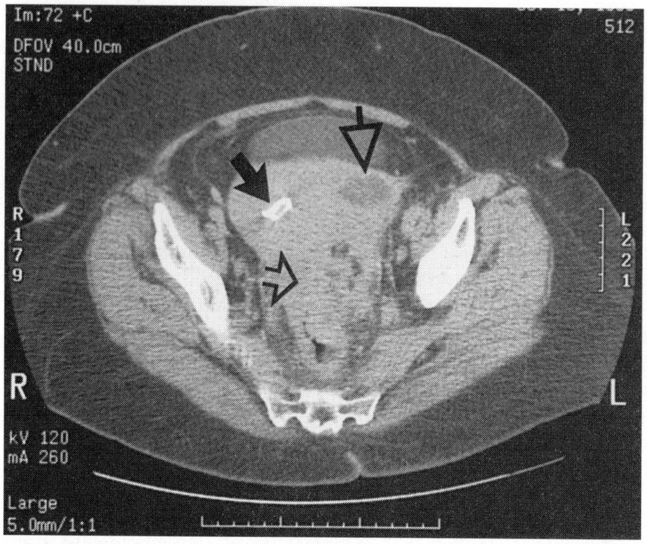

FIGURE 245–4. Intrauterine contraceptive device (IUCD)–associated pelvic actinomycosis. An IUCD encased by endometrial fibrosis *(solid arrowhead)*, paraendometrial fibrosis *(open arrow)*, and an area of suppuration *(open arrowhead)* can be appreciated.

seminated peritoneal lesions, pelvic bone involvement, extension to the thorax, or hematogenous dissemination may occur.[136, 139, 140]

One of the management issues that has received considerable attention is whether screening cervical or endometrial specimens for the presence of *Actinomyces* or *Actinomyces*-like organisms can lead to the prevention of IUCD-associated pelvic actinomycosis. Papanicolaou-stained specimens, direct immunofluorescence using fluorescein isothiocyanate–labeled antisera against the agents of actinomycosis, and culture have been assessed to varying degrees for the detection of *Actinomyces* or *Actinomyces*-like organisms.[136] Conflicting results from studies performed to date have made the sensitivity and specificity of these diagnostic modalities for the detection of *Actinomyces* unclear. Nonetheless, these studies have established that (1) in the presence of IUCDs the prevalence and probably the number of *Actinomyces* organisms increase, (2) the prevalence is greater in women with IUCDs in place for 2 or more years and probably increases with time thereafter, and (3) all types of IUCDs have been implicated.[136] However, it is not known whether the detection of *Actinomyces* represents early local disease versus colonization, nor has the rate of invasive disease development in women with detectable *Actinomyces* been established. Furthermore, a Papanicolaou smear may fail to detect *Actinomyces*-like organisms even in the presence of active actinomycosis.[136] Although it has not been proved, endometrial disruption and an increased prevalence of endometrial colonization with the agents of actinomycosis as a result of IUCDs are undoubtedly crucial and probably necessary factors in the development of this disease. In view of the overall women-years of IUCD use and the limited number of reported cases of pelvic actinomycosis, the risk appears to be small but the consequences of infection are significant. Therefore, in the absence of more quantitative data, it would appear prudent to remove IUCDs if symptoms of pain, abnormal bleeding, or discharge cannot be attributed to other pathogens, regardless of whether *Actinomyces* or *Actinomyces*-like organisms are detected. A 14-day course of a penicillin or tetracycline should be given for treatment of possible early pelvic actinomycosis. Detection of *Actinomyces* or *Actinomyces*-like organisms in the absence of symptoms warrants patient education and close follow-up but not removal of the IUCD unless an equally suitable means of contraception can be agreed on.

Central Nervous System Disease

Actinomycosis of the central nervous system is rare. The source may be hematogenous or through extension of oral-cervicofacial disease. In a recent review, the mean duration of symptoms before diagnosis was 2.1 months—longer than most causes of central nervous system infection.[61, 141] Brain abscess is the most common finding. Headache and focal neurologic findings are the most common clinical features. Fever is variably present. Single or multiple abscesses may be present. The most frequent CT appearance is a ring-enhancing lesion with a thick wall that may be irregular or nodular. Multiloculation, edema, and contiguous areas of low attenuation may be present. These findings are also consistent with brain abscess and tumor.[142] Less commonly, solid nodular or mass lesions termed actinomycetomas or actinomycotic granulomas occur. Chronic meningitis may develop as a consequence of spread from a parameningeal focus, most commonly the middle ear or paranasal sinuses. Manifestation of the disease may be acute, particularly with rupture of an abscess into the subarachnoid space, or chronic, with the cerebrospinal fluid having normal or low glucose levels, elevated protein, lymphocytic pleocytosis, and negative culture. Diagnosis can be made by microscopic examination or rarely by culture of cerebrospinal fluid.[143] Extension of disease from foci of cranial osteomyelitis or from sinus or middle ear disease can result in cranial epidural and subdural infection.[144, 145] Spinal epidural disease may occur from direct extension of abdominal, thoracic, or cervical disease, is usually associated with contiguous osteomyelitis, and may result in spinal cord compression.[146] Cavernous sinus syndrome and spinal intrathecal empyema have also been reported.[147, 148]

Musculoskeletal Disease

Actinomycotic infection of bone is usually a result of adjacent soft tissue infection (75%), but it may also be associated with trauma (e.g., fracture of the mandible) (19%) or hematogenous spread (3%).[71] In the preantibiotic era, the unchecked spread of thoracic or abdominal disease resulted in vertebral infection being the most common site for osseous actinomycosis (see "Thoracic Disease"). Less commonly, hematogenous vertebral osteomyelitis may originate from an occult source and clinically resemble skeletal tuberculosis. Presently, infection involving the facial bones, particularly the mandible, is most frequently noted.[71] Actinomycosis of the skull, ribs, clavicle, sternum, scapula, or pelvis may also occur from extension of orofacial, thoracic, or abdominal disease. The clinical and radiographic features of infection in these locations have been discussed earlier.

Infection of the extremities, although uncommon, often poses diagnostic difficulties. Blunt or penetrating trauma of the affected area is a frequent inciting event.[149] Some cases are a result of hematogenous dissemination from apparent or cryptic foci.[12, 48, 150–152] Skin, subcutaneous tissue, muscle, and bone may be involved alone or in various combinations. Cutaneous sinus tracts or abscesses are present in most cases, as is bony involvement in the form of periostitis or acute or chronic osteomyelitis.[151] The initial findings are usually indolent. Although actinomycotic infections of the lower extremities have been described as mycetomas, this term is best reserved for the group of infections designated as actinomycetoma.

Actinomycotic infection of hip prostheses has been described in several reports. Although one patient may have had *Actinomyces* introduced at the time of surgery,[45] two other cases occurring 10 and 16 years after total hip arthroplasty suggest hematogenous seeding from a cryptic distant site.[44, 46] Actinomycotic arthritis of the knee has developed in association with trauma or as a consequence of hematogenous seeding.[153] Actinomycosis is a rare result of closed-fist injury.[154]

Disseminated Disease

Although uncommon, all agents of actinomycosis are capable of hematogenous dissemination and subsequent multiorgan involvement. *A. meyeri* appears to have the greatest capability of causing this syndrome. Disease in any location may serve as the source for spread. The lungs and liver are the most commonly affected organs, and the presence of multiple nodules can mimic disseminated malignancy. The kidneys, brain, spleen, skin, soft tissues of the extremities, and less commonly the heart valves may also be infected in various combinations. The clinical course may be surprisingly indolent when the extent of disease is appreciated.[12, 48, 150, 155]

DIAGNOSIS

The diagnosis of actinomycosis, particularly when it mimics malignancy, is rarely considered. All too often the first mention of actinomycosis is from the pathologist after extensive surgery has been performed. An increasing body of evidence suggests that medical therapy alone is usually sufficient for cure, including cure of extensive invasive disease. Therefore, the challenge for the clinician is to consider the possibility of actinomycosis so that this unique infection can be diagnosed in the least invasive fashion and unnecessary surgery avoided. Even when this diagnosis is considered, suitable sampling and handling of clinical specimens are necessary for confirmation. A combination of appropriate microbiologic and pathologic studies will maximize the chances of success. The most important step for optimal microbiologic yield is the avoidance of any antimicrobial therapy before obtaining the specimen. The agents of actinomycosis are exceedingly sensitive to a wide variety of drugs, and even a single dose can interfere with their isolation. Fine-needle aspiration or biopsy and CT- or ultrasound-guided aspirations or biopsies are being successfully used to obtain clinical material for diagnosis.[141, 156–158] Transbronchial biopsies have been less successful in providing diagnostic material for thoracic actinomycosis.[35, 159] Surgery may be required for diagnostic purposes.

Bacteriologic identification of one of the agents of actinomycosis from a sterile site confirms the diagnosis. Because these organisms are normal inhabitants of the oral cavity and female genital tract, identification of the organisms alone, in the absence of sulfur granules, from sputum, bronchial washings, and cervicovaginal secretions is of little significance.[30, 160] However, microbiologic identification of the agents of actinomycosis occurs in only a minority of cases.[26]

Although most strains of *Actinomyces* are microaerophilic or facultative (except *A. meyeri*), strict anaerobic processing and growth in the presence of CO_2 result in optimal growth. The laboratory should receive specimens expeditiously or in anaerobic transport media. Tissue, pus, or sulfur granules are ideal, and swabs should be avoided. The microbiology laboratory should be alerted before receiving any specimen that may harbor agents of actinomycosis. A Gram stain of the specimen is usually more sensitive than culture, especially if the patient has received prior antibiotics. If granules are identified, they should be washed and crushed between two slides for examination. The agents of actinomycosis are non–spore-forming rods. Except for *A. meyeri*, which is small and nonbranching, their usual appearance is that of branching, filamentous rods. Growth usually appears within 5 to 7 days, but primary isolation may take up to 2 to 4 weeks. Although specialized media are not required, the use of semiselective media may increase isolation rates of *Actinomyces*, particularly when more rapidly growing organisms are also present.[161] *A. israelii* characteristically forms a "molar tooth" colony on agar and grows as clumps within broth. *A. odontolyticus* colonies usually appear rust-brown or red. *Actinomyces* species are indole negative. Traditional identification is based on these features in combination with tests for urease, catalase, gelatin hydrolysis, and fermentation of cellobiose, trehalose, and arabinose. Occasionally, metabolic products identified by gas-liquid chromatography are contributory. Suggestive organisms can also be confirmed by immunofluorescence testing, which may be a useful alternative[162] (available through the Centers for Disease Control and Prevention, 404-639-3156, 3355).

The single most helpful diagnostic maneuver for actinomycosis is the demonstration of grains (sulfur granules) in pus or histologic section of a surgical specimen (Fig. 245–5). Grains represent a conglomeration of microorganisms that forms only in vivo. Hematoxylin-eosin staining of tissue suffices to demonstrate the grain, but a special stain (e.g., Gram, silver) is needed to show that the grain is composed of branching bacteria and not fungi (eumycetoma), cocci, or bacilli (botryomycosis). If branching bacteria are seen on stain of the grain and the infection did not originate in subcutaneous tissue (a characteristic of mycetoma) or tonsillar tissue (see "Oral-Cervicofacial Disease"), the diagnosis of actinomycosis is established. Grains may be either microscopic or macroscopic and are usually yellow, hence their name, but they may be white, pinkish gray, gray, or brown. Grains may be identified grossly from draining sinus tracts, other purulent material, or sputum, but they may easily escape notice unless sought after. When pus is poured down the side of a glass tube, grains will adhere and can be identified more readily. A magnifying glass may aid in their identification. In tissue sections, sulfur granules are most commonly found within microabscesses. Although they may be abundant, they are usually scanty. Only a single granule was identified in 26% of specimens from one series.[26] Because grains are surrounded by neutrophils, several histologic

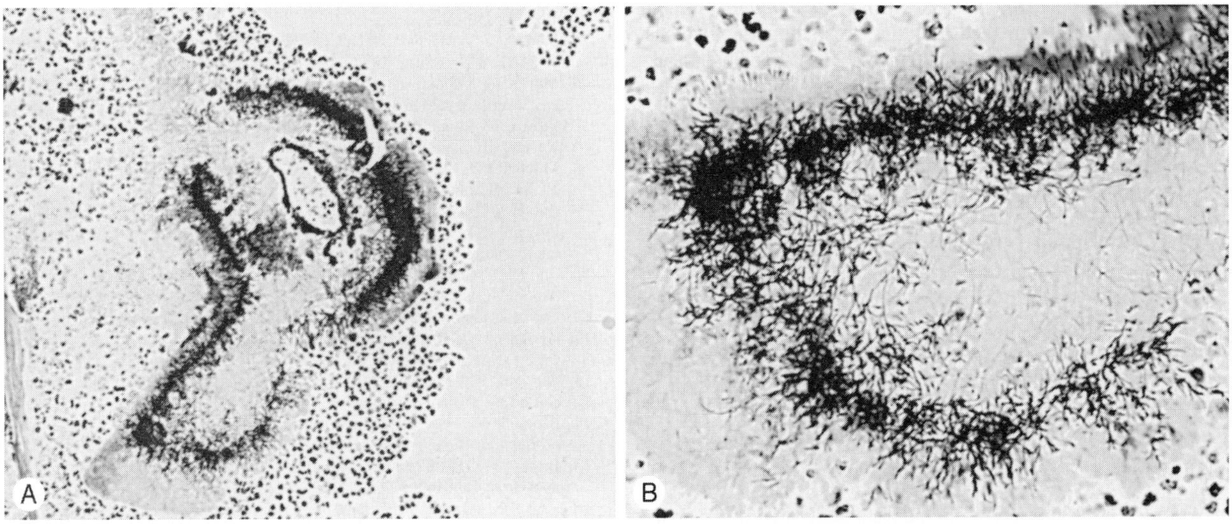

FIGURE 245–5. *A*, Actinomycotic sulfur granule surrounded by inflammatory cells (Brown-Brenn stain, ×250). *B*, Increased magnification (×1000) demonstrates the delicate, branched filaments of *Actinomyces.*

TABLE 245–1 Antibiotic Therapy for Actinomycosis

Group 1: Extensive successful clinical experience*
Penicillin
Erythromycin
Tetracycline
Doxycycline
Clindamycin
Group 2: Anecdotal successful clinical experience
Ceftriaxone
Imipenem
Ciprofloxacin
Group 3: Agents that should not be used
Metronidazole
Aminoglycosides
Oxacillin
Dicloxacillin
Cephalexin

*Controlled evaluations have not been performed. See the text for dosing, route of administration, and duration. These parameters will vary depending on the site and extent of infection. However, as a general rule, high doses are required for a prolonged duration (6 to 12 months) for most infections.

sections containing purulent foci need to be examined to find a grain. Microscopically, grains are round, oval, or horseshoe shaped. Although bacilli within the grain are rarely visible with hematoxylin-eosin stain, tissue Gram stains, Gomori methenamine silver, and Giemsa stains demonstrate gram-positive, filamentous, branching bacteria at its periphery[163] (see Fig. 245–4). On hematoxylin-eosin stain, the grains may be eosinophilic or variably surrounded by a radiating fringe of eosinophilic clubs. This eosinophilic, proteinaceous coating around organisms in tissue has been called the Splendore-Hoeppli phenomenon. It represents an ill-defined host response but may be accounted for, in part, by eosinophil granule major basic protein.[164] This coating is not specific for actinomycosis and can also be seen in schistosomiasis, sporotrichosis, subcutaneous zygomycosis, botryomycosis, mycetoma, and other indolent infections. A combination of the clinical scenario and stains of the grain can be used to distinguish actinomycotic sulfur granules from others. Clinically, nocardiosis may closely resemble actinomycosis but does not form grains in visceral lesions.[165] When *Nocardia* is the causative agent of mycetoma, granules are formed. On Gram stain the branching gram-positive bacilli are indistinguishable from *Actinomyces*, but they may be stained by a Fite-modified acid-fast stain whereas *Actinomyces* is not. The granules formed by the fungal agents of mycetoma show branching hyphae on periodic acid–Schiff or Gomori methenamine silver stain. Botryomycosis is a chronic bacterial soft tissue and rarely visceral infection that produces loose clumps of bacteria that resemble grains. Etiologic agents include *Staphylococcus*, *Streptococcus*, *Escherichia*, *Pseudomonas,* and *Proteus*, which are easily distinguished from the agents of actinomycosis by the presence of cocci or nonbranching bacilli.[166] Specimens obtained from mucus-producing locations, such as the endocervix, bronchus, or ventricular colloid cysts, may possess pseudoactinomycotic radiate granules. If hematoxylin-eosin stain alone is used, these pseudoactinomycotic granules may mimic actinomycotic granules in that the central region is bordered by the Splendore-Hoeppli phenomenon. However, special stains will reveal the absence of microorganisms.[167, 168] When the etiology of a sulfur granule is in question, specific immunofluorescent staining for *A. israelii*, *A. naeslundii*, *A. odontolyticus*, *A. viscosus,* and *P. propionicum* can be used.[163]

A variety of serologic assays have been developed for diagnostic purposes. However, improvement in sensitivity, specificity, or both is necessary before they can become useful tools in clinical practice.[163]

TREATMENT

The discovery and use of penicillin in the treatment of actinomycosis have dramatically altered the course of this disease.[36] Two principles of therapy based on the clinical experience of the last 50 years have evolved. It is necessary to treat this disease both with high doses and for a prolonged period. Although therapy needs to be individualized, 18 to 24 million units of penicillin intravenously per day for 2 to 6 weeks, followed by oral therapy with amoxicillin, ampicillin, or penicillin V, all administered at 500 mg four times daily for 6 to 12 months is a reasonable guideline. Cases with less extensive involvement, particularly in the oral-cervicofacial region, may require less intensive therapy.[169] If the duration of therapy is extended beyond the resolution of measurable disease, relapses, one of the clinical hallmarks of this infection, will be minimized. A similar approach is reasonable for immunocompromised patients, although refractory disease has been described in human immunodeficiency virus–infected individuals.[54] For patients who are allergic to penicillin, tetracycline has been used most extensively with success. Erythromycin, doxycycline, and clindamycin are other suitable alternatives.[170, 171] In pregnant, penicillin-sensitive patients, erythromycin is a safe alternative. Little clinical information is available on the newer antimicrobial agents except for anecdotal success with imipenem,[172] ceftriaxone,[173] and ciprofloxacin[174] (Table 245–1). In vitro data suggest that oxacillin, dicloxacillin, cephalexin, metronidazole, and aminoglycosides should be avoided.[175] Although the role that "companion" microbes play in actinomycosis is unclear, many of the isolates are pathogens in their own right. Designing a therapeutic regimen that includes coverage for these organisms during the initial treatment course is reasonable.

In the preantibiotic era, surgical removal of infected tissue was the only beneficial treatment. Despite the advent of efficacious antimicrobial therapy, combined surgical therapy is still advocated. An increasing body of literature now supports the approach of initially attempting a cure with medical therapy alone, including extensive disease.[121, 141, 156, 176, 177] CT and magnetic resonance imaging should be used to monitor the response to therapy.[108] In the setting of actinomycosis manifested as a well-defined abscess, percutaneous drainage in combination with medical therapy is a reasonable approach.[178] In a patient with disease in a critical location (e.g., epidural space, selected central nervous system disease) or if suitable medical therapy fails, surgical intervention may be appropriate.

REFERENCES

1. Weese WC, Smith IM. A study of 57 cases of actinomycosis over a 36-year period. Arch Intern Med. 1975;135:1562–1568.
2. Cope Z. Visceral actinomycosis. BMJ. 1949;1:1311–1316.
3. Coleman RM, Georg LK, Rozzell AR. *Actinomyces naeslundii* as an agent in human actinomycosis. Appl Microbiol. 1969;18:420–426.
4. Bonnez W, Lattimer G, Mohanraj NA. *Actinomyces naeslundii* as an agent of pelvic actinomycosis in the presence of an intra-uterine device. J Clin Microbiol. 1985;21:273–275.
5. Stenhouse D, MacDonald DG. Low grade osteomyelitis of the jaws with actinomycosis. Int J Oral Surg. 1974;3:60.
6. Morris JF, Kilbourn P. Systemic actinomycosis caused by *Actinomyces odontolyticus*. Ann Intern Med. 1974;81:700.
7. Peloux Y, Raoult D, Chardon H, et al. *Actinomycosis odontolyticus* infections: Review of six patients. J Infect. 1985;11:125–129.
8. Mitchell PD, Hintz CZ, Haselby RC. Malar mass due to *Actinomyces odontolyticus*. J Clin Microbiol. 1977;5:658–660.
9. Bassiri AG, Girgis RE, Theodore J. *Actinomyces odontolyticus* thoracopulmonary infections. Two cases in lung and heart-lung transplant recipients and a review of the literature. Chest. 1996;109:1109–1111.
10. Eng RHK, Corrado ML, Cleri D, et al. Infections caused by *Actinomyces viscosus*. Am J Clin Pathol. 1981;75:113–116.
11. Lewis R, Gorbach S. *Actinomyces viscosus* in man. Lancet. 1972;1:641.
12. Apothéloz C, Regamey C. Disseminated infection due to *Actinomyces meyeri*: Case report and review. Clin Infect Dis. 1996;22:621–625.
13. Albright JD, Toczek S, Brenner VJ, et al. Osteomyelitis and epidural abscess caused by *Arachnia propionica*. J Neurosurg. 1974;40:115.
14. Brock DW, Georg LK, Brown JM, et al. Actinomycosis caused by *Arachnia propionica*: Report of 11 cases. Am J Clin Pathol. 1973;59:66–77.
15. Brazier JS, Hall V. *Propionibacterium propionicum* and infections of the lacrimal apparatus. Clin Infect Dis. 1993;17:892–893.
16. Funke G, Alvarez N, Pascual C, et al. *Actinomyces europaeus* sp. nov. isolated from human clinical specimens. Int J Syst Bacteriol. 1997;47:687–692.
17. Reddy I, Ferguson DA Jr, Sarubbi FA. Endocarditis due to *Actinomyces pyogenes*. Clin Infect Dis. 1997;25:1476–1477.

18. Gahrn-Hansen B, Frederiksen W. Human infections with *Actinomyces pyogenes* (*Corynebacterium pyogenes*). Diagn Microbiol Infect Dis. 1992;15:349–354.
19. Funke G, Ramos CP, Fernandez-Garayzabal JF, et al. Description of human-derived Centers for Disease Control coryneform group 2 bacteria as *Actinomyces bernardiae* sp. nov. Int J Syst Bacteriol. 1995;45:57–60.
20. Ieven M, Verhoeven J, Gentens P, et al. Severe infection due to *Actinomyces bernardiae*: Case report. Clin Infect Dis. 1996;22:157–158.
21. Funke G, von Graevenitz A. Infections due to *Actinomyces neuii* (former "CDC coryneform group 1" bacteria). Infection. 1995;23:73–75.
22. Wust J, Stubbs S, Weiss N, et al. Assignment of *Actinomyces pyogenes*–like (CDC coryneform group E) bacteria to the genus *Actinomyces* as *Actinomyces radingae* sp. nov. and *Actinomyces turicensis* sp. nov. Lett Appl Microbiol. 1995;20:76–81.
23. Hill GB. *Eubacterium nodatum* mimics *Actinomyces* in intrauterine device–associated infections and other settings within the female genital tract. Obstet Gynecol. 1992;79:534–538.
24. Hill GB, Ayers OM, Kohan AP. Characteristics and sites of infection of *Eubacterium nodatum, Eubacterium timidum, Eubacterium brachy*, and other asaccharolytic eubacterium. J Clin Microbiol. 1987;25:1540–1545.
25. Garrod LP. Actinomycosis of the lung. Aetiology, diagnosis and chemotherapy. Tubercule. 1952;33:258–266.
26. Brown JR. Human actinomycosis. A study of 181 subjects. Hum Pathol. 1973;4:319–330.
27. Holm P. Studies on aetiology of human actinomycosis. II. Do the "other" microbes of actinomycosis possess virulence? Acta Pathol Microbiol Scand. 1951;28:391.
28. Holm P. Studies on aetiology of human actinomycosis. I. The "other" microbes of actinomycosis and their importance. Acta Pathol Microbiol Scand. 1950;27:736.
29. Pulverer G. Problems of human actinomycosis. Postepy Hig Med Dosw. 1974;28:253–260.
30. Persson E. Genital actinomycosis and *Actinomyces israelii* in the female genital tract. Adv Contracept. 1987;3:115–123.
31. Peabody JW, Seabury JH. Actinomycosis and nocardiosis. J Chronic Dis. 1957;5:374–403.
32. Bennhoff DF. Actinomycosis: Diagnostic and therapeutic considerations and a review of 32 cases. Laryngoscope. 1984;94:1198–1217.
33. Harvey JC, Cantrell JR, Fisher AM. Actinomycosis: Its recognition and treatment. Ann Intern Med. 1957;46:868–885.
34. Spilsbury BW, Johnstone FRC. The clinical course of actinomycotic infections: A report of 14 cases. Can J Surg. 1962;5:33–48.
35. Kinnear WJM, MacFarlane JT. A survey of thoracic actinomycosis. Respir Med. 1990;84:57–59.
36. Peabody JW, Seabury JH. Actinomycosis and nocardiosis. A review of basic differences in therapy. Am J Med. 1960;60:99–115.
37. Jordon HV, Kelly DM, Heeley JD. Enhancement of experimental actinomycosis in mice by *Eikenella corrodens*. Infect Immun. 1984;46:367–371.
38. Ochiai K, Kurita-Ochiai T, Kamino Y, et al. Effect of co-aggregation on the pathogenicity of oral bacteria. J Med Microbiol. 1993;39:183–190.
39. Weed LA, Baggenstoss AH. Actinomycosis: A pathologic and bacteriologic study of twenty-one fatal cases. Am J Clin Pathol. 1949;19:201–216.
40. Hennrikus EF, Pederson L. Disseminated actinomycosis. West J Med. 1987;147:201–204.
41. Figures KH, Douglas CWI. Actinomycosis associated with a root-treated tooth: Report of a case. Int Endod J. 1991;24:326–329.
42. Silbermann M, Chiminello FJ, Doku HC, et al. Mandibular actinomycosis: Report of case. J Am Dent Assoc. 1975;90:162–165.
43. Miller BJ, Wright JL, Colquhoun BPD. Some etiologic concepts of actinomycosis of the greater omentum. Surg Gynecol Obstet. 1978;146:412–414.
44. Cohen OJ, Keiser JK, Pollner J, et al. Prosthetic joint infection with *Actinomyces viscosus*. Infect Dis Clin Pract. 1993;2:349–351.
45. Petrini B, Welin-Berger T. Late infection with *Actinomyces israelii* after total hip replacement. Scand J Infect Dis. 1978;10:313–314.
46. Strazzeri JC, Anzel S. Infected total hip arthroplasty due to *Actinomyces israelii* after dental extraction. Clin Orthop. 1986;210:128–131.
47. Gaffney RJ, Walsh MA. Cervicofacial actinomycosis: An unusual cause of submandibular swelling. J Laryngol Otol. 1993;107:1169–1170.
48. Takeda H, Mitsuhashi Y, Kondo S. Cutaneous disseminated actinomycosis in a patient with acute lymphocytic leukemia. J Dermatol. 1998;25:37–40.
49. Rivera M, Marcen R, Aguilera A, et al. Facial actinomycosis in a renal transplant patient. Nephron. 1994;68:149–150.
50. Cendan I, Klapholz A, Talawera W. Pulmonary actinomycosis. A cause of endobronchial disease in a patient with AIDS. Chest. 1993;103:1886–1887.
51. Kingdom TT, Tami TA. Actinomycosis of the nasal septum in a patient infected with the human immunodeficiency virus. Otolaryngol Head Neck Surg. 1994;111:130–133.
52. Poles MA, McMeeking AA, Scholes JV, et al. *Actinomyces* infection of a cytomegalovirus esophageal ulcer in two patients with acquired immunodeficiency syndrome. Am J Gastroenterol. 1994;89:1569–1572.
53. Klapholz A, Talavera W, Rorat E, et al. Pulmonary actinomycosis in a patient with HIV infection. Mt Sinai J Med. 1989;56:300–303.
54. Manfredi R, Mazzoni A, Marinacci G, et al. Progressive intractable actinomycosis in patients with AIDS. Scand J Infect Dis. 1995;27:405–407.
55. Ossorio MA, Fields CL, Byrd RP, et al. Thoracic actinomycosis and human immunodeficiency virus infection. South Med J. 1997;90:1136–1138.
56. Watkins KV, Richmond AS, Langstein IM. Nonhealing extraction site due to *Actinomyces naeslundii* in a patient with AIDS. Oral Surg Oral Med Oral Pathol. 1991;71:675–677.
57. Yeager BA, Hoxie J, Weisman RA, et al. Actinomycosis in the acquired immunodeficiency syndrome–related complex. Arch Otolaryngol Head Neck Surg. 1986;112:1293–1295.
58. Sa'do B, Yoshiura K, Yuasa K, et al. Multimodality imaging of cervicofacial actinomycosis. Oral Surg Oral Med Oral Pathol. 1993;76:772–782.
59. Scott A, Stansbie JM. Actinomycosis presenting as a nasopharyngeal tumour: A case report. J Laryngol Otol. 1997;111:163–165.
60. Balatsouras DG, Kaberos AK, Eliopoulos PN, et al. Cervicofacial actinomycosis presenting as acute upper respiratory tract. J Laryngol Otol. 1994;108:801–803.
61. Smego RA. Actinomycosis of the central nervous system. Rev Infect Dis. 1987;9:855–865.
62. Freidman HD, Evangelisti PA, Emko P. Postoperative carotid artery rupture caused by *Actinomyces* infection. Otolaryngol Head Neck Surg. 1996;114:145–147.
63. Sakellariou PL. Periapical actinomycosis: Report of a case and review of the literature. Endod Dent Traumatol. 1996;12:151–154.
64. Bradley P. Actinomycosis of the temporomandibular joint. Br J Oral Surg. 1971;9:54–56.
65. Bramley P, Orton HS. Cervico-facial actinomycosis. A report on eleven cases. Br Dent J. 1960;109:235–238.
66. Nielsen PM, Novak A. Acute cervico-facial actinomycosis. Int J Oral Maxillofac Surg. 1987;16:440–444.
67. Samuels RHA, Martin MV. A clinical and microbiologic study of actinomycetes in oral and cervicofacial lesions. Br J Oral Maxillofac Surg. 1988;26:458–463.
68. Richtsmeier WJ, Johns ME. Actinomycosis of the head and neck. CRC Crit Rev Clin Lab Sci. 1979;11:175–202.
69. Friduss ME, Maceri DR. Cervicofacial actinomycosis in children. Henry Ford Hosp Med J. 1990;38:28–32.
70. Ohlms LA, Jones DT, Schreibstein J, et al. Sclerosing osteomyelitis of the mandible. Otolaryngol Head Neck Surg. 1993;109:1070–1073.
71. Lewis RP, Sutter SM, Finegold VL. Bone infections involving anaerobic bacteria. Medicine (Baltimore). 1978;57:279–305.
72. Liu CJ, Chang KM, Ou CT. Actinomycosis in a patient treated for maxillary osteoradionecrosis. J Oral Maxillofac Surg. 1998;56:251–253.
73. Roth M, Montone KT. Actinomycosis of the paranasal sinuses: A case report and review. Otolaryngol Head Neck Surg. 1996;114:818–821.
74. Vazquez AM, Marti C, Renaga I, et al. Actinomycosis of the tongue associated with human immunodeficiency virus infection: Case report. J Oral Maxillofac Surg. 1997;16:879–881.
75. Thomas R, Kameswaran M, Ahmed S, et al. Actinomycosis of the vallecula: Report of a case and review of the literature. J Laryngol Otol. 1995;109:154–156.
76. Nagral SS, Patel CV, Pathare PT, et al. Actinomycotic pseudo-tumor of the mid-cervical region. J Postgrad Med. 1990;37:62–64.
77. Appiah S, Tickke M. Actinomycosis—an unusual presentation. Br J Oral Maxillofac Surg. 1995;33:248–249.
78. Chuong R, Goldberg M. CPC, case 60: Preauricular mass. J Oral Maxillofac Surg. 1986;44:214–217.
79. Cobb RA, Ross HB. Actinomycosis in a persistent thyroglossal duct. Br J Surg. 1986;73:751.
80. Yiotakis J, Tzounakos P, Manolooulos L, et al. Actinomycosis of the thyroid gland masquerading as a neoplasm. J Laryngol Otol. 1997;111:172–174.
81. Adeniyi-Jones C, Minielly JA, Matthews WR, et al. *Actinomyces viscosus* in a branchial cyst. Am J Clin Pathol. 1973;60:711–713.
82. Hagan ME, Klotz SA, Bartholomew W, et al. Actinomycosis of the trachea with acute tracheal obstruction. Clin Infect Dis. 1996;22:1126–1127.
83. Gaffney R, Harrison M, Walsh M, et al. The incidence and role of *Actinomyces* in recurrent acute tonsillitis. Clin Otolaryngol. 1993;18:268–271.
84. Tarabichi M, Schloss M. Actinomycosis otomastoiditis. Arch Otolaryngol Head Neck Surg. 1993;119:561–562.
85. Roussel TJ, Olson R, Rice T, et al. Chronic postoperative endophthalmitis associated with *Actinomyces* species. Arch Ophthalmol. 1991;109:60–62.
86. McKellar MJ, Optom B, Aburn NS. Cast-forming *Actinomyces israelii* canaliculitis. Aust N Z J Ophthalmol. 1997;25:301–303.
87. Bates M, Cruickshank G. Thoracic actinomycosis. Thorax. 1957;12:99–124.
88. Heffner J. Pleuropulmonary manifestations of actinomycosis and nocardiosis. Semin Respir Infect. 1988;3:352–361.
89. Hsieh M-J, Liu H-P, Chang J-P, et al. Thoracic actinomycosis. Chest. 1993;104:366–370.
90. Flynn MW, Felson B. The roentgen manifestations of thoracic actinomycosis. AJR Am J Roentgenol. 1970;110:707–716.
91. Coodley EL, Yoshinaka R. Pleural effusion as the major manifestation of actinomycosis. Chest. 1994;106:1615–1617.
92. Pérez-Castrillon JL, Gonzalez-Castaneda C, del Campo-Matias F, et al. Empyema necessitatis due to *Actinomyces odontolyticus* (Letter). Chest. 1997;111:1144.
93. Kwong JS, Muller NL, Godwin JD, et al. Thoracic actinomycosis: CT findings in eight patients. Radiology. 1992;183:189–192.
94. Hinnie J, Jaques BC, Bell E, et al. Actinomycosis presenting as carcinoma. Postgrad Med J. 1995;71:749–750.
95. Neijens V, van Heerde P, van der Heijden A, et al. Actinomycosis, a sheep in wolves' clothes. Lung Cancer. 1996;15:131–135.
96. Fife TD, Finegold SM, Grennan T. Pericardial actinomycosis: Case report and review. Rev Infect Dis. 1991;13:120–126.
97. Lam S, Samraj J, Rahman S, et al. Primary actinomycotic endocarditis: Case report and review. Clin Infect Dis. 1993;16:481–485.
98. Prather JR, Eastridge CE, Hughes FA, et al. Actinomycosis of the thorax. Ann Thorac Surg. 1970;9:307–312.

99. Morgan DE, Nath H, Sanders C, et al. Mediastinal actinomycosis. AJR Am J Roentgenol. 1990;155:735–737.
100. Bentley E, Ostransky D. Unusual manifestations of thoracic actinomycosis. J Am Osteopath Assoc. 1994;94:249–253.
101. Spencer GM, Roach D, Skucas J. Actinomycosis of the esophagus in a patient with AIDS: Findings on barium esophagrams. AJR Am J Roentgenol. 1993;161:795–796.
102. Parker JS, deBoisblanc BP. Case report: Actinomycosis: Multinodular pulmonary involvement. Am J Med Sci. 1994;307:418–419.
103. Fisher MS. "Miliary" actinomycosis. J Can Assoc Radiol. 1980;31:149–150.
104. Dalhoff K, Wallner S, Finck C, et al. Endobronchial actinomycosis. Eur Respir J. 1994;7:1189–1191.
105. Jain BK, Sehgal VN, Jagdish S, et al. Primary actinomycosis of the breast: A clinical review and a case report. J Dermatol. 1994;21:497–500.
106. Berardi RS. Abdominal actinomycosis. Surg Gynecol Obstet. 1979;149:257–266.
107. Davies M, Keddie NC. Abdominal actinomycosis. Br J Surg. 1973;60:18–22.
108. Ko S-F, Ng S-H, Lee T-Y, et al. Retroperitoneal actinomycosis with intraperitoneal spread. Stellate pattern on CT. Clin Imaging. 1996;20:133–136.
109. Ha HK, Lee HJ, Kim H, et al. Abdominal actinomycosis: CT findings in 10 patients. AJR Am J Roentgenol. 1993;161:791–794.
110. Deshmukh N, Heaney SJ. Actinomycosis at multiple colonic sites. Am J Gastroenterol. 1986;81:1212–1214.
111. Skoutelis A, Panagopoulos C, Kalfarentzos F, et al. Intramural gastric actinomycosis. South Med J. 1995;88:647–650.
112. Putman HC, Dockerty MB, Waugh JM. Abdominal actinomycosis. An analysis of 122 cases. Surgery. 1950;28:781–800.
113. Alvardo-Cerna R, Bracho-Riquelme R. Perianal actinomycosis—a complication of a fistula-in-ano. Report of a case. Dis Colon Rectum. 1994;37:378–380.
114. Sarosdy MF, Brock WA, Parsons CL. Scrotal actinomycosis. J Urol. 1979;121:256–257.
115. Dayan K, Neufeld D, Zissin R, et al. Actinomycosis of the large bowel: Unusual presentations and their surgical treatment. Eur J Surg. 1996;162:657–660.
116. Miyamoto MI, Fang FC. Pyogenic liver abscess involving *Actinomyces*: Case report and review. Clin Infect Dis. 1993;16:303–309.
117. Ruutu P, Pentikainen PJ, Larinkari U, et al. Hepatic actinomycosis presenting as repeated cholestatic reactions. Scand J Infect Dis. 1982;14:235–238.
118. Ubeda B, Vilana R, Bianchi L, et al. Primary hepatic actinomycosis: Association with portal vein thrombosis. AJR Am J Roentgenol. 1995;164:231–232.
119. Kasano Y, Tanimura H, Yamaue H, et al. Hepatic actinomycosis infiltrating the diaphragm and right lung. Am J Gastroenterol. 1996;91:2418–2420.
120. Ellis LR, Kenny GM, Nellans RE. Urogenital aspects of actinomycosis. J Urol. 1979;122:132–133.
121. Khalaff H, Srigley JR, Klotz LH. Recognition of renal actinomycosis: Nephrectomy can be avoided. Report of a case. Can J Surg. 1995;38:77–79.
122. Piper JV, Stoner BA, Mitra SK, et al. Ileo-vesical fistula associated with pelvic actinomycosis. Br J Clin Pract. 1969;23:341–343.
123. Stringer MD, Cameron AEP. Abdominal actinomycosis: A forgotten disease? Br J Hosp Med. 1987;38:125–127.
124. Buckley P, McInerney PD, Stephenson TP. Actinomycotic vesico-uterine fistula from a wishbone pessary contraceptive device. Br J Urol. 1991;68:206–207.
125. Richards RJ, Grayer D. Actinomycosis: A rare cause of vesicocolic fistula. Am J Gastroenterol. 1989;84:677–679.
126. Guermazi A, de Kerviler E, Welker Y, et al. Pseudotumoral vesical actinomycosis. J Urol. 1996;156:2002–2003.
127. van Wijk FJ, Lodeer JV. Actinomycosis of urachal remnants. Eur Urol. 1991;19:339–340.
128. Jani AN, Casibang V, Mufarrij WA. Disseminated actinomycosis presenting as a testicular mass: A case report. J Urol. 1990;143:1012–1014.
129. Merle-Melet M, Mory F, Stempfel B, et al. *Actinomyces naeslundii*, acute cholecystitis and carcinoma of the gallbladder. Am J Gastroenterol. 1995;90:1530–1531.
130. Serrano-Rios M, Navarro V, Fontan J, et al. Isolated hepato-pancreatic actinomycosis. Digestion. 1969;2:262–271.
131. Nye FJ. Primary abdominal actinomycosis. J Infect. 1993;27:105–106.
132. DeSanto NG, Altucci P, Giordano C. *Actinomyces* peritonitis associated with dialysis. Nephron. 1976;16:236–239.
133. Henderson SR. Pelvic actinomycosis associated with an intrauterine device. Obstet Gynecol. 1973;41:726–732.
134. Nieman BH, Fahrner AH. Actinomycosis of the ovary. Am J Obstet Gynecol. 1943;45:534–538.
135. Brenner RW, Gehring SW. Pelvic actinomycosis in the presence of an endocervical contraceptive device. Obstet Gynecol. 1964;29:71–73.
136. Fiorino AS. Intrauterine contraceptive device–associated actinomycotic abscess and *Actinomyces* detection on cervical smear. Obstet Gynecol. 1996;87:142–149.
137. Schmidt WA, Webb JA, Bedrossian CWM, et al. Actinomycosis and intrauterine contraceptive devices. The clinicopathologic entity. Diagn Gynecol Obstet. 1980;2:165–177.
138. Spagnuolo PJ, Fransioli M. Intrauterine device–associated actinomycosis simulating pelvic malignancy. Am J Gastroenterol. 1981;75:144–147.
139. Dawson JM, O'Riordan B, Chopra S. Ovarian actinomycosis presenting as acute peritonitis. Aust N Z J Surg. 1992;62:161–163.
140. Perlow JH, Wigton T, Yordan EL, et al. Disseminated pelvic actinomycosis presenting as metastatic carcinoma: Association with the Progestasert intrauterine device. Rev Infect Dis. 1991;13:1115–1119.
141. Pauker SG, Kopelman RI. Clinical problem-solving. A rewarding pursuit of certainty. N Engl J Med. 1993;329:1103–1107.
142. Sharma BS, Banerjee AK, Sobti MK, et al. Actinomycotic brain abscess. Clin Neurol Neurosurg. 1990;92:373–376.
143. Bolton CF, Ashenhurst EM. Actinomycosis of the brain. Can Med Assoc J. 1964;90:922–928.
144. Louie JA, Kusske JA, Rush JL, et al. Actinomycotic subdural empyema. J Neurosurg. 1979;51:852–855.
145. Kirsch WM, Stears JC. Actinomycotic osteomyelitis of the skull and epidural space. J Neurol. 1970;33:347–351.
146. Muller PG. Actinomycosis as a cause of spinal cord compression: A case report and review. Paraplegia. 1989;27:390–393.
147. Holland NR, Deibert E. CNS actinomycosis presenting with bilateral cavernous sinus syndrome. J Neurol Neurosurg Psychiatry. 1998;64:4.
148. David C, Brasme L, Peruzzi P, et al. Intramedullary abscess of the spinal cord in a patient with a right-to-left shunt: Case report. Clin Infect Dis. 1997;24:89–90.
149. Vandevelde AG, Jenkins SG, Hardy PR. Sclerosing osteomyelitis and *Actinomyces naeslundii* of surrounding tissues. Clin Infect Dis. 1995;20:1037–1039.
150. Liaudet L, Erard P, Kaeser P. Cutaneous and muscular abscesses secondary to *Actinomyces meyeri* pneumonia. Clin Infect Dis. 1996;22:185–186.
151. Reiner SL, Harrelson JM, Miller SE, et al. Primary actinomycosis of an extremity: A case report and review. Rev Infect Dis. 1987;9:581–589.
152. Johnston JO. Case 29-1993. N Engl J Med. 1993;329:264–269.
153. Sherer PB, Dobbins J. Actinomycosis arthritis: A case report. Med Ann District Columbia. 1974;43:66–68.
154. Blinkhorn RJ, Strimbu V, Effron D, et al. 'Punch' actinomycosis causing osteomyelitis of the hand. Arch Intern Med. 1988;148:2668–2670.
155. Mesgarzadeh M, Bonakdarpour A, Redecki PD. Case report 365. Skeletal Radiol. 1986;15:584–588.
156. Cintron JR, Del Pino A, Duarte B, et al. Abdominal actinomycosis. Report of two cases and review of the literature. Dis Colon Rectum. 1996;39:105–108.
157. Hsu W-H, Chiang C-D, Chen C-Y, et al. Ultrasound-guided fine needle aspiration biopsy in the diagnosis of chronic pulmonary infection. Respiration. 1997;64:319–325.
158. Das DK. Actinomycosis in fine needle aspiration cytology. Cytopathology. 1994;5:243–250.
159. Lee C-H, Lin M-C, Tsai Y-H, et al. Thoracic actinomycosis—review of 9 cases. Chang Gung Med J. 1991;14:246–252.
160. Slack J. The source of infection in actinomycosis. J Bacteriol. 1942;43:193–209.
161. Lewis R, McKenzie D, Bagg J, et al. Experience with a novel selective medium for isolation of *Actinomyces* spp. from medical and dental specimens. J Clin Microbiol. 1995;33:1613–1616.
162. Hillier S, Moncla B. Anaerobic gram-positive nonsporeforming bacilli and cocci. In: Balows EIC, ed. Manual of Clinical Microbiology. Washington, DC: American Society for Microbiology; 1991.
163. Holmberg K. Diagnostic methods for human actinomycosis. Microbiol Sci. 1987;4:72–78.
164. Kephart GM, Andrade ZA, Gleich GJ. Localization of eosinophil major basic protein onto eggs of *Schistosoma mansoni* in human pathologic tissue. Am J Pathol. 1988;133:389–396.
165. Robboy SJ, Vickery AL. Tinctorial and morphologic properties distinguishing actinomycosis and nocardiosis. N Engl J Med. 1970;282:593–595.
166. Multz AS, Cohen R, Azeuta V. Bacterial pseudomycosis: A rare cause of haemoptysis. Eur Respir J. 1994;7:1712–1713.
167. Bhagavan BS, Ruffier J, Shinn B. Pseudoactinomycotic radiate granules in the lower female genital tract. Human Pathol. 1982;13:898–904.
168. Sobel RA. Pseudosulfur granules. Am J Clin Pathol. 1982;77:230.
169. Martin MV. The use of oral amoxicillin for the treatment of actinomycosis. Br Dent J 1984;156:252–254.
170. Fass RJ, Scholand JF, Hodges GR. Clindamycin in the treatment of serious anaerobic infections. Ann Intern Med. 1973;78:853–859.
171. Martin MV. Antibiotic treatment of cervicofacial actinomycosis for patients allergic to penicillin: A clinical and *in vitro* study. Br J Oral Maxillofac Surg. 1985;23:428–435.
172. Yew WW, Wong PC, Wong CF, et al. Use of imipenem in the treatment of thoracic actinomycosis. Clin Infect Dis. 1994;19:983–984.
173. Skoutelis A, Petrochilos J, Bassaris H. Successful treatment of thoracic actinomycosis with ceftriaxone. Clin Infect Dis. 1994;19:161–162.
174. Macfarlane DJ, Tucker G, Kemp RJ. Treatment of recalcitrant actinomycosis with ciprofloxacin. J Infect. 1993;27:177–180.
175. Lerner PI. Susceptibility of pathogenic actinomycetes to antimicrobial compounds. Antimicrob Agents Chemother. 1974;5:302–309.
176. Marty HU, Wust J. Disseminated actinomycosis caused by *Actinomyces meyeri*. Infection. 1989;17:154–155.
177. Schleck WF, Gelfand M, Alper B, et al. Medical management of visceral actinomycosis. South Med J. 1983;76:921–922.
178. Goldwag S, Abbitt PL, Watts B. Case report: Percutaneous drainage of periappendiceal actinomycosis. Clin Radiol. 1991;44:422–424.

SECTION G
MYCOSES

Chapter 246

Introduction to Mycoses

JOHN E. BENNETT

MYCOLOGY

Taxonomy, which is the science of classifying organisms, is drawing increasing reliance on genomic structure. A case in point is the reclassification of *Pneumocystis carinii* as a fungus based on sequences in one of the genes encoding ribisomal RNA (see Chapter 260). Taxonomy is always evolving as new relationships and modes of classification are found. However, each name change exacts a price. Infectious diseases are usually named by the organism, so a change in name makes it difficult for the clinician to locate prior published cases. Fungal names present an additional hurdle for the clinician in that many fungi have two names, a phenomenon described later. The guiding principle that will be used in this section is that advances in taxonomy do not necessarily need to be translated immediately into changes that can potentially baffle the clinician. Changes in names and groupings of fungi should be done only when the reasons are truly compelling.

It is important to understand that fungi can be divided into yeasts and molds. Yeastlike fungi are typically round or oval and reproduce by budding. Molds are composed of tubular structures called hyphae that grow by branching and longitudinal extension. Not all pathogenic fungi can be categorized neatly by their appearance in tissue as yeasts or molds. *Coccidioides immitis*, *Rhinosporidium seeberi*, and *P. carinii* are round in tissue but do not bud. Instead, the cytoplasm divides up to form numerous internal spores that, on rupture of the "mother" cell, are released to form new spherical structures. Some fungi can grow either yeastlike or as a mold. In candidiasis and tinea versicolor, the fungus is often seen in both tubular and rounded forms. The so-called dimorphic fungi grow in the host as yeastlike forms but grow at room temperature in vitro as molds. These fungi include the agents of histoplasmosis, blastomycosis, sporotrichosis, coccidioidomycosis, paracoccidioidomycosis, and chromoblastomycosis.

Virtually all fungi reproduce by forming spores through mitosis, a process in which the chromosome number remains the same. A fungal colony with only this asexual spore formation or with no spore formation is said to be an "anamorph," or "in the imperfect (asexual) state." Several decades ago, most fungi pathogenic for humans were found only in the imperfect state. Many have subsequently been induced to form sexual spores and have been given names. Fungi growing spores that have the specialized appearance known for "sexual spores" are said to be "telemorphs," or "in the perfect state." The name given to a fungus in the perfect state shows its similarity to other fungi in their perfect state. Although the fungus may have two names, the diagnostic laboratory uses the single name that is oldest and best established.

Sexual spores arise as a result of nuclear fusion followed by meiosis, a process that reduces the chromosome number by half. If the two nuclei are from the same colony (thallus), the fungus is said to be homothallic. If the nuclei are from different colonies that fuse their cytoplasm when grown adjacent to one another, the fungus is said to be heterothallic. Such fungi only join with colonies having a different, compatible mating type. Heterothallic fungi include the agents of histoplasmosis, blastoplasmosis, and cryptococcosis, as well as some fungi causing ringworm and mucormycosis.

Cells of fungi pathogenic for humans are nonmotile and have a rigid cell wall, usually containing chitin and polysaccharides. All fungal cell walls are stained by Gomori methenamine silver, and while the fungus remains viable, the periodic acid–Schiff reagent will also stain the cell wall. All fungi, including *P. carinii*, stain with calcofluor, which appears brilliant white under the fluorescent microscope. This stain has replaced the "wet mount" or KOH stain in many diagnostic laboratories because fungi are easier to see. Gram stain is not usually helpful because most fungi, except *Candida*, remain unstained. India ink smear of cerebrospinal fluid allows visualization of a polysaccharide capsule around the cell wall and is characteristic of only one pathogen for humans, the genus *Cryptococcus*. An India ink smear from a colony on a culture plate is less helpful because the capsule may be too thin to be seen. Inside the fungal cell wall is the sterol-containing cytoplasmic membrane, which is the site affected by azoles, allylamines, and the polyene macrolide antibiotics amphotericin B and nystatin. Fungi are not known to have important endotoxins. Exotoxins such as aflatoxin have been produced by certain fungi in vitro, but none are yet known to be produced in vivo.

Fungi can often be identified in tissue, even in the absence of culture, by taking into account the clinical findings, body site, inflammatory response, and fungal appearance (Table 246–1). Culture diagnosis is potentially more accurate than diagnosis by histologic features, but many smaller laboratories encounter difficulties in isolating and identifying fungi. The histologic features of a biopsy specimen can be more rapidly diagnostic than culture when mycoses are caused by slow-growing fungi. Biopsy slides are more readily mailed to consultants than cultures are, which may arrive nonviable or contaminated. Finally, biopsy may provide proof that the fungus is invading tissue and is not just a contaminant or saprophyte growing on debris in a lung cavity or skin ulcer. Ideally, both histologic examination and culture should be done together. As yet, detection of fungal DNA by polymerase chain reaction has not proved useful in detecting or identifying fungi in tissue. In contrast, luminescent DNA probes for hybridization to fungal RNA are commercially available and valuable for identifying colonies of *Histoplasma capsulatum*, *C. immitis*, *Blastomyces dermatitidis,* and *Cryptococcus neoformans*. Identification of fungi in tissue by immunohistochemistry remains experimental.

EPIDEMIOLOGY

With rare exception, mycoses are not transmissible from patient to patient. Gown, glove, or mask isolation of hospitalized patients with mycoses is not indicated. Ringworm of the scalp in children is transmissible to other children, so caps and combs should not be shared by infected children and playmates. Airborne transmission of *P. carinii* has been postulated, but isolation of these patients is not routine. Bandages or casts that become contaminated with draining pus from patients with coccidiodomycosis require care to see that the fungus does not remain on the fomite for several days because at room temperature the fungus will grow as the infectious, spore-bearing mold form.

The diagnostic laboratory should be alerted when specimens from patients suspected of having coccidiodomycosis or histoplasmosis

TABLE 246–1 Typical Appearance of Fungi in Tissue

Yeastlike fungi	
Histoplasma capsulatum	2–3 × 3–4-μm oval, budding uninucleate cells; often intracellular; granulomatous inflammation. Caseous necrosis can occur
Pneumocystis carinii	3.5–7-μm cysts resemble *H. capsulatum* on methenamine silver stain or calcofluor but do not bud. Clusters of cysts occur in alveoli surrounded by eosinophilic amorphous material
Candida glabrata	2.5–3 × 4–5-μm oval budding cells; pyogenic necrosis
Candida albicans	3 × 5-μm oval, budding cells usually by tubular structures (pseudohyphae), with constrictions at septae and branching only at septations
Cryptococcus neoformans	4–6-μm round uninucleate cell with large surrounding capsule; narrow pore between mother and daughter cell; daughter cell detached while small. Stains red with mucicarmine
Sporothrix schenckii	1–3 × 3–10-μm cigar-shaped cell or 2–10-μm round budding cell; pyogenic and granulomatous inflammation
Blastomyces dermatitidis	8–15-μm round multinucleate cell with large pore between mother and daughter cell; daughter cell remains attached until nearly size of mother cell; pyogenic and granulomatous inflammation
Paracoccidioides brasiliensis	2–30-μm multiple, budding, round cells with tiny pore between mother and daughter cell; daughter cell released when small
Coccidioides immitis	5–60-μm thick-walled, nonbudding, round cells that may contain endospores
Agents of chromoblastomycosis	4–12-μm round or oval, brown, thick-walled cells, often in clumps; hyphal forms may be seen in superficial crusts
Molds	
Aspergillus spp.	2–5-μm wide hyphae, frequently septate, even diameter, Y-shaped branching; vascular invasion; necrosis
Agents of mucormycosis	4–15-μm wide hyphae, rarely septate, uneven diameter, often branch at broad angles; vascular invasion; necrosis

are sent for culture. Once these cultures grow in the mold form, they can be hazardous to laboratory personnel.

BIBLIOGRAPHY

Connor D. Pathology of Infectious Diseases. Stamford, Conn: Appleton & Lange; 1997.

Howard DH, ed. Fungi Pathogenic for Humans and Animals. New York: Marcel Dekker; 1983.

Kwon-Chung KJ, Bennet JE. Medical Mycology. Philadelphia: Lee & Febiger; 1992.

Sugar SM. A Practical Guide to Medically Important Fungi and the Diseases They Cause. Philadelphia: Lippincott-Raven; 1997.

Chapter 247

Candida Species

JOHN E. EDWARDS, JR.

Written descriptions of oral lesions that were probably thrush date to the time of Hippocrates and Galen. Langenbeck, in 1839, found fungi in oral lesions of a patient.[1] By 1841, Berg established the fungal cause of thrush by inoculating healthy babies with aphthous "membrane material." In 1843, Robin attached to the organism the name *Oidium albicans*. There have been more than 100 synonyms for *Candida albicans*; the two that have persisted are *Monilia albicans*, originated by Zopf in 1890, and *C. albicans*, used by Berkhout in 1923.[2]

In 1861, Zenker described the first well-documented case of deep-seated *Candida*. The first case of *Candida*-induced endocarditis was described in 1940.[3] The most interesting period in the history of *Candida* infections began in the 1940s, when the widespread use of antibiotics was introduced. Since then, previously undocumented manifestations of *Candida* infections have occurred, and the incidence of practically all forms of *Candida* infections has risen abruptly. *Candida* spp. are now the fourth most common organisms recovered from blood of hospitalized patients in the United States.[4] The burden of this illness in terms of morbidity, mortality, and expense is considerable. The cost of an episode of candidemia in the United States in 1997 was estimated to be $34,123 per Medicare patient and $44,536 for a private insurance patient.[5] Excellent comprehensive reviews detailing the emergence of *Candida* as a common pathogen are now available.[6–12] These emerging infections have included arthritis, osteomyelitis, endophthalmitis, myocarditis, pericarditis, pacemaker endocarditis, meningitis, peritonitis, myositis, and others that are elaborated upon in detail in their respective sections of this chapter. The increasing incidence of human immunodeficiency virus–1 infection, the use of therapeutic modalities for advanced life support, and certain surgical procedures, such as organ transplantation and the implantation of prosthetic devices, have continued to be important in the expanding incidence of *Candida* infections.

PATHOGEN

Candida organisms are yeasts, that is, fungi that exist predominately in a unicellular form. Both sexual and asexual forms exist. They are small (4 to 6 μm), thin-walled, ovoid cells (blastospores) that reproduce by budding. They grow well in vented routine blood culture bottles and on agar plates and do not require special fungal media for cultivation. Several of the newer automated blood culture methods offer more rapid detection of *Candida*.[13, 14] Yeast forms, pseudohyphae, and hyphae may be found in microscopic examination of clinical specimens; identification of the hyphae and pseudohyphae is facilitated with 10% potassium hydroxide, which clears the epithelial cells, and with fluorescent microscopic examination of calcifluor white–stained smears. The organism also stains gram-positive.

Candida organisms form smooth, creamy white, glistening colonies that may resemble staphylococcal colonies. A rapid, presumptive identification of *C. albicans* can be made by placing the organism in serum and observing germ tube formation, small projections from the cell surface that appear within 90 minutes.[15] However, both false-negative and false-positive germ tube formation may occur. The remainder of the identification and speciation procedures are based primarily on physiologic parameters rather than on morphologic characteristics. Metabolic tests include carbohydrate assimilation and fermentation reactions, nitrate utilization, and urease production. Chlamydospore formation is also used to identify *C. albicans*. Because of variation in species pathogenicity, speciation is desirable. There are more than 150 species of *Candida,* but only nine are regarded as frequent pathogens for humans. They are *C. albicans, C. guilliermondii, C. krusei, C. parapsilosis, C. tropicalis, C. pseudotropicalis, C. lusitaniae, C. dubliniensis,* and *C. glabrata* (formerly classified as *Torulopsis glabrata*). *C. dubliniensis* is a newly described species that was formerly included within *C. albicans.*[16] *C. dubliniensis* forms germ tubes and chlamydospores and is identified as *C. albicans* by the most common methods. However, it will not grow at 45°C, is darker green when initially isolated on CHROMagar candida, and hybridizes poorly to the Ca3 probe.[17] Because it is not yet clear how the clinical features may differ from those of *C. albicans*, if at all, the two are considered synonymous in this chapter. Infections by other species are occasionally reported, such as the azole-resistant species *Candida inconspicua*.[18] The API Yeast 20C strip is a commercial kit that gives accurate identification of most *Candida* spp. in 2 to 5 days.[19]

EPIDEMIOLOGY AND ECOLOGY

C. albicans organisms have been recovered from soil, hospital environments, inanimate objects, and food. However, contamination from humans or animals is probable.[20] Other species may live in nonanimal environments, such as soil. Only rarely are *Candida* spp. laboratory contaminants.[21] That principle has not been generally appreciated, and interpretation of positive cultures as laboratory or skin contaminants has led to important errors in patient management.

The organisms are normal commensals of humans and are commonly found on skin, throughout the entire gastrointestinal (GI) tract, in expectorated sputum, in the female genital tract, and in the urine of patients with indwelling Foley catheters.[22] There is a relatively high incidence of carriage on the skin of health care workers.

Although the vast majority of *Candida* infections are of endogenous origin, human-to-human transmission is possible. Examples are thrush of the newborn, which may be acquired from the maternal vagina, and balanitis in the uncircumcised man, which may be acquired through contact with a partner having *Candida* vaginitis. There is also important, emerging evidence that *Candida* infection can be acquired from the hospital environment.[23–27] Molecular biology tools are improving the understanding of *Candida* epidemiology.[28–31]

PATHOGENESIS AND PATHOLOGIC FINDINGS

Normal defense mechanisms against *Candida* have been reviewed extensively.[32, 33] The defense mechanism of intact integument is of importance in maintaining resistance to cutaneous candidiasis; any process causing skin maceration leaves the involved site susceptible to *Candida* invasion, even in healthy individuals. Once the organism invades the dermis or enters the blood stream, polymorphonuclear leukocytes play a role in defense because they have the capacity to damage pseudohyphae and to phagocytize and to kill blastospores.[33, 34] Interestingly, in many instances, the phagocytic vacuoles around *Candida* remain unsealed.[35] In addition to neutrophils, monocytes and eosinophils also ingest and kill *Candida*.[36, 37] Monocyte killing in vitro is more efficient than polymorphonuclear killing. Platelets may also have anti-*Candida* activity.[38, 39] A platelet-derived factor stimulates germ tube production, and *Candida* cell wall fractions agglutinate platelets.[40, 41] Serum and plasma alone, even though they contain antibodies and complement components, are incapable of killing *Candida*.

Neutrophils and monocytes lacking myeloperoxidase or the capacity to generate hydrogen peroxide and superoxide anion fail to kill *C. albicans* effectively.[36, 37] This observation and additional related studies suggest that the myeloperoxidase, hydrogen peroxide, or superoxide anion system, or all of these, is a major mechanism responsible for intracellular killing of *C. albicans*. In addition, studies have identified a ferrous ion–hydrogen peroxide–iodide system that is operative in intracellular killing.[42] A further intracellular killing mechanism for phagocytes involves chymotrypsin-like cationic proteins.[43–45] These proteins probably act by increasing candidal membrane permeability. The role of macrophages and sessile reticuloendothelial cells has also been investigated. Rabbit and mouse alveolar and peritoneal and human lung macrophages have *Candida*-killing capacities.[46, 47] Of interest is a study of Taschdjian and colleagues that showed, by immunofluorescent techniques, organisms within tissue macrophages and sessile reticuloendothelial cells throughout the body in patients with disseminated candidiasis.[48] This observation suggests a defense role for these tissue macrophages.

The role of lymphocytes in defense against *Candida* and the development of *Candida*-induced cell-mediated immunity are exceptionally complex subjects that have been reviewed extensively[49] and can be only superficially summarized here. The importance of the defensive role of the lymphocyte can be gleaned from clinical observations. (1) Patients with chronic mucocutaneous candidiasis are afflicted with *Candida* infection as a result of dysfunction of their lymphocyte system.[50] (2) Patients with acquired immunodeficiency syndrome (AIDS) are highly susceptible to cutaneous candidiasis.[51, 52] However, it should be noted that there is experimental evidence for congenitally athymic (nude) mice having more resistance to *Candida* challenge than controls with normal T lymphocytes.[53, 54] Experimental evidence indicates that mannan is the important antigen influencing the lymphocyte responses.[55] Of interest also has been the identification of natural killer cells with anti-*Candida* activity.[56] Despite extensive experimental studies, there is no vaccine commercially available for the prevention of either mucocutaneous or systemic candidiasis. However, efforts are being made toward the development of a *Candida* vaccine.[57]

Several observations have substantiated the importance of humoral factors in *Candida* immune defense. The rate of ingestion of *C. albicans* by neutrophils is increased by both heat-labile and heat-stable serum opsonins.[58] Immunoglobulin G (IgG) and other serum constituents effectively opsonize *C. albicans*, and patients with disseminated candidiasis frequently have a high-titer antibody response. Although antibody is not required for the killing of partially ingested yeast cells,[59, 60] experimental studies have shown antibody-mediated protection.[61] Serum iron-binding proteins have been shown to inhibit the growth of *Candida*, presumably by binding iron, which is a *Candida* growth factor.[62] Finally, there are humoral substances that induce *C. albicans* to form pseudohyphae and to clump the organisms in vitro[63] and numerous other humoral substances that have inhibitory effects on *Candida* growth.

Complement is necessary for optimal opsonization of *Candida* blastospores[64] in vitro, and animals deficient in alternate pathway activation are more susceptible to *Candida* challenge.[65] Furthermore, C3b has been found to bind to *Candida* blastospores.[66] Also, evidence for an important role of complement is the finding of complement components deposited in the basement membrane of cutaneous lesions in patients with chronic mucocutaneous candidiasis.[67] Both the classic and the alternate pathways are activated by *Candida*. The weight of the evidence suggests that the alternate pathway is the most important. *Candida* cells, particularly pseudohyphae, have surface molecules that resemble human complement receptors CR2 and CR3.[68, 69]

The capabilities of *Candida* to adhere to vaginal and oral epithelial cells, fibronectin, platelet fibrin clots, acrylic, endothelium, and plastics have all been demonstrated.[68–73]

For this human commensal organism to become a pathogen, interruption of normal defense mechanisms is necessary. The factors responsible for this immunocompromise fall into two categories, naturally occurring and iatrogenic. Included in the first category is diabetes mellitus, which predisposes to cutaneous but not disseminated candidiasis.

The most important predisposing factors to *Candida* infection, and especially to disseminated candidiasis, are iatrogenic. The introduction of newer therapeutic modalities for advanced life support into clinical medicine has been primarily responsible for the dramatic change in incidence of this disease. Of these factors, probably the most important have been the introduction of antibiotics and the widespread use of indwelling intravenous catheters. Antibiotics suppress normal bacterial flora and allow *Candida* organisms to proliferate, especially in the GI tract. Sulfonamides decrease neutrophil *Candida* intracellular killing,[74] and tetracycline, doxycycline, and aminoglycosides have been shown to decrease neutrophil phagocytosis.[75, 76]

Factors that may provide a route for *Candida* to enter from the environment into the vascular system of susceptible patients include the use of heroin,[77] hyperalimentation fluids, polyethylene catheters,[78] and pressure-monitoring devices. The implantation of prosthetic materials, especially cardiac valves and the artificial heart, is also associated with an increased incidence of *Candida* infection. Clinical situations associated with general immune suppression may be further complicated by the use of antibiotics, hyperalimentation fluid, and the other therapeutic modalities mentioned earlier, usually in the setting of multiple abdominal surgeries, renal transplantation, neoplastic diseases, the use of steroids, and severe burns.

Two observations support the hypothesis that the GI tract is a likely source for entrance of *Candida* into the blood stream. Krause and associates reported drinking a suspension containing a massive amount of *Candida*.[79] Despite no recognizable GI disease, the investigator became candidemic and candiduric. Stone and coworkers have shown that yeasts can cross the GI tract of animals.[80] One would expect patients who have had abdominal surgery and therapy with multiple antibiotics to be at double risk for dissemination from the GI source by having both overgrowth of *Candida* in the GI tract and interruptions of the normal GI-tract mucosal integrity. GI-tract surgery is now a well-recognized predisposing factor to disseminated candidiasis.[81] It is possible that loss of integrity of the GI tract due to either the disease or the cytotoxic chemotherapy creates a portal by which *Candida* passes from the GI-tract lumen into the blood stream.[82] Alternatively, the growing body of literature regarding *Candida* as a cause of septic thrombophlebitis suggests that in many cases the skin site of vascular catheter entry, rather than the GI tract, is the most likely portal of entry.[83]

When the organism invades visceral tissue, microabscesses are formed, generally with normal parenchyma between the microabscesses. In tissue, both yeast forms and hyphal forms are present. Whether the formation of filamentous forms of *Candida* is a factor associated with virulence is one of the major unresolved controversies within the field.[84] The initial cellular reaction is granulocytic. Histiocytes, giant cells, and epithelioid cells appear early, and the reaction may take the form of a granulomatous response. Although organisms may be seen on hematoxylin-eosin stains, optimal staining is accomplished with period acid–Schiff or methenamine silver. In the severely immunocompromised patient, the inflammatory reaction may be minimal or almost nonexistent, leaving the abscess composed only of *Candida* and necrotic tissue.

In superficial candidiasis, the histopathologic change is a chronic dermatitis with the yeast confined to the stratum corneum. However, *Candida* granuloma (see "Clinical Manifestations") is characterized by invasion into both the epidermis and the dermis as well as by marked hyperkeratosis and acanthosis.

The factors associated with the organism rather than the host that are responsible for its virulence are under investigation.[33, 69, 85, 86] An incomplete list includes the germ tube, proteases, phospholipases, adherence capabilities, hydrophobicity, morphologic switching, the presence of human-like integrins, and resistance to platelet-derived microbicidal peptides.

CLINICAL MANIFESTATIONS

As the frequency of diseases due to *Candida* has increased, a relatively large number of manifestations, which were previously either not recognized or extremely infrequent, have become well documented. The discussion of these clinical manifestations is facilitated by their subdivision into mucocutaneous and deep organ involvement.

Mucous Membrane Infections

Thrush

Oral *Candida* infections are common and have been reviewed.[87–94] The term *thrush* is applied to a specific form of oral candidiasis characterized by creamy white, curdlike patches on the tongue (Fig. 247–1) and on other oral mucosal surfaces; the patches are removable by scraping and leave a raw, bleeding, and painful surface. The patches are actually a pseudomembrane consisting of *Candida*, desquamated epithelial cells, leukocytes, bacteria, keratin, necrotic tissue, and food debris.[95] The diagnosis can be made by the clinical appearance of the lesion and by scraping, using either a potassium hydroxide smear or Gram stain to show masses of hyphae, pseudohyphae, and yeast forms. Simple culturing does not solidify the diagnosis because *Candida* grows easily from normal mouths. In addition to the classic lesions, which have been described by Lehner,[95] other manifestations include (1) acute atrophic candidiasis, a nonspecific atrophy of the tongue that is thought to be a sequela of acute pseudomembranous candidiasis; (2) chronic atrophic candidiasis or "denture sore mouth," which is a chronic inflammatory reaction and epithelial thinning under the dental plates[90]; (3) angular cheilitis, an inflammatory reaction at the corners of the mouth (not due exclusively to *Candida*); and (4) *Candida* leukoplakia, firm, white plaques affecting the cheek, lips, and tongue that have a protracted course (and, in rare instances, may be precancerous).[96]

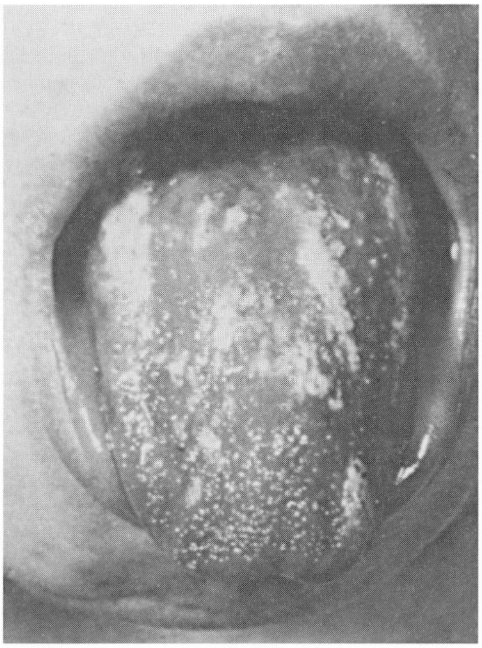

FIGURE 247–1. Typical oral thrush with curdlike white patches over the tongue. (Courtesy of Dr. Arnold Gurevitch.)

Since the introduction of inhaled steroids for the treatment of asthma, especially in children, oral thrush has been reported extensively in patients treated with these agents.[97] Incidence has ranged from 0 to 77%. Thrush developing in patients who use inhaled steroids usually resolves spontaneously without a change in the dosage of the agent or is successfully managed with topical nystatin or clotrimazole.

Other patients with a high incidence of thrush are cancer patients and those with AIDS.[98] Patients with thrush for no obvious reason should be evaluated for AIDS.[99] Because of the introduction of potent antiretroviral therapy, the incidence of thrush has declined in patients with AIDS.

Candida Esophagitis

Although there have been a small number of reports of *Candida* esophagitis occurring in patients with no known underlying illness, it is more commonly associated with treatment of malignancy of the hematopoietic or lymphatic systems (Fig. 247–2) and in AIDS patients. Esophageal disease was believed to occur by direct spread from oral disease (thrush), but reviews have shown that *Candida* esophagitis may occur frequently without thrush.[100–103] The most common symptoms of *Candida* esophagitis include painful swallowing, a feeling of obstruction on swallowing, and substernal chest pain. Nausea and vomiting may also occur. The diagnosis is made definitively by biopsy during endoscopy[104–106] (Fig. 247–3) or by brushing. However, the appropriate clinical settings, associated with

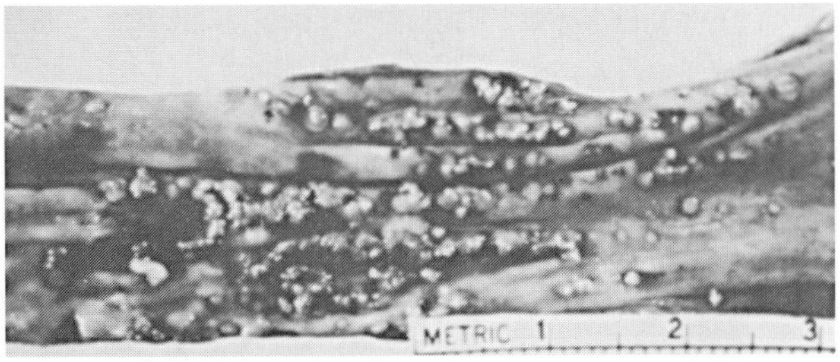

FIGURE 247–2. Severe *Candida* esophagitis at autopsy.

the endoscopic appearance of white patches resembling thrush that show masses of hyphae and pseudohyphae on scraping, are enough evidence to initiate therapy without a histopathologic demonstration of the organisms invading the mucosa.[100–102] It is important to recognize that *Candida* esophagitis can occur simultaneously with herpes simplex virus or cytomegalovirus infection in severely immunocompromised patients. Radiographic examination may be helpful in making a clinical diagnosis; irregularity of the esophageal mucosa as a result of ulcerations may be seen, as well as shoulder defects, diverticulae, fistulas, and dilatation of the esophagus from denervation.[107] Endoscopy is the preferred procedure for definitive diagnosis, however. The pseudomembrane that forms may become so extensive that it causes intraluminal protrusions and partial esophageal obstruction. Perforation of the esophagus due to esophageal candidiasis is very rare. Generally, if perforation occurs, it is in the lower two thirds of the esophagus. Some patients have had extensive esophageal disease and been almost asymptomatic, probably as a result of denervation of the esophagus from the disease.[108] Other complications include bleeding and, presumably, dissemination (see Chapter 82).

Nonesophageal, Mucous Membrane, Gastrointestinal Candidiasis

The most common clinical setting for GI-tract candidiasis is in patients with neoplastic disease. Eras and colleagues reviewed their autopsy experience with candidiasis in a cancer hospital and found that second only to esophageal candidiasis, involvement of the stomach was by far the next most common site.[109] The most frequent lesions were single or multiple ulcerations containing *Candida* deep in the ulcer beds. In addition, but with lesser frequency, chronic gastric ulcer, gastric perforation, and malignant gastric ulcer with concomitant *Candida* infection were seen. Small bowel and large bowel infection occur also.[110] Ulceration is the most common lesion. Pseudomembrane formation and ulceration in association with tumor occurs also. As in other mucous membrane *Candida* infections, white plaques may be seen on endoscopy of the duodenum, and there may be thickening of mucosal folds in the duodenum and jejunum.[110] Equal in frequency to the involvement of the small bowel is involvement of the large bowel, which again may be characterized by ulceration, superficial erosions, pseudomembrane formation, penetrating ulcers, and perforation. Gastric candidiasis has two forms: diffuse mucosal involvement (rare) and focal invasion of benign gastric ulcers.[111, 112]

Candida Vaginitis

This common infection is most frequently seen in a setting of diabetes mellitus, antibiotic therapy, and pregnancy (see Chapter 96).[113–115] In addition, the use of birth control pills may be a predisposing factor, although this association is controversial. However, estimates are that 75% of women have an episode of candidal vaginitis during their lifetime; many have no recognizable underlying predisposing factor.[116] *Candida* has assumed the role of the most common cause of vaginitis with higher frequency rates than those of

FIGURE 247–3. Numerous *Candida* plaques seen in the esophagus (panels 2 and 3) and the duodenum (panels 4 and 5) at endoscopy.

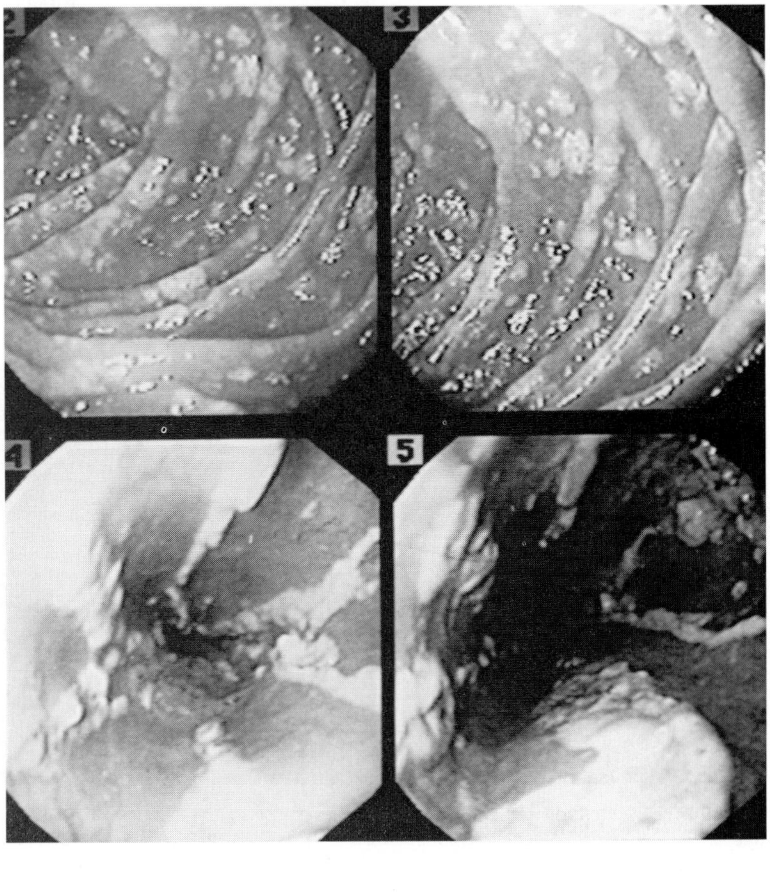

Trichomonas or bacterial vaginosis.[114] The widespread use of antibiotic therapy may be the most important factor responsible for the emergence of *Candida*-induced vaginitis.

Although *Candida*-induced vaginitis may be accompanied by a thick, curdlike discharge, scanty discharge may instead characterize the infection. Edema and intense pruritus of the vulva is almost always present. The discharge consists of epithelial cells and masses of hyphae and pseudohyphae; a polymorphonuclear leukocyte response is not a component of the inflammatory reaction. The vagina and labia are usually erythematous, and extension onto skin of the perineum can occur (Fig. 247–4). In addition, endometritis due to *Candida* has been reported, and the urethra may become secondarily infected.

Vaginal candidiasis is not clearly more common or more refractory to treatment in patients with AIDS.[117] The causes of recurrent vulvovaginal candidiasis may be related to deficiencies in both systemic cell-mediated immunity and local mucosal immunity.[118]

Cutaneous Candidiasis Syndromes

Generalized Cutaneous Candidiasis

This condition is an unusual form of cutaneous candidiasis and is characterized by widespread eruptions over the trunk, thorax, and extremities with increased severity in the genitocrural folds, anal region, axillae, hands, and feet (Fig. 247–5). The process begins as individual lesions that spread into large confluent areas. It occurs in both adults and children.[119, 120]

Erosio Interdigitalis Blastomycetica

This term applies to *Candida* infection occurring between the fingers or toes (Fig. 247–6). It has a red base, may extend onto the sides of the digits, is painful, and is predisposed to by maceration.[119]

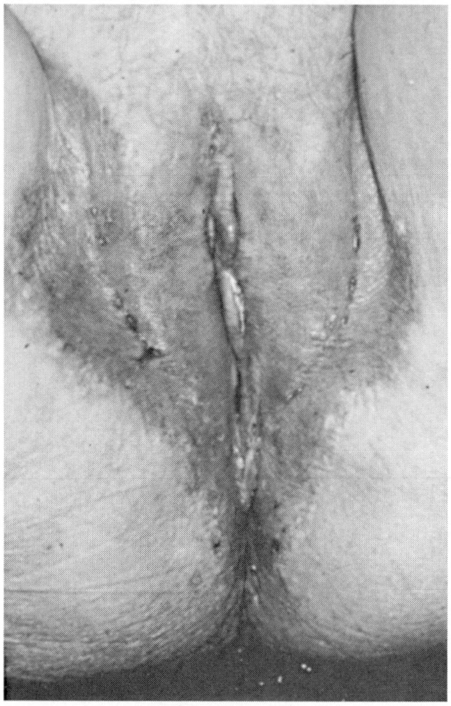

FIGURE 247–4. Extension of *Candida* vaginitis onto the perineum. (Courtesy of Dr. Victor Newcomer.)

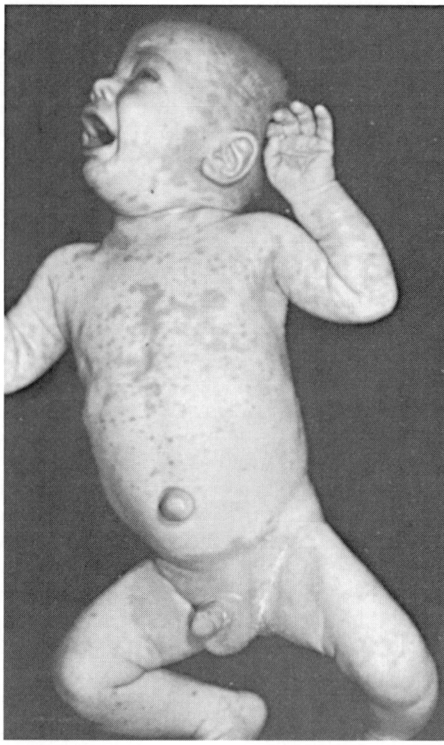

FIGURE 247–5. Generalized candidiasis. (Courtesy of Dr. Victor Newcomer.)

Candida Folliculitis

Infection at the hair follicles with *Candida* can occur (Fig. 247–7).[121, 122] Rarely, the condition may become extensive. It must be distinguished from folliculitis caused by the dermatophytes and tinea versicolor.

Candida Balanitis

This process begins as vesicles on the penis that develop into patches resembling thrush and are accompanied by severe itching and burning. It may spread to the thighs, gluteal folds, buttocks, and scrotum. It can be acquired through sexual intercourse with a partner having vaginal candidiasis.[123] *Candida* is one of the more common causes of balanitis.

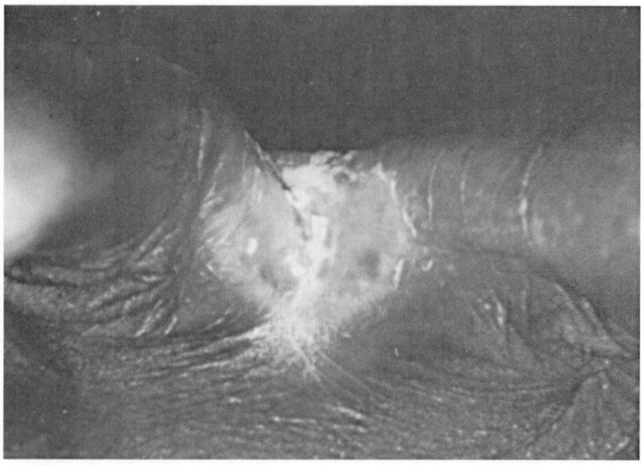

FIGURE 247–6. Erosio interdigitalis blastomycetica. (Courtesy of Dr. Arnold Gurevitch.)

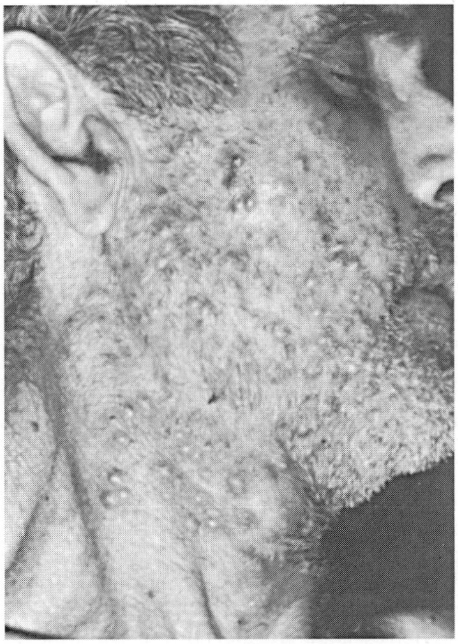

FIGURE 247–7. Severe *Candida* folliculitis in beard distribution. (Courtesy of Dr. Victor Newcomer.)

Cutaneous Lesions of Disseminated Candidiasis

Three distinct types of lesions associated with disseminated candidiasis have been described.[124–127] The macronodular lesions (Fig. 247–8) are 0.5 to 1 cm in diameter, pink to red, and may either be single or occur widely distributed over the entire body.[128, 129] The most accurate method of making a specific diagnosis is by punch biopsy and demonstration of organisms on histologic section. Most patients with these lesions are neutropenic, and all have disseminated candidiasis, not local inoculation. The lesions can resemble ecthyma gangrenosum[130] or purpura fulminans.[131] Chronic lesions of pyoderma gangrenosa may become superinfected with *Candida* and delay their diagnosis.[132]

Intertrigo

This common skin condition affects any site in which skin surfaces are in close proximity and provide a warm, moist environment. It begins as vesicopustules, which enlarge and rupture, causing maceration and fissuring. The area of involvement has a scalloped border with a white rim consisting of necrotic epidermis, which surrounds an erythematous, macerated base. Frequently, satellite lesions are found that may coalesce and extend the affected area. A variant form of cutaneous candidiasis in the intertriginous region has a miliary appearance resembling miliaria rubra with erythematous macules or vesicopustules.[133]

Paronychia and Onychomycosis

Candida is one of the most common causes of paronychia. Many skin bacteria, as well as *Candida*, can usually be recovered by culture of the infected area. The appearance of the reaction is that of a relatively well localized area of inflammation that becomes warm, glistening, and tense and may extend extensively under the nail (Fig. 247–9). Unless the disease process is stopped, secondary thickening, ridging, and discoloration occur, and nail loss may result.

Candida paronychia occurs in association with frequent immersion of the hands in water. People who may contract paronychia include dishwashers, laundry workers, and young mothers. There is also a higher incidence of paronychia among diabetic patients than in the nondiabetic population. Specific diagnosis is made by Gram stain or potassium hydroxide preparation and culture showing predominantly *Candida* organisms.

In addition to paronychia, *Candida* may cause infection in the nail itself and is a cause of onychomycosis.[134]

Diaper Rash

Candida is a common cause of diaper rash in infants. The condition generally starts in the perianal area and spreads over the perineum in the region of diaper contact (Fig. 247–10). The process is facilitated by maceration caused by wet diapers. The probable origin is the GI tract. Diagnosis is made by scraping the area and demonstrating the organisms on potassium hydroxide preparation.[135]

Perianal Candidiasis

Although numerous organisms and combinations of organisms have been associated with pruritus ani either alone or in combination, *Candida* is a frequent cause.[136] The perianal skin develops marked erythema and progresses to maceration (Fig. 247–11). Intense pruritus results. Complications include involvement of the anal canal and extensive spread over the perineum.

Chronic Mucocutaneous Candidiasis

The term *chronic mucocutaneous candidiasis* (CMC) is used to describe a heterogeneous group of *Candida* infections of the skin, mucous membranes, hair, and nails that have a protracted and persistent course despite what is usually adequate therapy. The subject has been the focus of several reviews.[50, 137, 138] *Candida* esophagitis can

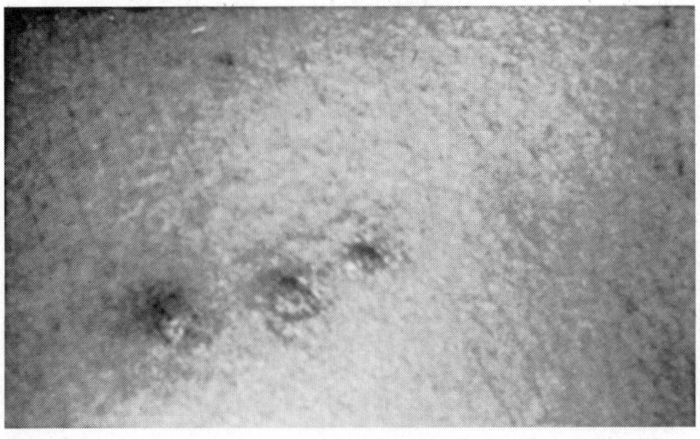

FIGURE 247–8. Macronodular lesions of disseminated candidiasis. (Courtesy of Dr. Richard Meyer.)

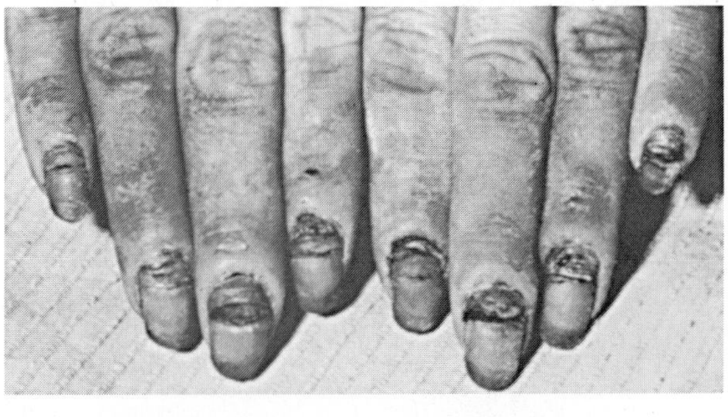

FIGURE 247–9. *Candida* paronychia and onychomycosis. (Courtesy of Dr. Victor Newcomer.)

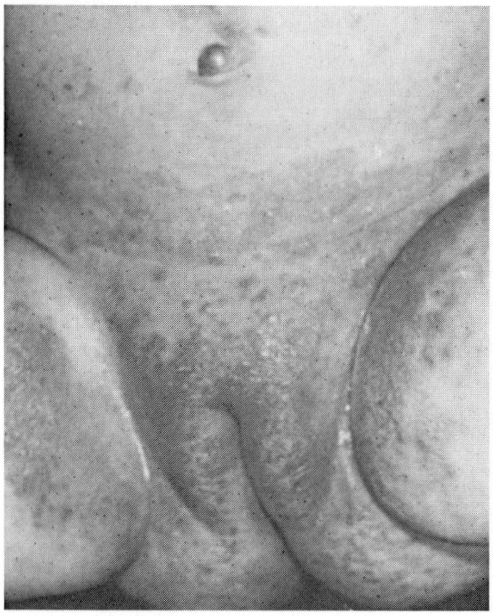

FIGURE 247–10. Severe *Candida* diaper rash. (Courtesy of Dr. Victor Newcomer.)

occur and, over the years, cause esophageal stenosis. The major problem, however, is disfiguring lesions of the face, scalp, and hands. Alopecia in areas of infection is common and may be permanent. These infections have been associated with definable, relatively specific, immunologic abnormalities, which may be responsible for their persistent nature.

The major immune defect associated with CMC is failure of T-cell lymphocytes (thymus derived) to respond to stimulation with *Candida* antigen in vitro by either lymphocyte transformation or the synthesis of macrophage inhibition factor. An in vivo manifestation of this abnormality is reflected in the cutaneous anergy found in approximately one half of the patients. Various combinations of the T-cell function abnormalities exist. Some patients' lymphocytes transform in vitro when stimulated by *Candida* antigen, but their skin tests remain negative to the antigen. Certain patients with positive transformations do not synthesize macrophage inhibition factor; virtually all patients with negative transformations lack macrophage inhibition factor production. Despite these abnormalities of T-cell function (T-cell numbers, lymphocyte proliferative responses to nonspecific mitogens such as phytohemagglutinins and allogenic cells), B-cell lymphocyte numbers and serum immunoglobulins are usually normal. However, some patients have other immune abnormalities, such as cutaneous anergy to such antigens as streptokinase-streptodornase, mumps virus, and tetanus toxoid; defective lymphocyte transformations to nonspecific mitogens (e.g., phytohemagglutinin); defective monocyte chemotaxis; a lack of anti-*Candida* antibody in salivary IgAs; plasma inhibitors to *Candida*-stimulated lymphocyte transformations; suppressor lymphocytes; and various degrees of thymic aplasia. Not all patients have these identifiable immune abnormalities.

Most forms of CMC begin in infancy or within the first 2 decades; rarely, the onset may be after the age of 30 years. The first manifestation is usually oral thrush followed by nail infections and then skin involvement. There is a considerable spectrum of severity, ranging from chronic involvement of an isolated nail to a severely disfiguring form (*Candida* granuloma) (Fig. 247–12). An additional facet of CMC is the association of several endocrine disorders in approximately one half of the patients. Endocrinopathy tends to follow, not precede, CMC, often after an interval of several years. The most common endocrinopathies are hypoparathyroidism and Addison's disease. Hypothyroidism and diabetes mellitus occur also. Autoimmune antibodies to adrenal, thyroid, and gastric tissues are present in approximately one half of the cases. Thymoma, chronic dermatophytosis, and dental dysplasia have also been associated with CMC. Associations have also been made with vitiligo, polyglandular autoimmune disease, and autoantibodies to melanin-producing cells.

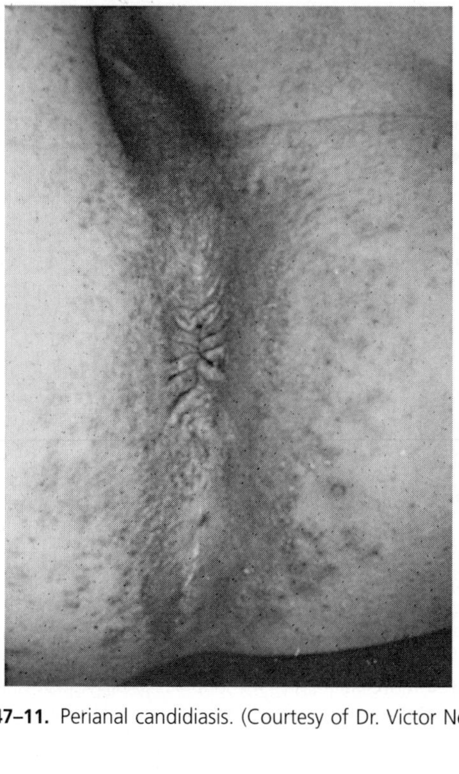

FIGURE 247–11. Perianal candidiasis. (Courtesy of Dr. Victor Newcomer.)

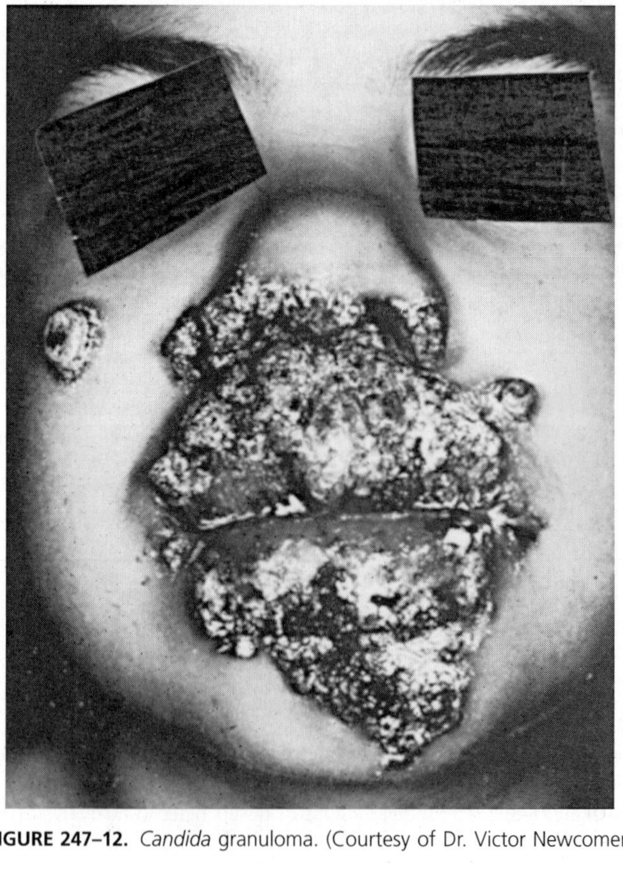

FIGURE 247–12. *Candida* granuloma. (Courtesy of Dr. Victor Newcomer.)

Although most patients with CMC survive for a prolonged period with their disease, patients may succumb if the cutaneous condition and immunodeficiencies are severe enough. Disseminated candidiasis has been a rare complication of this disease; the most common cause of death is bacterial sepsis.

The topic of *Candida* skin infection in general has been reviewed extensively.[139]

Deep Organ Involvement

Central Nervous System Candidiasis

Candida infects both parenchymal brain tissue and the meninges, usually as a complication of hematogenously disseminated candidiasis.[140–142] Approximately 50% of patients with *Candida* meningitis have had disseminated disease.[143] *Candida* has emerged as the dominant cerebral mycosis in autopsied patients.[140] When infection occurs in brain parenchyma, it generally forms multiple microabscesses and small macroabscesses scattered throughout the tissue.[144, 145] Rarely, larger abscesses have occurred and may be visualized by computed tomography.[146]

Virtually all patients with *Candida* meningitis have had cerebrospinal fluid pleocytosis. Fifty percent have had a lymphocyte pleocytosis with an average count of 600 cells/mm^3. Sixty percent have had hypoglycorrhachia and elevated protein levels; organisms have been present on wet mount or Gram stain in approximately 40%.[143] *C. albicans* has been the responsible pathogen in 90% of cases. Occasional cases due to *C. tropicalis* are being reported.

The clinical manifestations of central nervous system involvement with diffuse microabscesses may be variable. If the patient is comatose or noncommunicative, detection of abnormalities may be exceptionally difficult. When meningitis is present, the signs of meningeal irritation (headache, stiff neck, irritability), typical of any meningeal infection, are frequently present. In the newborn, particularly the very low birth weight neonate, diagnosis is often difficult and delayed, leading to permanent neurologic sequelae. Lumbar puncture should be considered when the blood culture of such infants contains *Candida*.

In addition to occurring as a complication of disseminated candidiasis,[147] *Candida* meningitis may result from infection of a ventricular shunt[148] or may be introduced by lumbar puncture,[149] trauma, or neurosurgery[150] or may complicate bacterial meningitis. The signs and symptoms are nonspecific. Untreated, the mortality rate is very high; it is reduced substantially with antifungal therapy. Hydrocephalus is a reasonably frequently occurring complication of the infection. An increase in the number of cases of *Candida* meningitis reported in neonates is occurring. AIDS is now considered a predisposing factor for *Candida* meningitis.[140, 151]

Respiratory Tract Candidiasis

In general, *Candida* pneumonia occurs in two forms: (1) either local or diffuse bronchopneumonia originating from endobronchial inoculation of the lung,[152, 153] a very rare event, or (2) as a hematogenously seeded, finely nodular, diffuse infiltrate, which in its early stages may be difficult to distinguish from congestive heart failure or *Pneumocystis* pneumonia.[154–157] Other forms of *Candida* pneumonia are very rare; those that have been described are necrotizing pneumonia,[155, 158] *Candida* pulmonary mycetoma,[159] and transient infiltrates due to *Candida*.[160] Radiographic and computed tomographic findings are nonspecific, and definitive diagnosis depends on biopsy-proven fungal invasion of pulmonary tissue.[161, 162] Because of a relatively high prevalence of yeasts colonizing the respiratory tract, especially in ill patients, a diagnosis of *Candida* pneumonia cannot be made on radiographic findings and recovery of yeasts from sputum or endotracheal tube aspirate.[163] *Candida* has also caused bronchial infection,[164] laryngitis,[165] epiglottitis,[166] and infection of laryngeal prostheses.[167]

Cardiac Candidiasis

In addition to causing endocarditis, *Candida* infects both the pericardium[168] and the myocardium. *Candida* myocarditis occurs as diffuse microabscesses scattered throughout the myocardium with normal intervening myocardial tissue. The relatively high incidence of myocarditis has been stressed by Franklin and coworkers, who found that 62% of their 50 patients with disseminated candidiasis had myocardial involvement.[169] Other retrospective autopsy studies have shown a range from 8.4 to 93%. *Candida* myocarditis is also occurring in AIDS patients.[170] Autopsy series of disseminated candidiasis reveal a surprisingly high incidence of myocarditis (without associated valvular involvement) and point to the importance of thorough cardiac evaluation in patients who may have disseminated candidiasis. Of interest has been the emergence of *Candida* organisms as a cause of pericarditis.[168, 171, 172] A review of purulent pericarditis spanning the years 1960 to 1974 revealed that *Candida* organisms were either the single cause or combined with *Aspergillus* in 15% of the 26 cases.[173] The association of *Candida* pericarditis with either cardiac surgery or burns has been emphasized.

Candida Endocarditis

This manifestation of *Candida* was once a distinctly rare phenomenon, but its true incidence has increased simultaneously with the generalized increase in *Candida* infections. Of all the forms of fungal endocarditis, *Candida* is by far the most common. In the last 4 decades, there have been well over 214 reported cases.[174–176] In a detailed review of 319 cases of fungal endocarditis, *Candida* accounted for 67% of the cases.[175] The entity of *Candida* endocarditis has been reviewed extensively.[177–181]

Candida endocarditis occurs in association with six clinical factors: (1) underlying valvular heart disease, (2) heroin addiction, (3) cancer chemotherapy, (4) implantation of prosthetic valves, (5) prolonged use of intravenous catheters (endocarditis, right atrial fungal masses, and infection of atrial myxomas have all been described), and (6) preexisting bacterial endocarditis, on which it is superimposed. Of these associations, by far the most frequent is the postoperative cardiac surgery, accounting for approximately 50% of the cases. Of interest is the frequency of species other than *C. albicans* that have caused endocarditis; a minimum of 41% of the cases have been due to organisms of other species. In heroin addicts, *C. parapsilosis* has been the most common causative organism.[182]

The pathogenic mechanisms for fungal endocarditis are not fully understood, but patients who undergo cardiac surgery are at risk for candidemia by being exposed to multiple antibiotics, prolonged intravenous fluid administration, and intravenous plastic catheters. Both the damaged endocardium and prosthetic material apparently serve as foci for the localization of *Candida* organisms. Also, contamination of suture material has been implicated in cases reported with concentration along the suture line. Contamination of homografts and heterografts before insertion has also been documented.[183] Experimental evidence for a role in the pathogenesis of adherence of *Candida* to platelet fibrin complexes and/or fibronectin is accumulating.[38, 184] The mechanisms for adherence and the potential for blocking the adherence are under investigation.

The most common valves involved in *Candida* endocarditis have been the aortic and the mitral. In postoperative *Candida* endocarditis, the type of surgery has not been as important as the length of the postoperative course and complications during the postoperative period. *Candida* infection has been seen in simple valvulotomies and in prosthetic material placement, heterografts, and homografts. Pacemaker endocarditis has also been described.[185] The physical findings and usual symptoms of *Candida* endocarditis are not significantly different from those of bacterial endocarditis with the exception of the occurrence of large emboli to major vessels. Osler's nodes, Janeway lesions, splinter hemorrhages, hepatosplenomegaly, hematuria, proteinuria, pyuria, and casts all can occur. In addition, although the lesions of hematogenous *Candida* endophthalmitis have been described much more frequently in the setting of disseminated candidiasis without endocarditis, they may also be seen with endocarditis.

The complications of *Candida* endocarditis are very similar to those of bacterial endocarditis and include valve perforation, myocarditis, congestive heart failure, and major emboli. Although most cases of postoperative *Candida* endocarditis occur in the first 2 postoperative months, some have occurred later,[180, 186] and some patients who have been treated have had recurrent active disease after 2 years[187] and perhaps as long as 8 years. Therefore, in following patients treated for postoperative endocarditis, careful follow-up must be extended over a prolonged period.

Most patients with *Candida* endocarditis have positive blood cultures. Seelig and associates, in their 1974 analysis of 91 published cases of *Candida* endocarditis following cardiac surgery, noted that only 24 patients (26%) had negative blood cultures.[188] Modern blood culture methods likely provide better sensitivity. Echocardiography is becoming progressively more helpful, and large vegetations may be detected with this technique. False-negative results are common, especially in cases of mural endocarditis without valvular involvement. Transesophageal echocardiography has improved the sensitivity, particularly in the mitral valve. Serologic tests for *Candida* antibodies are associated with a high incidence of false negatives and false positives and are not clinically useful in the diagnosis of *Candida* endocarditis.

The therapy for *Candida* endocarditis is discussed in detail in the section on therapy. Before the introduction of surgical procedures for the management of *Candida*-induced endocarditis, the mortality rate from this disease was approximately 90%. With combined surgical and medical therapy, this high mortality rate has dropped to approximately 45%.

Candida endocarditis has been seen in association with bacterial endocarditis. *Candida* is a superinfection introduced by prolonged intravenous catheterization for antibiotic treatment.

Urinary Tract Candidiasis

This topic has been reviewed comprehensively.[189–193] Urethral candidiasis can occur in both men and women. In men, it usually results from sexual contact with women with *Candida* vaginitis. In women, it is generally thought to be acquired from extension of *Candida* vaginitis. *Candida* prostatic infection has also been reported.[194–196] A history of previous antibiotic use has been frequent in most patients.

The presence of *Candida* in the urine is common and usually does not indicate renal tract infection. Antibiotics and Foley catheters have been associated with the acquisition of candiduria. Visualization (cystoscopy) or biopsy proof of either fungus balls or tissue invasion is requisite for linking candiduria to infection. Although the use of colony counting in urine has been attempted to separate colonization from infection, it is not useful.[197] However, finding *Candida* in urine casts may be helpful in diagnosing renal tissue invasion of the upper renal tract.[198] Most patients with iatrogenic candiduria have spontaneous resolution; however, long-term persistence or a bladder fungus ball may be a complication, particularly in patients with diabetes mellitus, urinary stones, or obstruction.[199] Hematogenous dissemination from the urinary tract may occur, usually with instrumention.[200]

Candida cystitis is most commonly a complication of an indwelling Foley catheter. In the absence of bladder instrumentation, *Candida* cystitis has been associated most often with diabetes mellitus. Symptoms may be absent or may be essentially identical to those of bacterial cystitis. The cystoscopic appearance of the condition is that of a chronic nonspecific cystitis. A typical thrush membrane has been observed; it resembles deposits of coagulated milk and bleeds on removal. The condition may be so severe that perforation occurs.[201]

Candida infection of the upper urinary tract has been classified into two distinct forms: primary, that is, presumably from an ascending route, and secondary, from hematogenous spread. Papillary necrosis,[202] calyceal invasion, fungus ball formation, and perinephric abscess[203] can result from ascending infection, particularly in the presence of urinary tract obstruction, renal stones, or diabetes mellitus.[204–207] The hematogenous form of the disease is by far the most common. The pathologic changes are those of multiple microabscesses, especially in the cortical areas. Of interest is one case of emphysematous pyelonephritis in a diabetic drug-addicted patient (and a case of cystitis emphysematosa[208, 209]). Pneumaturia has occurred.[210] The kidney is one of the organs most frequently involved in disseminated disease.

Candida Arthritis, Osteomyelitis, Costochondritis, and Myositis

These manifestations of *Candida* infections were once extremely rare; however, their true incidence has increased appreciably.[211–217] Sites of localization for hematogenous *Candida*–caused osteomyelitis include the spine (vertebrae and intervertebral disks (Fig. 247–13)), wrist, femur, cervical spine, and costochondral junctions of the ribs, scapula, and proximal humerus. Blood cultures have usually been negative, and diagnosis has been made by percutaneous needle aspiration of the involved area. In children, the long bones are generally affected, whereas in adults the axial skeleton predominates. Spinal involvement may be accompanied by disk infection.[218, 219] Bone infection may require surgery. Osteomyelitis may be a late complication of candidemia.[213] Radiographic examination findings are nonspecific.

Osteomyelitis as a result of contiguous spread from the skin has also been documented, and there is one reported case of extension of thrush of the mouth into the mandibular bone.

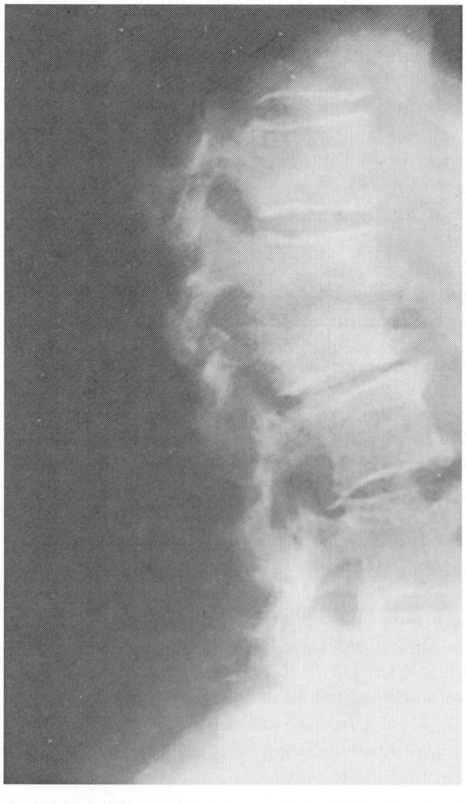

FIGURE 247–13. *Candida* spinal osteomyelitis. Note the involvement of the intervertebral disk and adjacent vertebrae. (Reprinted from Edwards JE Jr, Turkel SB, Elden HA, et al. Hematogenous candida osteomyelitis. Am J Med. 1975;59:89–94, with permission from Excerpta Medica Inc.)

Candida arthritis occurs most frequently as a complication of disseminated candidiasis.[220–222] It can also occur from trauma, surgery,[223] and intra-articular injections of steroids, and as a complication of heroin injection, rheumatoid arthritis, and AIDS.[224] The topic of fungal arthritis in general has been reviewed.[220] In *Candida* arthritis occurring unassociated with disseminated candidiasis, non-*albicans* species have been the most common. Although the majority of cases of *Candida* arthritis have been acute, chronic *Candida* arthritis has been reported, especially in leukemic patients. Generally, *Candida* arthritis has begun as a suppurative synovitis, and a high percentage of cases have extended to form osteomyelitis. *Candida* costochondritis can occur from hematogenous seeding or as a complication of median sternotomy wound infection.

Candida infection of muscle has been described. The majority of patients have been neutropenic, had hematogenously disseminated candidiasis, and had pain in the involved muscle.[225] The organisms may be seen on biopsy of the involved muscle. Generally, the muscle involvement is diffuse. However, a discrete muscle abscess may occur.[226]

Candida Infection of Peritoneum, Liver, Spleen, and Gallbladder

This infection is a complication of peritoneal dialysis, GI surgery, and perforation of an abdominal viscus.[227–239] Prior antibiotic administration has been an important predisposing factor. For reasons not completely understood, the peritoneal process usually remains localized to the abdomen; the incidence of dissemination is approximately 25% in patients acquiring the disease from GI-tract perforation. In patients with peritonitis caused by chronic ambulatory peritoneal dialysis, dissemination is distinctly uncommon. Infants disseminate more frequently.

Other GI organs infected with *Candida* that have been reported include the gallbladder,[240, 241] liver and spleen,[210, 242–247] spleen alone,[248, 249] and pancreas.[250–253] Hepatosplenic candidiasis has emerged as an important clinical problem in immunocompromised hosts and is particularly difficult to treat successfully. Most of these infections have occurred in severely immunocompromised patients and become manifest during their recovery from neutropenia. When the liver and spleen are involved, there is frequently involvement of other organs also, such as the kidney. Computed tomography, ultrasonography,[243] or magnetic resonance imaging may visualize liver, kidney, or spleen abscesses (Fig. 247–14).[254] Laparoscopic techniques have been used successfully for diagnosis.[246] Fungus balls may form in the gallbladder and bile ducts.[255–258]

Candida Infection of Vasculature

The incidence of *Candida* intravascular infection has increased significantly, probably due to the increased number of susceptible patients and the widespread increased use of indwelling intravascular devices for advanced life support.[83, 259–261] Both peripheral and deep vascular structures have been involved as well as both the venous and the arterial sides of the circulation and implanted prosthetic vascular materials.[262, 263] Although the exact pathogenesis is not known, presumably the damaged endothelium becomes susceptible to *Candida* invasion. *Candida* adherence to catheters may also play a role. Complications have included superior cava obstruction, mural endocarditis of the right atrium, tricuspid endocarditis, and pulmonary venous thrombosis. Of importance is that in patients with peripheral septic thrombophlebitis, there may be minimal symptoms and the extent of the disease may be greater than is apparent on initial clinical assessment. These patients require aggressive surgical exploration to determine the extent of the disease process. Culture of the blood and involved veins is frequently positive.[261]

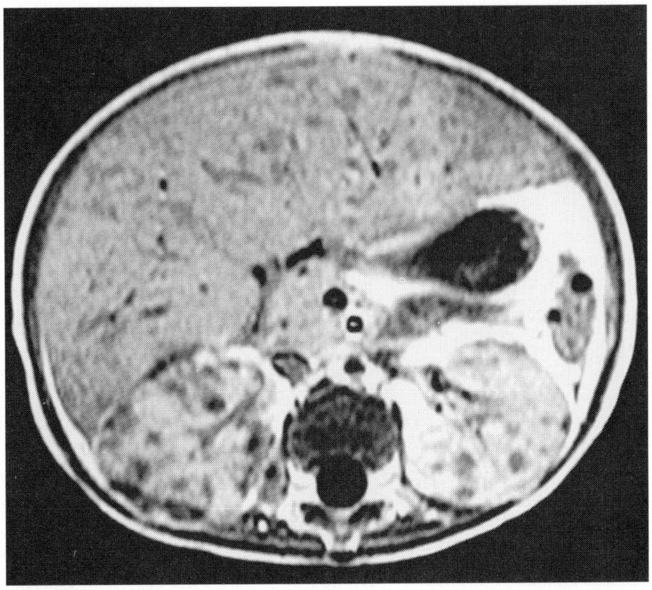

FIGURE 247–14. *Candida* abscesses in the liver, kidney, and spleen on magnetic resonance imaging.

Ocular Candidiasis

Candida can infect the eye by either hematogenous spread or direct inoculation, especially during eye surgery. *Candida* can infect virtually any eye structure, including conjunctiva, cornea, lens, ciliary body, vitreous humor, and the entire uveal tract. Once endophthalmitis occurs, therapy is difficult, and the incidence of permanent intraocular damage is high.

Through the 1970s there was increased reporting of hematogenous *Candida* endophthalmitis and an actual increase in incidence of this complication of candidemia.[264–277] Estimates of the incidence of the lesions in candidemic patients range as high as 28%.[278] The lesions are important because they can cause permanent blindness, and they may indicate underlying disseminated candidiasis. Lesions are white, cotton ball–like, and chorioretinal in origin and rapidly progress to involve the vitreous (Fig. 247–15). Use of the indirect ophthalmoscope facilitates visualization of their three-dimensional characteristics. Neutropenia inhibits the formation of ocular lesions in the experimental rabbit model[279] and may be associated with a lack of formation of easily seen lesions in some neutropenic patients. Diagnosis can be made by the characteristic fundoscopic picture plus, in half the cases, an episode of known candidemia. Aspiration of the anterior chamber is rarely diagnostic. However, elective vitrectomy may be helpful both diagnostically and therapeutically.[280–282] Symptoms include visual blurring, floating scotomas, and bulbar pain. Importantly, many patients in intensive care units are too ill to complain of symptoms. Although *C. albicans* has been the most frequent species causing endophthalmitis, other species have been reported with increasing frequency.

Syndrome of Disseminated Candidiasis and Candidemia

The problems of management of candidemia and detection of underlying disseminated candidiasis present major enigmas for clinicians dealing with patients who are predisposed to the disseminated form of this disease. The problem is compounded by the absence of positive blood cultures in many patients with disseminated disease. The interpretation of the significance of recovery of increased numbers of *Candida* from sites such as sputum, urine, feces, and skin is difficult, because the organisms can frequently be recovered from these sites without causing infection.

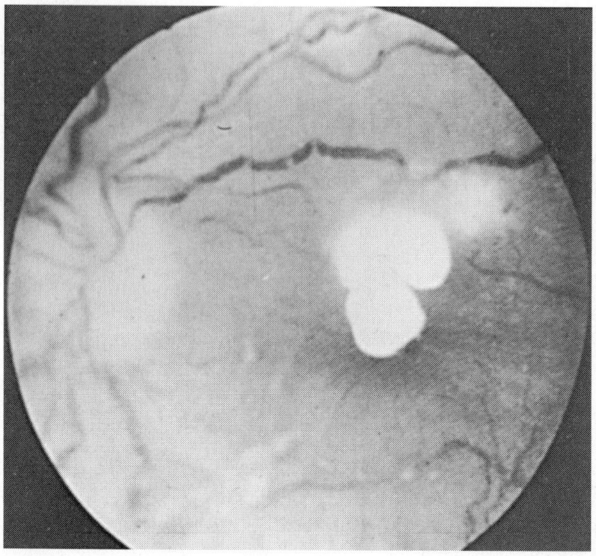

FIGURE 247–15. Advanced hematogenous *Candida* endophthalmitis. (From Fishman LS, Griffin JR, Sapico FL, et al. Hematogenous *Candida* endophthalmitis—a complication of candidemia. N Engl J Med. 1972;286:675. Copyright © 1972 Massachusetts Medical Society. All rights reserved.)

The clinical setting associated with disseminated candidiasis has been previously described. As expected, the populations of patients most commonly affected are those with neoplastic disease, patients who have had complicated postoperative courses, and burn patients. In the neoplastic group, the most common association has been with the acute leukemic population. In the postoperative group, the patients who have had organ transplantations, heart surgery, or GI-tract surgery are at greatest risk.

When *Candida* disseminates, multiple organs are usually involved, with the kidney, brain, myocardium, and eye the most common. In cancer patients receiving extensive immunosuppressive therapy, recognition of liver and spleen involvement has increased substantially. Other organs less frequently infected include the lungs, GI tract, skin, and endocrine glands. The hallmarks of the pathologic changes are diffuse microabscesses with a combined acute suppurative and granulomatous reaction and small macroabscesses. Macroabscesses more than a centimeter in diameter may also form, especially in the liver and spleen.

The rate of premortem diagnosis of disseminated candidiasis has been very low; only approximately 15 to 40% of cases have been diagnosed early enough for appropriate therapy. As an aid to earlier diagnosis, considerable attention has been focused on the detection of serum antibodies to *Candida* and the detection of *Candida* antigen. Despite the appearance of more than 100 publications on the serologic diagnosis of disseminated candidiasis, controversies exist regarding the value of various serodiagnostic procedures. Problems with the diagnostic tests have been reviewed in detail.[283–285]

The following conclusions can be drawn from available data: (1) the incidence of false-negative test results for antibody has been unacceptably high in most series (probably due to severe immunocompromise) and (2) techniques for antigen detection have been associated with a high incidence of false-negative results also (suggesting that antigen may not circulate or circulates in a nondetectable form).

A generalization regarding the application of these experimental serodiagnostic tests, which is an amplification of a similar statement made in 1976,[286] is still appropriate: a "positive" serodiagnostic test in a patient likely to have disseminated candidiasis increases the likelihood of the presence of disseminated disease, but a decision on treatment of a suspect patient cannot be made on serodiagnostic testing alone and must be made on the basis of a comprehensive, multifactorial, repetitive evaluation of the clinical circumstances.

The premortem diagnosis of disseminated candidiasis, therefore, remains a clinical diagnosis. Definitive diagnosis is made by histopathologic demonstration of the organism invading tissues. Of greatest importance in facilitating the diagnosis is awareness of, and persistent evaluation for, the variety of manifestations of disseminated candidiasis that serve as diagnostic clues.

Management of candidemia poses particularly difficult problems. Unquestionably, some patients who have candidemia, especially associated with an indwelling catheter or with the administration of intravenous fluids and competent immune status, have spontaneous resolution simultaneous with the removal of the catheter. Among severely immunosuppressed patients, almost all patients with candidemia have disseminated disease.[287] To assume that a positive blood culture for *Candida* represents "benign" candidemia may be extremely dangerous, and an extensive evaluation of such a patient should be undertaken to disprove the presence of disseminated disease. This evaluation should consist of repeated cultures and careful physical examinations for such manifestations as ocular involvement, osteomyelitis, cutaneous manifestations, and the other complications of disseminated disease that may be recognizable on physical examination. In the immunocompetent patient, the catheter, if present, should be removed,[8, 288, 289] and further blood cultures, as well as evaluation of peripheral smears (Fig. 247–16), should be performed. Interpretation of the ensuing resolution of the candidemia should be made with recognition that 50% of the patients with disseminated candidiasis have not had positive blood cultures, and if the patient is bacteremic also, concomitant fungi may not grow in culture.[290] Three factors have resulted in a consensus among clinical mycologists to treat candidemia, regardless of whether it occurs in a compromised host and regardless of whether it is associated with an indwelling intravenous catheter.[8] Those factors include (1) recognition that stratifying patients according to the likelihood of having "benign" candidemia has frequently been unsuccessful, (2) there is at least a 40% mortality rate associated with candidemia,[291] and (3) a less toxic antifungal, fluconazole, is now readily available for patients who would have otherwise not been treated. This increased aggressiveness is a change in approach from previous practices of withholding antifungals in selected patients with candidemia. Of growing concern is the number of patients who have had complications of candidemia, particularly arthritis, endophthalmitis, endocarditis, and osteomyelitis. The incidence of these complications is undefined. The occurrence of these complications is further reason for treating all candidemic patients with antifungals. Removal of an indwelling intravenous catheter is important in management, and a new catheter should not be inserted over a wire in the site of the old one.[288, 289]

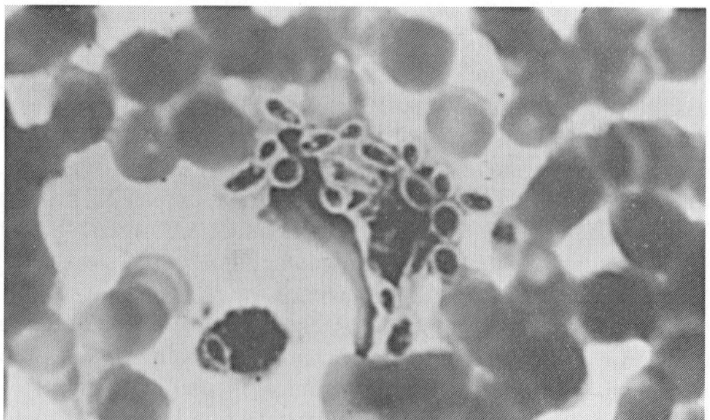

FIGURE 247–16. *Candida* seen on peripheral smear. (Courtesy of Dr. Jack Remington.)

Miscellaneous Candida Infections

Candida infections that have been described but are beyond the scope of this discussion include ear infections, nasal ulcers, lymphadenitis (in patients with leukemia), laryngeal infection, diarrhea, and the "drunken disease" syndrome described in Japan (thought to be due to *Candida* fermentation of carbohydrate in the GI tract). Also, *Candida* infections of numerous types have been reported with increasing frequency in antenates, neonates, and older children.[193, 292–296] The emergence of *C. tropicalis* as a progressively more frequent pathogen in a variety of *Candida* infections, including disseminated candidiasis,[297] should be noted. Additionally, the emergence of *C. glabrata* and *C. krusei*, which are relatively resistant to fluconazole, should be noted.[298, 299]

TREATMENT AND PROPHYLAXIS

Treatment strategies have been reviewed in detail for both neutropenic and non-neutropenic patients.[8, 81, 300] Nystatin has been the primary agent used for mucous membrane and cutaneous candidiasis, and most mild-to-moderate infections in these sites are treatable with it. Clotrimazole and miconazole have been efficacious for these mucocutaneous syndromes and are topical alternatives to nystatin, especially for vaginal infections. Oral clotrimazole has approximately equal efficacy as oral nystatin for thrush, but it is generally more palatable. Itraconazole (solution) is equal to fluconazole,[301] and the majority of patients with fluconazole-refractory infections at least initially respond to itraconazole solution.[302] Amphotericin B suspension or intravenous amphotericin B may be alternatives in refractory cases, but few data about their efficacy are available. Orally administered and absorbed, ketoconazole and fluconazole have been effective for mucocutaneous *Candida* infections, especially the chronic mucocutaneous candidiasis syndrome, thrush, and esophagitis. Superior efficacy of fluconazole over ketoconazole in AIDS patients with *Candida* esophagitis has been shown in one large, multicenter study of 169 patients.[303]

Amphotericin B remains the cornerstone of therapy for disseminated and deep organ *Candida* infection until more comparative data on the efficacy of amphotericin B versus the azoles is obtained. However, there have been an increasing number of reports of deep *Candida* infections successfully treated with fluconazole, and these reports were summarized in 1997.[304] Although these reports are encouraging, they generally lack a direct comparison with amphotericin B. These encouraging reports, the ease of administration, the availability of fluconazole in both oral and intravenous forms, and the relative lack of toxicity have been factors resulting in its emergence as the most attractive alternative to amphotericin B. Granulocyte transfusions have been given for *Candida* infection, but they are not used on a wide-scale basis, and their efficacy has not been established from the limited experience to date. Similarly, the role of human granulocytic colony–stimulating factor and other cytokines or immunomodulators has not been sufficiently evaluated in clinical settings

Prophylaxis of *Candida* infection has been highly controversial. However, prospective controlled trials have successful results in allogenic bone marrow transplant recipients.[305, 306] Although adequately controlled studies are not available, prophylaxis with fluconazole has also been used in high-risk autologous bone marrow transplantation and liver transplantation.[307] Large controlled trials in neutropenic leukemic patients have failed to show benefit from fluconazole prophylaxis. The possibility exists that there are subpopulations who are at high risk for deep candidiasis during neutropenia induced by cytotoxic chemotherapy for leukemia and may benefit. It should be noted that fluconazole prophylaxis does not provide protection against molds. There is no general consensus regarding prophylaxis in non-neutropenic surgery patients. Most experts do not recommend it. The subject was comprehensively reviewed in 1993.[308] The use of oral nystatin or ketoconazole has not been associated with an appreciable decrease in systemic candidiasis in leukemic patients.[309–311] However, there has been one successful trial in critically ill surgical patients.[312] Ketoconazole and fluconazole have been efficacious in preventing oral *Candida* infections in cancer patients and AIDS patients. Because these infections are easy to diagnose and treat, prevention must be weighed against the risk of inducing azole resistance in *Candida* strains carried by these patients.

Three lipid formulations of amphotericin B have been marketed in the United States: amphotericin B lipid complex (ABLC, Abelcet), amphotericin B colloidal dispersion (ABCD, Amphotec), and liposomal amphotericin B (AmBisome). The colloidal dispersion has substantial acute infusion-related reactions[313] and is not currently approved for *Candida* infection. All three lipid formulations are less nephrotoxic than the deoxycholate formulation, but their relative efficacy in candidiasis has not been studied.[314, 315] The approval stipulations by the Food and Drug Administration for use in patients refractory or intolerant to amphotericin B, high cost, and a lack of randomized trials relegate them to secondary use in candidiasis.

The total amount of amphotericin B needed to treat any form of *Candida* infection is not known. Derivation of a specific figure is complicated, because some forms of *Candida* infection resolve spontaneously (often correlated with improvement of the immune status of the host). Because the manifestations of *Candida* infections are so varied, their therapy is discussed individually.

Hematogenously Disseminated Candidiasis

The decision to administer treatment of candidemia has been discussed previously in this chapter, and the consensus that all candidemic patients should be treated with antifungals was described.[8] If the patient is neutropenic or the course is consistent with an acute sepsis causing the patient to be in an unstable or rapidly worsening condition, amphotericin B should be selected for initial therapy. Depending on the severity of the situation, 5-fluorocytosine (5-FC) can be added to the regimen to provide rapid attainment of therapeutic blood levels. However, bone marrow suppression or diarrhea may be complications of simultaneous use of these agents. Unfortunately, there are no controlled studies giving guidelines for the total dose of amphotericin B or 5-FC needed. If 5-FC is used, its serum levels should be monitored.[316] In patients who are clinically stable and in patients without neutropenia, fluconazole therapy is chosen by most experts.[8] The results of the large, multicenter clinical trial comparing fluconazole with amphotericin B in non-neutropenic patients has shown no statistically significant difference.[289] The choice of therapy also depends on the sensitivity of the isolate recovered, because *C. krusei* is resistant to fluconazole and *C. glabrata* is relatively resistant. A large, randomized trial comparing fluconazole at 12 mg/kg/day to amphotericin B at 0.7 mg/kg/day plus fluconazole at 12 mg/kg/day is in progress. Therapy is continued for 2 weeks past the last positive blood culture. In patients intolerant to amphotericin B, one of the lipid formulations is an alternative.

Candida Endocarditis

The mortality rate is lowest with combined medical and surgical therapy, compared with either medical or surgical treatment alone. McLeod and Remington have reviewed these data,[176] and current experience reflects the same concept.[179, 186] Once the diagnosis of *Candida*-caused endocarditis is made, the procedure of choice is to initiate amphotericin B therapy and to perform a surgical procedure as soon as possible. After surgery, amphotericin B should be given for 6 to 10 weeks because of the significant incidence of relapse. At the time of removal of the valve and surrounding vegetations, the area can be washed with an amphotericin-B–containing solution.[317] Some patients with *Candida* endocarditis have had relapses years after surgery. Patients with *Candida* endocarditis should be monitored for a minimum of 2 years postoperatively. Fluconazole is commonly used as long-term suppressive therapy.[179, 318]

Central Nervous System *Candida* Infection

Based on analysis of current literature, combined amphotericin B and 5-FC therapy, without intrathecal instillation, is the most rational treatment for both meningitis and diffuse parenchymal infection. If a shunt is in place, it should be removed, if possible.[150] In exceptionally severe cases, intrathecal antifungals should be considered. Indications for surgery of *Candida*-caused brain abscesses remain unclear.

Candida Peritonitis, Gallbladder Infection, and Intra-abdominal Abscesses

Candida peritonitis due to peritoneal dialysis of adults, if there is no evidence of spread to other organs, may respond to instillation of local amphotericin B at a concentration of 2 to 4 μg/ml in dialysate fluid.[230] However, many patients experience pain with this treatment. Successful treatment with fluconazole has been reported.[239, 319] Removal of the catheter is considered helpful whenever feasible.[319, 320] However, there are few reports of successful treatment without catheter removal.[321, 322]

Candida coming from an abdominal drain placed at the time of GI surgery should not ordinarily prompt antifungal therapy.[8] Discovery of *Candida* in ascites from an undrained abdomen usually means that therapy is required. Hematogenous dissemination from the peritoneum can occur. In general, the threshold for treating *Candida* isolated from the peritoneum is lowering.

The failure rate for the cure of hepatosplenic candidiasis has been high with both amphotericin B alone and in combination with 5-FC. Many experts recommend initial therapy with amphotericin B followed by long-term fluconazole therapy, or the use of fluconazole alone.[8] Reports of cures with liposomal amphotericin have appeared and are promising.[323, 324] Successful results have also been obtained with fluconazole, though not during periods of neutropenia.[325] In some instances splenectomy may be necessary for large or refractory abscesses. *Candida*-caused cholecystitis may respond to intravenous amphotericin B or fluconazole.[326] In candidiasis of the gall bladder or biliary tract, drainage may be necessary[241] in addition to antifungal therapy. *Candida* pancreatic abscess has been successfully drained with computed tomography–guided percutaneous aspiration.[252]

Urinary Candidiasis

Postcatheterization candiduria usually resolves without specific antifungal therapy. There are several conditions in which it should be treated: in renal transplantation patients, in neutropenic patients, in very low birth weight infants, and in patients undergoing urinary tract manipulations. Local amphotericin instillation is a desirable approach for patients with a Foley catheter. Usually a solution of 50 mg of amphotericin B in 1 liter of sterile water is infused at 40 ml/hour. In the absence of a Foley catheter, oral fluconazole is preferred by most experts.[8] Selected patients may require irrigation through nephrostomy tubes placed directly in the collecting systems. If fungus balls form, they require surgical removal. For kidney involvement, intravenous amphotericin B is indicated. However, oral fluconazole is an alternative to amphotericin B and is much more convenient.[8, 327] The drug is excreted in high concentration in the urine. Its role is under evaluation. 5-FC is another alternative.[328] However, it may be less attractive in renal insufficiency, and resistance may develop.[328] Any stents, catheters, or other prosthetic materials in the urinary tract should be removed in order to prevent recurrence.

Mucocutaneous Candidiasis

Oral thrush should be treated with topical agents whenever possible. The least expensive is nystatin. The usual adult dose is 4 to 6 ml of 100,000 units/ml four times daily. Clotrimazole 10-mg troches are also available. These can be sucked four times a day. Clotrimazole is approximately equally as effective as nystatin but is not bitter, as is nystatin. Gentian violet causes staining but is an effective topical agent, given as single treatment. However, newer agents have made it obsolete. Usually 7 to 10 days of therapy is sufficient; the patient should be treated for 48 hours after becoming asymptomatic. Therapy for denture sore mouth is the same as that for thrush, with the addition of meticulous cleaning of the dentures and correction of ill-fitting plates. Angular cheilitis, which is frequently associated with denture sore mouth, should be treated with either topical clotrimazole or miconazole cream. Oral, absorbable fluconazole, ketoconazole, and itraconazole are effective for thrush. Fluconazole is more expensive, is more effective, and has fewer side effects than ketoconazole.[329] Itraconazole capsules are approximately equal to ketaconazole,[330] and the oral solution of itraconazole is equal to fluconazole, because of better absorption of the solution than its capsules.[301, 331] Many patients with thrush unresponsive to fluconazole respond at least initially to itraconazole solution.[332]

The diagnosis of *Candida* esophagitis can be made presumptively on the basis of the presence of oral pharyngeal thrush and symptoms of esophagitis in patients with AIDS or cancer. Topical therapy with clotrimazole troches, amphotericin B suspension, or nystatin suspension usually fails. Fluconazole is superior to ketaconazole, itraconazole capsules, and flucytosine.[333–335] Itraconazole solution is approximately equal to fluconazole.[336] In one study, itraconazole solution plus 5-FC was approximately equal to fluconazole.[337] A last resort in refractory esophageal infections is low-dose (10 to 20 mg/day) intravenous amphotericin B.[338] Long-term suppressive therapy may be necessary in patients with AIDS.[339]

Candida intertrigo is most successfully managed by decreasing the moisture of the involved area and by the application of amphotericin B lotion or nystatin cream several times a day or topical miconazole or clotrimazole. Management of *Candida* diaper rash has been successful with nystatin powder or cream in combination with a corticosteroid, such as Mycolog-II cream. Amphotericin cream or lotion may also be used. The same agents used for diaper rash are generally successful for pruritus ani.

Uncomplicated *Candida* vaginitis responds to short courses of topical or oral therapy in the vast majority of patients. The following regimens used from 1 to 7 days are considered comparable: clotrimazole (over the counter); butoconazole (over the counter); miconazole (over the counter); tioconazole (over the counter); terconazole; oral azoles (ketoconazole, 500 mg twice daily for 5 days [not approved in the United States]); itraconazole, 200 mg twice daily for 1 day or 200 mg a day for 3 days (not approved in the United States); and fluconazole, 150 mg once.[340] Other regimens include nystatin, 100,000 units daily for 1 to 2 weeks; and boric acid, 600 mg in a gelatin capsule once daily (vaginal) for 14 days[341]). Recurrent *Candida* vaginitis requires eradication of causal factors as much as possible. Then treatment for 2 weeks with topical or oral azoles should be used, followed by 6 months of fluconazole—150 mg orally per week or itraconazole—100 mg every other day.

Candida-caused paronychia is best managed by preventing immersion of the hands in water as much as possible and applying clotrimazole or miconazole cream twice daily.

Chronic Mucocutaneous Candidiasis

Topical therapy to skin and mucous membranes achieves only slight improvement in this disease. Intravenous amphotericin B therapy has been effective, but nearly all patients relapse. Oral 5-FC has not been effective. The most important advance in the therapy of this disease is systemically administered azoles: ketoconazole, fluconazole, or itraconazole.[50] Numerous reports illustrate successful treatment. Therapy for months or years may be necessary.

Ocular Candidiasis

Treatment of intraocular *Candida* infections necessitates the use of parenteral antifungal agents, especially amphotericin B.[342–344] Because of the data demonstrating a synergistic effect of amphotericin B and 5-FC, combination therapy should be used in refractory cases, rapidly developing lesions, or lesions in the vicinity of the macula. There are now many reported successes with fluconazole.[266, 272, 345] Vitrectomy may be of value in patients with large abscesses in the vitreous, rapidly progessive disease, or lesions threatening the macula. Early consideration for vitrectomy is obligatory in such cases. In addition, vitrectomy may confirm the diagnosis.[266] Hematogenous *Candida* endophthalmitis not extensively involving the vitreous has occasionally healed spontaneously. The use of intraocular antifungals remains controversial.

Miscellaneous *Candida*-Caused Infections

Candida osteoarthritis has been successfully treated with azoles.[346] One case of successful treatment with antifungals but without removal of the prosthetic joint has been reported.[223] Usually, removal of the prosthetic material is necessary.[347] The topic of *Candida* laryngeal infection has been reviewed.[165] Most patients have been managed with intravenous amphotericin B. Fluconazole may be appropriate as follow-up therapy. The treatment of *Candida*-caused epididymo-orchitis has been reviewed.[348] Although success without surgery has occurred, most patients have required drainage or orchidectomy. Similarly, *Candida*-caused thrombophlebitis of peripheral veins usually requires surgery in addition to antifungals.[83, 259, 261]

REFERENCES

1. Langenbeck B. Auffingung von Pilzen aus der Schleimhaut der Speiserohre einer Typhus-Leiche. Neue Not Geb Natur Heilk (Froriep). 1839;12:145–147.
2. Rippon JW. Candidiasis and the pathogenic yeasts. In: Medical Mycology, the Pathogenic Fungi and the Pathogenic Actinomycetes. 3rd ed. Philadelphia: WB Saunders; 1988:532–581.
3. Joachim H, Polayes S. Subacute endocarditis and systemic mycosis (monilia). JAMA. 1940;115:205–208.
4. Pfaller MA, Jones RN, Messer SA, et al. National surveillance of nosocomial blood stream infection due to *Candida albicans*: Frequency of occurrence and antifungal susceptibility in the SCOPE Program. Diagn Microbiol Infect Dis. 1998;31:327–332.
5. Rentz AM, Halpern, MT Bowden R. The impact of candidemia on length of hospital stay, outcome and overall cost of illness. Clin Infect Dis. 1998; 27:781–788.
6. Anonymous. Candidiasis. In: Kwong-Chung KJ, Bennett JE, eds. Medical Mycology. Philadelphia: Lea & Febiger; 1992:280–336.
7. Bodey GP. Candidiasis. Pathogenesis, Diagnosis and Treatment. 2nd ed. New York: Raven; 1993.
8. Edwards JEJ, Bodey GP, Bowden RA, et al. International Conference for the Development of a Consensus on the Management and Prevention of Severe Candidal Infections (see Comments). Clin Infect Dis. 1997;25:43–59.
9. Viscoli C, Girmenia C, Marinus A, et al. A surveillance study of fungemia in cancer patients in Europe. Abstract 2. In: Invasive Fungal Infections Cooperative Group (IFIG of EORTC). Trends in Invasive Fungal Infections 3, Brussels, Belgium (Abstracts of Meeting). 1995.
10. Pfaller MA. Nosocomial candidiasis: Emerging species, reservoirs, and modes of transmission. Clin Infect Dis. 1996;22:S89–S94.
11. Anaissie EJ, Rex JH, Uzun O, Vartivarian S. Predictors of adverse outcome in cancer patients with candidemia. Am J Med. 1998;104:238–245.
12. Jarvis WR. Epidemiology of nosocomial fungal infections, with emphasis on *Candida* species. Clin Infect Dis. 1995;20:1526–1530.
13. Body BA, Pfaller MA, Durrer J, et al. Comparison of the lysis centrifugation and radiometric blood culture system for recovery of yeast. Eur J Clin Microbiol Infect Dis. 1988;7:417–420.
14. Yagupsky P, Nolte FS, Menegus MA. Enhanced detection of *Candida* in blood cultures with the BACTEC 460 system by use of the aerobic-hypertonic (8B) medium. Epidemiol Infect. 1990;105:553–558.
15. Reyolds R, Braude AI. The filament-inducing property of blood for *Candida albicans*: Its nature and significance. Clin Res Proc. 1956;7:417–420.
16. Kirkpatrick WR, Revankar SG, Mcatee RK, et al. Detection of *Candida dubliniensis* in oropharyngeal samples from human immunodeficiency virus–infected patients in North America by primary CHROMagar candida screening and susceptibility testing of isolates. J Clin Microbiol. 1998; 36:3007–3012.
17. Pinjon E, Sullivan D, Salkin I, et al. Simple, inexpensive, reliable method for differentiation of *Candida dubliniensis* from *Candida albicans*. J Clin Microbiol. 1998;36:2093–2095.
18. D'Antonio D, Violante B, Mazzoni A, et al. A nosocomial cluster of *Candida inconspicua* infections in patients with hematological malignancies. J Clin Microbiol. 1998;36:792–795.
19. Huppert M, Harper G, Sun SH, et al. Rapid methods for identification of yeasts. J Clin Microbiol. 1975;2:21–34.
20. Adhearn DG. Identification and ecology of yeasts of medical importance. In: Prier JE, Friedman H, eds. Opportunistic Pathogens. Baltimore: University Park Press; 1974:129–146.
21. Hurley R. Pathogenicity of the genus *Candida*. In: Winner HI, Hurley R, eds. Symposium on *Candida* Infections. Edinburgh: Churchill Livingstone; 1966.
22. Odds FC. *Candida* and Candidosis. A review and bibliography. 2nd ed. London: Bailliere-Tindall; 1988.
23. Fowler SL, Rhoton B, Springer SC, et al. Evidence for person-to-person transmission of *Candida lusitaniae* in a neonatal intensive-care unit. Infect Control Hosp Epidemiol. 1998;19:343–345.
24. D'Antonio D, Violante B, Mazzoni A, et al. A nosocomial cluster of *Candida inconspicua* infections in patients with hematological malignancies. J Clin Microbiol. 1998;36:792–795.
25. Branchini ML, Geiger DC, Fischman O, Pignatari AC. Molecular typing of *Candida albicans* strains isolated from nosocomial candidemia. Rev Inst Med Trop Sao Paulo. 1995;37:483–487.
26. Pertowski CA, Baron RC, Lasker BA, et al. Nosocomial outbreak of *Candida albicans* sternal wound infections following cardiac surgery traced to a scrub nurse. J Infect Dis. 1995;172:817–822.
27. Reagan DR, Pfaller MA, Hollis RJ, Wenzel RP. Evidence of nosocomial spread of *Candida albicans* causing bloodstream infection in a neonatal intensive care unit. Diagn Microbiol Infect Dis. 1995;21:191–194.
28. Zhang J, Hollis RJ, Pfaller MA. Variations in DNA subtype and antifungal susceptibility among clinical isolates of *Candida tropicalis*. Diagn Microbiol Infect Dis. 1997;27:63–67.
29. Pfaller MA. Epidemiology of fungal infections: The promise of molecular typing. Clin Infect Dis. 1995;20:1535–1539.
30. Joly S, Pujol C, Schroppel K, Soll DR. Development of two species-specific fingerprinting probes for broad computer-assisted epidemiological studies of *Candida tropicalis*. J Clin Microbiol. 1996;34:3063–3071.
31. Romano F, Ribera G, Giuliano M. A study of a hospital cluster of systemic candidosis using DNA typing methods. Epidemiol Infect. 1994;112:393–398.
32. Domer JE, Lehrer RI. Introduction to *Candida*. Systemic Candidiasis. In: Murphy JW, Friedman H, Bendinelli M, eds. Fungal Infections and Immune Response. New York: Plenum; 1993:49–116.
33. Calderone R, Diamond R, Senet JM, et al. Host cell–fungal cell interactions. J Med Vet Mycol. 1994;32(Suppl 1):151–168.
34. Lyman CA, Walsh TJ. Phagocytosis of medically important yeasts by polymorphonuclear leukocytes. Infect Immun. 1994;62:1489–1493.
35. Cech P, Lehrer RI. Heterogeneity of human neutrophil phagolysosomes: Functional consequences for candidacidal activity. Blood. 1984;64:147–151.
36. Lehrer RI. The fungicidal mechanisms of human monocytes. 1. Evidence for myeloperoxidase-linked and myeloperoxidase-independent candidacidal mechanisms. J Clin Invest. 1975;55:338–346.
37. Lehrer RI. Measurement of candidacidal activity of specific leukocyte types in mixed cell populations. II. Normal and chronic granulomatous disease eosinophils. Infect Immun. 1971;3:800–802.
38. Yeaman MR, Soldan SS, Ghannoum MA, et al. Resistance to platelet microbicidal protein results in increased severity of experimental *Candida albicans* endocarditis. Infect Immun. 1996;64:1379–1384.
39. Yeaman MR, Sullam PM, Dazin PF, et al. Fluconazole and platelet microbicidal protein inhibit *Candida* adherence to platelets in vitro. Antimicrob Agents Chemother. 1994;38:1460–1465.
40. Skerl KG, Calderone RA, Segal E, et al. In vitro binding of *Candida albicans* yeast cells to human fibronectin. Can J Microbiol. 1984;30:221–227.
41. Robert R, Senet JM, Mahaza C, et al. Molecular basis of the interactions between *Candida albicans*, fibrinogen, and platelets. J Mycol Med (France). 1992;2:19–25.
42. Levitz SM, Diamond RD. Killing of *Aspergillus fumigatus* spores and *Candida albicans* yeast phase by the iron-hydrogen peroxide-iodide cytotoxic system: Comparison with the myeloperoxidase-hydrogen peroxide-halide system. Infect Immun. 1984;43:1100–1102.
43. Selsted ME, Harwig SSL. Purification, primary structure, and antimicrobial activities of a guinea pig neutrophil defensin. Infect Immun. 1987;55:2281–2286.
44. Ganz T, Selsted ME, Szklarek D, et al. Defensins. Natural peptide antibiotics of human neutrophils. J Clin Invest. 1985;76:1427–1435.
45. Selsted ME, Szlarek D, Ganz T, et al. Activity of rabbit leukocyte peptides against *Candida albicans*. Infect Immun. 1985;49:202–206.
46. Patterson-Delafield J, Martinez RJ, Lehrer RI. Microbicidal cationic proteins in rabbit alveolar macrophages: A potential host defense mechanism. Infect Immun. 1980;30:180–192.
47. Lehrer RI. Host defense mechanisms against disseminated candidiasis. Ann Intern Med. 1978;89:91–106.
48. Taschdjian CL, Toni EF, Hsu KC, et al. Immunofluorescence studies of *Candida* in human reticuloendothelial phagocytes: Implications for immunogenesis and pathogenesis of systemic candidiasis. Am J Clin Pathol. 1971;56:50–58.
49. Odds FC. Pathogenesis of candidosis. In: Anonymous. *Candida* and Candidosis. A review and bibliography. 2nd ed. London: Bailliere-Tindall; 1988:236–278.
50. Kirkpatrick CH. Chronic mucocutaneous candidiasis. J Am Acad Dermatol. 1994;31:S14–S17.
51. Schmid J, Odds FC, Wiselka MJ, et al. Genetic similarity and maintenance of

Candida albicans strains from a group of AIDS patients, demonstrated by DNA fingerprinting. J Clin Microbiol. 1992;30:935–941.
52. Powderly WG. Fungal infections in patients infected with HIV. Mo Med. 1990;87:348–350.
53. Cutler JE. Acute systemic candidiasis in normal and congenitally thymic-deficient (nude) mice. J Reticuloendothel Soc. 1976;19:121–124.
54. Lee KW, Balish E. Systemic candidiasis in germ free, flora-defined and conventional mice. J Reticuloendothel Soc. 1981;29:71–77.
55. Domer JE, Garner RE. Immunomodulation in response to *Candida*. Immunol Ser. 1989;47:293–317.
56. Gulay Z, Imir T. Anti-candidial activity of natural killer (NK) and lymphokine activated killer (LAK) lymphocytes in vitro. Immunobiology. 1996;195:220–230.
57. Deepe JGS. Prospects for the development of fungal vaccines. Clin Microbiol Rev. 1997;10:585–596.
58. Solomkin JS, Mills EL, Giebink GS, et al. Phagocytosis of *Candida albicans* by human leukocytes: Opsonic requirements. J Infect Dis. 1978;137:30–37.
59. La Force FM, Mills DM, Iverson K, et al. Inhibition of leukocyte candidacidal activity by serum from patients with disseminated candidiasis. J Lab Clin Med. 1975;86:657–666.
60. Chilgren RA, Hong R, Quie PG. Human serum interactions with *Candida albicans*. J Immunol. 1968;101:128–132.
61. Han Y, Cutler JE. Antibody response that protects against disseminated candidiasis. Infect Immun. 1995;63:2714–2719.
62. Kirkpatrick CH, Rich RR, Bennett JE. Chronic mucocutaneous candidiasis: Model building in cellular immunity. Ann Intern Med. 1971;74:955–978.
63. Louria DB, Smith JK, Brayton RG, et al. Anti-*Candida* factors in serum and their inhibitors. I. Clinical and laboratory observations. J Infect Dis. 1972;125:102–114.
64. Kozel TR. Activation of the complement system by pathogenic fungi. Clin Microbiol Rev. 1996;9:34–46.
65. Gelfand JA, Hurley DL, Fauci AS, Frank MM. Role of complement in host defense against experimental disseminated candidiasis. J Infect Dis. 1978;139:9.
66. Kozel TR, Brown RR, Pformmer GS. Activation and binding of C3 by *Candida albicans*. Infect Immun. 1987;55:1890–1894.
67. Sohnle PG, Frank MM, Kirkpatrick CH. Deposition of complement components in the cutaneous lesions of chronic mucocutaneous candidiasis. Clin Immunol Immunopathol. 1976;5:340–350.
68. Hostetter MK. Adhesins and ligands involved in the interaction of *Candida* spp. with epithelial and endothelial surfaces. Clin Microbiol Rev. 1994;7:29–42.
69. Fukazawa Y, Kagaya K. Molecular bases of adhesion of *Candida albicans*. J Med Vet Mycol. 1997;35:87–99.
70. Calderone RA, Braun PC. Adherence and receptor relationships of *Candida albicans*. Microbiol Rev. 1991;55:1–19.
71. Klotz SA. Fungal adherence to the vascular compartment: A critical step in the pathogenesis of disseminated candidiasis. Clin Infect Dis. 1992;14:340–347.
72. Edwards JE Jr, Mayer CL. Adherence of *Candida albicans* to mammalian cells. In: Ayoub EM, Cassell GH, Branche WC Jr, Henry TJ, eds. Microbial Determinants of Virulence and Host Response. 1st ed. Washington, DC: American Society for Microbiology; 1990:179–194.
73. Ghannoum MA, Edwards JE Jr. *Candida* adherence to epithelial cells. J Mycol Med. 1992;2:10–13.
74. Lehrer RI. Inhibition by sulfonamides of the candidacidal activity of human neutrophils. J Clin Invest. 1971;50:2498–2505.
75. Forsgren A, Schmeling D, Quie PG. Effect of tetracycline on the phagocytic function of human leukocytes. J Infect Dis. 1974;130:412–415.
76. Ferrari FA, Pagani A, Marconi M, et al. Inhibition of candidacidal activity of human neutrophil leukocytes by aminoglycoside antibiotics. Antimicrob Agents Chemother. 1980;7:87–88.
77. Bisbe J, Miro JM, Latorre X, et al. Disseminated candidiasis in addicts who use brown heroin: Report of 83 cases and review. Clin Infect Dis. 1992;15:910–923.
78. Nielsen H, Stenderup J, Bruun B. Fungemia in a university hospital 1984–1988. Clinical and mycological characteristics. Scand J Infect Dis. 1991;23:275–282.
79. Krause W, Matheis H, Wulf K. Fungemia and funguria after oral administration of *Candida albicans*. Lancet. 1969;1:598–599.
80. Stone HH, Kolb LD, Currie CA, et al. *Candida* sepsis: Pathogenesis and principles of treatment. Ann Surg. 1974;697–711.
81. Edwards JEJ, Filler SG. Current strategies for treating invasive candidiasis: Emphasis on infections in nonneutropenic patients. Clin Infect Dis. 1992;14(Suppl 1):S106–S113.
82. Cole GT, Halawa AA, Anaissie EJ. The role of the gastrointestinal tract in hematogenous candidiasis: From the laboratory to the bedside. Clin Infect Dis. 1996;22(Suppl 2):S73–S88.
83. Benoit D, Decruyenaere J, Vandewoude K, et al. Management of candidal thrombophlebitis of the central veins: Case report and review. Clin Infect Dis. 1998;26:393–397.
84. Gow NA. Germ tube growth of *Candida albicans*. Curr Top Med Mycol. 1997;8:43–55.
85. Levy MY, Polacheck I, Barenholz Y, Benita S. Efficacy evaluation of a novel submicron miconazole emulsion in a murine cryptococcosis model. Pharm Res. 1995;12:223–230.
86. Agabian N, Odds FC, Poulain D, et al. Pathogenesis of invasive candidiasis. J Med Vet Mycol. 1994;32(Suppl 1):229–237.
87. Braun-Falco O. International Workshop on Oral and Gastrointestinal Candidosis: From Pathology to Therapy. Introduction. Mycoses. 1989;32(Suppl 2):6–8.
88. Fotos PG, Vincent SD, Hellstein JW. Oral candidosis. Clinical, historical, and therapeutic features of 100 cases. Oral Surg Oral Med Oral Pathol. 1992;74:41–49.
89. Peterson DE. Oral candidiasis. Clin Geriatr Med. 1992;8:513–527.
90. Nikawa H, Hamada T, Yamamoto T. Denture plaque—past and recent concerns. J Dent. 1998;26:299–304.
91. Rossie K, Guggenheimer J. Oral candidiasis: Clinical manifestations, diagnosis, and treatment. Pract Periodontics Aesthet Dent. 1997;9:635–641.
92. Allen CM. Animal models of oral candidiasis. A review. Oral Surg Oral Med Oral Pathol. 1994;78:216–221.
93. Challacombe SJ. Immunologic aspects of oral candidiasis. Oral Surg Oral Med Oral Pathol. 1994;78:202–210.
94. Fotos PG, Ray TL. Oral and perioral candidosis. Semin Dermatol. 1994;13:118–124.
95. Lehner T. Classification and clinico-pathological features of *Candida* infections in the mouth. In: Winner HI, Hurley R, eds. Symposium on *Candida* Infections. Edinburgh: Churchill Livingstone; 1966:119–137.
96. Field EA, Field JK, Martin MV. Does *Candida* have a role in oral epithelial neoplasia? J Med Vet Mycol. 1989;27:277–294.
97. Simon MR, Houser WL, Smith KA, Long PM. Esophageal candidiasis as a complication of inhaled corticosteroids. Ann Allergy Asthma Immunol. 1997;79:333–338.
98. Maenza JR, Merz WG, Romagnoli MJ, et al. Infection due to fluconazole-resistant *Candida* in patients with AIDS: Prevalence and microbiology. Clin Infect Dis. 1997;24:28–34.
99. Syrjanen D, Valle SL, Antonen J, et al. Oral candidal infection as a sign of HIV infection in homosexual men. Oral Surg. 1988;55:36–40.
100. Bonacini M, Laine L, Gal AA, et al. Prospective evaluation of blind brushing of the esophagus for *Candida* esophagitis in patients with human immunodeficiency virus infection. Am J Gastroenterol. 1990;85:385–389.
101. Porro GB, Parente F, Cernuschi M. The diagnosis of esophageal candidiasis in patients with acquired immune deficiency syndrome: Is endoscopy always necessary (see Comments)? Am J Gastroenterol. 1989;84:143–146.
102. Gould E, Kory WP, Raskin JB, et al. Esophageal biopsy findings in the acquired immunodeficiency syndrome (AIDS): Clinicopathologic correlation in 20 patients. South Med J. 1988;81:1392–1395.
103. Braegger CP, Albisetti M, Nadal D. Extensive esophageal candidiasis in the absence of oral lesions in pediatric AIDS. J Pediatr Gastroenterol Nutr. 1995;21:104–106.
104. Isaac DW, Parham DM, Patrick CC. The role of esophagoscopy in diagnosis and management of esophagitis in children with cancer. Med Pediatr Oncol. 1997;28:299–303.
105. Geisinger KR. Endoscopic biopsies and cytologic brushings of the esophagus are diagnostically complementary. Am J Clin Pathol. 1995;103:295–299.
106. Young JA, Elias E. Gastro-oesophageal candidiasis: Diagnosis by brush cytology. J Clin Pathol. 1985;38:293–296.
107. Yee J, Wall SD. Infectious esophagitis. Radiol Clin North Am. 1994;32:1135–1145.
108. Jones JM. Necrotizing *Candida* esophagitis. Failure of symptoms and roentgenographic findings to reflect severity. JAMA. 1980;244:2190–2191.
109. Eras P, Goldstein MJ, Sherlock P. *Candida* infections of the gastrointestinal tract. Medicine. 1972;51:367–379.
110. Prescott RJ, Harris M, Banerjee SS. Fungal infections of the small and large intestine. J Clin Pathol. 1992;45:806–811.
111. Trier JS, Bjorkman DJ. Esophageal, gastric, and intestinal candidiasis. Am J Med. 1984;30:39–43.
112. Minolig G, Terruzzi V, Ferrara A, et al. A prospective study of relationships between benign gastric ulcer, *Candida*, and medical treatment. Am J Gastroenterol. 1984;79:95–97.
113. Sobel JD. *Candida* vulvovaginitis. Semin Dermatol. 1996;15:17–28.
114. Sobel JD. Vaginitis. N Engl J Med. 1997;337:1896–1903.
115. Sobel JD, Faro S, Force RW, et al. Vulvovaginal candidiasis: Epidemiologic, diagnostic, and therapeutic considerations. Am J Obstet Gynecol. 1998;178:203–211.
116. Sobel JD. Genital candidiasis. In: Bodey GP, ed. Candidiasis: Pathogenesis, Diagnosis and Treatment. 2nd ed. New York: Raven; 1993:225–247.
117. Duerr A, Sierra MF, Feldman J, et al. Immune compromise and prevalence of *Candida* vulvovaginitis in human immunodeficiency virus–infected women. Obstet Gynecol. 1997;90:252–256.
118. Fidel PLJ, Sobel JD. Immunopathogenesis of recurrent vulvovaginal candidiasis. Clin Microbiol Rev. 1996;9:335–348.
119. Domonkos AN, Arnold HL Jr, Odom RB. Disease due to fungi. In: Domonkos AN, Arnold HL Jr, Odom RB, eds. Andrews' Diseases of the Skin. Clinical Dermatology. Philadelphia: WB Saunders; 1982:341–403.
120. Alteras I, Feverman EJ, David M, et al. Widely disseminated cutaneous candidosis in adults. Sabouraudia. 1979;17:383–388.
121. Kapdagli H, Ozturk G, Dereli T, et al. *Candida* folliculitis mimicking tinea barbae. Int J Dermatol. 1997;36:295–297.
122. Pierard GE, Pierard-Franchimont C. Candida folliculitis: Superficial dermatitis or septicemia? (In French: Folliculites à *Candida*: Dermatose superficielle ou septicemie? Rev Med Liège. 1996;51:565.
123. Edwards S. Balanitis and balanoposthitis: A review (see Comments). Genitourin Med. 1996;72:155–159.
124. McQuillen DP, Zingman BS, Meunier F, Levitz SM. Invasive infections due to *Candida krusei*: Report of ten cases of fungemia that include three cases of endophthalmitis. Clin Infect Dis. 1992;14:472–478.
125. Leibovitz E, Iuster-Reicher A, Amitai M, Mogilner B. Systemic candidal infections associated with use of peripheral venous catheters in neonates: A 9-year experience. Clin Infect Dis. 1992;14:485–491.

126. Marcus J, Grossman ME, Yunakov MJ, Rappaport F. Disseminated candidiasis, *Candida* arthritis, and unilateral skin lesions. J Am Acad Dermatol. 1992;26:295–297.
127. Lindblad R, al-Obaidy A, Mobacken H, Rodjer S. Diagnostically usable skin lesions in *Candida* septicaemia. Mycoses. 1989;32:416–420.
128. Darcis JM, Etienne M, Demonty J, et al. *Candida albicans* septicemia in heroin addicts. Am J Dermatopathol. 1986;8:501–504.
129. Bodey GP, Luna M. Skin lesions associated with disseminated candidiasis. JAMA. 1974;229:1466–1468.
130. Suster S, Rosen LB. Intradermal bullous dermatitis due to candidiasis in an immunocompromised patient. JAMA. 1987;258:2106–2107.
131. Silverman RA, Rhodes AR, Dennehy PH. Disseminated intravascular coagulation and purpura fulminans in a patient with *Candida* sepsis. Biopsy of purpura fulminans as an aid to diagnosis of systemic *Candida* infections. Am J Med. 1986;80:679–684.
132. Lysy J, Zimmerman J, Ackerman Z, Reifen E. Atypical auricular pyoderma gangrenosum simulating fungal infection. J Clin Gastroenterol. 1989;11:561–564.
133. Brophy MC, Dunagin WB. Intertriginous dermatoses. Common puzzling problems. Postgrad Med. 1985;78:105–115.
134. Hay RJ. Antifungal therapy of yeast infections. J Am Acad. Dermatol. 1994;31:S6–S9.
135. Rasmusson JE. Classification of diaper dermatitis: An overview. Pediatrician. 1987;14(Suppl 1):6–10.
136. Corno F, Caldart M, Toppino M, et al. Ano-rectal candidiasis. (In Italian: La candidosi ano-rettale.) Minerva Chir. 1989;44:2251–3.
137. Lilic D, Cant AJ, Abinun M, et al. Chronic mucocutaneous candidiasis. I. Altered antigen-stimulated IL-2, IL-4, IL-6 and interferon-gamma (IFN-gamma) production. Clin Exp Immunol. 1996;105:205–212.
138. Lilic D, Calvert JE, Cant AJ, et al. Chronic mucocutaneous candidiasis. II. Class and subclass of specific antibody responses in vivo and in vitro. Clin Exp Immunol. 1996;105:213–219.
139. Chapman SW, Daniel CR. Cutaneous manifestations of fungal infection. Infect Dis Clin North Am. 1994;8:879–910.
140. Chimelli L, Mahler-Araujo MB. Fungal infections. Brain Pathol. 1997;7:613–627.
141. Burgert SJ, Classen DC, Burke JP, Blatter DD. Candidal brain abscess associated with vascular invasion: A devastating complication of vascular catheter–related candidemia. Clin Infect Dis. 1995;21:202–205.
142. Voice RA, Bradley SF, Sangeorzan JA, Kauffman CA. Chronic candidal meningitis: An uncommon manifestation of candidiasis. Clin Infect Dis. 1994;19:60–66.
143. Lipton SA, Hickey VF, Morris JH, Loscalzo J. Candidal infection in the central nervous system. Am J Med. 1984;76:101–108.
144. Pendlebury WW, Perl DP, Munoz DG. Multiple microabscesses in the central nervous system: A clinicopathologic study. J Neuropathol Exp Neurol. 1989;48:290–300.
145. Lai PH, Lin SM, Pan HB, Yang CF. Disseminated miliary cerebral candidiasis. AJNR Am J Neuroradiol. 1997;18:1303–1306.
146. Hagensee ME, Bauwens JE, Kjos B, Bowden RA. Brain abscess following marrow transplantation: Experience at the Fred Hutchinson Cancer Research Center, 1984–1992. Clin Infect Dis. 1994;19:402–408.
147. Treseler CB, Sugar AM. Fungal meningitis. Infect Dis Clin North Am. 1990;4:789–808.
148. Sugarman B, Massanari RM. *Candida* meningitis in patients with CSF shunts. Arch Neurol. 1980;37:180–181.
149. Chmel H. *Candida albicans* meningitis following lumbar puncture. Am J Med Sci. 1973;266:465–467.
150. Nguyen MH, Yu VL. Meningitis caused by *Candida* species: An emerging problem in neurosurgical patients. Clin Infect Dis. 1995;21:323–327.
151. Casado JL, Quereda C, Oliva J, et al. Candidal meningitis in HIV-infected patients: Analysis of 14 cases. Clin Infect Dis. 1997;25:673–676.
152. Haron E, Vartivarian S, Anaissie E, et al. Primary *Candida* pneumonia. Experience at a large cancer center and review of the literature. Medicine (Baltimore). 1993;72:137–142.
153. Heurlin N, Bergstrom SE, Winiarski J, et al. Fungal pneumonia: The predominant lung infection causing death in children undergoing bone marrow transplantation. Acta Paediatr. 1996;85:168–172.
154. Armstrong D. Candida species. In: Sarosi GA, Davies SF, eds. Fungal Diseases of the Lung. Orlando, Fla: Grune & Stratton; 1986:167–173.
155. Cairns MR, Durack DT. Fungal pneumonia in the immunocompromised host. Semin Respir Infect. 1986;1:166–185.
156. Zeluff BJ. Fungal pneumonia in transplant recipients. Semin Respir Infect. 1990;5:80–89.
157. Xu XQ, Shi SY, Han TZ. A retrospective study of 115 cases of fungal pneumonia (in Chinese). Chinese Journal of Internal Medicine. 1989;28:7–10, 60.
158. Patriquin H, Lebowitz R, Perreault G, et al. Neonatal candidiasis: Renal and pulmonary manifestations. AJR Am J Roentgenol. 1980;135:1205–1210
159. Watanakunakorn C. Acute pulmonary mycetoma due to *Candida albicans* with complete resolution. J Infect Dis. 1983;148:1131.
160. Wengrower D, Or R, Segal E, et al. Bronchopulmonary candidiasis exacerbating asthma. Case report and review of the literature. Respiration. 1985;47:209–213.
161. McAdams HP, Rosado-de-Christenson ML, Templeton PA, et al. Thoracic mycoses from opportunistic fungi: Radiologic-pathologic correlation. Radiographics. 1995;15:271–286.
162. Von Eiff M, Zuhlsdorf M, Roos N, et al. Pulmonary fungal infections in patients with hematological malignancies—diagnostic approaches. Ann Hematol. 1995;70:135–141.
163. El-Ebiary M, Torres A, Fabregas N, et al. Significance of the isolation of *Candida* species from respiratory samples in critically ill, non-neutropenic patients. An immediate postmortem histologic study. Am J Respir Crit Care Med. 1997;156:583–590.
164. Wengrower D, Or R, Segal E, et al. Bronchopulmonary candidiasis exacerbating asthma. Respiration. 1985;47:209–213.
165. Wang JN, Liu CC, Huang TZ, et al. Laryngeal candidiasis in children. Scand J Infect Dis. 1997;29:427–429.
166. Walsh TJ, Gray WC. *Candida* epiglottis in immunocompromised patients. Chest. 1987;91:482–485.
167. Mahieu HF, van Saene HFK, Rosingh HJ, et al. *Candida* vegetations on silicone voice prostheses. Arch Otolaryngol. 1986;112:321–325.
168. Rabinovici R, Szewczyk D, Ovadia P, et al. *Candida* pericarditis: Clinical profile and treatment. Ann Thorac Surg. 1997;63:1200–1204.
169. Franklin WG, Simon AB, Sodeman TM. *Candida* myocarditis without valvulitis. Am J Cardiol. 1976;38:924–928.
170. Hofman P, Gari-Toussaint M, Bernard E, et al. Fungal myocarditis in acquired immunodeficiency syndrome (in French). Arch Mal Coeur Vaiss. 1992;85:203–208.
171. Canver CC, Patel AK, Kosolcharoen P, Voytovich MC. Fungal purulent constrictive pericarditis in a heart transplant patient. Ann Thorac Surg. 1998;65:1792–1794.
172. McNamee CJ, Wang S, Modry D. Purulent pericarditis secondary to *Candida parapsilosis* and *Peptostreptococcus* species. Can J Cardiol. 1998;14:85–86.
173. Rubin RH, Moellering RC. Clinical microbiologic and therapeutic aspects of purulent pericarditis. Am J Med. 1975;59:68–78.
174. McLeod R, Remington JS. Postoperative fungal endocarditis. In: Duma RJ, ed. Infections of Prosthetic Heart Valves and Vascular Grafts. Prevention, Diagnosis and Treatment. Baltimore: University Park Press; 1977:163–236.
175. Reyes MP, Lerner AM. Endocarditis caused by *Candida* species. In: Bodeg GP, Fainstein V, eds. Candidiasis. New York: Raven; 1985:203–209.
176. McLeod R, Remington JS. Infective Endocarditis. New York: Grune & Stratton; 1979:211–290.
177. Ellis M. Fungal endocarditis. J Infect. 1997;35:99–103.
178. Hallum JL, Williams TW Jr. *Candida* endocarditis. In: Bodey GP, ed. Candidiasis: Pathogenesis, Diagnosis and Treatment. 2nd ed. New York: Raven; 1993:357–369.
179. Melgar GR, Nasser RM, Gordon SM, et al. Fungal prosthetic valve endocarditis in 16 patients. An 11-year experience in a tertiary care hospital. Medicine (Baltimore). 1997;76:94–103.
180. Nasser RM, Melgar GR, Longworth DL, Gordon SM. Incidence and risk of developing fungal prosthetic valve endocarditis after nosocomial candidemia. Am J Med. 1997;103:25–32.
181. Nguyen MH, Nguyen ML, Yu VL, et al. *Candida* prosthetic valve endocarditis: Prospective study of six cases and review of the literature. Clin Infect Dis. 1996;22:262–267.
182. Odds FC. *Candida* endocarditis, myocarditis, and other cardiovascular *Candida* infections. In: Anonymous. *Candida* and Candidosis. A Review and Bibliography. 2nd ed. London: Bailliere-Tindall; 1988:175–180.
183. Anonymous. *Candida* albicans endocarditis associated with a contaminated aortic valve allograft—California, 1996. MMWR Morb Mortal Wkly Rep. 1997;46:261–263.
184. Calderone RA, Scheld WM. Role of fibronectin in the pathogenesis of candidal infections. Rev Infect Dis. 1987;9(Suppl 4):S400–S403.
185. Joly V, Belmatoug N, Leperre A, et al. Pacemaker endocarditis due to *Candida albicans*: Case report and review. Clin Infect Dis. 1997;25:1359–1362.
186. Gilbert HM, Peters ED, Lang SJ, Hartman BJ. Successful treatment of fungal prosthetic valve endocarditis: Case report and review (see Comments). Clin Infect Dis. 1996;22:348–354.
187. Galgiani JN, Stevens DA. Fungal endocarditis: Need for guidelines in evaluating therapy. J Thorac Cardiovasc Surg. 1977;73:293–296.
188. Seelig MS, Speth CP, Kozinn PJ, et al. Patterns of *Candida* endocarditis following cardiac surgery. Importance of early diagnosis and therapy (an analysis of 91 cases). Prog Cardiovasc Dis. 1974;27:125–160.
189. Fisher JF, Newman CL, Sobel JD. Yeast in the urine: Solutions for a budding problem. Clin Infect Dis. 1995;20:183–189.
190. Warren JW. Catheter-associated urinary tract infections. Infect Dis Clin North Am. 1997;11:609–622.
191. Phillips JR, Karlowicz MG. Prevalence of *Candida* species in hospital-acquired urinary tract infections in a neonatal intensive care unit. Pediatr Infect Dis J. 1997;16:190–194.
192. Oravcova E, Lacka J, Drgona L, et al. Funguria in cancer patients: Analysis of risk factors, clinical presentation and outcome in 50 patients. Infection. 1996;24:319–323.
193. Hitchcock RJ, Pallett A, Hall MA, Malone PS. Urinary tract candidiasis in neonates and infants. Br J Urol. 1995;76:252–256.
194. Williamson MR, Smith AY, Black WC, Rosenberg RD. Diagnosis of candidal infection of the prostate by transrectal ultrasonography and biopsy. J Clin Ultrasound. 1992;20:618–620.
195. Indudhara R, Singh SK, Vaidyanathan S, Banerjee CK. Isolated invasive candidal prostatitis. Urol Int. 1992;48:362–364.
196. Golz R, Mendling W. Candidosis of the prostate: A rare form of endomycosis. Mycoses. 1991;34:381–384.
197. Navarro EE, Almario JS, Schaufele RL, et al. Quantitative urine cultures do not reliably detect renal candidiasis in rabbits. J Clin Microbiol. 1997;35:3292–3297.
198. Gregory MC, Schumann GB, Schumann JL, et al. The clinical significance of *Candida* casts. Am J Kidney Dis. 1984;4:179–184.

199. Irby PB, Stoller ML, McAninch JW. Fungal bezoars of the upper urinary tract. J Urol. 1990;143:447–451.
200. Ang BSP, Telenti A, King B, et al. Candidemia from a urinary source: Microbiological aspects and clinical significance. Clin Infect Dis. 1993;17:662–666.
201. Aanestad O, Eilard T. Severe candida cystitis with perforation of the urinary bladder. Scand J Urol Nephrol. 1997;31:311–312.
202. Tomashefski JF Jr, Abramosky CR. *Candida*-associated renal papillary necrosis. Am J Clin Pathol. 1981;75:190–194.
203. High KP, Quagliarello VJ. Yeast perinephric abscess: Report of a case and review. Clin Infect Dis. 1992;15:128–133.
204. Eckstein CW, Kass EJ. Anuria in a newborn secondary to bilateral ureteropelvic fungus balls. J Urol. 1982;127:109–110.
205. Leiter E, Whitehead ED, Desai SB. Fungus balls in renal pelvis. N Y State J Med. 1982;82:64–66.
206. Biggers R, Edwards J. Anuria secondary to bilateral ureteropelvic fungus balls. Urology. 1980;15:161–163.
207. Tennant FS, Remmers AR, Perry JE. Primary renal candidiasis associated perinephric abscess and passage of fungus ball in the urine. Arch Intern Med. 1968;122:435–440.
208. Seidenfeld SM, Lemaistre CF, Setiawan H, et al. Emphymatous pyelonephritis caused by *Candida tropicalis*. J Infect Dis. 1982;146:569.
209. Singh CR, Lytle WF. Cystitis emphysematosa caused by *Candida tropicalis*. J Urol. 1983;130:1171–1173.
210. Sultana SR, McNeill SA, Phillips G, Byrne DJ. Candidal urinary tract infection as a cause of pneumaturia. J R Coll Surg Edinb. 1998;43:198–199.
211. McCullers JA, Flynn PM. *Candida tropicalis* osteomyelitis: Case report and review. Clin Infect Dis. 1998;26:1000–1001.
212. Jonnalagadda S, Veerabagu MP, Rakela J, et al. *Candida albicans* osteomyelitis in a liver transplant recipient: A case report and review of the literature. Transplantation. 1996;62:1182–1184.
213. Ferra C, Doebbeling BN, Hollis RJ, et al. *Candida tropicalis* vertebral osteomyelitis: A late sequela of fungemia. Clin Infect Dis. 1994;19:697–703.
214. Kerr J. Fungal osteomyelitis of the temporal bone: A review of reported cases (Letter; Comment). Ear Nose Throat J. 1994;73:339.
215. Lasday SD, Jay RM. *Candida* osteomyelitis. J Foot Ankle Surg. 1994;33:173–176.
216. Dan M, Priel I. Failure of fluconazole therapy for sternal osteomyelitis due to *Candida albicans* (Letter). Clin Infect Dis. 1994;18:126–127.
217. Heckenkamp J, Helling HJ, Rehm KE. Post-traumatic costochondritis caused by *Candida albicans*. Aetiology, diagnosis and treatment. Scand Cardiovasc J. 1997;31:165–167.
218. Collet P, Biron P, Larbre JP, et al. *Candida* spondylodiscitis. Report of 2 personal cases and 28 cases from the literature. (In French: Spondylodiscites à *Candida*. À propos de 2 observations personnelles et de 28 observations de la litterature). Rev Med Interne. 1989;10:413–419.
219. Herzog W, Perfect J, Roberts L. Intervertebral diskitis due to *Candida tropicalis*. South Med J. 1989;82:270–273.
220. Hansen BL, Andersen K. Fungal arthritis. A review. Scand J Rheumatol. 1995;24:248–250.
221. Silveira LH, Cuellar ML, Citera G, et al. *Candida* arthritis. Rheum Dis Clin North Am. 1993;19:427–437.
222. Murphy O, Gray J, Wagget J, Pedler SJ. *Candida* arthritis complicating long term total parenteral nutrition. Pediatr Infect Dis J. 1997;16:329.
223. Fukasawa N, Shirakura K. *Candida* arthritis after total knee arthroplasty—a case of successful treatment without prosthesis removal. Acta Orthop Scand. 1997;68:306–307.
224. Belzunegui J, Gonzalez C, Lopez L, et al. Osteoarticular and muscle infectious lesions in patients with the human immunodeficiency virus. Clin Rheumatol. 1997;16:450–453.
225. Arena FP, Perlin M, Brahman H. Fever, rash, and myalgias of disseminated candidiasis during antifungal therapy. Arch Intern Med. 1981;14:1233.
226. Fornadley JA, Parker GS, Rickman LS, Paparello S. *Candida* myositis manifesting as a discrete neck mass. Otolaryngol Head Neck Surg. 1990;102:74–76.
227. Sawyer RG, Rosenlof LK, Adams RB, et al. Peritonitis into the 1990s: Changing pathogens and changing strategies in the critically ill. Am Surg. 1992;58:82–87.
228. Levine J, Bernard DB, Idelson BA, et al. Fungal peritonitis complicating continuous ambulatory peritoneal dialysis: Successful treatment with fluconazole, a new orally active antifungal agent (see Comments). Am J Med. 1989;86:825–827.
229. Alden SM, Frank E, Flancbaum L. Abdominal candidiasis in surgical patients. Am Surg. 1989;55:45–49.
230. Bayer AS, Blumenkrantz MJ, Montgomerie JZ, et al. *Candida* peritonitis. Report of 22 cases and review of the English literature. Am J Med. 1976;61:832–840.
231. Solomkin JS, Flohr AB, Quie PG, et al. The role of *Candida* in intraperitoneal infections. Surgery. 1980;88:524–530.
232. Eisenberg ES, Leviton I, Soeiro R. Fungal peritonitis in patients receiving peritoneal dialysis: Experience with 11 patients and review of the literature. Rev Infect Dis. 1986;309–321.
233. Peoples JB. *Candida* and perforated peptic ulcers. Surgery. 1986;100:758–764.
234. Caesar-TonThat TC, Cutler JE. A monoclonal antibody to *Candida albicans* enhances mouse neutrophil candidacidal activity. Infect Immun. 1997;65:5354–5357.
235. Lo WK, Chan CY, Cheng SW, et al. A prospective randomized control study of oral nystatin prophylaxis for *Candida* peritonitis complicating continuous ambulatory peritoneal dialysis. Am J Kidney Dis. 1996;28:549–552.
236. Petri MG, Konig J, Moecke HP, et al. Epidemiology of invasive mycosis in ICU patients: A prospective multicenter study in 435 non-neutropenic patients. Paul-Ehrlich Society for Chemotherapy, Divisions of Mycology and Pneumonia Research. Intensive Care Med. 1997;23:317–325.
237. Michel C, Courdavault L, al Khayat R, et al. Fungal peritonitis in patients on peritoneal dialysis. Am J Nephrol. 1994;14:113–120.
238. Amici G, Grandesso S, Mottola A, et al. Fungal peritonitis in peritoneal dialysis: Critical review of six cases. Adv Perit Dial. 1994;10:169–173.
239. Goldie SJ, Kiernan-Tridle L, Torres C, et al. Fungal peritonitis in a large chronic peritoneal dialysis population: A report of 55 episodes. Am J Kidney Dis. 1996;28:86–91.
240. Takano H, Yoshikawa T, Nishida K, et al. *Candida* cholecystitis as an unusual complication of endoscopic retrograde cholangiography. Endoscopy. 1996;28:790–791.
241. Diebel LN, Raafat AM, Dulchavsky SA, Brown WJ. Gallbladder and biliary tract candidiasis. Surgery. 1996;120:760–764.
242. Chubachi A, Miura I, Ohshima A, et al. Risk factors for hepatosplenic abscesses in patients with acute leukemia receiving empiric azole treatment. Am J Med Sci. 1994;308:309–312.
243. Gorg C, Weide R, Schwerk WB, et al. Ultrasound evaluation of hepatic and splenic microabscesses in the immunocompromised patient: Sonographic patterns, differential diagnosis, and follow-up. J Clin Ultrasound. 1994;22:525–529.
244. Bjerke JW, Meyers JD, Bowden RA. Hepatosplenic candidiasis—a contraindication to marrow transplantation? Blood. 1994;84:2811–2814.
245. Anttila VJ, Ruutu P, Bondestam S, et al. Hepatosplenic yeast infection in patients with acute leukemia: A diagnostic problem. Clin Infect Dis. 1994;18:979–981.
246. Anttila VJ, Farkkila M, Jansson SE, et al. Diagnostic laparoscopy in patients with acute leukemia and suspected hepatic candidiasis. Eur J Clin Microbiol Infect Dis. 1997;16:637–643.
247. Chanock SJ, Pizzo PA. Infectious complications of patients undergoing therapy for acute leukemia: Current status and future prospects. Semin Oncol. 1997;24:132–140.
248. Vasquez TE, Evans DG, Schiffman H, et al. Fungal splenic abscesses in the immunosuppressed patient. Correlation of imaging modalities. Clin Nucl Med. 1987;12:30–38.
249. Helton WS, Carrico CJ, Zaveruha PA, et al. Diagnosis and treatment of splenic fungal abscesses in the immune-suppressed patient. Arch Surg. 1986;121:580–586.
250. Chia N, Clark R, Valainis GT. *Candida albicans* infected pseudocyst in a postpartum woman. South Med J. 1990;83:687–689.
251. Mannell A, Obers V. Pancreatic candidiasis. A case report. S Afr J Surg. 1990;28:26–27.
252. Foust RT. Infection of a pancreatic pseudocyst due to *Candida albicans*. South Med J. 1996;89:1104–1107.
253. Jalan R, Jones HL, Walker RJ. Multiple pancreatic abscesses due to *Candida albicans* following ERCP. Scott Med J. 1994;39:17–18.
254. Semelka RC, Shoenut JP, Greenberg HM, Bow EJ. Detection of acute and treated lesions of hepatosplenic candidiasis: Comparison of dynamic contrast-enhanced CT and MR imaging. J Magn Reson Imaging. 1992;2:341–345.
255. Uflacker R, Wholey MH, Amaral NM, et al. Parasitic and mycotic causes of biliary obstruction. Gastrointest Radiol. 1982;7:173–179.
256. Magnussen CR, Olson JP, Ona FV, et al. Candida fungus balls in the common bile duct. Unusual manifestations of disseminated candidiasis. Arch Intern Med. 1979;139:821–822.
257. Irani M, Truong LD. Candidiasis of the extrahepatic biliary tract. Arch Pathol Lab Med. 1986;110:1087–1090.
258. Morris AB, Sands ML, Shiraki M, et al. Gallbladder and biliary tract candidiasis: Nine cases and review (see Comments). Rev Infect Dis. 1990;12:483–489.
259. Garcia E, Granier I, Geissler A, et al. Surgical management of *Candida* suppurative thrombophlebitis of superior vena cava after central venous catheterization. Intensive Care Med. 1997;23:1002–1004.
260. Friedland IR. Peripheral thrombophlebitis caused by *Candida*. Pediatr Infect Dis J. 1996;15:375–377.
261. Khan EA, Correa AG, Baker CJ. Suppurative thrombophlebitis in children: A ten-year experience. Pediatr Infect Dis J. 1997;16:63–67.
262. Ward RA, Wellhausen SR, Dobbins JJ, et al. Thromboembolic and infectious complications of total artificial heart implantation. Ann N Y Acad Sci. 1987;516:638–650.
263. Doscher W, Krishnasastry KV, Deckoff SL. Fungal graft infections: Case report and review of the literature. J Vasc Surg. 1987;6:398–402.
264. Donahue SP, Greven CM, Zuravleff JJ, et al. Intraocular candidiasis in patients with candidemia. Clinical implications derived from a prospective multicenter study. Ophthalmology. 1994;101:1302–1309.
265. Chen SJ, Chung YM, Liu JH. Endogenous *Candida* endophthalmitis after induced abortion. Am J Ophthalmol. 1998;125:873–875.
266. Christmas NJ, Smiddy WE. Vitrectomy and systemic fluconazole for treatment of endogenous fungal endophthalmitis. Ophthalmic Surg Lasers. 1996;27:1012–1018.
267. Moller M, Althaus C, Sundmacher R. Bilateral candida endophthalmitis in two IV drug-dependent patients with oral L-methadone substitution. (In German: Beidseitige *Candida*-Endophthalmitis zweier i. v.-drogenabhngiger Patienten unter oraler L-Methadon-Substitution). Klin Monatsbl Augenheilkd. 1997;211:53–56.
268. Menezes AV, Sigesmund DA, Demajo WA, Devenyi RG. Mortality of hospitalized patients with *Candida* endophthalmitis. Arch Intern Med. 1994;154:2093–2097.
269. Coskuncan NM, Jabs DA, Dunn JP, et al. The eye in bone marrow transplantation. VI. Retinal complications. Arch Ophthalmol. 1994;112:372–379.
270. Widder RA, Bartz-Schmidt KU, Geyer H, et al. *Candida albicans* endophthalmitis after anabolic steroid abuse (Letter). Lancet. 1995;345:330–331.

271. Papanicolaou GA, Meyers BR, Fuchs WS, et al. Infectious ocular complications in orthotopic liver transplant patients. Clin Infect Dis. 1997;24:1172–1177.
272. Essman TF, Flynn HWJ, Smiddy WE, et al. Treatment outcomes in a 10-year study of endogenous fungal endophthalmitis. Ophthalmic Surg Lasers. 1997;28:185–194.
273. Nolla-Salas J, Sitges-Serra A, Leon C, et al. *Candida* endophthalmitis in non-neutropenic critically ill patients (see Comments). Eur J Clin Microbiol Infect Dis. 1996;15:503–506.
274. Shmuely H, Kremer I, Sagie A, Pitlik S. *Candida tropicalis* multifocal endophthalmitis as the only initial manifestation of pacemaker endocarditis. Am J Ophthalmol. 1997;123:559–560.
275. Wong VK, Tasman W, Eagle RCJ, Rodriguez A. Bilateral *Candida parapsilosis* endophthalmitis. Arch Ophthalmol. 1997;115:670–672.
276. Wolfensberger TJ, Gonvers M. Bilateral endogenous *Candida* endophthalmitis. Retina. 1998;18:280–281.
277. Stanbury RM, Chignell AH, Graham EM. Endogenous *Candida* endophthalmitis with no apparent predisposing factors (Letter). Eye. 1998;12:321–323.
278. Brooks RG. Prospective study of *Candida* endophthalmitis in hospitalized patients with candidemia. Arch Intern Med. 1989;149:2226–2228.
279. Henderson DK, Hockey LB, Vukalcic LJ, et al. Effect of immunosuppression on the development of experimental hematogenous *Candida* endophthalmitis. Infect Immun. 1980;27:628–631.
280. Barrie T. The place of elective vitrectomy in the management of patients with *Candida* endophthalmitis. Arch Clin Exp Ophthalmol. 1987;225:107–113.
281. Barrie T. The place of elective vitrectomy in the management of patients with *Candida* endophthalmitis. Graefes Arch Clin Exp Ophthalmol. 1987;225:107–113.
282. McDonald HR, De Bustros S, Sipperley JO. Vitrectomy for epiretinal membrane with *Candida* chorioretinitis. Ophthalmology. 1990;97:466–469.
283. Bennett JE. Rapid diagnosis of candidiasis and aspergilloses. Rev Infect Dis. 1987;9:398–402.
284. Edwards JE Jr. Invasive *Candida* infections. N Engl J Med. 1991;324:1060–1062.
285. Mitsutake K, Miyazaki T, Tashiro T, et al. Enolase antigen, mannan antigen, Cand-Tec antigen, and beta-glucan in patients with candidemia. J Clin Microbiol. 1996;34:1918–1921.
286. Krick JA, Remington JS. Opportunistic invasive fungal infections in patients with leukemia and lymphoma. Clin Hematol. 1976;5:249–310.
287. Young RC, Bennett JE, Geelhoed GW, et al. Fungemia with compromised host resistance. A study of 70 cases. Ann Intern Med. 1974;80:605–612.
288. Rex JH. Editorial response: Catheters and candidemia. Clin Infect Dis. 1996;22:467–470.
289. Rex JH, Bennett JE, Sugar AM, et al. A randomized trial comparing fluconazole with amphotericin B for the treatment of candidemia in patients without neutropenia. N Engl J Med. 1994;331:1325–1330.
290. Hockey LJ, Fujita NK, Gibson TR, et al. Detection of fungemia obscured by concomitant bacteremia: In vitro and in vivo studies. J Clin Microbiol. 1982;16:1080–1085.
291. Wey SB, Mori M, Pfaller MA, et al. Hospital-acquired candidemia. The attributable mortality and excess length of stay. Arch Intern Med. 1988;148:2642–2645.
292. MacDonald L, Baker C, Chenoweth C. Risk factors for candidemia in a children's hospital. Clin Infect Dis. 1998;26:642–645.
293. Khatib R, Thirumoorthi MC, Riederer KM, et al. Clustering of *Candida* infections in the neonatal intensive care unit: Concurrent emergence of multiple strains simulating intermittent outbreaks. Pediatr Infect Dis J. 1998;17:130–134.
294. Al Arishi H, Frayha HH, Kalloghlian A, al Alaiyan S. Liposomal amphotericin B in neonates with invasive candidiasis. Am J Perinatol. 1997;14:573–576.
295. Donowitz LG, Hendley JO. Short-course amphotericin B therapy for candidemia in pediatric patients. Pediatrics. 1995;95:888–891.
296. Stamos JK, Rowley AH. Candidemia in a pediatric population. Clin Infect Dis. 1995;20:571–575.
297. Wingard JR, Merz WG, Saral R. *Candida* tropicalis: A major pathogen in immunocompromised patients. Ann Intern Med. 1979;91:539–543.
298. Rex JH, Rinaldi MG, Pfaller MA. Resistance of *Candida* species to fluconazole. Antimicrob Agents Chemother. 1995;39:1–8.
299. Nguyen MH, Peacock JEJ, Morris AJ, et al. The changing face of candidemia: Emergence of non-*Candida albicans* species and antifungal resistance. Am J Med. 1996;100:617–623.
300. Rex JH, Walsh TJ, Sobel JD, et al. Treatment guidelines for candidiasis. Clin Infect Dis. 1998. In press.
301. Graybill JR, Vazquez J, Darouiche RO, et al. Randomized trial of itraconazole oral solution for oropharyngeal candidiasis in HIV/AIDS patients. Am J Med. 1998;104:33–39.
302. Eichel M, Just-Nubling G, Helm EB, Stille W. Itraconazole suspension in the treatment of HIV-infected patients with fluconazole-resistant oropharyngeal candidiasis and esophagitis. (In German: Itraconazol-Suspension in der Behandlung HIV-infizierter Patienten mit Fluconazol-resistenter oropharyngealer *Candida*-Infektion und Soorosophagitis.) Mycoses. 1996;39(Suppl 1):102–106.
303. Laine L, Dretler RH, Conteas CN, et al. Fluconazole compared with ketoconazole for the treatment of *Candida* esophagitis in AIDS. A randomized trial. Ann Intern Med. 1992;117:655–660.
304. Troke PF. Large-scale multicentre study of fluconazole in the treatment of hospitalised patients with fungal infections. Multicentre European Study Group. Eur J Clin Microbiol Infect Dis. 1997;16:287–295.
305. Slavin MA, Osborne B, Adams R, et al. Efficacy and safety of fluconazole prophylaxis for fungal infections after marrow transplantation—a prospective, randomized, double-blind study. J Infect Dis. 1995;171:1545–1552.
306. Goodman JL, Winston DJ, Greenfield RA, et al. A controlled trial of fluconazole to prevent fungal infections in patients undergoing bone marrow transplantation. N Engl J Med. 1992;326:845–851.
307. Collins LA, Samore MH, Roberts MS, et al. Risk factors for invasive fungal infections complicating orthotopic liver transplantation. J Infect Dis. 1994;170:644–652.
308. Reents S, Goodwin SD, Singh V. Antifungal prophylaxis in immunocompromised hosts. Ann Pharmacother. 1993;27:53–60.
309. De Gregorio MW, Lee WMF, Ries CA. *Candida* infections in patients with acute leukemia: Ineffectiveness of nystatin prophylaxis and relationship between oropharyngeal and systemic candidiasis. Cancer. 1982;50:2780–2784.
310. Hansen RM, Reinerio N, Sohnle PG, et al. Ketoconazole in the prevention of candidiasis in patients with cancer. A prospective, randomized, controlled, double-blind study. Arch Intern Med. 1987;147:710–712.
311. Meunier F. Prevention of mycosis in immunocompromised patients. Rev Infect Dis. 1987;9:408–416.
312. Slotman GJ, Burchard KW. Ketoconazole prevents *Candida* sepsis in critically ill surgical patients. Arch Surg. 1987;122:147–151.
313. White MH, Bowden RA, Sandler ES, et al. Randomized, double-blind clinical trial of amphotericin B colloidal dispersion vs. amphotericin B in the empirical treatment of fever and neutropenia. Clin Infect Dis. 1998;27:296–302.
314. Hiemenz JW, Walsh TJ. Lipid formulations of amphotericin B: Recent progress and future directions. Clin Infect Dis. 1996;22(Suppl 2):S133–S144.
315. Wong-Beringer A, Jacobs RA, Guglielmo BJ. Lipid formulations of amphotericin B: Clinical efficacy and toxicities. Clin Infect Dis. 1998;27:603–618.
316. Drutz DJ. In vitro antifungal susceptibility testing and measurement of levels of antifungal agents in body fluids. Rev Infect Dis. 1987;9:392–397.
317. Turnier E, Kay JH, Bernstein S, et al. Surgical treatment of *Candida* endocarditis. Chest. 1975;67:262–268.
318. Baddour LM. Long-term suppressive therapy for fungal endocarditis (Letter; Comment). Clin Infect Dis. 1996;23:1338–1340.
319. Montenegro J, Aguirre R, Gonzalez O, et al. Fluconazole treatment of candida peritonitis with delayed removal of the peritoneal dialysis catheter. Clin Nephrol. 1995;44:60–63.
320. Chan TM, Chan CY, Cheng SW, et al. Treatment of fungal peritonitis complicating continuous ambulatory peritoneal dialysis with oral fluconazole: A series of 21 patients (see Comments). Nephrol Dial Transplant. 1994;9:539–542.
321. Rodriguez-Perez JC. Fungal peritonitis in CAPD—which treatment is best? Contrib Nephrol. 1987;57:114–121.
322. Struijk DG, Krediet RT, Boeschoten EW, et al. Antifungal treatment of *Candida* peritonitis in continuous ambulatory peritoneal dialysis patients. Am J Kidney Dis. 1987;9:66–70.
323. Lopez-Berestin G, Bodeg GP, Frankel LS, et al. Treatment of hepatosplenic candidiasis with liposomal amphotericin B. J Clin Oncol. 1987;5:310–317.
324. Shirkhoda B, Lopez-Berestein G, Hlbert JM, et al. Hepatosplenic fungal infection: CT and pathologic evaluation after treatment with liposomal amphotericin B. Radiology. 1986;159:349–353.
325. Anaissie E, Bodey GP, Kantarjian H, et al. Fluconazole therapy for chronic disseminated candidiasis in patients with leukemia and prior amphotericin B therapy. Am J Med. 1991;91:142–150.
326. Bozzette SA, Gordon RL, Yen A, et al. Biliary concentrations of fluconazole in a patient with candidal cholecystitis: Case report. Clin Infect Dis. 1992;15:701–703.
327. Jacobs LG, Skidmore EA, Freeman K, et al. Oral fluconazole compared with bladder irrigation with amphotericin B for treatment of fungal urinary tract infections in elderly patients (see Comments). Clin Infect Dis. 1996;22:30–35.
328. Francis P, Walsh TJ. Evolving role of flucytosine in immunocompromised patients: New insights into safety, pharmacokinetics, and antifungal therapy. Clin Infect Dis. 1992;15:1003–1018.
329. DeWit S, Weerts D, Goossens H, Clumeck N. Comparisons of fluconazole and ketoconazole for oropharyngeal candidiasis in AIDS. Lancet. 1989;1:746–748.
330. Blatchford NR. Treatment of oral candidosis with itraconazole: A review. J Am Acad Dermatol. 1990;23:565–567.
331. Cartledge JD, Midgely J, Gazzard BG. Itraconazole solution: Higher serum drug concentrations and better clinical response rates than the capsule formulation in acquired immunodeficiency syndrome patients with candidosis. J Clin Pathol. 1997;50:477–480.
332. Phillips P, Zemcov J, Mahmood W, et al. Itraconazole cyclodextrin solution for fluconazole-refractory oropharyngeal candidiasis in AIDS: Correlation of clinical response with in vitro susceptibility. AIDS. 1996;10:1369–1376.
333. Laine L, Dretler RH, Conteas CN, et al. Fluconazole compared with ketoconazole for the treatment of *Candida* esophagitis in AIDS. A randomized trial (see Comments). Ann Intern Med. 1992;117:655–660.
334. Barbaro G, Barbarini G, Calderon W, et al. Fluconazole versus itraconazole for candida esophagitis in acquired immunodeficiency syndrome. *Candida* esophagitis. Gastroenterology. 1996;111:1169–1177.
335. Barbaro G, Barbarini G, Di LG. Fluconazole vs flucytosine in the treatment of esophageal candidiasis in AIDS patients: A double-blind, placebo-controlled study. Endoscopy. 1995;27:377–383.
336. Wilcox CM, Darouiche RO, Laine L, et al. A randomized, double-blind comparison of itraconazole oral solution and fluconazole tablets in the treatment of esophageal candidiasis. J Infect Dis. 1997;176:227–232.
337. Barbaro G, Barbarini G, Di LG. Fluconazole vs itraconazole-flucytosine association in the treatment of esophageal candidiasis in AIDS patients. A double-blind, multicenter placebo-controlled study. The *Candida* Esophagitis Multicenter Italian Study (CEMIS) Group. Chest. 1996;110:1507–1514.

338. Medoff G. Controversial areas in antifungal chemotherapy: Short-course and combination therapy with amphotericin B. Rev Infect Dis. 1987;9:403–407.
339. Agresti MG, De BF, Mondello F, et al. Clinical and mycological evaluation of fluconazole in the secondary prophylaxis of esophageal candidiasis in AIDS patients. An open, multicenter study. Eur J Epidemiol. 1994;10:17–22.
340. Reef SE, Levine WC, McNeil MM, et al. Treatment options for vulvovaginal candidiasis, 1993. Clin Infect Dis. 1995;20(Suppl 1):S80–S90.
341. Sobel JD, Chaim W. Treatment of *Torulopsis glabrata* vaginitis: Retrospective review of boric acid therapy. Clin Infect Dis. 1997;24:649–652.
342. Edwards JE Jr. *Candida* endophthalmitis. In: Bodey GP, Fainstein V, eds. Candidiasis. New York: Raven; 1985:211–225.
343. Jones DB. Chemotherapy of experimental endogenous *Candida albicans* endophthalmitis. Trans Am Opthalmol Soc. 1980;78:846–895.
344. Moyer DV, Edwards JE Jr. *Candida* endophthalmitis and central nervous system infection. In: Bodey GP, ed. Candidiasis: Pathogenesis, Diagnosis and Treatment. 2nd ed. New York: Raven; 1993:331–355.
345. Luttrull JK, Wan WL, Kubak BM, et al. Treatment of ocular fungal infections with oral fluconazole. Am J Ophthalmol. 1995;119:477–481.
346. Perez-Gomez A, Prieto A, Torresano M, et al. Role of the new azoles in the treatment of fungal osteoarticular infections. Semin Arthritis Rheum. 1998;27:226–244.
347. Dunkley AB, Leslie IJ. *Candida* infection of a silicone metacarpophalangeal arthroplasty. J Hand Surg Br. 1997;22:423–424.
348. Jenkin GA, Choo M, Hosking P, Johnson PD. Candidal epididymo-orchitis: Case report and review. Clin Infect Dis. 1998;26:942–945.

TABLE 248–1 Incidence of Invasive Aspergillosis in Different Host Groups

Group	Range (%)
Heart-lung or lung transplantation	19–26*
Chronic granulomatous disease	25–40†
Acute leukemia	5–24
Allogeneic bone marrow transplantation	4–9
Autologous bone marrow transplant without growth factors	0.5–6
AIDS	
Liver transplantation	0–12
Cardiac and renal transplantation	1.5–10
Severe combined immunodeficiency	0.5–10
Burns	3.5
Systemic lupus erythematosus	1–7
Autologous bone marrow transplant with growth factors	1
	<1

*Distinguishing colonization from disease is particularly difficult in these patients.
†Lifetime incidcence.
From Deming DW. Invasive aspergillosis. Clin Infect Dis. 1998;26:781–805.

Chapter 248

Aspergillus Species

DAVID W. DENNING

Aspergillus is a mold capable of causing several manifestations of disease both in healthy human (and other vertebrate) hosts and in immunocompromised patients. Previously, the term *aspergillosis* was used to mean any form of disease caused by *Aspergillus* or colonization with *Aspergillus*, but it is now used to mean either tissue invasive disease or allergic disease caused by *Aspergillus* and excludes colonization. The term *aspergilloma* is used to describe the occurrence of fungal balls in preexisting lung or sinus cavities.

Although *Aspergillus* as an organism was first recognized in 1729 by Micheli, the first cases in humans were not noted until the mid-19th century.[1] About 100 years later, invasive aspergillosis was first described as an opportunistic infection.[2] Since then, a substantial rise in the number of cases of invasive aspergillosis has been documented at autopsy in industrialized countries. The incidence of invasive aspergillosis varies substantially from center to center, and within centers it tends to occur sporadically. A recent study from Frankfurt, Germany, showed a 14-fold rise of invasive aspergillosis over the years 1978 to 1992.[3] These authors noted that 4% of all persons undergoing autopsy in their university hospital in 1992 had invasive aspergillosis. Rates of invasive aspergillosis vary substantially in different patient groups (Table 248–1). Data on the incidence of allergic aspergillosis are scanty, but increasing asthma rates may lead to more cases. Aspergillomas are much less common in the developed world than 2 decades ago.

Most species of *Aspergillus* reproduce only asexually, but those that have a telomorph are Ascomycetes.[4] *Aspergillus* taxonomy is gradually undergoing revision with the use of molecular taxonomic methods. The most common species of *Aspergillus* causing invasive disease include *Aspergillus fumigatus* (~90%), *Aspergillus flavus* (~10%), *Aspergillus niger* (~2%), *Aspergillus terreus* (~2%), and *Aspergillus nidulans* (<1%). *A. niger* is the predominant cause of otomycosis, and *A. flavus* is the principal cause of sinusitis. Other species of *Aspergillus* that have rarely caused disease include *Aspergillus amstelodami, Aspergillus avenaceus, Aspergillus caesiellus, Aspergillus candidus, Aspergillus carneus, Aspergillus chevalieri, Aspergillus clavatus, Aspergillus glaucus, Aspergillus granulosus, Aspergillus oryzae, Aspergillus quadrilineatus, Aspergillus restrictus, Aspergillus sydowi, Aspergillus ustus, Aspergillus versicolor, Aspergillus wentii, Aspergillus (Neosartorya) fisheri,* and others.

Pathogenic species of A*spergillus* generally grow easily and relatively quickly on routine bacteriologic and mycologic media in the clinical laboratory. A comparison of the yield from a large retrospective series established that mycologic media were superior to standard bacteriologic media in the clinical setting.[5] The organism appears after 36 to 90 hours as a small, fluffy white colony on the surface of agar. Sporulation usually occurs 36 to 48 hours later at 30°C to 37°C but can take longer in some rarer species, thus delaying identification. Potato dextrose agar is useful for inducing sporulation. Isolates of *A. fumigatus* grow at low oxygen tensions (0.1% O_2)[6] and occasionally anaerobically.

Identification of the common species of pathogenic *Aspergillus* is relatively straightforward by microscopic criteria and colony (conidial) color. Formal identification may require cultures on specialized media such as Czapek-Dox and malt extract. In the future, molecular methods will be increasingly used to formally identify unusual species. Susceptibility testing against azoles is now feasible with *Aspergillus*, and both agar dilution and microtiter methods have been reported.[7, 8] The clinical significance of susceptibility testing, however, remains to be established. Itraconazole resistance is described in isolates from the United States and Europe and is present in about 6% of U.K. isolates[9] but in less than 1% of Dutch isolates[10] and sporadically elsewhere.[11] Resistance to amphotericin B is also extant, but no in vitro susceptibility test is yet available.[12] Given the emerging development of resistance, a more aggressive approach to performing *Aspergillus* susceptibility testing is appropriate.

ECOLOGY AND EPIDEMIOLOGY

Environmental Location

A. fumigatus is a ubiquitous organism that is particularly found in and around human habitation,[13] particularly in cellars, potted plants, and pepper and spices.[14] *Aspergillus* is found in every country in the world, as well as Antarctica. Its primary ecologic niche is probably decomposing vegetable material,[15] and farms are a major source of organisms. Spore counts in hay barns are typically at least $10^6/m^3$. The incidence of colonization with *A. fumigatus* in patients with cystic fibrosis in rural locations is higher than the incidence in patients from urban locations.[16] Marijuana may yield substantial quantities of *Aspergillus* spores, and at-risk patients should be advised of this possibility.

Various molecular typing systems for *A. fumigatus* have been developed over the last 10 years. Genotypes of *A. fumigatus* are widely dispersed around the world, with identical genotypes causing disease in the United States and Europe.[17–21] Some patients colonized by *A. fumigatus* have single genotypes, but most have multiple types over time.[21] Likewise, patients with aspergilloma may carry more than one type.[18] The vast majority of invasive infections are caused by a single genotype of *A. fumigatus*, although occasionally two or more types have been implicated. It does not appear that any group of related genotypes is more or less pathogenic,[20] but such analyses have yet to examine isolates from patients in single host groups, with and without immunocompromising factors.

The size of the inoculum necessary for the development of any of the manifestations of aspergillosis is not known, but it is likely to be lower in the most immunocompromised patients. The incubation period between exposure to *Aspergillus* and invasive aspergillosis is variable and in two cases varied from 36 hours to 3 months.[1] In neutropenic patients, invasive aspergillosis is virtually never manifested before the 12th day of profound neutropenia,[22] although patients may have sinus or airway colonization of *Aspergillus* on arrival at the hospital.[23]

PATHOGENESIS AND PATHOLOGY

A classification of *Aspergillus*-induced diseases is shown in Table 248–2. Although *Aspergillus* species are unusual pathogens in nonimmunocompromised patients, many such cases are clearly documented.[1, 24–27] Infections include superficial infections such as onychomycosis and external otitis, as well as infection of damaged tissue as in keratitis or postoperative infections. Invasive disease also occurs. Thus, *A. fumigatus* is capable of being a primary pathogen in humans. *Aspergillus* infections also develop in many animals, including birds, dogs, and horses, further evidence that *Aspergillus* is an occasional primary pathogen.

Most species of *Aspergillus* are incapable of growth at 37°C, and this property is therefore a key characteristic that distinguishes pathogenic species from nonpathogenic species.[28] In vitro, *A. fumigatus* conidia germinate in 5 to 14 hours at 37°C, depending on the medium. In vitro, hyphal extension and overall fungal mass increase logarithmically until approximately 24 hours, when the growth rate starts to plateau. Physiologic and pharmacologic concentrations of hydrocortisone accelerate the growth rate of *A. fumigatus* and *A. flavus* by 30 to 40%.[29] Branching of hyphae occurs early, and in shaking conditions in vitro, the organism takes on the appearance of multiple small balls. At the liquid-air interface in static culture a mycelial mat is typically formed. These growth patterns probably reflect in part the branching characteristics of each isolate. *A. fumigatus* has a mass doubling time of 48 minutes and a hyphal extension rate of 1 to 2 cm/hour in vitro.[29] Growth rates among species of *Aspergillus* vary, with the most rapidly growing being *A. fumigatus*. The growth rate is probably one determinant of the rate of progression of disease and possibly pathogenicity. The very small spore size (3 to 5 μm) of *A. fumigatus,* which enables the spores to penetrate deep into the lung, may contribute to pathogenicity. The hydrophobic protein coat layer of conidia may help protect them from host defenses.[30–32] *A. fumigatus* binds laminin[33] and fibrinogen[34] more efficiently than other species do, presumably allowing greater adhesion in the airways before invasion. Pathogenic aspergilli produce several proteases.[35] Extensive work with the alkaline protease of *A. fumigatus* with the use of single or double gene deletants in carefully controlled animal model experiments has failed to show the importance of elastase (alkaline protease) in invasive aspergillosis.[36, 37] However, proteases are secreted during infection[38] and may induce pulmonary epithelial cell detachment and proinflammatory cytokine release,[39] but they do not appear to be responsible for invasion of blood vessels.[40] Several phospholipases are produced by *A. fumigatus*,[41] but their role in the pathogenesis of aspergillosis is as yet unknown.

Most species of *Aspergillus* produce a number of potentially toxic secondary metabolites, including aflatoxins, ochratoxin A, fumagillin, and gliotoxin. Gliotoxin has been shown to reduce macrophage and neutrophil phagocytosis[42] and exacerbate experimental invasive aspergillosis,[43] and it can also induce apoptosis.[44] Aflatoxin, produced by *A. flavus*, is immunosuppressive and carcinogenic but is not thought to be important in the pathogenesis of aspergillosis.[45] Phthioic acid is produced by a very small number of isolates of *A. fumigatus*[46] and could conceivably contribute to granuloma formation, as it may do in tuberculosis, but it is unlikely to be a major virulence determinant. However, these and other secondary metabolites could contribute to the systemic clinical features of patients with aspergillomas.

Aside from the mucous layer and ciliary action, the first line of defense against *Aspergillus* in the lungs is the macrophage, which is capable of attaching to, ingesting, and killing conidia.[47, 48] Both monocyte-derived and resident macrophages contribute to spore ingestion and killing. Hyphae are damaged and sometimes killed by neutrophils,[47, 49] with some contribution from monocytes[50] and possibly macrophages. Complement facilitates hyphal damage by neutrophils and monocyte killing of swollen conidia.[51, 52] Hyphae are damaged and killed extracellularly, unlike most bacteria, in which killing occurs intracellularly. Aspergilli produce several superoxide dismutases,[53] at least two catalases,[54–56] and mannitol.[57, 58] These substances may assist *Aspergillus* in minimizing damage from singlet oxygen, hydrogen peroxide, hydroxyl, and other free radicals produced by phagocytes during the respiratory burst.[52]

Oxidative killing by phagocytes is central to recovery from invasive aspergillosis. However, other factors impinge on the balance between phagocyte killing and organism survival. One important factor is corticosteroid use[59, 60] inasmuch as corticosteroids substantially impair macrophage killing of *Aspergillus* spores and neutrophil and mononuclear cell killing of *Aspergillus* hyphae.[61, 62] These detrimental effects are abrogated to a degree by granulocyte[61] and granulocyte-macrophage[62] colony-stimulating factor (in vitro), but any clinical impact has yet to be realized.[60] Interferon-γ also improves

TABLE 248–2 Classification of *Aspergillus* Infection

Allergic aspergillosis
Allergic bronchopulmonary aspergillosis
Allergic *Aspergillus* sinusitis
Saprophytic aspergillosis
Pulmonary aspergilloma
Fungal ball of the sinus (sinus aspergilloma)
Superficial aspergillosis
Otomycosis
Onychomycosis
Cutaneous aspergillosis (in nonimmunocompromised patients)
Infection associated with tissue damage, surgery, or foreign body
Keratitis and/or endophthalmitis
Cutaneous or soft tissue infection, e.g., burn wound aspergillosis
Operative site infection, e.g., prosthetic valve endocarditis, wound infection after liver transplantation, subdural empyema
Foreign body associated, e.g., Hickman or other intravenous line associated, vascular graft infection, and CAPD catheter
Infection predominantly in an immunocompromised host
Primary cutaneous or mucous membrane aspergillosis
Pulmonary aspergillosis
Acute invasive aspergillosis
Chronic necrotizing aspergillosis
Airway aspergillosis
Obstructing bronchial aspergillosis
Invasive *Aspergillus* tracheobronchitis
Nasal or paranasal sinusitis (rhinosinusitis)
Disseminated aspergillosis, especially cerebral aspergillosis

Abbreviation: CAPD, Continuous ambulatory peritoneal dialysis.

monocyte and neutrophil function.[56, 61, 63] The patient's underlying disease may also contribute directly to neutrophil dysfunction, as in acquired immunodeficiency syndrome (AIDS)[64] or chronic granulomatous disease.[65]

Emerging data also indicate that T-cell function may be important, particularly in the more chronic forms of invasive aspergillosis.[66] Recovery was prevented in mice with Th2 predominant responses, an outcome that was reversed with the administration of soluble interleukin-4 receptor and switching to a Th1 predominant response.[66] Some evidence also points to acquired immunity, possibly mediated in part by macrophages.[67] In more chronic forms of aspergillosis, including allergic disease and aspergilloma, precipitating antibodies are formed, thus implying antigen processing by T cells.

The pathology of invasive aspergillosis depends on the host. In immunosuppressed patients, vascular invasion is prominent, but not universal, and accompanied by necrotizing inflammation. Typically, this setting leads to infarction, necrosis, edema, and hemorrhage in distal tissues. Hyphae are abundant, even forming radially branching clusters in tissue. In chronic invasive aspergillosis, several pathologic features are seen.[68] Necrotizing granulomatous pneumonia may be present along with alveolar consolidation. The granulomas may be of the caseating type, and it is within these granulomas that fungal *Aspergillus* hyphae may be seen. In some cases, bronchiectatic cavities are seen along with invasion of the fibrous walls of the cavities by fungal hyphae, sometimes associated with granulomatous inflammation.

The pathogenesis of allergic forms of aspergillosis is incompletely understood but assumed to be akin to other forms of chronic respiratory allergy. Some distinctive features, however, include the appearance of central bronchiectasis in allergic bronchopulmonary aspergillosis and bronchocentric granulomatosis. Bronchocentric granulomatosis is characterized by granulomatous inflammation centered on the walls of bronchi and bronchioles. Exudative bronchiolitis and chronic eosinophilic pneumonia are the more common pathologic features of allergic bronchopulmonary aspergillosis. Hypersensitivity reactions to *Aspergillus* probably contribute in some way to the pathology in patients with aspergillomas. In addition, abnormal vascular connections appear in the lung tissue surrounding aspergillomas and may lead to hemoptysis. Pleural fibrosis is characteristic of aspergillomas (Fig. 248–1). The fungus does not invade lung tissue but remains confined to the cavity or the lumen of ectatic bronchi. The etiology of the hemoptysis and pleural fibrosis is unclear. Aspergillomas caused by *A. niger* can occasionally lead to oxalosis and renal failure, and birefringent crystals can be found in pulmonary and renal tissue.

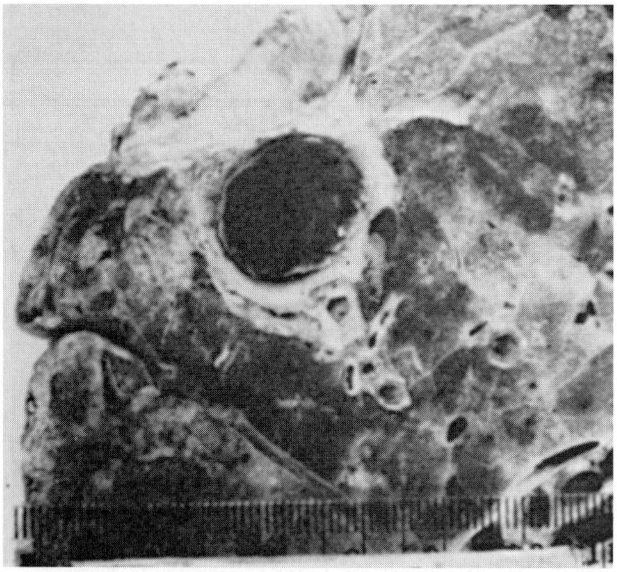

FIGURE 248–1. Aspergilloma in apex of lung at autopsy. Contiguous pleura is thickened.

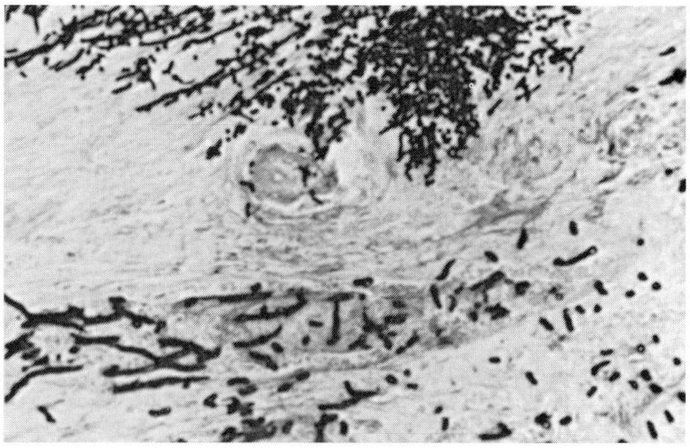

FIGURE 248–2. Aspergillosis in blood vessel and contiguous tissue of gastroesophageal junction. *Candida* pseudohyphae and yeastlike cells in contiguous lesion. (Methenamine silver, original magnification x375). (Photomicrograph courtesy of Nathaniel Young.)

Aspergillus hyphae are 2 to 4 μm wide, frequently septate, and branching at 45 degrees (Fig. 248–2). They are best visualized on silver stains and may be missed on routine hematoxylin-eosin stains, especially if sparse. In rapidly progressive infections the hyphae are of even diameter, whereas in more chronic cases they may have bulbous, widened areas. Sporulation is rarely observed in tissue, except for air-containing areas such as the lung or paranasal sinus. In the absence of sporulation, hyphae cannot be readily distinguished from a large number of pathogenic molds, and the mycologic differential diagnosis includes *Scedosporium, Fusarium, Scopulariopsis,* and many other rarer fungi.

CLINICAL MANIFESTATIONS

Allergic Disease

Patients with allergic bronchopulmonary aspergillosis have underlying asthma or cystic fibrosis and are hypersensitive to *Aspergillus* colonizing their airways. They present with worsening asthma or pulmonary function and eosinophilic pneumonia or mucoid impaction. Early in the course of disease they have peripheral eosinophilia, precipitating IgG and IgE antibodies against *Aspergillus.* Later, central bronchiectasis develops.[69] Exacerbations are best managed with oral corticosteroids and can be prevented in many cases by high-dose inhaled steroids.[70] Oral itraconazole therapy is useful for those who are corticosteroid dependent.[71]

Allergic *Aspergillus* sinusitis has many features in common with sinus aspergilloma.[72–74] It differs in that the sinus is filled with eosinophil-rich mucin that often contains Charcot-Leyden crystals. Management consists of aeration of the affected sinus. No convincing evidence of benefit from steroids has been demonstrated, and antifungal agents are unnecessary.

Aspergilloma

Fungal balls may develop in the maxillary and ethmoid sinus cavities, sometimes after endodontic treatment of the upper jaw.[75] In these cases no mucosal invasion is apparent, and good surgical drainage, including removal of the diseased ethmoid air cells, is usually curative. If pathologic specimens show hyphal invasion of mucosa or computed tomography (CT) shows bony erosion or involvement of the frontal or sphenoid sinus, medical therapy is also appropriate.[76]

Aspergillus may colonize preexisting pulmonary cavities or cysts or ectatic bronchi resulting from tuberculosis, sarcoidosis, and *Pneumocystis* infection in patients with AIDS. The vast majority of fungal balls in the lungs are due to *Aspergillus*, with rare cases caused by *Pseudallescheria boydii* or Mucorales. The risk of an aspergilloma developing within a tuberculous cavity 2 cm or larger in diameter is 15 to 25%.[77] Distinguishing chronic invasive aspergillosis from genuine aspergilloma is important because the former requires systemic antifungal therapy. Some patients with aspergillomas are asymptomatic, but most have persistent productive cough, hemoptysis, wheezing, weight loss, and finger clubbing. Masses of hyphae are visible on chest radiographs or CT scans of the lungs as a cavity surrounded by a rim of air. Sputum cultures yield *Aspergillus*, and precipitating IgG antibodies are present in the serum. Complications include mild or massive (and fatal) hemoptysis, spread of infection to the pleura and contiguous vertebral bodies, and rarely, dissemination to distant body sites. Invasive disease is more common in AIDS patients. Pulmonary aspergillomas are often difficult to treat. Approximately 10% of aspergillomas resolve spontaneously, which makes uncontrolled observations difficult to interpret. Intracavitary amphotericin B in the form of a thick paste has been given by transthoracic injection.[78–80] Surgical resection is useful if the aspergilloma is unilateral and pulmonary function is reasonable, although complications are frequent, particularly bronchopleural fistula.[81–83] Oral itraconazole has some symptomatic impact.[84] Embolization is sometimes valuable for significant hemoptysis in inoperable patients.

Superficial and Ear Aspergillosis

Otomycosis refers to the growth of usually *A. niger* in the external auditory canal. Patients always have underlying chronic otitis externa and complain of itching and discomfort or something blocking off the ear. Inspection of the ear may reveal a white mat of fungal mycelia with black conidiophores, but often the appearance is simply that of otitis externa. Thorough cleansing of the external auditory canal is very important. Topical thimerosal, amphotericin B (3%), flucytosine (10%), clotrimazole, or econazole usually effects a cure. Rarely, *Aspergillus* may cause onychomycosis or cutaneous infection.

Eye Infections

Aspergillus has been documented as a frequent cause of post-traumatic keratitis[85] and occasionally endophthalmitis. Smears from the cornea usually reveal hyphae and cultures are usually positive. Time between injury and recognition of fungal keratitis is a major determinant of success in the treatment of *Aspergillus* keratitis.

Aspergillus keratitis can be treated with topical amphotericin (0.15 to 1.0%), with a 27% response rate if administered hourly,[86] with natamycin (primaricin) (5%) for superficial infection, or with clotrimazole (1%) or miconazole (1%) solution. Oral itraconazole, 200 to 400 mg/day, is also effective in up to 75% of cases of *Aspergillus* keratitis.[86, 87]

Surgery is sometimes required in the management of cases of mycotic keratitis that fails to respond to medical therapy or when ocular perforation or the formation of a descemetocele is a possibility. Surgery should be preceded by medical therapy for as long as possible. Relevant surgical procedures include débridement or lamellar keratectomy, formation of a conjunctival flap over a severely ulcerated area of the cornea (in an attempt to save the eyeball), or penetrating keratoplasty if a donor cornea is available.[85]

Aspergillus endophthalmitis is uncommon but usually results in lost vision unless diagnosed rapidly and managed appropriately.[88] It occurs after penetrating eye surgery or trauma. Hematogenous endophthalmitis occurs in intravenous drug addicts and in the context of endocarditis or invasive aspergillosis. Ocular pain, photophobia, and impaired vision are typical, and the eye is inflamed to a greater or lesser extent. Partial or complete vitrectomy is necessary to establish the diagnosis and is therapeutically useful. Intraoperative microspore examination of the vitrectomy specimen, looking for hyphae, is helpful because intravitreal amphotericin B (5 to 7.5 μg) can be administered immediately. The whole vitrectomy specimen should be cultured, not a few drops. Parenteral amphotericin B and flucytosine are also recommended.[88]

Invasive Pulmonary Aspergillosis

Most patients with invasive aspergillosis have pulmonary disease (80 to 90%). Invasive pulmonary aspergillosis (IPA) is manifested differently in various patient groups.[89–109] Patients who are most immunocompromised, such as allogeneic bone marrow transplant recipients, have few symptoms initially and the progression rate is fast (acute IPA). Conversely, less immunocompromised patients, such as AIDS patients, usually have a more indolent, symptomatic manifestation that progresses slowly (chronic IPA).

Approximately 25 to 33% of patients with acute IPA have no attributable symptoms or signs initially. The earliest symptoms are a dry cough and low-grade fever. Pleuritic or nonspecific chest pain is common. Hemoptysis can occur, although it is rarely an initial feature. A pleural rub is sometimes heard. Dyspnea is more common in patients with diffuse bilateral disease. The findings in some patients are akin to those of pulmonary embolism. Pneumothorax is an occasional initial feature in neutropenic patients. The clinical features of pulmonary mucormycosis are indistinguishable from those of invasive aspergillosis.

Hypoxemia is usual in persons with bilateral diffuse IPA or in those with extensive consolidation. Patients may be neutropenic from prior chemotherapy, but if not, the white cell count may or may not be elevated. Serum fibrinogen and C-reactive protein levels are often elevated, but their specificity for either fungal infection or invasive aspergillosis is in doubt.[108]

The appearance of invasive aspergillosis on plain chest radiographs is heterogeneous.[89, 91, 97, 101–103, 107, 110–116] Consolidation is common. Cavitation and pleural-based wedge-shaped lesions are the most distinctive features of invasive aspergillosis. Nodular shadows, with and without cavitation, thick- or thin-walled cavities (in AIDS and chronic necrotizing pulmonary aspergillosis), and "alveolar" consolidation that coalesces over time to form small nodules and areas of consolidation are typical. Diffuse, usually lower lobe, fine shadowing is also seen. Pleural effusions are uncommon. In solid organ transplant recipients the major differential diagnoses of nodular disease are nocardiosis and lymphoma. Bilateral diffuse disease has a wide differential diagnosis, and further diagnostic studies are essential. Plain radiology results are falsely negative in about 10% of patients with IPA, and the size, number, and location of lesions are not well delineated. High-quality CT scans of the chest can play a major role in early diagnosis.[98, 108, 112, 113, 115, 117–121] The most distinctive early lesions are one or more small nodules and small pleural-based lesions with straight edges and surrounding low attenuation (the "halo" sign), particularly in neutropenic patients (Fig. 248–3). As IPA progresses, the nodules may cavitate (typically with neutrophil recovery) and reveal an "air-crescent" sign (Fig. 248–4). Both the "halo" and "air-crescent" signs are highly distinctive for invasive fungal disease of the lung and are usually caused by *Aspergillus*, occasionally by other molds, and rarely by *Pseudomonas aeruginosa*. These lesions represent infarcted lung tissue full of hyphae that extend beyond the area of infarction.

Focal and, in particular, nodular disease carries a more favorable outlook than does diffuse and bilateral IPA[91, 98, 110, 122] if diagnosed early. Nodules are resectable, whereas bilateral diffuse disease is not. The major problem for patients with focal disease is hemoptysis, which may be life threatening and occur without warning.[92, 101, 104, 111]

The incidence of chronic IPA is lower than that of acute disease. Underlying conditions include AIDS,[101, 123] chronic granulomatous disease,[124] alcoholism,[88] diabetes mellitus,[88] and corticosteroid therapy for chronic pulmonary disease.[125–127] A substantial minority of patients have no immunocompromising factors.[24–26] Pulmonary symp-

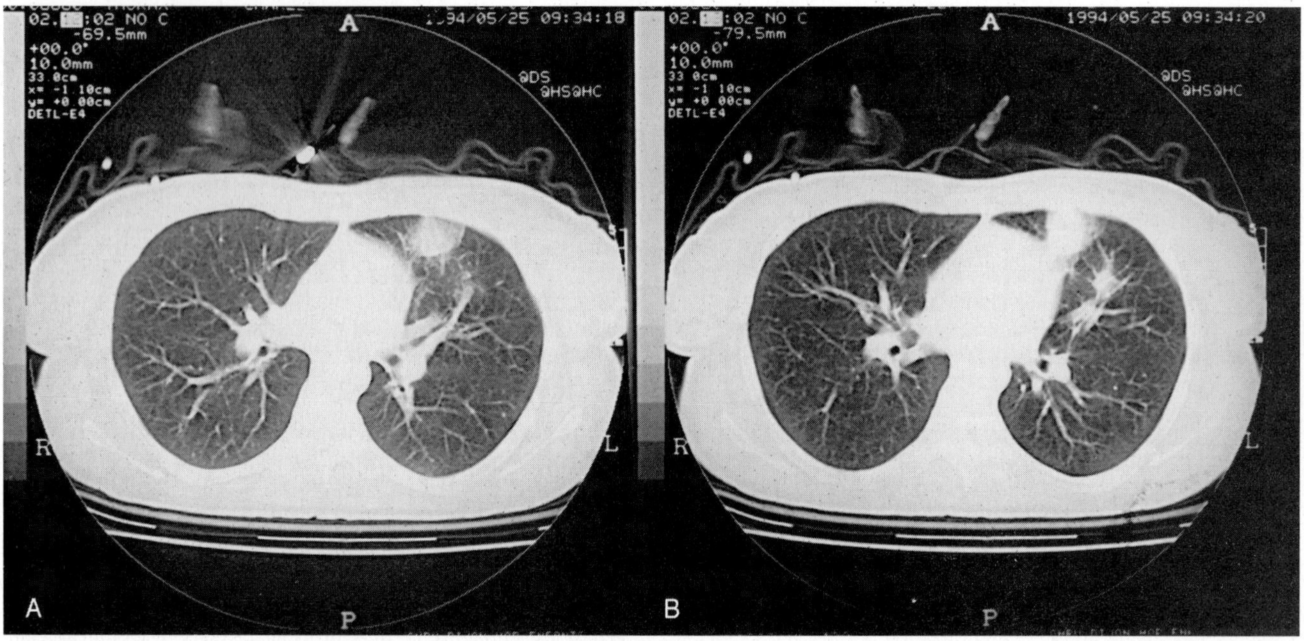

FIGURE 248–3. High resolution computed tomography scan of the chest after 12 days of empirical amphotericin B during neutropenia following an autologous bone marrow transplant. Panel *A* is 1 cm cranial to panel *B*. Panel *A* shows an ill-defined area of consolidation in the lingula with a clearly demarcated border of the oblique tissue. Panel *B* shows the same lesion as a nodule with surrounding low attenuation ("halo" sign) and two additional lesions in the left lower lobe, without distinctive features. The largest lesion was surgically removed 2 weeks later, and invasive pulmonary aspergillosis was confirmed on culture and histologic examination.

toms are more prominent in chronic IPA, and patients have typically been symptomatic for weeks or months. A chronic, productive cough is common, often with hemoptysis. Fever is occasionally present but is usually low grade. Malaise and weight loss are usual. Local extension of disease into the chest wall, brachial plexus, or vertebral column is occasionally seen, especially in patients with chronic granulomatous disease.

Chest radiographs show cavitation with surrounding consolidation in a previously normal lung or extending from a previous small cavity. Distinguishing an aspergilloma and chronic invasive pulmonary aspergillosis can be difficult, particularly if previous chest radiographs are not available. A cavitating lung tumor can have an appearance similar to *Aspergillus* that has invaded a solid tumor.

Definitive diagnosis requires demonstration of septate, hyaline branching hyphae in lung tissue with a concurrent positive culture of a respiratory specimen for *Aspergillus*. However, hyphae are often scant and only granulomas may be found. Patients with chronic IPA usually have strongly positive *Aspergillus* antibodies in serum (AIDS patients excepted—no data), which might be helpful in suggesting the diagnosis when biopsies are negative or contraindicated.

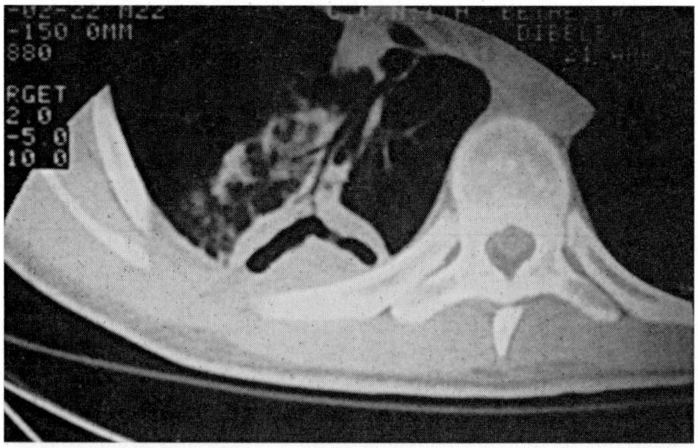

FIGURE 248–4. Cavitary pleural-based lung lesion in the right lower lobe of a patient with acute leukemia. *Aspergillus* pneumonia developed during remission induction and cavitated during marrow recovery.

Airways

Aspergillus tracheobronchitis is proportionately more common in patients with AIDS[27] and in lung transplant recipients,[107, 128] although 25% of patients are not apparently immunocompromised.[27, 129] The manifestations of *Aspergillus* tracheobronchitis vary from a mild tracheobronchitis, to ulcerative tracheobronchitis, to extensive pseudomembranous tracheobronchitis.[128] Distinguishing infection from colonization in lung transplant recipients can be problematic.[107, 128, 130]

In those who are symptomatic (80%), cough, fever, dyspnea (each present in less than 50%), chest pain, and hemoptysis occur but are often mild and reasonably attributable to another cause such as rejection in lung transplant recipients. Symptoms become more common and more severe with progression, and a unilateral monophonic wheeze or stridor may develop. Death may occur from respiratory insufficiency as a result of occlusion of the airway. Disseminated disease or perforation of the trachea or bronchi is common if the condition is untreated or diagnosed late.

Bronchoscopy with bronchial biopsy, microscopy, and culture is the only means of making the diagnosis antemortem. The trachea and bronchi show mucosal reddening, excess mucus, and ulcers, and patients with pseudomembranous *Aspergillus* tracheobronchitis can have a shaggy grayish lining of their whole trachea and bronchial wall. The chest radiograph is usually normal early in the course of disease, but consolidation may occur later. CT findings include peribronchial consolidation and centrilobular nodules,[131] but these entities are not specific. Biopsy of loose material in the tracheal lumen will often reveal necrotic cartilage invaded by hyphae.

Sinuses

Invasive *Aspergillus* sinusitis may be acute or chronic. About 10% of cases of invasive aspergillosis in neutropenic and bone marrow transplant patients are manifested as acute rhinosinusitis.[99,132–135] However, this form of aspergillosis is extremely rare in solid organ transplant patients.[136]

Early symptoms are nonspecific and consistent with possible bacterial infection.[133] Common features include fever, cough, epistaxis, and headache. More focal features are less common but include nasal discharge, sinus pain, and sore throat. The anterior nares may be apparently normal on initial examination; hence, a careful search for insensitive areas of decreased nasal blood flow, which precedes frank crusting or ulceration, is particularly important. Local extension to the palate,[137] orbit, or brain is common and relatively rapid.[132,133] Pulmonary and sinus aspergillosis may occur concurrently.

Plain radiographs of the sinuses are insensitive and do not distinguish bacterial from fungal infection.[133,135] CT and magnetic resonance imaging (MRI) show fluid opacification of the sinuses or nasal cavity and delineate the extent of disease.

The diagnosis can be inferred if typical clinical and radiographic features are accompanied by a positive culture from a lesion or characteristic hyphae in tissue, and the diagnosis is confirmed if both are present.

Chronic Invasive Aspergillus *Sinusitis*

Most patients with chronic invasive sinus aspergillosis have no discernible immunocompromising factors, although a substantial minority are diabetic, drink alcohol to excess, or have AIDS.[76,88,101,138–140] Any part of the nose may be involved, including the septum and floor of the nasal cavity. A variant of this condition, paranasal *Aspergillus* granuloma, is seen in the tropics.[141,142] The early clinical features of chronic invasive sinusitis include nasal stuffiness, loss of smell, headache, and nasal discharge. Fever is almost universally absent. Later, proptosis, blindness, pain in the eye, a stroke, and other features of local spread become apparent, particularly if the sphenoid sinus is involved. The early symptoms are similar to those of saprophytic *Aspergillus* sinusitis and can be distinguished only by scanning and histopathologic examination of the sinus mucosa, bone, or both. It cannot be clinically distinguished from other fungal causes of chronic sinusitis. The radiologic features of the disease are similar to those of acute disease.[143] Bony destruction may occur without direct fungal invasion, apparently as a result of either a "pressure" effect or local toxin production (speculative). However, bone invasion by hyphae may be under-recognized histopathologically because of the nature of the surgery to remove abnormal tissue.

Invasion of mucosa and other tissue by fungal hyphae is the hallmark of the disease, although in chronic invasive *Aspergillus* sinusitis few hyphae are seen and the diagnosis may be missed. Cultures are usually positive but may require multiple samples.

Brain

Cerebral aspergillosis occurs in about 10 to 20% of cases of invasive aspergillosis, usually as the worst manifestation of disseminated disease.[144–150] It is proportionately more common in allogeneic bone marrow transplant patients (25 to 50%). Rarely, it occurs in nonimmunocompromised patients, sometimes as a complication of neurosurgery.[151–153] The most immunocompromised patients present nonspecifically with alterations in mental status and seizures in the few days before death. Less immunocompromised patients are more likely to have focal neurologic features and headache. Fever sometimes occurs but may be attributable to other coexistent infections. Meningism (and *Aspergillus* meningitis) is rare.

The CT appearance of cerebral aspergillosis is either that of an infarction, sometimes with some contrast enhancement, or that of an abscess with ring enhancement and surrounding edema.[148,149,154–156] MRI often reveals additional lesions but without features diagnostic of aspergillosis[149,156] (Fig. 248–5). Many lesions are deep seated and therefore difficult or perilous to access surgically. Typically, contrast enhancement demonstrates a mass lesion with surrounding edema and a midline shift in nonimmunocompromised patients.[151,152]

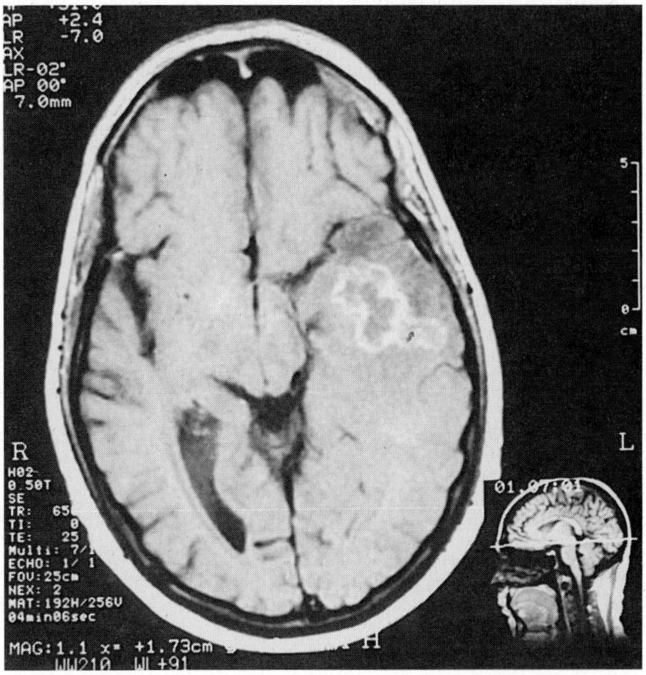

FIGURE 248–5. Magnetic resonance scan of the brain in a 24-year-old allogeneic bone marrow transplant recipient with severe graft-versus-host disease and steroid-induced diabetes mellitus. This T_2-weighted, gadolinium-enhanced scan shows an extensive left temporal lobe abscess with much surrounding edema.

Definitive diagnosis requires biopsy or aspiration of a cerebral lesion, but these procedures are often precluded by the state of the patient, coagulation problems, or the site of the lesion. The diagnosis can be presumptively made if invasive aspergillosis is documented elsewhere in an immunocompromised patient and a typical radiologic abnormality of the brain is observed.

Other Sites

At autopsy, many patients who die of or with invasive aspergillosis have disseminated disease. Antemortem, dissemination is often suspected but rarely proved unless cerebral or cutaneous aspergillosis is diagnosed. Jaundice and disseminated intravascular coagulation are often seen in the terminal stages of disseminated aspergillosis.

Cutaneous aspergillosis is most commonly seen in neutropenic patients at the site of insertion of intravenous catheters or is related to adhesive dressings applied to the skin[157–159] (Fig. 248–6). *Aspergillus* may cause invasive fungal dermatitis in premature neonates[160] and local lesions in patients with AIDS.[161] The clinical appearance of cutaneous aspergillosis is similar to that of pyoderma gangrenosum. *Aspergillus* may also invade burn wounds[162–164] and cause a rapidly progressive necrotic lesion that is usually refractory to amphotericin. Surgical or other wounds may also be infected with *Aspergillus* acquired either perioperatively or postoperatively.

Aspergillus may infect a healthy, a damaged, or a prosthetic heart valve as a sole manifestation of disease or as part of disseminated aspergillosis. Unfortunately, blood cultures are usually negative.[165] Valve replacement is almost always necessary for cure.[88] Pericarditis caused by *Aspergillus* may complicate invasive, usually disseminated aspergillosis and occasionally lead to cardiac tamponade.[166] Esophageal,[167] oral,[137,168] and intestinal[89] forms of aspergillosis are occasional manifestations of invasive aspergillosis; bleeding may or may

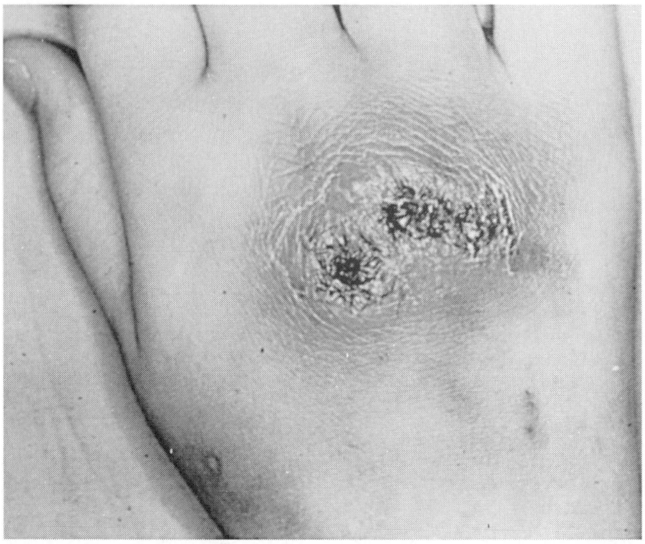

FIGURE 248–6. Cutaneous aspergillosis in a patient with acute leukemia and marked neutropenia. The lesion developed at the site where a steel needle had been left for several days of intravenous infusion.

not be present, as with ulcers, and occasionally perforation or infarction is seen. Many different manifestations of *Aspergillus* osteomyelitis have been described and should be managed differently according to the site of the disease and underlying conditions[88] (Table 248–3). *Aspergillus* infection of the renal pelvis is an occasional complication of diabetes and usually requires nephrectomy if unilateral.[169] Renal aspergillosis appears to be disproportionately more common in patients with AIDS. Many perioperative and postoperative infections with *Aspergillus* have been reported, including infection of prosthetic heart valves, aortic grafts, chronic ambulatory peritoneal dialysis equipment, port-A-Cath and Hickman catheters, neurosurgical sites, lumbar spine, pleural space, sternum, and other wound infections.[153] Virtually all body sites have been invaded by *Aspergillus*, and the diagnosis and therapeutic approach should be tailored to the patient and site affected.

DIAGNOSIS

Several parallel diagnostic approaches should be used rapidly if invasive aspergillosis is suspected. Detailed radiologic evaluation is essential for the lungs, sinuses, or brain. CT or MRI should be performed within 24 hours of suspicion of the diagnosis. The results of about 10% of chest radiographs are initially normal in patients with IPA.[170] Ultrasound or echocardiography is occasionally helpful. Bronchoscopy is essential if airway disease is possible but rarely yields *Aspergillus* on culture if the patient has peripheral, focal disease of the lungs. Nasal endoscopy is useful for patients with *Aspergillus* rhinosinusitis. Peripheral pulmonary lesions are best approached with a needle biopsy or surgical pulmonary resection of the lesion. Open lung biopsies have only a 50% yield,[170] probably because of sampling error, and pulmonary resection is superior.[108, 171] For focal lung lesions near the hilum and the great vessels, particularly in neutropenic patients, urgent thoracotomy and resection should be undertaken despite neutropenia and thrombocytopenia because the risk of life-threatening hemoptysis is high.[92, 101, 104, 110] Patients with bilateral consolidation or diffuse disease are best investigated by bronchoscopy, partly to rule out other likely causes of infection.

Bronchoalveolar lavage fluid, bronchial lavage fluid, endotracheal aspirates, and other fluids should be processed for microscopy (or cytology) and fungal culture, as well as any other appropriate diagnostic procedures. Microscopy has the virtue of being rapid and relatively sensitive, but it does not distinguish different species of fungi. The combination of microscopy and culture increases the diagnostic yield by about 15 to 20% when compared with culture alone,[172–174] particularly in patients receiving antifungal therapy (Fig. 248–7).[174] Concentration of fluids[174] and special stains for fungi (e.g., fluorescent brighteners such as calcofluor white) probably increase the sensitivity of microscopy. Sometimes, fruiting bodies are seen microscopically and thus allow direct identification of the pathogen. Encouraging data are emerging on the utility of *Aspergillus* antigen testing of bronchoalveolar lavage fluid.[108, 175]

Definitive proof of invasive aspergillosis requires culture of *Aspergillus* from a sterile site (e.g., a brain aspirate from an abscess). Histologic evidence of hyphal invasion of tissue with a concurrent positive culture of *Aspergillus* from the same organ (e.g., a transbronchial biopsy showing hyphae and a positive sputum culture for *Aspergillus*) is also definitive evidence of disease. Lesser degrees of diagnostic confidence accompany other combinations of positive findings because other molds may invade tissue and produce appearances similar to those of invasive aspergillosis. Occasionally, false-positive cultures of *Aspergillus* occur in heavily immunocompromised patients.[98, 106, 107, 109, 165] Use of fungal rather than bacterial media for culture increases the yield of *Aspergillus*.[5] Positive cultures from the respiratory tract, blood, wound, or other sites should alert clinicians to the possibility of invasive aspergillosis (or aspergilloma or allergic disease) and the need for thorough and urgent evaluation, especially in immunocompromised patients. Increasing numbers of

TABLE 248–3 *Aspergillus* Osteomyelitis (Osteitis)*

Manifestation	Underlying Cause	Surgical Approach
Invasive external otitis	None or immunocompromised	Local surgical débridement
Aspergillosis of the skull	Extension from sinusitis After neurosurgery	Surgical débridement if feasible, otherwise prolonged medical therapy
Aspergillosis of the sternum	After cardiac surgery	Removal of wires and débridement
Vertebral body/diskitis	Late manifestation of blood-borne spread, after laminectomy or back surgery	Débridement if possible, including intraoperative bone grafting; delayed surgery useful for instability or medical failure
	Chronic granulomatous disease	None other than for diagnosis, unless spinal cord compression is present
Long bone/rib aspergillosis	Chronic granulomatous disease	Diagnostic biopsy only

*All patients require medical therapy.

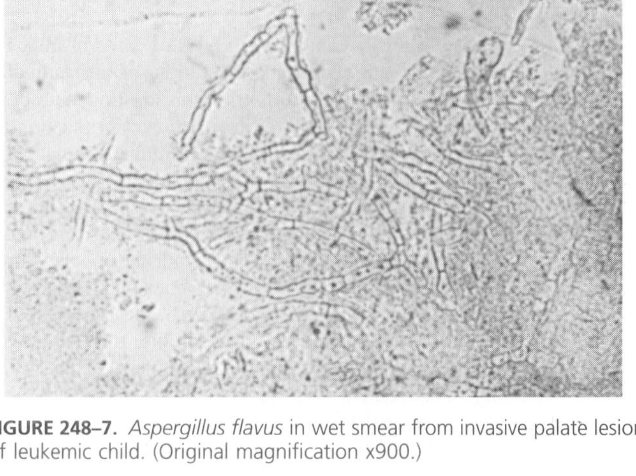

FIGURE 248–7. *Aspergillus flavus* in wet smear from invasive palate lesion of leukemic child. (Original magnification x900.)

cases of invasive aspergillosis are occurring in unusual risk groups, and a positive culture of *Aspergillus* may be the earliest clue to the diagnosis. Species of *Aspergillus* other than *A. fumigatus, A. flavus, A. terreus*, and *A. niger* are less likely to be significant.

Aspergillus antibody testing is useful in patients with allergic bronchopulmonary aspergillosis, aspergilloma, and chronic invasive aspergillosis. Although *Aspergillus* antibodies may be detectable in very immunocompromised patients with invasive aspergillosis, the sensitivity of such tests is poor, and in those instances in which the test is positive, typically the patient has already improved with therapy. Tests for circulating galactomannan antigen have until recently lacked sufficient sensitivity to be clinically useful. More recent assay procedures such as sandwich enzyme-linked immunosorbent assay are considerably more sensitive in hematology patients but have a low false-positive rate, particularly in children.[176] Routine testing of at-risk neutropenic or bone marrow transplant patients twice or three times weekly has been recommended. Detection of circulating 1,3-D-glucan is a new approach to the serologic diagnosis of fungal infection[177, 178] and requires further evaluation.

Detection of *Aspergillus* DNA in blood with molecular diagnostic approaches is possible[179, 179a] and also requires further evaluation.

TREATMENT

Invasive aspergillosis carries a nearly 100% mortality if untreated.[180] It progresses at a variable rate depending partly on the underlying disease. Outcomes are better if treatment is started early.[103] Response to treatment varies with the patient group, the organ affected, and, to a lesser extent, the choice of treatment (Table 248–4). The largest improvement in outcome follows an aggressive diagnostic approach in an at-risk patient population (e.g., serologic screening, CT scanning), combined with early empirical therapy, as well as change in therapy if the response is inadequate, and expeditious surgical resection of centrally located focal lesions in the lung.[108]

Only two antifungal agents with activity against *Aspergillus* are licensed—amphotericin B and itraconazole (Table 248–5). Three formulations of lipid-associated amphotericin have been licensed in the United States. In the absence of controlled trials, the comparative response rates of all these agents appear similar. Differences in open studies probably reflect differing patient populations and enrollment time and criteria. The initial choice of agent should be determined by issues of toxicity and (for itraconazole) factors affecting bioavailability. Itraconazole is a useful salvage agent,[108, 181] even in highly immunocompromised patients, as are the lipid-associated amphotericins.[182–186] Increasing data indicate a role for primary treatment of invasive aspergillosis with lipid-associated amphotericin B.[186–188] The major limitations of itraconazole are variable bioavailability and potential for drug interactions. An intravenous preparation of itraconazole is now available, but clinical response data are lacking.

However, if the patient has good intestinal function while eating and is not taking drugs that activate P-450 (e.g., rifampin, phenytoin, phenobarbital, carbamazepine), itraconazole is a reasonable first choice. Patients with intestinal problems (such as graft-versus-host disease) and patients with AIDS absorb itraconazole capsules poorly. Itraconazole suspension is better absorbed. Higher doses may be helpful for cerebral aspergillosis.[150] Serum concentrations of itraconazole should be measured after 5 to 10 days because the likelihood of a better outcome increases with increasing levels. Other drug interactions are problematic, including cyclosporine (halve the dose and measure levels), oral hypoglycemic agents (stop and observe), digoxin (monitor), antihistamines (stop), and protease inhibitors (observe carefully).

Recommended doses of conventional amphotericin B are 0.8 to 1.0 mg/kg/day and, for neutropenic patients, 1 to 1.25 mg/kg/day. If renal dysfunction is or is likely to be a major problem, the patient is intolerant of amphotericin B, or the fungal infection progresses despite treatment with an adequate dose of conventional amphotericin B, one of the lipid-associated preparations of amphotericin B (or itraconazole) is appropriate. The optimal dose of these agents has yet to be defined. Treatment at optimal dosage should be continued at least until disease progression has been arrested and certainly for at least 2 weeks. No a priori total dose of amphotericin B that should be given has been established. After intravenous therapy, continuation therapy with itraconazole is often appropriate while patients remain immunocompromised. Subsequent bone marrow transplantation or further cancer chemotherapy is possible in those with prior invasive aspergillosis as long as the disease is under control and secondary prophylaxis is administered.[189–192]

The less immunocompromised the patient, the longer it takes to make an evaluation of response. Inadequate response or failure requires an alternative agent.

Surgery (resection) has value in focal invasive pulmonary aspergillosis, for persisting lung shadows before bone marrow transplantation or more aggressive chemotherapy, for significant hemoptysis, or for lesions impinging on the great vessels or major airways. The cornerstone of treatment of acute invasive sinusitis is medical therapy with amphotericin B because itraconazole treatment appears to be less effective. Radical surgery during neutropenia may be associated with major complications such as hemorrhage[88] and appears to offer no survival advantage.[193] For chronic invasive *Aspergillus* sinusitis,

TABLE 248–4 Therapeutic Outcome of Invasive Aspergillosis in Immunocompromised Patients

Group	Response Rate (%)	Comment
Patient group*		
AIDS	27	Despite itraconazole and amphotericin in most cases
Leukemia†	39	Much better than this in some centers
Bone marrow transplantation†	21	Lower steroid dose for GVHD improves outcome
Liver transplantation†	14	
Heart transplantation†	80	Small numbers
Organs affected		
Lungs‡	37	Depends on host group
Sinus‡	37	Response and relapse common
Brain‡	0	A few survivors described
Drug		
Amphotericin B	38	
Itraconazole	39	Includes amphotericin B failures

*Patients with pulmonary disease.
†Amphotericin B therapy only.
‡Primarily amphotericin B therapy.
Abbreviation: AIDS, Acquired immunodeficiency disease; GVHD, graft-versus-host disease.
Data from refs. 180, 181.

TABLE 248–5 First- and Second-Line Therapy for Invasive Aspergillosis

Agent	Dose	Comments
Amphotericin B deoxycholate	0.8–1.25 mg/kg/d (IV)	First-line therapy, nephrotoxic, exacerbated by other nephrotoxic drugs
Itraconazole*	200 mg three times daily for 4 d, then 200 mg twice daily (PO)	First-line therapy if not taking P-450 inducers, increases cyclosporine levels, adequate absorption important for response, measurement of levels helpful; consider higher doses for cerebral aspergillosis
Lipid-associated amphotericin B	4–5 mg/kg/d (IV)	Less nephrotoxic than amphotericin B deoxycholate and fewer infusion-related side effects. Particularly useful in combination with nephrotoxic drugs

*Capsules are absorbed better with food; solution is absorbed better when fasting.

surgical débridement followed by prolonged antifungal therapy is required.[88] Chronicity and relapse characterize this disease. Surgery has no role other than diagnostic aspiration or biopsy for patients with cerebral aspergillosis, unless the lesion is superficial and single.

No definitive role for cytokines as adjunctive treatment with antifungal drugs has been established. Granulocyte colony-stimulating factor, granulocyte-macrophage colony-stimulating factor, and interferon-γ also increase both phagocytosis and damage to *Aspergillus* hyphae in vitro.[56, 61–63] However, no clinical benefit was demonstrated in phase I/II studies of macrocyte colony-stimulating factor[194] or in a retrospective series of invasive aspergillosis in which granulocyte colony-stimulating factor was used.[170]

A comprehensive literature database, images of aspergilli and aspergillosis, and detailed treatment recommendations are available on-line at www.aspergillus.man.ac.uk.

REFERENCES

1. Denning DW. Invasive aspergillosis. Clin Infect Dis. 1998;26:781–805.
2. Rankin NE. Disseminated aspergillosis and moniliasis associated with agranulocytosis and antibiotic therapy. BMJ. 1953;25:918–919.
3. Groll AH, Shah PM, Mentzel C, et al. Trends in the postmortem epidemiology of invasive fungal infections at a university hospital. J Infect. 1996;33:23–32.
4. Samson RA, Pitt JI, eds. Modern Concepts in *Penicillium* and *Aspergillus* Classification. New York: Plenum; 1990.
5. Horvath JA, Dummer S. The use of respiratory-tract cultures in the diagnosis of invasive pulmonary aspergillosis. Am J Med. 1996;100:171–178.
6. Hall LA, Denning DW. Oxygen requirements of *Aspergillus* species. J Med Microbiol. 1994;41:311–315.
7. Denning DW, Radford SA, Oakley KL, et al. Correlation between in-vitro susceptibility testing to itraconazole and in-vivo outcome of *Aspergillus fumigatus* infection. J Antimicrob Chemother. 1997;40:401–414.
8. Oakley KL, Moore CB, Denning DW. In vitro activity of SCH-56592 and comparison with amphotericin B and itraconazole against *Aspergillus* spp. Antimicrob Agents Chemother. 1997;41:1124–1126.
9. Oakley KL, Radford SA, Johnson EM, et al. Inter and intra-laboratory reproducibility of in vitro susceptibility testing for *Aspergillus* spp with itraconazole (ITR). Abstract D142. Presented at the Thirty-seventh Interscience Conference on Antimicrobial Agents and Chemotherapy, Toronto, September 28–October 1, 1997.
10. Verweij PE, Mensink M, Rijs AJ, et al. In vitro activity of amphotericin B, itraconazole and voriconazole against 151 clinical and environmental *Aspergillus fumigatus* isolates. J Antimicrob Chemother. 1998;42:389–392.
11. Chryssanthou E. In vitro susceptibility of respiratory isolates of *Aspergillus* species to itraconazole and amphotericin B. Acquired resistance to itraconazole. Scand J Infect Dis. 1997;29:509–552.
12. Verweij PE, Oakley KL, Morrissey J, et al. Efficacy of LY303,366 against amphotericin B "susceptible" and "resistant" *A. fumigatus* infection in a murine model of invasive aspergillosis. Antimicrob Agents Chemother. 1998;42:873–878.
13. Nolard N, Detand M, Beguin H. Ecology of *Aspergillus* species in the human environment. In: Vanden Bosche H, Mackenzie DWR, Cauwenbergh G, eds. Aspergillus and Aspergillosis. New York: Plenum; 1988:35–41.
14. Staib F. Ecological and epidemiological aspects of aspergilli pathogenic for man and animal in Berlin (West). Zentralbl Bakteriol 1984;257:240–245.
15. Mullins J, Harvey R, Seaton A. Sources and incidence of airborne *Aspergillus fumigatus* (Fres). Clin Allergy. 1976;6:209–217.
16. Simmonds EJ, Littlewood JM, Hopwood V, et al. *Aspergillus fumigatus* colonisation and population density of place of residence in cystic fibrosis. Arch Dis Child. 1994;70:139–140.
17. Denning DW, Clemons KV, Hanson LH, et al. Restriction endonuclease analysis of total cellular DNA of *Aspergillus fumigatus* isolates of geographically and epidemiologically diverse origin. J Infect Dis. 1990;162:1151–1158.
18. Denning DW, Shankland G, Stevens DA. DNA fingerprinting of *Aspergillus fumigatus* isolates from patients with aspergilloma. J Med Vet Mycol. 1991;29:339–345.
19. Anderson MJ, Gull K, Denning DW. Molecular typing by random amplification of polymorphic DNA and M13 Southern hybridisation of related paired isolates of *Aspergillus fumigatus*. J Clin Microbiol. 1996;34:87–93.
20. Debeaupuis JP, Sarfati J, Chazalet V, et al. Genetic diversity among clinical and environmental isolates of *Aspergillus fumigatus*. Infect Immun. 1997;19:3080–3085.
21. Latge JP, Neuveglise C, Sarfati J, et al. Longitudinal study of *Aspergillus fumigatus* strain isolated from cystic fibrosis patients. Eur J Clin Microbiol Infect Dis. 1997;16:747–750.
22. Gerson SL, Talbot GH, Hurwitz S, et al. Prolonged granulocytopenia: The major risk factor for invasive pulmonary aspergillosis in patients with acute leukemia. Ann Intern Med. 1984;100:345–351.
23. Martino P, Raccah R, Gentile G, et al. *Aspergillus* colonization of the nose and pulmonary aspergillosis in neutropenic patients: A retrospective study. Haematologica. 1989;74:263–265.
24. Gefter WB, Weingrad TR, Epstein DM, et al. "Semi-invasive" pulmonary aspergillosis: A new look at the spectrum of *Aspergillus* infections of the lung. Radiology. 1981;140:313–321.
25. Karam GH, Griffin FM Jr. Invasive pulmonary aspergillosis in nonimmunocompromised, nonneutropenic hosts. Rev Infect Dis. 1986;8:357–363.
26. Karim M, Alam M, Shah AA, et al. Chronic invasive aspergillosis in apparently immunocompetent hosts. Clin Infect Dis. 1997;24:723–733.
27. Kemper CA, Hostetler JS, Follansbee S, et al. Ulcerative and plaque-like tracheobronchitis due to infection with *Aspergillus* in patients with AIDS. Clin Infect Dis. 1993;17:344–352.
28. Pitt JI. The current role of *Aspergillus* and *Penicillium* in human and animal health. J. Med Vet Mycol. 1994;32(Suppl 1):S17–S21.
29. Ng TTC, Robson GD, Denning DW. Hydrocortisone-enhanced growth of *Aspergillus* spp: Implications for pathogenesis. Microbiology. 1994;140:2475–2480.
30. Parta M, Chang Y, Rulong S, et al. *HYP1*, a hydrophobin gene from *Aspergillus fumigatus*, complements the *rodletless* phenotype in *Aspergillus nidulans*. Infect Immun. 1994;62:4389–4395.
31. Thau N, Monod M, Crestani B, et al. Rodletless mutants of *Aspergillus fumigatus*. Infect Immun. 1994;62:4380–4388.
32. Penalver MC, Casanove M, Martinez JP, et al. Cell wall protein and glycoprotein constituents of *Aspergillus fumigatus* that bind to polystyrene may be responsible for the cell surface hydrophobicity of the mycelium. Microbiology. 1996;142:1597–1604.
33. Tronchin G, Bouchara J-P, Larcher G, et al. Interaction between *Aspergillus fumigatus* and basement membrane laminin: Binding and substrate degradation. Biol Cell. 1993;77:201–208.
34. Bouchara JP, Larcher G, Joubard F, et al. Extracellular fibrinogenolytic enzyme of *Aspergillus fumigatus*: Substrate-dependent variations in the proteinase synthesis and characterization of the enzyme. FEMS Immunol Med Microbiol. 1993;7:81–92.
35. Tang CM, Cohen J, Krausz T, et al. The alkaline protease of *Aspergillus fumigatus* is not a virulence determinant in two murine models of invasive pulmonary aspergillosis. Infect Immun. 1993;61:1650–1656.
36. Monod M, Fatih A, Jaton-Ogay K, et al. The secreted proteases of pathogenic species of *Aspergillus* and their possible role in virulence. Can J Bot. 1995;73(Suppl 1):S1081–S1086.
37. Jaton-Ogay K, Paris S, Huerre M, et al. Cloning and disruption of the gene encoding an extracellular metalloprotease of *Aspergillus fumigatus*. Mol Microbiol. 1994;14:917–928.
38. Markaryan A, Morozova I, Yu H, et al. Purification and characterization of an elastinolytic metalloprotease from *Aspergillus fumigatus* and immunoelectron microscopic evidence of secretion of this enzyme by the fungus invading the murine lung. Infect Immun. 1994;62:2149–2157.
39. Chris Tomee JF, Wierenhga ATJ, Hiemstra PS, et al. Proteases from *Aspergillus fumigatus* induce release of proinflammatory cytokines and cell detachment in airway epithelial cell lines. J Infect Dis. 1997;176:300–303.
40. Denning DW, Ward PN, Fenelon LE, et al. Lack of vessel wall elastolysis in human invasive pulmonary aspergillosis. Infect Immun. 1992;60:5153–5156.
41. Birch M, Robson G, Law D, et al. Evidence of multiple phospholipase activities of *Aspergillus fumigatus*. Infect Immun. 1996;64:751–755.
42. Müllbacher A, Waring P, Eichner RD. Identification of an agent in cultures of *Aspergillus fumigatus* displaying anti-phagocytic and immunomodulating activity in vitro. J Gen Microbiol. 1985;131:1251–1258.
43. Sutton P, Newcombe NR, Waring P, et al. Exacerbation of invasive aspergillosis by the immunosuppressive fungal metabolite, gliotoxin. Immunol Cell Biol. 1996;74:318–322.
44. Waring P. DNA fragmentation induced in macrophages by gliotoxin does not require protein synthesis and is preceded by raised inositol triphosphate levels. J Biol Chem. 1990;265:14476–14480.
45. Denning DW. Aflatoxin and human disease. A review. Adverse Drug React Acut Pois Rev. 1987;4:175–209.
46. Birch M, Drucker DB, Boote V, et al. Prevalence of phthioic acid in *Aspergillus* spp. J Met Vet Mycol. 1997;35:143–145.
47. Schaffner A, Douglas H, Braude A. Selective protection against conidia by mononuclear and against mycelia by polymorphonuclear phagocytes in resistance to *Aspergillus:* Observations on these two lines of defense in vivo and in vitro with human and mouse phagocytes. J Clin Invest. 1982;69:617–631.
48. Kan VL, Bennett JE. Lectin-like attachment sites on murine pulmonary alveolar macrophages bind *Aspergillus fumigatus* conidia. J Infect Dis. 1988;158:407–414.
49. Diamond RD, Krzesicki R, Epstein B, et al. Damage to hyphal forms of fungi by human leukocytes in vitro: A possible host defense mechanism in aspergillosis and mucormycosis. Am J Pathol. 1978;91:313–328.
50. Roilides E, Holmes A, Blake C, et al. Antifungal activity of elutriated human monocytes against *Aspergillus fumigatus* hyphae: Enhancement by granulocyte-macrophage colony-stimulating factor and interferon-γ. J Infect Dis. 1994;170:894–899.
51. Kozel TR, Wilson MA, Farrel TP, et al. Activation of C3 and binding to *Aspergillus fumigatus* conidia and hyphae. Infect Immun. 1989;57:3412–3417.
52. Washburn RG, Gallin JI, Bennett JE. Oxidative killing of *Aspergillus* proceeds by parallel myeloperoxidase-dependent and -independent pathways. Infect Immun. 1987;55:2088–2092.
53. Holdom MD, Hay RJ, Hamilton AJ. The Cu,Zn superoxide dismutases of *Aspergillus flavus, Aspergillus niger, Aspergillus nidulans, Aspergillus terreus*: Purification

and biochemical comparison with the *Aspergillus fumigatus,* Cu, Zn superoxide dismutase. Infect Immun. 1996;64:3326–3332.

54. Hearn VM, Wilson EV, MacKenzie DWR. Analysis of *Aspergillus fumigatus* catalases possessing antigenic activity. J Med Microbiol. 1992;36:61–67.
55. Takasuka T, Sayers NM, Anderson MJ, et al. *Aspergillus fumigatus* catalases: cloning of an *Aspergillus nidulans* catalase B homologue and evidence for at least three catalases. FEMS Immunol Med Microbiol. 1999;23:125–133.
56. Calera JA, Paris S, Monod M, et al. Cloning and disruption of the antigenic catalase gene of *Aspergillus fumigatus.* Infect Immun. 1997;65:4718–4724.
57. Wong, B, Brauer KL, Tsai RR, et al. Increased amounts of the *Aspergillus* metabolite D-mannitol in tissue and serum of rats with experimental aspergillosis. J Infect Dis. 1989;160:95–103.
58. Megson GM, Law D, Haynes KA, et al. The application of serum mannitol determinations for the diagnosis of invasive pulmonary aspergillosis in bone marrow transplant patients. Abstract. Presented at the Second Conference on Trends in Invasive Fungal Infections, Manchester, England, September 2–4, 1993.
59. Gustafson TL, Schaffner W, Lavely GB, et al. Invasive aspergillosis in renal transplant recipients: Correlation with corticosteroid therapy. J Infect Dis. 1983;148:230–234.
60. Denning DW, Marinus A, Cohen J, et al. Risk factors and outcome from invasive aspergillosis (IA). Presented at the Thirty-sixth Interscience Conference on Antimicrobial Agents and Chemotherapy, New Orleans, 1996.
61. Roilides E, Unlig K, Venzon D, et al. Prevention of corticosteroid-induced suppression of human polymorphonuclear leukocyte–induced damage of *Aspergillus fumigatus* hyphae by granulocyte colony-stimulating factor and gamma interferon. Infect Immun. 1993;61:4870–4877.
62. Roilides E, Blake C, Holmes A, et al. Granulocyte-macrophage colony-stimulating factor and interferon-γ prevent dexamethasone-induced immunosuppression of antifungal monocyte activity against *Aspergillus fumigatus* hyphae. J Med Vet Mycol. 1996;34:63–69.
63. Rex JH, Bennett JE, Gallin JI, et al. In vivo interferon-γ therapy augments the in vitro ability of chronic granulomatous disease neutrophils to damage *Aspergillus* hyphae. J Infect Dis. 1991;163:849–852.
64. Roilides E, Holmes A, Blake C, et al. Impairment of neutrophil antifungal activity against hyphae of *Aspergillus fumigatus* in children infected with human immunodeficiency virus. J Infect Dis. 1993;167:905–911.
65. Mouy R, Fischer A, Vilmer E, et al. Incidence, severity, and prevention of infections in chronic granulomatous disease. J Pediatr. 1989;114:555–560.
66. Cenci E, Perito S, Enssle KH, et al. Thl and TH2 cytokines in mice with invasive aspergillosis. Infect Immun. 1997;65:564–570.
67. de Repentigny L, Petitbois S, Boushira M, et al. Acquired immunity in experimental murine aspergillosis is mediated by macrophages. Infect Immun. 1993;61:3791–3802.
68. Yousem SA. The histological spectrum of chronic necrotizing forms of pulmonary aspergillosis. Hum Pathol. 1997;28:650–656.
69. Patterson R, Greenberger PA, Radin RC, et al. Allergic bronchopulmonary aspergillosis: Staging as an aid to management. Ann Intern Med. 1982;96:286–291.
70. Seaton A, Seaton RA, Wightman AJ. Management of allergic bronchopulmonary aspergillosis without maintenance oral corticosteroids: A fifteen year followup. Q J Med. 1994;87:529–537.
71. Stevens DA, Lee JY, Schwartz D, et al. Randomised double blind study of itraconazole in allergic bronchopulmonary aspergillosis. Abstract L-32. Presented at the Thirty-seventh Interscience Conference on Antimicrobial Agents and Chemotherapy, American Society for Microbiology, Toronto, September 28–October 1, 1997.
72. Katzenstein ALA, Sale SR, Greenberger PA. Pathologic findings in allergic *Aspergillus* sinusitis. A newly recognized form of sinusitis. Am J Surg Pathol. 1983;7:439–443.
73. Waxman JE, Spector JG, Sale SR. Allergic *Aspergillus* sinusitis: Concepts in diagnosis and treatment of a new clinical entity. Laryngoscope. 1987;97:261–265.
74. DeShazo RD, Swain RE. Diagnostic criteria for allergic fungal sinusitis. J Allergy Clin Immunol. 1995;96:24–35.
75. Stammberger H, Jakse R, Beaufort F. Aspergillosis of the paranasal sinuses: X-ray diagnosis, histopathology, and clinical aspects. Ann Otol Rhinol Laryngol. 1984;93:251–256.
76. de Carpentier J, Ramamurthy M, Taylor P, et al. An algorithmic approach to *Aspergillus* sinusitis. J Laryngol Otol. 1994;108:314–318.
77. British Tuberculosis Association. Aspergillosis in persistent lung cavities after tuberculosis. Tubercle. 1968;49:1–11.
78. Munk PL, Vellet AD, Rankin RN, et al. Intracavitary aspergilloma: Transthoracic percutaneous injection of amphotericin gelatin solution. Radiology. 1993;188:821–823.
79. Lee KS, Kim HT, Kim YH, et al. Treatment of hemoptysis in patients with cavitary aspergilloma of the lung: Value of percutaneous instillation of amphotericin B. AJR Am J Roentgenol. 1993;161: 727–731.
80. Giron J, Sans N, Poey C, et al. CT-guided percutaneous treatment of inoperable pulmonary aspergillomas: A study of 42 cases. J Radiol. 1998;79:139–145.
81. Daly RC, Pairolero PC, Piehler JM, et al. Pulmonary aspergilloma: Results of surgical treatment. J Thorac Cardiovasc Surg. 1986;92:981–988.
82. Massard G, Roeslin N, Wihelm JM, et al. Pleuropulmonary aspergilloma: Clinical spectrum and results of surgical treatment. Ann Thorac Surg. 1992;54:1159–1164.
83. El-Oakley R, Petrou M, Goldstraw P. Indications and outcome of surgery for pulmonary aspergilloma. Thorax. 1997;52:813–815.
84. Lebeau B, Pelloux H, Pinel C, et al. Itraconazole in the treatment of aspergillosis: A study of 16 cases. Mycoses. 1994;37:171–179.
85. Thomas PA. Mycotic keratitis an underestimated mycosis. J Med Vet Mycol. 1994;32:235–256.
86. Thomas PA, Rajasekaran J. Treatment of *Aspergillus* keratitis with imidazoles and related compounds. In: Vanden Bossche H, Mackenzie DWR, Cauwenbergh G, eds. *Aspergillus* & Aspergillosis. New York: Plenum; 1988:267–279.
87. Heidemann DG, Dunn SP, Watts JC. *Aspergillus* keratitis after radial keratotomy. Am J Ophthalmol. 1995;120:254–256.
88. Denning DW, Stevens DA. Antifungal and surgical treatment of invasive aspergillosis: Review of 2121 published cases. Rev Infect Dis. 1990;12:1147–1201.
89. Young RC, Bennett JE, Vogel CL, et al. Aspergillosis; the spectrum of the disease in 98 patients. Medicine (Baltimore). 1970;49:147–173.
90. Degregorio MW, Lee WMF, Linkera CA, et al. Fungal infections in patients with acute leukemia. Am J Med. 1982;73:543–548.
91. Weiland D, Ferguson RM, Peterson PK, et al. Aspergillosis in 25 renal transplant patients. Epidemiology, clinical presentation, diagnosis, and management. Ann Surg. 1983;198:622–629.
92. Abelda SM, Talbot H, Gerson SL, et al. Pulmonary cavitation and massive hemoptysis in invasive pulmonary aspergillosis. Influence of bone marrow recovery in patients with acute leukemia. Am Rev Respir Dis. 1985;131:115–120.
93. Gerson SL, Talbot H, Lusk E, et al. Invasive pulmonary aspergillosis in adult acute leukemia: Clinical clues to its diagnosis. J Clin Oncol. 1985;3:2209–2116.
94. Spearing RL, Pamphilon DH, Prentice AG. Pulmonary aspergillosis in immunosuppressed patients with haematological malignancies. Q J Med. 1986;59:611–625.
95. Martino P, Girmenia C, Venditti M. Spontaneous pneumothorax complicating pulmonary mycetoma in patients with acute leukemia. Rev Infect Dis. 1990;12:611–617.
96. Denning DW, Follansbee S, Scolaro M, et al. Pulmonary aspergillosis in AIDS. N Engl J Med. 1991;324:654–662.
97. Weinberger M, Elattar Inas PH, Marshall D, et al. Patterns of infection in patients with aplastic anemia and the emergence of *Aspergillus* as a major cause of death. Medicine (Baltimore). 1992;71:24–43.
98. McWhinney PHM, Kibbler CC, Hamon MD, et al. Progress in the diagnosis and management of aspergillosis in bone marrow transplantation: Thirteen years experience. Clin Infect Dis. 1993;17:397–404.
99. Morrison VA, Haake RJ, Weisdorf DJ. The spectrum of non-*Candida* fungal infections following bone marrow transplantation. Medicine (Baltimore). 1993;72:78–89.
100. Singh N, Mieles L, Yu VL, et al. Invasive aspergillosis in liver transplant recipients: Association with candidemia and consumption coagulopathy and failure of prophylaxis with low-dose amphotericin B. Clin Infect Dis. 1993;17:906–908.
101. Khoo S, Denning DW. *Aspergillus* infection in the acquired immune deficiency syndrome. Clin Infect Dis. 1994;19(Suppl 1):S541–S548.
102. End A, Helbich T, Wisser W, et al. The pulmonary nodule after lung transplantation; cause and outcome. Chest. 1995;107:1317–1322.
103. von Eiff M, Zuhlsdorf M, Roos N, et al. Pulmonary fungal infections in patients with hematological malignancies—diagnostic approaches. Ann Hematol. 1995;70:135–141.
104. Pagano L, Ricci P, Nosari A, et al. Fatal haemoptysis in pulmonary filamentous mycosis: An underevaluated cause of death in patients with acute leukemia in haematological complete remission. A retrospective study and review of the literature. Br J Haematol. 1995;89:500–505.
105. Guillemain R, Lavarde V, Amrein C, et al. Invasive aspergillosis after transplantation. Transplant Proc 1995;27:1307–1309.
106. Yelandi V, Laghi F, McCabe MA, et al. *Aspergillus* and lung transplantation. J Heart Lung Transplant. 1995;14:883–890.
107. Westney GE, Kesten S, de Hoyos A, et al. *Aspergillus* infection in single and double lung transplant recipients. Transplantation 1996;61:915–919.
108. Caillot D, Casasnovas O, Bernard A, et al. Improved management of invasive pulmonary aspergillosis in neutropenic patients using early thoracic computed tomographic scan and surgery. J Clin Oncol. 1997;15:139–147.
109. Wald A, Leisenring W, van Burik J, et al. Epidemiology of *Aspergillus* infections in a large cohort of patients undergoing bone marrow transplantation. J Infect Dis. 1997;175:1459–1466.
110. Miller WT Jr, Sais GJ, Frank I, et al. Pulmonary aspergillosis in patients with AIDS. Clinical and radiographic correlations. Chest. 1994;105:37–44.
111. Orr DP, Myerowitz RL, Dubois PJ. Patho-radiologic correlation of invasive pulmonary aspergillosis in the compromised host. Cancer. 1978;41:2028–2039.
112. Moro M, Galvin JR, Barloon TJ, et al. Fungal pulmonary infections after bone marrow transplantation: Evaluation with radiography and CT. Radiology. 1991;178:721–726.
113. Pasmans HLM, Loosveld OJL, Schouten HC, et al. Invasive aspergillosis in immunocompromised patients: Findings on plain film and (HR)CT. Eur J Radiol. 1992;14:37–40.
114. Sallustio G, Pagano L, La Barbera EO, et al. Pulmonary aspergillosis in patients with hematologic malignancies: Clinicoradiologic correlation. Rays. 1994;19:465–478.
115. Staples CA, Kang EY, Wright JL, et al. Invasive pulmonary aspergillosis in AIDS: Radiographic, CT, and pathologic findings. Radiology. 1995;196:409–414.
116. Logan PM, Primack SL, Staples C, et al. Acute lung disease in the immunocompromised host: Diagnostic accuracy of the chest radiograph. Chest. 1995;108:1283–1287.
117. Kuhlman JE, Fishman EK, Siegelman SS. Invasive pulmonary aspergillosis in acute leukemia: Characteristic findings on CT, the CT halo sign, and the role of CT in early diagnosis. Radiology. 1985;157:611–614.
118. Blum U, Windfuhr M, Buitrago-Tellez C, et al. Invasive pulmonary aspergillosis.

MRI, CT, and plain radiographic findings and their contribution for early diagnosis. Chest. 1994;106:1156–1167.
119. Taccone A, Occhi M, Garaventa A, et al. CT of invasive pulmonary aspergillosis in children with cancer. Pediatr Radiol. 1993;23:177–180.
120. Midiri M, Lo Casto A, Cascio A, et al. Invasive pulmonary aspergillosis—CT findings. Medit J Infect Parasitic Dis. 1994;9:59–62.
121. Primack SL, Hartman TE, Lee KS, et al. Pulmonary nodules and the CT halo sign. Radiology. 1994;190:513–515.
122. Tumbarello M, Tacconelli E, Pagano L, et al. Comparative analysis of prognostic indicators of aspergillosis in haematological malignancies and HIV infection. J Infect. 1997;34:55–60.
123. Lortholary O, Meyohas MC, Dupont B, et al. Invasive aspergillosis in patients with acquired immunodeficiency syndrome: Report of 33 cases. Am J Med. 1993;95:177–187.
124. Mouy R, Fischer A, Vilmer E, et al. Incidence, severity, and prevention of infections in chronic granulomatous disease. J Pediatr. 1989;114:555–560.
125. Binder RE, Faling LJ, Pugatch RD, et al. Chronic necrotizing pulmonary aspergillosis: A discrete clinical entity. Medicine (Baltimore). 1982;61:109–124.
126. Palmer LB, Greenberg HE, Schiff MJ. Corticosteroid treatment as a risk factor for invasive aspergillosis in patients with lung disease. Thorax. 1991;46:15–20.
127. Caras WE, Pluss JL. Chronic necrotizing pulmonary aspergillosis: Pathologic outcome after itraconazole therapy. Mayo Clin Proc. 1996;71:25–30.
128. Kramer MR, Denning DW, Marshall SE, et al. Ulcerative tracheobronchitis following lung transplantation: A new form of invasive aspergillosis. Am Rev Respir Dis. 1991;144:552–556.
129. Kac G, Roux P, Poirot JL, et al. Aspergillosis: Étude retrospective dans deux hôpitaux parisiens. J Mycol Med. 1995;5:75–85.
130. Flume PA, Egan TM, Paradowski LJ, et al. Infectious complications of lung transplantation. Impact of cystic fibrosis. Am J Respir Crit Care Med. 1994;149:1601–1607.
131. Logan PM, Primack SL, Miller RR, et al. Invasive aspergillosis of the airways: Radiographic, CT, and pathologic findings. Radiology. 1994;193:383–388.
132. Voillier AF, Peterson DE, de Jongh CA, et al. *Aspergillus* sinusitis in cancer patients. Cancer. 1986;58:366–371.
133. Talbot GH, Huang A, Provencher M. Invasive *Aspergillus* rhinosinusitis in patients with acute leukemia. Rev Infect Dis. 1991;13:219–232.
134. Drakos PE, Nagler A, Or R, et al. Invasive fungal sinusitis in patients undergoing bone marrow transplantation. Bone Marrow Transplant. 1993;12:203–208.
135. Choi SS, Milmoe GJ, Dinndorf PA, et al. Invasive *Aspergillus* sinusitis in pediatric bone marrow transplant patients. Evaluation and management. Arch Otolaryngol Head Neck Surg. 1995;121:1188–1192.
136. Iwen PC, Rupp ME, Hinrichs SH. Invasive mold sinusitis: 17 cases in immunocompromised patients and review of the literature. Clin Infect Dis. 1997;24:1178–1184.
137. Chambers MS, Lyzak WA, Martin JW, et al. Oral complications associated with aspergillosis in patients with hematologic malignancy. Presentation and treatment. Oral Surg Oral Pathol Oral Radiol Endod. 1995;79:559–563.
138. Jahrsdoerfer RA, Ejercito VS, Johns MME, et al. Aspergillosis of the nose and paranasal sinuses. Am J Otolaryngol. 1979;1:6–14.
139. Washburn RG, Kennedy DW, Begley MG, et al. Chronic fungal sinusitis in apparently normal hosts. Medicine (Baltimore). 1988;67:231–247.
140. Meyer RD, Gaultier CR, Yamashita JT, et al. Fungal sinusitis in patients with AIDS: Report of 4 cases and review of the literature. Medicine (Baltimore). 1994;73:69–78.
141. Milosev B, Davidson CM, Gentles JC, et al. *Aspergillosis* of paranasal sinuses and orbit in northern Sudanese. Lancet. 1966;1:746–747.
142. Gumaa SA, Mahgoub ES, Hay RJ. Post-operative responses of paranasal *Aspergillus* granuloma to itraconazole. Trans R Soc Trop Med Hyg. 1992;86:93–94.
143. Zinreich SJ, Kennedy DW, Malat J, et al. Fungal sinusitis: Diagnosis with CT and MR imaging. Radiology. 1988;169:439–444.
144. Darras-Joly C, Veber B, Bedos JP, et al. Noscomial cerebral aspergillosis: A report of 3 cases. Scand J Infect Dis. 1996;28:317–319.
145. Walsh TJ, Hier DB, Caplan LR. Aspergillosis of the central nervous system: Clinicopathological analysis of 17 patients. Ann Neurol. 1985;18:574–582.
146. Torre-Cisneros J, Lopez OL, Kusne S, et al. CNS aspergillosis in organ transplantation: A clinicopathological study. J Neurol Neurosurg Psychiatry. 1993;56:188–193.
147. Martinez AJ, Ahdab-Barmada M. The neuropathology of liver transplantation: Comparison of main complications in children and adults. Mod Pathol. 1993;6:25–32.
148. Boes B, Bashir R, Boes C, et al. Central nervous system aspergillosis. J Neuroimaging. 1994;4:123–129.
149. Hagensee ME, Bauwens JE, Kjos B, et al. Brain abscess following marrow transplantation: Experience at the Fred Hutchinson Cancer Research Center. 1984–1992. Clin Infect Dis. 1994;19:402–408.
150. Sanchez C, Mauri E, Dalmau D, et al. Treatment of cerebral aspergillosis with itraconazole: Do high doses improve the prognosis? Clin Infect Dis. 1995;21:1485–1487.
151. Haran RP, Chandy MJ. Intracranial *Aspergillus* granuloma. Br J Neurosurg. 1993;7:383–388.
152. Sharma BS, Khosla VK, Kak VK, et al. Intracranial fungal granuloma. Surg Neurol. 1997;47:489–497.
153. Denning DW. Postoperative or trauma-related *Aspergillus* infection. In: www.aspergillus.man.uk. June 1998.
154. Yuh WTC, Nguyen HD, Gao F, et al. Brain parenchymal infection in bone marrow transplantation patients: CT and MR findings. AJR Am J Roentgenol. 1994;162:425–430.
155. Ashdown BC, Tien RD, Felsberg GJ. Aspergillosis of the brain and paranasal sinuses in immunocompromised patients: CT and MR imaging findings. AJR Am J Roentgenol. 1994;162:155–159.
156. Miaux Y, Ribaud P, Williams M, et al. MR of cerebral aspergillosis in patients who have had bone marrow transplantation. Am J Neuroradiol. 1995;16:555–562.
157. Allo M, Miller J, Townsend T, et al. Primary cutaneous aspergillosis associated with Hickman intravenous catheters. N Engl J Med. 1987;317:1105–1108.
158. Walmsley S, Devi S, King S, et al. Invasive *Aspergillus* infections in a pediatric hospital: A ten-year review. Pediatr Infect Dis J. 1993;12:673–682.
159. Papouli M, Roilides E, Bibashi E, et al. Primary cutaneous aspergillosis in neonates: Case report and review. Clin Infect Dis. 1996;22:1102–1104.
160. Rowen JL, Atkins JT, Levy ML, et al. Invasive fungal dermatitis in the <1000-gram neonate. Pediatrics. 1995;95:682–687.
161. Shetty D, Giri N, Gonzalez CE, et al. Invasive aspergillosis in human immunodeficiency virus–infected children. Pediatr Infect Dis J. 1997;16:216–221.
162. Levenson C, Wohlford P, Djou J, et al. Preventing postoperative burn wound aspergillosis. J Burn Care Rehabil. 1991;12:132–135.
163. Stone HH, Cuzzell JZ, Kolb LD, et al. *Aspergillus* infection of the burn wound. J Trauma. 1979;19:765–767.
164. Becker WK, Cioffi WG Jr, McManus AT, et al. Fungal burn wound infection. A 10-year experience. Arch Surg. 1991;126:44–48.
165. Duthie R, Denning DW. *Aspergillus* fungemia. Two cases and review. Clin Infect Dis. 1995;20:598–605.
166. Moing VL, Lortholary O, Timsit JF, et al. *Aspergillus* pericarditis: Report of a successfully treated case with tamponade and literature review. Clin Infect Dis. 1998;26:451–460.
167. Choi JH, Yoo JH, Chung IJ, et al. Esophageal aspergillosis after bone marrow transplant. Bone Marrow Transplant. 1997;19:293–294.
168. Sugata T, Myoken Y, Kyo T, et al. Invasive oral aspergillosis in immunocompromised patients with leukaemia. J Oral Maxillofac Surg. 1994;52:382–386.
169. Irby PB, Stoller ML, McAninch JW. Fungal bezoars of the upper urinary tract. J Urol. 1990;143:447–451.
170. Denning DW, Marinus A, Cohen J, et al. An EORTC multicentre prospective survey of invasive aspergillosis in cancer patients: Diagnosis and therapeutic outcome. J Infect. 1998;37:173–180.
171. Habricht JM, Gratwohl A, Tamm M, et al. Diagnostic and therapeutic thoracic surgery in leukemia and severe aplastic anemia. J Thorac Cardiovasc Surg. 1997;133:982–988.
172. Levy H, Horak DA, Tegtmeier BR, et al. The value of bronchoalveolar lavage and bronchial washings in the diagnosis of invasive pulmonary aspergillosis. Respir Med. 1992;86:243–248.
173. Kahn FW, Jones JM, England DM. The role of bronchoalveolar lavage in the diagnosis of invasive pulmonary aspergillosis. Am J Clin Pathol. 1986;86:518–523.
174. Kwok-Yung Y, Woo CY, Ip MSM, et al. Stage-specific manifestations of mold infections in bone marrow transplant recipients: Risk factors and clinical significance of positive concentrated smears. Clin Infect Dis. 1997;25:37–42.
175. Verweij PE, Latge JP, Rijs AJMM, et al. Comparison of antigen detection and PCR assay using broncho-alveolar lavage fluid for diagnosing invasive pulmonary aspergillosis in patients receiving treatment for hematological malignancies. J Clin Microbiol. 1995;33:3150–3153.
176. Verweij PE, Denning DW. Diagnostic and therapeutic strategies for invasive aspergillosis. Semin Respir Crit Care Med. 1997;18:203–215.
177. Obayashi T, Yoshida M, Mori T, et al. Plasma (1,3)-β-D-glucan measurement in diagnosis of invasive deep mycosis and fungal febrile episodes. Lancet. 1995;345:17–20.
178. Yuasa K, Goto H, Iguchi M, et al. Evaluation of the diagnostic value of the measurement of (1,3)β-D-glucan in patients with pulmonary aspergillosis. Respiration. 1996;63:78–83.
179. Einsele H, Hebart H, Roller G, et al. Detection and identification of fungal pathogens in blood by using molecular probes. J Clin Microbiol. 1997;35:1353–1360.
179a. Bretagne S, Custa J-M, Bart-Delabesse E, et al. Comparison of serum galactomannan antigen detection and competitive polymerase chain reaction for diagnosing invasive aspergillosis. Clin Infect Dis. 1998;26:1407–1412.
180. Denning DW. Therapeutic outcome of invasive aspergillosis. Clin Infect Dis. 1996;23:608–615.
181. Denning DW, Lee JY, Hostetler JS, et al: NIAID Mycoses Study Group multicenter trial of oral itraconazole therapy of invasive aspergillosis. Am J Med. 1994;97:135–144.
182. Oppenheim BA, Herbrecht R, Kusne S. The safety and efficacy of amphotericin B colloidal dispersion in the treatment of invasive mycoses. Clin Infect Dis. 1995;21:1145–1153.
183. White MH, Anaissie EJ, Kusne S, et al. Amphotericin B colloidal dispersion vs amphotericin B as therapy for invasive aspergillosis. Clin Infect Dis. 1997;24:635–642.
184. Mehta J, Kelsey S, Chu P, et al. Amphotericin B lipid complex (ABLC) for the treatment of confirmed or presumed fungal infections in immunocompromised patients with hematologic malignancies. Bone Marrow Transplant. 1997;20:39–43.
185. Walsh TJ, Hiemenz JW, Seibel N, et al. Amphotericin B lipid complex in patients with invasive fungal infections: Analysis of safety and efficacy in 556 cases. Clin Infect Dis. 1998;26:1383–1396.
186. Mills W, Chopra R, Linch DC, et al. Liposomal amphotericin B in the treatment of fungal infections in neutropenic patients: A single-centre experience of 133 episodes in 116 patients. Br J Haematol. 1994;86:754–760.
187. Leenders ACAP, Daenen S, Jansen RLH, et al. Liposomal amphotericin B compared with amphotericin B deoxycholate in the treatment of documented and

suspected neutropenia-associated invasive fungal infections. Br J Haematol. 1998;103:205–212.
188. Myint H, Kyi AA, Winn RM. An open, non-comparative evaluation of the efficacy and safety of amphotericin B lipid complex as treatment of neutropenic patients with presumed or confirmed pulmonary fungal infections. J Antimicrob Chemother. 1998;41:424–426.
189. Karp JE, Burch PA, Merz WG. An approach to intensive antileukemia therapy in patients with previous invasive aspergillosis. Am J Med. 1998;85:203–206.
190. Hoover M, Morgan ER, Kletzel M. Prior fungal infection is not a contraindication to bone marrow transplant in patients with acute leukemia. Med Pediatr Oncol. 1997;28:268–273.
191. Krüger W, Stockschläder M, Sobottka I, et al. Antimycotic therapy with liposomal amphotericin B for patients undergoing bone marrow or peripheral blood stem cell transplantation. Leuk Lymphoma. 1997;24:491–499.
192. Martino R, Lopez R, Sureda A, et al. Risk of reactivation of a recent invasive fungal infection in patients with hematological malignancies undergoing further intensive chemo-radiotherapy. A single-center experience and review of the literature. Haematologia. 1997;82:297–304.
193. Kennedy CA, Adams GL, Neglia JP, et al. Impact of surgical treatment on paranasal fungal infections in bone marrow transplant patients. Otolaryngol Head Neck Surg. 1997;116:610–616.
194. Nemunaitis J, Shannon-Dorcy K, Appelbaum FR, et al. Long-term follow-up of patients with invasive fungal disease who received adjunctive therapy with recombinant human macrophage colony-stimulating factor. Blood. 1993;82:1422–1427.

Chapter 249

Agents of Mucormycosis and Related Species

ALAN M. SUGAR

Mucormycosis is the common name given to several different diseases caused by fungi of the order Mucorales. Many species have been implicated as etiologic agents of similar clinical syndromes. The taxonomy of this group is complicated not only by the number of fungi causing similar infections but also because of changes in the names of individual species that are made as new advances in classification are accepted. Table 249–1 summarizes the taxonomic relationships of those Zygomycetes known to be pathogenic. The details of the mycology of the Zygomycetes and problems in taxonomy are beyond the scope of this chapter but can be found elsewhere.[1]

This group of diseases has been known by other names in the past. For example, references can be found to *phycomycosis* and *zygomycosis.* The former is an allusion to an earlier and more imprecise classification scheme that is no longer used, and the latter reflects the class name of these fungi. As detailed later, not all of the Zygomycetes cause the same type of disease, so the term *zygomycosis* is too vague and does not accurately convey useful information to the physician. Furthermore, the designation *mucormycosis* is well ingrained in the medical literature and evokes certain useful associations, so it is best to continue to refer to the mycoses produced by the organisms in the order Mucorales by this name, a convention that is followed in this chapter.

In addition to the Mucorales, the fungi responsible for mucormycosis, the class Zygomycetes contains the Entomophthorales. The fungi in this order also cause distinctive clinical syndromes, but they usually are clearly separable from those produced by the agents causing mucormycosis. *Entomophthoramycosis* is the currently accepted general term used to describe disease caused by these fungi. Diseases caused by the Entomophthorales are extremely rare in North America; they are usually found in Africa, Southeast Asia, Indonesia, and South America. Because the clinical and pathologic manifestations of the diseases caused by this group of fungi are for the most part different from those produced by the agents of mucormycosis, they are discussed separately, after a discussion of the more common mucormycosis.

TABLE 249–1 Classification of the Agents of Mucormycosis and Related Diseases

- I. Zygomycotina
  - A. Zygomycetes
    - a. Mucorales
      - 1. Mucoraceae
        - i. *Absidia*
          - (a) *A. corymbifera*
          - (b) *A. ramosa*
        - ii. *Mucor*
          - (a) *M. circinelloides*
        - iii. *Rhizomucor*
          - (a) *R. pusillus*
        - iv. *Rhizopus*
          - (a) *R. oryzae* (*R. arrhizus*)*
          - (c) *R. rhizopodiformis*
      - 2. Cunninghamellacaeae
        - i. *Cunninghamella*
          - (a) *C. bertholletiae*
      - 3. Mortierellaceae
        - i. *Mortierella*
          - (a) *M. wolfii*
      - 4. Saksenaeaceae
        - i. *Saksenaea*
          - (a) *S. vasiformis*
      - 5. Syncephalastraceae
        - i. *Syncephalastrum*
      - 6. Apophysomyceae
        - i. *Apophysomyces*
          - (a) *A. elegans*
      - 7. Thamnidiaceae
        - i. *Cokeromyces*
          - (a) *C. recurvatus*
    - b. Entomophthorales
      - i. *Conidiobolus*
        - (a) *C. coronatus* (*Entomophthora coronata*)*
        - (b) *C. incongruans*
      - ii. *Basidiobolus*
        - (a) *B. haptosporus* (*B. meristosporus*; *B. ranarum*)*

*Obsolete synonyms.
Data from Howard DH. An introduction to the taxonomy and nomenclature of zoopathogenic fungi. In: Howard DH, ed. Fungi Pathogenic for Humans and Animals: Part A, Biology. New York: Marcel Dekker; 1983:3–7.

MUCORMYCOSIS

The Pathogens

The medically important Zygomycetes are molds that grow in the environment and in tissue as hyphal forms. The taxonomy of the Zygomycetes is based on a morphologic analysis of the fungus, which is reviewed later. Other taxonomically relevant features include carbohydrate assimilation and maximal temperature compatible with growth. These organisms typically grow in 2 to 5 days on most media. However, cycloheximide inhibits the growth of these fungi, and media that contain this compound, such as mycosel and mycobiotic agar, should not be used.

Rhizopus species are the most commonly isolated agents of mucormycosis, followed by *Rhizomucor.* Differentiation between these genera is accomplished by microscopic examination for the presence and location of rhizoids, the presence of apophyses, and the morphology of the columellae[1, 2] (Fig. 249–1). The capability to identify these strains to this level should be within the grasp of most tertiary-care hospital laboratories. Speciation of these organisms is desirable for many reasons, including monitoring of the progress of therapy (especially to document the eradication of the original fungus and to determine that a fungus growing from a subsequent clinical specimen is or is not a different contaminating organism) and elucidation of any species-specific responses to different antifungal drugs, an important consideration with the current emphasis on development of new classes of antifungal drugs. Disease caused by

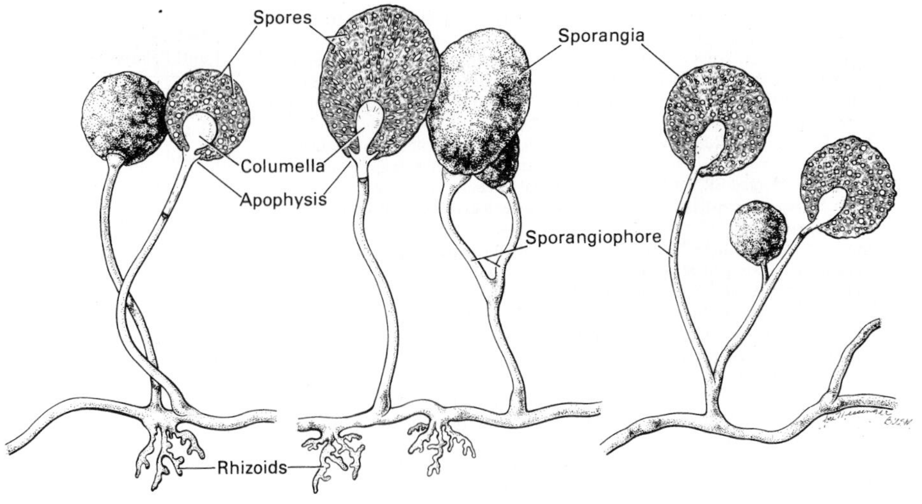

FIGURE 249–1. Diagram of major differentiating morphologic features of three of the most common Mucorales isolated from patients. Note the presence and location of the rhizoids, the columella, and the shape of the sporangia. The infectious spores reside within the sporangia. (Illustration by Lori Messenger.)

Cunninghamella,[2, 3] *Saksenaea*,[4, 5] and *Apophysomyces*[6, 7] is indistinguishable from that caused by the more common Mucorales, and these genera are more frequently being recovered in the laboratory as the etiologic agents of mucormycosis.[8] Laboratory confirmation of the identity of the organism is the only way to differentiate among the fungi.

Epidemiology

The Mucoraceae are ubiquitous fungi that are common inhabitants of decaying matter. For example, *Rhizopus* spp. frequently can be recovered from moldy bread. Because of their rapid growth and prolific spore-forming capacity, inhalation of conidia must be a daily experience. The presence of Mucorales spores on nonsterile adhesive tape has been shown to be the source of primary cutaneous mucormycosis.[9–11] Tongue depressors and wooden sticks used in the microbiology laboratory to prepare samples for culture have been found to harbor *Rhizopus* spp. In the former instance, clinical disease secondary to the use of the tongue depressor as a splint in neonates has occurred,[12] and in the latter, a pseudoepidemic was reported in immunocompromised patients.[13] Even though these fungi grow in many ecologic niches, the infrequency of disease caused by these organisms attests to their low virulence potential in the human host.

In contrast to the widespread distribution of these fungi, disease in humans is limited, in most cases, to people with severe immunocompromise, diabetes mellitus, or trauma. Solid organ transplant recipients represent a growing population at risk.[14] In these patients, the disease manifests in all of its diverse forms. More than half of patients have rhinocerebral disease; approximately 10% have pulmonary, cutaneous, or disseminated disease; and 2% have kidney or gastrointestinal involvement. Three quarters of these transplant patients also had diabetes or had received antirejection therapy. Scattered case reports of invasive mucormycosis in apparently normal hosts have appeared,[15–17] but the disease in the immunocompetent person remains a rarity.

Pathogenesis

Most commonly, the fungus gains entry to the body through the respiratory tract. The spores presumably are deposited in the nasal turbinates and may be inhaled into the pulmonary alveoli. In the case of primary cutaneous mucormycosis, spores are introduced directly into abraded skin. They then proliferate and can invade more widely.

To cause disease, spores must overcome the host's natural immunity and specific humoral and cell-mediated immune mechanisms. Most of our understanding of the pathogenesis of mucormycosis is derived from the mouse and rabbit models of infection. Normal animals inoculated with *Rhizopus* do not become ill.[18] However, inhalation of Mucorales spores by animals with diabetes mellitus or those receiving corticosteroids results in death from rapidly progressive pulmonary mucormycosis, often with hematogenous dissemination beyond the lungs.[19–21]

The initial event in fungal cell proliferation is spore germination. In the normal lung, *Rhizopus oryzae* spores are unable to germinate.[19, 20, 22] Bronchoalveolar macrophages harvested from normal mice readily ingest *Rhizopus* spores and inhibit their germination.[19, 23] However, the spores remain viable and can grow if removed from the phagolysosomes. In the lungs of mice with streptozotocin-induced diabetes and in steroid-treated mice, spore germination readily occurs.[19, 23] Bronchoalveolar macrophages recovered from these mice do not possess the normal ability to inhibit spore germination.

Neutrophils are prominent components of the host response to the Mucorales. Recruitment of neutrophils into areas of infection is accomplished by fungus-derived and serum-derived chemotactic factors.[24, 25] Activation of the alternative complement pathway is the source of the serum-induced chemotaxis.

The mechanisms responsible for the increased susceptibility to mucormycosis in various patient groups are not clear. Oxidative metabolites generated by the phagocyte respiratory burst (e.g., O_2^-, hydrogen peroxide, hypochlorous acid) have been shown to be fungicidal to *R. oryzae* hyphae.[26] How diabetes and steroids interfere with the ability of this fungus to elicit these toxic phagocyte products or with the activity of the oxidative metabolites is unknown. Defensins, cationic proteins obtained from mammalian phagocytic cells,[27] also have significant ability to kill *R. oryzae* spores and hyphae.[28] The relative importance of oxidative and nonoxidative fungicidal mechanisms in the normal state and in situations of immunosuppression or diabetes remains a mystery.

Hyperglycemia or acidosis per se is not sufficient to permit fungal replication within the alveolar macrophage,[1] although acidosis without hyperglycemia has been associated with invasive mucormycosis of humans on occasion.[29, 30] Normal human serum can inhibit the growth of *Rhizopus*.[24] In contrast, serum obtained from patients with diabetic ketoacidosis is not inhibitory and may actually enhance fungal growth.[31, 32] Although neither antibody nor complement is responsible for inhibition of growth of the Mucorales, interactions between transferrin and iron molecules and fungal spores have been described and may be important in determining the rate of fungal cell replication.[33, 34] Indeed, patients with renal failure who are receiving deferoxamine are at increased risk for developing a rapidly fatal case of mucormycosis, and the importance of iron in fostering growth of the Mucorales is clear.[35, 36] In a combination of in vitro and in vivo animal studies, Boelaert and colleagues showed that, in the presence of feroxamine complex (iron-loaded deferoxamine) and serum, the growth of *Rhizopus* is enhanced more than that of *Aspergillus,* and growth of *Candida* is unaffected.[36] Deferoxamine-treated guinea pigs infected with *Rhizopus, Aspergillus fumigatus,* or *Cryptococcus neoformans* died sooner than untreated animals, but survival of mice infected with *Candida albicans* was unchanged. The importance of the presence of serum, which is inherently fungistatic to *Rhizopus,* in the in vitro studies requires emphasis, because studies performed without the addition of serum fail to demonstrate the growth-enhancing effects of deferoxamine.[37] Feroxamine reverses this serum-associated fungistasis and augments fungal growth.[37]

It is still not possible to develop a unifying concept of the pathogenesis of mucormycosis. It is clear, however, that undefined defects of macrophages and neutrophils, present in diabetic and steroid-treated animals, are important in allowing the replication of the Mucorales. Moreover, immunologically healthy people can suppress the growth of the Mucorales and clear them from the lung with great efficiency. Finally, the relative paucity of cases of mucormycosis in patients with the acquired immunodeficiency syndrome (AIDS) attests to the importance of the neutrophil in inhibiting fungal spore development. However, cases of mucormycosis in AIDS patients do occur and may be secondary to quantitative and qualitative defects in neutrophils.[38–43]

Once the fungus begins to grow, the hyphae invade tissue and have a special affinity for blood vessels. Direct penetration and growth through the blood vessel wall explain the propensity for thrombosis and tissue necrosis, two major hallmarks of the histopathology of mucormycosis. *R. oryzae* spores have been shown to bind laminin and type IV collagen by a lectin-independent mechanism.[44] This binding occurred before spore germination and decreased as the spore germinated. These observations still do not explain the propensity of Mucorales hyphae to invade blood vessels.

Clinical Manifestations

The manifestations of mucormycosis can be arbitrarily divided into at least six separate entities, based on clinical presentation and involvement of a particular body site: (1) rhinocerebral, (2) pulmonary, (3) cutaneous, (4) gastrointestinal, (5) central nervous system, and (6) miscellaneous.[45] In general, the predilection for one of these types of presentation varies with the underlying or predisposing condition. For example, patients with diabetes most often develop rhinocerebral mucormycosis, neutropenic patients who have leukemia or who become neutropenic during bone marrow transplantation for other diseases develop rhinocerebral or pulmonary mucormycosis, and those with protein-calorie malnutrition most often present with gastrointestinal disease. Disseminated disease, resulting from progression from one of the primary anatomic locations, is particularly troublesome in patients with severe immunologic deficits, such as those with bone marrow transplants or acute leukemia.[46–48]

Rhinocerebral Mucormycosis. This form of mucormycosis is most often found in patients with diabetes mellitus, particularly in the presence of acidosis, and in patients with leukemia who have been neutropenic for long periods and who have been receiving broad-spectrum antibacterial drugs.[49–54] Occasional reports of this form of mucormycosis in organ transplant patients have appeared.[55, 56] Patients presenting with diabetic ketoacidosis and altered mental status should have an improvement in consciousness as the metabolic abnormalities are corrected. Persistence of mental status changes beyond the usual 24 to 48 hours after appropriate therapy is begun and metabolic abnormalities are resolving should alert the physician to the possibility that mucormycosis involving the brain may be responsible for the patient's condition.

Patients with this form of mucormycosis virtually always complain of facial pain or headache, or both. Fever and varying degrees of evidence of orbital cellulitis occur. With invasion of the orbit, loss of extraocular muscle function can develop and proptosis becomes evident (Fig. 249–2*A*). Marked swelling of the conjunctiva also occurs as the disease progresses (see Fig. 249–2*B*). Loss of vision may result from thrombosis of the retinal artery, presumably secondary to direct invasion by fungal elements. The development of cranial nerve dysfunction, especially of nerves V and VII, occurs with progression of the disease, is manifested by ptosis and pupillary dilatation, and represents a serious prognostic event. Cerebral abscess as a complication of mucormycosis involving the nose and eye can also occur.[57, 58] Cavernous sinus and internal carotid artery thrombosis[59] are additional complications that reflect the vascular tropism of the fungus. In the terminal stages of the disease, the underlying predisposing condition continues unabated, and patients may lose consciousness. The end result of such progression is death.

Laboratory studies are nonspecific, but suggestive evidence of the presence of disease can be found on roentgenograms of the sinuses. Plain roentgenograms of the sinuses and orbits can reveal sinusoidal mucosal thickening, with or without air-fluid levels.[60] Erosion of bone through the walls of the sinuses or into the orbit can be found as the disease progresses (Fig. 249–3). Destruction of bone in this region is often dramatically revealed by computed tomography (CT). Abnormalities in soft tissues involved in the disease process can also be visualized by CT scans[61] and can be used to guide surgical intervention. Similar changes have been demonstrated by magnetic resonance imaging (MRI) (Fig. 249–4).

Treatment with deferoxamine, usually for chelation therapy in patients receiving hemodialysis, is another risk factor for development of mucormycosis.[36, 62–67] Most of these patients died from aggressive infection with *Rhizopus* spp., but *Cunninghamella* spp. have also been recovered from such patients.[35, 67] However, iron overload per se may also be an important risk factor for the development of invasive mucormycosis.[63, 64]

Finally, chronic presentations or late sequelae after apparently successful therapy can be observed.[67–70] For this reason, all survivors of acute infection should be monitored for signs of indolent residual infection.

Pulmonary Mucormycosis. Most of the patients with this form of mucormycosis are seriously immunocompromised because of an absolute lack of circulating neutrophils. The cause of neutropenia is usually chemotherapy for hematologic malignancies. The patients often have been receiving broad-spectrum antibiotics for unremitting fever. Other than fever and perhaps dyspnea and cough, there usually are no other symptoms. With continued tissue necrosis, hemoptysis may develop; should a major blood vessel be eroded, fatal pulmonary hemorrhage can result.[71, 72] A chest roentgenogram shows evidence of infiltration or cavity formation, usually involving one anatomic segment but typically progressing to involve multiple contiguous areas in the same lung.[73] The most common finding on chest roentgenograms is consolidation (66%).[74] Cavitation occurs in about 40%, usually as neutropenia resolves. In one study, CT scans performed in patients with pulmonary mucormycosis revealed unsuspected abnormalities in 26%, including involvement of spleen, involvement of the kidney, and pulmonary artery pseudoaneurysm.[74] The disease most often begins with unilateral lung involvement but can disseminate more widely as the patient is dying. Patients in intensive care units for prolonged periods are often immunosuppressed as a result of malnutrition and medications (including corticosteroids) and may be hyperglycemic as a result of parenteral hyperalimentation or glucose intolerance. Therefore it is not surprising that nosocomial mucormycosis pneumonia occurs in such patients.

Scattered reports can be found of pulmonary mucormycosis with atypical presentations: as a solitary nodule in a diabetic[75]; in a patient with no underlying predisposing condition[76]; as a cavitary pneumonia in a patient without predisposing conditions[77]; as multiple mycotic

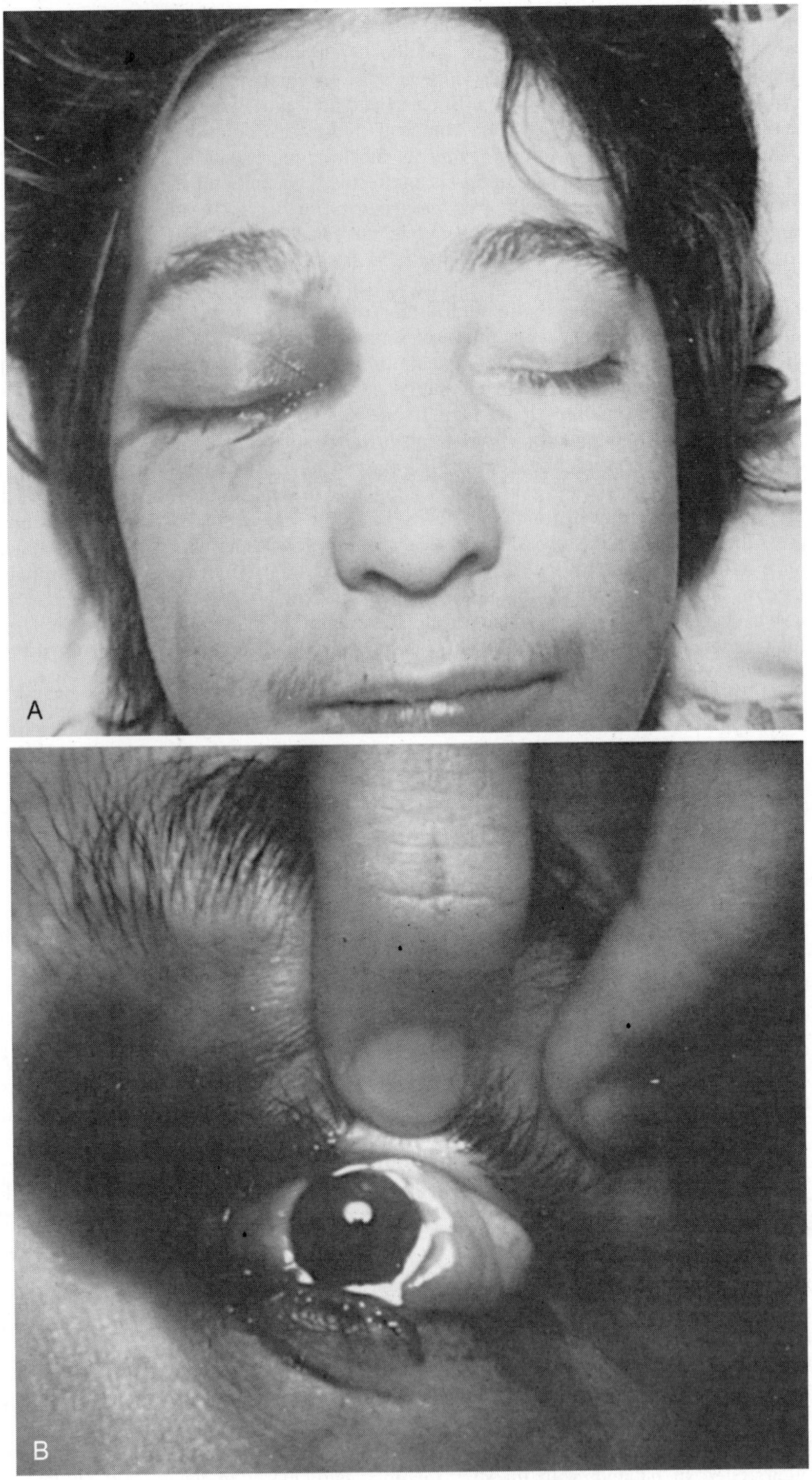

FIGURE 249–2. *A,* Orbital involvement in a diabetic patient. Note the periorbital ecchymosis, edema, and sanguineous discharge from the eye. *B,* Marked chemosis and proptosis secondary to retro-orbital invasion in rhinocerebral mucormycosis. (Courtesy of Prof. Bertrand Dupont, Paris, France.)

pulmonary artery aneurysms[78]; as bronchial obstruction[79]; as pseudoaneurysm of the pulmonary artery[80]; and even in a patient with a normal chest roentgenogram.[81] Patients with diabetes mellitus can also develop pulmonary mucormycosis with a less fulminant, more subacute course than is typically seen in patients with neutropenia.[82]

Cutaneous Mucormycosis. Sporadic cases of cutaneous mucormycosis continue to occur, but a nationwide epidemic that was caused by contaminated elastic bandages in the 1970s focused attention on primary cutaneous mucormycosis as a distinct entity. Patients presented with cellulitis under areas covered by the bandages, which presumably was caused by direct inoculation of fungi into skin occluded by the adhesive.[9–11] Failure to recognize the mycotic nature of the infection or to remove the bandages to inspect the area occasionally resulted in penetration of hyphae into areas below the skin, with subsequent infection of muscle, liver, or other viscera.

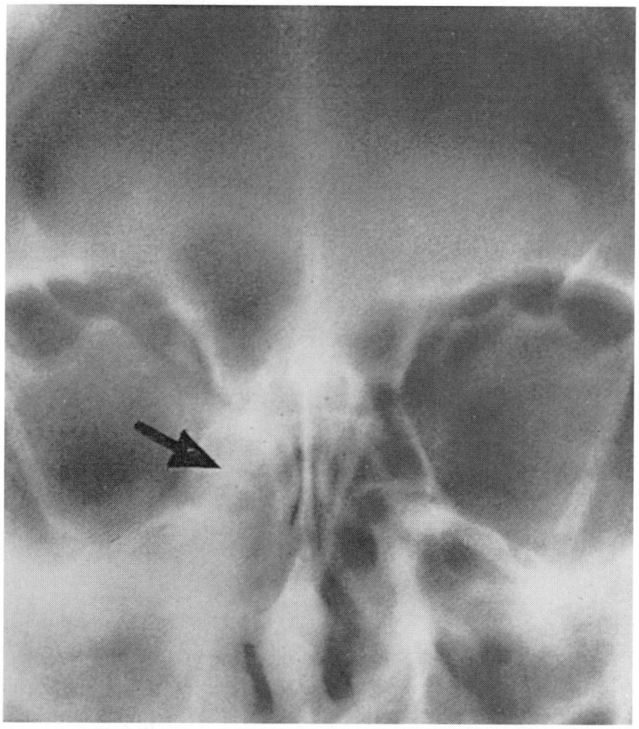

FIGURE 249–3. Tomogram of the head in a patient with rhinocerebral mucormycosis. Note the presence of clouding in the maxillary and ethmoid *(arrow)* sinuses. (Courtesy of Dr. David A. Stevens, San Jose, Calif.)

Use of sterilized bandages and dressings should eliminate this form of mucormycosis. Dissemination of the organism from the site of primary infection can occur.[83] Rarely, intramuscular injections have been reported to precede the development of this form of mucormycosis.[84] Cases of cutaneous mucormycosis have been described after minor trauma[85–87]; some of these patients may have had diabetes mellitus. A chronic, nonhealing ulcer at the site of a postoperative drain site has been reported.[88] Contamination of devitalized tissue during major traumatic accidents also can result in the appearance of this form of mucormycosis.[89] Extensive involvement of burn wounds can result in dissemination of the fungus throughout the body and death of the patient.[90]

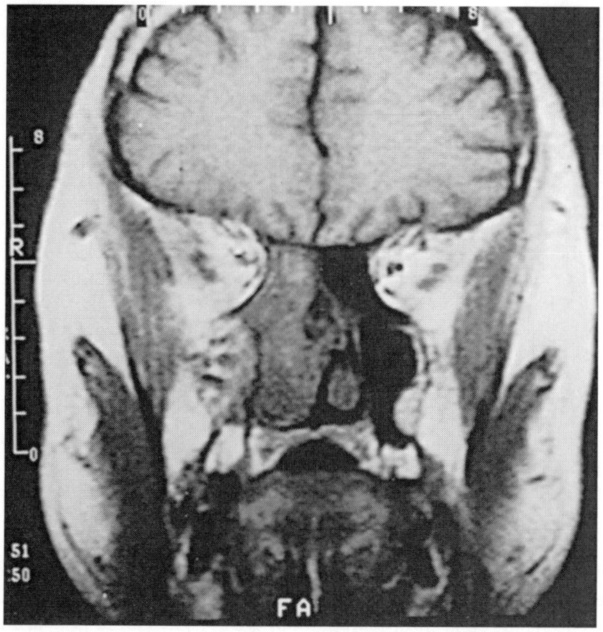

FIGURE 249–4. Magnetic resonance image of mucormycosis of the nasal cavity and ethmoid sinus. Note the contiguity of the frontal lobe to ethmoidal infection.

Cutaneous mucormycosis predominantly involves the epidermis and dermis, and necrosis develops secondary to vascular invasion. Cultures have yielded *R. oryzae* or *Rhizopus rhizopodiformis* in most cases. *Saksenaea vasiformis* was isolated from subcutaneous tissues of a child with thalassemia who sustained trauma and subsequently developed infection in the injured area.[91] *Mucor hiemalis,* a common soil inhabitant, was recovered from an otherwise healthy girl with cutaneous mucormycosis after an insect bite[92] and from a gardener with subcutaneous infection of a finger.[86]

Patients with pulmonary or other forms of mucormycosis can develop skin lesions distant from the site of primary pathology. This secondary cutaneous involvement of the skin is a result of fungemia, which is almost never documented by positive blood cultures and reflects the presence of widely disseminated disease.[47] The involved area is erythematous and painful, with varying degrees of central necrosis.

Gastrointestinal Mucormycosis. Mucormycosis of the gastrointestinal tract is found primarily in patients with extreme malnutrition and is thought to arise from fungi entering the body with food. Reports have highlighted the risk to kidney transplant recipients of gastric mucormycosis.[93, 94] All portions of the gastrointestinal tract are susceptible to infection, with the stomach, ileum, and colon being the sites most commonly infected.[95] Because this disease is acute and rapidly fatal, most of the reported cases were diagnosed after the patient died. The initial manifestations of gastrointestinal mucormycosis are abdominal pain and distention associated with nausea and vomiting. Fever and hematochezia may also be found. If the diagnosis is made before death, the patient is often thought to have an intra-abdominal abscess. Definitive diagnosis can be made only at surgery with appropriate examination of tissue (see later discussion).

Central Nervous System Mucormycosis. This rare manifestation of mucormycosis occurs in severely debilitated patients. Most often, extension of the fungus from its initial site of invasion in the nose or paranasal sinuses through adjacent bones into the brain is the mode of entry into the central nervous system.[57] This complication is recognizable by decreasing consciousness and development of multiple focal neurologic findings of cranial nerves and motor neurons to the rest of the body.

Occasionally, cerebral mucormycosis may occur after open head trauma, presumably as a result of direct implantation of the fungus at the time of injury,[96] or after intravenous injection of illicit drugs.[97–99] The appearance of a black discharge from the wound heralds necrosis of the underlying dura and brain and should suggest the diagnosis of mucormycosis. Occasional reports of isolated cerebral mucormycosis in patients with leukemia[100] or with no predisposing condition[101] have been published.

Isolated mucormycosis of the brain has also been described in two intravenous drug abusers with AIDS.[102] The appearance of mucormycosis in these patients may reflect the occurrence of cerebral mucormycosis in drug addicts,[97–99] but, as discussed previously, neutropenia complicating AIDS may increase the risk of mucormycosis.

Miscellaneous Forms. Sporadic reports can be found of mucormycosis involving other areas: heart (including endocarditis),[103–106] bones,[7, 107–111] kidney,[112] bladder,[113] arterial catheter site with extension to surrounding tissue,[114] mediastinum,[115, 116] and trachea.[117] Other conditions involving mucormycosis are osteomyelitis of the clivus resulting in chronic meningitis that is caused by parameningeal irritation,[118] superior vena cava syndrome,[119] and possibly bone marrow necrosis in a patient with a *Mucor*-infected renal cyst.[120] A case of allergic sinusitis caused by *Rhizomucor* species presented with a clinical syndrome similar to that of the more common *Aspergillus* sinusitis.[121]

There have been a number of case reports of mucormycosis in patients with AIDS. A review of 15 AIDS patients with mucormycosis illustrated the heterogeneity of presentations of the infection in this patient population. Nine patients had fungi recovered from biopsy specimens: 4 had *Absidia corymbifera*, 1 had *Absidia* sp., 3 had *Rhizopus* sp., and 1 had *Cunninghamella* sp.[43] The median $CD4^+$ T-lymphocyte count was 106/mm^3 (range, 0 to 387/mm^3). There were 4 patients with renal involvement, 4 with skin infection, and 3 with basal ganglia infection in this series.

Diagnosis

The hallmarks of disease caused by the Mucorales are vascular invasion and tissue necrosis; black eschars and discharges should be aggressively sought. The presence of a black nasal discharge should not be dismissed as merely dried blood. It may reflect tissue necrosis and may be an important sign of deep infection. Similarly, black necrotic lesions of the nasal mucosa or hard palate may reflect invasive mucormycosis. These manifestations occur only after some time, and attempts at making a diagnosis of mucormycosis should not await the development of necrotic areas. Diagnosis depends on demonstration of the organism in the tissue of a biopsy specimen. Swabs of discharge or abnormal tissue are not appropriate and often result in erroneous information. Fungal hyphae can be seen on potassium hydroxide preparations of touch slides prepared from the biopsy specimen. Fixed tissue can be stained with hematoxylin and eosin, and fungal hyphae can be seen with this routine histologic stain. Grocott methenamine–silver or periodic acid–Schiff (PAS) staining also adequately demarcates fungal elements in tissue in most cases (Fig. 249–5).

Typically, the fungi appear as broad (10 to 20 μm in diameter), nonseptate hyphae with branches occurring at right angles. Rarely, septae can be visualized. The appearance of Mucorales hyphae in tissue is different from that of *Aspergillus, Fusarium,* or *Pseudallescheria* spp., in that the latter organisms appear as thinner, more regularly shaped fungal elements with more frequent, acute-angle branching. These hyphae are also septate. Identification of the genus and species requires culture of tissue and assessment of the morphology of the fungal growth. For unclear reasons, agents of mucormycosis may be difficult to isolate from infected tissue and rarely appear in blood culture.

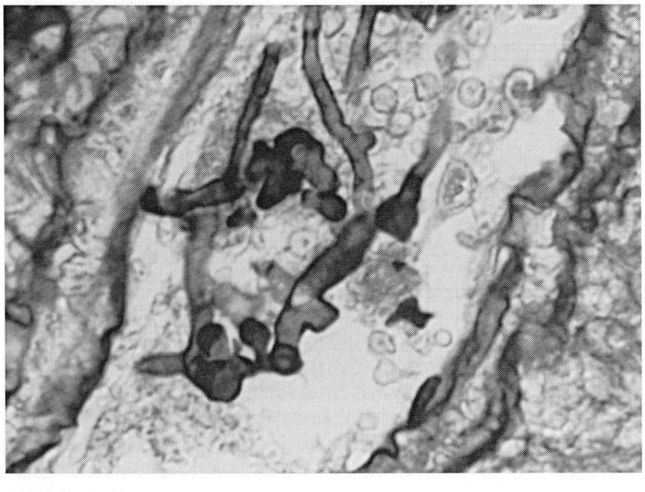

FIGURE 249–5. Photomicrograph of lung demonstrating typical broad, irregularly shaped hyphae with right angle branching, characteristic of the Mucorales (periodic acid–Schiff ×250). (Courtesy of Dr. Alayn Waldorf, Oakland, Calif.)

Affected tissue is typically infiltrated with neutrophils unless the patient is neutropenic. An inflammatory vasculitis involving both arteries and veins is the rule. Tissue necrosis as a result of blood vessel invasion is prominent. Thrombosis and hemorrhage are also commonly found. In more chronic cases, mononuclear cell infiltration is observed, and occasional giant cells may be seen if the infection has been present for a sufficient period.

Antigens that might be useful as reagents in serologic tests have been identified.[122–123] However, serodiagnosis of mucormycosis remains investigational and cannot yet be recommended for routine clinical use.

Differential Diagnosis

There are several other infectious diseases that produce manifestations of tissue necrosis and infarction secondary to direct invasion of the vasculature. Infection with *Aspergillus* is most likely to be confused with the rhinocerebral or pulmonary forms of mucormycosis. The only definitive method of differentiating between these two possibilities is by examination of tissue or culture of a biopsy specimen. Certain aggressive orbital tumors can produce some of the findings of rhinocerebral mucormycosis, but the rapid pace of mucormycosis, the presence of fever, and the evidence of necrosis all favor a fungal cause. Cavernous sinus thrombosis that is caused by extension of staphylococcal lesions of the face can resemble rhinocerebral mucormycosis, but there are no lesions in the nose or paranasal sinuses. Pulmonary mucormycosis can be mistaken for bland pulmonary embolism, but the progressive extension of the fungal lesion distinguishes the two. On rare occasions, patients with acute leukemia develop skin lesions identical to those of ecthyma gangrenosum, which more commonly is caused by *Pseudomonas aeruginosa.* Blood cultures are usually positive in the latter entity.

Therapy and Prevention

As with any opportunistic infection, the first therapeutic maneuver should be to correct the underlying disease. Aggressive correction of hyperglycemia and acidemia should be pursued. If possible, doses of immunosuppressive drugs, including steroids, should be decreased and the drugs stopped. The ultimate outcome of mucormycosis depends, in large part, on the prognosis of the underlying disease.

The standard therapy for invasive mucormycosis is treatment with amphotericin B. Because the fungus is relatively refractory to medical treatment, higher than usual doses of amphotericin B have been recommended. Doses typically range from 1.0 to 1.5 mg/kg/day in most patients. Once the patient has been stabilized, alternate-day amphotericin B can be considered. Higher doses of amphotericin B may be administered as lipid formulations, and several reports have described successful outcomes in patients with rhinocerebral mucormycosis who were treated with lipid preparations of amphotericin B.[124–126] The ultimate role of lipid formulation of amphotericin B in treatment of mucormycosis awaits further evidence of their efficacy and safety, compared with the standard preparation of amphotericin B (Fungizone). However, the lipid formulations may allow administration of very large amounts of amphotericin B over a short period. In an attempt to abruptly halt the proliferation of this rapidly growing fungus, the use of these formulations may offer an opportunity for more effective medical intervention. However, proof of this concept is still lacking, and the results of use of such high doses of the lipid formulations (e.g., 10 mg/kg/day) requires validation.

None of the currently available azoles (ketoconazole, itraconazole, or fluconazole) has a role in the treatment of mucormycosis. There is insufficient information about the activity of the new azoles, voriconazole and SCH 56592, against the Mucorales to suggest that they might be active. SCH 42427 is an experimental triazole that is no longer in development because it caused tumors in rodents. The drug was active in a mouse model of mucormycosis,[128] suggesting that broad-spectrum triazoles may offer some alternatives to amphotericin B in the future. However, amphotericin B remains the only proven effective therapy. The addition of other agents such as rifampin[129] to amphotericin B in an attempt to obtain synergistic antifungal activity is controversial and cannot be recommended. Likewise, the interpretation of in vitro susceptibility tests of single drugs[130] is problematic and adds little to the formulation of treatment plans in individual patients. Colony-stimulating factors have been employed on occasion,[131] but their role in neutropenic and non-neutropenic patients is not clear.

Although reports have appeared in the literature of recovery of patients with mucormycosis with antifungal therapy alone,[132–134] these are clearly the exception, and aggressive surgical débridement of necrotic tissue is advisable.[114, 136–142] Some patients may recover with minimally disfiguring surgery.[45, 52, 136–138, 143] These patients are probably in the minority, and a well-coordinated medical-surgical approach maximizes the chances of success. Repeated operations may be required for satisfactory removal of continuously appearing necrotic tissue. Frozen section–guided débridement has been advocated as a method for operative intervention and as an alternative to the extensive débridement that has traditionally been performed in patients with invasive mucormycosis.[135] Should the patient survive the acute episode, major reconstructive surgery may also be necessary.[144] Adjunctive oxygen therapy has been considered beneficial in a small number of patients.[145, 146] Because of the uncontrolled nature of the observations and the absence of a rationale for treating an obligate aerobic fungus with oxygen, this form of therapy cannot be routinely recommended at present.

In patients with primary cutaneous involvement, local débridement and topical administration of amphotericin B are satisfactory. However, with any evidence of progression of the disease beyond the skin into the subcutaneous tissue and muscle, or development of signs and symptoms distant to the focus of infection, systemically administered amphotericin B is advised. The duration of antifungal therapy depends on the response of the infection to treatment and success in resolving the underlying predisposing conditions.

It is almost impossible to determine accurately the effectiveness of any therapeutic approach to mucormycosis. The disease is too rare to warrant appropriately controlled comparative studies, and cases appear in the literature only if therapy is effective. This reporting bias makes generalization of findings in the published literature difficult when attempting to provide the best possible therapy for a given patient. One way of reconciling differences in approach is to assess the extent of infection at the time of diagnosis; early detection can mean less invasion and tissue destruction and therefore less need for extensive removal of devitalized tissue because there are fewer fungi in the tissue. Overall, the earlier the diagnosis of mucormycosis is made, the better the outcome. At present, no one approach is preferred over another, and treatment should be individualized.

It is apparent that two factors determine the outcome in all patients: early diagnosis and resolution of predisposing problems. The overall mortality rate has been about 50%, although higher survival rates (up to 85%) have been reported more recently.[45] Results of treating pulmonary mucormycosis have been poor, probably because diagnosis of this form of mucormycosis is so difficult. By the time the disease is suspected and the diagnosis is made, extensive tissue destruction has occurred, the pace of the disease is rapid, and the general condition of the patient is so poor that medical therapy has minimal effect and surgical options are not possible. Occasionally, surgery has appeared to be helpful.[147]

There is no recognized method for preventing systemic infection with the Mucorales. In patients with severe neutropenia, such as those with bone marrow transplant or leukemia, provision of care in rooms equipped with high-efficiency particulate air filters (HEPA) has been shown to reduce the risks of aspergillosis and mucormycosis.[132] However, because of the high cost of this approach and a lack of effect on eventual outcome, most centers do not use such filters in the routine care of these patients. Substitution of hydroxpyridinone chelators for deferoxamine may be one approach to decrease the risk of mucormycosis in patients who require such therapy.[148]

ENTOMOPHTHORAMYCOSIS

The Pathogens

Two genera of the Entomophthorales are responsible for human disease: *Conidiobolus* and *Basidiobolus* (see Table 249–1). Entomophthoramycosis has been arbitrarily subdivided into entomophthoramycosis conidiobolae and entomophthoramycosis basidiobolae on the basis of anatomic localization of the disease and the genus responsible for the pathology at the involved site. The former occurs in the head and face and the latter elsewhere in the body, usually the trunk and arms. This nosology is, however, clearly artificial, because reports of disseminated infection caused by *Conidiobolus* have been published.[149] These rare infections have been reported in the United States,[150–152] Central America,[153] and Australia.[154]

Epidemiology

These fungi are normal inhabitants of soil throughout the world, including the United States.[155] *Basidiobolus* spp. have also been isolated from the gut of amphibians and reptiles, including those found in Florida and other areas of the United States.[156] Isolation of *Basidiobolus* spp. from a variety of animals in Australia has been documented.[157] However, most reported cases are from Africa,[158] with cases also occurring in India and other parts of Asia.

Pathogenesis

These organisms are ubiquitous in the environment, even in regions where disease caused by the Entomophthorales is almost never found. Entrance into the body via inhalation or direct inoculation has been postulated,[158, 159] but proof for this hypothesis is lacking. Likewise, the mechanisms for host resistance to invasive disease are unknown; however, innate immunity must be fairly high, given the low incidence of disease in most areas of the world.

Echetebu and Ononogbu described lipase and proteinase activity in supernatants from *Basidiobolus haptosporus*.[160] They postulated that the liberation of lysolecithin from phosphatidylcholine by phospholipase A and a proteinase that can degrade serum proteins may be responsible for the invasive potential of the fungus. Lysolecithin is toxic to mammalian cell membranes, and this may enhance the invasive potential of the organism. However, the ability of the Entomophthorales to produce pathogenetically significant enzymes in vivo is unknown. Moreover, the rarity of disease caused by these agents attests to their low potential for virulence and indicates that some specific abnormality, as yet unknown, must be important in facilitating the initiation and maintenance of infection.

Clinical Manifestations

Entomophthoramycosis conidiobolae is characterized by swelling of the nose, perinasal tissues, and mouth. This is accompanied by symptoms of nasal stuffiness, drainage, and sinus pain. The infection begins as swelling of the inferior nasal turbinates, with subsequent extension into surrounding structures. Nodular subcutaneous masses can be palpated through intact skin. As the disease progresses, generalized facial swelling occurs and the patient may be unable to open the eyes as a result (Fig. 249–6). Systemic symptoms and signs are conspicuously absent. A particularly lucid and instructive summary of this disease has been published by Martinson.[158]

Entomophthoramycosis basidiobolae also begins as nodular sub-

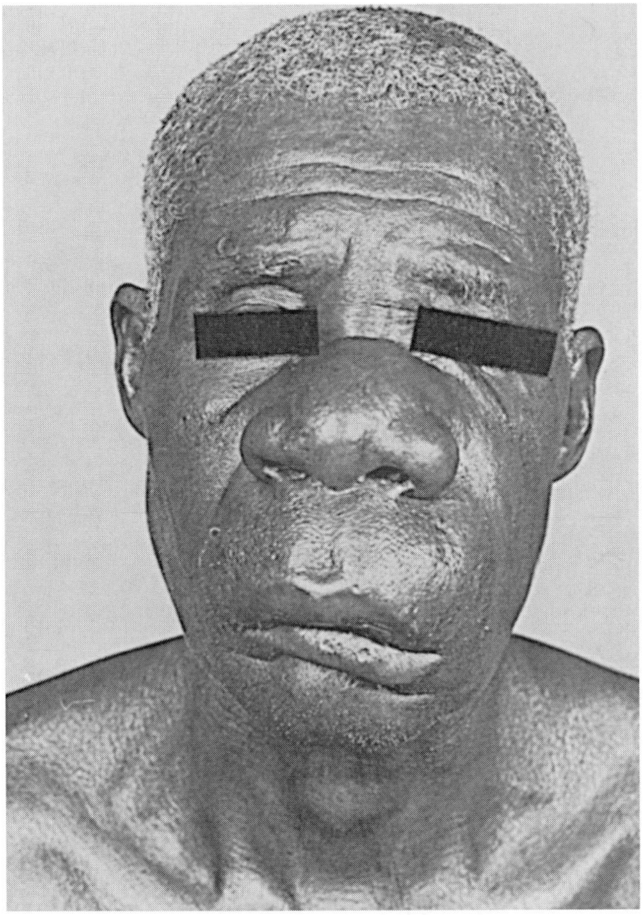

FIGURE 249–6. Photograph of a patient infected with *Conidiobolus* sp. Note the marked swelling of the nose and perinasal tissues extending to the periorbital region. (Courtesy of Dr. B. C. Okafor, Enugu, Nigeria.)

cutaneous lesions. The lesions are typically firm and are not painful. Most frequently, they are located on the trunk, arms, legs, or buttocks.[161] Deeper invasion of muscle underlying involved subcutaneous disease has been described,[162] as has gastrointestinal involvement.[163] Although the disease may resolve spontaneously, most cases are slowly progressive until appropriate therapy is administered.

Occasionally, disseminated infection occurs.[149] Both a chronic-appearing fibrotic reaction and angioinvasive disease reminiscent of the type of mucormycosis seen in diabetics and immunocompromised patients have been described.

Biopsy of the submucosal or subcutaneous masses of either form of entomophthoramycosis reveals similar histologic features. Acute and/or chronic inflammatory cells are found in the vicinity of the typical nonseptate, broad, thin-walled hyphae. Occasional hyphal septations can be observed. The hyphae are readily visible on routine hematoxylin and eosin staining but, in contrast to most other fungal pathogens, are not as well demonstrated by PAS or silver staining. Characteristically, the hyphae are surrounded by eosinophilic material, which can appear in a stellate formation or as a simple sheath surrounding the hyphae. This has been termed the *Splendore-Hoeppli phenomenon,* and it is an important histopathologic concomitant of this disease. However, similar perihyphal deposition of eosinophilic material can occur with other fungi or parasites. In contrast to the agents of mucormycosis, the Entomophthorales do not usually invade blood vessels; tissue infarction and necrosis are not part of the usual pathology seen in this disease. However, reports detail the rare case of invasive disease and tissue destruction that can be observed.[154, 164]

Diagnosis

In areas where entomophthoramycosis is relatively common, the diagnosis may be suspected from the clinical appearance of the patient and the lesions. Definitive diagnosis depends on biopsy of the involved site, with microscopic documentation of tissue invasion and the presence of typical hyphae of either genus. Culture of the fungus is the only way to identify correctly the species present in tissue. A preliminary report of an immunodiffusion test for making the diagnosis of *Basidiobolus haptosporus* and *Conidiobolus coronatus* infections has appeared,[165] but more work is needed to establish this serologic method as a useful clinical tool.

Differential Diagnosis

In tropical areas, a variety of diseases can present with submucosal or subcutaneous nodular lesions associated with swelling. Malignancy and abscess must be ruled out. The presentation in one patient was similar to that of Burkitt's lymphoma.[166] Similarly, pythiosis, onchocerciasis, and elephantiasis secondary to infection with filaria should be considered. Infection with *Sporothrix schenckii, Mycobacterium tuberculosis,* or *Mycobacterium ulcerans* also can mimic entomophthoramycosis. Biopsy of abnormal tissue, with pathologic and microbiologic evaluation, is the most efficient method for making the correct diagnosis.

Therapy and Prevention

Therapeutic recommendations for this disease can be made only on the basis of empirical observations. Potassium iodide, trimethoprim-sulfamethoxazole, imidazoles, triazoles, and amphotericin B have all been used. Anecdotal reports suggest that each of these remedies may work; however, the effect of reporting bias makes the determination of which agent is more efficacious and safer than the others an impossible task. Complicating such analysis of the efficacy of individual treatment regimens is the observation that some cases of entomophthoramycosis, especially those caused by *Basidiobolus* spp., may resolve spontaneously. In patients with chronic infection and without life-threatening complications, any of these antimicrobial agents could be considered for use.[167] Susceptibility testing, as with other fungi, is not reliable and has an uncertain place in guiding therapeutic decisions.[168] One patient infected with *C. coronatus* was apparently cured after receiving ketoconazole, 600 mg/day,[169] and others did well while receiving fluconazole[170, 171] or itraconazole.[172] However, failures of treatment with azoles have been noted.[164]

In addition to medical therapy, a surgical approach to this disease includes removal of accessible nodules and reconstructive surgery to restore a more normal appearance to tissues grossly swollen and deformed by the chronic inflammatory response to the fungus.

Currently, there are no means of preventing this infection or even of identifying those at risk for development of this disease. Therefore, there is no role for the use of prophylactic antifungal agents. Early detection of newly acquired infection seems to be the best hope of reducing the serious morbidity associated with long-standing disease.

REFERENCES

1. Kwon-Chung KJ, Bennett JE. Mucormycosis. In: Medical Mycology. Philadelphia: Lea & Febiger; 1992:524–559.
2. Kwon-Chung KJ, Young RC, Orlando M. Pulmonary mucormycosis caused by *Cunninghamella elegans* in a patient with chronic myelogenous leukemia. Am J Clin Pathol. 1975;64:544–548.
3. Kolbeck PC, Makhoul RG, Bollinger RR, et al. Widely disseminated *Cunninghamella* mucormycosis in an adult renal transplant patient: Case report and review of the literature. Am J Clin Pathol. 1985;83:747–753.
4. Torell H, Cooper BH, Helgeson NGP. Disseminated *Saksenaea vasiformis* infection. Am J Clin Pathol. 1981;76:116–121.

5. Gonis G, Starr M. Fatal rhinoorbital mucormycosis caused by *Saksenaea vasiformis* in an immunocompromised child. Pediatr Infect Dis J. 1997;16:714–716.
6. Lakshmi V, Rani TS, Sharma S, et al. Zygomycotic necrotizing fascitis caused by *Apophysomyces elegans.* J Clin Microbiol. 1993;31:1368–1369.
7. Huffnagle KE, Southern PM Jr, Byrd LT, et al. *Apophysomyces elegans* as an agent of zygomycosis in a patient following trauma. J Med Vet Mycol. 1992;30:83–86.
8. Holland J. Emerging zygomycoses of humans: *Saksenaea vasiformis* and *Apophysomyces elegans.* Curr Top Med Mycol. 1997;8:27–34.
9. Gartenberg G, Bottone EJ, Keusch GT, et al. Hospital-acquired mucormycosis *(Rhizopus rhizopodiformis)* of skin and subcutaneous tissue: Epidemiology, mycology and treatment. N Engl J Med. 1978;299:1115–1117.
10. Dennis JE, Rhodes KH, Cooney DR, et al. Nosocomial *Rhizopus* infection (zygomycosis) in children. J Pediatr. 1980;96:824–828.
11. Mead JH, Lupton GP, Dillavou CL, et al. Cutaneous *Rhizopus* infection: Occurrence as a postoperative complication associated with an elasticized adhesive dressing. JAMA. 1979;242:272–274.
12. Mitchell SJ, Gray J, Morgan MEI, et al. Nosocomial infection with *Rhizopus microsporus* in preterm infants: Association with wooden tongue depressors. Lancet. 1996;34:441–443.
13. Verweij PE, Voss A, Donnelly JP, et al. Wooden sticks as the source of a pseudoepidemic of infection with *Rhizopus microsporus* var. *rhizopodiformis* among immunocompromised patients. J Clin Microbiol. 1997;35:2422–2423.
14. Singh N, Gayowski T, Singh J, Yu VL. Invasive gastrointestinal zygomycosis in a liver transplant recipient: Case report and review of zygomycosis in solid-organ transplant recipients. Clin Infect Dis. 1995;20:617–620.
15. Al-Asiri RH, Van Dijken PJ, Mahmood MA, et al. Isolated hepatic mucormycosis in an immunocompetent child. Am J Gastroenterol. 1996;91:606–607.
16. Butala A, Shah B, Cho YT, Schmidt MF. Isolated pulmonary mucormycosis in an apparently normal host: A case report. J Natl Med Assoc. 1995;87:572–574.
17. Del Valle Zapico A, Rubio Suarez A, Mellado Encinas P, et al. Mucormycosis of the sphenoid sinus in an otherwise healthy patient: Case report and literature review. J Laryngol Otol. 1996;110:471–473.
18. Waldorf AR, Halde C, Vedros NA. Murine model of pulmonary mucormycosis in cortisone-treated mice. Sabouraudia. 1982;20:217–224.
19. Waldorf AR, Ruderman N, Diamond RD. Specific susceptibility to mucormycosis in murine diabetes and bronchoalveolar macrophage defense against *Rhizopus.* J Clin Invest. 1984;74:150–160.
20. Waldorf AR, Peter L, Polak A. Mucormycotic infection in mice following prolonged incubation of spores in vivo and the role of spore agglutinating antibodies on spore germination. Sabouraudia. 1984;22:101–108.
21. Reinhardt DJ, Licata I, Kaplan W, et al. Experimental cerebral zygomycosis in alloxan-diabetic rabbits: Variation in virulence among zygomycetes. Sabouraudia. 1981;19:245–255.
22. Schaffner A, Davis CE, Schaffner T, et al. In vitro susceptibility of fungi to killing by neutrophil granulocytes discriminates between primary pathogenicity and opportunism. J Clin Invest. 1986;78:511–524.
23. Waldorf AR, Levitz SM, Diamond RD. In vivo bronchoalveolar macrophage defense against *Rhizopus oryzae* and *Aspergillus fumigatus.* J Infect Dis. 1984;150:752–60.
24. Chinn RYW, Diamond RD. Generation of chemotactic factors by *Rhizopus oryzae* in the presence and absence of serum: Relationship to hyphal damage mediated by human neutrophils and effects of hyperglycemia and ketoacidosis. Infect Immun. 1982;38:1123–1129.
25. Marx RS, Forsyth KR, Hentz ZK. Mucorales species activation of a serum leukotactic factor. Infect Immun. 1982;38:1217–1222.
26. Diamond RD, Haudenschild CC, Erickson NF III. Monocyte-mediated damage to *Rhizopus oryzae* hyphae in vitro. Infect Immun. 1982;38:292–297.
27. Ganz T, Selsted ME, Szklarek D, et al. Defensins: Natural peptide antibiotics of human neutrophils. J Clin Invest. 1985;76:1427–1435.
28. Levitz SM, Selsted ME, Ganz T, et al. In vitro killing of spores and hyphae of *Aspergillus fumigatus* and *Rhizopus oryzae* by rabbit neutrophil cationic peptides and bronchoalveolar macrophages. J Infect Dis. 1986;154:483–489.
29. Espinoza CG, Halkias DG. Pulmonary mucormycosis as a complication of chronic salicylate poisoning. Am J Clin Pathol. 1983;80:508–511.
30. Wong KL, Tai YT, Loke SL, et al. Disseminated zygomycosis masquerading as cerebral lupus erythematosus. Am J Clin Pathol. 1986;86:546–549.
31. Gale GR, Welch A. Studies of opportunistic fungi: I. Inhibition of *R. oryzae* by human sera. Am J Med Sci. 1961;45:604–612.
32. Owens AW, Hacklette MS, Baker RD. An antifungal factor in human serum: I. Studies of *Rhizopus rhizopodiformis.* Sabouraudia. 1965;4:179.
33. Artis WM, Fountain JA, Delcher HK, et al. A mechanism of susceptibility to mucormycosis in diabetic ketoacidosis: Transferrin and iron availability. Diabetes. 1982;31:1109–1114.
34. Artis WM, Patrusky E, Rastinejad F, et al. Fungistatic mechanism of human transferrin for *R. oryzae* and *Trichophyton mentagrophytes:* Alternative to simple iron deprivation. Infect Immun. 1983;41:1269–1278.
35. Maloisel F, Dufour P, Waller J, et al. *Cunninghamella bertholletiae:* An uncommon agent of opportunistic fungal infection. Case report and review. Nouv Rev Fr Hematol. 1991;33:311–315.
36. Boelaert JR, de Locht M, Van Cutsem J, et al. Mucormycosis during deferoxamine therapy is a siderophore-mediated infection: In vitro and in vivo animal studies. J Clin Invest. 1993;91:1979–1986.
37. Vlasveld LT, van Asbeck BS. Treatment with deferoxamine: A real risk factor for mucormycosis? Nephron. 1991;57:487–488.
38. Smith AG, Bustamante CI, Gilmor GD. Zygomycosis (absidiomycosis) in an AIDS patient. Mycopathologia. 1989;105:7–10.
39. Vesa J, Bielsa O, Arango O, et al. Massive renal infarction due to mucormycosis in an AIDS patient. Infection. 1992;20:234–236.
40. Hopwood V, Hicks DA, Thomas S, et al. Primary cutaneous zygomycosis due to *Absidia corymbifera* in a patient with AIDS. J Med Vet Mycol. 1992;30:399–402.
41. Diamond HJ, Phelps RG, Gordon ML, et al. Combined *Aspergillus* and zygomycotic *(Rhizopus)* infection in a patient with acquired immunodeficiency syndrome: Presentation as inflammatory tinea capitis. J Am Acad Dermatol. 1992;26:1017–1018.
42. Blatt SP, Lucey DR, DeHoff D, et al. Rhinocerebral zygomycosis in a patient with AIDS. J Infect Dis. 1991;164:215–216.
43. Nagy-Agren SE, Chu P, Smith GJ, et al. Zygomycosis (mucormycosis) and HIV infection: Report of three cases and review. J Acquir Immune Defic Syndr Hum Retrovirol. 1995;10:441–449.
44. Bouchara J-P, Oumeziane NA, Lissitzky J-C, et al. Attachment of spores of the human pathogenic fungus *Rhizopus oryzae* to extracellular matrix components. Eur J Cell Biol. 1996;70:76–83.
45. Parfrey NA. Improved diagnosis and prognosis of mucormycosis: A clinicopathologic study of 33 cases. Medicine (Baltimore). 1986;65:113–123.
46. Myskowski PL, Brown AE, Dinsmore R, et al. Mucormycosis following bone marrow transplantation. J Am Acad Dermatol. 1983;9:111–115.
47. Meyer RD, Kaplan MH, Ong M, et al. Cutaneous lesions in disseminated mucormycosis. JAMA. 1973;225:737–738.
48. St-Germain G, Robert A, Ishak M, et al. Infection due to *Rhizomucor pusillus:* Report of four cases in patients with leukemia and review. Clin Infect Dis. 1993;16:640–645.
49. Peterson KL, Wang M, Canalis RF, Abemayor E. Rhinocerebral mucormycosis: Evolution of the disease and treatment options. Laryngoscope. 1997;107:855–862.
50. Yanagisawa E, Friedman S, Kundargi RS, et al. Rhinocerebral phycomycosis. Laryngoscope. 1977;87:1319–1335.
51. Pillsbury JC, Fischer ND. Rhinocerebral mucormycosis. Arch Otolaryngol. 1977;103:600–604.
52. Meyers BR, Wormser G, Hirschman SZ, et al. Rhinocerebral mucormycosis: Premortem diagnosis and therapy. Arch Intern Med. 1979;139:557–560.
53. England AC III, Weinstein M, Ellner JJ, et al. Two cases of rhinocerebral zygomycosis (mucormycosis) with common epidemiologic and environmental features. Am Rev Respir Dis. 1981;124:497–498.
54. Abedi E, Sismanis A, Choi K, et al. Twenty-five years' experience treating cerebro-rhino-orbital mucormycosis. Laryngoscope. 1984;94:1060–1062.
55. Morduchowicz G, Shmueli D, Shapira Z, et al. Rhinocerebral mucormycosis in renal transplant recipients: Report of three cases and review of the literature. Rev Infect Dis. 1986;8:441–446.
56. Torre Cisneros J, Kusne S, Martin M, et al. Rhinocerebral mucormycosis after liver transplantation. Transplant Sci. 1992;2:63–64.
57. Berthier M, Palmieri O, Lylyk P, et al. Rhino-orbital phycomycosis complicated by cerebral abscess. Neuroradiology. 1982;22:221–224.
58. Price DL, Wolpow ER, Richardson EP Jr. Intracranial phycomycosis: A clinicopathological and radiological study. J Neurol Sci. 1971;14:359–375.
59. Lowe JT Jr, Hudson WR. Rhinocerebral phycomycosis and internal carotid artery thrombosis. Arch Otolaryngol. 1975;101:100–103.
60. Lazo A, Wilner HI, Metes JJ. Craniofacial mucormycosis. Computed tomographic and angiographic findings in two cases. Radiology. 1981;139:623–626.
61. Greenberg MR, Lippman SM, Grinnell VS, et al. Computed tomographic findings in orbital *Mucor.* West J Med. 1985;143:102–103.
62. Boelaert JR, Vergauwe PL, Vandepitte JM. Mucormycosis infection in dialysis patients. Ann Intern Med. 1987;107:782–783.
63. McNab A, McKelvie P. Iron overload is a risk factor for zygomycosis. Arch Ophthalmol. 1997;115:919–921.
64. Gaziev D, Baronciani D, Galimberti M, et al. Mucormycosis after bone marrow transplantation: Report of four cases in thalassemia and review of the literature. Bone Marrow Transplant. 1996;17:409–414.
65. Windus DW, Stokes TJ, Julian BA, et al. Fatal *Rhizopus* infections in hemodialysis patients receiving deferoxamine. Ann Intern Med. 1987;107:678–680.
66. Kaneko T, Abe F, Ito M, et al. Intestinal mucormycosis in a hemodialysis patient treated with desferrioxamine. Acta Pathol Jpn. 1991;41:561–566.
67. Rex JH, Ginsberg AM, Fries LF, et al. *Cunninghamella bertholletiae* infection associated with deferoxamine therapy. Rev Infect Dis. 1988;10:1187–1194.
68. Finn DG, Farmer JC Jr. Chronic mucormycosis. Laryngoscope. 1982;92:761–763.
69. Ferstenfeld JE, Cohen SH, Rose HD, et al. Chronic rhinocerebral phycomycosis in association with diabetes. Postgrad Med J. 1977;53:337–342.
70. Harrison AR, Wirtschafter JD. Ocular neuromyotonia in a patient with cavernous sinus thrombosis secondary to mucormycosis. Am J Ophthalmol. 1997;124:122–123.
71. Harada M, Manabe T, Yamashita K, et al. Pulmonary mucormycosis with fatal massive hemoptysis. Acta Pathol Jpn. 1992;42:49–55.
72. Watts WJ. Bronchopleural fistula followed by massive fatal hemoptysis in a patient with pulmonary mucormycosis: A case report. Arch Intern Med. 1983;143:1029–1030.
73. Tedder M, Spratt JA, Anstadt MP, et al. Pulmonary mucormycosis: Results of medical and surgical therapy. Ann Thorac Surg. 1994;57:1044–1050.
74. McAdams HP, Rosado de Christenson M, Strollo DC, Patz EF Jr. Pulmonary mucormycosis: Radiologic findings in 32 cases. Am J Radiol. 1997;168:1541–1548.

75. Gale AM, Kleitsch WP. Solitary pulmonary nodule due to phycomycosis (mucormycosis). Chest. 1972;62:752–755.
76. Matsushima T, Soejima R, Nakashima T. Solitary pulmonary nodule caused by phycomycosis in a patient without obvious predisposing factors. Thorax. 1980;35:877–878.
77. Butala A, Shah B, Cho YT, Schmidt FJ. Isolated pulmonary mucormycosis in an apparently normal host: A case report. J Natl Med Assoc. 1995;87:572–574.
78. Loevner LA, Andrews JC, Francis IR. Multiple mycotic pulmonary artery aneurysms: A complication of invasive mucormycosis. Am J Radiol. 1992;158:761–762.
79. Brown RB, Johnson JH, Kessinger JM, et al. Bronchovascular mucormycosis in the diabetic: An urgent surgical problem. Ann Thorac Surg. 1992;53:854–855.
80. Coffey MJ, Fantone J III, Stirling MC, et al. Pseudoaneurysm of pulmonary artery in mucormycosis: Radiographic characteristics and management. Am Rev Respir Dis. 1992;145:1487–1490.
81. Aderka A, Sidi Y, Garfinkel D, et al. Roentgenologically invisible mucormycosis pneumonia. Respiration. 1983;44:158–160.
82. Rothstein RD, Simon GL. Subacute pulmonary mucormycosis. J Med Vet Mycol. 1986;24:391–394.
83. Wirth F, Perry R, Eskenazi A, et al. Cutaneous mucormycosis with subsequent visceral dissemination in a child with neutropenia: A case report and review of the pediatric literature. J Am Acad Dermatol. 1996;35:336–341.
84. Jain JK, Markowitz A, Khilanani PV, et al. Case report: Localized mucormycosis following intramuscular corticosteroid. Case report and review of the literature. Am J Med Sci. 1978;275:209–216.
85. Rothburn MM, Chambers DK, Roberts C, et al. Cutaneous mucormycosis: A rare cause of leg ulceration. J Infect. 1986;13:175–178.
86. Costa AR, Porto E, Tayah M, et al. Subcutaneous mucormycosis caused by *Mucor hiemalis* Wehmer f. luteus (Linnemann) Schipper 1973. Mycoses. 1990;33:241–246.
87. Hicks WL Jr, Nowels K, Troxel J. Primary cutaneous mucormycosis. Am J Otolaryngol. 1995;16:265–268.
88. Paparello SF, Parry RL, MacGillivray DC, et al. Hospital-acquired wound mucormycosis. Clin Infect Dis. 1992;14:350–352.
89. Vainrub B, Macareno H, Mandel S, et al. Wound zygomycosis (mucormycosis) in otherwise healthy adults. Am J Med. 1988;84:546–548.
90. Rabin ER, Lundberg GD, Mitchell ET. Mucormycosis in severely burned patients: Report of two cases with extensive destruction of the face and nasal cavity. N Engl J Med. 1961;264:1286–1289.
91. Tanphaichitr VS, Chaiprasert A, Suvatte V, et al. Subcutaneous mucormycosis caused by *Saksenaea vasiformis* in a thalassaemic child: First case report in Thailand. Mycoses. 1990;33:303–309.
92. Prevoo RLMA, Starink TM, de Haan P. Primary cutaneous mucormycosis in a healthy young girl. J Am Acad Dermatol. 1991;24:882–885.
93. Winkler S, Susani S, Willinger B, et al. Gastric mucormycosis due to *Rhizopus oryzae* in a renal transplant recipient. J Clin Microbiol. 1996;34:2585–2587.
94. Martinez EJ, Cancio MR, Sinnott JT IV, et al. Nonfatal gastric mucormycosis in a renal transplant recipient. South Med J. 1997;90:341–344.
95. Thomson SR, Bade PG, Taams M, Chrystal V. Gastrointestinal mucormycosis. Br J Surg. 1991;78:952–954.
96. Ignelzi RJ, VanderArk GD. Cerebral mucormycosis following open head trauma: Case report. J Neurosurg. 1975;42:593–596.
97. Hameroff SB, Eckholdt JW, Lindenberg R. Cerebral phycomycosis in a heroin addict. Neurology. 1970;20:261–265.
98. Pierce PF Jr, Soloman SL, Kaufman L, et al. Zygomycetes brain abscesses in narcotic addicts with serological diagnosis. JAMA. 1982;248:2881–2882.
99. Woods KF, Hanna BJ. Brain stem mucormycosis in a narcotic addict with eventual recovery. Am J Med. 1986;80:126–128.
100. Bachor R, Baczako K, Kern W. Isolated cerebral mucormycosis in a patient with leukemia. Mykosen. 1986;29:497–501.
101. Watson DF, Stern BJ, Levin ML, et al. Isolated cerebral phycomycosis presenting as focal encephalitis. Arch Neurol. 1985;42:922–923.
102. Cuadrado LM, Guerrero A, Lopez Garcia Asenjo JA, et al. Cerebral mucormycosis in two cases of acquired immunodeficiency syndrome. Arch Neurol. 1988;45:109–111.
103. Virmani R, Connor D, McAllister HA. A report of five patients and review of 14 previously reported cases. Am J Clin Pathol. 1982;78:42–47.
104. Merchant RK, Louria B, Geisler PH, et al. Fungal endocarditis: Review of the literature and report of three cases. Ann Intern Med. 1958;48:242–266.
105. Khica GJ, Berroya RB, Escano FB, et al. Mucormycosis in a mitral prosthesis. J Thorac Cardiovasc Surg. 1972;63:903–905.
106. Tuder RM. Myocardial infarct in disseminated mucormycosis: Case report with special emphasis on the pathogenic mechanisms. Mycopathologia. 1985;89:81–88.
107. Echols RM, Selinger DS, Hallowell C, et al. *Rhizopus* osteomyelitis: A case report and review. Am J Med. 1979;66:141–145.
108. Gussen R, Canalis RF. Mucormycosis of the temporal bone. Ann Otol Rhinol Laryngol. 1982;91:27–32.
109. Maliwan N, Reyes CV, Rippon JW. Osteomyelitis secondary to cutaneous mucormycosis: Report of a case and a review of the literature. Am J Dermatopathol. 1984;6:479–481.
110. Brown OE, Finn R. Mucormycosis of the mandible. J Oral Maxillofac Surg. 1986;44:132–136.
111. Pierce PF, Wood MB, Roberts GD Jr, et al. *Saksenaea vasiformis* osteomyelitis. J Clin Microbiol. 1987;25:933–935.
112. Davila R, Moser SA, Grosso LE. Renal mucormycosis: A case report and review of the literature. J Urol. 1991;145:1242–1244.
113. Axelrod P, Kwon-Chung KJ, Frawley P, et al. Chronic cystitis due to *Cokeromyces recurvatus:* A case report. J Infect Dis. 1987;155:1062–1064.
114. Oberle AD, Penn RL. Nosocomial invasive *Saksenaea vasiformis* infection. Am J Clin Pathol. 1983;80:885–888.
115. Leong ASY. Granulomatous mediastinitis due to *Rhizopus* species. Am J Clin Pathol. 1978;70:103–107.
116. Connor BA, Anderson RJ, Smith JW. Mucor mediastinitis. Chest. 1979;75:524–526.
117. Andrews DR, Allan A, Larbalestier RI. Tracheal mucormycosis. Ann Thorac Surg. 1997;63:230–232.
118. Jones PG, Gilman RM, Medeiros AA, et al. Focal intracranial mucormycosis presenting as chronic meningitis. JAMA. 1981;246:2063–2064.
119. Helenglass G, Elliott JA, Lucie NP. An unusual presentation of opportunistic mucormycosis. BMJ. 1981;282:108–109.
120. Caraveo J, Trowbridge AA, Amaral BW, et al. Bone marrow necrosis associated with a mucor infection. Am J Med. 1977;62:404–408.
121. Goldstein MF, Dvorin DJ, Dunsky EH, et al. Allergic *Rhizomucor* sinusitis. J Allergy Clin Immunol. 1992;90:394–404.
122. Levy SA, Schmitt KW, Kaufman L. Systemic zygomycosis diagnosed by fine needle aspiration and confirmed with enzyme immunoassay. Chest. 1986;89:146–148.
123. Wysong DR, Waldorf AR. Electrophoretic and immunoblot analyses of *Rhizopus arrhizus* antigens. J Clin Microbiol. 1987;25:358–363.
124. Strasser MD, Kennedy RJ, Adam RD. Rhinocerebral mucormycosis: Therapy with amphotericin B lipid complex. Arch Intern Med. 1996;156:337–339.
125. Munckhof W, Jones R, Tosolini FA, et al. Cure of *Rhizopus* sinusitis in a liver transplant recipient with liposomal amphotericin B. Clin Infect Dis. 1993;16:183.
126. Ericsson M, Anniko M, Gustafsson H, et al. A case of chronic progressive rhinocerebral mucormycosis treated with liposomal amphotericin B and surgery. Clin Infect Dis. 1993;16:585–586.
127. Barnert J, Behr W, Reich H. An amphotericin B–resistant case of rhinocerebral mucormycosis. Infection. 1985;13:134–136.
128. Goldani LZ, Sugar AM. Treatment of murine pulmonary mucormycosis with SCH 42427, a broad spectrum triazole antifungal drug. J Antimicrob Chemother. 1994;33:369–372.
129. Christenson JC, Shalit I, Welch DF, et al. Synergistic action of amphotericin B and rifampin against *Rhizopus* species. Antimicrob Agents Chemother. 1987;31:1775–1778.
130. Eng RHK, Person A, Mangura C, et al. Susceptibility of zygomycetes to amphotericin B, miconazole, and ketoconazole. Antimicrob Agents Chemother. 1981;20:688–690.
131. Fukushima T, Sumazaki R, Shibasaki M, et al. Successful treatment of invasive thoracopulmonary mucormycosis in a patient with acute lymphoblastic leukemia. Cancer. 1995;76:895–899.
132. Bogard BN. Pulmonary mucormycosis. N Engl J Med. 1972;286:606.
133. Hauch TW. Pulmonary mucormycosis: Another cure. Chest. 1977;72:92–93.
134. Brown JF Jr, Gottlieb LS, McCormick RA. Pulmonary and rhinocerebral mucormycosis: Successful outcome with amphotericin B and griseofulvin therapy. Arch Intern Med. 1977;137:936–938.
135. Langford JD, McCartney DL, Wang RC. Frozen section–guided surgical debridement for management of rhino-orbital mucormycosis. Am J Ophthalmol. 1997;124:265–267.
136. Henriquez M, Levy R, Raja RM, et al. Mucormycosis in a renal transplant recipient with successful outcome. JAMA. 1979;242:1397–1399.
137. Rosenberger RS, West BC, King JW. Case report: Survival from sino-orbital mucormycosis due to *Rhizopus rhizopodiformis.* Am J Med Sci. 1983;286:25–30.
138. Smith JL, Stevens DA. Survival in cerebro-rhino-orbital zygomycosis and cavernous sinus thrombosis with combined therapy. South Med J. 1986;79:501–504.
139. West BC, Kwon-Chung KJ, King JW, et al. Inguinal abscess caused by *Rhizopus rhizopodiformis:* Successful treatment with surgery and amphotericin B. J Clin Microbiol. 1983;18:1384–1387.
140. Hamill R, Oney LA, Crane LR. Successful therapy for rhinocerebral mucormycosis with associated bilateral brain abscesses. Arch Intern Med. 1983;143:581–583.
141. Breiman A, Sadowsky D, Friedman J. Mucormycosis: Discussion and report of a case involving the maxillary sinus. Oral Surg Oral Med Oral Pathol. 1981;52:375–378.
142. Rakover Y, Vered I, Garzuzi H, et al. Rhinocerebral phycomycosis: Combined approach therapy. Case Report. J Laryngol Otol. 1985;99:1279–1280.
143. Kohn R, Hepler R. Management of limited rhino-orbital mucormycosis without exenteration. Ophthalmology. 1985;92:1440–1444.
144. Kaplan AL, Huerta AR, Chiou SJ. Rhinocerebral mucormycosis. West J Med. 1981;135:326–329.
145. de la Paz MA, Patrinely JR, Marines HM, et al. Adjunctive hyperbaric oxygen in the treatment of bilateral cerebro-rhino-orbital mucormycosis. Am J Ophthalmol. 1992;114:208–211.
146. Ferguson BJ, Mitchell TG, Moon R, et al. Adjunctive hyperbaric oxygen for treatment of rhinocerebral mucormycosis. Rev Infect Dis. 1988;10:551–559.
147. Bribetz AR, Chuang MT, Burrows L, et al. *Rhizopus* lung abscess in renal transplant patient successfully treated by lobectomy. Chest. 1980;77:102–104.
148. Boelaert JR, VanCutsem J, deLocht M, et al. Deferoxamine augments growth and pathogenicity of *Rhizopus,* while hydroxypyridinone chelators have no effect. Kidney Int. 1994;45:667–671.

149. Walsh TJ, Renshaw G, Andrews J, et al. Invasive zygomycosis due to *Conidiobolus incongruus.* Clin Infect Dis. 1994;19:423–430.
150. Nathan MD Jr, Keller AR, Lerner CJ, et al. Entomophthorales infection of the maxillofacial region. Laryngoscope. 1982;92:767–769.
151. Dworzack DL, Pollock AS, Hodges GR, et al. Zygomycosis of the maxillary sinus and palate caused by *Basidiobolus haptosporus.* Arch Intern Med. 1978;138:1274–1276.
152. Akpunonu BE, Ansel G, Karurich JD, et al. Zygomycosis mimicking paranasal malignancy. Am J Trop Med Hyg. 1991;45:390–398.
153. Segura JJ, Gonzalez K, Berrocal J, et al. Rhinoentomophthoramycosis: Report of the first two cases observed in Costa Rica (Central America), and review of the literature. Am J Trop Med Hyg. 1981;30:1078–1084.
154. Davis SR, Ellis DH, Goldwater P, et al. First human culture-proven Australian case of entomophthoromycosis caused by *Basidiobolus ranarum.* J Med Vet Mycol. 1994;32:225–230.
155. Greer DL, Friedman L. Studies on the genus *Basidiobolus* with reclassification on the species pathogenic for man. Sabouraudia. 1966;4:231–241.
156. Okafor JI, Testrake D, Mushinsky HR, et al. A *Basidiobolus* sp. and its association with reptiles and amphibians in Southern Florida. Sabouraudia. 1984;22:47–51.
157. Zahari P, Hirst RG, Shipton WA, et al. The origin and pathogenicity of *Basidiobolus* species in northern Australia. J Med Vet Mycol. 1990;28:461–468.
158. Martinson FD. Clinical epidemiological and therapeutic aspects of entomophthoramycosis. Ann Soc Belg Med Trop. 1972;52:329–342.
159. Herstoff JK, Bogaars H, McDonald CJ. Rhinophycomycosis entomophtorae. Arch Dermatol. 1978;114:1674–1678.
160. Echetebu CO, Ononogbu IC. Extracellular lipase and proteinase of *Basidiobolus haptosporus:* Possible role in subcutaneous mycosis. Mycopathologia. 1982;80:171–177.
161. Antonelli M, Vignetti P, Dahir M, et al. Entomophthoramycosis due to *Basidiobolus* in Somalia. Trans R Soc Trop Med Hyg. 1987;81:186–187.
162. Kamalam A, Thambiah AS. Muscle invasion by *Basidiobolus haptosporus.* Sabouraudia. 1984;22:273–237.
163. Schmidt JR, Howard RJ, Chen JL, et al. First culture-proven gastrointestinal entomophthoromycosis in the United States: A case report and review of the literature. Mycopathologia. 1986;95:101–104.
164. Fournier S, Dupont B, Begue P, et al. Infection rhino-faciale a *Conidiobolus coronatus* avec lyse osseuse et adénomégalie: Difficultés thérapeutiques. J Mycol Méd. 1995;5(Suppl 1):35–39.
165. Kaufman L, Mendoza L, Standard PG. Immunodiffusion test for serodiagnosing subcutaneous zygomycosis. J Clin Microbiol. 1990;28:1887–1890.
166. Bittencourt AL, Serra G, Sadigursky M, et al. Subcutaneous zygomycosis caused by *Basidiobolus haptosporus:* Presentation of a case mimicking Burkitt's lymphoma. Am J Trop Med Hyg. 1982;31:370–373.
167. Taylor GD, Sekhon AS, Tyrrell DLJ, et al. Rhinofacial zygomycosis caused by *Conidiobolus coronatus:* A case report including in vitro sensitivity to antimycotic agents. Am J Trop Med Hyg. 1987;36:398–401.
168. Yangco BG, Okafor JI, TeStrake D. In vitro susceptibilities of human and wild-type isolates of *Basidiobolus* and *Conidiobolus* species. Antimicrob Agents Chemother. 1984;25:413–416.
169. Chauvin JL, Drouhet E, Dupont B. Nouveau cas de rhino-entomophthoramycose: Gueiron par le ketoconazole. Ann Otolaryngol (Paris). 1982;99:563–568.
170. Costa AR, Porto E, Pegas JRP, et al. Rhinofacial zygomycosis caused by *Conidiobolum* [sic] *coronatus.* A case report. Mycopathologia. 1991;115:1–8.
171. Gugnani HC. Fluconazole in the therapy of tropical deep mycoses. Abstracts of the XII Congress of the International Society for Human and Animal Mycology, PO2.59, Adelaide, Australia, March 1994.
172. Shaoxi W, Ningru G, Guixiz L, et al. Basidiobolomycosis in China successfully treated with itraconazole. J Mycol Méd. 1997;7:40–42.
173. Howard DH. An introduction to the taxonomy and nomenclature of zoopathogenic fungi. In: Howard DH, ed. Fungi Pathogenic for Humans and Animals: Part A, Biology. New York: Marcel Dekker; 1983:3–7.

Chapter 250

Sporothrix schenckii

JOHN H. REX
PABLO C. OKHUYSEN

Sporotrichosis is an endemic fungal infection caused by *Sporothrix schenckii.* Infection begins when the fungus is inoculated into a site of skin injury and produces an ulcerated, verrucous, or erythematous nodule, sometimes associated with local lymphatic spread. On rare occasion the fungus is inhaled and causes a granulomatous pneumonitis that often cavitates and produces a clinical pattern very similar to that of tuberculosis. The fungus may also disseminate hematogenously and cause isolated osteoarticular, central nervous system, or ocular lesions in healthy hosts or widespread, multifocal disease in immunosuppressed hosts.

MYCOLOGY

S. schenckii is a dimorphic fungus that exists in a hyphal form in vitro at temperatures lower than 37°C. Colonies are initially white but gradually become brown to black because of the production of pigmented conidia. In vivo or at 37°C on rich media such as brain-heart infusion, the organism converts to an oval- or cigar-shaped yeast. Along with the characteristic morphology of the sporulating mold, identification is based on demonstration of this conversion to a yeast form. The variety *S. schenckii* var. *luriei* has rarely been isolated from humans and differs by producing a variety of unusual forms in vivo.[1] Although nodular pulmonary lesions most likely caused by *Sporothrix cyanescens* were recently described in a heart transplant patient,[2] isolation of this low-virulence organism, even from skin or blood, is usually thought to represent skin contamination.[3]

EPIDEMIOLOGY

Sporotrichosis has been reported from locations around the globe, but most case reports come from the tropical and subtropical regions of the Americas.[4, 5] *S. schenckii* is most often isolated from soil, plants, or plant products such as straw and wood, and activities that involve exposure to these materials are frequently reported in cases of sporotrichosis. Epidemics caused by exposure to mine timbers, thorned plants (especially roses), hay, straw, sphagnum moss, and armadillos have all been described.[4, 6] Because most cases appear to be due to occupational or avocational exposure to these materials, typically in the form of gardening or farming, patients with suggestive syndromes should be asked about such activities. Cases of animal-to-human transmission involving squirrels, horses, dogs, cats, pigs, mules, and birds have been described,[7, 8] as well as one case in which sporotrichosis was apparently transmitted from the infected cheek of a mother to her infant.[9]

CLINICAL SYNDROMES

Infections due to *S. schenckii* can be broken down into several syndromes. The cutaneous forms are the most common.

Cutaneous Sporotrichosis

Cutaneous disease arises at sites of minor trauma and inoculation of the fungus into the skin. The initial lesion is most often on the distal end of an extremity, but almost any site may be involved, including such central locations as the nose and the ocular adnexa.[10, 11] This preference for cooler parts of the body corresponds to the known intolerance of some strains of *S. schenckii* to 37°C.[12] Initial lesions are papulonodular, are often erythematous, and range in size from a few millimeters to 2 to 4 cm. The lesions may be smooth or verrucous, and they often ulcerate and form raised erythematous borders.[10, 13, 14] Secondary lesions may develop proximally along lymphatic channels—these secondary lesions evolve in the same fashion as the primary lesion (Fig. 250–1). Secondary lesions do not usually involve a lymph node, although lymphadenopathy may develop. The lesions are typically painless, even after they ulcerate. The fixed, or plaque, form of sporotrichosis differs by not demonstrating any tendency to spread locally. Although spontaneous resolution of fixed sporotrichosis has been described,[10] the lesions of sporotrichosis usually wax and wane over months to years. The patient will not

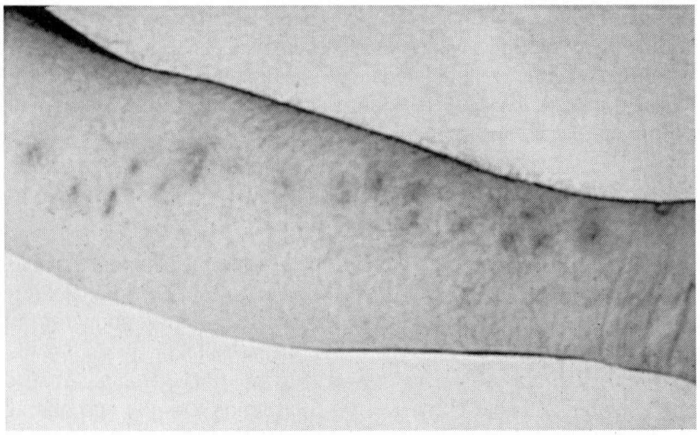

FIGURE 250–1. Cutaneous sporotrichosis. Lymphangitic spread of painless nodules is common. (Courtesy of Dr. Ronald Rapini, Houston, Tex.)

have systemic symptoms, and laboratory examinations will be normal.

Fixed sporotrichosis may be confused with bacterial pyoderma, foreign body granuloma, inflammatory dermatophyte infections (Majocchi's granuloma), blastomycosis, chromoblastomycosis, lobomycosis, and cutaneous tuberculosis. The nodular lymphangitis pattern of lymphocutaneous sporotrichosis may also be seen with nocardiosis, leishmaniasis, and nontuberculous mycobacterial infections, especially those caused by *Mycobacterium kansasii* and *Mycobacterium marinum*. The ulceroglandular form of tularemia may also be manifested as a nodular lymphangitis, but it is usually accompanied by systemic symptoms. Much less often, infections with such diverse organisms as *Blastomyces dermatitidis*, *Coccidioides immitis*, *Cryptococcus neoformans*, *Staphylococcus aureus*, *Streptococcus pyogenes*, *Burkholderia pseudomallei*, *Bacillus anthracis*, and vaccinia virus may also be characterized by nodular lesions that may resemble nodular lymphangitis.[15] Cultures of the drainage from skin lesions are occasionally helpful, but culture of biopsy material is preferred and is diagnostic when positive. Microscopic examination will reveal pyogranulomas in the mid and upper dermis, but examination of multiple sections may be required to demonstrate the organism.[16]

Extracutaneous Sporotrichosis

Osteoarticular involvement is the most common form of extracutaneous sporotrichosis.[17] The major joints of the extremities (hand, elbow, ankle, and knee) are involved; the hip, shoulder, and spine are not.[18] Most patients present with involvement of a single joint without previously having had sporotrichosis at any other site. The joint is swollen and painful on motion, an effusion is present, and a sinus tract may develop. The overlying skin may or may not be erythematous. Systemic symptoms are minimal, and other than elevation of the erythrocyte sedimentation rate, laboratory examinations are unrevealing. Untreated, other joints may become involved. Tenosynovitis associated with carpal tunnel syndrome or nerve entrapment has been reported.[19, 20] The radiologic changes of osteomyelitis develop slowly and include loss of articular cartilage, periosteal reaction, and periarticular osteopenia and cystic changes. Failure to consider the diagnosis has resulted in an average 25-month delay before diagnosis.[21] Repeated culture of fluid from joint aspiration, as well as culture and microscopic examination of tissue from synovial biopsies, is often required to make the diagnosis. Differential considerations include pigmented villonodular synovitis, tuberculosis, gout, and rheumatoid arthritis.

Pulmonary sporotrichosis is well described.[22] The typical patient is a 30- to 60-year-old male. Approximately one third of such patients are alcoholic; one third have another concomitant medical illness such as pulmonary tuberculosis, diabetes mellitus, sarcoidosis, or steroid use; and one third are apparently normal. Patients are occasionally asymptomatic but usually have a productive cough, low-grade fever, or weight loss. Other than elevation of the erythrocyte sedimentation rate, laboratory abnormalities are minimal. Chest radiographs reveal unilateral or bilateral cavitary lesions, usually with an associated parenchymal infiltrate (Fig. 250–2). Pleural effusion and hilar lymphadenopathy are occasionally noted. Gram stain or cytologic examination of sputum or bronchial washings will sometimes reveal characteristic yeast,[23] and sputum culture will usually yield the organism. With some patients, however, repeated cultures and long-term follow-up are necessary to make the diagnosis.[24] Untreated, the cavities of pulmonary sporotrichosis gradually enlarge and produce progressive pulmonary dysfunction. A single case of spontaneous resolution of noncavitary infection has been reported.[25] The differential diagnosis includes mycobacterial infections (*Mycobacterium tuberculosis* and the atypical mycobacteria), histoplasmosis, and coccidioidomycosis.

Meningitis caused by *S. schenckii* has been described in a small number of patients. These patients present with an indolent meningitis. Cerebrospinal fluid analysis demonstrates a lymphocytic pleocytosis, elevated protein levels, and hypoglycorrhachia. Culture of cerebrospinal fluid may be negative, and repeated cultures of large volumes of cerebrospinal fluid or serologic studies may be required to make the diagnosis.[26] The differential diagnosis is broad and includes tuberculosis, cryptococcosis, and histoplasmosis.

Infections of a variety of other sites have been reported but are uncommon. Involvement of the ocular adnexa has been described sometimes with spread to the eye.[11] Endophthalmitis may even occur without prior trauma or other evidence of sporotrichosis.[27] Cases of isolated involvement of the sinuses, kidney, testes, and epididymis have also been reported.[17, 28]

Multifocal Extracutaneous Sporotrichosis

In otherwise healthy patients with extracutaneous sporotrichosis, the lesions are generally restricted to a single site and are only locally

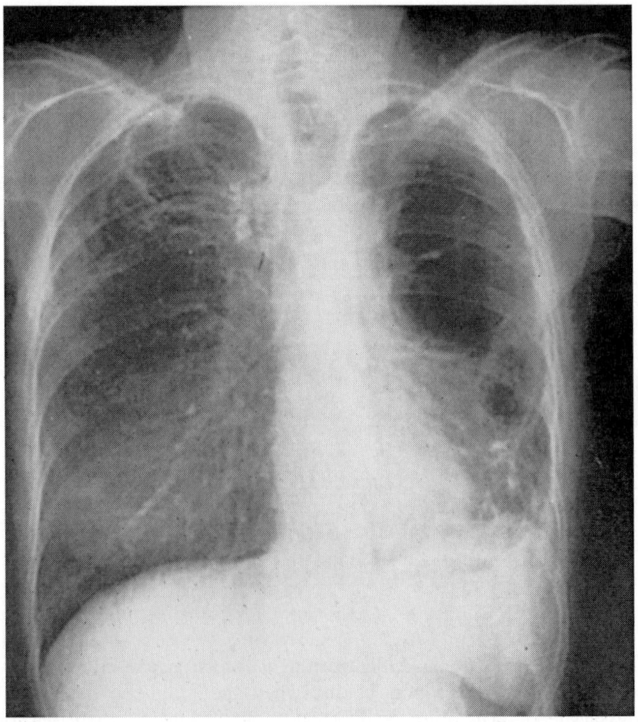

FIGURE 250–2. Chest roentgenogram demonstrating extensive bilateral cavitation due to sporotrichosis.

progressive. Occasionally a patient with osteoarticular sporotrichosis will have involvement of several joints, but the clinical picture is otherwise identical to that of patients with involvement of only a single joint. A much smaller group of patients, on the other hand, present with weight loss and variable low-grade fever and often have several widely scattered cutaneous lesions. Mild anemia, leukocytosis, and elevation of the erythrocyte sedimentation rate may be present. Osteolytic bone lesions and arthritis are common, and spread to the palate, eyes, and central nervous system may develop.[17, 29] Noncavitary lung lesions may also be seen. Untreated infection is ultimately fatal. Patients with this form of sporotrichosis almost always have some form of immunosuppression, commonly hematologic malignancy[17, 29] or human immunodeficiency virus (HIV) infection (see later). Cultures of skin lesions and joints are usually positive, whereas blood and bone marrow cultures are occasionally positive. Immunosuppressed patients who present with what appears to be simple cutaneous sporotrichosis should be carefully examined for other sites of infection and a technetium pyrophosphate bone scan performed.

CLINICAL MANIFESTATIONS OF SPOROTRICHOSIS IN PATIENTS INFECTED WITH HUMAN IMMUNODEFICIENCY VIRUS

As with other infections, infection with HIV predisposes to invasive, atypical, or disseminated manifestations of sporotrichosis. When CD4 counts are relatively well preserved, localized infection may follow direct cutaneous inoculation in a pattern analogous to that in immunocompetent patients.[30] However, widespread lymphocutaneous sporotrichosis or multifocal extracutaneous disease may be seen in patients with more advanced HIV infection. In a recent review of patients with acquired immunodeficiency syndrome (AIDS) and disseminated sporotrichosis,[31] all subjects were found to have less than 200 $CD4^{+}T$ cells $\times 10^6$/liter. The skin lesions may be widespread and ulcerative[32] and associated with arthritis.[33] Sporotrichosis may also be manifested as multifocal tenosynovitis and arthritis with or without overt cutaneous disease or systemic dissemination and may thus resemble disseminated gonococcal infection or seronegative spondyloarthropathies such as Reiter's syndrome or psoriatic arthritis (Fig. 250–3), which are seen with a higher frequency in the setting of AIDS.[34] Widespread visceral dissemination also occurs, as evidenced by reports of meningitis with parenchymal brain lesions[31, 35]; lung abscess, liver, and spleen involvement[36]; endophthalmitis[33, 37]; and fungemia with spread to the esophagus, colon, testes, bone marrow, and lymph nodes.[33] Sinusitis with invasion of contiguous bone and soft tissue has also been described,[38] which emphasizes the potential for the respiratory tract as the initial focus of infection in HIV-infected patients.

DIAGNOSIS

Diagnosis is best made by culture of the affected site, although repeated attempts at culture may have to be made. A positive culture from any site is ordinarily diagnostic of infection, although a case of saprophytic involvement of the respiratory tract has been described.[39] A positive blood culture strongly suggests the multifocal form of sporotrichosis seen in immunocompromised hosts, although newer, more sensitive blood culture systems such as the lysis-centrifugation system may detect fungemia in nonimmunocompromised patients.[40] Serologic techniques have been described and may be useful in such obscure forms of sporotrichosis as meningitis, but these techniques are confounded by the presence of antibody in individuals without evidence of sporotrichosis.[26, 41] No standard method of serologic testing is available.

Examination of biopsy specimens reveals a pyogranulomatous response and is diagnostic if characteristic 1- to 3-μm by 3- to 10-μm cigar-shaped yeast forms are seen. Unfortunately, the yeast may be difficult to detect unless multiple sections are examined,[16] although lesions from immunocompromised hosts may contain numerous yeasts (Fig. 250–4). In addition, *S. schenckii* often assumes a more rounded tissue form, which makes biopsy suggestive but not diagnostic. The organisms may be surrounded by a stellate, periodic acid–Schiff–positive eosinophilic material known as an asteroid body. In the brain or eye, a capsule has sometimes been demonstrable around the yeastlike cells.

As with other immunosuppressed patients, individuals with advanced AIDS may have a high fungal load that results in positive

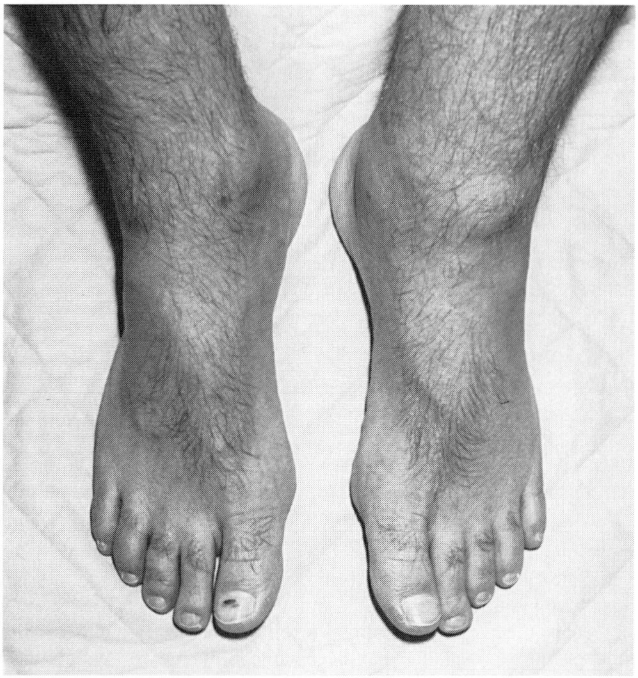

FIGURE 250–3. Extensive multifocal sporotrichosis with tenosynovitis of the toes, arthritis of the ankles, and associated lymphedema in a patient with advanced acquired immunodeficiency syndrome. This patient also had tenosynovitis of the wrists and hands along with arthritis of the wrists and knees.

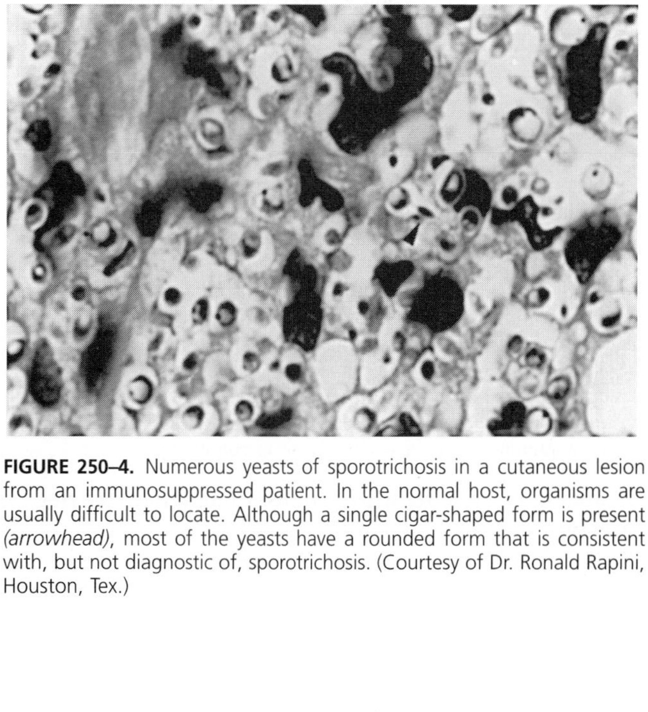

FIGURE 250–4. Numerous yeasts of sporotrichosis in a cutaneous lesion from an immunosuppressed patient. In the normal host, organisms are usually difficult to locate. Although a single cigar-shaped form is present *(arrowhead)*, most of the yeasts have a rounded form that is consistent with, but not diagnostic of, sporotrichosis. (Courtesy of Dr. Ronald Rapini, Houston, Tex.)

smears and cultures.[23] Skin biopsy may reveal fungal elements with a limited inflammatory response, which should prompt the clinician to initiate a search for a systemic immunodeficiency.[42]

THERAPY

Iodides are effective, inexpensive therapy for cutaneous sporotrichosis. A saturated solution of potassium iodide (SSKI) is prescribed, and therapy is begun with 5 to 10 drops taken orally three times per day. The dose is gradually advanced to 25 to 40 drops three times daily (for children) or 40 to 50 drops three times daily (for adults). SSKI has a bitter taste and is made more palatable by taking it in milk, juice, or a carbonated beverage. Side effects include nausea, anorexia, diarrhea, parotid or lacrimal gland enlargement, and an acneiform rash. These side effects will remit with reduction of the dose of SSKI or temporary cessation of therapy. Therapy at the maximal tolerated dose should be continued until the cutaneous lesions have resolved, a process that usually takes 6 to 12 weeks. Some patients are allergic to iodides, and in others, cutaneous disease may respond slowly to iodide therapy or rarely fail to respond at all. Because of the temperature sensitivity of this organism, heat is a useful adjunctive therapy and on occasion has been curative.[43] Ketoconazole has not proved to be very effective, and amphotericin B is too toxic to be used in this setting. Fluconazole has been shown to have some activity,[44, 45] but itraconazole at 100 to 200 mg/day appears more potent and has been quite effective for lymphocutaneous sporotrichosis.[46–48] Either SSKI or itraconazole can be used as initial therapy—selection between the two should weigh the greater cost and potential hepatotoxicity of itraconazole against the bitter taste and inconvenience of SSKI. As with SSKI, therapy with itraconazole usually requires 3 to 6 months to effect a clinical cure. Relapse has been observed on occasion after cessation of therapy. Should relapse develop, anecdotal reports suggest that a repeated, but more prolonged course of therapy will typically produce a permanent cure.

Treatment of extracutaneous sporotrichosis is often difficult. Osteoarticular sporotrichosis will often respond to amphotericin B, and a course of 2 to 2.5 g is curative in approximately two thirds of cases.[21] Relapse is unfortunately common, and such patients may be retreated with a longer course of amphotericin B. Intra-articular amphotericin B is sometimes given, although its role has not been clearly defined. Surgical débridement is often performed, but its utility is also uncertain. SSKI has rarely been reported to be effective, but usually it is not. Among the azole antifungal agents, itraconazole (200 to 400 mg/day) has activity, with ketoconazole (400 to 800 mg/day) and fluconazole (200 to 400 mg/day) appearing less efficacious.[44, 48, 49] Because of lower toxicity than amphotericin B and better efficacy than ketoconazole or fluconazole, itraconazole is appropriate as initial chemotherapy.

If diagnosed before the development of cavities, pulmonary sporotrichosis may be treated with SSKI or amphotericin B.[22] Cure of more advanced disease typically requires pulmonary resection plus a perioperative course of amphotericin B. Treatment failure is often associated with incomplete resection. Data on the use of ketoconazole, fluconazole, or itraconazole in this setting are as yet incomplete—both successes and failures have been reported with each.[22, 48]

S. schenckii meningitis does not consistently respond to amphotericin B, and the addition of 5-fluorocytosine may be warranted. No data on use of the azoles are available. The number of reported cases of involvement of other specific sites is too limited to permit generalization. Extracutaneous sporotrichosis in an immunocompromised host usually responds at least partially to either amphotericin B or itraconazole, although relapse is common.

Treatment of Patients with Acquired Immunodeficiency Syndrome

Therapy for sporotrichosis in patients with AIDS should be tailored to the initial syndrome. Itraconazole appears to be the drug of choice, and individuals with limited cutaneous disease can be treated with 200 mg twice daily. Lifetime suppressive itraconazole therapy should follow initial therapy given the likelihood of relapse and dissemination.[50] Monitoring of itraconazole levels is useful because of the potential for reduced drug absorption resulting from HIV-associated achlorhydria, malabsorption, or diarrhea caused by other opportunistic pathogens. Drug levels may also be altered as a result of drug interactions that interfere with drug metabolism. Levels of 1 to 2 μg/ml as detected by high-performance liquid chromatography are desirable. Although not approved for this indication, the increased bioavailability of the newer itraconazole cyclodextrin suspension is also helpful in achieving high blood levels.

Both anecdotal and published experience suggests that multifocal extracutaneous disease in HIV-infected patients may respond poorly, if at all, to current therapies.[31, 50] Therapy should be initiated with amphotericin B, followed by lifetime suppression with itraconazole. Progression may occur despite amphotericin therapy. Little information exists concerning the use of newer liposomal preparations in this setting. As has been demonstrated for other opportunistic pathogens, the use of potent new combination antiretroviral therapies with protease inhibitors may also assist in clearing the infection.[51]

PROGNOSIS

Cutaneous sporotrichosis responds well to therapy and has an excellent prognosis. Osteoarticular sporotrichosis may require prolonged therapy but is not life threatening. Other forms of extracutaneous sporotrichosis can be difficult to treat and may be associated with substantial morbidity and mortality.

REFERENCES

1. Ajello L, Kaplan W. A new variant of *Sporothrix schenckii*. Mykosen. 1969;12:633–644.
2. Tambini R, Farina C, Fiocchi R, et al. Possible pathogenic role for *Sporothrix cyanescens* isolated from a lung lesion in a heart transplant patient. J Med Vet Mycol. 1996;34:195–198.
3. Sigler L, Harris JL, Dixon DM, et al. Microbiology and potential virulence of *Sporothrix cyanescens*, a fungus rarely isolated from blood and skin. J Clin Microbiol. 1990;28:1009–1015.
4. Travassos LR, Lloyd KO. *Sporothrix schenckii* and related species of *Ceratocystis*. Microbiol Rev. 1980;44:683–721.
5. Restrepo A, Robledo J, Gomez I, et al. Itraconazole therapy in lymphangitic and cutaneous sporotrichosis. Arch Dermatol. 1986;122:413–417.
6. Hajjeh R, McDonnell S, Reef S, et al. Outbreak of sporotrichosis among tree nursery workers. J. Infect Dis. 1997;176:499–504.
7. Saravanakumar PS, Eslami P, Zar FA. Lymphocutaneous sporotrichosis associated with a squirrel bite: Case report and review. Clin Infect Dis. 1996;23:647–648.
8. Reed KD, Moore FM, Geiger GE, et al. Zoonotic transmission of sporotrichosis—case report and review. Clin Infect Dis. 1993;16:384–387.
9. Smith LM. Sporotrichosis: Report of four clinically atypical cases. South Med J. 1945;38:505–515.
10. Bargman HB. Sporotrichosis of the nose with spontaneous cure. Can Med Assoc J. 1981;124:1027.
11. Gordon D. Ocular sporotrichosis. Arch Ophthalmol. 1947;37:56–72.
12. Kwon-Chung KJ. Comparison of isolates of *Sporothrix schenckii* obtained from fixed cutaneous lesions with isolates from other types of lesions. J Infect Dis. 1979;139:424–431.
13. Chandler JW, Kriel RL, Tosh FE. Childhood sporotrichosis. Am J Dis Child. 1968;115:368–372.
14. Lynch PJ, Botero F. Sporotrichosis in children. Am J Dis Child. 1971;122:325–327.
15. Kostman JR, DiNubile MJ. Nodular lymphangitis: A distinctive but often unrecognized syndrome. Ann Intern Med. 1993;118:883–888.
16. Bullpitt P, Weedon D. Sporotrichosis: A review of 39 cases. Pathology. 1978;10:249–256.
17. Wilson DE, Mann JJ, Bennett JE, et al. Clinical features of extracutaneous sporotrichosis. Medicine (Baltimore). 1967;46:265–279.
18. Janes PC, Mann RJ. Extracutaneous sporotrichosis. J. Hand Surg [Am]. 1987;12:441–445.
19. Atdjian M, Granda JL, Ingberg HO, et al. Systemic sporotrichosis polytenosynovitis with median and ulnar nerve entrapment. JAMA. 1980;243:1841–1842.
20. Stratton CW, Lichtenstein KA, Lowenstein SR, Granulomatous tenosynovitis and carpal tunnel syndrome caused by *Sporothrix schenckii*. Am J Med. 1981;71:161–164.

21. Crout JE, Brewer NS, Tompkins RB. Sporotrichosis arthritis: Clinical features in seven patients. Ann Intern Med. 1977;86:294–297.
22. Pluss JL, Opal SM. Pulmonary sporotrichosis: Review of treatment and outcome. Medicine (Baltimore). 1986;65:143–153.
23. Gori S, Lupetti A, Moscato G, et al. Pulmonary sporotrichosis with hyphae in a human immunodeficiency virus–infected patient. A case report. Acta Cytol. 1997;41:519–521.
24. Khan FA, Guarneri JJ, Sierra MF. Primary pulmonary sporotrichosis complicated by perirectal abscess. Am Rev Respir Dis. 1975;112:119–123.
25. Pueringer RJ, Iber C, Deike MA, et al. Spontaneous remission of extensive pulmonary sporotrichosis. Ann Intern Med. 1986;104:366–367.
26. Scott EN, Kaufman L, Brown AC, et al. Serologic studies in the diagnosis and management of meningitis due to *Sporothrix schenckii*. N Engl J Med. 1987;317:935–940.
27. Font RL, Jakobiec FA. Granulomatous necrotizing retinochoroiditis caused by *Sporotrichum schenckii*. Arch Ophthalmol. 1976;94:1513–1519.
28. Friedman SJ, Doyle JA. Extracutaneous sporotrichosis. Int J Dermatol. 1983;22:171–173.
29. Lynch PJ, Voorhees JJ, Harrell ER. Systemic sporotrichosis. Ann Intern Med. 1970;73:23–30.
30. Keiser P, Whittle D. Sporotrichosis in human immunodeficiency virus–infected patients: Report of a case. Rev Infect Dis. 1991;13:1027–1028.
31. Donabedian H, O'Donnell E, Olszewski C, et al. Disseminated cutaneous and meningeal sporotrichosis in an AIDS patient. Diagn Microbiol Infect Dis. 1994;18:111–115.
32. Shaw JC, Levinson W, Montanaro M. Sporotrichosis in the acquired immunodeficiency syndrome. J Am Acad Dermatol. 1989;21:1145–1147.
33. Heller HM, Fuhrer J. Disseminated sporotrichosis in patients with AIDS: Case report and review of the literature. AIDS. 1991;5:1243–1246.
34. Oscherwitz SL, Rinaldi MG. Disseminated sporotrichosis in a patient infected with human immunodeficiency virus. Clin Infect Dis. 1992;15:568–569.
35. Penn CC, Goldstein E, Bartholomew WR. *Sporothrix schenckii* meningitis in a patient with AIDS. Clin Infect Dis. 1992;15:741–743.
36. Lipstein-Kresch E, Isenberg HD, Singer C, et al. Disseminated *Sporothrix schenckii* infection with arthritis in a patient with acquired immunodeficiency syndrome. J Rheumatol. 1985;12:805–808.
37. Kurosawa A, Pollock SC, Collins MP, et al. *Sporothrix schenckii* endophthalmitis in a patient with human immunodeficiency virus infection. Arch Ophthalmol. 1988;106:376–380.
38. Morgan M, Reves R. Invasive sinusitis due to *Sporothrix schenckii* in a patient with AIDS. Clin Infect Dis. 1996;23:1319–1320.
39. Lowenstein M, Markowitz SM, Nottebart HC, et al. Existence of *Sporothrix schenckii* as a pulmonary saprophyte. Chest. 1978;73:419–421.
40. Kosinski RM, Axelrod P, Rex JH, et al. *Sporothrix schenckii* fungemia without disseminated sporotrichosis. J Clin Microbiol. 1992;30:501–503.
41. Blumer SO, Kaufman L, Kaplan W, et al. Comparative evaluation of five serological methods for the diagnosis of sporotrichosis. Appl Microbiol. 1973;26:4–8.
42. Fitzpatrick JE, Eubanks S. Acquired immunodeficiency syndrome presenting as disseminated cutaneous sporotrichosis. Int J Dermatol. 1988;27:406–407.
43. Galiana J, Conti-Díaz IA. Healing effects of heat and a rubefacient on nine cases of sporotrichosis. Sabouraudia. 1963;3:64–71.
44. Kauffman CA, Pappas PG, McKinsey DS, et al. Treatment of lymphocutaneous and visceral sporotrichosis with fluconazole. Clin Infect Dis. 1996;22:46–50.
45. Castro LGM, Belda W, Cucé LC, et al. Successful treatment of sporotrichosis with oral fluconazole: A report of three cases. Br J Dermatol. 1993;128:352–356.
46. Conti Diaz IA, Civila E, Gezuele E, et al. Treatment of human cutaneous sporotrichosis with itraconazole. Mycoses. 1992;35:153–156.
47. Restrepo A. Treatment of tropical mycoses. J Am Acad Dermatol. 1994; 31(Suppl):S91–S102.
48. Sharkey-Mathis PK, Kauffman CA, Graybill JR, et al. Treatment of sporotrichosis with itraconazole. NIAID Mycoses Study Group. Am J Med. 1993;95:279–285.
49. Calhoun DL, Washkin H, White MP, et al. Treatment of systemic sporotrichosis with ketoconazole. Rev Infect Dis. 1991;13:47–51.
50. Kauffman CA. Old and new therapies for sporotrichosis. Clin Infect Dis. 1995;21:981–985.
51. Carr A, Marriott D, Field A, et al. Treatment of HIV-1–associated microsporidiosis and cryptosporidiosis with combination antiretroviral therapy. Lancet. 1998; 351:256–261.

Chapter 251

Agents of Chromomycosis

KENNETH F. WAGNER

Chromomycosis (also called chromoblastomycosis) is a chronic fungal infection that remains localized within cutaneous and subcutaneous tissue. The disease has been encountered on every continent and in all climates, but most cases occur in tropical and subtropical regions. Specimens from the verrucous cauliflower-like lesions demonstrate the fungus as sclerotic bodies, singly or in clusters. These sclerotic bodies separate chromomycosis from other related fungal diseases such as pheohyphomycosis. Histologically, hyperkeratotic pseudoepitheliomatous hyperplasia is seen along with keratolytic microabscess formation in the epidermis. Itraconazole has shown promise as an oral medical therapy for this disease, which is seldom life threatening but causes disfigurement and much discomfort to the patient. New antifungal agents such as voriconazole and the pneumocandins exhibit in vitro activity against the agents of chromomycosis. Future clinical studies will be needed to see whether these new agents have in vivo activity.

ETIOLOGY AND MYCOLOGY

Considerable confusion is apparent in the literature concerning the terminology of fungi that cause chromomycosis. I prefer the nomenclature and inclusion of fungi as suggested by McGinnis (common synonyms are shown in parentheses): *Fonsecaea pedrosoi (Hormodendrum pedrosoi, Phialophora pedrosoi, Rhinocladiella pedrosoi)*; *Fonsecaea compacta (Hormodendrum compactum, Phialophora compacta, Rhinocladiella compacta)*; *Phialophora verrucosa*; *Cladosporium carrionii (Cladophialophora ajelloi)*; *Botryomyces caespitosus*; and *Rhinocladiella aquaspersa (Acrotheca aquaspersa)*.[1] Recently, *Exophiala spinifera* and *Exophiala jeanselmei* have joined the list of etiologic agents of chromomycosis.[2]

In tissue and exudate, all species produce the same type of dark brown cells, which are septate (sclerotic bodies) and occur singly or in small clusters. On culture, all species form heaped-up dark colonies with short aerial hyphae producing a gray to green or brown to black velvety surface. Because most of the commonly isolated agents of chromomycosis grow slowly, cultures should be held at least 4 to 6 weeks. Specific identification of the various causal agents requires an experienced mycologist.

EPIDEMIOLOGY

Chromomycosis occurs worldwide and without racial predisposition, but it is most common in tropical and subtropical areas among barefooted agricultural workers.[3] These cosmopolitan opportunistic pathogens are among the more common fungi found in soil, rotting wood, and decaying vegetation. Traumatic inoculation of fungi into the skin is the main mode of infection. Handling lumber and sitting on wooden planks in Finnish sauna baths have also been implicated as point sources of infection with *F. pedrosoi*.[4] The lower extremities are the most frequently infected sites, with lesions occurring less frequently on the shoulders, chest, trunk, and face. In developed countries such as Japan and Australia, upper body sites predominate.[5, 6] The overwhelming preponderance of infection seen in males has been attributed to males having a greater opportunity for soil contact and predisposition to injury while working.[5] Contrary to this observation is a male-to-female ratio of 1:1.1 in 296 cases of chromomycosis in Japan.[6] Also, in drier climates, where *C. carrionii* is often the etiologic agent, reported series commonly demonstrate a higher incidence in women.[7]

F. pedrosoi is the most commonly isolated agent of chromomycosis throughout the world. *C. carrionii* is the major pathogen in Australia, Venezuela, and South Africa. Only a few cases in the literature have been attributed to *F. compacta*. Transmission has not been documented to occur from human to human or from animals to humans.

CLINICAL MANIFESTATIONS

In 1950, Carrion described five lesion types that appear to follow a relatively specific pattern as the disease progresses from a papule to cicatricial fibrosis: nodules, tumors, plaques, warty lesions, and scarring lesions.[3] The typical verrucous form of chromomycosis appears at a site where traumatic implantation of the fungus has occurred. However, the trauma may have been so long ago that the injury has been forgotten. The primary lesion begins as a small pink scaly papule that may be pruritic. In time (often months to years), a new crop of lesions appear in the same or adjacent areas that are warty, purplish, scaly nodules or can be smooth, firm tumors. Peripheral spread can occur with healing in the center as seen in cutaneous blastomycosis (Fig. 251–1). However, the lesions usually tend to enlarge and become grouped. Older lesions look like cauliflowers. On the warty surface are small ulcerations or "black dots" of hemopurulent material (Fig. 251–2). These lesions can be pruritic and are rarely painful. Satellite lesions may develop through scratching with subsequent autoinoculation or via the lymphatics. Lesions may coalesce and result in a large verrucous mass.

A second type of lesion is the annular, flattened, papular type with a raised active border (Fig. 251–3). Through healing the center becomes scarred. Sometimes, extensive keloid formation is noted in the healing lesions. In advanced cases, extensive fibrosis can cause lymphostasis and marked edema of the involved extremity.

The clinical history will usually reveal that the disease had been present for many years with minimal discomfort to the patient. Medical attention is usually sought because of secondary infection, cosmetic reasons, or lymphedema, which can result in elephantiasis. Fistula formation is not usually seen as in mycetomas or invasion of muscle or bone. In rare cases, hematogenous spread to the brain, lymph nodes, liver, lungs, and other organs has been reported.[6] Invasive *P. verrucosa* has been reported in a bone marrow transplant patient and led to fatal tracheal hemorrhage.[8] A major complication is the development of squamous carcinoma in long-standing lesions.[9]

The differential diagnosis of chromomycosis includes lobomycosis, blastomycosis, yaws, tertiary syphilis, tuberculosis verrucosa cutis, leishmaniasis, mycetoma, sporotrichosis, *Mycobacterium marinum* infection, phaeohyphomycosis, squamous carcinoma, leprosy, and bromide drug eruption.

PATHOLOGIC FINDINGS

The pathology of chromomycosis is highly reproducible and exists independently of the specific causative organism.[10] The tissue response in chromomycosis is a pyogranuloma, similar to that of blastomycosis, coccidioidomycosis, and sporotrichosis.[1] Numerous neutrophils cluster in the center of the granuloma. Foreign body giant cells, lymphocytes, eosinophils, and plasma cells are also present. Nonulcerated lesions that are not secondarily infected show a very high degree of pseudoepitheliomatous hyperplasia.[5] The hyperplasia is not as extreme as in cutaneous blastomycosis or coccidioidal granuloma, but it is considerable and would be termed extreme acanthosis.[5] Sclerotic cells are located in dermal microabscesses, whereas hyphal strands may be seen in the epidermis, particularly the stratum corneum. In older lesions and between nodular lesions, changes consistent with chronic fibrosis can be visualized. The process of transepithelial elimination, in which blood, foreign matter, and sclerotic bodies are expelled through the epidermis, results in "black dots" found on the lesion's surface[11, 12] (see Fig. 251–2). The fungus is visible in stained and unstained sections. The sclerotic bodies, referred to as copper pennies, medlar bodies, chromobodies, chlamydospores, and sclerotia, are 5 to 15 μm in diameter, have thick, planate, septal walls, and are often grouped or in chains. These pigmented organisms are easily seen in macrophages, in giant cells, or extracellularly on hematoxylin- and eosin-stained material. Sclerotic bodies are very hardy and can remain dormant, yet viable in tissue after inoculation for long periods in asymptomatic persons.[13] This property may explain reports of the development of chromomycosis in immunosuppressed and nonimmunosuppressed patients at the same sites from which previous splinter implantation preceded the development of clinical chromomycosis by some 2 to 3 years.[13]

DIAGNOSIS

In tissue and exudate, all types of chromomycosis produce the characteristic sclerotic bodies. These bodies are usually more abun-

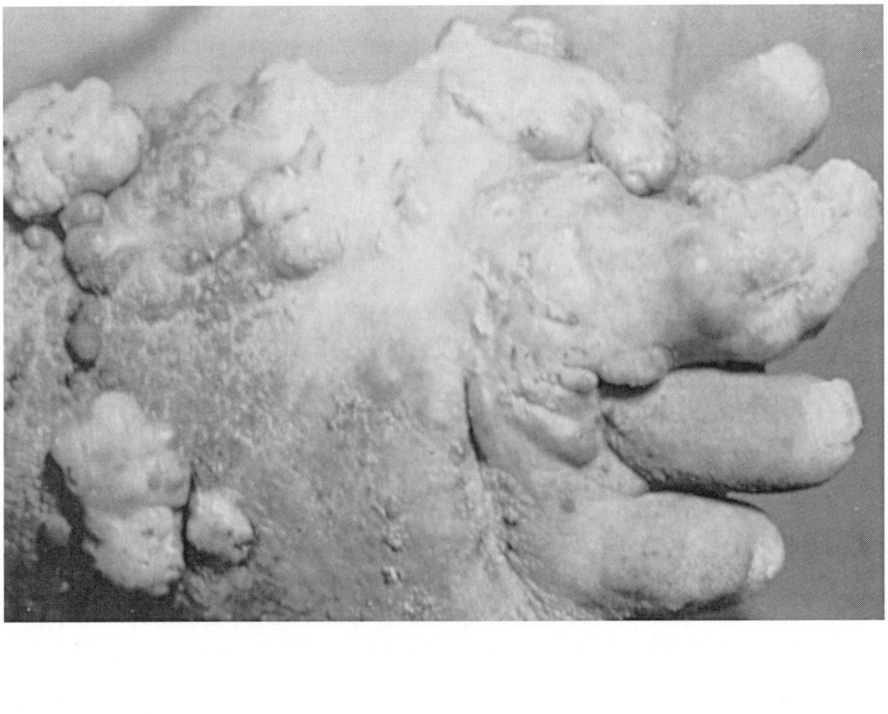

FIGURE 251–1. Verrucous lesions of chromomycosis demonstrate central healing on the foot of a patient in Panama.

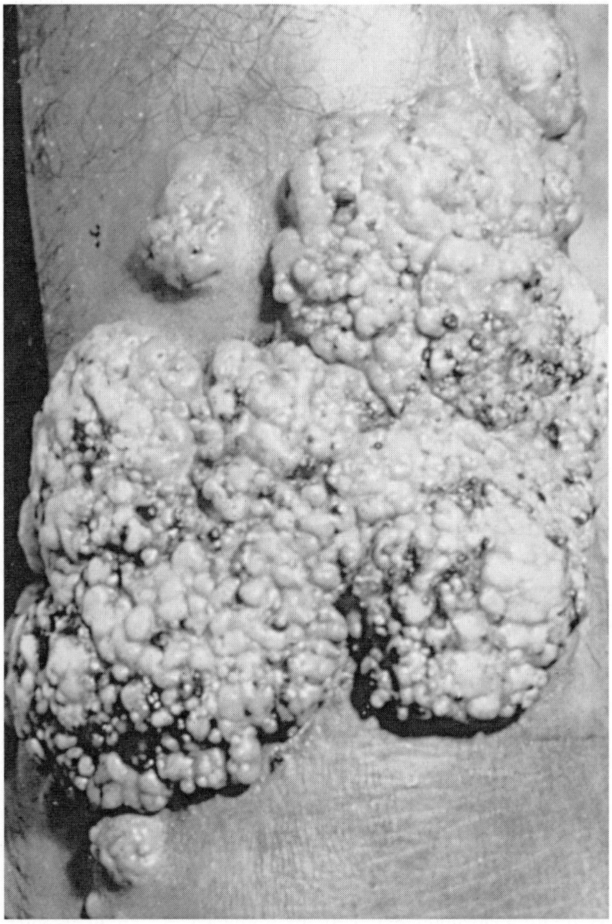

FIGURE 251–2. Pedunculated cauliflower-like chromomycosis lesions showing "black dots" at the apices of microabscesses on the leg of a Panamanian patient.

dant in specimens from verrucous lesions than in material from annular, flat lesions. On examination of the verrucous type of lesion, one can usually see "black dot" areas. Scrapings from these areas examined in 10 to 20% KOH on a microscopic slide will demonstrate the "copper pennies," which appear as pigmented sclerotic bodies. In crusts, pus, and exudate, the fungus may appear in the form of long, septate, branched, hyphal strands. Because of frequent contamination with bacteria and other fungi, direct examination of specimens should be confirmed by culture on Sabouraud glucose agar containing chloramphenicol and cycloheximide and kept at 25°C to 30°C for 4 to 6 weeks.[1] Skin testing and serologic evaluation are not helpful in making the diagnosis.

TREATMENT

In the early stages of the disease when the lesions are small and few, wide and deep surgical excision or cryosurgery with liquid nitrogen has been the most effective treatment.[14] Even with these therapies, relapse may occur if a lesion is not completely removed. However, most cases seen in clinical practice are advanced and require medical therapy, and cryosurgery should not be used in flexure areas. In general, medical therapy for chromomycosis has been disappointing. The combination of newer, more potent antifungal agents plus surgical excision or cryosurgery looks more promising. Drugs or procedures, including topical antifungals, potassium iodide, amphotericin B, thiabendazole, vitamin D_2, 5-fluorocytosine (5-FC), ketoconazole, fluconazole, itraconazole, and local heat, have all been reported to have varying degrees of success. Currently, itraconazole appears the most promising as medical therapy. Although saperconazole had good in vitro activity and showed promise in vivo, it will not be pursued for license in the United States because of toxicity.[15] At a daily oral dose of 100 to 200 mg/kg/day divided into 6-hour intervals for periods of up to 1 year, 5-FC has been successful in causing the rapid regression of lesions, symptoms, and organisms.[16] However, relapse, resistance, and partial cure are common with 5-FC. Lesions that recur after 5-FC therapy may grow rapidly and show resistance to this agent. Combination therapy with 5-FC and ketoconazole, 200 to 400 mg/day orally, was successful in a case in which ketoconazole alone failed.[17] Of eight patients treated with 200 to 600 mg/day of fluconazole for 2 to 19 months as monotherapy for *F. pedrosoi*, only one patient responded, but later relapsed.[18] In one study, apparent cure with itraconazole in doses of 100 to 400 mg/day orally for 4 to 8 months was achieved in eight of nine cases of chromomycosis caused by *C. carrionii* but in only two of five cases caused by *F. pedrosoi*.[19] Relapses also occurred after itraconazole. The duration of therapy in this study may not have been long enough. In another study, itraconazole, 100 to 200 mg/day, was given for *F. pedrosoi* infection to 10 patients with a mean duration of disease of 19 years (range, 1 to 42 years).[20] After 16 to 24 months of therapy, all severe lesions had transformed into moderate or minor lesions or had disappeared. These same investigators communicated that of 13 patients (including the 10 just mentioned) treated with only itraconazole, all patients responded after a mean duration of 17.9 months of

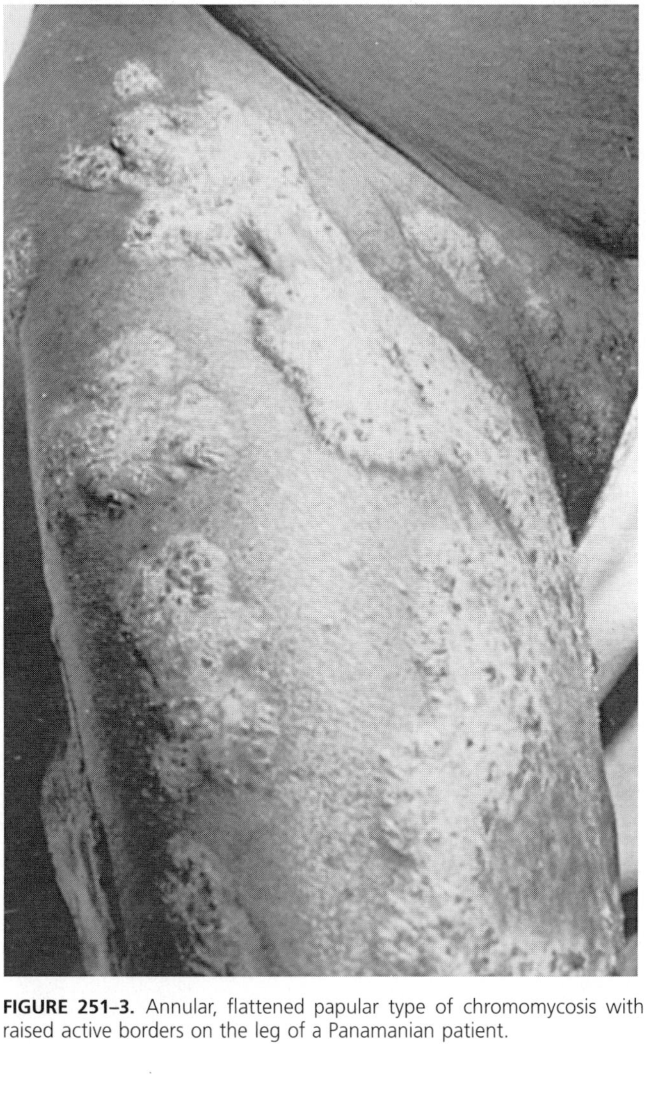

FIGURE 251–3. Annular, flattened papular type of chromomycosis with raised active borders on the leg of a Panamanian patient.

itraconazole therapy and suffered no side effects.[21] However, at the end of therapy, only 20% of the patients had no residual lesions, and the fungus was eradicated in only three patients. Marked improvement was reported when 5-FC and thermotherapy were used in combination with itraconazole in three patients.[18] In a recent study,[22] 12 patients with an average duration of disease of 7.2 years were put into three treatment groups: in group 1, patients with small lesions, not larger than 15 cm^2 in area, were treated with itraconazole, 300 mg/day; in group 2, patients were treated with one or more sessions of open-spray cryosurgery; and in group 3, patients with lesions larger than 15 cm^2 were treated with itraconazole, 300 mg/day, until maximal reduction of lesions, and then with one or several cryosurgery sessions. Two of four patients in groups 1 and 3 had clinical and fungal cure and the remaining patients experienced significant improvement. All four patients included in group 2 achieved cure. Eleven of the 12 patients had *F. pedrosoi* as the offending agent. Despite successful reports of intravenous amphotericin B plus 5-FC, I do not recommend its use because minimal inhibitory concentrations of amphotericin B tend to be high for these fungi. Despite large cumulative doses of liposomal amphotericin B in a bone marrow transplant patient with invasive *P. verrucosa*, the patient died.[8] Local thermal treatment as adjunctive therapy may be useful, especially with battery-driven pocket warmers.[23] Two investigational antifungal agents, voriconazole and pneumocandin L-743, 872, show promising in vitro activity against the agents of chromomycosis. Clear 80% minimal inhibitory concentration end points were observed for four *F. pedrosoi* and two *E. jeanselmei* isolates with pneumocandin L-743,872.[24] Voriconazole showed comparable or slightly better in vitro activity than did itraconazole against 13 *Exophiala* spp. and 6 *Fonsecaea* spp.[25] It remains to be seen whether the low minimal inhibitory concentrations seen in these studies will be predictive of good clinical outcome.

With only small series of chromomycosis patients studied, it appears that itraconazole may be more effective than fluconazole. Response rates of various agents of chromomycosis to the same antifungal agent may be different. The optimal dose and duration of therapy of the new triazoles must still be determined. The combination of itraconazole until maximum reduction in the size of lesions and subsequent cryosurgery may represent a new alternative in patients with large lesions, especially if *F. pedrosoi* is the offending agent. 5-FC may serve as an alternative for lesion reduction in some cases. More studies with 5-FC plus itraconazole, with or without cryosurgery, need to done.

REFERENCES

1. McGinnis MR. Chromoblastomycosis and phaeohyphomycosis: New concepts, diagnosis and mycology. J Am Acad Dermatol. 1983;8:1–16.
2. Barba-Gomez JF, Mayorga J, McGinnis MR, et al. Chromoblastomycosis caused by *Exophiala spinifera*. J Am Acad Dermatol. 1992;26:367–370.
3. Carrion A. Chromoblastomycosis. Ann N Y Acad Sci. 1950;50:1255–1281.
4. Sonck CE. Chromoblastomycosis in Finland. Dermatologia. 1975;19:189–193.
5. Kwon Chung KJ, Bennett JE. Medical Mycology. Philadelphia: Lea & Febiger; 1992.
6. Fukushiro R. Chromomycosis in Japan. Int J Dermatol. 1983;22:221–229.
7. Bayles M: Tropical mycosis. Chemotherapy. 1992;38(Suppl 1):S27–S34.
8. Lundstrom TS, Fairfax MR, Dugan MC et al. *Phialophora verrucosa* infection in a BMT patient. Bone Marrow Transplant. 1997;20:789–791.
9. Foster HM, Harris TJ. Malignant change (squamous carcinoma) in chronic chromoblastomycosis. Aust N Z Surg. 1987;57:775–777.
10. Elgart GW. Chromoblastomycosis. Dermatol Clin. 1996;14:77–83.
11. Fader RC, McGinnis MR. Infections caused by dematiaceous fungi: Chromoblastomycosis and phaeohyphomycosis. Infect Dis Clin North Am. 1988;2:925–938.
12. Batres E, Wolf J, Rudolph A, et al. Transepithelial elimination of cutaneous chromomycosis. Arch Dermatol. 1978;114: 1231–1232.
13. Rosen T, Overholt M. Persistent viability of the medlar body. Int J Dermatol. 1996;35:96–98.
14. Pimentel ERA, Castro LGM, Cuce LC, et al. Treatment of chromomycosis by cryosurgery with liquid nitrogen: A report on eleven cases. J Dermatol Surg Oncol. 1989;15:72–77.
15. Franco L, Gomez I, Restrepo A. Saperconazole in the treatment of systemic and subcutaneous mycoses. Int J dermatol. 1992;31:805–812.
16. Lopes CF, Alvarenga RJ, Cisalpeno EO, et al. Six years experience in treatment of chromomycosis with 5-fluorocytosine. Int J Dermatol. 1978;17:414–418.
17. Silber JG, Gombert ME, Green K, et al. Treatment of chromomycosis with ketoconazole and 5-fluorocytosine. J Am Acad Dermatol. 1983;8:236–238.
18. Diaz M, Negroni R, Montero-Gei F, et al. A pan-American 5-year study of fluconazole therapy for deep mycosis in the immunocompetent host. Clin Infect Dis. 1992;14 (Suppl): S568–S576.
19. Borelli D. A clinical trial of itraconazole in the treatment of deep mycosis and leishmaniasis. Rev Infect Dis. 1987;9(Suppl):S57–S63.
20. Restrepo A, Gonzalez A, Gomez I, et al. Treatment of chromoblastomycosis with itraconazole. Ann N Y Acad Sci. 1988;544:504–516.
21. Graybill J. Reply. Clin Infect Dis. 1992;15:553–554.
22. Bonifaz A, Martinez-Soto E, Carrasco-Gerard E, et al. Treatment of chromoblastomycosis with itraconazole, cryosurgery, and a combination of both. Int J Dermatol. 1997;36:542–547.
23. Kinbara T, Fukushiro R, Eryu Y. Chromomycosis—report of two cases successfully treated with local heat therapy. Mykosen. 1982;25:689–694.
24. Del Poeta M, Schell W, Perfect J. In vitro antifungal activity of pneumocandin L-743, 872 against a variety of clinically important molds. Antimicrob Agents Chemother. 1997;41:1837–1839.
25. Radford SA, Johnson EM, Warnock DW. In vitro studies of activity of voriconazole (UK-109, 496), a new triazole antifungal agent, against emerging and less-common mold pathogens. Antimicrob Agents Chemother. 1997;41:841–843.

Chapter 252

Agents of Mycetoma

EL SHEIKH MAHGOUB

Mycetoma (madura foot) is a local, chronic, slowly progressive, often painless destructive infection that begins in the subcutaneous tissue and spreads to contiguous structures. The organism is implanted in the subcutaneous tissue by minor trauma, often associated with plant debris or soil. The hands and feet are the most common sites, but any site exposed to trauma by lack of protective clothing can be involved. The defining characteristic is the presence of tiny "grains," which form in the tissue and can be seen in the serosanguineous drainage from sinus tracts.[1, 2] These grains are colonies of the organism.

DISTINCTION FROM OTHER ENTITIES

Use of the word *mycetoma* to refer to grossly visible clumps of fungus in a lung cavity, paranasal sinus, or renal pelvis is confusing and incorrect. Ringworm on the nape of the neck and occasionally elsewhere in persons of African descent can extend from the epidermis and hair follicles into the subcutaneous tissue. A chronic, indurated, painless subcutaneous granulomatous inflammation is formed, accompanied by grains composed of hyphae.[3, 4] This has been referred to as "dermatophyte mycetoma" but, unlike mycetoma, the lesion originates in the skin and does not extend into contiguous fascia and bone. Actinomycosis shares with mycetoma the ability to form grains in tissue, but it is caused by microaerophilic actinomycetes, which are normal flora in the mouth, gastrointestinal tract, and vagina.

ETIOLOGY

The term *actinomycetoma* refers to mycetoma caused by filamentous, branching bacteria. When the causative agent is a fungus, the infection is called *eumycetoma.* Agents of eumycetoma include *Pseudallescheria boydii, Madurella mycetomatis, Madurella grisea, Exophiala jeanselmei, Pyrenochaeta romeroi, Leptosphaeria senegalensis, Neotestudina rosatii, Arthrographis kalrae,*[5] and species of *Fusarium, Corynespora, Polycytella, Cylindrocarpon,*[6] *Curvularia,* and *Acremonium.* The agents of actinomycetoma include the following, all of which are aerobic actinomycetes: *Actinomadura madurae, Actinomadura pelletierii, Streptomyces somaliensis, Nocardia brasiliensis, Nocardia asteroides, Nocardia otitidis-caviarum,*[7] *Nocardia transvalensis,*[8] and *Nocardiopsis dassonvillei.* The organisms causing mycetoma vary in their geographic distribution, grain color, and, to a lesser extent, clinical manifestations.

EPIDEMIOLOGY

In 1842, Gill described the disease for the first time in patients in a dispensary located in the Madura District of India;[9] hence, the names Madura foot, maduromycetoma, and the genera *Madurella* and *Actinomadura.* Both Bidie[10] in 1862 and Carter[11] in 1874 independently gave a full description of the disease in India. Today, mycetoma is found worldwide in tropical zones and, less commonly, in temperate zones. The disease appears to be most common in India, Mexico,[12] Saudi Arabia, Venezuela, Yemen, and the so-called mycetoma belt of sub-Saharan Africa, which extends from Senegal on the west coast, across Mali,[13] Niger, Democratic Republic of Congo, and Sudan, to Somalia on the east coast.

The most common cause of the disease in the United States is *P. boydii,* which has been isolated frequently from soil in the United States and Canada.[14] *M. mycetomatis* and *S. somaliensis* predominate in tropical areas of Africa and India, and *N. brasiliensis* and *A. madurae* are the most common causes of mycetoma in Mexico and Central and South America.[15] *N. asteroides* is reported to predominate in Japan.

PATHOGENESIS AND PATHOLOGIC FINDINGS

Saprophytic soil fungi enter the tissues of the bare foot or hand after local trauma, most commonly from a thorn prick, wood splinter, or stone cut. The chest wall and back are infected by sacks contaminated with soil carried over the shoulders. The carrying of wood bundles on the head and shoulders leads to head and neck mycetoma.

The infection begins in the skin and subcutaneous tissues. Mycetoma tends to follow fascial planes in its proximal, lateral, and deep spread as it progressively involves and destroys connective tissue and bone.

The involved area is characterized by tumefaction, formation of multiple sinuses, and fistulous tracts that communicate with each other, with deep abscesses, and with ulcerated areas of the skin. The progressive proliferation of granulation and scar tissue leads to enlargement and disfigurement of the affected part.

In histologic sections stained with hematoxylin and eosin (H&E), involved tissue reveals a suppurative granuloma. Grains are seen embedded in an abscess composed of neutrophils accompanied by an outer epithelioid cell, plasma cell, and multinucleated giant cell reaction intermingled with areas of fibrosis. Within these suppurative foci, the grains are surrounded by an amorphous, eosinophilic, homogeneous, hyaline-like material termed the *Splendore-Hoeppli phenomenon.* Ultrastructural studies have revealed that this part of the grain matrix is host derived.[16]

The appearance of various grains in sections is so characteristic that it allows specific diagnosis of the causative organism.[17] Eumycetic hyphae within the grain are easy to see at 400× magnification, whereas those of actinomycetes are difficult to visualize even at 800×.

In electron micrographs, concentric rings of cell wall thickening and coarse cell wall fibrils around cells are seen within eumycetic grains.

Persons afflicted with mycetoma have deficient cell-mediated immunity, as evidenced by their inability to react to tuberculin or sensitization by dinitrochlorobenzine, and their lymphocytes fail to transform to lymphoblasts when challenged by phytohemagglutinin.[18] Immunoglobulins, particularly immunoglobulin G (IgG), are increased,[19] but they are of no protective value.

CLINICAL MANIFESTATIONS

Mycetoma is seen most frequently in men between the ages of 20 and 40 years. A true male-to-female ratio is 5:1. It occurs most often in farmers and other laborers in rural areas, bedouins, and nomads, who are frequently exposed to penetrating wounds by thorns and splinters. The most common site of infection is the foot, particularly on the dorsum of the forepart. A painless, massively swollen, indurated foot riddled with sinuses is the late presentation (Fig. 252–1). Constitutional complaints are rare, and pyrexia implies secondary bacterial infection. Extrapedal cases appear on other parts of the body that are in contact with soil during work, sitting, or lying, including the hand (Fig. 252–2), leg, torso, arm, head, thigh (Fig. 252–3), and buttocks. When the scalp is involved, the infection usually starts in the back of the head and neck or the frontal part.

The earliest manifestation is a small, painless papule or nodule on the sole or dorsum of the foot that progressively increases in size. Such development is usually quicker in actinomycetoma than in eumycetoma. The skin lesions swell and rupture, and sinus tracts form. As the infection spreads, similar lesions appear on adjacent parts. Old sinuses heal and close up, but new ones open at other sites. Therefore, an old mycetoma is characterized by healed scars

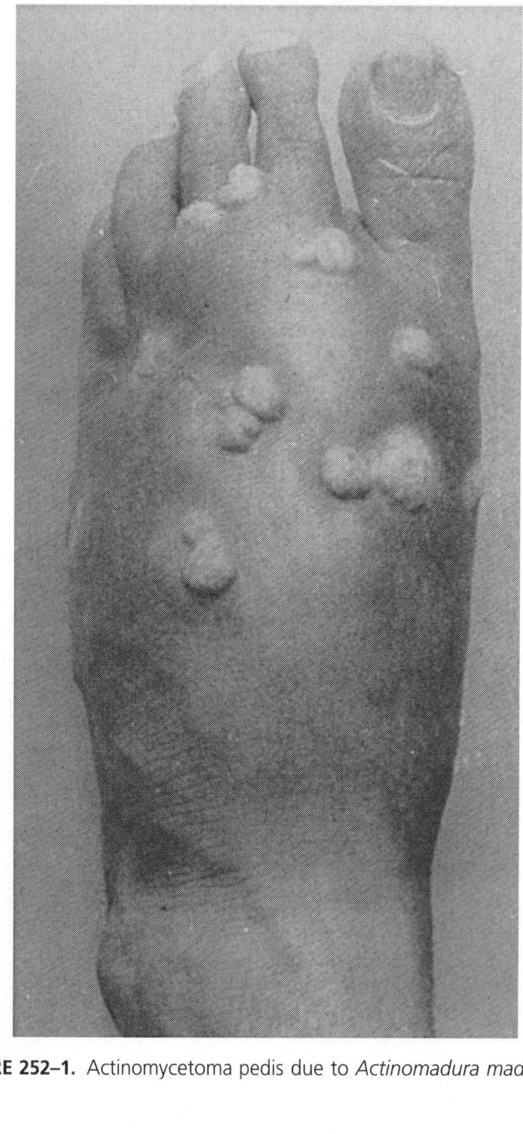

FIGURE 252–1. Actinomycetoma pedis due to *Actinomadura madurae.*

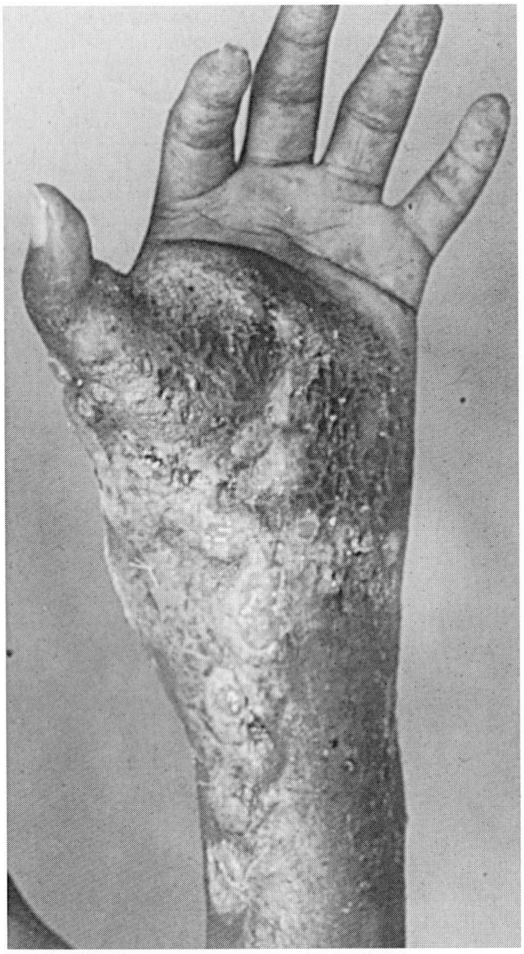

FIGURE 252–2. Extensive actinomycetoma of the hand.

in addition to sinuses. After months or years, destruction of deeper tissues, including bone, is manifested as generalized swelling that remains painless except in about 15% of patients, who report to the hospital primarily because of pain.

The course is progressive as local tissue undergoes a recurring cycle of swelling, suppuration, and scarring. Ultimately, an infected site becomes a swollen, deformed mass of destroyed tissue with many fistulas through which grains are discharged. The infection never spreads hematogenously, but lymphatic spread to regional lymph nodes and surrounding tissues may occur.[20] Such a phenomenon is often facilitated by repeated surgical intervention. Involved tissue may also become secondarily infected by bacteria. The extent of soft tissue invasion can best be appreciated on magnetic resonance imaging.[21]

In the bone, the cortex is invaded, and masses of grains gradually replace osseous tissue and marrow, providing support and preventing spontaneous pathologic fracture, which may however happen on rare occasions.[22] Radiographs reveal multiple osteolytic lesions called *cavities* (Fig. 252–4) and periosteal new bone formation.[23] Osteoporosis caused by pressure from surrounding swelling and disease atrophy is also seen at times. Joints are sometimes stiff because of chronic periarticular fibrosis.

Mycetomas of the skull show diffuse thickening of bones caused by dense bone formation and a loss of the trabecular pattern, but in a few sites there may be small osteolytic areas as well.[24] Pure osteolytic changes are not seen.

DIAGNOSIS

The triad of signs—indurated swelling, multiple sinus tracts draining grain-filled pus, and the usual localization on a foot—characterize a well-developed mycetoma. Characteristic grains in draining sinuses are 0.2 to 3.0 mm in diameter and may be black, white, yellow, pink, or red depending on the causal organism. Grains may be difficult to locate in histopathologic sections and require multiple cuts through the paraffin-embedded tissue. H&E stain is adequate to detect the grains (Fig. 252–5). Tissue Gram staining detects fine, branching hyphae within the actinomycetoma grain, and Gomori methenamine silver or periodic acid–Schiff stain, particularly in the case of pale grains, detects the larger hyphae of eumycetoma. Species of the agent can often be guessed by the color, size, compaction, and hematoxylin-staining character of the grain.

A more exact species diagnosis depends on culture of the grain and isolation of the organism. The grain obtained for culture must be as free as possible from bacterial and fungal contamination. A wedge-shaped, deep-seated biopsy provides a good specimen for both histologic and cultural diagnosis. Before being inoculated onto culture media, the grains should be rinsed quickly in 70% alcohol

FIGURE 252–3. Mycetoma of the thigh caused by *Streptomyces somaliensis*.

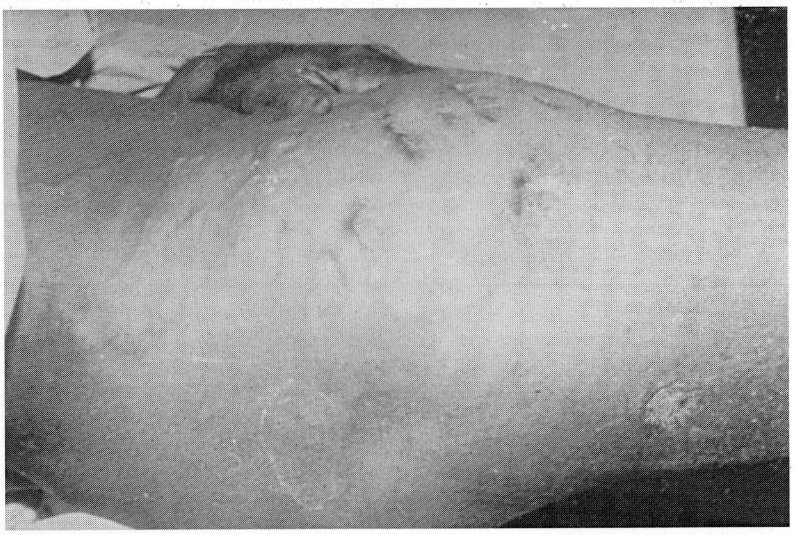

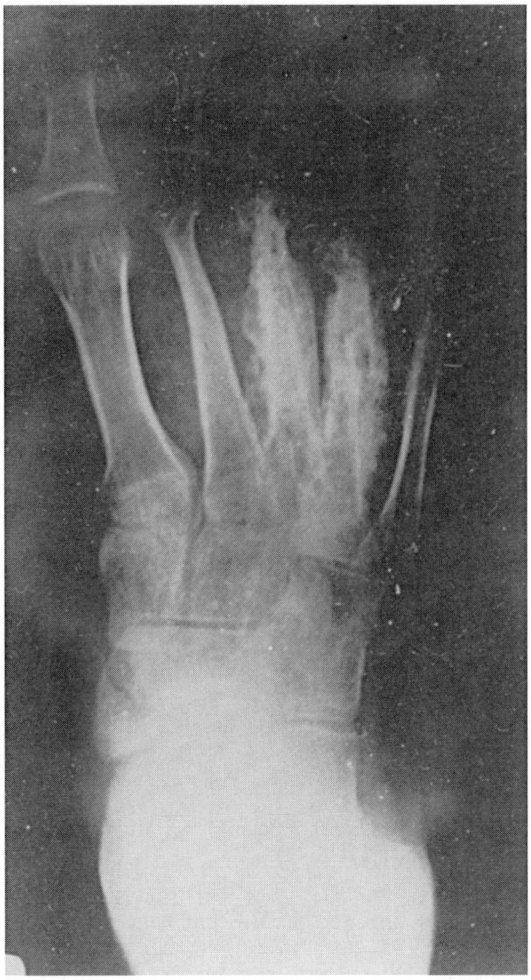

FIGURE 252–4. Radiograph showing small multiple cavities caused by *Streptomyces somaliensis.*

and washed several times in sterile saline. Biopsy specimens are preferred over grains discharged through sinuses, because such grains may be contaminated with surface organisms or may already be dead. For primary isolation, actinomycetoma grains are grown on Löwenstein-Jensen medium and fungal grains on blood agar. Sabouraud agar (2% glucose, 1% peptone agar) without antibacterial antibiotics is satisfactory for subcultures.

Two sets of cultures are prepared; one is inoculated at 37°C and the other at 26°C. Characteristic colonies are expected to develop within 10 days. Apart from *M. mycetomatis,* which secretes a brown pigment in the medium, all other organisms, both bacteria and fungi, tend to maintain the color of the original grain. Bacterial colonies are usually granular or cerebriform, whereas fungal colonies are either velvety or fluffy. Further identification is made by microscopic examination of fungi in lactophenol blue preparation and of bacteria after Gram and modified Zhiel-Neelsen stains.

Serologic diagnosis is routinely used in a few centers. Using cell extract antigens, antibodies are determined by means of immunodiffusion (ID) or counterimmunoelectrophoresis (CIE) for both serologic diagnosis and follow-up during medical treatment.[25]

Specific characterization of antibodies can be done by enzyme-linked immunosorbent assay (ELISA) and Western blotting.[26] Also by Western blot, three immunodominant antigens from extracts of *N. brasiliensis* were found to react with sera from patients having mycetoma caused by this organism.[27]

DIFFERENTIAL DIAGNOSIS

In endemic areas, a painless, firm, subcutaneous swelling should be regarded as a mycetoma until proved otherwise, even in the absence of sinuses. Once mycetoma has invaded bone, the entity is readily confused with chronic bacterial osteomyelitis. Botryomycosis is a chronic bacterial infection that manifests as an indurated fibrotic subcutaneous mass and draining sinuses resembling a mycetoma; grains (colonies of bacteria) are found in the purulent exudate and in tissue sections. Although botryomycosis is most commonly a disease of the skin and subcutaneous tissues, unlike mycetoma, it may also involve the viscera. The etiologic agents of botryomycosis include a number of gram-positive cocci (staphylococci, streptococci) and gram-negative bacilli (*Escherichia coli, Pseudomonas* species, *Proteus* species). In the absence of sinuses, mycetoma should be differentiated from benign or malignant tumors, a cold abscess, or a thorn granuloma.

TREATMENT AND PROGNOSIS

Through health education, patients are encouraged to report early to hospitals. Surgical treatment, which is still preferred by some doctors, leads either to immediate recurrence as a result of incomplete excision or to a mutilating result for a relatively painless disease. Mycetoma at all stages may be amenable to medical treatment alone or in combination with limited surgery. In a medicosurgical approach, only bulk reduction surgery is performed; amputation or disarticulation should be avoided. The success of treatment depends not only on the differentiation between actinomycetoma and eumycetoma but also on a definitive identification of the causal organism.

In all cases of actinomycetoma, a combination of two drugs is used.[28] One of these is always streptomycin sulfate, in a dose of 14 mg/kg daily for the first month and on alternate days thereafter. In patients with *A. madurae* mycetoma, dapsone (diaminodiphenylsulphone) is given orally, 1.5 mg/kg in the morning and evening. Similarly, *S. somaliensis* mycetoma is treated by dapsone first, but if no response appears after 1 month treatment is changed to trimethoprim-sulfamethoxazole tablets, 23 mg/kg/day of sulfamethoxazole and 4.6 mg/kg/day of trimethoprim (in two divided doses). *A. pelletierii* mycetoma responds better to streptomycin and trimethoprim-sulfamethoxazole; this was also our experience with *N. brasiliensis*

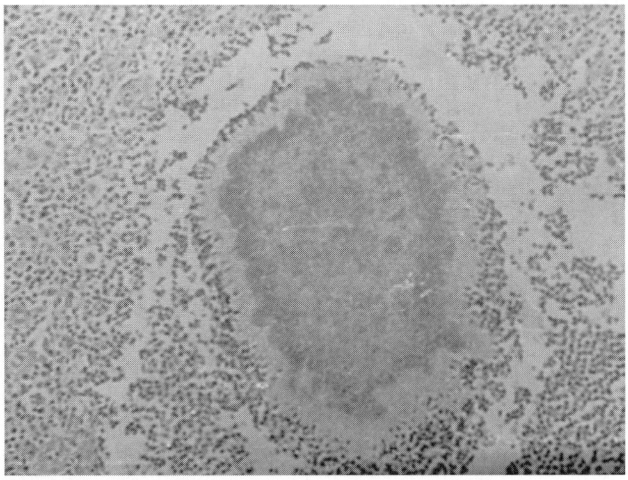

FIGURE 252–5. A young grain of *Actinomadura madurae* in the middle of an abscess composed mainly of polymorphonuclear leukocytes. Note the dark-colored basophilic center and pale eosinophilic border (H&E, ×200).

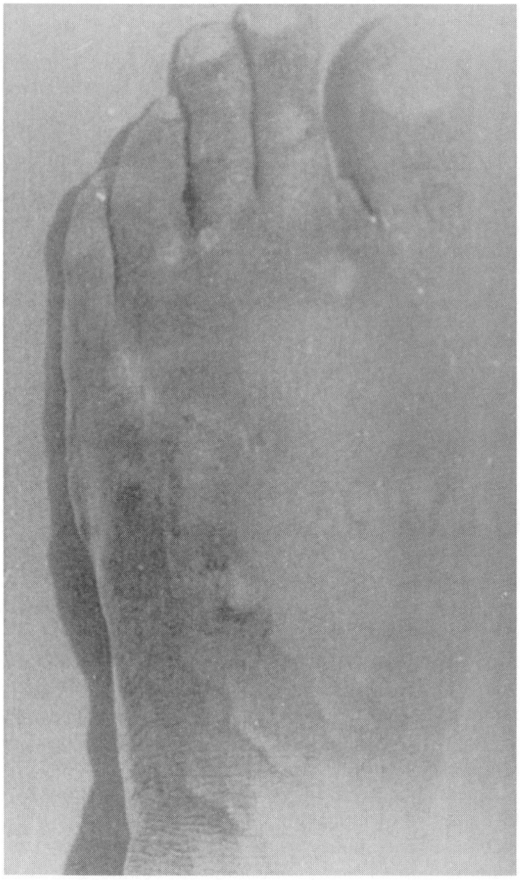

FIGURE 252–6. The same patient with *Actinomadura madurae* infection as in Figure 252–1 after the end of treatment.

in Sudan. However, such mycetoma caused by *Nocardia* in the Americas are treated with trimethoprim-sulfamethoxazole and dapsone[29] or trimethoprim-sulfamethoxazole and amikacin.[30] Because amikacin could have deleterious side effects in patients with renal disease and because of its high cost, it is kept as a second-line treatment when first-line treatment fails. Treatment is given in cycles of simultaneous administration of two divided doses of amikacin (15 mg/kg/day) for 3 weeks and trimethoprim-sulfamethoxazole (35 mg/kg/day) of the sulfamethoxazole component) for 5 weeks. The cycle is repeated a second and, rarely, for a third time as the need arises.[31]

Eumycetoma caused by *M. mycetomatis* often responds to ketoconazole, 200 mg twice daily, and bulk reduction of the lesion.[31–35] Itraconazole, 200 mg once or twice daily, has also been used successfully.[5, 35, 36] Rare cases of mycetoma caused by *Acremonium falciforme,*[37] *Aspergillus flavus,*[38] or *Fusarium* have responded well to itraconazole in a dose of 200 mg twice daily.

Intravenous liposomal amphotericin B has been tried in patients with mycetoma caused by *M. grisea* and *Fusarium* spp. in an average total dose of 3.5 g, with a maximum daily dose of 3 mg/kg body weight. Only temporary remission was obtained.[31]

In all cases of medical management, treatment is given for at least 10 months (Fig. 252–6). Although side effects are few, patients are regularly monitored to assess hematologic, kidney, or liver functions, depending on the drug used.

REFERENCES

1. Mahgoub ES, Murray IG. Mycetoma. London: Heinemann; 1973:1–97.
2. McGinnis MR. Mycetoma Dermatol Clin. 1996;14:97–104.
3. West BC, Kwon-Chung KJ. Mycetoma caused by *Microsporum audouinii:* First reported case. Am J Clin Pathol. 1980;73:447–455.
4. West BC. Five year follow up of a man with subcutaneous mycetomas caused by *Microsporum audouinii.* Am J Clin Pathol. 1982;77:767.
5. Degavre B, Joujoux JM, Dandurand M, et al. First report of mycetoma caused by *Arthrographis kalrae:* Successful treatment with itraconazole. J Am Acad Dermatol. 1997;37:318–320.
6. Zoutman DE, Sigler L. Mycetoma of the foot caused by *Cylindrocarpon destructans.* J Clin Microbiol. 1991;29:1855–1859.
7. Tight RR, Bartlett MS. Actinomycetoma in the United States. Rev Infect Dis. 1981;3:1139–1150.
8. Mirza SH, Campbell C. Mycetoma caused by *Nocardia transvalensis.* J Clin Pathol. 1994;47:85–86.
9. Gill. India Army Medical Reports. London: Churchill; 1874.
10. Bidie G. Notes on morbus pedis entophyticus. Madras Q J Med Sci. 1862;4:222–227.
11. Carter HV. On Mycetoma or the Fungus Disease of India. London: Churchill; 1874.
12. Southern PA. Mycetoma due to *Madurella grisea* acquired in Mexico. Trop Doct. 1996;26:187–188.
13. Mahe A, Develoux M, Lienhardt C, et al. Mycetomas in Mali: Causative agents and geographic distribution. Am J Trop Med Hyg. 1996;54:77–79.
14. Green WO, Adams TE. Mycetoma in the United States. Am J Clin Pathol. 1964;42:75–91.
15. Lavalle P. Micetomas: La experiencia mexicana: Problemas actuales. In: Libro de Resumens II Simposio Internacional de Micetomas. Taxco, Mexico; 1987.
16. Wethered DB, Markey MA, Hay RJ, et al. Ultrastructural and immunogenic changes in the formation of mycetoma grains. J Med Vet Mycol. 1987;25:39–46.
17. Mahgoub ES. Mycetoma. In: Mahgoub ES, ed. Tropical Mycoses. Beerse, Belgium: Janssen Research Council; 1989:57–74.
18. Mahboub ES, Gumaa SA, El Hassan AM. Immunological Status of mycetoma patients. Bull Soc Pathol Exot. 1997;70:48–54.
19. Mohamed AO, Fahal AH, Venge P. Immunoglobulin and inflammatory markers. Profiles in mycetoma. East Afr Med J. 1996;73:212.
20. El Hassan AM, Mahgoub ES. Lymph node involvement in mycetoma. Trans R Soc Trop Med Hyg. 1972;66:165–169.
21. Locken JA, Strong B, Martin TP. Mycetoma of the calf. Skel Radiol 1997;26:319–322.
22. Fahal AH, Sheikh HE, El Hassan AM. Pathological fracture in mycetoma. Trans R Soc Trop Med Hyg. 1996;90:675–676.
23. Corr P. Clinics in diagnostic imaging 26: Madura foot (or mycetoma). Singapore Med J. 1997;38:268–269.
24. Gumaa SA, Mahgoub ES, El Sid MA. Mycetoma of the head and neck. Am J Trop Med Hyg. 1986;35:594–600.
25. Gumaa SA, Mahgoub ES. Counterimmunoelectrophoresis in the diagnosis of mycetoma and its sensitivity as compared to immunodiffusion. Sabouraudia. 1975;13:309–315.
26. Wethered DB, Markey MA, Hay RJ, et al. Humoral immune response to mycetoma organisms: Characterization of specific antibodies by the use of enzyme-linked immunosorbent assay and immunoblotting. Trans R Soc Trop Med Hyg. 1988;82:918–923.
27. Salinas-Carmona MC, Vera L, Welsh O, et al. Antibody response to *Nocardia brasiliensis* antigens in man. Zbl Bakt. 1992;276:390–397.
28. Mahgoub ES. Medical management of mycetoma. Bull World Health Organ. 1976;54:303–310.
29. Caire P, Arenas R, Suchil P, et al. Tratamiento de micetomas por *Nocardia.* Experiencia en 50 pacientes. In: Libro de Resumenes II Simposio Internacional de Micetomas. Taxco, Mexico; 1987:49.
30. Welsh O, Sauceda E, Gonzalez J. Amikacin y trimetoprim sulphametoxazole el tratamiento de micetomas actinomicosicos. In: Libro de resumenes II Simposio Internacional de Micetomas. Taxco, Mexico; 1987:48.
31. Hay RJ, Mahgoub ES, Leon G, et al. Mycetoma. J Med Vet Mycol. 1992;30:41–49.
32. Mahgoub ES, Gumaa SA. Ketoconazole in the treatment of eumycetoma due to *Madurella mycetomatis.* Trans R Soc Trop Med Hyg. 1984;78:376–379.
33. Anreu JM. Traitement actuel des mycetomes fungiques: Intérêt du ketoconazole associé a la chirurgie conservatrice. Med Trop. 1986;46:293–297.
34. Mahgoub ES. Mycetoma. In: Jacobs PH, Nall L, eds. Antifungal Drug Therapy: A Complete Guide for the Practitioner. New York: Marcel Dekker, 1990:61–70.
35. Welsh O, Salinas MC, Rodriguez MA. Treatment of eumycetoma and actinomycetoma. Curr Top Med Mycol. 1995;6:47–71.
36. Paugram A, Tourte-Schaefer C, Keita A, et al. Clinical cure of fungal madura foot with oral itraconazole. Cutis. 1997;60:191–193.
37. Lee MW, Kim JC, Choi JS, et al. Mycetoma caused by *Acremonium falciforme:* Successful treatment with itraconazole. J Am Acad Dermatol. 1995;32:897–900.
38. Witzig RS, Greer DL, Hyslop NE. *Aspergillus flavus* mycetoma and epidural abscess successfully treated with itraconazole. J Med Vet Mycol. 1996;34:133–137.

Chapter 253

Cryptococcus neoformans

RICHARD D. DIAMOND

Cryptococcosis is a systemic infection caused by the yeastlike fungus *Cryptococcus neoformans.* Other species of *Cryptococcus* have been reported to cause infection, but the adequacy of documentation of these cases has been questioned.[1] Older names for this disease include *European blastomycosis* and *torulosis.* The latter name derives from *Torula histolytica,* an old and poorly chosen name for *C. neoformans.*

MYCOLOGY

C. neoformans is an encapsulated, yeastlike fungus that reproduces by budding. The cell is round or oval, usually 4 to 6 μm in diameter, although rarely, larger yeasts or pseudomycelial forms may develop. The surrounding capsule may vary greatly in size depending on genetic factors in different strains, but capsule size in any given strain can be altered by growth conditions such as carbon dioxide, ferric iron, glucose, glutamate, and thiamine concentrations, pH, temperature, and osmolarity.[2] Large capsules tend to form during infections, even by strains that have a tendency to form small capsules in vitro. At least in experimental studies in mice, the size of the capsule does not appear to be related to virulence, although virulence is reduced in totally unencapsulated mutants.[2, 3] In any case, the capsule confers several properties on the organism that affect the host response to infection (see "Pathophysiology" later).

IDENTIFICATION

C. neoformans colonies are smooth, convex, and yellow or tan on solid culture media. Several procedures can be used for differentiation from other yeastlike fungi. *C. neoformans* grows at 37°C, whereas most nonpathogenic species of *Cryptococcus* do not. In addition, *C. neoformans* is lactose negative and hydrolyzes starch, and all but rare strains hydrolyze urea during growth on Christensen agar.[4] For the latter, results of presumptive screening tests may be available in as few as 15 minutes. *C. neoformans* does not produce pseudomycelia on cornmeal or rice-Tween agar, but growth is slowed in vitro at 39°C to 40°C and aberrant budding or pseudohyphae may form.[2] Glucose is not fermented but is assimilated by the fungus. Dulcitol, inositol, maltose, and sucrose are assimilated, but lactose and nitrate are not.[2, 5] Many strains of *C. neoformans* can use creatinine as a nitrogen source, which may partially explain growth of the organism in creatinine-rich avian feces. Mouse pathogenicity has also been used as a specific procedure for identification of *C. neoformans.* Another useful procedure is based on the property of *C. neoformans* strains (but not nonpathogenic yeasts) to produce melanin. The fungal enzyme phenol oxidase acts on certain substrates such as caffeic acid and dihydroxyphenylalanine rather than tyrosine, in contrast to melanin synthesis in humans. *C. neoformans* strains produce dark brown pigment; only rare strains remain white. Agar around colonies of *C. neoformans* var. *gattii* (see later) may appear greenish. Rare *Cryptococcus laurentii* may produce brown pigment, and some turn the agar green. Melanin production appears to be related to the virulence of cryptococcosis in experimental murine infections, although the mechanism of this effect remains uncertain. To detect pigment production, agar medium made with glucose and creatinine is supplemented with niger seed (birdseed agar). Alternatively, chemically defined substrates are used (caffeic acid in cornmeal agar or paper strips saturated with a solution of L-β-3-dihydroxyphenylalanine-ferric citrate placed on standard agar plates.[6] Use of such media for primary isolation enables immediate separation and presumptive identification of *C. neoformans,* even if colonies of other fungi are present. Commercially available DNA probes for hybridization with RNA of organisms are sensitive, specific, and rapid and may therefore supplant biochemical procedures.[2]

SEROTYPES, PERFECT STATE, AND VARIETIES

Antigenic specificity of the capsular polysaccharide defines four different serotypes of *C. neoformans*—A, B, C, and D,[7] based on agglutination or immunofluorescence—although some strains react with antisera to serotypes A and D. Suitable strains of serotypes A and D, which include the large majority of clinical isolates of *C. neoformans,* can be mated to produce the perfect (sexual) state, *Filobasidiella neoformans* var. *neoformans*.[8] Of the two mating types, termed α and a, the α-type is 30- to 40-fold more frequent in environmental and clinical isolates and has greater virulence for mice.[9] Serotypes B and C are classified as *C. neoformans* var. *gattii* because of several characteristics that distinguish them from serotype A and D isolates. *F. neoformans* var. *neoformans* and *F. neoformans* var. *gattii* differ, but a few strains of serotypes A and D are able to mate with B and C organisms, albeit with a low survival rate.[9, 10] The epidemiology of infection and the ecology of *C. neoformans* var. *neoformans* and var. *gattii* also differ (see later).[11–14] Biochemical differences are also apparent among serotypes of *C. neoformans.* Most serotype B and C isolates assimilate 1-malic, fumaric, and succinic acids, produce green pigment on niger media, can assimilate tryptophan with production of a brown pigment, and can assimilate glycine as a sole carbon source, whereas serotype A and D isolates generally do not.[7, 15, 16] Agar containing L-canavanine, glycine, and bromothymol blue is useful in distinguishing serotypes B and C from A and D in that growth of the former turns the yellow agar alkaline and therefore blue, whereas the latter causes no color change.[17] Urease activity of the former is inhibited by 100 μmol/liter ethylenediamine tetra-acetic acid.[17] In addition, analysis of DNA base composition and sequence homology studies point to genetic differences between serotypes A and D versus B and C.[2, 10, 14] When compared with isolates of *C. neoformans,* environmental isolates of *C. neoformans* var. *gattii* are more virulent for mice, and cryptococcal meningitis caused by the varieties *gattii* and *neoformans* differ in host distribution and certain clinical manifestations.[18, 19]

ECOLOGY AND EPIDEMIOLOGY

C. neoformans is a saprobe in nature. Cryptococcal infections occur worldwide without any defined endemic areas, but the environmental distribution of the serotypes shows some differences. Serotypes A and D have been frequently found throughout the world in aged pigeon droppings or nesting places such as window ledges and barns. *C. neoformans* grows to high concentrations in pigeon feces, but the birds are not infected.[11] Soil or decayed wood chips may also contain the fungus, especially if contaminated with bird droppings. Survival of *C. neoformans* in soil may be affected by a variety of biotic factors; for example, soil bacteria, amebas, mites, and sow bugs are capable of inhibiting or killing the fungi.[20] Much less commonly, *C. neoformans* has also been isolated from fruits and a variety of other sources in nature.[11] Infections caused by serotype A strains are by far the most common. However, the prevalence of serotype D infections is increased in some areas (e.g., 21% of cases in France).[21] In addition, differences in predisposing factors and clinical manifestations of infection caused by serotype A versus D strains suggest that undefined environmental and host-related factors may affect the distribution of infections caused by these serotypes.[20] Cases of cryptococcosis caused by serotypes B and C are largely restricted in distribution to tropical and subtropical areas. Serotype B strains have been isolated from *Eucalyptus camaldulensis* (red river gum)[15] and *Eucalyptus tereticornis* (forest red gum)[16] trees and in air beneath them, especially when these trees are flowering.[11–13] However, some infections caused by serotype B and C strains occur in areas lacking these types of eucalyptus trees, so other environmental sources of these serotypes are still unidentified.[14]

Naturally acquired cryptococcosis occurs in animals as well as in humans, but animal-to-person transmission has not been documented,[11] even after heavy exposure from drinking nonpasteurized milk produced by cattle with cryptococcal mastitis. Rather, circumstantial evidence suggests that disease occurs after the organism is aerosolized and inhaled. In favor of this mechanism, viable particles of *C. neoformans* with a size compatible with alveolar deposition (<2 μm) have been isolated in nature from pigeon excreta and soil.[22] Furthermore, healthy persons with a history of heavy exposure to pigeons have a much higher rate of positive delayed skin tests to cryptococcal antigen, or cryptococcin.[23] However, unlike other aerosol-borne mycoses, cases of cryptococcosis rarely occur in clusters. No occupational predisposition is known, and a history of exposure to pigeons, dust, or eucalyptus trees is not helpful. Usually neither historical nor roentgenographic evidence of respiratory infection can be found at the time of diagnosis. Person-to-person transmission has not been documented by the pulmonary route but has occurred via transplanted tissues obtained from donors who had active cryptococcosis, including cases of systemic infection from a donor kidney and endophthalmitis from a corneal graft.[2] Furthermore, laboratory workers are frequently exposed to aerosols of the organism, as indicated by a high incidence of positive cryptococcin skin tests.[23] However, laboratory-acquired pulmonary or disseminated cryptococcosis has never been described. Rare instances of documented accidental cutaneous inoculation with *C. neoformans* have resulted in only localized cutaneous lesions without dissemination.[24]

Epidemiologic studies are now facilitated by a variety of modern genetic techniques, such as restrictive fragment polymorphism, karyotypic patterns, and specific DNA probes.[2, 25–31] *C. neoformans* may undergo rapid genotypic and phenotypic changes during in vitro culture and storage, thus indicating a need for care and consistency in maintenance conditions and cautious interpretation of data.[25] A broad range of studies have suggested diverse genomic patterns among clinical isolates from single geographic areas, extensive variation in specific allelic loci, karyotype changes during experimental infections, and potential for a clonal population structure of virulent *C. neoformans*.[25–31] Most studies suggest that infections of individual patients are caused by a single *C. neoformans* strain and that recurrences are due to persistence of the original infecting strain,[28, 29] but some data raise the possibility that multiple strains may occasionally be present in a single infection and that some recurrent infections may be caused by new strains.[30, 31]

FACTORS PREDISPOSING TO INFECTION

Because the organism is ubiquitous, it is presumed that exposure to *C. neoformans* is common. Skin test surveys of healthy subjects provide some support for this assumption.[2, 11, 23] Nevertheless, natural resistance to infection must be high because new cases were relatively rare before the advent of acquired immunodeficiency syndrome (AIDS). Patients with immunologic defects in T-cell–mediated host defense mechanisms appear to be at increased risk for progressive cryptococcosis.[11] Currently, AIDS is the predisposing factor in approximately 80 to 90% of cryptococcal infections. Patients with immunologic defects in T-cell–mediated host defense mechanisms appear to be at increased risk for progressive cryptococcosis. Among AIDS patients in the United States, cryptococcosis is the defining illness in 5% of patients,[32] with an overall 5 to 10% prevalence. The prevalence is even higher in central Africa,[11] and cryptococcosis was reported to be the initial defining illness in 88% of AIDS patients in Harare, Zimbabwe.[33] AIDS-associated cases usually occur when CD4 T-lymphocyte counts fall below 100/mm^3.[34] Cryptococcosis also occurs in patients with idiopathic CD4$^+$ lymphocytopenia who are not infected with human immunodeficiency virus (HIV),[35, 36] as well as in other patients with documented cell-mediated immune defects.[37–39] After AIDS, transplantation is the next most frequent risk factor for cryptococcosis, largely because the use of high-dose corticosteroids and other immunosuppressive agents for the treatment of chronic rejection is associated with a peak period of risk 4 to 6 weeks or more post-transplant.[40] Therapeutic doses of corticosteroids predispose to cryptococcal infection.[41] Although cyclosporine suppresses cellular host defense mechanisms, it also appears to inhibit the growth of *C. neoformans,* both in vitro and in vivo.[42] The incidence of cryptococcosis is also increased in patients with lymphoreticular malignancies (especially Hodgkin's disease), as well as sarcoidosis (even in the absence of corticosteroid therapy).[41] Other conditions such as diabetes mellitus have been cited as predisposing to cryptococcosis, but the association is less clear cut than for the aforementioned factors. In the absence of AIDS or transplant-related immunosuppression, more than half of cryptococcosis patients lack apparent predisposing factors. Among this latter group, males are affected more often than females,[41] but this trend may reflect the likelihood of exposure rather than a difference in host susceptibility.[11] The existence of a genetic predisposition to cryptococcosis in humans has not been established, but a single, brief report documented the onset of cryptococcosis 10 years apart in two previously healthy siblings,[43] and genetic factors have been described that increase susceptibility to experimental murine cryptococcosis.[2]

VIRULENCE AND CENTRAL NERVOUS SYSTEM LOCALIZATION

Cryptococcal Capsular Polysaccharide

Within the tissues of the host, *C. neoformans* has a large, distinctive capsule. The major constituent of the capsule appears to be a relatively unbranched chain of α1–3–linked mannose units substituted with xylosyl and β-glucuronyl groups. Serotype specificity appears to be determined by small structural differences in this glucuronoxylomannan (GXM), including the number of xylose residues and the degree of *O*-acetylation of hydroxyl groups.[2] A galactoxylomannan complex is also present as a minor capsular or cell wall constituent[44] along with one or more mannoproteins.[45] The capsular polysaccharide has a high negative cell surface charge,[46] perhaps because of sialoglycoconjugates, which may contribute to cryptococcal resistance to phagocytosis.[47] Cryptococcal polysaccharide also appears to be immunosuppressive. In mice injected with GXM, a T-cell–independent antigen, low-dose tolerance can occur by CD4$^+$ T-cell–dependent mechanisms, but high-dose tolerance is T cell independent.[48] In humans, long after being cured of cryptococcosis, patients often exhibit prolonged, specific immunologic unresponsiveness to cryptococcal polysaccharide both in vitro and in vivo, but responses to type III pneumococcal polysaccharide are not depressed when compared with responses to challenge in immune, healthy persons.[49] In addition, capsular polysaccharide suppresses leukocyte migration[50] and causes neutrophils to shed L-selectin, potentially preventing attachment to vascular endothelium and migration from the blood stream to sites of infections in tissues.[51] The diverse effects of the capsular polysaccharide on cell-mediated immunity include inhibition of human T-cell responses to disrupted cryptococci[52] and inhibition of the antigen-presenting capacity of macrophages.[53] Encapsulated or unencapsulated organisms and soluble capsular polysaccharide activate the alternative complement pathway in serum in vitro and in vivo.[55] Complement activation by the soluble capsular polysaccharide requires high concentrations[54] that are occasionally reached in some patients' sera,[34] and thus the potential is created for depletion of complement components during severe cryptococcosis and fungemia.[55] *C. neoformans* can also augment production of HIV in latently infected, cultured human monocytic cells, which raises the possibility of accelerating the progression of HIV infection.[56] In any case, the documented prolonged persistence of cryptococcal polysaccharide in tissues of infected animals[57] suggests that it might mediate long-term immunologic effects. Even patients with cryptococcosis who have no known predisposing factors often have a variety of defects in parameters of cell-mediated immunity. Patients with active disease or even those cured and tested several years after treatment often demonstrate persistent abnormalities in a variety of parameters. These abnormalities include delayed skin test and in vitro cellular immune responses, such as lymphocyte transformation or production of cytokines in response to cryptococcal antigens and, sometimes, to other antigens or to mitogens. Antigen-specific suppression of cell-mediated responses may contribute to such defects.[49] Genetic studies firmly establish that capsule production is essential for *C. neoformans* virulence in mice and requires at least three separate *C. neoformans* genes.[58]

Melanin Production

Genetic studies also suggest that melanin contributes to virulence.[3, 59] The enzyme laccase catalyzes the oxidation of L-dopa and other related aromatic compounds to quinones, which then polymerize to form melanin. Targeted disruption of the laccase gene eliminated melanin production and produced mutants with decreased virulence for mice. The virulence of a melanin-deficient strain was increased after restoration of laccase activity and melanin production by genetic complementation.[59] Melanin is densely deposited in the inner cell wall and may contribute to cell wall integrity,[60] resistance to oxidants or reactive nitrogen intermediates produced by phagocytes,[61] and decreased susceptibility to amphotericin B.[62] High central nervous system (CNS) dopamine levels might then foster the local growth of highly melanized, more virulent yeast.[3]

Other Potential Pathogenicity Factors

C. neoformans releases mannitol in vitro and in vivo in experimentally infected mice, which can serve as a quantitative marker for infection and, because of its hydrophilicity, may also contribute to cerebral edema.[63] Like the capsular polysaccharide, the hydrophilic nature of mannitol has the potential to contribute to brain swelling. In addition, mannitol can quench oxygen radicals and might inhibit killing by host phagocytic cells.[64]

Disruption of the gene for calcineurin results in loss of the ability to grow at 37°C.[65] Growth of *C. neoformans* in cerebrospinal fluid (CSF) in vivo has been shown to require the gene encoding phosphoribosylaminoimidazole carboxylase (*ADE2*).[66] Certain exoenzymes, such as proteases and phospholipases, have been suggested to contribute to pathogenicity, but their roles remain uncertain.[2]

CNS localization may be influenced by the ability of CSF to support active growth of *C. neoformans* inasmuch as CSF lacks the soluble anticryptococcal factors that are present in normal serum.[67] CSF and brain tissue are also deficient in chemotactic and opsonic factors such as complement components, which perhaps contributes to the usually minimal inflammatory response to cryptococci in the brain and might allow lesions to progress in the brain while large inflammatory reactions clear infectious foci outside the CNS.[68]

PATHOPHYSIOLOGY

Pathology

C. neoformans elaborates no known exotoxins. Tissue is only displaced by multiplying organisms, so little necrosis or organ dysfunction usually occurs until late in the course of most infections, although heavier infections may produce more rapid changes. Hemorrhage, infarction, calcification, and extensive fibrosis are extremely rare. The inflammatory response to infection is variable and ranges from minimal to strong. Macrophages and microglial cells may be present in and adjacent to perivascular spaces. Outside the CNS and to a lesser extent in the meninges, macrophages and giant cells are seen with ingested or adjacent cryptococci, together with plasma cells and lymphocytes, but well-formed granulomas are not generally present. Some inflammatory infiltrates are of mixed cell type or contain predominantly neutrophils. The characteristic lesion within the brain, also sometimes seen in other tissues as well, consists of cystic clusters of fungi with no inflammatory response (Fig. 253–1). These lesions are spread diffusely and prominently throughout the brain, so the disease would be more properly termed a *meningoencephalitis* rather than a *meningitis*. Typically, the basal ganglia and cortical gray matter are most heavily involved. Large focal collections of organisms with some inflammatory response may occur in the brain (cryptococcoma, cryptococcal granuloma), but infections are usually diffuse. In severe infections, the brain becomes swollen and soft. Leptomeninges are often thickened, with distention of the subarachnoid by a white, gelatinous material (largely attributable to the cryptococcal capsular polysaccharide).[69]

Cellular Host Defense Mechanisms

Effective cellular host defenses are required for clearance of cryptococci from tissues and development of protective immunity. It is known from experimental pulmonary infections in mice that neutrophils initially clear most of the cryptococci; then monocytes predominate in the later inflammatory infiltrates.[70] Human neutrophils and monocytes can ingest and kill cryptococci in vitro through oxidative[71] and perhaps nonoxidative killing mechanisms. Based on studies in transgenic mice, recruitment of inflammatory cells from the blood stream into infected lungs requires urokinase-mediated proteolysis.[72]

Monocyte-derived macrophages, macrophage-like microglial cells, natural killer cells, and T lymphocytes can kill or at least inhibit the growth of cryptococci in vitro.[73] Indirect evidence suggests that nitric oxide may contribute to clearance of cryptococci by alveolar macrophages.[74] Monocytes from HIV-infected patients have defective oxidant-dependent and oxidant-independent anticryptococcal mechanisms,[75] and HIV envelope protein gp120 inhibits killing by normal monocytes.[76] Clearance of cryptococci after initial infection requires mobilization and activation of macrophages and other effector cells. This process is not effective without the development of immune T cells mediating an effective Th1-type response. Cytokines released by phagocytic cells and lymphocytes have the potential to enhance the anticryptococcal responses of various effector cells. Tumor necrosis factor-α, interleukin-12, interleukin-18, granulocyte-macrophage

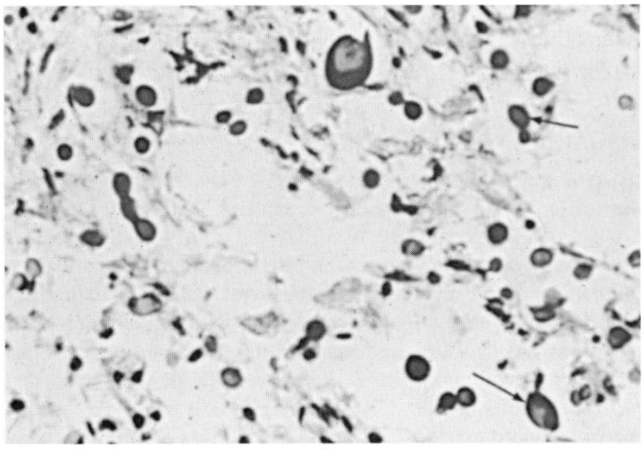

FIGURE 253–1. Cryptococci in brain, delineated by thin, dark-staining cell walls (periodic acid–Schiff). Some cells have characteristic narrow-based buds *(arrows)*. An artifactual halo is visible around organisms as a consequence of shrinkage of the capsule around the cell wall during fixation, rather than tissue necrosis. No inflammatory cells are visible (×800).

colony-stimulating factor, interferon-γ, macrophage inhibitory protein-1α, macrophage chemotactic protein-1, and other cytokines have been implicated in the development of protective Th1-type anticryptococcal immune responses and in the mobilization of inflammatory cells.[77–84] More virulent *C. neoformans* strains may fail to stimulate or block the formation of some of these key cytokines, and cryptococcal capsular polysaccharide can induce interleukin-10 production and a Th2-type response, which can downregulate cell-mediated immune responses.[85] These complex interactions between a broad range of host defense cell and cryptococcal components determine whether immune protection or suppression ultimately develops. Active cell-mediated immune responses indicated by anticryptococcal delayed-type hypersensitivity responses may sometimes reflect nonprotective rather than protective immunity.[86]

Humoral Host Defenses

The strong, natural host resistance to cryptococcosis depends heavily on cellular host defense mechanisms, but increasing data indicate that interactions with humoral defenses can be crucial in preventing and combating progressive infections. Anticryptococcal antibody and complement do not directly damage the organism, but they are key components of some of the cellular host defense mechanisms just described. In addition, anticapsular antibodies can play a crucial role by clearing circulating antigen.[87] Recent studies of monoclonal antibodies against the capsular GXM antigen explain earlier unpredictable results with polyclonal antiserum preparations. Some anti-GXM antibodies are protective when given to animals, but others are not or are even deleterious. Depending on structure, epitope specificity, or isotype, monoclonal antibodies given intravenously or intraperitoneally may vary in their ability to protect or prolong the survival of mice.[88–90] Besides clearing circulating cryptococcal antigen, protective anti-GXM antibodies can enhance opsonization, induce antibody-dependent cell-mediated killing of cryptococci, increase the rate of complement activation, augment the efficacy of antifungal chemotherapy, alter patterns of cytokine expression, enhance granuloma formation, and influence cell-mediated immunity.[87–91] Structural differences between anti-GXM antibodies may have enormous effects on complement deposition in the capsules of intact cryptococci. Some monoclonal antibodies actually decrease rates and total amounts of complement deposition, another mechanism by which certain antibodies might decrease rather than improve opsonization or chemotactic responses by host phagocytes.[91] A GXM–tetanus toxoid conjugate vaccine proved to be immunogenic in mice and humans and was protective in mice.[92, 93] The efficacy of potentially protective antibodies depends on an intact cell-mediated immune response, which emphasizes the complex potential for positive or negative host cellular and humoral interactions. Carefully chosen and tested antibodies have potential therapeutic value that is currently being studied.[89]

CLINICAL MANIFESTATIONS

Central Nervous System

The onset of CNS cryptococcosis may be acute or insidious. Acute manifestations are more common in immunosuppressed patients with AIDS[94] and in those receiving corticosteroid therapy or being treated for lymphoreticular malignancies. Those who have more chronic courses may have waxing and waning manifestations over weeks or months, often with completely asymptomatic periods. Complaints may be referable to the CNS, although they may be mild and nonspecific, such as headache, nausea, dizziness, irritability, somnolence, clumsiness, confusion, or obtundation. Careful questioning of the patient and family may uncover examples of impaired memory and judgment, as well as behavioral changes that affect relationships with others. Some HIV-positive patients have minimal or no symptoms when initially examined. If cranial nerves are involved, the patient may notice decreased visual acuity, diplopia, and facial numbness or weakness. Seizures usually occur only late in the course of infection. Like the history, physical findings do not provide specific clues to the diagnosis. Patients are often afebrile or have a mildly elevated temperature peaking at approximately 39°C, exaggerating the normal diurnal pattern. Most patients have minimal or no nuchal rigidity. Papilledema is noted in up to one third of cases and cranial nerve palsies in about one fifth. Visual loss may be total and attributable to direct fungal involvement of the optic tracts, adhesive arachnoiditis, chorioretinitis, or elevated intracranial pressure. In some patients, hyperreflexia, ankle clonus, or extensor plantar responses can be elicited. Choreoathetoid movements or myoclonic jerks may occur. Except for cranial nerve abnormalities, focal sensory or motor lesions are rare until late in the course of the disease. Large focal granulomas may produce focal neurologic findings, but such granulomas are rare. Whether an individual patient has an indolent or a rapidly progressive course seems to correlate with the degree of concomitant immunosuppression by HIV infection, corticosteroids, hematologic malignancy, or other factors. Dementia may develop because of direct involvement of the brain by the infection. However, late recrudescence of symptoms may indicate the presence of hydrocephalus.

Differences can be seen in clinical patterns of infection caused by the two varieties of *C. neoformans. C. neoformans* var. *gattii* tends to affect patients without evident predisposing factors and seldom affects HIV-infected patients.[18, 19] When compared with infections caused by *C. neoformans* var. *neoformans*, infections caused by *C. neoformans* var. *gattii* are more often associated with cerebral or pulmonary mass lesions, multiple enhancing lesions on imaging studies, papilledema, high CSF and serum cryptococcal antigen titers, and hydrocephalus. Although mortality tends to be lower, long-term neurologic sequelae are more common after cure of infections caused by *C. neoformans* var. *gattii* strains, even after prolonged courses of therapy. By comparison, the large majority of patients infected with *C. neoformans* var. *neoformans* strains are immunosuppressed and more frequently have diffusely disseminated lesions, as evidenced by positive blood or urine cultures, as well as higher fatality rates.

Respiratory System

Pulmonary cryptococcosis may be asymptomatic or may cause the production of only scant, sometimes blood-streaked sputum. Among HIV-positive patients, 5 to 25% of those with cryptococcosis present with cough and dyspnea. The patient may complain of a dull ache in the chest. More specific findings suggesting pulmonary pathologic changes such as rales or pleural friction rub are unusual. Pleural effusions may be present but are uncommon, and empyema is extremely rare. Cough and dyspnea have been the initial findings in 5 to 28% of HIV-positive patients with cryptococcosis[94–97] but are unusual in those who are nonimmunosuppressed. Adult respiratory distress syndrome may ensue. In nonimmunosuppressed patients, pulmonary cryptococcosis may progress or regress spontaneously or may remain stable for long periods. In most cases of CNS cryptococcosis in nonimmunosuppressed patients, pulmonary involvement is not apparent. Conversely, involvement of the respiratory tree often occurs alone, although it may also coexist with extrapulmonary cryptococcosis inside and outside the CNS. In patients with AIDS, cryptococcal pneumonia can be severe and rapidly progressive. A 42% acute-phase mortality was noted in one series.[97] Endobronchial obstruction and laryngeal involvement have also been rarely noted.

Other Sites

Besides the respiratory system, cryptococcosis may involve several other sites outside the CNS.[86] Single or multiple skin lesions may be found in 5 to 10% of patients, commonly as painless lesions of the face or scalp.[98–100] These nonspecific lesions are often ignored, although they are frequently the first signs of infection. Lesions may

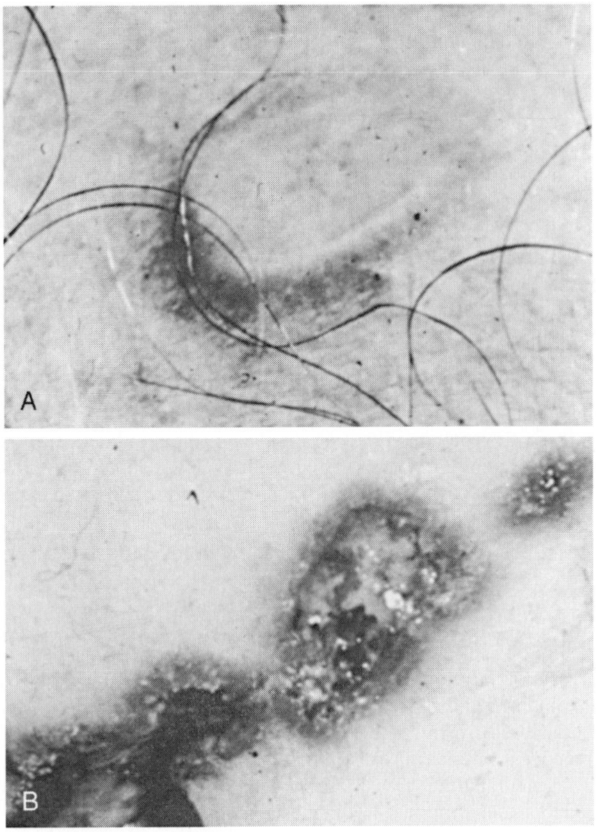

FIGURE 253–2. Nonspecific small lesion of cutaneous cryptococcosis. *A*, Papules and other small lesions can sometimes progress to large lesions. *B*, Unusual, extensive ulcerated lesion of the lower face from a different patient.

appear as small papules, pustules, erythematous indurated plaques, soft subcutaneous masses, draining sinus tracts, or larger ulcers with rolled, slightly undermined edges surrounding a base of granulation tissue (Fig. 253–2). Umbilicated papules in AIDS patients may resemble molluscum contagiosum. Cellulitis with necrotizing vasculitis has been observed in transplant recipients.[101] Oral mucosal and vulvar lesions occasionally occur. Bleeding into skin lesions may occur in patients with thrombocytopenia and result in palpable purpura. Regional lymph nodes are not involved. Bone lesions occur in as many as 5 to 10% of patients; they are usually osteolytic but may be asymptomatic or resemble cold abscesses such as those seen with tuberculosis.[102] Such lesions may be clinically mistaken for neoplasms. Joint, bursa, or muscle involvement is unusual. In post-transplant patients, cryptococcal pyelonephritis has been reported as a cause of renal allograft rejection.[103] Prostatic cryptococcosis occurs, especially in patients with AIDS, and may be manifested as peripheral nodules suggestive of tumor.[104] Other, less common forms of cryptococcosis include epididymo-orchitis, breast masses, otitis, chorioretinitis, conjunctivitis, endophthalmitis, sinusitis, adrenal involvement, myocarditis, endocarditis, pericarditis, esophagitis, gastroduodenitis, hepatitis, cholecystitis, peritonitis, arthritis, bursitis, renal abscess, and placental involvement. Rarely, localized extraneural lesions have occurred as primary infections attributed to direct inoculation, including "sporotrichoid" lymphadenitis, keratitis, peritonitis associated with continuous ambulatory peritoneal dialysis, or subcutaneous nodules resulting from laboratory accidents.[24]

DIAGNOSIS

Blood and Cerebrospinal Fluid Findings

Even with widespread cryptococcosis, usually no abnormalities are found in such routine laboratory test results as hematocrit, peripheral blood leukocyte count, and sedimentation rate, which are often abnormal in other infections. Eosinophilia is rarely present. Except for infections in severely immunosuppressed patients, such as those with AIDS, CNS involvement is almost always indicated by abnormalities in CSF. Opening pressure is often elevated, glucose is depressed, the protein concentration is usually increased, and leukocyte counts are 20/mm^3 or higher, with lymphocytes generally outnumbering neutrophils. An eosinophilic pleocytosis may occur rarely. CSF abnormalities are frequently minimal or absent in AIDS patients and occasionally so in others, but cryptococci grow in cultures.[94, 95] Besides those who have AIDS, this pattern is seen most often in patients with early, asymptomatic CNS disease when lumbar punctures are performed because of cryptococcosis at other sites or in patients who are immunosuppressed and have severe hematologic malignancies complicated by acute, rapidly progressing cryptococcosis. In the latter, the heavy infection may be reflected by the ease of finding the organism in India ink smears of CSF. In patients who have an indolent, waxing and waning course with asymptomatic periods, abnormalities in CSF persist and indicate continued activity of the disease.

Smear and Culture

Detection of the organism by culture is necessary for diagnosis. India ink smears cannot be used to definitely establish the presence of *C. neoformans,* but they can provide valuable support for a presumptive diagnosis that guides the direction of further diagnostic efforts. A drop of the sediment of 3 to 5 ml or more of CSF is mixed on a slide with an equal volume of India ink or nigrosin, and a coverslip is set in place. If correctly made, one should be able to barely read newsprint through the preparation. Because few cryptococci may be present, the entire slide should be examined. When the test is performed in this manner, cryptococci are seen in 25 to 50% of patients with cryptococcal meningitis.[94, 95] Strict criteria for identification of organisms should be used, especially for distinctness of the outline of the cell wall and capsule, because artifacts are often mistaken for cryptococci when details of cell structure are ignored (Fig. 253–3). Cryptococcosis has also been diagnosed with routine cytologic stains, although false-positive readings have occurred when this technique is used. Similarly, the appearance of cryptococci may vary considerably on Gram-stained smears of purulent specimens, so these smears may prove to be especially misleading for diagnostic use. Solutions

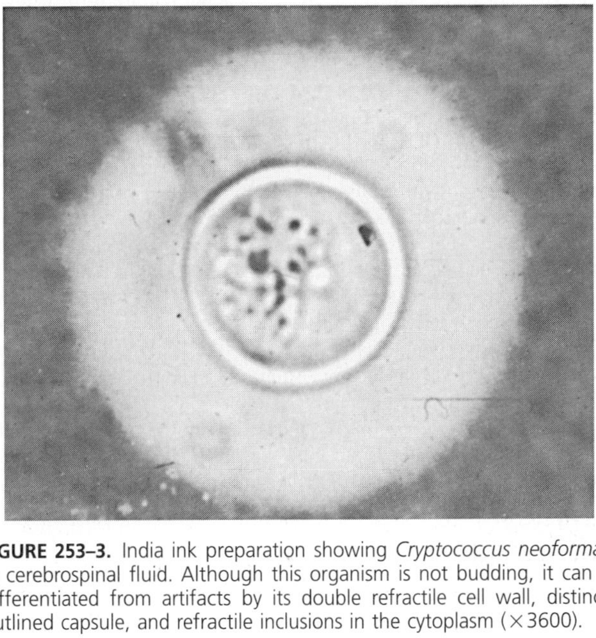

FIGURE 253–3. India ink preparation showing *Cryptococcus neoformans* in cerebrospinal fluid. Although this organism is not budding, it can be differentiated from artifacts by its double refractile cell wall, distinctly outlined capsule, and refractile inclusions in the cytoplasm (×3600).

used in the aforementioned procedures may also become contaminated with nonpathogenic cryptococci or other fungi. For these reasons, a positive smear must always be confirmed by culture. Centrifuged sediment from 5 to 10 ml or more of CSF should be cultured on three or more different occasions. Negative cultures do not absolutely rule out cryptococcosis because often only small numbers of organisms are present in some CSF and may be missed. Therefore, large specimens of CSF are occasionally required for diagnosis. To minimize desiccation of media over a 4- to 6-week incubation period and to increase the culture yield in difficult cases, large volumes of unsedimented CSF may be placed on large surfaces of Sabouraud agar on the bottoms of Erlenmeyer flasks. Besides repeated sampling of CSF, cultures should be made from any suspicious extraneural lesions. Urine and sputum should also be cultured, even without clinical or laboratory evidence suggesting involvement of the genitourinary or respiratory systems. Sputum cultures may be positive in the absence of roentgenographic evidence of pulmonary infection.[41] Similarly, urine cultures are commonly positive, although renal parenchymal involvement is rarely clinically detectable. Use of niger seed (birdseed) agar for primary isolation may increase the rate of detection of *C. neoformans* in sputum and urine specimens.[105] In AIDS patients with cryptococcal pneumonia, the combined sensitivity for smear and culture of specimens obtained by bronchoalveolar lavage and washings was noted to be as good or better than that of transbronchial biopsy.[106] Positive blood cultures occur most often in association with AIDS or rapid increases in corticosteroid doses or neutropenia and most often indicate extensive infection,[41] although some such patients with cryptococcosis can be cured.[107] Blood cultures may rarely become positive after urinary tract instrumentation in localized lesions of the genitourinary tract. In the occasional acute, extensive infection, cryptococci may be seen within leukocytes on peripheral blood smears or within bone marrow macrophages or megakaryocytes. Whenever cryptococcosis is documented at any site, a careful search is mandated for lesions elsewhere, both inside and outside the CNS. Isolation of *C. neoformans* should be performed on media without cycloheximide (Acti-Dione), which inhibits the growth of nonpathogens but also cryptococci. *C. neoformans* grows at 37°C but more rapidly at lower temperatures (e.g., 30°C); the latter should therefore be used for primary isolation. The lysis-centrifugation (isolator) method of blood culture is most rapid and sensitive. Because radiometric detection techniques may be less sensitive than standard procedures, negative bottles should be subcultured before being discarded. When compared with cultures, polymerase chain reaction methods have the potential to increase the sensitivity and speed of definitive diagnosis but require further development and testing to improve specificity and standardize procedures.

Histopathology

When tissue specimens are obtained, cryptococcosis may be diagnosed from the histologic sections. The organism is almost colorless and difficult to see with routine hematoxylin and eosin stains. Methenamine silver or periodic acid–Schiff stain clearly demarcates *C. neoformans* and permits recognition of its characteristic size and shape; it is seen as a yeastlike organism that reproduces by the formation of narrow-based buds (see Fig. 253–1). *C. neoformans* can then be distinguished from other yeastlike fungi, as well as from artifacts, by Mayer's mucicarmine stain, which colors the cryptococcal capsule rose red but does not stain other fungi that have similar morphologic characteristics. The Masson-Fontana silver stain for melanin also stains *C. laurentii* and is thus not completely specific for *C. neoformans*,[59] but it can be used for the histologic diagnosis of cryptococcosis.[108] Masson-Fontana staining may also be combined with capsular staining with mucicarmine or alcian blue.

Serologic Tests

Several serologic tests for cryptococcosis have been described. However, detection of cryptococcal polysaccharide capsular antigen is the only procedure that is clinically useful on a routine basis. Commercially available latex agglutination kits for detection of antigen generally use controls for nonspecific agglutination by rheumatoid factor in serum.[34, 109, 110] Pronase treatment or boiling of serum (but not CSF) improves the differentiation of positive and negative agglutination reactions while eliminating some false negatives and prozone-like reactions (positive specimens that fail to agglutinate unless diluted to higher titers). False-positive tests may also occur from contamination with soaps or detergents or by inadvertent transfer of surface fluid from agar culture media on wire loops. In addition, the test may detect cross-reactive antigens in disseminated infections with *Trichosporon beigelii* or *Capnocytophaga canimorsus (DF-2 bacillus)*. Titers of most false-positive results are 1:8 or less,[34, 110] but they may be even higher with some batches of commercial kits. In general, false-positive cryptococcal antigen test results are unusual if assays are performed carefully with proper controls, but a definitive diagnosis of cryptococcosis requires that positive antigen results be confirmed by culture. Latex agglutination detects antigen in CSF or serum (or both) from 90% or more of patients with cryptococcal meningitis, but CSF assays are more sensitive.[94–97, 109] Serum antigen tests are less often positive in extraneural cryptococcosis. However, testing of serum as well as CSF specimens can be useful if serum assays are positive in certain cases of cryptococcosis outside the CNS or remain high despite extended therapy. Lack of standardization among manufacturers of cryptococcal antigen tests means that titers cannot be compared without regard to which kit was used. Titers obtained at different times during the course of an infection are best compared by simultaneous testing of recent and prior samples. Cryptococcal antigen has also been detected in bronchoalveolar lavage or pleural fluid, transthoracic needle aspirates, and urine, but procedures and criteria for diagnosis are not standardized. Newer commercial antigen tests such as enzyme-linked antigen capture immunoassay appear sensitive and specific,[110] but experience in their use is more limited. As currently marketed, these enzyme-linked antigen detection kits are not useful for monitoring the results of therapy.

Because the cryptococcal antigen test is a sensitive and relatively specific indicator of CNS cryptococcosis, active cryptococcal infection may be present in some patients with negative cultures but positive CSF or serum antigen titers. Such patients should have CSF recultured as detailed before and be monitored closely. It has been suggested that persistently positive CSF or serum antigen titers signify cryptic infections that require treatment, even if therapy would be unnecessarily given to some patients who have false-positive antigen tests.[110] However, current data do not shed light on the likelihood that clinically apparent cryptococcosis will develop in culture-negative, antigen-positive patients. New studies would also be required to determine the efficacy of such presumptive therapy for preventing progressive cryptococcosis, the required duration of regimens, and relative risks in comparison to close follow-up observation.

Anticryptococcal antibodies are undetectable in most patients with cryptococcal meningitis, but low concentrations of antibody, principally IgM, are found in a significant percentage of healthy people. Therefore, the presence of antibody is not useful for diagnosis but may have slight value as a prognostic factor signaling a high likelihood for a favorable outcome in cryptococcal meningitis.[41] Several workers have made different preparations of cryptococcin for delayed skin testing,[23] but these are useful primarily in epidemiologic and immunologic studies and not at all in diagnosis.

Hydrocephalus

CNS cryptococcosis may be complicated by hydrocephalus. Hydrocephalus may be signaled by early or late clinical deterioration, with late development of increased intracranial pressure, or by a recrudescence of abnormalities after initial improvement. When hydrocephalus is suspected, computed tomography (CT) and magnetic

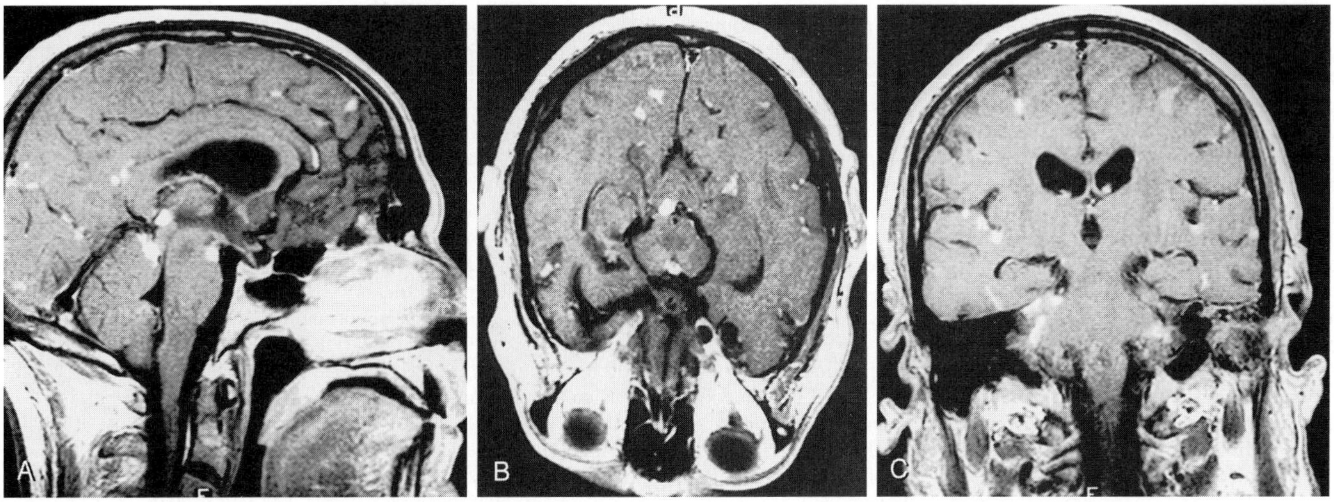

FIGURE 253–4. Sagittal *(A)*, coronal *(B)*, and cross-sectional *(C)* magnetic resonance imaging views showing multiple, widely scattered, small enhancing lesions (T_2-weighted image with gadopentetate dimeglumine enhancement). Most are subarachnoid, seen diffusely over the surface of the brain, including the brain stem and cerebellum, especially within fissures or sulci. Some are localized within cisterns or slightly dilated ventricles, but few parenchymal lesions can be seen. These enhancing lesions enlarged over a 4-month period during an extended course of antifungal therapy. Some neurologic deficits persisted after the patient's later cure, but he is ambulatory and functions independently. (Courtesy of Dr. S. Levitz, Boston, Mass., and Drs. C. Fenlon and M. Abdelazim, Binghamton, N.Y.)

resonance imaging (MRI) are the preferred methods for defining the ventricular system and confirming the diagnosis.

Differential Diagnosis

The differential diagnosis of cryptococcosis and other causes of chronic meningitis has been reviewed thoroughly by Ellner and Bennett.[111] Early CNS cryptococcosis may closely resemble other mycoses and tuberculosis, as well as viral meningoencephalitis or meningeal metastases. Elevated CSF adenosine deaminase levels were suggested as a useful diagnostic marker for tuberculous meningitis, but they may be elevated in cryptococcosis as well.[112] Cryptococcosis may resemble chronic meningitis that is due to treatable infections other than tuberculosis (e.g., coccidioidomycosis, histoplasmosis, other mycoses, brucellosis, syphilis) or to noninfectious causes (e.g., sarcoidosis, chronic benign lymphocytic meningitis).[111] The absence of definite localizing neurologic signs outside the distribution of cranial nerves reduces the likelihood of the diagnosis of intracranial neoplasm.

CT or MRI findings may be normal or reveal diffuse atrophy, cerebral edema, hydrocephalus, or focal mass lesions. Multiple nonenhancing lesions may be present, most often in the basal ganglia and thalamus, but sometimes at other sites, including infratentorial areas. These lesions are thought to correspond to the gelatinous pseudocysts seen in histopathologic specimens.[2, 113] On T_2-weighted MRI, nonenhancing parenchymal cryptococcomas may also be associated with nonenhancing, hyperintense, dilated perivascular Virchow-Robin spaces.[114] CT or MRI may demonstrate diffuse atrophy or cerebral edema, as revealed by focal homogeneous or doughnut-shaped, contrast-enhanced areas with or without surrounding circumferential areas of decreased density, even in asymptomatic patients. Cryptococcal masses must be distinguished from other causes of such intracranial mass lesions, including pyogenic, nocardial, or *Aspergillus*-associated abscesses, tuberculosis, toxoplasmosis, hemorrhage, lymphoma, or other neoplasms. MRI, particularly with gadopentetate dimeglumine enhancement, is more sensitive than CT scanning. Multiple small enhancing subarachnoid or parenchymal nodules may be present[2, 115] (Fig. 253–4). Focal cryptococcal lesions sometimes initially expand during the first few months of therapy,[2] as occurred in the patient whose MRI study is shown in Figure 253–4. In patients with dementia, progressive multifocal leukoencephalopathy can be detected by MRI. The possibility of mass lesions should be investigated by CT or MRI in patients with decreased mentation, who might have an increased risk of complications after lumbar puncture.

When pulmonary cryptococcosis occurs in patients without AIDS, the most common roentgenographic picture resembles tumor: single or multiple circumscribed masses or nodules without hilar involvement, more often in the upper lobes (Fig. 253–5).[116] Various other patterns are seen less often, including segmental pneumonia, thick-walled single cavities, lymphadenopathy, pleural effusion, and generalized miliary disease. Patients with AIDS usually manifest fever, cough, and dyspnea, often with pleuritic chest pain, sometimes with roentgenographic findings of lymphadenopathy or pleural effusions, and most often with diffuse mixed interstitial and intra-alveolar infiltrates.[96] The clinical findings in such patients are often indistinguishable from those of patients with acute pneumonia caused by *Pneumocystis carinii, Mycobacterium tuberculous, Histoplasma capsulatum,* or other organisms. Bronchoscopy with washings and brushings is usually diagnostic. Unusual patterns also include bronchiolitis obliterans, organizing pneumonia, and adult respiratory distress syn-

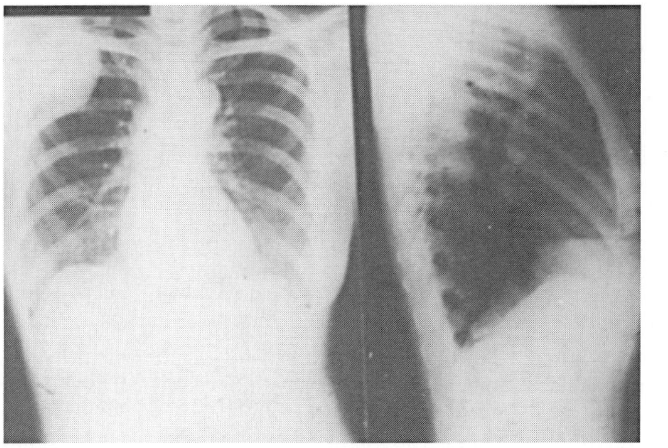

FIGURE 253–5. Chest roentgenogram from a patient with pulmonary cryptococcosis that manifested as a right upper lobe mass, simulating tumor.

drome. Cavitary lesions or asymptomatic solitary pulmonary nodules occasionally occur during the earlier phases of HIV infection.[117, 118] In patients without AIDS, the differential diagnosis is complicated by the fact that patients with pulmonary neoplasms or chronic lung disease may have repeated positive cultures of *C. neoformans* in sputum specimens, which is apparently due to saprophytic colonization rather than tissue invasion by the organisms in the lungs or elsewhere.[119] Because sputum cultures may be negative with invasive parenchymal cryptococcosis, demonstration of tissue invasion by cryptococci is usually necessary for the diagnosis of pulmonary cryptococcosis, sometimes requiring surgery. AIDS patients may also harbor one or more of the aforementioned or other conditions concomitant with cryptococcosis.

Cutaneous lesions of cryptococcosis are nonspecific and may be mistaken for a wide range of lesions, including those of comedo, acne, lipoma, syphilis, tuberculosis, sarcoidosis, molluscum contagiosum, or basal cell carcinoma. However, these lesions are readily accessible for biopsy and offer the opportunity for rapid diagnosis because cryptococci are present in large numbers and are easily identified. Bone lesions are usually round and lytic, without sclerosis at the margins, and resemble bone lesions caused by other fungi and by tuberculosis, especially if a cold abscess is present.

TREATMENT

Multiple studies have compared a variety of treatment regimens for cryptococcosis in patients with and without AIDS. Unlike the outcome in HIV-negative patients, cryptococcosis is seldom cured in patients with AIDS, and lifelong suppressive treatment is necessary. Differences in natural history and prognosis dictate caution in extrapolating the results of therapeutic trials in AIDS patients to treatment of non-AIDS patients and vice versa.

Patients Who Are Negative for the Human Immunodeficiency Virus

Initial prospective controlled studies of treatment of CNS cryptococcosis were performed in HIV-negative patients. One effective regimen for CNS cryptococcosis is a 6-week course of 0.3 mg/kg of amphotericin B administered intravenously plus 150 mg/kg of flucytosine in four divided oral doses daily.[120] Flucytosine resistance develops less often if amphotericin B is used in combination. Use of higher doses of amphotericin B increases the frequency of toxic reactions to flucytosine. It has been suggested that the doses of amphotericin used in this[120] and a follow-up study[121] were suboptimal.[122] Amphotericin B doses of 0.4 mg/kg/day or higher in combination with flucytosine are recommended empirically by some experts, especially during the first few weeks of therapy. Depression of the leukocyte or platelet count and diarrhea may be sufficiently severe to necessitate discontinuation of flucytosine treatment, but combination therapy with amphotericin B can be well tolerated even in myelosuppressed patients if dosages are regularly adjusted according to serum flucytosine levels. It is important to reduce the risk of flucytosine accumulation because amphotericin-induced azotemia develops by initiating therapy with only 75 to 100 mg/kg/day of flucytosine and continuing doses that sustain serum flucytosine levels between 25 and 60 μg/ml.[123, 124] Relapses are more common in chronically immunosuppressed patients, so prolongation of therapy beyond 6 weeks is often indicated. Nonimmunosuppressed patients can sometimes be cured after only 4 weeks of therapy,[121] but this abbreviated regimen should be limited to those who have negative cultures and India ink smears in large-volume CSF samples with 2 weeks or less of therapy, as determined weekly by an experienced laboratory.

If toxicity, vomiting, or confusion precludes flucytosine administration, amphotericin B can be used alone (0.5 to 0.7 mg/kg/day intravenously for at least 10 weeks). Double doses of amphotericin B can be substituted on alternate days for convenience. Febrile reactions to amphotericin B are not noted in all patients and are manageable by adjusting the dosage and administering low doses of corticosteroids. It should not be necessary to discontinue therapy because of severe fever, nausea, or early rapid progression of azotemia. Meperidine may be used to reduce the discomfort of severe chills. Therapy with any regimen is generally continued until weekly cultures are negative for 4 weeks. Positive India ink smears do not necessarily indicate continued active infection, although amphotericin B therapy is usually prolonged (to reach approximate total doses of 2.5 to 3.0 g) for persistently positive smears despite negative cultures. At the end of therapy, CSF glucose should be normal in most patients, but protein abnormalities (while improving) may be present for years and should not dictate prolongation of therapy. Intrathecal amphotericin B may be injected intracisternally or intraventricularly via an implanted subcutaneous reservoir but is rarely indicated.[125, 126]

Uncontrolled series and individual case reports suggest that oral fluconazole in doses ranging from 200 to 800 mg/day can be effective for many HIV-negative patients, has low toxicity, and facilitates outpatient management. One relatively small retrospective series reported equal efficacy of oral fluconazole and intravenous amphotericin B with or without flucytosine for the treatment of meningeal and nonmeningeal cryptococcosis in HIV-negative patients.[127] However, a higher percentage of patients with CNS involvement received amphotericin B, drug dosage and the duration of therapy varied widely, success was defined only as negative cultures at the end of therapy, relapse rates were not defined, and 1-year survival was unevaluable in 25% of patients. Ease of administration and relatively low toxicity suggest that oral fluconazole may be a logical first choice for some low-risk patients with no apparent predisposing factors or complications and minimal signs or symptoms. Even so, current data do not provide assurance that outcomes of treatment with oral fluconazole, including ultimate mortality and residual neurologic deficits, would be at least as good as with older, established alternative regimens. Likewise, it is unknown how long to treat and whether chronic maintenance suppressive therapy after the completion of initial treatment would benefit any group of severely immunosuppressed patients, such as certain types of transplant recipients. Because a relatively small percentage of patients with cryptococcosis are HIV negative, many decisions to use a particular drug, combination, dosage, or duration of therapy in individual HIV-negative patients must still be based on clinical judgment.

Treatment of Extraneural, Nonrespiratory Lesions

Presumably, therapy for cryptococcosis outside the respiratory system and CNS is analogous to that for meningitis, but series are too small to establish this point with certainty. Some isolated skin lesions appear to become inactive without therapy in nonimmunosuppressed patients. In the absence of AIDS, many cryptococcal lesions of skin, bone, or other organs have been treated with combined amphotericin B–flucytosine therapy or with a total adult dose of 2 to 3 g of amphotericin B intravenously. Case reports and small series suggest that oral fluconazole also can be effective, is easier to administer, and is much less toxic. Neither the optimum dosage nor the optimum duration of therapy is defined, but 400 to 800 mg/day for 8 to 12 weeks or more has been used successfully in individual cases. Surgical therapy is probably not helpful for most lesions, with the possible exception of curettage of bone lesions.

Special Considerations in Pulmonary Cryptococcosis

In patients who have no identifiable predisposing immunologic defects, considerations in the treatment of pulmonary cryptococcosis are different from those in meningeal or nonmeningeal nonpulmonary infection. Whereas the latter requires systemic drug treatment, most cases of pulmonary cryptococcosis occurring without concomitant immunosuppression or immunodeficiency resolve without antifungal therapy.[128] Because sputum cultures are often negative and may be falsely positive, diagnosis must often be made by surgical biopsy. The risk of meningitis as a postoperative complication is low. Total excision may be curative but is unnecessary if antifungal therapy is required. Antifungal therapy can probably be postponed during close observation for 2 to 3 months, as long as the CSF is normal and culture is negative, urine cultures are negative, the lesion is small and stable or decreasing in size, and the patient has no predisposing factors (corticosteroid therapy, lymphoreticular malignancy, or AIDS). Many such patients now are given oral fluconazole, but the dose, duration, and relative benefits are unknown. In general, the natural history of pulmonary cryptococcosis in abnormal hosts appears most often to consist of the development of disseminated infections in the absence of antifungal therapy.[128]

Patients with Acquired Immunodeficiency Syndrome

For initial therapy, results of a large, randomized trial of cryptococcal meningitis indicated that about 6 weeks of 200 to 400 mg/day of fluconazole was as effective as 0.4 to 0.6 mg/day of amphotericin B, except in patients with certain adverse prognostic features (e.g., positive blood cultures, CSF antigen titers greater than 128, positive CSF India ink smears, or impaired mental status).[129] Flucytosine was combined with amphotericin B in less than 15% of patients because earlier retrospective data suggested little or no benefit and greater toxicity if flucytosine were added to amphotericin B. Severely ill patients likely to die in 2 weeks were excluded. Even so, early deaths occurred more often among fluconazole-treated patients, which led investigators to recommend amphotericin B as the preferred choice for initial therapy. In a later double-blind multicenter trial, all patients were given a higher initial dose of amphotericin B (0.7 mg/kg/day) with or without flucytosine (100 mg/kg/day) for 2 weeks, followed by an additional 8 weeks of treatment with 400 mg/day of either fluconazole or itraconazole and then half that dose for maintenance.[130] No added toxicity or improved efficacy was noted in patients who received 2 weeks of 100 mg/kg/day of flucytosine. Itraconazole was not significantly worse than fluconazole during the subsequent 8 weeks but was less effective in preventing relapse during maintenance. A newer oral itraconazole solution formulation has improved bioavailability and might prove to be more effective.

Data are extremely limited about the efficacy of lipid preparations of amphotericin B in cryptococcosis.[131, 132] Liposomal amphotericin B (AmBisome) is approved for patients with cryptococcosis who have failed to respond or had unacceptable toxicity with amphotericin B deoxycholate, the approval based on noncomparative, open studies. Amphotericin B lipid complex did not appear promising in a small, short trial of cryptococcal meningitis in AIDS patients.[131] Current limited data do not warrant their routine use or substitution for amphotericin B deoxycholate, but they may be of value for situations in which amphotericin B is preferred but severe nephrotoxicity is a problem.

Higher doses of fluconazole (800 to 2000 mg/day) have been given to small numbers of AIDS patients after 2 weeks of amphotericin B therapy or to initiate anticryptococcal therapy with or without concomitant flucytosine. A prospective multicenter study of AIDS patients indicated that the addition of flucytosine (150 mg/kg/day) to fluconazole independently correlated with clearing of cultures by the end of a 10-week course of therapy. However, the addition of flucytosine to fluconazole did not improve clinical end points, and the daily dose of fluconazole (800 to 2000 mg/day) did not correlate with outcome.[133] The utility of higher fluconazole doses and utility of the flucytosine-fluconazole combination remains to be determined.

Lifelong maintenance therapy follows initial therapy in all patients. Fluconazole, 200 mg/day, proved superior to weekly amphotericin B.[134] Higher doses of fluconazole may be used if necessary. Fluconazole maintenance therapy has been well tolerated except for an occasional case of alopecia. Positive cultures persist or recur in some patients despite ongoing antifungal therapy. The prostate, in particular, represents a sequestered focus for active infection. Such sequestration is manifested by positive urine cultures, ideally obtained after prostatic massage. High levels of fluconazole may fail to sterilize urine,[135] but clinical relapse during full-dose maintenance therapy is unusual.

Susceptibility Testing

Fluconazole susceptibility was a partial predictor of CSF sterilization in one study,[132] but to date, recurrent positive CSF cultures in patients receiving fluconazole maintenance therapy have not been attributable to reduced susceptibility.[29] Marked differences between isolates in susceptibility to amphotericin B and fluconazole have been encountered with some assays, but the clinical significance is unknown.[136] At present, in vitro susceptibility testing of *C. neoformans* remains an investigational tool.

General Considerations in Therapy

HIV-negative patients with cryptococcosis involving any site should be evaluated every few months for at least 1 year after therapy, even if asymptomatic. Relapses in culture positivity usually occur in the first year after therapy, rarely later. Clinically apparent relapses become obvious much later, usually after significant organ damage has occurred. CSF should be monitored even if the original site of infection was outside the CNS. Conversely, cryptococcosis that originally involved the CNS may relapse with positive cultures in urine or sputum, in addition to CSF.[41] The increased use of CT and MRI scans of the brain has revealed mass lesions in many patients with CNS cryptococcosis, even in the absence of signs or symptoms of increased intracranial pressure.[114] These masses regress very slowly over months and years after treatment and may even enlarge initially.[2] However, no evidence indicates that such patients require either surgery or more prolonged courses of antifungal therapy. Death from cryptococcal meningitis often occurs early in the course of therapy and is frequently due to cerebral edema,[130] sometimes leading to brain stem compression. Opening pressure on lumbar puncture is high, sometimes over 500 mm H_2O. Ventricles are normal or small on CT or MRI scans, and cortical sulci may be flat. In general, ventricular drainage or shunting is not helpful. High doses of dexamethasone may provide temporary benefit, but long-term use interferes with clearance of organisms by antifungal therapy. In one multicenter trial, symptomatic patients with lumbar puncture opening pressures greater than 180 mm H_2O or asymptomatic patients with pressures greater than 320 received daily lumbar punctures, acetazolamide, and ventriculoperitoneal shunts.[130] Because no comparative trials have been completed, it is unknown whether these or any other measures can decrease mortality. Elevated CSF pressure in patients with cryptococcosis has also been linked to visual loss, but cerebral edema is sometimes not prominent when visual loss occurs.[137] Anecdotal reports suggest that some patients beginning to experience visual loss may benefit from reduction in intracranial pressure. Ventriculostomy, acetazolamide, and other measures have also been tried, but objective evidence to support their use is lacking.[138]

PROGNOSIS

Infections are rarely cured completely in patients with AIDS, and certain immunosuppressed patients with neoplastic disease are subject to even more rapid mortality or treatment failure.[139] In others, the mortality rate of treated cryptococcal meningitis is probably approximately 25 to 30%, although results in individual series may vary widely. After initial cure, at least with amphotericin B therapy, up to 20 to 25% of these patients relapse. Of those who are cured, 40% have significant residual neurologic deficits, including visual loss, cranial nerve palsies, significant motor impairment, or personality change and decreased mental function secondary to chronic brain syndrome or hydrocephalus. Hydrocephalus can cause late complications or death even when the infection is cured.[41] When severe enough to require shunting, hydrocephalus can lead to permanent loss of cognitive function.[41] Shunting can improve dementia and the device does not serve as a nidus of infection. Detection and relief of hydrocephalus are vital to ensure an optimum outcome. [1] In a large series of HIV-negative patients treated with amphotericin B, 55% died when predisposing factors (lymphoreticular malignancy or corticosteroid therapy) were present, as opposed to 25% in the absence of apparent predisposing factors. However, the worsened outcome was apparently eliminated when corticosteroid dosages were tapered and stopped or when patients were switched to an alternate-day regimen before the end of antifungal therapy. In addition, failure of antifungal therapy was more likely with certain CSF abnormalities, including an elevated opening pressure, a low glucose level, a leukocyte count less than 20/mm^3, and a positive India ink preparation. Not surprisingly, indications of extensive infection, such as culture of cryptococci from extraneural sites (especially blood) and high titers of cryptococcal antigen in blood or CSF, also signaled a poor outcome. However, prolonged positive cultures during therapy or a positive India ink smear with negative cultures after therapy were not necessarily bad prognostic signs.[41] In a more recent series of HIV-negative patients, besides neoplastic disease and disseminated infection at the time of diagnosis, abnormal mental status, age older than 60 years, and therapeutic failure were independent predictors of death.[127] Similar adverse signs have been reported in AIDS patients.[140] One report cites an association between diastolic hypertension and deaths from cryptococcal meningitis in AIDS patients.[141]

Poor prognostic features after combined amphotericin-flucytosine therapy appear similar to those with amphotericin B alone but also include the absence of headache and the presence of abnormal mental status on admission.[121] Certain subgroups of patients, particularly those who are immunosuppressed or have slow responses to antifungal therapy, may require more prolonged courses of treatment than the standard 6-week regimen. For example, based on the small numbers of patients evaluated, renal transplant recipients receiving continuing doses of azathioprine and prednisone have a high risk of treatment failure or relapse of cryptococcosis after completion of antifungal therapy. However, experience with assorted individual cases indicates that successful treatment of at least some such patients is possible and that repeated rounds of immunosuppression and even successful retransplantation of kidneys appear feasible without relapse after cure of cryptococcosis. Clinical judgment and periodic examinations of the CSF are required to determine whether treatment should deviate from standard regimens. Because cryptococcosis in association with AIDS is only rarely completely cured, objectives of therapy are directed toward defining effective, well-tolerated, long-term outpatient regimens that suppress recrudescence without interfering with the treatment of concomitant problems. Close follow-up throughout the course of maintenance, as well as during initial therapy, is crucial. Patients with AIDS-associated cryptococcal meningitis and rising CSF cryptococcal antigen titers during suppressive therapy are more likely to relapse, just as failure to respond during initial treatment is more likely if titers remain unchanged or increase.[111]

The significant mortality, morbidity, and prevalence of cryptococcosis in patients with AIDS has prompted studies of prevention. Cryptococcosis is unusual in patients whose CD4 lymphocyte counts are greater than 100. For more immunosuppressed patients, several studies suggest that fluconazole can provide effective primary prophylaxis in doses of 200 mg/day, 200 mg three times each week, or 400 mg once weekly.[142–144] However, data thus far have not established that prophylaxis decreases mortality, and cryptococcosis usually responds well to early therapy.[145] Potential benefits of prophylaxis are tempered by considerations of toxicity, interactions with antiretroviral agents and other essential drugs, the possibility of drug resistance, and cost. Thus, fluconazole prophylaxis is not recommended for routine use but might be considered an option for certain patients whose CD4 lymphocyte counts are less than 50.[145] A variety of newer approaches for prevention and adjunctive therapy are in very early stages of study. Preliminary basic experimental data suggest that some agents that alter host defenses may have sufficient promise to warrant pilot trials in humans, such as monoclonal antibodies,[89, 93] vaccines,[92, 93] cytokines, or chloroquine.[145]

REFERENCES

1. Krajden S, Summerbell RC, Kane J, et al. Normally saprobic cryptococci isolated from *Cryptococcus neoformans* infections. J Clin Microbiol. 1991;29:1883–1887.
2. Mitchell TG, Perfect JR. Cryptococcosis in the era of AIDS—100 years after the discovery of *Cryptococcus neoformans*. Clin Microbiol Rev. 1995;8:515–548.
3. Kwon-Chung KJ, Rhodes JC. Encapsulation and melanin formation as indicators of virulence in *Cryptococcus neoformans*. Infect Immun. 1986;51:218–223.
4. Bava AJ, Negroni R, Bianchi M. Cryptococcosis produced by a urease negative strain of *Cryptococcus neoformans*. J Med Vet Mycol. 1993;31:87–89.
5. Jennings A, Bennett JE, Young V. Identification of *Cryptococcus neoformans* in a routine clinical laboratory. Mycopathol Mycol Appl. 1968;35:256–264.
6. Kaufmann CS, Merz WG. Two rapid pigmentation tests for identification of *Cryptococcus neoformans*. J Clin Microbiol. 1982;15:339–341.
7. Wilson DE, Bennett JE, Bailey JW. Serologic grouping of *Cryptococcus neoformans*. Proc Soc Exp Biol Med. 1968;127:820–823.
8. Kwon-Chung KJ, Edman JC, Wickes BL. Genetic association of mating types and virulence in *Cryptococcus neoformans*. Infect Immun. 1992;60:602–605.
9. Kwon-Chung KJ. A new genus, *Filobasidiella*, the perfect state of *Cryptococcus neoformans*. Mycologia. 1975;67:1197–2000.
10. Aulakh HS, Straus SE, Kwon-Chung KJ. Genetic relatedness of *Filobasidiella neoformans* (*Cryptococcus neoformans*) and *Filobasidiella bacillispora* (*Cryptococcus bacillispora*) as determined by deoxyribonucleic acid base composition and sequence homology studies. J Syst Bacteriol. 1981;31:97–103.
11. Levitz SM. The ecology of *Cryptococcus neoformans* and the epidemiology of cryptococcosis. J Infect Dis. 1991;13:1163–1169.
12. Ellis DH, Pfeiffer TJ. Natural habitat of *Cryptococcus neoformans* var. *gattii*. J Clin Microbiol. 1990;28:1642–1644.
13. Pfeiffer TJ, Ellis DH. Environmental isolation of *Cryptococcus neoformans* var. *gattii* from *Eucalyptus tereticornis*. J Med Vet Mycol. 1992;30:407–408.
14. Chen SC, Currie BJ, Campbell HM, et al. *Cryptococcus neoformans* var. *gattii* infection in northern Australia: Existence of an environmental source other than known host eucalypts. *Trans R Soc Trop Med Hyg*. 1997;91:547–550.
15. Mukamurangwa P, Raes-Wuytack C, De Vroey C. *Cryptococcus neoformans* var. *gattii* can be separated from var. *neoformans* by its ability to assimilate D-tryptophan. J Med Vet Mycol. 1995;33:419–420.
16. Min KH, Kwon-Chung KJ. The biochemical basis for the distribution between the two *Cryptococcus neoformans* varieties with CGB medium. Zentralbl Bakteriol. 1986;261:471–480.
17. Kwon-Chung KJ, Wickes BL, Booth JL, et al. Urease inhibition by EDTA in the two varieties of *Cryptococcus neoformans*. Infect Immun. 1987;55:1751–1754.
18. Mitchell DH, Sorrell TC, Allworth AM, et al. Cryptococcal disease of the CNS in immunocompetent hosts: Influence of cryptococcal variety on clinical manifestations and outcome. Clin Infect Dis. 1995;20:611–616.
19. Speed B, Dunt D. Clinical and host differences between infections with the two varieties of *Cryptococcus neoformans*. Clin Infect Dis. 1995;21:28–36.
20. Ruiz A, Neilson JB, Bulmer GS. Control of *Cryptococcus neoformans* in nature by biotic factors. Sabouraudia. 1982;20:21–29.
21. Dromer F, Mathoulin S, Dupont B, et al. Epidemiology of cryptococcosis in France: A 9-year survey (1985–1993). French Cryptococcosis Study Group. Clin Infect Dis. 1996;23:82–90.
22. Neilson JB, Fromtling RA, Bulmer GS. *Cryptococcus neoformans:* Size range of infectious particles from aerosolized soil. Infect Immun. 1977;17:634–638.
23. Atkinson AJ Jr, Bennett JE. Experience with a new skin test antigen prepared from *Cryptococcus neoformans*. Am Rev Respir Dis. 1968;97:637–643.
24. Casadevall A, Mukherjee J, Yuan R, et al. Management of injuries caused by *Cryptococcus neoformans*–contaminated needles. Clin Infect Dis. 1994;19:951–953.
25. Franzot S, Mukherjee J, Cherniak R, et al. Microevolution of a standard strain of *Cryptococcus neoformans* resulting in differences in virulence and other phenotypes. Infect Immun. 1998;66:89–97.
26. Varma A, Swinne D, Staib F, et al. Diversity of DNA fingerprints in *Cryptococcus neoformans*. J Clin Microbiol. 1995;33:1807–1814.
27. Fries BC, Chen F, Currie BP, et al. Karyotype instability in *Cryptococcus neoformans* infection. J Clin Microbiol. 1996;34:1531–1534.
28. Brandt ME, Hutwagner LC, Klug LA, et al. Molecular subtype distribution of *Cryptococcus neoformans* in four areas of the United States. Cryptococcal Disease Active Surveillance Group. J Clin Microbiol. 1996;34:912–917.
29. Brandt ME, Pfaller MA, Hajjeh RA, et al. Molecular subtypes and antifungal susceptibilities of serial *Cryptococcus neoformans* isolates in human immunodeficiency virus–associated cryptococcosis. Cryptococcal Disease Active Surveillance Group. J Infect Dis. 1996;174:812–820.
30. Haynes KA, Sullivan DJ, Coleman DC, et al. Involvement of multiple *Cryptococ-*

cus neoformans strains in a single episode of cryptococcosis and reinfection with novel strains in recurrent infection demonstrated by random amplification of polymorphic DNA and DNA fingerprinting. J Clin Microbiol. 1995;33:99–102.
31. Sullivan D, Haynes K, Moran G, et al. Persistence, replacement, and microevolution of *Cryptococcus neoformans* strains in recurrent meningitis in AIDS patients. J Clin Microbiol. 1996;34:1739–1744.
32. HIV/AIDS Surveillance Report: U.S. HIV and AIDS Cases Reported through December 1996. Year-end edition, v. 8, no. 2. Atlanta: U.S. Dept. of Health and Human Services, Public Health Service, Centers for Disease Control and Prevention; 1996:17–18.
33. Heyderman RS, Gangaidzo IT, Hakim JG, et al. Cryptococcal meningitis in human immunodeficiency virus–infected patients in Harare, Zimbabwe. Clin Infect Dis. 1998;26:284–289.
34. Powderly WG, Cloud GA, Dismukes WE, et al. Measurement of cryptococcal antigen in serum and cerebrospinal fluid: Value in the management of AIDS-associated cryptococcal meningitis. Clin Infect Dis. 1994;18:789–792.
35. Smith DK, Neal JJ, Holmberg SD, et al. Unexplained opportunistic infections and CD4+ T-lymphocytopenia without HIV infection. An investigation of cases in the United States. N Engl J Med. 1993;328:373–379.
36. Duncan RA, Von Reyn F, Alliegro GM, et al. Idiopathic CD4+ T-lymphocytopenia—four patients with opportunistic infections and no evidence of HIV infection. N Engl J Med. 1993;328:393–398.
37. Sorenson RU, Boehm KD, Kaplan D, et al. Cryptococcal osteomyelitis and cellular immunodeficiency associated with interleukin-2 deficiency. J Pediatr. 1992;121:873–879.
38. Stone BD, Wheeler JG. Disseminated cryptococcal infection in a patient with hyperimmunoglobulinemia E syndrome. J Pediatr. 1990;117:92–95.
39. Dumler JS, Bakken JS. Ehrlichial diseases of humans: Emerging tick-borne infections. Clin Infect Dis. 1995;20:1102–1110.
40. Fishman JA, Rubin RH. Infections in organ transplant recipients. N Engl J Med. 1998;338:1741–1751.
41. Diamond RD, Bennett JE. Prognostic factors in cryptococcal meningitis. A study of 111 cases. Ann Intern Med. 1974;80:176–181.
42. Mody CH, Toews GB, Lipscomb MF. Cyclosporin A inhibits the growth of *Cryptococcus neoformans* in a murine mode. Infect Immun. 1988;56:7–12.
43. Krick JA. Familial cryptococcal meningitis. J Infect Dis. 1981;143:133.
44. James PG, Cherniak R. Galactoxylomannans of *Cryptococcus neoformans*. Infect Immun. 1992;60:1084–1088.
45. Hamilton AJ, Goodley J. Purification of the 115-kilodalton exoantigen of *Cryptococcus neoformans* and its recognition by immune sera. J Clin Microbiol. 1993;31:335–339.
46. Nosanchuk JD, Casadevall A. Cellular charge of *Cryptococcus neoformans*: Contributions from the capsular polysaccharide, melanin, and monoclonal antibody binding. Infect Immun. 1997;65:1836–1841.
47. Rodrigues ML, Rozental S, Couceiro JNSS, et al. Identification of *N*-acetylneuraminic acid and its 9-*O*-acetylated derivative on the cell surface of *Cryptococcus neoformans*: Influence on fungal phagocytosis. Infect Immun. 1997;65:4937–4942.
48. Sundstrom JB, Cherniak R. T-cell–dependent and T-cell–independent mechanisms of tolerance to glucuronoxylomannan of *Cryptococcus neoformans* serotype A. Infect Immun. 1993;61:1340–1345.
49. Henderson DK, Kan VL, Bennett JE. Tolerance to cryptococcal polysaccharide in cured cryptococcosis patients: Failure of antibody secretion in vitro. Clin Exp Immunol. 1986;65:639–646.
50. Dong ZM, Murphy JW. Intravascular cryptococcal culture filtrate (CneF) and its major component, glucuronoxylomannan, are potent inhibitors of leukocyte accumulation. Infect Immun. 1995;63:770–778.
51. Dong ZM, Murphy JW. Effects of the two varieties of *Cryptococcus neoformans* cells and culture filtrate antigens on neutrophil locomotion. Infect Immun. 1995;63:2632–2644.
52. Mody CH, Syme RM. Effect of the polysaccharide capsule and methods of preparation on human lymphocyte proliferation in response to *Cryptococcus neoformans*. Infect Immun. 1993;61:464–469.
53. Retini C, Vecchiarelli A, Monari C, et al. Encapsulation of *Cryptococcus neoformans* with glucuronoxylomannan inhibits the antigen-presenting capacity of monocytes. Infect Immun. 1998;66:664–669.
54. Kozel TR, Wilson MA, Welch WH. Kinetic analysis of the amplification phase for activation and binding of C3 to encapsulated and nonencapsulated *Cryptococcus neoformans*. Infect Immun. 1992;60:3122–3127.
55. Macher A, Bennett J, Gadek J, et al. Complement depletion in cryptococcal sepsis. J Immunol. 1978;120:1686–1690.
56. Harrison TS, Nong S, Levitz SM. Induction of human immunodeficiency virus type 1 expression in monocytic cells by *Cryptococcus neoformans* and *Candida albicans*. J Infect Dis. 1997;176:485–491.
57. Goldman DL, Lee SC, Casadevall A. Tissue localization of *Cryptococcus neoformans* glucuronoxylomannan in the presence and absence of specific antibody. Infect Immun. 1995;63:3448–3453.
58. Chang YC, Kwon-Chung KJ. Isolation of the third capsule-associated gene, *CAP60*, required for virulence in *Cryptococcus neoformans*. Infect Immun. 1998;66:2230–2236.
59. Salas SD, Bennett JE, Kwon-Chung KJ, et al. Effect of the laccase gene *CNLAC1*, on virulence of *Cryptococcus neoformans*. J Exp Med. 1996;184:377–386.
60. Wang Y, Aisen P, Casadevall A. Melanin, melanin "ghosts," and melanin composition in *Cryptococcus neoformans*. Infect Immun. 1996;64:2420–2424.
61. Wang Y, Aisen P, Casadevall A. *Cryptococcus neoformans* melanin and virulence: Mechanism of action. Infect Immun. 1995;63:3131–3136.
62. Wang Y, Casadevall A. Susceptibility of melanized and nonmelanized *Cryptococcus neoformans* to nitrogen- and oxygen-derived oxidants. Infect Immun. 1994;62:3004–3007.
63. Wong B, Perfect JR, Beggs S, et al. Production of the hexitol D-mannitol by *Cryptococcus neoformans* in vitro and in rabbits with experimental meningitis. Infect Immun. 1990;58:1664–1670.
64. Chaturvedi V, Wong B, Newman SL. Oxidative killing of *Cryptococcus neoformans* by human neutrophils. Evidence that fungal mannitol protects by scavenging reactive oxygen intermediates. J Immunol. 1996;156:3836–3840.
65. Odom A, Muir S, Lim E, et al. Calcineurin is required for virulence of *Cryptococcus neoformans*. Embo J. 1997;16:2576–2589.
66. Perfect JR, Toffaletti DL, Rude TH. The gene encoding phosphoribosylaminoimidazole carboxylase (*ADE2*) is essential for growth of *Cryptococcus neoformans* in cerebrospinal fluid. Infect Immun. 1993;61:4446–4451.
67. Igel JH, Bolande RP. Humoral defense mechanisms in cryptococcosis: Substances in normal human serum, saliva and cerebrospinal fluid affecting the growth of *Cryptococcus neoformans*. J Infect Dis. 1966;116:75–83.
68. Diamond RD, May JE, Kane MA, et al. The role of the classical and alternate complement pathways in host defenses against *Cryptococcus neoformans* infection. J Immunol. 1974;112:2260–2270.
69. Fetter BF, Klintworth GK, Hendry WS. Mycoses of the Central Nervous System. Baltimore: Williams & Wilkins; 1976:100.
70. Gadebusch HH. Mechanisms of native and acquired resistance to infection with *Cryptococcus neoformans*. CRC Crit Rev Microbiol. 1972;1:311–320.
71. Diamond RD, Root RK, Bennett JE. Factors influencing killing of *Cryptococcus neoformans* by human leukocytes in vitro. J Infect Dis. 1972;125:367–376.
72. Gyetko MR, Chen GH, McDonald RA, et al. Urokinase is required for the pulmonary inflammatory response to *Cryptococcus neoformans*. A murine transgenic model. J Clin Invest. 1996;97:1818–1826.
73. Levitz SM, Matthews HL, Murphy JW. Direct antimicrobial activity of T cells. Immunol Today. 1995;16:387–391.
74. Lovchik J, Lipscomb M, Lyons CR. Expression of lung inducible nitric oxide synthase protein does not correlate with nitric oxide production in vivo in a pulmonary immune response against *Cryptococcus neoformans*. J Immunol. 1997;158:1772–1778.
75. Harrison TS, Levitz SM. Mechanisms of impaired anticryptococcal activity of monocytes from donors infected with human immunodeficiency virus. J Infect Dis. 1997;176:537–540.
76. Pietrella D, Monari C, Retini C, et al. Human immunodeficiency virus type 1 envelope protein gp120 impairs intracellular antifungal mechanisms in human monocytes. J Infect Dis. 1998;177:347–354.
77. Dong ZM, Murphy JW. Cryptococcal polysaccharides induce L-selectin shedding and tumor necrosis factor receptor loss from the surface of human neutrophils. J Clin Invest. 1996;97:689–698.
78. Doyle HA, Murphy JW. MIP-1 alpha contributes to the anticryptococcal delayed-type hypersensitivity reaction and protection against *Cryptococcus neoformans*. J Leukoc Biol. 1997;61:147–155.
79. Hoag KA, Lipscomb MF, Izzo AA, et al. IL-12 and IFN-gamma are required for initiating the protective Th1 response to pulmonary cryptococcosis in resistant C.B-17 mice. Am J Respir Cell Mol Biol. 1997;17:733–739.
80. Huffnagle GB, Strieter RM, McNeil LK, et al. Macrophage inflammatory protein-1alpha (MIP-1alpha) is required for the efferent phase of pulmonary cell-mediated immunity to a *Cryptococcus neoformans* infection. J Immunol. 1997;159:318–327.
81. Huffnagle GB, Toews GB, Burdick MD, et al. Afferent phase production of TNF-alpha is required for the development of protective T cell immunity to *Cryptococcus neoformans*. J Immunol. 1996;157:4529–4536.
82. Kawakami K, Qureshi MH, Zhang T, et al. IL-18 protects mice against pulmonary and disseminated infection with *Cryptococcus neoformans* by inducing IFN-gamma production. J Immunol. 1997;159:5528–5534.
83. Kawakami K, Tohyama M, Xie Q, et al. IL-12 protects mice against pulmonary and disseminated infection caused by *Cryptococcus neoformans*. Clin Exp Immunol. 1996;104:208–214.
84. Levitz SM, North EA, Jiang Y, et al. Variables affecting production of monocyte chemotactic factor 1 from human leukocytes stimulated with *Cryptococcus neoformans*. Infect Immun. 1997;65:903–908.
85. Levitz SM, Tabuni A, Nong SH, et al. Effects of interleukin-10 on human peripheral blood mononuclear cell responses to *Cryptococcus neoformans*, *Candida albicans*, and lipopolysaccharide. Infect Immun. 1996;64:945–951.
86. Murphy JW, Schafer F, Casadevall A, et al. Antigen-induced protective and nonprotective cell-mediated immune components against *Cryptococcus neoformans*. Infect Immun. 1998;66:2632–2639.
87. Lendvai N, Casadevall A, Liang Z, et al. Effect of immune mechanisms on the pharmacokinetics and organ distribution of cryptococcal polysaccharide. J Infect Dis. 1998;177:1647–1659.
88. Yuan RR, Spira G, Oh J, et al. Isotype switching increases efficacy of antibody protection against *Cryptococcus neoformans* infection in mice. Infect Immun. 1998;66:1057–1062.
89. Casadevall A, Cleare W, Feldmesser M, et al. Characterization of a murine monoclonal antibody to *Cryptococcus neoformans* polysaccharide that is a candidate for human therapeutic studies. Antimicrob Agents Chemother. 1998;42:1437–1446.
90. Vecchiarelli A, Retini C, Monari C, et al. Specific antibody to *Cryptococcus neoformans* alters human leukocyte cytokine synthesis and promotes T-cell proliferation. Infect Immun. 1998;66:1244–1247.
91. Kozel TR, deJong BC, Grinsell MM, et al. Characterization of anticapsular mono-

clonal antibodies that regulate activation of the complement system by the *Cryptococcus neoformans* capsule. Infect Immun. 1998;66:1538–1546.
92. Devi SJN, Schneerson R, Egan W, et al. *Cryptococcus neoformans* serotype A glucuronoxylomannan-protein conjugate vaccines: Synthesis, characterization, and immunogenicity. Infect Immun. 1991;59:3700–3707.
93. Casadevall A. Antibody immunity and invasive fungal infections. Infect Immun. 1995;63:4211–4218.
94. Chuck SL, Sande MA. Infections with *Cryptococcus neoformans* in the acquired immunodeficiency syndrome. N Engl J Med. 1989;321:794–799.
95. Clark RA, Greer D, Atkinson W, et al. Spectrum of *Cryptococcus neoformans* infection in 68 patients infected with human immunodeficiency virus. Rev Infest Dis. 1990;12:768–777.
96. Meyohas MC, Roux P, Bollens D, et al. Pulmonary cryptococcosis: Localized and disseminated infections in 27 patients with AIDS. Clin Infect Dis. 1995;21:628–633.
97. Cameron ML, Bartlett JA, Gallis HA, et al. Manifestations of pulmonary cryptococcosis in patients with acquired immunodeficiency syndrome. Rev Infect Dis. 1991;13:64–67.
98. Hernandez AD. Cutaneous cryptococcosis. Dermatol Clin. 1989;7:269–274.
99. Dimino-Emme L, Gurevitch AW. Cutaneous manifestations of disseminated cryptococcosis. J Am Acad Dermatol. 1995;32:844–850.
100. Murakawa GJ, Kerschmann R, Berger T. Cutaneous *Cryptococcus* infection and AIDS. Report of 12 cases and review of the literature. Arch Dermatol. 1996;132:545–548.
101. Anderson DJ, Schmidt C, Goodman J, et al. Cryptococcal disease presenting as cellulitis. Clin Infect Dis. 1992;14:666–672.
102. Behrman RE, Masci JR, Nicholas P. Cryptococcal skeletal infections: Case report and review. Rev Infect Dis. 1990;12:181–190.
103. Hellman RN, Hinrichs J, Sicard G, et al. Cryptococcal pyelonephritis and disseminated cryptococcosis in a renal transplant recipient. Arch Intern Med. 1981;141:128–130.
104. Adams JR, Mata JA, Culkin DI, et al. Acquired immunodeficiency syndrome manifesting as prostate nodule secondary to cryptococcal infection. Urology 1992;39:289–291.
105. Denning DW, Stevens DA, Hamilton JR. Comparison of *Guizotia abyssinica* seed extract (birdseed agar) with conventional media for selective identification of *Cryptococcus neoformans* in patients with the acquired immunodeficiency syndrome. J Clin Microbiol. 1990;28:2565–2567.
106. Malabonga VM, Bast J, Kamholz SL. Utility of bronchoscopic sampling techniques for cryptococcal disease in AIDS. Chest. 1991;99:370–372.
107. Perfect JR, Durack DT, Gallis HA. Cryptococcemia. Medicine (Baltimore). 1983;62:98–109.
108. Kwon-Chung KJ, Hill WB, Bennett JE. New, special stain for histopathological diagnosis of cryptococcosis. J Clin Microbiol. 1981;13:383–387.
109. Bennett JE, Bailey JW. Control for rheumatoid factor in the latex test for cryptococcosis. Am J Clin Pathol. 1971;56:360–365.
110. Feldmesser M, Harris C, Reichberg S, et al. Serum cryptococcal antigen in patients with AIDS (Editorial). Clin Infect Dis. 1996;23:827–830.
111. Ellner JJ, Bennett JE. Chronic meningitis. Medicine (Baltimore). 1976;53:341–369.
112. Martinez E, Domingo P, Ris J, et al. Cerebrospinal fluid adenosine deaminase levels in a patient with cryptococcal meningitis. Clin Infect Dis. 1992;15:1061–1062.
113. Popovich MJ, Arthur RH, Helmer E. CT of intracranial cryptococcosis. AJR Am J Roentgenol. 1990;154:603–606.
114. Miszkiel KA, Hall-Craggs MA, Miller RF, et al. The spectrum of MRI findings in CNS cryptococcosis in AIDS. Clin Radiol. 1996;51:842–850.
115. Tien RD, Chu PK, Hesselink JR, et al. Intracranial cryptococcosis in immunocompromised patients: CT and MR findings in 29 cases. AJR Am J Roentgenol. 1991;156:1245–1251.
116. Gordonson J, Birnbaum W, Jacobson G, et al. Pulmonary cryptococcosis. Radiology. 1974;112:557–561.
117. Gallant JE, Ko AH. Cavitary pulmonary lesions in patients infected with human immunodeficiency virus. Clin Infect Dis. 1996;22:671–682.
118. Miller KD, Mican JA, Davey RT. Asymptomatic solitary pulmonary nodules due to *Cryptococcus neoformans* in patients infected with human immunodeficiency virus. Clin Infect Dis. 1996;23:810–812.
119. Duperval R, Hermans PE, Brewer NS, et al. Cryptococcosis, with emphasis on the significance of isolation of *Cryptococcus neoformans* from the respiratory tract. Chest. 1977;72:13–19.
120. Bennett JE, Dismukes WE, Duma RJ, et al. A comparison of amphotericin B alone and combined with flucytosine in the treatment of cryptococcal meningitis. N Engl J Med. 1979;301:126–131.
121. Dismukes WE, Cloud G, Gallis HA, et al. Treatment of cryptococcal meningitis with combination amphotericin B and flucytosine for four as compared with six weeks. N Engl J Med. 1987;317:334–341.
122. Powderly WG. Editorial response: Management of cryptococcal meningitis—have we answered all the questions? Clin Infect Dis. 1996;22:329–330.
123. Francis P, Walsh TJ. Evolving role of flucytosine in immunocompromised patients: New insights into safety, pharmacokinetics, and antifungal therapy. Clin Infect Dis. 1992;15:1003–1008.
124. Armstrong D. Treatment of opportunistic fungal infections. Clin Infect Dis. 1993;16:1–9.
125. Diamond RD, Bennett JE. A subcutaneous reservoir for intrathecal therapy of fungal meningitis. N Engl J Med. 1973;288:186–188.
126. Polsky B, Depman MR, Gold JWM, et al. Intraventricular therapy of cryptococcal meningitis via a subcutaneous reservoir. Am J Med. 1986;81:24–28.
127. Dromer F, Mathoulin S, Dupont B, et al. Comparison of the efficacy of amphotericin B and fluconazole in the treatment of cryptococcosis in human immunodeficiency virus–negative patients: Retrospective analysis of 83 cases. Clin Infect Dis. 1996;22(Suppl 2):S154–S160.
128. Kerkering TM, Duma RJ, Shadomy S. The evolution of pulmonary cryptococcosis: Clinical implications from a study of 41 patients with and without compromising host factors. Ann Intern Med. 1981;94:611–616.
129. Saag MS, Powderly WG, Cloud GA, et al. Comparison of amphotericin B with fluconazole in the treatment of acute AIDS-associated cryptococcal meningitis. N Engl J Med. 1992;326:83–89.
130. van der Horst CM, Saag MS, Cloud GA, et al. Treatment of cryptococcal meningitis associated with the acquired immunodeficiency syndrome. National Institute of Allergy and Infectious Diseases Mycoses Study Group and AIDS Clinical Trials Group. N Engl J Med. 1997;337:15–21.
131. Sharkey PK, Graybill JR, Johnson ES, et al. Amphotericin B lipid complex compared with amphotericin B in the treatment of cryptococcal meningitis in patients with AIDS. Clin Infect Dis. 1996;22:315–321.
132. Leenders AC, Reiss P, Portegies P, et al. Liposomal amphotericin B (AmBisome) compared with amphotericin B both followed by oral fluconazole in the treatment of AIDS-associated cryptococcal meningitis. AIDS. 1997;11:1463–1471.
133. Witt MD, Lewis RJ, Larsen RA, et al. Identification of patients with acute AIDS-associated cryptococcal meningitis who can be effectively treated with fluconazole: The role of antifungal susceptibility testing. Clin Infect Dis. 1996;22:322–328.
134. Powderly WG, Saag MS, Cloud GA, et al. A controlled trial of fluconazole or amphotericin B to prevent relapse of cryptococcal meningitis in patients with the acquired immunodeficiency syndrome. NIAID AIDS Clinical Trials Group and Mycoses Study Group. N Engl J Med. 1992;326:793–798.
135. Larsen RA, Bozzette S, McCutchan JA, et al. Persistent *Cryptococcus neoformans* infection of the prostate after successful treatment of meningitis. Ann Intern Med. 1989;111:125–128.
136. Venkateswarlu K, Taylor M, Manning NJ, et al. Fluconazole tolerance in clinical isolates of *Cryptococcus neoformans*. Antimicrob Agents Chemother. 1997;41:748–751.
137. Rex JR, Larsen RA, Dismukes WE, et al. Catastrophic visual loss due to *Cryptococcus neoformans* meningitis. Medicine (Baltimore). 1993;72:207–224.
138. Denning D, Armstrong RW, Lewis BH, et al. Elevated cerebrospinal fluid pressures in patients with cryptococcal meningitis and acquired immunodeficiency syndrome. Am J Med. 1991;91:267–272.
139. White M, Cirrincione C, Blevins A, et al. Cryptococcal meningitis: Outcome in patients with AIDS and patients with neoplastic disease. Clin Infect Dis. 1992;165:960–963.
140. Powderly WG. Therapy for cryptococcal meningitis in patients with AIDS. Clin Infect Dis. 1992;14(Suppl 1):S554–S559.
141. Fan-Havard P, Yamaguchi E, Smith SM, et al. Diastolic hypertension in AIDS patients with cryptococcal meningitis. Am J Med. 1992;93:347–348.
142. Singh N, Barnish MJ, Berman S, et al. Low-dose fluconazole as primary prophylaxis for cryptococcal infection in AIDS patients with CD4 cell counts of or = 100/mm^3: Demonstration of efficacy in a positive, multicenter trial. Clin Infect Dis. 1996;23:1282–1286.
143. Powderly WG, Finkelstein D, Feinberg J, et al. A randomized trial comparing fluconazole with clotrimazole troches for the prevention of fungal infections in patients with advanced human immunodeficiency virus infection. NIAID AIDS Clinical Trials Group. N Engl J Med. 1995;332:700–705.
144. Preface to the 1997 USPHS/IDSA guidelines for the prevention of opportunistic infections in persons infected with human immunodeficiency virus. USPHS/IDSA Prevention of Opportunistic Infections Working Group. Clin Infect Dis. 1997;25(Suppl 3):S299–S312.
145. Mazzolla R, Barluzzi R, Brozzetti A, et al. Enhanced resistance to *Cryptococcus neoformans* infection induced by chloroquine in a murine model of meningoencephalitis. Antimicrob Agents Chemother. 1997;41:802–807.

Chapter 254

Histoplasma capsulatum

GEORGE S. DEEPE, JR.

Among the microbes that have been designated as emerging or reemerging pathogens, *Histoplasma capsulatum* is one of the more common causes of infection in the midwestern and southeastern United States. Histoplasmosis, acquired by inhalation of mycelial fragments and microconidia, has become an increasingly frequent opportunistic infection among patients whose immune system is impaired either by pharmaceutical agents or by infection with human immunodeficiency virus (HIV). This accelerating trend is unlikely to abate because the reservoir of infection, the soil, will never disappear.

HISTORY

The discovery of *H. capsulatum* began in December 1905 when Samuel Darling, a pathologist stationed in Panama, examined visceral tissues and bone marrow from a young man from Martinique whose death was originally attributed to miliary tuberculosis.[1] Peering through his microscope, Darling was struck by the presence of many small bodies, most of which were intracellular. Having been influenced by reports from Leishman and Donovan, he mistakenly thought that this organism was a protozoan. Because it lacked a kinetoplast, Darling assumed that it was a different *Leishmania* sp. He termed it *H. capsulatum* by virtue of the fact that this new species exhibited what appeared to be a capsule. In 1912, after reviewing tissue specimens, da Rocha-Lima suggested that the organism resembled a yeast rather than a protozoan.[2] A little over 20 years later the organism was finally isolated on artificial medium and observed to grow as a mold at room temperature and as a yeast at 37°C.[3]

For many years, physicians considered the presence of pulmonary calcifications to be synonymous with healed tuberculosis. Amos Christie, a pediatrician at Vanderbilt University, dispelled that dictum.[4, 5] The presence of cutaneous reactivity to a skin test reagent prepared from the mycelial phase of the organism obtained from an infant with disseminated histoplasmosis prompted large-scale testing during the 1930s. This endeavor unearthed the surprising finding that histoplasmosis was highly prevalent in the Ohio and Mississippi River valleys.[4, 5] Moreover, many cases presumed to be tuberculosis on the basis of calcifications on chest roentgenograms were determined to be histoplasmosis instead.[6] Eventually, many individuals residing in tuberculosis sanatoriums in the midwestern and southeastern United States were found to be admitted mistakenly because they suffered from histoplasmosis, not tuberculosis. Some of these individuals acquired tuberculosis while they were housed in open wards with patients who had active pulmonary tuberculosis.

ECOLOGY AND EPIDEMIOLOGY

Cases of histoplasmosis have been reported from every continent except Antarctica. Although *H. capsulatum* has been detected in many areas of the world, the most endemic region is found in the Ohio and Mississippi River valleys[7–9] (Fig. 254–1). *H. capsulatum* is a soil-based fungus. The conditions that favor the growth of this fungus in soil are a mean temperature that ranges from 22°C to 29°C, an annual precipitation of 35 to 50 inches, and a relative humidity of 67 to 87%.[10] These conditions are typically found in the temperate zone between latitudes 45 degrees north and 30 degrees south.[8] The organism is typically found within 20 cm of the surface, and it prefers soil that is acidic, has a high nitrogen content, and is moist. In areas where birds roost, the fungus is found most often where the guano is decaying and mixed with soil.[11–13] In such areas, infectious particles can exceed 10^5 particles per gram of soil.[14] Fresh guano is less likely to contain many infectious particles. There is a strong association between the presence of bird and bat guano and the presence of *H. capsulatum*. In fact, the first isolation of the organism from an environmental source was from an area adjacent to a chicken house.[15, 16] Birds are not infected by the fungus, and attempts to isolate *H. capsulatum* from their cloacae have been unsuccessful.[12] Bats, on the other hand, carry the fungus in their gastrointestinal tracts and can shed it in their droppings.[17]

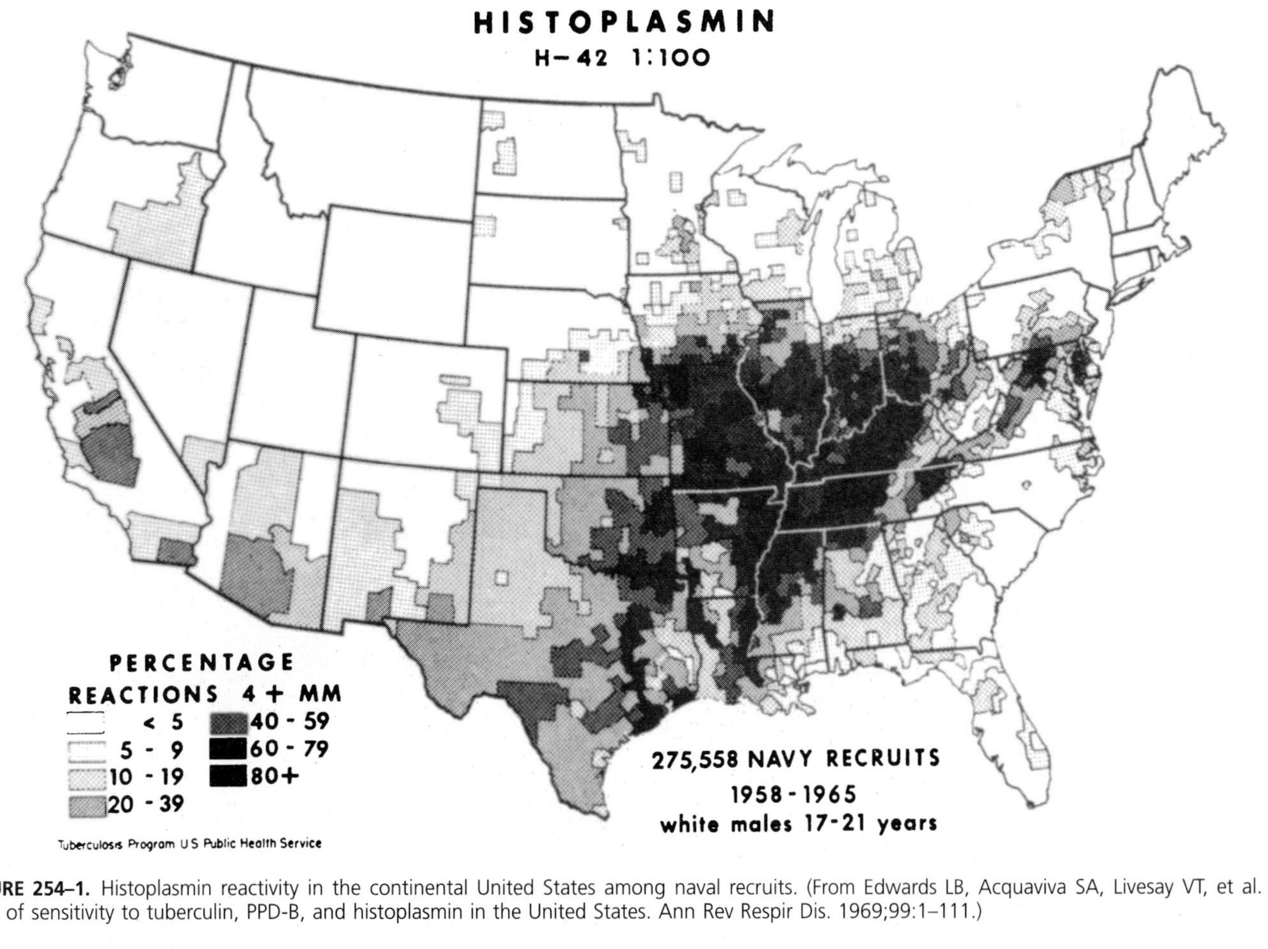

FIGURE 254–1. Histoplasmin reactivity in the continental United States among naval recruits. (From Edwards LB, Acquaviva SA, Livesay VT, et al. An atlas of sensitivity to tuberculin, PPD-B, and histoplasmin in the United States. Ann Rev Respir Dis. 1969;99:1–111.)

Disruption of the soil by excavation or construction is one of the most common means of releasing infectious particles, which are inhaled and eventually settle in the lungs. Those involved in recreational or work activities that expose them to disrupted soil are at highest risk for infection. Examples include spelunkers who roam caves where bats reside and those who are engaged in agriculture, outdoor construction, or rehabilitation of buildings that have been inhabited by birds or bats. Human-to-human transmission via the pulmonary route has not been reported and is unlikely to occur.

Although skin test reactivity to histoplasmin is equally distributed among men and women, disease develops in men more frequently than in women by a 4:1 ratio.[18] The disease incidence may be skewed because of the association of chronic pulmonary histoplasmosis with smoking, which for many years was a male-dominated activity. In histoplasmosis, unlike coccidioidomycosis, there are no known differences in susceptibility or resistance to infection among racial or ethnic groups. In contrast, inbred mouse strains vary in their susceptibility to infection, but there is no polarity in resistance and susceptibility.[19, 20] The difference in susceptibility among mouse strains disappears if they are depleted of lymphocytes, suggesting that the innate immune system handles *H. capsulatum* similarly among mouse strains.[21]

H. capsulatum contains four to seven chromosomes.[22] Differences in numbers of chromosomes are evident among strains, although no explanation for the finding has been proffered. Originally, the organism could be distinguished by two chemotypes, but the advent of molecular biology has improved methods for distinguishing strains of *H. capsulatum*. Restriction fragment length polymorphisms of mitochondrial DNA and of ribosomal and *yps-3* (a yeast phase–specific gene) nuclear genes have segregated *H. capsulatum* into six classes that correlate with geographic distribution and virulence.[23–26] The vast majority of North American and African *H. capsulatum* var. *duboisii* isolates belong to class 2, and those from Central America and South America are in class 3. A thermointolerant strain that is avirulent, the Down strain, has been assigned to class 3. Interestingly, many of the isolates recovered from patients with acquired immunodeficiency syndrome (AIDS) in St. Louis are found to be in class 3.[27] Genetic diversity within each restriction fragment length polymorphism group has been reported. In one study, 30 isolates from Indianapolis were analyzed, and each isolate contained a unique multilocus genotype. However, no association could be made with the clinical manifestations or the underlying disease condition of the patient from whom the isolate was recovered.[28] These findings indicate that each strain is genetically distinct. The basis for the differences may be the fact that *H. capsulatum* undergoes sexual recombination in nature, allowing exchange of genetic material.

MYCOLOGY

H. capsulatum is a member of the class Ascomycetes and has a heterothallic form that is designated *Ajellomyces capsulatum*. Mating types (+) and (−) have been described, and when combined on sporulating medium, they produce fruiting bodies containing asci. Isolates from patients carry the (−) mating type two to seven times more frequently than the (+) type, although the ratio of mating types in soil is 1:1.[29–31]

The organism has two forms, the mycelial phase and the yeast phase. The former is present at ambient temperature and the latter at 37°C or higher. The saprobic or mycelial phase can be divided into two colony types, brown (B) and albino (A). Type A organisms grow more rapidly in culture and lose the ability to produce spores after prolonged subculturing. Type B organisms generate a brown pigment. Yeast cells from the B type are more virulent than those from the A type.[12]

The basic elements of the nutritional needs of the organism are poorly defined because of lack of a standardized medium. The organism requires vitamins, thiamine, biotin, and iron. Sulfhydryl groups in the form of cysteine or cystine are necessary for growth and maintenance of the yeast phase. It has been demonstrated that the mycelial and yeast phases differ in their requirements for calcium. Chelation of calcium in a medium inhibits the growth of the mycelial but not the yeast phase. The transition from the mycelial to the yeast phase is associated with upregulation of the transcription of a calcium-binding protein messenger RNA and synthesis of the protein. This protein may act as a scavenger of calcium and may be synthesized by yeast cells in order to acquire calcium from intracellular environments that contain little of this element.[32, 33]

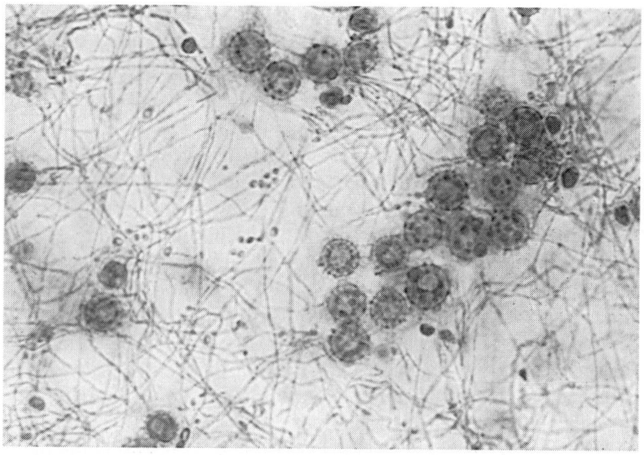

FIGURE 254–2. Mycelial phase of *Histoplasma capsulatum*. Both macroconidia and microconidia are evident.

Microscopic evaluation of the mycelial phase reveals two types of conidia. Macroconidia are large, ovoid bodies 8 to 15 μm in diameter. The surface is decorated with slender protrusions that are referred to as tuberculate. Microconidia are small, smooth oval bodies whose diameter ranges from 2 to 5 μm (Fig. 254–2). These forms are believed to be the infective phase because their size is small enough to lodge in the terminal bronchioles and alveoli.

The transition from the saprobic to the yeast phase is a critical step in infectivity of the fungus. At 37°C, the organism undergoes genetic, biochemical, and physical alterations that result in the production of yeast cells that are uninucleate.[34, 35] These forms are small, typically 2 to 5 μm in diameter, and reproduce by multipolar budding (Fig. 254–3). The stimulus for the transition is heat, and the shift in temperature may be sensed by a change in the fluidity of the yeast membrane. Genetically, the first genes that are upregulated upon

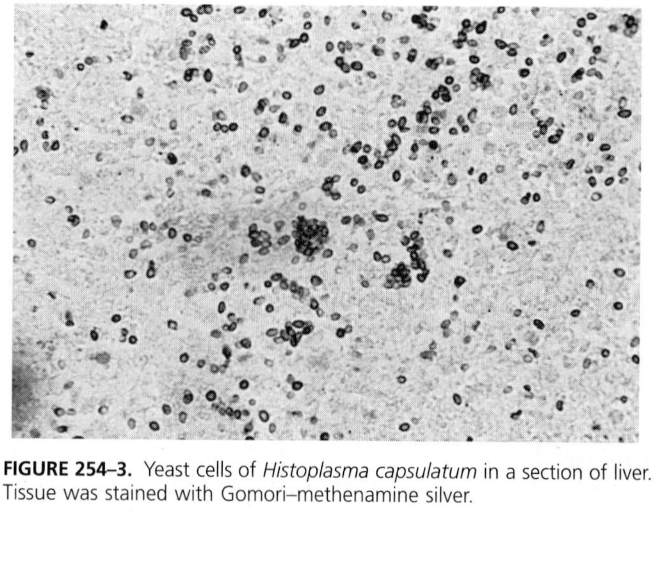

FIGURE 254–3. Yeast cells of *Histoplasma capsulatum* in a section of liver. Tissue was stained with Gomori–methenamine silver.

exposure to heat are *cdc2*,[36] a gene involved in cell cycle progression, followed by increased transcription within 24 hours of *yps-3*, a yeast phase–specific gene whose protein product is located within the cell membrane of yeast cells but whose function remains unknown.[37] There is also increased transcription of genes encoding heat shock proteins, especially heat shock protein 70.[38]

Three biochemical stages have been identified during the conversion after exposure to 37°C. Stage 1 is characterized by an uncoupling of oxidation and phosphorylation and a decrease in RNA and protein synthesis. In stage 2, no respiration is detectable, and in stage 3, there is a resumption of respiration. Chitin and α-glucan and β-glucan contents differ between the two phases.[34]

Within tissues, yeast cells may have a morphology that differs from the usual ovoid shape. Misshapen or large yeasts have been observed in tissues and in epithelial cells. These allomorphs may contain less α-1,3-glucan and appear to be less virulent than oval yeasts. It has been suggested that because of their reduced virulence potential the allomorphs may represent a persistent or dormant phase of the fungus.[39, 40]

PATHOGENESIS

Unlike prokaryotes or some eukaryotes, *H. capsulatum* has no single biochemical moiety that has been implicated as a virulence trait. The transition from the mycelial to the yeast phase is one of the most critical determinants of the establishment of infection.[34, 41] This contention is supported by the following findings. First, it is quite rare to find mycelial particles in tissues of humans or mammals with established infection. Rather, yeast cells are commonly detected. Second, exposure of *H. capsulatum* mycelia to *p*-chloromercuriphenylsulfonic acid, a sulfhydryl inhibitor, irreversibly blocks the conversion to yeasts but does not alter the growth of yeasts or mycelia. *p*-Chloromercuriphenylsulfonic acid–treated mycelia fail to infect animals, although these forms stimulate a protective immune response.[42]

After conidia settle into the alveoli, they bind to the CD11/CD18 family of integrins and are engulfed by both neutrophils and macrophages.[43–45] Hence, it is likely that the conversion of mycelia to the yeast phase transpires, at least partially if not entirely, intracellularly, although the biologic importance of this fact has not been explored.[46] The duration of the phase transition ranges from hours to days. After transformation of the conidia into yeasts within the pulmonary parenchyma, yeasts migrate, presumably intracellularly, to local draining lymph nodes and subsequently distant organs that are rich in mononuclear phagocytes such as liver and spleen. The yeasts grow quite readily within resting macrophages. Activation of cellular immunity is necessary for restricting growth, and in primary infection this arm of immunity is mature by 2 weeks.

In experimental pulmonary infection, neutrophils constitute one of the prominent cell populations that migrate early into infected foci of lungs.[47–49] These cells are capable of inhibiting the growth of yeast cells.[50, 51] Constituents of the azurophilic granules express fungistatic activity, and defensins also inhibit the growth of yeast cells.[50, 51] Elimination of murine neutrophils enhances considerably the susceptibility of mice to sublethal inocula with yeast cells.[52] Neutrophils mount a respiratory burst in response to the fungus, but the oxygen intermediates are trapped intracellularly. Despite the burst, there is little evidence that toxic oxygen intermediates contribute to the anti-*Histoplasma* activity of these phagocytes.

Macrophages are the principal effector cells in host resistance to this fungus. Yeast cells invade and proliferate within resting mononuclear phagocytes. Upon engulfment by murine macrophages, a high percentage of yeast cells are located within phagolysosomes.[53, 54] The fungus must contend with the inimical contents (e.g., acid proteinases) of this intensely hostile environment. One mechanism by which yeasts survive is alkalinization of the phagolysosome.[54] Yeast cells raise the pH of the phagocytic compartment to 6.0 to 6.5. Although yeast cells have the capacity to alkalinize media to a pH in excess of 8, the pH of the phagolysosome does not achieve this degree of alkalinity. One reason for keeping the pH within a narrow range is that yeast cells require iron to grow, and if the pH exceeds 6.5 they cannot acquire iron from the host.[56, 57] It is also possible that the vacuolar adenosine triphosphatase in macrophages may counterregulate the pH because production of highly alkaline products may damage the host cell contents.

Nitric oxide produced by activated murine macrophages is a major mediator of anti-*Histoplasma* activity. The ability of this nitrogen intermediate to chelate iron may explain its potent fungicidal activity.[58, 59] However, its influence in human infection remains controversial because it has been difficult to demonstrate that human macrophages produce nitric oxide in response to a variety of stimuli. Nevertheless, other sources of nitric oxide generated by human tissues such as endothelial cells may contribute to the antifungal host defense armamentarium.

The interaction between human macrophages and yeasts differs substantially from that found with murine macrophages. The human cell population mounts a vigorous respiratory burst in response to unopsonized yeasts,[43] whereas murine cells do not unless yeasts are opsonized with antibody and therefore engulfed through Fc receptors.[60, 61] Another contrast is that yeast cells reside predominantly not in phagolysosomes of plastic-bound macrophages but in endosomes. However, when human macrophages that are adherent to collagen gels are exposed to yeast cells, massive phagolysosomal fusion develops.[62] This process is correlated with a pronounced inhibition of growth of *H. capsulatum* yeasts.

Macrophages from HIV-infected individuals manifest defective activity in their interaction with *H. capsulatum*. These cells bind fewer yeasts than cells from uninfected individuals, and a direct correlation exists between the $CD4^+$ T-cell count and the capacity of macrophages to bind yeast cells.[63] Upon entry into cells, yeasts grow more rapidly within macrophages from HIV-infected individuals or macrophages that have been infected in vitro with a macrophage-tropic strain of HIV. The envelope glycoprotein 120 from the virus is responsible for the inhibition of binding yeasts to macrophages[64] but not the altered growth characteristics of the yeasts within phagocytes.

Among the elements of the acquired immune response, T cells are pivotal in clearance of the fungus. Experimental studies indicate that neither B cells nor antibodies influence host resistance, although the data are limited. Among T-cell populations, $CD4^+$ cells are vitally important because mice deficient in them died when challenged with a sublethal inoculum of yeasts.[65] As a corollary, transfer of $CD4^+$ cells from mice immunized with yeast cells or *H. capsulatum*–reactive T-cell clones reduced the fungal burden.[66] The central role of $CD4^+$ cells is supported by the finding that in HIV-infected individuals, most cases of histoplasmosis develop when the $CD4^+$ cell count is less than 200/μl.[67] Mice deficient in $CD8^+$ cells are impaired in their ability to reduce the fungal burden, but they can eventually eliminate the fungus. Likewise, β_2-microglobulin knockout mice that lacked $CD8^+$ T cells and major histocompatibility complex class I antigens were more susceptible to infection than littermate controls.[68] However, they were able to sterilize tissues. Thus, between the two major T-cell subpopulations a hierarchy exists in importance to host resistance, with $CD4^+$ cells being more important than $CD8^+$ cells.

Little information exists concerning natural killer cells. Although they are known to produce interferon-γ and tumor necrosis factor-α after exposure to various stimuli, their influence on the course of histoplasmosis is unclear. Beige mice with defective natural killer cells were not more susceptible to infection than control mice.[69] However, this fact does not preclude the possibility that this cell population can amplify the immune response to *H. capsulatum*.

The primary contribution of T cells to host defense is the release of cytokines that activate mononuclear phagocytes. There is convincing evidence that functional cytotoxic T cells are generated by *H. capsulatum*. The only lymphokine to date that has been shown to be

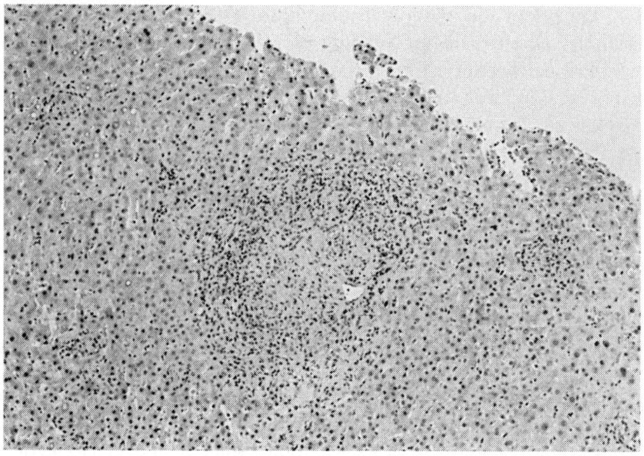

FIGURE 254–4. Granuloma in the liver of a patient with histoplasmosis.

active in vitro and in vivo against this fungus is interferon-γ. Thus, mice in which endogenous interferon-γ was blocked and mice congenitally deficient in this lymphokine were exceptionally susceptible to infection.[19, 52, 70] Other cytokines in mice that are necessary for host clearance are interleukin-12 and tumor necrosis factor-α. Blockade of endogenous production of either of these leads to the death of mice. The effect of interleukin-12 is mediated through the induction of interferon-γ generation.[71] Interestingly, interleukin-12 is important in primary infection but not in reexposure histoplasmosis.[72] Tumor necrosis factor-α and interferon-γ are both necessary for controlling primary as well as secondary infection.[52, 73–75]

In vitro, recombinant interferon-γ activates murine peritoneal macrophages to inhibit the growth of yeast cells. Macrophages from other tissue sources are either nonresponsive to this stimulus or require costimulation with lipopolysaccharide.[76] The anti-*Histoplasma* action of interferon-γ is mediated by limiting iron acquisition, and this effect can be reversed by exposure to additional iron.[57] Human macrophages, on the other hand, do not respond to human recombinant interferon-γ by inhibiting yeast cell growth.[77, 78] The cytokines that activate these cells are macrophage colony-stimulating factor, granulocyte-macrophage colony-stimulating factor, and interleukin-3,[78] but the mechanism by which these cytokines activate human macrophages to limit infection has not been established.

Although the infection is limited by cell-mediated immunity, tissues are not sterilized. Therefore, infected individuals contain yeasts for many years. The dormant organisms pose little risk to individuals unless they become immunosuppressed as a result of either potent immunosuppressive agents used to combat various clinical conditions or immunosuppressive viruses such as HIV. The metabolic state of *H. capsulatum* in tissues is unknown. It is likely that some of the yeasts remain viable because individuals who have moved from endemic to nonendemic areas may have reactivated infection many years later. Despite the frequency with which reactivation develops, the cascade of immunologic events that lead to this form of the infection remains unknown.

The hallmark of the tissue response to this fungus is the development of caseating or noncaseating granulomas in which calcium may be deposited (Fig. 254–4). The granuloma consists of an admixture of mononuclear phagocytes and lymphocytes, principally T cells. The putative function of the granuloma is to contain fungal growth. Although interferon-γ and tumor necrosis factor-α are important in the generation of granulomas formed in response to other microbes, neutralization of these two cytokines does not prevent granuloma formation in response to *H. capsulatum*.[70, 78] Organized granulomatous inflammation is typically observed in self-limited disease. Conversely, in progressive histoplasmosis, the more common histopathologic appearance of tissue is that of a massive influx of macrophages with scattered lymphocytes. Well-circumscribed granulomas are infrequently present,[79, 80] and the lack of an organized inflammatory response is indicative of a perturbed cellular immune response. Occasionally, the inflammatory response in mediastinal lymph nodes is exaggerated, resulting in excessive granuloma formation followed by fibrosis. The progressive scarring may affect the patency of the airways and major blood vessels.

In experimental infection, either cutaneous or in vitro delayed-type hypersensitivity responses to *H. capsulatum* antigens are detected approximately 2 weeks after exposure.[81] In humans, it is estimated that delayed-type hypersensitivity responses are manifest within 3 to 6 weeks after exposure.[82, 83] However, these values are simply approximations because the precise time at which individuals are exposed in endemic areas is exceptionally difficult to determine. Reexposure of previously sensitized individuals to *H. capsulatum* is characterized by a more rapid tissue response. This finding is not surprising because *H. capsulatum* induces a memory response in which the immune system reacts in a much shorter time frame.

Infection with *H. capsulatum* produces a broad array of clinical and pathologic manifestations that must be recognized for correct diagnosis and treatment of individuals afflicted with this fungus. A summary of the clinicopathologic manifestations is given in Table 254–1.

PULMONARY HISTOPLASMOSIS

Acute Primary Infection

The vast majority of primary infections (>90%) go unrecognized medically. Most often, they are either asymptomatic infections or a

TABLE 254–1 The Spectrum of *Histoplasma capsulatum*–Induced Disease

Manifestations	Acute Pulmonary Disease	Cavitary Pulmonary Disease	Acute Disseminated Disease
Clinical	Often asymptomatic	Fever, productive cough, chest pain	Fever, weight loss, hepatosplenomegaly, hematologic disturbances*
Immunologic			
Positive skin test	>90%	70–90%	30–55%
Lymphocyte transformation	+ + +†	+ to + + +	±
Antibody to *H. capsulatum*‡	25–85%§	75–95%	70–90%
Antigenuria	20%§	40%	60–90%
Pathologic			
Positive culture from lungs	<25%	50–70%	50–70%
Histology	Caseating and noncaseating granulomas, few yeasts, giant cells	Noncaseating granulomas, interstitial fibrosis, necrosis, cavities, few to moderate yeasts	Diffuse macrophage proliferation, abundant yeasts, few giant cells

*Hematologic disturbances include anemia, leukopenia, and thrombocytopenia.
†A proliferation response to antigen or mitogen that is 3- to 5-fold higher than background; + +, 5- to 10-fold higher than background; + + +, more than 10-fold higher.
‡Complement fixation titer ≥1:8.
§Higher incidence in those with symptomatic infection.
From Deepe GS Jr, Bullock WE. Histoplasmosis: A granulomatous inflammatory response. In: Gallin JI, Goldstein IM, Snyderman R, eds. Inflammation: Basic Principles and Clinical Correlates. 2nd ed. New York: Raven; 1992:943.

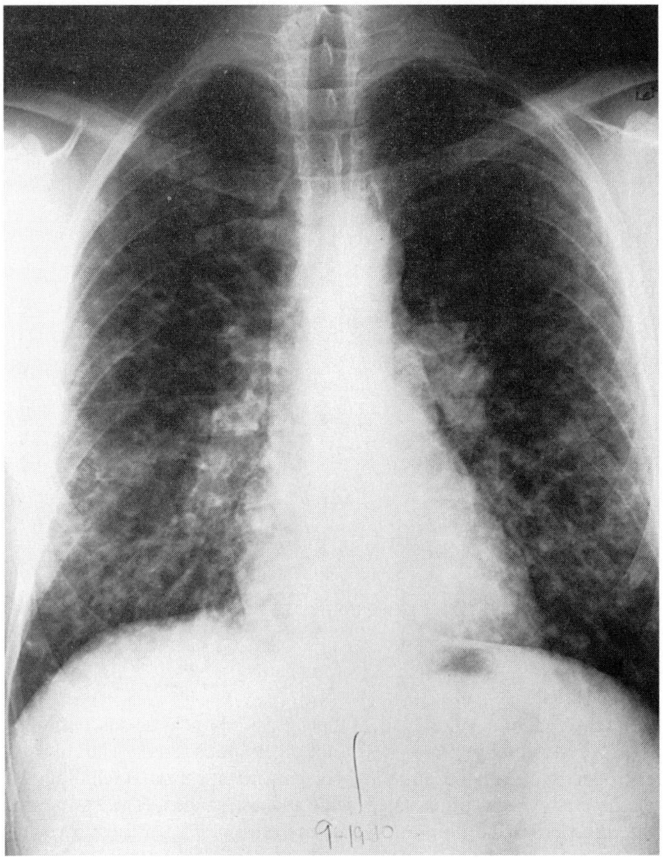

FIGURE 254–5. Chest roentgenogram of a patient with acute pulmonary histoplasmosis.

mild influenza-like illness for which individuals do not seek medical attention. However, a small proportion of patients become overtly ill. The major determinant of the development of symptoms is probably the inoculum size, although differences in strain virulence cannot be excluded.[84, 85] Other contributing factors include age and underlying diseases. Thus, the elderly, those younger than 2 years of age, and individuals whose immune systems are compromised are more likely to develop symptoms.

In those who become ill, the typical incubation time is 7 to 21 days, and most individuals manifest symptoms by day 14.[84–86] Fever with a temperature that may reach 42°C, headache, nonproductive cough chills, and chest pain are the most common symptoms. The chest pain is usually described as a substernal discomfort, although in an outbreak in children it was more often located in the anterior chest.[87] Pleuritic chest pain is uncommon. The chest pain is believed to be caused by enlargement of either mediastinal or hilar lymph nodes or both. Malaise, weakness, fatigue, and myalgia are observed in a distinctly smaller percentage of patients.[84, 88] Most symptoms resolve within 10 days, but they can persist for several weeks if there is exposure to a heavy inoculum. Acute pulmonary infection can be accompanied by a number of rheumatologic manifestations.[89, 90] Arthralgias, erythema nodosum, and erythema multiforme are present in approximately 6% of patients, the majority of whom are women.[89] In some, these manifestation of histoplasmosis may be the presenting complaint. Frank arthritis is distinctly uncommon.

Physical findings in acute pulmonary histoplasmosis are minimal. Rales may be detected and, rarely, hepatosplenomegaly. The common roentgenographic features are a patchy pneumonitis that eventually calcifies and hilar lymphadenopathy (Fig. 254–5). If a heavy exposure has occurred, numerous patches of pneumonitis that calcify may develop, and these produce the so-called buckshot appearance on the chest roentgenogram.[84] Pleural effusions are uncommon. The white blood cell count is usually within the normal range, but approximately 30% of patients have either leukocytosis or leukopenia during the course of this infection.[84, 85] Another laboratory abnormality is a transient increase in serum alkaline phosphatase. Pulmonary function studies have been performed in only a few patients, and the studies have demonstrated reversible restrictive defects, impaired single-breath carbon monoxide differing capacity, and obstructive defects.[91, 92]

At least 6% of patients who acquire histoplasmosis suffer from acute pericarditis.[93–96] This percentage may underestimate the true incidence because only the most seriously affected individuals seek medical attention. Precordial chest pain and fever are frequent. A high proportion of patients report a respiratory illness approximately 6 weeks before the onset of the pericarditis. A pericardial friction rub is auscultated in more than 75%, and pulsus paradoxus is present in a similar percentage. An enlarged cardiac silhouette is usually seen on the chest roentgenogram. Electrocardiographic abnormalities indicative of pericarditis, such as ST segment elevation, are often observed. Only a small percentage of individuals develop cardiac tamponade. The likely cause of the pericarditis is not direct invasion of the organism, because it is rarely found in tissue specimens or in pericardial fluid, but rather the granulomatous inflammatory response that is mounted in mediastinal lymph nodes adjacent to the pericardium.

Acute pulmonary histoplasmosis must be distinguished from influenza and from other forms of community-acquired pneumonia. This task is difficult unless a thorough exposure history is obtained. Of greater concern, however, are patients who present with mediastinal lymphadenopathy. This finding is often considered to be caused by a hematologic malignancy rather than histoplasmosis. In such cases, patients may undergo unnecessary surgical procedures in an attempt to establish a diagnosis. Sarcoidosis should also be considered, and distinguishing between histoplasmosis and sarcoidosis can be difficult at best. Both may have similar histopathologic features, and serum angiotensin-converting enzyme levels are elevated in each disease.[97, 98] Thus, for all patients who present with mediastinal or hilar lymphadenopathy and who reside in or have recently resided in an endemic region, it is critically important that histoplasmosis be considered in the differential diagnosis.

A Ghon complex and pulmonary calcifications are common in healed pulmonary histoplasmosis. Another characteristic feature of resolved primary infection is the presence of splenic or liver calcifications. In fact, the presence of these on a routine roentgenogram should be considered evidence of resolved histoplasmosis if the patient has resided in an endemic area. Although splenic and liver calcifications are also noted in healed tuberculosis, the most likely cause of these findings remains histoplasmosis because the incidence of tuberculosis in the United States is much lower than that of histoplasmosis.

Acute Reinfection Pulmonary Histoplasmosis

It is not uncommon for those who reside in endemic areas to be reexposed to *H. capsulatum*. Those who are reexposed to a large inoculum in heavily endemic areas present with a milder influenza-like illness. The onset can begin within 3 days, which is shorter than in primary infection. The characteristic chest roentgenogram shows numerous small nodules that are diffusely scattered throughout both lung fields. This feature has been referred to as miliary granulomatosis. Hilar or mediastinal lymphadenopathy is absent. The duration of illness is often briefer than in primary infection.[84, 99]

Histoplasmoma

An infrequent complication of primary histoplasmosis is the development of a mass lesion that resembles a fibroma.[85, 100–102] When it arises, it is found most often in the lung. Instead of resolving, a nidus of infection gradually enlarges over years to form a calcified mass. Presumably, the growth is caused by persistent antigenic stimulus from the yeasts. It is composed of active inflammation at the periphery and fibrous tissue within the inner sphere, and eventually the central portion calcifies. Roentgenographically, the histoplasmoma may have a central core of calcium, rings of calcium, or clusters ("mulberry" calcifications), and these findings are useful in distinguishing it from a neoplastic growth.

Mediastinal Granuloma and Fibrosis

Another complication of primary infection is a massive enlargement of the mediastinal lymph nodes that is caused by the granulomatous inflammation mounted in response to the fungus.[84, 103] The diameter of these nodes can reach 8 to 10 cm. The nodes are caseous and contain a fibrotic shell that may be up to 5 mm thick. Often, this process is asymptomatic. Occasionally, however, the nodes may impinge upon major airways and impair gas exchange. During the healing process, the fibrotic tissue can cause retraction of the airways, leading to postobstructive pneumonias, hypoxemia, and bronchiectasis. The fibrosis may also constrict the esophagus or the superior vena cava, resulting in dysphagia or superior vena cava syndrome or both.[103–105]

Calcific deposits that originate within the lungs occasionally produce lithoptysis. More common, however, is the penetration of enlarged, calcified nodes into the airways and the generation of particles of calcium that can be expectorated. If the calcific mass is large, airway obstruction may ensue. Another consequence of enlarged nodes is the creation of sinuses or fistulas between the airways and the pericardium or the esophagus.[105]

A rare but dire consequence of mediastinal involvement is mediastinal fibrosis.[106, 107] This syndrome is quite similar to that observed with tuberculosis in which the infection leads to a massive deposition of fibrotic tissue within the mediastinum (Fig. 254–6). The mechanism underlying this exuberant immune response is unknown. However, it appears not to be triggered by massive numbers of yeasts because they are observed infrequently in lesions. The reaction to the antigen(s) from *H. capsulatum* must be host specific on the basis of its infrequent development. If there exist any genetic susceptibility loci for this entity, they have not been uncovered. The fibrosis encroaches on all the structures of the mediastinum including the major airways, superior vena cava, and esophagus. The symptoms that arise from the fibrotic process are attributable to the narrowing of the patency of these structures. Hypoxemia, shortness of breath, superior vena cava syndrome, and dysphagia may ensue as the fibrotic process progresses.[108, 109]

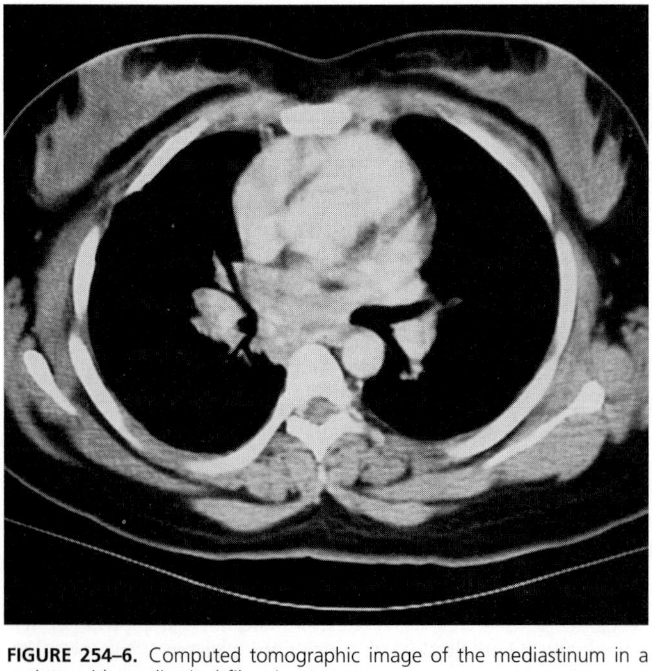

FIGURE 254–6. Computed tomographic image of the mediastinum in a patient with mediastinal fibrosis.

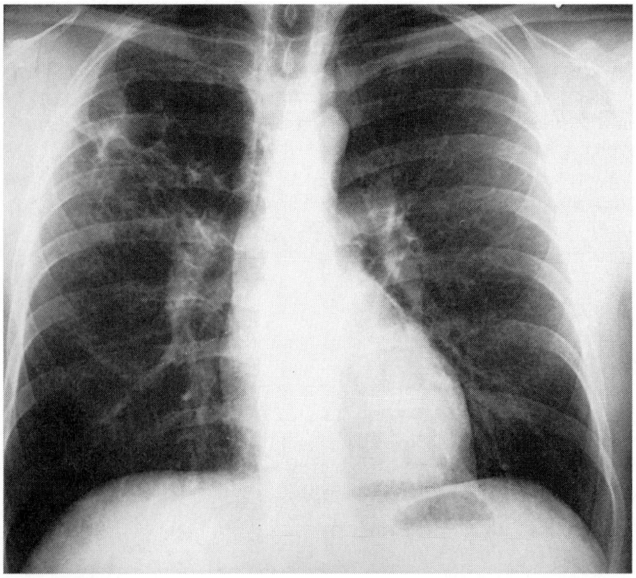

FIGURE 254–7. Chest roentgenogram of a patient with cavitary histoplasmosis.

Cavitary Pulmonary Histoplasmosis

Cavitary pulmonary histoplasmosis (also known as chronic pulmonary histoplasmosis) is a distinct clinical entity (Fig. 254–7). Although the precise incidence is not known because of the sporadic nature of the disease, approximately 8% of individuals developed this manifestation of disease after two large epidemics in Indianapolis.[110] Cavitary lesions are found in the upper lobes in more than 90% of cases. Males older than 50 years of age with preexisting chronic lung disease, usually emphysema, constitute the highest proportion of patients, and it is quite unusual in those younger than age 40 (<5% of all cases).[110, 111]

The most frequent symptoms are low-grade fever, productive cough, dyspnea, and weight loss. Night sweats, chest pain, hemoptysis, and malaise are less common. Both an early and a late stage have been described. The major difference between the two forms is the symptomatology. In the early stage, the illness, characterized by chest pain, productive cough, fever, and weakness, begins abruptly and persists for several weeks before medical attention is sought. In the late stage, the proportion of patients experiencing productive cough and hemoptysis is much higher, whereas chest pain and fever are much less frequent. Bronchogenic transmission from one segment of the lung to another may occur during cough or aspiration.[111]

Roentgenographically, cavitary lesions are present in the upper lobes. A high proportion of patients exhibit evidence of coexisting chronic obstructive pulmonary disease, and therefore the cavities must be distinguished from preexisting bullae. Thin-walled or thick-walled cavities may form in response to *H. capsulatum*. Enlarged hilar or mediastinal lymph nodes are notably absent, and distinctive laboratory features are not present. Leukocytosis and elevated alkaline phosphatase levels are detected in about one third of patients, and anemia is present in one half.[110, 111]

This form of histoplasmosis originates as an interstitial pneumonitis. The inflammatory infiltrate is composed primarily of lymphocytes and macrophages, and it is often found adjacent to bullae. The alveolar walls are thickened, and the peribronchial lymphatics contain a similar type of inflammatory infiltrate. Subsequently, necrosis develops, and it resembles that caused by infarction. Vascular compromise as denoted by subintimal thickening and vessel obliteration is present in inflamed regions. Proteinaceous exudate can be found within bullae, and yeasts are present within the necrotic lining of a cavity or within small encapsulated necrotic lesions. The healing phase is characterized by fibrosis and scarring of the involved parenchyma. After healing, cavitary lesions recur in approximately 20% of patients, but the prognosis for recurrence is not different from that in the initial infection.[111]

Spontaneous resolution of thin-walled and thick-walled cavities ranges from 10 to 60%, and thin-walled cavities have a higher healing rate. In individuals with chronic obstructive pulmonary disease, cavitary histoplasmosis can exacerbate the existing pulmonary dysfunction, and the destructive nature of the inflammation irreversibly compromises pulmonary function. Death caused by cavitary histoplasmosis is distinctly unusual but is attributable to respiratory failure, cor pulmonale, or secondary pneumonia.

The association between the presence of chronic obstructive pulmonary disease and cavitary histoplasmosis suggests that the anatomic defect present in these lungs promotes the formation of cavities. This intriguing postulate has been proposed and is most likely correct, although no experimental data exist to support it.[111] The difficulty in testing this hypothesis is that a suitable animal model has not been developed. In addition, the postulate does not explain the development of cavities in other patients. At present, *H. capsulatum* is not known to elaborate any elastinolytic or proteolytic enzymes that digest collagen.

Some have argued that most cases represent reinfection because there is no concomitant enlargement of intrathoracic lymph nodes. However, this finding may argue equally well for reactivation because nodal enlargement may not be expected in local reactivation disease. Until the tools are available to distinguish individual isolates of *H. capsulatum*, this controversy will not be settled.

PROGRESSIVE DISSEMINATED HISTOPLASMOSIS

Although all primary infections can be considered disseminated because yeast cells migrate from the lungs to organs rich in mononuclear phagocytes, the term progressive disseminated histoplasmosis (PDH) refers to the relentless growth of the organism in multiple organ systems. Because infection with *H. capsulatum* is not a reportable disease, only estimates of incidence or prevalence are available. The estimated incidence of histoplasmosis is 1 in 2000.[112] After the two Indianapolis epidemics, 8% of clinically recognized cases of histoplasmosis were PDH.[67] In those two epidemics, the major risk factors for this manifestation of histoplasmosis were age older than 54 years and immunosuppression. Among patients with AIDS, the incidence may approach 25%.[113, 114] In an analysis of 1074 renal allograft recipients, 0.4% developed clinically recognized PDH over a 25-year span.[115] This value is moderately different from the one reported during the Indianapolis epidemic, in which 2.1% of renal allograft recipients exhibited PDH.[116]

PDH can develop on reexposure to a large inoculum of the fungus or reactivation of dormant, endogenous foci. The vast majority of cases are believed to arise from endogenous reactivation because cases develop in those who remotely resided in an endemic area. Nevertheless, it is nearly impossible to distinguish reinfection from reactivation with the current diagnostic tools. In recent years, most cases have been observed in immunosuppressed individuals.[112–118] However, there are still cases in those who are not known to have preexisting immunologic dysfunction. The perturbations that cause a breach in the integrity of the immune system and therefore lead to reactivation of quiescent infected foci have not been delineated.

Although infection with *H. capsulatum* produces a broad range of disease, PDH can also be categorized by clinical and pathologic manifestations. The acute form is associated with a fulminant course. Histopathologically, massive macrophage infiltration and scattered lymphocytes are observed. Tissue macrophages are engorged with yeast cells, and tests of cellular immunity often reveal poor to absent responses. At the other extreme is the chronic form, characterized by an indolent course and the presence of well-circumscribed granulomas in involved tissues. In tissues, few yeasts are seen, and delayed-type hypersensitivity responses are intact in a high proportion of individuals.[80]

Acute Progressive Disseminated Histoplasmosis

In the era before aggressive immunosuppressive or cytotoxic therapy, this entity was seen principally in infants, hence the term infantile form. Today, however, it is most often observed in those who are severely immunosuppressed, especially those with AIDS and hematologic malignancies such as Hodgkin's and non-Hodgkin's lymphoma. In infants and young children, it is believed that this form of histoplasmosis is a progression of either a primary exposure or reinfection because pulmonary symptoms dominate the early phases of illness. The onset is usually abrupt. Fever and malaise are the two most common manifestations, followed by weight loss, cough, and diarrhea. Physical findings include hepatosplenomegaly in nearly all patients, lymphadenopathy especially of the cervical chain in about 30%, and rales. Jaundice is observed in a minority, and oropharyngeal ulcers develop in less than 20%.[80]

Hematologic disturbances are frequent. Anemia is present in more than 90%, the majority of whom have a hematocrit less than 20%. Leukopenia and thrombocytopenia are observed in more than 80% of children. Serum levels of the liver enzymes alanine aminotransferase and alkaline phosphatase are elevated in a high proportion. Chest roentgenograms most often reveal a patchy pneumonitis with mediastinal and hilar node enlargement. This finding supports the contention that acute PDH in children represents an extension of an exogenous exposure. When the condition is untreated the mortality is 100%, and before the introduction of effective antifungal agents most children died within 5 to 6 weeks after onset of symptoms. Terminal events include disseminated intravascular coagulation, gastrointestinal hemorrhage probably resulting from severe thrombocytopenia, and secondary bacterial sepsis associated with profound granulocytopenia.

In HIV-infected individuals, the risk factors for the development of histoplasmosis are a $CD4^+$ cell count fewer than 200 cells/μl, a history of exposure to chicken coops, and positive serology for complement-fixing antibodies before illness.[67, 119, 120] Most AIDS patients who develop PDH have had at least one opportunistic infection. Although PDH may develop in approximately 25% of AIDS patients residing in an endemic area, there is no comparable information for the era of potent combination antiretroviral therapy. Anecdotal reports suggest a decline in the incidence of cases. On seeking medical attention, nearly all patients manifest evidence of disseminated disease. Fever and weight loss are found in more than 90% of those with AIDS and PDH. The most common physical findings include rales, hepatosplenomegaly, and lymphadenopathy. Mucosal ulcers are distinctly uncommon, but as many as 10% of patients exhibit cutaneous lesions.[121, 122] The common cutaneous findings are a maculopapular eruption, petechiae, and ecchymosis. The maculopapular rash does not display any unique pattern of distribution. Histopathology of skin lesions reveals necrosis circumscribing the superficial dermal vessels. There is perivascular cuffing with lymphocytes and neutrophils, but the number of cells is very small. Yeasts are present both intra- and extracellularly. In addition to the skin findings, a number of other unusual manifestations have been reported, including colonic masses, perianal ulcers, chorioretinitis, meningitis, and encephalitis. It is estimated from results of one series that up to 20% of patients with PDH have central nervous system involvement.[123] The more aggressive forms include encephalitis, acute meningitis, and encephalopathy in acute PDH. Histoplasmoma of the central nervous system and chronic meningitis are manifestations of a more indolent form of PDH.

Anemia, thromobocytopenia, and leukopenia are common laboratory features of PDH in the immunosuppressed population. In AIDS patients, the alteration in the peripheral blood counts may be attributable, in part, to the disease or to the drugs the patients are receiving. Elevated serum levels of hepatic enzymes are frequently detected. Again, concomitant drugs may obscure the laboratory abnormalities caused strictly by *H. capsulatum*. Chest roentgenograms typically demonstrate widely scattered nodular opacities or a diffuse reticular pattern (Fig. 254–8). However, a substantial percentage (30%) of patients may present with a normal roentgenogram.[124]

The fatality rate of acute PDH in immunocompromised patients is 100% if untreated. With therapy, survival rates of the acute episode exceed 80%. Infrequently, patients exhibit a sepsis-like syndrome characterized by disseminated intravascular coagulation, encephalopathy, acute respiratory distress syndrome, vascular collapse, and, subsequently, multiorgan failure. In some patients, bone marrow biopsy has demonstrated the presence of histiocytes phagocytosing erythrocytes.[125] This form of PDH has been termed the reactive hemophagocytic syndrome, and despite aggressive management and therapy, the outcome is usually catastrophic.

Subacute Progressive Disseminated Histoplasmosis

Subacute PDH is distinguished from the acute form primarily by the more prolonged nature of the symptoms before patients seek medical attention. Fever and weight loss are common some time during the course of infection, but fever is a presenting complaint in only about 50%. Physical findings include hepatosplenomegaly and oropharyngeal ulcers. In contrast to the ulcers observed in acute PDH, these are deeper and more likely to be confused with malignancy. Laboratory abnormalities are much less striking than in acute PDH. Although anemia and leukopenia are noted in up to 40%, the percentage of patients with severe depression of either the hematocrit or leukocyte count is small. Thrombocytopenia is evident in about 20% and is usually mild. Rarely is the platelet count less than 20,000/μl.[80]

One of the notable features of subacute PDH is the presence of focal lesions in various organ systems, including the gastrointestinal tract, endovascular structures, central nervous system, and adrenal glands. Aside from liver and spleen, the gastrointestinal tract is one of the organs most commonly affected in subacute PDH. Yeast cells can be found in the bowel mucosa in up to 70% of autopsy cases. Macroscopic ulcerations of the small and large bowel are present in about 40%, and perforation by a penetrating ulcer has been reported.[80, 126] The terminal ileum and cecum are the sites most frequently involved. Symptoms referable to the bowel are not frequent, but when they are present, diarrhea and crampy abdominal pain are typical complaints. Intestinal obstruction of the ileum has also been reported.

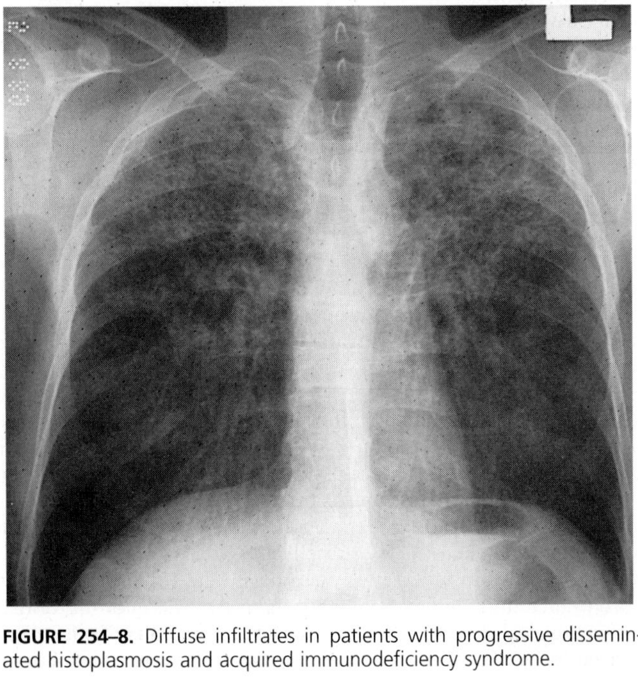

FIGURE 254–8. Diffuse infiltrates in patients with progressive disseminated histoplasmosis and acquired immunodeficiency syndrome.

Endocarditis and infection of other vascular structures may be manifestations of subacute PDH.[127] The aortic and mitral valves are affected more commonly than right-sided valves, and the aortic valve is most commonly involved. In about 50% of the cases, there is prior evidence of valvular disease. On echocardiography, the lesions tend to be extensive and large vessel embolization can be the presenting symptom. Clumps of yeasts embedded in a fibrin mesh are the characteristic histopathologic feature. Occasionally, allomorphs that are as large as 20 μm in diameter have been observed. In addition, hyphal forms of *H. capsulatum* have been detected in endocarditis.[128] If the condition is untreated, death usually ensues. Other endovascular manifestations include prosthetic valve endocarditis and infection of abdominal aortic aneurysms and prosthetic grafts.[129, 130] Early reports indicated that blood cultures are rarely positive; however, those reports preceded improved methods for isolating *H. capsulatum* from blood.

Central nervous system infection involves all age groups and causes a number of manifestations including chronic meningitis, mass lesion, and cerebritis. Among these, chronic meningitis is the most frequent.[123] Symptoms of central nervous system histoplasmosis may precede medical attention by several weeks, and they include headache, altered sensorium, and cranial nerve deficits. Seizures, ataxia, meningismus, and other focal deficits constitute much of the remaining symptomatology. It must be emphasized that only half of the patients may complain of symptoms localized to the central nervous system. Associated physical findings consist of hepatosplenomegaly in about a third, lymphadenopathy, and mucocutaneous lesions.

In cases of meningitis, pleocytosis of the cerebrospinal fluid is present in all patients. Cell counts usually range from 10 to 100 cells/μl with a preponderance of lymphocytes. Hypoglycorrhachia and elevated protein are detected in 80%. Histopathology of the brain parenchyma and meninges characteristically reveals granulomatous inflammation. A perivenous granulomatosis in which parasitized macrophages are observed beneath the intima of parenchymal and meningeal veins is commonly seen. The basilar meninges are the most severely affected area of the central nervous system.[123, 131] Hydrocephalus may contribute to the symptoms.

Histoplasmoma causes a mass effect and may initially be mistaken for a malignancy or abscess on computed tomography because it exhibits ring enhancement with the administration of contrast medium. Dense fibrotic tissue surrounds a caseous center in which yeasts are detected. Histoplasmomas may be associated with meningitis but are often independently present. Cerebrospinal fluid pleocytosis is common but hypoglycorrhachia is not.

Although symptoms arising from involvement of adrenal glands are not frequent, autopsy series indicate that yeasts invade this organ system in approximately 80% of cases.[80, 132] Macrophages containing yeasts are found scattered throughout the parenchyma of the adrenal gland. There is no particular predilection for either the cortex or the medulla. The severity of infection ranges from focal areas containing parasitized macrophages to diffuse involvement of the adrenal parenchyma. The former is more commonly detected. Tissue necrosis is seen but usually involves only a small portion of the gland. Grossly, the adrenal glands are enlarged. This postmortem discovery has been supported by computed tomographic findings of enlarged adrenals in

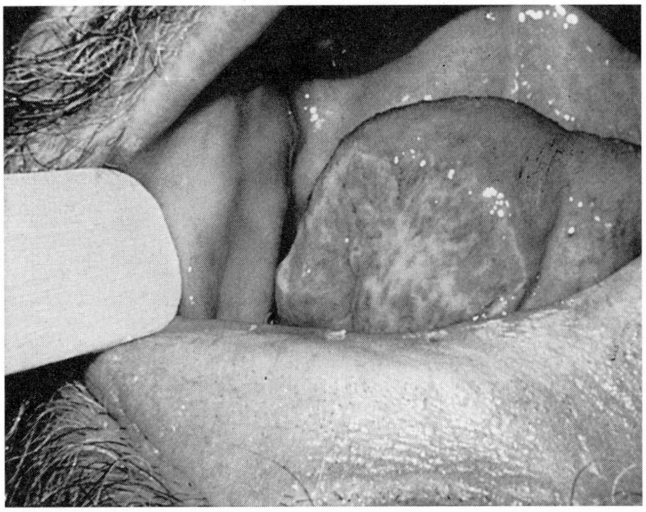

FIGURE 254–9. Tongue ulcer in a patient with chronic disseminated histoplasmosis.

a high percentage of patients with subacute PDH.[133] Overt Addison's disease is uncommon, occurring in less than 10%. There is little information concerning the incidence of an impaired pituitary-adrenal axis.[80, 132]

Chronic Progressive Disseminated Histoplasmosis

Chronic PDH can be distinguished from subacute PDH by the chronicity of symptoms that are often very mild. This form is seen almost exclusively in adults. Malaise and lethargy stand out as the most frequent complaints. Fever is much less frequent (<30%) and is often low grade. The most common physical finding (about 50%) is an oropharyngeal ulcer that is deep and painless (Fig. 254–9). The tongue, buccal mucosa, larynx, gums, and lips constitute the majority of affected structures. These lesions are often confused with an oral malignancy. Hence, it is incumbent upon the clinician to consider the diagnosis of histoplasmosis; otherwise, tissue will be sent only for histology. Histopathologically, the center of the lesion contains macrophages with many yeasts, but the number of such macrophages decreases in the periphery of the lesion. Unlike the histologic reaction in other viscera, the response in the mucosa is an admixture of acute and chronic inflammation. Thus, plasma cells, lymphocytes, eosinophils, and granulocytes are found infiltrating the ulcer, and fibrosis is a characteristic feature. Well-circumscribed granulomas are typically found, usually at the periphery.[80]

Other symptoms include hepatosplenomegaly in about one third of patients. Unlike the findings in subacute PDH, there is a notable absence of involvement of other organ systems including central nervous system, heart, and adrenals. Bone infection, Addison's disease, and endocarditis all have been described, but these entities are truly in the minority. Hematologic abnormalities are distinctly uncommon and often not significant. This illness may persist for years without being recognized. On occasion, there may be an abrupt worsening caused by involvement of a particular organ such as the central nervous system or heart. Usually, however, the illness remains undiagnosed until symptoms arising from a single organ are observed.

OCULAR HISTOPLASMOSIS

Two different syndromes of ocular involvement have been described. The less common is uveitis or panophthalmitis in association with active histoplasmosis. Granulomas are present in the uvea and yeasts are recovered from lesions. Much more frequent is the presumed ocular histoplasmosis syndrome, which consists of posterior uveitis or choroiditis in individuals who manifest skin test positivity to histoplasmin and intrathoracic calcifications.[134] However, it must be stressed that a skin test and the presence of intrathoracic calcifications do not prove cause and effect.

Typically, there are peripheral atrophic scars and a lack of vitreous or anterior segment inflammation. The scars or "histospots" are located posterior to the equator of the eye. They range in size from 0.2 to 0.7 disk diameter, and their number can vary from 1 to 70 in a single eye. Initial involvement of both eyes is uncommon (<10%). Most individuals are between 20 and 50 years of age when this syndrome is diagnosed, and the prevalence may be as high as 10% in endemic regions. The major destructive consequence of this lesion is macular hemorrhage, which develops 10 to 20 years after the appearance of scars. Neovascularization and scarring can lead to loss of vision in up to 60% of patients.[134] Because neovascularization can exert such devastating effects, efforts have been made to understand its etiology. It has been shown that the integrin $\alpha_v\beta_3$ is expressed on blood vessels from patients with presumed ocular histoplasmosis syndrome. Moreover, a peptide that blocks the effect of this integrin inhibits angiogenesis.[135] This finding raises hope for halting the possible progressive nature of this disease.

The histopathology of presumed ocular histoplasmosis syndrome reveals a lymphocytic infiltration in the scarred areas. Yeasts are rarely observed. A model for this syndrome has been developed in primates in order to define the cellular immunopathology. Chronic lesions contain a preponderance of B and $CD4^+$ cells. As in affected human eyes, yeasts are not found in the lesions. Within the choroidal lesions there is an increase in the percentage of $CD4^+$ cells and macrophages.[136, 137] There is no definitive proof that *H. capsulatum* causes the scars that are observed in humans, although the primate model establishes that this fungus can produce choroidal scars. The pathogenesis appears to be an exuberant cellular immune reaction to inert fungal antigens, which resembles to some degree the tissue response in mediastinal fibrosis.

AFRICAN HISTOPLASMOSIS

In Africa, the classical *H. capsulatum* var. *capsulatum* coexists with *H. capsulatum* var. *duboisii*. The yeast form of the latter is typically much larger, with a diameter up to 15 μm, and has a thicker wall. The mycelial forms of both are indistinguishable. This fungus is presumed to be inhaled from the soil, although a primary pulmonary infection has not been demonstrated. Cutaneous inoculation is certainly an alternative mode of acquisition of the infection. Spontaneous disease has been reported in baboons and cynocephalus monkeys. Most cases are reported from Uganda, Nigeria, Democratic Republic of Congo, and Senegal.

The clinical picture associated with infection by *H. capsulatum* var. *duboisii* is distinctly different from that associated with *H. capsulatum* var. *capsulatum*.[138] Skin and skeleton are the organs most frequently affected by this pathogen. In the skin, the usual findings are ulcers, nodules, or psoriasis-like lesions that may spontaneously resolve. Involvement of the subcutaneous tissue may be indicated by tender nodules ("cold" abscesses) in which the typical manifestations of inflammation are absent. Osteolytic bone lesions are fairly common and are noted in up to 50% of cases. The skull and ribs are the bones most frequently affected, followed by vertebrae. The organism produces granulomatous inflammation within the bone. This type of inflammation can lead to sinus formation and cystic bone lesions. In a high proportion of patients, multiple bones may be infected. Even in the presence of overt skin or bone lesions, chest roentgenograms are often free of evidence of previous exposure to *H. capsulatum*. Draining lymph nodes may also become inflamed.

A progressive disseminated disease has been recognized. Patients are febrile with hematologic abnormalities. There is multiorgan involvement including liver, spleen, kidney, and lung, and miliary lesions are observed in the latter. The histopathology resembles that induced by *Blastomyces dermatitidis* or *Coccidioides immitis*, that is, a pyogranulomatous reaction in which there is a combination of granulomas and suppuration. One likely reason for this pathologic reaction is that the large size of *H. capsulatum* var. *duboisii* prevents avid ingestion by macrophages. Thus, neutrophils may enter to assist in the clearance of the fungus.

Reports of African histoplasmosis in HIV-infected individuals are just emerging.[139] A variety of manifestations in individual patients have been observed. Disseminated infection with fever, cutaneous infection, and bone infection have been recognized. The outcome has been favorable only in a minority of patients.

DIAGNOSIS

Histoplasmosis can be established with assurance only by isolation of *H. capsulatum* from body fluids or tissues. The typical medium that is used to recover the fungus includes brain-heart infusion agar with a source of blood plus antibiotics and cycloheximide. The latter are included to inhibit the growth of saprophytic fungi and bacteria. Cultures are incubated at 30°C for up to 6 weeks. Often, growth is noted within 3 weeks, and more than 90% of cultures exhibit fungus within 7 days. Previously, confirmation that the fungus was *H. capsulatum* required exoantigen testing, but this step is no longer necessary. All mycelial isolates are confirmed using a DNA probe that recognizes ribosomal DNA.

The success rate varies considerably and is often correlated with the number of specimens collected, the source of the specimen, and the burden of infection. Recovery of *H. capsulatum* from sputa of patients with acute pulmonary histoplasmosis ranges from 10 to 15%, whereas in cavitary histoplasmosis cultures are positive in up to 60% of patients.[140] The yield of positive cultures increases with the number of specimens collected. Three or more specimens are more likely to display growth of *H. capsulatum*. In AIDS patients with pulmonary manifestations, up to 90% of cultures obtained from bronchoscopic samples from the lungs grow *H. capsulatum*.[141] Bone marrow and blood cultures are positive in up to 50%.[67] Yields for blood cultures are considerably higher if the lysis centrifugation technique is used.[142] The organism can be frequently isolated from oropharyngeal ulcers in patients with chronic PDH. In endocarditis, valve cultures are positive in a high percentage but blood cultures are often negative. However, much of the data concerning blood cultures was obtained with the biphasic medium, which may not be as sensitive as lysis centrifugation. In meningitis, the organism is recovered from the cerebrospinal fluid in 25 to 65% of patients,[125, 131] and the yield is improved if a large volume ($\geq$20 ml) is removed because *H. capsulatum* invades the basilar meninges. The organism is unlikely to be isolated from pericardial or pleural fluid but more likely to be isolated from their respective serosal tissues. Likewise, *H. capsulatum* is rarely isolated from mediastinal tissues in patients with mediastinal fibrosis.

Antigen Detection and Polymerase Chain Reaction Analysis

One of the major advances in the diagnosis of histoplasmosis has been the development and introduction of an antigen detection assay that identifies a polysaccharide antigen in either urine or serum. The test was done originally by radioimmunoassay and more recently by enzyme-linked immunosorbent assay, a test that may or may not be equivalent. The precise biochemical nature of the antigen is not known, nor are in vivo characteristics such as clearance by the kidney and half-life. Nevertheless, this assay has become a mainstay of diagnosis, especially for immunosuppressed patients with PDH. Antigen is detected in up to 90% of patients with PDH, 40% with cavitary disease, and 20% with acute pulmonary histoplasmosis.[143, 144] The test also has excellent utility in monitoring relapses of PDH, especially in immunosuppressed patients.[145] An increase in the arbitrary value of two units is significantly associated with relapse of infection. Antigen detection is much more sensitive than serology for identifying relapses, and it has been applied successfully to cerebrospinal fluid in patients with meningitis. In 14 cases, the test was positive in 12.[146] Thus, it has a high degree of sensitivity. The specificity of this test is also relatively good. However, in patients infected with *B. dermatitidis*, *Paracoccidioides brasiliensis*, or *Penicillium marneffie*, there is a high degree of cross-reactivity in the enzyme-linked immunosorbent assay urine antigen test.[147]

The introduction of the polymerase chain reaction in the diagnostic arena has allowed laboratories to make a rapid and specific diagnosis of infections using small samples, tissues, or fluids. A specific test using the polymerase chain reaction has been developed, and although it is not in clinical use yet, it shows promise.[148]

Serology

Since the late 1940s, serology has been a vital instrument in the diagnosis of infection with *H. capsulatum*. Complement-fixing (CF) antibodies and precipitin bands have been most commonly used in the clinical laboratory. For CF antibodies, a titer of 1:8 is considered positive and a titer of 1:32 is strongly suggestive of active infection. Titers that fall between these two values are less diagnostic of active disease, but they must be analyzed in the context of the clinical illness. A fourfold rise in titer is certainly indicative of infection. Moreover, rising titers in those who have been treated and presumably recovered are strongly suggestive of a relapse. On occasion, a result is returned that states that the test is anticomplementary. This result signifies that the serum contained a substance or substances that interfered with the CF test. Repeating the test with a new serum specimen quite frequently yields a result.

Low levels of CF antibodies are detected in approximately 10% of healthy individuals who reside in an endemic region. A low percentage of individuals with acute pulmonary histoplasmosis develop CF antibodies within the first 3 weeks of infection, but by 6 weeks at least 75% of patients manifest a positive CF antibody titer or a fourfold rise. Over the course of months, the antibody titer declines, although it may remain serofast for years, especially in those with cavitary pulmonary disease or with chronic PDH. The false-positive rate is estimated to be 15%, and false-positive results are most commonly observed in those with coccidioidomycosis or with blastomycosis.[149, 150] The reason for the cross-reactivity is the presence of a carbohydrate antigen common to the three fungi.

Another test involves the detection of H and M bands during the illness. These two precipitin bands were originally identified by Heiner[151] using immunodiffusion as specific to sera from patients with histoplasmosis. The H and M antigens are glycoproteins that are released by both mycelial and yeast phase cultures. The H antigen has been cloned and sequenced, and it demonstrates homology to β-glucosidases.[152] It is infrequently (<10%) detected in the sera of patients, but, when present, it signifies active infection. The M antigen has also been cloned and sequenced, and it has a high degree of homology to catalase.[153] Unlike the H antigen, it is detected in up to 80% of individuals after exposure to the fungus. However, it is present in patients who have recovered from infection or who have active disease. Therefore, it is not useful in discriminating remote from current infection. A major limitation of the serologic tests is that even in the presence of active infection, they are negative in up to 50% of immunosuppressed patients, especially those with AIDS. One explanation for the poor anti-*Histoplasma* antibody response is that the immunosuppressive agents or HIV induces dysfunctional B cells or $CD4^+$ T cells, or both, thus rendering serologic assays almost useless.

Histochemical Identification of *Histoplasma capsulatum*

Stains for the presence of *H. capsulatum* can be extremely useful in rapid identification of the fungus in various tissues or body fluids.

The yeast is visualized poorly by hematoxylin-eosin staining, but it is more apparent using the periodic acid–Schiff stain. The most useful stain is either the Gomori methenamine or Grocott silver stain. The organism can be detected in peripheral blood smears stained with Wright-Giemsa in up to 40% of cases of acute PDH (Fig. 254–10). The percentage is much less if the reader of the blood smear is scrutinizing the slide only to determine a differential. Examination of the peripheral blood smear can be useful if the clinician suspects PDH as the cause of a patient's illness. The yeast must be discriminated from *Pneumocytis carinii* in the lung. The latter is larger and usually extracellular. Moreover, it is exceedingly rare to find *P. carinii* in the same organs as *H. capsulatum*. Although *Leishmania* sp. and *Toxoplasma gondii* may on occasion be confused morphologically with *H. capsulatum*, neither stains with silver. One report described an immunohistochemical identification of yeast cells in tissues, but it has not gained wide acceptance.[154]

Skin Test

The histoplasmin skin test has been used for several decades to determine who has been exposed to *H. capsulatum*. The skin test reagent is prepared as the supernatant from the mycelial growth and has been standardized by the World Health Organization. This reagent has been exceptionally useful as an epidemiologic tool but has practically no value as a diagnostic tool. It must be stressed that the skin test indicates only past exposure. Moreover, in a high percentage of cases of PDH, the skin test result may be negative. In past surveys, the prevalence of skin test positivity among inhabitants of an endemic area was as high as 90%. More recent surveys have found that the prevalence is much lower, perhaps because of the changing nature of our society to become more urban.[87]

Miscellaneous Laboratory Tests

One retrospective study has suggested that patients with AIDS who are admitted to the hospital with pulmonary infiltrates, a temperature higher than 38°C, and serum lactate dehydrogenase values greater than 600 IU/ml are highly likely to have disseminated histoplasmosis.[155] Other studies have suggested that elevated serum ferritin levels are strongly suggestive of histoplasmosis.[156] Although these studies are small, they provide intriguing preliminary data that need to be expanded in larger clinical analyses.

TREATMENT

The increasing incidence of fungal infections has prompted the development and testing of numerous new antifungal agents, some of which have reached the marketplace. The introduction of azoles has moved the treatment of histoplasmosis from an inpatient to an outpatient setting. In the past, the clinician's principal option was amphotericin B. Now, ketoconazole, fluconazole, and itraconazole have been studied in clinical trials and found to have varying degrees of effectiveness in the treatment of this fungal infection. The addition of lipid-based preparations of amphotericin B to the clinician's therapeutic armamentarium has widened the options available for treatment.

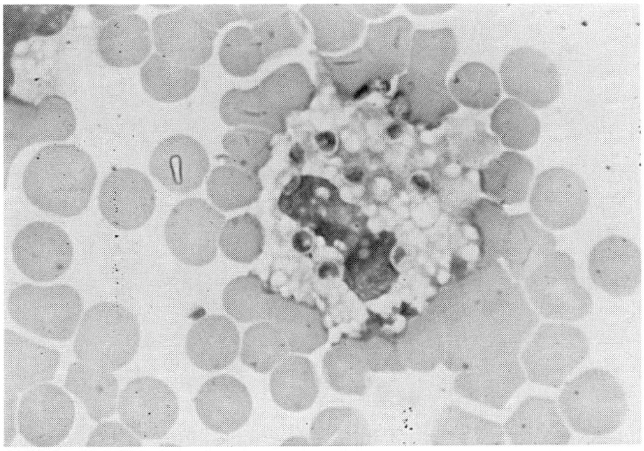

FIGURE 254–10. Wright-Giemsa stain of a circulating monocyte with intracellular yeast cells.

Acute Pulmonary Histoplasmosis

The vast majority of cases of acute pulmonary histoplasmosis do not require therapeutic intervention. Bed rest and antipyretics suffice for these individuals. Treatment should be instituted for those who have been exposed to a high inoculum and manifest fevers for more than a week associated with respiratory compromise, anorexia, and malaise. Itraconazole, 200 mg orally daily for 4 to 6 weeks, is sufficient for most patients.[157] Occasionally, longer therapy may be necessary. Ketoconazole, 400 mg orally daily, can also be used and is less expensive, but it has more side effects. Fluconazole is not as active as either itraconazole or ketoconazole.[158] If the patient cannot ingest an oral medication or tolerate an azole, amphotericin B is the preferred agent. A dosage of 0.4 to 0.5 mg/kg intravenously can be given every day until the symptoms subside, often within 2 weeks, and it is uncommon to administer more than 500 mg. No comparative trials of amphotericin B and azoles have been performed, but clinical experience suggests that resolution of symptoms is faster with the former.

Itraconazole and ketoconazole are lipophilic agents that potently inhibit the cytochrome P-450 system. Hence, there are a number of drug interactions with the antihistamines, terfenadine, and astemizole. Coadministration of azoles with either of these two drugs can lead to serious ventricular arrthymias because elevated levels of the antihistamines increase the QT interval. The azoles also increase the levels of cyclosporine, warfarin, and digoxin. Rhabdomyolysis has developed in patients taking the cholesterol-lowering agent simvastatin or lovastatin with azoles. Rifampin, isoniazid, phenytoin, and carbamazepine can lower concentrations of itraconazole and ketoconazole by increasing metabolism. Optimal itraconazole and ketoconazole absorption is dependent on gastric acidity, and agents that alkalinize the gastric pH may interfere. A suspension of itraconazole has been developed that has improved absorption by 50% and makes administration to young children much easier. It is possible that with the increased absorption, lower dosages may be used, but there is no clinical evidence to support this contention at this time.

Mediastinal Granuloma, Mediastinal Fibrosis, and Histoplasmoma

The confluence of mediastinal lymph nodes often does not cause sufficient symptoms to require therapeutic intervention. If the lymph nodes impinge upon major airways it is reasonable to treat with itraconazole at 200 mg per day for 3 to 6 months. If rapid resolution of symptoms is necessary, amphotericin B is preferable. Treatment with 300 to 500 mg of this antifungal suffices. Rarely, surgical extraction of the nodes is necessary to prevent serious sequelae.

Mediastinal fibrosis is an exceptionally difficult clinical problem for which there is no consensus on optimal management. Surgery, corticosteroids, and antifungal agents have been utilized in the treatment of this condition, and the success rate with a combination of two or more therapies has been minimal. Surgery to remove the fibrosis can alleviate the life-threatening situation, but the fibrosis often recurs. Moreover, the surgery is exceedingly difficult because of the nature of the disease and its location. Addition of azoles after surgery has been proposed, but the utility of this approach is debatable.[106, 159]

Histoplasmomas of the lung do not require any therapy unless they are expanding. Surgical resection is the definitive treatment. Additional azole therapy for 2 to 3 months may be beneficial, although there is little evidence that this step alters outcome. Histoplasmomas of the central nervous system that impinge on critical areas of the parenchyma should be surgically removed. Because itraconazole and ketoconazole do not penetrate the central nervous system well, fluconazole may be useful adjunctive therapy. The clinician must be cautious in using this drug because it has been only moderately effective against various form of histoplasmosis.

Cavitary Pulmonary Histoplasmosis

In most patients with thin-walled cavities, infection resolves spontaneously without therapeutic intervention. Patients can be followed with serial chest roentgenograms every 2 to 3 months. Those who have thick-walled cavities, progressive pulmonary infiltrates, or persistent cavities associated with declining respiratory function should be treated. Itraconazole at 400 mg per day or ketoconazole at 400 mg per day should be given for at least 6 months.[160, 161] This regimen leads to improvement in 75 to 85% of patients. Fluconazole is less effective for this clinical condition. The response rate is approximately 50%, but studies have been completed in only a small number of patients. If there is progression of infection during treatment with azoles or the patient is immunocompromised, amphotericin B is preferable. The total dose is 30 to 35 mg/kg, and amphotericin B can be given every day at 0.4 to 0.5 mg/kg.[162]

The adverse effects of amphotericin B are well known. The major inimical effects are a reversible nephrotoxicity and a decline in the hemoglobin concentration. Administration is often associated with fever and chills, which subside after the first few doses. Caution must be taken if other nephrotoxic agents are used. In addition, the clinician must be extremely cautious if administering other drugs that are cleared by the kidney and have a narrow therapeutic-to-toxic ratio.

The relapse rates for cavitary pulmonary histoplasmosis are as high as 20%. This value is observed most often in patients with thick-walled cavities. Yeasts are difficult to eradicate from these cavities. If there is a failure of antifungal therapy, surgical resection may be necessary, depending on the patient's underlying pulmonary function.

Acute Progressive Disseminated Histoplasmosis

Prompt institution of amphotericin B therapy is necessary for treatment of patients with acute, life-threatening PDH. Patients should receive 25 mg at the initial dose, followed by a rapid escalation to 0.7 to 1 mg/kg daily. Within a week, most patients are symptomatically improved and laboratory abnormalities begin to return to baseline values. When the patient has become afebrile and clinically stable, amphotericin B can be administered every day, but at a lower dose of 0.4 to 0.5 mg/kg. If amphotericin B is utilized throughout the illness, patients should receive a total dose of 30 to 35 mg/kg. Patients who demonstrate resolution of symptoms while receiving amphotericin B may be treated with itraconazole at 400 mg daily for up to 6 months. Ketoconazole should be avoided in immunosuppressed patients because of the high failure rate.[160] In acute PDH that is not associated with hemodynamic instability or severe illness, itraconazole may be administered. Therapy should begin with 300 mg twice a day for 3 days followed by 200 mg twice a day for at least 6 months.

For patients with AIDS, lifelong suppressive therapy with itraconazole is recommended.[163, 164] A dose of 200 mg per day should be given. It is not yet known whether potent antiretroviral therapy and consequent improvement in the number of $CD4^+$ cells will permit discontinuation of suppressive therapy. Other groups of patients who may benefit from long-term suppressive therapy are those who remain on immunosuppressive therapy indefinitely. Thus, after the acute infection, transplant recipients and patient's with chronic autoimmune diseases who are receiving potent immunosuppressives may be considered for indefinite suppressive therapy with itraconazole. If the patient has a relapse while receiving an azole, amphotericin B should be given.[165] After treatment of the relapse, the patient should receive 0.7 to 1 mg/kg once or twice a week.

One of the unresolved issues in the treatment of histoplasmosis, especially PDH, is the niche for the lipid-based preparations of amphotericin B. Three preparations are now approved by the Food and Drug Administration. They are modestly less nephrotoxic than amphotericin B deoxycholate but far more expensive. There is little clinical experience with them in the treatment of histoplasmosis, although they should be equally efficacious. Optimal dosing for histoplasmosis has not been established. Nevertheless, if renal dysfunction is a major concern, these agents should be considered in the initial management of the infection.

Subacute and Chronic Progressive Disseminated Histoplasmosis

Because many of these cases develop in patients whose immune system is intact, itraconazole, 400 mg daily, is highly efficacious. The success rate in these individuals approaches 90%. Ketoconazole has a similar success rate, but more side effects may be anticipated with this drug. If the patient fails to improve with azole therapy, is immunosuppressed, or demonstrates intolerance to azoles, amphotericin B, 0.4 to 0.5 mg/kg daily, should be given. The total amount that should be prescribed is 30 to 35 mg/kg. Selected patients whose infection is controlled by this drug may be switched to an azole for the completion of therapy.

Meningitis

Patients with meningitis should be given amphotericin B, 0.7 to 1 mg/kg. Total dosage is 30 to 35 mg/kg. Lumbar punctures should be performed approximately every week for the first 6 weeks and every 2 weeks thereafter to assess therapy. Although a high percentage of patients may respond initially to therapy, relapses occur frequently. Overall cure rates are no better than 50%, and immunocompetent patients respond much better to treatment than do immunosuppressed individuals. Itraconazole and ketoconazole do not penetrate the blood-brain barrier well and therefore should not be used. Fluconazole does cross this barrier, but this azole has not been as efficacious as itraconazole and whether fluconazole is useful for this particular condition is unresolved.

Endocarditis

As with bacterial causes of endocarditis, a microbicidal agent should be used. Therefore, amphotericin B, 0.7 to 1 mg/kg should be given. However, administration of an antifungal agent alone is not sufficient; it must be used in combination with surgical removal of the affected valve(s). One issue is how long to treat after the valve has been removed. If there are other foci of active histoplasmosis, the dosage should be 30 to 35 mg/kg. However, if the valve was the only site involved, treatment with amphotericin B for 2 weeks after surgical extraction may be sufficient. If the patient cannot undergo surgery, amphotericin B in the highest tolerated dose should be used on a daily basis.[166] The lipid-based formulations may be superior for this rare circumstance.

Pericarditis

Pericarditis after acute pulmonary histoplasmosis does not require antifungal therapy. Most patients can be treated symptomatically with nonsteroidal anti-inflammatory agents and bed rest.[95] If patients do not respond to these agents, corticosteroids are indicated. One must be cautious because if there are active lesions of histoplasmosis, the infection may become more aggressive. Cardiac tamponade associated with *H. capsulatum* pericarditis is uncommon, but when it occurs it must be treated as a medical emergency with pericardiocentensis. Despite the severity of illness, antifungal therapy is not indicated. Unlike tuberculous pericarditis, constrictive pericarditis rarely develops, but patients should be monitored for several years after the acute attack. In the uncommon situation in which the pericardium is infected as a manifestation of PDH, antifungal therapy with either amphotericin B or azoles is indicated, depending on the severity of illness.

Presumed Ocular Histoplasmosis

This condition does not require antifungal therapy. Laser therapy is used to prevent additional neovascularization within the choroid, but lesions that abut the fovea cannot be subjected to this treatment.[167] The role of local injection of corticosteroids is unclear.

Prevention and Vaccination

Educational efforts must be ongoing to alert those who work in areas in which a substantial risk of infection exists. For example, construction workers who are rehabilitating buildings that have served as homes for starlings and bats must be warned about the possibility of exposure and steps taken to remove the guano safely. Spraying 3% formalin on guano deposits kills the fungus within several days, and the material can then be removed.[168] However formaldehyde decontamination is rarely employed because the vapor is toxic, it can seep into ground water and thus poses an environmental hazard, and it does not penetrate dried guano uniformly.

There is a resurgent effort to develop preventive or therapeutic vaccines against pathogenic fungi because of their increasing incidence. Among those for which animal studies have defined a vaccine is *H. capsulatum*. Heat shock protein 60 from the fungus has been demonstrated to confer protection in three mouse strains.[169, 170] Furthermore, the domain of this protein that spans amino acids 174 to 445 appears to contain the protective activity of the entire protein.[171] Ongoing studies are examining the potential of this protein fragment to confer protection in humans.

REFERENCES

1. Darling ST. A protozoal general infection producing pseudotubercules in the lungs and focal necrosis in the liver, spleen, and lymph nodes. JAMA. 1906;46:1283–1285.
2. da Rocha-Lima H. Histoplasmose und epizootische Lymphangitis. Arch Schiffs Trop Hyg. 1912;16:79.
3. DeMonbreun WA. The cultivation and cultural characterisitics of Darling's *Histoplasma capsulatum*. Am J Trop Med Hyg. 1934;14:93–125.
4. Christie A. Peterson JC. Pulmonary calcification in negative reactors to tuberculin. Am J Public Health. 1945;35:1131–1147.
5. Christie A. Histoplasmosis and pulmonary calcification. Ann N Y Acad Sci. 1950;50:1283–1298.
6. Furcolow ML, Schubert J, Tosh FE, et al. Serologic evidence of histoplasmosis in sanitariums in the U.S. JAMA. 1962;180:109–114.
7. Palmer CE. Nontuberculous pulmonary calcification and sensitivity to histoplasmin. Public Health Rep. 1945;60:513–520.
8. Furculow ML, High RH, Allen MF. Some epidemiological aspects of sensitivity to histoplasmin and tuberculin. Public Health Rep. 1946;61:1132–1144.
9. Ajello L. Distribution of *Histoplasma capsulatum* in the United States. In: Ajello L, Chick W, Furculow MF, eds. Histoplasmosis. Springfield, Ill: Charles C Thomas; 1971:103–122.
10. Furculow ML. Recent studies on the epidemiology of histoplasmosis. Ann N Y Acad Sci. 1958;72:127–164.
11. Brandesberg JW. Fungi found in association with *Histoplasma capsulatum* in a naturally contaminated site in Clarksburg, Maryland. Sabouraudia. 1968;6:246–254.
12. Rippon JW. Histoplasmosis. In: Medical Mycology: The Pathogenic Fungi and the Pathogenic Actinomycetes. 2nd ed. Philadelphia: WB Saunders; 1982:342.
13. Zeidberg LD, Ajello L, Webster RH. Physical and chemical factors in relation to *Histoplasma capsulatum* in soil. Science. 1955;122:33–34.
14. Weeks RJ, Tosh FE, Chin TDY. Estimation of the number of viable particles of *Histoplasma capsulatum* in soil. Mycopathologia. 1968;35:233–238.
15. Emmons CW. Isolation of *Histoplasma capsulatum* from soil. Public Health Rep. 1949;64:892–896.
16. Zeidberg LD, Ajello L, Dillon A, Runyon EC. Isolation of *Histoplasma capsulatum* from soil. Am J Public Health. 1952;42:930–935.
17. DiSalvo AF, Ajello L, Palmer JW, Winkler WG. Isolation of *Histoplasma capsulatum* from Arizona bats. Am J Epidemiol. 1969;89:606–614.
18. Schwarz J. Immunity. In: Histoplasmosis. New York: Praeger; 1981:147.
19. Wu-Hsieh B. Relative susceptibilities of inbred mouse strains C57BL/6 and A/J to infection with *Histoplasma capsulatum*. Infect Immun. 1989;57:3788–3792.
20. Deepe GS. *Histoplasma capsulatum* and $V\beta^a$ mice: Cellular immune responses and susceptibility patterns. J Med Vet Mycol. 1993;31:181–188.
21. Patton RM. Riggs AR, Compton SB. Chick EW. Histoplasmosis in purebred mice: Influence of genetic susceptibility and immune depression on treatment. Mycopathologia. 1976;60:39–43.
22. Steele PE, Carle GF, Kobayashi GS, Medoff G. Electrophoretic analysis of *Histoplasma capsulatum* chromosomal DNA. Mol Cell Biol. 1989;9:983–987.
23. Vincent RD, Goewert R, Goldman WE, et al. Classification of *Histoplasma capsulatum* isolates by restriction fragment polymorphisms. J Bacteriol. 1986;165:813–818.
24. Spitzer ED, Lasker BA, Travis SJ, et al. Use of mitochondrial and ribosomal DNA polymorphisms to classify clinical and soil isolates of *Histoplasma capsulatum*. Infect Immun. 1989;57:1409–1412.
25. Keath EJ, Kobayashi GS, Medoff G. Classification of *Histoplasma capsulatum* by restriction fragment length polymorphisms in a nuclear gene. J Clin Microbiol. 1992;30:2104–2107.
26. Kersulyte D, Woods JP, Keath EJ, et al. Diversity among clinical isolates of *Histoplasma capsulatum* detected by polymerase chain reaction with arbitrary primers. J Bacteriol. 1992;174:7075–7079.
27. Spitzer ED, Keath EJ, Travis SJ, et al. Temperature-sensitive variants of *Histoplasma capsulatum* isolated from patients with acquired immunodeficiency syndrome. J Infect Dis. 1990;162:258–261.
28. Carter DA, Burt A, Taylor JW, et al. Clinical isolates of *Histoplasma capsulatum* from Indianapolis, Indiana, have a recombining population structure. J Clin Microbiol. 1996;34:2577–2584.
29. Kwon-Chung KJ. Sexual stage of *Histoplasma capsulatum*. Science. 1971;175:326.
30. Kwon-Chung KA, Weeks RJ, Larsh HW. Studies on *Emmonsiella capsulata (Histoplasma capsulatum)*. II. Distribution of the two mating types in 13 endemic states of the United States. Am J Epidemiol. 1974;99:44–49.
31. Kwon-Chung KJ, Bartlett MS, Wheat LJ. Distribution of the two mating types among *Histoplasma capsulatum* isolates obtained from an urban histoplasmosis outbreak. Sabouraudia. 1984;22:155–157.
32. Batanghari JW, Goldman WE. Calcium dependence and binding in cultures of *Histoplasma capsulatum*. Infect Immun. 1997;65:5257–5261.
33. Batanghari JW, Deepe GS Jr, Di Cera E, Goldman WE. *Histoplasma* acquisition of calcium and expression of *CBP1* during intracellular parasitism. Mol Microbiol. 1998;27:531–539.
34. Maresca B. Kobayashi GS. Dimorphism in *Histoplasma capsulatum*: A model for the study of cell differentiation in pathogenic fungi. Microbiol Rev. 1989;53:186–209.
35. Keath EJ, Painter AA, Kobayashi GS, Medoff G. Variable expression of a yeast-phase-specific gene in *Histoplasma capsulatum* strains differing in thermotolerance and virulence. Infect Immun. 1989;57:1384–1390.
36. Di Lallo G, Gargano S, Maresca B. The *Histoplasma capsulatum cdc2* gene is transcriptionally regulated during the morphologic transition. Gene. 1994;140:51–57.
37. Keath EJ, Abidi FE. Molecular cloning and sequence analysis of *yps-3*, a yeast-phase-specific gene in the dimorphic fungal pathogen *Histoplasma capsulatum*. Microbiology. 1994;140:759–767.
38. Shearer G Jr, Birge CH, Yuckenberg PD, et al. Heat-shock proteins induced during the mycelial-yeast transition of strains of *Histoplasma capsulatum*. J Gen Microbiol. 1987;133:3375–3382.
39. Schwarz J. Giant forms of *Histoplasma capsulatum* in tissue explants. Am J Clin Pathol. 1953;23:898–903.
40. Eissenberg LG, Poirier S, Goldman WE. Phenotypic variation and persistence of *Histoplasma capsulatum* yeasts in host cells. Infect Immun. 1996;64:5310–5314.
41. Medoff G, Kobayashi GS, Painter A, et al. Morphogenesis and pathogenicity of *Histoplasma capsulatum*. Infect Immun. 1987;55:1355–1358.
42. Medoff G, Sacco M, Maresca B, et al. Irreversible block of the mycelial to yeast phase transition of *Histoplasma capsulatum*. Science. 1986;23:476–479.
43. Bullock WE, Wright SD. The role of adherence-promoting receptors, CR3, LFA-1, and p150,95 in binding of *Histoplasma capsulatum* by human macrophages. J Exp Med. 1986;165:195–210.
44. Newman SL, Bucher C, Rhodes J, Bullock WE. Phagocytosis of *Histoplasma capsulatum* yeasts and microconidia by human cultured macrophages and alveolar macrophages. Cellular cytoskeleton requirement for attachment and ingestion. J Clin Invest. 1990;85:223–230.
45. Schnur RA, Newman SL. The respiratory burst response to *Histoplasma capsulatum* by human neutrophils. Evidence for intracellular trapping. J Immunol. 1990;144:4765–4772.
46. Kimberlin CL, Hariri AR, Hempel HO, Goodman NL. Interactions between *Histoplasma capsulatum* and macrophages from normal and treated mice: Comparison

of the mycelial and yeast phases in alveolar and peritoneal macrophages. Infect Immun. 1981;34:6–10.

47. Procknow JJ, Page MI, Loosli CG. Early pathogenesis of experimental histoplasmosis. Arch Pathol. 1960;69:413–426.
48. Schlitzer RL, Chandler FW, Larsh HW. Primary acute histoplasmosis in guinea pigs exposed to aerosolized *Histoplasma capsulatum*. Infect Immun. 1981;33:575–582.
49. Baughman RP, Kim CK, Vinegar A, et al. The pathogenesis of experimental pulmonary histoplasmosis. Correlative studies of histopathology, bronchoalveolar lavage, and respiratory function. Am Rev Respir Dis. 1986;134:771–776.
50. Newman SL, Gootee L, Gabay J. Human neutrophil-mediated fungistasis against *Histoplasma capsulatum*. Localization of fungistatic activity to the azurophil granules. J Clin Invest. 1993;92:624–631.
51. Couto MA, Liu L, Lehrer RI, Ganz T. Inhibition of intracellular *Histoplasma capsulatum* replication by murine macrophages that produce human defensin. Infect Immun. 1994;62:2375–2378.
52. Zhou P, Miller G, Seder RA. Factors involved in regulating primary and secondary immunity to infection with *Histoplasma capsulatum*: TNF-α plays a critical role in maintaining immunity in the absence of IFN-γ. J Immunol. 1998;160:1359–1368.
53. Eissenberg LG, Schlesinger PH, Goldman WE. Phagosome-lysosome fusion in P388D1 macrophages infected with *Histoplasma capsulatum*. J Leukoc Biol. 1988;43:483–491.
54. Eissenberg LG, Goldman WE, Schlesinger PH. *Histoplasma capsulatum* modulates the acidification of phagolysosomes. J Exp Med. 1993;177:1605–1611.
55. Newman SL, Gootee L, Morris R. Bullock WE. Digestion of *Histoplasma capsulatum* yeasts by human macrophages. J Immunol. 1992;149:574–580.
56. Newman SL, Gootee L, Brunner G, Deepe GS Jr. Chloroquine induces human macrophage killing of *Histoplasma capsulatum* by limiting the availability of intracellular iron and is therapeutic in a murine model of histoplasmosis. J Clin Invest. 1994;93:1422–1429.
57. Lane TE, Wu-Hsieh BA, Howard DH. Iron limitation and the gamma interferon-mediated antihistoplasma state of murine macrophages. Infect Immun. 1991;59:2274–2278.
58. Lane TE, Otero GC, Wu-Hsieh BA, Howard DH. Expression of inducible nitric oxide synthase by stimulated macrophages correlates with their antihistoplasma activity. Infect Immun. 1994;62:1478–1479.
59. Lane TE, Wu-Hsieh BA, Howard DH. Antihistoplasma effect of activated mouse splenic macrophages involves production of reactive nitrogen intermediates. Infect Immun. 1994;62:1940–1945.
60. Wolf JE, Kerchberger V, Kobayashi GS, Little JR. Modulation of the macrophage oxidative burst by *Histoplasma capsulatum*. J Immunol. 1987;138:582–586.
61. Eissenberg LG, Goldman WE. *Histoplasma capsulatum* fails to trigger release of superoxide from macrophages. Infect Immun. 1987;55:29–34.
62. Newman SL, Gootee L, Kidd C, et al. Activation of human macrophage fungistatic activity against *Histoplasma capsulatum* upon adherence to type 1 collagen matrices. J Immunol. 1997;158:1779–1786.
63. Chaturverdi S, Frame P, Newman SL. Macrophages from human immunodeficiency virus–positive persons are defective in host defense against *Histoplasma capsulatum*. J Infect Dis. 1995;171:320–327.
64. Chaturverdi S, Newman SL. Modulation of the effector function of human macrophages for *Histoplasma capsulatum* by HIV-1. Role of the envelope glycoprotein 120. J Clin Invest. 1997;100:1465–1474.
65. Gomez AM, Bullock WE, Taylor CL, Deepe GS Jr. Role of L3T4$^+$ T cells in host defense against *Histoplasma capsulatum*. Infect Immun. 1988;56:1685–1691.
66. Deepe GS Jr. Protective immunity in murine histoplasmosis: Functional comparison of adoptively transferred T-cell clones and splenic T cells. Infect Immun. 1988;56:2350–2355.
67. Wheat LJ, Connolly-Stringfield PA, Baker RL, et al. Disseminated histoplasmosis in the acquired immune deficiency syndrome: Clinical findings, diagnosis and treatment, and review of the literature. Medicine (Baltimore). 1990;69:361–374.
68. Deepe GS Jr. Role of CD8$^+$ T cells in host resistance to systemic infection with *Histoplasma capsulatum* in mice. J Immunol. 1994;152:3491–3500.
69. Patino MM, Williams DM, Ahrens J, Graybill JR. Experimental histoplasmosis in the beige mouse. J Leukoc Biol. 1987;41:228–235.
70. Allendoerfer R, Deepe GS Jr. Intrapulmonary response to *Histoplasma capsulatum* in gamma interferon knockout mice. Infect Immun. 1996;65:2564–2569.
71. Zhou P, Sieve MC, Bennett J, et al. IL-12 prevents mortality in mice infected with *Histoplasma capsulatum* through induction of IEN-γ. J Immunol. 1995;155:785–795.
72. Allendoerfer R, Boivin GP, Deepe GS Jr. Modulation of immune responses in murine pulmonary histoplasmosis. J Infect Dis. 1997;175:905–914.
73. Smith JG, Magee DM, Williams DM, Graybill JR. Tumor necrosis factor-α plays a role in host defense against *Histoplasma capsulatum*. J Infect Dis. 1990;162:1349–1353.
74. Wu-Hsieh BA, Lee GS, Franco M, Hofman FM. Early activation of splenic macrophages by tumor necrosis factor alpha is important in determining the outcome of experimental histoplasmosis in mice. Infect Immun. 1992;60:4230–4238.
75. Allendoerfer R, Deepe GS Jr. Blockade of endogenous TNF-α exacerbates primary and secondary pulmonary histoplasmosis by differential mechanisms. J Immunol. 1998;160:6072–6082.
76. Lane TE, Wu-Hsieh BA, Howard DH. Gamma interferon cooperates with lipopolysaccharide to activate mouse splenic macrophages to an antihistoplasma state. Infect Immun. 1993;61:1468–1473.
77. Fleischman J, Wu-Hsieh B, Howard DH. The intracellular fate of *Histoplasma capsulatum* in human macrophages is unaffected by recombinant human interferon-γ. J Infect Dis. 1990;161:143–145.
78. Newman SL, Gootee L. Colony-stimulating factors activate human macrophages to inhibit intracellular growth of *Histoplasma capsulatum* yeasts. Infect Immun. 1992;60:4593–4597.
79. Vaněk J, Schwarz J. The gamut of histoplasmosis. Am J Med. 1971;50:89–104.
80. Goodwin RA Jr, Shapiro JL, Thurman GH, et al. Disseminated histoplasmosis: Clinical and pathologic correlations. Medicine (Baltimore). 1980;59:1–31.
81. Artz RP, Bullock WE. Immunoregulatory responses in experimental disseminated histoplasmosis: Depression of T-cell–dependent and T-effector responses by activation of splenic suppressor cells. Infect Immun. 1979;23:893–902.
82. Loosli CG, Grayston JT, Alexander ER, Tanzi F. Epidemiological studies of pulmonary histoplasmosis in a farm family. Am J Hyg. 1952;55:392–401.
83. Murry JE, Lurie HI, Kaye J, et al. Benign pulmonary histoplasmosis (cave disease) in South Africa. S Afr Med J. 1957;31:245–253.
84. Goodwin RA Jr, Loyd JE, Des Prez RM. Histoplasmosis in normal hosts. Medicine (Baltimore). 1981;60:231–266.
85. Goodwin RA Jr, Des Prez RM. Histoplasmosis. Am Rev Respir Dis. 1978;117:929–956.
86. Storch G, Burford JG, George RB, et al. Acute histoplasmosis: Description of an outbreak in northern Louisiana. Chest. 1980;77:38–42.
87. Wergin WP. Outbreak of histoplasmosis associated with the 1970 Earth Day activities. Am J Med. 1973;54:333–342.
88. Goodwin RA Jr, Des Prez RM. Pathogenesis and clinical spectrum of hisplasmosis. South Med J. 1973;66:13–25.
89. Rosenthal J, Brandt KD, Wheat LJ, et al. Rheumatologic manifestations of histoplasmosis in the recent Indianapolis epidemic. Arthritis Rheum. 1983;26:1065–1070.
90. Wheat J. Histoplasmosis. Experience during outbreaks in Indianapolis and review of the literature. Medicine (Baltimore). 1997;76:339–353.
91. Ploy-song-sang YY, Loudon RG, Beach BC, Corbin RP. Pulmonary function studies in acute pulmonary histoplasmosis. South Med J. 1979;72:568–572.
92. Kritski AL, Lemle A, de Souza GRM, et al. Pulmonary function changes in acute stage of histoplasmosis, with follow-up. Chest. 1990;97:1244–1245.
93. Kaplan MM, Sherwood LM. Acute pericarditis due to *Histoplasma capsulatum*. Ann Intern Med. 1963;58:862–867.
94. Picardi JL, Kauffman CA, Schwartz J, et al. Pericarditis caused by *Histoplasma capsulatum*. Am J Cardiol. 1976;37:82–88.
95. Wheat LJ, Stein L, Corya BC, et al. Pericarditis as a manifestation of histoplasmosis during two large urban outbreaks. Medicine (Baltimore). 1983;62:110–119.
96. Wheat LJ, Slama TG, Eitzen HE, et al. A large urban outbreak of histoplasmosis: Clinical features. Ann Intern Med. 1981;94:331–337.
97. Ryder KW, Jay SJ, Kiblawi SO, Hull MT. Serum angiotensin converting enzyme in patients with histoplasmosis. JAMA. 1983;249:1888–1889.
98. Davies SF, Rohrbach MS, Thelen V, et al. Elevated serum angiotensin-converting enzyme (SACE) activity in acute pulmonary histoplasmosis. Chest. 1984;85:307–310.
99. Powell KE, Hammerman KJ, Dahi BA, Tosh FE. Acute reinfection pulmonary histoplasmosis. A report of six cases. Am Rev Respir Dis. 1973;107:374–378.
100. Puckett TF. Pulmonary histoplasmosis. Am Rev Tuberc. 1953;67:453–476.
101. Baum GL, Green RA, Schwarz J. Enlarging pulmonary histoplasmoma. Am Rev Respir Dis. 1960;82:721–726.
102. Goodwin RA, Snell JD. The enlarging histoplasmoma. Concept of a tumor-like phenomenon encompassing the tuberculoma and coccidioidoma. Am Rev Respir Dis. 1969;100:1–12.
103. Schowengerdt CG, Suyemoto R, Main FB. Granulomatous and fibrous mediastinitis: A review and analysis of 180 cases. J Thorac Cardiovasc Surg. 1969;57:365–379.
104. Garamella JJ, Stutzman FL, Varco RL, Jensen NK. Subcarinal mediastinal granulomas causing esophageal obstruction. J Thorac Surg. 1955;30:187–192.
105. Schwarz J, Schaen MD, Picardi JL. Complications of the arrested primary histoplasmic focus. JAMA. 1976;236:1157–1161.
106. Loyd JE, Tillman BF, Atkinson JB, Des Prez RM. Mediastinal fibrosis complicating histoplasmosis. Medicine (Baltimore). 1988;67:295–310.
107. Mathisen DJ, Grillo H. Clinical manifestations of mediastinal fibrosis and histoplasmosis. Ann Thorac Surg. 1992;54:1053–1058.
108. Peabody JW, Brown RB, Davis EW, et al. Surgical implications of mediastinal granulomas. Ann Surg. 1959;25:357–368.
109. Pate J, Hammon J. Superior vena cava syndrome due to histoplasmosis in children. Ann Surg. 1965;161:778–787.
110. Wheat LJ, Wass J, Norton J, et al. Cavitary histoplasmosis occurring during two large urban outbreaks: Analysis of clinical, epidemiologic, roentgenographic, and laboratory features. Medicine (Baltimore). 1984;63:201–209.
111. Goodwin RA, Owens FT, Snell JD, et al. Chronic pulmonary histoplasmosis. Medicine (Baltimore). 1976;55:413–452.
112. Wheat LJ, Slama TG, Norton JA, et al. Risk factors for disseminated or fatal histoplasmosis. Ann Intern Med. 1982;96:159–163.
113. Sarosi GA, Johnson PC. Disseminated histoplasmosis in patients infected with human immunodeficiency virus. Clin Infect Dis. 1992;14(Suppl):S60–S67.
114. Johnson PC, Khardori N, Najjar AF, et al. Progressive disseminated histoplasmosis in patients with acquired immunodeficiency syndrome. Am J Med. 1988;85:152–158.
115. Peddi VR, Hariharan S, First MR. Disseminated histoplasmosis in renal allograft recipients. Clin Transplant. 1996;10:160–165.

116. Wheat LJ, Smith EJ, Sathapatayavongs B, et al. Histoplasmosis in renal allograft recipients: Two large urban outbreaks. Arch Intern Med. 1983;143:703–707.
117. Kauffman CA, Israel KS, Smith JW, et al. Histoplasmosis in immunosuppressed patients. Am J Med. 1978;64:923–932.
118. Dismukes WE, Royal SA, Tynes BS. Disseminated histoplasmosis in corticosteroid-treated patients. Report of five cases. JAMA. 1978;240:1495–1498.
119. Nightingale SD, Parks JM, Pounders SM, et al. Disseminated histoplasmosis in patients with AIDS. South Med J. 1990;83:624–630.
120. McKinsey DS, Spiegel RA, Hutwagner L, et al. Prospective study of histoplasmosis in patients infected with human immunodeficiency virus: Incidence, risk factors, and pathophysiology. Clin Infect Dis. 1997;24:1195–1203.
121. Eidbo J, Sanchez RL, Tschen JA, Ellner KM. Cutaneous manifestations of histoplasmosis in the acquired immune deficiency syndrome. Am J Surg Pathol. 1993;17:110–116.
122. Krunic A, Calonje E, Jeftovic D, et al. Primary localized cutaneous histoplasmosis in a patient with acquired immunodeficiency syndrome. Int J Dermatol. 1995;34:558–562.
123. Wheat LJ, Batteiger BE, Sathapatayavongs B. *Histoplasma capsulatum* infections of the central nervous system: A clinical review. Medicine (Baltimore). 1990;69:244–260.
124. Conces DJ, Stockberger SM, Tarver RD, Wheat LJ. Disseminated histoplasmosis in AIDS: Findings on chest radiographs. AJR. 1993;160:15–19.
125. Koduri PR, Chundi V, DeMarais P, et al. Reactive hemophagocytic syndrome: A new presentation of disseminated histoplasmosis in patients with AIDS. Clin Infect Dis. 1995;21:1463–1465.
126. Sturim HS, Kouchoukos NT, Ahluvin RC. Gastrointestinal manifestations of disseminated histoplasmosis. Am J Surg. 1965;110:435–440.
127. Blair TP, Waugh RA, Pollack M, et al. *Histoplasma capsulatum* endocarditis. Am Heart J. 1980;99:783–788.
128. Svirbely JR, Ayers LW, Bueschlng WJ. Filamentous *Histoplasma capsulatum* endocarditis involving mitral and aortic valve porcine bioprostheses. Arch Pathol Lab Med. 1985;109:273–276.
129. Alexander WJ, Mowry RW, Gobbs CG, Dismukes WE. Prosthetic valve endocarditis caused by *Histoplasma capsulatum*. JAMA. 1979;242:1399–1400.
130. Miller BM, Waterhouse G, Alford RH, et al. *Histoplasma* infection of abdominal aortic aneurysms. Ann Surg. 1983;197:57–62.
131. Karalakulasingam R, Arora KK, Adams G, et al. Meningoencephalitis caused by *Histoplasma capsulatum*. Arch Intern Med. 1976;136:217–220.
132. Sarosi GA, Voth DW, Dahl BA, et al. Disseminated histoplasmosis: Results of long-term follow-up. A center for disease control cooperative mycoses study. Ann Intern Med. 1971;75:511–516.
133. Wilson DA, Muchmore HG, Tisdal RG, et al. Histoplasmosis of the adrenal glands studied by CT. Radiology. 1984;150:779–783.
134. Schlaegel TF. Ocular Histoplasmosis. New York: Grune & Stratton; 1977.
135. Friedlander M, Theesfeld CL, Sugita M, et al. Involvement of integrins $\alpha_v\beta_3$ and $\alpha_v\beta_5$ in ocular neovascular disease. Proc Natl Acad Sci U S A. 1996;93:9764–9769.
136. Anderson A, Clifford W, Palvolgyi I, et al. Immunopathology of chronic experimental histoplasmic choroiditis in the primate. Invest Opthalmol Vis Sci. 1992;33:1637–1641.
137. Palvolgyi I, Anderson A, Rife L, et al. Immunopathology of reactivation of experimental ocular histoplasmosis. Exp Eye Res. 1993;57:169–175.
138. Cockshott WP, Lucas AO. *Histoplasma duboisii*. Q J Med. 1964;33:223–238.
139. Chandenier J, Goma D, Moyen G, et al. Histoplasmose africaine a *Histoplasma capsulatum* var. *duboisii*: Liens avec le SIDA à propos de cas congolais récents. Sante. 1995;5:227–234.
140. Wheat LJ. Histoplasmosis. Infect Dis Clin North Am. 1988;2:841–859.
141. Baughman RP, Dohn MN, Loudon RG, Frame PT. Bronchoscopy with bronchoalveolar lavage in tuberculosis and fungal infections. Chest. 1991;99:92–97.
142. Bille J, Stockman L, Roberts GD, et al. Evaluation of a lysis-centrifugation system for recovery of yeasts and filamentous fungi from blood. J Clin Microbiol. 1983;18:469–471.
143. Wheat LJ, Kobler RB, Tewari RP. Diagnosis of disseminated histoplasmosis by detection of *Histoplasma capsulatum* antigen in serum and urine specimens. N Engl J Med. 1986;314:83–88.
144. Wheat LJ, Connolly-Stringfield P, Kohler RB, et al. *Histoplasma capsulatum* polysaccharide antigen detection in diagnosis and management of disseminated histoplasmosis in patients with acquired immunodeficiency syndrome. Am J Med. 1989;87:396–400.
145. Wheat LJ, Connolly-Stringfield P, Blair R, et al. Histoplasmosis relapse in patients with AIDS: Detection using *Histoplasma capsulatum* variety *capsulatum* antigen levels. Ann Intern Med. 1991;115:936–941.
146. Wheat LJ, Kohler RB, Tewari RP, et al. Significance of *Histoplasma* antigen in the cerebrospinal fluid of patients with meningitis. Arch Intern Med. 1989;149:302–304.
147. Wheat LJ, Wheat H, Connolly P, et al. Cross-reactivity in *Histoplasma capsulatum* variety *capsulatum* antigen assays of urine samples from patients with endemic mycoses. Clin Infect Dis. 1997;24:1169–1171.
148. Collins MH, Jiang B, Croffie JM, et al. Hepatic granulomas in children. A clinicopathologic analysis of 23 cases including polymerase chain reaction for *Histoplasma*. Am J Surg Pathol. 1996;20:332–338.
149. Davies SF. Serodiagnosis of histoplasmosis. Semin Respir Infect. 1986;1:9–15.
150. Terry PB, Rosenow EC, Roberts GD. False-positive complement fixation serology in histoplasmosis. A retrospective study. JAMA. 1978;239:2453–2456.
151. Heiner DC. Diagnosis of histoplasmosis using precipitin reactions in agar gel. Pediatrics. 1958;22:616–627.
152. Deepe GS Jr, Durose GG. Immunobiological activity of recombinant H antigen from *Histoplasma capsulatum*. Infect Immun. 1995;63:3151–3157.
153. Zancope-Oliveira RM, Mayer LW, Reiss E, Lott TJ. Isolation and characterization of the M antigen of *Histoplasma capsulatum*. Abstract F-35. Presented at the Ninety-seventh Meeting of the American Society for Microbiology, Miami, Fla, May 1997.
154. Klatt EC, Cosgrove M, Meyer PR. Rapid diagnosis of disseminated histoplasmosis in tissues. Arch Pathol Lab Med. 1986;110:1173–1175.
155. Corcoran GR, Al-Abdely H, Glanders CD. Markedly elevated serum lactate dehydrogenase levels are a clue to the diagnosis of disseminated histoplasmosis in patients with AIDS. Clin Infect Dis. 1997;24:942–944.
156. Kim DH, Fredericks D, McCutchan JA, et al. Serum ferritin levels correlate with disease activity in patients with AIDS and disseminated histoplasmosis. Clin Infect Dis. 1995;21:1048–1049.
157. Wheat LJ. Histoplasmosis: recognition and treatment. Clin Infect Dis. 1994;19(Suppl 1):S19–S27.
158. McKinsey DS, Kaufmann CA, Pappas PG, et al. Fluconazole therapy for histoplasmosis. Clin Infect Dis. 1996;23:996–1001.
159. Dines DE, Payne WS, Bernatz PE. Mediastinal granuloma and fibrosing mediastinitis. Chest. 1979;75:320–324.
160. National Institute of Allergy and Infectious Diseases Mycoses Study Group. Treatment of blastomycosis and histoplasmosis with ketoconazole: Results of a prospective randomized clinical trial. Ann Intern Med. 1985;103:861–872.
161. Dismukes WE, Bradsher RW Jr, Cloud GC, et al. Itraconazole therapy for blastomycosis and histoplasmosis: NIAID Mycoses Study Group. Am J Med. 1992;93:489–497.
162. Sutliff WD, Andrews CE, Jones E, et al. Histoplasmosis cooperative study. Am Rev Respir Dis. 1964;89:641–650.
163. Wheat J, Hafner R, Wulfsohn M, et al. Prevention of relapse of histoplasmosis with itraconazole in patients with the acquired immunodeficiency syndrome. Ann Intern Med. 1993;118:610–616.
164. Hecht FM, Wheat J, Korzun AH, et al. Itraconazole maintenance treatment for histoplasmosis in AIDS: A prospective, multicenter trial. J Acquir Immune Defic Syndr. 1997;16:100–107.
165. McKinsey DS, Gupta MR, Riddler SA, et al. Long-term amphotericin B therapy for disseminated histoplasmosis in patients with the acquired immunodeficiency syndrome (AIDS). Ann Intern Med. 1989;111:655–659.
166. Kanawaty DS, Stalker MJ, Munt PW. Nonsurgical treatment of *Histoplasma* endocarditis involving a bioprosthetic valve. Chest. 1991;99:253–256.
167. Macular Photocoagulation Study Group. Krypton laser photocoagulation for neovascular lesions of ocular histoplasmosis. Results of a randomized clinical trial. Arch Ophthalmol. 1987;105:1499–1507.
168. US Department of Health, Education and Welfare. Histoplasmosis Control: Decontamination of Bird Roosts, Chicken Houses and Other Sources. Bulletin HEW (CDC 80-8380). Atlanta: US Department of Health, 1979.
169. Gomez FJ, Gomez AM, Deepe GS Jr. Protective efficacy of a 62-kilodalton antigen, HIS-62, from the cell wall and cell membrane of *Histoplasma capsulatum* yeast cells. Infect Immun. 1991;59:4459–4464.
170. Gomez FJ, Allendoerfer R, Deepe GS Jr. Vaccination with recombinant heat shock protein 60 from *Histoplasma capsulatum* protects mice against pulmonary histoplasmosis. Infect Immun. 1995;63:2587–2595.
171. Deepe GS Jr, Gibbons R, Brunner GD, Gomez FJ. A protective domain of heat shock protein 60 from *Histoplasma capsulatum*. J Infect Dis. 1996;174:828–834.

Chapter 255

Blastomyces dermatitidis

STANLEY W. CHAPMAN

Blastomyces dermatitidis is the dimorphic fungus that causes the systemic pyogranulomatous disease blastomycosis. Initial infection is through the lungs and is often subclinical. Hematogenous dissemination may occur, culminating in a disease with protean manifestations. Clinical disease most often involves the lungs, skin, bones, and genitourinary system.

HISTORY

The first report of blastomycosis was in 1894 by Gilchrist,[1] who initially postulated that the disease was caused by a protozoan. In collaboration with Stokes, Gilchrist was subsequently able to isolate the organism, to establish that the disease was caused by a fungus, and, finally, to infect a dog with the newly isolated fungus.[2–4] Although blastomycosis was originally believed to involve only the skin, a number of cases of systemic disease were soon reported. Analysis of these early cases[5, 6] led to the concept that two forms of the disease existed, namely, cutaneous and systemic, and that they represented different portals of entry, skin and lung, respectively. This erroneous concept was not corrected until the work of Schwartz and Baum.[7] Through careful clinical and pathologic studies, they established that the lung was the primary route of infection and that skin disease or other organ involvement was secondary to dissemination.

THE ORGANISM

B. dermatitidis is the imperfect (asexual) stage of *Ajellomyces dermatitidis*. The imperfect stage exhibits dimorphism, growing as a mycelial form at room temperature and as a yeast form at 37°C.[8, 9] The mycelial form grows as a white mold that slowly turns light brown. On primary isolation, colonies appear in 1 to 3 weeks. The branching hyphae are usually 2 to 3 μm in diameter. Arising at right angles to the hyphae are conidiophores that produce single terminal conidia that vary from 2 to 10 μm in diameter and are round or oval in shape. The conidia are thought to be infectious for humans when the mycelia are disturbed. Conversion of the mycelial form to the yeast form at 37°C is necessary for definitive identification. The physiologic events associated with this phase shift are similar to those associated with *Histoplasma capsulatum* and include heat-related stress followed by uncoupling of oxidative phosphorylation.[10] Yeastlike colonies are wrinkled and cream or tan in color. The yeast cells (Fig. 255–1) may vary in diameter from 5 to 30 μm but are usually 8 to 15 μm, with a thick cell wall that is highly refractile. The yeast cells are multinucleate, containing 8 to 12 nuclei, and reproduce by single buds with a broad base between parent and bud. The daughter cell is often nearly as large as the mother cell before detachment. The same yeast cell in vitro characteristics are also noted in tissue or secretions and are used to distinguish *B. dermatitidis* from other fungi.

Two serotypes of *B. dermatitidis* have been identified by exoantigen analysis of yeast organisms.[11] Initial studies indicate that the A antigen–deficient serotypes are restricted to Africa.[12] The sexual form, *A. dermatitidis*, is heterothallic and requires opposite mating types (+ and −) for fertile cultures.[13, 14] Infection occurs with equal frequency with both mating types.[15] Both types are occasionally isolated from a single patient.

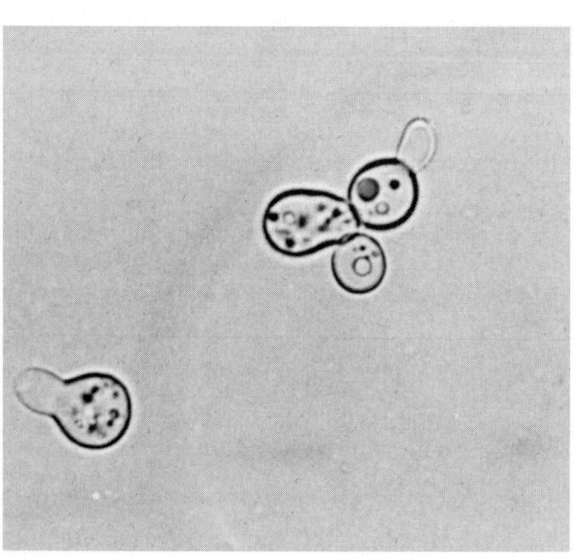

FIGURE 255–1. Yeast cells of *Blastomyces dermatitidis* in wet smear (×1000).

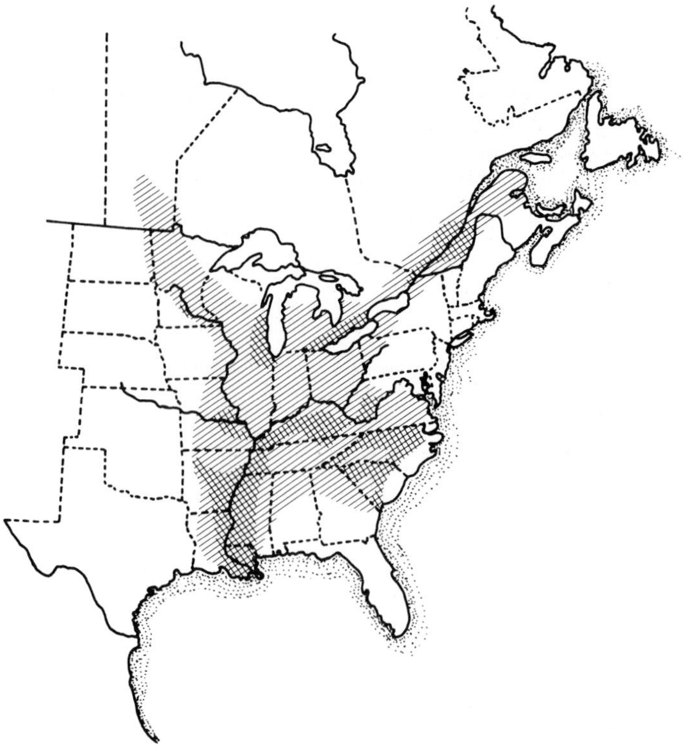

FIGURE 255–2. The incidence and prevalence of blastomycosis in North America. *Diagonal lines* indicate the known endemic region; *hatched areas* are those with the highest incidence. (From Rippon JW. Medical Mycology: The Pathogenic Fungi and Pathogenic Actinomycetes. 3rd ed. Philadelphia: WB Saunders; 1988:474.)

EPIDEMIOLOGY

A complete understanding of the incidence and epidemiology of blastomycosis has been hindered by the lack of a sensitive, specific skin test reagent and the difficulty in establishing the ecologic niche of *B. dermatitidis* in nature. Our knowledge of blastomycosis is based on the collected reports of sporadic cases in humans and dogs,[16–21] as well as the studies of 11 epidemics or clusters of disease.[22–31] On the basis of these data, the endemic area in North America (Fig. 255–2) includes the southeastern and south central states, especially those bordering the Mississippi and Ohio River basins; the midwestern states and Canadian provinces that border the Great Lakes; and a small area in New York and Canada along the St. Lawrence River. Outside North America, well-documented autochthonous cases have been most frequently reported in Africa.[32] Occasional cases have also been reported in Central America, South America, India, and the Middle East.[33]

Initial analysis of sporadic cases indicated that middle-aged men with outdoor occupations that exposed them to soil were at greatest risk for blastomycosis.[16, 17] These findings, however, may reflect only the demographics of the rural states from which most of the cases were reported. In contrast, review of the 11 case clusters reported to date[22–31] indicates that there is no sex, age, race, occupational, or seasonal predilection for blastomycosis. In six of the outbreaks, recreational activities in wooded areas along waterways were the major risk identified. Exposure to dust clouds associated with construction projects or crop harvesting was the only potential risk for infection identified in four of the outbreaks. Thus, exposure to soil, whether at work or at play, appears to be the common link in reports of sporadic disease and outbreaks.

Attempts to isolate the organism in nature have been difficult and the results inconsistent. Denton and coworkers[34–36] reported multiple isolations of *B. dermatitidis* from soil and rotting wood during environmental surveys between 1958 and 1963. Yeast phase organisms were purportedly recovered from pigeon manure after a single case of blastomycosis, but this report lacks crucial details.[37] Isolation from soil samples from an earthern floor was also reported after a single case of disease in Canada.[38] The environmental isolations of *B. dermatitidis* by Klein and coworkers[28, 29] in association with two outbreaks of disease represent an important breakthrough in defining the ecologic niche of the organism. In both instances, the organism was isolated from soil containing decayed vegetation or from decomposed wood. Humidity probably played an important role in promoting the growth of the organism because of the proximity to water and recent rainfall in both outbreaks. These studies, together with other in vitro work,[39] indicate that *B. dermatitidis* exists in nature in warm, moist soil of wooded areas that is also rich in organic debris, such as decaying vegetation. The conditions that support the growth of *B. dermatitidis* in these microfoci probably exist for only short periods of time. Thus, when a sporadic case or outbreak of blastomycosis is recognized, environmental isolation is often impossible because the appropriate local and environmental conditions may no longer exist at the site of exposure.

PATHOGENESIS AND PATHOLOGY

The studies of Schwartz and Baum[7] were the first to establish that the usual portal of entry for blastomycosis in humans is the lungs. Thus, disease at other body sites is the result of dissemination from a primary pulmonary infection, even if clinically undetected. Primary cutaneous blastomycosis has occurred after accidental inoculation in the laboratory or at autopsy[40] and after dog bites.[41] Person-to-person transmission of disease by yeast phase organisms has not been documented, except for a rare vaginal infection acquired from a man with genitourinary blastomycosis[42] and two instances of perinatal transmission.[43, 44]

Pulmonary infection occurs by inhalation of the conidia, which convert to the yeast phase in the lung. The usual inflammatory response consists of clusters of neutrophils and noncaseating granulomas with epithelioid and giant cells. This response is similar to that seen with coccidioidomycosis and sporotrichosis. Although this histopathologic picture is duplicated to a variable degree in extrapulmonary sites, the response in cutaneous disease is unique and shows prominent pseudoepitheliomatous hyperplasia with microabscess formation that clinically and histologically may mimic a variety of cutaneous diseases, including giant keratoacanthoma and squamous cell carcinoma of the skin.[45] The same pseudoepitheliomatous response may also be seen when mucosal surfaces of the mouth, oropharynx, or larynx are involved.[46] The gross and histopathologic appearance of laryngeal disease is similar to that of well-differentiated squamous cell carcinoma and is not infrequently misdiagnosed as such.

IMMUNITY

Our understanding of the immunologic defenses against *B. dermatitidis* is incomplete owing to the lack of appropriate antigens. Advances in characterizing specific yeast antigens have facilitated our study of both humoral and cellular immunity. Specific antibody against *B. dermatitidis* does not appear to confer resistance to or hasten recovery from disease. The major acquired host defense against *B. dermatitidis* is cellular immunity, mediated by antigen-specific T lymphocytes and lymphokine-activated macrophages.

Natural Immunity and Virulence

Investigations of point-source outbreaks indicate that infection rates are high but that symptomatic disease occurs in less than one half of infected individuals.[28] Studies using antigen-specific lymphocyte proliferation as a marker of remote infection suggest that subclinical cases of sporadic blastomycosis also occur, probably more commonly than symptomatic cases.[47] This high frequency of asymptomatic infection supports the concept that healthy people are fairly resistant to infection by *B. dermatitidis*. The presence of natural resistance may, in part, explain why blastomycosis is infrequently reported as an opportunistic infection in the immunocompromised host. When conidia are inhaled into the lungs, natural resistance is probably mediated by neutrophils, monocytes, and alveolar macrophages, which can phagocytize and kill the conidia of *Blastomyces*. Sugar and Picard[48] have also shown that alveolar macrophages inhibit transformation of conidia to the pathogenic yeast form. Once converted in tissue, the yeast forms are relatively resistant to phagocytosis and killing. This conidia-to-yeast conversion most likely results in a survival advantage for the organism when inhaled into the lungs and contributes to the pathogenicity of *B. dermatitidis*.

Although the thick cell wall of the yeast form has been proposed to be antiphagocytic, specific structural and chemical components of the cell wall have been associated with virulence. Early studies by DiSalvo and Denton[49] reported a higher concentration of lipid in the yeast cells of virulent strains of *B. dermatitidis* than in less virulent strains. Cox and Best,[50] in contrast, noted more phospholipid in a single virulent strain than in a less virulent strain. These two studies were limited by the genetic unrelatedness of the strains employed. The elegant work of Klein and coworkers[51–53] has defined other important virulence factors associated with the yeast form of *B. dermatitidis*. These investigators have identified a novel 120-kD glycoprotein antigen on the cell wall surface of the yeast form that serves as the major immunodominant epitope for both humoral and cellular immunity. This antigen, designated WI-1, also functions as an adhesin that binds to host cell receptors, including CR3 and CD14 of human macrophages.[54] This adhesin activity is mediated by a 24-amino-acid tandem repeat that shares 90% homology with the Yersinia adhesin invasin.[55] Binding to extracellular matrix may also be mediated by a cysteine-rich domain at the carboxyl-terminal end of WI-1 that is similar to epidermal growth factor.[55] Using three genetically related strains, Klein and colleagues[56] have shown that alterations in the quantity of WI-1 expressed on the cell surface, the amount of WI-1 shed, and the modification of shed WI-1 are different in two hypovirulent strains compared with the parental (virulent) strain. Using the same strains, Hogan and Klein[57] have also shown that the quantity and distribution of cell wall α-1,3-glucan are different in the hypovirulent and virulent strains. The sum of all these experiments indicates that the adhesin WI-1 is a major virulence factor of *B. dermatitidis* but that other cell wall components, such as α-1,3-glucan, may modulate the WI-1–mediated interactions between the yeast and host cell and thereby also modulate virulence.[58]

Polymorphonuclear Leukocytes

The histopathologic response previously noted implicates both a neutrophil response and a cellular immune response. The polymorphonuclear leukocyte reaction is probably initiated by the release of chemotactic factors from the organism.[59] Human neutrophils efficiently phagocytize and kill the conidia of *B. dermatitidis*. Phagocytosis of conidia of *B. dermatitidis*. Phagocytosis of conidia is optimal when complement and divalent cations are present, and killing is predominantly by oxidative mechanisms.[60, 61] To the contrary, phagocytosis and killing of yeast forms are inefficient; this is probably an important factor in disease progression.[60, 61] Despite activating the neutrophil NADPH oxidase system, yeast forms do not efficiently stimulate the production of myeloperoxidase-dependent microbicidal products.[62] The fungicidal activity of neutrophils can be enhanced by either lymphokine-rich supernatants from immunologically stimulated T lymphocytes or interferon-γ, providing a link between cellular immunity and neutrophil function.[63, 64]

Cellular Immunity

Delayed hypersensitivity can be induced in mice by subcutaneous injections of live or killed *B. dermatitidis*. Decreased susceptibility to infection parallels the development of the cellular immune response,[65, 66] and resistance to infection in mice has been transferred by T lymphocytes.[67] Macrophages harvested from mice with experimental blastomycosis have also been reported to inhibit the replication of *B. dermatitidis*, and both in vivo and in vitro interferon-γ treatment has been shown to enhance killing of *B. dermatitidis* by murine alveolar macrophages.[68, 69] Interestingly, therapeutic concentrations of hydrocortisone and cyclosporine do not inhibit macrophage activation by interferon-γ.[70]

The study of cellular immunity in humans has been hindered by the lack of a sensitive, specific antigen for both in vitro studies and skin testing. The development of specific cellular immunity, as monitored by antigen-induced lymphocyte proliferation, has been documented in patients with blastomycosis using whole yeast phase organisms; an alkali-soluble, water-soluble yeast extract; and the surface protein of yeast cells designated WI-1.[52, 71, 72] Macrophages from patients recovering from blastomycosis have also been shown to have enhanced inhibition of intracellular growth of *B. dermatitidis* compared with control macrophages.[73] Finally, supernatants of antigen-stimulated human lymphocytes have been shown to enhance phagocytosis and intracellular inhibition of the growth of *B. dermatitidis* by both alveolar and monocyte-derived macrophages.[73] Despite these advances, however, an antigen for skin testing is not yet available. Blastomycin, a culture filtrate of mycelial phase organisms, lacks both specificity and sensitivity. In the Veterans Administration Cooperative Study, only 40% of patients with blastomycosis had a positive skin test to blastomycin.[16] Further clarification of cellular immunity in human cases of blastomycosis awaits more definitive characterization of the fungal antigens.

Humoral Immunity

Yeast antigens have been used to evaluate humoral immunity in a variety of serologic tests of different sensitivities and specificities. The complement fixation test has not proved to be useful because it lacks both sensitivity and specificity. At most 50% of patients with blastomycosis have a positive complement fixation reaction to *B. dermatitidis* antigens.[22] Cross-reactivity with *H. capsulatum* and, to a lesser degree, *Coccidioides immitis* has also been a problem.

The immunodiffusion test, which detects precipitin antibodies to the A and B antigens located in the cell wall of the yeast, is more specific for blastomycosis. With the test modified by Kaufman and associates,[74, 75] the presence of antibody to the A antigen has been noted in up to 70 to 80% of patients with blastomycosis. However, patients with localized disease or those with symptoms of less than 50 days' duration are less likely to have a positive antibody response.[76, 77] Furthermore, the presence of detectable antibody is short lived after cure of disease. These finding emphasize the limitations of immunodiffusion serology for both clinical and epidemiologic studies. Using the A antigen in an enzyme immunoassay has improved sensitivity, but false-positive reactions, especially in patients with histoplasmosis and other fungal infections, are more common.[76–79] Studies by Klein and Jones[80] indicate that the cross-reactive determinants reside in the carbohydrate component of the A antigen. Commerical kits for both the immunodiffusion assay and enzyme immunoassay are available.

Klein and Jones[51] have identified the novel 120-kD surface protein of *B. dermatitidis* yeasts that they have designated WI-1. These investigators purified and characterized WI-1 and compared it immunologically with the commercially available A antigen.[80] The results of this study indicate that the tandem repeat of WI-1 is the major antibody recognition site of both WI-1 and A antigen. When used in a radioimmunoassay, antibody to WI-1 was detected in 85% of patients with blastomycosis and in only 3% of patients with other fungal infections.[51] In a second study from the same laboratory, similar sensitivity (83%) was noted for the detection of anti–WI-1 antibodies by radioimmunoassay.[81] All patients with proven blastomycosis whose serum was obtained within 60 days of onset of symptoms or diagnosis had at least one serum sample positive for anti–WI-1. Furthermore, anti–WI-1 antibody titers fell as the infection resolved and antibody titers in most patients were undetectable after 8 months from the onset of symptoms. Enhanced diagnostic sensitivity did not result from modification of the radioimmunoassay to detect immunoglobulin M antibody. Further studies, including the development of a nonradiometric test, are needed to clarify the role of the WI-1 antigen in the serodiagnosis of blastomycosis.

CLINICAL MANIFESTATIONS

Our knowledge of the clinical manifestations of blastomycosis is derived from careful studies of symptomatic, sporadic cases and the few case clusters reported. It must be emphasized that blastomycosis is a systemic disease with a wide variety of pulmonary and extrapulmonary manifestations. Pulmonary disease may be acute or chronic and mimics infection with pyogenic bacteria, tuberculosis, infection with other fungi, and malignancy. Cutaneous disease, the most common extrapulmonary manifestation, appears similar to disease seen with bromoderma, pyoderma gangrenosum, Majocchi's granuloma, leishmaniasis, *Mycobacterium marinum* infection, giant keratoacanthoma, and squamous cell carcinoma.

B. dermatitidis infection may involve almost every organ of the body (Table 255–1), resulting in the diversity of clinical manifestations. Skin, bone, and genitourinary sites of infection are the most common and are most likely to be clinically manifest. Extrapulmonary disease is seen most commonly during the chronic form of illness, in which approximately two thirds of patients have been reported with multiple-organ involvement. However, many of the reports noting this high frequency of extrapulmonary dissemination were autopsy based or appeared before the availability of effective treatments. In contrast to these earlier studies, later clinical experience in Arkansas,[88] Wisconsin,[89] and Mississippi,[90] three states in which blastomycosis is endemic, has indicated a lower frequency of extrapulmonary disease (Table 255–2). Approximately three fourths of the patients reported in these studies had isolated pulmonary disease.

Although a variety of clinical schemata may be used in discussing blastomycosis, that proposed by Sarosi and Davies[91] appears most comprehensive. A modification of this schema is presented in Figure 255–3. It should be noted that the occurrence of reactivation blastomycosis is a controversial issue, with only a few cases being suggestive.[92] Cases attributed to extrapulmonary reactivation may represent the late clinical manifestations of chronic, subclinical disease that remains active after pulmonary healing. The factors determining the clinical course after acute infection are not well defined but probably involve a complex interaction of pulmonary anatomy, host defenses, and microbial factors.

Acute Infection

Acute pulmonary infection is often unrecognized unless related to group exposure. Analysis of point-source outbreaks indicated that only about one half of infected individuals develop symptomatic disease and that the median incubation period is 30 to 45 days.[21, 26–29] Symptoms are nonspecific and tend to mimic those of influenza or bacterial infection with abrupt onset of myalgias, arthralgias, chills, and fever. Pleuritic pain may be prominent but is usually transient. Cough is initially nonproductive but in many cases becomes productive of purulent sputum. The radiologic findings in the acute stage of disease, whether symptomatic or asymptomatic, are also nonspecific but are usually those of lobar or segmental consolidation[93, 94] (Fig. 255–4). Pleural effusion is uncommon and, if pres-

TABLE 255-1 Organ Involvement in Blastomycosis from Clinical and Autopsy Findings in Seven Studies

Organ System Involved	Study*							
	Cherniss and Waisbren[82] [40]	*Abernathy[83] [35]*	*Veterans Administration Cooperative Study[16] [198]*	*Witorsch and Utz[84] [40]*	*Lockwood et al[85] [63]*	*Duttera and Osterhout[86] [63]*	*Busey and Veterans Administration Cooperative Study[87] [84]*	*Total†*
Lungs	28 (70)‡	27 (77)	118 (60)	28 (70)	59 (80)	33 (52)	76 (90)	369/534 (69)
Skin	30 (75)	28 (80)	118 (60)	29 (73)	33 (45)	36 (57)	32 (38)	306/534 (57)
Bone	19 (48)	12 (34)	46 (23)	11 (28)	10 (14)	12 (19)	6 (7)	116/534 (22)
Genitourinary	11 (28)	5 (14)	32 (16)	13 (33)	13 (18)	6 (10)	12 (14)	92/534 (17)
Reticuloendothelial system (liver, spleen, lymph nodes)	5 (13)	13 (37)	25 (13)	7 (18)	NS†	3 (5)	3 (4)	56/460 (12)
Central nervous system	4 (10)	1 (3)	9 (5)	1 (3)	5 (7)	4 (6)	4 (5)	29/534 (5)
Mucous membranes	3 (8)	2 (6)	11 (6)	10 (25)	NS	NS	NS	26/273 (10)
Subcutaneous	25 (63)	NS	NS	15 (38)	NS	NS	NS	40/80 (30)
Other§	5 (13)	9 (26)	18 (9)	5 (13)	NS	7 (11)	2 (2)	46/460 (10)

*Number of cases given in square brackets; reference numbers after authors.
†Total based on studies where stated; NS, not stated.
‡Number of cases followed by percentage in parentheses.
§Other: thyroid, 10; gastrointestinal, 8; larynx, 8; adrenal, 7; pleura, 6; joints, 5; heart, 2; peritoneum, 1; eye, 1; psoas, 1; retropharynx, 1.

FIGURE 255–3. Clinical classification of blastomycosis. (Adapted from Sarosi GA, Davies SF. Blastomycosis. Am Rev Respir Dis. 1979; 120:911–938.)

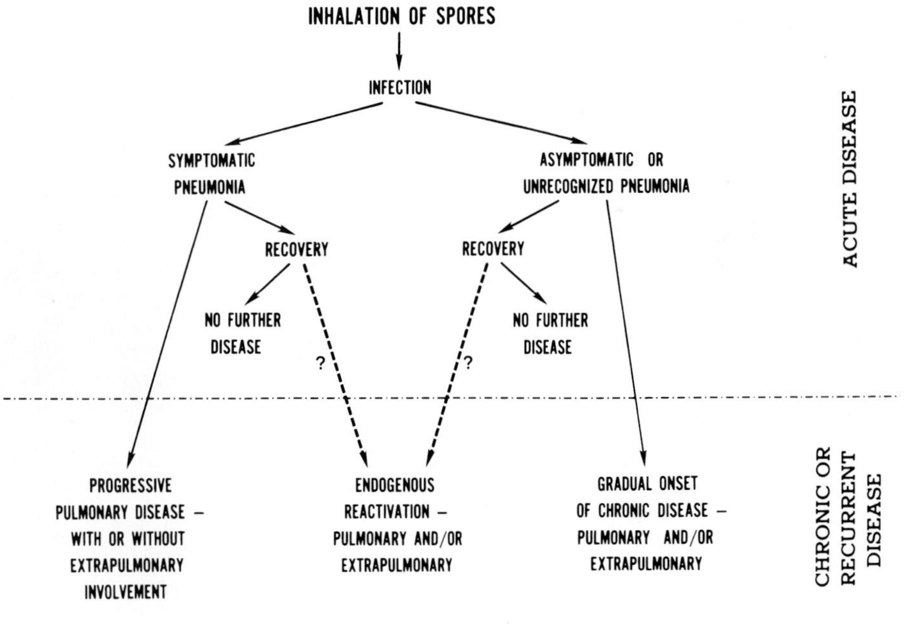

TABLE 255-2 Clinical Experience with Blastomycosis*

Involvement	Arkansas[88] [44]	Wisconsin[89] [73]	Mississippi[90] [326]	Total [443]
Single-organ disease	30 (69)†	62 (85)	270 (83)	362 (82)
Lung	26 (59)	56 (77)	245 (75)	327 (74)
Skin	2 (5)	3 (4)	16 (5)	21 (5)
Other	2 (5)	3 (4)	9 (3)	14 (3)
Multiorgan disease	14 (31)	11 (15)	56 (17)	81 (18)

*Number of cases given in square brackets; reference numbers after state names.
†Number of cases followed by percentage in parentheses.

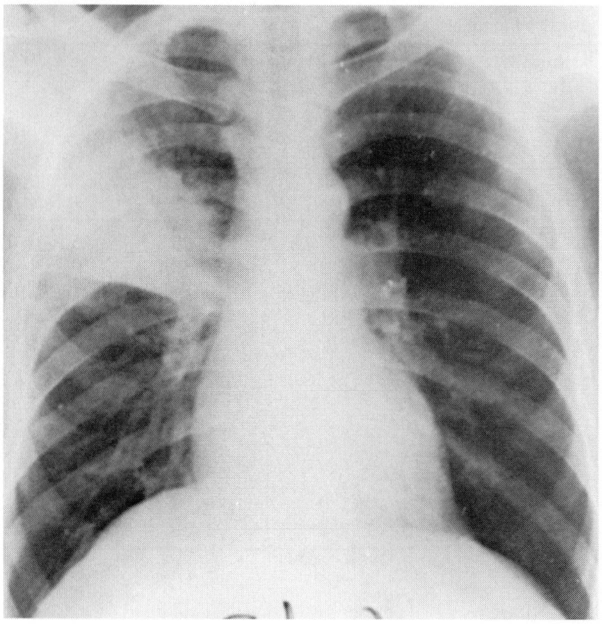

FIGURE 255–4. A confluent infiltrate with a segmental distribution in a patient with blastomycosis.

ent, is found only in small amounts. Hilar adenopathy is also uncommon.

Spontaneous resolution of symptomatic acute pneumonia has been recognized in a few sporadic cases, in case clusters, and after accidental laboratory infection.[95–97] How frequently this occurs has not been established. In these cases symptoms have usually resolved in less than 4 weeks, but radiologic abnormalities have taken longer to clear.

Chronic or Recurrent Infection

Most patients in whom blastomycosis is diagnosed have an indolent onset and progressive disease. The clinical manifestations are diverse, including pulmonary or extrapulmonary disease or both. For clarity, these are discussed separately.

Pulmonary Manifestations. The clinical manifestations of pulmonary disease are those of chronic pneumonia, including productive cough, hemoptysis, weight loss, and pleuritic chest pain. Fever, if present, tends to be low grade. The radiologic findings in these patients are variable. Lobar or segmental alveolar infiltrates, with or without cavitation, are most frequently reported[93, 94] (Fig. 255–5). The specific lobar distribution of infiltrates is not clinically helpful, although upper lobe infiltrates are reported more commonly. Mass lesions that mimic bronchogenic carcinoma occur almost as frequently as alveolar infiltrates[98] (Fig. 255–6). Other radiographic features include intermediate-sized nodules, solitary cavities, and fibronodular infiltrates, often with cavities (Fig. 255–7). Hilar adenopathy is variably reported. Postinfectious calcification of lymph nodes or pulmonary parenchyma is rare. An occasional patient has acute deterioration associated with miliary disease resulting from hematogenous spread[99] (Fig. 255–8) or diffuse pneumonitis from presumed endobronchial spread.[100] When either of these radiographic findings is accompanied by respiratory failure, mortality usually exceeds 50%.[100] Although pleural thickening and small pleural effusions may occur, large pleural effusions are uncommon. One report noted an unfavorable response to therapy in patients with major pleural disease.[101]

Skin. Skin disease is the most common extrapulmonary manifestation of blastomycosis, being reported in 40 to 80% percent of cases (See Table 255–1). Although extrapulmonary disease is usually seen in conjunction with active pulmonary disease, skin involvement may occur alone.[102] In some patients with skin disease, asymptomatic pulmonary disease is found. In my experience, skin disease is a marker for multiorgan infection, being present in three quarters of patients with disease in two or more organs.[90]

Two types of skin lesions may be seen. The first is the more characteristic verrucous lesions that usually appear on exposed body areas. These often begin as small papulopustular lesions (Fig. 255–9) and slowly spread to form crusted, heaped-up lesions that can vary in color from gray to a violaceous hue (Fig. 255–10). These lesions are often mistaken for squamous cell carcinoma. Older lesions may show central clearing with scar formation and depigmentation. Microabscess formation tends to occur at the periphery of such lesions, and removal of the eschar peripherally reveals purulent material in which the yeast forms are usually visible on wet preparation.

The second type of lesion is described as ulcerative (Fig. 255–11); the initial pustule spreads as a superficial ulcer or slightly raised lesion, with a bed of red friable granulation tissue that bleeds easily. Skin lesions of both types may be seen in the same patient. Lesions may also occur on the mucosa of the nose, mouth, and larynx. With skin lesions associated with a pulmonary pathogenesis there is little or no regional lymph node involvement or lymphadenitis, in contrast to that seen with inoculation blastomycosis.[40, 41]

Subcutaneous Nodules. Although subcutaneous nodules are often discussed as a skin manifestation, the clinical syndrome seen in patients with subcutaneous nodules is different from that associated with other skin lesions. Subcutaneous nodules are cold abcesses that

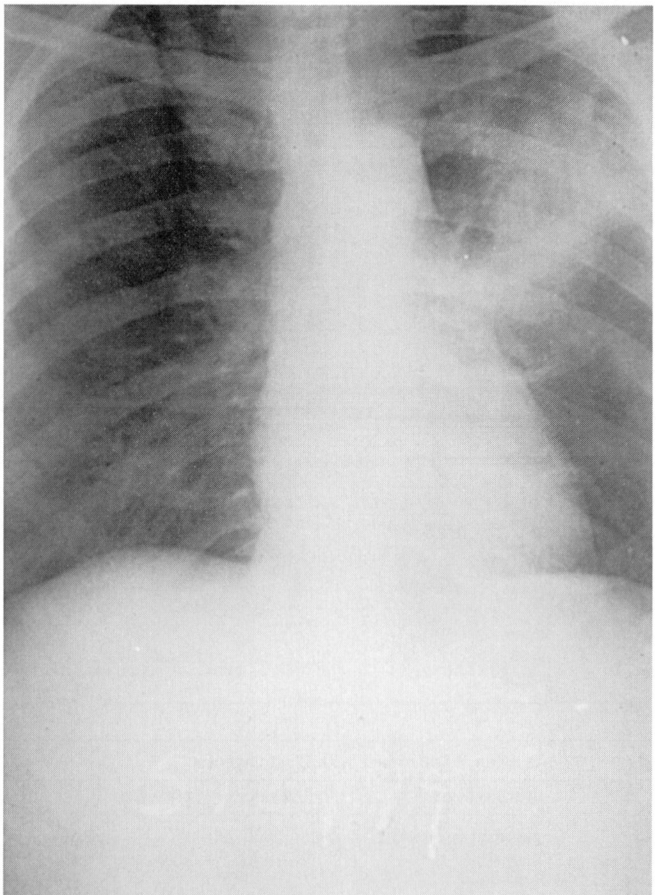

FIGURE 255–5. Multinodular densities with consolidation of the left upper lobe in a patient with blastomycosis.

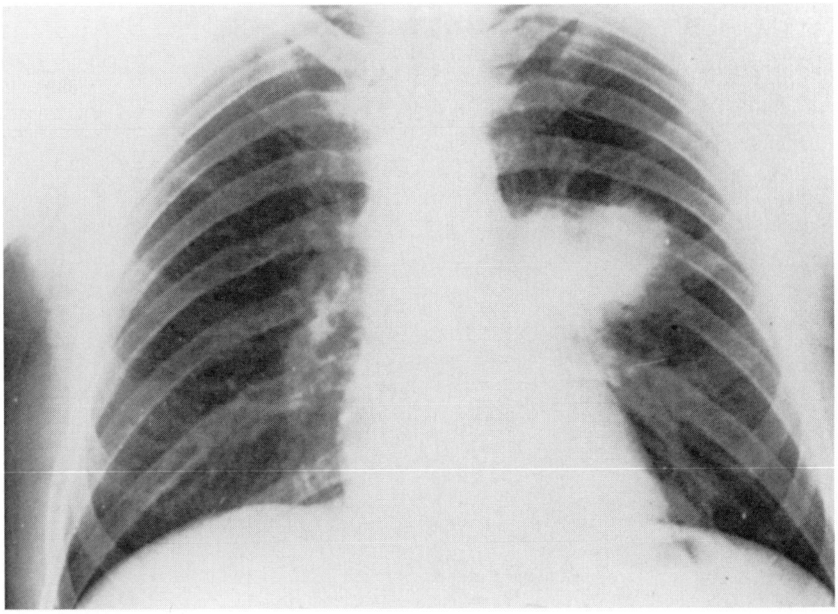

FIGURE 255–6. A perihilar mass lesion in a patient with blastomycosis. This radiograph appearance mimics that of carcinoma of the lung. To rule out a coexisting malignancy, patients with this radiographic picture should have bronchoscopy even if wet preparations of sputum reveal the organism.

are usually seen in conjunction with pulmonary and other extrapulmonary disease. The patient often appears acutely ill, systemic manifestations may be prominent, and rapid deterioration may result unless therapy is initiated promptly. Lesions sometimes drain spontaneously. Drainage or aspirated pus has abundant numbers of organisms that are readily visible on microscopic examination.

Bone and Joint. After skin disease, skeletal blastomycosis is next in frequency. Although almost any bone can be infected, the long bones, vertebrae, and ribs are most commonly involved.[103] A well-circumscribed osteolytic lesion is typical (Fig. 255–12). Patients with bone lesions rarely present with bone pain but instead present with contiguous soft tissue abscesses or chronic draining sinuses. Vertebral disease mimics tuberculosis, with anterior involvement of the vertebral body, destruction of the interspace, and development of large paraspinous abscesses.[104]

Arthritis usually occurs by extension from a contiguous osteomyelitis. Signs and symptoms may be acute or chronic. Synovial fluid is usually purulent, with organisms readily visible on wet preparation.[105]

Genitourinary Tract. From 10 to 30% of the cases in men have been reported to involve the genitourinary tract, primarily the prostate and epididymis.[106] Epididymal disease may spread to the testes. The variable incidence reported may reflect the respective authors' tenacity in pursuing the diagnosis. Prostatic involvement is most common and is usually manifested by symptoms of obstruction, an enlarged,

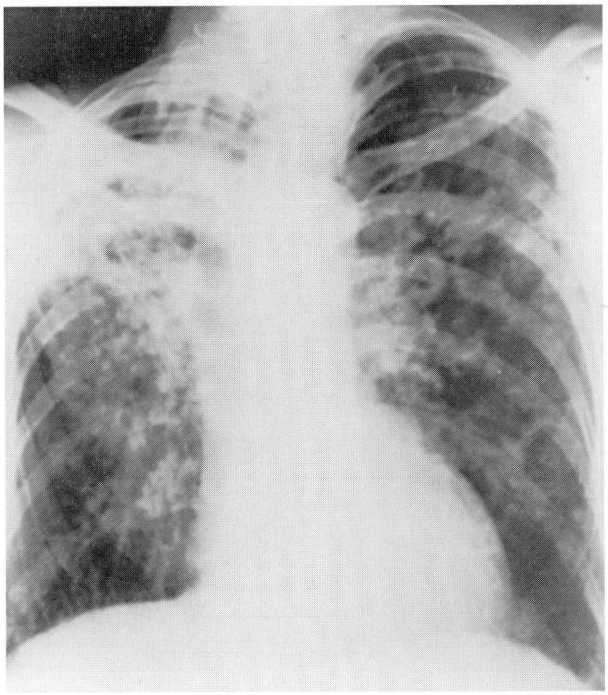

FIGURE 255–7. Bilateral fibronodular infiltrates with cavitation and volume loss in the right upper lobe. This radiographic appearance cannot be distinguished from that of tuberculosis or other granulomatous diseases.

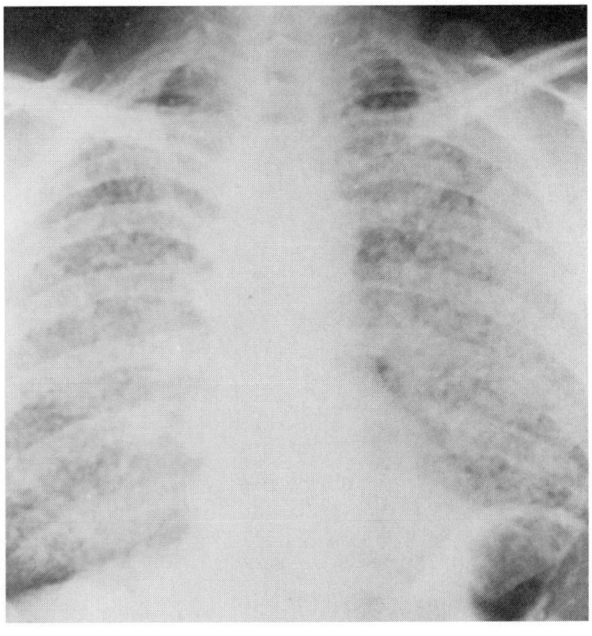

FIGURE 255–8. Miliary blastomycosis in a patient with respiratory failure. (Courtesy of Dr. Guy Campbell, Jackson, Miss.)

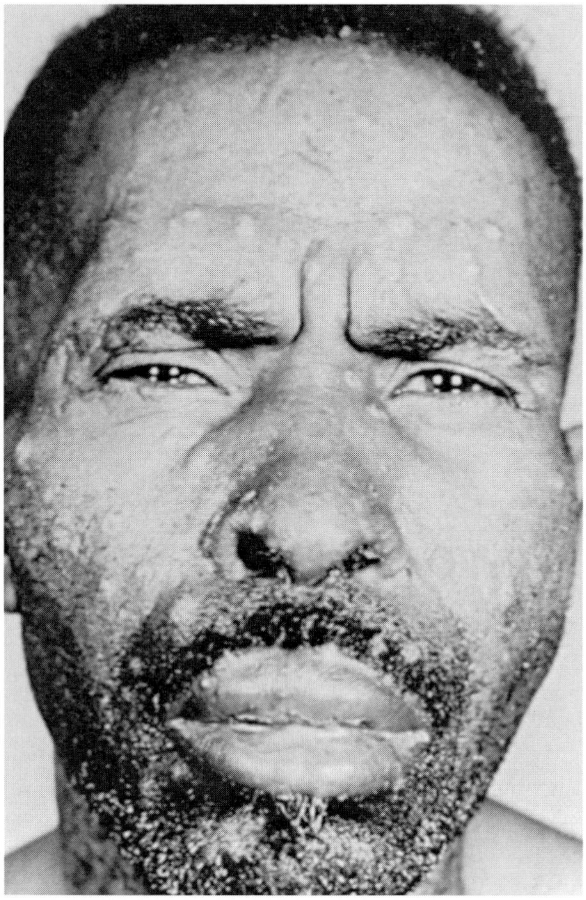

FIGURE 255–9. Multiple papulopustular lesions in a patient with blastomycosis. (Courtesy of Dr. Guy Campbell, Jackson, Miss.)

tender prostate, and pyuria. Urine cultures, especially after prostatic message, are often positive.

Central Nervous System. In the normal host, disease involving the central nervous system is uncommon, being reported in less than 5% of cases. In patients with acquired immunodeficiency syndrome (AIDS), however, central nervous system complications of blasto-

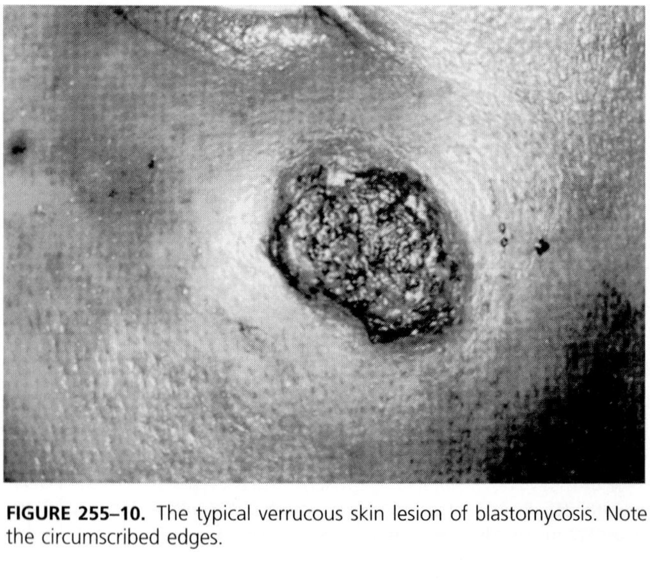

FIGURE 255–10. The typical verrucous skin lesion of blastomycosis. Note the circumscribed edges.

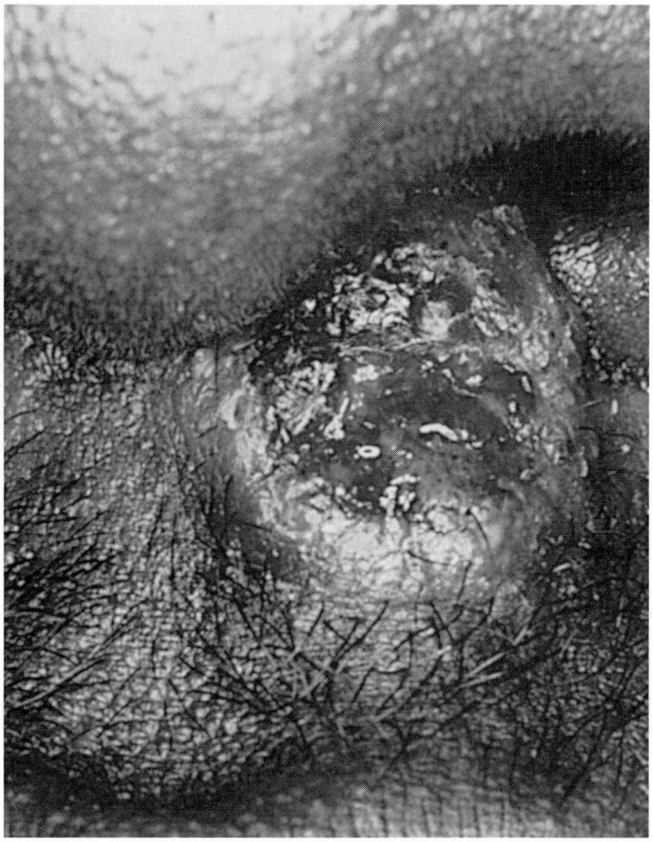

FIGURE 255–11. The ulcerative skin lesion of blastomycosis. These lesions bleed easily.

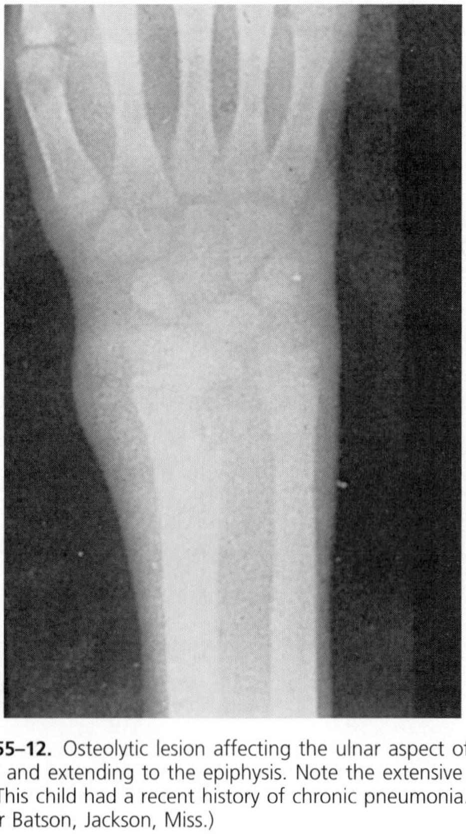

FIGURE 255–12. Osteolytic lesion affecting the ulnar aspect of the distal left radius and extending to the epiphysis. Note the extensive soft tissue swelling. This child had a recent history of chronic pneumonia. (Courtesy of Dr. Blair Batson, Jackson, Miss.)

mycosis are common. A review noted that 40% of AIDS patients with blastomycosis had central nervous disease, usually associated with dissemination to multiple organs.[107] When present, it is manifest as either an abscess or meningitis.[108–110] Abscesses present as mass lesions and may be intracranial (Fig. 255–13) or, occasionally, spinal in location. Surgical management of mass lesions may be necessary for diagnosis and to prevent progressive neurologic deterioration.[111] Meningitis is usually a late and fulminant complication of widely disseminated blastomycosis.

Other Sites. Blastomycosis may infrequently affect the liver, spleen, gastrointestinal tract, thyroid, pericardium, adrenal glands, and other sites (see Table 255–1). Most such reports represent findings at autopsy in patients with widely disseminated disease. Of note, gastrointestinal disease below the esophagus and overt adrenal insufficiency are rare.

Special Circumstances

Blastomycosis in Children. Although blastomycosis in children is considered rare by some authors, most reviews of blastomycosis note that 2 to 10% of the patients reported are younger than 15 years of age. In a large common-source outbreak of disease involving 46 children, the attack rate for infection was approximately 50%. Of the infected, about one half were symptomatic.[28] Pediatric patients manifest the full clinical spectrum of disease as outlined for adults.[112–114] However, a clinical review from Arkansas noted greater difficulty in establishing the diagnosis and a poorer response to oral azole treatment in children with blastomycosis.[115]

Blastomycosis in Pregnancy. Despite the depressed cellular immunity associated with pregnancy, blastomycosis has been reported only infrequently in pregnant women.[116] Disseminated disease is common, and a case of adult respiratory distress syndrome in a woman who developed blastomycosis in the third trimester of pregnancy is noteworthy.[117] Perinatal blastomycosis has been reported in two infants born to mothers with untreated blastomycosis.[43, 44] Both infants died as a result of overwhelming pulmonary disease. Infection of the infant may result from aspiration into the lungs of vaginal secretions colonized with *B. dermatitidis*, an ascending vaginal infection associated with partially ruptured membranes, or transplacental intrauterine infection.[44] Although a presumptive case of intrauterine transmission has been reported,[43] the placenta in this case was never examined. It is therefore not possible to state with certainty that the child acquired blastomycosis by intrauterine transmission. However, in a case reported by MacDonald and Alguire,[117] *B. dermatitidis* was demonstrated on both the maternal and fetal sides of the placenta. Irrespective of the pathogenesis of infection, perinatal transmission remains a definite possibility and all pregnant women with blastomycosis should be treated without delay. Amphotericin B has been used successfully for blastomycosis and other fungal infections during pregnancy, with no documented adverse outcome for the pregnancy or fetus.[116]

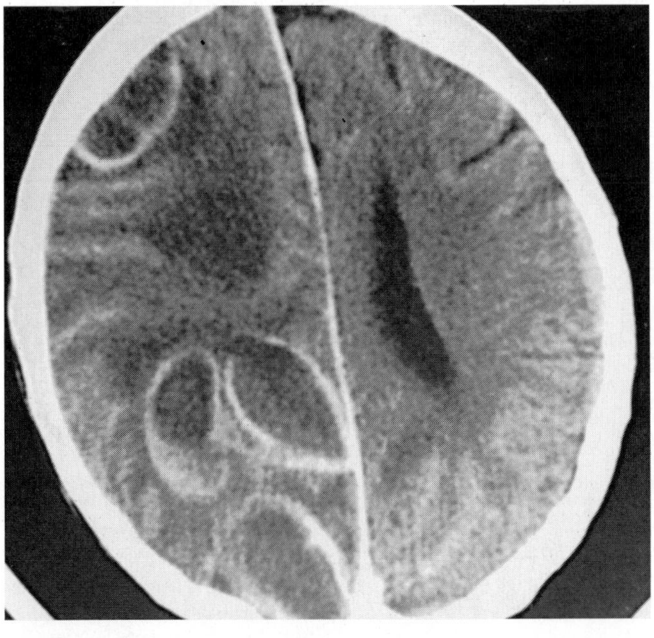

FIGURE 255–13. Multiple ring-enhancing lesions affecting the right frontal and parietal lobes. There is extensive surrounding edema with effacement of the sulci and right ventricle. This patient simultaneously had pulmonary blastomycosis.

Blastomycosis in the Compromised Host. Although invasive fungal diseases are common in the immunosuppressed host, only a few reports have indicated that *B. dermatitidis* can act as an opportunistic pathogen.[107, 118–120] As suggested previously, this may be related to natural host defenses that are active against the inhaled conidia.

Blastomycosis has been reported as a late infectious complication in AIDS patients.[107] Most patients have had previous AIDS-defining illnesses and their CD4 counts are usually less than 200 cells/mm^3. Disease, whether pulmonary or disseminated, is more aggressive and more often rapidly fatal than disease in the healthy host. Pulmonary disease is more likely to present with diffuse interstitial infiltrates or a miliary pattern on the chest radiograph. Central nervous system disease is especially common, being noted to occur in 40% of patients.[107]

Blastomycosis has also been reported in other immunocompromised hosts, including transplant recipients, patients receiving glucocorticosteroid therapy, and patients receiving cytotoxic chemotherapy for hematologic malignancies or solid tumors.[118–120] A large series of patients reported by Pappas and colleagues[120] has helped to clarify the clinical spectrum of blastomycosis in the immunocompromised host. Blastomycosis in these patients was more often disseminated, more aggressive, and associated with higher mortality than in the immunocompetent host. Diffuse pulmonary infiltrates, pleural effusions, and respiratory failure were common. Multiple visceral organ dissemination and central nervous system disease occurred frequently but not as often as in AIDS patients.

Mortality rates of 30 to 40% have been reported for immunocompromised patients with blastomycosis. In addition, most deaths attributed to blastomycosis occur within the first few weeks of disease. Thus, early aggressive therapy with amphotericin B is indicated. Frequent relapses have been noted in AIDS patients and those with continued immunosuppressive therapy. Chronic suppressive therapy with an oral azole should therefore be strongly considered for individuals who respond to a primary course of amphotericin.[107, 120, 121]

DIAGNOSIS

No clinical syndrome is characteristic of blastomycosis. Definitive diagnosis requires the growth of the organism from clinical specimens. A presumptive diagnosis may be made by visualization of the charactereistic yeast in pus, sputum, secretions, or histopathologic sections. In the appropriate clinical setting, visualization of the fungus can prompt the initiation of antimicrobial therapy.

Direct Examination of Secretions

Sputum or pus is easily examined by wet preparation. A drop of the specimen is placed on a microscope slide, covered with a coverslip, and examined under the high dry objective. Although 10% potassium hydroxide has been recommended to aid in finding the organism, it is usually not necessary, as the large, characteristic yeast cell is easily seen despite cellular debris. Sometimes it is also useful to digest sputum with trypsin and smear the centrifuged sediment. Body fluids such as urine, pleural fluid, or cerebrospinal fluid should be centrifuged and the sediment evaluated in the same way. Calcofluor white stain is particularly useful when organisms are sparse.

When visualized, the yeast cells are easily differentiated from others on the basis of their size, refractile cell wall, and single, broad-based buds (see Fig. 255–1). Occasionally the endospores of *C. immitis* may resemble single yeast cells, but the presence of budding can be used to distinguish *B. dermatitidis*. *Paracoccidioides brasiliensis*, rarely seen in the United States, is distinguished by the presence of multiple, narrow-based buds. *B. dermatitidis* may sometimes be as small as *Cryptococcus neoformans*, although the capsule and narrow-based bud of the latter aid in differentiation.

Although bronchoscopy has been recommended as a useful technique for obtaining specimens, the collective experience at the University of Mississippi and Jackson Veterans Affairs Medical Centers indicates that bronchoscopy is best reserved for patients who are not producing sputum or for whom the radiograph indicates the possibility of malignancy. Bronchial washings, lavage fluid, and postbronchoscopy sputum samples should be sent for cytology as well as smear and culture, because the organism is often visualized on Papanicolaou preparations.[122]

Histopathologic Examination

The presence of pyogranulomas should alert one to the possibility of blastomycosis. Yeast forms can be difficult to see with routine hematoxylin and eosin stains, and special stains should be used to enhance visualization. The Gomori methenamine silver stain is best used for screening tissue for the presence of fungal elements (Fig. 255–14). The Gomori methenamine silver counterstain does not allow evaluation of the inflammatory response in the tissue. The periodic acid–Schiff stain, which colors the cell wall pink or red, has a counterstain that does allow evaluation of cell morphology and tissue response. Mayer mucicarmine stains the cell wall of *B. dermatitidis* faintly or not at all, which may be useful in differentiating it from *C. neoformans* when necessary. A variety of fluorescent microscopic techniques and reagents have also been used to facilitate the histopathologic review of specimens.[123–125] Although these are occasionally helpful when fungal elements in a specimen are atypical or sparse, in my experience their routine use is not warranted because a presumptive diagnosis of *B. dermatitidis* can usually be made by review of GMS- or PAS-stained tissue sections.

Culture

Any material obtained should be placed on Sabouraud's or, preferably, more enriched agar (e.g., Sabhi, brain-heart infusion, Gorman's medium). Because initial growth is more dependable at 30°C, this temperature is recommended. Specimens contaminated with bacteria should also be cultured on medium containing an antibacterial antibiotic such as chloramphenicol. Cycloheximide can be incorporated in the medium to inhibit other fungal contaminants. However, this selective medium should never be used at 37°C because the yeast phase of *B. dermatitidis* (as well as some opportunistic fungi) is sensitive to cycloheximide, and growth may be inhibited. The mycelial form of *B. dermatitidis* is not diagnostic, and conversion to the yeast form is required for confirmation. Early identification of mycelial cultures is, however, possible with commercially available chemiluminescent DNA probes that recognize unique RNA sequences of *Blastomyces*.[126]

Serologic Methods

As mentioned previously, serum complement fixation tests are neither specific nor sensitive. The immunodiffusion test is more sensitive and specific than the complement fixation test.[12, 74–77] Antibody against A antigen has been reported in 52 to 80% of patients with blastomycosis, with almost no cross-reactivity with other fungi.[12] In one report, however, patients with localized disease had a lower rate of positivity (33%) than those with disseminated disease (88%).[76] Furthermore, immunodiffusion serology is of little help in the diagnosis of acute disease. In one large outbreak, only 28% of patients had a positive test and all but one of the positive sera were obtained 50 or more days after the onset of symptoms.[77]

A radioimmunoassay and an enzyme immunoassay employing commercial antigens have been used by George and coworkers[127, 128] as rapid screening tests for histoplasmosis and blastomycosis. Both tests are quite sensitive, but their specificity is no beter than that of complement fixation. A sensitive enzyme immunoassay using purified A antigen has been reported, but the specificity of this test varies depending on the cutoff titer employed.[129] When this assay was used in evaluating a large common-source outbreak, a positive test was noted in 77% of patients.[77] Although some positive results were noted in the first 2 weeks of illness, both the peak seroprevalence rate and peak geometric mean titer did not occur until 50 to 70 days after the onset of symptoms. A commercial enzyme-linked immunosorbent assay is now available and the use of this sensitive

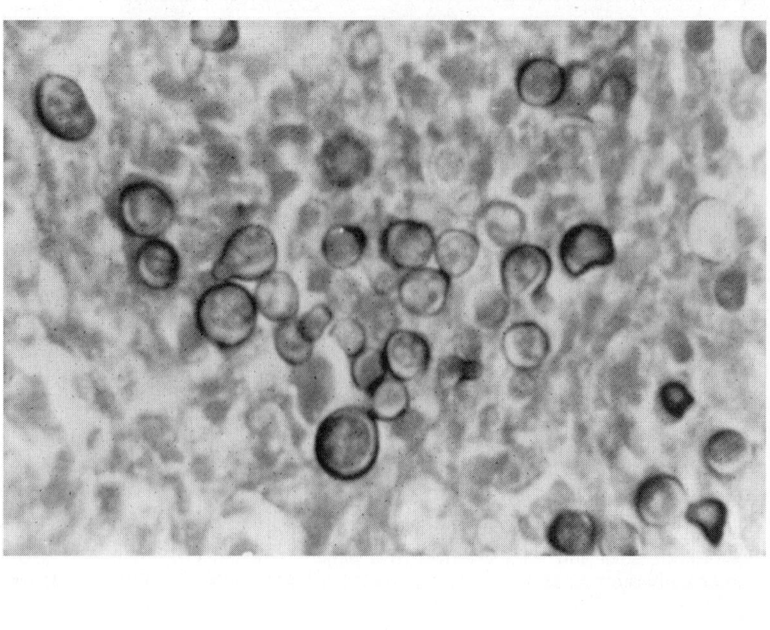

FIGURE 255–14. A Gomori–methenamine silver stain of a laryngeal biopsy specimen in a patient with suspected carcinoma of the larynx. (Courtesy of Mr. James Gorman, Jackson, Miss.)

test for initial screening in conjunction with the more specific immunodiffusion test may be helpful.[78, 79]

Klein and coworkers[51, 81] have utilized a 120-kD cell wall protein antigen (WI-1) to detect antibodies to *B. dermatitidis* in infected patients. When it was employed in a radioimmunoassay, antibodies to WI-1 were detected in 85% of patients with blastomycosis. Specificity was excellent, with positive tests being noted in only 3 to 5% of patients with other fungal infections or patients in whom infection could not be confirmed. Although the use of WI-1 in serologic testing appears promising, this test is not generally available and further studies are necessary to establish its role in the diagnosis of blastomycosis.

In summary, complement fixation, immunodiffusion, and enzyme-linked immunosorbent assay serologic tests are currently available to aid in the diagnosis of blastomycosis. Unfortunately, sensitivity and specificity vary with the test employed. Because false-positive and false-negative results occur commonly, a negative antibody titer, regardless of which test is used, should never be used to rule out disease. Neither should a positive titer alone be an indication for therapy; rather, it should stimulate the clinician to look carefully for the disease.

Cellular Immunity Testing

No reagent is currently available for skin testing patients with suspected blastomycosis. Lymphocyte transformation to yeast phase organisms, alkali-soluble, water-soluble antigens, and the WI-1 surface protein have been used as indicators of cell-mediated immunity in patients with blastomycosis.[52,71,72] In an outbreak, 81% of definite and probable cases of blastomycosis had positive lymphocyte transformation tests with the alkali-soluble, water-soluble antigen.[28] This test does not appear to be useful early in the acute disease, because positive tests are not obtained in the first 2 weeks of disease. Furthermore, because this immunity appears to be long lived, a positive test does not necessarily indicate recent infection.[72] Finally, there are only limited data on the specificity of this test. Lymphocyte transformation assays are therefore not yet clinically useful and should be considered investigational tests.

TREATMENT

Before the availability of chemotherapy for treatment of blastomycosis, the disease as reported had a progressive course with eventual extrapulmonary disease and a mortality exceeding 60%. Even though isolated cutaneous disease had a better prognosis, skin lesions were progressive and spontaneous recovery was uncommon. Thus, after the introduction of effective antifungal therapy, it was accepted that all patients with blastomycosis should be treated. This concept came under some question after the description of self-limited pulmonary blastomycosis.[95] The decision to withhold therapy for patients with acute pulmonary blastomycosis is difficult and remains a controversial issue. Although it is true that in some patients blastomycotic pneumonia may resolve without therapy, there is no way to determine which patients will present later with extrapulmonary disease, often with serious sequelae[130] Furthermore, some patients while under observation may suffer acute exacerbation with miliary disease or endobronchial spread, both associated with high mortality.[99, 100] For these reasons, it is the policy at my medical center that almost all patients with active disease are treated. If a cultural diagnosis is made after spontaneous recovery from blastomycotic pneumonia, patients are carefully evaluated for the presence of extrapulmonary disease before a decision is made to withhold treatment. If treatment is withheld, patients must be followed carefully for many years for evidence of reactivation or progressive disease.

Amphotericin B was previously considered the treatment of choice for all clinical forms of blastomycosis.[85, 87, 131] However, ketoconazole, itraconazole and fluconazole are now considered effective alternatives for immunocompetent patients with mild to moderate disease (Table 255–3). Azoles should not be used in patients with life-threatening disease or with central nervous system blastomycosis. Hydroxystilbamidine, the first effective drug available for the treatment of blastomycosis, is no longer used. Miconazole, as an intravenous formulation, has been infrequently used for blastomycosis.[132] No clinical trials with this drug in the treatment of blastomycosis have been published, and thus there is no currently defined role for miconazole in the management of this disease.

In a prospective, randomized multicenter trial of patients treated with ketoconazole for at least 6 months, the cure rates were 100% in patients treated with 800 mg/day and 79% in those treated with 400 mg/day.[133] Toxicity was greater with the higher dose. A second study noted a cure rate of 81% in 43 patients who completed at least 1 month of therapy with 400 mg/day.[88] A retrospective study documented a cure rate of 82% for patients treated with ketoconazole at a daily dose of 400 mg or greater.[90] Thus, a single daily 400-mg dose of ketoconazole is recommended as initial therapy. If the clinical response is not satisfactory, the dose should be increased in 200-mg increments to a maximum of 800 mg/day. Therapy should be continued for at least 6 months.[134, 135] Relapse rates of 10 to 14% have been reported after ketoconazole therapy.[88, 90, 133] Although in most cases relapses occur in the first few months after treatment is completed, careful follow-up is warranted for 1 to 2 years after ketoconazole therapy.

Itraconazole, an oral triazole, has excellent in vitro and in vivo activity against *B. dermatitidis*.[136, 137] In a prospective, phase II clinical trial, itraconazole at doses ranging from 200 to 400 mg/day was effective in 90% of patients.[138] For compliant patients with at least 2 months of therapy, a successful outcome was noted in 95%. Although the study design did not allow comparison of the relative efficacy of the different doses, most patients received 200 mg/day and no further improvement in outcome was noted in patients receiving a daily dose exceeding 200 mg. Itraconazole was well tolerated and only one patient had to discontinue therapy because of drug toxicity. When compared with ketoconazole in a similar study design,[133] itraconazole appeared to be better tolerated. Bradsher[139] noted similar success in 42 patients treated with itraconazole at a daily dose of 200 mg. Thus, the recommended initial dose of itraconazole is 200 mg/day, which should effect a cure in most patients with blastomycosis. For patients whose disease persists or progresses, the dose

TABLE 255–3 Treatment Guidelines for Blastomycosis

Type of Disease	Preferred	Alternative
Pulmonary*		
Serious	Amphotericin B, 0.3–0.6 mg/kg/d†	Change to itraconazole after the patient's condition has stabilized
Mild to moderate	Itraconazole, 200–400 mg/d‡	Ketoconazole, 400–800 mg/d or Fluconazole, 400–800 mg/d
Disseminated		
Central nervous system	Amphotericin B, 0.7–1.0 mg/kg/d	For patients unable to tolerate a full course of amphotericin B, consider fluconazole, 800 mg/d
Non–central nervous system		
Serious	Amphotericin B, 0.3–0.6 mg/kg/d	Change to itraconazole after the patient's condition has stabilized
Mild to moderate	Itraconazole, 200–400 mg/d	Ketoconazole, 400–800 mg/d or Fluconazole, 400–800 mg/d

*Some patients with acute pulmonary infection may have a spontaneous cure. Thus, patients with mild pulmonary disease may be monitored closely for resolution. Patients with extrapulmonary disease or progressive pulmonary disease should be treated.

†Some authors recommend higher initial doses of amphotericin B (0.7–1.0 mg/kg/d) for immunocompromised patients and patients with adult respiratory distress syndrome or central nervous system disease. For patients requiring a full course of amphotericin B, a total dose of 1.5 to 2.5 g is associated with the lowest relapse rates.

‡Treatment with an azole should be continued for at least 6 months.

should be increased in increments of 100 mg daily to a maximum daily dose of 400 mg. The optimal duration of therapy has not been determined, but it is recommended that treatment be continued for 6 months. It is my opinion that itraconazole, because of its equal or superior efficacy and lesser toxicity, should replace ketoconazole as the oral azole of choice for patients with blastomycosis.

Several caveats must be considered when using either ketoconazole or itraconazole as therapy. First, gastric acid is necessary for absorption of both agents, and the bioavailability of each drug is enhanced when taken with meals.[140, 141] Patients receiving antacid therapy or H_2 blockers may have subtherapeutic serum levels. Second, rifampin, phenytoin, and carbamazepine have been shown to increase the hepatic metabolism of ketoconazole and itraconazole.[142] The concurrent use of these drugs may result in treatment failure. Third, very little of either agent is excreted in the urine as active drug.[140, 141] It is possible that patients with genitourinary disease may be more resistant to therapy or more likely to have relapses after treatment.[143] Finally, life-threatening ventricular arrhythmias have occurred when either agent was given simultaneously with terfenadine.[144, 145] For a more extensive review of the role of azoles in antifungal therapy, the reader is referred to Chapter 35.

Fluconazole, a triazole that is available in both oral and intravenous preparations, has been used to treat only a small cohort of patients with blastomycosis. It is my opinion that, compared with ketoconazole and itraconazole, fluconazole has a limited role in the treatment of blastomycosis. The results of a pilot study employing lower dose fluconazole were disappointing, with a successful outcome noted in only 65% of the 23 patients treated with daily doses of 200 and 400 mg.[146] A study employing higher doses of fluconazole (400 to 800 mg daily) showed enhanced efficacy.[147] A successful outcome was noted in 87% of the 39 patients treated for a mean of 8.9 months. Adverse events were usually mild. Cessation of therapy owing to an adverse event was necessary in only 1 of 39 patients; a second patient required a dosage reduction. In both patients, however, treatment was successful. These results indicate that fluconazole is similar in efficacy to ketoconazole at equivalent doses but has less serious toxicity. However, fluconazole is not as efficacious as itraconazole for the treatment of patients with mild to moderate blastomycosis. Because fluconazole has excellent penetration into the central nervous system, it may have some role in the treatment of blastomycotic meningitis and cerebral abscesses, although clinical experience in treating these conditions is limited to only a few cases.

Amphotericin B remains the drug of choice for patients who are severely immunocompromised; for patients with life-threatening disease, central nervous system disease, or progression of disease during treatment with an azole; and for those who are unable to tolerate an azole because of toxicity.[120, 134, 135] Although the exact dose and optimal duration of therapy are uncertain, relapse appears to be more common if the total dose is less than 1.5 g. Most researchers, therefore, recommend a total dose of 1.5 to 2.5 g of amphotericin B. For seriously ill patients, 0.3 to 0.6 mg/kg (usually not exceeding 50 mg) should be administered daily until objective evidence of improvement is noted. Some authors recommend higher doses of amphotericin B (0.7 to 1.0 mg/kg/day) as initial therapy for patients with life-threatening disease (such as adult respiratory distress syndrome) or central nervous system disease (Chapman SW, Bradsher RW, Campbell GD, et al, submitted). Patients who are immunocompetent and do not have central nervous system disease have been successfully treated at our medical center by the substitution of itraconazole or ketoconazole in their treatment regimen. For patients who must continue to take amphotericin B, 0.6 to 0.8 mg/kg (usually 50 mg) may be administered thrice weekly or every other day on an outpatient basis.[148] Relapse rates of most patients treated with amphotericin B are less than 5%. Relapse is more common in immunocompromised patients, especially those with AIDS.[119–121] Some authorities recommend long-term suppressive therapy with an azole, and this practice seems prudent.[120, 121] These patients still require close follow-up for relapse of disease, especially in the central nervous system.

Lipid preparations of amphotericin B (Abelcet, Amphocil, AmBisome) have not been adequately evaluated in blastomycosis. Usage should be confined to patients who cannot tolerate conventional amphotericin B.

Apart from diagnosis, surgery has little role in the treatment of blastomycosis.[149, 150] In conjunction with antifungal therapy, surgery appears indicated for the drainage of large abscesses, for the rare patient with large accumulations of empyema fluid or bronchopleural fistula, and for the débridement of devitalized bone tissue in patients with osteomyelitis who are responding poorly to therapy. Unless patients have repeated relapses in the lung or remain culture positive with appropriate therapy, the surgical resection of large or residual lung cavities is not indicated. Although one report implied that surgical resection alone may be curative,[151] the likelihood of relapse must be considered. Furthermore, we have seen patients at my medical center who developed acute, life-threatening disease after surgical resection of lung tissue for diagnostic purposes when blastomycosis was left untreated.[148] Therefore, it is our policy to treat any patient whose resected lung tissue contains *B. dermatitidis* with itraconazole or ketoconazole.

REFERENCES

1. Gilchrist TC. Protozoan dermatitis. J Cutan Gen Dis. 1894;12:496–499.
2. Gilchrist TC. A case of blastomycetic dermatitis in man. Johns Hopkins Hosp Rep. 1896;1:269–283.
3. Gilchrist TC, Stokes WR. The presence of an oidium in the tissues of a case of pseudo-lupus vulgaris. Johns Hopkins Hosp Rep. 1896;7:129–133.
4. Gilchrist TC, Stokes WR. Case of pseudo-lupus vulgaris caused by *Blastomyces*. J Exp Med. 1898;3:53–78.
5. Martin DS, Smith DT. Blastomycosis I: A review of the literature. Am Rev Tuberc. 1939;39:275–304.
6. Martin DS, Smith DT. Blastomycosis II: A report of thirteen new cases. Am Rev Tuberc. 1939;39:488–515.
7. Schwartz J, Baum GL. Blastomycosis. Am J Clin Pathol. 1951;21:999–1029.
8. Kwon-Chung KJ, Bennett JE. Medical Mycology. Philadelphia: Lea & Febiger; 1992:248.
9. Rippon JW. Medical Mycology: The Pathogenic Fungi and Pathogenic Actinomycetes. 3rd ed. Philadelphia: WB Saunders; 1988:474.
10. Medoff G, Painter A, Kobayashi GS. Mycelial-to-yeast-phase transitions of the dimorphic fungi *Blastomyces dermatitidis* and *Paracoccidioides brasiliensis*. J Bacteriol. 1987;169:4055–4060.
11. Kaufman L, Standard PG, Weeks RJ, et al. Detection of two *Blastomyces dermatitidis* serotypes by exoantigen analysis. J Clin Microbiol. 1983;18:110–114.
12. Turner S, Kaufman L. Immunodiagnosis of blastomycosis. Semin Respir Infect. 1986;1:22–28.
13. McDonough ES, Lewis AL. *Blastomyces dermatitidis*: Production of the sexual state. Science. 1967;156:528–529.
14. McDonough ES, Lewis AL. The ascigerous state of *Blastomyces dermatitidis*. Mycologia. 1968;60:76–83.
15. McDonough ES, McNamara WJ, Chan DM, et al. Geographic distribution of "+" and "−" isolates of *Blastomyces (Ajellomyces) dermatitidis* in North America. Am J Epidemiol. 1973;98:63–67.
16. Blastomycosis Cooperative Study of the Veterans Administration. Blastomycosis I: A review of 198 collected cases in Veterans Administration Hospitals. Am Rev Respir Dis. 1964;89:659–672.
17. Menges RW, Doto IL, Weeks RJ. Epidemiologic studies of blastomycosis in Arkansas. Arch Environ Health. 1969;18:956–971.
18. Furcolow ML, Chick EW, Busey JF, et al. Prevalence and incidence studies of human and canine blastomycosis I: Cases in the United States, 1885–1968. Am Rev Respir Dis. 1970;102:60–67.
19. Furcolow ML, Busey JF, Menges RW, et al. Prevalence and incidence studies of human and canine blastomycosis II: Yearly incidence studies in three selected states, 1960–1967. Am J Epidemiol. 1970;92:121–131.
20. Sekshon AS, Borgorus MS, Sims HV. Blastomycosis: Report of three cases from Alberta with a review of Canadian cases. Mycopathologia. 1979;1:53–63.
21. Klein BS, Vergeront JM, Davis JP. Epidemiologic aspects of blastomycosis, the enigmatic systemic mycosis. Semin Respir Infect. 1986;1:29–39.
22. Smith JD Jr, Harris JS, Conant NF, et al. An epidemic of North American blastomycosis. JAMA. 1955;158:641–646.
23. Tosh FE, Hammerman KJ, Weeks RJ, et al. A common source epidemic of North American blastomycosis. Am Rev Respir Dis. 1974;109:525–529.
24. United States Department of Health, Education and Welfare, Public Health Service, Centers for Disease Control and Prevention. Blastomycosis: North Carolina. MMWR Morb Mortal Wkly Rep. 1976;25:205–206.
25. Kitchen MS, Reiber CD, Eastin GB. An urban epidemic of North American blastomycosis. Am Rev Respir Dis. 1977;115:1063–1066.

26. Cockerill FR III, Roberts GD, Rosenblatt JE, et al. Epidemic of pulmonary blastomycosis (Nanekagan fever) in Wisconsin canoeists. Chest. 1984; 86:688–692.
27. Armstrong CW, Jenkins SR, Kaufman L, et al. Common source outbreak of blastomycosis in hunters and their dogs. J Infect Dis. 1987;155:568–570.
28. Klein BS, Vergeront JM, Weeks RJ, et al. Isolation of *Blastomyces dermatitidis* in soil associated with a large outbreak of blastomycosis in Wisconsin. N Engl J Med. 1986;314:529–534.
29. Klein BS, Vergeront JM, DiSalvo AF, et al. Two outbreaks of blastomycosis along rivers in Wisconsin: Isolation of *Blastomyces dermatitidis* from riverbank soil and evidence of its transmission along waterways. Am Rev Respir Dis. 1987;136:1333–1338.
30. Baumgardner DJ, Burdick JS. An outbreak of human and canine blastomycosis. Rev Infect Dis. 1991;13:898–905.
31. Frye MD, Seifer FD. An outbreak of blastomycosis in eastern Tennessee. Mycopathologia. 1991;116:15–21.
32. Baily GG, Robertson VJ, Neill P, et al. Blastomycosis in Africa: Clinical features, diagnosis and treatment. Rev Infect Dis. 1991;13:1005–1008.
33. DiSalvo AF. The ecology of *Blastomyces dermatitidis*. In: Al-Doory Y, DiSalvo AF, eds. Blastomycosis. New York: Plenum; 1992:43.
34. Denton JF, McDonough ES, Ajello L, et al. Isolation of *Blastomyces dermatitidis* from soil. Science. 1961;133:1126–1127.
35. Denton JF, Disalvo AF. Isolation of *Blastomyces dermatitidis* from natural sites in Augusta, Georgia. Am J Trop Med Hyg. 1964;13:716–722.
36. Denton JF, Disalvo AF. Additional isolations of *Blastomyces dermatitidis* from natural sites. Am J Trop Med Hyg. 1979;28:697–700.
37. Sarosi GA, Serstock DA. Isolation of *Blastomyces dermatitidis* from pigeon manure. Am Rev Respir Dis. 1976;114:1179–1183.
38. Bakerspigel A, Kane J, Schaus D. Isolation of *Blastomyces dermatitidis* from an earthen floor in southwestern Ontario, Canada. J Clin Microbiol. 1986;24:890–891.
39. Dixon DM, Shadomy HJ, Shadomy S. In vitro growth and sporulation of *Blastomyces dermatitidis* on woody plant material. Mycologia. 1977;69:1193–1195.
40. Larson DM, Eckman MR, Alber RL, et al. Primary cutaneous (inoculation) blastomycosis: An occupational hazard to pathologists. Am J Clin Pathol. 1983;79:253–255.
41. Gnann JW Jr, Bressler GS, Bodet CA, et al. Human blastomycosis after a dog bite. Ann Intern Med. 1983;98:48–49.
42. Craig MW, Davey WN, Green RA. Conjugal blastomycosis. Am Rev Respir Dis. 1970;102:86–90.
43. Watts EA, Gard PD Jr, Tuthill SW. First reported case of intrauterine transmission of blastomycosis. Pediatr Infect Dis. 1983;2:308–310.
44. Maxson S, Miller SF, Tryka AF, et al. Perinatal blastomycosis: a review. Pediatr Infect Dis. 1992;11:760–763.
45. Daniel WP, Danaar SC, Perry HD. Blastomycosis-like pyoderma. Arch Dermatol. 1979;115:170–173.
46. Reder PA, Neel HB III. Blastomycosis in otolaryngology: Review of a large series. Laryngoscope. 1993;103:53–58.
47. Vaaler AK, Bradsher RW, Davies SF. Evidence of subclinical blastomycosts in forestry workers in northern Minnesota and northern Wisconsin. Am J Med. 1990;89:470–476.
48. Sugar AM, Picard M. Macrophage- and oxidant-mediated inhibition of the ability of live *Blastomyces dermatitidis* conidia to transform to the pathogenic yeast phase: Implications for the pathogenesis of dimorphic fungal infections. J Infect Dis. 1991;163:371–375.
49. DiSalvo AF, Denton JF. Lipid content of four strains of *Blastomyces dermatitidis* of different mouse virulence. J Bacteriol. 1963;85:927–931.
50. Cox RA, Best GK. Cell wall composition of two strains of *Blastomyces dermatitidis* exhibiting differences in virulence for mice. Infect Immun. 1972;5:449–453.
51. Klein BS, Jones JM. Isolation, purification, and radiolabeling of a novel 120-kD surface protein on *Blastomyces dermatitidis* yeasts to detect antibody in infected patients. J Clin Invest. 1990;85:152–161.
52. Klein BS, Sondel PM, Jones JM. WI-1, a novel 120-kilodalton surface protein on *Blastomyces dermatitidis* yeast cells, is a target antigen of cell-mediated immunity in human blastomycosis. Infect Immun. 1992;60:4291–4300.
53. Klein BS, Hogan LH, Jones JM. Immunologic recognition of a 25-amino acid repeat arrayed in tandem on a major antigen of *Blastomyces dermatitidis*. J Clin Invest. 1993;92:330–337.
54. Newman Sl, Chaturvedi S, Klein BS. The WI-1 antigen of *Blastomyces dermatitidis* yeast mediates binding to human macrophage CD11b/CD18 (CR3) and CD14. J Immunol. 1995;154:753–761.
55. Hogan LH, Josvai S, Klein BS. Cenomic cloning, characterization and functional analysis of the major surface adhesin WI-1 on *Blastomyces dermatitidis* yeasts. J Biol Chem. 1995;270:30725–30732.
56. Klein BS, Chaturvedi S, Hogan LH, et al. Altered expression of surface protein WI-1 in genetically related strains of *Blastomyces dermatitidis* that differ in virulence regulates recognition of yeasts by human macrophages. Infect Immun. 1994;62:3536–3542.
57. Hogan LH, Klein BS. Altered expression of surface α-1,3-glucan in genetically related strains of *Blastomyces dermatitidis* that differ in virulence. Infect Immun. 1994;62:3543–3546.
58. Klein BS, Newman SL. Role of cell-surface molecules of *Blastomyces dermatitidis* in host-pathogen interactions. Trends Microbiol. 1996;4:246–251.
59. Thurmond LM, Mitchell TG. *Blastomyces dermatitidis* chemotactic factor: Kinetics of production and biological characterization evaluated by a modified chemotaxis assay. Infect Immun. 1984;46:87–93.
60. Drutz DJ, Frey CL. Intracellular and extracellular defenses against *Blastomyces dermatitidis* conidia and yeasts. J Lab Clin Med. 1985;105:737–750.
61. Schaffner A, Davis CE, Schaffner T, et al. In vitro susceptibility of fungi to killing by neutrophil granulocytes discriminates between primary pathogenicity and opportunism. J Clin Invest. 1986;78:511–524.
62. Brummer E, Kurita N, Yoshida K, et al. A basis for resistance of *Blastomyces dermatitidis* killing by human neutrophils: Inefficient generation of myeloperoxidase system products. J Med Vet Mycol. 1992;30:233–243.
63. Brummer E, Stevens DA. Activation of murine polymorphonuclear neutrophils for fungicidal activity with supernatants from antigen-stimulated immune spleen cell cultures. Infect Immun. 1984;45:447–452.
64. Morrison CJ, Brummer E, Isenberg RA, et al. Activation of murine polymorphonuclear neutrophils for fungicidal activity by recombinant gamma interferon. J Leukoc Biol. 1987;41:434–440.
65. Cozad GC, Chang C. T-cell mediated immunoprotection in blastomycosis. Infect Immun. 1980;78:393–403.
66. Morozumi PA, Brummer E, Stevens DA. Protection against pulmonary blastomycosis. Infect Immun. 1982;37:670–678.
67. Brummer E, Morozumi PA, Vo PT, et al. Protection against pulmonary blastomycosis: Adaptive transfer with T lymphocytes, but not serum, from resistant mice. Cell Immunol. 1982;73:349–359.
68. Brummer E, Morozumi A, Philpott DE, et al. Virulence of fungi: Correlation of virulence of *Blastomyces dermatitidis* in vivo with escape from macrophage inhibition of replication in vitro. Infect Immunol. 1981;32:864–871.
69. Brummer E, Hanson LH, Restrepo A, et al. In vivo and in vitro activation of pulmonary macrophages by IFN-γ for enhanced killing of *Paracoccidioides brasiliensis* or *Blastomyces dermatitidis*. J Immunol. 1988;140:2786–2789.
70. Brummer E, Hanson LH, Stevens DA. Kinetics and requirements for activation of macrophages for fungicidal activity: Effect of protein synthesis inhibitors and immunosuppressants on activation and fungicidal mechanisms. Cell Immunol. 1991;132:236–245.
71. Bradsher RW. Live *Blastomyces dermatitidis* yeast-induced responses of immune and non-immune human mononuclear cells. Mycopathologia. 1984;87:159–166.
72. Klein PS, Bradsher RW, Vergeront JM, et al. Development of long-term specific cellular immunity after acute *Blastomyces dermatitidis* infection: Assessments following a large point-source outbreak in Wisconsin. J Infect Dis. 1990;161:97–101.
73. Bradsher RW, Balk RA, Jacobs RF. Growth inhibition of *Blastomyces dermatitidis* in alveolar and peripheral macrophages from patients with blastomycosis. Am Rev Respir Dis. 1987;135:412–417.
74. Kaufman L, McLaughlin DW, Clark MJ, et al. Specific immunodiffusion test for blastomycosis. Appl Microbiol. 1973;26:244–247.
75. Williams JE, Murphy R, Standard PG, et al. Serologic response in blastomycosis: Diagnostic value of double immunodiffusion assay. Am Rev Respir Dis. 1981;123:209–212.
76. Klein BS, Kuritsky WAC, Kaufman L, et al. Comparison of enzyme immunoassay, immunodiffusion and complement fixation in detecting antibody in human serum to the A antigen in *B. dermatitidis*. Am Rev Respir Dis. 1986;133:144–148.
77. Klein BS, Vergeront JM, Kaufman L, et al. Serological test for blastomycosis: Assessments during a large point-source outbreak in Wisconsin. J Infect Dis. 1987;155:262–268.
78. Bradsher RW, Pappas PG. Detection of specific antibodies in human blastomycosis by enzyme immunoassay. South Med J. 1995;88:1256–1259.
79. Sekhorn AS, Kaufman L, Kobayashi AS, et al. The value of the Premier enzyme immunoassay for diagnosing *Blastomyces dermatitidis* intections. J Med Vet Mycol. 1995;33:123–125.
80. Klein BS, Jones JM. Purification and characterization of the major WI-1 from *Blastomyces dermatitidis* yeast and immunological comparison with A antigen. Infect Immun. 1994;62:3890–3900.
81. Soufleris AJ, Klein BS, Courtney BT, et al. Utility of anti–WI-1 serological testing in the diagnosis of blastomycosis in Wisconsin residents. Clin Infect Dis. 1994;19:87–92.
82. Cherniss EI, Waisbren BA. North American blastomycosis: A clinical study of 40 cases. Ann Intern Med. 1956;44:105–123.
83. Abernathy RS. Clinical manifestations of pulmonary blastomycosis. Ann Intern Med. 1959;51:707–727.
84. Witorsch P, Utz JP. North American blastomycosis: A study of 40 patients. Medicine (Baltimore). 1968;47:169–200.
85. Lockwood WR, Allison F, Batson BE, et al. The treatment of North American blastomycosis: Ten years experience. Am Rev Respir Dis. 1969;100:314–320.
86. Duttera MJ, Osterhout S. North American blastomycosis: A survey of 63 cases. South Med J. 1969;62:295–301.
87. Busey JF, Veterans Administrative Cooperative Group. Blastomycosis: III. A comparative study of 2-hydroxystilbamidine and amphotericin B therapy. Am Rev Respir Dis. 1972;105:812–818.
88. Bradsher RW, Rice DC, Abernathy RS. Ketoconazole therapy for endemic blastomycosis. Ann Intern Med. 1985;103:872–879.
89. Baumgardner DJ, Buggy BP, Mattson BJ, et al. Epidemiology of blastomycosis in a region of high endemicity in north central Wisconsin. Clin Infect Dis. 1992;15:629–635.
90. Chapman SW, Lin AC, Hendricks KA, et al. Endomic blastomycosis in Mississippi: Epidemiological and clinical studies. Semin Respir Infect. 1997;12:219–228.
91. Sarosi GA, Davies SF. Blastomycosis. Am Rev Respir Dis. 1979;120:911–938.
92. Ehni W. Endogenous reactivation in blastomycosis. Am J Med. 1989;86:831–832.

93. Sheflin JR, Campbell JA, Thompson GP. Pulmonary blastomycosis: Findings on chest radiographs in 63 patients. AJR. 1990;154:1177–1180.
94. Brown LR, Sweasen SJ, VanScoy RE, et al. Roentgenologic features of pulmonary blastomycosis. Mayo Clin Proc. 1991;66:29–38.
95. Sarosi GA, Davies SF, Phillips JR. Self-limited blastomycosis: A report of 39 cases. Semin Respir Infect. 1986;1:40–44.
96. Sarosi GA, Hammerman KJ, Tosh FE, et al. Clinical features of acute pulmonary blastomycosis. N Engl J Med. 1974;290:540–543.
97. Baum GL, Lerner PI. Primary pulmonary blastomycosis. A laboratory acquired infection. Ann Intern Med. 1970;73:263–265.
98. Poe RH, Vassallo CL, Plessinger VA, et al. Pulmonary blastomycosis versus carcinoma. A challenging differential. Am J Med Sci. 1972;263:145–155.
99. Stelling CB, Woodring JH, Rehm SR, et al. Miliary pulmonary blastomycosis. Radiology. 1984;150:7–13.
100. Meyer KC, McManus EJ, Maki DG. Overwhelming pulmonary blastomycosis associated with the adult respiratory distress syndrome. N Engl J Med. 1993;329:1231–1236.
101. Kinasewitz GT, Penn RL, George RB. The spectrum and significance of pleural disease in blastomycosis. Chest. 1984;86:580–584.
102. Mercurio MG, Elewski BE. Cutaneous blastomycosis. Cutis. 1992;50:422–424.
103. MacDonald PB, Black GB, MacKenzie R. Orthopaedic manifestations of blastomycosis. J Bone Joint Surg [Am]. 1990;72:860–864.
104. Guler N, Palanduz A, Ones U, et al. Progressive vertebral blastomycosis mimicking tuberculosis. Pediatr Infect Dis J. 1995; 14:816–818.
105. Bayer AS, Scott VJ, Guze LB. Fungal arthritis IV. Blastomycotic arthritis. Semin Arthritis Rheum. 1979;9:145–151.
106. Eikenberg HA, Amin M, Lich RJ. Blastomycosis of the genitourinary tract. J Urol. 1975;113:650–652.
107. Pappas PG, Pottage JC, Powderly WG, et al. Blastomycosis in patients with acquired immunodeficiency syndrome. Ann Intern Med. 1992;116:847–853.
108. Gonyea EF. The spectrum of primary blastomycotic meningitis. A review of central nervous system blastomycosis. Ann Neurol. 1978;3:26–39.
109. Kravitz GR, Davies SF, Eckman MR, et al. Chronic blastomycotic meningitis. Am J Med. 1981;71:501–505.
110. Roos KL, Bryan JP, Maggio WW, et al. Intracranial blastomycoma. Medicine (Baltimore). 1987;66:224–235.
111. Ward BA, Parent AD, Raila F. Indications for the surgical management of central nervous system blastomycosis. Surg Neuol. 1995;43:379–388.
112. Laskey WK, Sarosi GA. Blastomycosis in children. Pediatrics. 1980;65:111–114.
113. Steele RW, Abernathy RS. Systemic blastomycosis in children. Pediatr Infect Dis. 1983;2:304–307.
114. Alkrinawi S, Reed MH, Pasterkamp H. Pulmonary blastomycosis in children: Findings on chest radiographs. AJR. 1995;165:651–654.
115. Schutze GE, Hickerson SL, Fortin EM, et al. Blastomycosis in children. Clin Infect Dis. 1996;22:496–502.
116. Ismail MA, Lerner SA. Disseminated blastomycosis in a pregnant woman: Review of amphotericin B usage in pregnancy. Am Rev Respir Dis. 1982;126:350–353.
117. MacDonald D, Alguire PC. Adult respiratory distress syndrome due to blastomycosis during pregnancy. Chest. 1990;98:1527–1528.
118. Recht AD, Davies SF, Eckman MR. Blastomycosis in immunosuppressed patients. Am Rev Respir Dis. 1982;125:359–362.
119. Serody JS, Mill MR, Detterbeck FC, et al. Blastomycosis in transplant recipients: Report of a case and review. Clin Infect Dis. 1993;16:54–58.
120. Pappas PG, Threlkeld MG, Bedsole GD, et al. Blastomycosis in immunocompromised patients. Medicine (Baltimore). 1993;72:311–325.
121. Wheat J. Endemic mycoses in AIDS: a clinical review. Clin Microbiol Rev. 1995;8:146–159.
122. Lemos LB, Baliga M, Taylor BD, et al. Bronchoalveolar lavage for diagnosis of fungal disease: Five years experience in a southern United States rural area with many blastomycosis cases. Acta Cytol. 1995;39:1101–1011.
123. Graham AR. Fungal autofluorescence with ultraviolet illumination. Am J Clin Pathol. 1983;79:231–234.
124. Monheit JG, Cowman DF, Moore DG. Rapid detection of fungi in tissues using calcofluor white and fluorescence microscopy. Arch Pathol Lab Med. 1984;108:616–618.
125. Kaplan W, Kaufman L. Specific fluorescent antiglobulins for the detection and identification of *Blastomyces dermatitidis* yeast phase cells. Mycopathologia. 1963;19:173–180.
126. Stockman L, Clark MA, Hunt JM, et al. Evaluation of commercially available acridine ester–labeled chemiluminescent DNA probes for culture identification of *Blastomyces dermatitidis*, *Coccidioides immitis*, *Cryptococcus neoformans* and *Histoplasma capsulatum*. J Clin Microbiol. 1993;31:845–850.
127. George RB, Lambert RS, Bruce MJ, et al. Radioimmunoassay: A sensitive screening test for histoplasmosis and blastomycosis. Am Rev Respir Dis. 1981;124:407–410.
128. Lambert RS, George RB. Evaluation of enzyme immunoassay as a rapid screening test for histoplasmosis and blastomycosis. Am Rev Respir Dis. 1987;136:316–319.
129. Turner SH, Kaufman L, Jalbert M. Diagnostic assessment of an enzyme-linked immunosorbent assay for human and canine blastomycosis. J Clin Microbiol. 1986;23:294–297.
130. Lagging LM, Breland CM, Kennedy DJ, et al. Delayed treatment of pulmonary blastomycosis causing vertical osteomyelitis, paraspinal abscess and spinal cord compression. Scand J Infect Dis. 1994;26:111–115.
131. Sarosi GA. Management of fungal disease. Am Rev Respir Dis. 1983;127:250–253.
132. Rose HD, Varkey B. Miconazole treatment of relapsed pulmonary blastomycosis. Am Rev Respir Dis. 1978;118:403–408.
133. National Institute of Allergy and Infectious Diseases Study Group. Treatment of blastomycosis and histoplasmosis with ketoconazole: Results of a prospective randomized trial. Ann Intern Med. 1985;103:861–872.
134. Sagg MS, Dismukes WE. Treatment of histoplasmosis and blastomycosis. Chest. 1988;93:848–851.
135. Johnson P, Sarosi G. Current therapy of major fungal diseases of the lung. Infect Dis Clin North Am. 1991;5:635–645.
136. Brummer E, Bhagavathula PR, Hanson LH, et al. Synergy of itraconazole with macrophages in killing *Blastomyces dermatitidis*. Antimicrob Agents Chemother. 1992;36:2487–2492.
137. Chapman SW, Rogers PD, Rinaldi MG, et al. Susceptibilities of clinical and laboratory isolates of *Blastomyces dermatitidis* to ketoconazole, itraconazole and fluconazole. Antimicrob Agents Chemother. 1998;42:978–980.
138. Dismukes WE, Bradsher RW, Cloud GC, et al. Itraconazole therapy for blastomycosis and histoplasmosis. Am J Med. 1992;93:489–497.
139. Bradsher RW. Histoplasmosis and blastomycosis. Clin Infect Dis. 1996;22:5102–5111.
140. Daneshmend TK, Warnock DW. Clinical pharmacokinetics of ketoconazole. Clin Pharmacokinet. 1988;14:13–34.
141. Cleary JD, Taylor JW, Chapman SW. Itraconazole in antifungal therapy. Ann Pharmacother. 1992;26:502–509.
142. Tucker RM, Denning DW, Hanson LH, et al. Interactions of azoles with rifampin, phenytoin, and carbamazepin: In vitro and clinical observations. Clin Infect Dis. 1992;14:165–174.
143. Wise GJ, Goldberg PE, Kozinin PJ. Do the imidazoles have a role in the management of genitourinary fungal infections? J Urol. 1985;133:61–64.
144. Honig PK, Wortham DC, Zamani K, et al. Terfenadine-ketoconazole interaction: Pharmacokinetic and electrocardiographic consequences. JAMA 1992;269:1513–1518.
145. Itraconazole. Med Lett Drugs Ther. 1993;35:7–9.
146. Pappas PG, Bradsher RW, Chapman SW, et al. Treatment of blastomycosis with fluconazole: A pilot study. Clin Infect Dis. 1995;20:267–271.
147. Pappas PG, Bradsher RW, Kaufman CA, et al. Treatment of blastomycosis with higher dose fluconazole. Clin Infect Dis. 1997;25:200–205.
148. Campbell GD, Chapman SW. Blastomycosis. Semin Respir Med. 1987;9:164–170.
149. Hammon JW, Prager RL. Surgical management of fungal diseases of the chest. Surg Clin North Am. 1980;60:897–912.
150. Newsom BD, Hardy JD. Pulmonary fungal infections: Survey of 159 cases with surgical implications. J Thorac Cardiovasc Surg. 1982;83:218–226.
151. Edson RS, Keys TF. Treatment of primary pulmonary blastomycosis: Results of long-term follow-up. Mayo Clin Proc. 1981;56:683–685.

Chapter 256

Coccidioides immitis

JOHN GALGIANI

Although the systemic fungal infection now known as coccidioidomycosis has been recognized for more than a century,[1] in the past decade its importance has increased throughout the nonendemic as well as the endemic regions of the world.[2, 3] A medical intern is credited with identifying in 1892 the first patient who had widespread disease.[4] Organisms seen microscopically were mistakenly thought to be parasites, and only several years later was its true mycotic etiology determined and the agent given the name *Coccidioides immitis*.[5] For 3 decades, coccidioidomycosis was thought to be a rare and nearly always fatal infection. However, in 1929 an accidental laboratory exposure of a medical student at Stanford University resulted in only a transient respiratory infection. His unexpected survival stimulated a reassessment of the natural history of coccidioidal infections, soon leading to the recognition that a common respiratory condition in the San Joaquin Valley of California ("valley fever") was the more usual result of infection.[6] This link was corroborated with the development by Charles E. Smith of a specific skin test and serologic assays for coccidioidomycosis,[7] tests still in clinical use to this day. With these tools the clinical spectrum was well described by the mid-1950s (an excellent monograph was published by Fiese[8] and remains a valuable contemporary reference on the disease).

That coccidioidomycosis is now a reemerging disease can be attributed to changes both in demography and in contemporary medicine. First, the populations at risk of exposure are greatly expanded. Regions in which *C. immitis* is endemic, which were previously sparsely populated, now encompass major metropolitan centers such as Phoenix, Arizona. With this growth has also come greatly increased tourism and movement of persons into and out of infected areas. As a result, coccidioidal infections occur in increased numbers. Second, there has emerged a major segment of the population with compromised cellular immunity because of either underlying diseases or immunosuppressive therapies to control other diseases.[9–20] Such patients are unusually susceptible to serious coccidioidal infections, and as a result the severity of coccidioidal infections as a public health problem has increased. Finally, advances in prevention and treatment of fungal infections have been made in the past two decades that offer new opportunities for management. These trends have made coccidioidomycosis more relevant to physicians everywhere.

MYCOLOGY

C. immitis is a dimorphic fungus that exists as either a mycelium or a unique structure known as a spherule.[21] Both forms of growth are asexual, and therefore it is not possible to classify *C. immitis* in relation to other fungi by classic taxonomy, which is based on the characteristics of sexual spores. However, by molecular analysis *C. immitis* appears most related to other ascomycetes, most closely to the medically important *Blastomyces dermatitidis* and *Histoplasma capsulatum*.[22] Moreover, population genetic studies suggest that a sexual phase does indeed exist and therefore may be identified in the future.[23]

Mycelial (Saprobic) Growth. On routine microbiologic nutrient agar media and presumably in the soil, *C. immitis* grows as mycelia by apical extension. Its wall contains both α-1,3-glucan and chitin, and true septa form along its course.[24] Maturation within a week of growth results in alternating mycelial cells undergoing a process of autolysis and thinning of their cell walls. The remaining cells (arthroconidia), which become barrel shaped and approximately 5 μm in length, develop a hydrophobic outer layer and become capable of remaining viable for long periods. Furthermore, the fragile attachments of arthroconidia to adjacent cell remnants make them prone to separation by physical disruption or even mild air turbulence. As a result, arthroconidia become airborne in a form capable of deposition in the lungs if inhaled.

Spherule (Parasitic) Growth. In the lungs, arthroconidia remodel into spherical cells, shedding their hydrophobic outer wall.[25] During this phase, nuclear division and cell multiplication occur and septa extend from the internal surface of the wall to transect the growing spherule into scores of subcompartments, each containing viable daughter cells or endospores. In tissue, spherules can become as large as 75 μm in diameter (Fig. 256–1). As a spherule matures, its outer wall thins and eventually ruptures to release its viable endospores to continue propagation in tissue or to revert to mycelial growth if removed from the site of an infection.

EPIDEMIOLOGY

Geographic Range. *C. immitis* is endemic to the soils of only certain regions of the Western Hemisphere, nearly all of which are within the north and south 40-degree latitudes. Well-described transport of arthroconidia, either in soil on fomites[26] or as the result of unusually severe dust storms,[27] has produced infections in persons without endemic exposure, but *C. immitis* has not established new areas of endemicity. Regions of the United States in which *C. immitis* is endemic are shown in Figure 256–2. These regions generally have the characteristics of the "lower Sonoran life zone," which include an arid climate, yearly rainfall of 5 to 20 inches, hot summers, winters with few freezes, and alkaline soil. Other areas where *C. immitis* has been identified include Mexico (adjacent to the U.S. border; western portions of Sonora, Nayarit, Jalisco, and Michoacan; central regions including Coahulia, Durango, and San Luis Potosi), Central America (Guatemala; Honduras; Nicaragua), and South America (Argentina; Paraguay; Venezuela; Colombia).

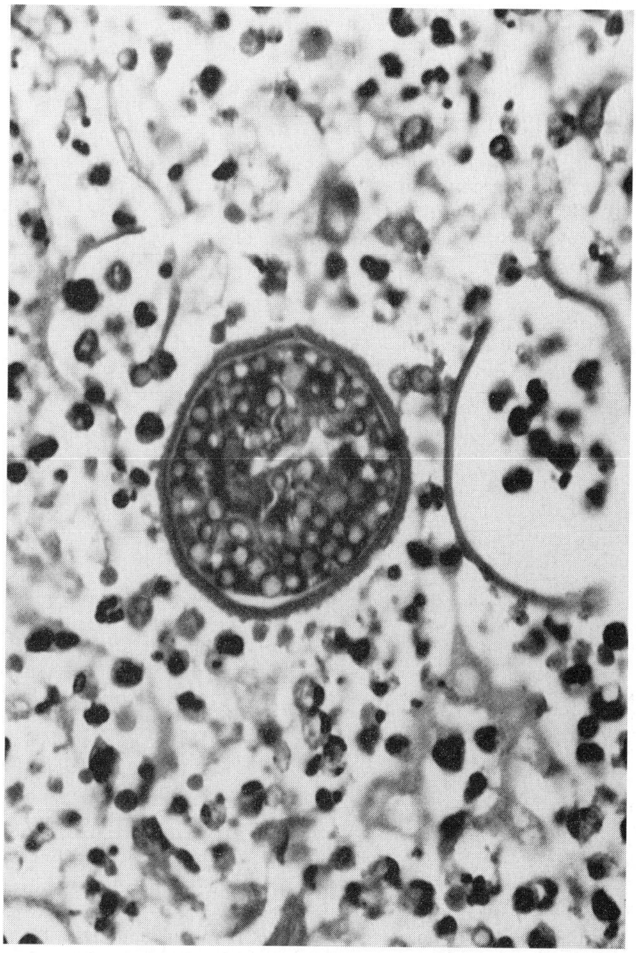

FIGURE 256–1. Photomicrograph of a spherule in tissue. Hematoxylin and eosin staining. (Courtesy of Richard Sobonya, M.D., University of Arizona.)

Within the endemic regions, the likelihood of finding *C. immitis* in soil samples varies considerably among different locations and different seasons. The fungus is most easily recovered toward the end of winter rains.[28] Of interest, this is opposite to the seasonal relationship for acquisition of new infections, which in both California and Arizona occur most frequently during the summer months after the soil has become dry. In Arizona, there is a second peak of new clinical infections in October, which corresponds to a similar dry period after the late summer rains in that region.[29]

Rates of Coccidioidal Infection. Prevalence surveys in the 1950s of skin test reactivity to coccidioidal antigens in school-aged children of California's central valley suggested that the annual risk of infection was approximately 15%. Smith and coworkers[30] also demonstrated that 25 to 50% of military personnel in the San Joaquin valley experienced conversion of their coccidioidal skin during a single year. More contemporary estimates from the same areas in California as well as from Tucson, Arizona, indicate that the risk has declined to approximately 3% per year.[31] Because of these lower rates and because of the large influx of new residents to the endemic regions from nonendemic locales (in the year 2000 estimated to total

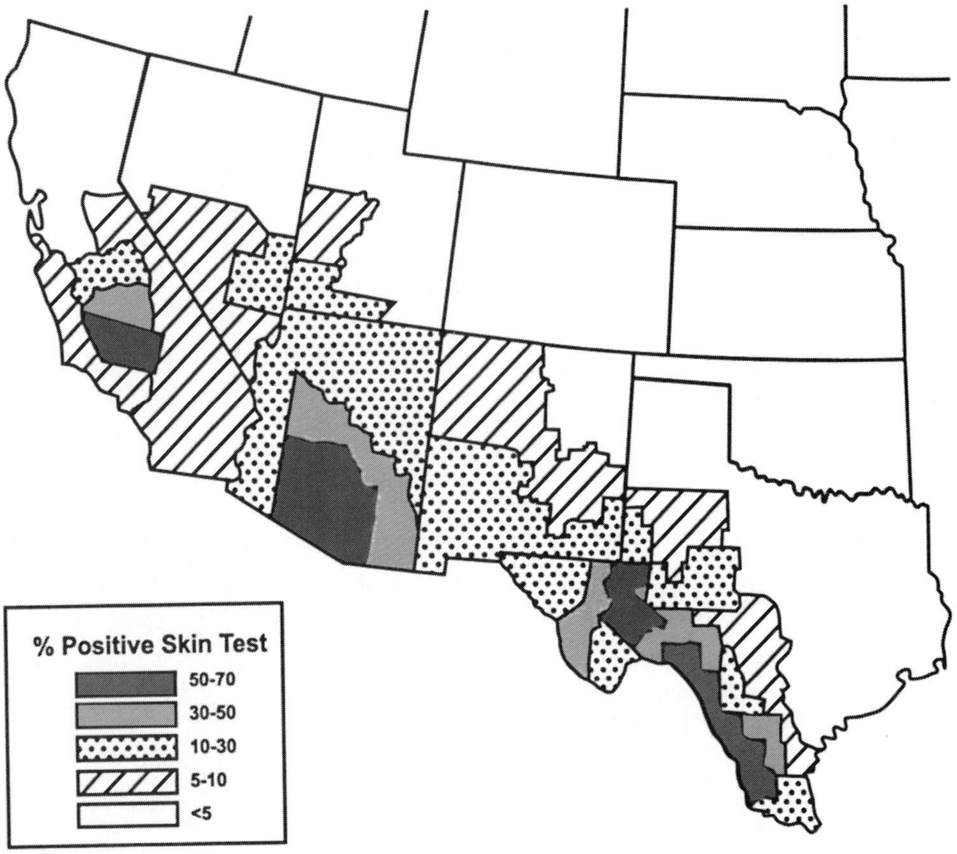

FIGURE 256–2. Map of the United States regions endemic for coccidioidomycosis as evidenced by a survey of skin test reactivity to coccidioidin. (From Edwards PQ, Palmer CE. Prevalence of sensitivity to coccidioidin, with special reference to specific and nonspecific reactions to coccidioidin and to histoplasmin. Dis Chest. 1957;31:35–60.)

more than 4.5 million persons for southern Arizona and the southern central valley of California), the proportion of persons within the endemic region with prior infection is approximately 30%. Thus, the expected number of infections is on the order of 100,000 annually.

The numbers of infections reported to state departments of public health show significant differences from year to year. Some variation has been associated with total winter rainfall, with more cases occurring in the summers after wetter winters. Occasionally, epidemics have also been associated with disruption of infected soil, either by human intent such as with archeologic excavation[32] or after natural events such as severe dust storms or earthquakes.[33] However, some fluctuations in rates of infections are not explained. Such is the case for an exceptionally large epidemic in California's Central Valley in the period 1992 to 1995, in which the incidence of infection at times was more than 10 times that normally reported.[34]

PATHOGENESIS AND CONTROL

Nearly all infections are the result of inhaling arthroconidia. Cutaneous inoculations have been reported, producing lymphatic extension to regional lymph nodes and resolving without treatment. However, such occurrences are exceedingly rare.[35] A single arthroconidium may be sufficient to produce a naturally acquired respiratory infection. This is certainly the case for experimental infections in mice,[36] and air sampling within coccidioidal endemic regions suggests that the ambient density of arthroconidia in the air is very low.[37, 38] The size of the arthroconidium would allow it to be deposited within the terminal bronchiole but probably not to reach the alveolar space directly. As an arthroconidium transforms into a spherule, inflammation ensues, forming a local pulmonary lesion. Extracts of *C. immitis* have been shown to react with complement, releasing mediators of chemotaxis for neutrophils.[39] In some infections, *C. immitis* leaves the lungs to establish disseminated lesions in other parts of the body. Clearly, in this sequence of events, fungal elements must somehow move from the distal bronchiole into the lung parenchyma, gain entry into the vascular space, and leave the vascular space to create extrapulmonary sites of infection. It is possible that endospores within macrophages travel through lymphatics to the blood stream, as has been described for dissemination of tuberculosis and histoplasmosis. This is also compatible with the common finding of infected hilar, peritracheal, and cervical lymph nodes in patients with extrapulmonary coccidioidal infections.[40] However, specific details of any of these events are unknown.

Histopathology. Microscopic examination of tissue infected with *C. immitis* demonstrates elements of both acute and chronic inflammation. Acute inflammation, including neutrophils and eosinophils, is associated with active infections and rupturing spherules.[40, 41] On the other hand, granulomatous lesions that include lymphocytes, histiocytes, and multinucleated giant cells are associated with chronic or arrested infections and with mature unruptured spherules. In patients with widespread infections, it is not uncommon to find both inflammatory responses represented concurrently at different anatomic sites.

Host Defenses. Control of coccidioidomycosis is critically dependent on T lymphocytes. This conclusion is supported both by studies of experimentally produced infections in mice[42–46] and by the increased severity of naturally acquired infections in T-cell–deficient patients.[10–20] Peripheral blood mononuclear cells from patients with disseminated coccidioidomycosis have virtually no interferon-γ response to coccidioidal antigens.[47] This is in contrast to the brisk stimulation of similar leukocyte preparations from persons in whom coccidioidal infections are competently controlled and who have delayed-type dermal hypersensitivity to coccidioidal skin-testing antigens.[48] This is consistent with an absent Th1-type response described in some experimental animal[49–51] and human infectious diseases in which cellular immunity plays a role. However, in humans, despite the observed depression of interferon-γ, interleukin-4 and interleukin-10 levels were not reciprocally elevated,[48] which would be indicative of a Th2 response.

In addition to T-cell–mediated control of infection, innate cellular responses may contribute to host defense. Inhibition of growth of *C. immitis* can be demonstrated in vitro by human neutrophils and mononuclear cells from persons with or without prior coccidioidal infection as judged by skin test reactivity to coccidioidal antigens.[52] Although neutrophils do not appear to be fungicidal against *C. immitis*, mononuclear cells or natural killer cells have been demonstrated to reduce fungal viability.[53, 54] These innate cellular inhibitory effects are most evident against arthroconidia or endospores and are lost as spherules increase in size and mature.[55] Extrapolating from these in vitro observations, innate defenses may serve primarily to slow fungal proliferation after infection, thus transforming what otherwise might be a more fulminant infection to a more subacute or chronic process.

Coccidioidal infections engender a variety of humoral responses to several different antigens in patients, and, as discussed subsequently, several are diagnostically useful. However, none have thus far been found to play a role in host defenses against *C. immitis*.

CLINICAL MANIFESTATIONS

At least one half to two thirds of all infections due to *C. immitis* are either inapparent or sufficiently mild not to prompt medical evaluation.[30] Many other coccidioidal infections produce a respiratory illness that is indistinguishable from a variety of other diseases without specific testing.[56] Misunderstandings of the manifestations of coccidioidomycosis or a mistaken belief that diagnosis of early infections is unimportant has led to gross disparities between the numbers of expected and reported coccidioidal infections. For example, public health statistics for Arizona represent only 1 to 2% of the expected 60,000 annual infections.[57] Underdiagnosis is even more likely for patients with coccidioidomycosis evaluated outside the endemic region.[58, 59] Whether detected or not, most infections follow a self-limited course with only a small number producing residual sequelae or chronic progressive infections. Although complications are typically manifest within weeks or up to 2 years after the original infection, the severity of the initial respiratory infection frequently does not correlate with the likelihood of complications. In this context, the identification of even mild primary infections takes on added significance and clinical relevance.

Early Respiratory Infection. The first symptoms of the primary infection usually appear between 7 and 21 days after exposure. Although most infections appear to develop as a result of exposure to small numbers of arthroconidia, where exposure is unusually intense symptoms are more likely to appear early. In an epidemic of coccidioidomycosis that occurred in the San Joaquin Valley of California between 1991 and 1994,[60] the findings for 536 patients with new infections included cough (73%), chest pain (44%), shortness of breath (32%), fever (76%), and fatigue (39%). These are typical of earlier reports. Although the infection is often subacute in development, patients occasionally report abrupt onset of symptoms, especially that of pleurisy. Weight loss is also a common sign and headache has been noted in as many as 21% of patients even in the absence of meningeal infection.[29] Skin manifestations develop as part of the primary illness. Most frequent and easily missed is a nonpruritic fine papular rash that occurs early and transiently during the illness. More striking are *erythema nodosum* and *erythema multiforme*, which have strong predilections for females. Migratory arthralgias are also common complaints, and the triad of fever, *erythema nodosum*, and arthralgias has been termed "desert rheumatism." Routine laboratory findings are usually normal except for an increase in the erythrocyte sedimentation rate or the peripheral blood eosinophil count, on occasion accounting for two thirds of the circulating leukocytes. Chest radiograph results are abnormal in more than half of patients. Common findings include unilateral infiltrates, hilar adenopathy, and effusions. Persistent hilar or peritracheal adenopathy is associated with extrathoracic spread of infection. Lung cavities are present initially in approximately 8% of adults but are less frequent in children.

Uncommonly, coccidioidal pneumonia presents as a diffuse process leading to respiratory failure, either because of high-inoculum exposure[61, 62] or because of fungi in the blood stream seeding the lung in many sites[18] (Fig. 256–3). The presentation is often fulminant, mimicking that of septic shock or a bacterial infection, and despite treatment mortality is high. Approximately one third of human immunodeficiency virus–infected patients present with this radiographic appearance. Fungemia associated with diffuse pulmonary infiltrates is nearly always due to a recognizable cellular immunodeficiency state.[17] In human immunodeficiency virus–infected patients the CD4 counts are typically below 100 cells/mm^3 and the viral load is probably high.[15]

Although some of the presenting symptoms are statistically more likely to occur with coccidioidal infections than with respiratory illness of other etiologies, the overlap of clinical syndromes is substantial.[56] For most patients, specific testing is required to secure a diagnosis.

Most respiratory infections resolve without complications, taking several week to several months to do so. A minority of patients with infections develop various pulmonary sequelae, and even fewer manifest disseminated infection outside the lungs. Despite their relative infrequency, these complications pose significant difficulties in diagnosis or management, as discussed in a later section.

Pulmonary Nodules and Cavities. Approximately 4% of pulmonary infections result in a nodule, ranging up to 5 cm in diameter. Typically, a nodule causes no symptoms but may be indistinguishable from a neoplasm without histologic examination.[63] Occasionally, nodules liquefy and drain into a bronchus to form a cavity (Fig. 256–4).

Pulmonary cavities may be present initially or in the later stages of the primary infection. They are usually peripheral and solitary, and with time most develop a distinctive thin wall.[64] Cavities may not cause any symptoms, and half close within 2 years. Others are

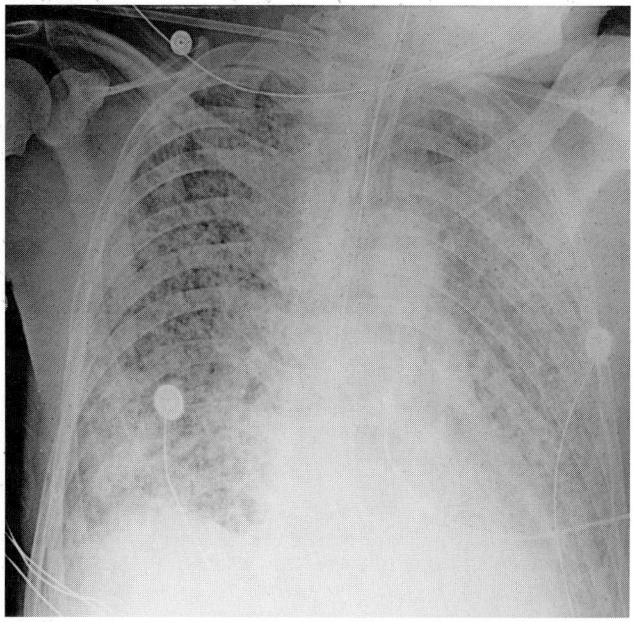

FIGURE 256–3. Diffuse reticulonodular infiltrates due to *Coccidioides immitis* in a patient with human immunodeficiency virus infection.

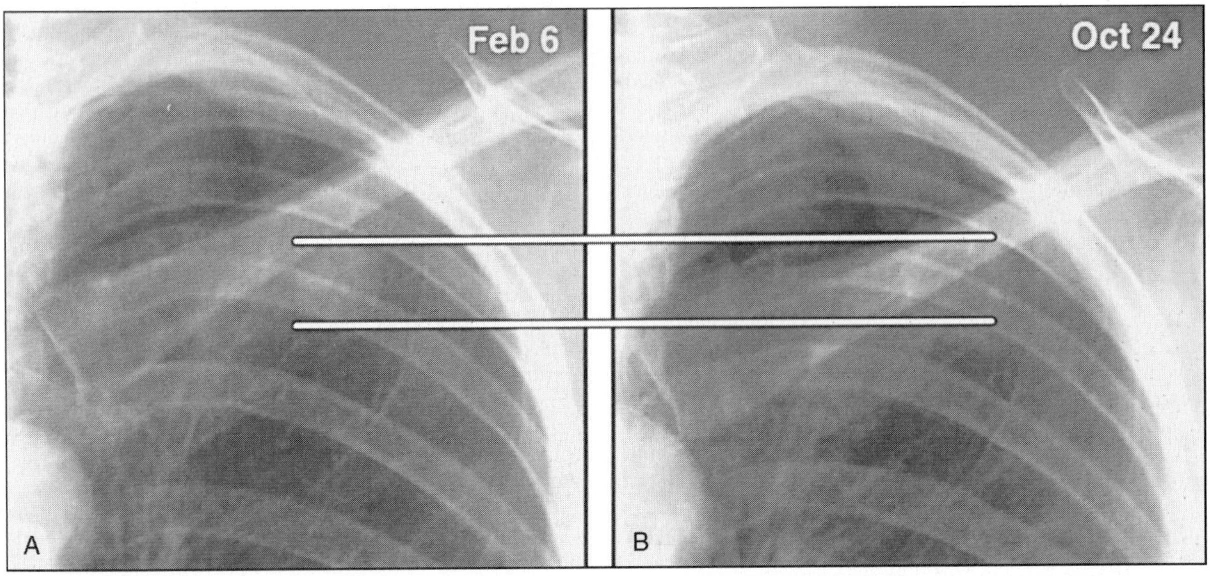

FIGURE 256–4. Cavitation of a coccidioidal nodule. A 1.8-cm nodule can be seen in *A*. Eight months later *(B)* this lesion has become a thin-walled cavity.

associated with local symptoms of pleuritic pain, cough, or hemoptysis (Figs. 256–5 and 256–6). Mycetoma may develop within cavities, either from mycelia of *C. immitis*[65] or with other species of fungi (Fig. 256–7). Another infrequent but well-recognized complication is that a peripheral coccidioidal cavity ruptures into the pleural space. This occurs most frequently in young athletic males and is not associated with underlying immunodeficiency. Usually a pyopneumothorax is present, and the presence of an air-fluid level within the pleural space is a clue that the process is not a spontaneous pneumothorax or a ruptured pulmonary bleb (Fig. 256–8). Prompt surgical correction of the defect is the preferred treatment unless there is a delay in diagnosis or other medical conditions preclude an operation.[66]

Chronic Fibrocavitary Pneumonia. In distinction from thin-walled coccidioidal cavities, some patients develop a chronic fibrotic pneumonia process that is characterized by both pulmonary infiltrates and pulmonary cavitation.[67] This form of infection is not common among persons with T-cell deficiencies but does appear to be associated with diabetes or preexisting pulmonary fibrosis related to smoking or other causes. Involvement of more than one lobe is more common, and such lesions may cause systemic symptoms such as night sweats and weight loss as well as local symptoms.

Extrapulmonary Dissemination. *C. immitis* spreads beyond the lungs in approximately 0.5% of all infections in the general population. However, several factors dramatically increase the risk of dissemination. Patients who have immunodeficiency conditions such as the later stages of human immunodeficiency virus infection, therapies to prevent solid organ rejection, high-dose corticosteroid therapy (equivalent to chronic prednisone doses greater than 20 mg/day), and Hodgkin's lymphoma are all at much greater risk of dissemination.[9–20] For example, two thirds of renal transplant recipients who

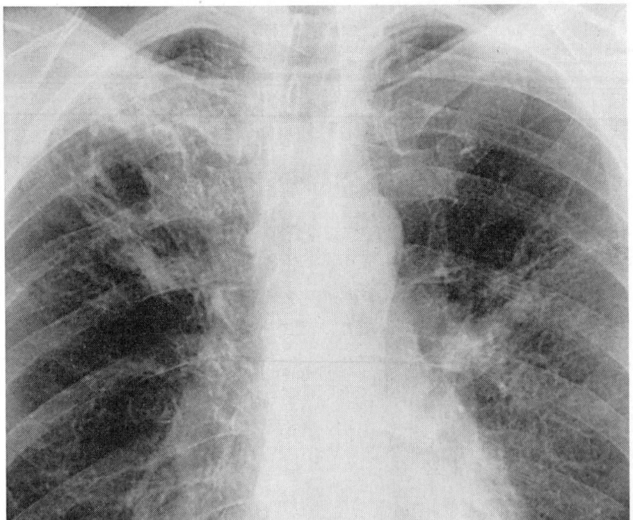

FIGURE 256–5. Pulmonary cavity in the right upper lobe with surrounding fibrosis.

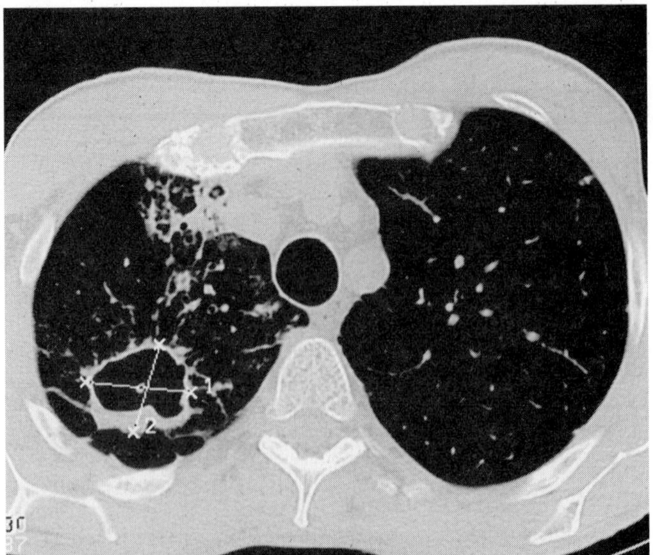

FIGURE 256–6. Computed tomography scan of the cavity shown in Figure 256–4.

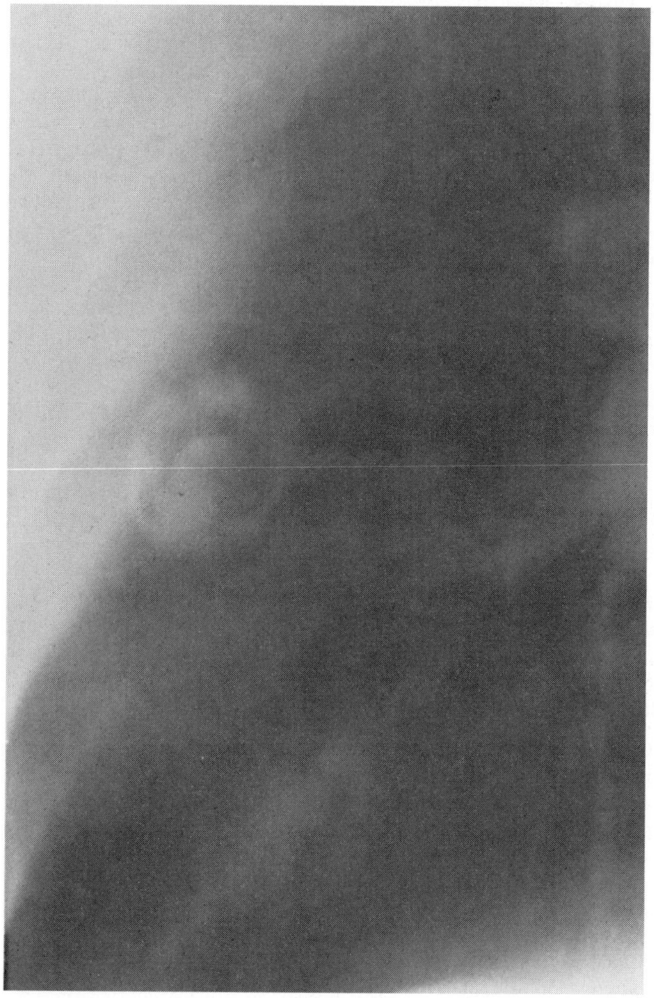

FIGURE 256–7. Mycetoma in the right lung of a coccidioidal cavity. Bronchoscopy specimens yielded *Coccidioides immitis* in culture. (From Winn RE, Johnson R, Galgiani JN, et al. Cavitary coccidioidomycosis with fungus ball formation. Chest. 1994;105:412–416.)

developed coccidioidal infection progressed to dissemination.[12] Men are more likely to develop dissemination than women.[28] However, dissemination is also more likely if infection is first diagnosed during pregnancy, especially during the third trimester or in the immediate postpartum period.[68, 69] There also appears to be an increased risk of dissemination among persons of African or Filipino ancestry, although the exact magnitude of the risk is controversial.[70, 71] Interestingly, extrapulmonary dissemination is not often associated with pulmonary complications. In fact, many patients with disseminated coccidioidal infection have entirely normal chest radiographs.

The most common site of dissemination is the skin. Lesions range from superficial maculopapular lesions to keratotic and verrucose ulcers to subcutaneous fluctuant abscesses. There is a predilection for lesions at the nasolabial fold (Fig. 256–9). Although most extrapulmonary dissemination is the result of hematogenous spread, supraclavicular and cervical lymphadenopathy is also a frequent presentation and probably represents lymphatic drainage from the primary pulmonary infection.

Joints and bones are also a common site of dissemination. Joint infections differ from "desert rheumatism" in that infections are typically associated with a prominent synovitis and effusion whereas the self-limited joint findings associated with the early infection are not. Although any joint can be involved, the knee is most frequently involved, and others commonly infected include the joints of the hands and wrists, the feet and ankles, and the pelvis.[72–74] Infection

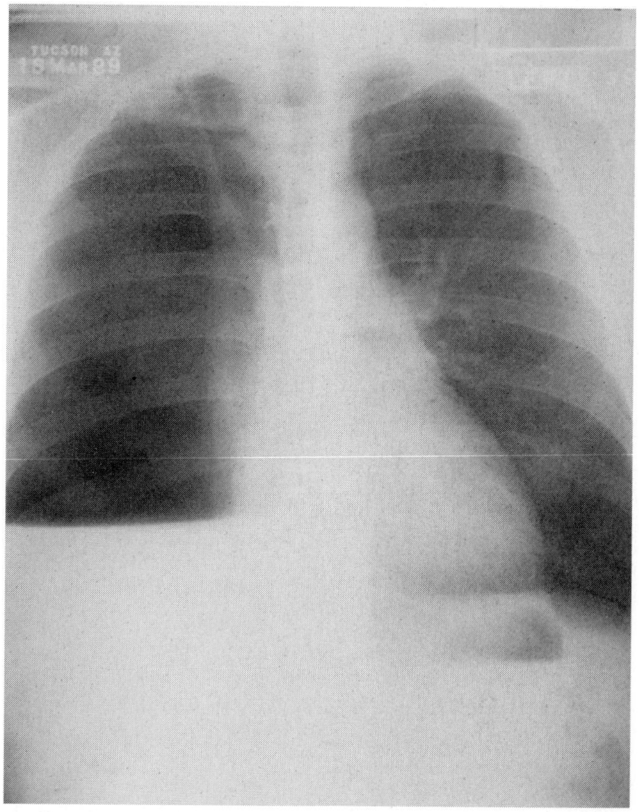

FIGURE 256–8. Pyopneumothorax resulting from a ruptured coccidioidal cavity. (From Snyder LS, et al. Semin Respir Crit Care Med. 1997;18:235–247.)

may be isolated in the synovium or may erode to involve the underlying bone as well. Alternatively, bones may be involved first with secondary extension into the joint.[75] Although long bones may be affected, vertebral infection is much more common. Involvement of multiple vertebrae is typical. These may coalesce to produce anterior or posterior paraspinous abscesses (Fig. 256–10). Magnetic resonance imaging is often helpful in defining the exact location of such lesions.[76]

Coccidioidal meningitis is the most serious form of disseminated infection. Untreated, it is nearly always fatal within 2 years of diagnosis.[77, 78] Like most other complications of coccidioidomycosis,

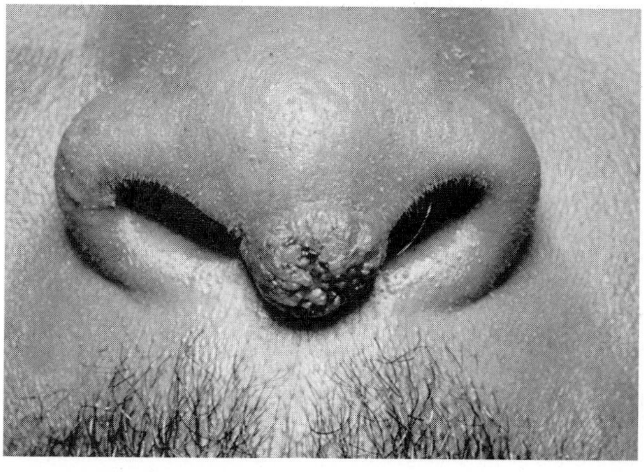

FIGURE 256–9. Ulcerative lesion of disseminated coccidioidal infection. (From Galgiani JN. Coccidioidomycosis. West J Med. 1993;159:153–171.)

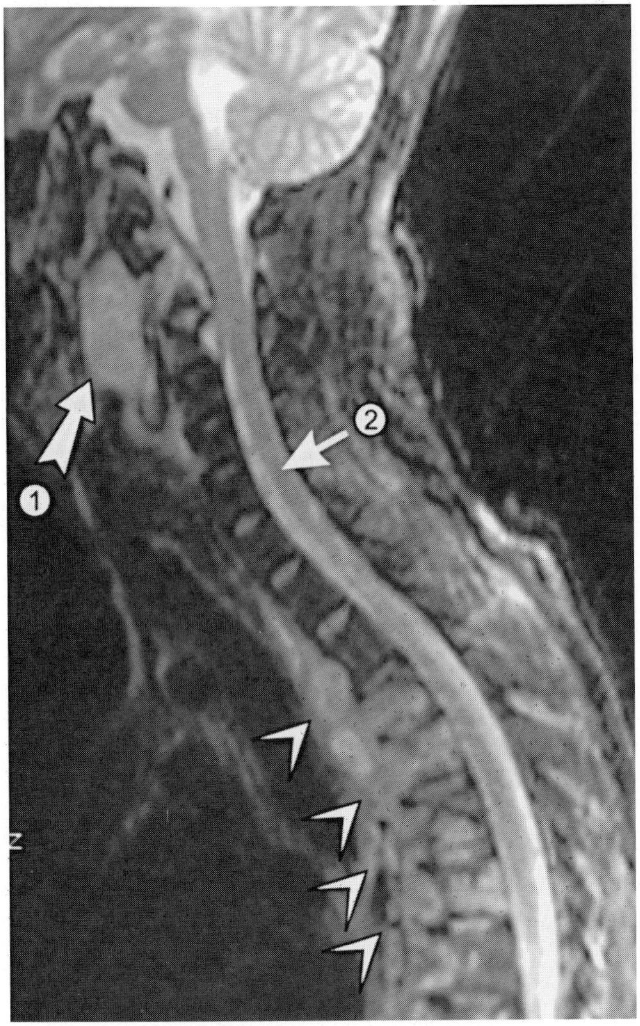

FIGURE 256–10. Sagittal magnetic resonance imaging scan demonstrating an anterior paraspinous abscess extending from the base of the skull to the midthoracic vertebrae. *Arrow 1* points to an abscess that orginated in a cervical vertebra and dissected anteriorly. *Arrow 2* identifies a normal spinal cord. The *other arrows* indicate abscesses anterior to the thoracic vertebrae. Multiple surgical procedures were required to control this infection.

meningitis usually develops relatively soon after the initial infection. For example, in one study all of 22 patients who developed meningitis after a large dust storm did so an average of 5.4 weeks after the onset of symptoms.[79] Similarly, a review of cases from Veterans Affairs and military records showed that 20 of 25 patients developed meningitis within 6 months of their first symptoms of infection.[77, 78] Common presenting symptoms are headache, vomiting, and altered mental status. In addition to an elevated cerebrospinal fluid, white blood cell count, elevated protein, and depressed glucose, eosinophils are occasionally prominent.[80] The main areas of involvement are the basilar meninges. Hydrocephalus is a common complication, especially in children.[81] Attention has been drawn to vasculitis and focal intracerebral coccidioidal abscesses as less frequent complications.[82–84]

DIAGNOSIS

The manifestations of most early coccidioidal infections overlap substantially with those of other respiratory infections.[56] Therefore, specific laboratory testing is usually required to establish a diagnosis of coccidioidomycosis. In regions where *C. immitis* is endemic, such testing is commonplace. In most of the rest of the country, the possibility of coccidioidomycosis is unlikely to be considered unless a geographic exposure is identified. It is hard to overestimate the importance of obtaining a detailed travel history as a critical first step in diagnosis. Because the incubation period usually ranges between 1 and 3 weeks, endemic exposure within this time period should raise the possibility of coccidioidomycosis to account for a respiratory condition of new onset. It should also be emphasized that exposure need not be extensive. Infections have occurred in patients whose only exposure occurred while changing airplanes at the Phoenix airport or during a single drive across California's Central Valley. Complications of the initial infection such as chronic pneumonia or extrathoracic dissemination may take longer to become apparent but nearly always emerge within 2 years after exposure. One exception to this rule is the detection of a pulmonary nodule, which may persist without symptoms for many years after the original infection. Another special case is the setting of waning immunity, such as after the development of acquired immunodeficiency syndrome or with immunosuppressive therapy associated with solid organ transplantation. In such circumstances, exposure to *C. immitis* in the distant past may be sufficient to account for the current clinical illness.[85]

When the possibility of coccidioidomycosis has been raised, diagnosis may be established in three ways: identifying spherules in or recovering *C. immitis* from a clinical specimen; detecting specific anticoccidioidal antibodies in serum, cerebrospinal fluid, or other bodily fluid; or detecting dermal delayed-type hypersensitivity to coccidioidal antigens by skin testing.

Direct Examination and Culture. Isolating *C. immitis* from a patient is definitive evidence of a coccidioidal infection, and this diagnostic approach is most frequently utilized for patients with complicated pulmonary or disseminated syndromes. Sputum or other clinical specimens can be collected at no risk to personnel because the infection is not transmitted from the primary specimen. Direct microscopic examination of secretions can be carried out immediately or after the addition of potassium hydroxide. Calcofluor staining of the cell wall may also help to distinguish spherules from leukocytes. *C. immitis* cannot be detected by Gram staining. Spherules can also be stained by cytology stains (e.g., in bronchoscopy specimens), by hematoxylin and eosin stains, and by other specialized procedures such as silver or periodic acid–Schiff staining. Hematoxylin and eosin staining of spherules also produces a distinctive autofluorescence that may help to identify small numbers of organisms in tissues.[86] Although culture results are more sensitive, identification of spherules by direct examination is more rapid and may speed diagnosis.

C. immitis grows well on most mycologic or bacteriologic media after 5 or 7 days of incubation. Aerobic conditions are required. When growth occurs, it is typically as a white (nonpigmented) mold. However, there are many exceptions to this general appearance and the morphologic appearance is not reliable in determining whether the fungus is *C. immitis*.[87] When growth is evident on culture medium, care should be taken not to open the culture container except in an appropriate biocontainment cabinet. Cultures at this stage are highly infectious, and infections have occurred in laboratory personnel when cultures have not been properly handled.[88]

The mycelial form of growth is not specific for *C. immitis* and further testing is required for species identification. The two most common ways for microbiologists to do this are to detect a specific coccidioidal antigen (exoantigen) in an extract of the fungus and to detect a specific ribosomal RNA sequence using a DNA probe.[89–91] In place of maintaining these capabilities, some smaller laboratories refer the culture to a reference laboratory where identification is completed.

Serologic Testing. This approach is the most frequent means of diagnosing primary coccidioidal infections because the patients may not be able to produce a sputum specimen and fungal cultures are often not practical in an ambulatory setting. It may also be indispensable in establishing the etiology of chronic meningitis, because cultures of cerebrospinal fluid are commonly negative in coccidioidal meningitis. Of the variety of tests available, most are highly specific for an active infection.[92] Even minimally reactive test results are often diagnostically important and should usually not be dismissed as insignificant. However, a negative serologic test never excludes the presence of a coccidioidal infection. Performing one or more repeated serologic tests over the course of 2 months increases the sensitivity of serologic diagnosis, especially for recently acquired infections.

Tube Precipitin Antibodies. Antibodies of this type were originally detected by the presence of a precipitin button that formed at the bottom of a test tube after overnight incubation of the patient's serum mixed with coccidioidal antigen.[93] Because immunoglobulin M (IgM) is most adept at forming such immune precipitins and these reactions were detected early after the onset of infection, this test is sometimes referred to as the IgM test. The antigen responsible for this reaction is a polysaccharide from the fungal cell wall. Up to 90% of patients have tube precipitin (TP) antibodies detected at some time within the first 3 weeks of symptoms, and this value declines to less than 5% more than 7 months after the onset of a self-limited illness.

Complement-Fixing Antibodies. When the patient's serum is mixed with coccidioidal antigen, an immune complex forms that consumes complement.[7] This event is detected by the subsequent addition of antibody-coated red blood cells, which normally lyse in the presence of complement but remain intact if the complement is depleted. Because immunoglobulin G (IgG) is the immunoglobulin class usually involved in such immune complexes, this test is sometimes referred to as the IgG test. Although this test was originally developed using various complex extracts of *C. immitis*, it is now known that the antigen involved in this reaction is a chitinase, and the gene encoding this enzyme has been cloned.[94–97] In early coccidioidal infections, complement-fixing (CF) antibodies are detected somewhat later and for longer periods than TP antibodies. CF antibodies can be detected in other body fluids, and their detection in the cerebrospinal fluid is an especially important aid to the diagnosis of coccidioidal meningitis. CF antibody concentration is expressed as a titer, such as 1:4 or 1:64, indicating the greatest dilution of serum at which complement consumption is still detected. Traditionally, a titer of 1:16 or greater has been frequently associated with extrathoracic dissemination. However, because of technical factors, end-point results for the same serum samples may vary considerably on testing by different laboratories. More useful are serial determinations of CF antibody concentrations performed by the same laboratory. In general, higher titers reflect more extensive coccidioidal infection and rising CF antibody concentrations are associated with worsening disease.

Immunodiffusion Tests. Antibodies that were detected by the original TP or CF tests can be detected by alternative procedures known as the immunodiffusion TP (IDTP) and immunodiffusion CF (IDCF) tests, respectively. Although the IDTP and IDCF tests are conducted quite similarly, they use different antigens in order to measure different types of antibodies. As with the original tests, the IDTP test result is reported by some laboratories as the IgM test result and the IDCF result as the IgG test result. Both tests have been found to be at least as sensitive as their original counterparts.[98, 99] Moreover, immunodiffusion tests are more amenable to being manufactured and distributed as commercially prepared kits, allowing the tests to be performed in laboratories not fully dedicated to a mycology specialty.

Enzyme-Linked Immunoassays. An enzyme immunoassay for coccidioidal antibodies is available commercially (Meridian Diagnostics, Cincinnati, Ohio). The test kit allows the specific detection of IgM or IgG antibodies. However, these results are not interchangeable with the IgM test or IgG test results. Positive results with this commercial kit are highly sensitive for coccidioidal infection. Occasionally false-positive results are noted, especially with the IgM enzyme immunoassay. At present, enzyme immunoassay results should normally be confirmed with IDTP, IDCF, or CF tests before they are considered diagnostic.[100–102]

Latex Tests. Latex tests for coccidioidal antibodies are also commercially available. They are attractive to clinical laboratories because they are easy to use and results are obtained rapidly. However, there are significant numbers of false-positive reactions and therefore the latex test is not as reliable as any of the other tests described in this section.[92]

Skin Testing. Dermal delayed-type hypersensitivity to coccidioidal antigens is highly specific for coccidioidal infection.[103] However, because skin tests remain positive after infection in most persons for life, a result may not be related to the current illness. In addition, some of the most serious infections may be associated with selective anergy and the skin test may not demonstrate reactivity. Therefore, as useful as skin test results are for epidemiologic studies, the test has important limitations as a screening procedure for recent infection. For patients in whom coccidioidomycosis has been diagnosed by other means, skin testing may have prognostic significance.[104]

Although the original skin testing reagent was prepared from mycelia of *C. immitis*, the only commercial reagent currently available is a spherule-derived coccidoidin, also referred to as spherulin (ALK Laboratories, Wallingford, Conn.). Results of skin tests are measured both 24 and 48 hours after the antigen is injected intradermally. An induration of more than 5 mm is considered reactive. Erythema at the injection site is not of diagnostic value. Coccidioidal skin testing does not influence subsequent coccidioidal serology results.

Other Approaches to Diagnosis. Antigenemia may occur either with early or with chronic coccidioidal infections and could be the basis of a diagnostic test.[105–108] The specific antigens responsible have not been characterized in any detail and currently antigen detection remains a research rather than a clinically applicable procedure. It is also possible that polymerase chain reaction methodology could be used to detect *C. immititis*–specific nucleic acid sequences in patients' specimens. Primers that appear to be specific for *C. immitis* are know to exist,[109] and a report has suggested that coccidioidal nuclei acid has been detected in a small number of tissue and fluid samples from patients.[110] However, this approach has not yet been implemented for clinical use.

MANAGEMENT

General Approaches. The three components of managing coccidioidal infections are assessment of the need for intervention, selection of antifungal agents for those who would benefit from treatment, and choice of surgical procedures for débridement and reconstruction of destructive lesions.

In patients with newly diagnosed coccidioidal infections, two critical assessments are the extent of disease at present and factors that increase the risk of future complications. Assessment of the current extent of disease usually can be based on a careful review of systems and physical examination. Where new focal complaints of discomfort or swelling are identified, these should be further evaluated with appropriate imaging or, if necessary, biopsy. For example, pain referable to bones might be assessed with a radionuclide bone scan,[111, 112] an effusion that develops in a joint could be aspirated for cell count and culture, a progressively severe headache may require magnetic resonance imaging and lumbar puncture to evaluate the possibility of meningitis, or a nonhealing skin lesion may need biopsy.

In the general population, pulmonary or extrapulmonary complications are uncommon. However, there is a special risk of disseminated infection with conditions that prominently suppress T-cell immunity. The best recognized of these are human immunodeficiency virus infection, immunosuppression to prevent rejection of a transplanted solid organ, and treatment with high doses of corticosteroids. Pregnancy, especially during the third trimester or the immediate peripartem period, also appears to predispose patients to a high risk of widespread dissemination. Patients with any of these risk factors should nearly always be treated with antifungal therapy even if there is no evidence of extrapulmonary spread. Patients with diabetes mellitus are not prone to extrapulmonary dissemination. However, they are more likely to develop pulmonary cavitation or chronic pneumonia and therefore may be more likely to require treatment.

Available antifungal agents include amphotericin B and the azole antifungal agents ketoconazole, fluconazole, and itraconazole. Their detailed pharmacology is described elsewhere (see Chapter 35). In coccidioidomycosis, selecting between amphotericin B and azole antifungals is based primarily on the degree of respiratory compromise in pulmonary infections or rate of progression of disseminated infections. Amphotericin B is perceived to have a more rapid onset of action, so despite its well-known toxicities it is the preferred initial therapy for patients who have developed respiratory compromise or who are deteriorating rapidly. There is no evidence that a lipid formulation of amphotericin B improves on the efficacy of amphotericin B suspended with deoxycholate. On the other hand, azole antifungals are often selected for patients with chronic processes because possible differences in rate of response to azole antifungals would be outweighed by their ease of administration and lack of toxicity. Ketoconazole is the only orally available azole antifungal approved by the Food and Drug Administration for the treatment of coccidioidomycosis, although several clinical trials have indicated that fluconazole and itraconazole are also efficacious.[113–121] There are no studies demonstrating superiority of one azole antifungal over another. In a comparison of fluconazole (400 mg/day) and itraconazole (200 mg twice daily), the primary analysis demonstrated that the two drugs were within 20% of each other in producing responses (Mycoses Study Group study 20).

Because the manifestations, locations, and severity of progressive forms of coccidioidomycosis vary a great deal among patients, the need for surgery is determined by the nature of specific lesions on a case-by-case basis. In some patients, especially where there is extensive skeletal involvement, débridement and drainage of infected sites may be critical to achieving control of the infection. One reason for this may be that the spherule wall, a strong stimulus of inflammation,[122] is not easily degraded and cleared from large coccidioidal lesions by macrophages and other elements of the reticuloendothelial system. Therefore, even if therapy is effective in arresting fungal proliferation, fungal debris already present may continue to produce tissue destruction until it is surgically removed. Patients with persistent fever and malaise may benefit from drainage of large collections of pus. Also, surgery may be needed to stabilize bones that are structurally unsound or may be needed when the spinal cord is at risk of compression. Advances in imaging using computed tomography or magnetic resonance imaging have aided greatly in the evaluation of specific lesions.[74, 76, 123] Repeated use of these modalities often helps to identify lesions that are progressing in spite of antifungal therapy and thus are likely to benefit from resection or drainage.

Early Uncomplicated Infections. For patients without either risk factors or evidence of extrapulmonary spread, treatment is of unproven benefit. To date, there have been no placebo-controlled trials concerning this self-limited form of infection to determine whether treatment hastens the resolution of symptoms or prevents the risk of complications. Not surprisingly, experts familiar with coccidioidomycosis vary widely in their recommendations for management of specific patients in this category. Although some physicians recommend treatment for all patients, others recommend treating only patients with more severe manifestations. Evidence that is often considered to indicate more severe infection includes loss of more than 10% of body weight, intense night sweats for more than 3 weeks, infiltrates involving more than half of one lung or portions of both lungs, prominent or persistent hilar or peritracheal adenopathy, anticoccidioidal CF antibody titer in excess of 1:16, failure to develop dermal hypersensitivity to coccidioidal antigens, inability to work, or symptoms that persist for more than 2 months. Because persons of African or Filipino descent appear to have some increased risk of dissemination, this factor sometimes also weighs in the decision for treatment. If treatment is recommended, commonly prescribed therapies include currently available oral azole antifungal agents such as ketoconazole, fluconazole, or itraconazole for courses of therapy ranging from 3 to 6 months.

Diffuse Pneumonia. Diffuse bilateral infiltrates represent either hematogenous infection of the lungs or multiple foci of infection resulting from exposure to a high inoculum of arthroconidia. In either case, even early infections are regarded as serious and warranting therapy. Initial therapy in such cases is usually with amphotericin B, at least for the first several weeks and until the illness appears to be improving. After this time, therapy is often switched to an antifungal azole agent for at least a year. Fungemia resulting in diffuse pulmonary infiltrates is often the consequence of severe immunodeficiency, and for such patients treatment may need to be continued indefinitely to prevent relapse.

Pulmonary Cavity. Cavitation as a sequela of coccidioidal pneumonia is often asymptomatic and may not need treatment. With the passage of time, some cavities disappear. Cavities that do not close spontaneously over a period from one to several years are sometimes resected to prevent future complications, especially if the cavity shows progressive enlargement or is immediately adjacent to the pleura. This potential benefit must be weighed against the risks of the surgical procedure, which vary according to the experience and skill of the surgeon.

Pulmonary cavities occasionally produce symptoms such as local pain, superinfection, or hemoptysis. When this occurs, treatment is usually instituted with oral antifungal azole therapy. Such therapy is often accompanied by a diminution of symptoms, but recurrences are frequent if therapy is stopped. For such patients, resection is a reasonable alternative to chronic suppressive medical therapy.

Chronic Fibrocavitary Pneumonia. Persistent coccidioidal pneumonia is normally treated with oral azole antifungal agents. Responses to these agents are approximately 55 to 60% as judged by improved symptoms and radiographic appearance. Treatment options for patients who do not respond include switching to an alternative antifungal azole, for fluconazole raising the dose, or instituting amphotericin B therapy.

Extrapulmonary Dissemination. For most patients with nonmeningeal dissemination, initial therapy is with an oral antifungal azole. Exceptional patients with rapidly progressive infection or infection in critical locations such as vertebrae may respond faster to initial therapy with amphotericin B, although this has not been proved. As discussed before, surgical débridement or drainage of lesions may be an important component of controlling infection. As with patients with chronic coccidioidal pneumonia, treatment is continued for at least a year and for 6 months past the point at which all evidence of further improvement has ceased. Even so, relapses occur in approximately a third of patients when therapy is stopped, and some patients may require suppressive therapy indefinitely.

In the management of coccidioidal meningitis, most patients are now treated initially with fluconazole. This is a major departure from therapy with intrathecal amphotericin B, which until the past several years was still standard treatment.[124] Although there have been no comparative trials of intrathecal amphotericin B and fluconazole, the response rate of approximately 70% with fluconazole at 400 mg/day is probably at least as good as that achieved with intrathecal amphotericin B, and use of fluconazole avoids most of the toxicity associated with amphotericin B. Higher doses of fluconazole have produced responses in some patients who did not initially respond to 400 mg/day. Similar results have been obtained in patients treated with itraconazole, although there is less clinical experience with this drug than with fluconazole. Ketoconazole in doses of at least 1200 mg/day has been effective in some patients,[125] although it has been largely superseded by the newer azoles.

Patients who do not respond to oral azole therapy may be helped with intrathecal amphotericin B. Routes of administration include repeated percutaneous intracisternal injection, injection into Ommaya's reservoirs that drain to either the cistern or a ventricle, lumbar puncture with medication in a hyperbaric glucose solution, and lateral cervical injection. The technique, frequency, and dosage of intrathecal amphotericin B have varied widely among practitioners. For some patients who could not tolerate intrathecal amphotericin B, miconazole administered intravenously or intrathecally has also been effective treatment.[126]

In addition to antifungal therapy to control the meningeal inflammation, interventions are required for two other manifestations. Hydrocephalus is a common complication of coccidioidal meningitis. Normally, hydrocephalus does not respond to antifungal therapy and requires a shunting procedure. Ventriculoperitoneal shunts become a conduit for *C. immitis* from the cerebrospinal space to the peritoneum, but this usually does not result in clinically apparent abdominal complications. Although infection predominantly affects the basilar meninges, intracerebral abscesses occasionally develop.[83] Such lesions may require drainage or resection in addition to systemic antifungal drug therapy.

PREVENTION

Developing a vaccine as a means of preventing coccidioidomycosis has been an attractive goal for many years. Such a strategy might be useful because immunity develops in most persons who are infected naturally. A formalin-killed whole-cell spherule vaccine was found to be exceptionally protective for mice against lethal intranasal infections.[36, 127–135] However, the whole-cell vaccine also induced a great deal of local inflammation at the injection site, limiting the dose in humans to 1.84 mg.[122] For an average human this is approximately 1/1000 of the vaccine dose (mg/kg) required for protection in mice. When this dose of formalin-killed spherule vaccine was used in a human field trial, vaccination failed to result in fewer symptomatic cases of coccidioidal pneumonia than were detected in placebo recipients.[136] One plausible explanation for the failure is that the inflammatory reactions to the whole-cell vaccine prevented use of a sufficient dose of the antigens responsible for protection. If this is the case, use of a purified or recombinant antigen might circumvent this limitation. Vaccination with the unsedimented fraction of disrupted formalin-killed spherules (termed the "27 K" fraction) was protective against intranasal infection in mice.[137] This demonstrates that the whole cell is not required for protection. Recombinant antigens have also shown varying degrees of protection.[138, 139] With continued development of purified or recombinant antigens, candidate subunit coccidioidal vaccines may be available for preliminary human trials within the next several years.

REFERENCES

1. Deresinski SC, Hector RF. The history of coccidioidomycosis. In: Einstein HE, Catanzaro A, eds. Coccidioidomycosis. Proceedings of the 5th International Conference on Coccidioidomycosis. Washington, DC: National Foundation for Infectious Diseases; 1996:48–76.
2. Centers for Disease Control and Prevention. Addressing Emerging Infectious Disease Threats: A Prevention Strategy for the United States. Rockville, Md: U.S. Department of Health and Human Services, Public Health Service; 1994:1–46.
3. Kirkland TN, Fierer J. Coccidioidomycosis: A reemerging infectious disease. Emerging Infect Dis. 1996;2:192–199.
4. Kovacs A, Forthal DN, Kovacs JA, et al. Disseminated coccidioidomycosis in a patient with acquired immune deficiency syndrome. West J Med. 1984;140:447–449.
5. Ophuls W, Moffitt HC. A new pathogenic mould (formerly described as a protozoon: *Coccidioides immitis*): Preliminary report. Phila Med J. 1900;5:1471–1472.
6. Gifford MA. San Joaquin fever. Kern County Dept Public Health Annu. Rep. 1936:22–23.
7. Smith CE, Saito MT, Simons SA. Pattern of 39,500 serologic tests in coccidioidomycosis. JAMA. 1956;160:546–552.
8. Fiese MJ. Coccidioidomycosis. Springfield, Ill: Charles C Thomas; 1958:3–253.
9. Riley DK, Galgiani JN, O'Donnell MR, et al. Coccidioidomycosis in bone marrow transplant recipients. Transplantation. 1994;56:1531–1533.
10. Hall KA, Sethi GK, Rosado LJ, et al. Coccidioidomycosis and heart transplantation. J Heart Lung Transplant. 1993;12:525–526.
11. Hall KA, Copeland JG, Zukoski CF, et al. Markers of coccidioidomycosis before cardiac or renal transplantation and the risk of recurrent infection. Transplantation. 1993;55:1422–1424.
12. Cohen IM, Galgiani JN, Potter D, et al. Coccidioidomycosis in renal replacement therapy. Arch Intern Med. 1982;142:489–494.
13. Huth RG. Concomitant systemic cryptococcosis and coccidioidomycosis in a patient with AIDS. Clin Infect Dis. 1994;18:262–263.
14. Ampel NM, Dols CL, Galgiani JN. Coccidioidomycosis during human immunodeficiency virus infection. Results of a prospective study in coccidioidal endemic area. Am J Med. 1993;94:235–240.
15. Fish DG, Ampel NM, Galgiani JN, et al. Coccidioidomycosis during human immunodeficiency virus infection. A review of 77 patients. Medicine (Baltimore). 1990;69:384–391.
16. Byrne WR, Dietrich RA. Disseminated coccidioidomycosis with peritonitis in a patient with acquired immunodeficiency syndrome. Prolonged survival associated with positive skin test reactivity to coccidioidin. Arch Intern Med. 1989;149:947–948.
17. Bronnimann DA, Adam RD, Galgiani JN, et al. Coccidioidomycosis in the acquired immunodeficiency syndrome. Ann Intern Med. 1987;106:372–379.
18. Ampel NM, Ryan KJ, Carry PJ, et al. Fungemia due to *Coccidioides immitis*. An analysis of 16 episodes in 15 patients and a review of the literature. Medicine (Baltimore). 1986;65:312–321.
19. Deresinski SC, Stevens DA. Coccidioidomycosis in compromised hosts. Experience at Stanford University Hospital. Medicine (Baltimore). 1974;54:377–395.
20. Rutala PJ, Smith JW. Coccidioidomycosis in potentially compromised hosts: The effect of immunosuppressive therapy in dissemination. Am J Med Sci. 1978;275:283–295.
21. Sun SH, Sekhon SS, Huppert M. Electron microscopic studies of saprobic and parasitic forms of *Coccidioides immitis*. Sabouraudia. 1979;17:265–273.
22. Bowman BH, Taylor JW, Brownlee AG, et al. Molecular evolution of the fungi: Relationship of the basidiomycetes, ascomycetes, and chytridiomycetes. Mol Biol Evol. 1992;9:285–296.
23. Burt A, Carter DA, Koenig GL, et al. Molecular markers reveal cryptic sex in the human pathogen *Coccidioides immitis*. Proc Natl Acad Sci U S A. 1996;93:770–773.
24. Hector RF, Pappagianis D. Enzymatic degradation of the walls of spherules of *Coccidioides immitis*. Exp Mycol. 1982;6:136–152.
25. Huppert M, Sun SH, Harrison JL. Morphogenesis throughout saprobic and parasitic cycles of *Coccidioides immitis*. Mycopathologia. 1982;78:107–122.
26. Ogiso A, Ito M, Koyama M, et al. Pulmonary coccidioidomycosis in Japan: Case report and review. Clin Infect Dis. 1997;25:1260–1261.
27. Pappagianis D, Einstein H. Tempest from Tehachapi takes toll or *Coccidioides* conveyed aloft and afar. West J Med. 1978;129:527–530.
28. Pappagianis D. Epidemiology of coccidioidomycosis. Curr Top Med Mycol. 1988;2:199–238.
29. Kerrick SS, Lundergan LL, Galgiani JN. Coccidioidomycosis at a university health service. Am Rev Respir Dis. 1985;131:100–102.
30. Smith CE, Beard RR, Whiting EG, et al. Varieties of coccidioidal infection in relation to the epidemiology and control of the disease. Am J Public Health. 1946;36:1394–1402.
31. Dodge RR, Lebowitz MD, Barbee RA, et al. Estimates of *C. immitis* infection by skin test reactivity in an endemic community. Am J Public Health. 1985;75:863–865.
32. Werner SB, Pappagianis D, Heindl I, et al. An epidemic of coccidioidomycosis among archeology students in northern California. N Engl J Med. 1972;286:507–512.
33. Schneider E, Hajjeh RA, Spiegel RA, et al. A coccidioidomycosis outbreak following the Northridge, Calif, earthquake. JAMA. 1997;277:904–908.
34. Centers for Disease Control and Prevention. Coccidioidomycosis—United States, 1991–1992. MMWR Morb Mortal Wkly Rep. 1993;42:21–24.
35. Winn WA. Primary cutaneous coccidioidomycosis. Reevaluation of its potentiality based on study of three new cases. Arch Dermatol. 1965;92:221–228.
36. Kong Y-C, Levine HB, Madin SH, et al. Fungal multiplication and histopathologic changes in vaccinated mice infected with *Coccidioides immitis*. J Immunol. 1964;92:779–790.
37. Hoggan MD, Ransom JP, Pappagianis D, et al. Isolation of *Coccidioides immitis* from the air (Abstract). Stanford Med Bull. 1956;14:190.
38. Ajello L, Maddy K, Crecelius G, et al. Recovery of *Coccidioides immitis* from the air. Sabouraudia. 1965;4:92–95.

39. Galgiani JN, Isenberg RA, Stevens DA. Chemotaxigenic activity of extracts from the mycelial and spherule phases of *Coccidioides immitis* for human polymorphonuclear leukocytes. Infect Immun. 1978;21:862–865.
40. Huntington RW Jr, Waldmann WJ, Sargent JA, et al. Pathologic and clinical observations on 142 cases of fatal coccidioidomycosis with necropsy. In: Ajello L, ed. Coccidioidomycosis. Tucson: University of Arizona Press; 1967:221–225.
41. Echols RM, Palmer DL, Long GW. Tissue eosinophilia in human coccidioidomycosis. Rev Infect Dis. 1982;4:656–664.
42. Beaman L, Pappagianis D, Benjamini E. Mechanisms of resistance to infection with *Coccidioides immitis* in mice. Infect Immun. 1979;23:681–685.
43. Beaman L, Benjamini E, Pappagianis D. Role of lymphocytes in macrophage-induced killing of *Coccidioides immitis* in vitro. Infect Immun. 1981;34:347–353.
44. Beaman L, Benjamini E, Pappagianis D. Activation of macrophages by lymphokines: Enhancement of phagosome-lysosome fusion and killing of *Coccidioides immitis*. Infect Immun. 1983;39:1201–1207.
45. Beaman L. Fungicidal activation of murine macrophages by recombinant gamma interferon. Infect Immun. 1987;55:2951–2955.
46. Beaman L. Effects of recombinant gamma interferon and tumor necrosis factor on in vitro interactions of human mononuclear phagocytes with *Coccidioides immitis*. Infect Immun. 1991;59:4227–4229.
47. Ampel NM, Christian L. *In vitro* modulation of proliferation and cytokine production by human peripheral blood mononuclear cells from subjects with various forms of coccidioidomycosis. Infect Immun. 1997;65:4483–4487.
48. Corry DB, Ampel NM, Christian L, et al. Cytokine production by peripheral blood mononuclear cells in human coccidioidomycosis. J Infect Dis. 1996;174:440–443.
49. Appelberg R, Castro AG, Pedrosa J, et al. Role of gamma interferon and tumor necrosis factor alpha during T-cell–independent and –dependent phases of *Mycobacterium avium* infection. Infect Immun. 1994;62:3962–3971.
50. Kauffman SH. Immunity to intracellular bacteria. Annu Rev Immunol. 1993;11:151–177.
51. Reiner SL, Locksley RM. The regulation of immunity to *Leishmania major*. Annu Rev Immunol. 1995;13:151–177.
52. Galgiani JN, Payne CM, Jones JF. Human polymorphonuclear-leukocyte inhibition of incorporation of chitin precursors into mycelia of *Coccidioides immitis*. J Infect Dis. 1984;149:404–412.
53. Ampel NM, Bejarano GC, Galgiani JN. Killing of *Coccidioides immitis* by human peripheral blood mononuclear cells. Infect Immun. 1992;60:4200–4204.
54. Petkus AF, Baum LL. Natural killer cell inhibition of young spherules and endospores of *Coccidioides immitis*. J Immunol. 1987;139:3107–3111.
55. Frey CL, Drutz DJ. Influence of fungal surface components on the interaction of *Coccidioides immitis* with polymorphonuclear neutrophils. J Infect Dis 1986;153:933–943.
56. Yozwiak ML, Lundergan LL, Kerrick SS, et al. Symptoms and routine laboratory abnormalities associated with coccidioidomycosis. West J Med. 1988;149:419–421.
57. Centers for Disease Control and Prevention. Coccidioidomycosis—Arizona, 1990–1995. MMWR Morb Mortal Wkly Rep. 1996;45:1069–1073.
58. Standaert SM, Schaffner W, Galgiani JN, et al. Coccidioidomycosis among visitors to a *Coccidioides immitis*–endemic area: An outbreak in a military reserve unit. J Infect Dis. 1995;171:1672–1675.
59. Cairns L, Blythe D, Kao A, et al. An outbreak of coccidioidomycosis in Washington State travelers returning from Mexico. Abstract K-661997. Presented at the Thirty-seventh Interscience Conference on Antimicrobial Agents and Chemotherapy.
60. Johnson RH, Caldwell JW, Welch G, et al. The great coccidioidomycosis epidemic: Clinical features. In: Einstein HE, Catanzaro A, eds. Coccidioidomycosis. Proceedings of the Fifth International Conference. Washington, DC: National Foundation for Infectious Diseases; 1996:77–87.
61. Lopez AM, Williams PL, Ampel NM. Acute pulmonary coccidioidomycosis mimicking bacterial pneumonia and septic shock: A report of two cases. Am J Med. 1993;95:236–239.
62. Arsura EL, Bellinghausen PL, Kilgore WB, et al. Septic shock in coccidioidomycosis. Crit Care Med. 1998;26:62–65.
63. Forseth J, Rohwedder JJ, Levine BE, et al. Experience with needle biopsy for coccidioidal lung nodules. Arch Intern Med. 1986;146:319–320.
64. Smith CE, Beard RR, Saito MT. Pathogenesis of coccidioidomycosis with special reference to pulmonary cavitation. Ann Intern Med. 1948;29:623–655.
65. Winn RE, Johnson R, Galgiani JN, et al. Cavitary coccidioidomycosis with fungus ball formation: Diagnosis by fiberoptic bronchoscopy with coexistence of hyphae and spherules. Chest. 1994;105:412–416.
66. Cunningham RT, Einstein H. Coccidioidal pulmonary cavities with rupture. J Thorac Cardiovasc Surg. 1982;84:172–177.
67. Sarosi GA, Parker JD, Doto IL, et al. Chronic pulmonary coccidioidomycosis. N Engl J Med. 1970;283:325–329.
68. Walker MP, Brody CZ, Resnik R. Reactivation of coccidioidomycosis in pregnancy. Obstet Gynecol. 1992;79:815–817.
69. Peterson CM, Schuppert K, Kelly PC, et al. Coccidioidomycosis and pregnancy. Obstet Gynecol Surv. 1993;48:149–156.
70. Huppert M. Racism in coccidioidomycosis? Am Rev Respir Dis. 1978;118:797–798.
71. Pappagianis D, Lindsay S, Beall S, et al. Ethnic background and the clinical course of coccidioidomycosis (Letter). Am Rev Respir Dis. 1979;120:959–961.
72. Bisla RS, Taber TH Jr. Coccidioidomycosis of bone and joints. Clin Orthop Relat Res. 1976;121:196–204.
73. Bried JH, Galgiani JN. *Coccidioides immitis* infections in bones and joints. Clin Orthop. 1986;211:235–243.
74. Lund PJ, Chan KM, Unger EC, et al. Magnetic resonance imaging in coccidioidal arthritis. Skeletal Radiol. 1996;25:661–665.
75. Dalinka MK, Dinnenberg S, Greendyke WH, et al. Roentgenographic features of osseous coccidioidomycosis and differential diagnosis. J Bone Joint Surg [Am] 1971;53-A:1157–1164.
76. Erly WK, Carmody RF, Seeger JF, et al. Magnetic resonance imaging of coccidioidal spondylitis. Int J Neuroradiol. 1997;3:385–392.
77. Einstein HE, Holeman CW Jr, Sandidge LL, et al. Coccidioidal meningitis. The use of amphotericin B in treatment. Calif Med. 1961;94:339–343.
78. Vincent T, Galgiani JN, Huppert M, et al. The natural history of coccidioidal meningitis: VA–Armed Forces Cooperative Studies, 1955–1958. Clin Infect Dis. 1993;16:247–254.
79. Pappagianis D. Coccidioidomycosis. In: Balows A, Hausler WJ Jr, Lennette EH, eds. Laboratory Diagnosis of Infectious Diseases. Berlin: Springer-Verlag; 1988:600–623.
80. Ismail Y, Arsura EL. Eosinophilic meningitis associated with coccidioidomycosis. West J Med. 1993;158:300–301.
81. Harrison HR, Galgiani JN, Reynolds AF Jr, et al. Amphotericin B and imidazole therapy for coccidioidal meningitis in children. Pediatr Infect Dis. 1983;2:216–221.
82. Mischel PS, Vinters HV. Coccidioidomycosis of the central nervous system: Neuropathological and vasculopathic manifestations and clinical correlates. Clin Infect Dis. 1995;20:400–405.
83. BaZuelos AF, Williams PL, Johnson RH, et al. Central nervous system abscesses due to *Coccidioides* species. Clin Infect Dis. 1996;22:240–250.
84. Williams PL, Johnson R, Pappagianis D, et al. Vasculitic and encephalitic complications associated with *Coccidioides immitis* infection of the central nervous system in humans: Report of 10 cases and review. Clin Infect Dis. 1992;14:673–682.
85. Hernandez JL, Echevarria S, Garcia-Valtuille A, et al. Atypical coccidioidomycosis in an AIDS patient successfully treated with fluconazole. Eur J Clin Microbiol Infect Dis. 1997;16:592–594.
86. Graham AR. Fungal autofluorescence with ultraviolet illumination. Am J Clin Pathol. 1983;79:231–234.
87. Huppert M, Sun SH, Bailey JW. Natural variability in Coccidioides immitis. In: Ajello L, ed. Coccidioidomycosis. The Second Symposium on Coccidioidomycosis. Tucson: University of Arizona Press; 1965:323–328.
88. Pappagianis D. Coccidioidomycosis (San Joaquin or valley fever). In: DiSalvo A, ed. Occupational Mycoses. Philadelphia: Lea & Febiger; 1983:13–28.
89. Huppert M, Sun SH, Rice EH. Specificity of exoantigens for identifying cultures of *Coccidioides immitis*. J Clin Microbiol. 1978;8:346–348.
90. Padhye AA, Smith G, Standard PG, et al. Comparative evaluation of chemiluminescent DNA probe assays and exoantigen tests for rapid identification of *Blastomyces dermatitidis* and *Coccidioides immitis*. J Clin Microbiol. 1994;32:867–870.
91. Sandhu GS, Kline BC, Stockman L, et al. Molecular probes for diagnosis of fungal infections. J Clin Microbiol. 1995;33:2913–2919.
92. Pappagianis D, Zimmer BL. Serology of coccidioidomycosis. Clin Microbiol Rev. 1990;3:247–268.
93. Smith CE, Whiting EG, Baker EE, et al. The use of coccidioidin. Am Rev Tuberc Pulm Dis. 1948;57:330–360.
94. Johnson SM, Pappagianis D. The coccidioidal complement fixation and immunodiffusion–complement fixation antigen is a chitinase. Infect Immun. 1992;60:2588–2592.
95. Pishko EJ, Kirkland TN, Cole GT. Isolation and characterization of two chitinase-encoding genes *(cts1, cts2)* from the fungus *Coccidioides immitis*. Gene. 1995;167:173–177.
96. Yang CM, Zhu YF, Magee DM, et al. Molecular cloning and characterization of the *Coccidioides immitis* complement fixation chitinase antigen. Infect Immun. 1996;64:1992–1997.
97. Zimmermann CR, Johnson SM, Martens GW, et al. Cloning and expression of the complement fixation antigen-chitinase of *Coccidioides immitis*. Infect Immun. 1996;64:4967–4975.
98. Huppert M, Bailey JW. The use of immunodiffusion tests in coccidioidomycosis. II. An immunodiffusion test as a substitute for the tube precipitin test. Am J Clin Pathol. 1965;44:369.
99. Wieden MA, Galgiani JN, Pappagianis D. Comparison of immunodiffusion techniques with standard complement fixation assay for quantitation of coccidioidal antibodies. J Clin Microbiol. 1983;18:529–534.
100. Kaufman L, Sekhon AS, Moledina N, et al. Comparative evaluation of commercial Premier EIA and microimmunodiffusion and complement fixation tests for *Coccidioides immitis* antibodies. J Clin Microbiol. 1995;33:618–619.
101. Wieden MA, Lundergan LL, Blum J, et al. Detection of coccidioidal antibodies by 33-kDa spherule antigen, *Coccidioides* EIA, and standard serologic tests in sera from patients evaluated for coccidioidomycosis. J Infect Dis. 1996;173:1273–1277.
102. Zartarian M, Peterson EM, De la Maza LM. Detection of antibodies to *Coccidioides immitis* by enzyme immunoassay. Am J Clin Pathol. 1997;107:148–153.
103. Drutz DJ, Catanzaro A. Coccidioidomycosis. Part I. Am Rev Respir Dis. 1978;117:559–585.
104. Oldfield EC, Bone WD, Martain CR, et al. Prediction of relapse after treatment of coccidioidomycosis. Clin Infect Dis. 1997;25:1205–1210.
105. Yoshinoya S, Cox RA, Pope RM. Circulating immune complexes in coccidioidomycosis. Detection and characterization. J Clin Invest. 1980;66:655–663.
106. Weiner MH. Antigenemia detected in human coccidioidomycosis. J Clin Microbiol. 1983;18:136–142.
107. Galgiani JN, Dugger KO, Ito JI, et al. Antigenemia in primary coccidioidomycosis. Am J Trop Med Hyg. 1984;33:645–649.

108. Galgiani JN, Grace GM, Lundergan LL. New serologic tests for early detection of coccidioidomycosis. J Infect Dis. 1991;163:671–674.
109. Bowman BH. Designing a PCR/probe detection system for pathogenic fungi. Clin Immunol. 1992;12:66–69.
110. Clark KA, McAllister D. Direct detection of *Coccidioides immitis* in clinical specimens using target amplification. In: Einstein HE, Catanzaro A, eds. Coccidioidomycosis. Proceedings of the 5th International Conference. Washington, DC: National Foundation for Infectious Diseases; 1996:129–136.
111. Stadalnik RC, Goldstein E, Hoeprich PD, et al. Diagnostic value of gallium and bone scans in evaluation of extrapulmonary coccidioidal lesions. Am Rev Respir Dis. 1980;121:673–676.
112. Boddicker JH, Fong D, Walsh TE, et al. Bone and gallium scanning in the evaluation of disseminated coccidioidomycosis. Am Rev Respir Dis. 1980;122:279–287.
113. Galgiani JN, Stevens DA, Graybill JR, et al. Ketoconazole therapy of progressive coccidioidomycosis. Comparison of 400- and 800-mg doses and observations at higher doses. Am J Med. 1988;84:603–610.
114. Tucker RM, Denning DW, Dupont B, et al. Itraconazole therapy for chronic coccidioidal meningitis. Ann Intern Med. 1990;112:108–112.
115. Graybill JR, Stevens DA, Galgiani JN, et al. Itraconazole treatment of coccidioidomycosis. Am J Med. 1990;89:282–290.
116. Tucker RM, Denning DW, Arathoon EG, et al. Itraconazole therapy for nonmeningeal coccidioidomycosis: Clinical and laboratory observations. J Am Acad Dermatol. 1990;23(Suppl):593–601.
117. Diaz M, Puente R, De Hoyos LA, et al. Itraconazole in the treatment of coccidioidomycosis. Chest. 1991;100:682–684.
118. Galgiani JN, Catanzaro A, Cloud GA, et al. Fluconazole therapy for coccidioidal meningitis. Ann Intern Med. 1993;119:28–35.
119. Stevens DA. Itraconazole and fluconazole for treatment of coccidioidomycosis. Clin Infect Dis. 1994;18:470–470.
120. Catanzaro A, Galgiani JN, Levine BE, et al. Fluconazole in the treatment of chronic pulmonary and nonmeningeal disseminated coccidioidomycosis. Am J Med. 1995;98:249–256.
121. Perez JA Jr, Johnson RH, Caldwell JW, et al. Fluconazole therapy in coccidioidal meningitis maintained with intrathecal amphotericin B. Arch Intern Med. 1995;155:1665–1668.
122. Williams PL, Sable DL, Sorgen D, et al. Immunologic responsiveness and safety associated with the *Coccidioides immitis* spherule vaccine in volunteers of white, black and Filipino ancestry. Am J Epidemiol. 1984;119:591–602.
123. Garvin GJ, Peterfy CG. Soft tissue coccidioidomycosis on MRI. J Comput Assist Tomogr. 1995;19:612–614.
124. Labadie EL, Hamilton RH. Survival improvement in coccidioidal meningitis by high-dose intrathecal amphotericin B. Arch Intern Med. 1986;146:2013–2018.
125. Craven PC, Graybill JR, Jorgensen JH, et al. High-dose ketoconazole for treatment of fungal infections of the central nervous system. Ann Intern Med. 1983;98:160–167.
126. Deresinski SC, Lilly RB, Levine HB, et al. Treatment of fungal meningitis with miconazole. Arch Intern Med. 1977;137:1180–1185.
127. Levine HB, Cobb JM, Smith CE. Immunity to coccidioidomycosis induced in mice by purified spherule, arthrospore, and mycelial vaccines. Trans NY Acad Sci. 1960;22:436–447.
128. Levine HB, Cobb JM, Smith CE. Immunogenicity of spherule-endospore vaccines of *Coccidioides immitis* for mice. J Immunol. 1961;87:218–227.
129. Levine HB, Miller RL, Smith CE. Influence of vaccination on respiratory coccidioidal disease in cynomolgus monkeys. J Immunol. 1962;89:242–251.
130. Kong Y-C, Levine HB, Smith CE. Immunogenic properties of nondisrupted and disrupted spherules of *Coccidioides immitis* in mice. Sabouraudia. 1963;2:131–142.
131. Levine HB, Kong Y-C, Smith CE. Immunization of mice to *Coccidioides immitis*: Dose, regimen and spherulation stage of killed spherule vaccines. J Immunol. 1965;94:132–142.
132. Levine HB. Purification of the spherule-endospore phase of *Coccidioides immitis*. Sabouraudia. 1961;1:112–115.
133. Kong Y-C, Savage DC, Levine HB. Enhancement of immune responses in mice by a booster injection of *Coccidioides* spherules. J Immunol. 1966;95:1048–1056.
134. Huppert M, Levine HB, Sun SH, et al. Resistance of vaccinated mice to typical and atypical strains of *Coccidioides immitis*. J Bacteriol. 1967;94:924–927.
135. Pappagianis D. Histopathologic response of mice to killed vaccines of *Coccidioides immitis*. J Invest Dermatol. 1967;49:71–77.
136. Pappagianis D. Valley Fever Vaccine Study Group: Evaluation of the protective efficacy of the killed *Coccidioides immitis* spherule vaccine in humans. Am Rev Respir Dis. 1993;148:656–660.
137. Zimmermann CR, Johnson SM, Martens GW, et al. Protection against lethal murine coccidioidomycosis by a soluble vaccine from spherules. Infect Immun. 1998;66:2342–2345.
138. Kirkland TN, Thomas PW, Finley F, et al. Immunogenicity of a 48-kilodalton recombinant T-cell–reactive protein of *Coccidioides immitis*. Infect Immun. 1998;66:424–431.
139. Kirkland TN, Finley F, Orsborn KI, et al. Evaluation of the proline-rich antigen of *Coccidioides immitis* as a vaccine in mice. Infect Immun. 1998;66:3519–3522.

Chapter 257

Dermatophytosis and Other Superficial Mycoses

RODERICK J. HAY

The superficial fungal infections include some of the most common infectious conditions such as ringworm or dermatophytosis and pityriasis versicolor as well as rare disorders including tinea nigra. Their prevalence varies in different parts of the world, but in many tropical countries they are the most common causes of skin disease. Dermatophyte infections and other superficial mycoses are described in this chapter. Superficial candidiasis is discussed in Chapter 247.

DERMATOPHYTOSIS

The dermatophytes are molds that can invade the stratum corneum of the skin or other keratinized tissues derived from epidermis, such as hair and nails. They may cause infections, dermatophytoses, at most skin sites, although the feet, groin, scalp, and nails are most commonly affected.[1] The dermatophytes are among the earliest microorganisms that were found to cause infections in humans. *Trichophyton schoenleinii*, the cause of the scalp infection favus, was isolated from a patient and the culture shown to reproduce the typical lesions after inoculation onto human skin as early as 1841. Dermatophyte infections had been described many years before this even though the identity of the cause had not been recognized. The ancient Greek physicians knew about ringworm, and there are descriptions of the manifestations of dermatophytosis in more unlikely sources such as the records of the early Dutch explorers of the 16th century who brought back reports of a strange disease of the skin, subsequently known as tinea imbricata caused by *Trichophyton concentricum*, in the islanders of the western Pacific.

The Dermatophytes

There are three genera of pathogenic dermatophyte fungi—*Trichophyton, Microsporum*, and *Epidermophyton*. The last genus is represented by only a single species, *Epidermophyton floccosum*. These keratinophilic organisms probably arose as saprophytic soil fungi, and some dermatophytes, which have been isolated only from soil, have not been shown to cause disease in either animals or humans. Most of the 39 dermatophyte species, however, are parasitic and can cause disease in either humans or animals, often being adapted to a single or narrow range of host species. The dermatophytes are referred to as either zoophilic, anthropophilic, or geophilic, depending on whether their primary source is an animal, human, or soil, respectively.

The taxonomy of these fungi is complicated by the fact that most clinical isolates are imperfect fungi, organisms that do not produce sexual structures in culture. However, sexual forms of many of these species are known and have been assigned to one of two genera, *Arthroderma* and *Nannizzia*, which correspond to the imperfect genera *Trichophyton* and *Microsporum*, respectively. The classification of these fungi is difficult, and their exact taxonomic status remains a subject of debate.[2]

The relationships among different dermatophytes are not simply a subject for intellectual dispute. It is important, for instance, to attempt to differentiate strains of the same species to understand the spread of infections. Studies of genomic or mitochondrial DNA of different species have not proved universally helpful, because the fungi are so closely related.[3] Attempts have also been made to classify the dermatophytes according to their protein composition[4] and production of antibiotics or enzymes such as urease. Both antibiotics and enzymes may play a role in determining pathogenicity. Proteinases produced by dermatophytes are inducible by, for instance, amino acids. *Trichophyton rubrum* secretes a number of enzymes with different protein affinities including keratin, the largest of which is a 200-kD glycosylated metalloprotease.[5] The production of elastase has also been proposed as a factor affecting the development of inflammatory responses in ringworm.[6] The significance of the production of antibiotics by dermatophytes is uncertain. The main groups detected have been the penicillins and fusidanes, and these are produced by dermatophytes not only under laboratory culture conditions but also after growth on epidermal sheets in vitro.

Epidemiology

The factors affecting the distribution and transmission of dermatophytosis are largely dependent on the source of the infection[7]—animal, soil, or human.

Zoophilic Dermatophyte Infections

The main zoophilic dermatophyte fungi are shown in Table 257–1. Each organism is primarily an animal pathogen that sometimes causes human infection. In each case there is usually a range of host specificities, from organisms such as *Microsporum nanum*, whose natural host is the pig and which does not infect other animals, to *Trichophyton mentagrophytes*, which affects a range of different rodent species as well as cats, dogs, and horses.

The host preferences of *T. mentagrophytes* coupled with small clinical and cultural differences have led many mycologists to subdivide this group into different species or subspecies (the *mentagrophytes* complex). Under this classification *T. mentagrophytes quinckeanum (Trichophyton quinckeanum)* is used to describe the fungus that causes the clinical pattern of favus in mice, an infection associated with the formation of epithelial crusts. In most temperate countries *Trichophyton verrucosum*, the cause of cattle ringworm, and *Microsporum canis*, a dermatophyte that causes infections in cats or dogs, are the most common zoophilic dermatophytes that cause human infections.

Of all the zoophilic dermatophytes, *M. canis* is probably the most prevalent throughout the world. Its appearance in the tropics is a comparatively recent event, and it is mainly found there as a cause of disease in urban communities.[7] Occasionally, the distribution of zoophilic dermatophytes may appear to be difficult to explain, but usually it reflects the distribution of the animal host. For instance, *Trichophyton erinacei (T. mentagrophytes)* is mainly confined to Europe and New Zealand. It is carried by hedgehogs, which were introduced into New Zealand in the 19th century from England. *Microsporum persicolor* is a rare cause of human infections in Europe, where it has been isolated from the bank vole, whose distribution is similarly restricted. *Trichophyton simii* is associated with monkeys in India and the Far East, and human infections are seen only in these areas.[8]

Geophilic Dermatophyte Infections

Dermatophytes originating from soil such as *Microsporum gypseum* are infrequent causes of human disease, although they may be seen more commonly in certain parts of the tropics such as the western Pacific and Central America. In other areas they usually cause sporadic infections, although occasionally they may be responsible for outbreaks of human disease in appropriately exposed occupational groups such as gardeners or farm workers.[8]

Anthropophilic Dermatophyte Infections

Dermatophytes that are natural pathogens of humans are the most common cause of human dermatophytosis. They include organisms that mainly cause infections of glabrous skin of the feet or hands as well as a range of pathogens whose invasion may involve penetration of the hair shaft. The most common of these organisms in most parts of the world is *T. rubrum*, which causes tinea pedis or tinea cruris in temperate climates and, particularly in the tropics, tinea corporis. Cases of infection that are due to *T. rubrum* were once rare in the Western Hemisphere, but the infection has spread rapidly during the past 40 years. The ability of this dermatophyte to cause noninflammatory chronic infections of the feet, among other sites, that are easily transmitted is probably an important factor that has determined its spread in recent years.[7] The large population movements during World War II are also thought to have contributed to the spread of the disease. Despite this, a variant with distinct morphologic appearances may be isolated from patients with tinea corporis in remote rural areas of the New World and Old World tropics, which suggests that although endemic disease caused by this species has been present for a considerable time, the key adaptation leading to spread was the appearance of strains capable of causing indolent and noninflammatory infections of peripheral skin sites.[9]

Spread of the organisms that infect glabrous skin is largely through contact with infected desquamated skin scales. Classically, this occurs in bathing areas or shower rooms where large numbers of individuals share common facilities, for instance, in military camps or factories.[10] In the U.K. coal mining industry as many as 30 to 35% of coal miners may have dermatophyte infections affecting their feet. In most cases this is due to *T. rubrum*, although *Trichophyton interdigitale (mentagrophytes)* may also be isolated.[11] Schools and public swimming baths are also sites for infection. By contrast, transmission within the home as a reflection of conjugal or familial

TABLE 257–1 Classification of the Main Dermatophytes *(Trichophyton, Microsporum,* and *Epidermophyton)* by Their Primary Reservoir(s)

Organism			
Anthropophilic	***Geophilic***	***Zoophilic***	***Source(s)***
Trichophyton concentricum	*Trichophyton ajelloi*	*Trichophyton erinacei**	Hedgehogs
Trichophyton gourvilii	*Trichophyton terrestre*	*Trichophyton equinum*	Horses
*Trichophyton mentagrophytes interdigitale**	*Microsporum fulvum*	*Trichophyton mentagrophytes mentagrophytes**	Rodents
Trichophyton megnini	*Microsporum gypseum*	*Trichophyton quinckeanum**	Mice
Trichophyton rubrum		*Trichophyton simii*	Monkeys
Trichophyton schoenleinii		*Trichophyton verrucosum*	Cattle
Trichophyton soudanense		*Microsporum canis*	Cats, dogs
Trichophyton tonsurans		*Microsporum gallinae*	Pigs
Trichophyton violaceum		*Microsporum nanum*	Bank voles
Trichophyton yaoundei		*Microsporum persicolor*	
Microsporum audouinii			
Microsporum ferrugineum			
Epidermophyton floccosum			

*These organisms are part of the "mentagrophytes" complex and may be classified as a single species.

TABLE 257–2 Distribution of *Trichophyton* and *Microsporum* Species Causing Tinea Capitis

Dermatophyte	Distribution
Trichophyton gourvilii	Central Africa
Trichophyton tonsurans	North America and Central America (Europe—some inner cities)
Trichophyton soudanense	West and central Africa
Trichophyton schoenleinii	North Africa (United States, Middle East, South Africa, South America—sporadic)
Trichophyton verrucosum	Europe
Trichophyton violaceum	Indian subcontinent, Middle East, North Africa
Trichophyton yaoundei	Central Africa
Microsporum audouinii	Central America, West Africa (Europe—uncommon)
Microsporum canis	Worldwide but uncommon in India and Far East
Microsporum ferrugineum	Central Africa, Far East

cases is not common.[12] *E. floccosum* may also cause foot infections, although it is particularly associated with tinea cruris either as a sporadic disease or in institutions such as prisons or military barracks. These infections are not geographically restricted, even though there are variations in different countries. In many tropical areas, particularly the Far East, *T. mentagrophytes* is less commonly a cause of interdigital foot disease, and patients are infected by the zoophilic variety of this species on sites other than the feet.[13]

Tinea corporis (tinea imbricata), caused by the anthropophilic dermatophyte *T. concentricum*, has an unusual distribution confined to remote parts of the humid tropics.[14] The main endemic areas are the western Pacific, Malaysia, Assam, and parts of the Amazon basin in Brazil. Infants may be affected shortly after birth, and spontaneous recovery is unusual. Large numbers of viable organisms can be cultured from the houses of infected families. Visitors to endemic areas are rarely infected. Cases have also been described in southern Mexico, where the disease appears to fluctuate in severity with the season.

The distribution of some of the other anthropophilic dermatophytes that cause tinea capitis in children as well as other clinical forms of disease such as tinea corporis or onychomycosis may be more restricted. The reasons for this are not entirely clear unless the prevalence of these infections in children, who form a relatively stable population with little opportunity for travel, limits the spread of the disease to certain localities. Whatever the reason, these scalp infections are often found in defined endemic areas (Table 257–2). The situation is best illustrated by the distribution of *Trichophyton* spp. causing tinea capitis in West Africa, where the endemic areas for *Trichophyton soudanense, Trichophyton yaoundei*, and *Trichophyton gourvilii* are distinct, although there is some overlap.[15] *Trichophyton tonsurans* in the United Kingdom, United States, and Mexico and *Trichophyton violaceum* in India, East Africa, and the Middle East are the predominant causes of scalp infection in some areas. The situation does not always remain stable, and the slow increase in numbers of *T. tonsurans* in the United States after its presumed introduction from Central America illustrates the point.[7] Endemic anthropophilic scalp infections that are due to *Microsporum* spp. are less common. For instance, *Microsporum ferrugineum* is found occasionally in the Far East or central Europe. *Microsporum rivalieri* is seen in Africa, Democratic Republic of Congo, and Angola. The most widely distributed of this genus is *Microsporum audouinii*. Once common throughout Europe, it is now rare in this area, but it is still an important cause of tinea capitis in West Africa and in parts of the United States and Latin America.

The infection caused by *T. schoenleinii*, favus, has characteristic clinical features. It was once common in Europe but has now largely disappeared from many areas, although there are still pockets of infection in parts of the United States, South America, South Africa (Botswana), and North Africa. One of the features of this disease is the development of crusts or scutula on the scalp. Hairs are invaded, but shedding is delayed because they are not structurally damaged until late in the course of the infection. Although tinea capitis is normally a disease of children, adult women with favus are occasionally seen.

Dermatophytes causing scalp disease may be carried on the skin surface without invading the skin or hair. A small proportion of carriers develop infections within 6 months, others lose the fungus, and the rest remain carriers.[16] The same can also be seen in foot infections, where carriage can also occur.

Age Incidence. Tinea capitis is mainly a disease of childhood, and cases are rare after puberty. Occasionally, this infection may occur in elderly women and is associated with scarring alopecia. The reason for the preponderance of the disease in children is thought to be the presence of medium-chain-length fatty (C_8 to C_{12}) acids in sebum that inhibit the growth of dermatophytes in postpubertal individuals. By contrast, tinea pedis is usually seen in adolescents or young adults.[17] Although foot infections can occasionally occur in young children, in this age group the nails may be invaded without concomitant skin infection.

Pathogenesis

Transfer of infecting organisms from soil, other animals, or humans is accomplished by means of arthrospores, which are vegetative cells with thickened cell walls formed by dermatophyte hyphae in vitro and vivo. It is likely that these structures are shed by the primary host with shed skin scales or hair. It has been shown that dermatophyte arthrospores can survive for considerable periods outside the host, in some cases for more than 15 months. Direct contact between the infected individual and another is not necessary for the development of dermatophytosis. The process of transfer itself is little understood, but invasion of the skin appears to follow adherence of fungal cells to keratinocytes in vitro, a process that is maximal after about 2 or 3 hours. Keratinocytes from different sites do not appear to differ in their binding capacity for arthrospores. Subsequent germination leads to invasion.[18]

Susceptibility to infection is not universal. Studies of mice experimentally infected with *T. quinckeanum* have shown considerable interstrain variation in susceptibility to dermatophytosis.[19] In humans it has been suggested that susceptibility to tinea imbricata is mediated through an autosomal recessive gene, the evidence being based on population studies among tribes of Papua, New Guinea.[20] Similar studies of the more common infections have not been carried out, but familial cases of tinea pedis are not common. The factors determining individual susceptibility to dermatophytosis are not understood, but variations in the composition of inhibitory fatty acids in sebum (see earlier) offer one explanation. Other skin surface factors thought to be important in determining the outcome of infection include the local carbon dioxide tension and the presence of surface moisture. Sweat and serum also contain inhibitory substances, one of which, transferrin, in its unsaturated state is inhibitory to the growth of dermatophytes.[21]

In experimentally infected mice and guinea pigs, the inflammatory response to dermatophytosis is maximal after 9 to 16 days, and after this stage there is resolution of the infection. The main efferent limb of immunologic resistance is the T lymphocyte. Studies of mice with *T. quinckeanum* infections have shown that resistance can be transferred to sublethally irradiated mice with T cells bearing the Thy-1 phenotype (helper-inducer T cells).[19] Suppressor lymphocyte activity can be detected in cells from the draining lymph nodes at the peak of infection. Immunity cannot be transferred to naive animals with antibody. Although it is difficult to extrapolate these data to infected humans, there is evidence that the kinetics of the immune response in humans are similar. For instance, the development of delayed-type hypersensitivity in children with naturally acquired scalp ringworm caused by *T. tonsurans* correlates with recovery. Experimentally infected humans develop both delayed-type skin reactions to trichophytin and T-lymphocyte blastogenic responses at the time of recovery.[22] Patients with chronic *T. rubrum* or *T. concentricum* infections appear to have defective T-lymphocyte–mediated responses suggestive of a Th2 response.[23] These observations suggest that appropriate T-lymphocyte activation is critical for recovery in dermatophytosis.

The afferent limb of the immune response is provided by epidermal Langerhans cells, which have been shown to act as antigen-presenting cells in mixed cultures with human lymphocytes. The mechanisms by which T lymphocytes affect recovery are less well understood. Phagocytes, mainly neutrophils and to a lesser extent macrophages, can kill dermatophytes both intracellularly and extracellularly, mainly via oxidative pathways.[19] Dermatophyte antigens have been shown to be chemotactic to human leukocytes and may activate the alternative pathway of complement activation. However, except in inflammatory ringworm, neutrophils are not commonly seen as part of the inflammatory infiltrate in dermatophytosis, and other mechanisms of fungal clearance must be involved. It has been shown that increased epidermal turnover occurs during infection. Although this also occurs in heterologous skin grafted onto *nu/nu* (T-cell–deficient) mice, suggesting that an intrinsic response is involved, it is maximal at the time of development of the maximal immune responses.[24] It is possible that elimination of dermatophytes is also accomplished by increased shedding of the stratum corneum and that the immune system amplifies an endogenous epidermal response to infection.

Different dermatophyte species vary in their ability to elicit an immune response, with some organisms such as *T. rubrum* causing chronic or relapsing infections and others, including *T. verrucosum*, leading to long-term resistance to reinfection. Some dermatophytes produce glycopeptides, which are capable of reversibly inhibiting T-lymphocyte blastogenesis in vitro.[5] This may account for in vivo modulation of immunity.

Clinical Features

The archetypal lesion of dermatophytosis is an annular scaling patch with a raised margin showing a variable degree of inflammation, the center usually being less inflamed than the edge. This clinical form is sometimes described as tinea circinata. The word *tinea* is used to refer to dermatophyte infections, and it is usually followed by the Latin description of the appropriate site. Hence, tinea pedis is an infection of the feet and tinea capitis, the scalp. The phrase *tinea incognito* is used to describe infections that do not show any of the usual characteristic features of dermatophytosis, often because of inappropriate application of corticosteroid creams.

The clinical appearances of the infection vary with the site, the fungal species involved, and the host's immune response. Zoophilic fungi often cause inflammatory lesions, and in some cases large pustular lesions (kerions) may develop. By contrast, lesions caused by anthropophilic dermatophytes often show little inflammation and may become chronic (see "Pathogenesis").

Dermatophytes cause infections irrespective of the patient's underlying immune status. However, in common with other infections, the clinical appearances are altered in immunocompromised individuals. Dermatophyte lesions are usually less inflamed in patients with diseases affecting T-lymphocyte function, but paradoxically, in some patients lesions are pustular as well as extensive. Often there is a marked follicular component of the rash in these individuals.

Tinea Pedis

Tinea pedis is usually caused by infection with either *T. rubrum* or *T. mentagrophytes (interdigitale)*, less commonly by *E. floccosum*. The infection usually starts in the lateral interdigital spaces of the foot or on the undersurface of the lateral aspects of the toes. The main symptom is itching, although this is variable. The skin usually cracks and may become severely macerated. In some cases, often where *T. mentagrophytes* is the causative organism, bullae are formed, and there is severe itching. The infection may also spread onto the dorsum of the feet, usually on the lateral side of the foot. Involvement of the sole is common in *T. rubrum* infections, and part of or the whole sole becomes erythematous and covered with dry scales. This is most noticeable along the lateral borders of the sole, where the appearance often leads to the term "moccasin" or "dry-type" infection. Blisters may also be formed in small clusters on the sole. The course of infection is variable. In noninflammatory forms the interdigital scaling is often chronic or intermittent, whereas if blisters are formed the infection usually resolves but may recur several months later. The main complications of tinea pedis are bacterial cellulitis and fungal invasion of the toenails (onychomycosis) or the skin of the dorsum of the foot and leg.

Tinea pedis is usually seen in young adults or teenage children. It is particularly common in institutions or places where common bathing facilities are used. The clinical manifestations of infection are altered in patients with T-lymphocyte abnormalities, including those with acquired immunodeficiency syndrome, in whom there is often extensive spread of the lesions onto the dorsal surface of the foot.

Scaling between the toes is often referred to as athlete's foot, but similar clinical signs may be produced by a variety of organisms. Erythrasma that is due to *Corynebacterium minutissimum* may present with scaling and, in particular, maceration between the toe webs. Gram-negative bacteria such as *Pseudomonas* and *Proteus* spp. may contribute to interdigital disease in patients with closely apposed web spaces or whose work involves immersion in water. These organisms may replace the original dermatophytes in this site, an infection known as dermatophytosis complex.[25] *Staphylococcus aureus* may cause secondary infections of foot eczema, but characteristically this starts on the dorsum of the foot over the first two digits. The mold fungi *Scytalidium dimidiatum (Hendersonula toruloidea)* and *Scytalidium hyalinum* may cause interdigital scaling as well as nail disease and sole involvement that is indistinguishable from dry-type infections caused by dermatophytes.

Tinea Cruris

The most common dermatophytes associated with groin infections are *T. rubrum* and *E. floccosum*. This infection is also called jock itch. The infection starts with scaling and irritation in the groin. The rash usually involves the anterior aspect of the thighs, less commonly the scrotum. The leading edge extending onto the thighs is prominent and may contain follicular papules and pustules. The infection may also spread to the anal cleft. Although tinea cruris is mainly a disease of young adult men, it may affect women, particularly in the tropics, where the infection is often less well delineated and spreads in a band around the waist area.

Tinea cruris is mainly seen in young adult men, and as with tinea pedis, there may be clustering of cases in institutionalized groups such as in military camps. The toe webs are also often infected in patients with tinea cruris.

Erythrasma of the groin may also cause a localized rash with itching. However, here the leading edge is less prominent than in tinea cruris, and the rash is covered with fine wrinkles. Erythrasma fluoresces pink under Wood's light. Candidiasis of the groin may also mimic tinea cruris, but an important clue to the presence of *Candida* is the appearance of small satellite pustules beyond the free margin of the rash. Flexural psoriasis causes a vivid red and uniformly scaling rash in the groin, and there is usually at least one other site with typical psoriatic plaques.

Tinea Corporis

Tinea corporis, or ringworm, is one of the most commonly misdiagnosed skin diseases. Cases of this infection are not common in temperate climates, although it is seen more frequently in the tropics. Generally there are various clinical presentations of this form of dermatophytosis. Most lesions have a prominent edge that may contain pustules or follicular papules, and the center of the lesion is often less inflamed and scaly (Fig. 257–1). Sites commonly involved are the trunk and legs. Itching is variable, and lesions may be single or multiple. Generally, infections caused by anthropophilic dermatophytes such as *T. rubrum* are less inflammatory and less clearly demarcated, and in some patients it is necessary to search for the margin carefully to delineate the rash. Lesions are usually hyperpigmented in pigmented skins. By contrast, zoophilic infections such as those caused by *M. canis* and *T. verrucosum* are more inflammatory, and lesions may become elevated and contain pustules. Infections caused by *M. gypseum* are also usually inflammatory and may have a brick-red appearance.

These clinical patterns vary with the site of infection. *T. rubrum* infections on the lower parts of the legs may lead to the formation of single or multiple deep nodules that may mimic erythema nodosum.[26] The overlying skin is dry, red, and scaly, which is a useful clue to the correct diagnosis. This form of infection, which is known as nodular folliculitis, follows follicular penetration of the hair follicles of the lower portions of the legs by the fungus. It is seen mainly in women. In patients with defective T-lymphocyte function, scaling is often minimal, and the rash of tinea corporis consists of grouped papules or pustules without significant erythema.

Tinea corporis can occur at any age, although in temperate countries it is most often seen in children and is associated with zoophilic infections.

A number of different conditions should be considered in the differential diagnosis of tinea corporis, ranging from eczema to psoriasis or annular erythema. The important points to look for are the annular scaling margin of lesions and follicular prominence, which are features of dermatophytosis. However, it may be necessary to take scrapings for laboratory culture where there is doubt.

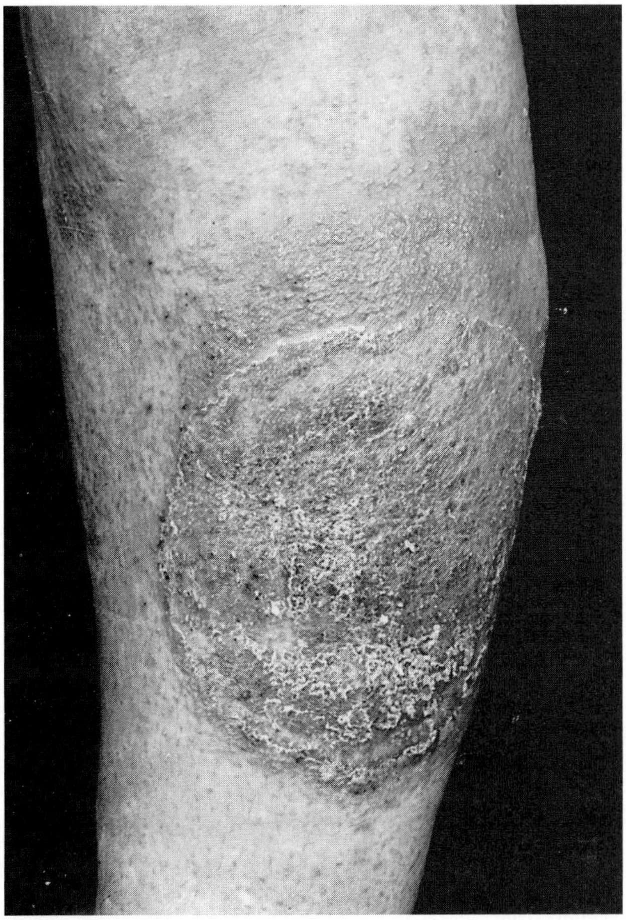

FIGURE 257–1. Inflammatory tinea corporis due to *Trichophyton erinacei* (mentagrophytes).

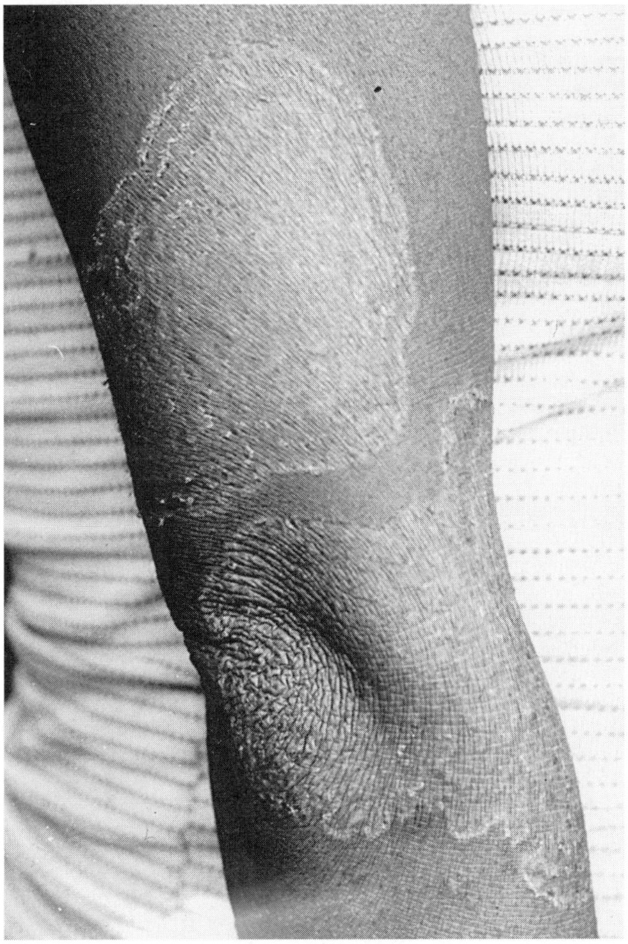

FIGURE 257–2. Early lesions of tinea imbricata showing the first signs of concentric rings.

Tinea Imbricata

Tinea imbricata is a variant of tinea corporis that is caused by *T. concentricum*. The geographic distribution of the disease is shown in Table 257–2. Patients may be infected at any age, although infants and young children are frequently affected. The main characteristic of the rash is the formation of concentric rings of scales (Fig. 257–2) over large parts of the body that amalgamate to form waves of scaling.[14] There are other clinical varieties of tinea imbricata, including the diffuse scaling variety, where large flakes of skin are prominent. The disease gets its name *imbricata* (Latin, "tiled") from this clinical pattern. Other patients may have itchy lichenified lesions on the forearms. The face may be affected, as well as the sides of the fingers, but the feet, scalp, axillae, and groin are usually spared. Tinea imbricata is seldom mistaken for other diseases, and the inhabitants of endemic areas easily recognize the appearance of the infection and have specific names for it. In Papua New Guinea, it is called *sipoma* or *grille*.

Dermatophytosis of the Hand (Tinea Manuum)

The term *tinea manuum* is used for dermatophyte infections involving the hand. In some patients the dorsum of the hand may be affected, but most commonly the disease occurs on the palmar surface. It is a characteristic of dry-type infections at this site to find that only one palm is involved, although in some patients both may be infected. The clinical features are identical to those seen with dry-type infections of the sole. The usual cause is *T. rubrum*, and the feet are often involved in addition to the hands.

Dermatophytosis affecting the palm may be confused with eczema, but the unilateral distribution of the infection and the common accompanying findings of onychomycosis and tinea pedis are helpful clues. Patients with palmoplantar keratoderma (tylosis) are particularly susceptible to superinfection of the palms and soles with dermatophytes.[27] This complication may be difficult to identify, but the skin may blister and the hand usually itches. In these patients fungi other than *T. rubrum* may be implicated.

Tinea Faciei

Dermatophyte infections of the face are usually caused by the same organisms associated with tinea corporis. Infections that are due to *T. rubrum* at this site are often particularly difficult to recognize (tinea incognito). The facial skin becomes itchy and red, but the margin of the rash may be difficult to discern (Fig. 257–3). Some patients report that the facial rash is exacerbated by sun exposure. In other instances lesions are more readily noticeable and affect the ears.

Tinea barbae, infection of the neck and beard area, may be pustular and inflamed because it is often caused by zoophilic organisms such as *T. verrucosum*. It is more localized than sycosis barbae caused by *S. aureus*, a helpful point in distinguishing the two conditions.

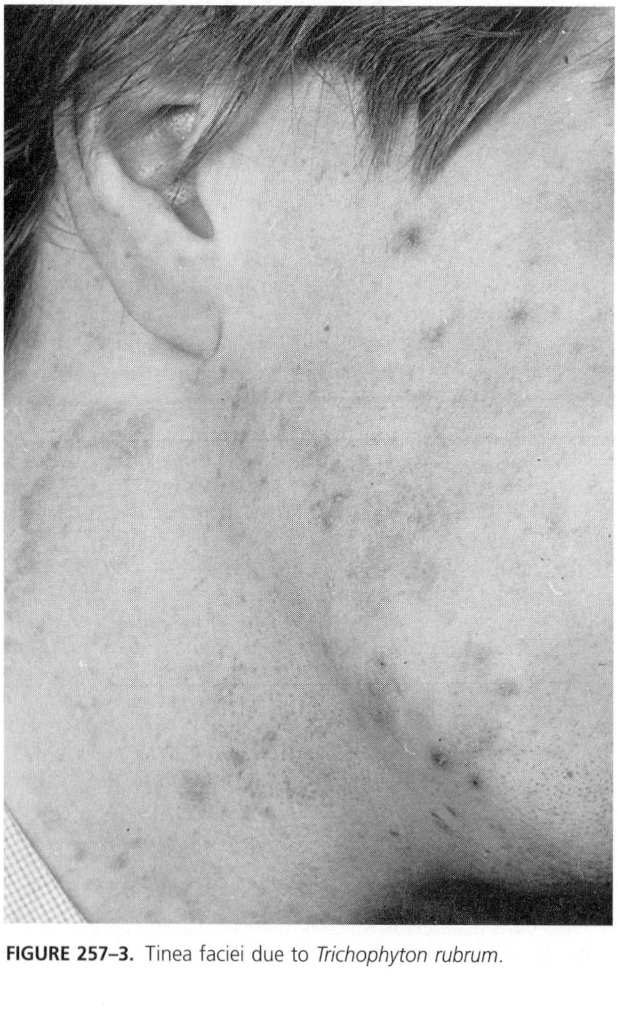

FIGURE 257–3. Tinea faciei due to *Trichophyton rubrum*.

Tinea Capitis

Scalp ringworm, or tinea capitis, is a disease of childhood. Its prevalence varies considerably in different parts of the world. The disease is widespread in some urban areas in the United States, Central America, and South America. Tinea capitis is also common in parts of Africa and India. In northern Europe the disease is sporadic. The main reasons for these differences in the prevalence of infection in different localities are the nature of the infecting organisms and the availability of control measures. Endemic infections affecting large numbers of children are associated with anthropophilic organisms, sporadic disease with zoophilic fungi. Tinea capitis is usually classified by the pattern of hair shaft invasion. Dermatophyte infections in which arthrospores are formed on the outside of the hair shaft are known as *ectothrix* infections and those in which the spores develop within the hair itself as *endothrix* infections. In *T. schoenleinii* infections the fungi invade the hair medulla but then regress and leave tunnels containing air within the hair shaft (the "favic" pattern).

The main clinical feature of scalp infections that are due to dermatophytes is the appearance of scaling of the scalp skin that is associated with a variable degree of erythema and inflammation and alopecia. In some cases the infection closely resembles seborrheic dermatitis or dandruff of the scalp. The infection is often accompanied by itching. A pathognomonic feature is hair loss. In ectothrix infections hairs often break a few millimeters or more above the skin surface (Fig. 257–4). Broken or infected hairs are also slightly swollen and have a dull appearance. In endothrix infections, parasitized hairs break at the skin level. In some endothrix infections scattered stumps can be seen within areas of hair loss (black-dot ringworm). In such cases inflammation may be minimal. A further element in tinea capitis is the variable amount of inflammation, but in some cases the whole area becomes pustular and covered with a thick scale or exudative crust. Often one of these elements dominates the clinical pattern. For instance, in some children there is little overt hair loss, the whole infection resembling seborrheic dermatitis. Likewise, in some ectothrix infections a pustular form of dermatophytosis, or kerion, develops. This is less common in endothrix infections. In most kerions the pustules are not a sign of secondary bacterial infection,[28] although this may occur under adherent crusts.

Tinea capitis is rare in adults, although it may occasionally be found in elderly patients and is caused by a variety of fungi such as *T. tonsurans*. It has been associated with scarring alopecia of unknown etiology, pseudopelade, in adults.

In favus the same processes occur, but an important clinical characteristic is the formation of an inflammatory crust, or scutulum, composed of neutrophils and serous exudate around individual hair shafts. With time these amalgamate over the surface of the scalp so that the hair appears to be matted together with a thick crust that is said to have a mousy odor. In many patients the signs are indistinguishable from those seen with other forms of scalp ringworm. Two other characteristics of favus are late shedding of hairs and a tendency to develop scarring alopecia. The infection may persist into adult life, particular in women.

Untreated scalp ringworm usually remits spontaneously after puberty. Permanent hair loss is uncommon unless there has been a severe inflammatory response or the patient has favus. A surprising degree of recovery of hair growth occurs, even in children with severe kerions.

Tinea capitis has to be distinguished from seborrheic dermatitis, which usually occurs in older children and does not cause hair loss. Alopecia areata also causes circumscribed areas of hair loss but does not scale, and the "exclamation mark" hairs seen in this condition—broken hairs tapering from the fractured end toward the skin surface—are pathognomonic.

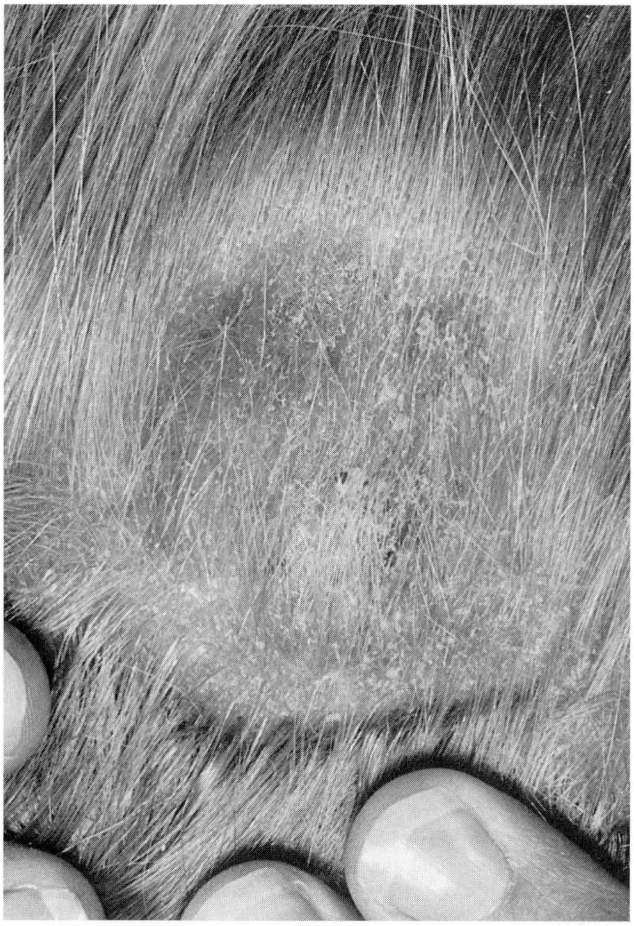

FIGURE 257–4. Scalp ringworm in which an ectothrix infection of the hair is caused by *Microsporum canis.*

Onychomycosis Caused by Dermatophytes

Onychomycosis, or fungal infection of the nails, usually occurs in individuals with infections of adjacent toe or palmar skin except in rare cases of childhood nail infection in which nail plate invasion may develop without skin involvement. There are several different patterns of nail plate invasion.[29]

The most common clinical pattern of onychomycosis is distal and subungual onychomycosis, in which the nail plate is invaded from the distal and lateral borders. There is usually associated thickening of the nail, which becomes white, yellow, or brown. The latter color is more common in the rare instances of *T. mentagrophytes* nail disease. In onychomycosis caused by endothrix scalp fungi such as *T. soudanense*, the thickening may be minimal, and the nail surface is pitted with small fissures.[30] The most common cause of onychomycosis is *T. rubrum*, which often accompanies long-standing disease, and the infection involves the entire nail plate.

Superficial white onychomycosis occurs where the nail plate is invaded from the top surface, which is eventually covered with white crumbly plaques. Other fungi, such as *Fusarium* species, more commonly cause this pattern of nail invasion. However, in its pure form superficial white onychomycosis can be seen with *T. mentagrophytes*, and it may also accompany distal and subungual onychomycosis in some *T. rubrum* infections.

Rarely, invasion appears to originate from the proximal nail plate. This is usually a feature of relapse of treated nails, but rapidly spreading proximal nail plate invasion has also been described in patients with acquired immunodeficiency syndrome.[31]

Onychomycosis can occur at any age, although it is more common with increasing age. Males and females are equally affected.

This infection has to be distinguished from onychomycosis caused by *Candida*, in which there is little nail plate thickening but toenail infection is rare. *Scytalidium* infections may also lead to nail plate invasion. These are difficult to distinguish from infections caused by dermatophytes, but the nail plate is often not grossly thickened and may be severely undermined, and invasion predominantly affects the lateral border of the plate in the early stages of disease. Psoriasis of the nail also causes onycholysis, but the nail plate is typically covered with fine pits.

Deep Dermatophyte Infections

On rare occasions patients known to be immunocompromised or apparently unselected individuals develop dermatophyte infections in which the fungi invade subcutaneous tissues via the lymphatics, usually causing clusters of granulomas, lymphedema (Fig. 257–5), and draining sinuses.[32] Sometimes aggregates of fungal hyphae resembling those found in eumycetomas may be seen in histologic sections. These dermatophyte "mycetoma" grains may be surrounded by neutrophil abscesses, but often the fungal hyphae are engulfed by giant cells in tissue sections. Deep dermatophyte infections may extend further to involve draining lymph nodes or other sites including the liver and brain, and they may be fatal.

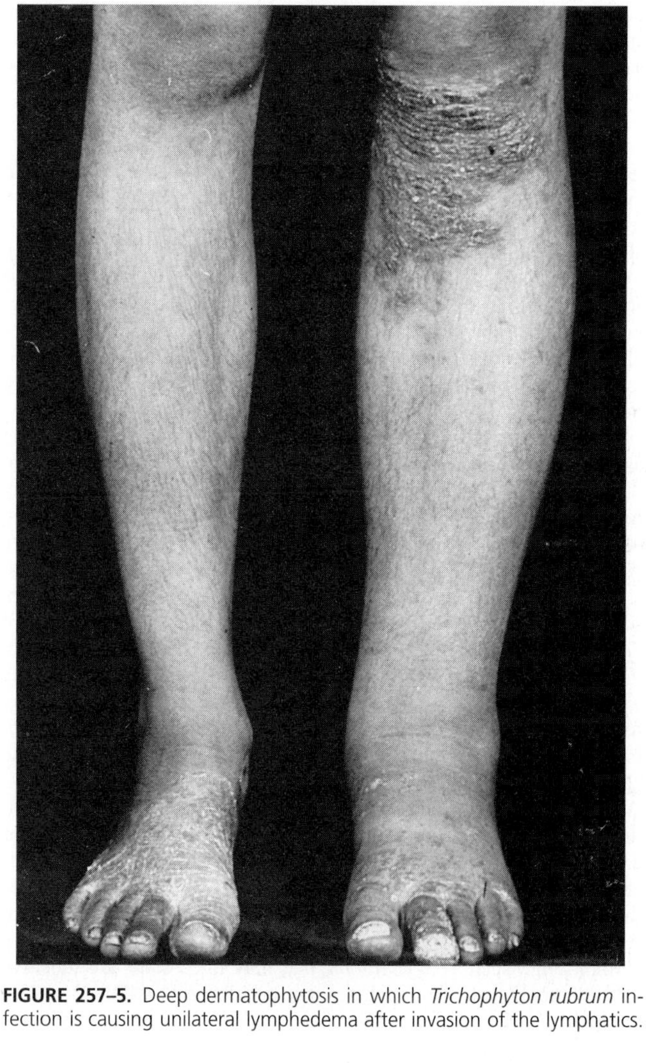

FIGURE 257–5. Deep dermatophytosis in which *Trichophyton rubrum* infection is causing unilateral lymphedema after invasion of the lymphatics.

Dermatophyte "Id" Reactions

The immune mechanisms in dermatophytosis may lead to the appearance of secondary rashes called *id reactions*. The most common of these is a type of acute vesicular eczema or pompholyx that occurs on the hands and feet in patients with inflammatory ringworm of the feet, mainly caused by *T. mentagrophytes*. These events are thought to be linked if the original dermatophyte infection becomes inflamed before the appearance of the secondary rash, the latter is maximal on the affected foot, and the patient has a strong delayed-type hypersensitivity reaction to intradermal trichophytin. The histology of this id reaction is that of eczema. A second form of id reaction is seen in patients with inflammatory tinea capitis or corporis and is usually caused by zoophilic organisms. It consists of small follicular papules, some of which appear necrotic. This is a form of cutaneous vasculitis that usually subsides spontaneously. Both reactions may be triggered by antifungal therapy. Other less common types of id reaction include annular erythema and erythema nodosum.

Patients with follicular invasion by dermatophytes may develop a residual granuloma in the late stages of the disease called Majocchi's granuloma. It is usually sterile, although sometimes fragments of mycelium can be seen in histologic sections, and resolves slowly with time.

Laboratory Diagnosis

In some cases it is possible to screen patients with scalp infections by using a filtered ultraviolet light source (Wood's light). Infections caused by *Microsporum* spp. fluoresce green. However, *Trichophyton* infections do not fluoresce, apart from favus, in which the hairs appear yellowish. Fluorescent hairs are infected, and apart from its use as a screening procedure, Wood's light examination may be helpful as a method of selecting hairs for microscopy and culture.

The laboratory diagnosis of dermatophytosis depends on the examination and culture of scrapings or clippings from lesions. It is important to sample the edge of skin lesions and infected nails. In the case of infected hairs, broken stubs are best selected and can be removed with forceps without undue trauma. Material should be allowed to soften in 10 to 20% potassium hydroxide before being examined under the microscope. Nails often take up to 2 hours to soften, although the process can be hastened by gentle warming. Fungal hyphae can be seen as chains of arthrospores in cleared scales or clippings. The fluorescent whitener calcoflour may also be used to stain fungi, but preparations have to be viewed using fluorescence microscopy.

Dermatophytes infecting hair show characteristic appearances that are helpful in recognition. Some form arthrospores on the outside of the hair shaft, ectothrix infections. The small spores can be seen by focusing the microscope on the edge of the epilated hair shaft. Most of the pathogenic *Microsporum* spp. that cause tinea capitis have small arthrospores clustered around the outside of hair. By contrast, few *Trichophyton* spp. form ectothrix spores, but those that do, such as *T. verrucosum*, produce large arthrospores. The majority of *Trichophyton* spp. causing scalp ringworm form arthrospores within the hair shaft (endothrix infection). With some practice it is possible to make a preliminary identification of the likely genus of invading fungus on the basis of the microscopy of infected hair. *T. schoenleinii* invades hair, but hyphae regress and leave airspaces within the hair shaft.

Scrapings or nail clippings may also be cultured. Primary isolation is carried out at room temperature, usually on Sabouraud's agar containing antibiotics (penicillin-streptomycin or choramphenicol) and cycloheximide (Actidione), an antifungal agent that suppresses the growth of environmental contaminant fungi. In the case of nail disease it is important to use media without cycloheximide because certain fungi, such as *Scytalidium*, that may infect nails are sensitive to the latter. Most dermatophytes can be identified within 2 weeks, although *T. verrucosum* grows best at 37°C and may only have formed into small and granular colonies at this stage. Identification depends on the gross colonial and microscopic morphology. In some cases, other tests involving nutritional requirements and hair penetration in vitro are necessary to confirm the identification.

Generally, the identification of dermatophytes in skin material is simple and worth the effort required to obtain samples. It is particularly helpful in scalp infections, where it is important to identify the likely source of infection.

Treatment

The usual approach to the management of dermatophyte infections is to treat with topical therapy if possible, but most nail and all hair infections and widespread dermatophytosis are best treated with oral drugs.[33]

The main topical agents used for dermatophytosis are the keratolytics and compounds with specific antifungal activity. The keratolytic agent used most frequently is Whitfield's ointment (salicylic and benzoic acid compound). This is particularly effective in infections confined to heavily keratinized areas such as the soles or palms. It is inexpensive but messy to use, although a cream formulation of benzoic acid compound is available in some countries.

In the past, therapy relied on the use of substances including dyes with weak antifungal activity such as brilliant green and Castellani Paint (magenta and resorcinol). There is now a large group of specific antifungals that may be used in dermatophytosis, although the use of some of these is largely confined to the treatment of tinea pedis. They include drugs such as chlorphenesin, undecylenate, and tolnaftate, which are available in cream or, in some cases, powder form. Few comparative studies have examined their relative merits. Nonetheless, they are effective in uncomplicated cases. More attention has been focused on one particular group of antifungal drugs, the azoles, which include miconazole, clotrimazole, econazole, tioconazole, ketoconazole, oxiconazole, bifonazole, isoconazole, and fenticonazole.[34] These are active against all the common skin fungi, and many can be given once daily. Other potent antifungals used in the treatment of dermatophytosis are cyclopiroxolamine, terbinafine, butenafine, and naftifine. It is difficult to choose between the different groups of these agents on the basis of well-constructed comparative studies.

Generally, topical therapy for tinea pedis has to be continued for at least 2 and possibly 4 weeks. The topical form of the allylamine terbinafine can be used to clear lesions of tinea pedis in 1 to 7 days. Dry-type infections of the sole respond poorly to topical application, although the topical medication may be useful in relieving the dryness and scaling. Tinea cruris usually responds within 2 or 3 weeks of the outset of treatment. Some of the azole agents can be used only once daily. Topical treatments for scalp and nail infections are generally ineffective, although cures of nail disease have been claimed for topically applied azoles and cyclopiroxolamine. Three other approaches are of potential value in the management of nail disease. The first, a topically applied nail solution containing 28% tioconazole, has been found to produce mycologic and clinical remission on its own or in conjunction with oral griseofulvin. The second such preparation used in nail disease is a combination of 40% urea and bifonazole. Urea is a potent hydrating agent and softens nails after application under occlusion. The 40% urea paste may be used to remove residual areas of infection after oral therapy for onychomycosis.[35] This combination may also prove useful in addition to oral therapy for nail disease. Finally, 5% amorolfine used as a nail lacquer is effective in a significant proportion of early cases of dermatophyte and *Candida* nail infection and can be applied once or twice weekly.[36]

The main oral antifungals used for dermatophytosis are terbinafine, itraconazole, and fluconazole. Griseofulvin is an alternative treatment but is still the treatment of choice for most cases of tinea capitis. Terbinafine is given in doses of 250 mg daily for 2 weeks for tinea cruris or corporis, 6 weeks for fingernail infections, and

12 weeks for toenail infections. It produces rapid and long-lasting remissions for dry-type dermatophytosis and other skin infections.[37] Itraconazole can be given continuously in doses of 200 mg daily and is curative for tinea cruris or corporis after 1 week.[38] There have been fewer clinical trials of fluconazole as a treatment for dermatophytosis, but current regimens use 150 to 300 mg weekly for infections of the skin. All three drugs are well tolerated and involve a low risk of hepatic injury (less than 1 in 70,000); rarely, terbinafine causes disturbance or loss of taste.

Griseofulvin is given in doses of 10 to 20 mg/kg daily in either tablet or syrup form and is the main treatment for tinea capitis. Adverse effects include headache, nausea, and abdominal discomfort. Less common reactions are urticaria, diarrhea, and photosensitivity. Griseofulvin may precipitate acute intermittent porphyria and systemic lupus erythemamatosus in predisposed subjects. Oral ketoconazole may also be used for dermatophytosis, although the risk of hepatitis, albeit rare, makes this a second choice for therapy in most instances.

Oral therapy is used for scalp ringworm and nail infections. Scalp infections take 6 to 12 weeks to respond to griseofulvin. Often it is useful to use a topical azole cream or shampoo in addition and, if crusts are present, to remove these with saline soaks. For the treatment of large numbers of infected children, intermittent therapy with up to 1 g of griseofulvin has been suggested, with possible retreatment after 6 weeks. A substantial percentage of those infected may respond to single-dose therapy. Itraconazole and terbinafine are also effective in scalp disease but there are no ideal paediatric formulations yet.[39] It is important to attempt to identify the organism causing scalp infection because if the infection is of human origin it can spread to other contacts and it may be necessary to screen classmates or members of the families of children with anthropophilic infections. Zoophilic infections do not usually spread from child to child, although several family members exposed to the same source of infection may develop scalp disease.

Onychomycosis caused by dermatophytes can be treated with oral therapy. Terbinafine and itraconazole have replaced griseofulvin for this indication. For instance, terbinafine produces 70 to 80% cure rates in 6 weeks for fingernails and 12 weeks for toenails.[40] Itraconazole is also effective at a dose of 200 mg daily for 3 months in toenail infections. But in nail infections it is usually administered as a "pulsed" treatment given for 1 week of each month at a dose of 400 mg daily, the week's course being repeated once more for fingernail infections (two pulses) and twice or three times for toenail disease (three or four pulses).[41] Reported remission rates are above 60%. Intermittent regimens using fluconazole (150, 300, and 450 mg weekly) in the treatment of onychomycosis have been compared.[42] There are no significant differences between the three dose regimens in overall efficacy, although with both higher doses, 300 and 450 mg, there is a trend to greater efficacy. There have been no large comparative studies of fluconazole versus the other two treatments for nail disease. However, one large double-blind comparative study of terbinafine given continuously at 250 mg daily for 12 or 16 weeks versus pulsed itraconazole at 200 mg twice a day for 1 week each month repeated three or four times in toenail onychomycosis showed significantly better responses for both terbinafine groups in both mycologic and clinical remission rates (LION Study results).[42a]

SCYTALIDIUM INFECTIONS

Infections caused by the pigmented fungus *S. dimidiatum (H. toruloidea)* closely resemble dry-type dermatophytosis caused by *T. rubrum. S. dimidiatum* was originally described as a plant pathogen, but it appears to be a genuine cause of human infection. A similar type of infection has been ascribed to a nonpigmented mold, *S. hyalinum.* In both cases the affected patients have originated from the tropics.

The precise mechanisms of infection with either organism are unknown. *S. hyalinum* has never been isolated from the environment, and although *S. dimidiatum* is a pathogen of certain plants such as fruit trees, patients do not usually give a specific history of exposure. It has been found that healthy individuals in some tropical areas carry these organisms on the feet but do not have overt disease, suggesting that asymptomatic carriage may be followed under the appropriate conditions by infection. Infections have been described in immigrants from tropical areas to the United Kingdom, Canada, and France. Patients have also been identified in the southern United States, Trinidad, Colombia, Ecuador, and India, and it is likely that the infection is more widespread. Occasionally, it may be seen in patients who have paid short visits to the tropics.

Clinical Features

The clinical signs of skin infection with both *Scytalidium* species are identical to those associated with dry-type *T. rubrum* infections.[43] There is scaling of the lateral interdigital spaces, over the soles, and on one or both palms. Itching is usually minimal. Onychomycosis may also develop. Often there is early invasion of the lateral border of the nail without significant thickening of the nail plate (Fig. 257–6), but eventually the whole nail plate may be undermined and onycholysis may lead to shedding of the complete nail. Hyperpigmented streaks may occur in the nails, although these are not pathognomonic for these infections and can be seen with other forms of inflammatory nail dystrophy.

Diagnosis

Scrapings or nail clippings examined after treatment with potassium hydroxide contain sinuous fungal hyphae. On close inspection the morphology is different from that normally seen with dermatophyte hyphae, but accurate discrimination requires experience. Both organisms grow on Sabouraud's agar but are inhibited if cycloheximide (Actidione) is incorporated in the medium.

Treatment

There is no satisfactory therapy for either infection. Whitfield's ointment may be used to treat *Scytalidium* infections of the sole or the palm. However, none of the specific antifungal drugs currently available produces consistent results.

OTHER FORMS OF ONYCHOMYCOSIS

A number of other fungi may cause onychomycosis. The most common of these is *Scopulariopsis brevicaulis*, which usually causes

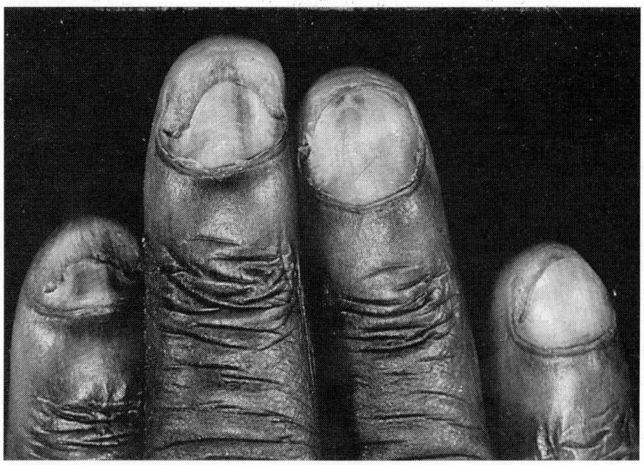

FIGURE 257–6. Onychomycosis due to *Scytalidium dimidiatum.*

infection of the great toenails. Some patients with this form of infection have previously abnormal toenails (e.g., onychogryphosis). *Scopulariopsis* infections of the nails have a typical cinnamon color that is caused by the presence of fungal spores seen on direct microscopy of the nail. The fungus is easy to isolate in culture. Treatment may be difficult, but chemical nail removal with 40% urea may be useful.

Superficial white onychomycosis may be caused by *Acremonium* or *Fusarium* species. These infections are similar to those caused by *T. mentagrophytes*, and the identity of the causative organisms should be confirmed by culture.

Occasionally, other fungi are isolated from nail material. In many cases they appear to be colonizing the undersurface of dystrophic nail plate. On rare occasions, however, they may contribute to the nail pathology by invasion. This is best established by repeated attempts at culture, and if the organism is isolated on numerous occasions and if hyphae are present in the nail, it is likely that the organism is implicated in the nail disease. Examples of infections caused by a range of different organisms such as *Aspergillus, Fusarium*, and *Acremonium* spp. have been recorded. There is seldom effective oral therapy for these infections, and nail removal with 40% urea is probably the best alternative treatment.

PITYRIASIS VERSICOLOR

Pityriasis or tinea versicolor is a superficial infection caused by *Malassezia* species, lipophilic yeasts, which are normal commensals on the skin surface.[44] The infection is confined to the trunk or proximal aspects of the limbs. Hair and nail plate invasions do not occur.

Organisms

The normal skin is colonized in late childhood and adult life by lipophilic yeasts. Morphologically, these are either oval, most common on the scalp, or round, mainly on the trunk, and they were previously called *Pityrosporum ovale* and *Pityrosporum orbiculare*, respectively. These organisms have now been reclassified as members of the genus *Malassezia* and there are seven pathogenic species: *Malassezia furfur, Malassezia pachydermatis* (not associated with human skin infections), *Malassezia sympodialis, Malassezia globosa, Malassezia restricta, Malassezia obtusa*, and *Malassezia slooffiae*.[44] Round yeasts, usually *M. globosa*, are seen in lesions of pityriasis versicolor accompanied by short stubby hyphae; *M. furfur* may produce filaments as well.

Pathogenesis

The infection is associated with transformation of yeast phase organisms into hyphal forms, although patients with pityriasis versicolor occasionally have only oval yeasts. The stimulus for this phase change is unknown. Infections are more common in the tropics and may appear after sun exposure, which may therefore be a trigger factor. Patients with Cushing's syndrome may also develop this infection,[45] but diseases related to T-lymphocyte suppression are not necessarily associated with pityriasis versicolor.

A carboxylic acid called *azaleic acid,* thought to be produced by the organism in the stratum corneum, is believed to lead to the depigmentation seen in lesions.[46] *Malassezia* yeasts grow in the presence of medium-chain-length fatty acids.

Clinical Features

Pityriasis versicolor is usually seen on the trunk or proximal portions of the limbs, although more extensive infections involving the face and waist area are seen in the tropics. Lesions may be hypopigmented or hyperpigmented macules that amalgamate to cover the affected area with scaling plaques. The lesions are usually not itchy. In some patients lesions may remit spontaneously.

The diagnosis can be confirmed by direct microscopy of lesions, with which the characteristic round yeast forms and short hyphae can be seen. The scrapings can be viewed after clearing with potassium hydroxide but are seen more clearly after staining with a mixture of Parker Quink ink and potassium hydroxide. Lesions fluoresce yellow-green under Wood's light, although this may not be seen on all affected areas. *Malassezia* yeasts are difficult to culture unless oil is added to the medium. An overlay of Tween 80 encourages growth.

Treatment

The most appropriate therapy for pityriasis versicolor is a topical azole, terbinafine cream, 2% selenium sulfide lotion, or 20% sodium thiosulfate applied daily for 10 to 14 days. The latter preparations may be irritative. In some cases intermittent applications of 50% propylene glycol in water prevents a relapse.[47] In severe cases, oral ketoconazole or itraconazole produces remissions. The exact doses of ketoconazole needed to induce a remission are not clear, but therapy for 5 to 10 days with 200 mg is usually sufficient, although mycologic recovery is not seen for about 30 days because the organisms can still be seen in skin scrapings. In some patients a single dose of 400 mg is effective. The effective dose of itraconazole is 200 mg daily for 5 days.

Patients usually have to be warned that the pigmentary changes may return to normal only after many months, even when the infection has been successfully treated.

OTHER *MALASSEZIA* INFECTIONS

Two other skin conditions are associated with *Malassezia* yeasts: *Malassezia* folliculitis and seborrheic dermatitis. In addition, this fungus has caused catheter-acquired sepsis (see Chapter 259).

Malassezia Folliculitis

There are three main forms of this condition. The first is a folliculitis on the back or upper part of the chest that consists of scattered follicular papules or pustules (LION Study results). These are itchy and often appear after sun exposure. In the second form, which is seen in patients with seborrheic dermatitis, there are numerous small follicular papules over the upper and lower portions of the back and chest. Erythema and greasy perifollicular scales are often seen in these patients. In the third form multiple pustules are seen on the trunk and face in patients with human immunodeficiency virus infection. This type is similar to the second form, and the patients usually have severe seborrheic dermatitis.

Scrapings or biopsy specimens from lesions show numerous yeasts occluding the mouths of follicles. Treatment with topical azole antifungals may be effective, but oral therapy with ketoconazole or itraconazole is often necessary.

Seborrheic Dermatitis

In the early part of the 20th century, seborrheic dermatitis and dandruff of the scalp were thought to be caused by *Malassezia* yeasts because numerous organisms are present in skin scales. This view was subsequently superseded by the belief that the yeasts were secondary to a hyperproliferative state. However, evidence suggests that *Malassezia* is implicated in the pathogenesis of the condition.[48]

In most cases, seborrheic dermatitis responds to oral ketoconazole or topical azole antifungals. Improvement is associated with disappearance of the organisms, and relapse is associated with recolonization. Furthermore, the clinical appearances can be mimicked in animals with the application of both live and killed organisms to the skin. Some patients with seborrheic dermatitis have high antibody titers to *Malassezia* species.

It is unlikely that invasion of the epidermis is responsible for the appearance of seborrheic dermatitis, but an indirect disease mechanism such as sensitization or toxic damage is possible.

Seborrheic dermatitis can appear in any individual, although it is said to be particularly common in patients with neurologic disease such as parkinsonism. In patients with acquired immunodeficiency syndrome the onset of seborrheic dermatitis may be sudden and the rash more extensive than in other individuals.[49] The histology of seborrheic dermatitis is similar in all groups. Acanthosis and hyperkeratosis with elongation of dermal papillae are seen. An infiltrate of polymorphs in the epidermis above the dermal papillae is also often seen. Human immunodeficiency virus–positive patients tend to have more plasma cells in the infiltrate. These changes are similar to those seen in some forms of psoriasis.

Clinical Features

The classic features of seborrheic dermatitis comprise a range of different clinical appearances. These include erythema and scaling of the central part of the anterior aspect of the chest and the upper part of the back that are accompanied by a variable degree of itching. On the face there is erythema with greasy scales in the eyebrows, around the alae nasi, behind the ears, and in the external ears. Scaling may also appear in the presternal areas of the chest and on the back. Scaling in the scalp is accompanied by the appearance of pustules in some patients. The clinical appearances are typical, and fungal scrapings are unnecessary.

Other forms of skin disease, including severe erythroderma in infants and an intertriginous rash in adults, have also been called seborrheic dermatitis, but these lesions do not appear to be related to the variety discussed here.

Treatment

The main therapy involves the use of topical azole creams and weak topical corticosteroids such as 1% hydrocortisone. Relapse is common, but retreatment when necessary is the simplest approach to management.

TINEA NIGRA

Tinea nigra is a superficial form of phaeohyphomycosis caused by *Hortaea (Exophiala) werneckii.* The infection is confined to the stratum corneum of the palms or soles and is mainly seen in the tropics or subtropics in children or young adults.

The typical lesion of tinea nigra is a superficial scaling macule that is brown or black on the palms or soles. The pigmentation is irregularly distributed over larger lesions. Spread of the infection to other sites is rare, and lesions remain asymptomatic.

The main differential diagnosis is a superficial form of melanoma or a pigmented nevus. The pigmented hyphae can be seen by direct microscopy of skin scrapings treated with potassium hydroxide. The organism can also be cultured from scrapings.

The best therapy is treatment with a keratolytic agent such as Whitfield's ointment or 5 to 10% salicylic acid ointment.

WHITE PIEDRA

White piedra is an uncommon infection caused by yeasts of the genus *Trichosporon,* namely, *Trichosporon beigelii, Trichosporon inkin, Trichosporon mucoides*, and *Trichosporon ovoides*. The infection occurs in both the tropics and temperate zones. It is a superficial infection of the hair shafts of the scalp, body, or pubic hair. *Trichosporon* species may also cause a systemic infection in neutropenic patients (see Chapter 259).

The organisms may be carried on the skin or around the anus. In some patients the infection appears to be sexually transmitted. White piedra is asymptomatic and presents with small yellow concretions on the hair shafts.[50] These are circumscribed and lesions appear as small nodules, unlike the more diffuse coating of axillary or pubic hair seen in trichomycosis axillaris, which is due to the presence of bacteria on the hair.

The diagnosis may be confirmed by examining an epilated hair mounted in potassium hydroxide. Each nodule contains fungal hyphae, and the organisms can be cultured from infected hairs without difficulty.

Treatment is difficult. Nodules may be removed simply by shaving. Otherwise, coating the hairs with an azole such as econazole or treating the patient with oral ketoconazole may cure the infection. Relapse is common after therapy.

BLACK PIEDRA

Black piedra is another infection of the hair shafts that is caused by a black yeast, *Piedraia hortae*. The disease is rare and mainly confined to parts of the humid tropics. The infection manifests with small black nodules on the hairs of the scalp, less commonly elsewhere. These have to be distinguished from pediculosis, but itching is usually absent in black piedra. With direct micrscopy these nodules can be shown to be composed of hyphal elements and small ascospores of the causative agent within a dark cement-containing stroma. Treating hairs with a topical salicylic acid, 2% formaldehyde, or an azole cream is usually sufficient, although relapse is common.

REFERENCES

1. Midgley M, Clayton YM, Hay RJ. Medical Mycology. London: Gower; 1997.
2. De Vroey C. Epidemiology of ringworm (dermatophytosis). Semin Dermatol. 1985;4:185–200.
3. Kawasaki M, Aoki M, Ishizaki H, et al. Phylogeny of *Epidermophyton floccosum* and other dermatophytes. Mycopathologia. 1996;134:121–128.
4. Jeffries CD, Reiss E, Ajello L. Analytical isoelectric focusing of secreted dermatophyte proteins applied to taxonomic differentiation of *Microsporum* and *Trichophyton* species (preliminary studies). J Med Vet Mycol. 1984;22:364–379.
5. MacGregor JM, Hamilton A, Hay RJ. Possible mechanisms of immune modulation in chronic dermatophytoses—An in vitro study. Br J Dermatol. 1992;127:233–238.
6. Rippon JW. Elastase production by ringworm fungi. Science. 1967;157:947.
7. Rippon JW. Epidemiology and emerging patterns of dermatophyte species. Curr Top Med Mycol. 1985;1:208–234.
8. Philpot CM. Geographical distribution of the dermatophytes—A review. J Hyg (Lond). 1978;80:301–313.
9. Smith JMB, Rush-Munro FM. An unusual strain of *Trichophyton rubrum* from Fiji. Sabouraudia. 1971;9:153–156.
10. Gentles JC, Evans EGV. Foot infections in swimming baths. Br Med J. 1973;3:260–262.
11. Hope YM, Clayton YM, Hay RJ, et al. Foot infection in coal miners: A reassessment. Br J Dermatol. 1985;112:405–413.
12. Rothman S, Knox G, Windhorst D. Tinea pedis, a source of infection in the family. Arch Dermatol. 1957;75:270–271.
13. Blank H, Taplin D, Zaias N. Cutaneous *Trichophyton mentagrophytes* infections in Vietnam. Arch Dermatol. 1969;99:135–144.
14. Hay RJ. Tinea imbricata. Curr Top Med Mycol. 1987;2:55–72.
15. Verhagen AR. Distribution of dermatophytes causing tinea capitis in Africa. Trop Geogr Med. 1973;26:101–120.
16. Ive FA. The carrier state of tinea capitis in Nigeria. Br J Dermatol. 1966;78:219–221.
17. Blank F, Mann SJ, Peak PA. Distribution of dermatophytosis according to age, ethnic group and sex. Sabouraudia. 1974;12:352–361.
18. Zurita J, Hay RJ. The adherence of dermatophyte microconidia and arthroconidia to human keratinocytes in vitro. J Invest Dermatol. 1987;89:529–534.
19. Hay RJ. Fungal infections. In: Bos JD, ed. Skin Immune System (SIS). Boca Raton, Fla: CRC Press; 1997:593–604.
20. Serjeantson S, Lawrence G. Autosomal recessive inheritance of susceptibility to tinea imbricata. Lancet. 1977;1:13–15.
21. King RD, Khan HA, Foye JC, et al. Transferrin, iron and dermatophytes 1. Serum dermatophyte inhibitory component definitely identified as unsaturated transferrin. J Lab Clin Med. 1975;86:204–212.
22. Jones HE, Reinhardt JH, Rinaldi MG. Acquired immunity to dermatophytosis. Arch Dermatol. 1974;109:840–848.
23. Hay RJ, Reid S, Talwet E, et al. Immune responses of patients with tinea imbricata. Br J Dermatol. 1983;108:581–589.
24. Green F, Lee KW, Balish E. Chronic *T. mentagrophytes* dermatophytosis of guinea pig skin grafts on nude mice. J Invest Dermatol. 1982;79:125–131.
25. Leyden JJ, Kligman AM. Interdigital athletes foot, the interaction of dermatophytes and residual bacteria. Arch Dermatol. 1978;114:1466–1472.
26. Wilson JW, Plunkett DA. Nodular granulomatous perifolliculitis due to *Trichophyton rubrum*. Arch Dermatol. 1954;64:258–277.
27. Elmros T, Liden S. Hereditary palmo-plantar keratoderma: Incidence of dermato-

phyte infections and the results of topical treatment with retinoic acid. Acta Derm Venereol. 1983;63:254–257.
28. Birt AR, Wilt JC. Mycology, bacteriology and histopathology of suppurative ringworm. Arch Dermatol. 1957;69:441–448.
29. Baran R, Hay RJ, Tosti A, Haneke E. A new classification of onychomycosis. Br J Dermatol. 1998;139:567–571.
30. Kalter DC, Hay RJ. Onychomycosis due to *Trichophyton soudanense*. Clin Exp Dermatol. 1988;13:221–227.
31. Weismann K, Knudsen EA, Pedersen C. White nails in AIDS/ARC due to *Trichophyton rubrum* infection. Clin Exp Dermatol. 1988;13:24–27.
32. Allen DE, Snyderman R, Meadows L, et al. Generalized *Microsporum audoninii* infection and depressed cellular immunity associated with a missing plasma factor required for lymphocyte blastogenesis. Am J Med. 1977;63:991–1000.
33. Gupta AK, Sauder DN, Shear NH. Antifungal agents: An overview. Parts I and II. J Am Acad Dermatol. 1994;30:911–918.
34. Hay RJ. Recent advances in the management of fungal disease. Q J Med. 1987;244:631–639.
35. Hay RJ, Roberts D, Richardson M, et al. The evaluation of bifonazole 1% and 40% urea paste in the management of onychomycosis. Clin Exp Dermatol. 1988;13:164–167.
36. Reinel D. Topical treatment of onychomycosis with amorolfine 5% nail lacquer: Comparative efficacy and tolerability of once and twice weekly use. Dermatology. 1992;182(Suppl):21–24.
37. Villars V, Jones TC. Clinical efficacy and tolerability of terbinafine (Lamisil)—A new topical and systemic fungicidal drug for treatment of dermatomycoses. Clin Exp Dermatol. 1989;14:101–103.
38. Grant SM, Clissold SP. Itraconazole: A review of its pharmacodynamic and pharmacokinetic properties and therapeutic use in superficial and systemic mycoses. Drugs. 1989;37:310–344.
39. Elewski B. Cutaneous mycoses in children. Br J Dermatol. 1996;134(Suppl 46):7–11.
40. Drake LA, Shear NH, Arlette JP, et al. Oral terbinafine in the treatment of toe nail onychomycosis; North American multicenter trial. J Am Acad Dermatol. 1997;37:740–745.
41. Odom RB, Aly R, Scher RK, et al. A multicenter, placebo-controlled, double-blind study of intermittent therapy with itraconazole for the treatment of onychomycosis of the finger nail. J Am Acad Dermatol. 1997;36:231–235.
42. Scher RK, Breneman D, Rich P, et al. Once-weekly fluconazole (150, 300 or 450 mg) in the treatment of distal subungual onychomycosis of the toenail. J Am Acad Dermatol. 1998;38:S77–S86.
42a. Evans EG, Sigurgeirsson B. Double blind, randomised study of continuous terbinafine compared with intermittent intraconazole in treatment of toenail onychomycosis. The LION study group. BMJ. 1999;318:1031–1035.
43. Hay RJ, Moore MK. The clinical features of superficial infections caused by *Hendersonula toruloidea* and *Scytalidium hyalinum*. Br J Dermatol. 1984;110:677–684.
44. Gueho E, Midgley G, Guillot J. The genus *Malassezia* with description of four new species. Antonie Van Leeuwenhoek. 1996;69:337–355.
45. Burke RC. Tinea versicolor: Susceptibility factors and experimental infections in human beings. J Invest Dermatol. 1961;36:389–402.
46. Nazzaro-Porro M, Passi S. Identification of tyrosinase inhibitors in cultures of *Pityrosporum*. J Invest Dermatol. 1978;71:205–208.
47. Faergemann J, Fredriksson T. Propylene glycol in the treatment of pityriasis versicolor. Acta Derm Venereol. 1980;60:92–93.
48. Shuster S. The aetiology of dandruff and the mode of action of therapeutic agents. Br J Dermatol. 1984;111:235–242.
49. Mathes BM, Douglas MC. Seborrheic dermatitis in patients with acquired immunodeficiency syndrome. J Am Acad Dermatol. 1985;13:947–951.
50. Kalter DCA, Tschen JA, Cernoch PL, et al. Genital white piedra: Epidemiology, microbiology and therapy. J Am Acad Dermatol. 1986;14:982–993.

Chapter 258

Paracoccidioides brasiliensis

ANGELA RESTREPO

Paracoccidioidomycosis is one of the most important systemic mycoses in Latin America. It is usually manifested as a chronic, progressive disease of adult men. Although the lungs are the site of primary infection, dissemination is common, mainly to the mucous membranes, skin, reticuloendothelial system, and adrenals.

DESCRIPTION OF THE PATHOGEN

The etiologic agent is a dimorphic fungus, *Paracoccidioides brasiliensis*. Microscopically, in cultures at 37°C as well as in tissues and exudates, the fungus appears as an oval to round yeast cell surrounded by a double-contoured cell wall and quite variable in size (4 to 40 μm); intracytoplasmic lipid globules are prominent. It reproduces by multiple budding, and the presence of the "pilot wheel" cell is characteristic (Fig. 258–1). Typically, numerous small (2 to 4 μm) blastoconidia surround the mother cell, to which they are connected by means of short cytoplasmic bridges. Colonies produced at 37°C grow in approximately 10 days and are soft and cream colored and have a cerebriform aspect.[1, 2] At lower temperatures (19°C to 28°C), the fungus develops as a slow-growing mold (20 to 30 days). Initially, colonies are provided with short tufts of white aerial mycelia, but the colonies become cottony and adhere strongly to the agar; the area beneath is often brownish. Few microscopic reproductive structures (chlamydospores, thin septate hyphae) are produced by the mold when grown in the regular mycologic media.[1, 2] When media with reduced carbohydrate content are used, arthroconidia and other types of conidia may be formed.[2–4] The size of these propagules varies from 4 to 5 μm, and when given to mice intranasally, they produce progressive disease as well as pulmonary fibrosis.[5, 6]

ECOLOGY AND EPIDEMIOLOGY

Perhaps the most notable ecologic characteristic of paracoccidioidomycosis is its restricted geographic distribution. It has been reported only in Latin America from Mexico (23 degrees north) to Argentina (34 degrees south); however, some countries within these latitudes are not affected (e.g., some of the Caribbean Islands and Chile); furthermore, the disorder does not afflict persons living in every region of the affected areas. Endemicity centers in regions with relatively well-defined ecologic characteristics, in the tropical and subtropical forests where temperatures are mild and humidity is relatively high and constant throughout the year.[2, 7] Although 50 cases have been reported in North America, Europe, and Asia,[2, 8, 9] patients in those cases had previously been residents in countries where paracoccidioidomycosis is endemic. Judging by the number of reported cases (more than 7000) Brazil constitutes the heart of the area of endemicity, with considerably fewer cases reported from Colombia, Venezuela, Ecuador, and Argentina.[2, 7]

Restricted geographic distribution indicates an equally limited ecologic niche for *P. brasiliensis*, one that has proved elusive. The

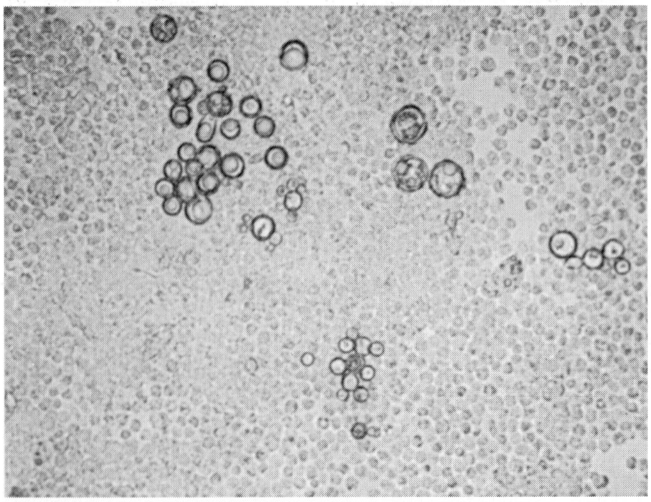

FIGURE 258–1. *Paracoccidioides brasiliensis*. KOH preparation from pus. Multiple budding and variation in cell size are apparent (×200).

fungus has been isolated from nonhuman sources only sporadically, three times from soils and once from a commercial chow contaminated with soil.[2, 10] Naturally acquired animal infection has been convincingly demonstrated only in armadillos *(Dasypus novemcinctus)*[10, 11]; in spite of the clue offered by such isolations, attempts to locate the precise microniche of the fungus have failed.[2, 7, 10] Skin tests surveys[10, 12] have revealed a significant prevalence of delayed hypersensitivity reactions to paracoccidioidin (close to 70%) among workers in coffee farms. In one study[10] *P. brasiliensis* was isolated from soil and armadillos in the same area, suggesting that coffee-growing lands were propitious for *P. brasiliensis*. In another study,[12] a cross-sectional epidemiologic survey of the indigenous population of the Brazilian Amazon basin, where an unusual number of paracoccidioidomycosis cases had been diagnosed, revealed that changes in the natives' traditional economic system and agricultural practices had resulted in increased contact with the fungus.[10, 12]

Paracoccidioidomycosis is not contagious from person to person. The route of infection is still a matter of debate. Initially, traumatic implantation was postulated; at present, however, the inhalation theory is accepted by most investigators.[2, 5, 9, 13]

The age and gender distribution of clinical cases is peculiar. Paracoccidioidomycosis is rare in children and teenagers, and most patients are 30 or more years of age.[2, 13, 14] Also, men are more commonly afflicted than women, at a mean ratio of 15:1. This is in contrast to the rate of infection, as determined by a paracoccidioidin skin test, which is similar for both genders. Of interest, too, is the fact that when the disease occurs in prepubertal patients this difference does not exist.[15] It has been suggested that the marked gender difference seen in adults could be explained by the inhibitory action of estrogens on the conidia or mycelium-to-yeast transition.[15] The occupational distribution reveals a predilection for agricultural workers.[2, 14] Alcoholism and smoking have been shown to be important predisposing factors.[16, 17]

The disease has long periods of latency, as demonstrated by the nonautochthonous cases reported outside the endemic area; some of these patients developed overt disease 30 or more years after leaving the endemic regions.[2, 8, 9] There is an indication that the fungus can remain dormant in residual lymph node lesions.[18] Dormancy may be the reason why outbreaks have not been reported.[7] Outbreaks, had they occurred, might have provided information on the ecologic niche of the fungus.

CLINICAL MANIFESTATIONS

It is now accepted that most primary infections are subclinical, with a reactive skin test being the only evidence of infection.[2, 14] Nonetheless, *P. brasiliensis* has the ability to remain dormant for long periods so that at a later date, if the formerly resistant host becomes immune depressed or acquires an underlying debilitating disease, the fungus multiplies and the mycosis becomes manifest.[9, 14, 18, 19] The host's immune defenses are directly related to the clinical form and the severity of the mycosis.[20] Cell-mediated immunity plays a crucial role; it is usually depressed at the peak of infection, partly because of the fungus itself; humoral immunity, on the other hand, is intact. Upon recovery, the immune balance tends to normalize.[14, 19–22] The dichotomy between humoral and cellular immune responses suggests a Th2 pattern of immune response.[23] A possible relationship between impaired cellular immunity and altered CD4/CD8 ratios has been shown to exist in patients with the juvenile form of the mycosis and has been strongly suggested in the chronic form of paracoccidioidomycosis.[14, 23–25] Furthermore, the capacity of lymphocytes to produce regulatory cytokines appeared to be altered.[23–26] Nonetheless, the mycosis is not markedly opportunistic as revealed by the relatively few immunosuppressed patients who develop *P. brasiliensis* disease, including those with acquired immunodeficiency syndrome.[27, 28]

Paracoccidioidomycosis is a polymorphic disease, often severe and progressive, although some self-limited cases have been reported.[14, 18, 21, 29, 30] In younger patients, the disorder is subcute and carries a severe prognosis; in adults, the course is chronic and the outcome better if appropriate therapy is given.[14, 19, 21, 22] The lungs are the site of the primary infection, but the patient's symptoms may not reflect this fact.[2, 21, 22, 31] In the juvenile form, for example, the mononuclear phagocyte system is the target organ, and respiratory complaints are minimal.[13] In the adult form, most patients present with a respiratory problem either as the sole manifestation of the disease or as pathology contributing to the overall clinical picture.[2, 19, 22, 29, 31–34] Such patients seek medical advice as a result of the following symptoms in order of decreasing frequency: (1) mucosal ulcerations occurring in the upper respiratory and digestive tracts, mostly in the mouth and nose; (2) difficulties in swallowing and changes in voice; (3) cutaneous lesions preferentially located on the face and limbs; (4) enlarged lymph nodes, especially those of the cervical area; and (5) respiratory problems such as shortness of breath, persistent cough, purulent or blood-tinged sputum, and chest pain. These symptoms are accompanied by weakness, malaise, fever, and weight loss; usually, more than one lesion is present at the time of the initial consultation.[2, 17, 22, 32, 35, 36]

CHARACTERISTICS OF THE LESIONS

Lungs

The auscultatory findings are minimal in comparison with the radiologic abnormalities.[22, 32] Gallium imaging has revealed the presence of radiologically and clinically unsuspected lesions.[34] Usually, there is some degree of dyspnea. In the active forms, radiographs reveal patchy or confluent nodular infiltrates or condensed lesions, very frequently bilateral and symmetric (Fig. 258–2). Most changes occur in the central and basal portions of the lungs; the apices usually remain clear. Cavities are frequent but hilar adenopathy is not too common. In cases of long duration, fibrosis, bullae, and presence of emphysematous areas are the rule. Right ventricular hypertrophy is present in some patients and is the most feared sequela.[19, 22, 32–34]

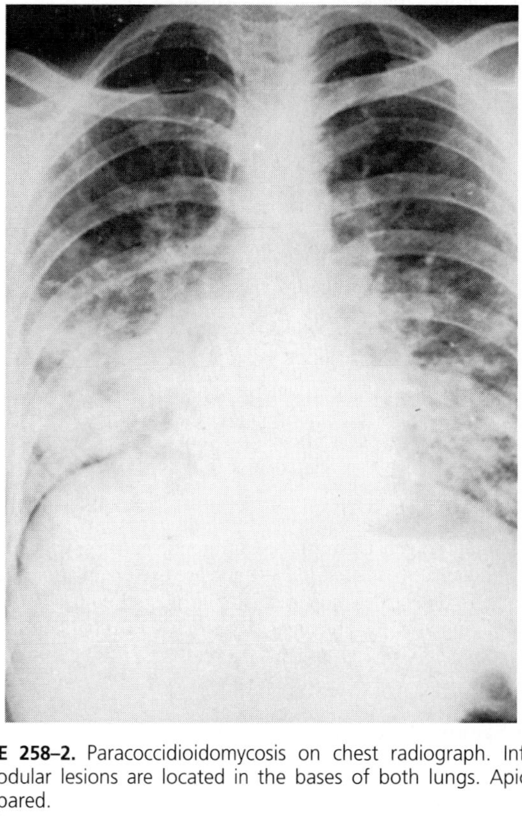

FIGURE 258–2. Paracoccidioidomycosis on chest radiograph. Infiltrates and nodular lesions are located in the bases of both lungs. Apices appear spared.

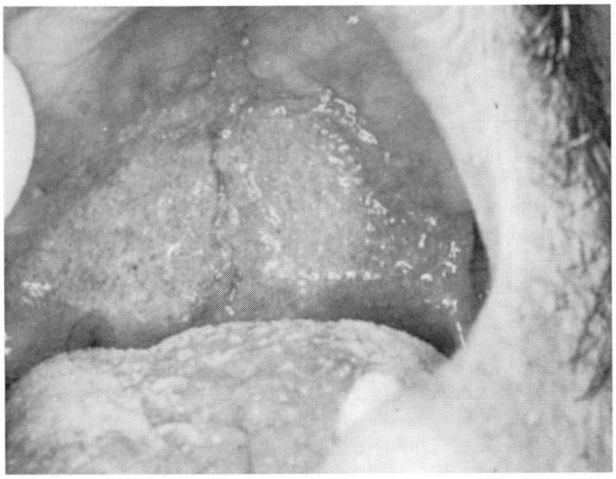

FIGURE 258–3. Paracoccidioidomycosis: lesions of the hard palate.

Mucosal Lesions

Infiltrated, ulcerated, and painful lesions are observed regularly in the mouth, lips, gingiva, tongue, and palate and to a lesser extent the nose, larynx, and pharynx. Tooth loss is common, as is vocal cord damage with dysphonia. Such lesions have a granulomatous appearance and may produce edema of the affected area. Ulcerated lesions have a mulberry-like aspect. Healing is accompanied by cicatricial lesions (Fig. 258–3).[17, 21, 22, 35]

Skin

Cutaneous lesions are variable in appearance;[36] they tend to appear around the natural orifices and the lower limbs. Most commonly, the lesions are warty, ulcerated, and crusted and infiltrate the subcutaneous tissues; they are also granulomatous. Often, lung, skin, and mucosal lesions coexist in the same patient.[22]

Lymph Node

Cervical, axillary, mesenteric, mediastinal, and other nodes are regularly involved and may become enlarged. Draining fistulas may form.[2, 13, 21, 22]

Adrenals

Diminished adrenal function or overt addisonian syndrome may occur. The adrenals are hypertrophied and show nodular lesions.[37, 38]

Other Lesions

The spleen, liver, gastrointestinal tract, vascular system, bones, central nervous system, and male genitourinary tract are occasionally involved.[9, 21, 22]

DIFFERENTIAL DIAGNOSIS

Paracoccidioidomycosis must be differentiated from tuberculosis, which can coexist in 15 to 20% of the cases.[17, 21, 22, 35] Other diseases to be taken into consideration are histoplasmosis, neoplastic disorders including lymphoma, leishmaniasis, leprosy, and syphilis.

LABORATORY DIAGNOSIS

Direct Examination

When such specimens as sputum, exudates, and pus are available, a simple KOH mount suffices to reveal *P. brasiliensis* in 93% of the patients. If results are negative, repeated samples should be collected; sputum should be digested and concentrated. The relative large size of the cells, their refractile wall, and multiple budding make diagnosis simple, especially if calcofluor preparations are examined.[1, 2]

Histologic Studies

Biopsy is often diagnostic. Gomori stain is recommended. If the typical multiple budding cells are not abundant, differentiation from other fungi *(Blastomyces dermatitidis, Histoplasma capsulatum,* and *Cryptococcus neoformans)* should be made. The histologic reaction corresponds to a mixed mycotic granuloma with neutrophils, epithelioid cells, and multinucleated giant cells. Fungi are often found inside the latter cells. A mixed pyogenic, inflammatory reaction is found in ulcerated mucocutaneous lesions and in ruptured lymph nodes. In the subacute progressive form, tissue reactions are diffuse and phagocytosis is sparse. Lymph nodes have hyperplastic germinal centers and increased numbers of plasmocytes. Skin lesions reveal pseudoepitheliomatous hyperplasia and intraepithelial microabscesses.[21]

Cultures

Culture should be attempted because isolation proves the activity of the process. With contaminated samples, room temperature incubation is preferred; Sabouraud-dextrose or yeast extract agar with antibacterial and antimycotic compounds (in Petri dishes) is recommended for this purpose. Cultures should be kept for 6 weeks.[1, 2]

Serologic Tests

Serology for antibody detection is useful not only for the diagnosis but also for follow-up studies; antibodies of the immunoglobulin G and immunoglobulin M classes predominate.[2, 39] The easiest method, the agar gel immunodiffusion test, demonstrates circulating antibodies in 95% of the cases. The test is also specific, and the presence of a precipitin band practically makes a diagnosis.[40] However, the activity of the process cannot be judged on this basis, because these antibodies can be detected years after apparent successful therapy. Another useful test, albeit a cumbersome one, is the complement fixation test. Its quantitative nature allows a better evaluation of the patient's response to treatment. In the complement fixation test, in contrast to the immunodiffusion test, cross-reactions with *H. capsulatum* antigens are important. Other tests, such as immunofluorescence, counterimmunoelectrophoresis, dot-blot, and enzyme-linked immunosorbent assay, are also currently used.[2, 40–42] Improvements in the field of serodiagnosis include the detection of antibodies against specific *P. brasiliensis* antigens[41, 42] as well as demonstration of circulating fungal antigens in patients' sera with monoclonal antibody–based techniques. Antigen is detected in more than 60% of all patients.[43] Production of recombinant antigens that can be used in Western blot and enzyme-linked immunosorbent assay tests has increased specificity and reproducibility.[44]

Skin Tests

Paracoccidioidin skin testing is not reliable for diagnosis, because many active cases (35 to 50%) are nonreactive at the time of diagnosis. However, during the course of treatment, some cases become reactive, and this can be taken as a good prognosis.[2, 14, 20] Cross-reactions with histoplasmin are to be expected, although the use of the purified antigen gp43 appears to be more specific.[2, 45]

TREATMENT

Paracoccidioidomycosis is the only mycosis amenable to treatment with sulfa drugs (alone or combined with trimethoprim). It can also be treated with amphotericin B and various imidazole derivatives.

Because in many cases the diagnosis is not established until late and the patients are usually malnourished, treatment directed merely at suppressing growth of the microorganism is not always successful. Appropriate supportive therapeutic measures (e.g., improved diet, rest, correction of anemia) are essential.[46, 47]

Sulfonamides

Either sulfadiazine or one of the long-acting compounds (sulfamethoxypyridazine, sulfadimethoxine) can be used. With sulfadiazine, the dosage is 4 g/day for adults and 60 to 100 mg/kg/day (in divided doses) for children. This dosage must be continued for several weeks to months, without interruption, until clinical and mycologic improvement is apparent. Then the dosage can be reduced by half. The long-acting compounds require 1 to 2 g/day for adults and half the dose for children during the first 2 to 3 weeks of treatment; after clinical improvement (approximately 4 weeks), 500 mg/day suffices. Most investigators agree that sulfonamide treatment should be continued for 3 to 5 years to avoid relapses, which occur in 20 to 25% of the cases.[47] Availability of more potent medications has curtailed the use of sulfonamides.[47, 47]

Amphotericin B

The dosage and administration pattern for amphotericin B in paracoccidioidomycosis are similar to those recommended for other systemic mycoses. Total dosages have varied from 1200 to 3000 mg; the latter require prolonged periods of hospitalization. Amphotericin B is not curative by itself, and all patients treated with it should also receive maintenance sulfonamide or azole therapy according to the indications previously given. Amphotericin B should be reserved for severe cases and for those unresponsive to other means of therapy.[47, 48]

The two therapeutic measures mentioned are not always successful, and the mortality rate is rather high (17 to 25%); improvement is obtained in 65 to 70% of the cases, and the remainder have relapses or fail to improve.[47–49] Mortality in Brazil has been estimated to be 1486 per 1 million inhabitants, according to a review of fatal cases during a 16-year period.[49]

Imidazole Compounds

The orally administered imidazole ketaconazole resulted in major improvement in 84 to 95% of the cases with only a 10% relapse rate after 5 years.[46, 47] Comparisons between amphotericin B plus sulfonamides and ketoconazole have favored the latter.[47] Ketoconazole should be given at a dose of 200 to 400 mg/day for a minimum of 6 months and for as long as 12 to 18 months, depending on the patient's response and the results of mycologic tests. Generally, patients unresponsive to other therapeutic regimens are successfully treated with ketoconazole.[46, 47]

Long-lasting ketoconazole therapy mandates regular checkups for hepatic dysfunction and gonadal alterations. In general, side effects of ketoconazole have been minor in paracoccidioidomycosis.[46, 47] This fact, the relatively short periods of therapy that are needed, and the facility for oral administration make ketoconazole an adequate drug for the treatment of this disorder. At present, however, most researchers agree that the newer triazole derivative itraconazole is superior to ketoconazole. This conclusion is based on the requirement for shorter treatment periods (6 months), lower daily doses (100 mg), lack of interference with endocrine metabolism, little or no liver toxicity,[46, 47, 50] and a lower relapse rate (3 to 5%).[46, 47, 50, 51] Experience to date indicates that itraconazole is both effective and safe, even in patients with the severe juvenile form.[46, 50]

In a limited trial,[52] fluconazole appeared effective as a therapeutic agent; however, the need for high doses (up to 600 mg/day) and longer periods of therapy and the frequent relapses have curtailed the use of this compound. The immunostimulatory role of glucan as adjunctive therapy has led to its recommendation.[53]

REFERENCES

1. Lacaz CS. *Paracoccidioides brasiliensis*: Morphology, evolutionary cycle, maintenance during saprophytic life, biology, virulence, taxonomy. In: Franco MF, Lacaz CS, Restrepo A, et al, eds. Paracoccidioidomycosis. Boca Raton, Fla: CRC Press; 1994:13–22.
2. Brummer E, Castañeda E, Restrepo A. Paracoccidioidomycosis: An update. Clin Microbiol Rev. 1993;6:89–117.
3. Edwards MR, Salazar ME, Samsonoff WA, et al. Electron microscopy study of conidia produced by the mycelium of *Paracoccidioides brasiliensis*. Mycopathologia. 1991;114:169–177.
4. Samsonoff WA, Salazar ME, McKee ML, et al. Scanning electron microscopy of conidia produced by the mycelium of *Paracoccidioides brasiliensis*. Mycopathologia. 1991;114:9–15.
5. McEwen JG, Bedoya V, Patiño MM, et al. Experimental murine paracoccidioidomycosis induced by the inhalation of conidia. J Med Vet Mycol. 1987;25:165–175.
6. Franco L, Navjar L, Gomez BL, et al. Experimental pulmonary fibrosis induced by *Paracoccidioides brasiliensis* conidia: Measurement of local host responses. Am J Trop Med Hyg. 1998;58:424–430.
7. Restrepo A. Ecology of *Paracoccidioides brasiliensis*. In: Fanco M, Lacaz CS, Restrepo A, et al, eds. Paracoccidioidomycosis. Boca Raton, Fla: CRC Press; 1994:121–130.
8. Ajello L, Polonelli L. Imported paracoccidioidomycosis: A public health problem in non-endemic areas. Eur J Epidemiol. 1985;1:160–165.
9. Manns BJ, Baylis BW, Urbanski JJ, et al. Paracoccidioidomycosis: Case report and review. Clin Infect Dis. 1996;23:1026–1032.
10. Silva-Vergara M. Contribution to the epidemiological study of paracoccidioidomycosis: A study at a coffee crops area. Rev Soc Bras Med Trop. 1997;30:83–86.
11. Gagagli E, Sano A, Coelho KI, et al. Isolation of *Paracoccidioides brasiliensis* from armadillo *(Dasypus novemcinctus)* captured in an endemic area for paracoccidioidomycosis. Am J Trop Med Hyg. 1998;58:505–512.
12. Coimbra CEA, Wanke B, Santos RV. Paracoccidioidin and histoplasmin sensitivity in Tupi-Mondé populations from Brazilian Amazonia. Ann Trop Med Parasitol. 1994;88:197–207.
13. Londero AT, Rios-Gonçalves AJ, Terra CMF, et al. Paracoccidioidomycosis in Brazilian children. A critical review (1911–1994). Arq Bras Med. 1996;70:197–203.
14. Franco MF, Peraçoli MT, Sõares A, et al. Host-parasite relationship in paracoccidioidomycosis. Curr Top Med Mycol. 1993;5:115–149.
15. Restrepo A, Salazar ME, Clemons KV, et al. Hormonal influences in the host interplay with *Paracoccidioides brasiliensis*. In: Vanden Bosche H, Stevens DA, Odds FS, eds. Host-fungus Interplay. Proceedings of the Fifth Symposium on Topics in Mycology. Bethesda, Md: National Foundation for Infectious Diseases; 1997:125–133.
16. Martinez R, Moya MJ. Associãção entre paracoccidioidomycose e alcoholism. Rev Saude Publica. 1992;26:12–16.
17. Valle ACF, Aprigliano Filho F, Moreira JS, et al. Clinical and endoscopic findings of the upper respiratory and digestive tracts in post-treatment follow-up of paracoccidioidomycosis patients. Rev Inst Med Trop Sao Paulo. 1995;37:407–413.
18. Restepo A, de Bedout C, Cano LE, et al. Recovery of *Paracoccidioides brasiliensis* from a calcified lymph node by micro-aerophilic incubation in liquid media. Sabouraudia. 1981;19:295–300.
19. Londero AT. Paracoccidioidomicose: Patogenia, formas clinicas, manifestações pulmonares e diagnóstico. J Pneumol (Bras). 1986;12:41–57.
20. Franco MF, Montenegro MRG, Mendes RP, et al. Paracoccidioidomycosis: A recently proposed classification of its clinical forms. Rev Soc Bras Med Trop. 1987;20:129–132.
21. Montenegro MR, Franco M. Pathology: In: Franco M, Lacaz CS, Restrepo A, et al, eds. Paracoccidioidomycosis. Boca Raton, Fla: CRC Press; 1994:131–150.
22. Londero AT, Ramos CD. Paracoccidioidomicose: Estudo clinico-micológico de 260 casos observados no interior do Estado do Rio Grande do Sul. J Pneumol (Bras). 1990;16:129–132.
23. Bernard G, Mendes-Giannini MJS, Juvenale M, et al. Immunosuppression in paracoccidioidomycosis. T cell hyporesponsiveness to two *Paracoccidioides brasiliensis* glycoproteins that elicit strong humoral immune response. J Infect Dis. 1997;175:1263–1267.
24. Calich VLG, Singer-Vermes LM, Russo M, et al. Immunogenetics in paracoccidioidomycosis. In: Paracoccidioidomycosis. Franco MF, Lacaz CS, Restrepo A, et al. Boca Raton, Fla: CRC Press; 1994:151–173.
25. Musatti CC, Peraçoli MTJ, Sõares AMVC, et al. Cell-mediated immunity in patients with paracoccidioidomycosis. In: Franco MF, Lacaz CS, Restropo A, et al, eds. Paracoccidioidomycosis. Boca Raton, Fla: CRC Press; 1994:175–186.
26. Cano LE, Kashino SS, Arruda C, et al. Protective role of gamma interferon in experimental pulmonary paracoccidioidomycosis. Infect Immun 1998;66:800–806.
27. Tobon AM, Orozco B, Estrada S, et al. Paracoccidioidomycosis and AIDS. Report of the first Colombian cases. Rev Inst Med Trop São Paulo. 1998;40:377–381.
28. Marques SA, Shikanai-Yasuda MA. Paracoccidioidomycosis associated with immunosuppression, AIDS and cancer. In: Franco MF, Lacaz CS, Restrepo A, et al, eds. Paracoccidioidomycosis. Boca Raton, Fla: CRC Press; 1994:393–405.
29. Restrepo A, Trujillo M, Gomez I. Inapparent lung involvement in patients with the subacute juvenile type of paracoccidioidomycosis. Rev Inst Med Trop Sao Paulo. 1989;31:18–22.
30. Ferreira-Cruz MF, Wanke B, Galvao-Castro B. Prevalence of paracoccidioidomycosis in hospitalized patients. Mycopathologia. 1987;97:61–64.
31. Correa AL, Restrepo A, Franco L, Gomez I. Paracoccidioidomicosis. Coexistencia

de lesiones extrapulmonares y patología pulmonar silente. Descripción de 64 pacientes. Acta Med Colomb. 1991;16:304–308.
32. Campos EP, Padovani CR, Cataneo AMJ. Paracoccidioidomicose: Estudo radiologico e pulmonar de 58 casos. Rev Inst Med Trop Sao Paulo. 1991;33:267–276.
33. Valle ACF, Guimaraes RR, Lopes DJ, et al. Thoracic radiologic aspects in paracoccidioidomycosis. Rev Inst Med Trop Sao Paulo. 1992;34:107–116.
34. Calegaro JUM, Gomes EF, Caravalho ACM, et al. 67-Gallium na blastomicose: Nossa experiencia. Radiol Bras. 1990;23:59–63.
35. Sposto MR, Almeida ODP, Jorge J, et al. Oral paracoccidioidomycosis. A study of 36 South American patients. Oral Surg Oral Med Oral Pathol. 1993;75:464–465.
36. Robledo MA, Restrepo A, Franco L, et al. Poliformismo de las lesiones cutáneas en la paracoccidioidomicosis. Rev Soc Colombiana Dermatol. 1992;2:5–8.
37. Tendrich MF, de Luca EK, Tourino B, et al. Computed tomography and ultrasonography of the adrenal glands in paracoccidioidomycosis. Comparison with cortisol and aldosterone responses to ACTH stimulation. Am J Trop Med Hyg. 1991;44:83–92.
38. Moreira AC, Martines R, Castro M, et al. Adrenocortical dysfunction in paracoccidioidomycosis: Comparison between plasma beta-lipotropin/adrenocorticotrophin levels and adrenocortical tests. Clin Endocrinol. 1992;36:545–551.
39. Taborda CP, Camargo ZP. Diagnosis of paracoccidioidomycosis by dot immunobinding assay for antibody detection using the purified and specific antigen gp43. J Clin Microbiol. 1994;32:554–556.
40. Del Negro GMB, Garcia NM, Rodrigues EG, et al. The sensitivity, specificity and efficiency value of some serological tests used in the diagnosis of paracoccidioidomycosis. Rev Ins Med Trop Sao Paulo. 1991;33:277–280.
41. Bueno JP, Mendes-Giannini MJS, del Negro GMB, et al. IgG, IgM and IgA antibody response for the diagnosis and follow-up of paracoccidioidomycosis: Comparison of counter immunoelectrophoresis and complement fixation. J Med Vet Mycol. 1997;35:213–217.
42. Mendes-Giannini MJS, del Negro GMB, Siqueira AM. Serodiagnosis. In: Franco MF, Lacaz CS, Restrepo A, et al, eds. Paracoccidioidomycosis. Boca Raton, Fla: CRC Press; 1994:345–363.
43. Gomez BL, Figueroa JI, Hamilton AJ, et al. Use of monoclonal antibodies in the diagnosis of paracoccidioidomycosis. New strategies for detection of circulating antigens. J Clin Microbiol. 1997;35:3278–3283.
44. Ortiz BL, García AM, Restrepo A, et al. Immunological characterization of recombinant 27 kDa antigenic protein from *P. brasiliensis*. Clin Diag Lab Immunol. 1996;3:239–241.
45. Saraiva ECO, Altemani A, Franco M, et al. *Paracoccidioidodes brasiliensis* gp43 used as paracoccidioidin. J Med Vet Mycol. 1996;34:115–161.
46. Restrepo A. Paracoccidioidomycosis (South American blastomycosis). In: Jacobs PH, Nall L, eds. Antifungal Drug Therapy: A Complete Guide for the Practitioner. New York: Marcel Dekker; 1990:181–205.
47. Mendes R, Negroni R, Arechavala A. Treatment and control of cure. In: Franco M, Lacaz CS, Restrepo A, et al, eds. Paracoccidioidomycosis. Boca Raton, Fla: CRC Press; 1994:373–392.
48. Dillon NL, Sampaio SAP, Habermann MC, et al. Delayed results of treatment of paracoccidioidomycosis with amphotericin B plus sulfonamides versus amphotericin B alone. Rev Inst Med Trop Sao Paulo. 1986;28:265–266.
49. Coutinho Z, Silva D, Lacera M, et al. Mortalidad por paracoccidioidomicose, Brasil 1980–1995. Abstract A57. Presented at II Congreso brasileiro de Micologia, Rio de Janeiro, April 17–21, 1998:72.
50. Naranjo MS, Trujillo M, Munera MI, et al. Treatment of paracoccidioidomycosis with itraconazole. J Med Vet Mycol. 1990;67–76.
51. Martins R, Marques S, Alves M, et al. Serological follow-up of patients with paracoccidioidomycosis treated with itraconazole using dot-blot, ELISA and Western blot. Rev Inst Med Trop Sao Paulo. 1997;39:261–269.
52. Diaz M, Negroni R, Montero-Gei F, et al. A Pan American five-year study of fluconazole therapy for deep mycoses in the immunocompetent host. Clin Infect Dis. 1992;14(Suppl 1):S68–S76.
53. Meira DA, Pereira PCM, Marcondes-Machado J, et al. The use of glucan as an immunostimulant in the treatment of paracoccidioidomycosis. Am J Trop Med Hyg. 1996;55:496–503.

Chapter 259

Miscellaneous Fungi and *Prototheca*

DUANE R. HOSPENTHAL
JOHN E. BENNETT

PSEUDALLESCHERIA BOYDII

Human infection with *Pseudallescheria boydii* (anamorph: *Scedosporium apiospermum*) can produce two distinct rare diseases: mycetoma and pseudallescheriasis. Mycetoma is a chronic subcutaneous infection characterized by the production of grains (see Chapter 252). Pseudallescheriasis includes all other infections caused by *P. boydii*. The most common sites of pseudallescheriasis are lung, bone, joints, and the central nervous system (CNS).[1] Sinusitis,[2] keratitis,[3, 4] endophthalmitis,[5] skin and soft tissue infections,[6, 7] prostatitis, and endocarditis[8–10] have also been described. The fungus is found in soil and fresh water, especially stagnant or polluted water, throughout the world. The portal of entry is by inhalation into the lungs or paranasal sinuses or through the skin by trauma. Invasive pulmonary disease similar to invasive pulmonary aspergillosis is seen predominantly in immunocompromised patients. Local trauma is the most common cause of the eye, soft tissue, and osteoarticular infections in previously healthy persons. CNS infection is seen in both immunocompromised and healthy individuals. Infections in immunocompetent patients usually have subacute to chronic courses, whereas those in immunocompromised patients are frequently more acute and severe.

P. boydii can colonize a bronchiectatic bronchial tree or an intermittently obstructed paranasal sinus. Masses of *P. boydii* hyphae (fungus balls) have been found in lung cavities.[11] *P. boydii* has also been reported as a cause of allergic bronchopulmonary disease (similar to allergic bronchopulmonary aspergillosis (ABPA),[12, 13] pleural space infection,[14] lung abscess,[15] pneumonia,[16] including aspiration pneumonia, and invasive sinusitis. Colonization is more likely than disease with this organism. Invasive sinus and pulmonary disease similar to aspergillosis is seen in immunocompromised patients. As with invasive aspergillosis, invasive pseudallescheriasis most commonly occurs in patients with prolonged neutropenia, those receiving prolonged high-dose corticosteroid therapy, or those who have undergone allogeneic bone marrow transplantation.[17–19] Invasive pulmonary disease with dissemination has also occurred in patients with acquired immunodeficiency syndrome (AIDS) and after solid organ transplantation.[10, 20, 21] Pulmonary disease in the severely immunocompromised patient usually manifests with fever, cough, pleuritic pain, and often hemoptysis. Chest films show areas of nodularity, alveolar infiltrate or, most commonly, consolidation.[18, 19, 22] Later, cavitation has been noted.[18, 19] Disseminated disease that manifests with only painful cutaneous nodules has also been described in this group of patients.[23] Invasive pulmonary disease with extension to the vertebrae has been described in a patient without apparent immunocompromise.[24]

Localized disease, including infections of the eye and cutaneous, subcutaneous (Fig. 259–1), and osteoarticular tissue may be seen both with and without immunocompromise. Infection is commonly initiated via traumatic implantation of the fungus from soil or water. Surgery, intravenous drug injection, and repeated corticosteroid injections have less frequently been associated with localized infections.[25] Osteoarticular infection in immunocompetent patients often appears as a painful, swollen joint with overlying erythema after penetrating joint injury. Occasionally, weeks or months may pass between antecedent trauma and the development of septic arthritis.[26–28]

Brain abscesses may result from a known or unsuspected lung

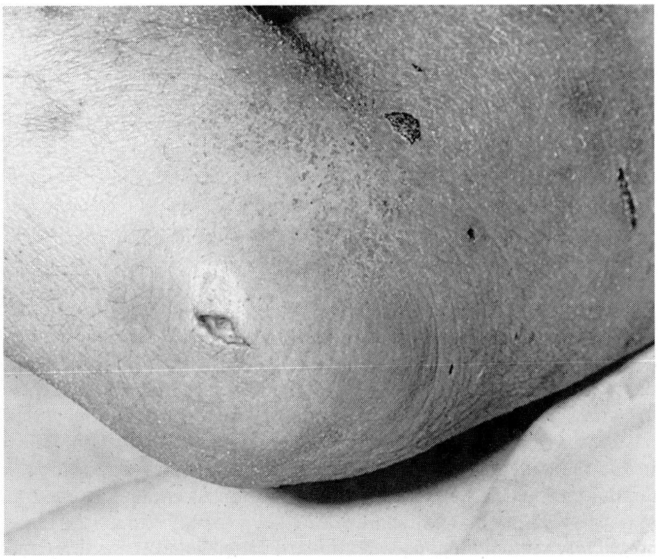

FIGURE 259–1. *Pseudallescheria boydii* olecranon bursitis in a corticosteroid-treated patient who fell on his elbow in his garden. Photograph shows the incision site over the subcutaneous abscess, which began in the bursa.

lesion in immunocompromised patients, including AIDS patients.[29, 30] CNS infection appears to be disproportionately increased in patients with pseudallescheriasis when compared with many other mycoses. Cerebral abscesses are usually multiple and in the immunocompetent host are often reported in association with near-drownings in polluted water, such as ponds, pig troughs, and roadside ditches.[31–36] CNS infection from contiguous spread of sinusitis[37] and after penetrating trauma[38] has also been described. An indolent, severe neutrophilic meningitis has been reported occasionally, usually in patients with intravenous drug abuse or human immunodeficiency virus (HIV) infection. Cerebrospinal fluid culture and smear have been negative, with the diagnosis made at autopsy.[29] The first described human case of pseudallescheriasis was a meningitis that was likely iatrogenic after a lumbar puncture for the administration of anesthesia.[39]

Isolation of *P. boydii* from normally sterile sites is diagnostic. Rarely, *P. boydii* may be cultured from blood.[8] Growth of the organism from sputum, bronchoalveolar lavage, draining wounds, or paranasal sinus aspirates is less convincing unless accompanied by hyphae on smear or biopsy. *P. boydii* resembles *Aspergillus*, with dichotomously branching septate hyphae. In neutropenic patients, blood vessel invasion and thrombosis are usual. The fungus grows well in standard mycologic media. In a few days, the mold colony takes on a tan color and has sporulating structures that are quite different from *Aspergillus*. No clinically useful serologic or other rapid identification tests are currently available.

Effective antifungal therapy of pseudallescheriasis has not been established. In vitro and clinical resistance to amphotericin B has been reported repeatedly. Surgical débridement has been an important adjunct in treatment of pseudallescheriasis of soft tissue, bone, joint and pleural and paranasal sinuses, although it is not curative in itself. Intra-articular instillation of amphotericin B may have contributed to success in a few patients.[27] Mortality with brain abscess is greater than 75%.[29, 38] Intravenous miconazole and surgery have been included in most regimens leading to successful outcome in CNS infection.[1, 29, 38, 40, 41] Success with intravenous miconazole has been reported in other types of infections as well, but this agent has been increasingly difficult to obtain. Successes have been reported with ketoconazole, although most were in patients with localized infection and in conjunction with débridement.[42] Itraconazole has also been used in focal infection in combination with débridement.[43] Successful therapy with itraconazole alone has been reported in a case of probable invasive pulmonary disease[22] and in conjunction with lobectomy in another.[18] In a recent report, voriconazole resulted in improvement of a case with disseminated disease.[44]

SCEDOSPORIUM PROLIFICANS (INFLATUM)

Scedosporium prolificans (*inflatum*) was first described in 1984 as an agent of human disease.[45] Since that time, several dozen cases have been reported from the United States, Spain, and Australia in both immunocompromised and immunocompetent patients. Patients with intact immunity most frequently have focal infections (usually osteoarticular), whereas immunocompromised persons more frequently have disseminated disease.

In immunocompetent patients, infection is usually localized and associated with trauma, including surgery.[46, 47] These cases have included infections of bone and joints (Fig. 259–2), onychomycosis, and endophthalmitis. Immunocompromised patients, commonly undergoing cytoreductive chemotherapy or bone marrow transplantation, present with fungemia and fever during neutropenia.[48–50] Skin lesions, myalgia, and pulmonary infiltrates have also been described in this setting.[51] Skin lesions have been described as a papular rash, later becoming necrotic. Disseminated disease without neutropenia has also been described in lung and kidney transplantation.[52] Fatal localized CNS infection has been reported in a child with acute leukemia who had received six intrathecal chemotherapeutic injections.[53] *S. prolificans* has also been recovered from the external ear and sputum of patients without apparent disease.[46, 47] This apparent colonization includes recovery from sputum of two patients with AIDS without evidence of infection.[47, 54]

Diagnosis is most commonly made by culturing the organism from infected sites, such as skin biopsy. Disseminated disease in the immunocompromised patient is usually diagnosed by blood culture.[49]

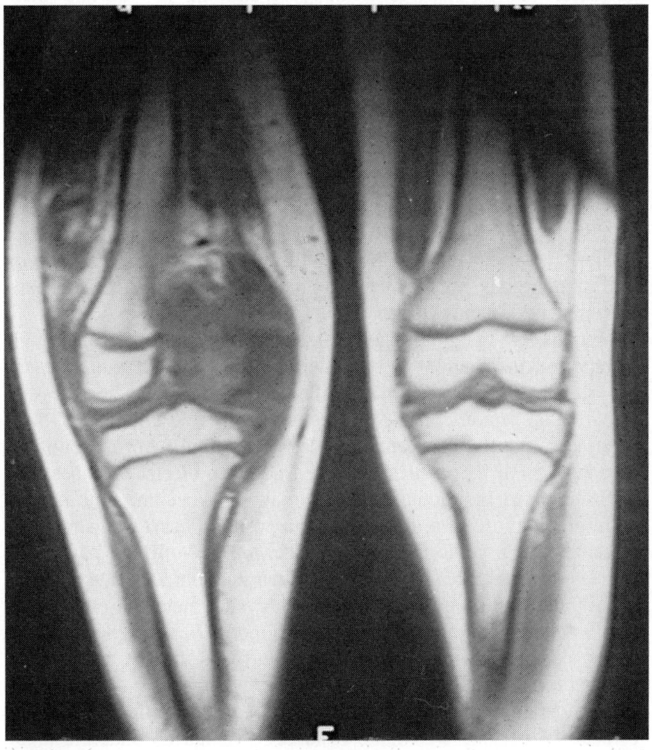

FIGURE 259–2. *Scedosporium inflatum* septic arthritis of the knee in a healthy 12-year-old African American boy who drove a splinter into his knee when he fell on the school playground. Magnetic resonance imaging with T2-weighted imaging shows osteomyelitis of the medial condyle.

Identification of *S. prolificans* is based chiefly on the morphologic characteristics of the asexual structures produced by the mold in culture.[55]

Currently, the treatment of choice for these infections is not known. *S. prolificans* appears to be intrinsically resistant to most currently available antifungals. Successful therapy of joint infections has been reported with the use of surgical débridement with or without intra-articular amphotericin B.[46] Disseminated infection is usually resistant to antifungal agents and carries a high mortality.[48] Survival has been reported in one patient with disseminated disease and neutropenia who received granulocyte colony-stimulating factor and amphotericin B followed by itraconazole.[49]

PENICILLIUM MARNEFFEI

Penicillium marneffei is a thermally dimorphic fungus that causes life-threatening disseminated infection (penicilliosis marneffei) in a geographically distinct area of the world. The rapid expansion of the AIDS epidemic in Thailand has led to a marked rise in the incidence of disseminated infection with *P. marneffei*. Before the first reports of this infection in HIV-infected patients in 1988,[56–58] only 29 patients had been described since the first human infection in 1959.[59, 60] In 1995, the annual incidence of this disease in Thailand had risen to 1300 cases.[61] In the mid-1990s, this infection was the third most common opportunistic infection seen in HIV-infected individuals in northern Thailand.[62] Infection with *P. marneffei* has a limited geographic distribution, affecting persons residing in or those who have visited Southeast Asia or southern China. Endogenous cases have been reported from Myanmar (Burma), Hong Kong, Indonesia, Laos, Malaysia, Singapore, Taiwan, Thailand, Vietnam, and the Guangxi province of China.[63–65] Although most commonly seen in young adults infected with HIV, disease has been reported in children[66, 67] and adults, both with and without detectable immunocompromise.[63, 64] *P. marneffei* has been isolated from the organs of apparently healthy bamboo rats (*Rhizomys pruinosis, Rhizomys sinensis, Rhizomys sumatrensis,* and *Cannomyus badius*)[68–71] and the soil around their burrows.[72] The role of these rats in human infection is unknown. A case control study of the disease in 80 persons with AIDS found an association with recent history of occupational or other exposure to soil.[73] In that study, no association between infection and exposure to bamboo rats was found. According to one report, infection occurs more commonly during the rainy season in northern Thailand.[74] It is likely that this infection is acquired by inhalation of conidia from an environmental source such as the soil.

Patients typically present with a chronic illness averaging 4 weeks in duration associated with low-grade fever, weight loss, and one or more skin lesions.[62] The most common clinical characteristics are fever, malaise, anemia, leukocytosis, weight loss, and, in 60 to 70%, skin lesions.[62, 64] Fungemia, generalized lymphadenopathy, and cough are reported in about 50% of patients. Subcutaneous and mucosal lesions, hepatomegaly with or without splenomegaly, hemoptysis, osteoarticular lesions, and pericarditis are also described.[63, 75] Skin lesions commonly occur on the face, upper trunk, and extremities. They may occur as papules, pustules, nodules, ulcers, or abscesses. In HIV-infected individuals, lesions commonly become umbilicated and resemble those of molluscum contagiosum. Pharyngeal and palatal lesions are also more commonly seen in HIV-infected patients.[75] Lung lesions can appear as reticulonodular, nodular, or diffuse alveolar infiltrates, but on occasion have been cavitary and caused hemoptysis.[76] Autopsy involvement of lymph nodes, liver, spleen, lung, kidney, skin, bone, bone marrow, adrenal, tonsil, bowel, and meninges has been reported.[63, 77]

Consideration of the diagnosis of *P. marneffei* infection should be made in persons who have resided or visited an endemic area. Laboratory exposure to the organism has been causally linked to disseminated infection in one immunocompromised individual.[78] The duration of incubation is not currently known, and reactivation disease may be possible. In one report, a severely immunocompromised individual acquired disseminated infection more than 10 years after visiting an endemic area.[79] Diagnosis is based on identification of the organism on smear, histopathologic studies, or culture. Diagnosis has most frequently been made from smears of skin lesions and biopsies of lymph node and bone marrow.[62] The organism has also been noted on peripheral blood smear in at least one report.[80] Isolation of *P. marneffei* from culture of bone marrow, blood, lymph node, skin lesions, sputum, bronchoalveolar lavage, or sputum can be diagnostic. Microscopic examination of clinical materials reveals yeast forms (2 to 3 $\times$ 2 to 6.5 μm) both within phagocytes and extracellularly.[63] The intracellular forms are smaller, resembling *Histoplasma capsulatum*, whereas the extracellular forms are larger and often have a transverse septum (asexual fission or schizogony). The extracellular forms may also appear as "sausage forms," consisting of three cells (8 to 13 μm in length) divided by two transverse septa, or rarely as short hyphae. Three types of histopathologic reactions have been noted in association with *P. marneffei* infection. They include granulomatous, suppurative, and necrotizing inflammation.[77] Granulomatous or suppurative changes are most commonly seen in patients with normal immunity. The necrotizing reaction is more commonly seen in immunocompromised patients and is characterized by focal necrosis with surrounding histiocytes and extracellular fungi. Culture at 30°C produces a mold with sporulating structures typical for *Penicillium*. Identification is aided by the formation of a soluble red pigment that diffuses into the agar. This mold form may be converted to a yeast form by incubation at 37°C.[81] This dimorphism is not found in other known members of the genus *Penicillium*. Because disease normally appears to result from inhalation of conidia, it seems reasonable to use biosafety level II precautions when working with the mold form. Diagnosis by immunologic techniques, including serum antibody and antigen tests, as well as identification of organisms in tissue to immunolabeling is still in the experimental stage.[82–86]

Successful treatment of disseminated infection has been reported with amphotericin B with or without the addition of flucytosine.[63] Therapy with itraconazole has also been successful. Fluconazole therapy has been associated with a high rate of failure. Although no randomized, comparative studies have been performed, the failure rates in a study of 86 HIV-infected patients were as follows: amphotericin B (8 of 35, 22.8%), itraconazole (3 of 12, 25%), and fluconazole (7 of 11, 63.6%).[87] Excellent response (97.3%) has been seen with a regimen of intravenous amphotericin B for 2 weeks (0.6 mg/kg/day) followed by oral itraconazole for 10 weeks (200 mg twice daily) in 74 HIV-infected patients.[88] This regimen allowed shortened hospital stays while producing a more rapid clearing of fungemia compared with that seen using itraconazole alone. Itraconazole has been shown to prevent relapses of this disease in patients with HIV infection.[89] Lifelong secondary prophylaxis in HIV-infected patients with itraconazole (200 mg once daily) or ketoconazole appears appropriate because relapse in this group of patients is common.[62]

FUSARIUM SPECIES

Species in the genus *Fusarium* are common in soil and organic debris and cause disease in plants. Disease in humans is rare, usually following traumatic inoculation in the healthy host. Inhalation or minor trauma can lead to fusariosis in immunocompromised patients. Fusarium, usually *Fusarium solani*, is one of the more common causes of fungal keratitis. *Fusarium* can also cause onychomycosis, endophthalmitis, and skin and musculoskeletal infections (including mycetoma).[90] Since the early 1970s, disseminated infection with *Fusarium* has become an increasingly common problem in persons with hematologic malignancy and other immunocompromising disorders (including AIDS).

Rare cases of dissemination have been described in the clinical setting of severe burns[91] and heat stroke.[92] Most commonly, however, fusariosis occurs in patients with acute leukemia (70 to 80% of cases)[93, 94] and prolonged neutropenia (more than 90% of cases).[93, 95]

In one review of 43 patients, the median duration of neutropenia was greater than 3 weeks.[93] Fusariosis is also increasingly reported in patients undergoing bone marrow transplantation.[96, 97] The portal of entry in the majority of these cases of disseminated infection is not known. Inhalation, ingestion, and entry through skin trauma have been suggested.[90] Sinusitis has preceded dissemination in a few reports.[98] Hematogenous spread attributed to indwelling intravascular catheters also has been reported.[99, 100] Onychomycosis has been postulated to be a source of this infection in some patients.[93, 101]

Infection commonly manifests with fever and myalgia that are unresponsive to broad-spectrum antibacterial antibiotics during periods of profound neutropenia. Disseminated fusariosis has been recognized in patients who have been receiving empirical or prophylactic antifungal therapy.[94, 96, 102] Skin lesions occur in 60 to 80% of infections, usually appearing as multiple papules or deeply set, painful nodules. They may initially be flat (macular) with a central pallor, but later become raised, erythematous, and necrotic (Fig. 259–3).[90, 93, 95, 97] Lesions are most commonly seen on the extremities but have been reported on the trunk and face as well.[96] In profoundly neutropenic patients, this infection can progress rapidly to death, in a manner similar to that seen in invasive aspergillosis. Skin lesions, denoting dissemination, can occur within a day of the onset of fever. In patients whose neutrophils start to return, the infection can progress slowly over weeks until death or can become controlled and eventually cured.

Recovery of the fungus from the blood and biopsy of suspicious skin lesions are the two most common and effective ways to diagnose this infection. In contrast to aspergillosis, in which blood cultures are nearly always negative, fusariosis is commonly (40 to 50%) accompanied by positive blood cultures.[95] Although nonspecific for *Fusarium*, finding septate hyphal elements in a skin biopsy specimen should aid in making rapid therapeutic decisions. *Fusarium* can usually be recovered in culture of skin biopsy tissue and seen in histopathologic studies. The hyphae resemble *Aspergillus. Fusarium* has a predilection for small blood vessels, resulting in angioinvasion and associated thrombosis, although not as prominently as *Aspergillus.* The septate hyphae of *Fusarium* species are difficult to visualize with routine hematoxylin and eosin staining but are easily identified when tissue is prepared with methenamine silver or periodic acid–Schiff stains. In culture, the characteristic feature of *Fusarium* is the production of sickle (banana)-shaped multiseptate macroconidia.[103] *F. solani* is the most common species recovered (when speciated), followed by *Fusarium oxysporum*, and *Fusarium moniliforme*.[93, 95] The fungi of the genus *Fusarium* are known to produce a variety of toxic metabolites.[103] Although it is not known whether these toxins are produced during the course of human infection, it has been suggested that they could possibly cause prolongation of myelosuppression or contribute to myalgia.[98] The optimal treatment for disseminated fusariosis has not been established. Amphotericin B has been included in the regimens of most successfully treated patients and thus high-dose amphotericin B is probably the drug of choice. Lipid-based amphotericin B formulations[93, 104] and combinations of other antifungal agents with amphotericin B have been reported; all with mixed success. The addition of colony-stimulating factors (granulocyte colony-stimulating factor or granulocyte-macrophage colony-stimulating factor) or granulocyte transfusions to specific antifungal therapy has also been used.[90, 93, 95, 105] The benefit of these latter therapies is not currently known. Removal of indwelling venous catheters have been associated with improvement and thus should be considered in cases of fungemia.[100] Overall mortality in this infection has been reported to range from 50 to 80%.[93, 95–97] Survival is almost always associated with the recovery from neutropenia.[93, 95, 96] Analysis of survivors versus nonsurvivors in one study of 43 patients noted an association with malignancy in remission (100% versus 10%), adequate neutrophil counts (100% versus 0%), and lack of significant (grade II or greater) graft-versus-host disease (0% versus 66%).[93]

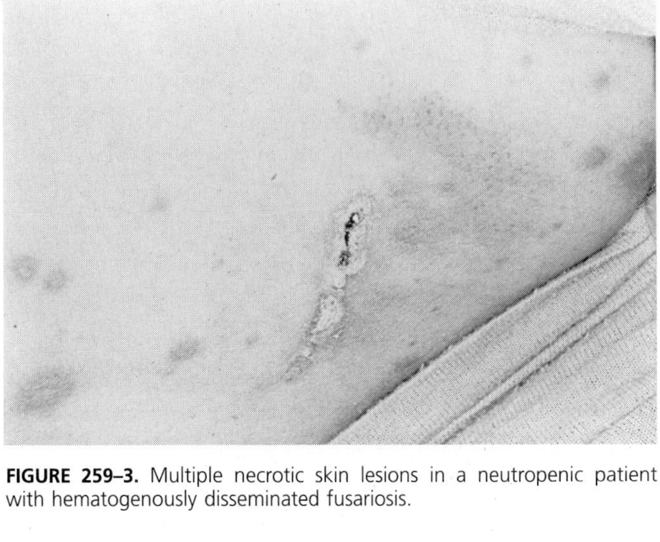

FIGURE 259–3. Multiple necrotic skin lesions in a neutropenic patient with hematogenously disseminated fusariosis.

DARK-WALLED FUNGI

Phaeohyphomycosis is a term introduced by Ajello in 1974 for hyphomycetous fungi with darkly pigmented (dematiaceous), septated hyphae. In 1981, he added Coelomycetes and Ascomycetes to the definition, a controversial expansion of the definition.[106] Phaeohyphomycosis remains a loosely defined term designating infections caused by molds with darks walls in culture but not necessarily in tissue. Melanin in the hyphal wall can be stained with Masson-Fontana, making it more obvious.[107] The number of species causing phaeohyphomycosis is quite broad.[106, 108] Frequent changes in species names has compounded the physician's difficulty in looking up similar cases in the literature. Some dark-walled molds cause chromoblastomycosis and black-grained mycetoma, names that designate a more distinctive entity. For most clinical purposes, it is preferable to describe the disease by the kind of infection and species name, such as "*Cladophialophora bantiana* brain abscess" and to reserve the term phaeohyphomycosis for patients who have no culture or whose culture has not yet been identified.

The most consistent syndrome caused by dark-walled molds is brain abscess.[106, 109] Patients have headache of indolent onset, low-grade or no fever, and eventual development of focal neurologic signs. They have no special history of exposure to dust or molds, no obvious pulmonary portal, and no evidence of dissemination to organs outside the central nervous system. Males have outnumbered females 3:1. Ages have ranged from 6 to 77 years. The abscess has a purulent center and a surrounding granuloma. On hematoxylin and eosin stain of the brain tissue, the fungus can be seen to have a golden brown hyphal wall. Hyphae are irregular in diameter and are septate. Chains of yeastlike cells may be seen with some species. A minority of patients have been immunocompromised.[110] Abscesses may be single or multiple and are well localized within the cerebral cortex on computed tomography or magnetic resonance imaging.[111] Purulent meningitis, with or without brain abscess, may be seen (Fig. 259–4).[112] In a recent tally, 38 cases were caused by *Cladophialophora bantiana*, 9 were caused by *Ramichloridium mackenziei*, 6 were caused by *Ochroconis gallopavum*, 5 were caused by *Exophiala dermatitidis*, 3 were caused by *Bipolaris spicifera*, 2 were caused by *Bipolaris hawaiiensis*, and 19 had histopathologic evidence of dark-walled fungi but no culture identification. *R. mackenziei* has so far been reported largely from the Middle East and India.[113, 114] *E. dermatitidis* cases have originated from the Far East. Surgical excision is the preferred therapy for single brain abscesses. Amphotericin B has been advocated,[115] but most patients have died despite chemotherapy.

Brain invasion also occurs by extension from the paranasal si-

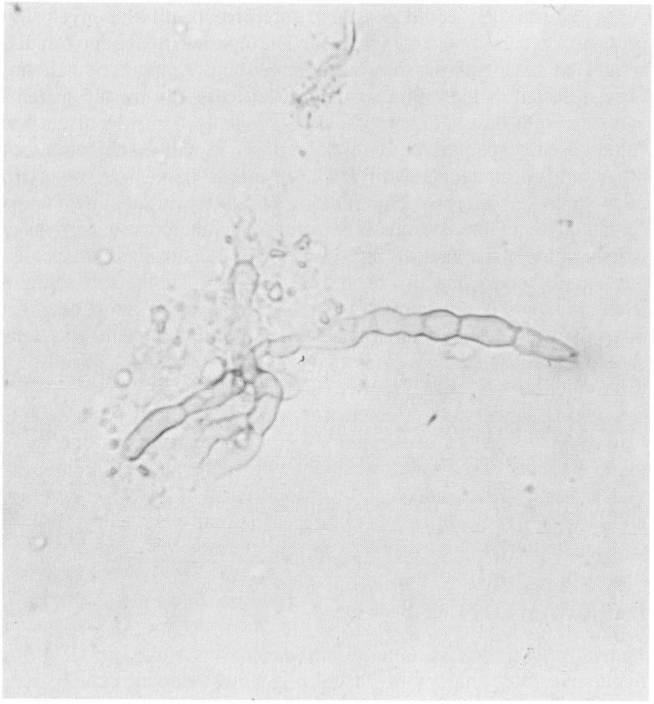

FIGURE 259–4. Weakly pigmented, segmented hyphae of *Cladophialophora bantiana* in wet mount of pus from the base of the brain.

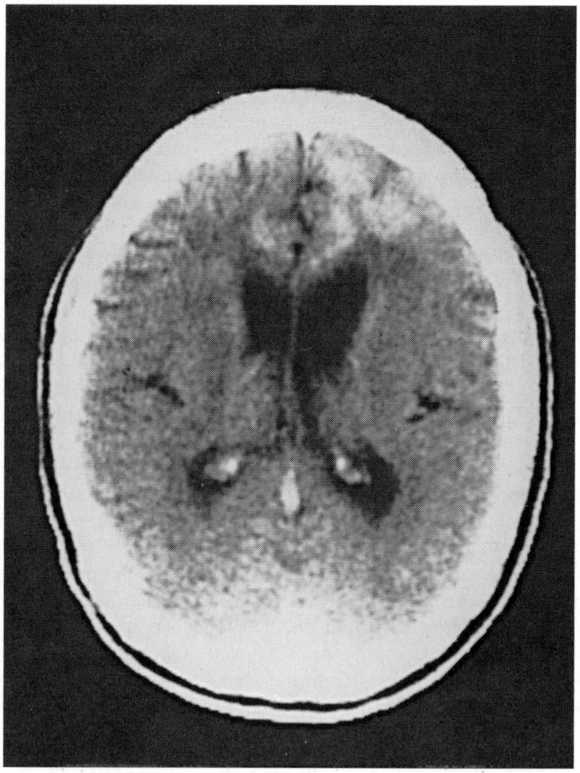

FIGURE 259–5. Magnetic resonance imaging with T2-weighted imaging showing extension into the frontal lobe of *Bipolaris hawaiiensis* sinusitis.

nuses and is the most serious sequela of allergic fungal sinusitis (Fig. 259–5). The number of species causing allergic fungal sinusitis is much broader than those causing brain abscess and includes some fungal species without dark walls. The most common species have been *Bipolaris, Exserohilum, Curvularia,* and *Alternaria.* The dark wall of the hyphae is apparent much less often than in brain abscess.[116] Patients present with an indolent onset of sinus pain or painless proptosis. A history of seasonal or allergic rhinitis is common and there may be a history of nasal polyps. On computed tomography or magnetic resonance imaging, one or more paranasal sinuses appears full of fluid, with outward pressure on the thinner bony sinus walls, such as the lamina papyracea, medial maxillary wall, or midline sphenoidal septum (Fig. 259–6). Maxillary and ethmoid sinuses are usually involved, but sphenoid and frontal sinuses may be diseased. Extension from the ethmoid or frontal sinus into the frontal lobe of the brain can be clinically silent. Erosion into the clivus, pterygoid space, or middle fossa occurs but is rare. Sudden blindness can occur from compression of the optic nerve posterior to the orbital fissure. Compression of the orbit by lateral bulging of the lamina papyracea does not decrease visual acuity but causes proptosis. Surgical débridement of the paranasal sinus removes dark, inspissated mucus that on histopathologic examination has strands of neutrophil and eosinophils with Charcot-Leyden crystals (degenerated eosinophils) and scattered septate hyphae. Irregular diameter and bulbous swellings may help distinguish these hyphae from *Aspergillus,* but culture is essential for diagnosis. Good surgical curettage often suffices if the cranial cavity has not been entered. Amphotericin B is probably the drug of choice for epidural or brain extension. In patients who have recurrent allergic fungal sinusitis, long-term itraconazole therapy may be used after repeat surgical drainage to help prevent another recurrence.

Cutaneous phaeohyphomycosis typically begins as a single red nodule. Among 47 cases, 21 were on the upper extremity, 16 were on the lower extremity, 6 were on the head or neck, and 4 were on the buttock. Indolent, painless expansion in the skin and subcutaneous tissue, sometimes with cyst formation, occurs in the immunocompetent patient. More rapid progression locally and, rarely, exten-

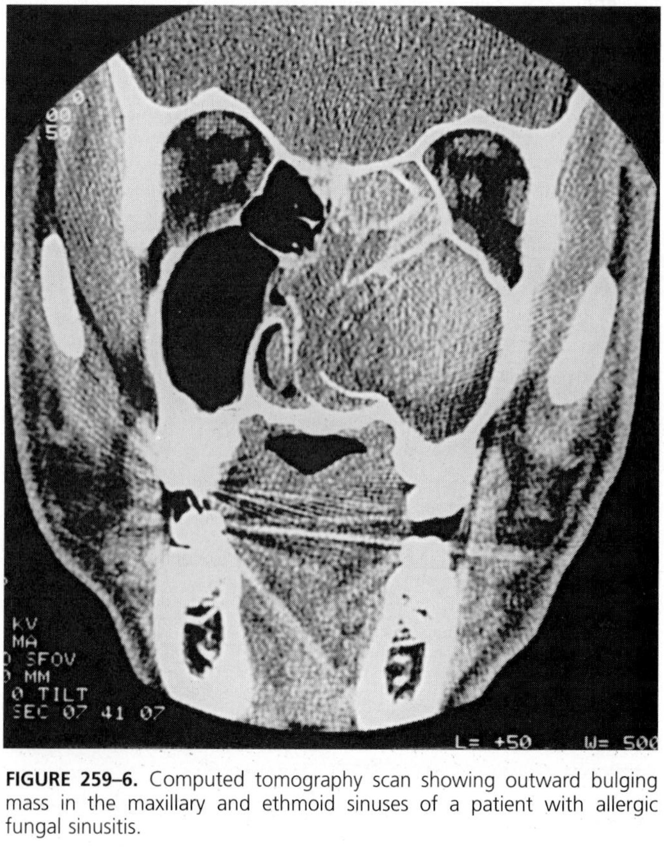

FIGURE 259–6. Computed tomography scan showing outward bulging mass in the maxillary and ethmoid sinuses of a patient with allergic fungal sinusitis.

sion to the brain, can occur in the immunosuppressed patient. A history of minor trauma may be obtained or a splinter may be found in the resected lesion. Among 80 patients, 69 were 30 years of age or older. The fungi causing subcutaneous phaeohyphomycosis are extraordinarily diverse, although species of *Exophiala* and *Phialophora* have been particularly common.[108] Surgical resection is often curative in the normal host, but itraconazole may be useful in patient whose lesions cannot be resected.[117, 118]

Other clinical entities have been reported, such as disseminated disease,[119] pneumonia,[120] endocarditis on a prosthetic valve, infection of a chronic ambulatory peritoneal dialysis catheter, osteomyelitis, and septic arthritis.[106]

PROTOTHECA

Prototheca are unicellular achloric algae that reproduce by endosporulation. The organisms are found in a wide range of environmental sites, including tree slime, sewage, fresh or marine water, soil, and foodstuffs. At least 71 cases have been reported,[106, 121, 122] almost all in adults and from widely scattered geographic areas.

The most common presentation of protothecosis is a single lesion of the skin or subcutaneous tissue. The typical skin lesion is a painless, slowly progressive, well-circumscribed plaque or papulonodular lesion that may become eczematoid or ulcerated. Soft tissue lesions favor the olecranon bursa, sites of minor trauma or corticosteroid injection,[123] or surgical wounds exposed to soil or water, such as a hand tendon repair. Gradual enlargement over weeks to months is the course of skin and soft tissue lesions, with no tendency for self-healing. A nasopharyngeal ulcerated lesion followed prolonged endotracheal intubation.[122] Infections of chronic ambulatory peritoneal catheters have been reported. Too few infections in other deep tissue have been reported to support any generalization.[116, 121, 124] Skin lesions in HIV-infected patients have not differed from those in previously normal patients.[125, 126]

Protothecosis is best diagnosed by biopsy for histologic study and culture. The inflammatory response shows both microabscesses and granulomas with multinucleate giant cells. *Prototheca* cells usually range from 8 to 20 μm in diameter, stain well with Gomori methenamine silver or periodic acid–Schiff, and often contain two to eight tightly packed endospores in each cell or sporangium. White opaque colonies appear in a few days on Sabouraud agar. Identification is by gross and microscopic appearance plus biochemical tests.

Protothecosis has little, if any, tendency toward self-healing. Surgical excision of lesions and intravenous amphotericin B have both been used successfully.[125] *Prototheca* spp. are resistant to flucytosine. Prolonged therapy with ketoconazole, itraconazole, or fluconazole has been reported to benefit some patients with skin lesions.[123, 127, 128]

ADIASPIROMYCOSIS

Adiaspiromycosis is known primarily as a disease of small burrowing rodents, which inhale *Emmonsia crescens* spores into the lung. The spores enlarge and become surrounded by dense pyogranulomatous inflammation. *E. crescens* has been found to have a teleomorph, named *Ajellomyces crescens.* The name was given because *A. crescens* closely resembles *Ajellomyces dermatitidis*, the teleomorph of the fungus causing blastomycosis.[129, 130] Humans can acquire a similar inhalation disease with scattered pulmonary granulomas. With the exception of one case caused by *E. crescens*, human cases appear to be caused by the closely related species *Emmonsia parva*. Although the teleomorph has not been demonstrated, *E. parva* is probably also a member of the *Ajellomyces* clade. The natural habitat of *E. crescens* and *E. parva* is soil. The fungus is widely distributed geographically, as are infections in humans and animals. In a report of 11 cases and a review of 35 other cases, 5 were from the United States, with the remaining 41 being from 12 different countries.[131] Adult men with outdoor occupations predominate. Symptoms seem to depend on the number of spores inhaled.[132]

A spore of *E. crescens* inhaled into the lung is capable of growing to a diameter of 200 to 700 μm. No dissemination or multiplication occurs in humans, but the huge spore becomes encased in a granuloma with epitheloid cells and multinucleated giant cells (Fig. 259–7). A patient may have one or many such granulomas. The infection is usually an incidental autopsy finding, but extensive infection can cause fever, cough, and dyspnea.[132] Diagnosis can be made by culture of lung tissue or by the appearance of the huge, thick-walled cysts in histopathologic section. Whether antifungal therapy alters the course of the inflammatory response is unknown.

RHINOSPORIDIUM SEEBERI

Rhinosporidiosis is a chronic, usually painless localized infection of the mucous membrane.[106] The lesion increases in size over months or years to form a friable pedunculated mass, typically in the nose, upper airway, or conjunctiva.[133] Nasal lesions appear as nasal obstruction or epistaxis.[134] One or more pedunculated or verrucous skin lesions, with or without nasal or conjunctival lesions, are seen occasionally.[135, 136] Rarely, polyps occur in the vagina, urethra, or penis. The causative agent, *Rhinosporidium seeberi,* has never been cultured but is thought to be a fungus. *R. seeberi* forms round, thick-walled cysts varying from 10 to 200 μm in the submucosa, often visible through the mucosa as white dots. Mature cysts become filled with numerous spores, which on release become new cysts (Fig. 259–8). The infection occurs throughout the world, although the greatest number of cases have been found in southern India and Sri Lanka. Lasser and Smith[137] reviewed 28 cases from the United States—19 in the nose and 9 in the conjunctiva. Twenty-four occurred in men and four in women. No state had an excess of cases. Treatment of choice is surgery.[133, 138]

LOBOA LOBOI

Lobomycosis (Lobo's disease, keloidal blastomycosis) is a chronic skin infection caused by a fungus never isolated in culture but called *Loboa loboi.* More than 100 cases have been reported from Latin America. The disease has not been acquired in the United States except in dolphins off the coast of Florida.[106] The diagnosis is made by finding the typical globose to lemon-shaped cells (about 9 μm in diameter), either singly or in short chains. The fungus remains confined to the skin, progressing slowly over decades. Lesions are nodular, red, hard, and shiny. Surgical excision is the only useful therapy.

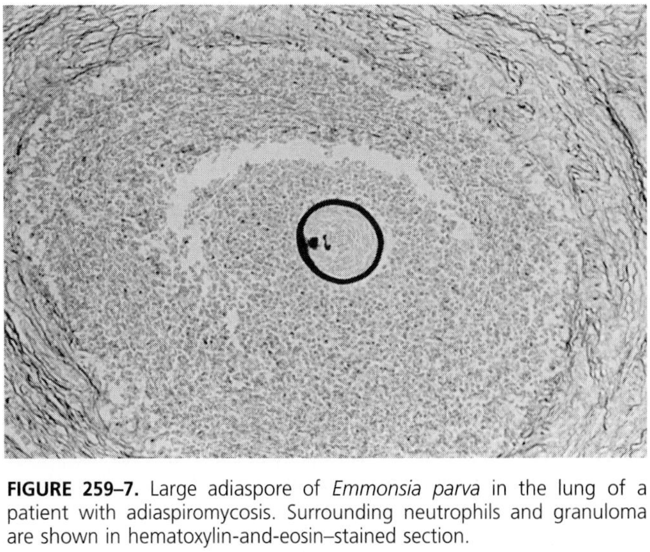

FIGURE 259–7. Large adiaspore of *Emmonsia parva* in the lung of a patient with adiaspiromycosis. Surrounding neutrophils and granuloma are shown in hematoxylin-and-eosin–stained section.

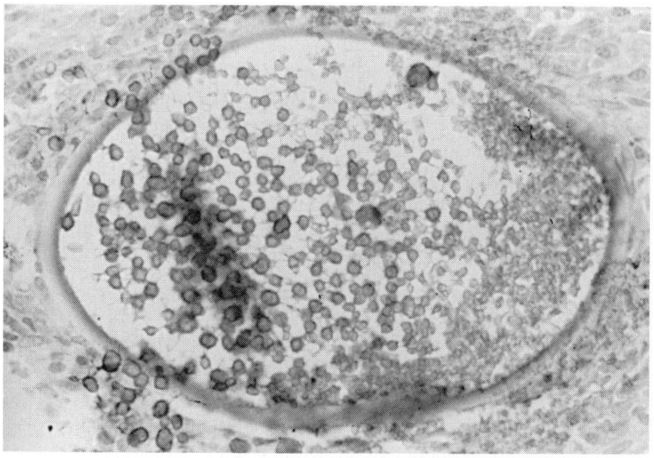

FIGURE 259–8. Histopathologic section showing *Rhinosporidium seeberi* in the nasal submucosa. Large sporangium is filled with spores.

TRICHOSPORON SPECIES

Recent revisions in the taxonomy have placed most of the agents of deeply invasive human *Trichosporon* infections into the species *Trichosporon asahii* or, less commonly, *Trichosporon mucoides.*[139, 140–142] According to this schema, *Trichosporon asteroides* and *Trichosporon cutaneum* cause superficial infections of humans. White piedra of the scalp is caused by *Trichosporon ovoides* and that of the pubic hair is caused by *Trichosporon inkin* (see Chapter 257). Because the bulk of the clinical data has identified the isolates as *Trichosporon beigelii,* this discussion retains the older nomenclature.

T. beigelii can be part of the normal human flora and appear in cultures of stool, skin, or urine.[143] At least 80 patients with deep trichosporonosis have been described, and approximately 60% have been severely neutropenic, usually with acute leukemia.[142, 144, 145] A few have had organ transplantation, HIV infection, burns, chronic ambulatory peritoneal dialysis, or catheter-acquired fungemia.[146] Seven patients had infections of the prosthetic cardiac valves.[143] Trichosporonosis is an acute, febrile, often fatal infection with dissemination to multiple deep organs. Pneumonia is not a consistent or early feature; the portal of entry is often not apparent. *T. beigelii* grows readily on ordinary culture media, but blood cultures tend to be positive late in the course. Multiple red papular skin lesions may occur earlier and assist diagnosis.[147, 148] On biopsy, a mixture of true hyphae, pseudohyphae, budding yeasts, and arthroconidia are seen, and are easily mistaken for candidiasis. Therapy with amphotericin B has been recommended, but there is no obviously effective drug.[143]

OTHER MYCOSES

Blastoschizomyces capitatus (Trichosporon capitatum) has caused severe infection in at least 28 patients, 22 of whom were severely neutropenic.[106, 149, 150] Blood cultures were positive in 23 of 25 cases. Six patients had papulonecrotic skin lesions similar to those seen in leukemic patients with disseminated candidiasis. Intravenous catheters have been a possible portal of entry.[151] Intravenous amphotericin B, with our without flucytosine, has been advocated, but neutrophil recovery determines outcome.[151]

Malassezia furfur, a lipophilic yeast, colonizes the normal human skin and causes the superficial mycosis, tinea versicolor. The fungus can also cause catheter-acquired sepsis. Almost all the septic cases have been receiving parenteral lipids through a central intravascular catheter such as a Broviac.[152] Most patients have been neonates with extended stays in intensive care units, although a few have been adults with malignancy or immunosuppression.[153] Fever has been the most common finding, but bradycardia, apnea, thrombocytopenia, and catheter blockage have been observed in some infants. In one autopsied case, the yeast was observed in lipid-containing areas of pulmonary vascular endothelium. *M. furfur* rarely is detected by conventional culture techniques because the yeast requires fatty acids for growth. Optimal recovery has been culture of blood drawn back through the catheter, using the lysis-centrifugation technique and lipid-enriched agar.[152, 154] The fungus adheres to the lumen of the catheter and has not been eradicated by discontinuing lipid infusions or administering miconazole or amphotericin B through the catheter.[155] Catheter removal and discontinuing parenteral lipids have been curative. In vitro, *M. furfur* appears to be susceptible to both amphotericin B and imidazoles.[156] Cultures or smears[157] of peripheral blood are occasionally positive. The yeast is identified on smear by its size, shape, and the distinctive collarette between mother and daughter cells. Lipid requirement for growth also aids identification. It seems likely that some cases reported as due to *M. furfur* have been due to other lipid-requiring species that can be termed the *Malassezia furfur* complex, including *Malassezia sympodialis, Malassezia globosa, Malassezia obtusa, Malassezia restricta,* or *Malassezia slooffiae.*[158] *Malassezia pachydermatis* has the same appearance, has caused similar infections, but does not require lipids for growth.

REFERENCES

1. Travis LB, Roberts GD, Wilson WR. Clinical significance of *Pseudallescheria boydii*: Review of 10 years' experience. Mayo Clin Proc. 1985;60:531–537.
2. Salitan ML, Lawson W, Som PM, et al. *Pseudallescheria* sinusitis with intracranial extension in a nonimmunocompromised host. Otolaryngol Head Neck Surg. 1990;102:745–750.
3. Bloom PA, Laidlaw DAH, Easty DL, Warnock DW. Treatment failure in a case of fungal keratitis caused by *Pseudallescheria boydii.* Br J Ophthalmol. 1992;76:367–368.
4. Ksiazek SM, Morris DA, Mandelbaum S, Rosenbaum PS. Fungal panophthalmitis secondary to *Scedosporium apiospermum (Pseudallescheria boydii)* keratitis. Am J Ophthalmol. 1994;118:531–533.
5. Bouchard CS, Chacko B, Cupples HP, et al. Surgical treatment for a case of postoperative *Pseudallescheria boydii* endophthalmitis. Ophthalmic Surg. 1991;22:98–101.
6. Sheftel TG, Mader JT, Cierny G. *Pseudallescheria boydii* soft tissue abscess. Clin Orthop. 1987;215:212–216.
7. Török L, Simon G, Scornai A, et al. *Scedosporium apiospermum* infection imitating lymphocutaneous sporotrichosis in a patient with myeloblastic-monocytic leukaemia. Br J Dermatol. 1995;133:805–809.
8. Davis WA, Isner JM, Bracey AW, et al. Disseminated *Petriellidium boydii* and pacemaker endocarditis. Am J Med. 1980;69:929–932.
9. Raffanti SP, Fyfe B, Carreiro S, et al. Native valve endocarditis due to *Pseudallescheria boydii* in a patient with AIDS: Case report and review. Rev Infect Dis. 1990;12:993–996.
10. Welty FK, McLeod GX, Ezratty C, et al. *Pseudallescheria boydii* endocarditis of the pulmonic valve in a liver transplant recipient. Clin Infect Dis. 1992;15:858–860.
11. Arnett JC, Hatch HB. Pulmonary allescheriasis. Report of a case and review of the literature. Arch Intern Med. 1975;135:1250–1253.
12. Lake FR, Tribe AE, McAleer R, et al. Mixed allergic bronchopulmonary fungal disease due to *Pseudallescheria boydii* and *Aspergillus*. Thorax. 1990;45:489–491.
13. Miller MA, Greenberger PA, Amerian R, et al. Allergic bronchopulmonary mycosis caused by *Pseudallescheria boydii.* Am Rev Respir Dis. 1993;148:810–812.
14. Bousley PH. Isolation of *Allescheria boydii* from pleural fluid. J Clin Microbiol. 1977;5:244.
15. Alture-Werber E, Edberg SC, Singer JM. Pulmonary infection with *Allescheria boydii.* Am J Clin Pathol. 1976;66:1019–1024.
16. Saadah HA, Dixon T. *Petriellidium boydii (Allescheria boydii)* necrotizing pneumonia in a normal host. JAMA. 1981;245:605–606.
17. Gluckman SJ, Ries K, Abrutyn E. *Allescheria* (*Petriellidium*) *boydii* sinusitis in a compromised host. J Clin Microbiol. 1977;5:481–484.
18. Walsh M, Atkinson K, White L, Enno A. Fungal *Pseudallescheria boydii* lung infiltrates unresponsive to amphotericin B in leukaemic patients. Aust N Z J Med. 1992;22:265–268.
19. Winer-Muram HT, Vargas S, Slobod K. Cavitary lung lesions in an immunosuppressed child. Chest. 1994;106:937–938.
20. Hofman P, Saint-Paul MC, Gari-Toussaint M, et al. Infection disséminée à *Scedosporium apiospermum* chez un transplanté hépatique. Un diagnostic différentiel de l'aspergillose invasive. Ann Pathol. 1993;13:332–335.
21. Patterson TF, Andriole VT, Zervos MJ, et al. The epidemiology of pseudallescheriasis complicating transplantation: Nosocomial and community-acquired infection. Mycoses. 1990;33:297–302.
22. Nomdedeu J, Brunet S, Martino R, et al. Successful treatment of pneumonia due

to *Scedosporium apiospermum* with itraconazole: Case report. Clin Infect Dis. 1993;16:731–733.
23. Bernstein EF, Schuster MG, Stieritz DD, et al. Disseminated cutaneous *Pseudallescheria boydii*. Br J Dermatol. 1995;132:456–460.
24. Hung CC, Chang SC, Yang PC, Hsieh WC. Invasive pulmonary pseudallescheriasis with direct invasion of the thoracic spine in an immunocompetent patient. Eur J Clin Microbiol Infect Dis. 1994;13:749–751.
25. Halpern AA, Nagel DA, Schurman DJ. *Allescheria boydii* osteomyelitis following multiple steroid injections and surgery. Clin Orthop. 1977;126:232–234.
26. Ansari RA, Hindson DA, Stevens DL, Kloss JG. *Pseudallescheria boydii* arthritis and osteomyelitis in a patient with Cushing's disease. South Med J. 1987;80:90–92.
27. Hayden G, Lapp C, Loda F. Arthritis caused by *Monosporium apiospermum* treated with intraarticular amphotericin B. Am J Dis Child. 1977;131:927.
28. Hung LHY, Norwood LA. Osteomyelitis due to *Pseudallescheria boydii*. South Med J. 1993;86:231–234.
29. Berenguer J, Diaz-Mediavilla J, Urra D, Mūnoz P. Central nervous system infection caused by *Pseudallescheria boydii*: Case report and review. Rev Infect Dis. 1989;11:890–896.
30. Montero A, Cohen JE, Fernandez MA, et al. Cerebral pseudallescheriasis due to *Pseudallescheria boydii* as the first manifestation of AIDS. Clin Infect Dis. 1998; 26:1476–1477.
31. Durieu I, Parent M, Ajana F, et al. *Monosporium apiospermum* meningoencephalitis: A clinico-pathological case. J Neurol Neurosurg Psychiatry. 1991;54:731–733.
32. Fisher JF, Shadomy S, Teabeaut R, et al. Near-drowning complicated by brain abscess due to *Petriellidium boydii*. Arch Neurol. 1982;39:511–513.
33. Gari M, Fruit J, Rousseaux P, et al. *Scedosporium (Monosporium) apiospermum*: Multiple brain abscesses. J Med Vet Mycol. 1985;23:371–376.
34. Hachimi-Idrissi S, Willemsen M, Desprechins B, et al. *Pseudallescheria boydii* and brain abscesses. Pediatr Infect Dis J. 1990;9:737–741.
35. Kershaw P, Freeman R, Templeton D, et al. *Pseudallescheria boydii* infection of the central nervous system. Arch Neurol. 1990;47:468–472.
36. Rüchel R, Wilichowski E. Cerebral *Pseudallescheria* mycosis after near-drowning. Mycoses. 1995;38:473–475.
37. Bryan CS, DiSalvo AF, Kaufman L, et al. *Petriellidium boydii* infection of the sphenoid sinus. Am J Clin Pathol. 1980;74:846–851.
38. Dworzack DL, Clark RB, Borkowski WJ, et al. *Pseudallescheria boydii* brain abscess: Association with near-drowning and efficacy of high-dose, prolonged miconazole therapy in patients with multiple abscesses. Medicine. 1989;68:218–224.
39. Benham RW, Georg LK. *Allescheria boydii*, causative agent in a case of meningitis. J Invest Dermatol. 1948;10:99–110.
40. Pérez RE, Smith M, McClendon J, et al. *Pseudallescheria boydii* brain abscess. Complication of an intravenous catheter. Am J Med. 1988;84:359–362.
41. Schiess RJ, Coscia MF, McClellan GA. *Petriellidium boydii* pachymeningitis treated with miconazole and ketoconazole. Neurosurgery. 1984;14:220–224.
42. Galgiani JN, Stevens DA, Graybill JR, et al. *Pseudallescheria boydii* infections treated with ketoconazole. Clinical evaluations of seven patients and in vitro susceptibility results. Chest. 1984;82:219–224.
43. Piper JP, Golden J, Brown D, Broestler J. Successful treatment of *Scedosporium apiospermum* suppurative arthritis with itraconazole. Pediatr Infect Dis J. 1990;9:674–675.
44. Girmenia C, Luzi G, Monaco M, Martino P. Use of voriconazole in treatment of *Scedosporium apiospermum*. J Clin Microbiol. 1998;36:1436–1438.
45. Malloch D, Salkin IF. A new species of *Scedosporium* associated with osteomyelitis in humans. Mycotaxon. 1984;21:247–255.
46. Wilson CM, O'Rourke EJ, McGinnis MR, Salkin IF. *Scedosporium inflatum*: Clinical spectrum of a newly recognized pathogen. J Infect Dis. 1990;161:102–107.
47. Wood GM, McCormack JG, Muir DB, et al. Clinical features of human infection with *Scedosporium inflatum*. Clin Infect Dis. 1992;14:1027–1033.
48. Alvarez M, Ponga BL, Rayon C, et al. Nosocomial outbreak caused by *Scedosporium prolificans* (*inflatum*): Four fatal cases in leukemia patients. J Clin Microbiol. 1995;33:3290–3295.
49. Bouza E, Muñoz P, Vega L, et al. Clinical resolution of *Scedosporium prolificans* fungemia associated with reversal of neutropenia following administration of granulocyte colony-stimulating factor. Clin Infect Dis. 1996;23:192–193.
50. Spielberger RT, Tegtmeier BR, O'Donnell MR, Ito JI. Fatal *Scedosporium prolificans* (*S. inflatum*) fungemia following allogeneic bone marrow transplantation: Report of a case in the United States. Clin Infect Dis. 1995;21:1067.
51. Farag SS, Firkin FC, Andrew JH, et al. Fatal disseminated *Scedosporium inflatum* infection in a neutropenic immunocompromised patient. J Infect. 1992;25:201–204.
52. Rabodonirina M, Paulus S, Thevenet F, et al. Disseminated *Scedosporium prolificans* (*S. inflatum*) infection after single-lung transplantation. Clin Infect Dis. 1994;19:138–142.
53. Madrigal V, Alonso J, Bureo E, et al. Fatal meningoencephalitis caused by *Scedosporium inflatum* (*Scedosporium prolificans*) in a child with lymphoblastic leukemia. Eur J Clin Microbiol Infect Dis. 1995;14:601–603.
54. Hopwood V, Evans EGV, Matthews J, Denning DW. *Scedosporium prolificans*, a multi-resistant fungus, from a UK AIDS patient. J Infect. 1995;30:153–155.
55. Salkin IF, McGinnis MR, Dykstra MJ, Rinaldi MG. *Scedosporium inflatum*, an emerging pathogen. J Clin Microbiol. 1988;26:498–503.
56. Ancelle T, Dupouy-Camet J, Pujol F, et al. Un cas de pénicilliose disséminée à *Penicillium marneffei* chez un malade atteint d'un syndrome immunodéficitaire acquis. Presse Med. 1988;17:1095–1096.
57. Peto TEA, Bull R, Millard PR, et al. Systemic mycosis due to *Penicillium marneffei* in a patient with antibody to human immunodeficiency virus. J Infect. 1988;16:285–290.
58. Piehl MR, Kaplan RL, Haber MH. Disseminated penicilliosis in a patient with acquired immunodeficiency syndrome. Arch Pathol Lab Med. 1988;112:1262–1264.
59. DiSalvo AF, Fickling AM, Ajello L. Infection caused by *Penicillium marneffei*: Description of first natural infection in man. Am J Clin Pathol. 1973;59:259–263.
60. Segretain G. *Penicillium marneffei* n. sp., agent d'une mycose du système réticulo-endothélial. Mycopathol Mycol Appl. 1959;11:327–353.
61. Phillips P. *Penicillium marneffei* part of southeast Asian AIDS. JAMA. 1996;276:86–87.
62. Supparatpinyo K, Khamwan C, Baosoung V, et al. Disseminated *Penicillium marneffei* infections in Southeast Asia. Lancet. 1994;344:110–113.
63. Drouhet E. Penicilliosis due to *Penicillium marneffei*: A new emerging systemic mycosis in AIDS patients traveling or living in Southeast Asia. Review of 44 cases reported in HIV infected patients during the last 5 years compared to 44 cases of non AIDS patients reported over 20 years. J Mycol Med. 1993;4:195–224.
64. Duong TA. Infection due to *Penicillium marneffei*, an emerging pathogen: Review of 155 reported cases. Clin Infect Dis. 1996;23:125–130.
65. Hung C, Hsueh P, Chen M, et al. Invasive infection caused by *Penicillium marneffei*: An emerging pathogen in Taiwan. Clin Infect Dis. 1998;26:202–203.
66. Kwan EYW, Lau YL, Yuen KY, et al. *Penicillium marneffei* infection in a non-HIV infected child. J Paediatr Child Health. 1997;33:267–271.
67. Sirisanthana V, Sirisanthana T. *Penicillium marneffei* infection in children infected with human immunodeficiency virus. Pediatr Infect Dis J. 1993;12:1021–1025.
68. Ajello L, Padhye AA, Sukroongreung S, et al. Occurrence of *Penicillium marneffei* infections among wild bamboo rats in Thailand. Mycopathologia. 1995;131:1–8.
69. Deng Z, Yun M, Ajello L. Human penicilliosis marneffei and its relation to the bamboo rat (*Rhizomys pruinosus*). J Med Vet Mycol. 1986;24:383–389.
70. Li JC, Pan LQ, Wu SX. Mycologic investigation on *Rhizomys pruinosus senex* in Guangxi as natural carrier with *Penicillium marneffei*. Chin Med J. 1989;102:477–485.
71. Cooper CR. From bamboo rats to humans: The odyssey of *Penicillium marneffei*. ASM News. 1998; 64:390–396.
72. Chariyalertsak S, Vanittanakom P, Nelson KE, et al. *Rhizomys sumatrensis* and *Cannomys badius*, new natural animal hosts of *Penicillium marneffei*. J Med Vet Mycol. 1996;34:105–110.
73. Chariyalertsak S, Sirisanthana T, Supparatpinyo K, et al. Case-control study of the risk factors for *Penicillium marneffei* infection in human immunodeficiency virus–infected patients in northern Thailand. Clin Infect Dis. 1997;24:1080–1086.
74. Chariyalertsak S, Sirisanthana T, Supparatpinyo K, Nelson KE. Seasonal variation of disseminated *Penicillium marneffei* infections in northern Thailand: A clue to the reservoir? J Infect Dis. 1996;173:1490–1493.
75. Wortmann PD. Infection with *Penicillium marneffei*. Int J Dermatol. 1996;35:393–399.
76. Cheng NC, Won WW, Fung CP, et al. Unusual pulmonary manifestations of disseminated *Penicillium marneffei* infection in three AIDS patients. Med Mycol. 1998;36:429–432.
77. Deng Z, Ribas JL, Gibson DW, Connor DH. Infections caused by *Penicillium marneffei* in China and southeast Asia: Review of eighteen published cases and report of four more Chinese cases. Rev Infect Dis. 1988;10:640–652.
78. Hilmarsdottir I, Coutellier A, Elbaz J, et al. A French case of laboratory-acquired disseminated *Penicillium marneffei* infection in a patient with AIDS. Clin Infect Dis. 1994;19:357–358.
79. Jones PD, See J. *Penicillium marneffei* infection in patients infected with human immunodeficiency virus: Late presentation in an area of nonendemicity. Clin Infect Dis. 1992;15:744.
80. Supparatpinyo K, Sirisanthana T. Disseminated *Penicillium marneffei* infection diagnosed on examination of a peripheral blood smear of a patient with human immunodeficiency virus infection. Clin Infect Dis. 1994;18:246–247.
81. Cooper CR, McGinnis MR. Pathology of *Penicillium marneffei*. An emerging acquired immunodeficiency syndrome–related pathogen. Arch Pathol Lab Med. 1997;121:798–804.
82. Imwidthaya P, Sekhon AS, Mastro TD, et al. Usefulness of a microimmunodiffusion test for the detection of *Penicillium marneffei* antigenemia, antibodies, and exoantigens. Mycopathologia. 1997;138:51–55.
83. Kaufman L, Standard PG, Anderson SA, et al. Development of specific fluorescent-antibody test for tissue form of *Penicillium marneffei*. J Clin Microbiol. 1995;33:2136–2138.
84. Kaufman L, Standard PG, Jalbert M, et al. Diagnostic antigenemia tests for penicilliosis marneffei. J Clin Microbiol. 1996;34:2503–2505.
85. Yuen KY, Wong SSY, Tsang DNC, Chau PY. Serodiagnosis of *Penicillium marneffei* infection. Lancet. 1994;344:444–445.
86. Hamilton AJ. Serodiagnosis of histoplasmosis, paracoccidioidomycosis and penicilliosis marneffei; current status and future trends. Med Mycol. 1998;36:351–364.
87. Supparatpinyo K, Nelson KE, Merz WG, et al. Response to antifungal therapy by human immunodeficiency virus–infected patients with disseminated *Penicillium marneffei* infections and in vitro susceptibilities of isolates from clinical specimens. Antimicrob Agents Chemother. 1993;37:2407–2411.
88. Sirisanthana T, Supparatpinyo K, Perriens J, Nelson KE. Amphotericin B and itraconazole for treatment of disseminated *Penicillium marneffei* infection in human immunodeficiency virus–infected patients. Clin Infect Dis. 1998;26:1107–1110.
89. Supparatpinyo K, Perriens J, Nelson KE, Sirisanthana T. A controlled trial of itraconazole to prevent relapse of *Penicillium marneffei* infection in patients in-

fected with the human immunodeficiency virus. N Engl J Med. 1998;339:1739–1743.
90. Guarro J, Gené J. Opportunistic fusarial infections in humans. Eur J Clin Microbiol Infect Dis. 1995;14:741–754.
91. Wheeler MS, McGinnis MR, Schell WA, Walker DH. *Fusarium* infection in burned patients. Am J Clin Pathol. 1981;75:304–311.
92. Strum AW, Grave W, Kwee WS. Disseminated *Fusarium oxysporum* infection in a patient with heat stroke. Lancet. 1989;1:968.
93. Boutati EI, Anaissie EJ. *Fusarium*, a significant emerging pathogen in patients with hematologic malignancy: Ten years' experience at a cancer center and implications for management. Blood. 1997;90:999–1008.
94. Krcmery V, Jesenska Z, Spanik S, et al. Fungaemia due to *Fusarium* spp. in cancer patients. J Hosp Infect. 1997;36:223–228.
95. Martino P, Gastaldi R, Raccah R, Girmenia C. Clinical patterns of *Fusarium* infections in immunocompromised patients. J Infect. 1994;28(Suppl 1):7–15.
96. Gamis AS, Gudnason T, Giebink GS, Ramsay NKC. Disseminated infection with *Fusarium* in recipients of bone marrow transplants. Rev Infect Dis. 1991;13:1077–1088.
97. Hennequin C, Lavarde V, Poirot JL, et al. Invasive *Fusarium* infections: A retrospective survey of 31 cases. J Med Vet Mycol. 1997;35:107–114.
98. Anaissie E, Kantarjian H, Ro J, et al. The emerging role of *Fusarium* infections in patients with cancer. Medicine. 1988;67:77–83.
99. Ammari LK, Puck JM, McGowan KL. Catheter-related *Fusarium solani* fungemia and pulmonary infection in a patient with leukemia in remission. Clin Infect Dis. 1993;16:148–150.
100. Raad I, Hachem R. Treatment of central venous catheter–related fungemia due to *Fusarium oxysporum*. Clin Infect Dis. 1995;20:709–711.
101. Girmenia C, Arcese W, Micozzi A, et al. Onychomycosis as a possible origin of disseminated *Fusarium solani* infection in a patient with severe aplastic anemia. Clin Infect Dis. 1992;14:1167.
102. Krcméry V, Spanik S, Kunova A, Trupl J. Breakthrough fungemia appearing during empiric therapy with amphotericin B. Chemotherapy. 1997;43:367–370.
103. Nelson PE, Dignani MC, Anaissie EJ. Taxonomy, biology, and clinical aspects of *Fusarium* species. Clin Microbiol Rev. 1994;7:479–504.
104. Wolff MA, Ramphal R. Use of amphotericin B lipid complex for treatment of disseminated cutaneous *Fusarium* infection in a neutropenic patient. Clin Infect Dis. 1995;20:1568–1569.
105. Spielberger RT, Falleroni MJ, Coene AJ, Larson RA. Concomitant amphotericin B therapy, granulocyte transfusions, and GM-CSF administration for disseminated infection with *Fusarium* in a granulocytopenic patient. Clin Infect Dis. 1993;16:528–530.
106. Kwon-Chung KJ, Bennett JE. Medical Mycology. Philadelphia: Lea & Febiger; 1992.
107. Oliveira Ramos AM, Oliveira Sales, A, Andrade MC, et al. A simple method for detecting subcutaneous phaeohyphomycosis with light colored fungi. Am J Surg Pathol. 1995;19:109–114.
108. Rinaldi MG. Phaeohyphomycosis. Dermatol Clin. 1996;14:147–153.
109. Rossman SNB, Cernoch PL, Davis JR. Dematiaceous fungi are an increasing cause of human disease. Clin Infect Dis. 1996;22:73–80.
110. Aldape KD, Fox HS, Roberts JP, et al. *Cladosporium trichoides* cerebral phaeohyphomycosis in a liver transplant recipient. Am J Clin Pathol. 1991;95:499–502.
111. Buxi TBS, Prakash K, Vohra R, et al. Imaging in phaeohyphomycosis of the brain. Case report. Neuroradiology. 1996;38:139–141.
112. Walz R, Bianchin M, Chaves ML, et al. Cerebral phaeohyphomycosis caused by *Cladophialophora bantiana* in a Brazilian drug abuser. J Med Vet Mycol. 1997;35:427–431.
113. Campbell CK, Al-Hedaithy SSA. Phaeohyphomycosis of the brain caused by *Ramichloridium mackenziei* sp nov in Middle Eastern countries. J Med Vet Mycol. 1993;31:325–332.
114. Sutton DA, Slifkin M, Yakulis R, et al. U.S. Case report of cerebral phaeohyphomycosis caused by *Ramichloridium obovoideum (R. mackenziei)*; criteria for identification, therapy, and review of other known dematiaceous neurotropic taxa. J Clin Microbiol. 1998;36:708–715.
115. Vukmir RB, Kusne S, Linder P, et al. Successful therapy for cerebral phaeohyphomycosis due to *Dactylaria gallopava* in a liver transplant recipient. Clin Infect Dis. 1994;19:714–719.
116. Washburn RG, Kennedy DW, Begley MG, et al. Chronic fungal sinusitis in apparently normal hosts. Medicine. 1988;67:231–247.
117. Whittle DI, Kominos S. Use of itraconazole for treating subcutaneous phaeohyphomycosis caused by *Exophiala jeanselmei*. Clin Infect Dis. 1995;21:1068.
118. Sharkey PK, Graybill JR, Rinaldi MG, et al. Itraconazole treatment of phaeohyphomycosis. J Am Acad Dermatol. 1990;23:577–586.
119. Karim M, Sheikh H, Alam M, et al. Disseminated bipolaris infection in an asthmatic patient: Case report. Clin Infect Dis. 1993;17:248–253.
120. Borges MC, Warren S, White W, et al. Pulmonary phaeohyphomycosis due to *Xylohypha bantiana*. Arch Pathol Lab Med. 1991;115:627–629.
121. Kaminski ZC, Kapila R, Sharer LR, et al. Meningitis due to *Prototheca wickerhamii* in a patient with AIDS. Clin Infect Dis. 1992;15:704–706.
122. Iacoviello VR, DeGirolami PC, Lucarini J, et al. Protothecosis complicating prolonged endotracheal intubation: Case report and literature review. Clin Infect Dis. 1992;15:959–967.
123. Kim ST, Suh KS, Chae YS, et al. Successful treatment with fluconazole of protothecosis at the site of an intralesional corticosteroid injection. Br J Dermatol. 1996;135:803–806.
124. Ras R, Rottem M, Bisharat N, et al. Intestinal protothecosis in a patient with chronic mucocutaneous candidiasis. Clin Infect Dis. 1998;27:399–400.
125. Carey WP, Kaykova Y, Bandres JC, et al. Cutaneous protothecosis in a patient with AIDS and severe functional defect: Successful therapy with amphotericin B. Clin Infect Dis. 1997;25:1265–1266.
126. Polk P, Sanders DY. Successful treatment with fluconazole of cutaneous protothecosis in association with the acquired immunodeficiency syndrome. South Med J. 1997;90:831–832.
127. Matsumoto Y, Shibata M, Adachi A, et al. Two cases of protothecosis in Nagoya, Japan. Australas J Dermatol. 1996;37(Suppl 1):S42–S43.
128. Tang WY, Lo KK, Lam WY, et al. Cutaneous protothecosis: Report of a case in Hong Kong. Br J Dermatol. 1995;133:479–482.
129. Sigler L. *Ajellomyces crescens sp. nov.*, taxonomy of *Emmonsia spp.*, and relatedness with *Blastomyces dermatitidis* (teleomorph *Ajellomyces dermatitidis*). J Med Vet Mycol. 1996;34:303–314.
130. Peterson SW, Sigler L. Molecular genetic variation in *Emmonsia crescens* and *Emmonsia parva*, etiologic agents of adiaspiromycosis, and their phylogenetic relationship to *Blastomyces dermatitidis (Ajellomyces dermatitidis)* and other systemic fungal pathogens. J Clin Microbiol. 1998;36:2918–2925.
131. England DM, Hochholzer L. Adiaspiromycosis: An unusual fungal infection of the lung. Am J Surg Pathol. 1993;17:876–886.
132. Nuorva K, Pitkanen R, Issakainen J, et al. Pulmonary adiaspiromycosis in a two year old girl. J Clin Pathol. 1997;50:82–85.
133. Reidy JJ, Sudesh S, Klafter AB, et al. Infection of the conjunctiva by *Rhinosporidium seeberi*. Surv Ophthalmol. 1997;41:409–413.
134. Snidvongs ML, Supanakorn S, Supiyaphun P. Severe epistaxis from rhinosporidiosis: A case report. J Med Assoc Thai. 1998;81:555–558.
135. Thappa DM, Venkatesan S, Sirka CS, et al. Disseminated cutaneous rhinosporidiosis. J Dermatol. 1998;25:527–532.
136. Ghorpade A, Ramanan C. Verrucoid cutaneous rhinosporidiosis. J Eur Acad Dermatol Venereol. 1998;10:269–270.
137. Lasser A, Smith HW. Rhinosporidiosis. Arch Otolaryngol. 1976;102:308–310.
138. Shrestha SP, Hennig A, Parija SC. Prevalence of rhinosporidiosis of the eye and its adnexa in Nepal. Am J Trop Med Hyg. 1998;59:231–234.
139. Gueho E, Improvisi L, de Hoog GS, et al. Trichosporon in humans, a practical account. Mycoses. 1994;37:3–10.
140. Sugita T, Nishikawa A, Shinoda T. Identification of *Trichosporon asahii* by PCR based on sequences of the internal transcribed spacer regions. J Clin Microbiol. 1998;36:2742–2744.
141. Sugita T, Nishikawa A, Shinoda T, et al. Taxonomic position of deep-seated, mucosa associated, and superficial isolates of *Trichosporon cutaneum* from trichosporonosis patients. J Clin Microbiol. 1995;33:1368–1370.
142. Itoh T, Hosokawa H, Kohdera U, et al. Disseminated infection with *Trichosporon asahii*. Mycoses. 1996;39:195–199.
143. Haupt HM, Merz WG, Beschorner WE, et al. Colonization and infection with *Trichosporon* species in the immunosuppressed host. J Infect Dis. 1983;147:199.
144. Hung CC, Chang SC, Chen YC, et al. *Trichosporon beigelii* fungemia in patients with acute leukemia: Report of three cases. J Formos Med Assoc. 1995;94:127–131.
145. Hajjeh RA, Blumberg HM. Bloodstream infection due to *Trichosporon beigelii* in a burn patient: Case report and review of therapy. Clin Infect Dis. 1995;20:913–916.
146. Mirza SH. Disseminated *Trichosporon beigelii* infection causing skin lesions in a renal transplant patient. J Infect. 1993;27:67–70.
147. Nahass GT, Rosenberg SP, Leonardi CL, et al. Disseminated infection with *Trichosporon beigelii*. Arch Dermatol. 1993;129:1020–1023.
148. Walsh TJ, Newman KR, Moody M, et al. Trichosporonosis in patients with neoplastic disease. Medicine. 1986;65:268–279.
149. Martino P, Venditti M, Micozzi A, et al. *Blastoschizomyces capitatus:* An emerging cause of invasive fungal disease in leukemia patients. Rev Infect Dis. 1990;12:570–582.
150. Polacheck I, Salkin IF, Kitzes-Cohen R, et al. Endocarditis caused by *Blastoschizomyces capitatus* and taxonomic review of the genus. J Clin Microbiol. 1992;30:2318–2322.
151. Sanz MA, Lopez FA, Martinez ML, et al. Disseminated *Blastoschizomyces capitatus* infection in acute myeloblastic leukemia. Support Care Cancer. 1996;4:291–293.
152. Dankner WM, Spector SA, Fierer J, et al. *Malassezia* fungemia in neonates and adults: Complication of hyperalimentation. Rev Infect Dis. 1987;9:743–753.
153. Barber GR, Brown AE, Kiehn TE, et al. Catheter-related *Malassezia furfur* fungemia in immunocompromised patients. Am J Med. 1993;95:365–370.
154. Azimi PH, Levernier K, Lefrak LM, et al. *Malassezia furfur*: A cause of occlusion of percutaneous central venous catheters in infants in the intensive care nursery. Pediatr Infect Dis J. 1988;7:100–103.
155. Powell DA, Marcon MJ. Failure to eradicate *Malassezia furfur* broviac catheter infection with antifungal therapy. Pediatr Infect Dis J. 1987;6:579–588.
156. Marcon MJ, Durrell DE, Powell DA, et al. In vitro activity of systemic antifungal agents against *Malassezia furfur*. Antimicrob Agents Chemother. 1987;31:951–953.
157. Brooks R, Brown L. Systemic infections with *Malassezia furfur* in an adult receiving long-term hyperalimentation therapy. J Infect Dis. 1987;156:410–411.
158. Boekhout T, Kamp M, Geuho E. Molecular typing of *Malassezia* species with PFGE and RAPD. Mol Mycol. 1998;36:365–372.

Chapter 260

Pneumocystis carinii

PETER D. WALZER

Pneumocystis carinii was discovered in 1909 by Chagas, who mistakenly interpreted the organism as a trypanosome. Several years later, the Delanöes identified *P. carinii* as a separate genus and species and named the organism in honor of Dr. Carini, another early worker. *P. carinii* first came to medical attention when it was implicated as the cause of interstitial plasma cell pneumonia, a disorder of institutionalized and debilitated infants in central and eastern Europe after World War II. In the 1960s, *P. carinii* became widely appreciated as an important cause of pneumonia in immunocompromised hosts; however, with the development of safe and effective antimicrobial drugs, interest in the organism waned. The dramatic rise in the incidence of pneumocystosis associated with human immunodeficiency virus (HIV) infection in the 1980s rekindled interest in *P. carinii* as a major medical and public health problem.[1] During the 1990s, advances in the treatment of HIV reduced the frequency of *P. carinii* pneumonia and other complications.[2] Nevertheless, *P. carinii* remains a leading cause of opportunistic infection, morbidity, and mortality in these patients.

THE PATHOGEN

P. carinii is an organism of low virulence found in the lungs of humans and a variety of animals in nature. Although organisms from these hosts have identical morphologic features, evidence accumulated since the late 1980s has shown that *P. carinii* has considerable genetic diversity and host specificity. Examples of these studies include chromosomal karyotyping, nucleotide sequence analysis, multilocus enzyme electrophoresis, antigenic characterization, and experimental transmission of infection.[1, 3–5] There are not only differences in *P. carinii* among different animal hosts but also species or strain differences, or both, in organisms from the same host. Molecular approaches have been used to analyze human *P. carinii* isolates.[6–11] The internal transcribed spacer regions of the nuclear rRNA gene and the large subunit mitochondrial rRNA gene have received the most attention, although other genes have also been compared. The data indicate that *P. carinii* isolates from HIV patients are similar to those from non-HIV patients; patients may harbor more than one strain of the organism; and some recurrent episodes of *P. carinii* pneumonia may represent new infection from an external source rather than relapse of an existing infection. A new nomenclature system based on the host of origin has been proposed to acknowledge the genetic diversity of *P. carinii*.[12]

For many years, the taxonomic status of *P. carinii* was a matter of controversy. However, analysis of the rRNA gene in the 1980s suggested that the organism is more closely related to fungi than to protozoa.[1] This conclusion has been strengthened by sequence analysis of genes encoding for dihydrofolate reductase, thymidylate synthetase, β-tubulin, and adenosine triphosphatase; the demonstration of the presence of elongation factor 3—a factor needed for protein synthesis that is found in fungi but not protozoa; the presence of β-1,3 glucan in the *P. carinii* cell wall and the susceptibility of the organism to β-glucan inhibitors, which were developed as antifungal drugs; and recent ultrastructural studies.[4, 13] Phylogenetic studies have suggested that the organism is closely related to Ascomycetes and Basidiomycetes; however, *P. carinii* is unusual among fungi in that the organism lacks ergosterol in its plasma membranes and is insensitive to antifungal drugs that target ergosterol biosynthesis.

Despite the strenuous efforts by many investigators, the lack of a reliable *P. carinii* in vitro cultivation system remains an intractable problem.[14, 15] Limited (up to 10-fold) replication of rat-derived organisms has been achieved in different cell lines and in axenic media, but attempts to cultivate human-derived organisms have been unsuccessful. Short-term culture has been used to study *P. carinii* metabolism and susceptibility to antimicrobial drugs, but standardization and reproducibility among laboratories have not yet been achieved.

Studies of the life cycle of *P. carinii* have been based mainly on light and electron microscopic analysis of forms seen in infected lungs or in short-term culture. Three developmental stages of the organism have been identified; the nomenclature used here includes both the older, more familiar protozoal terms as well as the newer fungal terminology (Fig. 260–1).[4, 16] The *trophozoite* or *trophic form* is small (1 to 4 μm) and pleomorphic and commonly exists in clusters; this stage can be identified on Giemsa stain by its reddish nucleus and blue cytoplasm (Fig. 260–2*A*). In the asexual phase of the life cycle, the trophic forms multiply by binary fission. In the sexual phase, the haploid trophic forms conjugate to form a diploid zygote that becomes a 4- to 6-μm *precyst* or *sporocyte*; this form is difficult to distinguish from the other developmental stages at the light microscopic level. The precyst undergoes meiosis, followed by mitosis, leading to the formation of the *cyst* or *spore case*, which contains eight haploid *intracystic bodies* or *spores*. The 5- to 8-μm cyst has a thick cell wall that stains well with stains such as methenamine silver (Fig. 260–2*B*). The intracystic bodies are formed by compartmentalization of nuclei and cytoplasmic organelles, exhibit different shapes, and appear to be released through a rent in the cell wall.

Biochemical and metabolic studies of *P. carinii* have been limited by the problems of culturing the organism.[17] The surface of *P. carinii* is rich in glucose and mannose, *N*-acetylglucosamine, and galactose/*N*-acetylgalactosamine residues. The cell wall of cysts and trophic forms contains a number of immunogenic glycoproteins that may be part of a large complex.[18] Lipids have received considerable attention.[19] Instead of ergosterol, *P. carinii* synthesizes distinct Δ 7, C-24 alkylated sterols. Coenzyme Q10 is the major ubiquinone homologue synthesized by the organism; CoQ homologues, such as 8-aminoquinolones and hydroxynaphthoquinones, have shown good activity against the organism. A variety of enzymes and other metabolic pathways have been identified.[4]

Two major groups of *P. carinii* antigens have been identified. The most widely studied is a 95- to 140-kD moiety, termed the *major surface glycoprotein (MSG)* or gpA, is highly immunogenic, exhibits shared and species-specific antigenic determinants, and contains protective B- and T-cell epitopes.[3, 20–25] Immunization with MSG also elicits a protective response in some, but not all, animal models.[26, 27] MSG actually represents a family of proteins encoded by multiple genes that are arranged in clusters at the ends of chromosomes.[28–31]

Recent studies have suggested that MSG undergoes antigenic variation.[3] Transcription of MSG genes occurs at a single expression site, termed the *upstream conserved sequence*, which is thought to result in only one MSG isoform being expressed on the surface of *P. carinii* at a time.[32–34] Changing the MSG gene at the upstream conserved sequence, which probably results from recombination, results in changing the surface MSG.

The ability of MSG to undergo antigenic variation may be an important mechanism by which *P. carinii* evades the host immune response. The other important function of MSG is to facilitate interaction with host cells by adherence to extracellular matrix proteins (fibronectin, vitronectin, possibly laminin), surfactant proteins A and D, and the mannose receptor.[35–41] MSG is composed of up to 10% of *N*-linked carbohydrates (particularly mannose), which participate in the binding to these proteins.

The other major antigen complex is a glycoprotein that migrates as a broad band of 45 to 55 kD and 35 to 45 kD in rat and human *P. carinii*, respectively.[42] Although this antigen has not been purified, evidence suggests that it resides in the cell wall.[43] The gene encoding the rat *P. carinii* 45- to 55-kD antigen (p55) has recently been cloned and sequenced; the 3′ end of the molecule stimulates a host immune

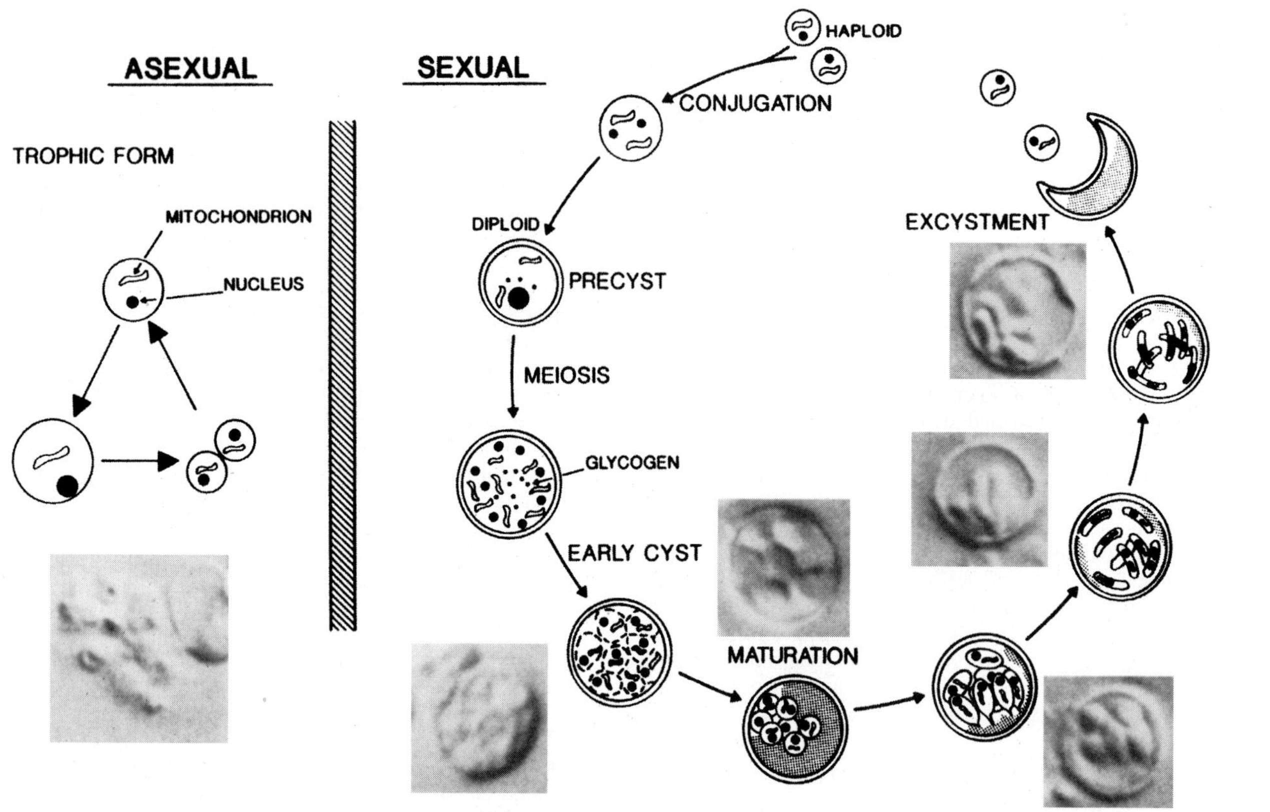

FIGURE 260–1. Proposed *Pneumocystis carinii* life cycle involving asexual and sexual stages. The photographs show living trophic and cyst forms of the organism by Nomarski interference microscopy. (From Cushion M. *Pneumocystis carinii*. In: Collier L, Balows A, Sussman M, eds. Topley and Wilson's Microbiology and Microbial Infections, v. 4. New York: Oxford University Press; 1998:645–683.)

response.[44, 45] The predicted amino acid sequence of p55 shows a repeated motif rich in glutamic acid residues that, in other microbes (e.g. *Plasmodia*), has been suggested as a mechanism to divert the host immune response.[46] The 35- to 45-kD band of human *P. carinii* is the principal antigen found in respiratory tract specimens and the moiety most frequently recognized by the host[42, 47–49]; thus, this antigen may serve as an important marker of *P. carinii* infection.

EPIDEMIOLOGY

Seroepidemiologic surveys have demonstrated that most healthy children have been exposed to *P. carinii* by an early age.[48] This primary infection is probably asymptomatic, although careful analysis has not been performed to determine if subtle clinical manifestations occur. The serologic studies have shown that *P. carinii* has a world-

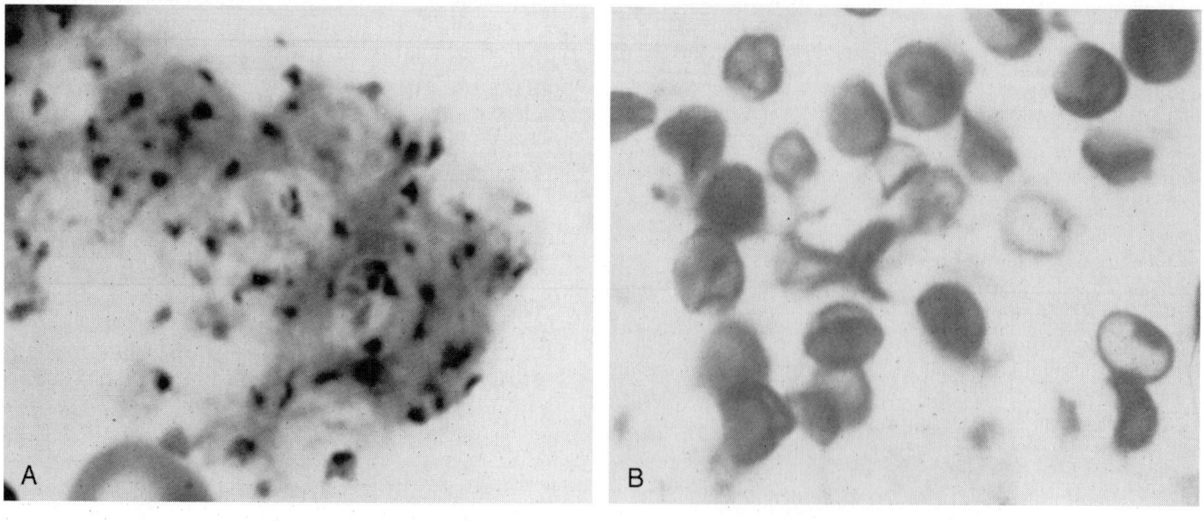

FIGURE 260–2. *A*, Cluster of *Pneumocystis carinii* trophozoites and cysts (Diff-Quik, ×2500). *B*, Cluster of *P. carinii* cysts (methenamine silver stain, ×1250).

wide distribution but that the prevalence of antibodies to specific antigens varies among different geographic regions.[49] The frequency with which *P. carinii* pneumonia is recognized among HIV patients in tropical and developing countries is generally much lower than that in industrialized nations.[50–52] This difference cannot be explained by differences in exposure to the organism; rather, it is likely due to the prevalence of more virulent infections that shorten life span (e.g., tuberculosis) and poor access to advanced diagnostic techniques in the developing world. The demographic features of patients with pneumocystosis generally reflect those of the underlying disease. Attempts to compare the frequency of *P. carinii* pneumonia among different racial and ethnic groups have been complicated by social and cultural factors.[53, 54] There have been conflicting reports about the seasonal occurrence of pneumocystosis.[55–57] Geographic clustering of pneumocystosis has been suggested in areas of Cincinnati, Ohio (Dohn M, Walzer PD, unpublished observations). Based on the high degree of host specificity of *P. carinii*, it is unlikely that animals serve as a reservoir of the infection in humans. Data suggesting the fungal nature of *P. carinii* have raised interest in looking for environmental sources and the infective stage of the organism.

Animal model studies have shown that *P. carinii* is communicable and that the principal mode of transmission is the airborne route.[1, 4, 57] Once *P. carinii* infection is acquired, there is debate about how long the organism resides in the host. One school of thought holds that *P. carinii* becomes part of the host's resident microbial flora and remains quiescent for long periods; as immune defenses become compromised, the organism causes disease by reactivation of latent infection. This view is supported by the presence of the same genetic strain of *P. carinii* in animal colonies for several years; the high host specificity of *P. carinii*, which implies coevolution of the organism and host; and the capability of MSG for antigenic variation.[1] In the pre-HIV era, the prevalence of latent *P. carinii* in immunocompromised patients autopsied varied from 0 to 8%; the frequency of *P. carinii* pneumonia at some institutions was related to the type or intensity of immunosuppressive therapy.[58] Subclinical *P. carinii* infection has been detected in HIV patients by the polymerase chain reaction (PCR) months before they acquired *P. carinii* pneumonia.[59]

The other view is that *P. carinii* infection is transient but that people are frequently exposed to sources of the organism throughout their lives. One line of support for this hypothesis comes from the limited duration of carriage in recent animal model studies.[1] Healthy adult mice inoculated with *P. carinii* clear the infection from the lungs within a short time; the process takes a bit longer in neonates.[60] Immunocompromised animals clear *P. carinii* from the lungs after normal immune function is restored. Other evidence supporting this concept comes from the occurrence of outbreaks or clusters of *P. carinii* pneumonia at orphanages and hospitals and in immunocompromised patients who had prolonged contact with each other; the demonstration that some recurrent episodes of pneumocystosis in HIV patients are due to different organism isolates; and the detection of *P. carinii* DNA in air samples.[1, 6, 7, 61–63] Conflicting results reported in surveys to detect subclinical infection in immunocompetent patients or in hospital workers may be due to differences in sample size.[64–66]

PATHOLOGY AND PATHOGENESIS

Once *P. carinii* is inhaled, it escapes the defenses of the upper respiratory tract and is deposited in alveoli. The tropic form preferentially attaches to the alveolar type I cell, and is thought to initiate infection by this act.[58] Ultrastructural analysis has shown that the adherence is characterized by close apposition of the cell surfaces without fusion of the membranes or changes in the intramembranous particles. Although the type I cell does not replicate, in vitro studies using different cell lives have enhanced our understanding about the interaction of the organism and the host. In one report, *P. carinii* attachment increased as cultured alveolar type II cells differentiated into a type I cell–like phenotype.[67] Other studies have shown that the adherence occurs via extracellular matrix glycoproteins (as mentioned previously) but involves different mechanisms.[68] For example, the *P. carinii* ligand proposed for fibronectin is MSG, whereas the ligand for vitronectin is β-glucan. A gene encoding a receptor for extracellular matrix proteins in *P. carinii* has been identified.[69]

The attachment for *P. carinii* to lung epithelial cells requires an intact cytoskeleton and results in changes in both the organism and the host.[68] One effect is to enhance *P. carinii* proliferation. Studies have analyzed *P. carinii* regulatory components in the cell division cycle, signal transduction pathways and other proteins, and organism ploidy.[70–74] The close relationship of *P. carinii* to fungi has been helpful in this work. *P. carinii* maintains an extracellular existence within alveoli and probably obtains essential nutrients from the alveolar fluid or living cells.[58, 75] Knowledge of how the organism responds to its alveolar microenvironment might lead to an in vitro culture system.

The adherence of *P. carinii* suppresses the growth of lung epithelial cells through cyclin-dependent kinase regulatory pathways.[76] Other reports have shown that the organism alters lung guanosine triphosphate–binding regulatory proteins and induces expression of the intracellular adhesion molecule-1.[77, 78] These properties may influence both the lung damage as well as the host inflammatory and reparative response in *P. carinii* pneumonia.

The host immune defects that lead to the unchecked replication of *P. carinii*, and hence to the development of pneumocystosis, are complex and incompletely understood. Accumulating evidence suggests that one important factor is impaired humoral immunity. *P. carinii* pneumonia has been reported in patients and mice with B-cell defects.[58, 79–81] A positive therapeutic effect has been found with the passive administration of hyperimmune serum or a monoclonal antibody to MSG in experimental models of pneumocystosis.[23, 82–84] Immunization with live *P. carinii* protects T-cell–depleted mice against challenge with the organism; this protection is mediated by antibodies that can be produced from Th1- or Th2-type responses.[85–87] In contrast to animal models, analysis of the role of antibodies in humans has been difficult because of the high prevalence of serum antibodies to *P. carinii* in the population and the lack of information about which antigen epitopes are protective. Serologic studies of HIV patients have demonstrated a variety of responses, ranging from a fall in serum antibody levels before an episode of pneumocystosis to the development of a vigorous antibody response after recovery.[48, 88–90] The role of local (bronchoalveolar lavage fluids; BALF) antibodies in host defenses against *P. carinii* in humans has received only limited attention.[91]

Impaired cellular immunity has long been considered to be an important predisposing factor in the development of pneumocystosis.[58] Naturally occurring outbreaks of *P. carinii* pneumonia have occurred in a variety of immunodeficient animals, particularly colonies of severe combined immunodeficiency disease (SCID) mice and athymic (nude) mice and rats.[92–94] The central role of CD4 cells in host defenses against this organism has been shown by cell depletion and reconstitution experiments.[25, 82, 83, 95, 96] Interaction of T cells with B cells and other cells via the CD40 to CD40L pathway is also important.[97] CD8 cells also participate in host defenses against *P. carinii*, although their precise role is less well defined.[98, 99] Pneumocystosis can be induced in animals by the administration of corticosteroids and is enhanced by protein malnutrition; the corticosteroid-treated rat has served as the standard animal model for more than 3 decades.[58] Immunization of rats with MSG induces a vigorous cellular and humoral response that persists despite corticosteroid immunosuppression and results in partial protection against the development of *P. carinii* pneumonia.[26]

Evidence supporting the role of impaired cellular immunity in the development of *P. carinii* pneumonia in humans has been based on analysis of the immune defects in the underlying disease. In the pre-AIDS era, the patient populations at risk for pneumocystosis included premature, debilitated infants; children with primary immunodeficiency diseases, particularly SCID; and patients receiving immunosuppressive drugs for the treatment of cancer, organ transplantation, and other disorders.[58] Protein malnutrition was an important risk factor for the development of *P. carinii* pneumonia, both by itself and as a complication of the patient's underlying disease or its chemotherapy.

Studies since the late 1980s have shown that *P. carinii* remains a threat, but there has been a shift in the populations at risk from patients with hematologic malignancies to those with solid tumors (e.g., brain tumors) or collagen-vascular diseases and transplant recipients.[100–111] Part of this change has been the more widespread use of cytotoxic and immunosuppressive therapy in diseases in which the risk of *P. carinii* infection was not thought to be of sufficient magnitude to warrant prophylaxis. Corticosteroids, used either alone or in combination with other agents, remain the most common immunosuppressive drugs implicated in the development of pneumocystosis. The relationship of corticosteroids to *P. carinii* infection has been emphasized by the occurrence of pneumocystosis in patients with Cushing's syndrome and children receiving corticosteroids for diseases (e.g., asthma) not known to predispose one to opportunistic infections.[112–114] Cases of *P. carinii* pneumonia occurring with chemotherapy regimens without corticosteroids have also been well documented.[108] Lymphopenia and lung factors (e.g., radiation, fibrosis) have been suggested as additional predisposing factors in non-HIV patients.[107, 109, 110, 115]

In the 1980s, HIV infection replaced all other conditions as the most common disease predisposing to the development of pneumocystosis.[58] The risk of the development of pneumocystosis in HIV patients can be directly correlated with the number of circulating CD4 cells; in adults, cell counts of 200/mm^3 or less have strong predictive value.[116] Because CD4 counts are much higher in young children than in adults, different criteria must be used. The presence of other clinical complications of HIV (e.g., fever, oral candidiasis) increases the risk of pneumocystosis independent of the CD4 count. Cases of pneumocystosis associated with low CD4 counts have been encountered in cancer patients receiving cytotoxic drugs, in adults with idiopathic CD4 T-lymphopenia, and in otherwise healthy individuals with subtle T-cell defects.[108, 117, 118] The issue of evaluating CD4 counts as a risk factor for *P. carinii* pneumonia in immunosuppressed patients has also been raised.[101] Of the few reports that have examined the frequency of T-cell subjects in BALF, the presence of low CD4 cells in HIV patients with pneumocystosis has been associated with an adverse prognosis.[119, 120]

Studies of cellular immune function have shown that HIV patients have a decline in peripheral blood lymphocyte proliferative responses to whole *P. carinii* or MSG with progression of the disease and a fall in the number of CD4 cells.[121, 122] A similar decline occurs in TH1-like cytokine response interferon (IFN)-α but not in the Th2-like cytokine response (interleukin [IL]-4). Patients who have recovered from pneumocystosis exhibit higher proliferative and IL-4 responses to MSG than do HIV patients at a similar stage of the infection who have never had pneumocystosis. Thus, *P. carinii* patients retain enough CD4 memory cells to recognize the organism, but exhibit a shift from a Th1- to a Th2-like response with progression of HIV.[122]

Alveolar macrophages are the first line of defense against *P. carinii* and the principal effector cell in clearing the organism from the lung.[123, 124] However, activated macrophages, in the absence of CD4 cells, are unable to control *P. carinii* infection.[125] Recognition and adherence of *P. carinii* to macrophages occur by multiple pathways involving MSG and β-glucan in the organism, extracellular matrix and surfactant proteins, mannose and Fc receptors on the cells.[35–41, 126, 127] Macrophages ingest, degrade, and kill *P. carinii*, releasing cytokines such as tumor necrosis factor (TNF)-α, eicosanoids, and reactive oxidants.[128–132] Although nitric acid is released by macrophages, it does not appear to play a major role in host defenses against *P. carinii*.[133, 134] The impact of HIV on the interaction of alveolar macrophages has received little attention; one report has shown that HIV modulates the cytokine response to the organism.[135]

The role of other cells in the host defenses against *P. carinii* is poorly understood. One study has shown that neutrophils from *P. carinii* patients stimulated with the organism have an impaired respiratory burst when compared with the cells of healthy controls.[136] A role for natural killer cells has been suggested by reports of the occurrence of pneumocystosis in HIV or other immunodeficient patients who have decreased natural killer cell numbers or function.[137–140]

Exposure of *P. carinii* or its antigens stimulate production of a multitude of cytokines. Two proinflammatory cytokines, TNF-α and IL-1, have been shown to be important in host defenses against the organism, particularly in the early stages of the infections.[141–144] These cytokines are not only potent recruiters of host inflammatory cells, but TNF-α may possibly act directly on *P. carinii*.[145] IL-6, another proinflammatory cytokine, has been produced in response to *P. carinii*, but its contributions to host resistance to the organism are unclear.[142, 146] The role of IFN-γ in host defenses is complex: on the one hand, IFN-γ is not crucial for resolution of pneumocystosis but influences the inflammatory response[147]; on the other hand, administration of IFN-α has a beneficial effect.[148–150] IL-4, a Th2-like cytokine, does not appear to contribute to host resistance.[87] The administration of granulocyte-macrophage–colony-stimulating factor (GM-CSF) but not granulocyte–colony-stimulating factor (G-CSF) has been correlated with a positive therapeutic response.[151, 152]

The pathologic changes that occur during the development of pneumocystosis in animal models and in humans are very similar.[58] As the host defenses become compromised, *P. carinii* organisms begin to proliferate and gradually fill alveolar lumens. In the corticosteroid-treated rat model, the organism number increases from 10^5 per lung or fewer to 10^9 to 10^{10} per lung after 8 to 10 weeks of corticosteroid administration. The principal histologic finding is the formation of a foamy, eosinophilic alveolar exudate (Fig. 260–3); as the pneumocystosis increases in severity, there may also be hyaline membrane formation along with interstitial fibrosis and edema. The host inflammatory response is usually inconspicuous and is characterized by type II cell proliferation (a typical reparative response) and scanty mononuclear cell infiltrate. SCID mice exhibit cytokine production only late in the course of pneumocystosis when elevated

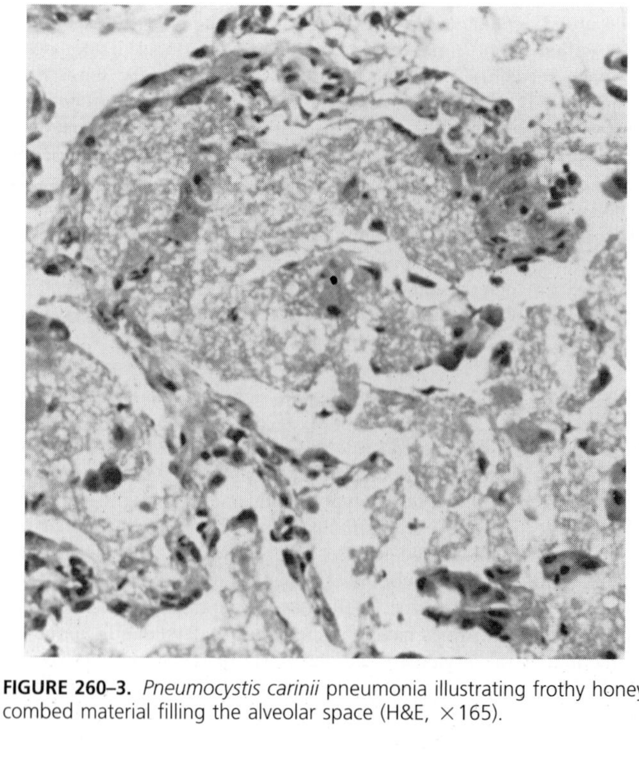

FIGURE 260–3. *Pneumocystis carinii* pneumonia illustrating frothy honeycombed material filling the alveolar space (H&E, ×165).

levels of TNF-α and IL-1 are found in the lungs.[153] Corticosteroid-treated rats have increased levels of proinflammatory cytokines in the respiratory tract but not in peripheral blood.[154] Some patients exhibit atypical findings such as the lack of the alveolar exudate or the development of cavitary lesions, granulomas, or microcalcifications.[155] On electron microscopy, there is increased alveolar-capillary permeability followed by evidence of damage to the type I cell; these changes are secondary to *P. carinii* attachment.[58, 156]

Physiologic changes include hypoxemia with an increased alveolar-arterial (PAO_2-PaO_2) oxygen gradient and respiratory alkalosis; impaired diffusing capacity, suggesting alveolar-capillary block; and alterations in lung compliance, total lung capacity, and vital capacity.[157–161] The resulting picture suggests diffuse lung damage similar to that seen in the adult respiratory distress syndrome.

The pathophysiologic changes described earlier are due not only to the effects of *P. carinii* on the type I cell but also to alterations in the surfactant system and host inflammatory response. There is a fall in surfactant phospholipids (mainly phosphatidylcholine) and a rise in surfactant proteins (notably SP-A and SP-D).[39, 157, 162–166] These abnormalities are due, in part, to suppression of surfactant phospholipid secretion, which is mediated by MSG.[167, 168] The pathogenic significance of these abnormalities is supported by reports that have shown that the administration of surfactant is of benefit in the treatment of *P. carinii* pneumonia.[169–172]

Studies in animal models and humans have shown that the inflammatory response to *P. carinii* can have harmful as well as helpful effects on the host. Immunologic reconstitution of infected SCID mice with splenocytes results in lung inflammation with elevated levels of multiple cytokines and clearance of *P. carinii*.[153, 173] By contrast, reconstitution with purified CD4 cells results in an exaggerated inflammatory response associated with high mortality; the surviving animals then clear the organism from the lung.[82, 83] Similar findings have been found in adoptive transfer of spenocytes and CD4 cells sensitized with MSG in corticosteroid-treated rats with pneumocystosis.[25] The harmful properties of the host inflammatory response in the mice and rats can be prevented by the addition of hyperimmune serum or CD8 cells to the CD4 cells.[82, 83, 99] Although the adverse effects of host inflammation may be mediated by cytokines, studies to address this question have not yet been performed.

The contribution of the host inflammatory response to lung damage in HIV patients with pneumocystosis has been suggested by studies that have correlated increased numbers of neutrophils and levels of IL-8 in BALF with more severe pneumonia and worse prognosis.[174–180] IL-8 functions as a potent chemoattractant, and its interaction with MSG is mediated by MSG.[181, 182] Alterations in eicosanoids, TNF-α, IL-1, other cytokines, and inflammatory mediators have also been noted in these studies and other reports; however, the pathogenic significance of these changes is unclear.[183–189] HIV patients with *P. carinii* pneumonia also frequently experience a worsening of respiratory function soon after receiving antimicrobial drugs; it is thought that the host response is triggered by products released from dying organisms. Corticosteroids, if given promptly, can ameliorate or prevent this effect and improve survival[190]; yet, the effects of corticosteroids on the cytokines and mediators mentioned in these studies has been inconsistent.[177, 185, 186, 189] Thus, the deleterious effects of the host inflammatory response to *P. carinii* in humans (steroid-responsive) and in rodents (steroid-unresponsive) appear to occur by different mechanisms. Some reports have suggested that the beneficial effects of corticosteroids may be due to their influence on surfactant phospholipid production rather than on the inflammatory response.[167, 170]

CLINICAL MANIFESTATIONS

Interstitial plasma cell pneumonia, which gets its name from the distinctive lung infiltrate, has occurred classically in debilitated infants aged 6 weeks to 4 months housed in orphanages or foundling homes under crowded conditions.[58] The disease begins insidiously with symptoms such as poor feeding and progresses gradually to overt respiratory distress and cyanosis. Cases sometimes occurred in explosive outbreaks, giving rise to the term *epidemic* form of *P. carinii* pneumonia. Interstitial plasma cell pneumonia has largely disappeared from industrialized countries but still exists in parts of the world (and in their refugees) where poor socioeconomic conditions abound.

The major presenting symptoms of *P. carinii* pneumonia in the compromised host are shortness of breath, fever, and a nonproductive cough.[58, 191] Occasionally, there is sputum production and, rarely, hemoptysis; chest pain may also occur. Patients receiving immunosuppressive drugs frequently have these clinical manifestations after the corticosteroid dose has been tapered and are typically sick for about 1 to 2 weeks before seeking medical attention. Pneumocystosis in HIV patients usually is a more subtle disease with symptoms lasting from weeks to months; the organism burden is higher but lung damage is less severe.[192–194] Recent studies have also compared the clinical features of pneumocystosis in adult HIV patients by age and underlying risk group.[195–197] Yet, in both acquired immunodeficiency syndrome (AIDS) and non-AIDS patients the clinical picture is quite variable, for example, lung allograft recipients who acquire pneumocystosis frequently are asymptomatic at the time of diagnosis.[198]

On physical examination, tachypnea and tachycardia are found in acutely ill patients. Children may demonstrate cyanosis, flaring of the nasal alae, and intercostal retractions in severe disease. Lung auscultation is usually not helpful, although rales can be heard in about one third of adults with the disease.

The chest radiograph classically exhibits bilateral diffuse infiltrates extending from the perihilar region (Fig. 260–4). Atypical manifestations have ranged from normal films to unilateral infiltrates, nodules, cavities, pneumatoceles, lymphadenopathy, and effusion.[58, 199] Patients receiving prophylactic aerosol pentamidine have an increased incidence of apical infiltrates and pneumothoraces.[200] Techniques such as ultrasonography and computed tomography have been helpful in studying mass lesions and extrapulmonary infection.[199, 201] High resolution computed tomography has shown promise in patients with normal or equivocal chest radiographs.[202] Nuclear medicine procedures have demonstrated increased lung uptake on scans using gallium-67 citrate, indium-111 human IgG, and technetium-99–labeled monoclonal antibody to *P. carinii* MSG.[199, 201, 203] Enhanced clearance of inhaled technetium-99m diethylentriamine pentaacetate, a marker for alveolar-capillary membrane permeability, has also been reported.[204]

Impaired oxygenation is the most frequent laboratory abnormality

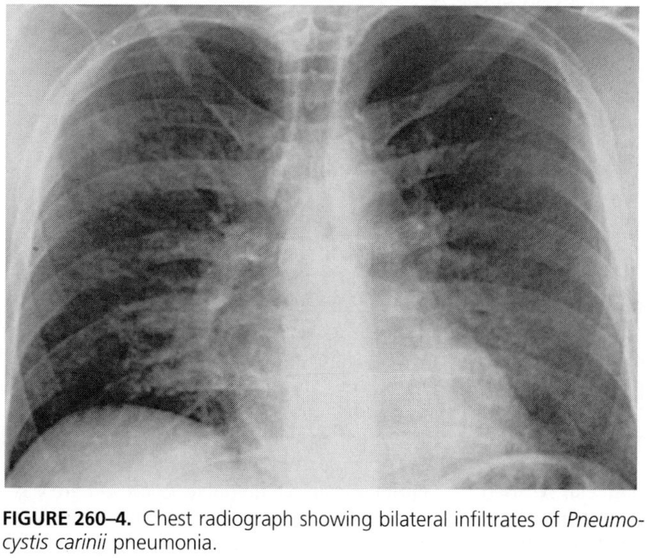

FIGURE 260–4. Chest radiograph showing bilateral infiltrates of *Pneumocystis carinii* pneumonia.

found in pneumocystosis; analysis of the magnitude of hypoxemia or the alveolar-oxygen gradient has been used to evaluate disease severity and monitor progression.[190] Serum lactic dehydrogenase levels, which appear to reflect lung injury, rise frequently in *P. carinii* pneumonia and fall with successful therapy; however, the usefulness of serum lactate dehydrogenase has been limited because there is much overlap among different patient groups and elevations can be produced by other diseases.[205, 206] Other laboratory tests studied in *P. carinii* pneumonia include hemoglobin, leukocyte, and lymphocyte counts and serum albumin, angiotensin-converting enzyme, thyroxine, triiodothyronine, and carcinoembryonic antigen levels.[191, 207] Unfortunately, none of these tests is specific for *P. carinii*.

Extrapulmonary Pneumocystosis

In the pre-HIV era, spread of *P. carinii* beyond the lungs was considered to be a rare event, with only 16 cases being reported; however, extrapulmonary pneumocystosis has received much more attention in HIV patients, with 90 cases or more being reported.[208] The precise frequency of this complication in HIV patients has been difficult to determine (estimates have ranged from negligible to 3%) because diagnosis was made by histologic demonstration of *P. carinii* at extrapulmonary locations where there were clinical manifestations or at autopsy.[208–210] A recent survey of autopsies of 233 HIV patients at two medical centers over a 12-year period revealed evidence of *P. carinii* pneumonia in 24% with extrapulmonary involvement in 13%.[211] Studies in animal models have demonstrated *P. carinii* outside the lungs histologically, and even more commonly, by PCR analysis; these reports raise the question of whether extrapulmonary dissemination of *P. carinii* is more common than generally realized.[212–214]

Extrapulmonary pneumocystosis occurs mainly in patients with advanced HIV infection who are taking no prophylaxis or only aerosolized pentamidine. The main sites of involvement are lymph nodes, spleen, liver, bone marrow, gastrointestinal tract, eyes, thyroid, adrenal glands, and kidneys. The clinical manifestations, which may occur with or without lung involvement, vary from incidental findings at autopsy to a rapidly progressive multisystem disease. Among the focal manifestations of extrapulmonary pneumocystosis are a rapidly enlarging thyroid mass, pancytopenia from bone marrow necrosis, retinal cotton wool spots, polypoid lesions in the external auditory canal, pleural effusion, numerous hypodense lesions in the spleen on computed tomography (Fig. 260–5), and punctate calcifications in the spleen, liver, adrenal, or kidney. Biopsy or fine needle aspiration shows areas of necrosis filled with foamy material. Gomori methenamine silver or fluorescent monoclonal antibody stain reveals numerous organisms.

DIAGNOSIS

Pneumocystosis should be considered in any immunocompromised patient who acquires respiratory symptoms, fever, and an abnormal chest radiograph. Because these clinical manifestations may be produced by a long list of infectious and noninfectious agents, diagnosis of *P. carinii* must be made by histopathologic demonstration of the organism. With extrapulmonary pneumocystosis, the diagnosis may be suspected by the presence of the typical eosinophilic, honeycombed material at the affected site.

A variety of stains have been used to identify *P. carinii* in respiratory tract secretions; in the hands of experienced microscopists, all are highly efficient in detecting the organism.[58, 207, 215, 216] Stains such as methenamine silver or one of its simpler variants (e.g. toluidine blue O, cresylecht violet), which selectively stain the wall of *P. carinii* cysts, have been popular among pathologists because they can be used on imprint smears or tissue sections and are easy to interpret. Reagents such as Wright-Giemsa or one of its more rapid variants (e.g., Diff-Quik) stain all *P. carinii* developmental

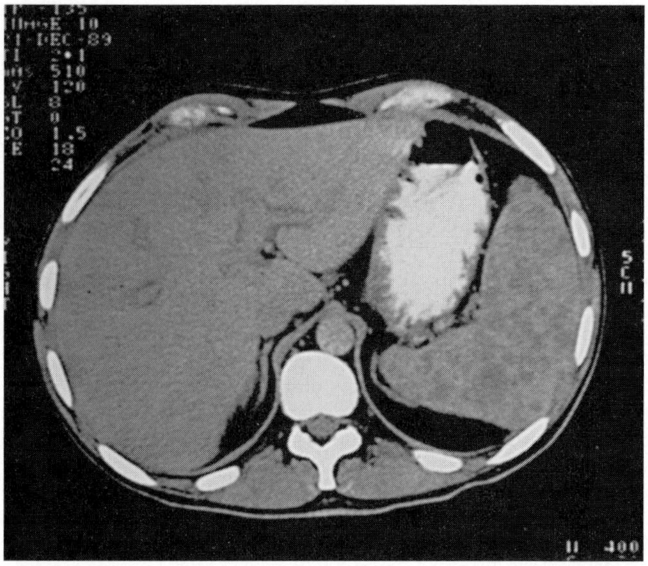

FIGURE 260–5. Abdominal computed tomography scan of a patient infected with human immunodeficiency virus with a history of *Pneumocystis carinii* pneumonia who was receiving aerosol pentamidine prophylaxis and presented with an acute abdomen. Note the enlarged and inhomogeneous spleen with multiple low-density areas. Microscopic examination revealed hemorrhagic abscesses with *P. carinii*. (Reprinted from Fishman JA. Radiological approaches to the diagnosis of *Pneumocystis carinii* pneumonitis. In: Walzer PD, ed. *Pneumocystis carinii* Pneumonia. New York: Marcel Dekker; 1994:415–436, by courtesy of Marcel Dekker, Inc.)

stages as well as host cells. Calcofluor white is a chemifluorescent agent that binds to β-linked polymers of fungi and *P. carinii*. The Papanicolaou stain, which is used by cytopathologists, is a very sensitive method to detect the foamy, eosinophilic material surrounding *P. carinii*, although individual organisms do not stain well. Laboratories may use a rapid staining technique to screen for *P. carinii*, which is then followed by a more time-consuming procedure for definitive identification.

Immunofluorescence has been the most widely used immunologic technique for *P. carinii* diagnosis.[217, 218] Commercial kits employing monoclonal antibodies have been shown to be somewhat more sensitive than histologic stains in detecting *P. carinii*; however, this has to be balanced against the need for specialized facilities and increased cost. Immunohistochemistry has been used to detect *P. carinii* in tissue sections.[219] Soluble *P. carinii* antigens have been found in patients with pneumocystosis by immunoblotting.[47] In some patients, the pattern of immunoreactivity changes after therapy of pneumocystosis or with recurrent episodes of the disease; these results suggest antigenic variation.[3]

The development of DNA amplification by PCR has introduced a new level of sensitivity in *P. carinii* detection. In recent years, PCR has proved to be a highly efficient method of detecting *P. carinii* in a variety of respiratory specimens; when performed under carefully controlled conditions, specificity has been reasonable.[59, 220–226] The presence of a positive PCR product in a specimen that cannot be confirmed by other methods of detection presents a diagnostic dilemma. Such a situation might result from the recent administration of anti–*P. carinii* drugs or may represent subclinical infection. In the latter case, some patients have gone on to acquire *P. carinii* pneumonia.[59, 220] PCR has been modified so that it can be used in clinical microbiology laboratories; if commercial kits become approved, PCR could gain acceptance as one of the standard techniques available for the diagnosis of pneumocystosis. In contrast to respiratory specimens, the results of PCR in detecting *P. carinii* in serum have been inconsistent.[227, 228]

The collection of specimens that accurately reflect the disease process in the lungs is an essential component of the diagnostic evaluation of patients with suspected pneumocystosis. The collection procedures used in adults can usually be performed in children, although infants present special problems.[229] In general, the more invasive the procedure the better the diagnostic yield. These procedures usually have a higher diagnostic yield in AIDS patients than in other immunocompromised hosts because of the higher organism burden. However, chemoprophylaxis (mainly aerosolized pentamidine) and the empirical treatment have made the diagnosis of pneumocystosis in AIDS patients more difficult.[200, 230–232]

Although *P. carinii* is rarely found in expectorated sputum, the organism can be frequently detected in sputum that has been induced by inhalation of a saline mist. Induced sputum has emerged as a simple, noninvasive technique that can be used to screen for the presence of *P. carinii*. The diagnostic yield from induced sputum ranges from less than 50 to 90% at different medical centers, depending on the level of interest and expertise in performing the procedure.[207, 215, 216] Success in the use of induced sputum requires a serious institutional commitment in terms of specially dedicated and trained personnel and care in the processing of specimens.

Fiberoptic bronchoscopy is the most commonly performed invasive procedure and results in the diagnosis of pneumocystosis in greater than 90% of the cases.[58, 215, 216] Bronchoalveolar lavage (BAL) is usually performed instead of washings and brushings because it has greater sensitivity and low morbidity. The diagnostic yield of BAL can be increased if multiple lobes are sampled or the procedure is directed toward the site or sites of greatest involvement.[233] BAL also provides information that cannot be obtained from induced sputum about *P. carinii* organism burden, the presence of other infectious agents, and the host inflammatory response.[234] In one report, the failure to achieve a 50% reduction in *P. carinii* burden in BAL after treatment was associated with an increased risk of recurrence of pneumocystosis.[235] Transbronchial biopsy may provide information not obtainable from a BAL but is associated with a higher rate of complications (e.g., pneumothorax, bleeding).

Open lung biopsy, which requires the use of operating room facilities and general anesthesia, has long served as the standard reference procedure for the diagnosis of *P. carinii* because it provides the greatest amount of tissue that can be obtained under direct visualization.[58] Open lung biopsy can be helpful when bronchoscopy is nondiagnostic and in evaluating another infection or condition complicating pneumocystosis and diagnosing Kaposi's sarcoma of the lung. Open lung biopsy is performed less frequently than it was in the past.

Since the onset of the HIV pandemic, pneumocystosis has placed a strain on health care facilities. As managed care with its singular focus on controlling costs has come to dominate health care, *P. carinii* has served as a model for articles examining the allocation of resources devoted to the care of HIV patients.[236–240] One way to reduce costs has been to replace invasive diagnostic procedures with algorithms and simple diagnostic techniques that are predictive of pneumocystosis.[191, 207, 215, 216] The major problem with this approach is that none of the tests can reliably distinguish *P. carinii* from multiple other causes of pulmonary infiltrates in HIV patients. Another way to lower costs has been to use empirical therapy.[241] This approach may be appropriate in tropical or developing countries: however, at hospitals in the United States, patients treated empirically for pneumocystosis had higher mortality than patients in whom a specific diagnosis was made by bronchoscopy.[242–244] Financial considerations were cited as a major contributing factor in the decision not to perform bronchoscopy. Empirical therapy may also impair later attempts to establish a specific causative diagnosis.[232]

COURSE AND PROGNOSIS

The natural history of untreated pneumocystosis in HIV patients and other immunocompromised hosts is characterized by progressive respiratory insufficiency, leading to death. Prognosis is related to the degree of hypoxemia at the time of presentation; an arterial oxygen pressure of 70 mm Hg while breathing room air has been established to separate the milder from the more serious forms of disease.[190] When this is expressed as the alveolar-arterial oxygen gradient, *P. carinii* pneumonia has been classified as mild (<35 mmHg), moderate (35 to 45 mmHg), and severe (>45 mmHg). Other prognostic indicators in HIV patients include extensive infiltrates on the chest radiograph, interstitial fibrosis and edema on biopsy, increased neutrophils and IL-8 levels in BALF, elevated lactate dehydrogenase levels and reduced albumin levels in serum, and general markers of disease severity.[103, 160, 174–176, 191, 205–207] CD4 cells in BALF and blood have also received recent attention.[119, 120, 245] Concurrent pulmonary infection with other microorganisms can complicate the management of all patients, but the presence of cytomegalovirus in the respiratory tract of HIV patients does not affect survival.[246] Other prognostic host factors in non-HIV patients include severity of the underlying disease and prior lung damage.

Optimal management of pneumocystosis depends on prompt diagnosis and institution of therapy. Early in the HIV epidemic, survival of *P. carinii* patients was better at hospitals with greater familiarity with the disease. Over time, improvement in management has occurred throughout the medical community so that the in-hospital or short-term (1 to 3 month) survival from an episode of pneumocystosis is about 10 to 20%.[247–251] Patients who have taken *P. carinii* prophylaxis medications or who have milder forms of the disease have a case fatality rate of less than 10%.[252–254] In contrast to HIV patients, the mortality of pneumocystosis in several large series of patients is 30 to 50%, a figure that has not changed appreciably in 2 decades.[100–105, 107, 192, 193] The lack of improvement in the survival in non-HIV patients probably reflects a lack of recognition and delays in diagnosis.

The development of severe pneumocystosis requiring mechanical ventilation or admission to the intensive care unit, or both, has presented vexing problems for patients, families and physicians. In the early and mid-1980s, the mortality from respiratory failure was so high (80 to 90%) that aggressive measures were often discouraged.[255] Improvements in the diagnosis and treatment of *P. carinii* pneumonia were accompanied by a reduction in the mortality rate to about 50% in patients admitted to the intensive care unit. During the 1990s, this progress resulted in fewer patients who required intensive care unit admission; however, the mortality rate rose again.[256–259]

Patients who recover from pneumocystosis are at risk for the development of recurrent episodes of the disease as long as the immunosuppressive conditions persist.[58] HIV patients are much more likely to experience recurrence than are non-HIV patients. Recent studies have shown that recurrent episodes occurring within 6 months of the first episode are more likely to be relapse, whereas episodes occurring more than 6 months after are more likely to represent a new episode of infection.[6, 7] The prognosis of recurrent episodes of pneumocystosis is similar to that of initial episodes.[260]

Another complication plaguing patients who recover from *P. carinii* pneumonia is pneumothorax.[160, 191, 261–263] Risk factors include a previous episode of pneumocystosis, the use of aerosol pentamidine, and cigarette smoking. Pneumatoceles, pneumomediastinum, and subcutaneous emphysema also occur. Management is difficult and should be individualized; measures have included chest tube, surgical, or chemical pleurodesis and thoracostomy with stapling. The previous use of corticosteroids may increase the risk of morbidity.[261]

TREATMENT

Trimethoprim-sulfamethoxazole (TMP-SMX) is the drug of choice for all forms of pneumocystosis.[264–266] This agent, which acts by inhibiting folic acid synthesis, has been used for 2 decades against *P. carinii* with a high degree of success.[267–270] Among the attractive features of TMP-SMX are its availability in oral and parenteral forms, well-known pharmacokinetics, antibacterial properties, and cost. TMP-SMX is administered orally or intravenously in a dosage of 15 to 20 mg/kg/day TMP and 75 to 100 mg/kg/day SMX in three or four divided doses. The parenteral preparation should be used in patients who are seriously ill or have gastrointestinal disturbances. As with all anti–*P. carinii* drugs, treatment should be continued for 21 days in HIV patients and 14 days in non-HIV patients. The longer duration in HIV patients is thought to be necessary because these individuals have a higher organism burden and respond more slowly.

TMP-SMX is well tolerated by non-HIV patients, with gastrointestinal symptoms and skin rashes being the most common complaints. By contrast, HIV patients experience a high frequency (up to 80% or more) of adverse reactions that usually begin during the second week of TMP-SMX therapy and may result in discontinuation of the drug in up to 50% of these persons.[265, 266, 271] The most frequent side effects are skin rash, fever, and cytopenias, but nausea and vomiting, hepatitis, pancreatitis, nephritis, hyperkalemia, metabolic acidosis, central nervous system manifestations, and an anaphylactoid reaction also occur.[272–274] Most of these reactions appear to be due to the sulfonamide component, but the mechanisms are not well understood. Among the possible contributing factors are elevated serum drug levels, the formation of hydroxylamine metabolites, glutathione deficiency, hypersensitivity, and CD4 counts.[271, 275, 276] Hyperkalemia has been attributed to trimethoprim, which acts like a potassium-sparing diuretic.[272, 277]

Some investigators have recommended adjusting the dose of TMP-SMX to achieve serum concentrations of 5 to 8 μg/ml TMP and 100 to 150 μg/ml SMX in order to achieve maximal efficacy and minimal toxicity[269, 271]; however, other workers have not found this approach to be beneficial.[278] *N*-acetylcysteine and folinic acid have not helped prevent side effects from TMP-SMX, and folinic acid may actually be harmful.[279–281] Skin reactions to TMP-SMX range from mild to life-threatening (e.g., toxic epidermal necrolysis, Stevens-Johnson syndrome, anaphylaxis). In some cases, the skin rash and manifestations such as fever may resolve spontaneously or respond to conservative measures, whereas in other instances they may require discontinuation of the drug. Corticosteroids may also be helpful.[282] Desensitization regimens have been successful in patients who have experienced non–life-threatening reactions to TMP-SMX but should be undertaken with caution.[265]

Several alternative regimens have been developed for the treatment of mild to moderate pneumocystosis.[264–266] Although these studies have mainly been performed in HIV patients, the results should be applicable to non-HIV patients with *P. carinii* pneumonia. TMP administered at a dose of 15 to 20 mg/kg/day orally combined with dapsone, 100 mg/day orally, has been shown to be as effective as TMP-SMX and less toxic.[283, 284] The major adverse reactions to dapsone are methemoglobinemia, rash, fever, nausea, and vomiting; hemolysis can occur in patients who have glucose-6-phosphate dehydrogenase deficiency. Dapsone can be administered to patients intolerant of sulfonamides but must be approached with caution because there are few reliable guidelines to predict who might experience a serious reaction.[265] The serum levels of dapsone and TMP are higher when these drugs are used together than when they are used alone and suggest bidirectional interference with clearance.[285] The anti–*P. carinii* activity of dapsone is reduced when the drug is administered with didanosine; this is probably due to buffer in the didanosine, which raises pH and interferes with dapsone absorption.[286]

Controlled studies have shown that the combination of clindamycin and primaquine exhibits efficacy and toxicity comparable to that of TMP-SMX and TMP and dapsone in the therapy of *P. carinii* pneumonia.[284, 287] The mechanism of action of clindamycin and primaquine against *P. carinii* is not known. The usual doses are clindamycin 600 mg every 6 hours intravenously or 300 to 450 mg every 6 hours orally and primaquine 15 to 30 mg base per day orally. Treatment may also be initiated with intravenous clindamycin and then switched to oral administration. Adverse effects include skin rash, fever, neutropenia, gastrointestinal complaints, and methemoglobinemia.[264–266] Primaquine also causes hemolysis in patients with glucose-6-phosphate dehydrogenase deficiency.

Atovaquone is a hydroxynaphthoquinone that was originally developed as an antimalarial agent.[265, 266] Atovaquone acts on the mitochondrial electron transport chain of Plasmodia, but its mechanism of action against *P. carinii* is unknown. One study compared atovaquone with TMP-SMX and another with pentamidine isethionate in the treatment of mild to moderate pneumocystosis in HIV patients.[288, 289] Atovaquone was less effective than TMP-SMX and about as effective as pentamidine; however, atovaquone was better tolerated in both studies. Adverse reactions to atovaquone include skin rash, fever, gastrointestinal symptoms, and abnormal liver function test results.[288, 289] The major limitation to atovaquone is its poor bioavailability. The drug must be given with food, but absorption is still erratic. An oral suspension, administered at a dose of 750 mg/5 ml twice daily with food, has been developed that results in better absorption. Further studies are needed to see if this preparation will be more effective against *P. carinii* than the original tablet preparation.

Two parenteral drugs, pentamidine isethionate and trimetrexate, are the major alternatives to TMP-SMX for the treatment of moderate to severe pneumocystosis in hospitalized patients. Clindamycin at doses of 600 to 900 mg every 6 to 8 hours intravenously has been used with primaquine in these patients, but experience is limited.[290, 291] Pentamidine, a diamidine, is an old drug that was first used to treat African trypanosomiasis; pentamidine appears to exert its antimicrobial activity by binding to DNA, but its precise mode of action against *P. carinii* is unknown. A number of reports have shown that pentamidine is about as effective as TMP-SMX in the therapy of *P. carinii* pneumonia in HIV and non-HIV patients.[267–270] Pentamidine is usually administered as a single daily dose of 4 mg/kg, although a dose of 3 mg/kg has been used in some studies. The intravenous route is preferred over the intramuscular route of administration; pentamidine is diluted in 50 to 250 ml of a 5% dextrose solution and infused over a period of at least 1 hour. Pentamidine administered by aerosol has also been used in the treatment of *P. carinii* pneumonia; however, since this form of administration is less effective than oral drugs, it is not recommeded.[265, 292]

Pharmacokinetic studies have shown that pentamidine follows a three-compartment model with rapid passage to tissues, secondary distribution, and a long (about 12 days) elimination half-life; only a small amount of the drug is cleared by the kidney.[271, 293, 294, 322] Pentamidine is a toxic drug: adverse reactions occur in 80% or more of HIV and non-HIV patients and are severe enough to necessitate discontinuation of the drug in about half the cases.[265–271] Side effects include hypotension, cardiac arrhythmias (e.g., torsades de pointes), azotemia, pancreatitis, dysglycemias, hyperkalemia, hypomagnesemia, hypocalcemia, neutropenia, hepatic disturbances, bronchospasm, and problems at intramuscular injection sites. Hypoglycemia, which is due to damage of pancreatic β cells with insulin release, occurs early in therapy, and may be followed later by diabetes mellitus. The frequency of hypoglycemia and azotemia has been correlated with high serum pentamidine levels, total drug dose, and duration of treatment.[295, 296] The mechanism of hyperkalemia caused by pentamidine is similar to that caused by TMP.[297]

Trimetrexate, a lipid-soluble derivative of methotrexate, is a highly potent inhibitor of *P. carinii* dihydrofolate reductase (DHFR). A controlled study showed that trimetrexate was less effective but better tolerated than TMP-SMX in the therapy of pneumocystosis in hospitalized patients.[298] Other studies have shown that trimetrexate may be valuable as "salvage" therapy in patients who cannot tolerate TMP-SMX or in whom it has failed.[265, 266] Trimetrexate is administered intravenously in a single daily dose of 45 mg/m^2. The principal side effect of trimetrexate is bone marrow suppression, which can be ameliorated or prevented by the administration of folinic acid at a dose of 20 mg/m^2 intravenously or orally every 6 hours. There is no evidence that folinic acid used at the recommended dose interferes with the therapeutic effect of trimetrexate. Other side effects of trimetrexate include skin rash, peripheral neuropathy, and liver function abnormalities.

The response to anti–*P. carinii* drugs generally mirrors other clinical features of the infection. Non-HIV patients, who become ill rather quickly, usually show a clinical response by 4 days of treatment; if there is no response by 5 to 6 days, it is wise to consider switching to another drug. HIV patients typically respond more slowly and take longer to clear *P. carinii* from their lungs; it is prudent to wait for at least 7 days before declaring a treatment failure. Adding other anti–*P. carinii* drugs to the regimen is no more effective than substituting one agent for another and may increase the risk of adverse reactions.

HIV patients frequently experience worsening of blood oxygenation during the first few days of therapy; such a clinical deterioration can be particularly dangerous if the initial hypoxemia is marked. Several studies have shown that the administration of corticosteroids during the first 72 hours of treatment can lessen the decline in oxygenation and improve survival.[265, 266] These studies led to a recommendation by an expert panel that steroids be added to treatment in all patients with moderate to severe pneumocystosis (i.e., an arterial oxygen pressure of <70 mm Hg or an alveolar-arterial oxygen gradient of >35 mm Hg) in the following dose regimen for adults: prednisone 40 mg orally twice daily, days 1 to 5; 40 mg once daily, days 6 to 10; and 20 mg once daily, days 11 to 20.[190] The use of corticosteroids became widely adopted by the medical community. A subsequent report showed that steroids did not improve the outcome of pneumocystosis other than reducing the frequency of hypersensitivity reactions to TMP-SMX.[299] However, a meta-analysis of published controlled studies continued to support the use of these agents.[300]

Corticosteroids used in the manner described have generally been well tolerated.[190] The principal side effects are oral candidiasis, mucocutaneous herpes simplex, and metabolic changes such as hyperglycemia. Concerns have been raised about increased frequency of cytomegalovirus, other fungi, and mycobacterial infections, but so far these concerns have not materialized.[300–304] Nevertheless, the lack of efficacy of steroids in some studies,[299, 300] along with the risk of other opportunistic infections and other possible complications (e.g., increased morbidity of pneumothorax) associated with the use of corticosteroids, emphasize the need for careful patient selection and follow-up.

Recommendations about the use of adjunctive corticosteroids in other *P. carinii* patient populations are difficult to formulate because of the limited information available. One report showed that steroids prevented early deterioration and impaired exercise tolerance in patients with mild pneumocystosis, as defined by pulse oximetry.[305] However, the low mortality rate in mild *P. carinii* pneumonia and the factors discussed earlier argue against the routine use of steroids in these patients. Corticosteroids have improved the survival in uncontrolled studies of pediatric HIV patients with pneumocystosis.[306–308] A retrospective study of adult non-HIV *P. carinii* patients showed that treatment with high-dose steroids resulted in faster recovery but no improved survival when compared with low-dose steroids.[309] The problem with non-HIV patients is that most of these individuals have been on corticosteroids shortly before or at the time they developed pneumocystosis. Rapid withdrawal of steroids may have serious adverse consequences, and thus it seems prudent either to maintain the current dose or return to the previous steroid dose when instituting anti–*P. carinii* therapy. The steroid dose can then be slowly tapered. The place of corticosteroids in non-HIV patients who have received immunosuppressive drugs other than steroids is unknown.

Future clinical advances in the treatment of pneumocystosis might come from several current lines of investigation. Although the development of a continuous culture system remains elusive, it might be possible to use molecular techniques to identify markers of virulence or antimicrobial resistance. The recent finding of sequence variation in dihydropteroate synthetase, the target enzyme of sulfonamides, in human *P. carinii* illustrates the potential importance of such a discovery.[310] New drugs with improved efficacy, less toxicity, and different mechanism of action are needed. Animal models, which are the principal test system, have identified several new types of drugs (e.g., papulocandins, 8-aminoquinolines, diamidines); however, clinical trials have been held up because of market considerations. Manipulation of the host immune or inflammatory response might improve defenses against *P. carinii* while lessening their deleterious effects on the host. These studies might develop drugs with greater specificity than corticosteroids. Finally, there is increasing evidence that the physiologic changes that accompany the development of *P. carinii* pneumonia and result in lung injury cannot be reversed by antimicrobial therapy alone; however, they can be improved by the administration of surfactant.[169–172] Clinical trials of surfactant or other agents that improve lung physiology are needed.

PREVENTION

Controlled studies demonstrating the safety and efficacy of daily or intermittent TMP-SMX in preventing pneumocystosis in pediatric cancer patients stimulated considerable interest in developing prophylactic regimens in HIV patients and other immunocompromised hosts.[265] Prophylaxis can be considered either primary (directed at the first bout of *P. carinii* pneumonia) or secondary (directed at recurrent episodes). The decision whether to institute chemoprophylaxis depends on factors such as the incidence of pneumocystosis in the target population as well as drug effectiveness, safety, ease of administration, and cost. Because none of the available anti–*P. carinii* drugs used in humans has proved to be lethal for *P. carinii*, they should be continued for as long as the immunosuppressive conditions exist.

An expert panel convened by the U.S. Public Health Service (USPHS) and Infectious Disease Society of America (IDSA) has existing data and has formulated general guidelines for the prevention of pneumocystosis in adult and pediatric HIV patients.[311] Chemoprophylaxis is indicated for all adolescents and adults (including those who are pregnant) with CD4 counts lower than 200/mm^3, with oropharyngeal candidiasis, or unexplained fever (>100°F or 37.7°C) for 2 weeks or more, or who have recovered from a previous episode of pneumocystosis. Chemoprophylaxis is continued for life. Chemoprophylaxis is also indicated for children born to HIV-infected mothers beginning at 4 to 6 weeks of age. Medication should be continued until the child's HIV status is determined. If the child is infected with HIV, prophylaxis should be continued through the first year of life. The subsequent need for chemoprophylaxis is determined by age-specific CD4 counts.

Three drug regimens are currently recommended for *P. carinii* prophylaxis,[311] and several reviews nicely summarize the clinical trials on which these recommendations are based.[312–314] The doses used here are for adults and adolescents; the USPHS/IDSA Guidelines should be consulted for doses in children. TMP-SMX, the drug of choice, is administered at a dose of one double-strength tablet (160 mg TMP and 800 mg SMX) per day. One single-strength tablet (80 mg TMP and 400 mg SMX) per day is very effective and one double-strength tablet three times per week is also acceptable. TMP-SMX not only protects against *P. carinii*, but also against *Toxoplasma gondii* and bacterial infections. Adverse reactions to TMP-SMX occur in up to 50% or more of the patients and require discontinuation of the drug in up to 30 to 40% of cases. The frequency of side effects is somewhat lower with the use of single-strength tablets or three times per week administration. Guidelines for desensitization or rechallenge with TMP-SMX in prophylaxis are similar to those for use of TMP-SMX in treatment.

Recommended drug regimens for HIV patients who cannot tolerate TMP-SMX include dapsone and aerosolized pentamidine. Dapsone may be administered alone at a dose of 100 mg/day or at a dose of 50 mg/day combined with pyrimethamine (a DHFR inhibitor)

50 mg/week and lencovorin 25 mg/week. Additional dose schedules have also been used. Overall, the dapsone regimens have shown similar efficacy and toxicity to the TMP-SMX regimens. Dapsone and pyrimethamine protect against *T. gondii* but not bacterial infections. Pentamidine is administered at a dose of 300 mg in a Respirgard nebulizer once per month. Aerosolized pentamidine is less effective, better tolerated, and much more expensive than TMP-SMX or dapsone. The major side effects are cough and bronchospasm, which can be controlled with a β-agonist. Aerosolized pentamidine requires a negative-pressure room with adequate ventilation and should not be used in patients with tuberculosis.

A number of other drug regimens have been considered as possible *P. carinii* prophylactic agents, but there is insufficient supportive information to recommend their use.[311, 314] Examples include pyrimethamine combined with sulfonamides (e.g., Fansidar) or clindamycin, pentamidine administered as an aerosol using other nebulizers or administered intravenously, clindamycin plus primaquine, atovaquone used alone or in combination with macrolides, or sulfonamides. Prophylactic regimens for *Mycobacterium avium* complex that contain azithromycin or clarithromycin lower the frequency of pneumocystosis. Mycophenylate mofetil, an immunosuppressive agent, has demonstrated anti–*P. carinii* activity in experimental models.

The widespread use of *P. carinii* chemoprophylaxis has had a major impact on the care of HIV patients.[312–316] This practice has not only reduced the incidence of pneumocystosis but also has improved survival and quality of life while decreasing resource utilization and cost. Despite this success, studies performed before the introduction of the protease inhibitors showed that breakthrough cases of *P. carinii* pneumonia occurred in about 20% of patients.[317] The most important predictor of failure was very low ($<$50 to 100/mm^3) CD4 counts.[317, 318] These breakthrough infections may also have atypical manifestations, particularly in patients taking aerosolized pentamidine.[319] Examples include upper lobe disease, pneumothorax, extrapulmonary pneumocystosis, and fever of unknown origin.

In contrast to HIV patients, there are no national guidelines for *P. carinii* prophylaxis in other immunocompromised hosts. The need for such guidelines is illustrated by the fact that cases of pneumocystosis continue to occur in non-HIV patients despite the availability of safe and effective drugs.[100, 101] Based on the available literature, chemoprophylaxis should be considered in patients with the following conditions: (1) primary immune deficiency diseases, (2) severe protein malnutrition, (3) organ transplantation, (4) persistent CD4 counts of less than 200/mm^3, (5) cytotoxic or immunosuppressive therapy for the treatment of cancer (all types), collagen vascular diseases, and other disorders. If a corticosteroid is the sole drug used, a reasonable guide for the need for *P. carinii* prophylaxis is the equivalent of 20 mg of prednisone for more than 1 month.[100] Some authors have excluded diseases (e.g. asthma) that are usually not associated with *P. carinii* from this recommendation[100]; however, in light of case reports of pneumocystosis in children with asthma[113, 114] this exclusion may become blurred.

TMP-SMX is the chemoprophylactic agent of choice and should be used in the same doses as those used in HIV patients. Although there is limited clinical experience with dapsone with or without pyrimethamine, and aerosolized pentamidine, there is no reason to doubt the effectiveness of these agents in non-HIV patients.

Another method of preventing pneumocystosis is to boost the host immune response. This could be done either by improving general immune function or by focusing on organism-specific immunity. In the latter case, MSG is an attractive potential candidate because it confers protection in experimental animals and elicits an immune response by patients with advanced HIV infection.[26, 122] Other *P. carinii* antigens might also be explored.[44, 45] Immunization of immunocompromised patients at an early stage of their disease (e.g., HIV patients with $>$500 CD4 cells, newly diagnosed cancer patients) might prevent, delay, or lessen the severity of pneumocystosis. Boosting the host immune response might also lessen the need for, or lower the dose of, antimicrobial drugs. Alternate approaches involve administration of specific antibodies or cytokines.

A third method of preventing pneumocystosis is by preventing exposure. The communicability of *P. carinii* has been shown in experimental animals.[57] However, infection control guidelines for health care facilities have not recommended isolating *P. carinii* patients because person-to-person transmission has never been convincingly demonstrated and the disease was thought to occur by reactivation of latent infection. This attitude seems to be changing because of the continued occurrence of outbreaks or clusters of pneumocystosis, the development of sensitive techniques to detect *P. carinii* DNA in asymptomatic individuals and the air, and the ability to distinguish among *P. carinii* isolates, particularly in patients with recurrent episodes of pneumocystosis.[1, 320] The practice of isolating *P. carinii* patients from direct contact with other immunocompromised hosts, which has long been advocated by myself and others, is now recommended by the Centers for Disease Control Hospital Infection Control Practice Advisory Committee[321] but not yet by the USPHS/IDSA Opportunistic Infections Working Group.[311] The conflicting results of studies of the presence of *P. carinii* in health care workers and other healthy persons illustrate the difficulties in investigating the transmission of this infection.[64–66] Little is also known about the behavior of the organism in the environment, although a recent study suggests *P. carinii* is susceptible to inactivation by common antiseptic agents.[322] Despite these limitations, recent advances in technology offer promise of providing valuable insight into the epidemiologic features of this interesting and enigmatic organism.

REFERENCES

1. Stringer JR, Walzer PD. Molecular biology and epidemiology of *Pneumocystis carinii* infection in AIDS. AIDS. 1996;10:561–571.
2. Palella FJ Jr, Delaney KM, Moorman AC, et al. Declining morbidity and mortality among patients with advanced human immunodeficiency virus infection. N Engl J Med. 1998;338:853–860.
3. Smulian AG, Keely SP, Sunkin SM, et al. Genetic and antigenic variation in *Pneumocystis carinii* organisms: Tools for examining the epidemiology and pathogenesis of infection. J Lab Clin Med. 1997;130:461–468.
4. Cushion M. *Pneumocystis carinii.* In: Collier L, Balows A, Sussman M, eds. Topley and Wilson's Microbiology and Microbial Infections, v. 4. New York: Oxford University Press; 1998:645–683.
5. Mazars E, Guyot K, Durand I, et al. Isoenzyme diversity in *Pneumocystis carinii* from rats, mice, and rabbits. J Infect Dis. 1997;175:655–660.
6. Keely SP, Stringer JR, Baughman RP, et al. Genetic variation among *Pneumocystis carinii* hominis isolates in recurrent pneumocystosis. J Infect Dis. 1995;172:595–598.
7. Keely SP, Stringer JR. Sequences of *Pneumocystis carinii* f. sp. hominis strains associated with recurrent pneumonia vary at multiple loci. J Clin Microbiol. 1997;35:2745–2747.
8. Tsolaki AG, Miller RF, Underwood AP, et al. Genetic diversity at the internal transcribed spacer regions of the rRNA operon among isolates of *Pneumocystis carinii* from AIDS patients with recurrent pneumonia. J Infect Dis. 1996;174:141–156.
9. Jiang B, Lu JJ, Li B, et al. Development of type-specific PCR for typing *Pneumocystis carinii* f. sp. hominis based on nucleotide sequence variations of internal transcribed spacer region of rRNA genes. J Clin Microbiol. 1996;34:3245–3248.
10. Latouche S, Poirot JL, Bernard C, et al. Study of internal transcribed spacer and mitochondrial large-subunit genes of *Pneumocystis carinii* hominis isolated by repeated bronchoalveolar lavage from human immunodeficiency virus–infected patients during one or several episodes of pneumonia. J Clin Microbiol. 1997;35:1687–1690.
11. Tsolaki AG, Beckers P, Wakefield AE. Pre-AIDS era isolates of *Pneumocystis carinii* f. sp. hominis: High genotype similarity with contemporary isolates. J Clin Microbiol. 1998;36:90–93.
12. Anonymous. Revised nomenclature for *Pneumocystis carinii*. The *Pneumocystis* Workshop. J Euk Microbiol. 1994;41:121S–122S.
13. Itatani CA. Ultrastructural morphology of intermediate forms and forms suggestive of conjugation in the life cycle of *Pneumocystis carinii*. J Parasitol. 1996;82:163–171.
14. Sloand E, Laughon B, Armstrong M, et al. The challenge of *Pneumocystis carinii* culture. J Euk Microbiol. 1993;40:188–195.
15. Armstrong MYK, Cushion MT. In vitro cultivation. In: Walzer PD, ed. *Pneumocystis carinii* Pneumonia. New York: Marcel Dekker; 1994:3–24.
16. Ruffolo JJ. *Pneumocystis carinii* cell structure. In: Walzer PD, ed. *Pneumocystis carinii* Pneumonia. New York: Marcel Dekker; 1994:25–42.

17. Kaneshiro ES. *Pneumocystis carinii* pneumonia: The status of *Pneumocystis* biochemistry. Int J Parasitol. 1998;28:65–84.
18. De Stefano JA, Myers JD, Du Pont D, et al. Cell wall antigens of *Pneumocystis carinii* trophozoites and cysts: Purification and carbohydrate analysis of these glycoproteins. J Euk Microbiol. 1998;45:334–343.
19. Kaneshiro ES. The lipids of *Pneumocystis carinii*. Clin Microbiol Rev. 1998;11:27–41.
20. Gigliotti F. Host species specific antigenic variation of mannosylated surface glycoprotein of *Pneumocystis carinii*. J Infect Dis. 1992;165:329–336.
21. Kovacs JA, Swann JC, Shelhammer J, et al. Monoclonal antibodies to *Pneumocystis carinii*: Identification of specific antigens and characterization of antigenic differences between rat and human isolates. J Infect Dis. 1989;159:60–70.
22. Linke MJ, Sunkin SM, Andrews RP, et al. Expression, structure, and location of Epitopes of the major surface glycoprotein of *Pneumocystis carinii* f. sp *carinii*. Clin Diagn Lab Immunol. 1998;5:50–57.
23. Gigliotti F, Hughes WT. Passive immunoprophylaxis with specific monoclonal antibody confers partial protection against *Pneumocystis carinii* pneumonitis in animal models. J Clin Invest. 1988;81:1666–1668.
24. Theus SA, Smulian AG, Sullivan D, et al. Cytokine responses to the native and recombinant forms of the major surface glycoprotein of *Pneumocystis carinii*. Clin Exp Immunol. 1997;109:255–260.
25. Theus SA, Andrews RP, Steele P, Walzer PD. Adoptive transfer of lymphocytes sensitized to the major surface glycoprotein confers protection in the rat. J Clin Invest. 1995;95:2587–2593.
26. Theus SA, Smulian AG, Steele P, et al. Immunization with the major surface glycoprotein of *Pneumocystis carinii* elicits a protective response in the rat. Vaccine. 1998;16:1149–1157.
27. Gigliotti F, Wiley JA, Harmsen AG. Immunization with *Pneumocystis carinii* gpA is immunogenic but not protective in a mouse model of *P. carinii* pneumonia. Infect Immun. 1998;66:3179–3182.
28. Kovacs JA, Powell F, Edman JC, et al. Multiple genes encode the major surface glycoprotein of *Pneumocystis carinii*. J Biol Chem. 1993;268:6034–6040.
29. Linke MJ, Smulian AG, Stringer JR, et al. Characterization of multiple unique cDNAs encoding the major surface glycoprotein of rat-derived *Pneumocystis carinii*. Parasitol Res. 1994;80:478–486.
30. Garbe TR, Stringer JR. Molecular characterization of clustered variants of genes encoding major surface antigens of human *Pneumocystis carinii*. Infect Immun. 1994;62:3092–3101.
31. Haidaris CG, Medzihradsky OF, Gigliotti F, et al. Molecular characterization of mouse *Pneumocystis carinii* surface glycoprotein A. DNA Res. 1998;5:77–85.
32. Wada M, Sunkin SM, Stringer JR, et al. Antigenic variation by positional control of major surface glycoprotein gene expression in *Pneumocystis carinii*. J Infect Dis. 1995;171:1563–1568.
33. Sunkin SM, Stringer JR. Residence at the expression site is necessary and sufficient for the transcription of surface antigen genes of *Pneumocystis carinii*. Mol Microbiol. 1997;25:147–160.
34. Sunkin SM, Linke MJ, McCormack FX, et al. Identification of a putative precursor to the major surface glycoprotein of *Pneumocystis carinii*. Infect Immun. 1998:66:741–746.
35. Pottratz ST, Paulsrud J, Smith JS, et al. *Pneumocystis carinii* attachment to cultured lung cells by pneumocystis gp 120, a fibronectin binding protein. J Clin Invest. 1991;88:403–407.
36. Limper AH. Vitronectin binds to *Pneumocystis carinii* and mediates organism attachment to cultured lung epithelial cells. Infect Immun. 1993;61:4302–4309.
37. Fishman JA, Samia JA, Fuglestad J, et al. The effects of extracellular matrix (ECM) proteins on the attachment of *Pneumocystis carinii* to lung cell lines in vitro. J Protozool. 1991;38:34S–37S.
38. McCormack FX, Festa AL, Andrews RP, et al. The carbohydrate binding domain of surfactant protein A mediates binding to the major surface glycoprotein of *Pneumocystis carinii*. Biochemistry 1997;36:8092–8099.
39. O'Riordan DM, Standing JE, Kwon KY, et al. Surfactant protein D interacts with *Pneumocystis carinii* and mediates organism adherence to alveolar macrophages. J Clin Invest. 1995;95:2699–2710.
40. Ezekowitz RAB, Williams DJ, Koziel H, et al. Uptake of *Pneumocystis carinii* mediated by the macrophage mannose receptor. Nature. 1991;351:155–158.
41. O'Riordan DM, Standing JE, Limper AH. *Pneumocystis carinii* glycoprotein A binds macrophage mannose receptors. Infect Immun. 1995:63:779–784.
42. Walzer PD, Linke MJ. A comparison of the antigenic characteristics of rat and human *Pneumocystis carinii* by immunoblotting. J Immunol. 1987;138:2257–2265.
43. Broomall KR, Morris RE, Walzer PD, et al. Zymolyase treatment exposes p55 antigen of *Pneumocystis carinii*. J Euk Microbiol. 1998;45:284–289.
44. Smulian AG, Stringer JR, Linke MJ, et al. Isolation and characterization of a recombinant antigen of *Pneumocystis carinii*. Infect Immun. 1992;60:907–915.
45. Theus SA, Sullivan DW, Walzer PD, et al. Cellular immune response to a 55 kilodalton recombinant *Pneumocystis carinii* antigen. Infect Immun. 1994;62:3479–3484.
46. Schofield L. On the function of repetitive domains in protein antigens of Plasmodium and other eukaryotic parasites. Parasitol Today. 1991;7:99–105.
47. Smulian AG, Linke MJ, Baughman RP, et al. Analysis of *Pneumocystis carinii* antigens in bronchoalveolar lavage fluid in patients with pneumocystosis. AIDS. 8:1555–1562, 1994.
48. Peglow SL, Smulian AG, Linke MJ, et al. Serologic responses to *Pneumocystis carinii* antigens in health and disease. J Infect Dis. 1990;161:296–306.
49. Smulian AG, Sullivan DW, Linke MJ, et al. Geographic variation in the humoral response to *Pneumocystis carinii*. J Infect Dis. 1993;167:1243–1247.
50. Russian DA, Kovacs JA. *Pneumocystis carinii* in Africa: An emerging pathogen? Lancet. 1995;346:1242–1243.
51. Malin AS, Lovemore KZ, Klein S, et al. *Pneumocystis carinii* pneumonia in Zimbabwe. Lancet. 1995;346:1258–1261.
52. Daley CL, Mugusi F, Chen LL, et al. Pulmonary complications of HIV infection in Dar es Salaam, Tanzania. Role of bronchoscopy and bronchoalveolar lavage. Am J Respir Crit Care Med. 1996;154:105–110.
53. Hu DJ, Fleming PL, Castro KG, et al. How important is race/ethnicity as an indicator of risk for specific AIDS-defining conditions? J Acquired Immun Def Syn Hum Retrovirol 1995;10:374–380.
54. Eckholdt H, Chin J. *Pneumocystis carinii* pneumonia in Asians and Pacific Islanders. Clin Infect Dis. 1997;24:1265–1267.
55. Hoover DR. Factors associated with the development of *Pneumocystis carinii* pneumonia. Clin Infect Dis. 1996;22:738.
56. Lundgren JD, Phillips AN. Letter to editor (reply). Clin Infect Dis. 1996;22:739.
57. Cushion MT. Transmission and epidemiology. In: Walzer PD, ed. *Pneumocystis carinii* Pneumonia. New York: Marcel Dekker; 1994:122–139.
58. Walzer PD, Kim CK, Cushion MT. *Pneumocystis carinii*. In: Walzer PD, Genta RM, eds. Parasitic Infections in the Compromised Host. New York: Marcel Dekker; 1989;83–178.
59. Olsson M, Elvin K, Lidman C, et al. A rapid and simple nested PCR assay for the detection of *Pneumocystis carinii* in sputum samples. Scand J Infect Dis. 1996;28:597–600.
60. Garvy BA, Harmsen AG. Susceptibility to *Pneumocystis carinii* infection: Host responses of neonatal mice from immune or naive mothers and of immune or naive adults. Infect Immun. 1996;10:3987–3992.
61. Wakefield AE. DNA sequences identical to *Pneumocystis carinii* f. sp. *carinii* and *Pneumocystis carinii* f. sp. *hominis* in samples of air spora. J Clin Microbiol. 1996;34:1754–1759.
62. Olsson M, Sukura A, Lindberg LA, et al. Detections of *Pneumocystis carinii* DNA by filtration of air. Scand J Infect Dis. 1996;28:279–282.
63. Bartlett MS, Vermund SH, Jacobs RL, et al. Detection of *Pneumocystis carinii* DNA in air samples: Likely environmental risk to susceptible persons. J Clin Microbiol. 1997;35:2511–2513.
64. Lundgren B, Elvin K, Rothman LP, et al. Transmission of *Pneumocystis carinii* from patients to hospital staff. Thorax. 1997;52:422–424.
65. Lidman C, Olsson M, Bjorkman A, et al. No evidence of nosocomial *Pneumocystis carinii* infection via health care personnel. Scand J Infect Dis. 1997;29:63–64.
66. Armbruster C, Hassl Al, Kriwanek S. *Pneumocystis carinii* colonization in the absence of immunosuppression. Scand J Infect Dis. 1997;29:591–593.
67. Pottratz ST, Weir AL. Attachment of *Pneumocystis carinii* to primary cultures of rat alveolar epithelial cells. Exp Cell Res. 1995;221:357–362.
68. Limper AH, Thomas CF Jr, Anders RA, et al. Interactions of parasite and host epithelial cell cycle regulation during *Pneumocystis carinii* pneumonia. J Lab Clin Med. 1997;130:132–138.
69. Narasimhan S, Armstrong MY, Rhee K, et al. Gene for an extracellular matrix receptor protein from *Pneumocystis carinii*. Proc Natl Acad Sci U S A. 1994;91:7440–7444.
70. Thomas CF, Anders RA, Gustafson MP, et al. *Pneumocystis carinii* contains a functional cell-division-cycle Cdc2 homologue. Am J Respir Cell Mol Biol 1998;18:297–306.
71. Narasimhan S, Armstrong M, McClung JK, et al. Prohibitin, a putative negative control element present in *Pneumocystis carinii*. Infect Immun. 1997;12:5125–5130.
72. Smulian AG, Ryan M, Staben C, et al. Signal transduction in *Pneumocystis carinii*: Characterization of the genes (pcgl) encoding the alpha subunit of the G protein (PCGl) of *Pneumocystis carinii carinii* and *Pneumocystis carinii ratti*. Infect Immun. 1996;64:691–701.
73. Stedman TT, Buck GA. Identification, characterization, and expression of BiP endoplasmic reticulum resident chaperonins in *Pneumocystis carinii*. Infect Immun. 1996;64:4463–4471.
74. Wyder MA, Rasch EM, Kaneshiro ES. Quantitation of absolute *Pneumocystis carinii* nuclear DNA content. Trophic and cystic forms isolated for infected rat lungs are haploid organisms. J Euk Microbiol. 1998;45:233–239.
75. Furlong ST, Koziel H, Bartlett MS, et al. Lipid transfer from human epithelial cells to *Pneumocystis carinii* in vitro. J Infect Dis. 1997;175:661–668.
76. Limper AH, Edens M, Anders RA, et al. *Pneumocystis carinii* inhibits cyclin-dependent kinase activity in lung epithelial cells. J Clin Invest. 1998;101:1148–1155.
77. Oz HS, Hughes WT. *Pneumocystis carinii* infection alters GRP-binding proteins in the lung. J Parasitol. 1997;83:679–685.
78. Yu ML, Limper AH. *Pneumocystis carinii* induces ICAM-1 expression in lung epithelial cells through a TNF-alpha-mediated mechanism. Am J Physiol. 1997;273:L1103–L1111.
79. Esolen LM, Fasano MB, Flynn J, et al. Brief report: *Pneumocystis carinii* osteomyelitis in a patient with common variable immunodeficiency. N Engl J Med. 1992;326:909–1001.
80. Marcotte H, Levesque D, Delanay K, et al. *Pneumocystis carinii* infection in transgenic B cell-deficient mice. J Infect Dis. 1996;173:1034–1037.
81. Walzer PD, Runck J, Steele P, et al. Immunodeficient and immunosuppressed mice as models to test anti-*Pneumocystis carinii* drugs. Antimicrob Agents Chemother. 1997;41:251–258.
82. Roths JB, Sidman CL. Both immunity and hyperresponsiveness to *Pneumocystis carinii* result from transfer of CD4+ but not CD8+ T cells into severe combined immunodeficiency mice. J Clin Invest. 1992;90:673–678.

83. Roths JB, Sidman CL. Single and combined humoral and cell-mediated immunotherapy of *Pneumocystis carinii* pneumonia in immunodeficient scid mice. Infect Immun. 1993;61:1641–1649.
84. Bartlett MS, Angus WC, Shaw MM, et al. Antibody to *Pneumocystis carinii* protects rats and mice from developing pneumonia. Clin Diagn Lab Immun. 1998:5:74–77.
85. Harmsen AG, Chen W, Gigliotti F. Active immunity to *Pneumocystis carinii* reinfection in T-cell-depleted mice. Infect Immun. 1995;63:2391–2395.
86. Gigliotti F, Harmsen AG. *Pneumocystis carinii* host origin defines the antibody specificity and protective response induced by immunization. J Infect Dis. 1997;176:1322–1326.
87. Garvy BA, Wiley JA, Gigliotti F, et al. Protection against *Pneumocystis carinii* pneumonia by antibodies generated from either T helper 1 or T helper 2 responses. Infect Immun. 1997;65:5052–5056.
88. Lundgren B, Kovacs JA, Mathiesen L, et al. IgM response to a human *Pneumocystis carinii* surface antigen in HIV-infected patients with pulmonary symptoms. Scand J Infect Dis. 1993;25:515–520.
89. Buhl L, Settnes OP, Andersen PL. Antibodies to *Pneumocystis carinii* in Danish blood donors and AIDS patients with and without *Pneumocystis carinii* pneumonia. APMIS. 1993;101:707–710.
90. Elvin K, Bjorkman A, Heurlin N, et al. Seroreactivity to *Pneumocystis carinii* in patients with AIDS versus other immunosuppressed patients. Scand J Infect Dis. 1994;26:33–40.
91. Laursen AL, Jensen BN, Andersen PL. Local antibodies against *Pneumocystis carinii* in bronchoalveolar lavage fluid. Eur Respir J. 1994;7:679–685.
92. Walzer PD, Kim CK, Linke MJ, et al. Outbreaks of *Pneumocystis carinii* pneumonia in colonies of immunodeficient mice. Infect Immun. 1989;57:62–70.
93. Hanano R, Reifenberg K, Stefan H, et al. Naturally acquired *Pneumocystis carinii* pneumonia in gene disruption mutant mice: roles in distinct T-cell populations in infection. Infect Immun. 1996;64:3201–3209.
94. Furuta T, Fujita M, Machii K, et al. Fatal spontaneous pneumocystosis in nude rats. Lab Animal Sci. 1993;43:551–556.
95. Harmsen AG, Stankiewicz M. Requirement to $CD4^+$ cells in resistance to *Pneumocystis carinii* pneumonia in mice. J Exp Med. 1990;172:937–945.
96. Shellito J, Suzara VV, Blumenfeld W, et al. A new model of *Pneumocystis carinii* infection in mice selectively depleted of help T lymphocytes. J Clin Invest. 1990;85:1686–1693.
97. Wiley JA, Harmsen AG. CD 40 ligand is required for resolution of *Pneumocystis carinii* pneumonia in mice. J Immunol. 1995;155:3525–3529.
98. Beck JM, Newbury RL, Palmer BE, et al. Role of $CD8^+$ lymphocytes in host defense against *Pneumocystis carinii* in mice. J Lab Clin Med. 1996;128:477–487.
99. Theus SA, Walzer PD. Adoptive transfer of specific lymphocyte populations sensitized to the major surface glycoprotein of *Pneumocystis carinii* decreases organism burden while increasing survival rate in the rat. J Euk Microbiol (Suppl) 1997;44:23–24.
100. Sepkowitz KA, Brown AE, Armstrong D. *Pneumocystis carinii* pneumonia without acquired immunodeficiency syndrome. More patients, same risk. Arch Intern Med. 1995;155:1125–1128.
101. Walzer PD. Editorial response: *Pneumocystis carinii* pneumonia in patients without human immunodeficiency virus infection. Clin Infect Dis. 1997;25:219–220.
102. Varthalitis I, Aoun M, Daneau D, et al. *Pneumocystis carinii* pneumonia in patients with cancer: An increasing incidence. Cancer. 1993;71:481–485.
103. Ewig S, Bauer T, Schneider C, et al. Clinical characteristics and outcome of *Pneumocystis carinii* pneumonia in HIV-infected and otherwise immunosuppressed patients. Eur Respir J. 1995;8:1548–1553.
104. Gerrard JG. *Pneumocystis carinii* pneumonia in HIV-negative immunocompromised adults. Med J Aust. 1995;162:233–235.
105. Yale SH, Limper AH. *Pneumocystis carinii* pneumonia in patients without acquired immunodeficiency syndrome: Associated illness and prior corticosteroid therapy. Mayo Clin Proc. 1996;71:5–13.
106. Byrd JC, Hargis JB, Kester KE, et al. Opportunistic pulmonary infections with fludarabine in previously treated patients with low-grade lymphoid malignancies: A role for *Pneumocystis carinii* pneumonia prophylaxis. Am J Hematol. 1995;49:135–142.
107. Schiff D. *Pneumocystis* pneumonia in brain tumor patients: Risk factors and clinical features. J Neurooncol. 1996;27:235–240.
108. Kulke MH, Vance EA. *Pneumocystis carinii* pneumonia in patients receiving chemotherapy for breast cancer. Clin Infect Dis. 1997;25:215–218.
109. Godeau B, Coutant-Perronne V, Le Thi Houng D, et al. *Pneumocystis carinii* pneumonia in the course of connective tissue disease: report of 34 cases. J Rheumatol. 1994;21:246–251.
110. Kadoya A, Okada J, Iikuni Y, et al. Risk factors for *Pneumocystis carinii* pneumonia in patients with polymyositis/dermatomyositis or systemic lupus erythematosus. J Rheumatol. 1996;23:1186–1188.
111. Munoz P, Munoz RM, Palomo J, et al. *Pneumocystis carinii* infection in heart transplant recipients. Efficacy of a weekend prophylaxis schedule. Medicine (Baltimore). 1997;76:415–422.
112. Graham BS, Tucker WS. Opportunistic infections in endogenous Cushing's syndrome. Ann Intern Med. 1984;101:334–338.
113. Abernathy-Carver KJ, Fan LL, Boguniewicz M, et al. *Legionella* and *Pneumocystis* pneumonias in asthmatic children on high doses of systemic steroids. Pediatr Pulmonol. 1994;18:135–138.
114. Sy ML, Chin TW, Nussbaum E. *Pneumocystis carinii* pneumonia associated with inhaled corticosteroids in an immunocompetent child with asthma. J Pediatr. 1995;127:1000–1002.
115. Tattevin P, Di Palma M, Vittecoq D. *Pneumocystis carinii* pneumonia in patients with breast cancer: Are there contributing local factors? Clin Infect Dis. 1998;26:1018–1019.
116. Phair J, Munoz A, Detels R, et al. The risk of *Pneumocystis carinii* pneumonia among men infected with immunodeficiency virus type 1. N Engl J Med. 1990;322:161–165.
117. Smith DK, Neal JJ, Holmberg SD, et al. Idiopathic $CD4^+$ T-lymphocytopenia Task Force. Unexplained opportunistic infections and $CD4^+$ T-lymphocytopenia without HIV infection. N Engl J Med. 1993;328:373–379.
118. Jacobs JL, Libby DM, Winters RA, et al. A cluster of *Pneumocystis carinii* pneumonia in adults without predisposing illnesses. N Engl J Med. 1991;324:246–250.
119. Sharma R, Herndon B, Dew M, et al. Survival benefits of pulmonary cellular activation in AIDS patients with *Pneumocystis* infection. South Med J. 1997; 90:531–534.
120. Agostini C, Adami F, Poulter LW, et al. Role of bronchoalveolar lavage in predicting survival of patients with human immunodeficiency virus infection. Am J Respir Crit Care Med. 1997;156:1501–1507.
121. Hagler DN, Deepe GS, Pogue CL, et al. Blastogenic responses to *Pneumocystis carinii* among patients with human immunodeficiency (HIV) infection. Clin Exp Immunol. 1988;74:7–13.
122. Theus SA, Sawhney N, Smulian AG, et al. Proliferation and cytokine responses of human T lymphocytes isolated from HIV patients to the major surface glycoprotein of *Pneumocystis carinii*. J Infect Dis. 1998;177:238–241.
123. Koziel H, O'Riordan D, Warner A. Alveolar macrophage interaction with *Pneumocystis carinii*. Immunol Series. 1994;60:417–436.
124. Limper AH, Hoyte JS, Standing JE. The role of alveolar macrophages in *Pneumocystis carinii* degradation and clearance from the lung. J Clin Invest. 1997;99:2110–2117.
125. Hanano R, Reifenberg K, Kaufmann SH. Activated pulmonary macrophages are insufficient for resistance against *Pneumocystis carinii*. Infect Immun. 1998;66:305–314.
126. Williams MD, Wright JR, March KL, et al. Human surfactant protein A enhances attachment of *Pneumocystis carinii* to rat alveolar macrophages. Am J Respir Cell Mol Biol. 1996;14:232–238.
127. Masur H, Jones TC. The interaction in vitro of *Pneumocystis carinii* with macrophage and L-cells. J Exp Med. 1978;147:157–170.
128. Kolls JK, Beck JM, Nelson S, et al. Alveolar macrophage release of tumor necrosis factor during murine *Pneumocystis carinii* pneumonia. Am J Respir Cell Mol Biol. 1993;8:370–376.
129. Hoffman OA, Standing JE, Limper AH. *Pneumocystis carinii* stimulates tumor necrosis factor-α release from alveolar macrophages through a β-glucan–mediated mechanism. J Immunol. 1993;150:3932–3940.
130. Neese LW, Standing JE, Olson EJ, et al. Vitronectin, fibronectin, and gp^{120} antibody enhance macrophage release of tumor necrosis factor-α in response to *Pneumocystis carinii*. J Immunol. 1994;152:4549–4956.
131. Castro M, Morgenthaler TI, Hoffman OA, et al. *Pneumocystis carinii* induces the release of arachidonic acid and its metabolites from alveolar macrophages. Am J Respir Cell Mol Biol. 1993;9:73–81.
132. Laursen AL, Moller B, Rungby J, et al. *Pneumocystis carinii*–induced activation of the respiratory burst in human monocytes and macrophages. Clin Exp Immunol. 1994;98:196–202.
133. Simonpoli AM, Rajagopalan-Levasseur P, Brun-Pascaud M, et al. Influence of *Pneumocystis carinii* on nitrite production by rat alveolar macrophages. J Euk Microbiol. 1996;43:400–403.
134. Shellito JE, Kolls JK, Olariu R, et al. Nitric oxide and host defense against *Pneumocystis carinii* infection in a mouse model. J Infect Dis. 1996;173:432–439.
135. Kandil O, Fishman JA, Koziel H, et al. Human immunodeficiency virus type 1 infection of human macrophages modulates the cytokine response to *Pneumocystis carinii*. Infect Immun. 1994;62:644–650.
136. Laursen AL, Rungby J, Andersen PL. Decreased activation of the respiratory burst in neutrophils from AIDS patients with previous *Pneumocystis carinii* pneumonia. J Infect Dis. 1995;172:497–505.
137. Guzman J, Wang YM, Teschler H, et al. Phenotypic analysis of bronchoalveolar lavage lymphocytes from acquired immunodeficiency patients with and without *Pneumocystis carinii* pneumonia. Acta Cytol. 1992;36:900–904.
138. Bonagura VR, Cunningham-Rundles S, Edwards BL, et al. Common variable hypogammaglobulinemia, recurrent *Pneumocystis carinii* pneumonia on intravenous γ-globulin therapy, and natural killer deficiency. Clin Immunol Immunopathol. 1995;51:216–223.
139. Bonagura VR, Cunningham-Rundles SL, Schuval S. Dysfunction of natural killer cells in human immunodeficiency virus-infected children with or without *Pneumocystis carinii* pneumonia. J Pediatr. 1992;121:195–201.
140. Duncan RA, Von Reyn CF, Alliegro GM, et al. Idiopathic CD4 T-lymphocytopenia: Four patients with opportunistic infections and no evidence of HIV infection. N Engl J Med. 1993;328:393–398.
141. Chen W, Havell EA, Harmsen AG. Importance of endogenous tumor necrosis factor alpha and gamma interferon in host resistance against *Pneumocystis carinii* infection. Infect Immun. 1992;60:1279–1284.
142. Kolls JK, Dinghua L, Vazquez C, et al. Exacerbation of murine *Pneumocystis carinii* infection by adenoviral-mediated gene transfer of a TNF inhibitor. Am J Respir Cell Mol Biol. 1997;16:112–118.
143. Limper AH. Tumor necrosis factor α-mediated host defense against *Pneumocystis carinii*. Am J Respir Cell Mol Biol. 1997;16:110–111.
144. Chen W, Havell EA, Moldawer L, et al. Interleukin 1: An important mediator of

host resistance against *Pneumocystis carinii* infection. J Exp Med. 1992;176:713–718.
145. Pesanti EL. Interaction of cytokines and alveolar cells with *Pneumocystis carinii* in vitro. J Infect Dis. 1994;163:611–616.
146. Chen W, Havell EA, Gigliotti F, et al. Interleukin-6 production in a murine model of *Pneumocystis carinii* pneumonia: Relation to resistance and inflammatory response. Infect Immun. 1992;61:97–102.
147. Garvy BA, Ezekowitz RAB, Harmsen AG. Role of gamma interferon in the host immune and inflammatory responses to *Pneumocystis carinii* infection. Infect Immun. 1997;65:373–379.
148. Beck JM, Liggitt HD, Brunette EN, et al. Reduction in intensity of *Pneumocystis carinii* pneumonia in mice by aerosol administration of interferon-gamma. Infect Immun. 1991;59:3859–3862.
149. Shear HL, Valladares G, Narachi MA. Enhanced treatment of *Pneumocystis carinii* pneumonia in rats with interferon-γ and reduced doses of trimethoprim/sulfamethoxazole. J Acquir Immun Defic Syndr Hum Retrovirol. 1990;3:943–948.
150. Ishimine T, Kawakami K, Nakamoto A, et al. Analysis of cellular response and gamma interferon synthesis in bronchoalveolar lavage fluid and lung homogenate of mice infected with *Pneumocystis carinii*. Microbiol Immunol. 1995;39:49–58.
151. Mandujano JF, Nympha B, D'Sousa B, et al. Granulocyte-macrophage colony stimulating factor and *Pneumocystis carinii* pneumonia in mice. Am J Respir Care Med. 1995;151:1233–1238.
152. Ikei R, Furuta T, Asano S. Effect of recombinant human granulocyte colony stimulating factor on *Pneumocystis carinii* infection in nude mice. Jpn J Exp Med. 1989;59:51–58.
153. Wright TW, Johnston CJ, Harmsen AG, et al. Analysis of cytokine mRNA profiles in the lungs of *Pneumocystis carinii*–infected mice. Am J Respir Cell Mol Biol. 1997;17:491–500.
154. Perenboom RM, Beckers P, Van Der Meer JW, et al. Pro-inflammatory cytokines in lung and blood during steroid-induced *Pneumocystis carinii* pneumonia in rats. J Leukoc Biol. 1996;60:710–715.
155. Travis WD, Pittaluga S, Lipschik GY, et al. Atypical pathologic manifestations of *Pneumocystis carinii* pneumonia in the acquired immune deficiency syndrome. Review of 123 lung biopsies from 76 patients with emphasis on cysts, vascular invasion, vasculitis, and granulomas. Am J Surg Pathol. 1990;14:615–625.
156. Benefield TL, Prento P, Junge J, et al. Alveolar damage in AIDS-related *Pneumocystis carinii* pneumonia. Chest. 1997;111:1193–1199.
157. Sheehan PM, Stokes DC, Yeh Y, et al. Surfactant phospholipids and lavage phospholipase A_2 in experimental *Pneumocystis carinii* pneumonia. Am Rev Respir Dis. 1986;134:526–531.
158. Coleman DL, Dodek PM, Golden JA, et al. Correlation between serial pulmonary function tests and fiberoptic bronchoscopy in patients with *Pneumocystis carinii* pneumonia and the acquired immune deficiency syndrome. Am Rev Respir Dis. 1984;129:491–493.
159. Sankary RM, Turner J, Lipavsky A, et al. Alveolar-capillary block in patients with AIDS and *Pneumocystis carinii* pneumonia. Am Rev Respir Dis. 1988;137:443–449.
160. Stansell JD, Hopewell PC. *Pneumocystis carinii* pneumonia: Risk factor, clinical presentation and natural history. In: Sattler FR, Walzer PD, eds. *Pneumocystis Carinii*. London: Bailliere Tindall; 1995:449–459.
161. D'Angelo E, Calderini E, Robatto FM, et al. Lung and chest wall mechanics in patients with acquired immunodeficiency syndrome and severe *Pneumocystis carinii* pneumonia. Eur Respir J. 1997;10:2343–2350.
162. Guo Z, Kaneshiro ES. Phospholipid composition of *Pneumocystis carinii* and effects of methylprednisolone immunosuppression on rat lung lipids. Infect Immun. 1995;63:1286–1290.
163. Su TH, Natarajan V, Kachel DL, et al. Functional impairment of bronchoalveolar lavage phospholipids in early *Pneumocystis carinii* pneumonia in rats. J Lab Clin Med. 1996;127:263–271.
164. Aliouat EM, Escamilla R, Cariven C, et al. Surfactant changes during experimental pneumocystosis are related to *Pneumocystis* development. Eur Respir J. 1998;11:542–547.
165. Hoffman AGD, Lawrence MG, Ognibene FP, et al. Reduction of pulmonary surfactant in patients with human immunodeficiency virus and *Pneumocystis carinii* pneumonia. Chest. 1992;102:1730–1736.
166. Steinberg RI, Whitsett JA, Hull WM, et al. *Pneumocystis carinii* alters surfactant protein A concentrations in bronchoalveolar lavage fluid. J Lab Clin Med. 1995;125:462–469.
167. Rice WR, Singleton FM, Linke MJ, et al. Regulation of surfactant phosphatidylcholine secretion from alveolar type II cells during *Pneumocystis carinii* pneumonia in the rat. J Clin Invest. 1993;92:2778–2882.
168. Lipschik GY, Treml JF, Moore SD, et al. *Pneumocystis carinii* glycoprotein A inhibits surfactant phospholipid secretion by rat alveolar type II cells. J Infect Dis. 1998;177:182–187.
169. Eijking EP, van Daal GJ, Tenbrinck R. Effect of surfactant replacement on *Pneumocystis carinii* pneumonia in rats. Intensive Care Med. 1991;17:475–478.
170. Hughes WT, Sillos E, LaFon S, et al. Effects of aerolized synthetic surfactant, atovaquone, and the combination of these on murine *Pneumocystis carinii* pneumonia. J Infect Dis. 1998;177:1046–1056.
171. Salter AJ, Nichani SH, Macrae D, et al. Surfactant adjunctive therapy for *Pneumocystis carinii* pneumonitis in an infant with acute lymphoblastic leukemia. Intensive Care Med. 1995;21:261–263.
172. Creery WD, Hashmi A, Hutchison JS, et al. Surfactant therapy improves pulmonary function in infants with *Pneumocystis carinii* pneumonia and acquired immunodeficiency syndrome. Pediatr Pulmonol. 1997;24:370–373.
173. Chen W, Mills JW, Harmsen AG. Development and resolution of *Pneumocystis carinii* pneumonia in severe combined immunodeficient mice; A morphological study of host inflammatory responses. Int J Exp Pathol. 1992;73:709–720.
174. Mason GR, Hashimoto CH, Dickman PS, et al. Prognostic implications of bronchoalveolar lavage neutrophilia in patients with *Pneumocystis carinii* pneumonia and AIDS. Am Rev Respir Dis. 1989;139:1336–1342.
175. Limper AH, Offord KP, Smith TF, et al. *Pneumocystis carinii* pneumonia. Am Rev Respir Dis. 1989;140:1204–1209.
176. Benefield TL, Vestbo J, Junge J, et al. Prognostic value of interleukin-8 in AIDS-associated *Pneumocystis carinii* pneumonia. Am J Respir Crit Care Med. 1995;151:1058–1062.
177. Benefield TL, van Steenwijk R, Nielsen TL, et al. Interleukin-8 and eicosanoid production in the lung during moderate to severe *Pneumocystis carinii* pneumonia in AIDS: A role of interleukin-8 in the pathogenesis of *P. carinii* pneumonia. Respir Med. 1995;89:285–290.
178. Lipschik GY, Doerfler ME, Kovacs JA, et al. Leukotriene B4 and interleukin-8 in human immunodeficiency virus-related pulmonary disease. Chest. 1993;104:763–769.
179. Denis M, Ghadirian E. Dysregulation of interleukin 8, interleukin 10, and interleukin 12 release by alveolar macrophages from HIV type 1-infected subjects. AIDS Res Hum Retrovirus 1994;10:1619–1627.
180. Villard J, Dayer-Pastore F, Hamacher J, et al. GRO alpha and interleukin-8 in *Pneumocystis carinii* or bacterial pneumonia and adult respiratory distress syndrome. Am J Respir Crit Care Med. 1995;152:1549–1554.
181. Benfield TL, Kharazmi A, Larsen CG, et al. Neutrophil chemotactic activity in bronchoalveolar lavage fluid of patients with AIDS-associated *Pneumocystis carinii* pneumonia. Scand J Infect Dis. 1997;29:367–371.
182. Benfield TL, Lundgren B, Levine SJ, et al. The major surface glycoprotein of *Pneumocystis carinii* induces release and gene expression of interleukin-8 and tumor necrosis factor alpha in monocytes. Infect Immun. 1997;65:4790–4794.
183. Krishnan VL, Meager A, Mitchell DM, et al. Alveolar macrophages in AIDS patients: Increased spontaneous tumour necrosis factor-alpha production in *Pneumocystis carinii* pneumonia. Clin Exp Immunol. 1990;80:156–160.
184. Millar AB, Miller RF, Foley NM, et al. Production of tumor necrosis factor-alpha by blood and lung mononuclear phagocytes from patients with human immunodeficiency virus–related lung disease. Am J Respir Cell Mol Biol. 1991;5:144–148.
185. Huang ZB, Eden E. Effect of corticosteroids on IL1 beta and TNF alpha release by alveolar macrophages from patients with AIDS and *Pneumocystis carinii* pneumonia. Chest. 1993;104:751–755.
186. Perenboom RM, Sauerwein RW, Beckers P, et al. Cytokine profiles in bronchoalveolar lavage fluid and blood in HIV-seropositive patients with *Pneumocystis carinii* pneumonia. Eur J Clin Invest. 1997;27:333–339.
187. De Benedetti E, Nicod L, Reber G, et al. Procoagulant and fibrinolytic activities in bronchoalveolar fluid of HIV-positive and HIV-negative patients. Eur Respir J. 1992;5:411–417.
188. Angelici E, Contini C, Romani R, et al. Production of plasminogen activator and plasminogen activator inhibitors by alveolar macrophages in control subjects and AIDS patients. AIDS. 1996;10:283–290.
189. Benfield TL, Schattenkerk JK, Hofmann B, et al. Differential effect on serum neopterin and serum beta 2-microglobulin is induced by treatment in *Pneumocystis carinii* pneumonia. J Infect Dis. 1994;169:1170–1173.
190. The National Institutes of Health—University of California Expert Panel for Corticosteroids as Adjunctive Therapy for *Pneumocystis Carinii* Pneumonia. Consensus statement on the use of corticosteroids as adjunctive therapy for *Pneumocystis* pneumonia in the acquired immunodeficiency syndrome. N Engl J Med. 1990;323:1500–1504.
191. Dohn MN, Frame PT. Clinical manifestations in adults. In: Walzer PD, ed. *Pneumocystis carinii* Pneumonia. New York: Marcel Dekker; 1994:331–359.
192. Haverkos HW. Assessment of therapy for *Pneumocystis carinii* pneumonia. Am J Med 1984;76:501–508.
193. Kovacs JA, Hiemenz JW, Macher AM, et al. *Pneumocystis carinii* pneumonia: A comparison between patients with the acquired immunodeficiency syndrome and patients with other immunodeficiencies. Ann Intern Med. 1984;100:663–671.
194. Ziefer A, Abramowitz JA. *Pneumocystis carinii* pneumonia in HIV-positive and HIV-negative patients. An epidemiological, clinical and histopathological study of 18 patients. S Afr Med J. 1989;76:308–313.
195. Keitz SA, Bastian LA, Bennett CL, et al. AIDS-related *Pneumocystis carinii* pneumonia in older patients. J Gen Intern Med. 1996;11:591–596.
196. Chen HX, Ryan PA, Ferguson RP, et al. Characteristics of acquired immunodeficiency syndrome in older adults. J Am Geriatr Soc. 1998;46:153–156.
197. Laing R, Brettle R, Leen C, et al. Features and outcome of *Pneumocystis carinii* pneumonia according to risk category for HIV infection. Scand J Infect Dis. 1997;29:57–61.
198. Gryzan S, Paradis IL, Zeevi A, et al. Unexpectedly high incidence of *Pneumocystis carinii* infection after lung-heart transplantation. Am Rev Respir Dis. 1988;137:1268–1274.
199. Fishman JA. Radiological approaches to the diagnosis of *Pneumocystis carinii* and pneumonitis. In: Walzer PD, ed. *Pneumocystis carinii* Pneumonia. New York: Marcel Dekker; 1994;415–436.
200. Fahy JV, Chin DP, Schnapp LM, et al. Effect of aerosolized pentamidine prophylaxis on the clinical severity and diagnosis of *Pneumocystis carinii* pneumonia. Am Rev Respir Dis. 1992;146:844–848.
201. Tumeh SS, Belville JS, Pugatch R, et al. Ga-67 scintigraphy and computed

tomography in the diagnosis of *Pneumocystis carinii* pneumonia in patients with AIDS. A prospective comparison. Clin Nucl Med. 1992;17:387–394.
202. Gruden JF, Huang L, Turner J, et al. High-resolution CT in the evaluation of clinically suspected *Pneumocystis carinii* pneumonia in AIDS patients with normal, equivocal, or nonspecific radiographic findings. AJR. 1997;169:967–975.
203. Goldenberg DM, Sharkey RM, Udem S, et al. *Pneumocystis carinii* pneumonia in AIDS patients: A new method of diagnosis by radioimmunodetection (immunoscintigraphy). J Nucl Med. 1994;35:1028–1034.
204. Monaghan P, Provan I, Murray C, et al. An improved radionuclide technique for the detection of altered pulmonary permeability. J Nucl Med. 1991;32:1945–1949.
205. Zaman MK, White DA. Serum lactate dehydrogenase levels and *Pneumocystis carinii* pneumonia: Diagnostic and prognostic significance. Am Rev Respir Dis. 1988;137:796–800.
206. Benson CA, Spear J, Hines D, et al. Combined APACHE II score and serum lactate dehydrogenase as predictors of in-hospital mortality caused by first episode *Pneumocystis Carinii* pneumonia in patients with acquired immunodeficiency syndrome. Am Rev Respir Dis. 1991;144:319–323.
207. Montaner JS, Zala C. The role of the laboratory in the diagnosis and management of AIDS-related *Pneumocystis carinii* pneumonia. In: Sattler FR, Walzer PD, eds. *Pneumocystis Carinii*. London: Bailliere Tindall; 1995:471–485.
208. Ng VL, Yajko DM, Hadley WK. Extrapulmonary pneumocystosis. Clin Microbiol Rev. 1997;10:401–418.
209. Telzak EE, Cote RJ, Gold JWM, et al. Extrapulmonary *Pneumocystis carinii* infections. Rev Infect Dis. 1990;12:380–386.
210. Raviglione MC. Extrapulmonary pneumocystosis: The first 50 cases. Rev Infect Dis. 1990;12:1127–1138.
211. Afessa B, Green W, Chiao J, et al. Pulmonary complications of HIV infection: Autopsy findings. Chest. 1998:113:1225–1229.
212. Oz HS, Hughes WT, Vargas SL. Search for extrapulmonary *Pneumocystis carinii* in an animal model. J Parasitol. 1996;82:357–359.
213. Chary-Reddy S, Graves DC. Identification of extrapulmonary *Pneumocystis carinii* in immnunocompromised rats by PCR. J Clin Microbiol. 1996;34:1660–1665.
214. Rabodonirina M, Wilmotte R, Dannaoui E, et al. Detection of *Pneumocystis carinii* DNA by PCR amplification in various rat organs in experimental pneumocystosis. J Med Microbiol. 1997;46:665–668.
215. Baughman RP. Current methods of diagnosis. In: Walzer PD, ed. *Pneumocystis carinii* Pneumonia. New York: Marcel Dekker; 1994:381–401.
216. Kroe DM, Kirsch CM, Jensen WA. Diagnostic strategies for *Pneumocystis carinii* pneumonia. Semin Respir Infect. 1997;12:70–78.
217. Cregan P, Yamamoto A, Lum A, et al. Comparison of four methods for rapid detection of *Pneumocystis carinii* in respiratory specimens. J Clin Microbiol. 1990;28:2432–2436.
218. Aslanzadeh J, Stelmach PS. Detection of *Pneumocystis carinii* with direct fluorescence antibody and calcofluor white stain. Infection. 1996;24:248–250.
219. Radio SJ, Hansen S, Goldsmith J, et al. Immunohistochemistry of *Pneumocystis carinii* infection. Mod Pathol. 1990;3:462–469.
220. Graves DC, Chary-Reddy S, Becker-Hapak M. Detection of *Pneumocystis carinii* in induced sputa from immunocompromised patients using a repetitive DNA probe. Molec Cell Probe. 1997;11:1–9.
221. Weig M, Kunker H, Bogner BH, et al. Usefulness of PCR for diagnosis of *Pneumocystis carinii* pneumonia in different patient groups. J Clin Microbiol. 1997;35:1445–1449.
222. Ribes JA, Limper AH, Espy MJ, et al. PCR detection of *Pneumocystis carinii* in bronchoalveolar lavage specimens: Analysis of sensitivity and specificity. J Clin Microbiol. 1997;35:830–835.
223. Helweg-Larsen J, Jensen JS, Lundgren B. Non-invasive diagnosis of *Pneumocystis carinii* pneumonia in haematological patients using PCR on oral washes. J Euk Microbiol. 1997;44:59S.
224. Mathis A, Weber R, Kuster H, et al. Simplified sample processing combined with a sensitive one-tube nested PCR assay for detection of *Pneumocystis carinii* in respiratory specimens. J Clin Microbiol. 1997;35:1691–1695.
225. Rabodonirina M, Raffenot D, Cotte L, et al. Rapid detection of *Pneumocystis carinii* in bronchoalveolar lavage specimens from human immunodeficiency virus–infected patients: Use of a simple DNA extraction procedure and nested PCR. J Clin Microbiol. 1997;35:2748–2751.
226. Caliendo AM, Hewitt PL, Allega JM, et al. Performance of a PCR assay for detection of *Pneumocystis carinii* from respiratory specimens. J Clin Microbiol. 1998;36:979–982.
227. Atzori C, Lu JJ, Jiang B, et al. Diagnosis of *Pneumocystis carinii* pneumonia in AIDS patients by using polymerase chain reactions on serum specimens. J Infect Dis. 1995;172:1623–1626.
228. Wagner D, Koniger J, Kern WV, et al. Serum PCR of *Pneumocystis carinii* DNA in immunocompromised patients. Scand J Infect Dis. 1997;29:159–164.
229. Birriel JA, Adams JA, Saldana MA, et al. Role of flexible bronchoscopy and bronchoalveolar lavages in the diagnosis of pediatric acquired immunodeficiency syndrome–related pulmonary disease. Pediatrics. 1991;87:897–899.
230. Levine SJ, Masur H, Gill VL, et al. Effect of aerosolized pentamidine prophylaxis on the diagnosis of *Pneumocystis carinii* pneumonia by induced sputum examination in patients infected with the human immunodeficiency virus. Am Rev Respir Dis. 1991;144:760–764.
231. Teuscher AU, Opravil M, Theiler R, et al. Predictive value of bronchoalveolar lavage in excluding a diagnosis of *Pneumocystis carinii* pneumonia during prophylaxis with aerosolized pentamidine. Clin Infect Dis. 1993;16:519–522.
232. Gracia JD, Miravitlles M, Mayordomo C, et al. Empiric treatments impair the diagnostic yield of BAL in HIV-positive patients. Chest. 1997;111:1180–1186.
233. Cadranel J, Gillet-Juvin K, Antoine M, et al. Site-directed bronchoalveolar lavage and transbronchial biopsy in HIV-infected patients with pneumonia. Am J Respir Crit Care Med. 1995;152:1103–1106.
234. Huang L, Hecht FM, Stansell JD, et al. Suspected *Pneumocystis carinii* pneumonia with a negative induced sputum examination. Is early bronchoscopy useful? Am J Respir Crit Care Med. 1995;151:1866–1871.
235. Colangelo G, Baughman RP, Dohn MN, et al. Follow-up bronchoalveolar lavage in AIDS patients with *Pneumocystis carinii* pneumonia: *Pneumocystis carinii* burden predicts early relapse. Am Rev Respir Dis. 1991;143:1067–1071.
236. Horner RD, Bennett CL, Achenbach C, et al. Predictors of resource utilization for hospitalized patients with *Pneumocystis carinii* pneumonia (PCP): A summary of effects from the multi-city study of quality of PCP care. J Acquir Immune Defic Syndr Hum Retrovirol 1996;12:379–385.
237. Bennett CL, Curtis JR, Achenbach C, et al. U.S. hospital care for HIV-infected persons and the role of public, private, and Veterans Administration hospitals. J Acquir Immune Defic Syndr Hum Retrovirol. 1996;13:416–421.
238. Cohn SE, Klein JD, Weinstein RA, et al. Geographic variation in the management and outcome of patients with AIDS-related *Pneumocystis carinii* pneumonia. J Acquir Immune Defic Syndr Hum Retrovirol. 1996;13:408–415.
239. Curtis JR, Ullman M, Collier, AC, et al. Variations in medical care for HIV-related *Pneumocystis carinii* pneumonia: A comparison of process and outcome at two hospitals. Chest. 1997;112:398–405.
240. Curtis JR, Bennett CL, Horner RD, et al. Variations in intensive care unit utilization for patients with human immunodeficiency virus-related *Pneumocystis carinii* pneumonia: Importance of hospital characteristics and geographic location. Crit Care Med. 1998;26:668–675.
241. Masur H, Shelhamer J. Empiric outpatient management of HIV-related pneumonia: Economical or unwise? Ann Intern Med. 1996;124:451–453.
242. Bennett CL, Horner RD, Weinstein RA, et al. Empirically treated *Pneumocystis carinii* pneumonia in Los Angeles, Chicago, and Miami: 1987–1990. J Infect Dis. 1995;172:312–315.
243. Horner RD, Bennett CL, Rodriguez D, et al. Relationship between procedures and health insurance for critically ill patients with *Pneumocystis carinii* pneumonia. Am J Respir Crit Care Med. 1995;152:1435–1442.
244. Glassroth J. Empiric diagnosis of *Pneumocystis carinii* pneumonia. Am J Respir Crit Care Med. 1995;152:1433–1434.
245. Kumar SD, Krieger BP. CD4 lymphocyte counts and mortality in AIDS patients requiring mechanical ventilator support due to *Pneumocystis carinii* pneumonia. Chest. 1998;113:430–433.
246. Bozzette SA, Arcia J, Bartok AE, et al. Impact of *Pneumocystis carinii* and cytomegalovirus on the course and outcome of atypical pneumonia in advanced human immunodeficiency virus disease. J Infect Dis. 1992;165:93–98.
247. Bauer T, Ewig S, Hasper E, et al. Predicting in-hospital outcome in HIV-associated *Pneumocystis carinii* pneumonia. Infection. 1995;23:272–277.
248. Fernandez P, Torres A, Miro JM, et al. Prognostic factors influencing the outcome in *Pneumocystis carinii* pneumonia in patients with AIDS. Thorax. 1995;50:668–671.
249. Bennett CL, Adams J, Bennett RL, et al. The learning curve for AIDS-related *Pneumocystis carinii* pneumonia: Experience from 3,981 cases in Veterans Affairs Hospitals 1987–1991. J Acquir Immune Defic Syndr Hum Retrovirol. 1995;8:373–378.
250. Lundgren JD, Barton SE, Katlama C, et al. Changes in survival over time after a first episode of *Pneumocystis carinii* pneumonia for European patients with acquired immunodeficiency syndrome. Multicentre Study Group on AIDS in Europe. Arch Intern Med. 1995;155:822–828.
251. Yarnold PR, Soltysik RC, Bennett CL. Predicting in-hospital mortality of patients with AIDS-related *Pneumocystis carinii* pneumonia: An example of hierarchically optimal classification tree analysis. Stat Med. 1997;16:1451–1463.
252. Gallant JE, McAvinue SM, Moore RD, et al. The impact of prophylaxis on outcome and resource utilization in *Pneumocystis carinii* pneumonia. Chest. 1995;107:1018–1023.
253. Hentzen BT, Schreij G. Patterns of morbidity and mortality in AIDS patients on *Pneumocystis carinii* prophylaxis who died during hospital admission: A report of 50 diseased patients. Neth J Med. 1996;49:101–105.
254. Safrin S, Finkelstein DM, Feinberg J, et al. Comparison of three regimens for treatment of mild to moderate *Pneumocystis carinii* pneumonia in patients with AIDS. Ann Intern Med. 1996;124:792–802.
255. Gatell JM, Marrades R, El-Ebiary M, et al. Severe pulmonary infections in AIDS patients. Semin Respir Infect. 1996;11:119–128.
256. Hawley PH, Ronco JJ, Guillemi SA, et al. Decreasing frequency but worsening mortality of acute respiratory failure secondary to AIDS-related *Pneumocystis carinii* pneumonia. Chest. 1994;106:1456–1459.
257. Torres A, El-Ebiary M, Marrades R, et al. Aetiology and prognostic factors of patients with AIDS presenting life-threatening acute respiratory failure. Eur Respir J. 1995;8:1922–1928.
258. De Palo VA, Millstein BH, Mayo PH, et al. Outcome of intensive care inpatients with HIV infection. Chest. 1995;107:506–510.
259. Rosen MJ, Clayton K, Schneider RF, et al. Intensive care of patients with HIV infection: Utilization, critical illnesses, and outcomes. Pulmonary Complications of HIV Infection Study Group. Am J Respir Crit Care Med. 1997;155:67–71.
260. Dohn MN, Baughman RP, Vigdorth EM, et al. Equal survival rates for first, second, and third episodes of *Pneumocystis carinii* pneumonia in AIDS patients. Arch Intern Med. 1992;152:2465–2470.
261. Metersky ML, Colt HG, Olson LH, et al. AIDS-related spontaneous pneumothorax. Risk factors and treatment. Chest. 1995;108:946–951.
262. Ingram RJ, Call S, Andrade A, et al. Management and outcome of pneumothoraces in patients infected with human immunodeficiency virus. Clin Infect Dis. 1996;23:624–627.

263. Tumbarello M, Tacconelli E, Pirronti T, et al. Pneumothorax in HIV-infected patients: Role of *Pneumocystis carinii* pneumonia and pulmonary tuberculosis. Eur Respir J. 1997;10:1332–1335.
264. Drugs for parasitic infections. Med Lett Drugs Ther. 1998;40:1–12
265. Warren E, George S, You J, et al. Advances in the treatment and prophylaxis of *Pneumocystis carinii* pneumonia. Pharmacotherapy. 1997;17:900–916.
266. Deresinski SC. Treatment of *Pneumocystis carinii* pneumonia in adults with AIDS. Semin Respir Infect. 1997;12:79–97.
267. Hughes WT, Feldman S, Chaudhary SC, et al. Comparison of pentamidine isethionate and trimethoprim-sulfamethoxazole in the treatment of *Pneumocystis carinii* pneumonia. J Pediatr. 1978;92:285–291.
268. Wharton JM, Coleman DL, Wofsy CB, et al. Trimethoprim-sulfamethoxazole or pentamidine for *Pneumocystis carinii* pneumonia in the acquired immunodeficiency syndrome: A prospective randomized trial. Ann Intern Med. 1986;105:37–44.
269. Sattler FR, Cowan R, Nielsen DM, et al. Trimethoprim-sulfamethoxazole compared with pentamidine for treatment of *Pneumocystis carinii* pneumonia in the acquired immunodeficiency syndrome: A prospective, noncrossover study. Ann Intern Med. 1988;109:280–287.
270. Klein NC, Duncanson FP, Lenox TH, et al. Trimethoprim-sulfamethoxazole versus pentamidine for *Pneumocystis carinii* pneumonia in AIDS patients: Results of a large prospective randomized treatment trial. AIDS. 1992;6:301–305.
271. Stein DS, Stevens RC. Treatment-associated toxicities: Incidence and mechanisms. In: Sattler FR, Walzer PD, eds. *Pneumocystis Carinii*. London: Bailliere Tindall; 1995:505–530.
272. Greenberg S, Reiser IW, Chou SY, et al. Trimethoprim-sulfamethoxazole induces reversible hyperkalemia. Ann Intern Med. 1993;119:291–295.
273. Porras MC, Lecumberri JN, Castrillon JL. Trimethoprim/sulfamethoxazole and metabolic acidosis in HIV-infected patients. Ann Pharmacother. 1998;32:185–189.
274. Kelly JW, Dooley DP, Lattuada CP, et al. A severe, unusual reaction to trimethoprim-sulfamethoxazole in patients infected with human immunodeficiency virus. Clin Infect Dis. 1992;14:1034–1039.
275. Carr A, Swanson C, Penny R, et al. Clinical and laboratory markers of hypersensitivity to trimethoprim-sulfamethoxazole in patients with *Pneumocystis carinii* pneumonia and AIDS. J Infect Dis. 1993;167:180–185.
276. Veenstra J, Veugelers PJ, Keet JP, et al. Rapid disease progression in human immunodeficiency virus type 1–infected individuals with adverse reactions to trimethoprim-sulfamethoxazole prophylaxis. Clin Infect Dis. 1997;24:936–941.
277. Velazquez H, Perazella MA, Wright FS, et al. Renal mechanism of trimethoprim-induced hyperkalemia. Ann Intern Med. 1993;119:296–301.
278. Joos B, Blaser J, Opravil M, et al. Monitoring of Co-trimoxazole concentrations in serum during treatment of *Pneumocystis carinii* pneumonia. Antimicrob Agent Chemother. 1995;39:2661–2666.
279. Akerlund B, Tynell E, Bratt G, et al. *N*-acetylcysteine treatment and the risk of toxic reactions to trimethoprim-sulphamethoxazole in primary *Pneumocystis carinii* prophylaxis in HIV-infected patients. J Infect. 1997;35:143–147.
280. Bozzette SA, Forthal D, Sattler FR, et al. The tolerance for zidovudine plus thrice weekly or daily trimethoprim-sulfamethoxazole with and without leucovorin for primary prophylaxis in advanced HIV disease. Am J Med. 1995;98:177–182.
281. Safrin L, Lee BL, Sande MA. Adjunctive folinic acid with trimethoprim-sulfamethoxazole for *Pneumocystis carinii* pneumonia in AIDS patient is associated with an increased risk of therapeutic failure and death. J Infect Dis. 1994;170:912–917.
282. Caumes E, Roudier CE, Rogeaux O, et al. Effect of corticosteroids on the incidence of adverse cutaneous reactions to trimethoprim-sulfamethoxazole during treatment of AIDS-associated *Pneumocystis carinii* pneumonia. Clin Infect Dis. 1994;18:319–323.
283. Medina I, Mills J, Leoung G, et al. Oral therapy for *Pneumocystis carinii* pneumonia in the acquired immunodeficiency syndrome: A controlled trial of trimethoprim-sulfamethoxazole versus trimethoprim-dapsone. N Engl J Med. 1990;323:776–782.
284. Safrin S, Finkelstein DM, Feinberg J, et al. Comparison of three regimens for treatment of mild to moderate *Pneumocystis carinii* pneumonia in patients with AIDS. Ann Intern Med. 1996;124:792–802.
285. Lee BL, Medina I, Benowitz NL, et al. Dapsone, trimethoprim, and sulfamethoxazole plasma levels during treatment of *Pneumocystis carinii* pneumonia in patients with the acquired immunodeficiency syndrome (AIDS). Evidence of drug interactions. Ann Intern Med. 1989;110:606–611.
286. Metroka CE, MeMechan MF, Andrada R, et al. Failure of prophylaxis with dapsone in patients taking dideoxyinosine. N Engl J Med. 1991;325:737.
287. Toma E, Founier S, Dumont M, et al. Clindamycin/primaquine versus trimethoprim-sulfamethoxazole as primary therapy for *Pneumocystis carinii* pneumonia in AIDS: A randomized, double-blind pilot trial. Clin Infect Dis. 1993;17:178–184.
288. Hughes W, Leoung G, Kramer F, et al. Comparison of atovaquone (566C80) with trimethoprim-sulfamethoxazole to treat *Pneumocystis carinii* pneumonia in patients with AIDS. N Engl J Med. 1993;328:1521–1527.
289. Dohn MN, Weinberg WG, Torres RA, et al. Oral atovaquone compared with intravenous pentamidine for *Pneumocystis carinii* pneumonia in patients with AIDS. Ann Intern Med. 1994;121:174–180.
290. Black JR, Feinberg J, Murphy R, et al. Clindamycin and primaquine therapy for mild-to-moderate episodes of *Pneumocystis carinii* pneumonia in patients with AIDS: AIDS clinical trials group 044. Clin Infect Dis. 1994;18:905–913.
291. Noskin GA, Murphy RL, Black JR, et al. Salvage therapy with clindamycin/primaquine for *Pneumocystis carinii* pneumonia. Clin Infect Dis. 1992;14:183–188.
292. Montgomery AB, Feigal DW Jr, Sattler F, et al. Pentamidine aerosol trimethoprim-sulfamethoxazole for *Pneumocystis carinii* in acquired immune deficiency syndrome. Am J Respir Crit Care Med. 1995;151:1068–1074.
293. Sattler FR, Jelliffe RW. Pharmacokinetic and pharmacodynamic considerations for drug dosing in the treatment of *Pneumocystis carinii* pneumonia. In: Walzer PD, ed. *Pneumocystis Carinii* Pneumonia. New York: Marcel Dekker; 1994:467–485.
294. Conte JE Jr. Pharmacokinetics of intravenous pentamidine in patients with normal renal function or receiving hemodialysis. J Infect Dis. 1991;163:169–175.
295. Comtois R, Pouliot J, Vinet B, et al. Higher pentamidine levels in AIDS patients with hypoglycemia and azotemia during treatment of *Pneumocystis carinii* pneumonia. Am Rev Respir Dis. 1992;146:740–744.
296. Bronner LC, Gustafsson LL, Rombo L, et al. Plasma pentamidine concentrations vary between individuals with *Pneumocystis carinii* pneumonia and the drug is actively secreted by the kidney. J Antimicrob Chemother. 1994;33:803–810.
297. Kleyman TR, Roberts C, Ling BN. A mechanism for pentamidine-induced hyperkalemia: Inhibition of distal nephron sodium transport. Ann Intern Med. 1995;122:103–106.
298. Sattler FR, Frame P, Davis R, et al. Trimetrexate with leucovorin versus trimethoprim-sulfamethoxazole for moderate to severe episodes of *Pneumocystis carinii* pneumonia in patients with AIDS: A prospective, controlled multicenter investigation of the AIDS clinical trials group protocol 029/031. J Infect Dis. 1994;170:165–172.
299. Walmsley S, Levinton C, Brunton J, et al. A multicenter randomized double-blind placebo-controlled trial of adjunctive corticosteroids in the treatment of *Pneumocystis carinii* pneumonia complicating the acquired immune deficiency syndrome. J Acquir Immune Defic Syndr Hum Retrovirol. 1995;8:348–357.
300. Bozzette SA, Morton SC. Reconsidering the use of adjunctive corticosteroids in *pneumocystis* pneumonia? J Acquir Immune Defic Syndr Hum Retrovirol. 1995;8:345–347.
301. Jensen AM, Lundgren JD, Benfield T, et al. Does cytomegalovirus predict a poor prognosis in *Pneumocystis carinii* pneumonia treated with corticosteroids? A note for caution. Chest. 1995;108:411–414.
302. Mahaffey KW, Hippenmeyer CL, Mandel R, et al. Unrecognized coccidiodomycosis complicating *Pneumocystis carinii* pneumonia in patients infected with the human immunodeficiency virus and treated with corticosteroids. A report of two cases. Arch Intern Med. 1993;153:1496–1498.
303. Jones BE, Taikwel EK, Mercado AL, et al. Tuberculosis in patients with HIV infection who receive corticosteroids for presumed *Pneumocystis carinii* pneumonia. Am J Respir Crit Care Med. 1994;149:1686–1688.
304. Marots A, Podzamczer D, Martinez-Lacasa J, et al. Steroids do not enhance the risk of developing tuberculosis or other AIDS-related diseases in HIV-infected patients treated for *Pneumocystis carinii* pneumonia. AIDS 1995;9:1037–1041.
305. Montaner JS, Guillemi S, Quieffin J, et al. Oral corticosteroids in patients with mild *Pneumocystis carinii* pneumonia and the acquired immune deficiency syndrome (AIDS). Tuber Lung Dis. 1993;74:173–179.
306. Sleasman JW, Hemenway C, Klein AS, et al. Corticosteroids improve survival of children with AIDS and *Pneumocystis carinii* pneumonia. Am J Dis Child. 1993;147:30–43.
307. Bye MR, Cairns-Bazarian AM, Ewig JM. Markedly reduced mortality associated with corticosteroid therapy of *Pneumocystis carinii* pneumonia in children with acquired immunodeficiency syndrome. Arch Pediatr Adolesc Med. 1994;148:638–641.
308. McLaughlin GE, Virdee SS, Schleien CL, et al. Effect of corticosteroids on survival of children with acquired immunodeficiency syndrome and *Pneumocystis carinii*–related respiratory failure. J Pediatr. 1995;126:821–824.
309. Pareja JG, Garland R, Koziel H. Use of adjunctive corticosteroids in severe adult non-HIV *Pneumocystis carinii* pneumonia. Chest. 1998;113:1215–1224.
310. Lane BR, Ast JC, Hossler PA, et al. Dihydropteroate synthase polymorphisms in *Pneumocystis*. J Infect Dis. 1997;175:482–485.
311. Centers for Disease Control and Prevention. 1997 USPHS/IDSA guidelines for the prevention of opportunistic infections in persons infected with human immunodeficiency virus. MMWR Morb Mortal Wkly Rep. 1997;46(RR-12):1–46.
312. Ioannidis JP, Cappelleri JC, Skolnik PR, et al. A meta-analysis of the relative efficacy and toxicity of *Pneumocystis carinii* prophylactic regimens. Arch Intern Med. 1996;156:177–188.
313. Bucher HC, Griggith L, Guyatt GH, et al. Meta-analysis of prophylactic treatments against *Pneumocystis carinii* pneumonia and toxoplasma encephalitis in HIV-infected patients. J Acquir Immune Defic Syndr Hum Retrovirol. 1997;15:104–114.
314. Fishman JA. Prevention of infection due to *Pneumocystis carinii*. Antimicrob Agents Chemother. 1998;42:995–1004.
315. Gallant JE, McAvinue SM, Moore RD, et al. The impact of prophylaxis on outcome and resource utilization in *Pneumocystis carinii* pneumonia. Chest. 1995;107:1018–1023.
316. Freedberg KA, Scharfstein JA, Seage GR 3rd, et al. The cost-effectiveness of preventing AIDS-related opportunistic infections. JAMA. 1998;279:130–136.
317. Saah AJ, Hoover DR, Peng Y, et al. Predictors for failure of *Pneumocystis carinii* pneumonia prophylaxis. Multicenter AIDS Cohort Study. JAMA. 1995;273:1197–1202.
318. Bozzette SA, Finkelstein DM, Spector SA, et al. A randomized trial of three antipneumocystis agents in patients with advanced human immunodeficiency virus infection. NIAID AIDS Clinical Trials Group. N Engl J Med. 1995;332:693–699.
319. Sepkowitz KA. Effect of prophylaxis on the clinical manifestations of AIDS-related opportunistic infections. Clin Infect Dis. 1998;26:806–810.
320. Beard CB, Navin TB. Molecular epidemiology for *Pneumocystis carinii* pneumonia. Emerg Infect Dis. 1996;2:147–150.
321. Centers for Disease Control and Prevention. Guideline for isolation precaution in hospitals. Am J Infect Control. 1996;24:24–52.
322. Kuramochi T, Hioki K, Ito M. *Pneumocystis carinii* cysts are susceptible to inactivation by chemical disinfectants. Exp Anim. 1997;46:241–245.

S E C T I O N H

PROTOZOAL DISEASES

Chapter 261

Introduction to Protozoal Diseases

JONATHAN I. RAVDIN

The protozoans known to infect humans are a diverse group, as indicated by phylogeny (Table 261–1), epidemiology (Table 261–2), clinical manifestations (Table 261–3), preferred diagnostic studies (Table 261–4), and chemotherapeutic agents effective in eradicating or arresting infection (Chapter 39). Protozoans such as *Plasmodium* spp., *Entamoeba histolytica, Trypanosoma* spp., and *Leishmania* spp. are major worldwide pathogens and are among the leading causes of disease and mortality in areas of Africa, Asia, and Central and South America. *Giardia lamblia* and *Cryptosporidium* are frequent causes of diarrhea in developing areas and established industrialized countries. *Toxoplasma gondii, Cryptosporidium* spp., *Microsporidia, Cyclospora, Trypanosoma cruzi,* and *Leishmania* spp. all have been noted to cause severe diseases in patients with acquired immunodeficiency syndrome. New molecular biology techniques are leading to better characterization of protozoans.[2]

The new or continued importance of protozoal pathogens has stimulated active research in all areas.[2] Clinicians are encouraged to familiarize themselves with the material in Tables 261–2 through 261–4, which is addressed in depth in the chapters that follow. The key to the recognition of protozoal infection is a knowledge of epidemiologic risk factors such as the parasites' geographic distribution (see Table 261–2) and the major modes of clinical presentation (see Table 261–3). The clinical diagnosis of protozoal infection presenting outside normal areas of high prevalence is usually dependent on physicians considering this possibility in their differential diagnosis. Given present levels of travel, changing immigration patterns, and the immunosuppressive effects of infection with human immunodeficiency virus, all clinicians need to have a heightened awareness of diseases due to the protozoans. Diagnosis and therapy often require a specialized expertise with the use of tests (see Table 261–4) or drugs with which most physicians lack experience. Infectious disease consultants will frequently be called on to diagnose and manage protozoal infection; this requires the maintenance of an updated, in-depth database as provided by the chapters within this section.

REFERENCES

1. Committee on Systematics and Evolution of the Society of Protozoologists. A newly revised classification of the protozoa. J Protozool. 1980;27:37–58.
2. Clark CG, Diamond LS. Intraspecific variation and phylogenetic relationships in the genus *Entamoeba* as revealed by riboprinting. M Euk Microbiol. 1997;44:143–154.
3. Ubelaker JE, ed. Stedman's American Society of Parasitology. Parasitic Names. Baltimore: Williams & Wilkins; 1993.
4. Tenter AM, Baverstock PR, Johnson AM. Phylogenetic relationships of *Sarcocystis* species from sheep, goats, cattle and mice based on ribosomal RNA sequences. Int J Parasitol. 1992;22:503–513.

TABLE 261–1 Classification of Protozoans That Infect Humans

- Phylum I. Sarcomastigophora (flagella, pseudopodia)
  - Subphylum I. Mastigophora (flagella)
    - Class 2. Zoomastigophorea
      - Order 2. Kinetoplastida
        - Suborder 2. Trypanosomatina
          - *Leishmania, Trypanosoma*
      - Order 5. Diplomonadida
        - Suborder 2. Diplomonadina
          - *Giardia*
      - Order 7. Trichomonadida
        - *Dientamoeba, Trichomonas*
  - Subphylum III. Sarcodina (pseudopodia)
    - Super class 1. Rhizopoda
      - Class 1. Lobosea
        - Subclass 1. Gymnamoebia
          - Order 1. Amoebida
            - Suborder 1. Tubulina
              - *Entamoeba*
            - Suborder 5. Acanthopodina
              - *Acanthamoeba*
          - Order 2. Schizopyrenida
            - *Naegleria*
- Phylum III. Apicomplexa (apical microtubule complex)
  - Class 2. Sporozoea
    - Subclass 2. Coccidia
      - Order 3. Eucoccidia
        - Suborder 2. Eimeriina
          - *Cryptosporidium, Isospora, Microsporidia, Sarcocystis,*[3,4] *Toxoplasma*
        - Suborder 3. Haemosporina
          - *Plasmodium*
        - Suborder 3. Piroplasmia
          - Order 1. Piroplasmida
            - *Babesia*
- Phylum VII. Ciliophora (ciliated)
  - Class I. Kinetofragminophorea
    - Subclass 2. Vestibuliferia
      - Order 1. Trichostomatida
        - Suborder 1. Trichostomatina
          - *Balantidium*

Data from ref 1.

TABLE 261–2 Geographic Distribution and Mechanism of Transmission of Protozoal Infections

Organism	Geographic Distribution	Means of Transmission
Acanthamoeba spp.	Undefined	Contact lens, ? airborne
Babesia spp.	North America, Europe	Tick-borne, blood transfusions
Balantidium coli	Worldwide	Zoonosis (pigs), water,* fecal-oral
Blastocystis hominis	Unknown	Fecal-oral, water
Cryptosporidium spp.	Worldwide	Water, fecal-oral, zoonosis
Dientamoeba fragilis	Worldwide	Water, fecal-oral
Entamoeba histolytica	Worldwide	Water, fecal-oral, foodborne
Giardia lamblia	Worldwide	Water, fecal-oral, foodborne
Isospora spp.	Worldwide	Fecal-oral, suspected zoonosis
Leishmania spp.†		Sand fly
L. donovani	India, Pakistan, East Africa, China	
L. tropica	Middle East, Central Asia	
L. major	Middle East, India, Pakistan	
L. aethiopica	Ethiopia, Kenya	
L. mexicana	Central America, Texas	
L. amazonensis	South America	
L. chagasi	Latin America	
L. viannia braziliensis	Latin America	
Naegleria spp.	Worldwide	Fresh water, intranasal exposure
Plasmodium spp.	Africa, Asia, South and Central America, Oceania	Female anopheline mosquitoes, inoculation of infected blood
Sarcocystis spp.	Unknown	Foodborne (meat)
Toxoplasma gondii	Worldwide	Zoonosis (cats), foodborne (meat), blood or organ transplant, congenital
Trichomonas vaginalis	Worldwide	Venereal, during birth, ? nonvenereal
Trypanosoma spp.		
T. cruzi	South and Central America	Reduviid bugs
T. brucei gambiense	West Africa	Tsetse fly
T. brucei rhodesiense	East Africa	Tsetse fly

*Ingestion of water contaminated with fecal material.
†Other *Leishmania* spp. also infect humans but are less common.

TABLE 261–3 Clinical Syndromes Due to Infection by Protozoans

Organism (Disease)	Major Clinical Syndrome	Organism (Disease)	Major Clinical Syndrome
Acanthamoeba spp.	Keratitis, granulomatous encephalitis	Leptomyxida	Granulomatous amebic encephalitis
Babesia spp. (babesiosis)	Fever, malaise, hepatosplenomegaly, and hemolytic anemia, especially in the asplenic	*Naegleria* spp.	Meningoencephalitis
Balantidium coli (balantidiosis)	Colitis	*Plasmodium* spp. (malaria)	Paroxysmal fever, chills, headache, hepatosplenomegaly
Blastocystis hominis (blastocystis)	Diarrhea, mild eosinophilia		
Cryptosporidium spp. (cryptosporidiosis)	Self-limiting noninflammatory diarrhea; chronic severe diarrhea and cholangitis in AIDS patients	*Sarcocystis* spp.	Myositis, fever, eosinophilia
		Toxoplasma gondii (toxoplasmosis)	Fever, malaise, lymphadenopathy; chorioretinitis; congenital abnormalities; in immunocompromised host: encephalitis, myocarditis, pneumonitis
Dientamoeba fragilis	Diarrhea, eosinophilia		
Entamoeba histolytica (amebiasis)	Rectocolitis, liver abscess		
Giardia lamblia (giardiasis)	Noninflammatory diarrhea with malabsorption	*Trichomonas vaginalis* (trichomoniasis)	Vaginitis, urethritis
Isospora spp. (isosporiasis)	Diarrhea in AIDS patients	*Trypanosoma* spp. (African sleeping sickness and Chagas' disease)	Fever, lymphadenopathy, meningoencephalitis, myocarditis; megaesophagus and megacolon, congestive cardiopathy
Leishmania spp. (cutaneous and visceral leishmaniasis)	Cutaneous or mucosal ulceration; visceral disease with fever, hepatosplenomegaly		

Abbreviation: AIDS, Acquired immunodeficiency syndrome.

TABLE 261–4 Diagnostic Tests for Protozoal Diseases

Disease	Preferred Diagnostic Tests	Disease	Preferred Diagnostic Tests
Amebiasis	Stool for ova and parasites, serologic tests	Malaria	Wright or Giemsa stain of thin and thick blood smear
Intestinal	Fecal antigen		
Liver	Ultrasound examination, serologic tests		
Amebic keratitis	Corneal scraping for microscopy and culture	Primary amebic meningitis	Cerebrospinal fluid examination, culture for amebae
Babesiosis	Thin and thick blood smears		
Cryptosporidiosis	Acid-fast and auramine-rhodamine staining of fecal samples, small bowel biopsy		
Giardiasis	Stool for ova and parasites, stool antigen detection, sampling of duodenal contents	Toxoplasmosis	Serologic tests, Wright-Giemsa stain of tissue, antigen detection
Granulomatous amebic encephalitis	Brain biopsy	Trichomoniasis	Microscopy, culture, or antigen detection in genital secretions
Leishmaniasis			
Cutaneous and mucocutaneous	Biopsy, touch preparation, culture, serologic tests	Trypanosomiasis	
Visceral	Bone marrow or splenic aspiration, touch preparation, culture, serologic tests, lymph node biopsy	Chagas' disease	Fresh blood or stained smear, blood culture, xenodiagnosis; serologic tests for chronic disease
		African sleeping sickness	Blood smear, serologic tests

Chapter 262

Entamoeba histolytica (Amebiasis)

JONATHAN I. RAVDIN

If there be among you any man that is not clean by reasons of uncleanness that chanceth him by night, then shall he go abroad out of the camp. . . . And thou shalt have a paddle upon thy weapon; and it shall be, when thou wilt ease thyself abroad, thou shalt dig therewith, and shalt turn back and cover that which cometh from thee.

Deuteronomy 23:10 and 23:13

Acute and chronic diarrhea has been of major concern to humans since earliest recorded history. The invasion of Russia by Napoleon was halted by widespread acute diarrhea. The atrocities affecting prisoners of war such as at Andersonville during the Civil War and the Bataan Death March in the Philippines during World War II were caused as much by *Entamoeba histolytica* as by prison officials. This protozoal organism is the third leading parasitic cause of death in developing nations[1] and is one of the important health risks to which travelers are exposed. New information has been acquired on the pathogenesis of invasive amebiasis and the host immune response to the parasite.[2–4]

There is overwhelming evidence that distinct pathogenic and nonpathogenic species of *Entamoeba* exist. Analyses of zymodemes, the patterns of electrophoretic mobility of certain parasite isoenzymes, revealed an association of distinct zymodemes with symptomatic invasive disease.[5] Studies with RNA and DNA probes have clearly indicated genetic differences between pathogenic *E. histolytica* and the nonpathogenic *Entamoeba dispar.*[6–8] Restriction enzyme polymorphism analysis of polymerase chain reaction (PCR)-amplified small-subunit ribosomal RNA genes (riboprinting) further defined *Entamoeba* into specific species.[9] Studies that indicate phenotypic transformation in vitro due to the influence of bacterial associates were apparently flawed by inadvertent contamination of the cultures. Genetic differences between *E. histolytica* and *E. dispar* have been extended to genes encoding important proteins involved in pathogenesis, such as adherence lectins[10] and cysteine proteinases.[11]

Disease caused by *E. histolytica* is expressed most often as ulcerative and inflammatory lesions of the colon resulting in a complete spectrum of colonic signs and symptoms. Occasionally, amebas gain access to extraintestinal sites, most commonly the liver, where marked tissue destruction occurs.

Losch, in St. Petersburg, Russia, in 1875, is credited with documenting amebas to be pathogenic by inducing lesions in a dog fed dysenteric stool.[12] Kartulis, in Egypt in 1886, settled the role of amebas as a cause of intestinal and hepatic lesions in patients with diarrhea, and Walker and Sellards dispelled all doubt of the pathogenicity of *E. histolytica* with their detailed studies in the Philippines in 1913.[13] Councilman and Lafleur, pathologists at Johns Hopkins University, provided the information in 1891 to allow a clear distinction between bacillary and amebic dysentery.[13] The history of amebiasis has been highlighted by a number of well-studied epidemics such as that at the Chicago Century of Progress Exposition in 1933[14] and that at the Singer Sewing Machine Plant in Indiana in 1950.[15] But its main impact has been the ability of *E. dispar* and *E. histolytica* to maintain infection in 20 to 30% of people living in areas of the tropics and in up to 5% of the people in temperate climate nations.[1] The most subtle break in personal sanitation allows the organisms to spread and initiate disease.

ORGANISM

E. histolytica belongs to the pseudopod-forming protozoal superclass Rhizopoda within the subphylum Sarcodina.[16] Within their family Entamoebidae, order Amoebida, and class Lobosea are many species that infect humans, including *E. histolytica, E. hartmanni, E. polecki, E. coli, E. gingivalis. E. hartmanni,* previously referred to as "small race" *E. histolytica,* is a distinct species by virtue of morphology, unique antigens, and riboprinting.[9] Most experts agree that the noninvasive *Entamoeba*-like Laredo strain, which grows in culture at a lower temperature (25°C), is a separate species. Classification of *Entamoeba* has been based on morphology, antigenic differences, DNA characterization, riboprinting isoenzyme analysis, drug susceptibility, host specificity, in vitro growth characteristics, and in vivo virulence.[7, 9–11, 17, 18]

The distinction between *E. dispar* and *E. histolytica* was first defined by the mobility of four isoenzymes (L-malate:NADP$^+$ oxidoreductase, glucose phosphate isomerase, phosphoglucomutase, and hexokinase) on starch gel electrophoresis. Sargeaunt and coworkers studied more than 6000 clinical isolates and noted more than 22 distinct isoenzyme patterns (zymodemes).[5] Studies have indicated that the true number of distinct zymodemes is much lower.[18a] Individual zymodemes have a clear association with the occurrence of asymptomatic infection or symptomatic highly invasive disease.[5]

Entamoeba histolytica spp. have numerous antigenic differences from *E. dispar.* Distinct epitopes of the 170-kD heavy subunit of the galactose-inhibitable adherence lectin exist in *E. histolytica* and are absent in *E. dispar.*[18] However, the gene for the *E. dispar* 170-kD lectin subunit contains all 97 cysteine residues and conserves the same sequence homology to CD59 found in the *hgl2* lectin gene of *E. histolytica.*[10] Several research groups have produced monoclonal antibodies that distinguish between *E. histolytica* and *E. dispar* by immunofluorescence methodology[19] and immunoblotting.[20–22] Tannich and coworkers were the first to demonstrate genomic DNA differences between *E. histolytica* and *E. dispar.*[23] A complementary DNA (cDNA) clone specific for pathogenic amebas was identified by screening for the expressed protein with pooled human immune sera. Southern blotting of the cDNA probe and restriction mapping of hybridization by an actin cDNA probe both revealed significant genomic DNA differences. These studies were extended by comparison of the restriction fragment pattern of specific PCR-amplified genomic DNA fragments to differentiate isolates. Additional cDNA clones have been identified that distinguish *E. dispar* from *E. histolytica*[24, 25]; studies of ribosomal RNA have also been successful in differentiating strains.[9, 26] Genetic distance analysis supports the existence of at least two distinct groups within the species *E. histolytica.*[27, 28]

E. histolytica and *E. dispar* trophozoites are morphologically indistinguishable, ranging in size from 10 to 60 μm, with an average of 25 μm. Trophozoites have a single 3- to 5-μm nucleus containing fine peripheral chromatin and a central nucleolus; *E. histolytica* trophozoites often have ingested erythrocytes (Fig. 262–1).[29] The cytoplasm consists of a clear ectoplasm and a granular endoplasm that contains numerous vacuoles (Fig. 262–2). Cysts of *E. histolytica* average 12 μm in diameter (range, 5 to 20 μm) and, depending on their maturity, contain one to four nuclei with morphology identical to that of trophozoite nuclei. As in other members of the order Amoebida, young *E. histolytica* cysts contain chromatoid bodies with smooth, rounded edges; these are composed of ribosome particles in crystalline arrays. Immature cysts may contain clumps of glycogen that stain with iodine (Fig. 262–3).

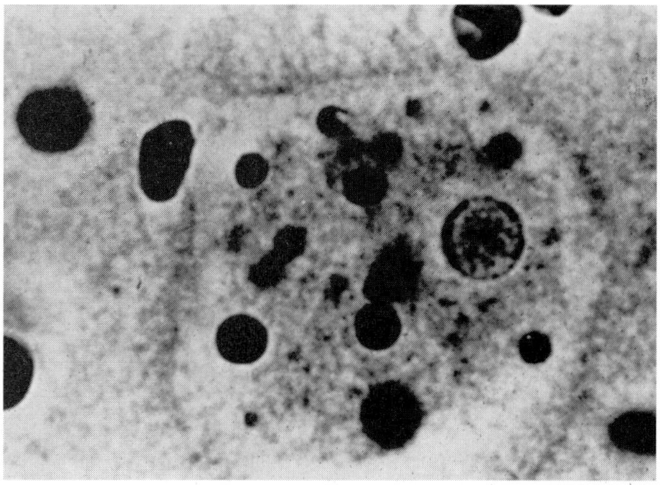

FIGURE 262–1. Trophozoite of *Entamoeba histolytica*. A delicate round nucleus with a small central chromatin dot is seen. The trophozoite contains dense ingested red blood cells.

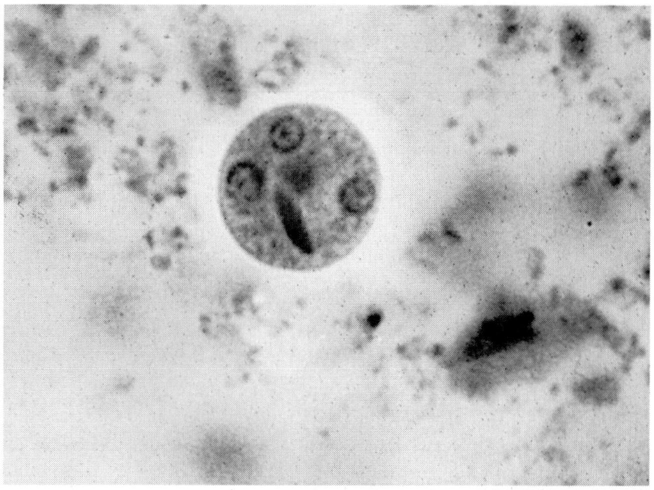

FIGURE 262–3. Mature cyst of *Entamoeba histolytica*. Three of the four nuclei are seen in the plane of focus of this photomicrograph.

LIFE CYCLE AND EPIDEMIOLOGY

The life cycles of *E. histolytica* and *E. dispar* are not complex; cysts are excreted and can survive for weeks in a hospitable environment. Ingestion of the cyst results in excystation in the small bowel and trophozoite infection of the colon. The trophozoite undergoes encystment only within the large bowel, possibly associated with conditions that are not ideal for continued activity of the trophozoite. Encystment of xenic cultures of *E. histolytica* can be induced in vitro by hypo-osmotic conditions resulting in the appearance of two sialylated glycoproteins and a chitinous cell wall (an *N-acetyl-*D-glucosamine polymer).[30] Cysts may remain viable for weeks or months in an appropriately moist environment; outside the body, trophozoites degenerate within minutes. In addition, trophozoites are rapidly destroyed by the low gastric pH and gastric enzymes; the encysted stage readily passes this barrier. The cyst, therefore, is the primary reason for the extensive prevalence of the infection throughout the world because it moves from one person to another through fecal contamination of water and vegetables or direct fecal-oral contact.

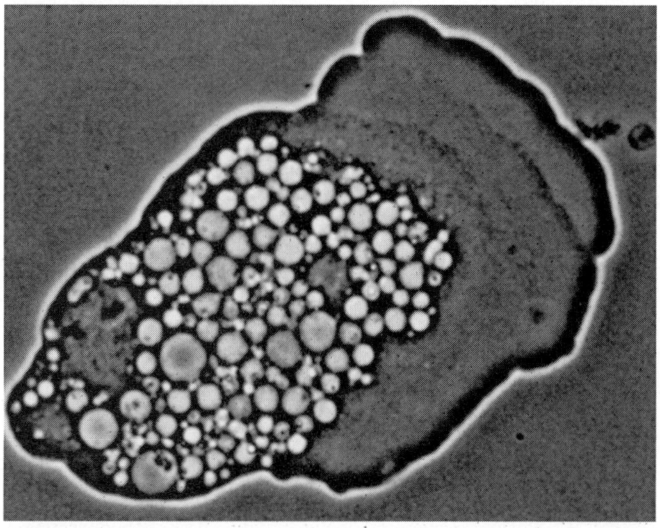

FIGURE 262–2. Phase micrograph of an axenic *Entamoeba histolytica* trophozoite strain HM1:IMSS; note that the cell is oriented with extension of pseudopodia and the highly vesiculated cytoplasm, which is characteristic of virulent axenic strains.

Knowledge of the epidemiologic risk factors for acquisition of *E. histolytica* infection and for increased severity of the disease (Table 262–1) is essential for the recognition of patients with amebiasis and an understanding of the importance of this parasite. Epidemiologic surveys for infection with *E. histolytica* are difficult to interpret owing to the low number of infected patients who demonstrate the organism on a single stool examination,[31, 32] frequent laboratory error in identification,[33] and the variability of detection of serum antiamebic antibodies after infection. Given these limitations, it is estimated that more than 10% of the world's population are infected by *E. dispar* and *E. histolytica.*[1] Excluding the People's Republic of China, approximately 50 million cases of invasive disease occur in the world each year and result in up to 100,000 deaths.[1] The prevalence of infection is as high as 50% in underdeveloped areas,[34–36] and, for example, serologic studies in Mexico City indicate that up to 5% of the population are infected with *E. histolytica* every 2 years.[37] Persistence of a high prevalence of amebic infection depends on cultural habits, sanitation, crowding, and socioeconomic status.[34, 37, 38] Asymptomatic intestinal infection occurs in 90 to 99% of infected individuals[39–41]; most eliminate the parasite from the gut within 12 months—the mechanisms of such are unknown. In a highly endemic area in Durban, South Africa, a 10% prevalence of *E. dispar* and *E. histolytica* infection resulted in 0.1% prevalence of amebiasis each year.[42, 43]

In one study by Gathiram and Jackson, there was a 10% risk per year of developing symptomatic invasive amebiasis after the acquisition of a pathogenic strain.[43] There is wide geographic variation in the percentage of asymptomatic intestinal amebic infections

TABLE 262–1 Epidemiologic Risk Factors That Apparently Predispose to *Entamoeba histolytica* Infection and Increased Severity of Disease

Prevalence	Increased Severity
Persons with lower socioeconomic status in endemic area including those with	Children, especially neonates
Crowding	Pregnancy and postpartum states
No indoor plumbing	Corticosteroid use
Immigrants from endemic area	Malignancy
Institutionalized populations, especially mentally retarded	Malnutrition
Persons living communally	
Promiscuous male homosexuals	

From Ravdin JI. Intestinal disease caused by *Entamoeba histolytica.* In: Ravdin JI, ed. Amebiasis: Human Infection with *Entamoeba histolytica.* New York: Churchill Livingstone. 1988:495–510.

that are *E. histolytica*, usually averaging 10% as in Durban, South Africa. It is the occurrence of asymptomatic infection with pathogenic *E. histolytica* in endemic areas that accounts for the high prevalence of serum anti-amebic antibodies; asymptomatic *E. dispar* infection does not elicit a serum antibody response.[39, 44, 45]

In the United States, the overall prevalence of *Entamoeba* infection is approximately 4%; however, certain high-risk groups have a much higher incidence of infection and disease. Institutionalized populations, especially the mentally challenged, have a very high incidence of *E. histolytica* infection (up to 73% by one serologic survey) with frequent invasive disease and significant mortality.[46–48] Attempts to eradicate amebic infection within individual institutions by the liberal use of anti-amebic drugs or isolation of stool carriers have been unsuccessful.[46, 49] Only improved housing and staffing of health care personnel appear to make a substantial impact.[50] In the late 1970s, there was an increased incidence of infection among sexually promiscuous male homosexuals. The prevalence of *E. dispar* and *E. histolytica* in the gay population of New York City and San Francisco approached 40 to 50% and was one of the many causes considered in the differential diagnosis of bloody diarrhea in these individuals.[51–55] Although the prevalence of amebic infection is undoubtedly declining with the change in sexual practices due to human immunodeficiency virus infection,[56] a continued high index of clinical suspicion is indicated.[57, 58] Amebiasis is a treatable cause of diarrhea in individuals with acquired immunodeficiency syndrome.[59, 60] Although only a few cases of invasive amebiasis have been reported to complicate acquired immunodeficiency syndrome worldwide, it is still an important differential diagnostic consideration.[60–63] Brown and associates have demonstrated that *E. histolytica* trophozoites took up human immunodeficiency virus in vitro but did not transfer it to uninfected human cells.[64] In addition, amebas isolated from two uninfected individuals were also positive for human immunodeficiency virus.

Many other factors are associated with risk for amebiasis, some unanticipated, such as colonic irrigation without proper sterilization of equipment at a chiropractic clinic in Colorado.[65] Recent immigrants or migrant workers from areas endemic for *E. histolytica* are an important focus of disease in the United States. The overwhelming majority of cases of invasive amebic disease reported from academic institutions in the southwestern United States in the 1980s occurred in Mexican Americans.[66–71] Increased risk of amebiasis is associated with foreign travel to any endemic area of the world, especially without taking precautions to avoid enteric infection.[72] The acquisition of *E. histolytica* infection is usually associated with long-term (greater than 1 month) residence in endemic areas and is usually detected only when symptomatic disease results.[73, 74] Additional high-risk groups include children in endemic areas, who suffer from fulminant invasive disease with a higher mortality than adults,[75, 76] and malnourished individuals at any age.[77]

PATHOLOGY AND PATHOGENESIS

Pathology

E. histolytica exerts a lytic effect on tissue, a characteristic for which the organism is named. Reports of initial invasion of amebas via mucosal crypts have not been confirmed; amebas appear to invade the colonic epithelium directly.[78, 79] Light and electron microscopic studies have been interpreted as showing lysis of mucosal cells on contact with amebas or, alternatively, diffuse mucosal damage before amebic invasion.[79–81] An amorphous, granular, eosinophilic material surrounds trophozoites in tissue, whether in colon, liver, lung, or brain.[78, 82, 83] Consistent with the fact that trophozoites have the capacity to destroy leukocytes,[84, 85] inflammatory cells are found only at the periphery of established amebic lesions.[78, 82] In vivo and in vitro studies demonstrate that lysis of host neutrophils by *E. histolytica* results in the release of toxic nonoxidative neutrophil products that contribute to the destruction of host tissues.[86, 87] However, in the severe combined immunodeficient mouse model of experimental amebic liver abscess, the absence of neutrophils resulted in larger abscesses, suggesting that neutrophils may play a protective role rather than exacerbating tissue destruction.[88]

A spectrum of colonic lesions ranging from nonspecific thickening of the mucosa to the classic flask-shaped ulcer may be associated with amebic infection (Fig. 262–4).[80, 82] In one study, only 20 of 53 patients had classic ulcers extending through the mucosa and muscularis mucosa into the submucosa.[82] Amebas can be recognized by a surrounding halo due to fixation artifact, the presence of characteristic nuclear morphology, ingested erythrocytes, and intense staining with periodic acid–Schiff stain or the Gridley stain to detect ingested erythrocytes.[89]

Liver abnormality in amebiasis consists of necrotic abscess or periportal fibrosis. The "abscess" contains acellular, proteinaceous debris rather than white cells and is surrounded by a rim of amebic trophozoites invading tissue.[78, 83] Amebas establish hepatic infection by ascending the portal venous system rather than the lymphatics.[90, 91] Triangular areas of hepatic necrosis, possibly due to ischemia from amebic obstruction of portal vessels, have been observed.[78, 90] Amebic liver abscesses probably result from the coalescence of small microabscesses.[90] Liver function abnormalities are frequently present with intestinal amebiasis and are associated with periportal inflammation without demonstrable trophozoites.[83, 92] Periportal fibrosis has been reported in such patients; whether this reflects past trophozoite invasion or host reaction to amebic antigens or toxins is unclear.

Pathogenesis

Knowledge of the pathogenic mechanisms of *E. histolytica* has been rapidly expanding; this has been due in part to the development of an axenic culture medium for the parasite.[93, 94] The pathogenesis of invasive amebiasis requires adherence of *E. histolytica* trophozoites to the luminal surface of the bowel, amebic cytolytic and proteolytic effects on tissue, and resistance of the parasite to host effector mechanisms.[2]

The in vitro adherence of *E. histolytica* trophozoites to Chinese hamster ovary cells and human colonic mucins is exclusively mediated by the parasite's galactose-inhibitable surface lectin.[95–98] The adherence lectin participates in the in vitro adherence of *E. histolytica* trophozoites to human leukocytes,[85, 99] rat and human colonic mucosa and submucosa,[98] human erythrocytes,[95, 100] Chang liver cells,[87] opsonized bacteria or bacteria with galactose-containing lipopolysaccharide, and rat colonic epithelial cells.[97] By taking advantage

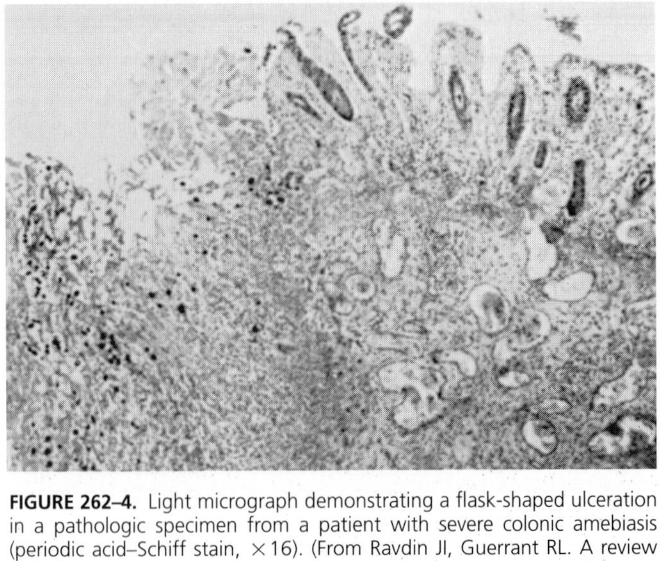

FIGURE 262–4. Light micrograph demonstrating a flask-shaped ulceration in a pathologic specimen from a patient with severe colonic amebiasis (periodic acid–Schiff stain, ×16). (From Ravdin JI, Guerrant RL. A review of the parasite cellular mechanisms involved in the pathogenesis of amebiasis. Rev Infect Dis. 1982;41:1185–1207.)

of its carbohydrate-binding activity and adherence-inhibitory monoclonal antibodies,[100, 101] Petri and coworkers isolated the *E. histolytica* galactose-inhibitable lectin.[96] The lectin is a 260-kD surface protein that consists of 170- and 35-kD subunits. The heavy subunit may mediate attachment as it is recognized by adherence-inhibitory monoclonal antibodies.[102] Direct galactose-binding activity by recombinant heavy subunit protein produced by expression-PCR methodology has been demonstrated. The heavy and light subunits are encoded by at least five genes[4, 103–105] that have unique promoter elements.[106] The heavy subunit has a short cytoplasmic domain, a transmembrane domain, and a large extracellular portion with a distinct cysteine-rich area. *Entamoeba dispar* also possesses a distinct gene encoding the functional subunit of the lectin.[10] The light subunit, in contrast, is attached to the membrane via a glycosyl-phosphatidylinositol anchor.[107] Petri and coworkers identified seven discrete epitopes in the heavy subunit using monoclonal immunoglobulin G (IgG) antibodies, all of which are located in the cysteine-rich domain.[108] Monoclonal antibodies to the lectin heavy subunit abrogate amebic resistance to the lytic effect of the human complement C5b–9 membrane attack complex at the steps of C8 and C9 assembly.[109] The lectin has sequence and antigenic similarities to the human CD59 inhibitor of C8 and C9.[109]

Axenic *E. histolytica* trophozoites kill target cells only on direct contact and not via secreted cytotoxins.[95, 110] Adherence mediated by the galactose lectin is absolutely required for the in vitro lysis of target cells.[85, 95] The death of a target cell may occur up to 20 minutes after amebic adherence; a lethal hit can be delivered within seconds by a trophozoite.[110, 111] Amebic cytolytic activity is dependent on parasite microfilament function,[95, 110] calcium,[111, 112] Ca^{2+}-dependent parasite phospholipase A enzyme activity,[112, 113] and maintenance of an acid pH in amebic endocytic vesicles.[114] The presence of a calcium signal pathway in *E. histolytica* is supported by the identification of Ca^{2+}-binding proteins,[115, 116] calcium-dependent protein kinases,[115] and a phosphoinositide 3-kinase.[117] Establishment of adherence by *E. histolytica* trophozoites is followed by a marked sustained elevation of the target cell-free intracellular calcium concentration, which contributes to, but may not be totally sufficient for, death of the target cell.[2] Phorbol esters, tumor-promoting agents, and protein kinase C activators specifically augment parasite cytolytic activity.[118] *Entamoeba histolytica* contains an ionophore-like protein of 77 amino acids with sequence homology to NK-lysin, a functionally equivalent protein in the cytotoxic T cells of swine.[119, 120] There are three isoforms of the protein, which have been well characterized by protein sequencing and molecular cloning of the cDNA.[120] The polypeptide chain folds into four helical elements; monomers oligomerize after insertion in the membrane to form an ion channel. Amebapore proteins possess potent antibacterial activity, comparable to the role of defensins in mammalian phagocytes, and have been found in the nonpathogenic *E. dispar* spp.[121] Whether these pre-forming proteins function solely as defensins or have a direct role in amebic cytolysis of host cells remains to be determined. Current evidence suggests that target cells undergo necrosis rather than apoptosis.[122]

E. histolytica contains numerous proteolytic enzymes, including collagenase and a well-characterized major neutral proteinase.[122, 123] Proteinases appear to be involved in dissolution of the extracellular matrix anchoring cells and tissue structure.[122] Kelsall and Ravdin demonstrated that parasite cysteine proteinases are responsible for degradation of human secretory IgA molecules, a possible means of immune evasion.[124] These proteinases have been found to also degrade IgG molecules and prevent their binding to trophozoites.[125] The 56-kD cysteine proteinase has been associated with activation of complement by cleavage of C3,[126] and pathogenic organisms release greater amounts of the enzyme.[127] Reed and coworkers succeeded in cloning the cysteine proteinase[128]; there are three genes encoding the cysteine proteinases, all of which have been well characterized.[11, 123] *E. histolytica* trophozoites contain more mRNA and secrete greater quantities of the proteinase than *E. dispar* amebas.[123] Amebic glycosidases, such as β-glucosaminidase[129] and a surface membrane–associated neuraminidase,[130] may be involved in the degradation of colonic mucins or alteration of target cell surface membrane glycoproteins.

In vivo models of amebic liver abscess[86] and in vitro studies[87] demonstrate that host polymorphonuclear leukocytes constitute the initial host response to *E. histolytica*. Neutrophils demonstrate chemotaxis to amebas,[131] and their lysis by *E. histolytica* enhances tissue destruction in vitro.[87]

HOST IMMUNITY

Anecdotal experience suggests that patients cured of amebic colitis or liver abscess are immune to a recurrence of invasive amebiasis. DeLeon followed 1021 patients with amebic liver abscess for 5 years in Mexico City; only five recurrent abscesses occurred.[132] A study of 982 subjects in a highly endemic area of India found that the rate of gut infection was lower in individuals who possessed serum anti-amebic antibodies.[36] In a longitudinal follow-up of over 1100 subjects in Durban, South Africa, for over 36 months, no recurrences of invasive amebiasis were found (Jackson TFGH, Lifson A, Ravdin JI, unpublished observations). Individuals asymptomatically infected with *E. dispar* spontaneously clear the parasite in 8 to 12 months[41]; it is unknown whether that is due to the acquisition of specific immunity or competition by other intestinal microflora. Patients cured of amebic liver abscess are immune to intestinal infection by *E. dispar* for up to 24 months.

By the seventh day of illness, patients with amebic liver abscess develop high titers of serum anti-amebic antibodies.[68] However, patients have progressive, unremitting disease despite possessing serum antibodies, which inhibit amebic adherence in vitro.[133] After cure of invasive amebiasis, serum anti-amebic antibodies persist for up to 10 years.[134] By immunoblotting human sera to total parasitic protein, we have demonstrated that there is a set of highly conserved *E. histolytica* antigens of approximately 37, 43, 59, 90, 110, and 170 kD.[133, 134] The 170-kD antigen was determined to be the heavy subunit of the galactose-specific lectin, recognized in native and recombinant protein by antibodies in over 95% of sera from patients with invasive amebiasis.[45, 135, 136] Convalescent sera from India, Mexico, Democratic Republic of Congo (formerly Zaire), Egypt, South Africa, and the United States all recognize epitopes on the lectin heavy subunit that was purified from a single *E. histolytica* clone of an axenic strain originally isolated in Mexico City (strain HMI:IMSS).[44, 45, 135–137] Highly conserved *E. histolytica* antigens include a 29-kD protein,[138] a 125-kD antigen,[139] a serine-rich surface antigen,[140, 141] cysteine proteinases,[25] and an asparagine-rich novel repeat protein.[142]

Serum from both healthy controls and infected patients (with high antibody titers to *E. histolytica*) are amebicidal to trophozoites through activation of the alternate and classic complement pathways.[143, 144] However, amebas isolated from a liver abscess or colonic lesions are resistant to complement-mediated lysis[144]; complement-resistant amebas can be selected in vitro by culture in normal human serum.[145] Trophozoites are lysed by the terminal complement components; complement activation occurs at least in part via cleavage of C3 by the parasite's 56-kD neutral cysteine proteinase.[126] As mentioned previously, the galactose-lectin heavy subunit inhibits the assembly of C8 and C9 into the membrane attack complex and apparently has a role in the parasite's resistance to complement-mediated lysis. Complement components present in the intestinal epithelium, therefore, may play a role in the prevention of the initial amebic invasion of the colonic mucosa as well as hematogenous dissemination to the liver.

Mucosal immune responses to *E. histolytica* have been characterized. Studies of colostral antibodies first demonstrated that anti-amebic secretory IgA is produced at mucosal surfaces during natural infection.[146, 147] Anti-lectin IgA has been found in the saliva, serum, and feces of subjects with amebic colitis and liver abscess.[136, 148, 149] Serum IgA antibody responses are found in subjects with asymptomatic *E. histolytica* infection, but not during infection with *E. dispar.*[136] Anti-lectin intestinal IgA responses persist for over 6 months in subjects with amebic liver abscess.[136] Oral challenge of BALB/c mice with a recombinant cysteine-rich portion of the lectin 170-kD subunit, designated LC3, with cholera holotoxin as adjuvant, resulted in a high level of intestinal anti-lectin IgA response, sufficient to block amebic adherence to target cells in vitro.[150] Many investigations are using numerous vaccine strategies and antigens to elicit mucosal immune responses to *E. histolytica*, including the use of an attenuated live *Salmonella* strain with amebic gene inserts or genetically engineered recombinant proteins containing amebic proteins linked to adjuvant proteins.[3]

Cell-mediated immune defense mechanisms probably have a role in limiting invasive disease and resisting a recurrence after pharmacologic cure. The cell-mediated response consists of antigen-specific lymphocyte blastogenesis with the production of lymphokines (including interferon-γ) capable of activating monocyte-derived macrophages to kill *E. histolytica* trophozoites in vitro.[99, 151] Macrophage cytotoxicity is primarily mediated by nitrous oxide (NO) with superoxide (O_2) and hydrogen peroxide (H_2O_2) as cofactors.[152] Colonic epithelial cells may have a role in eliciting cellular immune responses by the direct production of cytokines such as interleukin-1β and interleukin-8 on contact with *E. histolytica* trophozoites.[153, 154] In addition, in vitro incubation of immune T cells with *E. histolytica* antigen for 5 days elicits cytotoxic T-lymphocyte activity against *E. histolytica* trophozoites.[155] Purified native lectin is sufficient to elicit a competent amebicidal cell-mediated immune response in lymphocytes from subjects cured of invasive amebiasis.[156] However, in acute disease, the T-lymphocyte response to *E. histolytica* may be specifically depressed by a parasite-induced serum factor.[157] The lack of an increased incidence of severe invasive amebiasis in acquired immunodeficiency syndrome patients[56] suggests that host resistance to the initial amebic invasion of the colonic mucosa does not involve cell-mediated mechanisms. Clinical correlations relating the severity of established invasive disease with cell-mediated immune function include the numerous reports of severe exacerbation of intestinal amebiasis with the occurrence of toxic megacolon during corticosteroid therapy[158] and the fulminant amebic disease in young infants and pregnant women.[75, 76]

Nonimmune host defenses may be most important in resistance to symptomatic invasive amebiasis. In animal models, depletion of the colonic mucous blanket is always seen before parasite invasion.[159] Chadee and colleagues demonstrated that purified rat and human colonic mucins, rich in terminal galactose residues, act as high-affinity receptors for the *E. histolytica* galactose-inhibitable lectin.[97, 160] Colonic mucins inhibit amebic adherence to and lysis of colonic epithelial cells in vitro.[97, 161] *E. histolytica* possesses a potent mucus secretogogue activity, comparable to that found with cholera toxin.[162] Therefore, colonic mucin glycoproteins act as an important host defense by binding to the parasite's adherence lectin; however, this interaction probably facilitates intestinal colonization, thus promoting parasitism by *E. histolytica*.

Interruption of transmission of *E. histolytica* depends on complex socioeconomic problems or changes in human behavior. Clearly, applying to vaccine development our knowledge of the pathogenesis of the disease and the immunity of the host would be the most efficient and cost-effective means of preventing disease. The amebic native galactose lectin was demonstrated by Petri and Ravdin to be highly effective as a vaccine in an experimental model of amebic liver abscess in the gerbil.[162] The recombinant LC3 protein has also been found efficacious as a vaccine in the gerbil model of amebic liver abscess via systemic immunization.[135] The use of *Salmonella* expressing different fragments of the lectin 170-kD subunit provided partial protection.[163] Protective immunity in gerbils immunized with recombinant portions of the lectin 170-kD subunit was found to correlate with the induction of antibodies to a 25–amino acid region of the molecule.[164] Immunization with polyclonal antibodies to a recombinant serine-rich protein[3] or with monoclonal antibody to a lipophosphoglycan antigen provide protection against amebic liver abscess in the severe combined immunodeficient mouse model of amebic liver abscess.[165] Research on gene expression systems[166–168] and stable episomal transfection[169] provides opportunities to further study unique antigens and their relation to virulence, pathogenesis, and immunity. Numerous research groups are working on the development of different recombinant vaccines to induce amebicidal cell-mediated immunity, adherence-inhibitory secretory IgA responses, or humoral immunity that contributes to protection against invasive amebiasis.[3]

CLINICAL MANIFESTATIONS

The clinical syndromes associated with *E. histolytica* infection are summarized in Table 262–2; familiarity with these diverse manifestations and epidemiologic risk factors greatly facilitates a rapid, correct diagnosis.

Intestinal Disease

Noninvasive intestinal infection is established by a lack of hematophagous trophozoites, hemoccult-negative stools, and normal mucosa on colonoscopy. In contrast to infection with *E. dispar*, asymptomatic infection with *E. histolytica* is associated with a serum anti-amebic antibody response.[44, 45, 136] Patients with noninvasive luminal infection may manifest nonspecific gastrointestinal complaints, the cause of which is difficult to determine. We do not have a truly controlled prospective study available evaluating the outcome and clinical significance of "noninvasive" amebiasis. In New Delhi, India, a highly endemic area, Nanda and associates[41] studied a selected population of 184 patients who were referred, because of intestinal complaints, to a gastroenterology clinic. Because the total prevalence of symptoms was so high (42% with diarrhea), it was not surprising that there was no correlation between a positive stool culture for *E. histolytica* (found in 18.7%) and symptoms. Fifteen infected patients were followed in the clinic for a mean of 8.6 months, and all spontaneously cleared their infection. However, it is difficult to rule out unknown use of anti-amebic drugs. It is impossible to differentiate the clinical significance, if any, of asymptomatic *E. histolytica* compared with *E. dispar* infection without appropriate prospective studies.

The presentation of invasive intestinal disease due to *E. histolytica* has been reviewed extensively.[170–172] The signs and symptoms of acute amebic rectocolitis as reported in two large series are summarized in Table 262–3. Its onset is usually gradual over 1 to 3 weeks; although abdominal pain, tenderness, and bloody stools occur in most patients, only one third are febrile. The liver may be enlarged and exhibit percussion tenderness. When diarrhea is marked, the secondary signs of fluid loss and electrolyte imbalance are observed.[171]

Amebic colitis can affect all age groups and both sexes equally. A key point in the differential diagnosis is that virtually all patients have heme-positive stools.[171] Especially in children, colitis can present as rectal bleeding alone without evidence of diarrhea.[173, 174] Fecal leukocytes may not be present and are in reduced numbers when compared with patients with shigellosis,[175] presumably due to the

TABLE 262–2 Clinical Syndromes Associated with *Entamoeba histolytica* Infection

Intestinal disease	Extraintestinal disease
Asymptomatic infection	Liver abscess
Symptomatic noninvasive infection	Liver abscess complicated by
Acute rectocolitis (dysentery)	Peritonitis
Fulminant colitis with perforation	Empyema
Toxic megacolon	Pericarditis
Chronic nondysenteric colitis	Lung abscess
Ameboma	Brain abscess
Perianal ulceration	Genitourinary disease

TABLE 262-3 Clinical Presentation of Acute Amebic Rectocolitis

Signs and Symptoms	Adams and MacLeod[171] (1958–1972)	Juniper[172] (1957–1962)
Number of Cases	3013	55
History <4 wk	85%	71%
Onset	Gradual	Gradual
Abdominal pain	85%	NA
Diarrhea	100%	94%
Dysentery	99%	94%
Weight loss	NA	44%
Fever	38%	36%
Abdominal tenderness	83%	12%
Heme (+)	100%	100%
Case fatality	1.9%	9.1% (females, twice that of males)
Uncomplicated	10.5%	NA

Abbreviation: NA, Not available.

ability of amebic trophozoites to lyse human neutrophils.[84, 85] Charcot-Leyden crystals are often seen in the stool.

Fulminant colitis is an infrequent presentation of amebic infection that has a very high mortality[176] and a predisposition for occurring in malnourished[77] pregnant women,[75] recipients of corticosteroids,[158] or very young patients.[76] Such patients are severely ill with fever, leukocytosis, profuse bloody mucoid diarrhea, and widespread abdominal pain and are often hypotensive with signs of peritoneal irritation.[175] Fulminant colitis is often associated with liver abscess; segmental or total necrotic involvement of the colon is frequently present and may necessitate total colectomy and result in a fatal outcome despite anti-amebic and supportive therapy.[175] Intestinal perforation usually manifests as a slow leakage rather than an acute event; it is unclear whether surgical intervention is beneficial because attempts to suture such necrotic bowels are usually fruitless.[177]

Toxic megacolon is a well-described complication of acute amebic colitis, occurs in 0.5% of cases, and is a definite complication of inappropriate corticosteroid therapy.[178] Recognition is important because these patients do not respond to drug therapy and require colectomy.

Ameboma may be manifested as an annular lesion of the colon that is indistinguishable from colonic carcinoma or as an extrahepatic tender palpable mass, suggesting a pyogenic abscess.[170] Lesions may be single or multiple and are most common in the cecum and ascending colon. Serum anti-amebic antibodies are usually present in this form of amebiasis; in an endemic area, serologic examination or colonoscopy with biopsy should be performed before the surgeon explores the abdomen of such a patient.

Intestinal amebiasis can occur as a chronic nondysenteric syndrome. This was well documented in a series of 159 patients from Pakistan in which most had symptoms for more than 1 year (37% persisted more than 5 years) that consisted of intermittent diarrhea, mucus, abdominal pain, flatulence, and weight loss.[179] This disease is associated with less colonic inflammation and smaller ulcers than in inflammatory bowel disease; amebas are found in the stool, anti-amebic serologic tests are positive, and patients respond to anti-amebic drug therapy.[179] Chronic amebic infection may be misdiagnosed as inflammatory bowel disease with potentially disastrous consequences if corticosteroid therapy is begun. Examination of stools and serologic tests for amebic infection should be performed before a diagnosis of idiopathic inflammatory bowel disease is made.[178]

A chronic, irritative bowel syndrome may also follow acute amebic colitis. This illness usually subsides spontaneously. A more serious but similar illness is that referred to as ulcerative postdysenteric colitis.[171] Fortunately, this is not common. It has a pattern similar to that of ulcerative colitis, with recurrent signs and symptoms of mucus and bloody diarrhea that are unresponsive to anti-amebic therapy, but is associated with high antibody titers against *E. histolytica*. Occasionally this can be manifested as a granulomatous colitis with fistula formation.

Perianal amebiasis may result from extension of severe bowel disease to the skin and results from previous trauma, underlying abnormality of the squamous epithelium, or fistulous tracts.[180] Lesions can be ulcerative or condylomatous, slowly enlarge over weeks to months, and result in pain and bleeding. Trophozoites are found in the purulent exudate or on biopsy, and these lesions respond well to anti-amebic therapy.

Extraintestinal Amebiasis

An amebic liver abscess can appear concurrently with colitis, but more frequently there is no evidence or history of recent intestinal infection by *E. histolytica.*[181] In a study of 103 residents of Germany with amebic liver abscesses after exposure in endemic areas around the world, 95% presented with liver abscesses within 2 to 5 months (median of 3 months) after leaving the endemic area.[182]

Liver abscess can manifest with an acute onset (less than 10 days) with abdominal pain and fever or subacutely, with weight loss being prominent and less than half the patients having fever or abdominal pain.[68, 183–186] Concomitant diarrhea occurs in 30 to 40% of patients; amebas are found in stool by microscopic examination even less frequently.[68] However, Irusen and colleagues demonstrated by fecal culture a high incidence of intestinal colonization at presentation in patients with amebic liver abscess.[187] Failure to eradicate intestinal infection with therapy was associated with a recurrence of amebic liver abscess. Abdominal pain is usually localized to the right upper quadrant but can be referred to the shoulder and accompanied by a nonproductive cough.[69, 181] On physical examination there is exquisite point tenderness over the liver,[181] hepatomegaly is present in less than half, dullness and rales at the right lung base are common, and peritoneal signs or jaundice are unusual.[181–186] The presence of diffuse peritonitis or a pericardial friction rub indicates extension of the infection beyond the liver and increased mortality.

Laboratory findings include leukocytosis without eosinophilia in 80%, mild anemia in more than half, elevated alkaline phosphatase levels in 80%, elevated transaminase levels in more aggressive disease, and a high erythrocyte sedimentation rate.[68, 181–186] Serum cholesterol and albumin concentrations have been noted to be decreased in most patients; hyperbilirubinemia is uncommon and present in the setting of severe disease or peritonitis.[68, 181] Urinalysis frequently has abnormal findings in acute disease, with proteinuria common.[68]

Pleuropulmonary amebiasis is the most common complication of amebic liver abscess, usually due to the rupture of a superior right lobe abscess with erosion through the diaphragm to involve the pleural space or lung parenchyma.[181, 188] Serous pleural effusion and atelectasis are common accompaniments of liver abscesses and do not indicate extension of disease. Patients with pleuropulmonary complications present with cough, pleuritic pain, and dyspnea.[189–191] Empyema due to a rupture of the abscess into the pleural cavity presents with sudden respiratory distress and pain and has a substantial associated mortality (15 to 35%).[190, 192] Involvement of lung parenchyma may be by direct or hematogenous extension from the liver. Formation of a hepatobronchial fistula is not uncommon and has been associated with spontaneous cure. The sputum contains large amounts of necrotic material, with amebas often demonstrable.[189–191]

Intraperitoneal rupture of liver abscesses occurs in 2 to 7%,[181] with sudden perforation associated with a high mortality.[192] Left lobe abscesses are more likely to progress to rupture because of their later clinical presentation.[181] Such a febrile patient with a rigid distended abdomen may suggest an erroneous diagnosis of a perforated viscus. Pericardial amebiasis is an unusual but serious complication of liver abscesses. Although acute perforation with cardiac tamponade and shock can occur, the usual course is that of fever and abdominal pain progressing to substantial chest pain with signs of congestive heart failure.[181, 193] A correct diagnosis is usually dependent on the physician's consideration of the liver as the original source of infection.

Cerebral amebiasis is a rare cause of brain abscess; unfortunately, the onset is abrupt, with rapid progression to death over a period of 12 to 72 hours without adequate therapy.[194] Amebic brain abscesses must be considered in patients with known amebiasis and alteration of mental states or focal signs; on head computed tomography (CT), the lesions appear irregular without a capsule or surrounding enhancement.[195, 196] The diagnosis is made directly by examining tissue for amebic trophozoites; medical therapy with metronidazole and surgical decompression for increased intracranial pressure have improved the outcome of cerebral amebiasis.[194–197]

Genitourinary amebiasis is rare; rectovaginal fistulas in females can result in the spread of *E. histolytica* trophozoites to the genitourinary tract.[198, 199] Genital disease appears with painful granulation tissue or ulcers; malignancy is often suspected, and diagnosis is again made by biopsy. Penile amebiasis can result via acquisition from vaginal or anal intercourse.[200, 201] Medical therapy without surgery is adequate.[202]

DIAGNOSIS

Intestinal Amebiasis

The diagnosis of intestinal amebiasis continues to be made by identifying *E. histolytica* or *E. dispar* in the stool. The finding of either trophozoites or cysts confirms the diagnosis of intestinal infection. Substances that interfere with the stool examination should be avoided if possible; these include barium, bismuth, antimicrobials such as tetracyclines or erythromycin, antacids, laxatives, and soap or hypertonic enemas.[172] When a laboratory reports either trophozoites or cysts of *E. histolytica,* the physician should carefully review the patient's history, one should look for potential complications of amebic disease and then treat the patient accordingly. Laboratories vary tremendously in their ability to diagnose amebiasis.[33] Success depends on which techniques for identifying trophozoites are used, whether fixed and stained material is examined, whether concentration techniques are used to find cysts, the average specimen load on the laboratory, and the turnover rate of technicians. The best approaches for evaluating stool specimens for amebas are as follows:

1. A specimen obtained during endoscopy should be examined for motile, erythrocyte-containing amebas by direct mount in saline on a warm microscope stage. A small amount of liquid from an area of inflamed bowel is aspirated with a pipette passed through the sigmoidoscope. Liquid stool arriving in the laboratory within 30 minutes after passage can be examined by wet mount in a similar manner. The characteristic motility is that of a directed, linear movement across the microscope stage. Scraping of the ulcer edge or biopsy has a very high yield.
2. Fresh stool specimens should either be smeared and stained with iron hematoxylin or Wheatley Trichrome stain or remain fixed in polyvinyl alcohol for later staining (see Figs. 262–1 and 262–3). This allows the best identification of hematophagous *E. histolytica* trophozoites, the characteristic sign of invasive colonic disease. The nuclear morphology of *E. histolytica,* such as the central position of the nucleolus and the fine peripheral chromatic pattern, is key to differentiate it from commensals such as *Entamoeba coli.*
3. Stool specimens are suspended, after a 6% formalin wash and centrifugation, in formalin-ethyl acetate (9 ml 10% formalin, 3 ml ethyl acetate) to allow concentration of *E. histolytica* cysts at the bottom of the tube after centrifugation.[203] A drop of the sediment is then examined with a drop of dilute iodine solution (1 to 2% iodine in distilled water) to enhance the morphologic features of the cysts (see Fig. 262–3).
4. Because a single stool examination picks up only one third of infected patients, at least three specimens should be submitted before excluding the diagnosis of amebiasis.[31] A saline-purged specimen may increase the likelihood of diagnosis with less than three specimens. Stool culture for *E. histolytica* is more sensitive[187] and would decrease the need for multiple specimens; however, such cultures are generally not available in clinical practice. The culture media used are not selective for different species of intestinal amebas; therefore, skilled microscopy is still required to determine species identity. Stool culture may be a helpful diagnostic tool in chronic or asymptomatic colonic syndromes with low levels of cyst passage, especially to evaluate the efficacy of cure or the existence of infection when the presence or absence of serum anti-amebic antibodies is not definitive.

Endoscopy with scraping or biopsy is a valuable technique for the diagnostic evaluation of patients with diarrhea and suspected amebiasis (Table 262–4).[204] Amebic colitis is manifested as punctate hemorrhagic areas or small ulcers (a few millimeters to centimeters in diameter) with exudative centers and hyperemic borders. Rarely, large confluent ulcers are seen. The mucosa may be hyperemic and edematous because of the inflammatory process, and pseudomembranous changes can be present. In the early stage of the disease, endoscopy may be normal; therefore, amebiasis should not be excluded on this basis. In addition, disease may be localized to the cecum or ascending colon and be seen only by total colonoscopy.[177]

Serum anti-amebic antibody tests are very helpful in the diagnosis of invasive intestinal amebiasis.[45, 137, 205] Asymptomatic cyst passers infected by *E. dispar* have negative results by standard serologic methods. Eighty-five percent of the patients with biopsy-proven invasive intestinal amebiasis have serum anti-amebic antibodies as determined by various techniques.[45, 136, 137] Patients with symptoms for more than 1 week are much more likely to have serum anti-amebic antibodies.[137] Indirect hemagglutination anti-amebic antibody titers remain elevated (≥1:128) for years after invasive disease. Other available less sensitive studies such as counterimmunoelectrophoresis and gel diffusion precipitation become negative sooner after cure of invasive disease and are helpful in the diagnosis of active amebiasis in an endemic area.[205, 206]

Research has produced promising new diagnostic methodologies. Detection of serum antibodies to purified defined parasite antigens such as the galactose adhesin,[45, 137] a 29-kD surface antigen,[207] and recombinant LC3 subunit antigen[135, 136] provide specific and reproducible means to diagnose infection by *E. histolytica.* More exciting are the advances in direct detection of *E. histolytica* antigen in serum and feces. Numerous workers have reported the differentiation of cultivated isolates by binding of monoclonal antibodies to trophozoites.[20, 208] Abd-Alla and coworkers[209] and Haque and colleagues[210] (TechLab, Blacksburg, Va.) directly detected galactose inhibitable lectin antigen in fecal samples by enzyme-linked immunosorbent assay and used epitope-specific monoclonal antibodies to differentiate *E. histolytica* from *E. dispar* infection. In addition, Abd-Alla and coworkers[209] detected and characterized galactose lectin antigen in serum and found it to be highly specific for infection by *E. histolytica.* Levels of lectin antigen in feces and serum became undetectable after 7 days of treatment for amebic colitis or liver abscess.[136] Antigen detection provides great advantages in endemic areas where there is a high prevalence of serum anti-amebic antibodies (often

TABLE 262–4 Indications for Endoscopy with Biopsy or Scrapings in a Patient with a Clinical Syndrome and Risk Factors Consistent with Amebiasis

Stool exam (−), (+) serum anti-amebic antibody test
Stool exam (−), immediate diagnosis required
Stool exam (−), (−) serum anti-amebic antibody test, acute presentation with high suspicion
Chronic syndromes or mass lesions

From Ravdin, JI. Intestinal disease caused by *Entamoeba histolytica.* In: Ravdin JI, ed. Amebiasis: Human Infection with *Entamoeba histolytica.* New York: Churchill Livingstone. 1988:495–510.

25%[45]). In addition, antigen detection facilitates early diagnosis before an antibody response has occurred (<7 days) and differentiates pathogenic from nonpathogenic intestinal infection.[209, 210] There is a consensus that all *E. histolytica* infections should be treated; however, it is not common practice to treat asymptomatic *Entamoeba* infections in endemic areas. On the horizon are the use of strain-specific DNA probes and PCR to detect *E. histolytica* in feces. A new commercial, fecal antigen detection method has been developed using polyclonal antibodies (Prospect EIA, Alexon); this method was found in one study to be of comparable sensitivity and specificity to microscopy[211]; however, as zymodeme determination was not performed, it is unclear if this assay can differentiate *E. dispar* from *E. histolytica* infection. PCR may be so sensitive that it can detect a single trophozoite per gram of feces using amplification of DNA or ribosomal RNA with various methods for performing the study.[212, 213] PCR has been utilized successfully for detection of *Entamoeba* cysts[214] and trophozoites in liver aspirates[215] can differentiate *E. histolytica* from *E. dispar*.[212–215]

There is a broad differential diagnosis in patients presenting with a clinical syndrome consistent with intestinal amebiasis. In patients who excrete *Entamoeba* cysts and have nonspecific and episodic abdominal complaints such as bloating, cramps, and increased frequency of stools, the differential diagnosis includes giardiasis, viral gastroenteritis, enterotoxigenic *E. coli* infection, *Campylobacter* infection, *Salmonella* infection, cryptosporidiosis, isosporiasis, malabsorption syndromes, and functional bowel disease. Patients with acute amebic rectocolitis need to be differentiated from those with shigellosis, campylobacteriosis, *Salmonella* colitis, or infection with invasive vibrios, *Yersinia enterocolitica,* or invasive *E. coli* strains.[175] The most difficult distinction is the differentiation of amebiasis from an acute exacerbation of inflammatory bowel disease. A complete history with attention to epidemiologic risk factors, stool Gram stain (using carbol fuchsin for *Campylobacter*), and examination of stool for amebas are immediately useful. Appropriate culture of stool for bacterial pathogens and obtaining an amebic serologic examination, both of which usually take a few days to obtain results, can be definitive. Immediate endoscopy is recommended if the stool examination is negative and amebic colitis is suspected. A relative contraindication to endoscopy would be patients with fulminant colitis and toxic megacolon, in which there is a substantial risk of intestinal perforation during endoscopy. Patients with chronic nondysenteric amebiasis, which can be easily mistaken for inflammatory bowel disease, should have a positive serologic test for anti-amebic antibodies and colonic biopsy for trophozoites.[179] Amebomas must be differentiated from other localized processes such as carcinoma, lymphoma, tuberculosis, regional enteritis, or *Yersinia* infection. Toxic megacolon is a not-infrequent complication of inflammatory bowel disease. Ruling out colitis due to *E. histolytica* is imperative because corticosteroid therapy exacerbates colonic amebiasis.

Extraintestinal Amebiasis

The diagnosis of amebic liver abscess, pending serologic results, is based on the clinical presentation and recognition of epidemiologic risk factors, a lack of predisposing conditions for pyogenic liver abscess (such as biliary disease, prior appendicitis), and early use of noninvasive imaging studies.

Most important is performing an imaging technique to evaluate for the presence of a hepatic lesion versus biliary tract disease. In one study of 75 patients in an endemic area who presented with fever, right upper quadrant pain, nausea, and vomiting, 9 of the 75 had a liver abscess detected by hepatic sonography and hepatobiliary scans, and all were due to *E. histolytica*.[185] These patients were clinically indistinguishable from those with cholecystitis except for their younger age (younger than 45 years).[185] Imaging techniques available to establish the presence of cystic liver lesions include ultrasonography, ^{99m}Tc liver scanning, CT, magnetic resonance imaging, and ^{67}Ga scanning.[216] None of these methods is absolutely specific in differentiating an amebic liver abscess from a pyogenic abscess or tumor.[217] Sonography is rapid, low in cost, and only slightly less sensitive than CT; simultaneously evaluates the gallbladder; and lacks radiation exposure.[216, 217] Liver scans have been used successfully to diagnose amebic liver abscesses in many series[68] but have generally given way to CT in examination of hepatic abnormalities.[218] The CT scan is sensitive but not specific for amebic liver abscess (Fig. 262–5).[216–218] The use of injected contrast material may help differentiate hepatic abscesses from vascular tumors, an important point if liver aspiration is being contemplated. Magnetic resonance imaging is sensitive in the detection of amebic liver abscess but is no more specific than less costly technology.[219, 220] Due to the delay in imaging, gallium scans are not as helpful except if there is uncertainty in regard to a pyogenic versus an amebic abscess. Amebic liver abscesses do not contain leukocytes and therefore appear on gallium scans as cold areas, possibly having a "hot" rim. In contrast, a pyogenic abscess presents as an area of increased isotope concentration.[216]

The presence of serum anti-amebic antibodies is often the definitive study in the diagnosis of amebic liver abscess; such antibodies are present in up to 99% of patients.[45, 66, 68, 181] One pitfall is in patients with an acute presentation of less than 7 days: serologic studies may be negative.[68] If the diagnosis is still in question, a repeat serologic examination 5 to 7 days later should be positive.

The galactose lectin antigen is present in the serum of 75% of subjects with amebic liver abscess[209, 211] and may be an especially useful test in the future for patients who present acutely, before an IgG serum anti-amebic antibody response occurs.

The differential diagnosis for a cystic lesion in the liver that is accompanied by the signs, symptoms, and laboratory abnormalities seen in an amebic liver abscess might also include pyogenic abscess, echinococcal cyst, and hepatoma. Although older studies emphasize that an amebic liver abscess presents as a single large lesion in the right lobe of the liver, studies using modern imaging technology demonstrate a high frequency of multiple lesions.[68, 216, 220] Epidemiologic risk factors, serologic studies, and the presence of calcification aids in the diagnosis of echinococcal disease. If an amebic or pyogenic cause cannot be differentiated on clinical grounds and the patient is not stable enough to await serologic studies, liver aspiration with a "skinny needle" under CT or ultrasound guidance should be performed.[221, 222] Aspiration of an amebic liver abscess yields a sterile, odorless, brown or yellow liquid with amebas not commonly detected on microscopy. A culture of abscess fluid for *E. histolytica* may be helpful; however, most amebas are in the "wall" of the

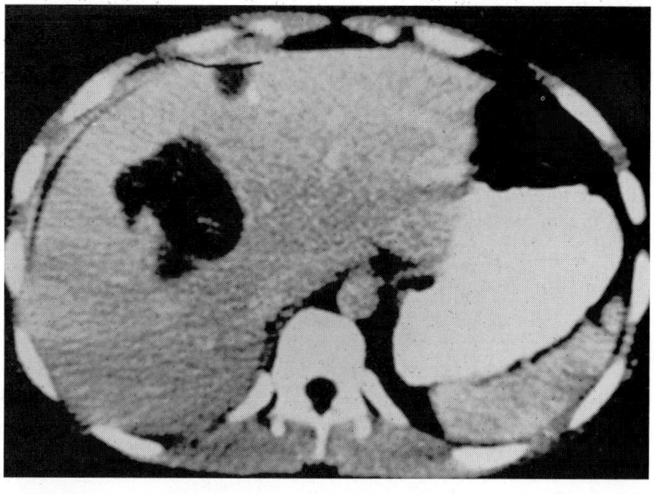

FIGURE 262–5. Abdominal computed tomography scan of a patient with an amebic liver abscess; the irregular multiple defects present in the right lobe of the liver cannot be differentiated from a pyogenic abscess or hepatocellular carcinoma.

abscess, and the yield of a culture can be low. As indicated, the use of antigen detection enzyme-linked immunosorbent assay on abscess contents could be diagnostic.[215] Aspiration of a pyogenic abscess is both diagnostic and therapeutic.[183, 184] The main risk of aspiration in all cases is peritoneal spillage; amebic peritonitis complicating a liver abscess markedly increases mortality. In addition, aspiration of an echinococcal cyst is to be avoided because of the anaphylactic reaction and seeding with scolices that may accompany leakage into the peritoneum.

Most cases of amebic liver abscess can be diagnosed and treated without aspiration. In some cases, antimicrobial therapy directed against enteric gram-negative organisms can be added to metronidazole therapy, pending the results of serologic studies. Therapeutic trials of specific anti-amebic therapy can be helpful diagnostically; most patients respond within 3 days with decreased pain and fever.[68] The liver abscess cavity usually resolves gradually over months, but persistent cystic lesions are not unusual.[223, 224]

TREATMENT

Therapy for amebiasis has been complicated by a number of factors including (1) variation of drug effects at the three different sites of amebic replication: the lumen of the bowel, the intestinal submucosa, and extraintestinal sites (Table 262–5); (2) the availability of different drugs in different countries; and (3) the development of new drugs and differences of opinion about side effects and efficacy.

It is controversial whether asymptomatic, apparently noninvasive *E. histolytica* infection merits therapy. There is sufficient information to conclude that treatment of *E. dispar* infection in a serum antibody–negative individual is not indicated, especially in an endemic area.[39, 40–43, 45] In contrast, all asymptomatic *E. histolytica* infections should be treated[40] because of the potential or real risks of invasive disease, antigenic exposure, and transmission to others. Availability of serum and fecal antigen detection allows differentiation of *E. histolytica* from *E. dispar* infection.[210, 211] Alternatively, serum anti-amebic antibody tests provide a reasonable screen because they are positive in almost all subjects with prior or current *E. histolytica* infection.[45] High-risk groups, who, once infected, suffer severe disease, include malnourished individuals,[77] pregnant women,[75] children,[76, 225] and patients being administered corticosteroids.[158] In addition, patients cured of luminal *E. histolytica* infection could be at least partially resistant to reinfection if they possess a secretory anti-amebic IgA response.

The following recommendations (summarized in Table 262–6) for treating amebiasis are a synthesis of opinions, with emphasis on the easiest, safest, and most effective combination likely to give maximal cure rates with a single course of therapy. Follow-up stool examination is always necessary because no regimen is completely effective in eradicating intestinal infection. Slightly different treatment regimens in addition to drug toxicities are also summarized in a 1998 *Medical Letter.*[226]

Intraluminal infection should be treated with diloxanide furoate, 500 mg three times a day for 10 days (this drug is available through the Centers for Disease Control and Prevention).[226–228] Paromomycin alone is also an effective treatment of intraluminal infection[229] and has the advantage of being a nonabsorbable agent.[230] Iodoquinol (diiodohydroxyquin, Yodoxin) is in limited supply in the United States.

Symptomatic amebiasis involving the intestine should be treated with a metronidazole or tinidazole, although tinidazole is not available in the United States.[172, 181, 231, 232] Metronidazole is administered in a dose of 750 mg three times a day for 5 to 10 days. This dose of metronidazole causes nausea and abdominal discomfort in a number of patients, but most can successfully complete the course of therapy. Therapy using 2.4 g/day for 2 days has also been reported to be effective in a small number of patients[233]; there is more extensive experience with single-dose therapy using tinidazole. In view of the side effects, which often begin on the second or third day, this short course may be more palatable to the patient.[234] Metronidazole therapy should be followed by an agent known to eradicate the intraluminal encysted organism (see Table 262–6).

Extraintestinal amebiasis should be treated with metronidazole and, to prevent continued intraluminal infection, paromomycin or diloxanide furoate (available from the Centers for Disease Control and Prevention).[187] In patients who are seriously ill due to complications of amebic infection such as peritonitis or a ruptured amebic abscess, some overseas physicians add parenteral emetine for the first few days (a total of two or three doses once a day, 65 mg/dose). This provides the rapid amebicidal action of emetine with a low incidence of cardiotoxicity; however, there is no published evidence of anti-amebic synergy when using these agents in combination. Neither emetine or its less toxic congener, dehydroemetine, is commercially available in the United States. Because of the few cases of incomplete therapy with metronidazole alone, the addition of chloroquine, 600 mg base/day for 2 to 3 days followed by 300 mg base/day for 2 to 3 weeks, can be considered but is usually unnecessary. There is no evidence of metronidazole-resistant *E. histolytica,* although in vitro metronidazole resistance can be induced by axenic culture of trophozoites in increasing concentrations of metronidazole, resulting in increased superoxide dismutase activity,[235] it has not ever been reported to be observed clinically.

The role of invasive procedures in the treatment of amebic abscesses has been an area of debate. Needle aspiration of the liver is a safe procedure in experienced hands,[181] but in most patients it is unnecessary for the relief of symptoms.[68, 221] Approximately 10 to

TABLE 262–6 Therapeutic Regimens for the Treatment of Amebiasis*

Type	Efficacy (%)
Cyst Passers	
Diloxanide fuorate,† 500 mg tid for 10 d	87–96
Paromomycin, 30 mg/kg/d in 3 divided doses for 5–10 d	85–90
Tetracycline, 250 mg qid for 10 d, then iodoquinol (Yodoxin), 650 mg tid for 20 d	95
Metronidazole, 750 mg tid for 10 d	90
Invasive Rectocolitis	
Metronidazole, 750 mg tid for 5–10 d	>90
Or 2.4 g qd for 2–3 d	>90
Or 50 mg/kg, 1 dose	>86
Plus diloxanide furoate† or paromomycin	
Tetracycline, 250 mg qid for 15 d, plus chloroquine (base), 600 mg, 300 mg, then 150 mg tid for 14 d	>94
Dehydroemetine,† 1–1.5 mg/kg/d IM or SC (max. 90 mg) for up to 5 d plus diloxanide furoate† or paromomycin	>90
Liver Abscess	
Metronidazole, 750 mg tid for 5–10 d or 2.4 g qd for 1–2 d plus diloxanide furoate† or paromomycin	>95
Dehydroemetine,† 1–1.5 mg/kg/d IM or SC (max. 90 mg) for up to 5 d plus diloxanide furoate or paromomycin	>90

*All dosages are for oral administration except dehydroemetine, which is administered intramuscularly; metronidazole can be used intravenously.
†Not commercially available in the United States. Diloxanide furoate is available from the Centers for Disease Control and Prevention.

TABLE 262–5 Antimicrobial Agents for Use in Treating Amebiasis

Luminal agents	Tissue agents
Diloxanide furoate	Bowel wall only
Paromomycin	Tetracycline
Iodoquinol	Erythromycin
	Liver only
	Chloroquine
	All tissues
	Metronidazole
	Tinidazole
	Emetine hydrochloride
	2-Dehydroemetine

15% of patients, however, are sufficiently ill to consider reducing the size of the abscess before a full therapeutic response is observed. In these patients, needle aspiration is helpful and indicated.[181] Open surgical drainage is not necessary and should be avoided unless the abscess is inaccessible to needle drainage and response to therapy has not occurred in 4 or 5 days. Percutaneous catheter drainage has a higher rate of initial success, compared with needle aspiration, but the ultimate outcome in successfully drained patients was no different.[236] Surgical attempts to correct amebic bowel perforation or peritonitis should be avoided, although some patients may benefit from peritoneal lavage.[237] Once a surgeon has performed a laparotomy on a patient with acute abdominal pain of unknown cause and found the damaged bowel of amebiasis, the temptation is to resect it. This is almost always unsuccessful. The surgeon would be better advised simply to obtain confirmatory specimens for examination and bacterial culture and to rely on antiprotozoal and antibacterial agents to control the infection. Maintaining drainage of the peritoneum plus antimicrobial therapy is optimal treatment. Maximal supportive care including meticulous fluid and electrolyte balance is essential in the seriously ill patient.

PREVENTION

Amebic infection is prevented by eradicating fecal contamination of food and water. The most commonly contaminated foods are fresh, ground-grown vegetables such as lettuce. Water is always a prime source of spread of infection. Amebic cysts are not killed by low doses of chlorine or iodine; therefore, simply relying on halide tablets in water as a means of preventing amebic infection is not adequate. Only boiling of water ensures the absence of amebas. Vegetables should be treated with a strong detergent soap and then soaked in acetic acid or vinegar for 10 to 15 minutes to ensure eradication of the cysts.

In general, in the tropics, unless the boiling of the water and the preparation of vegetables has been personally observed, these sources of food and refreshment should be omitted. Even in the finest hotels and restaurants, those preparing the food or placing water in bottles for drinking are often not aware of the potential danger of infection to the nonimmune traveler. Improvement in waste disposal and water purification is the most important factor in reducing the risk of acquiring amebiasis.

Avoiding sexual practices that allow fecal-oral contact can prevent infection in the male homosexual population. At present, there is not a clear means to prevent infection in institutionalized individuals, especially the mentally challenged, although case identification, therapy, improved supervision, and hygiene may be beneficial. Studies of the pathogenesis of amebiasis and host immunity may eventually lead to an immunologic or pharmacologic means to prevent invasive amebic disease.

REFERENCES

1. Walsh JA. Prevalence of *Entamoeba histolytica* infection. In: Ravdin JI, ed. Amebiasis: Human Infection by *Entamoeba histolytica.* New York: Churchill Livingstone; 1988:93–105.
2. Ravdin JI. Amebiasis, "State of the Art." Clin Infect Dis. 1995;20:1453–1466.
3. Stanley SL Jr. Progress toward development of a vaccine for amebiasis. Clin Microbiol Rev. 1997;10:637–649.
4. Leippe M. Amoebapores. Parasitol Today. 1997;13:178–183.
5. Sargeaunt PG, Williams JE, Greene JD. The differentiation of invasive and non-invasive *Entamoeba histolytica* by isoenzyme electrophoresis. Trans R Soc Trop Med Hyg. 1978;72:519–521.
6. Tannich E, Burchard GD. Differentiation of pathogenic from nonpathogenic *Entamoeba histolytica* by restriction fragment analysis of a single gene amplified in vitro. J Clin Microbiol. 1991;29:250–255.
7. Ortner S, Clark CG, Binder M, et al. Molecular biology of the hexokinase isoenzyme pattern that distinguishes pathogenic *Entamoeba histolytica* from nonpathogenic *Entamoeba dispar.* Mol Biochem Parasitol. 1997;86:85–94.
8. Diamond LS, Clark CG. A redescription of *Entamoeba histolytica* Schaudinn 1903 (Emended Walker 1911), separating it from *Entamoeba dispar* Brumpt 1925. J Eukaryot Microbiol. 1993;40:340–344.
9. Clark CG, Diamond LS. Intraspecific variation and phylogenetic relationships in the genus *Entamoeba* as revealed by riboprinting. J Eukaryot Microbiol. 1997;44:143–154.
10. Pillai DR, Britten D, Ackers JP, et al. A gene homologous to *hgl2* of *Entamoeba histolytica* is present and expressed in *Entamoeba dispar.* Mol Biochem Parasitol. 1997;87:101–105.
11. Bruchhaus I, Jacobs T, Leippe M, Tannich E. *Entamoeba histolytica* and *Entamoeba dispar*: Differences in numbers and expression of cysteine proteinase genes. Mol Microbiol. 1996;22:255–263.
12. Losch FA. Massive development of amebas in the large intestine. Am J Trop Med Hyg. 1875;24:383–392.
13. Kean BY, Mott KE, Russel AJ. Tropical Medicine and Parasitology: Classic Investigations. Ithaca, NY: Cornell University Press; 1978.
14. Select Committee. Amebiasis outbreak in Chicago: Report of a special committee. JAMA. 1934;102:369.
15. LeMaistre CA, Sappenfield R, Culbertson C, et al. Studies of a water-borne outbreak of amebiasis: South Bend, Indiana. Am J Hyg. 1956;64:30–45.
16. Levine ND, Corliss JO, Cox FEG. A newly revised classification of the protozoa. J Protozool. 1980;27:37–58.
17. Tachibana H, Ihara S, Kobayashi S, et al. Differences in genomic DNA sequences between pathogenic and nonpathogenic isolates of *Entamoeba histolytica* identified by polymerase chain reaction. J Clin Microbiol. 1991;29:2234–2239.
18. Petri WA Jr, Jackson TFHG, Gathiram V, et al. Pathogenic and nonpathogenic strains of *Entamoeba histolytica* can be differentiated by monoclonal antibodies to the galactose-specific adherence lectin. Infect Immun. 1990;58:1802–1806.
18a. Jackson TFHG. *Entamoeba histolytica* and *Entamoeba dispar* are distinct species; clinical, epidemiological and serelogical evidence. Int J Parasitol. 1998;28:181–186.
19. Tachibana H, Kobayashi S, Nagakura K. Reactivity of monoclonal antibodies to species-specific antigens of *Entamoeba histolytica.* J Protozool. 1991;38:329–334.
20. Tachibana H, Kobayashi S, Cheng X, Hiwatashi E. Differentiation of *Entamoeba histolytica* from *E dispar* facilitated by monoclonal antibodies against a 150-kDa surface antigen. Parasitol Res. 1997;83:435–439.
21. Bhattacharya S, Bhattacharya S, Sharma MP, et al. Metabolic labeling of *Entamoeba histolytica* antigens: Characterization of a 28-kDa major intracellular antigen. Exp Parasitol. 1990;70:255–263.
22. Reed SL, Flores BM, Batzer MA, et al. Molecular and cellular characterization of the 29-kilodalton peripheral membrane protein of *Entamoeba histolytica:* Differentiation between pathogenic and nonpathogenic isolates. Infect Immun. 1992;60:542–549.
23. Tannich E, Horstmann RD, Knobloch J, et al. Genomic DNA differences between pathogenic and nonpathogenic *Entamoeba histolytica.* Proc Natl Acad Sci U S A. 1989;86:5118–5122.
24. Tachibana H, Kobayashi S, Paz KC, et al. Analysis of pathogenicity by restriction-endonuclease digestion of amplified genomic DNA of *Entamoeba histolytica* isolated in Pernambuco, Brazil. Parasitol Res. 1992;78:433–436.
25. Burch DJ, Li E, Reed S, et al. Isolation of a strain specific *Entamoeba histolytica* cDNA clone. J Clin Microbiol. 1991;29:696–701.
26. Que X, Reed SL. Nucleotide sequence of a small subunit ribosomal RNA (16S-like rRNA) gene from *Entamoeba histolytica:* Differentiation of pathogenic from nonpathogenic isolates. Nucleic Acids Res. 1991;19:5438.
27. Blanc DS. Determination of taxonomic status of pathogenic and nonpathogenic *Entamoeba histolytica* zymodemes using isoenzyme analysis. J Protozool. 1992;39:471–479.
28. Baez-Camargo M, Riveron AM, Delgadillo DM, et al. *Entamoeba histolytica*: Gene linkage groups and relevant features of its karyotype. Mol Gen Genet. 1996;253:289–296.
29. Gonzalez-Ruiz A, Hague R, Aquirre A, et al. Value of microscopy in the diagnosis of dysentery associated with invasive *Entamoeba histolytica.* J Clin Pathol. 1994;4:236–239.
30. Chayen A, Avron B, Nuchamowitz Y, et al. Appearance of sialoglycoproteins in encysting cells of *Entamoeba histolytica.* Infect Immun. 1988;56:673–681.
31. Healy GR. Diagnostic techniques for stool samples. In: Ravdin JI, ed. Amebiasis: Human Infection by *Entamoeba histolytica.* New York: Churchill Livingstone; 1988:635–649.
32. Mathur TN, Kaur J. The frequency of excretion of cysts of *Entamoeba histolytica* in known cases of non-dysenteric amoebic colitis based on 21 stool examinations. Indian J Med Res. 1973;61:330–334.
33. Krogstad DJ, Spencer HC, Healy GR, et al. Amebiasis: Epidemiologic studies in the United States, 1971–1974. Ann Intern Med. 1978;88:89–97.
34. Cabellero-Salcedo A, Viveros-Rogel M, et al. Seroepidemiology of amebiasis in Mexico. Am J Trop Med Hyg. 1994;50:412–419.
35. Hossain MM, Ljungstrom I, Glass RI, et al. Amoebiasis and giardiasis in Bangladesh: Parasitological and serological studies. Trans R Soc Trop Med Hyg. 1983;77:552–554.
36. Choudhuri G, Prakash V, Kumar A, et al. Protective immunity to *Entamoeba histolytica* infection in subjects with antiamoebic antibodies residing in a hyperendemic zone. Scand J Infect Dis. 1991;23:771–776.
37. Gutierrez G, Ludlow A, Espinos G, et al. National serologic survey. II. Search for antibodies against *Entamoeba histolytica* in Mexico. In: Sepulveda B, Diamond LS, eds. Amebiasis. Proceedings of the International Conference on Amebiasis. Mexico City: Instituto Mexicano del Seguro Social; 1976:609–618.
38. Abdel Hafez MM, el Kady N, Bolbol AS, et al. Prevalence of intestinal parasitic

infections in Riyadh district, Saudi Arabia. Ann Trop Med Parasitol. 1986;80:631–634.
39. Jackson TFHG, Gathiram V, Simjee AE. Seroepidemiological study of antibody responses to the zymodemes of *Entamoeba histolytica*. Lancet. 1985;1:716–719.
40. Jackson TFHG. *Entamoeba histolytica* cyst passers—to treat or not to treat (Editorial)? S Afr Med J. 1987;72:657–658.
41. Nanda R, Baveja U, Anand BS. *Entamoeba histolytica* cyst passers: Clinical features and outcome in untreated subjects. Lancet. 1984;2:301–303.
42. Gathiram V, Jackson TFHG. Frequency distribution of *Entamoeba histolytica* zymodemes in a rural South African population. Lancet. 1985;1:719–721.
43. Gathiram V, Jackson TFHG. A longitudinal study of asymptomatic carriers of pathogenic zymodemes of *Entamoeba histolytica*. S Afr Med J. 1987;72:669–672.
44. Abd-Alla M, Jackson TGFH, Ravdin JI. Serum IgM antibody response to the galactose-inhibitable adherence lectin of *Entabmoeba histolytica*. Am J Trop Med Hyg. 1998;59:431–434.
45. Ravdin JI, Jackson TF, Petri WA Jr, et al. Association of serum antibodies to adherence lectin with invasive amebiasis and asymptomatic infection with *Entamoeba histolytica*. J Infect Dis. 1990;162:768–772.
46. Thacker SB, Simpson S, Gordon TJ, et al. Parasitic disease control in a residential facility for the mentally retarded. Am J Public Health. 1979;69:1279–1281.
47. Sexton DJ, Krogstad DJ, Spencer HC, et al. Amebiasis in a mental institution: Serologic and epidemiologic studies. Am J Epidemiol. 1974;100:414–423.
48. Petri WA, Ravdin JI. Amebiasis in institutionalized populations. In: Ravdin JI, ed. Amebiasis: Human Infection by *Entamoeba histolytica*. New York: Churchill Livingstone; 1988:576–581.
49. Thacker SB, Kimball AM, Wolfe M, et al. Parasitic disease control in a residential facility for the mentally retarded: Failure of selected isolation procedures. Am J Public Health. 1981;71:303.
50. Brooke MM. Epidemiology and control of amebiasis in institutions for the mentally retarded. Am J Ment Defic. 1963;68:187.
51. Kean BH, William DC, Luminais SK. Epidemic of amoebiasis and giardiasis in a biased population. Br J Vener Dis. 1979;55:375–378.
52. Quinn TC, Corey L, Chaffee RG, et al. The etiology of anorectal infections in homosexual men. Am J Med. 1981;71:395.
53. Phillips SC, Mildvan D, William DC, et al. Sexual transmission of enteric protozoa and helminths in a venereal-disease-clinic population. N Engl J Med. 1981;305:603–606.
54. Markell EK, Havens RF, Kuritsubo RA, et al. Intestinal protozoa in homosexual men of the San Francisco Bay area: Prevalence and correlates of infection. Am J Trop Med Hyg. 1984;33:239–245.
55. Ortega HB, Borchardt KA, Hamilton R, et al. Enteric pathogenic protozoa in homosexual men from San Francisco. Sex Transm Dis. 1983;11:59.
56. Druckman DA, Quinn TC. *Entamoeba histolytica* infection in homosexual men. In: Ravdin JI, ed. Amebiasis: Human Infection by *Entamoeba histolytica*. Edinburgh: Churchill Livingstone; 1988:563–575.
57. Peters CS, Sable R, Janda WM, et al. Prevalence of enteric parasites in homosexual patients attending an outpatient clinic. J Clin Microbiol. 1986;24:684–685.
58. Sorvillo FJ, Strassburg MA, Seidel J, et al. Amebic infections in asymptomatic homosexual men, lack of evidence of invasive disease. Am J Public Health. 1986;76:1137–1139.
59. Smith PD, Lane HC, Gill VJ, et al. Intestinal infections in patients with the acquired immunodeficiency syndrome (AIDS): Etiology and response to therapy. Ann Intern Med. 1988;108:328–333.
60. Fatkenheuer G, Arnold G, Steffen H, et al. Invasive amoebiasis in two patients with AIDS and cytomegalovirus colitis. J Clin Microbiol. 1997;35:2168–2169.
61. Blanshard C, Collins C, Francis N, Gazzard BG. Invasive amoebic colitis in AIDS patients. AIDS. 1992;6:1043–1044.
62. Reed SL, Wessel DW, Davis CE. *Entamoeba histolytica* infections and AIDS. Am J Med. 1991;90:269–271.
63. Ohnishi K, Murata M, Okuzawa E. Symptomatic amebic colitis in a Japanese homosexual AIDS patient. Intern Med. 1994;33:120–122.
64. Brown M, Reed S, Levy JA, et al. Detection of HIV-1 in *Entamoeba histolytica* without evidence of transmission to human cells. AIDS. 1991;5:93–96.
65. Istre GR, Kriess K, Hopkins RS, et al. An outbreak of amebiasis spread by colonic irrigation at a chiropractic clinic. N Engl J Med. 1982;309:339–342.
66. Shabot JM, Patterson M. Amebic liver abscess: 1966–1976. Dig Dis. 1978;23:110.
67. Abuabara SF, Barrett JA, Hau T, et al. Amebic liver abscess. Arch Surg. 1982;117:239–244.
68. Katzenstein D, Rickerson V, Braude A. New concepts of amebic liver abscess derived from hepatic imaging, serodiagnosis, and hepatic enzymes in 67 consecutive cases in San Diego. Medicine (Baltimore). 1982;61:237–246.
69. Thompson JE Jr, Forlenza S, Verma R. Amebic liver abscess: A therapeutic approach. Rev Infect Dis. 1985;7:171–179.
70. Barnes PF, DeCock KM, Reynolds TN, et al. A comparison of amebic and pyogenic abscess of the liver. Medicine (Baltimore). 1987;66:472–483.
71. Thompson JE Jr, Glasser AJ. Amebic abscess of the liver. Diagnostic features. J Clin Gastroenterol. 1986;8:550–554.
72. Pearson RD, Hewlett EL. Amebiasis in travelers. In: Ravdin JI, ed. Amebiasis: Human Infection by *Entamoeba histolytica*. New York: Churchill Livingstone; 1988:556–562.
73. Pehrson PO. Amoebiasis in a non-endemic country. Scand J Infect Dis. 1983;15:207–214.
74. Merson MH, Morris GK, Sack DA, et al. Traveler's diarrhea in Mexico: A prospective study. N Engl J Med. 1976;294:1299.
75. Lewis EA, Antia AU. Amoebic colitis: Review of 295 cases. Trans R Soc Trop Med Hyg. 1969;63:633–638.
76. Fuchs G, Ruiz Palacios G, Pickering LK. Amebiasis in the pediatric population. In: Ravdin JI, ed. Amebiasis: Human Infection by *Entamoeba histolytica*. New York: Churchill Livingstone; 1988:594–613.
77. Wanke C, Butler T, Islam M. Epidemiologic and clinical features of invasive amebiasis in Bangladesh: A case-control comparison with other diarrheal diseases and postmortem findings. Am J Trop Med Hyg. 1988;38:335–341.
78. Brandt H, Perez Tamayo R. Pathology of human amebiasis. Hum Pathol. 1970;1:351–385.
79. Griffin JL, Juniper K Jr. Ultrastructure of *Entamoeba histolytica* from human amebic dysentery. Arch Pathol. 1971;91:271–280.
80. Pittman FE, El Hashimi WK, Pittman JC. Studies of human amebiasis. II. Light and electromicroscopic observations of colonic mucosa and exudate in acute amebic colitis. Gastroenterology. 1973;65:588–603.
81. Takeuchi A, Phillips BP. Electron microscopic studies of experimental *Entamoeba histolytica* infection in the guinea pig. I. Penetration of the intestinal epithelium by trophozoites. Am J Trop Med Hyg. 1975;24:34–48.
82. Prathap K, Gilman R. The histopathology of acute intestinal amebiasis. Am J Pathol. 1970;60:229–239.
83. Chatgidakis CB. The pathology of hepatic amoebiasis as seen on the Witwatersrand. S Afr J Clin Sci. 1953;4:230.
84. Guerrant RL, Brush J, Ravdin JI, et al. Interaction between *Entamoeba histolytica* and human polymorphonuclear neutrophils. J Infect Dis. 1981;143:83–93.
85. Ravdin JI, Murphy CF, Salata RA, et al. The *N*-acetyl-D-galactosamine–inhibitable adherence lectin of *Entamoeba histolytica*. I. Partial purification and relation to amoebic virulence *in vitro*. J Infect Dis. 1985;151:804–15.
86. Tsutsumi V, Mena-Lopez R, Anaya-Velazquez F, et al. Cellular basis of experimental amebic liver abscess formation. Am J Pathol. 1984;117:81–91.
87. Salata RA, Ravdin JI. The interaction of human neutrophils and *Entamoeba histolytica* increases cytopathogenicity for liver cell monolayers. J Infect Dis. 1986;154:19–26.
88. Seydel KB, Zhang T, Stanley JR. Neutrophils play a critical role in early resistance to amebic liver abscesses in severe combined immunodeficient mice. Infect Immun. 1997;65:3951–3953.
89. Joyce MP, Ravdin JI. Pathology of human amebiasis. In: Ravdin JI, ed. Amebiasis: Human Infection by *Entamoeba histolytica*. New York: Churchill Livingstone; 1988:129–146.
90. Aikat BK, Bhusnurmath SR, Pal AK, et al. The pathology and pathogenesis of fatal hepatic amoebiasis: A study based on 79 autopsy cases. Trans R Soc Trop Med Hyg. 1979;73:188–192.
91. Gulati PD, Gupta DN, Chuttani HK. Amoebic liver abscess and disturbances of portal circulation. Am J Med. 1967;45:852–854.
92. Tandon BN, Tandon HD, Puri BK. An electron microscopic study of liver in hepatomegaly presumably caused by amebiasis. Exp Mol Pathol. 1975;22:118.
93. Diamond LS, Harlow DR, Cunnick CC. A new medium for the axenic cultivation of *Entamoeba histolytica* and other *Entamoeba*. Trans R Soc Trop Med Hyg. 1978;72:431–432.
94. Clark CG. Axenic cultivation of *Entamoeba dispar* Brumpt 1925, *Entamoeba insolita* Geiman and Wichterman 1937 and *Entamoeba ranarum* Grassi 1879. J Eukaryot Microbiol. 1995;42:590–593.
95. Ravdin JI, Guerrant RL. Role of adherence in cytopathogenic mechanisms of *Entamoeba histolytica*. J Clin Invest. 1981;68:1305–1313.
96. Petri WA, Smith RD, Schlesinger PH, et al. Isolation of the galactose-binding lectin which mediates the in vitro adherence of *Entamoeba histolytica*. J Clin Invset. 1987;80:1238–1244.
97. Chadee K, Petri WA, Innes DJ, et al. Rat and human colonic mucins bind to and inhibit the adherence of lectin of *Entamoeba histolytica*. J Clin Invest. 1987;80:1245–1254.
98. Ravdin JI, John JE, Johnston LI, et al. Adherence of *Entamoeba histolytica* trophozoites to rat and human colonic mucosa. Infect Immun. 1985;48:292–297.
99. Salata RA, Pearson RD, Ravdin JI. Interaction of human leukocytes with *Entamoeba histolytica*: Killing of virulent amebae by the activated macrophage. J Clin Invest. 1985;76:491–499.
100. Kain KC, Ravdin JI. Galactose-specific adhesion mechanisms of *Entamoeba histolytica*: Model for study of enteric pathogens. Methods Enzymol. 1995;253:424–439.
101. Ravdin JI, Petri WA, Murphy CF, et al. Production of mouse monoclonal antibodies which inhibit in vitro adherence of *Entamoeba histolytica* trophozoites. Infect Immun. 1986;53:1–5.
102. Petri WA Jr, Chapman MD, Snodgrass T, et al. Subunit structure of the galactose and *N*-acetyl-D-galactosamine–inhibitable adherence lectin of *Entamoeba histolytica*. J Biol Chem. 1989;264:3007–3012.
103. Ramakrishnan G, Ragland BD, Purdy JE, Mann BJ. Physical mapping and expression of gene families encoding the *N*-acetyl-D-galactosamine adherence lectin of *Entamoeba histolytica*. Mol Microbiol. 1996;19:91–100.
104. Tannich E, Ebert F, Horstmann RD. Primary structure of the 170-kDa surface lectin of pathogenic *Entamoeba histolytica*. Proc Natl Acad Sci U S A. 1991;88:1849–1853.
105. Mann BJ, Torian BE, Vedvick TS, et al. Sequence of a cysteine-rich galactose-specific lectin of *Entamoeba histolytica*. Proc Natl Acad Sci U S A. 1991;88:3248–3252.
106. Singh U, Rogers JB, Mann BJ, Petri WA. Transcription initiation is controlled by three core promoter elements in the *hgl5* gene of the protozoan parasite *Entamoeba histolytica*. Proc Natl Acad Sci U S A. 1997;94:8812–8817.

107. McCoy JJ, Mann BJ, Vedvick T, et al. Structural analysis of the light subunit of the *Entamoeba histolytica* galactose-specific lectin. J Biol Chem. 1993;24:223–231.
108. Petri WA, Jackson TFHG, Gathiram V, et al. Pathogenic and nonpathogenic strains of *Entamoeba histolytica* can be differentiated by monoclonal antibodies to the galactose-specific lectin. Infect Immun. 1990;58:1802–1806.
109. Braga LL, Ninomiya H, McCoy JJ, et al. Inhibition of the complement membrane attack complex by the galactose-specific adhesion of *Entamoeba histolytica.* J Clin Invest. 1992;90:1131–1137.
110. Ravdin JI, Croft BY, Guerrant RL. Cytopathogenic mechanisms of *Entamoeba histolytica.* J Exp Med. 1980;152:377–390.
111. Ravdin JI, Moreau F, Sullivan JA, et al. The relationship of free intracellular calcium ions to the cytolytic activity of *Entamoeba histolytica.* Infect Immun. 1988;56:1505–1512.
112. Ravdin JI, Murphy CF, Guerrant RL, et al. Effect of calcium and phospholipase A antagonists on the cytopathogenicity of *Entamoeba histolytica.* J Infect Dis. 1985;152:542–549.
113. Long-Krug SA, Hysmith RM, Fischer KJ, et al. The phospholipase A enzymes of *Entamoeba histolytica:* Description and subcellular localization. J Infect Dis. 1985;152:536–541.
114. Ravdin JI, Schlesinger PH, Murphy CF, et al. Acid intracellular vesicles and the cytolysis of mammalian target cells by *Entamoeba histolytica* trophozoites. J Protozool. 1986;33:478–486.
115. Yadava N., Chandok MR., Prasad J., Bhattacharya S., Sopory SK, Bhattacharya A. Characterization of EhCaBP, a calcium-building protein of *Entamoeba histolytica* and its binding proteins. Mol Biochem Parasitol. 1997;84:69–82.
116. Gopal B, Swaminathan CP, Bhattacharya S, et al. Thermondynamics of metal ion binding and denaturation of a calcium binding protein from *Entamoeba histolytica*. Biochemistry. 1997;36:10,910–10,916.
117. Ghosh SK, Samuelson J. Involvement of p21^{racA}, phosphoinositide 3-kinase, and vacuolar ATPase in phagocytosis of bacteria and erythrocytes by *Entamoeba histolytica*: Suggestive evidence for coincidental evolution of amebic invasiveness. Infect Immun. 1997;65:4243–4249.
118. Weikel CS, Murphy CF, Orozco ME, et al. Phorbol esters specifically enhance the cytolytic activity of *Entamoeba histolytica.* Infect Immun. 1988;56:1485–1491.
119. Leippe M, Tannich E, Nickel R, et al. Primary and secondary structure of the pore-forming peptide of pathogenic *Entamoeba histolytica.* EMBO J. 1992;11:3501–3506.
120. Leippe M. Amoebapores. Parasitol Today. 1997;13(5):178–183.
121. Leippe M, et al. Comparison of pore-forming peptides from pathogenic and nonpathogenic *Entamoeba histolytica*. Mol Biol Parasitol. 1997;59:101–110.
122. Berninghausen O, Leippe M. Necrosis versus apoptosis as the mechanism of target cell death induced by *Entamoeba histolytica*. Infect Immun. 1997;65:3615–3621.
123. Que X, Reed SL. The role of extracellular cysteine proteinases in pathogenesis of *Entamoeba histolytica* invasion. Parasitol Today. 1997;13:190–194.
124. Kelsall BL, Ravdin JI. Proteolytic degradation of human IgA by *Entamoeba histolytica.* J Infect Dis. 1993;168:1319–1322.
125. Tran VQ, Herdman DS, Torian BE, Reed SL. The neutral cysteine proteinase of *Entamoeba histolytica* degrades IgG and prevents its binding. J Infect Dis. 1998;177:508–511.
126. Reed SL, Gigli I. Lysis of complement-sensitive *Entamoeba histolytica* by activated terminal complement components. J Clin Invest. 1990;86:1815–1822.
127. Reed SL, Keene WE, McKerrow JH. Thiol proteinase expression and pathogenicity of *Entamoeba histolytica.* J Clin Microbiol. 1989;27:2772–2777.
128. Reed S, Bouvier J, Pollack AS, et al. Cloning of a virulence factor of *Entamoeba histolytica.* J Clin Invest. 1993;91:1532–1540.
129. Werries E, Nebinger P, Franz A. Degradation of biogene oligosaccharides by beta-*N*-acetylglucosaminidase secreted by *Entamoeba histolytica.* Mol Biochem Parasitol. 1983;7:127–140.
130. Udezulu IA, Leitch GJ. A membrane-associated neuraminidase in *Entamoeba histolytica* trophozoites. Infect Immun. 1987;55:181–186.
131. Salata RA, Ahmed P, Ravdin JI. *Entamoeba histolytica* contains a chemoattractant for human polymorphonuclear neutrophils. J Parasitol. 1989;75:644–646.
132. DeLeon A. Prognostico tardio en el absceso hepatico amibiano. Arch Invest Med (Mex). 1970;1(Suppl 1):205–206.
133. Petri WA, Joyce MP, Broman J, et al. Recognition of the galactose- or *N*-acetyl-galactosamine–binding lectin of *Entamoeba histolytica* by human immune sera. Infect Immun. 1987;55:2327–2331.
134. Joyce MP, Ravdin JI. Antigens of *Entamoeba histolytica* recognized by immune sera from liver abscess patients. Am J Trop Med Hyg. 1988;38:74–80.
135. Soong CJG, Kain KC, Abd-Alla M, Jackson TFHG, Ravdin JI. A recombinant cysteine-rich section of the *Entamoeba histolytica* galactose-inhibitable adherence lectin is efficacious as a subunit vaccine in the gerbil model of amebic liver abscess. J Infect Dis. 1995;171:645–651.
136. Abou-El-Magd I, Soong CG, El-Hawey AM, Ravdin JI. Humoral and mucosal IgA antibody response to a recombinant 52-kDa cysteine-rich portion of the *Entamoeba histolytica* galactose-inhibitable lectin correlates with detection of native 170-kDa lectin antigen in serum of patients with amebic colitis. J Infect Dis. 1996;174:157–162.
137. Abd-Alla M, El-Hawey AM, Ravdin JI. Use of an enzyme-linked immunosorbent assay to detect anti-adherence protein antibodies in sera of patients with invasive amebiasis in Cairo, Egypt. Am J Trop Med Hyg. 1992;47:800–804.
138. Torian BE, Flores BM, Stroeher VL, et al. cDNA sequence analysis of a 28 kDa cysteine-rich surface antigen of pathogenic *Entamoeba histolytica.* Proc Natl Acad Sci U S A. 1990;87:6358–6362.
139. Edman U, Meraz MA, Agabian N, et al. Characterization of an immunodominant variable surface antigen from pathogenic and nonpathogenic *E histolytica.* J Exp Med. 1990;172:879–888.
140. Stanley SL Jr, Becker A, Kunz-Jenkins C, et al. Cloning and expression of a membrane antigen of *Entamoeba histolytica* possessing multiple tandem repeats. Proc Natl Acad Sci U S A. 1990;87:4976–4980.
141. Stanley SL Jr, Tian K, Koester JP, Li E. The serine-rich *Entamoeba histolytica* protein is a phosphorylated membrane protein containing *O*-linked terminal *N*-acetylglucosamine residues. J Biol Chem. 1995;270:4121–4126.
142. Mai Z, Samuelson J. A new gene family (ariel) encodes asparagine-rich *Entamoeba histolytica* antigens, which resemble the amebic vaccine candidate serine-rich *E. histolytica* protein. Infect Immun. 1998;66:353–355.
143. Ortiz-Ortiz L, Capin R, Capin NR, et al. Activation of the alternative pathway of complement by *Entamoeba histolytica.* Clin Exp Immunol. 1978;34:10–18.
144. Reed SL, Sargeaunt PG, Braude AI. Resistance to lysis by human serum of pathogenic *Entamoeba histolytica.* Trans R Soc Trop Med Hyg. 1983;77:248–253.
145. Calderon J, Tovar R. Loss of susceptibility to complement lysis in *Entamoeba histolytica* HM1 by treatment with human serum. Immunology. 1986;58:467–471.
146. Grundy MS, Cartwright TL, Lundin L, et al. Antibodies against *Entamoeba histolytica* in human milk and serum in Kenya. J Clin Microbiol. 1983;17:753–758.
147. Islam A, Stoll BJ, Ljungstrom I, et al. The prevalence of *Entamoeba histolytica* in lactating women and in their infants in Bangladesh. Trans R Soc Trop Med Hyg. 1988;82:99–103.
148. Carrero JC, Diaz MY, Viveros M, et al. Human secretory immunoglobulin A anti-*Entamoeba histolytica* antibodies inhibit adherence of amebae to MDCK cells. Infect Immun. 1994;62:764–767.
149. Kelsall BL, Jackson TFHG, Gathiram V, et al. Secretory immunoglobulin A antibodies to the galactose-inhibitable adherence protein in the saliva of patients with amebic liver disease. Am J Trop Med Hyg. 1994;4:454–459.
150. Beving DE, Soong CJ, Ravdin JI. 1996. Oral immunization with a recombinant cysteine-rich section of the *Entamoeba histolytica* galactose-inhibitable lectin elicits an intestinal secretory immunoglobulin A response that has in vitro adherence inhibition activity. Infect Immun. 64;4:1473–1476.
151. Salata RA, Murray HW, Rubin BY, et al. The role of gamma interferon in the generation of human macrophages and T lymphocytes cytotoxic for *Entamoeba histolytica.* Am J Trop Med Hyg. 1987;37:72–78.
152. Campbell D, Chadee K. Survival strategies of *Entabmoeba histolytica*: Modulation of cell-mediated immune responses. Parasitol Today. 1997;13:184–190.
153. Yu Y, Chadee K. *Entamoeba histolytica* stimulates interleukin 8 from human colonic epithelial cells without parasite-enterocyte contact. Gastroenterology. 1997;112:1536–1547.
154. Seydel KB, Li E, Swanson PE, Stanley SL Jr. Human intestinal epithelial cells produce proinflammatory cytokines in response to infection in a SCID mouse-human intestinal xenograft model of amebiasis. Infect Immun. 1997;65:1631–1639.
155. Salata RA, Martinez-Palomo A, Murphy CF, et al. Patients treated for amebic liver abscess develop a cell-mediated immune response effective *in vitro* against *Entamoeba histolytica*. J Immunol. 1986;136:2633–2639.
156. Schain DS, Salata RA, Ravdin JI. Human T-lymphocyte proliferation, lymphokine production, and amebicidal activity elicited by the galactose-inhibitable adherence protein of *Entamoeba histolytica.* Infect Immun. 1992;60:2143–2146.
157. Salata RA, Martinez-Palomo A, Conales L, et al. Immune sera suppresses the antigen specific proliferative response in T lymphocytes from patients cured of amebic liver abscess. Infect Immun. 1990;58:3941–3946.
158. Kanani SR, Knight R. Relapsing amoebic colitis of 12 years' standing exacerbated by corticosteroids. BMJ. 1969;2:613–614.
159. Chadee K, Meerovitch E. *Entamoeba histolytica:* Early progressive pathology in the cecum of the gerbil (*Meriones unguiculatus*). Am J Trop Med Hyg. 1985;34:283–291.
160. Belley A, Keller K, Grove J, Chadee K. Interaction of LS174T human colon cancer cell mucins with *Entamoeba histolytica*: An *in vitro* model for colonic disease. Gastroenterology. 1996;111:1484–1492.
161. Chadee K, Innes DJ, Ravdin JI. Mucin and nonmucin secretagogue activity of *Entamoeba histolytica* and cholera toxin in rat colon. Gastroenterology. 1991;100:986–997.
162. Petri WA Jr, Ravdin JI. Protection of gerbils from amebic liver abscess by immunization with the galactose-specific adherence lectin of *Entamoeba histolytica.* Infect Immun. 1991;59:97–101.
163. Mann BJ, Burkholder BV, Lockhart LA. Protection in a gerbil model of amebiasis by oral immunization with *Salmonella* by expressing the galactose/*N*-acetyl D-galactosamine inhibitable lectin of *Entabmoeba histolytica*. Vaccine. 1997;15:659–663.
164. Lotter H, Zhang T, Seydel KB, et al. Identification of an epitope on the *Entamoeba histolytica* 170-kD lectin conferring antibody-mediated protection against invasive amebiasis. J Exp Med. 1997;185:1793–1801.
165. Marinets A, Zhang T, Guillen N, et al. Protection against invasive amebiasis by a single monoclonal antibody directed against a lipophosphoglycan antigen localized on the surface of *Entamoeba histolytica*. J Exp Med. 1997;186:1557–1565.
166. Nickel R, Tannich E. Transfection and transient expression of chloramphenicol acetyltransferase in the protozoan parasite *Entamoeba histolytica*. Proc Natl Acad Sci U S A. 1994;91:7095–7098.
167. Ramakrishnan G, Vines RR, Mann BJ, Petri WA Jr. A tetracycline-inducible gene expression system in *Entamoeba histolytica*. Mol Biochem Parasitol. 1996;84:93–100.

168. Gilchrist CA, Mann BJ, Petri WA Jr. Control of ferredoxin and Gal/GalNAc lectin gene expression in *Entamoeba histolytica* by a *cis*-acting DNA sequence. Infect Immun. 1998;66:2383–2386.
169. Moshitch-Moshkovitch S, Stolarsky T, Mirelman D, Alon RN. Stable episomal transfection and gene expression in *Entamoeba dispar*. Mol Biol Parasit. 1996;83:257–261.
170. Ravdin JI. Intestinal disease caused by *Entamoeba histolytica*. In: Ravdin JI, ed. Amebiasis: Human Infection by *Entamoeba histolytica*. New York: Churchill Livingstone; 1988:495–510.
171. Adams EB, MacLeod IN. Invasive amebiasis. I. Amebic dysentery and its complications. Medicine (Baltimore). 1977;56:315–323.
172. Juniper K. Parasitic diseases of the intestinal tract. In: Paulson M, ed. Gastroenterologic Medicine. Philadelphia: Lea & Febiger; 1969:172.
173. Jammal MA, Cox K, Ruebner B. Amebiasis presenting as rectal bleeding without diarrhea in childhood. J Pediatr Gastroenterol Nutr. 1985;4:294–296.
174. Merritt TJ, Coughlin E, Thomas DW, et al. Spectrum of amebiasis in children. Am J Dis Child. 1982;136:785.
175. Speelman P, McGlaughlin R, Kabir I, et al. Differential clinical features and stool findings in shigellosis and amoebic dysentery. Trans R Soc Trop Med Hyg. 1987;81:549–551.
176. Takahashi T, Gamboa-Dominguez A, Gomez-Mendez TJM, et al. Fulminant amebic colitis. Analysis of 55 cases. Dis Colon Rectum. 1997;40:1362–1367.
177. Monga NK, Sood S, Kaushik SP, et al. Amebic peritonitis. Am J Gastroenterol. 1976;67:366–373.
178. El-Hennawy M, Abd-Rabbo H. Hazards of cortisone therapy in hepatic amoebiasis. J Trop Med Hyg. 1978;81:71–73.
179. Haider Z, Rasul A. Chronic non-dysenteric intestinal amoebiasis. A review of 159 cases. J Pakistan Med Assoc. 1975;25:75–78.
180. Ruiz-Moreno F. Perianal skin amebiasis. Dis Colon Rectum. 1967;10:65.
181. Adams EB, MacLeod IN. Invasive amebiasis. II. Amebic liver abscess and its complications. Medicine (Baltimore). 1977;56:325–334.
182. Knobloch J, Mannweiler E. Development and persistence of antibodies to *Entamoeba histolytica* in patients with amebic liver abscess: Analysis of 216 cases. Am J Trop Med Hyg. 1983;32:727–732.
183. Conter RL, Pitt HA, Tompkins RK, et al. Differentiation of pyogenic from amebic hepatic abscesses. Surg Gynecol Obstet. 1986;162:114–120.
184. Greenstein AJ, Barth J, Dicker A, et al. Amebic liver abscess: A study of 11 cases compared with a series of 38 patients with pyogenic liver abscess. Am J Gastroenterol. 1985;80:472–478.
185. Boom RA, Fonseca L, Yãnez C, et al. Differential diagnosis between amoebic liver abscess and acute cholecystitis. J Med Syst. 1983;7:205–212.
186. Overbosch D, Stuiver PC, van der Kaay JH. Hepatic amoebiasis: Current concepts and a report of 25 cases in the Netherlands. Acta Leiden. 1983;51:3–17.
187. Irusen EM, Jackson TFGH, Simjee AE. Asymptomatic intestinal colonization by pathogenic *Entamoeba histolytica* in amebic liver abscess: Prevalence, response to therapy and pathogenic potential. Clin Infect Dis. 1992;14:889–893.
188. Rhode FC, Prieto O, Riveros O. Thoracic complications of amoebic liver abscess. Br J Dis Chest. 1979;73:302.
189. Adeyemo AO, Aderounmu A. Intrathoracic complications of amoebic liver abscess. J R Soc Med. 1984;77:17–20.
190. Kubitschek KR, Peters J, Nickeson D, et al. Amebiasis presenting as pleuropulmonary disease. West J Med. 1985;142:203–207.
191. Nwafo DC, Egbue MO. Intrathoracic manifestations of amoebiasis. Ann R Coll Surg Engl. 1981;63:126–128.
192. Eggleston FC, Handa AK, Verghese M. Amebic peritonitis secondary to amebic liver abscess. Surgery. 1982;91:46–48.
193. Wilmot AJ. Clinical Amebiasis. Oxford: Blackwell Scientific; 1962.
194. Orbison JA, Reeves N, Leedham CL, et al. Amebic brain abscess: Review of the literature and report of five additional cases. Medicine (Baltimore). 1951;30:247–282.
195. Becker GL Jr, Knep S, Lance KP, et al. Amebic abscess of the brain. Neurosurgery. 1980;6:192–194.
196. Schmutzhard E, Mayr U, Rumpl E, et al. Secondary cerebral amebiasis due to infection with *Entamoeba histolytica:* A case report with computer tomographic findings. Eur Neurol. 1986;25:161–165.
197. Banerjee AK, Bhatnagar RK, Bhusnurmath SR. Secondary cerebral amebiasis. Trop Geogr Med. 1983;35:333–336.
198. Grisby W. Surgical treatment of amebiasis. Surg Gynecol Obstet. 1969;128:609–627.
199. Heinz KPW. Amoebic infection of the female genital tract: A report of three cases. S Afr Med J. 1973;47:1795.
200. Mylius RE, Ten Seldam RE. Venereal infection by *Entamoeba histolytica* in a New Guinea native couple. Trop Geogr Med. 1962;14:20.
201. O'Leary RK, Posen J. Amoebiasis of the penis. S Afr Med J. 1984;65:113.
202. Purpon I, Jiminez D, Engelking RL. Amebiasis of the penis. J Urol. 1967;98:372.
203. Young KH, Ballock S, Melvin DM, et al. Ethyl acetate as a substitute for diethylether in the ether-formalin sedimentation technique. J Clin Microbiol. 1979;10:852–853.
204. Blumencranz H, Kasen L, Romeu J, et al. The role of endoscopy in suspected amebiasis. Am J Gastroenterol. 1983;78:15–18.
205. Patterson M, Healy GR, Shabot JM. Serologic testing for amoebiasis. Gastroenterology. 1980;78:136–141.
206. Healy GR, Sumner CK. The indirect hemagglutination test for amebiasis in patients with inflammatory bowel disease. Am J Dig Dis. 1972;17:97.
207. Reed SL, Flores BM, Batzer MA, et al. Molecular and cellular characterization of the 29-kilodalton peripheral membrane protein of *Entamoeba histolytica:* Differentiation between pathogenic and nonpathogenic isolates. Infect Immun. 1992; 60:542–549.
208. Gonzalez-Ruiz A, Haque R, Rehman T, et al. A monoclonal antibody for distinction of invasive and noninvasive clinical isolates of *Entamoeba histolytica*. J Clin Microbiol. 1992;30:2807–2813.
209. Abd-Alla MD, Jackson TFGH, Gatherim V, et al. Differentiation of pathogenic from nonpathogenic *Entamoeba histolytica* infection by detection of galactose-inhibitable adherence protein antigen in sera and feces. J Clin Microbiol. 1993;31:2845–2850.
210. Haque R, Kress K, Wood S, et al. Diagnosis of pathogenic *Entamoeba histolytica* infection using a stool ELISA based on monoclonal antibodies to the galactose-specific adhesin. J Infect Dis. 1993;167:247–249.
211. Jelinek T, Peyerl G, Löscher T, Nothdurft HD. Evaluation of an antigen capture enzyme immunoassay for detection of *Entamoeba histolytica* in stool samples. Eur J Clin Microbiol Infect Dis. 1996;15:752–755.
212. Britten D, Wilson SM, McNerney R, et al. An improved colorimetric PCR-based method for detection and differentiation of *Entamoeba histolytica* and *Entamoeba dispar* in feces. J Clin Microbiol. 1997;35:1108–1111.
213. Mirelman D, Nuchamowitz Y, Stolarsky T. Comparison of use of enzyme-linked immunosorbent assay-based kits and PCR amplification of rRNA genes for simultaneous detection of *Entamoeba histolytica* and *E dispar*. J Clin Microbiol. 1997;35:2405–2407.
214. Walderich B, Müller L, Bracha R, et al. A new method for isolation and differentiation of native *Entamoeba histolytica* and *E dispar* cysts from fecal samples. Parasitol Res. 1997;83:719–721.
215. Zengzhu G, Zhengyi W, Yijun A, Hong Z. Application of polymerase chain reaction for diagnosing amebic liver abscess. Chin Med Sci J. 1996;11:100–102.
216. Ralls PW, Colletti PM, Halls JM. Imaging in hepatic amebic abscess. In: Ravdin JI, ed. Amebiasis: Human Infection by *Entamoeba histolytica*. New York: Churchill Livingstone; 1988:664–704.
217. Halvorsen RA, Korobkin M, Foster WL, et al. The variable CT appearance of hepatic abscesses. AJR. 1984;142:941–946.
218. Siddiqui JH, Gharib M, Muscat-Baron J, et al. Liver abscess in Dubai: Analysis of 29 cases and an assessment of the value of CAT scan. Trop Med Parasitol. 1985;79:281–286.
219. Elizondo G, Weissleder R, Stark DD, et al. Amebic liver abscess: Diagnosis and treatment evaluation with MR imaging. Radiology. 1987;165:795–800.
220. Ralls PW, Henley DS, Colletti PM, et al. Amebic liver abscess: MR imaging. Radiology. 1987;165:801–804.
221. Ralls PW, Barnes PF, Johnson MB, et al. Medical treatment of hepatic amebic abscess: Rare need for percutaneous drainage. Radiology. 1987;165:805–807.
222. Van Sonnenberg E, Mueller PR, Schiffman RR, et al. Intrahepatic amebic abscesses: Indications for and results of percutaneous catheter drainage. Radiology. 1985;156:631–635.
223. Sharma MP, Dasarathy S, Sushma S, Verma N. Long term follow-up of amebic liver abscess: Clinical and ultrasound patterns of resolution. Trop Gastroenterol. 1995;16:24–28.
224. Simjee A, Patel A, Gathiram V, et al. Serial ultrasound in amoebic liver abscess. Clin Radiol. 1985;36:61–68.
225. Scragg J. Amoebic liver abscess in African children. Arch Dis Child. 1960;35:171–174.
226. Abramowicz M, ed. Drugs for parasitic infections. Med Lett. 1998;40:1–12.
227. McAuley JB, Herwaldt BL, Stokes SL, et al. Diloxanide furoate for treating asymptomatic *Entamoeba histolytica* cyst passers: 14 years' experience in the United States. Clin Infect Dis. 1992;15:464–468.
228. Qureshi H, Ali A, Baqai R, Ahmed W. Efficacy of a combined diloxanide furoate–metronidazole preparation in the treatment of amoebiasis and giardiasis. J Int Med Res. 1997;25:167–170.
229. Sullam PM, Slutkin G, Gottlieb AB, et al. Paromomycin therapy of endemic amebiasis in homosexual men. Sex Transm Dis. 1986;13:151–15 5.
230. Norris SM, Ravdin JI. The pharmacology of anti-amebic drugs. In: Ravdin JI, ed. Amebiasis: Human Infection by *Entamoeba histolytica*. New York: Churchill Livingstone; 1988:734–740.
231. Bhatia S, Karnad DR, Oak JL. Randomized double-blind trial of metronidazole versus secnidazole in amebic liver abscess. Indian J Gastroenterol. 1998;17:53–54.
232. Simjee AE, Gathiram V, Jackson TFHG, et al. A comparative trial of metronidazole v tinidazole in the treatment of amoebic liver abscess. S Afr Med J. 1985;68:923–924.
233. Powell SJ. Drug trials in amoebiasis. Bull World Health Organ. 1969;40:956.
234. Lasserre R, Jaroonvesama N, Kurathong S, et al. Single-day drug treatment of amebic liver abscess. Am J Trop Med Hyg. 1983;32:723–726.
235. Samarawickrema NA, Brown DM, Upcroft JA, et al. Involvement of superoxide dismutase and pyruvate: Ferredoxin oxidoreductase in mechanisms of metronidazole resistance in *Entamoeba histolytica*. J Antimicrob Chemother. 1997;40:833–840.
236. Rajak CL, Gupta S, Jain S, et al. Percutaneous treatment of liver abscesses: Needle aspiration versus catheter drainage. Am J Rad. 1998;170:1035–1039.
237. Kapoor OP, Joshi VR. Multiple amoebic liver abscess. A study of 56 cases. J Trop Med Hyg. 1972;75:4–6.

Chapter 263

Free-Living Amebas

UPINDER SINGH
WILLIAM A. PETRI, JR.

HISTORY

Infection of humans with free-living amebas is an infrequent but often life-threatening occurrence in both normal and immunocompromised individuals. Central nervous system (CNS) invasion by *Naegleria, Acanthamoeba*, and *Balamuthia mandrillaris* (formerly known as leptomyxid amebas) has been reported in approximately 400 patients worldwide with numerous cases of *Acanthamoeba* keratitis in the medical literature.[1, 2] Distinct from other pathogenic protozoa by nature of their free-living existence, these organisms have no known insect vectors, there are no human carrier states of epidemiologic importance, and there is little relationship of poor sanitation to the spread of infection. Three distinct clinical syndromes are caused by the species of free-living amebas that infect humans (1) primary amebic meningoencephalitis, (2) granulomatous amebic encephalitis, and (3) amebic keratitis. Primary amebic meningoencephalitis is caused by *Naegleria fowleri* and occurs in healthy children and young adults who usually have been recently swimming in fresh water. The *Naegleria* amoebas gain access to the CNS by direct invasion through the nasal mucosa and the cribriform plate and cause a rapidly fatal meningoencephalitis. Granulomatous amebic encephalitis, caused by *Acanthamoeba castellanii, Acanthamoeba culbertsoni, Acanthamoeba astronyxis, Acanthamoeba palestinensis*, and *B. mandrillaris*, is a subacute opportunistic infection that spreads hematogenously from pulmonary or skin lesions to the CNS, resulting in focal neurologic deficits that progress over days to weeks to a diffuse meningoencephalitis and death. *Acanthamoeba* causes a subacute to chronic keratitis that is associated with contact lens use, with rare reports of cases occurring after radial keratotomy.[3]

ORGANISMS

N. fowleri was named after the late Malcolm Fowler of Adelaide Children's Hospital of Australia, who with R.F. Carter described the initial cases of primary amebic meningoencephalitis.[4] *N. fowleri*, also called *Naegleria aerobia* and *Naegleria invadens*, is the only recognized pathogenic species of *Naegleria*. On transfer to distilled water or a non-nutrient medium, *Naegleria* spp. have the ability to transform rapidly from the trophozoite to a flagellate form.[5] The flagellate form can spontaneously revert to the trophozoite, the reproductive stage of the protozoan. The trophozoites are 10 to 30 μm in diameter and have a clear nucleus with a prominent dense central nucleolus, and pseudopodia (Fig. 263–1). The granular cytoplasm can contain ingested red blood cells and leukocytes along with cytoplasmic organelles including rough endoplasmic reticulum and mitochondria. The trophozoites feed predominantly on bacteria and have an aerobic metabolism. Division occurs with a unique nuclear mitosis with retention of the nuclear membrane and nucleolus during karyokinesis. Encystment of the trophozoite results in a 9-μm-diameter spherical cyst with a central nucleus and a single-layered wall containing an average of two pores. The pores, which are plugged with mucus in the cyst, serve as ports for the emergence of the trophozoite during excystation.[6] *N. fowleri* is thermophilic, with the trophozoite growing well at temperatures as high as 45°C.[7]

Acanthamoeba (earlier classified as *Hartmanella*)[7] species recognized as pathogenic for humans include *A. castellanii, A. polyphaga, A. culbertsoni, A. palestinensis, A. astronyxis, A. hatchetti* and *A. rhysodes*. Other species identified to cause disease are *A. divionesis* (CNS disease in an immunocompromised host)[8] and *A. griffini* (corneal disease).[9] The life cycle of *Acanthamoeba* consists of only the trophozoite and the cyst. Trophozoites are 14 to 40 μm in diameter, contain mitochondria and a single nucleus with a prominent central nucleolus, and have distinctive slender spinelike projections of the plasma membrane (Fig. 263–2). The cysts have a double-layered wall or envelope, are 12 to 16 μm in diameter, and also may contain pores in the cyst wall. *Acanthamoeba* has aerobic metabolism and grows best 25°C to 35°C.

B. mandrillaris, formerly referred to as leptomyxid ameba, is a free-living ameba identified as a cause of meningoencephalitis in animals and humans.[10–15] The trophozoites of *B. mandrillaris* have an average size of 30 μm (range 12 to 60 μm) and are uninucleate. Cysts have a mean diameter of 15 μm (range 6 to 30 μm) and a wavy and irregular outer wall that is composed of three layers.[15] On

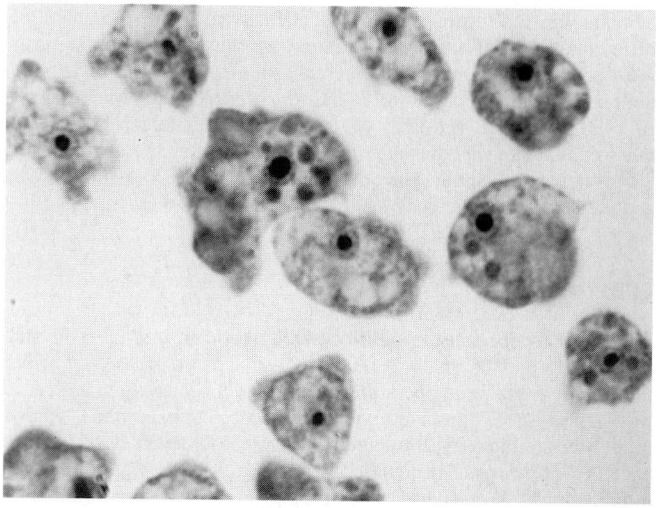

FIGURE 263–1. Trophozoites of *Naegleria fowleri* demonstrating the blunt pseudopodium or lobopodium. The characteristic nucleus contains a centrally placed dense nucleolus. (Iron-hematoxylin, ×800.) (From Martinez AJ. Free-Living Amebas: Natural History, Prevention, Diagnosis, Pathology, and Treatment of Disease. Boca Raton, Fla: CRC Press; 1985.)

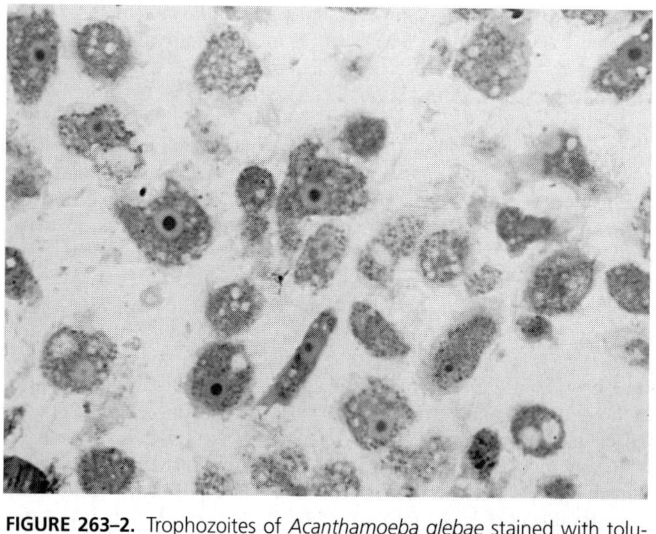

FIGURE 263–2. Trophozoites of *Acanthamoeba glebae* stained with toluidine blue, which demonstrates the round nucleolus surrounded by a nuclear halo and the granular and abundant cytoplasm (×600). (From Martinez AJ. Free-Living Amebas: Natural History, Prevention, Diagnosis, Pathology, and Treatment of Disease. Boca Raton, Fla: CRC Press; 1985.)

hematoxylin and eosin–stained specimens, the organism cannot be differentiated reliably from *Acanthamoeba*; thus, definitive diagnosis must be made using immunofluorescent staining with species-specific antibodies. The first case of *B. mandrillaris* encephalitis was reported in 1990.[11] To date, 63 cases of granulomatous amebic encephalitis due to this organism have been reported worldwide. The approximate 30 cases in the United States have included 7 cases in patients with acquired immunodeficiency syndrome (AIDS) and 8 in animals.[14]

EPIDEMIOLOGY

N. fowleri has been isolated all over the world from soil, river and lake water, and thermally polluted water.[5, 7] Pathogenic *N. fowleri* proliferate at higher temperatures, with growth occurring at temperatures up to 45°C, compared with pathogenic *Acanthamoeba*, whose growth is inhibited by temperatures above 35°C to 39°C. The presence of *N. fowleri* in fresh water is directly related to water temperature,[16] and *N. fowleri* has been frequently isolated from thermally polluted waters in temperate climates.[17] In semitropical locations such as Florida, thermal pollution of the already very warm freshwater lakes in summer and fall is less significant, with at least one *N. fowleri* per 25 ml of water frequently isolated.[16] In the winter as water temperatures drop, *Naegleria* can only be isolated from the lake bottom sediments. *Naegleria* cysts are stable up to 8 months at 4°C.[18] Wellings and colleagues estimated that there had been a billion exposures of people to *Naegleria*-contaminated fresh water with only seven cases of primary amebic meningoencephalitis in Florida over a 14-year period.[16] The factors that protect most individuals from invasive *Naegleria* infection are not understood. The presence of serum-agglutinating activity for *N. fowleri* in the majority of young adults, but not infants, tested from the southern United States indicates that subclinical infection or exposure to *Naegleria* is common.[19] Primary amebic meningoencephalitis has been reported to have occurred in the central and southern United States[20]; southern Australia; New Zealand; Europe; Africa; and Central America.[7] Clusters of cases of primary amebic meningoencephalitis with common environmental exposures have occurred.[4, 6, 7] As of 1997, approximately 179 cases of primary amebic meningoencephalitis have been reported worldwide with 81 cases in the United States.[21] The first case of CNS disease due to *N. fowleri* in an animal was reported in 1997,[22] although previous studies have demonstrated antibodies to *Naegleria* in wild mammals.[23]

Acanthamoeba spp. have also been isolated from soil, water, and air from diverse geographic locations.[7] *Acanthamoeba* spp. were cultured from pharyngeal swabs of 38 of 2289 individuals during a study of respiratory viruses in healthy families,[24] and serologic surveys have detected serum antibodies directed against *Acanthamoeba* in healthy people.[25] Despite such evidence of common exposure of the normal population to *Acanthamoeba*, granulomatous amebic encephalitis due to *Acanthamoeba* spp. occurs predominantly in debilitated or immunosuppressed individuals.[26, 27] Underlying illnesses in patients with granulomatous amebic encephalitis have included AIDS,[26, 28, 29] liver disease, diabetes mellitus, renal and bone marrow transplantation, steroid therapy, and chemotherapy.[30] *Acanthamoeba* keratitis, on the other hand, occurs in healthy people. Of the first 100 cases of amebic keratitis reported to the Centers for Disease Control and Prevention, 83% occurred in people who were contact lens wearers. Corneal infection was associated with the use of homemade saline to clean the lenses and with the wearing of lenses while swimming.[31] *Acanthamoeba* can survive in many contact lens solutions, which may result in transmission of the disease. Benzalkonium chloride–preserved saline and solutions containing thimerosal with edetate have rendered *A. polyphaga* nonviable and are recommended for cleaning and storing lenses.[32] With the advent of disposable soft contact lenses in the late 1980s, the risk of *Acanthamoeba* keratitis has not declined. The annual incidence during 1985 through 1987 was estimated at 1.65 to 2.01 cases per million contact lens wearers, and it is unclear whether the incidence has subsequently declined.[2]

B. mandrillaris, a soil inhabitant, was first reported to be isolated from water samples from the area around Tulsa, Oklahoma.[33] Water samples taken in the spring and autumn had the highest incidence of contamination with *B. mandrillaris*. The first human cases of infection with this organism were reported in 1990.[11] In contrast to CNS disease caused by *Acanthamoeba* spp., *Balamuthia* infections have been reported to occur in both immunocompetent and immunocompromised human hosts.

PATHOGENESIS AND PATHOLOGIC FINDINGS

Primary amebic meningoencephalitis occurs chiefly in healthy children and young adults who have recently swum in warm freshwater lakes or ponds. Animal models[34] and autopsy studies[4, 5, 7, 35] indicate that CNS invasion by *N. fowleri* occurs after nasal inoculation with the amebas by disruption of the olfactory mucosa. The amebas penetrate the submucosal nervous plexus and the cribriform plate and gain access to the CNS (Fig. 263–3). *N. fowleri* produces a diffuse meningoencephalitis and purulent leptomeningitis with severest involvement of the cortical gray matter. Cortical hemorrhages and edema with uncal or cerebellar herniation are seen, and the olfactory bulbs are hemorrhagic and necrotic. *Naegleria* trophozoites are found in the olfactory nerves and the adventitia and perivascular spaces of small to midsize arteries and arterioles. No amebic cysts are seen in the brain.[4, 5, 7, 35] A diffuse or focal myocarditis was present in 7 of 16 autopsies of patients with primary amebic meningoencephalitis. The inflammatory infiltrate was predominantly neutrophilic, and no amebae were seen in the myocardium. Retrospective chart review of the patients with primary amebic meningoencephali-

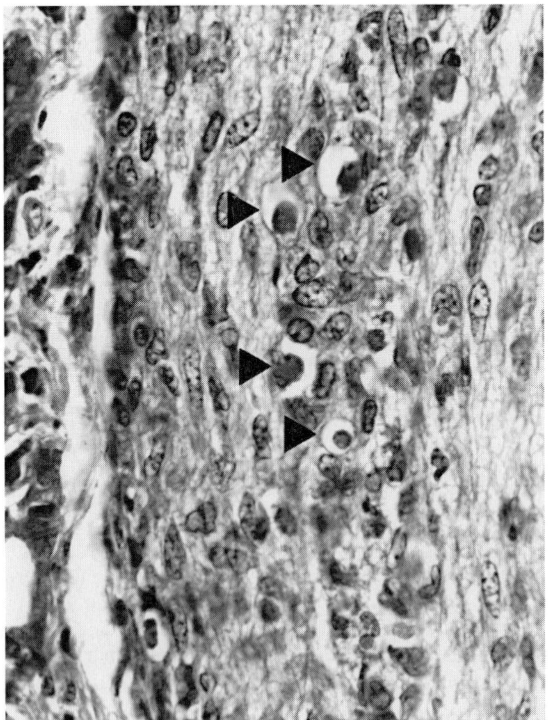

FIGURE 263–3. *Naegleria fowleri* trophozoites *(arrowheads)* within unmyelinated submucosal olfactory nerve bundles of a 27-year-old man who swam in fresh water 4 days before developing primary amebic meningoencephalitis. (H&E, ×500.) (From Martinez AJ. Free-Living Amebas: Natural History, Prevention, Diagnosis, Pathology, and Treatment of Disease. Boca Raton, Fla: CRC Press; 1985.)

tis and myocarditis did not reveal evidence of congestive heart failure or arrhythmias in the patients with myocarditis.[36] When looked for, *Naegleria* trophozoites have been identified in the cerebrospinal fluid (CSF) of patients with acute meningoencephalitis.[7, 37] The tissue necrosis elicited by *Naegleria* is speculated to be mediated in part by a secreted cysteine protease.[38] Interestingly, *Naegleria gruberi*, a nonpathogenic *Naegleria* that is not thermotolerant above 30°C, expresses a similar protease that is active in vitro at 37°C.[38]

Granulomatous amebic encephalitis with *Acanthamoeba* spp. occurs in immunocompromised patients, who present with focal neurologic deficits. On macroscopic examinations, the leptomeninges are spared except when directly overlying areas of cortical involvement. Moderate to severe cerebral edema occurs, with bilateral uncal or cerebellar tonsillar herniations occasionally seen. Necrotizing granulomatous lesions containing perivascular trophozoites and cysts are most frequently located in the cerebellum, midbrain, and brain stem. Multinucleated giant cells are occasionally present within the granulomas.[7] A granulomatous tissue reaction may not be present in some immunocompromised individuals with *Acanthamoeba* CNS infection.[13] The preferential location of amebic trophozoites and cysts perivascularly suggests a hematogenous dissemination of *Acanthamoeba* to the CNS. Hematogenous spread in patients with granulomatous amebic encephalitis is supported by identification of *Acanthamoeba* in the skin (Fig. 263–4), lung, adrenals, and lymph nodes. Amebic skin lesions have been present for weeks to months before the development of granulomatous amebic encephalitis[29, 39]; amebic sinusitis,[40] pneumonitis,[30] or skin infection may be sites of primary human infection that lead to hematogenous dissemination.[7]

Acanthamoeba keratitis is a corneal infection associated with minor corneal trauma and the use of soft contact lenses in otherwise healthy people. The histologic appearance of corneal infection is similar to *Acanthamoeba* infections of other organs. Both amebic cysts and trophozoites are found within the cornea. There is an acute or mixed inflammatory infiltrate that may contain epithelial and giant cells. However, amebae have also been found in tissue in the absence of an inflammatory infiltrate. Corneal neovascularization occurs to a variable extent.[41, 42] Involvement of the posterior chamber of the eye is a rare complication of amebic keratitis but has been observed in enucleation specimens. Sterile inflammation of the posterior segment occurs without isolation or visualization of amebic cysts or trophozoites.[41] The corneal ringlike infiltrate seen with keratitis caused by *Acanthamoeba* and occasionally with gram-negative bacterial, herpes simplex, or fungal causes appears to be due to the neutrophil chemoattractant effect of antigen-antibody complexes in the cornea.[41, 42]

Significant progress has been made toward understanding the molecular basis of pathogenesis in *Acanthamoeba* infections, and molecular techniques are being utilized to differentiate pathogenic from nonpathogenic *Acanthamoeba*.[43] The toxic effect of *Acanthamoeba* in corneal cells is attributed to the release of a variety of cytolytic factors that function by increasing free intracellular calcium levels.[44, 45] Studies have shown that *Acanthamoeba* keratitis does not stimulate a delayed-type hypersensitivity response or a serum immunoglobulin G (IgG) response perhaps due to the lack of resident antigen-presenting cells in the cornea.[46] It has long been appreciated that *Legionella* spp. can survive intracellularly within *Acanthamoeba*. Other intracellular bacteria are also being described with *Acanthamoeba* such as *Chlamydia* spp.,[47, 48] *Pseudomonas aeruginosa*,[49] and *Burkholderia pickettii*.[50] Models have been developed that can study the intracellular growth of *Legionella* in *Acanthamoeba*[51] as well as an immortalized hamster corneal epithelial cell line that is susceptible to *Acanthamoeba* infection.[52]

B. mandrillaris causes a subacute or chronic granulomatous meningoencephalitis clinically similar to that caused by *Acanthamoeba* spp. The CNS lesions demonstrate a chronic inflammatory process involving lymphocytes, monocytes, plasma cells, and giant cells.[53] Granulomas can be seen in both immunocompetent and immunocompromised patients with *B. mandrillaris* infection; however, they are often absent.[53] Cysts and trophozoites of *B. mandrillaris* are seen in a

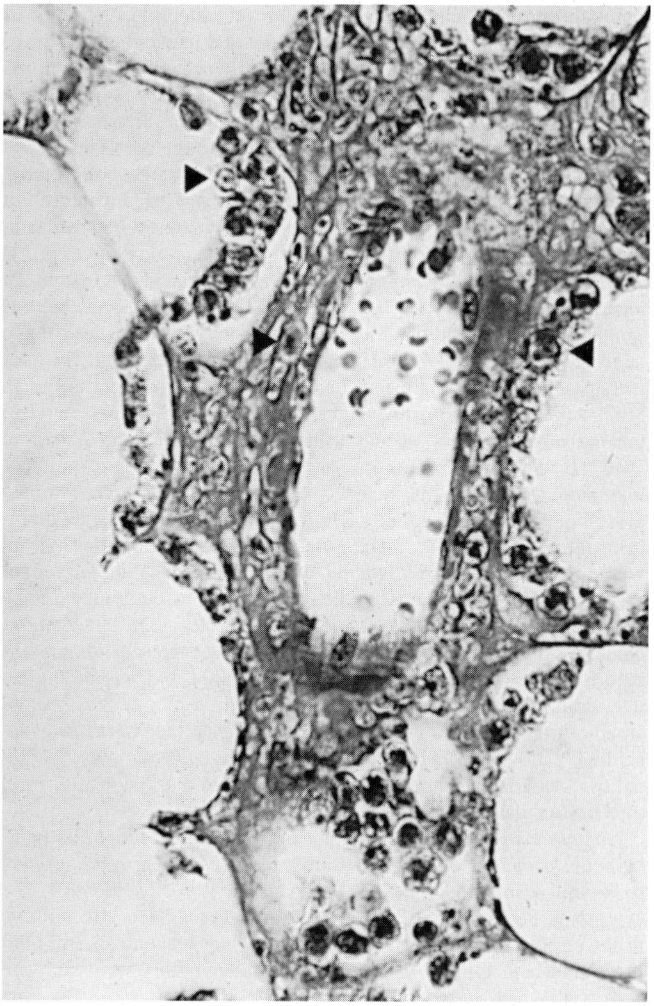

FIGURE 263–4. Skin biopsy from a skin nodule of a patient with granulomatous amebic encephalitis demonstrating perivascular amebic trophozoites *(arrowheads)*. (H&E, ×250.) (From Martinez AJ. Free-Living Amebas: Natural History, Prevention, Diagnosis, Pathology, and Treatment of Disease. Boca Raton, Fla: CRC Press; 1985.)

perivascular pattern and are associated with angiitis and hemorrhagic necrosis of the underlying meninges and brain tissue. The angiotrophic location as well as the fact that the organism has been isolated from other tissues (skin,[54] adrenals,[55] and kidneys[12]) suggests that it may be spread in a hematogenous manner. An animal model of encephalitis with *B. mandrillaris* has been developed[56] and may be useful in studying the pathogenesis of this infection. As is the case in humans, both immunocompetent and immunocompromised mice are susceptible to intranasal challenge with *B. mandrillaris*.[56]

CLINICAL MANIFESTATIONS

Primary amebic meningoencephalitis usually occurs in children and young adults who have previously been in excellent health. Most often the patients have been swimming in warm fresh water or have had other exposure to water within 1 week. Rarely will there be no history of water exposure: one episode of primary amebic meningoencephalitis in an arid region of Nigeria was thought to be due to inhalation of *Naegleria* cysts.[57] The onset of symptoms occurs on average 2 to 5 days after the last exposure to fresh water, but apparent incubation periods of up to 2 weeks have been reported. Very early in the illness, the patient may notice changes in taste or smell followed by an abrupt onset of fever, anorexia, nausea, and vomiting. On initial presentation, headache and meningismus is present in 86 to 100% of patients and mental status changes in two thirds of patients. Patients rapidly progress to coma and death within 1 week after the onset of illness, usually without ever developing focal neurologic signs.[7] Spinal cord involvement has been seen once,[58] and one AIDS patient with *Naegleria* CNS infection has been reported.[59] Myocarditis has been present in almost half of autopsied patients, but congestive heart failure or arrhythmias are uncommon before death.

Granulomatous amebic encephalitis with *Acanthamoeba* spp. is an illness of the immunocompromised and debilitated.[26, 27] In contrast to primary amebic meningoencephalitis, granulomatous amebic encephalitis has an insidious onset and presents with focal neurologic deficits. Presenting signs and symptoms of 15 patients with granulomatous amebic encephalitis included mental status abnormalities in 86%; seizures in 66%; fever, headache, and hemiparesis in 53%; meningismus in 40%; visual disturbances in 26%; and ataxia in 20%.[60] Underlying illnesses or conditions in patients with granulomatous amebic encephalitis included AIDS, liver disease, renal transplantation, neoplasm, steroid therapy, chemotherapy, diabetes mellitus, and pregnancy.[26, 28–30] The duration of CNS illness until death was 7 to 120 days (average: 39 days). The incubation period of granulomatous amebic encephalitis is difficult to determine as the disease is not associated with freshwater exposure, but *Acanthamoeba* skin ulcers and lesions have often been present for months before the onset of CNS disease.[7, 40] The skin lesions can be ulcerative, nodular, or subcutaneous abscesses and on biopsy demonstrate amebic granulomas.[40] Other clinical syndromes that have been described with *Acanthamoeba* infection include pneumonitis,[30] adrenalitis,[30] leukocytoclastic vasculitis,[61] osteomyelitis,[62] sinusitis,[41] and infection of a peptic ulcer.[63]

Acanthamoeba keratitis is frequently misdiagnosed initially as herpetic, bacterial, or fungal keratitis, resulting in an average delay to definitive treatment ranging from 11 days to 15 months. The symptoms begin with a foreign-body sensation in the affected eye followed by severe pain, photophobia, tearing, blepharospasm, conjunctivitis, and blurred vision. Periods of temporary remission are common, which lead to further delays in diagnosis since they are interpreted as responses to antibacterial or antiviral therapy. Signs of amebic keratitis in 36 eyes included iritis in 86%, a characteristic corneal ring infiltrate in 78% (Figs. 263–5 and 263–6), recurrent epithelial breakdown or cataracts in 44%, and, in the minority, hypopyon, elevated intraocular pressure, and anterior nodular scleritis. Most patients have an anterior uveitis of fluctuating severity.[41, 64] A dendriform epithelial pattern has been described in three patients as an early sign of *Acanthamoeba* keratitis before stromal involvement (Fig. 263–7). Recognition of this dendriform pattern enabled early and vision-saving therapy in three patients.[2, 65]

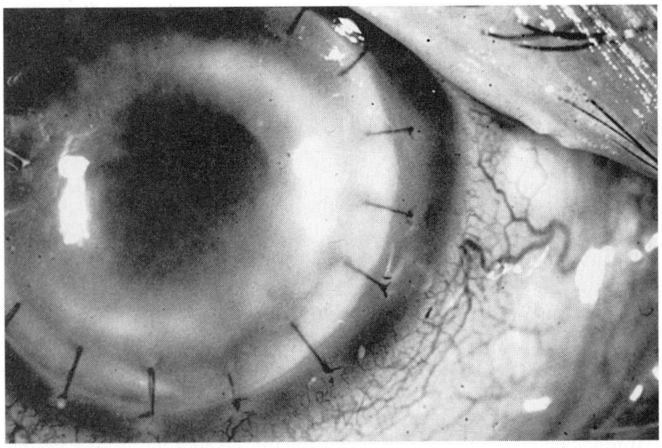

FIGURE 263–6. Progressive ring infiltrate in a corneal graft infected with *Acanthamoeba polyphaga*. (Reprinted from Cohen EJ, Parlato CJ, Arentsen JJ, et al. Medical and surgical treatment of *Acanthamoeba* keratitis. Am J Ophthalmol. 1987; 103: 615–625, with permission from Elsevier Science.)

Infection with *B. mandrillaris* is clinically dissimilar to CNS infection with *Acanthamoeba* spp. in that it can cause disease in both immunocompetent and immunocompromised hosts. Subacute or chronic granulomatous meningoencephalitis, similar to granulomatous amebic encephalitis due to *Acanthamoeba*, resulting in death within 1 week to several months after the onset of symptoms is the commonest clinical presentation. Important signs and symptoms include fever, headache, nausea, vomiting, seizure, and focal neurologic signs. Hydrocephalus as a complication[66] and initial misdiagnosis as an intracranial neoplasm[55] have been reported. Of the 63 cases reported worldwide, 7 have been in patients with AIDS. Other underlying illnesses include diabetes, renal failure, alcoholism, and intravenous drug abuse. In nonhuman primates, the disease can

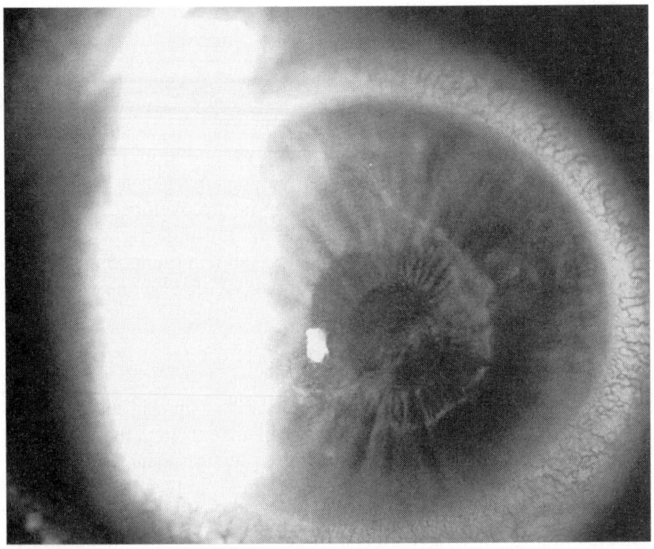

FIGURE 263–5. *Acanthamoeba* keratitis with an early and only partially ring-shaped infiltrate. (From Lindquist TD, Sher NA, Doughman DJ. Clinical signs and medical therapy of early *Acanthamoeba* keratitis. Arch Ophthalmol. 1988; 106: 73–77.)

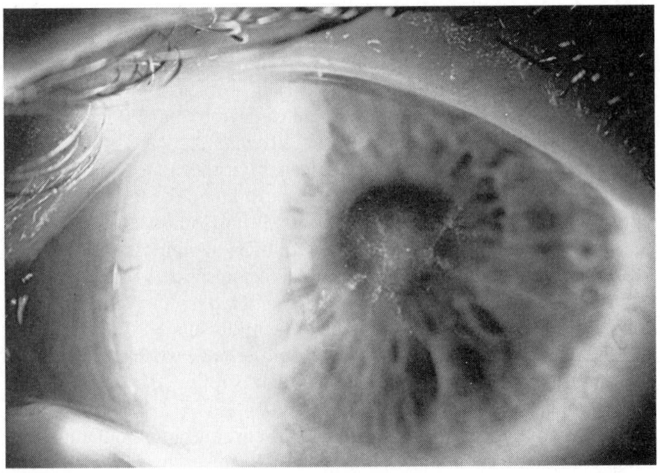

FIGURE 263–7. *Acanthamoeba* keratitis with dendriform epithelial pattern. Radial, linear anterior stromal infiltrates extend nearly to temporal periphery associated with dendriform epithelial irregularity. (From Lindquist TD, Sher NA, Doughman DJ. Clinical signs and medical therapy of early *Acanthamoeba* keratitis. Arch Ophthalmol. 1988; 106: 73–77.)

manifest in two clinically distinct patterns, one with a short clinical course as an acute necrotizing meningoencephalitis and the other with a more prolonged clinical course and granulomatous amebic meningoencephalitis.[67]

LABORATORY DIAGNOSIS

Primary amebic meningoencephalitis should be included in the differential diagnosis of children and young adults with meningoencephalitis. Recent exposure to fresh water should raise suspicions of *N. fowleri* infection. The peripheral white cell count is usually elevated, with a predominance of neutrophils. Head computed tomographic scans in one patient with primary amebic meningoencephalitis showed diffuse contrast enhancement of the gray matter and obliterated ambients, interpeduncular, and quadrigeminal cisterns.[7] The CSF pressure can be elevated, and the CSF is hemorrhagic. White blood cell counts in the CSF may be low early in disease but later range from 400 to 26,000 white blood cells/μl, with neutrophils predominating. The CSF glucose level is low to normal, and the CSF protein level is elevated. In patients with purulent CSF indices and no bacteria demonstrated on Gram stain of CSF sediment, it is very important to examine a wet mount of CSF for amebic trophozoites. These trophozoites are generally destroyed by the fixation procedure for Gram stain and missed if not looked for on a wet mount. Motile trophozoites in the CSF have been seen in 14 of 16 patients with primary amebic meningoencephalitis in which a wet mount of CSF was made.[4, 68–70] More recent methods to rapidly and specifically diagnose *Naegleria* infections include molecular methods such as monoclonal antibodies,[1] polymerase chain reaction,[71, 72] isoenzyme profile analysis,[1] and DNA probes.[73]

Granulomatous amebic encephalitis with *Acanthamoeba* in the past has frequently been diagnosed only at autopsy. Brain biopsy is the only way to make the diagnosis during life because *Acanthamoeba* spp. have never been isolated from the CSF of a patient with granulomatous amebic encephalitis. Head computed tomographic scans have shown multiple lucent nonenhancing lesions in the cortex.[7, 29] Lumbar puncture may be contraindicated in patients with granulomatous amebic encephalitis because of the risk of herniation. When it has been performed, the results have been nondiagnostic, with intermediate elevations in the white blood cell count (to 800/μl, lymphocyte predominance) and usually elevated protein and decreased glucose levels.[7, 29] *Acanthamoeba* infection of the skin frequently is present with granulomatous amebic encephalitis, and skin nodules or ulcers should be biopsied and examined for *Acanthamoeba* in patients suspected of having granulomatous amebic encephalitis. *Acanthamoeba* and *B. mandrillaris* amebae have been successfully cultured from brain and cutaneous biopsy specimens. Culture of *Acanthamoeba* is best accomplished by the use of tryptic soy agar with rabbit or horse blood, buffered charcoal yeast extract agar, and non-nutrient agar overlaid with live organisms such as *P. aeruginosa*, *Enterobacter aerogenes*, or *Stenotrophomonas maltophilia*.[74] Specimens should not be frozen and should not be fixed before culture.[13]

The successful treatment of *Acanthamoeba* keratitis depends on its early diagnosis and initiation of therapy. Patchy stromal infiltrates[75] and dendriform epithelial involvement without frank corneal ulcerations[65] can be early signs of amebic keratitis (see Figs. 263–5 through 263–7). The ring corneal infiltrate that is characteristic of this disease is a late sign of stromal involvement. Diagnosis rests on demonstrating *Acanthamoeba* in corneal scrapings or biopsy material by histopathologic examination or culture. Initial corneal scrapings, Gram stains, and cultures may be misleading because in one third of cases of amebic keratitis these grew *Staphylococcus epidermidis*, *Staphylococcus aureus*, α-hemolytic streptococcus, or *Propionibacterium*. A non-nutrient agar overlaid with *Escherichia coli* or *E. aerogenes* has been used to successfully culture *Acanthamoeba* from 10 of 15 amebic keratitis patients whose previous smear or biopsy had been negative.[41] Culture of the contact lenses and contact lens saline solution has also yielded *Acanthamoeba* when initial corneal scrapings were negative.[75] Corneal scrapings should be examined under wet mount for motile trophozoites. Spray fixatives may best preserve the morphology of the trophozoites before air drying occurs.[76] The cysts and trophozoites can be visualized with a number of different stains including hematoxylin-eosin, Wright, Giemsa, and periodic acid–Schiff.[41] Calcofluor white fluorescently stains the cysts and trophozoites in tissue section, facilitating their identification.[77] Molecular techniques that have been used to diagnose infection with *Acanthamoeba* include polymerase chain reaction and DNA probe.[78]

Several of the reported cases of *B. mandrillaris* had initially been described to be due to *Acanthamoeba* because of the inability of reliably distinguishing the two based on morphologic characteristics. Development of an immunofluorescence assay with the use of rabbit antiserum to the washed trophozoites and cysts from cultures has enabled definitive diagnosis of infection with this organism. Previously, the organism was able to be grown only on living tissue culture cells such as monkey kidney tissue lines; however, the recent development of a cell-free growth medium and axenization should make the clinical isolation of this organism much easier.[79] In brain biopsy specimens of patients with *B. mandrillaris* infection, both the cysts and trophozoites of the organism have been identified. To date *B. mandrillaris* has not been identified in the CSF; however, wet mount specimens should be examined if this entity is in the clinical differential. The CSF findings resemble that of *Acanthamoeba* infections and has a mononuclear pleocytosis (10 to 500 cells), moderate hypoglycorrachia, and an elevated protein level. Imaging studies often reveal multiple hypodense lesions that enhance with a mass effect, thus raising the spectrum of mass-occupying lesions from malignancy, tuberculosis, and toxoplasmosis. Radiographically, these entities cannot be differentiated reliably, and tissue is required for definitive diagnosis.

TREATMENT

Six patients are known to have survived primary amebic meningoencephalitis.[37, 80–83] Patients with well-documented primary amebic meningoencephalitis received high-dose systemic and intrathecal amphotericin B. One of the patients was also treated with systemic and intrathecal miconazole, systemic rifampin, and sulfisoxazole.[80] Other agents that have been investigated in animal models include artemisurin, β-arteether, and sodium artesunic acid; however, these have all been found to be inferior to amphotericin B.[84] Because of the overall 95% mortality of primary amebic meningoencephalitis, passive immunotherapy in animal models has been attempted. Intrathecal administration of anti-*Naegleria* immune serum or an anti-*Naegleria* monoclonal antibody prolonged the survival of rabbits inoculated intracisternally with *N. fowleri*.[85] Passive immunotherapy may one day prove to be a useful adjunct to antibiotic treatment of primary amebic meningoencephalitis.

Little is known about the treatment of granulomatous amebic encephalitis due to *Acanthamoeba*. Most cases have been diagnosed postmortem; premortem diagnosis has generally preceded death by only a few days, making evaluation of therapy difficult. In vitro testing of drug susceptibilities is complicated by interspecies and interstrain differences in antimicrobial sensitivities.[41] Each clinical isolate should be tested for drug sensitivities. In general the diamidine derivatives (propamidine, pentamidine, dibromopropamidine) have the greatest activity against *Acanthamoeba*. Other drugs active in vitro include ketoconazole, miconazole, paromomycin, neomycin, 5-flucytosine, and, to a lesser extent, amphotericin B.[41, 86, 87] A case of CNS disease reputedly successfully treated with trimethoprim-sulfamethoxazole has been reported.[88] In vitro data regarding the susceptibility of *Acanthamoeba* to trimethoprim-sulfamethoxazole are minimal, although in a case of *A. castellanii* keratitis, the organism was found to be resistant to this drug in vitro.[89]

Treatment of *Acanthamoeba* keratitis has been notably more successful than that of granulomatous amebic encephalitis or primary amebic meningoencephalitis.[90] This relates in large part to the accessibility of the infection to surgical débridement and high concentrations of topical antimicrobial drugs. Successful treatment requires early diagnosis and aggressive surgical and medical management. Recognition of the dendriform pattern on the corneal epithelium, the earliest recognized sign of *Acanthamoeba* keratitis, should be followed immediately with débridement of the abnormal epithelium and institution of antiamebic medical therapy.[41, 90, 91] Medical treatment with topical 1% miconazole nitrate, 0.1% propamidine isethionate, and neosporin should continue for a minimum of 3 to 4 weeks. Topical propamidine should be administered at least nine times a day, with some authorities recommending it to be administered as often as every 15 to 60 minutes for the first 3 days.[90, 92] Combination therapy with propamidine and polyhexamethyl biguanide[93] and chlorhexidine and propamidine[94] have been shown to be effective. Early recognition and treatment have eliminated the need in some patients for a late penetrating keratoplasty to restore vision and reduce pain.[41, 90, 91] Propamidine isethionate has caused a reversible epithelial keratopathy after prolonged treatment that can be confused with recurrent amebic keratitis.[95] Other agents with activity against *Acanthamoeba* include pentamidine[96] and ivermectin.[97] Crystalline keratopathy caused by viridans streptococci has occurred after topical corticosteroid therapy of *Acanthamoeba* keratitis in two patients, emphasizing both the risks of using topical steroids in this disease and the need for a complete diagnostic reevaluation of patients with amebic keratitis in whom therapy appears to be failing.[98] A more recent study revealed no increased risk of treatment failure in patients treated with adjuvant steroids, and prudent steroid treatment was felt to be justified for the treatment of severe pain or inflammation.[99]

At the present time, there is no known effective treatment for *B. mandrillaris* infections. Studies have found some efficacy with pentamidine isethionate,[79] but this drug was amebastatic in the axenic system tested. In the same study, fluconazole and ketoconazole were poor inhibitors of amebic growth, and amphotericin B was marginal, whereas azithromycin, clarithromycin, and trimethoprim-sulfamethoxazole had no effect.[79]

PREVENTION

Primary amebic meningoencephalitis occurs so rarely that active surveillance for *N. fowleri* in public swimming lakes is probably not justified as a public health measure. However, because of the occurrence of clusters of patients with primary amebic meningoencephalitis with common environmental exposures,[4, 35, 69] health officials should consider closing the implicated lake to swimming.

Acanthamoeba keratitis associated with contact lens use is preventable. Contact lenses should be heat disinfected or cleaned in benzalkonium-preserved saline, as hydrogen peroxide disinfection does not kill *Acanthamoeba*. Homemade saline solutions should not be used to clean or store contact lenses, and the lenses should not be worn while swimming in fresh water.[31, 32, 75, 100]

REFERENCES

1. Szenazi Z, Endo T, Yagita K, Nagy B. Isolation, identification and increasing importance of free-living amoebae causing human disease. J Med Microbiol. 1998;47:5–16.
2. Schaumberg DA, Snow KK, Dana MR. The epidemic of acanthamoeba keratitis—where do we stand. Cornea. 1998;17:3–10.
3. Friedman RF, Wolf TC, Chodosh J. Acanthamoeba infection after radical keratotomy. Am J Ophthalmol. 1997;123:409–410.
4. Fowler M, Carter RF. Acute pyogenic meningitis probably due to *Acanthamoeba* sp: A preliminary report. BMJ. 1965;2:740.
5. John DT. Primary amebic meningoencephalitis and the biology of *Naegleria fowleri*. Annu Rev Microbiol. 1982;36:101–123.
6. Schuster FL. Ultrastructure of cysts of *Naegleria* spp: A comparative study. J Protozool. 1975;22:352–359.
7. Martinez AJ. Free-Living Amebas: Natural History, Prevention, Diagnosis, Pathology and Treatment of Disease. Boca Raton, Fla: CRC Press; 1985.
8. Di Gregorio C, Rivasi F, Mongiardo N, et al. *Acanthamoeba* meningoencephalitis in a patient with acquired immunodeficiency syndrome. Arch Pathol Lab Med. 1992;116:1363–1365.
9. Ledee DR, Hay J, Byers TJ, et al. *Acanthamoeba griffini*. Molecular characterization of a new corneal pathogen. Invest Ophthalmol Vis Sci. 1996;37:544–550.
10. Visvesvara GS, Stehy-Green JK. Epidemiology of free-living ameba infections. J Protozool. 1990;37:25S–33S.
11. Visvesvara GS, Martinez AJ, Schuster FL, et al. Leptomyxid ameba, a new agent of amebic meningoencephalitis in humans and animals. J Clin Microbiol. 1990;28:2750–2756.
12. Anzil AP, Chandrakant R, Wrzolek AA, et al. Amebic meningoencephalitis in a patient with AIDS caused by a newly recognized opportunistic pathogen. Arch Pathol Lab Med. 1991;115:21–25.
13. Gordon SM, Steinberg JP, DuPuis MH, et al. Culture isolation of *Acanthamoeba* species and leptomyxid amebas from patients with amebic meningoencephalitis, including two patients with AIDS. Clin Infect Dis. 1992;15:1024–1030.
14. Denney CF, Iragui VJ, Uber-Zak LD, et al. Amebic meningoencephalitis caused by *Balamuthia mandrillaris*: Case report and review. Clin Infect Dis. 1997;25:1354–1358.
15. Visvesvara GS, Schuster FL, Martinez AJ. *Balamuthia mandrillaris*, NG, NSp, agent of amebic meningoencephalitis in humans and other animals. J Eukaryot Microbiol. 1993;40:504–512.
16. Wellings FM, Amuso PT, Chang SL, et al. Isolation and identification of pathogenic *Naegleria* from Florida lakes. Appl Environ Microbiol. 1977;34:661–667.
17. Sykora JL, Keleti G, Martinez AJ. Occurrence and pathogenicity of *Naegleria fowleri* in artificially heated waters. Appl Environ Microbiol. 1983;45:974–979.
18. Warhurst DC, Carman JA, Mann PG. Survival of *Naegleria fowleri* cysts at 4°C for eight months with retention of virulence. Trans R Soc Trop Med Hyg. 1980;74:832.
19. Marciano-Cabral F, Cline MC, Bradley SG. Specificity of antibodies from human sera for *Naegleria* species. J Clin Microbiol. 1987;25:692–697.
20. Anonymous. Primary amebic meningoencephalitis—North Carolina, 1991. MMWR. 1992;41:437–440.
21. Martinez AJ, Visvesvara GS. Free-living, amphozoic and opportunistic amebas. Brain Pathol. 1997;7:583–598.
22. Lozanoalarcon F, Bradley GA, Houser BS, Visvesvara GS. Primary amebic meningoencephalitis due to *Naegleria fowleri* in a South American tapir. Vet Pathol. 1997;34:239–243.
23. Kollars TM Jr, Wilhelm WE. The occurrence of antibodies to *Naegleria* species in wild mammals. J Parasitol. 1996;82:73–77.
24. Wang SS, Feldman HA. Isolation of *Hartmanella* species from human throats. N Engl J Med. 1967;277:1174–1179.
25. Cursons RTM, Brown TJ, Keys EA. Immunity to pathogenic free-living amoeba. Lancet. 1977;2:875–876.
26. Sison JP, Kemper CA, Loveless M, et al. Disseminated *Acanthamoeba* infection in patients with AIDS: Case reports and review. Clin Infect Dis. 1995:20:1207–1216.
27. Lowichik A, Siegel JD. Parasitic infections of the central nervous system in children. Part I. Congenital infections and meningoencephalitis. J Child Neurol. 1995:10:4–17.
28. Gonzalez MM, Gould E, Dickinson G, et al. Acquired immunodeficiency syndrome associated with *Acanthamoeba* infection and other opportunistic organisms. Arch Pathol Lab Med. 1986;110:749–751.
29. Wiley CA, Safrin RE, Davis CE, et al. *Acanthamoeba* meningoencephalitis in a patient with AIDS. J Infect Dis. 1987;155:130–133.
30. Anderlini P, Przepiorka D, Luna M, et al. *Acanthamoeba* meningoencephalitis after bone marrow transplantation. Bone Marrow Transplant. 1994;14:459–461.
31. Stehr-Green JK, Bailey TM, Brandt FH, et al. *Acanthamoeba* keratitis in soft contact wearers. A case-control study. JAMA. 1987;258:57–60.
32. Nauheim RC, Brockman RJ, Stopak SS, et al. Survival of *Acanthamoeba* in contact lens rinse solutions. Cornea. 1990;9:290–293.
33. John DT, Howard MJ. Seasonal distribution of pathogenic free-living amebae in Oklahoma waters. Parasitol Res. 1995;81:193–201.
34. Martinez AJ, Duma RJ, Nelson EC, et al. Experimental *Naegleria* meningoencephalitis in mice. Lab Invest. 1973;29:121–133.
35. Dos Santos JG. Fatal primary amebic meningoencephalitis. A retrospective study in Richmond, Virginia. Am J Clin Pathol. 1970;54:737–742.
36. Markowitz SM, Martinez AJ, Duma RJ, et al. Myocarditis associated with primary amebic *(Naegleria)* meningoencephalitis. Am J Clin Pathol. 1974;62:619–628.
37. Loschiavo F, Ventura-Spagnolo T, Sessa E, Bramanti P. Acute primary meningoencephalitis from entamoeba *Naegleria fowleri*. Report of a clinical case with a favourable outcome. Acta Neurol (Napoli). 1993;15:333–340.
38. Aldape K, Huizinga H, Bouvier J, McKerow J. *Naegleria fowleri*: Characterization of a secreted histolytic cysteine protease. Exp Parasitol. 1994;78:230–241.
39. Wortman PD. *Acanthamoeba* infection (Review). Int J Dermatol. 1996;35:48–51.
40. Dunand VA, Hammer SM, Rossi R, et al. Parasitic sinusitis and otitis in patients infected with human immunodeficiency virus: Report of five cases and review. Clin Infect Dis. 1997;25:267–272.
41. Auran JD, Starr MB, Jakobiec FA. *Acanthamoeba* keratitis. A review of the literature. Cornea. 1987;6:2–26.
42. Baum J. In: Case records of the Massachusetts General Hospital Case 10-1985. N Engl J Med. 1985;312:634–641.
43. Howe DK, Vodkin MH, Novak RJ, et al. Identification of two genetic markers that distinguish pathogenic and nonpathogenic strains of *Acanthamoeba* spp. Parasitol Res. 1997;83:345–348.
44. Leher H, Silvany R, Alizadeh H, et al. Mannose induces the release of cytopathic factors from *Acanthamoeba castellanii*. Infect Immun. 1998;66:5–10.

45. Mattana A, Bennardini F, Usai S, et al. *Acanthamoeba castellanii* metabolites increase the intracellular calcium levels and cause cytotoxicity in wish cells. Microb Pathol. 1997;23:85–93.
46. Vanklink F, Leher H, Jager MJ, et al. Systemic immune response to *Acanthamoeba* keratitis in the chinese hamster. Ocul Immunol Inflamm. 1997;5:235–244.
47. Amann R, Springer N, Schonhuber W, et al. Obligate intracellular bacterial parasites of *Acanthamoeba* related to *Chlamydia* spp. Appl Environ Microbiol. 1997;63:115–121.
48. Essig A, Heinemann M, Simnacher U, Marre R. Infection of *Acanthamoeba castellanii* by *Chlamydia pneumoniae*. Appl Environ Microbiol. 1997;63:1396–1399.
49. Michel R, Burghardt H, Bergmann H. *Acanthamoeba*, naturally intracellularly infected with *Pseudomonas aeruginosa*, after their isolation from a microbiologically contaminated drinking water system in a hospital. Zentralbl Hyg Umweltmed. 1995;196:532–544.
50. Michel R, Hauroder B. Isolation of an *Acanthamoeba* strain with intracellular *Burkholderia pickettii* infection. Zentralbl Bakteriol. 1997;285:541–557.
51. Moffat JF, Tompkins LS. A quantitative model of intracellular growth of *Legionella pneumophila* in *Acanthamoeba castellanii*. Infect Immun. 1992;60:296–301.
52. Halenda RM, Grevan VL, Hook RR, Riley LK. An immortalized hamster corneal epithelial cell line for studies of the pathogenesis of *Acanthamoeba* keratitis. Curr Eye Res. 1998;17:225–230.
53. Popek EJ, Neafie RC. Granulomatous meningoencephalitis due to leptomyxid amoeba. Pediatr Pathol. 1992;12:871–881.
54. Reed RP, Cooke-Yarborough CM, Jaquiery AL, et al. Fatal granulomatous amoebic encephalitis caused by *Balamuthia mandrillaris*. Med J Aust. 1997;167:82–84.
55. Riestra-Castaneda JM, Riestra-Castaneda R, Gonzalez-Garido AA, et al. Granulomatous amebic encephalitis due to *Balamuthia mandrillaris* (Leptomyxiidae): Report of four cases from Mexico. Am J Trop Med Hyg. 1997;56:603–607.
56. Janitschke K, Martinez AJ, Visvesvara GS, Schuster F. Animal model *Balamuthia mandrillaris* CNS infection: Contrast and comparison in immunodeficient and immunocompetent mice: A murine model of "granulomatous" amebic encephalitis. J Neuropathol Exp Neurol. 1996;55:815–821.
57. Lawande RV, John I, Dobbs RH, et al. A case of primary amebic meningoencephalitis in Zaria, Nigeria. Am J Clin Pathol. 1979;71:591–594.
58. Viriyavejakul P, Rochanawutanon M, Sirinavin S. *Naegleria* meningomyeloencephalitis. Southeast Asian J Trop Med Public Health. 1997;28:237–240.
59. Dejonckheere JF, Brown S. Primary amebic meningoencephalitis in a patient with AIDS—Unusual protozoological findings. Clin Infect Dis. 1997;25:943–944.
60. Martinez AJ. Is *Acanthamoeba* encephalitis an opportunistic infection? Neurology. 1980;30:567–574.
61. Helton J, Loveless M, White CR Jr. Cutaneous *Acanthamoeba* infection associated with leukocytoclastic vasculitis in an AIDS patient. Am J Dermatopathol. 1993;15:146–149.
62. Selby DM, Chandra RS, Rakusan TA, et al. Amebic osteomyelitis in a child with acquired immunodeficiency syndrome—A case report. Pediatr Pathol Lab Med. 1998;18:89–95.
63. Thamprasert K, Khunamornpong S, Morakote N. *Acanthamoeba* infection of peptic ulcer. Ann Trop Med Parasitol. 1993;87:403–405.
64. Heffler KF, Eckhardt TJ, Reboli AC, Stieritz D. *Acanthamoeba* endophthalmitis in acquired immunodeficiency syndrome. Am J Ophthalmol. 1996;122:584–586.
65. Lindquist TD, Sher NA, Doughman DJ. Clinical signs and medical therapy of early *Acanthamoeba* keratitis. Arch Ophthalmol. 1988;106:73–77.
66. Duke BJ, Tyson RW, DeBiasi R, et al. *Balamuthia mandrillaris* meningoencephalitis presenting with acute hydrocephalus. Pediatr Neurosurg. 1997;26:107–111.
67. Rideout BA, Gardiner CH, Stalis IH, et al. Fatal infections with *Balamuthia mandrillaris* (a free living amoeba) in gorillas and other Old World primates. Vet Pathol. 1997;34:15–22.
68. Lawande RV, Macfarlane JT, Weir WRC, et al. A case of primary amebic meningoencephalitis in a Nigerian farmer. Am J Trop Med Hyg. 1980;29:21–25.
69. Callicott JH Jr, Nelson EC, Jones MM, et al. Meningoencephalitis due to pathogenic free-living amoebae. Report of two cases. JAMA. 1968;206:579–582.
70. Duma RJ, Rosenblum WI, McGehee RF, et al. Primary amebic meningoencephalitis caused by *Naegleria*. Two new cases, responses to amphotericin B and a review. Ann Intern Med. 1971;74:923–932.
71. Sparagano O. Differentiation of *Naegleria fowleri* and other *Naegleriae* by polymerase chain reaction and hybridization methods. FEMS Microbiol Lett. 1993;110:325–330.
72. Sparagano O, Drouet E, Denoyel G, et al. Differentiation of *Naegleria fowleri* from other species of *Naegleria* using monoclonal antibodies and the polymerase chain reaction. Trans R Soc Trop Med Hyg. 1994;88:119–120.
73. Sparagano O. Detection of *Naegleria fowleri* cysts in environmental samples by using a DNA probe. FEMS Microbiol Lett. 1993;112:349–351.
74. Penland RL, Wilhelmus KR. Comparison of axenic and monoxenic media for isolation of *Acanthamoeba*. J Clin Microbiol. 1997;35:915–922.
75. Cohen EJ, Parlato CJ, Arentsen JJ, et al. Medical and surgical treatment of *Acanthamoeba* keratitis. Am J Ophthalmol. 1987;103:615–625.
76. Wright P, Warhurst D, Jones BR. *Acanthamoeba* keratitis successfully treated medically. Br J Ophthalmol. 1984;69:778–782.
77. Silvany RE, Luckenbach MW, Moore MB. The rapid detection of *Acanthamoeba* in paraffin-embedded sections of corneal tissue with Calcofluor white. Arch Ophthalmol. 1987;105:1366–1367.
78. Lai S, Asgari M, Henney HR Jr. Non-radioactive DNA probe and polymerase chain reaction procedures for the specific detection of *Acanthamoeba*. Mol Cell Probes. 1994;8:81–89.
79. Schuster FL, Visvesvara GS. Axenic growth and drug sensitivity studies of *Balamuthia mandrillaris*, an agent of amebic meningoencephalitis in humans and other animals. J Clin Microbiol. 1996;34:385–388.
80. Siedel JS, Harmatz P, Visvesvara GS, et al. Successful treatment of primary amebic meningoencephalitis. N Engl J Med. 1982;306:346.
81. Brown RL. Successful treatment of primary amebic meningoencephalitis. Arch Intern Med. 1991;151:1201–1202.
82. Anderson K, Jamieson A. Primary amoebic meningoencephalitis. Lancet. 1972;1:902–903.
83. Wang A, Kay R, Poon WS, Ng HK. Successful treatment of amoebic meningoencephalitis in a Chinese living in Hong Kong. Clin Neurol Neurosurg. 1993;95:249–252.
84. Gupta S, Ghosh PK, Dutta GP, Vishwakarma RA. In vivo study of artemisinin and its derivatives against primary amebic meningoencephalitis caused by *Naegleria fowleri*. J Parasitol 1995;81:1012–1013.
85. Lallinger GJ, Reiner SL, Cooke DW, et al. Efficacy of immune therapy in early experimental *Naegleria fowleri* meningitis. Infect Immun. 1987;55:1289–1293.
86. Duma RJ, Finley R. In vitro susceptibility of pathogenic *Naegleria* and *Acanthamoeba* species to a variety of therapeutic agents. Antimicrob Agents Chemother. 1976;10:370–376.
87. Nagington J, Richards JE. Chemotherapeutic compounds and *Acanthamoeba* from eye infections. J Clin Pathol. 1976;29:648–651.
88. Sharma PP, Gupta P, Murali MV, Ramachandran VG. Primary amebic meningoencephalitis caused by *Acanthamoeba*: Successfully treated with cotrimoxazole. Indian Pediatr. 1993;30:1219–2122.
89. Ma P, Willaert E, Jeuchter KB, Stevens AR. A case of keratitis due to *Acanthamoeba* in New York, New York and features of 10 cases. J Infect Dis. 1981;143:662–667.
90. Lindquist TD. Treatment of *Acanthamoeba* keratitis. Cornea. 1998;17:11–16.
91. Holland GN, Donzis PB. Rapid resolution of early *Acanthamoeba* keratitis after epithelial debridement. Am J Ophthalmol. 1987;104:87–89.
92. Moore MB, McCulley JP. Medical and surgical treatment of *Acanthamoeba* keratitis (Letter). Am J Ophthalmol. 1987;104:310–311.
93. Duguid IG, Dart JK, Morlet N, et al. Outcome of *Acanthamoeba* keratitis treated with polyhexamethyl biguanide and propamidine. Ophthalmology. 1997;104: 1587–1592.
94. Seal D, Hay J, Kirkness C, et al. Successful medical therapy of *Acanthamoeba* keratitis with topical chlorhexidine and propamidine. Eye. 1996;10:413–421.
95. Johns KJ, Head WS, O'Day DM. Corneal toxicity of propamidine. Arch Ophthalmol. 1988;106:68–69.
96. Alizadeh H, Silvany RE, Meyer DR, et al. In vitro amoebicidal activity of propamidine and pentamidine isethionate against *Acanthamoeba* species and toxicity to corneal tissues. Cornea. 1997;16:94–100.
97. Rain AN, Radzan T, Sajiri S, Mak JW. In vitro drug susceptibility of *Acanthamoeba castellanii* to chloroquine, ivermectin and fungizon. Southeast Asian J Trop Med Public Health. 1996;27:319–324.
98. Davis RM, Schroeder RP, Rowsey JJ, et al. *Acanthamoeba* keratitis and infectious crystalline keratopathy. Arch Ophthalmol. 1987;105:1524–1527.
99. Park DH, Palay DA, Daya SM, et al. The role of topical corticosteroids in the management of *Acanthamoeba* keratitis. Cornea. 1997;16:277–283.
100. Zanetti S, Fiori PL, Pinna A, et al. Susceptibility of *Acanthamoeba castellanii* to contact lens disinfecting solutions. Antimicrob Agents Chemother. 1995;39:1596–1598.

Chapter 264

Plasmodium Species (Malaria)

DONALD J. KROGSTAD

HISTORICAL

The word *malaria* is based on the association between the bad air of marshes (where the anopheline mosquito vector breeds) and human infection by malaria parasites, *Plasmodium* spp.[1] Malaria has afflicted humankind for millenia and continues to do so today. Examination of the primate malarias suggests that human plasmodia have evolved together with their hosts from the plasmodia of nonhuman primates.[2] This hypothesis is supported by the remarkable similarities between several primate malaria parasites *(Plasmodium reichenowi, Plasmodium cynomolgi,* and *Plasmodium brasilianum)* and their human counterparts (*Plasmodium falciparum, Plasmodium vivax,* and *Plasmodium malariae,* respectively).[3]

In terms of recorded history, the earliest references to malaria are descriptions of splenomegaly with fever from China in the Nei Ching Canon of Medicine in 1700 BC and from Egypt in the Ebers Papyrus in 1570 BC. Hippocrates clearly recognized the syndrome of malaria and its relationship to marshes. Literary references to malaria appear in Homer's *Iliad* and in the works of Chaucer and Shakespeare.[1] European travelers to India, sub-Saharan Africa, and South America were decimated by malaria from the 16th to the 19th centuries. Malaria was endemic in the United States and Canada during the 18th and 19th centuries. In fact, there were more than 500,000 malaria cases per year in the United States at the beginning of the 20th century, and the Centers for Disease Control and Prevention was actually founded as the Office of Malaria Control. Malaria was a major factor in the American Revolution, the Civil War, World Wars I and II, and the Korean and Vietnam Wars. In Vietnam, U.S. soldiers lost more combat days from malaria than from battle injuries. Today, malaria remains an overwhelming problem in tropical developing countries (with 300 to 500 million cases and 2 to 3 million deaths per year),[4] and a potentially life-threatening complication for nonimmune expatriate travelers to the tropics.

DESCRIPTION OF THE ORGANISM

Malaria and Plasmodia

Malaria is an illness caused by one or more of the four plasmodia that infect humans: *P. falciparum, P. vivax, Plasmodium ovale,* and *P. malariae. P. falciparum* is found primarily in tropical regions and poses the greatest risk of death for nonimmune persons because it can invade red blood cells of all ages and is often drug-resistant. However, *P. falciparum* produces no dormant liver stages (hypnozoites, Fig. 264–1) and thus does not cause late relapse. In contrast,

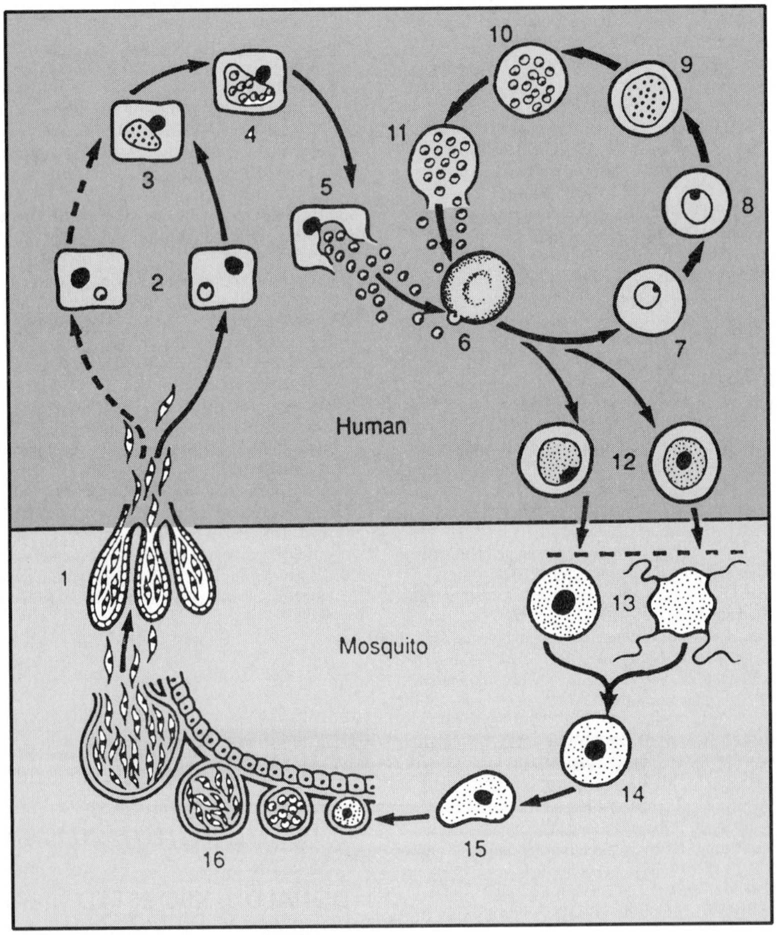

FIGURE 264–1. Life cycle of the malaria parasite. Sporozoites released from the salivary gland of the female *Anopheles* mosquito are injected under the skin when biting a human *(1)*. These sporozoites then travel through the blood stream and enter individual hepatocytes in the liver *(2)*. Within hepatocytes, they mature *(3)* to tissue schizonts *(4)*, which rupture to release merozoites *(5)* that reenter the blood stream and invade red blood cells (RBCs). Alternatively, some parasites remain dormant in the liver as hypnozoites (*dashed lines* from *1* to *3*) until they become active 6–11 months later, by generating the tissue schizonts *(4)* responsible for relapse in *Plasmodium vivax* and *Plasmodium ovale* infections. Once within the blood stream, merozoites *(5)* invade RBCs *(6)* and mature successively to ring *(7, 8)* trophozoite *(9)*, and schizont *(10)* stage asexual erythrocytic parasites. As schizont stage parasites complete their maturation, they lyse the host RBC, releasing the next generation of merozoites *(11)*, which invades previously uninfected RBCs.

Alternatively, some intraerythrocytic parasites differentiate to the sexual forms (male and female gametocytes, *12*) responsible for completing the life cycle in the mosquito vector. Within the mosquito midgut, the haploid male gametocyte loses its flagellum to become a male gamete *(13)*, and fertilizes a haploid female gamete to produce a diploid zygote *(14)*. The diploid zygote then transforms to an ookinete, invades the gut of the mosquito *(15)*, develops into an oocyst *(16)*, and undergoes a meiotic reduction division to produce the haploid sporozoites that migrate to the salivary gland to complete the cycle by infecting humans. The *dashed line* between *12* and *13* indicates that absence of the anopheline vector precludes natural transmission by this cycle. (From Krogstad DJ, Engleberg NC. Blood and tissue protozoa. In: Schaechter M, Engleberg NC, Eisenstein BI, Medoff G, eds. Mechanisms of Microbial Disease. 3rd ed. Baltimore: Williams & Wilkins; 1998:448–462.)

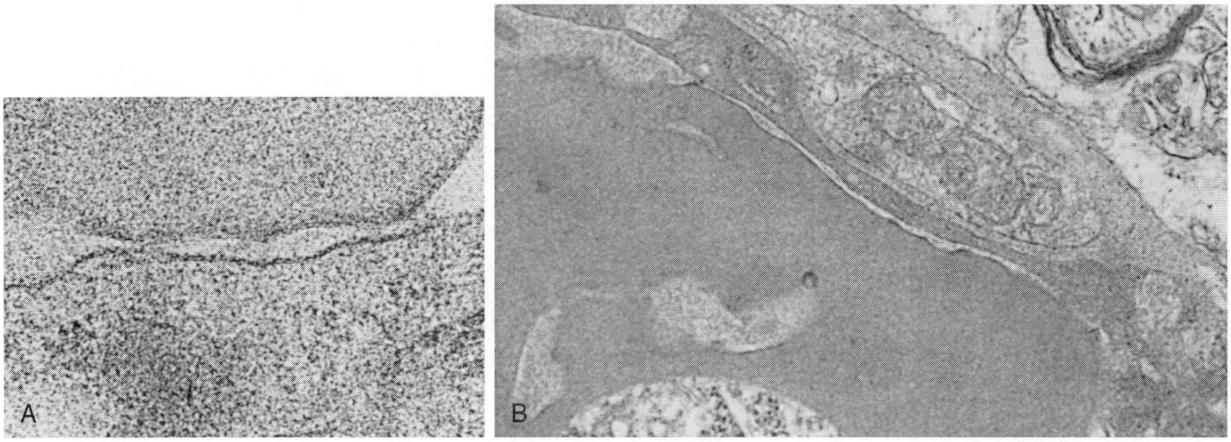

FIGURE 264–2. Cytoadherence of *Plasmodium falciparum*–infected red blood cells (RBCs) to endothelial cells. Knobs on the surface of *P. falciparum*–infected RBCs *(A)* mediate their adherence to endothelial cells *(B)*. (From Aikawa M, Iseki M, Barnwell JW, et al. The pathology of human cerebral malaria. Am J Trop Med Hyg. 1990;43:30–37.)

both *P. vivax*[5] and *P. ovale* produce hypnozoites and may thus cause late relapse 6 to 11 months or more after the initial infection. Although *P. malariae* infections may persist in the blood stream at low levels for 30 years or more, they do not produce hypnozoites and thus do not cause relapse from persistent liver stages.

Light microscopy of Giemsa-stained blood smears is the method used most frequently to diagnose malaria and identify the infecting species. Although malaria parasites are readily recognizable by experienced observers, inexperienced observers are often confused by platelets and may fail to use the oil immersion magnification (1000×) necessary for parasite identification. In addition, Giemsa staining is critically dependent on buffer pH for characteristic features such as Schüffner's dots in the cytoplasm of *P. vivax*- or *P. ovale*-infected red cells.

Acutely ill patients with malaria typically have either *P. falciparum* or *P. vivax* infections, although 5 to 7% of infections are due to more than one species (*P. ovale* is sufficiently similar to *P. vivax* clinically and morphologically that they can be considered identical for clinical purposes, whereas *P. malariae* rarely produces acute illness in normal hosts.) Thus, examination of the peripheral blood smear for multiply infected red blood cells, late-stage asexual parasites (trophozoites and schizonts), and enlarged parasitized red cells usually permits one to distinguish between *P. falciparum* and *P. vivax* (or *P. ovale*) (Table 264–1).[6] Identification of the infecting species is important clinically. Because *P. falciparum* may produce overwhelming parasitemias (by invading red cells of all ages)[7] and is often drug-resistant, *P. falciparum* infections pose a much greater risk of death than do *P. vivax, P. ovale,* or *P. malariae* infections.

Transmission electron microscopy has been extremely useful in defining the ultrastructural nature of interactions between the parasite and its host red cell and between the parasitized red cell and surrounding cells in vivo. Studies by Aikawa and colleagues have graphically demonstrated the events associated with parasite entry into the red blood cell, the endocytosis of red cell hemoglobin, and its degradation to malarial pigment in the food vacuole (the parasite secondary lysosome). In *P. falciparum* infection, the most important pathophysiologic event is the adherence of parasitized red blood cells via knobs on their surface to endothelial cells in capillaries and postcapillary venules (Fig. 264–2).[8, 9] This cytoadherence event is the basis of the microvascular pathology observed in the brain, kidneys, and other affected organs in severe, complicated, and cerebral *P. falciparum* malaria.[10]

Scanning electron microscopy has shown that plasmodial invasion and maturation dramatically change the human red blood cell from a doughnut-shaped 7- to 8-μm-diameter deformable cell (with more surface area than necessary for its volume) to a sphere-shaped 4- to 5-μm-diameter red blood cell so distended by the growth of the maturing parasite[11] and altered by cross-linking of red cell cytoskeletal proteins[12] that it is no longer deformable (Fig. 264–3).

TABLE 264–1 Differential Diagnosis of Malaria in the Acutely Ill Patient Based on Examination of the Peripheral Blood Smear

	P. falciparum	P. vivax (P. ovale)
Multiply infected red cells	Common	Rare
Mature (trophozoite and schizont) parasites	Absent*	Common
Red cell enlargement with later parasite stages	Absent	Common†

*Mature (trophozoite and schizont) stage *P. falciparum* parasites are not seen on the blood smear because they are typically sequestered in the peripheral microvasculature.

†Red cell enlargement in *P. vivax* typically occurs with later stage parasites that do not circulate in *P. falciparum* infection.

From Krogstad DJ, Engleberg NC. Blood and tissue protozoa. In: Schaechter M, Engleberg NC, Eisenstein BI, Medoff G, eds. Mechanisms of Microbial Disease. 3rd ed. Baltimore: Williams & Wilkins; 1998:448–462.

EPIDEMIOLOGY

The epidemiology of malaria results from the demands of its life cycle, which requires reservoirs of infected and uninfected humans, competent anopheline vectors, and multiple opportunities for contact between the vector and its human host.

Parasite Life Cycle

Humans acquire malaria from *sporozoites* transmitted by the bite of infected anopheline mosquitoes. The sporozoites then travel through the blood stream to the liver, where they invade hepatocytes and mature to *tissue schizonts* or become dormant *hypnozoites.* Tissue schizonts are a central feature of all four plasmodial species that infect humans; they amplify the infection by producing large numbers of merozoites (10,000 to 30,000) from each sporozoite-infected hepatocyte. Each merozoite released from the liver is capable of invading a human red blood cell and establishing the asexual cycle of replication in that red cell with the release of 24 to 32 merozoites at the conclusion of a 48- or 72-hour asexual cycle. Unlike tissue schizonts, hypnozoites are found only in relapsing malarias such as *P. vivax* or *P. ovale;* they remain dormant for up to 6 to 11 months after the initial blood stream infection and cause no symptoms during that time. When hypnozoites mature to tissue schizonts and release infectious merozoites, they produce a second symptomatic blood

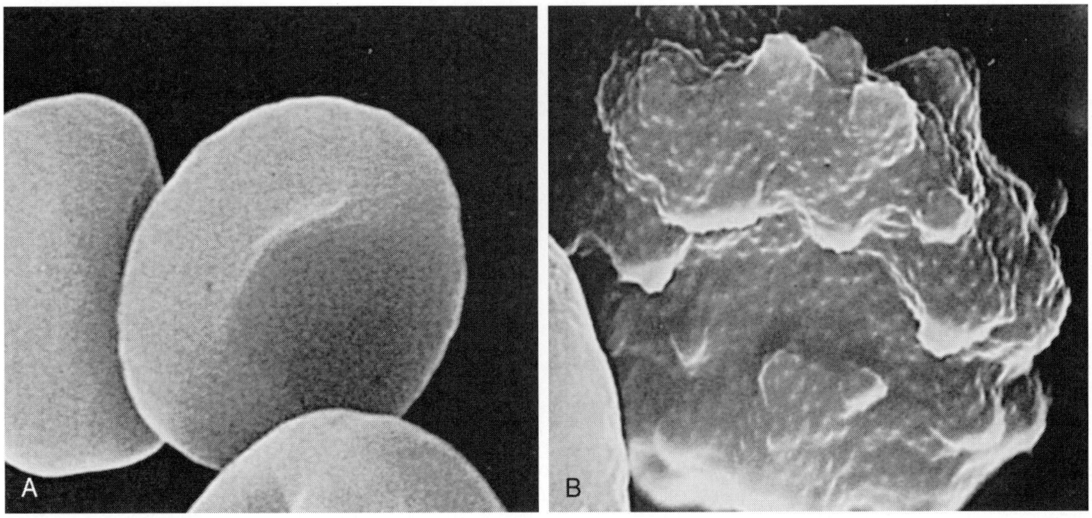

FIGURE 264–3. Effects of the malaria parasite on its host red blood cell (RBC). Distention from the presence and growth of the malaria parasite *(Plasmodium falciparum)* converts the RBC from a biconcave disk *(A)* to a distended sphere *(B)*, the shape that permits the greatest volume with the same (RBC membrane) surface area. (From Aikawa M, Rabbege JR, Udeinya IJ, et al. Electron microscopy of knobs in *Plasmodium falciparum*–infected erythrocytes. J Parasitol. 1983;69:435–437.)

stream infection or a delayed primary infection (if the first infection was suppressed by chemoprophylaxis). Alternatively, some intraerythrocytic parasites develop into the sexual *(gametocyte)* forms necessary to complete the life cycle in the anopheline vector. When infectious gametocytes are taken up by a female anopheline mosquito with a blood meal, micro- and macrogametocytes mature to form male and female *gametes;* they fertilize one another to produce a diploid *zygote* that matures to an *ookinete* and then undergoes a meiotic reduction division to produce the haploid sporozoites that migrate to the salivary gland and subsequently reinfect humans.

Adaptive Features of the Parasite Life Cycle: Hypnozoites, Relapse, and the External Environment

Plasmodial parasites endemic in tropical regions (e.g., *P. falciparum*) can survive by relying on the year-round presence of the mosquito vector and thus do not require dormant hypnozoite liver stages to sustain transmission. In contrast, plasmodia endemic in more temperate zones (e.g., *P. vivax*) benefit from dormant hypnozoite liver stages that permit parasite survival in the human host during the winter, followed by reemergence 6 to 11 months after the initial infection during the following spring or summer when the weather is warmer and mosquito vectors are abundant. Thus, the hypnozoite stage can be viewed as a plasmodial adaptation for survival in temperate zones.

Transmission by Transfusion or Sharing Needles (Induced Malaria)

Hypnozoites are not produced in induced malaria because the hypnozoite stage is produced only from natural mosquito-borne infection. Thus, relapses do not occur (even with *P. vivax* and *P. ovale* infections) after inadvertent transfusion of infected blood or needle sharing among drug addicts because the contaminated blood producing these infections contains asexual (or sexual) stage parasites, but not sporozoites.

The Anopheline Vector

The female anopheline mosquito is responsible for malaria transmission (only female mosquitoes take blood meals). For example, the intense transmission of malaria in sub-Saharan Africa may result primarily from efficient transmission by the *Anopheles gambiae* complex and *Anopheles funestus* vectors established in that region.[13] This hypothesis is also consistent with the lower intensity transmission observed in South America and Southeast Asia, where neither *A. gambiae* nor *A. funestus* is present. However, despite the importance of the anopheline vector, malaria control may be achieved without vector eradication. Thus, although malaria transmission is unusual in the United States, vectors that persist in the United States include *Anopheles albimanus, Anopheles quadrimaculatus,* and *Anopheles freeborni.* These anophelines are responsible for the outbreaks of malaria that occur when infected persons enter the United States and infect the mosquito pool, for example, after a war with the return of infected soldiers, or with the resettlement of refugees from malaria-endemic areas such as Southeast Asia.[14]

Human Evolution and Malaria: Sickle Cell Hemoglobin

In areas such as sub-Saharan Africa where *P. falciparum* malaria kills more than 2 million children a year, factors that enhance the ability of children to survive *P. falciparum* infection should have a strong selective advantage. This appears to be the case with sickle hemoglobin (a mutation in the β-chain that changes the glutamate at position 6 to a valine). Although the survival value (fitness) of homozygous (HbSS) children in most traditional African villages is close to zero, the prevalence of the sickle cell gene (as sickle cell trait, HbAS) is 25% or greater in many areas of sub-Saharan Africa. Thus, there must be a powerful factor such as surviving *P. falciparum* malaria that selects in favor of HbAS heterozygotes to maintain the prevalence of the sickle gene in the population.[15] That hypothesis is also consistent with in vivo observations by a number of investigators suggesting that HbAS children rarely have severe or complicated malaria, although they are infected with *P. falciparum* as frequently as their normal (HbAA) peers.[16] In contrast, the evidence for protection by glucose-6-phosphate dehydrogenase deficiency is less striking and is a subject of continuing controversy.[17]

Molecular Insights into the Plasmodial Life Cycle

Although the stages of the parasite life cycle have been known for almost 100 years, the bases (cell biology) of the individual interactions between the parasite and specific host cells are just beginning to be understood. For example, what parasite ligands and host receptors are responsible for sporozoite entry into the hepatocyte, merozoite entry into the red blood cell, and the cytoadherence of parasitized red cells to the endothelium of capillaries and postcapillary venules (Table 264–2)? Recent studies have shown that sporozoites invade hepatocytes using region II of the circumsporozoite protein on their surface as the ligand for binding to heparan sulfate proteoglycans and the low-density lipoprotein receptor on the hepatocyte surface.[18, 19]

Likewise, studies by Miller and colleagues at the National Institutes of Health have shown that a red blood cell antigen (Duffy factor) is necessary for invasion by *P. vivax* parasites and that *P. vivax* infection is uncommon among black populations because their red blood cells do not have Duffy factor.[20] Recent studies have expanded those observations to define a family of plasmodial genes that may encode proteins responsible for red blood cell entry by all malaria parasites, which function by binding to red cell chemokine receptors.[21, 22] Homologous proteins (ligands) have now been identified in *P. falciparum, P. vivax,* and in the nonhuman malarias *(Plasmodium knowlesi).*[23] Studies by other investigators have revealed reticulocyte-binding proteins in plasmodia that preferentially invade young red cells *(P. vivax)*[24] and thus explain that tropism.

The multiple molecules on the endothelial cell surface reported to function as receptors for *P. falciparum*–parasitized red blood cells include ICAM-1, CD36, VCAM1, ELAM1, E-selectin, and thrombospondin.[8, 25,26] Recent studies suggest that the molecule on the parasitized red blood cell surface that functions as the ligand in cytoadherence is *P. falciparum*–infected erythrocyte-binding protein 1 (*PfEMP1*). Within *PfEMP1,* conserved regions similar to the Duffy-binding domain are interspersed with variable regions, thus providing both cytoadherence and a means to evade the immune response in these variable (*var*) genes, of which there may be 50 to 150 copies per parasite.[27] *Var* genes may also be involved in rosetting (clusters of unparasitized red blood cells around *P. falciparum*–parasitized red blood cells), based on binding to complement-receptor 1 on the red cell surface.[28]

PATHOGENESIS

Disease due to *P. falciparum* infection is more severe and qualitatively different from disease caused by the other plasmodia that infect humans. For those reasons, it will be discussed first.

Pathogenesis of Disease Due to *Plasmodium falciparum* Infection (Cytoadherence)

P. falciparum is the only human malaria parasite that produces microvascular disease.[29] As *P. falciparum* parasites mature, knobs appear on the surface of the parasitized red cell that facilitate the cytoadherence of *P. falciparum*–parasitized red cells to endothelial cells in capillaries and postcapillary venules of the brain, kidneys, and other affected organs (see Fig. 264–2).[8, 9] This cytoadherence accounts for the observation that mature asexual *P. falciparum* parasites are not seen on the peripheral blood smear because they are sequestered in the peripheral microcirculation. Although the binding of *P. falciparum*–parasitized red blood cells to endothelial cells depends on specific endothelial receptors (see Table 264–2),[8, 25, 26] the expression of those receptors (and thus the extent of cytoadherence) may vary with cytokines such as tumor necrosis factor-α (TNF-α), which are increased in severe *P. falciparum* infection and may exacerbate the microvascular pathology by enhancing cytoadherence (Fig. 264–4).[30, 31] The peripheral sequestration resulting from cytoadherence shelters *P. falciparum* parasites from (1) removal from the circulation as they pass through the interendothelial cell slits of the spleen because their host red blood cells are no longer deformable[11, 12] and (2) oxidant damage caused by circulating repetitively through the capillary bed of the lung with its elevated Po_2.

TABLE 264–2 Ligands and Receptors in the Malaria Parasite Life Cycle

Life Cycle Event	Parasite Ligand	Host Receptor Molecule
Hepatocyte entry by sporozoites	Circumsporozoite protein[18]	Heparan sulfate proteoglycans, low-density lipoprotein receptor-related protein[19]
Red cell entry by merozoites		
P. vivax	Pv135[23]	Duffy factor[20]
P. falciparum	Erythrocyte-binding antigen 175 (EBA175)[23]	Glycophorin A[23]
Rosetting of *P. falciparum*–parasitized red cells	*P. falciparum*–infected erythrocyte membrane protein 1 (*PfEMP1*)[35]	Complement-receptor 1[35]
Cytoadherence of *P. falciparum*–parasitized red blood cells	*PfEMP1* (*var* genes)[27]	Thrombospondin, CD36, ICAM-1, VCAM-1, ELAM-1[8, 25, 26]

Peripheral Sequestration and the Protective Effects of Sickle Hemoglobin

Because sickling is enhanced by a reduced oxygen tension,[32] the sequestration of *P. falciparum*–parasitized red blood cells in the peripheral microvasculature increases the sickling of parasitized HbAS cells by trapping those cells where the oxygen tension is lower (Fig. 264–5). (The mechanisms by which sickling inhibits parasite growth may include physical disruption of the parasite and its host red blood cell.) By thus inhibiting parasite growth, sickle hemoglobin protects against severe, complicated, or cerebral *P. falciparum* infection but not against parasites that do not sequester (*P. vivax, P. ovale,* and *P. malariae*) nor against red blood cell invasion by merozoites.

Rosetting refers to the flower-like appearance of a parasitized red blood cell, surrounded by unparasitized red cells (petals). Although this phenomenon is real, its relationship to severe and cerebral malaria is controversial, and the pathogenic significance of rosetting is unclear.[33, 34] Recent data suggest that *PfEMP1* (the molecule encoded by *var* genes, which is responsible for cytoadherence to endothelial cells) is also the ligand involved in rosetting, and that the red blood cell receptor for rosetting is complement-receptor 1.[35]

Effects of Hyperparasitemia

There is a semiquantitative relationship between the magnitude of the parasitemia and the risk of death, especially among nonimmune expatriates with *P. falciparum* infection.[36] Reasons for this relationship may include more extensive microvascular disease and more severe metabolic effects (hypoglycemia, lactic acidosis)[37, 38] in persons with hyperparasitemia (>250,000/μl[>5% parasitemia]). In contrast, persons with partial immunity may tolerate substantial parasitemias (>5%) without evidence of disease.

Hypoglycemia has at least four causes in persons with severe *P. falciparum* malaria: (1) depletion of liver glycogen from decreased oral intake during 1 to 3 days of illness before obtaining medical attention,[38] (2) glucose consumption by the large numbers of parasites present in the blood stream that have a glycolytic (Embden-Meyerhof) pathway but not a Krebs cycle,[37–39] (3) the hypoglycemic effects of elevated levels of TNF-α (interleukin-1 and TNF-β),[40] and (4) release of insulin from the pancreatic β cell during treatment with quinine or quinidine, which stimulates insulin release in vivo as evidenced by elevated C-peptide levels in persons with hypoglycemia and hyperinsulinemia during severe *P. falciparum* infection.[37]

Lipid peroxidation has been suggested as a potentially important pathogenic mechanism, in part because studies have shown beneficial effects from the use of desferrioxamine (an iron chelator).[41] One hypothesis proposed to explain these effects is that free iron (from the heme in malarial pigment) may catalyze lipid peroxidation via

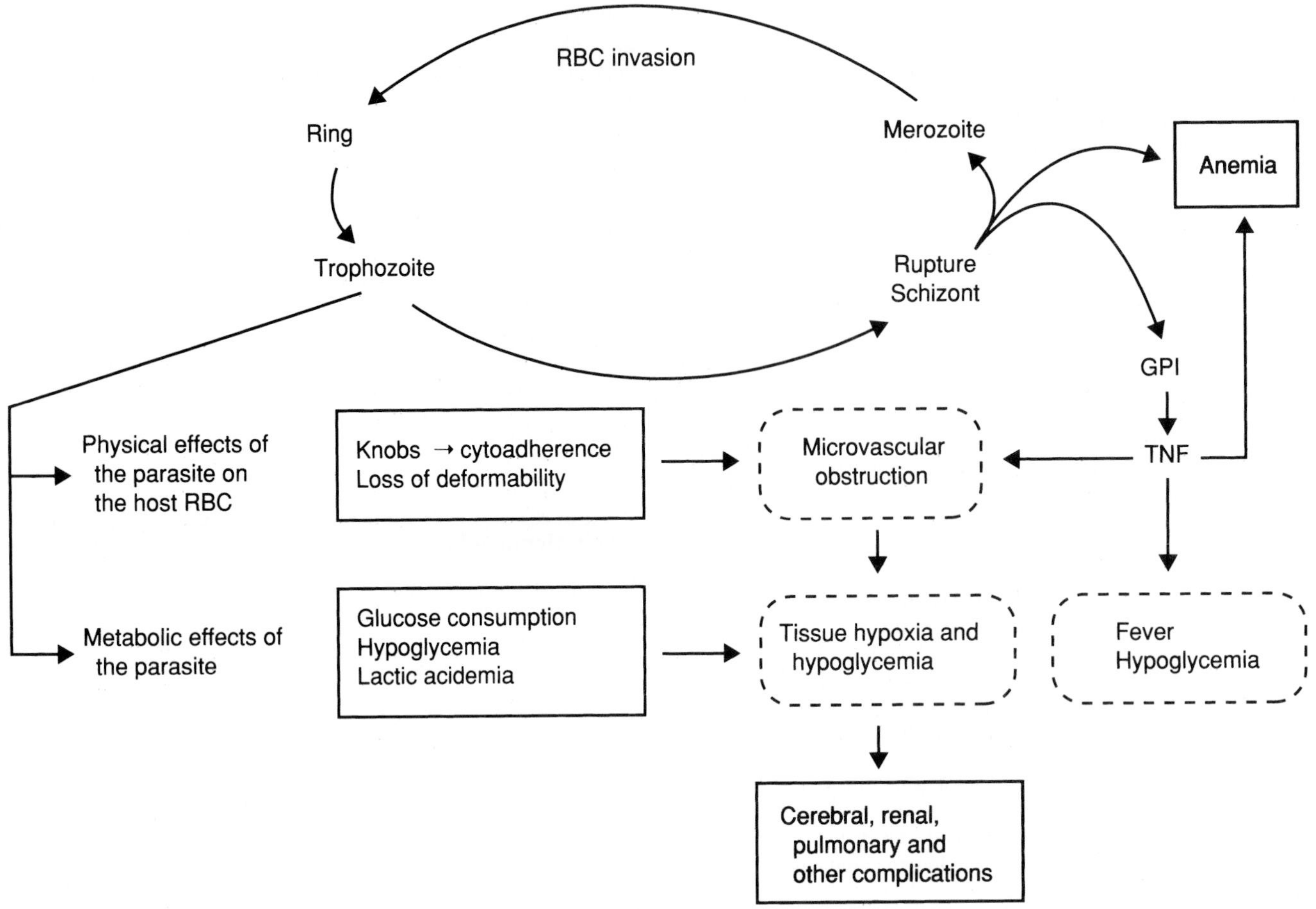

FIGURE 264–4. Pathogenesis of severe, complicated, and cerebral *Plasmodium falciparum* malaria. *P. falciparum* malaria is a microvascular disease with a strong metabolic component. It is a microvascular disease because cytoadherence of *P. falciparum*–infected red blood cells (RBCs) to endothelial cells in capillaries and postcapillary venules,[8–10] plus the nondeformable nature of those cells,[11, 12] produces functional microvascular obstruction. Cytokines such as tumor necrosis factor (TNF)-α contribute to the process by enhancing expression of receptor molecules on the endothelial cell surface[25, 26] and thus further increasing cytoadherence and obstruction to flow. It is a metabolic disease because consumption of glucose and production of lactate by the parasite plus the hypoglycemic effects of TNF-α (and possibly IL-1 and TNF-β)[40] and treatment with quinine (or quinidine)[37, 38] all contribute to glucose deprivation, lactate excess, and acidemia at the tissue level. Anemia results acutely from RBC lysis as schizont stage parasites mature and chronically from the effects of TNF-α.[48] Some studies have shown that rupture of schizont stage parasites exposes glycosylphosphatidylinositol (GPI) anchors on the parasite and RBC surface that elicit TNF-α and thus explains why the asexual erythrocytic cycle stimulates the release of TNF-α[31, 57] in the absence of the gram-negative endotoxin previously associated with the release of TNF-α from macrophages.[46]

the Haber-Weiss reaction and that superoxide or oxygen radicals from this reaction may then produce tissue damage, causing the pathologic features and symptoms of severe, complicated, and cerebral malaria. Reservations about this hypothesis include the observation that many persons with cerebral malaria respond rapidly to treatment, which would not be expected if tissue damage from lipid peroxidation were the basis of cerebral malaria and coma. Alternative explanations for the beneficial effects of desferrioxamine treatment include its antiparasite activity in vitro, which may result from inhibition of the iron-dependent enzyme ribonucleotide reductase.[42]

TABLE 264–3 Complications of Plasmodial Infection

Plasmodium falciparum
Cerebral malaria, including seizures and coma
Hypoglycemia, lactic acidosis
Severe anemia
Pulmonary edema
Tropical splenomegaly (chronic)
Plasmodium vivax
Late splenic rupture (2–3 mo after the initial infection)
Plasmodium malariae
Immune complex glomerulonephritis with parasite antigen and host IgG

Specific Complications (Table 264–3)

Cerebral Malaria. Despite the pathologic evidence for cytoadherence in the brains of persons dying of cerebral malaria,[8, 9, 43] the pathogenic mechanisms responsible for cerebral malaria remain unclear. These mechanisms must account for a devastating effect on brain function with modest histopathologic evidence of tissue damage and must permit rapid reversibility with treatment (although up to 10 to 12% of persons surviving cerebral malaria have persistent neurologic abnormalities at the time of discharge from the hospital). Microvascular obstruction that prevents the exchange of glucose and oxygen at the capillary level, hypoglycemia, lactic acidosis, and high-grade fever are all consistent with the principal manifestations of cerebral malaria: seizures and impaired consciousness. In contrast, the effects of nitric oxide are not yet clear. Because nitric oxide production is likely to be increased by the elevated circulating TNF-α levels in cerebral malaria, nitric oxide should produce vasodilation (and potentially improve brain function) by acting on the microvasculature. Conversely, nitric oxide that crosses from the microvasculature into the brain parenchyma may function as an inhibitory neurotransmitter.[44] Thus, the overall effect of nitric oxide on brain function in cerebral malaria is unclear. In addition, contrary to expectation, there is no evidence that malaria is more frequent or more severe in children with progressive human immunodeficiency virus infection.[45]

Renal Failure. Renal failure is a relatively common complication among patients with severe *P. falciparum* infection and no immunity. However, its pathogenesis is also unclear. A reasonable working hypothesis is that renal failure in severe *P. falciparum* infection may result from the combined effects of microvascular disease (particularly oxygen and glucose deprivation at the capillary-tissue level in the renal cortex) and hemolysis (due to circulating free hemoglobin and malarial pigment in the blood stream) on the kidneys (see Fig. 264–4).

Pulmonary Edema. Although parasitized red blood cells sequester in the pulmonary microvasculature, neither the extent of that sequestration nor its impact on oxygen and carbon dioxide exchange has been defined. In addition, the elevated TNF-α levels in the serum of persons with severe or complicated malaria raise the possibility that TNF-α alone may produce the pulmonary edema observed in severe malaria (as in gram-negative bacteremia).[46] This hypothesis is consistent with clinical studies that demonstrate normal or reduced, rather than elevated, pulmonary capillary wedge pressures in the pulmonary edema observed in malaria.[47]

Gastroenteritis. Gastroenteritis is common among young children with *P. falciparum* infection and is associated with the cytoadherence of parasitized red blood cells to endothelial cells in the microvasculature of the gastrointestinal tract.

Anemia. At least two factors contribute to the severe anemia seen in *P. falciparum* infection. The first is that the mature schizont physically destroys its host red blood cell as it matures and liberates merozoites. The second is that cytokines such as TNF-α released as a result of red blood cell rupture by the parasite (see Fig. 264–4) suppress hematopoiesis.[48]

Pathology of *Plasmodium falciparum* Infection

Pathologic studies have shown that 94% of cerebral microvessels have adherent parasitized red blood cells in persons dying of cerebral malaria (versus 13% in controls with noncerebral malaria).[43] However, the histopathologic evidence for tissue damage in the brain is modest; it is typically restricted to scattered ring hemorrhages and mild perivascular inflammation.[49] Based on those observations, the simplest explanation for multiorgan failure in severe and complicated malaria[50] is that diffuse microvascular disease resulting from large

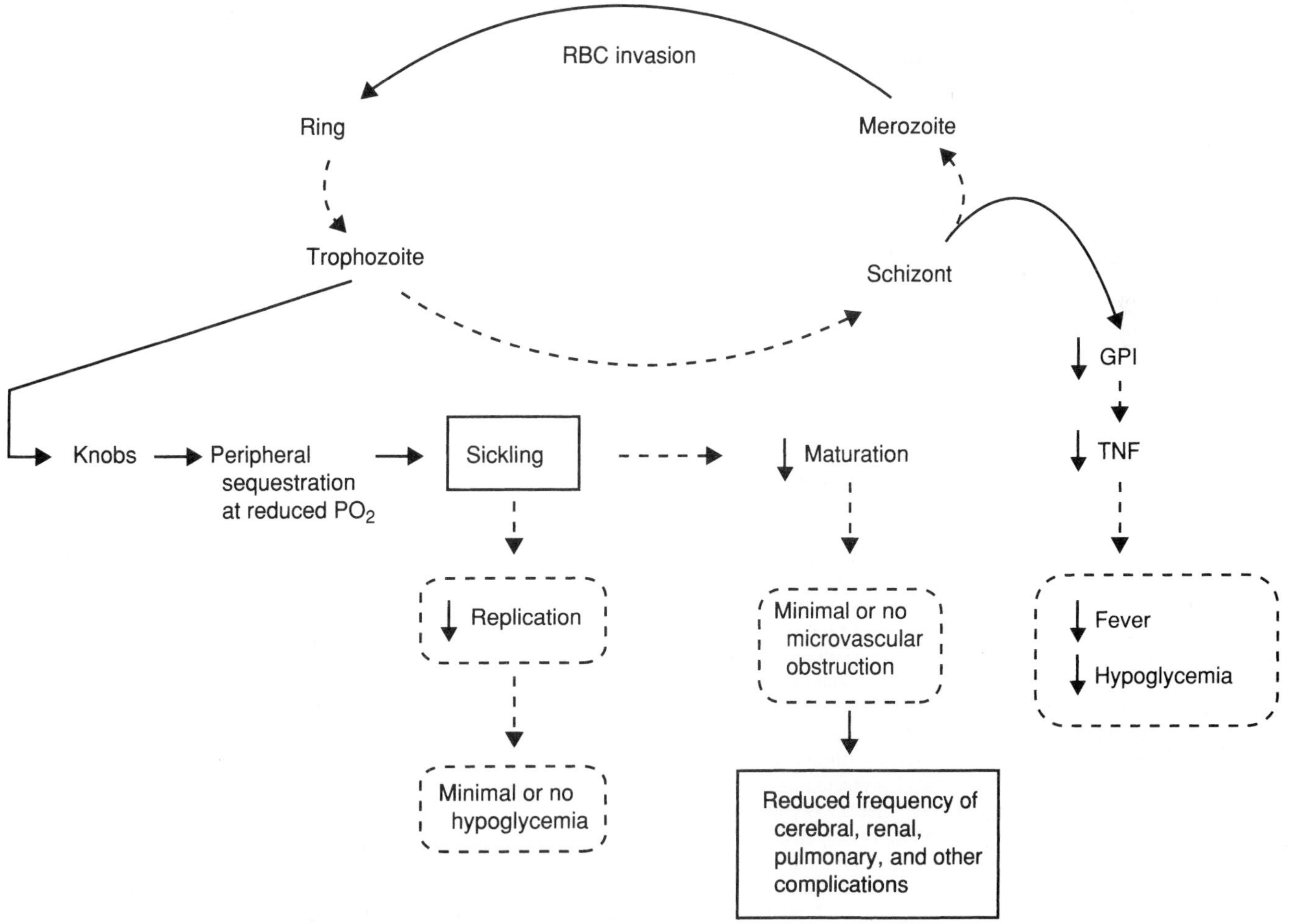

FIGURE 264–5. The relationship between the protective effect of sickle hemoglobin and peripheral sequestration of *Plasmodium falciparum*–parasitized red blood cells (RBCs). In contrast to the events in persons with normal (HbAA) hemoglobin, the difference in persons with sickle trait (HbAS) is that the reduced Po_2 in the peripheral microvasculature enhances sickling, which inhibits parasite growth.[32] Thus, cytoadherence via knobs (as in Fig. 264–4) places the *P. falciparum*–parasitized RBC in an environment that inhibits parasite maturation and replication (represented by the change from solid to dashed lines on the diagram) and its metabolic consequences.[15, 16]

numbers of adherent parasitized red blood cells produces functional obstruction to flow, with secondary organ dysfunction from hypoxia and hypoglycemia. (The severity of obstruction to flow is exacerbated by the loss of red cell deformability that accompanies parasite maturation.)[11, 12, 51] Note that this sequence of events (see Fig. 264–4) is hypothetical because there have as yet been no direct measurements of microvascular blood flow or capillary exchange in the brain during cerebral malaria, or in other organs during the development of renal, pulmonary, or cardiac complications. Additional, potentially relevant factors include the effects of elevated cytokine levels (TNF-α, interleukin-1, TNF-β) on endothelial cell and brain function.

Disease Due to *Plasmodium vivax* or *Plasmodium ovale* Infection

In contrast to *P. falciparum* infection, peripheral sequestration does not occur in *P. vivax* or *P. ovale* infection because neither *P. vivax*– nor *P. ovale*–parasitized red blood cells have knobs. Thus, all asexual stages of these parasites circulate in the peripheral blood and there are no microvascular complications in the brain, kidneys, lungs, or other organs damaged so severely in *P. falciparum* infection. Although the magnitude of the parasitemia is limited by the requirement for young red blood cells (reticulocytes) in *P. vivax* (or *P. ovale*) infection,[7, 24] the hemolysis associated with *P. vivax* (or *P. ovale*) infection may stimulate hematopoiesis enough to increase the number of reticulocytes and may thus permit parasitemias substantially greater than 1 to 2%.

Disease Due to *Plasmodium malariae* Infection

Because *P. malariae*–parasitized red blood cells likewise have no knobs, they do not sequester in the peripheral microvasculature and do not produce microvascular disease. The magnitude of the parasitemia is low and symptoms are typically mild. In fact, low-grade *P. malariae* blood stream infections may persist for 20 to 30 years or more after leaving the endemic area. *P. malariae* infection may also produce an immune complex glomerulonephritis in which the principal components are parasite *(P. malariae)* antigens, host antibody to those antigens, and complement. This syndrome is thought to result from continued antigenic stimulation (low-level parasitemia) and typically occurs 3 to 6 months after the peak of the malaria transmission season.[52]

Host Factors

In addition to antibodies and cell-mediated immunity, other host factors important in the response to plasmodial infection include age (duration of exposure), HLA determinants, and the natural filter function of the spleen. Although the risk of infection persists throughout life in endemic areas, the risk of severe disease is greatest among young children[16] and recent immigrants to malarious areas.[53] Although the host immune response is thought to be responsible for the decreased risk of severe complications and death among children who survive the first several years of life in endemic areas and among immigrants who survive their first several years after moving to endemic areas, no specific antibodies or cell-mediated responses have been shown to protect against disease. Although studies in Gambia initially suggested that HLA Bw53 protected against severe disease,[16] subsequent studies have shown that a polymorphism in the closely linked TNF-α promoter region is responsible for this protection.[54] Normal spleen function is an important host factor because of both the immunologic and filtering functions of the spleen. The spleen removes parasitized red cells and older red blood cells from the circulation because they are less deformable. In the person without a spleen, malaria is a rapidly progressive disease in which large numbers of parasitized cells circulate in the peripheral blood (including mature asexual-stage parasites normally not observed in vivo with *P. falciparum* infection).

CLINICAL MANIFESTATIONS

Cyclic fevers are the hallmark of malaria and typically occur shortly before or at the time of red blood cell lysis as schizonts rupture to release new infectious merozoites—every 48 hours with *P. vivax* or *P. ovale* infection (tertian malaria) and every 72 hours with *P. malariae* infection (quartan malaria). Although the parasite cycle is also 48 hours in *P. falciparum,* continuous fevers with intermittent irregular spikes are more characteristic of *P. falciparum* infection than a regular 48-hour cycle, especially in persons with no immunity, such as expatriate travelers.

The malarial paroxysm is so characteristic that it is the defining clinical feature of the disease. After a prodrome that may last several hours, the paroxysm typically has three stages. The first is an initial "cold or chilling stage" that lasts 15 minutes to several hours, during which the patient feels cold and has true shaking chills. The second "hot stage" lasts several hours and coincides with schizont rupture. During that time, the temperature rises and may reach 40°C (104°F) or higher with minimal diaphoresis and the attendant risks of febrile convulsions and hyperthermic brain damage. Clinical signs and symptoms include tachycardia, hypotension, cough, headache, backache, nausea, abdominal pain, vomiting, diarrhea, and altered consciousness. Within 2 to 6 hours, the patient enters the third "sweating" stage of the paroxysm with generalized diaphoresis, resolution of fever, and marked fatigue—usually giving way rapidly to sleep.

The cause of fever in malaria has been a matter of controversy for decades. Despite many efforts, lipopolysaccharide-like material similar to the bacterial cell wall has not been identified in either the parasite or in the blood stream at the time of red blood cell rupture. Thus, although TNF-α levels are increased in persons with severe and cerebral malaria,[55, 56] the reason for those increases has not been clear. The current hypothesis is that the glycosyl phosphatidylinositol anchor that connects parasite proteins to the parasite or red blood cell surface is exposed (or released) at the time of merozoite release and stimulates the production and release of TNF-α by macrophages.[31, 57] TNF-α then produces the fever associated with synchronous parasite release at the end of the asexual cycle.[46, 57] Chloroquine, which inhibits the release and the action of TNF-α in other systems,[58, 59] may act by these mechanisms (in addition to being an antiplasmodial drug) in persons with malaria.

Laboratory Findings

Abnormal laboratory findings in malaria typically reflect the severity of hemolysis. For example, massive *P. falciparum* infections produce acute decreases in hemoglobin, hematocrit, and haptoglobin, with increases in lactic dehydrogenase and a vigorous reticulocyte response. Thrombocytopenia is common. Renal disease, including acute renal failure, is a frequent complication of severe *P. falciparum* infection with proteinuria, hemoglobinuria, and an elevated serum creatinine level. Although liver involvement may occur, most hyperbilirubinemia results from intravascular hemolysis, and rises in serum enzymes such as alanine aminotransferase may result from the involvement of organs other than the liver. Although the laboratory findings may be consistent with disseminated intravascular coagulation, pathologic changes consistent with this syndrome are rarely observed at autopsy, and treatment with heparin typically increases complications (rather than reducing them).

Coma, Seizures, and Other Evidence of Central Nervous System Dysfunction

Central nervous system dysfunction is so common among children and other persons with no immunity with severe malaria that its presence is often regarded as diagnostic of malaria. (This is despite the fact that the same clinical picture may be produced by illnesses such as bacterial meningitis, which should be treated with antibiotics rather than antimalarial agents. Note that classic signs of meningismus associated with bacterial meningitis may disappear with deep coma from any cause.) The extent of central nervous system dysfunction in cerebral malaria may reflect parasite virulence, host immune status, the time from onset of symptoms to treatment, or a combination of these factors. Clinical manifestations vary from subtle central nervous system impairment (confusion, obtundation) to seizures and deep unrousable coma. From the therapeutic perspective, it is essential to remember that hypoglycemia alone may produce these findings and that hypoglycemia may result from other causes (e.g., insulin overdose), as well as from severe malaria.

Renal failure occurs in a substantial number of persons with severe or complicated malaria; it is especially frequent among persons without immunity with high parasitemias who have hemoglobinuria in the context of glucose-6-phosphate deficiency, often after treatment with quinine (blackwater fever).[60] Renal failure due to malaria is typically oliguric, although nonoliguric renal failure may also occur. A significant subset of persons with severe disease must undergo dialysis for several weeks in order to survive, as in other causes of acute renal failure, although many persons who have elevated serum creatinine levels improve with conservative fluid management alone.

Pulmonary edema is uncommon, even with severe or complicated *P. falciparum* infection. When pulmonary edema occurs in malaria, it typically results from capillary leak (rather than cardiac failure) and primarily affects persons with hyperparasitemia. Although pulmonary edema was once thought to be a universally fatal complication, it can be treated successfully with artificial ventilation using a positive-pressure respirator.

DIFFERENCES IN CLINICAL MANIFESTATIONS BETWEEN PERSONS WITH NO IMMUNITY (EXPATRIATES) AND RESIDENTS OF MALARIOUS AREAS WITH PARTIAL IMMUNITY

Plasmodium falciparum malaria is a markedly different disease in persons with no immunity and those with partial immunity. (The term *immune* is not used because natural infection does not elicit immune responses that prevent reinfection.) Among persons with no immunity, such as expatriate travelers, detectable parasitemias produce significant symptoms, and the magnitude of the parasitemia is related to the risk of death or complications.[36] In contrast, many infected persons with partial immunity have few or no symptoms (with even fewer complications). Thus, one child in an African village may be playing soccer while another child with the same parasitemia is severely ill and may go on to die. The mechanisms responsible for this discrepancy must be understood in order to produce a vaccine that reduces morbidity and mortality among African children.

ANTIMALARIAL DRUGS

Many of the greatest successes (and failures) of malaria control have resulted from the advantages (and limitations) of specific antimalarial agents (see Chapter 39). In fact, the single most important factor in the current worldwide resurgence of malaria is the increasing prevalence of antimalarial resistance.[61] The most important antimalarial agents are quinoline derivatives such as chloroquine, quinine, mefloquine, and halofantrine; antifolates such as pyrimethamine and sulfonamides that are used in the treatment of many bacterial pathogens; artemisinin derivatives such as qinghaosu; and ribosomal inhibitors such as tetracycline and clindamycin, which are also used against many bacterial pathogens.

Unique Targets for Antiplasmodial Drugs

As with other pathogens, rational development of antimalarial agents is based on identifying unique targets present in the parasite but not the host cell (thus limiting toxicity) that are essential for parasite growth and development (thus limiting the ability of the parasite to bypass that pathway). At least three potentially specific targets are present in plasmodia: (1) hemoglobin degradation in the plasmodial food vacuole,[62, 63] (2) orotic acid dehydrogenase activity in the mitochondrion, and (3) the purine salvage pathway.[64] In addition, iron chelation with desferrioxamine B may accelerate recovery from cerebral malaria (possibly by inhibiting ribonucleotide reductase), particularly in persons with elevated transferrin saturations.[65]

Mechanisms of Drug Action against Plasmodia

Aminoquinolines such as chloroquine, quinine, amodiaquine, and probably mefloquine and halofantrine act against the parasite by inhibiting the proteolysis of hemoglobin in the food vacuole.[62, 63] Because free heme from the proteolysis of hemoglobin is toxic (it lyses membranes), it must be sequestered in a nontoxic form (malarial pigment) to protect the parasite. Recent studies suggest that aminoquinolines may inhibit the heme polymerase activity responsible for polymerizing heme into malarial pigment[66] and that they may also inhibit the aspartic and cysteine proteases that degrade hemoglobin and alkalinize the plasmodial food vacuole (secondary lysosome).[67] Artemisinin and its derivatives are thought to act by binding to the iron in malarial pigment to yield free radicals that then react with and damage parasite proteins near the plasmodial food vacuole.[68, 69]

Mechanisms of Drug Resistance in Plasmodia

Although there are no known artemisinin-resistant plasmodia, resistance to chloroquine and antifolates is a major problem in the treatment and control of malaria (Fig. 264–6). In vivo, the response to chloroquine treatment is graded as S, RI, RII, or RIII based on whether standard doses of chloroquine (1.5 g base or 2.5 g salt over 3 days, Table 264–4) produce a cure (S = susceptible), clearance of the parasitemia followed by recrudescence within 28 days (RI = low-level resistance), a decrease in the parasitemia without parasite clearance from the blood stream (RII = intermediate-level resistance), or no detectable decrease (or an increase) in the parasitemia (RIII = high-level resistance). Although this nomenclature suggests variability in the level of resistance in *P. falciparum,* laboratory studies suggest that there is only one mechanism of chloroquine resistance and that all resistant parasites have the same energy-dependent chloroquine efflux mechanism (which leads to reduced chloroquine accumulation).[70] Recent studies suggest that the genetic basis of chloroquine resistance is a 300-kD protein on chromosome 7[71] and that chloroquine resistance is not genetically linked to either of the two multidrug resistance–like genes in *P. falciparum.*[72] In contrast, neither the nature nor the genetic basis of chloroquine resistance in *P. vivax* has been defined; it is not clear whether chloroquine-resistant *P. vivax* also has an energy-dependent efflux process or a different mechanism of chloroquine resistance.

In contrast to chloroquine, resistance to mefloquine and halofantrine has been associated with amplification of multidrug resistance–like genes but not with drug efflux (or reduced drug accumulation). Resistance to antifolates is based primarily on specific point mutations in the parasite dihydrofolate reductase thymidylate synthase enzyme that can be detected by polymerase chain reaction.[73, 74] The clustering of those amino acid changes at the enzyme's active site suggests that their effect is to decrease (or interfere with) drug binding at the active site.[75]

Chemoprophylaxis of Malaria

Drugs used for chemoprophylaxis should be started 2 weeks before departure to permit time to change the regimen if there are significant side effects. Chemoprophylaxis should continue for 4 weeks after

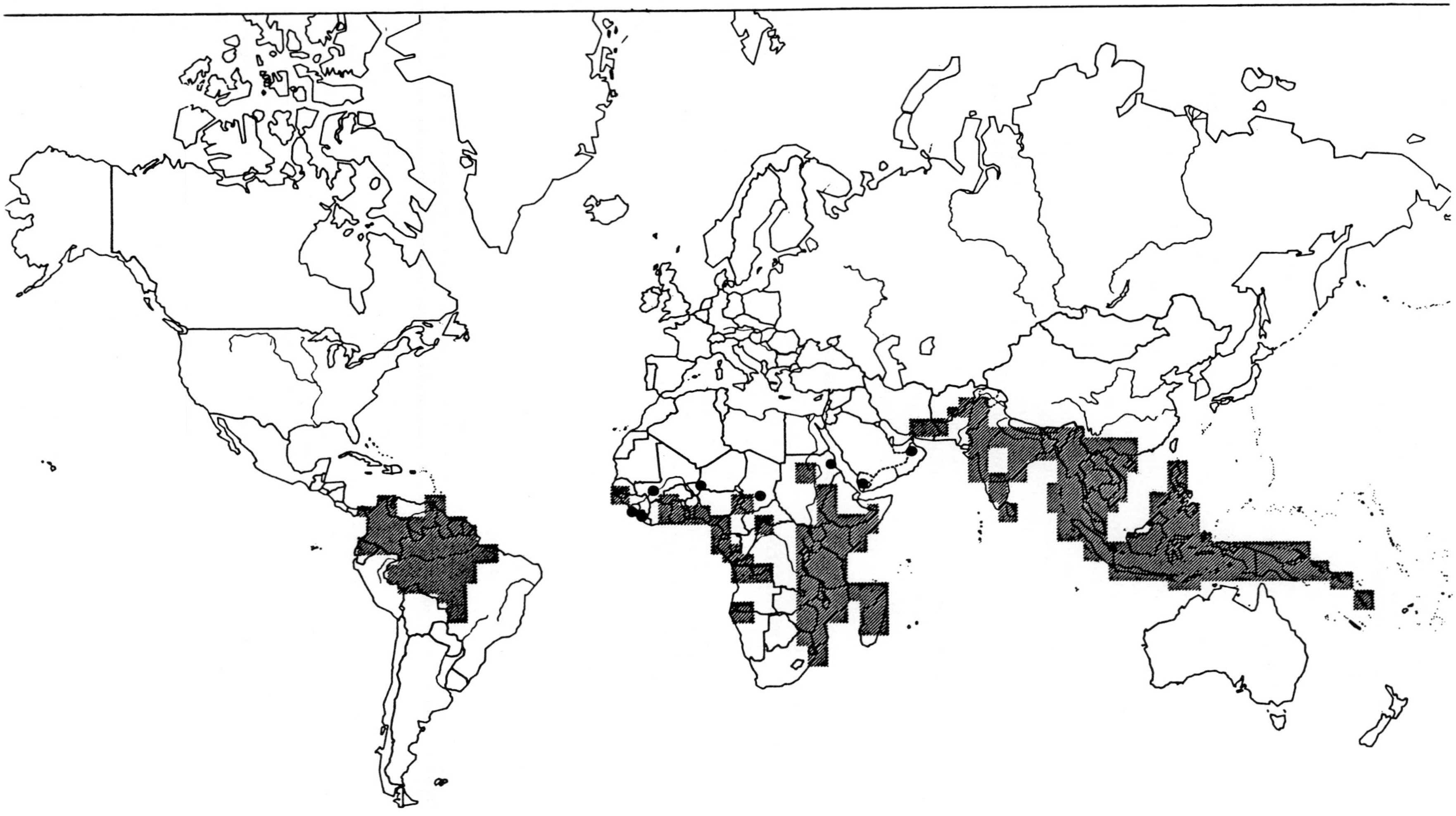

FIGURE 264–6. Areas with chloroquine-resistant *Plasmodium falciparum*. Areas of greatest interest to American physicians that do not have chloroquine-resistant *P. falciparum* are in Central America and the Caribbean, especially Haiti.[84, 85] Resistance is uncommon in the Middle East, although it is present. Although transmission is much less intense in Southeast Asia than in sub-Saharan Africa,[84, 85] drug resistance is quite prevalent and includes resistance to chloroquine, pyrimethamine-sulfadoxine, mefloquine, and halofantrine.[4, 98–103]

TABLE 264-4 Treatment of Malaria

Drug	Adult Dose	Pediatric Dose
P. vivax, P. ovale, P. malariae and chloroquine-susceptible *P. falciparum*	600 mg base (1000 mg chloroquine phosphate) PO initially, followed by an additional 300 mg base (500 mg salt) 6 hr later, and again on days 2 and 3	10 mg base/kg PO initially, followed by an additional 5 mg base/kg 6 hr later and on days 2 and 3 (total dose of 25 mg base/kg over 3 d)
Chloroquine-resistant *P. falciparum*		
Oral regimens		
Drugs of choice	Quinine sulfate 650 mg every 8 hr × 3–7 d	25 mg/kg/day in three divided doses × 3–7 d
	plus	*plus*
	Doxycycline 100 mg bid × 7 d	2 mg/kg/day up to 100 mg × 7 d
	or	*or*
	Quinine followed by pyrimethamine-sulfadoxine, 3 tablets on the last day of quinine treatment	Quinine as above followed by one dose of pyrimethamine-sulfadoxine: <1 yr: 0.25 tablet 1–3 yr: 0.5 tablet 4–8 yr: 1.0 tablet 9–14 yr: 2 tablets
Alternatives	Quinine followed by clindamycin 900 mg tid × 5 days	Quinine followed by clindamycin 20–40 mg/kg/day in 3 divided doses
	or	
	Mefloquine 1250 single dose	25 mg/kg single dose (<45 kg)
	or	*or*
	Halofantrine† 500 mg every 6 hr × 3 doses, repeat 1 wk later	8 mg/kg every 6 hr × 3 doses (<40 kg), repeat 1 wk later
	or	*or*
	Atovaquone 1000 mg daily × 3 d plus proguanil 400 mg daily × 3 d	Atovaquone: 11–20 kg: 250 mg; 21–30 kg: 500 mg; 31–40 kg: 750 mg plus proguanil: 11–20 kg: 100 mg; 21–30 kg: 200 mg; 31–40 kg: 300 mg
	or	*or*
	Atovaquone 1000 mg daily × 3 d plus doxycycline 100 mg bid × 3 days	Atovaquone (as above) plus doxycycline 2 mg/kg daily × 3 d
	or	
	Artesunate 4 mg/kg daily × 3 d plus mefloquine 1250 single dose (750 mg followed 12 hr later by 500 mg)	(no recommended dose)
Parenteral Regimens		
	Quinidine gluconate 10 mg salt/kg loading dose (max 600 mg) in normal saline infused slowly over 1–2 hr, followed by continuous infusion of 0.02 mg/kg/min until patient is able to begin oral treatment	Same as adult dose
or		
	Quinine dihydrochloride 20 mg salt/kg loading dose in 5% dextrose over 4 hr, followed by 10 mg salt/kg over 2–4 hr every 8 hr (max 1800 mg/d) until patient is able to begin oral treatment	Same as adult dose
	Artemether 3.2 mg/kg intramuscularly, then 1.6 mg/kg daily × 3 d	Same as adult dose
Prevention of Relapse Due to P. Vivax or P. Ovale		
	Primaquine phosphate 15.3 mg base (26.5 mg phosphate salt) per day PO for 14 days *or* 45 mg base (79 mg salt) per week × 8 wk	0.3 mg base (0.5 mg salt) per kg/day × 14 d

*Doxycycline and clindamycin are typically begun after 2 to 3 days of treatment with quinine to ensure that side effects from quinine are not confused with those of doxycycline or clindamycin.
†Halofantrine has not been approved by the U.S. Food and Drug Administration for use in the United States for either adults or children. Cardiac toxicity from halofantrine can be fatal.
Adapted from Drugs for parasitic infections. Med Lett Drugs Ther. 1998;40:1–12, with permission from the Medical Letter on Drugs and Therapeutics.

leaving the endemic area to cover infections acquired shortly before or at the time of departure.

Prevention of Infection Due to Chloroquine-Susceptible *Plasmodium vivax, Plasmodium ovale, Plasmodium malariae,* and *Plasmodium falciparum.* Chloroquine is the chemoprophylactic agent of choice for the prevention of infections due to susceptible plasmodia because it is effective against those parasites and is safe for pregnant women and young children (Table 264–5).[76–79] Although side effects occur (headache, dizziness, blurred vision), most are transient and can be controlled by taking half the dose twice a week (e.g., on Sunday and Wednesday) rather than the full dose once a week. Significant hazards include the arrhythmogenic effects of chloroquine, which are not seen at normal doses, but do occur with inadvertent rapid intravenous infusion or massive overdoses.[80, 81] For this reason, candy-coated chloroquine pills and chloroquine-containing syrups must be stored in areas where young children cannot reach them, or not used at all, to prevent accidental, potentially fatal ingestions. More subtle adverse effects include suppression of the immune response to rabies vaccine,[82] although the response to yellow fever vaccine is unimpaired.[83]

Prevention of Infection Due to Chloroquine-Resistant *Plasmodium falciparum.* Based on the increasing prevalence of chloroquine-resistant *P. falciparum* and on the experience with U.S. Peace Corps volunteers and Swiss travelers,[84, 85] mefloquine (Lariam) chemoprophylaxis is now recommended for travel to Southeast Asia, the Amazon region of South America, and sub-Saharan Africa.[78, 79] Although headache, dizziness, and visual symptoms occur with mefloquine prophylaxis, they are no more frequent than with chloroquine.[84] Pyrimethamine sulfadoxine (Fansidar) is not recommended for prophylaxis because of potentially fatal hypersensitivity reactions, such as the Stevens-Johnson syndrome. Daily doxycycline is an alternative for persons unable to tolerate these drugs, although it produces yeast vaginitis so frequently that women who take it should be supplied with nystatin suppositories; doxycycline may also produce a photosensitive drug eruption. Weekly chloroquine plus daily proguanil is less effective than mefloquine alone.[84, 85]

Prevention of Infection Due to Chloroquine-Resistant *Plasmodium vivax.* Although chloroquine-resistant *P. vivax* has been reported from Irian Jaya, Indonesia, Papua New Guinea, and possibly Colombia,[86–90] chemoprophylaxis recommendations for travel to those areas remain unchanged because of uncertainty about the relative prevalence of chloroquine-resistant versus chloroquine-susceptible *P. vivax.*

DIAGNOSIS OF MALARIA

The most critical factor in beginning malaria treatment is establishing the diagnosis. Although empirical treatment is a reasonable public

TABLE 264–5 Chemoprophylaxis of Malaria*

Species	Drug	Adult Dose	Pediatric Dose
P. vivax, P. ovale, P. malariae, and chloroquine-susceptible *P. falciparum*	Chloroquine	300 mg base (500 mg chloroquine phosphate) PO/wk†	5 mg base/kg (8.3 mg salt/kg) PO per week up to adult dose
Chloroquine-resistant *P. falciparum*	Mefloquine (Lariam)	250 mg (228 mg base) PO/wk†	5–9 kg: 0.125 tablet (31.25 mg) 10–19 kg: 0.25 tablet (62.5 mg) 20–30 kg: 0.50 tablet (125 mg) 31–45 kg: 0.75 tablet (187.5 mg) >45 kg: 1.0 tablet (250 mg)
	Or doxycycline (Vibramycin)	100 mg PO/d	Contraindicated in children less than 8 yr of age 2 mg/kg/d up to 100 mg/d PO
	Or primaquine	0.5 mg base/kg/d	Same as adult dose
	Or chloroquine plus proguanil	Chloroquine as above plus 200 mg proguanil/d PO	Chloroquine as above plus proguanil <2 yr: 50 mg/d 2–6 yr: 100 mg/d 7–10 yr: 150 mg/d >10 yr: 200 mg/d

*Updated malaria chemoprophylaxis recommendations may be obtained 24 hours a day by calling the Centers for Disease and Prevention Control Hot Line at 404-332-4555.
†Beginning 1 week before travel and continuing weekly for the duration of stay and for 4 weeks after leaving.
Adapted from Drugs for parasitic infections. Med Lett Drugs Ther. 1998;40:1–12, with permission from the Medical Letter on Drugs and Therapeutics.

health strategy for malaria control programs with limited diagnostic resources, symptoms and signs consistent with malaria are produced by a wide variety of infectious and noninfectious conditions in the tropics, including typhoid fever, rheumatic fever, and bacterial meningitis (due to meningococci, *Haemophilus*, or pneumococci). Thus, the differential diagnosis is sufficiently broad that failure to respond to treatment should suggest not only antimalarial resistance but also the possibility of an alternative diagnosis. Although malaria is typically diagnosed by microscopic examination of a thin or thick smear, alternative techniques of similar (or greater) sensitivity now available for the diagnosis of *P. falciparum* infection include an enzyme-linked immunosorbent assay for a histidine-rich *P. falciparum* antigen (histidine-rich protein 2), an immunoassay for species-specific parasite lactate dehydrogenase isoenzymes, DNA hybridization, and the amplification of parasite DNA or mRNA using the polymerase chain reaction. Of these three techniques, the ones most applicable in the field are enzyme-linked immunosorbent assay kits for histidine-rich protein 2 or parasite lactate dehydrogenase, which may be performed within 10 minutes in the field using reagents now available commercially.[91, 92]

TREATMENT OF MALARIA

Effective treatment of persons with malaria includes a full complement of supportive strategies in addition to antimalarial agents. Although hypoglycemia is discussed here, important issues not discussed include the management of seizures, pulmonary edema, renal failure, and lactic acidosis.[50] Exchange transfusion is a potentially useful adjunct in the treatment of hyperparasitemia, although there are no levels of parasitemia at which survival does not occur without exchange transfusion. In fact, survival has been reported without exchange transfusion despite parasitemias greater than 50%,[93] although some have recommended exchange transfusion for parasitemias greater than 15% in persons with no immunity.[94] Physicians in countries such as the United States should hospitalize persons with *P. falciparum* infection who have no immunity until a response to treatment has been observed and enough time has elapsed to be certain that cerebral, renal, pulmonary, or other complications are not likely. Persons with partial immunity and uncomplicated *P. falciparum* infection and some persons with no immunity and *P. vivax (P. ovale)* or *P. malariae* infection can be treated as outpatients if reliable follow-up is possible.

Treatment of Chloroquine-Susceptible Plasmodium vivax, Plasmodium ovale, Plasmodium malariae, *and* Plasmodium falciparum

Chloroquine-susceptible infections may be treated orally using a total dose of 25 mg chloroquine base/kg given over 3 days (see Table 264–4). Patients unable to take oral medications may be treated initially with parenteral chloroquine, and then switched to oral chloroquine when they are able to take oral medications. Even for persons with central nervous system involvement, there are no advantages of quinine (or other antimalarial agents) over chloroquine for infections due to chloroquine-susceptible parasites. Halofantrine is contraindicated in pregnant or lactating women. Because of its arrhythmogenic potential,[80, 81] intravenous chloroquine must be given as a carefully controlled infusion to avoid a large bolus in the heart. Pruritus is an important side effect of chloroquine (and halofantrine) and is particularly common in sub-Saharan Africa,[95] although its pathogenesis is unclear.

Treatment of Chloroquine-Resistant Plasmodium falciparum

Persons able to take oral medications may be treated with quinine, mefloquine,[96] halofantrine,[97] or pyrimethamine sulfadoxine, assuming that they did not receive the same drug for chemoprophylaxis. Because most parasites resistant to mefloquine are also resistant to halofantrine,[98, 99] halofantrine should not be used to treat persons who acquire *P. falciparum* infection while receiving mefloquine chemoprophylaxis. Halofantrine can result in prolongation of the QT interval and ventricular arrhythmias in susceptible persons receiving higher than recommended doses as well as in those with recent or concurrent mefloquine therapy, QT prolongation, or thiamine deficiency. Because fatalities have occurred with halofantrine, alternative drugs are preferred when possible.[100] Halofantrine is contraindicated in pregnant or lactating women. Because resistance to pyrimethamine sulfadoxine is common in areas with chloroquine resistance, persons given pyrimethamine sulfadoxine should be watched carefully to ensure that the drug is effective. Although quinine may often produce side effects, it is effective in vivo against all strains of *P. falciparum* studied thus far. Because quinidine is two- to threefold more active than quinine, because its serum and plasma levels can be measured in most American hospitals, and because parenteral quinine is no longer available in the United States, quinidine is preferable to quinine for parenteral use in the United States. Artemisinin derivatives such as artemether are effective in children with *P. falciparum* infection; they may clear parasitemia and coma more rapidly than does quinine. A controlled study in Thailand has suggested that intravenous artesunate followed by mefloquine is more effective than either artesunate or mefloquine alone and may prevent the late recrudescences typically observed with artesunate alone.[101] Additional controlled studies suggest that artemisinin suppositories may clear *P. falciparum* parasitemia as rapidly as intravenous artesunate,[102, 103] and that artemether is as effective as quinine for severe and cerebral malaria.[104, 105] Because artemisinin treatment is frequently associated with late recrudescences,[102, 103] additional drugs such as mefloquine, tetracycline, or pyrimethamine sulfadoxine are often given after the initial treatment with artemisinin to prevent recrudescence 3 to 4 weeks later. Anecdotal reports of embryo toxicity in rats and mice and pathologic evidence of neurotoxicity in dogs[106] suggest that artemisinin derivatives should not be given to pregnant women and should be used with caution until these issues have been resolved. Note that comparative studies of artemether and quinine have not found an increase in neurotoxicity with artemether.[104, 105] As with quinine, there is no evidence of high-level resistance to artemisinin or its derivatives.

Treatment of Chloroquine-Resistant Plasmodium vivax

Thus far, all persons with chloroquine-resistant *P. vivax* infection have responded to treatment with oral mefloquine or halofantrine.

Eradication of Persistent Hypnozoites in Plasmodium vivax *or* Plasmodium ovale *Infection*

Persons with *P. vivax* or *P. ovale* infection in nonendemic areas are usually treated with primaquine to eradicate hypnozoites (see Table 264–4) in order to prevent relapse.

USE OF ANTIMALARIAL AGENTS IN PREGNANT WOMEN

Chemoprophylaxis is an important issue for pregnant women because they are at increased risk of serious disease, especially primigravidas; because maternal malaria may decrease fetal survival; and because chloroquine is the only antimalarial agent known to be safe in pregnancy.[76, 77] This is a particularly difficult issue because of concern about teratogenicity during pregnancy. Although data suggest that mefloquine may also be safe,[107] the number of women studied thus far is limited, and mefloquine has not yet been approved by the U.S. Food and Drug Administration for chemoprophylaxis during pregnancy. In contrast to the concerns about chemoprophylaxis, treatment is essential for pregnant women with symptomatic malaria to save their lives and their pregnancies. In fact, despite the known abortifacient effects of quinine at higher doses, therapeutic doses of quinine intravenously decrease both premature uterine contractions and fever in pregnant women with *P. falciparum* infection.[108]

ANCILLARY MEASURES IN THE TREATMENT OF SEVERE MALARIA

Antibodies against Tumor Necrosis Factor-α

Despite the potentially critical importance of TNF-α in the pathogenesis of severe, complicated, and cerebral malaria,[55, 56] studies using monoclonal antibodies directed against TNF-α had no impact on mortality and may increase morbidity (neurologic sequelae), although they did reduce fever more rapidly than was seen in the controls.[109, 110] Potential explanations for these disappointing results include the participation of multiple cytokines (including interleukin-1 and lymphotoxin [TNF-β], as well as TNF-α)[40] in the pathogenesis of severe and complicated malaria.

Steroids and Cerebral Malaria

Although steroids were used empirically for many years to treat persons with cerebral malaria, a controlled trial has now shown that they are harmful. Patients who received dexamethasone had a longer duration of coma and worse outcomes than did patients who received quinine alone.[111]

REDUCING VECTOR-HUMAN CONTACT

Because of increasing drug resistance, alternative measures such as reducing vector-human contact are progressively more (rather than less) important. Insecticide-impregnated bed nets (with permethrin or deltamethrin) markedly reduce intradomiciliary vector populations and should protect against infection,[112] although protection against disease may be less in areas with more intense transmission.[113] In addition, insect repellents such as diethyltoluamide (DEET) may reduce the risk of transmission in areas in which mosquitoes are active before bedtime.

CANDIDATE MALARIA VACCINE ANTIGENS

Because natural infection with malaria parasites does not produce immunity, there is no model of effective immunity to plasmodial infection and no guarantee that humoral or cellular immune responses to specific antigens will protect against either infection or disease.[114, 115] New strategies, such as the DNA vaccines under study, and established methods, such as peptide-based vaccines, have had substantial difficulty.[116] In addition, a major unresolved question is whether different mechanisms may be necessary to provide protection against both infection and disease. Antigens currently under study as vaccine candidates include sporozoite antigens (circumsporozoite protein),[18, 19, 117] merozoite antigens (merozoite surface protein 1 [MSP1]),[118] erythrocyte-binding antigen 175 [EBA 175], rhoptry-associated protein 1 [RAP1], apical merozoite antigen [AMA1], and gametocyte antigens (Pfs25, Pfs230).[119] The antigens present on different parasite stages are sufficiently different from each other that antibodies directed against one stage do not cross-react with other stages. Thus, most investigators expect that an effective vaccine will require at least three antigens (sporozoite-, merozoite-, and gametocyte-stage antigens). Of these, the antigen with the best evidence for protection against blood-transmitted infection in primates is MSP1[117]; the antigen that should prevent initial infection from the anopheline mosquito is circumsporozoite protein[18, 19]; the antigen that should reduce transmission from humans to mosquitoes, but not transmission from mosquitoes to humans or the development of disease, is Pfs25.[119]

OVERALL PERSPECTIVE

Despite the progress that has been made against many other infectious diseases, several factors should temper optimism about the short-term control or eradication of malaria: (1) drug resistance is increasing in *P. falciparum,*[120] has spread to *P. vivax,* and is the principal reason that malaria is now a reemerging (resurgent) disease[61]; (2) neither the basis of protection against infection (the goal of immunization with sporozoite vaccines) nor the basis of protection against disease (the basis of the semi-immune state) is understood; (3) the biologic basis of the vector capacity responsible for mosquito-borne malaria transmission is unknown; and (4) insecticide resistance is increasing among the anophelines responsible for malaria transmission.

REFERENCES

1. Bruce-Chwatt LJ. History of malaria from prehistory to eradication. In: Wernsdorfer WH, MacGregor IA, eds. Malaria: Principles and Practice of Malariology. London: Churchill-Livingstone; 1988:1–59.

2. Bruce-Chwatt LJ. Paleogenesis and paleoepidemiology of primate malaria. Bull World Health Organ. 1965;32:363–387.
3. Coatney GR, Collins WE, Warren McW, et al. The Primate Malarias. Washington, DC: U.S. Dept of Health, Education and Welfare, U.S. Government Printing Office; 1971:1–340.
4. World malaria situation in 1994, Parts I–III. Wkly Epidemiol Rec. 1997;72:269–274, 277–283, 285–291.
5. Krotoski WA. The hypnozoite and malarial relapse. Prog Clin Parasitol. 1989;1:1–19.
6. Krogstad DJ, Engleberg NC. Blood and tissue protozoa. In: Schaechter M, Engleberg NC, Eisenstein BI, Medoff G, eds. Mechanisms of Microbial Disease. 3rd ed. Baltimore: Williams & Wilkins; 1998:448–462.
7. Neva FA. Observations on induced malaria: Looking back for a view of the future. Am J Trop Med Hyg. 1977;26(Suppl):211–216.
8. Aikawa M, Iseki M, Barnwell JW, et al. The pathology of human cerebral malaria. Am J Trop Med Hyg. 1990;43:30–37.
9. Aikawa M, Rabbege JR, Udeinya IJ, et al. Electron microscopy of knobs in *Plasmodium falciparum*–infected erythrocytes. J Parasitol. 1983;69:435–437.
10. Nagatake T, Hoang VT, Tegoshi T, et al. Pathology of *Plasmodium falciparum* malaria in Vietnam. Am J Trop Med Hyg. 1992;47:259–264.
11. Cranston HA, Boylan CW, Corroll GL, et al. *Plasmodium falciparum* maturation abolishes red cell deformability. Science. 1984;223:400–403.
12. Krogstad DJ, Sutera SP, Marvel JS, et al. Calcium and the malaria parasite: Parasite maturation and the loss of red cell deformability. Blood Cells. 1991;17:229–241, 242–248.
13. Touré YT. The current state of studies of malaria vectors and the antivectorial campaign in West Africa. Trans R Soc Trop Med Hyg. 1989;83(Suppl):39–41.
14. Zucker JR. Changing patterns of autochthonous malaria transmission in the United States: A review of recent outbreaks. Emerg Infect Dis. 1997;2:37–43.
15. Allison AC. Polymorphism and natural selection in human populations. Cold Spring Harb Symp Quant Biol. 1964;29:137–149.
16. Hill AV, Allsopp CE, Kwiatkowski D, et al. Common West African HLA antigens are associated with protection from severe malaria. Nature. 1991;352:595–600.
17. Ruwende C, Khoo SC, Snow RW, et al. Natural selection of hemi- and heterozygotes for G6PD deficiency in Africa by resistance to severe malaria. Nature. 1995;376:246–249.
18. Cerami C, Frevert U, Sinnis P, et al. The basolateral domain of the hepatocyte plasma membrane bears receptors for the circumsporozoite protein of *Plasmodium falciparum* sporozoites. Cell. 1992;70:1021–1033.
19. Sahkibaei M, Frevert U. Dual interaction of the malaria circumsporozoite protein with the low density lipoprotein receptor-related protein (LRP) and heparan sulfate proteoglycans. J Exp Med. 1996;184:1699–1711.
20. Miller LH, Mason SJ, Clyde DF, et al. The resistance factor to *Plasmodium vivax* in blacks. N Engl J Med. 1976;295:302–304.
21. Horuk R, Chitnis CE, Darbonne WC. A receptor for the malarial *parasite Plasmodium vivax:* The erythrocyte chemokine receptor. Science. 1993;261:1182–1184.
22. Hadley TJ, Peiper SC. From malaria to chemokine receptor: The emerging physiologic role of the Duffy blood group antigen. Blood. 1997;89:3077–3091.
23. Adams JH, Sim BK, Dolan SA, et al. A family of erythrocyte binding proteins of malaria parasites. Proc Natl Acad Sci U S A. 1992;89:7085–7089.
24. Galinski MR, Medina CC, Ingravallo P, et al. A reticulocyte binding protein complex of *Plasmodium vivax* merozoites. Cell. 1992;69:1213–1226.
25. Chulay JD, Ockenhouse CF. Host receptors for malaria infected erythrocytes. Am J Trop Med Hyg. 1990;43:6–14.
26. Ockenhouse CF, Tegoshi T, Maeon Y, et al. Human vascular endothelial cell adhesion receptors for *Plasmodium falciparum*–infected erythrocytes: Roles for endothelial leukocyte adhesion molecule 1 and vascular cell adhesion molecule 1. J Exp Med. 1992;176:1183–1189.
27. Su XZ, Heatwole VM, Wertheimer SP, et al. The large diverse gene family *var* encodes proteins involved in cytoadherence and antigenic variation of *Plasmodium falciparum*–infected erythrocytes. Cell. 1995;82:89–100.
28. Rowe JA, Moulds JM, Newbold CI, Miller LH. *P. falciparum* rosetting mediated by a parasite-variant erythrocyte membrane protein and complement-receptor 1. Nature. 1997;388:292–295.
29. Miller LH, Good MF, Milon G. Malaria pathogenesis. Science. 1994;264:1878–1883.
30. Barnwell JW. Cytoadherence and sequestration in *falciparum* malaria. Exp Parasitol. 1989;69:407–412.
31. Schofield L, Hackett F. Signal transduction in host cells by a glycosylphosphatidylinositol toxin of malaria parasites. J Exp Med. 1993;177:145–153.
32. Friedman MJ. Erythrocytic mechanism of sickle cell resistance to malaria. Proc Natl Acad Sci U S A. 1978;75:1994–1997.
33. Ho M, Davis TM, Silamut K, et al. Rosette formation of *Plasmodium falciparum*–infected erythrocytes from patients with acute malaria. Infect Immun. 1991;59:2135–2139.
34. Carlson J, Helmby H, Hill AV, et al. Human cerebral malaria: Association with erythrocyte rosetting and lack of anti-rosetting antibodies. Lancet. 1990;336:1457–1460.
35. Rowe JA, Moulds JM, Newbold CI, Miller LH. *P. falciparum* rosetting mediated by a parasite-variant erythrocyte membrane protein and complement-receptor 1. Nature. 1997;388:292–295.
36. Field JW. Blood examination and prognosis in acute *falciparum* malaria. Trans R Soc Trop Med Hyg. 1949;43:33–48.
37. White NJ, Warrell DA, Chanthavanich P, et al. Severe hypoglycemia and hyperinsulinemia in *falciparum* malaria. N Engl J Med. 1983;309:61–66.
38. Taylor TE, Molyneux ME, Wirima JJ, et al. Blood glucose levels in Malawian children before and during the administration of intravenous glucose for severe *falciparum* malaria. N Engl J Med. 1988;319:1040–1047.
39. Sherman IW. Biochemistry of *Plasmodium* (malaria parasites). Microbiol Rev. 1979;43:453–495.
40. Clark IA, Gray KM, Rockett EJ, et al. Increased lymphotoxin (TNF-β) in human malarial serum, and the ability of this cytokine to increase plasma interleukin-6 and cause hypoglycaemia in mice: Implications for malarial pathology. Trans R Soc Trop Med Hyg. 1992;86:602–607.
41. Gordeuk V, Thuma P, Brittenham G, et al. Effect of iron chelation therapy on recovery from deep coma in children with cerebral malaria. N Engl J Med. 1992;327:1473–1477.
42. Atkinson CT, Bayne MT, Gordeuk VR, et al. Stage-specific ultrastructural effects of desferrioxamine on *Plasmodium falciparum* in vitro. Am J Trop Med Hyg. 1991;45:593–601.
43. Riganti M, Pongponratn E, Tegoshi T, et al. Human cerebral malaria in Thailand: A clinicopathological correlation. Immunol Lett. 1990;25:199–205.
44. Clark IA, Rockett KA, Cowden WB. Possible central role of nitric oxide in conditions clinically similar to cerebral malaria. Lancet. 1992;340:894–896.
45. Greenberg AE, Nsa W, Ryder RW, et al. *Plasmodium falciparum* malaria and perinatally acquired human immunodeficiency virus type 1 infection in Kinshasa, Zaire: A prospective, longitudinal cohort study of 587 children. N Engl J Med. 1991;325:105–109.
46. Tracey KJ, Fong Y, Hesse DG, et al. Anti-cachectin/TNF monoclonal antibodies prevent septic shock during lethal bacteremia. Nature. 1987;330:662–664.
47. Charoenpan P, Indraprasit S, Kiatboonsri S, et al. Pulmonary edema in severe *falciparum* malaria: Hemodynamic study and clinicophysiologic correlation. Chest. 1990;97:1190–1197.
48. Moldawer LL, Marano MA, Wei H, et al. Cachectin/tumor necrosis factor-α alters red blood cell kinetics and induces severe anemia in vivo. FASEB J. 1989;3:1637–1643.
49. Turner G. Cerebral malaria. Brain Pathol. 1997;7:569–582.
50. Warrell DA, Molyneux ME, Beales PF, eds. Severe and complicated malaria. Trans R Soc Trop Med Hyg. 1990;84(Suppl 2):1–65.
51. Krogstad DJ, Sutera SP, Marvel JS, et al. Calcium and the malaria parasite: Parasite maturation and the loss of red cell deformability. Blood Cells. 1991;17:229–241, 242–248.
52. Kibukamusoke JW, Hutt MSR, Wilks NE. The nephrotic syndrome in Uganda and its association with quartan malaria. Q J Med. 1967;36:393–408.
53. Baird JK, Purnomo, Basri H, et al. Age-specific prevalence of *Plasmodium falciparum* among six populations with limited histories of exposure to endemic malaria. Am J Trop Med Hyg. 1993;49:707–719.
54. McGuire W, Hill AVS, Allsopp CEM, et al. Variation in the TNF-α promoter region associated with susceptibility to cerebral malaria. Nature. 1994;371:508–511.
55. Grau GE, Taylor TE, Molyneux ME, et al. Tumor necrosis factor and disease severity in children with *falciparum* malaria. N Engl J Med. 1989;320:1586–1591.
56. Kwiatkowski D, Hill AV, Sambou I, et al. TNF concentration in fatal cerebral, non-fatal cerebral, and uncomplicated *Plasmodium falciparum* malaria. Lancet. 1990;336:1201–1204.
57. Kwiatkowski D, Cannon JG, Manogue KR, et al. Tumor necrosis factor production in *falciparum* malaria and its association with schizont rupture. Clin Exp Immunol. 1989;77:361–366.
58. Picot S, Peyron F, Vuillez JP, et al. Chloroquine inhibits tumor necrosis factor production by human macrophages in vitro. J Infect Dis. 1991;164:830.
59. Kull FC Jr, Besterman JM. Drug-induced alterations of tumor necrosis factor–mediated cytotoxicity: Discrimination of early versus late stage action. J Cell Biochem. 1990;42:1–12.
60. Tran TH, Day NP, Ly VC, et al. Blackwater fever in southern Vietnam: A prospective descriptive study of 50 cases. Clin Infect Dis. 1996;23:1274–1281.
61. Krogstad DJ. Malaria as a re-emerging disease. Epidemiol Rev. 1996;18:77–89.
62. Goldberg DE, Slater AF, Beavis R, et al. Hemoglobin degradation in the human malaria pathogen *Plasmodium falciparum:* A catabolic pathway initiated by a specific aspartic protease. J Exp Med. 1991;173:961–969.
63. Rosenthal PJ, Nelson RG. Isolation and characterization of a cysteine proteinase gene of *Plasmodium falciparum.* Mol Biochem Parasitol. 1992;51:143–152.
64. Ring CS, Sun E, McKerrow JH, et al. Structure-based inhibitor design by using protein models for the development of antiparasitic agents. Proc Natl Acad Sci U S A. 1993;90:3583–3587.
65. Gordeuk VR, Thuma PE, McLaren CE, et al. Transferrin saturation and recovery from coma in cerebral malaria. Blood. 1995;85:3297–3301.
66. Slater AF, Cerami A. Inhibition by chloroquine of a novel haem polymerase enzyme activity in malaria trophozoites. Nature. 1992;355:167–169.
67. Krogstad DJ, Schlesinger PH. A perspective on antimalarial action: Effects of weak bases on *Plasmodium falciparum.* Biochem Pharmacol. 1986;35:547–552.
68. Meshnick SR, Yang YZ, Lima V, et al. Iron-dependent free radical generation from the antimalarial agent artemisinin (quinghaosu). Antimicrob Agents Chemother. 1993;37:1108–1114.
69. Zhang F, Gosser DK Jr, Meshnick SR. Hemin-catalyzed decomposition of artemisinin (quinghaosu). Biochem Pharmacol. 1992;43:1805–1809.
70. Krogstad DJ, Gluzman IY, Kyle DE, et al. Efflux of chloroquine from *Plasmodium falciparum:* Mechanism of chloroquine resistance. Science. 1987;238:1283–1285.
71. Su X-Z, Kirkman LA, Fujioka H, Wellems TE: Complex polymorphisms in a p330 kDa protein are linked to chloroquine-resistant *Plasmodium falciparum* in South-east Asia and Africa. Cell. 1997;91:591–603.

72. Wellems TE, Panton LJ, Gluzman IY, et al. Chloroquine resistance not linked to mdr-like genes in a *Plasmodium falciparum* cross. Nature. 1990;345:253–255.
73. Peterson DS, DiSanti SM, Povoa M, et al. Prevalence of the dihydrofolate reductase Asn-108 mutation as the basis for pyrimethamine-resistant *Plasmodium falciparum* malaria in the Brazilian Amazon. Am J Trop Med Hyg. 1991;45:492–497.
74. Gyang FN, Peterson DS, Wellems TE. *Plasmodium falciparum:* Rapid detection of dihydrofolate reductase mutations that confer resistance to cycloguanil and pyrimethamine. Exp Parasitol. 1992;74:470–472.
75. Peterson DS, Milhous WK, Wellems TE. Molecular basis of differential resistance to cycloguanil and pyrimethamine in *Plasmodium falciparum* malaria. Proc Natl Acad Sci U S A. 1990;87:3018–3022.
76. Levy M, Buskila D, Gladman DD, et al. Pregnancy outcome following first trimester exposure to chloroquine. Am J Perinatol. 1991;8:174–178.
77. Nyirjesy P, Kavasya T, Axelrod P, et al. Malaria during pregnancy: Neonatal morbidity and mortality and the efficacy of chloroquine chemoprophylaxis. Clin Infect Dis. 1993;16:127–132.
78. White NJ: The treatment of malaria. N Engl J Med. 1996;335:800–806.
79. Anonymous. Drugs for parasitic infections. Med Lett Drugs Ther. 1998;40:1–12.
80. Looareesuwan S, White NJ, Chanthavanich P, et al. Cardiovascular toxicity and distribution kinetics of intravenous chloroquine. Br J Clin Pharmacol. 1986;22: 31–36.
81. Jaeger A, Sauder P, Kopferschmitt J, et al. Clinical features and management of poisoning due to antimalarial drugs. Med Toxicol Adverse Drug Exper. 1987;2:242–273.
82. Pappaioanou M, Fishbein DB, Dreesen DW, et al. Antibody response to preexposure human diploid-cell rabies vaccine given concurrently with chloroquine. N Engl J Med. 1986;314:280–284.
83. Barry M, Patterson JE, Tirrell S, et al. The effect of chloroquine prophylaxis on yellow fever vaccine antibody response. Am J Trop Med Hyg. 1991;44:79–82.
84. Lobel HO, Miani M, Eng T, et al. Long-term prophylaxis with weekly mefloquine. Lancet. 1993;341:848–851.
85. Steffen R, Fuchs E, Schildknecht J, et al. Mefloquine compared with other malaria chemoprophylactic regimens in tourists visiting East Africa. Lancet. 1993; 341:1299–1303.
86. Rieckmann KH, Davis DR, Hutton DC. *Plasmodium vivax* resistant to chloroquine? Lancet. 1989;2:1183–1184.
87. Baird JK, Basri H, Purnomo, et al. Resistance to chloroquine by *Plasmodium vivax* in Irian Jaya, Indonesia. Am J Trop Med Hyg. 1991;44:547–552.
88. Murphy GS, Basri H, Purnomo, et al. Vivax malaria resistant to treatment and prophylaxis with chloroquine. Lancet. 1993;341:96–100.
89. Schuurkamp GH, Spicer PE, Kereu RK, et al. Chloroquine-resistant *Plasmodium vivax* in Papua New Guinea. Trans R Soc Trop Med Hyg. 1992;86:121–122.
90. Arias AE, Corredor A. Low response of Colombian strains of *Plasmodium vivax* to classical antimalarial therapy. Trop Med Parasitol. 1989;40:21–23.
91. Parra ME, Evans CB, Taylor DW. Identification of *Plasmodium falciparum* histidine-rich protein 2 in the plasma of humans with malaria. J Clin Microbiol. 1991;29:1629–1634.
92. Palmer CJ, Lindo JF, Klaskala WI, et al. Evaluation of the OptiMAL test for rapid diagnosis of *Plasmodium vivax* and *Plasmodium falciparum* malaria. J Clin Microbiol. 1998;36:203–206.
93. Marik PE. Severe *falciparum* malaria: Survival without exchange transfusion. Am J Trop Med Hyg. 1989;41:627–629.
94. Miller KD, Greenberg AE, Campbell CC. Treatment of severe malaria in the United States with a continuous infusion of quinidine gluconate and exchange transfusion. N Engl J Med. 1989;321:65–70.
95. Ezeamuzie IC, Igbibgi PS, Ambakederemo AW, et al. Halofantrine-induced pruritus amongst subjects who itch to chloroquine. J Trop Med Hyg. 1991;94:184–188.
96. Palmer KJ, Holliday SM, Brogden RN. Mefloquine: A review of its antimalarial activity, pharmacokinetic properties and therapeutic efficacy. Drugs. 1993;45: 430–475.
97. Anonymous. Halofantrine in the treatment of malaria. Lancet. 1989;2:537–538.
98. Shanks GD, Watt G, Edstein MD, et al. Halofantrine for the treatment of mefloquine chemoprophylaxis failures in *Plasmodium falciparum* infections. Am J Trop Med Hyg. 1991;45:488–491.
99. Ketrangsee S, Vijaykadga S, Yamokgul P, et al. Comparative trial on the response of *Plasmodium falciparum* to halofantrine and mefloquine in Trat Province, eastern Thailand. S E Asian J Trop Med Public Health. 1992;23:55–58.
100. Drug alert: Halofantrine. Change in recommendations for use. Wkly Epidemiol Rec. 1993;68:269–270.
101. Looareesuwan S, Wiravan C, Venijanonta S, et al. Randomised trial of artesunate and mefloquine alone and in sequence for acute uncomplicated *falciparum* malaria. Lancet. 1992;339:821–824.
102. Hien TT, Arnold K, Vinh H, et al. Comparison of artemisinin suppositories with intravenous artesunate and intravenous quinine in the treatment of cerebral malaria. Trans R Soc Trop Med Hyg. 1992;86:582–583.
103. Arnold K, Tran TH, Nguyen TC, et al. A randomized comparative study of artemisinin (qinghaosu) suppositories and oral quinine in acute *falciparum* malaria. Trans R Soc Trop Med Hyg. 1990;84:499–502.
104. van Hensbroek MB, Onyiorah E, Jaffar S, et al. A trial of artemether or quinine in children with cerebral malaria. N Engl J Med. 1996;335:69–75.
105. Tran TH, Day NP, Nguyen HP, et al. A controlled trial of artemether or quinine in Vietnamese adults with severe *falciparum* malaria. N Engl J Med. 1996;335:76–83.
106. Brewer TG, Grate SJ, Peggins JO, et al. Fatal neurotoxicity of arteether and artemether. Am J Trop Med Hyg. 1994;51:251–259.
107. Steketee RW, Wirima JJ, Slutsker L, et al. Malaria prevention in pregnancy: The effects of treatment and chemoprophylaxis on placental malaria infection, low birth weight and fetal, infant and child survival. CDC-ARTS Publication 0994048. Washington, DC: U.S. Dept of Health and Human Services; 1994.
108. Looareesuwan S, Phillips RE, White NJ, et al. Quinine in severe falciparum malaria in late pregnancy. Lancet. 1985;2:4–8.
109. Kwiatkowski D, Molyneux ME, Stephens S, et al. Anti-TNF therapy inhibits fever in cerebral malaria. Q J Med. 1993;86:91–98.
110. van Hoensbroek MB, Palmer A, Onyiorah E, et al. The effect of a monoclonal antibody to tumor necrosis factor on survival from childhood malaria. J Infect Dis. 1996;174:1091–1097.
111. Warrell DA, Looareesuwan S, Warrell MJ, et al. Dexamethasone proves deleterious in cerebral malaria: A double-blind clinical trial in 100 comatose patients. N Engl J Med. 1982;306:313–318.
112. Beach RF, Ruebush TK 2nd, Sexton JD, et al. Effectiveness of permethrin-impregnated bed nets and curtains for malaria control in a holoendemic area of western Kenya. Am J Trop Med Hyg. 1993;49:290–300.
113. Curtis CF. Impregnated bednets, malaria control and child mortality. Trop Med Intl Health. 1996;1:137–138.
114. Kwiatkowski D, Marsh K. Development of a malaria vaccine. Lancet. 1997;350:1696–1701.
115. Targett GAT. Malaria vaccines—now and the future. Trans R Soc Trop Med Hyg. 1995;89:585–587.
116. Riley E. Malaria vaccine trials: SPf66 and all that. Curr Opin Immunol. 1995;7:612–616.
117. Nardin EH, Nussenzweig RS. T cell responses to pre-erythrocytic stages of malaria: Role in protection and vaccine development against pre-erythrocytic stages. Annu Rev Immunol. 1993;11:687–727.
118. Siddiqui WA, Tam LQ, Kramer KJ, et al. Merozoite surface coat precursor protein completely protects monkeys against *Plasmodium falciparum* malaria. Proc Natl Acad Sci U S A. 1987;84:3014–3018.
119. Kaslow DC. Immunogenicity of *Plasmodium falciparum* sexual stage antigens: Implications for the design of a transmission blocking vaccine. Immunol Lett. 1990;25:83–86.
120. Tsai YL, Krogstad DJ. The resurgence of malaria. In: Scheld WM, Craig WA, Hughes JM, eds. Emerging Infections 2. Washington, DC: American Society for Microbiology; 1998:195–212.

Chapter 265

Leishmania Species: Visceral (Kala-Azar), Cutaneous, and Mucosal Leishmaniasis

RICHARD D. PEARSON
ANASTACIO DE QUEIROZ SOUSA
SELMA M. B. JERONIMO

Leishmaniasis refers to the spectrum of disease caused by *Leishmania* spp., which are protozoa of the order Kinetoplastida. Leishmanias live in macrophages as intracellular amastigotes in humans and other mammalian hosts and as extracellular promastigotes in the gut of their invertebrate sandfly vectors.[1, 2] Cell-mediated immune mechanisms are responsible for controlling leishmanial infections. The clinical manifestations of leishmaniasis depend on complex interactions resulting from the parasite's invasiveness, tropism, and pathogenicity, and the host's genetically determined immune responses. Clinically, leishmaniasis is divided into visceral, cutaneous, and mucosal syndromes. A single *Leishmania* sp. can produce different clinical syndromes, and each of the syndromes can be caused by more than one species. The *Leishmania* spp. that infect humans, their geographic distributions, and the clinical syndromes that they most commonly produce are summarized in Table 265–1.[2, 3]

A great deal of attention has focused on leishmaniasis during the past 2 decades. Major epidemics of visceral leishmaniasis have occurred in eastern India and Bangladesh[4, 5] and among refugees in Sudan.[6–8] Large urban outbreaks have been reported from cities in northeastern Brazil.[9, 10] A viscerotropic syndrome caused by *Leish-*

TABLE 265–1 Leishmaniasis*

Clinical Syndromes	*Leishmania* Spp.	Location
Visceral leishmaniasis (kala-azar): generalized involvement of the reticuloendothelial system (spleen, bone marrow, liver and so on)	*L. (Leishmania) donovani*	Indian subcontinent, northern and eastern China, Pakistan, Nepal, eastern Africa
	L. (L.) infantum	Middle East, Mediterranean littoral, Balkans, central and southwestern Asia, northern and western China, North and sub-Saharan Africa
	L. (L.) spp.	Kenya, Ethiopia, Sudan, Somalia
	L. (L.) chagasi	Latin America
	L. (L.) amazonensis	Brazil (Bahia state)
	L. (L.) tropica (rare)	Middle East, Saudi Arabia (U.S. troops), India, North Africa, Pakistan, Mediterranean littoral, central and western Asia
Post–kala-azar dermal leishmaniasis	*L. (L.) donovani*	Indian subcontinent
	L. (L.) spp.	Kenya, Ethiopa, and Somalia
Old World cutaneous leishmaniasis: Single or limited number of skin lesions	*L. (L.) major*	Middle East, India, Pakistan, Africa, central and western Asia, northern and western China
	L. (L.) tropica	Mediterranean littoral, Middle East, North Africa, India, Pakistan, central and western Asia
	L. (L.) aethiopica	Ethiopian highlands, Kenya, Yemen
	L. (L.) infantum (rare)	Middle East, Mediterranean littoral, central Asia, northern and western China, North and sub-Saharan Africa
	L. (L.) donovani	East Africa
	L. (L.) spp.	Kenya, Ethiopia, Somalia
Diffuse cutaneous leishmaniasis	*L. (L.) aethiopica*	Ethiopian highlands, Kenya, Yemen
New World cutaneous leishmaniasis: single or limited number of skin lesions	*L. (L.) mexicana* (chicle ulcer)	Central and South America, Texas
	L. (L.) amazonensis	Amazon Basin, neighboring areas, Bahia and other states of Brazil
	L. (L.) pifanoi	Venezuela
	L. (L.) garnhami	Venezuela
	L. (L.) venezuelensis	Venezuela
	L. (Viannia) braziliensis	Central and South America
	L. (V.) guyanensis (forest yaws)	Guyana, Surinam, northern Amazon Basin
	L. (V.) peruviana (uta)	Peru (western Andes) Argentinian highlands
	L. (V.) panamensis	Panama, Costa Rica, Colombia
	L. (V.) colombiensis	Colombia and Panama
	L. (L.) chagasi	Central and South America
Diffuse cutaneous leishmaniasis	*L. (L.) amazonensis*	Amazon Basin, neighboring areas, Bahia and other states of Brazil
	L. (L.) pifanoi	Venezuela
	L. (L.) mexicana	Central and South America, Texas
	L. (L.) spp.	Dominican Republic
Mucosal leishmaniasis	*L. (V.) braziliensis* (espundia)	Central and South America
	Other *Leishmania* spp. (rare)	Worldwide

*The taxonomy of *Leishmania* spp. is still in a state of flux.
Data from refs. 2, 3, 153, and 154.

mania (L.) tropica, a species that historically had been associated with cutaneous leishmaniasis, was identified among a small number of American military personnel who served in the Persian Gulf War.[11, 12] In addition, visceral leishmaniasis has emerged as an opportunistic disease in persons with human immunodeficiency virus (HIV) infection,[13–16] in persons who have had organ transplants,[17, 18] and in association with other conditions in which cell-mediated immunity is compromised. Cutaneous leishmaniasis is an important problem for farmers, settlers, troops, and tourists in the Middle East,[19] in Central and South America,[20] and in other endemic areas. Mucosal leishmaniasis is an important problem in Latin American countries. Finally, leishmaniasis has emerged as an ideal model system for the study of cell-mediated immune responses both in vivo and in vitro.[21, 22]

LEISHMANIA SPECIES

Leishmania spp. have a dimorphic life cycle.[2, 23] A sexual stage has not yet been identified. In humans and other susceptible mammals, leishmanias are found in cells of reticuloendothelial origin as intracellular amastigotes, which are 2 to 3 μm in length, oval or round, and lack an exteriorized flagellum (Figs. 265–1 and 265–2). In Wright- and Giemsa-stained preparations, the cytoplasm appears blue, and the nucleus is relatively large, eccentrically located, and red. The distinct, rod-shaped, red-staining kinetoplast is a specialized mitochondrial structure that contains a substantial amount of extranuclear DNA arranged as catenated minicircles and maxicircles. Parasite multiplication occurs by simple division within parasitophorous vacuoles in mononuclear phagocytes. Amastigotes are eventually released and go on to infect other mononuclear phagocytes.

In the digestive tract of the invertebrate vectors, female phlebotomine sandflies, leishmanias develop through a series of flagellated, intermediate stages[24–26] to become metacyclic promastigotes. Promastigotes can be grown in vitro in a number of culture media provided that the temperature is kept in the range of 22°C to 26°C. They have pear- or spindle-shaped bodies of variable dimensions, ranging from 10 to 15 μm in length to 1.5 to 3.5 μm in width. A single flagellum, which emerges from a basal body within the parasite, extends 15 to 28 μm and pulls the promastigote forward.

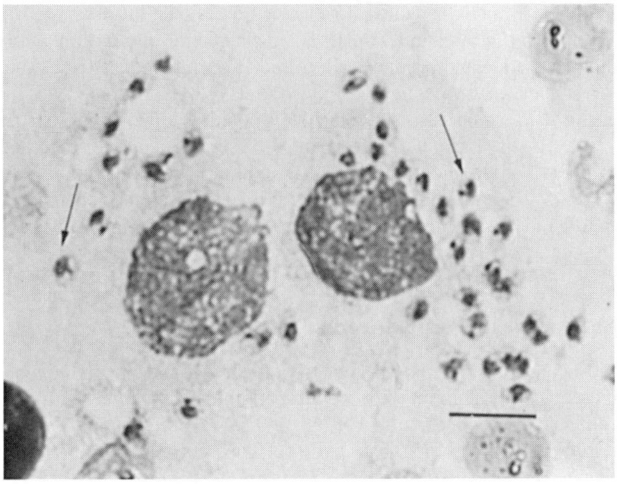

FIGURE 265–1. *Leishmania donovani* amastigotes *(arrows)* in a touch preparation made from the spleen of an infected hamster. The bar equals 10 μm. (From Pearson RD, Wheeler DA, Harrison LH, et al. The immunology of leishmaniasis. Rev Infect Dis. 1983;5:907–927.)

Female sandflies of the genus *Lutzomyia* in the Americas and *Phlebotomus* elsewhere transmit *Leishmania.*[2, 27] They are modified pool feeders. Sandflies breed in cracks in the walls of dwellings, in rubbish or rubble, or in rodent burrows. They are weak fliers and tend to remain close to the ground near their breeding sites. Sandflies ingest amastigotes when they feed on an infected mammalian reservoir. Amastigotes convert to promastigotes in the sandfly gut, replicate, and differentiate to metacyclic promastigotes in approximately 1 week. The life cycle is completed when the sandfly attempts to take its next blood meal. Saliva from the sandfly enhances the infectivity of promastigotes. Depending on the *Leishmania* sp. and the sandfly genus, the major reservoirs are canines, rodents, humans, or other animals.

Speciation was initially based on factors such as the parasites' behavior in humans, epidemiologic differences associated with geographic distribution, involvement of specific animal reservoirs, and transmission by different species of sandflies.[2, 3] Although minor ultrastructural variations exist among *Leishmania* spp., isolates cannot be differentiated on the basis of morphologic features in either the promastigote or amastigote form.

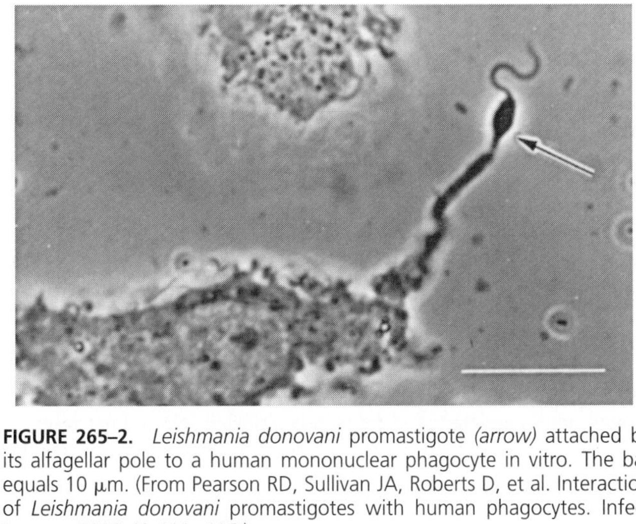

FIGURE 265–2. *Leishmania donovani* promastigote *(arrow)* attached by its alfagellar pole to a human mononuclear phagocyte in vitro. The bar equals 10 μm. (From Pearson RD, Sullivan JA, Roberts D, et al. Interaction of *Leishmania donovani* promastigotes with human phagocytes. Infect Immun. 1983;40:411–416.)

Lainson and Shaw[3] have divided the leishmanias into two subgenera, *Viannia* and *Leishmania,* based on their development in the sandfly. The *Viannia* subgenus includes *Leishmania (Viannia) braziliensis* and related species that develop in the hindgut before migrating to the midgut and foregut (peripylaria). Included in the subgenus *Leishmania* are species that have lost the primitive hindgut development and occupy only the midgut and foregut of the sandfly host (suprapylaria). Speciation within each of the subgenera is based on multiple factors.[3]

Several assays are now available to speciate isolates. They include isoenzyme analysis, which is available at a number of World Health Organization reference laboratories; species-specific monoclonal antibodies[28–30]; restriction endonuclease digestion and analysis of kinetoplast DNA[31, 32]; and polymerase chain reaction assays using *Leishmania* spp.–specific oligonucleotide primers,[33–35] which are available in research laboratories. Pulse-field gradient electrophoresis has been used to separate the 36 chromosomes. They are conserved across *Leishmania* spp., although there is substantial size polymorphism among the chromosomes of different species.[36, 37] Future revisions in taxonomy are likely as more is learned about the genetic diversity of the leishmanias.

IMMUNOLOGY

The interactions of promastigotes with mononuclear phagocytes that occur at the start of infection have been studied extensively in vitro using human monocyte-derived macrophages and rodent peritoneal macrophages.[23, 38] In the absence of serum, attachment is mediated by the macrophage complement type 3 receptor, the receptor for advanced glycosylation end products, and the mannose-fucose receptor, which is involved in the attachment of species such as *L. (L.) donovani* and *Leishmania (L.) mexicana* that have terminal exposed mannose on their surfaces.[39–46]

When serum is present, antileishmanial antibodies and complement are deposited on the parasite surface and contribute to attachment via macrophage Fc and the complement receptors complement type 1 receptor and complement type 3 receptor. Some *Leishmania* spp., *Leishmania major,* for example, activate complement through the alternative pathway,[42] whereas others such as *L. (L.) donovani* activate complement only when antibody is present.[47] Two parasite surface molecules play prominent roles in parasite-macrophage interactions: gp63, a glycoprotein that is a zinc metalloproteinase with a glycosylphosphatidylinositol anchor,[48–50] and a lipophosphoglycan.[51–53]

Once attached, promastigotes are phagocytosed by macrophages.[54] They reside in acidic parasitophorous vacuoles that fuse with lysosomes. Promastigotes convert within them to amastigotes. Parasite replication follows. Amastigotes are eventually released and infect other mononuclear phagocytes that are recruited to the site of infection.

The resolution of leishmanial infection and prevention of reinfection in genetically susceptible mammals depends on cell-mediated immune events.[21, 22] In inbred strains of mice, susceptibility to *L. (L.) donovani* is determined by *Nramp*, a single autosomal gene on murine chromosome 1, which was previously termed *Lsh.*[55] This locus also governs susceptibility to *Salmonella typhimurium* (*Ity*) and the Calmette-Guérin bacillus.[56] Different genes determine the susceptibility of mice to *L. (L.) major* and other *Leishmania* spp.[57] The genetic determinants of human leishmaniasis have not been defined, but human *Nramp-1* does not appear to be linked to visceral leishmaniasis.[58]

In genetically susceptible strains of mice, the outcome of leishmanial infection depends on a complex interplay between potentially protective cellular immune responses and disease-enhancing ones. Cytokines play a key role in mediating these responses, but despite substantial progress, the precise sequence of events that determines the outcome of infection has not been fully elucidated.

Interferon (INF)-γ activates human and murine macrophages to kill intracellular amastigotes.[59, 60] Initial studies suggested that oxidative microbicidal mechanisms were responsible, but more recent data indicate that the L-arginine–dependent production of nitric oxide, which follows induction of nitric oxide synthase by INF-γ, results in the death of intracellular amastigotes.[61, 62] Murine macrophages can also be activated to kill amastigotes in a genetically restricted manner by contact with leishmania-specific CD4+ T lymphocytes that have membrane-bound tumor necrosis factor (TNF)-α on their surface.[63]

The resolution of leishmanial infection in humans and animals is associated with expansion of leishmania-specific CD4+ T cells of the Th1 type, which secrete INF-γ and interleukin (IL)-2 in response to leishmanial antigens.[21, 22] IL-12 plays an important role in the development of protective Th1 responses.[64] In the murine model antigen-specific CD8+ cells also participate in the control of infection, probably by secreting INF-γ.[65] In addition, IL-1 and TNF-α prime macrophages for activation by INF-γ.

Leishmania spp. also elicit disease-enhancing immune responses that vary among mouse strains and humans. In inbred mice with progressive *L. (L.) major* infection, expansion of leishmania-specific, disease-enhancing CD4+ cells of the Th2 type, which produce IL-4, IL-5, and IL-10, but not INF-γ or IL-2, are associated with progressive disease.[21, 22, 66–69] IL-4, which can inhibit expansion of Th1 cells and activation of macrophages by INF-γ, was initially thought to be responsible for immune suppression, but infection progresses in susceptible mice in which the IL-4 gene has been knocked out.[70] Visceral leishmaniasis in humans caused by *L. (L.) donovani* or *Leishmania chagasi* is associated with secretion of IL-10, rather than IL-4.[71–73] IL-10 can inhibit expansion of potentially protective Th1 cells and the activation of macrophages by INF-γ.

Macrophages and their products also play a significant role in the outcome of infection.[74–79] IL-12 from macrophages supports the expansion of potentially protective Th1 cells.[64, 75] In contrast, transforming growth factor-β stimulates Th2 responses and the downregulation of Th1 responses.[76] Leishmanial infection also decreases expression of class I and class II histocompatibility antigens on macrophages[77] and stimulates macrophage secretion of potentially immune suppressive prostaglandins.[78] Finally, *L. donovani*–infected macrophages do not produce IL-1 or TNF-α in response to stimuli unless they are primed with INF-γ before leishmanial infection.[79]

It is still not clear why protective Th1 responses come to dominate in some humans and inbred strains of mice and not in others. Analysis of the T-cell receptor repertoires in mice infected with *L. (L.) major* suggests that the same immunodominant parasite epitope can drive a Th1 response in healing animals or a Th2 response in animals with progressive disease. [80] The sequence of early cytokine responses; the manner in which leishmanial antigens are presented by macrophages, Langerhans cells, or B cells in the context of histocompatibility antigens[81–83]; parasite virulence factors; and the size of the infecting inoculum[84] may all be important variables.

In persons with progressive visceral leishmaniasis, evidence of leishmania-specific Th1 responses is absent.[71] Peripheral blood mononuclear cells neither proliferate nor produce INF-γ or IL-2 in response to leishmanial antigens in vitro. There is no evidence of delayed-type hypersensitivity responses to leishmanial antigens that are inoculated intradermally (the leishmanin or Montenegro skin test). Paradoxically, antileishmanial antibodies are produced in high titer in progressive visceral leishmaniasis, and there is evidence of polyclonal B-cell activation.[85]

Persons with self-resolving infection with *L. (L.) donovani* or *L. (L.) chagasi* and those who have undergone successful chemotherapy usually manifest protective Th1 responses.[71] Their peripheral blood mononuclear cells produce INF-γ and IL-2 when exposed to leishmanial antigens in vitro, and in most cases they have positive leishmanin skin tests. They have protective immunity against visceral leishmaniasis, but disease can occur years later if they become immunocompromised.[86]

Persons with cutaneous or mucosal leishmaniasis have evidence of both Th1 and Th2 lymphocytes in their lesions, but their systemic response is predominantly Th1. Their peripheral blood mononuclear cells proliferate and produce INF-γ and IL-2 in response to leishmanial antigens in vitro, and they exhibit delayed-type cutaneous hypersensitivity responses as evidenced by positive leishmanin skin tests in vivo. In the rare anergic variant, diffuse cutaneous leishmaniasis, peripheral blood mononuclear cells neither proliferate nor produce INF-γ or IL-2 and the leishmanin skin test result is negative. The nonulcerative skin lesions of diffuse cutaneous leishmaniasis persist for decades and respond poorly to chemotherapy.

VISCERAL LEISHMANIASIS (KALA AZAR)

In visceral leishmaniasis, amastigotes are found in mononuclear phagocytes throughout the reticuloendothelial system.[1–3] The syndrome is most commonly caused by *L. (L.) donovani, Leishmania (L.) infantum,* and *L. (L.) chagasi* (see Table 265–1), but on occasion, other *Leishmania* spp. such as *Leishmania amazonensis* in Latin America[87] or *Leishmania tropica* in the Middle East[11] or Africa[88] are isolated from patients with typical visceral leishmaniasis.

The symptoms and findings in visceral leishmaniasis represent a spectrum of disease. At one extreme are patients with classic visceral leishmaniasis who present with fever, weight loss, hepatosplenomegaly, anemia, leukopenia, and hypergammaglobulinemia. The condition is known as *kala-azar, Dumdum fever, Assam fever,* or *infantile splenomegaly* in different areas of the world.

On the other extreme are persons with asymptomatic, self-resolving infections with *L.(L.) donovani, L. (L.) infantum,* or *L. (L.) chagasi.* The ratio of self-resolving infection to frank visceral leishmaniasis varies geographically and with a person's age; it has been reported to range from 6.5:1 to 18:1 with *L. (L.) chagasi* in northeastern Brazil.[89–91] Although many of those infected have no clinical manifestations of infection, some experience mild symptoms and a smoldering course[90] before either progressing to frank visceral leishmaniasis or undergoing spontaneous cure. Young children and those with concurrent HIV infection have the greatest likelihood of progressive disease developing.

Visceral leishmaniasis has emerged as an important opportunistic infection in persons with HIV infection in Spain, France, and Italy.[13–16] It may be the first opportunistic infection in a previously asymptomatic HIV-1–infected person, or it can occur in the advanced stages of the acquired immunodeficiency syndrome (AIDS). Visceral leishmaniasis can manifest in an atypical fashion in persons with HIV infection. However, not all persons concurrently infected with HIV and *Leishmania* spp. are symptomatic.[92] A number of cases of visceral leishmaniasis have been reported after organ transplantation[17, 18] and in other immunocompromised persons.

Epidemiology

Visceral leishmaniasis occurs in widely dispersed areas of the world (see Table 265–1).[1–18, 89–96] Transmission depends on a suitable reservoir and vector and a susceptible human host. *Lutzomyia* species are responsible for transmission in the Americas and *Phlebotomus* species facilitate transmission elsewhere in the world. On rare occasions, visceralizing *Leishmania* spp. cause congenital leishmaniasis.[97–99] Visceral leishmaniasis can also be acquired following transfusion of contaminated blood[100, 101] and accidental needle stick injuries in the laboratory.[102, 103]

L. (L.) donovani is responsible for visceral leishmaniasis in eastern India and Bangladesh.[4, 5] Large numbers of cases have been reported in India in the states of Assam and Bilhar. Children and young adults are the most frequently affected. No animal reservoir has been identified there. Transmission is by *Phlebotomus argentipes* and other anthropophilic *Phlebotomus* spp.

In East Africa, visceral leishmaniasis due to *L. (L.) donovani* often occurs in a sporadic manner among older children and young adults, but large epidemics can occur as reported among refugees in southern Sudan.[6–8] Putative reservoirs include rats, gerbils, other rodents, and small carnivores. Humans may also be a reservoir during epidemics.

Visceral leishmaniasis occurs sporadically in the Mediterranean littoral and the Middle East, where rodents such as the black rat and dogs are reservoirs for *L. (L.) donovani sensu lato* and *L. (L.) infantum,* respectively. Sporadic cases are encountered among children and immunocompromised persons, including those with AIDS and those who have undergone organ transplantation. Dogs, wild canines, and rodents serve as reservoirs.

Visceral leishmaniasis is endemic in areas of southern China and in central Asia, where dogs and other canines appear to be reservoirs. Disease is observed primarily in children. The number of cases in China is now small.[93]

In Latin America, *L. (L.) chagasi* produces sporadic cases in scattered rural areas.[89–91] Large outbreaks have been reported from cities in northeastern Brazil as the suburbs have extended into rural endemic areas.[9, 10] Children are most frequently affected. *Lutzomyia longipalpis* is the major vector. Domestic dogs and wild foxes have long been considered the major reservoirs of infection, but the clustering of cases in households suggests that humans may also be a reservoir.[91]

On occasion *L. (L.) amazonensis, L. (L.) tropica,* or other *Leishmania* spp. that are more commonly associated with cutaneous leishmaniasis are isolated from persons with visceral leishmaniasis. The epidemiology of these species is discussed later in this chapter. A small number of American military personnel who served in the Persian Gulf War acquired a "viscerotropic" form of *L. (L.) tropica* infection that did not progress to classic, progressive, visceral leishmaniasis.[11]

Pathogenesis

Promastigotes convert to amastigotes in macrophages in the skin, multiply, and eventually disseminate to mononuclear phagocytes throughout the reticuloendothelial system. The site where promastigotes are inoculated is often not apparent in persons who acquire visceral leishmaniasis, but a small papule may be noticed.[94–96] Large, ulcerative, skin lesions are rare but have been observed in persons with visceral leishmaniasis in East Africa.

Large numbers of amastigote-infected mononuclear phagocytes in the liver and spleen result in progressive hypertrophy. The spleen in particular may become massively enlarged as splenic lymphoid follicles are replaced by parasitized mononuclear cells. In the liver there is a marked increase in the number and size of Kupffer cells, many of which contain amastigotes. Infected mononuclear phagocytes are also found in the bone marrow, lymph nodes, skin, and other organs.

Many patients with visceral leishmaniasis become cachectic. This appears to be mediated in part by the secretion of TNF-α, which is known to have catabolic and anorectic effects.[104–106] Death in visceral leishmaniasis is often secondary to bacterial or viral infections in debilitated patients with advanced disease.[107, 108]

Clinical Manifestations

The clinical features of visceral leishmaniasis are remarkably similar in different areas of the world. The incubation period varies but is usually in the range of 3 to 8 months.[109–111] In one case, the time that elapsed from arrival in an endemic area to the onset of fever was less than 10 days.[111] Incubation periods as long as 34 months have also been reported.[112]

The onset of symptoms may be gradual or sudden. In subacute or chronic cases, there is an insidious onset of abdominal enlargement due to hepatosplenomegaly, fever, weakness, loss of appetite, pallor, and weight loss. The symptoms can persist for weeks to several months before patients come to medical attention. Fever may be intermittent, remittent with twice-daily temperature spikes or, less commonly, continuous, and it is relatively well tolerated. In acute cases, there is an abrupt onset of high fever and chills, sometimes with a periodicity that mimics malaria. Chills, but seldom rigors, accompany the temperature spikes. A patient subset has smoldering courses with mild symptoms or isolated splenomegaly; some then evolve into frank visceral leishmaniasis, whereas others have self-resolving courses.[90]

As time passes, the spleen can become massively enlarged. It is usually soft and nontender. The presence of a hard spleen suggests a hematologic disorder or another diagnosis such as schistosomiasis. The liver also enlarges; it usually has a sharp edge, soft consistency, and a smooth surface. Lymphadenopathy is common in patients in Sudan but uncommon in other geographic areas.[6–8] Elevated liver enzymes and bilirubin are observed occasionally.[113, 114] The skin in persons with visceral leishmaniasis often becomes dry, thin, and scaly, and hair may be lost. As the disease progresses, particularly in light-colored persons in India, the skin on the hands, feet, abdomen, and face may become grayish. This discoloration gave rise to the Indian name kala-azar, which means black fever. Peripheral edema may be seen late in disease, particularly in malnourished children. Hemorrhage can occur from one or more sites: epistaxis and gingival bleeding are most common. Petechiae and ecchymoses may be observed on the extremities. Interstitial pneumonia and periodontitis have been observed in a few cases.[115, 116]

Secondary bacterial infections of the skin, respiratory tract, and middle ear are common in persons with advanced visceral leishmaniasis.[107, 108] Death may result from bacterial pneumonia, septicemia, tuberculosis, dysentery, or measles or may be the consequence of malnutrition, severe anemia, or hemorrhage.

The laboratory findings include anemia, leukopenia, and hypergammaglobulinemia. Anemia is almost always present and may be severe. It is usually normocytic and normochromic. It appears to be due to a combination of factors, including hemolysis, marrow replacement with leishmania-infected macrophages, hemorrhage, splenic sequestration of erythrocytes, hemodilution, and effects of cytokines such as TNF-α.[117–119]

Leukopenia is also prominent, with white blood cell counts occasionally as low as 1000/mm^3.[120, 121] It is not known whether the observed neutropenia is due to increased margination, splenic sequestration, or an autoimmune process, or a combination of those factors. Of note, anemia and neutropenia have not been prominent in patients with visceral leishmaniasis who have undergone splenectomy.[121, 122]

Hypergammaglobulinemia, circulating immune complexes, and rheumatoid factors are present in the sera of most patients with visceral leishmaniasis.[123, 124] There is evidence of polyclonal B-cell activation. The globulin level may be as high as 9 g/dl; the ratio of globulin to albumin is typically high. The kidneys show evidence of immune complex deposition, and mild glomerulonephritis has been reported in humans[125] as well as in naturally infected dogs. Renal failure is rarely a feature of visceral leishmaniasis.[126]

Visceral Leishmaniasis in Patients with Human Immunodeficiency Virus. Visceral leishmaniasis may be the first opportunistic infection in persons with HIV, or it may complicate the terminal stages of AIDS. Studies in Spain indicate that the majority of HIV-infected persons with visceral leishmaniasis present with fever, hepatomegaly, splenomegaly, and pancytopenia, but atypical presentations are common.[13–16] Splenomegaly may be absent. Involvement of the lungs, pleura, oral mucosa, esophagus, stomach, small intestine, skin, or bone marrow presenting as aplastic anemia, have been reported.[127–135] Asymptomatic leishmanial infections have also been documented in persons with HIV.[92]

Viscerotropic Leishmaniasis. A viscerotropic syndrome due to *L. tropica* was observed among American troops who served in the Persian Gulf War.[11] The symptoms included chronic low-grade fever, malaise, fatigue, and in some cases, diarrhea. Mild splenomegaly was observed in some, but none of the troops developed classic, progressive visceral leishmaniasis.

Post–Kala-Azar Dermal Leishmaniasis. Post–kala-azar dermal leishmaniasis follows the treatment of visceral leishmaniasis in a subset of persons in Africa and India.[136–139] Lesions appear in India up to 2 years after treatment and may persist for as long as 20 years. In Africa they usually appear at the end of, or within several months of, therapy and persist for only a few months. The skin lesions vary from hyperpigmented macules to frank nodules. They may be confused clinically and pathologically with leprosy. They are found on the face, trunk, extremities, oral mucous membranes, and occasionally, on the genitals. In a few instances in India, visceral leishmaniasis has recurred in patients with post–kala-azar dermal leishmaniasis.

Diagnosis

In an endemic area, the constellation of prolonged fever, progressive weight loss, weakness, pronounced splenomegaly, hepatomegaly, anemia, leukopenia, and hypergammaglobulinemia is highly suggestive of visceral leishmaniasis. The diagnosis is more difficult in persons in whom fever, splenomegaly, or hypergammaglobulinemia is absent; in travelers who acquire symptoms after leaving endemic areas; and in those with concurrent HIV who have atypical presentations.

A definitive diagnosis depends on the demonstration of amastigotes in tissue or the isolation of promastigotes in culture. Splenic puncture[140] is the most sensitive diagnostic method and is routinely performed in many areas. It has been associated with life-threatening hemorrhage in a few cases, particularly in patients with advanced stages of disease who have undergone aspirations by inexperienced operators. The risk is less when aspiration is performed quickly with a small-bore needle by an experienced operator in patients with no laboratory evidence of coagulopathy. Bone marrow aspiration is less sensitive, but safer. Amastigotes are seen on Wright- and Giemsa–stained smears in 54 to 86% of cases.[141] Liver biopsy is less likely to yield the diagnosis than is splenic puncture or bone marrow biopsy and carries the risk of hemorrhage.

Lymph node aspiration or biopsy may be diagnostic when enlarged nodes are present, as is often the case in Sudan. In some cases, parasites can be cultured from the buffy coat or blood. On occasion, they are seen within mononuclear cells in Wright- and Giemsa–stained smears of the buffy coat or in biopsy specimens of various organs. This is particularly true in patients with concurrent HIV infection in whom amastigotes have been identified in macrophages in bronchoalveolar lavage fluid, pleural effusions, or biopsy specimens of the oropharynx, stomach, or intestine.[127–133]

Cultures of aspirates from the spleen, bone marrow, liver, lymph node and, in patients with concurrent HIV, blood may be positive. Specimens can be inoculated into Novy, McNeal, and Nicolle medium, a biphasic medium, or one of several liquid media with fetal calf serum (e.g., Schneider insect medium)[142] and maintained at 22°C to 26°C. Motile promastigotes develop from amastigotes and multiply. They may be identified in cultures within a few days, but it can take several weeks for the concentration to reach the level of detection. Species-specific isoenzyme profiles, monoclonal antibodies, or gene probes can be used to perform speciation in isolates.

Antileishmanial antibodies are usually present in high titer in immunocompetent patients with visceral leishmaniasis. Enzyme-linked immunosorbent assays (ELISAs), indirect immunofluorescent assays, and direct agglutination tests are sensitive,[141, 143–149] but false-positive test results can occur. Cross-reacting antibodies may be present in patients with leprosy, Chagas' disease, malaria, schistosomiasis, toxoplasmosis, or cutaneous leishmaniasis. Antileishmanial antibodies are frequently absent or of low titer in patients with concurrent HIV infection. Recent efforts have focused on the development of tests employing defined leishmanial antigens. An ELISA using recombinant *L. (L.) chagasi* antigen rk39, a kinesin-like antigen, appears to be highly sensitive and specific in detecting visceral leishmaniasis in immunocompetent persons.[150]

The leishmanin (Montenegro) skin test produces negative results in patients with progressive visceral leishmaniasis. The result becomes positive in the majority of persons in whom infection spontaneously resolves and in those who have undergone successful chemotherapy. It is useful in studies of epidemiology but has no value in the diagnosis of visceral leishmaniasis. The leishmanin skin test result may be negative or positive in persons with post–kala-azar dermal leishmaniasis.

Differential Diagnosis

The clinical picture of visceral leishmaniasis is often indistinguishable from that of other infectious diseases. Acute manifestations may be confused with those of malaria, typhoid fever, typhus, acute Chagas' disease, acute schistosomiasis, miliary tuberculosis, or amebic liver abscess. Subacute or chronic visceral leishmaniasis may be confused with brucellosis, prolonged *Salmonella* bacteremia, histoplasmosis, infectious mononucleosis, lymphoma, leukemia, agnogenic myeloid metaplasia, hepatosplenic schistosomiasis, and spleno-

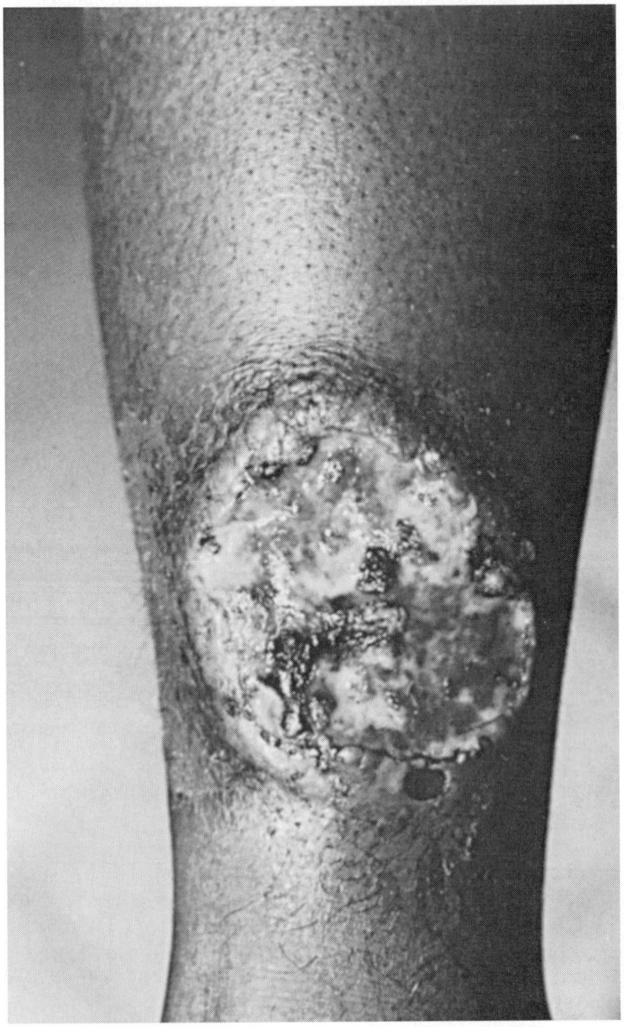

FIGURE 265–3. American cutaneous leishmaniasis. Single, large leg lesion. (Courtesy of Dr. Kurt L. Wiese.)

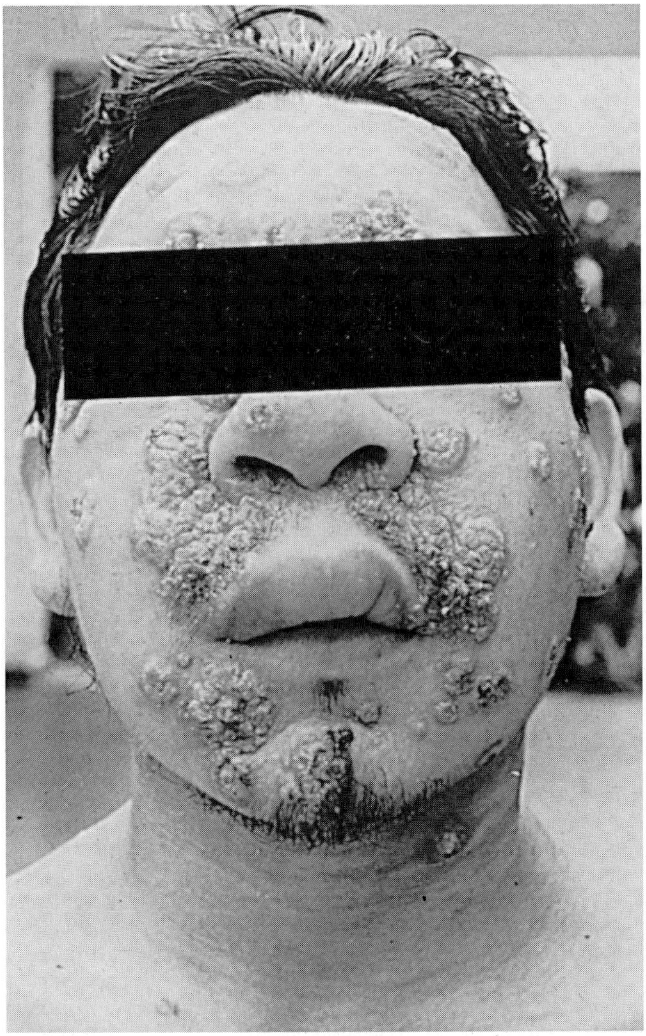

FIGURE 265–4. Brazilian patient with diffuse cutaneous leishmaniasis.

megaly due to chronic malaria. Post–kala-azar dermal leishmaniasis must be differentiated from leprosy, yaws, and syphilis.

CUTANEOUS LEISHMANIASIS

Cutaneous leishmaniasis is endemic in widely scattered areas throughout the world. The classic form of Old World cutaneous leishmaniasis is the "oriental sore."[1-3, 111, 151] It has also been termed *bouton d'orient, bouton de Crete, bouton d'Alep, bouton de Biskra, Aleppo evil, Baghdad boil,* and *Dehli boil* in various tropical and subtropical regions of the Middle East, the Mediterranean littoral, Africa, India, and Asia (see Table 265–1). It is most frequently caused by *L. (L.) major, L. (L.) tropica,* or *Leishmania (L.) aethiopica,* but *L. (L.) donovani* and *L. (L.) infantum* also produce simple cutaneous leishmaniasis on occasion.[152] In general, oriental sores are troublesome and unsightly but not a threat to life. Diffuse cutaneous leishmaniasis due to *L. (L.) aethiopica* infection occurs in Ethiopia and adjacent areas of Africa.

American cutaneous leishmaniasis is endemic in widespread areas of Latin America (see Table 265–1).[1-3, 153, 154] The causative agents include *L. (V.) braziliensis, L. (L.) mexicana, L. (V.) panamensis,* and related species. On occasion, *L. (L.) chagasi* causes simple cutaneous leishmaniasis.[1-3, 153, 154] Depending on the clinical presentation and geographic location, the disease has been variously called *pian bois* (bush yaws), *uta,* or *Chiclero's ulcer.* The spectrum of disease includes single, localized, cutaneous ulcers (Fig. 265–3); diffuse cutaneous leishmaniasis (Fig. 265–4); and mucosal disease (espundia) due to *L. (V.) braziliensis* and some other *Leishmania (Vianna)* subspecies (Fig. 265–5).[155, 156]

Epidemiology

Cutaneous leishmaniasis is usually a sporadic disease in endemic areas, but occasionally it occurs in an epidemic pattern, particularly when large groups of susceptible persons are exposed during road construction, refugee movements, or military activities. *Lutzomyia* species are the vectors in the Americas and *Phlebotomus* species elsewhere. A number of mammals serve as reservoirs in different regions.

L. (L.) major is an infection of desert rodents, primarily gerbils, and affects humans in uninhabited areas or in villages in arid regions of the Middle East, North Africa, and central Asia. It has been a major problem for troops operating in endemic regions. The lesions tend to be larger and "wet" with an overlying exudate. *Phlebotomus papatasi* and other *Phlebotomus* spp. are the vectors.

L. (L.) tropica infects dogs and humans in urban areas of the Middle East such as Baghdad, Teheran, and Damascus as well as cities in the Mediterranean littoral, India, and Pakistan. The lesions tend to be crusted and "dry." The vectors include *Phlebotomus sergenti* and *P. papatasi.*

L. (L.) aethiopica is endemic in Ethiopia, Kenya, and southwest Africa. The primary reservoirs are hyrax (a small mammal); rodents are secondary reservoirs. *Phlebotomus longipes* is one of the vectors. The epidemiology of *L. (L.) donovani* and *L. (L.) infantum,* which

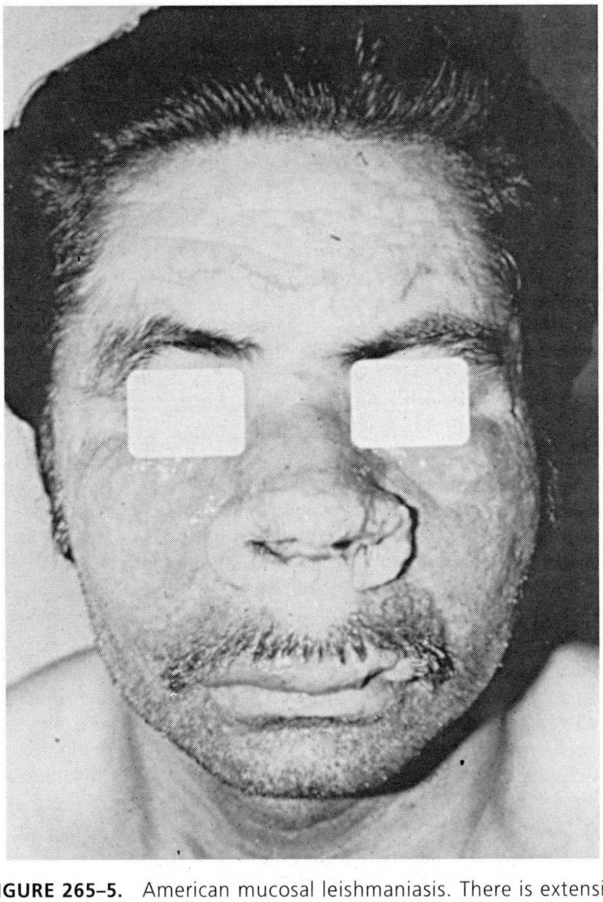

FIGURE 265–5. American mucosal leishmaniasis. There is extensive involvement of the nose and upper lip with destruction of the nasal septum. (From Pearson RD, Wheeler DA, Harrison LH, et al. The immunology of leishmaniasis. Rev Infect Dis. 1983;5:907–927.)

occasionally cause simple cutaneous leishmaniasis, was reviewed earlier in the discussion of visceral leishmaniasis.

L. (L.) mexicana is responsible for American cutaneous leishmaniasis from northern Argentina to Texas, where a small number of autochthonous cases have been reported.[111, 157–161] It is an occupational disease of gum, or chicle, collectors in Central America as well as persons living, working, or touring in endemic areas. Lesions typically appear on exposed areas of the extremities, face or ears. A number of sylvatic rodents are reservoirs. *Lutzomyia* species are vectors.

L. (L.) amazonensis produces a spectrum of disease in South America that includes simple cutaneous, diffuse cutaneous, and visceral leishmaniasis.[87] Several other *Leishmania (L.)* spp. are endemic in South America. The vectors are *Lutzomyia* spp., and the reservoirs are forest animals.

L. (V.) braziliensis is found in widely scattered areas of Central and South America.[153, 154] It is responsible for cutaneous as well as mucosal leishmaniasis. *L. (V.) panamensis* is found in Panama and adjacent countries. It has been an important problem for U.S. military personnel training in jungle areas. *Leishmania (V.) peruviana* is the cause of *uta* in Peru. It typically causes dry lesions. *Leishmania (V.) guyanensis* is responsible for *pian bois* or *bush yaws* in the Amazon basin. Regional lymphadenopathy frequently accompanies the skin lesions.

The main reservoirs for *L. (V.) braziliensis* and other *Leishmania (Vianna)* spp. are small forest rodents, except in the case of *L. (V.) peruviana,* in which dogs are the primary reservoirs. The vectors are ground-dwelling or arboreal *Lutzomyia* sandflies, which are abundant in the forest. Disease is most common in persons working at the edge of the forest and among rural settlers. Outbreaks develop when areas of forest are being cleared for roads, villages, or farms, as well as in military personnel and occasionally tourists. Disseminated cutaneous lesions have been reported in a small number of patients with concurrent HIV and in transplant recipients.[162–164]

Pathogenesis

The clinical manifestations of cutaneous leishmaniasis depend on the virulence factors of the infecting *Leishmania* spp. and the genetically determined immune responses of their human hosts. After promastigotes are inoculated into the skin, they convert to amastigotes and multiply within macrophages. A papule forms, enlarges, and, in most instances, ulcerates.

Cutaneous leishmaniasis is characterized by a mixed acute and chronic inflammatory infiltrate with infected and noninfected mononuclear phagocytes, lymphocytes, and plasma cells. There are areas of focal necrosis.[165, 166] Early in infection, amastigote-containing macrophages dominate. Eventually, parasitized mononuclear phagocytes are eliminated, lymphocytes become prevalent, and a granulomatous response containing epithelioid cells and giant cells evolves. Lesions heal slowly leaving a flat, atrophic, burnlike scar as evidence of disease. Recovery is associated with a high level of resistance to reinfection by the homologous *Leishmania* spp.

In some respects, the range of clinical features in cutaneous leishmaniasis parallels that of leprosy. At one end of the spectrum lies diffuse cutaneous leishmaniasis, a relatively uncommon syndrome, in which there is little evidence of effective cell-mediated immune responses. Heavily parasitized macrophages are abundant throughout the dermis, and few lymphocytes are present. Cutaneous delayed-type hypersensitivity reactions and in vitro Th1 responses to leishmanial antigen are absent. Diffuse cutaneous leishmaniasis is somewhat analogous to lepromatous leprosy in which there is a large number of mycobacteria in macrophages and no evidence of protective, Th1 cell–mediated immune responses.

At the other extreme lies leishmaniasis recidivans, a hyperergic variant of cutaneous leishmaniasis, in which chronic lesions slowly expand while healing at the center. Amastigotes are sparse and a mononuclear cell infiltrate predominates. This is clinically analogous to tuberculoid leprosy in which there is an intense mononuclear infiltrate with few mycobacteria.

Although the character and organization of the granuloma in leprosy are invariably characteristic of the position in the clinical spectrum, this is not true in simple cutaneous leishmaniasis in which lesions progress over time from a predominance of amastigote-containing macrophages and few lymphocytes to a granulomatous response with a predominance of lymphocytes and few parasites before healing.[165, 166]

Clinical Manifestations

The incubation period of cutaneous leishmaniasis varies from 2 weeks to several months and in one case was as long as 3 years.[111, 167] A wide variety of skin manifestations ranging from small, dry, crusted lesions to large, deep, mutilating ulcers may be seen. The characteristics vary among *Leishmania* spp. and from one geographic area to another, but overlap occurs. Lesions with different characteristics may be seen in the same patient. There may be a single lesion or multiple ones. They are usually found on exposed areas of the body. No characteristic of the skin lesion is pathognomonic for cutaneous leishmaniasis or can be used to identify the causative *Leishmania* spp.

In general *L. (L.) tropica* tends to cause "dry," crusted, slowly enlarging lesions that can persist for a year or more, whereas *L. (L.) major* and *L. (V.) braziliensis* are associated with "moist," exudative lesions that are larger, have a granulating base with overlying exudate, mature more rapidly, and typically heal after many months.

Ulcerative lesions are usually shallow and circular with well-defined, raised, borders and a bed of granulation tissue. They gradually increase in size and may develop a "pizza-like" appearance with a raised, circular outer margin, beefy red granulating base, and yellowish exudate on the surface. Satellite lesions may be present, and they may fuse with the original ulcer. The center of the granulating base of the ulcer may contain a hard excrescence. A cutaneous horn may arise. Secondary staphylococcal or streptococcal infection may occur. After a variable period ranging from several months to longer than a year, ulcers heal leaving flat, atrophic, depigmented, burnlike scars.

In *L. (V.) braziliensis* infection, regional lymphadenopathy often precedes the development of cutaneous lesions by 1 to 12 weeks.[168, 169] Patients may experience constitutional symptoms including malaise, anorexia, weight loss, and low-grade fever. As the skin ulcer develops, the lymphadenopathy and systemic symptoms subside. In *L. (V.) guyanensis* infection, a chain of nodules may develop along lymphatics proximal to the lesion, particularly if it is on an extremity, and mimic sporotrichosis.[156, 170]

Diffuse Cutaneous Leishmaniasis. The condition starts as a localized papule that does not ulcerate. Satellite lesions develop around the initial papule, and organisms gradually spread in the skin, resulting in disseminated nodules primarily on the face and extremities. It has a protracted course and may last for the patient's lifetime.[171]

Leishmaniasis Recidivans. This is a relapsing, tuberculoid form of cutaneous leishmaniasis caused by *L. (L.) tropica.* It is observed in Iran and elsewhere in Central Asia. The lesions are usually on the face. They spread outward while healing at the center. Leishmaniasis recidivans is chronic and can last 20 to 30 years in some cases.

Diagnosis

The development of one or more chronic skin lesions with the appropriate characteristics in an endemic area is suggestive of cutaneous leishmaniasis. A definite diagnosis depends on the identification of amastigotes in tissue or promastigotes in culture.

Punch or incisional biopsies should be taken from the border of the lesion. Biopsies of the surface of the ulcer are often not diagnostic because *Leishmania*-infected macrophages are rare there. Meticulous cleaning is necessary before biopsy to prevent bacterial and fungal contamination of cultures. Touch preparations are made from biopsy samples,[172–174] stained with a Wright-Giemsa preparation, and examined for amastigotes. A portion is fixed for histologic examination. Amastigotes can be seen in Giemsa-stained tissue sections. The diagnosis can also be made by culturing tissue or nonbacteriostatic saline that has been injected and aspirated from a nonulcerated site near the margin of the lesion. Specimens can be cultured using media and conditions described for *L. (L.) donovani*.[140–142]

The sensitivity of direct parasite identification and culture varies with the type and duration of the lesion and the infecting *Leishmania* spp. The combined sensitivity of these methods in leishmanin-positive patients is in the range of 50 to 70%.[173] Species-specific monoclonal antibodies and DNA probes have been used successfully to diagnose cutaneous leishmaniasis in tissue samples in experimental studies, [175] but they are not routinely available. They have the potential advantage of allowing immediate speciation, which has relevance for chemotherapy.

Antileishmanial antibodies are present in the serum of some patients with cutaneous leishmaniasis as detected by ELISA, immunofluorescent assays, direct agglutination tests or other assays,[149, 176] but the titers are usually low. Cross-reacting "natural" antibodies are present at low titer in the serum of some persons who have never been exposed to *Leishmania* spp. The leishmanin skin test result usually becomes positive during the course of the disease. When lymphadenopathy precedes or accompanies skin ulcers in *L. (V.) braziliensis* infection, the diagnosis may be made by aspirating an enlarged node. On rare occasions *L. (L.) major, L. (L.) tropica,* or *L. (V.) braziliensis* has been grown from blood or the buffy coat.[169, 177]

Cutaneous leishmaniasis must be differentiated from sporotrichosis, blastomycosis, chromomycosis, lobomycosis, cutaneous tuberculosis, atypical mycobacterial infection, syphilis, yaws, leprosy, sarcoidosis, lupus vulgaris, and neoplasms. Rarely, lesions may assume a keloidal form and give the appearance of lobomycosis.

MUCOSAL LEISHMANIASIS (ESPUNDIA)

A subset of persons infected with *L. (V.) braziliensis* or related *Leishmania (Vianna)* subspecies acquire mucous membrane involvement of the nose, oral cavity, pharynx, or larynx months to years after their skin lesions have healed.[178] The percentage of patients infected with *L. (V.) braziliensis* who acquire mucosal disease is relatively small. In one study, mucosal disease occurred in 2.7% of persons with primary skin lesions after a median duration of 6 years.[179] The time between the primary lesions and mucosal involvement may be as short as 1 month[180] or as long as 2 decades.[181]

The initial symptoms are often nasal stuffiness, discharge, discomfort, or epistaxis. Over time, the nasal septum may be destroyed, resulting in nasal collapse ("taper" nose). Perforation can occur through the skin of the nose or through the soft palate.[182, 183] The upper lip may be involved in addition to the buccal, pharyngeal, or laryngeal mucosa, in that approximate order. Involvement of the trachea[183, 184] as well as the genital mucosa has been reported.[183, 185] On rare occasions, the lesions are so extensive that the individual is unable to eat or experiences fatal aspiration pneumonia.[184] Histopathologically, chronic mucosal lesions are characterized by an intense mononuclear cell infiltrate with few parasites.[186, 187, 198, 201] Persons with mucosal leishmaniasis demonstrate strong systemic Th1 responses. Their peripheral blood mononuclear cells proliferate and produce INF in response to leishmanial antigens in vitro, and their leishmanin skin test results are positive.

Various reasons have been advanced for the predominance of nasal involvement. They include lower temperature, which favors parasite growth; failure of cell-mediated immune responses to be effective in cartilage; local trauma; and capillary plexus trapping of amastigotes. Spontaneous cure of mucosal leishmaniasis has been reported, but it is rare.[186] The lack of an appropriate animal model has hindered research on the immunopathology of *L. (V.) braziliensis* infection.

Mucosal involvement is seen on occasion because of the contiguous spread of cutaneous lesions caused by *L. (L.) tropica* or other *Leishmania* spp. It is also observed in some persons with visceral leishmaniasis, particularly those with concurrent HIV infection. The pathophysiology and natural history in those cases is thought to resemble cutaneous and visceral leishmaniasis, respectively.

Diagnosis

The diagnosis of mucosal leishmaniasis is confirmed when amastigotes are identified in touch preparations or tissue sections or when promastigotes are isolated in culture. However, the parasite burden is usually low, and *L. (V.) braziliensis* is relatively difficult to grow in vitro.

A putative diagnosis is often made on the basis of the clinical findings, a characteristic scar representing previous cutaneous infection, and a positive leishmanin skin test result or the presence of antileishmanial antibodies in serum. The leishmanin test result is positive in 86.5[186] to 100% of cases[187, 188] and the indirect fluorescent antibody test produces positive results in 62.5% when promastigotes are used as the antigen source[189] and up to 89 to 96% when amastigotes are the antigen.[189, 190] In one study an ELISA was positive in all those with mucosal leishmaniasis who were tested.[179] In general, mucosal disease due to *L. (V.) braziliensis* is associated with higher antileishmanial antibody titers and stronger delayed-type hypersensitivity responses than simple cutaneous leishmaniasis. Antibody studies may also be useful in evaluating the response to chemotherapy. The indirect fluorescent antibody titer falls after successful chemotherapy,[191] and a subsequent rise in titer suggests a relapse.

In mucosal disease, paracoccidioidomycosis, syphilis, tertiary yaws, histoplasmosis, sarcoidosis, basal cell carcinoma, and midline granuloma must be considered in the differential diagnosis.[182] The polyp-like nasal lesions that occur in some persons with mucosal leishmaniasis may occasionally mimic rhinosporidiosis.[192, 193]

TREATMENT OF LEISHMANIASIS

The treatment of leishmaniasis is in a state of flux. Pentavalent antimony–containing compounds have been used for decades, but drug resistance and treatment failures are becoming increasingly common, immunocompromised patients often fail to respond or relapse, and side effects are frequent.[194–196] Liposomal amphotericin B recently became the first drug licensed by the U.S. Food and Drug Administration for the treatment of visceral leishmaniasis. [197–201] Amphotericin B deoxycholate and pentamidine isethionate are effective but more toxic alternatives. Topical therapy with paromomycin and methylbenzethonium chloride has been used successfully for the treatment of Old World cutaneous leishmaniasis.[202] A number of other drugs are variably effective. As discussed further on, the treatment of choice depends on the infecting *Leishmania* spp., the clinical syndrome, the immunologic status of the host, and the availability and cost of drugs.

Two pentavalent antimony–containing drugs are used: stibogluconate sodium (Pentostam) is available in many English-speaking countries, and meglumine antimoniate (Glucantime)is available in Latin America and French-speaking countries. These compounds are chemically similar and have comparable toxicities. Their therapeutic efficacy is directly related to the content of pentavalent antimony (Sb^v). Meglumine antimoniate solution contains approximately 8.5% (85 mg/ml) Sb^v, whereas sodium stibogluconate solution contains about 10% Sb^v (100 mg/ml).

The dosage of these drugs is based on their Sb^v content. Both can be administered intramuscularly or intravenously. The recommended dose is Sb^v 20 mg/kg body weight/day. The duration of therapy varies from 20 to 28 days depending on the infecting *Leishmania* spp. and the clinical syndrome.[194–196] In general, doses lower than 20 mg of Sb^v/kg body weight/day should not be used to minimize the evolution of Sb^v resistance and the likelihood of treatment failure and relapse. Doses greater than 20 mg of Sb^v/kg body weight/day carry with them the risk of sudden death and are contraindicated.

Common side effects of these compounds include abdominal pain, anorexia, vomiting, nausea, myalgia, arthralgia, headache, and malaise, but these complications seldom prevent completion of therapy. Recent studies suggest that elevations of amylase and lipase are present in most recipients, but only a minority of patients manifest clinically apparent pancreatitis. Persons with renal insufficiency seem to be at increased risk of this complication.[203] Electrocardiographic changes are dose-dependent and include T-wave inversion and a prolonged QT interval.[204] Arrhythmias and sudden death have been reported with doses greater than 20 mg of Sb^v/kg body weight/day. Renal failure is a rarely reported toxicity.[205]

Liposomal amphotericin B (AmBisome) recently became the first, and is the only, drug approved by the U.S. Food and Drug Administration for the treatment of visceral leishmaniasis.[197–201] It is at least as effective as, and less toxic than, pentavalent antimony. Although the data are limited, amphotericin B lipid complex also appears to be effective.[206]

Conventional amphotericin B deoxycholate is also active against *Leishmania* spp. It has been used successfully to treat patients with visceral leishmaniasis who have failed to respond to or have relapsed after treatment with pentavalent antimony.[207–209] Its use has been limited because it causes nephrotoxicity and other side effects and requires parenteral administration over a prolonged period.

Pentamidine is another effective, but toxic, alternative.[209–211] Side effects are frequent and include headache, flushing, nausea, vomiting, abdominal discomfort and, more importantly, vascular collapse, if the drug is infused too rapidly. Hypoglycemia can develop during therapy because of insulin release from damaged pancreatic β cells. Some persons go on to acquire insulin-dependent diabetes mellitus.[211]

Recombinant INF-γ has been used on an experimental basis and appears promising as a supplement to pentavalent antimony therapy for persons who have failed pentavalent antimony alone.[212–213] The imidazoles ketoconazole and itraconazole have activity against some *Leishmania* spp. but not others. Finally, topical treatment has been used for cutaneous lesions caused by *Leishmania* spp. that are not associated with mucosal disease.

Visceral Leishmaniasis. Liposomal amphotericin B is the only drug currently approved by the U.S. Food and Drug Administration for the treatment of visceral leishmaniasis. It is less toxic than pentavalent antimony and at least, if not more, effective. Its cost and availability will probably limit its use in developing areas.

Several dosage regimens have been studied. For immunocompetent patients, 3.0 mg/kg body weight/day is given on days 1 to 5, 14, and 21. The course of therapy may be repeated in those who do not achieve parasite clearance. For immunocompromised patients, the dose is 4.0 mg/kg body weight/day on days 1 to 5, 10, 17, 24, 31, and 38. Relapses are common in persons with HIV. Amphotericin B lipid complex also appears to be effective for the treatment of visceral leishmaniasis, but the data are limited.

Pentavalent antimony remains the initial treatment of choice of visceral leishmaniasis in many areas. Either stibogluconate sodium or meglumine antimoniate can be used. The dosage recommended is 20 mg Sb^v/kg body weight/day for 28 days. Persons who do not respond to the initial course may respond to a second course. Primary failures and relapses are particularly common in patients with concurrent HIV infection.[13–16] Long-term therapy (up to 120 days) has been reported to be successful in the treatment of post–kala-azar dermal leishmaniasis in India.[214, 215]

Amphotericin B deoxycholate, 0.5 mg/kg given daily or 1 mg/kg every other day for up to 8 weeks, has been used successfully to treat patients who fail to respond to antimony compounds.[208–209] Pentamidine isethionate, 2 to 4 mg/kg body weight/day for up to 15 days, is an effective but potentially toxic alternative. It has been studied extensively in India.[209]

The combination of recombinant INF-γ and pentavalent antimony has been used successfully to treat patients who failed to respond to a pentavalent antimony alone or who relapsed after treatment,[212, 213] as well as in a limited number of patients with AIDS.[216] Although INF-γ is a useful adjunct to pentavalent antimony for the treatment of refractory visceral leishmaniasis, it is variably effective when used alone. Other drugs have been studied. Aminosidine, ketoconazole,[217] and itraconazole have been used in a limited number of cases, but failures occur. Clinical experience is currently insufficient to justify the routine use of these drugs.

Patients with visceral leishmaniasis should be hospitalized until they are stable. Their nutritional deficiencies must be addressed. Associated bacterial infections should be diagnosed and treated promptly. Splenectomy is not indicated except in the rare instance in which signs of hypersplenism persist after clinically successful chemotherapy.[218]

Unfortunately, there are no tests or rigid criteria to document cure after treatment of visceral leishmaniasis. The cessation of fever; weight gain; resolution of anemia, leukopenia, and thrombocytopenia; and the resolution of splenomegaly and hepatomegaly are suggestive. Viable amastigotes may persist even after clinically successful chemotherapy.

Relapses of visceral leishmaniasis usually occur within 6 months. They are more frequent in patients with HIV infection than in immunocompetent persons and occur after treatment with either pentavalent antimony or liposomal amphotericin B. Chronic suppressive therapy is probably advisable in persons with HIV, but the optimal drug and regimen have not been defined.

Cutaneous Leishmaniasis. The decision whether to treat cutaneous leishmaniasis depends on the location and extent of the lesion or lesions and on the infecting *Leishmania* spp. In geographic areas where there is no mucosal leishmaniasis and a cutaneous lesion is healing or is located at a cosmetically insignificant site, it can be followed without therapy or treated topically. Cutaneous lesions due to *L. (L.) mexicana* or *L. (L.) major* heal more rapidly than do those due to *L. (V.) braziliensis* or *L. (L.) tropica*.

Large or disfiguring lesions are often treated with pentavalent antimony. Although the optimal dosage and duration of therapy are uncertain and may vary from one location to another, 20 mg of Sb^v/kg body weight daily for 20 days have been recommended. Healing of cutaneous lesions occurs slowly over a period of weeks and is often incomplete at the end of therapy. In persons who fail to respond, a second or even third course of pentavalent antimony may be successful, or an alternative drug may be necessary. Secondary bacterial infections should be treated with local care and may require antibiotics.

Amphotericin B deoxycholate is an alternative for persons who fail to respond to pentavalent antimony. The efficacy of liposomal amphotericin B for cutaneous leishmaniasis has not yet been accessed. The combination of pentavalent antimony and concurrent INF-γ has been used successfully to treat patients with diffuse cutaneous leishmaniasis, which usually responds poorly to pentavalent antimony alone.[212] In the Ethiopian forms of cutaneous and diffuse cutaneous leishmaniasis caused by *L. (L.) aethiopica*, pentamidine (2 to 4 mg/kg body weight once or twice a week) has been used successfully,[219] but it is potentially toxic.[211]

Ketoconazole, 400 to 600 mg/day for 4 to 6 weeks, has been reported to be effective in approximately 70% of persons with *L. (L.) major* or *L. (V.) panamensis* lesions,[220] but it is not as effective against *L. (L.) tropica, L. (L.) aethiopica,* or *L. (V.) braziliensis.* There have been reports of cures with various antibiotics and antiprotozoal agents, but many of them have been uncontrolled observations, and generalizations are impossible because cutaneous leishmaniasis resolves spontaneously in time. Immunotherapy with live Calmette-Guérin bacillus administered with killed leishmania promastigotes has been used effectively in Latin America, but the clinical response is slow.[221]

The topical administration of 15% paromomycin and 12% methylbenzethonium chloride in soft white paraffin has been used successfully in the treatment of cutaneous *L. (L.) major* infections.[202]

Various forms of cryotherapy or local hyperthermic therapy have been studied. Patients with isolated lesions in Guatemala[222] and others with diffuse cutaneous leishmaniasis acquired in the Dominican Republic have been treated successfully with locally applied, controlled heat.

Leishmaniasis recidivans is relatively resistant to most forms of therapy, although some success has been achieved with intralesional infections of pentavalent antimony, with or without concomitant parenteral pentavalent antimony therapy.

Mucosal Leishmaniasis. Multiple treatment regimens have been used for mucosal leishmaniasis. Pentavalent antimony is administered at a dose of 20 mg Sb^v/kg body weight/day for 28 days. Some patients require longer courses. Unfortunately, there are no tests or rigid criteria to document cure. Some have advocated the addition of steroids in persons with laryngeal lesions.

The response of mucosal leishmaniasis to pentavalent antimony is frequently unsatisfactory.[223] In some regions of South America, relapse after apparent cure has been as high as 50 to 70%.[224, 225] Patients who do not respond or those who relapse can be treated with amphotericin B deoxycholate.[223, 226–229] Depending on the patient's tolerance, 0.5 or 1.0 mg/kg body weight is given intravenously daily or every other day, respectively. A reasonable total adult dose is 1.5 to 2 g. Alternatively, pentamidine isethionate, 2 to 4 mg/kg body weight, can be administered once or twice weekly. Recombinant INF-γ has been used successfully in association with pentavalent antimony to treat a limited number of persons with mucosal leishmaniasis who failed to respond to pentavalent antimony alone.[230, 231]

Plastic surgery may be necessary to ameliorate sequelae of mucosal leishmaniasis,[232, 233] but it should not be performed earlier than 1 year after successful chemotherapy because grafts may be lost if relapses occur.

PREVENTION

Despite recent advances in understanding the immunology and molecular biology of leishmaniasis, there is still no effective form of immunoprophylaxis. The basic approaches to prevention have been to control sandfly vectors, to detect and exterminate animal reservoirs, and to treat infected patients.[234] Residual insecticides have yielded good results in some situations in which peridomestic transmission occurs, but spraying is necessary at intervals. Of historical note, the cessation of dichlorodiphenyltrichloroethane spraying for malaria in India, Bangladesh, and southern Iran was followed by major epidemics of visceral leishmaniasis. In areas where transmission occurs away from dwellings, residual insecticides are obviously of no benefit. Permethrin applied to clothing, diethyltoluamide (DEET)-containing insecticides to skin, and fine mesh netting at night provide partial protection.[234, 235]

Control of the animal reservoirs of leishmaniasis is often difficult. In northeastern Brazil, infected domestic dogs have been identified by mass serologic testing and exterminated, but the efficacy has been debated. In addition, the risk of *L. (L.) chagasi* being reintroduced into domestic dogs from infected foxes remains. In epidemics in which there is person-sandfly-person transmission, case identification and treatment are important components in control schemes. Recent evidence suggests that persons with post–kala-azar dermal leishmaniasis are reservoirs for *L. (L.) donovani* in interepidemic periods in India.[4] In many areas leishmaniasis is a zoonosis involving sylvatic mammals, and reservoir control is impossible.

Spontaneous resolution of cutaneous leishmaniasis is associated with the development of high-level immunity against the infecting *Leishmania* spp. Historically, mothers living in endemic areas in the Middle East have exposed the buttocks of their children to sandflies to ensure that infection occurred at an inconspicuous site. Immunization has been performed in Israel and the former Soviet Union with live promastigotes taken from culture. Good results were obtained with the "Jericho" strain of *L. (L.) major.*[236] Although this practice was effective in preventing naturally acquired disease, it was discontinued in Israel because some of the resulting lesions healed slowly, others became secondarily infected, and parasites persisted at the site of inoculation even after the lesions had healed.

Based on experience with animal models and humans, it is likely that an effective form of immunoprophylaxis will eventually be developed. A vaccine composed of killed promastigotes of five *Leishmania* strains was administered to troops in Brazil.[237] It induced T-cell responses, but its efficacy in protecting against cutaneous leishmaniasis was not clearly documented. Efforts continue toward the development of a vaccine with defined, possibly recombinant, leishmanial antigens and the proper adjuvant to elicit protective immune responses. Another approach would be the development of a genetically engineered, live, avirulent promastigote vaccine. As promising as these seem, an effective human vaccine is probably years away.

REFERENCES

1. Pearson RD, Sousa AQ. Clinical spectrum of leishmaniasis. Clin Infect Dis. 1996;22:1–13.
2. Peters W, Killick-Kendrick R, eds. The Leishmaniases in Biology and Medicine. London: Academic Press; 1987.
3. Lainson R, Shaw JJ. Evolution, classification and geographic distribution. In: Peters W, Killick-Kendrick R, eds. The Leishmaniases in Biology and Medicine, v. 1. London: Academic Press; 1987:1–120.
4. Addy M, Nandy A. Ten years of kala-azar in west Bengal, Part I. Did post-kala-azar dermal leishmaniasis initiate the outbreak in 24-Parganas? Bull World Health Organ. 1992;70:341–346.
5. Elias M, Rahman AJ, Khan NI. Visceral leishmaniasis and its control in Bangladesh. Bull World Health Organ. 1989;67:43–49.
6. Perea WA, Ancelle T, Moren A, et al. Visceral leishmaniasis in southern Sudan. Trans R Soc Trop Med Hyg. 1991;85:48–53.
7. Zijlstra EE, Ali MS, el-Hassan AM, et al. Kala-azar in displaced people from southern Sudan: Epidemiological, clinical and therapeutic findings. Trans R Soc Trop Med Hyg. 1991;85:365–369.
8. Zijlstra EE, Ali MS, el-Hassan AM, et al. Clinical aspects of kala-azar in children from the Sudan: A comparison with the disease in adults. J Trop Pediatr. 1992;38:17–21.
9. Costa CH, Pereira HF, Araugo MV. Visceral leishmaniasis epidemic in the State of Piaui, Brazil, 1980–1986. Rev Saude Pulica. 1990;24:361–372.
10. Jeronimo SMB, Oliveira RM, Mackay S, et al. An urban outbreak of visceral leishmaniasis in Natal, Brazil. Trans R Soc Trop Med Hyg. 1994;88:386–388.
11. Magill AJ, Grogl M, Gasser RA, et al. Visceral infection caused by *Leishmania tropica* in veterans of Operation Desert Storm. N Engl J Med. 1993;328:1383–1387.
12. Gunby P. Desert Storm veterans now may donate blood; others call for discussion of donor tests. JAMA. 1993;269:451–452.
13. Alvar J, Canavate C, Gutierrez-Solar B, et al. Leishmania and human immunodeficiency virus coinfection: The first 10 years. Clin Microbiol Rev. 1997;10:298–319.
14. Montalban C, Calleja JL, Erice A, et al. Visceral leishmaniasis in patients infected with human immunodeficiency virus. Co-operative Group for the Study of Leishmaniasis in AIDS. J Infect. 1990;21:261–270.
15. Peters BS, Fish D, Golden R, et al. Visceral leishmaniasis in HIV infection and AIDS: Clinical features and response to therapy. Q J Med. 1990;77:1101–1111.
16. Medrano FJ, Hernandez-Quero J, Jimenez E, et al. Visceral leishmaniasis in HIV-1–infected individuals: A common opportunistic infection in Spain? AIDS. 1992;6:1499–1503.
17. Kher V, Ghosh AK, Gupta A, et al. Visceral leishmaniasis: An unusual case of fever in a renal transplant recipient. Nephrol Dial Transplant. 1991;6:736–768.
18. Moulin B, Ollier J, Bouchouareb D, et al. Leishmaniasis: A rare cause of unexplained fever in a renal graft recipient. Nephron. 1992;60:360–362.
19. Norton SA, Frankenburg S, Klaus SN. Cutaneous leishmaniasis acquired during military service in the Middle East. Arch Dermatol. 1992;128:83–87.
20. Hepburn NC, Tidman MJ, Hunter JA. Cutaneous leishmaniasis in British troops from Belize. Br J Dermatol. 1993;128:63–68.
21. Scharton-Kersten T, Scott P. The role of innate immune responses in Th1 cell development following *Leishmania major* infection. J Leukocyte Biol. 1995;57:515–522.
22. Reiner SL, Locksley RM. Cytokines in the differentiation of Th1/Th2 CD4+ subsets in leishmaniasis. J Cell Biol. 1993;53:323–328.

23. Jeronimo SMB, Pearson RD. The Leishmania: Protozoans adapted for intracellular survival. Subcell Biochem. 1992;18:1–37.
24. Giannini MS. Effects of promastigote growth phase, frequency of subculture, and host age on promastigote-initiated infections with *Leishmania donovani* in the golden hamster. J Protozool. 1974;21:521–527.
25. Sacks DL, Perkins PV. Identification of an infective stage of *Leishmania* promastigotes. Science. 1984;223:1417–1419.
26. Sacks DL, Hieny S, Sher A. Identification of cell surface carbohydrate and antigenic changes between noninfective and infective developmental stages of *Leishmania major* promastigotes. J Immunol. 1985;135:564–569.
27. Lewis DJ, Ward RD. Transmission and vectors. In: Peters W, Killick-Kendrick R, eds. The Leishmaniases in Biology and Medicine, v. 1. London: Academic Press; 1987:235–262.
28. Ebert F. Charakterisierung von *Leishmania donovani*-Stammen mit der Disk-Electrophorese. Z Tropenmed Parasitol. 1973;24:517–524.
29. Grimaldi G, McMahon-Pratt D. Monoclonal antibodies for the identification of New World Leishmania species. Memorias do Instituto Oswaldo Cruz. 1996;9: 37–42.
30. Pratt DM, David JR. Monoclonal antibodies that distinguish between new world species of *Leishmania.* Nature. 1981;291:581–583.
31. Arnot DE, Barker DC. Biochemical identification of cutaneous leishmanias by analysis of kinetoplast DNA. II. Sequence homologies in *Leishmania* kDNA. Mol Biochem Parasitol. 1981;3:47–56.
32. Jackson PR, Wohlhieter JA, Jackson JE, et al. Restriction endonuclease analysis of *Leishmania* kinetoplast DNA characterizes parasites responsible for visceral and cutaneous disease. Am J Trop Med Hyg. 1984;33:808–819.
33. de Bruijn MH, Barker DC. Diagnosis of new world leishmaniasis: Specific detection of species of the *Leishmania braziliensis* complex by amplification of kinetoplast DNA. Acta Trop. 1992;52:45–58.
34. Rodriquez N, Guzman B, Rodas A, et al. Diagnosis of cutaneous leishmaniasis and species discrimination of parasites by PCR and hybridization. J Clin Microbiol. 1994;32:2246–2252.
35. Nuzum E, White F III, Thakur C, et al. Diagnosis of symptomatic visceral leishmaniasis by the use of the polymerase chain reaction on patient blood. J Infect Dis. 1995;171:751–754.
36. Giannini SH, Schittini M, Keithly JS, et al. Karyotype analysis of *Leishmania* species and its use in classification and clinical diagnosis. Science. 1986;232:762–765.
37. Wincker P, Ravel C, Blaineau C, et al. The Leishmania genome comprises 36 chromosomes conserved across widely divergent pathogenic species. Nucleic Acids Res. 1996;24:1688–1694.
38. Wilson MW, Donelson JE, Pearson RD, et al. Macrophage receptors of *Leishmania.* In: Korkonen TK, Hovi T, Makela PH, eds. Molecular Recognition in Host-Parasite Interactions. New York: Plenum; 1992:17–30.
39. Blackwell JM, Ezekowitz RAB, Roberts MB, et al. Macrophage complement and lectin-like receptors bind *Leishmania* in the absence of serum. J Exp Med. 1985;162:324–331.
40. Wozencraft AO, Sayers G, Blackwell JM. Macrophage type 3 complement receptors mediate serum-independent binding of *Leishmania donovani.* J Exp Med. 1986;164:1332–1337.
41. Russell DG, Wilhelm H. The involvement of the major surface glycoprotein (gp63) of *Leishmania* promastigotes in attachment to macrophages. J Immunol. 1986;136:2613–2620.
42. Mosser DM, Edelson PJ. Activation of the alternative complement pathway by *Leishmania* promastigotes: Parasite lysis and attachment to macrophages. J Immunol. 1984;132:1501–1505.
43. Wilson ME, Pearson RD. Evidence that *Leishmania donovani* utilizes a mannose receptor on human mononuclear phagocytes to establish intracellular parasitism. J Immunol. 1986;136:4681–4688.
44. Wilson ME, Pearson RD. Roles of CR3 and mannose receptors in the attachment and ingestion of *Leishmania donovani* by human mononuclear phagocytes. Infect Immun. 1988;56:363–369.
45. Puentes SM, Sacks DL, da Silva RP, et al. Complement binding by two developmental stages of *Leishmania* major promastigotes varying in expression of a surface lipophosphoglycan. J Exp Med. 1988;167:887–902.
46. Mosser DM, Vlassara H, Edelson PJ, et al. *Leishmania* promastigotes are recognized by the macrophage receptor for advanced glycosylation end products. J Exp Med. 1987;165:140–145.
47. Pearson RD, Steigbigel RT. Mechanism of lethal effect of human serum upon *Leishmania donovani.* J Immunol. 1980;125:2195–2201.
48. Colomer-Gould V, Quintao LG, Keithly J, et al. A common major surface antigen on amastigotes and promastigotes of *Leishmania* species. J Exp Med. 1985;162:902–916.
49. Etges R, Bouvier J, Bordier C. The major surface protein of *Leishmania* promastigotes is a protease. J Biol Chem. 1986;261:9098–9101.
50. Joshi PB, Sacks DL, Modi G, McMaster WR. Targeted gene deletion of Leishmania major genes encoding development of stage-specific leishmanolysin (GP63). Mol Microbiol. 1998;27:519–530.
51. McConville MJ, Bacic A, Mitchell GF, et al. Lipophosphoglycan of *Leishmania major* that vaccinates against cutaneous leishmaniasis contains an alkylglycerophosphoinositol lipid anchor. Proc Natl Acad Sci U S A. 1987;84:8941–8945.
52. King DL, Chang Y-D, Turco SJ. Cell surface lipophosphoglycan of *Leishmania donovani.* Mol Biochem Parasitol. 1987;24:47–53.
53. Hatzigeorgiou DE, Geng J, Zhu B, et al. Lipophosphoglycan from *Leishmania* suppresses agonist-induced interleukin 1 beta gene expression in human monocytes via a unique promoter sequence. Proc Nat Acad Sci U S A. 1996;93:14708–14713.
54. Pearson RD, Sullivan JA, Roberts D, et al. Interaction of *Leishmania donovani* promastigotes with human phagocytes. Infect Immun. 1983;40:411–416.
55. Bradley DJ, Taylor BA, Blackwell J, et al. Regulation of *Leishmania* populations within the host. III. Mapping of the locus controlling susceptibility to visceral leishmaniasis in the mouse. Clin Exp Immunol. 1979;37:7–14.
56. Plant JE, Blackwell JM, O'Brien AD, et al. Are the *Lsh* and *Ity* disease resistance genes at one locus on mouse chromosome 1? Nature. 1982;297:510–511.
57. Mock BA, Fortier AH, Potter M, et al. Genetic control of systemic *Leishmania major* infections; dissociation of intrahepatic amastigote replication from control by the *Lsh* gene. Infect Immun. 1985;50:588–591.
58. Blackwell JM, Black GF, Peacock CS, et al. Immunogenetics of leishmanial and mycobacterial infections: The Belem Family Study. Philos Trans R Soc Lond B Biol Sci. 1997;352:1331–1345.
59. Murray HW, Rubin BY, Rothermel CD. Killing of intracellular *Leishmania donovani* by lymphokine-stimulated human mononuclear phagocytes. Evidence that interferon-gamma is the activating lymphokine. J Clin Invest. 1983;72:1506–1510.
60. Squires KE, Schreiber RD, McElrath MJ, et al. Experimental visceral leishmaniasis: Role of endogenous IFN-gamma in host defense and tissue granulomatous response. J Immunol. 1989;143:4244–4249.
61. Liew FY, Li Y, Moss D, et al. Resistance to *Leishmania major* infection correlates with the induction of nitric oxide synthase in murine macrophages. Eur J Immunol. 1991;21:3009–3014.
62. Green SJ, Meltzer MS, Hibbs JB, et al. Activated macrophages destroy intracellular *Leishmania major* amastigotes by an L-arginine-dependent killing mechanism. J Immunol. 1990;144:278–283.
63. Sypek JP, Wyler DJ. Antileishmanial defense in macrophages triggered by tumor necrosis factor expressed on CD4+ T lymphocyte plasma membrane. J Exp Med. 1991;174:755–759.
64. Heinzel FP, Schoenhaut DS, Rerko RM, et al. Recombinant interleukin 12 cures mice infected with *Leishmania major.* J Exp Med. 1993;177:1505–1509.
65. Murray HW, Squires KE, Miralles CD, et al. Acquired resistance and granuloma formation in experimental visceral leishmaniasis. Differential T cell and lymphokine roles in initial versus established immunity. J Immunol. 1992;148:1858–1863.
66. Heinzel FP, Sadick MD, Holaday BJ, et al. Reciprocal expression of interferon-gamma or interleukin 4 during the resolution or progression of murine leishmaniasis. Evidence for expansion of distinct helper T cell subsets. J Exp Med. 1989;169:59–72.
67. Scott P, Natovitz P, Coffman RL, et al. Immunoregulation of cutaneous leishmaniasis. T cell lines that transfer protective immunity or exacerbation belong to different T helper cell subsets and respond to distinct parasite antigens. J Exp Med. 1988;168:1675–1684.
68. Leal LM, Moss DW, Kuhn R, et al. Interleukin-4 transgenic mice of resistant background are susceptible to *Leishmania major* infection. Eur J Immunol. 1993;23:566–569.
69. Morris L, Troutt AB, Handman E, et al. Changes in the precursor frequencies of IL-4 and IFN-gamma secreting CD4+ cells correlate with resolution of lesions in murine cutaneous leishmaniasis. J Immunol. 1992;149:2715–2721.
70. Noben-Trauth N, Kropf P, Muller I. Susceptibility of Leishmania major infection in interleukin-4-deficient mice. Science. 1996;271:987–990.
71. Holaday BJ, Pompeu MML, Evans T, et al. Correlates of leishmania-specific immunity in the clinical spectrum of infection with *Leishmania chagasi.* J Infect Dis. 1993;167:411–417.
72. Karp CL, El-Safi SH, Wynn TA, et al. In vivo cytokine profiles in patients with kala-azar; marked elevation of both interleukin-10 and interferon-gamma. J Clin Invest. 1993;91:1644–1648.
73. Holaday BJ, Pompeu MML, Jeronimo S, et al. Potential role for interleukin-10 in the immunosuppression associated with kala-azar. J Clin Invest. 1993;92: 2626–2632.
74. Peterson EA, Neva FA, Barral A, et al. Monocyte suppression of antigen-specific lymphocyte responses in diffuse cutaneous leishmaniasis patients from the Dominican Republic. J Immunol. 1984;132:2603–2606.
75. Heinzel FP, Ahmed F, Hujer AM, Rerko RM. Immunoregulation of murine leishmaniasis by interleukin-12. Research Immunol. 1995;146:575–581.
76. Barral-Netto M, Barral A, Brownell CE, et al. Transforming growth factor–beta in leishmanial infection: A parasite escape mechanism. Science. 1992;247:545–548.
77. Reiner NE, Ng W, McMaster WR. Parasite-accessory cell interactions in murine leishmaniasis II. *Leishmania donovani* suppresses macrophage expression of class I and class II major histocompatibility complex gene products. J Immunol. 1987;138:1926–1932.
78. Reiner NE, Malemud CJ. Arachidonic acid metabolism by murine peritoneal macrophages infected with *Leishmania donovani:* In vitro evidence for parasite-induced alterations in cyclooxygenase and lipoxygenase pathways. J Immunol. 1985;134:556–563.
79. Reiner NE, Ng W, Wilson CB, et al. Modulation of in vitro monocyte cytokine responses to *Leishmania donovani.* Interferon-gamma prevents parasite-induced inhibition of interleukin 1 production and primes monocytes to respond to *Leishmania* by producing both tumor necrosis factor-alpha and interleukin 1. J Clin Invest. 1990;85:1914–1924.
80. Reiner SL, Wang ZE, Hatam F, et al. TH1 and TH2 cell antigen receptors in experimental leishmaniasis. Science. 1993;259:1457–1460.
81. Will A, Blank C, Rollinghoff M, et al. Murine epidermal Langerhans cells are potent stimulators of an antigen-specific T cell response to *Leishmania major,* the cause of cutaneous leishmaniasis. Eur J Immunol. 1992;22:1341–1347.

82. Scott P, Natovitz P, Sher A. B lymphocytes are required for the generation of T cells that mediate healing of cutaneous leishmaniasis. J Immunol. 1986;137:1017–1021.
83. Sacks DL, Scott PA, Asofsky R, et al. Cutaneous leishmaniasis in anti-IgM–treated mice: Enhanced resistance due to functional depletion of a B cell–dependent T cell involved in the supressor pathway. J Immunol. 1984;132:2072–2077.
84. Bretscher PA, Wei G, Menon JN, et al. Establishment of stable, cell-mediated immunity that makes "susceptible" mice resistant to *Leishmania major.* Science. 1992;257:539–542.
85. Campos-Neto A, Bunn-Moreno MM. Polyclonal B cell activation in hamsters infected with parasites of the genus *Leishmania.* Infect Immun. 1982;38:871–876.
86. Badaró R, Carvalho EM, Rocha H, et al. *Leishmania donovani:* An opportunistic microbe associated with progressive disease in three immunocompromised patients. Lancet. 1986;1:647–648.
87. Barral A, Pedral-Sampaio D, Grimaldi JG, et al. Leishmaniasis in Bahia, Brazil: Evidence that *Leishmania amazonensis* produces a wide spectrum of clinical diseases. Am J Trop Med Hyg. 1991;44:536–546.
88. Mebrahtu Y, Lawyer P, Githure J, et al. Visceral leishmaniasis unresponsive to pentostam caused by *Leishmania tropica* in Kenya. Am J Trop Med Hyg. 1989;41:289–294.
89. Badaró R, Jones TC, Lorenco R, et al. A prospective study of visceral leishmaniasis in an endemic area of Brazil. J Infect Dis. 1986;154:639–649.
90. Badaró R, Jones TC, Carvalho EM, et al. New perspectives on a subclinical form of visceral leishmaniasis. J Infect Dis. 1986;154:1003–1011.
91. Evans TG, Teixeira MJ, McAuliffe IT, et al. Epidemiology of visceral leishmaniasis in northeast Brazil. J Infect Dis. 1992;166:1124–1132.
92. Condom MJ, Clotet B, Sirera G, et al. Asymptomatic leishmaniasis in the acquired immunodeficiency syndrome (AIDS). Ann Intern Med. 1989;111:767–768.
93. Guan LR. Current status of kala-azar and vector control in China. Bull World Health Organ. 1991;69:595–601.
94. Marsden PD. Current concepts in parasitology: Leishmaniasis. N Engl J Med. 1979;300:350–352.
95. Manson-Bahr PEC. A primary skin lesion in visceral leishmaniasis. Nature. 1955;175:433–434.
96. Manson-Bahr PEC. East African kala-azar with special reference to the pathology, prophylaxis and treatment. Trans R Soc Trop Med Hyg. 1959;53:123–137.
97. Eltoum IA, Zijlstra EE, Ali MS, Ghalib HW, et al. Congenital kala-azar and leishmaniasis in the placenta. Am J Trop Med Hyg. 1992;46:57–62.
98. Yadav TP, Gupta H, Satteya U, et al. Congenital kala-azar. Ann Trop Med Parasitol. 1989;83:535–537.
99. Nyakundi PM, Muigai R, Were JB, et al. Congenital visceral leishmaniasis: Case report. Trans R Soc Trop Med Hyg. 1988;82:564.
100. Grogl M, Daugirda JL, Hoover DL, et al. Survivability and infectivity of viscerotropic *Leishmania tropica* from Operation Desert Storm participants in human blood products maintained under blood bank conditions. Am J Trop Med Hyg. 1993;49:308–315.
101. Shulman IA. Parasitic infections and their impact on blood donor selection and testing. Arch Pathol Lab Med. 1994;118:366–370.
102. Cummins D, Amin S, Halil O, et al. Visceral leishmaniasis after cardiac surgery. Arch Dis Child. 1995;72:235–236.
103. Herwaldt BL, Juranek DD. Laboratory-acquired malaria, leishmaniasis, trypanosomiasis and toxoplasmosis. Am J Trop Med Hyg. 1993;8:313–323.
104. Harrison LH, Naidu TG, Drew JS, et al. Reciprocal relationships between undernutrition and the parasitic disease visceral leishmaniasis. Rev Infect Dis. 1986;8:447–453.
105. Cerf BJ, Jones TC, Badaro R, et al. Malnutrition as a risk factor for severe visceral leishmaniasis. J Infect Dis. 1987;156:1030–1033.
106. Pearson RD, Cox G, Jeronimo SMB, et al. Visceral leishmaniasis: A model for infection-induced cachexia. Am J Trop Med Hyg. 1992;47(Suppl):8–15.
107. Andrade TM, Carvalho EM, Rocha H. Bacterial infections in patients with visceral leishmaniasis. J Infect Dis. 1990;162:1354–1359.
108. Garces JM, Tomas S, Rubies-Prat J, et al. Bacterial infection as a presenting manifestation of visceral leishmaniasis. Rev Infect Dis. 1990;12:518–519.
109. De Alencar JE, Neves J. Leishmaniose visceral (calazar). In: Veronesi R, ed. Doencas Infecciosas e Parasitarias. 7th ed. Rio de Janeiro: Editora Guanabara Koogan SA; 1982:724.
110. Manson-Bahr PEC, Southgate BA, Harvey AEC. Development of kala-azar in man after inoculation with a leishmania from a Kenyo sandfly. BMJ. 1963;1:1208–1210.
111. Manson-Bahr PEC, Apted FIC. Leishmaniasis. In: Manson-Bahr PEC, Apted FIC, eds. Manson's Tropical Diseases. 18th ed. London: Bailliere Tindall; 1982:93–115.
112. Stone HH, Tool CD, Pugsley WS. Kala-azar (visceral leishmaniasis): Report of a case with 34 month incubation period and positive Doan-Wright test. Ann Intern Med. 1952;36:686–693.
113. di Martino L, Vajro P, Nocerino A, et al. Fulminant hepatitis in an Italian infant with visceral leishmaniasis. Trans R Soc Trop Med Hyg. 1992;86:34.
114. Hervas JA, Alberti P, Ferragut J, et al. Acute hepatitis as a presenting manifestation of kala azar. Pediatr Infect Dis J. 1991;10:409–410.
115. Duarte MI, da Matta VL, Corbett CE, et al. Interstitial pneumonitis in human visceral leishmaniasis. Trans R Soc Trop Med Hyg. 1989;83:73–76.
116. Abbas K, el Toum IA, el Hassan AM. Oral leishmaniasis associated with kala-azar. A case report. Oral Surg Oral Med Oral Pathol. 1992;73:583–584.
117. Knight R, Woodruff AW, Pettitt LE. The mechanism of anaemia in kala-azar: A study of two patients. Trans R Soc Trop Med Hyg. 1967;61:701–705.
118. Woodruff AW, Topley E, Knight R, et al. The anaemia of kala azar. Br J Haematol. 1972;22:319–329.
119. Pippard MJ, Moir D, Weatherall DJ, et al. Mechanism of anaemia in resistant visceral leishmaniasis. Ann Trop Med Parasitol. 1986;80:317–323.
120. Most H, Lavietes PH. Kala-azar in American military personnel. Report of 30 cases. Medicine (Baltimore). 1947;26:221–284.
121. Musumeci S, D'Agata A, Schiliro G, et al. Studies of the neutropenia in kala-azar. Results in two patients. Trans R Soc Trop Med Hyg. 1976;70:500–503.
122. Burchenal JH, Bowers RF, Haedicke TA. Visceral leishmaniasis complicated by severe anemia—improvement following splenectomy. Am J Trop Med Hyg. 1947;27:699–709.
123. Carvalho EM, Andrews BS, Martinelli R, et al. Circulating immune complexes and rheumatoid factor in schistosomiasis and visceral leishmaniasis. Am J Trop Med Hyg. 1983;32:61–69.
124. Pearson RD, Alencar JE, Romito R, et al. Circulating immune complexes and rheumatoid factors in visceral leishmaniasis. J Infect Dis. 1983;147:1102.
125. De Brito T, Hoshino-Shimizu S, Neto VA, et al. Glomerular involvement in human kala-azar. Am J Trop Med Hyg. 1975;24:9–18.
126. Caravaca F, Munoz A, Pizarro JL, et al. Acute renal failure in visceral leishmaniasis. Am J Nephrol. 1991;11:350–352.
127. Chenoweth CE, Singal S, Pearson RD, et al. Acquired immunodeficiency syndrome–related visceral leishmaniasis presenting in a pleural effusion. Chest. 1993;103:648–649.
128. Matheron S, Cable A, Parquin F, et al. Visceral leishmaniasis and HIV infection: Unusual presentation with pleuropulmonary involvement, and effect of secondary prophylaxis. AIDS. 1992;6:238–240.
129. Datry A, Similowski T, Jais P, et al. AIDS-associated leishmaniasis: An unusual gastro-duodenal presentation. Trans R Soc Trop Med Hyg. 1990;84:239–240.
130. Altes J, Salas A, Llompart A, et al. Small intestine involvement in visceral leishmaniasis. Am J Gastroenterol. 1991;86:1283.
131. Delsedime L, Coppola F, Mazzucco G. Gastric localization of systemic leishmaniasis in a patient with AIDS. Histopathology. 1991;19:93–95.
132. Muigai R, Gatei DG, Shaunak S, et al. Jejunal function and pathology in visceral leishmaniasis. Lancet. 1983;2:476–479.
133. Sendino A, Barbado FJ, Mostaza JM, et al. Visceral leishmaniasis with malabsorption syndrome in a patient with acquired immunodeficiency syndrome. Am J Med. 1990;89:673–674.
134. Kumar PV, Sadeghi E, Torabi S. Kala azar with disseminated dermal leishmaniasis. Am J Trop Med Hyg. 1989;40:150–153.
135. Grau JM, Bosch X, Salgado AC, et al. Human immunodeficiency virus (HIV) and aplastic anemia. Ann Intern Med. 1989;110:576–577.
136. Kirk R. Studies in leishmaniasis in the Anglo-Egyptian Sudan: V. Cutaneous and mucocutaneous leishmaniasis. Trans R Soc Trop Med Hyg. 1942;35:257–270.
137. Sen Gupta PC, Bhattacharjee B. Histopathology of post-kala-azar dermal leishmaniasis. J Trop Med Hyg. 1953;56:110–116.
138. Muigai R, Gachihi GS, Oster CN, et al. Post kala-azar dermal leishmaniasis: The Kenyan experience. East Afr Med J. 1991;68:801–806.
139. el Hassan AM, Ghalib HW, Zijlstra EE, et al. Post kala-azar dermal leishmaniasis in the Sudan: Clinical features, pathology and treatment. Trans R Soc Trop Med Hyg. 1992;83:245–248.
140. Chulay JD, Bryceson ADM. Quantitation of amastigotes of *Leishmania donovani* in smears of splenic aspirates from patients with visceral leishmaniasis. Am J Trop Med Hyg. 1983;32:475–479.
141. Report of the informal meeting on the chemotherapy of visceral leishmaniasis. UNDP/World Bank/WHO Special Programme for Research and Training in Tropical Diseases. Nairobi, Kenya, June 1982.
142. Hockmeyer WT, Kager PA, Rees PH, et al. The culture of *Leishmania donovani* in Schneider's insect medium: Its value in the diagnosis and management of patients with visceral leishmaniasis. Trans R Soc Trop Med Hyg. 1981;75:861–863.
143. Badaró R, Reed SG, Carvalho EM. Immunofluorescent antibody test in American visceral leishmaniasis: Sensitivity and specificity of different morphological forms of two *Leishmania* species. Am J Trop Med Hyg. 1983;32:480–484.
144. Mohammed EAER, Wright EP, Rahman AMA, et al. Serodiagnosis of Sudanese visceral and mucosal leishmaniasis: Comparison of ELISA-immunofluorescence and indirect haemagglutination. Trans R Soc Trop Med Hyg. 1986;80:271–274.
145. Pearson RD, Evans T, Naidu TG, et al. Humoral responses during South American visceral leishmaniasis. Ann Trop Med Parasitol. 1986;80:465–468.
146. Zijlstra EE, Ali MS, el-Hassan AM, et al. Kala-azar: A comparative study of parasitological methods and the direct agglutination test in diagnosis. Trans R Soc Trop Med Hyg. 1992;86:505–507.
147. Pal A, Mukerji K, Basu D, et al. Evaluation of direct agglutination test (DAT) and ELISA for serodiagnosis of visceral leishmaniasis in India. J Clin Lab Anal. 1991;5:303–306.
148. Scott JM, Shreffler WG, Ghalib HW, et al. A rapid and simple diagnostic test for active visceral leishmaniasis. Am J Trop Med Hyg. 1991;44:272–277.
149. Kar K. Serological diagnosis of leishmaniasis. Crit Rev Microbiol. 1995;21:123–152.
150. Burns JM Jr, Shreffler WG, Benson DR, et al. Molecular characterization of a kinesin-related antigen of *Leishmania chagasi* that detects specific antibody in African and American visceral *leishmaniasis.* Proc Natl Acad Sci U S A. 1993;90:775–759.
151. Ashford RW, Bettini S. Ecology and epidemiology: Old World. In: Peters W, Killick-Kendrick R, eds. The Leishmaniases in Biology and Medicine, v. 1. London: Academic Press; 1987;365–424.
152. Gramiccia M, Ben-Ismail R, Gradoni L, et al. A *Leishmania infantum* enzymatic variant, causative agent of cutaneous leishmaniasis in north Tunisia. Trans R Soc Trop Med Hyg. 1991;85:370–371.

153. Grimaldi G Jr, Tesh RB, McMahon-Pratt DM. A review of the geographic distribution and epidemiology of leishmaniasis in the new world. Am J Trop Med Hyg. 1989;41:687–725.
154. Desjeux P. Information on the epidemiology and control of the leishmaniasis by country and territory. 1991. WHO/Leish/91.30 World Health Organization.
155. Marsden PD. Mucosal leishmaniasis ("espundia," Escomel, 1911). Trans R Soc Trop Med Hyg. 1986;80:859–876.
156. Marsden PD, Sampaio RNR, Rocha R, et al. Mucocutaneous leishmaniasis—an unsolved clinical problem. Trop Doct. 1977;7:7–11.
157. Shaw JJ, Lainson R. Ecology and epidemiology: New world. In: Peters W, Killick-Kendrick R, eds. The Leishmaniases in Biology and Medicine, v. 1. London: Academic Press; 1987:291–363.
158. Simpson MH, Mullins JF, Stone OJ. Disseminated anergic cutaneous leishmaniasis. An autochthonous case in Texas and the Mexican states of Tamaulipas and Nuevo Leon. Arch Dermatol. 1968;97:301–303.
159. Shaw PK, Quigg LT, Allain DS, et al. Autochthonous dermal leishmaniasis in Texas. Am J Trop Med Hyg. 1976;25:788–796.
160. Gustafson TL, Reed CM, McGreevy PB, et al. Human cutaneous leishmaniasis acquired in Texas. Am J Trop Med Hyg. 1985;34:58–63.
161. Nelson DA, Gustafson TL, Spielvogel RL. Clinical aspects of cutaneous leishmaniasis acquired in Texas. J Am Acad Dermatol. 1985;12:985–992.
162. Agostoni C, Dorigoni N, Malfitano A, et al. Mediterranean leishmaniasis in HIV-infected patients: Epidemiology, clinical and diagnostic features of 22 cases. Infection. 1998;26:93–99.
163. Moses AE, Maayan S, Rahav G, et al. HIV infection and AIDS in Jerusalem: A microcosm of illness in Israel. Isr J Med Sci 1996;32:716–721.
164. Golino A, Duncan JM, Zeluff B, et al. Leishmaniasis in a heart transplant patient. J Heart Lung Transplant. 1992;11:820–823.
165. Ridley DS. The pathogenesis of cutaneous leishmaniasis. Trans R Soc Trop Med Hyg. 1979;73:150–160.
166. Ridley MJ, Ridley DS. Cutaneous leishmaniasis: Immune complex formation and necrosis in the acute phase. Br J Exp Pathol. 1984;65:327–336.
167. Smith PAJ. Long incubation period in leishmaniasis. BMJ. 1955;2:1143.
168. Barral A, Guerreiro J, Bomfim G, et al. Lymphadenopathy as the first sign of human cutaneous infection by *Leishmania braziliensis*. Am J Trop Med Hyg. 1995;53:256–259.
169. Sousa AQ, Parise ME, Pompeu MM, et al. Bubonic leishmaniasis: A common manifestation of *Leishmania (Viannia) braziliensis* infection in Ceara, Brazil. Am J Trop Med Hyg. 1995;53:380–385.
170. Kerdel-Vegas F. American leishmaniasis. Int J Dermatol. 1982;21:291–303.
171. Bryceson ADM. Diffuse cutaneous leishmaniasis in Ethiopia. I: The clinical and histological features of disease. Trans R Soc Trop Med Hyg. 1969;63:708–737.
172. Berger RS, Perez-Figaredo, Spielvogel RL. Leishmaniasis: The touch preparation as a rapid means of diagnosis. J Am Acad Dermatol. 1987;16:1096–1105.
173. Weigle KA, de Davalos M, Heredia P, et al. Diagnosis of cutaneous and mucocutaneous leishmaniasis in Colombia: A comparison of seven methods. Am J Trop Med Hyg. 1987;36:489–496.
174. Pearson RD, Navin TR, Sousa AQ, et al. Leishmaniasis. In: Kass EH, Platt R, eds. Current Therapy in Infectious Diseases-3. Toronto: BC Decker; 1990:3384–3389.
175. Wirth DF, Rogers WO, Barker R Jr, et al. Leishmaniasis and malaria: New tools for epidemiologic analysis. Science. 1986;234:975–979.
176. Kalter DC. Laboratory tests for the diagnosis and evaluation of leishmaniasis. Dermatol Clin. 1994;12:37–50.
177. Martinez JE, Arias AL, Escobar MA, et al. Haemoculture of *Leishmania (Viannia) braziliensis* from two cases of mucosal leishmaniasis: Reexamination of haematogenous dissemination. Trans R Soc Trop Med Hyg. 1992;86:392–394.
178. Marsden PD. Mucosal leishmaniasis ("espundia," Escomel, 1911). Trans R Soc Trop Med Hyg. 1986;80:859–876.
179. Jones TC, Johnson WD Jr, Barretto AC, et al. Epidemiology of American cutaneous leishmaniasis due to *Leishmania braziliensis braziliensis*. J Infect Dis. 1987;156:73–83.
180. Villela F, Pestana BR, Pessoa SB. Presenca da *Leishmania brasiliensis* na mucosa nasal sem lešao aparente, em casos recentes de leishmaniose cutanea. O Hospital. 1939;16:953–960.
181. Walton BC, Chinel LV, Eguia OE. Onset of espundia after many years of occult infection with *Leishmania braziliensis*. Am J Trop Med Hyg. 1973;22:696–698.
182. Marsden PD, Nonata RR. Mucocutaneous leishmaniasis—a review of clinical aspects. Rev Soc Bras Med Trop. 1975;9:309–326.
183. Pupo JA. Estudo clinico da leishmaniose tegumentar Americans—*(Leishmania brazilliensis—viannia* (1911). Rev Hosp Clin Fac Med Sao Paulo. 1946;1:113–164.
184. Marsden PD, Sampaio RNR, Rocha R, et al. Mucocutaneous leishmaniasis—an unsolved clinical problem. Trop Doct 1977;7:7–11.
185. Aleixo J. Leishmaniose com localizacao genital. An Bras Dermatol Sifilolog. 1945;20:69–71.
186. Montenegro J. Cutaneous reaction in leishmaniasis. Arch Dermatol Syph. 1926;13:187–194.
187. Furtado T. Criterios para o diagnostico da leishmaniose tegumentar Americana. An Bras Dermatol. 1980;55:81–86.
188. Bonfante-Garrido R, Barreto T. Leishmaniasis tegumentaria Americana en el distrito undaneta. Venezuela Bol Sanit Panam. 1981;91:30–37.
189. Cuba CAC, Marsden PD, Barreto AC, et al. Parasitologic and immunologic diagnosis of American (mucocutaneous) leishmaniasis. Bull Pan Am Health Org. 1981:15:249–259.
190. Walton BC, Brooks WH, Arjona J. Serodiagnosis of American leishmaniasis by indirect fluorescent antibody test. Am J Trop Med Hyg. 1972;21:296–299.
191. Walton BC. Evaluation of chemotherapy of American visceral leishmaniasis by indirect fluorescent antibody test. Am J Trop Med Hyg. 1980:29:747–752.
192. Costa OG. American (mucocutaneous) leishmaniasis. Arch Dermatol Syph. 1944;49:194–196.
193. Jaffe L. Nasal leishmaniasis Americana in Panama. Arch Otolaryngol. 1954;60:601–611.
194. Berman JD. Human leishmaniasis: Clinical, diagnostic, and chemotherapeutic developments in the last 10 years. Clin Infect Dis. 1997;24:684–703.
195. Grogl M, Thomason TN, Franke ED. Drug resistance in leishmaniasis: Its implications in systemic chemotherapy of cutaneous and mucocutaneous disease. Am J Trop Med Hyg. 1992;47:117–126.
196. Herwaldt BL, Berman JD. Recommendations for treating leishmaniasis with sodium stibogluconate (Pentostam) and review of pertinent clinical studies. Am J Trop Med Hyg. 1992;46:296–306.
197. Torre-Cisneros J, Villanueva JL, Kindelan JM, et al. Successful treatment of antimony-resistant visceral leishmaniasis with liposomal amphotericin B in patients infected with human immunodeficiency virus. Clin Infect Dis. 1993;17:625–627.
198. Gokhale PC, Kshiragar NA, Khan MU, et al. Successful treatment of resistant visceral leishmaniasis with liposomal amphotericin B. Trans R Soc Trop Med Hyg. 1994;88:228.
199. Davidson RN, di Martino L, Gradoni L, et al. Liposomal amphotericin B (AmBisome) in Mediterranean visceral leishmaniasis: A multi-centre trial. Q J Med. 1994;87:75–81.
200. di Martiono L, Ramondi F, Scotti S, et al. Efficacy and tolerability of liposomal amphotericin B in Italian infants with visceral leishmaniasis. Trans R Soc Trop Med Hyg. 1993;87:477.
201. Seaman J, Boer C, Wilkerson R, et al. Liposomal amphotericin B (AmBisome) in the treatment of complicated kala-azar under field conditions. Clin Infect Dis. 1995;21:188–193.
202. El-On J, Harvey S, Grunwald MH, et al. Topical treatment of Old World cutaneous leishmaniasis caused by *Leishmania major*: A double-blind study. J Am Acad Dermatol. 1992;27:227–231.
203. Halim MA, Alfurayh O, Kalin ME, et al. Successful treatment of visceral leishmaniasis with allopurinol plus ketoconazole in a renal transplant recipient after the occurrence of pancreatitis due to stibogluconate. Clin Infect Dis. 1993;16:397–399.
204. Antezana G, Zeballos R, Mendoza C, et al. Electrocardiographic alterations during treatment of mucocutaneous leishmaniasis with meglumine antimoniate and allopurinol. Trans R Soc Trop Med Hyg. 1992;86:31–33.
205. Balzan M, Fenech F. Acute renal failure in visceral leishmaniasis treated with sodium stibogluconate. Trans R Soc Trop Med Hyg. 1992;86:515–516.
206. Sundar S, Agrawal NK, Sinha PR, et al. Short-course, low-dose amphotericin B lipid complex therapy for visceral leishmaniasis unresponsive to antimony. Ann Intern Med. 1997;127:133–137.
207. Prata A. Treatment of kala-azar with amphotericin B. Trans R Soc Trop Med Hyg. 1963;57:266–268.
208. Thakur CP, Sinha GP, Pandey AK, et al. Daily versus alternate-day regimen of amphotericin B in the treatment of kala-azar: A randomized comparison. Bull World Health Organ. 1994;72:931–936.
209. Mishra M, Biswas UK, Jha DN, et al. Amphotericin versus pentamidine in antimony-unresponsive kala-azar. Lancet. 1992;340:1256–1257.
210. Soto-Mancipe J, Grogl M, Berman JD. Evaluation of pentamidine for the treatment of cutaneous leishmaniasis in Colombia. Clin Infect Dis. 1993;16:417–425.
211. Wispelwey B, Pearson RD. Pentamidine: Risk-benefit analysis. Drug Safety. 1990;5:212–219.
212. Badaró R, Johnson WD Jr. The role of interferon-gamma in the treatment of visceral and diffuse cutaneous leishmaniasis. J Infect Dis. 1993;167(Suppl 1):S13–S17.
213. Badaró R, Falcoff E, Badaró FS, et al. Treatment of visceral leishmaniasis with pentavalent antimony and interferon gamma. N Engl J Med. 1990;322:16–21.
214. Thakur CP, Kumar K, Sinha PK, et al. Treatment of post–kala-azar dermal leishmaniasis with sodium stibogluconate. BMJ. 1987;295:886–887.
215. Thakur CP, Kumar K. Efficacy of prolonged therapy with stibogluconate in post kala-azar dermal leishmaniasis. Indian J Med Res. 1990;91:144–148.
216. Gorgolas M, Castrillo JM, Guerrero MLF. Visceral leishmaniasis in patients with AIDS: Report of three cases treated with pentavalent antimony and interferon-γ. Clin Infect Dis. 1993;17:56–58.
217. Wali JP, Aggarwal P, Gupta U, et al. Ketoconazole in the treatment of antimony- and pentamidine-resistant kala-azar. J Infect Dis. 1992;166:215–216.
218. Buchenal JH, Bowers RF, Haedicke TA. Visceral leishmaniasis complicated by severe anemia—improvement following splenectomy. Am J Trop Med Hyg. 1947;27:699–709.
219. Bryceson ADM. Diffuse cutaneous leishmaniasis in Ethiopia. II. Treatment. Trans R Soc Trop Med Hyg. 1970;64:369–393.
220. Weinrauch L, Livshin R, El-On J. Ketoconazole in cutaneous leishmaniasis. Br J Dermatol. 1987;117:666–668.
221. Convit J, Rondon A, Ulrich M, et al. Immunotherapy versus chemotherapy in localized cutaneous leishmaniasis. Lancet. 1987;1:401–405.
222. Navin TR, Arana BA, Arana FE, et al. Placebo-controlled clinical trial of meglumine antimonate (glucantime) vs. localized controlled heat in the treatment of cutaneous leishmaniasis in Guatemala. Am J Trop Med Hyg. 1990;42:43–50.
223. Rocha RAA, Sampaio RN, Guerra M, et al. Apparent glucantime failure in five patients with mucocutaneous leishmaniasis. Am J Trop Med Hyg. 1980;83:131–139.
224. Franke ED, Wignall S, Cruz ME, et al. Efficacy and toxicity of sodium stibogluconate for mucosal leishmaniasis. Ann Intern Med. 1990;113:934–940.

225. Report of the workshop on the chemotherapy of mucocutaneous leishmaniasis. UNDP/World Bank/Who Special Programme for Research and Training in Tropical Diseases, Brasilia, July 1979.
226. Furtado TA. Clinical results in the treatment of American leishmaniasis with oral and intravenous amphotericin. In: Welch H, Marti-Ibanez F, eds. Antibiotics Annual 1959–1960. New York: Antibiotica; 1960;631–637.
227. Sampaio SAP, Godoy JT, Paiva L, et al. The treatment of American (mucocutaneous) leishmanias with amphotericin B. Arch Dermatol. 1960;82:627–635.
228. Miranda JL, Lima NDS, Da Cuhna JF. A anfotericina B na terapeutic de leishmaniose tegumentar Americana. O Hosp. 1961;59:31–53.
229. Crofts MAJ. Use of amphotericin B in mucocutaneous leishmaniasis. J Trop Med Hyg. 1976;79:111–113.
230. Badaró R, Carvalho JS, Badaró F, et al. Cytokines in the management of leishmaniasis. In: Van Furth R, ed. Hemopoietic Growth Factors and Mononuclear Phagocytes. Basel: Karger; 1993;111–112.
231. Bottasso O, Cabrine J, Falcoff R. Successful treatment of antimony-resistant American mucocutaneous leishmaniasis. Arch Dermatol. 1992;128:996–997.
232. Farina R. Nose tip collapse through loss of chondro-mucous substance (repair of nasal lining). Plast Reconstr Surg. 1954;13:137–143.
233. Pitanguy I, Ribiero A. Leishmaniasis: Surgical treatment of its sequelae. Plast Reconstr Surg. 1965;30:565–572.
234. Schreck CE, Kline DL, Chaniotis BN, et al. Evaluation of personal protection methods against phlebotomine sand flies including vectors of leishmaniasis in Panama. Am J Trop Med Hyg. 1982;31:1046–1053.
235. Soto J, Medina F, Dember N, Berman J. Efficacy of permethrin-impregnated uniforms in the prevention of malaria and leishmaniasis in Colombian soldiers. Clin Infect Dis. 1995;21:599–602.
236. Greenblatt CL. The present and future of vaccination for cutaneous leishmaniasis. In: Mizrahi A, Hertman I, Klingberg MA, et al, eds. Progress in Clinical and Biological Research, v 47. New Developments with Human and Veterinary Vaccines. New York: Alan R Liss; 1980:259–285.
237. Antunes CM, Mayrink W, Magalhaes PA, et al. Controlled field trials of a vaccine against New World cutaneous leishmaniasis. Int J Epidemiol. 1986;15:572–580.

Chapter 266

Trypanosoma Species (American Trypanosomiasis, Chagas' Disease): Biology of Trypanosomes

LOUIS V. KIRCHHOFF

The genus *Trypanosoma* consists of approximately 20 species of protozoa.[1] Two of the three species that infect humans are pathogenic, and several other species cause severe and economically important diseases in domestic mammals. Broadly defined, the organisms belonging to this genus are protozoan flagellates of the family Trypanosomatidae, order Kinetoplastida, that pass through different morphologic stages (epimastigote, amastigote, and trypomastigote) in their vertebrate and invertebrate hosts.[2] The criterion of three morphologic stages, however, is not fulfilled by each species in the genus. For example, only *Trypanosoma cruzi,* the etiologic agent of American trypanosomiasis, or Chagas' disease, and one other species, multiply in mammalian hosts as intracellular amastigotes similar to those seen in infections caused by *Leishmania.* In contrast, African trypanosomes, which cause sleeping sickness in humans and varying degrees of morbidity in wild and domestic mammals, do not have an intracellular form and multiply as trypomastigotes that circulate in the mammalian blood stream and other extracellular spaces.

The trypomastigote form has a single flagellum originating near the kinetoplast, which is a DNA-containing structure located in the parasite's single, complex mitochondrion. The flagellum runs alongside the body of the parasite and is enveloped in an undulating membrane. It extends beyond the body as a free, threadlike structure. The undulating membrane and the free portion of the flagellum give the organism considerable motility.

According to their course of development in the vector, trypanosomes have been classified into two major groups:

1. *Stercoraria:* Multiplication in the mammalian host is discontinuous, taking place in the amastigote stage. Development in the vector (Triatominae, or kissing bug) is completed in the hindgut (posterior station), and mammalian hosts become infected by contaminative transmission. The subgenus *Schizotrypanum* belongs to this group and includes *T. cruzi.*
2. *Salivaria:* Multiplication in the mammalian host is continuous, taking place in the trypomastigote stage. Development in the vector (*Glossina,* or tsetse fly) is completed in the salivary glands (anterior station), and inoculative transmission to the mammalian host occurs. The subgenus *Trypanozoon* belongs to this group and includes, among others, *Trypanosoma brucei brucei,* which causes disease in animals but does not infect humans. *Trypanosoma brucei gambiense* and *Trypanosoma brucei rhodesiense,* the two causative agents of African sleeping sickness, or human African trypanosomiasis, are also found in this subgenus. As a group, these three organisms are often referred to as the *T. brucei* complex.

Endemic areas of Chagas' disease and African sleeping sickness do not overlap (Fig. 266–1). Moreover, there are such important differences in the transmission, pathogenesis, and clinical course of the two diseases that they have little in common except the morphologic similarities of the causative agents.

CHAGAS' DISEASE

Life Cycle and Transmission

T. cruzi, the causative agent of American trypanosomiasis, is transmitted by various species of bloodsucking triatomine insects, or kissing bugs (Fig. 266–2).[3] These vectors are found in large numbers in the wild, where the parasite is transmitted among many mammalian species that constitute the natural reservoir, and in endemic areas they live in the nooks and crannies of substandard dwellings. The insects become infected by sucking blood from animals or humans that have circulating trypomastigotes (Fig. 266–3). The ingested parasites multiply in the midgut of the insects as epimastigotes, which are flagellates of a distinct morphologic type, and in the hindgut transform into infective metacyclic trypomastigotes that are discharged with the feces at the time of subsequent blood meals. Transmission to a second vertebrate host occurs when mucous membranes, conjunctivae, or breaks in the skin are contaminated with bug feces containing the infective forms. The parasites then enter a variety of host cell types and multiply in the cytoplasm after transformation into amastigotes. When multiplying amastigotes fill the host cell, they differentiate into trypomastigotes, and the cell ruptures. The parasites released invade local tissues or spread hematogenously to distant sites, thus initiating further cycles of multiplication, primarily in muscle cells, and maintaining a parasitemia infective for vectors.

Transmission of *T. cruzi* also occurs through blood transfusions[4] and typically takes place in cities when infected but asymptomatic migrants from endemic rural areas donate blood. This mode of transmission constitutes a public health problem in some endemic areas. Congenital transmission has been reported as well and is associated with considerable fetal wastage as well as a high fatality rate and severe impairment in surviving infants.[5,6] Finally, numerous laboratory accidents resulting in acute Chagas' disease have occurred as a consequence of the facility with which infective forms of the parasite can be produced in the laboratory.[7,8]

FIGURE 266–1. Distribution of human trypanosomiasis.

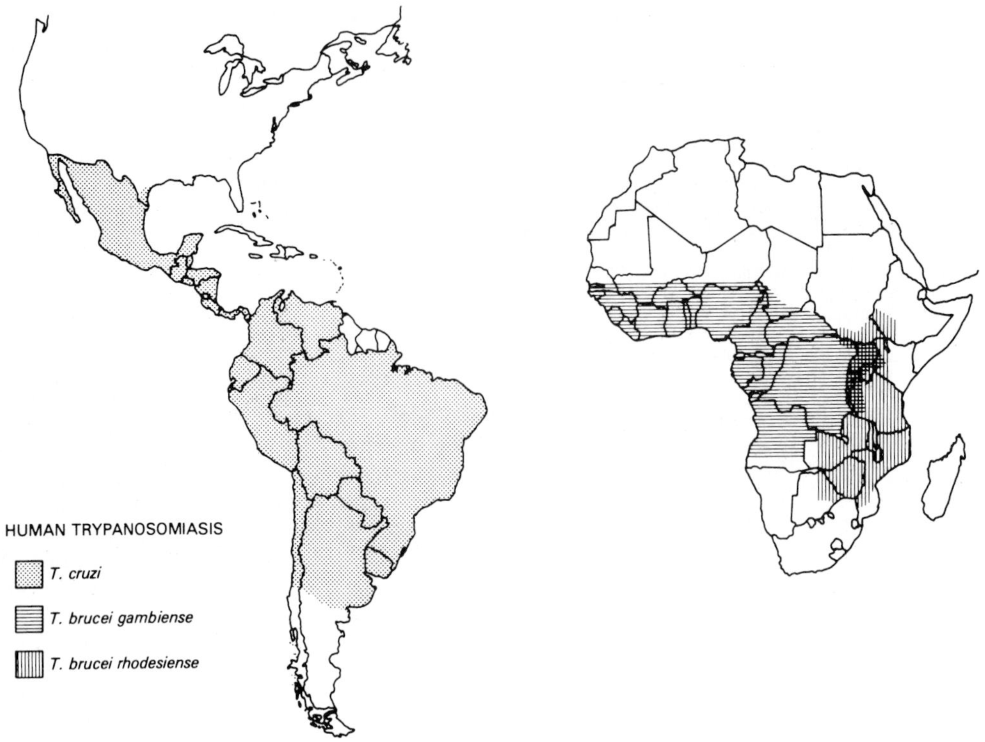

Pathology

In acute Chagas' disease, the inflammatory lesion caused by *T. cruzi* at the site of entry is called a *chagoma*.[9, 10] Local histologic changes include intracellular parasitism of muscle and other subcutaneous tissues, interstitial edema, lymphocytic infiltration, and reactive hyperplasia of adjacent lymph nodes. Trypomastigotes released when host cells rupture often can be detected by microscopic examination of fresh blood. Muscles, including the myocardium, are the most heavily parasitized tissues. Myocarditis may develop in association with patchy areas of infected cells and necrosis.[11] The characteristic pseudocysts seen in sections of infected tissues are intracellular aggregates of amastigotes (Fig. 266–4). A lymphocytosis accompanies the high parasitemias of the acute illness, and mild elevation of transaminase levels is occasionally seen. In some patients, parasites may be found in the cerebrospinal fluid.[12]

The heart is the organ most commonly affected in chronic Chagas' disease. Gross examination of the hearts of chronic chagasic patients who died of heart failure reveals marked bilateral ventricular enlargement, often involving the right side of the heart more than the left. Thinning of the ventricular walls is common, as are apical aneurysms and mural thrombi. Widespread lymphocytic infiltration is present, accompanied by diffuse interstitial fibrosis and atrophy of myocardial cells. Parasites are rarely seen in stained sections of myocardial tissue, but recent studies using polymerase chain reaction (PCR)–based assays have demonstrated the presence of parasites in areas of focal inflammation.[13]

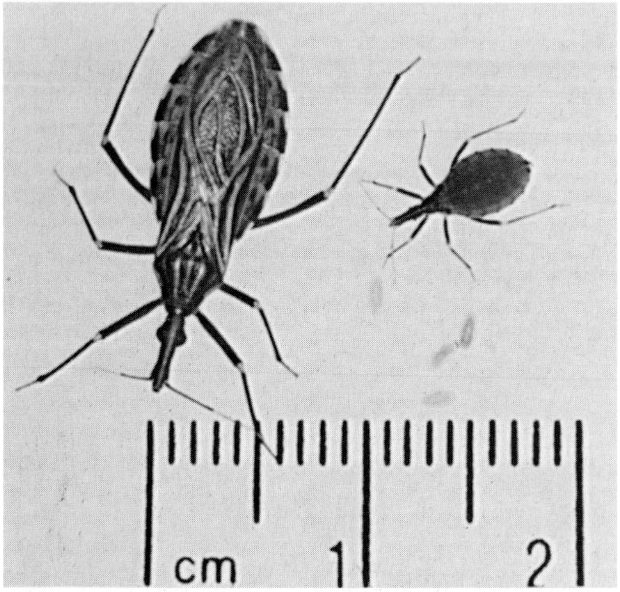

FIGURE 266–2. *Rhodnius prolixus*, a common vector of *Trypanosoma cruzi*. *Counterclockwise*, Eggs, second stage nymph, and adult.

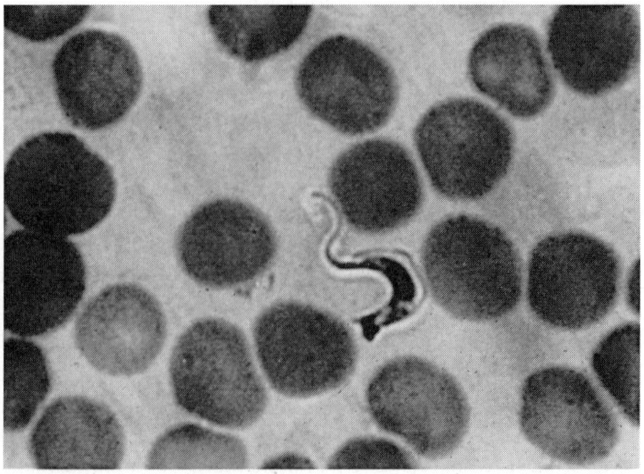

FIGURE 266–3. *Trypanosoma cruzi* trypomastigote in human blood smear (Giemsa, ×625). (Courtesy of Dr. Maria Shikanai Yasuda, São Paulo, Brazil.)

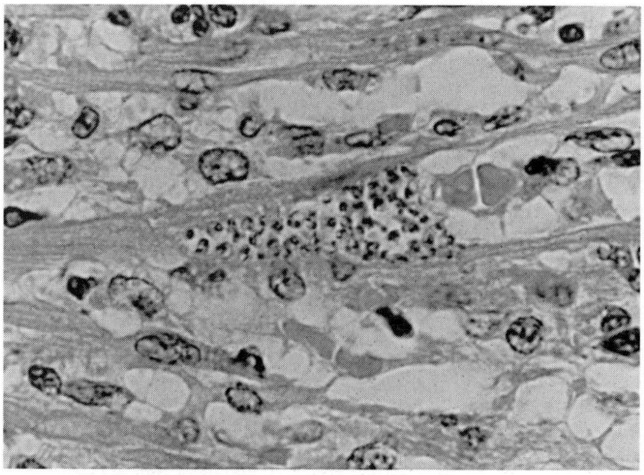

FIGURE 266–4. *Trypanosoma cruzi* in the cardiac muscle of a child who died of acute Chagas' disease. (H&E, ×900)

Pathologic changes are also common in the conduction system of chronic chagasic hearts and often correlate with premortem rhythm disturbances.[14] Dense fibrosis and chronic inflammatory lesions most frequently involve the right branch and the left anterior branch of the bundle of His, but lesions of this type are found in other parts of the conduction system as well.

The striking features apparent on gross examination of the esophagus or colon of a patient with chronic Chagas' disease of the digestive tract (megadisease) are the enormous dilation and muscular hypertrophy of the affected organs.[15] On microscopic examination, focal inflammatory lesions with lymphocytic infiltration are seen. A marked reduction in the number of neurons in the myenteric plexus is also apparent, and peri- and intraganglion fibrosis in the presence of Schwann cell proliferation and lymphocytosis is found. In most patients, the clinical effects of this parasympathetic denervation are confined to the esophagus or the colon, or both, but similar lesions have been observed in the biliary tree, the ureters, and other hollow viscera.

The pathogenesis of the cardiac and gastrointestinal lesions of chronic Chagas' disease is controversial and has been the subject of debate for many years. In the view of some investigators, tissue injury related to invasion by *T. cruzi* parasites during the acute and chronic phases of the infection initiates the processes that result in the lesions that develop over time.[13, 16, 17] A second mechanism, initially proposed by Cossio and colleagues[18] and Santos-Buch and Teixeira,[19] invokes autoimmune mechanisms in the lesions of chronic disease. Experimental work performed subsequent to these latter studies has failed to resolve the issue[20, 21]; thus, the pathogenesis of the lesions of chronic Chagas' disease continues to be the subject of debate.[22, 23]

Epidemiology

T. cruzi infection is a zoonosis, and humans are merely unfortunate hosts whose involvement in the cycle of transmission is not necessary for the perpetuation of the parasite in nature. The triatomine vectors necessary for natural transmission of *T. cruzi* are found in the Americas from the southern half of the United States to southern Argentina.[24, 25] Although infected insects have been found throughout this range, their distribution is uneven. Burrows, hollow trees, palm trees, and other animal shelters are sites where transmission of *T. cruzi* occurs among infected insects and nonhuman mammalian hosts. Vector transmission to humans occurs only in areas in which triatomine species that defecate during or immediately after blood meals are present. This limitation does not apply to the range of the infection in lower mammals, however, because they can acquire the infection by eating infected insects.[26]

T. cruzi has been isolated from more than 150 species of wild and domestic mammals. The ability of the parasite to adapt to such a wide variety of hosts, coupled with the long-term parasitemias in infected mammals, results in the presence of an enormous sylvatic and domestic reservoir in enzootic areas. Infected mammals have been found in the southern United States[27–29] and from there southward throughout all of Latin America to central Argentina.[30]

Historically, humans become involved in the cycle of transmission when land is opened up for farming in enzootic areas where vector species adaptable to living in human dwellings, such as *Rhodnius prolixus* and *Triatoma infestans,* are prevalent. As the natural habitat of the vectors and mammalian hosts is disrupted, the insects take up residence in the cracks and holes of the settlers' primitive wood, mud, and stone houses. In this way, the infected triatomine insects become domiciliary, and the domestic cycle of transmission is established to include domestic animals and humans.[31, 32] Thus, human trypanosomiasis in Latin America is primarily a public health problem among poor persons who live in rural areas. The mean age of infection in areas of intense transmission is thought to be around 4 years, and in one survey 85% of acute cases occurred in children younger than 10 years of age.[33] In this study of selected patients, the case fatality rate for acute Chagas' disease was 12%, but the rate for all new infections is probably less than 1%.

It is currently estimated by the World Health Organization that 16 to 18 million people are infected with *T. cruzi* and that up to 45,000 persons die each year of Chagas' disease.[34] However, in recent years the epidemiology of *T. cruzi* infection has been improving in several endemic countries as vector and blood bank control programs have been implemented successfully. As a consequence, prevalence rates have decreased in many areas in younger age groups. A major international control program in the "southern cone" nations of South America (Argentina, Bolivia, Brazil, Chile, Paraguay, and Uruguay), initiated in 1991, has provided the framework for much of the progress achieved to date. If current trends continue, by the year 2003, transmission will be essentially eliminated in much of the endemic range.[35–37] The barriers hindering the elimination of *T. cruzi* transmission to humans are economic and political, and no technical breakthroughs are necessary for its completion.

Only about 10 to 30% of persons with chronic *T. cruzi* infections will acquire symptomatic Chagas' disease.[38, 39] The age distribution of the onset of the two types of chronic disease is broad. The relatively high frequency of sudden death in young adults observed in some regions in the past was attributed to the disturbances of cardiac rhythm associated with Chagas' disease, and in one highly endemic area in Brazil, chagasic cardiac disease was found to be the leading cause of death in adults.[40] There is considerable geographic variation in the prevalence of symptomatic chronic Chagas' disease among infected persons. The prevalence of cardiac disease among persons who harbor the parasite chronically is lower in Venezuela, Colombia, Central America, and Mexico than in the rest of the endemic range. Similarly, megaesophagus and megacolon in association with *T. cruzi* infection are virtually unknown in the northern endemic range, whereas they reach 15 to 20% in the southern endemic regions. It is not known whether host factors or parasite strain differences are the primary determinants of this geographic variation in the patterns of clinical disease.[41, 42]

Despite the presence of *T. cruzi*–infected triatomine vectors in many parts of the southern and western United States, only four autochthonous cases of Chagas' disease have been reported: three cases in Texas and one case in California.[43, 44] The rarity of transmission of *T. cruzi* to humans in the United States probably results from the relatively high housing standards and the low overall vector density. Since 1973, seven confirmed laboratory-acquired infections and nine imported cases of acute Chagas' disease have been reported to the Centers for Disease Control and Prevention (CDC), but none in the latter group occurred in returning tourists (T. A. Navin, personal communication). However, two instances of tourists returning to Europe from Latin America with acute *T. cruzi* infections have been reported.[45, 46] Although the number of autochthonous and imported cases of acute *T. cruzi* infection that go unrecognized may be several times the number reported, the fact remains that acute Chagas' disease is rare in the United States.

In contrast, in recent years the number of persons in the United States with chronic *T. cruzi* infections has grown considerably. Between 1971 and 1996 more than 6 million persons emigrated to the United States legally from endemic areas, and an estimated 3.4 million illegal immigrants from Mexico and Central America alone now reside in the United States.[47] A sizable proportion of these immigrants have come from Central America, a region in which the prevalence of *T. cruzi* infection is high.[4, 48] A study of Salvadoran and Nicaraguan immigrants in Washington, D.C., found a 5% prevalence of *T. cruzi* infection.[49] Seroprevalence studies carried out in a Los Angeles hospital in which 50% of the blood donors are Hispanic have shown that between 1 in 1000 and 1 in 500 donors harbor *T. cruzi*.[50–52] In another investigation performed in seven blood banks in three southwestern states, 1 in 603 donors with Hispanic surnames was determined to be infected.[53] Finally, in a study of 300,000 donors in Los Angeles and Miami, the prevalence of *T. cruzi* infection was found to be 1 in 8800 in the general donor population and 1 in 710 among donors who had spent a month or more in an area in which Chagas' disease is endemic.[54]

These findings and census data suggest that there are at least 50,000 to 100,000 *T. cruzi*–infected persons now living in the United States. The presence of these immigrants poses a risk of transfusion-associated transmission of *T. cruzi* in the United States,[55] and to date six such cases have occurred in the United States and Canada.[56–58] The course of acute Chagas' disease in these patients was particularly fulminant because of immunosuppressive therapy they were receiving, and this certainly contributed to the definitive diagnoses. Because most transfusions are given to immunocompetent persons in whom acute Chagas' disease would be a mild illness, it is reasonable to infer that many other instances of transfusion-associated transmission of *T. cruzi* have occurred in the United States but have not been noticed. Recently, however, the U.S. Food and Drug Administration has recommended screening prospective blood donors with questions relating to residence in endemic countries, and this may have reduced the risk.[51]

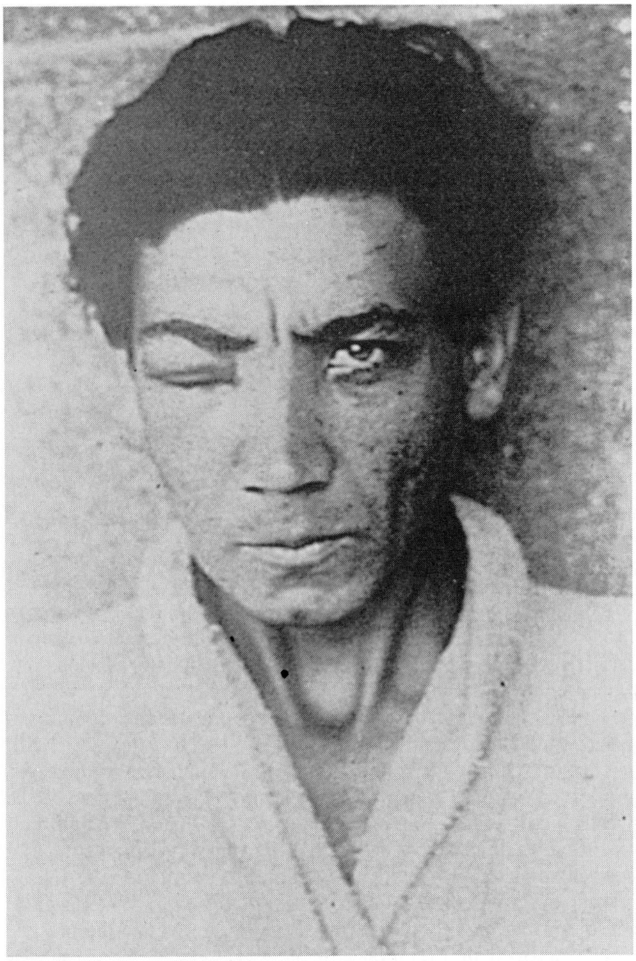

FIGURE 266–5. Romaña sign in a Brazilian patient with acute Chagas' disease. (Courtesy of Dr. Mário Shiroma, São Paulo, Brazil.)

Clinical Course

The clinical syndromes of acute *T. cruzi* infection and chronic Chagas' disease are quite different. The acute illness results from the first encounter of the host with the parasite, and chronic disease involves late sequelae.

Acute Chagas' disease[59] is usually an illness of children, but it can occur at any age. Only a small portion of acute infections caused by *T. cruzi* are recognized as such because of the mild and nonspecific nature of the symptoms in most patients and the lack of access to medical care. The first signs of illness occur at least 1 week after invasion by the parasites. When the parasite has entered through a break in the skin, a chagoma may be formed, consisting of an indurated area of erythema and swelling accompanied by local lymph node involvement. The Romaña sign (Fig. 266–5), the classic sign of acute Chagas' disease, consists of painless edema of the palpebrae and periocular tissues and may appear when the conjunctiva is the portal of entry. These initial local signs are followed by fever, malaise, anorexia, and edema of the face and lower extremities. Generalized lymphadenopathy and mild hepatosplenomegaly also may appear.

Overt central nervous system signs are not common, but meningoencephalitis develops in some patients and is associated with a very poor prognosis.[60, 61] Severe myocarditis also develops in a small proportion of patients with acute disease, and most deaths are due to the resultant congestive heart failure.[44] Nonspecific electrocardiographic changes are seen, but the life-threatening arrhythmias that are frequent in chronic Chagas' disease generally do not occur. In untreated patients, symptoms resolve gradually over a period of weeks to months. Areas of local reaction around the eye or other sites of parasite entry can persist for several weeks, as can the lymphadenopathy and splenomegaly. After the spontaneous resolution of the acute illness, the patient enters what is called the *indeterminate phase* of Chagas' disease, which is characterized by asymptomatic and subpatent parasitemia and antibodies to a variety of *T. cruzi* antigens.

Chronic Chagas' disease becomes apparent years or even decades after the initial infection. The heart is the organ most commonly involved, and symptoms reflect the rhythm disturbances, congestive heart failure, and thromboembolism that are characteristic of the chronic illness.[62–64] Dizziness, syncope, and, less commonly, seizures result from a wide variety of arrhythmias. The cardiomyopathy that develops insidiously often primarily affects the right ventricle, and the classic signs of right-sided heart failure are frequently present. As in patients with arrhythmias, the progression of symptoms related to the cardiomyopathy may be gradual, but once congestive heart failure develops, death often occurs in a matter of months.[40] The clinical course is frequently complicated by emboli to the brain or other areas.

In patients with megaesophagus, symptoms are similar to those of idiopathic achalasia and may include dysphagia, odynophagia, chest pain, cough, and regurgitation.[65, 66] Hypersalivation and salivary gland hypertrophy have been observed. Aspiration can occur, especially during sleep, and repeated episodes of aspiration pneumonitis are common. Weight loss and even cachexia in patients with megaesophagus can combine with pulmonary infection to result in death. As in idiopathic achalasia, an increased incidence of cancer of the esophagus has been reported in patients with chagasic esophageal disease.[67]

Patients with chagasic megacolon are plagued by chronic constipation and abdominal pain. Individuals with advanced disease can go for several weeks between bowel movements, and acute obstruction, occasionally with volvulus, can lead to perforation, septicemia, and death.[62, 68]

Immunosuppression and Transplantation in *Trypanosoma cruzi*–Infected Patients

When persons who harbor *T. cruzi* chronically become immunosuppressed, reactivation of the infection can occur, often with a severity that is greater than is typical of acute Chagas' disease in immunocompetent patients. The incidence of reactivation in *T. cruzi*–infected patients who become immunosuppressed is not known, and descriptions of its occurrence[69–71] and absence[72–76] have been published. There have been several reports of reactivations of chronic *T. cruzi* infections after renal transplantation, and in two of these instances the central nervous system was involved.[70, 77, 78] In my view, *T. cruzi* infection should not be a contraindication for kidney transplantation. In infected patients who do undergo the procedure, however, periodic monitoring for signs and symptoms of chronic Chagas' disease should be carried out, and a specific search for *T. cruzi*, including careful neurologic evaluation, should be performed when acute illnesses occur postoperatively.

Immunosuppression caused by the human immunodeficiency virus can also lead to recrudescence of chronic *T. cruzi* infection. To date, several dozen such patients have been described,[79–81] one of whom was a Latin American immigrant living in the United States.[82] It is noteworthy that most of these patients developed *T. cruzi* brain abscesses, which do not occur in immunocompetent *T. cruzi*–infected patients.

Heart transplantation is an option in patients with end-stage Chagas' cardiac disease. Several dozen *T. cruzi*–infected persons have undergone the procedure in Brazil, and about a dozen such patients have undergone cardiac transplantation in the United States.[83–86] Reactivated acute Chagas' disease occurred frequently in the Brazilian patients as a consequence of the postoperative immunosuppression, and this was thought to have contributed to the deaths of several patients, despite treatment with benznidazole. An additional problem is the fact that the parasitologic approaches usually used to detect acute *T. cruzi* infections were not sensitive detectors of the reactivations. Moreover, a higher than expected incidence of malignant neoplasms was observed in the Brazilian patients.[87] In several of the patients who underwent transplantation in the United States, nifurtimox given prophylactically was effective in preventing recrudescence of acute Chagas' disease. The frequency of reactivation of *T. cruzi* infection in the patients who underwent transplantation in Brazil may have resulted from the relatively high doses of immunosuppressive drugs they were given. Since 1991, however, reactivation of *T. cruzi* infection has been less of a problem among chagasic patients who have undergone transplantation in Brazil because reduced doses of cyclosporine have been used.[88, 89]

The question of whether immigrants in the United States with *T. cruzi* infections should be considered for heart transplantation will arise with increasing frequency as they age and develop end-stage chagasic cardiac disease in increasing numbers. It is not yet known if the long-term viability of the transplanted hearts will be affected by the persistent *T. cruzi* infections in the recipients. Almost all the Brazilian patients who suffered acute reactivation of *T. cruzi* after transplantation had clear histologic evidence of parasitization of the new hearts. These problems and uncertainties, when considered in light of the fact that the overall number of acceptable candidates for heart transplantation is many times the number of available donor hearts, suggest that heart transplantation in *T. cruzi*–infected patients be approached with caution. This perspective should not be applied to kidney transplantation, however, because postoperative immunosuppressive therapy is less intense and the risk of acute reactivation of *T. cruzi* is minimal.

Diagnosis

The first consideration in the diagnosis of acute Chagas' disease is a history consistent with exposure to *T. cruzi*. This includes residence in an environment in which transmission occurs, a recent blood transfusion in an endemic area, or a laboratory accident. It is important to keep in mind, moreover, that autochthonous *T. cruzi* infections in the United States are extremely rare and that imported cases among tourists returning to the United States have not been reported.

The diagnosis of acute Chagas' disease is made by detecting parasites, and serologic tests for anti–*T. cruzi* IgM, which are not widely available and are not standardized, play a limited role. Circulating parasites are motile and can often be seen in wet preparations of anticoagulated blood or buffy coat. In many cases, the parasites can also be seen in Giemsa-stained smears. In acutely infected immunocompetent patients, examination of blood preparations is the cornerstone of detecting *T. cruzi*. In immunocompromised patients suspected of having acute Chagas' disease, however, other specimens such as lymph node and bone marrow aspirates, pericardial fluid, and cerebrospinal fluid should be examined microscopically. When these methods fail to detect *T. cruzi* in a patient whose clinical and epidemiologic histories suggest that the parasite is present, as is often the case,[90] efforts to grow the organism can be undertaken. This can be attempted by culturing blood or other specimens in liquid media,[91] or by xenodiagnosis,[92] which is a method involving laboratory-reared insect vectors. A major problem with the use of these two methods for diagnosing acute disease is the fact that they take at least a month to complete, and this is far beyond the time at which decisions regarding drug treatment must be made. Furthermore, although it is thought that xenodiagnosis and culture are more sensitive than microscopic examination of blood and other specimens, their sensitivities may be no greater than 50%. In view of these considerations, it is obvious that improved methods for diagnosing acute *T. cruzi* infections are needed, and PCR-based assays may fulfill this role (see farther on).

Chronic *T. cruzi* infection is usually diagnosed by detecting IgG antibodies that bind specifically to parasite antigens, and demonstration of the presence of the organism is not of primary importance. Several sensitive serologic tests are used widely in Latin America, such as complement fixation, indirect immunofluorescence, indirect hemagglutination, and enzyme-linked immunosorbent assay.[93, 94] A persistent problem with these conventional serodiagnostic assays has been the occurrence of false-positive results. These occur typically with specimens from patients having illnesses such as malaria, leishmaniasis, syphilis, and other parasitic and nonparasitic diseases. Because of this lack of specificity, most authorities recommend that sera be tested in two or three conventional tests before being accepted as positive. This latter approach carries with it an enormous economic and logistical burden, particularly for blood banks. For example, in the largest blood donor center in São Paulo, Brazil, three serologic tests for antibodies to *T. cruzi* are employed, and 3.4% of donated units are thrown out because of reactivity in one or more of the assays. As many as two thirds of these may in fact not come from *T. cruzi*–infected donors but must be discarded because of inconsistent test results.[94] Thus, as is the case with acute *T. cruzi* infection, improved tests for chronic Chagas' disease are needed.

Numerous test kits for detecting antibodies to *T. cruzi* are available commercially in Latin America. These assays are used widely for clinical testing and for screening donated blood, but in some endemic areas screening of the blood supply is limited by financial constraints and a lack of appreciation of the problem of transfusion-associated transmission of *T. cruzi*.[95] In the United States, there are a number of options for testing for *T. cruzi* infection. Abbott Laboratories has received U.S. Food and Drug Administration clearance for marketing an enzyme-linked immunosorbent assay for clinical testing but not blood bank screening (Chagas EIA, Abbott Laboratories, Abbott Park, Ill.).[93] In addition, similar clearance for clinical use has been obtained for tests manufactured by Gull Laboratories (Chagas' IgG ELISA, Gull Laboratories, Salt Lake City, Utah), and Hemagen Diagnostics (Chagas' Kit [EIA method], Waltham, Mass.). Limited comparative studies of the Gull and Abbott assays suggest that the latter may have a slight advantage in terms of sensitivity and specificity.[94, 96] Finally, in our laboratory we perform a radioimmune precipitation assay that was shown to be highly sensitive and specific when used to test a geographically diverse group of sera from *T. cruzi*–infected patients and controls.[97]

In response to the need for better tests for detecting both acute and chronic *T. cruzi* infection, considerable research has been invested in the development of new assays. Through the application of recombinant DNA methods, cloned segments of *T. cruzi* genes have been used to produce portions of antigenic proteins in bacteria, and several of these, singly and in combination, have been used as target antigens in serologic tests.[94, 98–100] When taken together, the findings of these studies suggest that it is likely that recombinant tests will be developed that have higher specificities than do the conventional assays, while still maintaining high sensitivities. It must be kept in mind, however, that the tests described to date have not been evaluated in large field trials, and none is available commercially.

The possibility of using PCR-based assays for detecting *T. cruzi* infection has also been investigated.[101, 102] The numbers of parasites circulating in the blood of patients with chronic *T. cruzi* infections is extremely low, but PCR-based assays have the potential for detecting such low numbers because the organisms have highly repetitive nuclear and kinetoplast DNA (kDNA) sequences that can be amplified by PCR. Moser and colleagues[103] described a PCR-based assay in which a 188–base pair repetitive nuclear DNA sequence is amplified. Each parasite contains approximately 100,000 copies of this sequence, and in contrived experiments as little as 0.5% of the genome of a single parasite gave a positive result. Studies in mice with acute and chronic *T. cruzi* infections indicated clearly that this PCR-based assay is much more sensitive than microscopic examination of blood.[104] Russomando and associates[105] confirmed this sensitivity in a study of patients with both acute and chronic *T. cruzi* infections, and other studies have obtained similarly encouraging results.

In a second PCR-based test, described by Sturm and coworkers,[106] a 330–base pair segment of the *T. cruzi* kinetoplast minicircle is amplified. Each parasite is thought to have approximately 120,000 copies of this sequence, and in mixing experiments the authors were able to detect 0.1% of one parasite genome. The results obtained in several subsequent studies performed in humans suggest that this test may be useful for definitive diagnoses of *T. cruzi* infection.[107–109] In view of the results obtained in the various studies using these two approaches, it appears that there may be a useful role for PCR-based assays for the detection of *T. cruzi*. However, potential problems that may limit their widespread use include the occurrence of false-positive results due to contamination of reaction mixtures with amplicons and the complexity of the technology that may not be appropriate for the developing countries in which Chagas' disease is endemic. At the present time no PCR-based test for the detection of *T. cruzi* is available commercially.

Treatment

Unfortunately, *T. cruzi* is not susceptible to most of the long list of drugs tested for activity over the past several decades, including those that are effective against African trypanosomes, *Leishmania* spp., and other parasitic protozoans, and thus current therapy is unsatisfactory. Two drugs are currently being used to treat patients infected with *T. cruzi*.[110–112] The first of these, the nitrofuran derivative nifurtimox (Lampit, Bayer 2502), has been in use for more than 2 decades, and extensive clinical experience has accumulated. In acute and congenital Chagas' disease, nifurtimox markedly reduces the duration and severity of the illness and decreases mortality. However, it results in parasitologic cure in only about 70% of treated patients, can cause severe side effects, and must be taken for prolonged periods.[113, 114] Cure rates with nifurtimox are higher in Argentina and Chile than in Brazil and some other countries. Therapy with nifurtimox should be initiated as early as possible in cases of acute or congenital Chagas' disease. Moreover, when laboratory accidents occur in which there is a reasonable likelihood that *T. cruzi* infection will become established, therapy should be initiated without waiting for clinical or parasitologic indications of infection.

A large proportion of patients treated with nifurtimox experience adverse side effects. Gastrointestinal complaints include abdominal pain, nausea, vomiting, anorexia, and weight loss. Possible neurologic symptoms include restlessness, insomnia, twitching, paresthesias, and seizures. These symptoms generally disappear when the dosage is reduced or therapy is discontinued.

Nifurtimox is supplied as 30- and 120-mg tablets. The recommended oral dosage for adults is 8 to 10 mg/kg body weight/day. The dose for adolescents is 12.5 to 15 mg/kg/day, and for children 1 to 10 years of age it is 15 to 20 mg/kg/day. The drug should be given in four divided doses each day, and therapy should be continued for 90 to 120 days. Nifurtimox can be obtained from the Drug Service of the Centers for Disease Control (770-639-3670 [weekdays]; 770-639-2888 [off hours]).

Benznidazole (Rochagan, Roche 7-1051), a nitroimidazole derivative, is the second agent used to treat patients with Chagas' disease. The efficacy of this drug is similar to that of nifurtimox, with the exception that geographic differences in its efficacy have not been observed.[114] Side effects include peripheral neuropathy, rash, and granulocytopenia. The recommended oral dosage of benznidazole is 5 mg/kg/day for 60 days. Benznidazole is used widely in Latin America, where it is viewed as the drug of choice by many specialists. It also can be obtained from the Centers for Disease Control Drug Service.

The question of whether patients in the indeterminate or chronic symptomatic phases of *T. cruzi* infection should be treated with nifurtimox or benznidazole has been debated for many years. Evidence from studies of *T. cruzi*–infected humans and laboratory animals has accumulated, indicating that the presence of parasites in cardiac muscle is specifically associated with inflammation, thus implicating the organisms in the chronic pathology.[13, 17, 115] Moreover, in several long-term follow-up studies the appearance or progression of cardiac pathology in treated patients was significantly less than in untreated controls.[116–118] In view of these findings, an international panel of experts recently recommended that all *T. cruzi*–infected patients be treated with either nifurtimox or benznidazole regardless of their clinical status or the time elapsed since infection (Dr. Anis Rassi, personal communication).

The use of two compounds, developed for other purposes, to treat acute *T. cruzi* infections merits comment. In 1988 Reed reported that the severity of acute *T. cruzi* infection in mice was reduced by exogenous recombinant interferon-γ (IFN-γ).[119] I am aware of two patients with acute Chagas' disease to whom recombinant IFN-γ has been given. One was an immunosuppressed cancer patient who acquired the parasite from a contaminated transfusion,[56] and the other had become infected through laboratory work with *T. cruzi* (H. B. Tanowitz, personal communication). Both patients were given IFN-γ as well as nifurtimox and recovered. It has been established that one of these patients was cured parasitologically, and this issue has not been addressed in the other. Because the parasites are successfully controlled in a matter of weeks in most patients with acute *T. cruzi* infections, even without drug treatment, my view is that in immunocompetent patients with acute *T. cruzi* infections, nifurtimox or benznidazole should be used alone. Whether recombinant IFN-γ should also be given to immunocompromised patients with acute Chagas' disease infections is an open question that merits further investigation.

The usefulness of itraconazole, fluconazole, and allopurinol has been studied extensively in laboratory animals and to a lesser extent in persons with acute Chagas' disease. None of these three drugs has shown a level of anti–*T. cruzi* activity that warrants its use in humans. Finally, bis-triazole (D0807) was identified recently as a promising agent that cures acute *T. cruzi* infections in mice,[120, 121] but unfortunately, development of this drug has been discontinued.

Most patients with acute Chagas' disease require no therapy other than benznidazole or nifurtimox because symptoms are generally self-limited even in the absence of drug treatment. The management of the occasional severely ill acute-phase patient with myocarditis or meningoencephalitis is largely supportive. The treatment of patients with chronic chagasic heart disease is also supportive. Chronically infected persons should have electrocardiograms performed every 6 months or so because pacemakers have been shown to be useful in the management of bradyarrhythmias seen in chronic Chagas' disease.[122] The congestive heart failure of cardiomyopathic Chagas' disease is generally treated with measures used in patients with cardiomyopathies due to other causes.[63, 64, 123, 124]

Megaesophagus associated with Chagas' disease should be managed as is idiopathic achalasia. The first approach to relieving symptoms is balloon dilation of the lower esophageal sphincter.[124] Patients who fail to respond to repeated attempts at this approach are treated surgically.[125, 126] The procedure used most frequently is wide esophagocardiomyectomy of the anterior gastroesophageal junction, combined with valvuloplasty to reduce reflux. Patients with extreme megaesophagus are often treated with esophageal resection with reconstruction using an esophagogastroplasty. In industrialized countries, laparoscopic myotomy is being used with increasing frequency to treat idiopathic achalasia. This relatively simple procedure may become the approach of choice for both idiopathic achalasia and Chagas' megaesophagus if the encouraging results achieved to date are borne out in larger numbers of patients.

Patients in the early stages of colonic dysfunction associated with chronic Chagas' disease can be managed with a high-fiber diet and occasional laxatives and enemas. Fecal impaction necessitating manual disimpaction may occur, as can toxic megacolon, which requires surgical treatment.[68] Another complication of chagasic megacolon that requires immediate attention is volvulus. This usually occurs when the lengthened and enlarged sigmoid colon twists and folds on itself, causing a constellation of symptoms resulting from the obstruction. Endoscopic emptying can be performed initially in patients without radiographic, clinical, or endoscopic signs of ischemia in the affected area. Complicated cases should be treated with surgical decompression. In either event, however, surgical treatment of the megacolon is eventually necessary because of the high probability of recurrence of the volvulus. A number of surgical procedures have been used to treat advanced chagasic megacolon, and all include resection of the sigmoid colon as well as removal of part of the rectum. The latter is performed to avoid recurrence of megacolon in the segment of the colon that is anastomosed to the rectum. The Haddad modification[127] of the procedure described by Duhamel[128] has been used with considerable success.

Prevention

In view of the possible serious consequences of chronic *T. cruzi* infection, I feel that all immigrants from endemic regions should be screened for serologic evidence of infection with the parasite. Identification of infected persons is important because the implantation of pacemakers has been shown to benefit some patients who acquire rhythm disturbances. The possibility of congenital transmission is another justification for screening.[129]

As noted earlier, several cases of transfusion-associated transmission of *T. cruzi* have occurred in the United States, and the question as to how best to avoid this is not easily answered. Because no test has received clearance from the U.S. Food and Drug Administration for use in blood banks, serologic screening currently is not a possibility. An alternative approach is to defer from donation prospective donors whose answers to a questionnaire indicate they are at high risk for *T. cruzi* infection. In a recent study in a Los Angeles blood bank in which the percentage of Hispanic donors is about 50%, my coworkers and I assessed the usefulness of such a questionnaire in identifying high-risk prospective donors and the impact of their deferral on the blood supply.[51] We found that deferring donors found to be at high risk for *T. cruzi* infection as a consequence of prolonged residence in endemic areas under conditions favoring exposure to insect vectors or a history of transfusion or seroreactivity in those areas reduced the blood supply by only 2.0 percent. Furthermore, the proportion of individuals in the deferred group found to be positive in later serologic testing was consistent with our previous estimate of *T. cruzi* infection among donors in that blood bank (~1 in 1000).[50] These findings suggest that a questionnaire-based approach for avoiding transfusion-associated transmission of *T. cruzi* may be effective and may not reduce the blood supply intolerably. It is important to keep in mind, however, that approaches based solely on questionnaires have not been entirely successful at eliminating transfusion-associated transmission of other infectious agents.

Laboratory personnel should wear gloves and eye protection when working with *T. cruzi,* and suitable containment should be used when dealing with infected insects.[130] Persons traveling in endemic areas should avoid sleeping in dilapidated dwellings and should use insect repellent and mosquito nets to reduce exposure to vectors. No vaccine is available for the prevention of transmission of *T. cruzi.* Special precautions for campers, hunters, and others engaging in outdoor activities in the United States are not warranted.

REFERENCES

1. Levine ND, Corliss JO, Cox FEG, et al. A newly revised classification of the protozoa. J Protozool. 1980;27:37–58.
2. Hoare CA, Wallace FG. Developmental stages of trypanosomatid flagellates: A new terminology. Nature. 1966;212:1385–1386.
3. Brener Z. Biology of *Trypanosoma cruzi*. Ann Rev Microbiol. 1973;27:347–382.
4. Schmunis GA. *Trypanosoma cruzi*, the etiologic agent of Chagas' disease: Status in the blood supply in endemic and nonendemic countries. Transfusion. 1991;31:547–557.
5. Azogue E, La Fuente C, Darras CH. Congenital Chagas' disease in Bolivia: Epidemiological aspects and pathological findings. Trans R Soc Trop Med Hyg. 1985;79:176–180.
6. Freilij H, Altcheh J. Congenital Chagas' disease: Diagnostic and clinical aspects. Clin Infect Dis. 1995;21:551–555.
7. Hofflin JM, Sadler RH, Araujo FG. Laboratory-acquired Chagas' disease. Trans R Soc Trop Med Hyg. 1987;81:437–440.
8. Herwaldt BL, Juranek DD. Laboratory-acquired malaria, leishmaniasis, trypanosomiasis, and toxoplasmosis. Am J Trop Med Hyg. 1993;48:313–323.
9. Santos-Buch CA. American trypanosomiasis: Chagas' disease. Int Rev Exp Pathol. 1979;19:63–100.
10. Andrade ZA, Andrade SG. Patologia. In: Brener Z, Andrade ZA, eds. *Trypanosoma cruzi* e Doença de Chagas. Rio de Janeiro: Guanabara Koogan; 1979:199–248.
11. Parada H, Carrasco HA, Anez N, et al. Cardiac involvement is a constant finding in acute Chagas' disease: a clinical, parasitological and histopathological study. Int J Cardiol. 1997;60:49–54.
12. Hoff R, Teixeira RS, Carvalho JS, Mott KE. *Trypanosoma cruzi* in the cerebrospinal fluid during the acute stage of Chagas' disease. N Engl J Med. 1978;298: 604–606.
13. Jones EM, Colley DG, Tostes S, et al. Amplification of a *Trypanosoma cruzi* DNA sequence from inflammatory lesions in human chagasic cardiomyopathy. Am J Trop Med Hyg. 1993;48:348–357.
14. Andrade ZA, Andrade SG, Oliveira GB, Alonso DR. Histopathology of the conducting tissue of the heart in Chagas' myocarditis. Am Heart J. 1978;95:316–324.
15. Tanowitz HB, Kirchhoff LV, Simon D, et al. Chagas' disease. Clin Microbiol Rev. 1992;5:400–419.
16. Koberle F. Chagas' disease and Chagas' syndromes: The pathology of American trypanosomiasis. Adv Parasitol. 1968;6:63–116.
17. Bellotti G, Bocchi EA, de Moraes AV, et al. In vivo detection of *Trypanosoma cruzi* antigens in hearts of patients with chronic Chagas' heart disease. Am Heart J. 1996;131:301–307.

18. Cossio PM, Diez C, Szarfman A. Chagasic cardiopathy—demonstration of a serum gamma globulin factor which reacts with endocardium and vascular structures. Circulation. 1974;49:13–21.
19. Santos-Buch CA, Teixeira ARL. The immunology of experimental Chagas' disease. III. Rejection of allogeneic heart cells in vitro. J Exp Med. 1974;140:38–53.
20. Van Voorhis WC, Eisen H. A surface antigen of *Trypanosoma cruzi* that mimics mammalian nervous tissue. J Exp Med. 1989;169:641–652.
21. Tarleton RL, Zhang L, Downs MO. "Autoimmune rejection" of neonatal heart transplants in experimental Chagas' disease is a parasite-specific response to infected host tissue. Proc Natl Acad Sci U S A. 1997;94:3932–3937.
22. Kaplan D, Ferrari I, Bergami PL, et al. Antibodies to ribosomal P proteins of *Trypanosoma cruzi* in Chagas' disease possess functional autoreactivity with heart tissue and differ from anti-P autoantibodies in lupus. Proc Natl Acad Sci U S A. 1997;94:10301–10306.
23. Reed SG. Immunology of *Trypanosoma cruzi* infections. Chem Immunol. 1998;70:124–143.
24. Lent H, Wygodzinsky P. Revision of the Triatominae (Hemiptera, Reduviidae), and their significance as vectors of Chagas' disease. Bull Am Museum Nat Hist. 1979;163:123–520.
25. Beard CB, Young DG, Butler JF, Evans DA. First isolation of *Trypanosoma cruzi* from a wild-caught *Triatoma sanguisuga* (LeConte) (Hemiptera: Triatominae) in Florida, U.S.A. J Parasitol. 1988;74:343–344.
26. Ryckman RE, Olsen LE. Epizootiology of *Trypanosoma cruzi* in Southwestern North America. Part VI. Insectivorous hosts of Triatominae—the perizootiological relationship to *Trypanosoma cruzi*. J Med Entomol. 1965;2:99–106.
27. Karsten V, Davis C, Kuhn R. *Trypanosoma cruzi* in wild raccoons and opossums in North Carolina. J Parasitol. 1992;78:547–549.
28. Meurs KM, Anthony MA, Slater M, Miller MW. Chronic *Trypanosoma cruzi* infection in dogs: 11 cases (1987–1996). JAVMA. 1998;213:497–500.
29. Pietrzak SM, Pung OJ. Trypanosomiasis in raccoons from Georgia. J Wildlife Dis. 1998;34:132–136.
30. Wisnivesky-Colli C, Schweigmann NJ, Alberti A, et al. Sylvatic American trypanosomiasis in Argentina. *Trypanosoma cruzi* infection in mammals from the Chaco forest in Santiago del Estero. Trans R Soc Trop Med Hyg. 1992;86:38–41.
31. Starr MD, Rojas JC, Zeledon R, et al. Chagas' disease: Risk factors for house infestation by *Triatoma dimidiata*, the major vector of *Trypanosoma cruzi* in Costa Rica. Am J Epidemiol. 1991;133:740–747.
32. Gurtler RE, Cohen JE, Cecere MC, et al. Influence of humans and domestic animals on the household prevalence of *Trypanosoma cruzi* in *Triatoma infestans* populations in northwest Argentina. J Med Entomol. 1998;35:99–103.
33. Laranja FS, Dias E, Nobrega G, Miranda A. Chagas' disease: A clinical, epidemiologic, and pathologic study. Circulation. 1956;14:1035–1060.
34. Anonymous. Chagas' disease—interruption of transmission, Brazil. Wkly Epidemiol Rec. 1997;72:1–8.
35. Schmunis GA, Zicker F, Moncayo A. Interruption of Chagas' disease transmission through vector elimination. Lancet. 1996;348:1171–1172.
36. Moncayo A. Progress toward elimination of transmission of Chagas' disease in Latin America. World Health Stat Q. 1997;50:195–198.
37. Anonymous. Chagas' disease—interruption of transmission, Uruguay. Wkly Epidemiol Rec. 1998;73:1–4.
38. Mota EA, Guimaraes AC, Santana OO, et al. A nine year prospective study of Chagas' disease in a defined rural population in Northeast Brazil. Am J Trop Med Hyg. 1990;42:429–440.
39. Goldsmith RS, Zarate RJ, Zarate LG, et al. Clinical and epidemiologic studies of Chagas' disease in rural communities of Oaxaca, Mexico, and an eight-year followup: II. Chila. Bull Pan Am Health Org. 1992;26:47–59.
40. Amorim DS. Chagas' disease. Prog Cardiol. 1979;8:235–279.
41. de Diego JA, Palau MT, Gamallo C, Penin P. Are genotypes of *Trypanosoma cruzi* involved in the challenge of chagasic cardiomyopathy? Parasitol Res. 1998;84:147–152.
42. Reis DD, Jones EM, Tostes S, et al. Expression of major histocompatibility complex antigens and adhesion molecules in hearts of patients with chronic Chagas' disease. Am J Trop Med Hyg. 1993;49:192–200.
43. Schiffler RJ, Mansur GP, Navin TR, Limpakarnjanarat K. Indigenous Chagas' disease (American trypanosomiasis) in California. JAMA. 1984;251:2983–2984.
44. Ochs DE, Hnilica V, Moser DR, et al. Postmortem diagnosis of autochthonous acute chagasic myocarditis by polymerase chain reaction amplification of a species-specific DNA sequence of *Trypanosoma cruzi*. Am J Trop Med Hyg. 1996;34:526–529.
45. Brisseau JM, Cebron JP, Petit T, et al. Chagas' myocarditis imported into France. Lancet. 1988;7:1046.
46. Crovato F, Rebora A. Chagas' disease: A potential problem for Europe? Dermatology. 1997;195:184–185.
47. Bureau of Census. Statistical Abstract of the United States. The National Data Book. 118 ed. Washington, DC: United States Department of Commerce; 1998:11.
48. Rivera T, Palma-Guzman R, Morales W. Seroepidemiological and clinical study of Chagas' disease in Nicaragua. Rev Inst Med Trop Sao Paulo. 1995;37:207–213.
49. Kirchhoff LV, Gam AA, Gilliam FC. American trypanosomiasis (Chagas' disease) in Central American immigrants. Am J Med. 1987;82:915–920.
50. Kerndt PR, Waskin HA, Kirchhoff LV, et al. Prevalence of antibody to *Trypanosoma cruzi* among blood donors in Los Angeles, California. Transfusion. 1991;31:814–818.
51. Appleman MD, Shulman IA, Saxena S, Kirchhoff LV. Use of a questionnaire to identify potential donors at risk for infection with *Trypanosoma cruzi*. Transfusion. 1993;33:61–64.
52. Shulman IA, Appleman MD, Saxena S, et al. Specific antibodies to *Trypanosoma cruzi* among blood donors in Los Angeles, California. Transfusion. 1997;37:727–731.
53. Winkler MA, Brashear RJ, Hall HJ, et al. Detection of antibodies to *Trypanosoma cruzi* among blood donors in the southwestern and western United States. II. Evaluation of a supplemental enzyme immunoassay and radioimmunoprecipitation assay for confirmation of seroreactivity. Transfusion. 1995;35:219–225.
54. Leiby DA, Read EJ, Lenes BA, et al. Seroepidemiology of *Trypanosoma cruzi*, etiologic agent of Chagas' disease, in U.S. blood donors. J Infect Dis. 1997;176:1047–1052.
55. Kirchhoff LV. Is *Trypanosoma cruzi* a new threat to our blood supply? Ann Intern Med. 1989;111:773–775.
56. Grant IH, Gold JWM, Wittner M, et al. Transfusion-associated acute Chagas' disease acquired in the United States. Ann Intern Med. 1989;111:849–851.
57. Nickerson P, Orr P, Schroeder M-L, et al. Transfusion-associated *Trypanosoma cruzi* infection in a non-endemic area. Ann Intern Med. 1989;111:851–853.
58. Cimo PL, Luper WE, Scouros MA. Transfusion-associated Chagas' disease in Texas: Report of a case. Texas Med. 1993;89:48–50.
59. Rassi A. Clínica: Fase aguda. In: Brener Z, Andrade ZA, eds. *Trypanosoma cruzi e Doença de Chagas*. Rio de Janeiro: Guanabara Koogan; 1979:249–264.
60. Villanueva MS. Trypanosomiasis of the central nervous system. Semin Neurol. 1993;13:209–218.
61. Pentreath VW. Trypanosomiasis and the nervous system. Trans R Soc Trop Med Hyg. 1995;89:9–15.
62. Kirchhoff LV, Neva FA. Chagas' disease in Latin American immigrants. JAMA. 1985;254:3058–3060.
63. Hagar JM, Rahimtoola SH. Chagas' heart disease in the United States. N Engl J Med. 1991;325:763–768.
64. Hagar JM, Rahimtoola SH. Chagas' heart disease. Curr Probl Cardiol. 1995;20:825–924.
65. Kirchhoff LV. American trypanosomiasis (Chagas' disease). Gastroenterol Clin North Am. 1996;25:517–533.
66. de Oliveira RB, Troncon LE, Dantas RO, Menghelli UG. Gastrointestinal manifestations of Chagas' disease. Am J Gastroenterol. 1998;93:884–889.
67. Camara-Lopes LH. Carcinoma of the esophagus as a complication of megaesophagus. An analysis of seven cases. Am J Dig Dis. 1961;6:742–756.
68. Kobayasi S, Mendes EF, Rodrigues MAM, Franco MF. Toxic dilatation of the colon in Chagas' disease. Br J Surg. 1992;79:1202–1203.
69. Rivero I, Moravenik M, Morales J, et al. Chagas' disease—another hazard in acute leukemia. N Engl J Med. 1974;290:285.
70. Leiguarda R, Roncoroni A, Taratuto AL, et al. Acute CNS infection by *Trypanosoma cruzi* (Chagas' disease) in immunosuppressed patients. Neurology. 1990;40:850–851.
71. Kohl S, Pickering LK, Frankel LS, Yaeger RG. Reactivation of Chagas disease during therapy of acute lymphocytic leukemia. Cancer. 1982;50:827–828.
72. Barousse AP, Costa JA, Esposto M, et al. Enfermedad de Chagas e inmunosupresión. Medicina (B Aires). 1980;40(Suppl)1:17–26.
73. Lopez-Blanco OA, Cavalli NH, Jasovich A, et al. Chagas' disease and kidney transplantation—follow-up of nine patients for 11 years. Transplant Proc. 1992;24:3089–3090.
74. de Arteaga J, Massari PU, Galli B, et al. Renal transplantation and Chagas' disease. Transplant Proc. 1992;24:1900–1901.
75. Luders C, Caetano MA, Ianhez LE, et al. Renal transplantation in patients with Chagas' disease: A long-term follow-up. Transplant Proc. 1992;24:1878–1879.
76. Blanche C, Aleksic I, Takkenberg JJ, et al. Heart transplantation for Chagas' cardiomyopathy. Ann Thorac Surg. 1995;60:1406–1408.
77. Pizzi TP, De Criozret VA, Smok G, Diaz M. Enfermedad de Chagas en un paciente con transplante renal y tratamiento inmunosupresor. Rev Med Chile. 1982;110:1207–1211.
78. Mocelin AJ, Brandina L, Gordon PA, et al. Immunosuppression and circulating *Trypanosoma cruzi* in a kidney transplant recipient. Transplantation. 1977;23:163.
79. Rocha A, Oliveira de Meneses AC, da Silva AM, et al. Pathology of patients with Chagas' disease and acquired immunodeficiency syndrome. Am J Trop Med Hyg. 1994;50:261–268.
80. Cohen JE, Tsai EC, Ginsberg HJ, Godes J. Pseudotumoral chagasic meningoencephalitis as the first manifestation of acquired immunodeficiency syndrome. Surg Neurol. 1998;49:324–327.
81. Sartori AM, Shikanai-Yasuda MA, Amato Neto V, Lopes MH. Follow-up of 18 patients with human immunodeficiency virus infection and chronic Chagas' disease, with reactivation of Chagas' disease causing cardiac disease in three patients. Clin Infect Dis. 1998;26:177–179.
82. Gluckstein D, Ciferri F, Ruskin J. Chagas' disease: Another cause of cerebral mass in the acquired immunodeficiency syndrome. Am J Med. 1992;92:429–432.
83. Stolf NAG, Higushi L, Bocchi E, et al. Heart transplantation in patients with Chagas' disease cardiomyopathy. J Heart Transplant. 1987;6:307–312.
84. Bocchi EA, Bellotti G, Uip D, et al. Long-term follow-up after heart transplantation in Chagas' disease. Transplant Proc. 1993;25:1329–1330.
85. Libow LF, Beltrani VP, Silvers DN, Grossman ME. Post-cardiac transplant reactivation of Chagas' disease diagnosed by skin biopsy. Cutis. 1991;48:37–40.
86. Kirchhoff LV. American trypanosomiasis (Chagas' disease)—a tropical disease now in the United States. N Engl J Med. 1993;329:639–644.
87. Bocchi EA, Higuchi ML, Vieira ML, et al. Higher incidence of malignant neoplasms after heart transplantation for treatment of chronic Chagas' heart disease. J Heart Lung Transplant. 1998;17:399–405.

88. Bocchi EA, Bellotti G, Mocelin AO, et al. Heart transplantation for chronic Chagas' heart disease. Ann Thorac Surg. 1996;61:1727–1733.
89. de Carvalho VB, Sousa EF, Vila JH, et al. Heart transplantation in Chagas' disease. 10 years after the initial experience. Circulation. 1996;94:1815–1817.
90. Shikanai-Yasuda MA, Lopes MH, Tolezano JE, et al. Doença de Chagas aguda: Vias de transmissao, aspectos clínicos e resposta à terapêutica específica em casos diagnosticados em um centro urbano. Rev Inst Med Trop Sao Paulo. 1990;32: 16–27.
91. Chiari E, Dias JCP, Lana M, Chiari CA. Hemocultures for the parasitological diagnosis of human chronic Chagas' disease. Rev Soc Bras Med Trop. 1989;22: 19–23.
92. Marsden PD, Barreto AC, Cuba CC, et al. Improvements in routine xenodiagnosis with first instar *Dipetalogaster maximus* (Uhler 1894)(Triatominae). Am J Trop Med Hyg. 1979;28:649–652.
93. Pan AA, Rosenberg GB, Hurley MK, et al. Clinical evaluation of an EIA for the sensitive and specific detection of serum antibody to *Trypanosoma cruzi* (Chagas' disease). J Infect Dis. 1992;165:585–588.
94. Carvalho MR, Krieger MA, Almeida E, et al. Chagas' disease diagnosis: Evaluation of several tests in blood bank screening. Transfusion. 1993;33:830–834.
95. Carrasco R, Miguez H, Camacho C, et al. Prevalence of *Trypanosoma cruzi* infection in blood banks of seven departments of Bolivia. Mem Inst Oswaldo Cruz. 1990;85:69–73.
96. Barrett VJ, Leiby DA, Odom JL, et al. Negligible prevalence of antibodies against *Trypanosoma cruzi* among blood donors in the southeastern United States. Am J Clin Pathol. 1997;108:499–503.
97. Kirchhoff LV, Gam AA, Gusmao RD, et al. Increased specificity of serodiagnosis of Chagas' disease by detection of antibody to the 72- and 90-kilodalton glycoproteins of *Trypanosoma cruzi*. J Infect Dis. 1987;155:561–564.
98. Frasch ACC, Reyes MB. Diagnosis of Chagas' disease using recombinant DNA technology. Parasitol Today. 1990;6:137–139.
99. Luquetti AO. Use of *Trypanosoma cruzi* defined proteins for diagnosis-multicentre trial: Serological and technical aspects. Mem Inst Oswaldo Cruz. 1990;85:497–505.
100. Burns JM Jr, Shreffler WG, Rosman DE, et al. Identification and synthesis of a major conserved antigenic epitope of *Trypanosoma cruzi*. Proc Natl Acad Sci U S A. 1992;89:1239–1243.
101. Kirchhoff LV, Donelson JE. PCR detection of *Trypanosoma cruzi*, African trypanosomes, and *Leishmania* species. In: Persing DH, Smith TF, Tenover FC, White TJ, eds. Diagnostic Molecular Microbiology—Principles and Applications. Washington, DC: American Society for Microbiology; 1993:443–455.
102. Kirchhoff LV. Chagas' disease. American trypanosomiasis. Infect Dis Clin North Am. 1993;7:487–502.
103. Moser DR, Kirchhoff LV, Donelson JE. Detection of *Trypanosoma cruzi* by polymerase chain reaction gene amplification. J Clin Microbiol. 1989;27:1744–1749.
104. Kirchhoff LV, Votava JR, Ochs DE, Moser DR. Comparison of PCR and microscopic methods for detecting *Trypanosoma cruzi*. J Clin Microbiol. 1996;34:1171–1175.
105. Russomando G, Figueredo A, Almiron M, et al. Polymerase chain reaction–based detection of *Trypanosoma cruzi* DNA in serum. J Clin Microbiol. 1992;30:2864–2868.
106. Sturm NR, Degrave W, Morel C, Simpson L. Sensitive detection and schizodeme classification of *Trypanosoma cruzi* cells by amplification of kinetoplast minicircle DNA sequences: Use in diagnosis of Chagas' disease. Mol Biochem Parasitol. 1989;33:205–214.
107. Avila HA, Pereira JB, Thiemann O, et al. Detection of *Trypanosoma cruzi* in blood specimens of chronic chagasic patients by polymerase chain reaction amplification of kinetoplast minicircle DNA: Comparison with serology and xenodiagnosis. J Clin Microbiol. 1993;31:2421–2426.
108. Britto C, Cardoso MA, Monteiro Vanni CM, et al. Polymerase chain reaction detection of *Trypanosoma cruzi* in human blood samples as a tool for diagnosis and treatment evaluation. Parasitology. 1995;110:241–247.
109. Gomes ML, Macedo AM, Vago AR, et al. *Trypanosoma cruzi:* Optimization of polymerase chain reaction for detection in human blood. Exp Parasitol. 1998;88:28–33.
110. Marr JJ, Docampo R. Chemotherapy for Chagas' disease: A perspective on current therapy and considerations for future research. Rev Infect Dis. 1986;8:884–903.
111. Levi GC, Lobo IM, Kallas EG, Amato Neto V. Etiological drug treatment of human infection by *Trypanosoma cruzi*. Rev Inst Med Trop Sao Paulo. 1996;38:35–38.
112. Coura JR. Current prospects of specific treatment of Chagas' disease [Spanish]. Bol Chil Parasitol. 1996;51:69–75.
113. Rassi A, Ferreira HO. Tentativas de tratamento específico da fase aguda da doença de Chagas com nitrofuranos em esquemas de duração prolongada. Rev Soc Bras Med Trop. 1971;5:235–262.
114. Ferreira HO. Tratamento específico da fase aguda da doença de Chagas. J Pediatr. 1988;64:1–3.
115. Andrade SG, Stocker-Guerret S, Pimentel AS, Imaud JA. Reversibility of cardiac fibrosis in mice chronically infected with *Trypanosoma cruzi*, under specific chemotherapy. Mem Inst Oswaldo Cruz. 1991;86:200.
116. Andrade ALSS, Zicker F, Oliveira RM, et al. Randomised trial of efficacy of benznidazole in treatment of early *Trypanosoma cruzi* infection. Lancet. 1996;348:1413.
117. Fragata Filho AA, Boianain E, Silva MAD, et al. Validade do tratamento etiológico da fase crônico da doença de Chagas com benznidazol. Arq Bras Cardiol. 1995;65(Suppl 1):71.
118. Viotti R, Vigliano C, Armenti H, Segura E. Treatment of chronic Chagas' disease with benznidazole: Clinical and serologic evolution of patients with long-term follow-up. Am Heart J. 1994;127:151–162.
119. Reed SG. In vivo administration of recombinant IFN-gamma induces macrophage activation, and prevents acute disease, immune suppression, and death in experimental *Trypanosoma cruzi* infections. J Immunol. 1988;140:4342–4347.
120. Urbina JA, Payares G, Molina J, et al. Cure of short- and long-term experimental Chagas' disease using D0870. Science. 1996;273:969–971.
121. Liendo A, Lazardi K, Urbina JA. In-vitro antiproliferative effects and mechanism of action of the bis-triazole D0870 and its S(-) enantiomer against *Trypanosoma cruzi*. J Antimicrob Chemother. 1998;41:197–205.
122. Chuster M. Implante de marcapasso nas bradiarritmias chagásicas. In: Cançado JR, Chuster M, eds. Cardiopatia Chagásica. Belo Horizonte, Brazil: Fundação Carlos Chagas; 1985:289–297.
123. Cançado JR, Chuster M, eds. Cardiopatia Chagásica. Belo Horizonte: Fundação Carlos Chagas; 1985.
124. Salis GB, Chiocca JC, Perisse E, et al. Veinte años de experiencia en el tratamiento no quirúrgico. Braz J Med Biol Res. 1991;25:145–148.
125. Pinotti HW, Felix VN, Zilberstein B, Cecconello I. Surgical complications of Chagas' disease: Megaesophagus, achalasia of the pylorus, and cholelithiasis. World J Surg. 1991;15:198–204.
126. Pinotti HW, Habr-Gama A, Cecconello I, et al. The surgical treatment of megaesophagus and megacolon. Dig Dis. 1993;11:206–215.
127. Haddad J, Raia A, Correa Neto A. Abaixamento retroretal do colon com colostomia perineal no tratamento do megacolon adqurido: Operaçao de Duhamel modificada. Rev Assoc Med Bras. 1965;11:83–88.
128. Duhamel B. Une nouvelle opération de mégacôlon congénital. Presse Med. 1956;64:2249–2250.
129. Gilson GJ, Harner KA, Abrams J, et al. Chagas' disease in pregnancy. Obstet Gynecol. 1995;86:646–647.
130. Hudson L, Grover F, Gutteridge WE, et al. Suggested guidelines for work with live *Trypanosoma cruzi*. Trans R Soc Trop Med Hyg. 1983;77:416–419.

Chapter 267

Agents of African Trypanosomiasis (Sleeping Sickness)

LOUIS V. KIRCHHOFF

PARASITES AND THEIR TRANSMISSION

The agents of African sleeping sickness are flagellated protozoan parasites that belong to the genus *Trypanosoma*, subgenus *Trypanozoon*.[1, 2] A general description of the members of this genus and specific characteristics of the subgenus are presented in the introduction to Chapter 266. Three trypanosome subspecies, *T. brucei brucei*, *T. brucei rhodesiense*, and *T. brucei gambiense*, are considered here. They are indistinguishable morphologically, and as a group they are often referred to as the *T. brucei* complex. *T. b. brucei* is a parasite of wild and domestic animals that is not infectious for humans. In contrast, *T. b. rhodesiense*, which is primarily a parasite of wild game, can infect humans, and this difference in host specificity forms the basis of the distinction between the two subspecies. *T. b. gambiense* primarily infects humans, and infections of wild and domestic animals are of limited importance.

The members of the *T. brucei* complex are transmitted by various species of tsetse flies that belong to the genus *Glossina*.[3] These bloodsucking insects are found only in Africa, where their range covers millions of square kilometers of rain forest and savanna. The parasites undergo a developmental cycle in the insect vectors. Tsetse flies of both sexes become infected with trypanosomes when they ingest blood from infected mammalian hosts that contains trypomastigotes, the form of the parasite that circulates in the blood stream. There are two forms of circulating trypomastigotes: long, slender organisms that are capable of dividing and short, stumpy forms thought to be nondividing parasites that are infective for the insect vectors. Once in the midgut of the tsetse flies, stumpy trypomastigotes transform into relatively long, slender procyclic trypomastigotes. After many cycles of multiplication, the procyclic forms migrate to the salivary glands, where they differentiate into epimastigotes and continue to multiply. A final transformation occurs as the epimastigotes become nondividing metacyclic trypomastigotes. Transmission takes place when these infective forms are inoculated during a subsequent blood meal. The cycle is completed when the injected metacyclic forms become blood stream trypomastigotes and begin to multiply in the blood or other extracellular spaces.

The capacity of African trypanosomes to multiply in the blood stream of their mammalian hosts, where they are continually exposed to humoral defenses, constitutes a fundamental difference between the agents of sleeping sickness and *Trypanosoma cruzi*, the cause of Chagas' disease in the Americas. The African trypanosomes are able to evade immune destruction indefinitely because they undergo antigenic variation, a process in which they periodically change the antigenic structure of the coat of glycoproteins that covers the surface of the parasite. The molecular mechanisms that control this complex process have been studied intensively.[4–6] When epimastigotes transform into metacyclic trypomastigotes in the salivary glands of the tsetse fly, each parasite synthesizes a surface coat made up of one of about a dozen types of antigenic glycoproteins, called variant antigen types (VATs). Presumably, this occurs as a preadaptation to the relatively hostile environment of the mammalian host into which the metacyclics must be inoculated if they are to survive. After injection into a mammalian host, the parasites express metacyclic VATs for approximately 5 days, after which they switch to the expression of blood stream VATs. Over time, the host sequentially mounts specific humoral responses directed against the predominantly expressed VATs. The population of parasites survives because an intrinsic rate of VAT switching provides an apparently endless supply of parasites that have surface glycoprotein coats to which the host has not been exposed previously.

Virtually all transmission of African trypanosomes to both wild and domestic animals, as well as to humans, takes place in the cyclic fashion just described. There is no evidence that these parasites can be transmitted by insects other than tsetse flies, and mechanical transmission by vectors is not important, although it may occur occasionally. Congenital transmission can occur, but in humans it is extremely rare,[7] as is transmission by blood transfusion. A small number of laboratory accidents resulting in infection with African trypanosomes have been reported.[8]

PATHOGENESIS AND PATHOLOGY

The pathogenesis of African sleeping sickness is complex, and many aspects of the process are poorly understood.[9–11] The first sign of infection with African trypanosomes is the acute inflammatory lesion (trypanosomal chancre) that appears a week or so after the bite of an infected tsetse fly and resolves spontaneously over several weeks. Interstitial multiplication of the trypanosomes takes place within the chancre, and there is an intense mononuclear cell reaction to the parasites, as well as edema and local tissue destruction.

After this initial local response, the infection evolves over weeks and months into a systemic hemolymphatic illness as the parasites disseminate widely through the lymphatics and the blood stream. Systemic African trypanosomiasis without central nervous system (CNS) involvement is generally referred to as stage I disease. The parasites first travel from the site of inoculation to regional lymph nodes, where they proliferate and cause an inflammatory response. They then move through the lymphatics into the blood stream, where multiplication continues. Egress of trypanosomes from vessels into interstitial spaces, where multiplication also takes place, is thought to be facilitated by increased vascular permeability.

In stage I trypanosomiasis, there is widespread lymphadenopathy and histiocytic proliferation, which may be followed by fibrosis. Morular cells (Mott cells) are also often present in tissue. These cells are plasmacytes with vacuolated cytoplasm and pyknotic nuclei that are thought to play a role in the production of immunoglobulin M (IgM).[12] The spleen may be enlarged, with generalized cellular proliferation, congestion, and focal necrosis. As the disease evolves, an endarteritis with perivascular infiltration of both parasites and lymphocytes may develop in lymph nodes and the spleen.

The heart is frequently involved in this stage of the disease, especially with *T. b. rhodesiense* infections. A pancarditis may develop involving all layers of the heart, including the mural and valvular endocardia.[13] The conduction system may also be affected, and involvement of the autonomic innervation of the heart has also been reported.[14] At the cellular level, pathologic changes include intense mononuclear infiltration consisting of lymphocytes, plasmacytes, and morular cells. As the infection progresses, myocytolysis and fibrosis may develop.

A number of hematologic manifestations accompany the development of stage I disease. Normocytic anemia is a regular feature in this phase of the illness and is usually accompanied by a brisk reticulocytosis. Several factors are thought to contribute to the anemia, and immune-medicated hemolysis may be important.[12] Platelet counts are often reduced, especially in infections with *T. b. rhodesiense*,[15] and disseminated intravascular coagulation before and during therapy has also been described.[16] A moderate degree of leukocytosis is usually present, especially in the early months of the infection, and this is accompanied by polyclonal B-cell activation.[17] High titers of immunoglobulins are a striking and constant feature of the illness. They consist primarily of polyclonal IgM that, for the most part, is not directed against specific parasite antigens. A number of other factors, including heterophile antibodies, rheumatoid factor, and anti-DNA antibodies, are often detectable. In addition, high levels of circulating antigen-antibody complexes are uniformly present, and these may play a role in the anemia, tissue damage, and increased vascular permeability that facilitate the dissemination of the parasites. Erythrocyte sedimentation rates are elevated, and hypocomplementemia has also been noted.

Stage II African trypanosomiasis involves invasion of the CNS. Parasites reach the brain and meninges via the blood stream and cause meningoencephalitis or meningomyelitis, or both. In the brain, they are found mainly in the frontal lobes, the pons, and the medulla, but other areas may be parasitized as well. Edema and hemorrhages may be evident on gross examination of affected areas at autopsy. Trypanosomes are present in perivascular areas, and nests of organisms can be found without apparent relation to blood vessels. The presence of parasites in the CNS is associated with infiltration of mononuclear cells that are predominantly lymphocytes, plasmacytes, and morular cells. The presence of parasites in the CNS is heralded by abnormal findings in the cerebrospinal fluid (CSF). The CSF may be under increased pressure, and the total protein concentration is elevated, with mononuclear cells predominating in addition to small numbers of morular cells and eosinophils. Trypanosomes are frequently present in the CSF as well.

EPIDEMIOLOGY

Sleeping sickness was a much greater problem in the past than it is at present.[3, 18] Approximately 50 million individuals are at risk for acquiring the disease, and tens of thousands of new cases of human African trypanosomiasis occur each year. Exact figures are not available because the acquisition of reliable health statistics is difficult in the developing countries where the human trypanosomiases are endemic. Sleeping sickness has undergone a resurgence, and major epidemics have occurred in the Sudan, Côte d'Ivoire, Chad, the Central African Republic, and several other endemic countries. West African (gambiense) trypanosomiasis and East African (rhodesiense) trypanosomiasis are epidemiologically distinct diseases. The general geographic distributions of these two illnesses are presented in Figure

266–1, and foci where transmission is known to occur are distributed throughout the indicated areas. Distinguishing epidemiologic and clinical features of the two diseases are presented in Table 267–1.

West African Trypanosomiasis

West African trypanosomiasis is caused by *T. b. gambiense*, which is transmitted primarily by tsetse flies belonging to the *palpalis* group: *Glossina palpalis*, *Glossina tachinoides*, and *Glossina fuscipes*. These vectors inhabit forests and wooded areas along rivers, where favorable conditions of temperature, moisture, and darkness are combined with the availability of mammalian blood. This distribution of the vectors restricts the occurrence of human infection to the tropical rain forests of Central and West Africa. Despite the fact that these tsetse flies adapt to feeding on a variety of mammals, infected humans constitute the only major reservoir of *T. b. gambiense*. The primary determinant of the risk of acquiring the infection is the frequency of contact with the vector. This risk increases during the dry season, when the density of both vectors and humans increases around limited numbers of water holes. Because of this pattern of transmission, West African trypanosomiasis is primarily a problem in rural populations, and tourists rarely become infected with *T. b. gambiense*. The illness caused by *T. b. gambiense* is less severe than that caused by *T. b. rhodesiense*. Thus, many infected persons are asymptomatic for long periods and continue to have contact with the vectors. This may be an important element in the persistence of the infection in the reservoir between epidemics.

East African Trypanosomiasis

The etiologic agent of East African trypanosomiasis is *T. b. rhodesiense*. This subspecies is transmitted by tsetse flies of the *morsitans* group, principally *Glossina morsitans*, *Glossina pallidipes*, and *Glossina swynnertoni*. These vectors are widely distributed in savanna and woodland areas of central and East Africa. Wild animals are the reservoir of this organism, principally antelope such as the bushbuck and hartebeest. These animals are trypanotolerant and generally do not suffer significant morbidity unless weakened by other illnesses. Cattle are the only domestic animals that can serve as a reservoir of *T. b. rhodesiense*, and infection with the parasite usually causes death if left untreated. Many other wild and domestic animals can be infected with this parasite, but their importance as reservoirs is minimal either because parasitemias are quite low or because they succumb quickly to the infection. The presence of the reservoir of *T. b. rhodesiense* in wild game in vast areas of Africa precludes the opening of these lands for cattle grazing.[19] Humans become infected with *T. b. rhodesiense* only incidentally, because for the most part risk results from contact with tsetse flies that principally feed on wild animals. Thus, the illness is an occupational hazard for individuals such as game wardens who work in areas where infected wild animals and vectors are present. In addition, sporadic cases of *T. b. rhodesiense* infection occur among tourists returning from game parks of East Africa.

The natural cycle of the African trypanosomes does not exist outside Africa, and human African trypanosomiasis in the United States is limited to an occasional imported cause. During the past 25 years, roughly two dozen cases of imported African trypanosomiasis have been reported to the Centers for Disease Control and Prevention.[20–22] Most of these cases were caused by *T. b. rhodesiense*, and several patients had CNS involvement. Despite the serious nature of the infection, all the patients were treated effectively.

TABLE 267–1 Comparisons of West African and East African Trypanosomiasis

	West African (gambiense)	East African (rhodesiense)
Organism	*Trypanosoma brucei gambiense*	*Trypanosoma brucei rhodesiense*
Vectors	Tsetse flies (*palpalis* group)	Tsetse flies (*morsitans* group)
Primary reservoir	Humans	Antelope and cattle
Human illness	Chronic (late CNS disease)	Acute (early CNS disease)
Duration of illness	Months to years	<9 mo
Lymphadenopathy	Prominent	Minimal
Parasitemia	Low	High
Diagnosis by rodent inoculation	No	Yes
Epidemiology	Rural populations	Tourists in game parks Workers in wild areas Rural populations

CLINICAL COURSE

West African Trypanosomiasis

An indurated, painful trypanosomal chancre may develop at the site where parasites were inoculated by an infected tsetse fly. This lesion usually appears 1 to 2 weeks after the bite of the infected fly and resolves spontaneously over several weeks. The chancre may ulcerate and reach a diameter of several centimeters; regional lymphadenopathy may also develop. However, the trypanosomal chancre is seldom seen in clinical practice. Thus, most patients may develop systemic trypanosomiasis without experiencing the symptoms of localized disease.

The development of stage I (hemolymphatic) disease with dissemination of the parasites is marked by the onset of fever, which may appear weeks or months after the acquisition of the infection. The fever is characterized by intermittent bouts of high temperatures lasting for several days, and extended periods may intervene during which the patient is afebrile. As the chronic illness evolves, a wide variety of other signs and symptoms develop. Lymphadenopathy is a fairly constant feature of gambiense trypanosomiasis. The nodes are typically discrete, movable, rubbery, and nontender. With time they frequently become indurated as fibrosis occurs. Supraclavicular and cervical nodes are often visibly discernible, and enlargement of the nodes of the posterior cervical triangle, or Winterbottom's sign, is a classic finding in persons infected with *T. b. gambiense*. Mild hepatosplenomegaly may be present as well.

Transient edema is a frequent sign during this phase of the illness and can occur in the face as well as in the hands, feet, and other periarticular areas. Pruritus is common, and an irregular circinate rash is often present. The rash is typically located on the trunk, shoulders, buttocks, and thighs and consists of erythematous areas 5 to 10 cm in diameter with clear centers.[23] Other inconstant findings include malaise, headache, weakness, weight loss, arthralgias, and tachycardia. Amenorrhea and infertility in women as well as a loss of libido and impotence in men as a consequence of neuroendocrine dysfunction have been documented.[24, 25]

Stage II (meningoencephalitic) disease is characterized by the insidious development of protean neurologic manifestations, accompanied by progressive alterations in the composition of the CSF.[26] In gambiense trypanosomiasis, CNS findings may develop months or even years after the initiation of the infection. Irritability, a personality change, and a loss of the ability to concentrate may develop before changes in the CSF become evident, and this underscores the arbitrary nature of the distinction between the hemolymphatic and CNS stages of the illness. A picture of progressive indifference develops, associated with daytime somnolence, sometimes alternating with restlessness and insomnia at night. The frequency and progressive nature of the somnolence result in the use of the term *sleeping sickness*. A listless gaze reflects a loss of spontaneity, and speech may become indistinct. Extrapyramidal signs often develop and may include choreiform movements of the trunk, neck, and extremities, tremors of the tongue and fingers, and fasciculations of a variety of muscle groups. Ataxia is a frequent sign, and the patient may appear to have Parkinson's disease as a shuffling gait, hypertonia, tremors, and slurred speech develop.[22] The final phase of the CNS disease is one of progressive neurologic impairment ending in coma and death.

Trypanosomiasis in children, which is uncommon because of their relatively limited exposure to the vectors, does not differ greatly from the clinical illness seen in adults. However, the illness tends to run a more acute course, and the distinction between the hemolymphatic and CNS stages is difficult to make.[27] Moreover, due to the protean nature of the symptoms and the lack of pathognomonic signs, the diagnosis is often missed in the early stages of the infection and is made only after neurologic impairment has developed.[28]

East African Trypanosomiasis

The most striking general difference between West African and East African trypanosomiases is that the latter illness tends to follow a more acute course, reflecting a relatively less effective adaptation of *T. b. rhodesiense* to humans.[29, 30] The onset of symptoms usually occurs a few days after the patient has been bitten by an infected tsetse fly, but the incubation period may be as long as several weeks. Typically in tourists, systemic signs of infection such as fever, malaise, and headache may appear before the end of the trip or shortly after their return home. As the illness progresses, the pattern of intermittent fever develops, and rash is a nearly constant feature of the early weeks of the illness. Lymph node swelling is not prominent in rhodesiense trypanosomiasis, and thus Winterbottom's sign is generally absent. Persistent tachycardia unrelated to the fevers is frequently present early in the course of the illness, and in some patients death may result from arrhythmias and congestive heart failure due to pancarditis even before CNS disease develops. In general, untreated rhodesiense trypanosomiasis usually leads to death in a matter of weeks to months, without a clear distinction between the hemolymphatic and CNS stages.

DIAGNOSIS

Epidemiologic information and clinical findings often combine to suggest the diagnosis of African trypanosomiasis, and a high index of suspicion should be maintained with persons who have been in endemic areas. However, there are numerous other illnesses common in the tropics that cause symptoms similar to those seen in both the early and the late stages of sleeping sickness, and a definitive diagnosis of African trypanosomiasis requires demonstration of the parasite.[31]

If a chancre is present, fluid should be expressed and examined directly under light microscopy for the highly motile trypanosomes. Part of the specimen should be fixed and stained with Giemsa. Aspiration of soft lymph nodes early in the course of the infection can also be used to demonstrate the presence of parasites. This method is more effective in patients with West African trypanosomiasis because of the prominence of lymphadenopathy, but even in such patients, multiple aspirates are sometimes necessary before parasites are found. An enlarged node should be punctured and kneaded gently during aspiration, and the sample obtained should be examined directly and also after staining.

Examination of wet preparations and Giemsa-stained thin and thick smears of peripheral blood is also a sensitive method for detection of infection with African trypanosomes (Fig. 267–1). This approach is more likely to be successful in the hemolymphatic stage of the illness, and it is much more useful in patients infected with *T. b. rhodesiense* because of the relatively high parasitemias. Because parasitemia levels vary considerably from one day to the next, serial specimens should be examined. If parasites are not seen in blood from a patient whose history and clinical findings point to African trypanosomiasis as a possible diagnosis, efforts should be made to concentrate the organisms. This can be done most simply by using

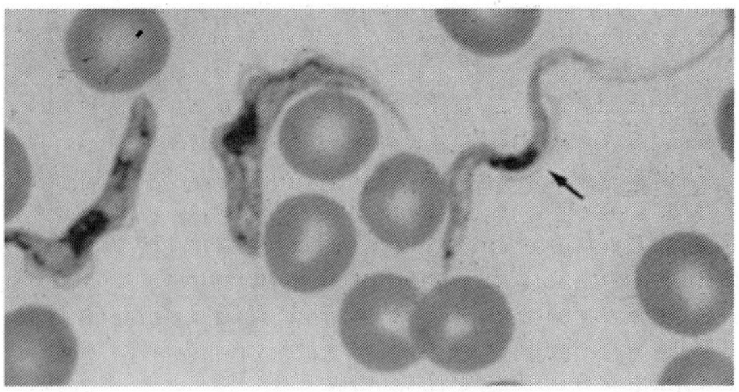

FIGURE 267–1. *Trypanosoma brucei rhodesiense* trypomastigotes in rat blood. The parasite indicated by the arrow is typical of the long, slender forms capable of multiplying in the mammalian host. The other two organisms represent the stumpy, nondividing forms infective for the insect vector. (Giemsa, ×1250.) (Courtesy of Dr. G.A. Cook, Madison, Wis.)

quantitative buffy coat analysis tubes (QBC, Becton-Dickenson, Franklin Lakes, NJ).[32, 33] In these tubes, which are coated with acridine orange, the parasites are separated from blood components by centrifugation and are easily seen under light microscopy because of the stain. Alternatively, the buffy coat obtained by centrifuging 10 to 15 ml of anticoagulated blood can be examined microscopically as a wet preparation and after Giemsa staining.

Examination of the CSF is mandatory in all patients suspected of having African trypanosomiasis.[34] An increase in the CSF cell count is the first abnormality to be detected. Increased opening pressure of the fluid develops later, as do an elevated IgM level and total protein concentration. Examination of the CSF processed by a double-centrifugation technique often reveals trypanosomes in patients with CNS involvement.[35] Any CSF abnormality in a patient in whom trypanosomes have been found in specimens from other sites must be viewed as indicative of CNS involvement, and this has implications for treatment that are discussed later. CSF IgM levels may remain elevated for long periods after effective therapy.

An additional approach to patients in whom parasites cannot be demonstrated by the previously described methods is bone marrow aspiration. Trypanosomes may be found by careful examination of Giemsa-stained specimens. Moreover, material aspirated from the bone marrow can be inoculated into special liquid culture medium, as can blood, CSF, or lymph node aspirates obtained from the patient in whom trypanosomiasis is suspected.[36] Finally, a highly sensitive method for the detection of infection with *T. b. rhodesiense* is inoculation of specimens obtained from the patient into mice or rats. Patent parasitemias usually develop within a week or two in animals inoculated with specimens from infected persons. Unfortunately, due to host specificity, it is very difficult to isolate *T. b. gambiense* by this method.

Several serologic assays are available to aid in the diagnosis of African trypanosomiasis, but the variable sensitivity and specificity of these tests mandate that treatment decisions still be based on demonstration of the parasite. Nonetheless, these assays are useful in epidemiologic surveys. Detection of elevated serum IgM levels was used for many years as a screening procedure. Simple direct agglutination tests for trypanosomes performed on cards (CATT, TrypTect CIATT)[37, 38] have been developed and are available commercially. A role for polymerase chain reaction–based assays for detecting African trypanosomes has not yet been defined.[22, 39, 40]

TREATMENT

The drugs classically used for the therapy of African trypanosomiasis are suramin, pentamidine, and organic arsenicals. More recently, eflornithine has been shown to be effective in both the hemolymphatic and the CNS stages of West African trypanosomiasis. Therapy of gambiense and rhodesiense trypanosomiases must be individualized based on the presence or absence of CNS disease, side reactions, and occasionally drug resistance of the infecting organisms. Suramin and pentamidine do not penetrate the CNS adequately. Thus eflornithine should be used in patients with gambiense trypanosomiasis who have CNS disease, but because the response of *T. b.* rhodesiense to this drug has been variable,[41] patients with stage II rhodesiense trypanosomiasis must be treated with the more toxic arsenicals (Table 267–2). In the United States these drugs must be obtained from the Drug Service of the Centers for Disease Control and Prevention in Atlanta, Georgia (770-639-3670 [weekdays]; 770-639-2888 [off hours]). Currently recommended treatment protocols are summarized in two publications.[42, 43]

Patients with the hemolymphatic stage of gambiense trypanosomiasis and normal CSF should be given either suramin (Bayer 205, Naphuride, Antrypol) or eflornithine, whereas suramin is the only first-choice drug for stage I rhodesiense disease. In the case of suramin, a 100- to 200-mg test dose should be given. The dosage for adults is 1 g intravenously on days 2, 3, 7, 14, and 21. The dosage for children is 20 mg/kg intravenously on days 1, 3, 7, 14, and 21. The drug is administered by slow intravenous infusion of a freshly prepared 10% aqueous solution. Suramin causes a number of side effects and must be administered under the close supervision of a physician. Approximately 1 patient in 20,000 has an immediate, severe, and potentially fatal reaction to the drug consisting of nausea, vomiting, seizures, and shock. A number of less severe reactions can also occur, including fever, pruritus, photophobia, arthralgias, and skin eruptions. The most important side effect of suramin is renal damage. Transient proteinuria is often seen during treatment. Urinalysis should be done before giving each dose, and if proteinuria increases or casts and red cells appear in the urine sediment, the drug should be discontinued. Suramin should not be used in patients with preexisting renal insufficiency.

In 1990 eflornithine (difluoromethylornithine, DFMO, Ornidyl) was approved by the U.S. Food and Drug Administration for treatment of patients infected with *T. b. gambiense*.[42] Eflornithine is highly effective in both the hemolymphatic and the CNS stages of gambiense trypanosomiasis. This drug produces a dramatic reduction of symptoms and rapid clearing of parasites from blood and CSF. The recommended dosage is 400 mg/kg/day intravenously in four divided doses for 14 days, followed by 300 mg/kg/day orally, also in four divided doses, for 30 days. Frequent side effects include diarrhea and anemia. Thrombocytopenia has been observed, and seizures and hearing loss have been reported rarely. A major disadvantage is the amount of drug that must be given, the variable drug availability, and the duration of therapy, and these factors may make widespread use difficult.

For patients with gambiense CNS disease who cannot tolerate eflornithine, the alternative therapeutic approach is the combination of the arsenical tryparsamide (Tryparsone, Novatoxyl) and suramin. Tryparsamide is effective against *T. b.* gambiense but not against *T. b. rhodesiense*. It crosses the blood-brain barrier and thus can be used in stage II disease. The dosage of tryparsamide is one injection of 30 mg/kg every 5 days for a total of 12 injections, and that for suramin is 10 mg/kg intravenously every 5 days, also for a total of 12 injections. The courses of both drugs may be repeated after 1 month. Tryparsamide may also cause encephalopathy; other side effects include fever, abdominal pain, vomiting, rash, tinnitus, and a variety of ocular symptoms.

TABLE 267–2 Drugs Recommended for Treatment of the African Trypanosomiases

Causative Agent	Clinical Stage I	Clinical Stage II
Trypanosoma brucei gambiense	Suramin Or: Eflornithine Alt: Pentamidine	Eflornithine Alt: Tryparsamide + suramin
Trypanosoma brucei rhodesiense	Suramin Alt: Pentamidine	Melarsoprol

Pentamidine isoethionate (Lomidine) is the alternative drug recommended for patients with hemolymphatic African trypanosomiasis.[44] The drug is effective in treatment of the early stages of gambiense trypanosomiasis, but it has a lower cure rate than suramin. In addition, some *T. b. rhodesiense* infections do not respond to pentamidine. The dosage for both adults and children is 4 mg/kg/day intramuscularly for 10 days. Frequent, immediate side effects of pentamidine include nausea, vomiting, hypotension, and tachycardia. These reactions are generally transient and do not warrant discontinuation of therapy. Other side effects include nephrotoxicity, abnormal liver function tests, neutropenia, rashes, hypoglycemia, and sterile abscesses.

The drug of choice for rhodesiense trypanosomiasis with CNS involvement is the arsenical melarsoprol (mel B, Arsobal). Melarsoprol cures both stages of the disease. Thus, it is also indicated for treatment of the hemolymphatic stage in patients in whom suramin or pentamidine, or both, has failed or could not be tolerated. However, it should never be the first choice for therapy of stage I trypanosomiasis because of its relatively high toxicity. In adults the drug is given in three courses of 3 days each. The recommended dosage is 2 to 3.6 mg/kg/day intravenously in three divided doses for 3 days, followed 1 week later by 3.6 mg/kg/day, also in three divided doses for 3 days. This latter course is then repeated 10 to 21 days later. In debilitated patients, treatment with suramin for 2 to 4 days before starting melarsoprol therapy and an 18-mg initial dose of the latter drug, followed by progressive drug increases, have been recommended. For pediatric patients, 18 to 25 mg/kg total should be given over 1 month. An initial dose of 0.36 mg/kg intravenously should be increased gradually to a maximum of 3.6 mg/kg at 1- to 5-day intervals for a total of 9 to 10 doses.

Melarsoprol is a highly toxic drug and should be administered with great care. The most important side effects involve the CNS. Reactive encephalopathy is a frequent occurrence, and its incidence has been reported to be as high as 18% in some series. It is thought to result from the interaction of the drug with diseased brain tissue and trypanosomes, and it is rare in patients with minimal CNS involvement. It generally occurs during the first course, and its onset may be sudden or insidious. Clinical indications of reactive encephalopathy include high fever, headache, tremor, impaired speech, seizures, and finally coma. The reaction may be fatal, but death rates have been reduced as experience with the drug has accumulated. Melarsoprol should be discontinued at the first sign of encephalopathy. It may be restarted cautiously with small doses a few days after the signs have resolved.

A number of other side effects are associated with melarsoprol therapy. Extravasation of the drug results in intense local reactions and, as with administration of other heavy metals, abdominal pain and vomiting are commonly observed. Jarisch-Herxheimer–type reactions have been reported, as have nephrotoxicity, abnormal liver function tests, and myocardial damage.

PREVENTION

The trypanosomiases constitute complex public health and epizootic problems in many developing countries in Africa. Control programs that focus on eradication of vectors and drug treatment of infected humans and animals have been in operation in some regions for decades. Considerable progress has been made in a number of areas, but the lack of a consensus on the best approach to solving the overall problem of African trypanosomiasis and a paucity of resources stand in the way of effective control.[45, 46] Individuals can reduce their risk of acquiring infections with trypanosomes by avoiding areas known to harbor infected insects, by wearing clothing that reduces the biting of the flies, and by using insect repellent. Chemoprophylaxis is not recommended because of the high toxicity of the drugs that are active against African trypanosomes, and no vaccine is available to prevent transmission of the parasites.

REFERENCES

1. Hoare CA. The Trypanosomes of Mammals: A Zoological Monograph. Oxford: Blackwell; 1972.
2. Vickerman K. Developmental cycles and biology of pathogenic trypanosomes. Br Med Bull. 1985;41:105–114.
3. Jordan AM. Trypanosomiasis Control and African Rural Development. London: Longmans; 1986.
4. Cross GA. Antigenic variation in trypanosomes: Secrets surface slowly. Bioessays. 1996;18:283–291.
5. Borst P, Rudenko G, Blundell PA, et al. Mechanisms of antigenic variation in African trypanosomes. Behring Inst Mitt. 1997;99:1–15.
6. Donelson JE, Hill KL, El-Sayed NMA. Multiple mechanisms of immune evasion by African trypanosomes. Mol Biochem Parasitol. 1998;91:51–66.
7. Mbala L, Matendo R, Kinkela T, et al. Congenital African trypanosomiasis in a newborn child with current neurologic symptomatology. Trop Doct. 1996;26: 186–187.
8. Herwaldt BL, Juranek DD. Laboratory-acquired malaria, leishmaniasis, trypanosomiasis, and toxoplasmosis. Am J Trop Med Hyg. 1993;48:313–323.
9. Poltera AA. Pathology of human African trypanosomiasis with reference to experimental African trypanosomiasis and infections of the central nervous system. Br Med Bull. 1985;41:169–174.
10. Hunter CA, Kennedy PGE. Immunopathology in central nervous system human African trypanosomiasis. J Neuroimmunol. 1992;36:91–95.
11. Sternberg JM. Immunobiology of African trypanosomiasis. Chem Immunol. 1998;70:186–199.
12. Wery M, Mulumba PM, Lambert PH, Kazyumba L. Hematologic manifestations, diagnosis, and immunopathology of African trypanosomiasis. Semin Hematol. 1982;19:83–92.
13. Poltera AA, Cox JN, Owor R. Pancarditis involving the conducting system and all valves in human African trypanosomiasis. Br Heart J. 1976;38:827–837.
14. Poltera AA, Owor R, Cox JN. Pathological aspects of human African trypanosomiasis (HAT) in Uganda. A post-mortem survey of fourteen cases. Virchows Arch Pathol Histol. 1997;373:249–265.
15. Robins-Browne RM, Schneider J, Metz J. Thrombocytopenia in trypanosomiasis. Am J Trop Med Hyg. 1975;24:226–231.
16. Barrett-Connor E, Ugoreta RJ, Braude I. Disseminated intravascular coagulation in trypanosomiasis. Arch Intern Med. 1973;131:574–577.
17. Lambert PH, Berney M, Kazyumba GL. Immune complexes in serum and in cerebrospinal fluid in sleeping sickness. Correlation with polyclonal B-cell activation and with intracerebral immunoglobulin synthesis. J Clin Invest. 1981;67:77–85.
18. Ekwanzala M, Pepin J, Khonde N, et al. In the heart of darkness: Sleeping sickness in Zaire. Lancet. 1996;348:1427–1430.
19. D'Ieteren GD, Authie E, Wissocq N, Murray M. Trypanotolerance, an option for sustainable livestock production in areas at risk from trypanosomiasis. Rev Sci Tech. 1998;17:154–175.
20. Bryan RT, Waskin HA, Richards FO, et al. African trypanosomiasis in American travelers: A 20 year review. In: Steffen R, Lobel HO, Haworth J, Bradley DJ, eds. Travel Medicine. Berlin: Springer-Verlag; 1989:
21. Panosian CB, Cohen L, Bruckner D, et al. Fever, leukopenia, and a cutaneous lesion in a man who had recently traveled in Africa. Rev Infect Dis. 1991;13:1131–1138.
22. Kirchhoff LV. Use of a PCR assay for diagnosing African trypanosomiasis of the CNS. Cent Afr J Med. 1998;44:134–136.
23. McGovern TW, Williams W, Fitzpatrick JE, et al. Cutaneous manifestations of African trypanosomiasis. Arch Dermatol. 1995;131:1178–1182.
24. Reincke M, Arlt W, Heppner C, et al. Neuroendocrine dysfunction in African trypanosomiasis. The role of cytokines. Ann N Y Acad Sci. 1998;840:809–821.
25. Petzke F, Heppner C, Bulamberi D, et al. Hypogonadism in Rhodesian sleeping sickness: Evidence for acute and chronic dysfunction of the hypothalamic-pituitary-gonadal axis. Fertil Steril. 1996;65:68–75.
26. Haller L, Adams A, Merouze F, Dago A. Clinical and pathological aspects of human African trypanosomiasis *(T. b. gambiense)* with particular reference to reactive arsenical encephalopathy. Am J Trop Med Hyg. 1986;35:94–99.
27. Buyst H. Sleeping sickness in children. Ann Soc Belge Med Trop. 1977;57:201–212.
28. Koko J, Dufillot D, Gahouma D, et al. Human African trypanosomiasis in children. A pediatrics service experience in Libreville, Gabon (in French). Bull Soc Pathol Exot. 1997;90:14–18.
29. Gear JHS, Miller B. The clinical manifestations of rhodesiense trypanosomiasis: An account of cases contracted in the Okavango swamps of Botswana. Am J Trop Med Hyg. 1986;35:1146–1152.
30. Odiit M, Kansiime F, Enyaru JC. Duration of symptoms and case fatality of sleeping sickness caused by *Trypanosoma brucei rhodesiense* in Tororo, Uganda. East Afr Med J. 1997;74:792–795.
31. Van Meirvenne N. Diagnosis of human African trypanosomiasis. Ann Soc Belge Med Trop. 1992;72(Suppl 1):53–56.
32. Bailey JW, Smith DH. The use of the acridine orange QBC technique in the diagnosis of African trypanosomiasis. Trans R Soc Trop Med Hyg. 1992;86:630.
33. Truc P, Jamonneau V, N'Guessan P, et al. Parasitological diagnosis of human African trypanosomiasis: A comparison of the QBC® and miniature anion-exchange centrifugation techniques. Trans R Soc Trop Med Hyg. 1998;92:288–289.
34. Miezan TW, Meda HA, Doua F, et al. Assessment of central nervous system involvement in gambiense trypanosomiasis: Value of the cerebro-spinal white cell count. Trop Med Int Health. 1998;3:571–575.
35. Cattand P, Miezan BT, deRaadt P. Human African trypanosomiasis: Use of double centrifugation of cerebrospinal fluid to detect trypanosomes. Bull World Health Organ. 1988;66:83–86.
36. Truc P, Aerts D, McNamara JJ, et al. Direct isolation *in vitro* of *Trypanosoma brucei* from man and other animals, and its potential value for the diagnosis of gambian trypanosomiasis. Trans R Soc Trop Med Hyg. 1992;86:627–629.
37. Zillmann U, Albiez EJ. The Testryp CATT (card agglutination test for trypanosomiasis): A field study on gambiense sleeping sickness in Liberia. Trop Med Parasitol. 1986;37:390–392.
38. Nantulya VM. *Tryp*Tect CIATT®—a card indirect agglutination trypanosomiasis test for diagnosis of *Trypanosoma brucei gambiense* and *T. b. rhodesiense* infections. Trans R Soc Trop Med Hyg. 1997;91:551–553.
39. Schares G, Mehlitz D. Sleeping sickness in Zaire: A nested polymerase chain reaction improves the identification of *Trypanosoma (Trypanozoon) brucei gambiense* by specific kinetoplast DNA probes. Trop Med Int Health. 1996;1:59–70.
40. Kanmogne GD, Asonganyi T, Gibson WC. Detection of *Trypanosoma brucei gambiense*, in serologically positive but aparasitemic sleeping-sickness suspects in Cameroon, by PCR. Ann Trop Med Parasitol. 1996;90:475–483.
41. Iten M, Mett H, Evans A, et al. Alterations in ornithine decarboxylase characteristics account for tolerance of *Trypanosoma brucei rhodesiense* to D, L-alpha-difluoromethylornithine. Antimicrob Agents Chemother. 1997;41:1922–1925.
42. Pepin J, Milord F. The treatment of human African trypanosomiasis. Adv Parasitol. 1995;33:1–47.
43. Anonymous. Drugs for parasitic infections. Med Lett Drugs Ther. 1998;40:1–12.
44. Doua F, Miezan TW, Sanon Singaro JR, et al. The efficacy of pentamidine in the treatment of early-late stage *Trypanosoma brucei gambiense* trypanosomiasis. Am J Trop Med Hyg. 1997;55:586–588.
45. Molyneux DH. Vector-borne parasitic diseases—an overview of recent changes. Int J Parasitol. 1998; 28:927–934.
46. Holmes PH. New approaches to the integrated control of trypanosomiasis. Vet Parasitol. 1997;71:121–135.

Chapter 268

Toxoplasma gondii

JOSE G. MONTOYA
JACK S. REMINGTON

Although *Toxoplasma gondii* infects a large proportion of the world's human populations, it is an uncommon cause of disease. Certain individuals, however, are at high risk for severe or life-threatening disease due to this parasite. These include congenitally infected fetuses and newborns and immunologically impaired individuals. Congenital toxoplasmosis is the result of maternal infection acquired during gestation, an infection that is most often clinically inapparent. In immunodeficient patients, toxoplasmosis most often occurs in persons with defects in T-cell–mediated immunity such as those with hematologic malignancies, bone marrow and solid organ transplants, or acquired immunodeficiency syndrome (AIDS). In the vast majority of otherwise immunocompetent individuals, primary or chronic (latent) infection with *T. gondii* is asymptomatic; after the acute infection, a small percentage suffer chorioretinitis, lymphadenitis, or, even more rarely, myocarditis and polymyositis.

T. gondii was first observed in the North African rodent (*Ctenodactylus gundi*) by Nicolle and Manceaux in 1908[1] and as a cause of human disease in an 11-month-old congenitally infected child by Janku in 1923.[2] It was reported as a cause of encephalitis by Wolf, Cowen, and Paige, who in 1939 observed it in a newborn who presented with seizures, intracranial calcifications, hydrocephalus, and chorioretinitis.[3] Although relatively few cases of severe toxoplasmosis in adults were reported during the ensuing years, the remarkable 1968 report by Vietzke and his colleagues from the National Cancer Institute of the National Institutes of Health highlighted *T.*

This work was supported by National Institutes of Health Grant AI04717.

gondii as a cause of life-threatening infection in patients with malignancy, predominantly in those with hematologic malignancies.[4] Since that time, more than 200 such cases in non-AIDS immunodeficient patients have been recorded in the literature.[5] With the advent of the AIDS epidemic, toxoplasmic encephalitis (TE) was recognized as the major cause of space-occupying lesions in the brains of patients with advanced human immunodeficiency virus (HIV) infection and serologic evidence of prior exposure to the parasite.[6, 7] Despite significant advances during the past 2 decades, major challenges remain in the areas of prevention and management of the acute infection in pregnancy, the fetus, and the newborn[8] and in the understanding and treatment of the reactivated infection in chronically infected immunocompetent[9] and immunocompromised individuals.[5]

ETIOLOGY

T. gondii is a coccidian parasite of felids with humans and other warm-blooded animals as intermediate hosts. It belongs to the subphylum Apicomplexa, class Sporozoa and exists in nature in three forms: the oocyst (which releases sporozoites), the tissue cyst (which contains and may release bradyzoites), and the tachyzoite (Fig. 268–1).[10]

Evidence that more than one strain of *T. gondii* exists has been based on different isolates' differences in virulence for laboratory animals and with the generation time in tissue culture.[11] Efforts to explain these differences in virulence using protein and antigen analyses were unrevealing.[12] In contrast, genetic variation among strains of *T. gondii* has been demonstrated by the use of molecular techniques including isoenzyme analysis[13] and restriction fragment length polymorphism.[14] Population genetic analysis based on the latter technique in both animals and humans indicated that strains of the parasite isolated from a variety of mammals have a perfect correlation between virulence for mice and a single clonal lineage that is geographically widespread and found in both domestic animals and humans.[14] Clear differences were observed in the frequency of parasite genotypes when *T. gondii* isolates from animals were compared with those of humans. Type III strains were common in animals but observed significantly less often in cases of human toxoplasmosis; most cases in humans were caused by type II strains. Type II strains were significantly more often associated with reactivation of chronic infections and accounted for 65% of strains isolated from AIDS patients. Type I strains were significantly more often associated with human congenital toxoplasmosis.[15]

Oocyst

Cats shed oocysts after they ingest any of the three forms of the parasite at which time an enteroepithelial cycle begins. The organ-

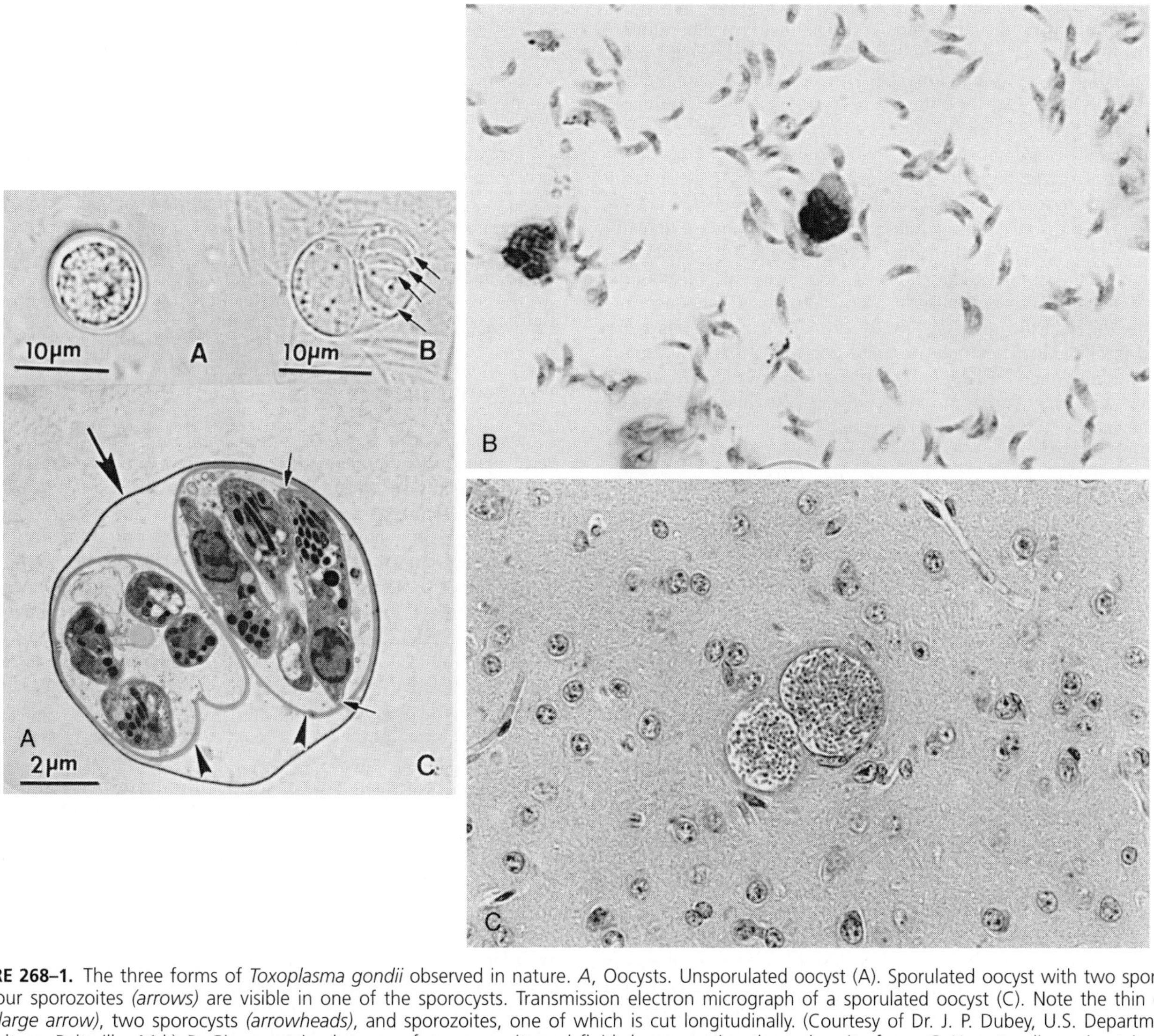

FIGURE 268–1. The three forms of *Toxoplasma gondii* observed in nature. *A*, Oocysts. Unsporulated oocyst (A). Sporulated oocyst with two sporocysts (B). Four sporozoites *(arrows)* are visible in one of the sporocysts. Transmission electron micrograph of a sporulated oocyst (C). Note the thin oocyst wall *(large arrow)*, two sporocysts *(arrowheads)*, and sporozoites, one of which is cut longitudinally. (Courtesy of Dr. J. P. Dubey, U.S. Department of Agriculture. Beltsville, Md.) *B*, Giemsa-stained smear of mouse peritoneal fluid demonstrating the tachyzoite form. *C*, Hematoxylin-eosin stain of the cyst form in brain. The adjacent smaller cyst illustrates the "daughter" cyst phenomenon (see text).

isms penetrate the epithelial cells of the small intestine and initiate the development of asexual and sexual (gametogony) forms of the parasite. Oocyst wall formation begins around the fertilized gamete, and when mature, oocysts are discharged into the intestinal lumen by rupture of intestinal epithelial cells.[10] Unsporulated oocysts are subspheric to spheric and measure 10 × 12 μm in diameter (see Fig. 268–1*A* [A]). Oocysts are formed in the small intestine only in members of the cat family and are excreted in the feces for periods varying from 7 to 20 days. As many as 10 million oocysts may be shed in the feces in a single day.[10] Sporulation, required for oocysts to become infectious, occurs outside the cat within 1 to 5 days depending on temperature and the availability of oxygen. Sporulated oocysts contain two sporocysts (see Fig. 268–1*A* [B and C]), each of which contains four sporozoites. This maturation process occurs after excretion of the oocysts into the environment. Maturation is more rapid at warm temperatures (2 to 3 days at 24°C compared with 14 to 21 days at 11°C).[16] Oocysts may remain viable for as long as 18 months in moist soil; this results in an environmental reservoir from which incidental hosts may be infected.

Tachyzoite

The tachyzoite form (see Fig. 268–1*B*) is crescentic and measures 2 to 4 μm wide and 4 to 8 μm long; it requires an intracellular habitat to survive and multiply despite having its own Golgi apparatus, ribosomes, and mitochondria. Tachyzoites are seen in the primary or reactivated infection; their presence is the hallmark of active infection. They reside and multiply within vacuoles in their host's cells, can infect all phagocytic and nonphagocytic cell types,[17] and multiply approximately every 4 to 6 hours to form rosettes. Continuous multiplication leads to cell disruption and release of organisms that go on to invade contiguous cells or are phagocytosed and transported to other areas of the body by blood and lymph.[10, 17] At the anterior end of the tachyzoite, there is a cone-shaped structure termed the *conoid.* It is protruded during the parasite's entry into host cells. *Rhoptries*, numbering four to eight, are club-shaped organelles that terminate in the conoid. The rhoptries, together with surrounding small, rod-shaped organelles, most likely have important secretory functions for parasitic invasion. *Dense granules* are organelles distributed throughout the cytoplasm. Their contents are released into a vacuole, termed the *parasitophorous vacuole*, that is formed around the parasite during entry into the cell and also into the external environment as excreted-secreted antigens.[17]

Tachyzoites cannot survive desiccation, freezing and thawing, or extended exposure to gastric digestive juices.[8] They are propagated in the laboratory in the peritoneum of mice and in tissue cultures of mammalian cells. Tachyzoites can be visualized in sections stained with hematoxylin and eosin but are better visualized with Wright-Giemsa and immunoperoxidase stains.[18]

Cyst

After entry into the cell and replication, encystation and the formation of tissue cysts may occur. The factors that result in cyst formation are not known. These cysts grow and remain within the host cell cytoplasm as the intracystic form wherein the bradyzoites continue to divide. Tissue cysts vary in size from younger ones that contain only a few bradyzoites to older cysts that contain several thousand bradyzoites and may reach more than 100 μm (see Fig. 268–1*C*). They appear spheric in the brain and conform to the shape of muscle fibers in heart and skeletal muscles. The central nervous system (CNS), eye, and skeletal, smooth, and heart muscles appear to be the most common sites of latent infection.[19] Because of this persistence in tissues, the demonstration of cysts in histologic sections does not necessarily mean that the infection was recently acquired or that it is clinically relevant. Cysts stain well with periodic acid–Schiff, Wright-Giemsa, Gomori–methenamine silver, and immunoperoxidase stains. Cysts in meat are rendered nonviable by γ-irradiation (0.4 kGy),[20] heating meat throughout to 67°C, and freezing to −20°C for 24 hours and then thawing.[21, 22]

Although the tachyzoite form appears to be indiscriminate in the type of host cell parasitized, it has been suggested that in brain tissue there is a predilection for cyst formation to occur predominantly within neurons.[23, 24] However, it has been shown that cysts can form within astrocytes cultured in vitro.[25] In an electron microscopic study of the pathologic changes in brains of infected mice, cysts were observed to remain intracellular throughout the period of study (22 months).[26] The observation that cysts persist only within cells is, however, controversial.[27] It has been proposed that the growth of cysts results in the degeneration and death of the host cell[25, 28] and thus that the majority of cysts in the brain are located extracellularly. Whether cysts are intracellular or extracellular in the brain is important for the design of drugs against this form of the parasite. There is compelling evidence to suggest that bradyzoites can exit otherwise intact cysts and invade contiguous cells (where they convert to the tachyzoite form). This is the likely explanation for the appearance of "daughter" cysts or clumps of cysts in the brain (see Fig. 268–1*C*).[29] In addition, it has been demonstrated that parasites with morphologic characteristics of tachyzoites exist in tissue cysts along with organisms that have the characteristic morphology of bradyzoites.[30, 31]

Stage Conversion

Tachyzoites and bradyzoites are phenotypically different.[17] Tachyzoites multiply rapidly and synchronously, forming rosettes and lysing the cell, whereas the more slowly replicating bradyzoites form tissue cysts. Molecules are expressed in a stage-specific manner and are responsible for certain of the phenotypic differences between tachyzoites and bradyzoites. There are major differences in the energy metabolism and antigenic structure of tachyzoites and bradyzoites that suggest the existence of stage-specific metabolic pathways and other molecules that allow the parasite to be maintained in the host.[32, 33] Interferon-γ (IFN-γ) and nitric oxide (NO) are triggers for the conversion of tachyzoites to bradyzoites in vitro and perhaps in vivo as well.[34, 35]

TRANSMISSION AND EPIDEMIOLOGY

T. gondii infection is a worldwide zoonosis. The organism infects herbivorous, omnivorous, and carnivorous animals, including birds. Infection in humans most commonly occurs through the ingestion of raw or undercooked meat that contains cysts, through the ingestion of water or food contaminated with oocysts, or congenitally through transplacental transmission from a mother who acquired her infection during gestation (Fig. 268–2). Less common are transmission by transplantation of an infected organ or transfusion of contaminated blood cells. Transmission has also occurred by accidental sticks[36] with contaminated needles or through exposing open lesions or mucosal surfaces to the parasite.[37] Coprophagous invertebrates, including cockroaches, filth flies, earthworms, snails, and slugs, may serve as transport hosts for the oocyst to reach the gastrointestinal tract of animals or humans.

Because the sexual cycle of the parasite takes place in the small bowel of members of the cat family, cats play a significant role as powerful amplifiers of the infection in nature (see "Oocyst").[37] Epidemiologic surveys have revealed that in most areas of the world, the presence of cats is of primary importance for the transmission of the parasite. *T. gondii* infection in humans has been found to be absent in studies of geographic locales where there are no cats. The excretion of oocysts has been reported to occur in approximately 1% of cats in diverse areas of the world.[37]

Although the ingestion of raw or undercooked meat that contains viable *T. gondii* cysts will result in infection, the relative frequency

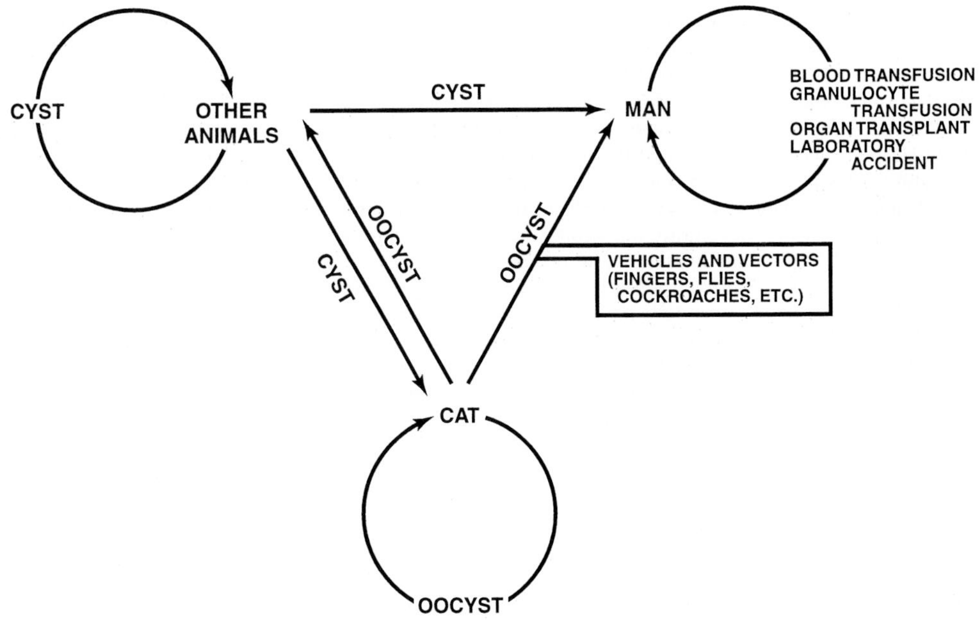

FIGURE 268–2. Transmission and life cycle of *Toxoplasma gondii.* (From Knick JA, Remington JS. Toxoplasmosis in the adult—an overview. N Engl J Med. 1978; 298:550–553. Copyright © 1978 Massachusetts Medical Society. All rights reserved.)

with which this occurs in relation to the frequency of infection due to ingestion of oocysts is unclear. For instance, in countries such as France, where eating undercooked meat is common and the prevalence of the infection is high, meat may be an important cause of the infection. (It was in Paris, France, that the meat-to-human hypothesis of spread of *T. gondii* was proved.[38]) In contrast are countries such as those in Central America, where the prevalence of the infection in humans is high but the ingestion of undercooked meat is uncommon.

The ingestion of tissue cysts in infected pork may be one of the major sources of the infection in humans.[39] The only study on the prevalence of *T. gondii* in samples of meat used for human consumption (obtained from grocery stores) was performed in the United States in the 1960s.[40] The parasite was isolated from 32% of pork chops and 4% of lamb chops; there were no isolations from beef.[40] The actual prevalence of the infection in various types of meat is presently unknown. Serologic surveys indicate that *T. gondii* antibodies are widely prevalent in swine in the United States.[41] Little is known about the prevalence of *T. gondii* infection in lambs. Although *T. gondii* infection of sheep is widely prevalent, the public health importance of the infection in adult sheep is not known; in the United States, meat from adult sheep is not usually used for human consumption.[37]

Although *T. gondii* cysts may be found in edible tissues of chickens, poultry products are probably not important in the transmission of *T. gondii* to humans because they are usually frozen for storage and are thoroughly cooked to avoid diseases that could be caused by contamination by other organisms.[37] The parasite has been isolated from chicken eggs.[42] Reports of suspect transmission by unpasteurized goat's milk have appeared.[43, 44] Venison and meat from other wild animals have also been the source of infection in humans. The parasite has been found in muscles of naturally infected deer, bear, moose, and pronghorn, and *T. gondii* can encyst in elk. The prevalence of *T. gondii* antibodies among black bears in the United States has been found to be as high as 80%. Thus, wild animal meat can serve as a source of organisms for hunters and their families, especially when care is not taken while eviscerating and handling the game or when meat from these animals is served undercooked or uncooked.[37]

The ingestion of vegetables and other food products contaminated with oocysts probably accounts for infection in seropositive vegetarians. Although the isolation of tachyzoites from secretions of people with the acute infection has been claimed, human-to-human transmission of infection by this route has not been established. Outbreaks within families and other groups are common,[45–47] but there is no evidence of direct human-to-human transmission other than from mother to fetus.

In humans, the incidence of *T. gondii* antibodies increases with increasing age; the incidence does not vary significantly between sexes. The incidence tends to be less in cold regions, in hot and arid areas, and at high elevations. Slaughterhouse workers may have an increased risk for infection. In many populations such as in El Salvador and France, the prevalence of seropositivity is as high as 75% by the fourth decade of life. Serologic surveys indicate that 3 to 70% of healthy adults in the United States have been infected with *T. gondii.* In general, the incidence of the infection varies with the population group and geographic locale. The prevalence of *T. gondii* antibodies in U.S. military recruits decreased by one third between 1965 and 1989;[48] the crude seropositivity rate among recruits from 49 states was 9.5% in 1989 compared with 14.4% in 1965.[48]

For discussion of congenital transmission, see "*Toxoplasma gondii* Infection in Pregnancy."

The seroprevalence of antibodies among different populations may change significantly with time. This is of particular importance in women of childbearing age. For example, in the 1970s, 24% of women in the childbearing age group in the Palo Alto, California, area were seropositive. The prevalence rate in 1998 was 10% (seroprevalence rates in the United States among such women range from 3% to greater than 35%). Seroprevalence rates greater than 50% are present in women of childbearing age in much of Western Europe, Africa, and South and Central America.[49–51] An individual moving from an area of low prevalence of infection to an area of high prevalence at or before the time of childbearing potential may be at increased risk.[52]

T. gondii may survive in citrated blood at 4°C for as long as 50 days, and infection has been transmitted by the transfusion of whole blood or white blood cells. Blood and blood products from patients with chronic myelogenous leukemia (e.g., for leukocyte transfusions) may pose a special risk.[53] The transmission of infection by organ transplantation has been documented and may result from the transplantation of an organ (e.g., heart) from a seropositive donor to a seronegative recipient.[54, 55] In bone marrow transplant recipients, toxoplasmosis almost always is a result of recrudescence of a latent infection rather than from the transplant.[5, 56–58]

The incidence of TE among HIV-infected individuals directly correlates with the prevalence of *T. gondii* antibodies among the general HIV-infected population, the degree of immunosuppression in the HIV-infected individuals, and the institution of effective prophylactic treatment regimens against the development of TE. In the United States, *T. gondii* seropositivity among HIV-infected patients varies from 10 to 45%.[6] In contrast, the seropositivity rate is approximately 50 to 78% in certain areas of Western Europe and Africa.[59, 60] In a study by Belanger and colleagues in France between 1988 and 1996, 1215 of 1683 (72.2%) HIV-infected patients had serologic evidence of exposure to *T. gondii* (personal communication to JSR, 1998). During the study period, the overall incidence of toxoplasmosis was estimated to be 1.53 per 100 patient-years (py). The incidence of toxoplasmosis increased from 0.68 per 100 py in 1988 to 2.1 per 100 py in 1992 and fell thereafter to 0.19 per 100 py in 1995. A similar decrease in the incidence of toxoplasmosis in AIDS patients has been observed in other countries including the United States, most likely due to the routine use of prophylactic drug regimens and in some countries due to the use of highly active antiretroviral therapy. For example, only 3 (3.8%) of 80 patients receiving trimethoprim-sulfamethoxazole (TMP-SMX) for primary prophylaxis of toxoplasmosis developed TE, whereas 72 (17.2%) of 419 patients without TMP-SMX developed TE.[61]

In the United States, TE has been reported in 1 to 5% of patients with AIDS.[62, 63] TE has been reported to be the index AIDS diagnosis in 44 to 58% of HIV-infected patients with TE.[62, 63] These figures are considerably higher in geographic locales that have populations with a higher prevalence of *T. gondii* seropositivity. Such surveillance data likely underestimate the true prevalence of toxoplasmosis in AIDS patients because they frequently do not include all AIDS-related illnesses in a single patient.

In the AIDS population in the United States, TE and toxoplasmosis involving other organs are almost always due to reactivation of a chronic (latent) infection that results from the progressive immune dysfunction that develops in these patients.[6] Thus, the incidence of TE is directly related to, or directly correlates with, the prevalence of *T. gondii* antibodies in a given population and the stages of HIV infection in individuals in that population. It is estimated that 20 to 47% of HIV-infected, *T. gondii*–seropositive individuals will ultimately develop TE.[6, 64–66] Thus, in geographic locales with a high *T. gondii* seroprevalence, 25 to 50% of all AIDS patients who do not receive appropriate prophylactic drugs will develop TE.[6] For example, in France, TE was the AIDS-defining diagnosis in 16% of patients reported with AIDS,[67] and 37% of AIDS patients had evidence of TE at autopsy.[68]

Within the United States, there are significant differences in the incidence of TE both in different geographic regions and among various ethnic groups.[62, 69] Toxoplasmosis in AIDS patients was reported to occur three times more frequently in Florida than in other areas of the United States[62]; in AIDS patients of Haitian origin in Florida, 12 to 40% developed TE.[6, 62] These differences in incidence rates reflect regional and ethnic population differences in the prevalence of *T. gondii* seropositivity.[6, 62]

Of interest is the low reported incidence of TE from Africa despite *T. gondii* seroprevalence rates of 32 to 75%. A lack of autopsy data and a lack of neuroimaging studies may contribute to the low incidence reported. It has also been suggested that because of poor access to medical care, many HIV-infected patients in Africa succumb to infection with organisms such as *Mycobacterium tuberculosis* before they develop the opportunistic infections associated with the advanced stage of HIV infection, including toxoplasmosis. However, in one autopsy series of 175 patients with AIDS-defining abnormalities from the Ivory Coast, the prevalence of TE was 21%.[70]

The risk of toxoplasmosis among HIV-infected patients who have antibodies against *T. gondii* can be estimated by their CD4$^+$ T-cell count. In a study in France, in patients not receiving prophylaxis against *T. gondii* infection whose CD4$^+$ T-cell counts were greater than 100/mm^3, 18% developed toxoplasmosis by 12 months and 28% by 18 months.[71] In contrast, the figures were 47 and 70%, respectively, if the CD4$^+$ T-cell counts were below 100/mm^3.

T. gondii infection may be acquired after the acquisition of HIV infection. Seroconversion rates between 2 and 5.5% have been reported in patients followed for periods up to 28 months.

Even before the emergence of AIDS, TE had been recognized as a cause of incapacitating disease and death among immunosuppressed patients,[5, 72] especially in those whose underlying disease or therapy caused a deficiency in cell-mediated immunity. Patients with hematologic malignancies, especially those with Hodgkin's disease, are at a particularly higher risk to develop recrudescence of the infection. Among organ transplantation patients, those with heart, lung, kidney, and bone marrow transplants develop toxoplasmosis at a higher rate.[5, 56, 57, 72]

PATHOGENESIS AND IMMUNITY

T. gondii multiplies intracellularly at the site of invasion (the gastrointestinal tract appears to be the major route for and the initial site of infection in nature); bradyzoites released from tissue cysts or sporozoites released from oocysts penetrate and multiply within intestinal epithelial cells. Organisms may spread first to the mesenteric lymph nodes and then to distant organs by invasion of lymphatics and blood.[10] *T. gondii* infects all cell types, and cell invasion occurs as an active process.[73] Survival of tachyzoites is due to the formation of a parasitophorous vacuole that protects against lysosomal fusion [74] with the vacuole, and consequent acidification does not occur.[75] Active invasion of macrophages by tachyzoites does not trigger oxidative killing mechanisms.[7] With the appearance of humoral and cellular immunity, only those parasites protected by an intracellular habitat or within cysts survive. An effective immune response significantly reduces the number of tachyzoites in all tissues.[11] Tachyzoites are killed by reactive oxygen intermediates,[77] acidification,[75] osmotic fluctuations, reactive nitrogen intermediates,[78] intracellular tryptophan depletion,[79] and specific antibody combined with complement.[80, 81] Thereafter, tachyzoites are rarely demonstrable histologically in tissues of infected humans.

Cyst formation takes place in multiple organs and tissues during the first week of infection. Despite the ability to isolate *T. gondii* from normal brains of chronically infected humans, the cyst form is rarely observed in histologic preparations; it has been isolated from both brain and skeletal muscle in 10% of 52 *T. gondii*–seropositive patients who at autopsy had no clinical or pathologic evidence of the infection.[19] The cyst form is responsible for residual (chronic or latent) infection and persists primarily in brain, skeletal and heart muscle, and eye.[19, 82, 83]

Although residual infection is higher in brains of laboratory mice and rats than in other tissues, experimental data do not support the concept that *T. gondii* is neurotropic. It is unclear whether *T. gondii* penetrates the brain more easily than other organs of some animals or whether it is more difficult for their brains, as an immunologically privileged site, to eradicate the organism during the initial acute infection and once residual infection has been established.[84]

In immunocompetent individuals, the initial infection and the resultant seeding of different organs leads to a chronic or latent infection without clinical significance. This chronic stage of infection corresponds to the asymptomatic persistence of the cyst form in multiple tissues. It is believed that periodically, bradyzoites are released from cysts or that cysts "rupture"; cyst disruption in this setting is a clinically silent process effectively contained by the immune system and likely results in small inflammatory nodules, with a limited degree of neuronal cell death and architectural damage.[85]

Whereas toxoplasmosis in severely immunodeficient individuals may be caused by primary infection, it most often is the result of recrudescence of a latent infection. It is widely held that reactivation is the result of disruption of the cyst form followed by the uncontrolled proliferation of organisms and tissue destruction. In individuals with deficient cell-mediated immunity, rapid, uncontrolled proliferation of *T. gondii* results in progressively enlarging necrotic lesions.[86, 87] It has been postulated that damage of any organ in these patients including the brain, eye, heart, lung, skeletal muscle, gastrointestinal tract, and pancreas can result directly from cyst disruption in the parenchyma of the organ itself or from cyst disruption elsewhere in the body followed by subsequent spread to that organ.[88] Hematogenous spread is supported by the observation of the development of simultaneous lesions in the brain and the presence of parasitemia in 14 to 38% of patients.[89, 90] Lymphocytes obtained from patients with AIDS have impaired production of IFN-γ [91] and interleukin-2 (IL-2)[92] in response to stimulation with *T. gondii* antigens. Serum IFN-γ levels have been reported to be lower in AIDS patients with TE than in immunocompetent patients with toxoplasmic lymphadenopathy.[93] Treatment of monocytes and monocyte-derived macrophages from AIDS patients with IFN-γ enhances their activity against *T. gondii*.[94, 95] Coinfection with other opportunistic pathogens may predispose to reactivation; murine cytomegalovirus (CMV) induces reactivation of latent *T. gondii* infection in the lung.[96]

Infection with *T. gondii* induces both humoral and cell-mediated immunity responses. A well-orchestrated and effective systemic immune response is responsible for the early disappearance of *T. gondii* from peripheral blood during the acute infection and limits the parasite burden in other organs. Immunity in the immunocompetent host is lifelong. Reinfection, which likely occurs in humans, does not appear to result in clinically apparent disease.[11]

Adoptive transfer experiments in murine models have revealed that immune T cells (primarily a helper T cell 1 [Th1] response) confer resistance against *T. gondii*.[97–101] $CD8^+$ T cells are primarily responsible for this resistance, although significant protection is also conferred by $CD4^+$ T lymphocytes.[100, 101] Both immune $CD4^+$ and $CD8^+$ T cells can lyse *T. gondii*–infected cells.[102–105] These T-cell subsets synergize with macrophages and natural killer and lymphokine-activated killer cells in protective mechanisms.

A rapid and remarkable αβ T-cell response plays an important role in the early events of the immune response against the parasite.[106] Both $CD4^+$ αβ T cells with naive ($CD45RA^+$) and memory ($CD45RO^+$) phenotypes from seronegative individuals have been shown to proliferate after incubation with *T. gondii*.[106] Costimulatory ligands such as CD80 and CD86 play a crucial role in the initiation and maintenance of the immune response.[107] A remarkable γδ T-cell response occurs in the infection in humans and may also be an important component of the early immune response.[108–111] Human γδ T cells can be cytotoxic for *T. gondii*–infected cells and produce IFN-γ, IL-2, and tumor necrosis factor-α when incubated with cells infected with the parasite.[108]

Cytokines play a critical role in defense against the infection and are important in the pathogenesis of toxoplasmosis and TE.[112, 113] Tumor necrosis factor-α is required for triggering of IFN-γ–mediated activation of macrophages for *T. gondii*–cidal activity[114] and for NO (an inhibitor of *T. gondii* replication) production by macrophages.[115] IL-10 has been shown to deactivate macrophages and result in reduced in vitro killing of *T. gondii*. IL-12 enhances survival of T-cell–deficient mice during *T. gondii* infection, possibly through increased production of IFN-γ by natural killer cells.[116] IFN-γ has been shown to play a significant role in the prevention or development of TE in mice.[117–119] The administration of monoclonal antibody against IFN-γ to chronically infected mice resulted in a dramatic worsening in the degree of encephalitis.[117] In mice with active TE, treatment with IFN-γ significantly reduced the inflammatory response and numbers of tachyzoites.[119]

Several hypotheses have been proposed to explain the role of IFN-γ in host resistance to *T. gondii*. Involvement of reactive nitrogen intermediates (including NO) is suggested by the observation that L-NMMA, a competitive analogue of L-arginine, simultaneously inhibits NO synthesis and intracellular tachyzoite killing by cytokine-activated peritoneal macrophages and microglial cells.[78, 120, 121] In addition, mice in which NO synthesis is impaired as a result of genetic disruptions of the IFN-γ or interferon regulatory factor-1 genes succumb to the acute infection.[122, 123] Similar enhanced susceptibility was observed in mice treated with the reactive nitrogen intermediate inhibitor aminoguanidine[124] and in nitric oxide synthase–deficient mice.[125] The protective role of NO appears to be tissue-specific rather than systemic.[125] Because control of the acute infection in vivo was unaffected by nitric oxide synthase deficiency, the major role of reactive nitrogen intermediates appears to be to maintain control of established infections in this mouse model.[125]

The administration of tumor necrosis factor-α–neutralizing antibody to infected mice caused the death of the mice and an increase in the number of *T. gondii* cysts in the brains of survivors.[126, 127] IL-4 and IL-6, which are usually considered downregulatory cytokines, have been shown to be important in resistance against TE in the murine model.[128, 129] IL-7 has also been shown to have a protective role against *T. gondii* in mice.[130] During the early stages of the infection, IL-12, IL-1, and tumor necrosis factor act in concert with IL-15 to stimulate natural killer cells to produce IFN-γ.

Immunoglobulin G (IgG), IgM, IgA, and IgE antibodies are produced in response to the infection. Extracellular tachyzoites are lysed by specific antibody when it is combined with complement[80, 81]; this phenomenon is used in the Sabin-Feldman dye test.[80] In mice, humoral immunity results in limited protection against less virulent strains of *T. gondii,* but not against virulent strains.[131]

Both astrocytes and microglia likely play important roles in the immune response against *T. gondii* within the CNS. In the early stages of TE in both humans and mice, there is a remarkable and widespread astrocytosis restricted to areas in which the parasite is detected.[132] Whereas *T. gondii* can invade, survive, and multiply within astrocytes, they are killed by activated microglia.[120, 133, 134]

GENETIC SUSCEPTIBILITY

The observations in mice that genetic factors in the host contribute to the development and severity of TE[135–142] and the fact that not all HIV-infected patients with positive *T. gondii* serologic findings develop TE suggested the possibility that genetic factors may also play a role in the predisposition of AIDS patients for this disease.[143] HLA-DQ3 was found to occur significantly more frequently in white North American AIDS patients with TE (85%) than in the general white population (51.8%; $p = 0.007$, corrected $p = 0.028$) or randomly selected control AIDS patients who had not developed TE (40%; $p = 0.016$).[143] In contrast, the frequency of HLA-DQ1 was lower in TE patients than in healthy controls (40% versus 66.5%, $p = 0.027$); this difference, however, did not reach statistical significance when corrected for the number of variables tested. Thus, HLA-DQ3 appears to be a genetic marker of susceptibility to the development of TE in AIDS patients, and DQ1 may be a resistance marker. These HLA associations with disease suggest that the development of TE in HIV-infected patients is regulated by genes in or near the HLA complex. Studies will be required to determine if genetic control of susceptibility to TE is similar in white individuals from countries outside North America and in other racial groups.

PATHOLOGY

Our knowledge of the pathology of infection in humans has come largely from autopsy studies in severely infected infants and immunodeficient patients. Data in immunocompetent adults are limited almost entirely to results obtained from biopsy specimens from lymph nodes.

Damage to the CNS by *T. gondii* is characterized by multiple foci of enlarging necrosis and microglia nodules.[8] Necrosis is the most prominent feature of the disease because of vascular involvement by the lesions. In infants, periaqueductal and periventricular vasculitis and necrosis are distinctive of toxoplasmosis. The necrotic areas may calcify and lead to striking radiographic findings suggestive but not pathognomonic of toxoplasmosis. Hydrocephalus may result from obstruction of the aqueduct of Sylvius or foramen of Monro. Tachyzoites and cysts are seen in and adjacent to necrotic foci near or in glial nodules, in perivascular regions, and in cerebral tissue uninvolved by inflammatory change. Periaqueductal and periventricular vasculitis with necrosis has been reported to be pathognomonic of toxoplasmosis.[144] The necrotic brain tissue autolyzes and is gradually shed into the ventricles. The protein content of such ventricular fluid may be in the range of grams per deciliter and has been shown to contain significant amounts of *T. gondii* antigens.

The presence of multiple brain abscesses is the most characteristic feature of TE in severely immunodeficient patients and particularly characteristic in patients with AIDS.[5, 145] Brain abscesses in AIDS patients are characterized by three histologic zones. The central area is avascular. Surrounding this is an intermediate hyperemic area with a prominent inflammatory infiltrate and perivascular cuffing by lymphocytes, plasma cells, and macrophages. Many tachyzoites and, at times, cysts as well, appear at the margins of necrotic areas. An outer peripheral zone contains *T. gondii* cysts.[146] In the areas around the abscesses, edema, vasculitis, hemorrhage and cerebral infarction secondary to vascular involvement may also be present.[147] Important associated features in TE are the presence of arteritis, perivascular cuffing, and astrocytosis. Because these findings may also be present in patients with viral encephalitis, immunoperoxidase staining is important for differentiating these pathologic processes. Widespread, poorly demarcated, and confluent areas of necrosis with minimal inflammatory response are seen in some patients.[147] Identification of tachyzoites is pathognomonic of active infection, but their visualization may be difficult in hematoxylin-and-eosin–stained sections. The use of immunoperoxidase staining markedly improves the identification of both cyst and tachyzoite forms and highlights the presence of *T. gondii* antigens (Fig. 268–3*A*).[18] *T. gondii* DNA can be amplified from cerebrospinal fluid (CSF) or brain biopsy specimens of patients with TE.[148]

At autopsy in AIDS patients with TE, there is almost universal involvement of the cerebral hemispheres and a remarkable predilection for the basal ganglia.[6] In a consecutive autopsy study of 204 patients who died of AIDS, 46 (23%) had morphologic evidence of cerebral toxoplasmosis. In 38 (83%) of the 46 cases, histologic evidence of toxoplasmosis was restricted to the CNS. The cerebral hemispheres were affected in 91% of cases and the rostral basal ganglia in 78%.[147] In cases of congenital toxoplasmosis, necrosis of the brain is most intense in the cortex and basal ganglia and at times in the periventricular areas.[8]

A "diffuse form" of TE has been described with histopathologic findings of widespread microglial nodules without abscess formation in the gray matter of the cerebrum, cerebellum, and brain stem.[149] In these patients, involvement by *T. gondii* was confirmed by immunoperoxidase stains that demonstrated cysts and tachyzoites. In diffuse TE, the clinical course progresses rapidly to death. It has been postulated that in such cases, the lack of characteristic findings on computed tomography (CT) or magnetic resonance imaging (MRI) studies is due to insufficient time for abscesses to form before death occurs. Leptomeningitis is infrequent and, when present, occurs over adjacent areas of encephalitis. Spinal cord necrotizing lesions are seen at autopsy in approximately 6% of patients with TE.[147] The differential diagnosis of TE lesions includes CNS lymphoma, progressive multifocal leukoencephalopathy, and infection with CMV, *Cryptococcus neoformans, Aspergillus* spp., and *M. tuberculosis.* More than one agent may be present.

Pulmonary toxoplasmosis in the immunodeficient patient may appear in the form of interstitial pneumonitis, necrotizing pneumonitis, consolidation, or pleural effusion, or all of these.[150] The pneumonitis is associated with the development of fibrinous or fibrinopurulent exudate. Tachyzoites may be found in alveolocytes, alveolar macrophages, pleural fluid, or extracellularly within alveolar exudate. *T. gondii* DNA may be demonstrated in bronchoalveolar lavage (BAL) fluid by the polymerase chain reaction (PCR).[151]

Chorioretinitis in AIDS patients is characterized by segmental panophthalmitis and areas of coagulative necrosis associated with cysts and tachyzoites.[9] Numerous organisms in the absence of remarkable inflammation may be seen around thrombosed retinal vessels adjacent to necrotic areas. Multiple and bilateral lesions may occur.[9] Amplification of parasite DNA in both aqueous humor and vitreous fluid has confirmed or supported the diagnosis of toxoplasmic chorioretinitis in AIDS patients.[152]

Toxoplasmic myocarditis is frequently noted at autopsy in AIDS patients but is usually clinically inapparent,[153] with CNS manifestations predominating.[154] Focal necrosis with edema and an inflammatory infiltrate is typical,[153] although abscesses may also be noted.[153, 154] Similar histologic findings are seen in the non-AIDS immunodeficient population,[5] and in both groups cardiac myocytes may be packed with tachyzoites (to produce pseudocysts) in the absence of an inflammatory response.

Myositis due to *T. gondii* has been reported in as high as 4% of HIV-infected patients who present with neuromuscular symptoms, and the same percentage has been observed in autopsy series of AIDS patients in whom a systematic histologic evaluation of the skeletal muscle was performed.[155] Successful isolation from skeletal muscle biopsies has been reported.[156] Microscopy has revealed necrotic muscle fibers with a variable inflammatory reaction. Skeletal muscle involvement has also been reported in the non-AIDS immunodeficient patient.[5, 157]

Extensive involvement of the gastrointestinal tract in AIDS patients may occur with tremendous variation in the inflammatory response.[158–160] Hemorrhagic gastritis and colitis have been described.[161] Other organs reported to be involved during toxoplasmosis include the liver,[162] pancreas,[163] seminiferous tubules,[164] prostate,[164] adrenals,[165] kidneys,[166] and bone marrow.[167]

The histopathologic changes in toxoplasmic lymphadenitis in immunocompetent individuals are frequently distinctive and often diagnostic (see Fig. 268–3*B*).[168] There is a typical triad of findings: a reactive follicular hyperplasia (see Fig. 268–3*B* [A]), irregular clusters of epithelioid histiocytes encroaching on and blurring the margins of the germinal centers (see Fig. 268–3*B* [B]), and focal distention of sinuses with monocytoid cells (see Fig. 268–3*B* [C]). Langhans giant cells, granulomas, microabscesses, and foci of necrosis are not typically seen. Rarely, tachyzoites or cysts are demonstrable. *T. gondii* DNA has infrequently been amplified from lymph node tissue.[169]

Eye infection in immunocompetent patients produces acute chorioretinitis characterized by severe inflammation and necrosis.[9] Granulomatous inflammation of the choroid is secondary to the necrotizing retinitis. There may be exudation into the vitreous or invasion of the vitreous by a budding mass of capillaries. Although rare, tachyzoites and cysts may be demonstrated in the retina. The pathogenesis of recurrent chorioretinitis is controversial. One school proposes that rupture of cysts releases viable organisms that induce necrosis and inflammation, whereas another school contends that chorioretinitis results from a hypersensitivity reaction triggered by unknown causes.[9]

Biopsy-proven toxoplasmic myocarditis and polymyositis in the setting of acute toxoplasmosis have been reported in otherwise immunocompetent individuals and in patients on corticosteroids (see Fig. 268–3*C* and 3*D*).[157]

CLINICAL MANIFESTATIONS

Toxoplasmosis describes the clinical or pathologic disease caused by *T. gondii* and is distinct from *T. gondii* infection, which is asymptomatic in the vast majority of immunocompetent patients.

Toxoplasmosis is conveniently considered in five categories: (1) acquired in the immunocompetent patient, (2) acquired or reactivated in the immunodeficient patient, (3) ocular, (4) in pregnancy, and (5) congenital. In any category, the clinical presentations are not specific for toxoplasmosis, and a wide differential diagnosis must be entertained. Furthermore, methods of diagnosis and their interpretations may differ for each clinical category.

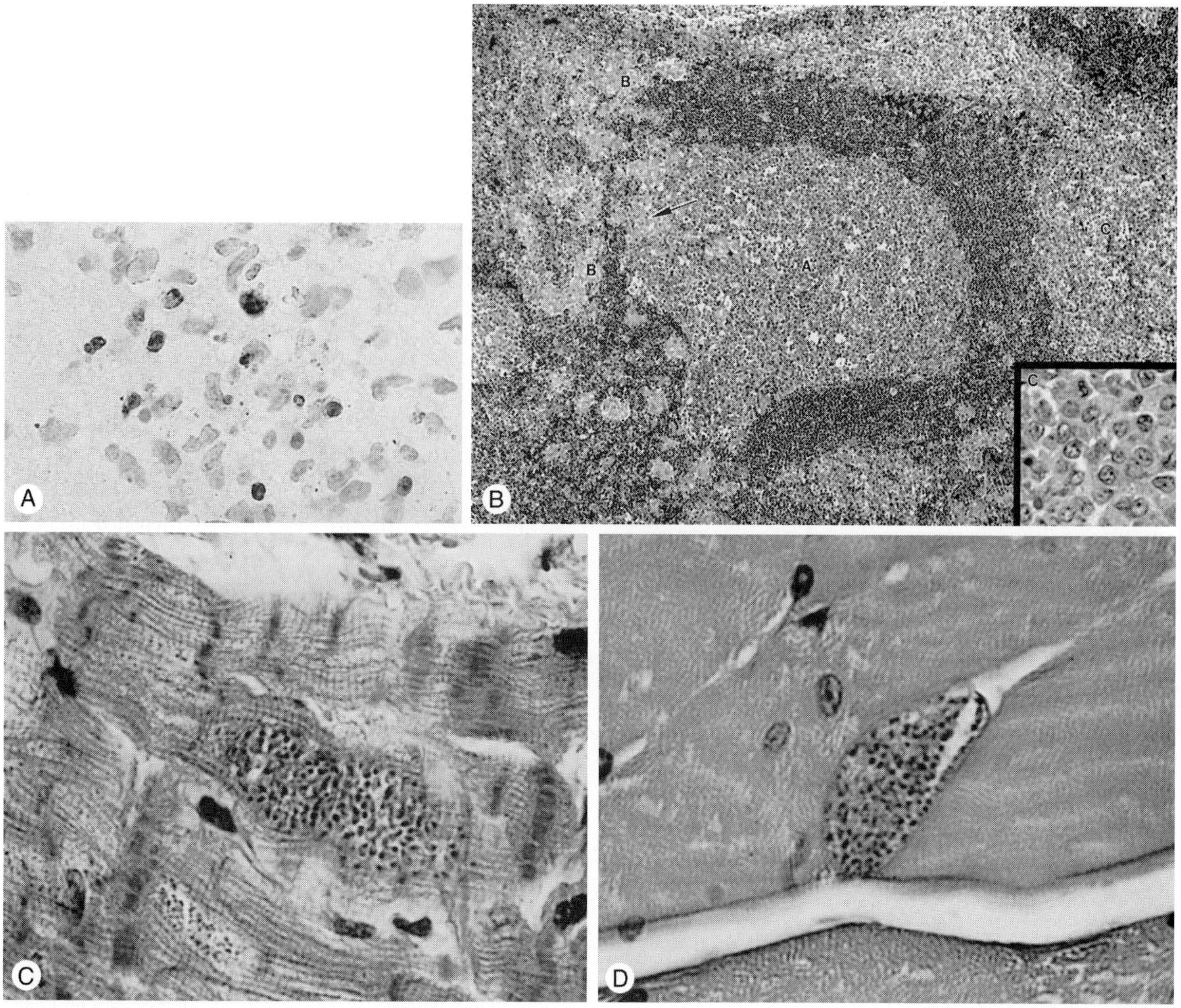

FIGURE 268–3. Histologic features of *Toxoplasma gondii* in humans. *A*, Positive immunoperoxidase stain of a brain biopsy specimen in a patient with acquired immunodeficiency syndrome and toxoplasmic encephalitis. *B*, Hematoxylin and eosin (H&E) stain of a lymph node biopsy specimen from an immunocompetent patient demonstrating the classic morphologic triad of toxoplasmic lymphadenitis. Reactive germinal center (A). Epithelioid histiocytes encroaching on the germinal center *(arrow)* (B). Sinus distended by monocytoid B cells (C) (see insert) (see text under "Pathology"). (Courtesy of Dr. Ronald F. Dorfman, Department of Pathology, Stanford University, Palo Alto, Calif.) *C*, H&E stain of a right ventricle endomyocardial biopsy specimen from a patient with toxoplasmic myocarditis. Organisms are seen within myocytes (see text under "Clinical Manifestations"). *D*, H&E stain of a right quadriceps muscle biopsy specimen depicting tissue cyst from the same patient as shown in *B*. She also developed toxoplasmic polymyositis.

Toxoplasmosis in the Immunocompetent Patient

Only 10 to 20% of cases of *T. gondii* infection in adults and children are symptomatic.[170] Most often, toxoplasmosis manifests as asymptomatic cervical lymphadenopathy, but any or all lymph node groups may be enlarged. On palpation, the nodes are usually discrete and nontender, rarely more than 3 cm in diameter, may vary in firmness, and do not suppurate.[171] However, the nodes may be tender or matted. Fever, malaise, night sweats, myalgias, sore throat, maculopapular rash, hepatosplenomegaly, or small numbers of atypical lymphocytes (less than 10%) may be present. The clinical picture may resemble infectious mononucleosis or CMV infection, but toxoplasmosis probably causes no more than 1% of mononucleosis syndromes.[172] Retroperitoneal or mesenteric lymphadenopathy may produce abdominal pain.

It appears that toxoplasmic chorioretinitis as a manifestation of the acute acquired infection is more common than previously recognized.[173, 174] Chorioretinitis in the setting of acute acquired toxoplasmosis can occur either sporadically or in the context of an epidemic of acute toxoplasmosis.[46, 47, 173–176] For further discussion of this clinical entity, see "Ocular Toxoplasmosis in Immunocompetent Patients."

In most cases the clinical course of toxoplasmosis in the immunocompetent patient is benign and self-limited. Symptoms, if present, usually resolve within a few months and rarely persist beyond 12 months. Lymphadenopathy may wax and wane for months and, in unusual cases, for 1 year or longer. A form of the disease characterized by chronic lymphadenopathy has been described.[171, 177] Rarely, an apparently healthy person develops clinically overt, potentially fatal disseminated disease, with myocarditis, pneumonitis, hepatitis, or encephalitis. None of the clinical presentations of acquired toxoplasmosis is distinctive; the differential diagnosis of toxoplasmic lymphadenitis includes lymphoma, infectious mononucleosis, CMV "mononucleosis," cat-scratch disease, sarcoidosis, tuberculosis, tularemia, metastatic carcinoma, and leukemia. Acute acquired toxoplasmosis associated with multiple-organ involvement has been reported to mimic other causes of pneumonitis, hepatitis, myocarditis, polymyositis, or fever of unknown origin in apparently immunocompetent patients.[170]

T. gondii has been estimated to cause 3 to 7% of clinically significant lymphadenopathy.[171] The major diagnostic confusion with toxoplasmic lymphadenopathy occurs with Hodgkin's disease and the lymphomas. The diagnosis of recently acquired toxoplasmic lymphadenopathy is easily made serologically, but unfortunately, physicians often do not consider this diagnosis in patients with lymphadenopathy. Serologic test titers diagnostic of acute *T. gondii* infection are often obtained after histologic examination of a biopsied node has suggested the possibility of toxoplasmosis.[178]

Myocarditis as a manifestation of acute toxoplasmosis has been reported in relatively few patients.[157, 179, 180] It may occur clinically as an isolated disease process or as part of a variety of manifestations of the disseminated infection. Manifestations include arrhythmias, pericarditis, and heart failure.[157]

Myositis resembling polymyositis as a manifestation of acute toxoplasmosis has also been reported infrequently.[157, 181–183] Dermatomyositis has been associated with toxoplasmosis, although a cause-and-effect relationship has not been proved.[184, 185]

The clinical features of toxoplasmic myocarditis and polymyositis are illustrated by a case in which both were present in the same individual.[157] A 43-year-old woman presented with cardiogenic pulmonary edema followed by progressive sinus bradycardia and subsequent complete heart block; viral myocarditis was considered the most likely diagnosis. During the ensuing months, she developed proximal muscle weakness while being treated with corticosteroids; an endomyocardial biopsy (see Fig. 268–3*C*) and a quadriceps muscle biopsy (see Fig. 268–3*D*) revealed *T. gondii.*[157] Her symptoms improved on pyrimethamine-sulfadiazine. One year after her initial presentation with myocarditis, retinal lesions characteristic of toxoplasmic chorioretinitis were observed in her right eye. Serologic test results and follow-up were consistent with recently acquired toxoplasmosis.[157]

Toxoplasmosis in the Immunodeficient Patient

The course of toxoplasmosis in almost all immunocompetent individuals is relatively benign, but it is a serious and often life-threatening disease in immunodeficient patients.

Toxoplasmosis in the non-AIDS immunodeficient patient has been reviewed in detail elsewhere.[5] A total of 121 patients with organ transplants or underlying malignancy (mainly Hodgkin's disease and other lymphomas) has been reported in the literature; 76% had CNS, 38% myocardial, and 23% pulmonary involvement. A total of 58% of the organ transplant recipients had myocardial involvement with *T. gondii*. Death or serious deterioration was almost universal if treatment was not instituted (i.e., 99% of 89 patients). These data highlight the need for a high index of suspicion for toxoplasmosis in immunodeficient patients. Toxoplasmosis in these patients may be due to either newly acquired or reactivated latent infection.[5] Studies in bone marrow transplant recipients suggest that in the vast majority of cases, toxoplasmosis results from reactivation of a latent infection; a small number of cases have been reported in *T. gondii*–seronegative recipients of bone marrow from seropositive donors.[186] Most patients with toxoplasmosis after bone marrow transplantation have had an allogenic transplant and graft-versus-host disease.[57, 186] In heart transplant recipients, toxoplasmosis may result when a seronegative recipient receives a heart from a seropositive donor. Seropositive heart transplant recipients frequently exhibit IgM and IgG antibody titer rises after transplantation without evidence of clinical disease.[187, 188] In the heart transplant recipient, toxoplasmosis may simulate organ rejection. In such cases, toxoplasmosis has been established by endomyocardial biopsy.

Clinical manifestations of toxoplasmosis in AIDS patients commonly reflect involvement of the brain (i.e., TE), the lung (pneumonitis), and the eye (chorioretinitis). Toxoplasmosis with multiorgan involvement manifesting with acute respiratory failure and hemodynamic abnormalities similar to septic shock in these cases has been reported, although septic shock has not been definitely proved to be due to *T. gondii.*[189] TE is the most common presentation of toxoplasmosis in AIDS patients[6] and is a frequent cause of focal CNS lesions in AIDS.[6] A wide range of clinical findings including altered mental state, seizures, weakness, cranial nerve disturbances, sensory abnormalities, cerebellar signs, meningismus, movement disorders, and neuropsychiatric manifestations are seen in TE. The characteristic presentation usually has a subacute onset with focal neurologic abnormalities in 58 to 89% of patients.[145] However, in 15 to 25% of cases, the clinical presentation may be more abrupt, with seizures or cerebral hemorrhage. Most commonly, hemiparesis or abnormalities of speech, or both, are the major initial manifestations. Brain stem involvement often produces cranial nerve lesions, and many patients exhibit cerebral dysfunction with disorientation, altered mental state, lethargy, and coma.[145] Less commonly, parkinsonism, focal dystonia, rubral tremor, hemichorea-hemiballismus, panhypopituitarism, diabetes insipidus, or the syndrome of inappropriate antidiuretic hormone secretion may dominate the clinical picture.[145] In some patients, neuropsychiatric symptoms such as paranoid psychosis, dementia, anxiety, and agitation may be the major manifestations. Similar manifestations of TE are seen in non-AIDS immunodeficient patients, except for a tendency for a higher incidence of nonfocal signs with disseminated disease.[5]

Diffuse TE in AIDS patients[149] has been reported in relatively few patients; its actual incidence is unknown. This form of TE may manifest acutely and can be fatal rapidly; generalized cerebral dysfunction without focal signs is the most common manifestation, and CT scans are within normal limits or reveal cerebral atrophy.

Spinal cord involvement by *T. gondii* in AIDS patients manifests as motor or sensory disturbances of single or multiple limbs, bladder or bowel dysfunctions, or both, and local pain. Patients may present with a clinical syndrome resembling a spinal cord tumor. Reports of cervical myelopathy,[190] thoracic myelopathy,[191] and conus medullaris syndrome[192–194] have been published.

Pulmonary disease due to toxoplasmosis is being increasingly recognized in patients with AIDS who are not receiving appropriate anti-HIV drugs or primary prophylaxis for toxoplasmosis (see "Treatment").[150, 195, 196] The diagnosis may be made by demonstration of the parasite in BAL fluid. In France, the prevalence of pulmonary toxoplasmosis in patients dually infected with HIV and *T. gondii* has been estimated to be approximately 5%.[197] Pulmonary toxoplasmosis occurs mainly in patients with advanced AIDS (mean CD4 count = 40 cells/mm^3 ± 75 SD) and primarily presents as a prolonged febrile illness with cough and dyspnea.[196] Illness may be clinically indistinguishable from *Pneumocystis carinii* pneumonia (PCP), and the mortality even when treated appropriately may be as high as 35%. Extrapulmonary disease may be present in about 50% of cases with toxoplasmic pneumonitis.[189] Often, pulmonary toxoplasmosis is not associated with TE; however, TE may develop after successful treatment of pulmonary toxoplasmosis when therapy is discontinued. The differential diagnosis of toxoplasmic pneumonitis includes PCP and infection with *M. tuberculosis*, *C. neoformans*, *Coccidioides immitis*, and *Histoplasma capsulatum*.

Toxoplasmic chorioretinitis is seen relatively infrequently in AIDS patients[198–200]; it commonly manifests with ocular pain and loss of visual acuity. Funduscopic examination usually demonstrates necrotizing lesions that may be multifocal or bilateral.[198, 201, 202] Overlying vitreal inflammation is often present and may be extensive. The optic nerve may be involved in as many as 10% of cases. Toxoplasmic chorioretinitis in AIDS patients is associated with concurrent TE in up to 63% of patients. The differential diagnosis of toxoplasmic chorioretinitis in AIDS patients includes CMV retinitis, syphilis, herpes simplex, varicella zoster, and fungal infections. The diagnosis relies primarily on clinical findings and the response to anti–*T. gondii* therapy, although definitive diagnosis may be made by demonstration of the organism in retinal biopsies,[201] isolation of the parasite from vitreous aspirates,[203] or amplification of the parasite DNA by PCR.[152]

Other uncommon manifestations of toxoplasmosis in AIDS patients include panhypopituitarism, diabetes insipidus, syndrome of inappropriate antidiuretic hormone secretion, and orchitis. Gastrointestinal involvement may result in abdominal pain, ascites (due to involvement of the stomach, peritoneum, or pancreas) or diarrhea. Acute hepatic failure[162] due to *T. gondii* has been reported as has musculoskeletal involvement.[155]

Ocular Toxoplasmosis in Immunocompetent Patients

T. gondii infection is an important cause of retinitis and probably accounts for at least 25% of posterior uveitis cases in the United States[9] and more than 85% of posterior uveitis cases in southern Brazil.[176] Retinochoroidal lesions may result from congenital or postnatally acquired infection. In both these situations, lesions may occur during the acute or latent (chronic) stage of the infection.[173–176, 204, 205] Patients who present with chorioretinitis as a late sequela of the infection acquired in utero are more frequently in the second and third decades of life (it is rare after the age of 40 years); bilateral disease, old retinal scars, and involvement of the macula are hallmarks of the retinal disease in these cases.[8] By contrast, patients who present with toxoplasmic chorioretinitis in the setting of acute toxoplasmosis are more often between the fourth and sixth decades of life and most often have unilateral involvement, and the eye lesions usually spare the macula and do not present with associated old scars.[174]

Whereas acquired *T. gondii* infection in otherwise healthy adults is most often subclinical, toxoplasmic chorioretinitis in these individuals may result in complete or partial loss of vision, or in glaucoma, and may necessitate enucleation.[8, 206] Acute chorioretinitis may produce symptoms of blurred vision, scotoma, pain, photophobia, and epiphora. Impairment or a loss of central vision occurs when the macula is involved. As inflammation resolves, vision improves, frequently without complete recovery of visual acuity. In most cases, toxoplasmic chorioretinitis is diagnosed by ophthalmologic examination, and empirical therapy directed against the organism is often instituted based on clinical findings and serologic test results. Typical features of toxoplasmic chorioretinitis include intensely white focal lesions with an overlying, intense, vitreous inflammatory reaction (Fig. 268–4). Focal necrotizing retinitis initially appears in the fundus as a yellowish-white, elevated cotton patch with indistinct margins, usually on the posterior pole. The lesions are often in small clusters, and individual lesions in the cluster may be of varied ages. With healing, the lesions pale, atrophy, and develop black pigment (see Fig. 268–4). There can also be an associated, secondary iridocyclitis and increased intraocular pressure.[9] The classic "headlight in the fog" appearance is due to the presence of active retinal lesions with severe vitreous inflammatory reaction. The choroid is secondarily inflamed. Recurrent lesions tend to occur at the borders of chorioretinal scars, and scars are often found in clusters. Panuveitis may accompany chorioretinitis, but isolated anterior uveitis has never been proved to occur.

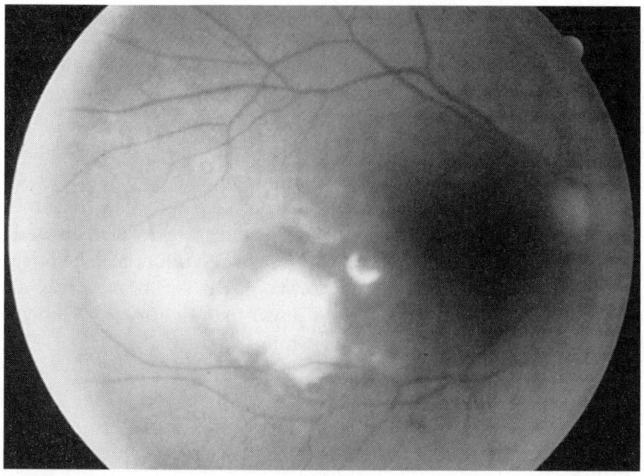

FIGURE 268–4. Toxoplasmic chorioretinitis in an immunocompetent adult. Note the macular scar with dense pigmentation at its borders and a "soft" area of recurrence with overlying inflammatory haze at the temporal (left) border. (Courtesy of Dr. Gary N. Holland, Jules Stein Eye Institute, Los Angeles, Calif.)

Although the morphology of the lesions of acute toxoplasmic chorioretinitis in the setting of postnatally acquired disease may be indistinguishable from the those observed in patients who suffer acute eye disease in later life due to a congenitally acquired infection, it is important to attempt to establish which type of the infection (postnatally acquired or congenital) is occurring in a given patient.[174] It appears that the congenitally acquired disease has a more guarded prognosis. From the public health perspective, it is important epidemiologically to establish whether the patient has the acute acquired infection to initiate efforts to identify the possible source of *T. gondii* infection and whether other individuals who may be at high risk for developing severe, life-threatening disease (i.e., fetuses of serologically negative pregnant women or immunodeficient individuals) shared the same exposure as the individual with acute acquired toxoplasmic chorioretinitis.[46, 47, 174, 207] Serologic tests have been useful in establishing whether such patients have been infected recently.[173, 174] In patients with chorioretinitis and IgG antibodies, additional serologic tests should be performed to determine whether the patient's infection is recently acquired.[174]

T. gondii chorioretinitis may resemble the posterior uveitis of tuberculosis, syphilis, leprosy, or presumed ocular histoplasmosis syndrome.

Atypical clinical and serologic manifestations of toxoplasmic chorioretinitis have been reported most commonly in elderly and in immunodeficient individuals.[152, 208] Patients are considered to have atypical-appearing lesions when one or more of the following features are present: multiple foci of active retinitis, acute retinal necrosis syndrome (vitritis, peripheral retinitis, retinal vasculitis), significant intraretinal hemorrhage, an absence of ophthalmoscopically visible chorioretinal scarring. In patients with atypical lesions or an inadequate clinical response to antitoxoplasma therapy or in whom other diagnostic procedures have not proved helpful, obtaining vitreous fluid (in some cases indicated for therapeutic reasons as well) for PCR should be considered early in the workup (see "Diagnosis").[209]

Congenital Toxoplasmosis

Congenital *T. gondii* infection or toxoplasmosis results from an acute infection, usually asymptomatic, that is acquired by the mother during gestation. A few cases of congenital toxoplasmosis are now known to have occurred in immunocompetent women when they acquired their infection within 6 to 8 weeks before conception.[210–212] Chronically infected women who are immunodeficient (e.g., patients with systemic lupus erythematosus who are being treated with corticosteroids) may transmit the infection to their fetus; the risk of this occurrence is difficult to quantify, but it is probably low. The risk to the fetus does not correlate with whether the infection in the mother was symptomatic or asymptomatic during gestation.

The data accumulated from prospective studies in France indicate that the incidence and severity of congenital toxoplasmosis vary with the trimester during which the infection was acquired by the mother.[8] There is an inverse relationship between the frequency of transmission and the severity of disease. Infants born of mothers who acquire their infection in the first and second trimester more frequently show severe congenital toxoplasmosis.[213] In contrast, the majority of children born of women who acquire their infection during the third trimester are born with the subclinical form of the infection. However, if left untreated, as many as 85% of these latter children develop signs and symptoms of the disease, in most cases chorioretinitis or delays in development.[8, 214, 215] The period of highest risk for the development of clinically apparent congenital infection was shown to be weeks 10 to 24; the low-risk period was 26 to 40 weeks.[216–218]

Infection acquired in the first trimester by women who were not treated with anti–*T. gondii* drugs resulted in congenital infection in 10 to 25% of cases.[213] For second- and third-trimester infections, the incidences of fetal infection ranged between 30 and 54% and 60 and 65%, respectively.[213] Treatment of the mother with spiramycin appears to reduce the incidence of congenital infection by about 60%.[219–222] Maternal infection acquired around the time of conception and within the first 2 weeks of gestation and treated with spiramycin usually does not result in transmission.[221]

Clinical manifestations of congenital toxoplasmosis vary. There may be no sequelae, or sequelae may develop or be evident at various times after birth. Most signs and clinical presentations are nonspecific and may mimic disease due to organisms such as herpes simplex virus, CMV, and rubella virus. Signs include chorioretinitis, strabismus, blindness, epilepsy, psychomotor or mental retardation, anemia, jaundice, rash, petechiae due to thrombocytopenia, encephalitis, pneumonitis, microcephaly, intracranial calcification, hydrocephalus, diarrhea, hypothermia, and nonspecific illness.[8] *T. gondii* infection is not known to cause fetal malformations by affecting the host's DNA.

A detailed examination may be necessary to detect signs of the infection.[8] In one prospective study,[223] 210 congenitally infected infants were identified: 2 patients (0.9%) died, 21 (10.9%) had severe disease, 71 (33.8%) were mildly afflicted, and 116 (54.4%) were without signs of the infection. More intensive examination of the latter 116 infants revealed abnormalities in 39; abnormal CSF was detected in 22 infants, chorioretinitis was seen in 17, and intracranial calcifications were found in 10. Premature infants often suffer CNS disease and ocular disease in the first 3 months of life. Full-term infants frequently develop a milder disease manifested by hepatosplenomegaly and lymphadenopathy that usually appear in the first 2 months of life. In these infants, disease reflecting damage to the CNS may occur later, and eye disease may occur months to years after birth.

Most infants with subclinical infection at birth subsequently develop signs or symptoms of congenital toxoplasmosis.[215] In one study, clinical evaluation at a mean age of 8.3 years showed that 11 of the 13 infected children who had no signs of the disease after detailed examination in the newborn period suffered sequelae. Some of these children were treated with specific therapy in the newborn period. In each child, the initial manifestation was chorioretinitis, which appeared at a mean age of 3.7 years. Three children had unilateral blindness, whereas the other eight children had no loss of visual function. Five children developed neurologic sequelae, including one child with delayed psychomotor development, microcephaly, and seizure disorder and two children with minor cerebellar signs. Sensorineural hearing loss occurred in 3 of 10 children evaluated. A study from The Netherlands[224] reported that five of nine congenitally infected, untreated children followed for up to 14 years developed chorioretinitis. Information from prospective studies being performed in France and the United States suggests that early instigation of specific therapy in those infants with congenital infection but without clinical signs will markedly reduce untoward sequelae.[225, 226]

Latent *T. gondii* infection may reactivate in HIV-infected women and result in congenital transmission of the parasite. Congenital toxoplasmosis appears to occur more frequently in the offspring of women infected with both HIV and *T. gondii* than in those of women who are infected with *T. gondii* but not with HIV.[227] Infants with congenital toxoplasmosis born to HIV-infected mothers are also infected with HIV (suggesting that factors that predispose to the vertical transmission of HIV also favor the transmission of *T. gondii*, or vice versa). Congenital toxoplasmosis in the HIV-infected infant appears to run a more rapid course than that in the non–HIV-infected infant, with the development of failure to thrive, fever, hepatosplenomegaly, chorioretinitis, and seizures. Most children have multiorgan involvement, including CNS, cardiac, and pulmonary disease.

Congenital toxoplasmosis must be differentiated from rubella virus, CMV, and herpes simplex virus infections; syphilis, listeriosis, and other bacterial infections; other infectious encephalopathies; erythroblastosis fetalis; and sepsis. Herpes simplex virus, CMV, rubella virus, and syphilis may cause chorioretinitis; both CMV and rubella have been associated with hydrocephalus, microcephaly, and cerebral calcification. A markedly elevated CSF protein concentration is a hallmark of congenital toxoplasmosis.

T. gondii infection acquired during pregnancy has been implicated in spontaneous abortion, stillbirth, and premature births. On rare occasion, *T. gondii* has been isolated from the abortuses of women with chronic infection, but the frequency of *T. gondii* infection as a cause of abortion is unknown and controversial.

DIAGNOSIS

When considering toxoplasmosis in the differential diagnosis of a patient's illness, emphasis should not be placed on whether the patient has been exposed to cats. Transmission of oocysts virtually always occurs without knowledge of the patient and may be unrelated to direct exposure to a cat (e.g., transmission by contaminated vegetables or water). Patients with an indoor cat or cats that are fed only cooked food are not at risk of acquiring the infection from that cat. Serologic investigation of a cat to establish whether it is a potential source of the infection should be discouraged; the prevalence of *T. gondii* antibodies among cats in a given locale is usually similar to their prevalence in humans. Seropositivity does not predict shedding of oocysts.

Because the clinical manifestations of *T. gondii* infection may be protean and nonspecific, toxoplasmosis must be carefully considered in the differential diagnosis of a large variety of clinical presentations. The correct diagnostic tests must be performed and appropriately interpreted in light of the patient's clinical presentation. The usefulness of a given diagnostic method may differ considerably with the clinical entity, which can be toxoplasmosis in the immunocompetent and immunodeficient patient, ocular toxoplasmosis, toxoplasmosis in pregnancy, and congenital toxoplasmosis. Later we describe some of the most common methods used for diagnosis of the infection and disease (toxoplasmosis) and discuss diagnoses in specific clinical situations.

Acute infection is diagnosed by the isolation of *T. gondii* or amplification of its DNA in blood or body fluids; demonstration of tachyzoites in histologic sections of tissue or in cytologic preparations of body fluids; the demonstration of a characteristic lymph node histologic appearance or of characteristic serologic test results or demonstration of *T. gondii* tissue cysts in the placenta, fetus, or neonate.[8] Rarely, asymptomatic patients with latent infection have recurrent parasitemia.[228] Isolation of *T. gondii* from the tissues of older children or adults may only reflect the presence of cysts. Finding numerous cysts in tissue sections suggests but does not prove the presence of active infection.

Isolation of *Toxoplasma gondii*

Isolation of *T. gondii* from blood or body fluids establishes that the infection is acute. In neonates, isolation of the organism from the placenta is usually diagnostic; isolation from fetal tissues is diagnostic of congenital infection.[8] Attempts at isolation of the parasite can be performed by mouse inoculation[229] or inoculation of tissue cell cultures.[230] In tissue cell cultures, parasite-laden cells can be demonstrated with appropriate staining, and plaques are formed in which tachyzoites are easily recognized.[231] Tissue cell culture has the advantage of widespread availability (e.g., virology laboratories) and yields results more rapidly (within 3 to 6 days) than does mouse inoculation. However, mouse inoculation is more sensitive.

Histologic Diagnosis

Demonstration of tachyzoites in tissue sections or smears of body fluid (e.g., CSF, amniotic fluid, or BAL) establishes the diagnosis of the acute infection.[232] Multiple tissue cysts near an inflammatory necrotic lesion probably establish the diagnosis.[233] It is often difficult to demonstrate tachyzoites in stained tissue sections. Fluorescent antibody staining may be useful, but this method often yields nonspecific results.[234] The immunoperoxidase technique, which uses antisera to *T. gondii*, has proved both sensitive and specific; it has been used successfully in clinical settings to demonstrate the organisms in the CNS of patients with AIDS.[18, 235] Both the fluorescent antibody and immunoperoxidase methods are applicable to unfixed or formalin-fixed paraffin-embedded tissue sections.[18] An enzyme-linked immunosorbent assay (ELISA) has been reported to detect *T. gondii* antigen in unfixed tissues.[236] The use of fluorescein-labeled monoclonal antibodies to *T. gondii* for touch preparations of specimens[237] and rapid electron microscopy[238] have been used successfully to diagnose TE.

A rapid, technically simple, and underused method is the detection of *T. gondii* in air-dried, Wright-Giemsa–stained slides of centrifuged (e.g., cytocentrifuge) sediment of CSF or of brain aspirate or in impression smears of biopsy tissue.

Endomyocardial biopsy has been used successfully to diagnose toxoplasmosis in heart transplant recipients.[188] Characteristic histologic criteria alone are probably sufficient to establish the diagnosis of toxoplasmic lymphadenitis in older children and adults.[168]

Polymerase Chain Reaction

PCR amplification for the detection of *T. gondii* DNA in body fluids and tissues has successfully diagnosed congenital,[239, 240] ocular,[152, 208, 241–243] cerebral, and disseminated toxoplasmosis.[244–246] PCR has revolutionized the diagnosis of intrauterine *T. gondii* infection by enabling an early diagnosis to be made, thereby avoiding the use of invasive procedures on the fetus. PCR has enabled the detection of *T. gondii* DNA in brain tissue,[247] CSF,[148, 248] vitreous and aqueous fluids,[152, 208] BAL,[151, 249, 250] and blood[246, 251–254] in patients with AIDS. The sensitivity of PCR in CSF varies between 11 and 77%, whereas the specificity is close to 100%.[148, 253, 255, 256] PCR may also detect the parasite in buffy coat specimens of AIDS patients with TE.[246, 257] The sensitivity of PCR on whole blood or buffy coat ranges from 15 to 85%. PCR on blood appears to be a valuable tool primarily in patients with disseminated disease; it is less sensitive in the detection of TE because a relatively low percentage of AIDS patients with TE have parasitemia.[258, 259] Therapy for toxoplasmosis appears to influence the sensitivity of the method; sensitivity is higher in CSF or blood samples collected within the first week of or before therapy.[246, 260–262] When PCR is used, we recommend that the specimen be split in separate aliquots to allow repeated testing to be performed on independent aliquots. This protocol allows one to reconfirm ambiguous results and to avoid false positives.

Antigen-Specific Lymphocyte Transformation and Lymphocyte Typing

Lymphocyte proliferation in response to exposure to *T. gondii* antigens is a specific and sensitive indicator of previous infection in adults. It has been used successfully to diagnose the congenital infection in infants 2 months of age or older.[263] Specific lymphocyte anergy to the organism may also occur in congenitally infected infants.[264]

Adults with toxoplasmic lymphadenopathy may have abnormal $CD4^+/CD8^+$ ratios of T lymphocytes in their peripheral blood.[265] A marked increase in $CD8^+$ T cells may correlate with the presence of symptoms in acute acquired infection in immunocompetent patients. These abnormalities may persist for months after the acquisition of the infection and are not specific for infection with *T. gondii*. Similar abnormalities in T-cell subsets have been reported in congenitally infected fetuses.[266]

Serologic Tests for Demonstration of Antibody

The use of serologic tests for the demonstration of specific antibody to *T. gondii* is the primary method of diagnosis. The problem with serologic diagnosis is that antibody to *T. gondii* is present in relatively high numbers of individuals in most human populations. These antibody titers may persist at high levels for years in healthy people. A large number of tests have been described, some of which are still in the experimental stage or are available only in highly specialized laboratories. Different serologic tests often measure different antibodies that possess unique patterns of rise and fall with the time after infection. False-positive and false-negative results (or both) have been a problem with certain commercial kits and laboratories in the United States and Europe.[267, 268] There is no single serologic test that can be used to support the diagnosis of acute or chronic infection by *T. gondii*. The clinician must be familiar with these problems and consult reference laboratories if the need arises.

A panel of tests (the *T. gondii* serologic profile [TSP]) consisting of the Sabin-Feldman dye test (IgG), the IgM-, IgA-, and IgE-ELISAs, the IgE immunosorbent agglutination assay (IgE-ISAGA), and the differential agglutination test (measures IgG antibody and is also known as the AC/HS test) is used successfully by our group to determine whether serologic test results are more likely consistent with infection acquired in the recent or more distant past.[174, 178, 269]

Immunoglobulin G Antibodies

The most widely used tests for the measurement of IgG antibody are the Sabin-Feldman dye test,[80] ELISA,[270, 271] the indirect fluorescent antibody (IFA) test,[272] and the modified direct agglutination test.[273] In these tests, IgG antibodies usually appear within 1 to 2 weeks of acquisition of the infection, peak within 1 to 2 months, fall at variable rates, and usually persist for life.

Sabin-Feldman Dye Test

The Sabin-Feldman dye test is the reference serologic test against which other methods have been evaluated.[80] It is a sensitive and specific neutralization test in which the organisms are lysed in the presence of antibody and complement. It measures primarily IgG antibodies that usually appear 1 to 2 weeks after the initiation of infection, reach peak titers in 6 to 8 weeks, and then gradually decline over 1 to 2 years.[8] Titers, usually at low levels, probably persist for life. Some patients have high titers for years. The titer does not correlate with the severity of illness.[274] This test is available in only a few reference laboratories, primarily because live organisms are required. A negative Sabin-Feldman dye test practically rules out prior exposure to *T. gondii*. However, although rare, cases of documented TE and chorioretinitis have been reported in dye test–negative patients.

Indirect Fluorescent Antibody Test

The IFA test is widely used; it is easier and safer to perform and is more economical than the dye test. It appears to measure the same antibodies as the dye test, and its titers tend to parallel dye test titers.[8] False-positive results may occur with sera that contain antinuclear antibodies,[275] and false-negative results may occur in sera with low IgG antibody titers.

Agglutination Test

The agglutination test using formalin-preserved whole tachyzoites is available commercially (Bio-Mérieux, Lyon, France) and detects IgG antibody. The test is very sensitive to IgM antibody, and "natural" IgM antibody causes nonspecific agglutination in sera that yield negative results when tested in the dye test and the IFA test. This problem is avoided by including 2-mercaptoethanol in the test. The method is accurate, simple to perform, inexpensive, and excellent for screening pregnant women.[276] This method should not be used for the measurement of IgM antibodies.

When two different compounds (i.e., acetone and formalin) are used to fix parasites for use in the agglutination test, a "differential" agglutination test (AC/HS test) results because the different antigenic preparations vary in their ability to recognize sera obtained during the acute and chronic stages of the infection. This test has proved useful in helping differentiate acute from chronic infections[277] but is best used in combination with a panel of other tests (e.g., the TSP).

Immunoglobulin G Enzyme-Linked Immunosorbent Assay

The IgG-ELISA method is now the most widely used for the demonstration of IgG antibodies to *T. gondii.* Most commercial IgG antibody test kits are accurate for the demonstration of IgG antibodies; however, it is important to recognize that one cannot use a single IgG titer, no matter what its level, to predict whether the infection was recently acquired or acquired in the distant past. A single titer of 150 IU/ml or greater in patients with AIDS has been found to be a predictor of TE[278] (see "Diagnosis of Specific Clinical Entities").

Immunoglobulin G Avidity Test

At present, the IgG avidity test is not available in the United States. It is marketed in an ELISA format in Europe and is based on the observation that during acute *T. gondii* infection, IgG antibodies bind antigen weakly (i.e., have low avidity), whereas chronically infected patients have antibody of high avidity.[279] As the change from low to high avidity occurs within 6 months in most patients, the test may be able to discriminate those with acute from those with chronic infections better than alternative assays such as those that measure IgM antibodies. At present the test appears to be most useful if significant amounts of high-avidity antibody are demonstrable early in gestation. Such high-avidity antibody titers reflect the fact that primary infection occurred in the more distant past (more than 3 to 5 months). This method cannot be used to determine whether the infection was acquired recently because low-avidity antibody may persist for 3 to 5 months.[280, 281] As is true for IgM-antibody tests, the avidity test is most useful when performed early in gestation because a "chronic" pattern occurring late in pregnancy does not rule out the possibility that the acute infection may have occurred during the first months of gestation.

Immunoglobulin M Antibodies

IgM antibodies may appear earlier and decline more rapidly than IgG antibodies. IgM antibody tests have been widely used for the diagnosis of acute infection and to determine whether a pregnant woman has been infected during gestation or before conception. There has been a heightened awareness of the fact that titers in tests for IgM antibodies may persist for years after the acute infection and that the reliability of commercially available assays varies considerably.[267, 282–284] Both the laboratory performing the test and the physician requesting the test should be aware of this problem. The U.S. Food and Drug Administration has issued a health advisory to obstetricians, gynecologists, pediatricians, clinical pathologists, and infectious diseases specialists warning about the use of *T. gondii* IgM commercial test kits as the sole determinant of recent infection in pregnant women. At present, the decision to treat or undertake other medical interventions, including the termination of pregnancy, should be based on clinical evaluation and additional testing performed in reference or research laboratories with experience in the diagnosis of toxoplasmosis. (For further discussion, see *"Toxoplasma gondii* Infection in Pregnancy."[285])

Indirect Fluorescent Antibody Test

IgM-IFA antibody appears within the first week of infection; titers rise rapidly and then fall to low titers and usually disappear within a few months. Low titers may persist 1 year or longer.[286] Antinuclear antibodies and rheumatoid factor may cause false-positive results.[287] IgG-blocking antibodies can cause false-negative results in this test when IgG is not removed.[288]

Immunoglobulin M Enzyme-Linked Immunosorbent Assay

False-positive results due to rheumatoid factor and antinuclear antibodies in some IgM-IFA tests are not detected in the most commonly used commercial "double-sandwich" or "capture" IgM-ELISA kits.[287] In the conventional IgM-ELISA, false-positive results may occur in sera that contain rheumatoid factor.[289] IgM-capture ELISA kits are most commonly used. Despite the wide distribution of commercial tests kits to measure IgM antibodies, these kits often have low specificity and the reported results are frequently misinterpreted. False-positive results and the problems associated with the persistence of positive titers even years after the initial infection remain major obstacles to correct interpretation of the results obtained in these tests.[267, 282, 283]

Immunoglobulin M Immunosorbent Agglutination Assay

The IgM-ISAGA (available from Bio-Mérieux), which binds the patient's IgM to a solid surface and uses intact tachyzoites to detect IgM antibodies, is both sensitive and specific.[290] The test is simple to perform, does not require the use of enzyme conjugate, and is read in the same manner as the agglutination test. It is more sensitive and specific than the IgM-IFA test. The presence of rheumatoid factor or antinuclear antibodies does not cause false-positive results in the IgM-ISAGA. The ISAGA method has also been used to detect IgA and IgE antibodies.[291, 292]

Immunoglobulin A Antibodies

IgA antibodies may be detected in sera of acutely infected adults and congenitally infected infants using ELISA or ISAGA.[293–295] As is true for IgM antibodies to the parasite, IgA antibodies may persist for many months or more than 1 year. For this reason they are of little additional assistance for the diagnosis of the acute infection in the adult. In contrast, the increased sensitivity of IgA assays over IgM assays for the diagnosis of congenital toxoplasmosis represents a major advance in the diagnosis of the infection in the fetus and newborn.[294] IgA antibodies are rarely detectable by ELISA in sera of AIDS patients with TE.[294] Immunoblotting was reported to be more sensitive for the detection of IgA antibodies in a small number of AIDS patients with toxoplasmosis.[296] If IgA antibodies are detected in the newborn, the test should be repeated at approximately 10 days after birth to make certain that what is being measured is not contaminating maternal IgA antibodies. The possibility that such contamination might occur is the reason we recommend that under most circumstances, peripheral blood rather than cord serum be used to measure IgM, IgA, or IgE antibodies in the newborn.

Immunoglobulin E Antibodies

IgE antibodies are detectable by ELISA in sera of acutely infected adults,[291, 292] congenitally infected infants,[291, 292, 297] and children with congenital toxoplasmic chorioretinitis.[298] Their demonstration does not appear to be particularly useful for diagnosis of *T. gondii* infection in the fetus or newborn when compared with IgA tests. The duration of IgE seropositivity is briefer than that with IgM or IgA antibodies and hence appears useful for identifying recently acquired infections.[178, 292] *T. gondii*–specific IgE antibody has been detected in patients with TE and may be useful as a marker for TE in this population of patients.[292]

Radiologic Methods

Radiologic studies are of particular help in patients with toxoplasmosis of the CNS. The presence of calcifications in the brain of a newborn, detected by radiography, ultrasonography, or CT, should heighten the suspicion of *T. gondii* as the cause of the disease. In severely affected infants with congenital toxoplasmosis, unilateral or, more often, bilateral and symmetric dilatation of the ventricles is a common finding.[8]

In the majority of immunodeficient patients with TE, CT scans show multiple bilateral cerebral lesions. Although multiple lesions are more common in toxoplasmosis, they also may be solitary; a single lesion should not exclude TE as a diagnostic possibility. Clinicians should be aware that toxoplasmosis may manifest as an encephalitis that at autopsy is "diffuse," in which case the neuroimaging study results may appear normal or reveal findings suggestive of HIV encephalopathy.[149]

CT scans in AIDS patients with TE reveal multiple ring-enhancing lesions in 70 to 80% of the cases.[145] In AIDS patients with detectable *Toxoplasma* IgG and multiple ring-enhancing lesions on CT or MRI, the predictive value for TE is approximately 80%.[299] Lesions tend to occur at the corticomedullary junction (frequently involving the basal ganglia) and are characteristically hypodense.[300–303] The number of lesions is frequently underestimated by CT,[87] although delayed imaging after a double dose of intravenous contrast material may improve the sensitivity of this modality.[300, 301] An enlarging hypodense lesion that does not enhance is a poor prognostic sign.[301] TE lesions on MRI studies appear as high signal abnormalities on T_2-weighted studies and reveal a rim of enhancement surrounding the edema on T_1-weighted contrast-enhanced images (Fig. 268–5). MRI has superior sensitivity (particularly if gadolinium is used for contrast) compared with CT and often demonstrates a lesion or lesions or more extensive disease not shown by CT.[304, 305] Hence, MRI should be used as the initial procedure when feasible (and especially if a single lesion is demonstrated by CT). Nevertheless, even characteristic lesions on CT or MRI studies are not pathognomonic of TE. The major differential diagnosis of focal CNS lesions in AIDS patients is CNS lymphoma, which may manifest with multiple enhancing lesions in 40% of cases. The probability of TE falls and the probability of lymphoma rises in the presence of single lesions on MRI.[62] A brain biopsy may therefore be required in the patient with a solitary lesion (especially if confirmed by MRI) to obtain a definitive diagnosis.[62, 305, 306]

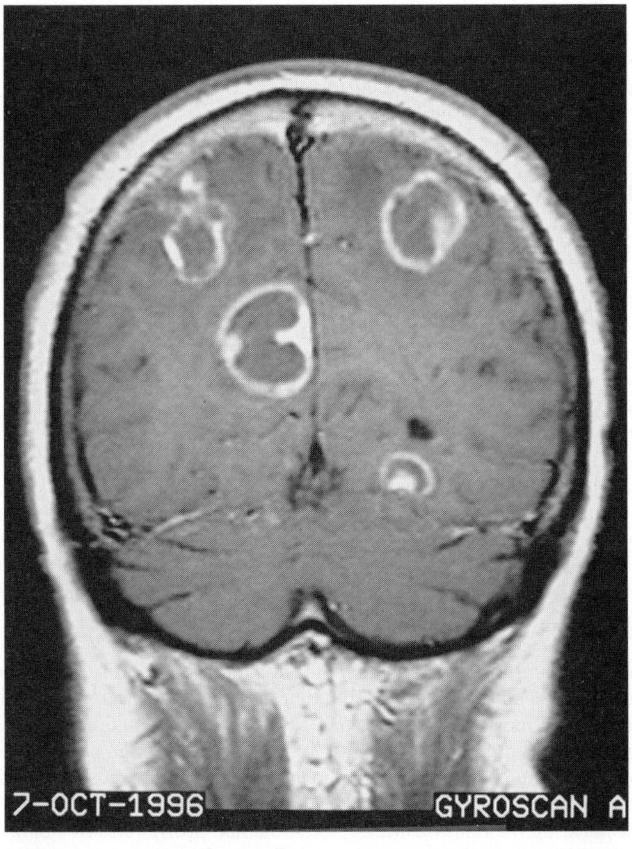

FIGURE 268–5. Magnetic resonance imaging scan of the brain of a patient with acquired immunodeficiency syndrome with toxoplasmic encephalitis. Note the multiple ring-enhancing lesions.

In AIDS patients with TE, CT-scan improvement is seen in up to 90% of patients after 2 to 3 weeks of treatment.[62, 302] Complete resolution takes from 6 weeks to 6 months; peripheral lesions resolve more rapidly than deeper ones. Smaller lesions usually resolve completely on MRI studies within 3 to 5 weeks, but lesions with a mass effect tend to resolve more slowly and leave a small residual lesion.[303] A radiologic response to therapy lags behind the clinical response with better correlation between them observed by the end of acute therapy.[307]

CT and MRI in toxoplasmic myelopathy usually demonstrates localized enlargement of the spinal cord,[191, 192] which may result in obstruction to dye flow on myelography.[191] Gadolinium enhancement of MRI studies usually highlights as an intramedullary lesion at the site of spinal cord enlargement.[192]

A variety of positron emission tomography (PET) scanning,[308] radionuclide scanning,[309] and MR techniques[310] have been used to evaluate AIDS patients with focal CNS lesions and specifically to differentiate between toxoplasmosis and primary CNS lymphoma.[310] [^{18}F]Fluorodeoxyglucose PET scanning is now widely used in the evaluation of patients with tumors. There is a significantly higher uptake of [^{18}F]fluorodeoxyglucose in patients with cerebral lymphoma than in patients with TE.[308, 311] Radionuclide scanning has also been used to differentiate between CNS toxoplasmosis and lymphoma. Neoplasms usually demonstrate increased uptake of thallium 201 on both early and late scanning.[310] MR spectroscopy using the proton brain evaluation has been used in a small number of patients. MR spectroscopy in patients with TE reveals an elevation in the lactate and lipid contents[310] and a decrease in the levels of choline. In contrast, MR spectroscopy in patients with CNS lymphoma reveals mildly elevated levels of choline.[310]

Cerebrospinal Fluid Abnormalities

CSF abnormalities in patients with TE are nonspecific; mild mononuclear pleocytosis and mild to moderate elevations in CSF protein are often observed; hypoglycorrhachia is uncommon.[87, 167] Almost unique to infants with neonatal toxoplasmosis, however, is the very high protein content of the ventricular fluid. Although in some infants the protein level is just slightly above normal, in others it can be measured in grams per deciliter rather than in milligrams per deciliter.[8] Demonstration of intrathecal production of *T. gondii* IgG supports the diagnosis of TE.[312, 313] It is not known whether this method is as useful when serologic methods other than the Sabin-Feldman dye test are used.

Diagnosis of Specific Clinical Entities

The initial step in pursuing the diagnosis of *T. gondii* infection or toxoplasmosis is to determine whether the patient has been exposed to the parasite. In virtually all cases, tests for IgG antibodies reliably establish the presence or absence of the infection; a negative IgG test essentially rules out prior or recent exposure to the parasite. However, clinicians should be aware that cases of documented toxoplasmic chorioretinitis and TE have been observed in which IgG antibodies were not demonstrable; such cases are very uncommon In the presence of clinical illness, it is important to establish whether the patient's condition is due to a recently acquired infection or to recrudescence of latent infection (chronic infection) or is unrelated to the infection. A true negative IgM test essentially rules out that the infection has been acquired in recent months. A positive IgM test is more difficult to interpret correctly. One must not assume that a positive IgM test result is diagnostic of recently acquired infection. The presence of *T. gondii*--specific IgM antibodies can be interpreted as a true positive result consistent with recently acquired infection; a true positive result consistent with a chronic infection (IgM antibodies have been shown to persist for as long as 5 years after the acute infection); or a false-positive result. To establish which of these is most likely in a given case, confirmatory testing in a reference laboratory should be performed whenever feasible.[267, 285] The TSP has been useful for determining whether the patient has been recently infected or infected in the more distant past.[178, 269] Clinicians and laboratories should consider confirmatory testing in all patients in whom IgM test results are positive.[267, 285] If the patient has received a blood transfusion, serologic tests may measure exogenously administered rather than endogenous antibody. The use of serologic tests to evaluate the response to therapy should be discouraged.

Toxoplasmosis in the Immunocompetent Patient

Tests for IgG and IgM antibodies should be used for initial evaluation of immunocompetent patients. Testing of serial specimens obtained 3 weeks apart (in parallel) provides the best discriminatory power if the results in the initial specimen are equivocal. Negative results in either of these tests virtually rules out the diagnosis of toxoplasmosis. Rarely, early in infection, IgG antibodies may not be detectable whereas IgM antibodies are present (hence the need for both tests to be performed). Acute infection is supported by documented seroconversion of IgG or IgM antibodies or a greater than two-tube rise in antibody titer in sera run in parallel. A single high titer of any immunoglobulin antibodies is insufficient to make the diagnosis; IgG antibodies may persist at high titers for many years,[8] and IgM antibodies may be detectable for more than 12 months. The TSP, performed on a single serum sample, is useful in determining the likelihood that the infection is acute.

Toxoplasmosis should be considered in the differential diagnosis of lymphadenopathy, whether or not symptoms are present and especially in those without symptoms. Confirmatory serologic tests should be obtained in such patients. The sensitivity of serologic tests performed in these patients is time-dependent from the clinical onset of lymphadenopathy. Thus, the interval between the clinical onset of lymphadenopathy and the date that the specimen is drawn is critical for interpretation of the test results.[178] In patients whose serum is available during the first 3 months after the clinical onset, at least the dye test and the IgM-ELISA are positive. In those patients in whom sera are obtained more than 3 months after the clinical onset, the IgM-ELISA is most likely to be negative but the dye test and at least one of the following tests are positive: IgA-ELISA, IgE-ELISA, IgE-ISAGA, or AC/HS test.[178]

Histologic diagnosis can be useful in some cases of suspected toxoplasmosis in the immunocompetent patient. The histologic criteria for the diagnosis of toxoplasmic lymphadenitis has been well established (see Fig. 268–3*B*) (see "Histologic Diagnosis").[168] In this setting, there is no need to visualize the parasite. Endomyocardial biopsy and biopsy of skeletal muscle have been successfully used to establish *T. gondii* as the etiologic agent of myocarditis and polymyositis in the rare cases in immunocompetent patients.[157] Isolation studies and PCR have rarely proved useful in immunocompetent patients.

Toxoplasmosis in the Immunodeficient Patient

Because reactivation of the chronic infection is the most common cause of toxoplasmosis in patients with AIDS, patients with malignancies, or recipients of organ transplants, initial assessment of these patients should routinely include an assay for *T. gondii* IgG antibodies. Those with a positive result are at risk of reactivation of the infection; those with a negative result should be instructed on how they can prevent becoming infected (see "Prevention"). Those at highest risk (e.g., HIV-infected and AIDS patients) who are initially seronegative should be retested on an annual basis to determine whether they have seroconverted. Seronegative organ transplant recipients should be identified before transplantation to avoid, when feasible, their receiving an organ from a seropositive donor, particularly if it is a heart.[55, 314]

In patients with AIDS and toxoplasmosis, the IgG titer may be relatively low, and tests for IgM, IgA, and IgE antibodies may be negative.[145] In HIV-infected patients with $CD4^+$ counts less than 200 cells/mm^3, the IgG antibody titer is prognostic of the occurrence of TE, with a higher risk for titers of 150 IU/ml or greater.[278, 315]

In the early postoperative period in heart transplant recipients who present with a clinical illness, serologic test results may be misleading.[187, 188] In these patients, results indicating apparent reactivation (a rising IgG and IgM titer) may be present in the absence of clinically apparent infection. In addition, serologic test results consistent with chronic infection may be seen in the presence of toxoplasmosis.[5, 188] In heart transplant recipients in whom toxoplasmosis is suspected as a cause of altered myocardial function, endomyocardial biopsy has proved useful.[188] The parasite has been demonstrated in the myocardium of patients in whom the biopsy was performed because of a suspicion of rejection.[188]

Serologic tests in patients with B-cell disorders such as hypo- or agammaglobulinemia may not be useful to diagnose toxoplasmosis; active infection can occur in these patients in the setting of negative IgG titers.

A definitive diagnosis of toxoplasmosis in the immunodeficient patient relies on histologic demonstration of the parasite, usually in association with an inflammatory process. The presence of tachyzoites is diagnostic of active infection. The presence of a solitary *T. gondii* cyst may only reflect chronic infection unless it is associated with an area of inflammation (e.g., as seen in myocardial biopsy); visualization of several *T. gondii* cysts virtually always means that active infection is present. In these patients, other means of diagnosis are by detection of *T. gondii* DNA by PCR or by isolation of the parasite.

When clinical signs suggest involvement of the CNS or spinal cord, the workup should include CT or MRI (see "Radiologic Methods") of the brain. These studies should be performed even if the neurologic examination does not reveal focal deficits.

Empirical anti–*T. gondii* therapy for patients with multiple ring-enhancing brain lesions (usually established by MRI), positive IgG antibody titers against *T. gondii,* and advanced immunodeficiency (e.g., patients with a CD4 count under 200 or patients receiving intensive immunosuppressive therapy) is accepted practice; a clinical and radiologic response to specific anti–*T. gondii* therapy is considered supportive of the diagnosis of TE.

Brain biopsy should be considered in immunodeficient patients with presumed TE if there is a single lesion on MRI, a negative IgG antibody test, or an inadequate clinical response to an optimal treatment regimen, or in patients who the physician considers have adhered to an effective prophylactic regimen against *T. gondii* (e.g., TMP-SMX). An impression smear of the brain biopsy specimen can be made and immediately examined for the presence of tachyzoites using the conventional Wright-Giemsa stain employed for blood smears in most laboratories. The brain specimen should then be submitted to the pathology and microbiology departments for appropriate workup. In addition to hematoxylin and eosin staining, *T. gondii*–specific immunoperoxidase staining should be performed.[18] Because the amount of brain tissue obtained at aspiration or biopsy is usually small, sufficient tissue for mouse inoculation may not be available; however, this should be performed whenever feasible. A positive result may often be obtained with far less than 1 g of brain tissue. PCR has been used successfully in brain tissue to diagnose TE.[247]

If *T. gondii* serologic and radiologic studies are nonconclusive or do not support a recommendation for empirical treatment, and if brain biopsy is not feasible, a lumbar puncture should be considered if it is safe to perform; PCR can then be performed on the CSF specimen; CSF can also be sent for isolation studies, although *T. gondii* has uncommonly been isolated from the CSF of these patients. PCR examination of the CSF can also be used for the detection of Epstein-Barr virus, JC virus, or CMV DNA in patients in whom primary CNS lymphoma, progressive multifocal leukoencephalopathy or CMV ventriculitis, respectively, have been entertained in the differential diagnosis. The intrathecal production of *T. gondii*–specific antibody within the CSF may help confirm the diagnosis.[312] Unless sufficient CSF is available, we suggest that the highest priority be for PCR and an attempt at isolation of the parasite.

In the appropriate clinical setting, it is important to include toxoplasmosis in the differential diagnosis of pulmonary symptoms, particularly in those individuals with interstitial infiltrates. Wright-Giemsa stain and PCR of BAL specimens are useful for the diagnosis of pulmonary toxoplasmosis.[151, 249, 316]

In patients with visual symptoms in whom toxoplasmic chorioretinitis is a possibility, PCR examination of vitreous fluid can be considered and is particularly helpful in patients with atypical clinical features of toxoplasmic chorioretinitis.[152, 208] Of note, PCR examination of the vitreous fluid can also be helpful when other etiologic agents such as herpes simplex virus, varicella-zoster virus, or CMV are considered in the differential diagnosis.

PCR and isolation studies in peripheral blood can help establish *T. gondii* as the etiologic agent of a febrile syndrome or systemic symptoms of unclear cause.[246, 317] These studies tend to have a higher yield early in the disease and before or shortly after specific anti–*T. gondii* therapy is initiated.[246]

In pursuing the diagnosis, histologic examination with the appropriate stains and mouse inoculation can be attempted in virtually any tissue suspected of being involved by *T. gondii*. Body fluids that should be considered for examination by PCR include CSF, blood, vitreous, and BAL specimens. Reference laboratories should be contacted before diagnostic procedures to optimize the handling of the specimens and their yield.

Ocular Toxoplasmosis

Low titers of IgG antibody are usual in patients with active chorioretinitis due to reactivation of congenital *T. gondii* infection; IgM antibodies are not usually detected. When sera from such patients are examined in the dye test, they should be titered beginning with undiluted serum because in some cases the conventional initial dilution of 1:16 may be negative.

In most cases, toxoplasmic chorioretinitis is diagnosed by ophthalmologic examination, and empirical therapy directed against the organism is often instituted based on clinical findings and serologic test results. In a number of patients, the morphology of the retinal lesion or lesions may be nondiagnostic, or the response to treatment may be suboptimal, or both. In such cases (unclear clinical diagnosis or inadequate clinical response, or both), the detection of an abnormal *T. gondii*–antibody response in ocular fluids (immune load) or demonstration of the parasite by isolation or histopathologic examination has been used successfully to establish the diagnosis.[9, 205, 318–321] PCR has been employed in an attempt to support or confirm the diagnosis of *T. gondii* as the cause of the retinal lesions. It has been used to detect *T. gondii* DNA in both aqueous and vitreous fluids.[152, 208] In patients in whom toxoplasmosis is considered in the differential diagnosis but in whom the presentation is atypical, PCR is a useful diagnostic aid.[209] However, vitreous biopsy is a potentially hazardous procedure, and its use should be considered only when other diagnostic measures have not revealed a cause.

Toxoplasma gondii Infection in Pregnancy

Acute acquired *T. gondii* infection is diagnosed serologically by the same methods used for immunocompetent adults discussed earlier. Special care is taken to determine whether the infection was acquired before or after conception. This determination is frequently difficult because routine serologic screening is not conducted in pregnant women in the United States. Repeat serologic tests in a pregnant woman who has been previously shown to have *T. gondii* antibodies are not helpful.

The diagnosis of acute *T. gondii* infection or toxoplasmosis in most cases requires demonstration of a rise in titers in serial serum samples (either conversion from a negative to a positive titer or a significant rise from a low to a higher titer).[8] These specimens should be obtained at least 3 weeks apart and be tested in parallel. Because the diagnosis is frequently considered relatively late in the course of the patient's pregnancy, serologic test titers may already have reached their peak at the time the first serum is obtained for testing. It therefore is often difficult to discriminate between infections acquired recently (possibly during pregnancy) and those acquired in the more distant past. Thus, the initial serum should be obtained as early as possible during gestation.

Initial screening of maternal serum involves testing for IgG and IgM antibodies; a lack of both immunoglobulins essentially excludes active infection but identifies the patient as being at risk for acquisition of the infection (and hence in need of instruction about primary prevention). The presence of IgG antibodies in the absence of IgM antibodies in the first two trimesters almost always indicates chronic maternal infection with essentially no risk to the fetus (the exceptions are severely immunodeficient patients). In the third trimester, a negative IgM test titer is most likely consistent with a chronic maternal infection but does not exclude the possibility of an acute infection acquired early in pregnancy; this is especially true in those patients who exhibit a rapid decline in their IgM titers during the acute infection. In these cases, the use of other serologic tests (e.g., IgA, IgE, AC/HS, avidity) may be of particular help (Fig. 268–6).

A positive IgM test result requires further assessment with confirmatory testing at a reference laboratory (see also "Diagnosis of Specific Clinical Entities").[267, 285, 322] The use of confirmatory testing with a panel of serologic tests (e.g., TSP) in a reference laboratory has proved helpful in discriminating between recently and more distantly acquired infections, and having an expert interpret the results to the patient's physician has been shown to reduce unnecessary induced abortions among pregnant women reported to have IgM antibodies.[269] Women who are informed that they have a positive IgM test titer and that it signifies that their offspring will or might be infected often choose abortion. Unfortunately, a positive IgM test may not necessarily indicate infection acquired during gestation (a false-positive result), and thus the abortion may not be indicated. It is for this reason that confirmatory testing in a reference laboratory has been recommended by many experts and most recently by the U.S. Food and Drug Administration.[285]

Once the diagnosis of acute acquired infection during pregnancy has been presumptively established, diagnostic efforts should focus on determining whether the fetus has been infected.

Congenital Infection in the Fetus and Newborn

Prenatal diagnosis of fetal infection is advised when a diagnosis of acute infection is established or highly suspected in a pregnant woman. Methods to obtain fetal blood such as periumbilical fetal blood sampling have been largely abandoned because of the rate of false-negative prenatal diagnoses, the risk involved for the fetus, and the delay in obtaining definitive results with conventional parasitologic tests.[221]

Prenatal diagnosis of congenital toxoplasmosis is presently based on ultrasonography and amniocentesis. PCR on amniotic fluid for the detection of *T. gondii*–specific DNA performed at 18 weeks of

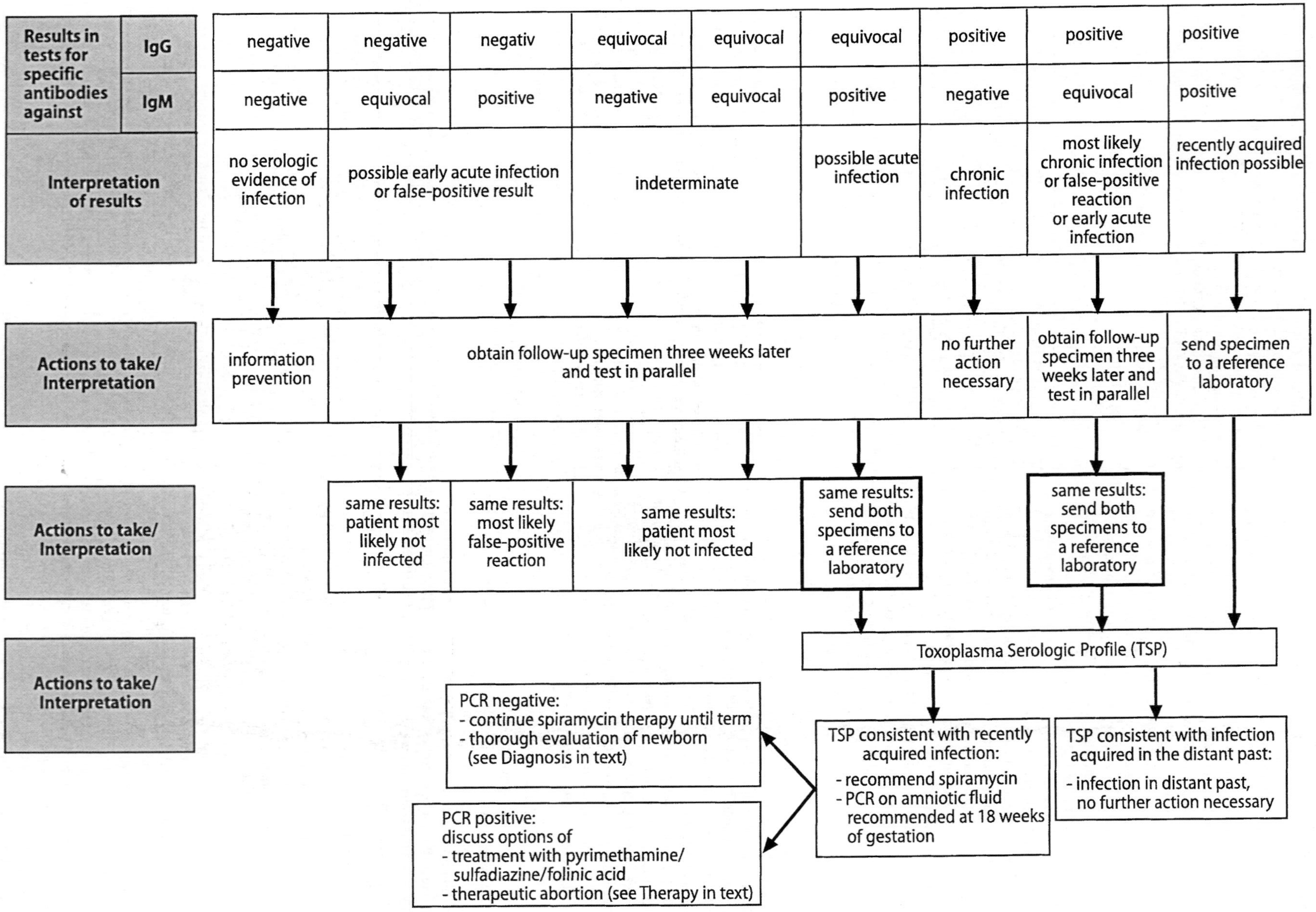

FIGURE 268–6. Guidelines for interpretation of serologic tests for IgG and IgM antibodies in pregnant women.

gestation is more sensitive, more rapid, and safer than conventional diagnostic procedures involving fetal blood sampling.[221] PCR on amniotic fluid should be used in all cases of established maternal infection or cases with serologic test results highly suggestive of acute acquired infection during pregnancy. PCR in amniotic fluid has a positive predictive value of 100% and a negative predictive value of 99.7%.[221] The reliability of the PCR test before 18 weeks of gestational age is unknown.[221] Prenatal diagnosis should not be attempted until at least 4 weeks after acute disease has been diagnosed in the mother because of the possibility of a false-negative result.[221]

Maternal IgG antibodies present in the newborn may reflect either past or recent infection in the mother. For this reason, tests for the detection of IgA and IgM antibodies are commonly employed for the diagnosis of infection in the newborn. It is essential that maternal contamination of blood obtained at birth be excluded; serum samples obtained from peripheral blood and not from the umbilical cords are preferred. The demonstration of IgA antibodies appears to be more sensitive than the detection IgM antibodies for establishing infection in the newborn.[294] If IgG antibodies are detected but serologic tests for IgM and IgA antibodies are negative and *T. gondii* is not isolated, follow-up serologic testing in suspect cases is indicated in order to attempt to establish the diagnosis. Maternally transferred antibodies usually decline and disappear within 6 to 12 months. Use of the protein blot technique has shown that maternal and infant sera may recognize different *T. gondii* antigens when the infant is congenitally infected.[323] This method has proved useful in the early diagnosis of congenital infection.[226]

Additional diagnostic methods that have been used successfully to diagnose the infection in infants are direct demonstration of the organism by isolation in mice or cell culture (e.g., placental tissue, body fluid) and PCR in body fluids (e.g., CSF, blood, and urine).[240, 324, 325] Evaluation of infants with suspected congenital toxoplasmosis should always include ophthalmologic examination, radiologic studies (particularly to detect the presence of cerebral calcifications), and examination of CSF. A more detailed discussion of diagnostic procedures in congenitally infected infants is available in a chapter by Remington and colleagues.[8]

Because it is not feasible to screen of all pregnant women, a secondary prevention program that consists of serologic testing of all newborns for IgM antibodies against *T. gondii* has been implemented in Massachusetts.[326] Using routine screening of all newborns, congenital infection was confirmed in approximately 1 in 12,000 infants. More than 90% of these were identified only through neonatal screening and not through initial clinical examination. Because testing for IgM antibodies in newborns is only 25 to 75% sensitive, this program does not detect a number of subclinically infected infants or those infected late in the third trimester (when the frequency of transmission is highest but antibody formation has not yet occurred).

In infants with congenital toxoplasmosis or congenital infection, a rebound in IgG- and IgM-antibody titers is frequently observed after discontinuation of therapy. In our experience, such a serologic rebound has not been shown to be clinically significant.[226]

TREATMENT

Currently recommended drugs against *T. gondii* act primarily against the tachyzoite form and thus do not eradicate the encysted form (bradyzoite). Pyrimethamine is considered to be the most effective anti-*Toxoplasma* agent and if feasible should always be included in drug regimens used against the parasite. Folinic acid should be administered concomitantly to avoid bone marrow suppression. Unless there are circumstances that preclude the use of more than one drug, there is no role for monotherapy in the treatment of toxoplasmosis. A second drug such as sulfadiazine or clindamycin should be added. The role of other drugs including azithromycin, clarithromycin, atovaquone, dapsone, and TMP-SMX is less clear; they should only be used as alternatives and should be used in combination with pyrimethamine.

Although drugs used to treat toxoplasmosis in the setting of different clinical entities are basically the same, careful attention should be given to the dosing and dosing regimen. Recommended doses in immuncompromised patients are usually higher than those in immunocompetent patients. For instance, the recommended dose of pyrimethamine for patients with TE is 50 to 75 mg/day after a loading dose of 200 mg, whereas the dose to treat fetal infection during pregnancy is 25 to 50 mg/day after a loading dose of 100 mg in the mother.

Treatment Regimens in Specific Clinical Entities

Toxoplasmosis in the Immunocompetent Patient

Immunocompetent adults with the lymphadenopathic form are usually not treated unless visceral disease is clinically overt or symptoms are severe or persistent. Treatment is usually administered for 2 to 4 weeks, followed by reassessment of the patient's condition. Infections acquired by laboratory accident or transfusion of blood products are potentially more severe, and patients who have been infected in these ways probably should be treated.[36]

Toxoplasmosis in the Immunodeficient Patient

If left untreated, toxoplasmosis in immunodeficient patients is often lethal. Treatment is recommended for 4 to 6 weeks after the resolution of all signs and symptoms (often for 6 months or longer). At one medical center, 80% of non-AIDS immunodeficient patients with toxoplasmosis improved with specific therapy.[327] This rate of improvement is similar to that observed in appropriately treated AIDS patients with TE.[307] Chronic (latent) asymptomatic infection in immunodeficient patients is not treated.

At present, the exact dosing schedule for the treatment of toxoplasmosis in non-AIDS immunocompromised patients has not been defined.[5] However, a great deal of useful information in this regard has resulted from studies performed in AIDS patients with toxoplasmosis.[145]

A detailed review of the management of TE has been published[145] and is summarized in Fig. 268–7. Algorithms for empirical treatment of TE have developed because a definitive diagnosis can only be made by brain biopsy, a procedure that carries a recognized complication rate and is not always feasible.[6, 145, 306]

Therapy for toxoplasmosis in AIDS patients includes acute (primary or induction) treatment, maintenance treatment (secondary prophylaxis), and primary prophylaxis. Because relapse occurs in up to 80% of cases[328] after the discontinuation of primary therapy, maintenance therapy is recommended for the life of the patient. There are as yet no convincing data from prospective, carefully designed trials to allow the recommendation of monotherapy for induction, maintenance, or primary prophylaxis.

Acute therapy should be for at least 3 weeks,[6] and up to 6 weeks or more may be required for more severely ill patients who have not achieved a complete response. Pyrimethamine combined with sulfadiazine and folinic acid is the therapy of choice for AIDS patients with toxoplasmosis and is the standard by which experimental regimens should be compared. This regimen was associated with clinical response in 68 to 95% of patients with TE.[62, 87, 167, 299, 329] Unfortunately, up to 40% of patients develop side effects from one or more of the drugs, requiring discontinuation of therapy.[62, 167] Pyrimethamine-clindamycin and folinic acid appear comparable in efficacy to pyrimethamine-sulfadiazine,[330, 331] but this combination also has comparable toxicity. Alternative regimens used for acute therapy and their dosage schedules are listed in Table 268–1.

Corticosteroids are often given to patients with TE for the reduction of cerebral edema and raised intracranial pressure. The clinical response and survival in patients with TE who received corticoster-

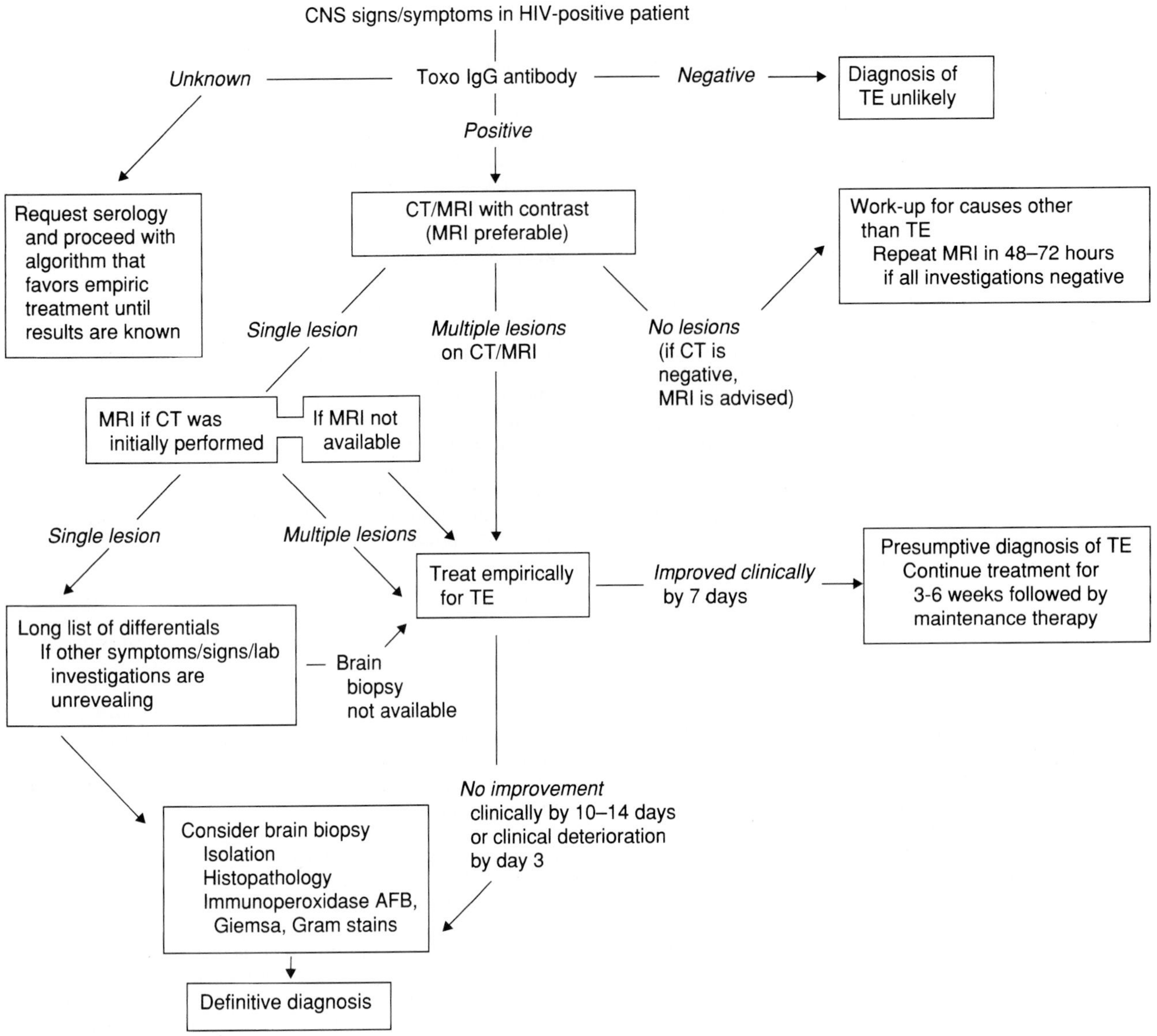

FIGURE 268–7. Treatment algorithm for human immunodeficiency virus–infected patients with central nervous system symptoms or signs that might potentially be toxoplasmic encephalitis.

oids in addition to antimicrobial therapy has been reported to be no different from that of those who received antimicrobial agents alone.[307] The use of these agents may complicate the interpretation of empirical therapy of TE because partial clinical and radiologic improvement may be seen solely due to a reduction in cerebral edema and inflammation or a response of CNS lymphoma.

The time to clinical response in AIDS patients with TE who were receiving appropriate anti-*Toxoplasma* therapy has been evaluated in a study that included an objective, graded neurologic examination.[307] Of those with a response, 91% improved with respect to at least half of their baseline abnormalities by day 14.[307] AIDS patients with presumed TE had some degree of improvement within 7 to 10 days of the initiation of appropriate anti-*Toxoplasma* therapy. By contrast, a significant number of patients with an alternate diagnosis, including lymphoma, exhibited signs of clinical deterioration as early as 3 to 5 days after the initiation of the empirical regimen for presumed TE.[307] Headaches and seizures were insensitive indicators for a response to therapy. In some cases, toxoplasmosis has progressed to death despite the use of appropriate drug regimens.[330, 331]

After successful primary therapy, drug dosages are generally decreased for lifelong maintenance therapy. No single maintenance regimen that is efficacious with an acceptable adverse reaction profile has yet been identified. Relapse of TE occurs in approximately 20 to 30% of patients who are receiving maintenance therapy, in part because of nonadherence to and patient intolerance of the prescribed regimen.[167] Maintenance regimens, their dosages, and dosing intervals have not been studied in a systematic fashion. Hence, it is difficult to provide unqualified recommendations.[332] Pyrimethamine (25 mg/day) plus sulfadiazine (500 mg four times daily) has been associated with the lowest relapse rate[331] and is recommended unless there are contraindications to its use. When daily therapy with pyrimethamine-sulfadiazine was compared with a twice-weekly regimen for the prevention of recurrence of TE, the latter was found to be less effective.[333, 334] Patients receiving the pyrimethamine-sulfadiazine combination most likely do not require another regimen for PCP prophylaxis. Whereas 25% of patients receiving pyrimethamine-clindamycin subsequently developed PCP,[335] no patient receiving pyrimethamine-sulfadiazine developed PCP.[334, 335] Because of drug toxicity, many patients are unable to continue taking the combination pyrimethamine-sulfadiazine for maintenance therapy. A higher re-

TABLE 268–1 Guidelines for Acute (Primary) Therapy of Toxoplasmic Encephalitis in Patients with Acquired Immunodeficiency Syndrome

Drug	Dosage Schedule
Standard regimens	
Pyrimethamine	PO 200-mg loading dose then 50–75 mg qd
plus	
Folinic acid (leucovorin)*	PO, IV, or IM 10–20 mg qd (up to 50 mg qd)
plus one of the following:	
Sulfadiazine	PO 1–1.5 g q6h
or	
Clindamycin	PO or IV 600 mg q6h (up to IV 1200 mg q6h)
Possible alternative regimens†	
1. Trimethoprim-sulfamethoxazole	PO or IV 3–5 mg (trimethoprim component)/kg q6h
2. Pyrimethamine and folinic acid as in standard regimens *plus* one of the following:	
Clarithromycin	PO 1 g q12h
Atovaquone	PO 750 mg q6h
Azithromycin	PO 1200–1500 mg qd
Dapsone	PO 100 mg qd

* The dose of folinic acid can be titrated based on the hemogram to reduce pyrimethamine-associated myelotoxicity.
† These agents have been used in clinical studies with small numbers of patients and have response rates lower than the standard regimens (see text for references). They should be used only in patients who are intolerant of the standard regimens. Alternative agents must be used in combination with another antimicrobial agent (most frequently, pyrimethamine with folinic acid) that has proven clinical activity against *Toxoplasma gondii.*

lapse rate has been reported with the use of pyrimethamine-clindamycin compared with pyrimethamine-sulfadiazine for secondary prophylaxis of TE; hence, it is recommended that the clindamycin dose be at least 1200 mg/day.[336] Encouraging results have been reported with other drug combinations. These include Fansidar (pyrimethamine-sulfadoxine), which has been used in a dose of one tablet every 2 weeks,[337] and pyrimethamine-dapsone administered on an intermittent schedule (2 to 3 times a week).[338–340] The long half-life of these agents allowed the longer dosing interval.

When pyrimethamine was used alone as maintenance therapy at 50 mg/day[341, 342] and 100 mg/day,[341] the relapse rates were 10 to 28% and 5%, respectively. The efficacy of TMP-SMX for maintenance therapy has not been sufficiently investigated. Further studies are required before specific recommendations can be made for other drug combinations.

Primary prophylaxis against *T. gondii* in patients with AIDS has been shown to be effective in preventing acute TE.[343, 344] In addition, the use of new highly active antiretroviral therapies in HIV-infected patients has had a profound effect in decreasing the incidence of TE in these patients.[345] Primary prophylaxis is recommended for patients who have detectable *Toxoplasma* IgG antibodies and whose lowest $CD4^+$ count has been below 100/mm^3 (many experts use less than 200/mm^3 as the cutoff rather than 100/mm^3), regardless of the HIV RNA viral load.[346] It is not known whether the recovery of the $CD4^+$ count above 100/mm^3 observed in a significant number of patients on highly active antiretroviral therapies would constitute an indication to discontinue the primary prophylactic regimen being administered against the development of toxoplasmosis.[346] TMP-SMX (1 double-strength or single-strength tablet/day),[343, 344] dapsone (50 mg/day) plus pyrimethamine (50 mg/week),[339, 340, 343, 347] and Fansidar[337, 348] have been reported to be effective in preventing the first episode of TE.[346]

Roxithromycin administered at 900 mg once a week (may be given in three divided doses)[349] has been reported to be effective for primary prophylaxis. A number of investigators have studied pyrimethamine for primary prophylaxis and have come to different conclusions regarding dosing and efficacy.[71, 350, 351] In one study, pyrimethamine actually was associated with a higher death rate,[351] whereas in another no such correlation was found.[71] Patients who developed a rash while receiving prophylactic therapy with pyrimethamine were also noted to be at higher risk of TE.[352] At this time, pyrimethamine alone for primary prophylaxis cannot be recommended. Clarithromycin[353, 354] and spiramycin[355] have been ineffective for primary prophylaxis when they were used alone. A randomized, placebo-controlled trial demonstrated that when clindamycin was administered at 600 mg/day for primary prophylaxis, it was associated with an unacceptably high rate of associated gastrointestinal disease, in particular diarrhea, suggesting that poor patient tolerance will prevent its further study for this purpose.[356]

It must be emphasized that in a number studies of TMP-SMX,[357] pyrimethamine-dapsone,[347] and Fansidar[337, 348] for primary prophylaxis, discontinuation of therapy as a result of adverse effects was reported in 29 to 39% of the patients. Thus, on an intent-to-treat basis, these regimens are not satisfactory for a significant number of AIDS patients.

Seizures occur in up to 35% of patients with TE.[62, 358] One retrospective study demonstrated a poorer outcome in those patients who received anticonvulsant therapy compared with those who did not.[328] Whether this result represents a true drug effect or a selection bias (given that those receiving anticonvulsant therapy are likely to be more severely ill) is unclear. Anticonvulsant agents may be responsible for numerous side effects and drug interactions; for instance, potentially serious interactions can occur between agents such as carbamazepine, phenobarbital, or phenytoin and other drugs to treat HIV infection such as protease inhibitors. Anticonvulsant therapy is probably best administered when seizures have occurred.[328]

Data on the outcome of treatment of AIDS patients with toxoplasmosis outside the CNS are limited; available information on the therapy of ocular[198, 201, 202] and pulmonary involvement[189, 359] indicates that these forms of toxoplasmosis are also responsive to treatment. A favorable response to therapy in cases of ocular toxoplasmosis has been the rule.[198, 201, 202] Therapy was successful in 50 to 77% of patients with pulmonary toxoplasmosis.[189, 196, 359]

The hematologic toxicity associated with zidovudine and the high doses of pyrimethamine used for the treatment of TE are additive. Other drugs used in treating HIV-infected patients that cause myelosuppression include ganciclovir, flucytosine, trimethoprim, trimetrexate, pentamidine, chemotherapy agents, and IFN-α.

Ocular Toxoplasmosis

The decision to treat active toxoplasmic chorioretinitis should be made based on a complete ophthalmologic evaluation. Treatment is most likely indicated in the following settings: any decrease in visual acuity, macular or peripapillary lesions, lesions greater than one optic disk diameter, lesions associated with a moderate-to-severe vitreous inflammatory reaction, the presence of multiple active lesions, the persistence of active disease for greater than 1 month, and any ocular lesions associated with recently acquired infection. Because the disease can be self-limited, many clinicians may not treat small, peripheral retinal lesions that are not immediately vision-threatening in immunocompetent patients.[9]

The reported benefits of medical therapy are based primarily on the clinical presentation.[9] Because there is so much variation in the clinical manifestations of the retinal disease, and because the disease may be self-limited even without treatment, the response to therapy is difficult to interpret. The combination of pyrimethamine (100-mg loading dose given over 24 hours, followed by 25 to 50 mg daily) and sulfadiazine (2- to 4-g loading dose initially, followed by 1 g given four times daily) for 4 to 6 weeks depending on the clinical response, which is considered "classic" therapy for ocular toxoplasmosis, is the most common drug combination used.[9]

Clindamycin (300 mg orally every 6 hours for a minimum of 3 weeks) has also been used with favorable clinical results.[360] Systemic corticosteroids are indicated when lesions involve the macula, optic nerve head, or papillomacular bundle. Photocoagulation has been used both for the treatment of active lesions and for prophylaxis against the spread of lesions because new lesions appear contiguous to old lesions.[361] In some patients, vitrectomy and lentectomy may be necessary.[362]

For the approach to ocular toxoplasmosis during pregnancy see "Acute Acquired *Toxoplasma* Infection in Pregnant Women."

Acute Acquired Toxoplasma *Infection in Pregnant Women*

Treatment of the acutely infected pregnant woman does not eliminate but does appear to decrease the incidence of fetal infection. Because there is usually a delay between the acquisition of acute maternal infection, infection of the placenta, and subsequent infection of the fetus, identification of acute maternal infection necessitates immediate institution of treatment of the mother. Most experience of maternal treatment to prevent transmission to the fetus has been with spiramycin (3 g/day, obtainable in the United States from the Food and Drug Administration, telephone 301-827-2335). Spiramycin has been accepted by most investigators as being effective in reducing the frequency of maternal transmission of *T. gondii* to the fetus by approximately 60%.[220] If spiramycin cannot be used or is not available, it may be replaced by sulfadiazine alone with appropriate precautions at term. However, there are no data on the efficacy of sulfonamides, including sulfadiazine, when these drugs are used for this purpose.

Because spiramycin does not reliably cross the placenta,[363] if fetal infection is documented, the recommended therapeutic regimen is the combination of sulfadiazine (4 g/day), pyrimethamine (25 mg/day), and folinic acid (5 to 15 mg/day). Such treatment might be an alternative to the termination of pregnancy when abortion is not allowed by law or for women who desire to continue their pregnancy. Pyrimethamine should not be used in the first 12 to 14 weeks of pregnancy because of a concern for teratogenicity (in this circumstance we recommend that sulfadiazine be administered alone although there are no data on its efficacy in this situation).[8]

Pregnant women with toxoplasmic chorioretinitis as a result of reactivation of chronic disease do not have a higher risk to transmit the parasite to their offspring than do pregnant women who have been infected before pregnancy and do not have ocular disease. Their eye disease should be treated according to the indications discussed in the section "Ocular Toxoplasmosis," page 2877. Pregnant women with toxoplasmic chorioretinitis thought to be a manifestation of recently acquired infection should be treated because of both the eye disease and the risk of transmission of the infection to their fetus.

Congenital Infection

Detailed information on and recommendations for the postnatal treatment of congenital toxoplasmosis are reviewed elsewhere,[8] but we favor continuous sulfadiazine (50 mg/kg twice daily), pyrimethamine (2 mg/kg/day for 2 days, then 1 mg/kg/day for 2 to 6 months, then 1 mg/kg/day three times a week), and folinic acid (10 mg three times weekly) for a minimum of 12 months. Other groups have used pyrimethamine–sulfadiazine–folinic acid alternated with spiramycin (100 mg/kg/day).[8, 223] Serial follow-up to gauge the response of the infant to therapy should include neuroradiology, ophthalmologic examinations, and CSF analysis if indicated.[8]

For guidance on therapy in congenital cases we recommend that physicians contact Dr. Rima McLeod at the University of Chicago, where a major study, the National Collaborative Treatment Trial, on the appropriate management of these cases is being performed (telephone 773-834-4152).[226] Physicians who are treating patients with congenital toxoplasmosis who are younger than 2.5 months of age may wish to contact this multidisciplinary group regarding potential enrollment of their patients in that study.[226] This study has shown that outcomes are substantially better for most, but not all, infants treated from the neonatal period for 12 months with pyrimethamine-sulfadiazine and leucovorin, compared with historical controls receiving no or short-course therapy.[226, 364–368] Improvement in intellectual function, regression of retinal lesions, reduction in anticonvulsant drug requirements, and prevention of auditory sequelae appear to be the major benefits of such treatment, which was combined with CSF shunting if required.[226] Signs of active infection resolved within weeks of initiation of treatment. In a significant number of treated children, cerebral calcifications diminished in size or resolved.[368]

Drugs

The most effective available therapeutic regimen is the combination of pyrimethamine plus sulfadiazine (or trisulfapyrimidines-sulfamerazine, sulfamethazine, and sulfapyrazine). These agents are active against tachyzoites and are synergistic when used in combination. Readers are encouraged to refer to the drug package inserts for each of the antimicrobial agents for a complete description of the adverse effects and drug interactions that may occur.

Pyrimethamine

Pyrimethamine is lipid-soluble, is readily absorbed from the gastrointestinal tract, and has a half-life of 4 to 5 days. CSF concentrations have been reported to be 10 to 25% of simultaneous plasma concentrations.[369, 370] A study in patients with TE revealed that serum levels varied markedly between patients receiving similar dosages, that toxoplasmacidal levels can be but probably are not always attained in the CSF (especially when pyrimethamine is used without sulfadiazine), and that measurement of serum levels could be useful.[370] The loading regimen of pyrimethamine for adults is 100 to 200 mg/day in two divided doses for 1 day. Sulfadiazine, as described later, is used along with pyrimethamine. Regimens after loading doses of pyrimethamine and sulfadiazine depend on the severity of disease and the immunocompetence of the patient. For immunocompetent patients, pyrimethamine is usually given for 2 to 4 weeks at 25 to 50 mg/day (for treatment of the fetus see "Treatment Regimens in Specific Clinical Entities"). Administration of pyrimethamine at 2- to 4-day intervals has been suggested by some workers in view of pyrimethamine's 4- to 5-day half-life. For non-AIDS immunodeficient patients, pyrimethamine is given for a minimum of 4 to 6 weeks at 25 to 50 mg/day. For AIDS patients, 50 to 75 mg/day is being used for 3 to 6 weeks, followed by maintenance therapy. For ocular toxoplasmosis, pyrimethamine is used at doses of 25 to 50 mg/day. Pyrimethamine is available only in 25-mg tablets; there is no parenteral form.

Pyrimethamine is a folic acid antagonist. The most common side effect is dose-related suppression of the bone marrow. A peripheral blood cell and platelet count should be performed twice weekly. The risk of this adverse effect may be decreased by concomitant administration of folinic acid (calcium leucovorin). The parenteral form of folinic acid is well absorbed orally, and 5 to 10 mg of folinic acid (up to 50 mg/day is being used in AIDS patients) may be given orally (e.g., with orange juice at the same time as the pyrimethamine). Folinic acid does not inhibit the action of pyrimethamine on tachyzoites. Less serious side effects of pyrimethamine include gastrointestinal distress, rash, headaches, and a bad taste in the mouth.

Sulfadiazine

Because sulfadiazine acts synergistically with pyrimethamine, the drugs are given in combination. Most other sulfonamides have inferior activity. The half-life of sulfadiazine is approximately 10 to 12 hours. A loading dose of 75 mg/kg up to 4 g is given. Thereafter, 1 to 1.5 gm is given every 6 hours. The patient must maintain a good urine output to prevent crystalluria and oliguria. Alkalinization of the urine with oral sodium bicarbonate reduces the chance of crystalluria. The maintenance dose of sulfadiazine for AIDS patients is 500 mg orally four times daily; it is given with pyrimethamine (25 mg/day). Tablets and a liquid oral form of sulfadiazine are available. The most common side effects associated with sulfadiazine are skin rashes (which may be life-threatening)[328] and crystal-induced nephrotoxicity.[371] Worsening encephalopathy, hallucinations, or a new onset of psychiatric symptoms in patients with AIDS may be sulfadiazine induced and must be considered in the patient who is nonresponsive to otherwise appropriate antitoxoplasma treatment.[372] A drug rash with sulfonamide therapy does not necessarily preclude its use because successful desensitization protocols have been reported.[373–375]

Clindamycin

Clindamycin is a lincosamide that inhibits protein synthesis in bacteria, but its mechanism of action in *T. gondii* is unknown. In combination with pyrimethamine, it has comparable efficacy and toxicity when compared with pyrimethamine-sulfadiazine.[330, 331] The recommended dose is 600 mg every 6 hours in either an oral or intravenous formulation[336]; an intravenous dose of 1200 mg every 6 hours has also been used with success in TE.[330] Adverse reactions to clindamycin include rash, nausea, vomiting, and diarrhea. Myopathy with electromyographic abnormalities and elevated serum creatine phosphokinase levels have been described.[376]

Spiramycin

Spiramycin has been used effectively for the treatment of pregnant women to reduce transmission to the fetus and is given orally, 3 g/day in two to four divided doses. It has not been shown to be effective for acute therapy, maintenance therapy, or primary prophylaxis of TE in AIDS patients. There is no evidence that spiramycin is teratogenic.

Trimethoprim and Trimethoprim-Sulfamethoxazole

Trimethoprim is less active than pyrimethamine against *T. gondii*.[377] In experimental toxoplasmosis, pyrimethamine-sulfadiazine has greater efficacy than TMP-SMX.[377, 378] Retrospective studies of small numbers of patients suggest that TMP-SMX is effective for the treatment of TE in AIDS patients,[379–381] but because data on its use for TE are limited compared with those available for pyrimethamine-sulfadiazine, we recommend use of the latter regimen. TMP-SMX is the drug of choice for primary prophylaxis of toxoplasmosis in patients with AIDS.

Dapsone

This sulfone in combination with pyrimethamine has been reported to be effective for the treatment of TE when used in an oral dose of 100 mg/day with 25 mg/day of oral pyrimethamine.[382] Adverse reactions are frequent and include skin rash, hematologic abnormalities, fever, and nausea.[347, 383] It has also been used successfully in combination with pyrimethamine for primary prophylaxis and maintenance therapy (secondary prophylaxis) for toxoplasmosis in AIDS patients.

Pyrimethamine-Sulfadoxine (Fansidar)

This drug combination in its oral form is used in many areas of Europe for the treatment and prevention of toxoplasmosis in AIDS patients and in congenitally infected patients. When administered intramuscularly, this combination has provided responses in 80% of patients with TE.[384] Adverse reactions are common and include skin rashes, Stevens-Johnson syndrome, and hematologic and gastrointestinal side effects that resulted in discontinuation in up to 39% of patients.[348]

Trimetrexate

This folate antagonist has been used alone as salvage therapy of TE with initial clinical responses but subsequent relapses observed during therapy, raising the possibility of the development of drug resistance.[385]

Macrolides-Azalides and Ketolides

Newer macrolide-azalide antibiotics such as azithromycin,[386] clarithromycin,[387] and roxithromycin[388, 389] have been found to be effective in the treatment of toxoplasmosis in murine models. Azithromycin has activity against both tachyzoite and cyst forms.[386, 390] Initial analysis of data from a trial (ACTG 156) that investigated the use of azithromycin (900 to 1500 mg every day) plus pyrimethamine (25 to 50 mg) for the treatment of TE revealed a response rate of 31% (data provided by B. Luft).[391] In this study, 9% of patients were classified as potential responders and 50% as relapse and induction failures, and in another 9%, the response was indeterminate. It is evident from this study that azithromycin is effective (when used in combination with pyrimethamine) for the treatment of some cases of TE in AIDS patients. A final conclusion in regard to the effectiveness of the azithromycin-pyrimethamine combination cannot yet be made. A single case report described a dramatic response to azithromycin in a patient with TE who was allergic to sulfonamide and pyrimethamine and in whom clindamycin and doxycycline were not effective.[392]

Promising results have been reported in a pilot study for the treatment of TE in AIDS patients with the combination of pyrimethamine 75 mg/day and clarithromycin 1 g every 12 hours by the oral route. 62% of patients had a complete and 23% a partial clinical response; 15% died by week 3 of therapy.[393] Adverse events associated with therapy in this study included nausea and vomiting (38%), skin rash (38%), hepatic enzyme abnormalities (24%), hematologic abnormalities (31%), and hearing loss (15%). Of the surviving patients, 27% had clarithromycin discontinued because of drug toxicity that resulted in thrombocytopenia or liver enzyme abnormalities, or both.

Ketolides are a new class of macrolide antibiotics that have been shown to be active against a variety of bacteria including macrolide-resistant bacteria and mycobacteria. The ketolide antibiotics HMR 3647 and HMR 3004 have been shown to possess excellent in vitro activity against *T. gondii* and provided remarkable protection against death in infected mice.[394]

Tetracyclines

Doxycycline has had success in the treatment of TE in a few patients when used at 300 mg/day intravenously in three divided doses.[395] A dosage of 100 mg twice a day was given to six patients intolerant to pyrimethamin-/sulfadiazine, but five had associated neurologic and radiologic recurrences while receiving the drug.[396] Further study of the use of tetracyclines in combination with other agents in the treatment of toxoplasmosis is warranted.

Atovaquone

Atovaquone has been approved by the U.S. Food and Drug Administration for use in patients with mild to moderate PCP. Atovaquone has potent in vitro and in vivo (in a murine model of the disease) activity against both tachyzoite and cyst forms.[390, 397] It has been administered alone in AIDS patients with TE with varied results. In studies that included small numbers of patients,[398, 399] clinical response rates of 75 and 66% were reported with atovaquone alone in tablet form. In a large series of patients with AIDS-related TE, the use of atovaquone alone in tablet form as salvage therapy was successful in 37% of those intolerant to standard therapy.[400] Unfortunately, relapse occurred in approximately 50% of patients in whom atovaquone was used for acute therapy and continued alone as maintenance therapy.[398, 400] In another study, 17 (26%) of 65 patients treated with atovaquone in tablet form as a single agent for the maintenance therapy of TE experienced a relapse.[401] The combination of pyrimethamine and atovaquone may prove more useful.[402] Serum levels of atovaquone in patients treated with TE were not predictive of clinical response or failure in one study[399]; in another more extensive study, a direct correlation was noted between clinical and radiologic responses and median atovaquone plasma concentrations.[400] There continues to be a problem with the reliability of absorption of this drug. The bioavailability of atovaquone is highly dependent on formulation and diet.[403] The suspension formulation of microfine particles provides an approximately twofold increase in atovaquone bioavailability in the fasting or fed state compared with the previously marketed tablet formulation. The absolute bioavailability of a 750-mg dose of atovaquone suspension administered under fed conditions in HIV-infected (CD4 >100 cells/mm^3) volunteers was 47 ± 15%.[403] The bioavailability of a 750-mg dose of the previously marketed tablet formulation was 23 ± 11%. Administering atovaquone with food (e.g., after a standard breakfast containing 23 g of fat) enhances its absorption by approximately twofold. A better survival time among patients with higher steady-state plasma concentrations of the drug has been reported.[400] Prospective trials are needed to assess the efficacy of the new suspension formulation of the drug. This drug should not be used alone for the treatment of the acute infection but rather should be used in combination with drugs such as pyrimethamine. The use of atovaquone with or without pyrimethamine in AIDS patients with TE has been well tolerated. The adverse events observed in these studies included hepatic enzyme abnormalities (50%), rash (25%), nausea (21%), and diarrhea (19%).[399] Between 3 and 10% of patients treated with atovaquone discontinued the drug because of rash, hepatic enzyme abnormalities, nausea, or vomiting.[399, 401, 402] Leukopenia associated with the combination of pyrimethamine and atovaquone has responded to folinic acid (leucovorin) and granulocyte colony-stimulating factor therapy.[402]

Other Antimicrobial Agents

Other antimicrobial agents that have demonstrable activity against *T. gondii* include arprinocid, a purine analogue,[404] qinghaosu,[405] and pentamidine.[406] Arprinocid has not been used in humans; the latter two agents are of particular interest because of the considerable experience that has accumulated in their use for other infectious diseases. The antimetabolite 5-fluorouracil has in vitro activity against *T. gondii*[407] at doses approximately 10-fold less than those used for cancer chemotherapy. There are two reports of the successful use of the combination of 5-fluorouracil and clindamycin for treatment of TE in AIDS patients. Severe toxicity was not observed.[408, 409] Rifabutin, a derivative of rifamycin, has remarkable activity against acute toxoplasmosis in mice,[410] and rifapentine, another derivative of rifamycin, was noted to be active in vitro and in vivo against *T. gondii.*[411] Trovafloxacin, a fluoroquinolone,[412] has been shown to be effective against *T. gondii* in vitro and in vivo in a mouse model of the infection.[412]

Immunotherapy

Because of the severely impaired immune function in patients with AIDS, immunotherapy has been proposed as adjunctive treatment for life-threatening toxoplasmosis. Of particular interest is IFN-γ, which has previously been identified as the most important mediator of resistance against *T. gondii.*[118] In murine models of toxoplasmosis, the administration of IFN-γ in concert with antimicrobial agents has resulted in synergistic or additive toxoplasmacidal activity. These include IFN-γ in combination with roxithromycin,[413] pyrimethamine,[414] azithromycin,[415] and clindamycin.[416] The combination of IL-12 plus atovaquone or IL-12 plus clindamycin has also proved useful in a mouse model of acute toxoplasmosis.[417]

PREVENTION

General Methods

Prevention is most important in seronegative pregnant women and in immunodeficient patients. It is most readily accomplished through education of these patients by their personal physicians (Table 268–2). The goal is to avoid the ingestion of and contact with cysts or sporulated oocysts. Cysts in meat are made noninfectious by heating the meat to 66°C (meat should be cooked to "well done" with no pink meat visible in the center), by smoking or curing it, or by freezing it to −20°C (which is not attainable in most home freezers). Hands should be washed thoroughly after handling raw meat or vegetables, eggs should not be eaten raw, and unpasteurized milk (particularly milk from goats) should be avoided. Vectors such as flies and cockroaches should be controlled. Areas contaminated with cat feces should be avoided altogether. Disposable gloves should be worn while disposing of cat litter material, working in the garden, or cleaning a child's sandbox. Oocysts are killed if the cat litter pan is soaked in nearly boiling water for 5 minutes. If the litter pan is cleaned every day, oocysts will not have a chance to sporulate. Serologic testing of cats is unwarranted because testing does not demonstrate whether the infected cat is excreting oocysts.

Serologic Screening

Acute Toxoplasma gondii *Infection or Toxoplasmosis in the Immunodeficient Patient*

Transmission of *T. gondii* and death due to the infection have resulted from the transfusion of leukocyte-rich blood products and by organ transplantation in immunodeficient patients. Transmission of infection by these routes may occur frequently enough to warrant screening for antibody to *T. gondii* in blood product donors and possibly to exclude seropositive people as organ donors to seronegative potential recipients whenever feasible. Prophylactic treatment (pyrimethamine 25 mg orally every day for 6 weeks after transplantation) has been used with apparent success in seronegative recipients of hearts transplanted from seropositive donors.[5, 418, 419] Primary prophylaxis can prevent toxoplasmosis in patients dually infected with HIV and *T. gondii* (see "Toxoplasmosis in the Immunodeficient Patient" in the "Treatment" section).

Congenital Toxoplasma gondii *Infection or Toxoplasmosis*

Congenital toxoplasmosis is a preventable disease. It is threfore the responsibility of physicians who care for pregnant women to educate

TABLE 268–2 Measures to Prevent Primary *Toxoplasma gondii* Infection

Avoid contact with materials potentially contaminated with cat feces, especially handling of cat litter and gardening. Gloves are advised when these activities are necessary.
Disinfect cat litter box with near-boiling water for 5 minutes before handling.
Avoid mucous membrane contact when handling raw meat.
Wash hands thoroughly after contact with raw meat.
Wash kitchen surfaces and utensils that have come in contact with raw meat.
Cook meat to 66°C or "well done" (meat that is smoked or cured in brine may be infectious).
Avoid ingestion of dried meat.
Wash fruits and vegetables before consumption.
Refrain from skinning animals.

TABLE 268–3 Incidence of Congenital Toxoplasmosis in 2243 Fetuses According to Gestational Age at the Time of Maternal Infection*

Week of Gestation	Infected Fetuses	All Fetuses	Incidence (%)
0–2	0	100	0
3–6	6	384	1.6
7–10	9	503	1.8
11–14	37	511	7.2
15–18	49	392	13
19–22	44	237	19
23–26†	30	116	26
Total	175	2243	7.8

* Maternal Infection was treated with spiramycin at a dose of 1 g three times daily.
† Insufficient data were available after the 32nd week.
Adapted from Hohlfeld P, Daffos F, Costa J-M, et al. Prenatal diagnosis of congenital toxoplasmosis with polymerase-chain-reaction test or amniotic fluid. N Engl J Med. 1994;331:695–699. Copyright © 1994 Massachusetts Medical Society. All rights reserved.

them on how they can prevent themselves from becoming infected (and thereby not place their fetus at risk). A lack of adoption of a systematic serologic screening program in the United States leaves education as the principal means of preventing this tragic disease. If physicians choose to screen their patients serologically, the appropriate tests must be used, the laboratory performing the tests must be competent, and the test results must be interpreted correctly. In some countries (e.g., France and Austria), initially seronegative pregnant women are tested monthly during gestation; this schedule is optimal for detecting infection early enough to institute proper medical management. For further discussion and recommendations regarding serologic screening, see Remington and colleagues[8] and Liesenfeld and Remington.[322] Women identified as possibly having acquired the infection during gestation can be considered for prenatal diagnosis (see "Congenital Infection in the Fetus and Newborn" in "Diagnosis of Specific Clinical Entities."). The appropriate use of prenatal diagnosis can markedly reduce the incidence of clinically significant congenital toxoplasmosis.[217, 218, 221]

Women with positive results in the initial IgG-antibody test should have a test for IgM antibody performed on the same serum. If the IgM assay is positive, the specimen should be sent to a reference laboratory for confirmatory testing (see "*Toxoplasma gondii* Infection in Pregnancy" and Fig. 268–6).[267, 285, 322] In patients with IgG antibodies at any titer, a negative IgM-antibody test result in the first trimester, and no clinical signs of acute toxoplasmosis, no further testing would be necessary because the probability of acute acquired infection in these women is extremely low. Given the same circumstances in the second trimester of pregnancy, a negative IgM test result rules out, for practical purposes, recent acquisition of acute infection. A negative IgM test in the third trimester may occur in a patient who acquired the infection earlier in gestation.

The incidence of congenital toxoplasmosis has been shown to be lower in infants born of women who acquire the infection during gestation and are treated with spiramycin.[213, 220] Results of a study in France[221] on the incidence of *T. gondii* infection in the fetus of women whose date of acquiring the infection during the gestation was known and who were treated with spiramycin are shown in Table 268–3.

Until further information is available to quantify the risk of reactivation in pregnant women who are dually infected with HIV and *T. gondii,* we recommend that primary prophylaxis against *T. gondii* be introduced when their CD4 T-cell count falls below 200/mm^3. If the patient is receiving TMP/SMX, additional prophylaxis is probably unnecessary. Otherwise, spiramycin can be used at a dose of 3 g/day.

REFERENCES

1. Nicolle C, Manceaux L. Sur une infection à corps de Leishman (ou organismes voisins) du gondi. Compte rendu hebdomadaire des seances de l'Academie des sciences. 1908;146:207–209.
2. Janku J. Pathogenesa a pathologicka anatomie tak nazvaneho vrozeneho kolobomu zlute skvrny v oku normalne velikem a mikrophthalmickem s nalezem parazitu v sitnici. Cas Lek Cesk. 1923;62:1021–1027, 1054–1059, 1081–1085, 1111–1115, 1138–1144.
3. Wolf A, Cowen D, Paige BH. Toxoplasmic encephalomyelitis. III. A new case of granulomatous encephalomyelitis due to a protozoon. Am J Pathol. 1939;15:657–694.
4. Vietzke WM, Gelderman AH, Grimley PM, Valsamis MP. Toxoplasmosis complicating malignancy. Experience at the National Cancer Institute. Cancer. 1968;21:816–827.
5. Israelski DM, Remington JS. Toxoplasmosis in the non-AIDS immunocompromised host. In: Remington J, Swartz M, eds. Current Clinical Topics in Infectious Diseases, v. 13. London: Blackwell Scientific; 1993:322–356.
6. Luft BJ, Remington JS. Toxoplasmic encephalitis in AIDS (AIDS Commentary). Clin Infect Dis. 1992;15:211–222.
7. Luft BJ, Conley F, Remington JS, et al. Outbreak of central-nervous-system toxoplasmosis in western Europe and North America. Lancet. 1983;1:781–784.
8. Remington JS, McLeod R, Desmonts G. Toxoplasmosis. In: Remington JS, Klein JO, eds. Infectious Diseases of the Fetus and Newborn Infant. 4th ed. Philadelphia: WB Saunders; 1995:140–267.
9. Holland GN, O'Connor GR, Belfort R Jr, Remington JS. Toxoplasmosis. In: Pepose JS, Holland GN, Wilhelmus KR, eds. Ocular Infection and Immunity. St Louis: Mosby–Year Book; 1996:1183–1223.
10. Dubey J. *Toxoplasma, Neospora, Sarcocystis,* and other tissue cyst-forming coccidia of humans and animals. In: Kreier J, ed. Parasitic Protozoa, v. 6. San Diego: Academic; 1993:1–57.
11. Krahenbuhl JL, Remington JS. The immunology of *Toxoplasma* and toxoplasmosis. In: Cohen S, Warren KS, eds. Immunology of Parasitic Infections. 2nd ed. London: Blackwell Scientific; 1982:356–421.
12. Handman E, Goding JW, Remington JS. Detection and characterization of membrane antigens of *Toxoplasma gondii*. J Immunol. 1980;124:2578–2583.
13. Dardé M, Bouteille B, Pestre-Alexandre M. Isoenzyme analysis of 35 *Toxoplasma gondii* isolates and the biological and epidemiological implications. J Parasitol. 1992;78:786–794.
14. Sibley LD, Boothroyd JC. Virulent strains of *Toxoplasma gondii* comprise a single clonal lineage. Nature. 1992;359:82–85.
15. Howe DK, Sibley DL. *Toxoplasma gondii* comprises three clonal lineages: Correlation of parasite genotype with human disease. J Infect Dis. 1995;172:1561–1566.
16. Frenkel JK, Dubey JP, Miller NL. *Toxoplasma gondii* in cats: Fecal stages identified as coccidian oocysts. Science. 1970;167:893–896.
17. Smith JE. A ubiquitous intracellular parasite: The cellular biology of *Toxoplasma gondii*. Int J Parisitol. 1995;25:1301–1309.
18. Conley FK, Jenkins KA, Remington JS. *Toxoplasma gondii* infection of the central nervous system. Use of the peroxidase-antiperoxidase method to demonstrate toxoplasma in formalin fixed, paraffin embedded tissue sections. Hum Pathol. 1981;12:690–698.
19. Remington JS, Cavanaugh EN. Isolation of the encysted form of *Toxoplasma gondii* from human skeletal muscle and brain. N Engl J Med. 1965;273:1308–1310.
20. Dubey J, Thayer D. Killing of different strains of *Toxoplasma gondii* tissue cysts by irradiation under defined conditions. J Parasitol. 1994;80:764–767.
21. Dubey J, Kotula A, Sharar A, et al. Effect of high temperature on infectivity of *Toxoplasma gondii* tissue cysts in pork. J Parasitol. 1990;76:201.
22. Jacobs L, Remington JS, Melton ML. The resistance of the encysted form of *Toxoplasma gondii*. J Parasitol. 1960;46:11–21.
23. Sims TA, Hay J, Talbot IC. An electron microscope and immunohistochemical study of the intracellular location of *Toxoplama* tissue cysts within the brains of mice with congenital toxoplasmosis. Br J Exp Pathol. 1989;70:317–325.
24. Ferguson DJ, Hutchison WM. The host-parasite relationship of *Toxoplasma gondii* in the brains of chronically infected mice. Virchows Arch A. 1987;411(1):39–43.
25. Jones TC, Bienz KA, Erb P. In vitro cultivation of *Toxoplasma gondii* cysts in astrocytes in the presence of gamma interferon. Infect Immun. 1986;51:146–156.
26. Ferguson DJP, Graham DI, Hutchinson WM. Pathological changes in the brains of mice infected with *Toxoplasma gondii*: A histological immunocytochemical and ultra structural study. Int J Exp Pathol. 1991;72:463–474.
27. Ferguson DJ, Hutchison WM. An ultrastructural study of the early development and tissue cyst formation of *Toxoplasma gondii* in the brains of mice. Parasitol Res. 1987;73:483–491.
28. Van Der Zypen E. Light and electronmicroscopic studies on the development of toxoplasma cysts in the brain of the white mouse. Z Parasitenkunde. 1966;28:31–44.
29. Stahl W, Matsubayashi H, Akao S. Murine toxoplasmosis: Development of bizarre clusters of cysts. Jpn J Parasitol. 1966;15(1):44–47.
30. Ferguson DJ, Huskinson-Mark J, Araujo FG, Remington JS. A morphological study of chronic cerebral toxoplasmosis in mice: Comparison of four different strains of *Toxoplasma gondii*. Parasitol Res. 1994;80:493–501.
31. Ferguson DJ, Huskinson-Mark J, Araujo FG, Remington JS. An ultrastructural study of the effect of treatment with atovaquone in brains of mice chronically infected with the ME49 strain of *Toxoplasma gondii*. Int J Exp Pathol. 1994;75:111–116.
32. Gross U, Bohne W, Sôete M, Dubremetz JF. Developmental differentiation between tachyzoites and bradyzoites of *Toxoplasma gondii*. Parasitol Today. 1996;12(1):30–33.
33. Parmley SF, Yang S, Harth G, et al. Molecular characterization of a 65-kilodalton *Toxoplasma gondii* antigen expressed abundantly in the matrix of tissue cysts. Mol Biochem Parasitol. 1994;66:283–296.
34. Bohne W, Roos DS. Stage-specific expression of a selectable marker in *Toxoplasma*

gondii permits selective inhibition of either tachyzoites or bradyzoites. Mol Biochem Parasitol. 1997;88:115–126.
35. Soete M, Dubremetz JF. *Toxoplasma gondii*: Kinetics of stage-specific protein expression during tachyzoite-bradyzoite conversion in vitro. In: Gross U, ed. Current Topics in Microbiology and Immunology: *Toxoplasma gondii, v.* 219. New York: Springer; 1996:75–80.
36. Neu HC. Toxoplasmosis transmitted at autopsy. JAMA. 1967;202:284–285.
37. Dubey J. Toxoplasmosis. Am Vet Med Assoc. 1994;205:1593–1598.
38. Desmonts G, Couvreur J, Alison F, et al. Étude épidémiologique sur la toxoplasmose: L'influence de la cuisson des viandes de boucherie sur la fréquence de l'infection humaine. Rev Fr Étud Clin. 1965;10:952–958.
39. Dubey JP. A review of toxoplasmosis in pigs. Vet Parasitol. 1986;19:181–223.
40. Remington JS. Toxoplasmosis and congenital infection. Intra-uterine infection. 1968;4:47–56.
41. Dubey JP, Leighty JC, Beal VC, et al. National seroprevalence of *Toxoplasma gondii* in pigs. J Parasitol. 1991;77:517–521.
42. Swartzberg JE, Remington JS. Transmission of *Toxoplasma*. Am J Dis Child. 1975;129:777–779.
43. Riemann HP, Meyer ME, Theis JH, et al. Toxoplasmosis in an infant fed unpasteurized goat milk. J Pediatr. 1975;87:573–576.
44. Sacks JJ, Roberto RR, Brooks NF. Toxoplasmosis infection associated with raw goat's milk. JAMA. 1982;248:1728–1732.
45. Luft BJ, Remington JS. Acute *Toxoplasma* infection among family members of patients with acute lymphadenopathic toxoplasmosis. Arch Intern Med. 1984;144:53–56.
46. Masur H, Jones TC, Lempert JA, Cherubini TD. Outbreak of toxoplasmosis in a family and documentation of acquired retinochoroiditis. Am J Med. 1978;64:396–402.
47. Bowie WR, King AS, Werker DH, et al. Outbreak of toxoplasmosis associated with municipal drinking water. Lancet. 1997;350:173–177.
48. Smith KL, Wilson M, Hightower AW, et al. Prevalence of *Toxoplasma gondii* antibodies in US military recruits in 1989: Comparison with data published in 1965. Clin Infect Dis. 1996;23:1182–1183.
49. Remington JS, Efron B, Cavanaugh E, et al. Studies on toxoplasmosis in El Salvador. Prevalence and incidence of toxoplasmosis as measured by the Sabin-Feldman dye test. Trans R Soc Trop Med Hyg. 1970;64:252–267.
50. Sinibaldi J, De Ramirez I. Incidence of congenital toxoplasmosis in live Guatemalan newborns. Eur J Epidemiol. 1992;8:516–520.
51. Ndumbe PM, Andela A, Nkeumnkeng-Asong J, et al. Prevalence of infections affecting the child among pregnant women in Yaounde, Cameroon. Med Microbiol Immunol (Berl). 1992;181:127–130.
52. Papoz L, Simondon F, Saurin W, Sarmini H. A simple model relevant to toxoplasmosis applied to epidemiologic results in France. Am J Epidemiol. 1986;123(1): 154–161.
53. Siegel SE, Lunde MN, Gelderman AH, et al. Transmission of toxoplasmosis by leukocyte transfusion. Blood. 1971;37:388–394.
54. Britt RH, Enzmann DR, Remington JS. Intracranial infection in cardiac transplant recipients. Ann Neurol. 1981;9:107–119.
55. Ryning FW, McLeod R, Maddox JC, et al. Probable transmission of *Toxoplasma gondii* by organ transplantation. Ann Intern Med. 1979;90:47–49.
56. Derouin F, Devergie A, Auber P, et al. Toxoplasmosis in bone marrow–transplant recipients: Report of seven cases and review. Clin Infect Dis. 1992;15:267–270.
57. Slavin MA, Meyers JD, Remington JS, Hackman RC. *Toxoplasma gondii* infection in marrow transplant recipients: A 20 year experience. Bone Marrow Transplant. 1994;13:549–557.
58. Chandrasekar PH, Momin F. Disseminated toxoplasmosis in marrow recipients: A report of three cases and a review of the literature. Bone Marrow Transplant. 1997;19:685–689.
59. Zumla A, Savva D, Wheeler RB, et al. *Toxoplasma* serology in Zambian and Ugandan patients infected with the human immunodeficiency virus. Trans R Soc Trop Med Hyg. 1991;85:227–229.
60. Clumeck N. Some aspects of the epidemiology of toxoplasmosis and pneumocystosis in AIDS in Europe. Eur J Clin Microbiol Infect Dis. 1991;10:177–178.
61. Oksenhendler E, Charreau I, Tournerie C, et al. *Toxoplasma gondii* in advanced HIV infection. AIDS. 1994;8:483–487.
62. Porter SB, Sande M. Toxoplasmosis of the central nervous system in the acquired immunodeficiency syndrome. N Engl J Med. 1992;327:1643–1648.
63. Levy RM, Janssen RS, Bush TJ, Rosenblum ML. Neuroepidemiology of acquired immunodeficiency syndrome. J Acquir Immune Defic Syndr. 1988;1:31–40.
64. Grant IH, Gold JWM, Rosenblum M, et al. *Toxoplasma gondii* serology in HIV-infected patients: The development of central nervous system toxoplasmosis. AIDS. 1990;4:519–521.
65. Matheron S, Dournon E, Garakhanian S, et al. Prevalence of toxoplasmosis in 365 AIDS and ARC patients before and during zidovudine treatment (Abstract). Sixth International Conference on AIDS. San Francisco, Calif, 1990:B.476.
66. Zangerle R, Allerberger F, Pohl P, et al. High risk of developing toxoplasmic encephalitis in AIDS patients seropositive to *Toxoplasma gondii*. Med Microbiol Immunol. 1991;180:59–66.
67. Leport C, Remington JS. Toxoplasmose au cours du SIDA. Presse Med. 1992;21:1165–1171.
68. Khuong MA, Matheron S, Marche C, et al. Diffuse toxoplasmic encephalitis (DTE) without abscess in AIDS patients. Abstract 1157. 30th Interscience Conference on Antimicrobial Agents and Chemotherapy. Atlanta, Ga, 1990.
69. Moore RD, Chaisson R, McArthur J. Abstract—Natural history of central nervous system toxoplasmosis. VIII International Conference on AIDS. Amsterdam, The Netherlands; 1992: B124.
70. Lucas S, Hounnou A, Peacock C, et al. The mortality and pathology of HIV infection in a West African city. AIDS. 1993;7:1569–1579.
71. Leport C, Chêne G, Morlat P, et al. Pyrimethamine for primary prophylaxis of toxoplasmic encephalitis in patients with human immunodeficiency virus infection: A double-blind, randomized trial. J Infect Dis. 1996;173:91–97.
72. Ruskin J, Remington JS. Toxoplasmosis in the compromised host. Ann Intern Med. 1976;84:193–199.
73. Aikawa M, Komata Y, Asai T, Midorikawa O. Transmission and scanning electron microscopy of host cell entry by *Toxoplasma gondii*. Am J Pathol. 1977;87:285–296.
74. Jones TC, Hirsch JG. The interaction between *Toxoplasma gondii* and mammalian cells. II. The absence of lysosomal fusion with phagocytic vacuoles containing living parasites. J Exp Med. 1972;136:1173–1194.
75. Sibley LD, Weidner E, Krahenbuhl JL. Phagosome acidification blocked by intracellular *Toxoplasma gondii*. Nature. 1985;315:416–419.
76. Wilson CB, Tsai V, Remington JS. Failure to trigger the oxidative metabolic burst by normal macrophages: Possible mechanism for survival of intracellular pathogens. J Exp Med. 1980;151:328–346.
77. Murray HW, Juangbhanich CW, Nathan CF, Cohn ZA. Macrophage oxygen-dependent antimicrobial activity. II. The role of oxygen intermediates. J Exp Med. 1979;150:950–964.
78. Adams LB, Hibbs JB Jr, Taintor RR, Krahenbuhl JL. Microbiostatic effect of murine-activated macrophages for *Toxoplasma gondii*. J Immunol. 1990;144:2725–2729.
79. Pfefferkorn ER. Interferon gamma blocks the growth of *Toxoplasma gondii* in human fibroblasts by inducing the host cells to degrade tryptophan. Proc Natl Acad Sci U S A. 1984;81:908–912.
80. Sabin AB, Feldman HA. Dyes as microchemical indicators of a new immunity phenomenon affecting a protozoan parasite (toxoplasma). Science. 1948;108:660–663.
81. Schreiber RD, Feldman HA. Identification of the activator system for antibody to *Toxoplasma* as the classical complement pathway. J Infect Dis. 1980;141:366–369.
82. Remington JS, Jacobs L, Kaufman HE. Studies on chronic toxoplasmosis: The relation of infective dose to residual infection and to the possibility of congenital transmission. Am J Ophthalmol. 1958;46:261–267.
83. Ruchman I, Fowler JC. Localization and persistence of toxoplasma on tissues of experimentally infected white rats. Proc Soc Exp Biol Med. 1951;76:793–796.
84. Montoya JG, Remington JS. Toxoplasmosis of the central nervous system. In: Peterson PK, Remington JS, eds. In Defense of the Brain: Current Concepts in the Immunopathogenesis and Clinical Aspects of CNS Infections. Boston: Blackwell Scientific; 1997:163–188.
85. Ferguson DJ, Hutchison WM, Pettersen E. Tissue cyst rupture in mice chronically infected with *Toxoplasma gondii*. Parasitol Res. 1989;75:599–603.
86. Frenkel JK, Nelson BM, Arias SJ. Immunosuppression and toxoplasmic encephalitis: Clinical and experimental aspects. Hum Pathol. 1975;6:97–111.
87. Navia BA, Petito CK, Gold JW, et al. Cerebral toxoplasmosis complicating the acquired immune deficiency syndrome: Clinical and neuropathological findings in 27 patients. Ann Neurol. 1986;19:224–238.
88. Hofflin JM, Conley FK, Remington JS. Murine model of intracerebral toxoplasmosis. J Infect Dis. 1987;155:550–557.
89. Tirard V, Niel G, Rosenheim M, et al. Diagnosis of toxoplasmosis in patients with AIDS by isolation of the parasite from the blood. N Engl J Med. 1991;324:632.
90. Hofflin JM, Remington JS. Tissue culture isolation of *Toxoplasma* from blood of a patient with AIDS. Arch Intern Med. 1985;145:925–926.
91. Murray H, Rubin BY, Masur H, Roberts RB. Impaired production of lymphokines and immune (gamma) interferon in the acquired immunodeficiency syndrome. N Engl J Med. 1984;310:883.
92. Murray H, Welte K, Jacobs J, et al. Production and in vitro response to interleukin-2 in the acquired immunodeficiency syndrome. J Clin Invest. 1985;76:1959–1964.
93. Canessa A, Del Bono V, Miletich F, Pistoia V. Serum cytokines in toxoplasmosis: Increased levels of interferon-γ in immunocompetent patients with lymphadenopathy but not in AIDS patients with encephalitis (Letter). J Infect Dis. 1992;165:1168–1170.
94. Murray HW, Gellene RA, Libby DM, et al. Activation of tissue macrophages from AIDS patients: In vitro response of AIDS alveolar macrophages to lymphokines and interferon-gamma. J Immunol. 1985;135:2374–2377.
95. Murray HW, Scavuzzo D, Jacobs JL, et al. In vitro and in vivo activation of human mononuclear phagocytes by interferon-gamma. Studies with normal and AIDS monocytes. J Immunol. 1987;138:2457–2462.
96. Pomeroy C, Filice G, Hitt J, Jordan M. Cytomegalovirus-induced reactivation of *Toxoplasma gondii* in mice: Lung lymphocyte phenotypes and suppressor function. J Infect Dis. 1992;166:677–681.
97. Duquesne V, Auriault C, Darcy F, et al. Protection of nude rats against *Toxoplasma* infection by excreted-secreted antigen-specific helper T cells. Infect Immun. 1990;58:2120–2126.
98. Beaman MH, Araujo FG, Remington JS. Protective reconstitution of the SCID mouse against reactivation of toxoplasmic encephalitis. J Infect Dis. 1994;169:375–383.
99. Johnson LL. SCID mouse models on acute and relapsing chronic *Toxoplasma gondii* infections. Infect Immun. 1992;60:3719–3724.
100. Gazzinelli RT, Hakim FT, Hieny S, et al. Synergistic role of $CD4^+$ and $CD8^+$ T lymphocytes in IFN-γ production and protective immunity induced by an attenuated *Toxoplasma gondii* vaccine. J Immunol. 1991;146:286–292.

101. Suzuki Y, Remington JS. Dual regulation of resistance against *Toxoplasma gondii* infection by Lyt-2+ and Lyt-1+, L3T4+ T cells in mice. J Immunol. 1988;140:3943–3946.
102. Subauste CS, Koniaris AH, Remington JS. Murine CD8+ cytotoxic T lymphocytes lyse *Toxoplasma gondii*--infected cells. J Immunol. 1991;147:3955–3959.
103. Hakim FT, Gazzinelli RT, Denkers E, et al. CD8+ T cells from mice vaccinated against *Toxoplasma gondii* are cytotoxic for parasite-infected or antigen-pulsed host cells. J Immunol. 1991;147:2310–2316.
104. Yano A, Aosai F, Ohta M, et al. Antigen presentation by *Toxoplasma gondii*–infected cells to CD4+ proliferative T cells and CD8+ cytotoxic cells. J Parasitol. 1989;75:411–416.
105. Montoya JG, Lowe KE, Clayberger C, et al. Human CD4+ and CD8+ T lymphocytes are both cytotoxic to *Toxoplasma gondii*–infected cells. Infect Immun. 1996;64:176–181.
106. Subauste CS, Fuh F, de Waal Malefyt R, Remington JS. αβ T cell response to *Toxoplasma gondii* in previously unexposed individuals. J Immunol. 1998;160:3403–3411.
107. Subauste CS, de Waal Malefyt R, Fuh F. Role of CD80 (B7.1) and CD86 (B7.2) in the immune response to an intracellular pathogen. J Immunol. 1998;160:1831–1840.
108. Subauste CS, Chung JY, Do D, et al. Preferential activation and expansion of human peripheral blood γδ T cells in response to *Toxoplasma gondii* in vitro and their cytokine production and cytotoxic activity against *T gondii*–infected cells. J Clin Invest. 1995;96:610–619.
109. Hara T, Ohashi S, Yamashita Y, et al. Human V02+ Y0 T-cell tolerance to foreign antigens of *Toxoplasma gondii*. Proc Natl Acad Sci U S A. 1996;93:5136–5140.
110. De Paoli P, Basaglia G, Gennari D, et al. Phenotypic profile and functional characteristics of human gamma and delta T cells during acute toxoplasmosis. J Clin Microbiol. 1992;30:729–731.
111. Scalise F, Gerli R, Castellucci G, et al. Lymphocytes bearing the γδ T-cell receptor in acute toxoplasmosis. Immunology. 1992;76:668–670.
112. Beaman MH, Wong SY, Remington JS. Cytokines, *Toxoplasma* and intracellular parasitism. Immunol Rev. 1992;127:97–117.
113. Hunter CA, Subauste CS, Remington JS. The role of cytokines in toxoplasmosis. Biotherapy. 1994;7:237–247.
114. Sibley LD, Adams LB, Fukutomi Y, Krahenbuhl JL. Tumor necrosis factor-α triggers antitoxoplasmal activity of IFN-γ primed macrophages. J Immunol. 1991;147:2340–2345.
115. Langermans JAM, Van Der Hulst MEB, Nibbering PH, et al. Interferon-γ L-arginine–dependent toxoplasmastatic activity in murine peritoneal macrophages is mediated by endogenous tumor necrosis factor. J Immunol. 1992;148:568–574.
116. Gazzinelli R, Hieny S, Wynn T, et al. Interleukin 12 is required for the T-lymphocyte–independent induction of interferon γ by an intracellular parasite and induces resistance in T-cell–deficient hosts. Proc Natl Acad. Sci USA. 1993;90:6115–6119.
117. Suzuki Y, Conley FK, Remington JS. Importance of endogenous IFN-γ for prevention of toxoplasmic encephalitis in mice. J Immunol. 1989;143:2045–2050.
118. Suzuki Y, Orellana MA, Schreiber RD, Remington JS. Interferon-γ: The major mediator of resistance against *Toxoplasma gondii*. Science. 1988;240:516–518.
119. Suzuki Y, Conley FK, Remington JS. Treatment of toxoplasmic encephalitis in mice with recombinant gamma interferon. Infect Immun. 1990;58:3050–3055.
120. Chao C, Gekker G, Hu S, Peterson P. Human microglial cell defense against *Toxoplasma gondii*. J Immunol. 1994;152:1246–1252.
121. Bohne W, Hessemann J, Gross U. Reduced replication of *Toxoplasma gondii* is necessary for induction of bradyzoite-specific antigens: A possible role for nitric oxide in triggering stage conversion. Infect Immun. 1994;62:1761–1767.
122. Scharton-Kersten TM, Wynn TA, Denkers EY, et al. In the absence of endogenous IFN-γ mice develop unimpaired IL-12 responses to *Toxoplasma gondii* while failing to control acute infection. J Immunol. 1996;157:4045–4054.
123. Khan IA, Matssuura T, Fonseka S, Kasper LH. Production of nitric oxide (NO) is not essential for protection against acute *Toxoplasma gondii* infection in IRF-1 −/− mice1. J Immunol. 1996;156:636–643.
124. Hayashi S, Chan C, Gazzinelli R, Roberge FG. Contribution of nitric oxide to the host parasite equilibrium in toxoplasmosis. J Immunol. 1996;156:1476–1481.
125. Scharton-Kersten TM, Yap G, Magram J, Sher A. Inducible nitric oxide is essential for host control of persistent but not acute infection with the intracellular pathogen *Toxoplasma gondii*. J Exp Med. 1997;185:1261–1273.
126. Johnson L. A protective role for endogenous tumor necrosis factor in *Toxoplasma gondii* infection. Infect Immun. 1992;60:1979–1983.
127. Chang H, Pechere J, Piguet P. Role of tumour necrosis factor in chronic murine *Toxoplasma gondii* encephalitis. Immunol Infect Dis. 1992;2:61–68.
128. Suzuki Y, Yang Q, Yang S, et al. IL-4 is protective against development of toxoplasmic encephalitis. J Immunol. 1996;157:2564–2569.
129. Suzuki Y, Rani S, Liesenfeld O, et al. Impaired resistance to the development of toxoplasmic encephalitis in interleukin-6-deficient mice. Infect Immun. 1997;65:2339–2345.
130. Kasper LH, Matsuura T, Khan IA. IL-7 stimulates protective immunity in mice against the intracellular pathogen, *Toxoplasma gondii*. J Immunol. 1995;155:4798–4804.
131. Pavia CS. Protection against experimental toxoplasmosis by adoptive immunotherapy. J Immunol. 1986;137:2985–2990.
132. Hunter CA, Remington JS. Immunopathogenesis of toxoplasmic encephalitis. J Infect Dis. 1994;170:1057–1067.
133. Peterson P, Gekker G, Hu S, Chao C. Human astrocytes inhibit intracellular multiplication of *Toxoplasma gondii* by a nitric oxide–mediated mechanism. J Infect Dis. 1995;171:516–518.
134. Peterson P, Gekker G, Hu S, Chao C. Intracellular survival multiplication of *Toxoplasma gondii* in astrocytes. J Infect Dis. 1993;168:1472–1478.
135. Suzuki Y, Yang Q, Remington JS. Genetic resistance against acute toxoplasmosis depends on the strain of *Toxoplasma gondii*. J Parasitol. 1995;81:1032–1034.
136. Suzuki Y, Joh K, Kwon O-C, et al. MHC class I gene(s) in the D/L region but not the TNF-α gene determines development of toxoplasmic encephalitis in mice. J Immunol. 1994;153:4649–4654.
137. Suzuki Y, Yang Q, Conley F, Remington J. The L gene of the MHC class I antigens but not the TNF-α gene determines development of toxoplasmic encephalitis in mice. 47th Annual Meeting of Opportunistic Protozoan Pathogens. Cleveland: Society of Protozoologists; 1994:66.
138. Suzuki Y, Joh K, Orellna MA, et al. A gene(s) within the H-2D region determines the development of toxoplasmic encephalitis in mice. Immunology. 1991;74:732–739.
139. Brown C, Estes R, Beckmann E, et al. Definitive identification of a gene that confers resistance against Toxoplasmosis. 47th Annual Meeting Opportunistic Protozoan Pathogens. Cleveland: Society of Protozoologists; 1994:65.
140. Brown C, David C, Khare S, McLeod R. Effects of human class I transgenes on *Toxoplasma gondii* cyst formation. 47th Annual Meeting Opportunistic Protozoan Pathogens. Cleveland: Society of Protozoologists; 1994:65.
141. Brown CR, McLeod R. Class I MHC genes and CD8+ T cells determine cyst number in *Toxoplasma gondii* infection. J Immunol. 1990;145:3438–3441.
142. Deckert-Schlüter M, Schlüter D, Schmidt D, et al. *Toxoplasma* encephalitis in congenic B10 and BALB mice: Impact of genetic factors in the immune response. Infect Immun. 1994;62:221–228.
143. Suzuki Y, Wong S-Y, Grumet FC, et al. Evidence for genetic regulation of susceptibility to toxoplasmic encephalitis in AIDS patients. J Infect Dis. 1996;173:265–268.
144. Frenkel JK. Pathology and pathogenesis of congenital toxoplasmosis. Bull N Y Acad Med. 1974;50:182–91.
145. Liesenfeld O, Wong SY, Remington JS. Toxoplasmosis in the Setting of AIDS. In: Bartlett JG, Merigan TC, Bolognesi D, eds. Textbook of AIDS Medicine. 2nd ed. Baltimore: Williams & Wilkins; 1999:225–259.
146. Post MJ, Chan JC, Hensley GT, et al. *Toxoplasma* encephalitis in Haitian adults with acquired immunodeficiency syndrome: A clinical-pathologic-CT correlation. AJR. 1983;140:861–868.
147. Strittmatter C, Lang W, Wiestler OD, Klleihues P. The changing pattern of human immunodeficiency virus associated cerebral toxoplasmosis: A study of 46 postmortem cases. Acta Neuropathol. 1992;83:475–481.
148. Parmley SF, Goebel FD, Remington JS. Detection of *Toxoplasma gondii* DNA in cerebrospinal fluid from AIDS patients by polymerase chain reaction. J Clin Microbiol. 1992;30:3000–3002.
149. Gray F, Gherardi R, Wingate E, et al. Diffuse "encephalitic" cerebral toxoplasmosis in AIDS. J Neurol. 989;236:273–277.
150. Mariuz P, Bosler EM, Luft BJ. *Toxoplasma* pneumonia. Semin Respir Infect. 1997;12(1):40–43.
151. Bretagne S, Costa J-M, Fleury-Feith J, et al. Quantitative competitive PCR with bronchoalveolar lavage fluid for diagnosis of toxoplasmosis in AIDS patients. J Clin Microbiol. 1995;33:1662–1664.
152. Danise A, Cinque P, Vergani S, et al. Use of the polymerase chain reaction assays of aqueous humor in the differential diagnosis of retinitis in patients infected with human immunodeficiency virus. Clin Infect Dis. 1997;24:1100–1106.
153. Roldan EO, Moskowitz L, Hensley GT. Pathology of the heart in acquired immunodeficiency syndrome. Arch Pathol Lab Med. 1987;111:943–946.
154. Adair OV, Randive N, Krasnow N. Isolated *Toxoplasma* myocarditis in acquired immune deficiency syndrome. Am Heart J. 1989;118:856–857.
155. Gherardi R, Baudrimont M, Lionnet F, et al. Skeletal muscle toxoplasmosis in patients with acquired immunodeficiency syndrome: A clinical and pathological study. Ann Neurol. 1992;32:535–542.
156. Calico I, Caballero E, Martinez O, et al. Isolation of *Toxoplasma gondii* from immunocompromised patients using tissue culture. Infection. 1991;19:340–342.
157. Montoya JG, Jordan R, Lingamneni S, et al. Toxoplasmic myocarditis and polymyositis in patients with acute acquired toxoplasmosis diagnosed during life. Clin Infect Dis. 1997;24:676–683.
158. Mishra G, Curry NS, Lewin DN, Hoffman BJ. Computerized tomography presentation of toxoplasma colitis. J Clin Gastroenterol. 1997;25:702–703.
159. Pauwels A, Meyohas MC, Eliaszewicz M, et al. *Toxoplasma* colitis in the acquired immunodeficiency syndrome. Am J Gastroenterol. 1992;87:518–519.
160. Smart PE, Weinfeld A, Thompson NE, Defortuna SM. Toxoplasmosis of the stomach: A cause of antral narrowing. Radiology. 1990;174:369–370.
161. Garcia LW, Hemphill RB, Marasco WA, Ciano PS. Acquired immunodeficiency syndrome with disseminated toxoplasmosis presenting as an acute pulmonary and gastrointestinal illness. Arch Pathol Lab Med. 1991;115:459–463.
162. Brion J-P, Pelloux H, Le Marc'hadour F, et al. Acute toxoplasmic hepatitis in a patient with AIDS. Clin Infect Dis. 1992;15:183–184.
163. Bergin C, Murphy M, Lyons D, et al. *Toxoplasma* pneumonitis: Fatal presentation of disseminated toxoplasmosis in a patient with AIDS. Eur Respir J. 1992;5:1018–1020.
164. Crider SR, Horstman WG, Massey GS. *Toxoplasma* orchitis: Report of a case and a review of the literature. Am J Med. 1988;85:421–424.
165. Groll A, Schneider M, Althoff PH, et al. Morphology and clinical significance of AIDS-related lesions in the adrenals and pituitary. Dtsch Med Wochenschr. 1990;115:483–488.

166. Patrick AL, Roberts LA, Burton EN, et al. Focal and segmental glomerulosclerosis in the acquired immunodeficiency syndrome. West Indian Med J. 1986;1986:200–202.
167. Renold C, Sugar A, Chave J-P, et al. *Toxoplasma* encephalitis in patients with the acquired immunodeficiency syndrome. Medicine. 1992;71:224–239.
168. Dorfman RF, Remington JS. Value of lymph-node biopsy in the diagnosis of acute acquired toxoplasmosis. N Engl J Med. 1973;289:878–881.
169. Weiss L, Chen Y, Berry G, et al. Infrequent detection of *Toxoplasma gondii* genome in toxoplasmic lymphadenitis: A polymerase chain reaction study. Hum Pathol. 1992;23:154–158.
170. Remington JS. Toxoplasmosis in the adult. Bull N Y Acad Med. 1974;50:211–227.
171. McCabe RE, Brooks RG, Dorfman RF, Remington JS. Clinical spectrum in 107 cases of toxoplasmic lymphadenopathy. Rev Infect Dis. 1987;9:754–774.
172. Remington JS, Barnett CG, Meikel M, Lunde MN. Toxoplasmosis and infectious mononucleosis. Arch Intern Med. 1962;110:744–753.
173. Couvreur J, Thulliez P. Acquired toxoplasmosis with ocular or neurologic involvement (in French: Toxoplasmose acquise à localisation oculaire ou neurologique). Presse Med. 1996;25:438–442.
174. Montoya JG, Remington JS. Toxoplasmic chorioretinitis in the setting of acute acquired toxoplasmosis. Clin Infect Dis. 1996;23:277–282.
175. Silveira C, Belfort R Jr, Burnier M Jr, Nussenblatt R. Acquired toxoplasmic infection as the cause of toxoplasmic retinochoroiditis in families. Am J Ophthalmol. 1988;106:362–364.
176. Glasner PD, Silveira C, Kruszon-Moran D, et al. An unusually high prevalence of ocular toxoplasmosis in Southern Brazil. Am J Ophthal. 1992;114:136–144.
177. Sheagren JN, Lunde MN, Simon HB. Chronic lymphadenopathic toxoplasmosis. A case with marked hyperglobulinemia and impaired delayed hypersensitivity responses during active infection. Am J Med. 1976;60:300–305.
178. Montoya JG, Remington JS. Studies on the serodiagnosis of toxoplasmic lymphadenitis. Clin Infect Dis. 1995;20:781–790.
179. Cunningham T. Pancarditis in acute toxoplasmosis. Am J Clin Pathol. 1982;78:403–405.
180. Prado SP, Pacheco VC, Noemi IH, et al. *Toxoplasma* pericarditis and myocarditis (in Spanish: Pericarditis y miocarditis por toxoplasma). Rev Chil Pediatr. 1978;49:179–185.
181. Greenlee JE, Johnson WD Jr, Campa JF, et al. Adult toxoplasmosis presenting as polymyositis and cerebellar ataxia. Ann Intern Med. 1975;82:367–371.
182. Behan WM, Behan PO, Draper IT, Williams H. Does *Toxoplasma* cause polymyositis? Report of a case of polymyositis associated with toxoplasmosis and a critical review of the literature. Acta Neuropathol (Berl). 1983;61:246–252.
183. Samuels BS, Rietschel RL. Polymyositis and toxoplasmosis. JAMA. 1976;235:60–61.
184. Pollock JL. Toxoplasmosis appearing to be dermatomyositis. Arch Dermatol. 1979;115:736–737.
185. Palma S, Reyes H, Guzman L, Cartier L. Dermatomyositis and toxoplasmosis (in Spanish: Dermatomiositis y toxoplasmosis). Rev Med Chil. 1984;111:164–167.
186. Derouin F, Gluckman E, Beauvais B, et al. *Toxoplasma* infection after human allogeneic bone marrow transplantation: Clinical and serological study of 80 patients. Bone Marrow Transplant. 1986;1:67–73.
187. Luft BJ, Naot Y, Araujo FG, et al. Primary and reactivated toxoplasma infection in patients with cardiac transplants. Clinical spectrum and problems in diagnosis in a defined population. Ann Intern Med. 1983;99:27–31.
188. Luft BJ, Billingham M, Remington JS. Endomyocardial biopsy in the diagnosis of toxoplasmic myocarditis. Transplant Proc. 1986;18:1871–1873.
189. Oksenhendler E, Cadranel J, Sarfati C, et al. *Toxoplasma gondii* pneumonia in patients with the acquired immunodeficiency syndrome. Am J Med. 1990;88:5-18N–5-21N.
190. Mehren M, Burns PJ, Mamani F, et al. Toxoplasmic myelitis mimicking intramedullary spinal cord tumor. Neurology. 1988;38:1648–1650.
191. Herskovitz S, Siegel SE, Schneider AT, et al. Spinal cord toxoplasmosis in AIDS. Neurology. 1989;39:1552–1553.
192. Harris TM, Smith RR, Bognanno JR, Edwards MK. Toxoplasmic myelitis in AIDS: Gadolinium-enhanced MR. J Comput Assist Tomogr. 1990;14:809–811.
193. Kayser C, Campbell R, Sartorious C, Barlett M. Toxoplasmosis of the conus medullaris in a patient with hemophilia A–associated AIDS. J Neurosurg. 1990;73:951–953.
194. Overhage JM, Greist A, Brown DR. Conus medullaris syndrome resulting from *Toxoplasma gondii* infection in a patient with the acquired immunodeficiency syndrome. Am J Med. 1990;89:814–815.
195. Campagna AC. Pulmonary toxoplasmosis. Semin Respir Infect. 1997;12:98–105.
196. Rabaud C, May Th, Amiel C, et al. Pulmonary toxoplasmosis in patients infected with human immunodeficiency virus: A French national study. Clin Infect Dis. 1996;23:1249–1254.
197. Derouin F, Sarfati C, Beauvais B, et al. Prevalence of pulmonary toxoplasmosis in HIV-infected patients. AIDS. 1990;4:1036.
198. Friedman AH, Orellana J, Gagliuso DJ, Teich SA. Ocular toxoplasmosis in AIDS patients. Trans Am Ophthalmol Soc. 1990;88:63–88.
199. Schuman JS, Friedman AH. Retinal manifestations of the acquired immune deficiency syndrome (AIDS): Cytomegalovirus, *Candida albicans*, cryptococcus, toxoplasmosis and *Pneumocystis carinii*. Trans Ophthalmol Soc U K. 1983;103:177–190.
200. Friedman AH. The retinal lesions of the acquired immune deficiency syndrome. Trans Am Ophthalmol Soc. 1984;82:447–491.
201. Holland G, Engstrom R Jr, Glasgow B, et al. Ocular toxplasmosis in patients with acquired immunodeficiency syndrome. Am J Opthalmol. 1988;106:653–667.
202. Cochereau-Massin I, LeHoang P, Lautier-Frau M, et al. Ocular toxoplasmosis in human immunodeficiency virus-infected Patients. Am J Ophthalmol. 1992;114:130–135.
203. Heinemann MH, Gold JM, Maisel J. Bilateral toxoplasma retinochoroiditis in a patient with acquired immune deficiency syndrome. Retina. 1986;6:224–227.
204. Nussenblatt R, Belfort R Jr. Ocular toxoplasmosis. JAMA. 1994;271:302–307.
205. Perkins ES. Ocular toxoplasmosis. Br J Ophthalmol. 1973;57(1):1–17.
206. Remington JS, Gentry LO. Acquired toxoplasmosis: Infection versus disease. Ann N Y Acad Sci. 1970;174:1006–1017.
207. Akstein RB, Wilson LA, Teutsch SM. Acquired toxoplasmosis. Ophthalmology. 1982;89:1299–1302.
208. Johnson MW, Greven CM, Jaffe GJ, et al. Atypical, severe toxoplasmic retinochoroiditis in elderly patients. Ophthalmology. 1997;104:48–57.
209. Montoya JG, Parmley S, Liesenfeld O, et al. Use of the polymerase chain reaction for diagnosis of ocular toxoplasmosis. Ophthalmol. 1999;106:1554–1563.
210. Vogel N, Kirisits M, Michael E, et al. Congenital toxoplasmosis transmitted from an immunologically competent mother infected before conception. Clin Infect Dis. 1996;23:1055–1060.
211. Hennequin C, Dureau P, N'Guyen L, et al. Congenital toxoplasmosis acquired from an immune woman. Pediatr Infect Dis. 1997;16:75–76.
212. Gavinet MF, Robert F, Firtion G, et al. Congenital toxoplasmosis due to maternal reinfection during pregnancy. J Clin Microbiol. 1997;35:1276–1277.
213. Desmonts G, Couvreur J. Congenital toxoplasmosis. A prospective study of the offspring of 542 women who acquired toxoplasmosis during pregnancy. Pathophysiol Congenital Dis. 1979:51–60.
214. Koppe JG, Loewer-Sieger DH, De Roever-Bonnet H. Results of 20-year follow-up of congenital toxoplasmosis. Am J Ophthalmol. 1986;101:248–249.
215. Wilson CB, Remington JS, Stagno S, Reynolds DW. Development of adverse sequelae in children born with subclinical congenital *Toxoplasma* infection. Pediatrics. 1980;66:767–774.
216. Desmonts G. Acquired toxoplasmosis in pregnant women. Evaluation of the frequency of transmission of toxoplasma and of congenital toxoplasmosis. Lyon Med. 1982;248:115–123.
217. Desmonts G, Daffos F, Forestier F, et al. Prenatal diagnosis of congenital toxoplasmosis. Lancet. 1985;1:500–504.
218. Daffos F, Forestier F, Capella-Pavlovsky M, et al. Prenatal management of 746 pregnancies at risk for congenital toxoplasmosis. N Engl J Med. 1988;318:271–275.
219. Desmonts G, Couvreur J. Congenital toxoplasmosis: A prospective study of the offspring of 542 women who acquired toxoplasmosis during pregnancy. Pathophysiology of congenital disease. In: Thalhammer O, Baumgarten K, Pollak A, eds. Perinatal Medicine. Sixth European Congress. Stuttgart: Georg Thieme Verlag; 1979:51–60.
220. Forestier F. Fetal diseases, prenatal diagnoses and practical measures (in French: Les foetopathies infectieuses—Prevention, diagnostic prenatal, attitude pratique). Presse Med. 1991;20:1448–1454.
221. Hohlfeld P, Daffos F, Costa J-M, et al. Prenatal diagnosis of congenital toxoplasmosis with polymerase-chain-reaction test on amniotic fluid. N Engl J Med. 1994;331:695–699.
222. Hohlfeld P, Daffos F, Thulliez P, et al. Fetal toxoplasmosis: Outcome of pregnancy and infant follow-up after in utero treatment. J Pediatr. 1989;115:765–769.
223. Couvreur J, Desmonts G, Tournier G, Szusterkac M. A homogeneous series of 210 cases of congenital toxoplasmosis in 0 to 11-month-old infants detected prospectively (in French: Étude d'une série homogène de 210 cases de toxoplasmose congénitale chez des nourrissons âgés de 0 à 11 mois et dépistes de façon prospective). Ann Pediatr (Paris). 1984;31:815–9.
224. De Roever-Bonnet H, Koppe JG, Loewer-Sieger DH. Follow-up of children with congenital *Toxoplasma* infection and children who become serologically negative after 1 year of age, all born in 1964–1965. Pathophysiology of congenital disease. In: Thalhammer O, Baumgarten K, Pollak A, eds. Perinatal Medicine. Sixth European Congress. Stuttgart: Georg Thieme Verlag; 1979:61–75.
225. Labadie MD, Hazemann JJ. Contribution of health check-ups in children to the detection and epidemiologic study of congenital toxoplasmosis (in French: Apport des bilans de santé de l'énfant pour le dépistage et l'étude épidémiologique de la toxoplasmose congénitale). Ann Pediatr (Paris). 1984;31:823–8.
226. McAuley J, Boyer KM, Patel D, et al. Early and longitudinal evaluations of treated infants and children and untreated historical patients with congenital toxoplasmosis: The Chicago collaborative treatment trial. Clin Infect Dis. 1994;18:38–72.
227. Mitchell CD, Erlich SS, Mastrucci MT, et al. Congenital toxoplasmosis occurring in infants perinatally infected with human immunodeficiency virus 1. Pediatr Infect Dis J. 1990;9:512–518.
228. Miller MJ, Aronson WJ, Remington JS. Late parasitemia in asymptomatic acquired toxoplasmosis. Ann Intern Med. 1969;71:139–45.
229. Jacobs L. The biology of toxoplasma. Am J Trop Med Hyg. 1953;2:365–389.
230. Cook MK, Jacobs L. Cultivation of *Toxoplasma gondii* in tissue cultures of various derivations. J Parasitol. 1958;44:172–182.
231. Shepp D, Hackman R, Conley F, et al. *Toxoplasma gondii* reactivation identified by detection of parasitemia in tissue culture. Ann Intern Med. 1985;103:218–221.
232. Remington JS, McLeod R. Toxoplasmosis. In: Gorbach SL, Bartlett JG, Blacklow NR, eds. Infectious Diseases. 2nd ed. Philadelphia: WB Saunders; 1998:1620–1640.
233. Levy RM, Bredesen DE, Rosenblum ML. Opportunistic central nervous system pathology in patients with AIDS. Ann Neurol. 1988;23(Suppl):S70–S12.
234. Frenkel JK, Piekarski G. The demonstration of *Toxoplasma* and other organisms by immunofluorescence: A pitfall (Editorial). J Infect Dis. 1978;138:265–266.
235. Moskowitz LB, Hensley GT, Chan JC, et al. The neuropathology of acquired immune deficiency syndrome. Arch Pathol Lab Med. 1984;108:867–872.
236. Van Knapen F, Panggabean SO. Detection of toxoplasma antigen in tissues by

means of enzyme-linked immunosorbent assay (ELISA). Am J Clin Pathol. 1982;77:755–757.
237. Sun T, Greenspan J, Tenenbaum M, et al. Diagnosis of cerebral toxoplasmosis using fluorescein-labeled antitoxoplasma monoclonal antibodies. Am J Surg Pathol. 1986;10:312–316.
238. Cerezo L, Alvarez M, Price G. Electron microscopic diagnosis of cerebral toxoplasmosis. Case report. J Neurosurg. 1985;63:470–472.
239. Grover CM, Thulliez P, Remington JS, Boothroyd JD. Rapid prenatal diagnosis of congenital *Toxoplasma* infection by using polymerase chain reaction and amniotic fluid. J Clin Microbiol. 1990;28:2297–2301.
240. Van de Ven E, Melchers W, Galama J, et al. Identification of *Toxoplasma gondii* infections by BI gene amplification. J Clin Microbiol. 1991;19:2120–2124.
241. De Boer JH, Verhagen C, Bruinenberg M, et al. Serologic and polymerase chain reaction analysis of intraocular fluids in the diagnosis of infectious uveitis. Am J Opthalmol. 1996;121:650–658.
242. Brézin A, Kasner L, Thulliez P, et al. Ocular toxoplasmosis in the fetus immunohistochemistry analysis and DNA amplification. Retina. 1994;14(1):19–26.
243. Verbraak FD, Galema M, Hans van den Horn G, et al. Serological and polymerase chain reaction–based analysis of aqueous humour samples in patients with AIDS and necrotizing retinitis. AIDS. 1996;10:1091–1099.
244. Brezin AP, Egwuagu CE, Burnier M, et al. Identification of *Toxoplasma gondii* in paraffin-embedded sections by the polymerase chain reaction. Am J Ophthalmol. 1990;110:599–604.
245. Cinque P, Scarpellini P, Vago L, et al. Diagnosis of central nervous system complications in HIV-infected patients: Cerebrospinal fluid analysis by the polymerase chain reaction. AIDS. 1997;11:1–17.
246. Dupouy-Camet J, Lavareda de Souza L, Maslo C, et al. Detection of *Toxoplasma gondii* in venous blood from AIDS patients by polymerase chain reaction. J Clin Microbiol. 1993;31:1866–1869.
247. Holliman RE, Johnson JD, Savva D. Diagnosis of cerebral toxoplasmosis in association with AIDS using the polymerase chain reaction. Scand J Infect Dis. 1990;22:243–244.
248. Schoondermark–van de Van E, Galama J, Kraaijeveld C, et al. Value of the polymerase chain reaction for the detection of *Toxoplasma gondii* in cerebrospinal fluid from patients with AIDS. Clin Infect Dis. 1993;16:661–666.
249. Roth A, Roth B, Höffken G, et al. Application of the polymerase chain reaction to diagnosis of pulmonary toxoplasmosis in immunocompromised patients. Eur J Clin Microbiol Infect Dis. 1992;11:1177–1181.
250. Lavrard I, Chouaid C, Roux P, et al. Pulmonary toxoplasmosis in HIV-infected patients: Usefulness of polymerase chain reaction and cell culture. Eur Respir J. 1995;8:697–700.
251. Lavareda DS, De Souza S, Maslo C, et al. PCR in blood for diagnosis of toxoplasmosis in AIDS patients. Abstract 45. Third European Conference Clinical Aspects and Treatment of HIV Infection. Paris, France, 1992.
252. Khalifa K, Roth A, Roth B, et al. Value of PCR for evaluating occurrence of parasitemia in immunocompromised patients with cerebral and extracerebral toxoplasmosis. J Clin Microbiol. 1994;32:2813–2819.
253. Foudrinier F, Aubert D, Puygauthier-Toubas D, et al. Detection of *Toxoplasma gondii* in immunodeficient subjects by gene amplification: Influence of therapeutics. Scand J Infect Dis. 1996;28:383–386.
254. Lamoril J, Molina J-M, Gouvello AD, et al. Detection by PCR of *Toxoplasma gondii* in blood in the diagnosis of cerebral toxoplasmosis in patients with AIDS. J Clin Pathol. 1996;49:89–92.
255. Dupon M, Cazenave J, Pellegrin J-L, et al. Detection of *Toxoplasma gondii* by PCR and tissue culture in cerebrospinal fluid and blood of human immunodeficiency virus–seropositive patients. J Clin Microbiol. 1995;33:2421–2426.
256. Eggers C, Grob U, Klinker H, et al. Limited value of cerebrospinal fluid for direct detection of *Toxoplasma gondii* in toxoplasmic encephalitis associated with AIDS. J Neurol. 1995;242:644–649.
257. Robert F, Ouatas T, Blanche P, et al. Évaluation rétrospective de la détection de *Toxoplasma gondii* par réaction de polymérisation en chaîne chez des patients sidéens. Presse Med. 1996;25:541–545.
258. Dannemann BR, Israelski DM, Leoung GS, et al. *Toxoplasma* serology, parasitemia and antigenemia in patients at risk for toxoplasmic encephalitis. AIDS. 1991;5:1363–1365.
259. Pelloux H, Dupouy-Camet J, Derouin F, et al. A multicentre prospective study for the polymerases chain reaction detection of *Toxoplasma gondii* DNA in blood samples from 186 AIDS patients with suspected toxoplasmic encephalitis. AIDS. 1997;11:1888–1890.
260. Franzen C, Altfeld M, Hegener P, et al. Limited value of PCR for detection of *Toxoplasma gondii* in blood from human immunodeficiency virus–infected patients. J Clin Microbiol. 1997;35:2639–2641.
261. Cingolani A, De Luca A, Ammassari A, et al. PCR detection of *Toxoplasma gondii* DNA in CSF for the differential diagnosis of AIDS-related focal brain lesions. J Med Microbiol. 1996;45:472–476.
262. Novati R, Castagna A, Morsica G, et al. Polymerase chain reaction for *Toxoplasma gondii* DNA in the cerebrospinal fluid of AIDS patients with focal brain lesions. AIDS. 1994;8:1691–1694.
263. Wilson CB, Desmonts G, Couvreur J, Remington JS. Lymphocyte transformation in the diagnosis of congenital *Toxoplasma* infection. N Engl J Med. 1980;302:785–788.
264. McLeod R, Mack DG, Boyer K, et al. Phenotypes and functions of lymphocytes in congenital toxoplasmosis. J Lab Clin Med. 1990;116:623–635.
265. Luft BJ, Pedrotti PW, Engleman EG, Remington JS. Induction of antigen-specific suppressor T cells during acute infection with *Toxoplasma gondii*. J Infect Dis. 1987;155:1033–1037.
266. Lecolier B, Marion S, Derouin F, Sarrot G. T-Cell subpopulations of fetuses infected by *Toxoplasma gondii*. Eur J Clin Microbiol Infect Dis. 1989;8:572–573.
267. Liesenfeld O, Press C, Montoya JG, et al. False-positive results in immunoglobulin M (IgM) toxoplasma antibody tests and importance of confirmatory testing: The Platelia toxo IgM test. J Clin Microbiol. 1997;35:174–178.
268. Wilson M, Remington JS, Clavet C, et al. Evaluation of six commercial kits for detection of human immunoglobulin M antibodies to *Toxoplasma gondii*. J Clin Microbiol. 1997;35:3112–3115.
269. Liesenfeld O, Montoya JG, Tathineni NJ, et al. Confirmatory serological testing results in remarkable decrease in unnecessary abortion among pregnant women in the United States with positive toxoplasma serology (Abstract). 35th Annual Meeting of the Infectious Diseases Society of America. San Francisco, Calif; 1997:76.
270. Balsari A, Poli G, Molina V, et al. ELISA for toxoplasma antibody detection: A comparison with other serodiagnostic tests. J Clin Pathol. 1980;33:640–643.
271. Walls KW, Bullock SL, English DK. Use of the enzyme-linked immunosorbent assay (ELISA) and its microadaptation for the serodiagnosis of toxoplasmosis. J Clin Microbiol. 1977;5:273–277.
272. Walton BC, Benchoff BM, Brooks WH. Comparison of the indirect fluorescent antibody test and methylene blue dye test for detection of antibodies to *Toxoplasma gondii*. Am J Trop Med Hyg. 1966;15:149–152.
273. Thulliez P, Remington JS, Santoro F, et al. A new agglutination test for the diagnosis of acute and chronic toxoplasma infection. Pathol Biol (Paris). 1986;34:173–177.
274. Anderson SE, Remington JS. The diagnosis of toxoplasmosis. South Med J. 1975;68:1433–1443.
275. Araujo FG, Barnett EV, Gentry LO, Remington JS. False-positive anti-*Toxoplasma* fluorescent-antibody tests in patients with antinuclear antibodies. Appl Microbiol. 1971;22:270–275.
276. Desmonts G, Remington JS. Direct agglutination test for diagnosis of *Toxoplasma* infection: Method for increasing sensitivity and specificity. J Clin Microbiol. 1980;11:562–568.
277. Dannemann BR, Vaughan WC, Thulliez P, Remington JS. Differential agglutination test for diagnosis of recently acquired infection with *Toxoplasma gondii*. J Clin Microbiol. 1990;28:1928–1933.
278. Derouin F, Leport C, Pueyo S, et al. Predictive value of *Toxoplasma gondii* antibody titres on the occurrence of toxoplasmic encephalitis in HIV-infected patients. AIDS. 1996;10:1521–1527.
279. Hedman K, Lappalainen M, Seppala I, Makela O. Recent primary *Toxoplasma* infection indicated by a low avidity of specific IgG. J Infect Dis. 1989;159:736–739.
280. Hedman K, Lappalainen M, Söderlund M, Hedman L. Avidity of IgG in serodiagnosis of infectious diseases. Rev Med Microbiol. 1993;4:123–129.
281. Lappalainen M, Koskela P, Koskiniemi M, et al. Toxoplasmosis acquired during pregnancy: Improved serodiagnosis based on avidity of IgG. J Infect Dis. 1993;167:691–697.
282. Bobic B, Sibalic D, Djurkovic-Djakovic O. High levels of IgM antibodies specific for *Toxoplasma gondii* in pregnancy 12 years after primary toxplasma infection. Gynecol Obstet Invest. 1991;31:182–184.
283. Del Bono V, Canessa A, Bruzzi P, et al. Significance of specific immunoglobulin M in the chronological diagnosis of 38 cases of toxoplasmic lymphadenopathy. J Clin Microbiol. 1989;27:2133–2135.
284. Ashburn D, Evans R, Skinner LJ, et al. Comparison of relative uses of commercial assays for *Toxoplasma gondii* IgM antibodies. J Clin Pathol. 1992;45:483–486.
285. FDA public health advisory: Limitations of toxoplasma IgM commercial test kits. 1997July 25:1–3.
286. Welch PC, Masur H, Jones TC, Remington JS. Serologic diagnosis of acute lymphadenopathic toxoplasmosis. J Infect Dis. 1980;142:256–264.
287. Naot Y, Barnett EV, Remington JS. Method for avoiding false-positive results occurring in immunoglobulin M enzyme-linked immunosorbent assays due to presence of both rheumatoid factor and antinuclear antibodies. J Clin Microbiol. 1981;14:73–78.
288. Filice GA, Yeager AS, Remington JS. Diagnostic significance of immunoglobulin M antibodies to *Toxoplasma gondii* detected after separation of immunoglobulin M from immunoglobulin G antibodies. J Clin Microbiol. 1980;12:336–342.
289. Camargo ME, Ferreira AW, Mineo JR, et al. Immunoglobulin G and immunoglobulin M enzyme–linked immunosorbent assays and defined toxoplasmosis serological patterns. Infect Immun. 1978;21:55–58.
290. Remington JS, Eimstad WM, Araujo FG. Detection of immunoglobulin M antibodies with antigen-tagged latex particles in an immunosorbent assay. J Clin Microbiol. 1983;17:939–941.
291. Pinon JM, Toubas D, Marx C, et al. Detection of specific immunoglobulin E in patients with toxoplasmosis. J Clin Microbiol. 1990;28:1739–1743.
292. Wong SY, Hadju M-P, Ramirez R, et al. The role of specific immunoglobulin E in diagnosis of acute toxoplasma infection and toxoplasmosis. J Clin Microbiol. 1993;31:2952–2959.
293. Pinon JM, Thoannes H, Pouletty PH, et al. Detection of IgA specific for toxoplasmosis in serum and cerebrospinal fluid using a non-enzymatic IgA-capture assay. Diagn Immunol. 1986;4:223–227.
294. Stepick-Biek P, Thulliez P, Araujo FG, Remington JS. IgA antibodies for diagnosis of acute congenital and acquired toxoplasmosis. J Infect Dis. 1990;162:270–273.
295. Decoster A, Slizewicz B, Simon J, et al. Platelia-toxo IgA, a new kit for early

diagnosis of congenital toxoplasmosis by detection of anti-P30 immunoglobulin A antibodies. J Clin Microbiol. 1991;29:2291–2295.
296. Gross U, Roos T, Appoldt D, Heesemann J. Improved serological diagnosis of *Toxoplasmosis gondii* infection by detection of immunoglobulin A (IgA) and IgM antibodies against P30 by using the immunoblot technique. J Clin Microbiol. 1992;30:1436–1441.
297. Pinon JM, Thoannes H, Gruson N. An enzyme-linked immuno-filtration assay used to compare infant and maternal antibody profiles in toxoplasmosis. J Immunol Methods. 1985;77(1):15–23.
298. Poirriez J, Toubas D, Marx-Chemia C, et al. Isotypic characterization of anti–*Toxoplasma gondii* antibodies in 18 cases of congenital toxoplasmic chorioretinitis. Acta Ophthalmol. 1988;67:164–168.
299. Haverkos HW. Assessment of therapy for toxoplasma encephalitis. The TE Study Group. Am J Med. 1987;82:907–914.
300. Post MJ, Kursunoglu SJ, Hensley GT, et al. Cranial CT in acquired immunodeficiency syndrome: Spectrum of diseases and optimal contrast enhancement technique. AJR. 1985;145:929–940.
301. Post MJ, Chan JC, Hensley GT, et al. Toxoplasmosis encephalitis in Haitian adults with acquired immunodeficiency syndrome: A clinical-pathologic-CT correlation. Am J Neuroradiol. 1983;4:155–162.
302. Levy RM, Rosenbloom S, Perrett LV. Neuroradiologic findings in AIDS: A review of 200 cases. AJNR Am J Neuroradiol. 1986;147:977–983.
303. De La Paz R, Enzmann D. Neuroradiology of acquired immunodeficiency syndrome. In: Rosenblum ML, ed. AIDS and the Nervous System. New York: Raven; 1988:121–154.
304. Levy RM, Mills CM, Posin JP, et al. The efficacy and clinical impact of brain imaging in neurologically symptomatic AIDS patients: A prospective CT/MRI study. J Acquir Immune Defic Syndr. 1990;3:461–471.
305. Ciricillo SF, Rosenblum ML. Use of CT and MR imaging to distinguish intracranial lesions and to define the need for biopsy in AIDS patients. J Neurosurg. 1990;73:720–724.
306. Holloway RG, Mushlin AI. Intracranial mass lesions in acquired immunodeficiency syndrome: Using decision analysis to determine the effectiveness of stereotactic brain biopsy. Neurology. 1996;46:1010–1015.
307. Luft BJ, Hafner R, Korzun AH, et al. Toxoplasmic encephalitis in patients with the acquired immunodeficiency syndrome. N Engl J Med. 1993;329:995–1000.
308. O'Doherty MJ, Barrington SF, Campbell M, et al. PET scanning and the human immunodeficiency virus–positive patient. J Nucl Med. 1997;38:1575–1583.
309. Naddaf SY, Akisik MF, Aziz M, et al. Comparison between 201Tl-chloride and 99Tc(m)-sestamibi SPECT brain imaging for differentiating intracranial lymphoma from non-malignant lesions in AIDS patients. Nucl Med Commun. 1998;19(1):47–53.
310. Ramsey RG, Gean AD. Central nervous system toxoplasmosis. Neuroimaging Clin N Am. 1997;7:171–186.
311. Rosenfeld SS, Hoffman JM, Coleman RE, et al. Studies of primary central nervous system lymphoma with [18F]-fluorodeoxyglucose (FDG) PET. J Nucl Med. 1992;33:532–536.
312. Potasman I, Resnick L, Luft BJ, Remington JS. Intrathecal production of antibodies against *Toxoplasma gondii* in patients with toxoplasmic encephalitis and the acquired immunodeficiency syndrome (AIDS). Ann Intern Med. 1988;108:49–51.
313. Orefice G, Carrieri PB, de Marinis T, et al. Use of the intrathecal synthesis of antitoxoplasma antibodies in the diagnostic assessment and in the follow-up of AIDS patients with cerebral toxoplasmosis. Acta Neurol (Napoli). 1990;12(1):79–81.
314. McGregor CG, Fleck DG, Nagington J, et al. Disseminated toxoplasmosis in cardiac transplantation. J Clin Pathol. 1984;37:74–77.
315. Hellerbrand C, Goebel FD, Disko R. High predictive value of *Toxoplasma gondii* IgG antibody levels in HIV-infected patients for diagnosis of cerebral toxoplasmosis. Eur J Clin Microbiol Infect Dis. 1996;15:869–872.
316. Lavrard I, Roux P, Poirot Jf, et al. Pulmonary toxoplasmosis: Detection of *Toxoplasma gondii* DNA by polymerase chain reaction in bronchoalveolar lavage and induced sputum. VIII International Conference on AIDS. Amsterdam, The Netherlands; 1992: B121.
317. Bretagne S, Costa JM, Keuntz M, et al. Late toxoplasmosis evidenced by PCR in marrow transplant recipient. Bone Marrow Transplant. 1995;15:809–811.
318. Desmonts G. Definitive serological diagnosis of ocular toxoplasmosis. Arch Ophthalmol. 1966;76:839–851.
319. Greven C, Teot L. Cytologic identification of *Toxoplasma gondii* from vitreous fluid. Arch Ophthalmol. 1994;112:1086–1088.
320. Diaz MG, Miller D, Perez E, et al. Recovery and identification of *Toxoplasma gondii* in cell culture as a causative agent of necrotizing retinitis (Abstract). Abstract for the 97th General Meeting of the American Society for Microbiology. May 4–8, 1997, Miami Beach, Fla; 1997:204.
321. Turunen HJ, Leinikki PO, Saari KM. Demonstration of intraocular synthesis of immunoglobulin G toxoplasma antibodies for specific diagnosis of toxoplasmic chorioretinitis by enzyme immunoassay. J Clin Microbiol. 1983;17:988–992.
322. Liesenfeld O, Remington JS. Toxoplasmosis. In: Martens MG, Faro S, Soper D, eds. Infectious Diseases in Women's Health: Philadelphia: WB Saunders. In press.
323. Remington JS, Araujo FG, Desmonts G. Recognition of different *Toxoplasma* antigens by IgM and IgG antibodies in mothers and their congenitally infected newborns. J Infect Dis. 1985;152:1020–1024.
324. Cazenave J, Forestier F, Bessieres M, et al. Contribution of a new PCR assay to the prenatal diagnosis of congenital toxoplasmosis. Prenat Diagn. 1992;12:119–127.
325. Fuentes I, Rodriguez M, Domingo CJ, et al. Urine sample used for congenital toxoplasmosis diagnosis by PCR. J Clin Microbiol. 1996;34:2368–2371.
326. Guerina N, Hsu H-W, Meissner H, et al. Neonatal serologic screening and early treatment for congenital *Toxoplasma gondii* infection. N Engl J Med. 1994;330:1858–1863.
327. Carey RM, Kimball AC, Armstrong D, Lieberman PH. Toxoplasmosis. Clinical experiences in a cancer hospital. Am J Med. 1973;54:30–38.
328. Cohn J, McMeeking A, Cohen W, et al. Evaluation of the policy of empiric treatment of suspected *Toxoplasma* encephalitis in patients with the acquired immunodeficiency syndrome. Am J Med. 1989;86:521–527.
329. Luft BJ, Remington JS. AIDS commentary. Toxoplasmic encephalitis. J Infect Dis. 1988;157:1–6.
330. Dannemann BR, McCutchan JA, Israelski DA, et al. Treatment of toxoplasmic encephalitis in patients with AIDS: A randomized trial comparing pyrimethamine plus clindamycin to pyrimethamine plus sulfadiazine. Ann Intern Med. 1992;116:33–43.
331. Katlama C, De Wit S, O'Doherty E, et al. Pyrimethamine-clindamycin vs. pyrimethamine-sulfadiazine as acute and long-term therapy for toxoplasmic encephalitis in patients with aids. Clin Infect Dis. 1996;22:268–275.
332. Beaman M, Luft B, Remington J. Prophylaxis for toxoplasmosis in AIDS. Ann Intern Med. 1992;117:163–164.
333. Pedrol E, Gonzales-Clemente JM, Gatell JM, et al. Central nervous system toxoplasmosis in AIDS patients: Efficacy of an intermittent maintenance therapy. AIDS. 1990;4:511–517.
334. Podzamczer D, Miró J, Bolao F, et al. Twice-weekly maintenance therapy with sulfadiazine-pyrimethamine to prevent recurrent toxoplasmic encephalitis in patients with AIDS. Ann Intern Med. 1995;123:175–180.
335. Heald A, Flepp M, Chave J-P, et al. Treatment for cerebral toxoplasmosis protects against *Pneumocystis carinii* pneumonia in patients with AIDS. Ann Intern Med. 1991;115:760–763.
336. Remington JS, Vilde JL, Antunes F, et al. Clindamycin for toxoplasmosis encephalitis in AIDS (Letter). Lancet. 1991;338:1142–1143.
337. Köppen S, Grunewald T, Jautzke G, et al. Prevention of *Pneumocystis carinii* pneumonia and toxoplasmic encephalitis in human immunodeficiency virus infected patients: A clinical approach comparing aerosolized pentamidine and pyrimethamine/sulfadoxine. Clin Invest. 1992;70:508–512.
338. Opravil M, Hirschel B, Lazzarin A, et al. Once-weekly administration of dapsone/pyrimethamine vs. aerosolized pentamidine as a combined prophylaxis for *Pneumocystis carinii* pneumonia and toxoplasmic encephalitis in human immunodeficiency virus-infected patients. Clin Infect Dis. 1995;20:531–41.
339. Clotet B, Sirera G, Romeu J, et al. Twice-weekly dapsone-pyrimethamine for preventing PCP and cerebral toxoplasmosis. AIDS. 1991;5:601–602.
340. Torres R, Barr M, Thorn M, et al. Randomized trial of dapsone and aerosolized pentamidine for the prophylaxis of *Pneumocystis carinii* pneumonia and toxoplasmic encephalitis. Am J Med. 1993;95:573–583.
341. Maslo C, Matheron S, Saimot AG. Cerebral toxoplasmosis: Assessment of maintenance therapy. VIII International Conference on AIDS. Amsterdam, The Netherlands; 1992:B123.
342. De Gans J, Portegies P, Reiss P, et al. Pyrimethamine alone as maintenance therapy for central nervous system toxoplasmosis in 38 patients with AIDS. J Acquir Immune Defic Syndr. 1992;5:137–142.
343. Podzamczer D, Salazar A, Jiménez J, et al. Intermittent trimethoprim-sulfamethoxazole compared with dapsone-pyrimethamine for the simultaneous primary prophylaxis of pneumocystis pneumonia and toxoplasmosis in patients infected with HIV. Ann Intern Med. 1995;122:755–761.
344. Bozzette S, Finkelstein D, Spector S, et al. A randomized trial of three antipneumocystis agents in patients with advanced human immunodeficiency virus infection. N Engl J Med. 1995;332:693–699.
345. Update: Trends in AIDS incidence, deaths, and prevalence—United States, 1996. MMWR 1997;46:165–173.
346. 1997 USPHS/IDSA guidelines for the prevention of opportunistic infections in persons infected with human immunodeficiency virus. USPHS/IDSA Prevention of Opportunistic Infections Working Group. MMWR Morb Mortal Wkly Rep. 1997;46:1–46.
347. Girard P-M, Landman R, Gaudebout C, et al. Dapsone-pyrimethamine compared with aerosolized pentamidine as a primary prophylaxis against *Pneumocystis carinii* pneumonia and toxoplasmosis in HIV infection. N Engl J Med. 1993;328:1514–1520.
348. Partisani M, De Mautort E, Hassairi N, et al. Primary prophylaxis of cerebral toxoplasmosis with pyrimethamine-sulfadoxine in human immunodeficiency virus-infected individuals seropositive to toxoplasma (Abstract). VIII International Conference on AIDS. Amsterdam, The Netherlands; 1992:B125.
349. Durant J, Hazime F, Carles M, et al. Prevention of *Pneumocystis carinii* pneumonia and of cerebral toxoplasmosis by roxithromycin in HIV-infected patients. Infection. 1995;23(Suppl 1):S33–S38.
350. Klinker H, Langmann P, Richter E. Pyrimethamine alone as prophylaxis for cerebral toxoplasmosis in patients with advanced HIV infection. Infection. 1996;4:324–328.
351. Jacobson M, Besch C, Child C, et al. Primary prophylaxis with pyrimethamine for toxoplasmic encephalitis in patients with advanced human immunodeficiency virus disease: Results of a randomized trial. J Infect Dis. 1994;169:384–394.
352. Rousseau F, Pueyo S, Morlat P, et al. Increased risk of toxoplasmic encephalitis in human immunodeficiency virus–infected patients with pyrimethamine-related rash. Clin Infect Dis. 1997;24:396–402.
353. Ruf B, Schurmann D, Pohle H. Failure of clarithromycin in preventing toxoplasmic

encephalitis in AIDS patients (Letter). J Acquir Immune Defic Syndr. 1992;5:530–531.
354. Raffi F, Struillou L, Ninin E, et al. Breakthrough cerebral toxoplasmosis in patients with AIDS who are being treated with clarithromycin. Clin Infect Dis. 1995;20:1076–1077.
355. Leport C, Vilde JL, Katlama C, et al. Failure of spiramycin to prevent neurotoxoplasmosis in immunosuppressed patients (Letter). JAMA. 1986;255:2290.
356. Jacobson M, Besch C, Child C, et al. Toxicity of clindamycin as prophylaxis for AIDS-associated toxoplasmic encephalitis. Lancet. 1992;339:333–334.
357. Carr A, Tindall B, Brew BJ, et al. Low-dose trimethoprim-sulfamethoxazole prophylaxis for toxoplasmic encephalitis in patients with AIDS. Ann Intern Med. 1992;117:106–111.
358. Navia BA, Petito CK, Gold J, et al. Central nervous system (CNS) toxoplasmosis complicating AIDS: Analysis of 20 patients. International Conference on Acquired Immunodeficiency Syndrome (AIDS). Atlanta, Ga; 1985:43.
359. Schnapp L, Geaghan S, Campagna A, et al. *Toxoplasma gondii* pneumonitis in patients infected with the human immunodeficiency virus. Arch Intern Med. 1992;152:1073–1076.
360. Tabbara KF, O'Connor GR. Treatment of ocular toxoplasmosis with clindamycin and sulfadiazine. Ophthalmology. 1980;87:129–134.
361. Ghartey K, Brockhurst R. Photocoagulation of acute toxoplasmic retinochoroiditis. Am J Ophthalmol. 1980;89:858–864.
362. Fitzgerald CR. Pars plana vitrectomy for vitreous opacity secondary to presumed toxoplasmosis. Arch Ophthalmol. 1980;98:321–323.
363. Forestier F, Daffos F, Rainaut M, et al. Suivi thérapeutique foetomaternel de la spiramycine en cours de grossesse. Arch Fr Pediatr. 1987;44:539–544.
364. Roizen N, Swisher CN, Stein MA, et al. Neurologic and developmental outcome in treated congenital toxoplasmosis. Pediatrics. 1995;95:11–20.
365. Wolters C, Stein L, Johnson D, et al. Absence of sensorineural hearing impairment in treated children with congenital toxoplasmosis. Pediatr Res. 1990;27:278A.
366. McGee T, Wolters C, Stein L, et al. Absence of sensorineural hearing loss in treated infants and children with congenital toxoplasmosis. Otolaryngol Head Neck Surg. 1992;106(1):75–80.
367. Mets MB, Holfels E, Boyer KM, et al. Eye manifestations of congenital toxoplasmosis. Am J Opthalmol. 1996;122:309–324.
368. Roizen N, Swisher CN, Stern MA, et al. Neurologic and developmental outcome in treated congenital toxoplasmosis. Pediatrics. 1995;95:11–20.
369. McLeod R, Mack D, Foss R, et al. Levels of pyrimethamine in sera and cerebrospinal and ventricular fluids from infants treated for congenital toxoplasmosis. Antimicrob Agents Chemother. 1992;36:1040–1048.
370. Weiss LM, Harris C, Berger M, et al. Pyrimethamine concentrations in serum and cerebrospinal fluid during treatment of acute *Toxoplasma* encephalitis in patients with AIDS. J Infect Dis. 1988;157:580–583.
371. Carbone LG, Bendixen B, Appel GB. Sulfadiazine-associated obstructive nephropathy occurring in a patient with the acquired immunodeficiency syndrome. Am J Kidney Dis. 1988;12(1):72–75.
372. Reboli AC, Mandler HD. Encephalopathy and psychoses associated with sulfadiazine in two patients with AIDS and CNS toxoplasmosis. Clin Infect Dis. 1992;15:556–557.
373. Torgovnick J, Arsura E. Desensitization to sulfonamides in patients with HIV infection. Am J Med. 1990;88:548–549.
374. Tenant-Flowers M, Boyle MJ, Carey D, et al. Sulphadiazine desensitization in patients with AIDS and cerebral toxoplasmosis. AIDS. 1991;5:311–315.
375. Gluckstein D, Ruskin J. Rapid oral desensitization to trimethoprim-sulfamethoxazole (TMP-SMZ): Use in prophylaxis for *Pneumocystis carinii* pneumonia in patients with AIDS who were previously intolerant to TMP-SMZ. Clin Infect Dis. 1995;20:849–853.
376. Coppola S, Angarano G, Monno L, et al. Adverse effects of clindamycin in the treatment of cerebral toxoplasmosis in AIDS patients. (Abstract). VII International Conference on AIDS. Florence, Italy; 1991:265.
377. Grossman PL, Remington JS. The effect of trimethoprim and sulfamethoxazole on *Toxoplasma gondii* in vitro and in vivo. Am J Trop Med Hyg. 1979;28:445–455.
378. Feldman HA. Effects of trimethoprim and sulfisoxazole alone and in combination on murine toxoplasmosis. J Infect Dis. 1973;128(Suppl):S774–S776.
379. Solbreux P, Sonnet J, Zech F. A retrospective study about the use of cotrimoxazole as diagnostic support and treatment of suspected cerebral toxoplasmosis in AIDS. Acta Clin Belg. 1990;45(2):85–96.
380. Canessa A, Del Bono V, De Leo P, et al. Cotrimoxazole therapy of *Toxoplasma gondii* encephalitis in AIDS patients. Eur J Clin Microbiol Infect Dis. 1992;11:125–130.
381. Herrera G, Villalta O, Visona K. Trimethoprim-sulfamethoxazole treatment of *Toxoplasma* encephalitis in AIDS patients. (Abstract). VII International Conference on AIDS. Florence, Italy; 1991:262.
382. Ward DJ. Dapsone/pyrimethamine for the treatment of toxoplasmic encephalitis (Abstract). VIII International Conference on Aids. Amsterdam, The Netherlands; 1992:B133.
383. Clotet B, Romeu J, Sirera G. Cerebral toxoplasmosis and prophylaxis for *Pneumocystis carinii* pneumonia. Ann Intern Med. 1992;117:169.
384. Paulic P, Pestre P, Bonnet E, et al. Treatment of brain toxoplasmosis by Fansidar (Abstract). Sixth International Conference on AIDS. San Francisco, Calif; 1990:Th.B.478.
385. Masur H, Polis M, Tuazon C, et al. Salvage trial of Trimetrexate-leucovorin for the treatment of cerebral toxoplasmosis in patients with AIDS. J Infect Dis. 1993;167:1422–1426.
386. Araujo FG, Guptill DR, Remington JS. Azithromycin, a macrolide antibiotic with potent activity against *Toxoplasma gondii*. Antimicrob Agents Chemother. 1988;32:755–757.
387. Chang HR, Rudareanu FC, Pechere JC. Activity of A-56268 (TE-031), a new macrolide, against *Toxoplasma gondii* in mice. J Antimicrob Chemother. 1988;22:359–361.
388. Luft BJ. In vivo and in vitro activity of roxithromycin against *Toxoplasma gondii* in mice. Eur J Clin Microbiol. 1987;6:479–481.
389. Chang HR, Pechere JC. Activity of roxithromycin against *Toxoplasma gondii* in murine models. J Antimicrob Chemother. 1987;20(Suppl B):69–74.
390. Huskinson-Mark J, Araujo FG, Remington JS. Evaluation of the effect of drugs on the cyst form of *Toxoplasma gondii*. J Infect Dis. 1991;164:170–177.
391. Remington JS. Macrolides, azalides, and streptogramins in treatment of opportunistic infections in immunocompromised patients. In: Zinner SH, Young LS, Acar JF, Neu HC, eds. Expanding Indications for the New Macrolides, Azalides, and Streptogramins. New York: Marcel Dekker; 1997:189–204.
392. Farthing C, Rendel M, Currie B, Seidlin M. Azithromycin for cerebral toxoplasmosis. Lancet. 1992;339:437.
393. Fernandez-Martin J, Leport C, Morlat P, et al. Pyrimethamine-clarithromycin combination for therapy of acute *Toxoplasma* encephalitis in patients with AIDS. Antimicrob Agents Chemother. 1991;35:2049–2052.
394. Araujo FG, Khan AA, Slifer TL, et al. The ketolide antibiotics HMR 3647 and HMR 3004 are active against *Toxoplasma gondii* in vitro and in murine models of infection. Antimicrob Agents Chemother. 1997;41:2137–2140.
395. Pope-Pegram L, Gathe J Jr, Bohn B, et al. Treatment of presumed central nervous system toxoplasmosis with doxycycline (Abstract). In: Program and Abstracts of VII International Conference on AIDS. Florence, Italy; 1991:188.
396. Turett G, Pierone G, Masci J, Nicholas P. Failure of doxycycline in the treatment of cerebral toxoplasmosis. Sixth International Conference on AIDS (Abstract). San Francisco, Calif; 1990:Th.B.479.
397. Araujo FG, Huskinson J, Remington JS. Remarkable in vitro and in vivo activities of the hydroxynaphthoquinone 566C80 against tachyzoites and tissue cysts of *Toxoplasma gondii*. Antimicrob Agents Chemother. 1991;35:293–299.
398. Kovacs JA. Efficacy of atovaquone in treatment of toxoplasmosis in patients with AIDS. Lancet. 1992;340:637–638.
399. Clumeck N, Katlama C, Ferrero T, et al. Atovaquone (1.4 hydroxynaphthoquinone, 566C80) in the treatment of acute cerebral toxoplasmosis (CT) in AIDS patients (Abstract). 32nd Interscience Conference on Antimicrobial Agents and Chemotherapy. Anaheim, Calif; 1992:313.
400. Torres R, Weinberg W, Stansell J, et al. Atovaquone for salvage treatment and suppression of toxoplasmic encephalitis in patients with AIDS. Clin Infect Dis. 1997;24:422–429.
401. Katlama C, Mouthon B, Gourdon D, et al. Atovaquone as long-term suppressive therapy for toxoplasmic encephalitis in patients with AIDS and multiple drug intolerance. AIDS. 1996;10:1107–1112.
402. Kovacs JA, Polis MA, Blaird B, et al. Evaluation of azithromycin or the combination of 566C80 and pyrimethamine in the treatment of Toxoplasmosis (Abstract). VIII International Conference on AIDS. Amsterdam, The Netherlands; 1992:B120.
403. Dixon R, Pozniak AL, Watt HM, et al. Single-dose and steady-state pharmacokinetics of a novel microfluidized suspension of atovaquone in human immunodeficiency virus–seropositive patients. Antimicrob Agents Chemother. 1996;40:556–560.
404. Luft BJ. Potent in vivo activity of arprinocid, a purine analogue, against murine toxoplasmosis. J Infect Dis. 1986;154:692–694.
405. Ou-yang K, Krug EC, Marr JJ, Berens RL. Inhibition of growth of *Toxoplasma gondii* by Quinghaosu and derivatives. Antimicrob Agents Chemother. 1990;34:1961–1965.
406. Lindsay DS, Blagburn BL, Hall JE, Tidwell RR. Activity of pentamidine and pentamidine analogs against *Toxoplasma gondii* in cell cultures. Antimicrob Agents Chemother. 1991;35:1914–1916.
407. Harris C, Salgo MP, Tanowitz HB, Wittner M. In vitro assessment of antimicrobial agents against *Toxoplasma gondii*. J Infect Dis. 1988;157:14–22.
408. Eliaszewicz M, Kirstetter M, Meyohas M, Frottier J. Traitement de la toxoplasmose cerebrale par la clindamycin et le 5-fluorouracile (Abstract). V International Conference on AIDS, The Scientific and Social Challenge. Montreal, Quebec, Canada; 1989:193.
409. Dhiver C, Milandre C, Poizot-Martin I, et al. 5-fluro-uracil-clindamycin for treatment of cerebral toxoplasmosis. AIDS. 1993;7:143–144.
410. Araujo FG, Slifer T, Remington JS. Rifabutin is active in murine models of toxoplasmosis. Antimicrob Agents Chemother. 1994;38:570–575.
411. Araujo FG, Khan AA, Remington JS. Rifapentine is active in vitro and in vivo against *Toxoplasma gondii*. Antimicrob Agents Chemother. 1996;40:1335–1337.
412. Khan AA, Slifer T, Araujo FG, Remington JS. Trovafloxacin is active against *Toxoplasma gondii*. Antimicrob Agents Chemother. 1996;40:1855–1859.
413. Hofflin JM, Remington JS. In vivo synergism of roxithromycin (RU 965) and interferon against *Toxoplasma gondii*. Antimicrob Agents Chemother. 1987;31:346–348.
414. Derouin F, Almadany R, Chau F, et al. Synergistic activity of azithromycin and pyrimethamine or sulfadiazine in acute experimental toxoplasmosis. Antimicrob Agents Chemother. 1992;36:997–1001.
415. Araujo FG, Remington JS. Synergistic activity of azithromycin and gamma interferon in murine toxoplasmosis. Antimicrob Agents Chemother. 1991;35:1672–1673.
416. Israelski DM, Remington JS. Activity of gamma interferon in combination with

pyrimethamine or clindamycin in treatment of murine toxoplasmosis. Eur J Clin Microbiol Infect Dis 1990;9:358–360.
417. Araujo FG, Hunter CA, Remington JS. Treatment with interleukin 12 in combination with atovaquone or clindamycin significantly increases survival of mice with acute toxoplasmosis. Antimicrob Agents Chemother. 1997;41:188–190.
418. Hakim M, Esmore D, Wallwork J, English TA. Toxoplasmosis in cardiac transplantation. BMJ. 1986;292:1108.
419. Wreghitt TG, Hakim M, Gray JJ, et al. Toxoplasmosis in heart and heart lung transplant recipients. J Clin Pathol. 1989;42:194–199.

Chapter 269

Giardia lamblia

DAVID R. HILL

Giardia lamblia, a flagellated enteric protozoan, is a common cause of endemic and epidemic diarrhea throughout the world. It is particularly seen in waterborne outbreaks of diarrhea, in children in daycare centers, and increasingly in foodborne outbreaks. It also contributes to chronic diarrhea in both the developed and developing world. In the United States and Canada, it is the most prevalent enteric parasite.

DESCRIPTION OF THE PATHOGEN

The genus *Giardia* belongs to the class Zoomastigophorea, the order Diplomonadida, and the family Hexamitidae. Based on its small subunit ribosomal RNA sequence and the absence of many organelles such as mitochondria and a typical Golgi apparatus, it is one of the most primitive eukaryotes, and can be used as a model to understand the development of eukaryotic cells.[1, 2] The differentiation of *Giardia* into species has traditionally relied on morphology and the host of origin, with only a few species described. However, *Giardia* species may now be classified according to antigen, isoenzyme, and genetic analysis in addition to their morphology and host range.[1, 3–7] *G. lamblia* (also called *intestinalis* or *duodenalis*) is the species infecting humans. The information from laboratory analysis and the clinical differences between isolates in both experimental human and animal infection indicate that there is marked heterogeneity within a given species.[8, 9] In addition, an individual isolate may undergo antigenic variation by changing a cysteine-rich surface protein termed the variant specific surface protein.[7] These variant specific surface proteins may help to protect the parasite against the activity of intestinal proteases, as well as play a role in immune evasion.

The life cycle of *G. lamblia* is composed of two stages: the trophozoite, or freely living stage, and the cyst. The trophozoite is 9 to 21 μm long and 5 to 15 μm wide (Fig. 229–1*A*) and has a convex dorsal surface and a flat ventral surface containing the disk, which is often referred to as the *sucking* or *adhesive disk*. There are four pairs of posteriorly directed flagellae that are involved in locomotion and perhaps attachment. Their intracytoplasmic projections are termed *axonemes*. The disk cytoskeleton is composed of a clockwise spiral array of microtubules joined by vertical microribbons.[1, 2, 10] Within these structural components are important antigens: tubulin within microtubules and giardins within microribbons.[1, 11, 12] The protozoan has two nuclei, each with a prominent central karyosome. On stained preparations, these create the characteristic facelike image. Median bodies, tight collections of microtubules, are placed transversely in a clawlike manner in *G. lamblia* and may be helpful in species differentiation.

Of the *Giardia* species, only *G. lamblia* has been successfully cultured in vitro. Growth is enhanced by the presence of biliary lipids, intestinal mucous and epithelial cells, and low oxygen tension, thus helping to explain the predilection of *Giardia* to colonize the upper small bowel.[2] The trophozoite divides by longitudinal binary fission and has a doubling time in culture of 9 to 12 hours. It is an aerotolerant anaerobe; metabolizes glucose to ethanol, acetate, and CO_2; may generate ATP via the arginine dihydrolase pathway; and scavenges phospholipids, fatty acids, cholesterol, and purines and pyrimidines from the environment.[1–3, 13] It requires exogenous cysteine. The total genome size is about 1.2×10^7 base pairs, and efforts are under way to sequence and clone its genes.[1, 2, 6, 7, 10]

G. lamblia trophozoites encyst to form smooth, oval-shaped, thin-walled cysts 8 to 12 μm long and 7 to 10 μm wide (see Fig. 269–1*B*). Encystation is enhanced by multiple factors, including cholesterol starvation followed by an alkaline pH and excess bile salts.[2, 7, 14] After encystment is initiated, specific encystment vesicles are formed, followed by transcription and secretion into the encystment vesicles of cyst wall proteins.[2, 15] On ultrastructural analysis, the cyst wall is found to have a fibrous character.[16] The major sugar associated with the cyst wall proteins is *N*-acetylgalactosamine.[2] As the cyst matures, trophozoite division may occur, forming two daughter trophozoites. Excystation follows exposure of cysts to gastric acid and pancreatic enzymes and the stimulation of a parasite-derived cysteine protease.[2, 17]

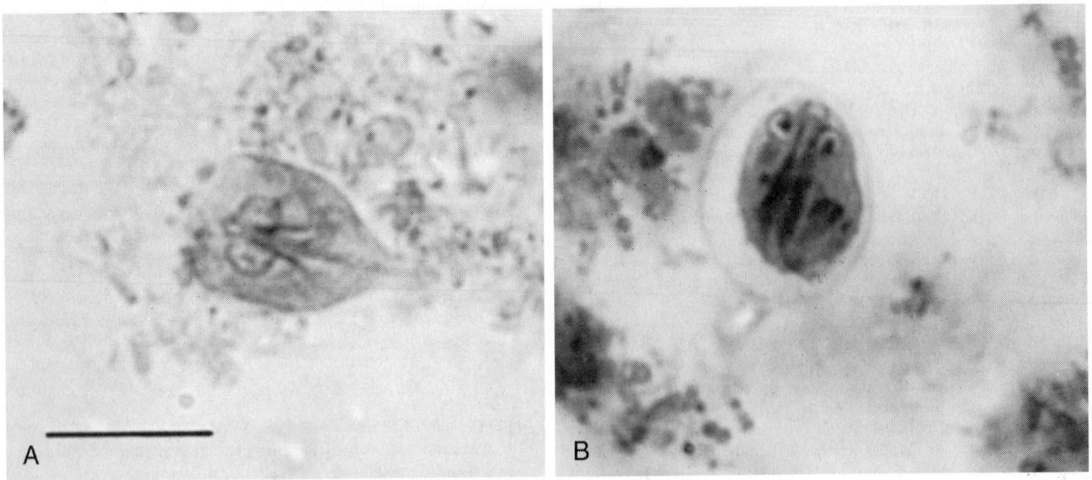

FIGURE 269–1. *Giardia lamblia* trophozoite *(A)* and cyst *(B)* are demonstrated in a trichrome stain of fecal material. Note the prominent nuclei in the trophozoite. In the cyst the cytoplasm has separated from the cyst wall; centrally located axonemes, a clawlike median body, and two eccentrically located nuclei can be detected. (Bar = 10 μm.)

EPIDEMIOLOGY

G. lamblia is distributed throughout the world. In the United States, from 1979 to 1991, *Giardia* was demonstrated in 4 to 7% of stool specimens,[18] making it the most commonly identified intestinal parasite. In the developing world, *Giardia* is one of the first enteric pathogens to infect infants,[19, 20] with peak prevalence rates of 15 to 30% occurring in children younger than 10 years.[19, 21, 22] Nearly all children in these settings become infected.[20, 23]

Acquisition of the parasite requires oral ingestion of *Giardia* cysts. Although this usually occurs after the ingestion of contaminated water, person-to-person and foodborne transmission are also important. In the United States from 1965 to 1994, *G. lamblia* has been the most commonly identified pathogen in outbreaks of waterborne diarrheal illness, accounting for 132 outbreaks that have affected over 27,000 persons.[24–26] The first documented outbreak occurred in Aspen, Colorado, in 1965–1966, where it affected 11% of more than 1000 skiers.[27] Many subsequent waterborne outbreaks have occurred in the mountainous regions of the Northeast, the Northwest, and the Rocky Mountain states of the United States, and British Columbia in Canada.[24, 28, 29] Surface water can easily become contaminated by human or animal sources, and *Giardia* cysts survive well in the environment, particularly in cold water.[30, 31] Common to most waterborne outbreaks has been the use of untreated surface water, or water treated by a faulty purification system or by inadequate chlorination and not subjected to flocculation, sedimentation, and filtration.[25, 32] Water used for recreation has also been associated with outbreaks.[25, 33, 34] Overseas travelers or hikers to wilderness areas may be at risk for waterborne giardiasis.[35]

Person-to-person transmission is now the second most commonly identified mode of acquisition and occurs in groups with poor fecal-oral hygiene, such as small children in daycare centers, sexually active male homosexuals, and persons in custodial institutions.[36] In children in daycare centers, the prevalence of *Giardia* cyst passage has been as high as 20 to 50%.[37–40] Many of these children are symptomatic, have been shown to spread the disease within their homes, and may contribute to high endemic rates in their communities.[38, 41, 42] Sexually active gay men have cyst passage rates as high as 20%, frequently with symptoms.[43] Reports that have documented the transmission of *Giardia* in commercial food establishments, corporate office settings, and small gatherings indicate that foodborne transmission is more common than previously recognized.[43–48]

Natural or experimental infection with *G. lamblia*–type parasites has been documented for many mammalian species including gerbils, mice, beavers, sheep, cattle, dogs, and cats. Analysis of these isolates by morphology, by the ability to be cultured in vitro, and by their genetic, isoenzyme, and antigenic makeup confirms their similarity to human isolates.[1, 5, 49–54] Whether animals act as an important reservoir for transmission to humans is less clear.[55] However, a study that rigorously analyzed a Canadian waterborne outbreak of giardiasis linked the outbreak to beavers.[29, 52] This emphasizes the importance of adequate purification of public water supplies.

PATHOGENESIS AND IMMUNE RESPONSE

Giardia was once thought to be a harmless commensal, but its association with symptomatic diarrhea, malabsorption in children,[56, 57] and disease after waterborne outbreaks, travel, and experimental human infection[8] has clearly established its pathogenicity. The production of diarrhea, and occasionally malabsorption, is the result of a complex interaction of *Giardia* with the host, with the outcome related to the number and strain of *Giardia* ingested and the host's immune response to the parasite.

Infection occurs after oral ingestion of as few as 10 to 25 cysts.[58] Although virulence characteristics of individual strains have not been clearly determined, the ability to establish infection and to cause diarrhea can vary between strains.[7, 8, 59] After excystation, trophozoites colonize and multiply in the upper small bowel. Adherence of *G. lamblia* in the human gut may be via the disk, with attachment at the brush border of enterocytes by either a suction or a clasping mechanism, but may also involve specific receptor-ligand interactions.[60] The parasite may avoid peristalsis by becoming trapped in intestinal mucus or between villi.

Several pathogenic mechanisms have been postulated: disruption of the brush border, mucosal invasion, elaboration of an enterotoxin, and stimulation of an inflammatory infiltration leading to fluid and electrolyte secretion and occasionally to villous changes.[6] This last mechanism is discussed later in this section. Electron microscopy has documented disruption of the brush border in some patients, which could lead to the disaccharidase deficiencies commonly seen in giardiasis.[61, 62] Mucosal invasion is rare, and there is no evidence for the production of an enterotoxin. Simultaneous colonization of the small bowel with *Giardia* and Enterobacteriaceae or yeast may contribute to malabsorption in some patients by the deconjugation of bile salts.

The host immune response is the other important component of the host-parasite relationship.[1, 63–65] Host immunity plays a role in providing protection from disease, in clearance of the parasite, and, in certain instances, in production of disease. Several observations indicate that partially protective immunity may develop to *Giardia*. In animal models of giardiasis, animals clear infection and become resistant to reinfection. These experimental observations of the development of immunity are supported by epidemiologic studies of human giardiasis. The prevalence of *Giardia* in developing countries is higher in younger age groups,[19, 66] and in endemic areas of North America, lower rates of symptomatic disease have occurred in long-term residents of the area than in visitors or short-term residents.[27, 67, 68]

The components of host immunity are humoral and cellular including lymphocyte- and macrophage-mediated mechanisms.[63, 64] A systemic antibody response occurs in patients with *Giardia*, and it has been useful in seroprevalence studies.[19, 66, 69, 70] Although serum immunoglobulin M (IgM) and IgG antibodies develop and with complement can be lethal to *Giardia* trophozoites, it is likely that gastrointestinal, secretory IgA antibodies play a more important role because of the luminal location of the trophozoites.[59, 69, 71–77] In mice, IgA has been the predominant antibody class detected in gut secretions; its development correlates temporally with clearance of the parasite, and its absence is associated with a failure to resolve infection.[64, 73, 76] The failure to develop IgA against specific *Giardia* antigens has been suggested to correlate with chronic giardiasis in humans.[71] The mechanism by which IgA prevents or helps to clear infection is probably by binding to trophozoites and preventing a critical adherence step. There is no evidence that IgA can kill trophozoites. *Giardia* spp. can produce an IgA protease.[6]

The cellular immune response helps to clear parasites by coordinating the production of anti-*Giardia* secretory IgA[64, 78, 79] and perhaps by engaging in specific anti-*Giardia* cytotoxicity. Athymic, T-cell–deficient mice are unable to clear infection with *Giardia muris* until the mice are reconstituted with lymphoid cells, particularly the $CD4^+$ helper T lymphocyte.[79] After reconstitution, animals develop an abnormal intestinal histologic appearance that parallels the changes seen in some humans with giardiasis: spruelike lesions with marked flattening of the villi, crypt hypertrophy, and a dense mononuclear cell infiltration of the submucosa.[56, 80, 81] The presence of intraepithelial lymphocytes has also been shown to correlate with adverse histologic changes.[82]

This immune response is likely to be initiated when *Giardia* is taken up and processed by macrophages residing in Peyer's patches. Parasite antigen alone may be sufficient to initiate inflammation.[83, 84] Although it is clear that *Giardia* organisms change their variant specific suface proteins in vivo, the role that this plays in avoiding immune recognition and allowing persistent infection is speculative.[7, 85, 86] Under immune pressure, however, parasites do change their variant specific surface proteins.[76]

The inflammatory response with damage to enterocytes and the mucosa could initiate a cytokine reaction leading to diarrhea, similar to the proposed mechanism for diarrhea production in adherent or minimally invasive coccidians such as *Cyclospora* and *Cryptosporidium*.[87] It could also stimulate increased epithelial cell turnover in the crypt region, changing the bowel's absorptive capacity.[82, 83]

Human milk may also play a role in protection of the host against *Giardia*. Milk is cytotoxic to trophozoites when free fatty acids are released from milk triglycerides by the action of bile salt–stimulated lipase.[88] Both human and animal breast milk have been found to contain anti-*Giardia* antibodies, and three studies have demonstrated protection of breast-feeding infants from symptomatic infection.[89–91]

Predisposition to giardiasis has been documented in patients with common variable immunodeficiency and in children with X-linked agammaglobulinemia.[43] These patients have symptomatic disease with prolonged diarrhea, malabsorption, and marked changes on small bowel biopsy, as described previously, which can include nodular lymphoid hyperplasia. On administration of anti-*Giardia* therapy, their symptoms improve and the histologic changes resolve. It remains unclear if selective IgA deficiency is a predisposing factor. Susceptibility to giardiasis has also been seen in patients with previous gastric surgery and reduced gastric acidity. There appears to be no association of giardiasis with blood group specificity. Patients with acquired immunodeficiency syndrome do not appear to have more severe illness with *Giardia*; however, they do exhibit impaired immune responses to the parasite.[92]

Small bowel biopsy may demonstrate spruelike lesions or may be normal[93]; two studies have correlated the severity of diarrhea with the degree of histologic abnormality on biopsy.[57, 81] The variation in the histologic appearance supports the multiple potential mechanisms for the production of diarrhea.

CLINICAL MANIFESTATIONS

Infection with *G. lamblia* includes asymptomatic cyst passage, acute self-limited diarrhea, and a chronic syndrome of diarrhea, malabsorption, and weight loss. Of 100 people ingesting *Giardia* cysts, an estimated 5 to 15% become asymptomatic cyst passers, 25 to 50% become symptomatic with an acute diarrheal syndrome, and the remaining 35 to 70% have no trace of infection. Although many symptomatic patients spontaneously clear their infection, most develop a diarrheal syndrome lasting 1 to several weeks and come to antimicrobial therapy. For children in daycare centers, asymptomatic cyst passage has been documented to last as long as 6 months.[37]

After the ingestion of *G. lamblia* cysts, there is an incubation period of 1 to 2 weeks before the onset of symptoms. The time from ingestion of cysts to detection of cysts in the stool may be longer than the incubation period.[8] Thus, a stool examination at the time of the onset of symptoms might well be negative.

Symptomatic giardiasis is characterized by the acute onset of diarrhea, abdominal cramps, bloating, and flatulence (Table 269–1). The patient usually expresses feelings of malaise, nausea, and anorexia and may complain of sulfuric belching. Vomiting, fever, and tenesmus occur less commonly. Initially, stools may be profuse and watery, but later they are commonly greasy, and foul-smelling and may float. Gross blood, pus, and mucus are usually absent, and if examined microscopically, the stool is found to be free of polymorphonuclear cells.

TABLE 269–1 Symptoms of Giardiasis

	Percentage	Range
Diarrhea	89	64–100
Malaise	84	72–97
Flatulence	74	35–97
Foul-smelling, greasy stools	72	57–79
Abdominal cramps	70	44–85
Bloating	69	42–97
Nausea	68	59–79
Anorexia	64	41–82
Weight loss	64	56–73
Vomiting	27	17–36
Fever	13	0–21
Urticaria	9	4–14
Constipation	9	0–17

Data from refs. 27, 35, 45, and 47.

One of the most important distinguishing features is the prolonged duration of diarrhea with giardiasis. At the time of presentation, most patients have been symptomatic for more than 1 week to 10 days. Weight loss of about 10 pounds occurs more than 50% of the time and is another useful clinical feature.[27, 35, 45, 47] Unusual features include urticaria, reactive arthritis, biliary tract disease, and gastric infection.[94–96] Gastric infection occurs exclusively in the presence of achlorhydria and may be seen in conjunction with *Helicobacter pylori* infection.

Although most persons with giardiasis have a relatively benign course, some persons, particularly children younger than 5 years and pregnant women, may have a severe illness characterized by volume depletion and require hospitalization.[97, 98]

Patients who develop chronic diarrhea have profound malaise, lassitude, occasional headache, and diffuse abdominal and epigastric discomfort often exacerbated by eating. Stools may again be greasy and foul-smelling or frothy, yellowish, occurring in small volume, and frequently passed. Weight loss is usually present. Periods of diarrhea may be interrupted by periods of constipation or normal bowel habits, with the syndrome waxing and waning over months until therapy is given or spontaneous resolution occurs.

Various degrees of malabsorption may be present. Children who present for evaluation for failure to thrive or with a spruelike illness have been found to have giardiasis.[56, 57] Steatorrhea and malabsorption of vitamins A and B_{12}, protein, *D*-xylose, and iron have been documented.[57, 99, 100] The most common disaccharidase deficiency has been that of lactase, occurring in 20 to 40% of cases,[61, 82] with post-*Giardia* lactose intolerance sometimes persisting for several weeks after treatment. This is often confused with relapse or reinfection.

The role that chronic infection with *Giardia* plays in the growth and development of children in the developing world has been controversial.[99, 101, 102] It is clear that high prevalence rates of *Giardia* exist in both symptomatic and asymptomatic children.[19–22, 56, 57, 103, 104] Some studies point to a deleterious effect on growth,[21, 99, 101] arguing for the need to treat recurrent disease to allow catch-up growth. Others emphasize the high prevalence of *Giardia* infection in asymptomatic children living in areas of poor sanitation and suggest that reinfection occurs so rapidly that repeated therapy is impractical and not indicated.[22, 102] In addition, many children may be simultaneously infected with other bacterial, viral, and parasitic infections, making the contribution that *Giardia* makes to their illness less clear. These issues are not likely to be resolved until adequate sanitation is provided for persons in the developing world.

DIAGNOSIS

The diagnosis of giardiasis should be considered in all patients with prolonged diarrhea, particularly that which is associated with malabsorption or weight loss. If there is a history of recent travel to an endemic area, the presence of small children in the home who attend daycare centers, or an active homosexual lifestyle, giardiasis is also more likely. Other diarrheal syndromes caused by viruses, noninvasive bacteria, and protozoans such as *Cryptosporidium* and *Cyclospora*,[26, 87] as well as tropical sprue, can be considered in the differential diagnosis.

The traditional method of diagnosis is a stool examination for trophozoites or cysts and is the assay with which other tests are compared.[43, 105] Antigen detection assays are now available and have frequently become the tests of choice.[106, 107] In the stool ova and parasite examination, the stool should be examined fresh and after preservation. A saline wet mount of fresh liquid stool in the acute stages of illness may yield motile trophozoites. In semiformed stool, trophozoites are usually not found, and the stool should be examined fresh for cysts after iodine staining or after preservation in 10% buffered formalin or polyvinyl alcohol and subsequent trichrome or iron hematoxylin staining.[108] Formalin-ether or zinc sulfate flotation concentration techniques may increase the yield. *Giardia* should be identified 50 to 70% of the time after one stool, and some report over 90% identification after three stools.[43, 105] Examination of a purged sample does not increase the yield.

Antigen assays detect *Giardia* by immunofluorescence or enzyme-linked immunosorbent assay. They are most helpful when giardiasis is the leading diagnosis such as during an outbreak, when screening children in daycare, or when testing patients after the completion of treatment.[43, 105] They are comparable in cost to a stool ova and parisite examination and are 85 to 98% sensitive and 90 to 100% specific.[106, 107, 109, 110] One of the best-studied assays detects a 65-kD *Giardia* cyst wall glycoprotein by enzyme-linked immunosorbent assay (ProSpecT, *Giardia* Assay, Alexon, Inc., Mountain View, Calif.[109, 111] An immunofluorescence assay detecting *Giardia* and *Cryptosporidium* is also available (Merifluor, Meridian Diagnostics, Inc., Cincinnati, Ohio).[106, 112, 113]

Between a carefully performed stool ova and parasite examination or an antigen assay, sampling of duodenal contents by string or biopsy is generally not needed. However, in particularly difficult cases, these procedures may be helpful. Three methods have been used: the string test or Entero-Test (HDC Corporation, San Jose, Calif.), duodenal aspiration, and duodenal biopsy. The string test should yield bile-stained mucus from the duodenum that can be examined for trophozoites in a wet mount or after staining.[114, 115] Duodenal aspiration and biopsy are more invasive. Biopsies require touch preparations, Giemsa staining, and a careful search for trophozoites. An advantage of biopsy, particularly in patients infected with human immunodeficiency virus or persons with malabsorption, is the identification of histologic abnormality that is not due to giardiasis; an aspirate could be sampled for small bowel overgrowth.

Testing for systemic anti-*Giardia* antibody, although not widely available, has been useful in seroepidemiologic studies throughout the world.[19, 66, 69, 70] The IgG antibodies remain elevated for long periods of time, making them less helpful diagnostically in areas endemic for giardiasis. Serum anti-*Giardia* IgM, however, may be useful in distinguishing current from past giardiasis.[116]

Although in vitro culture is available in research settings, it is not routinely used because of the difficulty in reproducibly isolating *Giardia* from patient samples.[117, 118] Detection of *Giardia* nucleic acid by polymerase chain reaction or by gene probes is a highly sensitive methodology but experimental at this point.[5, 119] The white blood cell count is usually normal, and eosinophilia is absent. Barium studies are generally nonspecific, showing an increased transit time and irregular thickening of small bowel folds and may interfere with the examination of stools.

TREATMENT

The routine isolation, culture, and susceptibility testing of *Giardia* have been difficult, with a lack of standardization and variable results.[120–122] Drug resistance can be induced in vitro; however, the clinical significance of this is not known.[123] In addition, some isolates that appear clinically resistant are susceptible in vitro and vice versa.[43, 105, 121, 124, 125] Most information on drug efficacy, therefore, relies on clinical experience.[105, 126–128]

The drug of choice for the therapy of giardiasis is metronidazole. Quinacrine is also effective, but production in the United States was discontinued in 1992. Although it has never received a Food and Drug Administration indication for giardiasis, most physicians have been treating giardiasis with metronidazole because of their familiarity with using it for other infections, its favorable side-effect profile, and its ready availability. Metronidazole, a nitroimidazole, is given in divided doses for 7 days (Table 269–2), with an efficacy of 80 to 95%. It is tolerated reasonably well in the pediatric age group.

TABLE 269–2 Treatment of Giardiasis

Drug	Dosage: Adult	Dosage: Pediatric
Metronidazole	250 mg tid × 5–7 d	5 mg/kg tid × 7 d
Quinacrine	100 mg tid × 5–7 d	2 mg/kg tid × 7 d
Furazolidone	100 mg qid × 7–10 d	2 mg/kg qid × 10 d
Paromomycin	25–30 mg/kg/d in 3 doses × 5–10 d	
Tinidazole	2 g × 1 dose	

From Hill DR. Giardiasis: Issues in management and treatment. Infect Dis Clin North Am. 1993;7:503–525.

Although concerns about potential mutagenicity make its routine use in children debatable, this has never been documented in humans.[129] Side effects that may be noted are a metallic taste in the mouth, some nausea, dizziness, headache, and, rarely, reversible neutropenia. When taken with alcohol, it can give a disulfiram-like effect. High-dose, short-course regimens have lower efficacy rates and may be poorly tolerated. Although not available in the United States, another nitroimidazole, tinidazole, has shown excellent efficacy (approximately 90%) when given in a single 2-g dose.[130]

If quinacrine can be obtained through alternative sources, it is given in divided doses for 5 to 7 days (see Table 269–2) and should have an efficacy of about 90%. The most common side effects are nausea, vomiting, and abdominal cramping. Yellow discoloration of the skin, urine, and sclerae can occasionally occur, and exfoliative dermatitis is a rare side effect.

Furazolidone, a nitrofuran, has been advocated as an alternative drug in the pediatric age group because of its availability in liquid suspension. It has a lower efficacy rate of about 80% and may cause gastrointestinal side effects, turn urine brown, and cause mild hemolysis in glucose-6-phosphate dehydrogenase–deficient individuals. For patients in whom one drug course fails or who infrequently relapse, a second course of the same drug or a switch to a drug from a different class is generally effective. Rare patients may require combination therapy.[124, 131]

There is increasing experience with the benzimidazoles. Although efficacy with mebendazole is generally disappointing,[132] several studies have demonstrated success with albendazole in a single daily dose of 400 mg for 5 days.[133, 134] The actual role that albendazole will have in therapy remains to be determined. Bacitracin has also shown limited efficacy.[135]

For pregnant women with giardiasis, there is no consistently recommended therapy because of the theoretical adverse effects of anti-*Giardia* drugs on the fetus.[43] In women for whom disease is mild and hydration and nutrition can be maintained, therapy may be delayed until after delivery, or at least until after the first trimester. If treatment is necessary, paromomycin, an oral aminoglycoside, may be tried. In limited clinical experience, it has an efficacy rate of 60 to 70% but has the advantage of not being measurably absorbed from the intestine in persons with normal renal function.[43, 136] It is given in divided doses for 5 to 10 days. Metronidazole has been used extensively in pregnancy for the treatment of trichomoniasis. The teratogenic effect appears to be minimal and, if present, greatest during the first trimester, when the drug should not be used.[136–139] If therapy cannot be avoided, then it can probably be used safely in the last two trimesters of pregnancy.

PREVENTION

The prevention of giardiasis requires proper handling and treatment of water used for communities and good personal hygiene on an individual basis. Although chlorination alone is sufficient to kill *G. lamblia* cysts, important variables, such as water temperature, clarity, pH, and contact time, alter the efficacy of chlorine, and higher chlorine levels (4 to 6 mg/liter) may be required.[32, 140] Thus, in addition to chlorination, public water supplies should also be subjected to flocculation, sedimentation, and filtration.[32] For travelers to the developing world or to wilderness areas, all water should be considered potentially contaminated because of the wide animal and human reservoirs of giardiasis. Bringing water to a boil is sufficient to kill all protozoal cysts; at high altitudes, boiling for longer periods may be necessary. If boiling is impossible, halogenation is generally effective for *Giardia*, but *Cryptosporidium* may be resistant,[141, 142] and the sensitivity of *Cyclospora* is not known. Chlorine-based (halazone, 5 tablets/liter for 30 minutes; chlorine bleach, 5.25%, 5 ml/gallon) or iodine-based (Potable Aqua, 1 tablet/liter for 30 minutes; saturated crystalline iodine, 12.5 ml/liter for 30 minutes) preparations may be used.[140] Contact time should be increased for water that is turbid or cold. Small-volume personal water filters with pore sizes of 1 μm or less may also be used. Uncooked foods that may have been washed or prepared in contaminated water should be avoided.

The endemic foci present in day care centers are a major problem. It is also not clear if chronic, asymptomatic carriage of *Giardia* in otherwise well-nourished children is deleterious to their health.[143] For these reasons and because of potential side effects of treatment, some recommend that only symptomatic children be treated.[37, 143] On the other hand, infected children transmit *Giardia* to parents and family members and may contribute to high endemic infection rates in communities.[34, 38] Because of these conflicting issues, each situation requires an individual decision. However, if strict hand washing and treatment of symptomatic children fail to control an outbreak of diarrhea, consideration can be given to treating all infected children.[144] Venereal transmission of *Giardia* can be decreased by avoidance of oral-anal and oral-genital sex. At present there is no immuno- or chemoprophylactic strategy for giardiasis.

REFERENCES

1. Adam RD. The biology of *Giardia* spp. Microbiol Rev. 1991;55:706–732.
2. Gillin FD, Reiner DS, McCaffery JM. Cell biology of the primitive eukaryote *Giardia lamblia*. Ann Rev Microbiol. 1996;50:679–705.
3. Thompson RCA, Reynoldson JA, Mendis AH. *Giardia* and giardiasis. Adv Parasitol. 1993;32:71–160.
4. Meloni BP, Lymbery AJ, Thompson RCA. Genetic characterization of isolates of *Giardia duodenalis* by enzyme electrophoresis: Implications for reproductive biology, population structure, taxonomy, and epidemiology. J Parasitol. 1995;81:368–383.
5. Weiss JB. DNA probes and PCR diagnosis of parasitic infection. Clin Microbiol Rev. 1995;8:113–130.
6. Farthing MJG. The molecular pathogenesis of giardiasis. J Pediatr Gastroenterol Nutr. 1997;24:79–88.
7. Nash TE. Antigenic variation in *Giardia lamblia* and the host's immune response. Philos Trans R Soc Lon B Biol Sci. 1997;352:1369–1375.
8. Nash TE, Herrington DA, Losonsky GA, Levine MM. Experimental human infections with *Giardia lamblia*. J Infect Dis. 1987;156:974–984.
9. Visvesvara GS, Dickerson JW, Healy GR. Variable infectivity of human-derived *Giardia lamblia* cysts for Mongolian gerbils *(Meriones unguiculatus)*. J Clin Microbiol. 1988;26:837–841.
10. Feely DE, Holberton DV, Erlandsen SL. The biology of *Giardia*. In: Meyer EA, ed. Giardiasis. The Netherlands: Elsevier Science; 1990:11–49.
11. Peattie DA. The giardins of *Giardia lamblia*: Genes and proteins with promise. Parasitol Today. 1990;6:52–56.
12. Holberton D, Baker DA, Marshall J. Segmented alpha-helical coiled-coil structure of the protein giardin from the *Giardia* cytoskeleton. J Mol Biol. 1988;204:789–795.
13. Stevens TL, Gibson GR, Adam R, et al. Uptake and cellular localization of exogenous lipids by *Giardia lamblia*, a primitive eukaryote. Exp Parasitol. 1997;86:133–143.
14. Schupp DG, Januschka MM, Sherlock LAF, et al. Production of viable *Giardia* cysts in vitro: Determination by fluorogenic dye staining, excystation, and animal infectivity in the mouse and mongolian gerbil. Gastroenterology. 1988;95:1–10.
15. Mowatt MR, Lujan HD, Cotten DB, et al. Developmentally regulated expression of a *Giardia lamblia* cyst wall protein gene. Mol Microbiol. 1995;15:955–963.
16. Erlandsen SL, Macechko PT, van Keulen H, Jarroll EL. Formation of the *Giardia* cyst wall: Studies on extracellular assembly using immunogold labeling and high resolution field emission SEM. J Eukaryot Microbiol. 1996;43:416–429.
17. Ward W, Alvarado L, Rawlings ND, et al. A primitive enzyme for a primitive cell: The protease required for excystation of *Giardia*. Cell. 1997;89:437–444.
18. Kappus KD, Lundgren RGJ, Juranek DD, et al. Intestinal parasitism in the United States: Update on a continuing problem. Am J Trop Med Hyg. 1994;50:705–713.
19. Gilman RH, Brown KH, Visvesvara GS, et al. Epidemiology and serology of *Giardia lamblia* in a developing country: Bangladesh. Trans R Soc Trop Med Hyg. 1985;79:469–473.
20. Fraser D, Dagan R, Naggan L, et al. Natural history of *Giardia lamblia* and *Cryptosporidium* infections in a cohort of Israeli Bedouin infants: A study of a population in transition. Am J Trop Med Hyg. 1997;57:544–549.
21. Farthing MJG, Mata L, Urrutia JJ, Kronmal RA. Natural history of *Giardia* infection of infants and children in rural Guatemala and its impact on physical growth. Am J Clin Nutr. 1986;43:395–405.
22. Gilman RH, Miranda E, Marquis GS, et al. Rapid reinfection by *Giardia lamblia* after treatment in a hyperendemic Third World community. Lancet. 1988;1:343–345.
23. Mahmud MA, Chappell C, Hossain MM, et al. Risk factors for development of first symptomatic *Giardia* infection among infants of a birth cohort in rural Egypt. Am J Trop Med Hyg. 1995;53:84–88.
24. Craun GF. Waterborne giardiasis in the United States 1965–1984. Lancet. 1986;2:513–514.
25. Kramer MH, Herwaldt BL, Craun GF, et al. Surveillance for waterborne-disease outbreaks—United States, 1993–1994. CDC Surveillance Summaries, April 12, 1996. MMWR Morb Mortal Wkly Rep. 1996;45:1–30.
26. Marshall MM, Naumovitz D, Ortega Y, Sterling CR. Waterborne protozoan pathogens. Clin Microbiol Rev. 1997;10:67–85.
27. Moore GT, Cross WM, McGuire D, et al. Epidemic giardiasis at a ski resort. N Engl J Med. 1968;282:402–407.
28. Birkhead G, Vogt RL. Epidemiologic surveillance for endemic *Giardia lamblia* infection in Vermont. The roles of waterborne and person-to-person transmission. Am J Epidemiol. 1989;129:762–768.
29. Isaac-Renton JL, Cordeiro C, Sarafis K, Shahriari H. Characterization of *Giardia duodenalis* isolates from a waterborne outbreak. J Infect Dis. 1993;167:431–440.
30. LeChevallier MW, Norton WD, Lee RG. Occurrence of *Giardia* and *Cryptosporidium* spp. in surface water supplies. Appl Environ Microbiol. 1991;57:2610–2616.
31. Wallis PM, Erlandsen SL, Isaac-Renton JL, et al. Prevalence of *Giardia* cysts and *Cryptosporidium* oocysts and characterization of *Giardia* spp. isolated from drinking water in Canada. Appl Environ Microbiol. 1996;62:2789–2797.
32. Jakubowski WS. Purple burps and the filtration of drinking water supplies (Editorial). Am J Public Health. 1988;78:123–125.
33. Porter JD, Ragassoni HP, Buchanon JD, et al. *Giardia* transmission in a swimming pool. Am J Public Health. 1988;78:659–662.
34. Dennis DT, Smith RP, Welch JJ, et al. Endemic giardiasis in New Hampshire: A case-control study of environmental risks. J Infect Dis. 1993;167:1391–1395.
35. Barbour AG, Nichols CR, Fukushima T. An outbreak of giardiasis in a group of campers. Am J Trop Med Hyg. 1976;25:384–389.
36. Brannan DK, Greenfield RA, Owen WL, et al. Protozoal colonization of the intestinal tract in institutionalized Romanian children. Clin Infect Dis. 1996;22:456–461.
37. Pickering LK, Woodward WE, DuPont HL, Sullivan P. Occurrence of *Giardia lamblia* in children in day care centers. J Pediatr. 1984;104:522–526.
38. Polis MA, Tuazon CU, Alling DW, Talamis E. Transmission of *Giardia lamblia* from a day care center to the community. Am J Public Health. 1986;76:1142–1144.
39. Addiss DG, Stewart JM, Finton RJ, et al. *Giardia lamblia* and *Cryptosporidium* infections in child day-care centers in Fulton County, Georgia. Pediatr Infect Dis J. 1991;10:907–911.
40. Thompson SC. *Giardia lamblia* in children and the child care setting: A review of the literature. J Paediatr Child Health. 1994;30:202–209.
41. Addiss DG, Davis JP, Roberts JM, Mast EE. Epidemiology of giardiasis in Wisconsin: Increasing incidence of reported cases and unexplained seasonal trend. Am J Trop Med Hyg. 1992;47:13–19.
42. Overturf GD. Endemic giardiasis in the United States—role of the daycare center (Editorial). Clin Infect Dis. 1994;18:764–765.
43. Hill DR. Giardiasis: Issues in management and treatment. Infect Dis Clin North Am. 1993;7:503–525.
44. Porter JDH, Gaffney C, Heymann D, Parkin W. Foodborne outbreak of *Giardia lamblia*. Am J Public Health. 1990;80:1259–1260.
45. Mintz ED, Hudson-Wragg M, Mshar P, et al. Foodborne giardiasis in a corporate office setting. J Infect Dis. 1993;167:250–253.
46. Quick R, Paugh K, Addiss D, et al. Restaurant-associated outbreak of giardiasis. J Infect Dis. 1992;166:673–676.
47. Petersen LR, Cartter MC, Hadler JL. A food-borne outbreak of *Giardia lamblia*. J Infect Dis. 1988;157:846–848.
48. White KE, Hedberg CW, Edmonson LM, et al. An outbreak of giardiasis in a nursing home with evidence for multiple modes of transmission. J Infect Dis. 1989;160:298–304.
49. Erlandsen S, Sherlock LA, Januschka M, et al. Cross-species transmission of *Giardia* spp: Inoculation of beavers and muskrats with cysts of human, beaver, mouse, and muskrat origin. Appl Environ Microbiol. 1988;54:2777–2785.
50. Buret A, denHollander N, Wallis PM, et al. Zoonotic potential of giardiasis in domestic ruminants. J Infect Dis. 1991;162:231–237.
51. Capon AG, Upcroft JA, Boreham PFL, et al. Similarities of *Giardia* antigens derived from human and animal sources. Int J Parasitol. 1989;19:91–98.
52. Baruch AC, Isaac-Renton J, Adam RD. The molecular epidemiology of *Giardia lamblia*: A sequence-based approach. J Infect Dis. 1996;174:233–236.
53. Thompson RCA, Lymbery AJ. Genetic variability in parasites and host-parasite interactions. Parasitology. 1996;112(Suppl):S7–S22.

54. Ey PL, Bruderer T, Wehrli C, Kohler P. Comparison of genetic groups determined by molecular and immunological analyses of *Giardia* isolated from animals and humans in Switzerland and Australia. Parasitol Res. 1996;82:52–60.
55. Bemrick WJ, Erlandsen SL. Giardiasis—is it really a zoonosis? Parasitol Today. 1988;4:69–71.
56. Burke JA. Giardiasis in childhood. Am J Dis Child. 1975;129:1304–1310.
57. Hjelt K, Poerregaard A, Krasilnikoff PA. Giardiasis causing chronic diarrhoea in suburban Copenhagen: Incidence, physical growth, clinical symptoms and small intestinal abnormality. Acta Paediatr. 1992;81:881–886.
58. Rendtorff RC. The experimental transmission of human intestinal protozoan parasites. II. *Giardia lamblia* cysts given in capsules. Am J Hyg. 1954;59:209–220.
59. Nash TE. Immunology of *Giardia lamblia*. In: Warren KS, Agabian N, eds. Immunology and Molecular Biology of Parasitic Infections. 3rd ed. Boston: Blackwell Scientific; 1993:157–169.
60. Lev B, Ward H, Keusch GT, Pereira MEA. Lectin activation in *Giardia lamblia* by host protease: A novel host-parasite interaction. Science. 1986;232:71–73.
61. Welsh JD, Poley JR, Hensley J, Bhatia M. Intestinal disaccharidase and alkaline phosphatase activity in giardiasis. J Pediatr Gastroenterol Nutr. 1984;3:37–40.
62. Chávez B, González-Mariscal L, Cedillo-Rivera R, Martínez-Palomo A. *Giardia lamblia*: In vitro cytopathic effect of human isolates. Exp Parasitol. 1995;80:133–138.
63. DenHollander N, Riley D, Befus D. Immunology of giardiasis. Parasitol Today. 1988;4:124–131.
64. Heyworth MF. Immunology of *Giardia* and *Cryptosporidium* infections. J Infect Dis. 1992;166:465–472.
65. Roberts-Thomson IC. Genetic studies of human and murine giardiasis. Clin Infect Dis. 1993;16(Suppl 2):S98–S104.
66. Miotti PPG, Gilman RH, Santosham M, et al. Age-related rate of seropositivity of antibody to *Giardia lamblia* in four diverse populations. J Clin Microbiol. 1986;24:972–975.
67. Istre GR, Dunlop TS, Gaspard B, Hopkins RS. Waterborne giardiasis at a mountain resort: Evidence for acquired immunity. Am J Public Health. 1984;74:602–604.
68. Isaac-Renton JL, Lewis LF, Ong CS, Nulsen MF. A second community outbreak of waterborne giardiasis in Canada and serological investigation of patients. Trans R Soc Trop Med Hyg. 1994;88:395–399.
69. Ljungström I, Castor B. Immune response to *Giardia lamblia* in a water-borne outbreak of giardiasis in Sweden. J Med Microbiol. 1992;36:347–352.
70. Soliman MM, Taghi-Kilani R, Abou-Shady AF, et al. Comparison of serum antibody response to *Giardia lamblia* of symptomatic and asymptomatic patients. Am J Trop Med Hyg. 1998;58:232–239.
71. Char S, Cervallos AM, Yamson P, et al. Impaired IgA response to *Giardia* heat shock antigen in children with persistent diarrhoea and giardiasis. Gut. 1993;34:38–40.
72. Birkhead G, Janoff EN, Vogt RL, Smith PD. Elevated levels of immunoglobulin A to *Giardia lamblia* during a waterborne outbreak of gastroenteritis. J Clin Microbiol. 1989;27:1707–1710.
73. Underdown BJ, Skea DL, Loney GM, Snider DP. Murine giardiasis and mucosal immunity: A model for the study of immunity to intestinal protozoan parasites. Monogr Allergy. 1988;24:287–296.
74. Heyworth MF, Vergara JA. *Giardia muris* trophozoite antigenic targets for mouse intestinal IgA antibody. J Infect Dis. 1994;169:395–398.
75. Rosales-Borjas DM, Diaz-Rivadeneyra J, Dona-Leyva A, et al. Secretory immune response to membrane antigens during *Giardia lamblia* infection in humans. Infect Immun. 1998;66:756–759.
76. Stager S, Muller N. *Giardia lamblia* infections in B-cell–deficient transgenic mice. Infect Immun. 1997;65:3944–3946.
77. Gottstein B, Deplazes P, Tanner I. In vitro synthesized immunoglobulin A from nu/+ and reconstituted nu/nu mice against a dominant surface antigen of *Giardia lamblia*. Parasitol Res. 1993;79:644–648.
78. Hill DR. Lymphocyte proliferation in Peyer's patches of *Giardia muris* infected mice. Infect Immun. 1990;58:2683–2685.
79. Heyworth MF, Carlson JR, Ermak TH. Clearance of *Giardia muris* infection requires helper/inducer T lymphocytes. J Exp Med. 1987;165:1743–1748.
80. Ridley MJ, Ridley DS. Serum antibodies and jejunal histology in giardiasis. J Clin Pathol. 1976;29:30–34.
81. Duncombe VM, Bolin TD, Davis AE, Crouch RL. Histopathology in giardiasis: A correlation with diarrhea. Aust N Z J Med. 1978;8:392–396.
82. Buret A, Gall DG, Nation PN, Olson ME. Intestinal protozoa and epithelial kinetics, structure and function. Parasitol Today. 1990;12:375–380.
83. Buret A, Hardin JA, Olson ME, Gall DG. Pathophysiology of small intestinal malabsorption in gerbils infected with *Giardia lamblia*. Gastroenterology. 1992;103:506–513.
84. Mohammed SR, Faubert GM. Disaccharidase deficiencies in Mongolian gerbils *(Meriones unguiculatus)* protected against *Giardia lamblia*. Parasitol Res. 1995;81:582–590.
85. Nash TE, Herrington DA, Levine MM, et al. Antigenic variation of *Giardia lamblia* in experimental human infections. J Immunol. 1990;144:4362–4369.
86. Byrd LG, Conrad JT, Nash TE. *Giardia lamblia* infections in adult mice. Infect Immun. 1994;62:3583–3585.
87. Goodgame RW. Understanding intestinal spore-forming protozoa: Cryptosporidia, microsporidia, isospora, and cyclospora. Ann Intern Med. 1996;124:429–441.
88. Reiner DS, Wang CS, Gillin FD. Human milk kills *Giardia lamblia* by generating toxic lipolytic products. J Infect Dis. 1986;154:825–832.
89. Nayak N, Ganguly NK, Walia BNS, et al. Specific secretory IgA in the milk of *Giardia lamblia*–infected and uninfected women. J Infect Dis. 1987;155:724–727.
90. Morrow AL, Reves RR, West MS, et al. Protection against infection with *Giardia lamblia* by breast feeding in a cohort of Mexican infants. J Pediatr. 1992;121:363–370.
91. Walterspiel JN, Morrow AL, Guerrero ML, et al. Secretory anti-*Giardia lamblia* antibodies in human milk: Protective effect against diarrhea. Pediatrics. 1994;93:28–31.
92. Janoff EN, Smith PD, Blaser MJ. Acute antibody responses to *Giardia lamblia* are depressed in patients with AIDS. J Infect Dis. 1988;157:798–804.
93. Oberhuber G, Kastner N, Stolte M. Giardiasis: A histologic analysis of 567 cases. Scand J Infect Dis. 1997;32:48–51.
94. Shaw RA, Stevens MB. The reactive arthritis of giardiasis. JAMA. 1987;258:2734–2735.
95. Clyne CA, Eliopoulos GM. Fever and urticaria in acute giardiasis. Arch Intern Med. 1989;149:939–940.
96. Quincey C, James PD, Steele RJ. Chronic giardiasis of the stomach. J Clin Pathol. 1992;45:1039–1041.
97. Lengerich EJ, Addiss DG, Juranek DD. Severe giardiasis in the United States. Clin Infect Dis. 1994;18:760–763.
98. Robertson LJ. Severe giardiasis and cryptosporidiosis in Scotland, UK. Epidemiol Infect. 1996;117:551–561.
99. Solomons NW. Giardiasis: Nutritional implications. Rev Infect Dis. 1982;4:859–869.
100. Gillon J. Clinical studies in adults presenting with giardiasis to a gastrointestinal unit. Scott Med J. 1985;30:89–95.
101. Gupta MC, Urrutia JJ. Effect of periodic antiascaris and antigiardia treatment on nutritional status of preschool children. Am J Clin Nutr. 1982;36:79–86.
102. Sullivan PS, DuPont HL, Arafat RR, et al. Illness and reservoirs associated with *Giardia lamblia* infection in rural Egypt: The case against treatment in developing world environments of high endemicity. Am J Epidemiol. 1988;127:1272–1281.
103. Sullivan PB, Marsh MN, Phillips MB, et al. Prevalence and treatment of giardiasis in chronic diarrhoea and malnutrition. Arch Dis Child. 1991;66:304–306.
104. Islam A, Stoll BJ, Ljungström I, et al. *Giardia lamblia* infections in a cohort of Bangladeshi mothers and infants followed for one year. J Pediatr. 1983;103:996–1000.
105. Wolfe MS. Giardiasis. Clin Microbiol Rev. 1992;5:93–100.
106. Zimmerman SK, Needham CA. Comparison of conventional stool concentration and preserved-smear methods with Merifluor Cryptosporidium/Giardia Direct Immunofluorescence Assay and ProSpecT Giardia EZ Microplate Assay for the detection of *Giardia lamblia*. J Clin Microbiol. 1995;33:1942–1943.
107. Garcia LS, Shimizu RY. Evaluation of nine immunoassay kits (enzyme immunoassay and direct fluorescence) for detection of *Giardia lamblia* and *Cryptosporidium parvum* in human fecal specimens. J Clin Microbiol. 1997;35:1526–1529.
108. Thornton SA, West AH, DuPont HL, Pickering LK. Comparison of methods for identification of *Giardia lamblia*. Am J Clin Pathol. 1983;80:858–860.
109. Addiss DG, Mathews HM, Stewart JM, et al. Evaluation of a commercially available enzyme-linked immunosorbent assay for *Giardia lamblia* antigen in stool. J Clin Microbiol. 1991;29:1137–1142.
110. Aldeen WE, Hale D, Robison AJ, Carroll K. Evaluation of a commercially available ELISA assay for detection of *Giardia lamblia* in fecal specimens. Diagn Microbiol Infect Dis. 1995;21:77–79.
111. Rosoff JD, Sanders CA, Sonnad SS, et al. Stool diagnosis of giardiasis using a commercially available enzyme immunoassay to detect *Giardia*-specific antigen 65 (GSA 65). J Clin Microbiol. 1989;27:1997–2002.
112. Alles AJ, Waldron MA, Sierra LS, Mattia AR. Prospective comparison of direct immunofluorescence and conventional staining methods for detection of *Giardia* and *Cryptosporidium* spp in human fecal specimens. J Clin Microbiol. 1995;33:1632–1634.
113. Grigoriew GA, Walmsley S, Law L, et al. Evaluation of the Merifluor immunofluorescent assay for the detection of *Cryptosporidium* and *Giardia* in sodium acetate formalin-fixed stools. Diagn Microbiol Infect Dis. 1994;19:89–91.
114. Rosenthal P, Liebman WM. Comparative study of stool examinations, duodenal aspiration, and pediatric Entero-Test for giardiasis in children. J Pediatr. 1980;96:278–279.
115. Goka AKJ, Rolston DDK, Mathan VI, Farthing MJG. The relative merits of faecal and duodenal juice microscopy in the diagnosis of giardiasis. Trans R Soc Trop Med Hyg. 1990;84:66–67.
116. Sullivan PB, Neale G, Cevallos AM, Farthing MJG. Evaluation of specific serum anti-*Giardia* IgM antibody response in diagnosis in children. Trans R Soc Trop Med Hyg. 1991;85:748–749.
117. Korman SH, Hais E, Spira DT. Routine in vitro cultivation of *Giardia lamblia* by using the string test. J Clin Microbiol. 1990;28:368–369.
118. Isaac-Renton JL, Shahriari H, Bowie WR. Comparison of an in vitro method and an in vivo method of *Giardia* excystation. Appl Environ Microbiol. 1992;58:1530–1533.
119. Mayer CL, Palmer CJ. Evaluation of PCR, nested PCR, and fluorescent antibodies for detection of *Giardia* and *Cryptosporidium* species in wastewater. Appl Environ Microbiol. 1996;62:2081–2085.
120. Gordts B, Hemelhof W, Asselman C, Butzler JP. In vitro susceptibilities of 25 *Giardia lamblia* isolates of human origin to six commonly used antiprotozoal agents. Antimicrob Agents Chemother. 1985;28:378–380.
121. McIntyre P, Boreham PFL, Phillips RE, Shepard RW. Chemotherapy in giardiasis: Clinical responses and in vitro drug sensitivity of human isolates in axenic culture. J Pediatr. 1986;108:1005–1010.
122. Crouch AA, Seow WK, Whitman LM, Thong YH. Sensitivity in vitro of *Giardia*

intestinalis to dyadic combinations of azithromycin, doxycycline, mefloquine, tinidazole and furazolidone. Trans R Soc Trop Med Hyg. 1990;84:246–248.
123. Upcroft JA, Upcroft P. Drug resistance and *Giardia*. Parasitol Today. 1993;9:187–190.
124. Smith PD, Gillin FD, Spira WM, et al. Chronic giardiasis: Studies on drug sensitivity, toxin production, and host immune response. Gastroenterology. 1982;83:797–803.
125. Majewska AC, Kasprzak W, De Jonckheere JF, Kaczmarek E. Heterogeneity in the sensitivity of stocks and clones of *Giardia* to metronidazole and ornidazole. Trans R Soc Trop Med Hyg. 1991;85:67–69.
126. Medical Letter. Drugs for parasitic infections. Med Lett Drug Ther. 1998;40:1–12.
127. Lerman SJ, Walker RA. Treatment of giardiasis. Literature review and recommendations. Clin Pediatr. 1982;21:409–414.
128. Davidson RA. Issues in clinical parasitology: The treatment of giardiasis. Am J Gastroenterol. 1984;79:256–261.
129. Beard CM, Noller KL, O'Fallon WM. Cancer after exposure to metronidazole. Mayo Clin Proc. 1988;63:147–153.
130. Speelman P. Single-dose tinidazole for the treatment of giardiasis. Antimicrob Agents Chemother. 1985;27:227–229.
131. Taylor GD, Wenman WM, Tyrrell DLJ. Combined metronidazole and quinacrine hydrochloride therapy for chronic giardiasis. Can Med Assoc J. 1987;136:1179–1180.
132. Bulut BU, Gulnar SB, Aysev D. Alternative treatment protocols in giardiasis: A pilot study. Scand J Infect Dis. 1996;28:493–495.
133. Hall A, Nahar Q. Albendazole as a treatment for infections with *Giardia duodenalis* in children in Bangladesh. Trans R Soc Trop Med Hyg. 1993;87:84–86.
134. Dutta AK, Phadke MA, Bagade AC, et al. A randomised multicentre study to compare the safety and efficacy of albendazole and metronidazole in the treatment of giardiasis in children. Indian J Pediatr. 1994;61:689–693.
135. Andrews BJ, Panitescu D, Jipa GH, et al. Chemotherapy for giardiasis: Randomized clinical trial of bacitracin, bacitracin zinc, and a combination of bacitracin zinc with neomycin. Am J Trop Med Hyg. 1995;52:318–321.
136. Rotblatt MD. Giardiasis and amebiasis in pregnancy. Drug Intell Clin Pharm. 1983;17:187–188.
137. Briggs GG, Freeman RK, Yaffe SJ. Metronidazole. In: Briggs GG, Freeman RK, and Yaffe SJ, eds. Drugs in Pregnancy and Lactation. 3rd ed. Baltimore: Wiliams & Wilkins; 1990:430–433.
138. Burton P, Taddio A, Ariburno O, et al. Safety of metronidazole in pregnancy: A meta-analysis. Am J Obstet Gynecol. 1995;172:525–529.
139. Rosa FW, Baum C, Shaw M. Pregnancy outcomes after first-trimester vaginitis drug therapy. Obstet Gynecol. 1987;69:751–755.
140. Backer HD. Field water disinfection. In: Auerbach P, ed. Wilderness Medicine. Management of Wilderness and Environmental Emergencies. 3rd ed. St. Louis: CV Mosby; 1995:1060–1110.
141. Centers for Disease Control and Prevention. Assessing the public health threat associated with waterborne cryptosporidiosis: Report of a workshop. MMWR Morb Mortal Wkly Rep. 1995;44(RR-6):1–19.
142. Juranek DD. Cryptosporidiosis: Sources of infection and guidelines for prevention. Clin Infect Dis. 1995;21(Suppl 1):S57–S61.
143. Ish-Horowicz M, Korman SH, Shapiro M, et al. Asymptomatic giardiasis in children. Pediatr Infect Dis J. 1989;8:773–339.
144. Bartlett AV, Englender SJ, Jarvis BA, et al. Controlled trial of *Giardia lamblia*: Control strategies in day care centers. Am J Public Health. 1991;81:1001–1006.

Chapter 270

Trichomonas vaginalis

MICHAEL F. REIN

Trichomonas vaginalis was first described by Donné in 1836.[1] Its acceptance as a primary pathogen was gradual, and the older literature frequently refers to it as a harmless commensal.[2] Closely related organisms are widespread in nature and are important pathogens of cattle, among which they are venereally transmitted, and fowl. Other organisms in the same family also infect humans. *Trichomonas tenax* resides in the anaerobic, periodontal crevices of some patients with pyorrhea[3] and occasionally appears to cause respiratory tract infection in patients with underlying pulmonary disease.[4–6] *Pentatrichomonas hominis* can be recovered from the lower gastrointestinal tract, more frequently from patients with symptomatic bowel disease.[4] Trichomonads are highly site-specific, and infection has never followed attempts to inoculate one species into an anatomic site usually inhabited by another.[2] Infected vaginal discharge contains 10^1 to 10^5 protozoans/ml, with most women carrying the larger numbers.[7] In fresh preparations, *T. vaginalis* is actively motile and usually pear-shaped, with average dimensions of approximately 10×7 μm. The organisms vary somewhat in size and shape and are most easily identified by their characteristic twitching motility. There are four free anterior flagella that appear to arise from a single stalk and a fifth flagellum, which is embedded in the undulating membrane that extends about half way across the organism. *T. vaginalis* can use a variety of carbohydrates.[8] All areas of the cell surface are capable of phagocytosis and can ingest bacteria, leukocytes, erythrocytes, and epithelial cells.[9] The organism generates metabolic energy with unique organelles called *hydrogenosomes*,[10] reproduces by binary fission, and exists only as a vegetative cell, no cyst forms having been described. Some isolates appear to contain viral particles.[11]

Strains vary with respect to serotype,[2, 12] size, surface carbohydrates and proteins,[12–16] enzyme complement,[17, 18] hemolytic activity,[19, 20] and experimental virulence.[2, 8, 20–22] The severity of clinical disease can be correlated with some laboratory characteristics[20–22] but not with others.[23] Trichomonads appear to damage genital epithelium by direct contact,[24–27] which is mediated by surface proteins[26, 28, 29] and results in microulcerations. Although a good deal is now known about many characteristics of *T. vaginalis*, specific virulence factors that could serve as points of therapeutic attack have not yet been convincingly and reproducibly defined, and the immune response is poorly understood.[30] *T. vaginalis* activates the alternative complement pathway[31] and attracts polymorphonuclear neutrophils,[32] which can kill the protozoans.[33] On the other hand *T. vaginalis* moves away from the products of polymorphonuclear neutrophil oxidative metabolism.[34] Monocytes and macrophages can also kill trichomonads in vitro, but their role in natural infection is uncertain.[35] Local and systemic humoral responses and delayed hypersensitivity are seen in human infection,[2, 12, 36–39] but they have insufficient sensitivity and specificity to permit serologic diagnosis in the clinical setting.

EPIDEMIOLOGY

An estimated 3 million American women contract trichomoniasis every year, and the infection rate in men is unknown. The incidence of trichomoniasis appears to be declining in the United States and Western Europe, possibly because of the widespread use of metronidazole for bacterial vaginosis. Trichomoniasis is reported in 17% of human immunodeficiency virus–positive women and 9 to 22% of pregnant women attending inner-city clinics[40, 41] and in 12% of men attending sexually transmitted disease clinics.[42]

The venereal nature of trichomoniasis is well established.[2, 8] Its incidence is highest among women with multiple sexual partners[43–46] and in groups with high rates of other sexually transmitted diseases.[8, 46] Thus, patients found to harbor *T. vaginalis* should always be screened for infections with other sexually transmitted pathogens, such as *Neisseria gonorrhoeae, Chlamydia trachomatis*, or human immunodeficiency virus[8, 47, 48] which may be clinically silent but of far greater medical consequence than is the protozoan. Current opinion favors the presumption that the inflammatory response to trichomonal infection increases the risk of transmitting or acquiring human immunodeficiency virus.[49–52]

The organism is recovered from 66 to 100% of the female partners of infected men[8] and from 22 to 80% of the male sexual partners of infected women.[8, 53] The infection appears to be self-limited in only about 20% of women[54] but in at least 40% of men,[53] possibly due to the trichomonacidal action of prostatic secretions or to the mechanical elimination of urethral protozoa during micturition.

Trichomoniasis is occasionally acquired nonvenereally. The organism survives for several hours in moist environments, including moist cloths.[8] Thus, the potential for nonvenereal transmission clearly exists,[8, 46] and trichomoniasis is found with high prevalence in some institutionalized populations. Transmission via the fingers during

TABLE 270–1 Sensitivity of Clinical and Laboratory Features in Vaginal Trichomoniasis

	Clinical Feature	Percentage Positive
Symptoms	None	9–56
	Discharge	50–75
	Malodorous	~10
	Irritating, pruritic	23–82
	Dyspareunia	10–50
	Dysuria	30–50
	Lower abdominal discomfort	5–12
Signs	None	~15
	Vulvar erythema	10–20
	Excessive discharge	50–75
	Yellow, green	5–20
	Frothy	10–50
	Vaginal wall inflammation	40–75
	Strawberry cervix (direct visualization)	1–2
	Colpitis macularis (colposcope)	45
Laboratory Findings	pH >4.5	66–91
	Positive whiff test	~75
	Excess polymorphonuclear neutrophils on wet mount	~75

Data from refs. 8, 59, 118, 119.

mutual masturbation has been suggested,[55] and transmission by sexual toys or shared douche equipment seems a possibility.

Like the other genital infections, trichomoniasis may be transmitted to neonates during passage through an infected birth canal and is acquired by 2 to 17% of the female offspring of infected women.[8, 56] Pulmonary infection is rarely acquired by this route.[56] Thereafter, trichomoniasis is rare until menarche. Genital trichomoniasis in an older child should raise the question of sexual abuse,[57] but, because of the possibility of nonvenereal transmission, the diagnosis does not prove that abuse has occurred.[58]

CLINICAL FEATURES

The incubation period in women ranges from about 5 to 28 days.[8, 48, 59] Symptoms often begin or exacerbate during the menstrual period. Clinical features are summarized in Table 270–1. Approximately 10 to 50% of infected women attending sexually transmitted disease clinics carry the organism asymptomatically.[59] Infected women usually note vaginal discharge and vulvovaginal soreness or irritation.[8, 48, 59] Dysuria may be perceived as internal or external, and dyspareunia is common. Although up to two thirds of infected women complain of a disagreeable odor, this symptom may actually be more suggestive of bacterial vaginosis (see Chapter 95).[59] Abdominal discomfort is described by 5 to 12% of infected women[8] but should still prompt careful evaluation of a second process, such as pelvic inflammatory disease. Unfortunately, none of these symptoms alone or in combination is sufficient to diagnose trichomoniasis reliably because all can accompany other genital infections.[40]

Examination usually reveals a copious, rather loose discharge that pools in the posterior vaginal fornix. Only about 5 to 40% of the women have a discharge that is distinctly yellow or green, but the presence of a yellow vaginal discharge should prompt a careful evaluation for trichomoniasis.[48] A yellow discharge may, however, accompany other processes, such as mucopurulent cervicitis.[48, 59] Bubbles are observed in the discharge of 10 to 33% of the patients.[8, 48, 59] Although protozoans can be recovered by culture from the endocervix in 90% of infected women,[60, 61] endocervical disease is not caused by *T. vaginalis*.[62] Symptomatic women usually manifest inflammation of the vaginal walls and the exocervix. Punctate hemorrhages (colpitis macularis), including the so-called strawberry cervix, are observed colposcopically in 45% of infected women but in only 2% by visual inspection alone.[22, 48, 59] Trichomonal vaginitis is a superficial infection, and invasion of the vaginal walls by the parasite has not been observed.[8] Vaginal discharge from 66 to 91% of women with trichomoniasis has a pH level elevated above the normal value of 4.5. An elevated pH level determined with indicator paper suggests trichomoniasis or bacterial vaginosis rather than vulvovaginal candidiasis (see Chapter 95).

Trichomonads can be recovered from the urethra and paraurethral glands in more than 95% of the women with trichomoniasis, which may explain the association of the infection with urinary frequency and internal dysuria.[48]

Complications of trichomonal vaginitis include vaginitis emphysematosa, an uncommon condition in which gas-filled blebs occur in the vaginal wall. If associated with trichomoniasis, the condition resolves when the infection in eradicated.[63] Women with trichomoniasis are more likely to suffer vaginal cuff cellulitis afier abdominal hysterectomy.[64] Gestational trichomoniasis has been associated with premature labor and low birth weight[40, 65] and less strikingly with postabortal infection and with premature rupture of the membranes. There has been speculation that bacterial or viral pathogens might be carried into the fallopian tubes by trichomonads,[66] but spread of trichomonads beyond the lower urogenital tract is extremely rare.

The clinical picture of trichomoniasis in men is clouded by the failure of many studies to control observations for the simultaneous presence of *C. trachomatis* and *Ureaplasma urealyticum*. In any case, most men carrying trichomonads are asymptomatic.[53] Organisms can, however, be isolated from 5 to 15% of patients with nongonococcal urethritis, particularly from men with nonchlamydial nongonococcal urethritis.[53] These men have a syndrome that is not clinically distinguishable from nongonococcal urethritis of other causes, although the discharge from trichomonal urethritis is usually somewhat milder than with other infections,[53] often so scant that it is noticed only as a small bead at the meatus on arising in the morning. *T. vaginalis*, as well as some isolates of *U. urealyticum*, should be considered in cases of tetracycline-unresponsive nongonococcal urethritis (see Chapter 94).[67] Trichomoniasis occasionally causes epididymitis and superficial penile ulcerations, often beneath the prepuce, and may involve the prostate gland.[53, 68]

DIAGNOSIS

Clinical differentiation of various forms of infectious vaginitis is unreliable, and the accurate diagnosis of trichomoniasis in patients of either sex depends on demonstrating the organism in genital specimens. The sensitivity of various techniques is summarized in Table 270–2; each is relatively specific. Trichomonads may be identified in vaginal secretions using the wet mount technique (described in Chapter 95), which will detect them, in most series, in about 60% of infected women.[8, 48, 59, 69–73] *T. vaginalis* is most easily recognized by its characteristic movements. The wet mount generally also reveals large numbers of white blood cells,[8, 43, 48] although asymptomatic women may have very few. In trichomonal infection, epithelial

TABLE 270–2 Sensitivity of Techniques for Identifying *Trichomonas vaginalis* in Genital Specimens

Technique	Sensitivity (%)
Wet mount	49–80
Fluorescent antibody	64–90
Gram stain	<1
Acridine orange stain	~66
Giemsa stain	35–60
Latex fixation	56–90
Enzyme-linked immunosorbent assay	77–93
DNA probe	86–91
Polymerase chain reaction	92–100
Cervical cytologic appearance	56–70
Vaginal culture	85–98
Male urethral culture	80
Male first-void urine culture	68

Data from refs. 8, 53, 59, 61, 71–76, and 118–120.

cells appear normal on wet mount, and the bacterial flora consists of either rods or coccobacilli.[8] The presence of clue cells suggests coincident bacterial vaginosis. Although culture from the endocervix is usually positive, endocervical specimens should not be used for the microscopic diagnosis of trichomoniasis, because only small numbers of organisms are present therein.[60, 61]

Wet mount examination of material obtained with a platinum loop from the anterior urethra reveals the organism in 50 to 90% of infected men.[8, 53] Culture of a urethral scraping has a sensitivity of about 80%, and culture of a first-void urine sediment reveals the organism in 70%.[53] Prostatic massage before collecting the urine increases the sensitivity, possibly to 95%.[8, 53]

The Gram, Giemsa, Pappenheim, and acridine orange stains are less useful than the wet mount in diagnosing trichomoniasis in patients of either gender. Direct fluorescent antibody staining,[69, 70] latex agglutination,[71] enzyme-linked immunosorbent assay techniques,[72, 73] DNA probe,[74] and polymerase chain reaction[75, 76] are more sensitive than wet mount (80 to 90%) but less sensitive than culture.

Trichomonads can be cultured on a number of liquid and semisolid media,[48, 59, 69, 70, 77] with modified Diamond's medium[23, 78, 79] or thioglycolate medium preferred.[23, 78–80] The organism can also be recovered in tissue culture.[81] Culture remains the most sensitive (>95%) technique for the diagnosis of trichomoniasis, and commercially available kits have increased the ease with which the organism can be cultured.[82]

Serodiagnosis is plagued by a lack of specificity, particularly in high risk-populations in which antibody may persist from prior infections. Sensitivity is also low. Serologic testing has no current role in the evaluation of the individual patient.

THERAPY

General

The development of metronidazole in the early 1960s revolutionized the treatment of trichomoniasis. The drug is activated with reduction of the nitro group by ferredoxin-like proteins possessed only by anaerobic organisms.[83] Short-lived metabolites are felt to act primarily by combining with DNA. Other 5-nitroimidazoles used to treat trichomoniasis outside the United States (see Table 270–3) have somewhat different pharmacologic properties but do not vary much in effectiveness or toxicity.[83] Systemic therapy eradicates trichomonads from the urinary tract as well as from the vagina, thereby reducing the risk of relapse. Obviously, only systemic therapy is capable of eradicating trichomonads from the male urogenital tract.

Numerous studies have confirmed the efficacy of a single oral 2-g dose of metronidazole in women,[84, 85] but doses of less than 1.5 g are associated with higher failure rates.[54, 86, 87] Data on men are limited and poorly controlled for reinfection, but it is reasonable to assume that the single-dose regimen is effective in men as well as in women. An alternative regimen for either gender consists of either 250 mg orally three times daily or 500 mg twice daily for 7 days.[84] The single-dose regimen provides freedom from problems with patient compliance. The lower dose reduces cost and, theoretically, the risk of toxicity. An apparent disadvantage of the single-dose regimen is a higher rate of reinfection if sexual partners are not treated simultaneously.[86, 88] In theory, any marginally effective regimen might select for metronidazole-resistant organisms.

TABLE 270–3 Therapy of Trichomoniasis

Drug	Regimen
Metronidazole	2 g as single oral dose
	250 mg PO tid for 7 d
	500 mg PO bid for 7 d
Nimorazole	2 g as single oral dose
Tinidazole	2 g as single oral dose
Ornidazole	1.5 g as single oral dose
	1 g as single oral dose along with 500-mg vaginal suppository *per vaginum*
	500 mg po bid for 5 d

Data from ref 113.

The disadvantages of systemic metronidazole are several: Many people taking the drug complain of mild nausea or bad taste, which is more frequent after the administration of a large single dose. Metronidazole blocks the metabolism of alcohol, and patients consuming the two concurrently may suffer nausea, vomiting, and flushing.[89] Not merely a narrow-spectrum trichomonacide, metronidazole is active against most anaerobic bacteria and may alter the normal vaginal flora, occasionally causing candidal vaginitis to supervene. Metronidazole may increase the anticoagulatory effect of warfarin.

Intolerance of metronidazole is not common. Desensitization has been successfully employed in a small number of cases,[90] and paromomycin has been used topically in a few women as well.[91, 92] Metronidazole vaginal gel (0.5%) is inadequate therapy for trichomoniasis.[93] Alternatives to the 5-nitroimidazoles are discussed in more detail in the section on metronidazole resistance.

Attention has been called to the capacity of high-dose, long-term metronidazole to induce lung tumors in animals. However, data linking clinical use of metronidazole to cancer in humans are weak,[84, 94, 95] and its advantages in treating trichomoniasis outweigh its risks. The drug should not be administered indiscriminately, and the doses given should be kept as small as possible.

A single 2-g dose of metronidazole can be used to treat trichomoniasis in any stage of pregnancy.[95–97]

As a public health measure, asymptomatically infected women should be treated because they represent an important reservoir of the disease. In addition, about one third of them will become symptomatic during the following few months. The long-term effects of chronic, asymptomatic trichomoniasis are unknown. Initial simultaneous treatment of male sexual partners is particularly important if the single-dose regimen is used.

The number of cases of putative metronidazole treatment failure appears to be increasing. When confronted with a woman who presents with recurrent infection, the clinician should consider the following possibilities. (1) Reinfection from an untreated sexual partner remains the most common cause of recurrent disease, especially if the patient received a single-dose regimen.[84, 86, 88] Nonjudgmental questioning regarding sexual activity may provide necessary information. It is useful to remind women that infected male sexual partners are usually completely asymptomatic. (2) Noncompliance with multidose regimens may be revealed by careful questioning. (3) Very rarely, metronidazole treatment failures have been attributed to increased hepatic inactivation of the drug[98] or even, theoretically, to competitive inactivation by bacteria. (4) Finally, one must consider the possibility of true metronidazole resistance.

Metronidazole Resistance

Metronidazole-resistant *T. vaginalis* has been reported for some years, and its prevalence seems to be increasing.[83, 84, 99–101a] Standard regimens fail to cure infections with some of these resistant strains. Methods for determining the antimicrobial sensitivity of *T. vaginalis* are not standardized, and the apparent level of resistance depends markedly on assay conditions (e.g., oxygen concentration),[99, 100, 102–104] but assays are becoming more widely available,[105] and suspect organisms should be cultured and tested. In vitro data suggest that resistance may develop during exposure to metronidazole.[104] Infections with moderately resistant strains might be treated with oral doses of 2 g of metronidazole administered daily for 3 to 7 days, and more resistant infections may require the same oral dose for 7 to 14 days along with a 500-mg tablet broken and inserted intravaginally each day.[84, 99, 100, 106, 107] Some resistant cases have been cured with intravenous metronidazole, administered in high doses of 2 g every 6 to 8 hours for 3 days,[107, 108] but the minimal effective dose has not been determined. Surprisingly, tinidazole, which is available outside the

United States, has cured some cases of metronidazole-resistant trichomoniasis.[109, 110] High-dose metronidazole cream is available in some countries, including Canada. Limited observations suggest that vaginal application of a spermacide containing nonoxynol-9[110, 111] or douching with a 1% solution of zinc sulfate[112] may serve as an adjunct to metronidazole therapy.

A few infections with resistant trichomonads have been cured with the nightly vaginal application of 250 mg of paromomycin for 2 weeks, but reversible vaginal ulceration occurred in some women.[91, 92, 110] Pessaries containing arsenic[113] have been used in a small number of cases with varied success.[114, 115] Furazolidone is active in vitro[116] and may prove useful therapeutically.

Postmenopausal women may perhaps be cured by temporarily discontinuing estrogen replacement therapy.[117]

REFERENCES

1. Kampmeier RH. Description of *Trichomonas vaginalis* by MA Donné. Sex Transm Dis. 1978;5:119–122.
2. Honigberg BM, ed. Trichomonads Parasitic in Humans. New York: Springer-Verlag; 1990.
3. Mahdi NK, al-Saeed AT. *Trichomonas tenax* in Barash, Iraq. JPMA J Pak Med Assoc. 1993;43:261–262.
4. Honigberg BM. Trichomonads found outside the urogenital tract in humans. In: Honigberg BM, ed. Trichomonads Parasitic in Humans. New York: Springer-Verlag; 1990:342–393.
5. Hersh SM. Pulmonary trichomoniasis and *Trichomonas tenax*. J Med Microbiol. 1985;20:1–10.
6. El Kamel A, Rouetbi N, Chakroun M, Battikh M. Pulmonary eosinophilia due to *Trichomonas tenax*. Thorax. 1996;51:554–555.
7. Philip A, Carter-Scott P, Rogers C. An agar culture technique to quantitate *Trichomonas vaginalis* from women. J Infect Dis. 1987;155:304–308.
8. Müller M, Rein ME. *Trichomonas vaginalis*. In: Holmes KK, Mardh P-A, Sparling PF, et al, eds. Sexually Transmitted Diseases. 2nd ed. New York: McGraw-Hill; 1990:481–492.
9. Rendon-Maldonado JG, Espinosa-Cantellano M, Gonzalez-Robles A, Martinez-Palomo A. *Trichomonas vaginalis*: In vitro phagocytosis of lactobacilli, vaginal epithelial cells, leukocytes, and erythrocytes. Exp Parasitol. 1998;89:241–250.
10. Biagini GA, Finlay BJ, Lloyd D. Evolution of the hydrogenosome. FEMS Microbiol Lett. 1997;155:133–140.
11. Provenzano D, Khoshnan A, Alderete JF. Involvement of dsRNA virus in the protein composition and growth of host *Trichomonas vaginalis*. Arch Virol. 1997;142:939–952.
12. Garber GE, Proctor EM, Bowie WR. Immunogenic proteins of *Trichomonas vaginalis* as demonstrated by the immunoblot technique. Infect Immun. 1986;51:250–253.
13. Warton A, Honigberg BM. Analysis of surface saccharides of *Trichomonas vaginalis* strains with various pathogenicity levels by fluorescein-conjugated plant lectins. Z Parasitenkd. 1983;69:149–159.
14. Krieger JN, Holmes KK, Spence MR, et al. Geographic variation among *Trichomonas vaginalis*: Demonstration of antigenic heterogeneity using monoclonal antibodies and the indirect immunofluorescent technique. J Infect Dis. 1985;5:979–984.
15. Alderete JF, Demes P, Gombosova A, et al. Phenotypes and protein-epitope phenotypic variation among fresh isolates of *Trichomonas vaginalis*. Infect Immun. 1987;55:1037–1041.
16. Alderete JF, Kasmala L, Metcalfe E, et al. Phenotypic variation and diversity among *Trichomonas vaginalis* isolates and correlation of phenotype with trichomonal virulence determinants. Infect Immun. 1986;53:285–293.
17. Irvine JW, North MJ, Coombs GH. Use of inhibitors to identify essential proteinases of *Trichomonas vaginalis*. FEMS Microbiol Lett. 1997;149:45–50.
18. Arroyo R, Alderete JF. Two *Trichomonas vaginalis* surface proteinases bind to host epithelial cells and are related to levels of cytoadherence and cytotoxicity. Arch Med Res. 1995;26:279–285.
19. Fiori PL, Rappelli P, Addis MF, et al. *Trichomonas vaginalis* haemolysis: pH regulates a contact-independent mechanism based on pore-forming proteins. Microb Pathogen. 1996;20:109–118.
20. Krieger JN, Poisson MA, Rein MF. Beta-hemolytic activity of *Trichomonas vaginalis* correlates with virulence. Infect Immun. 1983;41:1291–1295.
21. Graves A, Gardner WA Jr. Pathogenicity of *Trichomonas vaginalis*. Clin Obstet Gynecol. 1993;36:145–152.
22. Garber GE, Lemchuk-Favel LT. Association of production of cell detaching factor with the clinical presentation of *Trichomonas vaginalis*. J Clin Microbiol. 1990;28:2415–2417.
23. Krieger JN, Wolner-Hanssen P, Stevens C, et al. Characteristics of *Trichomonas vaginalis* isolates from women with and without colpitis macularis. J Infect Dis. 1990;161:307–311.
24. Krieger JN, Ravdin JI, Rein MF. Contact-dependent cytopathogenic mechanisms of *Trichomonas vaginalis*. Infect Immun. 1985;50:778–786.
25. Arroyo R, Gonzalez-Robles A, Martinez-Palomo A, et al. Signaling of *Trichomonas vaginalis* for amoeboid transformation and adhesin synthesis follows cytoadherence. Mol Microbiol. 1993;7:299–309.
26. Arroyo R, Engbring J, Alderete JF. Molecular basis of host epithelial cell recognition by *Trichomonas vaginalis*. Mol Microbiol. 1992;6:853–862.
27. Nielsen MH, Nielsen R. Electron microscopy of *Trichomonas vaginalis* Donné: Interaction with vaginal epithelium in human trichomoniasis. Acta Pathol Microbiol Scand B. 1975;83:305–320.
28. Mirhaghani A, Warton A. An electron microscope study of the interaction between *Trichomonas vaginalis* and epithelial cells of the human amnion membrane. Parasitol Res. 1996;82:43–47.
29. O'Brien JL, Lauriano CM, Alderete JF. Molecular characterization of a third malic enzyme–like *AP65* adhesin gene of *Trichomonas vaginalis*. Microb Pathog. 1996;20:335–349.
30. Petrin D, Delgaty K, Bhatt K, Garber G. Clinical and microbiological aspects of *Trichomonas vaginalis*. Clin Microbiol Rev. 1998;11:300–317.
31. Shaio MF, Chang FY, Hou SC, et al. The role of immunoglobulin and complement in enhancing the respiratory burst of neutrophils against *Trichomonas vaginalis*. Parasite Immunol. 1991;13:241–250.
32. Shaio MF, Lin PR, Lee CS, et al. A novel neutrophil activating factor released by *Trichomonas vaginalis*. Infect Immun. 1992;60:4475–4482.
33. Rein MF, Sullivan JA, Mandell GL. Trichomonacidal activity of polymorphonuclear neutrophils: Killing by disruption and fragmentation. J Infect Dis. 1980;142:575–585.
34. Styrt B, Sugarman B, Mummaw N, et al. Chemorepulsion of trichomonads by products of neutrophil oxidative metabolism. J Infect Dis. 1991;163:176–179.
35. Mantovanic A, Polentaruttic N, Pen G, et al. Cytotoxicity of human peripheral blood monocytes against *Trichomonas vaginalis*. Clin Exp Immunol. 1981;46:391.
36. Bozner R, Gambosova A, Valent M, et al. Proteinases of *Trichomonas vaginalis*: Antibody response in patients with urogenital trichomoniasis. Parasitology. 1992;105:387–391.
37. Bhatt R, Penditt D, Deodhar L. Detection of serum antitrichomonal antibodies in urogenital trichomoniasis by immunofluorescence. J Postgrad Med. 1992;38:72–74.
38. Skerma P, Malla N, Gupta I, et al. Antitrichomonad IgA antibodies in trichomoniasis before and after treatment. Folia Microbiol (Praha). 1991;36:302–304.
39. Alderete JF, Newton E, Dennis C, et al. Antibody in sera of patients infected with *Trichomonas vaginalis* is to trichomonad proteases. Genitourin Med. 1991:67:331–334.
40. Pastorek JG II, Cotch MF, Martin DH, et al. Clinical and microbiological correlates of vaginal trichomoniasis during pregnancy. Clin Infect Dis. 1996;23:1075–1080.
41. Sorvillo F, Kovacs A, Kerndt P, et al. Risk factors for trichomoniasis among women with human immunodeficiency virus (HIV) infection at a public clinic in Los Angeles County, California: Implications for HIV prevention. Am J Trop Med Hyg. 1998;58:495–500.
42. Borchardt KA, al-Haraci S, Maida N. Prevalence of *Trichomonas vaginalis* in a male sexually transmitted disease clinic population by interview, wet mount microscopy, and the InPouch TV test. Genitourin Med. 1995;71:405–406.
43. McLellan R, Spence MR, Brockman M, et al. The clinical diagnosis of trichomoniasis. Obstet Gynecol. 1982;60:30.
44. Cotch MF, Pastorek JG 2nd, Nugent RP, et al. Demographic and behavioral predictors of *Trichomonas vaginalis* infection among pregnant women. Obstet Gynecol. 1991;78:1087–1092.
45. Barbone F, Austin H, Louv WC, et al. A follow-up study of methods of contraception, sexual activity, and rates of trichomoniasis, candidiasis, and bacterial vaginosis. Am J Obstet Gynecol. 1990;163:510–514.
46. Lossick JG. Epidemiology of urogenital trichomoniasis. In: Honigberg BM, ed. Trichomonads Parasitic in Humans. New York: Springer-Verlag; 1990:311–323.
47. Reynolds M, Wilson J. Is *Trichomonas vaginalis* still a marker for other sexually transmitted infections in women? Int J STD AIDS. 1996;1:131–132.
48. Wolner-Hanssen P, Krieger JN, Stevens CE, et al. Clinical manifestations of vaginal trichomoniasis. JAMA. 1989;264:571–576.
49. Laga M, Manoka A, Kivuvu M, et al. Non-ulcerative sexually transmitted diseases as risk factors for HIV-1 transmission in women. AIDS. 1993;7:95–102.
50. Wasserheit JN. Epidemiological synergy: Interrelationship between HIV infection and other STDs. Sex Transm Dis. 1992;19:61–77.
51. Levine WC, Pope V, Bhoomkar A, et al. Increase in endocervical CD4 lymphocytes among women with nonulcerative sexually transmitted diseases. J Infect Dis. 1998;177:167–174.
52. Cohen MS, Hoffman IF, Royce RA, et al. Reduction of concentration of HIV-1 in semen after treatment of urethritis: Implications for prevention of sexual transmission of HIV-1. Lancet. 1997;349:1868–1873.
53. Krieger JN. Trichomoniasis in men: Old issues and new data. Sex Transm Dis 1995;22:83–96.
54. Gulmezoglu AM. Treating trichomoniasis in women. The Cochrane Database of Systematic Reviews (online database), Cochrane Collaboration, Oxford, England, 1998;3.
55. Kellock D, O'Mahony CP. Sexually acquired metronidazole-resistant trichomoniasis in a lesbian couple. Genitourin Med. 1996;72:60–61.
56. Danesh IS, Stephen JM, Gorbach J. Neonatal *Trichomonas vaginlis* infection. J Emerg Med. 1995;13:51–54.
57. Jones JG, Yamaguchi T, Lambert B. *Trichomonas vaginalis* infestation in sexually abused girls. Am J Dis Child. 1985;139:846–847.
58. Ross JD, Scott GR, Busuttil A. *Trichomonas vaginalis* infection in pre-pubertal girls. Med Sci Law. 1993;33:82–85.
59. Rein MF. Clinical manifestations of urogenital trichomoniasis in women. In:

Honigberg BM, ed. Trichomonads Parasitic in Humans. New York: Springer-Verlag; 1990:225–234.
60. Herzberg AJ, Silverman JF. Detection of *Trichomonas vaginalis* in endocervical and ectocervical smears. Diagn Cytopathol. 1996;14:273–276.
61. Ohlemeyer CL, Hornberger LL, Lynch DA, Swierkosz EM. Diagnosis of *Trichomonas vaginalis* in adolescent females: InPouch TV culture *versus* wet-mount microscopy. J Adolesc Health. 1998;22:205–208.
62. Kiviat NB, Paavonen JA, Wolner-Hanssen P, et al. Histopathology of endocervical infection caused by *Chlamydia trachomatis*, herpes simplex virus, *Trichomonas vaginalis*, and *Neisseria gonorrhoeae*. Hum Pathol. 1990;21:831–837.
63. Josey WE, Campbell WG Jr. Vaginitis emphysematosa. A report of four cases. J Reprod Med. 1990;35:974–977.
64. Soper DE, Bump RC, Hurt WG. Bacterial vaginosis and trichomoniasis vaginitis are risk factors for cuff cellulitis after abdominal hysterectomy. Am J Obstet Gynecol. 1990;163:1016–1021.
65. Cotch MF, Pastorek JG II, Nugent RP, et al. *Trichomonas vaginalis* associated with low birth weight and preterm delivery. Sex Transm Dis. 1998, 24:353–360.
66. Paisarntantiwong R, Brockman S, Clarke L, et al. The relationship of vaginal trichomoniasis and pelvic inflammatory disease among women colonized with *Chlamydia trachomatis*. Sex Transm Dis. 1995;22:344–347.
67. Centers for Disease Control and Prevention. 1998 guidelines for the treatment of sexually transmitted diseases. MMWR Morb Mortal Wkly Rep. 1998;47:52.
68. Krieger JN, Riley DE, Roberts MC, Berger RE. Prokaryotic DNA sequences in patients with chronic idiopathic prostatitis. J Clin Microbiol. 1996;34:3120–3128.
69. Smith RF. Detection of *Trichomonas vaginalis* in vaginal specimens by direct immunofluorescence assay. J Clin Microbiol. 1986;24:1107–1108.
70. Krieger JN, Tam MR, Stevens CE, et al. Diagnosis of trichomoniasis: Comparison of conventional wet-mount examination with cytologic studies, cultures, and monoclonal antibody straining of direct specimens. JAMA. 1988;259:1223–1227.
71. Carney JA, Unadkat P, Yule A, et al. A new rapid agglutination test for the diagnosis of *Trichomonas vaginalis* infection. J Clin Pathol. 1988;41:806–808.
72. Yule A, Gellan MCA, Oriel JD, et al. Detection of *Trichomonas vaginalis* antigen in women by enzyme immunoassay. J Clin Pathol. 1987;40:566–568.
73. Wan RM, Philip A, Wos SM, et al. Rapid assay for immunological detection of *Trichomonas vaginalis*. J Clin Microbiol. 1986;24:551–555.
74. DeMeo LR, Draper DL, McGregor JA, et al. Evaluation of a deoxyribonucleic acid probe for the detection of *Trichomonas vaginalis* in vaginal secretions. Am J Obstet Gynecol. 1996;174:1339–1342.
75. Heine RP, Wiesenfeld HC, Sweet RL, Witkin SS. Polymerase chain reaction analysis of distal vaginal specimens: A less invasive strategy for detection of *Trichomonas vaginalis*. Clin Infect Dis. 1997;24:985–987.
76. Shaio MF, Lin PR, Liu JY. Colorimetric one-tube nested PCR for detection of *Trichomonas vaginalis* in vaginal discharge. J Clin Microbiol. 1997;35:132–138.
77. Gelbart SM, Thomason JL, Osypowski PJ, et al. Growth of *Trichomonas vaginalis* in commercial culture media. J Clin Microbiol. 1990;28:962–964.
78. Schmid GP, Matheny LC, Zaidi AA, et al. Evaluation of six media for the growth of *Trichomonas vaginalis* from vaginal secretions. J Clin Microbiol. 1989;27:1230–1233.
79. Gelbart SM, Thomason JL, Osypowski PJ, et al. Comparison of Diamond's medium modified and Kupferberg medium for detection of *Trichomonas vaginalis*. J Clin Microbiol. 1989;27:1095–1096.
80. Poch F, Levin D, Levin S, Dan M. Modified thioglycolate medium: A simple and reliable means for detection of *Trichomonas vaginalis*. J Clin Microbiol. 1996;34:2630–2631.
81. Meysick KC, Garber GE. Growth of *Trichomonas vaginalis* in a serum free McCoy cell culture system. J Parasitol. 1990;76:926–928.
82. Levi MH, Torres J, Pina C, Klein RS. Comparison of the InPouch TV culture system and Diamond's modified medium for detection of *Trichomonas vaginalis*. J Clin Microbiol. 1997;35:3308–3310.
83. Müller M. Mode of action of metronidazole on anaerobic bacteria and protozoa. Surgery. 1983;93:165.
84. Lossick JG. Therapy of urogenital trichomoniasis. In: Honigberg BM, ed. Trichomonads Parasitic in Humans. New York: Springer-Verlag; 1990:324–341.
85. Tidwell BH, Lushbaugh WB, Laughlin M, et al. A double-blind placebo-controlled trial of single-dose intravaginal versus single-dose oral metronidazole in the treatment of *Trichomonas* vaginitis. J Infect Dis. 1994;170:242–246.
86. Austin TW, Smith EA, Darwish R, et al. Metronidazole in a single dose for the treatment of trichomoniasis: Failure of a 1-g single dose. Br J Vener Dis. 1982;58:121.
87. Spence MR, Harwell TS, Davies MC, Smith JL. The minimum oral metronidazole dose for treating trichomoniasis: A randomized blinded study. Obstet Gynecol. 1997;89:699–703.
88. Lyng J, Christensen J. A double-blind study of the value of treatment with a single dose tinidazole of partners to females with trichomoniasis. Acta Obstet Gynecol Scand. 1981;60:199.
89. Goodwin DW, Reinhard J. Disulfiramlike effects of trichomonacidal drugs: A review and double blind study. Q J Stud Alcohol. 1972;33:734.
90. Pearlman MD, Yashar C, Ernst S, Solomon W. An incremental dosing protocol for women with severe vaginal trichomoniasis and adverse reactions to metronidazole. Am J Obstet Gynecol. 1996;174:934–936.
91. Nyirjesy P, Sobel JD, Weitz MV, et al. Difficult to treat trichomoniasis: Results with paromomycin cream. Clin Infect Dis. 1998;26:986–988.
92. Coelho DD. Metronidazole resistant trichomoniasis successfully treated with paromomycin. Genitourin Med. 1997;73:397–398.
93. DuBouchet L, McGregor JA, Ismail M, McCormack WM. A pilot study of metronidazole vaginal gel versus oral metronidazole for the treatment of *Trichomonas vaginalis* vaginitis. Sex Transm Dis. 1998;25:176–179.
94. Beard CM, Noller KL, O'Fallon WM, et al. Cancer after exposure to metronidazole. Mayo Clin Proc. 1988;63:147–153.
95. Schwebke JR. Metronidazole: Utilization in the obstetric and gynecologic patient. Sex Transm Dis. 1995;22:370–376.
96. Centers for Disease Control and Prevention. 1998 guidelines for the treatment of sexually transmitted diseases. MMWR Morb Mortal Wkly Rep. 1998;47:74–75.
97. Caro-Paton T, Carvajal A, Martin de Diego I, et al. Is metronidazole teratogenic? A meta-analysis. Br J Clin Pharmacol. 1997;44:179–182.
98. Robertson DHH, Heyworth R, Harrison C, et al. Treatment failure in *Trichomonas vaginalis* infections in females. 1. Concentrations of metronidazole in plasma and vaginal content during normal and high dosage. J Antimicrob Chemother. 1988;21:373–378.
99. Lossick JG, Müller M, Gorrell TE. In vitro drug susceptibility and doses of metronidazole required for cure in cases of refractory vaginal trichomoniasis. J Infect Dis. 1986;153:948–955.
100. Müller M, Lossick JG, Gorrell TE. In-vitro susceptibility of *Trichomonas vaginalis* to metronidazole: Treatment outcome in vaginal trichomoniasis. Sex Transm Dis. 1988;15:17–24.
101. Grossman JH 3rd, Galask RP. Persistent vaginitis caused by metronidazole-resistant *Trichomonas*. Obstet Gynecol. 1990;76:521–522.
101a. Sobel JD, Nagappan V, Nyirjesy P. Metronidazole-resistant vaginal trichomoniasis—an emerging problem. N Engl J Med. 1999;341:292–293.
102. Krieger JN, Dickens CS, Rein ME. Susceptibility testing of *Trichomonas vaginalis*: Use of a time kill technique. Antimicrob Agents Chemother. 1985;27:332–336.
103. Sears SD, O'Hare J. In vitro susceptibility of *Trichomonas vaginalis* to 50 antimicrobial agents. Antimicrob Agents Chemother. 1988;32:144–146.
104. Tachezy J, Kulda J, Tomkova F. Aerobic resistance of *Trichomonas vaginalis* to metronidazole induced in vitro. Parasitology. 1993;106:31–37.
105. Borchardt KA, Li Z, Zhang MZ, Shing H. An in vitro metronidazole susceptibility test for trichomoniasis using the InPouch TV test. Genitourin Med. 1996;72:132–135.
106. Lossick JG. Treatment of sexually transmitted vaginosis/vaginitis. Rev Infect Dis. 1990;12(Suppl 6):S665-S681.
107. Lossick JG, Kent HL. Trichomoniasis: Trends in diagnosis and management. Am J Obstet Gynecol. 1991;165:1217–1222.
108. Dombrowski MP, Sokol RJ, Brown WJ, et al. Intravenous therapy of metronidazole-resistant *Trichomonas vaginalis*. Obstet Gynecol. 1987;69:524–525.
109. Hamed KA, Studemeister AE. Successful response of metronidazole-resistant trichomonal vaginitis to tinidazole. A case report. Sex Transm Dis. 1992;19:339–340.
110. Lewis DA, Habgood I, White R, et al. Managing vaginal trichomoniasis resistant to high-dose metronidazole therapy. Int J STD AIDS. 1997;8:780–784.
111. Livengood CH, Lossick JG. Resolution of resistant vaginal trichomoniasis associated with the use of intravaginal nonoxynol-9. Obstet Gynecol. 1991;7:995–997.
112. Houang ET, Ahmet Z, Lawrence AG. Successful treatment of four patients with recalcitrant vaginal trichomoniasis with a combination of zinc sulfate douche and metronidazole therapy. Sex Transm Dis. 1997;24:116–119.
113. Reynolds JEF, ed. Martindale The Extra Pharmacopoeia. London: Pharmaceutical; 1993:509.
114. Walker PP, Hall RE, Wilson JD. Arsenical pessaries in the treatment of metronidazole-resistant *Trichomonas vaginalis*. Int J STD AIDS. 1997;8:473.
115. Watson PG, Pattman RS. Arsenical pessaries in the successful elimination of metronidazole-resistant *Trichomonas vaginalis*. Int J STD AIDS. 1996;7:296–297.
116. Narcisi EM, Secor WE. In vitro effect of tinidazole and furazolidone on metronidazole-resistant *Trichomonas vaginalis*. Antimicrob Agents Chemother. 1996; 40:1121–1125.
117. Sharna R, Pickering J, McCormack WM. Trichomoniasis in a postmenopausal woman cured after discontinuation of estrogen replacement therapy. Sex Transm Dis. 1997;24:543–545.
118. Bickley LS, Krisher KK, Punsalang A Jr, et al. Comparison of direct fluorescent antibody, acridine orange, wet mount, and culture for detection of *Trichomonas vaginalis* in women attending a public sexually transmitted disease clinic. Sex Transm Dis. 1989;16:127–131.
119. Rein MF. Uncertainties and controversies in trichomoniasis. In: Sobel JD, ed. Vulvovaginal Infections: Current Concepts in Diagnosis and Therapy. New York: Academy Professional Information Services; 1990:73–85.
120. Ferris DG, Hendrich J, Payne PM, et al: Office laboratory diagnosis of vaginitis. Clinician-performed tests compared with a rapid nucleic acid hybridization test. J Fam Pract. 1995;41:575–581.

Chapter 271

Babesia

JEFFREY A. GELFAND
DEBRA POUTSIAKA

Babesiosis is an infection by malaria-like protozoans *(Babesia)* that parasitize erythrocytes of wild and domestic animals and may cause fever, hemolysis, and hemoglobinuria. Although babesiosis has long been an economically important disease of cattle, only in the last 30 years has *Babesia* been appreciated to be an occasional pathogen in humans. Typically a mild illness in healthy people, in the asplenic or immunocompromised patient, disease may be overwhelming.

The first recorded reference to babesiosis is probably the plague ("murrain") visited upon the cattle of Pharaoh Rameses II (Exodus 9:3).[1] In 1888, during investigations ot febrile hemoglobinuria in Romanian cattle, V. Babes described an intraerythrocytic pathogen that he thought to be a bacterium. In 1893, Theobald Smith and F. L. Kilbourne demonstrated that the organism causing "Texas cattle fever" was a protozoan transmitted by a bloodsucking tick—the first demonstration of an arthropod vector. In 1957, babesiosis was described in the former Yugoslavia by Skrabalo as a disease of humans.[1] Subsequent, early reports involved splenectomized individuals with fulminant disease. In 1969, infection with *Babesia microti* was described in a patient from the island of Nantucket off the Massachusetts coast who had an intact spleen. In the decades since, more than 100 cases have been reported in the literature, and the disease has spread from the islands off the northeast coast of the United States to the northeast mainland and has also appeared in the upper Midwest and West Coast.[2]

PATHOGEN

There are more than 70 species worldwide in the genus *Babesia*, and they infect numerous mammals and birds. Originally thought to be host-specific, some species can infect a wide range of hosts. Only the rodent strain *B. microti* (in the United States) and the cattle strains *Babesia divergens* and *Babesia bovis* (in Europe) have been positively identified as causing disease in humans.[1] Other species of *Babesia* have been implicated in sporadic instances of disease in humans. A hitherto unknown species of *Babesia*, designated WA-1, was isolated from an immunocompetent man in Washington state with clinical babesiosis. Several additional cases of WA-1 infection have been reported from California. DNA-hybridization patterns with a *Babesia*-specific ribosomal DNA probe, as well as antigenic differences, suggest that WA-1 is either a new species distinct from either *B. microti* or *B. bovis*, or a strain whose infectious potential for humans had been previously unrecognized.[2] When genetic sequence analysis (with amplification by polymerase chain reaction) was performed on the WA-1 strain parasites recovered from the four California patients, it revealed piroplasm-specific, small-subunit ribosomal DNA. The organisms from all four patients were essentially identical. Phylogenetic analysis of the sequences suggested that this strain is closely related to a know canine pathogen, *Babesia gibsoni*, and is closer to *Theileria* spp. than to many members of the genus *Babesia*. Serum from the California patients was unreactive with *B. microti* antigen.[3]

Persing and Conrad have suggested that many of the small *Babesia* species, including *B. microti*, *B. equi*, *B. gibsoni*, and WA-1 may be phylogenetically related to the genus *Theileria*.[4] This hypothesis raises the possibility that these piroplasms might undergo an exoerythrocytic stage of development, implying that it might add to their potential to produce chronic infection, immunosuppression, and even lymphoproliferation.[4]

The first case of babesiosis in Missouri, a fatal one, was reported in 1996.[5] Serologic studies, a series of animal inoculations, and molecular analysis were performed. Indirect immunofluorescent antibody testing showed that the patient's serum strongly reacted with *B. divergens*, the strain that causes babesiosis in cattle and humans in Europe. Sequencing of small-subunit ribosomal DNA recovered from the patient's blood and amplified by polymerase chain reaction suggested that this strain, MO-1, was closely related to *B. divergens*. The authors made the important point that in the United States, life-threatening babesiosis can occur in patients seronegative to both *B. microti* and WA-1 antigens.[5]

Babesia spp. in the host erythrocyte vary from 1 to 5 μm in length. *B. microti* is 2 by 1.5 μm; *B. divergens*, 4 by 1.5 μm; and *B. bovis*, 2.4 by 1.5 μm. They are pear-shaped, oval, or round.[1] Their ring conformation and peripheral location in the erythrocyte frequently lead to their being mistaken for *Plasmodium falciparum*.

Most cases of human babesiosis have occurred in the northeastern coastal region of the United States, particularly Nantucket Island, Martha's Vineyard, Cape Cod (Massachusetts); Block Island (Rhode Island); eastern Long Island, Shelter Island, and Fire Island (New York); and, most recently, the Connecticut mainland and Washington state.[2] Cases have also been reported from Wisconsin, Georgia, and Mexico. This is likely due to the increasing numbers and proximity of reservoir, vector, and host. Babesiosis is a zoonotic disease and requires transmission from an animal reservoir to humans via a tick vector. *Ixodes scapularis* (also called *Ixodes dammini*), the tick vector of Lyme disease, Rocky Mountain spotted fever, and ehrlichiosis, transmits the disease to humans from rodents (primarily the white-footed deer mouse, but also the field mouse, vole, rat, and chipmunk) in the United States.[6] The northern form of this tick was originally thought to be a distinct species, *I. dammini*. *I. dammini* is now thought to be the same as *I. scapularis* on the grounds of genetic similarity and mating compatibility with the southern form of *I. scapularis*.[7] The hard-bodied cattle tick *Ixodes ricinus* is thought to transmit bovine babesiosis to humans in Europe.

The tick *I. scapularis* has three developmental stages (larva, nymph, adult). In each of these stages, the tick requires a blood meal to mature to the next stage. Blood meals may come from different species. White-tailed deer are the preferred host for the adult tick (but they are not infected with *B. microti*), and it is the reemergence of this host for the tick that appears to be responsible for the spread of *I. scapularis*.[8] While obtaining their blood meal on the deer, female ticks are impregnated, with the formation of up to 20,000 eggs. The larval phase requires a blood meal to develop into the next phase, the nymph, which in turn requires another blood meal to become an adult. Rodents, especially the white-footed deer mouse, are the preferred hosts of larval and nymphal phases of the tick.[8]

B. microti is enzootic in the white-footed mouse, which acts as the reservoir. The tick larva becomes infected with *B. microti* after feeding on an infected mouse. In endemic areas, rodent infection may be heavy (60% on Nantucket Island),[8] and *B. microti* is transmitted from the larval phase of the tick to the nymphal phase (transstadial transmission). There is no evidence that *B. microti* can be transmitted transovarially in *I. scapularis* (as may occur with *Babesia bigemina*). The infected nymph then seeks a blood meal and infects another rodent—or a human. Larvae, nymphs, or adult ticks can all feed on humans, but it is the nymph that is the primary vector of *B. microti* to humans. All three stages of tick may feed on the deer, which is not infected by *B. microti*. Thus, the deer appears to be a necessary host for the (adult) tick, whereas the parasite is maintained in a rodent reservoir. The coming together of all three in large numbers—deer, mouse, and tick—create the conditions for infection in humans.[8]

After passage of the sporozoites from the salivary glands of the tick into the mammalian blood stream, erythrocytes are penetrated and infected. There is evidence that in one babesial species, *Babesia rodhaini*, penetration of rat erythrocytes requires an intact host alternative complement pathway and an erythrocyte C3b receptor.[9] The parasite activates complement and fixes C3b to its surface, which in turn presumably binds to the rat erythrocyte C3b receptor and infects the cell. Additionally, erythrocytes with C3 on their surface are infected, thus suggesting that complement somehow facilitates the parasite-erythrocyte interaction.[9] There are no data on the involvement of these factors in the interaction between *B. microti* and human erythrocytes.

On infection of the host erythrocyte, mature *B. microti* trophozoites undergo asynchronous, asexual budding and divide into two or four merozoites (daughter cells). As parasites exit the erythrocyte, the membrane is damaged, with perforations, protrusions, and inclusions.[10] The actual mechanism of hemolysis is unknown. Because schizogony is asynchronous, massive hemolysis does not occur as it does in *Plasmodium* (with synchronous schizogony).

EPIDEMIOLOGY

There have been more than 100 documented human infections with *Babesia*, with additional cases being reported constantly.[11] Babesiosis is still a rarity in Europe, with cases reported from the former Yugoslavia, France, Russia, Sweden, Ireland, and Scotland. Cases have been reported from Asia, Africa, and South America as well.[12] European cases usually occurred in splenectomized individuals, and involved bovine *Babesia*.[11] Infection with *B. microti* is no longer a rarity in the coastal areas and islands of Massachusetts, Rhode Island, Connecticut, and New York, and infections with *Babesia* spp. have also been reported in Maryland, Virginia, California, Wisconsin, Minnesota (strain MO-1), Washington state (strain WA-1), Georgia, and Mexico.[2, 8, 11, 13] Restocking of deer populations and curtailment of hunting has increased deer herds in certain areas of the northeastern United States, and the proximity of mouse reservoirs to human habitats favors further spread of the disease. The tick vector *I. scapularis* now ranges from New Hampshire to Maryland and west to Wisconsin and Minnesota.[8, 13]

Most infections with *B. microti* appear to be subclinical. This is borne out by the finding that the seroprevalence (using an immunofluorescent antibody assay) for *B. microti* on Cape Cod was 3.7%,[14] whereas on Shelter Island, in individuals with a high risk of exposure to ticks, it was 4.4% in June and reached 6.9% by October.[14] Nymphs, the primary vector, feed from May through September, and clinical infection usually occurs 1 to 3 weeks later.

With asymptomatic infection the rule and a high seroprevalence rate in certain areas, transfusion-associated babesiosis cases have occurred.[14] Sources of transfusion-associated cases have included platelets and frozen erythrocytes.[14] The incubation period in transfusion-associated disease appears to be longer (6 to 9 weeks).[14] Finally, transplacental or perinatal transmission of the disease has been described.[15]

CLINICAL MANIFESTATIONS

The clinical manifestations of babesiosis differ markedly between the European and the North American cases. Virtually all the European cases have involved splenectomized individuals, and bovine *Babesia* was involved *(B. bovis, B. divergens)*.[11, 16] Seven of the first nine cases were fatal, and all presented with fulminant, febrile, hemolytic disease.[1, 11, 16]

In contrast, epidemiologic data from the United States suggest a high incidence of infection of the rodent strain *B. microti* that is either subclinical or mild.[11, 14, 17] A seroprevalence study of residents of a semirural community in Sonoma County (northern), California, found that 18% of sera were positive for the Babesia-like piroplasm WA-1.[18] The incubation period after the tick bite is usually 1 to 3 weeks but occasionally may be as long as 6 weeks.[19] Because the nymph is the primary vector and when engorged is only 2 mm in diameter, most patients do not recall a tick bite.[20] In contradistinction to the European cases, most patients reported in the United States have had intact spleens—only 30% have been asplenic—and almost all of the more than 120 patients with clinical disease have survived (several have not).[11] The patients with clinical illness and intact spleens are usually 50 years old or older—suggesting that age plays a factor in the severity of the clinical response.[20] This is similar to the findings in animals. In cattle and horses, babesiosis is mild in younger animals and more severe in older animals. Previously healthy individuals with babesiosis are generally older (mean, >60 years) than are babesiosis patients with antecedent medical problems (mean, 48 years).[20] A 1998 report suggests that persistent babesial infection may be more common than previously supported.[21]

Initial symptoms begin gradually and are nonspecific. Malaise, fatigue, anorexia, shaking chills, fever, headache, myalgias, arthralgias, nausea, vomiting, abdominal pain, depression and emotional lability, and dark urine are all common. Photophobia, conjunctival injection, sore throat, and cough have been described as well. Fevers may be sustained or intermittent, and temperatures may reach levels of 40°C. Nonetheless, babesiosis has been associated with the adult respiratory distress syndrome,[22] and at our institution, three patients with babesiosis and shock, two with adult respiratory distress syndrome, were seen in a 14-month period. Rash similar to erythema migrans has been described, but this probably represents intercurrent Lyme disease because the same tick is the vector for *Borrelia burgdorferi*; 54% of one group of patients with babesiosis had antibodies to the Lyme spirochete.[23] Intercurrent Lyme disease should be suspected in any patient with suspected babesiosis. Petechiae, splinter hemorrhages, and ecchymoses have occasionally been noted. Splenomegaly and occasionally hepatomegaly are described in some patients, but lymphadenopathy is absent.

Hemolytic anemia, decreased serum haptoglobin levels, and elevated reticulocyte counts are noted, and the anemia may occasionally be severe. The percentage of erythrocytes parasitized in clinical cases is usually 1 to 10% but has ranged from less than 1 to 85%. The total leukocyte count may be normal or mildly decreased, and thrombocytopenia is common. The erythrocyte sedimentation rate may be elevated, and the direct Coombs' test may react positively. Urinalysis reveals proteinuria and hemoglobinuria, and blood urea nitrogen and serum creatinine levels may be elevated. Mild elevations of the levels of serum bilirubin, alkaline phosphatase, serum aspartate aminotransferase, serum alanine aminotransferase, and lactic dehydrogenase levels are usually found. On one occasion, bone marrow examination of a patient with babesiosis revealed macrophages exhibiting hemophagocytosis.

In one series of 17 patients with symptomatic *B. microti* infection, the mean duration of hospitalization was 19.1 days (±2.9), with convalescence lasting zero to 18 months.[20] All patients regarded the disease as having been severe. As in other series, patients without preexisting medical conditions were older.[20] In the recent report of Krause and coworkers, it was observed that when left untreated, babesiosis symptoms may last for months in some patients, whereas sublinical infection may recrudesce spontaneously or after splenectomy or immunosuppressive therapy.[21] Underscoring the potential severity of this infection were reports of two deaths from babesiosis in Massachusetts within a 2-week period in August 1998, one in a splenectomized patient, the other aged 67 years.[24]

Thus, *B. microti* produces a high incidence of subclinical infections, but clinical infections are likely in asplenic patients, patients with Lyme disease in endemic areas, older individuals, and individuals with preexistent medical disease (including human immunodeficiency virus infection).[25, 26] In patients with clinical disease, symptoms may be severe and even life-threatening, but the disease is still only occasionally fatal. In contrast, bovine babesiosis, as seen in Europe, occurs in asplenic patients and is always fulminant and usually fatal.

PATHOGENESIS

The critical role of the spleen in the host defense against this disease is emphasized by the higher incidence and greater severity of this disease in asplenic patients and animals. In fact, animals that have recovered from babesiosis can recrudesce after splenectomy, and steroid treatment, which reduces splenic function, can increase infection. Blood percolates through the spleen in intimate contact with splenic endothelium, macrophages, and macrophage products. Erythrocytes must squeeze through intraendothelial spaces. Infected, deformed, and potentially more rigid erythrocytes are more likely to be retained in the spleen,[27] where ingestion by macrophages or the action of macrophage products may control the infection. Complement-sensitized erythrocytes would likely bind under these circumstances. Furthermore, complement activation by *Babesia* could theoretically lead to the generation of tumor necrosis factor and interleukin-1.[28] Decreased complement levels, presumably secondary to activation, are frequently found in babesiosis.[29] In addition, increased circulating C1q-binding activity, presumably due to immune complexes, with decreased C4, C3, and CH_{50} levels is seen in patients.[29] The generation of these primarily macrophage-produced mediators (tumor necrosis factor and interleukin-1) in turn could explain many of the clinical features (fever, anorexia, arthralgias, myalgias) of babesiosis, especially the fulminant shock syndrome of bovine babesiosis. A similar pathogenesis has been proposed for malaria.[30] It is likely that, in the less fulminant situation, tumor necrosis factor enhances killing of *Babesia*, as in malaria.

In addition to macrophage factors, other cellular immune functions appear to be important in the host response to *Babesia*. Nude mice and mice with T-lymphocyte hypofunction due to thymectomy, lethal irradiation, or anti-T-lymphocyte serum develop significantly greater parasitemia. The disease itself alters cellular immune function. Patients with acute babesiosis have an increase in T-suppressor–cytotoxic lymphocytes and decreased responses to lymphocyte mitogens with a polyclonal hypergammaglobulinemia.[29]

DIAGNOSIS

Babesiosis is usually diagnosed by microscopic examination of Giemsa- or Wright-stained thin or thick blood smears. The predominant forms seen strongly resemble the ring forms of *P. falciparum*. They may have a single chromatic dot or two or more chromatic masses. With older stages of *P. falciparum*, there are brownish pigment deposits (hemozoin).[1] These are absent in babesiosis. *Babesia* spp. also lack the synchronous stages, schizonts, and gametocytes seen with *Plasmodium* spp. A rare diagnostic feature of *Babesia* is the presence of tetrads of merozoites (Fig. 271–1). Larger rings may have a central white vacuole that is absent in malaria. Trophozoites may be seen outside erythrocytes with heavier infestation.

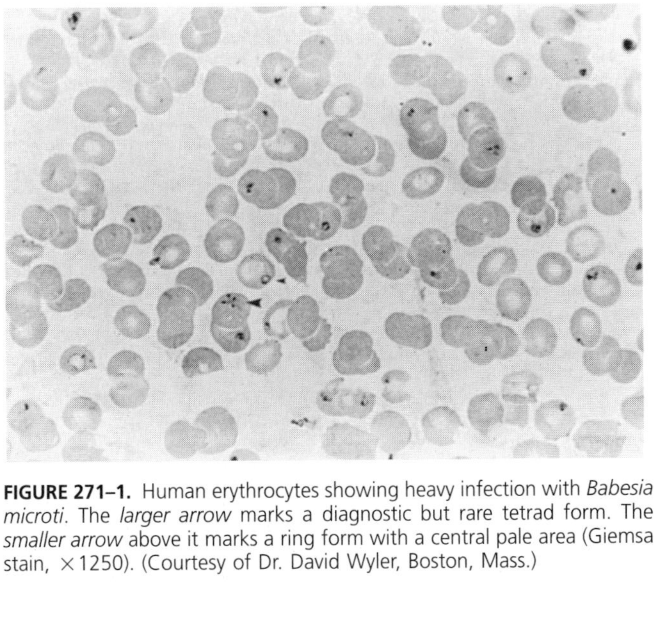

FIGURE 271–1. Human erythrocytes showing heavy infection with *Babesia microti*. The *larger arrow* marks a diagnostic but rare tetrad form. The *smaller arrow* above it marks a ring form with a central pale area (Giemsa stain, ×1250). (Courtesy of Dr. David Wyler, Boston, Mass.)

An indirect immunofluorescent antibody titer for *B. microti* is available through the Centers for Disease Control and Prevention (Atlanta). Patients with active infection usually have serum titers of 1024 or greater within a few weeks that fall slowly over months to 1:256 or less. A titer of 1:256 or greater is diagnostic for *B. microti* infection. Titers of 1:32 or higher are generally considered indicative of prior infection; titers as low as 1:16 have been accepted as positive by some.[31] Assay for antibody to *B. microti* cannot be used to detect infection with the WA-1 piroplasm or vice versa.[32] A polymerase chain reaction–based diagnostic assay was reported in 1992 and holds great promise for increasing the detection of very low level parasitemia.[33] In a 1998 report by Krause and colleagues on chronic babesiosis, the persistence of antibody titers for *B. microti* correlated well with the detection of babesial DNA by PCR.[21] In fact, in untreated, asymptomatic patients, babesial DNA could be detected for as long as 27 months. Currently, confirmation of suspected *B. microti* infection can be made with intraperitoneal inoculation of 1 ml of edetate–whole blood into the peritoneum of golden hamsters. *B. divergens* replicates readily in gerbils. Within 2 to 4 weeks, smears are positive in the infected animals.

TREATMENT

Most patients infected by *B. microti* appear to have a mild illness and recover without specific chemotherapy. Splenectomized patients are more likely to have high-level parasitemia and be severely ill, but patients with intact spleens may have severe infection. In patients with serious disease, a combination of clindamycin (in children, 20 mg/kg/day; in adults, 300 to 600 mg every 6 hours intravenously or intramuscularly) and oral quinine (in children, 25 mg/kg/day; in adults, 650 mg every 6 to 8 hours) taken for 7 to 10 days appears to be an effective regimen.[34] Chloroquine, frequently given because of confusion of *B. microti* with *P. falciparum*, is not effective therapy. A number of other antimalarial and antiprotozoal therapies have likewise been largely unsuccessful, including primaquine, quinacrine, pyrimethamine, pyrimethamine-sulfadoxine, sulfadiazine, tetracycline, minocycline, pentamidine isethionate, and trimethoprim-sulfamethoxazole.[35] Despite the usual success of the clindamycin-quinine combination, failure of this therapy has been reported.[35]

Atovaquone is a potent antiprotozoal agent. Atovaquone has been used along with and in combination with azithromycin for treatment of experimental *B. microti* infection in hamsters.[36] These studies showed atovaquone and azithromycin to be an effective combination for the treatment of experimental babesiosis. Atovaquone monotherapy resulted in recrudescence and resistance. A recent abstract from Krause and colleagues compared atovaquone and azithromycin to clindamycin and quinine, both for 7 days.[37] Both regimens were effective in clearing parasitemia. Clindamycin-quinine caused untoward drug reactions in 67% of patients, with atovaquone-azithromycin–caused drug reactions in 12% of patients. The atovaquone-azithromycin regimen may not be as rapidly effective but appears preferable because of fewer side effects. The long-term efficacy remains to be validated. The usual dose of atovaquone is 750 mg orally (as suspension), taken with a meal two times daily. Although the pediatric dose has not been established, doses of 40 mg/kg/day have been used in children. The dose of azithromycin in adults is 500 mg on day 1 and 250 mg daily thereafter. Higher doses (500 mg daily) could be employed but have not yet been tested in babesiosis. A patient with acquired immunodeficiency syndrome has been treated successfully with a combination of clindamycin, doxycycline, and azithromycin after becoming allergic to quinine.[38] The antitrypanosomal drug diminazene aceturate (Berenil, Hoechst-Roussel Pharmaceuticals, Inc., Somerville, NJ) is effective against *B. microti* infections in animals and has been given to one patient who recovered from *B. microti* infection. This patient developed a Guillian-

Barré–like disorder.[39] Diminazene was also used unsuccessfully in a fatal case of babesiosis due to *B. divergens*.[16] The combination of pentamidine with trimethoprim-sulfamethoxazole was reported to be successful in the treatment of *B. divergens* infection in a splenectomized patient in France.[16] Exchange transfusions are used in profoundly ill patients with high levels of parasitemia and hemolysis.[25] Used concurrently with chemotherapy, exchange transfusion reduces the level of parasitemia and may remove toxic erythrocyte, babesial, or macrophage-produced factors.[40]

PREVENTION

The prevention of babesiosis requires avoidance of areas endemic for *I. scapularis* between May and September. This is especially important for splenectomized individuals and others who are immunocompromised. It is quite possible that babesiosis may become a greater problem in the future for patients with acquired immunodeficiency syndrome. In endemic areas, clothing should be worn to cover the lower portion of the body (long pants and socks). Because ticks may crawl up pants legs, tucking pants into boots or socks or cinching the legs at the ankles is helpful. Wearing light-colored clothes enables the ticks to be spotted more easily. Diethyltoluamide ("deet") insect repellent applied to the skin or clothes is only partially repellent for hours. A spray containing permethrin (Duranon; Permanone) is far more effective but should be applied only to clothes (pants bottoms, socks, shirt sleeves). Ultrasonic insect repellents have not been shown to ward off ticks.

Pets should be inspected carefully for ticks before allowing them inside the home. In endemic areas, one should avoid tall grass and brush and keep to well-worn roads or paths. If a tick is found, speedy removal is indicated. The tick should be grasped below the mouth, where it attaches to the skin, with a small forceps or tweezers and pulled off steadily.

Transfusion-associated babesiosis can be reduced by discouraging blood donors from endemic areas between May and September, by avoiding donors with fevers during the 2 months before the intended donation, and by not accepting those with a history of tick bites. It is unlikely that screening of blood for *Babesia* will be adopted in the near future, and thus it is anticipated that increases in transfusion-associated babesiosis are likely, given the spread of the tick—and the parasite—into ever-enlarging areas. Clinicians will therefore have to be increasingly alert to the possibility of this once arcane and relatively unimportant disease, babesiosis.

REFERENCES

1. Dammin GJ. Babesiosis. In: Weinstein L, Fields B, eds. Seminars in Infectious Disease. New York: Stratton; 1978:169–199.
2. Quick RE, Herwaldt BL, Thomford JW, et al. Babesiosis in Washington State: A new species of *Babesia*? Ann Intern Med. 1993;119:284–290.
3. Persing DH, Herwaldt BL, Glaser C, et al. Infection with a *Babesia*-like organism in northernCalifornia. 1995;332:298–303.
4. Persing DH, Conrad PA. Babesiosis: New insights from phylogenetic analysis. Infect Agents Dis. 1995;4:182–195.
5. Herwaldt B, Persing DH, Precignout EA, et al. A fatal case of babesiosis in Missouri: Identification of another piroplasm that infects humans. Ann Intern Med. 1996;124:643–650.
6. Spielman A, Etkind P, Piesman J, et al. Reservoir hosts of human babesiosis on Nantucket Island. Am J Trop Med Hyg. 1981;30:560–565.
7. Barbour AG, Fish D. The biological and social phenomenon of Lyme disease. Science. 1993;260:1610–1616.
8. Spielman A, Wilson ML, Levine JF, et al. Ecology of *Ixodes dammini*–borne human babesiosis and Lyme disease. Ann Rev Entomol. 1985;30:439–460.
9. Jack RM, Ward PA. *Babesia rodhaini* interactions with complement: Relationship to parasitic entry into red cells. J Immunol. 1980;124:1566–1573.
10. Sun T, Tenenbaum MJ, Greenspan J, et al. Morphologic and clinical observations in human infection with *Babesia microti*. J Infect Dis. 1983;148:239–248.
11. Dammin GJ, Spielman A, Benach JL, et al. The rising incidence of clinical *Babesia microti* infection. Hum Pathol. 1981;12:398–400.
12. Gorenflot A, Moubri K, Precigout E, et al. Human babesiosis. Ann Trop Med Parasitol. 1998;92:489–501.
13. Steketee RW, Eckman MR, Burgess EC, et al. Babesiosis in Wisconsin: A new focus of disease transmission. JAMA. 1985;253:2675–2678.
14. Popovsky MA, Lindberg LE, Syrek AL, et al. Prevalence of *Babesia* antibody in a selected blood donor population. Transfusion. 1988;28:59–61.
15. Esernio-Jenssen D, Scimeca PG, Benach JL, et al. Transplacental/perinatal babesiosis. J Pediatr. 1987;110:570–572.
16. Raoult D, Soulayrol L, Toga B, et al. Babesiosis, pentamidine, and cotrimoxazole. Ann Intern Med. 1987:107:944.
17. Ruebush TK II, Juranek DD, Chisholm ES, et al. Human babesiosis on Nantucket Island: Evidence for self-limited and subclinical infections. N Engl J Med. 1977;297:825–827.
18. Fritz CL, Kjemtrup AM, Conrad PA, et al. Seroepidemiology of emerging tickborne infectious diseases in a Northern California community. J Infect Dis. 1997;175:1432–1439.
19. Ruebush TK II, Juranek DD, Spielman A, et al. Epidemiology of human babesiosis on Nantucket Island. Am J Trop Med Hyg. 1981;30:937–941.
20. Benach JL, Habicht GS. Clinical characteristics of human babesiosis. J Infect Dis. 1981;144:481.
21. Krause PJ, Spielman A, Telford SR III, et al. Persistent parasitemia after acute babesiosis. N Engl J Med. 1998;339:160-165.
22. Iacopino V, Earnhart T. Life-threatening babesiosis in a woman from Wisconsin. Arch Intern Med. 1990;150:1527-1528.
23. Benach JL, Coleman JL, Habicht GS, et al. Serological evidence for simultaneous occurrences of Lyme disease and babesiosis. J Infect Dis. 1985;152:473–477.
24. LaSalandra M. Tick sickness fatal for 2. Boston Herald. 1998;Aug 14:5.
25. Machtinger L, Telford SR III, Inducil C, et al. Treatment of babesiosis by red blood cell exchange in an HIV-positive splenectomized patient. J Clin Apheresis. 1993;8:78–81.
26. Benezra D, Brown AL, Polsky B, et al. Babesiosis and infection with human immunodeficiency virus (HIV). Ann Intern Med. 1987;107:944.
27. Looareesuwan S, Ho M, Wattanagoon MB, et al. Dynamic alteration in splenic function during acute falciparum malaria. N Engl J Med. 1987;312:675–679.
28. Okusawa S, Yancey KB, van der Meer JWM, et al. C5a stimulates secretion of tumor necrosis factor from human mononuclear cells in vitro: Comparison with secretion of interleukin-1-beta and interleukin-1-alpha. J Exp Med. 1988;168:443–448.
29. Benach JL, Habicht GS, Hamburger MI. Immunoresponsiveness in acute babesiosis in humans. J Infect Dis. 1982;146:369–380.
30. Taverne J, Matthews N, Depledge P, et al. Malarial parasites and tumor cells are killed by the same component of tumor necrosis serum. Clin Exp Immunol. 1984;57:293–300.
31. Krause PJ, Telford SR III, Ryan R, et al. Geographical and temporal distribution of babesial infection in Connecticut. J Clin Microbiol. 1991;29:1–4.
32. Herwaldt BL, Kjemtrup AM, Conrad PA, et al. Transfusion-transmitted babesiosis in Washington State: First reported case caused by a WA-1-type parasite. J Infect Dis. 1997;175:1259–1262.
33. Persing DH, Mathiesen D, Marshall WF, et al. Detection of *Babesia microti* by polymerase chain reaction. J Clin Microbiol. 1992;30:2097–2103.
34. Wittner M, Rowin KS, Tanowitz HB, et al. Successful chemotherapy of transfusion babesiosis. Ann Intern Med. 1982;96:601–604.
35. Centers for Disease Control and Prevention. Clindamycin and quinine treatment for *Babesia microti* infections. MMWR Morb Mortal Wkly Rep. 1983;32:65–71.
36. Wittner M, Lederman J, Tanowitz HB, et al. Atovaquone in the treatment *Babesia microti* infections in hamsters. Am J Trop Med. 1996;55:219–222.
37. Krause PJ, Telford S, Spielman A, et al. Treatment of babesiosis: Comparison of atovaquone and azithromycin with clindamycin and quinine (Abstract). In: Program and Abstracts of the 46th Annual Meeting of the American Society of Tropical Medicine and Hygiene, Lake Buena Vista, Fla, December 7–11, 1997. Northbrook. Ill: American Society of Tropical Medicine and Hygiene; 1997;247.
38. Falagas ME, Klempner MS. Babesiosis in patients with AIDS: A chronic infection presenting as fever of unknown origin. Clin Infect Dis. 1996;22:809–812.
39. Ruebush TK II, Rubin RH, Wolpow ER, et al. Neurologic complications following the treatment of human *Babesia microti* infection with diminazene aceturate. Am J Trop Med. 1979;28:184–189.
40. Jacoby GA, Hunt JV, Kosinski KS, et al. Treatment of transfusion-transmitted babesiosis by exchange transfusion. N Engl J Med. 1980;303:1098–1100.

Chapter 272

Cryptosporidium

BETH L. P. UNGAR

Cryptosporidium is an intracellular protozoan parasite first described in 1907 in mice but thought rare and insignificant for nearly 50 years.[1] It was linked to gastrointestinal disease in young turkeys in 1955, associated with bovine diarrhea in 1971, and found in two cases of human diarrhea in 1976.[2–4] Sporadic human cases were reported over the next few years, but with the onset of the acquired immunodeficiency syndrome (AIDS) epidemic, these numbers increased dramatically, leading to improved diagnostic techniques and recognition of *Cryptosporidium* as a ubiquitous enteric pathogen. Scattered reports of waterborne outbreaks and, in 1993, one affecting at least 400,000 persons in Milwaukee, Wisconsin,[5] gave human *Cryptosporidium* infection a new meaning as a threat to the general public and as an extremely difficult pathogen to control. It is now considered one of the most common enteric pathogens in humans and domesticated animals worldwide, and it may cause biliary tract and respiratory disease as well. The absence of reliable palliative or curative therapy increases the magnitude and significance of cryptosporidiosis. Guidelines for prevention from both the Centers for Disease Control and Prevention (CDC) and Environmental Protection Agency have been issued.[6–9]

PARASITE

Taxonomically, *Cryptosporidium* is one genus of the protozoan phylum Apicomplexa, class Sporozoasida, subclass Coccidiasina referred to as coccidians.[10] *Plasmodium*, *Babesia*, *Sarcocystis*, and *Toxoplasma* are other coccidians, as are *Isospora* and *Eimeria*, which also develop in gastrointestinal and respiratory epithelium.[10] Recent RNA-based studies suggest that *Cryptosporidium* may be more closely related to malarial organisms, and this has implications for prevention and therapy.[11] The parasite is known to infect and reproduce in epithelial cells lining the digestive or respiratory tracts of most vertebrates, including fish, birds, reptiles, and mammals.[4] Twenty species of *Cryptosporidium* were originally named based on morphologic features and the host from which they were isolated, although the majority are now considered misidentified.[4] It is commonly accepted that *Cryptosporidium baileyi* and *Cryptosporidium meleagridis* are valid species infecting birds, and *Cryptosporidium parvum* and *Cryptosporidium muris* valid species infecting mammals, the former responsible for clinical illness in humans and most other mammals.[2, 4] Some *Cryptosporidium* isolates may be able to infect both avian and mammalian hosts.[12]

Although subspecies of *Cryptosporidium* are not recognized, *C. parvum* isolates vary in their ability to infect and cause clinical illness in different hosts. Variation has been demonstrated using two-dimensional electrophoresis, isozyme typing, DNA sequencing, surface labeling of oocysts, restriction fragment length analysis, and immunoblotting.[11]

The life cycle of *Cryptosporidium* (Fig. 272–1) is completed within a single host. Ingestion of oocysts, generally transmitted from an infected person or animal, or from a fecally contaminated environment, is followed by excystation, usually after exposure to reducing agents such as bile salts and digestive enzymes but sometimes spontaneously. Four banana-shaped motile sporozoites are released and attach to the epithelial cell wall. Most later development occurs within a superficial parasitophorous vacuole, composed of two host cell–and two parasite-derived membranes, making *Cryptosporidium* intracellular but extracytoplasmic.[13] This location may be critical in preventing effective drug delivery.[12] In guinea pigs, organisms have also been identified in M-cell cytoplasm adjacent to Peyer's patches and in macrophages.[13]

Sporozoites mature asexually into meronts. Meronts release merozoites intraluminally, some of which reinvade the host cell and produce a powerful autoinfectious cycle and others of which begin sexual maturation leading to zygote formation. The oocyst, containing four new sporozoites, is excreted fully infectious and may excyst within the host intestinal tract, initiating another autoinfectious cycle, or may pass into the environment, where it can remain viable over a wide temperature range for many months.

Autoinfectious cycles are clinically important, explaining why the ingestion of only a few oocysts can lead to severe disease and why persistent infections may develop in immunodeficient persons. Spontaneous excystation may explain why autoinfection from endogenous oocysts and primary respiratory infection are possible.

EPIDEMIOLOGY

In humans, *Cryptosporidium* is a ubiquitous enteric pathogen of all age groups. Factors facilitating this include multiple animal and environmental reservoirs, especially water; a low infectious dose; and resistance to therapy and disinfection.[14, 15] Most general population prevalence data are based on the detection of active *Cryptosporidium* oocyst excretion in fecal specimens from geographic surveys. This leads to underdiagnosis, because oocysts may be shed sporadically and because specialized staining of stool samples is necessary for detection. Rates generally range between 1 and 3% in the more industrialized countries of Europe and North America, and between 5% (Asia) and 10% (Africa) in less industrialized nations.[14, 16] Cryptosporidiosis may be seasonal, occurring more in warmer humid months in communities where outdoor living is common. Oocysts can survive and be infectious for up to 18 months at 4°C, and they remain infectious at −10°C for a week but must be heated to 72°C for 1 minute to be inactivated.[16, 17]

In the United States, national reporting for cryptosporidiosis began in 1995, when 27 states reported 2972 cases. A year later, 42 states reported 2426 cases.[18] The CDC was notified of 969 cases by the 33rd week of 1999, with cases defined by the demonstration of *Cryptosporidium* oocysts or antigen (immunodiagnostic test) in stool specimens or the organism in intestinal fluid or biopsy specimens.[19, ,19a, 20] Surveillance on a smaller scale has been stimulated by a need to determine whether oocysts found routinely in drinking water are associated with an increased risk of infection. New York City initiated active surveillance in 1994 with cases identified by monthly contact with clinical laboratories and case follow-up by telephone or chart review. The investigation followed an increase in diagnosis in one laboratory and showed that the laboratory was inaccurate—a cautionary note.[21]

Seroprevalence studies using immunofluorescent antibody or enzyme-linked immunosorbent assay (ELISA) techniques to detect specific anti-*Cryptosporidium* immunoglobulin M (IgM), IgG, or IgA, suggest that *Cryptosporidium* infections sometime in life may, in fact, be more common than surveys of fecal oocyst excretion can demonstrate.[14] In Europe and North America, for example, the seroprevalence ranged between 25 and 35% in several studies, whereas in urban slum areas in Venezuela, Brazil, Peru, and rural China, 42 to 64% of those surveyed were seropositive.[22–26] A group of Peace Corps volunteers with 32% seroprevalence before their departure for West Africa showed more than 13% seroconversion while there.[22] More than 90% of children were seropositive in a slum area in Brazil and in an orphanage in Thailand.[26–28] In a serologic survey of Peruvian children, 33% were infected during the first 2 years of life, rising to 73% between 2 and 5 years of age.[25] In the United States, in Oklahoma, 38% of children and 58% of adolescents were seropositive; in dairy farmers in Wisconsin, 44% were seropositive compared with 24% of other residents.[29, 30]

Data on the prevalence of *Cryptosporidium* infection in human immunodeficiency virus (HIV)-infected patients are limited. In 1986,

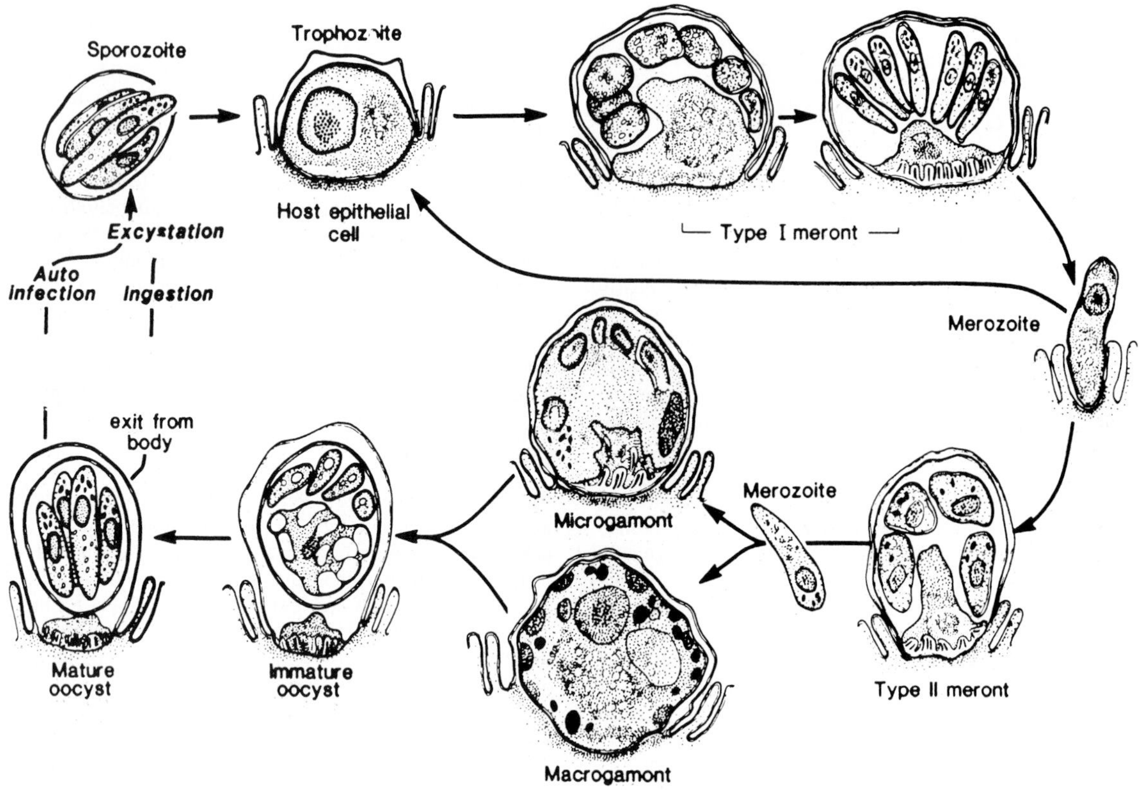

FIGURE 272–1. *Cryptosporidium* life cycle. (From Fayer R, Ungar BLP. *Cryptosporidium* spp and cryptosporidiosis. Microbiol Rev. 1986;50:458–483.)

the CDC reported that 3.6% of the first 19,182 AIDS patients had cryptosporidiosis at the time of CDC notification, with a case-fatality rate said to be 61%.[31] A retrospective analysis of data on 16,953 persons in an AIDS surveillance registry used from 1983 to 1992 in Los Angeles found that 3.8% had cryptosporidiosis.[32] In 1995, 2.2% of all AIDS patients reported to the CDC had cryptosporidiosis as an AIDS-defining illness with an annual rate estimated between 5 and 10%.[33] Similarly, in 17 countries in Europe, in an inception cohort study of 6548 patients with AIDS, 3.3% had cryptosporidiosis at the time of diagnosis and another 3.3% later developed it.[34] Between 11 and 37% of AIDS patients with diarrhea in the United States and Europe excreted *Cryptosporidium* oocysts, the most common enteropathogen in two series.[16, 33, 35, 36] In the less developed world, comparable prevalences range from 9 to 48% in Africa, Latin America, Asia, and elsewhere.[16, 37–40] The extent to which cryptosporidiosis is a significant cause of morbidity and mortality over the life span of HIV-infected persons remains unclear. Homosexual men may be more likely to have cryptosporidiosis than women or people who use illicit intravenous drugs.[32, 37]

TRANSMISSION

Cryptosporidium infection occurs after person-to-person, animal-to-person, and environmental, particularly waterborne, transmission. Persons at particular risk include those living in custodial or group settings, including families; travelers to endemic areas; secondary contacts of infected individuals; and immunosuppressed persons. Ingestion of as few as 10 oocysts resulted in infection in one primate model.[41] A human volunteer study of 29 healthy adults without serologic evidence of past *Cryptosporidium* infection showed that all who received at least 1000 calf-derived oocysts and one of five individuals who received 30 oocysts became infected. The 50% infectious dose was around 132 oocysts, and mathematical modeling suggests that even one oocyst might cause infection.[15]

Transmission between household and family members, sexual partners, children in daycare centers and their caretakers, and health care workers and their patients has been well established and may be underappreciated because clinical symptoms may be mild and oocyst excretion may last well beyond symptoms.[14, 42] Spread may be hand-to-mouth or through contact with contaminated items, such as diapers or linens. Infected family members are often detected after an index case: in one daycare center outbreak, for example, 71% of families with a symptomatic child had additional infected family members.[43] Probable intrafamilial spread to a mother and sibling occurred 16 days after the initial infection in three family members exposed to a presumed infected calf[44]; a bone marrow transplant recipient became infected after caring for her two infected toddlers[45]; and in two families traveling in Africa, cryptosporidiosis in children was followed by probable infection in other family members.[46] Household transmission occurred in 58% of 31 households followed prospectively in Brazil, with the index case involving a child younger than 3 years; there was a 19% secondary transmission rate.[27] The secondary transmission rate was 15% after a foodborne epidemic in Maine, but only 4.2% after the waterborne outbreak in Milwaukee, perhaps because the index case generally involved an adult.[47, 48] Spread of *Cryptosporidium* between sexual partners, both heterosexual and homosexual, has been reported[14, 35, 49]

Outbreaks of cryptosporidiosis in child care centers in the United States, Australia, Chile, France, Israel, Portugal, and Spain have been described.[14, 43, 50–55] Relative immunosuppression may predispose to outbreaks, suggested by the association with chickenpox in one center and malnutrition in another.[51, 52] Many cases in child care centers probably remain undetected: in a random survey of children from 30 home daycare centers in Grand Junction, Colorado, 30% excreted *Cryptosporidium* oocysts and only three of these were symptomatic.[53] In Fulton County, Georgia, in a random survey of 17 daycare centers, eight infected children, six without symptoms, were found in two centers.[54] In a survey of asymptomatic children in an upper-middle-class daycare center in New York City, 27% excreted oocysts.[55]

Hospital-associated infection in health care providers and patients has occurred.[14, 56–61] For example, in Denmark, 18 of 60 HIV-infected inpatients developed cryptosporidiosis, as did the departmental secretary and a visitor, after exposure to ice from an ice machine contaminated by a psychotic incontinent patient, and eight died after severe diarrhea.[57] In Italy, six patients on a bone marrow transplant unit acquired cryptosporidiosis, and ultimately *Cryptosporidium* was found in water from floor-cleaning machines and toilet-cleaning rags.[58] Shared toilet facilities were thought to be the source of infection in 11 of 14 Italian dialysis patients with diarrhea, in several asymptomatic patients, and in a nurse and her husband.[56] Poor hand washing and nasogastric feeding tubes may have been the key in the transmission of infection in a Mexican pediatric hospital.[60] Outbreaks have also been described pediatric wards and in a residential care home for people with AIDS.[59, 60, 62]

Animal-to-person (zoonotic) transmission may occur from household pets and from laboratory and farm animals. Since *C. parvum* has been identified in over 75 mammalian species, the zoonotic reservoir is large. In 1982, the first outbreak of *Cryptosporidium*-associated diarrhea was described in personnel handling infected calves.[63] More than 20 instances of laboratory animal–acquired infection have been reported, most from infected calves, but also from infected rodents and rabbits.[14, 64] In one instance, presumed inhalation of aerosolized *Cryptosporidium* rather than oral ingestion of organisms was the putative route of infection.[64] Farm animals, particularly cattle and sheep, have been implicated either directly or through a contaminated environment, in individual cases, such as those first reported in 1976, and in surveys of farming communities in Bangladesh, Canada, and Finland.[14] The role of household pets remains equivocal: two possible cases have been reported, but the direction of spread is impossible to ascertain.[33] In one serologic survey of cats, anti-*Cryptosporidium* IgG was detected in serum from 15.3% (26 of 170) of naturally exposed animals.[65] In an animal shelter in Atlanta, 10% of the puppies actively shed oocysts.[33]

Waterborne transmission was initially suspected in 1983, from travel-connected cases, first when 12 of 14 unrelated Finnish patients excreting *Cryptosporidium* oocysts were retrospectively found to have become ill within 12 days of independent visits to Leningrad and later, in a prospective study, when 9 of 34 Finnish students screened for cryptosporidiosis before traveling to Leningrad were found to be infected on their return.[66, 67] Additional travel-related cases have been described in visitors to the Caribbean, Egypt, Mauritius, Mexico, Nepal, Pakistan, and New Guinea.[14, 22, 46, 68]

As techniques for identifying *Cryptosporidium* oocysts in water have improved, outbreaks associated with drinking or swimming water have been increasingly documented. Endemic infection from persistent or low numbers of *Cryptosporidium* in the water supply is likely in some communities. Surface water (lakes, ponds, rivers, and streams) may be contaminated by infected humans, wildlife, and livestock, the latter particularly important as water drains from fields containing animal feces after a rainfall. In 28 states surveyed in the United States in 1991 to 1992, more than 90% of farms had animals excreting *Cryptosporidium*.[9] In turn, surface water can contaminate recreational water, irrigation water in direct contact with agricultural produce, and water that ultimately becomes domestic and institutional, used for drinking, food preparation, and hygiene. From 65 to 97% of surface water supplies in North America identified *Cryptosporidium* with concentrations up to 240 oocysts per liter.[8, 69] Maximal oocyst densities were found in the Mississippi, Ohio, and Missouri rivers and ranged from 10 to 4840 oocysts per liter.[69] Between 1988 and 1990, oocysts were detected in 87% of 85 raw water sources, although their viability and ability to infect is unclear.[70, 71]

Oocysts—with their small size and thick outer wall—are resistant to most standard water purification techniques used in the United States. Filtration may be more effective than chlorination or other disinfectants, although filters may actually concentrate oocysts, and backwashing filters without recycling the backwash through the water treatment plant may actually increase contamination. A surge of contaminated water after a heavy rain, high agricultural runoff, or a sewage disposal leak can overwhelm any large-scale purification system. A recent survey found *Cryptosporidium* oocysts in 27 to 54% of drinking water samples from 66 surface water treatment plants, 78% of which met relevant U.S. Environmental Protection Agency regulations.[70, 71] In 82 treatment plants in 39 states, 73% of raw water and 17% of finished water had *Cryptosporidium*, with greater numbers related to the original source water—creeks more than rivers more than lakes.[9]

The Safe Water Drinking Act of 1974 led to the development of drinking water standards for more than 80 potential contaminants; this was amended in 1986 to include a maximal level for all human pathogens. To implement this, the Surface Water Treatment Rule (in effect in 1993)—and subsequently the Enhanced Surface Water Treatment Rule directed at a few specific pathogens including *Cryptosporidium*—requires filtration and disinfection of all surface water and groundwater with a surface water origin without documentation that the putative contaminant is actually present.[72] There are neither infectivity data nor reliable and practical removal techniques for *Cryptosporidium*. In 1996, the Information Collection Rule was enacted to determine the prevalence of *Cryptosporidium* in all surface water treatment utilities serving 100,000 or more. The eventual goal is the removal of this pathogen from drinking water. The uncertainty of how important and how achievable *Cryptosporidium*-free water may be makes this undertaking a potentially enormous expense to the water industry and its consumers. Large volumes of water must be concentrated and separated from other debris before examination for *Cryptosporidium*, and this does not include assessment of the viability of organisms and their infectious ability.[9, 72, 73] Conclusions from a 1994 CDC workshop suggested that the magnitude of the problem posed by small numbers of oocysts in drinking water can be addressed only when there are appropriate methods for assessing the viability of oocysts and information on the minimal infectious dose and on the differential ability of different strains to cause disease.[74]

The first recognized waterborne outbreak in San Antonio, Texas, in 1984, had a 34% attack rate of gastroenteritis and was linked to sewage contamination of a chlorinated but unfiltered well water sample.[75] An estimated 13,000 persons experienced gastrointestinal illness in Carroll County, Georgia, in 1987, and illness was significantly correlated with the consumption of water from the filtered, chlorinated public water supply that met established Environmental Protection Agency guidelines.[23] Oocysts were identified in water samples from the water treatment plant, in streams serving the treatment plant, and in cattle grazing in the watershed area. Another large outbreak in Oxfordshire-Swinton, England, in 1989, resulted in a "boil water" advisory to 600,000 people after oocysts were detected in the public water supply.[76] After this outbreak, 3 of 28 renal transplant patients studied excreted oocysts asymptomatically and 5 of 14 AIDS patients studied developed severe cryptosporidiosis.[77]

The largest waterborne outbreak of cryptosporidiosis, and, in fact, of any pathogen since such record keeping began in 1920, occurred in the spring of 1993, when an estimated 403,000 residents of Milwaukee, Wisconsin, developed gastrointestinal symptoms associated with drinking presumably contaminated water (4400 were ultimately hospitalized).[5, 8, 48] An increase in water turbidity (retrospectively identified) approximately 10 days earlier was thought to be secondary to a decrease in the purity of the source water and in filtration effectiveness in one of two facilities treating Lake Michigan water for drinking. Heavy rain and snow runoff into the two major rivers feeding this region of the lake, whose watersheds have plentiful livestock, abattoirs, and human sewage discharge, were thought responsible for the decreased purity.[72] All state and federal standards were met, although the water quality would not meet Environmental Protection Agency standards set since then.[72] Oocysts were ultimately found in ice made in southern Milwaukee during the outbreak, but *Cryptosporidium* was not identified until at least 2 weeks after the outbreak began, with a 100-fold increase in its detection in affected persons.[5] Predominant symptoms were diarrhea (ranging from 1 to 90 stools daily, median 12), abdominal cramps (84%), fever (57%), and vomiting (48%).[5] There was a greater than 20% recurrence rate, generally 5 or more days after the initial recovery. A clear increase in morbidity and mortality was noted in HIV-infected patients with CD4 T-lymphocyte cell counts below 50; severe biliary and intestinal disease was observed. A citywide shortage of antidiarrheal agents, increased numbers of emergency room visits, and increased absenteeism among hospital employees, students, and schoolteachers led to recognition that an outbreak was in progress and ultimately led to the CDC workshop and initiative to improve surveillance, prevention, and the response to potential outbreaks.[74] Point-of-use filters with a submicron pore size were associated with significantly less disease during the Milwaukee outbreak (18% compared with 50%).[73] An outbreak of gastrointestinal illness occurred on a U.S. Coast Guard vessel that filled its water tanks in Milwaukee during the outbreak: of 58 crew members, 20 had confirmed or probable cases, and an additional 22 were suspected of having cryptosporidiosis.[78]

In Washington state, contamination of two deep unchlorinated groundwater wells with presumed treated wastewater from a nearby piped irrigation system in one area and surface water in another caused two outbreaks.[79, 80] Groundwater—untreated water—outbreaks have almost always been associated with sewage or surface water contamination, which in turn occurs because of infected source water or problems arising from antiquated treatment and distribution systems.[9] In Clark County, Nevada, a review of the first two years of *Cryptosporidium* surveillance records documented 104 cases with a 53% mortality rate within 6 months among AIDS patients identified in 1994 (although 1 year mortality rates were not increased); a case-control study showed that drinking unboiled tap water rather than bottled water was statistically significant.[81] Water treatment was well monitored and adequate—both filtered and chlorinated as was the Lake Michigan water, and both the source and the finished drinking water were negative for oocysts.[74, 81]

More than 20 additional waterborne outbreaks have been reported in the United States and Britain, probably due to increased awareness and proficiency in detection.[9] Elsewhere, in one drug rehabilitation community in Italy, the attack rate from waterborne cryptosporidiosis was 13.6% in HIV-negative and 30.7% in HIV-positive persons with clinical symptoms correlated with CD4 cell counts.[82] In Zambia, adults with persistent diarrhea in townships with higher *Cryptosporidium* contamination of the water supply were more likely to have cryptosporidiosis than those with diarrhea living in areas with lower levels of water contamination.[83] In Brazil, the association of infection in HIV-infected patients was greater in the rainy season, suggesting that rainwater is another potential source of *Cryptosporidium*.[84] Protection of source waters, removal of oocysts by filtration, and research into disinfection procedures should be high priorities.

Other outbreaks have been associated with swimming in pools containing oocyst-contaminated water. The first, in Los Angeles, affected 44 persons (73% attack rate) after a fecal accident and malfunctioning filters.[85] Additional swimming pool outbreaks have occurred in London, British Columbia, Wisconsin, and Oregon.[9, 14, 86] In 1993–1994, six outbreaks of cryptosporidiosis associated with recreational water were reported, five associated with motel or community swimming pools that were adequately filtered and chlorinated.[8] In 1994, exposure to water from a recreational lake in a state park in New Jersey led to cryptosporidiosis in an estimated 2070 persons over a 4-week period; contamination was thought to have come from infected bathers and runoff rainwater.[87]

Foodborne cryptosporidiosis has been recognized. After drinking hand-pressed apple cider at an agricultural fair in Maine, 54% of 284 exposed, compared with 2% of 292 unexposed persons, developed illness.[47] From 160 primary cases, there were 53 secondary cases with symptoms beginning about 6 days after the exposure (range 1 to 13) and lasting about 6 days (range 1 to 16). Oocysts were detected in the feces of calves from the farm supplying apples as well as from the cider press and the cider.[47] Another outbreak in 1995 affecting 50 attendees at a social event in Minnesota was linked to chicken salad prepared by a woman who also operated a daycare facility at her home.[88] In Cortland County, New York, in 1996, there were 20 confirmed cases of cryptosporidiosis in 19 households, which compared with neighborhood-matched control households had a statistically significant history of drinking unpasteurized apple cider from a mill across the road from a dairy farm.[89] In 1997, a number of banquet attendees in Spokane, Washington, became ill with cryptosporidiosis 10 days after the event, with a case-controlled study showing an association with unwashed green onions; two food handlers had *Cryptosporidum* in their stools.[19] *Cryptosporidium* was found in 14.5% of vegetables from markets at a periurban slum in Peru through examination of the water used to wash them.[90] Oocysts do not survive cooking, but infected food handlers with poor hygiene are potential vehicles of transmission. Although other outbreaks have been described, the difficulty in identifying *Cryptosporidium* in food products may make this an underrecognized source of infection.[9, 91]

Other routes of transmission such as airborne or insect-borne are theoretically possible but have not been conclusively documented.

PATHOGENESIS AND PATHOLOGY

How *Cryptosporidium* causes disease is unknown, although clinical manifestations seem to correlate with the anatomic location of the organism: diarrhea with intestinal infection and respiratory symptoms with pulmonary infection. The voluminous watery diarrhea that may accompany cryptosporidiosis is reminiscent of cholera and a toxin-mediated process causing hypersecretion of fluids and electrolytes, but cytopathic changes in cell lines sensitive to toxins have not been demonstrated.[11] Two studies, one using piglet ileal mucosa and the other using human jejunum, suggest that *Cryptosporidium* affects intestinal ion transport.[11, 12, 92, 93] Sodium chloride transport is disrupted in a piglet model; ion transport and sodium-glucose absorption is disrupted in an adult immunocompromised mouse model.[93, 94] Damage to the epithelial cell intestinal barrier and intestinal villi may cause malabsorptive diarrhea with impaired digestion, bacterial overgrowth, a change in osmotic fluid flux, and possibly altered immunologic cell function.[12, 92, 95, 96] Both secretory diarrhea, unaffected by fasting, and malabsorptive diarrhea, with abnormal D-xylose and vitamin B_{12} absorption and with steatorrhea, have been reported in HIV-infected patients.[97, 98]

Gross pathologic lesions are unremarkable, with *Cryptosporidium* found on biopsy or autopsy of immunocompromised patients throughout the intestinal tract from esophagus to rectum, the hepatobiliary system, and the respiratory tree; in immunologically healthy patients where there are fewer data, organisms are usually limited to the intestine, including the appendix in one child.[14] Histologically, *Cryptosporidium* is found within epithelial cells (Fig. 272–2). In the intestines, there may be atrophy, blunting, fusion or loss of villi, and crypt hyperplasia; inflammatory changes include infiltration of the lamina propria with lymphocytes, neutrophils, plasma cells, and macrophages.[14] In one study of hyperinfected piglets, only 2% of intestinal villi were disrupted.[93]

LABORATORY RESEARCH

A lack of excellent in vitro and in vivo models have limited progress in understanding the basic biology and biochemistry of *Cryptosporidium*, its pathophysiology, and the host immune responses—normal and abnormal. Current areas of interest include identification of parasite molecular targets for drug action and elucidation of the role of humoral, especially secretory, antibody for vaccine development.[12, 17]

The full life cycle of *Cryptosporidium* can be produced in chick

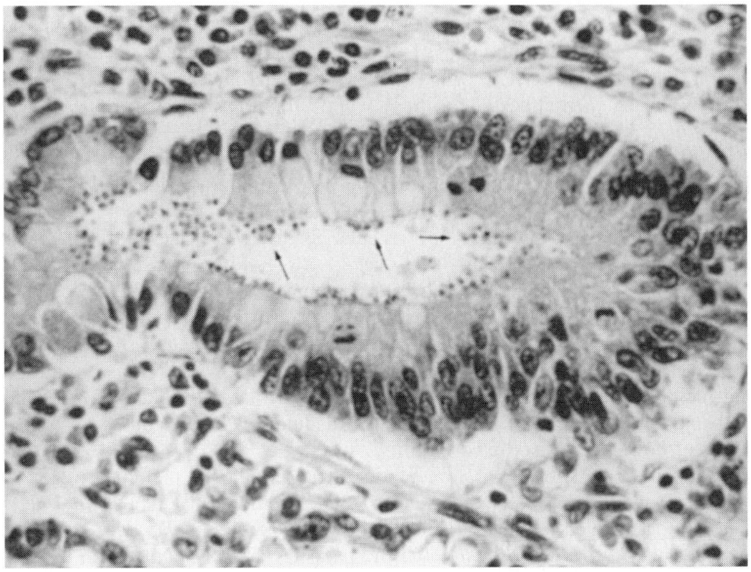

FIGURE 272–2. Duodenal biopsy from a patient with acquired immunodeficiency syndrome cryptosporidiosis. Numerous parasites *(arrows)* are seen in the microvillous border. (Hematoxylin and eosin stain, light microscopic examination.) (Courtesy of Dr. T. Flanigan.)

embryos, but not in those from every flock, and in human fetal lung and in porcine kidney cells, although minimal numbers of oocysts are retrieved.[14] Growth in cell culture was first described in 1984 with more than two dozen reports of successful cultivation since then; the most successful hosts have been epithelial-like cells and generally only the asexual portion of the *Cryptosporidium* life cycle is reproducible.[12, 17] A differentiated human enterocyte cell line, HT29.74, which only permits asexual development of *Cryptosporidium*, has been used to evaluate therapeutic modalities including paromomycin and hyperimmune bovine colostrum; a human colon carcinoma cell line, Caco-2, yields scant oocysts and has been used to screen pharmacologic agents.[99–101] Infection of human biliary cells is consistently achievable.[102] Madin-Darby canine kidney cells support the development of asexual and sexual stages but not sporulated oocysts.[103] Large-scale production of oocysts has not been possible in any of these systems, and an adequate supply of oocysts is still best obtained after labor-intensive purification from infected calf feces. Storage is problematic since oocyst infectivity begins to decline after 6 weeks, although some remain infectious for as long as 12 months.

Laboratory animal models are critical to immunologic and pathophysiologic studies of cryptosporidiosis as well as the development of therapeutic and preventative modalities. Many neonatal animals—including mice, rats, guinea pigs, hamsters, opossums, pigs, lambs, goats, calves, and nonhuman primates—develop spontaneously remitting cryptosporidiosis, making them unsuitable for prolonged investigations.[104] Protracted *Cryptosporidium* infection occurs in some genetically immunodeficient mice, athymic mice and rats, some immunosuppressed rodents, and some immunologically suppressed or depleted mice.[105–119] At least 10 studies have evaluated more than 50 artificially manipulated mouse strains for suitability as a model of persistent cryptosporidiosis.[104–119] In primates, pigtailed macaques just after weaning develop disease similar to that in healthy humans, and simian immunodeficiency virus–infected rhesus monkeys and macaques develop diarrhea and widespread *Cryptosporidium* infection.[104] Animal studies have also, however, been limited by an inadequate oocyst supply.

More than 30 cellular and molecular studies of *Cryptosporidium* have been published.[120] Antigenic composition of *Cryptosporidium* is being defined, primarily through sporozoite and merozoite protein and epitope recognition by antisera and monoclonal antibodies.[109, 121–123] Two major highly antigenic surface antigens have been identified at the 17- and 27-kD masses and have been useful in diagnostic techniques. Some antigens have been genetically analyzed and cloned.[120] Between five and eight chromosomes are likely, and approximately 30 gene sequences are available in gene banks.[120, 124]

CLINICAL FEATURES

Cryptosporidiosis has been reported without predisposition to either gender in individuals of all ages, from a vaginally delivered 3-day-old infant whose mother had cryptosporidiosis to a 95-year-old patient. Young children, particularly those younger than 2 years, may be more susceptible to infection, perhaps reflecting increased fecal-oral transmission in this age group, a lack of protective immunity from prior exposure, or relative immunologic immaturity.[14] The role of breast-feeding in human cryptosporidiosis remains controversial but did not prevent infection in one primate model.[14, 125] A review of several human population–based studies suggested a protective role, although a single prospective study showed no significant difference in the prevalence or duration of cryptosporidiosis in children nursing from mothers with different colostral antibody levels.[16, 126, 127] Like children, elderly persons may be at increased risk for *Cryptosporidium* infection, perhaps related to normal immunosenescence.[14]

The prepatent period, the interval from the oral ingestion of oocysts to the development of symptoms, is 7 to 10 days (range 5 to 28 days).[14, 15, 42, 44, 49, 57, 68] In four veterinary students exposed to one infected calf on the same day, all became symptomatic 6 to 7 days later, although the severity and duration of illness varied.[49] In HIV-infected patients exposed to a presumed small *Cryptosporidium* inoculum in contaminated ice, the mean time to symptoms was 13 days.[57] It is not known whether the time to infection varies with virulence or strain differences of *Cryptosporidium* or with the immunologic health of the patient. There is no evidence that second symptomatic infections occur if the initial infection is completely eradicated. In the human volunteer study, reinfection a year later required a 10-fold greater inoculum size and was asymptomatic.[128] Whether there is a latent state that can be reactivated is not known.

Diarrhea, with or without crampy abdominal pain, may be intermittent and scant, or continuous, watery, and voluminous, as much as 12 to 17 liters/day.[4, 14, 97, 129] Its severity varies considerably from individual to individual and may wax and wane or be relentlessly persistent in any patient, although the latter is more common in immunologically impaired persons. For example, in 20 patients with hematologic malignancies, 5 had severe and 10 had moderate diarrhea whereas the remaining 5 were asymptomatic.[130] In 50 immunologically healthy patients, diarrhea ranged from 2 to 26 days.[42] However, severe diarrhea has persisted from 42 to 85 days in at least two cases reported in immunologically healthy men.[131, 132] Whether diarrhea correlates with the intensity of oocyst shedding is uncertain, although human volunteers with diarrhea shed significantly more oocysts during their illness than those without diarrhea.[15] Diarrhea may contain mucus but rarely blood or leukocytes.

Low-grade (<39°C) fever, general malaise, weakness, fatigue, loss of appetite, nausea, and vomiting may accompany diarrhea.[14] Toxic megacolon complicated the course of one HIV-infected patient with severe diarrhea, and an enterovesicular fistula complicated another.[133, 134]

There are no characteristic laboratory features of enteric cryptosporidiosis other than the identification of organisms. Leukocytosis is uncommon, although eosinophilia has been reported.[14] Malabsorption of fat, D-xylose, and vitamin B_{12} has been noted.[14, 97, 135] Abdominal radiographic and computed tomographic studies are nonspecific and may show prominent mucosal folds, air-fluid levels, distended loops of bowel, and disordered motility.[4]

The differential diagnosis for enteric cryptosporidiosis, particularly relevant to HIV-infected patients, includes some easily identified pathogens such as the bacteria *Shigella*, *Salmonella*, *Campylobacter*, and *Clostridium difficile*, and the parasites *Giardia lamblia*, *Cyclospora cayetanesis*, *Entamoeba histolytica*, and *Isospora belli*. Other pathogens, however, are more difficult to exclude, particularly cytomegalovirus, *Mycobacterium avium*, and *Microsporidia*.

Other clinical manifestations associated with cryptosporidiosis include cholecystitis, hepatitis, pancreatitis, reactive arthritis, and a variety of respiratory problems. The causal role of *Cryptosporidium* for these symptoms has not been as well established as for diarrheal disease. Because diagnostic proficiency varies substantially with experience, and because oocysts are more easily recognized in persons with diarrhea than in those without, other clinical presentations may be underrecognized.

Gallbladder infection, first reported in 1981, may affect as many as 10% of AIDS patients with cryptosporidiosis.[14, 16, 136–138] Patients present with acalculous cholecystitis or sclerosing cholangitis, with fever, right upper quadrant nonradiating pain, nausea, and vomiting, but not necessarily with simultaneous diarrhea. Alkaline phosphatase and bilirubin levels may be elevated. Sonographic or computed tomographic imaging shows an enlarged gallbladder with a thickened wall, dilated or irregular intra- and extrahepatic biliary ducts, and a normal or stenotic distal common bile duct.[14, 16, 136, 137] Cholangiograms may show beading of the common bile duct or papillary stenosis.[136]

Diagnosis is made histologically after cholecystectomy or ampullary biopsy, or by examination of the bile for oocysts. Even when present in bile, oocysts are not necessarily detectable in fecal specimens. Liver biopsy has shown *Cryptosporidium* attached to bile duct epithelial cells.[14, 16, 138] Concurrent infection with cytomegalovirus, *Enterobacter cloacae*, and *Microsporidia* has been frequently noted.[14, 16, 139] Papillotomy, sphincterotomy, T-tube drainage, and cholecystectomy have had variable therapeutic success.[14, 136, 138, 140, 141] There is a single case report of successful treatment of sclerosing cholangitis with paromomycin followed by letrazuril.[142] The prognosis is usually poor, with pancreatitis, cholangitis, and hepatitis as possible sequellae.[14] Of 82 HIV-infected persons with cryptosporidiosis after the Milwaukee outbreak, only 4 of 24 with biliary involvement were alive 1 year later compared with 30 of 58 without gallbladder disease, although the latter tended to have higher CD4 cell counts.[16] Chronic gallbladder carriage may be responsible for the inability to eradicate intestinal cryptosporidiosis.

Pancreatitis associated with cryptosporidiosis has been described.[14, 143–145] In one case, an otherwise healthy 14-year-old farmer's daughter developed severe abdominal pain, an enlarged pancreas, ascites, and a serum amylase level of 14,400 U/liter (normal <300) 1 week after being diagnosed with intestinal cryptosporidiosis without another cause and with spontaneous resolution over 6 weeks.[143] In another case, a patient with AIDS had severe abdominal pain, elevated alkaline phosphatase and amylase levels, an enlarged head of the pancreas, and a dilated and beaded main pancreatic duct and had *Cryptosporidium* oocysts in her biliary drainage for more than 36 hours.[14] In another instance, an otherwise healthy 23-year-old man developed diarrhea and pancreatitis with a positive enzyme immunoassay for *Cryptosporidium* in a stool specimen.[145]

Cryptosporidium in the respiratory tract may represent aspirated organisms or true infection.[14, 130, 146] Symptoms are nonspecific and do not reflect severe pulmonary dysfunction: shortness of breath, hoarseness, wheezing, croup, and, most often, cough. Laryngotracheitis and sinusitis have also occurred.[147, 148] Chest radiographic findings have been unremarkable, usually with modest infiltrates or increased bronchial markings. Organisms have been identified in sputum; in tracheal aspirates; in bronchoalveolar lavage fluid; in brush biopsy and lung biopsy specimens; in alveolar exudate; attached to the surface of bronchial mucosal cells; or in macrophages.[14] Eight of 86 bronchoscopic biopsies in one group of Danish patients with AIDS had *Cryptosporidium*.[149] In most instances, another pulmonary pathogen has been concurrently detected, such as cytomegalovirus or *Pneumocystis carinii*, although in one series of four HIV-infected patients, *Cryptosporidium* was the only pathogen identified for at least 9 months after the initial diagnosis.[146] Clear association with intestinal cryptosporidiosis or diarrhea has not been shown, although respiratory symptoms were threefold more frequent in children with diarrhea due to *Cryptosporidium* rather than other pathogens in three case-controlled studies.[16] Successful treatment has been reported in isolated cases with azithromycin and inhaled paramomycin.[150, 151] *Cryptosporidium baileyi* involving the trachea, larynx, and lungs as well as the intestines was found in one kidney transplant recipient with AIDS.[152]

Reactive arthritis affecting the wrists, hands, knees, ankles, and feet has been described in three immunologically healthy patients concurrent with *Cryptosporidium* enteritis and without other apparent cause; complete spontaneous resolution occurred in all patients, in one case over a 4-month period.[153, 154] Association with Reiter's syndrome has also been described.[155]

Disseminated cryptosporidiosis has not been described, although one adult leukemic patient with disseminated candidiasis was found to have *Cryptosporidium* in the intestinal epithelium and respiratory parenchyma at autopsy, as well as in the lumen of submucosal colonic vessels, suggesting possible hematogenous spread.[156]

Asymptomatic intestinal infections, usually uncovered during epidemiologic surveys, are thought to be infrequent but may be underestimated because small numbers of oocysts are hard to find.[14] As many as 30% of childhood infections, however, have been reported to be asymptomatic in Bolivia, Peru, Chile, and Gabon[16, 25, 51, 157]; 20 and 27% of those surveyed in daycare settings in Grand Junction, Colorado, and New York City, respectively, excreted *Cryptosporidium* without symptoms.[53, 55] In a prospective study in Bronx, New York, 5 of 78 (6.4%) immunologically healthy children were asymptomatic carriers.[158] Of 154 adults undergoing endoscopy for abdominal symptoms other than diarrhea, 11.7% had *Cryptosporidium* in duodenal aspirates, suggesting a gallbladder reservoir.[159] There have been individual case reports of asymptomatic cryptosporidiosis in patients with HIV infection or with leukemia.[14, 160, 161] In studies of HIV-infected drug users in Malaysia and Cuba, 23 and 45%, respectively, had asymptomatic cryptosporidiosis.[16, 162] Whether asymptomatic infections actually represent oocyst detection sometime after a brief, mild, or atypical clinical illness remains speculative. They do increase the potential for inadvertent transmission.

Recovery from *Cryptosporidium* infection depends on the immune status of the host. Immunologically healthy persons usually experience full spontaneous symptomatic recovery within a few weeks and parasitologic cure within a few months; all participants in the human volunteer study recovered fully.[14, 15, 42, 163] An acquired immune response may limit the duration and perhaps the severity of infection.

The ability of an immunocompromised patient to eliminate *Cryptosporidium* varies with the nature of the immune deficit. Unless immunosuppression is alleviated, clearance of *Cryptosporidium* infection is unlikely although possible.[14] Immune deficiencies associated with cryptosporidiosis include a variety of immune globulin disorders (congenital hypogammaglobulinemia, IgA deficiency); intercurrent viral infections such as measles and chickenpox; thalassemia major; insulin-dependent diabetes mellitus; bone marrow, renal, or liver transplantation; hematologic malignancies; and other cancers or exogenous immunosuppression.[14, 45, 58, 130, 147, 148, 160, 164–168] Persons with AIDS remain the largest group of immunologically impaired persons affected. Malnourished children, well described in Chile, Israel, Jamaica, Mexico, Peru, the Philippines, and South Africa, also appear more susceptible to severe cryptosporidiosis, likely related to an inadequate immune system.[14, 51, 60, 169–172] Pregnancy may predispose to *Cryptosporidium* infection as well.[14]

In HIV-infected individuals, cryptosporidiosis lasting more than 30 days is part of the CDC's case definition of AIDS.[173] Although it is not certain that HIV-infected patients are ever able to eliminate the organism completely, the majority with CD4 cell counts above 180 to 200 cells/mm^3 have clinical resolution.[140, 174, 175] Some with CD4 cell counts below 50 cells/mm^3 occasionally clear their infection.[140] In late-stage HIV infections, cryptosporidiosis rarely remits and often contributes to death.

IMMUNE RESPONSE

The host immune responses that prevent initial infection with *Cryptosporidium*, limit its spread, and ultimately facilitate its clearance are poorly understood but probably include both B- and T-lymphocyte—mediated processes. In humans, prolonged cryptosporidiosis develops in patients with a variety of immune deficiencies, T-cell abnormalities, and diffuse or selective immune globulin deficiencies. It is plausible that secretory antibody interferes with sporozoite and merozoite attachment and therefore the initiation of initial infection and completion of the extracellular life cycle. Many classes of serum antibody, however, may be present in HIV-infected hosts unable to clear *Cryptosporidium* infection.[176–179] Cell-mediated responses, perhaps a cytotoxic effect, perhaps an antibody- or cytokine-dependent effect, are likely to influence the intracellular life cycle. Effector cells such as macrophages are capable of engulfing extracellular *Cryptosporidium* life-cycle stages but have not yet been studied.[13] Young mammals may be more susceptible because they lack fully developed immunologic abilities.

Immunologic studies in humans have determined that specific anti-*Cryptosporidium* IgM, IgG, or fecal or salivary IgA, or all of these, develop within 3 months of infection and persist for varied lengths of time even in HIV-infected persons.[14, 22, 25, 109, 177–179] Functional capacity is impaired in HIV-infected persons since high levels of both serum and secretory antibodies are found coincident with severe cryptosporidiosis. In one study, 41 patients with cryptosporidiosis, both with and without concomitant HIV infection, all had detectable specific anti-*Cryptosporidium* IgG or IgM antibodies at the time of medical presentation.[176] In another, anti-*Cryptosporidium* antibodies were detected in two of seven animal workers within 6 days of the onset of infection and in all within 3 months; antibodies lasted for at least a year in five patients.[180] Persistent serum antibodies may represent the normal duration of antibody response or, alternatively, continuous antigenic stimulation from undetected or sequestered infections, such as in the gallbladder, potentially with separate antibodies produced to different life-cycle stages. Alternatively, they may represent the ingestion of oocysts without infection including with antigenically dissimilar *Cryptosporidium* isolates.

Acquired immunity is presumed to limit the initial and perhaps subsequent *Cryptosporidium* infection in immunologically healthy human hosts. *Macaca nemestrina* infant monkeys develop self-limited *Cryptosporidium*-associated diarrhea, although older animals are refractory to infection,[41] and many other species, particularly ruminants and rodents, are most susceptible to infection as neonates.[4] Many immunogenic *Cryptosporidium* antigens, including some shared by sporozoites and merozoites, have been identified, although antibody to individual antigens has not been correlated with immunity. In mice, researchers have identified at least seven neutralization-sensitive antigens, some of which are conserved between various *Cryptosporidium* life-cycle stages.[109] In one human example, sera from 93% of 40 patients with cryptosporidiosis reacted with a 23-kD cell-derived *Cryptosporidium* oocyst antigen.[122] In another, advanced AIDS patients produced serum and fecal antibodies that recognized the same antigen. One 17-and another 27-kD antigen have been repeatedly identified, with the latter localized to the sporozoite surface.[181] Western blot analysis of sera from crew members affected by a waterborne outbreak of cryptosporidiosis on a Coast Guard cutter showed an antibody response to both antigens in persons with confirmed and suspected disease.[182]

CD4 cells, involved in both cellular and humoral responses, are important immunologic mediators of *Cryptosporidium* infection in humans.[109, 112, 119, 174, 175, 183] Several animal models—athymic mice and rats, immunologically depleted mice, retrovirus-infected mice, aged hamsters, and primates—also show an association between the loss of T-lymphocyte function and prolonged cryptosporidiosis.[105–109, 112] For example, experimentally infected neonatal and adult congenitally athymic mice develop a chronic symptomatic infection including the hepatobiliary tree, which is cured by reconstitution with histocompatible lymphoid cells.[105] T-cell–independent mechanisms also exist, since adult athymic mice and severe combined immunodeficient mice develop infection more slowly than neonates.[105–109, 114] In a selectively depleted adult BALB/c mouse model, both CD4 cells and interferon-γ (IFN-γ) are required to prevent the initiation of *Cryptosporidium* infection, whereas CD4 cells limit the duration of infection, and INF-γ limits its intensity.[106] Adult BALB/c mice, normally resistant to infection, shed larger numbers of oocysts when CD8 cells are depleted along with CD4 cells, suggesting a yet-undefined role for these cells.[106] Severe combined immunodeficient mice, which lack functional T and B cells and have impaired macrophage function, develop more severe disease if also depleted of INF-γ.[107,-109, 111–114, 119] Reconstitution experiments suggest that CD4 cells plus INF-γ are both necessary for complete recovery.[105, 109, 112, 115] Possible mechanisms of action of INF-γ include macrophage activation, direct toxicity, and inhibition of invasion and intracellular development, perhaps cytokine mediated. Some cytokines do appear important: Depletion of both interleukin-5 (IL-5) and IL-12 intensifies infection in some mouse models, whereas IL-2 and IL-4 depletion has no effect.[105, 109, 119] Exogenous IL-2 prevents infection in a severe combined immunodeficient mouse model through an INF-γ–dependent mechanism.[119]

Use of $\alpha\beta$ T-cell–deficient and $\gamma\delta$ T-cell–deficient mice demonstrate persistent infections in the former (MHC class II) and complete resistence in the latter (MHC class I). The role of these cell types is also being studied in calves.[116, 117, 118] Cell types such as natural killer and mast cells do not appear to mediate resistance to cryptosporidiosis.[106–109]

DIAGNOSIS

Diagnosis of enteric cryptosporidiosis has progressed from histologic identification of developmental stages in intestinal biopsy sections to examination of stool specimens for oocysts or parasite antigens. Biopsy, an invasive procedure that relies on sampling an affected portion of the intestine, yields tissue sections that are difficult to fix without separation of the organism from the cell surface; it is now rarely used. Organisms appear basophilic with hematoxylin and eosin staining and seem to project into the lumen because of their intracellular but extracytoplasmic location (see Fig. 272–2). Electron microscopy shows cellular detail. Because of the relative simplicity and well-developed methods of the fecal diagnosis, the detection of cryptosporidiosis has improved greatly, although health care personnel may be reluctant to request diagnostic tests since there is no effective therapy, short-sighted given the secondary transmission potential.

With the use of Giemsa stain, *Cryptosporidium* oocysts were first identified by microscopic examination of feces from calves in 1978 and from humans in 1980.[14] The small oocysts, generally 4 to 6 μm in diameter, stain purple, as do similarly sized yeast cells. Many techniques have been developed to maximize the detection of oocysts in stool samples as well as in duodenal aspirates, bile, or respiratory secretions. Most laboratories process every sample by at least two separate methods, generally a concentration technique and a staining procedure for confirmation and permanent record. Examination of multiple stool specimens may be necessary due to intermittent shedding of oocysts, although experienced laboratory personnel rarely have difficulty identifying even small numbers of oocysts. During one waterborne outbreak, a single stool specimen, however, identified only 50% of those infected.[23] In another study, 53% of single stool specimens compared with 73% of multiple stool specimens were diagnostic. Sensitivity of small intestinal biopsy varied from 53 to 91%.[184]

Specimens may be examined fresh or formalin-fixed, by light or phase-contrast microscopy. For long-term preservation, fecal samples may be stored in 2.5% (weight/volume) potassium dichromate, in which oocysts may remain viable for as long as 6 months.[14] Floatation or sedimentation concentration of fecal samples is particularly helpful in recovering oocysts from a nonliquid stool specimen. Oocysts float easily in Sheather's sucrose solution, in zinc sulfate (33% saturated), and in sodium chloride (36% saturated). They pellet with formalin ethyl acetate or formalin ether. There is no consensus as to the best concentration method.[181, 185] Phase- or interference-contrast microscopy of concentrated specimens may show bright, birefringent oocysts containing up to four sporozoites and a dark granular oocyst residual body.

For staining before direct microscopy, modified acid-fast procedures, first described in 1981, have become the mainstay of diagnosis in most laboratories.[4, 181, 185] Round oocysts stain red or pink, whereas yeast cells and fecal debris assume the color of the blue or green counterstain (Fig. 272–3). The red color may be unevenly distributed due to variable carbol-fuchsin uptake by the oocyst wall, especially in rapidly shed young oocysts with less mature walls.[4] Although sometimes sporozoites can be clearly seen within the oocyst, size is important in differentiating oocysts from other organisms with similar staining properties, such as *Cyclospora cayetanesis*.

Other available staining techniques include safranin–methylene blue (malachite green), which colors *Cryptosporidium* oocysts orange-pink and other fecal organisms blue-green. There are also negative stains, such as methenamine silver and nigrosin, which cause background darkening while oocysts remain clear. Fluorescent stains, which are good for screening, neither provide a permanent record nor allow visualization of internal oocyst structure.[4] Fluorescent stains include acridine orange, which causes both oocysts and yeast cells to fluoresce, and, auramine-rhodamine and auramine–carbol-fuchsin, which cause oocysts but not yeast to fluoresce.[4]

Both polyclonal and monoclonal antibodies raised to *Cryptosporidium* antigens have been used in immunologically based fluorescent assays and ELISA tests that are routinely used for oocyst detection in clinical and research laboratories as well as in water supplies.[181, 186, 187] At least three commercial immunofluorescent antibody tests and four ELISA tests are available with ELISA sensitivities and specificities ranging from 66 to 100% and 93 to 100%, respectively.[181, 185, 188] Antisera-coated latex beads and a flow cytometry–based assay have also been described.[181, 189]

Although no single universally appropriate diagnostic technique is accepted, most clinical laboratories rely on an acid-fast staining procedure with or without fecal concentration.[181] Antibody-based detection systems may be most useful in settings where cryptosporidiosis is rare, oocysts are few, and expense is not a barrier.

Serologic detection of specific anti-*Cryptosporidium* antibodies, using immunofluorescent antibody assays with oocysts or infected intestinal mucosal tissue, ELISA tests, or Western blot assays with

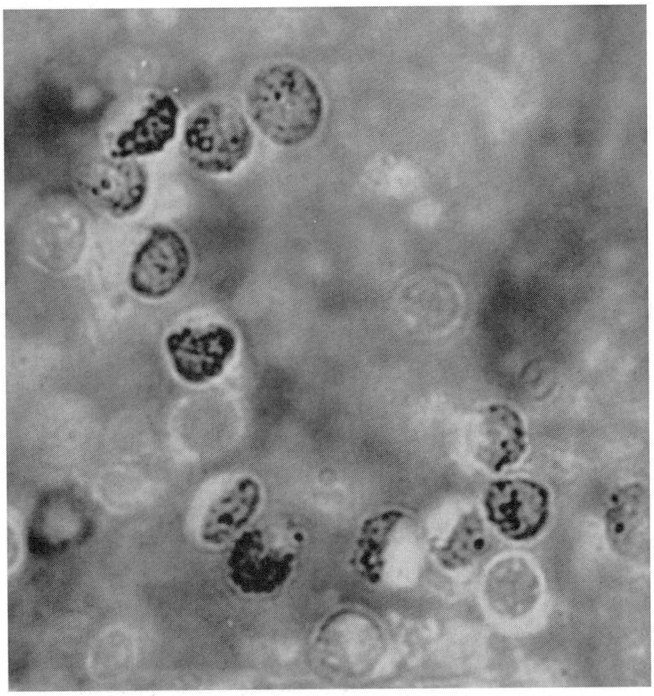

FIGURE 272–3. *Cryptosporidium* oocysts stained using modified acid-fast technique. Oocysts are round and often color pink or red unevenly. Yeast and other fecal debris (blue or green depending on the counterstain) appear unstained. (From Fayer R, Ungar BLP. *Cryptosporidium* spp and cryptosporidiosis. Microbiol Rev. 1986;50:458–483.)

sonicated oocysts or sporozoites as antigen, is primarily used as an investigational or epidemiologic tool because antibody persistence limits its usefulness in the diagnosis of acute infection.[22, 25, 122, 176, 181, 182] For example, in a study comparing serologic responses to the 17- and 27-kD antigens among persons whose municipal water supply is filtered surface water compared with those drinking groundwater, individuals from the former had a higher seroprevalence, a higher intensity of response, and a higher rate of seroconversion (Floyd Frost, Southwest Center for Managed Care Research, Albuquerque, New Mexico, personal communication).

Polymerase chain reaction assays have been developed, but not yet tested in large trials. One chemiluminescent-based assay appears at least two orders of magnitude more sensitive than other means of identifying the parasite in fecal specimens, and another reproducibly detected as few as 20 oocysts.[190–193] Polymerase chain reaction has been used to assess the viability of the organism and to detect oocysts in water.[194–198] Polymerase chain reaction detection methods that require amplification of *Cryptosporidium* DNA have been used to detect organisms in parafin-fixed tissue and to distinguish live from dead organisms.[120] The development and application of these techniques is likely to be increasingly important.

TREATMENT

There is no reliable palliative or curative treatment for cryptosporidiosis. In immunocompetent or temporarily immunocompromised patients, the disease is self-limited, but dehydration may necessitate hospitalization. For irreversibly immunocompromised patients, therapy may be critical. Some nonspecific antidiarrheal agents, including bismuth subsalicylate, kaolin and pectin, diphenoxylate, opiates, and loperamide, provide temporary relief to individual patients, but supportive care with parenteral nutrition and hydration remains the backbone of treatment. A lack of either a full in vitro cultivation system or a simple small model of disease has greatly hampered the discovery and development of drugs, particularly the study of biochemical and metabolic requirements of *Cryptosporidium* and host cell–parasite interaction. Continuous movement of intestinal contents, increased in diarrhea, exacerbates the difficulty of achieving high luminal concentrations of a therapeutic agent before *Cryptosporidium* becomes intracellular; why intracellular forms are so difficult to eradicate remains elusive.

Early evaluation of many pharmacologic agents in mice, lambs, calves, and pigs did not show any one to be efficacious.[4] Among the first 21 AIDS patients with cryptosporidiosis reported by the CDC, only 7 treated with multiple agents experienced transitory symptomatic improvement.[129] By 1983, anecdotal reports of putative cure or symptomatic improvement with oral spiramycin, a macrolide antibiotic with more than 2 decades of use in Europe for respiratory illness and toxoplasmosis, led to initial optimism.[14, 199] Compassionate use of spiramycin increased, but its safety and efficacy were never demonstrated in controlled clinical trials in immunologically healthy children or in HIV-infected patients using both oral and intravenous formulations.[60, 199]

By 1990, more than 100 investigational agents had been tried with rare and inconsistent success.[14, 16, 199, 200] These included drugs effective against other parasites, such as quinine, chloroquine, mefloquine, atovaquone, Qinghaosu (artemisinin), metronidazole, pyrimethamine, trimethoprim-sulfamethoxazole, and difluoromethylornithine.[14, 16, 199] Others receiving attention have been (1) octreotide acetate, a synthetic analogue of somatostatin, which inhibits intestinal secretory diarrhea and has been associated with symptomatic improvement but not parasitologic cure in a few patients[201–203]; (2) diclazuril sodium, a benzeneacetonitrile derivative used as an anticoccidial agent in poultry, which has also caused subjective improvement but proved ineffective when tested in a dose-escalating placebo-controlled phase I/II trial; the diclazuril congener letrazuril, which has greater bioavailability, had no better clinical effect.[199, 204]; (3) azithromycin, another macrolide antibiotic, which achieves good biliary concentrations but, has not been shown to be significantly therapeutic or curative in a double-blind study of 85 AIDS patients, a compassionate-use program, and a case-control study of the intravenous preparation[199, 205–209]; (4) clarithromycin, another macrolide antibiotic that achieves high intracellular levels and reduces parasite burden in a rodent model; in a retrospective chart review of AIDS patients receiving clarithromycin prophylactically, none developed clinical cryptosporidiosis[210, 211]; (5) paromomycin, a poorly absorbed antibiotic active against *E. histolytica*, widely used as a first-line agent, although the data from three placebo-controlled trials have demonstrated temporary amelioration and not eradication of infection.[16, 150, 151, 199, 200, 212–221]; and (6) nitazoxanide, a nitrothiazole compound with broad antiparasitic activity, currently undergoing an open-label safety and efficacy study in New York and an National Institutes of Health AIDS Clinical Trial Group (ACTG) randomized trial.[16, 199] In a study in Mali, oocyst shedding was reduced by at least 95% in 7 of 12 AIDS patients with symptoms eradicated in 4, for up to 2 weeks after the treatment.[222]

Zidovudine has been associated with improvement, perhaps due to general augmentation of immune function or a direct effect on HIV-infected intestinal cells in some AIDS patients, even with absolute CD4 counts less than 100 cells/mm^3.[16, 140, 223, 224] An HIV protease inhibitor has been reported to cure cryptosporidiosis in one patient, likely due to improved immune competence. Whether the overall failure of therapeutic agents is due to true resistance, metabolic or structural, of *Cryptosporidium*, or to a drug-delivery problem, either to the intracellular life stages or to inaccessible organisms, for example in the biliary tree, remains unclear.

The biologic immunomodulators, immune serum, immunoglobulins from bovine colostrum and from humans, monoclonal antibodies, bovine transfer factor (or bovine dialyzable leukocyte extract), and hyperimmune bovine colostrum (HBC), have been discussed in more than 40 publications.[183] Although some may be promising therapeutic modalities, they are difficult to prepare and standardize, although at least five commercial immunoglobulin preparations are in production.[183] Pooled human donor immunoglobulins with anticryptosporidial activity has been approved by the Food and Drug Administration for human use and has had anecdotal success.[183, 225, 226] HBC has been administered by direct duodenal infusion to 16 AIDS patients in Australia and the United States, with a dramatic rapid decrease in stool volume early in therapy, lasting up to 3 months, but without parasitologic cure (B Ungar, unpublished data; S Tzipori, personal communication).[227, 228] One child with leukemia did have complete clinical and parasitologic cure.[227] HBC-derived immunoglobulin has been administered in powder form to infected patients with AIDS with a decrease in oocyst shedding but no statistically significant clinical benefit.[183, 229, 230] The protective factor, not yet identified, may be antibody or a critical substance, absent because of deficient T-cell responses or diminished CD4 cells, that activates other intact portions of the immune system. Nonhyperimmune bovine colostrum or bovine colostrum from animals with previous natural *Cryptosporidium* infection have not been therapeutically useful.[183] DNA injection of sheep has produced specific serum and colostrum antibody responses and may hold promise.[230]

PREVENTION

Since there is no option to prevent disease, prevention of exposure through increased education about modes of transmission is critical. control measures are limited by oocyst resistance to common disinfectants: ammonia, sodium hypochlorite, and formalin have been advocated in the laboratory setting.[4] Enteric precautions and good hygiene such as hand washing and proper disposal of contaminated material are universally important when in contact with an infected person.

In 1995, with 1997 modification, the U.S. Public Health service issued guidelines for the prevention of opportunistic infections, including *Cryptosporidium*, in persons with HIV.[6, 7] Contact with human and animal feces should be avoided, and immediate hand washing or use of disposable gloves is prudent if contact with human feces (for example, changing diapers), pet handling, gardening, or other contact with soil does occur. Although the removal of healthy pets is not thought necessary, new pets should be more than 6 months old, should not have diarrhea, should not be stray, and should have their stools examined for *Cryptosporidium* before contact with the patient. Exposure to calves and lambs or their homes should be avoided.[6, 7, 33]

Water should never be drunk directly from rivers or lakes. The risk of cryptosporidiosis from drinking water in nonoutbreak settings is uncertain, and data are considered inadequate to recommend general avoidance of tap water. For routine drinking water, personal-use water filters that remove particles 1 μm or less labeled as absolute (not nominal 1 μm filters only, which may not be standardized), operating by reverse osmosis and meeting National Sanitation Foundation Standard 53 for cyst removal, may be considered. Other 1 μm filters may not be standardized. Adequate filter cleaning and replacement of filters where *Cryptosporidium* may concentrate is necessary, but only if gloves are used. Bottled water should not be assumed to be free from oocyst contamination; the source and methods of disinfecting the bottled water would need to be carefully scrutinized to ensure its safety, which may only be possible by direct contact with the vendor. There are no standardized labeling requirements. During outbreaks, boiling water for 1 minute will eliminate organisms. Products using potentially contaminated water should be avoided, such as ice, fountain beverages, and unpasteurized drinks (some refrigerated fruit juices). Carbonated drinks and noncarbonated drinks that can be stored without refrigeration are considered safe.[6, 7]

Because oocysts may be shed asymptomatically for long periods after illness, and disintection of swimming pools requires high concentrations of chlorine for prolonged periods, swallowing water in swimming pools and recreational water parks or in some lakes and rivers during recreational activities may also lead to infection.[33]

In the hospital setting, the use of gloves with hand washing after their removal should avoid transmission from an infected person, but sharing a room or bathroom, because of the unknown potential of fomite transmission, should be avoided.[6, 7, 33]

Future research that should help refine future prevention guidelines includes better understanding of the role of low numbers of oocysts in drinking water in new infections; the frequency of asymptomatic *Cryptosporidium* carriage in HIV-infected persons and how disease manifestations correlate with CD4 cell counts; better diagnostic techniques for both animal and environmental sources; better reporting systems to identify the magnitude of cryptosporidiosis; and a continued search for a prophylactic or therapeutic agent.

REFERENCES

1. Tyzzer EE. A sporozoan found in the peptic glands of the common mouse. Proc Soc Exp Biol Med. 1907;5:12–13.
2. Slavin D. *Cryptosporidium meleagridis* (sp nov). J Comp Pathol. 1955;65:262–266.
3. Panciera RJ, Thomassen RW, Garner FM. Cryptosporidial infection in a calf. Vet Pathol. 1971;8:479–484.
4. Fayer R, Ungar BLP. *Cryptosporidium* spp and cryptosporidiosis. Microbiol Rev. 1986;50:458–483.
5. MacKenzie W, Hoxie N, Proctor M, et al. A massive outbreak in Milwaukee of *Cryptosporidium* infection transmitted through the public water supply. N Engl J Med. 1994;331:161–167.
6. Centers for Disease Control and Prevention. 1997 USPHS/IDSA guidelines for the prevention of opportunistic infections in persons infected with human immunodeficiency virus. MMWR Morb Mortal Wkly Rep. 1997;46:7–9.
7. Centers for Disease Control and Prevention. 1995 USPHS/IDSA guidelines for the prevention of opportunistic infections in persons infected with human immunodeficiency virus. MMWR Morb Mortal Wkly Rep. 1995;44:8–9.
8. Centers for Disease Control and Prevention. Surveillance for waterborne-disease outbreaks, United States, 1993–1994. MMWR Morb Mortal Wkly Rep. 1996;45:6–11.
9. Fricker C, Crabb J. Waterborne cryptosporidiosis: Detection methods and treatment options. Adv Parasitol. 1998;40:242–280.
10. Ma P. *Cryptosporidium* spp and *Isospora belli*. In: Leoung G, Mills J, eds. Opportunistic Infections in Patients with the Acquired Immunodeficiency Syndrome. New York: Marcel Dekker; 1989:355–377.
11. Tilley M, Upton S. Biochemistry of *Cryptosporidium*. In: Fayer R, ed. *Cryptosporidium* and cryptosporidiosis. Boca Raton, Fla: CRC Press; 1997:163–180.
12. Tzipori S, Griffiths J. Natural history and biology of *Cryptosporidium parvum*. Adv Parasitol. 1998;40:6–37.
13. Marcial MA, Madara JL. *Cryptosporidium*: Cellular localization, structural analysis of absorptive cell-parasite membrane-membrane interactions in guinea pigs, and suggestion of protozoan transport by M cells. Gastroenterology. 1986;90:583–594.
14. Ungar BLP. Cryptosporidiosis in humans. In: Dubey JP, Speer CA, Fayer R, eds. Cryptosporidiosis of Man and Animals. Boca Faton, Fla: CRC Press; 1990:59–82.
15. Dupont H, Chappell C, Sterling C, et al. The infectivity of *Cryptosporidium parvum* in healthy volunteers. N Engl J Med. 1995;332:855–859.
16. Griffiths J. Human cryptosporidiosis: Epidemiology, transmission, clinical disease, treatment and diagnosis. Adv Parasitol. 1998;40:38–87.
17. Tzipori S. Cryptosporidiosis: Laboratory investigations and chemotherapy. Adv Parasitol. 1998;40:188–223.
18. Centers for Disease Control and Prevention. Summary of notifiable diseases, United States. MMWR Morb Mortal Wkly Rep. 1997;45:7.
19. Centers for Disease Control and Prevention. Summary—provisional cases of selected notifiable diseases; foodborne outbreak of cryptosporidiosis—Spokane, Washington, 1997. MMWR Morb Mortal Wkly Rep. 1998;47:577; 565–567.

19a. Centers for Disease Control and Prevention. Provisional cases of selected notifiable diseases. MMWR Morb Mortal Wkly Rep. 1999;48:740.

20. Centers for Disease Control and Prevention. Case definitions for infectious conditions under public health surveillance. MMWR Morb Mortal Wkly Rep. 1997;46:11.
21. Centers for Disease Control and Prevention. Outbreaks of pseudoinfection with *Cyclospora* and *Cryptosporidium*. MMWR Morb Mortal Wkly Rep. 1997;46:354–358.
22. Ungar BLP, Mulligan M, Nutman TB. Serologic evidence of *Cryptosporidium* infection in US volunteers before and after Peace Corps service in Africa. Arch Intern Med. 1989;149:894–897.
23. Hayes EB, Matte TD, O'Brien TR, et al. Contamination of a conventionally treated filtered public water supply by *Cryptosporidium* associated with a large community outbreak of cryptosporidiosis. N Engl J Med. 1989;320:1372–1376.
24. Koch KL, Phillips DJ, Aber RC, et al. Cryptosporidiosis in hospital personnel: Evidence for person-to-person transmission. Ann Intern Med. 1984;102:593–596.
25. Ungar BLP, Gilman RH, Lanata CF, et al. Seroepidemiology of *Cryptosporidium* infection in two Latin American populations. J Infect Dis. 1988;157:551–555.
26. Zu S, Li J, Barrett L, et al. Seroepidemiologic study of *Cryptosporidium* infection in children from rural communities of Anhui, China and Fortaleza, Brazil. Am J Trop Med Hyg. 1994;51:1–10.
27. Newman R, Zu S, Wuhib T, et al. Household epidemiology of *Cryptosporidium parvum* infection in an urban community in Northeast Brazil. Ann Intern Med. 1994;120:500–505.
28. Janoff E, Mead P, Mead J, et al. Endemic *Cryptosporidium* and *Giardia* infections in a Thai orphanage. Am J Trop Med Hyg. 1990;43:248–256.
29. Kuhls T, Mosier D, Crawford D, et al. Seroprevalence of cryptosporidial antibodies during infancy, childhood and adolescence. Clin Infect Dis. 1994;18:731–735.
30. Lengerich E, Addiss D, Marx J, et al. Increased exposure to cryptosporidia among dairy farmers in Wisconsin. J Infect Dis. 1993;167:1252–1255.
31. Selik RM, Starcher ET, Curran JW. Opportunistic diseases in AIDS patients: Frequencies, associations and trends. AIDS. 1987;1:175–182.
32. Sorvillo F, Lieb L, Kerndt, et al. Epidemiology of cryptosporidiosis among persons with AIDS in Los Angeles County. Epidemiol Infect. 1994;113:313–320.
33. Juranek D. Cryptosporidiosis: Sources of infection and guidelines for prevention. Clin Infect Dis. 1995;21:S57–S61.
34. Pederson C, Danner S, Lazzarin A, et al. Epidemiology of cryptosporidiosis among European AIDS patients. Genitourin Med. 1996;72:128–131.
35. Laughon BE, Druckman DA, Vernon A, et al. Prevalence of enteric pathogens in homosexual men with and without acquired immunodeficiency syndrome. Gastroenterology. 1988;94:984–993.
36. Smith PD, Lane HC, Gill VJ, et al. Intestinal infections in patients with the acquired immunodeficiency syndrome. Ann Intern Med. 1988;108:328–333.
37. Moolasart P, Eampokalap B, Ratanasrithong M, et al. Cryptosporidiosis in HIV infected patients in Thailand. Southeast Asian J Trop Med Public Health. 1995;26:335–338.
38. Sewankambo N, Mugerwa RD, Goodgame R, et al. Enteropathic AIDS in Uganda. AIDS. 1987;1:9–13.
39. Colebunders R, Lusakumuni K, Nelson AM, et al. Persistent diarrhoea in Zairean AIDS patients. Gut. 1988;29:1687–1691.
40. Dias RMDS, Mangini ACS, Torres D, et al. Cryptosporidiosis among patients with acquired immunodeficiency syndrome in the county of Sao Paulo, Brazil. Rev Inst Med Trop Sao Paulo. 1988;30:310–312.
41. Miller RA, Bronsdon MA, Morton WR. Experimental cryptosporidiosis in a primate model. J Infect Dis. 1990;161:312–315.
42. Jokipii L, Jokipii AMM. Timing of symptoms and oocyst excretion in human cryptosporidiosis. N Engl J Med. 1986;315:1643–1647.
43. Combee CL, Collinge ML, Britt EM. Cryptosporidiosis in a hospital-associated day care center. Pediatr Infect Dis. 1986;5:528–532.
44. Ribiero CD, Palmer SR. Family outbreak of cryptosporidiosis. BMJ. 1986;292:377–380.
45. Collier AC, Miller RA, Meyers JD. Cryptosporidiosis after marrow transplantation: Person-to-person transmission and treatment with spiramycin. Ann Intern Med. 1984;101:205–206.
46. Soave R, Ma P. Cryptosporidiosis: Traveler's diarrhea in two families. Arch Intern Med. 1985;145:70–72.
47. Millard P, Gensheimer K, Addiss D, et al. An outbreak of cryptosporidiosis from fresh-pressed apple cider. JAMA. 1994;272:1592–1596.
48. MacKenzie W, Schell W, Blair K, et al. Massive outbreak of waterborne *Cryptosporidium* infection in Milwaukee, Wisconsin: Recurrence of illness and risk of secondary transmission. Clin Infect Dis. 1995;21:57–62.
49. Pohjola S, Oksanen H, Jokipii L, et al. Outbreak of cryptosporidiosis among veterinary students. Scand J Infect Dis. 1986;18:173–178.
50. Miron D, Kenes J, Dagan R. Calves as a source of an outbreak of cryptosporidiosis among young children in an agricultural closed community. Pediatr Infect Dis J. 1991;10:438–441.
51. Weitz JC, Tassara R, Mercado TMR, et al. Brote de cryptosporidiosis en un centro de recuperacion nutricional. Rev Chil Pediatr. 1987;58:50–53.
52. Stehr-Green JK, Juranek DJ, McCaig L, et al. Chickenpox and infection with cryptosporidiosis. Am J Dis Child. 1986;140:1213.
53. Diers J, McCallister GL. Occurrence of *Cryptosporidium* in home daycare centers in west-central Colorado. J Parasitol. 1989;75:637–638.
54. Addiss DG, Stewart JM, Finton RJ, et al. *Giardia lamblia* and *Cryptosporidium* infections in child day-care centers in Fulton County, Georgia. Pediatr Infect Dis J. 1991;10:907–911.
55. Crawford FG, Vermund SH, Ma JY, et al. Asymptomatic cryptosporidiosis in a New York City day care center. Pediatr Infect Dis. 1988;7:806–807.
56. Roncoroni AJ, Gomez MA, Mera J, et al. *Cryptosporidium* infection in renal transplant patients. J Infect Dis. 1989;160:559.
57. Ravn P, Lundgren JD, Kjaeldgaard P, et al. Nosocomial outbreak of cryptosporidiosis in AIDS patients. BMJ. 1991;302:277–280.
58. Martino P, Gentile G, Caprioli A, et al. Hospital-acquired cryptosporidiosis in a bone marrow transplantation unit. J Infect Dis. 1988;158:647–648.
59. Navarrete S, Stetler HC, Avila C, et al. An outbreak of *Cryptosporidium* diarrhea in a pediatric hospital. Pediatr Infect Dis J. 1991;10:248–250.
60. Wittenberg DF, Miller NM, Van den Ende J. Spiramycin is not effective in treating diarrhea in infants: Results of a double-blind randomized trial. J Infect Dis. 1989;159:131–132.
61. Foot A, Oakhill A, Mott M. Cryptosporidiosis and acute leukaemia. Arch Dis Child. 1990;65:236–238.
62. Heald A, Bartlett J. *Cryptosporidium* spread in a group residential home. Ann Intern Med. 1994;121:467–469.
63. Current WL, Reese NCV, Ernst JV, et al. Human cryptosporidiosis in immunocompetent and immunodeficient persons. N Engl J Med. 1983;308:1252–1257.
64. Hojlyng N, Holten-Anderson W, Jepsen S. Cryptosporidiosis: A case of airborne transmission. Lancet. 1988;2:271–272.

65. Lappin M, Ungar B, Brown-Hahn B, et al. Enzyme-linked immunosorbent assay for the detection of *Cryptosporidium parvum* IgG in the serum of cats. J Parasitol. 1997;83:957–960.
66. Jokipii L, Pohjola S, Jokipii A. *Cryptosporidium*: A frequent finding in patients with gastrointestinal symptoms. Lancet. 1983;2:358–360.
67. Jokipii AMM, Hemila M, Jokipii L. Prospective study of acquisition of *Cryptosporidium, Giardia lamblia*, and gastrointestinal illness. Lancet. 1985;2:487–489.
68. Gatti S, Cevini C, Bruno A, et al. Cryptosporidiosis in tourists returning from Egypt and the island of Mauritius. Clin Infect Dis. 1993;16:344–345.
69. Rose J, Gerba C, Jakubowski W. Survey of potable water supplies for *Cryptosporidium* and *Giardia*. Environ Sci Technol. 1991;25:1393–1400.
70. Le Chevallier M, Moser R. Occurrence of *Giardia* and *Cryptosporidium* in raw and finished drinking water. J Am Water Works Assoc. 1995;87:54–68.
71. Le Chevallier M, Norton W, Lee R. Occurrence of *Giardia* and *Cryptosporidium* spp in surface water supplies. Appl Environ Microbiol. 1991;57:2610–2616.
72. Rose J, Lisle J, LeChevallier M. Waterborne cryptosporidiosis: Incidence, outbreaks, and treatment strategies. In: Fayer R, ed. *Cryptosporidium* and cryptosporidiosis. Boca Raton, Fla: CRC Press; 1997:93–109.
73. Addiss D, Pond R, Remshak M, et al. Reduction of risk of watery diarrhea with point-of-use water filters during a massive outbreak of waterborne *Cryptosporidium* infection in Milwaukee, Wisconsin, 1993. Am J Trop Med Hyg. 1998;58:110–118.
74. Centers for Disease Control and Prevention. Assessing the public threat associated with waterborne cryptosporidiosis: Report of a workshop. MMWR Morb Mortal Wkly Rep. 1995;44:1–19.
75. D'Antonio RG, Winn RE, Taylor JP, et al. A waterborne outbreak of cryptosporidiosis in normal hosts. Ann Intern Med. 1985;103:886–888.
76. Richardson AJ, Frankenberg RA, Buck AC, et al. An outbreak of waterborne cryptosporidiosis in Swinton and Oxfordshire. Epidemiol Infect. 1991;107:485–495.
77. Clifford CP, Crook DWM, Conlon CP, et al. Impact of waterborne outbreak of cryptosporidiosis in AIDS and renal transplant patients. Lancet. 1990;335:1455–1456.
78. Moss D, Bennett S, Arrowood M, et al. Kinetic and isotypic analysis of specific immunoglobulins from crew members with cryptosporidiosis on a US Coast Guard cutter. J Eukaryot Microbiol. 1994;41:52S–55S.
79. Moore AC, Herwaldt BL, Craun GF, et al. Surveillance for waterborne disease outbreaks—United States, 1991–1992. MMWR Morb Mortal Wkly Rep. 1993;42(Suppl SS-5):1–22.
80. Dworkin M, Goldman D, Wells T, et al. Cryptosporidiosis in Washington state: An outbreak associated with well water. J Infect Dis. 1996;174:1372–1376.
81. Goldstein S, Juranek D, Ravenholt O, et al. Cryptosporidoiosis: An outbreak associated with drinking water despite state-of-the-art water treatment. Ann Intern Med. 1996;124:459–468.
82. Pozio E, Rezza G, Boschini A, et al. Clinical cryptosporidiosis and human immunodeficiency virus (HIV)-induced immunosuppression: Findings from a longitudinal study of HIV-positive and HIV-negative former injection drug users. J Infect Dis. 1997;176:969–975.
83. Kelly P, Baboo K, Ndubani P, et al. Cryptosporidiosis in adults in Lusaka, Zambia, and its relationship to oocyst contamination of drinking water. J Infect Dis. 1997;176:1120–1123.
84. Wuhib T, Silva T, Newman R, et al. Cryptosporidial and microsporidial infections in human immunodeficiency virus–infected patients in northeastern Brazil. J Infect Dis. 1994;170:494–497.
85. Centers for Disease Control and Prevention. Swimming-associated cryptosporidiosis—Los Angeles County. MMWR Morb Mortal Wkly Rep. 1990;39:343–345.
86. Centers for Disease Control and Prevention. *Cryptosporidium* infections associated with swimming pools Dane County, Wisconsin, 1993. MMWR Morb Mortal Wkly Rep. 1994;43:561–563.
87. Kramer M, Sorhage F, Goldstein S, et al. First reported outbreak in the United States of cryptosporidiosis associated with a recreational lake. Clin Infect Dis. 1998;26:27–33.
88. Centers for Disease Control and Prevention. Foodborne outbreak of diarrheal illness associated with *Cryptosporidium parvum*—Minnesota, 1995. MMWR Morb Mortal Wkly Rep. 1996;45:783–784.
89. Centers for Disease Control and Prevention. Outbreaks of *Escherichia coli* O157: H7 infection and cryptosporidiosis associated with drinking unpasteurized apple cider—Connecticut and New York, October, 1996. MMWR Morb Mortal Wkly Rep. 1997;46:4–8.
90. Ortega Y, Roxas C, Gilman R, et al. Isolation of *Cryptosporidium parvum* and *Cyclospora cayetanesis* from vegetables collected in markets of an endemic region in Peru. Am J Trop Med Hyg. 1997;57:683–686.
91. Laberge I, Griffiths M, Griffiths M. Prevalence, detection and control of *Cryptosporidium parvum* in food. Int J Food Microbiol. 1996;32:1–26.
92. Guarino A, Canani R, Casola A, et al. Human intestinal cryptosporidiosis: Secretory diarrhea and enterotoxic activity in Caco-2 cells. J Infect Dis. 1995;171:976–983.
93. Moore R, Tzipori S, Griffiths J, et al. Temporal changes in permeability and structure of piglet ileum after site-specific infection by *Cryptosporidium parvum*. Gastroenterology. 1995;108:1030–1039.
94. Kapel N, Huneau J, Magne D, et al. Cryptosporidiosis-induced impairment of ion transport and Na^+-glucose absorption in adult immunocompromised mice. J Infect Dis. 1997;176:834–837.
95. Adams R, Guerrant R, Zu S, et al. *Cryptosporidium parvum* infection of intestinal epithelium: Morphologic and functional studies in an in vitro model. J Infect Dis. 1994;169:170–177.
96. Griffiths J, Moore R, Dooley S, et al. *Cryptosporidium parvum* infection of Caco-2 cell monolayers induces an apical monolayer defect, selectively increases transmonolayer permeability, and causes epithelial cell death. Infect Immun. 1994;62:4506–4514.
97. Soave R, Danner RL, Honig CL, et al. Cryptosporidiosis in homosexual men. Ann Intern Med. 1984;100:504–511.
98. Modigliani R, Bories C, Charpentier YL, et al. Diarrhoea and malabsorption in acquired immune deficiency syndrome: A study of four cases with special emphasis on opportunistic protozoan infestations. Gut. 1985;26:179–187.
99. Buraud M, Forget E, Favennec L, et al. Sexual stage development of cryptosporidia in the Caco-2 cell line. Infect Immun. 1991;59:4610–4613.
100. Flanigan TP, Aji T, Marshall R, et al. Asexual development of *Cryptosporidium* within a differentiated human enterocyte cell line. Infect Immun. 1991;59:234–239.
101. Flanigan T, Marshall R, Redman D, et al. In vitro screening of therapeutic agents against *Cryptosporidium*: Hyperimmune cow colostrum is highly inhibitory. J Protozool. 1991;38:225S–227S.
102. Verdon R, Keusch G, Tzipori S, et al. An in vitro model of infection of human biliary epithelial cells by *Cryptosporidium parvum*. J Infect Dis. 1997;175:1268–1272.
103. Gut J, Petersen C, Nelson R, et al. *Cryptosporidium parvum* in vitro cultivation in Madin-Darby canine kidney cells. J Protozool. 1991;38:72S–73S.
104. Lindsay D. Laboratory models of cryptosporidiosis. In: Fayer R, ed. *Cryptosporidium* and cryptosporidiosis. Boca Raton, Fla: CRC Press; 1997:209–224.
105. Ungar BLP, Burris JA, Quinn CA, et al. New mouse models for chronic *Cryptosporidium* infection in immunodeficient hosts. Infect Immun. 1990;58:961–969.
106. Ungar BLP, Kao TC, Burris JA, et al. *Cryptosporidium* infection in an adult mouse model: Independent roles for IFN-gamma and $CD4^+$ T lymphocytes in protective immunity. J Immunol. 1991;147:1014–1022.
107. Mead JR, Arrowood MJ, Sidwell RW, et al. Chronic *Cryptosporidium parvum* infections in congenitally immunodeficient SCID and nude mice. J Infect Dis. 1991;163:1297–1304.
108. Mead J, Ilksoy N, You X, et al. Infection dynamics and clinical features of cryptosporidiosis in SCID mice. Infect Immun. 1994;62:1691–1695.
109. Riggs M. Immunology: Host response and development of passive immunotherapy and vaccines. In: Fayer R, ed. *Cryptosporidium* and cryptosporidiosis. Boca Raton, Fla: CRC; 1997:129–162.
110. Rehg J. Effect of interferon-gamma in experimental *Cryptosporidium parvum* infection. J Infect Dis. 1996;174:229–232.
111. Chen W, Harp J, Harmsen A, et al. Gamma interferon functions in resistance to *Cryptosporidium parvum*. Infection in severe combined immunodeficient mice. Infect Immun. 1993;61:3548–3551.
112. Chen W, Harp J, Harmsen A, et al. Requirements for CD4 cells and gamma interferon in resolution of established *Cryptosporidium parvum* infection in mice. Infect Immun. 1993;61:3928–3931.
113. Tzipori S, Rand W, Theodos C. Evaluation of a two-phase SCID mouse model preconditioned with anti–interferon-gamma monoclonal antibody for drug testing against *Cryptosporidium parvum*. J Infect Dis. 1995;172:1160–1164.
114. McDonald V, Bancroft G. Mechanisms of innate and acquired resistance to *Cryptosporidium parvum* infection in SCID mice. Parasite Immunol. 1994;16:315–317.
115. Perryman L, Mason P, Chrisp C. Effect of spleen cell populations on resolution of *Cryptosporidium parvum* infection in SCID mice. Infect Immun. 1994;62:1474–1478.
116. Waters W, Harp J. Infection in T-cell receptor-(TCR) alpha and TCR-delta–deficient mice. Infect Immun. 1996;64:1854–1857.
117. Aguirre S, Mason P, Perryman L. Susceptibility of major histocompatibility complex (MHC) class I–and MHC class-II–deficient mice to *Cryptosporidium parvum* infection. Infect Immun. 1994;62:697–699.
118. Abrahamsen M, Lancto C, Walcheck B, et al. Localization of alpha/beta and gamma/delta T-lymphocytes in *Cryptosporidium parvum*–infected tissues in naïve and immune calves. Infect Immun. 1997;65:2428–2433.
119. Urban J, Fayer R, Chen S, et al. IL-12 protects immunocompetent and immunodeficient neonatal mice against infection with *Cryptosporidium parvum*. J Immunol. 1996;156:263–268.
120. Jenkins M, Petersen C. Molecular biology of *Cryptosporidium*. In: Fayer R, ed. *Cryptosporidium* and cryptosporidiosis. Boca Raton, Fla: CRC Press; 1997:225–232.
121. Riggs MW, McGuire TC, Mason PH, et al. Neutralization-sensitive epitopes are exposed on the surface of infectious *Cryptosporidium parvum* sporozoites. J Immunol. 1989;143:1340–1345.
122. Ungar BLP, Nash TE. Quantification of specific antibody response to *Cryptosporidium* antigens by laser densitometry. Infect Immun. 1986;53:124–128.
123. Bjorneby JM, Riggs MW, Perryman LE. *Cryptosporidium parvum* merozoites share neutralization-sensitive epitopes with sporozoites. J Immunol. 1990;145:298–304.
124. Blunt D, Khramtsov N, Upton S, et al. Molecular karyotype analysis of *Cryptosporidium parvum*: Evidence for eight chromosomes and a low-molecular-size molecule. Clin Diagn Lab Immunol. 1997;4:11–13.
125. Miller RA, Bronsdon MA, Morton WR. Failure of breast-feeding to prevent *Cryptosporidium* infection in a primate model. J Infect Dis. 1991;164:826–827.
126. Sterling C, Gilman R, Sinclair N, et al. The role of breast milk in protecting urban Peruvian children against cryptosporidiosis. J Protozool. 1991;38:23S–25S.
127. Molbak K, Aaby P, Hojlyng N, et al. Risk factors for *Cryptosporidium* diarrhea in early childhood: A case-control study from Guinea-Bissau, West Africa. Am J Epidemiol. 1994;139:734–740.

128. Chappell C. Susceptibility and serologic response of healthy adults to reinfection with *Cryptosporidium parvum*. Infect Immun. 1998;66:441–443.
129. Centers for Disease Control and Prevention. Cryptosporidiosis: An assessment of chemotherapy of males with acquired immune deficiency syndrome (AIDS). MMWR Morb Mortal Wkly Rep. 1982;31:589–592.
130. Gentile G, Venditti M, Micozzi A, et al. Cryptosporidiosis in patients with hematologic malignancies. Rev Infect Dis. 1991;13:842–846.
131. Fafard J, Lalonde R. Long-standing symptomatic cryptosporidiosis in a normal man: Clinical response to spiramycin. J Clin Gastroenterol. 1990;12:190–191.
132. Edelman MJ, Oldfield EC. Severe cryptosporidiosis in an immunocompetent host. Arch Intern Med. 1988;148:1873–1874.
133. Connolly GM, Gazzard BG. Toxic megacolon in cryptosporidiosis. Postgrad Med J. 1987;63:1103–1104.
134. Meyers SA, Kuhlman JE, Fishman EK. Enterovesical fistula in a patient with cryptosporidiosis and AIDS. Clin Imaging. 1990;14:143–145.
135. Bartlett JG, Belitsos PC, Sears C, et al. AIDS enteropathy. Clin Infect Dis. 1992;15:726–735.
136. Teixidor HS, Godwin TS, Ramirez EA. Cryptosporidiosis of the biliary tract in AIDS. Radiology. 1991;180:51–56.
137. Benhamou Y, Caumes E, Gerosa Y, et al. AIDS-related cholangiopathy. Dig Dis Sci. 1993;38:1113–1115.
138. Margulis SJ, Honig CL, Soave R, et al. Biliary tract obstruction in the acquired immunodeficiency syndrome. Ann Intern Med. 1986;105:207–210.
139. Pol S, Romana C, Richard S, et al. Microsporidia infection in patients with the human immunodeficiency virus and unexplained cholangitis. N Engl J Med. 1993;328:95–99.
140. Blanshard C, Jackson A, Shanson D, et al. Cryptosporidiosis in HIV-seropositive patients. Q J Med. 1992;85:813–823.
141. Forbes A, Blanshard C, Gazzard B. Natural history of AIDS-related sclerosing cholangitis: A study of 20 cases. Gut. 1993;34:116–121.
142. Hamour A, Bonnington A, Hawthorne B, et al. Successful treatment of AIDS-related cryptosporidial sclerosing cholangitis. AIDS. 1993;7:1449–1451.
143. Hawkins SP, Thomas RP, Tesdate C. Acute pancreatitis: A new finding in *Cryptosporidium* enteritis. BMJ. 1987;294:483–484.
144. Miller TL, Winter HS, Luginbuhl LM, et al. Pancreatitis in pediatric human immunodeficiency virus infection. J Pediatr. 1992;120:223–227.
145. Fredenucci I, Chomarat N, Boucaud C, et al. Acute pancreatitis associated with *Cryptosporidium parvum* enteritis in an immunocompetent man. Clin Infect Dis. 1998;27:233–234.
146. Hojlyng N, Jensen BN. Respiratory cryptosporidiosis in HIV-positive patients. Lancet. 1987;1:590–591.
147. Davis JJ, Heyman MB. Cryptosporidiosis and sinusitis in an immunodeficient adolescent. J Infect Dis. 1988;158:649.
148. Harari MD, West B, Dwyer B. *Cryptosporidium* as a cause of laryngotracheitis in an infant. Lancet. 1983;1:1207.
149. Jensen B, Gerstoft J, Hojlyng N, et al. Pulmonary pathogens in HIV-infected patients. Scand J Infect Dis. 1990;22:413–420.
150. Mohri H, Fujita H, Asakura Y, et al. Inhalation therapy of paromomycin is effective for respiratory infection and hypoxia by *Cryptosporidium* with AIDS. Am J Med Sci. 1995;309:60–62.
151. Dupont C, Bougnoux M, Turner L, et al. Microbiological findings about pulmonary cryptosporidiosis in two AIDS patients. J Clin Microbiol. 1996;34:227–229.
152. Ditrich O, Palkovic L, Sterba J, et al. The first finding of *Cryptosporidium baileyi* in man. Parasitol Res. 1991;77:44–47.
153. Hay EM, Winfield J, McKendrick MW. Reactive arthritis associated with *Cryptosporidium* enteritis. BMJ. 1987;295:248.
154. Shepherd RC, Smail PJ, Sinha GP. Reactive arthritis complicating cryptosporidial infection. Arch Dis Child. 1989;64:743–744.
155. Cron R, Sherry D. Reiter's syndrome associated with cryptosporidial gastroenteritis. J Rheumatol. 1995;10:1962–1963.
156. Gentile G, Baldassarri L, Caprioli A, et al. Colonic vascular invasion as a possible route of extraintestinal cryptosporidiosis. Am J Med. 1987;82:574–575.
157. Esteban J, Aguirre C, Flores A, et al. High *Cryptosporidium* prevalences in healthy Aymara children from the northern Bolivian altiplano. Am J Trop Med Hyg. 1998;58:50–55.
158. Pettoello-Mantovani M, Di Martino L, Dettori G, et al. Asymptomatic carriage of intestinal *Cryptosporidium* in immunocompetent and immunodeficient children: A prospective study. Pediatr Infect Dis J. 1995;14:1042–1047.
159. Roberts WG, Green PH, Ma J, et al. Prevalence of cryptosporidiosis in patients undergoing endoscopy: Evidence for an asymptomatic carrier state. Am J Med. 1989;87:537–539.
160. Gentile G, Caprioli A, Donelli G, et al. Asymptomatic carriage of *Cryptosporidium* in two patients with leukemia. Am J Infect Control. 1990;18:127–128.
161. Saltzberg DM, Kotloff KL, Newman JL, et al. *Cryptosporidium* infection in acquired immunodeficiency syndrome: Not always a poor prognosis. J Clin Gastroenterol. 1991;13:94–97.
162. Kamel A, Maning N, Arulmainathan S. Cryptosporidiosis among HIV-positive intravenous drug users in Malaysia. Southeast Asian J Trop Med Public Health. 1994;25:650–653.
163. Chappell C, Okhuysen P, Sterling C, et al. *Cryptosporidium parvum*: Intensity of infection and oocyst excretion patterns in healthy volunteers. J Infect Dis. 1996;173:232–236.
164. Vajro P, Martino L, Scotti S, et al. Intestinal *Cryptosporidium* carriage in two liver-transplanted children. J Pediatr Gastroenterol Nutr. 1991;12:139.
165. Van Deutekom H. Immunodeficiency with hyper-immunoglobulin M in an infant who had cryptosporidiosis associated with interferon-gamma deficiency. Clin Infect Dis. 1996;23:1337–1338.
166. Gledhill JA, Porter J. Diarrhoea due to *Cryptosporidium* infection in thalassaemia major. BMJ. 1990;301:212–213.
167. Chan AW, MacFarlane IA, Rhodes JM. Cryptosporidiosis as a cause of chronic diarrhoea in a patient with insulin-dependent diabetes mellitus. J Infect. 1989;19:293.
168. Gomez Morales M, Ausiello C, Guarino A, et al. Severe, protracted intestinal cryptosporidiosis associated with interferon gamma deficiency: Pediatric case report. Clin Infect Dis. 1996;22:848–850.
169. Sarabia-Arce S, Salazar-Lindo E, Gilman RH, et al. Case-control study of *Cryptosporidium parvum* infection in Peruvian children hospitalized for diarrhea. Pediatr Infect Dis J. 1990;9:627–631.
170. Molbak K, Andersen M, Aaby P, et al. *Cryptosporidium* infection in infancy as a cause of malnutrition: A community study from Guinea-Bissau, West Africa. Am J Clin Nutr. 1997;65:149–152.
171. MacFarlane DE, Horner-Bryce J. Cryptosporidiosis in well-nourished and malnourished children. Acta Paediatr Scand. 1987;76:474–477.
172. Sallon S, Deckelbaum RJ, Schmid II, et al. *Cryptosporidium*, malnutrition, and chronic diarrhea in children. Am J Dis Child. 1988;142:312–315.
173. Centers for Disease Control and Prevention. Classification system for human T-lymphotrophic virus type III/lymphadenopathy-associated virus infections. MMWR Morb Mortal Wkly Rep. 1986;35:334–339.
174. Flanigan T, Whalen C, Turner J, et al. *Cryptosporidium* infection and CD4 counts. Ann Intern Med. 1992;116:840–842.
175. Crowe SM, Carlin JB, Stewart KI, et al. Predictive value of CD4 lymphocyte numbers for the development of opportunistic infections and malignancies in HIV-infected persons. J AIDS. 1991;4:770–776.
176. Ungar BLP, Soave R, Fayer R, et al. Enzyme immunoassay detection of immunoglobulin M and G antibodies to *Cryptosporidium* in immunocompetent and immunocompromised persons. J Infect Dis. 1986;153:570–578.
177. Cozon G, Biron F, Jeannin M, et al. Secretory IgA antibodies to *Cryptosporidium parvum* in AIDS patients with chronic cryptosporidiosis. J Infect Dis. 1994;169:696–699.
178. Flanigan T. Human immunodeficiency virus infection and cryptosporidiosis protective immune responses. Am J Trop Med Hyg. 1994;50:29–34.
179. Benhamou Y, Kapel N, Hoang C, et al. Inefficacy of intestinal secretory immune response to *Cryptosporidium* in acquired immunodeficiency syndrome. Gastroenterology. 1995;108:627–633.
180. Campbell PN, Current WL. Demonstration of serum antibodies to *Cryptosporidium* sp in normal and immunodeficient humans with confirmed infections. J Clin Microbiol. 1983;18:165–169.
181. Arrowood M. Diagnosis. In: Fayer R, ed. *Cryptosporidium* and cryptosporidiosis. Boca Raton, Fla.: CRC Press; 1997:43–64.
182. Moss D, Bennett S, Arrowood M, et al. Enzyme-linked immunoelectrotransfer blot analysis of a cryptosporidiosis outbreak on a United States Coast Guard cutter. Am J Trop Med Hyg. 1998;58:110–118.
183. Crabb J. Antibody-based immunotherapy of cryptosporidiosis. Adv Parasitol. 1998;40:122–151.
184. Greenberg P, Koch J, Cello J. Diagnosis of *Cryptosporidium parvum* in patients with severe diarrhea and AIDS. Dig Dis Sci. 1996;41:2286–2290.
185. Ma P, Soave R. Three-step stool examination for cryptosporidiosis in 10 homosexual men with protracted watery diarrhea. J Infect Dis. 1983;147:824–828.
186. Ungar BLP. Enzyme-linked immunoassay for detection of *Cryptosporidium* antigens in fecal specimens. J Clin Microbiol. 1990;28:2491–2495.
187. Sterling CR, Arrowood MJ. Detection of *Cryptosporidium* sp infections using a direct immunofluorescent assay. Pediatr Infect Dis. 1986;5:139–142.
188. Weber R, Bryan RT, Bishop HS, et al. Threshold of detection of *Cryptosporidium* oocysts in human stool specimens: Evidence for low sensitivity of current diagnostic methods. J Clin Microbiol. 1991;29:1323–1327.
189. Valdez L, Dang H, Okhuysen P, et al. Flow cytometric detection of *Cryptosporidium* oocysts in human stool samples. J Clin Microbiol. 1997;35:2013–2017.
190. Laxer MA, Timblin BK, Patel RJ. DNA sequences for the detection of *Cryptosporidium parvum* by the polymerase chain reaction. Am J Trop Med Hyg. 1991;45:688–694.
191. Webster K, Smith H, Giles M, et al. Detection of *Cryptosporidium parvum* oocysts in faeces: Comparison of conventional coproscopical methods and the polymerase chain reaction. Vet Parasitol. 1996;61:5–9.
192. Leng X, Mosier D, Oberst R. Simplified method for recovery and PCR detection of *Cryptosporidium* DNA from bovine feces. Appl Environ Microbiol. 1996;62:643–646.
193. Zhu G, Marchewka M, Ennis J, et al. Direct isolation of DNA from patient stools for polymerase chain reaction detection of *Cryptosporidium parvum*. J Infect Dis. 1998;177:1443–1446.
194. Mayer C, Palmer C. Evaluation of PCR, nested PCR, and fluorescent antibodies for the detection of *Giardia* and *Cryptosporidium* species in wastewater. Appl Environ Microbiol. 1996;62:2081–2084.
195. Sluter S, Tzipori S, Widmer G. Parameters affecting polymerase chain reaction detection of waterborne *Cryptosporidium parvum* oocysts. Appl Microbiol Biotechnol. 1997;48:325–330.
196. Johnson D, Pieniazek N, Griffin D, et al. Development of a PCR protocol for sensitive detection of *Cryptosporidium* oocysts in water samples. Appl Environ Microbiol. 1995;61:3849–3851.
197. Wagner-Wiening C, Kimmig P. Detection of viable *Cryptosporidium parvum* oocysts by PCR. Appl Environ Microbiol. 1995;61:4514–4516.

198. Johnson D, Pieniazek N, Griffin D, et al. Development of a PCR protocol for sensitive detection of *Cryptosporidium* oocysts in water samples. Appl Environ Microbiol. 1995;61:3849–3851.
199. Blagburn B, Soave R. Prophylaxis and chemotherapy: Human and animal. In: Fayer R, ed. *Cryptosporidium* and cryptosporidiosis. Boca Raton, Fla: CRC Press; 1997:111–128.
200. Woods K, Nesterenko M, Upton S. Efficacy of 101 antimicrobials and other agents on the development of *Cryptosporidium parvum* in vitro. Ann Trop Med Parasitol. 1996;6:603–615.
201. Cello JP, Grendell JH, Basuk P, et al. Effect of octreotide on refractory AIDS-associated diarrhea—a prospective, multicenter clinical trial. Ann Intern Med. 1991;115:705–710.
202. Clotet B, Sirera G, Cofan F, et al. Efficacy of the somatostatin analogue, sandostatin, for cryptosporidial diarrhea in patients with AIDS. AIDS. 1989;3:857–858.
203. Romeu J, Miro JM, Sirera G, et al. Efficacy of octreotide in the management of chronic diarrhea in AIDS. 1991;5:1495–1499.
204. Connolly GM, Youle M, Gazzard BG. Diclazuril in the treatment of severe cryptosporidial diarrhoea in AIDS patients. AIDS. 1990;4:700–701.
205. Vargas S, Shenep J, Flynn P, et al. Azithromycin for treatment of severe *Cryptosporidium* diarrhea in two children with cancer. J Pediatr. 1993;1:154–156.
206. Bessette R, Amsden G. Treatment of non-HIV cryptosporidial diarrhea with azithromycin. Ann Pharmacother. 1995;10:991–993.
207. Hicks P, Zweiner R, Squires J, et al. Azithromycin therapy for *Cryptosporidium parvum* infection in four children infected with human immunodeficiency virus. J Pediatr. 1996;129:297–300.
208. Dunne M, Williams D, Young L. Azithromycin and the treatment of opportunistic infections. Rev Contemp Pharmacother. 1994;5:373–378.
209. Blanshard C, Shanson D, Gazzard B. Pilot studies of azithromycin, letrazuril, and paromomycin in the treatment of cryptosporidiosis. Int J STD AIDS. 1997;8:124–129.
210. Cama V, Marshall M, Shubitz L, et al. Treatment of acute and chronic *Cryptosporidium parvum* infections in mice using clarithromycin and 14-OH clarithromycin. J Eukaryot Microbiol. 1994;41:25S.
211. Jordan E. Clarithromycin prophylaxis against *Cryptosporidium* enteritis in patients with AIDS. J Natl Med Assoc. 1996;88:425–427.
212. Bissuel F, Cotte L, Rabodonirina M, et al. Paromomycin: An effective treatment for cryptosporidial diarrhea in patients with AIDS. Clin Infect Dis. 1994;18:447–449.
213. Flanigan T, Ramratnam B, Graeber C, et al. Prospective trial of paromomycin for cryptosporidiosis in AIDS. Am J Med. 1996;100:370–372.
214. Scaglia M, Atzori C, Marchetti G, et al. Effectiveness of aminosidine (paromomycin) sulfate in chronic *Cryptosporidium* diarrhea in AIDS patients: An open, uncontrolled, prospective, clinical trial. J Infect Dis. 1994;170:1349–1350.
215. Rehg J. Comparison of anticryptosporidial activity of paromomycin with that of other aminoglycosides and azithromycin in immunosuppressed rats. J Infect Dis. 1994;170:934–938.
216. Tzipori S, Rand W, Griffiths J, et al. Evaluation of an animal model system for cryptosporidiosis: Therapeutic efficacy of paromomycin and hyperimmune bovine colostrum-immunoglobulin. Clin Diagn Lab Immunol. 1994;1:450–463.
217. Tzipori S, Griffiths J, Theodos C. Paromomycin treatment against cryptosporidiosis in patients with AIDS. J Infect Dis. 1995;171:1069–1070.
218. Armitage K, Flanigan T, Carey J, et al. Treatment of cryptosporidiosis with paromomycin. Arch Intern Med. 1992;152:2497–2499.
219. Fichtenbaum CJ, Ritchie DJ, Powderly WG. Use of paromomycin for treatment of cryptosporidiosis in patients with AIDS. Clin Infect Dis. 1993;16:298–300.
220. Clezy K, Gold J, Blaze J, et al. Paromomycin for the treatment of cryptosporidial diarrhea in AIDS patients. AIDS. 1991;5:1146–1147.
221. White A, Chappell C, Hayat C, et al. Paromomycin for cryptosporidiosis in AIDS: A prospective, double-blind trial. J Infect Dis. 1994;170:419–422.
222. Duombo O, Rossignol J, Pichard E, et al. Nitazoxanide in the treatment of cryptosporidial diarrhea and other intestinal parasitic infections associated with aquired immunodeficiency syndrome in tropical Africa. Am J Trop Med Hyg. 1997;56:637–639.
223. Greenberg RE, Mir R, Bank S, et al. Resolution of intestinal cryptosporidiosis after treatment of AIDS with AZT. Gastroenterology. 1989;97:1327–1330.
224. Chandrasekar PH. "Cure" of chronic cryptosporidiosis during treatment with azidothymidine in a patient with the acquired immune deficiency syndrome. Am J Med. 1987;83:187.
225. Kuhls T, Orlicek S, Mosier D, et al. Enteral human serum immunoglobulin treatment of cryptosporidiosis in mice with severe combined immunodeficiency. Infect Immun. 1995;63:3582–3586.
226. Borowitz S, Saulsbury F. Treatment of chronic cryptosporidial infection with orally administered human serum immune globulin. J Pediatr. 1991;119:593–595.
227. Tzipori S, Robertson D, Cooper DA, et al. Chronic cryptosporidial diarrhoea and hyperimmune cow colostrum. Lancet. 1987;2:344–345.
228. Ungar BLP, Ward DJ, Fayer RF, et al. Cessation of *Cryptosporidium*-associated diarrhea in an acquired immunodeficiency patient after treatment with hyperimmune bovine colostrum. Gastroenterology. 1990:98:486–489.
229. Greenberg PD, Cello J. Treatment of severe diarrhea caused by *Cryptosporidium parvum* with oral bovine immunoglobulin concentrate in patients with AIDS. J Acquir Immune Defic Syndr Hum Retrovirol. 1996;13:348–354.
230. Okhuysen P, Chappell C, Crabb J, et al. Prophylactic effect of bovine anti-*Cryptosporidium* hyperimmune colostrum immunoglobulin in healthy volunteers challenged with *Cryptosporidium parvum*. Clin Infect Dis. 1998;26:1324–1329.

Chapter 273

Isospora belli, Sarcocystis Species, *Blastocystis hominis,* and *Cyclospora*

JAY S. KEYSTONE
PHYLLIS KOZARSKY

ISOSPORA BELLI

Isospora belli, first described in 1915,[1, 2] is a coccidian protozoal parasite taxonomically related to *Cryptosporidium, Toxoplasma,* and *Cyclospora.* This enteric pathogen is thought to be the only *Isospora* species that infects humans, the organism's only known host.[3] Ingestion of infectious sporulated oocysts results in the release of sporozoites that penetrate mucosal epithelial cells of the proximal small intestine, where they develop into trophozoites.[4–6] Asexual multiplication is followed by a sexual cycle in which immature, unsporulated oocysts are passed in the feces. Within 2 to 3 days, oocysts are infective as sporulation occurs, resulting in a mature elliptic oocyst (22 to 33 × 12 to 15 μm) that contains two sporocysts each with four sporozoites.[7] Oocysts can remain viable in the environment for months. Infection is presumed to result from the ingestion of food and water contaminated with human feces.

Isospora is found predominantly in tropical and subtropical climates, especially in South America, Africa, and Southeast Asia.[7–9] In the United States, isosporiasis has been associated with human immunodeficiency virus infection, immigration from Latin America,[10, 11] daycare centers, and mental institutions.[7, 9] In patients with acquired immunodeficiency syndrome (AIDS), *I. belli* infection accounts for approximately 2 to 3% of AIDS-defining illness and is rarely identified as a cause of chronic diarrhea in this population,[12, 13] likely because of the widespread use of trimethoprim-sulfamethoxazole used to prevent *Pneumocystis carinii* pneumonia.[10] In contrast, in developing countries, *I. belli* infections are frequently associated with chronic diarrhea in AIDS patients, occurring in 17 to 19% of these patients in Haiti,[14, 15] 19% in Democratic Republic of Congo (formerly Zaire),[13, 16] 14 to 16% in Zambia,[17, 18] and 10% in Brazil.[19]

As a rule, the clinical illness resulting from *I. belli* infection is dependent on the competence of the host's immune system. In immunocompetent hosts, illness is indistinguishable from other noninflammatory intestinal infections such as giardiasis, cryptosporiasis, cyclosporiasis, and enterotoxigenic *Escherichia coli* infection. After an incubation period of approximately 1 week, patients present with self-limited diarrheal illness (lasting 2 to 3 weeks) characterized by malaise, anorexia, weight loss, abdominal cramps, and profuse watery diarrhea without blood.[20, 21] Fever is uncommon and is usually low grade. Oocyst shedding may persist for several weeks after recovery.[22, 23] Rarely, in the immunocompetent patient, chronic persistent or intermittent symptoms may continue for many years.[5, 24] In contrast, in immunocompromised hosts, including patients with AIDS,[25–27] patients with a malignancy,[28, 29] and patients on cytotoxic therapy,[30] protracted, severe diarrheal illness, including hemorrhagic colitis,[31] may result; dehydration and debilitation may be life-threatening. Disseminated extraintestinal disease has occurred in two patients.[32, 33] Other rare, atypical presentations include acalculous cholecystitis and reactive arthritis.[34, 35]

The pathogenesis of isosporiasis has not been determined but may be due to cell damage from direct consequences of parasite invasion, cell-mediated inflammation, or proteins and oxidants released from mast cells.[36] Histologic examination of the small bowel of infected patients is relatively nonspecific and reveals villous atrophy, crypt hyperplasia, and lamina propria infiltration with inflammatory cells, particularly eosinophils.[4, 5] Asexual and sexual stages of the parasite are identified within parasitophorous vacuoles of enterocytes. Damage to villous absorptive cells has been associated with reports of malabsorption.[5, 25, 27]

Typically, *I. belli* infection is diagnosed by identification of oocysts in stool in wet mounts[8, 24] or acid-fast stained fecal smears[37] made from stool concentrates using flotation or sedimentation methods.[38] Direct or concentrated wet mounts are preferable to permanent stain smears because oocysts are difficult to detect in polyvinyl alcohol–preserved stool specimens.[39, 40] Auramine-rhodamine and heated safranin-methylene blue stains may also be used.[38, 41] Ultraviolet autofluorescence microscopy is a simple, rapid, and sensitive diagnostic method that is based on the detection of *Isospora* oocyst (blue) autofluorescence when a 330- to 380-mm ultraviolet filter is used.[42] Because *I. belli* parasites are shed intermittently in low numbers, multiple stool examinations may be required for diagnosis.[8, 24] Duodenal aspirates,[43] the string test,[25] and small bowel biopsies[4] may be helpful. Peripheral blood eosinophilia and Charcot-Leyden crystals in stool have been reported.[4, 5]

AIDS patients with isosporiasis usually respond to antimicrobial therapy within several days.[14, 15] Trimethoprim-sulfamethoxazole (160 mg of trimethoprim and 800 mg of sulfamethoxazole), the drug of choice, is administered four times daily for 10 days.[14, 15] In patients with AIDS, lifelong suppressive therapy is recommended because of the 50% chance of recurrence within 6 to 8 weeks of discontinuing initial treatment.[10] Long-term trimethoprim-sulfamethoxazole therapy is efficacious when taken daily or three times each week.[10] When sulfamethoxazole intolerance is present, pyrimethamine alone (75 mg/day) together with folinic acid (10 to 25 mg/day) has been used successfully.[44] Anecdotal case reports suggest that diclazuril,[45, 46] roxithromycin,[47] nitazoxanide,[48] and a combination of albendazole and ornidazole[49] may be effective. Isolated reports indicating that metronidazole, quinacrine, and furazolidone may be effective have not yet been substantiated.[25, 26, 29]

SARCOCYSTIS SPECIES

Sarcocystis is a zoonotic coccidian protozoal parasite that has an obligatory two-host cycle. In the definitive host (usually a carnivore) sexual reproduction occurs in the intestinal mucosa and results in the shedding of oocysts and infective sporocysts in the feces. After the ingestion of sporocysts by the intermediate host (usually a herbivore) and gut penetration, asexual multiplication occurs in vascular endothelial cells. Subsequent hematogenous dissemination leads to invasion of cardiac or striated muscle cells, where characteristic septate cysts (sarcocysts) develop. The cycle is complete when muscle cysts are eaten by an appropriate definitive host. Although more than 120 species of *Sarcocystis* have been reported from a wide range of domestic and wild animals, the definitive and intermediate hosts are known for only 56[50] through the ingestion of poorly cooked or raw meat. Humans may serve as definitive hosts for pork and cattle *Sarcocystis*, excreting fecal oocysts, previously incorrectly referred to as *Isospora hominis*. Humans may also serve as incidental intermediate hosts when food or water contaminated with fecal sporocysts is ingested.[51]

Although worldwide in distribution, most human cases have been reported from Southeast Asia.[51–55] Muscle *Sarcocystis* is most often an incidental finding[51, 53]; however, clinical manifestations consisting of myalgia, fever, and associated eosinophilia have been reported rarely[55, 56] Muscle cysts vary greatly in size, with diameters from below 50 to 325 μm, and cyst lengths up to 5 cm.[51, 57] Differentiation from morphologically indistinguishable *T. gondii* has been achieved by riboprint analysis and a surface antigen gene polymerase chain reaction.[58] Naturally occurring gastrointestinal illness, when humans act as definitive hosts, is also rare. In human volunteers, mild self-limited gastrointestinal illness has resulted from the ingestion of pork or beef containing *Sarcocystis* spp.[57] Segmental eosinophilic and necrotizing enteritis due to sexual forms of *Sarcocystis* has been reported; however, the cause was not clear-cut owing to the rarity of the organisms and the inability to exclude *I. belli* in these cases.[59] No specific treatment for *Sarcocystis* infection is known. In acute disease of sheep and goats, oxytetracycline, but not cotrimoxazole, prevented death.[56] Corticosteroids should provide symptomatic relief in cases of eosinophilic myositis.

BALANTIDIUM COLI

Balantidium coli, a ciliate, is the largest and possibly least common protozoal pathogen of humans.[60] In its usual habitat, the colon, it is found as a trophozoite and cyst; the latter is the infective form that resists the external environment.[61] The oval trophozoite usually measures 10 to 15 μm, but may reach 200 μm in length. Its surface is covered with tiny cilia that propel it through the intestinal lumen. Although *B. coli* is found in many mammals, pigs are considered to be the main reservoir for human infection, with prevalence rates of 40 to 90%.[61, 62] The infection is often acquired from the ingestion of pig excrement used in fertilizer, contaminating water supplies, or during handling of the animal. *B. coli* has a worldwide distribution but is most frequently reported from Latin America, Southeast Asia, and Papua New Guinea.[61, 62] In humans, the prevalence is usually less than 1%; high rates have been reported in hyperendemic areas and residential institutions.

Poor nutrition and achlorhydria appear to be predisposing factors, because humans are usually resistant to infection.[61–63] Disease results when the organism invades the colonic mucosa, producing necrosis and ulceration similar to that found in invasive amebiasis.

Although most infections are asymptomatic, clinical manifestations usually include a chronic course characterized by intermittent diarrhea, abdominal pain, and weight loss or, rarely, a more fulminant colitis in which stools contain blood and mucus.[61, 64, 65] The latter may result in intestinal perforation and extraintestinal spread to liver and mesenteric lymph nodes[61, 62, 66] The differential diagnosis includes amebic colitis, bacterial dysentery, and inflammatory bowel disease. Infection can be diagnosed by finding the rapidly motile trophozoite in fresh or preserved stool or from scrapings of the periphery of ulcers detected on sigmoidoscopic examination. Cysts are infrequently detected in stool.[61, 62] Tetracycline is the treatment of choice, but other drugs such as iodoquinol, metronidazole, paromomycin, and nitazoxanide have been used successfully.[67–69]

BLASTOCYSTIS HOMINIS

Despite many years of debate since *Blastocystis hominis* was first described, not a single issue about this protozoal intestinal infection has been satisfactorily resolved.[70, 71] The taxonomy of the organism remains controversial, and it is still unclear whether more than one species is present in humans and animals.[72–74] Morphologically, considerable variability occurs, with the organism measuring 3 to 30 μm. In culture, three major forms predominate: vacuolar, granular, and ameboid.[70] Although previously the vacuolated form (usually 10 to 15 μm) was detected most frequently in fecal specimens, more recent studies suggest that smaller forms, including a multivacuolar and cyst form, may be more common.[75–77] The newly described multilayered, thick-walled cyst measures 3 to 10 μm.[73, 78]

The prevalence of blastocystosis appears to be higher in developing countries (30 to 50%) than in developed countries (1.5 to 10%) and has been associated with travel.[79–83] Evidence that *B. hominis* is causally linked to intestinal disease is based on numerous case reports and uncontrolled or retrospective series in which infection was associated with acute or chronic diarrhea, bloating, flatulence, abdominal cramps, and fatigue.[79, 84–86] The few studies in which asymptomatic controls were included have provided little support for a pathogenic role of the parasite.[80, 87–91] However, several experimental studies support its pathogenicity including work in animal models[92, 93] and cell cultures.[94] Also, it has been hypothesized that there may be virulent and avirulent strains of *B. hominis* on the basis of antigen, isoenzyme, and DNA analysis.[74, 88, 95–98] In spite of numerous studies, the pathogenicity of the organism remains in doubt because of the difficulty in applying the results of animal models to humans, the uncertainty that other causes of symptoms have been eliminated in case series, and the inability of case-control studies to determine the association of a low-grade pathogen with disease.[84] Diagnosis is based on stool examination, preferably using permanent smears for microscopic diagnosis.[99, 100] Concentration methods have been shown to cause disruption of the organism, which also may be difficult to find in wet mounts.[71, 101] Symptomatic infections do not correlate with the concentration of organisms in stool.[79, 80, 102]

Although treatment of asymptomatic infections is unnecessary, until more is known about the virulence of the organism, therapy for "symptomatic" infections should be withheld until a thorough search has been made to rule out other causes of intestinal symptoms.

Treatment of blastocystosis is unsatisfactory; anecdotal studies in which metronidazole and iodoquinol, the most commonly recommended therapies, were used showed variable results.[71, 80, 102–107] In vitro studies have shown that emetine dihydrochloride, furazolidone, metronidazole, iodoquinol, and trimethoprim-sulfamethoxazole were inhibitory.[108, 109] Adding to the difficulty in the assessment of therapy is the evidence that *B. hominis* is often a self-limited infection.[80, 102, 103, 105]

CYCLOSPORA

Cyclosporiasis is an emerging infectious disease that was first described in humans living in Papua New Guinea in 1977.[110] Over the subsequent 15 years, additional cases of diarrheal illness were reported as being caused by the same organism. It eluded taxonomic classification, however, being labeled fungal spores, cyanobacterium-like bodies,[111] blue-green algae,[112–116] and large cryptosporidia,[117] until 1993, when Ortega and colleagues succeeded in inducing sporulation and thus confirmed its genus, *Cyclospora.*[118, 119] It was then named *Cyclospora cayetanensis* after the Universidad Peruana Cayetano Heredia in Lima, Peru, a major site of research on the infection. Phylogenetic analysis[120] confirmed that *Cyclospora* and *Eimeria* belong to the same family, though no other known *Eimeria* species have been identified as causing human illness.[121] These organisms were first noted by Eimer in the intestine of a mole and since then have been found in snakes, insectivores, rodents, and poultry,[119, 122] though the entire host range is still unknown[123] and it is unclear whether animals are a source of human infection.[122, 124, 125]

Cyclospora oocysts are spheric, measure 8 to 10 μm in diameter, contain two sporocysts that each hold two sporozoites, and are variably acid-fast. A skilled microscopist can identify the organisms in wet mounts of stool.[126] Ultrastructural studies of the unsporulated oocyst reveals an outer fibrillar coat, cell wall, and membrane; within the sporulated oocyst, sporozoites within sporocysts contain a membrane-bound nucleus and micronemes. In vitro sporulation at 27 to 32°C takes from 8 to 11 days. Oocysts in the environment are quite resistant, surviving freezing, 2% formalin, 2% potassium dichromate, and even chlorination.[127–130]

Transmission occurs by contaminated food and water,[125, 127, 129, 131–133] and probably not person to person because human *Cyclospora* oocysts, like those of *Isospora* spp., require time outside the host to sporulate and become infective.[123]

Cyclospora infections occur worldwide[123, 131, 134–136] in clusters and sporadically, with a major increase in reported cases since 1997. The organism has been found in travelers[117, 137–139] and in children[119, 140] and can act as an opportunistic infection in those with human immunodeficiency virus infection.[111, 112, 134, 141, 142] In travelers, it has been described even in those on usual tourist routes who stay in deluxe facilities.[137]

Most of the earlier cases were described in Nepal, Peru, and Haiti, as most research on the organism took place in these areas before the mid 1990s.[113, 115, 118, 119, 127, 131, 140–144] Though isolated cases of community-acquired cyclosporiasis are being reported in the United States in patients who have no history of travel,[128] more intensive study of the organism was prompted by the occurrence of large outbreaks in North America. The first occurred in 1990 in a hospital dormitory in Chicago, where an investigation implicated tap water contaminated from transient pump failure in a storage tank.[114, 129] During spring and summer 1996, almost 1500 cases were reported in the United States and Canada,[145] followed by a similar number of cases in 1997.[146–149] Illness was both sporadic and social event–related and was epidemiologically linked primarily to the consumption of imported, contaminated fresh raspberries; it was postulated that the illness was caused by spraying fruit, before harvest, with fungicide that contained contaminated surface waters.

The prevalence of *Cyclospora* infection in the United States is not known, though it is thought to be low. Surveys of stool samples and screening studies from various cities within the United States and other developed countries reveal *Cyclospora* in 0.1 to 0.5% of samples,[117, 123, 128, 138, 143, 150, 151] although it may now be found more frequently than *Isospora* infection.[116] It does not yet appear to be a major cause of traveler's diarrhea.[139] There are few data on the prevalence among indigenous populations of developing countries, although in Nepal, the highest risk of diarrhea is in children between the ages of 18 months and 5 years[140]; in Peru, the prevalence decreases with age as well.[152] Infants may be protected by breast-feeding.

The epidemiology of disease appears different for the residents of endemic areas as opposed to travelers to these regions. Whereas the duration of illness in endemic areas is short-lived and many are asymptomatic carriers, diarrhea has averaged over 1 month in visitors to Nepal and in upper-class Peruvians.[118, 153, 154] Studies from Peru appear to confirm that rates of symptomatic diarrhea are lower in the indigenous population of endemic areas and particularly in adults from these areas.[118, 152] In general, infection occurs seasonally, with spring and summer (May through July) being the peak seasons in the United States; in Peru, the incidence is highest in the warm season (April through June), and in Katmandu, the infection rate is highest before and during the monsoon (May through October).[151]

Asymptomatic infection has been reported in those native to endemic regions,[118] though it may occur rarely in others, and even in those who are infected with human immunodeficiency virus or human T-lymphotropic virus-1.[155] The incubation period is between 1 and 11 days, with the average about 1 week. The onset of illness is often abrupt but may be preceded by a flulike illness.[117, 138] Watery diarrhea is invariably present with a median of six stools per day, but in some patients, upper gastrointestinal symptoms predominate.[137, 138, 156] Fatigue, anorexia, myalgia, abdominal cramps, flatus, and nausea occur frequently.[154] Fever occurs in about 25% of cases. Illness lasts from 2 to 7 weeks or longer,[123] may be cyclic or relapsing, and may result in dehydration and significant weight loss.[117, 134, 135, 157] Clinical signs and symptoms do not distinguish cyclosporiasis from illness due to cryptosporidia, microsporidia, or *Isospora*. In patients with AIDS, illness tends to be even more severe and last longer.[142] In these patients, as with *Cryptosporidium* infection, biliary tract disease has been described.[156]

The diagnosis of cyclosporiasis requires microscopic identification of the oocysts, which are roughly twice the size of cryptosporidia oocysts. Shedding of oocysts in stool can precede the onset of clinical illness, and the disappearance of symptoms and oocysts usually occurs simultaneously.[115, 131] Abnormalities in the physical examination or routine laboratory testing are nondiagnostic. With severe diarrhea, xylose absorption may be decreased.[115, 158] Though the organism is variably acid-fast using the modified Ziehl-Neelsen or Kinyoun stains, these techniques are superior to the examination of routine wet mounts, which require a trained eye for identification of the organism.[159] If available, the demonstration of blue autofluorescence of the oocysts under ultraviolet epifluorescence microscopy is both rapid and sensitive, though not specific.[118, 160] Another fast, reliable technique is the use of safranin staining of fecal smears.[161] Sporulation assays provide a definitive diagnosis, as does confirmation with electron microscopy, but these means are not routinely available. Molecular diagnostic techniques have been developed and are undergoing further evaluation and refinement, as cross-amplification with other coccidian parasites may occur.[120, 121] Antibodies to *Cyclospora* can be detected, though it is unclear whether they play a role in immunity,[131, 162] and reinfection has occurred.[150]

Cyclospora may also be detected in jejunal aspirates or in biopsy specimens, though it is controversial whether routine hematoxylin and eosin staining of the biopsy material permits adequate visualization of the organisms.[116, 163] Tissue sections reveal *Cyclospora* in a supranuclear location of the cytoplasm that distinguishes them from *Cryptosporidium*, which are on the surface of the enterocytes.[164] Electron microscopy reveals the presence of the organisms and its various stages[164] in the cytoplasm of the jejunal epithelial cells.[116] Upper endoscopy appears normal, yet the histologic architecture of the small bowel is altered, with villous atrophy, infiltration of the lamina propria by inflammatory cells, and vascular dilatation.[113, 157] It is unknown whether the pathogenesis of infection is due to enterocyte dysfunction or whether toxins are secreted.

The only treatment known at this time is trimethoprim-sulfamethoxazole twice daily for 7 days: 160 mg trimethoprim and 800 mg sulfamethoxazole in adults, and 5 mg/kg trimethoprim and 25 mg/kg sulfamethoxazole in children.[144, 152, 165] For patients with human immunodeficiency virus infection, because relapse is common, the recommendation is four times daily dosing for 10 days followed by chronic prophylaxis three times per week.[142, 166] Treatment with other antimicrobial agents has not been successful. There continue to be unanswered questions regarding the extent of reservoirs, the infectious dose, and the pathogenesis of *Cyclospora*.[146] Better diagnostic techniques are required along with prevention and control measures. *Cyclospora* cases should be reported to the Centers for Disease Control and Prevention Division of Parasitic Diseases, telephone 770-488-7760.[146]

REFERENCES

1. Ledingham JCG, Penfold WJ, Woodcock HM. Recent bacteriological experiences with typhoidal disease and dysentery: With notes on the protozoan parasites in the excreta. BMJ. 1915;2:704–711.
2. Wenyon CM. Observations on the common intestinal protozoa of man: Their diagnosis and pathogenicity. Lancet. 1915;2:1178–1183.
3. Kirkpatrick CE. Animal reservoirs of *Cryptosporidium* spp and *Isospora belli*. J Infect Dis. 1988;158:909.
4. Trier JS, Moxey PC, Schimmel EM, et al. Chronic intestinal coccidiosis in man: Intestinal morphology and response to treatment. Gastroenterology. 1974;66:923–935.
5. Brandborg LL, Goldberg SB, Breidenbach WC. Human coccidiosis—a possible cause of malabsorption. N Engl J Med. 1970;24:1306–1313.
6. Lindsay DS, Dubey JP, Blagburn BL. Biology of *Isospora* spp from humans, nonhuman primates and domestic animals. Clin Microbiol Rev. 1997;10:19–34.
7. Faust EC, Giraldo, LE, Caicedo G, et al. Human isosporosis in the Western Hemisphere. Am J Trop Med Hyg. 1961;10:343–349.
8. Smitskamp H, Dey-Muller E. Geographic distribution and clinical significance of human coccidiosis. Trop Geogr Med. 1966;18:133–136.
9. Sauve R, Johnson WD. *Cryptosporidium* and *Isospora belli* infections. J Infect Dis. 1988;157:255–259.
10. Sorvillo FJ, Lieb LE, Seidel J, et al. Epidemiology of isosporiasis among persons with acquired immunodeficiency syndrome in Los Angeles County. Am J Trop Med Hyg. 1995;53:656–659.
11. Sorvillo F, Leib L, Iwaskoshi K, et al. *Isospora belli* and the acquired immunodeficiency syndrome. N Engl J Med. 1990;332:131.
12. Bartlett JG, Belitsos PC, Sears CL. AIDS enteropathy. Clin Infect Dis. 1992;15:726–735.
13. Colebunders R, Lusakumuni K, Nelson AM, et al. Persistent diarrhoea in Zairian AIDS patients: An endoscopic and histological study. Gut. 1988;29:1687–1691.
14. DeHovitz JA, Pape JW, Boncy M, et al. Clinical manifestations and therapy of *Isospora belli* infection in patients with acquired immunodeficiency syndrome. N Engl J Med. 1986;315:87–90.
15. Pape JW, Verdier RI, Johnson WD Jr. Treatment and prophylaxis of *Isospora belli* infection in patients with acquired immunodeficiency syndrome. N Engl J Med. 1989;320:1044–1047.
16. Henry MC, de Clercq D, Lokombe B, et al. Parasitological observations of chronic diarrhoea in suspected AIDS adult patient Kinshasa (Zaire). Trans R Soc Trop Med Hyg. 1986;80:309–310.
17. Hunter G, Bagshave AF, Baboo KS, et al. Intestinal parasites in Zambian patients with AIDS. Trans R Soc Trop Med Hyg. 1992;86:543–545.
18. Conlon CP, Pinching AJ, Perera CU, et al. HIV-related enteropathy in Zambia: A clinical, microbiological and histological study. Am J Trop Med Hyg. 1990;42:83–88.
19. Sauda FC, Zamarioli LA, Filho WE, et al. Prevalence of *Cryptosporidium* sp and *Isospora belli* among AIDS patients attending Santos Reference for AIDS, Sao Paulo, Brazil. J Parasitol. 1993;79:454–456.
20. Henderson HE, Gillepsie, GW, Kaplan P, et al. The human *Isospora*. Am J Hyg. 1963;78:302–309.
21. Leibman WM, Thaler MM, Delorimier A, et al. Intractable diarrhea of infancy due to intestinal coccidiosis. Gastroenterology. 1980;78:579–584.
22. La Via WV. Parasitic gastroenteritis. Pediatr Ann. 1994:556–560.
23. Matsubayashi H, Nozawa T. Experimental infection of *Isospora hominis* in man. Am J Trop Med Hyg. 1948;28:633–637.
24. Shaffer N, Moore L. Chronic travelers' diarrhea in a normal host due to *Isospora belli*. J Infect Dis. 1989;159:596–597.
25. Whiteside ME, Barkin JS, May RG, et al. Enteric coccidiosis among patients with the acquired immunodeficiency syndrome. Am J Trop Med Hyg. 1984;33:1065–1072.
26. Forthal DN, Guest SS. *Isospora belli* enteritis in three homosexual men. Am J Trop Med Hyg. 1984;33:1060–1064.
27. Modigliani R, Bories C, Le Charpentier Y, et al. Diarrhea and malabsorption in acquired immune deficiency syndrome: A study of four cases with special emphasis on opportunistic protozoan infestations. Gut. 1985;26:179–187.
28. Greenberg SJ, Davey MP, Zierdt WS, et al. *Isospora belli* infections in patients with human T-cell leukemia virus type 1–associated adult T-cell leukemia. Am J Med. 1988;85:435–438.
29. Hallak A, Yust I, Ratan Y, et al. Malabsorption syndrome, coccidiosis, combined immune deficiency and fulminant lymphoproliferative disease. Arch Intern Med. 1982;142:196–197.
30. Westerman EL, Christensen RP. Chronic *Isospora belli* treated with cotrimoxazole. Ann Intern Med. 1979;91:413–414.
31. Alfandari S, Ajana F, Senneville E, et al. Haemorrhagic ulcerative colitis due to *Isospora belli* in AIDS. Int J STD AIDS. 1995;6:216.
32. Michiels JF, Hofman P, Bernard E, et al. Intestinal and extraintestinal *Isospora belli* infection in an AIDS patient. Pathol Res Pract. 1994;190:1089–1093.
33. Restrepo C, Macher AM, Radany EH. Disseminated extraintestinal isosporiasis in a patient with acquired immune deficiency syndrome. Am J Clin Pathol. 1987;87:536–542.
34. Benator DA, French AL, Beaudet LM, et al. *Isospora belli* infection associated with acalculous cholecystitis in a patient with AIDS. Ann Intern Med. 1994;121:663–664.
35. Gonzalez-Dominguez J, Roldan R, Villanueva JL, et al. *Isospora belli* reactive arthritis in a patient with AIDS (Letter). Ann Rheum Dis. 1994;53:618–619.
36. Goodgame RW. Understanding intestinal spore-forming protozoa: *Cryptosporidia, Microsporidia, Isospora* and *Cyclospora*. Ann Intern Med. 1996;124:429–441.
37. Ng E, Markell EK, Fleming RL, et al. Demonstration of *Isospora belli* by acid-fast stain in a patient with acquired immune deficiency syndrome. J Clin Microbiol. 1984;20:384–386.
38. Ma P, Kaufman D, Montana J. *Isospora belli* diarrheal infection in homosexual men. AIDS Res. 1984;1:327–338.
39. Garcia LS, Bruckner. Diagnostic Medical Parasitology. Washington, DC: American Society for Microbiology; 1993.
40. Wittner M, Tanowitz HB, Weiss LM. Parasitic infections in AIDS patients. Cryptosporidiosis, isosporosis, microsporidiosis, cyclosporiasis. Infect Dis Clin North Am. 1993;7:569–586.
41. Bush JB, Markus MB. Staining of *Isospora belli* oocysts (Letter). Trans R Soc Trop Med. 1987;81:244.
42. Berlin OGW, Conteas CN, Sowerby TM. Detection of *Isospora* in the stools of AIDS patients using a new rapid autofluorescence technique. AIDS. 1996;10:442–443.
43. Limbos P, VanRos G, DeMuynck A. Deux noveaux cas de coccidiose à *Isospora belli* observés in Belgique. Bull Soc Pathol Exot. 1972;65:288–292.
44. Weiss LM, Perlman D, Sherman J, et al. *Isospora belli* infection: Treatment with pyrimethamine. Ann Intern Med. 1988;109:474–475.
45. Kayembe K, Desmet P, Henry MC, et al. Diclazuril for *Isospora belli* infection in AIDS. Lancet. 1989;1:1397–1398.
46. Limson-Pobre RNR, Merrick S, Gruen D, et al. Use of diclazuril for the treatment of isosporiasis in patients with AIDS. Clin Infect Dis. 1995;20:201–202.
47. Musey KL, Chidiac C, Beaucaire G, et al. Effectiveness of roxithromycin for treating *Isospora belli* infection. J Infect Dis. 1988;158:646.
48. Doumbo O, Rossignol JF, Pichard E, et al. Nitazoxanide in the treatment of cryptosporidial diarrhea and other intestinal parasitic infections associated with acquired immunodeficiency syndrome in tropical Africa. Am J Trop Med Hyg. 1997;56:637–639.
49. Dionisio D, Sterrantino M, Meli M, et al. Treatment of isosporiasis with combined albendazole and ornidazole in patients with AIDS. AIDS. 1996;10:1301–1302.
50. Levine ND. The Protozoan Phylum Apicomplexa, v. 2. Bocca Raton, Fla: CRC Press; 1988:1–8.

51. Beaver PC, Gadgil RK, Morera P. *Sarcocystis* in man: A review and report of five cases. Am J Trop Med Hyg. 1979;22:819–844.
52. Greve E. Sarcosporidiosis—an overlooked zoonosis. Dan Med Bull. 1985;32:228–230.
53. Wong KT, Pathmananthan R. Review of human skeletal muscle sarcocystosis in Southeast Asia. Trans R Soc Trop Med Hyg. 1992;86:631–632.
54. Kan SP, Pathmananthan R. Review of sarcocystosis in Malaysia. Southeast Asian J Trop Med Public Health. 1991;22(Suppl):129–134.
55. Van den Enden E, Praet M, Joos R, et al. Eosinophilic myositis resulting from sarcocystosis. J Trop Med Hyg. 1995;98:273–276.
56. Pamphlett R, O'Donoghue P. *Sarcocystis* infection of human muscle. Aust N Z J Med. 1990;20:705–707.
57. Jeffrey HC. Sarcosporidiosis in man. Trans R Soc Trop Med Hyg. 1974;68:17–29.
58. Brindley PJ, Ricardo T, Gazzinelli EY, et al. Differentiation of *Toxoplasma gondii* from closely related coccidia by riboprint analysis and a surface antigen gene polymerase chain reaction. Am J Trop Med Hyg. 1993;48:447–456.
59. Bunyaratvej S, Bunyawongwiroj P, Nitiyanant P. Human intestinal sarcosporidiosis: Report of six cases. Am J Trop Med Hyg. 1982;31:36–41.
60. Woody NC, Woody HB. Balantidiasis in infancy: Review of the literature and report of a case. J Pediatr. 1960;56:485–489.
61. Arean VM, Koppisch E. Balantidiasis—a review and report of cases. Am J Pathol. 1956;32:1089–1108.
62. Walzer PD, Judson FN, Murphy KB, et al. Balantidiasis outbreak in Truk. Am J Trop Med Hyg. 1973;22:33–41.
63. Young MD. Attempts of transmit human *Balantidium coli.* Am J Trop Med. 1950;30:71–72.
64. Swartzwelder JC. Balantidiasis. Am J Dig Dis. 1950;17:173–179.
65. Baskerville L. *Balantidium* colitis. Report of a case. Am J Dig Dis. 1970;15:727–731.
66. Ladas SD, Savva S, Frydas A, et al. Invasive balantidiasis presented as chronic colitis and lung involvement. Dig Dis Sci. 1989;34:1621–1623.
67. Abaza H, El-Zayadi AR, Kabil SM, et al. Nitazoxanide in the treatment of patients with intestinal protozoan and helminthic infections: A report of 546 patients in Egypt. Curr Therapeutic Res. 1998;59:116–121.
68. Drugs for parasitic infections. Med Lett. 1998;40:1–12.
69. Garcia-Laverde A, De Bonilla L. Clinical trials with metronidazole in human balantidiasis. Am J Trop Med Hyg. 1975;24:781–783.
70. Zierdt CH. *Blastocystis hominis*—past and future. Clin Microbiol Rev. 991;4:61–79.
71. Stenzel DJ, Boreham PFL. *Blastocystis hominis* revisited. Clin Microbiol Rev. 1996;9:563–584.
72. Stenzel DJ, Boreham PFL. A cyst-like stage of *Blastocystis hominis.* Int J Parasitol. 1991;21:613–615.
73. Zaman V, Howe J, Ng M. Ultrastructure of *Blastocystis hominis* cysts. Parasitol Res. 1995;81:465–469.
74. Stenzel DJ, Lee MG, Boreham PFL. Morphological differences in *Blastocystis cysts*—an indication of different species. Parasitol Res. 1997;83:452–457.
75. Boreham PFL, Stenzel DJ. *Blastocystis* in humans and animals: Morphology, biology and epizootiology. Adv Parasitol. 1993;32:1–70.
76. Stenzel DJ. Ultrastructural and cytochemical studies of *Blastocystis* sp. PhD thesis. Queensland University of Technology, Brisbane, Australia, 1995.
77. Stenzel DJ, Boreham PFL, McDougall R. Ultrastructure of *Blastocystis hominis* in human stool samples. Int J Parasitol. 1991;21:807–812.
78. Stenzel DJ, Boreham PFL. A cyst-like stage of *Blastocystis hominis.* Int J Parasitol. 1991;21:613–615.
79. Doyle PW, Helgason MM, Mathias RG, et al. Epidemiology and pathogenicity of *Blastocystis hominis.* J Clin Microbiol. 1990;28:116–121.
80. Kain KC, Noble MA, Freeman HJ, et al. Epidemiology and clinical features associated with *Blastocystis hominis* infection. Diagn Microbiol Infect Dis. 1987;8:235–244.
81. Puga SL, Figueroa, Navarrette N. Protozoos y helmintos intestinales en la poblacion prescolar y escolar de la cuidad de Valdivia, Chile. Parasitol Dia. 1991;15:57–58.
82. Torres PJ, Miranda L, Flores J, et al. *Blastocystis* and other intestinal protozoan infections in human riverside communities from Valdiva River Basin, Chile. Rev Inst Med Trop Sao Paulo.1992;34:557–564.
83. Yamada, MH, Matsumoto Y, Tegoshi T, et al. The prevalence of *Blastocystis hominis* infection in humans in Kyoto City, Japan. Jpn J Trop Med Hyg. 1987;15:158–159.
84. Keystone JS. *Blastocystis hominis* and traveler's diarrhea. Clin Infect Dis. 1995;21:102–103.
85. O'Gorman MA, Orenstein SR, Proujansky R, et al. Prevelance and characteristics of *Blastocystis hominis* infection in children. Clin Pediatr. 1993;32:91–96.
86. Wilson KW, Winget D. *Blastocystis hominis*: Infection, signs and symptoms in patients at Wilford Hall Medical Center. Mil Med. 1990;155:394–396.
87. Udkow MP, Markell EK. *Blastocystis hominis:* Prevalence in asymptomatic versus symptomatic hosts. J Infect Dis. 1993;168:242–244.
88. Kukoschke KG, Muller HE. Varying incidence of *Blastocystis hominis:* In culture from faeces of patients with diarrhoea and from healthy persons. Int J Med Microbiol Virol Parasitol Infect Dis. 1992;277:112–118.
89. Herwaldt BL, de Arroyave KR, Wahlquist SP, et al. Infections with intestinal parasites in Peace Corps volunteers in Guatemala. J Clin Microbiol. 1994;32:1376–1378.
90. Nimri LF. Evidence of an epidemic of *Blastocystis hominis* infections in preschool children in northern Jordan. J Clin Microbiol. 1993;31:2706–2708.
91. Shlim DR, Hoge CW, Rajah R, et al. Is *Blastocystis hominis* a cause of diarrhea in travelers? A prospective controlled study in Nepal. Clin Infect Dis. 1995;21:97–101.
92. Phillips PB, Zierdt CH. *Blastocystis hominis:* Pathogenic potential in human patients and gnotobiotes. Exp Parasitol. 1976;39:358–364.
93. Moe KT, Singh M, Howe J, et al. Experimental *Blastocystis hominis* infection in laboratory mice. Parasitol Res. 1997;83:319–325.
94. Walderich B, Bernauer S, Renner M, et al. Cytopathic effects of *Blastocystis hominis* on Chinese hamster ovary (CHO) and adeno carcinoma HT29 cell cultures. Trop Med Int Health. 1998;3:385–390.
95. Bohm-Gloning B, Knobloch J, Walderich B. Five subgroups of *Blastocystis hominis* isolates from symptomatic and asymptomatic patients revealed by restriction site analysis of PCR-amplified I6S-like rDNA. Trop Med Int Health. 1997;2:771–778.
96. Boreham PFL, Upcroft JA, Dunn LA. Protein and DNA evidence for two demes of *Blastocystis hominis* from humans. Int J Parasitol. 1992;22:49–53.
97. Muller HE. Four serologically different groups within the species *Blastocystis hominis.* Int J Med Microbiol Virol Parasitol Infect Dis. 1994;280:403–408.
98. Gericke AS, Burchard GD, Knobloch J, et al. Isoenzyme patterns of *Blastocystis hominis* patient isolates derived from symptomatic and healthy carriers. Trop Med Int Health. 1997;2:245–253.
99. Garcia LS, Bruckner DA. Diagnostic Medical Parasitology. 2nd ed. Washington, DC: American Society for Microbiology; 1993.
100. Markell EK, Udkow MP. Association of *Blastocystis hominis* with human disease (Letter)? J Clin Microbiol. 1990;28:1085.
101. Boreham RE. Unpublished data.
102. Senay H, MacPherson D. *Blastocystis hominis:* Epidemiology and natural history. J Infect Dis. 1990;162:987–990.
103. Grossman I, Weiss LM, Simon D, et al. *Blastocystis hominis* in hospital employees. Am J Gastroenterol. 1992;87:729–732.
104. Quadris SMH, Al-Okaili GA, Al-Dayel F. Clinical significance of *Blastocystis hominis.* J Clin Microbiol. 1989;27:2407–2409.
105. Markell EK, Udkow MP. *Blastocystis hominis:* Pathogen or fellow traveler? Am J Trop Med Hyg. 1986;35:1023–1026.
106. Babb RR, Wagener S. *Blastocystis hominis:* A potential intestinal pathogen. West J Med. 1989;151:518–519.
107. Sun T, Katz S Tanenbaum B, et al. Questionable clinical significance of *Blastocystis hominis* infection. Am J Gastroenterol. 1989;84:1543–1547.
108. Zierdt CH, Swan JC, Hosseini J. *In vitro* response of *Blastocystis hominis* to antiprotozoal drugs. J Protozool. 1983;30:332–334.
109. Dunn LA Boreham PFL. The *in vitro* activity of drugs against *Blastocystis hominis.* J Antimicrob Chemother. 1991;27:507–516.
110. Ashford RW. Occurrence of an undescribed coccidian in man in Papua New Guinea. Ann Trop Med Parasitol. 1979;73:497–500.
111. Hart AS, Ridinger MR, Soundarajan R, et al. Novel organism associated with chronic diarrhoea in AIDS (Letter). Lancet. 1990;335:169–170.
112. Long EG, Ebrahimzadeh A, White EH, et al. Alga associated with diarrhoea in patients with acquired immunodeficiency syndrome and in travelers. J Clin Microbiol. 1990;28:1101–1104.
113. Connor BA, Shlim DR, Scholes JV, et al. Pathogenic changes in the small bowel in nine patients with diarrhoea associated with a coccidia-like body. Ann Intern Med. 1993;119:377–382.
114. Centers for Disease Control. Outbreaks of diarrhoeal illness associated with cyanobacteria (blue-green algae)–like bodies: Chicago and Nepal. MMWR Morb Mortal Wkly Rep. 1991;40:325–327.
115. Shlim DR, Cohen MT, Eaton M, et al. An alga-like organism associated with an outbreak of prolonged diarrhoea among foreigners in Nepal. Am J Trop Med Hyg. 1991;45:383–389.
116. Bendall RP, Luca S, Moody A, et al. Diarrhoea associated with cyanobacterium-like bodies: A new coccidian enteritis of man. Lancet. 1993;341:590–592.
117. Soave R. *Cyclospora*: An overview. Clin Infect Dis. 1996;23:429–435.
118. Ortega YR, Sterling CR, Gilman RH, et al. *Cyclospora* species—a new protozoan pathogen of humans. N Engl J Med. 1993;328:1308–1312.
119. Ortega YR, Gilman RH, Sterling CR. A coccidian parasite (Apidocomplexa: Eimeriidae) from humans. J Parasitol. 1994;80:625–629.
120. Relman DA, Schmidt TM, Gajadhar A, et al. Molecular phylogenetic analysis of *Cyclospora*, the human intestinal pathogen, suggests that it is closely related to *Eimeria* species. J Infect Dis. 1996;173:440–445.
121. Pieniazek NJ, Herwaldt BL. Reevaluating the molecular taxonomy: Is human-associated *Cyclospora* a mammalian *Eimeria* species? Emerg Infect Dis. 1997;3:381–383.
122. Garcia-Lopez HL, Rodriguez-Tovar LE, Medina de la Garza CE. Identification of *Cyclospora* in poultry. Emerg Infect Dis. 1996;2:356–357.
123. Taylor AD, Davis LJ, Soave R. *Cyclospora*—review. Curr Clin Top Infect Dis. 1997;17:256–268.
124. Zerpa R, Uchima N, Huicho L. *Cyclospora cayetanensis* associated with water diarrhoea in Peruvian patients. J Trop Med Hyg. 1995;98:325–329.
125. Connor BA, Shlim DR. Food borne transmission of *Cyclospora*. Lancet. 1995;345:1634.
126. Goodgame RW. Understanding intestinal spore-forming protozoa: *Cryptosporidia, Microbporidia, Isospora* and *Cyclospora*. Ann Intern Med. 1996;124:429–441.
127. Rabold JG, Hoge CW, Shlim DR, et al. *Cyclospora* outbreak associated with chlorinated drinking water (Letter). Lancet. 1994;344:1360–1361.
128. Ooi WW, Zimmerman SK, Needham CA. *Cyclospora* species as a gastrointestinal pathogen in immunocompetent hosts. J Clin Microbiol. 1995;33:1267–1269.

129. Huang P, Weber JT, Sosin DM, et al. The first reported outbreak of diarrheal illness associated with *Cyclospora* in the United States. Ann Intern Med. 1995;123:409–414.
130. Steiner TS, Thielman NM, Guerrant RL. Protozoal agents: What are the dangers for the public water supply? Annu Rev Med. 1997;48:329–340.
131. Hoge CW, Shlim DR, Rajah R, et al. Epidemiology of diarrhoeal illness associated with coccidian-like organisms among travellers and foreign residents in Nepal. Lancet. 1993;341:1175–1179.
132. Ortega YR, Roxas CR, Gilman RH, et al. Isolation of *Cryptosporidium parvum* and *Cyclospora cayetanensis* from vegetables collected in markets of an endemic region in Peru. Am J Trop Med Hyg. 1997;57:683–686.
133. Brennan MK MacPherson DW, Palmer J, Keystone JS. Cyclosporiasis: A new cause of diarrhea. Can Med Assoc J. 1996;155:1293–1296.
134. Farthing MJG, Kelly MP, Veitch AM. Recently recognised microbial enteropathies and HIV infection. J Antimicrob Chemother. 1996;37(Suppl B):61–70.
135. Chiodini PL. A "new" parasite: Human infection with *Cyclospora cayetanensis*. Trans R Soc Med Hyg. 1994;88:369–371.
136. Markus MB, Frean JA. Occurrence of human *Cyclospora* infection in sub-Saharan Africa. S African Med J. 1993;83:862–863.
137. Berlin OGW, Novak SM, Porschen RK, et al. Recovery of *Cyclospora* organisms from patients with prolonged diarrhea. Clin Infect Dis. 1994;18:606–609.
138. Wurtz R. *Cyclospora*: A newly identified intestinal pathogen of humans. Clin Infect Dis. 1994;18:620–623.
139. Jelinek T, Lotze M, Eichenlaub S, et al. Prevalence of infection with *Cryptosporidium parvum* and *Cyclospora cayetanensis* among international travellers. Gut. 1997;41:801–804.
140. Hoge CW, Echeverria P, Rajah R, et al. Prevalence of *Cyclospora* species and other enteric pathogens among children less than 5 years of age in Nepal. J Clin Microbiol. 1995;33:3058–3060.
141. Pape JW, Levine E, Beaulieu ME, et al. Cryptosporidiosis in Haitian children. Am J Trop Med Hyg. 1987;36:333–338.
142. Wurtz RM, Kocka FE, Peters CS, et al. Clinical characteristics of seven cases of diarrhea associated with novel acid-fast organism in the stool. Clin Infect Dis. 1993;16:136–138.
143. Pape JW, Verdier, Boncy M, et al. *Cyclospora* infections in adults with HIV: Clinical manifestations, treatment and prophylaxis. Ann Intern Med. 1994;121:654–657.
144. Hoge CW, Shlim DR, Ghirire M, et al. Placebo controlled trail of co-trimoxazole for *Cyclospora* infections among travellers and foreign residents in Nepal. Lancet. 1995;345:691–693.
145. Herwaldt BL, Ackers M-L, *Cyclospora* Working Group. An outbreak in 1996 of cyclosporiasis associated with imported rasberries. N Engl J Med. 1997;336:1548–1556.
146. Centers for Disease Control and Prevention. Update: Outbreaks of *Cyclospora cayetanensis* infection—United States and Canada. MMWR Morb Mortal Wkly Rep. 1996;45:611–612.
147. Centers for Disease Control and Prevention. Outbreaks of cyclosporiasis—United States, 1997. MMWR Morb Mortal Wkly Rep. 1997;46:451-452.
148. Centers for Disease Control and Prevention. Update: outbreaks of cyclosporiasis—United States and Canada. MMWR Morb Mortal Wkly Rep. 1997;45:521–3.
149. Centers for Disease Control and Prevention. Outbreak of cyclosporiasis—United States and Canada. MMWR Morb Mortal Wkly Rep. 1997;46:689.
150. Clarke SC, McIntyre M. The incidence of *Cyclospora cayetanensis* in stool samples submitted to a district general hospital. Epidemiol Infect. 1996;117:189–193.
151. Soave R, Herwaldt BLL, Relman DA. *Cyclospora*. Emerging Infectious Diseases. Infect Dis Clin North Am. 1998;12:1–12.
152. Madico G, McDonald J, Gilman RH, et al. Epidemiology and treatment of *Cyclospora cayatenensis* infection in Peruvian children. Clin Infect Dis. 1997;24:977–981.
153. Taylor DN, Houston R, Shlim DR, et al. Etiology of diarrhea among travelers and foreign residents in Nepal. JAMA. 1988;260:1245–1248.
154. Hoge CW, Shlim D, Echeverria P. Cynaobacterium-like *Cyclospora* species (Letter). N Engl J Med. 1993;329:1504–1505.
155. Schubach TM, Neves ES, Leite AC, et al. *Cyclospora cayetanensis* in an asymptomatic patient infected with HIV and HTLV-1. Trans R Soc Trop Med Hyg. 1997;91:175.
156. Sifuentes-Osornio J, Porras-Cortes G, Bendall RP, et al. *Cyclospora cayetanensis* infection in patients with and without AIDS: Biliary disease as another clinical manifestation. Clin Infect Dis. 1995;21:1092–1097.
157. Ortega YR, Nagle R, Gilman RH, et al. Pathologic and clinical findings in patients with cyclosporiasis and a description of intracellular parasite life-cycle stages. J Infect Dis. 1997;176:1584–1589.
158. Pollock RCG, Bendall RP, Moody A, et al. Travellers' diarrhoea associated with cyanobacterium-like bodies. Lancet. 1992;340:556–557.
159. Eberhard ML, Pieniazek NJ, Arrowood MJ. Laboratory diagnosis of *Cyclospora* infections (Review). Arch Pathol Lab Med. 1997;121:792–797.
160. Berlin OGW, Peter JB, Gagne C, et al. Autofluorescence and the detection of *Cyclospora* oocysts. Emerg Infect Dis. 1998;4:127–128.
161. Visvesvara GS, Moura H, Kovacs-Nace E, et al. Uniform staining of *Cyclospora* oocysts in fecal smears by a modified safranin technique with microwave heating. J Clin Microbiol. 1992;35:730–733.
162. Long EG, White EH, Carmichael WW, et al. Morphologic and staining characteristics of a cyanobacterium-like organism associated with diarrhea. J Infect Dis. 1991;164:199–202.
163. Tran Van Nhieu J, Nin F, Fleury-Feith J, et al. Identification of intracellular stages of *Cyclospora* species by light microscopy of thick sections using hematoxylin. Hum Pathol. 1996;27:1107–1109.
164. Sun T, Ilardi CF, Asnis D, et al. Light and electron microscopic identification of *Cyclospora* species in the small intestine. Evidence of the presence of asexual life cycle in human host. Am J Clin Pathol. 1996;105:216–220.
165. Fryauff DJ, Krippner R, Purnomo, et al. Short report: Case report of *Cyclospora* infection acquired in Indonesia and treated with cotrimoxazole. Am J Trop Med Hyg. 1996;55:584–585.
166. Soave R, Johnson WD Jr. *Cyclospora:* Conquest of an emerging pathogen. Lancet. 1995;345:667–668.
167. Colley DG. Widespread foodborne cyclosporiasis outbreaks present major challenges. Emerg Infect Dis. 1996;2:354–356.

Chapter 274

Microsporidia

RAINER WEBER
DAVID A. SCHWARTZ
RALPH T. BRYAN

The term *microsporidia* is a nontaxonomic designation commonly used to describe organisms belonging to the order Microsporida of the phylum Microspora. Contained in this phylum are more than 1000 species, at least 11 of which are known to infect humans. These unique protozoa should not be confused with the more familiar coccidia (e.g., *Cryptosporidium, Isospora*), which belong to the phylum Apicomplexa. First identified in 1857, microsporidia have long been recognized as a cause of disease in many nonhuman hosts. Historically, these organisms have caused serious economic problems for the silkworm, honeybee, and commercial fishing industries. They have also been shown to infect laboratory rodents, rabbits, furbearing animals, and primates.[1–5] Molecular phylogeny researchers, in addition to debating the ancient origins of these parasites, are poised to restructure an already complex and rapidly changing taxonomy that has traditionally been based on ultrastructure, method of cell division, and parasite relationships to host cell cytoplasm.[6–10] The role of microsporidia as important emerging pathogens in humans is being increasingly recognized.[1–3, 11]

DESCRIPTION OF THE PATHOGEN

The microsporidia are a unique group of obligately intracellular, spore-forming protozoa. They are true eukaryotes because they have a membrane-bound nucleus, an intracytoplasmic membrane system, and chromosome separation on mitotic spindles but are unusual among the eukaryotes in that they have 70S ribosomes, no mitochondria, and simple vesicular Golgi membranes. Microsporidia are diverse organisms that are capable of infecting a wide variety of both vertebrate and invertebrate hosts.[1–5] These unusual protozoa are truly ubiquitous in our environment and infect familiar insects such as mosquitoes, fleas, grasshoppers, and honeybees; common food fish such as salmon, flounder, and monkfish; and freshwater snails. They can also be found in common environmental sources such as ditch water and, in the western United States, certain species are intentionally released into the environment for the biologic control of destructive grasshoppers and locusts.[12–14]

The microsporidial spore is a highly specialized, environmentally resistant structure that varies in size and shape according to species. The species infecting mammals, including humans, tend to be smaller, ranging in size from 1.0 to 3.0 $\mu m \times 1.5$ to 4.0 μm, and are usually ovoid. The ultrastructural characteristics of microsporidial spores are distinctive (Figs. 274–1 and 274–2).[1–3, 15–17]

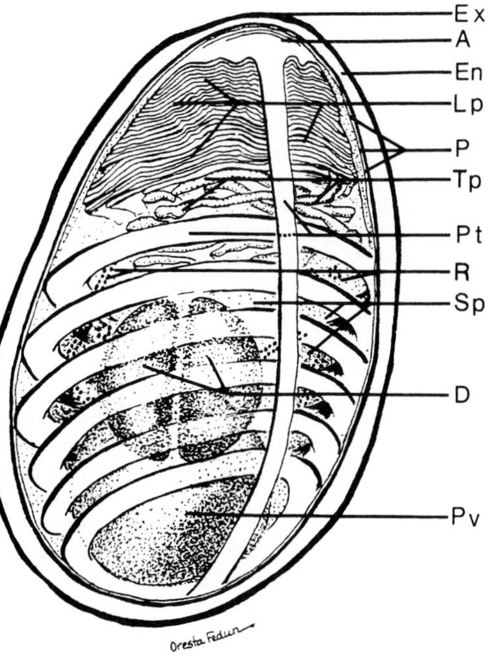

FIGURE 274–1. Diagram of the internal structure of a microsporidial spore. The spore coat has an outer electron-dense exospore and an inner, thicker, electron-lucent endospore. The extrusion apparatus (anchoring disk, polar filament, lamellar polaroplast, and tubular polaroplast) dominates the spore contents and is diagnostic of microsporidia. The number of polar filament coils depends on the particular species and can vary from a few to more than 30. *Abbreviations:* A, Anchoring disk; D, diplokaryon nuclei; En, endospore; Ex, exospore; LP, lamellar polaroplast; P, unit membrane; Pt, polar filament; Pv, posterior vacuole; R, ribosomes; Sp, sporoplasm; Tp, tubular polaroplast. (From Cali A, Owen R. Microsporidiosis. In: Balows A, ed. The Laboratory Diagnosis of Infectious Diseases: Principles and Practice. New York: Springer Verlag; 1988;929–950.)

Although different microsporidial genera can display significant variation in their methods of cell division, their life cycles share several general features that can be described in three phases. Phase I, the infective phase, begins with the ingestion or possibly inhalation of spores by a susceptible host. Thereafter, the spore is stimulated by conditions such as shifting pH or ionic concentrations to evert its coiled polar filament, which is actually a tubular structure analogous to a telescoping fishing rod or radio antenna. On eversion, this filament becomes a tubule through which the infective sporoplasm is injected into a host cell. During phase II, the injected sporoplasm develops into proliferative stages, or meronts, which multiply, depending on the species, by either repeated binary fission or by multiple fission with the formation of multinucleate plasmodial forms. This process, also known as merogony, is followed by phase III, or sporogony, which begins as meront cell membranes thicken to form sporonts. After subsequent divisions, sporonts give rise to sporoblasts, which develop into mature spores without undergoing further multiplication. As mature spores accumulate in an infected cell, that cell eventually expands to the point of rupture, thereby releasing infectious spores and completing the life cycle. This combination of merogonous and sporogonous multiplication gives the microsporidia enormous reproductive potential, with resultant heavy host infestations and environmental contamination. Released spores may infect nearby host cells or escape into the environment via stool, urine, or respiratory secretions.[17, 18]

Among the numerous microsporidial species, at least 11 have been implicated in human disease (Table 274–1).[19–38] There are also other human-infecting microsporidia for which appropriate genera and species have not been determined, such as those termed *Nosema-like* or assigned to the "collective group" Microsporidium. *Nosema* and *Pleistophora* are generally considered to be pathogens of insects

TABLE 274–1 Microsporidia Implicated in Human Disease

Genus	Species
Enterocytozoon	*Ent. bieneusi*
Encephalitozoon	*Enc. hellem*
	Enc. intestinalis (formerly *Septata intestinalis*)
	Enc. cuniculi
Pleistophora	*Pleistophora* spp.
Trachipleistophora	*T. hominis*
	T. anthropophthera
Nosema	*N. connori*
	N. ocularum
Brachiola	*B. vesicularum*
Vittaforma	*V. corneae* (formerly *Nosema corneum*)
Microsporidia, not specified	"Microsporidium ceylonensis"*
	"Microsporidium africanum"

* "Microsporidium" is a collective term for microsporidia that cannot be classified because of insufficient information.

and fish, respectively, whereas *Encephalitozoon cuniculi* usually infects nonhuman mammals and, occasionally, birds.[1–3] *Enterocytozoon bieneusi, Encephalitozoon hellem, Encephalitozoon intestinalis, Trachipleistophora* spp., *Vittaforma corneae,* and *Brachiola vesicularum* were all originally described in humans, but animal hosts have recently been identified for *Ent. bieneusi*, *Enc. hellem*, and *Enc. intestinalis.*[39–44]

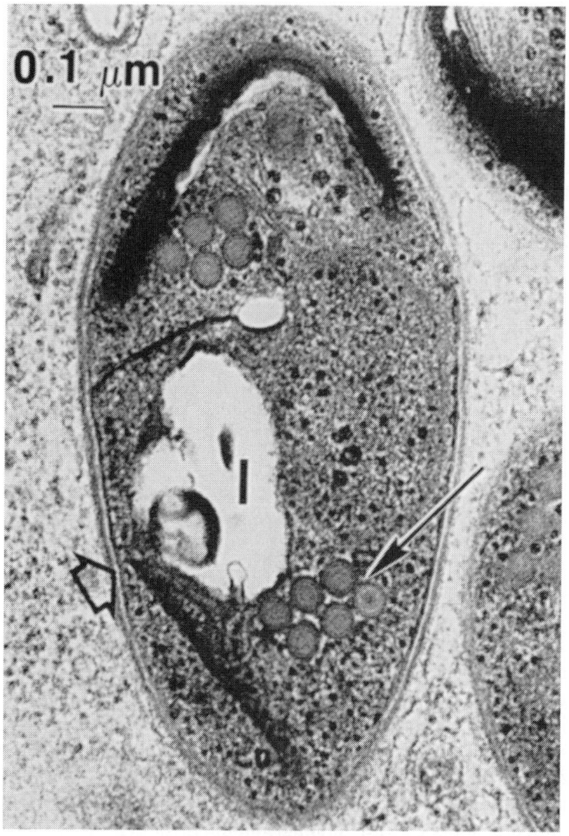

FIGURE 274–2. Transmission electron micrograph of an individual spore of *Enterocytozoon bieneusi* in a small bowel biopsy specimen. Spores are characterized by polar filaments seen in cross-section *(solid arrow)* that are coiled around electron-lucent inclusions (I). Outside the plasma membrane of the spore, an electron-lucent endospore layer *(open arrow)* and a dense outer spore coat are present. (From Weber R, Bryan RT, Owen RL, et al. Improved light microscopic detection of microsporidia spores in fecal specimens and duodenal aspirates from HIV-infected persons with intestinal microsporidiosis. N Engl J Med. 1992;326:161–166. Copyright © 1992 Massachusetts Medical Society. All rights reserved.)

EPIDEMIOLOGY

Persons suffering from a variety of microsporidial disease manifestations have been identified from all continents except Antarctica, but these persons are predominantly from Europe and North America. With new interest in the organisms and improved diagnostic approaches, case recognition in the developing regions of the world is increasingly common. Human infections are now well documented in several African nations,[45–52] Southeast Asia,[53] and South America.[54–56]

Serious illness due to microsporidial infections appears to occur predominantly in adults suffering from immunosuppression, especially that associated with human immunodeficiency virus (HIV) infection and acquired immunodeficiency syndrome (AIDS).[1, 2, 57, 58] Human microsporidiosis, however, is being increasingly recognized in persons with other forms of immunosuppression. Infections with *Ent. bieneusi* have been confirmed in HIV-negative liver and heart-lung transplant recipients,[59–61] as well as in at least one patient with unexplained immunosuppression.[62] *Enc. cuniculi* was identified in a kidney-pancreas transplant recipient,[63] and a case of pulmonary microsporidial infection (presumably an *Encephalitozoon* spp.) was confirmed at autopsy in a patient with chronic myeloid leukemia who had undergone bone marrow transplantation.[64] In addition to transplant recipients, chronic bilateral microsporidial keratoconjunctivitis occurred in a patient taking systemic prednisone (20 mg/day) for severe asthma.[65]

Although most recognized cases of human microsporidiosis are associated with some form of immunosuppression, reports describing microsporidial infections in HIV-negative, immunocompetent patients are also increasing. These reports have included instances of *Ent. bieneusi* infections in travelers as well as in adult and children residents of various tropical countries.[47, 49, 51, 60, 62, 66–70] *Enc. intestinalis* infection with associated chronic diarrhea has recently been observed in immunocompetent travelers.[71]

Of the at least 11 species of microsporidia known to cause human disease, *Ent. bieneusi* appears to be the most common. Since 1985 and the first recognition of *Ent. bieneusi* as an AIDS-associated opportunistic infection,[19] several hundred patients with chronic diarrhea attributed to this organism have been reported. Worldwide, between 1989 and 1998, at least 25 published studies of *Ent. bieneusi* in AIDS patients with chronic diarrhea have reported prevalences ranging from 4 to 50%. Combined, these studies have evaluated more than 2400 patients and confirmed some 375 cases of *Ent. bieneusi* infection, for an overall prevalence of approximately 15%. These observations suggest that we can reasonably expect that *Ent. bieneusi* accounts for a significant proportion of the chronic diarrheal disease observed in patients with AIDS. Although further studies are needed, at present there appears to be no consistent trends or variations in prevalence based on country of origin or other demographic characteristics.[1, 48, 52, 54, 56–58, 72–75]

Surveys for antibodies to microsporidia in human sera have focused exclusively on human exposure to *Encephalitozoon* spp. Studies published before 1991 have been summarized previously.[72] These earlier studies failed to produce any definitive epidemiologic conclusions. Although earlier studies targeted (presumably) *Enc. cuniculi*, recent publications have reported results based on human immunoreactivity to *Enc. intestinalis* and *Enc. hellem* as well. Human sera from France, the Netherlands, Slovakia, and the Czech Republic were variably screened for antibodies to *Encephalitozoon* spp. using techniques such as the enzyme-linked immunosorbent assay, indirect fluorescent antibody test, counterimmunoelectrophoresis, and complement fixation. Antibodies to *Enc. intestinalis* were found among pregnant French women (5%) and Dutch blood donors (8%).[76] Also, 5.3% of screened HIV-infected Czech patients were seropositive to *Enc. cuniculi,* whereas 1.3% showed seropositivity to *Enc. hellem.*[77] In Slovakia, 5.1% of screened slaughterhouse workers were seropositive for *Encephalitozoon* spp. (species not specified), but 92 forestry workers, 22 dog breeders, and 150 blood donors were all seronegative.[78] These more recent studies suffer from many of the same limitations as those of earlier years, including the use of convenience rather than random sampling techniques, but they do suggest that human infections with *Encephalitozoon* spp. may be more common than previously recognized.

Transmission of microsporidia occurs by several potential mechanisms. Waterborne transmission is an increasingly likely possibility given reports confirming the isolation of human-infecting microsporidia from surface water, tertiary sewage effluent, and ground water.[79, 80] Further, several groups of investigators have found that water contact may be an independent risk factor for intestinal microsporidiosis.[60, 81–83] Although two studies failed to show an association of water with intestinal microsporidiosis,[55, 84] the balance of evidence strongly suggests that the microsporidia are, in at least some instances, waterborne pathogens.

The well-documented presence of viable, infective spores in multiple body fluids and excreta suggests that person-to-person transmission is possible for most forms of human microsporidiosis. Extensive genitourinary tract involvement, including prostatic and urethral disease, is seen in disseminated infections with *Encephalitozoon* spp, indicating that person-to-person transmission by sexual means is at least anatomically feasible.[21, 85–87] Person-to-person transmission is also supported by observations of concurrent microsporidial infections in cohabitating homosexual men.[57] In addition, recent case-control studies have implicated male homosexuality[82] and having an HIV-infected cohabitant[81] as risk factors for acquiring intestinal microsporidiosis. Interestingly, in the mouse, rectal installation of *Enc. cuniculi* has been shown to cause disseminated infections.[88]

The occurrence of upper and lower respiratory tract infections suggests that microsporidiosis can be acquired by inhalation or transmitted via aerosolized infected materials. Transmission via the aerosol route has been implicated as a likely route of infection in reported cases of *Enc. hellem* infection.[21] The presence of *Encephalitozoon* spp. spores in respiratory secretions as well as in urine suggests that ocular infections with these agents may be acquired by external autoinoculation, perhaps by contaminated fingers.[89] Ingestion or inhalation of spore-laden urine contaminating animal cages is an established means of *Enc. cuniculi* transmission in rabbits and other laboratory animals, suggesting that comparable forms of environmental exposure could lead to human infection.[90, 91]

Substantial evidence is also accumulating to support the long-held contention that human microsporidiosis is often a zoonotic infection. Potential zoonotic sources have been identified for *Enc. cuniculi, Enc. hellem, Enc. intestinalis,* and *Ent. bieneusi.* Animal reservoirs identified thus far include dogs (*Enc. cuniculi* III), rabbits (*Enc. cuniculi* I), psittacine birds (*Enc. hellem*), a diverse group of farm animals—donkeys, pigs, dogs, cows, and goats (*Enc. intestinalis*), and pigs (*Ent. bieneusi*)—and rhesus macaque monkeys (*Ent. bieneusi*).[40–44, 92–97]

PATHOLOGY AND PATHOGENESIS

Eye and Ocular Adnexae

All three species of *Encephalitozoon* have been found in the eyes of patients with AIDS, and ocular disease is often the presenting manifestation of systemic encephalitozoonosis.[20, 22, 27, 89, 97–99] Infection with *Encephalitozoon* spp. often results in keratoconjunctivitis that is characterized clinically by numerous minute corneal ulcers (punctate epithelial keratopathy). Characteristic microsporidial spores are present in the corneal and conjunctival epithelium of ocular biopsies or cytologic specimens. The organisms do not invade the corneal stroma and are limited to the epithelium.

In contrast to *Encephalitozoon* keratoconjunctivitis, ocular infections due to *V. corneae* and *Nosema* spp. have been reported almost exclusively in immunocompetent persons, and these invade beyond the lining epithelium into the corneal stroma.[100]

Respiratory Tract

Respiratory tract infection due to microsporidia is associated with disseminated disease produced by all three members of the genus *Encephalitozoon*.[101] Infections may be limited to the upper or lower respiratory tract or may involve both. The pathologic features of sinonasal microsporidiosis are nonspecific and include rhinitis, sinusitis, and nasal polyposis, and patients frequently have all these entities simultaneously.[11, 101, 102]

Microsporidial infection of the lower respiratory tract, either with or without symptoms, appears to be a common component of disseminated microsporidiosis.[103] In one study of patients presenting with keratoconjunctivitis due to *Enc. hellem,* a significant number of persons had microsporidial spores present in sputum even though they had no pulmonary symptoms.[89] In the initial patient who underwent autopsy with disseminated *Enc. hellem* infection, massive numbers of gram-positive microsporidial spores were present diffusely throughout the entire length of the tracheobronchial tree, extending into terminal bronchioles, associated in some areas with an erosive tracheitis, bronchitis, and bronchiolitis.[21] This confluent pattern of microsporidial colonization of the superficial tracheobronchial mucosa, extending into terminal bronchioles, was suggestive of a respiratory mechanism of acquisition. Reports from additional patients have confirmed that all three species of *Encephalitozoon* can cause bronchiolitis with or without pneumonia.[101] Large numbers of gram-positive ovoid spores are abundant in epithelial cells lining bronchi and bronchioles, neutrophils within the bronchiolar wall, cells lining the alveoli, and extracellularly in alveolar spaces.

Genitourinary Tract

Urinary tract microsporidiosis appears to be common in patients with *Encephalitozoon* infections.[1, 11, 103–105] In HIV-infected patients, there is frequently simultaneous infection of the eyes, urinary tract, and bronchial tree, although many persons do not have symptoms referable to the kidneys or bladder. With *Enc. hellem* infections, the urinary tract may be the most severely affected organ system.[21] The kidneys show a geographic pattern of chronic and granulomatous interstitial nephritis, composed mostly of plasma cells and lymphocytes, with lesser numbers of histiocytes and neutrophils. Extensive tubular necrosis is present, and the lumina of many necrotic tubules are filled with amorphous, granular material. Coalescence of inflammatory cells around some necrotic tubules may result in microabscesses and poorly formed granulomas. Using tissue Gram stain, microsporidial spores are often seen concentrated in necrotic renal tubules and, to a lesser extent, in the interstitium. The glomeruli are almost always spared in microsporidial nephritis. Non–HIV-infected immunosuppressed recipients of organ transplants can also acquire *Encephalitozoon* infections. The pathologic features of renal infection due to *Enc. cuniculi* in one such patient did not differ significantly from the histologic appearance of microsporidial nephritis in patients with AIDS.[63]

Because of the propensity for *Encephalitozoon* spp. to infect renal tubular epithelium, spores are carried in the direction of urine flow from the kidneys through the ureters and into the bladder, infecting the urothelial lining epithelium of those structures and resulting in necrotizing ureteritis and cystitis.[106] Microsporidial spores can be identified in macrophages, urothelial cells, and extracellularly in the bladder and ureteral mucosa.

Genital tract involvement by *Encephalitozoon* has been reported to occur in association with urinary tract infection. In one patient, a large, central prostatic abscess was present at time of autopsy for disseminated *Enc. hellem*.[85] This abscess probably resulted from extension into the prostatic tissue from an initial focus in the prostatic urethral mucosa. Spores were present within necrotic abscess material, adjacent granulation tissue, and inflamed prostatic glands. The frequency of prostatic involvement in persons with disseminated microsporidiosis is not known.

Gastrointestinal and Hepatobiliary Tracts

Intestinal epithelium is the most prevalent site of human microsporidial infection (Fig. 274–3).[11, 100] Three microsporidial agents have been described from the intestinal tract—*Ent. bieneusi, Enc. intestinalis* and, in at least one patient, *Enc. cuniculi.*

The vast majority of microsporidial intestinal infections are caused by *Ent. bieneusi*.[11, 107, 108] Organisms tend to be present throughout the length of the small intestine, occurring within the cytoplasm of superficial lining enterocytes. *Ent. bieneusi* does not produce active enteritis, ulceration, or other histologic abnormalities specific for this infection. Using Gram staining, the spores appear smaller than those of *Encephalitozoon* and are usually present in the supranuclear portion of the cytoplasm. *Ent. bieneusi* infection is usually focal and, unlike *Encephalitozoon* infections, spores may be scarce and difficult to locate. In biopsy tissues, several levels of tissue sections should be examined using Gram or other appropriate stains before a biopsy result is diagnosed as negative.[106] In rare instances, spores are present beneath the epithelium in the lamina propria, but this has not been shown to represent a risk factor for disseminated infection.[109]

The intestines are frequently, if not always, involved in cases of *Enc. intestinalis* infection. Similar to *Ent. bieneusi*, this microsporidian does not produce any specific endoscopic or tissue abnormality. Unlike *Ent. bieneusi*, however, *Enc. intestinalis* is invasive, infecting not only enterocytes but also cells in the lamina propria including endothelial cells, fibroblasts, and macrophages.[110, 111] This pattern of

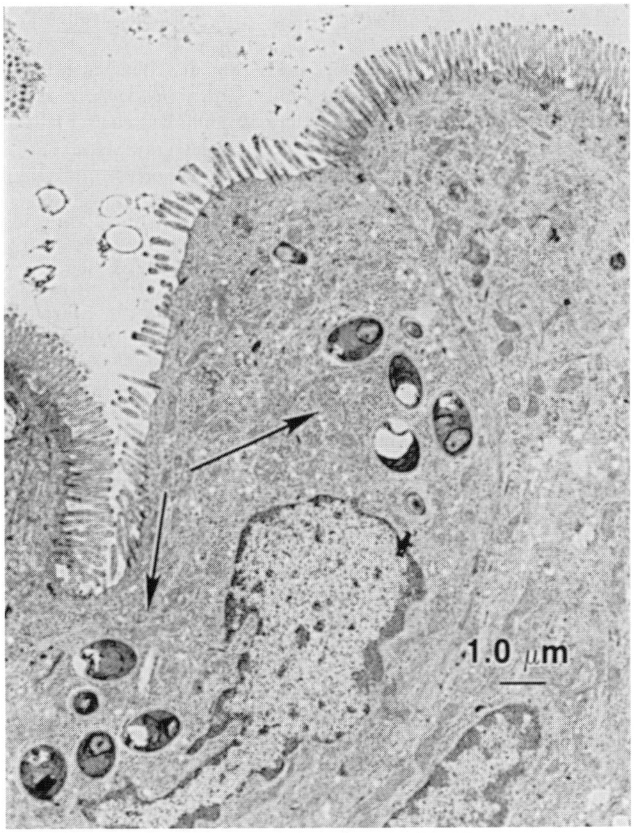

FIGURE 274–3. Low-power electron micrograph showing spores of *Enterocytozoon bieneusi (arrows)* in the cytoplasm of a jejunal enterocyte of a man infected with human immuno deficiency virus who had intractable diarrhea. Note the disrupted microvilli in the infected cell compared with those in the adjacent uninfected cells. (From Current WL, Owen RL. Cryptosporidiosis and microsporidiosis. In: Farthing JMG, Keusch GT, eds. Enteric Infection: Mechanisms, Manifestations, and Management. London: Chapman and Hall Medical; 1989:223–249.)

intestinal mucosal invasion presumably accounts for its capability to produce disseminated disease. *Enc. intestinalis* can also infect the large bowel.[112] In well-prepared, paraffin-embedded sections and in plastic-embedded, semithin sections the parasitophorous vacuole can often be seen surrounding the developing spores and separating them from the host cell cytoplasm. The biopsy finding of an intestinal microsporidian with a parasitophorous vacuole can permit a tentative diagnosis of *Enc. intestinalis* infection.

Microsporidia, usually *Ent. bieneusi* but also *Enc. intestinalis*, can infect the biliary tract.[11, 106, 113–115] Infections of nonparenchymal liver cells and the epithelium of bile ducts and, rarely, gallbladder have been reported. Infected biliary or gallbladder epithelial cells are often seen budding off and detaching from the underlying basement membrane. Granulomatous hepatitis due to *Encephalitozoon* spp. has been reported in patients with AIDS.[22] In recently described spontaneous infections of rhesus macaques (*Macacca mulatta*) with *Ent. bieneusi*, the gallbladder was the most heavily parasitized organ, raising the possibility of this anatomic site as a possible reservoir of infection in humans.[39]

Central Nervous System

Cerebral microsporidiosis has been described in several patients with AIDS. Disseminated disease with a "dog strain" of *Enc. cuniculi*, involving almost all organs, was identified at the time of autopsy in one female patient.[116] Spores were present in the cerebral parenchyma, in perivascular spaces, and within macrophages. No microsporidia were present in neurons, oligodendrocytes, astrocytes, or meningeal cells. In another patient with cerebral *Enc. cuniculi* infection due to a "rabbit strain," brain tissue was not available for study.[117]

Two patients with AIDS died following disseminated infection with the newly described microsporidian, *Trachipleistophora anthropophthera*.[33] Both patients, a child and an adult, had central nervous system infection with multiple ring-enhancing gray matter lesions shown by computed tomography. These lesions consisted of central areas of necrosis filled with free spores and spore-laden macrophages surrounded by microsporidia-filled astrocytes.

Musculoskeletal System

Inflammatory myositis has been attributed to three different microsporidial agents—*Pleistophora* sp., *Trachipleistophora hominis*, and *B. vesicularum*.[28, 30, 37, 38, 118, 119] Biopsies from three persons with myositis due to *Pleistophora* sp. revealed atrophic and degenerating skeletal muscle fibers, which were focally infiltrated by clusters of microsporidia measuring up to 3.4 μm in length. There was an associated mild inflammatory infiltrate composed of plasma cells, lymphocytes, eosinophils, and histiocytes in the two patients with AIDS, and in an HIV-seronegative person the inflammatory response was severe.[28, 119] A deltoid muscle biopsy from a patient with AIDS and *T. hominis* infection showed discrete lesions consisting of a central zone of fibrosis and degenerated skeletal muscle fibers, surrounded by myofibers containing variable numbers of sporophorous vesicles. The vesicles contained up to 32 spores or spore precursors.[30]

Other Tissues

Microsporidial infection of the peritoneum has been described due to *Enc. cuniculi*.[120] At autopsy, a 20-cm lobulated inflammatory mass of the omentum was found that contained focal necrosis, nongranulomatous inflammation, and microsporidial spores. The species identity of this microsporidian was not confirmed using antigenic or nucleic acid methods.

Rare microsporidial spores were identified in the soft tissues beneath a tongue ulcer in an AIDS patient with disseminated, confirmed *Enc. cuniculi* infection[23]; it is not known whether or not the microsporidia were the direct cause of ulceration.

CLINICAL MANIFESTATIONS

Microsporidiosis in Persons Not Infected with Human Immunodeficiency Virus (Table 274–2)

Intestinal Infections. Spores of *Ent. bieneusi* and *Enc. intestinalis* have been detected in stool specimens from HIV-negative, immunocompromised hosts as well as from a few otherwise healthy, immunocompetent children and adults. Although case reports of intestinal microsporidial infections in organ transplant recipients, patients with other forms of immunosuppression, and immunocompetent travelers have suggested a clinical association with diarrhea, a definitive causal link has not yet been firmly established. Among these case reports, clinical manifestations of intestinal microsporidiosis have included watery, nonbloody diarrhea; nausea; diffuse abdominal pain; and fever. Diarrhea was always self-limited in immunocompetent persons but tended to persist in those who were immunocompromised.[46, 57, 49, 59, 61–66, 68, 70, 71, 83, 121]

Ocular Infections. Four patients without overt evidence of underlying immunodeficiency have been observed with deep corneal stroma infection or a corneal ulcer due to different microsporidia. In addition, superficial keratoconjunctivitis has been reported in one HIV-negative, immunocompromised patient. These case reports are summarized in Table 274–2.[72, 98, 122–124, 127] Of note, one of these cases resulted in the first successful isolation of a microsporidian (*V. corneae*, formerly *Nosema corneum*) from human tissues.[35–36]

Cerebral Infections. Cerebral infections in nonimmunocompromised hosts appear to be extremely rare. The two probable cases found in the literature are summarized in Table 274–2.[125–126] Although both patients were thought at the time to be infected with *Enc. cuniculi*, there is no way to confirm this assumption because the knowledge and techniques needed to distinguish this microsporidian from *Enc. hellem* or *Enc. intestinalis* were not available in 1959 or 1984 when these cases were observed.

Systemic Infections in Human Immunodeficiency Virus–Negative Immunocompromised Hosts. At least two cases of severe microsporidial disease have been observed in HIV-negative, immunocompromised patients. In the first, fatal, disseminated infection with *Nosema connori* occurred in a 4-month-old boy with thymic alymphoplasia.[26] The second case involved a 20-year-old male prisoner with diffuse myopathy in whom muscle biopsy demonstrated scarring and fibrosis with an intense inflammatory reaction. Atrophic and degenerating muscle β-fibers were extensively infiltrated with microsporidial spores consistent with *Pleistophora* spp. Muscle enzyme levels, however, were normal. Immunologic evaluation showed depressed cell-mediated immunity, but test results for HIV were repeatedly negative.[119, 128]

Microsporidiosis in Persons Infected with Human Immunodeficiency Virus (Table 274–3)

Intestinal Infections with *Enterocytozoon bieneusi*. Chronic diarrhea, anorexia, and weight loss are the most common manifestations of *Ent. bieneusi* infections in the HIV-infected population. Patients typically report from 3 to 10 bowel movements per day (ranging from 1 to more than 20). Stools are loose to watery and, unless coinfected with invasive intestinal pathogens, nonbloody and without fecal leukocytes.[1, 16, 17, 72, 107, 137, 144–148] Diarrhea seems to be worsened by most foods and tends to be more frequent in the mornings.[1, 11, 107, 158, 159] Laboratory evidence for intestinal malabsorption is common and CD4 lymphocyte counts are usually low (<100 cells/mm^3). The increased stool frequency (with incontinence in severe cases), malabsorption, and weight loss associated with *Ent. bieneusi* infections often result in a protracted debilitating illness that has a severe impact on the infected person's quality of life.[137, 158, 160] Prolonged diarrhea for up to 48 months has been reported.[137, 160, 161]

Other signs and symptoms reported in association with *Ent. bie-*

TABLE 274–2 Summary of Microsporidiosis in Persons Not Infected with Human Immunodeficiency Virus

Clinical Syndrome	Microsporidial Species	Patients and Location	Clinical Manifestations	Immune Status	Parasite Detection	Year (References)
			Intestinal Infection			
Tropical countries	*Enterocytozoon bieneusi*	8 children, 3–26 mo old, Niger	Diarrhea (2 asymptomatic carriers)	Not assessed*	Stool examination	1993 (46)
	Encephalitozoon intestinalis	20 (7.8% of 255 examined) children and adults, Mexico	Not assessed	Not assessed	Stool examination, IF	1998 (83)
	Enterocytozoon bieneusi	Child, Zambia	Asymptomatic	HIV-seronegative	Stool examination	1997 (49)
	Enterocytozoon bieneusi	35-yr-old man, Mali	Hemiplegia, wasting syndrome, cough, diarrhea	HIV-seronegative, immune status not assessed	Duodenal biopsy	1998 (121)
	Microsporidia (not specified)	22- and 32-yr-old man, Mali	Fever, chronic diarrhea	HIV-seronegative, immune status not assessed	Stool examination	1998 (121)
Travelers	*Enterocytozoon bieneusi*	26-yr-old men, Germany	Diarrhea (self-limited) after travel to Egypt, Jordan	Normal	Stool examination	1993 (69)
	Enterocytozoon bieneusi	3-yr-old girl, Germany	Chronic diarrhea after travel to Turkey	Normal		1995 (70)
	Encephalitozoon intestinalis	4 travelers	Chronic diarrhea, travel to Africa, Nepal, Asia	Normal	Stool exam, PCR	1998 (71)
Immunocompetent persons	*Enterocytozoon bieneusi*	26-yr-old woman, Switzerland (nurse)	Acute diarrhea	Normal	Stool examination	1995 (68)
	Enterocytozoon bieneusi	24-yr-old woman, Spain	Chronic diarrhea	Normal	Stool examination	1998 (66)
Organ transplant recipients	*Enterocytozoon bieneusi*	32-yr-old woman, U.S.	Diarrhea	Liver transplant, immunosuppressed	Stool examination	1995 (61)
	Enterocytozoon bieneusi	48-yr-old woman, France	Diarrhea	Heart-lung transplant, immunosuppressed	Stool examination	1996 (59)
Otherwise immunocompromised hosts	*Enterocytozoon bieneusi*	42-yr-old man, U.S.	Chronic diarrhea	CD4 cells 0.52 × 10⁹/L, HIV-seronegative	Stool examination	1996 (62)
	Enterocytozoon bieneusi	66-yr-old man, Spain	Chronic diarrhea	CD4 cells 0.32 × 10⁹/L, HIV-seronegative	Stool examination	1998 (66)
			Ocular Infections			
Corneal stroma infection	*Microsporidium ceylonensis*	11-yr-old boy, Sri Lanka	Corneal scarring	Unknown	Corneal histology	1973 (122)
	Microsporidium africanum	26-year-old woman, Botswana	Corneal ulcer	Unknown	Corneal histology	1981 (123)
	Nosema corneum	45-year-old man, U.S.	Keratitis/iritis	Normal	Corneal histology	1990 (35, 124)
	Nosema ocularum	39-year-old man, U.S.	Corneal ulcer	Normal	Corneal histology	1991 (72, 98)
Keratoconjunctivitis	Microsporidia (not specified)	35-year-old woman, U.S.	Bilateral keratotoconjunctivitis	HIV seronegative, immunocompromised, oral prednisone (20 mg/d)	Corneal scraping	1997 (65)
			Central Nervous System Infections			
	Encephalitozoon cuniculi	9-year-old boy, Japan	Seizures	Unknown; anergy after BCG	CSf examination, urine examination	1959 (125)
	Encephalitozoon cuniculi	2-year-old boy, Colombia†	Seizures	Low CD4⁺/CD8⁺ cell ratio	Serum Ab, urine examination	1984 (126)
			Various Opportunistic Infections			
Systemic infection	*Nosema connori*	4-month-old boy, U.S.	Diarrhea, systemic disease	Thymic alymphoplasia	Autopsy	1973 (26)
Myositis	*Pleistophora* spp.	20-year-old man, U.S.	Myositis	HIV seronegative, cellular immunodeficiency	Muscle biopsy	1985 (119, 128)
Pulmonary infection in bone marrow transplant recipient	Microsporidia (not specified)	27-yr-old woman, India	Pneumonitis	Allogeneic bone marrow transplant, immunosuppressed	Autopsy	1997 (64)
Renal infection in kidney-pancreas transplant recipient	*Encephalitozoon cuniculi*	40-yr-old woman, U.S.	Renal failure, renal graft infection, presumably systemic infection	Kidney-pancreas transplant, immunosuppressed (HIV-seronegative)	Renal biopsy, urine examination	1998 (63)

* HIV status was not evaluated. Because the HIV seroprevalence among pregnant women was only 0.5%, it is unlikely that many children were infected with HIV.
† Diagnosed in Sweden.
Abbreviations: BCG, Calmette-Guérin bacillus vaccine; CSF, cerebrospinal fluid; HIV, human immunodeficiency virus; IF, immunofluorescence detection procedures; PCR, polymerase chain reaction.

TABLE 274-3 Microsporidiosis in Persons Infected with Human Immunodeficiency Virus

Microsporidial Species	Clinical Manifestations*	Diagnostic Techniques	Pertinent References
Enterocytozoon bieneusi	Enteritis, chronic diarrhea	Stool examination, duodenal lavage, small bowel biopsy	15, 16, 19, 107, 137, 144–148
	Cholangitis, "AIDS cholangiopathy," acalculous cholecystitis	Cholecystectomy, autopsy, biliary fluid examination	113–115
	(Chronic) rhinosinusitis, bronchitis, pneumonitis	Nasal biopsy, sputum examination, BAL, transbronchial biopsy	130, 134, 149
Encephalitozoon hellem	Systemic infection	Urine examination, respiratory specimens, autopsy	21, 94, 104, 150, 151
	Keratoconjunctivitis	Corneal-conjunctival smear, scraping, or biopsy	72, 89, 99, 152–156
	(Chronic) rhinosinusitis, nasal polyposis, bronchiolitis, pneumonitis	Nasal smear, sinunasal lavage, sinus biopsy, sputum examination, BAL, transbronchial biopsy, autopsy	21, 102–103, 132, 138–139, 153, 157
	Nephritis, ureteritis, cystitis, prostatitis, urethritis	Urine examination bladder biopsy, autopsy	21, 85, 87, 94, 150–151
Encephalitozoon intestinalis (formerly *Septata intestinalis*)	Enteritis, chronic diarrhea, small bowel perforation	Stool examination, intestinal biopsy, autopsy	24, 105, 110–112, 141
	Biliary tract infection	Cholecystectomy, autopsy, biliary fluid examination	24, 105, 110–111
	Conjunctivitis	Corneal-conjunctival smear, scraping, or biopsy	105
	Rhinosinusitis, bronchitis	Nasal smear, sinunasal lavage, sinus biopsy	112, 131, 142
	Nephritis	Urine examination, autopsy	24, 110–112
	Bone infection	Biopsy	129
Encephalitozoon cuniculi	Disseminated infection	Urine examination, respiratory specimens, CSF examination	23, 92, 94, 95, 117, 133, 143
	Keratoconjunctivitis	Corneal-conjunctival smear, scraping, or biopsy	23, 117
	Rhinosinusitis, bronchiolitis, pneumonitis	Sinunasal smear-lavage, sputum, BAL	23, 94, 117, 143
	Nephritis, ureteritis, cystitis	Urine examination	23, 94, 135
	Hepatitis, peritonitis	Liver biopsy, autopsy	22, 120
	Encephalitis	CSF examination	116–117
Encephalitozoon spp.	Cutaneous infection	Skin biopsy	136
	Fulminant hepatic failure	Autopsy	140
Pleistophora spp.	Myositis	Muscle biopsy	28
Trachipleistophora hominis	Myositis	Muscle biopsy	31
	Keratoconjunctivitis, sinusitis	Sinunasal aspirate	31
Trachipleistophora anthropophthera	Disseminated infection including almost all organs including brain	Autopsy	32–33
Brachiola vesicularum	Myositis	Muscle biopsy	37–38
Vittaforma corneae (formerly *Nosema corneum*)	Urinary tract infection, possibly disseminated infection	Urine examination	34

* asymptomatic carriers described for *Ent. bieneusi, Enc. hellem, Enc. cuniculi.*
Abbreviations: BAL, Bronchoalveolar lavage; CSF, cerebrospinal fluid.

neusi intestinal infections include abdominal pain, nausea, vomiting, and fever. These findings, however, may represent concomitant biliary infection that typically produces clinical manifestations consistent with cholangitis or cholecystitis. *Ent. bieneusi* is now recognized as at least one cause of AIDS-related sclerosing cholangitis.[113–115] Clinical jaundice is rarely evident. Imaging procedures (abdominal ultrasonography and computed tomography, endoscopic ultrasonography, and endoscopic retrograde cholangiopancreatography) often reveal dilatation of both intrahepatic and common bile ducts, irregularities of the bile duct wall, and gallbladder abnormalities such as wall thickening, distention, or the presence of sludge. Papillary stenosis may also be present. Laboratory values for serum alkaline phosphatase, gamma-glutamyltransferase, and aspartate and alanine aminotransferases are usually elevated (two to three times upper limit of normal), but bilirubin is usually normal.[113–115]

Intestinobiliary coinfections with *Ent. bieneusi* and other enteric pathogens are being recognized with increasing frequency, emphasizing the need to perform thorough diagnostic evaluations for dual or even multiple parasitic infections in persons with HIV-associated chronic diarrhea.[162, 163]

Respiratory tract involvement with *Ent. bieneusi* was observed in two patients with chronic diarrhea, persistent cough, dyspnea, and wheezing. Chest radiographs revealed interstitial infiltrates. Spores of *Ent. bieneusi* were detected in bronchoalveolar lavage fluid, transbronchial biopsy specimens, and stool.[130, 149] A single case of rhinosinusitis attributed to *Ent. bieneusi* has also been reported.[134]

Reports of deaths directly attributable to *Ent. bieneusi* are rare, but reported mortality rates in patients with intestinal *Ent. bieneusi* have been as high as 56%.[114, 147, 164] Although therapeutic options are limited, recent studies have found that improvements in immune function can result in significant clinical improvement and normalization of intestinal architecture.[165–168]

Intestinal and Systemic Infections with *Encephalitozoon intestinalis*. Diarrheal illness associated with enteric *Enc. intestinalis* infection appears to be similar to that associated with *Ent. bieneusi*. Also similar is the ability of *Enc. intestinalis* to infect biliary epithelium. *Enc. intestinalis*, however, has been shown to disseminate to distant organs where the most predominant histopathology appears to occur in the kidneys.[24, 110, 111] In addition to enteritis, clinical manifestations of *Enc. intestinalis* may include signs and symptoms of cholecystitis, renal failure, and upper respiratory infections.[111, 112, 132] Bony destruction of the maxillary antra[129] and ocular involvement have also been reported.[11, 105, 112]

Systemic Infections with *Encephalitozoon hellem* and *Encephalitozoon cuniculi*. Keratoconjunctivitis has generally been the first and most commonly recognized clinical manifestation of these infections. Symptoms include dry eyes, foreign body sensation, ocular pain, excessive tearing, blurred vision, and photophobia—all of which may range from mild to severe. On physical examination, conjunctival hyperemia is common. Ophthalmologic slit lamp examination often reveals a characteristic diffuse, superficial punctate keratopathy (Fig. 274-4). Infection is frequently bilateral, but not all patients exhibit keratopathy. Cases with only mild conjunctivitis have been reported.[89, 151] Corneal ulceration rarely, if ever, occurs. Retinal involvement with *Encephalitozoon* has not been reported.[72, 89, 99, 154]

Although most known cases of HIV-associated infection with *Encephalitozoon* were initially diagnosed because of symptomatic keratoconjunctivitis, it now appears that ocular disease rarely, if ever, occurs in the absence of systemic microsporidial infection. In almost

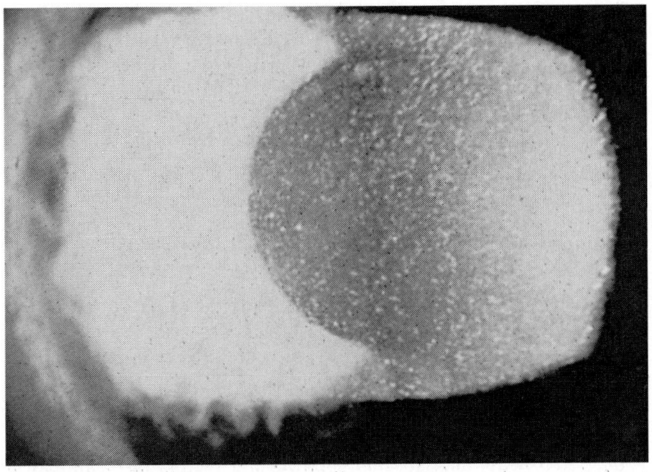

FIGURE 274–4. Slit-lamp photograph showing *Encephalitozoon*-associated diffuse superfical punctate keratopathy.

every patient with *Encephalitozoon* infection in whom ocular, respiratory, and urinary specimens were available, microsporidia were detected in at least two of three specimens.[21, 23, 102, 103, 117, 143, 151] As with *Enterocytozoon,* CD4 lymphocyte counts are generally low in AIDS patients with encephalitozoonosis. In addition to keratoconjunctivitis, the spectrum of recognized *Encephalitozoon*-associated disease includes bronchiolitis, sinusitis, nephritis, cystitis-ureteritis, urethritis, prostatitis, hepatitis, fulminant hepatic failure, and peritonitis.[1, 11, 21, 22, 85, 103, 120, 140] Also, symptomatic cerebral infection was recently documented.[116, 117] In one of these patients, the cranial computed tomographic and magnetic resonance imaging scans showed multiple small, contrast-enhancing, ringlike (or micronodular) lesions in hippocampal, mesencephalic, and intracortical regions.[117] In addition, an *Encephalitozoon*-like microsporidian has been associated with nodular skin infection.[136] *Encephalitozoon* infections may exhibit a wide range of severity, from essentially asymptomatic infection to chronic rhinosinusitis to lethal respiratory or renal failure.

Myositis. Myositis in patients with AIDS has been attributed to several microsporidial species (*Pleistophora* spp., *T. hominis*, *B. vesicularum*).[28–30, 37–38] Prominent clinical manifestations include diffuse myalgias and muscular weakness. Laboratory tests are notable for elevated serum levels of creatinine phosphokinase and aldolase. Electromyography often shows a diffuse, active myopathic process with denervation characteristic of inflammatory myopathy. Muscle biopsies demonstrate focal areas of atrophic muscle fibers containing clusters of microsporidia and scant inflammatory infiltrates.

Systemic Infections with Other Microsporidia. Infections due to other microsporidial species have been described in isolated case reports. *T. anthropophthera* was identified at autopsy in multiple organs, including brain, of patients presenting with seizures.[32–33] A computed tomographic scan of one of these patients showed similar findings as those observed in a patient with cerebral *Enc. cuniculi* infection,[117] that is, multiple, ring-enhancing lesions of less than 1 cm in diameter.

V. corneae was recently isolated from the urine of an HIV-infected patient with signs and symptoms of urinary tract infection and chronic prostatitis.[34]

DIAGNOSIS

Stool Examination

Microscopic examination of stool is the easiest and most practical method for diagnosis of intestinal microsporidiosis caused by *Ent. bieneusi* and *Enc. intestinalis.* Several staining techniques are currently used by laboratories throughout the world, but experience is greatest with Weber chromotrope-based stain and its modifications, as well as various chemofluorescent stains.[16, 169, 170] Because of clinical and therapeutic differences, it is important to distinguish between the two aforementioned species. The spores of *Enc. intestinalis* are larger than those of *Ent. bieneusi*, permitting a tentative genus-level diagnosis when stool smears are well prepared and the observers are experienced. Spores of *Ent. bieneusi* measure approximately 1.5 × 0.9 μm, whereas those of *Encephalitozoon* spp. measure 2.5 to 3.0 × 1.0 to 1.5 μm. However, in many cases it is necessary to confirm the identity of the agent using either intestinal biopsy with electron microscopy or, when available, molecular techniques such as polymerase chain reaction. Using chromotrope-based staining methods, microsporidial spore walls stain bright pink-red, and although some spores appear transparent, others have a distinctive equatorial beltlike stripe. A new modification of this technique, the rapid Gram-chromotrope method, combines the chromotrope stain with a Gram-staining step, resulting in rapid (11 minutes) crisp violet staining of microsporidial spores.[171]

Chemofluorescent optical brightening agents, which require examination using a fluorescence microscope, stain microsporidial spores by adherence to the chitinous spore wall. Fungi and other fecal elements may also be brightened, leading some investigators to recommend that stool screening be performed with a chemofluorescent stain and results confirmed using a chromotrope-based stain.[172]

Cytologic Diagnosis

Cytologic techniques are easily performed, inexpensive, and rapid methods for diagnosis of microsporidiosis in most organ systems. Although there are some important exceptions, microsporidial infections in humans generally affect mucosal and epithelial-lined tissues, and are thus amenable to relatively safe, noninvasive cytologic techniques. Cytologic methods are particularly useful for the diagnosis of microsporidial infections of intestinal and biliary epithelium, epithelium of the cornea and conjunctivae, epithelium of the sinonasal and tracheobronchial region, and renal tubular epithelium and urothelium. Body fluids that may be useful for diagnosis of microsporidiosis include urine, cerebrospinal fluid, bile, duodenal aspirates, bronchoalveolar lavage fluid, and sputum.[106, 118, 173]

Cytologic studies are especially suited for screening patients who are at high risk for microsporidial infection and for evaluating the efficacy of novel treatment of microsporidiosis. The specific technique (e.g., lavage, scrape, smear, swab, fluid concentrate) used for obtaining cytologic material for diagnosis is dependent on the site of infection.

The laboratory technique for preparing glass slides for microsporidial examination, which is similar for all cytologic specimens, has recently been reviewed.[1, 118] Microsporidial spores are difficult to identify using conventional hematoxylin and eosin and Papanicolaou stains. In most laboratories, Gram stain and chromotrope-based staining methods are used with excellent results. Using Gram stain, the microsporidial spores of *Encephalitozoon* spp. usually appear purple or light violet. *Ent. bieneusi* spores have greater variability in their Gram-staining features, appearing gram-positive, -negative, or -intermediate. In general, Weber original chromotrope-based stain is preferable to the Gram stain in specimens that contain large numbers of bacteria, such as stool. Other cytologic stains used to identify microsporidial spores include Giemsa, Steiner silver, trichrome-blue, and chemofluorescent optical brightening agents.[170, 174] When using any of the staining techniques, it is important that microsporidial spores not be confused with yeast or bacteria. Microsporidial spores have a uniform oval shape, are nonbudding, and many contain an equatorial belt across the midline of the spore, or polar granules.

Histologic Diagnosis

Histologic examination of biopsy and autopsy tissues continues to be one of the most important methods for routine diagnosis of microsporidiosis. Similar to cytologic specimens, spores cannot be readily identified in tissue sections stained with hematoxylin and eosin. The tissue Gram stain, using either Brown and Brenn or Brown and Hopp modifications, is the preferred stain in most pathology laboratories (Fig. 274–5). Because intestinal microsporidial infections usually produce no characteristic inflammatory response, the pathologist must maintain a high index of suspicion to request Gram stains on intestinal biopsies of patients who are at risk for this infection. Microsporidial spores in Gram-stained tissue sections have a similar appearance to those in cytologic specimens—they are usually gram-positive, but may be gram-negative or Gram-variable, and are distinguished from similar-sized yeasts, bacteria, or nuclear debris by having an equatorial beltlike stripe. Other histochemical stains that may be useful include period acid–Schiff, Steiner silver stain, and Giemsa. Because the parasite burden in infected tissues may be low, especially in intestinal biopsies with *Ent. bieneusi*, several tissue sections (serial sections or levels) should be examined when there is a strong suspicion of infection.[106, 118]

Biopsy or autopsy tissues can be fixed for microsporidial examination using routine fixatives. When a definitive genus- or species-level identification is required, tissues well fixed in formalin can be used for ultrastructural analysis by electron microscopy without significant loss of the diagnostic features of the parasites.[175] Species-specific fluorescent antibody stains can also be performed on formalin-fixed, paraffin-embedded tissue sections (see farther on).[106, 118, 173]

Ultrastructure, Nucleic Acid–Based Methods, Immunofluorescence, Serologic Studies, and Tissue Culture

Electron microscopy is a useful technique that is currently the most widely available of the specialized methods for confirmation of microsporidial infections. Although most easily performed in tissue specimens, it has also proved useful, but time-consuming, for analysis of stool and body fluid specimens in selected situations. Ultrastructural examination in well-fixed specimens can often provide a genus-specific, and often a species-level, diagnosis of many microsporidial infections including *Ent. bieneusi, Enc. intestinalis, Pleistophora* spp., *Trachipleistophora* spp., *Nosema* spp., and *V. corneae. Enc. hellem* and *Enc. cuniculi* cannot be reliably distinguished from one another by morphologic criteria. Ultrastructure can also identify coinfections with other agents[162] and can be used to assess the effects of medications on microsporidial viability.[176]

There has been great attention paid to the development of a battery of nucleic acid-based methods for species-specific diagnosis of microsporidiosis. The great advantage of these methods is their sensitivity and specificity. They are also useful for taxonomic classification and phylogenetic analysis. Several polymerase chain reaction assays that target small ribosomal subunit genes have been successfully used to diagnose *Ent. bieneusi*, all three species of *Encephalitozoon, V. corneae*, and *Nosema* spp. Several factors have limited the clinical utility of molecular testing for microsporidial agents, including the restriction of these methods to a few research laboratories and the requirement for special handling and fixation of the diagnostic specimens.[118]

Immunodetection of microsporidia in tissue sections or cytologic specimens can be performed by most laboratories when the appropriate immunologic reagents are available. Unlike histologic methods, which stain only the spore or sporoblast walls, immunofluorescent detection procedures, especially using polyclonal antisera, visualize spores as well as extruded polar tubules and immature developmental stages. Immunofluorescent detection of microsporidia can be performed with most clinical specimens, including formalin-fixed, paraffin-embedded tissues. It is not very useful for stool diagnosis because of high background staining. Antisera are available in research laboratories for many microsporidial pathogens. Unfortunately, no effective antibody has yet been developed for the most prevalent agent, *Ent. bieneusi*.[100, 118, 177]

Serologic tests of various types have been used to detect antibodies to microsporidia in several serosurveys. The specificity of such assays, however, remains unknown, and it is unclear whether the presence of antibodies to microsporidia represents true previous infections. Thus, serologic studies are not a clinically useful technique at the present time.[118]

The tissue culture and propagation of microsporidial agents that infect humans has been of enormous benefit, both in understanding the biologic aspects of the host cell–parasite relationship and in the development of immunologic reagents for use in clinical diagnosis. Microsporidial tissue culture is available in only a few specialized laboratories, and it is not practical to use this method for routine clinical diagnosis. Microsporidia that have been successfully cultivated from human specimens include *Enc. hellem, Enc. cuniculi, Enc. intestinalis, V. corneae, Pleistophora* sp., and *T. hominis. Ent. bieneusi* has been propagated only in short-term culture.[177]

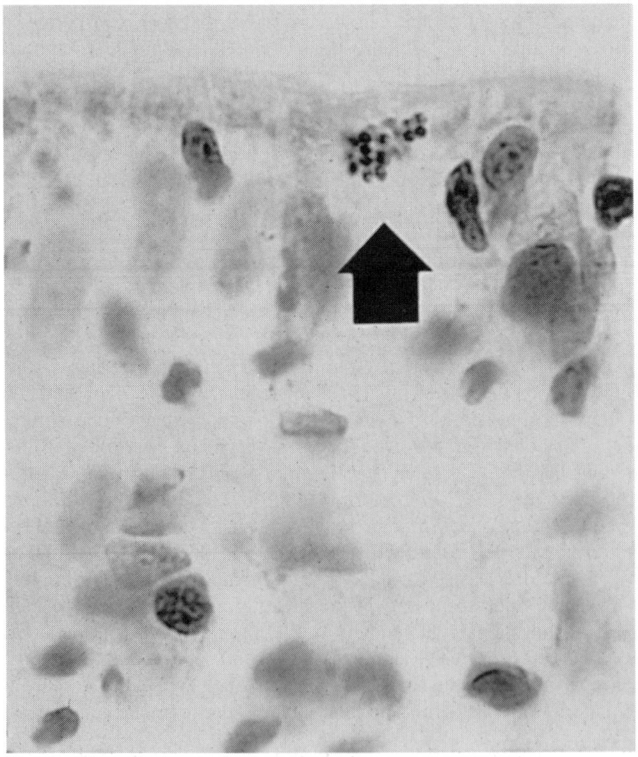

FIGURE 274–5. Small bowel biopsy specimen containing a cluster gram-positive *Enterocytozoon bieneusi* spores near the luminal surface of an enterocyte (Brown-Hopp, ×1000.)

TREATMENT

In vitro susceptibility testing for microsporidia is hampered because these protozoa do not grow on axenic media. Propagation in cell culture and drug susceptibility testing has been accomplished with some human-infecting species (including *Encephalitozoon* spp., *Vittaforma*).[178, 179] Albendazole, as well as other benzimidazole derivatives, has been shown to cause growth deformities of *Encephalitozoon* spp. and to reduce or eradicate the parasites propagated in cell cultures.[180–182] Other in vitro studies, however, suggest that albendazole does not destroy mature microsporidial spores so that these may sustain infection.[181, 183] Fumagillin has been shown to inhibit replication of *Enc. cuniculi* in infected cell cultures,[178, 180, 181, 183, 184] but lasting eradication of the parasites has not been achieved. In addition, the semisynthetic fumagillin analogue, TNP-470, appears to have similar in vitro activity against *Enc. intestinalis* and *V.*

corneae.[184, 185] Other substances, among them 5-fluorouracil, sparfloxacin,[180] propamidine isethionate, thiabendazole and oxibendazole,[181] sinefungin,[186] the calcium channel blocker nifedipine, and two nitric oxide donors (S-nitroso-*N*-acetylpenicillamine and sodium nitroprusside),[187] have been shown to inhibit replication or spore germination of *Encephalitozoon* spp. in vitro. Furthermore, chloroquine,[180, 188] perfloxacin, azithromycin, and rifabutin were partially effective at high concentrations.[180] Cytochalasin D, demecolcine, nifedipine and itraconazole were found to inhibit spontaneous and H_2O_2-stimulated polar filament extrusion.[189]

Little information on clinical experience in the therapy of human microsporidiosis is available, and blinded, placebo-controlled comparative treatment trials are, with one exception, lacking. Most published studies to date have involved severely immunocompromised, HIV-infected patients. An increasing number of case observations indicate that a 2- to 4-week course of oral albendazole, 400 mg twice daily, leads to clinical improvement and apparent parasite eradication from stool, urine, respiratory specimens, or conjunctival scrapings in HIV-infected patients with *Enc. intestinalis*, *Enc. hellem*, and *Enc. cuniculi* infections.[105, 190, 191] Case reports of a response to albendazole included patients with chronic sinusitis or lower respiratory tract infections,[94, 102, 117] urethritis,[87] renal failure,[192] cerebral encephalitozoonosis,[117] and disseminated infection.[23, 112, 132] Complete treatment failures were rare, but at least one fatal treatment failure in a patient with cerebral *Enc. cuniculi* infection has been reported.[117] A double-blind, placebo-controlled trial including eight patients with AIDS and diarrhea due to *Enc. intestinalis* infection has confirmed that treatment with albendazole, 400 mg twice daily for 3 weeks, results in clinical improvement as well as clearance of microsporidia from the intestine in all patients.[105]

In contrast, no therapy has been proved effective for *Ent. bieneusi* infection. Preliminary reports of a clinical response among patients treated with metronidazole,[164] azithromycin,[193] atovaquone,[194] and various other antibiotics or antiprotozoal drugs could not be substantiated.[195, 196] Some reports have suggested that treatment with albendazole may lead to clinical improvement in some patients, although parasites were still present in intestinal biopsy specimens, and microsporidial spores were still detected in stool specimens obtained after treatment.[197] In an open-label prospective trial conducted before potent antiretroviral therapy was available, 400 mg albendazole (twice daily for 4 weeks or longer) was used. In 13 of 26 patients, there was a greater than 50% reduction in bowel movements, and in 9 patients there was a partial response. Repeat small bowel biopsy revealed persistent microsporidial infection in all patients, irrespective of their clinical response to albendazole.[198] Thalidomide was studied in 18 severely immunodeficient HIV-infected patients with chronic diarrhea due to *Ent. bieneusi* that had not responded to albendazole.[176] After a 1-month course of 100 mg thalidomide, complete clinical response was observed in seven and partial clinical response in three patients, but parasite load as determined in biopsy specimens did not decrease in any patient. Transient clinical remission was reported in single patients treated with furazolidone.[199] Oral purified fumagillin was recently used in a pilot study to treat 9 HIV-infected patients with *Ent. bieneusi*–associated chronic diarrhea.[196] The investigators reported a rapid eradication of the parasite, but a follow-up study found frequent relapses.[200] Furthermore, the drug caused severe thrombocytopenia in many patients.

An HIV-infected patient with myositis due to *T. hominis*, was successfully treated with a combination of albendazole (400 mg twice daily), sulfadiazine (1 g four times daily), pyrimethamine (50 mg daily), and folinic acid (7.5 mg daily).[30]

Because microsporidial infections are observed mainly in severely immunodeficient patients, it was hypothesized that such patients could benefit from highly active antiretroviral therapy. Clinical studies indeed have shown that an improvement in immune function can result in complete clinical response and normalization of intestinal architecture in conjunction with clearance of the parasites.[165–168, 201] However, recurrent diarrhea and parasitologic relapse was observed in patients with failure of antiretroviral therapy associated with declining blood CD4 lymphocyte counts.[167] Also, these observations indicated that intestinal parasites can probably not be eradicated in immunodeficient patients by transient improvement of immune functions.

PREVENTION

Although data to support effective preventive strategies are limited, the presence of infective spores in body fluids and feces suggests that body substance precautions in health care and other institutional settings, general attention to hand washing, and other personal hygiene measures may be helpful in preventing primary infections. Meticulous hand washing may be of particular importance in preventing ocular infection, which may occur as a result of inoculation of conjunctival surfaces by fingers contaminated with respiratory fluids or urine. Whether respiratory precautions might be efficacious for persons documented to have spores in sputum or other respiratory secretions is unknown. Prevention strategies pertinent to environmental or zoonotic exposure to microsporidia have not yet been developed, but existing guidelines for the prevention of opportunistic infections that address food, water, and animal (pet) contact may be helpful in preventing microsporidiosis as well.[202] In addition, infected patients should be warned that sexual transmission of microsporidiosis cannot be excluded. Cohabitating sexual partners of infected patients should be offered screening for microsporidiosis regardless of their HIV status.[57]

Whether primary prophylaxis with antimicrobials is possible remains to be determined. Cotrimoxazole and atovaquone (for *Pneumocystis carinii*, *Toxoplasma gondii*) and azithromycin (for mycobacteria) are effective or are currently under investigation for prophylactic treatment of other opportunistic infections in patients with AIDS. It is possible that the use of these agents could potentially also reduce the incidence of microsporidiosis. *Ent. bieneusi* infection, however, has been detected in patients receiving clindamycin, trimethoprim-sulfamethoxazole (TMP-SMX), dapsone, pyrimethamine, and itraconazole,[203] and *Enc. intestinalis* infections appeared unaffected by TMP-SMX prophylactic regimens.[105] Finally, although its efficacy as a therapeutic agent for *Encephalitozoon* infections is well established,[23, 87, 105, 112] rigorous clinical trials using albendazole for primary or secondary prophylaxis have yet to be performed.

As noted earlier, several studies have now shown that administration of highly active antiretroviral therapy can produce remission of diarrheal symptoms in patients with microsporidia-associated diarrhea.[166, 168, 201] Although highly active antiretroviral therapy is a promising treatment regimen for microsporidiosis in patients with AIDS, its potential role in preventing *infection* requires further evaluation.

Microsporidial spores can survive and remain infective in the environment for extended periods of time. In vitro data evaluating the potential efficacy of preventive measures have been published for *Enc. cuniculi* only.[188] These experiments indicate that spores can survive in the environment for months to years depending on humidity and temperature. Even in a typical dry hospital environment (22°C) spores can survive for at least a month. Exposure to recommended working concentrations of most disinfectants for 30 minutes, boiling for 5 minutes, and autoclaving at 120°C was reported to kill the spores. Freezing may not be an effective means of disinfection because it has been possible to grow *Enc. hellem* successfully after storing it at −70°C for months.

REFERENCES

1. Weber R, Bryan RT, Schwartz DA, et al. Human microsporidial infections. Clin Microbiol Rev. 1994;7:426–461.
2. Didier ES. Microsporidiosis. Clin Infect Dis. 1998;27:1–8.
3. Wittner M, ed. The Microsporidia and Microsporidiosis. Washington, DC: ASM Press; 1999.

4. Spraque V, Becnel JJ, Hazard EI. Taxonomy of the phylum Microspora. Crit Rev Microbiol. 1992;18:285–395.
5. Gannon J. A survey of *Encephalitozoon cuniculi* in laboratory animals colonies in the United Kingdom. Lab Anim. 1980;14:91–94.
6. Vossbrinck CR, Maddox JV, Friedman S, et al. Ribosomal RNA sequence suggests microsporidia are extremely ancient eukaryotes. Nature. 1987;326:411–414.
7. Müller M. What are the microsporidia? Parasitol Today. 1997;13:455–456.
8. Germot A, Philippe H, Leguyader H. Evidence for loss of mitochondria in microsporidia from a mitochondrial-type HSP70 in *Nosema locustae*. Mol Biochem Parasitol. 1997;87:159–168.
9. Li J, Katiyar SK, Hamelin A, et al. Tubulin genes from AIDS-associated microsporidia and implications for phylogeny and benzimidazole sensitivity. Mol Biochem Parasitol. 1996;78:289–295.
10. Keeling PJ, McFadden GI. Origins of the microsporidia. Trends Microbiol. 1998;6:19–23.
11. Schwartz DA, Bryan RT. Microsporidia. In: Horsburgh CR Jr, Nelson AM, eds. Pathology of Emerging Infections. Washington, DC: ASM Press; 1997:61–93.
12. Beard CB, Butler JF, Becnel JJ. *Nolleria pulicis* n.sp. (Microsporida: Chytridiopsidae), a microsporidian parasite of the cat flea, *Ctenocephalides felis* (Siphonaptera: Pulicidae). J Protozool. 1990;37:90–99.
13. Avery SW, Undeen AH. The isolation of microsporidia and other pathogens from concentrated ditch water. J Am Mosq Control Assoc. 1987;3:54–58.
14. Hazard EI. Microsporidia (Microspora) (Protozoa). In: Chapman HC, Barr AR, Laird M, et al, eds. Biological Control of Mosquitoes. Fresno, CA: American Mosquito Control Association; 1985:51–55.
15. Cali A, Owen RL. Intracellular development of *Enterocytozoon,* a unique microsporidian found in the intestine of AIDS patients. J Protozool. 1990;37:145–155.
16. Weber R, Bryan RT, Owen RL, et al. Improved light microscopic detection of microsporidia spores in fecal specimens and duodenal aspirates from HIV-infected persons with intestinal microsporidiosis. N Engl J Med. 1992;326:161–166.
17. Cali A, Owen R. Microsporidiosis. In: Balows A, ed. The Laboratory Diagnosis of Infectious Diseases: Principles and Practice. New York: Springer Verlag; 1988;929–950.
18. Bryan RT. Critical commentary to "Intestinal microsporidiosis in a Chilean patient with AIDS." Path Res Pract. 1993;189:215–216.
19. Desportes I, Le Charpentier Y, Galian A, et al. Occurrence of a new microsporidian: *Enterocytozoon bieneusi* n.g., n. sp., in the enterocytes of a human patient with AIDS. J Protozool. 1985;32:250–254.
20. Didier ES, Didier PJ, Friedberg DN, et al. Isolation and characterization of a new human microsporidian, *Encephalitozoon hellem* (n. sp.), from three AIDS patients with keratoconjunctivitis. J Infect Dis. 1991;163:617–621.
21. Schwartz DA, Bryan RT, Hewan-Lowe KO, et al. Disseminated microsporidiosis and AIDS: Pathologic evidence for respiratory acquisition of *Encephalitozoon* infection. Arch Pathol Lab Med. 1992;116:660–668.
22. Terada S, Reddy R, Jeffers LJ, et al. Microsporidian hepatitis in the acquired immunodeficiency syndrome. Ann Intern Med 1987;107:61–62.
23. De Groote MA, Visvesvara G, Wilson ML, et al. Polymerase chain reaction and culture confirmation of disseminated *Encephalitozoon cuniculi* in a patient with AIDS: Successful therapy with albendazole. J Infect Dis. 1995;171:1375–1378.
24. Cali A, Kotler DP, Orenstein JM. *Septata intestinalis* N.G., N. Sp., and intestinal microsporidian associated with chronic diarrhea and dissemination in AIDS patients. J Euk Microbiol. 1993;40:101–112.
25. Hartskeerl RA, Van Gool T, Schuitema ARJ, et al. Genetic and immunologic characterization of the microsporidian *Septata intestinalis* Cali, Kotler, and Orenstein, 1993: reclassification to *Encephalitozoon intestinalis*. Parasitology. 1995;110:277–285.
26. Margileth AM, Strano AJ, Chandra R, et al. Disseminated nosematosis in an immunologically compromised infant. Arch Pathol. 1973;95:145–150.
27. Cali A, Meisler D, Lowdes CY, et al. Corneal microsporidiosis, characterization and identification. J Protozool. 1991;38:105S–111S.
28. Chupp GL, Alroy J, Adelman LS, et al. Myositis due to *Pleistophora* (microsporidia) in a patient with AIDS. Clin Infect Dis. 1993;16:15–21.
29. Grau A, Valls ME, Williams JE, et al. [Myositis caused by *Pleistophora* in a patient with AIDS]. Miositis por *Pleistophora* en un paciente con sida. Med Clin Barc. 1996;107:779–781.
30. Field AS, Marriott DJ, Milliken ST, et al. Myositis associated with a newly described microsporidian, *Trachipleistophora hominis*, in a patient with AIDS. J Clin Microbiol. 1996;34:2803–2811.
31. Hollister WS, Canning EU, Weidner E, et al. Development and ultrastructure of *Trachipleistophora hominis* n.g., n.sp. after in vitro isolation from an AIDS patient and inoculation into athymic mice. Parasitology. 1996;112:143–154.
32. Vávra J, Yachnis AT, Shadduck JA, Orenstein JM. Microsporidia of the genus *Trachipleistophora*—causative agents of human microsporidiosis: Description of *Trachipleistophora anthropophthera* n.sp. (Protozoa: Microsporidia). J Eukaryot Microbiol. 1998;45:273–283.
33. Yachnis AT, Berg J, Martinez-Salazar A et al. Disseminated microsporidiosis especially infecting the brain, heart, and kidneys—report of a newly recognized pansporoblastic species in two symptomatic AIDS patients. Am J Clin Pathol. 1996;106:535–543.
34. Deplazes P, Mathis A, van Saanen M, et al. Dual microsporidial infection due to *Vittaforma corneae* and *Encephalitozoon hellem* in an AIDS patient. Clin Infect Dis. 1998;27:1521–1524.
35. Shadduck JA, Meccoli RA, Davis R, Font RL. First isolation of a microsporidian from a human patient. J Infect Dis. 1990;162:773–776.
36. Silveira H, Canning EU. *Vittaforma corneae* n.comb. for the human microsporidium *Nosema corneum* Shadduck, Meccoli, Davis, & Font, 1990, based on its ultrastructure in the liver of experimentally infected athymic mice. J Euk Microbiol. 1995;42:158–65.
37. Cali A, Takvorian PM, Lewin S, et al. Identification of a new *Nosema*-like microsporidian associated with myositis in an AIDS patient. J Euk Microbiol. 1996;43:S108.
38. Cali A, Takvorian PM, Lewin S, et al. *Brachiola vesicularum*, n.g, n.sp., a new microsporidium associated with AIDS and myositis. J Eukaryot Microbiol. 1998;45:240–251
39. Schwartz DA, Anderson DC, Klumpp SA, McClure HM. Ultrastructure of atypical (teratoid) developmental stages of *Enterocytozoon bieneusi* in naturally-infected rhesus monkeys *(Macacca mulatta)*. Arch Pathol Lab Med 1998;122:423–429.
40. Mansfield KG, Carville A, Shvetz D, et al. Identification of an *Enterocytozoon bieneusi*–like microsporidian parasite in simian-immunodeficiency-virus–inoculated macaques with hepatobiliary disease. Am J Pathol. 1997;150:1395–1405.
41. Deplazes P, Mathis A, Müller C, Weber R. Molecular epidemiology of *Encephalitozoon cuniculi* and first detection of *Enterocytozoon bieneusi* in faecal samples of pigs. J Eukaryot Microbiol. 1996;43:93S.
42. Black SS, Steinohrt LA, Bertucci DC, et al. *Encephalitozoon hellem* in Budgerigars (*Melopsittacus undulatus*). Vet Pathol. 1997;34:189–198.
43. Pulparampil N, Graham D, Phalen D, Snowden K. *Encephalitozoon hellem* infection in an Eclectus parrot—zoonotic potential? In: Proceedings of the International Conference on Emerging Infectious Diseases. Atlanta, GA: March, 1998:64.
44. Bornay-Linares FJ, da Silva AJ, Moura H, et al. Immunologic, microscopic, and molecular evidence of *Encephalitozoon intestinalis (Septata intestinalis)* infection in mammals other than humans. J Infect Dis. 1998;178:820–826.
45. Aoun K, Bouratbine A, Datry A, et al. [Presence of intestinal microsporidia in Tunisia; apropos of 1 case]. Bull Soc Pathol Exot. 1997;90:176.
46. Bretagne S, Foulet F, Alkassoum W, et al. Prévalence des spores d'*Enterocytozoon bieneusi* dans les selles de patients sidéens et d'enfants Africains non infectés par le VIH. Bull Soc Pathol Exot. 1993;86:351–357.
47. Cegielski JP, Ortega YR, McKee S, et al. *Cryptosporidium, Enterocytozoon,* and *Cyclospora* infections in pediatric and adult patients with diarrhea in Tanzania. Clin Infect Dis. 1999;28:314–321.
48. Drobniewski F, Kelly P, Carew A, et al. Human microsporidiosis in African AIDS patients with chronic diarrhea. J Infect Dis. 1995;171:515–516.
49. Hautvast JLA, Tolboom JJM, Derks TJMM, et al. Asymptomatic intestinal microsporidiosis in a human immunodeficiency virus-seronegative, immunocompetent Zambian child. Pediatr Infect Dis J. 1997;16:415–416.
50. Lucas SB, Papadaki L, Conlon C, et al. Diagnosis of intestinal microsporidiosis in patients with AIDS. J Clin Pathol. 1989;42:885–890.
51. Maiga I, Doumba O, Dembele M, et al. [Human intestinal microsporidiosis in Bamako (Mali): the presence of *Enterocytozoon bieneusi* in HIV seropositive patients]. Sante. 1997;7:257–262.
52. Van Gool T, Luderhoff E, Nathoo KJ, et al. High prevalence of *Enterocytozoon bieneusi* infections among HIV-positive individuals with persistent diarrhea in Harare, Zimbabwe. Trans R Soc Trop Med Hyg. 1995;89:478–480.
53. Morakote N, Siripraset P, Piangjai S, et al. Microsporidium and Cyclospora in human stools in Chiang Mai, Thailand. SE Asian J Trop Med Hyg Pub Hlth. 1995;26:799–800.
54. Brasil P, Sodre FC, Cuzzi-Maya T, et al. Intestinal microsporidiosis in HIV-positive patients with chronic unexplained diarrhea in Rio de Janeiro, Brazil: Diagnosis, clinical presentation, and follow-up. Rev Inst Med Trop Sao Paulo. 1996;38:97–102.
55. Wuhib T, Silva TMJ, Newman RD, et al. Cryptosporidial and microsporidial infections in HIV-infected patients in northeastern Brazil. J Infect Dis. 1995;170:494–497.
56. Weitz JC, Botehlo R, Bryan RT. Microsporidiosis in patients with chronic diarrhea and AIDS, in HIV. Rev Med Chil. 1995;123:849–856.
57. Bryan RT, Schwartz DA. Epidemiology of microsporidiosis. In: Wittner M, ed. The Microsporidia and Microsporidiosis. Washington, DC: ASM Press. 1999:502–516.
58. Bryan RT. Microsporidiosis as an AIDS-related opportunistic infection. Clin Infect Dis. 1995;21(Suppl):S62–S65.
59. Rabodonirina M, Bertocchi M, Desportes-Livage I, et al. *Enterocytozoon bieneusi* as a cause of chronic diarrhea in a heart-lung transplant recipient who was seronegative for human immunodeficiency virus. Clin Infect Dis. 1996;23:114–117.
60. Cotte L, Rabodonirina M, Raynal C, et al. Outbreak of intestinal microsporidiosis in HIV-infected and non-infected patients (Abstract No. 483). In: Abstracts of the 5th Conference on Retroviruses and Opportunistic Infections. Chicago, February 1–5, 1998.
61. Sax PE, Rich JD, Pieciak WS, Trnka YM. Intestinal microsporidiosis occurring in a liver transplant recipient. Transplantation. 1995;60:617–618.
62. Wanke CA, DeGirolami P, Federman M. *Enterocytozoon bieneusi* infection and diarrheal disease in patients who were not infected with human immunodeficiency virus: Case report and review. Clin Infect Dis. 1996;23:816–818.
63. Dalal AA, Melzer J, Friese CE, et al. Disseminated microsporidiosis in a kidney-pancreas transplant recipient. Manuscript submitted.
64. Kelkar R, Sastry PS, Kulkarni SS, et al. Pulmonary microsporidial infection in a patient with CML undergoing allogenic marrow transplant. Bone Marrow Transplant. 1997;19:179–182.
65. Silverstein BE, Cunningham ET, Margolis TP, et al. Microsporidial keratoconjunctivitis in a patient without human immunodeficiency virus infection. Am J Ophthalmol. 1997;124:395–396.
66. Gainzarain JC, Canut A, Lozano M, et al. Detection of *Entercytozoon bieneusi* in two human immunodeficiency virus–negative patients with chronic diarrhea by

polymerase chain reaction in duodenal biopsy specimens and review. Clin Infect Dis. 1998;27:394–398.
67. Albrecht H, Sobottka I. *Enterocytozoon bieneusi* infection in patients who are not infected with human immunodeficiency virus. Clin Infect Dis. 1997;25:344.
68. Bryan RT, Weber R, Schwartz DA. Microsporidiosis in persons without HIV (Letter). Clin Infect Dis. 1997;24:534–535.
69. Sandfort J, Hannerman A, Gelderblom H, et al. *Enterocytozoon bieneusi* infection in an immunocompetent patient who had acute diarrhea and who was not infected with the human immunodeficiency virus. Clin Infect Dis. 1994;19:514–516.
70. Sobottka I, Albrecht H, Schottelius J, et al. Self-limited traveller's diarrhea due to a dual infection with *Enterocytozoon bieneusi* and *Cryptosporidium parvum* in an immunocompetent HIV-negative child. Eur J Clin Microbiol Infect Dis. 1995;14:919–920.
71. Raynaud L, Delbac F, Broussolle V, et al. Identification of *Encephalitozoon intestinalis* in travelers with chronic diarrhea by specific PCR amplification. J Clin Microbiol. 1998;36:37–40.
72. Bryan RT, Cali A, Owen RL, Spencer HC. 1991. Microsporidia: Opportunistic pathogens in patients with AIDS. In Sun T, ed. Progress in Clinical Parasitology, 2. Philadelphia: Field & Wood; 1991:1–26.
73. Coyle CM, Wittner M, Kotler DP, et al. Prevalence of microsporidiosis due to *Enterocytozoon bieneusi* and *Encephalitozoon intestinalis* among patients with AIDS-related diarrhea: Determination by polymerase chain reaction to the microsporidian small-subunit rRNA gene. Clin Infect Dis. 1996;23:1002–1006.
74. Voglino MC, Donelli G, Rossi P, et al. Intestinal microsporidiosis in Italian individuals with AIDS. Ital J Gastroenterol. 1996;28:381–386.
75. Kyaw T, Curry A, Edwards-Jones V, et al. The prevalence of *Enterocytozoon bieneusi* in acquired immunodeficiency syndrome (AIDS) patients from the north west of England: 1992–1995. Br J Biomed Sci. 1997;54:186–191.
76. Van Gool T, Vetter JCM, Weinmayr B, et al. High seroprevalence of *Encephalitozoon* species in immunocompetent subjects. J Infect Dis. 1997;175:1020–1024.
77. Pospisilova Z, Ditrich O, Stankova M, Kodym P. Parasitic opportunistic infections in Czech HIV-infected patients—a prospective study. Cent Eur J Public Health. 1997;5:208–213.
78. Cislakova L, Prokopcakova H, Stefkovic M, Halanova M. [*Encephalitozoon cuniculi*—clinical and epidemiologic significance. Results of a preliminary serologic study in humans]. Epidemiol Mikrobiol Imunol. 1997;46:30–33.
79. Sparfel JM, Sarfati C, Ligoury O, et al. Detection of microsporidia and identification of *Enterocytozoon bieneusi* in surface water by filtration followed by specific PCR. J Euk Microbiol. 1997;44:78S.
80. Dowd SE, Gerba CP, Pepper IL. Confirmation of the human-pathogenic microsporidia *Enterocytozoon bieneusi, Encephalitozoon intestinalis, and Vittaforma corneae* in water. Appl Environ Microbiol. 1998;64:3332–3335
81. Watson DAR, Asmuth D, Wanke CA. Environmental risk factors for acquisition of microsporidia in HIV-infected persons. Abstract 235. Presented at the 34th annual meeting of the Infectious Diseases Society of America, New Orleans, 1996.
82. Hutin YJF, Sombardier M-N, Liguory O, et al. Risk factors for intestinal microsporidiosis in patients with human immunodeficiency virus infection: A case-control study. J Infect Dis. 1998;178:904–907.
83. Enriquez FJ, Taren D, Cruz-López A, et al. Prevalence of intestinal encephalitozoonosis in Mexico. Clin Infect Dis. 1998;26:1227–1229.
84. Conteas CN, Berlin OGW, Lariviere MJ, et al. Examination of the prevalence and seasonal variation of intestinal microsporidiosis in the stools of persons with chronic diarrhea and human immunodeficiency virus infection. Am J Trop Med Hyg. 1998;58:559–561.
85. Schwartz DA, Visvesvara G, Weber R, Bryan RT. Male genital tract microsporidiosis and AIDS: Prostatic infection with *Encephalitozoon hellem*. J Euk Microbiol. 1994;41:61S.
86. Birthistle K, Moore P, Hay P. Microsporidia: A new sexually transmissible cause of urethritis. Genitourin Med. 1996;72:445.
87. Corcoran GD, Isaacson JR, Daniels C, Chiodini PL. Urethritis associated with disseminated microsporidiosis: Clinical response to albendazole. Clin Infect Dis. 1996;22:592–593.
88. Fuentealba IC, Mahoney NT, Shadduck JA, et al. Hepatic lesions in rabbits infected with *Encephalitozoon cuniculi* administered per rectum. Vet Pathol. 1992;29:536–540.
89. Schwartz DA, Visvesvara GS, Diesenhouse MC, et al. Ocular pathology of microsporidiosis: Role of immunofluorescent antibody for diagnosis of *Encephalitozoon hellem* in biopsies, smears, and intact globes from seven AIDS patients. Am J Ophthalmol. 1993;115:285–292.
90. Cox JC, Hamilton RC, Attwood HD. An investigation of the route and progression of *Encephalitozoon cuniculi* infection in adult rabbits. J Protozool. 1979;26:260–265.
91. Wicher V, Baughn RE, Fuentealba C, et al. Enteric infection with an obligate intracellular parasite, *Encephalitozoon cuniculi*, in an experimental model. Infect Immun. 1991;59:2225–2231.
92. Didier ES, Visvesvara GS, Baker MD, et al. A microsporidian isolated from an AIDS patient corresponds to *Encephalitozoon cuniculi* III, originally isolated from domestic dogs. J Clin Microbiol. 1996;34:2835–2837.
93. Didier ES, Vossbrinck CR, Baker MD, et al. Identification and characterization of three *Encephalitozoon cuniculi* strains. Parasitology 1995;111:411–421.
94. Deplazes P, Mathis A, Baumgartner R, et al. Immunologic and molecular characteristics of *Encephalitozoon*-like microsporidia isolated from humans and rabbits indicate that *Encephalitozoon cuniculi* is a zoonotic parasite. Clin Infect Dis. 1996;22:557–559.
95. Mathis A, Michel M, Kuster H, et al. Two *Encephalitozoon cuniculi* strains of human origin are infectious to rabbits. Parasitology. 1997;114:29–35.
96. Anderson DC, Klumpp SA, Da Silva AJ, et al. Naturally-acquired *Enterocytozoon bieneusi* (Microsporida) hepatobiliary infection in rhesus monkeys with simian immunodeficiency virus (SIV): A possible animal model of disease {Abstract No. K-120b). In: Abstracts of the 37th Interscience Conference on Antimicrobial Agents and Chemotherapy (ICAAC), Toronto, 1997:349.
97. Yee RW, Fermon OT, Alberto Martinez J, et al. Resolution of microsporidial epithelial keratopathy in a patient with AIDS. Ophthalmology. 1991;98:196–201.
98. Cali A, Meisler DM, Lowder CY, et al. Corneal microsporidioses: Characterization and identification. J Protozool. 1991;38:215S.
99. Cali A, Meisler DM, Rutherford I, et al. Corneal microsporidiosis in a patient with AIDS. Am J Trop Med Hyg. 1991;44:463.
100. Bryan RT, Weber R, Schwartz DA. Microsporidiosis. In: Guerrant RL, Krogstad DJ, Maguire JH, et al, eds. Tropical Infectious Diseases: Principles, Pathogens and Practice. New York: Churchill Livingstone; 1999.
101. Haselton PS, Schwartz DA, Lucas SB. Pulmonary parasitic infections. In: Haselton PS, ed. Spencer's Pathology of the Lung. 4th ed. McGraw Hill; 1996:305–356.
102. Lacey CJN, Clark A, Frazer P, et al. Chronic microsporidian infection in the nasal mucosae, sinuses, and conjunctivae in HIV disease. Genitourin Med. 1992;68:179–181.
103. Schwartz DA, Visvesvara GS, Leitch GJ, et al. Pathology of symptomatic microsporidial (*Encephalitozoon hellem*) bronchiolitis in the acquired immunodeficiency syndrome: A new respiratory pathogen diagnosed from lung biopsy, bronchoalveolar lavage, sputum, and tissue culture. Hum Pathol. 1993;24:937–943.
104. Gunnarsson G, Hurlbut D, DeGirolami PC, et al. Multiorgan microsporidiosis: Report of five cases and review. Clin Infect Dis. 1995;21:37–44.
105. Molina J-M, Oksenhendler E, Beauvais B, et al. Disseminated microsporidiosis due to *Septata intestinalis* in patients with AIDS: Clinical features and response to albendazole therapy. J Infect Dis. 1995;171:245–249.
106. Schwartz DA, Sobottka I, Leitch GJ, et al. Pathology of microsporidiosis— emerging parasitic infections in patients with AIDS. Arch Pathol Lab Med. 1996;120:173–188.
107. Orenstein JM, Chiang J, Steinberg W, et al. Intestinal microsporidiosis as a cause of diarrhea in human immunodeficiency virus–infected patients. Hum Pathol. 1990;21:475–481.
108. Orenstein JM, Tenner M, Kotler DP. Localization of infection by the microsporidian *Enterocytozoon bieneusi* in the gastrointestinal tract of AIDS patients with diarrhea. AIDS. 1992;6:195–197.
109. Schwartz DA, Abou-Elella A, Wilcox CM, et al. The presence of *Enterocytozoon bieneusi* spores in the lamina propria of small bowel biopsies with no evidence of disseminated microsporidiosis. Arch Pathol Lab Med. 1995;119:424–428.
110. Orenstein JM, Tenner M, Cali A, Kotler DP. A microsporidian previously undescribed in humans, infecting enterocytes and macrophages, and associated with diarrhea in an acquired immunodeficiency syndrome patient. Hum Pathol. 1992;23:722–728.
111. Orenstein JM, Dieterich DT, Kotler DP. Systemic dissemination by a newly recognized intestinal microsporidia species in AIDS. AIDS. 1992;6:1143–1150.
112. Dore GJ, Marriott DJ, Hing MC, et al. Disseminated microsporidiosis due to *Septata intestinalis* in nine patients infected with the human immunodeficiency virus: Response to therapy with albendazole. Clin Infect Dis. 1995;21:70–76.
113. McWhinney PHM, Nathwani D, Green ST, et al. Microsporidiosis detected in association with AIDS-related sclerosing cholangitis. AIDS. 1991;5:1394–1395.
114. Pol S, Romana CA, Richard SR, et al. Microsporidia infection in patients with the human immunodeficiency virus and unexplained cholangitis. N Engl J Med. 1993;328:95–99.
115. Beaugerie L, Teilhac MF, Deluol AM, et al. Cholangiopathy associated with microsporidia infection of the common bile duct mucosa in a patient with HIV infection. Ann Intern Med. 1992;117:401–402.
116. Mertens RB, Didier ES, Fishbein MC, et al. *Encephalitozoon cuniculi* microsporidiosis: Infection of the brain, heart, kidneys, trachea, adrenal glands, and urinary bladder in a patient with AIDS. Mod Pathol. 1997;10:68–77.
117. Weber R, Deplazes P, Flepp M, et al. Cerebral microsporidiosis due to *Encephalitozoon cuniculi* in a patient with human immunodeficiency virus infection. N Engl J Med. 1997;336:474–478.
118. Weber R, Schwartz DA, Deplazes P. Laboratory diagnosis of microsporidiosis. In: Wittner M, ed. The Microsporidia and Microsporidiosis. Washington, DC: American Society of Microbiology Press; 1999:315–362.
119. Ledford DK, Overman MD, Gonzalvo A, et al. Microsporidiosis myositis in a patient with acquired immunodeficiency syndrome. Ann Intern Med. 1985;102:628–630.
120. Zender HO, Arrigoni E, Eckert J, Kapanci Y. A case of *Encephalitozoon cuniculi* peritonitis in a patient with AIDS. Am J Clin Pathol. 1989;92:352–356.
121. Livage I, Doumbo O, Pichard E, et al. Microsporidiosis in HIV-seronegative patients in Mali. Trans R Soc Trop Med Hyg. 1998;92:423–424.
122. Ashton N, Wirasinha PA. Encephalitozoonosis (nosematosis) of the cornea. Br J Ophthalmol. 1973;57:669–674.
123. Pinnolis M, Egbert PR, Font RL, et al. Nosematosis of the cornea. Arch Ophthalmol. 1981;99:1044–1047.
124. Davis RM, Font RL, Keisler MS, et al. Corneal microsporidiosis: A case report including ultrastructural observations. Ophthalmology. 1990;97:953–957.
125. Matsubayashi H, Koike T, Mikata T, Hagiwara S. A case of *Encephalitozoon*-like body infection in man. Arch Pathol. 1959;67:181–187.
126. Bergquist NR, Stintzing G, Smedman L, Waller T. Diagnosis of encephalitozoonosis in man by serological tests. BMJ. 1984;288:902.

127. Cali A. General microsporidian features and recent findings on AIDS isolates. J Protozool. 1991;38:625–630.
128. Macher AM, Neafie R, Angritt P, et al. Microsporidial myositis and the acquired immunodeficiency syndrome (AIDS): A four-year follow-up (Letter). Ann Intern Med. 1988;109:343.
129. Belcher JW Jr, Guttenberg SA, Schmookler BM. Microsporidiosis of the mandible in a patient with acquired immunodeficiency syndrome. J Oral Maxillofac Surg. 1997;55:424–426.
130. Del Aguila C, Lopez Velez R, Fenoy S, et al. Identification of *Enterocytozoon bieneusi* spores in respiratory samples from an AIDS patient with a 2-year history of intestinal microsporidiosis. J Clin Microbiol. 1997;35:1862–1866.
131. Del Aguila C, Croppo CP, Moura H, et al. Ultrastructure, immunofluorescence, Western blot, and PCR analysis of eight isolates of *Encephalitozoon (Septata) intestinalis* established in culture from sputum and urine samples and duodenal aspirates of five patients with AIDS. J Clin Microbiol. 1998;36:1201–1208.
132. Didier ES, Rogers LB, Orenstein JM, et al. Characterization of *Encephalitozoon (Septata) intestinalis* isolates cultured from nasal mucosa and bronchoalveolar lavage fluids of two AIDS patients. J Eukaryot Microbiol. 1996;43:34–43.
133. Franzen C, Schwartz DA, Visvesvara GS, et al. Disseminated antibody-confirmed *Encephalitozoon cuniculi* with asymptomatic infection of the gastrointestinal tract in a patient with AIDS. Clin Infect Dis. 1995;21:1480–1484.
134. Hartskeerl RA, Schuitema ARJ, van Gool T, Terpstra WJ. Genetic evidence for the occurrence of extra-intestinal *Enterocytozoon bieneusi* infections. Nucleic Acids Res. 1993;21:4150.
135. Hollister WS, Canning ES, Colbourn NI, Aarons EJ. *Encephalitozoon cuniculi* isolated from the urine of an AIDS patient, which differs from canine and murine isolates. Nucleic Acids Res. 1993;21:4150.
136. Kester KE, Turiansky GW, McEvoy PL. Nodular cutaneous microsporidiosis in a patient with AIDS and successful treatment with long-term oral clindamycin therapy. Ann Intern Med. 1998;128:911–914.
137. Navin TR, Weber R, Rimland D, et al. Declining CD4 T lymphocyte counts are associated with increasing likelihood of enteric parasitosis and chronic diarrhea: Results of a 3-year longitudinal study. J Acquir Immune Defic Syndr. 1999;20:154–159.
138. Rossi RM, Wanke C, Federman M. Microsporidian sinusitis in patients with acquired immunodeficiency syndrome. Laryngoscope. 1996;106:966–971.
139. Scaglia M, Gatti S, Sacchi L, et al. Asymptomatic respiratory tract microsporidiosis due to *Encephalitozoon hellem* in three patients with AIDS. Clin Infect Dis. 1998;26:174–176.
140. Sheth SG, Bates C, Federman M, Chopra S. Fulminant hepatic failure caused by microsporidial infection in a patient with AIDS. AIDS. 1997;11:553–554.
141. Soule JB, Halverson AL, Becker RB, et al. A patient with acquired immunodeficiency syndrome and untreated *Encephalitozoon (Septata) intestinalis* microsporidiosis leading to small bowel perforation. Response to albendazole. Arch Pathol Lab Med. 1997;121:880–887.
142. Visvesvara GS, da Silva AJ, Croppo GP, et al. In vitro culture and serologic and molecular identification of *Septata intestinalis* isolated from urine of a patient with AIDS. J Clin Microbiol. 1995;33:930–936.
143. Weber R, Flepp M, Wichmann W. Cerebral microsporidiosis due to Encephalitozoon cuniculi (Letter). New Engl J Med. 1997;337:640–641.
144. Weber R, Ledergerber B, Zbinden R, et al. Diarrhea and enteric pathogens in HIV infected patients: Prospective community based cohort study. Arch Intern Med. 1999;159:1473–1480.
145. Modigliani R, Bories C, Le Charpentier Y, et al. Diarrhea and malabsorption in acquired immune deficiency syndrome: A study of four cases with special emphasis on opportunistic protozoan infestations. Gut. 1985;26:179–187.
146. Rijpstra AC, Canning EU, van Ketel RJ, et al. Use of light microscopy to diagnose small-intestinal microsporidiosis in patients with AIDS. J Infect Dis. 1988;157:827–831.
147. Molina J-M, Sarfati C, Beauvais B, et al. Intestinal microsporidiosis in human immunodeficiency virus–infected patients with chronic unexplained diarrhea: Prevalence and clinical and biologic features. J Infect Dis. 1993;167:217–221.
148. Field AS, Hing MC, Milliken ST, et al. Microsporidia in the small intestine of HIV-infected patients. Med J Aust. 1993;158:390–394.
149. Weber R, Kuster H, Keller R, et al. Pulmonary and intestinal microsporidiosis in a patient with the acquired immunodeficiency syndrome. Am Rev Respir Dis. 1992;146:1603–1605.
150. Visvesvara GS, Leitch GJ, Moura HM, et al. Culture, electron microscopy, and immunoblot studies on a microsporidian parasite isolated from the urine of a patient with AIDS. J Protozool. 1991;38:105S–111S.
151. Weber R, Kuster H, Visvesvara GS, et al. Disseminated microsporidiosis due to *Encephalitozoon hellem:* Pulmonary colonization, microhematuria, and mild conjunctivitis in a patient with AIDS. Clin Infect Dis. 1993;17:415–419.
152. Diesenhouse MC, Wilson LA, Corrent GF, et al. Treatment of microsporidial keratoconjunctivitis with topical fumagillin. Am J Ophthalmol. 1993;115:293.
153. Rosberger DF, Serdarevic ON, Erlandson RA, et al. Successful treatment of microsporidial keratoconjunctivitis with topical fumagillin in a patient with AIDS. Cornea. 1993;12:261–265.
154. Centers for Disease Control and Prevention. Microsporidian keratoconjunctivitis in patients with AIDS. MMWR Morb Mortal Wkly Rep. 1990;39:188–189.
155. Friedberg DN, Stenson SM, Orenstein JM, et al. Microsporidial keratoconjunctivitis in acquired immunodeficiency syndrome. Arch Ophthalmol. 1990;108:504–508.
156. Yee RW, Tio FO, Martinez A, et al. Resolution of microsporidial epithelial keratopathy in a patient with AIDS. Ophthalmology. 1991;98:196–201.
157. Michiels JF, Hofman P, Saint Paul MC, et al. Pathological features of intestinal microsporidiosis in HIV positive patients: A report of 13 new cases. Pathol Res Pract. 1993;189:377–383.
158. Asmuth DM, DeGirolami PC, Federman M, et al. Clinical features of microsporidiosis in patients with AIDS. Clin Infect Dis. 1994;18:819–825.
159. Orenstein JM. Microsporidiosis in the acquired immunodeficiency syndrome. J Parasitol. 1991;77:843–864.
160. Weber R, Muller A, Spycher MA, et al. Intestinal *Enterocytozoon bieneusi* microsporidiosis in an HIV-infected patient: Diagnosis by ileo-colonoscopic biopsies and long-term follow-up. Clin Invest. 1992;70:1019–1023.
161. Svenson J, MacLean JD, Kokoskin-Nelson E, et al. Microsporidiosis in AIDS patients. Can Commun Dis Rep. 1993;19:13–15.
162. Hewan-Lowe K, Furlong B, Sim, M, Schwartz DA. Co-infection with *Giardia lamblia* and *Enterocytozoon bieneusi* in a patient with AIDS and chronic diarrhea. Arch Pathol Lab Med. 1997;121:417–422.
163. Weber R, Sauer B, Luthy R, et al. Intestinal coinfection with *Enterocytozoon bieneusi* and *Cryptosporidium* in a human immunodeficiency virus–infected child with chronic diarrhea. Clin Infect Dis. 1993;17:480–483.
164. Eeftinck Schattenkerk JKM, Van Gool T, Van Ketel RJ, et al. Clinical significance of small-intestinal microsporidiosis in HIV-1–infected individuals. Lancet. 1991;337:895–898.
165. Benhamou Y, Bochet MV, Carriere J, et al. Effects of triple antiretroviral therapies including a HIV protease inhibitor on chronic intestinal cryptosporidiosis and microsporidiosis in HIV-infected patients (Abstract). Fourth Conference on Retroviruses and Opportunistic Infections, Washington, DC, 1997.
166. Goguel J, Katlama C, Sarfati C, et al. Remission of AIDS-associated intestinal microsporidiosis with highly active antiretroviral therapy (Letter). AIDS. 1997;11:1658–1659.
167. Carr A, Marriott D, Field A, et al. Treatment of HIV-associated microsporidiosis and cryptosporidiosis with combination antiretroviral therapy. Lancet. 1998;351:256–261.
168. Foudraine NA, Weverling GJ, Vangool T, et al. Improvement of chronic diarrhoea in patients with advanced HIV-1 infection during antiretroviral therapy. AIDS. 1998;12:35–41.
169. Van Gool T, Hollister WS, Efttinck Schattenkerk JE, et al. Diagnosis of *Enterocytozoon bieneusi* microsporidiosis in AIDS patients by recovery of spores from faeces. Lancet. 1990;336:697–698.
170. Van Gool T, Snijders R, Reiss P, et al. Diagnosis of intestinal and disseminated microsporidial infections in patients with HIV by a new rapid fluorescence technique. J Clin Pathol. 1993;46:694–699.
171. Moura H, Schwartz DA, Bornay-Linnares F, et al. A new and improved "quick-hot Gram-chromotrope" technique that differentially stains micropsoridian spores in clinical samples including paraffin-embedded tissue sections. Arch Pathol Lab Med. 1997;121:888–893.
172. Didier ES, Orenstein JM, Aldras A, et al. Comparsion of three staining methods for detecting microsporidia in fluids. J Clin Microbiol. 1995;33:3138–3145.
173. Schwartz DA, Visvesvara GS, Weber R, et al: Microsporidiosis in HIV positive patients: current methods for diagnosis using biopsy, cytologic, ultrastructural, immunological and tissue culture techniques. Folia Parasitol. 1994;41:91–99.
174. Van Gool T, Canning EU, Dankert J. An improved practical and sensitive technique for the detection of microsporidian spores in stool samples. Trans R Soc Trop Med Hyg. 1994;88:189–190.
175. Joste N, Rich JD, Busam KJ, Schwartz DA. Autopsy verification of *Encephalitozoon intestinalis* (microsporidiosis) eradication following albendazole therapy. Arch Pathol Lab Med. 1996;120:199–203.
176. Sharpstone D, Rowbottom A, Francis N, et al. Thalidomide: A novel therapy for microsporidiosis. Gastroenterology. 1997;112:1823–1829.
177. Visvesvara GS, Moura H, Schwartz DA. Culture and propagation of microsporidia. In: Wittner M, ed. The Microsporidia and Microsporidiosis. Washington, DC: American Society of Microbiology Press. 1999:363–392.
178. Shadduck JA. Effect of fumagillin on in vitro multiplication of *Encephalitozoon cuniculi.* J Protozool. 1980;27:202–208.
179. Silveira H, Canning EU. In vitro cultivation of the human microsporidium *Vittaforma corneae*: Development and effect of albendazole. Folia Parasitol (Praha). 1995;42:241–250.
180. Beauvais B, Sarfati C, Challier S, Derouin F. In vitro model to assess effect of antimicrobial agents on *Encephalitozoon cuniculi.* Antimicrob Agents Chemother. 1994;38:2440–2448.
181. Franssen FF, Lumeij JT, van Knapen F. Susceptibility of *Encephalitozoon cuniculi* to several drugs in vitro. Antimicrob Agents Chemother. 1995;39:1265–1268.
182. Katiyar SK, Edlind TD. In vitro susceptibilities of the AIDS-associated microsporidian *Encephalitozoon intestinalis* to albendazole, its sulfoxide metabolite, and 12 additional benzimidazole derivates. Antimicrob Agents Chemother. 1997;41:2729–2732.
183. Colbourn NI, Hollister WS, Curry A, Canning EU. Activity of albendazole against *Encephalitozoon cuniculi* in vitro. Eur J Protistol. 1994;30:211–220.
184. Didier ES. Effects of albendazole, fumagillin, and TNP 470 on microsporidial replication in vitro. Antimicrob Agents Chemother. 1997;41:1541–1546.
185. Coyle C, Kent M, Tanowitz HB, et al. TNP-470 is an effective antimicrosporidial agent. J Infect Dis. 1998;177:515–518.
186. Canning EU, Curry A, Lacey CJN, et al. Ultrastructure of *Encephalitozoon* sp. infecting the conjunctival, corneal, and nasal epithelia of a patient with AIDS. Eur J Protistol. 1992;28:226–237.
187. He Q, Leitch GJ, Visvesvara GS, Wallace S. Effects of nifedipine, metronidazole, and nitric oxide donors on spore germination and cell culture infection of the

microsporidia *Encephalitozoon hellem* and *Encephalitozoon intestinalis*. Antimicrob Agents Chemother. 1996;40:179–185.
188. Waller T. Sensitivity of *Encephalitozoon cuniculi* to various temperatures, disinfectants and drugs. Lab Anim. 1979;13:227–230.
189. Leitch GJ, He Q, Wallace S, Visvesvara GS. Inhibition of the spore polar filament extrusion of the microsporidium, *Encephalitozoon hellem*, isolated from an AIDS patient. J Eukaryot Microbiol. 1993;40:711–717.
190. Orenstein JM, Dieterich DT, Lew EA, Kotler DP. Albendazole as a treatment for disseminated microsporidiosis due to *Septata intestinalis* in AIDS patients: A report of four patients. AIDS. 1993;7(Suppl 3):S40–2.
191. Weber R, Sauer B, Spycher MA, et al. Detection of *Septata intestinalis* (Microsporidia) in stool specimens, and coprodiagnostic monitoring of successful treatment with albendazole. Clin Infect Dis. 1994;19:342–345.
192. Aarons EJ, Woodrow D, Hollister WS, et al. Reversible renal failure caused by a microsporidian infection. AIDS. 1994;8:1119–1121.
193. Hing M, Marriott D, Verre J, et al. Enteric microsporidiosis—response to azithromycin therapy (Abstract). Workshop on Intestinal Microsporidia in HIV Infection, Paris, December 15–16, 1992.
194. Anwar Bruni DM, Hogan SE, Schwartz DA, et al. Atovaquone is effective treatment for the symptoms of gastrointestinal microsporidiosis in HIV-1-infected patients. AIDS. 1996;10:619–623.
195. Kotler DP, Orenstein JM. Clinical syndromes associated with microsporidiosis. In: Wittner M, ed. The Microsporidia and Microsporidiosis. Washington, DC: American Society of Microbiology Press; 1999:258–292.
196. Molina JM, Goguel J, Sarfati C, et al. Potential efficacy of fumagillin in intestinal microsporidiosis due to *Enterocytozoon bieneusi* in patients with HIV infections—results of a drug screening study. AIDS. 1997;11:1603–1610.
197. Blanshard C, Hollister WS, Peacock CS, et al. Simultaneous infection with two types of intestinal microsporidia in a patient with AIDS. Gut. 1992;33:418–420.
198. Dieterich DT, Lew EA, Kotler DP, et al. Treatment with albendazole for intestinal disease due to *Enterocytozoon bieneusi* in patients with AIDS. J Infect Dis. 1994;169:178–183.
199. Dionisio D, Manneschi LI, Dilollo S, et al. *Enterocytozoon bieneusi* in AIDS: Symptomatic relief and parasite changes after furazolidone. J Clin Patohol. 1997;50:472–476.
200. Molina JM, Goguel J, Sarpati C, et al. Efficacy and safety of intermittent oral fumagillin for the treatment of *Enterocytozoon bieneusi* infections in patients with AIDS (ANRS 054) (Abstract). Twelfth World AIDS Conference, Geneva, Switzerland, 1998.
201. Conteas CN, Berlin OGW, Speck CE, et al. Modification of the clinical course of intestinal microsporidiosis in acquired immunodeficiency syndrome patients by immune status and anti–human immunodeficiency virus therapy. Am J Trop Med Hyg. 1998;58:555–558.
202. USPHS/IDSA Prevention of Opportunistic Infections Working Group. 1997 USPHS/IDSA guidelines for the prevention of opportunistic infections in persons infected with human immunodeficiency virus. MMWR Morb Mortal Wkly Rpt. 1997;46(RR-12):1–46.
203. Albrecht H, Sobottka I, Stellbrink HJ, Greten H. Does the choice of *Pneumocystis carinii* prophylaxis influence the prevalence of *Enterocytozoon bieneusi* microsporidiosis in AIDS patients? AIDS. 1995;9:302–303.

SECTION I

DISEASES DUE TO TOXIC ALGAE

Chapter 275

Human Illness Associated with Harmful Algal Blooms

J. GLENN MORRIS, JR.

During the past several decades, recognition of human health and environmental problems associated with harmful and toxic algae has been increasing.[1–3] Toxic species constitute a very small percentage of the thousands of species of microscopic algae at the base of the marine food chain. However, when these species proliferate, they may cause massive kills of fish and shellfish, the death of marine mammals and seabirds, alterations in marine habitats, and with appropriate exposure, human illness and death. Although blooms of certain species such as *Gymnodinium breve* may be manifested as "red tides," adverse events often occur in the absence of visible discoloration of water.

It is generally perceived that harmful algal blooms are increasing in frequency; in the United States, problems that in the past were confined to a few geographic locations are now being seen at multiple sites along the U.S. coastline[1–3] (Fig. 275–1). The factors leading to this apparent increase in incidence are not well understood, although it has been postulated that human-related phenomena such as nutrient enrichment of waterways, climatic change, and disruption of ecosystems play some role.[1–6]

Six clinical syndromes/illnesses are currently linked with harmful algal blooms (Table 275–1).[6a] Ciguatera fish poisoning, paralytic shellfish poisoning, and neurotoxic shellfish poisoning are described in Chapter 87 and are only briefly discussed in this chapter. Diarrhetic shellfish poisoning, amnesic shellfish poisoning, and *Pfiesteria*-associated syndrome are presented in greater detail in later sections.

CIGUATERA FISH POISONING

Worldwide, ciguatera fish poisoning (see Chapter 87) is the most common of the clinical syndromes associated with marine biotoxins. It is a major public health problem in the Caribbean and south Pacific, particularly in areas with tropical reefs.[7, 8] Illness is caused by toxins that are passed up the marine food chain, with large predatory reef fish (such as barracuda or jacks) having the greatest risk of toxicity. Gastrointestinal symptoms are the first manifestation of illness and usually occur within 24 hours of eating a toxic fish. These symptoms are followed by neurologic sequelae, which may persist for weeks to months.[8, 9]

PARALYTIC SHELLFISH POISONING

Paralytic shellfish poisoning (see Chapter 87) is the most common cause of marine biotoxin-associated illness in the continental United

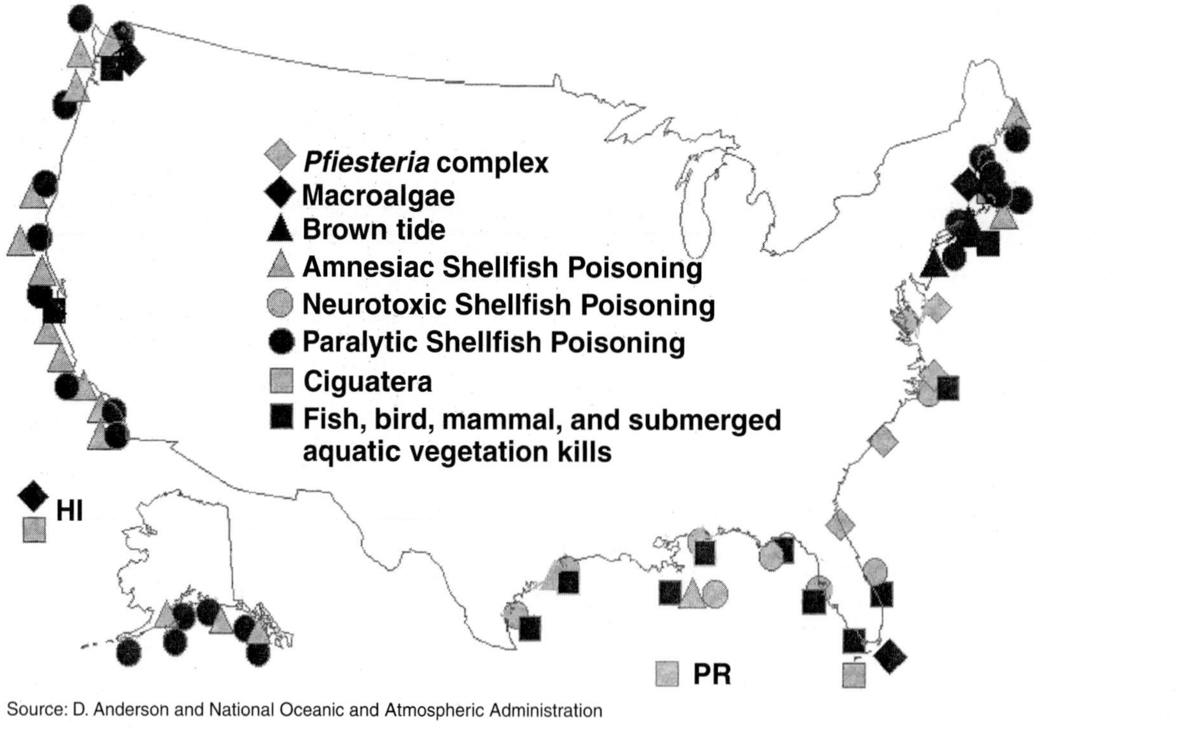

FIGURE 275–1. Sites of harmful algal blooms along U.S. coast. (From Boesch DE, Anderson DM, Horner RA, et al. Harmful Algal Blooms in Coastal Waters: Options for Prevention, Control, and Mitigation. NOAA Coastal Oceans Program Decision Analysis Series No. 10. Silver Spring, Md: NOAA Coastal Oceans Office; 1996: 1–46.)

TABLE 275–1 Human Illness Associated with Harmful Algal Blooms

Syndrome	Causative Organisms	Toxin Produced	Clinical Manifestations
Ciguatera fish poisoning	*Gambierdiscus toxicus* and others	Ciguatoxin, maitotoxin	Acute gastroenteritis followed by paresthesias and other neurologic symptoms
Paralytic shellfish poisoning	*Alexandrium* spp. and others	Saxitoxins	Acute paresthesias and other neurologic manifestations; may progress rapidly to respiratory paralysis
Neurotoxic shellfish poisoning	*Gymnodinium breve*	Brevetoxins	Gastrointestinal and neurologic symptoms; formation of toxic aerosols by wave action can produce respiratory irritation and asthma-like symptoms
Diarrhetic shellfish poisoning	*Dinophysis* spp.	Okadaic acid and others	Acute gastroenteritis
Amnesic shellfish poisoning	*Pseudo-nitzschia* spp.	Domoic acid	Gastroenteritis, followed by neurologic manifestations, leading in severe cases to amnesia, coma, and death
Pfiesteria-associated syndrome	*Pfiesteria piscicida;* ? other species	Unidentified to date	Deficiencies in learning and memory, acute respiratory and eye irritation, acute confusional syndrome

States and Alaska.[10, 11] Illness is associated with eating clams and mussels containing saxitoxins produced by *Alexandrium* spp. and related dinoflagellates. Neurologic manifestations predominate; paresthesias are most common, although severe cases may progress to respiratory paralysis. Prevention is linked with regular monitoring of shellfish populations for saxitoxin by public health authorities.[10]

NEUROTOXIC SHELLFISH POISONING

Illness is caused by brevetoxins produced by *G. breve*, a major cause of red tides along the Florida coast. Ingestion of shellfish containing the toxin causes gastrointestinal and neurologic symptoms (see Chapter 87). Aerosolization of toxins by heavy wave action on the Atlantic coast of Florida can result in respiratory irritation and asthma-like symptoms in persons walking along affected beaches.[12]

DIARRHETIC SHELLFISH POISONING

Illness results from eating mussels, scallops, or clams that have been feeding on *Dinophysis fortii* or *Dinophysis acuminata*. In addition to diarrhea, symptoms of diarrhetic shellfish poisoning include nausea, vomiting, and abdominal pain. Although okadaic acid appears to be the primary toxin responsible for the observed clinical syndrome, other toxic compounds have been isolated from these species. Case reports came initially from Japan; however, diarrhetic shellfish poisoning has occurred in France and other parts of Europe, and *Dinophysis* spp. are spreading along the French and Spanish coasts. One episode of diarrhetic shellfish poisoning has occurred in Nova Scotia in association with eating cultured mussels.[2] No U.S. cases have been confirmed although the causative organisms have been identified in U.S. coastal waters.[1, 2]

AMNESIC SHELLFISH POISONING

Amnesic shellfish poisoning results from the ingestion of shellfish containing domoic acid produced by the diatom *Pseudo-nitzschia pungens*.[2] A series of outbreaks caused by this toxin were reported in the Atlantic provinces of Canada in 1987.[2, 13] Symptoms included vomiting, abdominal cramps, diarrhea, headache, and loss of short-term memory. On neuropsychological testing several months after the acute intoxication, patients were found to have severe antegrade memory deficits with relative preservation of other cognitive functions; patients also had clinical and electromyographic evidence of pure motor or sensorimotor neuropathy or axonopathy. Neuropathologic studies in four patients who died demonstrated neuronal necrosis and loss, predominantly in the hippocampus and amygdala.[14] Canadian authorities now analyze mussels and clams for domoic acid and close shellfish beds to harvesting when levels exceed 20 μg/g.

In September 1991, more than 100 brown pelicans and cormorants were found dead or suffering from unusual neurologic symptoms in Monterey Bay, California. An investigation implicated *Pseudo-nitzschia* species present in the bay (ingested by anchovies, which in turn were consumed by the seabirds) as the cause of the outbreak. Subsequent studies have demonstrated the persistence of *Pseudo-nitzschia* in this area, with low levels of domoic acid detectable in the marine food web.[3] Although no clear-cut human cases of amnesic shellfish poisoning have been identified in California, the clinical significance of the ingestion of low levels of domoic acid (as may be occurring in persons eating shellfish and anchovies from Monterey Bay) is unknown.

PFIESTERIA-ASSOCIATED SYNDROME

Pfiesteria piscicida was identified in the early 1990s as a cause of massive fish kills in the New River and the Albemarle-Pamlico estuarine system of North Carolina.[15, 16] Toxin production is triggered by the presence of fish (or fish feces); toxins kill fish, cause sloughing of fish skin, and may affect fish behavior. Fish in affected areas frequently have a characteristic "punched out" skin lesion that occurs most often in the anal region[17]; in many instances these lesions result from secondary fungal infection, possibly at sites of toxin-mediated skin damage. Nutrient loading of waterways appears to play a role in promoting the growth of *Pfiesteria*, with recent concerns focused on the impact of estuarine runoff of animal feces from large-scale commercial hog and chicken production.

Shortly after identification of the organism, laboratory investigators working with toxic *Pfiesteria* cultures began to note problems with respiratory irritation, skin rashes, and most disturbingly, cognition.[18] In subsequent studies conducted in the Chesapeake Bay region,[19] a significant association was found between the degree of exposure to waterways where *Pfiesteria* was known to be present and objective deficiencies in learning, memory, and higher-order cognitive function (divided attention). Seventy-five percent of persons with high levels of exposure to affected waterways (daily exposure, 6 to 8 hours per day over a period of months) scored below the second percentile on tests of learning ability as compared with national age and educationally matched norms. Six months after the cessation of exposure, scores of all affected persons had returned to within normal ranges. Exposed persons also complained of headaches, skin lesions,[20] and at times, a burning sensation in skin directly exposed to water where *Pfiesteria* organisms appeared to be active. Persons with exposure to waterways with findings suggestive of very high levels of *Pfiesteria* activity (as seen during active fish kills) have reported acute respiratory and eye irritation; an acute, transient confusional syndrome has also been reported in this setting.

In contrast to syndromes associated with other marine biotoxins, *Pfiesteria*-associated illness is not connected with eating fish or shellfish. Although exposure routes are not clearly defined, it appears likely that the toxins are transmitted either through aerosols (analogous to what is seen at times with *G. breve* toxins) or by direct contact of skin with water in which toxin is present. Maryland and other mid-Atlantic states have developed policies for closure of waterways when the organism appears to be active. Until we have a better understanding of *Pfiesteria* toxins and their mode of action, it would appear prudent for persons who must come in contact with such waterways, particularly in the midst of an active *Pfiesteria*-related fish kill, to wear protective clothing and respiratory protective gear.

REFERENCES

1. Boesch DE, Anderson DM, Horner RA, et al. Harmful Algal Blooms in Coastal Waters: Options for Prevention, Control, and Mitigation. NOAA Coastal Oceans Program Decision Analysis Series No. 10. Silver Spring, Md: NOAA Coastal Oceans Office; Md. 1996: 1–46.
2. Todd ECD. Emerging diseases associated with seafood toxins and other water-borne agents. Ann N Y Acad Sci. 1994;740:77–94.
3. ECOHAB. The ecology and oceanography of harmful algal blooms: A national research agenda. Http://www.redtide.whoi.edu/hab/nationplan/ECOHAB/ECOHA-BExecSummary.html.
4. Ruff TA. Ciguatera in the Pacific: A link with military activities. Lancet. 1989;1:201–205.
5. Thomassin BA, Ali Halidi ME, Quod JP, et al. Evolution of *Gambierdiscus toxicus* populations in the coral reef complex of Mayotte Island (SW Indian Ocean) during the 1985–1991 period. Bull Soc Pathol Exot. 1992;85:449–452.
6. Tester PA. Harmful marine phytoplankton and shellfish toxicity. Potential consequences of climatic change. Ann N Y Acad Sci. 1994;740:69–76.

6a. Morris JG Jr. *Pfiesteria,* "the cell from hell," and other toxic algal nightmares. Clin Infect Dis. 1999;28:1191–1198.

7. Morris JG Jr, Lewin P, Smith CW, et al. Ciguatera fish poisoning: Epidemiology of the disease on St. Thomas, U.S. Virgin Islands. Am J Trop Med Hyg. 1982;31:574–578.
8. Bagnis R, Kuberski T, Lugier S. Clinical observations on 3009 cases of ciguatera (fish poisoning) in the South Pacific. Am J Trop Med Hyg. 1979;28:1067–1073.
9. Morris JG Jr, Lewin P, Hargrett NT, et al. Clinical features of ciguatera fish poisoning: A study of the disease in the U.S. Virgin Islands. Arch Intern Med. 1982;142:1090–1092.
10. Centers for Disease Control. Paralytic shellfish poisoning—Massachusetts and Alaska, 1990. MMWR Morb Mortal Wkly Rep. 1991;40:157–161.
11. Gessner BD, Middaugh JP. Paralytic shellfish poisoning in Alaska: A 20-year retrospective. Am J Epidemiol. 1995;141:766–770.
12. Music SI, Howell JT, Brumback CL. Red tide: Its public health implications. J Fla Med Assoc. 1973;60:27–29.
13. Perl TM, Bedard L, Kosatsky T, et al. An outbreak of toxic encephalopathy caused by eating mussels contaminated with domoic acid. N Engl J Med. 1990;322:1775–1780.
14. Teitelbaum JS, Zatorre RJ, Carpenter S, et al. Neurologic sequelae of domoic acid intoxication due to ingestion of contaminated mussels. N Engl J Med. 1990;322:1781–1787.
15. Burkholder JM, Noga EJ, Hobbs CH, et al. New "phantom" dinoflagellate is the causative agent of major estuarine fish kills. Nature. 1992;358:407–410.
16. Noga EJ, Smith SA, Burkholder JM, et al. A new ichthyotoxic dinoflagellate: Cause of acute mortality in aquarium fishes. Vet Rec. 1993;133:96–97.
17. Kane AS, Oldach D, Reimschuessel R. Fish lesions in the Chesapeake Bay: *Pfiesteria*-like dinoflagellates and other etiologies. Md Med J. 1998;47:106–112.
18. Glasgow HB Jr, Burkholder JM, Schmechel DE, et al. Insidious effects of a toxic estuarine dinoflagellate on fish survival and human health. J Toxicol Environ Health. 1995;46:501–522.
19. Grattan LM, Oldach D, Perl TM, et al. Learning and memory difficulties after environmental exposure to waterways containing toxin-producing *Pfiesteria* or *Pfiesteria*-like dinoflagellates. Lancet. 1998;352:532–539.
20. Lowitt MH, Kauffman L. *Pfiesteria* and the skin: A practical update for clinicians. Md Med J. 1998;47:124–126.

SECTION J

DISEASES DUE TO HELMINTHS

Chapter 276

Introduction to Helminth Infections

ADEL A. F. MAHMOUD

Worm infections in humans and other animals constitute a significant contributor to the global burden of illness caused by infectious diseases in general. The major pathogens that are included in this group are the roundworms (nematodes), flukes (trematodes), and tapeworms (cestodes). As shown in Table 276–1, these pathogens infect humans by several different routes. Worms as infectious agents are classified as macroparasites, a group that also contains orthopod causes of disease. Macroparasites are unique because of their biologic structure (multicellular), complex antigenic constituents, and life cycle. These features along with immunologic and other host responses result in a set of complex host-parasite interactions and multiple clinical syndromes.

BIOLOGY OF HELMINTHS

Worms, in contrast to all other infectious agents, are large in size, varying from 1 cm to 10 m. The size of these infectious agents poses a challenge in relation to mechanisms of invasion of mammalian hosts and taxes the immune response of their respective hosts. The size of these organisms also reflects their multicellular complex structure and physiologic system differentiation. Worms are usually encased by a cuticle or outer membrane that protects their internal structures. Inside this protective coating, several differentiated organ systems are present, including digestive, neuromuscular, excretory, and reproductive organs.

The life cycle of worms is complex and may involve two or more hosts. In general, infection in humans is initiated by ingestion of helminth eggs or penetration of intact skin by infective larvae. In some worm infections, the infective stage gains entry via bites of insect vectors. Within the human host, worms undergo maturation and differentiation into adult sexually mature organisms. These are usually of separate sex, but in some species adult worms are hermaphroditic. Mature worms perpetuate their life cycle by producing eggs or larvae that are responsible for transmission of infection outside the human host. In the environment, the organisms invade specific intermediate hosts (e.g., snails, fish). Inside, the worm larvae undergo asexual multiplication and maturation into the stage infective to humans. In some worm infections, a simpler life cycle exists in which the transmission stages of the organisms undergo changes upon leaving the human host that make them infective to humans without the need for an intermediate host.

The most significant feature of the biology of worm infections is the inability of the worms to reproduce and multiply in numbers within the definitive human host. This means that an individual human harboring a pair of worms cannot develop an infection with four worms unless he or she is exposed again to the infective stage of the pathogen. Therefore, the only way for intensity of infection of any individual to increase is by further exposure to the infective stage. (There are, however, two clinically relevant exceptions to this feature, strongyloidiasis and echinococcosis.) Because of this inability of worms to multiply in the human host, the concept of quantification of infection becomes of central importance in appreciating worm infections and their clinical and epidemiologic impact.

EPIDEMIOLOGY

The classic parameters that are used to evaluate infectious diseases such as prevalence, intensity, and incidence apply equally well to worm infections in human populations. Measurements of intensity of infection are inexact in most circumstances.

Most epidemiologic studies have demonstrated that worm infections are distributed in an overdispersed manner in the population of areas of endemicity, which fits a negative binomial distribution. This

TABLE 276–1 Major Helminth Infections of Humans

Group or Class	Infection	Organism	Mode of Transmission to Humans
Nematodes (roundworms)	Trichuriasis	*Trichuris trichiura*	Ingestion of embryonated eggs
	Enterobiasis	*Enterobius vermicularis*	Ingestion of eggs
	Ascariasis	*Ascaris lumbricoides*	Ingestion of embryonated eggs
	Hookworm	*Ancylostoma duodenale, Necator americanus*	Skin penetration by larvae
	Strongyloidiasis	*Strongyloides stercoralis*	Larva penetration of skin or colon
	Trichinosis	*Trichinella spiralis*	Ingestion of muscle larvae
	Lymphatic filariasis	*Wuchereria bancrofti, Brugia malayi*	Injection of larvae during mosquito bite
	Onchocerciasis	*Onchocerca volvulus*	Injection of larvae during blackfly bite
Trematodes (flukes)	Schistosomiasis	*Schistosoma haematobium, Schistosoma mansoni, Schistosoma japonicum, Schistosoma intercalatum, Schistosoma mekongi*	Penetration of intact human skin by cercariae
	Clonorchiasis	*Clonorchis sinensis*	Ingestion of metacercariae in freshwater fish
	Fascioliasis	*Fasciola hepatica*	Ingestion of metacercariae on aquatic plants
	Paragonimiasis	*Paragonimus westermani*	Ingestion of metacercariae in crayfish or freshwater crabs
Cestodes (tapeworms)	Echinococcosis	*Echinococcus granulosus, Echinococcus multilocularis*	Ingestion of eggs
	Taeniasis saginata	*Taenia saginata*	Ingestion of cysticerci in beef
	Taeniasis solium	*Taenia solium*	Ingestion of cysticerci in pork
	Cysticercosis	*Taenia solium*	Ingestion of eggs
	Diphyllobothriasis	*Diphyllobothrium latum*	Ingestion of cysts in freshwater fish

means that most infected individuals harbor low worm burdens and only a minority show evidence of high intensity. The aggregation of parasite load in the population, therefore, results in 80% of the pathogens being found in approximately 20% of the population. The basis of aggregation of helminths in human populations is unknown; it may be related to heterogeneity of the parasites, differences in susceptibility of the human or intermediate hosts, or differences in the patterns of exposure of human populations. Furthermore, the predisposition for light or heavy infection in any specific individual may be related to social, behavioral, genetic, or nutritional factors.

HOST-PARASITE RELATIONSHIP

Disease related to worm infection may occur by direct mechanisms, such as blood loss in hookworm infection. Alternatively, host responses may lead to immunopathologic lesions such as schistosome egg granulomas, which contribute significantly to disease. In other circumstances, several mechanisms may contribute to disease and chronic sequelae such as bladder cancer and cholangiocarcinoma associated, respectively, with schistosomiasis haematobia and opisthorchiasis viverrini. Basic to our understanding of pathogenesis of helminthiasis is an appreciation of the size, antigen multiplicity, and chronicity of these infections. Consequently, host responses are composed of a myriad of immunologic and nonimmunologic factors. Some contribute to disease as outlined in individual chapters. On the other hand, worms have successfully developed multiple strategies to evade host protective responses. Suggested mechanisms include encapsulation within a host fibrous reaction (hydatid cyst), intraluminal location *(Ascaris)*, generalized or specific immunosuppression (filariasis), and acquisition of host antigens (schistosomes). The question of whether worm infections lead to specific resistance to subsequent reinfection has not been settled. A degree of acquired immunity has been shown in infected individuals who were cured chemotherapeutically and lived under the same conditions of exposure to infection. These findings are encouraging in that induction of resistance by vaccines may be a viable control strategy.

Eosinophilia is a characteristic phenomenon related to helminth infection. Peripheral blood, bone marrow, and tissue eosinophilias are associated with the tissue migratory stages of worm infections. Eosinophilia is not observed in infections with helminths that reside in the human gut (e.g., tapeworms). Eosinophils have been demonstrated to play a significant role in host resistance to worm infections, as well as in protection against the tissue stages of these parasites. Although other cells of the immune system may contribute to acquired resistance, the close association of eosinophilia and helminths points to a specific set of interactions and adaptation to this particular class of infectious agents.

Human infection with parasitic helminths is undergoing changes similar to those of infections with other emerging and reemerging pathogens. The spectrum of infectious agents is expanding (e.g., capillariasis, baylisascariasis, anisakiasis) and the interaction with new infectious agents such as human immunodeficiency virus may change the clinical presentation and management of worm infections such as strongyloidiasis. The global nature of the food industry has added new dimensions to the epidemiology and distribution of some helminth infections such as clonorchiasis. Finally, with chemotherapy as the most relied upon treatment and control modality, the threat of development of drug resistance is real.

APPROACH FOR THE PATIENT WITH HELMINTHIASIS

The presenting clinical features of helminthiasis may not differ from those of many other clinical conditions. Two features may be of significance: (1) a history of possible exposure under the correct circumstances, for example, swimming in fresh water in areas where schistosomiasis is endemic or eating undercooked pork or bear meat when trichinosis is suspected, and (2) the presence of eosinophilia. Knowledge of the geographic distribution of these infections and their general clinical manifestations is necessary to direct the physician to the correct diagnostic approach. In general, most individuals infected with worms harbor low burdens and are asymptomatic. The only clue to diagnosis may be eosinophilia or a positive serologic test. For symptomatic patients, however, a systematic approach to history, physical examination, and appropriate imaging and laboratory tests is necessary. Physicians need to have a higher index of suspicion because of the ever-expanding scope of clinical conditions that are encountered. Consultation with experts in this field may save unnecessary diagnostic procedures and define the etiologic diagnosis. Physicians may also be called upon to advise individuals or groups traveling to areas where these infections are endemic or to consult with such groups upon their return. In either case, knowledge of the biology, geographic distribution, and preventive measures is necessary.

Bibliography

Anderson RM, May RM. Infectious Diseases of Humans, Dynamics and Control. New York: Oxford University Press; 1991:433–606.

Schistosome, liver flukes and *Helicobacter pylori*. IARC Monogr Eval Carcinog Risks Hum. 1994;61:1–270.

Lederberg J, Shope RE, Oaks SC, eds. Emerging Infections: Microbial Threats to Health in the United States. Washington, DC: Institute of Medicine, National Academy Press; 1992:1–294.

Mahmoud AAF. Tropical and Geographical Medicine Companion Hand Book. 2nd ed. New York: McGraw Hill; 1993:75–154.

Warren KS, Mahmoud AAF. Tropical and Geographical Medicine. 2nd ed. New York: McGraw-Hill; 1990:368–556.

Chapter 277

Intestinal Nematodes (Roundworms)

ADEL A. F. MAHMOUD

The phylum Nematoidea, or roundworms, is the second largest phylum in the animal kingdom, encompassing as many as 500,000 species. Members of this phylum are elongated, with bilaterally symmetric bodies containing an intestinal tract and a large body cavity. Many roundworm species are free-living, but few are parasites of humans. Infection with intestinal roundworms, however, constitutes the largest group of helminthic infections of humans. For example, it is estimated that worldwide there are 1 billion cases of ascariasis and 800 million of trichuriasis. The life cycle of parasitic nematodes is important clinically because some of these infections can be transmitted directly from infected to uninfected people, whereas in others, eggs must undergo a process of maturation outside the human host, and in a third category the parasites may spend a part of their life cycle in the soil before becoming infective to humans. As with other parasitic infections, definitive diagnosis depends on demonstration of the stage of the life cycle in the host. Serologic or molecular probes are increasingly being used as diagnostic methodologies. Nematodes, like most other worms infectious to humans, do not multiply in the host; the exception is strongyloidiasis in the immunosuppressed person, in which the parasite is capable of increasing its larval stage in the host in the absence of exposure to infective larvae from the environment. The major parasitic nematodes with their mode of infection and final habitat in the host are outlined in Table 277–1.

TABLE 277–1 Important Intestinal Roundworm Infections of Humans

Infection	Mode of Transmission	Superfamily	Species Infecting Humans	Infective Stage	Final Habitat
Trichuriasis	Direct	Trichuroidea	*Trichuris trichiura*	Eggs	Large intestines
Enterobiasis	Direct	Oxyuroidea	*Enterobius vermicularis*	Eggs	Cecum
Ascariasis	Modified direct	Ascaroidea	*Ascaris lumbricoides*	Mature eggs	Small intestines
Hookworm	Skin penetration	Strongyloidea	*Ancylostoma duodenale*	Larvae	Small intestines
			Necator americanus	Larvae	Small intestines
Strongyloidiasis	Skin penetration	Rhabditoidea	*Strongyloides stercoralis*	Larvae	Small intestines

TRICHURIASIS

Infection with the nematode *Trichuris trichuria* is among the most prevalent human helminthiases; approximately 800 million cases occur worldwide, most abundantly in warm, moist regions.[1] In the United States, it has been estimated that 2.2 million people are infected with *T. trichiura*, mainly in the rural Southeast. Infection rates up to 75% were found in young schoolchildren in Puerto Rico.

The normal habitat of *T. trichiura* adults in humans is in the cecum and ascending colon. The body of the pinkish-gray adult worms (mean length 40 mm) is divided into an attenuated whiplike anterior part that is three fifths its length and a more robust posterior part. The head or anterior part of the worm penetrates and anchors itself to the intestinal mucosa.

Life Cycle

Humans are the principal hosts for *T. trichiura*, and infection is transmitted directly (Fig. 277–1). The mean expected life span of adult worms is 1 year, and during this period each female worm produces 5000 to 20,000 eggs/day. The ova (50 to 54 × 22 μm) are barrel-shaped, with a thick shell and translucent polar prominences, and are unsegmented at oviposition. After excretion in the feces, embryonic development takes place under optimal conditions of moisture and shade in 2 to 4 weeks. When the embryonated egg is ingested by humans, the larva escapes from the shell in the upper small intestine. These larval worms penetrate the intestinal villi, where they lie for 3 to 10 days before slowly moving downward into the lumen of the cecum, where the anterior three quarters of the worms remain within the superficial mucosa and the short posterior end is free in the lumen. Worms develop to mature ovipositing adults in 1 to 3 months.

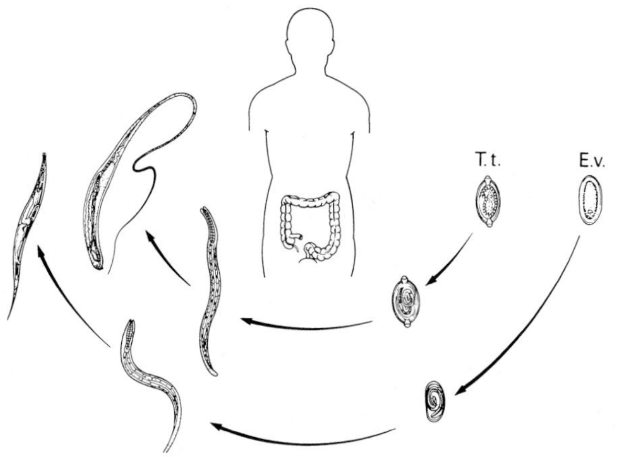

FIGURE 277–1. Life cycle of direct infecting nematodes. Eggs are passed with stools in *Trichuris trichiura* (T.t.) or are deposited at the perianal region in *Enterobius vermicularis* (E.v.). They embryonate in a short time and infection is acquired by ingestion. Eggs hatch in the intestine, and larvae migrate to their final habitat in the colon (T.t.) or cecum (E.v.).

Epidemiology

Trichuriasis has a worldwide prevalence; it is most common, however, in poor rural communities and areas in which sanitary facilities are lacking. The intensity of infection is usually light; children in the 5- to 15-year age group have the highest prevalence and probably have heavier worm loads than adults. Infection results from the ingestion of embryonated ova by direct contamination of hands, food, or drink or indirectly through flies and other insects.

Humans are the principal host of *T. trichiura*, but the parasite has also been found in monkeys, lemurs, and hogs. Soil pollution by human or animal feces, therefore, constitutes the major determining factor in the spread of infection.

The morbidity due to trichuriasis in endemic communities is not fully understood. Although most infected people harbor low worm burdens, a small proportion acquire heavy infections. Clinical impressions point to this subpopulation of heavily infected people (mainly children) as most likely to suffer from disease.

Clinical Syndromes

Infection with *T. trichiura* in humans is mainly asymptomatic; however, several clinical features have been described on the basis of uncontrolled morbidity surveys. Adult worms embed their heads in the intestinal mucosa, and in heavily infected individuals, an association with iron-deficiency anemia has been demonstrated.[2] Although a plethora of abdominal signs and symptoms have been associated with *T. trichiura* infections, the underlying mechanisms are unknown. In heavily infected people,[3] it appears that infection may manifest itself as mild anemia, bloody diarrhea (classic *Trichuris* dysentery syndrome), growth retardation (chronic *Trichuris* colitis with growth retardation), or rectal prolapse. Associated conditions such as malnutrition and other geohelminthiases[4] seem to play a significant role in the pathogenesis of the previously mentioned symptoms and signs. Although a portion of the worms are embedded in the mucosa of the large bowel, no significant eosinophilia has been reported in trichuriasis.

Diagnosis

Fecal examination by the simple smear technique is sufficient because the level of egg output is so high (about 200 eggs/g of feces per worm pair). Diagnosis is made by finding the characteristic lemon-shaped ova.

Management

Mebendazole (Vermox) is essentially nontoxic, is highly effective, and gives a cure rate of 70 to 90% and a reduction in egg output of 90 to 99%. Mebendazole is administered in a dosage of 100 mg twice a day for 3 days regardless of body weight.[5] The drug is poorly absorbed from the gastrointestinal tract and has very few side effects.

ENTEROBIASIS

Enterobiasis, or pinworm, is also highly prevalent throughout the world, particularly in countries of the temperate zone. In the United

States, it is the most common of all helminthic infections, with an estimated 42 million cases. Pinworm infection is particularly common among children and is not associated with any specific socioeconomic levels.[6] Enterobiasis is most prevalent in congested districts, in institutionalized groups, and among members of the same family.

Life Cycle

Enterobius vermicularis is a small (1 cm in length) white threadlike worm inhabiting the cecum and adjacent gut (see Fig. 277–1). A gravid female worm contains an average of 11,100 ova and has a life span of 11 to 35 days. The gravid females migrate at night to the perianal and perineal regions for oviposition; ova are infrequently laid in the intestines. The stimulus for oviposition seems to be a subclinical temperature and an aerobic environment. Ova are laid either in clusters or in a stream but are not widely distributed in the perianal region. *Enterobius* ova are ovoid but flattened on one side and measure approximately 56×27 μm. The eggs embryonate within 6 hours and are transferred from the perianal region to night clothes, bedding, and dust and air. The most common mode of transmission, however, is via the hands of the patient, particularly beneath the fingernails, through scratching or handling clothes and bed linen. On ingestion, the embryos hatch in the duodenum, molt twice, and develop into adult worms in 36 to 53 days.

Epidemiology

The prevalence of pinworm infection is lowest in nurslings and reaches its maximum in schoolchildren 5 to 14 years old.[6] The absence of an extended extracorporeal development stage favors direct transmission. Eggs are infective within 6 hours of ovideposition and may remain so for 20 days.

Pinworm is primarily a familial or institutional infection, with no predilection to specific socioeconomic conditions.[7] Because the life span of the worms is relatively brief, long-standing infections must be due to continuous reinfection.[8] Estimates of worm burdens in infected people have shown an average of 58 worms in the 4- to 10-year-old group, compared with 16 worms in the 11- to 16-year-old group. No data are available, however, on the intensity of infections in adults.

Clinical Syndromes

The clinical presentations in enterobiasis are related largely to perianal and perineal pruritis. Although various classifications of symptoms into local, secondary, and reflex nervous symptoms have been proposed, it is important to realize that a large proportion of pinworm infections are essentially asymptomatic. In a hospital-based study of children 2 to 12 years old, none of the signs and symptoms largely ascribed to enterobiasis was significantly more common in infected than in uninfected children.[9]

The most common complaints are local itching and restless sleep due to nocturnal anal pruritis.[10] Occasionally, the migration of the parasite may produce ectopic disease such as appendicitis, chronic salpingitis, or ulcerative lesions in the small or large bowel. There is no evidence that enterobiasis is associated with significant eosinophilia or elevated serum immunoglobulin E (IgE) levels.

Diagnosis

Although pinworms can be seen by the naked eye, they may easily be confused with bits of white thread. Diagnosis is readily made by examination of an adhesive cellophane tape pressed against the perianal region early in the morning. A single examination detects 50% of infections, three examinations detect 90%, and five examinations detect 99%. Because the infection usually runs in families, diagnosis in one person necessitates examination of all members.

Management

Drug therapy is recommended for all infected members of families with symptomatic infections. Mebendazole (Vermox) in a single oral dose of 100 mg, repeated in 2 weeks, results in a cure rate of 90 to 100%.[5] Albendazole, in a single oral dose of 400 mg, repeated in 2 weeks, may also be used. Although personal cleanliness is a useful general principle, its role in the management of enterobiasis is trivial, and emphasis on cleanliness tends only to enhance the psychological trauma and stigmas associated with this infection.

ASCARIASIS

Ascaris, or roundworm, is the most common helminthic infection of humans, with an estimated worldwide prevalence of more than 1 billion.[10] The causative organism, *Ascaris lumbricoides*, is cosmopolitan in distribution, being most abundant in tropical countries. In the United States, it has been estimated that 4 million people, mainly in the southeast, have *Ascaris* infection.[11]

The white or reddish-yellow adult worms (15 to 35 cm in length) live in the lumen of the small intestine, most commonly in the jejunum and middle ileum. Infection with *Ascaris* appears to be asymptomatic in the vast majority of cases but may produce serious pulmonary disease or obstruction of biliary or intestinal tracts in a small proportion of infected people.

Life Cycle

A. lumbricoides is a parasite of humans; adult worms inhabit the lumen of the small intestine and have a life span of approximately 10 to 24 months. Eath female worm produces a daily output of 200,000 ova. The fertile ovum is broadly oval, has a thick shell with an outer, coarse, mammillated albuminous covering, and measures 45 to 70 μm in length by 35 to 50 μm in breadth (Fig. 277–2). After their passage with feces and under favorable environmental conditions, fully developed infective embryos are formed within the eggs in 5 to 10 days. When ingested by humans, they hatch in the small intestine; the embryos penetrate the intestinal wall and migrate via venous blood to the heart and reach the lungs, where they break into the alveoli and pass up through the bronchi and trachea. They are then swallowed to return to the intestines and become mature

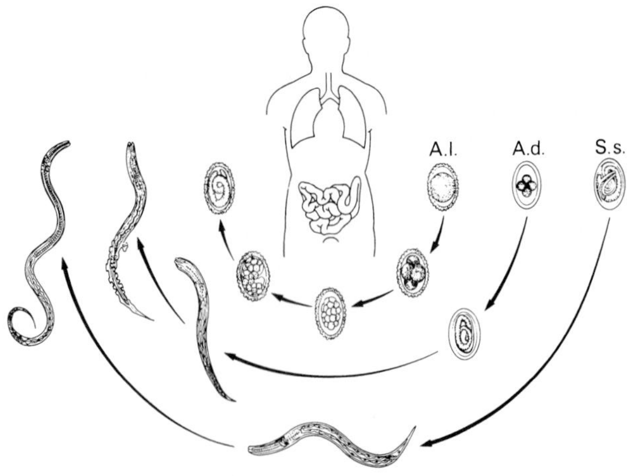

FIGURE 277–2. Life cycle of modified direct and skin penetrating nematodes. Eggs are passed with stools in *Ascaris lumbricoides* (A.l.), *Necator americanus*, or *Ancylostoma duodenale* (A.d.), or they hatch on their way out in *Strongyloides stercoralis*. *Ascaris* eggs mature in soil, and humans are infected on ingestion of these eggs. In hookworm and strongyloidiasis, humans are infected by skin penetration by filariform larvae. In all three infections, larvae pass through a migratory phase via the lungs before reaching maturity at their final habitat in the small intestine.

worms. The time required to produce a gravid female has been estimated to be 2 months.

Epidemiology

Ascaris infection occurs at all ages but is most common in preschool and young school-aged children.[12] The incidence is approximately the same for both sexes, but in blacks of the southeastern United States, it is over three times that in whites. Transmission of *A. lumbricoides* is usually hand to mouth. It is enhanced by the extremely high output of eggs by fecund female worms and the ability of ova to resist unfavorable external environments. *Ascaris* eggs can live for 2 years at 5 to 10°C, can survive for 3 months in the absence of oxygen, and can resist desiccation for 2 to 3 weeks at 22°C.[13] In moist, loose, sandy soil, ova remain viable up to 6 years and can survive freezing winter temperatures.

In endemic areas, most people have light to moderate worm burdens. For example, a recent survey in Colombia reported that 72% of the infected people had less than 1 to 19 eggs/mg of feces and only 5% had more than 200 eggs/mg of feces.

Recent molecular studies on the patterns of variation in ribosomal RNA of *Ascaris* worms isolated in North America were compared with those of worms obtained from pigs and humans from worldwide locations. Repeats bearing specific restriction sites were found in most parasites from humans in North America and pigs, whereas they were rarely detected in parasites obtained from infected humans worldwide. This evidence raises the question of the source of infection in humans in North America and whether we actually are dealing with a reservoir of infection or whether most cases in humans are *Ascaris suum* and not *A. lumbricoides*.[14]

Clinical Syndromes

The pathologic lesions encountered in ascariasis depend on the intensity of infection and the organs involved. Although overt disease is rare in roundworm infection, the more common problems are pulmonary and nutritional disorders and obstruction of the intestinal or biliary tract. The pulmonary manifestations of ascariasis occur during the stage of larval migration through the lungs and resemble Löffler's syndrome. Transient respiratory symptoms associated with pulmonary infiltration and peripheral blood eosinophilia are the main features of this syndrome. Considering the endemicity and prevalence of *Ascaris* infections, it is amazing that only a very small proportion of infected people have pulmonary symptoms. In some endemic areas such as Saudi Arabia, where transmission of *Ascaris* is seasonal, the so-called seasonal pneumonitis has frequently been reported.[15]

Children with moderately heavy *Ascaris* infection were shown to have impairment of digestion or absorption of dietary proteins.[16] In one study, children with an average worm burden of 71 had a 72% impairment of dietary nitrogen absorption, and two thirds had moderate steatorrhea. Some of these studies were performed in areas in the developing world in which additional nutritional deficiencies cannot be excluded. In contrast, a controlled study performed in the southern United States on the nutritional status of children with *Ascaris* infection revealed no significant difference between uninfected and infected groups.[17]

A more serious complication of *Ascaris* infection is encountered when a mass of worms obstructs the lumen of the small bowel. This acute abdominal condition is commonly seen in children with heavy infections.[18–20] The presentation is similar to that of acute intestinal obstruction, with vomiting, abdominal distention, and cramps. These patients may pass worms in vomitus or in stools during an attack. Another obstructive syndrome is encountered when *Ascaris* worms invade the biliary duct causing pancreatic-biliary ascariasis. The most common presenting feature is abdominal pain, seen in 98% of patients. Less common features include ascending cholangitis, acute pancreatitis, and rarely obstructive jaundice.[21] Ultrasonography is becoming an important method for diagnosis of this clinical presentation of ascariasis.[22]

Because of the great prevalence of ascariasis, aberrant ascarids situated at different tissue sites in infected people have been described. Worms were found escaping through umbilical and hernial fistulas, in the fallopian tubes and urinary bladder, and in the lungs and heart. These ectopic locations of ascarids may give rise to difficult diagnostic problems, but fortunately they are very rare.

Diagnosis

Because of the enormous daily output of eggs by gravid ascarids, direct smear examination of stools is sufficient for diagnosis.

Management

The drug of choice for treatment of intestinal infections with *A. lumbricoides* is mebendazole (Vermox).[5] It is given as 100 mg twice daily for 3 days. Pyrantel pamoate (Antiminth) at a dose of 11 mg/kg orally (maximum of 1 g) can also be used. Chemotherapy is the currently recommended method of controlling ascariasis in endemic areas.[23] In cases in which intestinal or biliary obstruction is suspected, piperazine citrate (Antepar) is recommended.[5] It is administered as piperazine syrup by instillation through a nasogastric tube, 150 mg/kg initially, followed by six doses of 65 mg/kg at 12-hour intervals. Piperazine narcotizes the worms and helps relieve the obstruction of the intestinal or biliary tract.

HOOKWORM

Human infection with the two species of hookworm, *Ancylostoma duodenale* and *Necator americanus*, is estimated to affect approximately one fourth of the world's population. The present geographic distribution of hookworm infection lies in the tropical and subtropical zones between 45 degrees north and 30 degrees south latitude.[24] The remarkable success in controlling hookworm infection in the United States during the early part of this century has not, however, occurred in other parts of the world. Iron-deficiency anemia due to hookworms and other nutritional factors looms across most of the developing world. A low degree of prevalence of the infection still exists in the southeastern United States. A newly recognized syndrome of eosinophilic enteritis has been linked to enteric infection with *Ancylostoma caninum*.[25] Human infection with this canine hookworm has been known previously to cause cutaneous larva migrans but not to disseminate systemically.

Life Cycle

Adult hookworms are small, cylindrical (approximately 1 cm long), grayish-white nematodes. Hookworms live chiefly in the upper small intestine, attached to the mucosa by their strong buccal capsules. The average daily blood loss for *N. americanus* worm is about 0.03 ml and for *A. duodenale* is 0.2 ml. Human hookworms have a mean life span of approximately 5 years, although it is probable that most worms disappear within 2 years.

Adult worms lay an average of 7000 eggs daily. The eggs are ovoid and thin-shelled and measure 58×36 μm. They pass out with the stools, and under suitable conditions of soil humidity and temperature, the eggs hatch into larvae that molt once to become infective for humans (see Fig. 277–2). Contact with contaminated soil for 5 to 10 minutes is required for skin penetration. The larvae are carried by the circulation to the lungs, penetrate the alveolar walls, and make their way up the trachea to be swallowed and carried to their final habitat in the small intestine. Gravid females start egg deposition 4 to 6 weeks after skin penetration.

Epidemiology

The distribution and prevalence of hookworm infections are limited by environmental conditions. Ova fail to develop at temperatures below 13°C. Although larvae require relatively little moisture, drying and direct sunlight are destructive. The superficial position of infective larvae on the topsoil affords easy access for the penetration of human skin. Other major epidemiologic features of hookworm transmission concern methods of disposal or fecal waste and the human habit of walking barefoot. Transmission also is suspected to occur through transplacental or transmammary routes from infected mothers to their infants.[24]

Clinical Syndrome

Disease manifestations may occur early during the course of infection, with "ground itch," intense pruritus, erythema, and a papular, vesicular rash at the site of larval penetration. The migration of the larvae through the lungs may produce a Löffler-like syndrome with transitory chest symptoms, diffuse opacities on radiographs, and eosinophilia in sputum and peripheral blood. The major manifestations of hookworm disease, however, are iron-deficiency anemia[26] and chronic protein energy malnutrition. The development of these clinical features depends not only on the worm burden but on the amount of absorbable dietary iron.

Along with the phase of worm attachment to the small intestine mucosa, abdominal pain, diarrhea, and weight loss may be noted. In addition, malabsorption has been reported in children and, less commonly, in adults.[24]

Diagnosis

Direct fecal smear examination is adequate for diagnosis of clinically significant hookworm infections. This technique identifies egg counts of more than 1200 eggs/ml.

Management

Mebendazole (Vermox) is the current drug of choice.[5] It is administered as 100 mg twice a day for 3 days regardless of the patient's body weight. This regimen results in a 95% cure rate and a 99.9% reduction of egg counts. Albendazole in a single dose can also be used. Anemia should be corrected by iron therapy.

STRONGYLOIDIASIS

Infection with the nematode *Strongyloides stercoralis* is potentially lethal because of its capacity to cause an overwhelming autoinfection, particularly in the immunosuppressed host.[27] Strongyloidiasis, although uncommon in comparison with the other major intestinal nematodes, is widely distributed in the tropics. In the United States, a prevalence of 0.4 to 4% has been estimated in the southern states.

S. stercoralis worms can survive and reproduce as parasitic forms in humans or as free-living forms in soil.[28] The parasitic female is a colorless semitransparent nematode 2.2 mm in length, whereas the male is considerably shorter (0.7 mm). Adult worms inhabit the upper small intestine, where the females burrow through the mucosa but usually not through the muscularis mucosa.

Life Cycle

The life cycle of *S. stercoralis* is complex and is not fully understood. Parasitic forms that exist in humans, the principal host, deposit ova as they burrow their way into the intestinal mucosa (Fig. 277–2). Eggs ordinarily hatch in the mucosa, releasing larvae that bore through the epithelium to the intestinal lumen and are passed in the feces. They can either molt and differentiate into free-living adult males and females or metamorphose into the filariform infectious forms. The free-living adults either continue their life cycles in the soil or produce filariform infective larvae. The usual route of infection in humans is through skin contact with soil contaminated with the infective filariform larvae. Humans may also be infected via the lower gastrointestinal tract or perianal region from larvae that transform into infective organisms during their passage with feces. This "autoinfection" cycle explains the overwhelming larval invasion seen in strongyloides hyperinfection syndrome. The larvae then pass by way of the blood stream to the lungs, break into the alveolar spaces, and ascend to the glottis, where they are swallowed to their final habitat in the small intestines. Deposition of eggs begins about 28 days after the initial infection.

Epidemiology

Transmission of *S. stercoralis* depends on the suitability of the soil, climatic conditions, and sanitation. In temperate zones, the incidence is highest in institutions (5 to 35%) reflecting the need for close contact transmission. Autochthonous cases have been reported in the United States and may be due to autoinfection. Contrary to most other worm infections, the patient's worm burden in strongyloidiasis is dependent not only on the size of the larval inoculum but also on the degree of autoinfection. This process is enhanced in people with compromised immune systems and may lead to a fatal outcome from an overwhelming infection.

Clinical Syndromes

The symptoms of strongyloidiasis correspond to the three stages of infection: invasion of the skin, migration of larvae, and penetration of the intestinal mucosa by adults. Although approximately one third of people with strongyloidiasis are asymptomatic, the remainder may have symptoms related to one or more of the stages of parasite migration in the host. The skin and pulmonary symptoms resemble those encountered in hookworm disease: pruritic papular erythematous rash and a Löffler-like syndrome with eosinophilia.[28, 29]

The more characteristic clinical features are, however, seen simultaneously with the intestinal phase of strongyloidiasis. Burning or colicky abdominal pain, often epigastric, occurs and is associated with diarrhea and the passage of mucus. Some patients may complain of nausea, vomiting, and weight loss with evidence of malabsorption or of protein-losing enteropathy. Eosinophilia is a prominent feature of this infection.[27] In addition, 5 to 22% of patients may develop a generalized or localized urticarial rash beginning perianally and extending to the buttocks, abdomen, and thighs.

Massive larval invasion of the lungs and other tissue may occur with autoinfection, particularly in immunocompromised hosts.[30] Hyperinfection strongyloidiasis has been described in patients with lymphomas, leukemias, and lepromatous leprosy, and in those treated with corticosteroids; more recently it has been reported in association with human immunodeficiency virus infection.[31] Severe generalized abdominal pain, diffuse pulmonary infiltrates, ileus, shock, and meningitis or sepsis from gram-negative bacilli may occur. Eosinophilia may be absent.

Diagnosis

Definitive diagnosis depends on the demonstration of *S. stercoralis* larvae in the feces or duodenal fluid. Sampling of duodenal contents can easily be accomplished by the use of Entero-Test. A modified agar plate method has recently been shown to be superior to other techniques used for stool examination.[32] Repeated examinations may be necessary to exclude the diagnosis. Serodiagnosis[33] or the use of molecular probes[34] may help solve the difficulties associated with parasitologic examination of stool or other samples.

Management

All people infected with *S. stercoralis* should be treated with the aim of eradicating the infection. Thiabendazole (Mintezol) is an effective agent that can be given in a dose of 25 mg/kg twice a day for 2 days (maximum of 3 g/day).[5] Albendazole, although currently not approved by the Food and Drug Administration for this purpose, may also be used at a dose of 200 μg/kg/day for 1 to 2 days. In the hyperinfection syndrome, early diagnosis and treatment for 2 to 3 weeks may be lifesaving, but the mortality is very high despite treatment. Patients with a past history of exposure to *S. stercoralis* should be thoroughly examined and treated before undergoing any immunosuppressive therapy.

REFERENCES

1. Bundy DAP, Cooper ES. Trichuriasis. In: Warren KS, Mahmoud AAF, eds. Tropical and Geographical Medicine. 2nd ed. New York: McGraw-Hill; 1990:399–404.
2. Ramdath DD, Simeon DT, Wong MS, Grantham-McGregor SM. Iron status of school children with varying intensities of *Trichuris trichiura* infection. Parasitology. 1995;110:347–351.
3. Gilman RH, Chong UH, Davis C, et al. The adverse consequences of heavy *Trichuris* infection. Trans R Soc Trop Med Hyg. 1983;77:432–438.
4. Booth M, Bundy DA, Albonico M, et al. Associations among multiple geohelminth species infections in school children from Pemba Island. Parasitology. 1998;116:85–93.
5. Drugs for Parasitic Infections. Med Lett Drug Ther. 1998;40:1–8.
6. Pawlowski, ZS. Enterobiasis. In: Pawlowski ZS, ed. Clinical Tropical Medicine and Communicable Diseases, v. 3. London: Bailliere Tindall; 1987;667–676.
7. Grencis RK, Cooper ES. *Enterobius, Trichuris, Capillaria* and hookworm including *Ancylostoma caninum*. Gastroenterol Clin North Am. 1996;25:579–597.
8. Nunez FA, Hernandez M, Finlay CM. A longitudinal study of enterobiasis in three day care centers of Havana City. Rev Inst Med Trop Sao Paulo. 1996;38:129–132.
9. Welsh NM. Recent insights into childhood "social diseases" gonorrhea, scabies, pediculosis, pinworms. Clin Pediatr. 1978;17:318–322.
10. DeSilva NR, Chan MS, Bundy DA. Morbidity and mortality due to ascariasis: Reestimation and sensitivity analysis of global numbers at risk. Trop Med Int Health. 1997;2:519–528.
11. Khuroo MS. Ascariasis. Gastroenterol Clin North Am. 1996;25:553–577.
12. Crampton DWT, Nesheim MC, Pawlowski ZS, eds. Ascariasis and Its Public Health Significance. London: Taylor and Francis; 1985.
13. Sinniah B. Daily egg production of *Ascaris lumbricoides*: The distribution of eggs in the feces and the variability of egg counts. Parasitology. 1982;84:167.
14. Anderson TJ. *Ascaris* infections in humans from North America: Molecular evidence for cross infection. Parasitology. 1995;110:215–219.
15. Gelpi AP, Mustafa A. *Ascaris* pneumonia. Am J Med. 1968;44:377.
16. Strephenson LS. The contribution of *Ascaris lumbricoides* to malnutrition in children. Parasitology. 1980;81:221–233.
17. Blumenthal DS, Schults MG. Effects of *Ascaris* infection on nutritional status in children. Am J Trop Med Hyg. 1976;25:682.
18. Blumenthal DS, Schultz MG. Incidence of intestinal obstruction in children infected with *Ascaris lumbricoides*. Am J Trop Med Hyg. 1974;24:801.
19. Wasadikar PP, Kulkami AB. Intestinal obstruction due to ascariasis. Br J Surg. 1997;84:410–412.
20. DeSilva NR, Guyatt HL, Bundy DA. Morbidity and mortality due to *Ascaris*-induced intestinal obstruction. Trans R Soc Trop Med Hyg. 1997;91:31–36.
21. Sandouk F, Haffar S, Zada M, et al. Pancreatic-biliary ascariasis: Experience of 300 cases. Am J Gastroenterol. 1997;92:2264–2267.
22. Ali M, Khan AN. Sonography of hepatobiliary ascariasis. J Clin Ultrasound. 1996;24:235–241.
23. Guyatt HL, Chan MS, Medley GF, Bundy DA. Control of *Ascaris* infection by chemotherapy: Which is the most cost-effective option? Trans R Soc Trop Med Hyg. 1995;89:16–20.
24. Schad GA, Banwell JG. Hookworms. In: Warren KS, Mahmoud AAF, eds. Tropical and Geographical Medicine. 2nd ed. New York: McGraw-Hill; 1990;379–393.
25. Prociv P, Croese J. Human enteric infection with *Ancylostoma caninum*: hookworms reappraised in the light of a "new" zoonosis. Acta Tropica. 1996;62:23–44.
26. Stoltzfus RJ, Albonico M, Chawaya HM, et al. Hemoquant determination of hookworm-related blood loss and its role in iron deficiency in African children. Am J Trop Med Hyg. 1996;55:399–404.
27. Mahmoud AAF. Strongyloidiasis. Clin Infect Dis. 1996;23:949–952.
28. Grove DI. Human strongyloidiasis. Adv Parasitol. 1996;38:251–309.
29. Wehner JH, Kirsch CM. Pulmonary manifestations of strongyloidiasis. Semin Respir Infect. 1997;12:122–129.
30. Heyworth MF. Parasitic diseases in immunocompromised hosts. Cryptosporidiosis, isosporiasis and strongyloidiasis. Gastroenterol Clin North Am. 1996;25:691–707.
31. Gompels MM, Todd J, Peters BS, et al. Disseminated strongyloidiasis in AIDS: Uncommon but important. AIDS. 1991;5:329.
32. Sato Y, Kobayashi J, Tona H, Shiroma Y. Efficacy of stool examination for detection of strongyloides infection. Am J Trop Med Hyg. 1995;53:248–250.
33. Sato Y, Kobayashi J, Shiroma Y. Serodiagnosis of strongyloidiasis. The application and significance. Rev Inst Med Crop Sao Paulo. 1995;37:35–41.
34. Ramachandran S, Thompson RW, Gam AA, Neva FA. Recombinant cDNA clones for immunodiagnosis of strongyloidiasis. J Infect Dis. 1998;177:196–203.

Chapter 278

Tissue Nematodes (Trichinosis, Dracunculiasis, Filariasis)

DAVID I. GROVE

The tissue-dwelling roundworms constitute a major global health problem. They are widely scattered around the world, especially in the tropics, and infect millions of people. Some are parasites of humans only, whereas others have an animal reservoir. All these parasites have complex life cycles involving arthropod intermediate hosts except for *Trichinella spiralis*, which is transmitted directly from one host to the next by ingestion of infective larvae. Like most helminths, the adult worms do not multiply within the human host; therefore, the worm load and severity of disease depend in large measure on the intensity and frequency of exposure to the infective forms. The relative pathogenicity of the adult worms versus the larval forms varies according to the species of infecting worm. Definitive diagnosis requires isolation and identification of the parasite, but in some infections this may be difficult. Effective therapy is available for only some of these infections. Some parasites present almost insurmountable control problems, but others can be avoided by simple preventive measures. Infections acquired by ingestion of contaminated food or water are considered first, and then those transmitted by blood-sucking flies are discussed. Historical information concerning all of these parasites, including the circumstances of their discovery and elucidation of their life cycles, together with the clinical illness they cause as well as modes of treatment that have been developed may be found elsewhere.[1]

TRICHINOSIS

Trichinosis develops when undercooked flesh contaminated with infective larvae of *Trichinella* spp. is eaten. Most infections are asymptomatic, but heavy exposure may lead to diarrhea, periorbital edema, myositis, fever, and prostration.

T. spiralis is the species that has been recognized for years, but the genus has been revised taxonomically. Five species have now been described on the basis of genetic, biochemical, and biologic data (Table 278–1). In addition, three other phenotypes are acknowledged in the genus, but their taxonomic level is uncertain at present.[2, 3]

TABLE 278–1 Species within the Genus *Trichinella*

Species Name	Code	Distribution	Common Hosts
T. spiralis	T1	Worldwide	Pigs, rats, horses, bears, foxes
T. nativa	T2	Arctic, subarctic	Bears, horses
T. britovi	T3	Temperate, subarctic	Boar, horses, foxes
T. pseudospiralis	T4	Arctic, Tasmania	Birds, omnivorous mammals
	T5	Temperate, subarctic	Bears
	T6	Subarctic	Bears
T. nelsoni	T7	Southern Africa	Hyenas
	T8	Tropical Africa	Lions, panthers

Life Cycle

When raw or inadequately cooked meat containing viable larvae of *Trichinella* spp. is eaten, the organisms are freed from the cyst walls by acid-pepsin digestion in the stomach and pass into the small intestine. Larvae invade the columnar epithelium at the bases of the villi of the small intestine and then develop into adult worms. These are obligate intracellular parasites occupying the cytoplasm of a row of enterocytes. The males are about 1.5 × 0.05 mm and the females 3.5 × 0.06 mm in size. The number of larvae released by a fertilized female varies with the species of both parasite and host. *T. spiralis* probably produces about 500 larvae over a period of 2 weeks and then the fertilized female is expelled in the feces. The newborn larvae seed the skeletal muscles via the blood stream. They burrow into individual muscle fibers and then over the next 3 weeks increase 10 times in length, coil, and become capable of infecting a new host. A cyst wall develops around the larva and may eventually calcify. Larvae may remain viable for several years.

Epidemiology

Trichinella spp. are distributed throughout the world and are widely spread in nature among a large number of carnivorous animals, humans being an incidental host (see Table 278–1). Most human infections are due to *T. spiralis*; a few are due to *Trichinella britovi, Trichinella nativa*, and *Trichinella nelsoni*. Only one case of human infection with *Trichinella pseudospiralis* has been reported.[4] *T. spiralis* is the only species with good infectivity for swine and rats. For most of the other species, the different reservoir hosts reflect primarily the fauna present in the region. The vast majority of swine in the United States are fed with grain and are generally uninfected. The small proportion fed with garbage may become infected when given uncooked trichinous scraps, usually pig meat, or when the carcasses of infected wild animals such as rats are eaten. In Europe, the fox is the primary reservoir of the sylvatic cycle of *Trichinella* and human infections usually occur in rural areas where traditional swine-rearing practices are used.[5]

Fewer than 100 human cases are usually reported each year in the United States. About three quarters of these are due to inadequately processed pork; most of the rest have been due to ingestion of poorly cooked bear meat, walrus meat, or cougar jerky.[6, 7] Some epidemics in Europe have followed the consumption of infected horse meat[8] and in Canada the ingestion of wild boar meat.[9] Epidemics occur when families or small communities consume trichinous meat from a common source.

Pathologic Characteristics

There have been indications that the various species have different pathogenicities for humans and other hosts.[2] For example, trichinosis in the Inuit population in Canada after ingestion of infected walrus seems to be associated with prolonged diarrhea and few muscle symptoms. *T. nativa* produces primarily an enteral illness, whereas *T. britovi* causes few if any intestinal symptoms. *T. nelsoni* is of relatively low pathogenicity in both its enteral and parenteral phases.[3]

During the first 2 to 3 weeks after infection, the small intestine shows a mild, partial villous atrophy and an inflammatory infiltrate of polymorphs, eosinophils, lymphocytes, and macrophages in the mucosa and submucosa. Adult worms may be seen in the epithelial layer near the bases of the villi. The most striking changes are in the skeletal muscles. The fibers become edematous, lose their cross-striations, undergo basophilic degeneration, and their nuclei proliferate. The typical coiled worm, the cyst wall derived from the host cell, and the surrounding lymphocytic and eosinophilic infiltrate may be seen within the muscle fiber. In severe cases, focal interstitial myocarditis, meningitis, and encephalitis may occur.

Clinical Features

Most infections are subclinical. The development of symptoms depends mainly on the size of the inoculum of viable larvae. Consequently, the frequencies of the symptoms and signs of trichinosis vary widely from outbreak to outbreak. Their relative frequencies are shown in Table 278–2.

Symptoms attributable to adult worms in the intestines may be found during the first week after infection. Diarrhea is the most common symptom, but patients may also complain of abdominal discomfort and vomiting. Patients with extremely heavy worm burdens may develop a fulminant enteritis. Symptoms associated with systemic invasion by larvae are much more common and usually appear during the second week after infection. Fever is frequently present, although it is of variable intensity and duration. Periorbital edema may be associated with subconjunctival hemorrhages and chemosis. Myositis with pain, swelling, and weakness is also common; it usually develops first in the extraocular muscles and then involves the masseters, neck muscles, limb flexors, and lumbar muscles. Some patients may complain of headache, cough, shortness of breath, hoarseness, and dysphagia. Occasionally, a rash that may be macular or petechial is observed. Retinal or subungual splinter hemorrhages are sometimes seen. These systemic symptoms usually peak 2 to 3 weeks after infection and then slowly subside, although malaise and weakness may persist for weeks. Occasionally, a patient dies, usually from myocarditis but sometimes from encephalitis or pneumonia. It has been claimed that there may be long-lasting sequelae of infection including muscle aches, eye disturbances, cardiac complaints, and headaches.[10]

Diagnosis

Trichinosis should be suspected in a patient who has any of the cardinal features of periorbital edema, myositis, fever, and eosinophilia. If questioning reveals the recent consumption of poorly cooked meat, particularly pork products, the likelihood of the diagnosis is greatly increased. Further confirmation is provided if others who have eaten the same meat have similar symptoms. An eosinophilia is often found: it begins about the 10th day and may reach very high levels. The erythrocyte sedimentation rate is usually normal. Elevated serum creatine phosphokinase and lactic dehydrogenase levels indicate considerable muscle involvement.

Antibodies are not detectable until at least 3 weeks after infection. They may be measured by a variety of techniques including enzyme-linked, immunofluorescent, indirect hemagglutinin, precipitin, and bentonite flocculation assays. A rising titer may help establish the diagnosis.[3] Tests for detection of *Trichinella* DNA in muscle or blood using the polymerase chain reaction are being developed.[11] The skin test for *Trichinella* remains positive for years after exposure; therefore, it does not differentiate between past and recent infections. Muscle biopsy is usually unnecessary; if doubt remains,

TABLE 278–2 Frequencies of Symptoms and Signs of Trichinosis Condensed from Nine Reported Outbreaks

Symptoms or Sign	Mean	Range
Fever	91	(71–100)
Myalgia	89	(68–100)
Weakness and malaise	82	(50–94)
Periorbital edema	77	(29–100)
Headache	52	(0–100)
Cutaneous rash	20	(0–67)
Trunk and limb edema	18	(0–75)
Diarrhea	16	(0–48)
Nausea	15	(0–67)
Subconjunctival hemorrhages	9	(0–65)
Subungual splinter hemorrhages	9	(0–60)
Cough	6	(0–40)
Vomiting	3	(0–13)

a sample taken from a tender swollen muscle may confirm the diagnosis.

The protean manifestations of trichinosis require differentiation of this infection from a large number of other diseases. The gastrointestinal symptoms may mimic those of gastroenteritis. Systemic symptoms may cause confusion with influenza, typhoid fever, sinusitis, dermatomyositis, glomerulonephritis, and angioneurotic edema. The rash may resemble that found in measles, scarlet fever, and typhus.

Treatment

There is no satisfactory treatment for trichinosis. In the rare case that a patient is known to have ingested trichinous meat within a week or so, thiabendazole should be administered in an oral dose of 25 mg/kg/day for 1 week. This drug is active against intestinal worms but has little effect on muscle larvae and has not been shown to alter the course of the disease in established infections. The mainstays of treatment are bed rest and salicylates. Corticosteroids may be used for critically ill patients, but the evidence for benefit is equivocal. It was claimed that mebendazole was effective when given 5 months after the onset of infection;[12] this uncontrolled, single case report must be viewed with some skepticism. Albendazole has been compared with a combination of thiabendazole and flubendazole, and a marginal benefit was claimed for albendazole; however, no untreated control group was available for comparison.[13] A subsequent study suggested that the efficacy of thiabendazole and albendazole is similar but that albendazole is better tolerated.[14] Albendazole may be given in a dose of 400 mg/day for 5 days.

Prevention

The most effective method of killing *Trichinella* larvae is by proper cooking: the thermal death point is 55°C, so meat should be cooked until there is no trace of pink fluid or flesh. Storage in a home freezer (−15°C) for 3 weeks usually sterilizes meat, but smoking, salting, and drying are unreliable.

DRACUNCULIASIS

Dracunculiasis (dracontiasis, guinea worm infection) develops after drinking water containing crustaceans infected with *Dracunculus medinensis*. It is characterized by a chronic cutaneous ulcer from which the worm protrudes.

Life Cycle

When water containing infected copepods is drunk, larvae are released in the host stomach, pass into the small intestine, penetrate the mucosa, and reach the retroperitoneum, where they mature and mate. The female worm (1 to 2 mm in diameter and up to 1 m long) migrates to the subcutaneous tissue, usually of the legs, about 1 year later. The overlying skin ulcerates, and a portion of the worm protrudes. On contact with water, large numbers of larvae are released from a loop of uterus prolapsed through either the mouth or a rupture in the body wall. These are in turn ingested by crustaceans, in which they undergo further development whereby the life cycle is continued.

Epidemiology

D. medinensis is now found mostly in tropical Africa. Shallow ponds, cisterns, and wells are the usual habitat of the crustacean intermediate hosts. The disease is prevalent in areas where people bathe or wade in water used for drinking purposes. Manifestations in a community are markedly seasonal. This reflects both the developmental cycle of the parasite, which requires an incubation period of about 1 year, and the influence of climate on the types of water sources used. The disability resulting from infection may be of great economic importance if the timing of clinical manifestations coincides with a busy period of the agricultural year and causes a significant loss of time in school for children.[15, 16]

Clinical Features

There are often no clinical signs until the worm reaches the surface and is ready to discharge larvae. A stinging papule develops at this point, usually on the lower portions of the legs. At this time, some patients may have a generalized reaction with urticaria, nausea, vomiting, diarrhea, and dyspnea. Over the next few days the lesion vesiculates, and then the blister ruptures and forms a painful ulcer within which part of the worm is often visible. If the area is douched with fluid, a milky fluid containing larvae wells up. Discharge continues intermittently, and the worm is slowly absorbed or extruded over the next few weeks, after which the ulcer heals. Multiple ulcers are common, and secondary infection is frequent. In endemic areas, patients are often bedridden for a month or so. Immunity to reinfection does not develop.

Diagnosis

The clinical picture is characteristic. Larvae can be found on microscopic examination of the discharge fluid.

Treatment

Thiabendazole, 25 mg/kg twice daily for 2 days, and metronidazole, 5 mg/kg twice daily for 1 week, have no effect on the worms themselves but produce resolution of inflammation within several days. This permits easy removal of the worm over a week or so by progressively rolling out the emerging worm onto a small stick. Corticosteroid ointments shorten the time to complete healing, and the addition of topical antibiotics reduces the risk of secondary bacterial infection.[17]

Ivermectin has no effect on prepatent guinea worms.[18] Mebendazole in high dosage is not recommended, because it does not lessen the duration of disease or disability but increases the incidence of nonemerged worms, thus exacerbating the danger of release of larvae into joints.[19] Alternatively, unerupted worms may be removed completely and painlessly in several minutes by surgical means with local anesthesia.[20] Secondary bacterial infection should be treated as necessary.

Prevention

Guinea worm infection can be prevented by boiling or chlorinating drinking water or by sieving it through a cloth. Control on a public health scale requires health education and improved water supplies. In 1986, the World Health Organization initiated a program to eradicate dracunculiasis by 1995. Strategies include documentation of the extent of the disease as a national problem, demonstration that it can be prevented by targeted provision of protected rural water supplies, mobilization of community participation and political support, and then implementation of interventions nationwide.

Although success has not yet been achieved, dramatic progress has been made. The number of cases has fallen from an estimated 4 million in 1981 to 150,000 in 1996, 120,000 of whom were in the Sudan, where civil war was raging. Infection has been eradicated from Kenya and Pakistan, and only nine cases were reported in 1996 in India, once the home of countless cases of dracunculiasis. Guinea worm disease may soon become the second human infection to be eradicated.[21]

BANCROFTIAN AND BRUGIAN FILARIASIS

Bancroftian filariasis and brugian (Malayan) filariasis are similar clinical conditions resulting from the transmission of *Wuchereria bancrofti, Brugia malayi*, and *Brugia timori* to humans by mosquitoes. Symptomatic patients have acute lymphatic inflammation or the effects of chronic lymphatic obstruction such as hydrocele, elephantiasis of the limbs, and chyluria.

Life Cycle

After the bite of an infected mosquito, infective larvae pass into the lymphatics and lymph nodes, where they mature over the next few months into white, threadlike adult worms, the males being about 40 × 0.1 mm and the females 100 × 0.25 mm in size. The adults live for 5 years or more, and the fertilized females discharge microfilariae approximately 150 × 7 μm in size via the lymphatics into the blood stream. The number of microfilariae found in the peripheral blood varies. There is usually a surge of microfilariae into the blood during the middle of the night, a phenomenon known as *nocturnal periodicity*. Patients from the South Pacific with *W. bancrofti* infection have a much less pronounced peak that is maximal during the day. *B. malayi* infections produce nocturnal peaks of varying intensity. If microfilariae are ingested by a mosquito during feeding, the organisms develop into infective larvae over the next 2 weeks and are ready to repeat the cycle.

Epidemiology

W. bancrofti is distributed widely throughout the tropics and subtropics; *B. malayi* is restricted to South and Southeast Asia. *B. timori* is restricted to the eastern Indonesian archipelago. It is estimated that 120 million people are infected with these parasites. There is no animal reservoir for *W. bancrofti*, but *B. malayi* has been found in felines and primates. Even in endemic areas, only a small proportion (less than 1%) of mosquito bites are infective. It is probable that patent infections are produced only when a susceptible person receives a large number of infective larvae and that obstructive disease develops only when exposure continues for many years. Filariasis is mainly a disease of adults and is more common in men.[22, 23]

Pathologic Characteristics

Lymphatics harboring adult worms display endothelial proliferation, fibrin deposition, and a granulomatous inflammatory infiltrate of eosinophils, lymphocytes, and macrophages. Molting and the death of worms probably exacerbate the inflammation, which is succeeded by fibrosis and obstruction of lymph flow. All of these processes are associated with complex immunologic events.

It is possible that a proportion of the population in endemic areas generates protective immunity that may be T cell mediated.[24] Secondary bacterial infection may be an important cofactor in the development of elephantiasis.[25]

Clinical Features

Many patients are asymptomatic despite the presence of a microfilaremia. Clinical manifestations are due either to acute inflammation or to chronic lymphatic obstruction. Attacks of lymphangitis or lymphadenitis with fever, headache, backache, and nausea occasionally occur. Acute funiculitis, epididymitis, or orchitis may be seen. These acute episodes usually subside after a few days to several weeks but may recur.[26] Chronic lymphadenopathy is frequently found and may be the only manifestation of filariasis. In long-standing cases lymphedema may develop. Chronic hydrocele is the most common feature and may cause considerable sexual disability. The lower limbs are involved less frequently; at first there is pitting edema that is most marked pretibially, but eventually nonpitting edema may involve the whole limb. In elephantiasis, the skin of the leg or scrotum becomes thickened, fissured, and warty. Ulceration and secondary infection may occur.[27] Occasionally, lymph varices may be seen, especially in the genital region. Chyluria develops when swollen lymphatics burst into the urinary tract.

Diagnosis

The definitive diagnosis of bancroftian filariasis and brugian filariasis depends on demonstration of the parasite. Unfortunately, microfilariae are frequently absent from the blood in both the early and late stages of the disease. A blood sample should be taken around midnight unless the patient is from the South Pacific. The smear is stained and examined for microfilariae (Fig. 278–1). If none is found, a concentration method should be used.

Microfilariae may occasionally be found in hydrocele fluid or chylous urine. Eosinophilia is usually absent except during episodes of acute inflammation. Serologic tests for antibody such as bentonite flocculation, indirect hemagglutination, enzyme-linked immunosorbent assay, and indirect fluorescent antibody tests may be of some help but do not differentiate among the various forms of filariasis or between past and current infection. Immunoassays to measure filarial antigen in serum have been described.[28] Polymerase chain reaction tests to detect *W. bancrofti* in blood are being developed.[29]

Adult worms can sometimes be found in lymph node biopsy specimens, but this procedure is not generally justified. Microfilariae or worm fragments may be seen with fine-needle aspiration cytology.[30] Ultrasonography of the lymphatic vessels in the spermatic cord may reveal motile adult worms in dilated lymphatics.[31] Abnormal lymphatic drainage in the legs may be demonstrated by lymphoscintigraphy.[32] If microfilariae cannot be found, the diagnosis must be made on clinical grounds by the exclusion of other causes.

Treatment

There is no satisfactory treatment for filariasis. Diethylcarbamazine citrate has been used for 50 years. Given in an oral dose of 6 mg/kg daily for 2 weeks, it reduces the number of microfilariae in the peripheral blood. Diethylcarbamazine kills some adult worms but

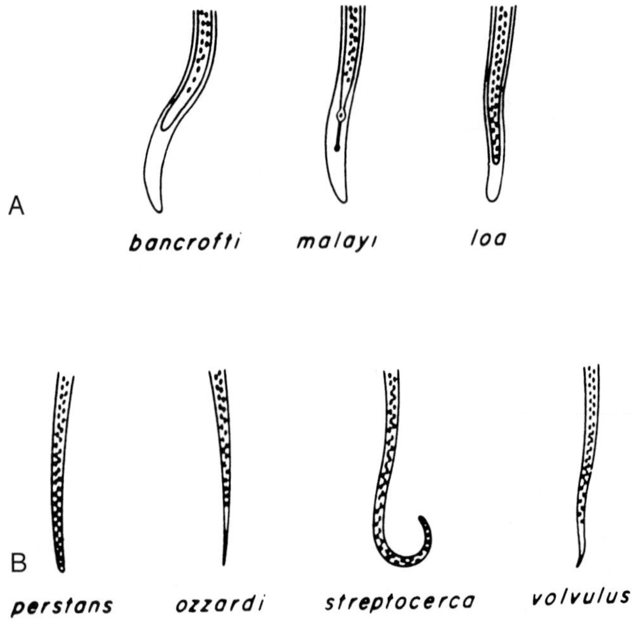

FIGURE 278–1. Comparative features of sheathed *(A)* and unsheathed *(B)* microfilariae.

not others. When it does kill worms, it may precipitate acute inflammation that culminates in an exuberant granulomatous process with progressive fibrosis. Ivermectin in a single dose of 200 to 400 μg/kg has been shown to have a microfilaricidal effect similar to that of diethylcarbamazine. Ultrasonography showed that it has no effect on adult worms, and microfilariae often reappear in the peripheral blood after a few months.[33] Even if patients remain amicrofilaremic after diethylcarbamazine or ivermectin treatment, *Wuchereria* antigens persist in the serum for at least 2 to 3 years.[34] Although diethylcarbamazine and ivermectin have no or limited therapeutic value for the individual patient, repeated administration of either or both drugs every 6 to 12 months may reduce transmission in a community.[33] Single-dose therapy with ivermectin at 200 to 400 μg/kg plus albendazole at 400 mg may be even more effective.[35] Rarely, repeated treatment with diethylcarbamazine has succeeded in eradicating infection. This was achieved in Kinmen Island; acute inflammatory filarial illnesses disappeared but, as expected, chronic obstructive disease persisted for the next 2 decades.[36]

Acute inflammatory reactions should be treated with anti-inflammatory agents. Mild lymphedema may be controlled with elastic stockings. Surgery is useful in the management of hydrocele but has little place for patients with elephantiasis of the legs. Laparoscopic ligation of lymphatic vessels has been used successfully to treat recalcitrant chyluria.[37]

Prevention

The most effective preventive measure is avoidance of mosquitoes by the use of screens, nets, and insect repellents.

LOIASIS

Loiasis is caused by *Loa loa* and is transmitted to humans by tabanid flies. It is characterized by transient subcutaneous swellings. Occasionally, the worm is seen migrating through the subconjunctiva or other tissues.

Life Cycle

The white, threadlike adult worms, measuring 30 to 70 × 0.3 mm, migrate through the connective tissues. The sheathed microfilariae, 300 × 8 μm, appear in the blood during the day and may be ingested by tabanid (horse) flies, in which they develop into infective larvae.

Epidemiology

L. loa is irregularly distributed in West and central Africa. The vectors are diurnally biting flies (*Chrysops* spp.) that live in the canopy of the rain forest. They are attracted by people moving through open spaces in the jungle. Infection rates in populations and parasite loads in individuals change little over time in endemic areas.[38]

Clinical Features

Many patients are asymptomatic, although they may have high eosinophil levels in the peripheral blood. Transient swellings of localized subcutaneous edema, called *Calabar swellings*, may develop.[39] Usually only one swelling occurs at a time. The onset may be preceded by localized pain and itching for several hours. It is nonerythematous, 10 to 20 cm in diameter, and lasts for several days to weeks. Calabar swellings are commonly seen around joints such as the wrist or the knee and recur irregularly at either the same or different sites. Other patients complain of pruritus or have urticaria. (Occasionally, a worm may be seen passing through the subconjunctiva, where it produces an intense conjunctivitis lasting several days. Worms have also been seen in the penis or around the nipple.) Infected visitors to areas of endemicity may have a hyperreactive state characterized by more frequent recurrences of fugitive swellings, greater eosinophilia, increased debilitation, and more complications, particularly the development of renal disease, either before or after treatment with diethylcarbamazine.[40] These features are associated with differences in immunologic responses from those of people living in endemic areas.[41]

Other complications that may be seen are endomyocardial fibrosis, retinopathy, encephalopathy, peripheral neuropathy, arthritis, pleural effusion, and breast calcification. Pulmonary infiltrates have also been ascribed to loiasis, but it is difficult to differentiate this condition from tropical pulmonary eosinophilia. Splenectomy has been performed on patients with suspected lymphoma that turned out to be granulomas associated with *L. loa* microfilariae.[42]

Diagnosis

The disease should be suspected in a patient with a typical history who has lived in West or central Africa. The diagnosis is established by finding microfilariae in the daytime blood as described under "Bancroftian and Brugian Filariasis." Failure to find microfilariae does not rule out the diagnosis, and the diagnosis is usually made on clinical grounds. A polymerase chain reaction test has been described that is positive in some amicrofilaremic individuals but is not generally available.[43] Occasionally, the adult worm can be extracted from the eye.

Treatment

Diethylcarbamazine eliminates microfilariae from the blood and often does not kill adult worms.[44] It is administered as described under "Onchocerciasis." Encephalitis may be precipitated by treatment, especially if microfilarial loads are high.[45] Treatment with ivermectin in a single dose of 200 μg/kg decreases microfilarial densities in the peripheral blood.[46] Patients with high microfilarial counts (>30,000/ml) often experience fever, pruritus, headache, and arthralgia within 36 hours of ivermectin therapy.[47] Albendazole at 200 mg twice daily for 3 weeks slowly reduced microfilarial levels, possibly as a result of an embryotoxic effect on the adult worms.[48]

Prevention

Personal protection depends on avoiding places where biting flies are numerous, wearing protective clothing, and using insect repellents. Mass treatment of villages interrupts transmission; diethylcarbamazine is administered in doses of 5 mg/kg/day for 3 consecutive days each month, or ivermectin may be given at 3-monthly intervals.[49] Diethylcarbamazine in a dose of 300 mg once weekly is effective in preventing loiasis in persons resident temporarily in endemic regions.[50]

ONCHOCERCIASIS

Onchocerciasis (river blindness) is caused by *Onchocerca volvulus* and is transmitted to humans by blackflies. It is characterized by an itchy dermatitis, subcutaneous nodules, keratitis, and chorioretinitis.

Life Cycle

After the bite of an infected *Simulium* blackfly, larvae penetrate the skin and migrate into the connective tissues. They develop into white filiform adults, the males being 3 × 0.2 mm and the females 400 × 0.3 mm in size. The worms are often found tangled together in nodules of fibrous tissue, where they may live for years. Each female produces large numbers of unsheathed microfilariae 200 to 300 × 6 to 8 μm in size that migrate through the skin and connective tissues.

The life cycle is continued when they are ingested by female blackflies and develop into infective larvae.

Epidemiology

O. volvulus infects 20 million people in West, central, and East Africa and another 1 million people in scattered foci in Central America and South America. There is no known animal reservoir. Onchocerciasis tends to be focal in distribution within areas in which it is endemic. In Africa, the flies breed in fast-flowing streams in both the savannah and rain forest and tend to bite low on the body. In America, the flies breed in small streams on the hillsides and bite more frequently around the head. Heavy parasite loads and severe disease require repeated infection.

Pathologic Characteristics

A granulomatous inflammatory reaction followed by fibrosis develops around the adult worms. The microfilariae in the subcutaneous tissues may produce a low-grade inflammatory reaction, destruction of the elastic fibers, and fibrosis. Different patterns of cell-mediated and humoral immunity are seen in patients with different clinical syndromes and in the presence or absence of microfilaridermia.[51]

Clinical Features

Early skin lesions produce an itchy, erythematous, papular rash. In severe infections, cutaneous lymphedema with leathery thickening and depigmentation may be seen.[52] Ultimately, loss of elasticity with chronic lymphadenopathy may produce pendulous sacs containing inguinal and femoral lymph nodes. Firm, nontender, freely mobile fibrous nodules that may be several millimeters to centimeters in size and may contain the adult worms may be found. They are more commonly located over bony prominences. In addition, there may be systemic features including weight loss and musculoskeletal pains.[53] Impaired visual acuity is the most serious complication. The most common lesion is punctate keratitis followed by pannus formation and corneal fibrosis. Microfilariae can often be seen in the cornea and anterior chamber with a slit lamp. Iridocyclitis, glaucoma, choroiditis, and optic atrophy may develop.[54, 55] Not surprisingly, blindness in endemic areas is associated with a three- to fourfold increase in the mortality rate. It has been suggested that onchocerciasis may be associated with an increased prevalence of epilepsy.[56]

Diagnosis

The diagnosis is made either by demonstrating microfilariae in skin snips or in the cornea or anterior chamber on slit-lamp examination or by finding adult worms in a nodule biopsy specimen. Impalpable nodules can sometimes be demonstrated by ultrasound techniques.[57] Bloodless skin snips are taken without anesthesia by raising small cones of skin about 3 mm in diameter with the tip of a needle and then cutting them off with a razor blade. Snips should be taken from over the scapulas and iliac crests and from the buttocks and thighs. They are allowed to stand for half an hour in a drop of 0.9% saline and are then examined under a microscope for microfilariae.

Microfilariae are sometimes found in urine. A red-dot card test has been proposed as a useful aid in screening for the presence of optic nerve disease.[58] Ultrasound detection of changes in the vitreous humor has been described.[59] Eosinophilia is common. Reliable immunodiagnostic tests are not yet generally available, but molecular techniques are under development.[60]

If the diagnosis is strongly suspected but parasites cannot be found, a single oral test dose of 50 mg of diethylcarbamazine can be given. If an exacerbation of the rash occurs within a few hours, the diagnosis is likely (Mazzotti reaction).

Treatment

Traditionally, patients with skin disease have been treated with diethylcarbamazine. This drug kills microfilariae but has little effect on the adult worm. Severe reactions such as rash, fever, generalized body pains, keratitis, and iritis may occur, so the dose must be built up gradually as follows: day 1, 50 mg; day 2, 50 mg three times; day 3, 100 mg three times; and days 4 to 21, 3 mg/kg three times a day.

In the past few years, many studies have shown that ivermectin is safer and more effective than diethylcarbamazine.[33, 61] The rates of decrease in numbers of microfilariae in the skin and anterior chamber of the eye and the severity of Mazzotti reactions are less and the duration of the reduction in microfilarial loads is greater with ivermectin than with diethylcarbamazine. Ivermectin is now the drug of choice. Unfortunately, like diethylcarbamazine, ivermectin primarily kills microfilariae but not adult worms. When given in a single dose, it has little effect on the viability or fertility of adult worms, but courses of treatment with 150 μg/kg repeated at 3-month intervals for 2 to 3 years prevent embryogenesis to the microfilarial stage and may cause slow but steady attrition of adult worms.[62, 63] Both single and repeated courses of treatment result in marked reductions in microfilarial skin densities and the numbers of microfilariae in the anterior chamber of the eye, and there is a significant reduction in transmission of infection. Ivermectin therapy leads to improvement in severe skin disease and regression of early lesions of the anterior segment of the eye, especially iridocyclitis, but posterior segment lesions remain stable.[64, 65] A practical approach to treatment is to administer ivermectin, 150 μg/kg orally once, and repeat at 3-monthly intervals if there are continuing symptoms or evidence of eye infection. Side effects appear to be relatively mild in patients in endemic areas but may be more severe in infected expatriates, who often develop fever, pruritus, and an urticarial rash.[66] However, patients with concurrent onchocerciasis and loiasis may develop an encephalopathy when treated with ivermectin.[67] Inadvertent administration of ivermectin during pregnancy was not associated with an increased number of birth defects.

Adult worms can be killed by suramin, but this drug is not generally recommended.[61] Albendazole does not kill microfilariae but interferes with embryogenesis.[68] Amocarzine is a novel drug still under development that appears to have both macro- and microfilaricidal effects. Unfortunately, it does not prevent the evolution of chorioretinopathy.[69] Surgical removal of nodules should be performed whenever practical. Expert ophthalmologic advice should be sought before the treatment of eye lesions.

Prevention

Personal protection depends on avoiding places where biting flies are numerous and on wearing protective clothing. A major control program is in progress in West Africa. The vector is being attacked by larvicides applied to breeding places; the onchocerciasis-infected population is gradually being replaced by a healthy population.[70, 71] In 1991 a program was set in motion to eradicate onchocerciasis from the Americas, and there is hope that one of the three major foci of infection will shortly be eliminated.[72]

MANSONELLA INFECTIONS

Mansonella ozzardi, transmitted by blackflies and midges, is found in Latin America. Adult worms are found in the visceral fatty issues. Unsheathed microfilariae that are not periodic may be found in the peripheral blood. Most patients are asymptomatic.

Mansonella perstans, also transmitted by midges, is found in Africa and South America. Adult worms live in the body cavities. Unsheathed microfilariae may be found in the peripheral blood, especially at night. Most patients are asymptomatic, although some have conjunctival nodules.[73] If treatment is required, diethylcarbamazine should be tried because ivermectin does not appear to be effective.[74] Albendazole may be of some value when given at a dose of 400 mg twice daily for at least 1 month.[75]

Mansonella streptocerca is transmitted to humans by biting midges. It is found in central Africa and is characterized by dermatitis. Microfilariae are found in skin snips, and treatment is with diethylcarbamazine;[76] the value of ivermectin is unproved.

TROPICAL PULMONARY EOSINOPHILIA

Tropical pulmonary eosinophilia is a disease syndrome caused by microfilariae in the tissues, especially the lungs. It is probably due to immunologic hyperresponsiveness to *W. bancrofti* or *B. malayi*. It is scattered throughout the tropics but is most commonly seen in southern Asia. Patients have recurrent episodes of a paroxysmal, dry cough, wheezing, and dyspnea. Malaise, anorexia, and weight loss are frequently seen. Physical examination often reveals scattered wheezes and crackles. Some patients may have hepatomegaly and lymphadenopathy. The symptoms usually fluctuate in severity over many months. The absence of microfilariae from the blood makes a definitive diagnosis difficult. Eosinophilia is almost always present, often at extremely high levels. Chest radiographs usually reveal scattered reticulonodular opacities. Antibodies to filarial worms are found in the serum. A presumptive clinical diagnosis can usually be made without recourse to lung biopsy, and the diagnosis is established by a successful response to therapy. The administration of diethylcarbamazine orally in a dose of 3 mg/kg three times daily for 2 weeks is an effective treatment. There may be an initial exacerbation of symptoms, but the eosinophil level falls, and the chest radiograph clears over a few weeks. A small proportion of patients, however, have persistent subtle clinical, radiologic, or functional abnormalities indicating chronic low-grade alveolitis;[77] in such instances, it may be appropriate to repeat the course of treatment with diethylcarbamazine. The role of ivermectin in the treatment of tropical pulmonary eosinophilia has not yet been determined.

REFERENCES

1. Grove DI. A History of Human Helminthology. Wallingford, UK: CAB International; 1990:1–848; compact disk version obtainable from the author.
2. Wakelin D, Goyal PK. *Trichinella* isolates: Parasite variability and host responses. Int J Parasitol. 1996;26:471–481.
3. Capo V, Despommier DD. Clinical aspects of infection with *Trichinella* spp. Clin Microbiol Rev. 1996;9:47–54.
4. Andrews JRH, Ainsworth R, Abernethy D. *Trichinella pseudospiralis* in humans: Description of a case and its treatment. Trans R Soc Trop Med Hyg. 1994;88:200–203.
5. Pozio E, La Rosa G, Serrano FJ, et al. Environmental and human influence on the ecology of *Trichinella spiralis* and *Trichinella britovi* in Western Europe. Parasitology 1996;113:527–533.
6. McAuley JB, Michelson MK, Schantz PM. Trichinosis surveillance, United States, 1987–1990. MMWR Morb Mortal Wkly Rep. 1991;40:35–42.
7. Dworkin MS, Gamble HR, Zarlenga DS, Tennican PO. Outbreak of trichinellosis associated with eating cougar jerky. J Infect Dis. 1996;174:663–666.
8. Laurichesse H, Cambon M, Perre D, et al. Outbreak of trichinosis in France associated with eating horse meat. Commun Dis Rep CDR Rev. 1997;7:69–73.
9. Greenbloom SL, Martin-Smith P, Isaacs S, et al. Outbreak of trichinosis in Ontario secondary to ingestion of wild boar meat. Can J Public Health. 1997;88:52–56.
10. Harms G, Binz P, Feldmeier H, et al. Trichinosis: A prospective controlled trial of patients ten years after acute infection. Clin Infect Dis. 1993;17:637–647.
11. Uparanukraw P, Morakote N. Detection of circulating *Trichinella spiralis* larvae by polymerase chain reaction. Parasitol Res. 1997;83:52–56.
12. Levin ML. Treatment of trichinosis with mebendazole. Am J Trop Med Hyg. 1983;32:980–983.
13. Fourestie V, Bougnoux ME, Ancelle T, et al. Randomized trial of albendazole versus tiabendazole plus flubendazole during an outbreak of human trichinellosis. Parasitol Res. 1988;75:36–41.
14. Cabie A, Bouchaud O, Houze S, et al. Albendazole versus thiabendazole as therapy for trichinosis: A retrospective study. Clin Infect Dis. 1996;22:1033–1035.
15. Chippaux JP, Banzou A, Agbede K. Impact social et economique de la dracunculose: Une étude longitudinale effectuée dans deux villages du Benin. Bull World Health Organ. 1992;70:73–78.
16. Hours M, Cairncross S. Long-term disability due to guinea worm disease. Trans R Soc Trop Med Hyg. 1994;88:559–560.
17. Magnussen P, Yakuba A, Bloch P. The effect of antibiotic- and hydrocortisone-containing ointments in preventing secondary infections in guinea worm disease. Am J Trop Med Hyg. 1994;51:797–799.
18. Issaka-Tinorgah A, Magnussen P, Bloch P, Yakuba A. Lack of effect of ivermectin on prepatent guinea-worm: A single-blind, placebo-controlled trial. Trans R Soc Trop Med Hyg. 1994;88:346–348.
19. Chippaux JP. Mebendazole treatment of dracunculiasis. Trans R Soc Trop Med Hyg. 1991;85:280.
20. Rohde JE, Sharma BL, Patton H, et al. Surgical extraction of guinea worm: Disability reduction and contribution to disease control. Am J Trop Med Hyg. 1993;48:71–76.
21. Hopkins DR, Ruiz-Tiben E, Ruebush TK. Dracunculiasis eradication: Almost a reality. Am J Trop Med Hyg. 1997;57:252–259.
22. Michael E, Bundy DA, Grenfell BT. Re-assessing the global prevalence and distribution of lymphatic filariasis. Parasitology 1996;112:409–428.
23. Kazura JW, Bockarie M, Alexander N, et al. Transmission intensity and its relationship to infection and disease due to *Wuchereria bancrofti* in Papua New Guinea. J Infect Dis. 1997;176:242–246.
24. Steel C, Guinea A, Ottesen EA. Evidence for protective immunity to bancroftian filariasis in the Cook Islands. J Infect Dis. 1996;174:598–605.
25. Olszewski WL, Jamal S, Manokaran G, et al. Bacteriologic studies of skin, tissue fluid, lymph and lymph nodes in patients with filarial lymphedema. Am J Trop Med Hyg. 1997;57:7–15.
26. Ramaiah KD, Ramu K, Kumar KN, Guyatt H. Epidemiology of acute filarial episodes caused by *Wuchereria bancrofti* infection in two rural villages in Tamil Nadu, south India. Trans R Soc Trop Med Hyg. 1996;90:639–643.
27. Burri H, Loutan L, Kumaraswami V, Vijayasekaran V. Skin changes in chronic filariasis. Trans R Soc Trop Med Hyg. 1996;90:671–674.
28. Freedman DO, de Almeida A, Miranda J, et al. Field trial of a rapid card test for *Wuchereria bancrofti*. Lancet. 1997;350:1681.
29. Ramzy RM, Farid HA, Karnal IH, et al. A polymerase chain reaction–based assay for detection of *Wuchereria bancrofti* in human blood and *Culex pipiens*. Trans R Soc Trop Med Hyg. 1997;91:156–160.
30. Arora VK, Singh N, Bhatia A. Cytomorphologic profile of lymphatic filariasis. Acta Cytol. 1996;40:948–952.
31. Noroes J, Addiss D, Santos A, et al. Ultrasonographic evidence of abnormal lymphatic vessels in young men with adult *Wuchereria bancrofti* infection in scrotal areas. J Urol. 1996;156:409–412.
32. Dissanayake S, Watana L, Piessens WF. Lymphatic pathology in *Wuchereria bancrofti* microfilaraemic infections. Trans R Soc Trop Med Hyg. 1995;89:517–521.
33. Grove DI. Chemotherapy of the filariases. Curr Concepts Infect Dis. 1996;9:439–443.
34. Eberhard ML, Hightower AW, Addiss DG, Lammie PJ. Clearance of *Wuchereria bancrofti* antigen after treatment with diethylcarbamazine or ivermectin. Am J Trop Med Hyg. 1997;57:483–486.
35. Addiss DG, Beach MJ, Streit TG, et al. Randomised placebo-controlled comparison of ivermectin and albendazole alone and in combination for *Wuchereria bancrofti* microfilaraemia in Haitian children. Lancet. 1997;350:480–484.
36. Fan PC, Peng HW, Chen CC. Follow-up investigations on clinical manifestations after filariasis eradication by diethylcarbamazine medicated common salt on Kinmen (Quemoy) Island, Republic of China. J Trop Med Hyg. 1995;98:461–464.
37. Chiu AW, Chen MT, Chang LS. Laparoscopic nephrolysis for chyluria: Case report of long-term success. J Endourol. 1995;9:319–322.
38. Garcia A, Abel L, Ranque S. Longitudinal survey of *Loa loa* filariasis in southern Cameroon: Long-term stability and factors influencing individual microfilarial status. Am J Trop Med Hyg. 1995;52:370–375.
39. Noireau F, Apembet JD, Nzoulani A, et al. Clinical manifestations of loiasis in an endemic area in the Congo. Trop Med Parasitol. 1990;41:37–39.
40. Churchill DR, Morris C, Fakoya A, et al. Clinical and laboratory features of patients with loiasis (*Loa loa* filariasis) in the U.K. J Infect. 1996;33:103–109.
41. Klion AD, Massougbodji A, Sadeler BC, et al. Loiasis in endemic and nonendemic populations: Immunologically mediated differences in clinical presentation. J Infect Dis. 1991;163:1318–1325.
42. Burchard GD, Reimold-Jehle U, Burkle V, et al. Splenectomy for suspected malignant lymphoma in two patients with loiasis. Clin Infect Dis. 1996;23:979–982.
43. Toure FS, Bain O, Nerrienet E, et al. Detection of *Loa loa*–specific DNA in blood from occult-infected individuals. Exp Parasitol. 1997;86:163–170.
44. Klion AD, Ottesen EA, Nutman TB. Effectiveness of diethylcarbamazine in treating loiasis by expatriate visitors to endemic regions: Long-term follow-up. J Infect Dis. 1994;169:604–610.
45. Carme B, Boulesteix J, Boutes H, et al. Five cases of encephalitis during treatment of loiasis with diethylcarbamazine. Am J Trop Med Hyg. 1991;44:684–690.
46. Gardon J, Kamgno J, Folefack G, et al. Marked decrease in *Loa loa* microfilaraemia six and twelve months after a single dose of ivermectin. Trans R Soc Trop Med Hyg. 1997;91:593–594.
47. Ducorps M, Gardon-Wendel N, Ranque S, et al. Effets sécondaires du traitement de la loase hypermicrofilarémique par l'ivermectine. Bull Soc Pathol Exot. 1995;88:105–112.
48. Klion AO, Massougbodji A, Horton J, et al. Albendazole in human loiasis: Results of a double-blind, placebo-controlled trial. J Infect Dis. 1993;168:202–206.
49. Ranque S, Garcia A, Boussinesq M, et al. Decreased prevalence and intensity of *Loa loa* infection in a community treated with ivermectin every three months for two years. Trans R Soc Trop Med Hyg. 1996;90:429–430.
50. Nutman TB, Miller KD, Mulligan M, et al. Diethylcarbamazine prophylaxis for human loiasis. Results of a double-blind study. N Engl J Med. 1988;319:752–756.

51. Soboslay PT, Geiger SM, Weiss N, et al. The diverse expression of immunity in humans at distinct states of *Onchocerca volvulus* infection. Immunology 1997;90:592–599.
52. Murdoch ME, Hay RJ, Mackenzie CD, et al. A clinical classification and grading system of the cutaneous changes in onchocerciasis. Br J Dermatol. 1993;129:260–269.
53. Burnham GM. Onchocerciasis in Malawi. 2. Subjective complaints and decreased weight in persons infected with *Onchocerca volvulus* in the Thyolo highlands. Trans R Soc Trop Med Hyg. 1991;85:497–500.
54. Semba RD, Murphy RP, Newland HS, et al. Longitudinal study of lesions of the posterior segment in onchocerciasis. Ophthalmology. 1990;97:1334–1341.
55. Newland HS, White AT, Greene BM, et al. Ocular manifestations of onchocerciasis in a rain forest area of west Africa. Br J Ophthalmol. 1991;75:163–169.
56. Kaiser C, Kipp W, Asaba G, et al. The prevalence of epilepsy follows the distribution of onchocerciasis in a west Ugandan focus. Bull World Health Organ. 1996;74:361–367.
57. Poltera AA, Reyna O, Zea-Flores G, et al. Use of an ophthalmologic ultrasound scanner in human onchocercal skin nodules for non-invasive sequential assessment during a macrofilaricidal trial with amocarzine in Guatemala. The first experiences. Trop Med Parasitol. 1991;42:303–307.
58. Murdoch I, Jones BR, Babalola OE, et al. Red-dot card test of the paracentral field as a screening test for optic nerve disease in onchocerciasis. Bull World Health Organ. 1996;74:573–576.
59. Reyna O, Zea Flores, Nowell de Arevalo AM, et al. Ultrasound detection of changes in the vitreous humor of onchocerciasis patients from Guatemala. Trans R Soc Trop Med Hyg. 1988;82:606.
60. Bradley JE, Unnasch TR. Molecular approaches to the diagnosis of onchocerciasis. Adv Parasitol. 1996;37:57–106.
61. Van Laetham Y, Lopes C. Treatment of onchocerciasis. Drugs. 1996;52:861–869.
62. Plaisier AP, Alley ES, Boatin BA, et al. Irreversible effects of ivermectin on adult parasites in onchocerciasis patients in the onchocerciasis control programme in West Africa. J Infect Dis. 1995;172:204–210.
63. Klager S, Whitworth JA, Downham MD. Viability and fertility of adult *Onchocerca volvulus* after 6 years of treatment with ivermectin. Trop Med Int Health 1996;1:581–589.
64. Whitworth JA, Maude GH, Downham MD. Clinical and parasitological responses after up to 6.5 years of ivermectin treatment for onchocerciasis. Trop Med Int Health 1996;1:786–793.
65. Mabey D, Whitworth JA, Eckstein M, et al. The effects of multiple doses of ivermectin on ocular onchocerciasis. A six-year follow-up. Ophthalmology 1996;103:1001–1008.
66. Davidson RN, Godfrey-Faussett P, Bryceson ADM. Adverse reactions in expatriates treated with ivermectin. Lancet. 1990;336:1005.
67. Gardon J, Gardon-Wendel N, Demanga-Ngangue, et al. Serious reactions after mass treatment of onchocerciasis with ivermectin in an area endemic for *Loa loa* infection. Lancet. 1997;350:18–22.
68. Cline BL, Hernandez JL, Mather FJ, et al. Albendazole in the treatment of onchocerciasis: Double-blind clinical trial in Venezuela. Am J Trop Med Hyg. 1992;47:512–520.
69. Cooper PJ, Proano R, Beltran C, et al. Onchocerciasis in Ecuador: Evolution of chorioretinopathy after amocarzine treatment. Br J Ophthalmol. 1996;80:337–342.
70. Davies JB. Sixty years of onchocerciasis vector control: A chronological summary with comments on eradication, reinvasion, and insecticide resistance. Annu Rev Entomol. 1994;39:23–45.
71. Anonymous. Onchocerciasis and its control. World Health Organ Tech Rep Ser. 1995;852:1–104.
72. Anonymous. Onchocerciasis: Progress towards elimination in the Americas. Wkly Epidemiol Rec. 1996;71:277–279.
73. Baird KJ, Neafie RC, Connor DH. Nodules in the conjunctiva, bung-eye, and bulge-eye in Africa caused by *Mansonella perstans*. Am J Trop Med Hyg. 1988;38:553–557.
74. Fischer P, Kilian AH, Bamuhiiga J, et al. Prevalence of *Mansonella perstans* in western Uganda and its detection using the QBC-fluorescence method. Appl Parasitol. 1996;37:32–37.
75. Lipani F, Caramello P, Biblioni A, Sacchi C. Albendazole for the treatment of *Mansonella perstans* filariasis. Trans R Soc Trop Med Hyg. 1997;91:221.
76. Meyers WM, Connor DH, Harman LE, et al. Human streptocerciasis. Am J Trop Med Hyg. 1972;21:528–545.
77. Ottesen EA, Nutman TB. Tropical pulmonary eosinophilia. Annu Rev Med. 1992;43:417–424.

Chapter 279

Trematodes (Schistosomiasis) and Other Flukes

ADEL A. F. MAHMOUD

Flukes are parasitic worms of the class Trematoda. The classic shape of a digenetic trematode is that of a thick, oval leaf, although there are many variations in both shape and size. The length of different fluke species varies from less than 1 mm to several centimeters. An oral and, in most species, a ventral sucker are characteristic external features. The principal internal organs are a blind bifurcate intestinal tract and prominent reproductive organs, which are arranged in a specific manner in each species.

All species parasitic in humans belong to the digenetic group in which sexual reproduction in the adult worms is followed by asexual multiplication in the larval stages (alternation of generations). Most flukes infecting humans are hermaphrodites, with the exception of the schistosomes. The more important parasitic trematodes of humans are summarized in Table 279–1. Because some of these species have a tissue migratory stage in the host, eosinophilia is a prominent clinical sign of trematode infections.

BLOOD FLUKES

Schistosomiasis

The five human blood flukes, *Schistosoma mansoni*, *Schistosoma japonicum*, *Schistosoma mekongi*, *Schistosoma haematobium*, and *Schistosoma intercalatum*, make up the group of major importance in flatworm infections of humans, because they currently infect more than 200 million people.[1] The major areas of agricultural and freshwater development are occurring in Africa, South America, and Asia, where infection is endemic. Schistosomiasis may cause a severe degree of morbidity and pathologic changes that, if left undiagnosed and untreated, may result in major disability, or death.

In the United States, infection with human schistosomes has been estimated to exceed 400,000 persons.[2] These are mainly immigrants from endemic areas, particularly Puerto Rico, Brazil, the Middle East, and the Philippines. Fortunately, infection cannot be transmitted in this country because of the absence of the appropriate snail intermediate host. Recently, several epidemics of acute schistosomiasis have been reported in Americans traveling or returning from endemic areas.[3]

Adult schistosome worms are distinct from most other flukes in that they exist as separate sexes. In *S. japonicum, S. mekongi, S. mansoni*, and *S. intercalatum* infection, mature worms inhabit the portal and mesenteric vessels; in *S. haematobium*, the vesical plexus. The lateral edges of the body of the male worm are folded to enclose a groove where the female usually lies. It has been estimated that each female produces 300 eggs daily in *S. mansoni* and *S. haematobium* and 3000 eggs in *S. japonicum* infections, but the consistency and stability of these rates have been challenged.

Life Cycle

Humans are the principal definitive host for the five schistosome species. Adult worms (1 to 2 cm in length) living in the venous system of the intestines or the urinary bladder start their sexual reproduction by mating and passing characteristically shaped eggs (approximately 145×55 μm but smaller in *S. japonicum* and *S. mekongi*) that find their way to the outside via the host excreta (Fig. 279–1). In fresh water, the eggs hatch and release ciliated motile

TABLE 279–1 Important Parasitic Trematodes of Humans

Type of Flukes	Disease	Species Infecting Humans	Intermediate Hosts		Final Habitat
			Primary	*Secondary*	
Blood	Schistosomiasis	*Schistosoma haematobium*	Snails	None	Vesical plexus
		Schistosoma japonicum	Snails	None	Superior mesenteric veins
		Schistosoma mansoni	Snails	None	Inferior mesenteric veins
		Schistosoma mekongi	Snails	None	Mesenteric veins
		Schistosoma intercalatum	Snails	None	Mesenteric veins
Liver	Clonorchiasis	*Chlonorchis sinensis*	Snails	Fish	Bile ducts
	Opisthorchiasis	*Opisthorchis felineus*	Snails	Fish	Bile ducts
		Opisthorchis viverrini			
	Fascioliasis	*Fasciola hepatica*	Snails	Watercress	Bile ducts
Intestinal	Fasciolopsiasis	*Fasciola buski*	Snails	Aquatic plants	Small intestines
Lung	Paragonimiasis	*Paragonimus westermani*	Snails	Crabs	Lungs

miracidia that soon penetrate into the body of the snail intermediate host. For each species and for each geographic strain of the schistosomes, there is a specific snail intermediate host. Inside the snail, the miracidia multiply asexually, and in 4 to 6 weeks hundreds of motile, forked-tail cercariae emerge. These are the forms that infect humans. On encountering human skin, the cercariae penetrate with the help of their glandular secretions. In the process of invasion of the human host, the cercariae lose their tails and change into schistosomulae; this process of transformation occurs in the absence of new protein synthesis and is associated with a unique formation of a heptalaminate membrane.[4] The schistosomulae migrate to the lungs and the liver, and in about 6 weeks they mature to adult worms and descend via the venous system to their final habitat. The life span of the schistosome worms has been the subject of controversy. On the basis of data obtained from persons who left an endemic area and who years later were found to be still passing eggs, a claim has been made that the worms can live up to 30 years. The mean life span of the worms, however, seems to be much shorter, in the order of 5 to 10 years.

Epidemiology

Each of the five species of schistosomes that infect humans has a specific geographic distribution.[5] *S. mansoni* occurs in Arabia, Africa, South America, and the Caribbean; *S. japonicum*, in China and the Philippines; *S. mekongi*, in Southeast Asia; *S. haematobium*, in Africa and the Middle East; and *S. intercalatum*, in West and central Africa. Two major factors are responsible for the endemicity of schistosomiasis in specific geographic areas: the presence of the snail intermediate host and the method of disposal of human excreta.

The specificity of the snail intermediate host is remarkable in regard not only to the species of schistosomes but also to the geographic strain of the parasites. The dynamics of snail infections are important; at any one time period, the infection rate of snails in an endemic area is very low, and although they shed an enormous number of cercariae, the latter also have extremely low counts in bodies of water.[6] Attempts to measure cercarial density in the field by filtration techniques have resulted in an extremely low recovery of organisms from large volumes of water. Adding to these findings the diurnal, seasonal, and yearly variations in snail infection rates, it would appear that the rate of exposure of persons in endemic areas to schistosome infections must be low. This is contrary to the old belief that the frequent contact with schistosome-infected water provides an ample opportunity for continual infection.

The distribution of the infection in endemic communities fits a negative binomial curve, with most infected persons harboring low worm burdens and only a small proportion having heavy infections.

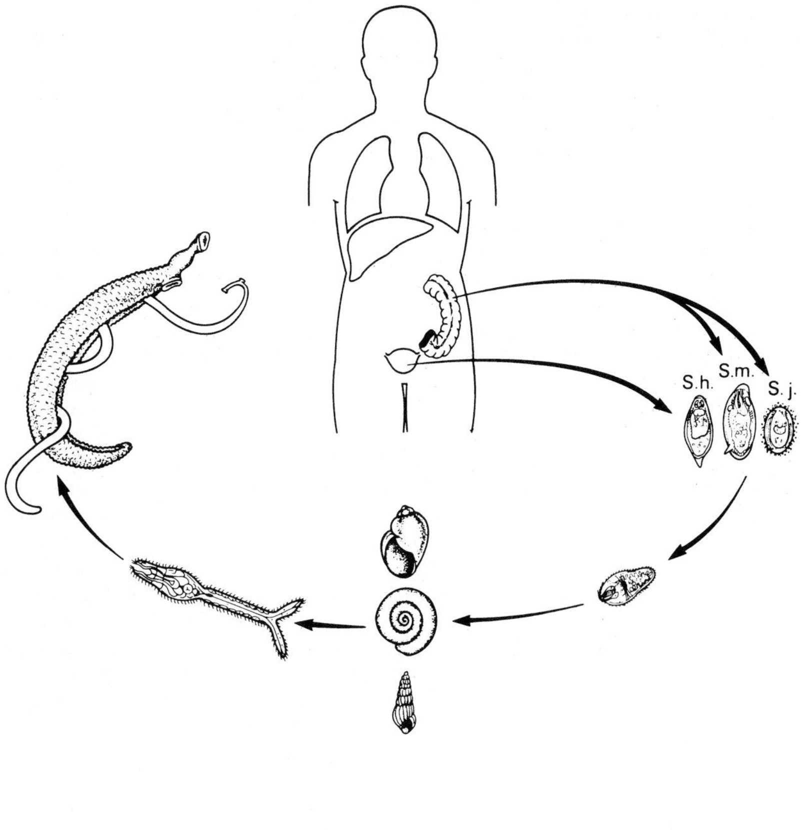

FIGURE 279–1. Life cycle of schistosomes. Eggs are passed with stools in *Schistosoma mansoni* (S.m.) and *Schistosoma japonicum* (S.j.) and with urine in *Schistosoma haematobium* (S.h.). The eggs hatch in fresh water, miracidia invade specific snail intermediate hosts, and in a few weeks forked-tail cercariae are liberated. These infective forms penetrate human skin, pass through a migratory phase in the lung and the liver, and then pass to their final habitat in the portal venous system (S.m. and S.j.) or in the urinary bladder venous plexus (S.h.) Two other species infect humans, although less frequently. *Schistosoma intercalatum* produces terminal spined eggs that may be found in feces, whereas *Schistosoma mekongi* produces eggs similar to but smaller than those of *S. japonicum*, which may also be found in stools. Both of these two species of schistosomes have characteristic snail intermediate hosts.

Aggregation of worm burden in a small proportion of infected individuals may have multiple explanations including genetic susceptibility.[7–9] The implications of these epidemiologic findings are relevant to our understanding of the dynamics of the infection in communities and the role of immunity or ecology in its control.

The prevalence and degree of morbidity in schistosomiasis have been shown to correlate with worm burdens as estimated by fecal or urinary egg counts; this relationship is, however, not exact, and other variables such as age and viral hepatitides may be involved.[10] In addition, information published in 1998 points to a possible link between human leukocyte antigens and the development of hepatosplenomegaly or urinary tract disease in schistosomiasis.[11]

Pathogenesis

Three major disease syndromes occur in schistosomiasis. In their chronologic order they are dermatitis, Katayama fever, and the chronic fibro-obstructive sequelae. These syndromes coincide with and are related to the three different stages of development of the parasite within the host: cercariae, mature worms, and eggs. The penetrating cercariae have been associated with a papular pruritic rash called swimmer's itch, or schistosome dermatitis. Although this reaction is seen occasionally in infections with human schistosomes, it occurs most often and is most severe when nonhuman (bird) cercariae penetrate the skin. Almost all these organisms die in the dermis, which results in the typical skin rash. Schistosome dermatitis is a sensitization phenomenon because it occurs in previously exposed persons; the papules are delayed in onset, and skin biopsy specimens have revealed edema and massive cellular infiltrate in the dermis and epidermis.

When the worms have matured and egg deposition begins, a condition known as Katayama fever, or acute schistosomiasis,[12] may be noticed. It is a serum sickness–like syndrome that is usually seen in primary heavy infections, particularly those due to *S. japonicum.* It may be due to immune complex formation initiated by the massive antigenic challenge produced by the eggs.[13]

During the chronic stages of infection, the mature worms produce large numbers of eggs, some of which remain in the body. Because of the habitat of *S. mansoni*, *S. intercalatum*, *S. japonicum*, and *S. mekongi*, the intestines are involved primarily, and egg embolism results in secondary involvement of the liver.[1] In *S. haematobium* infection, the main system involved is the urinary tract.[1] The host response to eggs retained in the tissues results in granuloma formation consisting mainly of lymphocytes, macrophages, and eosinophils. In *S. mansoni* and *S. haematobium* infections, the granulomatous response has been shown to be an immunologic reaction of the delayed-hypersensitivity type.[14, 15] The host granulomatous response in schistosomiasis has been shown to be tightly regulated by several immunologic mechanisms. These involve the development of helper-T-cell-1 and helper-T-cell-2 responses and the production of several cytokines locally within the granulomas and systemically[16]; these responses are regulated by multiple mechanisms.[17]

Tissue injury in chronic schistosomiasis is initiated by the egg-induced granulomas.[18] The inflammatory infiltrate leads to replacement of normal tissue followed by extensive collagen deposition and scarring. The large granulomas and the residual fibrosis cause the major pathologic lesions in chronic schistosomiasis: obstruction to portal blood flow in the liver, to pulmonary blood flow in the lungs, and to urine flow through the ureters and bladder. During the early stages of schistosome infection in humans and in experimental animals, the granulomatous response is exuberant, but it later modulates.[17] The occurrence of this modulation of granulomatous hypersensitivity is an important factor in protecting the host against its immunopathologic response to schistosome eggs and appears to play a significant role in limiting the progress of disease.

Schistosomiasis in humans and in experimental animals seems to be associated with a partial degree of resistance to reinfection.[19] Although the evidence for immunity in humans is controversial, several mechanisms for acquired resistance against schistosomiasis have been demonstrated in animals and humans.[20] One form of acquired resistance has been shown to depend on antibodies, is mediated by eosinophils, and is directed against the invading immature worms.[21]

Clinical Syndromes

Acute Schistosomiasis. Schistosome dermatitis occurs occasionally within 24 hours after penetration of the cercariae. It is a pruritic papular skin rash known as swimmer's itch. This syndrome appears to be a sensitization phenomenon because it rarely occurs on primary exposure. Swimmer's itch has been demonstrated in infected persons experimentally reexposed to *S. mansoni* and *S. haematobium* cercariae. The more severe form of schistosome dermatitis follow infection with avian schistosomes and is common in the region of the Great Lakes of the northern central United States.

The next clinical phase of schistosomiasis coincides with the beginning of oviposition, 4 to 8 weeks after infection.[1] Katayama fever was described in Japan, where it used to occur and has been known to be most severe after *S. japonicum* infections.[22] A few reports have described a similar syndrome in Puerto Rico and other areas endemic for *S. mansoni*, usually in patients with heavy infections. Patients with Katayama fever have an acute onset of fever, chills, sweating, headache, and cough. On physical examination, enlargement of the liver, spleen, and lymph nodes is noted. Eosinophilia occurs in most cases. Symptoms and signs usually disappear within a few weeks, but death may occur, particularly in acute schistosomiasis due to *S. japonicum*. At postmortem examination, massive infection is invariably found, with large numbers of eggs in the intestines and liver.

Chronic Schistosomiasis. Most persons with schistosomiasis harbor a low to moderate worm load, and a good proportion of these persons are asymptomatic. In patients with heavy worm loads, however, the chronic characteristic sequela of the disease eventually reveals itself.

Patients with chronic schistosomiasis caused by *S. mansoni*, *S. japonicum*, or *S. mekongi* may complain of fatigue and colicky abdominal pain with intermittent diarrhea or dysentery.[10] The two most commonly affected sites are the intestines and the liver. Intestinal schistosomiasis results from the chronic granulomatous lesions in the bowel wall. Polyps have been observed, but only in some endemic areas in Egypt.[21] Blood loss from ulcerations may lead to a moderate degree of anemia. In *S. mansoni*, *S. japonicum*, and *S. mekongi* infections, many eggs remain in the venous portal circulation and are carried into the liver. The eggs with their associated granulomas result in a presinusoidal block to portal blood flow and in the development of portal hypertension and portosystemic collateral circulation.[22] Hemodynamic studies of hepatic schistosomiasis reveal that both intrasplenic and portal pressures are markedly elevated, whereas the wedge hepatic vein pressure is normal. The total volume of hepatic blood remains within the normal range by increasing the arterial blood flow.[23] Liver cell perfusion is not reduced; consequently, liver function tests remain normal for a long time. These circulatory and immunologic processes also lead to enlargement of the spleen. Clinically, the earliest sign of chronic schistosomiasis due to *S. mansoni*, *S. japonicum*, or *S. mekongi* is enlargement of the liver. With progression of liver disease, splenomegaly develops. The spleen may reach massive dimensions and is usually firm. The hepatosplenic stage may be associated with abdominal pain or dragging pain in the left upper quadrant. Sudden episodes of hematemesis from bleeding esophageal varices may occur, but they are associated with low mortality. Patients may not bleed again for many years, or bleeding may recur at fairly frequent intervals. Persons with compensated liver disease have relatively normal hepatic function with normal serum albumin and elevated immune globulin levels. The white blood cell count may show a moderate degree of eosinophilia. Intestinal and esophageal blood losses and the development of hypersplenism may lead to a moderate degree of anemia in some patients. The terminal stage of hepatosplenic schistosomiasis is heralded by the development of decompensated liver disease. Jaundice, ascites, and liver failure may follow. It is not known, however, whether this is a natural progression of the schistosomal disease or whether it is related to additional factors such as nutritional deficiencies or hepatic viral infections.[24]

Evaluation of liver enlargement in areas endemic for schistosomiasis has been a difficult objective because of possible multiple causes. In the 1990s, ultrasonographic assessment has become the standard for diagnosing and assessing the extent of liver fibrosis in schistosomiasis,[25, 26] as definitive staging criteria are being worked out.

In *S. haematobium* infection, the initial pathologic lesions are located in the ureters and bladder.[27] Exuberant granulomatous reactions to the eggs may lead to obstruction of urinary flow or papillomatous irregularities of the bladder wall. On intravenous pyelography or ultrasonography, obstruction, hydronephrosis, hydroureters, and filling defects in the bladder may be demonstrated.[28] Patients usually complain of terminal hematuria and dysuria. The end stages of schistosomiasis due to *S. haematobium* progress through hydronephrosis, secondary infections, and uremia. In some endemic areas, an association has been demonstrated between *S. haematobium* infection and both the *Salmonella* urinary carrier state[29] and bladder cancer.[30–32]

In some parts of West and Central Africa, *S. intercalatum* parasitizes the mesenteric veins of humans; terminal spine eggs are passed in stools of infected individuals. The clinical syndromes caused by *S. intercalatum* infection in humans are poorly defined. Infected individuals may complain of abdominal pain and bloody diarrhea.[32]

S. japonicum had been considered the only species of schistosomes that infected humans in the Far East. A new species, *S. mekongi*,[33] reported in 1978, is now considered to be the main human pathogen in mainland Indochina. The parasite differs from *S. japonicum* by its smaller eggs and its specific intermediate snail host. There are no controlled studies that describe the specific clinical features of human infection with *S. mekongi*. On the basis of examining a small number of Laotian immigrants with *S. mekongi* infection, hepatomegaly was, however, the main clinical finding.[34]

The previous clinical descriptions have concentrated on the major organ systems affected by the five human schistosomes. Other syndromes that are occasionally seen will be outlined briefly. Pulmonary schistosomiasis is manifested by symptoms and signs of cor pulmonale and may occur as a complication of hepatosplenic disease.[35] Patent portosystemic collateral circulation in these patients enables the schistosome eggs to bypass the liver, and they are then trapped in the pulmonary capillaries. This syndrome may also be seen in schistosomiasis due to *S. haematobium* because the eggs can escape from the vesical plexus via the inferior vena cave to the lungs. Obstruction to pulmonary blood flow follows because of arteritis and granuloma formation. Pulmonary hypertension may be demonstrated, but the cardiac output usually remains within normal values.[36]

Central nervous system schistosomiasis is rare but constitutes 3% of the complications of *S. japonicum* infections.[22] In these cases, the brain is the usual site of disease, which is manifested as a space-occupying lesion or as a generalized encephalopathy. Furthermore, schistosomiasis caused by *S. japonicum* is considered one of the important causes of focal epilepsy in the Far East. In *S. haematobium* and *S. mansoni* infections, granulomatous lesions around ectopic eggs have been described in the spinal cord.[37] These patients have a transverse myelitis-like syndrome, and diagnosis may be difficult because active intestinal or urinary tract infection may not be easy to demonstrate. Reproductive tract involvement has been reported.[38]

Diagnosis

The geographic distribution of schistosomiasis is well defined.[5] Therefore, an important step in establishing the diagnosis is to inquire about the travel history of the patient. Detailed information should also be obtained about the history of water contact, skin rash, or an acute febrile episode (Katayama fever). A definitive diagnosis can be made by finding schistosome eggs in feces or urine or in a biopsy specimen, usually from the rectum. Because assessing the intensity of infection in schistosomiasis is an essential part of the clinical evaluation, quantitative techniques for stool and urine examination are strongly recommended.[39] At present, the Kato thick smear is the procedure of choice for the determination of eggs in the feces. Urine for the diagnosis of *S. haematobium* infection is best collected between noon and 2 PM. Counts can be made by passing a 10 ml aliquot of the urine sample through a Nuclepore filter.

A variety of immunologic diagnostic techniques are now available and play an important role in diagnosing early or light infections. They are particularly helpful in assessing individuals with less clear-cut clinical presentations in nonendemic areas.[40] Crude antigenic extracts of schistosomal materials are used in these tests, and this compromises their specificity and sensitivity.

Management

Drug management of schistosomiasis has changed drastically over the past few years. Safe, effective, and orally administered chemotherapeutic agents are now available for the treatment of major human schistosomal infections. Praziquantel is a broad-spectrum antihelminthic agent that is effective against all five human schistosomal species.[41] It is administered as two oral doses of 20 mg/kg body weight in 1 day for individuals with *S. mansoni* or *S. haematobium* infection. In subjects with schistosomiasis japonica, praziquantel is administered as 20 mg/kg body weight three times for 1 day. Praziquantel has also been found to be effective against *S. mekongi* (20 mg/kg × three doses in 1 day). The drug results in a remarkable degree of parasitologic cure and reduction of egg counts. Side effects are mild and include abdominal discomfort, fever, and headache. In addition, vigilance must be exercised to evaluate the possibility of drug resistance developing in the schistosomal populations, particularly in countries practicing mass chemotherapy as a control measure.[42, 43]

Several other oral compounds have been proved just as effective but with a limited range of parasite specificity.[41] Metrifonate (Bayer, Germany) is effective against *S. haematobium* infection. It is given orally at 7.5 mg/kg body weight, to be repeated twice at 2-week intervals. Oxamniquine (Pfizer) is effective against *S. mansoni* infection. The recommended dose is 15 to 20 mg/kg body weight given once. Individuals who were infected in Egypt or East Africa may need higher doses, up to 60 mg/kg body weight, given in divided doses over 2 to 3 days.

LIVER FLUKES

The major liver flukes of humans are *Clonorchis sinensis*, the Chinese liver fluke, and various species of *Opisthorchis*, which are largely found in Southeast Asia and Russia. *Fasciola hepatica* is one of the most important disease-causing organisms in sheep and cattle that, incidentally, infects humans; several hundred cases have been reported in Latin America, Europe, Asia, and North Africa.

Clonorchiasis

The Chinese or oriental liver fluke, *C. sinensis*, is a parasite of fish-eating mammals in the Far East. Although humans are incidental hosts, millions of persons are infected, mainly in China, Hong Kong, Vietnam, and Korea. The adult flukes are flat, elongated worms (approximately 15 × 3 mm). They inhabit the distal biliary capillaries, where they deposit relatively small, yellow operculated eggs (30 × 14 μm) that are fully embryonated when they pass out of the body in feces (Fig. 279–2). The eggs are then ingested by specific

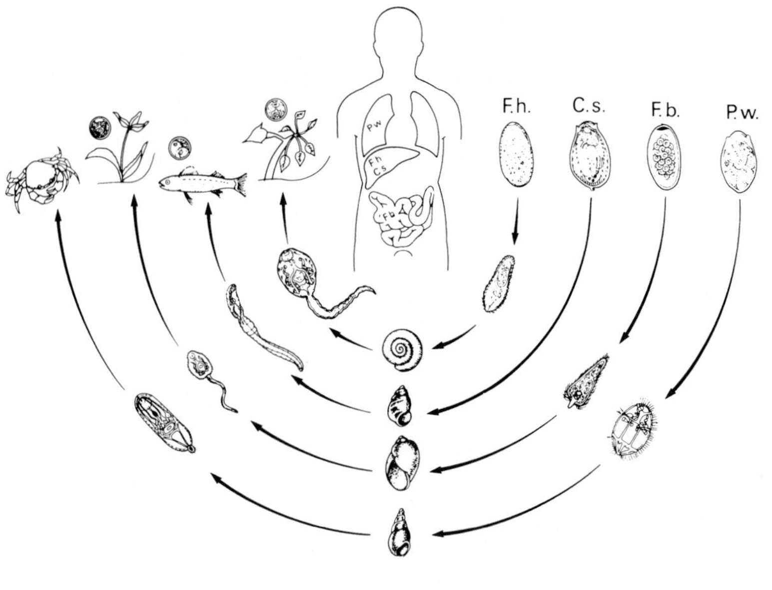

FIGURE 279–2. Life cycle of important parasitic flukes. Eggs are passed with stools in *Fasciola hepatica* (F.h.), *Clonorchis sinensis* (C.s.), and *Fasciolopsis buski* (F.b.) or in sputum in *Paragonimus westermani* (P.w.) infections. The next stage of multiplication occurs in specific snail intermediate hosts, followed by liberation of cercariae, which encyst on the second intermediate hosts (aquatic plants, fish, or crabs). These metacercariae are the infective stage, and humans develop the infection after consumption of the second intermediate hosts. The final habitats of these flukes are the liver (F.h. and C.s.), intestines (F.b.), or lungs (P.w.).

snails, inside which they hatch into miracidia. These organisms multiply enormously into large numbers of cercariae that pass into the water. On coming into contact with certain freshwater fish, the cercariae penetrate under the scales or into the skin, where they encyst as metacercariae, which are the forms that infect humans. Humans acquire clonorchiasis by the ingestion of raw or inadequately cooked fish; the metacercariae excyst in the duodenum and pass through the ampulla of Vater, where adult worms mature inside the bile ducts.

Clinical Syndromes

Controlled studies have revealed that most persons with *C. sinensis* infections are asymptomatic.[44] No gross changes can be detected in the liver in mild or early infection, but localized obstruction of bile ducts and thickening of their walls may be seen in heavy infection. Clinically, persons with heavy worm loads may suffer from cholangitis and cholangiohepatitis.[45] An increased incidence of cholangiocarcinoma has been associated with *C. sinensis* infections.[46] Pathologically, these tumors are adenocarcinomas originating from the hyperplastic epithelial lining of the bile ducts.

Diagnosis and Management

A definitive diagnosis of clonorchiasis depends on demonstration of the characteristic eggs in the feces. To improve the chance of finding eggs, a stool-concentration technique such as formol ether may be necessary. Praziquantel is now the drug of choice for the treatment of clonorchiasis (75 mg/kg/day in three doses for 1 day).[41] Albendazole in a dose of 10 mg/kg for 7 days may also be used. Surgery to relieve biliary tract obstruction may rarely be needed.[47]

Opisthorchiasis

Human infections with *Opisthorchis felineus* and *Opisthorchis viverrini* are significant clinical problems in defined geographic areas.[45] These two parasites are common liver flukes of cats and dogs that can occasionally be transmitted to humans. Infection with *O. felineus* is endemic in Southeast Asia and eastern Europe, whereas *O. viverrini* infection is commonly found in Thailand. The life cycle is similar to that of *C. sinensis* infection. Mild or moderate infection is not usually associated with specific symptoms or signs. Clinical symptoms and ultrasonographic changes of the biliary tract and gall bladder are more common in persons in the age group of 21 to 40 years[48] and older, who may have had heavy infection previously. A significant association between *O. viverrini* and cholangiocarcinoma has been documented in endemic areas, particularly northeastern Thailand.[46, 47] The diagnosis is established by fecal examination. Praziquantel is the drug of choice for treating infected individuals.[41]

Fascioliasis

Infection with the liver fluke *F. hepatica* is a cosmopolitan zoonosis throughout the sheep-raising areas of the world. Human infections have been reported, particularly from South America, Europe, Africa, China, and Australia. The adult fluke is large, flat, brownish, and leaf-shaped and measures approximately 2.5 × 1 cm. The final habitat of mature worms in their natural hosts (mainly sheep and cattle) or in humans is the biliary system, where they deposit their eggs (see Fig. 279–2). The large oval, yellowish-brown, operculate ova (140 × 75 μm) pass to the intestines, are evacuated in the feces, and complete their development in water. In a few days, mature miracidia hatch and must reach their specific snail intermediate host within 8 hours. Inside the lymph spaces of the snail, multiplication takes place, and unforked-tail cercariae emerge and undergo encystment into metacercariae on aquatic grasses, plants, and sometimes soil. When swallowed, the infective metacercariae excyst, and the larvae penetrate the intestinal wall into the peritoneum, whence they usually pass through the liver capsule and tissues to the biliary tract. Approximately 12 weeks are needed from infection to oviposition in humans.

Clinical Syndromes

Infection with *F. hepatica* has two distinct clinical phases corresponding to the hepatic migratory phase of its life cycle and to the presence of the worms in their final habitat in the bile ducts.[44] The early phase is characterized by fever and pain in the right upper quadrant that are associated with enlargement of the liver and positive serologic testing.[49] Marked eosinophilia is usually seen. Computed tomographic examination of the liver may show small nodules or tortuous linear tracks.[50, 51] A few weeks after this acute episode and as the worms enter the bile canaliculi, the symptoms may decline or disappear completely. Individual cases with obstruction of bile ducts and biliary cirrhosis have been reported, but they are extremely rare. Recently, magnetic resonance examination was found to be useful as an adjunct investigative tool in fascioliasis.[52]

Diagnosis and Management

Laboratory diagnosis is based on finding the characteristic ova in the feces or bile. A concentration method such as formol ether is necessary to enhance the chance of finding eggs. New improved serologic tests may help in establishing the diagnosis.[53] Bithionol (30 to 50 mg/kg on alternate days for 10 to 15 doses) is the drug of choice for treating fascioliasis.[41]

INTESTINAL FLUKES

Fasciolopsiasis

Human infection with the large intestinal fluke *Fasciolopsis buski* is endemic in the Far East and Southeast Asia. Adult worms are thick and fleshy and range in length from 2 to 7.5 cm and in breadth from 0.8 to 2 cm. These flukes inhabit the duodenum and jejunum and produce large operculated eggs (135 × 80 μm) (see Fig. 279–2). On reaching fresh water, the eggs develop into miracidia that hatch and must reach a specific snail intermediate host to multiply and to develop into free-living cercariae. These organisms will, in turn, encyst into metacercariae on almost any aquatic plant. The metacercariae, or infective forms, can survive in most environments for periods up to 1 year. When the infected plants are ingested by humans, the metacercariae excyst in the intestines, and the parasites develop into mature worms within 3 months.

Clinical Syndromes

Adult flukes live in the upper portion of the small intestine and are usually attached to its mucosa. Fasciolopsiasis appears to be mostly asymptomatic.[44] Controlled field studies demonstrated no significant difference between infected and control persons as regards their development or intestinal absorption capabilities. In heavy infections, however, the major symptoms relate to the presence of the worms in the intestines. Diarrhea, abdominal pain, and signs of malabsorption in the stools (undigested food) may be encountered.

Diagnosis and Management

A definitive diagnosis depends on demonstration of adult worms or eggs in stools. Adult worms recovered from feces should be examined by an experienced parasitologist. Eggs that resemble those of *F. hepatica* can be demonstrated by fecal smear examination or by the use of a concentration technique such as formol ether. The treatment of choice of symptomatic fasciolopsiasis is praziquantel. It is administered orally at 25 mg/kg body weight three times per day for 1 day.[41]

Heterophyiasis

Human infection with the minute intestinal fluke *Heterophyes heterophyes* is common in the Nile delta, the Far East, and Southeast Asia. These flukes are small, less than 2 mm in length, and they inhabit the small intestines. The life cycle is similar to that of *F. buski*, but the metacercariae encyst in freshwater or brackish water fish. Infection is acquired by consumption of undercooked or salted fish. Adult worms deposit small operculate eggs (30 × 15 μm) that can be detected in the stools. Clinically, heterophyiasis is manifested as abdominal pain associated with mucous diarrhea. There are no controlled studies to indicate the specificity of these symptoms and the relationship of morbidity to worm loads. Treatment is recommended for symptomatic patients; the drug of choice is praziquantel, as described previously for fasciolopsiasis.

LUNG FLUKES

Paragonimiasis

Human infection by the lung fluke *Paragonimus westermani* and several other related species is widely distributed over three continents. Endemic foci have been found in West Africa, in almost every country in the Far East and the Indian subcontinent, and in several parts of Central and South America.[54] Adult worms measuring 7 to 12 × 4 to 7 mm encapsulate within the parenchyma of the lung, usually close to bronchioles. On reaching maturity, the worm deposits golden brown operculate eggs (100 × 10 μm) that pass into the bronchioles and are coughed up (see Fig. 279–2). Eggs can be detected in the sputum of infected persons or in their feces if they swallow their sputum. In fresh water, the eggs mature and liberate free-swimming miracidia that infect the specific snail intermediate host. After a rather protracted period of development and reproduction in the snail (3 to 5 months), stumpy-tailed cercariae emerge. They encyst in the muscles and viscera of crayfish and freshwater crabs. Human infection is initiated by consumption of these freshwater crustaceans, either raw or pickled. Metacercariae excyst in the duodenum, penetrate the intestinal wall, and enter the peritoneal cavity. The next migratory phase takes the metacercariae through the diaphragm to the pleural cavities and then into the lungs, where they finally lodge. Egg deposition starts 5 to 6 weeks after infection. Infection with either *P. westermani* or other related species may localize in several sites such as the brain or peritoneal cavity.

Clinical Syndromes

Most light and moderate infections are asymptomatic. The important clinical manifestations of paragonimiasis are eosinophilia and chest complaints.[55] Cough productive of brownish sputum with intermittent hemoptysis is the initial manifestation. The condition then evolves to a picture of chronic bronchitis or bronchiectasis with profuse expectoration and pleuritic chest pain. Radiographic and computed tomographic changes are thought to be specific enough for diagnostic purposes.[56] Lung abscesses, pleural effusion, and, rarely, masses due to ectopic worms in the abdomen or central nervous system may be encountered. The clinical picture of cerebral paragonimiasis may resemble that of epilepsy, cerebral tumors, or embolism of the brain.

Diagnosis and Management

Examination of the sputum or feces provides the opportunity for finding the characteristic operculated eggs. In cases of ectopic paragonimiasis, serologic examination may be helpful.[54] Once the diagnosis is established, therapy should be initiated. Praziquantel is given orally in a dosage of 25 mg/kg body weight three times per day for 1 day.[41]

REFERENCES

1. Mahmoud AAF, Abdel Wahab MF. Schistosomiasis. In: Warren KS, Mahmoud AAF, eds. Tropical and Geographical Medicine. 2nd ed. New York: McGraw-Hill; 1990:458–473.
2. Warren KS. Helminthic diseases endemic in the United States. Am J Trop Med Hyg. 1974;23:723.
3. Centers for Disease Control and Prevention. Schistosomiasis in US Peace Corps Volunteers Malawi, 1992. MMWR Morb Mortal Wkly Rep. 1993;42:464–470.
4. Weist PM, Tartakoff AM, Aikawa M, et al. Inhibition of surface membrane maturation in schistosomula of *Schistosoma mansoni*. Proc Natl Acad Sci USA. 1988;85:3825–3829.
5. World Health Organization. Atlas of the Global Distribution of Schistosomiasis. Parasitic Diseases Programme. Geneva: World Health Organization; 1987.
6. Sturrock RF. Biology and ecology of human schistosomes. In: Mahmoud AAF, ed. Clinical Tropical Medicine and Communicable Diseases. London: Bailliere-Tindall; 1987;249–266.
7. Margnet S, Abel L, Hillaire D, et al. Genetic localization of a locus controlling the intensity of infection by *Schistosoma mansoni* on chromosome Sq31-q33. Nat Genet. 1996;181–184.
8. Abdel Salam E, Abdel Fattah M. Prevalence and morbidity of *Schistosoma haematobium* in Egyptian children. A controlled study. Am J Trop Med Hyg. 1977;26:463.
9. Secor WE, del Corral H, dos Reis MG, et al. Association of hepatosplenic schistosomiasis with HLA-DQB1*0201. J Infect Dis. 1996;174:1131–1135.
10. Siongok TKA, Mahmoud AAF, Ouma JH, et al. Morbidity in schistosomiasis

mansoni in relation to intensity of infection: Study of a community in Machakos, Kenya. Am J Trop Med Hyg. 1976;25:273.
11. May J, Kremsner PG, Milovanovic D, et al. HLA-DP control of human *Schistosoma haematobium* infection. Am J Trop Med Hyg. 1998;59:302–306.
12. Doherty JF, Moody AH, Wright SG. Katayama fever: An acute manifestation of schistosomiasis. BMJ. 1996;313:1071–1072.
13. Bethlem EP, Schettino G de P, Carvalho CR. Pulmonary schistosomiasis. Curr Opin Pulmon Med. 1997;3:361–365.
14. Warren KS, Domingo EO, Cowan RBT. Granuloma formation around schistosome eggs as a manifestation of delayed hypersensitivity. Am J Pathol. 1967;51:735.
15. Kassis AI, Warren KS, Mahmoud AAF. The *Schistosoma haematobium* egg granuloma. Cell Immunol. 1978;38:310.
16. Mwatha JK, Kimani G, Kamau T. High levels of TNF, soluble TNF receptors, soluble ICAM-1 and IFN-gamma but low levels of IL-5 are associated with hepatosplenic disease in human schistosomiasis mansoni. J Immunol. 1998;160:1992–1999.
17. King D, Mahmoud AAF. Schistosomiasis. In: Blaser M, Smith P, Ravdin J, et al, eds. Infections of the gastrointestinal tract. New York: Raven; 1995:1209–1222.
18. Chikunguwo SM, Quinn JJ, Horn DA, et al. The cell-mediated response to schistosome antigens at the clonal level. III. Identification of soluble egg antigens recognized by cloned specific granulomagenic murine CD4+ TH1-type lymphocytes. J Immunol. 1993;150:1413.
19. Chan MS, Anderson RM, Medley GI, Bundy DA. Dynamic aspects of morbidity and acquired immunity in schistosomiasis control. Acta Trop. 1996;62:105–117.
20. Butterworth AE. Immunology of schistosomiasis. In: Jordan P, Webbe G, Sturrock RE, eds. Human Schistosomiasis. United Kingdom; 1993:331–366.
21. Mahmoud AAF. Eosinophilia. In: Warren KS, Mahmoud AAF, eds. Tropical and Geographical Medicine. 2nd ed. New York: McGraw-Hill; 1990:65–70.
22. Olveda RM, Domingo EO. Schistosomiasis japonica. In: Mahmoud AAF, ed. Clinical Tropical Medicine and Communicable Diseases. London: Bailliere-Tindall; 1987;397–418.
23. Mies S, Neto OB, Beear A Jr. Systemic and hepatic hemodynamics in hepatosplenic Manson's schistosomiasis with and without propranolol. Dig Dis Sci. 1997;42:751–761.
24. Angelico M, Renganathan E, Gandin C, et al. Chronic liver disease in the Alexandria governorate, Egypt: Contribution of schistosomiasis and hepatitis virus infection. J Hepatol. 1997;26:236–243.
25. Gerapacher-Lara R, Pinto-Silva RA, Rayes AA, et al. Ultrasonography of periportal fibrosis in schistosomiasis mansoni in Brazil. Trans R Soc Trop Med Hyg. 1997;91:307–309.
26. Thomas AK, Dittrich M, Kardorff R, et al. Evaluation of ultrasonographic staging systems for the assessment of *Schistosoma mansoni* induced hepatic involvement. Acta Trop. 1997;68:347–356.
27. King OH, Lombardi G, Lombardi C, et al. Chemotherapy-based control of schistosomiasis haematobia. I. Metrifonate versus praziquantel in control of intensity and prevalence of infection. Am J Trop Med Hyg. 1988;39:295–305.
28. Medhat A, Zarzoura A, Nafeh M, et al. Evaluation of an ultrasonographic score for urinary bladder morbidity in *Schistosoma hematobium* infection. Am J Trop Med Hyg. 1997;57:16–19.
29. Young SW, Higashi G, Kamel R, et al. Interaction of salmonellae and schistosomes in host parasite relations. Trans R Soc Trop Med Hyg. 1973;67:797.
30. Bedwani R, Renegenathan E, El Kwhsky F, et al. Schistosomiasis and the risk of bladder cancer in Alexandria, Egypt. Br J Cancer. 1998;77:1186–1189.
31. Badawi AF. Molecular and genetic events in schistosomiasis-associated human bladder cancer: Role of oncogenes and tumor suppressor genes. Cancer Lett. 1996;105:123–138.
32. Bofetta P. Infection with *Helicobacter pylori* and parasites, social class and cancer. IARC Sci Publ. 1997;138:325–329.
33. Voge M, Bruckner D, Bruce JI. *Schistosoma mekongi* sp *n* from man and animals compared with four geographic strains of *Schistosoma japonicum*. J Parasitol. 1978;64:577.
34. Hofstetter M, Nash TE, Cheever AW, et al. Infection with *Schistosoma mekongi* in Southeast Asian refugees. J Infect Dis. 1981;144:420.
35. Morris W, Knaur CM. Cardiopulmonary manifestations of schistosomiasis. Semi Resp Infect. 1997;12:159–170.
36. King CL. Schistosomiasis. In: Mahmoud AAF, ed. Parasitic Lung Diseases. Lung Biology in Health and Disease, v. 101. New York: Marcel Dekker; 1997:135–155.
37. Pittella JE. Neuroschistosomiasis. Brain Pathol. 1997;7:649–662.
38. Helling-Giese G, Kjetland EF, Gundersen SG, et al. Schistosomiasis in women: Manifestations in the upper reproductive tract. Acte Trop. 1996;62:225–238.
39. Peters PAS, Kazura JW. Update on diagnostic methods for schistosomiasis. In: Mahmoud AAF, ed. Clinical Tropical Medicine and Communicable Diseases. London: Bailliere-Tindall; 1987:419–434.
40. Tsang VC, Wilkins PP. Immunodiagnosis of schistosomiasis. Immunol Invest. 1997;26:175–186.
41. Drugs for Parasitic Infection. Med Lett. 1998;40:1–12.
42. Ismail M, Metwally A, Fargholy A, et al. Characterization of isolates of *Schistosoma mansoni* from Egyptian villagers that tolerate high doses of praziquantel. Am J Trop Med Hyg. 1996;55:214–218.
43. Bennett JL, Dan T, Liang FT, et al. The development of resistance to antihelminthics: A perspective with an emphasis on the antischistosomal drug praziquantel. Exp Parasitol. 1997;87:260–267.
44. Liu LX, Harinasuta KT. Liver and intestinal flukes. Gastroenterol Clin North Am. 1996;25:627–636.
45. Harinasuta T, Bunnag D. Liver, lung and intestinal trematodiasis. In: Warren KS, Mahmoud AAF, et al, eds. Tropical and Geographical Medicine. 2nd ed. New York: McGraw-Hill; 1990:473–489.
46. Noller H, Heseltine E, Vainio H. Working group report on schistosomes, liver flukes and *Helicobacter pylori*. Int J Cancer. 1995;60:587–598.
47. Leung JW, Yu AS. Hepatolithiasis and biliary parasites. Baillieres Clin Gastroenterol. 1997;11:681–706.
48. Pungpak S, Viravan C, Radomyos B, et al. Opisthorciasis viverrini infection in Thailand: Studies on the morbidity of the infection and resolution following praziquantel treatment. Am J Trop Med Hyg. 1997;56:311–314.
49. Wutanapa P. Cholangiocarcinoma in patients with opisthorchiasis. Br J Surg. 1996;83:1062–1064.
50. Pulpeiro JR, Armesto V, Varela J, et al. Fascioliasis: Findings in 15 patients. Br J Radiol. 1991;64:798.
51. Van Beers B, Pringot C, Geuber A, et al. Hepatobiliary fascioliasis: Noninvasive imaging findings. Radiology. 1990;174:809.
52. Han JK, Han D, Choi BL, Han MC. MR findings in human fascioliasis. Trop Med Int Health. 1996;1:367–372.
53. Hillyer GV, De Galanes MS, Rodriguez Perez J, et al. Use of the Falcon assay screening test enzyme-linked immunosorbent assay (FASTelisa and the enzyme-linked immunoelectrotransfer blot (E1TB) to determine the prevalence of human fascioliasis in the Bolivian altiplano. Am J Trop Med Hyg. 1992;46:603.
54. Kagawa FT. Pulmonary paragonimiasis. Semin Respir Infect. 1997;12:149–158.
55. King CH. Pulmonary flukes. In: Mahmoud AAF, ed. Parasitic Lung Diseases. Lung Biology in Health and Disease, v. 101. New York, Marcel Dekker; 1997:157–169.
56. Im JG, Chang KH, Reeder MM. Current diagnostic imaging of pulmonary and cerebral paragonimiasis with pathologicla correlation. Semin Roentgenol. 1997;32:301–324.

Chapter 280

Cestodes (Tapeworms)

CHARLES H. KING

In humans, parasitic cestode infections occur in either of two forms—as mature tapeworms residing within the gastrointestinal tract or as one or more larval cysts (variously called hydatidosis, cysticercosis, coenurosis, or sparganosis) embedded in liver, lung, muscle, brain, eye, or other tissues.[1, 2] The form taken by the infecting parasite depends on which cestode species causes the infection and, to a lesser extent, on the route by which the infection was acquired. Table 280–1 summarizes the common cestode parasites of humans, their typical vectors, and their usual symptoms.

This chapter begins with a discussion of parasite biology and the immunology of cestode infection, followed by a description of individual parasite species: intestinal tapeworms (e.g., *Diphyllobothrium latum, Hymenolepis nana, Taenia saginata, Taenia solium*) and invasive cestode parasites (cysticercosis *[T. solium]*, hydatid and alveolar cyst disease [*Echinococcus* spp.], sparganosis, and coenurosis *[Taenia multiceps]*). Diagnosis and therapy, outlined briefly under the individual parasite headings, are discussed in greater detail at the end of each section.

CESTODE BIOLOGY

The Parasite Life Cycle

The parasitic cestodes discussed in this chapter are flatworms (platyhelminths) of the orders Pseudophyllidea *(Diphyllobothrium, Spirometra)* and Cyclophyllidea (other species) that divide their life cycle between two animal hosts (Fig. 280–1).[1, 2] As mature tapeworms, these parasites reside in the intestinal tract of a definitive host, which is a carnivorous mammal. Depending on the parasite species, mature tapeworms vary in size from several millimeters (*Echinococcus* spp.) to 25 m *(Diphyllobothrium)*.[1]

The tapeworm consists of several parts—a head or scolex, a neck, and a tail. The head has two or more suckers and in some cases a *rostellum*, or knob of small hooks, used to attach to the wall of the

TABLE 280–1 Common Cestode Parasites of Humans, Their Typical Vectors, and Their Usual Symptoms

Parasite Species	Developmental Stage Found in Humans	Common Name	Transmission Source	Symptoms Associated with Infection
Diphyllobothrium latum	Tapeworm	Fish tapeworm	Plerocercoid cysts in freshwater fish	Usually minimal; with prolonged or heavy infection, vitamin B_{12} deficiency
Hymenolepis nana	Tapeworm, cysticercoids	Dwarf tapeworm	Infected humans	Mild abdominal discomfort
Taenia saginata	Tapeworm	Beef tapeworm	Cysts in beef	Abdominal discomfort, proglottid migration
Taenia solium	Tapeworm	Pork tapeworm	Cysticerci in pork	Minimal
Taenia solium (*Cysticercus cellulosae*)	Cysticerci	Cysticercosis	Eggs from infected humans	Local inflammation, mass effect; if in CNS, seizures, hydrocephalus, arachnoiditis
Echinococcus granulosus	Larval cysts	Hydatid cyst disease	Eggs from infected dogs	Mass effect leading to pain, obstruction of adjacent organs; less commonly, secondary bacterial infection, distal spread of daughter cysts
Echinococcus multilocularis	Larval cysts	Alveolar cyst disease	Eggs from infected canines	Local invasion and mass effect leading to organ dysfunction; distal metastasis possible
Taenia multiceps	Larval cysts	Coenurosis, bladder worm	Eggs from infected dogs	Local inflammation and mass effect
Spirometra mansonoides	Larval cysts	Sparganosis	Cysts from infected copepods, frogs, snakes	Local inflammation and mass effect

Abbreviation: CNS, Central nervous system.

host's intestine (Fig. 280–2*A*).[3] The scolex is connected by a short neck to the lower portion of the tapeworm, the strobila, which is a ribbonlike chain of independent, but connected, segments called *proglottids* (Fig. 280–2*B*). Each proglottid has both male and female sexual organs and is responsible for production of parasite eggs. Proglottids begin to develop in the neck region of the parasite, then mature and move downward in the strobila as new segments are added from above. The hermaphroditic proglottids become gravid and eventually break free of the tapeworm. Proglottids may degenerate in the stool, releasing eggs (thousands to millions per day) into the feces. Alternatively, intact proglottids may be passed in the stool, with egg release occurring outside the body. In some cases, a section of strobila may be passed in a single day, with no further release of proglottids for several days thereafter. In practical terms, this means that although the number of tapeworm eggs in the stool is usually high, detection of parasite eggs by standard stool examination may be sporadic, and it may require multiple stool samples, rectal swabs, and visual examination of stool and perineum for proglottids to detect tapeworm infection. For some species of tapeworm (e.g., *T. saginata*), the proglottids are motile. They may migrate within the gastrointestinal tract, causing biliary or appendiceal obstruction, or out of the body, to be found in the perineum.

At the point at which eggs are released, two effective biotypes of

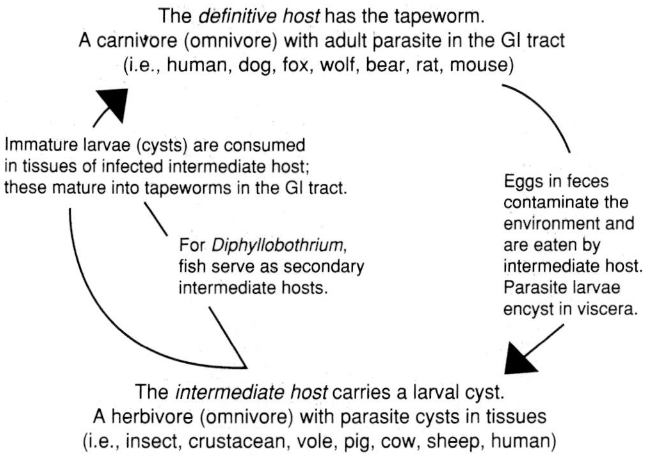

The *definitive host* has the tapeworm.
A carnivore (omnivore) with adult parasite in the GI tract
(i.e., human, dog, fox, wolf, bear, rat, mouse)
Immature larvae (cysts) are consumed
in tissues of infected intermediate host;
these mature into tapeworms in the GI tract.
For *Diphyllobothrium*,
fish serve as secondary
intermediate hosts.
Eggs in feces
contaminate the
environment and
are eaten by
intermediate host.
Parasite larvae
encyst in viscera.
The *intermediate host* carries a larval cyst.
A herbivore (omnivore) with parasite cysts in tissues
(i.e., insect, crustacean, vole, pig, cow, sheep, human)

FIGURE 280–1. Cestode parasites alternate larval and adult stages in two different hosts.

parasite can be defined. If the eggs released from the parasite are partially developed, they are called *embryonated*. If the egg embryo has not yet begun its differentiation, the egg is referred to as *nonembryonated*. In biologic terms, the embryonated egg can immediately infect the next intermediate mammalian or insect host, typically a herbivore or omnivore, through ingestion in food.[1] Such eggs, typical of *Echinococcus* spp., *Taenia* spp., and *H. nana*, may lie dormant in grazing areas or become scattered in the home environment and remain infectious for several months to years.[1, 4] Once ingested, the egg hatches in the intermediate host's intestine, releasing an *oncosphere*, which penetrates the gut mucosa to reach the circulation. The oncosphere passes to any of several organs to form a parasite cyst, which is variously called a cysticercoid, cysticercus, alveolar cyst, or hydatid cyst, depending on its morphology. The life cycle of these parasites is completed when the carnivorous definitive host consumes the cyst-infected tissues of the intermediate host and the cyst develops into a mature tapeworm within the lumen of the definitive host's intestine.

For nonembryonated eggs, such as those of the fish tapeworm *D. latum*, initial development takes place outside the body in water, after which the eggs hatch to release a free-swimming *coracidium* larva.[1] In time, the coracidium is ingested by a small crustacean called a copepod and then develops into a procercoid larva within the copepod's tissues. When the copepod is, in turn, ingested by a fish or other intermediate host, the procercoid infects its musculature, developing into the next larval stage, the *plerocercoid* cyst, or *sparganum*. If an uncooked plerocercoid of *D. latum* is ingested by a human, its definitive host, it develops into a mature, intraluminal "fish tapeworm." However, if the fish containing the plerocercoid is ingested by another, larger fish, it does not become a tapeworm. It reencysts instead as a plerocercoid in the muscles of the second, larger fish.

Plerocercoid encystment or reencystment is significant in terms of human disease (as *sparganosis*) for cestode species for which humans cannot serve as the definitive host (e.g., *Spirometra mansonoides*, a tapeworm of dogs and felines). Plerocercoids can develop in human tissues if *Spirometra*-infested copepods are ingested in drinking water. Alternatively, human plerocercoid cysts may be acquired via the intestine from another intermediate host (e.g., tadpole, frog, snake) if the meat of that aquatic host is eaten uncooked. Migrating plerocercoid cysts can also transfer directly into the skin or the eye if raw flesh of an aquatic intermediate host is used as a poultice in traditional healing.[1]

As a rule, humans are either definitive or intermediate hosts for a given cestode parasite, but not both. For example, humans are

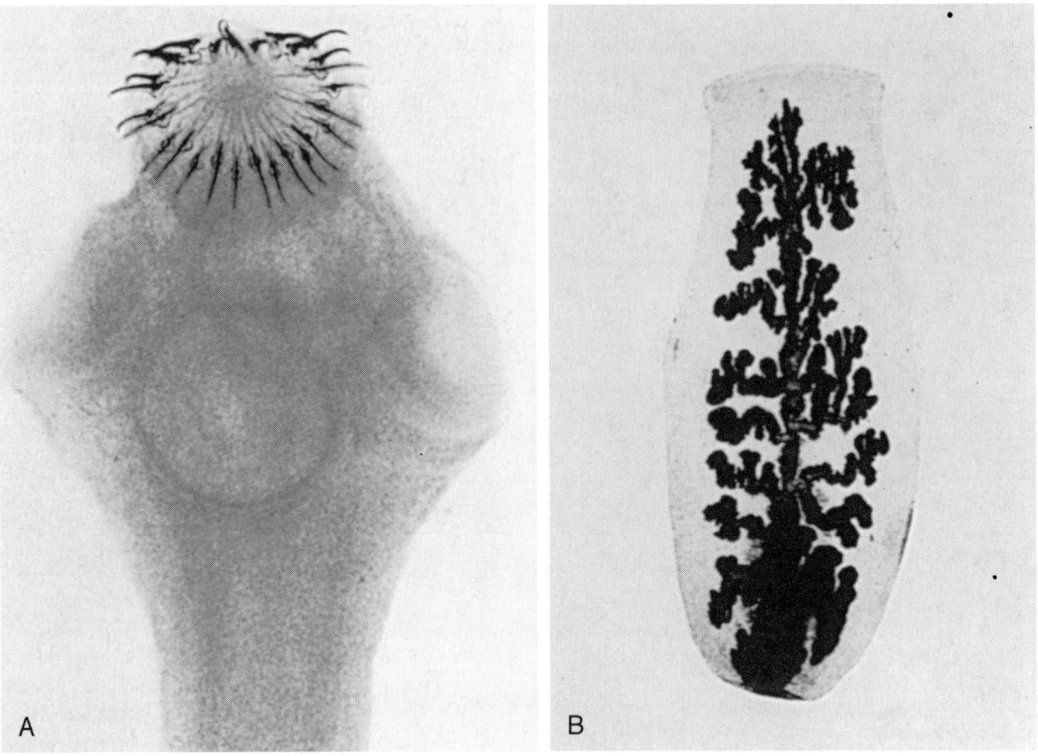

FIGURE 280–2. The scolex *(A)* and a proglottid *(B)* of the cestode *Taenia solium*. (From Ash LR, Orihel TC. Atlas of Human Parasitology. 3rd ed. Chicago: ASCP; 1990.)

solely definitive hosts (i.e., with tapeworms) for *D. latum* (the fish tapeworm) and *T. saginata* ("beef tapeworm"). Humans are solely intermediate hosts for *Echinococcus* spp. (hydatid cysts, alveolar cysts), *Spirometra* (sparganosis), and *T. multiceps* (coenurosis). There are two exceptions to this rule. The first is *T. solium*, which develops in humans as a cysticercus if ingested as an egg or as a tapeworm if ingested as a cysticercus in infected pork. It is thus possible for one patient to harbor both cyst and tapeworm forms of *T. solium*, and such dual infection is seen in about 25% of cysticercosis cases. The second exception is the dwarf tapeworm, *H. nana*, whose eggs, after ingestion, hatch in the gut to encyst within the wall of the human intestine. After 5 to 7 days, the cyst breaks open and the larva develops (within the same host) to become a mature tapeworm. The fertile eggs of this tapeworm may directly infect the mucosa, permitting continued increase in tapeworm numbers within the affected host, without further exposure to environmental egg contamination. In this fashion, humans serve as both intermediate and definitive hosts for *H. nana*. It should be stressed that single-host proliferation like that of *H. nana* is highly unusual among human cestode infections and helminth infections in general and that, normally, heavy cestode infections can be acquired only by repeated environmental exposure to eggs or infectious parasite cysts.

Disease Pathogenesis and Immunology

Adult tapeworms in the intestinal tract generally cause minimal local pathology. Reduced nutrient absorption and alteration of gut motility have been described, but there is no firm association of adult tapeworm infection with specific bowel symptoms. Immune response to adult tapeworm may provoke eosinophilia and immunoglobulin E elevation in some patients, but the immune response does not appear to alter the course of intraluminal tapeworm infection. In light of the limited range of potential hosts observed for most adult tapeworms, it has been suggested that host factors, including the presence or absence of specific immunoreactivity, may determine the success of parasite infection in various potential host species.[1]

Immune response to invasive cyst infection is more pronounced, but is often unsuccessful in eradicating the cyst in susceptible hosts.[5] Infiltration with neutrophils and eosinophils is followed by local fibrosis, leading to cyst encapsulation, and macrophage infiltration. Once the cyst is encapsulated, antigen release may be quite limited, leading to a reduction in local inflammatory response. Specific antibody production remains detectable in the serum, however, and delayed-type hypersensitivity may be detected on skin testing.[6] Immune response often increases at a later point in time, as the cyst begins to die and leak antigen or as the cyst erodes into a body cavity, duct, or vessel, increasing local or systemic exposure to antigen. Experimentally, anticyst immune response appears to limit dissemination of *Echinococcus* spp. after initial infection.[7, 8] Anticyst immunity is also likely to contribute to the spontaneous clearance of *H. nana* infection in older children.[6]

INTESTINAL TAPEWORM INFECTIONS

Diphyllobothrium latum

D. latum, or fish tapeworm, is one of the pseudophyllidean cestodes transmitted via aquatic species.[1] Human infection with *D. latum* is acquired by eating uncooked freshwater fish containing the parasite's plerocercoid cysts. Some traditional modes of infection include consumption of dried or smoked fish, which can contain viable cysts if not further cooked, or tasting of flavored freshwater fish (e.g., gefilte fish) before cooking. The enthusiasm for "raw bar" foods such as ceviche, sushi, and sashimi prepared from freshwater fish, especially salmon, has increased the transmission potential for *D. latum* in developed areas of North America.[9, 10] Areas of the world in which *D. latum* is highly endemic (>2% prevalence) include specific lake and delta areas of Siberia, Europe (especially Scandinavia and other Baltic countries), North America, Japan, and Chile. Endemicity in rural areas is favored by stable zoonotic transmission through alternative nonhuman definitive hosts. These include seals, cats, bears, minks, foxes, and wolves.

Human *D. latum* tapeworms are large, reaching up to 25 m (3000 to 4000 proglottids) in length. It takes 3 to 6 weeks after exposure for the tapeworm to mature. Once established, a *D. latum* parasite may survive for 30 years or more. Multiple tapeworms in the same patient are common. Normally, infection is asymptomatic, but a proportion of infected individuals report nonspecific symptoms of weakness (66%), dizziness (53%), salt craving (62%), diarrhea (22%), and intermittent abdominal discomfort.[1]

Prolonged (>3 to 4 years) or heavy *D. latum* infection may lead to megaloblastic anemia caused by vitamin B_{12} deficiency. The B_{12} deficiency is a consequence of two factors: parasite-mediated dissociation of the vitamin B_{12}–intrinsic factor complex within the gut lumen (making B_{12} unavailable to the host) and heavy vitamin uptake and use by the parasite. Megaloblastic anemia may be worsened by concurrent folate deficiency, which also occurs as a consequence of *D. latum* infection.[1] B_{12} deficiency may be sufficiently severe to cause injury to the nervous system, including peripheral neuropathy and severe combined degeneration of the central nervous system (CNS).

For diagnosis, tapeworm infection may first be suspected on the basis of the patient's history or when contrast studies of the intestine show an intraluminal, ribbon-like filling defect. Definitive diagnosis of *D. latum* infection is made by detection of 45 by 65 μm operculated parasite eggs on stool examination.[11, 12] Recovery of proglottids (with a characteristic central uterus) also establishes the diagnosis. Treatment is with a single course of niclosamide or praziquantel, as described in detail later.[13, 14] Mild B_{12} deficiency is reversed by eradication of the tapeworm. Severe vitamin B_{12} deficiency should be treated with parenteral vitamin injections.

Hymenolepis nana

H. nana, also known as dwarf tapeworm, is a cyclophyllidean tapeworm having embryonated eggs.[1] It is the only tapeworm that can be transmitted directly from human to human. Areas of endemicity (up to 26% prevalence) include Asia, southern and eastern Europe, Central and South America, and Africa. In North America, infection is most frequently found among institutionalized populations (up to 8% prevalence),[15] and among malnourished or immunocompromised patients.

Ingestion of parasite eggs on fecally contaminated food or fomites allows initial infection. Once in the intestine, the eggs hatch to form oncospheres that penetrate the mucosa to encyst as cysticercoid larvae. Four to 5 days later, the larval cyst ruptures into the lumen to form the relatively small, adult *H. nana* tapeworm (15 to 50 mm in length). Internal autoinfection may occur as parasite eggs are released from gravid proglottids in the ileum. In addition, poor sanitary practices promote external (fecal-oral) autoinfection as well as transmission to others sharing the same living quarters. Heavy infection is common among children and may be associated with abdominal cramps, anorexia, dizziness, and diarrhea.

Diagnosis of *H. nana* infection is made by identification of 30- to 47-μm parasite eggs, having a characteristic double membrane, in the stool.[11, 12] Treatment is with praziquantel or niclosamide as described in detail later.[13, 14] It is important to note that developing *H. nana* cysticercoids are not as susceptible to drug therapy as adult tapeworms. Because these cysts can emerge several days later to form new tapeworms, effective therapy of *H. nana* requires either higher than usual doses of praziquantel to reach cysticidal levels or more prolonged therapy with niclosamide (to eliminate emerging tapeworms) for a period of 5 to 7 days to eradicate infection.

Taenia saginata

T. saginata, known as the beef tapeworm, is transmitted to humans in the form of infectious larval cysts found in the meat of cattle, which serve as the parasite's usual intermediate host.[1] The *T. saginata* tapeworm is common in cattle-breeding areas of the world. The areas with highest prevalence (>10%) are in central Asia, the Near East, and central and eastern Africa. Areas of lower prevalence (<1%) are found in Europe, Southeast Asia, Central America, and South America. Consumption of "measly" (i.e., cyst infected) uncooked or undercooked beef is the usual means of transmission. Rare steak or kebabs and steak tartare are dishes typically associated with *T. saginata* tapeworm infection. In the definitive human host, adult *T. saginata* tapeworms are large (10 m in length) and can contain more than 1000 proglottids, each capable of producing thousands of eggs. If, through poor sanitary practices, eggs released in the feces are allowed to reach grazing areas, cattle are subsequently infected with *T. saginata* cysticerci. Alternative intermediate hosts include llamas, buffalo, and giraffes.

Symptoms are absent in most patients with *T. saginata* infection. A minority report mild abdominal cramps or malaise. The proglottids of *T. saginata* are motile and occasionally migrate out of the anus, to be found in the perineum or on clothing. The patient may report seeing moving segments in the feces or passing several feet of strobila at one time. These events are often psychologically distressing and are associated with significant anxiety-associated symptoms.

Specific diagnosis of *T. saginata* infection can be established by recovery of parasite proglottids.[1, 11, 12] If only eggs are found in the stool, it is important to note that *T. saginata* eggs are morphologically indistinguishable from those of *T. solium*. With *T. solium* tapeworms there is potential for autoinfection with cysticercosis, and thus if any *Taenia* spp. eggs are detected, treatment should be given without delay for further speciation. Effective oral treatment for either *Taenia* spp. is obtained with praziquantel or niclosamide,[13, 14] as described subsequently.

Taenia solium

Humans can serve as either intermediate or definitive hosts for *T. solium*. Individuals who ingest *T. solium* eggs develop tissue infection with parasite cysts, a condition known as cysticercosis (details of this illness are included later under "Cysticercosis"). Patients who consume raw or undercooked pork containing infectious larval cysts (cysticerci) acquire the "pork tapeworm," that is, the adult form of *T. solium*, which resides in the intestinal tract.[1] These tapeworms develop to approximately 2 to 8 m in length and may survive for 10 to 20 years. Some patients harbor both cysticerci and *T. solium* tapeworms, and it is possible for a tapeworm-carrying individual to develop cysticercosis by autoinfection. Areas in which *T. solium* infection is endemic include Mexico, Central America, South America, Africa, Southeast Asia, India, the Philippines, and southern Europe.

Infection with *T. solium* tapeworms is generally asymptomatic, unless cysticercosis, caused by autoinfection with parasite eggs, supervenes. The proglottids of *T. solium* are not motile (unlike those of *T. saginata*) and do not migrate. *Taenia* spp. infection is readily diagnosed by detection of eggs on stool examination,[11, 12] but *T. solium* eggs are indistinguishable from those of *T. saginata*. If a proglottid is recovered, the species can be identified on the basis of characteristic features of the uterine canals within the segment.[1, 3, 11, 12] Species identification is not required for therapy, which can be achieved with either praziquantel or niclosamide (see later).[13, 14]

Other Species Causing Tapeworm Infection in Humans

Human tapeworm infection may also be caused by *Dipylidium caninum*, a more frequent parasite of dogs and cats, or by *Hymenolepis diminuta*, a tapeworm that usually infects rats.[1] Such infections are acquired by consumption of insects (fleas or beetles) containing the larval cysticercoids of these species and are most commonly seen among children. Human infection with tapeworm species related to *D. latum*, called *Diphyllobothrium klebanovskii, Diphyllobothrium dendriticum, Diphyllobothrium ursi*, and *Diphyllobothrium dalliae*, has been described in the Arctic and parts of Siberia.[16, 17] Rarely, other tapeworm species may infect humans, particularly individuals with unusual dietary habits, such as the consumption of uncooked animal viscera.[18] Infection is diagnosed by identification of characteristic parasite eggs in the stool,[11] and effective treatment is obtained with praziquantel or niclosamide.

Diagnosis of Tapeworm Infection

Because mature tapeworm infection is strictly an intraluminal intestinal infection, the most practical approach to diagnosis is parasitologic examination of the feces for parasite eggs or proglottids.[11, 12] As discussed under "Cestode Biology" earlier, egg release in the stool may be variable because of an irregular rate of proglottid detachment and degeneration. Thus, examination of stool samples from several different days may be required to establish a diagnosis. Sensitivity for egg detection may be improved by formyl-ethyl acetate or other concentration techniques.[11] Because cestode eggs are relatively heavy, sedimentation procedures (and not flotation) provide a more efficient means of isolating tapeworm eggs.[11] In handling specimens, it is important to remember that *T. solium* eggs are infective for humans as a cause of cysticercosis. For this reason, precautions should be taken to avoid any potential contamination of fingers or clothing with parasite eggs.

In some cases, intact proglottids are passed in the stool. This is most common with *D. latum, T. saginata, T. solium*, and *D. caninum*. Expelled proglottids tend to degenerate over time, so fixation and staining of specimens are recommended to allow effective microscopic speciation.[11] Although species identification is not essential for treatment, identification of *T. solium* infection is significant and should prompt consideration of possible cysticercosis in the index patient or among his or her household contacts.[19–21] Proglottids of *D. latum* (fish tapeworm) often pass as short chains of grayish white connected segments, each 11 mm wide by 3 mm long, with a central uterine structure.[3, 11] Proglottids of the pork tapeworm, *T. solium*, are longer than they are wide (11 by 5 mm), with a lateral genital pore and 7 to 13 branches on either side of the central uterine canal. Proglottids of *T. saginata*, the beef tapeworm, have a similar appearance but may be distinguished by the greater number of lateral uterine branches (15 to 20) in the proglottid.[1, 3, 11, 12] *T. saginata* proglottids are motile and may emerge spontaneously from the anus to be found on the perineum, on the legs, or on clothing. Proglottids of *D. caninum* (23 mm long by 8 mm wide) are also motile and may be described by the patient (or parent) as whitish, moving cucumber seed–like objects in the stool. *D. caninum* proglottids may also become adherent to perianal hairs, then dry to form a whitish yellow object resembling a small grain of rice.

Treatment of Tapeworm Infection

Tapeworm infection should be treated whenever diagnosed. Safe and effective treatment of intestinal tapeworm infection may be achieved with either praziquantel or niclosamide. Both are well tolerated oral agents that have direct cidal effects on intraluminal cestode parasites.

Niclosamide

Niclosamide is a poorly absorbed, narrow-spectrum anthelmintic, available as 500-mg chewable tablets (Niclocide, Miles, West Haven, Conn.).[13, 14] The drug is normally taken as a 2-g (four-tablet) single dose for adults, as a 1.5-g (three-tablet) dose for children weighing more than 34 kg (75 pounds), or as a 1-g (two-tablet) dose for children weighing 11 to 34 kg (25 to 75 pounds). A single treatment is effective therapy for *D. latum, T. saginata, D. caninum*, and *T. solium* tapeworms.

Eradication of *H. nana* tapeworm infection requires a more prolonged course of therapy (repeat daily doses for 1 week) because of concomitant infection with maturing *H. nana* cysts, which are not affected by the drug. It is normally recommended that after the first dose, subsequent doses for *H. nana* (i.e., days 2 through 7) be reduced to 1 g daily for adults and larger children (>34 kg) and to 0.5 g daily for smaller children. These follow-up doses are intended to kill any newly emerging *H. nana* tapeworms and should completely eliminate the infection. Nevertheless, it is appropriate to rescreen the patient's stool for parasite eggs at 1 and 3 months after therapy to ensure cure. A repeated cycle of standard dosing (as just outlined) is usually sufficient to eliminate persistent infection.

Niclosamide must be thoroughly chewed before swallowing to obtain the maximal anthelmintic effect. Because the drug is poorly absorbed, the typical side effects of niclosamide are mild, occurring at a rate of approximately 10%.[13] These include malaise, mild abdominal pain, and nausea on the day of administration. High doses of niclosamide have not been shown to have mutagenic effects in animals, and the drug has been placed in Food and Drug Administration Pregnancy Category B. Normally, treatment should be delayed until after pregnancy, but with *T. solium* there is concern that patients may develop cysticercosis through autoinfection with parasite eggs. Considering the relative risks and benefits, it may be appropriate to treat pregnant women who have *T. solium* tapeworms at the time of diagnosis and not delay therapy. Concern has also been raised about the possibility of internal autoinfection during *T. solium* therapy because of the release and possible retrograde intestinal movement of eggs during therapy. Although such autoinfection has not been documented to occur, some experts recommend a mild laxative 1 to 2 hours after niclosamide treatment to avoid this possibility in *T. solium*–infected patients.[13]

Praziquantel

Praziquantel is a broad-spectrum anthelmintic used for treatment of both trematodes and cestodes.[13, 14] It is available as a scored, 600-mg coated tablet (Biltricide, Miles, West Haven, Conn.), has excellent activity against all tapeworms, and is given as a single dose of 5 to 10 mg/kg for both children and adults. The exception to this regimen is *H. nana* infection, in which a higher dose of 25 mg/kg is recommended. If the *H. nana* infection is heavy, a repeated dose is recommended 1 week after initial therapy. Follow-up stool screening is recommended at 1 and 3 months to ensure eradication of infection.

Mild side effects occur in 10 to 50% of those treated, depending on the population studied. These include transient dizziness, headache, malaise, abdominal pain, and nausea. Moderate side effects, including sedation, vomiting, diarrhea, urticaria, rash, fever, and mild transaminitis, are less common (<10%) but are also transient. Like niclosamide, praziquantel is classified in Food and Drug Administration Pregnancy Category B and should be used in pregnancy only if clearly needed. Praziquantel is well absorbed from the gastrointestinal tract and enters breast milk. Because the safety of praziquantel in children younger than 4 years of age is not known, women who are breast-feeding infants should not allow them to nurse for 72 hours after treatment is given.[13]

INVASIVE CESTODE INFECTIONS

Cysticercosis

Cysticercosis is tissue infection with larval cysts of the cestode *T. solium*, in which the patient serves as an intermediate host for the parasite. Infection is acquired by consumption of *T. solium* eggs. Prevalence is high wherever *T. solium* tapeworms are common (i.e., in Mexico, Central America, South America, the Philippines, and Southeast Asia). Infected subjects normally harbor multiple cysts in many parts of the body. In areas of endemicity, the cumulative infection risk increases with age, frequent consumption of pork, and poor household hygiene.[22] Symptoms may develop because of local inflammation at the site of involvement, but apart from CNS and cardiac involvement, serious disease is rare.

Neurocysticercosis is the term used for human CNS involvement with *T. solium* cysts.[23, 24] Infection may involve any part of the CNS, but symptomatic disease is most often related to intracerebral lesions (causing mass effects, seizures, or both) (Fig. 280–3), intraventricular cysts (causing hydrocephalus), subarachnoid lesions (causing chronic meningitis), and spinal cord lesions (causing cord compression syndrome or meningitis).[24] Intraparenchymal cerebral cysts typically enlarge slowly, causing minimal symptoms until years or decades after the onset of infection, when the cysts begin to die. At this point, cysts may lose osmoregulation and begin to swell. They may also leak antigenic material that provokes a severe inflammatory response (cerebritis, meningitis). Both processes contribute to symptoms of focal or generalized seizures, sensorimotor deficits, intellectual impairment, psychiatric disorders, and symptoms of hydrocephalus. In regions where *T. solium* is endemic, up to 33% of patients with seizures have antibodies to *T. solium*, compared with 2 to 11% prevalence in the general population, suggesting the likelihood that neurocysticercosis is an underlying cause of their disease.[22]

Because of their critical location, intraventricular cysts and basilar cysts tend to cause symptoms earlier during the course of infection. Symptoms are caused by obstruction of cerebrospinal fluid flow or by local meningeal irritation, which lead to injury to local blood vessels, cranial nerves, or brain stem.[24, 25] An aggressive form of basilar neurocysticercosis, called *racemose cysticerosis*, has been described in which proliferation of cysts occurs at the base of the brain, resulting in mental deterioration, coma, and death. Intraparenchymal spinal cord lesions are often symptomatic early because of direct local pressure effects. When spinal column cysts develop outside the cord itself, the onset of symptoms may be more gradual.

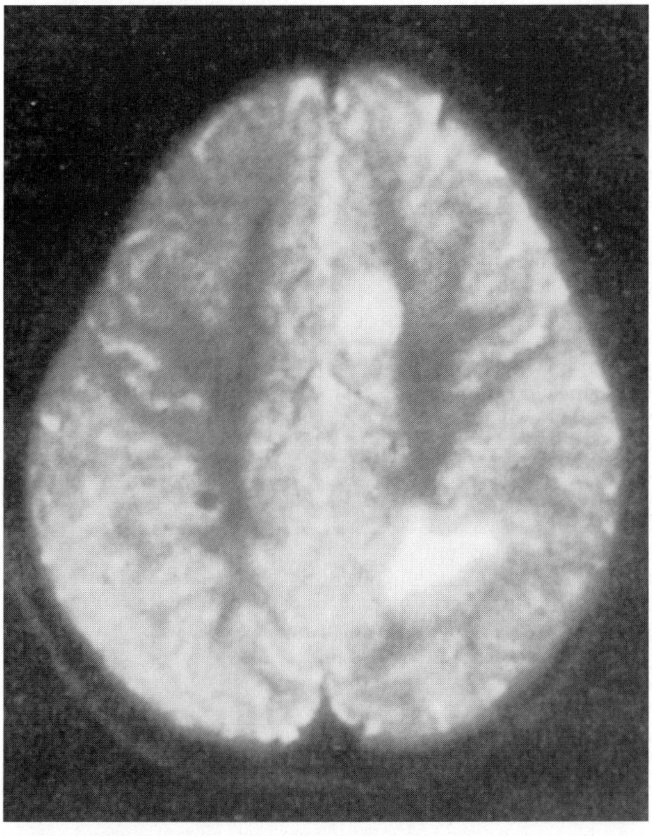

FIGURE 280–3. MRI of a child with neurocysticercosis. (From Kruskal BA, Moths L, Teele DW. Neurocysticercosis in a child with no history of travel outside the continental United States. Clin Infect Dis. 1993; 16:290–292.)

The slow onset of external cord compression, arachnoiditis, or radiculopathy may result in a confusing progression of symptoms. In the CNS, multiple cysticerci are the rule, and active symptoms may refer to one or several different locations.

Diagnosis and treatment of cysticercosis depend on the site of involvement and the symptoms experienced. Travel to or residence in an endemic area significantly increases the likelihood of the diagnosis, although transmission has been documented to occur within the United States in persons sharing the same household with a *T. solium*–infected immigrant.[19–21] Cysts outside the CNS tend not to be symptomatic. These eventually die and calcify, to be detected incidentally on plain radiographs of the limbs.

For symptomatic cysts outside the CNS, the optimal approach is surgical resection. Medical therapy, with praziquantel or albendazole, may also be employed.[13, 14, 24] Deep tissue and CNS lesions are more difficult to diagnose and treat surgically.[23, 24] Lesions may involve critical organs, making surgical removal technically infeasible. Presenting symptoms often suggest tumor, and a specific diagnosis of cysticercosis is often first suspected on the basis of imaging studies (computed tomography or magnetic resonance imaging) that show multiple enhancing and nonenhancing unilocular cysts.[26–28] Cerebral cysts are usually multiple (an average of 7 to 10 per patient). Cerebrospinal fluid examination may show lymphocytic or eosinophilic pleocytosis, hypoglycorrhachia, and elevation of protein levels. A suspected diagnosis may be strengthened by serology (available commercially or through the Centers for Disease Control and Prevention, Atlanta, Ga.) indicating prior exposure to *T. solium* antigens. Patients infected with other helminths, particularly other cestodes, may have circulating antibodies that cross react with antigens of *T. solium* in some assays (enzyme-linked immunosorbent assay).[29] However, immunoblotting techniques with the purified glycoprotein fraction of cyst fluid appear to offer both sensitive and specific diagnosis.[29, 30] Sensitivity of antibody testing tends to be high for patients with multiple cysts (94%) but substantially lower for patients with single cysts or calcified cysts (28%).[31] Computed tomography and magnetic resonance imaging remain the most effective means of diagnosis, however, and in the presence of a characteristic scan[25] negative serology should not exclude the diagnosis of cysticercosis.[32]

The utility of drug therapy for neurocysticercosis is currently controversial. Initially, a number of nonrandomized case series (each involving small numbers of treated patients who were compared with historical control subjects) suggested that both praziquantel and albendazole hastened the clearance of cysticercal lesions seen on computed tomography or magnetic resonance imaging.[33] Since these initial reports, concurrently controlled, randomized trials have indicated that anthelmintic therapy given with corticosteroids is not superior to corticosteroid therapy alone for long-term control of seizures or resolution of *intraparenchymal* CNS cysticerci.[24, 34] Other reports have indicated that anthelmintic therapy may exacerbate obstruction of cerebrospinal fluid flow, enhance eye inflammation in ocular disease, and increase the risk of pericystic vasculitis, with increased risk of stroke.[24, 35, 36] Thus, the risk-benefit ratio for treating disease limited to the CNS parenchyma appears unfavorable. Still, randomized, well-controlled trials have not yet been done for treatment of other forms of neurocysticercosis (i.e., intraventricular, basilar, and spinal cysticercosis), and the true value of drug treatment for these forms of the disease is not known. However, because drug treatment of *intraventricular* cysts may prove efficacious and because of the higher risk for disease progression, therapy for this form of the disease is currently recommended by experienced groups.

If, on the basis of a review of the latest literature, the decision is made to treat an individual patient with complicated neurocysticercosis medically, then treatment should generally be given with high doses of either praziquantel (50 mg/kg/day for 15 to 30 days)[14, 26, 33, 37] or albendazole (10 to 15 mg/kg/day for 8 days)[38] with the goal of achieving drug levels sufficient to kill remaining living cysts. As noted earlier, cyst death is often accompanied by increased local inflammation, leading to an increase in symptoms. Before, during, and after drug therapy, seizures should be controlled with appropriate antiepileptic medications, and symptomatic hydrocephalus should be relieved by shunting. Shunt complications caused by blockage and bacterial infection are common in patients with neurocysticercosis.[39] CNS inflammation can be reduced by concurrent administration of pharmacologic doses of corticosteroids (dexamethasone);[40] however, corticosteroids do not necessarily eliminate the risk of serious complications such as infarction[36, 41] or intracranial pressure elevation.[42] Limited pharmacologic evidence suggests that concurrent corticosteroid therapy lowers serum praziquantel levels.[43] In contrast, corticosteroid therapy may (variably) increase circulating levels of albendazole and its active metabolites in some patients.[44] On this basis, some experts favor the use of albendazole for medical treatment of neurocysticercosis.[38, 42]

A poor response to either surgical or drug therapy is more common with intraventricular or cisternal cysts and with racemose neurocysticercosis.[33] For these lesions, the drug levels achieved in the cerebrospinal fluid and cyst during medical therapy are likely to be lower than for parenchymal CNS cysts, making drug failure more likely. Surgical approaches to these areas are difficult, and local inflammation may prevent easy removal of the cyst. Retained cyst material may result in postoperative recurrence. Nevertheless, successful therapy of ventricular and basilar cysts has been achieved in a minority of patients by either medical or surgical means.[45, 46] Individualized therapy, possibly including a combined surgical-medical approach, is recommended in such cases.[24]

Echinococcosis (Hydatid and Alveolar Cyst Disease)

When humans serve as inadvertent intermediate hosts for cestodes of *Echinococcus* spp., which are carried as tapeworms by canines such as dogs, wolves, and foxes, disease may result from the development of expanding parasite cysts in visceral organs.[2, 47] This condition, termed *echinococcosis*, has two forms: hydatid or unilocular cyst disease, caused by *Echinococcus granulosus* or *Echinococcus vogeli*, and alveolar cyst disease, caused by *Echinococcus multilocularis*. Sheep, goats, camels, and horses are among the usual intermediate hosts for *E. granulosus*, but because *E. granulosus* is transmitted by domestic dogs in livestock-raising areas, hydatid disease is prevalent worldwide (Africa, Middle East, southern Europe, Latin America, southwestern United States). Infections with *E. multilocularis*, found in northern forest areas of Europe, Asia, and North America, and in the Arctic regions, and infections with *E. vogeli*, found in South American highlands, are transmitted by wild canines and are much less common.

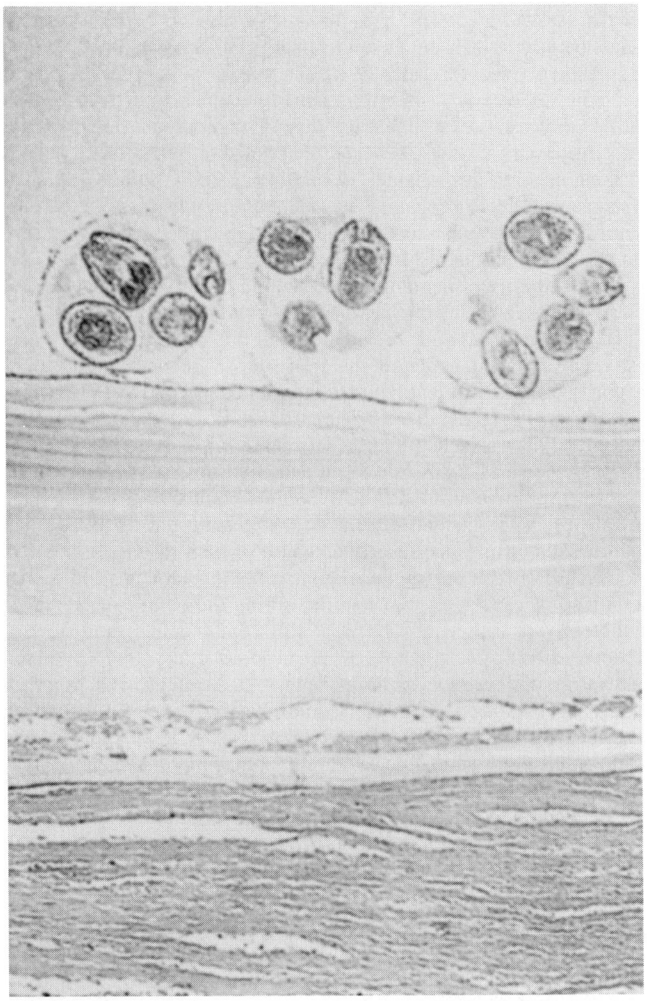

FIGURE 280–5. Daughter cyst formation from the germinal membrane of a hydatid cyst. (From Ash LR, Orihel TC. Atlas of Human Parasitology. 3rd ed. Chicago: ASCP; 1990.)

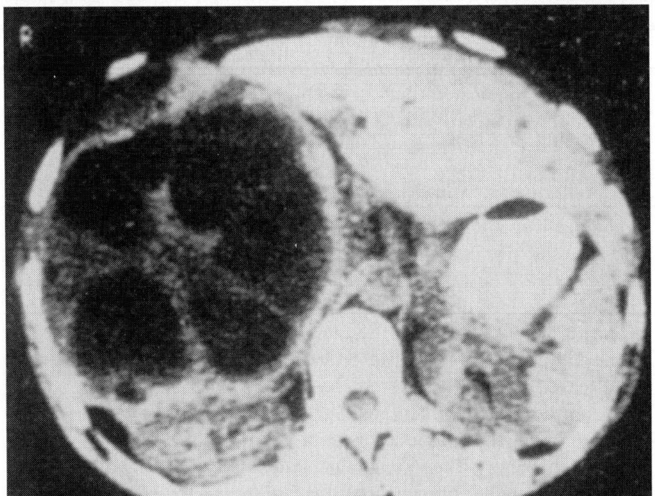

FIGURE 280–4. Hydatid cyst of the liver detected on computed tomographic scanning. Note the well-demarcated wall and characteristic septate internal structures (daughter cysts).

Humans acquire echinococcosis by ingesting viable parasite eggs with their food.[2, 47] The parasite eggs are distributed via local environmental contamination by the feces of tapeworm-infected canines. Eggs are partially resistant to desiccation and remain viable for many weeks,[4] allowing delayed transmission to individuals with no direct contact with vector animals. Once in the intestinal tract, the eggs hatch to form oncospheres that penetrate the mucosa and enter the circulation. Oncospheres then encyst in host viscera, developing over time to form mature larval cysts (Fig. 280–4).

The hydatid cysts of *E. granulosus* tend to form in the liver (50 to 70% of patients) or lung (20 to 30%) but may be found in any organ of the body, including brain, heart, and bones (<10%). These grow to 5 to 10 cm in size within the first year and can survive for years or even decades. Symptoms are often absent and, in many cases, infection is detected only incidentally by imaging studies. When symptoms do occur, they are usually due to the mass effect of the enlarging cyst in a confined space. Hydatid cysts contain a germinal layer that allows asexual budding to form "daughter" cysts within the primary cyst (Fig. 280–5). If a cyst erodes into the biliary tree or a bronchus, the cyst contents, including daughter cysts, may enter the lumen and cause obstruction or postobstructive bacterial infection. Bacteria may enter the cyst, causing pyogenic abscess formation within the cyst. Cyst leakage or rupture may be associated with a severe allergic reaction to parasite antigens; in the most extreme cases, patients may have anaphylactoid reactions, including hypotension, syncope, and fever, after cyst rupture. A dangerous complication of cyst rupture is secondary seeding of daughter cysts into other areas of the body. Their subsequent enlargement may be associated with critical failure of one or more organs, associated with significant morbidity and mortality. Less than 10% of patients develop such complications; because the infection is normally self-limited, it is likely that most infections never come to medical attention.[48] Nevertheless, symptomatic cysts should be treated and asymptomatic cysts carefully observed over a number of years to avert complications of infection.

Infection suspected on the basis of imaging studies (ultrasonography, computed tomography, magnetic resonance imaging) may be confirmed by specific enzyme-linked immunosorbent assay and Western blot serology (available in the United States through the Centers for Disease Control and Prevention), confirming exposure to the parasite.[49–51] Serology is 80 to 100% sensitive and 88 to 96% specific for liver cyst infection but less sensitive for lung (50 to 56%) or other organ involvement (25 to 56%). Assays are under development using recombinant *Echinococcus* antigens, which may provide better specificity for diagnosis.[52, 53] Imaging remains more sensitive than serodiagnosis, and a characteristic scan in the presence of negative serologic results should still suggest the diagnosis of echinococcosis.[48]

Optimal treatment of symptomatic cysts is by surgical resection to remove the cyst in toto. For surgical removal of hydatid cysts, because there is risk of spreading infection if the cyst ruptures, the recommended approach is to visualize the cyst, remove a fraction of the fluid, and instill a cysticidal agent, hypertonic (30%) saline, iodophor, or 95% ethanol, to kill the germinal layer and daughter cysts before resection.[2] Thirty minutes after instillation, the cyst should be totally removed, leaving a number of drains in the cyst bed to limit the risk of secondary bacterial infection. Cysts communicating with the biliary tree or branches should not have a cysticidal agent instilled because of the risk of postoperative sclerosing cholangitis.[47, 54] It may be prudent to treat the patient perioperatively with anthelmintic active against *Echinococcus* cysts (albendazole, mebendazole)[55–57] to limit further the risk of intraoperative dissemination of daughter cysts. Medical therapy for inoperative cysts with either albendazole or mebendazole has provided improvement in most patients (55 to 79%) and cure in a minority (29%).[55–57] The preferred agent is albendazole: three or more cycles of 400 mg of albendazole twice a day for 4 weeks, followed by a 2-week rest period without therapy, because of its greater absorption from the gastrointestinal tract and higher plasma levels. The alternative agent, mebendazole, is poorly absorbed and must be taken at higher doses (50 to 70 mg/kg/day) for several months to achieve a therapeutic effect.[56, 57] Response to drug therapy depends on the cyst size and location.[56, 58] Unfortunately, bone cysts, which are frequently not amenable to surgery, respond less well to drug treatment than other cysts. Response to drug therapy is best monitored by serial imaging studies; cyst disappearance, or shrinkage along with increasing cyst density, is thought to indicate a positive response.

An intermediate intervention for inoperable cysts has been developed, known as the PAIR procedure (for puncture, aspiration, injection, and reaspiration).[47, 57, 59, 60] While the patient is receiving anthelmintics to reduce the risk of cyst dissemination, the hydatid cyst may be aspirated with a thin needle under computed tomographic guidance. Approximately 30% of the cyst fluid volume is removed. Detection of protoscolices in the cyst fluid allows confirmation of cyst viability. An equal volume of 95% ethanol or other scolicidal agent is then instilled into the cyst cavity and allowed to react for 30 minutes before removal of the needle. Results indicate arrest or involution of cysts after treatment. Although this approach offers possible treatment for inoperable cysts, experience with the procedure is limited and the risks remain incompletely defined.

Alveolar cyst disease caused by *E. multilocularis* is more aggressive. *E. multilocularis* cysts reproduce asexually by lateral budding. Their gradual invasion of adjacent tissue is tumorlike, and sections of the parasite may "metastasize" to distal parts of the body.[2, 47] Symptoms are usually of gradual onset, referring to the organ of involvement, which is most commonly the liver. Complications include biliary tract disease, portal hypertension, and Budd-Chiari syndrome. Initial imaging studies are usually highly suspicious for carcinoma or sarcoma, and biopsy may provide the first indication of infection. Serology, available from the Centers for Disease Control and Prevention, combined with characteristic imaging studies, is an alternative means of establishing the diagnosis.[61, 62] For operable cases, wide surgical resection (e.g., hepatic lobectomy or liver transplantation) is recommended to ensure total removal of the cyst.[57, 63] Adjuvant albendazole therapy, either to reduce worm size before surgery or to limit intraoperative spread, has been reported to be beneficial in case series.[55, 61, 62] For inoperable cases, drug therapy with mebendazole or albendazole has provided arrest or cure of disease in some patients.[55, 57] Efficacy of surgical or drug therapy may be monitored by serial imaging and serology.

Other Invasive Cestodes

Human tissue infection with plerocercoid cysts of several different cestode species is referred to, collectively, as *sparganosis*. These parasites, like *D. latum*, pass through several developmental stages in copepods and vertebrates.[1] The definitive host forms of tapeworms of these species are usually canines or felines. Humans acquire inadvertent parasite infection by ingestion of copepods (in water) or by consumption of or prolonged exposure to uncooked meat of plerocercoid-infected animals.[64–66] Sparganosis has been reported in South America, Japan, China, and other parts of Asia in association with traditional use of frog- or snake-meat poultices. Infection has rarely been reported from Europe and North America. Sparganosis may be of the proliferating or nonproliferating type. Infection acquired in the United States is usually due to the species *S. mansonoides*, which is nonproliferating. In other areas of the world, proliferating forms are more common. These branch by lateral division and may detach to spread to other, distal areas of the body.[64] Clinical presentation typically involves local inflammation at the site of invasion (skin and eye are the most common sites with poultice application). There is local lymphocytic and eosinophilic inflammation surrounding the parasite(s). Tissue injury may be particularly severe in the eye. Diagnosis is usually by biopsy, although serologic testing is under development.[67] Treatment is by injection with ethanol, surgical resection, or both. Medical therapy with various anthelmintics has not shown a beneficial effect.

Coenurosis is human cyst infection with the cestodes *T. multiceps, Taenia crassiceps*, and *Taenia serialis*, which cause tapeworms in dogs.[1] The cysts are unilocular, with multiple protoscolices, but do not contain daughter cysts. Symptomatic disease is usually associated with involvement of the eye or the CNS. Clinically, the cysts may be difficult to distinguish from cysticercosis or hydatid disease. Basal arachnoiditis and hydrocephalus are common. Surgical resection is the recommended mode of therapy.[68]

PREVENTION OF CESTODE INFECTION

Prevention of cestode infection depends on interruption of the parasite life cycle. Transmission of human tapeworm infection can be reduced or eliminated by the following sanitary measures: (1) careful disposal of human sewage to limit environmental spread of parasite eggs; (2) limitation of forage areas and use of safe feeds for vector animals such as cattle or swine that serve as common intermediate hosts; (3) meat inspection before marketing to exclude cyst-infested carcasses; and (4) prolonged freezing (<18°C) or thorough cooking of meat (>50°C), or both, to kill any cysts in the tissues. Control of fish tapeworm is more difficult to achieve, because the fish vectors can range freely, and there are nonhuman reservoirs for the tapeworm (e.g., bear, seals) that can continue to infect vector fish despite the presence of good human sanitation.

Prevention of invasive cestode infection is more complex. Because this form of human infection results from egg ingestion and eggs may have been spread throughout an area by free-ranging definitive hosts such as dogs or humans, infection may be difficult to avoid. It is significant that half of patients with hydatid cysts do not recall specific exposure to dogs, although they may have resided in or visited an area of endemicity. Successful control of *E. granulosus* transmission has been achieved by regular screening and treatment of dogs in areas of endemicity in New Zealand, Tasmania, and the British Isles[69] to eliminate adult tapeworm carriage and local release of eggs. Treatment of human carriers in areas in which *T. solium* is endemic has proved effective in controlling transmission of cysticercosis.[70] Field trials also indicate that anti-*Echinococcus* and anti-cysticercus vaccines can significantly reduce infection in farm animals (sheep, pigs), which may further lower the level of peridomestic transmission.[71, 72]

In areas of good sanitation (e.g., the United States) autochthonous transmission of cysticercosis is rare but can occur in settings in which a *T. solium* tapeworm–carrying individual shares living or cooking quarters with susceptible individuals.[19–21] Screening of immigrants from *T. solium*–endemic areas and treatment of identified tapeworm infections would eliminate the risk of cysticercosis transmission to nontravelers.[19]

REFERENCES

1. Schantz PM. Tapeworms (cestodiasis). Gastroenterol Clin North Am. 1996;25:637–653.
2. Schantz PM, Okelo GBA. Echinococcosis (hydatidosis). In: Warren KS, Mahmoud AAF, eds. Tropical and Geographical Medicine. 2nd ed. New York: McGraw-Hill; 1990:505.
3. Ash LR, Orihel TC. Atlas of Human Parasitology. 3rd ed. Chicago: ASCP; 1990.
4. Wachira TM, Macpherson CN, Gathuma JM. Release and survival of *Echinococcus* eggs in different environments in Turkana, and their possible impact on the incidence of hydatidosis in man and livestock. J Helminthol. 1991;65:55–61.
5. Bresson-Hadni S, Liance M, Meyer JP, et al. Cellular immunity in experimental *Echinococcus multilocularis* infection. II. Sequential and comparative phenotypic study of the periparasitic mononuclear cells in resistant and sensitive mice. Clin Exp Immunol. 1990;82:378–383.
6. Williams JF. Cestode infections. In: Cohen S, Warren KS, eds. Immunology of Parasitic Infections. 2nd ed. London: Blackwell; 1982:676.
7. Baron RW, Tanner CE. The effect of immunosuppression on secondary *Echinococcus multilocularis* infections in mice. Int J Parasitol. 1976;6:37–42.
8. Rau ME, Tanner CE. BCG suppresses growth and metastasis of hydatid infections. Nature. 1975;256:318–319.
9. Deardorff TL, Kent ML. Prevalence of larval *Anisakis simplex* in pen-reared and wild-caught salmon (Salmonidae) from Puget Sound, Washington. J Wildl Dis. 1989;25:416–419.
10. Ebe T, Matsumura M, Mori T, et al. Eight cases of diphyllobothriasis. Kansenshogaku Zasshi. 1990;64:328–334.
11. Ash LR, Orihel TC. Parasites, a Guide to Laboratory Procedures and Identification. Chicago: ASCP Press; 1987.
12. See Centers for Disease Control and Prevention Internet site, www.dpd.cdc.gov/dpdx.
13. Anthelmintics. In: Drug Evaluations Subscription. Chicago: American Medical Association; III/INFM-4, Winter 1992.
14. Drugs for parasitic infections. Med Lett Drugs Ther 1998;40:1–12.
15. Yoeli M, Most H, Hammond J, et al. Parasitic infections in a closed community. Results of a 10-year survey in Willowbrook State School. Trans R Soc Trop Med Hyg. 1972;66:764–766.
16. Muratov IV, Posokhov PS, Romanenko NA, et al. The infectivity of the population with the tapeworm *Diphyllobothrium klebanovskii* in an area of infection drift in the Khabarovsk Territory. Med Parazitol (Mosk). 1992;2:30–32.
17. Curtis MA, Bylund G. Diphyllobothriasis: Fish tapeworm disease in the circumpolar north. Arctic Med Res. 1991;50:18–24.
18. Eom KS, Kim SH, Rim HJ. Second case of human infection with *Mesocestoides lineatus* in Korea. Kisaengchung Hak Chapchi. 1992;30:147–150.
19. Schantz PM, Moore AC, Munoz JL, et al. Neurocysticercosis in an Orthodox Jewish community in New York City. N Engl J Med. 1992;327:692–695.
20. Centers for Disease Control and Prevention. Locally acquired neurocysticercosis—North Carolina, Massachusetts, and South Carolina 1989–1991. MMWR Morb Mortal Wkly Rep 1992;41:1–4.
21. Kruskal BA, Moths L, Teele DW. Neurocysticercosis in a child with no history of travel outside the continental United States. Clin Infect Dis. 1993;16:290–292.
22. Sarti E, Schantz PM, Plancarte A, et al. Prevalence and risk factors for *Taenia solium* taeniasis and cysticercosis in humans and pigs in a village in Morelos, Mexico. Am J Trop Med Hyg. 1992;46:677–685.
23. Salata RA, King CH, Malmoud AAF. Parasitic infections in the central nervous system. In: Aminoff MJ, ed. Neurology and General Medicine. New York: Churchill Livingstone; 1989:643.
24. White AC Jr. Neurocysticercosis: A major cause of neurological disease worldwide. Clin Infect Dis. 1997;24:101–115.
25. Case Records of the Massachusetts General Hospital. Case 8–1993. N Engl J Med. 1993;328:566–573.
26. Sotelo J, Escobedo F, Rodriguez-Carbajal J, et al. Therapy of parenchymal brain cysticercosis with praziquantel. N Engl J Med. 1984;310:1001–1007.
27. Teitelbaum GP, Otto RJ, Lin M, et al. MR imaging of neurocysticercosis. AJR. 1989;153:857–866.
28. Rajshekar V, Chandy MJ. Comparative study of CT and MRI in patients with seizures and a solitary cerebral cysticercus granuloma. Neuroradiology. 1996;38:542–546.
29. Diaz JF, Verastegui M, Gilman RH, et al. Immunodiagnosis of human cysticercosis (*Taenia solium*): A field comparison of an antibody-enzyme-linked immunosorbent assay (ELISA), an antigen-ELISA, and an enzyme-linked immunoelectrotransfer blot (EITB) assay in Peru. The Cysticercosis Working Group in Peru (CWG). Am J Trop Med Hyg. 1992;46:610–615.
30. Tsang VCW, Brand JA, Boyer AE. An enzyme-linked immunoelectrotransfer blot assay and glycoprotein antigens for diagnosing human cysticercosis (*Taenia solium*). J Infect Dis. 1989;159:50–59.
31. Wilson M, Bryan RT, Fried JA, et al. Clinical evaluation of the cysticercosis enzyme-linked immunoelectrotransfer blot in patients with neurocysticercosis. J Infect Dis. 1991;164:1007–1009.
32. Richards F Jr, Schantz PM. Laboratory diagnosis of cysticercosis. Clin Lab Med. 1991;11:1011–1028.
33. Del Brutto OH, Sotelo J. Neurocysticercosis: An update. Rev Infect Dis. 1988;10:1075–1087.
34. Carpio A, Santillan F, Leon P, et al. Is the course of neurocysticercosis modified by treatment with antihelminthic agents? Arch Intern Med. 1995;155:1982–1988. [See comment by Del Brutto OH and reply by Carpio A et al. Arch Intern Med. 1997;157:128–130.]
35. Evans C, Garcia HH, Gilman RH, Friedland JS. Controversies in the management of cysticercosis. Emerg Infect Dis. 1997;3:403–405.
36. Bang OY, Heo JH, Choi SA, Kim DI. Large cerebral infarction during praziquantel therapy in neurocysticercosis. Stroke. 1997;28:211–213. [See comment by Del Brutto OH. Stroke. 1997;28:1088.]
37. Vasconcelos D, Cruz-Segura H, Mateos-Gomez H, et al. Selective indications for the use of praziquantel in the treatment of brain cysticercosis. J Neurol Neurosurg Psychiatry. 1987;50:383–388.
38. Sotelo J, Escobedo F, Penagos P. Albendazole vs pranziquantel for therapy for neurocysticercosis: A controlled trial. Arch Neurol. 1988;45:532–534.
39. Sotelo J, Marin C. Hydrocephalus secondary to cysticercotic arachnoiditis: A long-term follow-up review of 92 cases. J Neurosurg. 1987;66:686–689.
40. deGhetaldi LD, Norman RM, Douville AW. Cerebral cysticercosis treated biphasically with dexamethasone and pranziquantel. Ann Intern Med. 1983;99:179–181.
41. Woo E, Yu YL, Huang CY. Cerebral infarct precipitated by pranziquantel in neurocysticercosis—A cautionary note. Trop Geogr Med. 1988;40:143–146.
42. Takayangui OM, Jardim E. Therapy for neurocysticercosis: Comparison between albendazole and pranziquantel. Arch Neurol. 1992;49:290–294.
43. Vazquez ML, Jung H, Sotelo J. Plasma levels of pranziquantel decrease when dexamethasone is given simultaneously. Neurology. 1987;37:1561–1562.
44. Jung H, Hurtado M, Medina MT, et al. Dexamethasone increases plasma levels of albendazole. J Neurol. 1990;237:279–280.
45. Del Brutto OH, Sotelo J. Albendazole therapy for subarachnoid and ventricular cysticercosis: A case report. J Neurosurg. 1990;72:816–817.
46. Cuetter AC, Garcia-Bobadilla J, Guerra LG, et al. Neurocysticercosis: Focus on intraventricular disease. Clin Infect Dis. 1997;24:157–164.
47. Ammann RW, Eckert J. Cestodes. *Echinococcus*. Gastroenterol Clin North Am. 1996;25:655–689.
48. MacPherson CNL, Romig T, Zeyhle E, et al. Portable ultrasound scanner versus serology in screening for hydatid cysts in a nomadic population. Lancet. 1987;2:259–261.
49. Force L, Torres JM, Carrillo A, et al. Evaluation of eight serological tests in the diagnosis of human echinococcosis and follow-up. Clin Infect Dis. 1992;15:473–480.
50. Leggatt GR, Yang W, McManus DP. Serological evaluation of the 12 kDa subunit of antigen B in *Echinococcus granulosus* cyst fluid by immunoblot analysis. Trans R Soc Trop Med Hyg. 1992;86:189–192.
51. Verastegui M, Moro P, Guevara A, et al. Enzyme-linked immunoelectrotransfer blot test for diagnosis of human hydatid disease. J Clin Microbiol. 1992;30:1557–1561.
52. Blanton RE, Okelo GBA, Kijobe J, et al. Antibody responses to in vitro translation products following albendazole therapy for *Echinococcus granulosus*. Antimicrob Agents Chemother. 1991;35:1674–1676.
53. Chamekh M, Gras-Masse H, Bossus M, et al. Diagnostic value of a synthetic peptide derived from *Echinococcus granulosus* recombinant protein. J Clin Invest. 1992;89:458–464.
54. Teres J, Gomez J, Bouguera M, et al. Sclerosing cholangitis after surgical treatment of hepatic echinococcal cysts: Report of three cases. Am J Surg. 1984;148:694–697.
55. Ammann RW. Improvement of liver resectional therapy by adjuvant chemotherapy

in alveolar hydatid disease. Swiss Echinococcosis Study Group (SESG). Parasitol Res. 1991;77:290–293.
56. Davis A, Dixon H, Pawlowski ZS. Multicentre clinical trials of benzimidazole-carbamates in human cystic echinococcus (phase 2). Bull World Health Organ. 1989;67:503–508.
57. WHO. Guidelines for treatment of cystic and alveolar echinococcosis in humans. Bull World Health Organ. 1996;74:231–242.
58. Todorov T, Mechkov G, Vutova K, et al. Factors influencing the response to chemotherapy in human cystic echinococcus. Bull World Health Organ. 1992;70:347–358.
59. Filice C, Di Perri G, Strosselli M, et al. Parasitologic findings in percutaneous drainage of human hydatid liver cysts. J Infect Dis. 1990;161:1290–1295.
60. Mawhorter S, Temeck B, Chang R, et al. Nonsurgical therapy for pulmonary hydatid cyst disease. Chest. 1997;112:1432–1436.
61. Gottstein B, Tschudi K, Eckert J, et al. Em2-ELISA for the follow-up of alveolar *Echinococcus* after complete surgical resection of liver lesions. Trans R Soc Trop Med Hyg. 1989;383:389–393.
62. Wilson JF, Rausch RL, McMahon BJ, et al. Albendazole therapy in alveolar hydatid disease: A report of favorable results in two patients after short-term therapy. Am J Trop Med Hyg. 1987;37:162–168.
63. Mboti B, Van de Stadt J, Carlier Y, et al. Long-term disease-free survival after liver transplantation for alveolar echinococcosis. Acta Chir Belg. 1996;96:229–232.
64. Kim DG, Paek SH, Chang KH, et al. Cerebral sparganosis: Clinical manifestations, treatment and outcome. J Neurosurg. 1996;85:1066–1071.
65. Kron MA, Guderian R, Guevara A, et al. Abdominal sparganosis in Ecuador: A case report. Am J Trop Med Hyg. 1991;44:146–150.
66. Nakamura T, Hara M, Matsuoka M, et al. Human proliferative sparganosis. A new Japanese case. Am J Clin Pathol. 1990;94:224–228.
67. Cho SY, Kang SY, Kong Y. Purification of antigenic protein of sparganum by immunoaffinity chromatography using a monoclonal antibody. Kisaengchung Hak Chapchi. 1990;28:135–142.
68. Pau A, Perria C, Turtas S, et al. Long-term follow-up of the surgical treatment of intracranial coenurosis. Br J Neurosurg. 1990;4:39–43.
69. Gemmell MA. Australasian contributions to an understanding of the epidemiology and control of hydatid disease caused by *Echinococcus granulosus*—past, present and future. Int J Parasitol. 1990;20:431–456.
70. Cruz M, Davis A, Dixon H, et al. Operational studies on the control of *Taenia solium* taeniasis/cysticercosis in Ecuador. Bull World Health Organ. 1989;67:401–407.
71. Molinari JL, Rodriguez D, Tato P, et al. Field trial for reducing porcine *Taenia solium* cysticercosis in Mexico by systematic vaccination of pigs. Vet Parasitol. 1997;69:55–63.
72. Heath DD, Holcman B. Vaccination against *Echinococcus* in perspective. Acta Trop. 1997;67:37–41.

Chapter 281

Visceral Larva Migrans and Other Unusual Helminth Infections

THEODORE E. NASH

EOSINOPHILIA: CLINICAL SIGNIFICANCE

Eosinophilia is commonly, but not always, associated with invasive helminth infections and, when encountered, suggests their presence. The degree of eosinophilia can vary dramatically and is influenced by a number of factors. Helminths whose migrations through tissues are limited, such as infections localized to the skin or intestinal lumen, are associated with little or no eosinophilic response. However, helminths that migrate through the internal or visceral organs, either as part of their normal life cycle or ectopically, usually cause eosinophilia. Once the migration is completed and the tissues are no longer exposed to the parasite, eosinophilia wanes. In some helminth infections, the parasites are effectively separated from the host by encystment or a walling off process that limits the eosinophilic response. Acute, compared with chronic, infections tend to provoke higher responses, as do heavy compared with light infections. Eosinophilia also depends on the ability of the host to respond. Expected responses may not be found in septic patients or in some immunologically impaired patients. Although many helminths may cause eosinophilia, in most instances the possibilities can be narrowed by understanding the possible exposures; life cycle; prepatent and incubation periods; usual disease manifestations; and expected laboratory findings. The diagnostic procedures used to detect infections differ for each parasite, so that a clear idea of the potential causes is essential. The physician must understand the sensitivity of the diagnostic procedures and the abilities of the laboratory personnel performing them. For example, intestinal ascaris infections are readily detected. On the other hand, some parasitic infections, such as infection with the larvae of strongyloides or the ova of intestinal schistosomes, may be difficult to detect, and special stool concentration methods may be needed. Patients may present during the prepatent period before the parasite can be detected, such as in ascariasis or schistosomiasis. Repeated stool examinations eventually diagnose both infections. The usefulness of serologic testing varies, but serologic tests can be very helpful both in suggesting diagnoses and in ruling out infections. Few serologic tests for parasitic infections have been standardized, so the sensitivity and specificity may differ from published values and from laboratory to laboratory.

Most helminths that infect humans are relatively host-specific to humans, undergo characteristic migration and development, and are found in typical anatomic locations. However, these helminths may at times undergo atypical or aborted migrations and cause symptoms or signs because of their unusual or ectopic location. A good example of this is the deposition of schistosomal ova and the subsequent granulomatous, inflammatory lesions in the spinal cord or brain in schistosomal infections. Helminths of animals can also infect humans. Some helminths, such as *Echinococcus granulosus* and *Trichinella spiralis,* commonly infect humans, migrate and develop normally, and reside in similar locations as in the usual host. In contrast, other helminths of animals are unable to develop or migrate normally. Commonly, they undergo prolonged, aberrant migrations or locate abnormally in the tissues as underdeveloped larvae, inciting an eosinophilic inflammation that is responsible for many of the symptoms and signs of these infections. Although a large number of animal parasites may infect humans, most do so rarely. In contrast, some helminths of animals infect humans more commonly and cause distinctive clinical syndromes (Table 281–1) sometimes associated with characteristic epidemiology, exposure history, and geographic locations. More often than not, similar clinical syndromes are caused by a group of related parasites. The diagnosis is suggested on clinical and epidemiologic grounds. Although pathologic examination of tissue can sometimes establish the diagnosis, the detection of larvae is commonly unrewarding. Serologic tests are at times helpful (see "Visceral Larva Migrans [Toxocariasis]"), but usually are either not fully evaluated, are experimental, or are unavailable.

Visceral Larva Migrans (Toxocariasis)

Visceral larva migrans (VLM) is a syndrome characterized in its most florid state by eosinophilia, fever, and hepatomegaly. It is caused primarily by infection with *Toxocara canis* but also by *Toxicara cati* and other helminths less frequently.[1–3]

Life Cycle in the Dog

T. canis infects dogs and related mammals by a number of mechanisms.[1] Most commonly, ingested eggs hatch in the small intestine, and the resulting larvae migrate to the liver, lung, and trachea. They are then swallowed and mature in the lumen of the small intestine, where eggs are shed. Other larvae migrate to and remain dormant in the muscles but are capable of development even years after the primary infection, particularly in pregnant bitches. During pregnancy, larvae again develop and infect the pups transplacentally and transmammarily. Not uncommonly, infective larvae are found in the feces

TABLE 281–1 Clinical Syndromes Associated with Unusual Helminth Infections in Humans

Clinical Syndromes	Parasite	Usual Host
Visceral larva migrans	*Toxocara canis*	Dogs
	Toxocara cati	Felines
	Balyisascaris procyonis	Raccoon
Eosinophilic gastroenteritis	*Anisakis* spp.	Sea mammals
	Phocanema spp.	Sea mammals
	Ancylostoma caninum	Canines
Cutaneous larva migrans	*Ancylostoma braziliense*	Canines, felines
	Ancylostoma caninum	Dogs and cats
Eosinophilic meningitis	*Angiostrongylus cantonensis*	Rat
	Gnathostoma spinigerum	Feline, other mammals
Pulmonary or cutaneous nodules	*Dirofilaria* spp.	Dog, other mammals
Abdominal angiostrongyliasis	*Angiostrongylus costaricensis*	Cotton rat
Capillariasis	*Capillaria philippinensis*	?
Diarrhea	*Nanophyetus salmincola*	Mammals, birds
Swimmer's itch	*Trichobilharzia* spp.	Birds

of the pups. Eggs are not infectious when passed in the feces and take 3 to 4 weeks to develop. They are hardy and often remain viable for months. Large numbers of viable eggs contaminate the environment because of the high prevalence of infection in dogs and the ability of eggs to survive relatively harsh environmental conditions.

Infection in Humans

Prevalence. Toxocariasis is prevalent wherever dogs are found and *Toxocara* eggs are able to survive. The prevalence of infection or disease in humans is not known, but seroepidemiologic studies show wide differences in prevalence depending on the population tested. In the United States, seropositivity ranged from 2.8%[4] in an unselected population to 23.1%[5] in a kindergarten population in the southern United States to 54%[6] in a selected rural community. None of the seropositive persons had recognizable disease.

Clinical Manifestations. VLM occurs most commonly in children younger than 6 years.[3, 4] Disease manifestations vary and range from asymptomatic infection to fulminant disease and death, but it is increasingly appreciated that most infections are asymptomatic. Those who come to medical attention most commonly complain of cough, fever, wheezing, and other generalized symptoms.[3–7] The liver is the organ most frequently involved, and hepatomegaly is a common finding, although almost any organ can be affected. Splenomegaly occurs in a minority, and lymphadenopathy has been noted. Lung involvement with radiologic findings has been documented in 32 to 44%, but respiratory distress occurs rarely. Skin lesions such urticaria and nodules have also been described. Seizures have been noted to occur with increased frequency in VLM, but severe neurologic involvement is infrequent. Eye involvement in VLM is unusual but has been documented (see "Ocular Larva Migrans"). Eosinophilia, usually accompanied by leukocytosis, is the hallmark of VLM. Other laboratory findings include hypergammaglobulinemia and elevated isohemagglutinin titers to A and B blood group antigens, which are due to the host's immune response to cross-reacting antigens on the surface of *T. canis* larvae.

Diagnosis. The diagnosis of VLM is usually suggested clinically by the presence of eosinophilia or leukocytosis, or both, in a young child accompanied by hepatomegaly or signs and symptoms of other organ involvement. A history of pica and exposure to puppies is common. Patients are more commonly black and from rural areas. The diagnosis is definitively confirmed by finding larvae in the affected tissues by histologic examination or by digestion of tissue; however, larvae are frequently not found. The enzyme-linked immunosorbent assay (ELISA) employing extracts or excretory or secretory products of *T. canis* larvae appears specific and useful in confirming the clinical diagnosis.[8] However, *toxocara* antibody titers in populations without clinically apparent VLM vary dramatically, and elevated titers cannot definitively establish the diagnosis.

Differential Diagnosis. Eosinophilia, fever, and hepatomegaly are caused by other parasitic infections. *Balyisascaris procyonis* (an ascarid of raccoons) infection can cause a severe form of VLM commonly with incapacitating or mortal involvement of the central nervous system.[9] Others include acute schistosomiasis, *Fasciola hepatica* infections, *Ascaris lumbricoides* abscess of the liver, acute liver fluke infections (*Clonorchis sinensis* and *Opisthorchis viverrini*), complications from *Echinococcus* infection of the liver, *Capillaria hepatica*, and other invasive helminths. Diseases not caused by parasitic infections should also be considered. Children with mild disease may manifest only eosinophilia.

Treatment and Management. Most patients recover without specific therapy. Treatment with anti-inflammatory or anthelmintic drugs may be considered with severe complications that are usually due to involvement of the brain, lungs, or heart. There is no proven effective therapy, although albendazole, thiabendazole, mebendazole, diethylcarbamazine, and other anthelmintics have been used. Indeed, injury to the parasite may provoke a more intense inflammatory response leading to worsening of the clinical picture. Corticosteroids have been used with and without specific antilarval therapy, with some reports of improvement.

Prevention. VLM can be easily prevented by a number of simple but effective measures that prevent *T. canis* eggs from contaminating the environment and children from ingesting eggs. Dogs, particularly puppies, should be periodically tested and treated for *T. canis* and other worms. Pica should be prevented.

OCULAR LARVA MIGRANS

Ocular larva migrans is caused by an infection of the eye with *T. canis* larvae.[10] Although a present or past history of clinically recognized VLM has occasionally been noted, almost all patients present with unilateral eye involvement without a past history or present systemic symptoms or signs. Presumably, a larva by chance becomes entrapped in the eye, resulting in an eosinophilic inflammatory mass. Children are most commonly affected and, on the average, are older (mean, 8.6 years in one study) than those diagnosed with VLM. The findings are most commonly those of a posterior or peripheral inflammatory mass. In fact, this entity was first recognized after examination of eyes enucleated for the treatment of presumed retinoblastoma.[10]

Eosinophilia, hepatomegaly, and other signs and symptoms of VLM are lacking. The diagnosis is established clinically. Although the serum titers to *Toxocara* larvae are higher than those of a control population,[11] many patients with ocular larva migrans have low or negative titers. However, elevated vitreous[12] and aqueous fluid titers[13] to *Toxocara* larvae compared with serum levels have been documented and appear to be useful in establishing the diagnosis. There is no specific therapy.

A characteristic clinically recognizable syndrome, diffuse unilateral subacute neuroretinitis, is caused by infection with helminth larvae of uncertain species.[14, 15] A motile larva can commonly be found in or below the retina. Photocoagulation is curative. Anthelmintic therapy such as albendazole or thiabendazole may be effecitve.[15]

ANISAKIASIS

Anisakiasis is caused by the accidental infection of humans by larvae found in saltwater fish and squid. Definitive hosts are marine mammals. The clinical syndrome, caused by penetration of larvae into the stomach or small intestine and characterized by upper or lower, or both, abdominal symptoms, is suggested by a history of ingestion of raw, salted, pickled, smoked, or poorly cooked fish.

Life Cycle in Marine Mammals

Larvae of *Anisakis, Phocanema*, and occasionally other genera can accidentally infect humans.[1, 16–18] The adults are found in the stomach of marine mammals. The eggs, passed in the feces, hatch as free-swimming larvae, are ingested by certain crustaceans, and are eaten by fish and squid. When ingested by appropriate marine mammals, such as dolphins, seals, and whales, the larvae burrow head first into the stomach. When consumed by humans, the larvae attempt and many times succeed in burrowing into the stomach or intestine, resulting in typical symptoms.

Clinical Syndrome

Anisakiasis occurs after the ingestion of raw or improperly cooked marine fish. The disease, initially recognized in The Netherlands after the ingestion of raw herring, is most frequently reported from Japan, where raw fish are commonly eaten. In the United States, infection is still uncommon but is now more frequently recognized because of increased ingestion of raw fish, particularly salmon. Cod, halibut, pollock, greenling, herring, and mackerel are other implicated fishes.

Clinical manifestations are caused by penetration of worms into the gastrointestinal tract, usually the stomach or lower small intestine, most commonly the ileum.[17–19] Occasionally, throat irritation is followed by coughing up the characteristic worm. Initial invasion is associated with acute symptoms, whereas the presence of worms for longer periods causes chronic symptoms. The location of the worms and symptoms depend somewhat on the genus, with *Phocanema* more commonly associated with infection of the stomach and *Anisakis* with the intestine. Symptoms usually occur within 48 hours after ingestion, but this pattern is variable. In gastric anisakiasis, patients complain of intense abdominal pain, nausea, and vomiting. Small intestinal involvement results in lower abdominal pain and signs of obstruction mimicking appendicitis. Symptoms may be chronic, sometimes lasting for months and, rarely, for years. These symptoms are associated with intestinal masses containing the parasite and are sometimes confused with tumor, regional enteritis, or diverticulitis. *Anisakis* larvae present in seafood have been implicated as a cause of acute allergic manifestations such as urticaria and anaphylaxis with or without accompanying abdominal gastrointestinal symptoms in patients who ingest raw fish.[20–23] In vitro studies and skin tests indicate that sensitization to *Anisakis* antigen is common in this population, whereas sensitization to fish is uncommon.[20, 22, 23]

Laboratory Findings. Eosinophilia is usually not present in either gastric or intestinal anisakiasis. Leukocytosis has been noted in almost two thirds of cases in one series with intestinal involvement.

Diagnosis. Anisakiasis should be considered in anyone with a history of ingestion of raw marine fish and suggestive abdominal symptoms. A definitive diagnosis can be established by endoscopy, radiographic studies, or pathologic examination of tissue. In the upper gastrointestinal tract, worms are found partially embedded in any area of the stomach and may be associated with localized mucosal edema, erosions, or mass lesions.[24, 25] Upper gastrointestinal radiographic studies may note the outline of a worm associated with mucosal edema or tumor formation. Removal of the worm during endoscopy definitively establishes the diagnosis and is curative.[19] Intestinal anisakiasis is diagnosed clinically. Varied degrees of thickening of the walls and narrowing of the lumen of the ileum or jejunum are found on radiographic studies.[24, 25] High-resolution ultrasonography has demonstrated small intestinal wall thickening and localized ascites around the involved section of bowel. Examination of aspirated ascites has revealed a preponderance of eosinophils.[26] Lesions resolve within 2 to 3 weeks.[24] Occasionally, removal of the intestinal mass is required to establish the diagnosis and effectively treat the patient. Tissues show inflammatory masses, many eosinophils, and the characteristic helminth. Serologic tests are not generally available and are of limited usefulness.

Treatment. Symptoms improve spontaneously in most patients without specific therapy, but treatment is hastened by removing worms lodged in the stomach during endoscopy. In one series of intestinal anisakiasis, all 12 patients became asymptomatic by 2 weeks.[24] One Japanese investigator commonly uses antacids after removal of stomach worms.

Prevention. Larvae resist heating up to 50°C, as well as pickling, salting, and some methods of smoking. Infection can be prevented by cooking or freezing fish for 24 hours before ingestion.

CUTANEOUS LARVA MIGRANS (CREEPING ERUPTION)

Cutaneous larva migrans is characterized as serpiginous, reddened, elevated, pruritic skin lesions usually caused by *Ancylostoma braziliense*, the dog and cat hookworm.[1, 27] Other animal hookworms including *Ancylostoma caninum, Uncinaria stenocephala, Bunostomum phlebotomum*, and others; the human hookworms, *Strongyloids stercoralis* and *Gnathostoma spinigerum*; and, rarely, insect larvae can cause similar findings. Like human hookworms, *A. braziliense* larvae infect dogs and cats by burrowing through the skin. The adults reside in the intestine and shed eggs, which undergo development into infectious larvae outside the body in places protected from desiccation and temperature extremes, such as sandy, shady areas around beaches or under houses. Infections are most common in warmer climates such as the southeastern United States and occur in children more commonly than in adults. Larvae penetrate the skin, causing tingling followed by itching, vesicle formation, and typically raised, reddened, serpiginous tracks that mark the prior route of the parasite.[1, 27, 28] In severe infections, persons may have hundreds of tracks. Little further development of the parasite occurs. Usually there are few, if any, systemic symptoms, but some reports have documented lung infiltrates and, rarely, severe lung dysfunction and recovery of parasites in the sputum. Eosinophilia has been noted in some infections.[28] The skin lesions are readily recognized, and the diagnosis is made clinically. Biopsy specimens usually show an eosinophilic inflammatory infiltrate, but the migrating parasite is usually not identified. For this reason, biopsies are usually not indicated to establish the diagnosis. Without treatment, skin lesions gradually disappear.[29] Both topical (10% aqueous suspension four times daily)[30] thiabendazole and oral administration (25 mg/kg twice daily for 2 days)[30] are effective. In one study, most patients treated with thiabendazole responded within the first week compared with the more than 4 weeks required for comparable improvement in the placebo-treated group.[29] Highly successful treatment with albendazole[31] (400 mg/kg for 3 to 7 days) or invermectin[32] (150 to 200 μg/kg given once) has been reported.

EOSINOPHILIC MENINGITIS THAT IS DUE TO HELMINTHS

Infection of humans with larvae of *Angiostrongylus cantonensis*, the rat lung worm, is characterized by invasion of the brain leading to signs and symptoms of meningitis associated with an eosinophilic pleocytosis in the cerebrospinal fluid (CSF) and peripheral eosinophilia.[33] The adults of *A. cantonensis* reside in the lungs of rats.[1] Eggs hatch in the lungs, and the larvae are swallowed, are expelled in the feces, and seek an appropriate molluscan intermediate host, where the parasite develops into the infective third-stage larva. Infective larvae are found in a number of mollusks including slugs, land snails, and a land planarian, but are also found in a number of unrelated animals including freshwater prawns, land and coconut crabs, and frogs. After ingestion by rats, the infective larvae migrate to the brain and eventually to the lungs. In humans, the migration of the larvae to the brain causes eosinophilic meningitis. Although adult worms do not develop in humans, it is unclear if the larvae remain in the central nervous system or are killed elsewhere.

Epidemics and sporadic infections occur most commonly in the South Pacific,[34] Southeast Asia,[35] and Taiwan.[36] The most commonly recognized sources of human infection are raw or undercooked snails, prawns, or crabs. Contamination of foods such as leafy vegetables by larvae deposited by slugs or snails may also occur. Clinical manifestations vary, and although fatalities occur, particularly in massive infections, most patients have a relatively uncomplicated course.[33–36] In one well-characterized epidemic, the incubation period ranged from 1 to 6 days after the ingestion of infected snails.[34] Symptoms include headache, stiff neck, fever, rash, pruritus, abdominal pain, constitutional complaints, nausea, and vomiting. Neurologic involvement varies from no complaints to paresthesias and pain, weakness, various focal neurologic findings (sixth and fourth cranial nerve palsies are frequently noted), coma, and death. In general, the patients do not appear to be as ill as in bacterial meningitis. Signs of meningitis are frequent but nonspecific. CSF leukocytosis with more than 10% eosinophils is always present. CSF glucose values are usually normal, but depressed values have been noted. A fall followed by a rise in the number of eosinophils in the CSF at 50 to 90 days has been documented in some patients, although they are usually asymptomatic.

The diagnosis is established clinically, but occasionally a characteristic larva is found in the CSF at the time of lumbar puncture. The diagnosis is suggested by a history of eating raw or partially cooked implicated foods and recent travel to endemic areas. Serologic tests have not been fully evaluated, nor are they readily available.

There is no proven therapy. Repeated CSF lumbar punctures appear to be helpful in treating associated headaches, presumably by decreasing CSF pressure. Recovery usually occurs by 2 months, although prolonged symptoms and signs have occasionally been noted.

Infection with *G. spinigerum* may also cause eosinophilic meningitis.[37, 38] Infections occur mostly in Southeast Asia, particularly in Thailand and Japan. The larvae migrate in the tissues and clinically cause intermittent swellings that are most noticeable in the subcutaneous tissues. Occasionally, the larvae find their way into the nervous system and cause a myeloencephalitis. Permanent neurologic deficits and death are more common than with *A. cantonensis*, and red blood cells are more likely to be found in the CSF. The diagnosis is established clinically, and serologic tests are not generally available. Other helminth infections such as cysticercosis and paragonimiasis can result in eosinophilic meningitis. Fatal eosinophilic meningoencephalitis due to infection with the raccoon ascarid *B. procyonis* has been described. Infection occurs after the accidental ingestion of *B. procyonis* eggs, which are found in raccoon feces.[39]

ABDOMINAL ANGIOSTRONGYLIASIS

Clinical manifestations of human infections of *Angiostrongylus costaricensis* are due to penetration and development of the parasite in the lower small bowel and adjacent colon and are characterized by abdominal pain, vomiting, and a right lower quadrant mass.[40] In the normal host, the rat, adult parasites reside in the arteries and arterioles of the ileocecal area of the intestine. Eggs are deposited in the tissue hatch, and the larvae escape in the feces. They are then ingested by the slug intermediate host and after further development become infectious for rats after ingestion. After maturation in the lymphatics, the larvae penetrate the arterioles and arteries in the ileocecal area of the rat, where they reside as adults. In humans, the parasite follows a similar pattern of migration, except that eggs are retained in the tissues and larvae do not appear in the feces. Adults are found most commonly in the arteries and arterioles around the ileocecum and deposit eggs there. Both the eggs and worms provoke an inflammatory response resulting in occluded vessels, an accompanying vasculitis, and an eosinophilic, granulomatous, edematous mass. Infections of humans, most commonly children, have been recognized in Central and South America and, rarely, Africa. The manner of human infection is not usually known, but it may occur after accidental ingestion of infected slugs or after ingestion of foods contaminated with larvae deposited in the mucous slime trail of slugs. Patients are mild to moderately ill and complain of abdominal pain and tenderness, vomiting, and fever, and in about 50% of the cases,[41] a right lower quadrant mass is noted. Surgery reveals that the cecum, ascending colon, ileum, and appendix are involved to varied degrees. The syndrome resembles appendicitis, except for the presence of eosinophilia and leukocytosis. The diagnosis is suspected clinically and confirmed by examination of biopsied or excised areas. Radiographic findings are nonspecific and show filling defects and spasticity of the ileum, cecum, or colon. Serologic tests are not generally available. Most patients undergo laparotomy with removal of the inflamed areas; the natural history of infected children is unclear. Some clinically diagnosed children are treated with diethylcarbamazine and thiabendazole (75 mg/kg/day for 3 days, maximum 3 g/day, which may be toxic) without undergoing surgery. An alternative treatment can be mebendazole, 200 to 400 mg three times a day for 10 days. It is not known whether specific anthelmintic therapy is effective. Massive ascaris infections may present with intestinal masses and may be confused with infections that are due to *A. costaricensis*.

EOSINOPHILIC GASTROENTERITIS

One cause of eosinophilic gastroenteritis is infection of humans with *A. canium*, a hookworm of dogs.[42, 43] Most of the cases have been recognized in northeastern Australia, but because of the ubiquity of the parasite in dogs in temperate and tropical climates worldwide, the syndrome will likely be more commonly recognized elsewhere. Animals and presumably humans are infected by larvae that enter the skin, and after a migratory phase or possibly a dormant intracellular stage in muscle, or both, the adults reside in the small intestines. Clinical manifestations are caused by an intense focal response to the worm, which is usually found in single or multiple locations in the ileum primarily, but also in the colon.[43] Endoscopic or surgical findings in the most florid cases include ulceration, inflammatory nodules, inflammation, and thickening, and stricture formation at times is associated with a single adult larva. In one early description,[44] 97% of the patients presented with gastrointestinal pain usually accompanied by nausea and vomiting. Bowel obstruction was present in 45% and diarrhea and melena occurred in 18 and 3%, respectively. Eosinophilia was always detected, and an increased white blood cell count was found in about three quarters of the patients. Other patients with diagnosed *A. canium* infections presented with less severe, vague, or mildly suggestive symptoms and signs. Characteristically, an elevated immunoglobulin E level and increased antibodies to hookworm antigens can be detected in most patients. The diagnosis is suggested by the clinical presentation and definitively established by the detection of the worm in the intestine. No eggs are found in the feces because the adult parasites are not patent and do not produce eggs. Patients respond to a standard course of mebendazole, 100 mg three times daily for 3 days.

DIROFILARIASIS

Accidental human infections with *Dirofilaria* result most commonly in a lung nodule or subcutaneous mass. Two groups of parasites of the genus *Dirofilaria* accidentally infect humans.[1] The clinical presentations are generally different, reflecting the final location of the adults in the usual animal host. The adult worms of *Dirofilaria immitis*, the dog heartworm and the only important parasite in the first group, reside in the right side of the heart and the right pulmonary vessels and are usually located in the lungs in humans. *D. immitis* is transmitted by a mosquito to its most common host, the domesticated dog, and other related mammals. After development in the subcutaneous tissues, the parasites migrate as young adults to the right side of the heart and the right pulmonary vessels. In humans, the immature filariae migrate similarly but do not develop and instead die, causing a local vasculitis leading to pulmonary infarcts. Histologic examination usually reveals a dead worm in an infarct with vasculitis and with granulomatous and sometimes eosinophilic inflammation. Most infections occur in the southeastern United States, where infections and transmission to dogs and accidental transmission to humans are most likely to occur. Persons are asymptomatic in more than half of the infections and show a coin lesion on a routine chest radiograph.[45, 46] Others complain of cough, chest pain, or hemoptysis, which most likely are due to pulmonary infarction. In some instances, lung infiltrates are noted that resolve into nodules.[47] Eosinophilia occurs in less than 15% of cases. The diagnosis can be made with certainty only by biopsy. Although serologic tests are available, their sensitivity and specificity are not adequate to rule out other potential life-threatening conditions such as a tumor.

Adults of the second group of filariae (subgenus *Nochtiella*) reside in the subcutaneous tissue of various mammals and cause inflammatory subcutaneous masses in humans.[48] These parasites include *D. tenuis* (raccoon), *D. ursi* (bear), *D. subdermata* (porcupines), and *D. repens* (dog and cat in Europe and Asia). Patients present with inflammatory subcutaneous masses containing increased numbers of eosinophils. As in infections with *D. immitis*, there are few if any systemic symptoms, and eosinophilia is not usually present. The diagnosis is established by biopsy. However, careful inspection of the entire tissue may be needed to find the parasite.

CAPILLARIASIS

Capillaria philippinensis inhabits the small bowel of humans, causing diarrhea and malabsorption.[49] Infections have been recognized in the Philippines, primarily in northern Luzon, and in Thailand, and two cases have been reported from the Middle East. The life cycle is incompletely understood; however, fresh fish contain larvae infectious for humans and birds.[50] The latter may be an important reservoir host. After raw freshwater fish are eaten, the larvae invade the jejunum and ileum, and the resulting adults produce both eggs and larvae. Unlike almost all helminths that infect humans, with the exception of *S. sterocoralis*, the parasite multiplies in the gut, a process known as *autoinfection*, resulting in an overwhelming infection. In fulminant cases, autopsies reveal a thickened, edematous small bowel with a flattened mucosa containing a mononuclear infiltrate. Numerous adults, larvae, and eggs are present in both the lumen and the mucosa. Larvae infectious for birds, humans, and other mammals develop in certain freshwater fish after ingestion of eggs.[49, 50] Almost all the signs and symptoms are related to progressive diarrhea and malabsorption. Patients complain of borborygmi, abdominal pain, vomiting, weight loss, and malaise resulting in wasting, abdominal distention, and edema. Laboratory examinations document the typical findings of protein-losing enteropathy; fat, mineral, and vitamin malabsorption; and electrolyte loss.[49, 50] Fever and eosinophilia are uncommon, although eosinophilia has been noted after therapy. The diagnosis is established by detecting the characteristic *Trichuris trichiuria*-like ova or larvae in the stool. No serologic tests are available. In untreated patients, mortality rates of up to one third have been documented, but specific anthelmintic therapy is effective and lifesaving. Therapy in the past included thiabendazole, 25 mg/kg for 30 days, but mebendazole, 200 mg orally twice daily for 20 days, or albendazole[50] has largely supplanted thiabendazole treatment. Relapses should be treated with prolonged courses of therapy. Infection is prevented by eating properly cooked freshwater fish.

NANOPHYETIASIS

Human infections with *Nanophyetus salmincola*, a diminutive small intestine–dwelling trematode, have been increasingly recognized in the Pacific Northwest of the United States.[51] Humans as well as other mammals and birds become infected after the ingestion of raw or undercooked freshwater fish (most commonly salminoid fish) or their eggs. Gastrointestinal symptoms including diarrhea, abdominal pain, and gas or bloating in the presence of eosinophilia should suggest the diagnosis. However, asymptomatic infections are not uncommon. The diagnosis is established by finding the characteristic operculated ova in the feces. They measure 64 to 97 μm by 34 to 55 μm and are nonembryonated when shed. Because the numbers of ova shed may be small, methods that concentrate ova in stool should be employed. Praziquantel, 20 mg/kg three times for 1 day, is effective treatment.

SWIMMER'S ITCH

Cercariae, the infective form of a large number of blood flukes of birds (commonly *Trichobilharzia*), nonhuman mammals, and, less commonly, human schistosomes, can cause a characteristic dermatitis in humans associated with penetration of the cercariae into the skin.[1] Unlike human schistosomes, cercariae from animals do not develop further in humans, and their clinical manifestations are almost always limited to the skin. Infections are frequent in many areas of the world but are particularly common in persons exposed to the freshwater lakes of the northern United States. However, infections also occur after exposure to salt water (clam digger's itch). Although there is variation in the clinical manifestations after the initial exposure, symptoms are typically mild and sometimes go unnoticed.[52, 53] The patient complains of itching followed by the appearance of macules at the site of penetration of the cercariae. By 24 hours, the macules have disappeared and begin to be replaced by papules. After repeated exposures, reactions occur earlier than 24 hours after exposure and are more severe. Papules are larger and associated with erythema, itching, and edema. By 4 to 7 days, symptoms subside, but in severe cases they may last for weeks.

Cercariae are produced by various species of mollusks, which are the intermediate hosts of these parasites. Control of infection can be obtained by ridding bathing areas of the molluscan intermediate host or the definitive host or by avoiding infected bodies of water. There is no specific anthelmintic therapy.

REFERENCES

1. Beaver PC, Jung RC, Cupp EW. Clinical Parasitology. Philadelphia: Lea & Febiger; 1984.
2. Beaver PC, Snyder CH, Carrera GM, et al. Chronic eosinophilia due to visceral larva migrans. Report of three cases. Pediatrics. 1952;9:7.
3. Huntley CC, Costas MC, Lyerly BS. Visceral larva migrans syndrome: Clinical characteristics and immunologic studies in 51 patients. Pediatrics. 1965;36:523.
4. Glickman LT, Schantz PM. Epidemiology and pathogenesis of zoonotic toxocariasis. Epidemiol Rev. 1981;3:230.
5. Worley G, Green JA, Frothingham TE, et al. *Toxocara canis* infection: Clinical and epidemiological associations with seropositivity in kindergarten children. J Infect Dis. 1984;159:591.

6. Jones WE, Schantz PM, Foreman K, et al. Human toxocarias in a rural community. Am J Dis Child. 1980;134:967.
7. Mok CH. Visceral larva migrans. A discussion based on review of the literature. Clin Pediatr. 1968;7:565.
8. Glickman L, Schantz P, Dombroske R, et al. Evaluation of serodiagnostic tests for visceral larva migrans. Am J Trop Med Hyg. 1978;27:492.
9. Cunningham CK, Kazacos KR, McMillan JA, et al. Diagnosis and management of *Baylisascaris procyonis* infection in an infant with nonfatal meningoencephalitis. Clin Infect Dis. 1994:18:868–872.
10. Wilder HC. Nematode endophthalmitis. Trans Am Acad Ophthalmol Otolaryngol. 1950;55:99.
11. Schantz PM, Meyer D, Glickman LT. Clinical, serologic, and epidemiologic characteristics of ocular toxocariasis. Am J Trop Med Hyg. 1979;28:24.
12. Biglan AW, Glickman LT, Lobes LA. Serum and vitreous *Toxocara* antibody in nematode endophthalmitis. Am J Opthalmol. 1979;88:898.
13. Felberg NT, Shields JA, Federman JL. Antibody to *Toxocara canis* in the aqueous humor. Arch Ophthalmol. 1981;99:1563.
14. Gass JD, Braunstein RA. Further observations concerning the diffuse unilateral subacute neuroretinitis syndrome. Arch Ophthalmol. 1983;101:1689–1697.
15. Gass JD, Callanan DG, Bowman CB. Oral therapy in diffuse unilateral subacute neuroretinitis. Arch Ophthalmol. 1992;110:675–690.
16. Smith JW, Wootten R. *Anisakis* and anisakiasis. In: Lumsden WHR, Muller R, Baker JR, eds. Advances in Parasitology. v. 16. London: Academic Press; 1978:93–163.
17. Van Thiel PH, Kuipers FC, Roskam RTH. A nematode parasitic to herring, causing acute abdominal syndromes in man. Trop Geogr Med. 1960;2:97.
18. Yokogawa N, Yoshimura H. Clinicopathologic studies of larval anisakiasis in Japan. Am J Trop Med Hyg. 1967;16:723.
19. Sugimachi K, Inokuchi K, Ooiwa T, et al. Acute gastric anisakiasis. Analysis of 178 cases. JAMA. 1985;253:1012.
20. Montoro A, Perteguer MJ, Chivato T, et al. Recidivous acute urticaria caused by *Anisakis simplex*. Allergy. 1997;52:985–991.
21. Alonso A, Daschner A, Moreno-Ancillo A. Anaphylaxis with *Anisakis simplex* in the gastric mucosa. N Engl J Med. 1997;337:350–351.
22. Del Pozo MD, Audicana M, Diez JM, et al. *Anisakis simplex*, a relevant etiologic factor in acute urticaria. Allergy. 1997;52:576–579.
23. Moreno-Ancillo A, Caballero MT, Cabanas R, et al. Allergic reactions to *Anisakis simplex* parasitizing seafood. Ann Allergy Asthma Immunol. 1997;79:246–250.
24. Matsui T, Iida M, Murakami M, et al. Intestinal anisakiasis: Clinical and radiologic features. Radiology. 1985;157:299.
25. Kusuhara T, Watanabe K, Fukuda M. Radiographic study of acute gastric anisakiasis. Gastrointest Radiol. 1984;9:305.
26. Shirahama M, Koga T, Ishibashi H, et al. Intestinal anisakiasis: US in diagnosis. Radiology. 1991;185:789.
27. KirbySmith JL, Dove WE, White GF. Some observations on creeping eruption. Am J Trop Med Hyg. 1929;9:179.
28. Hitch JM. Systemic treatment of creeping eruption. Arch Dermatol Syph. 1947;55:664.
29. Katz R, Ziegler J, Blank H. The natural course of creeping eruption and treatment with thiabendazole. Arch Dermatol. 1965;91:420.
30. Davis CM, Israel RM. Treatment of creeping eruption with topical thiabendazole. Arch Dermatol. 1968;97:325.
31. Jones SK, Reynolds NJ, Oliwiecki S, Harman RRM. Oral albendazole for the treatment of cutaneous larva migrans. Br J Dermatol. 1990;122:99.
32. Caumes E, Datry A, Paris L, et al. Efficacy of ivermectin in the therapy of cutaneous larva migrans. Arch Dermatol. 1992;128:994.
33. Rosen L, Chappell R, Laqueur GL, et al. Eosinophilic meningoencephalitis caused by a metastrongylid lungworm of rats. JAMA. 1962;179:620.
34. Kliks MM, Kroenke K, Hardman JM. Eosinophilic radiculomyeloencephalitis: An angiostrongyliasis outbreak in American Samoa related to ingestion of *Achatina fulica* snails. Am J Trop Med Hyg. 1982;31:1114.
35. Punyagupta S, Juttijudata P, Bunnag T. Eosinophilic meningitis in Thailand: Clinical studies of 484 typical cases probably caused by *Angiostrongylus cantonensis*. Am J Trop Med Hyg. 1975;24:921.
36. Yii CY. Clinical observations on eosinophilic meningitis and meningoencephalitis caused by *Angiostrongylus cantonensis* on Taiwan. Am J Trop Med Hyg. 1976;25:233.
37. Chitanondh H, Rosen L. Fatal eosinophilic encephalomyelitis caused by the nematode *Gnathostoma spinigerum*. Am J Trop Med Hyg. 1967;16:638.
38. Punyagupta S, Juttijudata P. Two fatal cases of eosinophilic myeloencephalitis, a newly recognized disease caused by *Gnathostoma spinigerum*. Trans R Soc Trop Med Hyg. 1968;62:801.
39. Fox AS, Kazacos KR, Gould NS. Fatal eosinophilic meningoencephalitis and visceral larva migrans caused by the raccoon ascarid *Bayliscaris procyonis*. N Engl J Med. 1985;312:1619.
40. Morera P, Cepedes R. *Angiostrongylus costaricensis* n sp (Nematoda: metastrongyloidea), a new lungworm occurring in man in Costa Rica. Rev Biol Trop. 1971;18:173.
41. LoriaCortes R, LoboSanahuga JF. Clinical abdominal angiostrongylosis: A study of 116 children with intestinal eosinophilic granuloma caused by *Angiostrongylus costaricensis*. Am J Trop Med Hyg. 1980;29:538.
42. Provic P, Croese J. Human eosinophilic enteritis caused by dog hookworm *Ancylostoma caninum*. Lancet. 1990;335:1299–1302.
43. Croese J, Loukas A, Opdebeeck J, et al. Human enteric infection with canine hookworms. Ann Intern Med. 1994;120:369–374.
44. Croese TJ. Eosinophilic enteritis—a recent North Queensland experience. Aust N Z J Med. 1988;18:848–853.
45. Beaver PC, Orihel TC. Human infection with filariae of animals in the United States. Am J Trop Med Hyg. 1965;14:1010.
46. Cifferri F. Human pulmonary dirofilariasis in the United States: A critical review. Am J Trop Med Hyg. 1982;31:302.
47. Kochar AS. Human pulmonary dirofilariasis: Report of three cases and brief review of the literature. Am J Clin Pathol. 1985;84:19.
48. Beaver PC, Wolfson JS, Waldron MA. *Dirofilaria ursi*-like parasites acquired by humans in the northern United States and Canada: Report of two cases and brief review. Am J Trop Med Hyg. 1987;37:357.
49. Whalen GE, Strickland GT, Cross HJ, et al. Intestinal capillariasis: A new disease in man. Lancet. 1969;1:13.
50. Cross JH. Intestinal capillariasis. Clin Microbiol Rev. 1992;5:120.
51. Fritsche TR, Eastburn RL, Wiggens LH, et al. Praziquantel for treatment of human *Nanophyetus salmincola (Troglotrema salmincola)* infection. J Infect Dis. 1989;160:896.
52. Olivier L. Schistosome dermatitis, a sensitization phenomenon. Am J Hyg. 1949;49:290.
53. MacFarlane MV. Schistosome dermatitis in New Zealand. Part II. Pathology and immunology of cercarial lesions. Am J Hyg. 1949;50:152.

SECTION K

ECTOPARASITIC DISEASES

Chapter 282

Introduction to Ectoparasitic Diseases

MICHAEL ERIC MATHIEU
BARBARA BRAUNSTEIN WILSON

An ectoparasite is an organism that derives benefit or fulfills a life cycle requirement through interaction with the outer, or cutaneous, surface of the host. Such organisms are generally members of the Arthropoda, a phylum of more than 1 million species. The term ectoparasite can include organisms that live on the host only long enough to obtain a blood meal as well as those that burrow into the superficial layers of the skin and remain there for weeks to months or even years if left untreated.

Arthropods are invertebrates with a chitinous exoskeleton, an internal cavity containing a hemolymph-filled hemocoele and internal organs, a segmented body, and jointed appendages. There are five classes of arthropods that may affect the skin: Hexapoda, Arachnida, Diplopoda (millipedes), Chilopoda (centipedes), and Crustacea. Selected arthropods from Hexapoda and Arachnida are discussed in the following chapters. The class Hexapoda comprises insects, which are six-legged arthropods, and includes lice, bugs (e.g., bedbugs and kissing bugs), beetles, butterflies and moths, flies (including mosquitoes), fleas, ants, bees, and wasps. The class Arachnida comprises arachnids, which have eight legs, and include mites, spiders, and ticks.

Stinging or vesicating arthropods, such as spiders, bees, ants, and caterpillars, inflict injury on the skin but do not obtain a blood meal and are therefore not considered true ectoparasites. Although adult flies do not parasitize the skin, their larval forms (maggots) can live off living or necrotic tissue, resulting in a condition known as *myiasis*.

Although ectoparasitic infestations remain a more frequent health problem in nonindustrialized tropical nations of the world, a variety of vector-borne zoonoses are of increasing concern in the United States.[1] In particular, tick-borne bacterial diseases including Lyme disease, human monocytic ehrlichiosis, and human granulocytic ehrlichiosis cause increasing morbidity, occasional mortality, and considerable anxiety among both patients and physicians. *Bartonella henselae* and *Bartonella quintana*, the etiologic agents of bacillary angiomatosis-peliosis in patients with acquired immunodeficiency syndrome, have been linked to the age-old ectoparasites fleas and lice, respectively.[2] In tropical climates, few natives escape some type of ectoparasitic disease, and the consequences of such disease can be mutilating, incapacitating, debilitating, or fatal. Not only do ectoparasites cause enormous economic losses to humans by virtue of human parasitism, they also parasitize domestic animals used for food and contribute greatly to the malnutrition found in underdeveloped countries.

Many bacterial, spirochetal, viral, rickettsial, helminthic, and protozoal diseases can be transmitted to humans by arthropod vectors. Table 282–1 lists some arthropod-borne diseases.

ERADICATION, CONTROL, AND PREVENTION

For most ectoparasites, eradication is not a practical approach because of the substantial reservoir of wild animals, which allows perpetuation of the species. Elimination of some species from domestic animals is reasonable in certain climates but is a virtual impossibility in other regions of the world. In many instances, improvements in sanitation and improved socioeconomic factors will do more to reduce parasitism for humans than will attempts to eliminate the arthropods.

It is sometimes possible, however, to control important diseases in humans and livestock by controlling the arthropod vectors responsible for the transmission of those diseases. Such large-scale programs often require cooperation between governmental agencies at various levels for effective implementation. Methods used to control arthropod vectors include the use of insecticides, biologic interference with the arthropod's life cycle, and environmental manipulations that limit breeding and spread of the undesirable arthropod species. Unfortunately, the widespread use of insecticides may induce the development of resistance in the arthropods, thereby requiring the development of new and different toxic agents. Extensive use of insecticides may create anxiety and controversy because of the possible hazardous effects they may have on people, animals, and the environment.

Diseases spread by arthropods can be limited not only by controlling the arthropod vector but also by preventing access of the arthropod to its host. When possible, fine screening should be used on windows and doors to prevent entrance of flying arthropods into dwellings. Homes built above the ground are less accessible to crawling arthropods. Regular grooming and treatment of infested animals can reduce animal reservoirs of arthropods. Protective clothing and insect repellents that are applied to the skin or clothes are also effective means of protecting humans from arthropods. The active ingredient in most of the insect repellents available in the United States is either *N,N*-diethyl-*m*-toluamide (DEET) or ethyl hexanediol.

TABLE 282–1 Selected Diseases Transmitted by Arthropods

Infectious Disease	Vector
Arbovirus diseases (including yellow fever, dengue fever, and encephalitis)	Mosquitoes and ticks
Babesiosis	Hard ticks
Boutonneuse fever (tick bite fever) *(Rickettsia conorii)*	Rabbit flea
Colorado tick fever	Hard ticks
Ehrlichiosis	Hard ticks
Endemic relapsing fever *(Borellia duttonii)*	Soft ticks
Epidemic relapsing fever *(Borrelia recurrentis)*	Human body lice
Epidemic typhus *(Rickettsia prowazekii)*	Human body lice
Filiariasis *(Wuchereria bancrofti, Brugia malayi)*	Mosquitoes
Leishmaniasis (*Leishmania* spp.)	Phlebotomid flies
Loiasis *(Loa loa)*	Tabanid flies
Lyme disease *(Borrelia burgodorferi)*	Hard ticks
Malaria (*Plasmodium* spp.)	Mosquitoes
Murine typhus *(Rickettsia mooseri)*	Rat fleas, lice
Onchocerciasis *(Onchocerca volvulus)*	Black flies
Plague *(Yersinia pestis)*	Rat fleas
Q fever *(Coxiella burnetii)*	Hard ticks, fleas
Rickettsialpox *(Rickettsia akari)*	Mouse mites
Rocky Mountain spotted fever *(Rickettsia rickettsii)*	Hard ticks
Scrub typhus *(Rickettsia tsutsugamushi)*	Mites (chiggers)

REFERENCES

1. Walker DH, Barbour AG, Oliver JH, et al. Emerging bacterial zoonotic and vector-borne diseases: Ecological and epidemiological factors. JAMA 1996;275:463–469.
2. Koehler JE, Sanchez MA, Garrido CS, et al. Molecular epidemiology of *Bartonella* infections in patients with bacillary angiomatosis-peliosis. N Engl J Med 1997;337:1876–1883.

Bibliography

Alexander JO. Arthropods and Human Skin. New York: Springer-Verlag; 1984.
Derbes VJ. Injurious effects in man induced by animals. In: Demis DJ, ed. Clinical Dermatology. Philadelphia: JB Lippincott; 1991.
Honig PJ. Arthropod bites, stings, and infestations: Their prevention and treatment. Pediatr Dermatol. 1986;3:189–197.
James MT. Herm's Medical Entomology. 7th ed. New York: Macmillan; 1969.

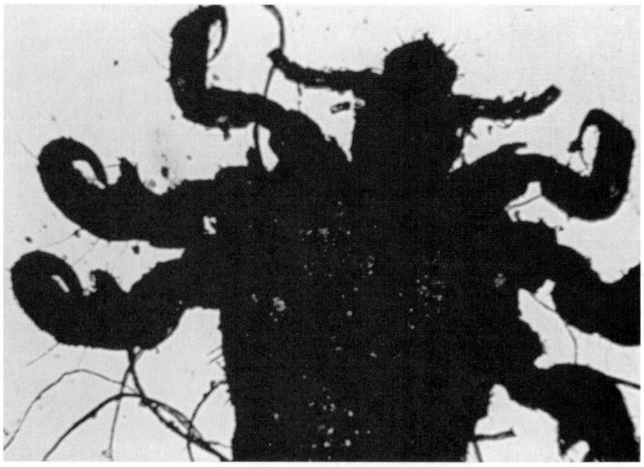

FIGURE 283–2. *Phthirus pubis* (pubic louse).

Chapter 283

Lice (Pediculosis)

MICHAEL ERIC MATHIEU
BARBARA BRAUNSTEIN WILSON

THE ORGANISMS

The order Anoplura (sucking lice) contains more than 200 species, of which only two genera, *Pediculus* and *Phthirus*, are parasitic for humans. The species of medical importance are *Pediculus humanus* var. *corporis*, the human body louse; *Pediculus humanus* var. *capitis*, the human head louse; and *Phthirus pubis*, the pubic or crab louse.

The body louse and the head louse are morphologically similar small (2 to 4 mm), grayish white, flattened, wingless, and elongated insects with pointed heads. From each segment of the fused triple-segmented thorax, a pair of jointed legs protrudes that end in clawlike projections (Fig. 283–1). The pubic louse is distinctively different in shape, being much wider and shorter than its cousins and resembling a crab, whence its nickname (Fig. 283–2).

Eggs laid by the fertilized adult female are firmly glued to body hairs or fibers of clothing and appear as small globoid or oval protrusions called nits (Fig. 283–3). Approximately 7 to 10 days after deposition, small voracious nymphs emerge that must feed within 24 hours to survive. After 2 to 3 weeks and three successive molts, the mature adult mate. The fertilized females produce 250 to 300 eggs over the next 20 to 30 days before death.

Lice pierce the skin, inject saliva, and then defecate while obtaining a blood meal. The pruritic papules that follow are secondary to the hypersensitivity reaction of the host to antigens present in the saliva.

EPIDEMIOLOGY

Lice infestations have been observed in virtually every inhabited area of the world. At times of war, overcrowding, or widespread inattention to personal hygiene, major epidemics have occurred.

Lice are medically important not only because they can cause significant cutaneous disease but also because they may serve as vectors for infectious diseases. The body louse is a known vector for epidemic typhus *(Rickettsia prowazekii)*, trench fever *(Bartonella quintana)*, and relapsing fever *(Borrelia recurrentis)*.

PEDICULOSIS CAPITIS

Persons from all social and economic backgrounds can become infested with head lice, and infestations can reach epidemic proportions, especially among schoolchildren. The disease is more common in whites than blacks, females than males, and children than adults. Lice are transferred by close personal contact and possibly by the sharing of hats, combs, and brushes.

PEDICULOSIS CORPORIS

Pediculosis corporis (body lice) is seen primarily where there is overcrowding and poor sanitation. The body louse lays its eggs (nits) and resides in the seams of the clothing rather than on the skin of

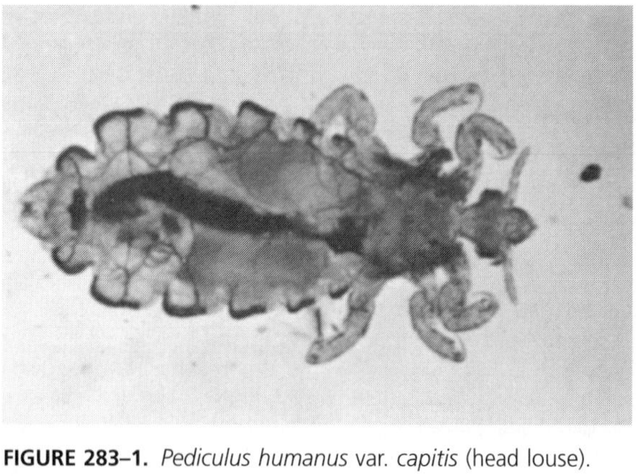

FIGURE 283–1. *Pediculus humanus* var. *capitis* (head louse).

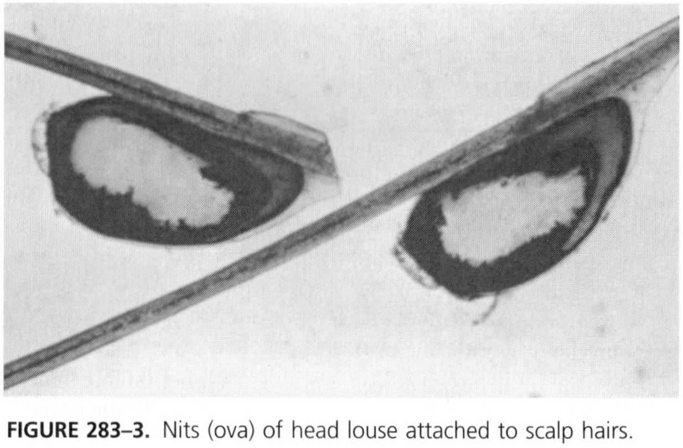

FIGURE 283–3. Nits (ova) of head louse attached to scalp hairs.

its host. The body louse leaves the clothing only to obtain a blood meal from its host. Nits present in the clothing are viable for up to 1 month.

PHTHIRUS PUBIS

P. pubis (pubic lice) infestation is transmitted by sexual or close body contact. The pubic louse resides primarily in the pubic hair but can also be seen in the eyebrows, eyelashes, axillary hair, and coarse hair on the back and chest of males. The pubic louse may also occasionally infest scalp hair.[1] As many as one third of individuals infested with pubic lice may harbor another sexually transmitted disease.[2]

CLINICAL MANIFESTATIONS

Pediculosis Capitis

Adult head lice and nits localize primarily in the temporal and occipital areas of the scalp; however, the entire scalp as well as the beard area may be involved. The adult lice may be difficult to observe, but the nits that are firmly attached to the base of the hair shaft are easily seen. The major complaint of persons afflicted with head lice is severe pruritus of the scalp. Scratching leads to excoriations and secondary bacterial infection that is manifested by weeping and crusting of the scalp as well as tender occipital and cervical adenopathy.

Pediculosis Corporis

Except in cases of severe infestations, the adult body louse is not seen on the skin but can be found in the seams of clothing. Patients complain of pruritus and develop small erythematous macules, papules, and excoriations that are located primarily on the trunk. Secondary impetiginization may occur. Persons with long-standing untreated pediculosis corporis may develop generalized hyperpigmentation and thickening of the skin with evidence of numerous healed excoriations, an entity known as vagabonds' disease.

Phthirus pubis

The primary complaint of persons infested with *P. pubis* is marked pruritus of all affected areas, which may include axillary and coarse truncal hairs and eyelashes as well as pubic hair. Erythematous macules and papules with excoriations and secondary infection may be seen, but the cutaneous findings are less severe than those seen in patients with pediculosis capitis and corporis. The nits and occasionally the adult pubic lice can be seen attached to the base of the hairs.

Small gray to bluish macules measuring less than 1 cm in diameter may be seen on the trunk, thighs, and upper parts of the arms. These lesions, known as maculae ceruleae (blue spots), are thought to be caused by an anticoagulant that is injected into the skin by the biting louse. Infestations of the eyelashes by pubic lice can cause crusting of the lid margins. In such cases, the nits are readily seen at the base of the lashes.

THERAPY

Pediculosis Capitis

Standard pediculicides include 1% lindane, gamma benzene hexachloride shampoo (Kwell), pyrethrins with piperonyl butoxide solution (RID, A-200 pyrinate liquid), 1% permethrin cream rinse (Nix), and 0.5% malathion lotion (Prioderm). Although these are generally still effective, reports of permethrin-resistant head lice in Israel and the Czech Republic suggest that global dissemination of resistant organisms may eventually occur.[3, 4]

Malathion lotion, which is no longer available in the United States, has been shown to be more effective than lindane and the pyrethrins; of the three, it is the only product with excellent ovicidal activity.[5] Objections to malathion include an unpleasant odor and a treatment time of 8 to 10 hours compared with 10 minutes for the other agents. All of the other available pediculicides are comparable in efficacy. They are all cosmetically acceptable and easy to use, each requiring only a 10-minute application to the scalp. This treatment is repeated in 1 week.

Lindane is the only pediculicide that requires a prescription, but it offers no advantage over the other agents. Although toxicity resulting from lindane has been reported when it has been improperly used for the treatment of scabies, toxicity is not a problem when treating pediculosis because the short treatment time minimizes the likelihood of systemic absorption of the agent through the skin.

Pyrethrins are extracts of the plant chrysanthemum. Permethrin is a synthetic pyrethroid with even greater insecticidal activity.[3]

Nits should be removed from the hairs by applying a solution of equal parts of vinegar and water and then combing the hair with a fine-tooth comb that has been dipped in vinegar. Combs and brushes should be soaked in a pediculicide for 1 hour.

Alternative therapeutic approaches that may be particularly useful for resistant organisms include application of petrolatum under a shower cap overnight, which is thought to cause asphyxiation of lice; oral trimethoprim/sulfamethoxazole, which is believed to deplete lice of a critical bacterial food source; and application of 5% permethrin cream to dry hair under a shower cap overnight, avoiding eye contact.[5, 6]

Pediculosis Corporis

The patient with body lice does not require treatment, but the patient's clothes must be treated. Body lice can be eradicated by either discarding the clothing, when practical, or laundering clothes in the hot cycle and then carefully ironing the seams of clothing. Body lice can also be eliminated by dusting the clothing with either 1% malathion powder or 10% DDT powder.

Phthirus pubis

P. pubis may be treated with lindane, permethrin, pyrethrin, or malathion, as described for pediculosis capitis. The pediculicides should be applied to all affected areas except the eyelids. Eyelid infestation can be effectively treated by applying a thick layer of petrolatum to the eyelid margins twice a day for 8 days or 1% yellow oxide of mercury four times daily for 2 weeks.[7] Sexual contacts should be treated when possible.

Symptomatic treatment of pruritus in all three types of infestation consists of adequate doses of antihistamines such as hydroxyzine, 25 to 50 mg three to four times daily. Medium- to high-potency topical corticosteroids such as triamcinolone or fluocinolone cream should be applied to affected areas two to three times daily. When secondary bacterial infection is present, *Staphylococcus aureus* is a frequent cause, and patients should be treated with a systemic antibiotic such as dicloxacillin, 250 mg four times a day for 10 days.

PREVENTION

The spread of pediculosis capitis can be minimized by improving living conditions such as overcrowding and by avoiding the sharing of hats, combs, and hairbrushes. Classroom epidemics are best prevented by periodic examination of the scalps of the students. Body lice are rarely seen in those with good personal hygiene who change their clothes frequently. Pubic lice are best prevented by avoiding sexual or close body contact with infested individuals.

REFERENCES

1. Mueller JF. Pubic lice from the scalp hair: A report of two cases. J Parasitol. 1973;59:943–4.
2. Chapel TA, Katta T, Kusamar T, et al. Ped. pubis in a clinic for treatment of sexually transmitted diseases. Sex Transm Dis. 1979;6:257.
3. Mumcuoglu KY, Hemingway J, Miller J, et al: Permethrin resistance in the head louse Pediculus capitis from Israel. Medical and Veterinary Entomology. 1995;9:427–432.
4. Rupes V, Moravec J, Chmela J, Ledvinka J, Zelenkova J: A resistance of head lice (Pediculus capitis) to permethrin in Czech Republic. Central Eur J Public Health. 1995;3:30–32.
5. Anonymous: Drugs for head lice. Med Let. 1997;39:6–7.
6. DiLiddo AP and Schachner LA: Scabies and lice infestations. Dermatol Ther. 1997;2:41–50.
7. Ashkenazi L, Desatnik HR, Abraham FA: Yellow mercuric oxide: A treatment of choice for phthriasis palpebrum. Br J Ophthalmol. 1991;75:356–8.

Bibliography

Alexander JO. Arthropods and Human Skin. New York: Springer-Verlag; 1984.
Hogan DJ, Schachner L, Tanglertsampan C: Diagnosis and treatment of childhood scabies and pediculosis. Pediatr Dermatol. 1991;38:941–57.
Honig PJ. Arthropod bites, stings and infestations: Their prevention and treatment. Pediatr Dermatol 1986;3:189–97.

Chapter 284

Scabies

MICHAEL ERIC MATHIEU
BARBARA BRAUNSTEIN WILSON

THE ORGANISMS

Human scabies is a highly contagious infestation caused by the "itch mite," *Sarcoptes scabiei* var. *hominis*, which belongs to the class Arachnida. The scabies mite is an obligate parasite that burrows into and resides and reproduces in human skin.

Two to three eggs are laid daily by the fertilized female in burrows several millimeters in length created at the base of the stratum corneum of the epidermis. After 72 to 84 hours larvae emerge and, after several molts, become adult mites and mate after about 17 days. The males die shortly, but the gravid females live for 4 to 6 weeks.[1] The full-grown adult female measures about 0.35 mm in length, is rounded, and has four pairs of short stubby legs (Fig. 284–1).

EPIDEMIOLOGY

Scabies is worldwide in distribution and occurs in all races and social classes. Epidemics have been associated with war, and conditions of poverty, poor hygiene, overcrowding, malnutrition, and sexual promiscuity are probably contributory factors. Although the scabies mite can cause significant cutaneous disease, it is not a vector for infectious diseases.

Scabies is transmitted by intimate personal contact, often sexual in nature, but casual contact, including that of nursing attendants, may be adequate for transmission, and institutional epidemics can occur. Live mites can be found in dust samples from homes of infested persons, suggesting that fomites may be an important factor in the transmission of scabies.[2] Studies suggest that an impregnated female mite can survive on human hosts for up to 2 days.[3]

The clinical picture of scabies is usually fairly characteristic but is extremely variable, depending on the degree and duration of the infestation. Fastidious individuals who wash frequently may have fewer and more subtle lesions, and those who neglect themselves are more likely to have extensive cutaneous disease.

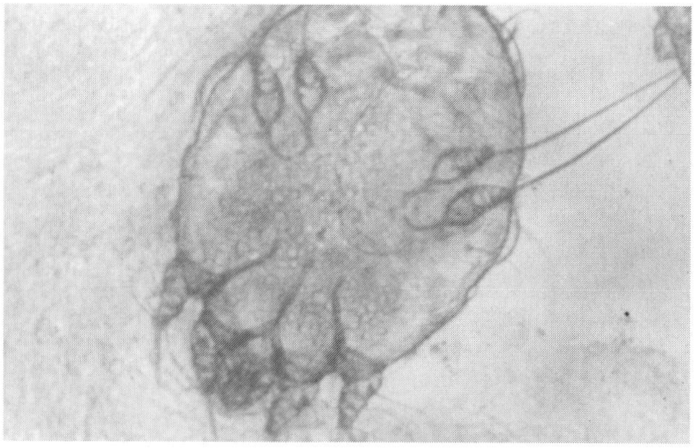

FIGURE 284–1. Scabies organism in a wet mount preparation.

CLINICAL MANIFESTATIONS

Human Scabies

Most individuals infested with the scabies mite complain of intense itching that is usually more severe at night. Erythematous papules and excoriations and occasionally vesicles are noted in areas of predilection such as the interdigital web spaces, wrists, anterior axillary folds, periumbilical skin, pelvic girdle, penis, and ankles. In infants and small children the palms, soles, face, neck, and scalp are often involved. One should look carefully for classic linear burrows, particularly in the interdigital spaces and on the wrists and ankles.

Infested males may have pruritic, erythematous papules and nodules on the scrotum and penis (Fig. 284–2). The diagnosis is confirmed microscopically by demonstrating the organism, eggs, or feces in skin scrapings. Skin samples are obtained by scraping or shaving the superficial layers of skin over a burrow with a No. 15 scalpel blade to a depth at which pinpoint bleeding occurs. In the normal host there are usually no more than 5 to 10 adult mites present, most of which reside on the hands and wrists.

Secondary impetiginization, usually caused by *Staphylococcus aureus*, may develop and obscure the underlying condition. A background eczematous eruption may be present and is probably related to the development of hypersensitivity of the host to the scabies mite. Treatment with topical or systemic corticosteroids may alter the clinical picture so that the disease remains unrecognized, an entity known as scabies incognito. Chronic infestations, especially in children, may lead to the development of pruritic reddish brown nodules, especially on the penis and scrotum and in the axillae (Fig. 284–3). These lesions are thought to be a manifestation of strong delayed hypersensitivity to retained mite products and may take weeks or months to disappear after adequate therapy.

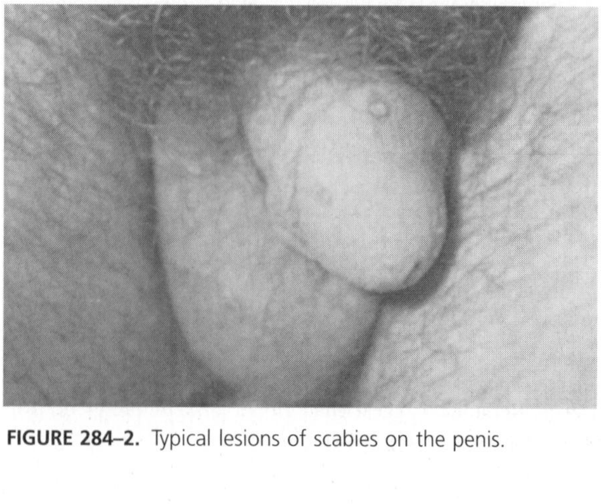

FIGURE 284–2. Typical lesions of scabies on the penis.

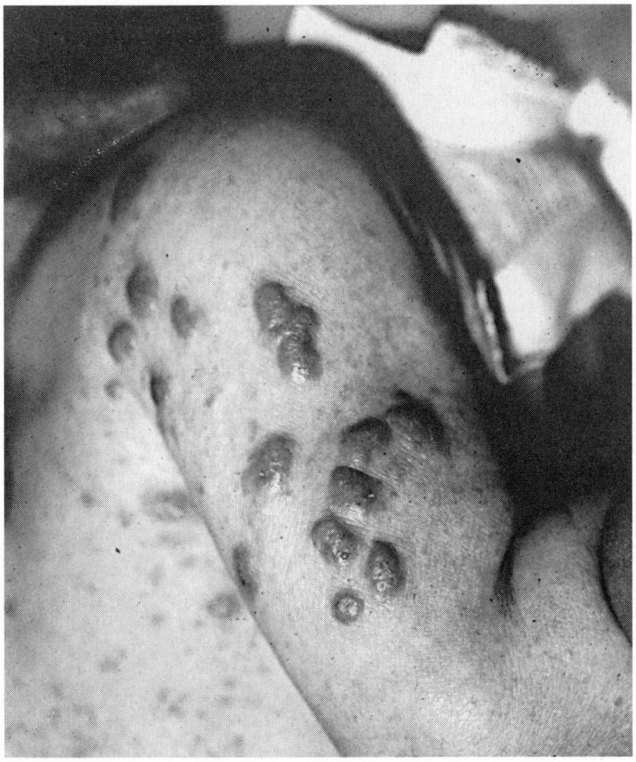

FIGURE 284–3. Nodular scabies on the arm of an infant.

Norwegian Scabies

A severe variant of scabies known as *Norwegian* or *crusted scabies* can occur, usually in institutionalized persons, particularly those with Down syndrome, and in individuals who are debilitated or immunosuppressed, including patients with acquired immunodeficiency syndrome.[4, 5] Cutaneous lesions consist of widespread, hyperkeratotic, crusted nodules and plaques. The nails are frequently involved and demonstrate thickening and subungual debris. Secondary bacterial infection, septicemia, and death have been reported.[5] Patients with Norwegian scabies are heavily infested with mites and harbor tens of thousands of organisms, compared with the 5 or 10 present in immunocompetent hosts with scabies. Patients are therefore highly contagious and require special control measures to prevent transmission of the disease.

Animal Scabies

Occasionally, dogs with sarcoptic mange caused by *S. scabiei* var. *canis* can be responsible for minor epidemics of mite bites, usually in members of a family. The lesions are pruritic, papular, or urticarial and are located primarily on the trunk, arms, axillae, and breasts. No burrows are seen because the organisms cannot complete their life cycle on humans. Eradication of the infestation of the animal produces prompt subsidence of the condition.

TREATMENT AND PREVENTION

Lindane 1% lotion is highly effective against scabies and has been the treatment of choice for many years. Permethrin 5% cream has become available and has been shown to have an even higher cure rate for scabies than lindane.[6, 7] Lindane is not recommended for pregnant women or very young children, especially premature infants, because it is absorbed through the skin and can cause side effects such as irritability, seizures, and even death.[6] In most instances, such side effects have been attributed to overuse or accidental ingestion of the medication. Lindane is applied to the entire skin surface from the chin to the tips of the toes and left on for 8 to 12 hours. Lindane should not be applied immediately after a bath because this increases systemic absorption and possible toxicity.[2] In children, the head is also treated, and the medication is left on for only 6 to 8 hours to minimize transcutaneous absorption. The treatment is repeated in 1 week. Fingernails should be trimmed because they may harbor mites. If the hands are washed for any reason, medication should be reapplied. Patients should be forewarned that even after adequate therapy, they may experience pruritus for up to 2 weeks.

Permethrin 5% cream is a cosmetically acceptable cream that is poorly absorbed by the skin and is therefore less likely to cause systemic side effects.[7] One application is usually curative. It is applied as described for lindane and is washed off after 8 to 10 hours. It is safe for use in children 2 months and older; although it may be safe to use during pregnancy, no confirmatory controlled studies have been performed. Pregnant women and infants can be treated with 6 to 10% precipitated sulfur in petrolatum daily for 3 days.[2]

If there is any evidence of secondary bacterial infection, patients should be treated with an antistaphylococcal antibiotic. Pruritus is treated with antihistamines and a topical lotion containing an antipruritic medication such as pramoxine or menthol.

Norwegian scabies is more difficult to treat because of the high mite population as well as a decreased immune response by the host. In such cases, the cure rate may be improved by hydrating the skin through soaking a tube of lukewarm water for 10 minutes before therapy. Permethrin or lindane is applied immediately after the bath, again in 12 hours, and then left on for another 12 hours. This regimen should be repeated in 1 week. One week after therapy, skin scrapings should be performed, and the patient should be retreated if mites are still present. Secondary bacterial infection should be treated.

A significant new treatment for human scabies is oral administration of the antiparasitic drug ivermectin, an agent approved by the U.S. Food and Drug Administration for the treatment of strongyloidiasis and onchocerciasis. Early anecdotal reports from Mexico noted eradication of coincidental scabies in patients with onchocerciasis treated with ivermectin. Placebo-controlled trials confirmed the efficacy of single-dose treatment in otherwise normal hosts and in most patients infected with human immunodeficiency virus, the latter group often being more difficult to treat with standard therapy. In addition to eradication of mites, patients noted rapid resolution of pruritus soon after taking invermectin.[8] Invermectin, in combination with topical therapy, was also effective against crusted scabies in normal and human immunodeficiency virus–infected individuals.

The extensive experience with ivermectin for the treatment of other diseases suggests that the drug is safe. A single report of increased mortality in elderly institutionalized patients over a 6-month period after treatment for an outbreak of scabies, however, questioned the safety of ivermectin, but other investigators have refuted such as association.[9, 10] The optimal dose of ivermectin has not been firmly established, but the published experience suggests that a single dose of 200 to 250 μg/kg is effective for uncomplicated cases. Patients with more severe disease may require a second or even third treatment, and patients with crusted disease should be treated simultaneously with topical therapy such as 5% permethrin cream. Although ivermectin is promising, particularly for the treatment of human immunodeficiency virus–infected patients and institutional outbreaks, its precise role as therapy for scabies has not been fully established; its use must therefore be considered experimental.

It is important that not only the patient but also household members and close contacts be treated at the same time. Any clothes worn or bed linens used during the 3 days before therapy should be laundered in hot, soapy water and dried in the hot cycle of the dryer. Such high temperatures should be sufficient to kill mites and their eggs.

Institutional Scabies

Scabies outbreaks are a major problem in hospitals and nursing homes where patients require much hands-on nursing care, leading to transmission of disease between patients and nursing personnel.[7]

Juranek and colleagues[11] made several recommendations for control measures to be followed if scabies occurs in a hospitalized patient or hospital employee. The management of scabies outbreaks in institutions depends on whether the index case has typical scabies or Norwegian scabies. If a patient has typical scabies, for at least 8 hours after treatment, nursing personnel should wear gloves while caring for that patient or handling the patient's clothes or bed linens. Close contacts should be treated prophylactically.

Patients with Norwegian scabies are highly contagious and require isolation. When possible, the nurse in charge of the patient with Norwegian scabies should have no other responsibilities for patients. Nursing personnel as well as visitors should wear disposable gowns, gloves, and shoe covers when in contact with the patient. The gown may be sprayed with an insect repellent such as Off or Cutter brand if lifting or handling the patient is required. The protective disposable clothing should be discarded in a plastic bag. Clothes and bed linens should be placed in a plastic laundry bag and handled only by personnel wearing gloves.

REFERENCES

1. Alexander JO. Arthropods and Human Skin. New York: Springer-Verlag; 1984.
2. Hogan DJ, Schachner L, Tanglertsampan C. Diagnosis and treatment of childhood scabies and pediculosis. Pediatr Dermatol. 1991;38:941–957.
3. Arlian LG, Estes SA, Vyszenski-Moher DL. Prevalence of sarcoptes scabiei in the homes and nursing homes of scabietic patients. J Am Acad Dermatol. 1988;19:806–811.
4. Glover R, Young L, Goltz RW. Norwegian scabies in acquired immunodeficiency syndrome: Report of a case resulting in death from associated sepsis. J Am Acad Dermatol. 1987;16:396–399.
5. Orkin M. Scabies in AIDS. Semin Dermatol. 1993;12:9–14.
6. Haustein UF, Hlawa B. Treatment of scabies with permethrin vs lindane and benzyl benzoate. Acta Derm Venereol (Stockh). 1989;69:348–351.
7. Taplin D, Meinking TL, Porcelain SL, et al. Permethrin 5% dermal cream: A new treatment for scabies. J Am Acad Dermatol. 1986;15:995–1001.
8. Meinking TL, Taplin D, Hermida JL, et al. The treatment of scabies with ivermectin. N Engl J Med. 1995;333:26–30.
9. Barkwell R, Shields S. Deaths associated with ivermectin treatment of scabies. Lancet. 1997;349:1144–1145.
10. Coyne PE, Addiss DG. Deaths associated with ivermectin for scabies (Correspondence). Lancet. 1997;350:215–216.
11. Juranek DD, Currier RW, Milikan LE. Scabies control in institutions. In: Orkin M, Maibach HI, eds. Cutaneous Infestations and Insect Bites. New York: Marcel Dekker; 1985;139–156.

Chapter 285

Myiasis

MICHAEL ERIC MATHIEU
BARBARA BRAUNSTEIN WILSON

Myiasis is the infestation of living vertebrates by the larvae (maggots) of dipterous (two-winged) flies, a disease that occurs more frequently, although not exclusively, in tropical climates. Disease of domestic animals is a global agricultural problem. Nosocomial infestation has been reported rarely. The appropriate travel or exposure history in a compatible clinical setting should alert the clinician to the possibility of myiasis.

CLASSIFICATION

Myiasis is enormously important in veterinary medicine, and human disease is due to parasites that usually interact with an animal host. Cutaneous myiasis is the most frequently encountered clinical form. Cutaneous disease is further subclassified according to the nature of the manifestation, such as furunculoid, subcutaneous infestation with tunnel formation, wound infestation, and subcutaneous infestation with migratory swellings. Nasopharyngeal myiasis has been reported to include infestation of the nose, mouth, sinuses, ear, or eye (ophthalmomyiasis). Intestinal myiasis includes enteric disease caused by ingestion of organisms and anal disease. Urogenital myiasis encompasses urethral, vaginal, and bladder infestations.

MYIASIS-ASSOCIATED SPECIES

Myiasis-inducing flies are members of the superfamily Oestrodiae. Oestrodiae consists of three major families: Oestridae, which includes four subfamilies (Oestrinae, Gasterophiliane, Hypodermatinae, and Cuterebrinae); Calliphoridae, or blow flies; and Sarcophagidae, or flesh flies. All Oestridae, at least 151 species, are obligate parasites. The families Calliforidae, greater than 1000 species, and Sarcophagidae, greater than 2000 species, contain both obligate and facultative organisms.

Despite the staggering number of potential agents, a limited number of species actually cause disease (Table 285–1). Travelers returning from the tropics are likely to harbor infestation with *Dermatobia hominis* or *Cordylobia anthropophaga*. Other species may infest humans when recreational or occupational activities unite human host and parasite, interactions that can also occur in temperate regions. The reader is referred to an excellent discussion for more detail regarding other potential agents of myiasis in both animals and humans.[1]

D. hominis, also known as human or tropical botfly, berne, and many other local names, is an Oestridae fly of the Cuterebrinae subfamily, which is endemic to tropical Mexico, South America, Central America, and Trinidad. *Bot* is a term sometimes used for the invading larva. *D. hominis* is an obligate parasite found in humid tropical forests and wooded lowlands. Adults have a blue-black thorax with a metallic violet abdomen and can grow to 2 cm in length. Domesticated animals, especially cattle, and humans may become infested. The ecology of the fly is fascinating in that egg-bearing female flies intercept blood-sucking arthropods, such as mosquitoes, and attach the eggs to the abdomen of the carrier insect. When the mosquito takes a blood meal from a warm-blooded animal, local heat induces larvae to hatch and drop to the skin of the mammalian host as cylindrical first-instar, or stage I, larvae. Larvae painlessly penetrate the skin of the mammal directly or through the defect produced by the insect proboscis and gain access to the dermis and subcutaneous tissue. Within 5 to 10 weeks, the organisms mature to flask-shaped second-instar, or stage II, larvae then fusiform third-instar, or stage III, larvae. Second and third instars have sickle-shaped hooks on the bulbous heads and rows of smaller concentric, backward-facing hooks and spines. Eventually, if the cycle is unperturbed, larvae emerge from the host, drop to the ground, and pupate to form flies in 2 to 3 weeks. Adult flies are short lived, surviving little more than a week.[2] Human and animal disease results from development of larvae within the skin of the infested host.

C. anthropophaga, the tumbu fly, is a member of the family Calliphoridae that is endemic to sub-Saharan Africa. The flies are 8 to 11 mm in length and dull yellow with two broad dark longitudinal stripes. Occasional case reports of disease apparently acquired in Europe have suggested the possibility of a more extended range. Female flies deposit eggs on shaded soil or drying clothes, preferably contaminated with urine or feces. Within 1 to 3 days, larvae hatch and remain near the soil surface until activated by heat, such as the body heat of a potential host, human or animal. Larvae from eggs deposited on clothes have direct access to the host when the clothes

TABLE 285-1 Summary of Common Myiasis-Associated Species

Taxonomic Classification, Common Name	Distribution	Mode of Infestation	Disease
OESTRODIAE			
Oestridae			
Oestrinae	Worldwide	Obligate	Ophthalmomyiasis
Oestrus ovis, sheep nasal botfly			
Gastrophilinae, horse botfly	Worldwide	Obligate	
Hypodermatinae	Worldwide	Obligate	Furunculoid and creeping eruption
Hypoderma bovis (cattle botfly)			
Cuterebrinae			
Dermatobia hominis (botfly)	Tropical Latin America, Trinidad	Obligate	Furunculoid
Cuterebra species (North American botfly)	North America	Obligate	Furunculoid, rarely ophthalmomyiasis
Calliphoridae (blowflies)			
Calliphorinae			
Cordylobia anthropophaga (tumbu fly)	Tropical Africa	Obligate	Furunculoid
Cordylobia rodhaini	Tropical Africa	Obligate	Furunculoid
Cochliomyia homnivorax (New World screwworm)	Tropical Latin America	Obligate	Wound
Chrysomya bezziana (Old World screwworm)	Tropical Africa and Asia	Obligate	Wound
Lucilia species (green bottle fly)	Worldwide	Facultative	Wound
Calliphora species (blue bottle fly)	Worldwide	Facultative	Wound
Phormia regina (black blowfly)	Worldwide	Facultative	Wound
Aucheromyia senegalensis (Congo floor maggot)	Tropical Africa	Obligate	Bites
Sarcophagidae (fleshflies)			
Wohlfahrtia species			
Wohlfahrtia magnifica	Mediterranean basin, Eastern Europe, near East	Obligate	Wound
Muscidae			
Musca domestica	Worldwide	Facultative	Wound

are worn. As with *D. hominis*, larvae pass through three stages. *Cordylobia rodhaini*, a related species also known as Lund's fly, is similar to *C. anthropophaga* in distribution and disease manifestations.

Rarely, humans in North America and elsewhere can become infested with horse or cattle botflies, *Gasterophilus* spp. and *Hypoderma bovis*, respectively, both Oestridae flies. These organisms produce migratory erythematous lesions. *Cuterebra* spp., large rabbit-parasitizing Oestridae flies, occur in North America and occasionally cause cutaneous myiasis and ophthalmomyiasis in humans, especially children.[3]

Several species occasionally cause wound myiasis by laying eggs directly on compromised tissue. Such parasites are found both in the tropics and in warm temperate zones such as southern North America. Some of the relevant organisms are obligatory species, such as New World and Old World screwworms. *Cochliomyia hominivorax* and *Chrysomyia bezziana*, respectively, both being Calliphoridae flies. New World screwworms are endemic in the southern United States, Caribbean, and most of Latin America. Old World screwworms are found in Africa, the subcontinent of India, the Arabian peninsula, and the archipelagos of Indonesia, the Philippines, and New Guinea. *Wohlfahrtia magnifica*, an obligate flesh fly Sarcophagidae species of the Mediterranean basin, Near East, and Eastern and central Europe, can also cause severe wound myiasis in animals and humans. Facultative wound myiasis, typical maggot-infested wounds, may be due to several frequent Calliphoridae animal pests: *Lucilia* spp., the ubiquitous greenbottle flies; *Calliphora* spp., the ubiquitous bluebottle flies; and *Phormia regina*, the black blow fly of North America. *Musca domestica*, the house fly found throughout the world, may also infest wounds.

Auchmeromyia senegalensis, the Congo floor maggot, is a unique Calliphoridae obligate parasite of sub-Saharan Africa that is primarily a human parasite. Eggs are laid in the soil or sand floors of traditional huts. The larvae hatch in 1 to 3 days to emerge at night, seeking a blood meal from sleeping human hosts. All three larval stages are blood sucking. The bite may be slightly painful and some patients experience considerable local edema.

Oestrus ovis, the Oestridae sheep nasal botfly found in all major sheep-raising regions, has been particularly implicated in ophthalmomyiasis. The species is found in all areas where shepherding is a major agricultural pursuit. Female flies directly deposit first-instar larvae in the nostrils of sheep for obligate development in the upper respiratory tract.

CLINICAL MANIFESTATIONS

Furunculoid Disease

In temperate North America and Europe, the occasional patient presenting with myiasis is likely to be a traveler who has recently returned from tropical Latin America or equatorial Africa. Both *D. hominis* and *C. anthropophaga*, the most common offending agents, cause furunculoid myiasis. As the term implies, furunculoid disease is characterized by cutaneous nodules, occurring singly or multiply, each containing one larva. The term *warble* is synonymous with a furunculoid lesion. A central punctum usually develops that may exude serosanguineous or purulent fluid (Fig. 285–1). Frequently, patients are aware of movement within the nodule; pruritus is common. The tail of the larva may be observed to extrude from the punctum intermittently, the two spiracles simulating tiny black eyes. *D. hominis* infestations are associated with local pain, perhaps because of the larval hooklets, which are believed to assist the organism in boring through tissue to exit.[4] *D. hominis* favors the scalp, face, and extremities, whereas *C. anthropophaga* is more likely to affect the trunk, buttocks, and thighs. *C. rodhaini* is similar to *C. anthropophaga*, but lesions are larger and more painful.

Associated findings include regional lymphadenopathy, malaise, and fever. Secondary bacterial infection may be present and a thick purulent discharge may suggest typical staphylococcal furunculosis. Tungiasis, a cutaneous disease caused by the chigoe flea, *Tunga penetrans*, may also be confused with myiasis, particularly because this infestation is also acquired in New World and Old World tropics. The female flea burrows into a distal extremity of and feeds on host blood until mature eggs are extruded through the punctum. Tungiasis may be differentiated clinically from myiasis by being virtually confined to the distal extremities, especially the toes, and by the presence of pruritic papules with a central punctum.

Rarer causes of furunculoid disease may be rodent and rabbit botflies of the genus *Cuterebra*. This form of myiasis is generally not of tropical origin but has been reported from many regions of the United States. Hypodermatinae species and *W. magnifica* have also occasionally caused furunculoid disease.

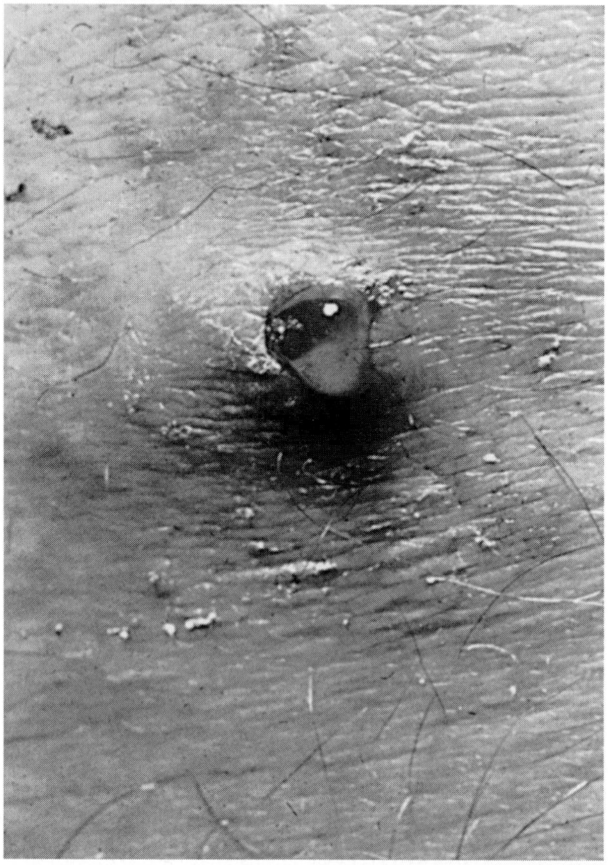

FIGURE 285–1. Typical lesion of furunculoid myiasis consisting of an erythematous nodule draining serosanguinous material from an overlying punctum.

Subcutaneous Infestation with Tunnel Formation

Although they infrequently affect humans, North American *Gasterophilus* species, horse botflies, cause significant morbidity among horses as these larvae normally develop within the gastrointestinal tract of equine hosts. *Gasterophilus intestinalis* and *Gasterophilus hemorrhoidalis* are responsible for migratory integumomyiasis in humans, the so-called creeping eruption as larvae slowly migrate through the skin. The clinical correlate is the development of pruritic, painful, erythematous lesions in a serpiginous configuration. Recurrent disease tends to form large pustules or nodules. Rarely, larvae may appear in the lungs and produce nodular parenchymal lesions. The burden of the clinician is to differentiate this disease from cutaneous larva migrans, a helminthic disease caused by animal intestinal nematode larvae, such as those of *Ancylostoma* species of dogs and cats, which cannot complete their life cycle in humans. The latter condition occurs at sites where skin has been in contact with contaminated warm sandy soil, such as the lower extremity, and consists of a thin, erythematous, intensely pruritic, rapidly moving (1 to 2 cm/day) serpiginous eruption that may induce systemic effects such as eosinophilia.

Subcutaneous Infestation with Migratory Swellings

The cattle botfly, or cattle grub, *H. bovis*, an obligate Oestridae species found in temperate regions including North America and Europe, is a major cause of morbidity in cattle. Humans are occasionally infested, causing disease that may be similar to that caused by *Gasterophilus* infestations but more characteristically involves formation of furunculoid lesions as larvae mature. Mature larvae may thus emerge through puncta as with *D. hominis* infestation. Rarely, cattle botfly disease may lead to severe ophthalmomyiasis, even blindness, or invasion of the central nervous system. As with other invasive parasites too large to be phagocytized, peripheral eosinophilia may occur.

Wound Myiasis

C. hominivorax and *C. bezziana*, New World and Old World screwworms, respectively, may cause an obligatory wound myiasis. More mature larvae are often more invasive, readily leaving necrotic tissue for viable tissue, leading to significant local destruction and secondary bacterial infection. Similarly, *W. magnifica* may parasitize wounds in an obligatory manner. *Lucilia sericata* and *M. domestica* may facultatively infest wounds when gravid females deposit eggs in and around wounds. Clinical manifestations include secondary bacterial infection and occasional fistula formation.

Other Manifestations

Ophthalmomyiasis is usually caused by *O. ovis*. Ophthalmomyiasis interna involves the globe, whereas ophthalmomyiasis externa is a relatively mild disease, characterized by conjunctivitis, lid edema, and superficial punctate keratopathy in response to movement of larvae across the external surface of the globe.[5] Patients commonly complain of an acute foreign body sensation with lacrimation, often of abrupt onset. Invasion of the globe and severe external inflammation occur occasionally. Non–*O. ovis* eye disease may be more severe.[6] Larvae may appear within the cornea, lens, anterior chamber, or vitreous but rarely undergo continued development when the globe has been entered. A rare devastating consequence is retinitis involving the macula with fibrosis leading to blindness. Occasionally, enucleation or exenteration is required.

Rarely, other body sites may become infested with dipterous larvae. Virtually any accessible cavity or tissue may provide an environment hospitable for facultative or obligate parasitism. Reported cases have involved the urethra, penis, vagina, bladder, colon, upper respiratory tract, oral cavity, and brain.

TREATMENT

Furunculoid and Migratory Myiasis

The goal of treatment is complete removal of larvae from parasitized tissue. *C. anthropophaga* is reportedly easier to remove than *D. hominis*.[4] Manual expression of *C. anthropophaga* may be adequate, this procedure being commonly performed by the patient before or in lieu of seeking medical attention. Numerous reports have noted successful eradication of *D. hominis* by occlusion of the punctum with a substance to prevent gas exchange. To avoid asphyxiation, the organism emerges far enough to be grasped by the forceps of a vigilant physician or patient. Occluding substances have included petrolatum, fingernail polish, makeup cream, adhesive tape, and bacon.[7] Reportedly, occlusion may have to be maintained for 24 hours or more to have the desired effect. The risk of attempted occlusion is that the organism may asphyxiate without emerging through the punctum and the retained larva may elicit an inflammatory response. Surgical excision is therefore often necessary for treatment. In our experience with several cases of furunculoid myiasis in patients returning from tropical Latin America, occlusion alone was unsuccessful and a surgical procedure was required (Fig. 285–2). Surgical excision is almost always required for the migratory forms of the disease, the formation of furunculoid lesions facilitating localization of the organism. Antibiotic therapy may be necessary for secondary bacterial infection.

Wound Myiasis

Treatment of wound myiasis requires manual removal of all visible larvae followed by débridement. Irrigation may be particularly use-

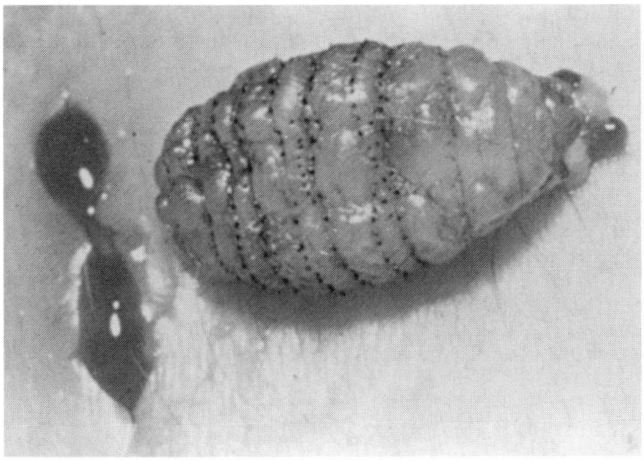

FIGURE 285–2. Larva removed from skin of a patient with furunculoid myiasis.

ful. Fifteen percent chloroform in olive or other oil or ether may help to immobilize the larvae. Extensive wound exploration may be mandated by the degree of involvement.

Ophthalmomyiasis

External infestation is managed by mechanical removal of larvae from the surface of the anesthetized globe using fine, nontoothed, forceps. Slit-lamp examination facilitates the process, but viable larvae have a tendency to avoid bright light. The use of lidocaine or cocaine as an anesthetic has the additional benefit of maggot immobilization, which facilitates removal. As with furuncular myiasis, occlusion with a thick ointment may assist removal by encouraging egress of organisms from the conjunctival sac, if involved.[6, 8] Careful follow-up examination is necessary to ensure complete removal of larvae.

The management of internal infestation is more variable and highly dependent on the clinical situation. Dead larvae unassociated with significant inflammation can usually be left in place and eventually regress. Inflammation requires management with topical corticosteroids and mydriatics with close follow-up. The presence of persistently viable larvae may require surgical removal, particularly when critical structures are at risk. Living organisms in the appropriate location, such as the subretinal space, may be amenable to destruction by laser photocoagulation. Ivermectin has been used for the treatment of myiasis in animals and in at least one human with subcutaneous *Hypoderma lineatum* infestation.[4]

PREVENTION

D. hominis infestation might be thwarted by the application of insect repellents containing diethyltoluamide (DEET) and the use of mosquito netting. Ironing is an effective method for destroying occult eggs laid in clothing by *C. anthropophaga*. Other general precautions include wearing of long-sleeved clothing, covering wounds, and avoiding falling asleep out of doors.

REFERENCES

1. Hall M, Wall R. Myiasis of humans and domestic animals. Adv Parasitol. 1995;35:257–334.
2. Gordon PM, Hepburn NC, Williams AE, Bunney MH. Cutaneous myiasis due to *Dermatobia hominis*: A report of six cases. Br J Dermatol. 1995;132:811–814.
3. Baird JK, Baird CR, Sabrosky CW. North American cuterebrid myiasis. J Am Acad Dermatol. 1989;21:673–772.
4. Jelinek T, Nothdurft HD, Rieder N, Löscher T. Cutaneous myiasis: Review of 13 cases in travelers returning from tropical countries. Int J Dermatol. 1995;34:624–626.
5. Harvey JT. Sheep botfly: Ophthalmomyiasis externa. Can J Ophthalmol. 1986;21(3):92–95.
6. Chodosh J, Clarridge J. Ophthalmomyiasis: A review with special reference to *Cochliomyia hominivorax*. Clin Infect Dis. 1992;14:444–449.
7. Brewer TF, Wilson ME, Gonzalez E, Felsenstein D. Bacon therapy and furuncular myiasis. JAMA. 1993;270:2087–2088.
8. Hira PR, Hajj B, al-Ali, Hall MJ. Ophthalmomyiasis in Kuwait: First report of infections due to the larvae of *Oestrus ovis* before and after the Gulf conflict. J Trop Med Hyg. 1993;96:241–244.

Bibliography

Canizares O. Myiasis and leeches. In: Canizares O, Harman RRM, eds. Clinical Tropical Dermatology. 2nd ed. Boston: Blackwell Scientific; 1992:404–412.
Garcia LS, Bruckner DA. Medically important arthropods. In: Diagnostic Medical Parasitology. 3rd ed. Washington, DC: American Society for Microbiology; 1997:523–563.
Rossignol PA, Feinsod FM. Arthropods directly causing human injury. In: Warren KS, Mahmoud AAE, eds. Tropical and Geographic Medicine. 2nd ed. New York: McGraw-Hill; 1990:519–522.

Chapter 286

Mites (Including Chiggers)

MICHAEL ERIC MATHIEU
BARBARA BRAUNSTEIN WILSON

THE ORGANISM

Mites belong to the order Acarina, of the class Arachnida. Mites are worldwide in distribution and may be free living or may parasitize plants, insects, animals, or humans.[1] Adult mites have a fused head and thorax and four pairs of legs. The size of the mites varies with the species.

Mites are medically important not only because they can cause significant cutaneous disease in humans but also because some species are known vectors of infectious diseases such as rickettsialpox, scrub typhus, murine typhus, Q fever, tularemia, plague, and tsutsugamushi fever.

The mites that may affect humans include chiggers (harvest mites), animal mites, bird mites, food mites, grain mites, follicle mites, and scabies. Except for the mite *Sarcoptes scabiei* var. *hominis* (see Chapter 284) and *Demodex* mites (see "Follicle Mites" later), which parasitize only humans, mites are only occasional predators of humans. Unlike the scabies mites, the occasional predators do not burrow into their hosts' skin, and they may remain attached to the skin surface only long enough to obtain a blood meal.

CHIGGERS

The common chigger, also known as the harvest mite or red bug, belongs to the family Trombiculidae and is prevalent in the southern United States, especially during the summer and fall months. Chiggers live on grasses and shrubs, and it is the larval form that attaches itself to passing animals or humans. After obtaining a blood meal, the larvae drop off, and, within hours, extremely pruritic, erythematous papules appear (Fig. 286–1). Occasionally, the larvae may be seen in the center of the lesions, but these have usually dropped off or have been scratched off by the time the eruption appears. Lesions are most frequent on the legs and are especially likely to occur where clothing is snug against the skin and may impede the migration of the larvae. The severity of the eruption depends on the allergic sensitivity of the host to the mite's oral secretions. If the reaction is severe, fever or a background eczematous eruption, or both, may develop. Secondary bacterial infection may also develop.

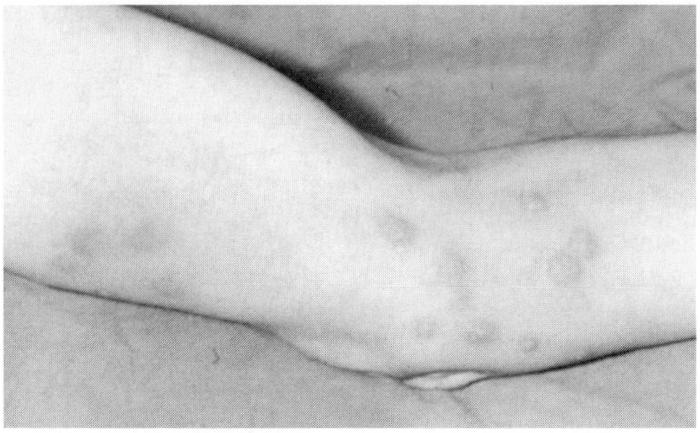

FIGURE 286–1. Intense reaction to chigger bites.

ANIMAL MITES

Humans may be the occasional hosts of mites that are the usual parasites of birds and mammals. Canine mites *(Sarcoptes scabiei* var. *canis)* from infested dogs and *Cheyletiella* spp. infesting the coats of dogs, cats, and rabbits can bite humans. *Dermanyssus gallinae* is a common ectoparasite of fowl and other birds. The mouse mite, *Liponyssoides sanguineus*, parasitizes mice and rats and has been documented as a vector for rickettsialpox. *Ornithonyssus bacoti* is an ectoparasite of certain species of rats as well as mice, hamsters, and guinea pigs and is a probable vector of murine typhus.[2]

FOOD, GRAIN, AND STRAW MITES

Grocery and warehouse workers who handle food such as cheese, flour, or vegetables infested with mites and farmers exposed to grain or straw mites may likewise develop pruritic eruptions as a result of mite bites. The clinical appearance of these as well as the animal mite bites consists of pruritic erythematous macules and papules that may show a central red punctum with vesiculation or crusting.

FOLLICLE MITES

Demodex folliculorum and *Demodex brevis* are mites that inhabit the pilosebaceous follicles, especially of the face and eyelids of humans and some animals. Although usually considered harmless saphrophytes, *Demodex* spp. can cause "red mange" in dogs, which is manifested by scaling, erythema, nodules, and alopecia.[2] *Demodex* spp. are present in large numbers and may be pathogenic in some people with rosacea and blepharitis. Skin lesions of demodicidosis do not resemble insect bite reactions, as seen with bites of other mites discussed earlier, but instead appear as erythematous follicular papulopustules, usually on the face. Treatment with topical sulfur preparations, lindane, or permethrin is often effective for *Demodex* spp. infestations.[3]

HOUSE DUST MITES

There is increasing evidence that hypersensitivity to house dust mites can cause flares in atopic diseases such as asthma, allergic rhinitis, and atopic dermatitis.[4] The most common species of dust mite in North America are *Dermatophagoides pteronyssinus* and *Dermatophagoides farinae.*[4]

TREATMENT AND PREVENTION

Treatment of mite bites is symptomatic. Oral antihistamines such as hydroxyzine, 25 to 50 mg by mouth three to four times daily, and the application of potent topical steroids such as fluocinonide cream twice a day give temporary relief of pruritus. Secondary bacterial infection should be treated with appropriate antibiotics. Most lesions resolve spontaneously within a week. Elimination of animal or plant sources of infestation or spraying an infested area with chemicals may reduce or eliminate human mite infestations. Protective clothing and insect repellents are useful for prevention.

REFERENCES

1. Moschella SL, Hurley JH, eds. Dermatology. Philadelphia: WB Saunders; 1986.
2. Alexander JO. Arthropods and Human Skin. New York: Springer-Verlag; 1984.
3. Bonnar E, Eustace P, Powell FC. The demodex mite population in rosacea. J Am Acad Dermatol. 1993;28:443–448.
4. Platts-Mills TAE, Chapman MD. Dust mites: Immunology, allergic disease and environmental control. J Allergy Clin Immunol. 1987;80:755–775.

Bibliography

Alexander JO. Arthropods and Human Skin. New York: Springer-Verlag; 1984.
Hewitt M, Barrow GI, Miller DC, et al. Mites in the personal environment and their role in skin disorders. Br J Dermatol. 1973;89:401.

Chapter 287

Ticks (Including Tick Paralysis)

MICHAEL ERIC MATHIEU
BARBARA BRAUNSTEIN WILSON

Ticks are vectors of bacterial, viral, and protozoal diseases throughout the world. Globally, ticks are second only to mosquitoes as vectors of infectious diseases, but in North America ticks are the leading perpetrator of vector-borne infections. A number of tick-borne diseases are recognized in the United States, including Lyme disease, Rocky Mountain spotted fever, human monocytic and granulocytic ehrlichiosis, tularemia, relapsing fever, Colorado tick fever, babesiosis, and tick paralysis, nearly all of which are zoonoses. Humans thus become infected with microbes usually found in wild animals when an ecologic niche involving mammals and ticks is violated. Ticks may also simply bite without transmitting disease and cause generally benign, but annoying, cutaneous inflammatory reactions.

BIOLOGY AND ECOLOGY

Ticks are bloodsucking arthropods of the class Arachnida. Three families are recognized: Ixodidae, hard ticks; Argasidae, soft ticks; and Nuttalliellidae, a less well-known group with characteristics of both hard and soft ticks. Hard ticks contain a dorsal plate known as the scutum, and adults have mouth parts that extend anteriorly from the head region when viewed from above. In contrast to soft ticks, male and female hard ticks also exhibit distinguishing morphologic characteristics. Some hard ticks have a one host life cycle with larva, nymph, and adult acquiring blood meals from the same host. Many *Ixodes* species, however, require three separate hosts. Adult mating occurs on the first host, and the fully engorged female drops off to lay eggs on the ground and then die. Six-legged larvae hatch in about 1 month and are sometimes referred to as seed ticks. Larval forms generally feed on small animals such as rodents and, when fully fed, drop to the ground and molt into eight-legged nymphs. Adults similarly develop from nymphs after obtaining a complete blood meal from another host. Ixodidae ticks generally require prolonged attachment to the host, feeding slowly and continuously at first and then rapidly engorging over approximately 24 hours. Hard ticks encounter hosts, including humans, by so-called questing, wherein ticks climb to the top of vegetation and await a potential host. Vibration or carbon dioxide stimulates the tick to wave its legs or move about to facilitate attachment to a passing host. Hard ticks favor brushy, wooded, or weedy areas populated by a variety of mammals. The interface between forest and field is an ideal habitat for most hard ticks. Desiccation is a constant threat that influences activity.

Soft ticks favor animal dwellings such as burrows, dens, or human-made animal or human shelters in endemic areas. Soft ticks are relatively unaffected by arid conditions. Females often have several opportunities to lay eggs and many ticks of the family Argasidae undergo several nymphal molts before achieving adult status. Nymphal and adult forms tend to feed rapidly and leave the host quickly.

Ticks penetrate the host epidermis by insertion and lateral motion of chelicerae, sharp structures located on the distal segments of the mouth parts. The hypostome, the tubelike central component of the mouth parts, is inserted into the defect for withdrawal of blood. The depth of penetration of the mouth parts varies with the species. Hard ticks generally elaborate a liquid cement from the salivary glands that hardens and holds the mouth parts in place for the 7 to 14 days required for blood meals. Transmission of tick-borne diseases occurs only after attachment has proceeded for several hours (Table 287–1).

Ticks are important vectors for the transmission of rickettsial, viral, and bacterial diseases (see Table 287–1). Rocky Mountain spotted fever is caused by *Rickettsia rickettsii*, which is transmitted primarily by *Dermacentor andersoni* (wood tick) in the western United States and *Dermacentor variabilis* (dog tick) (Fig. 287–1) in the eastern United States and Canada.[1]

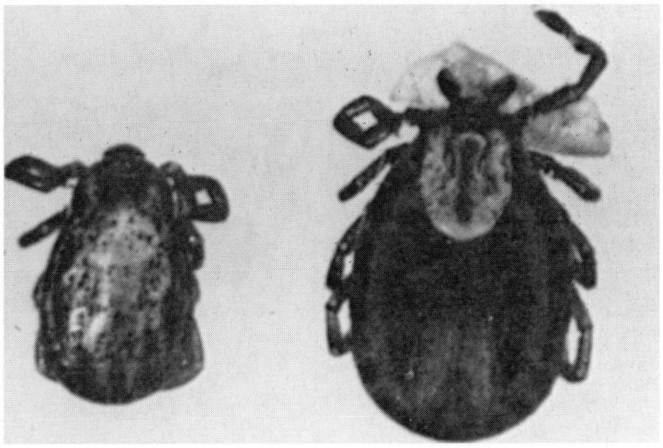

FIGURE 287–1. Nymph and adult dog ticks *(Dermacentor variabilis)*. The adult female dog tick is approximately twice as large as the adult female deer.

Lyme disease is a zoonosis caused by infection by the spirochete *Borrelia burgdorferi* and is the most common vector-borne disease in the United States. In 1996, 16,461 cases from 45 states and the District of Columbia were reported to the Centers for Disease Control and Prevention.[3] *Ixodes scapularis* (also known as *Ixodes dammini*) (deer tick) (Fig. 287–2) is believed to be the principal vector for Lyme disease in the northeastern and midwestern United States and *Ixodes pacificus* is the principal vector in the western United States.[2] The nymph stage of *I. scapularis* is approximately the size of a poppy seed and is therefore frequently overlooked. The adult deer tick, however, can also transmit Lyme disease and can be distinguished from the dog tick by its smaller size (approximately one

TABLE 287–1 Some Ticks of Medical Importance in the United States

Species Name, Common Name	Description	Distribution	Diseases	Comments
Ixodidae, hard ticks				
Ixodes scapularis, black-legged tick	Dark brown with long mouth parts	Northern form from southern Ontario south through eastern and central United States to Virginia; southern form to northern Mexico	Northern form transmits Lyme disease, babesiosis, and human granulocytic ehrlichiosis; Lyme transmission requires >24 h for nymphs, 36 h for adults	Adults active in fall, winter, and spring; immature forms active in spring and summer; favors edges of paths, roads; nymphs important vectors
Ixodes pacificus, western black-legged tick	Similar to *I. scapularis*	Canadian Pacific coast south through California to Mexico	Lyme disease; Lyme transmission requires 96 h for nymphs	May cause type I sensitivity reactions
Dermacentor variabilis, American dog tick	Dark brown with rounded mouth parts	Throughout United States except Rocky Mountains; southern Canada; northern Mexico	RMSF, tularemia; RMSF transmission requires ≥24 h	Handling ticks picked off dogs may be risky; favor trails or roadsides near clearings
Dermacentor andersoni, Rocky Mountain wood tick	Dark brown with white markings on scutum	Rocky Mountains and adjacent areas of United States and Canada	RMSF, Colorado tick fever, tularemia, tick paralysis	Favors brushy vegetation
Ambylomma americanum, Lone Star tick	Red-brown with long mouth parts; females have white spot on back	Central Texas north and east to Iowa and New York; northern Mexico	Tularemia, human monocytic ehrlichiosis, ?Lyme or Lyme-like disease in southeastern United States	Bites aggressively in southern areas; nymphs are common seed ticks
Ambylomma maculatum, Gulf Coast tick	Brown females have metallic markings on scutum; long mouth parts	Southeastern Atlantic and Gulf coasts, south to South America	None	Bites aggressively
Argasidae, soft ticks				
Ornithodoros hermsi	Characteristic soft tick morphology, gray, mammalated, up to 1 cm	Western United States and Canada	Relapsing fever	Painless bite; often found in cabins
Ornithodoros turicata, relapsing fever tick	Similar to *O. hermsi*	Southwestern and south-central United States to northern Florida, eastern Mexico	Relapsing fever	Painless bite but intense local reaction may occur

Abbreviation: RMSF, Rocky Mountain spotted fever.

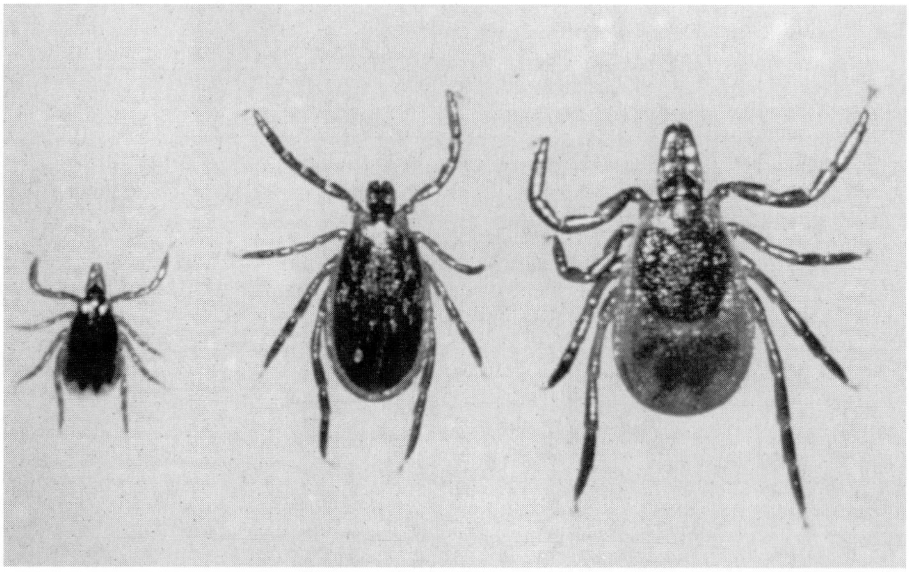

FIGURE 287–2. Nymph, adult male, and adult female ticks *(Ixodes scapularis [dammini])*. (Courtesy of Dr. Willy Burgdorfer, Hamilton, Mont.)

half) and the presence of an orange crescent along the posterior dorsal plate.

Human ehrlichioses are potentially life-threatening zoonoses transmitted by ticks. Human monocytic ehrlichiosis (HME) is due to *Ehrlichia chaffeensis; Amblyomma americanum*, the Lone Star tick, is the putative vector. Human granulocytic ehrlichiosis (HGE) is caused by an agent very similar to *Ehrlichia phagocytophila* and *Ehrlichia equi*. The hard tick *I. scapularis*, the most important vector in Lyme disease, is the probable vector of human granulocytic ehrlichiosis.[2] The vector for *Ehrlichia sennetsu* is unknown.

Other human diseases that may be transmitted by hard ticks include arboviruses, Colorado tick fever, tularemia, Q fever, babesiosis, and boutonneuse fever. Hard ticks emerge in early spring and summer, and sometimes a second peak occurs in autumn.

Tick infestation can cause great economic losses to industries dependent on domestic animals such as cattle and sheep by causing damage to hides or decreases in an animals' market weight. Ticks can also transmit infectious diseases such as babesiosis or rickettsial diseases to domestic animals.

CLINICAL MANIFESTATIONS

Uncomplicated Bites

Most tick bites are asymptomatic. Attached ticks should be removed as soon as possible because of the relation between feeding interval and disease transmission. Unprotected fingers should not be used to remove ticks, and one should avoid crushing or puncturing the tick. The standard method of removal is to grasp the anterior aspect of the arthropod with blunt, rounded forceps as close to the skin surface as possible and pull upward in a continuous motion. Instruments designed specifically to remove ticks are commercially available and may confer an advantage over standard forceps for the removal of nymphal forms.[2] Note that the ease of removal varies with the species; *D. variabilis*, for example, attaches superficially and *A. americanum* attaches more deeply.[2] If necessary, the tick may be removed by performing a small shave excision.

After removal, in uncomplicated bites, a pruritic erythematous papule or plaque may be present for 1 to 2 weeks. Sometimes, a persistent, firm, pruritic, erythematous papule or nodule known as a tick bite granuloma may develop. Microscopically, this lesion demonstrates a granulomatous reaction, which is thought to represent a response to retained foreign material at the bite site. If a granuloma persists, intralesional corticosteroids and occasionally surgical excision may be required for relief of pruritus.

TICK PARALYSIS

A rare but alarming reaction may occasionally occur in which prolonged attachment (5 to 7 days) of certain species of ticks may result in paralysis of the host. The paralysis begins in the lower extremities and ascends symmetrically to involve the trunk, upper extremities, and head within a few hours. A neurotoxin isolated from the tick salivary gland is thought to be responsible for the neurologic symptoms. Forty-three species of ticks have been found to cause tick paralysis, but the ticks most often responsible are *Ixodes holocyclus* in Australia, *D. andersoni* in western North America, and *D. variabilis* in eastern North America.[1] A seasonal incidence of tick paralysis corresponds to the breeding season of relevant ticks. In most cases, removal of the tick leads to rapid resolution of symptoms; however, the response may be slow and associated with electromyographic evidence of denervation. Tick paralysis caused by *L. holocyclus* can be especially severe, and the host may die despite removal of the tick. A hyperimmune serum against *I. holocyclus* has been developed and is an effective treatment for tick paralysis caused by this species of tick; however, it is ineffective against other species.

CLINICAL MANIFESTATIONS

Human Ehrlichioses

Bacteria of the genus *Ehrlichia* are rickettsia-like obligatory intracellular organisms found within the cytoplasmic vacuoles of host phagocytic leukocytes. White-tailed deer and dogs appear to be important reservoir species for *E. chaffeensis*, the agent implicated in HME. Lone Star tick larvae or nymphs presumably acquire the organisms from infected reservoir species and then transmit the disease to humans. Most patients with clinical disease are middle-aged men presenting during spring or summer. Missouri, Tennessee, Oklahoma, Texas, Arkansas, Virginia, and Georgia have the highest number of serologically confirmed cases in the United States.[10] Fever, myalgia, headache, nausea, and other nonspecific symptoms are frequent. An exanthem develops in up to 36% of patients. Leukopenia, thrombocytopenia, and elevation of hepatic transaminases are common laboratory abnormalities. Delay in diagnosis and institution of appropriate therapy increases the risk of fatal complications.[8] Diagnosis is based largely on clinical suspicion, but detection of organism-specific nucleic acids in body fluids by polymerase chain reaction amplification and serologic testing are available. Doxycycline, 100 mg twice a day is the treatment of choice.

HGE was initially described in the upper Midwest but cases have since been reported from several states in the eastern United States and California. The epidemiologic features resemble those of Lyme disease because *I. scapularis* is the principal vector and white-footed mice and deer are likely reservoirs.[9] Patients with concurrent Lyme disease and HGE have been reported, and ticks from an area in which Lyme disease is endemic have a high prevalence of the HGE agent. Other important mammalian reservoirs include sheep, goats, cattle, horses, and dogs. As with HME, adult men presenting in the spring or summer are most frequently affected.[10] Clinical features are generally similar to those of HME except that cutaneous findings are much less frequent. Thrombocytopenia, leukopenia, and transaminase elevation are usual and intracellular inclusions may be observed in peripheral blood neutrophils. HGE is potentially more severe than HME. Diagnosis and treatment are identical to those of HME.

Lyme Disease

The most common tick-borne disease in the United States is Lyme disease, a multisystem disorder caused by the spirochete *B. burgdorferi* (see Chapter 231). As already mentioned, species of *Ixodes* are the primary vectors for Lyme disease. The seasonal occurrence of Lyme disease parallels the emergence of *Ixodes* ticks between May and November, with most cases occurring during June and July. At the site of a tick bite, within 4 to 20 days an erythematous papule may develop and expand into an erythematous annular lesion with central clearing, an eruption known as erythema chronicum migrans (Fig. 287–3). Secondary annular lesions may also develop weeks to months later at locations distant from the original tick bite. Patients with Lyme disease may also have internal involvement, primarily of the heart, joints, and nervous system. Treatment options for early disease include doxycycline and amoxicillin.[4] The use of prophylactic antibiotics after tick bites is controversial, but most authorities advise against this practice even in highly endemic areas.[4, 6, 7]

ERADICATION AND PREVENTION

A well-organized and carefully implemented program can successfully control medically or economically important ticks in a limited geographic area. Such programs include the widespread use of acarricides in domestic animals and the breeding of domestic animals that are resistant to tick infestation. Spraying an area with appropriate chemicals may temporarily reduce the tick population.

Persons exposed to ticks should wear protective clothing and insect repellents and examine themselves for ticks. Children should be examined periodically by their parents during the tick season (midspring to midsummer). Periodic removal of ticks from household pets is important to prevent spread within the household.

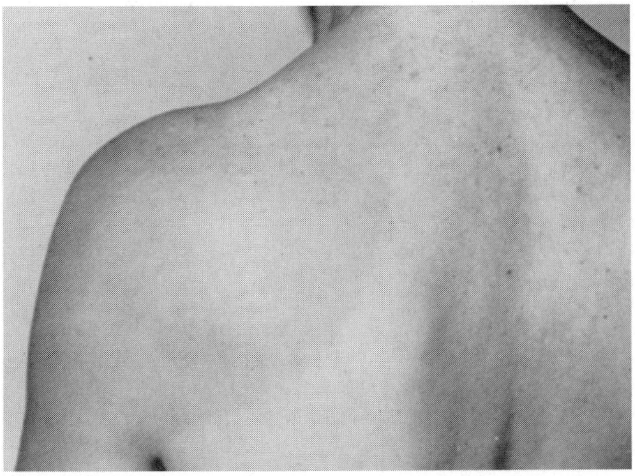

FIGURE 287–3. Expanding erythematous annular lesion of erythema migrans on the shoulder of a patient with Lyme disease.

REFERENCES

1. Spach DH, Liles WC, Campbell GL, et al. Medical progress: Tick-borne diseases in the United States. N Engl J Med. 1993;329:939–947.
2. Stewart RL, Burgdorfer W, Needham GR. Evaluation of three commercial tick removal tools. Wilderness Environ Med. In press.
3. Matuschka F-R, Spielman A. The vector of the Lyme disease spirochete. N Engl J Med. 1992;327:542.
4. Anonymous. Lyme Disease—United States. 1996. JAMA. 1997;278:112.
5. Anonymous. Treatment of Lyme disease. Med Lett Drugs Ther. 1997;39:47–48.
6. Shapiro ED, Gerber MA, Holabird NB, et al. A controlled trial of antimicrobial prophylaxis for Lyme disease after deer-tick bites. N Engl J Med 1992;327:1769–1773.
7. Dennis DT, Meltzer MI. Antibiotic prophylaxis after tick bites. Lancet. 1997;350:1191–1192.
8. Fix AD, Strickland GT, Grant J. Tick bites and Lyme disease in an endemic setting: Problematic use of serologic testing and prophylactic antibiotic therapy. JAMA. 1998;279:206–210.
9. Fishbein DB, Dawson JE, Robinson LE. Human ehrlichiosis in the United States, 1985 to 1990. Ann Intern Med. 1994;120:736–743.
10. Bakken JS, Kreuth J, Wilson-Nordskog RL, et al. Human granulocytic ehrlichiosis (HGE): Clinical and laboratory characteristics of 41 patients from Minnesota and Wisconsin. JAMA. 1996;275:199–205.
11. Walker DH. Emerging human ehrlichiosis: Recently recognized, widely distributed, life-threatening tick-borne diseases. In: Scheld WM, Armstrong D, Hughes JM, eds. Emerging Infections. Washington, DC: ASM Press; 1998:81–91.

Bibliography

Goddard J. Physician's Guide to Arthropods of Medical Importance. 2nd ed. Boca Raton, Fla: CRC; 1996.
Sonenshine DE. Biology of Ticks, v. 1. New York: Oxford University Press; 1991.
Sonenshine DE. Biology of Ticks, v. 2. New York: Oxford University Press; 1993.
Sonenshine DE, Mather TN, eds. Ecological Dynamics of Tick-Borne Zoonoses. New York: Oxford University Press; 1994.

Chapter 288

Kawasaki Syndrome

FRANK T. SAULSBURY

Kawasaki syndrome is an acute systemic vasculitis that affects primarily infants and young children. It was first reported in the Japanese literature in 1967 by Dr. Tomisaku Kawasaki.[1] The initial reports in the English literature appeared in the 1970s under the designation "mucocutaneous lymph node syndrome."[2, 3] Kawasaki syndrome is not a new disease; earlier descriptions of infantile periarteritis nodosa almost certainly represented examples of Kawasaki syndrome.[4] Kawasaki syndrome is now recognized throughout the world, but the prevalence is noticeably increased in Japan, where more than 100,000 cases have been reported. In the United States, 3000 to 5000 cases occur annually, and Kawasaki syndrome has replaced acute rheumatic fever as a leading cause of acquired heart disease in children.[5]

EPIDEMIOLOGY

Although Kawasaki syndrome has been reported in a few adults,[6, 7] it is overwhelmingly a disease of children, particularly children of Asian ancestry.[8] The peak age of onset is 1 to 2 years, and 80% of patients are younger than 4 years of age. The male-to-female ratio is 1.5:1. Not only are males affected more frequently, but they are at greater risk of developing coronary artery aneurysms, the most serious complication of the disease.[9]

Kawasaki syndrome occurs sporadically and in miniepidemics. Both endemic and epidemic diseases occur more commonly in late winter and spring. Despite the epidemic nature of the illness, person-to-person spread has not been documented, and secondary cases in contacts of affected patients are unusual.

Nevertheless, Kawasaki syndrome occurs in siblings (especially twins) of affected patients more frequently than in the general population.[10] More than half of the secondary cases in siblings develop within 10 days after the first case, suggesting a common exposure to an infectious agent.

CLINICAL FEATURES

The diagnosis of Kawasaki syndrome is established by the presence of the clinical criteria listed in Table 288–1.[11] Fever is usually the initial feature of Kawasaki syndrome. It is characteristically high, spiking and prolonged, and persisting for 1 to 2 weeks in untreated patients. Bilateral, nonpurulent conjunctivitis ensues shortly after the onset of fever and lasts 1 to 2 weeks in untreated patients. The conjunctival involvement is characterized by hyperemia and injection of the bulbar conjunctivae. Changes of the oropharyngeal mucosa consisting of (1) erythema progressing to fissuring, cracking, and bleeding of the lips; (2) strawberry tongue; and (3) diffuse erythema of the oropharynx are prominent during the acute febrile period. Changes of the extremities include erythema of the palms and soles accompanied by firm, indurative edema. The swollen extremities may be quite painful.

During recovery, a distinctive pattern of skin desquamation develops. Desquamation begins in the periungual region and often extends to involve the entire palms and soles. Approximately 1 to 2 months after the onset of the illness, transverse grooves across the nails (Beau's lines) appear in some patients. The erythematous rash of Kawasaki syndrome usually appears shortly after the onset of fever and it persists during the febrile period. Most often, the rash is a raised, deep red plaquelike eruption. A morbilliform maculopapular rash with multiforme-like target lesions, a scarlatiniform erythroderma, and rarely a fine pustular eruption have also been observed in Kawasaki syndrome. Typically, there is widespread involvement of the trunk and extremities with accentuation in the perineal area. Cervical lymphadenopathy is the least common of the principal diagnostic criteria. At least one lymph node more than 1.5 cm in diameter is necessary to fulfill this criterion. Usually there is enlargement of a single cervical lymph node; the nodes are firm, nonfluctuant, and only moderately tender.

In addition to the clinical features that constitute the diagnostic criteria, there is a wide variety of associated findings in Kawasaki syndrome, owing to the systemic nature of the vasculitis. Some of the more common associated features are listed in Table 288–2.[12]

Up to 10% of patients do not meet the clinical criteria, and they are designated as having atypical Kawasaki syndrome. Atypical disease is especially common in young infants. Patients with atypical Kawasaki syndrome remain at risk for coronary artery aneurysms.[13]

TABLE 288–1 Diagnostic Criteria for Kawasaki Syndrome

A. Fever of at least 5 days duration (100%)
B. Presence of at least four of the following five conditions:
  1. Bilateral conjunctivitis (85%)
  2. Changes of the lips and oral mucosa (90%)
    - Dry, red, fissured lips
    - Strawberry tongue
    - Oropharyngeal erythema
  3. Changes of the extremities (75%)
    - Erythema of palms and soles
    - Edema of hands and feet
    - Periungual desquamation
  4. Polymorphous rash (80%)
  5. Cervical lymphadenopathy (70%)
C. Illness not explained by other known disease processes

TABLE 288–2 Associated Features of Kawasaki Syndrome

- Cardiac disease
  - Coronary artery aneurysms
  - Myocarditis
  - Pericarditis
  - Mitral or aortic regurgitation
  - Dysrhythmias
- Irritability
- Arthralgia, arthritis
- Aseptic meningitis
- Urethritis with sterile pyuria
- Hepatitis
- Hydrops of the gallbladder
- Pneumonitis
- Anterior uveitis
- Sensorineural hearing loss
- Peripheral ischemia

The clinical course of untreated Kawasaki syndrome is triphasic. The acute febrile phase, lasting 7 to 14 days, is dominated by the features constituting the diagnostic criteria. Irritability, anorexia, aseptic meningitis, and hepatic dysfunction are also prominent features of the acute phase. During the subacute phase, which lasts 2 to 4 weeks, fever, rash, and lymphadenopathy resolve, but irritability and conjunctival injection may persist. Arthritis and desquamation of the fingers and toes occur during the subacute phase. Thrombocytosis, often reaching very high levels, is seen during the subacute phase. This is the time in which patients are at greatest risk for coronary artery thrombosis. The convalescent phase of Kawasaki syndrome begins when all clinical signs have disappeared and continues until the sedimentation rate and platelet count return to normal, usually 6 to 10 weeks after the onset of illness.

Recurrent Kawasaki syndrome after apparent resolution is rare, occurring in only 1 to 3% of patients.[14] Most recurrences develop within a few weeks of the original episode.

CARDIAC INVOLVEMENT

Although carditis is not included in the diagnostic criteria, cardiac involvement is the hallmark of Kawasaki syndrome, and it is the major source of morbidity and mortality. During the acute phase, up to 50% of patients have myocarditis manifested by tachycardia and gallop rhythms. Occasionally, myocarditis is severe enough to produce overt congestive heart failure. Pericarditis, conduction disturbances, and regurgitation of the mitral and aortic valves are less frequent manifestations of cardiac involvement during the acute phase.[15]

The most serious cardiac complication of Kawasaki syndrome is aneurysmal dilatation of the coronary arteries, which occurs in approximately 20% of untreated patients.[15] Dilatation of the proximal coronary arteries may be detected as early as 7 days after the onset of fever, and the peak frequency of coronary aneurysm formation occurs within 4 weeks of the onset of illness. If unrecognized and untreated, the coronary aneurysms are prone to clot during the subacute phase of the illness, when the patients are hypercoagulable because of the extreme thrombocytosis. Sudden death resulting from coronary thrombosis and myocardial infarction occurs in 1 to 2% of untreated patients.

The coronary aneurysms regress within 1 to 2 years in the majority of patients.[16] However, even with echocardiographic resolution of the aneurysms, there may be persistent coronary artery stenosis and cardiac ischemia in some patients.[17] The long-term consequences of coronary arteritis are unclear. However, ischemic heart disease, myocardial infarction, and sudden death have been reported in young adult survivors of childhood Kawasaki syndrome.[18, 19]

LABORATORY FEATURES

The laboratory features of Kawasaki syndrome are nonspecific and nondiagnostic. The acute phase of the illness is characterized by marked inflammation and immune activation. Most patients have a moderate leukocytosis with a left shift. The sedimentation rate and other acute-phase reactants are almost universally elevated during the acute febrile period. The platelet count, which is normal in the first few days of Kawasaki syndrome, begins to rise in the second week of the illness and may exceed 1 million/mm^3. Tests for antinuclear antibody and rheumatoid factor are routinely negative. A number of immunoregulatory abnormalities have been described in patients with Kawasaki syndrome. These include increased proportions of activated $CD4^+$ lymphocytes, decreased numbers of $CD8^+$ lymphocytes, polyclonal B-cell activation, and increased production of a number of proinflammatory cytokines.[20]

PATHOLOGY

Kawasaki syndrome is a generalized vasculitis involving small and medium-size arteries, with a predilection for the coronary arteries. Histologically, Kawasaki syndrome is characterized by endothelial cell necrosis, leukocyte infiltration of the media and adventitia, medial disruption, aneurysmal dilatation, and intraluminal thrombosis.[21]

ETIOLOGY AND PATHOGENESIS

The clinical and epidemiologic features of Kawasaki syndrome clearly suggest an infectious etiology. However, intensive efforts during the past 25 years have failed to identify a single, verifiable infectious cause of Kawasaki syndrome. Evidence suggests that Kawasaki syndrome may be caused by superantigen bacterial toxins.[22] Superantigens stimulate large populations of T cells expressing particular T-cell receptor β-chain variable gene segments.[23] The immunologic consequences of superantigen stimulation include massive proliferation and expansion of the target T cells with resultant production of proinflammatory cytokines.[23] The pathologic consequences of uncontrolled activation of the immune system include the recruitment of endothelial cells into the inflammatory process with resultant vascular damage.[20, 22]

A number of toxins elaborated by *Staphylococcus aureus* and *Streptococcus pyogenes* are known to have superantigen properties.[23] Several lines of evidence support a role for staphylococcal or streptococcal superantigen toxins in the pathogenesis of Kawasaki syndrome. First, selective expansion of $V_\beta 2^+$ and $V_\beta 8^+$ T cells in the peripheral blood of patients with Kawasaki syndrome provides indirect evidence of exposure to superantigens.[24–26] Second, selective expansion of $V_\beta 2^+$ T cells has been found in the myocardium, coronary arteries, and small intestinal mucosa of patients with Kawasaki syndrome.[27, 28] Third, staphylococci and streptococci elaborating superantigen toxins (toxic shock syndrome toxin-1 and streptococcal pyrogenic exotoxin, respectively) have been cultured from patients with Kawasaki syndrome.[29, 30] However, other studies have not confirmed the expansion of $V_\beta 2^+$ or $V_\beta 8^+$ T cells in the peripheral blood of patients with Kawasaki syndrome, and suggest that conventional antigens rather than superantigens are involved in the etiology of Kawasaki syndrome.[31–33] Moreover, culture and serologic data have disputed the role of staphylococcal or streptococcal superantigen toxins in the pathophysiology of Kawasaki syndrome.[34, 35] Thus, the hypothesis that Kawasaki syndrome is caused by bacterial exotoxins possessing superantigen properties requires confirmation. Nevertheless, it represents the first putative etiology put forth in the past 30 years that explains not only the clinical and epidemiologic features of Kawasaki syndrome but also the immunoregulatory abnormalities that characterize the disease.

THERAPY

Despite incomplete knowledge concerning the etiology and pathogenesis, there has been effective therapy for Kawasaki syndrome for more than 10 years. Several randomized studies in Japan and the United States have demonstrated that high-dose intravenous immune globulin (IGIV) is extremely effective therapy for Kawasaki syndrome.[36–38] The use of IGIV has resulted in a substantial decrease in the morbidity and mortality associated with Kawasaki syndrome. IGIV produces rapid resolution of fever and other clinical manifestations of the acute febrile phase and reverses the laboratory indices of systemic inflammation. More important, when IGIV is administered within the first 10 days of the illness, the incidence of coronary artery aneurysms is reduced from approximately 20% in untreated patients to 3 to 4%.[37] In addition to preventing coronary aneurysms, IGIV is effective in promoting the resolution of established aneurysms.[39] A number of dosage schedules have been studied, but the most effective regimen is a single infusion of IGIV at a dose of 2 g/kg given over 10 hours.[38]

The mechanisms by which IGIV produces the dramatic beneficial effects remain unclear. IGIV is a powerful immunomodulating agent,[40] and it may directly reverse a number of the immunologic abnormalities associated with Kawasaki syndrome.[41, 42] The rapidity with which it works suggests toxin neutralization as a possible mechanism of action of IGIV. Indeed, commercial IGIV contains specific antibodies to bacterial toxin superantigens.[43] These findings support the theory of a superantigen toxin etiology of Kawasaki syndrome and provide a plausible explanation for the rapid, dramatic benefit of IGIV therapy.

Aspirin is used as adjunctive therapy in Kawasaki syndrome. Traditionally, aspirin is administered in anti-inflammatory doses (80 to 100 mg/kg/day) until day 14 of the illness. The dose is then reduced to 3 to 5 mg/kg/day in order to provide an antiplatelet effect during the period of thrombocytosis when patients are at risk for clotting coronary artery aneurysms.[44]

Because IGIV therapy aborts the acute phase of the illness so rapidly, treatment with low-dose aspirin from the outset seems reasonable, but this regimen has not been studied prospectively.[44] Nevertheless, a meta-analysis of published data found no significant difference in the incidence of coronary artery disease between patients treated with IGIV plus high-dose aspirin and patients treated with IGIV and low-dose aspirin.[45]

In patients with no evidence of coronary artery disease, low-dose aspirin is continued until the platelet count returns to normal. In patients with coronary aneurysms despite IGIV therapy, low-dose aspirin should be continued indefinitely or until 1 year after the aneurysms resolve. Echocardiography at the time of diagnosis provides valuable baseline information. All patients should have repeated echocardiography 3 to 6 weeks after therapy in order to guide the duration of aspirin therapy.

REFERENCES

1. Kawasaki T. Acute febrile mucocutaneous syndrome with lymphoid involvement with specific desquamation of the fingers and toes in children: Clinical observations of 50 cases. Jpn J Allerg. 1967;16:178–222.
2. Kawasaki T, Kosaki F, Okawa S, et al. A new infantile acute febrile mucocutaneous lymph node syndrome (MLNS) prevailing in Japan. Pediatrics. 1974;54:271–276.
3. Melish ME, Hicks RM, Larson EJ. Mucocutaneous lymph node syndrome in the United States. Am J Dis Child. 1976;130:599–607.
4. Landing BH, Larson EJ. Are infantile periarteritis nodosa with coronary artery involvement and fatal mucocutaneous lymph node syndrome the same? Comparison of 20 patients from North America with patients from Hawaii and Japan. Pediatrics. 1977;59:651–662.
5. Taubert KA, Rowely AH, Shulman ST. Nationwide survey of Kawasaki disease and acute rheumatic fever. J Pediatr. 1991;119:279–282.
6. Paira SO, Roverano S. Kawasaki syndrome in a young adult. J Rheumatol. 1992;19:488–490.
7. Jackson JL, Kunkel MR, Libow L, et al. Adult Kawasaki disease. Arch Intern Med. 1994;154:1398–1405.
8. Yanagawa H, Kawasaki T, Shigematsu I. Nationwide survey of Kawasaki disease in Japan. Pediatrics. 1987;80:58–62.
9. Beiser AS, Takahashi M, Baker AL, et al. A predictive instrument for coronary artery aneurysms in Kawasaki disease. Am J Cardiol. 1998;81:1116–1120.
10. Fugita Y, Nakamura Y, Sakata K, et al. Kawasaki disease in families. Pediatrics. 1989;84:666–669.

11. Rauch A, Hurwitz E. Centers for Disease Control case definition of Kawasaki syndrome. Pediatr Infect Dis J. 1985;4:702–703.
12. Baron KS. Kawasaki disease in children. Curr Opin Rheumatol. 1998;10:29–37.
13. Fukushige J. Takahashi N, Ueda Y, et al. Incidence and clinical features of incomplete Kawasaki disease. Acta Paediatr. 1994;83:1057–1060.
14. Nakamura Y, Yanagawa H. A case-control study of recurrent Kawasaki disease using the database of the nationwide surveys in Japan. Eur J Pediatr. 1996;155:303–307.
15. Rose V. Kawasaki syndrome—Cardiovascular manifestations. J Rheumatol. 1990;17(Suppl 24):11–14.
16. Kato H, Ichinose E, Yoskioka F, et al. Fate of coronary aneurysms in Kawasaki disease: Serial coronary angiography and long-term follow-up study. Am J Cardiol. 1982;49:1758–1766.
17. Tanaka N, Naoe S, Masuda H, et al. Pathological study of sequelae of Kawasaki disease (MCLS) with special reference to the heart and coronary arterial lesions. Acta Pathol Jpn. 1986;36:1513–1527.
18. Burns JC, Shike H, Gordon JB, et al. Sequelae of Kawasaki disease in adolescents and young adults. J Am Coll Cardiol. 1996;28:253–257.
19. Kato H, Sugimura T, Akagi T, et al. Long-term consequences of Kawasaki disease. A 10 to 21 year follow-up study of 594 patients. Circulation. 1996;94:1379–1385.
20. Leung DYM. Immunologic aspects of Kawasaki syndrome. J Rheumatol. 1990;17(suppl 24):15–18.
21. Landing BH, Larson EJ. Pathologic features of Kawasaki disease (mucocutaneous lymph node syndrome). Am J Cardiovasc Pathol. 1987;1:215–229.
22. Leung DYM, Meissner C, Fulton DR, et al. Superantigens in Kawasaki syndrome. Clin Immunol Immunopathol. 1995;77:119–126.
23. Drake CG, Kotzin BL. Superantigens: Biology, immunology, and potential role in disease. J Clin Immunol. 1992;12:149–162.
24. Abe J, Kotzin BL, Jujo K, et al. Selective expansion of T cells expressing T-cell receptor variable regions $V_{\beta}2$ and $V_{\beta}8$ in Kawasaki disease. Proc Natl Acad Sci U S A. 1992;89:4066–4070.
25. Abe J, Kotzin BL, Meissner C, et al. Characterization of T cell repertoire changes in acute Kawasaki disease. J Exp Med. 1993;177:791–796.
26. Curtis N, Zheng R, Lamb JR, et al. Evidence for a superantigen mediated process in Kawasaki disease. Arch Dis Child. 1995;72:308–311.
27. Leung DYM, Giorno RC, Kazemi LV, et al. Evidence for superantigen involvement in cardiovascular injury due to Kawasaki syndrome. J Immunol. 1995;155:5018–5021.
28. Yamashiro Y, Nagata S, Oguchi S, et al. Selective increase of $V_{\beta}2^+$ T cells in the small intestinal mucosa in Kawasaki disease. Pediatr Res. 1996;39:264–266.
29. Leung DYM, Meissner HC, Fulton DR, et al. Toxic shock syndrome toxin–secreting *Staphylococcus aureus* in Kawasaki syndrome. Lancet. 1993;342:1385–1388.
30. Leung DYM, Sullivan KE, Brown-Whitehorn TF, et al. Association of toxic shock syndrome toxin–secreting and exfoliative toxin–secreting *Staphylococcus aureus* with Kawasaki syndrome complicated by coronary artery disease. Pediatr Res. 1997;42:268–272.
31. Pietra BA, De Inocencio J, Giannini EH, et al. TCR Vβ family repertoire and T cell activation markers in Kawasaki disease. J Immunol. 1994;153:1881–1888.
32. Choi IH, Chwae YJ, Shim WS, et al. Clonal expansion of $CD8^+$ T cells in Kawasaki disease. J Immunol. 1997;159:481–486.
33. Jason J, Montana E, Donald JF, et al. Kawasaki disease and the T cell antigen receptor. Hum Immunol. 1998;59:29–38.
34. Terai M, Miwa K, Williams T, et al. The absence of evidence of staphylococcal toxin involvement in the pathogenesis of Kawasaki disease. J Infect Dis. 1995;172:558–561.
35. Morita A, Imada Y, Igarashi H, et al. Serologic evidence that streptococcal superantigens are not involved in the pathogenesis of Kawasaki disease. Microbiol Immunol. 1997;41:895–900.
36. Furusho K, Kamiya T, Nakano H, et al. High-dose intravenous gammaglobulin for Kawasaki disease. Lancet. 1984;2:1055–1058.
37. Newburger JW, Takahashi M, Burns JC, et al. The treatment of Kawasaki syndrome with intravenous gamma globulin. N Engl J Med. 1986;315:341–347.
38. Newburger JW, Takahashi M, Beiser AS, et al. A single intravenous infusion of gamma globulin as compared with four infusions in the treatment of acute Kawasaki syndrome. N Engl J Med. 1991;324:1633–1639.
39. Saalouke MG, Venglarick JS, Baker DR, et al. Rapid regression of coronary dilatation in Kawasaki disease with intravenous gamma globulin. Am Heart J. 1991;121:905–909.
40. Dwyer JM. Manipulating the immune system with immune globulin. N Engl J Med. 1992;326:107–116.
41. Leung DYM, Burns JC, Newburger JW, et al. Reversal of lymphocyte activation in vivo in the Kawasaki syndrome by intravenous gammaglobulin. J Clin Invest. 1987;79:468–472.
42. Saulsbury FT. The effect of intravenous immunoglobulin on lymphocyte populations in children with Kawasaki syndrome. Clin Exp Rheumatol. 1992;10:617–620.
43. Takei S, Arora YK, Walker SM. Intravenous immunoglobulin contains specific antibodies inhibitory to activation of T cells by staphylococcal toxin superantigens. J Clin Invest. 1993;91:602–607.
44. Rowley AH, Shulman ST. Current therapy for acute Kawasaki syndrome. J Pediatr. 1991;118:987–991.
45. Durongpisitkul K, Gururaj VJ, Park JM, et al. The prevention of coronary artery aneurysm in Kawasaki disease: A meta-analysis on the efficacy of aspirin and immunoglobulin treatment. Pediatrics.1995;96:1057–1061.

PART IV

Special Problems

SECTION A

NOSOCOMIAL INFECTIONS

Chapter 289

Organization for Infection Control

MICHAEL B. EDMOND
RICHARD P. WENZEL

Infection control as a formal discipline in the United States developed in the late 1950s primarily to address the problem of nosocomial staphylococcal infection. Over the ensuing years, the field of infection control, through the incorporation of epidemiologic principles and the application of statistical analysis, emerged as one facet of the broader discipline of hospital epidemiology. The lessons learned from the development of infection-control programs are now being used to forge new territory, with infection control serving as a paradigm for other programs that monitor clinical performance.

The primary role of an infection-control program is to reduce the risk of hospital-acquired infection, thereby protecting patients, employees, health care students, and visitors. Nosocomial infections develop in at least 5% of patients admitted to hospitals in the United States[1] and account for 88,000 deaths yearly.[2] In 1992, these infections were estimated to add $4.5 billion to the annual expenditures for health care in the United States.[3] In the era of managed care with an intense focus on cost control, the value of effective infection control is obvious.

The functions of a hospital epidemiology program vary from institution to institution but can generally be divided into the following areas: surveillance, outbreak investigation, education, the health of health care employees, the monitoring and management of institutional antibiotic utilization, the development of infection-control policies and procedures, and new-product evaluation. In some hospitals, quality improvement is also performed through the hospital epidemiology program. In the academic setting, additional functions of the program may include research and the provision of consultative services to other acute care and long-term care facilities, public health agencies, and the university campus. The major functions of the effective hospital epidemiology program are discussed later.

SURVEILLANCE

The first aim of surveillance is to determine endemic rates of infection. Once endemic rates have been established, outbreaks can then be identified when a particular rate differs significantly from the endemic rate. The importance of surveillance was demonstrated by the Study on the Efficacy of Nosocomial Infection Control, which found a 32% reduction in nosocomial infections in hospitals with active surveillance programs compared with hospitals without such programs.[4]

Surveillance for nosocomial infections is generally targeted to areas of the hospital where the highest rates of infection and antibiotic resistance are likely to be found. These areas include intensive care units, cardiothoracic surgery units, and hematology and oncology units. Hospital-wide surveillance (i.e., concurrent surveillance throughout the entire hospital) is rarely practiced today because the resources required are prohibitive. Surveillance for some types of infections (e.g., blood stream infections, infections with antimicrobial-resistant organisms) is primarily microbiology-based; therefore, hospital-wide surveillance can be implemented relatively easily.

The use of the hospital information system can streamline the work of surveillance, because pharmacy, radiology, and laboratory (including microbiology) data can be obtained quickly. These data, along with fever charts and the nursing plan, can identify patients for whom chart reviews should be performed. Such a system has been found to be 81% sensitive and 97% specific.[5]

Unit-based surveillance trends should be periodically reported back to the health care workers in the unit. It is important that the data be delivered in a nonconfrontational manner. Infectious diseases of public health importance should be reported to public health agencies.

OUTBREAK INVESTIGATION

Data accumulated by ongoing surveillance allow the detection of nosocomial outbreaks. When the monthly rate for a particular infection exceeds the 95% confidence interval based on the previous years' rates for that month, the possibility of an outbreak exists and an investigation is warranted. At other times, an astute observation of a potential cluster of infections by physicians, nurses, or the microbiology laboratory technologists should prompt at least an initial investigation. The primary investigating team should include the hospital epidemiologist, the director of employee health, and the infection-control practitioners. External consultants may be necessary in some cases. Table 289–1 summarizes the steps of an outbreak investigation.

EDUCATION

The importance of the educational function of the hospital epidemiology program cannot be overstated. A substantial role for the infection-control practitioner is to educate hospital personnel in the areas of communicable disease control, sterilization, disinfection, and insti-

TABLE 289–1 Steps for Investigating an Outbreak

1. Develop a case definition.
2. Using the case definition, show statistically that current rates are significantly higher than preoutbreak rates.
3. Review the relevant medical literature.
4. Plot an epidemic curve with the number of cases on the Y-axis and time on the X-axis.
5. Review the charts of case patients, and develop line lists containing demographic data (dates of admission and procedures, ward locations and dates) and exposure to potential risk factors.
6. Plot a time line with data for all common events. The number of cases is plotted on the Y-axis, and the time interval between infection and potential risk factor (e.g., procedure, medication, contact with potentially infected patient or health care worker) is plotted on the X-axis.
7. Formulate a hypothesis regarding the source of infection and mechanism of transmission.
8. Perform a case-control study, comparing infected patients of the same age, gender, and service with exposure to potential risk factors.
9. Institute temporary infection-control measures.
10. Obtain cultures of suspected common sources.
11. Continue surveillance to document the efficacy of control measures.
12. Write a report of the investigation for the infection-control committee. Review infection-control policies related to the outbreak and revise if necessary.

tutional infection-control policies. In many hospitals, the hospital epidemiology team is responsible for blood-borne pathogen training, which is mandated by the Occupational Safety and Health Administration for all employees,[6] and in some hospitals may be responsible for airborne-isolation-mask training and fit testing. Unfortunately, educational efforts aimed at modifying the behavior of health care workers (e.g., increasing hand washing, eliminating needle recapping) have in general had little success.

HOSPITAL EMPLOYEE HEALTH

The hospital epidemiology program must work very closely with the employee health service. Issues such as postexposure prophylaxis of sharps injuries, and the management of exposures to communicable diseases such as varicella, influenza, meningococcal disease, and tuberculosis require the concerted effort of the two groups. In addition, the employee health service is responsible for ensuring that health care workers are free of communicable diseases. At the time of employment, workers should be reviewed to ensure that they have adequate immunity against illnesses such as rubella, measles, tetanus, hepatitis B, and varicella. In addition, baseline and periodic skin testing for tuberculosis should be performed, as well as postexposure testing. The employee health service should proactively and creatively devise delivery systems that encourage compliance with annual influenza vaccination by all health care workers.

ANTIMICROBIAL UTILIZATION

Nearly one half of hospitalized patients receive antimicrobial agents.[7] The hospital epidemiology program should monitor the antimicrobial susceptibility profiles produced by the microbiology laboratory on a regular basis to observe for trends in the development of antimicrobial resistance. This should be correlated with the antimicrobial agents currently used in the institution. The best data are obtained if nosocomial isolates are distinguished from community-acquired isolates, if only blood stream isolates are tested (true pathogens with high mortality), and if only one isolate per patient is counted in the numerator and denominator. To identify the nature of the relationship between antibiotic use and resistance, a graph could be plotted with the proportion of unique nosocomial blood stream isolates that were resistant to the drug on one axis and the total grams of usage for that drug by year on the other axis. Efforts should be made to optimize antimicrobial prophylaxis for operative procedures, optimize the choice and duration of empiric antimicrobial therapy, and improve antimicrobial prescribing practices by educational and administrative means.[8]

POLICY DEVELOPMENT

The primary administrative function of the infection-control program is to develop, implement, and continually evaluate policies and procedures designed to minimize the risk of nosocomial infection. Some policies are designed to be implemented institution-wide, whereas others apply to specific areas of the hospital. Policies are generally developed by the infection-control committee after a review of data generated in-house as well as information gleaned from the medical literature. Recommendations from the infection-control committee may then need to be forwarded to other committees for review and approval before dissemination of the new policy.

NEW-PRODUCT EVALUATION

A large number of new medical products are marketed each year. These products may be introduced into the hospital setting with few data to support their efficacy or their advantage over existing products. Often the newer products are significantly more costly. The hospital epidemiology program should evaluate existing data on new products designed to reduce infections or protect health care workers and make recommendations regarding their introduction to the hospital.

QUALITY ASSESSMENT

The components of quality monitoring include data collection and analysis, interpretation, remedial action to correct poor quality, and verification that remedial actions have actually improved quality.[9] Optimally, the assessment of quality should occur at every stage of health care delivery, from access to the hospital through hospitalization and postdischarge follow-up. The determinants of the quality of medical care have been categorized by Donabedian into structure, process, and outcome.[10] Structure refers to the set of actions required to provide care to the patient, and outcome is the result of those actions. Assessment of quality can be aimed at structure, process, or outcome, although assessment of outcome usually is the most meaningful. Efforts at monitoring and improving quality should focus on high-volume diagnoses and procedures as well as high-cost procedures.[11]

Organization of the Hospital Epidemiology Program

The organizational structure for infection control should be tailored to meet the demands of the hospital and to use available resources optimally. Larger hospitals with a high proportion of tertiary care patients require a more complex system to meet their needs.

Hospital Epidemiologist

The hospital epidemiologist occupies a unique position. He or she must interface with many hospital departments and extramural agencies, provide direct supervision of the infection-control program, and in some hospitals direct the quality assessment program. In areas where subspecialists are available, the position is generally held by a physician who is trained in infectious diseases. Unfortunately, however, many of these physicians have little or no training in the area of epidemiology.

There has been a trend for hospitals to recognize the importance of the role of the hospital epidemiologist and to compensate physicians for this work. In a 1996 survey of the membership of the Society for Healthcare Epidemiology of America, 50% of hospital epidemiologists were compensated for their infection-control activities.[12] The implementation of a prospective payment system for medical services placed a new emphasis on the avoidance of complications that prolong hospital stays (e.g., nosocomial infections) and provided an economic impetus for focusing on the quality of medical care. Preventing nosocomial infection is financially advantageous to the hospital because only 1 to 5% of the cost of treating the infection is reimbursed under the prospective payment system.[13]

Before assuming a hospital epidemiologist position, the physician should meet with key hospital administrators to discuss the responsibilities and expectations of the position, and to negotiate the human and material resources, including salary support, that will be made available to implement the infection-control program. An excellent review of resources necessary to operate an infection-control program is found in the Society for Healthcare Epidemiology of America position paper on infrastructure for infection control.[14]

Infection-Control Professionals

Talented infection-control professionals (ICPs) are essential for the operation of an excellent infection-control program. These individuals are usually registered nurses with clinical experience or medical technologists with experience in microbiology. The effective ICP must possess a working knowledge of epidemiologic principles and basic microbiology, and a sound understanding of the operations of the health care institution. Hoffmann has estimated that 30% of the

ICP's time should be devoted to surveillance activities, 25% to education, 15% to communication and consultation, and 10% each to quality assurance investigational studies, outbreak investigations, and exposure work-ups.[15]

Since the 1980s, the Centers for Disease Control and Prevention has recommended that hospitals should have one ICP for every 250 beds.[4] However, during the 1990s, the number of hospital beds has decreased, while the severity of illness of hospitalized patients has markedly increased. In response, the Society for Healthcare Epidemiology of America has recommended that the Centers for Disease Control and Prevention ratio is no longer valid.[14] In 1996, the Joint Commission of Accreditation of Healthcare Organizations suggested that hospitals should employ one ICP full-time equivalent for every 133 beds.[16] In a survey of University HealthSystem Consortium hospitals, a median of one ICP full-time equivalent per 137 occupied beds was documented. Other parameters were also evaluated and revealed a median of 28 intensive care unit beds, 1118 hospital staff, 6686 admissions, and 104,426 outpatient visits per ICP full-time equivalent.[17]

Infection-Control Committee

A multidisciplinary infection committee that meets at least quarterly is recommended. This committee should include representatives from the medical and nursing staffs, hospital administration, and the person or persons directly responsible for management of the infection-control program. The committee also typically includes the infection-control practitioners and representatives from the microbiology laboratory, pharmacy, operating room, and departments of employee health, housekeeping, central services, and engineering and maintenance. The ideal characteristics of committee members include the following: an interest in infection control, representation of a large group within the hospital, authority in their given specialty, tact, and charisma.

The bulk of the committee's work is best accomplished by a core that includes the hospital epidemiologist, infection-control professionals, the microbiologist, and the director of employee health. Policy formulations should be developed by this subgroup and after thoughtful consideration brought to the entire committee for review, ratification, and support from political and administrative standpoints. Thus, the purpose of the full infection-control committee is to provide the political support that allows the core members to implement policy.[18]

The chair of the committee should have expertise in hospital epidemiology and infection control. We recommend that the chair be either a physician trained in infectious diseases or a practicing physician trained in clinical epidemiology, because it is generally easier for a clinician to communicate effectively with the hospital staff. Usually it is best if the hospital epidemiologist functions as the committee chair.

In most hospitals the infection-control committee meets monthly. For greatest success, the meeting should be held on the same day and time each month. The meeting's agenda should be well planned and circulated to committee members before the meeting. In addition, the committee members should receive by mail all policies to be reviewed before the meeting to allow adequate time for review by individual committee members and to improve the efficiency of the meeting.

The agenda should begin with approval of the minutes of the previous meeting. This is followed by brief reports by representatives of the pharmacy, employee health department, and clinical microbiology laboratory. In addition, all communicable disease exposure work-ups from the previous month are summarized. Ideally, old business should be kept to a minimum. The monthly infection rates and trends should be reviewed. The focus of the meeting then turns to more in-depth reports of a few current issues, including outbreak investigations. Invited guests may discuss various aspects of these issues. In addition, we review and approve several policies at each meeting, obviating the need for a mass of policy approvals near the time of Joint Commission on Accreditation of Healthcare Organizations on-site survey.

Joint Commission on Accreditation of Healthcare Organizations

The Joint Commission on Accreditation of Healthcare Organizations is a nongovernmental, nonprofit organization that develops standards of quality used to accredit hospitals. The commission requires that health care organizations use a coordinated process to reduce the risks of endemic and epidemic nosocomial infections in patients and health care workers.[16] Accreditation is voluntary, although most hospitals view it as mandatory. It is important for the hospital epidemiologist to know and understand the Joint Commission on Accreditation of Healthcare Organizations standards and to work continually toward achieving compliance with them.

FUTURE CHALLENGES

The expected changes in the American health care system have presented the hospital epidemiologist with new challenges and opportunities. These reforms have prompted a renewed emphasis on efficiency, quality, and accountability. In the future, an increased reliance on scientific methods should be expected, including mathematical models to predict risks and outcomes, a greater need for information support, and rapid microbiologic techniques for molecular typing and antimicrobial resistance. The major shift of medical care to the outpatient setting requires the development of new methods to evaluate clinical performance. As the number and proportion of patients in the inpatient setting who are immunocompromised increases, environmental risks become more problematic and monitoring the environment will assume a high priority. Providing a safe workplace for health care workers will necessitate the development of innovative injury-prevention programs. The hospital epidemiologist will likely assume greater management responsibilities as programs expand and new roles are assumed. Lastly, the hospital epidemiologist will need to continue to ensure that institutional directives are based on sound epidemiologic principles, methods, and data and that the overarching goal is to improve the quality of patient care, not solely the control of resource utilization.

REFERENCES

1. Haley RW, Culver DH, White JW, et al. The nationwide infection rate: A new need for vital statistics. Am J Epidemiol. 1985;121:159–167.
2. Jasny BR, Bloom FE. It's not rocket science—but it can save lives. Science. 1998;280:1507.
3. CDC. Public health focus: Surveillance, prevention, and control of nosocomial infections. MMWR Morb Mortal Wkly Rep. 1992;41:783–787.
4. Haley RW, Culver DH, White JW, et al. The efficacy of infection surveillance and control programs in preventing nosocomial infections in US hospitals. Am J Epidemiol. 1985;121:183–205.
5. Broderick A, Mori M, Nettleman MD, et al. Nosocomial infections: Validation of surveillance and computer modeling to identify patients at risk. Am J Epidemiol. 1990;131:734–742.
6. Department of Labor. Occupational Safety and Health Administration. Occupational exposure to bloodborne pathogens: Final rule. Fed Reg. 1991;56:64,175–182.
7. Pallares, Dick R, Wenzel RP, et al. Trends in antimicrobial utilization at a tertiary teaching hospital during a 15-year period (1978–1992). Infect Control Hosp Epidemiol. 1993;14:376–382.
8. Goldmann DA, Weinstein RA, Wenzel RP, et al. Strategies to prevent and control the emergence and spread of antimicrobial-resistant microorganisms in hospitals: A challenge to hospital leadership. JAMA. 1996;275:234–240.
9. Donabedian A. Contributions of epidemiology to quality assessment and monitoring. Infect Control Hosp Epidemiol. 1990;11:117–121.
10. Donabedian A. The quality of care: How can it be assessed? JAMA. 1988;260:1743–1748.
11. Gross PA. The future of the hospital epidemiologist in the 1990s. Infect Control Hosp Epidemiol. 1995;16:179–182.
12. Membership survey. SHEA Newslett. 1996;6:5.
13. Haley RW, White JW, Culver DH, et al. The financial incentive for hospitals to

prevent nosocomial infections under the prospective payment system: An empirical determination from a nationally representative sample. JAMA. 1987;257:1611–1614.
14. Scheckler WE, Brimhall D, Buck AS, et al. Requirements for infrastructure and essential activities of infection control and epidemiology in hospitals: A consensus panel report. Infect Control Hosp Epidemiol. 1998;19:114–124.
15. Hoffmann KK. The modern infection control practitioner. In: Wenzel RP, ed. Prevention and Control of Nosocomial Infections, 3rd ed. Baltimore: Williams & Wilkins; 1997:33–45.
16. Joint Commission on Accreditation of Healthcare Organizations. Surveillance, prevention and control of infection. In: Comprehensive Accreditation Manual for Hospitals: The Official Handbook. Chicago: Joint Commission on Accreditation of Healthcare Organizations; 1998:IC1–IC24.
17. Friedman C, Chenoweth C, A survey of infection control professional staffing patterns at University Health System Consortium Institutions. Am J Infect Control. 1998;26:239–244.
18. Wiblin RT, Wenzel RP. The infection control committee. In: Herwaldt LA. A Practical Handbook for Hospital Epidemiologists. Thorofare, NJ: The Society for Healthcare Epidemiology of America; 1998:29–32.

Chapter 290

Isolation

MICHAEL B. EDMOND
RICHARD P. WENZEL

The purpose of isolating patients is to prevent the transmission of microorganisms from infected or colonized patients to other patients, hospital visitors, and health care workers (who may subsequently transmit them to other patients or become infected or colonized themselves). Because of the resurgence of tuberculosis and the increasing prevalence of colonization and infection with antibiotic-resistant organisms, a sizable fraction of hospitalized patients require isolation at any given time. Although isolation guidelines are based on current understanding of the mechanism of the transmission of organisms, few well-controlled studies have been performed to demonstrate their efficacy. Because nosocomial infections are relatively uncommon events, any study designed to demonstrate efficacy requires sample sizes that are often prohibitively large. Thus, studies evaluating the efficacy of infection-control measures often lack the power to allow one to confidently conclude a lack of effect (i.e., such studies have a high probability of type II error).

Because the process of isolating patients is expensive and time-consuming and may impede the care of the patient, it should be implemented only when necessary; conversely, failure to isolate a patient with a transmissible disease may lead to morbidity and mortality and may ultimately be quite expensive when one considers both the direct costs of an investigation of an outbreak and an excess length of stay and the indirect costs of lost productivity. Over the past 125 years, the practice of isolating patients has moved from the requirement for separate infectious disease hospitals to separate wards for these patients, and ultimately to providing precautions in the general hospital environment. In 1996, the Centers for Disease Control and Prevention and the Hospital Infection Control Practices Advisory Committee issued a revision of the recommended guidelines for isolation.[1] The new guidelines outline a two-tiered approach—standard precautions (which apply to all patients) and transmission-based precautions, which apply to patients with documented or suspected infection or colonization with certain microorganisms. These guidelines are summarized in Figure 290–1.

STANDARD PRECAUTIONS

Standard precautions have replaced universal precautions. These guidelines apply to all patients and stipulate that gloves should be worn to touch any of the following: blood; all body fluids, secretions, and excretions except sweat, whether or not they are visibly bloody; nonintact skin; and mucous membranes.[1] Hands should be washed immediately after gloves are removed and between patients. For procedures that are likely to generate splashes or sprays of body fluid, a mask with eye protection or a face shield and a gown should be worn. Gowns should be constructed of an impervious material to prevent penetration and subsequent contamination of the skin or clothing. Disposable, 100% polypropylene gowns have been demonstrated to be superior to reusable gowns in the prevention of both blood penetration and bacterial passage by the aerosol or blood-borne route.[2] Needles should not be recapped, bent, or broken but should be disposed of in puncture-resistant containers.[1]

Hand Washing

Because the majority of nosocomial infections are transmitted by the contact route, primarily by the hands of health care workers,[3] hand washing remains the single most important means to prevent the transmission of nosocomial pathogens. Nonetheless, observational studies in intensive care units have found that hand-washing compliance by health care workers is generally less than 50%.[4–9] It has been estimated that an increase in hand-washing compliance by 1.5- to twofold would result in a 25 to 50% decrease in the incidence of nosocomial infections,[6] but most studies designed to improve hand-washing compliance have not demonstrated a lasting positive effect.[10]

The microorganisms on the hand can be divided into transient flora and resident flora.[11] The resident flora includes organisms of low virulence (coagulase-negative staphylococci, *Micrococcus*, and *Corynebacterium*) that are rarely transmitted to patients except when introduced by invasive procedures.[12] They are not easily removed through hand washing. The transient flora, however, is an important cause of nosocomial infections. These organisms are acquired primarily by contact, are loosely attached to the skin, and are easily washed off. Thus, the purpose of hand washing in the hospital is to remove the transient flora recently acquired by contact with patients or environmental surfaces.[12]

Health care workers should wash their hands thoroughly before and after contact with patients and immediately after the removal of gloves.[1] In hospital units with high rates of antibiotic-resistant organisms, medicated hand-washing agents instead of bland soap should be used. Chlorhexidine and isopropyl alcohol are superior to bland soap and water in the removal of vancomycin-resistant enterococci and multiply-resistant gram-negative organisms from the hands.[13] Moreover, chlorhexidine has the advantage of producing a residual antibacterial effect.[14] In a large clinical trial comparing chlorhexidine to 60% isopropyl alcohol as hand-washing agents, Doebbeling and colleagues demonstrated that chlorhexidine resulted in a significantly lower nosocomial infection rate.[6]

In areas in which sinks are not readily accessible, wall-mounted dispensers with medicated, alcohol-based waterless agents should be installed. Alternatively, individual health care workers may carry small containers of waterless hand-washing agents. However, when the hands are visibly soiled, waterless agents alone are not adequate.

Gloves

Gloves should be worn by health care workers to prevent contamination of the hands with microorganisms, to prevent exposure of the health care worker to blood-borne pathogens, and to reduce the risk of transmission of microorganisms from the hands of the health care worker to the patient. However, gloves do not replace the need for hand washing. Contamination of the hands may occur with organisms on the surface of the gloves when they are removed,[15] and some gloves have small perforations that may allow organisms to contaminate the hands. Thus, gloves should be viewed as an adjunctive protective barrier but not as a substitute for hand washing.

	Airborne	Droplet	Contact	
Room	Negative pressure, private room with air exhausted to the outdoors or through high-efficiency filtration; door kept closed	Private room; door may remain open	Private room; dedicate use of noncritical patient-care items to a single patient	**Room**
	Private room for patients who contaminate the environment or cannot maintain appropriate hygiene			
Mask	N95 mask or portable respirator for those entering room; surgical mask should be placed on patient for transport outside of isolation room	For entering room; surgical mask should be placed on patient for transport outside of isolation room		**Mask**
	For procedures/activities likely to generate splashes/sprays of blood, body fluids, secretions, excretions			
Face shield/ eye protection	*For procedures/activities likely to generate splashes/sprays of blood, body fluids, secretions, excretions*			**Face shield/ eye protection**
Gown			If clothing will contact patient, surfaces, items in room; if patient has diarrhea, ileostomy, colostomy, uncontained wound drainage; remove gown before leaving room	**Gown**
	For procedures/activities likely to generate splashes/sprays of blood, body fluids, secretions, excretions			
Gloves			When entering room	**Gloves**
	When touching blood, body fluids, secretions, excretions, contaminated items, mucous membranes, nonintact skin. Remove promptly after use, before touching noncontaminated items, and before next patient			
Handwashing			Use medicated handwashing agent	**Handwashing**
	After touching blood, body fluids, secretions, excretions, contaminated items; immediately after glove removal; between patients			

FIGURE 290–1. Essential elements of isolation precautions. Standard precautions are shown in italics in the shaded areas.

TRANSMISSION-BASED PRECAUTIONS

Transmission-based precautions are a streamlined update of the previous category-specific precautions. These precautions apply to selected patients, based on either a suspected or confirmed clinical syndrome, a specific diagnosis, or colonization or infection with epidemiologically important organisms. It is important to note that transmission-based precautions are always implemented in conjunction with standard precautions. Three types of transmission-based precautions have been developed for the major modes of transmission of infectious agents in the health care setting: airborne, droplet, and contact.[1] A few diseases (e.g., varicella) require more than one isolation category. Essential elements of each isolation category are outlined in Figure 290–1, and indications for implementation are delineated in Table 290–1.

Airborne Precautions

Airborne precautions are designed to prevent the transmission of diseases by droplet nuclei (particles ≤ 5 μm) or dust particles containing the infectious agent.[1] These particles can remain suspended in the air and travel long distances. If the particles are inhaled, a susceptible host may develop infection. Airborne precautions are indicated for patients with documented or suspected tuberculosis (pulmonary or laryngeal), measles, varicella, or disseminated zoster. Patients who are infected with (or at high risk for infection with) human immunodeficiency virus with fever, cough, and a pulmonary infiltrate should be empirically placed under airborne precautions until tuberculosis can be ruled out.[1] Although open tuberculous skin wounds are uncommon, they have been presumptively associated with nosocomial transmission after manipulation of the wound (surgical débridement, dressing changes, irrigation).[16–18] Therefore, placement of such patients under airborne precautions should be considered. Patients with nontuberculous (atypical) mycobacterial pulmonary disease need not be isolated because person-to-person transmission does not occur.

Under airborne precautions, patients should be placed in a private room with monitored negative air pressure in relation to surrounding areas, and the room air must undergo at least six exchanges per hour.[19] The door to the isolation room must remain closed. Air from the isolation room should be exhausted directly to the outside, away from air intakes, and not recirculated. If outdoor exhaust is not possible, air should be exhausted through high-efficiency filters before it is returned to the general ventilation system.[19]

All persons entering the room of patients with suspected or confirmed tuberculosis must wear a personal respirator that filters 1-μm particles with an efficiency of at least 95%. These special masks must fit different facial sizes and characteristics, be fit-tested to obtain a leakage of 10% or less, and be able to be checked for fit each time the health care worker puts on the mask. The Occupational

TABLE 290–1 Indications for Transmission-Based Precautions

	Airborne	Droplet	Contact
Scenarios requiring empirical implementation of precautions	Vesicular rash* Maculopapular rash with coryza and fever Cough, fever, upper lobe pulmonary infiltrate Cough, fever, any pulmonary infiltrate in an HIV-infected patient (or patient at risk for HIV infection)	Meningitis Petechial or ecchymotic rash with fever Paroxysmal or severe persistent cough during periods of pertussis activity	Acute diarrhea with likely infectious cause in incontinent or diapered patient Diarrhea in adult with history of recent antibiotic use Vesicular rash Respiratory infections in infants and young children History of infection or colonization with MDR organisms Skin, wound, or urinary tract infection in patient with recent hospital or nursing home stay in facility where MDR organisms are prevalent Abscess or draining wound that cannot be covered
Known or suspected diseases or pathogens	Measles Tuberculosis, pulmonary or laryngeal Varicella* Zoster (disseminated or immunocompromised patient)*	Adenovirus (infants, children)* Diphtheria, pharyngeal *Haemophilus influenzae* meningitis, epiglottitis *Haemophilus influenzae* pneumonia (infants, children) Influenza Meningococcal infections Mumps *Mycoplasma* pneumonia Parvovirus B19 Pertussis Plague, pneumonic Rubella Streptococcal (group A) pharyngitis, pneumonia, scarlet fever (infants or young children)	Abscess, not covered or drainage not contained Adenovirus (infants, children)* Cellulitis, uncontrolled drainage Decubitus ulcer, infected and drainage not contained *Clostridium difficile* enterocolitis Conjunctivitis, acute viral Diphtheria, cutaneous *Escherichia coli* O157:H7 colitis (diapered or incontinent patients) Enteroviral infections (infants, young children) Furunculosis (infants, young children) Group A streptococcal major skin, burn, or wound infection Hemorrhagic fevers (Lassa, Marburg, Ebola) Hepatitis A (diapered or incontinent patients) HSV (neonatal; disseminated; severe primary mucocutaneous) Impetigo Lice Major (noncontained) abscess, cellulitis or decubitus MDR bacteria (e.g., MRSA, VRE, GISA, GRSA) infection or colonization Parainfluenza infection (infants, children) Pediculosis, scabies Rotavirus (diapered or incontinent patients) RSV infection (infants, children, immunocompromised) Rubella, congenital Scabies Streptococcal (group A) major skin, wound, or burn infection *Staphylococcus aureus* major skin, wound, or burn infection *Shigella* (diapered or incontinent patients) Varicella* *Yersinia enterocolitica* enteritis, disseminated or immunocompromised Zoster (disseminated or immunocompromised patient)*

*Condition requires two types of precautions.

Abbreviations: GISA, Glycopeptide-intermediate *S. aureus;* GRSA, glycopeptide-resistant *S. aureus;* HIV, human immunodeficiency virus; HSV, herpes simplex virus; MDR, multidrug-resistant; MRSA, methicillin-resistant *Staphylococcus aureus;* RSV, respiratory syncytial virus; VRE, vancomycin-resistant enterococci.

Safety and Health Administration requires that health care workers who manage patients with tuberculosis undergo fit-testing and training for self-fit checking.[19] Transportation of the patient from the isolation room should be limited, and the patient should be fitted with a standard surgical mask before leaving the room.[1] Before transport, hospital personnel in the area receiving the patient should be notified so that proper precautions can be implemented. Gowns and gloves are used as dictated by standard precautions.

Any patient with confirmed or suspected tuberculosis should be instructed to cover his or her mouth and nose with a tissue when coughing or sneezing. Patients should remain in isolation until tuberculosis can be ruled out. Isolation can generally be discontinued for patients with confirmed tuberculosis who are receiving effective antituberculous therapy and clinically improving when three consecutive sputum smears on separate days have no detectable acid-fast bacilli.[19] For patients with severe cavitary disease, persistent cough, or laryngeal tuberculosis, and possibly those who will return to an environment with high-risk individuals (e.g., children, immunosuppressed persons), we recommend the maintenance of isolation for at least 1 month. Patients with multidrug-resistant disease should remain in isolation for the duration of their hospital stay.[19] Hospitalization is unwarranted solely to provide isolation for clinically stable patients who are compliant with antituberculous therapy and agree to stay in their homes.

Patients with known or suspected measles, varicella, or disseminated zoster require airborne isolation, as do immunocompromised patients with localized zoster. Nonimmune health care workers should avoid entering the room of these patients when possible; if they are required to enter the room, they should wear a mask.[1]

Droplet Precautions

To prevent transmission by large-particle (droplet) aerosols, droplet precautions are used. Unlike droplet nuclei, droplets are larger, do not remain suspended in the air, and do not travel long distances. They are produced when the infected patient talks, coughs, or sneezes, and during some procedures (e.g., suctioning and bronchoscopy). A susceptible host may become infected if the infectious droplets land on the mucosal surfaces of the nose, mouth, or eye.

Droplet precautions require patients to be placed in a private room, but no special air handling is necessary.[1] Alternatively, patients with the same disease can be placed in the same room if private rooms are not available. Because droplets do not travel long distances (generally no more than 3 feet), the door to the room may remain open. Health care workers should wear standard surgical masks when working within 3 feet of the patient, although to improve compliance some hospitals require masks on entry into the room. Gowns and gloves should be worn when dictated by standard precautions. When transported out of the isolation room, the patient should be fitted with a standard surgical mask.[1]

Some illnesses that require droplet precautions include invasive *Haemophilus influenzae* type B and meningococcal infections, multidrug-resistant pneumococcal disease, *Mycoplasma* pneumonia, pertussis, influenza, mumps, rubella, and parvovirus B19 infections.

Contact Precautions

Contact precautions are implemented to prevent the transmission of epidemiologically important organisms from an infected or colonized patient through direct (touching the patient) or indirect (touching contaminated objects or surfaces in the patient's environment) contact. Patients in contact precautions should be placed in a private room, although patients infected with the same organism may be placed in the same room when private rooms are not available.[1] A number of studies have shown that multidrug-resistant organisms, such as vancomycin-resistant enterococci[20–25] and methicillin-resistant *Staphylococcus aureus*[26, 27] contaminate the environment (surfaces and items) in the vicinity of the infected or colonized patient. Therefore, barrier precautions to prevent the contamination of exposed skin and clothing should be employed. Gloves should be worn when entering the patient's room and removed before leaving the room. After the removal of gloves, the hands must be washed immediately with a medicated hand-washing agent and care should be taken to prevent recontamination of the hands before leaving the room.[1] Gowns should be worn if the health care worker anticipates substantial contact of his or her clothing with the patient or surfaces in the patient's environment. They should also be worn in situations in which there is an increased risk of contact with potentially infective material (e.g., the patient is incontinent, has diarrhea, colostomy, ileostomy, or uncontrolled wound drainage). Gowns should be removed before leaving the isolation room, and care should be taken to prevent contamination of clothing while removing the gown before leaving the room.[1] Numerous studies have documented contamination of noncritical patient care equipment (e.g., stethoscopes, blood pressure cuffs) with vancomycin-resistant enterococci and methicillin-resistant *Staphylococcus aureus*. Thus, these items should remain in the isolation room and not be used for other patients. If these items must be shared, they should be cleaned and disinfected before reuse. Transport of the patient from the isolation room should be kept to a minimum.

Contact precautions are indicated for patients infected or colonized with multidrug-resistant bacteria (e.g., methicillin-resistant *S. aureus*, vancomycin-resistant enterococci, glycopeptide-resistant *S. aureus*).[1] Other indications include *Clostridium difficile* enteritis, infections transmitted by the fecal-oral route (e.g., *Shigella*, rotavirus, hepatitis A virus infections) in patients who are diapered or incontinent, as well as acute diarrheal diseases likely to be infectious in origin. Infants and young children with respiratory syncytial virus, parainfluenza, or enteroviral infections and patients with neonatal, disseminated, or severe primary mucocutaneous herpes simplex virus infections should also be placed under contact precautions. Ectoparasitic infestations (lice and scabies) are additional indications. Patients with varicella or disseminated zoster require both contact and airborne precautions. Infants and children with adenovirus infection require contact and droplet precautions.[1]

Special Guidelines for Glycopeptide-Resistant *Staphylococcus aureus*

In the 1990s, vancomycin-resistant enterococci emerged and have become endemic in many American hospitals. Patients infected or colonized with these pathogens should be placed under contact precautions.[28] The increasing prevalence of vancomycin resistance among the enterococci coupled with the experimental transfer of vancomycin resistance genetic elements to *S. aureus* in both in vitro and in vivo models[29] raised concerns that vancomycin-resistant *S. aureus* strains would emerge in the clinical setting. Fortunately, such *vanA* strains have not been detected to date, but *S. aureus* strains with intermediate susceptibility to vancomycin have emerged in Japan and the United States.[30–35] Special isolation guidelines for this organism have been developed because the implications of a virulent pathogen with limited therapeutic options and the capacity for easy spread in the hospital setting are significant.[36–38]

In addition to contact precautions, we recommend limiting the number of health care workers caring for the infected or colonized patient and recording their names so that follow-up surveillance nasal cultures can be obtained. Health care workers with conditions predisposing to colonization with *S. aureus* (e.g., extensive dermatitides, insulin-requiring diabetes mellitus) should be restricted from the care of these patients.[37] To the greatest possible extent, diagnostic and therapeutic procedures should be performed in the patient's room to limit the need for the patient to leave the isolation room.[37] We recommend placing a monitor at the doorway to remind health care workers of appropriate infection control practices.[38] Isolation precautions should continue for the duration of hospitalization. After the patient is discharged, the room should undergo terminal disinfection with a quaternary ammonium compound and remain closed to new admissions until environmental cultures are found to be negative. If nosocomial transmission is documented, the hospital unit should be closed to new admissions.[37]

REFERENCES

1. Garner JS, Hospital Infection Control Practices Advisory Committee. Guideline for isolation precautions in hospitals. Infect Control Hosp Epidemiol. 1996;17:53–80.
2. Granzow JW, Smith JW, Nichols RL, et al. Evaluation of the protective value of hospital gowns against blood strike-through and methicillin-resistant *Staphylococcus aureus* penetration. Am J Infect Control. 1998;26:85–93.
3. Bauer TM, Ofner E, Just HM, et al. An epidemiological study assessing the relative importance of airborne and direct contact transmission of microorganisms in a medical intensive care unit. J Hosp Infect 1990;15:301.
4. Sproat LJ, Inglis TJJ. A multicentre survey of hand hygiene practice in intensive care units. J Hosp Infect. 1994;26:137.
5. Conley JM, Hill S, Ross J, et al. Handwashing practices in an intensive care unit: The effects of an educational program and its relationship to infection rates. Am J Infect Control. 1989;17:330.
6. Doebbeling BN, Stanley GL, Sheetz CT, et al. Comparative efficacy of alternative hand-washing agents in reducing nosocomial infections in intensive care units. N Engl J Med. 1992;327:88.
7. Kaplan LM, McGuckin M. Increasing handwashing compliance with more accessible sinks. Infect Control. 1986;7:408.
8. Albert RK, Condie F. Hand-washing patterns in medical intensive-care units. N Engl J Med. 1981;304:1465.
9. Graham M. Frequency and duration of handwashing in an intensive care unit. Am J Infect Control. 1990;18:77.
10. Larson E, Kretzer EK. Compliance with handwashing and barrier precautions. J Hosp Infect. 1995; 30(Suppl):88–106.
11. Price PB. The bacteriology of normal skin: A new quantitative test applied to a study of the bacterial flora and the disinfectant action of mechanical cleaning. J Infect Dis. 1938;63:301.
12. Steere AC, Mallison GF. Handwashing practices for the prevention of nosocomial infections. Ann Intern Med. 1975;83:683–690.
13. Wade JJ, Desai N, Casewell MW. Hygienic hand disinfection for the removal of epidemic vancomycin-resistant *Enterococcus faecium* and gentamicin-resistant *Enterobacter cloacae*. J Hosp Infect. 1991;18:211–218.
14. Wade JJ, Casewell MW. The evaluation of residual antimicrobial activity on hands and its clinical relevance. J Hosp Infect. 1991;18(Suppl B):23–28.
15. Doebbeling BN, Pfaller MA, Houston AK, et al. Removal of nosocomial pathogens from the contaminated glove: Implications for glove reuse and handwashing. Ann Intern Med. 1988;109:394–398.
16. Framptom MW. An outbreak of tuberculosis among hospital personnel caring for a patient with a skin ulcer. Ann Intern Med. 1992;117:312–313.
17. Hutton MD, Stead WW, Cauthen GM, et al. Nosocomial transmission of tuberculosis associated with a draining abscess. J Infect Dis. 1990;161:286–295.
18. Stead WW. Skin ulcers and tuberculosis outbreaks. Ann Intern Med. 1993;118:474.
19. Centers for Disease Control and Prevention. Guidelines for preventing the transmission of *Mycobacterium tuberculosis* in health-care facilities, 1994. MMWR Morb Mortal Wkly Rep. 1994;43:1–132.
20. Karanfil LV, Murphy M, Josephson A, et al. A cluster of vancomycin-resistant *Enterococcus faecium* in an intensive care unit. Infect Control Hosp Epidemiol. 1992;13:195–200.
21. Boyce JM, Mermel LA, Zervos JM, et al. Controlling vancomycin-resistant enterococci. Infect Control Hosp Epidemiol. 1995;16:634–637.
22. Boyce JM, Opal SM, Chow JW, et al. Outbreak of multidrug-resistant *Enterococcus faecium* with transferable *vanB* class vancomycin resistance. J Clin Microbiol. 1994;32:1148–1153.

23. Morris JG, Shay DK, Hebden JN, et al. Enterococci resistant to multiple antimicrobial agents, including vancomycin: Establishment of endemicity in a university medical center. Ann Intern Med. 1995;123:250–259.
24. Edmond MB, Ober JF, Weinbaum DL, et al. Vancomycin-resistant *Enterococcus faecium* bacteremia: Risk factors for infection. Clin Infect Dis. 1995;20:1126–1133.
25. Slaughter S, Hayden MK, Nathan N, et al. A comparison of the effect of universal use of gloves and gowns with that of glove use alone on acquisition of vancomycin-resistant enterococci in a medical intensive care unit. Ann Intern Med. 1996;125:448–456.
26. Blythe D, Keenlyside D, Dawson SJ, et al. Environmental contamination due to methicillin-resistant *Staphylococcus aureus* (MRSA). J Hosp Infect. 1998;38:67–70.
27. Boyce JM, Potter-Bynoe G, Chenevert C, et al. Environmental contamination due to methicillin-resistant *Staphylococcus aureus*: Possible infection control implications. Infect Control Hosp Epidemiol. 1997;18:622–627.
28. Hospital Infection Control Practices Advisory Committee. Recommendations for preventing the spread of vancomycin resistance: Recommendations of the Hospital Infection Control Practices Advisory Committee (HICPAC). Am J Infect Control. 1995;23:87–94.
29. Noble WC, Virani Z, Cree RG. Co-transfer of vancomycin and other resistance genes from *Enterococcus faecalis* NCTC 12201 to *Staphylococcus aureus*. FEMS Microbiol Lett. 1992;72:195–198.
30. Hiramatsu K, Hanaki H, Ino T, et al. Methicillin-resistant *Staphylococcus aureus* clinical strain with reduced vancomycin susceptibility. J Antimicrob Chemother. 1997;40:135–136.
31. Hiramatsu K, Aritaka N, Hanaki H, et al. Dissemination in Japanese hospitals of strains of *Staphylococcus aureus* heterogeneously resistant to vancomycin. Lancet. 1997;350:1670–1673.
32. Centers for Disease Control and Prevention. Reduced susceptibility of *Staphylococcus aureus* to vancomycin—Japan, 1996. MMWR Morb Mortal Wkly Rep. 1997;46:624–626.
33. Centers for Disease Control and Prevention. *Staphylococcus aureus* with reduced susceptibility to vancomycin—United States, 1997. MMWR Morb Mortal Wkly Rep. 1997;46:765–766.
34. Centers for Disease Control and Prevention. Update: *Staphylococcus aureus* with reduced susceptibility to vancomycin—United States, 1997. MMWR Morb Mortal Wkly Rep. 1997;46:813–815.
35. Tenover FC, Lancaster MV, Hill BC. Characterization of staphylococci with reduced susceptibilities to vancomycin and other glycopeptides. J Clin Microbiol. 1998;36:1020–1027.
36. Centers for Disease Control and Prevention. Interim guidelines for prevention and control of staphylococcal infection associated with reduced susceptibility to vancomycin. MMWR Morb Mortal Wkly Rep. 1997;46:626–628, 635.
37. Edmond MB, Wenzel RP, Pasculle AW. Vancomycin-resistant *Staphylococcus aureus*: Perspectives on measures needed for control. Ann Intern Med. 1996;124:329–334.
38. Wenzel RP, Edmond MB. Vancomycin-resistant *Staphylococcus aureus*: Infection control considerations. Clin Infect Dis. 1998; 27:245–249.

Chapter 291

Disinfection, Sterilization, and Control of Hospital Waste

MUSSARET ZAIDI
RICHARD P. WENZEL

Sound disinfection and sterilization policy is an essential element of a successful hospital infection control program. The potential for transmission of infection to patients and hospital personnel through contaminated medical devices is always present. The focus of sterilization and disinfection strategies includes medical equipment (surgical instruments, endoscopes, and ventilator circuits), nonsterile items (bedpans and urinals), and environmental surfaces (patients, chart covers and sinks).

DEFINITIONS[1–3]

Sterilization. The use of a physical or chemical procedure to destroy all microbial life, including bacterial endospores.

The authors are indebted to Dr. Martin Favero for kindly reviewing the manuscript.

Disinfection. A physical or chemical procedure performed on inanimate objects such as instruments and environmental surfaces that destroys most pathogenic microorganisms. High-level disinfection is a procedure that destroys all microorganisms except high numbers of bacterial endospores.

Antisepsis. This term is erroneously used interchangeably with disinfection. This procedure refers to the use of a germicide *on skin or living tissue* for the purpose of inhibiting or destroying microorganisms. Antiseptics are not designed to be used on medical devices, instruments, or environmental surfaces and should not be confused with disinfectants that are too irritating to be used on tissue or skin.

Germicide. A chemical agent that destroys microorganisms on either inanimate objects or living tissue.

Decontamination. The removal of pathogenic organisms from objects in order to make them safe to handle.[1, 2]

The selection of a sterilization or disinfection procedure depends on the type of item to be processed. A useful classification devised by Spaulding[1–3] stratifies medical equipment into critical, semicritical, and noncritical devices on the basis of the risk of infection involved with their use.

Critical Devices. These are instruments that have contact with the blood stream or sterile areas of the body. Examples are catheters, implants, and needles. Because the risk of acquiring infection is significant if these items are contaminated, critical devices should receive a sterilization process only.

Semicritical Devices. This term refers to devices that come in contact with mucous membranes. Examples include endoscopes, respiratory therapy equipment, and urinary catheters. For processing this equipment, sterilization is preferred over disinfection whenever possible. However, high-level disinfection preceded by proper physical cleaning of the instruments offers an acceptable margin of security.

Noncritical Devices. These include devices that come into contact with the patient's intact skin, such as stethoscopes, cardiac electrodes, and sphingomanometer cuffs. Environmental surfaces such as floors, walls, and surfaces of medical equipment also fall into this category. The risk of acquiring infection from these devices is minimal. The disinfection strategy for these depends on the particular surface but ranges from low-level disinfection to simple soap-and-water cleaning.

METHODS OF STERILIZATION

All critical and some semicritical devices require a sterilization procedure. Both physical and chemical methods exist to achieve sterilization. For instruments that can withstand high temperatures, either moist heat or dry heat is an excellent option. Instruments that are damaged by high temperatures can be sterilized with ethylene oxide (ETO) gas, gaseous formaldehyde, gas plasma, or a liquid sterilant such as peracetic acid or glutaraldehyde.

Steam and Dry Heat

Steam (moist heat under pressure) and dry heat autoclaves are inexpensive and effective devices for sterilization. Both may be used for linens, metallic surgical instruments, glass, fluids, and some plastics. Moist heat has the advantage of quickly penetrating all types of materials and is relatively unaffected by the presence of organic material. Steam autoclaves are routinely used at 121°C for time intervals that range from 15 to 30 minutes depending on the items to be sterilized.[1, 2] For emergencies, a cycle temperature of 132°C may be used to shorten sterilization times, a procedure known as flash sterilization.[4] The Association of Operating Room Nurses has established the following minimal parameters for flash sterilization at 132°C (1) 3 minutes for nonporous items and 10 minutes for porous items in gravity displacement autoclaves and (2) 4 minutes for both nonporous and porous items in prevacuum autoclaves.[5] Flash sterilization has a lower margin of safety because minimal times are used and items are unwrapped. Therefore, its use should be restricted to emergency situations only and it should never be used for sterilization of implantable devices.[6]

Dry heat sterilizers function at temperatures ranging from 121°C to 171°C. Their main disadvantages are that the time cycles are considerably longer than those of steam sterilizers, ranging from 16 hours at 121°C to 1 hour at 171°C, and their load capacity is smaller than that of steam autoclaves. For this reason, dry heat sterilizers are rarely used in the hospital setting, but they are useful for an office practice.[4]

Monitoring of the sterilization procedure in heat autoclaves is performed during each cycle with the use of Bowie-Davies tape. The tape undergoes a color change that indicates that the proper temperature was reached during the cycle. More accurate monitoring of the sterilization process is performed with the use of biologic indicators that are sold commercially. Because of their resistance to heat, *Bacillus stearothermophilus* spores are used for steam autoclaves and *Bacillus subtilis* spores are used for dry heat sterilizers. Most authorities recommend biologic monitoring of autoclaves at least once a week.[1] However, biologic indicator tests for steam and dry heat sterilizers should always be accompanied by measurements of time, temperature, and pressure and vacuum readings. When these measurements are consistently registered in an accurate manner, biologic tests may be performed with less frequency.[7]

For the sterilization of temperature-labile medical devices, available options include the use of a sterilization system (ETO, gaseous formaldehyde with steam, plasma gas, or peracetic acid) and immersion of the instruments in a liquid sterilant. If financially feasible, a sterilization system is preferred. Its use eliminates the potential for human error during the preparation, handling, or exchanges of the chemical sterilants. It also reduces possible toxicity to the health care workers in charge of the process.

Ethylene Oxide

ETO is a gas that can be used on a wide diversity of medical devices such as plastics, rubber, linens, endoscopes, surgical instruments, and fluids.[8] ETO's main form of cellular destruction is through a reaction with nucleic acids. It is known to alkylate the N position of guanine in DNA directly. Its major drawback is that it is carcinogenic and mutagenic. Chronic exposure to ETO has been associated with bone marrow carcinogenesis and axonal degeneration. Acute toxicity has occurred in health care workers. The symptoms and signs range from headache, dizziness, tachypnea, and vomiting to cyanosis, loss of motor coordination, convulsions, and coma. Because of the toxicity, carcinogenicity, and mutagenicity of ETO, all medical equipment sterilized with ETO requires an aeration period (8 to 24 hours) to reduce the amount of residual gas. Strict regulations have been imposed by the Environmental Protection Agency and the Occupational Safety and Health Administration to protect health care workers. The maximal permissible level of ETO in expired air is 0.5 mg/m^3, and the maximal acceptable blood level is 0.8 μg/100 ml. Hospitals that use ETO must install a special extraction system to reduce air emissions. Restrictions have also been imposed on the amount of ETO permitted to exit the sterilizers into the atmosphere.[8, 9] The standard cycle time for an ETO sterilizer is approximately 285 minutes, but sterilized items may not be used before adequate aeration, which is usually for a 24-hour period. All items processed in ETO sterilizers are wrapped and may be stored for future use. Biologic monitoring of the process is performed with *B. subtilis* spores, which must be used during every cycle when sterilizing implantable devices; otherwise, monitoring may be performed weekly.

Low-Temperature Steam with Gaseous Formaldehyde

Low-temperature steam with gaseous formaldehyde is a system that has been widely used in Europe for more than 30 years as an alternative to ETO for the sterilization of heat-labile equipment. Sterilization is achieved with a combination of gaseous formaldehyde and saturated steam at 65°C. Both of these are essential components for successful functioning of the process. Low-temperature steam with gaseous formaldehyde is suitable for all heat-labile material that can withstand a temperature of 65°C, such as nonflexible endoscopes, electric equipment, and most plastics. The total cycle including aeration takes approximately 2 hours. Biologic monitoring is performed with both *B. stearothermophilus* and *B. subtilis* to evaluate formaldehyde resistance and adequate hydration, both of which are necessary for full penetration of the steam. Because formaldehyde is known to be toxic and potentially carcinogenic, limits have been set for hospital worker exposure and residuals in sterilized equipment. The occupational exposure threshold limit is 0.6 mg/m^3, and the maximal acceptable residual on equipment is 5 μg/cm^2 measured on a filter paper.[9, 10] More information on formaldehyde is given later in the section on disinfection.

Gas Plasma Sterilization

Gas plasma sterilization is a technology that is well suited for temperature- and moisture-sensitive materials (Fig. 291–1). The gas

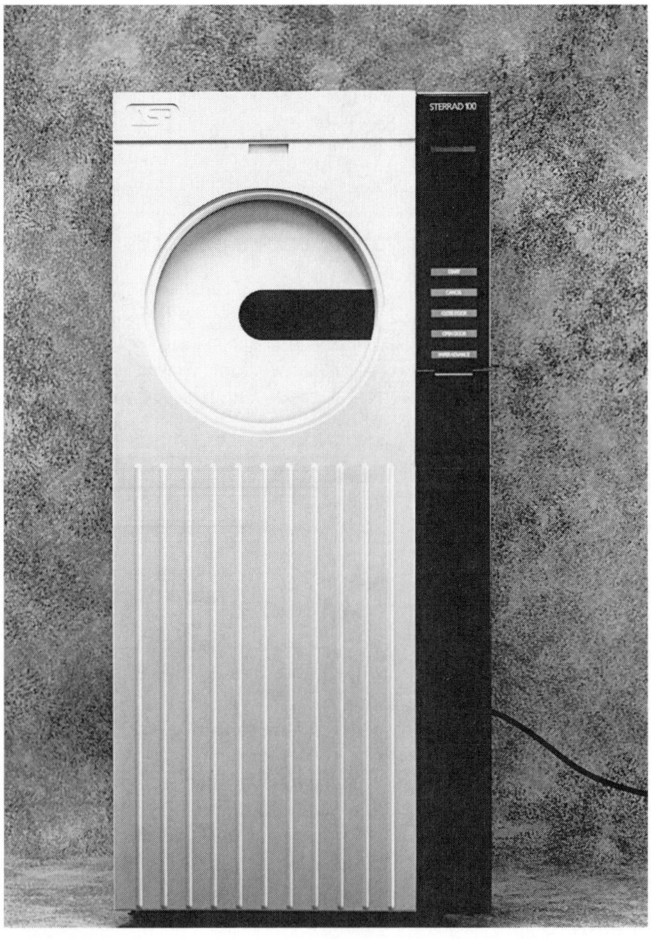

FIGURE 291–1. Gas plasma is an ecologically safe option for hospitals that require sterilization of large volumes of temperature-labile items. The equipment shown is a gas plasma sterilizer (STERAD, Advanced Sterilization Products, Johnson & Johnson, Calif.). The sterilizer weighs approximately 350 kg and requires a total of 9 m^2 for installation.

plasma is formed by applying a strong electric field to hydrogen peroxide vapor. In the plasma state, the hydrogen peroxide vapor is converted to hydroxyl and hydroperoxy free radicals, water, and oxygen. The free radicals in this plasma cloud disrupt cell membranes, enzymes, and nucleic acids and produce cell death. When the electric field is turned off, the activated components recombine to form oxygen and water vapor as by-products. This system has been approved by the Food and Drug Administration for use in sterilizing (1) metal and plastic instruments, including heat- and moisture-sensitive equipment and devices with internal lumina not less than 6 mm in diameter and not more than 310 mm in length, and (2) stainless steel devices with lumina not less than 3 mm in diameter and not more than 400 mm in length. Linens, powders, and liquids cannot be processed in this system. The standard cycle times range from 55 to 75 minutes. Because there are no toxic by-products, no aeration period is needed and sterilized items are immediately ready for use. Items are wrapped for the process and therefore may be stored for future use. The system is monitored with a chemical and biologic indicator (*B. subtilis* spore test pack), which is to be used at least once a day.

Sterilization with Liquid Germicides

Sterilization may also be achieved by immersion of medical equipment in chemical germicides. The most widely used liquid sterilants are peracetic acid and glutaraldehyde. A specific sterilization system using peracetic acid is available on the market (STERIS, Mentor, Ohio). The peracetic acid sterilization system is designed for most immersible medical devices. During a 30-minute cycle, the equipment to be sterilized is completely submerged in peracetic acid within a tabletop-sized chamber and subsequently rinsed thoroughly with sterile water. The system is especially apt for endoscopes and their accessories. Other devices such as ventilator circuits or surgical instruments may also be processed in this system. The major disadvantage of the system is that the final product is unwrapped and wet and, therefore, cannot be stored for future use. The by-products of the process, acetic acid, water, and oxygen, are nontoxic; therefore, there are no concerns regarding toxic residuals for patients or personnel.[11, 12] Biologic monitoring of the process can be performed with paper spore strips containing either *B. subtilis* or *B. stearothermophilus*. There is some debate about the validity of using biologic indicators to insure the sterility of liquid germicides. Studies have shown a good margin of overkill with no sterility failures. However, because the strip is submerged with the instruments in the liquid sterilant, a small number of spores (0.2 to 1.8%) are released from the strip into the solution, raising concerns about safety.[13] Further studies are clearly needed to achieve a consensus on the subject.

Other liquid sterilants are described in detail in the following section. For further information on sterilization systems, the reader may consult excellent reviews on the subject.[4, 7, 8, 12]

METHODS OF DISINFECTION

A wide variety of germicides exist for the disinfection of medical equipment and hospital surfaces. The compounds differ in their spectrum of activity against microorganisms. Some microorganisms, such as bacterial spores or parasite cysts, are innately highly resistant to disinfectants; others, such as viruses with lipid envelopes, are extremely sensitive. This variation among groups of microorganisms is related to the chemical composition and structure of the outer cell layers, which restrict the uptake of the germicide. The resistance of groups of microorganisms to germicides is shown in descending order in Figure 291–2.[1, 14]

HIGHEST

PRIONS
↓
BACTERIAL SPORES
↓
MYCOBACTERIA
↓
PARASITIC CYSTS
↓
SMALL NON-ENVELOPED VIRUSES
↓
TROPHOZOITES
↓
NON-SPORULATING GRAM-NEGATIVE BACTERIA
↓
FUNGI
↓
LARGE NON-ENVELOPED VIRUSES
↓
NON-SPORULATING GRAM-POSITIVE BACTERIA
↓
ENVELOPED VIRUSES

LOWEST

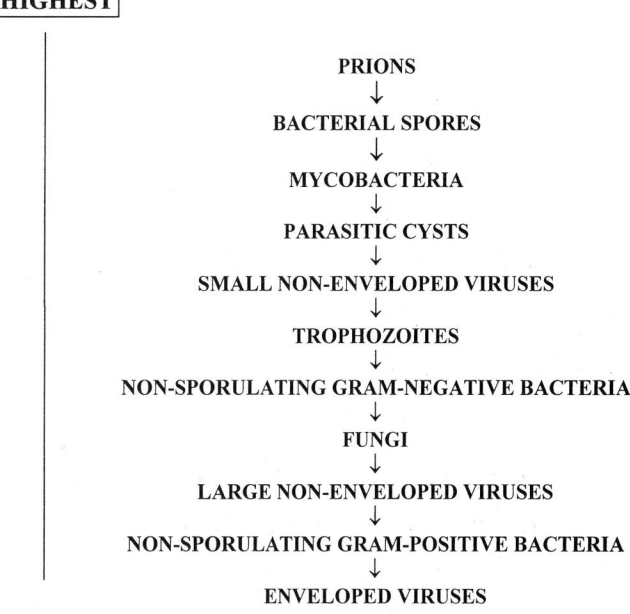

FIGURE 291–2. Resistance of microorganisms to disinfectants, in descending order. (Adapted From Russell AD, Furr JR, Maillard JY. Microbial susceptibility and resistance to biocides. ASM News. 1997;63:481–487.)

On the basis of the cidal activity for each group of microorganisms, the disinfection process can be classified into low, intermediate, and high levels. (Table 291–1).[1] These levels of disinfection provide hospital personnel with a practical guideline for selecting appropriate germicides for the disinfection of medical equipment and hospital surfaces. From an academic standpoint, however, the susceptibility of potential pathogens to disinfectants may vary considerably within these groups. Among vegetative bacteria, for example, gram-positive bacteria are generally more susceptible than gram-negative bacteria.[2] *Pseudomonas* spp., *Enterococcus* spp., and *Staphylococcus aureus* are considered to be comparatively more resistant to liquid germicides. *Staphylococcus epidermidis* and *Escherichia coli* O157-H7 are examples of organisms with medium-level resistance, and *Listeria monocytogenes* and *Vibrio cholerae* are extremely susceptible to germicides.[15]

Some general principles must be followed when using disinfectants. Every hospital should implement a formal written policy for its disinfection and sterilization procedures. Among other things, the policy should specify what disinfectant should be used for a particular purpose, safety aspects when using a particular disinfectant, methods for preparing an accurate use dilution, and the correct exposure time for each disinfectant and procedure.[16] The contact times and concentrations recommended by the manufacturer must be strictly followed. Some disinfectants, such as alcohols and phenols, are strongly affected by dilution. Others, such as formaldehyde and quaternary ammonium compounds (QACs), are less affected. Frequency of use is also a factor to consider. All disinfectants that are used more than once for disinfection or sterilization lose their potency, mainly because of the dilution resulting from immersion of precleaned wet instruments and the accumulation of organic material. The frequency of use should determine the periodicity with which the disinfectant needs to be replaced.

High-Level Disinfectants

Glutaraldehyde

Glutaraldehyde is a saturated dialdehyde that destroys microorganisms through alkylation of their sulfhydryl, hydroxyl, carboxyl, and amino groups. Glutaraldehyde has efficient bactericidal, fungicidal,

TABLE 291-1 Levels of Disinfectant Action According to Type of Microorganism

Disinfectant Level	Killing Effect*					
	Bacteria				Virus	
	Spores	Tubercle Bacillus	Vegetative Cells	Fungi†	Nonlipid and Small	Lipid and Medium Size
High	+‡	+	+	+	+	+
Intermediate	−§	+	+	+	±‖	+
Low	−	−	+	±	±	+

*+, Killing effect can be expected; −, little or no killing effect.
†Includes asexual spores but not necessarily chlamydospores or sexual spores.
‡Only with extended exposure times are high-level disinfectants capable of killing high numbers of bacterial spores in laboratory tests; they are, however, capable of sporicidal activity.
§Some intermediate-level disinfectants (e.g., hypochlorites) may exhibit some sporicidal activity, whereas others (e.g., alcohols or phenolic compounds) have no demonstrated sporicidal activity.
‖Some intermediate-level disinfectants, although tuberculocidal, may have limited virucidal activity.
From Favero NS, Bond WW. Sterilization, disinfection, and antisepsis in the hospital. In: Balows A, Hausler WJ, Herrmann KL, et al, eds. Manual of Clinical Microbiology. 5th ed. Washington, DC: American Society for Microbiology; 1991:183–200.

and virucidal activity but slow mycobactericidal activity (>30 minutes). In order to improve tuberculocidal activity, compounds can be mixed with phenols or alcohol. The contact times necessary for achieving high-level disinfection vary according to the formulation, ranging from 20 to 90 minutes. At longer contact times (6 to 10 hours), glutaraldehyde is also a sterilant. Once activated, these solutions have a shelf life of 14 to 28 days, depending on intensity of use, accumulation of organic material, and innate degradation of the germicide mixture. Glutaraldehyde-based germicides have broad applications in the hospital setting. They are widely used for the disinfection or sterilization of endoscopes, respiratory therapy and anesthesia equipment, and sharp surgical instruments.[1, 3, 17, 18]

Formaldehyde

Formaldehyde is a compound chemically similar to glutaraldehyde but a less potent germicide. It is a high-level disinfectant at 8% combined with 70% alcohol and an intermediate-level disinfectant when used at 4 to 8% in water. It inactivates microorganisms by alkylation of amino and sulfhydryl groups of proteins and ring nitrogen atoms of purinebases. Although it is bactericidal, tuberculocidal, fungicidal, virucidal, and sporicidal, its applications in the hospital setting are limited because of its carcinogenic potential and the irritating fumes associated with its use. Aside from the gaseous formaldehyde system mentioned earlier, its main application is in the disinfection of dialysis systems and hemodialysis filters. For optimal disinfection of these systems, a 4% formaldehyde solution with a minimal contact time of 24 hours is recommended. Extreme precautions must be taken to rinse the dialysis equipment thoroughly before use to avoid potential health hazards for patients.[1, 3, 17]

Peracetic Acid

Peracetic acid is becoming increasingly popular as a hospital disinfectant. It is sporicidal, bactericidal, virucidal, fungicidal, and tuberculocidal at relatively low concentrations (less than 1%). It is effective in the presence of organic matter and at low temperatures and has no harmful decomposition products (acetic acid, water, and oxygen). Its mode of action is believed to be the disruption of sulfhydryl and sulfur bonds in proteins and enzymes. Several formulations available on the market are combinations of low concentrations of peracetic acid (<1.0%) and hydrogen peroxide (1.0%). The result is a rapid, broad-spectrum germicide that may be used for the disinfection or sterilization of critical and semitcritical items. Contact time for these formulations is approximately 25 minutes and the maximal reuse period is 14 days. Peracetic acid alone is available with the STERIS system described earlier. Peracetic acid may also be used at low concentrations (50 ppm) as a laundry disinfectant instead of chlorine.[12, 19]

Hydrogen Peroxide

Hydrogen peroxide is a bactericidal, virucidal, and fungicidal agent. At high concentrations it is also sporicidal. Its mode of action involves the production of hydroxyl free radicals that destroy membrane lipids, DNA, and other essential cell components. Its has been used in the hospital as both a disinfectant and an antiseptic. However, unsatisfactory results have been reported with the use of pure preparations of hydrogen peroxide. The presence of inactivating levels of catalase in tissue and the cytotoxicity of 3% hydrogen peroxide have rendered it ineffective as an antiseptic. As a disinfectant, it provides good disinfection of surfaces and medical equipment from a microbiologic standpoint. Its major disadvantage is that residuals of the disinfectant have been reported to cause adverse effects in patients. Hemolysis has occured in hemodialysis patients who were exposed to residual hydrogen peroxide in their equipment, and peroxide enteritis associated with faulty rinsing procedures has been reported among patients in a gastrointestinal endoscopy unit. Available formulations are hydrogen peroxide in a concentration of 7.5% or mixtures with peracetic acid (0.08% peroxyacetic acid and 1.0% hydrogen peroxide). Both can be used for the sterilization or disinfection of critical and semicritical items. Contact time is 30 minutes for the 7.5% hydrogen peroxide formulation and 25 minutes for the mixture. If the pure hydrogen peroxide formulation is used, all equipment must be thoroughly rinsed before being used for patients.[1, 3, 17, 20]

Intermediate and Low-Level Disinfectants

Chlorine Compounds

The most commonly used chlorine disinfectants in the hospital are the hypochlorites, mainly sodium hypochlorite, and the organic chlorine–releasing agents such as sodium dichloroisocyanurate. Their advantages are low cost, rapidity of action, and broad antimicrobial activity; their disadvantages, particularly for the hypochlorites, are their corrosiveness, inactivation by organic matter, and chemical instability. Chlorine compounds are powerful oxidizing agents that oxidize thiol groups and halogenate amino groups in proteins. The biocidal component of all chlorine compounds is hypochlorous acid (HOCl), which dissociates in a pH-dependent manner into H^+ and OCl^-. Sodium dichloroisocyanurate has a more stable and prolonged effect, because it produces acidic solutions (pH 5.5 to 6.5) with about 90% undissociated HOCl, whereas inorganic hypochlorites release only 10% undissociated HOCl.[1, 3, 17, 21]

From a strictly microbiologic point of view, chlorine compounds are actually sterilants, because their spectrum includes vegetative bacteria, mycobacteria, bacterial spores, viruses, protozoa, and fungi. However, they are extremely corrosive and irritating to personnel at high concentrations. Moreover, no proprietary chlorine formulation has been formally registered with the Environmental Protection Agency. Their applications are limited to situations requiring an intermediate level of activity such as the decontamination of blood and body fluid spills; items such as bedpans, urinals, and kidney bowls; and culture spills in the microbiology laboratory. They are also useful for routine disinfection of hospital surfaces.[1, 3, 17] The applications of chlorine compounds are discussed further in the sections on decontamination of medical equipment and disinfection of the hospital environment.

Alcohol

Ethyl alcohol and isopropyl alcohol at a concentration of 70% are intermediate-level disinfectants. They are bactericidal, fungicidal, and virucidal and have excellent activity against *Mycobacterium tuberculosis.* Their activity is extremely rapid, and their mode of action is denaturation of proteins. Because they lack sporicidal activity, alcohols are not recommended for sterilizing critical medical devices. Rapid evaporation makes them inadequate for use on environmental surfaces. Alcohol may be used for the disinfection of noncritical and some semicritical devices such as thermometers and stethoscopes by submerging precleaned items for at least 10 minutes. Because alcohols cause damage to lensed instruments and tend to harden rubber materials, they should not be used to disinfect these items.[1, 3, 17]

Phenol Compounds

Phenol and its derivatives are intermediate- to low-level disinfectants that are useful primarily for the disinfection of environmental surfaces and noncritical devices. They are tuberculocidal, fungicidal, virucidal, and bactericidal but have no activity against spores. The mode of action of phenol at high concentrations is that of a protoplasmic poison that penetrates and destroys the cell wall and precipitates cellular protein. In lower concentration, this disinfectant inactivates essential enzyme systems. Important features of phenol are that it remains active when in contact with organic material and it is difficult to rinse from most materials. Because the residuals may cause irritation, these compounds are not suitable for the disinfection of medical devices that come in contact with living tissue.[1, 3, 17] Moreover, the use of phenolic detergents on infant bassinets and incubators has been associated with hyperbilirubinemia,[22] which precludes the use of phenol in nurseries. As discussed later, the primary use of phenol compounds is as environmental and laboratory detergents and disinfectants.

Iodophors

An iodophor is a combination of iodine and a carrier that allows continuous release of small amounts of iodine in solution. The cidal effects of iodine involve the disruption of protein and nucleic acid structure and synthesis. These compounds are intermediate- to low-level disinfectants but are mainly used as antiseptics. Their hospital applications for disinfection are limited because they may corrode certain metallic instruments that are disinfected for long periods. Also, nonmetallic items such as plastics and rubber may be discolored or stained when disinfected with these compounds.[1, 3, 17]

Quaternary Ammonium Compounds

A number of QACs are formulated for use in hospitals; most contain benzalkonium chloride and cetylpyridinium chloride. These germicides are low-level disinfectants that are bactericidal, fungicidal, and virucidal against viruses with lipid envelopes. Their mode of action involves disruption of the cell membrane, denaturation of essential cell proteins, and inactivation of enzymes. In the laboratory, these compounds initially appeared to be rapidly bactericidal against test bacteria in suspension tests. However, subsequent studies showed that contact with hard water, soap, protein, cotton, or gauze reduced or nullified the germicidal properties of QACs. Moreover, gram-negative bacteria, particularly *Pseudomonas* and *Proteus* spp., are capable of growing in these solutions.[1, 3, 17] Because contaminated solutions were implicated in several outbreaks, the Centers for Disease Control recommended the withdrawl of QACs as hospital antiseptics and disinfectants in 1976.[23] Today, QACs are used only for cleaning hospital environmental surfaces.

DECONTAMINATION

The term "decontamination" is frequently used interchangeably with "disinfection." Although they are indeed similar, it is important to underscore the differences between the two. Decontamination is a process that renders instruments or devices safe to handle and ranges from sterilization to soap-and-water cleaning. Decontamination is often required when items and surfaces have been contaminated with blood, feces, urine, and other body fluids containing potentially dangerous pathogens. These situations entail a far greater risk of transmission than the disinfection of clean items and medical equipment. In some cases, such as those involving blood spills, the large amount of microorganisms that need to be inactivated requires the use of germicides at a higher concentration than used for routine disinfection of the hospital environment. Therefore, the main objective of decontamination is to minimize the number of pathogenic organisms on contaminated medical equipment in order to reduce the risk of their transmission to health workers and patients. Decontamination is performed before routine disinfection and sterilization procedures or simultaneously, as is the case with automatic cleaner-disinfectors. Examples of equipment and situations requiring decontamination are the following:

1. Bedpans containing feces with pathogens such as salmonellae, shigellae, *V. cholerae,* or *Clostridium difficile.*
2. Respiratory therapy equipment and kidney bowls contaminated with sputum of patients with active tuberculosis.
3. Medical equipment contaminated with blood possibly containing or known to contain hepatitis B virus (HBV) or human immunodeficiency virus (HIV).
4. Blood spills from HIV- or HBV-positive patients on hospital surfaces.
5. Surgical instruments and medical equipment contaminated with tissues and fluids from patients with Creutzfeldt-Jakob disease (procedures are discussed in a separate section).

For reusable items, the preferred method for decontamination is thermal disinfection with flusher-disinfectors or washer-disinfectors. This equipment, widely used for many years in Europe, employs warm water with or without a detergent for cleaning followed by a high-level disinfection with hot water at 90°C. Flusher-disinfectors are designed mainly for bedpans, urinals, and suction drainage bowls. The total cycle takes approximately 4 minutes. A washer-disinfector has been designed for more complex equipment such as anesthesia and respiratory therapy equipment and surgical instruments and has a longer cycle of 20 to 30 minutes. These disinfectors have many advantages. By eliminating manual cleaning, this equipment reduces the risk of exposure to dangerous pathogens; it also curtails the consumption of chemical disinfectants, some of which are potential carcinogens that are ultimately released into the environment. They save time by decontaminating and disinfecting in one cycle. Their use in surgical departments, intensive care units, and otherwise busy wards may limit transmission of hospital pathogens by avoiding the transport of contaminated items to another part of the hospital for cleaning and disinfection.[10, 24]

Decontamination may also be performed with chemical germicides. The most appropriate compounds for this purpose are phenols and chlorine compounds. A chlorine compound is the best choice for decontamination of equipment and surfaces contaminated with blood. For heavy contamination, 5000 to 10,000 ppm available chlorine (i.e., a 1:10 dilution of a commercially sold 5% sodium hypochlorite) is recommended. For less contaminated equipment and surfaces, 500 ppm available chlorine or a phenol compound can be used. Because chlorine compounds are corrosive, a 2% glutaraldehyde or a peracetic acid mixture can be used for the decontamination of HIV- or HBV-contaminated surgical instruments and medical equipment. For situations involving, for example, bedpans with feces containing dangerous enteropathogens, kidney bowls with *M. tuberculosis*–containing sputum, or secretions or excretions from patients infected with methicillin-resistant *S. aureus* or Vancomycin-resistent enterococci (VRE), inactivation may be achieved with 500 ppm available chlorine. Hospital personnel handling contaminated items or performing decontamination procedures should wear gloves and gowns at all times; the minimal contact time for disinfectants should be 10 minutes.[17, 21, 25, 26]

Decontamination of medical equipment possibly contaminated with prions deserves special mention. Prions are proteinaceous, infectious particles that produce progressive, neurologic disorders in humans and a range of animals. The disorders are known as the transmissible spongiform encephalopaties. These pathogens have recently received considerable attention by the media owing to the association of the ingestion of beef contaminated with the bovine spongiform encephalopathy agent and the development of variant Creutzfeldt-Jakob disease (CJD) in humans. Nosocomial transmission of prions in humans has occurred with the CJD agent, and therefore further discussion is limited to this disease.

Iatrogenic episodes of CJD have been reported to occur through cornea transplants, dura mater grafts, contaminated neurosurgical instruments, and the administration of human cadaveric growth hormone and cadaveric pituitary gonadotropin. Tissues from the central nervous system have the highest concentration of prion proteins, and therefore carry the highest risk of transmission. Accordingly, the concentration of the CJD agent is less in cerebrospinal fluid, lymph node, spleen, pituitary gland, and tonsils, which are considered medium risk, and even lower in bone marrow, liver, lung, thymus, kidney, blood, and other organ systems.[27, 27a]

Although there is an obvious necessity to decontaminate the instruments and medical equipment used by a patient with CJD, considerable debate exists regarding the proper procedures for such decontamination. Prions are the most resistant infectious agents known in nature. Studies on prion inactivation have found only three methods to inactivate them: (1) extended steam sterilization, (2) chemical disinfection with sodium hypochlorite or sodium hydroxide, and (3) chemical disinfection followed by steam sterilization.[27] However, the success rates of each method have varied from one study to another. Moreover, some experiments suggest that decontamination procedures that involve initial protein fixation actually enhance the resistance of prion proteins and therefore should be avoided.[27b]

It is difficult to draw valid conclusions from many of the lethality studies because the element of cleaning has not been taken into consideration and because protocols frequently use large inocula of prion-containing material. For example, prion survival was observed after sterilization at 134 to 138°C for 18 minutes when brain macerate sample sizes as large as 340 mg were used, but not with 50-mg macerates.[27b] In a real life situation, 340 mg of tissue are probably far greater than the amount that would be found on a given surgical instrument or brain electrode. After these instruments were subjected to decontamination and cleaning, the amount of tissue would be reduced even further in such a manner that the risk of transmission would be significantly diminished.

Given the intrinsic resistance of the agent, the conflicting results from decontamination protocols, and the poor prognosis of the disease, recommendations for sterilization and disinfection of medical equipment used in patients with CJD tend to be very conservative.[27, 27b] It must be stressed, however, that because the concentration of the agent is not equal in all tissues, these stringent procedures are probably not necessary for processing all items that have been in contact with an infected patient.

To date, all documented cases of iatrogenic CJD have occurred through tissues within or directly connected to the central nervous system. As mentioned previously, the CJD agent is present in other body tissues, but the concentrations are vastly lower than in the CNS. Hypothetically, the potential threat for transmission through other tissues exists, but no case has ever been reported. Likewise, the probability of transmitting CJD through noncritical items and environmental surfaces is very remote.[27c, d]

A major consideration when choosing the proper decontamination procedure is the type of instrument involved. It is well known that instruments that are difficult to clean, such as those with narrow lumens, represent a serious challange to any sterilization procedure. Such instruments that have been in contact with high-risk tissues should probably be discarded until more scientific data are available. At the present time, it appears safe to subject instruments in contact with medium- or low-risk tissues to regular cleaning and sterilization procedures.

In summary, although it is clear that more data are needed to establish procedures for decontamination, sterilization, and disinfection of medical equipment used on patients with CJD, these can reasonably be based on the concentration of prions in the particular tissue and the kind of instrument involved. Suggested procedures for inactivating prions on medical equipment and hospital surfaces are shown in Table 29–2. These recommendations will surely need to be revised as more studies are conducted.

DISINFECTION OF THE HOSPITAL ENVIRONMENT

The role of the hospital environment in nosocomial infections is a subject of considerable controversy. Traditionally, environmental surfaces have been considered relatively unimportant because of the absence of an association between the pathogens found on these surfaces and the transmission of infections to patients and person-

TABLE 291–2 Suggested Procedures for Inactivating Prions on Instruments Potentially Contaminated with Creutzfeldt-Jakob Disease Agent

Type of Tissue Involved	Type of Medical Instrument Involved	Method	Temperature	Time (min)
High risk*	Small lumen, difficult to clean	Discard after single use		
	Critical and semicritical items	Sodium hydroxide (1 M NaOH)		60
		and		
		Prevacuum steam sterilization	132–134°C	18
		or		
		Gravity steam sterilization	121°C	60
	Environmental surfaces	5000–10,000 ppm available chlorine (1 : 10 dilution of household bleach)		10
Medium to low risk	Critical and semicritical items	Mechanical cleaning followed by conventional sterilization or high-level disinfection procedures		

*For medical instruments, the decontamination procedure should be followed by cleaning and the use of a conventional disinfection or sterilization procedure. For environmental surfaces, decontamination should be followed by a normal cleaning and disinfection procedure.

nel.[28] However, several reports have documented the extended survival of certain pathogens on dry surfaces, as well as the necessity to modify environmental disinfection procedures in order to control epidemics caused by these agents.

These findings, however, are still a matter of debate. Elements necessary for environmental transmission of infectious agents include the presence of the pathogen in high numbers in a viable and virulent state and a mechanism for transmission from an environmental niche to the correct portal of entry in a patient who is susceptible to infection by the pathogen. The best evidence for environmentally mediated transmission is an epidemiologic study in which an environmental factor has been shown to be associated with transmission. Least convincing are data from studies showing that a pathogen can be cultured or amplified or can survive in the environment.

Because of the enhanced capacity of certain pathogens to survive on inanimate surfaces, their environmental transmission is considered likely. Information relevant for the hospital epidemiologist today is discussed in Chapter 289.

Vancomycin-Resistant Enterococci

There is growing evidence that inanimate surfaces may play a significant role in the transmission of VRE. High frequencies (7 to 37%) of environmental contamination have been found in the rooms of patients with VRE,[29] and experimental studies have shown that *Enterococcus* spp. may survive up to 45 days on a dry surface when suspended with organic material.[30] In one outbreak,[31] the epidemic strain was isolated from 15% of the bedside rails, gowns, and bed linens of the patients without diarrhea. In the patients with diarrhea, the epidemic strain was recovered from 46% of the environmental samples. The strain was also isolated from equipment such as intravenous pumps and electrocardiogram monitors, as well as from floors and doors. The epidemic was not controlled until special measures designed to avoid cross-transmission from these surfaces were implemented. In addition, enterococci, particularly *Enterococcus faecium,* have enhanced resistance to diverse environmental stresses. In one study,[32] all six test strains of *E. faecium* survived at 75°C for 3 minutes and four of six strains survived at 80°C for 3 minutes. Three of 12 *E. faecium* and *Enterococcus faecalis* strains were able to survive exposure to 150 ppm available chlorine for 10 minutes, but none survived 500 ppm for 5 minutes. However, all strains survived exposure to 150 and 500 ppm available chlorine for 10 minutes in the presence of organic matter.

These studies suggest that transmission of VRE may occur through the persistence of organisms on inanimate surfaces, linen, and items such as bedpans that have been improperly disinfected. Proper disinfection of environmental surfaces, particularly during outbreaks, is of paramount importance. Saurina and colleagues[33] found that some strains of *E. faecium* may resist a 3-minute exposure to phenol and QACs. Although the conventional contact time is 10 minutes, the true drying times in the hospital setting are probably closer to the 3 minutes used in this study. Other important findings in this study were that 70% isopropyl alcohol and 500 ppm available chlorine were highly effective against VRE, whereas 3% hydrogen peroxide showed extremely poor activity. One could therefore surmise that when dealing with VRE, chlorine compounds are probably a better option for environmental disinfection than QACs or phenols. A reasonable strategy for hospitals that use phenols or QACs and are having problems with VRE would be to reapply these disinfectants after drying to ensure adequate contact time.

Clostridium difficile

C. difficile is another important nosocomial pathogen for which a strong linkage between environmental contamination, personnel hand carriage, and nosocomial transmission has been established. Environmental contamination is frequently found in areas surrounding cases (up to 58% in outbreaks), and the degree of contamination is directly associated with the severity of diarrhea. *C. difficile* is most commonly cultured from floors, bedpans, windowsills, toilets, and bathroom surfaces.[34–36] Even in areas with no known cases, *C. difficile* has been isolated from 2.5 to 4.3% of environmental sites, raising the possibility of spread through the shoes or cleaning items of hospital personnel.[33, 34] Because *C. difficile* is capable of sporulation, sporicidal disinfectants such as chlorine compounds theoretically have superiority over others. One study found that 500 ppm available chlorine achieved only 79.4% reduction of *C. difficile* colony-forming units on environmental surfaces. A concentration of 1600 ppm was required to achieve 98% reduction, which was necessary to contain the outbreak.[36] More studies are clearly needed to determine the best disinfectants for areas contaminated with *C. difficile.* Current recommendations include the use of a detergent-germicide or a chlorine solution.

Hepatitis B Virus

HBV warrants special mention because of the risk of its transmission for hospital personnel as well as patients. HBV is unique in that the blood of acutely infected patients or chronic carriers of hepatitis B surface antigen who are positive for hepatitis B early antigen have incredibly high titers of infective virus. Because of this, even in the absence of visible or chemically detectable blood, HBV can be present in relatively small inocula or on environmental surfaces. It is capable of surviving drying and storage at 25°C and 42% relative humidity for at least 7 days. Although the probability of disease transmission via environmental surfaces with a single exposure might be remote, the frequency of such exposures in busy hemodialysis units, laboratories, and surgical suites with HBV-infected patients makes this mechanism of transmission a potentially efficient one over a long period of time. For routine cleaning of areas where HBV is common, surfaces should be cleaned with a detergent followed by disinfection with 500 to 1000 ppm available chlorine or an intermediate-level phenol compound.[25, 37]

Acinetobacter Species

Several investigations have shown that certain common nosocomial pathogens such as *Acinetobacter baumannii* may survive much longer on inanimate environmental surfaces[30, 38] than most other gram-negative bacilli (> 7 versus 1 to 2 days). One study demonstrated survival of certain *Acinetobacter* strains up to 60 days when suspended with organic material on a dry surface and up to 30 days when suspended with distilled water.[30] *Acinetobacter* spp. also have an enhanced capacity for survival on human skin and may be spread by the airborne route.[39, 40] These features of *Acinetobacter* spp. might explain their high prevalence in nosocomially acquired infections and the difficulties encountered in eradicating them from the hospital environment. Although no specific recommendations have been made for the disinfection of surfaces contaminated with this pathogen, these findings strongly suggest that the use of a detergent followed by an intermediate-level disinfectant would be most adequate.

General Guidelines for Environmental Disinfection

Aside from the controversial issues already discussed, to which hospital epidemiologists may choose to respond on an individual basis, environmental surfaces may generally be separated into densely contaminated surfaces and sparsely contaminated surfaces. Densely contaminated surfaces such as doorknobs, sinks, patients' chart covers, and bed rails are usually located in busy high-risk areas such as intensive care units, surgical suites, and nurseries. They are the most critical because they are frequently touched by medical and nursing personnel after handling patients and, therefore, may function as temporary reservoirs of pathogenic organisms, which may be carried by other hospital workers to patients.

Most environmental surfaces in high-risk areas can be adequately disinfected with chlorine, phenol, or QACs. Because the presence of organic matter significantly increases the survival of pathogens in the inanimate environment, thorough cleaning is recommended before application of the disinfectant. Free available chlorine at 500 ppm is the most effective against most nosocomial pathogens, including those that are capable of surviving long periods in the hospital environment.

For sparsely contaminated surfaces such as walls and windows and for housekeeping in intermediate- and low-risk hospital areas, cleaning with a detergent alone is usually sufficient. In special situations, such as outbreaks, a cleaner-disinfectant may used. Phenols, QACs, and chlorine compounds with 100 to 200 ppm available chlorine are all satisfactory options.

Resistance to Disinfectants

Although resistance to disinfectants exists, it is not as serious a problem as resistance to antibiotics. Resistance to disinfectants is mainly intrinsic in nature, whereas antimicrobial resistance is frequently conferred by plasmids or transposons, which have allowed rapid and extensive spread throughout the globe. Furthermore, disinfectants have multiple targets for their cidal effects, whereas antibiotics usually have one specific target site.[2, 14]

Resistance to disinfectants may be intrinsic or extrinsic. The main mechanism of intrinsic resistance to disinfectants in gram-negative bacteria, fungi, parasite cysts, mycobacteria, and spores is impaired uptake of the germicide because of specific constituents of the cell wall or membrane. Another important form of intrinsic resistance involves the production of biofilms, a phenomenon that has been well studied in gram-negative bacteria, particularly *Pseudomonas* spp. and *Candida albicans*

A biofilm is a consortium of bacteria adhered to a surface and organized within an extensive glycocalyx.[2, 41] The efficiencies of germicides, antibiotics, and even antibodies are much reduced when they are used against biofilms rather than planktonic cells (floating cells with no biofilm). Several hypotheses have been postulated to explain this protection. It is believed that the biofilm matrix interferes with the germicide reaching the bacterial cell surface via chemical, ionic, and hydrophilic-hydrophobic interactions.[41, 42] One study demonstrated that in the presence of a biofilm the resistance of *E. coli* increased 25-fold against a peracetic acid–hydrogen peroxide mixture, 5-fold against sodium hypochlorite, and more than 400-fold against benzalkonium chloride.[42] This has obvious implications for the control of nosocomial infections.

In addition, the production of biofilm can confer protection against biocides such that the sessile bacteria are capable of surviving within a germicide solution. Several years ago, reports emerged on the intrinsic contamination of iodophor antiseptic solutions by *Pseudomonas cepacia* and *Pseudomonas aeruginosa,* which caused peritoneal infections in infants and pseudobacteremia in patients in intensive care units. The organisms that were protected by a biofilm matrix showed long-term survival within the antiseptic solutions (up to 68 weeks) and had an apparent level of resistance that would be expected of bacterial spores. In these investigations, the original source of the contaminating organisms appeared to be water pipe systems colonized with biofilm-containing pseudomonads that were used to distribute or store the iodophor solution during the manufacturing process.[43, 44]

Biofilms are also an important issue for surgery involving implantable devices. In patients with prostheses, for example, only 32% of infections caused by slime-producing coagulase-negative staphylococci resolved with antibiotics, compared with 100% recovery in patients with non–slime-producing strains.[45] For the infection to resolve, the implant and its adherent biofilm must be removed because recurrent acute infections or disseminated persistent infection may ensue if these reservoirs are allowed to persist.[41] Little is known about the epidemiology and pathogenesis of these infections. Experiments using slime-producing *S. aureus* in vitro with materials used in orthopedic surgery have found that within 6 hours these strains preferentially ahdere to metal and glass over bone and polymers such as polymethyl methacrylate.[46] It has already been mentioned that biofilms confer resistance to the cidal effect of chemical germicides. Considering the therapeutic implications of an infection by these organisms, it is obvious that strict protocols should be followed for sterilizing implants. As further research is conducted in this field, biofilms will surely be identified as an important mechanism of bacterial resistance to disinfectants in the hospital.

Aside from intrinsic mechanisms of resistance, bacteria may acquire plasmids or transposons that confer resistance to germicides. Resistance may occur through inactivation of compounds, as has been described for mercurials and formaldehyde. Resistance to organomercurials has been well studied in *P. aeruginosa* and *S. aureus.* A plasmid-mediated enzyme system reduces the toxic Hg^{2+} to the nontoxic, volatile Hg^{0}.[47–49] The high frequencies of bacterial resistance to mercury found in certain hospitals have been directly attributed to widespread usage of mercurial disinfectants.[50]

Formaldehyde-resistant strains have been isolated from patients with nosocomial infections and from disinfectant solutions. The species include *Pseudomonas* spp. and Enterobacteriaceae such as *Serratia marcescens, Citrobacter freundii, Klebsiella pneumoniae,* and *E. coli.* Resistance is conferred by a plasmid-mediated, nicotinamide adenine dinucleotide–dependent formaldehyde dehydrogenase enzyme that catalyzes the formation of *S*-formylglutathione and reduced nicotinamide adenine dinucleotide[51, 52]

Another form of acquired resistance to antiseptics and disinfectants involves efflux pumps. This mechanism has been described in *S. aureus* and coagulase-negative staphylococci.[53, 54] Three separate multidrug resistance determinants, designated *qacA, qacB,* and *qacC,* have been described. The *qacA* gene confers the broadest resistance phenotype, which includes four types of compounds, the most important of which are QACs such as benzalkonium chloride and biguanidines such as chlorhexidine. These genes are located predominantly on disinfectant-resistance plasmids but may also be found on β-lactamase or heavy-metal resistance plasmids. The *qacA* gene has been found in strains associated with hospital outbreaks of *S. aureus* infection in Australia and the United Kingdom since the 1980s. The *qacC* gene has been found in *S. aureus* strains from hospitals in Europe, the United States, Australia, and Japan. Both the *qacA* and the *qacC* genes have been identified in coagulase-negative staphylococci from Australian hospitals. The prevalence of these strains is extremely high in certain countries, where up to 40% of all clinical staphylococcal isolates are resistant to at least one disinfectant. Of additional concern is the fact that many of these strains are methicillin resistant. As with mercury resistance, selection of these strains is believed to occur through the widespread use of QACs and chlorhexidine in the hospital setting, because these strains frequently encode multiple antibiotic resistance and are rarely found in community isolates.[53]

With the exception of biofilms, which have caused well-documented outbreaks, it is difficult to determine the clinical relevance of many studies of bacterial resistance to disinfectants. Rutala and colleagues[55] have pointed out that the minimal inhibitory concentrations used in most of these studies are far lower than the concentrations of disinfectants used in the hospital. Even so, the importance of these emerging strains should not be underestimated. Several studies have shown that many of these strains have multiple drug resistance and that they are maintained in the hospital environment through the selective pressure exerted by the use of the disinfectants to which they are resistant.

CONTROL OF HOSPITAL WASTE

The control of hospital waste has been the subject of considerable debate in the past decade. *Hospital waste* refers to all waste, biologic or nonbiologic, that is discarded and not intended for future use. *Medical waste* is a subset of hospital waste and refers to the materials generated as a result of diagnosis and treatment of patients. *Infectious waste* is the subset of medical waste that is capable of transmitting an infectious disease.[56] From a regulatory perspective, only infectious waste requires special procedures for its handling, transport, and storage, and therefore further discussion is limited to infectious waste.

The definition of infectious waste has been a subject of great controversy for many years. It is commonly defined as "waste capable of producing an infectious disease."[57] The main difficulty in establishing an accurate definition is that several conditions must be present before infections are transmitted by means of contact with infectious waste: (1) pathogens that can initiate infection and are sufficiently virulent, (2) the number of microorganisms necessary to produce infection, (3) a mechanism to bring the pathogen in contact with the portal of entry, and (4) susceptibility of the host to the pathogen.

Because there are no tests that can objectively determine whether exposure to a particular waste may result in an infectious disease, the Centers for Disease Control and Prevention and the Environmental Protection Agency have defined waste as infectious when it is suspected to contain pathogens in sufficient numbers to cause disease. This has led to conflicting definitions from these agencies of what kind of waste is infectious and, consequently, what waste needs to be regulated.[56] As shown in Table 291–3, there is agreement on five types of waste–microbiologic, pathologic, blood and blood products, contaminated animal carcasses, and sharps—but disagreement on other types.

These conflicting opinions are further augmented by the paucity of microbiologic and epidemiologic evidence that such waste actually represents a threat to the community. First, no study has demonstrated that medical waste is more infective than residential waste. In fact, the few existing studies show that residential waste contains a higher number of microorganisms than hospital waste and that common nosocomial pathogens such as *P. aeruginosa, Klebsiella* sp., *Proteus* sp., and *Enterobacter* sp. were more commonly found in the former than in the latter.[58] Moreover, the number of pathogenic bacteria and viruses is significantly reduced when the waste is deposited in properly operated landfills through a combination of thermal inactivation, antimicrobial characteristics of the leachate, and adsorption to organic material in solid waste.[59, 60]

Most important, scientific evidence indicates that except for sharps, the potential for infection resulting from contact with medical waste is extremely remote. The absence of a portal of entry significantly reduces the possibility of tranmission. In fact, the only reports in the international scientific literature that document cases of disease acquired through contact with medical waste are precisely about sharps, and all of these cases have occurred in the hospital setting.[56] (As discussed in the following, a press release has suggested that *M. tuberculosis* can be transmitted through medical waste.)

A major public concern is the possibility of transmission of HIV through medical waste. Fortunately, HIV has extremely limited viability outside a living host. Thus, persons coming in contact with medical waste outside the health care setting have a very low risk of acquiring HIV infection. In a 1990 report to Congress on the public health implications of medical waste[61] it was calculated that at most less than one to four cases of acquired immunodeficiency syndrome per year could occur as a result of contact with medical waste sharps. As of 1989, these cases would have represented only 0.003 to 0.01% of the total cases of acquired immunodeficiency syndrome in the United States. On the other hand, HBV is capable of extended survival outside a host, particularly when protected by organic matter.[37] Therefore, it has greater potential to cause infections associated with medical waste. The report mentioned previously[61] estimated a theoretical maximum of 162 to 321 HBV infections and 81 to 160 hepatitis B disease cases per year related to medical waste sharps. These would account, respectively, for 0.05 to 0.1% of the HBV infections and 0.05 to 0.1% of the identified hepatitis B disease cases that occur annually in the United States. Most of these cases would probably occur in the hospital setting.

A news release from the Washington State Department of Health that reported that three workers at a medical waste processing facility acquired tuberculosis is reason for serious concern.[62] These workers' diseases were diagnosed during the previous 8 months. Laboratory tests confirmed that one of the workers had the same strain as a patient treated for tuberculosis at a hospital that sends waste to this facility. Preliminary investigations suggested that culture plates of *M. tuberculosis* were added to a grinding machine in which the filter failed and aerosols were produced. Workers handling this waste did not use any respiratory protection.

It is important to limit the number and types of medical waste

TABLE 291–3 Medical Waste Designated as Infectious and Recommended Disposal or Treatment Methods: Centers for Disease Control and Prevention and Environmental Protection Agency*

	CDC		EPA		MWTA
Source or Type of Medical Waste	*Infectious Waste*	*Disposal or Treatment Methods*	*Infectious Waste*	*Disposal or Treatment Methods*	*Infectious Waste†*
Microbiologic (e.g., stocks and cultures of infectious agents)	Yes‡	S, I	Yes	S, I, TI, C	Yes
Blood and blood products	Yes	S, I, Sew	Yes	S, I, Sew, C	Yes
Pathologic (e.g., tissue, organs)	Yes	I	Yes	I, SW, CB	Yes
Sharps (e.g., needles)	Yes	S, I	Yes	S, I	Yes§
Communicable disease isolation	No	—	Yes	S, I	Yes§
Contaminated animal carcasses, body parts, and bedding	Yes	S, I (carcasses)	Yes	I, SW (not bedding)	Yes
Contaminated laboratory wastes	No	—	Optional‖	If considered IW, use S or I	No
Surgery and autopsy wastes	No	—	Optional	If considered IW, use S or I	No
Dialysis unit	No	—	Optional	If considered IW, use S or I	No
Contaminated equipment	No	—	Optional	If considered IW, use S or I	No

*The Joint Commission for the Accreditation of Healthcare Organizations requires that there be a hazardous waste system designed and operated in accordance with applicable law and regulations.
†The act went into effect on June 22, 1989 and expired June 22, 1991. It affected only four states (New Jersey, New York, Connecticut, and Rhode Island). The act required both treatment (any method, technique, or process designed to change the biologic character or composition of medical waste so as to eliminate or reduce its potential for causing disease) and destruction (waste is ruined, torn apart, or mutilated so that it is no longer generally recognizable as medical waste).
‡The CDC guidelines specify "microbiology laboratory waste" as an infectious waste. This term includes stocks and cultures or etiologic agents and microbiology laboratory waste contaminated with etiologic agents (e.g., centrifuge tubes, pipettes, tissue culture bottles).
§MWTA specified used and unused sharps. The act regulated wastes from persons with highly communicable diseases such as class 4 etiologic agents (e.g., Marburg, Ebola, Lassa).
‖Optional infectious waste: EPA states that the decision to handle these wastes as infectious should be made by a responsible, authorized person or committee at the individual facility.
Abbreviations: C, Chemical disinfection for liquids only; CB, cremation or burial by mortician; CDC, Centers for Disease Control and Prevention; EPA, Environmental Protection Agency; I, incineration; IW, infectious waste; MWTA, Municipal Waste Tracking Act; S, steam sterilization; Sew, sanitary sewer (EPA requires secondary treatment); SW, steam sterilization with incineration or grinding; TI, thermal inactivation.
From Rutala WA, Mayhall CG. SHEA position paper: Medical Waste. Infect Control Hosp Epidemiol. 1992;13:38–48.

classified as infectious in order to reduce the economic burden for hospitals. In the United States, hospitalized patients generate about 15 pounds of hospital waste per day. Approximately 6700 tons are generated by U.S. hospitals daily, which constitutes 1% of the 158 million tons of municipal solid waste produced annually. U.S. hospitals designate about 15% of their total hospital waste as infectious waste. This percentage obviously depends on the number of categories of medical waste classified as infectious waste. For example, if the guidelines of the Centers for Disease Control and Prevention were followed, only 6% of hospital waste would be treated as infectious, in contrast to 45% if one followed the classification established by the Medical Waste Tracking Act.[63] In 1992, the cost of disposing of regulated medical waste was about 10 times (0.20 to $0.60 per pound) the cost of disposing of nonregulated medical waste ($0.02 to $0.05 per pound). The total cost for U.S. hospitals to comply with the Medical Waste Tracking Act was estimated to be $1.3 billion a year.[56]

Because the economic burden is considerable, the management of medical waste must be based on scientific evidence and not irrational fears. There is no justification for unnecessarily diverting limited financial resources to treat garbage that is probably a nonexistent threat to the community.

MANAGEMENT OF INFECTIOUS WASTE

The basic principles to be followed when managing infectious waste are segregation at the point of origin and treatment of the waste to reduce the hazard associated with the presence of infectious agents. In addition, in the United States medical waste must be rendered unrecognizable before being discarded.

Segregation of waste includes the use of distinctive, clearly marked containers or plastic bags. Plastic bags are usually red or orange. Sharps should be disposed of in rigid, puncture-resistant containers. All infectious waste should be labeled with the universal biologic hazard symbol.

The most inexpensive and efficient methods for treatment of infectious waste are steam sterilization and incineration. Steam sterilization is ideal for waste of low density that can be adequately penetrated by steam. Infectious wastes that contain hazards such as antineoplastic drugs or radioactive materials should not be steam sterilized because of the potential for exposure of equipment operators. Incineration is a suitable treatment technique for all types of infectious waste. It is ideal for pathologic waste and sharps because it renders these unrecognizable and unusable. Drainage into the sewer may be an acceptable practice for liquid wastes, which should be chemically treated before disposal.

A more detailed discussion of the procedures for treatment, storage, and disposal of infectious waste can be found elsewhere.[57]

REFERENCES

1. Favero MS, Bond WW. Sterilization, disinfection, and antisepsis in the hospital. In: Balows A, Hausler WJ, Herrmann KL, et al, eds. Manual of Clinical Microbiology. 5th ed. Washington, DC: American Society for Microbiology; 1991:183–200.
2. Rutala WA, ed. Chemical Germicides in Health Care. Association for Professionals in Infection Control and Epidemiology, Inc. Washington, DC; 1995.
3. Favero MS, Bond WW. Chemical disinfection of medical and surgical materials. In: Block SS, ed. Disinfection, Sterilization, and Preservation. 4th ed. Philadelphia: Lea & Febiger; 1991:617–641.
4. Perkins JJ. Principles and Methods of Sterilization in Health Sciences. Springfield, Va: Charles C Thomas; 1983.
5. Howard WJ. The controversy of flash sterilization. Today's OR Nurse 1991;13:24–27.
6. Rutala WA. Disinfection in the OR. Today's OR Nurse 1990;12:30–38.
7. Gardner JF, Peel MM. Introduction to Sterilization and Disinfection. New York: Churchill Livingstone; 1986.
8. Pausi AN, Young WE. Sterilization with ethylene oxide and other gases. In: Block SS, ed. Disinfection, Sterilization, and Preservation. 4th ed. Philadelphia: Lea & Febiger; 1991:580–595.
9. Casarett and Doull's Toxicology: The Basic Science of Poisons. 5th ed. New York: McGraw-Hill; 1996.
10. Nystrom B. New technology for sterilization and disinfection. Am J Med. 1991;91:264–266.
11. Crow S. Peracetic acid sterilization: A timely development for a busy healthcare industry. Infect Control Hosp Epidemiol. 1992;13:111–113.
12. Malchesky PS. Peracetic acid and its application to medical instrument sterilization. Artif Organs. 1993;17:147–152.
13. Kralovic RC. Use of biological indicators designed for steam or ethylene oxide to monitor a liquid chemical sterilization process. Infect Control Hosp Epidemiol. 1993;14:313–319.
14. Russell AD, Furr JR, Maillard JY. Microbial susceptibility and resistance to biocides. ASM News. 1997;63:481–487.
15. Sagripanti JL, Eklund CA, Trost PA, et al. Comparative sensitivity of 13 species of pathogenic bacteria to seven chemical germicides. Am J Infect Control. 1997;25:335–339.
16. Coates D, Hutchinson DN. How to produce a hospital disinfection policy. J Hosp Infect. 1994;26:57–68.
17. Rutala WA. APIC guidelines for selection and use of disinfectants. Am J Infect Control. 1990;18:99–117.
18. Ascenzi JM. Glutaraldehyde-based disinfectants. In: Ascenzi JM, ed. Handbook of Disinfectants and Antiseptics. New York: Marcel Dekker; 1996:111–132.
19. Block SS. Peracetic acid. In:Block SS, ed. Disinfection, Sterilization, and Preservation. 4th ed. Philadelphia: Lea & Febiger;1991:172–179.
20. Lever AM, Sutton SV. Antimicrobial effects of hydrogen peroxide as an antiseptic and disinfectant. In: Ascenzi JM, ed. Handbook of Disinfectants and Antiseptics. New York: Marcel Dekker; 1996:159–176.
21. Bloomfield SF. Chlorine and iodine formulations. In: Ascenzi JM, ed. Handbook of Disinfectants and Antiseptics. New York: Marcel Dekker; 1996:133–158.
22. Guidelines for Perinatal Care. 3rd ed. Elk Grove Village, Ill: American Academy of Pediatrics, American College of Obstetricians and Gynecologists; 1992.
23. Dixon RE, Kaslow RA, Mackel DC, et al. Aqueous quaternary ammonium antiseptics and disinfectants: Use and misuse. JAMA 1976;236:2415–2417.
24. Fryklund B, Marland M. Cleaning and disinfection of reusable items in Swedish hospitals. Today's OR Nurse 1994;16(5):20–24.
25. Favero MS, Bond WW. Transmission and control of laboratory-acquired viral hepatitis infection. In: JH Richardson, ed. Laboratory Safety—Principles and Practices. Washington, DC: American Society for Microbiology; 1995:19–32.
26. Sattar SA, Springthorpe VS. Survival and disinfectant inactivation of the human immunodeficiency virus: A critical review. Rev Infect Dis. 1991; 13:430–447.
27. Steelman VM. Activity of sterilization processes and disinfectants against prions (Creutzfeldt-Jakob disease agent). In: Rutala WA, ed. Disinfection, Sterilization, and Antisepsis in Health Care. Champlain, NY: Association for Professionals in Infection Control and Polyscience Publications; 1998:255–271.
27a. Brown P. Iatrogenic Creutzfeldt-Jakob disease. In: Morrisey R, Kowalski JB, eds. Sterilization of Medical Products. Champlain, NY: Johnson & Johnson and Polyscience Publications, 1998:212–218.
27b. Taylor DM. Inactivation of the causal agents of transmissible spongiform encephalopathies. In: Morrisey R, Kowalski JB, eds. Sterilization of Medical Products. Champlain, NY: Johnson & Johnson and Polyscience Publications, 1998:219–228.
27c. Favero M. Current status of sterilization technology. Cent Steril. 1998;6:159–164.
27d. Geertsma RE, van Asten JA. Sterilization of prions. Cent Steril. 1995;3:385–394.
28. Garner JS, Favero MS. Guideline for Handwashing and Hospital Environmental Control. Springfield, Va: National Technical Information Service; 1985.
29. Weber DJ, Rutala WA. Role of environmental contamination in the transmission of vancomycin-resistant enterococci. Infect Control Hosp Epidemiol. 1997; 18:306–309.
30. Jawad A, Heritage J, Snelling AM, et al. Influence of relative humidity and suspending menstrua on survival of *Acinetobacter* spp. on dry surfaces. J Clin Microbiol. 1996;34:2881–2887.
31. Boyce JM, Opal SM, Chow JW, et al. Outbreak of multidrug-resistant *Enterococcus faecium* with transferable *vanB* class vancomycin resistance. J Clin Microbiol. 1994;32:1148–1153.
32. Kearns AM. Freeman R, Lightfoot NF. Nosocomial enterococci: Resistance to heat and sodium hypochlorite. J Hosp Infect. 1995;30:193–199.
33. Saurina G, Landman D, Quale JM. Activity of disinfectants against vancomycin-resistant *Enterococcus faecium.* Infect Control Hosp Epidemiol. 1997;18:345–347.
34. Samore MH, Venkataraman L, De Girolami PC, et al. Clinical and molecular epidemiology of sporadic and clustered cases of nosocomial *Clostridium difficile* diarrhea. Am J Med. 1996;100:32–40.
35. Fekety R, Kim K, Brown D, et al. Epidemiology of antibiotic-associated colitis. Am J Med. 1981;70:906–908.
36. Kaatz GN, Gitlin SD, Schaberg DR, et al. Acquisition of *Clostridium difficile* from the hospital environment. Am J Epidemiol. 1988;6:1289–1294.
37. Bond WW, Favero MS, Petersen NJ, et al. Survival of hepatitis B virus after drying and storage for one week. Lancet 1981;1:550–551.
38. Getchell-White SI, Donowitz LG, Gröschel DHM. The inanimate environment of an intensive care unit as a potential source of nosocomial bacteria: Evidence for long survival of *Acinetobacter calcoaceticus.* Infect Control Hosp Epidemiol. 1989;10:402–407.
39. Allen KD, Green HT. Hospital outbreak of multiresistant *Acinetobacter anitratus*: An airborne mode of spread? J Hosp Infect. 1987;9:110–119.
40. Musa EK, Desai N, Casewell MN. The survival of *Acinetobacter calcoaceticus* inoculated on fingertips and on formica. J Hosp Infect. 1990;15:219–227.
41. Costerton JW, Lappin-Scott HM. Behavior of bacteria in biofilms. ASM News 1989;55:650–654.
42. Ntsama-Essomba C, Bouttier S, Ramaldes M, et al. Resistance of *Escherichia coli* growing as biofilms to disinfectants. Vet Res. 1997;28:353–363.
43. Anderson RL, Vess RW, Carr JH, et al. Investigations of intrinsic *Pseudomonas cepacia* contamination in commercially manufactured providone-iodine. Infect Control Hosp Epidemiol. 1991;12:297–302.

44. Berkelman RL, Anderson RL, Davis BJ, et al. Intrinsic bacterial contamination of a commercial iodophor solution: Investigation of the implicated manufacturing plant. Appl Environ Microbiol. 1984;47:752–756.
45. Davenport DS, Massanari RM, Pfaller MA, et al. Usefulness of a test for slime production as a marker for clinically significant infections with coagulase-negative staphylococci. J Infect Dis. 1986;1532:332–336.
46. Gracia E, Fernandez A, Conchello P, et al. Adherence of *Staphylococcus aureus* slime-producing strain variants to biomaterials used in orthopaedic surgery. Int Orthop. 1997;21:41–51.
47. Schottel J, Mandal A, Clark D, Silver S. Volatilisation of mercury and organomercurials determined by inducible R-factor systems in enteric bacteria. Nature 1974;251:335–337.
48. Weiss AA, Murphy SD, Silver S. Mercury and organomercurial resistances determined by plamids in *Staphylococcus aureus.* J Bacteriol. 1997;132:197–208.
49. Clark D, Weiss AA, Silver S. Mercury and organomercurial resistances determined by plasmids in *Pseudomonas.* J Bacteriol. 1977;132:186–196.
50. Porter FD, Silver S, Ong C, Nakahara H. Selection for mercurial resistance in hospital settings. Antimicrob Agents Chemother. 1982;22:852–858.
51. Kaulfers PM, Wollmann A. Demonstration of formaldehyde dehydrogenase activity in formaldehyde resistant Enterobacteriaceae. FEMS Microbiol Lett. 1991;79:335–338.
52. Kummerle N, Feucht HH, Kaulfers PM. Plasmid-mediated formaldehyde resistance in *Escherichia coli*: Characterization of resistance gene. Antimicrob Agents Chemother. 1996;40:2276–2279.
53. Leelaporn A, Paulsen H, Tennent JM, et al. Multidrug resistance to antiseptics and disinfectants in coagulase-negative staphylococci. J Med Microbiol. 1994;40:214–220.
54. Townsend DE, Ashdown N, Momoh M, Grubb WB. Distribution of plasmid-borne resistance to nucleic acid binding compounds in methicillin-resistant *Staphylococcus aureus.* J Antimicrob Chemother. 1985; 15:417–434.
55. Rutala WA, Stiegel MM, Sarrubi FA, Weber DJ. Susceptibility of antibiotic-susceptible and antibiotic-resistant hospital bacteria to disinfectants. Infect Control Hosp Epidemiol. 1997;18:417–421.
56. Rutala WA, Mayhall CG. The Society for Hospital Epidemiology of America. Position paper: Medical waste. Infect Control Hosp Epidemiol. 1992;13:38–48.
57. EPA Guide for Infectious Waste Management. Springfield, Va: National Technical Information Service; 1986.
58. Kalnowski G, Wiegand H, Ruben H. The microbial contamination of hospital waste. zentralbl Bakteriol Mikrobiol Hyg [B]. 1983;178:364–379.
59. Cooper RC, Potter JL, Leong C. Virus survival in solid waste leachates. Water Res. 1975;9:733–739.
60. Pahren HR. Microorganisms in municipal solid waste and public health implications. CRC Crit Rev Environ Control 1987;17:187–228.
61. The Public Health Implications of Medical Waste: A Report to Congress. Atlanta, Ga: U.S. Department of Health and Human Services; 1990.
62. Washington State Department of Health. Press release: Probable transmission of occupationally-acquired tuberculosis at Stericycle Inc., a medical waste processing facility in Morton, WA. Olympia: Washington State Department of Health; March 4, 1998.
63. Rutala WA, Weber DJ. Infectious waste: Mismatch between science and policy. N Engl J Med 1991;325:578–582.

Chapter 292

Infections Due to Percutaneous Intravascular Devices

DAVID K. HENDERSON

The relentless progress of medical science and technology has been accompanied by the development of a host of new diagnostic and therapeutic medical devices, each of which is associated with its own complications. Included in the list of devices to be discussed in this chapter are peripheral and central intravenous catheters, total parenteral nutrition (TPN) catheters, peripherally inserted central venous catheters, totally implanted intravascular access devices, flow-directed balloon-tipped pulmonary artery catheters, arterial lines, and catheters placed to afford long-term central venous access such as Hickman or Broviac catheters.

As early as 1977 Maki suggested that device-related bacteremia develops in more than 25,000 patients in the United States each year.[1] The burgeoning use of an ever-expanding array of vascular access devices in medicine has resulted in even more complications associated with their use. The incidence of bacteremia associated with the use of intravascular devices has increased significantly. In one center the rate of catheter-associated bacteremia rose from 20 episodes per 1000 admissions in 1986 to 50 episodes per 1000 admissions in 1993.[2] Such device-associated infections occur as sporadic cases, as well as in case clusters caused by the same organism. Most sporadic nosocomial bacteremias, however, are not device related but occur as a result of distant localized infection, which then seeds the blood stream.[3] Primary bacteremias (i.e., those without an obvious infected focus outside the blood stream) account for only one fourth of sporadic nosocomial bacteremias. The problem of iatrogenic, device-associated bacteremia is not unique to the United States; in one prospective study of bacteremia from Australia, nosocomial bacteremias accounted for 40% of all cases of bacteremia, and half of the nosocomial cases were device associated.[4]

Conversely, more than three fourths of the nosocomial bacteremias occurring in case clusters are primary bacteremias, and more than 75% of these primary bacteremias are device associated.[3] Much of what we know about the epidemiology and pathogenesis of device-associated infections has been learned from careful study of these case clusters of device-associated infection.

Both local and systemic infection may result from contamination of intravascular devices. Local cellulitis, abscess formation, septic thrombophlebitis, device-associated bacteremia, and endocarditis all occur as complications of intravascular therapy and monitoring.

PATHOGENESIS

Bacteria may gain access to an intravascular device at several points (Fig. 292–1). Each of the potential access sites depicted in Figure 292–1 has been associated with both sporadic cases and case clusters of nosocomial bacteremia. Whereas the skin entry site has long been thought to be the most important portal of entry for invading microorganisms, over the past 15 years the relative importance of the various potential portals of entry has been the focus of attention of several investigators. Discussion of the current state of these investigations is perhaps most easily accomplished through assessment of each potential portal of entry.

Contamination of the Infusate

Infusion-related sepsis has been reviewed in detail,[3, 5] and both manufacture-related[6, 7] and in-use contamination of infusate[3, 8, 9] have been documented as causes of device-associated sepsis.

Another factor influencing the pathogenesis of infusate-associated infection is the composition of the fluid. Different infusion fluids support the growth of different pathogens. The microbiology of outbreaks of infusate-related sepsis is somewhat monotonous; pathogens such as *Enterobacter*, *Citrobacter*, and *Serratia* predominate. No infusate is entirely free of risk; even distilled water can support the growth of *Burkholderia (Pseudomonas) cepacia.*[10] Parenteral nutrition solutions are superb substrates for the growth of certain microorganisms.[11] Casein hydrolysate solutions support the growth of many bacteria and fungi.[12] Lipid emulsions support bacterial growth extremely well,[13, 14] and their use has also been associated with a risk for fungemia caused by the lipid-dependent yeast *Malassezia furfur.*[15] This latter risk has been identified primarily in the neonatal intensive care setting and has been less commonly seen in adults.[15] More recently, the risk for coagulase-negative staphylococcal bacteremia in neonates has been directly linked to the administration of lipid infusions.[16, 17]

Parenteral nutrition solutions may also become contaminated during compounding in the hospital pharmacy.[18, 19] Two similar outbreaks of *Candida parapsilosis* infection were linked to the backflow of yeast into TPN solution because vacuum pumps were used improperly.[18, 19]

The composition of the infusate also influences the degree of irritation of the vascular intima at the site of infusion. Fluids that are not isotonic, those at nonphysiologic pH, and those containing particulates may all irritate the vascular wall, thus provoking throm-

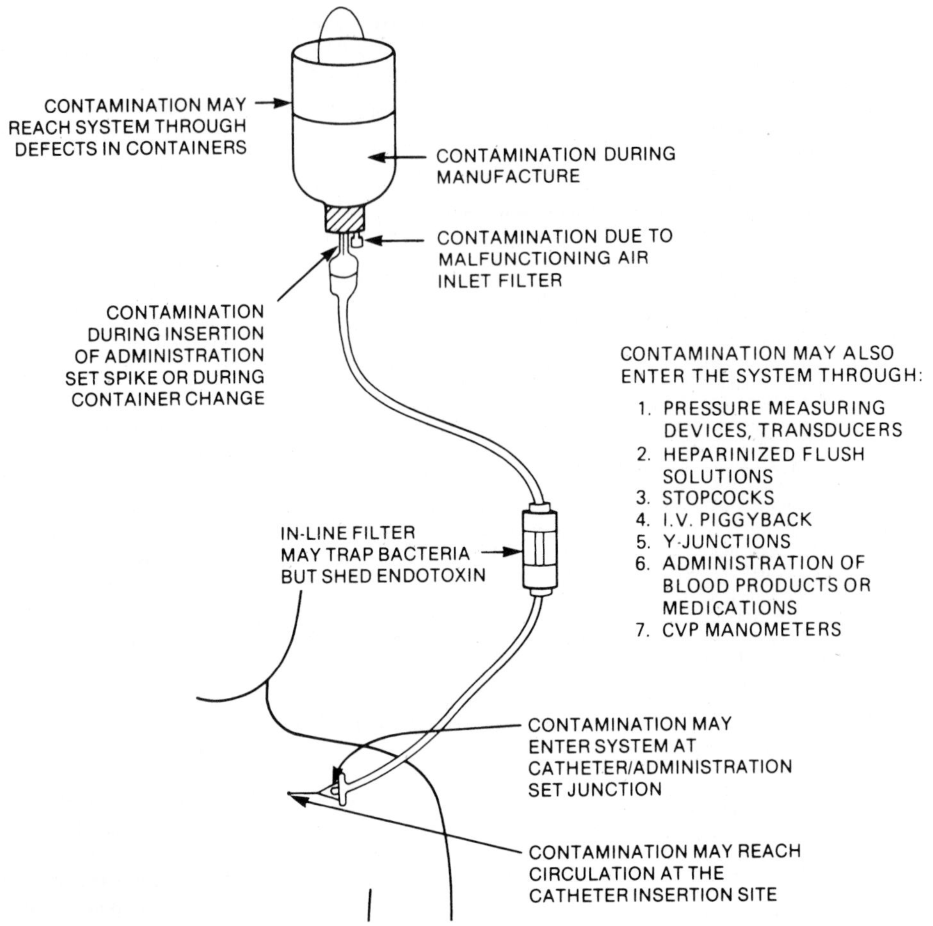
CONTAMINATION MAY
REACH SYSTEM THROUGH
DEFECTS IN CONTAINERS
CONTAMINATION DURING
MANUFACTURE
CONTAMINATION DUE TO
MALFUNCTIONING AIR
INLET FILTER
CONTAMINATION
DURING INSERTION
OF ADMINISTRATION
SET SPIKE OR DURING
CONTAINER CHANGE
CONTAMINATION MAY ALSO
ENTER THE SYSTEM THROUGH:
1. PRESSURE MEASURING
DEVICES, TRANSDUCERS
2. HEPARINIZED FLUSH
SOLUTIONS
3. STOPCOCKS
4. I.V. PIGGYBACK
5. Y-JUNCTIONS
6. ADMINISTRATION OF
BLOOD PRODUCTS OR
MEDICATIONS
7. CVP MANOMETERS
IN-LINE FILTER
MAY TRAP BACTERIA
BUT SHED ENDOTOXIN
CONTAMINATION MAY
ENTER SYSTEM AT
CATHETER/ADMINISTRATION
SET JUNCTION
CONTAMINATION MAY REACH
CIRCULATION AT THE
CATHETER INSERTION SITE

FIGURE 292–1. Points of access for microbial contamination in infusion therapy.

bus formation. Such thrombi may be seeded either hematogenously or by direct extension.

Contamination at Junctions

Contamination of the catheter hub–infusion tubing junction as a significant contributor to device-associated infection has been championed by Sitges-Serra and colleagues.[20–27] These investigators have suggested that endemic coagulase-negative staphylococcal bacteremias often arise as a result of contamination of the catheter hub with these organisms. Other investigators have incriminated the hub-tubing junction (particularly when it does not allow a good fit) in the pathogenesis of epidemics of coagulase-negative staphylococcal infection.[28, 29] Maki and Ringer found hub contamination to be the second most heavily weighted risk factor for catheter-associated infection in a large, prospective study.[30] Salzman and colleagues noted that more than 50% of episodes of central venous catheter–related sepsis occurring in a neonatal intensive care unit were preceded by colonization of the catheter hub with the incriminated organism.[31] In a subsequent experimental study, these investigators found that swabbing the catheter hub with disinfectant substantially reduced the hub's microbial burden and that preparations containing 70% ethanol were both more effective and more likely to be safer for the patient than preparations containing chlorhexidine.[32] Finally, several outbreaks of bacteremia have been traced to contaminated medications—either those added directly to the system or those piggybacked into a side port. Recent clusters of infection have been linked to flushing catheters with fluids from a contaminated common source.[33, 34]

Contamination at the Device Insertion Site

Many authorities believe that the catheter insertion tract provides the major avenue for the ingress of microbial.[1, 3–5, 20, 26, 28–30, 35, 36] Several studies have focused on microbial colonization around the catheter insertion site as a significant risk factor for catheter-associated infection.[37, 38] Supporting this contention are studies by Cooper and Hopkins, which demonstrated organisms on the exterior surface of catheters rather than within the catheter lumen.[39] In the prospective study of Maki and Ringer, colonization around the catheter insertion site was the most strongly associated risk factor for local catheter infection.[30] Nonetheless skin colonization is a dynamic process. Atela and coworkers conducted a prospective study to assess the turnover of superficial skin colonization.[36] Serial quantitative cultures of skin and the catheter hub were performed. Strains recovered from the targeted superficial skin sites demonstrated a poor correlation both with strains from previous skin cultures and with catheter tip isolates.[36] Others have found similar results.[40]

Numerous additional factors influence the risk for device-associated infection. Because of methodological difficulties in performing appropriate scientific studies to characterize relative risk, many of these risk factors have been identified either retrospectively or in the epidemic setting. Still, each of the patient-related factors identified in Table 292–1 has been associated with an increased risk of device-associated infection.[3] Several additional factors have been incriminated as increasing the risk for device-associated infection and bac-

TABLE 292–1 Patient-Related Risk Factors for Device-Associated Bacteremia

Age 1 yr or younger, 60 yr or older
Granulocytopenia
Immunosuppressive chemotherapy
Loss of skin integrity (e.g., burns, psoriasis)
Severity of underlying illness
Presence of distant infection

teremia (Table 292–2). Of these factors, a few deserve special mention.

Alteration of the patient's skin flora, either as a result of antimicrobial therapy or by colonization with an epidemic strain carried on the hands of hospital personnel, is a common event preceding catheter site infection. In addition, certain therapeutic devices (e.g., semipermeable membrane dressings) may actually increase the cutaneous microbial burden surrounding the catheter insertion site.[41, 42]

Failure of hospital personnel to perform appropriate hand-washing technique, particularly in the intensive care unit setting, has been well documented.[43, 44] Numerous epidemics of device-associated bacteremia have been linked to hospital personnel carrying the epidemic strain on their hands.

A few outbreaks of infection have been linked to the application of contaminated antiseptic ointment or disinfection solutions onto the skin of patients.[45, 46] Even the iodophors have been found to contain viable organisms.[47, 48]

Manipulating the system for repositioning, for obtaining a sample, or for any other reason increases the likelihood that the catheter may become contaminated.[49] This point has been best illustrated in studies of infectious complications associated with catheters used for TPN (discussed later).

Several catheter characteristics or properties have been suggested to be associated with an increased risk for catheter-associated infection. Catheters that irritate the vascular intima and provoke thrombogenesis and catheters that are made of materials that are intrinsically thrombogenic are likely to be associated with an increased risk for device-associated infection. Older studies suggested that stiff catheters were associated with higher infection rates.[50] Such catheters are likely to be more mobile in the insertion tract and are thought to be more thrombogenic. Stillman and colleagues demonstrated a clear association between the thrombogenicity of a catheter and the risk for device-associated infection.[51] Subsequently, Linder and coworkers have confirmed these observations by demonstrating that flexible silicone elastomer and polyurethane catheters are less thrombogenic than polyvinyl chloride catheters.[52] Despite differences in thrombogenicity, some authorities believe that all catheters become coated with a fibrin sheath shortly after placement.[53, 54] In the 1990s, use of catheters manufactured of stiffer and more thrombogenic materials was decreasing, along with an increase in the use of more pliable, less thrombogenic materials (e.g., silicone elastomer).

Catheter composition may influence the risk for infection in another way. Sheth and coworkers have shown that certain microorganisms, most notably staphylococci, are able to adhere better to a catheter made of polyvinyl chloride than to a Teflon catheter.[55] Rotrosen and colleagues demonstrated increased adherence of *Candida* spp. to polyvinyl chloride catheters when compared with Teflon catheters.[56] One might hypothesize that materials that facilitate microbial adherence may be associated with an increased risk for device-associated infection. Newer therapeutic interventions have focused on diminishing adherence to the catheter by a variety of different mechanisms.

The physical size of the catheter (and therefore the size of the defect in the skin's intrinsic host defenses) is also likely to be correlated with increased risk. Similarly, increasing the number of lumina in a catheter has been suggested to increase the risk for catheter-associated infections. Several studies have now suggested that the use of triple-lumen catheters is associated with an increased risk for catheter-associated infection when compared with single-lumen catheters.[57–63] Not all studies have found this difference.[64, 65]

TABLE 292–2 Additional Factors Associated with Increased Risk for Device-Associated Infection

Alteration in patient's cutaneous microflora
Health care provider hygiene (hand washing)
Contaminated ointment or cream
Catheter composition/construction
Flexibility/stiffness
Thrombogenicity
Microbial adherence properties
Size of catheter
Number of catheter lumina
Distant infection (hematogenous seeding)
Catheter function/use
Catheter management: entry into the system

TABLE 292–3 Hospital-Related Risk Factors for Catheter-Acquired Infection

Type of catheter (more risk with plastic than with steel)
Location of catheter (central more than peripheral[3, 78]; femoral more than jugular/subclavian)
Type of placement (cutdown associated with greater risk than percutaneous[78–80] placement)
Duration of placement (at least 72 hr is associated with greater risk than placement less than 72 hr[3, 30, 78, 79])*
Emergent placement is a greater risk factor than is elective placement
Skill of venipuncturist (others associated with greater risk than the IV team[3, 72])
Type/use of catheter (balloon-tipped, flow directed catheters are associated with greater risk than are percutaneously placed central venous catheters, which in turn are greater risk factors than implanted central venous catheters)

*Although several studies support this precept; one recent study has questioned it.[81]

The presence of distant infection resulting in hematogenous seeding of the intravascular device has been incriminated in the pathogenesis of device-associated infection in some series.[37, 66, 67] Several factors may influence the risk for catheter seeding, including catheter composition, local thrombus formation at the catheter insertion site, intensity of bacteremia, the pathogen, duration of catheterization, duration of bacteremia, and the patient's ability to mount an immunologic response to the infection.

Finally, the manner in which the catheter is used may influence risk. For example, the risk of infection with flow-directed, balloon-tipped pulmonary artery catheters may be higher because of the manner in which these catheters are used.[68] In critically ill patients, these catheters are used intensively; they are frequently repositioned to obtain accurate readings, they are used to obtain samples for the measurement of cardiac output, and they are often used to obtain mixed venous blood to measure oxygen and carbon dioxide tensions. Catheter management, including both insertion and maintenance, may also influence risk for infection. Several studies[69–71] have shown that catheters placed by less experienced personnel are at increased risk for infection. A recent study analyzed the efficacy of using a skilled team for the placement of peripheral intravenous catheters.[72] In this study, an intravenous therapy team significantly reduced both local and bacteremic complications associated with the placement of peripheral intravenous catheters, in part related to timely replacement of the catheters. Several studies have suggested that the number of times the system is entered also influences the risk for infection.[49, 73–77] In addition to the factors just outlined, the risk of development of catheter-associated bacteremia is related to the patient's intrinsic host defense mechanisms, as well as to factors related to the patient's hospital environment or therapy (see Table 292–1). The physician cannot alter most such patient-related factors; however, these data can be used when deciding on the necessity for and duration of intravenous therapy.

In addition to patient-related risk factors, several hospital-related risk factors for catheter-acquired bacteremia have been either identified or proposed (Table 292–3). In contraposition to the patient-related factors, such hospital-related factors can often be altered for patient benefit.

MICROBIOLOGY

Staphylococci continue to predominate as the most frequently encountered pathogens in device-related infections. Although *Staphylococcus aureus* is a frequent cause of device-associated infection, coagulase-negative staphylococci have become the most common causes of these infections in the past 20 years—especially in immunocompromised patients and those in whom long-term central venous access is required.[5, 78, 82–84]

Although the devices or therapies under discussion have some minor microbiologic differences, as a genus, staphylococci account for one half to two thirds of the episodes of bacteremia associated with these devices. Recent studies have suggested that coagulase-negative staphylococci may be able to adhere to plastic catheters more aggressively than other organisms can.[82, 83] This property would result in a selective advantage for coagulase-negative staphylococci in causing device-associated infection.

Other commonly encountered isolates are listed in Table 292–4. Some institutions have observed a recent increase in catheter-associated infection caused by gram-negative bacilli.[85, 86] The occurrence of some of the more unusual isolates (e.g., *Enterobacter* spp., *B. cepacia, Citrobacter freundii*) as a clear cause of device-associated infection should at least suggest the possibility of a contaminated infusion product[3] or an aqueous environmental reservoir for these pathogens.[3, 33, 34, 87, 88]

Other organisms may cause such infections (e.g., *Flavobacterium, Acinetobacter* spp.); however, such organisms have been infrequently associated with either infusion-related or cannula-related infections.[9, 89] Concomitant with the increasing empirical use of broad-spectrum antimicrobials in severely immunosuppressed patients, cases of device-associated blood stream infection caused by a variety of unusual bacterial and fungal pathogens have been reported with increasing frequency.[4, 90–114]

DIAGNOSIS

Clinical detection of catheter-associated septicemia is sometimes difficult. Signs of local inflammation are present in only about half of the cases.[3] Maki has summarized key issues in the diagnosis of device-associated bacteremia.[3] In addition to the presence of one of the indwelling intravascular devices listed earlier, several clinical features should alert the physician to the possibility of device-associated bacteremia. Salient features of device-associated sepsis that help distinguish it from other bacteremic syndromes are listed in Table 292–5. Although none of these criteria specifically identifies the intravascular device as the source of sepsis, the presence of these clinical findings should at least raise the possibility of device-associated bacteremia.

Culture of the catheter tip itself has been reported to be of variable value. Before development of the semiquantitative culturing technique reported by Maki and colleagues,[119, 120] most clinical microbiology laboratories used broth culture of catheter tips in an attempt to detect contaminated catheters. This technique yielded results that were highly variable and unreliable.[119, 120, 122]

Using the semiquantitative culture technique, which defines a positive catheter tip culture as yielding 15 or more colonies,[119, 120] in combination with a relatively strict definition of catheter-associated sepsis,[3] Maki and colleagues have reported a specificity ranging between 76 and 96% and a positive predictive value of a positive catheter tip culture ranging between 16[120] and 31%[119] in four studies.[115, 119–121] Data regarding the sensitivity of the semiquantitative culture technique are not available because the authors incorporated the presence of a positive culture as part of their definition of both local catheter infection and catheter-acquired bacteremia.[3, 115, 119–121] The cutoff point of 15 colonies per catheter as a definition for "infection" appears to have been somewhat arbitrary in these studies. The authors note that most infected catheters yield confluent growth when using the semiquantitative technique.[3] Because staphylococci predominate in these infections, early work with the semiquantitative method was focused on staphylococcal infection. Recent experience suggests that the semiquantitative method may also be valid for infections caused by other organisms as well.[123]

To culture a catheter by the semiquantitative technique, the point at which the catheter enters the skin should be marked and the catheter removed aseptically. Sterile scissors (plastic catheters) or a sterile hemostat (steel needles) should be used to sever the catheter distal to the skin entry site (Fig. 292–2).

Several investigators have tried to modify Maki's technique to improve the predictability of the procedure. Cleri and coworkers reported a technique for quantitatively culturing catheters in broth.[124] This system, which is a bit more cumbersome for the laboratory to use, was believed by these authors to have three advantages over the system described by Maki and associates: (1) the ability to detect organisms within the lumen of the insert, (2) the ability to evaluate relative numbers of organisms from different catheter segments, and (3) the ability to compare relative numbers of organisms present in mixed infections.[124] Brun-Buisson and colleagues used a simplified quantitative broth dilution tip culture to evaluate catheters as potential sources for infection and found this technique to be 97.5% sensitive and 88% specific for the diagnosis of device-associated bacteremia when a strict clinical definition of device-associated bacteremia was used.[125] Subsequently, Gutierrez and coworkers found a modified broth dilution technique to be only slightly more sensitive, but substantially more labor intensive than the semiquantitative technique.[100] These latter investigators advocate the use of semiquantitative cultures because of the ease with which this test is performed. More recently, Hnatiuk and coworkers demonstrated a substantial increase in sensitivity of the semiquantitative technique when catheter tip cultures are plated at the patient's bedside rather than cutting the tip into a sterile tube and sending the tip to the laboratory for culture.[126]

Farr and coworkers conducted a meta-analysis of catheter culturing techniques and suggested that accuracy increases for catheter segment cultures with increasing quantitation (i.e., the qualitative technique is less accurate than the semiquantitative technique, which is less accurate than the quantitative technique).[122] The increase in accuracy is primarily due to the increased specificity of the more quantitative tests. They found that quantitative catheter segment culture was the only method associated with sensitivity and specificity above 90%.[122] Similarly, Sheretz and associates suggested that the common practice of culturing a single segment of a central vascular catheter is inadequate.[127]

TABLE 292–5 Factors Differentiating Device-Associated Bacteremia from Other Septic Syndromes

Local phlebitis or inflammation at the catheter insertion site
Lack of other source for the bacteremia
Sepsis occurring in a patient not otherwise at high risk for bacteremia[3]
Localized embolic disease distal to a cannulated artery[115, 116]
Hematogenous *Candida* endophthalmitis in patients receiving total parenteral nutrition[117, 118]
Presence of ≥15 colonies of bacteria on semiquantitative culture of the catheter tip[115, 119–121]
Sepsis apparently refractory to "appropriate" antimicrobial therapy
Resolution of febrile syndrome after device removal
Typical (*Staphylococcus aureus, Staphylococcus epidermidis*) or unusual (*Burkholderia cepacia, Enterobacter agglomerans, Enterobacter cloacae*) microbiology
Clustered infections caused by infusion-related organisms

TABLE 292–4 Microbiology of Device-Associated Bacteremia

Staphylococcus aureus
Staphylococcus epidermidis, other coagulase-negative staphylococci*
Klebsiella spp.†
Enterobacter spp.†
Serratia marcescens†
Candida albicans‡
Candida spp.‡
Pseudomonas aeruginosa§
Burkholderia cepacia§
Citrobacter freundii†
Corynebacteria (especially *Corynebacterium jeikeium*)‖

*Most common pathogen for long-term lines; also associated with lipid infusions in neonates.
†Frequently associated with contaminated infusate.
‡Most often associated with total parenteral nutrition; usually along the catheter path, but occasionally as a result of contaminated infusate.
§May arise from a water source (e.g., infusate) or may reflect cutaneous colonization.
‖*C. jeikeium* bacteremia occurs almost exclusively in severely immunosuppressed patients who are or have been receiving broad-spectrum antibiotics and who have indwelling intravascular devices.

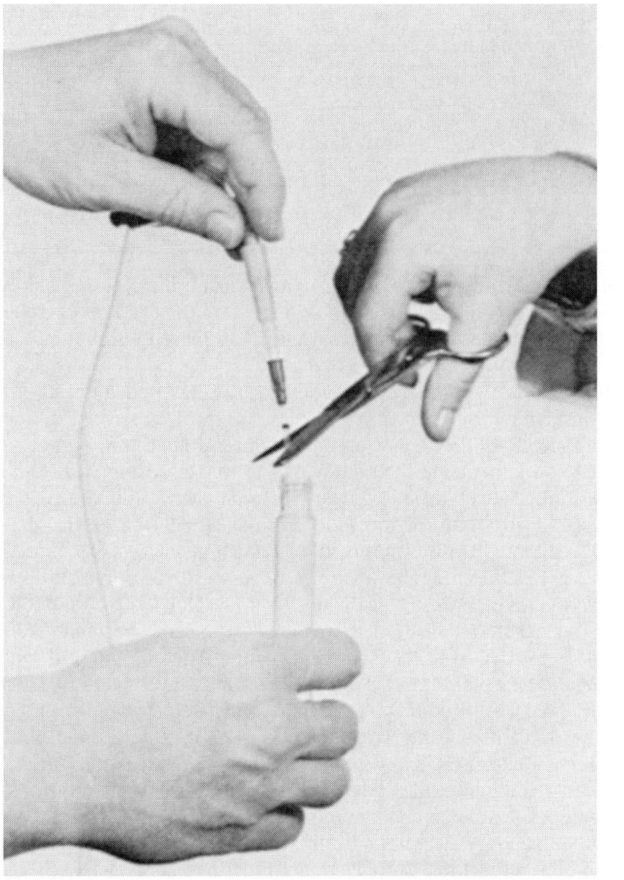

FIGURE 292–2. Procedure for culturing an intravenous catheter when a blood stream infection is thought to result from contamination of the catheter itself. The black band on the catheter above the scissors indicates the former skin surface-catheter interface. Using sterile scissors, cut the catheter as shown and allow the catheter tip to drop into the sterile screw-capped container.

Although the relative merits of these various procedures remain to be definitively delineated, the ease of performing the semiquantitative technique described by Maki and coworkers[119, 120] has brought it into widespread clinical use.

Other investigators have suggested alternative techniques for diagnosing catheter-associated infections.[122, 128–132] Cooper and Hopkins evaluated directly Gram staining of the catheter segment and found this technique to be more rapid and at least as sensitive and specific as semiquantitative cultureing.[39] Collignon and coworkers[128] advocated Gram staining of "impression smears" from the catheter, whereas Zuffrey and coworkers used direct acridine orange staining of the catheter.[131] Spencer and Kristinsson reported that the Gram-stain technique failed to diagnose infection adequately.[133] Although some experience is being gained with the direct Gram stain, none of these newer techniques appear to be effective enough to supplant the semiquantitative method. More recently, Kite and coworkers have suggested the use of an endoluminal brush method.[132] These authors suggest that the endoluminal brush method can be used without sacrificing the intravascular line and argue that the procedure is substantially more sensitive and more specific than the semiquantitative technique.[132] Some authors have recommended a combination of direct and microbiologic techniques.[122, 128]

Mosca and coworkers have emphasized the benefits of obtaining blood cultures by using the Isolator system, which allows for a quantitative estimate of microbial burden in the specimen.[134] Although several additional studies have underscored the usefulness of the Isolator system, one study has suggested that results obtained with traditional blood cultures may be complementary to those obtained with the Isolator system and that whenever feasible, both approaches should be used.[135] Kaditis and colleagues have argued that pediatric institutions should develop a standardized method of blood culture collection and suggest that consistent volumes of blood be drawn for each sample and that a minimum of two cultures be obtained for each febrile episode.[136] Blot and colleagues have suggested that the speed with which bacterial isolates can be detected in the microbiology laboratory may distinguish catheter-associated from non–catheter-associated infection.[137] Presumably because of a higher bacterial concentration, blood cultures from patients with device-associated infection often demonstrate growth much more rapidly than do those not associated with an intravascular device.[137]

Occasionally, intracellular bacteria may be identified in routine differential blood smears. The finding of intracellular bacteria in such routine studies on a central venous catheter blood specimen often indicates active infection. In one study, six such patients were asymptomatic at the time that bacteria were detected on their differential blood smears; nonetheless, all six had blood cultures positive for coagulase-negative staphylococci.[138] Identification of intracellular bacteria on differential blood smears from patients who have vascular access devices should prompt consideration for catheter removal, even if the patient is asymptomatic.[138]

On the basis of currently available data, conclusions cannot be drawn regarding the relative merits of various blood culturing techniques in confirming the diagnosis of catheter-acquired sepsis. Wing and colleagues used a comparison of quantitative cultures obtained peripherally and quantitative cultures obtained by drawing blood back through the putatively contaminated catheter to document the occurrence of catheter-acquired sepsis.[139] Subsequent studies have recommended a differential quantitative culturing technique (i.e., obtaining simultaneous quantitative cultures both from peripheral sites and through the line to determine whether the line is the source of the bacteremia).[140, 141] More recently, Quilici and colleagues have underscored the utility of obtaining "differential" blood cultures.[142] In their study, differential cultures had an overall sensitivity of 92.8% and a specificity of 98.8%. In instances in which the catheters were removed because of suspected infection, the differential cultures exhibited a sensitivity of 92.8% and a specificity of 100%.[142] Because of the complexity of the epidemiology of device-associated bacteremia and the increased technical complexity of the differential blood culturing procedure, the broad applicability of these and the earlier findings nonetheless remains unclear.

The usefulness of "through the line" cultures has been questioned repeatedly because these cultures may become contaminated easily. Tonnesen and associates reported that blood drawn through venous or arterial catheters gave concordant results with cultures obtained by peripheral venipuncture in 92% of cases.[143] In 5% of cases, results of catheter pullback cultures were considered to represent false positives (most were *Staphylococcus epidermidis*), and in an additional 2% catheter-drawn cultures were reported to be falsely negative.[143] Similar results were reported by Felices and colleagues,[144] who compared the results of cultures obtained by peripheral venipuncture with cultures obtained through central venous catheters. The incidence of false-positive drawback cultures may greatly depend on the type of access port used to draw the cultures and the care taken in obtaining the specimen. If the details of the method used to obtain the culture are unknown, relying entirely on cultures obtained by drawing blood through an indwelling catheter may be imprudent. In well-defined circumstances in which device-associated bacteria is an important consideration in the patient's differential diagnosis, however, these cultures may provide valuable information.[67, 100, 124, 125, 134, 135, 139–141, 145]

Over the past several years, molecular methods have begun to play an increasingly prominent role in the diagnostic microbiology laboratory. Linares has recently summarized the importance of molecular techniques in the laboratory.[27] Examples of the usefulness of these new techniques include the use of randomly amplified polymorphic DNA analysis for the rapid fingerprinting of coagulase-negative staphylococci,[146] the use of other molecular typing methods (e.g., pulsed-field electrophoresis, localization and probing the vicinity of the *mecA* gene),[27, 147] and molecular identification of antimicrobial resistance even before speciation can be completed. These molecular techniques are particularly valuable in epidemiologic investigations.

DEVICE-SPECIFIC ISSUES

Peripheral Intravenous Cannulization

In general, peripheral catheters are associated with much lower infection risks than are central catheters. Steel needles have been associated with lower rates of local infection, bacteremic infection, and local phlebitis than have plastic catheters.[78, 79] Tully and coworkers, however, demonstrated that steel catheters placed by an intravenous team nurse were associated with significantly less phlebitis but significantly more episodes of infiltration than were Teflon catheters.[148] In this study, all catheters were removed in less than 72 hours; infection rates for both catheter types were extremely low, and no differences, were seen in local or systemic infection rates between the two groups.[148] More recently, Bregenzer and colleagues have demonstrated that the risk of catheter-related complications—phlebitis, catheter-related infections, and mechanical complications—did not increase during extended (i.e., longer than 72 hours) catheterization.[81] These authors suggest that the Centers for Disease Control and Prevention's recommendation for routine replacement of peripheral intravenous catheters be reevaluated, particularly in view of the additional costs associated with routine catheter replacement, as well as the additional discomfort for the patient.[81]

The location of catheter placement also may influence subsequent infection rates. Catheters placed in the lower extremities, particularly in the femoral veins, are associated with increased risk for many complications, including infection.[78, 79, 148–153] Martin and coworkers evaluated axial vein cannulization as an alternative to the internal jugular insertion site and found that the rate of catheter-related infection and other complications was similar to that observed after internal jugular vein catheterization.[154]

If data are evaluated on the basis of infection per number of catheters placed, central lines are associated with higher infection rates than are peripheral catheters. If, on the other hand, data are assessed on the basis of infections (both local and systemic) per day of catheterization, central lines are associated with lower sepsis rates than peripheral catheters are.[3] For several reasons, including the increased risk of serious complications such as pneumothorax, hemothorax, puncture of the great arteries, and thrombosis and thrombophlebitis of the great veins, central catheter placement should be reserved for situations in which a peripheral catheter either cannot be placed or cannot be used.

Catheters placed percutaneously are associated with lower infection rates than are those placed by cutdown.[78–80] As noted earlier, the older literature suggests that leaving any peripheral catheter in place for longer than 72 hours significantly increases the risk of infection.[3, 30, 78, 79] One study has challenged this tenet.[81] Catheters placed emergently are also at higher risk for infection, presumably because of breaks in technique at the time of placement. Several investigators have suggested that catheters placed by members of an intravenous therapy team are associated with lower complication rates than are those placed by other health care professionals.[72]

Techniques for the placement and care of indwelling venous cannulas have been reviewed in detail.[78, 79] Several aspects of catheter maintenance and care are controversial and await definitive studies to document their efficacy. Issues that are the focus of such controversy are listed in Table 292–6. Several of these issues deserve further comment.

Although some authorities have recommended the routine use of an antimicrobial skin ointment to cover the catheter insertion site,[3, 78, 79, 155] no definitive study has documented the efficacy of such substances in preventing catheter-acquired bacteremia. Rhame and colleagues reviewed the composite experience of six different studies that were designed to address this issue.[78] Five of these studies did not find any differences between topical antimicrobial agents and placebo. In the smallest series in this review (a study of 78 catheter insertions), three infections occurred in the placebo group and none in the therapy group.[78] Maki and Band[156] prospectively studied the following three regimens of catheter care: (1) application of polymyxin-neomycin-bacitracin ointment at insertion and every 48 hours, (2) application of iodophor ointment at insertion and every 48 hours, or (3) no ointment. In their study of 827 random catheter insertions, no differences could be found in either catheter-acquired sepsis two cases in each group) or local inflammation (38.9 versus 41.9 versus 41.7). The only difference noted was in semiquantitative cultures of catheter tips.[156] The polymyxin-neomycin-bacitracin ointment group had 6 positive cultures, the iodophor group had 10, and the control group had 18. This difference was greatest in catheters that were left in place for over 4 days. Thus, information regarding the efficacy of these antimcrobial ointments or creams for intravascular cannulas is contradictory and confusing, and the clinical utility of these compounds remains questionable.

TABLE 292–6 Factors Not Definitively Documented to Affect Risk for Catheter-Acquired Infection

Topical antimicrobial ointment
In-line membrane filters
Dressing materials
Antimicrobial bonding to intravascular devices
Frequent changes of administration sets

Techniques used for skin preparation before catheter insertion may also influence the risk for infection. In a recent study, skin preparation and decontamination with 0.5% chlorhexidine gluconate in 70% isopropyl alcohol was more effective than 10% povidone-iodine in preventing colonization of peripheral catheters in neonates.[157]

The use of in-line membrane filters has also been advocated as a mechanism for reducing the incidence of catheter-acquired infection.[158] Because, as was pointed out earlier, the major points of entry are the skin insertion site and perhaps the catheter hub, one might suspect that such devices would be of limited usefulness in preventing most catheter-acquired septicemias. No investigators have recommended the routine inclusion of such filters in all intravenous setups, nor has any study demonstrated conclusive evidence that the routine use of such filters results in lowering of the infusion-related bacteremia rate.

In isolated situations (e.g., if particulate matter is present in the infusate, if the solution must hang for an extended period, or perhaps in a situation in which an infusate such as TPN solution supports the growth of microorganisms extremely well), the addition of these filters to the system is of theoretical value. However, even in cases in which the infusion fluid is contaminated, organisms trapped on the filter may shed endotoxins into the patient's circulation.[159]

In the past, several authorities have recommended placement of a sterile dressing over the catheter entry site,[78, 79] and others have made recommendations for routine care (usually on a daily or every-other-day basis) of the entry site. Maki and Ringer compared the efficacy of a sterile, dry gauze dressing with two semipermeable membrane dressings, one of which was impregnated with an iodophor.[30] No difference was seen among the four groups: (1) gauze changed every 48 hours, (2) gauze left in place for the life of the catheter, (3) transparent membrane left in place for the life of the catheter, and (4) iodophor membrane left on for the life of the catheter. Hoffmann and coworkers performed a meta-analysis of studies in an attempt to assess the use of semipermeable membrane dressing materials at catheter insertion sites.[160] These investigators found a significantly increased risk of cathetert tip colonization when transparent versus gauze dressings were used to dress either central or peripheral catheter insertion sites. In addition, they found a trend although not statistically significant in their meta-analysis) toward an increased risk for bacteremia and catheter sepsis associated with the use of semipermeable dressings as insertion-site dressings for central venous catheters.[160]

Finally, two studies have demonstrated that routinely changing intravenous admistration sets at 48 rather than 24 hours was not associated with a significant increase in the infusion-related bacteremia rate.[161, 162] Snydman and coworkers[163] and Maki and colleagues[164] compared the relative safety of changing administration sets at 72-hour intervals with changing them at 48 hours. Neither study identified an increased risk with the 72-hour interval.

Thus, inserting a peripheral catheter, dressing it, hooking up the administration set, and changing all three at 72-hour intervals now seem both safe and practical and reasonable.

Central Venous Catheters

Because central venous catheters frequently remain in place longer than peripheral catheters, certain problems either occur with more frequency or are unique to these catheters. In addition, because of the placement of these catheters in the great veins, complications of placement such as infective endocarditis and suppurative thrombophlebitis of the great veins represent life-threatening events.

Michel and colleagues studied 390 catheters placed into the subclavian vein by identical technique in an attempt to determine risk factors associated with microbial colonization.[165] In this study, the presence of distant infection, bacteremia, or tracheostomy was associated with an increased risk for catheter colonization.[165] Unfortunately, these authors chose to culture the catheters by using the broth culture technique, which yields notoriously unreliable results.[3, 78, 79]

The presence of either intraluminal or extraluminal fibrin has been proposed as predisposing to the development of catheter-associated infection.[3, 35, 51–54, 166–168] Stillman and colleagues studied 94 central catheters and found that all 11 catheters categorized as infected in their study and 30 of 83 not found to be either infected or colonized had gross visible evidence of either intraluminal or surface thrombin at the time of removal.[51] Lloyd and coworkers failed to find a deleterious effect associated with the so-called fibrin-sheath when evaluating a rat model of device-associated bacteremia.[169]

As with peripheral catheters, the use of antiseptic or antibiotic ointments on central venous catheter insertion sites has been recommended by several authorities;[3, 78, 79, 155] however, proof of the efficacy of these compounds in reducing infection remains to be demonstrated. In a study by Prager and Silva,[170] antiseptic cream was of no benefit in preventing either infection or colonization of central catheters.

The issue of whether central catheters should be changed over a guide wire remains controversial. Although the guide wire technique is commonly used, little scientific evidence supports its use if catheter-associated infection is suspected. Maher and colleagues used this technique successfully for catheter exchange in situations assessed as "low risk for infection."[171] Two additional studies suggest that guide wire exchange may not be particularly useful if device-associated infection is suspected.[172, 173] Use of a guide wire obviates the need for a second percutaneous puncture of the great veins and may be preferable for catheter exchanges judged routine or mandated by some reason other than suspected infection. In one of the two recently published studies, guide wire catheter exchange was associated with an increased risk of blood stream infection but a lower risk of mechanical complications.[173] In one experimental study, replacement of a biofilm-colonized central venous catheter over a guide wire was associated with an increased risk for colonization of the new catheter, as well as an increased risk for production of detached, slime-enclosed, antibiotic-resistant aggregates that may disseminate the infection to other sites.[141]

Although guide wire exchange of central venous catheters may be associated with a greater risk for catheter-related infection, this technique may result in many fewer mechanical complications than would be the case for repuncture.[174] Specifically, exchange over a guide wire is associated with lower risks for some complications (e.g., bleeding, pneumothorax).[172, 173] If a guide wire is to be used for catheter exchange, culture of the removed or "old" catheter tip should be performed. In addition, blood cultures should be drawn through the "old" line before removal. If either of these cultures becomes positive, the most conservative approach would be to remove the "replacement" catheter and perform appropriate cultures. If central access is still desired, a third catheter should be placed at a new puncture site. In situations in which the catheter is being removed for suspected sepsis, in my opinion, exchange over a guide wire should not be attempted. Conversely, one recent study suggested a possible benefit of guide wire exchange for patients who have catheter-associated candidemia.[175]

The umbilical vein catheter that is commonly used for vascular access in neonates presents some unique problems. Because of the extensive microbiologic flora of the umbilical stump,[176] these catheters are at high risk for both colonization and infection.[177–179] Although high rates of umbilical catheter–associated infection have been reported in several studies,[177–179] not all centers report such high rates.[180–182] One study has reported a much lower incidence of infectious complications when the umbilical artery (rather than the umbilical vein) was cannulated for infusion.[182]

Another approach that has recently been advocated to reduce the risk for central venous catheter–associated infection is bonding of an antimicrobial agent or antiseptic to the device itself or the addition of a subcutaneous catheter cuff impregnated with an antiseptic or antimicrobial. Following the hypothesis that the major microbial access to the intravascular device is along the insertion site (see "Pathogenesis," earlier), a cuff that provides both a physical and an antimicrobial barrier might well reduce the risk for infection. Several studies have found the use of such catheters to be associated with lower catheter infection rates.[183–189] Conversely, some studies have failed to find a benefit of catheters with antimicrobial or antiseptic substances bonded to them.[190–195] Thus, the benefit of this technology remains to be definitively established. Whether the added expense of bonding antimicrobial substances to intravascular devices provides any clinical benefit and whether the clinical benefit outweighs the additional expense associated with this process remain to be delineated.

Use of heparin or other anticoagulants has also been advocated as a method for reducing both thrombotic and infectious complications of central venous catheterization. In one small study, the addition of 1 unit/ml of heparin to the infusate decreased septic complications; however, a subsequent study failed to demonstrate a benefit from adding heparin to the infusate.[168] A more recent study found a clear benefit of covalently bonding heparin to catheters.[196] In this study, the use of catheters to which heparin had been covalently bonded decreased bacterial colonization in vitro as well as decreased the device-associated infection rate in vivo.[196] Randolph and associates concluded that heparin administration effectively reduces thrombus formation and may reduce catheter-related infections in patients who have central venous and pulmonary artery catheters in place.[197] Several anticoagulants have been suggested for use in this setting, and Randolph and coworkers point out that cost-effectiveness comparisons of these several preparations (e.g., unfractionated heparin, low-molecular-weight heparin, and warfarin) are needed.[197] Goey and colleagues ascribed the relatively low incidence of thrombosis and infection in their large series of catheters placed in patients receiving interleukin-2 infusions (a population of patients known to be at substantially increased risk for catheter-associated infection) to the use of tunneled catheters and prophylactic heparin.[198]

Thrombosis of the great veins, with the attendant risk of suppurative thrombophlebitis, is a major complication of central catheter placement.[152] Thrombosis occurs with increased frequency in patients with malignancies[151] (particularly those who have mediastinal lymphadenopathy) and in patients with sickle cell disease.[199, 200] In instances in which central catheters are placed in patients with these underlying illness, thrombotic and infectious complications should be anticipated, prevented (when possible), diagnosed early, and treated aggressively.

Additional issues relating to catheter composition, effectiveness of subcutaneous tunneling of catheters, and risks associated with electronic monitoring devices will be discussed in later sections.

Total Parenteral Nutrition

Several aspects of the delivery of TPN separate this mode of intravascular therapy from others. First, the composition of the infusate supports the growth of different microorganisms, most notably certain of the *Candida* spp.[11, 12] Second, TPN catheters are often required to remain in place much longer than either peripheral or other central venous cannulas. For this reason, problems with catheter contamination become much more of a concern. Third, the hypertonicity of the solution tends to cause thrombosis, which may result in an increased risk of infection. Fourth, because patients who require TPN are frequently severely ill with neoplasms, trauma, or inflammatory bowel disease, the risk for bacteremia is higher. Therefore, the potential for hematogenous seeding of the catheter is high.

For these and other reasons, the placement, management, and care of catheters used for TPN have received a great deal of attention. Ryan and colleagues, in a prospective study of 200 catheters, documented that the risk of catheter-associated infection increased significantly when the integrity of the delivery system was interrupted.[74] Numerous other studies support this concept.[75–77] Snydman and colleagues subsequently found that the occurrence of so-called line violations was highly associated with the development of TPN catheter–associated sepsis.[73] For these reasons, the Centers for Disease Control and Prevention have recommended that the administration of TPN be supervised and conducted by members of a team[201] (Table 292–7). In their study, Snydman and colleagues also attempted to correlate the results of twice-weekly 1-ml pour-plate blood cultures with the subsequent development of catheter colonization and sepsis. Similar to the previously cited studies,[143, 144] although concordance was high among blood cultures, catheter tip cultures, and peripheral blood cultures, cultures obtained through the TPN catheter demonstrated a reasonably high incidence of false positivity, primarily because of *S. epidermidis* contamination.[73]

TABLE 292–7 Prevention of Infusion-Related Infection in Total Parenteral Nutrition

Administration of TPN should be under the supervision of a team of health care professionals (usually a nurse, pharmacist, and physician). Both the decision for appropriateness of TPN therapy and protocols for catheter insertion and maintenance and for delivery of TPN should be the responsibility of this team

TPN solution should be prepared with sterile or aseptic technique when possible in a laminar flow hood. Once prepared, the solution should be infused immediately or stored at 4°C

Placement of the catheter should be performed by using sterile technique including, at a minimum, mask, gloves, drapes, and appropriate skin preparation (preferably with chlorhexidine[157, 202, 203] or 1% iodine)

Once placed, the catheter should be anchored to avoid movement, which may result in local irritation of the insertion site or transport of organisms along the insertion path

If possible, the system should be kept closed and unnecessary entry for blood drawing and administration of other fluids or blood products via the TPN line avoided

Other aspects of TPN administration are either of empirical or theoretical value, have shown equivocal or borderline results in studies, have shown conflicting results in studies, or have been demonstrated to be of value in small studies. Definitive studies to document the merit of the following techniques are needed before they are routinely implemented:

- Routine application of antiseptic cream at the site of catheter insertion (either at the time of venipuncture or at routine dressing change)
- Routine dressing changes, skin defatting with acetone, and skin preparation with antiseptics[157, 202, 203]
- Routine use of semipermeable dressing materials (a meta-analysis of data from several studies suggests that these dressings may actually play a detrimental role in catheter infections[160])
- Routine use of in-line membrane filters (no benefit demonstrated)
- Use of silicone or other less traumatic, nonthrombogenic catheters; use of heparin-bonded catheters; use of low-dose heparin infusions
- Tunneling the catheter subcutaneously to increase the anatomic distance between the catheter insertion site and the point at which the catheter enters the vessel (appeared to be useful in several small studies)

Modified from Goldman D, Maki D. Infection control in total parenteral nutrition. JAMA. 1973;223:1360–1364. Copyright 1973, American Medical Association.

Candida infection has been a particular problem in patients receiving TPN.[117, 118, 204] Curry and Quie reported a 16% incidence of candidemia among patients receiving TPN in a prospective study in a hospital that did not have a TPN team.[204] In another prospective study of 131 postoperative patients who were receiving TPN, chorioretinal lesions consistent with hematogenous *Candida* endophthalmitis were developing in 13 patients; 7 of the patients had positive blood cultures for *Candida*.[118] Although most of these infections are presumed to arise as a result of yeast contamination at the catheter entry site, occasional outbreaks of *Candida* infection from a TPN solution that was intrinsically contaminated have been reported.[18, 19] Because of the risk of intrinsic as well as in-use contamination of TPN solutions with *Candida* or other microorganisms, some authorities have recommended the routine use of an in-line membrane filter to prevent infusion-related sepsis.[158] Such filters have been implicated as a cause of device-associated infection or device-associated endotoxemia; however, the risk-benefit ratio for their use has not been established.

Because a TPN catheter must frequently be left in place for an extended period and because of the increased thrombogenicity of the TPN fluid, several modifications of the delivery system of the catheter itself have been advocated. Among the suggested mechanisms for decreasing infections in TPN catheters are (1) either bonding heparin or a heparin-like substance to the catheter or infusing heparin with the infusate in an attempt to minimize fibrin sheath formation[168, 205]; (2) constructing the catheter with a more flexible substance, thereby producing less trauma to the vascular endothelium[206, 207]; and (3) tunneling the catheter under the skin in an attempt to decrease access of pathogens to the circulation.[207, 208]

Several papers have reported lower infectious complication rates with silicone elastomer catheters.[206, 207] Two small studies have failed to show any benefit of increasing the distance between the anatomic insertion site and the site at which the catheter enters the vessel,[207, 208] although tunneling remains a standard practice, both with some types of catheters and in some institutions.

The routine use of antibiotic cream at the insertion site under the dressing may promote colonization of the skin (and ultimately the catheter) with *Candida*.[155] For this reason, many authorities recommend the use of antiseptic ointment (such as an iodophor). As noted earlier, no controlled study has demonstrated the efficacy of these ointments in preventing catheter-acquired sepsis. Similarly, several authorities recommend routinely changing the dressing, preparing the skin, and inspecting the catheter insertion site either daily,[155] every other day,[74] three times weekly,[207] or at longer intervals.[76] Although the use of antimicrobial creams and visualization of the insertion site to look for signs of local infection would seem reasonable, the theoretical possibility exists that the additional manipulations of the line caused by these procedures might actually be detrimental.[209] Topical antimicrobials have also been shown to invalidate cultures of the catheter insertion site and may potentially invalidate cultures of catheter segments upon removal.

A final and often difficult issue is deciding when to remove a TPN catheter for suspected sepsis. In the past, most authorities recommended the removal of a TPN line whenever infection was suspected. In separate studies, Ryan and colleagues[74] and Maher and coworkers[171] have suggested that nearly 70% of catheters removed for suspected sepsis are apparently removed unnecessarily. Thus, the TPN team is often faced with the dilemma of whether to remove the catheter from a patient in whom the evidence for infection is equivocal. Such a patient may have many reasons for fever; therefore, the diagnosis of infection may be difficult. Often, patients are severely immunosuppressed or thrombocytopenic, and the risks associated with catheter replacement may be quite high. Several clinical features may help the physician decide how to manage the catheter.[3, 35] The presence of positive blood cultures (particularly colonization by *Candida* or *S. epidermidis*) in the absence of another source for the infection or in the presence of hemodynamic instability, embolic phenomena, leukocytosis, or profound leukopenia may herald the onset of catheter-associated sepsis. In addition, the development of new glucose intolerance in a TPN patient whose carbohydrate metabolism had previously been well regulated may be an early subtle sign of bacteremia.[35, 118]

Long-Term Central Venous Access—Catheters and Ports

In 1973, Broviac and colleagues reported their initial experience with the use of a chronic indwelling right atrial catheter for the delivery of long-term parenteral nutrition.[210] Since this initial report, modifications of the catheter system have been published, and situations in which these catheters are used have broadened considerably. Initial reports suggested that the rate of catheter infection in non-neutropenic patients was approximately one infection per 5.5 patient years.[211] Venous access has long been a problem for patients receiving chemotherapy for malignancy. Hickman and colleagues modified the Broviac catheter for use in patients undergoing bone marrow transplantation.[212] This catheter can be used for the administration of intensive chemotherapy, administration of other medicines and fluids, transfusion, and phlebotomy. These catheters spare the patient both physical and psychological trauma. In the ensuing years a number of additional modifications of these catheters have been devised. These modified catheters and implanted infusion ports represent a major step forward in the management of all patients who require long-term central venous access, but they have been especially useful in the management of immunosuppressed patients and particularly in immunosuppressed children, in whom venous access is frequently problematic. Use of these devices in a variety of clinical settings has become the standard of care for more than 20 years.

Several centers have reported their experience with these catheters, and many series report remarkably low rates of infection. Press and colleagues summarized 1088 catheter placements from 18 studies in their literature review. In their summary data, these authors report approximately 0.14 infections per 100 catheter-days.[213] Table 292–8 presents a similar summary, including several published studies evaluating infection and bacteremia risk associated with the use of implanted catheters and infusion ports.[84, 110, 214–223, 225–227, 229, 231] The slightly elevated rate of all infections (0.15 infections for each 100 catheter-days), as well as the elevated risk for bacteremia (0.11 infections for each 100 catheter-days), may be more of a reflection of both the severity of the patients' illnesses, the increasing immunosuppression associated with their therapies, and the increasingly invasive care provided to critically ill patients. The differences noted between totally implanted ports and Hickman-Broviac catheters may also be a reflection of the populations being treated.

The use of peripherally inserted central catheters for long-term access has increased dramatically.[232–237] These catheters have several advantages over some of the other long-term access devices. Peripherally inserted central venous catheters may be inserted at the bedside,[232, 238] they are placed in children under fluoroscopic guidance with relative ease,[233] they are useful for administration of chemotherapy or antimicrobial agents,[233] and they are effective in the administration of TPN,[233, 237, 239–241] particularly in pediatric patients requiring long-term nutritional support.[237, 239, 240] Skilled interventional radiology is needed for difficult insertions and catheter salvage and to make certain that the catheter is not misplaced or misdirected.[232, 235] A major problem is device failure, with as many as 10% of these catheters subject to mechanical malfunction.[234, 239] Several institutions, including my own, have elected to develop a skilled team approach to the insertion and management of these catheters.[236]

Maki has argued that intraluminal contamination may represent the most important route of infection for implanted catheters and ports, further suggesting that strategies aimed at decreasing the risk of intraluminal contamination could substantially lower infection rates with these types of intravascular devices.[202]

Several issues regarding the care and maintenance of these catheters remain unsettled, including (1) whether a dressing should be placed over the exit site (and if so, what dressing materials should be used and how frequently should the dressing be changed), (2) whether the system should be routinely flushed (and if so, how frequently and with what), (3) whether blood cultures obtained through the catheter are reliable indicators of catheter contamination, and (4) what are the indications for catheter removal and can either or both local infection and bacteremia be treated with the catheter in place?

Although definitive answers to these questions remain elusive, at the Warren G. Magnuson Clinical Center of the National Institutes

TABLE 292–8 Infectious Complications Associated with Implanted Catheters in Immunosuppressed Patients

Authors	Number of Patients	Type of Catheter	Exit Site/Tunnel Infections (%)	Catheter-Associated Bacteremia (%)	Days of Catheterization (Range)	Infections per 100 Catheter-Days	Bacteremias per 100 Catheter-Days
Blacklock et al.[211]	25	H	14 (56)	2 (8)	70 (5–256)	0.91	0.11
Larson et al.[214]	34	H	4 (11.8)	4 (11.8)	110.3 (3–355)	0.23	0.12
Wade et al.[84]	51	H	5 (9.8)	3 (5.9)	91 (4–457)	0.17	0.06
Rizzari et al.[110]	125	H/B	3 (2.4)	106 (85)	134 (6–488)	0.53	0.51
Viscoli et al.[215]	145	B	6 (4.1)	57 (39)	171 (2–647)	0.26	0.19
Hogan and Pulito[216]	84	B	6 (7.1)	9 (10.7)	33.4 (2–119)	0.39	0.29
Alurkar et al.[217]	91	H/B	6 (6.6)	31 (34)	74.6 (NG)	0.54	0.41
Wacker et al.[218]	44	B	NG	15 (34)	236 (15–806)	NG	0.06
	33	P	NG	6 (18)	316 (12–1294)	NG	0.10
Johnson et al.[219]	64	B	25 (39)	33 (51.6)	251 (NG)	0.28	0.19
Lokich et al.[220]	92	P	6 (6.5)	2 (2.2)	127 (7–450)	0.06	0.02
Shulman et al.[221]	31	P	1 (3.2)	4 (12.9)	232 (14–607)	0.07	0.05
Cairo et al.[222]	46	H/B	14 (30)	23 (50)	163 (9–365)	0.48	0.30
Hockenberry et al.[223]	82	P	8 (10)	4 (4.9)	168 (7–1030)	0.06	0.02
van Hoff et al.[224]	59	H/B	7 (12)	30 (51)	220 (NG)	0.28	0.23
Ulz et al.[225]	111	H/B	3 (2.7)	63 (57)	81 (1–167)	0.69	0.66
Kappers-Klunne et al.[226]	23	H	0 (0)	19 (83)	166 (10–605)	0.50	0.50
	20	P	2 (10)	9 (45)	164 (1–971)	0.33	0.27
Ross et al.[227]	39	H/B	11 (28)	4 (10)	365 (30–426)	0.13	0.03
	49	P	7 (14)	0 (0)	350 (7–395)	0.07	0.00
Biffi et al.[228]	175	P	1 (0.6)	4 (2.3)	180 (4–559)	0.02	0.003
Elishoov et al.[229]	242	H/B	28 (12)	46 (19)	40 (7–187)	0.79	0.52
Schwarz et al.[230]	680	P	31 (4.6)	31 (4.6)	310 (2–1960)	0.02	0.01
Subtotal (by catheter type)	1183	H/B	132 (11)	445 (38)	147 (1–806)	0.40	0.26
	1162	P	56 (4.8)	60 (5.2)	231 (1–1960)	0.12	0.08
Total	2345	—	188 (8)	505 (21.5)	147 (1–1960)	0.15	0.11

Abbreviations: B, Broviac; H, Hickman; NG, not given; P, totally implantable port (e.g., Port-A-Cath, Infus-A-Port, Mediport).

of Health, a sterile dry gauze dressing or a semipermeable membrane is kept in place over the exit site. These dressings are changed at least twice weekly. We also use an every-other-day heparin flush (5 ml of 100 units/ml) in an attempt to keep the catheters open.

The issue of "pullback" blood cultures has been discussed earlier. Repeated isolation of the same organism from cultures drawn through the catheter indicates a need for therapy. Individual positive cultures and sporadic positive cultures are difficult to interpret in the absence of clinical or laboratory correlates. As noted before, some workers believe that quantitative cultures may prove particularly helpful in establishing a diagnosis in this setting.

The problem of how best to treat an infection in a patient with a long-term venous access catheter in place is a difficult one. Hiemenz and colleagues reported success in treating 90% of proven bacteremias while leaving the catheter in place.[242] Others have reported similar successes.[243–245] Some organisms (e.g., *Bacillus* spp., *Candida* spp.) may be difficult to eradicate,[246] although Hartman and Shuchat had some success in treating *Candida* infections.[243] Guidelines for managing these infections have been summarized by Hiemenz and colleagues.[246] Several studies have advocated the use of thrombolytic agents (e.g., urokinase) in combination with appropriate antimicrobials to treat both thrombosis and infections associated with implanted catheters.[166, 167, 247, 248] These studies suggest that eradicating the fibrin sheath that forms around the catheter may make treatment of catheter-associated infection much more likely to succeed. Benoit and colleagues have suggested that intraluminal treatment of infections of subcutaneously tunneled central venous catheters can be effective against selected bacterial infections.[249] These investigators also found that intraluminal therapy may suppress, but not eradicate *Candida* infections in tunneled catheters.[249] Raad and colleagues treated three patients with recurrent vascular catheter–related bacteremia by allowing a solution of minocycline and ethylenediaminetetraacetate to dwell in the lumen of the indwelling catheter or by coating polyurethane catheters with minocycline/ethylenediaminetetraacetate and flushing the lumen with this solution.[250] Similarly, McCarthy and colleagues successfully treated gram-positive catheter infections by instilling teicoplanin daily into "infected" central catheters for 4 to 9 days and allowing the drug to dwell in the lumen of the catheter.[251] Finally, Lai reported that catheter-associated bacteremia caused by vancomycin-resistant enterococci can be treated effectively by line removal alone.[252] Thus, additional experience has suggested that perhaps with the exception of true tunnel infections, many, if not most infections of indwelling central catheters may be amenable to therapy with the device left in place.

Several centers have reported remarkable success—few infections and few other complications as well—with totally implantable access devices.[253–258] In one of the earliest of these studies, the rate of infection for each 100 catheter-days was 0.43—comparable to other implantable catheters.[254] Subsequent studies have demonstrated even lower infection risk.[218, 220, 221, 223, 226, 227, 256–258] Finally, one epidemiologic study found in multiple logistic regression analysis that the only factor associated with risk for infection of these devices was the number of times that the system was entered.[259]

Use of catheters placed for long-term central venous access has also fostered some new kinds of complications. For example, use of these catheters has been associated with the fortunately rare complication of septic thrombosis of the atrium.[260–262]

Long-term central venous access devices have been used for pheresis for stem cell harvesting.[263–266] Contrasted with the reasonably benign experience with "short-term" catheters,[267, 268] more infectious, mechanical, and thrombotic complications than were anticipated occurred in two of these studies.[263, 266] In one study the investigators suggested that complications associated with using implanted catheters for pheresis for stem cell harvest might be reduced by proper placement of the catheter closer to the right atrial/superior vena cava junction.[263] In the other study, a central catheter infection rate nearly four times higher than the overall rate was identified in bone marrow transplant patients whose central catheters were used for stem cell harvest.[266]

Flow-Directed, Balloon-Tipped Pulmonary Artery Catheters

The use of indwelling, balloon-tipped pulmonary artery catheters[269] has revolutionized the management of hemodynamically unstable, critically ill patients. Placement of such a catheter in one of the great veins, across the tricuspid and pulmonic valves, and into the pulmonary vasculature is not without complications, however. Michel and associates demonstrated that 29 of 153 pulmonary artery catheter tips produced microbial growth in thioglycolate broth.[270] Although it was thought that sepsis did not develop in any patient in this study secondary to the contaminated catheter, other studies have suggested a reasonably high rate of contamination with occasional episodes of catheter-related sepsis and nosocomial endocarditis.[271]

Katz and colleagues retrospectively studied complications associated with the placement of 392 balloon-tipped catheters; of these, 17 (4.3%) were believed to be associated with bacteremia.[271] Maki has estimated that 3 to 5% of these catheters in place for more than 72 hours will result in bacteremia.[3] One recent study has evaluated the complications associated with the use of a new, "hands-off" pulmonary artery catheter that is completely shielded during balloon testing, preparation, and insertion.[272] Use of this catheter was associated with a substantial reduction in systemic infections related to the catheter.[272]

Another problem relatively unique to the flow-directed, balloon-tipped pulmonary artery catheter is that such catheters may traumatize the right-sided heart valves and the right-sided endocardium. In a study of 102 consecutive autopsies of patients who died in the hospital, 26 (25.5%) had had an indwelling intracardiac catheter inserted before death.[273] Six of these patients were excluded from analysis (four patients died 48 hours or less after catheter placement; two patients had permanent transvenous pacemakers in place for many years with the anticipated endocardial fibrosis). Of the remaining 20 patients, 6 had vegetations present, and 88% of the patients had some evidence of intracardiac damage.[273] One patient had infective endocarditis on the tricuspid valve. Other studies have reported slightly lower, but significant incidences of right-sided heart vegetations among monitored patients coming to autopsy.[274] Greene and colleagues noted a 10-fold increase in the incidence of valvular vegetations when they compared a period of time before the introduction of balloon-tipped pulmonary artery catheters with a time in which the catheters were in wide use.[274] Severely burned patients may be at even higher risk for this complication.[275] Nosocomial endocarditis is increasing in frequency; in one recent study, 9.3% of cases of endocarditis diagnosed in a referral hospital were both nosocomial in origin and unrelated to prior cardiac surgery.[276]

No prospective study has addressed risk factors associated with infection of these catheters, nor have studies assessed the efficacy of devices designed to decrease the risk of catheter-associated infection (e.g., leaving the introducer sheath in the vein to protect the catheter).[270] Maki has suggested that changing these catheters over a guide wire may be a major risk factor for infection.[202] In his studies, flow-directed, balloon-tipped catheters may be kept in place safely for up to 5 days; when replacement is necessary, Maki recommends repuncture rather than catheter exchange.[202] Infection risks associated with other aspects of monitoring equipment (e.g., transducer domes, heparin flush solution) will be discussed in the next section.

Arterial Lines, Transducers, and Transducer Domes

The widespread use of arterial lines for blood pressure monitoring or for obtaining arterial samples for blood gas determinations has yielded yet another source of device-associated infection. In addition, the technical electronic equipment used for hemodynamic monitoring—transducers and their associated paraphernalia—has also been cited as a source of device-associated infection.

Stamm and colleagues reported an outbreak of *Flavobacterium* bacteremia among monitored patients in an intensive care unit.[9] Ultimately, these organisms were cultured from in-use radial artery

TABLE 292–9 Prevention of Infection Associated with Hemodynamic Monitoring

Place arterial lines, central venous lines, and flow-directed, balloon-tipped catheters with sterile technique. Mask and sterile gloves should be worn at a minimum. The skin should be prepared with an effective antiseptic solution (e.g., 1% iodine in alcohol or chlorhexidine[157, 202, 203]
Place the catheters percutaneously and anchor well to avoid catheter movement. Dress the insertion site appropriately.
Use heparinized saline (not glucose) for continuous flush solutions.
Do not reuse transducer domes; sterilize the reusable part of the transducer setup with either glutaraldehyde or ethylene oxide between patients.
Replace chamber domes and continuous-flow devices every 48–72 hr[278]; if possible, replace arterial lines every 96 hr.[115]
Use sterile fluid to fill the chamber dome; use aseptic technique in the assembly.
Avoid placing unnecessary junctions or stopcocks in the apparatus; minimize manipulation of the system.
Whenever possible, avoid exchanging arterial catheters over guide wires; use of the guide wire exchange technique for arterial catheters is associated with an increased risk of infection.[202]

catheters, from stopcocks, and from ice used to cool syringes for blood gas determinations.[9] Adams and coworkers reported a series of 147 radial artery cannulizations in infants in whom umbilical artery cannulization failed.[116] In this series, two episodes of catheter-related sepsis occurred. Band and Maki used the semiquantitative catheter tip culture technique to study 130 arterial catheters in 95 patients.[115] In their series, 23 catheters were classified as "local infection" (e.g., ≥15 colonies per semiquantitative culture), and five episodes of sepsis were noted.[115] Factors associated with increased risk infection were (1) duration of catheterization (especially longer than 96 hours), (2) placement by cutdown rather than percutaneously, and (3) clinical signs of local inflammation.

Several years later, Maki and Hassemer reported a prospective study designed to assess the endemic rate of bacteremia associated with arterial monitoring.[277] Transducer chamber fluid was demonstrated to be contaminated in nearly 12% of cases. Eight cases of bacteremia were detected—four definitely related and four possibly related to the extrinsic contamination.[277] Maki has also identified an increased risk for infection of arterial catheters associated with replacing the catheter over a guide wire.[202]

Several epidemics of infection from improper sterilization of reusable transducer domes have been reported.[161, 278, 279] However, with the introduction of disposable transducer domes, one might assume that these problems would be overcome. Buxton and colleagues reported an epidemic of *Enterobacter* infection that was associated with the contamination of disposable transducer domes during their initial setup.[161] The chambers and domes were apparently contaminated by the hands of hospital personnel who had handled heavily contaminated transducer heads.[161] West and colleagues also reported *Serratia* sepsis caused by transducer dome cracks.[280] In this latter study, supposedly disposable transducer domes were being resterilized with resultant cracks or breaks in the dome membrane.[280]

Another potential reservoir for nosocomial bacteremia is the heparin flush solution used to continually irrigate certain intravascular devices. This fluid has been implicated as a reservoir for outbreaks of device-associated bacteremia in several instances.[34, 281, 282]

Several authors have made recommendations regarding the prevention of infection associated with intravascular monitoring devices.[3, 45, 115, 277, 278, 282, 283] A summary of these recommendations is presented in Table 292–9.

PREVENTION OF DEVICE-ASSOCIATED BACTEREMIA

Techniques to be used to prevent device-associated bacteremia have been reviewed by Maki[3] and by Murphy and Lipman[284] and have been outlined elsewhere in this chapter. Several additional points should be emphasized. First, a systematic approach to this issue, including the development of a standard approach, is likely to be beneficial.[285–287] For insertion and management of central venous catheters, TPN catheters, and peripherally inserted central venous catheters, the development of a multidisciplinary team approach has been advantageous.[201, 288]

Emphasis should be placed on attention to detail, including hand washing,[43, 44, 289] adherence to guidelines for catheter insertion and maintenance,[286, 287] appropriate use of antiseptic solutions such as chlorhexidine[157, 203] or iodine to prepare the skin around the catheter insertion site, use of sterile technique for central catheter insertion,[202, 290] optimal management of the insertion site, limitations of entry into the system,[259] careful management of the administration set and the catheter itself,[291] maintenance of a high index of suspicion for infectious complications, and once both safety and efficacy have been appropriately established, the application of new technologies. One example of a technological improvement based in science is the recently marketed modified catheter hub. Segura and coworkers reported that this modified catheter hub reduced the risk for endoluminal bacterial colonization and catheter-related sepsis in subclavian lines that were left in place for a mean of 2 weeks.[292] Others have reported similar success with modified catheter hubs.[24, 25] Conversely, some new technologies may be associated with an increased risk for catheter-associated infection. Although the implementation of needleless intravenous admixture systems provided a safer workplace environment for health care providers, some recent data suggest that the use of these devices may be associated with an increased risk for device-associated infection. Arduino and coworkers emphasized the importance of meticulous aseptic technique in the use of these devices,[293] and both Chodoff[294] and Danzig[295] and their colleagues investigated clusters of catheter-related infections linked to the needleless systems. In the former cluster, a point source for the cluster was identified (a bag of flush solution that was used for several different catheters)[295]; in the latter, an epidemic of catheter-associated infections in home infusion therapy patients was linked to the conjoint use of TPN and the needleless system.[295]

Some investigators have advocated using prophylactic antimicrobials in specific, defined circumstances to prevent catheter-associated infection. For example, Baier and colleagues found that the administration of vancomycin as prophylactic treatment of neonates with central catheters effectively prevented coagulase-negative staphylococcal bacteremia associated with the use of these catheters.[296] The vancomycin effect was greatest for very low birth weight infants.[296] Raad and coworkers used novobiocin and rifampin in an attempt to prevent catheter-associated infections in patients receiving interleukin-2.[297] Although the antimicrobial prophylaxis was poorly tolerated (and had to be discontinued in nearly a third of the patients), the regimen was believed to be successful.[297] Others have reported success in preventing catheter-associated infections in interleukin-2 recipients without using antimicrobial prophylaxis.[198, 298]

Finally, the role of appropriate nurse staffing in preventing catheter-associated infection deserves attention. In one recent study, nursing staff reductions during a period of increased TPN use was directly associated with an increase in catheter-associated bacteremias in a surgical intensive care unit.[299] In this era of health care downsizing, the impact of staffing reductions on untoward outcomes is deserving of careful scrutiny.[299]

New scientific approaches are needed to help establish better techniques for catheter management,[38, 41, 164, 202, 300] and further technological advances such as bonding antimicrobial and antiseptic agents to the intravascular device[184, 187–189, 301] may also reduce the risk of device-associated infection. Increased attention to such details can significantly lower the endemic rate of device-associated infection, as well as decrease the number of epidemics of such infections.

REFERENCES

1. Maki D. Sepsis arising from extrinsic contamination of the infusion and measures for control. In: Phillips I, ed. Microbiologic Hazards of Intravenous Therapy. Lancaster, England: MTP; 1977:99–114.
2. Gonzalez-Barca E, Fernandez-Sevilla A, Carratala J, et al. Prospective study of 288 episodes of bacteremia in neutropenic cancer patients in a single institution. Eur J Clin Microbiol Infect Dis. 1996;15:291–296.

3. Maki D. Epidemic nosocomial bacteremias. In: Wenzel R, ed. Handbook of Hospital Acquired Infections. Boca Raton, Fla: CRC Press; 1981:371–512.
4. McGregor AR, Collignon PJ. Bacteraemia and fungaemia in an Australian general hospital—associations and outcomes. Med J Aust. 1993;158:671–674.
5. Maki D. Nosocomial bacteremia: An epidemiologic overview. Am J Med. 1981;70:719–732.
6. Maki D, Rhame F, Mackel D, et al. Nationwide epidemic of septicemia caused by contaminated intravenous products: I: Epidemiologic and clinical features. Am J Med. 1976;60:471–475.
7. Felts S, Schaffner W, Melly M, et al. Sepsis caused by contaminated intravenous fluids: Epidemiologic, clinical and laboratory investigation of an outbreak in one hospital. Ann Intern Med. 1972;77:881–890.
8. Holmes CJ, Allwood MC. The microbial contamination of intravenous infusions during clinical use. J Appl Bacteriol. 1979;46:247–267.
9. Stamm W, Collella J, Anderson M, et al. Indwelling arterial catheters as a source of nosocomial bacteremia: An outbreak caused by *Flavobacterium* species. N Engl J Med. 1975;292:1099–1102.
10. Carson L, Favero M, Bond W, et al. Morphological biochemical and growth characteristics of *Pseudomonas cepacia* from distilled water. Appl Microbiol. 1973;25:476–483.
11. Goldmann D, Martin W, Worthington J. Growth of bacteria and fungi in total parenteral nutrition solutions. Am J Surg. 1973;126:314–318.
12. Maki D. Growth properties of microorganisms in infusion fluid and method of detection. In: Phillips I, ed. Microbiologic Hazards of Intravenous Therapy. Lancaster, England: MTP; 1977:13–47.
13. Crocker K, Noga R, Filibeck D, et al. Microbial growth comparisons of five commercial parenteral lipid emulsions. JPEN J Parenter Enteral Nutr. 1984;8:391–395.
14. Jarvis W, Highsmith A. Bacterial growth and endotoxin production in lipid emulsion. J Clin Microbiol. 1984;19:17–20.
15. Dankner WM, Spector SA, Fierer J. *Malassezia* fungemia in neonates and adults: Complication of hyperalimentation. Rev Infect Dis. 1987;9:743–753.
16. Avila-Figueroa C, Goldmann DA, Richardson DK, et al. Intravenous lipid emulsions are the major determinant of coagulase-negative staphylococcal bacteremia in very low birth weight newborns. Pediatr Infect Dis J. 1998;17:10–17.
17. Shiro H, Muller E, Takeda S, et al. Potentiation of *Staphylococcus epidermidis* catheter-related bacteremia by lipid infusions. J Infect Dis. 1995;171:220–224.
18. Plouffe J, Brown D, Silva J, et al. Nosocomial outbreak of *Candida parapsilosis* fungemia related to intravenous infusions. Arch Intern Med. 1977;137:1686–1689.
19. Solomon S, Khabbaz R, Parker R, et al. An outbreak of *Candida parapsilosis* bloodstream infections in patients receiving parenteral nutrition. J Infect Dis. 1984;149:98–102.
20. Salzman MB, Rubin LG. Relevance of the catheter hub as a portal for microorganisms causing catheter-related bloodstream infections. Nutrition. 1997;13(Suppl 4):S15–S17.
21. Sitges-Serra A, Puig P, Jaurrieta E, et al. Catheter sepsis due to *Staphylococcus epidermidis* during parenteral nutrition. Surg Gynecol Obstet. 1980;151:481–483.
22. Sitges-Serra A, Puig P, Jaurrieta E, et al. Hub colonization as the initial step in an outbreak of catheter-related sepsis due to coagulase negative staphylococci during parenteral nutrition. JPEN J Parenter Enteral Nutr. 1984;8:668–672.
23. Sitges-Serra A, Linares J, Perez J, et al. A randomized trial on the effect of tubing changes on hub contamination and catheter sepsis during parenteral nutrition. JPEN J Parenter Enteral Nutr. 1985;9:322–325.
24. Sitges-Serra A, Pi-Suner T, Garces JM, et al. Pathogenesis and prevention of catheter-related septicemia. Am J Infect Control. 1995;23:310–316.
25. Sitges-Serra A, Hernandez R, Maestro S, et al. Prevention of catheter sepsis: The hub. Nutrition. 1997;13(4 Suppl 4):S30–S35.
26. Linares J, Sitges-Serra A, Garau J, et al. Pathogenesis of catheter sepsis: A prospective study with quantitative and semiquantitative cultures of catheter hub and segments. J Clin Microbiol. 1985;21:357–360.
27. Linares J, Dominguez MA, Martin R. Current laboratory techniques in the diagnosis of catheter-related infections. Nutrition. 1997;13(Suppl 4):S10–S14.
28. Dietel M, Krajden S, Saldanha C, et al. An outbreak of *Staphylococcus epidermidis* septicemia. JPEN J Parenter Enteral Nutr. 1983;7:569–572.
29. Pemberton L, Lyman B, Mandal J, et al. Outbreak of *Staphylococcus epidermidis* nosocomial infections in patients receiving total parenteral nutrition. JPEN J Parenter Enteral Nutr. 1984;8:325–326.
30. Maki D, Ringer M. Evaluation of dressing regimens for prevention of infection with peripheral intravenous catheters: Gauze, a transparent polyurethane dressing, and an iodophor-transparent dressing. JAMA. 1987;258:2396–2403.
31. Salzman MB, Isenberg HD, Shapiro JF, et al. A prospective study of the catheter hub as the portal of entry for microorganisms causing catheter-related sepsis in neonates. J Infect Dis. 1993;167:487–490.
32. Salzman M, Isenberg H, Rubin L. Use of disinfectants to reduce microbial contamination of hubs of vascular catheters. J Clin Microbiol. 1993;31:475–479.
33. Goetz AM, Rihs JD, Chow JW, et al. An outbreak of infusion-related *Klebsiella pneumoniae* bacteremla in a liver transplantation unit. Clin Infect Dis. 1995;21:1501–1503.
34. van Laer F, Raes D, Vandamme P, et al. An outbreak of *Burkholderia cepacia* with septicemia on a cardiology ward. Infect Control Hosp Epidemiol. 1998;19:112–113.
35. Henderson DK, Myers RF, Laniak JM. Catheter-acquired infection in total parenteral nutrition. NITA. 1982;5:62–68.
36. Atela I, Coll P, Rello J, et al. Serial surveillance cultures of skin and catheter hub specimens from critically ill patients with central venous catheters: Molecular epidemiology of infection and implications for clinical management and research. J Clin Microbiol. 1997;35:1784–1790.
37. Bjornson H, Colley R, Bower R, et al. Association between microorganism growth at the catheter insertion site and colonization of the catheter in patients receiving total parenteral nutrition. Surgery. 1982;92:720–727.
38. Maki D, McCormack K. Defatting catheter insertion sites in total parenteral nutrition is of no value as an infection control measure. Am J Med. 1987;83:833–840.
39. Cooper G, Hopkins C. Rapid diagnosis of intravascular catheter–associated infection by direct Gram-staining of catheter segments. N Engl J Med. 1985;18:1142–1150.
40. Eastick K, Leeming JP, Bennett D, et al. Reservoirs of coagulase negative staphylococci in preterm infants. Arch Dis Child Fetal Neonatal Ed. 1996;74:F99–F104.
41. Kelsey M, Gosling M. A comparison of the morbidity associated with occlusive and non-occlusive dressings applied to peripheral intravenous devices. J Hosp Infect. 1984;5:313–321.
42. Craven D, Lichtenberg A, Kunches L, et al. A randomized study comparing a transparent polyurethane dressing to a dry gauze dressing for peripheral intravenous catheter sites. Infect Control. 1985;6:361–366.
43. Preston G, Larson E, Stamm W. The effect of private isolation rooms on patient care practices, colonization, and infection in an intensive care unit. Am J Med. 1981;70:641–645.
44. Albert R, Condie F. Hand-washing patterns in medical intensive care units. N Engl J Med. 1981;304:1465–1466.
45. Weinstein R, Emori T, Anderson R, et al. Pressure transducers as a source of bacteremia after open heart surgery: Report of an outbreak and guidelines for prevention. Chest. 1976;69:338–344.
46. Frank M, Schaffner W. Contaminated aqueous benzalkonium chloride: An unnecessary hospital infection hazard. JAMA. 1976;236:2418–2419.
47. Berkelman R, Lewin S, Allen J, et al. Pseudobacteremia attributed to contamination of povidone-iodine with *Pseudomonas cepacia*. Ann Intern Med. 1981;95:32–36.
48. Craven D, Moody B, Connolly M, et al. Pseudobacteremia caused by povidone-iodine solution contaminated with *Pseudomonas cepacia*. N Engl J Med. 1981;305:621–623.
49. Lucas JW, Berger AM, Fitzgerald A, et al. Nosocomial infections in patients with central catheters. J Intraven Nurs. 1992;15:44–48.
50. Welch G, McKeel D Jr, Silverstein P, et al. The role of catheter composition in the development of thrombophlebitis. Surg Gynecol Obstet. 1974;138:421–424.
51. Stillman R, Soliman S, Garcia L, et al. Etiology of catheter associated sepsis. Arch Surg. 1977;112:1497–1499.
52. Linder L, Curelaru I, Gustavsson B, et al. Material thrombogenicity in central venous catheterization: A comparison between soft, antebrachial catheters of silicone elastomer and polyurethane. JPEN J Parenter Enteral Nutr. 1984;8:399–406.
53. Bozzetti F. Central venous catheter sepsis. Surg Gynecol Obstet. 1985;161:293–301.
54. Peters W, Bush W, McIntyre R, et al. The development of fibrin sheath on indwelling venous catheters. Surg Gynecol Obstet. 1973;137:43–47.
55. Sheth N, Franson T, Rose H, et al. Colonization of bacteria on polyvinyl chloride and Teflon intravascular catheter in hospitalized patients. J Clin Microbiol. 1983;18:1061–1063.
56. Rotrosen D, Calderone R, Edwards J Jr. Adherence of *Candida* species to host tissues and plastic surfaces. Rev Infect Dis. 1986;8:73–85.
57. Wolfe B, Ryder M, Nishikawa R, et al. Complications of parenteral nutrition. Am J Surg. 1986;152:93–99.
58. Pemberton L, Lyman B, Lauder V, et al. Sepsis from triple- vs. single-lumen catheters during total parenteral nutrition in surgical or critically ill patients. Arch Surg. 1986;121:591–594.
59. Appelgran K. Triple-lumen catheters. Technologial advance or setback? Arch Surg. 1987;53:113–116.
60. Hilton E, Haslett TM, Borenstein MT, et al. Central catheter infections: Single- vs. triple-lumen catheters. Influence of guide wires on infection rates when used for replacement of catheters. Am J Med. 1988;84:667–672.
61. Vo N, Waycaster M, Godfrey J. Triple-lumen catheters for parenteral nutrition. South Med J. 1988;81:214–217.
62. Yeung C, May J, Hughes R. Infection rate for single-lumen vs. triple-lumen subclavian catheters. Infect Control Hosp Epidemiol. 1988;9:154–158.
63. Mantese V, German D, Kruminski D, et al. Colonization and sepsis from triple-lumen catheters in critically ill patients. Am J Surg. 1987;154:597–601.
64. Miller J, Venus B, Matthew M. Comparison of the sterility of long-term central catheterization using single-lumen, triple-lumen and pulmonary artery catheters. Crit Care Med. 1984;12:634–637.
65. Kelly C, Ligas J, Smith C, et al. Sepsis due to triple-lumen central venous catheters. Surg Gynecol Obstet. 1986;163:14–16.
66. Kovalevich D, Faubion W, Bender J, et al. Association of parenteral nutrition catheter sepsis with urinary tract infections. JPEN J Parenter Enteral Nutr. 1986;10:639–646.
67. Pettigren R, Lang D, Haycock D, et al. Catheter-related sepsis in patients on intravenous nutrition: A prospective study of quantitative catheter cultures and guideline changes for suspected sepsis. Br J Surg. 1985;72:52–55.
68. Hampton A, Sheretz R. Vascular-access infections in hospitalized patients. Surg Clin North Am. 1988;68:57–71.
69. Bernard R, Stahl W, Chase R Jr. Subclavian vein catheterizations: A prospective study. II. Infectious complications. Ann Surg. 1971;173:191–200.
70. Armstrong C, Mayhall C, Miller K, et al. Prospective study of catheter replacement and other risk factors for infection of hyperalimentatian catheters. J Infect Dis. 1986;154:808–816.
71. Sitzmann J, Townsend T, Siler M, et al. Septic and technical complications of central venous catheterization: A prospective study of 200 consecutive patients. Ann Surg. 1985;202:766–770.

72. Soifer NE, Borzak S, Edlin BR, et al. Prevention of peripheral venous catheter complications with an intravenous therapy team: A randomized controlled trial. Arch Intern Med. 1998;158:473–477.
73. Snydman D, Murray S, Kornfeld S, et al. Total parenteral nutrition–related infections: Prospective epidemiologic study using semiquantitative methods. Am J Med. 1982;73:695–699.
74. Ryan J, Abel R, Abbott W, et al. Catheter complications in total parenteral nutrition: A prospective study of 200 consecutive patients. N Engl J Med. 1974;290:757–761.
75. Sanderson I, Deitel M. Intravenous hyperalimentation without sepsis. Surg Gynecol Obstet. 1973;136:577–585.
76. Powell-Tuck J, Lennard-Jones J, Lowes J, et al. Intravenous feeding in a gastroenterological unit: A prospective study of infective complications. J Clin Pathol. 1979;32:549–555.
77. Sanders R, Sheldon G. Septic complications of total parenteral nutrition. Am J Surg. 1976;132:214–220.
78. Rhame F, Maki D, Bennett J. Intravenous cannula–related infections. In: Bennett J, Brachman P, eds. Hospital Infections. Boston: Little, Brown; 1979.
79. Maki D, Goldmann D, Rhame F. Infection control in intravenous therapy. Ann Intern Med. 1973;79:867–887.
80. Moran J, Atwood R, Rowe M. A clinical and bacteriologic study of infections associated with venous cutdowns. N Engl J Med. 1965;272:554–560.
81. Bregenzer T, Conen D, Sakmann P, et al. Is routine replacement of peripheral intravenous catheters necessary? Arch Intern Med. 1998;158:151–156.
82. Christensen G, Simpson A, Bisno A, et al. Adherence of slime-producing strains of *Staphylococcus epidermidis* to smooth surfaces. Infect Immun. 1982;37:318–326.
83. Peters G, Locci R, Pulverer G. Adherence and growth of coagulase-negative staphylococci on surfaces of intravenous catheters. J Infect Dis. 1982;146:479–482.
84. Wade JC, Schimpff SC, Newman KA, et al. *Staphylococcus epidermidis*: An increasing cause of infection in patients with granulocytopenia. Ann Intern Med. 1982;97:503–508.
85. Castagnola E, Garaventa A, Viscoli C, et al. Changing pattern of pathogens causing Broviac catheter–related bacteraemias in children with cancer. J Hosp Infect. 1995;29:129–133.
86. Castagnola E, Conte M, Venzano P, et al. Broviac catheter–related bacteraemias due to unusual pathogens in children with cancer: Case reports with literature review. J Infect. 1997;34:215–218.
87. Henderson DK, Baptiste RF, Parrillo J, et al. Indolent epidemic of *Pseudomonas cepacia* bacteremia and pseudobacteremia in an intensive care unit traced to a contaminated blood gas analyzer. Am J Med. 1988;84:75–81.
88. Pegues DA, Carson LA, Anderson RL, et al. Outbreak of *Pseudomanas cepacia* bacteremia in oncology patients. Clin Infect Dis. 1993;16:407–411.
89. Smith P, Massanari R. Room humidifiers as the source of *Acinetobacter* infections. JAMA. 1977;237:795–797.
90. Ammari LK, Puck JM, McGowan KL. Catheter-related *Fusarium solani* fungemia and pulmonary infection in a patient with leukemia in remission. Clin Infect Dis. 1993;16:148–150.
91. Ashkenazi S, Leibovici L, Samra Z, et al. Risk factors far mortality due to bacteremia and fungemia in childhood. Clin Infect Dis. 1992;14:949–951.
92. Bollet C, Elkouby A, Pietri P, et al. Isolation of *Enterobacter amnigenus* from a heart transplant recipient. Eur J Clin Microbiol Infect Dis. 1991;10:1071–1073.
93. Brown NM, Blundell EL, Chown SR, et al. *Acremonium* infection in a neutropenic patient. J Infect. 1992;25:73–76.
94. Buchman AL, McNeil MM, Brown JM, et al. Central venous catheter sepsis caused by unusual *Gordona* (*Rhodococcus* species: Identification with a digoxigenin-labeled rDNA probe. Clin Infect Dis. 1992;15:694–697.
95. Cieslak TJ, Robb ML, Drabick CJ, et al. Catheter-associated sepsis caused by *Ochrobactrum anthropi*: Report of a case and review of related nonfermentative bacteria. Clin Infect Dis. 1992;14:902–907.
96. Conlu A, Rothman J, Staszewski H, et al. *Flavimonas oryzihabitans* (CDC group Ve-2) bacteraemia associated with Hickman catheters. J Hosp Infect. 1992;20:293–299.
97. D'Antonio D, Pizzigallo E, Iacone A, et al. Occurrence of bacteremia in hematologic patients. Eur J Epidemiol. 1992;8:687–692.
98. Goodwin CS, Nsanze H, Worsley BW, et al. Umbilical catheter–related resistant *Klebsiella* septicaemia in a pre-term infant successfully treated with imipenem via the catheter. J Infect. 1992;25:237–238.
99. Gransden WR, Eykyn SJ. Seven cases of bacteremia due to *Ochrobactrum anthropi*. Clin Infect Dis. 1992;15:1068–1069.
100. Gutierrez J, Leon C, Matamoros R, et al. Catheter-related bacteremia and fungemia. Reliability of two methods for catheter culture. Diagn Microbiol Infect Dis. 1992;15:575–578.
101. Gucalp R, Ciobanu N, Sparano J, et al. Disseminated aspergillosis after fungemia in a patient with extragonadal germ cell tumor undergoing autologous bone marrow transplantation. Cancer. 1991;68:1842–1844.
102. Idemyor V, Cherubin CE. Retroperitoneal abscess caused by *Mycabacterium chelonae* and treatment. Ann Pharmacother. 1993;27:178–179.
103. Kiehn TE, Gorey E, Brown AE, et al. Sepsis due to *Rhodotorula* related to use of indwelling central venous catheters. Clin Infect Dis. 1992;14:841–846.
104. Lecciones JA, Lee JW, Navarro EE, et al. Vascular catheter–associated fungemia in patients with cancer: Analysis of 155 episodes. Clin Infect Dis. 1992;14:875–883.
105. Legrand C, Anaissie E. Bacteremia due to *Achromobacter xylosoxidans* in patients with cancer. Clin Infect Dis. 1992;14:479–484.
106. Leibovici L, Konisberger H, Pitlik SD, et al. Bacteremia and fungemia of unknown origin in adults. Clin Infect Dis. 1992;14:436–443.
107. Qureshi MN, Lederman J, Neibart E, et al. *Bordetella bronchiseptica* recurrent bacteraemia in the setting of a patient with AIDS and indwelling Broviac catheter. Int J STD AIDS. 1992;3:291–293.
108. Rello J, Quintana S, Mirelis B, et al. Polymicrobial bacteremia in critically ill patients. Intensive Care Med. 1993;19:22–25.
109. Rello J, Coll P, Net A, et al. Infection of pulmonary artery catheters. Epidemiologic characteristics and multivariate analysis of risk factors. Chest. 1993;103:132–136.
110. Rizzari C, Palamone G, Corbetta A, et al. Central venous catheter–related infections in pediatric hematology-oncology patients: Role of home and hospital management. Pediatr Hematol Oncol. 1992;9:115–123.
111. Shapiro CL, Haft RF, Gantz NM, et al. *Tsukamurella paurometabolum*: A novel pathogen causing catheter-related bacteremia in patients with cancer. Clin Infect Dis. 1992;14:200–203.
112. Sycova MZ, Sufliarsky J, Trupl J, et al. Catheter-associated septicaemia due to *Trichosporon capitatum*. J Hosp Infect. 1992;22:257–258.
113. Tan TQ, Ogden AK, Tillman J, et al. *Paecilomyces lilacinus* catheter-related fungemia in an immunocompromised pediatric patient. J Clin Microbiol. 1992;30:2479–2483.
114. Walsh TJ, Gonzalez C, Roilides E, et al. Fungemia in children infected with the human immunodeficiency virus: New epidemiologic patterns, emerging pathogens, and improved outcome with antifungal therapy. Clin Infect Dis. 1995;20:900–906.
115. Band J, Maki D. Infections caused by arterial catheters used for hemodynamic monitoring. Am J Med. 1979;67:735–741.
116. Adams J, Speer M, Rudolph A. Bacterial colonization of radial artery catheters. Pediatrics. 1980;65:94–97.
117. Montgomerie J, Edwards J Jr. Association of infection due to *Candida albicans* with intravenous hyperalimentation. J Infect Dis. 1978;127:197–201.
118. Henderson D, Edwards J Jr, Montgomerie J. Hematogenous *Candida* endophthalmitis in patients receiving parenteral hyperalimentation fluids. J Infect Dis. 1981;143:655–661.
119. Maki D, Jarrett F, Sarafin H. A semiquantitative method for identification of catheter-related infection in the burn patient. J Surg Res. 1977;22:513–520.
120. Maki D, Weisa C, Sarafin H. A semiquantitative method for identifying intravenous-catheter–related infection. N Engl J Med. 1977;296:1305–1309.
121. Band J, Maki D. Steel needles used for intravenous therapy: Morbidity in patients with hematologic malignancy. Arch Intern Med. 1980;140:31–34.
122. Siegman-Igra Y, Anglim AM, Shapiro DE, et al. Diagnosis of vascular catheter–related bloodstream infection: A meta-analysis. J Clin Microbiol. 1997;35:928–936.
123. Dooley DP, Garcia A, Kelly JW, et al. Validation of catheter semiquantitative culture technique far nonstaphylococcal organisms. J Clin Microbiol. 1996;34:409–412.
124. Cleri D, Corrado M, Seligman S. Quantitative culture of intravenous catheters and other intravascular inserts. J Infect Dis. 1980;141:781–786.
125. Brun-Buisson C, Abrouk F, Legrand P, et al. Diagnosis of central venous catheter–related sepsis. Critical level of quantitative tip cultures. Arch Intern Med. 1987;147:873–877.
126. Hnatiuk O, Pike J, Stolzfus D, et al. Value of bedside plating of semiquantitative cultures for diagnosis of central venous catheter–related infections in ICU patients. Chest. 1993;103:896–899.
127. Sherertz RJ, Heard SO, Raad II. Diagnosis of triple-lumen catheter infection: Comparison of roll plate, sonication, and flushing methodologies. J Clin Microbiol. 1997;35:641–646.
128. Collignon P, Chan R, Munro R. Rapid diagnosis of intravascular catheter-related sepsis. Arch Intern Med. 1987;147:1609–1612.
129. McGeer A, Righter J. Improving our ability to diagnose infections associated with central venous catheters: Value of Gram's staining and culture of entry site swabs. Can Med Assoc J. 1987;137:1009–1015.
130. Vanhuynegen L, Parmentier P, Porvliege C. In situ bacteriologic diagnosis of total parenteral nutrition catheter infection. Surgery. 1988;103:174–177.
131. Zuffrey J, Rime B, Franciou P, et al. Simple method for rapid diagnosis of catheter-associated infection by direct acridine orange staining of catheter tips. J Clin Microbiol. 1988;26:175–177.
132. Kite P, Dobbins BM, Wilcox MH, et al. Evaluation of a novel endoluminal brush method for in situ diagnosis of catheter related sepsis. J Clin Pathol. 1997;50:278–282.
133. Spencer R, Kristinsson K. Failure to diagnose intravascular associated infection by direct Gram-staining of catheter segments. J Hosp Infect. 1986;7:305–306.
134. Mosca R, Curtas S, Forbes B, et al. The benefits of isolator cultures in the management of suspected catheter sepsis. Surgery. 1987;102:718–723.
135. Ascher DP, Shoupe BA, Robb M, et al. Comparison of standard and quantitative blood cultures in the evaluation of children with suspected central venous line sepsis. Diagn Microbiol Infect Dis. 1992;15:499–503.
136. Kaditis AG, O'Marcaigh AS, Rhodes KH, et al. Yield of positive blood cultures in pediatric oncology patients by a new method of blood culture collection. Pediatr Infect Dis J. 1996;15:615–620.
137. Blot F, Schmidt E, Nitenberg G, et al. Earlier positivity of central-venous- versus peripheral-blood cultures is highly predictive of catheter-related sepsis. J Clin Microbiol. 1998;36:105–109.
138. Torlakovic E, Hibbs JR, Miller JS, et al. Intracellular bacteria in blood smears in patients with central venous catheters. Arch Intern Med. 1995;155:1547–1550.
139. Wing E, Norden C, Shadduck R, et al. Use of quantitative bacteriologic techniques to diagnose catheter-related sepsis. Arch Intern Med. 1979;139:482–488.
140. Capdevila JA, Planes AM, Palomar M, et al. Value of differential quantitative blood cultures in the diagnosis of catheter-related sepsis. Eur J Clin Microbiol Infect Dis. 1992;11:403–407.
141. Olson IE, Lam K, Bodey GP, et al. Evaluation of strategies for central venous catheter replacement. Crit Care Med. 1992;20:797–804.

142. Quilici N, Audibert G, Conroy MC, et al. Differential quantitative blood cultures in the diagnosis of catheter-related sepsis in intensive care units. Clin Infect Dis. 1997;25:1066–1070.
143. Tonnesen A, Peuler M, Lockwood W. Cultures of blood drawn by catheters vs. venipuncture. JAMA. 1976;235:1877.
144. Felices F, Hernandez J, Ruiz J, et al. Use of the central venous pressure catheter to obtain blood cultures. Crit Care Med. 1979;7:78–79.
145. Smyth EG, Keane NA, Lane BE, et al. Vascular catheter–related sepsis: Diagnosis and prevention. J Hosp Infect. 1992;22:81.
146. Bingen E, Barc MC, Brahimi N, et al. Randomly amplified polymorphic DNA analysis provides rapid differentiation of methicillin-resistant coagulase-negative staphylococcus bacteremia isolates in pediatric hospital. J Clin Microbiol. 1995;33:1657–1659.
147. Dominguez MA, Linares J, Pulido A, et al. Molecular tracking of coagulase-negative staphylocaccal isolates from catheter-related infections. Microb Drug Resist. 1996;2:423–429.
148. Tully J, Friedland G, Baldini M, et al. Complications of intravenous therapy with steel needles and Teflon catheters. Am J Med. 1981;70:702–706.
149. Crane D. Venous interruption for septic thrombophlebitis. N Engl J Med. 1962;262:947–951.
150. Munster A. Septic thrombophlebitis: A surgical disorder. JAMA. 1974;230:1010–1011.
151. De Cicco M, Matovic M, Balestreri L, et al. Central venous thrombosis: An early and frequent complication in cancer patients bearing long-term Silastic catheter. A prospective study. Thromb Res. 1997;86:101–113.
152. Khan EA, Correa AG, Baker CJ. Suppurative thrombophlebitis in children: A ten-year experience. Pediatr Infect Dis J. 1997;16:63–67.
153. Harden JL, Kemp L, Mirtallo J. Femoral catheters increase risk of infection in total parenteral nutrition patients. Nutr Clin Pract. 1995;10(2):60–66.
154. Martin C, Bruder N, Papazian L, et al. Catheter-related infections following axillary vein catheterization. Acta Anaesthesiol Scand. 1998;42:52–56.
155. Jarrard M, Freeman J. The effects of antibiotic ointments and antiseptics on the skin flora beneath subclavian catheter dressings during intravenous hyperalimentation. J Surg Res. 1977;22:521–526.
156. Maki D, Band J. A comparative study of polyantibiotic and iodophor ointments in prevention of vascular catheter–related infection. Am J Med. 1981;70:739–744.
157. Garland JS, Buck RK, Maloney P, et al. Comparison of 10% povidone-iodine and 0.5% chlorhexidine gluconate for the prevention of peripheral intravenous catheter colonization in neonates: A prospective trial. Pediatr Infect Dis J. 1995;14:510–516.
158. Wilmore D, Dudrick S. An in-line filter for intravenous solutions. Arch Surg. 1969;99:462–463.
159. Rusmin S, DeLuca P. Effect of antibiotics and osmotic change on the release of endotoxin by bacteria retained on intravenous in-line filters. Am J Hosp Pharm. 1975;32:378–380.
160. Hoffmann KK, Weber DJ, Samsa GP, et al. Transparent polyurethane film as an intravenous catheter dressing. A meta-analysis of the infection risks. JAMA. 1992;267:2072–2076.
161. Buxton A, Anderson K, Klimek J, et al. Failure of disposable domes to prevent septicemia from contaminated pressure transducers. Chest. 1978;74:508–518.
162. Band J, Maki D. Safety of changing intravenous delivery systems at longer than 24-hour intervals. Ann Intern Med. 1979;91:173–178.
163. Snydman D, Reidy M, Perry L, et al. Safety of changing intravenous (IV) administration sets containing burettes at longer than 48 hour intervals. Infect Control 1987;8:113–116.
164. Maki D, Boiticelli J, LeRoy M, et al. Prospective study of replacing administration sets for intravenous therapy at 48 vs. 72 hour intervals: 72 hours is safe and cost-effective. JAMA. 1987;258:1777–1781.
165. Michel L, McMichan J, Bachy J. Microbial colonization of indwelling central venous catheters: Statistical evaluation of potential contaminating factors. Am J Surg. 1979;137:745–748.
166. Jones GR, Konsler GK, Dunaway RP, et al. Prospective analysis of urokinase in the treatment of catheter sepsis in pediatric hematology-oncology patients. J Pediatr Surg. 1993;28:350–355.
167. Jones GR, Konsler GK, Dunaway RP. Urokinase in the treatment of bacteremia and candidemia in patients with right atrial catheters. Am J Infect Control. 1996;24:160–166.
168. Ruggiero R, Aisenstein T. Central catheter fibrin sleeve; heparin effect. JPEN J Parenter Enteral Nutr. 1983;7:270–273.
169. Lloyd DA, Shanbhogue LK, Doherty PJ, et al. Does the fibrin coat around a central venous catheter influence catheter-related sepsis? J Pediatr Surg. 1993;28:345–348.
170. Prager R, Silva J Jr. Colonization of central venous catheters. South Med J. 1984;77:458–461.
171. Maher M, Henderson D, Brennan M. Central venous catheter exchange in cancer patients during total parenteral nutrition. NITA. 1982;5:54–60.
172. Bach A, Bohrer H, Geiss HK. Safety of guidewire technique for replacement of pulmonary artery catheters. J Cardiothorac Vasc Anesth. 1992;6:711–714.
173. Cobb DK, High KP, Sawyer RG, et al. A controlled trial of scheduled replacement of central venous and pulmonary-artery catheters. N Engl J Med. 1992;327:1062–1068.
174. Cook D, Randolph A, Kernerman P, et al. Central venous catheter replacement strategies: A systematic review of the literature. Crit Care Med. 1997;25:1417–1424.
175. Anaissie EJ, Rex JH, Uzun O, et al. Predictors of adverse outcome in cancer patients with candidemia. Am J Med. 1988;104:238–245.
176. Fairchild J, Graber C, Vogel E. Flora of the umbilical stump. J Pediatr. 1958;53:538–546.
177. Anagnostakis D, Kamba A, Petrochilou V, et al. Risk of infection associated with umbilical vein catheterization: A prospective study in 75 newborn infants. J Pediatr. 1973;86:759–765.
178. Balagtas R, Bell C, Edwards L, et al. Risk of local and systemic infections associated with umbilical vein catheterization: A prospective study in 86 newborn patients. Pediatrics. 1971;48:359–367.
179. Hall R, Rhodes P. Total parenteral alimentation via indwelling umbilical catheters in the newborn period. Arch Dis Child. 1976;51:929–934.
180. Munson D, Thompson T, Johnson D, et al. Coagulase-negative staphylococcal septicemia: Experience in a newborn intensive care unit. J Pediatr. 1982;101:602–605.
181. Powers W, Tooley W. Contamination of umbilical vessel catheters: Encouraging information. Pediatrics. 1972;49:470–471.
182. Symansky M, Fox H. Umbilical vessel catheterization: Indications, management, and evaluation of the technique. J Pediatr. 1972;80:820–826.
183. Goldschmidt H, Hahn U, Salwender HJ, et al. Prevention of catheter-related infections by silver coated central venous catheters in oncological patients. Zentralbl Bakteriol. 1995;283:215–223.
184. Kamal GD, Divishek D, Kumar GC, et al. Reduced intravascular catheter–related infection by routine use of antibiotic-bonded catheters in a surgical intensive care unit. Diagn Microbiol Infect Dis. 1998;30:145–152.
185. Maki DG, Stolz SM, Wheeler S, et al. Prevention of central venous catheter–related bloodstream infection by use of an antiseptic-impregnated catheter. A randomized, controlled trial. Ann Intern Med. 1997;127:257–266.
186. Raad I, Hachem R, Zermeno A, et al. Silver iontophoretic catheter: A prototype of a long-term antiinfective vascular access device. J Infect Dis. 1996;173:495–498.
187. Sampath LA, Chowdhury N, Caraos L, et al. Infection resistance of surface modified catheters with either short-lived or prolonged activity. J Hosp Infect. 1995;30:201–210.
188. Bach A, Geiss M, Geiss HK, et al. Prevention of catheter-related colonization by silver-sulfadiazine-chlorhexidine bonding: Results of a pilot study in critical care patients. In: Thirty-third Interscience Conference on Antimicrobial Agents and Chemotherapy. New Orleans: American Society for Microbiology; 1993:415.
189. Clemence MA, Jernigan JA, Titus MA, et al. A study of an antiseptic impregnated central venous catheter for prevention of bloodstream infection. In: Thirty-third Interscience Conference on Antimicrobial Agents and Chemotherapy. New Orleans: American Society for Microbiology; 1993:416.
190. Bach A, Darby U, Bottiger B, et al. Retention of the antibiotic teicoplanin on a hydromer-coated central venous catheter to prevent bacterial colonization in postoperative surgical patients. Intensive Care Med. 1996;22:1066–1069.
191. Bach A, Schmidt H, Bottiger B, et al. Retention of antibacterial activity and bacterial colonization of antiseptic-bonded central venous catheters. J Antimicrob Chemother. 1996;37:315–322.
192. Ciresi DL, Albrecht RM, Volkers PA, et al. Failure of antiseptic bonding to prevent central venous catheter–related infection and sepsis. Am Surg. 1996;62:641–646.
193. Hasaniya NW, Angelis M, Brown MR, et al. Efficacy of subcutaneous silver-impregnated cuffs in preventing central venous catheter infections. Chest. 1996;109:1030–1032.
194. Logghe C, Van Ossel C, D'Hoore W, et al. Evaluation of chlorhexidine and silver-sulfadiazine impregnated central venous catheters for the prevention of bloodstream infection in leukaemic patients: A randomized controlled trial. J Hosp Infect. 1997;37:145–156.
195. Loo S, van Heerden PV, Gollege CL, et al. Infection in central lines: Antiseptic-impregnated vs standard non-impregnated catheters. Anaesth Intensive Care. 1997;25:637–639.
196. Appelgren P, Ransjo U, Bindslev L, et al. Surface heparinization of central venous catheters reduces microbial colonization in vitro and in vivo: Results from a prospective, randomized trial. Crit Care Med. 1996;24:1482–1489.
197. Randolph AG, Cook DJ, Gonzales CA, et al. Benefit of heparin in central venous and pulmonary artery catheters: A meta-analysis of randomized controlled trials. Chest. 1998;113:165–171.
198. Goey SH, Verweij J, Bolhuis RL, et al. Tunnelled central venous catheters yield a low incidence of septicaemia in interleukin-2–treated patients. Cancer Immunol Immunother. 1997;44:301–304.
199. Abdul-Rauf A, Gauderer M, Chiarucci K, et al. Long-term central venous access in patients with sickle cell disease. Incidence of thrombotic and infectious complications. J Pediatr Hematol Oncol. 1995;17:342–345.
200. McCready CE, Doughty HA, Pearson TC. Experience with the Port-A-Cath in sickle cell disease. Clin Lab Haematol. 1996;18(2):79–82.
201. Goldmann D, Maki D. Infection control in total parenteral nutrition. JAMA. 1973;223:1360–1364.
202. Maki D. Pathogenesis and strategies for prevention. In: Thirty-third Interscience Conference on Antimicrobial Agents and Chemotherapy. New Orleans: American Society for Microbiology; 1993:451.
203. Sheehan G, Leicht K, O'Brien M, et al. Chlorhexidine versus povidone-iodine as cutaneous antisepsis for prevention of vascular catheter infections. In: Thirty-third Interscience Conference on Antimicrobial Agents and Chemotherapy. New Orleans: American Society for Microbiology; 1993:414.
204. Curry C, Quie P. Fungal septicemia in patients receiving parenteral hyperalimentation. N Engl J Med. 1971;285:1221–1225.
205. Bailey M. Reduction of catheter-associated sepsis in parenteral nutrition using low-dose intravenous heparin. BMJ. 1979;1:1671–1673.
206. Bottino J, McCredie K, Groschel D, et al. Long-term intravenous therapy with

peripherally inserted silicone elastomer central venous catheters in patients with malignant diseases. Cancer. 1979;43:1937–1943.
207. Mitchell A, Atkins S, Royle G, et al. Reduced catheter sepsis and prolonged catheter life using a tunnelled silicone rubber catheter for total parenteral nutrition. Br J Surg. 1982;69:420–422.
208. Meyenfeldt M, Stapert J, deJone P, et al. TPN catheter sepsis: Lack of effect of subcutaneous tunneling of PVC catheters on sepsis rate. JPEN J Parenter Enteral Nutr. 1980;4:514–517.
209. Burke J, Garibaldi R, Britt M, et al. Prevention of catheter-associated urinary tract infections: Efficacy of daily meatal care regimens. Am J Med. 1981;70:655–658.
210. Broviac J, Cole J, Scribner B. A silicone rubber atrial catheter for prolonged parenteral alimentation. Surg Gynecol Obstet. 1973;136:602–606.
211. Blacklock H, Hill R, Clarke A, et al. Use of modified subcutaneous right-atrial catheter for venous access in leukaemic patients. Lancet. 1980;1:993–995.
212. Hickman R, Buckner C, Clift R, et al. A modified right atrial catheter for access to the venous system in marrow transplant recipients. Surg Gynecol Obstet. 1979;148:871–875.
213. Press O, Ramsey P, Larson E, et al. Hickman catheter infections in patients with malignancies. Medicine (Baltimore). 1984;63:189–200.
214. Larson EB, Wooding M, Hickman RO. Infectious complications of right atrial catheters used for venous access in patients receiving intensive chemotherapy. Surg Gynecol Obstet. 1981;153:369–373.
215. Viscoli C, Garaventa A, Boni L, et al. Role of Broviac catheters in infections in children with cancer. Pediatr Infect Dis J. 1988;7:556–560.
216. Hogan L, Pulito AR. Broviac central venous catheters inserted via the saphenous or femoral vein in the NICU under local anesthesia. J Pediatr Surg. 1992;27:1185–1188.
217. Alurkar SS, Dhabhar BN, Pathak AB, et al. Long-term right atrial catheters in patients with malignancies: An Indian experience. J Surg Oncol. 1992;51:183–187.
218. Wacker P, Bugmann P, Halperin DS, et al. Comparison of totally implanted and external catheters in paediatric oncology patients. Eur J Cancer. 1992;28A:841–844.
219. Johnson PR, Decker MD, Edwards KM, et al. Frequency of Broviac catheter infections in pediatric oncology patients. J Infect Dis. 1986;154:570–578.
220. Lokich JJ, Bothe A Jr, Benotti P, et al. Complications and management of implanted venous access catheters. J Clin Oncol. 1985;3:710–717.
221. Shulman RJ, Rahman S, Mahoney D, et al. A totally implanted venous access system used in pediatric patients with cancer. J Clin Oncol. 1987;5:137–140.
222. Cairo MS, Spooner S, Sowden L, et al. Long-term use of indwelling multipurpose Silastic catheters in pediatric cancer patients treated with aggressive chemotherapy. J Clin Oncol. 1986;4:784–788.
223. Hockenberry MJ, Schultz WH, Bennett B, et al. Experience with minimal complications in implanted catheters in children. Am J Pediatr Hematol Oncol. 1989;11:295–299.
224. van Hoff J, Berg AT, Seashore JH. The effect of right atrial catheters on the infectious complications of chemotherapy in children. J Clin Oncol. 1990;8:1255.
225. Ulz L, Petersen FB, Ford R, et al. A prospective study of complications in Hickman right-atrial catheters in marrow transplant patients. JPEN J Parenter Enteral Nutr. 1990;14:27–30.
226. Kappers-Klunne MC, Degener JE, Stijnen T, et al. Complications from long-term indwelling central venous catheters in hematologic patients with special reference to infection. Cancer. 1989;64:1747–1752.
227. Ross MN, Haase GM, Poole MA, et al. Comparison of totally implanted reservoirs with external catheters as venous access devices in pediatric oncologic patients. Surg Gynecol Obstet. 1988;167:141–144.
228. Biffi R, Corrado F, de Braud F, et al. Long-term, totally implantable central venous access ports connected to a Groshong catheter for chemotherapy of solid tumours: Experience from 178 cases using a single type of device. Eur J Cancer. 1997;33:1190–1194.
229. Elishoov H, Or R, Strauss N, et al. Nosocomial colonization, septicemia, and Hickman/Broviac catheter–related infections in bone marrow transplant recipients. A 5-year prospective study. Medicine (Baltimore). 1998;77:83–101.
230. Schwarz RE, Groeger JS, Coit DG. Subcutaneously implanted central venous access devices in cancer patients: A prospective analysis. Cancer. 1997;79:1635–1640.
231. Holloway RW, Orr JW. An evaluation of Groshong central venous catheters on a gynecologic oncology service. Gynecol Oncol. 1995;56:211–217.
232. Cardella JF, Cardella K, Bacci N, et al. Cumulative experience with 1,273 peripherally inserted central catheters at a single institution. J Vasc Interv Radiol. 1996;7:5–13.
233. Chait PG, Ingram J, Phillips-Gordon C, et al. Peripherally inserted central catheters in children. Radiology. 1995;197:775–778.
234. Hoch JR. Management of the complications of long-term venous access. Semin Vasc Surg. 1997;10:135–143.
235. Kearns PJ, Coleman S, Wehner JH. Complications of long arm-catheters: A randomized trial of central vs peripheral tip location. JPEN J Parenter Enteral Nutr. 1996;20:20–24.
236. Parkinson R, Gandhi M, Harper J, et al. Establishing an ultrasound guided peripherally inserted central catheter (PICC) insertion service. Clin Radiol. 1998;53:33–36.
237. Yeung CY, Lee HC, Huang FY, et al. Sepsis during total parenteral nutrition: Exploration of risk factors and determination of the effectiveness of peripherally inserted central venous catheters. Pediatr Infect Dis J. 1998;17:135–142.
238. Frey AM. Pediatric peripherally inserted central catheter program report: A summary of 4,536 catheter days. J Intraven Nurs. 1995;18:280–291.
239. Loughran SC, Borzatta M. Peripherally inserted central catheters: A report of 2506 catheter days. JPEN J Parenter Enteral Nutr. 1995;19:133–136.
240. Alhimyary A, Fernandez C, Picard M, et al. Safety and efficacy of total parenteral nutrition delivered via a peripherally inserted central venous catheter. Nutr Clin Pract. 1996;11:199–203.
241. Chung DH, Ziegler MM. Central venous catheter access. Nutrition. 1998;14:119–123.
242. Hiemenz J, Robichaud K, Johnston M, et al. Bacteremia in patients with indwelling Silastic catheters. Proc Am Soc Clin Oncol. 1982;1:57.
243. Hartman G, Shuchat S. Management of septic complications associated with Silastic catheters in childhood malignancies. Pediatr Infect Dis J. 1987;6:1042–1047.
244. Olson T, Fischer G, Lupo M, et al. Antimicrobial therapy of Broviac catheter infections in pediatric hematology oncology patients. J Pediatr Surg. 1987;22:839–842.
245. Prince A, Heller B, Levy J, et al. Management of fever in patients with central vein catheters. Pediatr Infect Dis. 1986;5:20–24.
246. Hiemenz J, Skelton J, Pizzo P. Perspective on the management of catheter-related infections in cancer patients. Pediatr Infect Dis. 1987;5:6–11.
247. Ascher DP, Shoupe BA, Maybee D, et al. Persistent catheter-related bacteremia: Clearance with antibiotics and urokinase. J Pediatr Surg. 1993;28:627–629.
248. Wever ML, Liem KD, Geven WB, et al. Urokinase therapy in neonates with catheter related central venous thrombosis. Thromb Haemost. 1995;73:180–185.
249. Benoit JL, Carandang G, Sitrin M, et al. Intraluminal antibiotic treatment of central venous catheter infections in patients receiving parenteral nutrition at home. Clin Infect Dis. 1995;21:1286–1288.
250. Raad I, Buzaid A, Rhyne J, et al. Minocycline and ethylenediaminetetraacetate for the prevention of recurrent vascular catheter infections. Clin Infect Dis. 1997;25:149–151.
251. McCarthy A, Byrne M, Breathnach F, et al. "In-situ" teicoplanin for central venous catheter infection. Ir J Med Sci. 1995;164:125–127.
252. Lai KK. Safety of prolonging peripheral cannula and i.v. tubing use from 72 hours to 96 hours. Am J Infect Control. 1998;26:66–70.
253. Becton D, Kletzel M, Golladay E, et al. An experience with an implanted port system in 66 children with cancer. Cancer. 1988;61:376–378.
254. Brothers T, VanMoll L, Niederhuber J, et al. Experience with subcutaneous infusion ports in three hundred patients. Surg Gynecol Obstet. 1988;166:295–301.
255. Strum S, McDermed J, Korn A, et al. Improved methods far venous access: The Port-a-cath, a totally implanted catheter system. J Clin Oncol. 1986;4:596–603.
256. Schuman E, Ragsdale J. Peripheral ports are a new option for central venous access. J Am Coll Surg. 1995;180:456–460.
257. Puig-la Calle J Jr, Lopez Sanchez S, Piedrafita Serra E, et al. Totally implanted device for long-term intravenous chemotherapy: Experience in 123 adult patients with solid neoplasms. J Surg Oncol. 1996;62:273–278.
258. Poorter RL, Lauw FN, Bemelman WA, et al. Complications of an implantable venous access device (Port-a-Cath) during intermittent continuous infusion of chemotherapy. Eur J Cancer. 1996;32A:2262–2266.
259. Duthoit D, Devleeshouwer C, Paesmans M, et al. Infection of totally implantable chamber catheters in cancer patients: Multivariate analysis of risk factors. In: Thirty-third Interscience Conference on Antimicrobial Agents and Chemotherapy. New Orleans: American Society for Microbiology; 1993:416.
260. Hollingsed MJ, Morales JM, Roughneen PT, et al. Surgical management of catheter tip thrombus: Surgical therapy for right atrial thrombus and fungal endocarditis *(Candida tropicalis)* complicating paediatric sickle-cell disease. Perfusion. 1997;12:197–201.
261. Horner SM, Bell JA, Swanton RH. Infected right atrial thrombus—an important but rare complication of central venous lines. Eur Heart J. 1993;14:138–140.
262. Haddad W, Idowu J, Georgeson K, et al. Septic atrial thrombosis. A potentially lethal complication of Broviac catheters in infants. Am J Dis Child. 1986;140:778–780.
263. Meisenberg BR, Callaghan M, Sloan C, et al. Complications associated with central venous catheters used for the collection of peripheral blood progenitor cells to support high-dose chemotherapy and autologous stem cell rescue. Support Care Cancer. 1997;5:223–227.
264. Madero L, Diaz MA, Benito A, et al. Non-tunneled catheters for the collection and transplantation of peripheral blood stem cells in children. Bone Marrow Transplant. 1997;20:53–56.
265. Leibundgut K, Muller C, Muller K, et al. Tunneled, double lumen Broviac catheters are useful, efficient and safe in children undergoing peripheral blood progenitor cell harvesting and transplantation. Bone Marrow Transplant. 1996;17:663–667.
266. Keung YK, Watkins K, Chen SC, et al. Increased incidence of central venous catheter–related infections in bone marrow transplant patients. Am J Clin Oncol. 1995;18:469–474.
267. Alegre A, Requena MJ, Fernandez-Villalta MJ, et al. Quinton-Mahurkar catheter as short-term central venous access for PBSC collection: Single-center experience of 370 aphereses in 110 patients. Bone Marrow Transplant. 1996;18:865–869.
268. Hahn U, Goldschmidt H, Salwendar H, et al. Large-bore central venous catheters for the collection of peripheral blood stem cells. J Clin Apheresis. 1995;10:12–16.
269. Swan H, Ganz W, Forrester J. Catheterization of the heart in a man with the use of a flow-directed balloon-tipped catheter. N Engl J Med. 1970;283:447–451.
270. Michel L, Marsh M, McMichan J, et al. Infection of pulmonary artery catheters in critically ill patients. JAMA. 1981;245:1032–1036.
271. Katz J, Cronan L, Barash P, et al. Pulmonary artery flow-guided catheters in the perioperative period. JAMA. 1977;237:2832–2834.
272. Cohen Y, Fosse JP, Karoubi P, et al. The "hands-off" catheter and the prevention

of systemic infections associated with pulmonary artery catheter: A prospective study. Am J Respir Crit Care Med. 1998;157:284–287.
273. Ford S, Manley P. Indwelling cardiac catheters. An autopsy study of associated endocardial lesions. Arch Pathol Lab Med. 1982;106:314–317.
274. Greene J Jr, Fitzwater J, Clemmer T. Septic endocarditis and indwelling pulmonary artery catheters. JAMA. 1975;233:891–892.
275. Ehrie M, Morgan A, Moore F, et al. Endocarditis with the indwelling balloon-tipped pulmonary artery catheter in burn patients. J Trauma. 1978;18:664–666.
276. Fernandez-Guerrero ML, Verdejo C, Azofra J, et al. Hospital-acquired infectious endocarditis not associated with cardiac surgery: An emerging problem. Clin Infect Dis. 1995;20:16–23.
277. Maki D, Hassemer C. Endemic rate of fluid contamination and related septicemia in arterial pressure monitoring. Am J Med. 1981;70:733–738.
278. Weinstein R, Stamm W, Kramer L, et al. Pressure monitoring devices: Overlooked source of nosocomial infection. JAMA. 1976;236:936–938.
279. Phillips I, Eykyne S, Curtis M, et al. *Pseudomonas cepacia (multivorans)* septicemia in an intensive care unit. Lancet. 1971;1:375–377.
280. West C, Wayle B, Touneson A, et al. Nosocomial *Serratia marcescens* bacteremia associated with reuse of disposable monitoring domes. In: Seventeenth Interscience Conference on Antimicrobial Agents and Chemotherapy. Washington, DC: American Society for Microbiology; 1977.
281. Walton J, Shapiro B, Harrison R. *Serratia* bacteremia from mean arterial pressure monitors. Anesthesiology. 1975;43:113–114.
282. Donowitz L, Marsik F, Hoyt J, et al. Control of nosocomial *Serratia marcescens* bacteremia traced to contaminated pressure transducers. JAMA. 1979;242:1749–1751.
283. Hawley H. Bacterial infection from intravascular monitoring devices. Infect Control. 1983;4:399–401.
284. Murphy L, Lipman T. Central venous catheter care in parenteral nutrition: A review. JPEN J Parenter Enteral Nutr. 1987;11:190–201.
285. Wyatt T, Timoney R. The effect of introducing a policy for catheter care on the catheter infection rate in a small hospital. J Hosp Infect. 1987;9:230–234.
286. Pearson ML. Guideline for prevention of intravascular device–related infections. Hospital Infection Control Practices Advisory Committee. Infect Control Hosp Epidemiol. 1996;17:438–473.
287. Gaynes RP, Edwards JR, Jarvis WR, et al. Nosocomial infections among neonates in high-risk nurseries in the United States. National Nosocomial Infections Surveillance System. Pediatrics. 1996;98:357–361.
288. Faubion W, Wesley J, Khalidi N, et al. Total parenteral nutrition catheter sepsis: Impact of the team approach. JPEN J Parenter Enteral Nutr. 1986;10:642–645.
289. Steere A, Mallison G. Handwashing practices for the prevention of nosocomial infections. Ann Intern Med. 1975;83:683–690.
290. Raad I, Gilbreath J, Suleiman N, et al. Maximal sterile barriers during the insertion of central venous catheters for the prevention of infection: A prospective, randomized study. In: Thirty-second Interscience Conference on Antimicrobial Agents and Chemotherapy. Anaheim, Calif: American Society for Microbiology; 1992:154.
291. Stotter A, Ward H, Waterfield A, et al. Junctional care: The key to prevention of catheter sepsis in intravenous feeding. JPEN J Parenter Enteral Nutr. 1987;11:159–162.
292. Segura M, Alvarez-Lerma F, Tellado JM, et al. A clinical trial on the prevention of catheter-related sepsis using a new hub model. Ann Surg. 1996;223:363–369.
293. Arduino MJ, Bland LA, Danzig LE, et al. Microbiologic evaluation of needleless and needle-access devices. Am J Infect Control. 1997;25:377–380.
294. Chodoff A, Pettis AM, Schoonmaker D, et al. Polymicrobial gram-negative bacteremia associated with saline solution flush used with a needleless intravenous system. Am J Infect Control. 1995;23:357–363.
295. Danzig LE, Short LJ, Collins K, et al. Bloodstream infections associated with a needleless intravenous infusion system in patients receiving home infusion therapy. JAMA. 1995;273:1862–1864.
296. Baier RJ, Bocchini JA Jr, Brown EG. Selective use of vancomycin to prevent coagulase-negative staphylococcal nosocomial bacteremia in high risk very low birth weight infants. Pediatr Infect Dis J. 1998;17:179–183.
297. Raad II, Hachem RY, Abi-Said D, et al. A prospective crossover randomized trial of novobiocin and rifampin prophylaxis for the prevention of intravascular catheter infections in cancer patients treated with interleukin-2. Cancer. 1998;82:403–411.
298. Escudier B, Lethiec JL, Angevin E, et al. Totally implanted catheters to reduce catheter-related infections in patients receiving interleukin-2: A 2-year experience. Support Care Cancer. 1995;3:297–300.
299. Fridkin SK, Pear SM, Williamson TH, et al. The role of understaffing in central venous catheter–associated bloodstream infections. Infect Control Hosp Epidemiol. 1996;17:150–158.
300. Gabel K, Geelhoed G, Zalkind D. A comparative study of a new skin preparation method for peripheral intravenous lines. Am J Surg. 1988;54:307–310.
301. Trooskin S, Donetz A, Harvey R, et al. Prevention of catheter sepsis by antibiotic bonding. Surgery. 1985;97:547–551.

Chapter 293

Nosocomial Respiratory Infections

LARRY J. STRAUSBAUGH

Virtually any respiratory infection may arise in the hospital setting, but the adjective nosocomial applies to those acquired or transmitted in the facility. Influenza and infections caused by respiratory syncytial virus and parainfluenza virus have afflicted both patients and health care workers occasionally. *Legionella* has caused outbreaks and endemic disease in a number of facilities during the past two decades. Tuberculosis may enter and spread within hospitals. Respiratory infections caused by *Aspergillus,* herpesviruses, and other opportunistic pathogens may originate in hospitalized transplant recipients and other immunocompromised patients (e.g., neutropenic patients with cancer). Nosocomial respiratory infections caused by these diverse etiologic agents as well as nonpulmonary infections (e.g., sinusitis) are reviewed elsewhere in this text and receive minimal attention here. Instead, this chapter focuses on the far more prevalent and universal problem of hospital-acquired pneumonia, which is usually a bacterial infection.

In hospitalized patients, pneumonia continues to be a common, serious, and costly problem. Overall, it is second only to urinary tract infection as a nosocomial infection, accounting for 15 to 20% of the total.[1–11] In intensive care units (ICUs) it usually ranks number one.[12, 13] Hospital-acquired pneumonias account for the majority of deaths attributed to nosocomial infections. Case-fatality rates have been as high as 70% in some series of ventilator-associated pneumonia (VAP). Finally, hospital stays for patients with nosocomial pneumonia average 1 to 2 weeks longer than those for appropriate control subjects, resulting in higher costs. Excess costs in the United States have been estimated to range from $1.2 to billion to 2.0 billion per year.

DEFINITION

Conceptually, nosocomial pneumonias are inflammatory conditions of the lung parenchyma caused by infectious agents not present or incubating at the time of admission, that is, conditions that develop 48 to 72 hours after admission to the hospital.[7, 8] Despite the clarity of this conception, the past three decades have witnessed the appearance of numerous operational definitions, none of which are universally accepted. Even definitions based on histopathologic findings at autopsy may fail to find consensus or provide certainty. Pneumonia in focal areas of a lobe may be missed, microbiologic studies may be negative despite the presence of inflammation in the lung, and pathologists may disagree about the findings.[14–17] The absence of a "gold standard" continues to fuel controversy about the adequacy and relevance of many studies in this field. For example, authors who require quantitative cultures of protected specimen brush (PSB) or bronchoalveolar lavage (BAL) specimens with the number of organisms above a certain threshold in conjunction with clinical criteria for diagnosis argue that results from studies using less strict criteria should be questioned or considered tentative at best.[3]

Despite some persisting uncertainty and ongoing controversy, the First International Consensus Conference on the Clinical Investigation of VAP in 1992 forged agreement on a number of important methodologic issues and helped define a research agenda.[18–22] Definitions that include quantitative PSB or BAL results received strong emphasis, and they have permeated subsequent reports. Nevertheless, their utility in care of patients and effect on outcomes await confirmation.[23] Because collection of PSB and BAL specimens requires bronchoscopy, their use remains circumscribed, and less cumbersome diagnostic modalities continue to be evaluated. In this context it is worth remembering, as Craven and Steger[2] have suggested, that operational definitions of nosocomial pneumonia should match the purposes for which they are selected. For example, definitions used for infection control surveillance differ from those used for diagnosing lobar disease after surgery or VAP occurring in mechanically ventilated patients with the acute respiratory distress syndrome (ARDS). Regardless, the level of diagnostic certainty clearly varies with the operational definition, as the examples in Table 293–1 illustrate. Several reviews of these examples and other criteria are available.[1–4, 9, 18, 19, 24]

EPIDEMIOLOGY

Nosocomial pneumonia is a common disease. Recurrent episodes are not uncommon, especially in ventilated patients. They may be either relapses or reinfections. The reported frequency varies with the operational definition, the hospital population, the hospital setting, and the type of rate calculated. A number of studies from the past two decades using surveillance or clinical definitions have identified cumulative incidence rates of 0.5 to 1.0% for U.S. hospitals.[4, 8–10] Extrapolations of these figures to hospital admission data suggest that 250,000 to 300,000 cases of nosocomial pneumonia occur annually. Hospital-acquired pneumonia also occurs commonly in other Western countries. A 1-day European study in April 1992 found a point prevalence rate of almost 10% (967 cases) for pneumonia acquired in critical care units.[13] Of note, this study, which utilized definitions, of the Centers for Disease Control and Prevention, surveyed 1417 units in 17 countries.

Hospital-wide surveillance studies utilizing clinical or surveillance definitions and preferred expressions of rates have identified incidences averaging 0.8 cases per 1000 patient-care days.[9] These rates tend to be higher in elderly patients. They are substantially higher in patients undergoing abdominal and thoracic surgery and in patients requiring intensive care. In patients requiring mechanical ventilation, rates are 6- to 20-fold higher.[7] The 1995 summary of the National Nosocomial Infections Surveillance (NNIS) system of the Centers for Disease Control and Prevention reported pooled mean VAP rates ranging from 6.7 to 24.1 cases per 1000 ventilator days in respiratory ICUs, and burn ICUs, respectively.[6] Not surprisingly, rates for nonventilated ICU patients in earlier reports from the NNIS system were considerably lower.[10] One would expect rates of lower magnitude in studies that use definitions with criteria that include quantitative PSB or BAL results. However, the one reported study using such criteria prospectively in a medical ICU found incidence rates of 0.9 cases per 1000 patient-days in nonventilated patients and 20.6 cases per 1000 patient-ventilator days.[9] The latter rate exceeds the 90th percentile for the rates from medical ICUs reported in 1997 from the NNIS system, suggesting that differences in the populations of patients may be more important than case definitions in some comparisons.[12]

Crude mortality rates for nosocomial pneumonia range from 20 to 70%.[1–4, 9, 10, 25–30] They are lowest for patients without VAP, intermediate for those with VAP not associated with ARDS, and highest for those with VAP and ARDS. Nationwide, hospital-acquired pneumonias are estimated to be a primary or contributing cause of death for 20,000 to 30,000 persons each year. Poor prognostic factors include advanced age, severe underlying disease, high Acute Physiology and Chronic Health Evaluation II (APACHE II) scores or other indicators of disease severity, multiple organ system failure, shock, and infection with certain gram-negative bacilli, especially *Pseudomonas aeruginosa.* The actual role that pneumonia plays remains controversial. Do patients die *of* pneumonia or *with* pneumonia?

Several studies suggest that pneumonia per se is an important cause of death. In one well-controlled hospital-wide study, the crude mortality for nosocomial pneumonia was 33% whereas the attributable mortality was 7%.[4] In a similar study involving ICU patients with VAP as defined by criteria including quantitative PSB or BAL cultures, the crude mortality was 54.2% and attributable mortality was 27.1%.[30] In a related study that used a stepwise logistic regression model, nosocomial pneumonia was found to be an independent risk factor for death (odds ratio 2.08; 95% confidence interval 1.55 to 2.80).[28]

In four other studies,[25–27, 29] however, VAP defined by similar criteria was not associated with excess mortality. In one study, patients with suspected VAP not confirmed by BAL or PSB cultures (control subjects) had mortality rates similar to those of patients with confirmed VAP, 58% and 57%, respectively.[26] Severity of illness was the most important determinant of death in another study, although VAP caused by *P. aeruginosa* was an independent risk factor for mortality.[25] In yet another study, which evaluated patients with VAP occurring after 5 or more days of mechanical ventilation, mortality rates were similar to those of subjects control.[29] Again, VAP caused by *P. aeruginosa* as well as *Acinetobacter* spp. and *Stenotrophomonas maltophilia* was associated with excess mortality. So, the contribution of nosocomial pneumonias to mortality remains unclear.

RISK FACTORS

Despite the variety and limitation of numerous studies performed to establish risk factors for nosocomial pneumonia, a reasonably clear

TABLE 293–1 Examples of Operational Definitions Used to Diagnose Nosocomial Pneumonias

Source	Examples of Operational Definitions	Comment
Centers for Disease Control and Prevention definitions for surveillance[9]	Rales or dullness to percussion plus any of the following: (1) new onset of purulent sputum or change in character of sputum, (2) organism isolated from blood culture, or (3) isolation of pathogen from specimen obtained by transtracheal aspirate, bronchoscopy, or biopsy. (Three other definitions are also provided.)	Probably sensitive but nonspecific; may require invasive procedure; may be poor for establishing etiologic diagnosis if culture is not obtained.
Conventional criteria for clinical diagnosis, case series, and other types of studies[18]	New or progressive pulmonary infiltrate on chest radiograph not otherwise explained, fever, leukocytosis, and purulent tracheal secretions. (Some investigators stipulate Gram stain findings as well: >25 leukocytes and <10 epithelial cells per low-power field ± bacteria.)	Data readily available; does not require invasive procedure; relatively inexpensive; poor sensitivity and specificity, especially for VAP and in immunocompromised hosts.
1992 Consensus Conference criteria for clinical investigation of VAP[18]	*Definite:* Radiographic evidence of abscess and positive needle aspirate culture from abscess. (One other definition is provided.) *Probable:* New (progressive) or persistent infiltrate and purulent tracheal secretions plus one of four other criteria, such as positive quantitative culture of a sample of secretions from the lower respiratory tract obtained by a technique that minimizes contamination with upper respiratory tract flora (PSB, BAL, protected BAL).	Good sensitivity and specificity; requires invasive procedures with attendant costs and risks; procedures may not always be available; requires quantitative bacteriology for optimal performance; and may miss early cases.

Abbreviations: BAL, Bronchoalveolar lavage; PSB, protected specimen brush; VAP, ventilator-associated pneumonia.

picture of predisposed individuals has emerged.[2–4, 7–11, 31–35] As a rule, these are persons at the extremes of age who are moderately to severely ill. They have noteworthy compromises in respiratory tract function. These may be due to intrinsic respiratory, neurologic, or other disease states that result in respiratory tract obstruction, diminished lung volumes, decreased filtration of inspired air, or decreased clearance of secretions. Trauma, surgery, medications, and respiratory therapy devices may interfere similarly with defenses of the lung.

Insertion of an endotracheal tube bypasses many layers of host defenses, allowing microorganisms direct access to the lower respiratory tract.[8] Insertion of the tube may injure the tracheal mucosa and permit pathogens to gain a foothold. Not surprisingly, endotracheal intubation and mechanical ventilation are the most important risk factors for development of nosocomial pneumonia. Specfic examples of additional risk factors are listed by category in Table 293–2 for both VAP and pneumonia occurring in more heterogeneous hospital populations that include both ventilated and nonventilated patients. For the most part, examples given were established in studies using clinical criteria to define disease and multivariate statistical analysis. Several reviews of these and other risk factors are available.[2–4, 7–11] Prospective studies of large cohorts defined by PSB or BAL cultures and multivariate statistical methods are a current research priority.[3]

Poor infection control practices also put patients at risk for nosocomial pneumonia. The role of poor hand-washing practices in cross-infection is undisputed.[10, 36] Outbreaks of nosocomial pneumonia caused by contaminated respiratory therapy equipment (e.g., nebulizers) have demonstrated repeatedly the potential hazards of inadequate disinfection.[3, 9, 10, 37] At present, hand washing, glove and other barrier use, tracheal suction practices, management of tubing condensate, and disinfection of in-line nebulizers head the list of infection control concerns.[2, 10] In some situations, failure to attend properly to such considerations may facilitate not only cross-infection but also delivery of large bacterial inocula to the lower airway.

PATHOGENESIS

Nosocomial pneumonias develop most frequently after the inapparent aspiration or so-called microaspiration of upper airway secretions into the lower respiratory tract.[1–4, 7–11] This paradigm applies to patients who are not intubated and to those who are. In intubated patients, secretions pool above the inflated cuff of the endotracheal tube.[8, 9] With changes in airway caliber associated with swallowing or breathing, secretions leak around the cuff, gaining entry to the lower respiratory tract. This phenomenon occurs in most intubated patients, and the supine position may facilitate its occurrence. Upper airway secretions, which are predominantly from the oropharynx, contain mixtures of pathogenic microorganisms. In previously healthy, newly hospitalized patients, normal mouth flora or pathogens associated with community-acquired pneumonia may predominate. In sicker patients who have been hospitalized more than a 5 days, gram-negative bacilli and *Staphylococcus aureus* frequently colonize the upper airway. Because microaspiration occurs commonly in intubated and nonintubated patients,[3, 4, 7–9, 11] the development of pneumonia probably requires adequate numbers of sufficiently virulent microbes entering the distal airways at a time when phagocytic, humoral, and other defenses are unable to eradicate or contain them. Microbial proliferation and the ensuing inflammatory response then produce the clinical syndrome of pneumonia.[5]

Uncommonly, nosocomial pneumonia may arise in other ways.[1–4, 7–11] Observed "macroaspirations" of esophageal or gastric material initiate the process in some patients. Allowing condensates in ventilator tubing to drain into the patient's airway may have the same effect. Bronchoscopy, tracheal suctioning, manual ventilation, or spirometry employing contaminated equipment may also bring pathogens to the lower respiratory tract.[2–4, 8–10, 38] In an earlier era, infected aerosols from contaminated nebulizers and other respiratory therapy equipment played an important role in pathogenesis.[3] More recently, concerns have focused on the potential role of contaminated in-line medication nebulizers, but these devices are infrequently associated with nosocomial pneumonia.[2, 3, 8, 11, 37, 39] Rarely, hematogenous dissemination of *S. aureus* or gram-negative uropathogens may seed the lung.

Although aerobic gram-negative bacilli frequently cause nosocomial pneumonia, they are isolated uncommonly from the respiratory tract of healthy individuals. Accordingly, considerable attention has focused on the source of gram-negative bacilli causing pneumonia and on their colonization of the respiratory tract in hospitalized patients.[1–5, 7–11, 40–45] The oropharynx and trachea continue to garner most of the attention. Colonization of these sites with gram-negative bacilli occurs within a few days after admission to ICUs, and colonization often precedes the development of pneumonia. Sophisticated typing techniques used in a prospective study demonstrated that oropharyngeal colonization was a predominant factor in the development of nosocomial pneumonia.[40] Many of the risk factors for colonization parallel those for pneumonia.[43] In vitro research has related some of these risk factors to changes in adherence of gram-negative bacilli to respiratory epithelial cells. Although formerly attributed to losses of cell surface fibronectin, these changes in adherence more likely reflect alterations in cell surface carbohydrates.[11] Bacterial adhesins and prior antimicrobial therapy appear to facilitate the process.[43] Of interest, Enterobacteriaceae usually appear in the oropharynx first, whereas *P. aeruginosa* more often appears first in tracheal secretions.[9]

Other sources of pathogens causing nosocomial pneumonia include the paranasal sinuses, dental plaque, and the subglottic area between the true vocal cords and the endotracheal tube cuff.[8, 9] The role of the stomach as a bacterial reservoir in patients receiving antisecretory therapy or antacids is more controversial.[3, 40–42, 44, 45] Those who champion the gastric reservoir hypothesis point to the large quantities of bacteria in the stomachs of patients rendered

TABLE 293–2 Examples of Risk Factors for Nosocomial Pneumonia

Category	Examples of Risk Factors in Category: *In Unventilated or Broad Mixtures of Hospital Patients*	*In Patients Receiving Mechanical Ventilation*
Host related	Advanced age, severity of illness, trauma or head injury, poor nutritional status, coma, impaired airway reflexes, and neuromuscular disease	Advanced age, chronic lung disease, severity of illness, depressed consciousness or coma, organ failure, severe head trauma, shock, blunt trauma, and stress ulceration
Device related	Endotracheal intubation, nasogastric tube, and bronchoscopy	Duration of mechanical ventilation, reintubation or self-extubation, ventilator cicuit changes at intervals <48 h; emergent intubation after trauma, positive end-expiratory pressure, and tracheostomy
Drug related	Immunosuppressive therapy	Prior antimicrobial therapy, antacid or histamine type 2 blocker therapy, and barbiturate therapy after head trauma
Miscellaneous	Thoracic or upper abdominal surgery; duration of surgery, duration of hospitalization, and large volume aspiration	Thoracic or upper abdominal surgery; gross aspiration of gastric contents, supine head position, and fall-winter season

Extracted from refs. 2–4, 7–11, and 31–35.

TABLE 293-3 Etiology of Nosocomial Pneumonia

Organism	Percentage of All Microbes Recovered in Aerobic Cultures in Study or Compilation: *NNIS System Hospital-Wide Component 1990–1996*[47]	*Bacteremic Cases from One Tertiary Care Hospital in Alberta, Canada: ICU and Non-ICU Cases 1986–1993*[46]	*Pooled Results from 10 Studies; PSB and/or BAL Techniques for Diagnosis; 544 Episodes of Predominantly VAP*[25–27, 40, 48–53]
Staphylococcus aureus	19	27	20.1
Streptococcus pneumoniae	0	1	1.8
Haemophilus spp. (predominantly *H. influenzae*)	5	2	9.1
Moraxella catarrhalis	0	0	0.8
Enterobacteriaceae	31	34	19.2
Pseudomonas spp. (predominantly *P. aeruginosa*)	17	12	20.1
Acinetobacter spp.	4	0	11.6
Other enteric gram-negative bacilli	0	0	1.5
Fungi (predominantly *Candida* spp.)	7	4	0.7
Assorted other bacteria*	10	21	14

* Includes coagulase-negative staphylococci, enterococci, viridans streptococci, *Neisseria* spp., and other unidentified bacteria.
Abbreviations: BAL, Bronchoalveolar lavage; ICU, intensive care unit; NNIS, National Nosocomial Infections Surveillance; PSB, protected specimen brush; VAP, ventilator-associated pneumonia.

achlorhydric as well as to the potential for reflux of gastric contents into the esophagus of patients in the supine position, particularly when enteral tubes compromise the function of the gastroesophageal sphincter. Lower incidences of pneumonia in some studies comparing sucralfate with histamine type 2 (H_2) blocker therapy have also been used to support this contention.

On the other hand, strong arguments have been mustered against the gastric reservoir hypothesis.[3, 41] Gastric isolates from patients receiving H_2 blocker therapy uncommonly cause VAP. The proposed sequence of gastric colonization first and subsequent development of nosocomial pneumonia has not been confirmed in studies using appropriate diagnostic and molecular typing techniques. The results with sucralfate therapy have been very inconsistent, and documented increases in gastric pH with sucralfate therapy have raised questions about the proposed rationale for its effect. Lastly, efforts to eliminate the gastric reservoir with antimicrobial therapy, that is, selective decontamination of the digestive tract, have generally failed to prevent pneumonia.

The frequency of nosocomial pneumonia caused by antimicrobial-resistant organisms, such as methicillin-resistant *S. aureus,* and multidrug-resistant gram-negative bacilli indicates that cross-colonization and cross-infection contribute to pathogenesis.[36] Infected or colonized patients usually constitute the most important reservoir for resistant organisms. Cross-infection and cross-colonization probably arise from patient contact with the contaminated hands of health care workers. Activities in patient care such as bathing, oral care, tracheal suctioning, enteral feeding, and tube manipulations provide ample opportunities for transmission of resistant pathogens when infection control practices are substandard.

ETIOLOGY

The operational definition of nosocomial pneumonia affects the determination of its microbial causation. Ideally, histopathologic evidence of pneumonia with isolation of organisms from biopsy specimens that correspond to microbes visualized with Gram stains of the tissue specimen establish the etiologic diagnosis. Blood cultures positive for pathogens also isolated from the respiratory tract, compatible smears and cultures from needle aspirates or biopsies of pulmonary lesions, and compatible smears and cultures from empyema specimens inspire confidence too.[18]

Blood cultures are positive in only 11% of patients, and empyema is less commonly present.[9, 24, 46] In addition, many patients with nosocomial pneumonia are too sick to undergo aspiration or biopsy procedures, which may be catastrophic in the setting of mechanical ventilation. Consequently, those using surveillance or clinical definitions for pneumonia usually have only Gram stain and culture results for expectorated sputum or tracheal secretions upon which to base etiologic diagnoses. In the aggregate, the results of these microbiologic tests have told a consistent story, suggesting that various gram-negative bacilli and *S. aureus* account for a majority of nosocomial pneumonia cases (Table 293–3).[25–27, 40, 46–53]

For example, data from the hospital-wide component of the NNIS system for the period 1990 to 1996 indicated that various groups of gram-negative bacilli and *S. aureus* accounted for 52% and 19% of all isolates from patients with pneumonia, respectively.[47] *Haemophilus* spp. accounted for 5% of the pneumonia isolates, and data for *Streptococcus pneumoniae* were not recorded. Data from the ICU component for the period 1986 to 1997 appeared to yield similar results.[12] In an abbreviated presentation of the data, *S. aureus* was listed as the pathogen in 17.4% of cases, *P. aeruginosa* in 17.4%, *Klebsiella pneumoniae* and *Enterobacter* spp. in 18.1%, and *Haemophilus influenzae* in 4.9%. In the NNIS system pneumonia is diagnosed with surveillance criteria. Although not delineated in later NNIS surveillance reports, cultures of expectorated sputum or tracheal secretions probably account for most of these statistics. Case series of nosocomial pneumonia requiring positive blood cultures for inclusion have yielded a similar range of pathogens.[9, 46]

Within the past decade, diagnostic methods using bronchoscopy coupled with quantitative techniques for microbiologic study of PSB and BAL specimens have been increasingly used to establish an etiologic diagnosis. Results obtained with these methods correlate well with those obtained using histopathologic criteria and cultures of tissue specimens.[3, 16, 17, 19, 24] Microbiologic results obtained with these methods for unselected patients have been discordant with those obtained from cultures of expectorated sputum or tracheal secretions, suggesting, in the setting of confirmative data from other sources, that they are indeed superior for etiologic diagnoses. Notwithstanding the diagnostic value that they may offer the individual patient, the overall results obtained with quantitative PSB and BAL cultures parallel those obtained with the older microbiologic methods (see Table 293–3).

Ten studies employing quantitative PSB and BAL cultures to diagnose VAP that were published during the period 1995 to 1997 indicated that various enteric gram-negative bacilli and *S. aureus* account for the majority of diagnosed cases.[25–27, 40, 48–53] PSB and BAL specimens yielded significant colony counts of more than one pathogen in 20 to 50% of cases, indicating that a polymicrobic etiology is more common than was previously thought. The higher frequency of pneumonia caused by *S. pneumoniae, H. influenzae,* and *Moraxella catarrhalis* noted in some of these studies probably reflects the onset of disease within 3 to 5 days of admission (or intubation), before colonization with enteric gram-negative bacilli occurred.[2, 7, 54] Similarly, studies of "late-onset" pneumonia developing more than 5 days after intubation generally yield few of these bacteria traditionally associated with community-acquired pneumonia. Longer duration of mechanical ventilation and prior antimicrobial therapy, especially broad-spectrum therapy, make it more likely that VAP is due to *P. aeruginosa, Acinetobacter* spp., or other highly resistant organisms such as methicillin-resistant *S. aureus.*[54]

Occasionally, other etiologic considerations arise. The isolation of coagulase-negative staphylococci, enterococci, *Neisseria* spp., or viridans streptococci in high concentrations from PSB or BAL specimens is of unknown significance.[3] Generally, the first two are ignored, but additional study is needed to evaluate the potential pathogenicity of these agents. All have occasionally been isolated from blood cultures from patients with nosocomial pneumonia.[46]

Isolation of fungi, most frequently *Candida* spp., in significant numbers poses interpretative problems too. Cases of invasive disease have been reported in VAP, but, more frequently, yeasts are isolated from respiratory tract specimens in the apparent absence of disease. One prospective study examined the relevance of isolating *Candida* spp. in 25 non-neutropenic patients who had been mechanically ventilated for more than 72 hours.[55] Just after death, multiple culture and biopsy specimens were obtained with bronchoscopic techniques. Ten patients had at least one biopsy specimen positive for *Candida* spp. However, only two patients had evidence of invasive disease. Many of the endotracheal aspirates, PSB specimens, and BAL specimens from the 10 patients also yielded positive cultures for *Candida* spp. Quantitative cultures of various samples from these patients were not helpful in the diagnosis of invasive disease.

The role of anaerobic bacteria needs additional study.[3] In one report they were isolated from 23% of the patients with VAP whose diagnoses were made with quantitative PSB and BAL techniques and special attention to the isolation of anaerobes.[50] Of note, the recovered anaerobes mirrored the bacteriology of the oropharynx, and they were the sole isolates in only four cases. None were isolated from blood or associated with necrotizing disease. These observations and the results of older studies imply that anaerobes are not noteworthy causes of VAP. Their role in other groups of patients with poor dentition may be more significant.[7]

In any particular facility, the etiologic considerations for nosocomial pneumonia are altered from time to time by the occurrence of outbreaks. These often occur in ICUs and involve patients being sustained with mechanical ventilation. Multidrug-resistant gram-negative bacilli and methicillin-resistant *S. aureus* are frequent offenders. *Burkholderia cepacia* and *S. maltophila* are the newest agents to appear in this setting.[37, 39, 54] Nosocomial outbreaks caused by *H. influenzae* and *M. catarrhalis* have been described on a few occasions.[56] Two reports indicate that *Chlamydia psittaci* and *Mycoplasma pneumoniae* may rarely cause nosocomial outbreaks of pneumonia.[57, 58]

DIAGNOSIS

The diagnostic process for nosocomial pneumonia runs the gamut from being fairly easy and uncomplicated to being extremely difficult, if not impossible.[24] Young patients without underlying lung disease who aspirate after surgery and then develop fever, leukocytosis, purulent sputum, and a new lobar infiltrate on chest radiographs pose few diagnostic difficulties, especially when blood and sputum cultures yield the same pathogen. At the other extreme, elderly patients with chronic obstructive pulmonary disease and congestive heart failure who have been intubated and ventilated mechanically for 2 weeks for ARDS developing after abdominal surgery may challenge and defeat all attempts at antemortem diagnosis. Although the latter patients often have fever, leukocytosis, and purulent tracheal aspirates, less than half may have pneumonia.[3] During febrile episodes, they usually have negative blood cultures, positive tracheal aspirates, and chest radiographs with unchanging, bilateral diffuse infiltrates. In practice, the majority of patients fall on the continuum between these two extremes. Their diagnosis depends on the operational definitions employed.

Pneumonia should be suspected in hospitalized patients, especially those with risk factors, when signs and symptoms of respiratory disease or unexplained fever appear[1, 7, 11, 24] Suspicion mounts in the presence of systemic toxicity, objectives measures of respiratory dysfunction (e.g., decreased O_2 saturation), the finding of a new or progressing infiltrate on a chest radiograph, and a rising leukocyte count. The differential diagnosis includes other consideration. For example, pulmonary findings might reflect atelectasis, pulmonary embolism, or congestive heart failure.[24] Similarly, fever might reflect extrapulmonary infection, drug reactions, or transfusion reactions. If the initial clinical evaluation points away from noninfectious causes, the search for information to support the "pneumonia hypothesis" continues.

Gross inspection of respiratory secretions and examination of a Gram-stained smear can be quite helpful, especially when the samples are obtained from nonintubated patients.[1, 7, 11, 24] Large numbers of neutrophils and macrophages plus high concentrations of a single morphologic form of bacteria can offer strong support for the diagnosis in nonventilated patients without underlying lung disease. Cultures of sputum or tracheal aspirates are advised despite their obvious limitations. Blood cultures should also be obtained. Thoracentesis to obtain pleural fluid for examination and culture should be considered if an effusion is present. Information from the history or medical record may prove valuable, such as a witnessed aspiration, a spouse's comment about respiratory disease in the family, or infection control surveillance data about high prevalences of resistant microbes in certain units or recent cases of unusual nosocomial infections (e.g., legionellosis or tuberculosis). This information may prompt orders for viral cultures, tests for legionella antigen in urine, or smears and cultures for acid-fast bacilli.

If, during the clinical appraisal, the diagnosis of nosocomial pneumonia comes to the fore, questions about the role of bronchoscopy become important, especially in patients with VAP.[1, 7, 11, 24] Emphasizing the imprecision and pitfalls of clinical diagnoses, some authorities have argued vigorously that all patients suspected of having VAP should undergo bronchoscopy to obtain specimens for quantitative PSB or BAL cultures.[59, 60] They argue that this approach is most likely to yield correct etiologic diagnoses for individual patients, to maximize their antimicrobial therapy, and to minimize unnecessary antimicrobial therapy.

Strong arguments are heard on the other side of the bronchoscopy issue.[61, 62] It is not always available, it is expensive, and it may be risky for hemodynamically unstable patients. Quantitative bacteriology of PSB and BAL specimens has yielded a broad range of sensitivity and specificity values. Many clinicians further recognize that antimicrobial therapy for nosocomial pneumonia necessarily commences on an empirical basis and often continues unchanged regardless of the bacteriologic findings. The same clinicians judge that they know enough about the microbial targets in general (see Table 293–3) to prescribe antimicrobial therapy prudently for the individual patient. Lastly, critics of universal bronchoscopy want to see outcome studies that vindicate its use, demonstrations of improved outcomes or reduced antimicrobial use.

On a practical level, the question often comes down to availability. Can an experienced bronchoscopist with the requisite technical support perform the procedure within an hour or two, before starting antibiotics becomes imperative? At the same time, it is essential to have laboratory services to back up the procedure—to perform quantitative tests on PSB and BAL specimens and additional studies, if indicated.[22, 63] When the procedure and the laboratory support are available, bronchoscopic studies should be strongly considered for the following individuals: immunocompromised patients, patients with VAP, and patients who have not responded to 48 to 72 hours of empirical antimicrobial therapy. Relative indications would include severe disease as judged by APACHE scores or similar indicators, an exceptionally broad range of etiologic considerations, and high levels of diagnostic uncertainty.

Part of the controversy about the use of bronchoscopic techniques derives from concerns about their diagnostic precision. The need for quantitative bacteriology to establish thresholds indicative of infection immediately identifies one concern. Insertion of a bronchoscope into the tracheobronchial tree literally pushes down nasopharyngeal, oropharyngeal, or endotracheal flora and contaminates the lower airway. Hence, quantitative thresholds are used to differentiate infection from contamination during the procedure. The current consensus recognizes 10^3 or more colony-forming units (CFUS) for microbes grown from PSB specimens and 10^4 or more CFUS for microbes grown from BAL specimens as clinching the diagnosis for patients with certain clinical features (see Table 293–1). In most studies focusing only on patients with VAP, sensitivities range from 65 to 100% for PSB cultures and from 80 to 100% for BAL cultures.[3, 4, 9, 19, 24] Specificities range from 60 to 100% for PSB cultures and from 75 to 100% for BAL cultures. Because the operational definition of VAP and experimental methods have varied somewhat from study to study, controversy persists about the breadth of these ranges and, hence, about the value of the tests.[3, 59–66] The greatest difficulties are encountered for patients with VAP who have received antibiotics, especially when the regimen has been altered in the 3-day period before to bronchoscopy.[3, 59, 62, 67]

A number of modifications and variations on the basic diagnostic approaches have appeared in the literature, but none are well enough established to recommend their general use.[3] Protected BAL, that is, lavage performed using a catheter equipped with a balloon to seal off the orifice of the bronchial subsegment to be sampled, appears to enhance performance of the BAL technique.[3, 59] Microscopic examination of BAL specimens and quantitation of intracellular organisms may also enhance test performance.[68] Both PSB and BAL techniques have been used with protected catheters that are inserted into the airway without bronchoscopic guidance.[3] To date, results have been inconsistent. Quantitative cultures of tracheal aspirates, tests to detect elastin fibers in tracheal secretions, and tests to detect antibody-coated bacteria have received some attention, but the results have failed to spark general interest. Finally, the role of high-resolution computed tomography, if any, remains to be established.[69]

THERAPY

Decisions about empirical antimicrobial therapy for nosocomial pneumonia commence during the clinical evaluation. Clinical and epidemiologic features suggestive of influenza would prompt consideration of empirical therapy with amantadine or rimantadine. Likewise, clinical features suggestive of legionellosis would warrant therapy with erythromycin, another macrolide, or a fluoroquinolone. Empirical therapy for patients with neutropenia or other forms of immunosuppression might involve amphotericin B or ganciclovir. Regardless of the likely pathogen, all patients with nosocomial pneumonia, especially those with VAP, require a lavish amount of supportive care directed not only at eradication of infection and maintenance of oxygenation but also at nutrition, skin care, and avoidance of iatrogenic complications.

In patients without notable forms of immunosuppression or unusual etiologic considerations, microbial targets are less diverse. In some cases, the availability of Gram-stained sputum or endotracheal aspirate specimens permits reasonable antimicrobial choices. In other situations in which such information is unavailable, empirical therapy may be based on guidelines such as those assembled by an expert committee of the American Thoracic Society and others.[7, 70] The examples of empirical antimicrobial regimens in Table 293–4 follow those of the American Thoracic Society guidelines. They reflect the useful concepts of core microorganisms, early- and late-onset disease, risk factors for certain pathogens, combination therapy for more resistant gram-negative bacilli, and severity of illness categorizations.

Of note, there are many variations on the examples given in Table 293–4. Individual medical centers and ICUs necessarily adapt such guidelines to their own situations, considering the characteristics of their population of patients, local patterns of antimicrobial resistance, pharmacy acquisition costs, and so forth. For example, in centers with increasing frequencies of pneumococci exhibiting high-level penicillin resistance, the consideration of vancomycin therapy for patients with early-onset disease arises more frequently. Physicians also make additional modifications on the basis of specific considerations for individual patients, such as the risk of anaphylaxis after β-lactam antibiotic administration or the likelihood of anaerobic disease in someone with poor dentition.[7]

The results of microbiologic studies (e.g., positive blood cultures or positive pleural fluid cultures), ordinarily permit reductions in the scope of antimicrobial therapy. It is hoped that the results of quantitative cultures of PSB and BAL specimens will promote the use of more specific therapies or even the discontinuation of therapy for patients with negative cultures.[22, 60] But this practice has not yet become widespread. Too often, physicians find it difficult to discontinue empirical regimens that appear to be working or to withhold antimicrobial therapy from extremely-ill, febrile patients in the ICU, even when their bacteriologic studies are negative. Additional studies to evaluate the timing and effect of discontinuing antimicrobial therapy are needed to bolster physicians' confidence in this area. More study is also needed to clarify the role of aerosolized or intratracheally administered antimicrobial therapy. Although these approaches have received some attention over the past two decades, definitive proof of their value has yet to appear.[71, 72]

Although sometimes difficult to measure, especially in VAP, clinical improvement usually requires at least 48 to 72 hours of antimicrobial therapy.[7] The duration of antimicrobial therapy for nosocomial pneumonia remains unsettled. As the American Thoracic Society guidelines indicate, courses of 7 to 10 days often suffice for infections caused by *S. aureus* and *H. influenzae,* but courses of at least 14 to 21 days are recommended for more serious infections caused

TABLE 293–4 Examples of Antimicrobial Agents Recommended for Empirical Therapy of Nosocomial Pneumonia by Microbial Targets and Clinical Settings*

Microbial Targets	Clinical Setting	Examples
Core organisms	Severe disease with onset before day 5 in the absence of certain risk factors†	Cefotaxime or ceftriaxone
Staphylococcus aureus		*or*
Streptococcus pneumoniae	*or*	Ampicillin-sulbactam
Haemophilus influenzae	Mild to moderate disease at any time in the absence of certain risk factors†	*or*
Enterobacteriaceae		Clindamycin and aztreonam
Core organisms *plus*	Severe disease with onset at any time in the presence of certain risk factors†	Gentamicin or ciprofloxacin
Pseudomonas aeruginosa		*plus*
Acinetobacter spp.	*or*	Piperacillin or piperacillin-tazobactam
Stenotrophomonas maltophila	Mild to moderate disease with onset after 5 days in presence of certain risk factors†	*or*
Burkholderia cepacia		Ceftazidime, cefepime, meropenem, or imipenem-cilastatin
Methicillin-resistant *Staphylococcus aureus*		± vancomycin (if methicillin-resistant *S. aureus* likely)

* Not for immunocompromised patients.
† Abdominal surgery, aspiration, coma, head trauma, diabetes mellitus, renal failure, high-dose or prolonged therapy with corticosteroids, prolonged ICU stay, underlying lung disease, and prior antimicrobial therapy.
Data from American Thoracic Society Ad Hoc Committee of the Scientific Assembly on Microbiology, Tuberculosis and Pulmonary Infections. Hospital-acquired pneumonia in adults: Diagnosis, assessment of severity, initial antimicrobial therapy, and preventative strategies. Am J Respir Crit Care Med. 1995;153:1711.

TABLE 293–5 Summary of HICPAC Recommendations for Prevention of Nosocomial Pneumonia*

1. Educate staff about pneumonia and preventive measures.	10. Use appropriate hand-washing practices, barrier precautions, and aseptic technique to prevent person-to-person transmission of bacteria.
2. Monitor pneumonia rates in ICU patients at high risk.	11. Remove invasive devices, such as enteral and tracheal tubes, as rapidly as feasible.
3. Do not routinely perform surveillance cultures of patients, equipment, or devices.	12. Elevate head of bed to 30–45 degrees if not contraindicated.
4. Clean and sterilize or disinfect† all reusable equipment or devices used in respiratory therapy or anesthesia between patients and at recommended intervals. Use sterile water for rinsing after chemical disinfection. Follow manufacturer's recommendations for use.	13. Monitor intestinal motility and enteral feedings to avoid regurgitation and aspiration.
5. Do not routinely change ventilator breathing circuits and components more frequently than every 48 h.	14. Remove subglottic secretions before deflating cuff and removing endotracheal tube.
6. Drain or discard ventilator tubing condensate away from patient.	15. Educate preoperative patients about respiratory hygiene.
7. Between treatments on the same patient, disinfect, rinse with sterile water, or air-dry small volume medication nebulizers.	16. Manage postoperative analgesia to avoid compromise of respiratory excursions and cough reflex.
8. Use only sterile fluids for nebulization and dispense aseptically.	17. Vaccinate patients at high risk for serious pneumococcal disease.
9. Avoid use of large-volume room air humidifiers unless recommended precautions can be implemented.	18. Do not routinely administer systemic antimicrobial agents to prevent nosocomial pneumonia.

* Includes only category IA and IB recommendations—strongly recommended for all hospitals.
† High-level disinfection.
Abbreviations: HICPAC, Hospital Infection Control Practices Advisory Committee; ICU, intensive care unit.
Adapted from Tablan OC, Anderson LJ, Arden NH, et al. Guidelines for prevention of nosocomial pneumonia—1994. Infect Control Hosp Epidemiol. 1994;15:587.

by *P. aeruginosa* and *Acinetobacter* spp. When patients do not improve, a number of noninfectious and infectious possibilities require consideration and evaluation.[7] Noninfectious considerations include development of ARDS, congestive heart failure, and pulmonary embolism. Infectious considerations include inappropriate initial antimicrobial selection, superinfection with resistant bacteria or fungi, development of pulmonary abscess or empyema, and onset of a nonpulmonary nosocomial infection. When patients are not improving, bronchoscopy to obtain PSB and BAL specimens for quantitative cultures may be helpful.

PREVENTION

In 1994, the Hospital Infection Control Practices Advisory Committee (HICPAC) of the Centers for Disease Control and Prevention published extensive recommendations for the prevention of nosocomial pneumonia.[10] The key functional components were (1) staff education and infection surveillance, (2) interruption of transmission of microorganisms via appropriate use of equipment and prevention of person-to-person spread, and (3) modification of risk factors for infection of bacteria (Table 293–5). The American Thoracic Society has provided compatible, albeit less comprehensive, guidelines for the prevention of nosocomial pneumonia,[7] and other reviews are available too.[2, 73, 74]

Many of the HICPAC guidelines are devoted to the use of equipment and devices for respiratory care. A number of outbreaks and high endemic rates of nosocomial pneumonia have resulted from contamination of humidifiers and nebulizers.[3] Although most believe this to be a problem of the past, reports of outbreaks associated with contaminated nebulizers and other items periodically surface.[2, 37, 39] In the interest of prevention and improvement in the quality of respiratory care, evaluation of new equipment and old practices continues. For example, a review of eight studies concluded that ventilator breathing circuits should be changed every 7 days.[75] Another review of airway management and VAP indicated that specific endotracheal suction systems do not appear to influence the frequency of VAP.[76] It further indicated that lower rates of VAP may be associated with avoidance of heated humidifiers, use of heat and moisture exchangers, use of oral intubation, subglottic secretion drainage, and use of kinetic beds. But the authors concluded that additional studies of such strategies are needed before endorsements can be made.

The HICPAC guidelines contain additional recommendations that may be useful in some hospitals as well as specific guidelines for prevention of nosocomial legionellosis, influenza, respiratory syncytial virus infection, and aspergillosis.[10] Moreover, they identified a number of unresolved issues for which there was no consensus. Chief among these was the use of selective digestive tract decontamination, the latest and best studied attempt to prevent nosocomial pneumonia using antimicrobial prophylaxis. Fundamentally, selective digestive tract decontamination utilizes antimicrobial agents, such as polymyxin and an aminoglycoside with or without amphotericin B or nystatin, applied to the oral cavity in a paste and to the gastrointestinal tract via oral suspensions in order to diminish concentrations of pathogenic bacteria at these sites in ventilator-dependent patients.[77, 78] A broad-spectrum parenteral antibiotic (e.g., cefotaxime) is frequently administered concurrently for the first 3 to 5 days. Despite more than 40 clinical trials of the selective digestive tract decontamination approach in ICUs and four meta-analyses, there is still conroversy about its benefit.[79, 80] Inconsistent results and concerns about emerging resistance in pathogens isolated from ICU patients persuasively argue against its general use and prompt calls for more study. More limited uses of antimicrobial prophylaxis to prevent nosocomial pneumonia in specific settings, such as after cardiac surgery or in patients with structural coma, continued to be studied.[81, 82]

The HICPAC guidelines left unresolved the issue of prophylaxis for stress ulcers using agents that do not raise gastric pH, such as sucralfate.[10] Here again the published results are quite mixed, and there is no consensus about the benefit of this approach.[83, 84] The pendulum, however, has swung against the use of sucralfate. In a well-designed trial involving more than 1200 patients requiring mechanical ventilation, rates of VAP were comparable in the ranitidine and sucralfate groups.[85] This result was consistant with that of a previous meta-analysis. Recipients of ranitidine in the large study had significantly lower rates of gastrointestinal hemorrhage. Because the role of the gastric reservoir in pathogenesis has also come under attack,[41] the sucralfate approach is in decline.

Lastly, the HICPAC guidelines also left unresolved a number of issues related to enteral feeding.[10] Should enteral feeding tubes have small or large diameters? Should tubes be placed in stomachs or distal to the pylorus? Should tube feedings be given intermittently or continuously? Should enteral feedings be acidified to reduce gastric pH? The influence of these factors on rates of VAP remains to be determined.

REFERENCES

1. Lode HM, Schaberg T, Raffenberg M, Mauch H. Nosocomial pneumonia in the critical care unit. Crit Care Clin. 1998;14:119.
2. Craven DE, Steger KA. Hospital-aquired pneumonia: Perspectives for the healthcare epidemiologist. Infect Control Hosp Epidemiol. 1997;18:783.
3. Mayhall CG. Nosocomial pneumonia—Diagnosis and prevention. Infect Dis Clin North Am. 1997;11:427.

4. Wiblin RT. Nosocomial pneumonia. In: Wenzel RP, ed. Prevention and Control of Nosocomial Infections. 3rd ed. Baltimore: Williams & Wilkins;1997:807.
5. Polk HC Jr, Heinzelmann M, Mercer-Jones MA, et al. Pneumonia in the surgical patient. Curr Probl Surg. 1997;34:117.
6. CDC NNIS System. National Nosocomial Infections Surveillance (NNIS) semi-annual report, May 1995. Am J Infect Control. 1995;23:377.
7. American Thoracic Society Ad Hoc Committee of the Scientific Assembly on Microbiology, Tuberculosis and Pulmonary Infections. Hospital-acquired pneumonia in adults: Diagnosis, assessment of severity, initial antimicrobial therapy, and preventative strategies. Am J Respir Crit Care Med. 1995;153:1711.
8. Craven DE, Steger KA. Epidemiology of nosocomial pneumonia—New perspectives on an old disease. Chest. 1995;108(2 Suppl):1S.
9. George, DL. Nosocomial pneumonia. In: Mayhall CG, ed. Hospital Epidemiology and Infection Control. Baltimore: Williams & Wilkins;1996:175.
10. Tablan OC, Anderson LJ, Arden NH, et al. Guidelines for prevention of nosocomial pneumonia—1994. Infect Control Hosp Epidemiol. 1994;15:587.
11. Dal Nogare AR. Nosocomial pneumonia in the medical and surgical patient—Risk factors and primary management. Med Clin North Am. 1994;78:1081.
12. CDC NNIS System. National Nosocomial Infections Surveillance (NNIS) report, data summary from October 1986–April 1997, issued May 1997. Am J Infect Control. 1997;25:477.
13. Vincent J-L, Bihari DJ, Suter PM, et al. The prevalence of nosocomial infection in intensive care units in Europe—Results of the European Prevalence of Infection in Intensive Care (EPIC) Study. JAMA. 1995;274:639.
14. Corley DE, Kirtland SH, Winterbauer RH, et al. Reproducibility of the histologic diagnosis of pneumonia among a panel of four pathologists: Analysis of a gold standard. Chest. 1997;112:458.
15. Kirtland SH, Corley DE, Winterbauer RH, et al. The diagnosis of ventilator-associated pneumonia: A comparison of histologic, microbiologic, and clinical criteria. Chest. 1997;112:445.
16. Marquette CH, Copin M-C, Wallet F, et al. Diagnostic tests for pneumonia in ventilated patients: Prospective evaluation of diagnostic accuracy using histology as a diagnostic gold standard. Am J Respir Crit Care Med. 1995;151:1878.
17. Rouby J-J, De Lassale EM, Poete P, et al. Nosocomial bronchopneumonia in the critically ill—Histologic and bacteriologic aspects. Am Rev Respir Dis. 1992;146:1059.
18. Pingleton SK, Fagon J-Y, Leeper KV Jr. Patient selection for clinical investigation of ventilator-associated pneumonia: Criteria for evaluating diagnostic techniques. Infect Control Hosp Epidemiol. 1992;13:635.
19. Meduri GU, Chastre J. The standardization of bronchoscopic techniques for ventilator-associated pneumonia. Infect Control Hosp Epidemiol. 1992;13:640.
20. Winer-Muram HT, Rubin SA, Miniati M, Ellis JV. Guidelines for reading and interpreting chest radiographs in patients receiving mechanical ventilation. Infect Control Hosp Epidemiol. 1992;13:650.
21. Baselski VA, El-Torky M, Coalson JJ, Griffin JP. The standardization of criteria for processing and interpreting laboratory specimens in patients with suspected ventilator-associated pneumonia. Infect Control Hosp Epidemiol. 1992;13:657.
22. Wunderink RG, Mayhall CG, Gibert C. Methodology for clinical investigation of ventilator-associated pneumonia: Epidemiology and therapeutic intervention. Infect Control Hosp Epidemiol. 1992;13:667.
23. Sanchez-Nieto JM, Torres A, Garcia-Cordoba F, et al. Impact of invasive and noninvasive quantitative culture sampling on outcome of ventilator-associated pneumonia. Am J Respir Crit Care Med. 1998;157:371.
24. Griffin JJ, Meduri GU. New approaches in the diagnosis of nosocomial pneumonia. Med Clin North Am. 1994;78:1091.
25. Rello J, Rue M, Jubert P, et al. Survival in patients with nosocomial pneumonia: Impact of the severity of illness and the etiologic agent. Crit Care Med. 1997;25:1862.
26. Timsit JF, Chevret S, Valcke J, et al. Mortality of nosocomial pneumonia in ventilated patients: Influence of diagnostic tools. Am J Respir Crit Care Med. 996;154:1161.
27. Baker AM, Meredith JW, Haponik EF. Pneumonia in intubated trauma patients—Microbiology and outcomes. Am J Respir Crit Care Med. 1996;153:343.
28. Fagon J-Y, Chastre J, Vuagnat A, et al. Nosocomial pneumonia and mortality among patients in intensive care units. JAMA. 1996;275:866.
29. Kollef MH, Silver P, Murphy DM, Trovillion E. The effect of late-onset ventilator-associated pneumonia in determining patient mortality. Chest. 1995;108:1655.
30. Fagon J-Y, Chastre J, Hance AJ, et al. Nosocomial pneumonia in ventilated patients: A cohort study evaluating attributable mortality and hospital stay. Am J Med. 1993;94:281.
31. Talon D, Mulin B, Rouget C, et al. Risks and routes for ventilator-associated pneumonia with *Pseudomonas aeruginosa.* Am J Respir Crit Care Med. 1998;157:978.
32. Baraibar J, Correa H, Mariscal D, et al. Risk factors for infection by *Acinetobacter baumannii* in intubated patients with nosocomial pneumonia. Chest. 1997;112:1050.
33. Beck-Sague CM, Sinkowitz RL, Chinn RY, et al. Risk factors for ventilator-associated pneumonia in surgical intensive care-unit patients. Infect Control Hosp Epidemiol. 1996;17:374.
34. Bonten MJ, Bergmans DC, Ambergen AW, et al. Risk factors for pneumonia, and colonization of respiratory tract and stomach in mechanically ventilated ICU patients. Am J Respir Crit Care Med. 1996;154:1339.
35. Cunnion KM, Weber DJ, Broadhead WE, et al. Risk factors for nosocomial pneumonia: Comparing adult critical-care populations. Am J Respir Crit Care Med. 1996;153:158.
36. Flaherty JP, Weinstein RA. Nosocomial infection caused by antibiotic-resistant organisms in the intensive-care unit. Infect Control Hosp Epidemiol. 1996;17:236.
37. Hamil RJ, Houston ED, Georghiou PR, et al. An outbreak of *Burkholderia* (formerly *Pseudomonas*) *cepacia* respiratory tract colonization and infection associated with nebulized albuterol therapy. Ann Intern Med. 1995;122:762.
38. Spach DH, Silverstein FE, Stamm WE. Transmission of infection by gastrointestinal endoscopy and bronchoscopy. Ann Intern Med. 1993;118;117.
39. Reboli AC, Koshinski R, Arias K, et al. An outbreak of *Burkholderia cepacia* lower respiratory tract infection associated with contaminated albuterol nebulization solution. Infect Control Hosp Epidemiol. 1996;17:741.
40. Garrouste-Orgeas M, Chevret S, Arlet G, et al. Oropharyngeal or gastric colonization and nosocomial pneumonia in adult intensive care unit patients—A prospective study based on genomic DNA analysis. Am J Respir Crit Care Med. 1997;156:1647.
41. Bonten MJM, Gaillard CA, de Leeuw PW, Stobberingh EE. Role of colonization of the upper intestinal tract in the pathogenesis of ventilator-associated pneumonia. Clin Infect Dis. 1997;24:309.
42. Niederman MS, Craven DE. Editorial response: Devising strategies for preventing nosocomial pneumonia—Should we ignore the stomach? Clin Infect Dis. 1997;24:320.
43. Bonten MJM, Weinstein RA. The role of colonization in the pathogenesis of nosocomial infections. Infect Control Hosp Epidemiol. 1996;17:193.
44. File TM, Tan JS, Thomson RB, et al. An outbreak of *Pseudomonas aeruginosa* ventilator-associated respiratory infections due to contaminated food coloring dye—Further evidence of the significance of gastric colonization preceding nosocomial pneumonia. Infect Control Hosp Epidemiol. 1995;16:417.
45. Torres A, El-Ebiary M, Gonzalez J, et al. Gastric and pharyngeal flora in nosocomial pneumonia acquired during mechanical ventilation. Am Rev Respir Dis.1993;148:352.
46. Taylor GD, Buchanan-Chell M, Kirkland T, et al. Bacteremic nosocomial pneumonia—A 7-year experience in one institution. Chest. 1995;108:786.
47. CDC NNIS System. National Nosocomial Infections Surveillance (NNIS) report, data summary from October 1986–April 1996, issued May 1996. Am J Infect Control. 1996;24:380.
48. Luna CM, Vujacich P, Niederman MS, et al. Impact of BAL data on the therapy and outcome of ventilator-associated pneumonia. Chest. 1997;111:676.
49. Bonten MJ, Bergmans DC, Stobberingh EE, et al. Implementation of bronchoscopic techniques in the diagnosis of ventilator-associated pneumonia to reduce antibiotic use. Am J Respir Crit Care Med. 1997;156:1820.
50. Dore P, Robert R, Grollier G, et al. Incidence of anaerobes in ventilator-associated pneumonia with use of a protected specimen brush. Am J Respir Crit Care Med. 1996;153:1292.
51. Timsit JF, Misset B, Goldstein FW, et al. Reappraisal of distal diagnostic testing in the diagnosis of ICU-acquired pneumonia. Chest. 1995;108:1632.
52. Kolleff MH, Bock KR, Richards RD, et al. The safety and diagnostic accuracy of minibronchoalveolar lavage in patients with suspected ventilator-associated pneumonia. Ann Intern Med. 1995;122:743.
53. Valles J, Artigas A, Rello J, et al. Continuous aspiration of subglottic secretions in preventing ventilator-associated pneumonia. Ann Intern Med. 1995;122:179.
54. Trouillet JL, Chastre J, Vuagnat A, et al. Ventilator-associated pneumonia caused by potentially drug-resistant bacteria. Am J Respir Crit Care Med. 1998;157:531.
55. El-Ebiary M, Torres A, Fabregas N, et al. Significance of the isolation of *Candida* species from respiratory samples in critically ill, non-neutropenic patients—An immediate postmortem histologic study. Am J Respir Crit Care Med. 1997;156:583.
56. Goetz MB, O'Brien H, Musser JM, et al. Nosocomial transmission of disease caused by nontypeable strains of *Haemophilus influenzae.* Am J Med. 1994;96:342.
57. Hughes C, Maharg P, Rosario P, et al. Possible nosocomial transmission of psittacosis. Infect Control Hosp Epidemiol. 1997;18:165.
58. Casalta JP, Piquet P, Alazia M, et al. *Mycoplasma pneumoniae* pneumonia following assisted ventilation. Am J Med. 1996;101:165.
59. Allen RM, Dunn WF, Limper AH, et al. Diagnosing ventilator-associated pneumonia: The role of bronchoscopy. Mayo Clin Proc. 1994;69:962.
60. Chastre J, Fagon JY. Invasive diagnostic testing should be routinely used to manage ventilated patients with suspected pneumonia. Am J Respir Crit Care Med. 1994;150:570.
61. Niederman MS, Torres A, Summer W. Invasive diagnostic testing is not needed routinely to manage suspected ventilator-associated pneumonia. Am J Respir Crit Care Med. 1994;150:565.
62. Bonten MJ, Gaillard CA, Wouters EF, et al. Problems with diagnosing nosocomial pneumonia in mechanically ventilated patients: A review. Crit Care Med. 1994;22:1683.
63. Reimer LG, Carroll KC. Role of the microbiology laboratory in the diagnosis of lower respiratory tract infections. Clin Infect Dis. 1998;26:742.
64. Chastre J, Fagon J-Y, Bornet-Lesco M, et al. Evaluation of bronchoscopic techniques for the diagnosis of nosocomial pneumonia. Am J Respir Crit Care Med. 1995;152:231.
65. Jourdain B, Joly-Guillou ML, Dombret MC, et al. Usefulness of quantitative cultures of BAL fluid for diagnosing nosocomial pneumonia in ventilated patients. Chest. 1997;111:411.
66. Timsit JF, Misset B, Renaud B, et al. Effect of previous antimicrobial therapy on the accuracy of the main procedures used to diagnose nosocomial pneumonia in patients who are using ventilation. Chest. 1995;108:1036.
67. Souweine B, Veber B, Bedos JP, et al. Diagnostic accuracy of protected specimen brush and bronchoalveolar lavage in nosocomial pneumonia: Impact of previous antimicrobial treatments. Crit Care Med. 1998;26:236.
68. Sole-Violan J, Rodriguez de Castrol F, Rey A, et al. Usefulness of microscopic

examination of intracellular organisms in lavage fluid in ventilator-associated pneumonia. Chest. 1994;106:889.
69. Lipchik RJ, Kuzo RS. Nosocomial pneumonia. Radiol Clin North Am. 1996;34:47.
70. Niederman MS. An approach to empiric therapy of nosocomial pneumonia. Med Clin North Am. 1994;78:1123.
71. Palmer LB, Smaldone GC, Simon SR, et al. Aerosolized antibiotics in mechanically ventilated patients: Delivery and response. Crit Care Med. 1998;26:31.
72. Itokazu GS, Weinstein RA. Aerosolized antimicrobials: Another look. Crit Care Med. 1998;26:5.
73. Bergogne-Berezin E. Treatment and prevention of nosocomial pneumonia. Chest. 1995;108(2 Suppl):26S.
74. Thompson R: Prevention of nosocomial pneumonia. Med Clin North Am. 1994;78:1185.
75. Stamm AM. Ventilator-associated pneumonia and frequency of circuit changes. Am J Infect Control. 1998;26:71.
76. Cook D, De Jonghe B, Brochard L, Brun-Buisson C. Influence of airway management on ventilator-associated pneumonia. JAMA. 1998;279:781.
77. Ferrer M, Torres A, Gonzalez J, et al. Utility of selective digestive decontamination in mechanically ventilated patients. Ann Intern Med. 1994;120:389.
78. Quinio B, Albanese J, Bues-Charbit M, et al. Selective decontamination of the digestive tract in multiple trauma patients. A prospective double-blind, randomized, placebo-controlled study. Chest. 1996;109:765.
79. Bonten MJM, Weinstein RA. Selective decontamination of the digestive tract: A measure whose time has passed? Curr Opin Infect Dis. 1996;9:270.
80. Hurley JC. Prophylaxis with enteral antibiotics in ventilated patients: Selective decontamination or selective cross-infection? Antimicrob Agents Chemother. 1995;39:941.
81. DeRiso AJ, Ladowski JS, Dillon TA, et al. Chlorhexidine gluconate 0.12% oral rinse reduces the incidence of total nosocomial respiratory infection and nonprophylactic systemic antibiotic use in patients undergoing heart surgery. Chest. 1996;109;1556.
82. Sirvent JM, Torres A, El-Ebiary M, et al. Protective effect of intravenously administered cefuroxime against nosocomial pneumonia in patients with structural coma. Am J Respir Crit Care Med. 1997;155:1729.
83. Thomason MH, Payseur ES, Hakenewerth AM, et al. Nosocomial pneumonia in ventilated trauma patients during stress ulcer prophylaxis with sucralfate, antacid, and ranitidine. J Trauma. 1996;41:503.
84. Prod'hom G, Leuenberger P, Koefer J, et al. Nosocomial pneumonia in mechanically ventilated patients receiving antacid, ranitidine, or sucralfate as prophylaxis for stress ulcer. Ann Intern Med. 1994;120:653.
85. Cook D, Guyatt G, Marshall J, et al. A comparison of sucralfate and ranitidine for the prevention of upper gastrointenstinal bleeding in patients requiring mechanical ventilation. N Engl J Med. 1998;338:791.

Chapter 294

Nosocomial Urinary Tract Infections

JOHN W. WARREN

Urinary tract infection (UTI) is the most common nosocomial infection, both in hospitals where it represents about 40%[1, 2] and in nursing homes where it makes up about 34%[3] of nosocomial infections. In both types of institutions, UTIs are usually associated with devices intended to assist in the drainage of urine. In hospitals, where the epidemiology has been better investigated, about 80% of nosocomial UTIs are associated with the use of urethral catheters.[4–7] Another 5 to 10% occur after other genitourinary manipulations.[4] The emphasis of this chapter is on catheter-associated bacteriuria.

CATHETER-ASSOCIATED BACTERIURIA

Each year millions of urinary catheters are placed in patients in acute care hospitals, rehabilitation units, and chronic care facilities. With the exception of nonbacterial urethritis, urethral strictures, and mechanical trauma,[8–10] virtually all complications of urinary catheterization result from bacteriuria.

The urethral catheter is one of the most venerable of medical devices, having been used to relieve urine retention on an intermittent or indwelling basis for centuries.[11] In the 1920s, Foley introduced a catheter that could be held in place with an intrabladder balloon.[12] Although initially used as a means to exert mechanical pressure against the prostate to stop bleeding after surgery, this innovation was soon recognized to be useful for holding in place indwelling urethral catheters inserted for other indications. For the first several decades of use, Foley catheters were attached to collecting tubes that drained rather unceremoniously into buckets sitting on the floor beside the bed, the so-called open catheter system. Bacteriuria was virtually universal by the end of 4 days of such catheterization.[13]

The 1950s saw the progressive development of "closed" catheter systems, and plastic collection bags fused to the distal end of the tubes began to be used in the 1960s.[14–18] This arrangement allows drainage through a tube into a receptacle so that the urine is always contained within a lumen protected from the contaminated environment. The onset of universal bacteriuria now occurs after more than 30 days in closed catheter systems.[18, 19] Although no well-designed, controlled trials comparing open with closed catheters have been performed, reports have been sufficiently persuasive that the closed system has become the standard for patients requiring indwelling urethral catheters.[18–22]

PATHOGENESIS

A symptomatic UTI results not just from bacteria being in urine but from these bacteria in some way perturbing urinary epithelium.[23] Fortunately, the normal, noncatheterized urinary tract has a number of defense mechanisms that prevent or minimize bacteria–epithelial cell interactions that are disadvantageous to the host. Although most organisms causing UTI have previously colonized the periurethral area, the urethra itself is an effective obstacle to bladder inoculation. Moreover, even if organisms traverse the urethra and enter the bladder, the next urination clears 99.9% of these bacteria,[24–26] a process enhanced by Tamm-Horsfall protein and oligosaccharides, which are suspended in urine and which bind bacteria.[27–29] Even after the most effective micturition, however, a film of urine remains coating the bladder mucosa. Fortunately, glycosaminoglycan overlays bladder epithelium and inhibits bacterial adherence to epithelial cells.[30–34] Moreover, there appears to be a poorly understood bacteriocidal mechanism closely associated with bladder mucosa[24, 35–37]; this is effective even in the absence of polymorphonuclear leukocytes or antibodies. The last protective effort of an epithelial cell is a sacrificial one: exfoliation of the cell allows associated organisms to be voided from the host.[38–41] Polymorphonuclear leukocytes arrive within hours and ingest infecting bacteria; they either kill them or carry them into the urine, where the phagocytes are voided with their captured prey.[42] Antibodies[43] and cell-mediated immunity[44, 45] are part of a slower response and perhaps useful in the later stages of the acute infection.

The use of a urethral catheter can thwart some of these defense mechanisms. Insertion of a catheter may carry urethral organisms into the bladder, the incidence of bacteriuria ranging from about 1% in healthy persons to 20% in elderly, hospitalized patients.[5, 46]

Once in place, the indwelling, closed catheter system may be opened at two sites. Although contrary to appropriate hygiene, the junction between the catheter and the collection tube may be disconnected for catheter irrigation or urine collection; bacteriuria has been associated with such interruptions.[21, 47] The second site, the drainage tube of the collection bag, is one that must be opened periodically to drain the accumulated urine. If the lumen of the drainage tube is contaminated with bacteria (e.g., from an unwashed container previously used to collect urine from a bacteriuric patient[48]), organisms may enter the drainage bag and before the next emptying multiply to high concentrations. Even after the bag is drained, organisms may persist in the film of urine coating its inner surface and multiply as it refills. Such bacteria may ascend the collection tube and catheter through the urine itself[49] or by growth along internal surfaces.[50]

The closed catheter system is successful because it greatly limits intraluminal entry of organisms and the pathways to the bladder just described. However, even with meticulous attention to maintenance of the closed system, the space between the external catheter and the urethral mucosa offers opportunity for bacterial entry directly into the bladder. Garibaldi and colleagues[51] demonstrated that periurethral colonization with gram-negative rods or enterococci was associated with bacteriuria significantly more often than when patients were not so colonized. Furthermore, Schaeffer and Chmiel[52] and Kunin and Steele[53] demonstrated progressive uropathogen colonization of the urethra in catheterized patients, particularly women. Such colonization precedes bacteriuria with the same strain in up to two thirds of patients.[19, 52, 54] This may be the route of entry in 70 to 80% of episodes of bacteriuria in women and 20 to 30% in men.[54] Even after removal of a catheter, the patient remains at risk of bacteriuria for at least 24 hours,[55] possibly because of the increased urethral colonization associated with the indwelling catheter.

Once inside the catheterized urinary tract, bacteria apparently find a hospitable environment. In marked contrast to the noncatheterized urinary tract, where small numbers of organisms introduced in the bladder are eliminated efficiently,[56, 57] the catheterized urinary tract allows bacteria that gain entry to multiply to high concentrations within a day or so.[19, 58] Specific adhesins enable fimbria to bind to uroepithelial cells and possibly to the catheter surface.[59–61] Uroepithelial cells of catheterized patients may transiently allow greater numbers of bacteria to adhere to their surfaces.[59] Among nonspecific mechanisms, glycocalyx, or biofilm, which covers and secures bacteria against a mucosal or catheter surface, has been demonstrated on drainage bags, catheters, and uroepithelium.[50, 62] Organisms contained within the biofilm appear to be well protected from the mechanical flow of urine, other host defenses, and even antibiotics.[63] The biofilm may allow the contained sessile organisms to establish a microenvironment from which some may move into the urine; these planktonic microbes are those that are voided and enumerated as bacteriuria by the diagnostic microbiology laboratory. Additionally, the catheter may mechanically damage urinary epithelium and the glycosaminoglycan layer.[64] As a foreign body, the catheter may blunt adequate antibacterial polymorphonuclear leukocyte function.[65, 66] Finally, catheter drainage is often imperfect and volumes of urine may remain in the bladder, allowing some stability to the residence of bacteria.

With time, the presence of bacteria elicits an inflammatory response, resulting in acute and chronic cystitis with pyuria and production of antibodies.[67–69] Organisms may move up the ureters to the kidneys, where a similar biofilm microenvironment may develop within the pelvis or the tubular system. Perturbation of the unicellular epithelium[70] may allow entry of bacteria into the renal interstitium; the subsequent inflammatory response is recognized pathologically and clinically as acute pyelonephritis.[71–73] With continued catheterization and bacteriuria, chronic renal inflammation may develop, and, particularly with stone formation, chronic pyelonephritis may follow.[74, 75] Although the conventional wisdom is that bacteremia associated with UTI is from a renal site, the presence of acute and chronic cystitis in long-term catheterized patients provokes the thought that bacteremia may occasionally follow invasion of bladder mucosa.

The majority of organisms causing catheter-associated bacteriuria are from the patient's own colonic flora[54]; they may be native inhabitants or new immigrants, that is, exogenous organisms from the hospital environment.[76–78] Just as with the pathogenesis of UTI in noncatheterized patients, colonic bacteria may colonize the periurethral area, especially in women.[51] Additionally, exogenous organisms may colonize catheter equipment, transferred there by the hands of health care personnel[48,79–82] or, infrequently, by contaminated products or containers.[48]

RISK FACTORS FOR BACTERIURIA

Multivariate analyses have clarified risk factors for catheter-associated bacteriuria.[83–85] Platt and colleagues' study of 1474 catheterizations[84] revealed nine independent risk factors for bacteriuria:

1. Duration of catheterization
2. Absence of use of a urinometer (drip chamber)
3. Microbial colonization of the drainage bag
4. Diabetes mellitus
5. Absence of antibiotic use
6. Female patient
7. Indications for other than drainage during surgery or output measurement
8. Abnormal serum creatinine
9. Errors in catheter care.

Shapiro and associates[85] revealed many of the same risk factors and additionally that patients catheterized relatively late in their hospitalization had an increased rate of bacteriuria. They further found that, among those patients who were to undergo prolonged catheterization, the risk of bacteriuria was higher in the first days than it was for patients catheterized for only short periods. This suggested to the authors that the need for prolonged catheterization is a marker for patients at higher risk of bacteriuria and that this risk is present even in the early catheterization period.

A risk factor that was not sought in these multivariate studies but that appears to be important is periurethral colonization with potential uropathogens. Garibaldi and colleagues[51] demonstrated that 18% of 612 patients colonized in the periurethral area with gram-negative rods or enterococci developed bacteriuria, compared with 5% of 601 patients not so colonized ($p<0.0001$).

DURATION OF CATHETERIZATION

Duration of catheterization is the most important risk factor for the development of catheter-associated bacteriuria (Table 294–1).[18, 21, 55, 83, 84] Duration is a general result of the indications for urethral catheterization, which in the hospital can be grouped into four categories[86–88]: (1) surgery (generally 1 to 7 days' duration); (2) urine output measurement, a proxy for cardiac output in seriously ill patients (7 to 30 days); (3) urine retention (1 to more than 30 days); and (4) urinary incontinence (more than 30 days).

A graph of patients by duration of their catheterization would show a bimodal frequency, with peaks at 2 to 4 days and at 3 to 6 months or more. The first peak would represent hospitalized patients with transient indications for catheterization; the second would be composed of nursing home patients with indications perceived to be permanent. Once a urethral catheter is in place in patients in a hospital or a nursing home, the daily increase in prevalence of bacteriuria is 3 to 10%.[18, 21, 47, 55, 89] The great majority of catheterized patients are bacteriuric by the end of 30 days,[18, 19, 69] a convenient dividing line between short-term and long-term catheterization (see Table 294–1).

The definitions used by the Centers for Disease Control and Prevention for its National Nosocomial Infection Surveillance System distinguish symptomatic UTI from asymptomatic bacteriuria.[90] As noted later, most studies of UTIs associated with catheters over the last several decades have looked at the development of bacteriuria, with or without symptoms. The focus of this chapter is the development of bacteriuria and the clinical manifestations of bacteriuria.

Short-Term Catheterization

Between 15 and 25% of patients in general hospitals have a catheter in place at some time during their stay.[5] Most are in place for only a short time, up to one third for less than a day,[21, 89] and both the mean and median durations are between 2 and 4 days.[5, 18, 21, 47, 55] Nevertheless, between 10 and 30% of these catheterized patients develop bacteriuria,[5, 18, 21] significantly more than the 1% found among noncatheterized hospital patients.[5]

Among short-term catheterized patients, *Escherichia coli* is the bacteriuric species most frequently isolated. Other common organisms are *Pseudomonas aeruginosa, Klebsiella pneumoniae, Proteus*

TABLE 294–1 Comparison of Short-Term and Long-Term Urethral Catheterization

Characteristic	Short-Term (<30 Days)	Long-Term (≥30 Days)
Patient		
Type of illness	Acute, surgical	Chronic, neurologic
Location	Hospital	Nursing home
Indications	Output measurement Surgery Urine retention Incontinence	Incontinence Urine retention
Usual catheter duration	2–4 d	Months to years
Bacteriuria		
Incidence	3–10%/d	3–10%/d
Prevalence	15%	90%
Number of species/patient	Single	Polymicrobial
Common species	*Escherichia coli* *Klebsiella pneumoniae* *P. mirabilis* *Pseudomonas aeruginosa*	*Providencia stuartii* *Proteus mirabilis* *E. coli* *Morganella morganii*
Proved prevention of bacteriuria	Closed catheter system Systemic antibiotic	None
Complications	Fevers Acute pyelonephritis Bacteremia Death	Fevers Acute pyelonephritis Bacteremia Death Catheter obstruction Urinary stones Chronic renal inflammation Periurinary infections Renal failure Bladder cancer
Medical goal	Postpone bacteriuria	Prevent complications of bacteriuria
Options	Diapers and pads External collection devices Intermittent catheterization Suprapubic catheterization	Diapers and pads External collection devices Intermittent catheterization Suprapubic catheterization Urinary diversions Prosthetic bladder sphincters

mirabilis, Staphylococcus epidermidis, enterococci, and *Candida* species[4, 18, 47, 84, 91, 92] (Table 294–2). Most bacteriuric episodes in short-term catheterization are manifestations of single organisms. However, as many as 15% may be polymicrobial.[7, 93] To establish a diagnosis, many investigators have required organism concentrations of at least 100,000 colony-forming units (cfu) per milliliter of urine[94]; others have selected lower concentrations.[95] It is worth noting that organisms isolated from the catheter itself are sometimes not found in the urine, a phenomenon attributed to sequestration of the bacteria under a biofilm on the catheter surface.[96] Most catheter-associated bacteriurias have accompanying pyuria.[97]

A word of caution is in order here. Because the kidney receives 20 to 25% of the cardiac output, certain hematogenous organisms may seed the kidney and subsequently appear in the urine. Two of these organisms are *Staphylococcus aureus* and *Candida* species; some investigators consider *Salmonella* and *Pseudomonas* species to have similar properties.[98] Two studies attempted to determine what proportion of *S. aureus* nosocomial bacteriuria resulted from bacteremia and yielded results ranging from 1 of 12 to 10 of 16 cases of *S. aureus* bacteriuria.[99, 100] The role of disseminated candidiasis in seeding the kidney with resulting candiduria is discussed later.

TABLE 294–2 Organisms Isolated from Catheter Bacteriuria (% of Total)

Organism	Catheterization: Short-Term* (Incidence)	Catheterization: Long-Term† (Weekly Prevalence)
Providencia stuartii	—	384 (24)
Proteus spp.	8 (6)	232 (15)
Escherichia coli	33 (24)	228 (14)
Pseudomonas aeruginosa	12 (9)	188 (12)
Enterococcus	9 (7)	179 (11)
Morganella morganii	—	118 (7)
Klebsiella spp.	11 (8)	68 (4)
Coagulase-negative staphylococci	11 (8)	53 (3)
Other gram-negative bacilli	10 (7)	93 (6)
Other gram-positive bacteria	6 (4)	56 (4)
Yeast	35 (26)	—
TOTAL	135 (99)	1599 (100)

*Data from Platt et al.[84]
†Data from Warren et al.[116]

Complications. Most episodes of short-term catheter-associated bacteriuria are asymptomatic.[5, 55, 89, 101] Indeed, among catheterized patients, the incidence of dysuria, pain, and urgency is not significantly different between those who develop bacteriuria and those who do not.[101] However, fevers may develop in 5% or more of patients with catheter-associated bacteriuria[5, 55, 89, 101]; daily cultures of urine indicate that many of these febrile UTIs occur on the first day of bacteriuria.[6, 89]

Less than 5% of catheter-associated bacteriuric patients are identified as having bacteremia caused by organisms in the urine.[4, 6, 72, 73, 89, 101] However, because of the large number of catheterized patients, these bacteremias constitute up to 15% of nosocomial blood-stream infections.[6, 72] The incidence of bacteremia is significantly higher when patients with catheter-associated bacteriuria undergo instrumentation such as prostatectomy.[102] Additionally, even without this provocation, men appear to be at greater risk for bacteremia.[6]

The relatively low incidence of febrile UTI and bacteremia may be a result of the types of organisms causing catheter-associated UTI. *E. coli*, the most common cause of cystitis and acute pyelonephritis in the uncatheterized urinary tract, causes only a minority of catheter-associated bacteriurias (see Table 294–2). Furthermore, of those *E. coli* causing nosocomial UTIs, most do not possess recognized virulence factors for acute pyelonephritis and bacteremia, such as P fimbriation.[103] Nevertheless, some non–*E. coli* organisms can be troublesome. For instance, *Serratia marcescens* may be more likely to cause bacteremia than other bacteriuric organisms.[4, 6] Furthermore, catheter-associated bacteriuria may predispose the patient to postoperative wound and intravenous line infections caused by the bacteriuric organisms.[104, 105]

The contribution of catheter-associated UTI to mortality is unclear. At autopsy, patients with catheter-associated bacteriuria dying in a hospital may have acute pyelonephritis, urinary stones, or perinephric abscesses.[72, 73] However, in prospective or case-controlled studies, catheter-associated UTIs are often not found to be associated with excess mortality[101, 106–108]; one study, however, has suggested an increased risk of death associated with catheter-associated bacteriuria.[109]

Minimal estimates are that catheter-associated bacteriuria adds 1 day of hospitalization for the bacteriuric patient. The significance of this figure is magnified by the large number of catheters in use and the high incidence of infection: in the United States, catheter-associated bacteriuria is estimated to cause 900,000 additional hospital days per year. This represents an additional medical cost of $615 million (in 1992 dollars) per year. Finally, certain estimates suggest that nosocomial UTIs directly cause almost 1000 deaths (about 1 death per 1000 episodes of catheter-associated bacteriuria) and contribute to an additional 6500 deaths annually in the United States.[110]

Studies over the last several decades suggest that the incidence of bacteriuria once a catheter is in place may be decreasing.[88, 111] Whether this is a result of shorter durations of catheter use, more attention to catheter hygiene, increased antibiotic use, or other factors is not clear.

Long-Term Catheterization

Although the magnitude of long-term urethral catheter use has not been directly measured, extrapolations from several studies[112–115] suggest that at any given time more than 100,000 patients in American nursing homes have urethral catheters in place. Many of these patients have been catheterized for months and in some cases years. The two most frequent indications are urinary incontinence (mostly women) and bladder outlet obstruction (mostly men).[115]

Even with excellent care, all patients, if catheterized long enough, become bacteriuric. This universal prevalence of bacteriuria is a function of two related phenomena.[116–118] The first is an incidence of new episodes of bacteriuria similar to that seen in short-term catheterized patients, although caused by a wider variety of gram-negative and gram-positive bacterial species.[117] The result is bacteriuria with a new organism somewhat more often than every 2 weeks. The second phenomenon is the ability of some of these strains to persist for weeks and months in the catheterized urinary tract.[117, 119] Two of the most persistent species are *E. coli* and *Providencia stuartii*. Persistence of *E. coli* is related to type 1 pilus, a well-studied adhesin for uroepithelium and Tamm-Horsfall protein.[60] For *P. stuartii*, persistence is associated with another adhesin, MR/K.[61]

These data suggest that two types of bacteria inhabit the long-term catheterized urinary tract. The first comprises common uropathogens such as *E. coli*, which, after easy access into the bladder, have bound to uroepithelium just as they would in the noncatheterized urinary tract. On the other hand, certain organisms such as *P. stuartii* are rarely found outside the catheterized urinary tract and may use the catheter itself, at least transiently, as a niche.[120, 121] Bergquist and associates[122] reported that about one quarter of organisms found in catheter urines were not present in simultaneously obtained bladder urine, suggesting that these organisms were colonizing only the catheter.

These phenomena result in polymicrobial bacteriuria in up to 95% of urine specimens from long-term catheterized patients. Such specimens commonly have two to four bacterial species, each at concentrations of 10^5 cfu/ml or higher[116–118]; some may have up to six to eight species at that concentration.[116] As noted, these include common uropathogens such as *E. coli*, *P. aeruginosa*, and *P. mirabilis*, as well as less familiar species such as *P. stuartii* and *Morganella morganii*[69, 112, 116, 117, 123–128] (see Table 294–2).

Complications. Complications of long-term catheter-associated bacteriuria fall into two categories. The first includes symptomatic UTIs such as those seen with short-term catheterization (i.e., fever, acute pyelonephritis, and bacteremia); some of these episodes may end in death. The second group is more often associated with long-term catheterization: obstruction, urinary tract stones, local periurinary infections, chronic renal inflammation, renal failure and, over years, bladder cancer.

Febrile Urinary Tract Infection. Although two thirds of febrile episodes in aged, long-term catheterized patients arise from the urinary tract,[116] the incidence is surprisingly low, about one febrile episode per 100 days of catheterization.[116, 129] Studied in women, most such episodes are of low-grade fever, last for 1 day or less, and resolve without antibiotic therapy or catheter change.[116]

However, UTIs are the most common source of bacteremias in nursing homes,[130] and the indwelling urethral catheter is the leading risk factor for bacteremia. Rudman and colleagues[127] demonstrated that patients with a catheter in place were 59 times more likely to be bacteremic over a 1-year period than patients without a catheter.[127] Although *E. coli* is significantly more likely than other bacteriuric organisms to cause bacteremia,[123] other bacteria, even supposedly nonuropathogens such as *P. stuartii* and *M. morganii*, can also do so.[116, 121, 130] Additionally, catheter removal or replacement is associated with bacteremia in 4 to 10% of incidents[131, 132]; most such episodes are transient and asymptomatic.

Acute pyelonephritis is undoubtedly the source of many of these febrile episodes. Moreover, autopsies have revealed acute pyelonephritis in more than one third of patients dying with long-term catheters in place,[71] many of whom were afebrile at the time of death. This suggests that, in the aged, debilitated patients who often are the users of long-term urethral catheters, serious bacterial infection of the kidneys may occur in the absence of fever.

The incidence of death during febrile episodes attributed to the catheterized urinary tract is 60 times the incidence in patients who are afebrile.[116] Bacteremia was not identified preceding most of these deaths.

Catheter Obstructions. In long-term catheterized patients, a catheter obstruction can be a problem, and in some patients it is a recurrent one.[133, 134] The complex material that obstructs urinary catheters is composed of bacteria, glycocalyx, Tamm-Horsfall protein, and precipitated crystals.[50, 135–137] *P. mirabilis* bacteriuria is associated with catheter obstruction,[136, 137] probably because of its potent urease,[138–140] which hydrolyzes urea to ammonia, increasing urine pH and causing crystallization of struvite and apatite in the catheter lumen. Electron microscopy has demonstrated these crystals within the bacterial biofilm.[62, 135] Although some catheter obstructions are associated with the onset of fever, most are not,[116] possibly because of early detection and removal of the obstructed catheter.

Urinary Stones. A similar bacterial process may occur in the urinary tract itself, resulting in the crystallization of struvite and apatite in the form of so-called infection stones, a common problem in long-term catheterized patients.[141–145] Such stones in the bladder, often crusting around the catheter balloon and tip, are relatively benign.[146] However, renal stones may be more serious and are associated with chronic pyelonephritis and renal dysfunction.[74, 75]

Chronic Renal Inflammation. Chronic renal inflammation, common in long-term catheterized persons,[69, 74, 75, 147–149] is related directly to the duration of catheterization.[69, 75] Chronic pyelonephritis (i.e., chronic renal inflammation with the additional components of deformed calyces and overlying parenchymal scarring) is also associated with duration of catheterization but is found in only a minority of long-term catheterized patients with bacteriuria, usually with renal stones.[74, 75]

Other Complications. More frequently in the past, additional complications were seen in long-term catheterized spinal-injured patients, mostly men, who are now usually managed with intermittent catheterization. These complications included periurinary infections such as urethritis, urethral fistula, epididymitis, scrotal abscess, prostatitis, and prostatic abscess.[74] Chronic renal failure was often diagnosed in catheterized spinal-injured patients and was frequently associated with intrarenal stones and chronic pyelonephritis.[74, 147, 148, 150–157] Among those catheterized for years, bladder metaplasia and cancer occurred more frequently than in noncatheterized populations.[153, 154]

PREVENTION

Prevention can be addressed in three stages: prevention of catheterization; once the catheter is in place, prevention of bacteriuria; and once bacteriuria occurs, prevention of complications.

Prevention of Catheterization

Obviously, the most direct method to prevent catheter-associated bacteriuria is to prevent catheterization. The last several decades have seen major advances in understanding the complications of catheterization, in weighing its risks and benefits, and in determining appropriate indications for catheter insertion.[22, 110, 155–163] This understanding has prompted increasing attention to the use of alternatives to the urethral catheter. For instance, for incontinent patients, the medical team might encourage a greater use of patient training, biofeedback, medications, surgery, and special clothes and bedclothes. Additionally, several devices have been explored as options to the urethral catheter. Encouragement of such options may yield a diminished use of urethral catheters.[164]

External Collection Devices. For men with urinary incontinence, external collectors applied about the penis that empty through a collection tube into a drainage bag have been widely used. Although these avoid the problems of a tube in the urinary tract, urine within these condom catheters may develop high concentrations of organisms, the urethra and skin may be colonized with uropathogens, and bladder bacteriuria may develop.[165–167] To distinguish bladder bacteriuria from skin contamination, careful collection of urine in a new condom by well-trained caregivers is necessary.[168, 169] Although no properly designed, controlled trials have been performed, parallel studies of condom catheters and urethral catheters in the same institution suggest a substantially lower incidence of bacteriuria with condom catheters.[170, 171] However, these contaminated devices can be reservoirs for the spread of nosocomial infections.[165, 167, 172] Complications include local problems such as skin breakdown, maceration, and ulceration; urethral diverticuli; and penile gangrene from constriction by the condom's roller ring.[173–176]

Intermittent Catheterization. This has been a venerable method for managing urinary retention, possibly going back for centuries.[177] After its re-introduction by Guttmann and Frankel in the 1940s,[178] by the 1970s intermittent catheterization had become the standard of urinary care for spinal-injured patients. Increasingly, clinicians dealing with other types of patients with chronic urine retention have used intermittent catheterization as the method of choice for urinary tract management.[179] Insertion of a catheter every 3 to 6 hours by caregivers or the patient, drainage of urine, and immediate removal of the catheter provide periodic bladder emptying. The incidence of bacteriuria is about 1 to 3% per catheterization. At four catheterizations a day, a new episode of bacteriuria occurs every 1 to 3 weeks.[179, 180]

Clean rather than sterile catheters have been used widely.[177, 179, 180] A randomized study comparing clean versus sterile intermittent catheterization showed no difference in symptomatic UTIs but did show that the clean catheterization was associated with diminished costs.[181] Oral antibiotics and methenamine compounds as well as instillations of povidone-iodine and chlorhexidine preparations have been used to postpone bacteriuria for short periods in intermittently catheterized patients[177, 182–186]; whether such practices would be beneficial over months and years has not been shown. Bacteriuria is usually asymptomatic and, although no well-designed comparisons have been performed, intermittent catheterization may be an improvement over indwelling catheterization in regard to local periurethral infections, febrile episodes, bacteremia, bladder and renal stones, and deterioration of renal function.[177, 187–189] Complications do occur, however, and may include bleeding; urethral inflammation, stricture, and false passage; epididymitis; bladder stones; and hydronephrosis.[177, 179, 188]

Experience with long-term intermittent catheterization has led to assessments of the technique for acute urinary retention, particularly in postoperative patients. Systematic evaluations of intermittent catheterization after total hip replacements, repair of hip fractures, and cesarean sections have been reported.[190, 191] More frequent use of intermittent catheterization in a variety of acute clinical situations can be anticipated; controlled studies comparing it with urethral catheterization for bacteriuria and its complications will be important.

Suprapubic Catheterization. Suprapubic catheterization has been used increasingly in several types of surgery.[192] The impetus is threefold. The first is the concept that the lower density of bacteria on the anterior abdominal skin might yield lower rates of bacteriuria with suprapubic catheterization than with a catheter in the urethra. The second is the realization that in some patients urethral strictures are sequelae of indwelling urethral catheters in place for even a few days.[193–196] The third feature is that clamping of the suprapubic catheter allows testing of voiding per urethra, obviously an advantage not shared with urethral catheterization. Studies have randomly assigned patients to suprapubic or urethral catheterization,[195–199] and some have shown significant benefits with the suprapubic catheter in terms of lower incidences of bacteriuria,[197] urethral strictures,[195, 196] or pain.[199] Complications include infection, leakage, and hematoma at the puncture site and occasional catheter prolapse through the urethra. Suprapubic catheterization is promising; well-designed trials should evaluate the effectiveness and the incidence of bacteriuria and bacteriuric complications in different populations now requiring short- and long-term urethral catheterization.

Intraurethral Catheters. Over the last decade, the concept of an entirely intraurethral device to relieve urinary retention secondary to benign prostatic hypertrophy has been introduced.[200, 201] Two such devices are used; one is an iron, gold-coated spiral tube, the other a polyurethane Malecot-type catheter. Each is intended to be totally contained within the urethra, spanning the prostate in order to relieve obstruction. These devices have remained in place for weeks and months until or instead of surgery. Early reports have suggested low incidences of bacteriuria and symptomatic infection. These appear to be promising devices for some patients and could diminish infectious complications of transurethral catheters.

Urinary Diversions. Bladder diseases, especially cancer and occasionally intractable incontinence, have been treated by structuring a nonbladder storage unit for urine. These are usually ileal or colonic segments that either require collection bags on the abdominal wall or are continent and emptied by intermittent catheterization through the stoma. Although not strictly options to the urethral catheter, these urologic modifications predispose to UTI. Bacteriologic investigations of these diversions have shown that bacteriuria is common, perhaps more in ileal than in colonic devices and more in those that require a collection bag than in those that do not.[202, 203] Acute pyelonephritis, chronic pyelonephritis, and renal dysfunction are complications, particularly in conduits in which ureteral reflux is a consequence.[203] These and orthopedic complications resulting from abnormalities in bone metabolism[204] suggest prudent use of these procedures.

Prevention of Bacteriuria

Once a urethral catheter is in place, only two principles are universally recommended for prevention of bacteriuria: keep the closed catheter system closed and remove the catheter as soon as possible.[155–161]

Maintain a Closed System. Urine specimens should be obtained without opening the catheter–collection tube junction.[21, 47] However, sealing this junction before or soon after placement of the catheter has inconsistent impact on subsequent bacteriuria.[205–207] The only point at which the system must be opened is at the bag drainage tube; personnel must avoid touching the end of the drainage tube to possibly contaminated containers.[48] Communication of appropriate techniques to caregivers must continue to be an important objective of infection control teams.[163] Longitudinal studies in the same institution suggest that continued attention has resulted in fewer errors of catheter hygiene.[89, 208]

Minimize Duration. If the catheter can be removed before bacteriuria develops, postponement becomes prevention. At least two groups of investigators, using lists of durations predetermined to be appropriate for each indication for catheterization, found that more than one third of days late in catheterization courses were unnecessary.[55, 88] Importantly, many bacteriurias occurred after the catheter would have been removed had the appropriate catheter durations been observed.[55] A reasonable management tool would be daily review of the necessity to continue catheterization in any given patient.[163] Randomized trials to ascertain appropriate durations of catheterization for various indications should be encouraged.[209]

Additional Efforts. The summary statement of this section is that, although many logical modifications have been attempted, none has markedly improved on the ability of the closed catheter system to postpone bacteriuria. Small trials and ones with historical controls have not demonstrated differences in bacteriuria after insertion of the catheter using sterile or clean techniques or an antiseptic gel.[210, 211] A common attempt to prevent bacteriuria has been the use of antibiotics instilled into the lumen of the catheter system. However, irrigation of the catheter and bladder with antibacterial solutions has not postponed bacteriuria.[47, 212, 213] Additionally, antimicrobials in the collection bag have generally had no effectiveness in curtailing bacteriuria[214–216]; in two studies that did show effectiveness,[217, 218] the rate of bag contamination in control patients was several times higher than that reported in other studies. These adaptations in which organisms entering the lumen of the indwelling catheter system encounter an antimicrobial might be of value for those systems in which the integrity of the closed catheter has been compromised. However, with appropriate attention to maintenance of the closed system, bacterial entry into the lumen of the catheter is minimal and such efforts should be superfluous.[219]

Another modification has been to manipulate the composition of the catheter material. Generally these have been attempts to decrease bacterial adherence or to incorporate antibacterial agents[220–222]; none has appeared to represent a breakthrough in preventive techniques. One variation of this theme is the use of silver-coated catheters, which are intended to exploit the antibacterial effect of silver ions. Several randomized trials have been performed and have yielded conflicting results.[19, 223–227] The smaller trials, in the same institution and using silver alloy–coated catheters, showed a beneficial effect.[223–225] However, the two largest trials, using silver oxide–coated catheters, revealed no overall effect.[226, 227] Cost analyses have not been performed.

Given that the potential space between the urethra and the external catheter surface is probably the most common source of entry for organisms into the catheterized urinary tract, numerous investigators have attempted to block this entry by the application of topical antibacterial agents. However, studies have shown little if any postponement of bacteriuria with such techniques. Indeed, several studies revealed that patients receiving such agents actually tended to have an increased incidence of bacteriuria, a finding attributed to easier bladder ingress of urethral and periurethral bacteria as a result of physical manipulation of the urethra.[228, 229]

However, one clinical practice has had a universal effect on postponement of bacteriuria. Virtually every study of systemic antibiotics, retrospective or prospective, has demonstrated effectiveness in initially diminishing the incidence of bacteriuria in catheterized patients.[19, 21, 51, 55, 84–86, 89, 230, 231] Because of the nature of catheterization in hospitals, up to 80% of catheterized patients are given antibiotics during, but not usually because of, catheterization. However, those studies that observed patients long enough revealed that antibiotics were effective for the first several days and then resistant organisms began to appear in the urine.[230–232] Most authorities believe that antibiotics to postpone bacteriuria are not indicated because of side effects, cost, and emergence of resistant bacteria in the patient and in the medical unit.[157, 158, 160, 161] However, there may be exceptions to this generalization. For instance, patients at high risk for the complications of catheter-associated bacteriuria (e.g., renal transplantation patients, granulocytopenic patients) might benefit from antibiotic use during short-term catheterization.

Prevention of Complications of Bacteriuria

Treatment with antibiotics of asymptomatic bacteriuria in catheterized patients may seem a logical measure to prevent its complications (e.g., fever, urinary symptoms, acute pyelonephritis, bacteremia). However, the data that are available suggest that this approach is not particularly useful. Garibaldi and colleagues[89] noted in hospitalized patients that symptomatic catheter-associated UTIs tended to occur on the first day of bacteriuria. These patients would be precluded from effective preventive treatment with antibiotics. Furthermore, even if antibiotics prescribed for asymptomatic bacteriuria were 100% effective in preventing the delayed symptomatic UTI, for each one prevented, 250 urine cultures would be required to identify the asymptomatic bacteriurias precipitating treatment. Other studies tend to confirm these findings.[5, 55, 233]

In long-term catheterized patients, the hypothesis that antibiotic treatment of catheter-associated bacteriuria will prevent symptomatic UTI has been tested in a prospective trial. In this study, cephalexin was administered whenever a susceptible organism appeared in the urine. There was no effect on incidence of new bacteriuria, number of bacterial strains per urine specimen, or, most importantly, incidence of febrile episodes.[232] The only change was a marked increase in antibiotic-resistant organisms, a finding of others as well.[234]

These investigations suggest that asymptomatic bacteriuria need not be treated as long as the catheter (short-term or long-term) remains in place.[55, 158–161] However, several exceptions may pertain. One is for particular bacterial strains that are causing a high incidence of bacteremia from catheter-associated bacteriuria in a given institution; *Serratia marcescens* has been such an organism.[4, 6] The second is if such therapy is part of a plan to control a cluster of infections by a particular organism in a medical unit. The third is for those patients who may be at high risk of serious complications; these include granulocytopenic patients, solid-organ transplantation patients, and pregnant women. The fourth exception includes patients undergoing urologic surgery. The final possible group consists of patients undergoing other types of surgery, particularly those in whom prostheses may be left in place. These possibilities should be evaluated by controlled trials.

A final idea for prevention of complications of catheter-associated bacteriuria is antibiotic treatment after the catheter is removed. Harding and coworkers[235] performed a controlled trial of patients who had bacteriuria after catheter removal, distributing them into three groups: no antibiotics, single-dose trimethoprim/sulfamethoxazole (TMP/SMZ), and 10 days of TMP/SMZ.[235] By monitoring the placebo group for 14 days after the catheter was removed, they observed over this short period the natural history of catheter-associated bacteriuria. They found that 7 (17%) of 42 developed symptoms of UTI, most of which were lower urinary tract in nature. Second, they found that 15 (36%) of 42 patients resolved their bacteriuria spontaneously. In this latter outcome there was a marked distinction by age: 74% of women 65 years of age or younger resolved their bacteriuria spontaneously, compared with only 4% of older women. Each of the two antibiotic therapies only marginally, and nonsignificantly, improved the resolution rate in the younger women, but each markedly and significantly improved the resolution of bacteriuria in the older women, the single dose to 56% and the 10-day course to 71%. Although the authors recommended that women with asymptomatic catheter-associated bacteriuria be treated with antibiotics after catheter removal, other interpretations of these data are possible. One is that older women with catheter-associated bacteriuria should be treated after removal of the catheter, yet the majority of younger women will clear their bacteriurias spontaneously; a urine culture from them at 2 or 3 weeks after catheter removal would identify those with persistent bacteriuria, for whom a decision about therapy could be made. A second possible interpretation is that the long-term natural history of bacteriuria after catheter removal is not clear. Objectives for postcatheterization bacteriuria probably should not be eradication of asymptomatic bacteriuria but rather prevention of complications such as cystitis, acute pyelonephritis, and bacteremia. Natural history studies and antibiotic trials of these theories would be welcomed.

Some patients undergoing long-term catheterization have recurrent obstructions of the catheter, which in many is associated with infections by *P. mirabilis* and subsequent encrustation with struvite and apatite crystals. Daily catheter irrigation with normal saline appears to be ineffective in diminishing obstructions.[236] Methenamine preparations may diminish the incidence of obstruction, possibly because of biochemical alteration of salt solubility.[237–239]

TREATMENT OF COMPLICATIONS

For the patient who develops fever or signs of bacteremia, the clinician should rule out sources outside the urinary tract, catheter obstruction, and, especially among men, periurethral infection; cultures of urine and blood should be obtained. Many clinicians would empirically treat such patients with parenteral antibiotics at doses high enough to achieve concentrations in the serum adequate to treat bacteremia from a known or suspected bacteriuric species. The selection of antibiotics should be based on knowledge of organisms common in the medical unit and Gram staining of the patient's urine. Antibiotics should be modified on notification of antibiotic susceptibility patterns of the urine and blood isolates. Seven to 10 days of therapy is usually sufficient and need not all be parenteral. The occasional catheterized patient with bladder symptoms such as lower abdominal pain and without fever or other evidence of systemic infection may benefit from an oral antibiotic active *in vitro*. Because of the likelihood of bacteria sequestered in a biofilm on the catheter surface, a reasonable decision might be to replace or remove the catheter during treatment for symptomatic catheter-associated bacteriuria,[163, 240] although the few data available are not particularly supportive of this concept.[241] For patients with increasing renal dysfunction or recalcitrant or recurring bacteremia or fever, a search for urinary stones may be helpful.

Candiduria. Candiduria may develop in catheterized patients. Its incidence is directly related to the durations of catheterization and hospitalization and to antibiotic use.[92, 242] The incidence of catheter-associated candiduria appears to be increasing.[243] Investigators have used a variety of concentrations of organisms for the definition of candiduria.[244, 245]

Catheter-associated candiduria is generally asymptomatic, and because its natural history is not well understood, its management is unclear. Removal of the catheter results in the disappearance of candiduria in up to 40% of patients; simply changing the catheter results in a 20% decrease in candiduria.[246] For asymptomatic patients whose candiduria persists or who must remain catheterized, appropriate management is problematic. Although 14 days of oral fluconazole therapy yielded a significantly higher eradication rate short-term than placebo, patients receiving placebo remained asymptomatic.[246] A randomized trial of fluconazole versus irrigation of the bladder with amphotericin B revealed similar eradication rates.[245] A group of investigators of candidal diseases reached consensus that, if possible, catheters should be removed from the urinary tract of patients with candiduria; such patients should be treated before undergoing a genitourinary tract operative procedure; and that, if non-*krusei* candidal cystitis were to be treated, oral fluconazole should be the treatment.[247] Amphotericin B irrigation of the bladder is a consideration if the catheter must be left in place. Flucytosine is potentially toxic in azotemic patients and is poorly effective. Ketoconazole is not excreted in a bioactive form in the urine and is ineffective.[245, 248]

Complications of candiduria can develop and include fever,[245, 249, 250] renal infection resulting in renal and perirenal abscesses,[251] fungus balls in the bladder or renal pelvis,[252] and particularly in patients with genitourinary abnormalities or associated with a genitourinary operative procedure, disseminated candidiasis.[251, 253] In these situations, systemic therapy with intravenous amphotericin B or intravenous or oral fluconazole and appropriate surgical procedures are indicated.

A note of caution should be introduced here: although the indwelling catheter does increase the risk of ascending candiduria, it is also a marker for patients who are at risk for disseminated candidiasis from other sources and in whom the observed candiduria may be caused by seeding of the kidney by blood-borne candida.

PREVENTION OF PATIENT-PATIENT TRANSMISSION

Once bacteriuria has developed, its consequences may extend beyond the individual patient. The periurethral bacterial flora, surfaces of the catheter system,[48, 80] and the "persistent, huge reservoir of contaminated urine,"[157] as well as the skin of the patient,[254] are sources for contamination of the hands of medical personnel who may carry the bacteria to other patients.[48, 79–82] Such patient-to-patient transmission leads to clusters of nosocomial bacteriurias; those most often recognized are multiple-drug–resistant nosocomial pathogens such as *Serratia*, *Pseudomonas*, and *Citrobacter* spp.[80, 172, 255–257] Schaberg and associates[257] found that 15% of nosocomial bacteriurias occurred in such clusters. Outbreaks must be recognized to be controlled, so some type of surveillance system, usually targeted at high-risk areas such as intensive care units, should be developed at each institution. Patients transferred from one medical facility to another have been the source of outbreaks in the second institution.[256, 258, 259]

Furthermore, plasmids encoding antibiotic resistance can move among bacteria[78, 254–257, 259, 260]; the transfer of such plasmids has been a phenomenon suspected to occur in urine of catheterized patients.[254, 255, 261] Such conjugation has been demonstrated in vitro in urine held at room temperature for 4 to 8 hours[262]; these are the conditions in the collection bag of the patient with polymicrobial bacteriuria.

To prevent or control such outbreaks, a number of techniques can be used. One is to diminish contact spread by treating the catheterized urinary tract as an open wound,[79] using gloves and washing hands between patients.[81, 82, 163] Antiseptic solutions are necessary to adequately kill gram-negative rods transiently colonizing the hand; bland soap may be inadequate.[81] The transmission of bacteriuric strains is significantly higher between patients in the same room than between those in different rooms;[263] therefore, segregation of catheterized patients in different rooms is suggested.[263, 264] Although not recommended for medical treatment of the individual patient, systemic antimicrobials might be considered for some outbreaks. Additionally, to minimize concentration of organisms in the collection bag, bag antimicrobials or oral methenamine preparations, which result in formaldehyde concentrations in the bag, might be useful.

Oral nonabsorbable antibiotics might diminish intestinal colonization.[265] To limit the number of patients at risk, urethral catheterization and its duration should be minimized and excellent catheter hygiene, maintaining the integrity of the closed catheter system, should be practiced.

NOSOCOMIAL BACTERIURIA NOT ASSOCIATED WITH INSTRUMENTATION

The pathogenesis of the 10% of nosocomial UTIs not associated with any urinary tract instrumentation is not well understood. A partial explanation may be that the natural history of asymptomatic bacteriuria in these patients simply has continued and an episode has occured in the hospital rather than in the community. Boscia and colleagues,[266] studying ambulatory, aged, noncatheterized women, found that 30% were transiently bacteriuric during a 12-month period.[266] These findings may explain why nosocomial UTIs in the absence of instrumentation are significantly associated with increasing age, female gender, and history of previous UTIs.[83] These characteristics define a population group, hospitalized or not, that has a relatively high incidence and prevalence of asymptomatic bacteriuria.

SUMMARY

Nosocomial bacteriuria is the most common infection acquired in both hospitals and nursing homes and is usually associated with catheterization. This infection would be even more common but for the use of the closed catheter system. Most modifications have not improved on the closed catheter itself. However, even with meticulous care, this system will not prevent bacteriuria forever. After bacteriuria develops, the ability to limit its complications is minimal. Additionally, the catheterized urinary tract becomes a reservoir of bacteria that can be transferred to other patients.

Once a catheter is put in place, the clinician must keep two important concepts in mind: keep the catheter system closed to postpone the onset of bacteriuria, and remove the catheter as soon as possible. If the catheter can be removed before bacteriuria develops, postponement becomes prevention.

However, the best prevention is not to use a urethral catheter at all. Other devices are increasingly used. For incontinent men, a condom catheter is a very useful alternative; an analogous device for women would be much welcomed. For patients with urinary retention, intermittent, suprapubic, and possibly intraurethral catheterization may be options for both short-term and long-term needs. The roles of these alternatives to urethral catheters need to be defined by controlled trials.

REFERENCES

1. Haley R, Culver D, White J, et al. The nationwide nosocomial infection rate: A new need for vital statistics. Am J Epidemiol. 1985;121:159–167.
2. Emori T, Banerjee S, Culver D, et al. Nosocomial infections in elderly patients in the United States, 1986–1990. Am J Med. 1991;91:289S–293S.
3. Beck-Sague C, Villarino E, Giuliano D, et al. Infectious diseases and death among nursing home residents: Results of surveillance in 13 nursing homes. Infect Control Hosp Epidemiol. 1994;15:494–496.
4. Stamm WE, Martin SM, Bennett JV. Epidemiology of nosocomial infections due to gram-negative bacilli: Aspects relevant to development and use of vaccines. J Infect Dis. 1977;136S:S151–S160.
5. Hale RW, Hooton TM, Culver DH, et al. Nosocomial infections in U.S. hospitals, 1975–1976: Estimated frequency by selected characteristics of patients. Am J Med. 1981;70:947–959.
6. Krieger JN, Kaiser DL, Wenzel RP. Urinary tract etiology of bloodstream infections in hospitalized patients. J Infect Dis. 1983;148:57–62.
7. Asher EF, Oliver BG, Fry DE. Urinary tract infections in the surgical patient. Am Surg. 1988;54:466–469.
8. Talja M, Korpela A, Järvi K. Comparison of urethral reaction to full silicone, hydrogen-coated and siliconised latex catheters. Br J Urol. 1990;66:652–657.
9. Robertson GS, Everitt N, Burton PR, et al. Effect of catheter material on the incidence of urethral strictures. Br J Urol. 1991;68:612–617.
10. Barnes-Snow E, Luchi R, Doig R. Penile laceration from a Foley catheter. J Am Geriatr Soc. 1985;33:712–714.
11. Clark A. Remarks on catheter fever. Lancet. 1883;1:1075–1077.
12. Foley F. Cystoscopic prostatectomy: A new procedure and instrument. Preliminary report. J Urol. 1929;21:289–306.
13. Kass EH. Asymptomatic infections of the urinary tract. Trans Assoc Am Phys. 1956;69:56.
14. Pyrah LN, Goldie W, Parsons FM, et al. Control of *Pseudomonas pyocyanea* infection in a urological ward. Lancet. 1955;2:314–317.
15. Gillespie WA. Infection in urological patients. Proc R Soc Med. 1956;49:1045–1047.
16. Gillespie WA, Linton KB, Miller A, et al. The diagnosis, epidemiology and control of urinary infection in urology and gynecology. J Clin Pathol. 1960;13:187–194.
17. Gillespie WA, Lennon GG, Linton KB, et al. Prevention of urinary infection in gynecology. B M J. 1964;2:423.
18. Kunin CM, McCormack RC. Prevention of catheter-induced urinary-tract infections by sterile closed drainage. N Engl J Med. 1966;274:1155.
19. Schaeffer AJ, Story KO, Johnson SM. Effect of silver oxide/trichloroisocyanuric acid antimicrobial urinary drainage system on catheter-associated bacteriuria. J Urol. 1988;139:69–73.
20. Thornton GF, Andriole VT. Bacteriuria during indwelling catheter drainage: II. Effect of a closed sterile drainage system. JAMA. 1970;214:339–342.
21. Garibaldi RA, Burke JP, Dickman ML, et al. Factors predisposing to bacteriuria during indwelling urethral catheterization. N Engl J Med. 1974;291:215.
22. Stamm WE. Guidelines for prevention of catheter-associated urinary tract infections. Ann Intern Med. 1975;82:386–390.
23. Warren JW. Host-parasite interactions and host defense mechanisms. In: Schrier RW, Gottschalk CW, eds. Diseases of the Kidney. 6th ed. Boston: Little, Brown; 1997;1:873–893.
24. Cox C, Hinman F Jr. Experiments with induced bacteriuria, vesical emptying and bacterial growth on the mechanism of bladder defense to infection. J Urol. 1961;86:739–748.
25. O'Grady F, Cattell W. Kinetics of urinary tract infection: II. The bladder. Br J Urol. 1966;38:156–162.
26. Norden C, Green G, Kass E. Antibacterial mechanisms of the urinary bladder. J Clin Invest. 1968;47:2689–2700.
27. Orskov I, Ferencz A, Orskov F. Tamm-Horsfall protein or uromucoid is the normal urinary slime that traps Type 1 fimbriated *Escherichia coli*. Lancet. 1980;1:887.
28. Reinhart H, Obedeanu N, Sobel J. Quantitation of Tamm-Horsfall protein binding to uropathogenic *Escherichia coli* and lectins. J Infect Dis. 1990;162:1335–1340.
29. Parkkinen J, Virkola R, Korhonen T. Identification of factors in human urine that inhibit the binding of *Escherichia coli* adhesins. Infect Immun. 1988;56:2623–2630.
30. Shrom S, Parsons C, Mulholland S. Role of urothelial surface mucoprotein in intrinsic bladder defense. Urology. 1977;9:526–533.
31. Parsons C, Mulholland S, Anwar H. Antibacterial activity of bladder surface mucin duplicated by exogenous glycosaminoglycan (heparin). Infect Immun. 1979;24:552–557.
32. Parsons C, Pollen J, Anwar H, et al. Antibacterial activity of bladder surface mucin duplicated in the rabbit bladder by exogenous glycosaminoglycan (sodium pentosanpolysulfate). Infect Immun. 1980;27:876–881.
33. Parsons C, Stauffer C, Schmidt J. Bladder-surface glycosaminoglycans: An efficient mechanism of environmental adaptation. Science. 1980;208:605–607.
34. Parsons C, Stauffer C, Schmidt J. Impairment of antibacterial effect of bladder surface mucin by protamine sulfate. J Infect Dis. 1981;144:180.
35. Gillenwater J, Cardozo N, Tyrone N, et al. Antibacterial activity of rat vesical mucosa. J Urol. 1970;104:687–692.
36. Hand W, Smith J, Sanford J. The antibacterial effect of normal and infected urinary bladder. J Lab Clin Med. 1971;77:605–615.
37. Schlager T, Lohr J, Hendley J. Antibacterial activity of the bladder mucosa. Urol Res. 1993;21:313–317.
38. Elliott T, Slack C, Bishop M. Scanning electron microscopy and bacteriology of the human bladder in acute and chronic urinary tract infections. In: Asscher AW, Brumfitt W, eds. Microbial Diseases in Nephrology. New York: John Wiley & Sons; 1986.
39. Fukushi Y, Orikasa S, Kagayama M. An electron microscopic study of the interaction between vesical epithelium and *E. coli*. Invest Urol. 1979;17:61–68.
40. McTaggart L, Ribgy R, Elliott T. The pathogenesis of urinary tract infections associated with *Escherichia coli, Staphylococcus saprophyticus* and *S. epidermidis*. Med Microbiol. 1990;32:135–141.
41. Orikasa S, Hinman F Jr. Reaction of the vesical wall to bacterial penetration: Resistance to attachment, desquamation, and leukocytic activity. Invest Urol. 1977;15:185–193.
42. Fukushi Y, Orikasa S. The role of intravesical polymorphonuclear leukocytes in experimental cystitis. Invest Urol. 1981;18:471–474.
43. Kantele A, Papunen R, Virtanen E, et al. Antibody-secreting cells in acute urinary tract infection as indicators of local immune response. J Infect Dis. 1994;169:1023–1028.
44. Hjelm E. Local cellular immune response in ascending urinary tract infection: Occurrence of T-cells, immunoglobulin-producing cells, and Ia-expressing cells in rat urinary tract tissue. Infect Immun. 1984;44:627–632.
45. Kurnick J, McCluskey R, Bhan A, et al. *Escherichia coli*–specific T lymphocytes in experimental pyelonephritis. J Immunol. 1988;141:3220–3226.
46. Turck M, Goffe B, Petersdorf RG. The urethral catheter and urinary tract infection. J Urol. 1962;88:834–837.

47. Warren JW, Platt R, Thomas RJ, et al. Antibiotic irrigation and catheter-associated urinary-tract infections. N Engl J Med. 1978;299:570.
48. Rutala WA, Kennedy VA, Loflin HB, et al. *Serratia marcescens* nosocomial infections of the urinary tract associated with urine measuring containers and urinometers. Am J Med. 1981;70:659–663.
49. Weyrauch HM, Bassett JB. Ascending infection in an artificial urinary tract: An experimental study. Stanford Med Bull. 1951;9:25.
50. Nickel JC, Gristina P, Costerton JW. Electron microscopic study of an infected Foley catheter. Can J Surg. 1985;28:50–52.
51. Garibaldi RA, Burke JP, Britt MR, et al. Meatal colonization and catheter-associated bacteriuria. N Engl J Med. 1980;303:316–318.
52. Schaeffer AJ, Chmiel J. Urethral meatal colonization in the pathogenesis of catheter-associated bacteriuria. J Urol. 1983;130:1096–1099.
53. Kunin CM, Steele C. Culture of the surface of urinary catheters to sample urethral flora and study the effect of antimicrobial therapy. J Clin Microbiol. 1985;21:902–908.
54. Daifuku R, Stamm W. Association of rectal and urethral colonization with urinary tract infection in patients with indwelling catheters. JAMA. 1984;252:2028–2030.
55. Hartstein AI, Garber SB, Ward TT, et al. Nosocomial urinary tract infection: A prospective evaluation of 108 catheterized patients. Infect Control. 1981;2:380–386.
56. Bran JL, Levison ME, Kaye D. Entrance of bacteria into the female urinary bladder. N Engl J Med. 1972;286:626.
57. Buckley RM, McGucken M, MacGregor RR. Urine bacterial counts following sexual intercourse. N Engl J Med. 1978;298:321.
58. Stark RP, Maki DG. Bacteriuria in the catheterized patient. What quantitative level of bacteriuria is relevant? N Engl J Med. 1984;311:560–564.
59. Daifuku R, Stamm W. Bacterial adherence to bladder uroepithelial cells in catheter-associated urinary tract infection. N Engl J Med. 1986;314:1208–1213.
60. Mobley HLT, Chippendale MG, Tenney JH, et al. Expression of type 1 fimbriae may be required for persistence of *E. coli* in the catheterized urinary tract. J Clin Microbiol. 1987;25:2253–2257.
61. Mobley HLT, Chipendale GR, Tenney JH, et al. MR/K hemagglutination of *Providencia stuartii* correlates with catheter adherence and with persistence in catheter-associated bacteriuria. J Infect Dis. 1988;157:264–271.
62. Cox AJ, Hukins DWL, Sutton TM. Infection of catheterised patients: Bacterial colonisation of encrusted Foley catheters shown by scanning electron microscopy. Urol Res. 1989;17:349–352.
63. Ladd TI, Schmiel D, Nickel JC, et al. The use of a radiorespirometric assay for testing the antibiotic sensitivity of catheter-associated bacteria. J Urol. 1987;138:1451–1456.
64. Isaacs J, McWhorter D. Foley catheter drainage systems and bladder damage. In: The Surgeon At Work. 889–891.
65. Zimmerli W, Lew PD, Waldvogel FA. Pathogenesis of foreign body infection: Evidence for a local granulocyte defect. J Clin Invest. 1984;73:1191–1200.
66. Zimmerli W, Waldvogel FA, Vaudaux P, et al. Pathogenesis of foreign body infection: Description and characteristics of an animal model. J Infect Dis. 1982;146:487–497.
67. Kostiala AAI, Nyren P, Jokinen EJ, et al. Prospective study on the appearance of antibody-coated bacteria in patients with an indwelling urinary catheter. Nephron. 1981;30:279–285.
68. Hulter H, Borchardt K, Mahood J, et al. Localization of catheter-induced urinary tract infections: Interpretation of bladder washout and antibody-coated bacteria tests. Nephron. 1984;38:48–53.
69. Nyren P, Runeberg L, Kostiala AI, et al. Prophylactic methenamine hippurate or nitrofurantoin in patients with an indwelling urinary catheter. Ann Clin Res. 1981;13:16–21.
70. Warren JW, Mobley HLT, Trifillis AL. Internalization of *Escherichia coli* into human renal tubular epithelial cells. J Infect Dis. 1988;158:221–223.
71. Warren JW, Muncie HL Jr, Hall-Craggs M. Acute pyelonephritis associated with the bacteriuria of long-term catheterization: A prospective clinico-pathological study. J Infect Dis. 1988;158:1341–1346.
72. Bryan C, Reynolds K. Hospital-acquired bacteremic urinary tract infection: Epidemiology and outcome. J Urol. 1984;132:494–498.
73. Gordon D, Bune A, Grime B, et al. Diagnostic criteria and natural history of catheter-associated urinary tract infections after prostatectomy. Lancet. 1983;1:1269–1271.
74. Tribe CR, Silver JR. Renal failure in paraplegia. London: Pitman Medical Publishing; 1969.
75. Warren JW, Muncie HL Jr, Hebel JR, et al. Long-term urethral catheterization increases risk of chronic pyelonephritis and renal inflammation. J Am Geriatr Soc. 1994;42:1286–1290.
76. Donovan WH, Hull R, Cifu DX, et al. Use of plasmid analysis to determine the source of bacterial invasion of the urinary tract. Paraplegia. 1990;28:573–582.
77. Selden R, Lee S, Wang WLL, et al. Nosocomial *Klebsiella* infections: Intestinal colonization as a reservoir. Ann Intern Med. 1971;74:657–664.
78. Brun-Buisson C, Philippon A, Ansquer M, et al. Transferable enzymatic resistance to third-generation cephalosporins during nosocomial outbreak of multiresistant *Klebsiella pneumoniae*. Lancet. 1987;2:302–306.
79. Schaberg DR, Weinstein RA, Stamm WE. Epidemics of nosocomial urinary tract infection caused by multiply resistant gram-negative bacilli: Epidemiology and control. J Infect Dis. 1976;133:363–366.
80. Maki DG, Hennekens CG, Phillips CW, et al. Nosocomial urinary tract infection with *Serratia marcescens*: An epidemiologic study. J Infect Dis. 1973;128:579–587.
81. Ehrenkranz NJ, Alfonso BC. Failure of bland soap handwash to prevent hand transfer of patient bacteria to urethral catheters. Infect Control Hosp Epidemiol. 1991;12:654–662.
82. Casewell M, Phillips I. Hands as route of transmission for *Klebsiella* species. BMJ. 1977;2:1315–1317.
83. Hooton TM, Haley RW, Culver DH, et al. The joint associations of multiple risk factors with the occurrence of nosocomial infection. Am J Med. 1981;70:960–970.
84. Platt R, Polk BF, Murdock B, et al. Risk factors for nosocomial urinary tract infection. Am J Epidemiol. 1986;124:977–985.
85. Shapiro M, Simchen E, Izraeli S, et al. A multivariate analysis of risk factors for acquiring bacteriuria in patients with indwelling urinary catheters for longer than 24 hours. Infect Control. 1984;5:525–532.
86. Hustinx W, Mintjes-de Groot A, Verkooyen R, et al. Impact of concurrent antimicrobial therapy on catheter-associated urnary tract infection. J Hosp Infect. 1991;18:45–56.
87. Burman L, Fryklund B, Nyström B. Use of indwelling urinary tract catheters in Swedish hospitals. Infect Control. 1987;8:507–511.
88. Jain P, Parada JP, David A, et al. Overuse of the indwelling urinary tract catheter in hospitalized medical patients. Arch Intern Med. 1995;155:1425–1429.
89. Garibaldi RA, Mooney BR, Epstein BJ, et al. An evaluation of daily bacteriologic monitoring to identify preventable episodes of catheter-associated urinary tract infection. Infect Control. 1982;3:466–470.
90. Garner J, Jarvis W, Emori T, et al. CDC definitions for nosocomial infections, 1988. J Infect Control. 1988;16:128–140.
91. Morrison AJ, Wenzel RP. Nosocomial urinary tract infections due to *Enterococcus*. Arch Intern Med. 1986;146:1549–1551.
92. Hamory BH, Wenzel RP. Hospital-associated candiduria: Predisposing factors and review of the literature. J Urol. 1978;120:444–448.
93. Siegman-Igra Y, Kulka T, Schwartz D, et al. Polymicrobial and monomicrobial bacteraemic urinary tract infection. J Hosp Infect. 1994;28:49–56.
94. U.S. Department of Health and Human Services. NNIS Manual: National Nosocomial Infections Surveillance System. U.S. Government Printing Office. Washington, DC: Public Health Service, Centers for Disease Control and Prevention; 1988;XIII-5–XIII-9.
95. Warren JW, Muncie HL Jr, Bergquist EJ, et al. Sequelae and management of urinary infection in the patient requiring chronic catheterization. J Urol. 1981;125:1–8.
96. Ramsay J, Garnham A, Mulhall A, et al. Biofilms, bacteria and bladder catheters. Br J Urol. 1989;64:395–398.
97. Musher D, Thorsteinsson S, Airola V II. Quantitative urinalysis: Diagnosing urinary tract infection in men. JAMA. 1976;236:2069–2072.
98. Rubin R, Tolkoff-Rubin N, Cotran R. Urinary tract infection, pyelonephritis, and reflux nephropathy. In: Brenner BM, Rector FC Jr, eds. Brenner and Rector's The Kidney, v. 2. 3rd ed. Philadelphia: WB Saunders, 1986;1085–1141.
99. Lee B, Crossley K, Gerding D. The association between *Staphylococcus aureus* bacteremia and bacteriuria. Am J Med. 1978;65:303–306.
100. Arpi M, Renneberg J. The clinical significance of *Staphylococcus aureus* bacteriuria. J Urol. 1984;697–700.
101. Tambyah PA, Knasinski V, Maki DG. Catheter-associated UTI (CAUTI) is rarely symptomatic and an infrequent cause of nosocomial bloodstream infection (NBSI): A prospective study of 1035 catheterized hospitalized patients. Program and Abstracts of the Infectious Diseases Society of America 35th Annual Meeting. 1997;45:79.
102. Ibrahim AIA. Hospital acquired pre-prostatectomy bacteriuria: Risk factors and implications. East Afr Med J. 1996;73:107–110.
103. Ikaheimo R, Siitonen A, Karkkainen U, et al. Virulence characteristics of *Escherichia coli* in nosocomial urinary tract infection. Clin Infect Dis. 1993;16:785–791.
104. Krieger JN, Kaiser DL, Wenzel RP. Nosocomial urinary tract infections cause wound infections postoperatively in surgical patients. Surg Gynecol Obstet. 1983;156:313–318.
105. Koracevich DS, Faubion WC, Bender JM, et al. Association of parenteral nutrition catheter sepsis with urinary tract infections. JPEN J Parenter Enteral Nutr. 1986;10:639–641.
106. Gross PA, Van Antwerpen C. Nosocomial infections and hospital deaths: A case-control study. Am J Med. 1983;75:658–662.
107. Daschner F, Nadjem H, Langmaack H. Surveillance, prevention and control of hospital-acquired infections. III. Nosocomial infections as cause of death: Retrospective analysis of 1000 autopsy reports. Infection. 1978;6:261–265.
108. Bueno-Cavanillas A, Delgado-Rodriguez M, Lopez-Luque A, et al. Influence of nosocomial infection on mortality rate in an intensive care unit. Crit Care Med. 1994;22:55–60.
109. Platt R, Polk BF, Murdock B, et al. Mortality associated with nosocomial urinary tract infection. N Engl J Med. 1982;307:637.
110. Stamm WE. Catheter-associated urinary tract infections: Epidemiology, pathogenesis, and prevention. Am J Med. 1991;91(Suppl 3B):65S–71S.
111. Martone W, Jarvis W, Culver D, et al. Incidence and nature of endemic and epidemic nosocomial infections. In: Bennett JV, Brachman PS, eds. Endemic and Epidemic Hospital Infections. Boston: Little, Brown 1992;577–594.
112. Garibaldi RA, Brodine S, Matsumiya S. Infections among patients in nursing homes: Policies, prevalence and problems. N Engl J Med. 1981;305:731–735.
113. Kunin CM, Chin QF, Chambers S. Indwelling urinary catheters in the elderly. Am J Med. 1987;82:405–411.
114. Ribeiro BJ, Smith SR. Evaluation of urinary catheterization and urinary incontinence in a general nursing home population. J Am Geriatr Soc. 1985;33:479–482.
115. Warren JW, Steinberg L, Hebel JR, et al. The prevalence of urethral catheterization

in Maryland nursing homes: Estimates for the United States. Arch Intern Med. 1989;149:1535–1537.
116. Warren JW, Damron D, Tanney JH, et al. Fever, bacteremia, and death as complications of bacteriuria in women with long-term urethral catheters. J Infect Dis. 1987;155:1151–1158.
117. Warren JW, Tenney JH, Hoopes JM, et al. A prospective microbiologic study of bacteriuria in patients with chronic indwelling urethral catheters. J Infect Dis. 1982;146:719–723.
118. Steward DK, Wood GL, Cohen RL, et al. Failure of the urinalysis and quantitative urine culture in diagnosing symptomatic urinary tract infections in patients with long-term urinary catheters. Am J Infect Control. 1985;13:154–160.
119. Rahav G, Pinco E, Silbaq F, et al. Molecular epidemiology of catheter-associated bacteriuria in nursing home patients. J Clin Microbiol. 1994;32:1031–1034.
120. Tenney JH, Warren JW. Bacteriuria in women with long-term catheters: Paired comparison of the indwelling and replacement catheter. J Infect Dis. 1988;157:199–202.
121. Warren JW. *Providencia stuartii*: A common cause of antibiotic-resistant bacteriuria in patients with long-term indwelling catheters. Rev Infect Dis. 1986;8:61–67.
122. Bergquist D, Bronnestam R, Hedelin H, et al. The relevance of urinary sampling methods in patients with indwelling Foley catheters. Br J Urol. 1980;52:92–95.
123. Senay H, Goetz MB. Epidemiology of bacteremic urinary tract infections in chronically hospitalized elderly men. J Urol. 1991;145:1201–1204.
124. Alling B, Brandberg A, Seeberg S, et al. Aerobic and anaerobic microbial flora in the urinary tract of geriatric patients during long-term care. J Infect Dis. 1973;127:34–39.
125. McLeod JW, Glasg MB, Mason JM, et al. Survey of the different urinary infections which develop in the paraplegic and their relative significance. Microbiology. 1965;3:124–143.
126. Damron D, Warren J, Chippendale M, et al. Do clinical microbiology laboratories accurately report bacteriology in urine from patients with long-term urinary catheters? J Clin Microbiol. 1986;24:400–404.
127. Rudman D, Hontanosas A, Cohen Z, et al. Clinical correlates of bacteremia in a Veterans Administration extended care facility. J Am Geriatr Soc. 1988;36:726–732.
128. Tenney JH, Warren JW. Long-term catheter-associated bacteriuria: Species at low concentration. Urology. 1987;30:444–446.
129. Ouslander JG, Greengold B, Chen S. Complications of chronic indwelling urinary catheters among male nursing home patients: A prospective study. J Urol. 1987;138:1191–1195.
130. Muder R, Brennen C, Wagener M, et al. Bacteremia in a long-term care facility: A five year prospective study of 163 consecutive episodes. Clin Infect Dis. 1992;14:647–654.
131. Polastri F, Auckenthaler R, Loew F, et al. Absence of significant bacteremia during urinary catheter manipulation in patients with chronic indwelling catheters. J Am Geriatr Soc. 1990;38:1208.
132. Jewes L, Gillespie W, Leadbetter A, et al. Bacteriuria and bacteraemia in patients with long-term indwelling catheters: A domiciliary study. J Med Microbiol. 1988;26:61–65.
133. Kunin CM, Chin QF, Chambers S. Formation of encrustations on indwelling urinary catheters in the elderly: A comparison of different types of catheter materials in "blockers" and "nonblockers." J Urol. 1987;138:899–902.
134. Muncie HL Jr, Warren JW. Reasons for replacement of long-term urethral catheters: Implications for randomized trials. J Urol. 1990;143:507–509.
135. Ohkawa M, Sugata T, Sawaki M, et al. Bacterial and crystal adherence to the surfaces of indwelling urethral catheters. J Urol. 1990;143:717–721.
136. Mobley HLT, Warren JW. Urease-positive bacteriuria and obstruction of long-term urinary catheters. J Clin Microbiol. 1987;25:2216–2217.
137. Kunin CM. Blockage of urinary catheters: Role of microorganisms and constituents of the urine on formation of encrustations. J Clin Epidemiol. 1989;42:835–842.
138. Mobley HLT, Hausinger RP. Microbial ureases: Significance, regulation, and molecular characterization. Microbiol Rev. 1989;53:85–108.
139. Jones B, Mobley H. Genetic and biochemical diversity of ureases of *Proteus*, *Providencia* and *Morganella* species isolated from urinary tract infection. Infect Immun. 1987;55:2198–2203.
140. Mobley HLT, Jones B, Jerse AE. Cloning of urease gene sequences from *Providencia stuartii*. Infect Immun. 1986;54:161–169.
141. Nemoy NJ, Stamey TA. Surgical, bacteriological, and biochemical management of "infection stones." JAMA. 1971;215:1470.
142. Williams HE. Nephrolithiasis. N Engl J Med. 1974;290:33.
143. Takeuchi H, Takayama H, Konishi T, et al. Scanning electron microscopy detects bacteria within infection stones. J Urol. 1984;132:67–69.
144. McLean R, Nickel JC, Noakes VC, et al. An in vitro ultrastructural study of infectious kidney stone genesis. Infect Immun. 1985;49:805–811.
145. Nikakhtar B, Vaziri ND, Khonsari F, et al. Urolithiasis in patients with spinal cord injury. Paraplegia. 1981;19:363–366.
146. Hardy AG. Complications of the indwelling urethral catheter. Paraplegia. 1968;6:5.
147. Dietrick RB, Russi S. Tabulation and review of autopsy findings in fifty-five paraplegics. JAMA. 1958;166:41.
148. Talbot HS. Renal disease and hypertension in paraplegics and quadriplegics. Med Serv J Can. 1966;22:570.
149. Carty M, Brocklehurst J, Carty J. Bacteriuria and its correlates in old age. Gerontology. 1981;27:72–75.
150. Najenson T, Mendelson L, Sabransky H, et al. Upper urinary tract in patients after traumatic spinal cord injury. Paraplegia. 1969;7:85.
151. Donnelly J, Hackler RH, Bunts RC. Present urologic status of the World War II paraplegic: 25-year followup. Comparison with status of the 20-year Korean War paraplegic and 5-year Vietnam paraplegic. J Urol. 1972;108:558.
152. Jousse AT, Wynne-Jones M, Breithaupt DJ. A followup study of life expectancy and mortality in traumatic transverse myelitis. Proceedings of the 16th Veterans Administration Spinal Cord Injury Conference; 1967;198–202.
153. Kaufman JM, Fam B, Jacobs S, et al. Bladder cancer and squamous metaplasia in spinal cord injury patients. J Urol. 1977;118:967–971.
154. Locke JR, Hill DE, Walzer Y. Incidence of squamous cell carcinoma in patients with long-term catheter drainage. J Urol. 1985;133:1034–1035.
155. Garibaldi RA. Hospital-acquired urinary tract infections. In: Wenzel RP, ed. Prevention and Control of Nosocomial Infections. 2nd ed. Baltimore: Williams & Wilkins; 1993:600–613.
156. Wong ES. Guideline for prevention of catheter-associated urinary tract infections. Am J Infect Control. 1983;11:28–36.
157. Kunin CM. Detection, prevention and management of urinary tract infections. 5th ed. Baltimore: Williams & Wilkins; 1997:226–278.
158. Slade N, Gillespie WA. The urinary tract and the catheter: Infection and other problems. New York: John Wiley & Sons, 1985.
159. Schaeffer AJ. Catheter-associated bacteriuria. Urol Clin North Am. 1986;13:735–747.
160. Schaberg DR, Zervos MJ. Nosocomial urinary tract infection. Compr Ther. 1986;12:8–11.
161. Warren JW. Catheter-associated urinary tract infections. Infect Dis Clin North Am. 1997;11:609–622.
162. Nordqvist P, Ekelund P, Edouard L, et al. Catheter-free geriatric care: Routines and consequences for clinical infection, care and economy. J Hosp Infect. 1984;5:298–304.
163. Zimakoff JDA, Pontoppidan B, Larsen SO, et al. The management of urinary catheters: Compliance of practice in Danish hospitals, nursing homes and home care to national guidelines. Scand J Urol Nephrol. 1995;29:299–309.
164. Zimakoff J, Pontoppidan B, Larsen S, et al. Management of urinary bladder function in Danish hospitals, nursing homes and home care. J Hosp Infect. 1993;24:183–199.
165. Fierer J, Ekstrom M. An outbreak of *Providencia stuartii* urinary tract infections: Patients with condom catheters are a reservoir of the bacteria. JAMA. 1981;245:1553–1555.
166. Hirsh DD, Fainstein V, Musher DM. Do condom catheter collecting systems cause urinary tract infection? JAMA. 1979;242:340–341.
167. Montgomerie JZ, Morrow JW. *Pseudomonas* colonization in patients with spinal cord injury. Am J Epidemiol. 1978;108:328–336.
168. Ouslander JG, Greengold BA, Silverblatt FJ, et al. An accurate method to obtain urine for culture in men with external catheters. Arch Intern Med. 1987;147:286–288.
169. Nicolle LE, Harding GKM, Kennedy J, et al. Urine specimen collection with external devices for diagnosis of bacteriuria in elderly incontinent men. J Clin Microbiol. 1988;26:1115–1119.
170. Ouslander JG, Greengold B, Chen S. Complications of chronic indwelling urinary catheters among male nursing home patients: A prospective study. J Urol. 1987;138:1191–1195.
171. Ouslander J, Greengold B, Chen S. External catheter use and urinary tract infections among incontinent male nursing home patients. J Am Geriatr Soc. 1987;35:1063–1070.
172. Shlaes DM, Currie CA. Endemic gentamicin resistance R factors on a spinal cord injury unit. J Clin Microbiol. 1983;18:236–241.
173. Golji H. Complications of external condom drainage. Paraplegia. 1981;19:189–197.
174. Jayachandran S, Mooppan U, Kim H. Complications from external (condom) urinary drainage devices. Urology. 1985;25:31–34.
175. Melekos M, Asbach HW. Complications from urinary condom catheters. Urology. 1986;27:88.
176. Steinhardt G, McRoberts JW. Total distal penile necrosis caused by condom catheter. JAMA. 1980;244:1238–1244.
177. Bakke A. Physical and psychological complications in patients treated with clean intermittent catheterization. Scand J Urol Nephrol Suppl. 1993;150:1–61.
178. Guttmann L, Frankel H. The value of intermittent catheterization in the early management of traumatic paraplegia and tetraplegia. Paraplegia. 1966;4:63.
179. Webb RJ, Lawson AL, Neal DE. Clean intermittent self-catheterisation in 172 adults. Br J Urol. 1990;65:20–23.
180. King RB, Carlson CE, Mervine J, et al. Clean and sterile intermittent catheterization methods in hospitalized patients with spinal cord injury. Arch Phys Med Rehabil. 1992;73:798–802.
181. Duffy LM, Cleary J, Ahern S, et al. Clean intermittent catheterization: Safe, cost-effective bladder management for male residents of VA nursing homes. J Am Geriatr Soc. 1995;43:865–870.
182. Van Den Broek PJ, Dahha TJ, Mouton RP. Bladder irrigation with povidone-iodine in prevention of urinary-tract infections associated with intermittent urethral catheterization. Lancet. 1985;11:563–565.
183. Kuhlemeier K, Stover S, Lloyd L. Prophylactic antibacterial therapy for preventing urinary tract infections in spinal cord injury patients. J Urol. 1985;134:514–517.
184. Pearman JW, Bailey M, Riley LP. Bladder instillations of trisdine compared with catheter introducer for reduction of bacteriuria during intermittent catheterisation of patients with acute spinal cord trauma. Br J Urol. 1991;67:483–490.
185. Mohler JL, Cowen DL, Flanigan RC. Suppression and treatment of urinary tract infection in patients with an intermittently catheterized neurogenic bladder. J Urol. 1987;138:336–340.

186. Krebs M, Halvorsen R, Fishman I, et al. Prevention of urinary tract infection during intermittent catheterization. J Urol. 1983;131:82–85.
187. Pearman JW. Urological follow-up of 99 spinal cord injured patients initially managed by intermittent catheterisation. Br J Urol. 1976;48:297.
188. Wyndaele J-J, Maes D. Clean intermittent self-catheterization: A 12-year followup. J Urol. 1990;143:906–908.
189. Diokno A, Sonda L, Hollander J, et al. Fate of patients started on clean intermittent self-catheterization therapy 10 years ago. J Urol. 1983;129:1120–1122.
190. Michelson JD, Lotke PA, Steinberg ME. Urinary-bladder management after total joint-replacement surgery. N Engl J Med. 1988;319:321–326.
191. Skelly JM, Guyatt GH, Kalbfleisch R, et al. Management of urinary retention after surgical repair of hip fracture. Can Med Assoc J. 1992;146:1185–1189.
192. Hodgkinson CP, Hodari AA. Trocar suprapubic cystostomy for postoperative bladder drainage in the female. Am J Obstet Gynecol. 1966;96:773–783.
193. Horgan AF, Prasad B, Waldron DJ, et al. Acute urinary retention: Comparison of suprapubic and urethral catheterisation. Br J Urol. 1992;70:149–151.
194. Dinneen MD, Wetter LA, May AR. Urethral strictures and aortic surgery: Suprapubic rather than urethral catheters. Eur J Vasc Surg. 1990;4:535–538.
195. Hammarsten J, Lindqvist K, Sunzel H. Urethral strictures following transurethral resection of the prostate: The role of the catheter. Br J Urol. 1989;63:397–400.
196. Hammarsten J, Lindqvist K. Suprapubic catheter following transurethral resection of the prostate: A way to decrease the number of urethral strictures and improve the outcome of operations. J Urol. 1992;147:648–652.
197. Andersen JT, Heisterberg L, Hebjorn S, et al. Suprapubic versus transurethral bladder drainage after colposuspension/vaginal repair. Acta Obstet Gynecol Scand. 1985;64:139–143.
198. Schiøtz HA, Malme PA, Tanbo TG. Urinary tract infections and asymptomatic bacteriuria after vaginal plastic surgery: A comparison of suprapubic and transurethral catheters. Acta Obstet Gynecol Scand. 1989;68:453–435.
199. O'Kelly TJ, Mathew A, Ross S, et al. Optimum method for urinary drainage in major abdominal surgery: A prospective randomized trial of suprapubic *versus* urethral catheterization. Br J Surg. 1995;82:1367–1368.
200. Nielsen KK, Klarskov P, Nordling J, et al. The intraprostatic spiral: New treatment for urinary retention. Br J Urol. 1990;65:500–503.
201. Nissenkorn I, Richter S, Slutzker D. A simple, self-retaining intraurethral catheter for treatment of prostatic obstruction. Eur Urol. 1990;18:286–289.
202. Mansson W, Colleen S, Mardh P-A. The microbial flora of the continent cecal urinary reservoir, its stoma and the peristomal skin. J Urol. 1986;135:247–250.
203. Hill MJ, Hudson MJ, Stewart M. The urinary bacterial flora in patients with three types of urinary tract diversion. J Med Microbiol. 1983;16:221–226.
204. Koch MO, McDougal WS, Hall MC, et al. Long-term metabolic effects of urinary diversion: A comparison of myelomeningocele patients managed by clean intermittent catheterization and urinary diversion. J Urol. 1992;147:1343–1347.
205. Platt R, Murdock B, Polk BF, et al. Reduction of mortality associated with nosocomial urinary tract infection. Lancet. 1983;1:1893–1897.
206. DeGroot-Kosolcharoen J, Guse R, Jones JM. Evaluation of a urinary catheter with a preconnected closed drainage bag. Infect Control Hosp Epidemiol. 1988;9:72–76.
207. Huth TS, Burke JP, Larsen RA, et al. Clinical trial of junction seals for the prevention of urinary catheter-associated bacteriuria. Arch Intern Med. 1992;152:807–812.
208. Burke J, Larsen R, Stevens L. Nosocomial bacteriuria: Estimating the potential for prevention by closed sterile urinary drainage. Infect Control. 1986;7:96–99.
209. Irani, J, Fauchery A, Dore B, et al. Systematic removal of catheter 48 hours following transurethral resection and 24 hours following transurethral incision of prostate: A prospective randomized analysis of 213 patients. J Urol. 1995;153:1537–1539.
210. Carapeti EA, Bentley PG, Andrews SM. Randomized study of sterile *versus* non-sterile urethral catheterization. Ann R Coll Surg Engl. 1994;76:59–60.
211. Schiotz HA. Antiseptic catheter gel and urinary tract infection after short-term postoperative catheterization in women. Arch Gynecol Obstet. 1996;258:97–100.
212. Bastable JRG, Peel RN, Birch DM, et al. Continuous irrigation of the bladder after prostatectomy: Its effect on post-prostatectomy infection. Br J Urol. 1977;49: 689–693.
213. Savage, JE, Phillips B, Lifshitz S, et al. Bacteriuria in closed bladder drainage versus continuous irrigation in patients undergoing intracavitary radium for treatment of gynecologic cancer. Gynecol Oncol. 1982;13:26.
214. Gillespie W, Jones J, Teasdale C, et al. Does the addition of disinfectant to urine drainage bags prevent infection in catheterized patients? Lancet. 1983;1:1037–1039.
215. Sweet DE, Goodpasture HC, Holl K, et al. Evaluation of H_2O_2 prophylaxis of bacteriuria in patients with long-term indwelling Foley catheters: A randomized controlled study. Infect Control. 1985;6:263–266.
216. Thompson RL, Haley CE, Searcy MA, et al. Catheter-associated bacteriuria: Failure to reduce attack rates using periodic instillations of a disinfectant into urinary drainage systems. JAMA. 1984;251:747–751.
217. Maizels M, Schaeffer AJ. Decreased incidence of bacteriuria associated with periodic instillations of hydrogen peroxide into the urethral catheter drainage bag. J Urol. 1980;123:841–845.
218. Al-Juburi AZ, Cicmanec J. New apparatus to reduce urinary drainage associated with urinary tract infections. Urology. 1989;33:97–101.
219. Kunin CM: The drainage bag additive saga. Infect Control. 1985;6:261–262.
220. Martinez-Martinez L, Pascual A, Perea E. Effect of three plastic catheters on survival and growth of *Pseudomonas aeruginosa*. J Hosp Infect. 1990;16:311–318.
221. Bibby J, Cox A, Hukins DW. Feasibility of preventing encrustation of urinary catheters. Cells and Materials. 1995;2:183–195.
222. Johnson J, Berggren T, Conway A. Activity of nitrofurazone matrix urinary catheter against catheter-associated uropathogens. Antimicrob Agents Chemother. 1993;2033–2036.
223. Lundeberg T. Prevention of catheter-associated urinary-tract infections by use of silver-impregnated catheters. Lancet. 1986;2:1031.
224. Liedberg H, Lundeberg T. Silver alloy coated catheters reduce catheter-associated bacteriuria. Br J Urol. 1990;65:379–381.
225. Liedberg H, Lundeberg T, Ekman P. Refinements in the coating of urethral catheters reduces the incidence of catheter-associated bacteriuria. Eur Urol. 1990;17: 236–240.
226. Johnson JR, Roberts PL, Olsen RJ, et al. Prevention of catheter-associated urinary tract infection with a silver oxide-coated urinary catheter: Clinical and microbiologic correlates. J Infect Dis. 1990;162:1145–1150.
227. Riley D, Classen D, Stevens L, et al. A large randomized clinical trial of a silver-impregnated urinary catheter: Lack of efficacy and staphylococcal superinfection. Am J Med. 1995;98:349–356.
228. Classen DC, Larsen RA, Burke JP, et al. Daily meatal care for prevention of catheter-associated bacteriuria: Results using frequent applications of polyantibiotic cream. Infect Control Hosp Epidemiol. 1991;12:157–162.
229. Huth TS, Burke JP, Larsen RA, et al. Randomized trial of meatal care with silver sulfadiazine cream for the prevention of catheter-associated bacteriuria. J Infect Dis. 1992;165:14–18.
230. Britt MR, Garibaldi RA, Miller WA, et al. Antimicrobial prophylaxis for catheter-associated bacteriuria. Antimicrob Agents Chemother. 1977;11:240.
231. Mountokalakis T, Skounakis M, Tselentis J. Short-term versus prolonged systemic antibiotic prophylaxis in patients treated with indwelling catheters. J Urol. 1985;134:506–508.
232. Warren JW, Anthony WC, Hoopes JM, et al. Cephalexin for susceptible bacteriuria in afebrile, long-term catheterized patients. JAMA. 1982;248:454–458.
233. Sweet DE, Goodpasture HC, Holl K, et al. Evaluation of H_2O_2 prophylaxis of bacteriuria in patients with long-term indwelling Foley catheters: A randomized controlled study. Infect Control. 1985;6:263–266.
234. Bjork DT, Pelletier LL, Tight R. Urinary tract infections with antibiotic resistant organisms in catheterized nursing home patients. Infect Control. 1984;5:173–176.
235. Harding GKM, Nicolle LE, Ronald AR, et al. How long should catheter-acquired urinary tract infection in women be treated? A randomized controlled study. Ann Intern Med. 1991;114:713–719.
236. Hoopes J, Muncie H, Warren J, et al. Once-daily irrigation of long-term urethral catheters with normal saline: Lack of benefit. Arch Intern Med. 1989;149:441–443.
237. Norrman K, Wibell L. Treatment with methenamine hippurate in the patient with a catheter. J Int Med Res. 1976;4:115–117.
238. Wibell L, Scheynius A, Norrman K. Methenamine-hippurate and bacteriuria in the geriatric patient with a catheter. Acta Med Scand. 1980;207:469–473.
239. Norberg A, Norberg B, Parkhede U, et al. Randomized double-blind study of prophylactic methenamine hippurate treatment of patients with indwelling catheters. Eur J Clin Pharmacol. 1980;18:497–500.
240. Peloquin C, Cumbo T, Schentag J. Kinetics and dynamics of tobramycin action in patients with bacteriuria given single doses. Antimicrob Agents Chemother. 1991;35:1191–1195.
241. Kumazawa J, Matsumoto T. The dipstick test in the diagnosis of UTI and the effect of pretreatment catheter exchange in catheter-associated UTI. Infection 20. 1992;3:S157–S159.
242. Febore N, Silva V, Medeiros EA. Microbiological characteristics of yeasts isolated from urinary tracts of intensive care unit patients undergoing urinary catheterization. J Clin Microbiol. 1999;37:1584–1586.
243. Bonsema D, Adams, J, Pallares R, et al. Secular trends in rates and etiology of nosocomial urinary tract infections at a university hospital. J Urol. 1993;150: 414–416.
244. Goldberg P, Kozinn P, Wise G, et al. Incidence and significance of candiduria. JAMA. 1979;241:582–584.
245. Jacobs L, Skidmore E, Freeman K, et al. Oral fluconazole compared with bladder irrigation with amphotericin B for treatment of fungal urinary tract infections in elderly patients. Clin Infect Dis. 1996;22:30–35.
246. Sobel JD, McKinsey D, Zervos M, et al. Candiduria: A randomized, double blind study of treatment with fluconazole and placebo. Ann Intern Med. 1999. In press.
247. Edwards JE Jr, Bodey GP, Bowden RA, et al. International conference for the development of a consensus on the management and prevention of severe candidal infections. Clin Infect Dis. 1997;25:43–59.
248. Wong-Beringer A, Jacobs R, Guglielmo J. Treatment of funguria. JAMA. 1992;267:2780–2785.
249. Sanford J. The enigma of candiduria: Evolution of bladder irrigation with amphotericin B for management from anecdote to dogma and a lesson from Machiavelli. Clin Infect Dis. 1993;16:145–147.
250. Nassoura Z, Ivtury R, Simon R, et al. Candiduria as an early marker of disseminated infection in critically ill surgical patients: The role of fluconazole therapy. J Trauma. 1993;35:290–295.
251. Wainstein M, Graham R, Resnick M. Predisposing factors of systemic fungal infections of the genitourinary tract. J Urol. 1995;154:160–163.
252. Fisher J, Mayhall G, Duma R, et al. Fungus balls of the urinary tract. South Med J. 1979;72:1281–1284.
253. Ang BSP, Telenti A, King B, et al. Candidemia from a urinary tract source: Microbiological aspects and clinical significance. Clin Infect Dis. 1993;17: 662–666.
254. Casewell MW, Phillips I. Aspects of the plasmid-mediated antibiotic resistance and epidemiology of *Klebsiella* species. Am J Med. 1981;70:459–462.

255. Shlaes DM, Lehman M-H, Currie-McCumber CA, et al. Prevalence of colonization with antibiotic resistant gram-negative bacilli in a nursing home care unit: The importance of cross-colonization as documented by plasmid analysis. Infect Control. 1986;7:538–545.
256. Penner JL, Hinton NA, Hamilton LJ, et al. Three episodes of nosocomial urinary tract infections caused by one O-serotype of *Providencia stuartii*. J Urol. 1981;125:668–671.
257. Schaberg DR, Haley RW, Highsmith AK, et al. Nosocomial bacteriuria: A prospective study of case clustering and antimicrobial resistance. Ann Intern Med. 1980;93:420–424.
258. Bjork DT, Pelletier LL, Tight R. Urinary tract infections with antibiotic resistant organisms in catheterized nursing home patients. Infect Control. 1984;5:173–176.
259. Schaberg DR, Alford RH, Anderson R, et al. An outbreak of nosocomial infection due to multiply resistant *Serratia marcescens*: Evidence of interhospital spread. J Infect Dis. 1976;134:181–188.
260. Rubens CE, Farrar WE Jr, McGee ZA, et al. Evolution of a plasmid mediating resistance to multiple antimicrobial agents during a prolonged epidemic of nosocomial infections. J Infect Dis. 1981;143:170–181.
261. Thompkins LS, Plorde JJ, Falkow S. Molecular analysis of R-factors from multiresistant nosocomial isolates. J Infect Dis. 1980;141:625–636.
262. Schaberg DR, Highsmith AK, Wachsmith IK. Resistance plasmid transfer by *Serratia marcescens* in urine. Antimicrob Agents Chemother. 1977;11:449–450.
263. Fryklund B, Haeggman S, Burman LG. Transmission of urinary bacterial strains between patients with indwelling catheters: Nursing in the same room and in separate rooms compared. J Hosp Infect. 1997;36:147–153.
264. Maki D, Hennekens C, Bennet J. Prevention of catheter-associated urinary tract infection. JAMA. 1972;221:1270–1271.
265. Vollaard E, Clasener H, Zambon J, et al. Prevention of catheter-associated gram-negative bacilluria with norfloxacin by selective decontamination of the bowel and high urinary concentration. J Antimicrob Chemother. 1989;23:915–922.
266. Boscia JA, Kobasa WD, Knight RA, et al. Epidemiology of bacteriuria in an elderly ambulatory population. Am J Med. 1986;80:208–214.

Chapter 295

Nosocomial Hepatitis and Other Infections Transmitted by Blood and Blood Products

KENT A. SEPKOWITZ

NOSOCOMIAL HEPATITIS

The potential for blood-borne transmission of hepatitis B was first noted in 1885, when Lurman described jaundice in factory workers who had received smallpox vaccination prepared from "human lymph."[1] More reports appeared in the 1930s and 1940s, when human serum was used to vaccinate against such infections as measles,[1] yellow fever,[2–5] mumps,[6] and polio.[7] In addition, more frequent use of phlebotomy equipment,[8] insulin therapy,[9] and intramuscular injection of penicillin for syphilis[10] led to small outbreaks of jaundice, ascribed to a transmissible "icterogenic" agent.

By the late 1940s, studies to clarify the modes of transmission were undertaken. Central to these was the use of human volunteers who were given putatively infectious material intradermally, intranasally, or by ingestion of feces and then observed for development of jaundice.[1, 11–15] From this landmark work arose our current understanding of the basic principles of transmission of serum and of infectious hepatitis.

The first report of occupational disease in health care workers (HCWs) was provided by Leibowitz and colleagues,[16] who described a blood bank nurse who sustained frequent needle pricks on her hands and fingers. There soon followed a spate of similar reports describing occupationally acquired hepatitis among nurses, blood bank workers, phlebotomists, and house staff, among others.[17–19] Soon, the workers' compensation boards of certain states ruled that viral hepatitis was a compensable occupational hazard.[19] Improved understanding of routes of transmission, more comprehensive and rigorous infection control including needle disposal, and, for hepatitis B, vaccination of workers at risk have helped to decrease, but not eliminate, this occupational risk. In addition, transmission of hepatitis B[20, 21] and hepatitis C[22] from HCWs to patients continues. The Centers for Disease Control and Prevention (CDC) has published guidelines for infection control in health care personnel.[23]

Fecal-Oral Transmission

Hepatitis A

Epidemiology

Cases of hepatitis A virus (HAV) infection gradually increased in the United States in the 1980s, peaking in 1989.[24] Common risk factors have traditionally included contact with a case (26%), employment or attendance at a daycare center (14%), and injecting drug use (11%).[24] More than a third of the U.S. population has antibody against HAV, similar to the prevalence among HCWs (35 to 54%).[25–27] A few reports have suggested ongoing occupational risk: in one, nurses older than 30 years of age had significantly higher rates of HAV antibody than office workers,[26] and in another, cleaning personnel had a high rate.[27] However, most series demonstrate no occupation-specific risk.[28]

Reported Outbreaks

Nosocomial transmission of hepatitis A most commonly occurs via the fecal-oral route, although transfusion-associated cases have also been described.[29] The majority of reports are from pediatric or neonatal intensive care units.[30–36] In one, a neonate who acquired HAV via transfusion spread disease to 10 (16%) of 61 susceptible nurses[32] (Table 295–1). In another, an HAV-infected child who, because of an immune defect, could not mount antibody to HAV remained undiagnosed for a protracted period, transmitting HAV to 15 of 102 staff members.[36] Adults with diarrhea have also transmitted disease to workers.[37, 38]

Despite appropriate infection control measures, HAV in a burn unit spread to 11 (19%) of 59 susceptible nurses.[35] Eating on the hospital ward was the most important risk factor. Other hospital outbreaks have also resulted from consumption of contaminated food, including orange juice[39] and sandwiches.[40] The latter report included 66 clinical or subclinical cases.[40]

Intervention

Administration of intramuscular immune globulin to contacts has been used effectively for many years[28] (see Table 295–1). Current Advisory Committee on Immunization Practices recommendations for vaccinations of health care workers consider that vaccination with newly available vaccines for hepatitis A "is or might be" indicated.[28] Currently, few employee health services routinely provide the vaccine.

Hepatitis E

Many outbreaks of hepatitis E, which is responsible for the majority of non-A, non-B hepatitis transmitted by the fecal-oral route, have occurred in communities in developing countries. However, nosocomial transmission has not been described from the West. Early reports[41] suggested increased seroprevalence among dialysis patients and intravenous drug users,[42] suggesting potential blood-borne transmission. However, subsequent studies from Spain, France, Sweden, and other European countries[43] demonstrated no increased seroprevalence among dialysis patients. Rather, the elevated seroprevalence in the preliminary studies was considered a consequence of the confounding effect of age[43] (see Table 295–1).

TABLE 295–1 Nosocomial Hepatitis: Transmission Rates and Interventions

Hepatitis	Outbreak or Needlestick Exposure Transmission Rate (%)	Prevention	Comment
A	10–30	Vaccine not routinely given Immune globulin in outbreak setting	ACIP advises vaccine "is or might be" indicated
B			
e Ag^-	3	HBV vaccination HBIG if appropriate	HB_SAg prevalence in U.S. dialysis units: 1.1% (patients) and 0.4% (staff)
e Ag^+	20–40	HBV vaccination HBIG if appropriate	
C	1–10	Immunoglobulin not recommended No known prophylaxis or therapy	Prevalence in U.S. dialysis units: >10% (patients) and 1–2% (staff)
Delta	Unknown rate; outbreaks described only in dialysis units	HBV vaccination	Segregate HB_SAg-positive dialysis patients by delta antibody status
E	None described	Unknown	Probably no increased seroprevalence among dialysis patients
G	None described	Unknown	Clinical implications of HGV seropositivity unknown

Abbreviations: ACIP, Advisory Committee on Immunization Practices; Ag, antigen; HBV, hepatitis B virus; HBIG, hepatitis B immune globulin; HB_SAg, hepatitis B surface antigen; HGV, hepatitis G virus.

Blood-Borne Transmission

Hepatitis B

Epidemiology

Hepatitis B was the first blood-borne disease recognized to pose occupational risk.[16–19] An early review found a preponderance of cases among pathologists, laboratory workers, and blood bank workers, alerting investigators to the risk of blood exposure.[17] Vaccine to prevent hepatitis B infection became available in the United States in 1982, resulting in a recommendation from the Advisory Committee on Immunization Practices that health care workers at occupational risk receive vaccine.[44] The plasma-derived vaccine, however, proved unpopular because of (unfounded) safety concerns.

In 1987, growing attention to potential nosocomial spread of the human immunodeficiency virus (HIV) led the Department of Labor, in conjunction with Health and Human Services, to recommend "universal precautions" to protect against exposure to body fluids.[23, 28, 44] Finally, in 1991, the Occupational Safety and Health Administration published the Federal Blood Borne Pathogens Standard, which went into effect in early 1992.[45] This mandated that all HCWs with potential exposure to blood or other potentially infectious materials either be offered the hepatitis B vaccine series free of charge, demonstrate immunity to hepatitis B, or formally decline vaccination.[45] Compliance with this recommendation has resulted in decreased rates of occupationally acquired hepatitis B.[44, 46–48]

Despite these regulations, the CDC estimated that in 1993, 1450 HCWs became infected with hepatitis B virus (HBV) after occupational exposure.[28] Another CDC estimate placed the incidence in 1994 at 1012 HCWs.[49] Although this is an alarming number, it represents a 90% decrease compared with 1985, when vaccination programs had just been introduced.[28] According to the natural history of HBV, up to 10% of newly infected persons become chronic carriers for hepatitis B surface antigen (HB_sAg), and among carriers, the lifetime risk of fatal complications of cirrhosis is about 20% and of fatal hepatoma is 6%.[49] Using these estimates, the CDC projected that 100 to 200 HCWs die annually because of complications of occupationally acquired HBV.[28] Another analysis suggested that 22 HCWs would die because of occupational HBV infections acquired in 1994.[49]

Seroprevalence

In general, HCWs have a seroprevalence two to four times higher (6 to 15%) than that of the U.S. general population (<5%).[29, 50] Among HCWs, dentists, physicians, laboratory workers, dialysis workers, cleaning service employees, and nurses[29, 50–68] have the highest prevalence. In addition, workers in facilities for the chronically mentally handicapped have increased seroprevalence.[69–71] Differences in seroprevalence are related to extent of exposure to blood rather than frequency of contact with patients.[50, 72] Assessment of risk among medical students,[73–75] dentists,[76] and surgeons[77–79] continues.

Incidence

Before the availability of vaccine, the incidence of hepatitis B was 5 to 10 times increased among physicians and dentists and more than 10 times increased among surgeons, dialysis workers, those caring for the mentally handicapped, and laboratory workers with blood exposure.[44, 56, 67]

The risk of transmission from a single needlestick exposure varies according to the e antigen status of the source case: 1 to 6% for e antigen–negative blood versus 22 to 40% for e antigen–positive blood[50, 80, 81] (see Table 295–1). Occupationally acquired e antigen–negative infection may rarely cause fulminant disease.[82] Transmission rates for mucocutaneous and other exposures are not known but are presumably lower. Not all cases of hepatitis B transmission are explained by specific exposures, suggesting other modes of spread.[50, 83, 84] Environmental contamination is strongly suggested by the high prevaccination seroprevalence among dialysis patients and personnel.[50, 60, 85–87] The quality-adjusted loss of life expectancy is similar for a single exposure involving a source case with HBsAg and one with HIV.[88, 89]

A CDC study documented a decreased incidence of occupational hepatitis B among U.S. HCWs from 386 per 100,000 in 1983 to 9.1 per 100,000 in 1995.[44] In addition, the rate in the U.S. general population declined from 122 to 50 per 100,000 in the same interval. A similar decrease has been described from the Czech Republic, which implemented a mandatory vaccination program in 1986 despite limited resources and ongoing political turmoil.[90] Between 1982 and 1995, rates decreased sharply, from 174 to 17 per 100,000 among all HCWs. The reduction among "higher risk" workers, including phlebotomists, laboratory workers, infectious disease staff, and others, was even more dramatic: 587 per 100,000 in 1982 to 23 per 100,000 in 1995.

In some countries, nosocomial transmission continues to account for a significant proportion of overall hepatitis rates.[91, 92] In addition, outbreaks related to such devices as the spring-loaded finger stick device,[93, 94] endoscopy devices,[95] acupuncture needles,[96] multidose medication vials,[97] and jet injections[98] have been reported.

Reported Transmissions

Worker-to-Patient Transmission. From 1972 to 1997, at least 47 instances of HCW-to-patient transmission of hepatitis B were reported from Western countries, resulting in more than 400 secondary cases (range 1 to 55 secondary cases per source case).[20, 21, 99–103] In a series of 10 clusters reported from the United Kingdom, the transmission rate ranged from 0.3 to 9%.[102, 103] At least 42 of the 47 HCWs were dentists or surgeons. No cases of transmission from dentists have been reported since 1987, suggesting that universal precautions and worker vaccination have been effective in limiting risk in this setting.[103] In response to this issue, in 1991, the CDC promulgated recommendations for preventing transmission of HIV and HBV to patients during exposure-prone invasive procedures.[104] Some have thought the recommendations too restrictive.[105]

In an outbreak in Los Angeles, 19 (13%) of 144 susceptible patients became infected from an e antigen–positive thoracic surgery resident.[20] This occurred despite appropriate infection control techniques. Molecular analysis of 13 available strains showed identity with the surgeon's strain. Examination of his surgical technique suggested that small cuts in his fingers, sustained by tying sutures, led to exposure of patients' open wounds to his blood. The index case had chosen to decline hepatitis B vaccine 2 years before himself becoming infected as the result of an occupational exposure.

In most but not all instances, the source worker has been HBV e antigen positive. In a series of transmissions from four different surgeons to at least four separate patients,[21] each surgeon was e antigen negative. The cases occurred in England, where restriction of e antigen–positive surgeons (principally cardiothoracic, gynecologic, orthopedic, and abdominal) is strictly enforced. Investigation of the transmission was greatly enhanced by HBV DNA sequencing of both putative source and secondary cases, which demonstrated near homology. This led to a recommendation that a history of any surgery in the previous 6 months of illness be included as a routine question for patients newly identified with HBV. Such an approach also demonstrates that the introduction of a novel technique—molecular typing—may reveal previously undiscerned transmission and force a reconsideration of current policy, although the United Kingdom has not revised restriction policies on the basis of this report.

Patient-to-Worker Transmission. Widespread transmission from a single patient to several HCWs has rarely been reported.[106] In one instance, a patient in the preclinical window period for hepatitis B sustained severe trauma and underwent several surgeries. At least four HCWs, including nurses and physicians, developed acute hepatitis that was temporally consistent with transmission from the putative source case.

Dialysis Setting. For many years, dialysis patients and staff were at high risk for nosocomial transmission of hepatitis B,[60, 85–87] given the frequency of blood exposure via sharp injury or mucocutaneous exposure (5 per 10,000 dialysis procedures[107]), the high titers of HBV in blood ($\geq 10^9$/ml), and the ability of HBV to survive well in the environment.[108] However, with segregation of patients by room, staff, and machine according to surface antigen status; institution of active vaccination programs; monthly serologic testing of susceptible patients; and attention to disinfection, equipment, and cleaning procedures,[108] this rate has decreased sharply. In a classic study from the CDC spanning 1976 to 1983, before the availability of vaccine, the incidence of new surface antigen among patients decreased from 3 to 0.5% and the prevalence from 7.8 to 2.4%. In the same period, the incidence among staff decreased from 2.6% to 0.5%.[109] Follow-up studies have shown continued improvement[86, 87] (see Table 295–1).

Application of this approach has contributed to a remarkable reduction in risk for patients and staff alike, although outbreaks continue in centers that fail to identify HBV-infected patients, that share staff and equipment, or that fail to vaccinate susceptible patients.[108] It is a model of a multifaceted approach to controlling nosocomial spread. In many dialysis centers, the once large risk of nosocomial hepatitis B has been replaced by similar problems with nosocomial hepatitis C (see later).

Interventions and Management

Management of exposed or susceptible workers has been well summarized in several documents[23, 28, 81, 110–113] (Table 295–2). Intramuscular hepatitis B immune globulin (HBIG) was the original intervention for postexposure prophylaxis.[114–118] It is still used in conjunction with initiation of a vaccine series in a postexposure circumstance for unvaccinated HCWs and vaccine nonresponders.[23, 28, 81, 119] Treatment should be given within 24 hours after exposure. Vaccine nonresponders should receive a second dose 1 month later (HBIG dose 0.06 ml/kg).[28, 119] Vaccine and HBIG may be given at the same time but should be administered with separate needles and syringes and at separate anatomic sites.[28, 81] Plain immune globulin does not contain sufficient titers of HBIG and should not be given.[119]

The introduction of plasma-derived vaccine for hepatitis B in the early 1980s and a recombinant form in 1990 profoundly changed the epidemiology of hepatitis B.[44, 120] Several series have shown significant decreases in rates of hepatitis B, including those among HCWs, which will translate to fewer deaths related to the long-term complications of hepatitis B.[44, 46, 47] Both failure to seroconvert after vaccination and HCW declination of vaccination contribute to the continued susceptibility of many HCWs to this occupational disease.

The durability of vaccine-induced immunity is not known.[44, 121, 122] Vaccine-induced antibody predictably wanes in many initial responders. However, in longitudinal reports to date, persons with waning antibody (to a level below 10 mIU/ml) have not developed active clinical hepatitis.[44, 122] Rather, those newly infected develop core antibody with subclinical disease; in addition, none have progressed to chronic complications.[122] Therefore, the CDC does not recommend routine revaccination of HCWs or patients, except for dialysis patients.[23, 28]

Because of cost, the CDC does not recommend routine prevacci-

TABLE 295–2 Recommended Postexposure Prophylaxis for Percutaneous or Permucosal Exposure to Hepatitis B Virus, United States

Vaccination and Antibody Response Status of Exposed Person	Treatment When Source Is		
	HB_sAg Positive	*HB_sAg Negative*	*Not Tested or Status Unknown*
Unvaccinated	HBIG* × 1; initiate HB vaccine series	Initiate HB vaccine series	Initiate HB vaccine series
Previously vaccinated:			
Known responder†	No treatment	No treatment	No treatment
Known nonresponder	HBIG × 2 or HBIG × 1 and initiate revaccination	No treatment	If known high-risk source, treat as if source were HB_sAg positive
Antibody response unknown	Test exposed person for anti-HB_sAg‡ If adequate†, no treatment If inadequate†, HBIG × 1 and vaccine booster	No treatment	Test exposed person for anti-HB_sAg If adequate†, no treatment If inadequate†, initiate revaccination

*Dose 0.06 ml/kg intramuscularly.
†A responder is defined as a person with adequate levels of serum antibody to HB_sAg (i.e., 10 mIU/ml); inadequate response to vaccination is defined as serum antibody to HB_2Ag < 10 mIU/ml.
‡Antibody to HB_sAg.
Abbreviations: HB, Hepatitis B; HBIG, hepatitis B immune globulin; HB_sAg, hepatitis B surface antigen.
Adapted from Centers for Disease Control and Prevention. Immunization of health-care workers: Recommendations of the Advisory Committee on Immunization Practices (ACIP) and the Hospital Infection Control Practices Advisory Committee (HICPAC). MMWR Morb Mortal Wkly Rep. 1997;46(RR-18):1–42.

nation serologic screening for prior HBV infection among those being vaccinated because of occupational risk.[23] Postvaccination testing should be routinely provided to all HCWs with an anticipated risk of occupational exposure. Knowledge of serostatus assists management of subsequent exposures[23, 28] (see Table 295–2). For vaccine responders, no postexposure intervention is required, regardless of the surface or e antigen status of the source. For those unvaccinated and for vaccine nonresponders, treatment upon exposure to a HB_sAG-positive source includes HBIG given within 24 hours of exposure and, if appropriate, initiation of a three-dose vaccine series.[23, 28] Vaccinated HCWs with an unknown response to vaccine should have their serostatus checked immediately after exposure and be treated according to serostatus[23, 28] (see Table 295–2). Vaccine is generally well tolerated.[123]

The best long-term management of vaccine nonresponder is not known. This is of particular importance because up to 10% of vaccinated persons fail to seroconvert.[48, 124, 125] Risk factors for a suboptimal response include cigarette smoking, increasing age, obesity, and, in some series, male sex.[23, 48, 124, 125] Persons who do not seroconvert after the initial three-dose series should receive a second three-dose series or be evaluated for HB_sAg carrier state.[23, 81, 126] Among those receiving a second course, up to half seroconvert after the second series.[126] Intradermal injection results in inadequate titers and is not recommended.[127] A third series for nonresponders is not recommended. Trials of a new vaccine utilizing pre-S1 and -S2 components[128, 129] appear promising; in one series, 69% of previous nonresponders seroconverted.[128]

The effectiveness of vaccine in preventing long-term complications was demonstrated in a study from Taiwan in which there was a significant decrease in the incidence of hepatocellular carcinoma among children who had received vaccine (from 0.70 per 100,000 to 0.36 to 100,000).[130] The role of antiviral agents such as lamivudine with activity against HBV in the management of nosocomial exposure has not been determined.

Vaccine Acceptance Rates

Despite the risk, and despite the 1991 mandate of the Occupational Safety and Health Administration for vaccination[45] or declination of all health care workers with risk, vaccination rates are suboptimal. A 1992 CDC-led study, conducted soon after the Occupational Safety and Health Administration regulations went into effect, examined acceptance rates at 96 hospitals throughout the United States.[47] The authors found that 51% of 77,302 eligible employees had completed a three-vaccine series, with a trend toward improving acceptance rates. In another CDC-led survey from 1994 to 1995, 113 randomly selected hospitals were surveyed and charts of 2532 employees reviewed.[44] Of these, 66.5% had received a complete series, with highest coverage for higher risk personnel, such as phlebotomists, laboratory personnel, and nursing staff. Other series have demonstrated the same results. In U.S. dialysis centers, only 31% of patients and 79% of staff have been vaccinated.[87]

Numerous other hospital- or occupation-specific studies have appeared.[48, 131–133] In one, the decision of workers to initiate the vaccine series was associated with younger age and occupation, including house staff, nurses and nurses' aides, and laboratory technicians.[133] Vaccine initiation was also higher among those who more frequently accepted annual influenza vaccination.[133] In the United States vaccination of children with a three-vaccine series will eventually result in a health care workforce with a high rate of immunity, ensuring additional protection against this occupational risk.

Hepatitis C

Epidemiology

The CDC estimated that 180,000 cases of hepatitis C virus (HCV) infection occurred in the United States in 1984.[134] With the introduction of the antibody test in 1990, implementation of universal precautions, and better screening of the blood donor pool, this was reduced to about 28,000 infections in 1995, including 560 cases (2%) in HCWs.[134] Because of the lack of effective treatment and the predictable long-term consequences of chronic HCV infection,[135, 136] effective control of nosocomial HCV has become a major goal for hospitals and workers.[134]

Prevalence

In most series, seroprevalence studies of HCW groups at increased risk for hepatitis B, including dialysis workers, laboratory workers, surgeons, nurses, and workers with the mentally impaired, have demonstrated no increased seroprevalence of hepatitis C,[107, 137–150] although a few reports demonstrate increased seroprevalence.[151–154] A 1995 survey of U.S. dialysis staff demonstrated 2% seroprevalence, similar to the overall prevalence in the United States (1 to 2%). Only 16% of centers routinely determined the HCV serostatus of staff, however.[87] Dialysis workers have not shown increased risk in other series.[107, 145, 149, 150] Dentists, particularly oral surgeons, have an elevated risk in some[155, 156] but not all series.[157] Seroprevalence in oral surgeons has ranged from 2% in Baltimore[155] to 9% in New York City.[156]

Reports of Transmission

Worker to Patient. A cardiac surgeon transmitted HCV to at least five patients during valve replacement surgery.[22] In this study, molecular analysis showed significant homology between the surgeon's and the patients' virus. The surgeon was treated with interferon-alfa-2b and ribavirin until his HCV RNA level became undetectable. At that point, he was allowed to resume performing surgery. His serum is rechecked monthly and, as of the 1996 report, he remains without detectable HCV RNA.

A preliminary report from Spain described a staggering outbreak: at least 217 secondary cases associated with a single HCV-infected anesthesiologist.[158] Initial investigation has suggested that the physician was a morphine addict who gave patients therapeutic opioids only after first injecting himself with the drug.

Rare cases of non-needlestick transmission include spread from a splash,[159] a retrograde cholangiogram,[160] and colonoscopy.[161] In the colonoscopy report, two secondary cases were shown by genetic sequencing to have an identical strain of hepatitis C. The two had undergone colonoscopy on the same day as the putative source case. Investigation suggested that inadequate cleaning of the biopsy suction channel and failure to autoclave some equipment, such as biopsy forceps, contributed to the transmission.

Dialysis. With improved control of nosocomial HBV, transmission of HCV has emerged as a significant problem in dialysis centers.[162] The renal literature is replete with reports on the incidence, prevalence, and small outbreaks, mostly from Europe and Japan.[150, 163–179] These studies typically utilize molecular fingerprinting techniques to suggest person-to-person transmission of HCV.[173–178]

In most series, HCV seroprevalence among dialysis patients is 2- to 10-fold higher than in the general population. The CDC reports regularly on dialysis-associated diseases in the United States.[86, 87] In 1995, information from 96% of all U.S. centers, representing 224,954 patients and 54,194 staff members, was presented.[87] About 40% of centers routinely tested for HCV. The prevalence of HCV infection among dialysis patients was 10.4% (range per center, 0 to 64%) and among staff, 2%[87] (see Table 298–1).

Outside the United States, seroprevalence of HCV among dialysis patients has ranged from about 20% in Israel[180] and Bari, Italy,[173] 32% in Marseilles,[178] and 40% in Rome[107] and Croatia,[149] to as high as 71% in Venezuela.[181] Incidence estimates have ranged from 0.6 to 2%.[87, 173, 182, 183] The prevalence of HCV among peritoneal dialysis patients, in contrast, is not elevated.[162]

Because of their compromised immune system, dialysis patients may fail to mount a significant antibody response to HCV. This was particularly apparent with the first-generation test because only about half of dialysis patients, subsequently shown to have HCV, were seropositive. The sensitivity of second- and third-generation tests is much improved, although one study found HCV RNA in 28% of dialysis patients with negative second-generation HCV enzyme-linked immunosorbent assay tests.[184] Routine use of HCV RNA has therefore been advocated by some.[184] However, this is mitigated by the substantial cost as well as the well-established difficulties in performing the test and reproducing the result.[134, 162] Regular surveillance of serum alanine aminotransferase levels has been recommended by some as a less costly, more reproducible approach for screening dialysis patients for new HCV infections.[182]

Early reports demonstrated that nosocomial spread was associated with overt interruptions in infection control.[185] In subsequent studies, however, obvious breaches of infection control in dialysis centers and elsewhere[186] have not been identified, suggesting that either subtle interruptions are responsible for spread or HCV transmission is incompletely understood. Supporting the latter, some studies utilizing genotypic analysis have not demonstrated spread among persons treated in the same or adjacent beds; rather, linked cases have been located throughout the dialysis center, suggesting widespread transmission by an unclear mechanism.[183]

Recognized risk factors for acquisition of HCV include blood transfusion and duration of dialysis time,[187] with the latter the more significant.[150] The widespread use of erythropoietin has resulted in a significant decrease in transfusion requirements and therefore transfusion-related infection.[167] However, even nontransfused dialysis patients have an elevated incidence and prevalence of HCV.[183] As already noted, the route of transmission is not established. Sharing of dialysis machines by HCV-infected and uninfected patients and, possibly, reprocessing of dialyzers from HCV-infected patients have been suggested,[188] although this is controversial.[187] In addition, a possible genetic predisposition has been theorized.[180]

Some have advocated keeping HCV-infected dialysis patients together, similar to the successful approach taken with HBV-infected patients.[174] The CDC, however, does not advocate this approach[134] because of the lack of sensitivity of the anti-HCV test, which means that not all infectious persons would be isolated; and the risk to already infected persons of superinfection.[162]

Solid Tumor Transplantation. Increasing use of solid organ transplantation has forced a consideration of the approach to transplantation of HCV-infected organs into HCV-infected or uninfected hosts.[162] Prevention of graft rejection requires ongoing immunosuppression, thereby compromising host control of HCV as well. In addition, nearly all susceptible recipients of HCV-positive organs develop HCV infection,[189] which may be severe.[189, 190] In most series, however, no adverse effect on overall survival of patients or grafts has been found, although recipients of HCV-positive organs had a higher rate of liver-related morbidity and mortality.[189, 190] Many organ banks now restrict the use of organs from HCV-positive donors except for lifesaving procedures, such as heart, lung, and liver transplants.[162]

Seroconversion

Seroconversion occurs in 0 to 10% of nonimmune HCWs who sustain needlesticks from a source case with hepatitis C[23, 107, 134, 151, 191–198] (see Table 295–1). Maternal-fetal transmission rates are similar (5 to 9%).[134] Reports vary owing to differences in the diagnostic test used (antibody or HCV RNA). The highest transmission rate (10%) was from a study using HCV RNA to detect infection in exposed workers.[194] This high rate has not been duplicated, and most studies place the transmission rate below 3%. A correlation between the HCV RNA quantitative level in the source patient and the risk of transmission has not been established. The annual cost of follow-up testing in the United States after potential exposure is $2 million to $4 million.[134]

One report of simultaneous transmission of HCV and HIV from a single needlestick was remarkable for the delayed time to seroconversion against each virus and the fulminantly fatal course of the HCV infection.[199] The frequency of this phenomenon is not known.

Management

For potential exposures, the CDC recommends determining the serostatus of the source case.[134] For the exposed HCW, baseline and follow-up (at 6 month) testing for HCW antibody (second-generation test) and alanine aminotransferase is recommended. Because of the poor specificity of the antibody test (enzyme immunoassay; as low as 50% in some series), a confirmatory recombinant immunoblot is recommended.[134] In addition, up to 10% of infections are not detected by enzyme immunoassay and require HCV RNA polymerase chain reaction (PCR) for diagnosis. Earlier testing with polymerase chain reaction–based assays has been useful in some instances; however, because of poor standardization of this technique and concerns about false positive results, the CDC does not recommend its routine use.[23, 134]

Optimal management of a needlestick exposure is unknown, but immune globulin is not recommended.[23, 134] Immediate prospects for an effective vaccine appear limited.[200] An Italian study demonstrated protection for HCV-discordant couples with unscreened intramuscular immune globulin,[201] suggesting that, in some settings, immune globulin offers some protection against HCV transmission. However, the preparation of immune globulin used in this trial had antibody to HCV glycoproteins E1 and E2, which may have some neutralizing activity.[201] In the United States, the presence of such antibody would result in rejection of the donated unit.

Several preliminary studies have suggested activity of interferon-alfa in HCWs or patients who have seroconverted acutely after nosocomial exposure.[202, 203] Small sample size and short follow-up have limited the applicability of these findings.

Because of the risk of fulminant hepatitis A infection in persons with underlying chronic liver disease, such as those with HCV,[204, 205] HAV vaccination should be considered for all persons, including HCWs, chronically infected with HCV.[206]

Hepatitis D

Delta virus is a defective RNA virus that requires the presence of active HBV infection (acute HBV or HB_sAg carrier state) to infect the liver productively.[110] Transmission of the delta agent has been reported from a dialysis center.[207] In this report, a dually infected source patient regularly shared a dialysis machine with an asymptomatic HB_sAg carrier, who subsequently developed acute delta hepatitis. A surgeon may also have become dually infected after a deep needlestick sustained while operating on the same source patient.[207] Review identified several additional possible instances of delta hepatitis transmission in dialysis centers.[207] This led to the current recommendation that patients and staff be vaccinated against HBV and that dialysis patients be separated according to delta virus status. Specifically, delta-positive, HB_sAg-positive patients should receive dialysis in a separate room from delta-negative, HB_sAg-positive patients.[207]

Hepatitis G (Hepatitis BG-C) (see Chapter 144)

In 1995, a novel flavivirus was identified and considered as a cause of non-A–E hepatitis, particularly among persons with post-transfusion hepatitis. Subsequent studies, however, have demonstrated no clear role for hepatitis G virus (HGV) as a cause of viral hepatitis.[208, 209] Despite this, because of the observed increased seroprevalence of the virus among transfusion recipients, analysis and surveillance for HGV in the dialysis setting are continuing.[210–215] One study demonstrated that among dialysis patients, HGV is found in patients not coinfected with HCV, suggesting that HGV transmission occurs independently of HCV and, more disturbingly, that measures to limit HCV transmission may be ineffective for HGV.[215] The implications of this finding are unknown.

TRANSFUSION-ASSOCIATED INFECTIONS

Beeson[216] reported the first cases of transfusion-associated infection in 1943, describing seven patients who developed hepatitis 33 to 119 days after receiving a red blood cell or plasma transfusion. Broader recognition of this and the related phenomenon of jaundice after serum injections to prevent various illnesses such as yellow fever, mumps, or polio[1–7] soon followed.[217, 218] Various regulations then arose to ensure an increasingly safe blood supply.[219] Surveys to determine blood product use, led by the National Heart and Lung Institute (now Heart, Lung, and Blood Institute), began in 1971.[219] By 1987, the cost of collecting, processing, and transfusing patients exceeded $3 billion.[219]

The advent of the epidemic of acquired immunodeficiency syndrome in the 1980s and the subsequent focus on hepatitis C have drawn medical and public attention to the safety of the blood supply.[220–223] Although less dramatic than the viral agents, bacteria may also be transmitted by transfusion, often with catastrophic results. In addition, spirochetal, rickettsial, and parasitic disease may rarely be transmitted by transfusion of blood products. Current concerns in the blood banking community center on how best to reconcile the high cost of excluding infections with the need to guarantee a maximally safe blood supply.

Scope of Transfusions, United States

Several surveys have reported the frequency of blood collection and utilization in the United States in the late 1980s and early 1990s.[219, 224–227] Between 12 million and 14 million units are collected annually for donation and given to millions of recipients.[220, 226] In 1992, 11.3 million red blood cell units were given to 3.7 million patients; 2.3 million units of plasma were administered, as were 8.3 million units of platelets and 939,000 units of cryoprecipitate.[225] The amounts of blood collected and of red cells transfused have slowly decreased, while the number of transfused platelets has increased.[225] In addition to contributions from the voluntary donor pool, 12 million units of plasma are collected from paid donors and are used to prepare immunoglobulin, albumin, and various other plasma-derived products.[220]

The likelihood of an individual receiving a transfusion is about 0.89% per year and increases dramatically with the age of the person.[227] Because of concern about contracting an infectious disease, there has been a dramatic shift toward autologous and donor-directed blood donation over the past decade.[219, 224, 225] Donor-directed units, usually given by family members for a specific patient, have not been shown to have lower rates of various infectious agents.[228] However, viral infections are about half as common among apheresis donors (generally donor-directed) as among whole blood donors.[229]

In 1992, 625,000 units, or about 4.5% of the donated allogeneic blood supply, were discarded on testing, less than in 1989 (675,000 units).[225] Many but not all of these units were discarded because of detection of a potentially transmissible agent.

Currently, seven tests are required for screening. In 1990, the rates of donated units discarded per test were as follows: syphilis (0.2%), HB_sAg (0.04%), HIV antibody (0.02%), hepatitis B core antibody (2.15%), elevated alanine aminotransferase (0.17%) human T-cell lymphotropic virus type I (HTLV-I) antibody (0.05%), and HCV antibody (0.29%).[226] A survey of blood banks in 1991 found that there were 1263 reported cases of transfusion-related hepatitis (0.008%), including 44% who had HB_sAg and 80% with HCV antibody.[230] Because of ongoing risk, strategies have been developed to retain uninfected donors.[231]

Viral Pathogens

A transfusion-associated transmission risk persists for HIV, hepatitis B, hepatitis C, and HTLV-1 for two distinct reasons: (1) the incomplete sensitivity of the available screening tests, which ranges from about 90% for hepatitis C to more than 99% for HIV, and (2) the "window" period (Table 295–3), which is defined as the period between acute infection (and potential infectivity) and the time when available tests are able to detect the infection reliably.

A U.S. study examined the risk of transmission of these four viruses[232] (Table 295–4). The study examined more than 580,000 persons who had each donated blood more than once at different blood centers throughout the United States. The rate of seroconversion to a viral infection was then established for persons who had initially been seronegative. Using this approach, the risk of a donor giving blood during an infectious window period was determined to be 1 in 493,000 for HIV, 1 in 641,000 for HTLV, 1 in 103,000 for hepatitis C, and 1 in 63,000 for hepatitis B. Similar rates have been found in studies conducted in France[233] and Australia[234] (see Table 295–4). These reports demonstrate that, although HIV draws the most attention, transmission of hepatitis B and hepatitis C is more common.

Human Immunodeficiency Virus Type I

More than 8000 persons in the United States have developed acquired immunodeficiency syndrome from receipt of blood or tissue, including 39 who received blood that had tested negative for HIV.[235] In addition, at least 50% of all hemophiliacs in the United States and Europe became infected with HIV from 1978 to 1985,[236] with the highest incidence in 1982, when there were 22 infections per 100 person-years.[236] The screening test was introduced in 1985, and since 1987 few new infections among hemophiliacs have been reported.[236]

In addition to these findings,[232–234] a U.S. study that corrected for laboratory and clerical errors found a risk of 1 case of HIV per 450,000 to 660,000 transfused units[237] (see Table 295–4). Because

TABLE 295–3 Current Window Period for Four Viral Infections and Potential Reduction Using Newer Tests for Detection

Virus	Current Test	Current Window Period	New Test	Potential Reduction in Window Period (d)	Potential Number of Additional Infected Donors Identified per Year*
HIV	ELISA or WB	22–25	p24 antigen	5†	7
			RNA PCR	11	12
HTLV	Antibody	51	N/A	N/A	N/A
HCV	Second-generation ELISA	82	Third-generation ELISA	12	15–20
			RNA PCR	59	84
HBV	HB_sAg	59	DNA PCR	25	81

*Based on 12 million donated units per year.
†Instituted for all blood banks in the United States in March 1996.
Abbreviations: ELISA, Enzyme-linked immunosorbent assay; HB_sAg, hepatitis B surface antigen; HBV, hepatitis B virus; HCV, hepatitis C virus; HIV, human immunodeficiency virus; HTLV, human T-cell lymphotropic virus; N/A = not available; PCR, polymerase chain reaction; WB, Western blot.

TABLE 295–4 Rate of Seroconversion in Blood Donor Population and Projected Rate of Infected Units per Unit of Transfused Blood in the Four Viral Infections Screened in the United States

	United States, 1991–1993[232]		United States, 1992–1993[236]		France, 1993–1995[233]		Australia, 1994–1995[234]	
Virus	*Seroconversion per 100,000*	*Per Unit of Blood*	*Seroconversion per 100,000*	*Per Unit of Blood*	*Seroconversion per 100,000*	*Per Unit of Blood*	*Seroconversion per 100,000*	*Per Unit of Blood*
HIV	3.37	1 per 493,080	3.4	1 per 450,000 to 1 per 650,000	2.90	1 per 571,000	1.31	1 per 1,265,822
HTLV	1.12	1 per 641,000	N/A	N/A	0.12	1 per 5 million	N/A	N/A
HCV	4.32	1 per 103,000	N/A	N/A	2.48	1 per 233,214*	1.89	1 per 234,000
HBV	9.80	1 per 63,000	N/A	N/A	5.51	1 per 118,343	1.67	1 per 155,038

*†Third-generation enzyme immunoassay used for screening.
Abbreviations: HBV, Hepatitis B virus; HCV, hepatitis C virus; HIV, human immunodeficiency virus; HTLV, human T-cell lymphotropic virus; N/A = not available.
Data from refs. 232–234 and 236.

12 million donations are collected annually in the United States, this projects to 18 to 27 transmissions annually, assuming a window period of about 25 days.[237] In the hope of decreasing the window period to 19 days and thereby decreasing risk, in August 1995 the Food and Drug Administration recommended donor screening for HIV-1 p24 antigen, even though many projections suggested the intervention would not be cost-effective.[238, 239] Others argued that the improving sensitivity of available tests rendered the p24 antigen test unnecessary.[240] The first licensed test became available in March 1996.

Projections had suggested that four to six infections not identified by routine testing would be diagnosed annually using the additional p24 antigen screening. However, in the first 6 months of the program, the yield was well below expectations[241, 242]: with 40 p24 antigen–positive, HIV antibody–negative specimens, only one acute infection was detected[242]; the other 39 were considered false-positive reactions. This technique and PCR for HIV RNA detection, however, have been useful in clarifying the HIV serostatus of persons with indeterminate results of Western blot tests.[243–245] These reactions occur in about 1 per 5000 donations[246] and are generally found to be HIV negative.

Human Immunodeficiency Virus Type 1 O Strain

In 1994, a new strain of HIV, the so-called group O strain, which appears to be endemic to western and central Africa, was identified.[247] This virus posed, and continues to pose, a new problem for blood banks, because the currently available Enzyme-linked immunosorbent assay does not predictably detect the virus[247, 248] To date, no transfusion-related cases of group O HIV-1 have been described, and attempts to screen for the infection continue.[249]

Human Immunodeficiency Virus Type 2

In June 1992, the Food and Drug Administration mandated screening for HIV-2.[250] Since then, only three HIV-2–positive donors have been identified and no cases of transmission have been described in the United States.[220] Transfusion-related cases have occurred in Europe, however.[220]

Human T-Cell Lymphotropic Virus Types I and II

HTLV-I and HTLV-II, unlike HIV-1 and HIV-2, are cell associated and therefore transmissible only with blood component transfusions.[220] The rate of transmission of HTLV-I decreased almost 10-fold (from 1 per 8500 to 1 per 69,000) after introduction of the screening test.[251, 252] Attempts continue to develop a single test for detection of both HTLV-I and HTLV-II.[253]

Hepatitis A Virus

Transmission of hepatitis A via transfusion of blood has been described with red cells, particularly in infants,[32, 33, 254] and with factor VIII concentrate.[255, 256] Factor VIII–associated transmission has occurred despite appropriate use of organic solvent and detergent to inactivate the virus. The lack of an envelope around HAV may have contributed to incomplete virus killing during preparation of the concentrate. Because of this small but persistent risk, vaccination for hepatitis A of chronic recipients of products made from pooled plasma has been recommended.[257]

Hepatitis B and D Viruses

As noted earlier, one study calculated that hepatitis B is transmitted in about 1 of every 63,000 transfusions,[232] although some CDC estimates place the rate much lower, at about 1 in 500,000[220] (see Table 295–4). This persistent risk derives from the prolonged window period and the incomplete sensitivity of the surface antigen (HB_sAg) test for identifying all potentially infectious persons.[258, 259] A mutant HBV not detected in many approved HB_sAg assays has been identified.[260] The implications of this finding for blood banking are unknown.

Screening donors for HB_sAg excludes most, but not all, carriers of delta virus.[261] Screening donors for antibody to the delta agent is not done routinely, so there is a residual risk of transmission of delta virus to HB_sAg-positive recipients.

A consensus panel considered several issues regarding infectious disease testing for blood transfusions pertinent to hepatitis B screening.[221] They addressed the continued need for alanine aminotransferase testing, given the development of other screens for hepatitis C. They weighed the potential benefit of the test (detection of some HB_sAg-negative cases, detection of persons at risk for other blood-borne diseases such as hepatitis C and HIV) against the cost of the test and the cost of evaluating individuals with nonspecific elevations. They also considered the loss of potentially transfusable units (200,000 units discarded annually; 150,000 donors deferred or excluded) and donor anxiety initiated by identification of the medical problem. They concluded that the test should be discontinued.[221]

They also reviewed the continued need for hepatitis B core antibody testing, which remains valuable for detecting patients with hepatitis B who are in the window period (before developing surface antibody) as well as HB_sAg-negative persons who remain infectious. Another benefit was the use of the test in identifying persons at risk for other blood-borne infections. Factors opposing continuation included the deferral of tens of thousands of donors and confusion of the donors regarding their medical "condition." The panel recommended continuation of the test.[221]

Hepatitis C Virus

Hepatitis C, then known as non-A, non-B hepatitis, was transmitted to as many as 7 to 10% of transfusion recipients in the late 1970s and early 1980s.[262, 264] More than 90% of recipients of HCV-contaminated blood products develop HCV infection.[264] A survey using the second-generation test found that 3.6 per 1000 U.S. donors were positive for HCV,[265] below the prevalence in the U.S. population of about 10 to 20 per 1000. Associations with seropositivity include intravenous drug use (denied at initial donor screening), prior blood transfusion, intranasal cocaine use, sexual promiscuity, and ear piercing in men.[266]

The rate of infection with hepatitis C has decreased with the introduction of tests to identify the virus.[267] Before any testing, 0.45% of all transfusions transmitted HCV; with the introduction in 1986 of surrogate marker testing alanine aminotransferase and hepatitis B core antibody,[262, 263] the rate decreased to 0.19%, and with the introduction of the first-generation antibody test for HCV in 1990, the rate fell to 0.03%.[269] The second-generation test has lowered the rate further (by about 1.2 donors per 1000),[238, 268–270] mostly by identifying chronic infections rather than by shortening the window period.

As with the other viral infections, risk for transmission persists for two reasons: a relatively long window period (about 82 days with second-generation testing) and the incomplete sensitivity of the second-generation test (see Table 295–3): about 10% of infected persons are HCV antibody negative but positive on other tests, such as PCR for HCV RNA.[270] This has resulted in a rate of HCV transmission at about 1 per 103,000 transfusions[232–234] (see Table 295–4), similar to that in Sweden.[271] The third-generation test may further improve screening to about 1 in 121,000 units by shortening the window period[272] by about 12 days.[238] Use of PCR for HCV RNA among HCV-negative donors with abnormal liver function tests has not identified additional cases.[273] Additional studies to determine the optimal screening and diagnostic tests for donors and recipients are ongoing.[274]

An outbreak of HCV related to contaminated immune globulin demonstrated a potential problem engendered by use of more sensitive screening test.[275] Transmission of hepatitis C was reported among children with primary immune deficiency who were receiving intravenous immune globulin on a regular basis. At least 23 (11%) of 210 children became infected after receiving Gammagard (Baxter Healthcare Corporation, Deerfield, Ill.), compared with none of 52 children who received other intravenous immune globulin products.

The investigators speculated that, because of the increased sensitivity of the second-generation test for hepatitis C antibody, additional antibody was eliminated from the vat of untreated donor plasma.[275] Presumably, this antibody had contributed in some measure to controlling virus introduced into the vat by additional viremic, but still antibody-negative, donors in the window period for acute hepatitis C. A similar report has come from Europe.[276] The product preparation did not involve a step of heat inactivation, which is used for some but not all other commercial products. As a result, the Food and Drug Administration now requires a heat inactivation step in the preparation of all intravenous immune globulin products. In addition, all immunoglobulin products, even intramuscular products (which have never been associated with transfusion of any infectious agent), are now screened by PCR for hepatitis C.

Hepatitis G Virus

HGV has been found in 1[277] to 7%[278] of donors and can be transmitted by transfusion.[279] The risk of transmission is in the range of 5.3 per 10,000 units.[280] HGV, however, is not responsible for non-A, non-B, non-C post-transfusion hepatitis, and the clinical implictions of hepatitis G infection remain undetermined.[208, 209] Hepatitis G does not influence the course of infection with HCV, a related flavivirus.[279]

Other Viruses

Several other viruses may be transmitted via transfusion[281] (Table 295–5), and for others, such as human herpesvirus types 6 and 8 and dengue, a theoretical potential exists. Transmission of cytomegalovirus (CMV) has been well summarized.[282] CMV is highly cell associated and is transmitted with white blood cells, which may be present in red cell, platelet, or white cell transfusions.[283] Transmission of CMV from fresh frozen plasma or cryoprecipitate has not been reported. The insensitivity of the serologic test has resulted in a residual risk of transmission of 0 to 6%, even when CMV-seronegative donors are used.[282] Because the demand for CMV-seronegative blood is outstripping the supply, use of leukocyte filtration of CMV-seropositive blood is being studied to provide CMV-safe blood.[284]

Screening for Epstein-Barr virus is not performed routinely, despite older reports of transfusion-associated transmission. A subsequent study found no transmission among 11 seronegative children who had received seropositive blood products.[285] Parvovirus B19 has been transmitted in coagulation factor concentrates. One report found that the risk of transmission to hemophiliac recipients persisted despite solvent and detergent treatment and heating to 100°C after lyophilization.[286]

Transfusion-transmitted virus (TTV) is a single-stranded, unencapsulated DNA virus discovered in 1997 in Japan, where 10% of blood donors were TTV DNA positive.[287] Using the same primers in PCR, TTV DNA was detected in the blood of 17 of 1000 Scottish blood donors.[288] The prevalence of TTV DNA was 10 to 38% in blood of various diagnostic groups studied in London[289] with a similar but not identical assay. Circumstantial evidence points to transfusion as the mode of transmission.[290] No clinical consequences of TTV infection have been described.

Bacterial Pathogens

Transfusion of bacterially contaminated blood products continues to be an infrequent but potentially lethal risk of blood transfusion. Contamination may arise from donation, processing, storage, or transfusion. In the United States from 1986 to 1991, 29 deaths were caused by transfusion of bacterially contaminated blood products: 21

TABLE 295–5 Infectious Agents Transmitted by Blood or Blood Products

Organism Category	Specific Organisms
Viruses	Hepatitis A virus
	Hepatitis B virus
	Hepatitis C virus
	Hepatitis D virus (delta agent)
	Cytomegalovirus
	Epstein-Barr virus
	Human immunodeficiency virus type 1
	Human immunodeficiency virus type 2
	Human T-cell leukemia virus type 1
	Human T-cell leukemia virus type 2
	Parvovirus B19
Parasites	Malaria
	Babesiosis
Rickettsiae	Rocky Mountain spotted fever
	Q fever
Spirochetes	Syphilis
	Relapsing fever
Bacteria	*Yersinia enterocolitica*
	Pseudomonas fluorescens
	Escherichia coli
	Serratia liquefaciens
	Serratia marcescens
	Brucella spp.
	Bacillus spp.
	Coagulase-negative *Staphylococcus*

Adapted from Doebbeling EN, Wenzel RP. Nosocomial viral hepatitis and infections transmitted by blood and blood products. In: Mandell G, Bennett J, Dolon R, eds. Principles and Practice of Infectious Diseases. 4th ed. New York: Churchill Livingston;1995:2616–2632.

from contaminated platelets and 8 from contaminated erythrocytes.[291–293] Another calculation projected transfusion-associated sepsis resulted in 1 death per 1 million transfused platelet units and 1 per 10 million erythrocyte units.[294]

The frequency of nonfatal outcomes is even less well characterized but ranges from 0.003 to 0.14% of all febrile reactions among recipients.[295] The U.S. General Accounting Office has estimated the rate of bacteria-associated adverse reactions to pooled platelets as 0.6 per 1000 pooled units and of *Yersinia*-associated erythrocyte reactions as 1 per 500,000.[296] Enhanced surveillance may result in an apparent increase in contamination rates.[297] In an attempt to better define rates and risks of bacteria-associated transfusion reactions in the United States, a national prospective study has been initiated.[296]

For both erythrocytes and platelets, longer storage time is well established as a risk factor for bacterial contamination. Further shortening the current storage times, however, would probably result in discarding too many uninfected units, exacerbating the nation's chronic blood supply shortage. In addition, contamination may occur during production and packaging of blood bags.[298] Because routine tests such as Gram staining appear ineffective,[295] development of additional screening tests, such as nucleic acid hybridization and PCR, to identify contaminated units in a cost-effective manner is a high priority.[238] Investigation of the potentially immunosuppressive consequences of blood transfusion is ongoing.[299]

Red Blood Cells

Two bacteria, *Yersinia enterocolitica* and *Pseudomonas fluorescens,* account for about 75% of all reported cases of transfusion of contaminated red blood cells[293] (see Table 295–5). Storage of red blood cells may extend 35 to 42 days depending on the type of additive used. Almost all instances of infection are associated with erythrocytes stored longer than 25 days and appear to derive from enhanced growth of these organisms at cold storage (4°C) temperatures. This is best exemplified by a case of transfusion-associated *Y. enterocolitica* in an autologous blood donor, who became bacteremic after receiving his own stored blood 41 days after donation.[300]

Donors with *Y. enterocolitica* are typically symptom free at the time of blood donation, although about two thirds recall a diarrheal illness a month before donation.[293] Addition of a donor question regarding diarrheal illness has not been adopted because of the commonness of the complaint. If it were used as a screening question, up to 10% of donors would be excluded.[293]

Platelets

A different spectrum of bacteria is associated with transfusion of platelets, possibly because they are stored at room temperature.[301,302] Coagulase-negative *Staphylococcus* are the most commonly recovered bacteria (about 25% of cases). Transfusion of *Salmonella choleraesuis* (13.5%) and a host of other organisms, including *Escherichia coli, Serratia marcescens, Bacillus* species, and *Enterobacter cloacae,* has also been reported[293] (see Table 295–5).

A patient may receive pooled platelets from 6 to 10 donors, any one of which may be contaminated, thereby increasing the risk per transfusion. One study found bacterial contamination in 1 of 4200 transfusions of pooled platelets.[302] Increasing use of single-donor platelets (via apheresis) decreases this risk.

As with erythrocytes, transmission of infection via platelet transfusion tends to occur with older platelets (4 or 5 days), although a survey of outdated platelets found a low rate of contamination.[303] Because of this, the Food and Drug Administration, in 1985, shortened the acceptable storage time for platelets from 7 days to the current 5 days. Apheresis platelets are typically stored for a briefer period, further reducing risk of using this product.

Parasites, Protozoa, Spirochetes, and Rickettsiae

Trypanosoma cruzi, which causes Chagas' disease, is endemic in certain areas of South America and Central America. Rare cases of *T. cruzi* transmitted by blood transfusion have been reported by U.S. investigators.[220] It is estimated that up to 100,000 persons with *T. cruzi* infection reside in the United States. A study by the Red Cross in Los Angeles and Miami found *T. cruzi* antibody in 34 (0.0014%) of 23,278 donors.[304] No transmission was identified in 11 recipients of *T. cruzi*–infected blood.[304] Because of the low prevalence of the disease among donors and the absence of an approved reliable test, as well as a transmission rate that may be as low as 10%, the CDC currently does not recommend routine screening for the infection.

At least 25 cases of transfusion-associated babesiosis have been reported.[220] Donor screening for the disease is performed by questionnaire only. The risk of acquiring a related tick-borne organism, *Borrelia burgdorferi,* from a transfusion appears to be low.[305] Rickettsiae may rarely be transmitted by blood transfusion.[306] Transfusion-related transmission of two venerable infections, syphilis[307] and malaria,[308] has long been reported. The risk of transmission of Creutzfeldt-Jakob disease via transfusion is unknown but appears low.[309] No cases have been reported.

A recent review of blood transfusion–related complications has appeared.[310]

REFERENCES

1. MacCallum FO, Bauer DJ. Homologous serum jaundice: Transmission experiments with human volunteers. Lancet. 1944;5:622–627.
2. Findlay GM, MacCallum FO. Hepatitis and jaundice associated with immunization against certain virus diseases. Proc R Soc Med. 1938;31:799–806.
3. Sawyer WA, Meyer KF, Eaton MD et al. Jaundice in army personnel in the western region of the United States and its relation to vaccination against yellow fever. Am J Hyg. 1944;40:35–107.
4. Turner RH, Snavely JR, Grossman EB, et al. Some clinical studies of actue hepatitis occurring in soldiers after inoculation with yellow fever vaccine; with especial consideration of severe attacks. Ann Intern Med. 1944;20:193–218.
5. Seeff LB, Beebe GW, Hoofnagle JH, et al. A serologic follow-up of the 1942 epidemic of post-vaccination hepatitis in the United States Army. N Engl J Med. 1987;316:965–970.
6. Beeson, PB, Chesney G, McFarlan AM. Hepatitis following injection of mumps convalescent plasma. Lancet. 1944;1:814–817.
7. Propert SA. Hepatitis after prophylactic serum. BMJ. 1938;9:677–678.
8. Mendelssohn K, Witts LJ. Transmission of infection during withdrawal of blood. BMJ. 1945;5:625–626.
9. Droller H. An outbreak of hepatitis in a diabetic clinic. BMJ. 1945;5:623–625.
10. Turner RH. Hepatitis following penicillin injections. Lancet. 1946;1:108–109.
11. Neefe JR, Stokes J, Gellis SS. Homologous serum hepatitis and infectious (epidemic) hepatitis: Experimental study of immunity and cross immunity in volunteers, a preliminary report. Am J Med Sci. 1945;210:561–575.
12. MacCallum FO, Bradley WH. Transmission of infective hepatitis to human volunteers. Lancet. 1944;2:228–231.
13. Neefe JR, Stokes J Jr, Reinhold JG, Lukens FDW. Hepatitis due to the injection of homologous blood products in human volunteers. J Clin Invest. 1944;23:836–853.
14. Neefe JR, Stokes J Jr, Reinhold JG. Oral administration to volunteers of feces from patients with homologous serum hepatitis and infectious (epidemic) hepatitis. Am J Med Sci. 1945;210:29–32.
15. Paul JR, Havens WP Jr, Sabin AB. Transmission experiments in serum jaundice and infectious hepatitis. JAMA. 1945;128:911–915.
16. Liebowitz S, Greenwald L, Cohen I, Litwins J. Serum hepatitis in a blood bank worker. JAMA. 1949;140:1331–1333.
17. Trumbull ML, Greiner DJ. Homologous serum jaundice: An occupational hazard to medical personnel. JAMA. 1951;145:965–967.
18. Kuh, C, Ward WE. Occupational virus hepatitis: An apparent hazard for medical personnel. JAMA. 1950;143:631–635.
19. Byrne EB. Viral hepatitis: An occupational hazard of medical personnel. JAMA. 1966;195:362–364.
20. Harpaz R, Von Seidlein L, Averhoff FM, et al. Transmission of hepatitis B virus to multiple patients from a surgeon without evidence of inadequate infection control. N Engl J Med. 1996;334:549–554.
21. The Incident Investigation Team and Others. Transmission of hepatitis B to patients from four infected surgeons without hepatitis B e antigen. N Engl J Med. 1997;336:178–184.
22. Esteban JI, Gomez J, Martell M, et al. Transmission of hepatitis C by a cardiac surgeon. N Engl J Med. 1996;334:555–560.
23. Bolyard EA, Tablan OC, Williams WW, et al. Guideline for infection control in health care personnel, 1998. Infect Control Hosp Epidemiol. 1998;19:407–463.
24. Shapiro CN, Coleman PJ, McQuillan GM, et al. Epidemiology of hepatitis A: Seroepidemiology and risk groups in the USA. Vaccine. 1992;10(Suppl):S59–S62.
25. Germamaud J, Causse X, Barthez JP. Prevalence of antibodies to hepatitis A virus in health care workers. Eur J Clin Microbiol Infect Dis. 1993;12:572–573.
26. Domart M, Milka-Cabanne N, Pouliquen A, et al. Seroprevalence of hepatitis A among hospital workers in Paris (implications for HAV vaccination). Abstract J68, p 269. Presented at the Thirty-fifth Interscience Conference on Antimicrobial

Agents and Chemotherapy, San Francisco, Calif, September 17–20, 1995. Washington, DC: American Society for Microbiology.
27. Hofmann F, Wehrle G, Berthold H, Koster D. Hepatitis A as an occupational hazard. Vaccine. 1992;10(Suppl):S82–S84.
28. Centers for Disease Control and Prevention. Immunization of health-care workers: Recommendations of the Advisory Committee on Immunization Practices (ACIP) and the Hospital Infection Control Practices Advisory Committee (HICPAC). MMWR Morb Mortal Wkly Rep. 1997;46(RR-18):1–42.
29. Sepkowitz KA. Occupationally acquired infections in health care workers. Part II. Ann Intern Med. 1996;125:917–928.
30. Centers for Disease Control. Outbreak of viral hepatitis in the staff of a pediatric ward—California. MMWR Morb Mortal Wkly Rep. 1977;26:77–78.
31. Klein BS, Michaels JA, Rytel MW, et al. Nosocomial hepatitis A: A multinursery outbreak in Wisconsin. JAMA. 1984;252:2716–2721.
32. Noble RC, Kane MA, Reeves SA, Rockel I. Posttransfusion hepatitis A in a neonatal intensive care unit. JAMA. 1984;252:2711–2715.
33. Azimi PH, Roberto RR, Guralnik J, et al. Transfusion-acquired hepatitis A in a premature infant with secondary nosocomial spread in an intensive care unit. Am J Dis Child. 1986;140:23–27.
34. Drusin LM, Sohmer M, Groshen SL, et al. Nosocomial hepatitis A infection in a paediatric intensive care unit. Arch Dis Child. 1987;62:690–695.
35. Doebbeling BN, Li N, Wenzl RP. An outbreak of hepatitis A among health care workers: Risk factors for transmission. Am J Public Health 1993;83:1679–1684.
36. Burkholder BT, Coronado VG, Brown J, et al. Nosocomial transmission of hepatitis A in a pediatric hospital traced to an anti–hepatitis A virus–negative patient with immunodeficiency. Pediatr Infect Dis J. 1995;14:261–266.
37. Goodman RA, Carder CC, Allen JR, et al. Nosocomial hepatitis A transmission by an adult patient with diarrhea. Am J Med. 1982;73:220–226.
38. Baptiste R, Koziol D, Henderson DK. Nosocomial transmission of hepatitis A in an adult population. Infect Control. 1987;8:364–370.
39. Eisenstein AB, Aach RD, Jacobsohn W, Goldman A. An epidemic of infectious hepatitis in a general hospital. JAMA. 1963;185:171–174.
40. Myers JD, Romm FJ, Tihen WS, Bryan JA. Food-borne hepatitis A in a general hospital: Epidemiologic study of an outbreak attributed to sandwiches. JAMA. 1975;231:1049–1053.
41. Halfon P, Ouzan D, Chanas M, et al. High prevalence of hepatitis E virus antibody in haemodialysis patients. (Letter) Lancet 1994;344:746.
42. Pisanti FA, Coppola A, Galli C. Association between hepatitis C and hepatitis E viruses in southern Italy (Letter). Lancet 1994;344:746–747.
43. Sylvan SP, Jacobson SH, Christenson B. Prevalence of antibodies to hepatitis E virus among hemodialysis patients in Sweden. J Med Virol. 1998;54:38–43.
44. Mahoney FJ, Stewart K, Hu H, et al. Progress toward the elimination of hepatitis B virus transmission among health care workers in the United States. Arch Intern Med. 1997;157:2601–2605.
45. Department of Labor, OSHA. Occupational exposure to bloodborne pathogens: Final rule. Fed Regist. 1991;56:64175–182.
46. Lanphear BP, Linnemann CC, Cannon CG, DeRonde MM. Decline of clinical hepatitis B in workers at a general hospital: Relation to increasing vaccine-induced immunity. Clin Infect Dis. 1993;16:10–14.
47. Agerton TB. Mahoney FJ, Polish LB, Shapiro CN. Impact of the bloodborne pathogens standard on vaccination of healthcare workers with hepatitis B vaccine. Infect Control Hosp Epidemiol. 1995;16:287–291.
48. Louther J, Rivera P, Villa N, et al. Hepatitis B vaccination program at a New York City hospital: Seroprevalence, seroconversion, and declination. Am J Infect Control. 1998;26:423–427.
49. Shapiro CN. Occupational risk of infection with hepatitis B and hepatitis C virus. Surg Clin North Am. 1995;75:1047–1056.
50. Mast EE, Alter MJ. Prevention of hepatitis B virus infection among health-care workers. In: Ellis RW, ed. Hepatitis B Vaccines in Clinical Practice. New York: Marcel Dekker; 1993:295–307.
51. Lewis TL, Alter HJ, Chalmers TC, et al. A comparison of the frequency of hepatitis-B antigen and antibody in hospital and non-hospital personnel. N Engl J Med. 1973;289:647–651.
52. Feldman RE, Schiff ER. Hepatitis in dental professionals. JAMA. 1975;232:1228–1230.
53. Denes AE, Smith JL, Maynard JE, et al. Hepatitis B infection in physicians: Results of a nationwide seroepidemiologic survey. JAMA. 1978;239:210–212.
54. Janzen J, Tripatzis I, Wagner U, et al. Epidemiology of hepatitis B surface antigen (HBsAg) and antibody to HBsAg in hospital personnel. J Infect Dis. 1978;137:261–265.
55. Deinstag JL, Ryan DM. Occupational exposure to hepatitis B virus in hospital personnel: Infection or immunization? Am J Epidemiol. 1982;115:26–39.
56. West DJ. The risk of hepatitis B infection among health professionals in the United States: A review. Am J Med Sci. 1984;287:26–33.
57. Smith CET. A study of prevalence of markers of hepatitis B infection in hospital staff. J Hosp Infect. 1987;9:39–42.
58. Segal HE, Evans LC, Irwin GA, Callahan MC. Hepatitis B antigen and antibody in the United States Army: Two-year follow-up of health care personnel. Mil Med. 1979;144:792–795.
59. Hadler SC, Doto IL, Maynard JE, et al. Occupational risk of hepatitis B infection in hospital workers. Infect Control. 1985;6:24–31.
60. Osterholm MT, Garayalde SM. Clinical viral hepatitis B among Minnesota hospital personnel. JAMA. 1985;254:3207–3212.
61. Hicks CG, Hargiss CO, Harris JR. Prevalence survey for hepatitis B. Am J Infect Control. 1985;13:1–6.
62. Snydman DR, Munoz A, Werner BG, et al. A multivariate analysis of risk factors for hepatitis B virus infection among hospital employees screened for vaccination. Am J Epidemiol. 1984;120:684–693.
63. Kalish SB, Fisher B, Wallemark CB, et al. Prevalence of antibody to hepatitis B virus in foreign-born hospital employees. Am J Med. 1987;83:824–828.
64. Thomas DL, Factor SH, Kelen GD, et al. Viral hepatitis in health care personnel at The Johns Hopkins Hospital: The seroprevalence of and risk factors for hepatitis B and hepatitis C virus infection. Arch Intern Med. 1993;153:1705–1712.
65. Petrosillo N, Puro V, Ippolito G, et al. Hepatitis B virus, hepatitis C virus and human immunodeficiency virus infection in health care workers: A multiple regression analysis of risk factors. J Hosp Infect. 1995;30:273–281.
66. Herruzo-Cabrera R, Malo-Gonzalez L, Calle Puron ME, et al. Predictive equation for acquisition of hepatitis B in hospital workers in a general hospital. Eur J Epidemiol. 1993;9:442–446.
67. Gibas A, Blewett DR, Schoenfeld DA, Dienstag JL. Prevalence and incidence of viral hepatitis in health workers in the prehepatitis B vaccination era. Am J Epidemiol. 1992;136:603–610.
68. Weiss Y, Rabinovich M, Cahane Y, et al. Prevalence of hepatitis B virus markers among hospital personnel in Israel: Correlation with some risk factors. J Hosp Infect. 1994;26:211–218.
69. Lohiya G, Lohiya S, Caires S, Nizibian R. Occupational risk of hepatitis B from institutionalized mentally retarded HBsAg carriers: A prospective study. J Infec Dis. 1986;154:990–995.
70. Cancio-Bello TP, de Medina M, Shorey J, et al. An institutional outbreak of hepatitis B related to a human biting carrier. J Infect Dis. 1982;146:652–656.
71. Remis RS, Rossignol MA, Kane MA. Hepatitis B infection in a day school for mentally retarded students: Transmission from students to staff. Am J Public Health. 1987;77:1183–1186.
72. Guillen Solvas J, Luna del Castillo J, Maroto Vela MC, et al. The risk of infection with hepatitis B virus in relation to length of hospital employment. J Hosp Infect. 1987;9:43–47.
73. Resnic FS, Noerdlinger MA. Occupational exposure among medical students and house staff at a New York City medical center. Arch Intern Med. 1995;155:75–80.
74. Koenig S, Chu J. Medical student exposure to blood and infectious body fluids. Am J Infect Control. 1995;23:40–43.
75. Tereskerz PM, Pearson RD, Jagger J. Occupational exposure to blood among medical students. N Engl J Med. 1996;335:1150–1153.
76. Ramos-Gomez F, Ellison J, Greenspan D, et al. Accidental exposures to blood and body fluids among health care workers in dental teaching clinics: A prospective study. J Am Dent Assoc. 1997;128:1253–1261.
77. Panlilio AL, Shapiro CN, Schable CA, et al. Serosurvey of human immunodeficiency virus, hepatitis B virus, and hepatitis C virus infection among hospital-based surgeons. J Am Coll Surg. 1995;180:16–24.
78. Shapiro CN, Tokars JI, Chamberland ME. Use of the hepatitis-B vaccine and infection with hepatitis B and C among orthopaedic surgeons. J Bone Joint Surg Am. 1996;78:1791–1800.
79. Lyerly HK. Transmissible agents and the surgeon. J Am Coll Surg. 1995;180:91–92.
80. Werner BG, Grady GF. Accidental hepatitis-B-surface-antigen–positive inoculations: Use of e antigen to estimate infectivity. Ann Intern Med. 1982;97:367–369.
81. Gerberding JL. Management of occupational exposures to blood-borne viruses. N Engl J Med. 1995;332:444–451.
82. Reiss-Levy EA, Wilson CM, Hedges MJ, McCaughan G. Acute fulminant hepatitis B following a spit in the eye by a hepatitis B e antigen negative carrier (Letter). Med J Aust. 1994;160:524–525.
83. Bond WW, Favero MS, Petersen NJ, et al. Survival of hepatitis B virus after drying and storage for one week. Lancet. 1981;1:550–551.
84. Petersen NJ. An assessment of the airborne route in hepatitis B transmission. Ann N Y Acad Sci 1980;353:157–166.
85. Garibaldi RA, Forrest JN, Bryan JA, et al. Hemodialysis-associated hepatitis. JAMA. 1973;224:384–389.
86. Tokars JI, Alter MJ, Favero MS, et al. National surveillance of dialysis associated diseases in the United States, 1992. ASAIO J. 1994;40:1020–1031.
87. Tokars JI, Miller ER, Alter MJ, Arduino MJ. National surveillance of dialysis associated diseases in the United States, 1995. ASAIO J. 1998;44:98–107.
88. Owens DK, Nease RF. Occupational exposure to human immunodeficiency virus and hepatitis B virus: A comparative analysis of risk. Am J Med. 1992;92:503–512.
89. Zuckerman AJ. Occupational exposure to hepatitis B virus and human immunodeficiency virus: A comparative risk analysis. Am J Infect Control. 1995;23:286–289.
90. Sepkowitz KA, Helcl J, Castkova J, et al. Control of hepatitis B among health care workers in the Czech Republic. Abstract 31. Eighth Annual Meeting of the Society for Healthcare Epidemiology of America, Orlando, Fla, April 4–7, 1998, p 31.
91. Narendranathan M, Philip M. Reusable needles—A major risk factor for acute virus B hepatitis. Trop Doct. 1993;23:64–66.
92. Sikorska K, Laniec M, Buraczewska A, et al. Iatrogenic hepatitis B, non-A non-B, and C virus infections acquired in health service institutions of the Gdansk province in 1986–1995. (in Polish). Przegl Epidemiol. 1997;51:229–237.
93. Polish LB, Shapiro CN, Bauer F, et al. Nosocomial transmission of hepatitis B virus associated with the use of a spring-loaded finger-stick device. N Engl J Med. 1992:326:721–725.
94. Centers for Disease Control and Prevention. Nosocomial hepatitis B virus infection associated with reusable fingerstick blood sampling devises—Ohio and New York City. MMWR Morb Mortal Wkly Rep. 1997;46:217–221.
95. Morris IM, Cattle DS, Smits BJ. Endoscopy and transmission of hepatitis B (Letter). Lancet. 1975;2:1152.

96. Kent GP, Brondum J, Keenlyside RA, et al. A large outbreak of acupuncture-associated hepatitis B. Am J Epidemiol. 1988;127:591–598.
97. Oren I, Hershow RC, Ben-Porath E, et al. A common-source outbreak of fulminant hepatitis B in a hospital. Ann Intern Med. 1989;110:691–698.
98. Canter J, Mackey K, Good LS, et al. An outbreak of hepatitis B associated with jet infections in a weight reduction clinic. Arch Intern Med. 1990;150:1923–1927.
99. Garibaldi RA, Rasmussen CM, Holmes AW, Gregg MB. Hospital-acquired serum hepatitis: Report of an outbreak. JAMA. 1972;219:1577–1580.
100. Gerety RJ. Hepatitis B transmission between dental or medical workers and patients. Ann Intern Med. 1981;95:229–231.
101. Lettau LA, Smith JD, Williams D, et al. Transmission of hepatitis B with resultant restriction of surgical practice. JAMA. 1986;255:934–937.
102. Weber DJ, Hoffmann KK, Rutala WA. Management of the healthcare worker infected with human immunodeficiency virus: Lessons from nosocomial transmission of hepatitis B virus. Infect Control Hosp Epidemiol. 1991;12:625–630.
103. Bell DM, Shapiro CN, Ciesielski CA, Chamberland ME. Preventing bloodborne pathogen transmission from health-care workers to patients. Surg Clin North Am. 1995;75:1189–1203.
104. Centers for Disease Control. Recommendations for preventing transmission of human immunodeficiency virus and hepatitis B virus to patients during exposure-prone invasive procedures. MMWR Morb Mortal Wkly Rep. 1991;40(RR-8):1–9.
105. Gerberding JL. The infected health care worker. N Engl J Med. 1996;334:594–595.
106. Shanson DC. Hepatitis B outbreak in operating-theatre and intensive care staff (Letter). Lancet. 1980;2:596.
107. Petrosillo N, Puro V, Jagger J, Ippolito G. The risks of occupational exposure and infection by human immunodeficiency virus, hepatitis B virus, and hepatitis C virus in the dialysis setting. Italian Multicenter Study on Nosocomial and Occupational Risk of Infections in Dialysis. Am J Infect Control. 1995;23:278–285.
108. Centers for Disease Control and Prevention. Outbreaks of hepatitis B virus infection among hemodialysis patients—California, Nebraska, and Texas, 1994. MMWR Morb Mortal Wkly Rep. 1996;45:285–289.
109. Alter MJ, Favero MS, Maynard JE. Impact of infection control strategies on the incidence of dialysis-associated hepatitis in the United States. J Infect Dis. 1986;153:1149–1151.
110. Lettau LA. The A, B, C, D, and E of viral hepatitis: Spelling out the risk for healthcare workers. Infect Control Hosp Epidemiol. 1992;13:77–81.
111. Diekema DJ, Doebbeling BN. Employee health and infection control. Infect Control Hosp Epidemiol. 1995;16:292–301.
112. Duthie R, Morgan-Capner P, Wilson M, Hitchen L. Problems in management of health care workers exposed to HBeAg positive body fluids. J Hosp Infect. 1994;26:129–132.
113. AIDS/TB Committee of the Society for Healthcare Epidemiology of America. Management of healthcare workers infected with hepatitis B virus, hepatitis C virus, human immunodeficiancy virus, or other bloodborne pathogens. Infect Control Hosp Epidemiol. 1997;18:349–363.
114. Stokes J, Blanchard M, Neefe JR, et al. Methods of protection against serum hepatitis. 1. Studies on the protective value of gamma globulin in homologous serum hepatitis SH virus. JAMA. 1948;138:336–343.
115. Beasley RP, Hwang LY, Stevens CE, et al. Efficacy of hepatitis B immune globulin for prevention of perinatal transmission of the hepatitis B virus carrier state: Final report of a randomized double-blind, placebo-controlled trial. Hepatology. 1983;3:135–141.
116. Lo KJ, Tsai YT, Lee SD, et al. Immunoprophylaxis of infection with hepatitis B virus in infants born to hepatitis B surface antigen–positive carrier mothers. J Infect Dis. 1985;152:817–822.
117. Stevens CE, Taylor PE, Ton MJ, et al. Yeast-recombinant hepatitis B vaccine: Efficacy with hepatitis B immune globulin in prevention of perinatal hepatitis B virus transmission. JAMA. 1987;257:2612–2616.
118. Stevens CE, Toy PT, Myron JT, et al. Perinatal hepatitis B virus transmission in the United States. JAMA. 1985;253:1740–1745.
119. Centers for Disease Control. Protection against viral hepatitis: Recommendations of the Immunization Practices Advisory Committee (ACIP). MMWR Morb Mortal Wkly Rep. 1990;39(Suppl):1–26.
120. Alter MJ, Hadler SC, Margolis HS, et al. The changing epidemiology of hepatitis B in the United States. JAMA. 1990;263:1218–1222.
121. Horowitz MM, Ershler WB, McKinney WP, Battiola RJ. Duration of immunity after hepatitis B vaccination: Efficacy of low-dose booster vaccine. Ann Intern Med. 1988;108:185–189.
122. Wainwright RB, Bulkow LR, Parkinsin AJ, et al. Protection provided by hepatitis B vaccine in a Yupik Eskimo population—Results of a 10-year study. J Infect Dis. 1997;175:674–677.
123. McMahon BJ, Helminiak C, Wainwright RB, et al. Frequency of adverse reactions to hepatitis B vaccine in 43,618 persons. Am J Med. 1992;92:254–256.
124. Roome AJ, Walsh SJ, Cartter ML, Hadler JL. Hepatitis B vaccine responsiveness in Connecticut public safety personnel. JAMA. 1993;270:2931–2934.
125. Wood RC, MacDonald KL, White KE, et al. Risk factors for lack of detectable antibody following hepatitis B vaccination of Minnesota health care workers. JAMA. 1993;270:2935–2939.
126. Hollinger FB. Factors influencing the immune response to hepatitis B vaccine, booster drug guidelines, and vaccine protocol recommendations. Am J Med. 1989;87(Suppl 3A):3A-36S–3A-40S.
127. Centers for Disease Control and Prevention. Inadequate immune response among public safety workers receiving intradermal vaccination against hepatitis B—United States—1990–1991. MMWR Morb Mortal Wkly Rep. 1991;40:569–572.
128. Zuckerman JN, Sabin C, Craig FM, et al. Immune response to a new hepatitis B vaccine in healthcare workers who had not responded to standard vaccine: Randomised double blind dose-response study. BMJ. 1997;314:329–333.
129. Bertino JS Jr, Tirrell P, Greenberg RN, et al. A comparative trial of standard or high-dose S subunit recombinant hepatitis B vaccine versus a vaccine containing S subunit, pre-S1, and pre-S2 particles for revaccination of healthy adult nonresponders. J Infect Dis. 1997;175:678–681.
130. Chang, MH, Chen CJ, Lai MS, et al. Universal hepatitis B vaccination in Taiwan and the incidence of hepatocellular carcinoma in children. N Engl J Med. 1997;336:1855–1859.
131. Israsena S, Kamolratanakul P, Sakulramrung R. Factors influencing acceptance of hepatitis B vaccination by hospital personnel in an area hyperendemic for hepatitis B. Am J Gastroenterol. 1992;87:1807–1809.
132. Karpuch J, Scapa E, Eshchar J, et al. Vaccination against hepatitis B in a general hospital in Israel: Antibody level before vaccination and immunogenicity of vaccine. Isr J Med Sci. 1993;29:471–472.
133. Doebbeling BN, Ferguson KJ, Kohout FJ. Predictors of hepatitis B vaccine acceptance in health care workers. Med Care. 1996;34:58–72.
134. Centers for Disease Control and Prevention. Recommendations for follow-up of health-care workers after occupational exposure to hepatitis C. MMWR Morb Mortal Wkly Rep. 1997;46:603–606.
135. Alter MJ. The detection, transmission, and outcome of hepatitis C virus infection. Infect Agents Dis. 1993;2:155–166.
136. Sharara AI, Hunt CM, Hamilton JD. Hepatitis C. Ann Intern Med. 1996;125:658–668.
137. Polywka S, Laufs R. Hepatitis C virus antibodies among different groups at risk and patients with suspected non-A, non-B hepatitis. Infection. 1991;19:81–84.
138. Zuckerman J, Clewley G, Griffiths P, Cockcroft A. Prevalence of hepatitis C antibodies in clinical health-care workers. Lancet. 1994;343:1618–1620.
139. Polish LB, Tong MJ, Co RL, et al. Risk factors for hepatitis C among health care personnel in a community hospital. Am J Infect Control. 1993;21:196–200.
140. Campello C, Majori S, Poli A, et al. Prevalence of HCV antibodies in health-care workers from northern Italy. Infection. 1992;20:224–226.
141. Struve J, Aronsson B, Frenning B, et al. Prevalence of antibodies against hepatitis C virus infection among health care workers in Stockholm. Scand J Gastroenterol. 1994;29:360–362.
142. De Luca M, Ascione A, Vacca C, Zarone A. Are health-care workers really at risk of HCV infection? (Letter). Lancet. 1992;339:1364–1365.
143. Cooper BW, Krusell A, Tilton RC, et al. Seroprevalence of antibodies to hepatitis C virus in high-risk hospital personnel. Infect Control Hosp Epidemiol. 1992;13:82–85.
144. Neal KR, Dornan J, Irving WL. Prevalence of hepatitis C antibodies among healthcare workers of two teaching hospitals: Who is at risk? BMJ. 1997;314:179–80.
145. Forester G, Wormser GP, Adler S, et al. Hepatitis C in the health care setting. Seroprevalence among hemodialysis staff and patients. Am J Infect Control. 1993;21:5–8.
146. Stellini R, Calzini AS, Gussago A, et al. Low prevalence of anti-HCV antibodies in hospital workers. Eur J Epidemiol. 1993;9:674–675.
147. Puro V, Petrosillo N, Ippolito G, Jagger J. Hepatitis C virus in healthcare workers (Letter). Infect Control Hosp Epidemiol. 1995;16:324–325.
148. Cunngingham SJ, Cunngingham R, Izmeth MGA, et al. Seroprevalence of hepatitis B and C in a Merseyside hospital for the mentally handicapped. Epidemiol Infect. 1994;112:195–200.
149. Jankovic N, Cala S, Nadinic B, et al. Hepatitis C and hepatitis B virus infection in hemodialysis patients and staff: A two year follow-up. Int J Artif Organs. 1994;17:137–140.
150. Niu MT, Coleman PJ, Alter MJ. Multicenter study of hepatitis C virus infection in chronic hemodialysis patients and hemodialysis center staff members. Am J Kidney Dis. 1993;22:568–573.
151. Lamphear BP, Linnemann CC, Cannon CG, et al. Hepatitis C virus infection in healthcare workers: Risk of exposure and infection. Infect Control Hosp Epidemiol. 1994;15:745–750.
152. Jochen ABB. Occupationally acquired hepatitis C virus infection (Letter). Lancet 1992;339:304.
153. Stroffolini T, Marzolini A, Palumbo F, et al. Incidence of non-A, non-B and HCV positive hepatitis in healthcare workers in Italy. J Hosp Infect. 1996;33:131–137.
154. De Mercato R, Guarnaccia D, Ciannella G, et al. Hepatitis C virus among health care workers. Minerva Med. 1996;87:501–504.
155. Thomas DL, Gruninger SE, Siew C, et al. Occupational risk of hepatitis C infections among dentists and oral surgeons in North America. Arch Intern Med. 1996;100:41–45.
156. Klein RS, Freeman K, Taylor PE, Stevens CE. Occupational risk for hepatitis C virus infection among New York City dentists. Lancet. 1991;338:1539–1542.
157. Herbert AM, Walker DM, Davies KJ, Bagg J. Occupationally acquired hepatitis C virus infection (Letter). Lancet. 1992;339:305.
158. Bosch H. Hepatitis C outbreak astounds Spain. Lancet. 1998;351:1415.
159. Sartori M, La Terra G, Aglietta M, et al. Transmission of hepatitis C via blood splash into conjunctiva. Scand J Infect Dis. 1993;25:270–271.
160. Tennenbaum R, Colardelle P, Chochon M, et al. Hepatitis C after retrograde cholangiography (in French). Gastroenterol Clin Biol. 1993;17:763–764.
161. Bronowicki JP, Venard V, Botte C, et al. Patient-to-patient transmission of hepatitis C virus during colonoscopy. N Engl J Med. 1997;337:237–240.
162. Pereira BJ, Levey AS. Hepatitis C virus infection in dialysis and renal transplantation. Kidney Int. 1997;51:981–999.
163. Petrarulo F, Maggi P, Sacchetti A, et al. HCV infection occupational hazard at

dialysis units and virus spread, among relatives of dialyzed patients. Nephron. 1992;61:302–303.
164. Besso L, Rovere A, Peano G, et al. Prevalence of HCV antibodies in a uraemic population undergoing maintenance dialysis therapy and in the staff members of the dialysis unit. Nephron. 1992;61:304–306.
165. Chan TM, Lok AS, Cheng IK, Chan RT. Prevalence of hepatitis C virus infection in hemodialysis patients: A longitudinal study comparing the results of RNA and antibody assays. Hepatology. 1993;17:5–8.
166. Jadoul M, Cornu C, van Ypersele de Strihou C. Incidence and risk factors for hepatitis C seroconversion in hemodialysis: A prospective study. Kidney Int. 1993;44:1322–1326.
167. Simon N, Courouce AM, Lemarrec N, et al. A twelve year natural history of hepatitis C virus infection in hemodialyzed patients. Kidney Int. 1994;46:504–511.
168. Morales MF, Lossi JS, Alderete TN, Noli D. Prevalence and seroconversion to HCV in hemodialyzed patients, and epidemiological factors. Transplant Proc. 1996;28:3402–3405.
169. Nakayama E, Liu JH, Akiba T, et al. Low prevalence of anti–hepatitis C virus antibodies in female hemodialysis patients without blood transfusion: A multicenter analysis. J Med Virol. 1996;48:284–288.
170. Bosmans JL, Nouwen EJ, Behets G, et al. Prevalence and clinical expression of HCV-genotypes in haemodialysis-patients of two geographically remote countries: Belgium and Saudi-Arabia. Clin Nephrol. 1997;47:256–262.
171. Watanabe T, Ishiguro M, Kametani M, et al. GB virus C and hepatitis C virus infections in hemodialysis patients in eight Japanese centers. Nephron. 1997;76:171–175.
172. Abdelnour GE, Matar GM, Sharara HM, Abdelnoor AM. Detection of anti–hepatitis C-virus antibodies and hepatitis C-virus RNA in Lebanese hemodialysis patients. Eur J Epidemiol. 1997;13:863–867.
173. Dentico P, Buongiorno R, Volpe A, et al. Prevalence and incidence of hepatitis C virus (HCV) in hemodialysis patients: Study of risk factors. Clin Nephrol. 1992;38:49–52.
174. Stuyver L, Claeys H, Wyseur A, et al. Hepatitis C virus in a hemodialysis unit: Molecular evidence for nosocomial transmission. Kidney Int. 1996;49:889–895.
175. Fabrizi F, Lunghi G, Pagliari B, et al. Molecular epidemiology of hepatitis C virus infection in dialysis patients. Nephron. 1997;77;190–196.
176. Cendoroglo Neto M, Manzano SI, Canziani ME, et al. Environmental transmission of hepatitis B and hepatitis C viruses within the hemodialysis unit. Artif Organs. 1995;19:251–255.
177. Seme K, Poljak M, Zuzek-Resek S, et al. Molecular evidence for nosocomial spread of two different hepatitis C virus strains in one hemodialysis unit. Nephron. 1997;77:273–278.
178. Olmer M, Bouchouareb D, Zandotti C, et al. Transmission of the hepatitis C virus in an hemodyalysis unit: Evidence for nosocomial infection. Clin Nephrol. 1997;47:263–270.
179. McLaughlin KJ, Cameron SO, Good T, et al. Nosocomial transmission of hepatitis C virus within a British dialysis centre. Nephrol Dial Transplant. 1997;12:304–309.
180. Golan E, Korzets A, Cristal-Lilov A, Ben-Tovim T, Bernheim J. Increased prevalence of HCV antibodies in dialyzed Ashkenazi Jews: A possible ethnic predesposition. Nephrol Dial Transplant. 1996;11:684–686.
181. Pujol FH, Ponce JG, Lema MG, et al. High incidence of hepatitis C virus infection in hemodialysis patients in units with high prevalence. J Clin Microbiol. 1996;34:1633–1636.
182. Fabrizi F, Martin P, Dixit V, et al. Acquisition of hepatitis C virus in hemodialysis patients: A prospective study by branched DNA signal amplification assay. Am J Kidney Dis. 1998;31:647–654.
183. Forns X, Fernandez-Llama P, Pons M, et al. Incidence and risk factors of hepatitis C virus infection in a haemodialysis unit. Nephrol Dial Transplant. 1997;12:736–740.
184. Caramelo C, Bartolome J, Albalate M, et al. Undiagnosed hepatitis C virus infection in hemodialysis patients: Value of HCV RNA and liver enzyme levels. Kidney Int. 1996;50:2027–2031.
185. Niu MT, Alter MJ, Kristensen C, Margolis HS. Outbreak of hemodialysis-associated non-A, non-B hepatitis and correlation with antibody to hepatitis C virus. Am J Kidney Dis. 1992;19:345–352.
186. Allander T, Gruber A, Naghavi M, et al. Frequent patient-to-patient transmission of hepatitis C virus in a haematology ward. Lancet. 1995;345:603–607.
187. Hardy NM, Sandroni S, Danielson S, Wilson WJ. Antibody to hepatitis C virus increases with time on hemodialysis. Clin Nephrol. 1992;38:44–48.
188. Hayashi H, Okuda K, Yokosuka O, et al. Adsorption of hepatitis C virus particles onto the dialyzer membrane. Artif Organs. 1997;21:1056–1059.
189. Pereira BJ, Milford EL, Kirkman RL, Levey AS. Transmission of hepatitis C virus by organ transplantation. N Engl J Med. 1991;325:454–460.
190. Pereira BJ, Milford EL, Kirkman RL, et al. Prevalence of hepatitis C virus RNA in organ donors positive for hepatitis C antibody and in the recipients of their organs. N Engl J Med. 1992;327:910–915.
191. Perez-Trallero E, Cilla G, Saenz JR. Occupational transmission of HCV. Lancet. 1994;344:548.
192. Puro V, Petrosillo N, Ippolito G. Risk of hepatitis C seroconversion after occupational exposures in health care workers. Italian Study Group on Occupational Risk of HIV and Other Bloodborne Infections. Am J Infect Control. 1995;23:273–277.
193. Kiyosawa K, Sodeyama T, Tanaka E, et al. Hepatitis C in hospital employees with needlestick injuries. Ann Intern Med. 1991;115:367–369.
194. Mitsui T, Iwano K, Masuko K, et al. Hepatitis C virus infection in medical personnel after needlestick accident. Hepatology. 1992;16:1109–1114.
195. Marranconi F. HCV infection following accidental needlestick injury in health-care workers. Infection. 1992;20:111.
196. Sodeyama T, Kiyosawa K, Urushihara A, et al. Detection of hepatitis C virus markers and hepatitis C virus genomic-RNA after needlestick accidents. Arch Intern Med. 1993;153:1565–1572.
197. Hernandez ME, Bruguera M, Puyuelo T, et al. Risk of needlestick injuries in the transmission of hepatitis C virus in hospital personnel. J Hepatol. 1992;16:56–58.
198. Puro V, Petrosillo N, Ippolito G, et al. Occupational hepatitis C virus infection in Italian health care workers. Am J Public Health. 1995;85:1272–1275.
199. Ridzon R, Gallagher K, Ciesielski C, et al. Simultaneous transmission of human immunodeficiency virus and hepatitis C virus from a needle-stick injury. N Engl J Med. 1997;33:919–922.
200. Lemon SM, Thomas DL. Vaccines to prevent viral hepatitis. N Engl J Med. 1997;336:196–203.
201. Piazza M, Sagliocca L, Tosone G, et al. Sexual transmission of the hepatitis C virus and efficacy of prophylaxis with intramuscular immune serum globulin. Arch Intern Med. 1997;157:1537–1544.
202. Noguchi S, Sata M, Suzuki H, et al. Early therapy with interferon for acute hepatitis C acquired through a needlestick. Clin Infect Dis. 1997;24:992–994.
203. Viladomiu L, Genesca J, Esteban JI, et al. Interferon in acute posttransfusion hepatitis C: A randomized controlled trial. Hepatology. 1992;15:767–769.
204. Vento S, Garofano T, Renzini C, et al. Fulminant hepatitis associated with hepatitis A virus superinfection in patients with chronic hepatitis C. N Engl J Med. 1998;338:286–290.
205. Mele A, Tosti ME, Stroffolini T. Hepatitis associated with hepatitis A superinfection in patients with chronic hepatitis C (Letter). N Engl J Med. 1998;338:1771–1773.
206. Koff RS. Should health care workers exposed to hepatitis C routinely receive hepatitis A vaccine? (Letter). JAMA. 1998;279:195.
207. Lettau LA, Alfred HJ, Glew RH, et al. Nosocomial transmission of delta hepatitis. Ann Intern Med. 1986;104:631–635.
208. Alter MJ, Gallagher M, Morris TT, et al. Acute non-A–E hepatitis in the United States and the role of hepatitis G virus infection. N Engl J Med. 1997;336:741–746.
209. Alter HJ, Nakatsuji Y, Melpolder J, et al. The incidence of transfusion-associated hepatitis G virus infection and its relation to liver disease. N Engl J Med. 1997;336:747–754.
210. Masuko K, Mitsui T, Iwano K, et al. Infection with hepatitis GB virus C in patients on maintenance hemodyalisis. N Engl J Med. 1996;334:1485–1490.
211. Cornu C, Jadoul M, Loute G, Goubau P. Hepatitis G virus infection in haemodialysed patients: Epidemiology and clinical relevance. Nephrol Dial Transplant. 1997;12:1326–1329.
212. Bjorkman P, Sundstrom G, Widell A. Hepatitis C virus and GB virus C/hepatitis G virus viremia in Swedish blood donors with different alanine aminotransferase levels. Transfusion. 1998;38:378–384.
213. Kallinowski B, Ahmadi R, Seipp S, et al. Clinical impact of GB-C virus in haemodialysis patients. Nephrol Dial Transplant. 1998;13:93–98.
214. Okuda K, Kanda T, Yokusura O, et al. GB virus-C infection among chronic haemodialysis patients: Clinical implications. J Gastroenterol Hepatol. 1997;12:766–770.
215. Sheng L, Widyastuti A, Kosala H, et al. High prevalence of hepatitis G virus infection compared with hepatitis C virus infection in patients undergoing chronic hemodialysis. Am J Kidney Dis. 1998;31:218–223.
216. Beeson PB. Jaundice occurring one to four months after transfusion of blood or plasma. JAMA. 1943;121:1332–1334.
217. Brightman J, Korns RF. Homologous serum jaundice in recipients of pooled plasma. JAMA. 1947;165:268–272.
218. Scheinberg IH, Kinney TD, Janeway CA. Homologous serum jaundice: A problem for the operation of blood banks. JAMA. 1947;134:841–848.
219. Surgenor DM, Wallace EL, Hao SHS, Chapman RH. Collection and transfusion of blood in the United States, 1982–1988. N Engl J Med. 1990;322:1646–1651.
220. Chamberland M, Khabbaz RF. Emerging issues in blood safety. Infect Dis Clin North Am. 1998;12:217–229.
221. NIH Consensus Conference. Infectious disease testing for blood transfusions. JAMA. 1995;274:1374–1379.
222. Sloand EM, Pitt E, Klein HG. Safety of the blood supply. JAMA. 1995;274:1368–1373.
223. Williams AE, Thomson RA, Schreiber GB, et al. Estimates of infectious disease risk factors in US blood donors. JAMA. 1997;277:967–972.
224. Wallace EL, Surgenor DM, Hao HS, et al. Collection and transfusion of blood and blood components in the United States, 1989. Transfusion. 1993;33:139–144.
225. Wallace EL, Churchill WH, Surgenor DM, et al. Collection and transfusion of blood and blood components in the United States, 1992. Transfusion. 1995;35:802–812.
226. McCullough J: The nation's changing blood supply system. JAMA. 1993;269:2239–2245.
227. Vamvakas EC, Taswell HF. Epidemiology of blood transfusion. Transfusion. 1994;34:464–470.
228. Starkey JM, MacPherson JL, Bolgiano DC, et al. Markers for transfusion-transmitted disease in different groups of blood donors. JAMA. 1989;262:34552–34554.
229. Glynn SA, Schreiber GB, Busch MP, et al. Demographic characteristics, unreported risk behaviors, and the prevalence and incidence of viral infections: A comparison of apheresis and whole-blood donors. Transfusion. 1998;38:350–358.
230. Devine P, Linden JV, Hoffstadter LK, et al. Blood donor–, apheresis-, and transfusion-related activities: Results of the 1991 American Association of Blood Banks Institutional Membership Questionnaire. Transfusion. 1993;33:779–782.

231. Thomson RA, Bethel J, Lo AY, et al. Retention of "safe" blood donors. Transfusion. 1998;38:359–367.
232. Schreiber GB, Busch MP, Kleinman SH, Korelitz JJ. The risk of transfusion-transmitted viral infections. N Engl J Med. 1996;334:1685–1690.
233. Courouce AM, Pillonel J. Transfusion-transmitted viral infections. Retrovirus and Viral Hepatitis Working Groups of the French Society of Blood Transfusion. N Engl J Med. 1996;335:1609–1610.
234. Whyte GS, Savoia HF. The risk of transmitting HCV, HBV or HIV by blood transfusion in Victoria. Med J Aust. 1997;166:584–586.
235. Centers for Disease Control and Prevention. HIV/AIDS surveillance report, 1997;9(2):10.
236. Kroner BL, Rosenberg PS, Aledort LM, et al. HIV-1 infection incidence among persons with hemophilia in the United States and western Europe, 1978–1990. Multicenter Hemophilia Cohort Study. J Acquir Immune Defic Syndr. 1994;7:279–286.
237. Lackritz EM, Satten GA, Aberle-Grasse J, et al. Estimated risk of transmission of the human immunodeficiency virus by screened blood in the United States. N Engl J Med. 1995;333:1721–1725.
238. Kleinman S, Busch MP, Korelitz JJ, Schreiber GB. The incidence/window period model and its use to assess the risk of transfusion-transmitted human immunodeficiency virus and hepatitis C virus infection. Transtus Med Rev. 1997;11:155–172.
239. AuBuchon JP, Birkmeyer JD, Busch MP. Cost-effectiveness of expanded human immunodeficiency virus–testing protocols for donated blood. Transfusion. 1997;37:45–51.
240. Busch MP, Lee LL, Satten GA, et al. Time course of detection of viral and serologic markers preceding human immunodeficiency virus type 1 seroconversion: Implications for screening of blood and tissue donors. Transfusion. 1995;35:91–97.
241. Stramer SL, Salemi BL, Sievert WS, et al. Evaluation of U.S. blood donations testing positive for HIV-1 p24 antigen (p24) (Abstract S151). Transfusion. 1996;36:38S.
242. Lackritz EM, Stramer SL, Jacobs TA, et al. Results of national testing of US blood donations for HIV-1 p-24 antigen (Abstract 751). Programs and Abstracts of the Fourth Conference on Retroviruses and Opportunistic Infections, Washington DC, 1997, p 203.
243. Brown AE, Jackson B, Fuller SA, et al. Viral RNA in the resolution of human immunodeficiency virus type 1 diagnostic serology. Transfusion. 1997;37:926–929.
244. Leitman SF, Klein HG, Melpolder JJ, et al. Clinical implications of positive tests for antibodies to human immunodeficiency virus type 1 in asymptomatic blood donors. N Engl J Med. 1989;321:917–924.
245. Sayre KR, Dodd RY, Tegtmeier G, et al. False-positive human immunodeficiency virus type 1 Western blot tests in noninfected blood donors. Transfusion. 1996;36:45–52.
246. Busch MP, Kleinman SH, Williams AE, et al. Frequency of human immunodeficiency virus (HIV) infection among contemporary anti–HIV-1 and anti–HIV-1/2 supplemental test–indeterminate blood donors. Transfusion. 1996;36:37–44.
247. Loussert-Ajaka I, Ly TD, Chaix ML, et al. HIV-1/HIV-2 seronegativity in HIV-1 subtype 0 infected patients. Lancet. 1994;343:1393–1394.
248. Schable C, Zekeng L, Pau CP, et al. Sensitivity of United States HIV antibody tests for detection of HIV-1 group O infections. Lancet. 1994;344:1333–1334.
249. Jongerius JM, van der Poel CL, van Loon AM, et al. Human immunodeficiency virus (HIV) antibodies detected by new assays that are enhanced for HIV-1 subtype O. Transfusion. 1997;37:841–844.
250. Centers for Disease Control and Prevention. Update: HIV-2 infection among blood and plasma donors—United States, June 1992–June 1995. MMWR Morb Mortal Wkly Rep. 1995;44:603–606.
251. Nelson KE, Donahue JG, Muñoz A, et al. Transmission of retroviruses from seronegative donors by transfusion during cardiac surgery. A multicenter study of HIV-1 and HTLV I/II infections. Ann Intern Med. 1992;117:554–559.
252. Vrielink H, Zaaijer HL, Reesink HW. The clinical relevance of HTLV type I and II in transfusion medicine. Transfus Med Rev. 1997;11:173–179.
253. Gallo D, Yeh ET, Moore ES, Hanson CV. Comparison of four enzyme immunoassays for detection of human T-cell lymphotropic virus type 2 antibodies. J Clin Microbiol. 1996;34:213–215.
254. Giacoia GP, Kasprisin DO. Transfusion-acquired hepatitis A. South Med J. 1989;82:1357–1360.
255. Mannucci PM, Gdovin S, Gringeri A, et al. Transmission of hepatitis A to patients with hemophilia by factor VIII concentrates treated with organic solvent and detergent to inactivate viruses. Ann Intern Med. 1994;120:1–7.
256. Kedda MA, Kew MC, Cohn RJ, et al. An outbreak of hepatitis A among South African patients with hemophilia: Evidence implicating contaminated factor VIII concentrate as the source. Hepatology. 1995;22:1363–1367.
257. Centers for Disease Control and Prevention. Prevention of hepatitis A through active or passive immunization: Recommendations of the Advisory Committee of Immunization Practices. MMWR Morb Mortal Wkly Rep. 1996;45(RR-4):1–30.
258. Brechot C, Degos F, Lugassy C, et al. Hepatitis B virus DNA in patients with chronic liver disease and negative tests for hepatitis B surface antigen. N Engl J Med. 1985; 312:270–276.
259. Dodd RY. Transfusion-transmitted hepatitis virus infection. Hematol Oncol Clin North Am. 1995;9:137–154.
260. Jongerius JM, Wester M, Cyupers HTM, et al. New hepatitis B virus mutant form in a blood donor that is undetectable in several hepatitis B surface antigen screening assays. Transfusion. 1998;38:56–59.
261. Rosina F, Saracco G, Rizzetto M. Risk of post-transfusion infection with the hepatitis delta virus. N Engl J Med. 1985;312:1488–1491.
262. Alter HJ, Purcell RH, Holland PV, et al. Donor transaminase and recipient hepatitis. Impact on blood transfusion services. JAMA. 1981;246:630–634.
263. Aach RD, Szmuness W, Mosley JW, et al. Serum alanine aminotransferase of donors in relation to the risk of non-A, non-B hepatitis in recipients. N Engl J Med. 1981;304:989–994.
264. Goldman M, Juodvalkis S, Gill P, Spurll G. Hepatitis C lookback. Transfus Med Rev. 1998;12:84–93.
265. Murphy EL, Bryzman S, Williams AE, et al. Demographic determinants of hepatitis C virus seroprevalence among blood donors. JAMA. 1996;275:995–1000.
266. Conry-Cantilena C, VanRaden M, Gibble J, et al. Routes of infection, viremia, and liver disease in blood donors found to have hepatitis C virus infection. N Engl J Med. 1996;334:1691–1696.
267. Donahue JG, Muñoz A, Ness PM, et al. The declining risk of post-transfusion hepatitis C virus infection. N Engl J Med. 1992;327:369–373.
268. Camps J, Gonzalez A, Esteban JI, et al. Towards zero risk of posttransfusion hepatitis with 2nd generation anti-HCV screening of blood donors. Hepatology. 1994;20:200A.
269. Kleinman S, Alter H, Busch M, et al. Increased detection of hepatitis C virus (HCV)-infected blood donors by a multiple-antigen HCV enzyme immunoassay. Transfusion. 1992;32:805–813.
270. Alter MJ, Margolis HS, Krawczynski K, et al. The natural history of community-acquired hepatitis C in the United States. N Engl J Med. 1992;327:1899–1905.
271. Lindholm A. Epidemiology of viral infections in the Swedish blood-donor program. Blood Coagul Fibrinolyses. 1994;5:S13–S17.
272. Vrielink H, Reesink HW, van den Burg PJ, et al. Performance of three generations of anti–hepatitis C virus enzyme-linked immunosorbent assays in donors and patients. Transfusion. 1997;37:845–849.
273. Prince AM, Scheffel JW, Moore B. A search for hepatitis C virus polymerase chain reaction–positive but seronegative subjects among blood donors with elevated alanine aminotransferase. Transfusion. 1997;37:211–214.
274. Henrard DR, Berthillon P, Scheffel JW, et al. Lack of evidence of hepatitis C infection in 290 blood component recipients, demonstrated by several single-antigen research immunoassays. Transfusion. 1998;38:194–198.
275. Bresee JS, Mast EE, Coleman PJ, et al. Hepatitis C virus infection associated with administration of intravenous immune globulin. JAMA. 1996;276:1563–1567.
276. Widell A, Zhang Y-Y, Andersson-Gare B, Hammarstrom L. At least three hepatitis C virus strains implicated in Swedish and Danish patients with intravenous immunoglobulin associated hepatitis C. Transfusion. 1997;37:313–320.
277. Yoshikawa A, Fakuda S, Itoh K, et al. Infection with hepatitis G virus and its strain variant, the GB agent (GBV-C) among blood donors in Japan. Transfusion. 1997;37:657–663.
278. Tacke M, Kiyosawa K, Stark K, et al. Detection of antibodies to a putative hepatitis G virus envelope protein. Lancet. 1997;349:318–320.
279. Alter HJ, Nakatsuji Y, Melpolder J, et al. The incidence of transfusion-associated hepatitis G virus infection and its relation to liver disease. N Engl J Med. 1997;336:747–754.
280. Prati D, Zanella A, Bosoni P, et al. The incidence and natural course of transfusion-associated GB virus C/hepatitis G virus infection in a cohort of thalassemic patients. Blood. 1998;91:774–777.
281. Sayers MH. Transfusion-transmitted viral infections other than hepatitis and human immunodeficiency virus infection: Cytomegalovirus, Epstein-Barr virus, human herpesvirus 6 and human parvovirus B19. Arch Pathol Lab Med. 1994;118:346–349.
282. Bowden RA. Transfusion-transmited cytomegalovirus infection. Hematol Oncol Clin North Am. 1995;9:155–166.
283. Hersman J, Meyers JD, Thomas ED, et al. The effect of granulocyte transfusions on the incidence of cytomegalovirus infection after allogeneic marrow transplantation. Ann Intern Med. 1982;96:149–152.
284. Bowden R, Slichter S, Sayers M, et al. A comparison of filtered leukocyte-reduced and cytomegalovirus (CMV) seronegative blood products for the prevention of transfusion-associated CMV infection after marrow transplant. Blood. 1995;86:3598–3603.
285. Wagner HJ, Klüter H, Kruse A, Kirchner H. Relevanz der übertragung des Epstein-Barr-Virus durch Bluttransfusionen. Beitr Infusionsther Transfusionsmed. 1994;32:138–141.
286. Santagostino E, Mannucci PM, Gringeri A, et al. Transmission of parvovirus B19 by coagulation factor concentrates exposed to 100 C heat after lyophilization. Transfusion. 1997;37:517–522.
287. Nishizawa T, Okamoto H, Konishi K, et al. A novel DNA virus (TTV) associated with elevated transaminase levels in posttransfusion hepatitis of unknown etiology. Biochem Biophys Res Commun. 1997;241:92–97.
288. Simmonds P, Davidson F, Lycett C, et al. Detection of a novel DNA virus (TTV) in blood donors and blood products. Lancet. 1998;352:191–195.
289. Naoumov NV, Petrova EP, Thomas MG, et al. Presence of a newly described human DNA virus (TTV) in patients with liver disease. Lancet. 1998;352:195–197.
290. Cossar Y. TTV a common virus, but pathogenic? Lancet. 1998;352:164.
291. Krishnan LAG, Brecher ME. Transfusion-transmitted bacterial infection. Hematol Oncol Clin North Am. 1995;9:167–185.
292. Klein HG, Dodd RY, Ness PM, et al. Current status of microbial contamination of blood components: Summary of a conference. Transfusion. 1997;37:95–101.
293. Wagner SJ, Friedman LI, Dodd RY. Transfusion-associated bacterial sepsis. Clin Microbiol Rev. 1994;7:290–302.
294. Wagner S. Transfusion-related bacterial sepsis. Curr Opin Hematol. 1997;4:464–469.

295. Barrett BB, Andersen JW, Anderson KC. Strategies for the avoidance of bacterial contamination of blood components. Transfusion. 1993;33:228–233.
296. Centers for Disease Control and Prevention. Red blood cell transfusions contaminated with *Yersinia enterocolitica*—United States, 1991–1996, and initiation of a national study to detect bacteria-associated transfusion reactions. MMWR Morb Mortal Wkly Rep. 1997;46:553–555.
297. Zaza S, Tokars JI, Yomtovian R, et al. Bacterial contamination of platelets at a university hospital: Increased identification due to intensified surveillance. Infect Control Hosp Epidemiol. 1994;15:82–87.
298. Heltberg O, Skov F, Gerner-Smidt P, et al. Nosocomial epidemic of *Serratia marcescens* septicemia ascribed to contaminated blood transfusion bags. Transfusion. 1993;33:221–227.
299. Houbiers JG, van de Velde CJ, van de Watering LM, et al. Transfussion of red cells is associated with increased incidence of bacterial infection after colorectal surgery: A prospective study. Transfusion. 1997;37:126–134.
300. Richards C, Kolins J, Trindade CD. Autologous transfusion–transmitted *Yersinia enterocolitica* (Letter). JAMA. 1992;268:1541–1542.
301. Buchholz DH, Young VM, Friedman NR, et al. Bacterial proliferation in platelet products stored at room temperature: Transfusion-induced *Enterobacter* sepsis. N Engl J Med. 1971;285:429–433.
302. Morrow JF, Braine HG, Kickler TS, et al. Septic reactions to platelet transfusion: a persistent problem. JAMA 1991;266:555–58.
303. Leiby DA, Kerr KL, Campos JM, Dodd RY. A retrospective analysis of microbial contaminants in outdated random-donor platelets from multiple sites. Transfusion. 1997;37:259–263.
304. Leiby DA, Read EJ, Lenes BA, et al. Seroepidemiology of *Trypanosoma cruzi*, etiologic agent of Chagas' disease, in US blood donors. J Infec Dis. 1997;176:1047–1052.
305. Gerber MA, Shapiro ED, Krause PJ, et al. The risk of acquiring Lyme disease or babesiosis from a blood transfusion. J Infect Dis. 1994;170:231–234.
306. Wells GM, Woodward TE, Fiset P, Hornick RB. Rocky Mountain spotted fever caused by blood transfusion. JAMA. 1978;239:2763–2765.
307. De Schryver A, Meheus A. Syphilis and blood transfusion: A global perspective. Transfusion. 1990;30:844–847.
308. Lettau LA. Nosocomial transmission and infection control aspects of parasitic and ectoparasitic diseases. Part II. Blood and tissue parasites. Infect Control Hosp Epidemiol. 1991;12:111–121.
309. Brown P. Can Creutzfeldt-Jakob disease be transmitted by transfusion? Curr Opin Hematol. 1995;2:472–477.
310. Goodnough L, Brecher ME, Kanter MH, et al. Blood transfusion. N Engl J Med. 1999;340:438–447.

Chapter 296

Human Immunodeficiency Virus in Health Care Settings

LINDA A. CHIARELLO
JULIE LOUISE GERBERDING

TRANSMISSION OF HIV IN HEALTH CARE SETTINGS

Transmission of human immunodeficiency virus (HIV) from patient to health care worker, from health care worker to patient, and from one patient to another can occur in health care settings.[1] Needle punctures or similar percutaneous injuries inflicted by contaminated sharp instruments account for most cases of occupational HIV infection among health care personnel. Transmission from an infected health care worker to a patient is unusual, but possible when an infected clinician is injured by a sharp object, which then recontacts a patient's tissues. Transmission between patients is usually attributable to breaches in infection-control practices such as reuse of contaminated equipment or injection of contaminated material. Fortunately, all these modes of transmission are rare. More importantly, both occupational and nosocomial HIV transmission can be prevented. In this chapter, the epidemiology of HIV infections acquired in health care settings, methods to prevent these infections, and principles of postexposure care when exposures do occur will be detailed.

Occupational HIV Transmission from Infected Patients to Health Care Personnel

Reported Cases of Occupational HIV/AIDS

As of December 1998, 54 cases of occupational HIV transmission to health care workers in the United States were detected through surveillance activities conducted by the Centers for Disease Control and Prevention (CDC).[2, 3] In all but one of these cases, occupational transmission was documented by demonstrating HIV antibody seroconversion temporally related to a discreet HIV exposure. In the single exception, infection in a laboratory worker was proved to be occupationally acquired by demonstrating close similarity between the HIV genetic sequence of the worker's virus isolate and that of the laboratory strain used. Most occupational HIV infections were caused by injuries inflicted by hollow-bore needles used in a vein or artery, but other sharp instruments were also involved in transmission. Breaks in the skin or mucous membrane inoculation was the most likely route of transmission in only five cases; each of these involved a large volume extended duration of blood exposure.

In addition to these 54 documented cases of occupational infection, 134 health care providers with possible occupational infection have been reported to the CDC.[3] These individuals did not have a baseline HIV antibody test performed at the time of known or potential exposure to HIV, so the temporal relationship between exposure and seroconversion could not be established with certainty. However, none reported nonoccupational behavior associated with HIV infection, and all recalled at least one exposure to blood or body fluids before their HIV infection was diagnosed.

All but 4 of the 54 documented occupational infections in the United States followed exposure to infected blood; 1 exposure involved bloody pleural fluid, 2 involved exposure to HIV concentrates in laboratories, and for 1 the source material was not reported. Contamination of intact skin with blood or other infectious material, close personal contact with infected patients, or contact with contaminated environmental surfaces or fomites has not been linked to occupational HIV transmission. Aerosolization of blood can occur during dental, pathology, laboratory, and surgical procedures, and inhalation of aerosols is not prevented by conventional surgical masks. However, no data support aerosol exposure as a route of HIV transmission in any setting.

Definition of Occupational HIV Exposure

The reported cases of occupational HIV transmission have been helpful in developing a definition of what constitutes an exposure that could result in HIV transmission. Exposure routes implicated in occupational HIV transmission include (1) percutaneous injury (e.g., needle puncture, cut caused by a needle or other sharp object), (2) mucous membrane contamination, and (3) nonintact skin (e.g., chapped, abraded, or afflicted with dermatitis) contamination.[2] Contact of intact skin when the duration of contact is prolonged (i.e., several minutes or more) or involves an extensive area has not been associated with HIV transmission but is considered a potential exposure, in part because the skin may have unrecognized areas of disruption that could serve as portals of entry.

Sources of HIV that may pose a risk of transmission through these routes include blood, visibly bloody fluids, tissues, and other body fluids including semen, vaginal secretions, and cerebrospinal, synovial, pleural, peritoneal, pericardial, and amniotic fluids.[2] In addition, any direct cutaneous or mucosal contact (i.e., without barrier protection) to concentrated HIV in a research laboratory or production facility is considered to be an exposure.

Although one nonoccupational episode of HIV transmission has been attributed to contact with blood-contaminated saliva, this incident was not analogous to the contact with saliva that occurs during dental or medical care.[4] In the absence of visible blood in the saliva, exposure to saliva from a person infected with HIV is not thought to pose a risk for HIV transmission. Exposure to tears, sweat, or nonbloody urine or feces from infected patients does not constitute exposure to HIV. Human breast milk has been implicated in perinatal transmission of HIV, but breast-feeding is not analogous to occupational exposure. Hence, occupational exposure to breast milk does not constitute an exposure.[2]

Occupational HIV Exposure Transmission Risk

Assessing Infection Risk in Populations of Exposed Health Care Personnel

Worldwide, more than 20 prospective studies have quantified the transmission risk associated with a discrete occupational HIV exposure.[5–16] In these studies, health care workers are tested for HIV antibody at the time of HIV exposure (baseline) and thereafter at regular follow-up intervals to detect new infections. Because both the numerator (number of infections) and the denominator (number of HIV exposures) are known, the probability of transmission through various exposure routes can be estimated.

Pooled data from these studies indicate that the average risk of HIV transmission associated with needle punctures or similar percutaneous injuries involving HIV-contaminated sharp objects is 0.32% (21 infections after 6498 exposures; 95% confidence interval, 0.18 to 0.46%).[1, 2, 5, 17] The estimated mucocutaneous transmission risk is 0.03% (1 infection after 2885 HIV exposures through mucous membranes or nonintact skin), but this estimate may be biased because the single transmission event in the numerator was actually reported before prospective data were collected from the involved institution. The risk of infection, if any, associated with intact skin exposure to HIV is too low to be detected in these studies.[18]

Assessing Infection Risk to Exposed Individuals

The average risk of transmission derived from prospective studies is helpful in evaluating populations of exposed persons but does not necessarily accurately reflect the risk of a specific exposure experienced by an individual. Many factors are known or suspected to affect the infection risk in specific cases, including the route of transmission (see earlier), the inoculum of infectious virus, and the host's immune response to the exposure.

The inoculum of virus is related to both the volume of material involved in the exposure and the titer of virus in that material. Laboratory models of needlestick exposure demonstrate that exposure volume increases with needle size and depth of penetration and that hollow needles usually transmit more blood than do comparably sized suture needles.[19, 20] In one model, the volume of blood transferred to skin was reduced by more than 50% for hollow needles and more than 80% for suture needles when the needle passed through one or more layers of latex or vinyl gloves before contacting the skin.[19] However, under all experimental conditions, the blood volume transferred to skin varied by a single order of magnitude. Large volumes of blood with or without prolonged duration of contact and a portal of entry are common features in the reported cases of infection through mucosal surfaces or skin, but the number of cases is too small to identify and quantity risk factors for mucocutaneous infection.

The titer of infectious virus present in the source material may vary by several logs, depending on the patient's stage and severity of HIV infection and the effect of antiretroviral treatments, and may therefore be a very important predictor of transmission risk.[21–23] In general, the titer of HIV circulating in the blood compartment is highest at the time of seroconversion and during advanced stages of acquired immunodeficiency syndrome (AIDS). The total titer of infectious virus circulating in the blood includes cell-free HIV plus cell-associated HIV. Tests to quantify cell-free HIV RNA (viral load) in plasma are in widespread use and provide a convenient measure of virus replication. However, these tests do not determine what proportion of the plasma virus titer is actually infectious. It is much more difficult to quantify the cell-associated titer of HIV, although HIV DNA in peripheral blood monocytes can be quantified in a few specialized laboratories. In some studies, higher viral load has been associated with an increased risk for perinatal transmission.[24, 25] On the other hand, HIV transmission from persons with a plasma viral load below the limits of quantification (based on the assay used at the time that the data were collected) has been reported in instances of mother-to-infant transmission and in one occupational infection[24, 25] (Gerberding, unpublished data). In general, the amount of cell-free and cell-associated virus in a given patient is correlated, but more data are needed to determine which component is more important in predicting transmission risk.

Factors associated with transmission risk have been evaluated in a retrospective case-control study of percutaneous exposure to HIV among health care personnel.[26, 27] Deep injuries, visibly bloody sharp devices, and devices that had been used in blood vessels were independent predictors of HIV transmission in this study. These factors are likely to reflect high exposure volume. In this same study, the odds of acquiring infection after percutaneous exposure were six times higher when the source patient had preterminal AIDS (defined by death within 2 months) than when the source had earlier stages of infection (Table 296–1). This difference may be a consequence of the very high titers of circulating HIV usually found among patients with advanced disease. However, the virus strains found in these patients have both phenotypic (syncytium induction, macrophage tropism) and genotypic (large numbers of HIV quasispecies) characteristics that could also account for the association of advanced disease with transmission risk. The fact that most cases of documented occupational transmission involve exposure to patients with advanced HIV infection is consistent with the hypothesis that the quantitative or qualitative differences present in these patients do increase the risk. However, patients with advanced disease are also more likely to be hospitalized and undergo procedures that pose an exposure risk to health care personnel.

The immunologic response of the exposed health care worker must also affect the probability of HIV transmission. At least three outcomes are believed to follow HIV exposure: (1) infection (HIV

TABLE 296–1 Logistic-Regression Analysis of Risk Factors for HIV Transmission after Percutaneous Exposure to HIV-Infected Blood

Risk Factor	U.S. Cases*	All Cases†
Deep injury	13 (4.4–42)‡	15 (6.0–41)
Visible blood on device	4.5 (1.4–16)	6.2 (2.2–21)
Procedure involving needle in artery or vein	3.6 (1.3–11)	4.3 (1.7–12)
Terminal illness in source patient§	8.5 (2.8–28)	5.6 (2.0–16)
Postexposure use of zidovudine	0.14 (0.03–0.47)	0.19 (0.06–0.52)

*All were significant at $p < .02$.
†All were significant at $p < .01$
‡Adjusted odds ratios (95% confidence interval) for the odds of seroconversion after exposure in workers with the risk factor versus those without it.
§Terminal illness was defined as disease leading to death of the source patient from acquired immunodeficiency syndrome within 2 months after the health care worker's exposure.
Reprinted, by permission, from Cardo DM, Culver DH, Ciesielski CA, et al. A case-control study of HIV seroconversion in health care workers after percutaneous exposure. Centers for Disease Control and Prevention Needlestick Surveillance Group. N Engl J Med. 1997;337:1485–1490. Copyright © 1997 Massachusetts Medical Society. All rights reserved.

antibody seroconversion and long-term systemic infection); (2) no infection, no immunologic response; and (3) "aborted infection" (limited cellular infection detected by T-cell response to HIV antigens, no long-term systemic infection, no HIV antibody seroconversion). Immunologic evidence supporting the concept of "aborted infection" has been found in uninfected prostitutes, in sexual partners of infected persons, in children born to HIV-infected mothers, and more recently, in some exposed but uninfected health care workers.[28–35] T lymphocytes derived from the peripheral blood of some uninfected health care workers who were exposed to HIV through needle injuries can be stimulated to proliferate and secrete cytokines when exposed to HIV antigens in vitro.[28, 29] The cellular immune response associated with HIV exposure among uninfected persons, including health care workers, is not known to be a manifestation of a protective host response. Nevertheless, the observation is consistent with the hypothesis that the cellular immune system is one important determinant of exposure outcome.

HIV Seroconversion among Health Care Workers

The characteristics and timing of HIV seroconversion among occupationally infected health care workers reported to the CDC have been evaluated. In the 51 cases for which data are available, 81% were associated with an illness compatible with primary HIV infection at a median of 25 days after exposure.[2, 36, 37] The clinical syndrome was indistinguishable from that observed in persons with primary HIV infection acquired via nonoccupational exposure. The median interval from exposure to documentation of a positive HIV antibody test was 46 days (mean of 65 days). This estimate is limited by the fact that testing is performed at variable intervals after exposure and the exact date of seroconversion is not usually known with certainty. Overall, at least 95% of infected health care workers are expected to seroconvert by 6 months after the exposure.[37] This estimate is identical to that associated with infection through other exposure routes.

Three cases of delayed HIV seroconversion among health care workers have been reported[36, 38] (Gerberding, unpublished data). These health care workers had a negative HIV antibody test 6 months after an occupational exposure but had a positive test sometime in the next 1 to 7 months. DNA sequencing confirmed that the infection was occupational in one instance. Two of these health care workers were also infected with hepatitis C virus during the index needlestick. In both, hepatitis C infection was unusually severe and, in one case, was associated with a rapidly fatal disease course. At this time it is not clear whether coinfection with these two viruses directly influences the timing or severity of either HIV or hepatitis C virus infection. However, most experts agree that until more data are available, health care workers who are exposed to both viruses and in whom serologic evidence of hepatitis C virus infection develops after exposure should be carefully monitored for up to a year after exposure to detect late HIV seroconversion.

Nosocomial HIV Transmission from Infected Health Care Personnel to Patients

Case Reports of HIV Transmission from Infected Providers to Patients

Since the onset of the AIDS epidemic almost 20 years ago, only two reports of HIV transmission from an infected health care worker to one or more patients have been published: one in the United States in 1990 and the other in France in 1997. The episode in the United States involved a cluster of six patients whose HIV infections were linked epidemiologically and through DNA sequencing to a dentist with AIDS.[39–43] Although the investigation indicated that HIV transmission occurred in the dental office and was most likely from dentist-to-patient rather than from patient-to-patient exposure, the precise mechanism of transmission was not determined. Although the dentist was a patient in his own practice, no deficiency of infection control that would readily explain HIV transmission to the six patients was identified. The dentist did not report occupational injuries that could create an opportunity for cross-contamination, nor was it proved that the infections were intentionally transmitted.

The second episode of nosocomial HIV transmission from an infected health care worker involved an orthopedic surgeon in France whose HIV transmission to one patient was confirmed through DNA sequence analysis of viral isolates obtained from the surgeon and the patient.[44–46] The surgeon in this case most likely became infected by an occupational injury sustained during a surgical procedure performed in 1983. However, the surgeon was not aware of his infection until AIDS was diagnosed in 1994. A retrospective ("look-back") investigation of 3004 patients who had undergone at least one invasive procedure performed by the infected surgeon since 1983 was initiated. The HIV infection status of 983 of the 2458 patients who were contacted was determined. One patient, who had a negative HIV antibody test before undergoing the first of three procedures performed by the index surgeon, was found to be infected with HIV when she underwent preoperative testing before a third procedure. Although the precise mechanism of transmission is unknown, the duration of the procedure (10 hours) and possible high viral titer in the surgeon are hypothesized as contributing factors. No breaches in recommended infection-control practices were identified.

Investigations of Patients Treated by HIV-Infected Health Care Personnel

In March 1992 the CDC developed a database to monitor the results of retrospective investigations of health care workers infected with HIV to assess the risk for this mode of HIV transmission. Excluding the patients in the Florida dental practice, as of December 1998, the CDC has obtained information from the investigations of 66 HIV-infected health care workers in the United States.[47, 48] HIV test results were available for 22,759 patients of 53 of these health care workers, including 29 dentists and dental students, 7 physicians and medical students, 16 surgeons/obstetricians, and 1 podiatrist. No HIV infections were reported among 13,667 tested from the practices of 40 health care providers. For the remaining 13 HIV-infected providers (7 dentists and 6 surgeons/obstetricians), 9108 patients were tested and 113 HIV-infected patients were identified. Of these 113 infected patients, follow-up investigations have been completed for all but 3. No infections have been linked to the infected health care provider. Genetic sequence analysis was done on HIV strains from three of the infected clinicians and 30 of their patients who were infected with HIV, including 3 of the 5 patients who had no identified risk. In no instances were the viral strains of patients and the infected workers genetically related (Table 296–2). These retrospective studies have important limitations, including incomplete follow-up evaluation and testing for some patients. Regardless, these data are consistent with previous assessments that the risk of HIV transmission from infected health care personnel to patients is extremely low.

U.S. HIV/AIDS Surveillance Data

In the United States, persons with AIDS or, in some states, those infected with HIV who are reported to state and local health departments with no identified risk for HIV infection are investigated to determine the likely mode of HIV acquisition.[3, 49] These investigations include a review of medical records, contact with health care providers, and interviews with the patients. Approximately 10% of persons with no reported risk for HIV are lost to follow-up, have died, or are otherwise unable to be interviewed. For the remainder, case investigations are successful in identifying established modes of infection in more than 95%. With the exception of the Florida dental investigation, no other cases of HIV transmission from an infected health care provider have been identified through this nationwide surveillance system.

TABLE 296-2 Epidemiologic and Laboratory Follow-up of Patients Infected with HIV, January 1995

Characteristic	Total	With Viral Strains Sequenced	With Sequences Related to Those of the Health Care Worker's Virus
Infected before treatment	28	0	—
Established risk factors	62	14	0
Other potential for exposure to HIV	15	13	0
No identified risk	5	3	0
Investigation incomplete	3	0	—
Total	113	30	0

From Robert LM, Chamberland ME, Cleveland JL, et al. Investigations of patients of health-care workers infected with HIV. Ann Intern Med. 1995;22:654.

Provider-to-Patient Nosocomial Transmission Risk Assessment

In general, three conditions are necessary to create a risk for provider-to-patient HIV transmission. First, the health care provider must be infected with HIV and have infectious HIV circulating in the blood stream. Second, the provider must be injured or have a condition (e.g., weeping dermatitis) that provides some other source of direct exposure to infected blood or body fluids. Third, the injury mechanism or condition must present an opportunity for the provider's blood or body fluids to directly contact a patient's mucous membranes, wound, or traumatized tissue (recontact). As stated earlier, currently no data can reliably estimate the infectivity of individuals infected with HIV, and for now, all infected persons are assumed to be infectious (condition 1). However, the vast majority of infected health care personnel pose no risk to patients because they do not perform procedures where they risk penetrating injuries and have no dermatologic conditions that present a source of exposure to infected body fluids (condition 2). In addition, most do not perform the kind of invasive procedures, such as surgical or obstetric interventions, in which an injury could expose the patient to infected blood (condition 3).

The risk of blood-borne pathogen transmission to patients during recontacts is not known but is believed to be lower than that associated with most occupational exposures. Most provider injuries potentially associated with blood exposure to the patient that have been reported in observational studies involved the penetration of a surgeon's glove by a solid sharp (e.g., suture needle, bone spicule).[50–52] Often, no wound or bleeding was evident at the site of the provider's injury. In one study, many of these events were not even associated with a detectable perforation in the provider's glove by the water distention leak test.[50] In a laboratory investigation, suture needle punctures transferred a much smaller volume of blood to the skin, even less when the needle passed through glove material, than did punctures caused by hollow-bore needles.[19]

After 2 decades of experience with the HIV epidemic, a convergence of epidemiologic evidence demonstrates that the risk of nosocomial HIV transmission to patients from an infected provider is extremely low, even when all three conditions associated with transmission may be present. In addition, risk can be made even smaller by adherence to standard infection-control practices, prevention of percutaneous injuries during invasive procedures, and changes in surgical practice (see later).[46, 52, 53]

Nosocomial HIV Transmission from Infected Patients to Other Patients

Episodes of nosocomial HIV transmission from one patient to another have involved breaches in protocol, improper infection-control practices, and inadequate disinfection procedures. Reuse of blood-contaminated hypodermic needles was linked to HIV transmission to at least 41 hospitalized children in the Soviet Union.[54] In three separate locales (two in the United States and one in The Netherlands), patients were inadvertently injected with blood from an HIV-infected patient during nuclear medicine procedures.[55]

Five patients in Australia who underwent minor outpatient surgical procedures requiring local anesthesia performed on the same day by an HIV-negative surgeon were subsequently found to be HIV positive.[56] The first infected patient had known risk factors for HIV and was the probable source of infection in the other four patients. The exact mode of patient-to-patient transmission in this practice has not been elucidated. No cases of patient-to-patient transmission of HIV have been reported from hemodialysis centers in the United States. However, HIV transmission to at least nine patients in a hemodialysis center in Colombia has been reported and was attributed to inadequate disinfection and reuse of contaminated access needles; similar cases have been reported from Argentina and Egypt.[57, 58]

PRIMARY HIV PREVENTION: EXPOSURE PREVENTION IN HEALTH CARE SETTINGS

Standard (Universal) Precautions to Prevent HIV Exposure

In 1985 the CDC recommended that the blood of all persons be regarded as infectious because it was not always possible to know who might be carrying a blood-borne pathogen. In 1987 the term universal precautions was used to communicate this concept.[59, 60] Universal precautions were designed to prevent direct contact with blood, bloody body fluids, and certain other fluids (amniotic fluid, semen, vaginal fluid, cerebrospinal fluid, serous transudates/exudates, and inflammatory exudates) that were known or likely to be associated with blood-borne pathogen transmission. Barrier precautions included the use of gloves for procedures imparting a risk of contact with these fluids, tissues, and materials, the use of masks and protective eyewear when splash or splatter was anticipated, and the use of gowns or other protective garments when clothing was likely to be soiled. Body substance isolation (or body substance precautions) is an alternative system of infection control practiced by many institutions.[61–63] In this approach, the decision about barrier protection is based on the degree of anticipated contact with all body fluids and tissues, regardless of the patient's diagnosis. Both universal precautions and body substance isolation include measures to prevent needle injuries.

In 1991 the Occupational Safety and Health Administration (OSHA) implemented a federal standard designed to enforce compliance with universal precautions (or body substance isolation) for health care personnel.[64] In addition, many states enacted legislation requiring that universal precautions be implemented as a condition of funding. The OSHA standard presented a hierarchy of control measures that institutions should incorporate into their blood-borne pathogen exposure control plan. These measures included engineering controls (use of equipment and devices designed to be inherently safer), work practice controls (safety procedures), and personal protective equipment.

In 1996 the CDC announced a new system of infection control, standard precautions, that includes features of both body substance isolation and universal precautions.[65] Standard precautions apply to all patients and require the use of gloves, protective clothing, and other barriers as needed to prevent direct contact with all body fluids (except sweat). Percutaneous injury prevention is a key component of standard precautions. These guidelines also reinforce infection-control practices to prevent infection transmission from patient to patient, including standards for cleaning and reprocessing patient care equipment.

In several studies that evaluated the efficacy of universal precautions in preventing blood contact, implementation and enforcement resulted in a significant reduction in exposure frequency.[66–68] Factors associated with efficacy include training, enforcement, and feedback about exposure mechanisms to managers and front-line workers. Implementation of universal precautions has also been associated with a reduction in the frequency of percutaneous injuries caused by needles and other sharp instruments. However, because the frequency of occupational and nosocomial HIV infection is so low, the impact of implementing universal precautions or any other intervention program on the incidence of occupational HIV infection is not known.

Injury Prevention during Routine Patient Care

Needle punctures are the most frequent cause of occupational HIV infection and the highest priority for prevention. All health care workers, including those who actually perform or assist with procedures, those employed as housekeepers and laundry workers, and other nonclinicians, are at risk for injury and infection. Hence, prevention efforts must include strategies to prevent injuries while the needle is being used for its intended purpose, as well as injuries occurring after use or disposal.

One component of injury prevention that may be overlooked is avoidance of unnecessary needle use. Phlebotomy procedures are a common indication for using needles and are also the most common procedure associated with occupational HIV infection. Avoiding "routine" blood drawing that does not contribute to patient care, better planning to minimize the number of phlebotomies required to obtain the necessary blood tests, and using needleless vascular access ports for blood withdrawal and injection of medication will reduce opportunities for injury. Likewise, avoiding unnecessary placement of intravenous catheters when alternative routes are available for administering therapy would also decrease the opportunity for needle injuries.

Implementation of needleless or protected needle infusion systems can reduce the frequency of needle injuries.[69, 70] The effect of this intervention on disease transmission is less certain because most needles used for intravenous infusion are not contaminated with blood. Needles used for heparin flushes and those in contact with ports close to the site of intravenous line insertion are more likely to be blood contaminated and hence more hazardous. In reality, it is hard to determine whether an infusion needle is or has been contaminated. Preventing injuries associated with intravenous infusions is therefore an important component of risk management, even though such injuries may be less prone to transmit disease.

Safer needle devices that have been engineered to retract, cover, or blunt the needle are now in widespread use. Some of these devices have safety features that are activated while the needle is being used for its intended purpose. Others are activated after withdrawal from the patient. The most effective devices are passive (do not require any action on the part of the user to activate the safety feature), do not require extensive training, and are cost-effective. Most importantly, improving worker safety must not increase the risk of infection or complications among patients. A multicentered study from the CDC has demonstrated that implementing safer needle devices for phlebotomy procedures is an effective strategy for preventing percutaneous injuries.[71] Improved product design and lower cost may lead to even more effective programs for protecting workers during procedures that require the use of needles.

All needles and other sharp instruments, with or without safety features, should be discarded in puncture-resistant containers. Such containers should be located as close as possible to the point of use in emergency rooms, in operating rooms, and in other patient care areas. Proper disposal will also prevent injuries caused by needles that have been carelessly discarded. Needle disposal programs can significantly reduce the incidence of injury. In one study, a sustained reduction in the needle injury rate occurred after needle disposal containers were placed at all points of needle use and after feedback from the infection-control staff about exposure risk was provided to those concerned.[60]

Injury Prevention during Invasive Surgical, Obstetric, and Gynecologic Procedures

Preventing intraoperative injuries that confer a risk of blood exposure is an important priority for preventing HIV transmission among health care providers and their patients. Data from observational studies indicate that the risk of provider injury is highest during procedures lasting longer than 2.5 to 3.0 hours, when intraoperative blood loss exceeds 250 to 300 ml, and during certain categories of major procedures (e.g., intra-abdominal gynecologic procedures, vaginal hysterectomies, major vascular procedures, and orthopedic procedures).[51, 72–79]

Prevention priorities in the operating room are based on the same principles used in other health care settings.[80–87] The least invasive surgical approach that will achieve the desired patient outcome is preferable. For example, fiber-optic techniques usually pose a lower risk of injury and blood exposure than do more invasive surgical approaches. Likewise, when patient safety permits, alternatives to needles and other sharp implements (e.g., use of adhesive tape, staples, and tissue glue rather than sutures, electrocautery rather than scalpels) should be used.

Suture needles are the most frequent cause of injuries in operating and delivery rooms. Curved suture needles with blunted tips are now available and appear to be an acceptable replacement to standard curved suture needles for suturing many types of tissue.[88–95] Use of these needles is effective in preventing intraoperative injuries. In one study conducted in three hospitals, 1.9 injuries per 1000 curved suture needles were observed during gynecologic surgery, but no injuries were associated with the use of blunted suture needles.[88] The estimated odds of sustaining an injury with a curved suture needle were reduced by 87% when 50% of the suture needles used during a procedure were blunted. Use of blunted suture needles is also associated with a lower incidence of glove perforation. Surgeons involved in these studies were overall accepting of the blunted needle, and no adverse patient outcomes were noted.

"No-touch" technique includes using instruments rather than hands for retracting and exploring tissue and avoiding the simultaneous presence of the hands of two or more operators in the surgical field. Avoiding hand passage of sharp instruments by use of a "neutral zone" (emesis basin, Mayo stand, or magnetic pad) and announcing the transfer of sharp instruments from person to person are among many new strategies to prevent intraoperative injuries that have been adopted by surgical personnel.

Gloves provide an important barrier between patients and health care providers. Sterile surgical gloves prevent microbial contamination of patient wounds and sterile instruments, as well as protect surgical personnel from cutaneous blood contact. Surgical gloves do not provide a barrier to sharp object penetration, but they may reduce the volume of blood transferred to the skin and hence decrease the risk of blood-borne pathogen infection.

Unfortunately, glove perforation is extremely common, especially during major surgical procedures of long duration.[96–102] Breakdown in glove integrity can cause contamination of exposed tissue and blood contamination of the provider's hands, and if the provider sustains an injury that results in bleeding (needle puncture) or tissue trauma (suture-induced "shear injury"), the patient may be exposed to the provider's blood or interstitial fluids. Double gloving is one strategy that may attenuate these problems. Without exception, in all studies of double gloving, the prevalence of inner glove perforation was significantly lower than that of the outer glove.[102–114] In addition, double gloving reduces the frequency of visible blood contamination of providers' hands.

Overall, the thumb, index, and middle fingers of the nondominant hand are the most common glove perforation sites.[51, 72, 113] Reinforcement of these areas is one approach to prevent perforation. The use of gloves that increase the thickness of the barrier between a patient and the provider creates concern about manual dexterity and tactile sensitivity.[115–120] In a study that measured two-point discrimination and the ability to tie surgical knots, double gloving did not affect performance. Some measures of tactile sensitivity are reduced, but not the ability to discriminate between suture pairs. In a subjective assessment, surgeons reported that double gloving did impair comfort, sensitivity, and dexterity, but acceptance was better if the inner glove was larger than the outer glove.[117]

The benefit of double gloving, glove reinforcement, and new glove materials in preventing disease transmission has not been proved. Nevertheless, double gloving greatly decreases perforation of the inner glove and reduces blood contamination of the operator's hands. Most authorities now recommend routine double gloving during invasive surgical and obstetric procedures.[53, 80]

As emphasized earlier, preventing intraoperative injuries to surgical care providers is the most important strategy for preventing the transmission of HIV and other blood-borne pathogens to patients. In two studies of intraoperative provider injuries, 11.4 to 29% of the sharp objects that injured the provider subsequently recontacted the patient.[50, 51] These exposures are preventable by immediately replacing the contaminated suture needle or other sharp object before reuse. Recontacts can also occur when the provider is injured by bone spicules or materials permanently embedded in the patient's body.[50, 51] These sources of potential exposure might be prevented by the use of reinforced gloves or other materials to protect the provider's hands. Gloves constructed of monofilament polymers or other materials resistant to tears have become available for use when manipulation of bone fragments or suture wires is needed, but as noted earlier, their use is not universal because of the associated decrease in tactile sensation.

Injury Prevention during Dental Procedures

The frequency of blood exposure among dental personnel has declined in the past decade. Surveys conducted at annual meetings of the American Dental Association found that the mean number of injuries involving blood or body fluid contact reported by dentists decreased from 12.0 to 2.2 per year between 1986 and 1993.[121] This impressive decline may be due to the widespread implementation of universal precautions in dental practices, safer instrumentation, and educational programs for dental professionals and patients.

Specific practices designed to prevent injuries include use of the one-handed "scoop" technique and mechanical devices for recapping needles used for local anesthetic administration, restricting the use of fingers during suturing and administration of anesthesia, controlling the placement of sharp instruments (such as scalers and laboratory knives), and improvements in the ergonomic design of dental operatories.[122] Safer devices such as self-sheathing anesthetic needles, dental units designed to shield burs in handpieces, and plastic finger guards might also contribute to safer dental care.

Today, most injuries to dental personnel actually occur outside the patient's mouth, involve very small amounts of blood, and are unlikely to pose a risk to patients.[122–124] In a 7-month observational study of dentists and oral and maxillofacial surgical residents in two New York City teaching hospitals, injuries were observed during 0.1% of dental procedures, and 86% of these injuries occurred outside the patient's mouth.[123] Only one needle puncture was observed during 16,000 anesthetic injections.

Low exposure rates have been observed during outpatient oral surgical procedures as well. However, oral procedures performed in the operating room are associated with injuries caused by surgical wires during fracture reduction.[125–127] The use of small plates instead of wires during the surgical treatment of some mandibular fractures, as well as reinforced gloves, may help prevent some of these injuries.

HIV Testing to Prevent Occupational/Nosocomial HIV Transmission

HIV testing of patients is not recommended as an infection-control procedure because current standards of practice are designed to prevent the transmission of blood-borne pathogens from all patients, whether HIV infection is known or not. No data have demonstrated that preprocedure identification of infected patients will reduce the chance of exposure; in one study, the exposure risk was not affected by knowledge of the patient's HIV infection status.[72] Researchers at Johns Hopkins University, an institution where HIV is highly prevalent among emergency department patients, evaluated preoperative testing of elective surgical patients.[128] Consecutive patients were tested for HIV, and 18 were infected. Ten of these patients knew their HIV status before the preoperative test was performed, and all provided a history of risk factors for infection. The prevalence of HIV infection was too low to justify routine preoperative testing in this institution, and the practice was abandoned. The advent of rapid HIV tests may allow reliable preoperative screening of patients requiring emergency surgery. However, this practice cannot be recommended unless it is demonstrated to result in reduced exposure risk without adverse patient outcomes.

Although HIV testing is not a useful strategy for preventing occupational and nosocomial HIV transmission, it is important for clinicians to address HIV risk in the context of the health care delivery system. Some patients at risk for HIV infection lack access to HIV testing in the community, and HIV infection is not diagnosed until they have advanced complications. HIV risk assessment should be conducted as a routine component of patient care, even in the emergency department and acute care settings. Patients at risk should be encouraged to consent to an HIV test. Of course, prevention counseling should also be available. If the responsible clinician is not prepared to offer prevention counseling at the time that testing is requested, an appropriate referral should be arranged.

Routine HIV testing of health care personnel is not recommended. Health care personnel who sustain blood exposures, including those who perform invasive procedures, are advised to seek postexposure testing for HIV and other blood-borne pathogens when indicated by the exposure circumstances.

Management of Infected Health Care Providers

In 1991 the CDC recommended that invasive surgical and dental procedures that had been implicated in hepatitis B virus transmission from infected health care workers to patients be considered "exposure prone."[129] The characteristics of these procedures included digital palpation of a needle tip in a body cavity or the simultaneous presence of a clinician's fingers and a needle or other sharp object in a poorly visualized or highly confined anatomic site. The CDC also recommended that invasive procedures associated with an increased risk for provider injury in observational studies be considered exposure prone. These exposure-prone procedures were to be identified by medical, surgical, and dental organizations with input from institutions where these procedures are performed. (Efforts to create a list of exposure-prone procedures were not successful.) Infected health care personnel who performed exposure-prone procedures were to be reviewed by an advisory panel to determine under what circumstances, if any, they would be allowed to practice. In addition, allowed procedures could be performed only after informed consent was obtained from the patient.

All states were required by Congress to implement these recommendations or their equivalent. However, considerable variability in interpretation and implementation of the guidelines has emerged. As a result, decisions about managing infected health care workers are currently inconsistent and often influenced by court decisions rather than epidemiologic science. In 1998 the CDC began the process of updating its guidelines for managing health care personnel infected with HIV or other blood-borne pathogens. This effort is intended to reflect the growing body of evidence that demonstrates the extremely low risk of nosocomial HIV transmission, as well as the proven efficacy of strategies to prevent injuries and exposures that place health care providers and their patients (albeit rarely) at risk. The new guidelines are expected before 2000 but are not complete at the time of this writing.

In the interim, most experts agree that practice restrictions are appropriate when an infected health care worker is impaired and cannot safely practice, when a pattern of substandard infection-control practice is demonstrated, or when HIV transmission to a patient has occurred or is suspected.[53] If transmission is suspected, the state or local health department should be contacted for consultation about the need for a more extensive investigation.

SECONDARY HIV PREVENTION: POSTEXPOSURE PROPHYLAXIS IN HEALTH CARE SETTINGS

In June 1996, a U.S. Public Health Service interagency working group, with input from other experts, published recommendations for providing antiretroviral treatment after occupational HIV exposure to prevent infection.[132] These recommendations and a more recent update[2] were based on data from several sources that strongly suggest that antiretroviral treatment soon after occupational HIV exposure could prevent infection. In effect, these recommendations (and a more recent update) established a standard of care for managing occupational HIV exposure among health care personnel that includes access to postexposure antiretroviral chemoprophylactic treatment. Specific recommendations for managing nosocomial HIV exposure in patients were not included in these guidelines. In this section, treatment recommendations and exposure management advice relevant to occupational exposure in health care workers will be presented, but the same principles and approach would also apply to nosocomial exposure to HIV among patients.

Rationale for Chemoprophylaxis after Occupational Exposure to HIV

The rationale for postexposure chemoprophylaxis is based on the pathogenesis of HIV infection and the biologic plausibility of treatment efficacy, studies of antiretroviral prophylaxis in experimental animals, clinical trials demonstrating the efficacy of HIV chemoprophylaxis in other clinical settings, and epidemiologic data from studies of exposed health care personnel.[1, 2, 133] Together, these data support the administration of antiretroviral drugs after HIV exposure associated with a transmission risk in health care settings.

Biologic Plausibility of Chemoprophylaxis

The hypothesis underlying chemoprophylaxis is that postexposure treatment during a "window of opportunity" will attenuate initial HIV replication and prevent systemic HIV infection. Dendritic cells in the mucosa and skin are believed to be the initial target for HIV infection or capture.[134] These cells also play a role in initiating HIV infection of $CD4^+$ T cells in regional lymph nodes. In a primate model of simian immunodeficiency virus (SIV) infection, SIV remained localized in association with dendritic cells underlying the site of vaginal inoculation for the first 24 hours after exposure to cell-free virus.[135] Over the next 24 to 48 hours, these cells appeared to migrate to regional lymph nodes and present SIV to T lymphocytes. Cell-free and cell-associated SIV was detected in the peripheral blood within 5 days after inoculation.

More recent in vitro studies have further characterized the earliest events in HIV exposure and infection. "Immature" dendritic cells in the skin and mucous membranes function to capture and process foreign antigens.[136] These cells also express important HIV coreceptors (CD4 and the chemokine receptor CCR5), but not the surface molecules required for potent T-lymphocyte activation (CD40, CD54, CD86). Immature dendritic cells selectively capture macrophage-tropic strains of HIV, the phenotype that usually predominates during transmission. These dendritic cells then mature to express the receptors required to stimulate T cells and migrate via the lymphatics to the regional lymph nodes. In tissue culture, HIV can replicate in immature dendritic cells, but replication in mature dendritic cells is blocked unless T cells are present. Mature dendritic cells in contact with T cells (probably via CD40–CD40 ligand interaction) undergo a single round of HIV replication and transfer HIV to T lymphocytes. Productive T-cell infection then ensues, with a strong burst of HIV replication. In this tissue culture system, zidovudine treatment does not prevent HIV replication in dendritic cells or transfer of HIV to T cells, but it will completely prevent productive T-cell infection.

These and other experiments support the concept that productive HIV infection occurs in a stepwise series of events involving initial infection of dendritic target cells near the exposure site and then productive T-lymphocyte infection in regional lymph nodes. Early antiretroviral treatment appears most likely to prevent infection by blocking productive T-lymphocyte infection in the regional lymph nodes. Unfortunately, the available data do not allow prediction of the maximum time interval after exposure in which prophylaxis might work or the factors that might affect the timing of these events in individual cases.

Efficacy of Antiretroviral Chemoprophylaxis in Experimental Animals

Antiretroviral chemoprophylaxis is effective in many murine and feline models of retrovirus infection, but these models may not be relevant to human HIV infection.[137] Most early studies designed to evaluate the efficacy of antiretroviral chemoprophylaxis in nonhuman primates exposed to SIV did not demonstrate complete protection.[137, 138] These experiments almost always entailed intravenous injection of very high inocula of HIV-2 or SIV (to ensure infection in 100% of control animals), an exposure route that would bypass the cellular events at the aforementioned exposure site.

Benefits associated with preexposure or postexposure prophylaxis in these and more recent experiments in animal models include (1) delay or suppression of viremia; (2) inhibition of viral replication and development of a long-lasting, protective cellular immune response; and (3) complete protection (i.e., chemoprophylactic efficacy).[139–142]

In general, postexposure prophylaxis is most likely to be effective in animal models when the exposure inoculum is relatively low, when treatment is started soon after exposure (usually within 24 hours), and when treatment is continued for at least several days to weeks after inoculation.[137, 143] For occupational HIV exposure, the viral inoculum is very low in comparison to that used in animal experiments, and current recommendations emphasize the importance of initiating treatment immediately after exposure and continuing it for 4 weeks. If the animal models are relevant to occupational HIV transmission prevention, the current recommendations should maximize the potential for postexposure treatment to be an effective prevention strategy.

Clinical Trials Evaluating the Efficacy of Chemoprophylaxis

In a randomized, controlled, prospective trial (AIDS Clinical Trial Group protocol 076), zidovudine or placebo was administered to HIV-infected pregnant women during the second and third trimesters of pregnancy and to newborns for 6 weeks after birth.[144] The infection rate among infants in the treatment arm of the study was 67% lower than that observed in the control group. Less than 20% of the protective effect of zidovudine was attributable to a reduction in maternal HIV titer, which suggests that additional mechanisms contributed to the observed benefit of therapy.[24, 25] In a more recent study, treatment of newborns of infected mothers who were not treated prepartum was also effective in preventing perinatal infection, an observation that strongly supports a direct postexposure prophylactic effect of antiretroviral treatment in this clinical context.[145]

It is not feasible to evaluate the efficacy of postexposure chemoprophylaxis in health care workers exposed to HIV because infection is so infrequent that a prospective clinical trial would need to enroll many thousands of exposed persons to achieve the statistical power necessary to directly demonstrate efficacy. Between 1987 and 1989, the Burroughs-Wellcome Company sponsored a prospective placebo-controlled clinical trial to evaluate the efficacy of postexposure zidovudine therapy among exposed health care workers.[146, 147] This trial was stopped prematurely because of low enrollment. In view of the evidence supporting a benefit from prophylaxis, it is now unlikely that a placebo-controlled trial of prophylactic treatment in health care workers can be justified.

Epidemiologic Evidence Supporting Chemoprophylaxis Efficacy

In the CDC's retrospective case-control study of health care workers (see Table 296–1), postexposure treatment with zidovudine was associated with an 81% reduction in the odds of infection (95% confidence interval, 43 to 94%) after adjustment for relevant exposure risk factors.[26, 27] This relatively small study was not designed to evaluate treatment, so the effect of the drug regimen (dose, time to initiation, duration) on efficacy could not be determined. The study does not prove that treatment is effective, and limitations inherent in the design, including the small number of cases and the fact that cases and controls were not from the same cohort, must be considered. Nevertheless, it provides very suggestive epidemiologic evidence that zidovudine offers protection to exposed health care workers and can prevent at least some infections.

Failure of Chemoprophylaxis after Occupational Exposure

As of August 1999, the CDC was aware of 18 health care workers from several countries who were infected with HIV despite postexposure zidovudine treatment.[148, 149] At least eight of the exposures implicated in these occupational infections involved blood from source patients who had taken zidovudine. Three of four source HIV isolates evaluated for zidovudine susceptibility demonstrated evidence of resistance, but one appeared to be fully susceptible. Factors besides drug resistance that could contribute to prophylaxis failure include exposure to a high inoculum of HIV, delayed initiation of treatment or failure to achieve adequate drug concentrations, short treatment duration (less than 4 weeks), and many other characteristics affecting immune-response or viral infectivity. It is also possible that antiretroviral prophylactic therapy may not always work.

Antiretroviral Drugs for Chemoprophylaxis

Choosing a Treatment Regimen

At least three major factors influence the selection of antiretroviral drugs for prophylaxis: (1) the estimated risk of HIV transmission associated with the exposure; (2) the probability that drug-resistant virus strains are currently circulating in the source patient and are likely to be present in the exposure inoculum; and (3) the safety, tolerance, and cost of proposed treatment regimens. Several antiretroviral agents from at least three classes of drugs are available for the treatment of HIV disease.[150–152] These agents include nucleoside reverse transcriptase inhibitors, non-nucleoside reverse transcriptase inhibitors, and protease inhibitors. Among these drugs, zidovudine (a nucleoside reverse transcriptase inhibitor) is the only agent proven to prevent HIV transmission in humans to date.

The "basic regimen" currently recommended by the CDC for treatment after most occupational HIV exposures that confer an infection risk includes both zidovudine and lamivudine[2] (Table 296–3). Combinations of antiretroviral drugs are more effective than single agents for treating established HIV infection. However, no data demonstrate that combinations of drugs are more effective for prophylaxis than is zidovudine (or other agents) used alone. The main reason for including lamivudine as a second drug in the basic regimen is that zidovudine resistance in patients with HIV infection is relatively high and even increasing in many communities.[153–158] In addition, the combination has greater antiretroviral activity than either drug does alone (and is active against some zidovudine-resistant HIV strains), but little or no additional toxicity.[159] These two drugs are now available in a single formulation that may be more convenient for health care workers.

The CDC recommends an "expanded regimen" that includes a protease inhibitor in addition to zidovudine and lamivudine after exposures in which the risk of HIV infection is increased (high volume/high HIV titer).[2] Indinavir and nelfinavir are active protease inhibitors, are available in formulations with excellent bioavailability, and do not require dose escalation. Therefore, at the present time, either drug is appropriate for inclusion in expanded treatment regimens. The final choice is largely influenced by differences in expected side effects. Non-nucleoside reverse transcriptase inhibitors are also used by some clinicians, but these drugs are associated with serious and sometimes life-threatening toxicities that are more probable than the infection risk associated with most exposures.

The basic and expanded drug regimens described by the CDC are good choices when the source patient is unlikely to harbor virus isolates that are resistant to the drugs included in the chosen regimen. Resistance to all antiretroviral drugs has been reported, and transmission of resistant strains can occur.[153–158] Drug resistance is most likely among patients with high viral loads who are not responding to treatment or do not adhere to the treatment regimen. Unfortunately, clinical predictions about drug resistance are neither sensitive nor specific. Special genotypic and phenotypic tests to detect HIV resistance are not readily available to affect prophylactic treatment decisions.

Empirical prophylactic treatment regimens when drug resistance is suspected are usually based on the same principles used to select drugs for HIV-infected patients who are failing treatment.[151] Use of

TABLE 296–3 Chemoprophylactic Treatment Regimens: Basic and Expanded Postexposure Prophylaxis Regimens

Regimen Category	Application	Drug Regimen
Basic	Occupational HIV exposure with a recognized transmission risk	4 wk (28 d) of both zidovudine, 600 mg/d in divided doses (i.e., 300 mg bid, 200 mg tid, or 100 mg q4h), *and* lamivudine, 150 mg bid
Expanded	Occupational HIV exposure that poses an increased risk for transmission (e.g., larger volume of blood and/or higher virus titer)	Basic regimen plus *either* indinavir, 800 mg q8h, *or* nelfinavir, 750 mg tid*

*Indinavir should be taken on an empty stomach, that is, without food or with a light meal, and with increased fluid consumption, such as drinking six 8-oz glasses of water throughout the day; nelfinavir should be taken with meals.

at least two drugs that the source patient has not taken in the recent past (i.e., prior 30 days) is recommended by many experts. For example, treatment with didanosine and stavudine (with or without a protease inhibitor) may be appropriate when the source patient is failing treatment with zidovudine plus lamivudine. Likewise, stavudine plus lamivudine is a reasonable choice when the source patient is failing zidovudine therapy or is deemed likely to have a predominance of zidovudine-resistant strains circulating in the blood stream at the time that exposure occurred.[1] If the resistance is likely to involve an entire class of antiretroviral drugs (e.g., protease inhibitors), inclusion of a drug from another class is sensible.[1]

Given all the complexities inherent in selecting antiretroviral drugs, consultation with an expert in HIV treatment is recommended when exposure to drug-resistant HIV is a concern. However, treatment should not be delayed to obtain such consultation. If local expertise is not available, clinicians in the United States who seek consultation about prophylaxis for occupational HIV exposure can also contact the "National Clinicians' Post-exposure Hotline (PEP-Line)" (Table 296–4).

Treatment Side Effects

Adverse side effects are associated with all antiretroviral drugs.[160–163] The frequency, severity, duration, and reversibility of side effects are important considerations when formulating a prophylactic treatment regimen. Unusual or serious and unexpected toxicity from antiretroviral drugs should be reported to the manufacturer and the Food and Drug Administration (see Table 296–4).

Most of the information about prophylactic treatment side effects was derived from studies of health care workers who took zidovudine alone, usually at doses of 1000 to 1200 mg/day (i.e., higher than the currently recommended dose).[164–168] More than 50% of those treated reported at least one side effect, and about 30% stopped treatment because of these symptoms. Nausea, vomiting, malaise or fatigue, headache, and insomnia were the most common complaints. Laboratory abnormalities, including decreases in hemoglobin and the absolute neutrophil count, have also been observed. Side effects were reversible when treatment was stopped.

Preliminary information about health care workers who took two or more antiretroviral drugs (usually zidovudine and lamivudine with or without a protease inhibitor) suggests that side effects are common.[169–171] More than 50 to 90% reported one or more symptoms, and at least 24% stopped treatment as a result. Serious side effects, including nephrolithiasis complicated by sepsis, hepatitis, pancytopenia, and Stevens-Johnson syndrome, have been reported with the use of combination drugs for prophylaxis.

The adverse side effects associated with HIV chemoprophylaxis are similar to those observed in HIV-infected patients. Most can be managed with relatively simple remedies such as acetaminophen (headache, myalgia), prochlorperazine (Compazine) (nausea), antimotility drugs (diarrhea), and so forth. Nephrolithiasis and urinary tract obstruction associated with indinavir can be prevented by increasing fluid intake to at least six 8-oz glasses a day.

Because drug interactions are especially common with protease inhibitors, careful evaluation to identify other drugs used by the exposed health care worker is essential. Protease inhibitors can inhibit the metabolism of nonsedating antihistamines and other hepatically metabolized drugs. Some (e.g., nelfinavir, ritonavir) accelerate the clearance of certain drugs, including oral contraceptives. Women taking these protease inhibitors should use alternative or additional contraceptive measures.

TABLE 296–4 Management of HIV Exposure and Chemoprophylactic Treatment: HIV Postexposure Prophylaxis Resources and Registries

National Clinicians' Post-exposure Hotline	Phone: (888) 448-4911
Antiretroviral Pregnancy Registry	Phone: (919) 488-9437 or (800) 722-9292, Ext. 39437 Fax: (919) 315-8981 Write: Post Office Box 13398, Research Triangle Park, NC 27709
Food and Drug Administration (reporting unusual or severe toxicity to antiretroviral agents - MedWatch)	Phone: (800) 332-1088
Reporting to the CDC HIV seroconversions in health care workers who received postexposure prophylaxis	Phone: (404) 639-6425

Antiretroviral Drugs for Pregnant Women

Antiretroviral chemoprophylaxis for pregnant women who sustain an occupational exposure is not contraindicated.[1, 2] The decision to offer treatment should be based on the same considerations that apply to other health care personnel. However, the potential risks and benefits to the fetus must also be addressed. Specifically, the risk of HIV transmission to the mother and the fetus, the stage of pregnancy in the context of potential teratogenicity, and the pharmacokinetics, safety, and tolerability of the antiretroviral drugs in pregnancy must be considered.[2, 172–183] In addition, antiretroviral drugs may cause or exacerbate conditions that are especially serious during pregnancy (e.g., nausea, nephrolithiasis, hyperbilirubinemia, and hyperglycemia). Given these complexities, input from experts in managing antiretroviral drugs during pregnancy may be helpful to the woman and her physician when treatment is elected.

Treating clinicians are also encouraged to report instances of prenatal antiretroviral therapy to the confidential Antiretroviral Pregnancy Registry (see Table 296–4). The registry is designed to help evaluate the safety of these drugs during pregnancy and detect evidence suggestive of teratogenicity. To date, zidovudine use appears safe in women and their infants, who have been observed for several years.[176] Data from the Antiretroviral Pregnancy Registry have shown no increased risk of birth defects in infants with in utero exposure to zidovudine. Less information is available for other antiretroviral drugs.

Initial Exposure Management

Exposure Reporting

Employers of health care workers and other employees at risk for occupational HIV infection are required to provide a system for reporting exposure and prompt access to medical care.[64] Many institutions have developed "needlestick hotlines" or other rapid-response systems to triage exposed persons and initiate immediate treatment.[184] However, even in facilities with excellent reporting mechanisms and on-site clinical expertise, many exposures are not reported.[185–187] All persons at risk must be informed of the importance of immediate exposure reporting to ensure that preventive care can be initiated in time to be effective.

Immediate Decontamination

Wounds and skin sites that have been in contact with blood or body fluids should be washed with soap and water.[2] Exposed mucous membranes should be flushed with tap water. Eyes should be flushed with sterile water or a commercial eye irrigant when available or else with clean tap water. Antiseptics are not known to reduce the incidence of infection, and decontamination should not be delayed until they are obtained. Application of caustic agents such as bleach is not recommended.

Immediate Counseling and Triage

The emotional impact of a known or suspected HIV exposure is usually significant, especially in the first hours to days after the episode.[188, 189] Access to supportive counseling by an experienced clinician who is familiar with the special medical and psychological needs of exposed persons is helpful during this time. The clinician must function as an effective translator. Objective information about exposure risk and the pros and cons of chemoprophylaxis must be communicated to an individual who is usually preoccupied with very subjective emotions.[184] Although it may be tempting to try to talk the worker out of "irrational" fear when objective data indicate that the risk is low, such reassurance is rarely successful. To the worker, the exposure risk may feel like 100%, and no amount of epidemiologic data is likely to change this impression in the short run. The most important initial messages to communicate are probably empathy ("I can see how frightening this is for you"), validation ("most people in your situation feel the way you do now"), and reassurance ("this is difficult, but I'll help you get through it").

Those who are too upset or confused to make a decision about chemoprophylaxis can sometimes be helped by suggesting that treatment be started immediately with the option to stop it later ("start treatment now and then tomorrow we can decide if continuing is your best option"). Buying some time in this manner alleviates the additional pressure to make an immediate decision about initiating the full 4-week course of treatment and gives workers permission to change their mind about treatment when they are able to more objectively evaluate the risks and benefits.[184]

Exposure History

When an exposure is reported, the first priority is to evaluate the risk of infection and the need for immediate wound care and prophylactic treatment. Additional details about the exposure can be elicited when these issues are addressed and the exposed worker is calm enough to engage in a more detailed discussion. A thorough exposure history can help troubleshoot problems that led to the exposure and, in aggregate form, monitor trends relevant to ongoing exposure prevention efforts.

If exposure to HIV (or hepatitis B or C virus infection [see Chapter 295]) has occurred, the risk of transmission should be assessed. If the source patient is known to be infected by HIV, the stage of illness, recent viral load test results (if available), and recent antiretroviral treatment history should be elicited.[2, 184] If the source's HIV status is not known, information relevant to the probability of infection (e.g., risk behavior) and clinical clues that suggest undiagnosed HIV infection should be recorded.

For needle punctures or similar percutaneous injuries, the source material and exposure characteristics known to be associated with an increased risk of HIV transmission (deep injury, visibly bloody device, device used in an artery or vein) should be described.[2] In addition, factors likely to increase the risk of transmission (actual injection of blood, hollow-bore needle, large-gauge needle) should also be reviewed.

For mucosal exposure, the body fluid or material involved and the exposed site, volume of material, and duration of contact before decontamination should be recorded. In addition to these data, for reported skin contacts, the condition of the skin at the site of contact should be evaluated to detect lesions that could provide a portal of entry and affect the risk of infection. In the absence of an obvious portal of entry, infection is so unlikely that further evaluation and treatment are not necessary unless the contact is prolonged or involves a large area of intact skin. Even then, the risk of HIV infection is negligible.

Human bites rarely transmit HIV.[190, 191] The person who inflicted the bite may sustain a mucosal blood exposure to HIV, but only if the skin was penetrated, the bite wound bled, or both. The person who is bitten is usually not at risk for HIV infection unless blood or visibly bloody saliva was in direct contact with the bite wound. Penetrating bite wounds do pose a risk for bacterial wound infection, and appropriate wound care and antibacterial prophylaxis should be provided, when indicated (see Chapter 311).

When the exposure risk is assessed and urgent treatment provided and when the health care worker is able and willing to cooperate, further history should be obtained. Information should be recorded about when, where, and how the exposure occurred, the type of device involved, the presence or absence of safety features (and if present, their state of activation), and when in the course of handling the device the exposure occurred (during use, after use, during disposal, etc.).

Evaluating the Exposure Source

The person who is the source of an occupational exposure, when known, should be evaluated for HIV and hepatitis B and C virus infection (see Chapter 295). The medical record is a useful source of information, but often interviewing the source patient provides the most accurate data about infection risks. If the HIV infection status of the source is unknown, consent to test for HIV antibodies should be requested. If consent is not obtained, further evaluation of HIV status should comply with applicable state laws and local policies.[2] The privacy of the source patient should be protected regardless of the decision to test or the test result.

HIV testing of the exposure source should be performed as soon as possible. In many facilities, conventional HIV tests (e.g., enzyme immunoassay) can be completed very quickly. A Food and Drug Administration–approved rapid HIV antibody test is an acceptable alternative, especially if conventional tests cannot be completed within 24 to 48 hours. In general, repeatedly reactive HIV test results obtained with enzyme immunoassay or a rapid test are highly suggestive of infection, but false positives do occur.[192] Reactive tests should be confirmed by Western blot or immunofluorescent antibody before disclosure to the exposure source. A negative conventional enzyme immunoassay is sufficient to exclude a diagnosis of HIV unless the source patient has clinical evidence of primary HIV infection or HIV-related disease. A negative rapid test is also very reliable in excluding infection, but false negatives have been reported, especially from laboratories that have little experience with the available test kits.

If the source cannot be tested, the "pretest" probability of infection should be assessed by using available clinical and laboratory information and, most importantly, common sense.[1, 2, 184] A similar approach applies to situations when the exposure source is not known. HIV testing of needles, syringes, or other sharp instruments associated with an exposure is dangerous and not recommended.

Evaluating the Exposed Health Care Worker

Health care personnel who report occupational exposure should be evaluated for susceptibility to infection by blood-borne pathogens.[2] Baseline testing (i.e., testing to establish infection status at the time of exposure) for HIV antibody should be performed. If the exposure source is seronegative for HIV, baseline testing or further follow-up of the worker is not normally necessary unless the source has clinical evidence of primary HIV infection. Without a negative baseline HIV test, proving that infection was temporally related to the exposure event is extremely difficult. In rare cases, demonstrating close genetic similarity in virus sequences obtained from the source patient and the infected health care provider can confirm the source of exposure, but these studies are expensive, difficult to obtain, and sometimes difficult to interpret. The evaluation should also include information about the use of medications and underlying medical conditions or circumstances (pregnancy, breast-feeding) that could affect the choice of drugs used for prophylaxis. Pregnancy testing should be offered to all nonpregnant women of childbearing age.

Indications for Chemoprophylaxis

Current U.S. Public Health Service guidelines for postexposure chemoprophylaxis reflect a balance between the estimated risk of HIV transmission associated with specific exposures and the potential risks associated with treatment.[2] In general, chemoprophylaxis is "recommended" for exposures known to confer a transmission risk, is "considered" for exposures with a "negligible risk," and "may not be warranted" for exposures that do not pose a known transmission risk. In this framework, treatment is recommended for all percutaneous exposures to HIV and for large-volume or long-duration mucosal and nonintact skin exposures that involve higher-titer HIV exposures (blood from patients with advanced AIDS, high viral load, or low CD4 counts). Treatment should be considered for small-volume, short-duration mucosal and nonintact skin exposure when the source is known or likely to involve a high HIV titer. Treatment may not be warranted for other mucosal exposures and is not indicated for most intact skin contacts.

Other strategies to stratify exposure risk and indications for treatment have been devised.[1, 184] The actual risk associated with exposure to HIV is difficult to predict; all treatment schemes must be implemented with caution (and humility) until better data are available. It is especially important to remember that the current U.S. Public Health Service guidelines are based on exposure to blood or other potentially infectious materials known to contain HIV, not materials of uncertain HIV status. Unfortunately, the guidelines have been interpreted to imply that antiretroviral chemoprophylaxis should be started for all blood exposures, unless HIV infection is specifically excluded with a negative source test.

Decisions about treatment when the source material is not known to contain HIV should be based on three factors: (1) the probability of HIV infection in the source, (2) the risk of HIV transmission if HIV was in fact present, and (3) the risks associated with treatment. In most of these cases, the risk of transmission is negligible, and treatment is not indicated. Only if the assessment suggests that the risk of HIV transmission outweighs the risk of treatment is it reasonable to initiate the basic treatment regimen until test results or other data become available. This statement reflects the experience of many institutions with comprehensive source patient testing programs that demonstrate a very low probability of undiagnosed HIV infection among source patients without obvious behavioral risks for HIV. For example, at San Francisco General Hospital, where the prevalence of HIV among adult inpatients usually exceeds 20%, in the past 5 years no previously undiagnosed HIV infections have been detected among source patients who did not use injection drugs or who were not men who had sex with other men.[193]

Health care workers who are facing a decision about chemoprophylactic treatment should be apprised that (1) the vast majority of persons exposed to HIV will not be infected even if no treatment is taken, (2) treatment can be stopped at any time, (3) data about the efficacy and safety of chemoprophylactic regimens are incomplete, (4) to date, zidovudine is the only drug proven to prevent HIV transmission, and (5) no data prove that combination treatment is more effective than single-drug therapy for HIV prevention.

Timing and Duration of Chemoprophylaxis

Treatment should begin as soon as possible after exposure. In most animal studies, efficacy is reduced when treatment is delayed for more than 24 hours, but the relevance of this observation to low-inoculum transcutaneous and transmucosal HIV exposure is not known. Regardless, an occupational exposure to HIV should be regarded as an urgent medical concern.[2] When indicated, chemoprophylaxis should be started immediately (i.e., within a few hours rather than days). When consultation is needed to select the best regimen, it is probably better to start the basic or expanded regimen than to delay treatment. In cases in which the risk of transmission is very high, treatment even after a long interval (e.g., 1 to 2 weeks) should still be considered. Even if infection is not prevented, early treatment of acute HIV infection may be beneficial. The optimal duration of chemoprophylaxis is not known. A 4-week regimen is currently recommended because that was the most common treatment duration reported in the CDC's case-control study that suggested a protective benefit.[27]

Subsequent Management of Occupational Exposure

Postexposure Medical Evaluation and HIV Testing

In addition to baseline HIV testing, follow-up testing, usually performed 6 weeks, 3 months, and 6 months after exposure, is recommended when exposure to HIV is documented or suspected. Sequential testing is useful in allaying fears, in documenting seronegativity, and rarely, in diagnosing HIV infection. Testing for more than 6 months is not routinely recommended.[2] In cases in which the exposure was especially risky (e.g., actual injection of blood), hepatitis C virus was transmitted during the index exposure, or symptoms of primary HIV infection appear, extending the testing interval for several more months may be appropriate.

Symptoms of acute retroviral infection (fever, lymphadenopathy, pharyngitis, rash, headache, profound fatigue) are associated with approximately 80% of reported occupational infections, even when chemoprophylaxis is taken.[36] All HIV-exposed persons should be advised to return for evaluation and HIV testing if such an illness occurs, even though drug reactions or other intercurrent illnesses can mimic primary HIV infection. HIV antibody tests may be negative or indeterminate during the early phases of seroconversion illness. Immunoblot, viral load tests (quantitative HIV RNA polymerase chain reaction), or virus cultures may be more sensitive methods for detecting early infection. However, these tests are not indicated in the routine management of exposed persons, in part because their sensitivity and, more important, their specificity have not been established.[2]

Monitoring Chemoprophylactic Treatment

Health care workers who elect to take chemoprophylaxis after HIV exposure should return in 2 weeks for evaluation of drug toxicity. A careful history, focused examination, and laboratory tests appropriate to the drug regimen should be obtained. A complete blood count and renal and hepatic chemical function tests are usually indicated. A random blood glucose test should be included when protease inhibitor therapy is prescribed.[161–163]

Exposed health care workers who choose to take chemoprophylaxis should be advised of the importance of completing the prescribed regimen. Information should be provided about potential drug interactions and the drugs that should not be taken with the prophylactic drug regimen, the side effects of the drugs that have been prescribed, measures to minimize these effects, and methods of clinical monitoring for toxicity during the follow-up period. They should be alerted to the need for immediate evaluation of symptoms suggestive of serious toxicity (e.g., back or abdominal pain, pain on urination or blood in the urine, and symptoms of hyperglycemia such as increased thirst or frequent urination).

Health care workers who fail to complete the recommended regimen often do so because of the side effects that they experience (e.g., nausea, and diarrhea). These symptoms can often be managed without changing the regimen by prescribing antimotility and antiemetic agents or other medications that target the specific symptoms. In other situations, modifying the dose interval (i.e., giving a lower dose of drug more frequently throughout the day, as recommended by the manufacturer) may help promote adherence to the regimen.

Counseling

Health care workers who sustain exposure to HIV should be counseled to avoid transmission to others during the follow-up period, especially the first 6 to 12 weeks after exposure, when seroconversion is most likely.[2] Such practices include sexual abstinence or condoms to prevent sexual transmission and avoidance of blood and organ donation. If the exposed person is breast-feeding, discontinuation of breast-feeding should be considered, especially for high-risk exposures. It is not necessary to modify an exposed health care worker's patient care responsibilities to prevent transmission to patients.

Counseling should also provide reassurance, review information about the degree of risk present, and inform the worker about procedures to protect the confidentiality of the exposure medical records. Counselors should be alert to the concerns of sexual partners, coworkers, family, and friends of the exposed worker. Referral for ongoing supportive therapy during the follow-up interval is helpful for the minority of exposed persons who experience difficulty in adjusting to the stress inherent in waiting the 6 months for testing to be complete.

The single most important message to communicate to most workers is that occupational HIV transmission is very unlikely—99.7% of exposures do not result in HIV infection, even if chemoprophylactic treatment is not used. Continued reassurance from a supportive clinician, coupled with practical advice about measures to prevent future exposure, will allow the worker to successfully cope with the exposure and its aftermath.

REFERENCES

1. Gerberding JL. HIV exposure risk assessment and prophylactic treatment. In: Sande MA, Volberding P, eds. The Medical Management of AIDS. Philadelphia: WB Saunders; 1999.
2. Centers for Disease Control and Prevention. Public Health Service guidelines for the management of health-care worker exposures to HIV and recommendations for post-exposure prophylaxis. MMWR Morb Mortal Wkly Rep. 1998;47:1–33.
3. Centers for Disease Control and Prevention. HIV/AIDS Surveillance Report. 1998;10:26.
4. Centers for Disease Control and Prevention. Transmission of HIV possibly associated with exposure of mucous membrane to contaminated blood. MMWR Morb Mortal Wkly Rep. 1997;46:620–623.
5. Heptonstall J, Porter K, Gill ON. Occupational HIV: Summary of Published Reports. London: Public Health Laboratory Services Communicable Disease Surveillance Centre; December 1995.
6. Gerberding JL. Incidence and prevalence of human immunodeficiency virus, hepatitis B virus, hepatitis C virus, and cytomegalovirus among health care personnel at risk for blood exposure: Final report from a longitudinal study. J Infect Dis. 1994;170:1410–1417.
7. Ippolito G, Puro V, DeCarlt G, Italian Study Group on Occupational Risk of HIV. The risk of occupational human immunodeficiency virus infection in health care workers. Arch Intern Med. 1993;153:1431–1438.
8. Bowden FJ, Pollett B, Birrell F, Dax EM. Occupational exposure to the human immunodeficiency virus and other blood-borne viruses: A six-year prospective study. Med J Aust. 1993;158:810–812.
9. Tokars JI, Marcus R, Culver DH, et al. Surveillance of human immunodeficiency virus infection and zidovudine use among health care workers after occupational exposure to HIV-infected blood: The CDC Cooperative Needlestick Group. Ann Intern Med. 1993;118:913–919.
10. Centers for Disease Control. Surveillance for occupationally acquired HIV infection—United States, 1981–1992. MMWR Morb Mortal Wkly Rep. 1992;41:823–835.
11. Cavalcante NJF, Abreu ES, Fernandes ME, et al. Risk of health care professionals acquiring HIV infection in Latin America. AIDS Care. 1991;3:311–316.
12. Pereira LIA, Souza LCS, Souza MA, et al. Acidentes profissionais com material biologico de paclantes com sindrome da immunodeficiencia adquirida-accompanhamento clinico-serologico. Rev Soc Bras Med Trop. 1991;24:169.
13. Henderson DK, Fahey BJ, Willy M, et al. Risk for occupational transmission of human immunodeficiency virus type-1 (HIV-1) associated with clinical exposures. A prospective evaluation. Ann Intern Med. 1990;113:740–746.
14. Josephson A, Bottone M, Gerber M, Oppermann N. Blood and body fluid exposure followup in the AIDS era: A two year experience. Am J Infect Control. 1990;18:136.
15. Wormser GP, Joline C, Sivak S, Arlin ZA. Human immunodeficiency virus infection: Considerations for health care workers. Bull N Y Acad Med. 1988;64:203–215.
16. Kuhls TL, Viker S, Parris NB, et al. Occupational risk of HIV, HBV and HSV-2 in health care personnel caring for AIDS patients. Am J Public Health. 1987;77:1306–1309.
17. Gerberding JL. Management of occupational exposures to blood-borne viruses. N Engl J Med. 1995;332:444–451.
18. Fahey BJ, Koziol DE, Banks SM, Henderson DK. Frequency of nonparenteral occupational exposure to blood and body fluids before and after universal precautions training. Am J Med. 1991;90:145–153.
19. Mast S, Woolwine J, Gerberding JL. Efficacy of gloves in reducing blood volumes transferred during simulated needlestick injury. J Infect Dis. 1993;168:1589–1592.
20. Bennett NT, Howard RJ. Quantity of blood inoculated in a needlestick injury from suture needles. J Am Coll Surg. 1994;178:107–110.
21. Daar ES, Moudgil T, Meyer RD, Ho DD. Transient high levels of viremia in patients with primary human immunodeficiency virus type 1 infection. N Engl J Med. 1991;325:733–735.
22. Saag MS, Crain MJ, Decker WD, et al. High-level viremia in adults and children infected with human immunodeficiency virus: Relation to disease stage and CD4+ lymphocyte levels. J Infect Dis. 1991;164:72–80.
23. Ho DD, Moudgil T, Alam M. Quantitation of human immunodeficiency virus type 1 in the blood of infected persons. N Engl J Med. 1989;321:1622–1625.
24. Cao Y, Krogstad P, Korber BT, et al. Maternal HIV-1 viral load, zidovudine treatment, and the risk of transmission of human immunodeficiency virus type 1 from mother to infant. N Engl J Med. 1997;3:549–552.
25. Sperling RS, Shapiro DE, Coombs RW, et al. Maternal viral load, zidovudine treatment, and the risk of transmission of human immunodeficiency virus type 1 from mother to infant. N Engl J Med. 1996;335:1621–1624.
26. Case-control study of HIV in health-care workers after percutaneous exposure to HIV-infected blood—France, United Kingdom, and United States, January 1988–August 1994. MMWR Morb Mortal Wkly Rep. 1995;44:929–933.
27. Cardo DM, Culver DH, Ciesielski CA, et al. A case-control study of HIV seroconversion in health care workers after percutaneous exposure. Centers for Disease Control and Prevention Needlestick Surveillance Group. N Engl J Med. 1997;337:1485–1440.
28. Pinto LA, Landay AL, Berzofsky JA, et al. Immune response to human immunodeficiency virus (HIV) in healthcare workers occupationally exposed to HIV-contaminated blood. Am J Med. 1997;102(Suppl 5B):S21–S24.
29. Clerici M, Levin JM, Kessler HA, et al. HIV-specific T-helper activity in seronegative health care workers exposed to contaminated blood. JAMA. 1994;271:42–46.
30. Langlade-Demoyen P, Ngo-Giang-Huong N, Ferchal F, Oksenhendler E. Human immunodeficiency virus (HIV) nef-specific cytotoxic T lymphocytes in noninfected heterosexual contacts of HIV-infected patients. J Clin Invest. 1994;93:1293–1297.
31. Kelker HC, Seidlin M, Vogler M, Valentine FT. Lymphocytes from some long-term seronegative heterosexual partners of HIV-infected individuals proliferate in response to HIV antigens. AIDS Res Hum Retroviruses. 1992;8:1355–1359.
32. Rowland-Jones S, Sutton J, Ariyoshi K, et al. HIV-specific cytotoxic T-cells in HIV-exposed but uninfected Gambian women. Nat Med. 1995;1:59–64.
33. Clerici M, Giorgi JV, Gudeman VK, et al. Cell-mediated immune response to human immunodeficiency virus (HIV) type 1 in seronegative homosexual men with recent sexual exposure to HIV-1. J Infect Dis. 1992;165:1012–1019.
34. Cheynier R, Langlade-Demoyen P, Marescot MR, et al. Cytotoxic T lymphocyte responses in the peripheral blood of children born to human immunodeficiency virus-1–infected mothers. Eur J Immunol. 1992;22:2211–2217.
35. Ranki AM, Mattinen S, Yarchoan R, et al. T-cell response towards HIV in infected individuals with and without zidovudine therapy, and in HIV-exposed sexual partners. AIDS. 1989;3:63–69.
36. Ciesielski CA, Metler RP. Duration of time between exposure and seroconversion in healthcare workers with occupationally acquired infection with human immunodeficiency virus. Am J Med. 1997;102(Suppl 5B):S115–S116.
37. Busch MP, Satten GA. Time course of viremia and antibody serconversion following human immunodeficiency virus exposure. Am J Med. 1997;102(Suppl 5B):S117–S124.
38. Ridzon R, Gallagher K, Ciesielski C, et al. Simultaneous transmission of human immunodeficiency virus and hepatitis C virus from a needle-stick injury. N Engl J Med. 1997;336:919–922.
39. Centers for Disease Control. Possible transmission of human immunodeficiency virus to a patient during an invasive dental procedure. MMWR Morb Mortal Wkly Rep. 1990;39:489–493.
40. Centers for Disease Control. Update: Transmission of HIV during invasive dental procedures—Florida. MMWR Morb Mortal Wkly Rep. 1991;40:21–27, 33.
41. Centers for Disease Control. Update: Transmission of HIV infection during invasive dental procedures—Florida. MMWR Morb Mortal Wkly Rep. 1991;40:377–381.
42. Ciesielski C, Marianos D, Ou CY, et al. Transmission of human immunodeficiency virus in a dental practice. Ann Intern Med. 1992;116:798–805.
43. Ciesielski CA, Marianos DW, Schoechetman G, et al. The 1990 Florida dental investigation: The press and the science. Ann Intern Med. 1994;121:886–888.
44. Blanchard A, Ferris S, Chamaret S, et al. Molecular evidence for nosocomial transmission of human immunodeficiency virus from a surgeon to one of his patients. J Virol. 1998;72:4537–4540.
45. Lot F, Seguier JC, Fegueux S, et al. HIV transmission from an orthopedic surgeon to a patient in France. Ann Intern Med. 1999;130:1–6.
46. Gerberding JL. Provider-to-patient HIV transmission: How to keep it exceedingly rare. Ann Intern Med. 1999;130:64–65.
47. Centers for Disease Control and Prevention. Update: Investigations of persons treated by HIV-infected health-care workers. MMWR Morb Mortal Wkly Rep. 1993;42:329–331, 337.
48. Robert LM, Chamberland ME, Cleveland JL, et al. Investigations of patients of health-care workers infected with HIV. Ann Intern Med. 1995;122:653–657.
49. Castro KG, Lifson AR, White CR, et al. Investigations of AIDS patients with no previously identified risk factors. JAMA. 1988;259:1338–1342.
50. Gerberding JL, Rose DA, Ramiro NZ, et al. Intraoperative provider injuries and potential patient recontacts at San Francisco General Hospital (Abstract). Infect Control Hosp Epidemiol. 1994;344:20.

51. Tokars JI, Bell DM, Culver DM, et al. Percutaneous injuries during surgical procedures. JAMA. 1992;267:2899–2904.
52. Gerberding JL. The infected health care provider. N Engl J Med. 1996;334:594–595.
53. Management of healthcare workers infected with hepatitis B virus, hepatitis C virus, human immunodeficiency virus, or other bloodborne pathogens. AIDS/TB Committee of the Society for Healthcare Epidemiology of America. Infect Control Hosp Epidemiol. 1997;18:349–363.
54. Pokrovsky VV, Eramova EU. Nosocomial outbreak of HIV infection in Elista USSR. Presented at the Fifth International Conference on AIDS, Montreal, June 4–9, 1989.
55. Centers for Disease Control. Patient exposures to HIV during nuclear medicine procedures. MMWR Morb Mortal Wkly Rep. 1992;41:575–578.
56. Chant K, Lowe D, Rubin G, et al. Patient-to-patient transmission of HIV in private surgical consulting room. Lancet. 1993;342:1548–1549.
57. Centers for Disease Control and Prevention. HIV transmission in a dialysis center—Colombia, 1991–1993. MMWR Morb Mortal Wkly Rep. 1995;44:404–405, 411–412.
58. Hassan NF, El Ghorab NM, Abdel Rehim MS, et al. HIV infection in renal dialysis patients in Egypt (Letter). AIDS. 1994;8:853.
59. Centers for Disease Control. Recommendations for prevention of HIV transmission in health-care settings. MMWR Morb Mortal Wkly Rep. 1987;36(Suppl 2S):S1–S18.
60. Centers for Disease Control. Update: Universal precautions for prevention of transmission of human immunodeficiency virus, hepatitis B virus, and other blood-borne pathogens in health care settings. MMWR Morb Mortal Wkly Rep. 1988;37:377–382, 387–388.
61. Gerberding JL, University of California, San Francisco Task Force on AIDS. Recommended infection-control policies for patients with human immunodeficiency virus infection: An update. N Engl J Med. 1986;315:1562–1564.
62. Lynch P, Jackson MM, Cummings MJ, et al. Rethinking the role of isolation practices in the prevention of nosocomial infections. Ann Intern Med. 1987;107:243–246.
63. Gerberding JL, Henderson DK. Design of rational infection control guidelines for human immunodeficiency virus infection. J Infect Dis. 1987;156:861–864.
64. Department of Labor Occupational Safety and Health Administration. Occupational exposure to bloodborne pathogens: Final rule. Fed Register. 1991;56:64004–64182.
65. Garner JL. Guidelines for isolation precautions in hospitals. Infect Control Hosp Epidemiol. 1996;17:54–80.
66. Kristensen MS, Wernberg NM, Anker-Moller E: Healthcare workers' risk of contact with body fluids in a hospital: The effect of complying with the universal precautions policy. Infect Control Hosp Epidemiol. 1992;13:719–724.
67. Wong ES, Stotka JL, Chinchilli VM, et al. Are universal precautions effective in reducing the number of occupational exposures among health care workers? JAMA. 1991;265:1123–1128.
68. Haiduven DJ, DeMaio TM, Stevens DA. A five-year study of needlestick injuries: Significant reduction associated with communication, education, and convenient placement of sharps containers. Infect Control Hosp Epidemiol. 1992;13:265–271.
69. Jagger J, Hunt EH, Bland-Elnaggar J, Pearson RD. Rates of needlestick injury caused by various devices in a university hospital. N Engl J Med. 1988;319:284–288.
70. Mendelson MH, Short LJ, Schechter CB. Study of a needleless intermittent intravenous-access system for peripheral infusions: Analysis of staff, patient, and institutional outcomes. Infect Control Hosp Epidemiol. 1998;19:401–406.
71. Evaluation of safety devices for preventing percutaneous injuries among health-care workers during phlebotomy procedures—Minneapolis–St. Paul, New York City, and San Francisco. MMWR Morb Mortal Wkly Rep. 1997;46:21–25.
72. Gerberding JL, Littell C, Tarkington A, et al. Risk of exposure of surgical personnel to patient's blood during surgery at San Francisco General Hospital. N Engl J Med. 1990;322:1788–1793.
73. Panlilio AL, Foy DR, Edwards JR, et al. Blood contacts during surgical procedures. JAMA. 1991;265:1533–1537.
74. Popejoy SL, Fry DE. Blood contact and exposure in the operating room. Surg Gynecol Obstet 1991;172:480–483.
75. Panlilio AL, Welch BA, Bell DM, et al. Blood and amniotic fluid contact sustained by obstetric personnel during deliveries. Am J Obstet Gynecol. 1992;167:703–708.
76. Quebbeman EJ, Telford GL, Hubbard S. Risk of blood contamination and injury to operating room personnel. Ann Surg. 1992;214:614–620.
77. White MC, Lynch P. Blood contact and exposures among operating room personnel: A multicenter study. Am J Infect Control. 1993;21:243–248.
78. Robert L, Short L, Chamberland M, et al. Percutaneous injuries sustained during gynecologic surgery (Abstract). Infect Control Hosp Epidemiol. 1994;15:349.
79. Folin AC, Nordström GM. Accidental blood contact during orthopedic surgical procedures. Infect Control Hosp Epidemiol. 1997;18:244–246.
80. Gerberding JL. Procedure-specific infection control for preventing intra-operative blood exposures. Am J Infect Control. 1992;21:364–367.
81. Hester RA, Nelson CL. Methods to reduce intraoperative transmission of blood-borne disease. J Bone Joint Surg Am. 1991;73:1108–1111.
82. American Academy of Orthopaedic Surgeons Task Force on AIDS and Orthopaedic Surgery. Recommendations for the Prevention of Human Immunodeficiency Virus (HIV) Transmission in the Practice of Orthopaedic Surgery. American Academy of Orthopaedic Surgeons; 1989.
83. Raahave D, Bremmelgaard A. New operative technique to reduce surgeons' risk of HIV infection. J Hosp Infect. 1991;18:177–183.
84. Davis JM, Demling RH, Lewis FR, et al. The Surgical Infection Society's policy on human immunodeficiency virus and hepatitis B and C infection. Arch Surg. 1992;127:218–221.
85. Lewis JFR, Short LJ, Howard RJ, et al. Epidemiology of injuries by needles and other sharp instruments: Minimizing sharp injuries in gynecologic and obstetric operations. Surg Clin North Am. 1995;75:1105–1121.
86. Smoot CE. Practical precautions for avoiding sharp injuries and blood exposure. Plast Reconstr Surg. 1998;101:528–534.
87. Loudon MA, Stonebridge PA. Minimizing the risk of penetrating injury to surgical staff in the operating theatre: Towards sharp-free surgery. J R Coll Surg Edinb. 1998;43:6–8.
88. Evaluation of blunt suture needles in preventing percutaneous injuries among health-care workers during gynecologic surgical procedures—New York City, March 1993–June 1994. MMWR Morb Mortal Wkly Rep. 119;46:25–29.
89. Wright KU, Moran CG, Briggs PJ. Glove perforation during hip arthroplasty: A randomized prospective study of a new taperpoint needle. J Bone Joint Surg Br. 1993;75:918–920.
90. Mingoli A, Sapienza P, Giovanna S, et al. Influence of blunt needles on surgical glove perforations and safety for the surgeon. Am J Surg. 1996;172:512–517.
91. Hartley JE, Ahmed S, Milkins R, et al. Randomized trial of blunt-tipped versus cutting needles to reduce glove puncture during mass closure of the abdomen. Br J Surg. 1996;83:1156–1157.
92. Davis MS. A blunt proposal for a safer surgical environment. South Med J. 1994;87:1193–1194.
93. Montz FJ, Fowler JM, Farias-Eisner R, Nash TJ. Blunt needles in fascial closure. Surg Gynecol Obstet. 1991;173:147–148.
94. Miller SS, Sabharwal A. Subarticular skin closure using a "blunt" needle. Ann R Coll Surg. 1994;76:281.
95. Rice JJ, McCabe JP, McManus F. Needle stick injury: Reducing the risk. Int Orthop. 1996;20:132–133.
96. Brough SJ, Hunt TM, Barrie WW. Surgical glove perforations. Br J Surg. 1988;75:317.
97. McLeod GG. Needlestick injuries at operations for trauma: Are surgical gloves an effective barrier? J Bone Joint Surg Br. 1989;71:489–491.
98. Cole RP, Gault DT. Glove perforation during plastic surgery. Br J Plastic Surg. 1989;42:481–483.
99. Serrano CW, Wright JW, Newton ER. Surgical glove perforation in obstetrics. Obstet Gynecol. 1991;77:525–528.
100. Green SE, Gompertz RHK. Glove perforation during surgery: What are the risks? Ann R Coll Surg Engl. 1992;74:306–308.
101. Chapman S, Duff P. Frequency of glove perforations and subsequent blood contact in association with selected obstetric surgical procedures. Am J Obstet Gynecol. 1993;168:1354–1357.
102. Rose DA, Ramiro N, Perlman J, et al. Usage patterns and perforation rates for 6396 gloves from intra-operative procedures at San Francisco General Hospital (Abstract). Infect Control Hosp Epidemiol. 1994;15:349.
103. Gani JS, Anseline PF, Bissett RL. Efficacy of double versus single gloving in protecting the operating team. Aust N Z J Surg. 1990;60:171–175.
104. Doyle PM, Alvi S, Johanson R. The effectiveness of double-gloving in obstetrics and gynaecology. Br J Obstet Gynaecol. 1992;99:83–84.
105. Matta H, Thompson AM, Rainey JB. Does wearing two pairs of gloves protect operating theatre staff from skin contamination? BMJ. 1988;297:597–598.
106. Cohen MS, Do JT, Tahery DP, Moy DL. Efficacy of double gloving as a protection against blood exposure in dermatologic surgery. J Dermatol Surg Oncol. 1992;18:873–874.
107. Chiu KY, Fung B, Lau SK, et al. The use of double latex gloves during hip fracture operations. J Orthop Trauma. 1993;4:354–356.
108. Cohn GM, Seifer DB. Blood exposure in single versus double gloving during pelvic surgery. Am J Obstet Gynecol. 1990;162:715–717.
109. Jensen SL, Kristensen B, Fabrin K. Double gloving as self protection in abdominal surgery. Eur J Surg. 1997;163:163–167.
110. Bennett B, Duff P. The effect of double gloving on frequency of glove perforations. Obstet Gynecol. 1991;78:1019–1022.
111. Dodds RDA, Barker SGE, Morgan NH, et al. Self protection in surgery: The use of double gloves. Br J Surg. 1990;77:219–220.
112. Schwimmer A, Massoumi M, Barr CE. Efficacy of double gloving to prevent inner glove perforation during outpatient oral surgical procedures. J Am Dent Assoc. 1994;125:196–198.
113. Quebbeman EJ, Telford GL, Wadsworth K, et al. Double gloving: Protecting surgeons from blood contamination in the operating room. Arch Surg. 1992;127:213–217.
114. Sanders R, Fortin P, Ross E, Helfet D. Outer gloves in orthopaedic procedures: Cloth compared with latex. J Bone Joint Surg Am. 1990;72:914–917.
115. Webb JM, Pentlow BD. Double gloving and surgical technique. Ann R Coll Surg Engl. 1993;75:291–292.
116. Watts D, Tassler PL, Dellon AL. The effect of double gloving on cutaneous sensibility, skin compliance, and suture identification. Contemp Surg. 1994;44:289–292.
117. Wilson SJ, Uy A, Sellu D, Ali Jaffer M. Subjective effects of double gloves on surgical performance. Ann R Coll Surg Engl. 1996;78:20–22.
118. Phillips AM, Ribbans WJ, Birch NC. Protective gloves for use in high-risk patients: How much do they affect the dexterity of the surgeon? Ann R Coll Surg Engl. 1997;79:124–127.
119. Leslie LF, Woods JA, Thacker JG, et al. Needle puncture resistance of surgical gloves, finger guards, and glove liners. J Biomed Mater Res. 1996;33:41–46.
120. Woods JA, Leslie LF, Drake DB, Edlich RF. Effect of puncture resistant surgical gloves, finger guards, and glove liners on cutaneous sensibility and surgical psychomotor skills. J Biomed Mater Res. 1996;33:47–51.

121. Cleveland JL, Gooch BF, Lockwood SA. Occupational blood exposures, in dentistry: A decade in review. Infect Control Hosp Epidemiol. 1997;18:717–721.
122. Ramos-Gomez F, Ellison J, Greenspan D, et al. Accidental exposures to blood and body fluids among dental health care workers in dental teaching clinics in San Francisco: A prospective study. J Am Dent Assoc. 1997;128:1253–1261.
123. Cleveland JL, Lockwood SA, Gooch BF, et al. Percutaneous injuries in dentistry: An observational study. J Am Dent Assoc. 1995;126:745–751.
124. Siew C, Gruninger SE, Miaw C, Neidle EA. Percutaneous injuries in practicing dentists. J Am Dent Assoc. 1994;126:1227–1234.
125. Carlton JE, Dodson TB, Cleveland JL, Lockwood SA. The risk of percutaneous injury in oral and maxillofacial surgery. J Oral Maxillofac Surg. 1997;55:553–556.
126. Gooch BF, Siew C, Cleveland JL, et al. Occupational blood exposure and HIV infection among oral and maxillofacial surgeons. Oral Surg Oral Med Oral Pathol Oral Radiol Endod. 1998;85:128–134.
127. Avery CME, Johnson PA. Surgical glove perforation and maxillofacial trauma: To plate or wire? Br J Oral Maxillofac Surg. 1992;30:31–35.
128. Charache P, Cameron JL, Maters AW, Frantz EI. Prevalence of infection with human immunodeficiency virus in elective surgery patients. Ann Surg. 1991;214:562–568.
129. Centers for Disease Control. Recommendations for preventing transmission of human immunodeficiency virus and hepatitis B virus infection to patients during exposure-prone invasive procedures. MMWR Morb Mortal Wkly Rep. 1991;40:1–9.
130. No reference provided.
131. Centers for Disease Control and Prevention. Update: Provisional Public Health Service recommendations for chemoprophylaxis after occupational exposure to HIV. MMWR Morb Mortal Wkly Rep. 1996;45:468–472.
132. No reference provided.
133. Gerberding JL. Prophylaxis for occupational exposures to HIV. Ann Intern Med. 1996;125:497–501.
134. Blauvelt A. The role of skin dendritic cells in the initiation of human immunodeficiency virus infection. Am J Med. 1997;102(Suppl 5B):S16–S20.
135. Spira AI, Marx PA, Patterson BK, et al. Cellular targets of infection and route of vital dissemination after an intravaginal inoculation of simian immunodeficiency virus into rhesus macaques. J Exp Med. 1996;183:215–225.
136. Granelli-Piperno A, Finkel V, Delgado E, Steinman RM. Virus replication begins in dendritic cells during the transmission of HIV-1 from mature dendritic cells to T cells. Curr Biol. 1999;9:21–29.
137. Black RJ. Animal studies of prophylaxis. Am J Med. 1997;102:39–44.
138. Fazely F, Haseltine WA, Rodger RF, Ruprecht RM. Postexposure chemoprophylaxis with ZDV or ZDV combined with interferon-γ. Failure after inoculating rhesus monkeys with a high dose of SIV. J AIDS. 1991;4:1093–1097.
139. Van Rompay KK, Marthas ML, Ramos RA, et al. Simian immunodeficiency virus (SIV) infection of infant rhesus macaques as a model to test antiretroviral drug prophylaxis and therapy: Oral 3′azido-3′-deoxythymidine prevents SIV infection. Antimicrob Agents Chemother. 1992;36:2381–2386.
140. Tsai C-C, Follis KE, Sabo A, et al. Prevention of SIV infection in macaques by (R)-9-(2-phosphonylmethoxypropyl)adenine. Science. 1995;270:1197–1199.
141. Böttiger D, Johansson N-G, Samuelsson B, et al. Prevention of simian immunodeficiency virus, SIV_{sm}, or HIV-2 infection in cynomolgus monkeys by pre- and postexposure administration of BEA-005. AIDS. 1997;11:157–162. Lundgren B, Böttiger D, Ljungdahl-Ståhle E, et al. Antiviral effects of 3′fluorothymidine and 3′azidothymidine in cynomolgus monkeys infected with simian immunodeficiency virus. J AIDS. 1991;4:489–498.
142. Böttiger D, Putkonen P, Oberg B. Prevention of HIV-2 and SIV infections in cynomolgus macaques by prophylactic treatment with 3′-fluorothymidine. AIDS Res Hum Retroviruses. 1992;8:1235–1238.
143. Böttiger D, Oberg B. Influence of the infectious dose of SIV on the acute infection in cynomolgus monkeys and on the effect of treatment with 3′-fluorothymidine. Abstract 81. Presented at the Ninth Symposium on Nonhuman Primate Models for AIDS, November 6–9, 1991.
144. Connor EM, Sperling RS, Gelber R, et al. Reduction of maternal-infant transmission of human immunodeficiency virus type 1 with zidovudine treatment. N Engl J Med. 1994;331:1173–1180.
145. Wade NA, Birkhead GS, Warren BL, et al. Abbreviated regimens of zidovudine prophylaxis and perinatal transmission of the human immunodeficiency virus. N Engl J Med. 1998;339:1409–1414.
146. LaFon SW, Mooney BD, McMullen JP, et al. A double-blind, placebo-controlled study of the safety and efficacy of Retrovir (zidovudine, ZDV) as a chemoprophylactic agent in health care workers exposed to HIV (Abstract 489). In: Program and Abstracts, 30th Interscience Conference on Antimicrobial Agents and Chemotherapy in Atlanta. Washington, DC: American Society for Microbiology; 1990:167.
147. LaFon SW, Lehrman SN, Barry DW. Prophylactically administered Retrovir in health care workers potentially exposed to the human immunodeficiency virus. J Infect Dis. 1988;158:503.
148. Jochimsen EM. Failures of zidovudine postexposure prophylaxis. Am J Med. 1997;102:52–55.
149. Jochimsen EM. Failures of postexposure prophylaxis after occupational human immunodeficiency virus exposure (Abstract 523). Program and Abstracts of the National HIV Prevention Conference. Atlanta, GA, August 29–September 1, 1999.
150. Anonymous. New drugs for HIV infection. Med Lett Drugs Ther. 1996;38:35–37.
151. Centers for Disease Control and Prevention. Report of the NIH Panel to Define Principles of Therapy of HIV Infection and Guidelines for the Use of Antiretroviral Agents in HIV-infected Adults and Adolescents. MMWR Morb Mortal Wkly Rep. 1998;47(RR-5):1–82.
152. Saag MS. Candidate antiretroviral agents for use in postexposure prophylaxis. Am J Med. 1997;102(Suppl 5B):S25–S30.
153. Mayers DL. Prevalence and incidence of resistance to zidovudine and other antiretroviral drugs. Am J Med. 1997;102(Suppl 5B):S70–S75.
154. Imrie A, Beveridge A, Genn W, et al. Transmission of human immunodeficiency virus type 1 resistant to nevirapine and zidovudine. J Infect Dis. 1997;175:1502–1506.
155. Veenstra J, Schuurman R, Cornelissen M, et al. Transmission of zidovudine-resistant human immunodeficiency virus type 1 variants following deliberate injection of blood from a patient with AIDS: Characteristics and natural history of the virus. Clin Infect Dis. 1995;21:556–560.
156. Erice A, Mayers DL, Strike DG, et al. Brief report: Primary infection with zidovudine-resistant human immunodeficiency virus type 1. N Engl J Med. 1993;328:1163–1165.
157. Fitzgibbon JE, Gaur S, Frenkel LD, et al. Transmission from one child to another of human immunodeficiency virus type 1 with a zidovudine-resistance mutation. N Engl J Med. 1993;329:1835–1841.
158. Larder BA. Viral resistance and the selection of antiretroviral combinations. J AIDS. 1995;10(Suppl 1):S28–S33.
159. Katlama C, Ingrand D, Loveday C, et al. Safety and efficacy of lamivudine-zidovudine combination therapy in antiretroviral naive patients: A randomized controlled comparison with zidovudine monotherapy. JAMA. 1996;276:118–125.
160. Struble KA, Pratt RD, Gitterman SR. Toxicity of antiretroviral agents. Am J Med. 1997;102(Suppl 5B):S65–S67.
161. Food and Drug Administration. Protease inhibitors may increase blood glucose in HIV patients. FDA Med Bull. 1997;27.
162. Dever LL, Oruwari PA, O'Donovan CA, Eng RHK. Hyperglycemia associated with protease inhibitors in HIV-infected patients (Abstract LB-4). In: Abstracts of the 37th Interscience Conference on Antimicrobial Agents and Chemotherapy in Toronto. September 28–October 1, 1997. Washington, DC: American Society for Microbiology; 1997.
163. Dube MP, Johnson DL, Currier JS, Leedom JM. Protease inhibitor–associated hyperglycaemia (Letter). Lancet. 1997;350:713–714.
164. Tokars JL, Marcus R, Culver DH, et al. Surveillance of HIV infection and zidovudine use among health care workers after occupational exposure to HIV-infected blood. Ann Intern Med. 1993;118:913–919.
165. Forseter G, Joline C, Wormser GP. Tolerability, safety, and acceptability of zidovudine prophylaxis in health care workers. Arch Intern Med. 1994;154:2746–2749.
166. Puro V, Ippolito G, Guzzanti E, et al. Zidovudine prophylaxis after accidental exposure to HIV: The Italian experience. The Italian Study Group on Occupational Risk of HIV Infection. AIDS. 1992;6:963–969.
167. Beekmann SE, Fahrner R, Henderson DK, Gerberding JL. Zidovudine safety and tolerance among uninfected health care workers: A brief update. Am J Med. 1997;102:63–64.
168. Ippolito G, Puro V, Italian Registry of Antiretroviral Prophylaxis. Zidovudine toxicity in uninfected healthcare workers. Am J Med. 1997;102(Suppl 5B):S58–S62.
169. Wang SA, HIV PEP Registry Group. Human immunodeficiency virus (HIV) postexposure prophylaxis (PEP) following occupational HIV exposure: Findings from the HIV PEP registry (Abstract 482). In: Program and Abstracts of the Infectious Diseases Society of America 35th Annual Meeting in San Francisco. September 13–16, 1997. Alexandria, Va: Infectious Diseases Society of America; 1997:161.
170. Steger KA, Swotinsky R, Snyder S, Craven DE. Recent experience with post-exposure prophylaxis (PEP) with combination antiretrovirals for occupational exposure (OE) to HIV (Abstract 480). In: Program and Abstracts of the Infectious Diseases Society of America 35th Annual Meeting in San Francisco. September 13–16, 1997. Alexandria, Va: Infectious Diseases Society of America; 1997:161.
171. Henry K, Acosta EP, Jochimsen E. Hepatotoxicity and rash associated with zidovudine and zalcitabine chemoprophylaxis (Letter). Ann Intern Med. 1996;124:855.
172. Public Health Service Task Force recommendations for the use of antiretroviral drugs in pregnant women infected with HIV-1 for maternal health and for reducing perinatal HIV-1 transmission in the United States. Centers for Disease Control and Prevention. MMWR Morb Mortal Wkly Rep. 1998;47(RR-2):1–30.
173. O'Sullivan MJ, Boyer P, Scott GB et al. The pharmacokinetics and safety of zidovudine in the third trimester of pregnancy for women infected with human immunodeficiency virus and their infants: Phase I acquired immunodeficiency syndrome clinical trials study group (protocol 082). Zidovudine Collaborative Working Group. Am J Obstet Gynecol. 1993;168:1510–1516.
174. Birth outcomes following zidovudine therapy in pregnant women. MMWR Morb Mortal Wkly Rep. 1994;43:409, 415–416.
175. White A, Eldridge R, Andrews E, Antiretroviral Pregnancy Registry Advisory Committee. Birth outcomes following zidovudine exposure in pregnant women: The Antiretroviral Pregnancy Registry. Acta Paediatr Suppl 1997;421:86–88.
176. Culnane M, Fowler MG, Lee S, et al. Evaluation for late effects of in utero (IU) ZDV exposure among uninfected infants born to HIV+ women enrolled in ACTG 076 & 219 (Abstract 485). Clin Infect Dis. 1997;25:445.
177. Anonymous. Antiretroviral Pregnancy Registry International Interim Report for Didanosine (VIDEX, ddl), Lamivudine (EPIVIR, 3TC), Saquinavir (INVIRASE, SAQ), Stavudine (ZERIT, d4t), Zalcitabine (HIVID, ddC), and Zidovudine (RET-

ROVIR, ZDV), 1 January 1989–30 June 1996. Research Triangle Park, NC: Antiretroviral Pregnancy Registry; 1997.
178. Johnson MA, Goodwin C, Yuen GJ, et al. The pharmacokinetics of 3TC administered to HIV-1–infected women (pre-partum, during labour and post-partum) and their offspring. Abstract Tu.C.445. Presented at the Eleventh International Conference on AIDS, Vancouver, Canada, July 7–12, 1996.
179. Moodley J, Moodley D, Pillay K, et al. Antiviral effect of lamivudine alone and in combination with zidovudine in HIV-infected pregnant women. Abstract 607. Presented at the Fourth Conference on Retroviruses and Opportunistic Infections, Washington, DC, January 22–26, 1997.
180. Ayers KM, Clive D, Tucker WE Jr, et al. Nonclinical toxicology studies with zidovudine: Genetic toxicity tests and carcinogenicity bioassays in mice and rats. Fundam Appl Toxicol. 1996;32:148–158.
181. Ayers KM, Torrey CD, Reynolds DJ. A transplacental carcinogenicity bioassay in CD-1 mice with zidovudine. Fundam Appl Toxicol. 1997;38:195–198.
182. Olivero OA, Anderson LM, Diwan BA, et al. AZT is a genomic transplacental carcinogen in animal models (Abstract 52). J AIDS. 1997;14:29.
183. National Institutes of Health. Summary of the meeting of a panel to review studies of transplacental toxicity of AZT. January 14, 1997.
184. Gerberding JL. Post-exposure prophylaxis for human immunodeficiency virus at San Francisco General Hospital. Am J Med. 1997;102:85–89.
185. Mangione CM, Gerberding JL, Cummings SR. Occupational exposure to HIV: Frequency and rates of underreporting of percutaneous and mucocutaneous exposures by medical housestaff. Am J Med. 1991;90:85–90.
186. Osborn EH, Papadakis MA, Gerberding JL. Occupational exposures to body fluids among medical students. A seven-year longitudinal study. Ann Intern Med. 1999;130:45–51.
187. Henry K, Campbell S. Needlestick/sharps injuries and HIV exposure among health care workers. National estimates based on a survey of U.S. hospitals. Minn Med. 1995;78:41–44.
188. Dilley JW. Counseling health care workers after accidental exposures. Focus. 1990;5:3–4.
189. Armstrong K, Gorden R, Santorella G. Occupational exposures of health care workers (HCWs) to human immunodeficiency virus (HIV): Stress reactions and counseling interventions. Social Work Health Care. 1995;21(3):61–80.
190. Richman KM, Rickman LS. The potential for transmission of human immunodeficiency virus through human bites. J AIDS. 1993;6:402–406.
191. Vidmar L, Poljak M, Tomazic J, et al. Transmission of HIV-1 by human bite (Letter). Lancet. 1996;347:1762.
192. Rich JD, Merriman NA, Mylonakis E, et al. Misdiagnosis of HIV infection by HIV-1 plasma viral load testing: A case series. Ann Intern Med. 1999;130:37–39.
193. Fahrner R, Humphrey E, Perlman J, Gerberding JL. Source patient testing at SFGH. In: Program and Abstracts, 30th Interscience Conference on Antimicrobial Agents and Chemotherapy in Atlanta. Washington, DC: American Society for Microbiology; 1997.

Chapter 297

Nosocomial Herpesvirus Infections

DAVID K. HENDERSON

Eight herpesviruses commonly infect humans (Table 297–1). In addition to the two *herpes simplex* viruses (HSV-1 and HSV-2), varicella-zoster virus (VZV), cytomegalovirus (CMV), and Epstein-Barr virus (EBV), two recently identified and characterized herpesviruses (human herpesvirus 6 [HHV-6] and HHV-7) cause a spectrum of illness from the acute childhood febrile illness roseola (exanthem subitum) to demyelinating disease, lymphoproliferative syndromes, and systemic infections in immunocompromised patients.[1–20] An eighth herpesvirus, a B-cell–tropic agent that is in many aspects similar to EBV, appears to contribute to the occurrence of both body cavity B-cell lymphomas and Kaposi's sarcoma in humans.[6, 21–25] A ninth herpesvirus, *Herpesvirus simiae*, is a rare cause of human infection (see Chapter 131). With the clear exception of VZV and the possible exceptions of HHV-6 and HHV-7, the remaining herpesviruses infecting humans apparently require close personal contact for person-to-person spread and are therefore not classified as highly contagious.

Two properties shared by members of this family of viruses are important to emphasize: (1) all these viruses can, after causing a primary infection, persist in a latent state in the body and subsequently cause recrudescent or reactivated infection, and (2) differentiation of recrudescent infection from primary infection is often difficult and makes identification of true nosocomial infections problematic. Historically, this distinction has often been made on the basis of serologic evidence, the reliability of which may be questionable. Because recrudescent infections are common among immunosuppressed patients, they are discussed in detail in the chapters of this book dealing with each of the different viruses.

Herpesviruses have become important nosocomial pathogens for several reasons, including the presence of some of these agents in blood, blood products, and organ transplants and the high prevalence of these infections in the population at large. This chapter discusses the risk of nosocomial transmission of each of these agents and appropriate techniques to be used to prevent transmission of these agents to patients and personnel in the hospital.

HERPES SIMPLEX VIRUSES

Risk of Nosocomial Transmission

Transmission of HSV-1 and HSV-2 from infected patients to staff has been well documented.[26–37] Both HSV-1 and HSV-2 have been associated with the occurrence of herpetic whitlow.[29–31, 36, 38–40] Primary HSV-1 infection has also been reported after mouth-to-mouth resuscitation.[31] Amir and colleagues reported an apparent cluster of primary oral HSV infections in four pediatric care providers.[41] The authors argue that these infections were probably acquired in the workplace, although no point source was identified and molecular techniques were not used to assess whether all were infected with similar isolates.[41] Although a great deal of attention has been focused on the problem of HSV-2 infection in obstetric and neonatal intensive care unit (ICU) settings, HSV-1 has also been associated with outbreaks of infection in hospital personnel and their families.[36] Once in a nursery or an ICU, for example, an infant with HSV infection may serve as a reservoir for transmission to other infants, although the risk of such transmission appears to be small.[36] Whereas HSV infection occurring as a result of the infant acquiring infection during delivery has been well documented, postpartum acquisition of HSV has been much less common and more difficult to document, and the diagnosis has been made most often on empirical grounds.[42]

Transmission of HSV-1 from staff to patients has also been reported. Linneman and colleagues used restriction enzyme analysis to demonstrate that two cases of HSV-1 infection in neonates in the same nursery were caused by viruses with identical DNA "fingerprints."[43] Sakadka and associates reported two clusters of HSV-1 infection at two separate hospitals.[44] Both clusters involved three neonates, and in both instances all three infants had HSV-1 isolates that produced virtually identical endonuclease cleavage profiles.[44] Although not proved definitively, an environmental reservoir (radiant warmer) was incriminated in one cluster. In the other, three infants born at one hospital approximately 1 year apart were infected with strains of HSV-1 that yielded identical restriction endonuclease patterns. The investigators postulated that periodic reactivation of HSV-1 infection in health care workers providing care for these infants

TABLE 297–1 Herpesviruses Infecting Humans

Herpes simplex viruses (HSV-1 and HSV-2)
Varicella-zoster virus
Cytomegalovirus
Epstein-Barr virus
Human herpesvirus 6
Human herpesvirus 7
Human herpesvirus 8 (also known as Kaposi's sarcoma–associated herpesvirus)
Herpesvirus simiae (herpesvirus subtype B) (rare)

TABLE 297–2 Recommendations for Peripartum Care of Pregnant Women with Herpes Simplex Virus Infections*

Genital Lesions Present at Term	Primary Genital Lesions	Secondary Genital Lesions	Status of Membranes	Recommended Route of Delivery
Yes	+	−	Intact or ruptured <4–6 hr	Cesarean section
	+	−	Ruptured >4–6 hr	Vaginally
	+	±	Baby has been delivered vaginally	—
	−	+	Ruptured >4–6 hr	Vaginally
	−	+	Intact or ruptured <4–6 hr	Cesarean section
No, cervical culture positive at term	−	−	Intact or ruptured <4–6 hr	Cesarean section
	−	−	Ruptured >4–6 hr	Vaginally
No, positive history, inactive	−	−	Intact or ruptured	Vaginally
No, active nongenital HSV	−	−	Intact or ruptured	Vaginally
No, history of nongenital HSV, inactive	−	−	Intact or ruptured	Vaginally

* To attempt to decrease the rate of caesarean section, some authorities recommend administering acyclovir prophylaxis, beginning at 38 weeks' gestation, to women with past histories of recurrent genital herpes, thereby permitting vaginal delivery.[288]

Modified from Kilbrick S. Herpes simplex infection at term: What to do with mother, newborn, and nursery personnel. JAMA. 1980;243:157–160. Copyright 1980, American Medical Association.

resulted in transmission to the infants.[44] Despite these anecdotal reports and despite the fact that the risk has not yet been measured, the risk of nosocomial transmission of HSV to susceptible patients, including neonates, appears to be quite small.

Mechanism of Nosocomial Transmission

The frequent occurrence of whitlow in ICU personnel, respiratory care personnel, and dentists argues in favor of a primary role for cutaneous inoculation of HSV-1 from oral secretions of infected patients directly into the skin of health care providers. Although many, if not most cases of whitlow represent primary infection with HSV, reactivation infection or recrudescence can occur,[28, 30, 38] and one experimental study has demonstrated the possibility of reinfection.[45]

Oral lesions caused by HSV-1 contain large quantities of virus and represent a potential reservoir for nosocomial transmission. For this reason, dental practitioners are at increased risk for occupational infections.[46–49] In one study, oral lesions were found to have an average of greater than 10^8 plaque-forming units per milliliter of vesicular fluid.[50] Moreover, high titers of virus remained in lesions of severely immunocompromised patients for 3 weeks or longer.[50] Turner and coworkers demonstrated that HSV-1 could be cultured from the hands of six of nine adults with oral lesions.[51] In addition, in the same study HSV-1 isolates were shown to survive drying on skin, plastic, and cloth for up to 4 hours. Both patients and hospital personnel can harbor inapparent reactivation infections. In one prospective study, 9.6% of asymptomatic staff members of an obstetric hospital were found to have HSV in saliva.[52] In a study cited earlier, Amir and colleagues reported four cases of primary HSV gingivostomatitis that occurred in pediatric care providers.[41] Each of these health care workers contracted primary oral HSV infection in their fourth decade of life. The investigators concluded that the development of acute pharyngitis in pediatric health care personnel who do not relate a history of either herpetic gingivostomatitis or herpes labialis may indicate primary infection. HSV infection should be considered in the differential diagnosis of acute pharyngitis in such individuals. They emphasize that early diagnosis is important to prevent the spread of infection to patients.[41]

HSV-contaminated breast milk has been inferentially incriminated as being responsible for the postpartum transmission of HSV in one instance[53]; however, HSV infection of either mother or child is not a contraindication to breast-feeding.

Prevention of Nosocomial Transmission

Use of universal or standard infection control precautions[54–56] should minimize the risk for transmission of HSV-1. By following these infection control precautions, health care workers should avoid direct cutaneous exposure to HSV-1 lesions. Special attention should be paid to patients who have extensive oral, genital, or cutaneous disease; such patients may require more stringent isolation precautions. All personnel having skin-to-skin contact with an HSV-infected patient should practice careful hand washing. Personnel performing procedures involving oral or genital secretions (e.g., suctioning, placement of an oral airway, dental work, irrigation of a Foley catheter, dressing changes) should wear gloves. Such patients are a reservoir for whitlow but probably represent minimal risk to other patients, with only the following few exceptions. Patients with extensive HSV lesions should not be roomed with immunocompromised patients or with patients who have severe atopic histories or defects in skin integrity (burn patients, eczema, etc.). Alternatively, in a nursery, a neonatal ICU, or a burn ward, such patients are optimally managed by strict isolation or, when possible, cohort nursing.

A special problem arises when the mother of a newborn has active nongenital HSV infection. Kibrick has recommended that the newborn be placed in a private room, that the mother be allowed to handle or feed the baby only after her lesions have crusted over, and that once the mother has had contact with the baby, the baby be placed on contact isolation.[57] Treatment with acyclovir or other effective antivirals may hasten clearing of the lesions. Management of mothers and babies exposed to mothers with genital infections is outlined in Table 297–2 and is also discussed in detail in the literature.[58–65] Optimal care of infants born to infected mothers would include placing the infant in a "special" nursery during hospitalization (for up to 14 days). Such infants should be evaluated frequently for signs of HSV infection. Depending on the stage of the mother's disease (i.e., primary versus secondary) and the extent of disease at delivery (i.e., modest versus extensive), empirical antiviral treatment of the newborn may be appropriate. Many authorities would empirically treat infants exposed to the birth canal of a mother who has active HSV infection acquired late in the course of her pregnancy with acyclovir.[59]

Because the efficacy of antiviral therapy in the setting of neonatal infection is increased when therapy is administered early in the course of the infection, caregivers must maintain a high index of suspicion for neonatal HSV infection—in children born to both symptomatic and asymptomatic mothers. Strikingly, in one series from a large Australian teaching hospital, none of the six infants with neonatal HSV infection identified in a retrospective review was born to a mother who had a history of past or recent genital HSV infection.[66] The authors of this study also offer a standard protocol for managing herpesvirus infections in pregnancy.[66] Brown and coworkers have shown that the approximately one third of women who shed HSV in early labor have recently acquired genital HSV.[62] Their infants are 10 times more likely to acquire neonatal HSV infection than are infants of women who have asymptomatic reactivation.[62] In this study, infants of mothers who had antibodies specific to HSV-2 (but not to HSV-1) had lower rates of HSV-2 infection.[62] Other investigators have described similar findings.[67]

Infants in whom signs or symptoms of active infection are developing should initially be managed according to strict principles of "standard" precautions; if more extensive disease develops, strict isolation or cohort nursing in a private room or in an isolation room in the ICU may be more effective. If such a room is not available, the infant should be separated from other infants in the nursery or ICU. Placing the infant in an incubator or isolette may raise the consciousness of the staff regarding the potential for transmission.[57] Gibbs has recommended a similar approach.[68, 69]

Mothers who have active genital lesions should be allowed to feed or handle infants. However, before handling her baby, the mother should cover all lesions, carefully wash her hands, and put on clean hospital garb. If an infant is restricted to an ICU or nursery for life support purposes, the mother may only visit that area after all lesions are crusted over and covered. Additionally, in circumstances in which vaginal delivery is attempted by a mother known or suspected of having active genital HSV infection, fetal scalp monitoring should not be performed because of the risk of infection from inoculation.[70]

Management of Infected or Exposed Personnel

Hospital personnel who have active oral or other cutaneous infection should not be permitted to care for high-risk patients until the lesions are entirely crusted and dry. Examples of such high-risk patients include premature infants, newborns, severely immunocompromised patients, burn patients, and patients with diseases that affect skin integrity. In the event that an infected individual must work to provide adequate care in a high-risk area, the provider should ensure that dressings (or a mask) cover all lesions. When practical, gloves should be worn. Particularly in situations in which the health care provider has active lesions on the hands, double-gloving may further reduce the risk for exposure.[71] Most importantly, frequent glove changes and strict hand-washing techniques should be used.

In the event of an apparent outbreak or cluster of infections caused by HSV-1, restriction enzyme analysis of DNA from viral isolates has proved to be an extremely useful epidemiologic tool.[44, 72]

VARICELLA-ZOSTER VIRUS

Risk of Transmission

Of the members of the herpesvirus family, VZV is by far the most contagious. For this reason, most adults have been exposed to the virus and have a prior history of chickenpox (varicella). The risk of transmission is highest in pediatric populations. Among adults, patients and staff from rural areas and locales where the incidence of VZV infection is lower (e.g., Pacific islands, tropical climates) are at highest risk for acquisition.[73]

The major problems with nosocomial transmission of VZV infection occur in areas housing potentially susceptible immunosuppressed patients (e.g., pediatric oncology ward). In immunocompetent patients, both primary infections (varicella) and recrudescent VZV infections (herpes zoster) are usually benign, self-limited infections. Although the development of effective antiviral therapy has substantially reduced the risk of severe morbidity and mortality from VZV infection for patients who are immunosuppressed, both primary[74–76] and recrudescent VZV infections[76–78] continue to be associated with increased morbidity and the potential for mortality in immunosuppressed patients. Finally, some authors have reported that varicella occurring during pregnancy is associated with increased severity.[79, 80] Others have stressed that this increase in severity is typical of varicella in an adult population[81, 82] and that complications of VZV infection in pregnancy occur no more frequently than in the entire adult population. The extent to which immunocompromised patients who have had chickenpox are at risk for exogenous reinfection is a matter of some controversy. Several investigators have suggested that immunocompromised patients may be at risk to acquire exogenous reinfection with VZV, either in the form of a second case of varicella or chickenpox[83, 84] or as atypical generalized zoster,[85] a syndrome reported to resemble disseminated zoster without an antecedent dermatome. One epidemiologic study has suggested such a possibility[83]; however, this study has considerable shortcomings,[86, 87] and molecular epidemiologic information regarding this outbreak is not available. Conversely, Gershon and coworkers have demonstrated definitively the presence of reinfection varicella in immunosuppressed patients.[84] Currently, most authorities believe that primary VZV infection generally produces lifetime protection against exogenous reinfection.

Mechanisms of Transmission

Nosocomial transmission of VZV infection does occur. Several studies have clearly demonstrated airborne transmission from an index case with varicella to susceptible children.[88–84] Also, a susceptible patient or staff member may acquire primary infection as a result of direct contact with lesions from a patient with dermatomal zoster.[82, 88] Despite some published evidence suggesting that dermatomal zoster may be transmitted from patient to patient,[82, 88, 95–97] most authorities believe that dermatomal zoster represents recrudescent infection rather than a transmissible illness.[82, 98–101] One report suggested that a patient with localized zoster was the index case in a nosocomial outbreak of VZV infection.[102] Because the index case was bedfast and several of the secondary cases were younger than 1 year (and therefore not ambulatory), the authors postulated that the transmission must have occurred either via the airborne route or via the hands of hospital personnel. In any event, such occurrences would appear to be extremely uncommon.

Garnett and Grenfell have argued that the presence of varicella in the community may reduce the incidence of zoster among individuals who have latent infection, presumably as a result of an immunologic "boosting" phenomenon arising from exposure to patients who have varicella.[101]

Prevention of Nosocomial Transmission

Because VZV is highly contagious and VZV infection may be life threatening in certain patient populations,[74–76] many authorities have made recommendations regarding techniques to be used to prevent nosocomial transmission of VZV infection.[56, 83, 87, 89–92, 94, 103–127] Whenever practical, patients who have active VZV infections should not be hospitalized. If patients with active infection must be hospitalized, most authorities recommend that patients with dermatomal zoster be managed with appropriate barriers (e.g., gloves when touching the patient or the patient's lesions) and that the patient's door be labeled with a sign warning people who have not had chickenpox to not enter the patient's room. Use of the so-called standard infection control precautions should be adequate for managing patients who have localized zoster.[56] Severely immunocompromised patients in whom dermatomal zoster develops (i.e., those with hematologic or reticuloendothelial malignancies, those with the acquired immunodeficiency syndrome [AIDS], and those receiving high-dose corticosteroids or multidrug chemotherapy) should be placed in strict isolation until the effects of antiviral therapy can be detected because of the high incidence of dissemination. In such instances, if the primary dermatome begins to heal without signs of dissemination, the patients may be managed with simple barrier (i.e., "standard") precautions.[56] Patients with varicella or disseminated zoster should be managed with strict isolation precautions. Because of the airborne transmission of VZV,[91, 93] Gustafson and colleagues have recommended that hospitalized patients with varicella be placed downwind from other potentially susceptible patients. Anderson and coworkers documented the absence of VZV transmission over a 1-year period in a pediatrics hospital with negative-pressure ventilation rooms.[104]

If a susceptible immunocompromised patient is exposed to a patient with VZV infection, transmission of the infection can be prevented (or the severity of infection reduced) by the administration of hyperimmune globulin (varicella-zoster immune globulin [VZIG]). To be effective, VZIG should be administered as soon as possible after exposure. The Centers for Disease Control and Prevention (CDC) recommends that VZIG be given within 96 hours of exposure.[103] VZV infections are common, and in spite of good infection control procedures, VZV is frequently introduced into the hospital environment in an uncontrolled fashion.[87, 91–93, 96, 97, 103, 109, 116, 124, 128–130] Over the past several years, the use of antiviral agents (e.g., acyclovir, famciclovir) has been shown to be of benefit in patients who have primary or recrudescent VZV infection.[115, 131–149] Especially in immunocompromised patients, acyclovir should be begun as early as the first symptoms of infection arise. In addition to the obvious benefit to the infected patient, antiviral therapy will reduce the risk for nosocomial spread of this airborne pathogen. Because of the urgency involved in identifying exposed, susceptible, immunosuppressed patients,[96] an organized approach to a potential outbreak is advisable. We have developed a flow chart to manage potential nosocomial outbreaks of VZV infection[109] (Fig. 297–1). Others have used a similar approach.[108, 113, 118]

Investigating a Potential Nosocomial Epidemic of Varicella-Zoster Virus Infection

Cases of VZV infection are identified by routine ward rounds, by routine surveillance activities, and by referrals from patient care areas. Once a suspected case is identified, the diagnosis is confirmed, either by hospital epidemiology service staff members or by staff of the clinical virology laboratory. If the suspected diagnosis is incorrect, the investigation is aborted. Once the diagnosis is confirmed, the investigation is divided into two separate areas: (1) patient-related epidemiologic investigation and (2) staff-related epidemiologic investigation. Because of the necessity for administering passive immune globulin prophylaxis to exposed, susceptible, immunocompromised children within 96 hours of exposure to be effective, the initial focus of the investigation is on patients. Similarly, if antiviral prophylaxis is chosen, prompt administration of the agent is important to success. In the event that immunosuppressed staff members are potentially exposed, they should be managed in the same expeditious manner as immunosuppressed patients.

An in-hospital "travel history" is first obtained from the index case. Because in-hospital exposure may take place in any of a number of patient-related areas, several diverse areas must be considered in history taking (see Fig. 297–1). When any of these areas is included in the patient's travel history, the departmental records from that area are examined. Patients documented to be in that area at the same time as the index case are included in the population at risk.

The second component of the patient-related investigation is direct identification of patients at high risk for severe complications of primary VZV infection (see Fig. 297–1). We use three methods to identify such patients: (1) compiling a computer list of all hospitalized pediatric, oncology, and transplant patients; (2) maintaining a list of all ambulatory care patients, including those children and severely immunosuppressed adults who might be staying outside the hospital but returning daily for chemotherapy or blood drawing; and (3) questioning the inpatient pediatrics, oncology, and transplant staff.

Once the population at risk has been determined, the immunologic status of all patients on the list is assessed. If a patient is found to be potentially immunosuppressed (i.e., hematologic malignancy receiving chemotherapy, high-dose steroid therapy, congenital or acquired immunodeficiency), the patient and the medical staff are questioned regarding the potential for exposure and for a prior history of chickenpox or prior varicella immunization. If the patient is potentially exposed and has a negative or equivocal history of VZV infection, baseline serologic analysis is performed and VZIG is administered. If VZIG is not available,[150] many blood banks may be able to prepare plasma from patients recovering from zoster (zoster immune plasma) that contains high-titer antivaricella antibody.[151] Depending on the patient's underlying status, some authorities recommend immunization in this setting.

If a patient is determined to have had primary VZV infection or is determined not to have been exposed, no further follow-up is needed.

If patients on the potentially exposed list are found to be immunocompetent, exposure and VZV histories are obtained after workup of the immunocompromised patients. Exposed, susceptible immunocompetent patients have serologic studies performed and, when possible, are discharged. In general, those with negative exposure histories or positive histories of prior VZV infection need no further follow-up.

If patients must remain hospitalized, serologic determination of immunity by using a sensitive technique such as fluorescent antimembrane antibody assay,[152] immune adherence hemagglutination inhibition assay,[153] or enzyme-linked immunosorbent assay[154] may help determine which exposed patients are susceptible. Less sensitive tests such as the complement fixation test are not reliable indicators of immunity.[155]

Exposed, susceptible, immunocompetent patients should be placed in strict isolation from 9 days after the first possible exposure until 21 days after the last possible exposure. Exposed, susceptible, immunosuppressed patients (even those receiving VZIG or zoster immune plasma) should be placed in strict isolation at the time that the patient is identified as being at risk until at least 21 days after the last possible exposure. Some studies have suggested that administration of zoster immune plasma or earlier preparations of VZIG to exposed, susceptible, immunosuppressed patients may actually lengthen the incubation period for such patients. Although instances of lengthened incubation periods have not been reported with newer preparations of VZIG, physicians responsible for the care of such patients should be mindful of this possibility when planning extended in-hospital care for the patient. Exposed, susceptible, immunosuppressed patients and patients who may become immunosuppressed as a result of either disease progression or therapy may be candidates for the varicella vaccine.[101, 102, 114, 115, 124–127, 131, 132, 136, 147, 156–167] Acyclovir should be administered to susceptible, exposed immunosuppressed patients at the first suggestion of clinical illness caused by VZV,[147] and some investigators have argued for its prophylactic use in susceptible individuals.[139, 168–170] A substantial amount of literature describes the use of this agent in immunocompetent patients as well, particularly for adolescents and adults who acquire varicella.[59, 114, 131, 138, 139, 146, 148, 149, 168, 169, 171–173]

Management of Infected or Exposed Personnel

The other major aspect of the workup of a potential nosocomial outbreak of VZV infection is the assessment of potentially exposed staff (see Fig. 297–1). Exposure and VZV histories are taken from all potentially exposed staff. Potentially exposed staff members who relate negative or equivocal histories of VZV infection should have serologic assessment of immunity with a sensitive test.[152–154] Immunocompromised employees should be managed with the same sense of urgency that is used for immunosuppressed patients.

Exposed, susceptible employees should be reassigned to a low-risk area or placed on administrative leave from 8 days after the first possible exposure until 21 days after the last possible exposure, although others have advocated a more liberal approach.[95] If employees desiring to work in an area with a high prevalence of VZV infection are found to be susceptible on the basis of assessment of humoral[152–154] and, possibly, cell-mediated[153] immunity to VZV, such employees may be candidates for the varicella vaccine.[101, 102, 114, 115, 124–127, 131, 132, 136, 147, 156–167]

Employees in whom primary VZV infection or zoster develops should not care for or be in the same area with patients until the last lesion is crusted over (usually 7 or 8 days after appearance of the last lesion). Employees who have zoster should be reassigned so

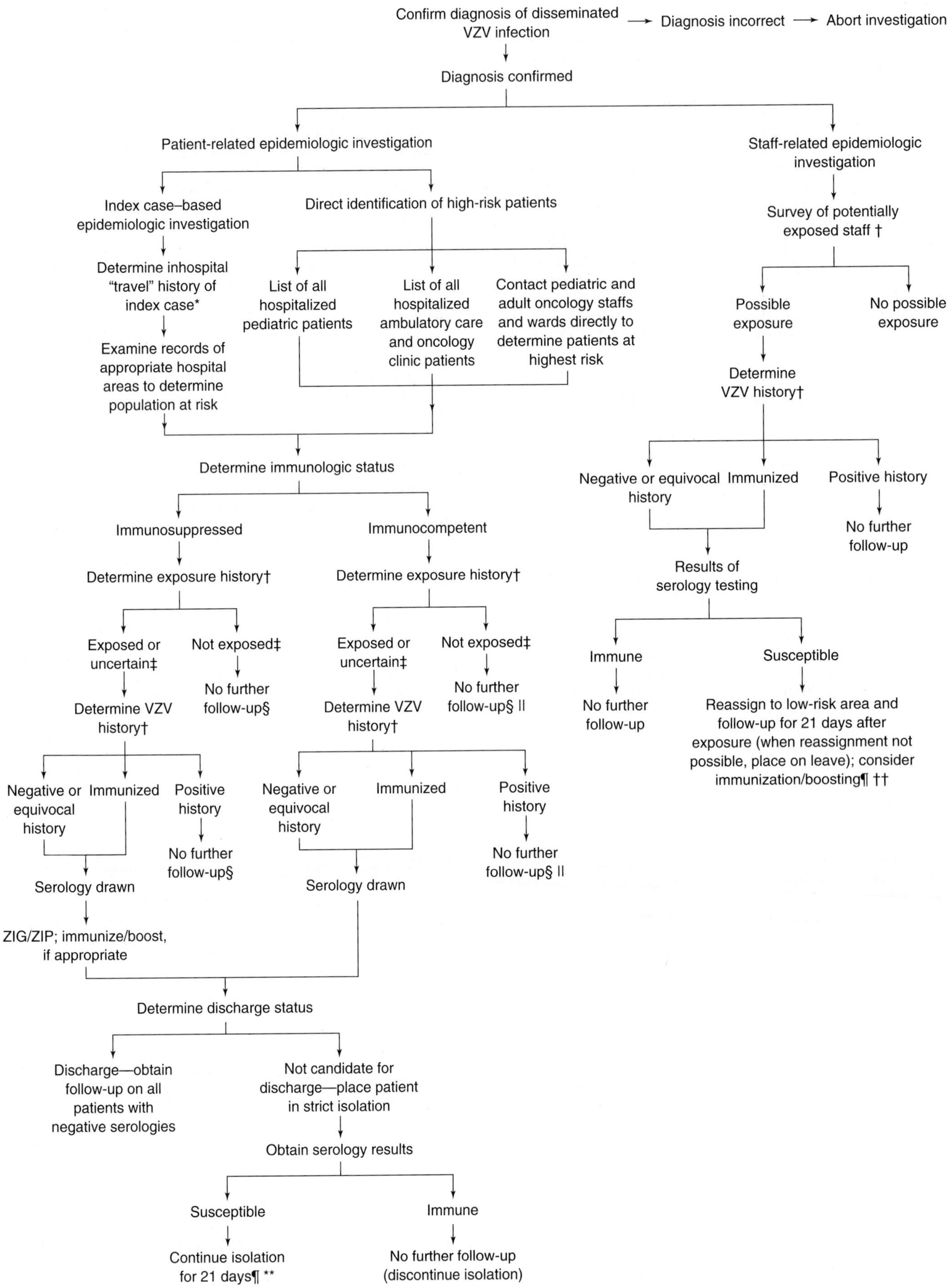

FIGURE 297–1. *See legend on opposite page*

that they also not work in high-risk areas until all lesions have crusted over.

CYTOMEGALOVIRUS

Risk for Nosocomial Transmission

The nosocomial epidemiology of CMV infection is incompletely understood. Part of the problem in assessing the magnitude of risk for nosocomial transmission lies in the difficulty in discriminating between endogenous reactivation infection and exogenous reinfection (i.e., infection with a second strain of CMV). The term *secondary infection* will be used here to encompass both possibilities. In several settings, the risk of an individual patient acquiring CMV infection, either in the hospital or as a result of iatrogenic intervention, appears to be quite high. Premature infants and infants in newborn nurseries are at increased risk for CMV acquisition.[174–181] Studies have suggested that from 14 to 30% of infants residing in a neonatal ICU for more than 1 month acquire CMV infection.[174, 176, 177]

Recipients of organ transplants are also at high risk for both primary and secondary CMV infection. As the required immunosuppressive regimens have become more powerful, secondary CMV infections have become increasingly more common. Recently, however, investigators have used newer immunosuppressive regimens in combination with appropriate antiviral chemoprophylaxis to reduce the incidence of CMV infection in this population.[182] A summary of 12 studies that used various techniques to assess CMV infection in renal transplant recipients demonstrated that 53% of seronegative transplant recipients acquired infection and 85% of seropositive transplant recipients either shed virus or had a fourfold rise in anti-CMV antibody titer.[183] Because these results include some studies that used only complement fixation to document infection, these numbers are probably conservative estimates of the risk of a renal transplant recipient acquiring CMV infection. Heart transplant recipients are also at high risk for CMV infection.[184–187] In an early study, 62% of seronegative heart transplant patients seroconverted post-transplant, and 60% of patients who were seropositive before heart transplantation had fourfold rises in antibody titer after transplantation.[184] Recipients of heterologous bone marrow infusions or grafts are also at increased risk for CMV infection.[188, 189] In one study, 39% of all seronegative patients acquired primary infection, and evidence of secondary CMV infection developed in 61% of seropositive bone marrow recipients.[189] Allogeneic stem cell infusions are associated with similar risks.

Recipients of granulocyte transfusions have also been demonstrated to be at risk for acquiring CMV infection. In the study just cited,[189] 48% of seronegative bone marrow recipients who received granulocyte transfusions seroconverted as compared with 33% of seronegative recipients who did not receive granulocyte transfusions. In an earlier study, Winston and colleagues reported that evidence of CMV infection developed in 61% of patients receiving granulocyte transfusions as compared with 26% of age- and disease-matched recipients.[190]

Several studies have suggested that the transfusion of fresh whole blood is implicated in the transmission of CMV. The risk for acquisition of CMV has been shown to be associated with increasing numbers of units transfused. The risk of acquiring CMV infection has been estimated to be between 2.4 and 2.7% per unit of transfused whole blood.[191, 192]

Even though the risk for CMV transmission by parenteral exposure seems clear, the issue of whether hospital patients or hospital personnel are at risk for acquiring CMV by nonparenteral routes of exposure is less clear. Although apparently uncommon, nonparenteral transmission of CMV from patient to patient has been reasonably well documented.[193–196] Breast milk has been implicated as a source of primary neonatal infection.[193–195, 197, 198] Two studies have reported clustering of CMV infections in neonatal nurseries, apparently from nonparenteral transmission.[193, 194] One of these studies used restriction endonuclease analysis to document nonparenteral spread of CMV among three infants in a neonatal ICU.[194] The author concluded, however, that such common-source outbreaks are apparently uncommon. In a similar, but more recent study, Aitken and colleagues evaluated a cluster of five CMV infections in a special care nursery and concluded that the infections were not epidemiologically linked.[199] In a study using similar technology, Demmler and coworkers demonstrated patient-to-patient transmission of a single strain of CMV in a busy chronic care pediatrics hospital.[196] The investigators isolated CMV from patients' hands, health care workers' hands, and hospitalized infants' diapers.[197]

The issue of whether hospital personnel are at risk for acquiring

FIGURE 297–1. Algorithm for the evaluation of a potential nosocomial outbreak of varicella-zoster virus (VZV) infection.

*That is, ward exposure, playroom, recreation, school classroom, radiology, nuclear medicine, physical therapy, occupational therapy, radiation oncology, pulmonary function.

†VZV history and exposure history are usually obtained simultaneously in the clinical center.

‡*Exposed* = one of the following types of exposure to chickenpox or zoster patient(s):

a. Playmate contact (>1 hour of play indoors)
b. Hospital contact (in same two- to four-bed room or adjacent beds in a large ward)
c. Newborn contact (newborn of mother who had onset of chickenpox <5 days before delivery or within 48 hours after delivery

Uncertain = in same location in the hospital as the patient (e.g., radiology waiting room, elevators) but exposure not documented

Not Exposed = not meeting criteria listed above

§Exposed, severely compromised patients with positive histories may be at risk, and obtaining serologic confirmation of immunity may be advisable. Exposed, immunosuppressed patients who are thought to be capable of mounting a response to immunization, and immunocompetent patients who are likely to become immunosuppressed as a result of an underlying disease or immunosuppressive therapy may be candidates for immunization.

‖ Discharged immunocompetent exposed patients in this category should be advised regarding VZV infections, and both the patients and their physicians should be advised that the patient should not be readmitted to the hospital unless absolutely essential. If readmitted, the patient should be placed in strict isolation until 21 days after exposure. Immunocompetent patients who are likely to become immunosuppressed may be candidates for immunization.

¶Some controversy exists regarding the absolute efficacy of zoster immunoglobulin (ZIG) or zoster immune plasma (ZIP). Some authorities have suggested that ZIG/ZIP may delay onset of VZV and may diminish the severity of symptoms. Clinicians should keep this in mind when assessing duration of isolation or work reassignment. For immunocompetent patients and immunosuppressed patients thought to be capable of mounting a response, consider immunization.

** Usual incubation period for VZV is 9 to 21 days; hence, the immunocompetent, susceptible, exposed patient should be placed in strict isolation 8 days following exposure. Isolation should be continued until 22 days following exposure. In an immunocompromised patient the incubation period may be shorter. Therefore, an exposed, susceptible, immunocompromised patient who did not receive prophylaxis should be placed in isolation immediately after the patient is identified as being at risk. If the patient did not receive prophylaxis, isolation should be continued for 21 days following exposure.

†† Several authorities, including the Centers for Disease Control and Prevention, recommend immunization of susceptible providers. For immunosuppressed providers VZIG may be appropriate.

CMV infection is controversial. Some investigators have suggested that hospital personnel are at slightly higher risk for seroconversion than are age-matched controls who did not have patient contact.[200] Intensive studies by Ahlfors and colleagues in Sweden, however, found little evidence that nurses were at greater risk to acquire CMV infection than other age-matched Swedish women.[201, 202] A study using restriction enzyme analysis of CMV DNA demonstrated no correlation between the CMV strain infecting a neonate and the strain of CMV found to be infecting a nurse who cared for the infant.[203] In a second study using similar technology, significant differences were found in DNA from CMV isolates obtained from a physician who became infected while caring for a CMV-infected child and the isolate from the child.[204] In both studies the health care professionals were pregnant, and both elected to have abortions. CMV with restriction patterns identical to those of the maternal isolates was detected in each of the infected fetuses.[203, 204]

Several other studies have suggested minimal or negligible risk for patient-to-staff transmission of CMV.[196, 205–213] Balfour and Balfour compared CMV infection rates in three groups of nurses—those working in neonatal ICUs, those working in renal transplant/dialysis units, and student nurses—with age-matched blood donors.[205] No association was found between the prevalence of infection in patients and seroconversion, and these authors concluded that nurses were no more likely to acquire CMV infection than were the age-matched blood donor controls.[205]

Demmler and colleagues[196] also found no association between CMV seroconversion and occupational exposure to CMV in two pediatric hospitals in Texas. In addition, this study found no correlation between the prevalence of infection in patients and seroconversion in health care providers.[196] Adler and coworkers used restriction endonucleases to evaluate CMV isolates from 34 hospitalized newborn infants and from the one seronegative health care worker in whom primary CMV infection developed during the 3-year study period.[208] No two isolates were identical.

Brady and colleagues demonstrated annual seroconversion rates for CMV-serosusceptible pediatric house staff of 3.8%.[207] Although appropriate controls were not available for this study, similar rates have been documented for other medical and nonmedical personnel.[196, 201, 214]

Hatherly found no seroconversions among obstetrics staff members caring for CMV-infected patients,[212] and Blackman and coworkers concluded that the risk of CMV transmission from infected disabled children to educational and health care personnel providing care for these children is low.[209] A more recent epidemiologic study failed to demonstrate an increased risk for congenital CMV infection in women who are health care workers.[215]

Finally, because patients who are infected with human immunodeficiency virus (HIV) (particularly those who have AIDS) are known to harbor and shed large quantities of herpesviruses, both Gerberding and colleagues[210, 211] and Kuhls and colleagues[213] evaluated health care workers providing care for HIV-1–infected patients for serologic evidence of CMV infection. Neither study found an elevated rate of CMV acquisition.

Conversely, other investigators, although failing to demonstrate patient-to-staff transmission of CMV, have postulated that the risk for transmission is likely to be higher for personnel working with patients who have a high prevalence of CMV infection.[214, 216] Although such a hypothesis seems plausible, to my knowledge no direct evidence supports this contention.

At this time, no instances of patient-to-staff transmission of CMV have been documented by restriction enzyme analysis of CMV isolates. One investigator has, however, used endonuclease analysis to document apparent nonparenteral transmission of CMV from an infected infant to his seronegative mother.[194] Thus, the magnitude of the risk of patient-to-staff transmission of CMV, especially when appropriate isolation procedures are observed, would appear to be small.[217]

Mechanisms of Nosocomial Transmission

In instances in which primary infection with CMV is documented to have occurred in the hospital setting, the parenteral route of transmission has almost always been implicated.

Most primary infections in the neonatal ICU can be traced to the transfusion of whole blood contaminated with CMV.[174, 176–181] Consumption of breast milk contaminated with CMV has been suggested to be an important nonparenteral mechanism of transmission of CMV to neonates.[176, 195, 197, 198] The possibility has also been raised, but not to my knowledge documented, that fomites[195] or health care professionals[194–196] may be vectors for nonparenteral transmission of CMV in unusual circumstances.

Renal transplant recipients can acquire primary CMV infection from blood transfusions,[183, 217–219] from leukocyte infusions, or from the transplanted organ itself.[218, 220–222] Recipients of bone marrow allografts can acquire CMV infection through receipt of an infected allograft, through transfused blood or platelets, or through infected leukocyte infusions.[194, 195] Weller[223] and others have postulated that intimate contact is required for the transmission of CMV infection. If nonparenteral transmission is occurring in the hospital, it must be due to exposure of a susceptible individual (patient or employee) to contaminated excreta or secretions, presumably via the oral or respiratory routes.

Prevention of Nosocomial Transmission

Several precautionary measures can be implemented to minimize the risk of CMV transmission in a high-risk setting in the hospital. Choosing organ donors who are seronegative for renal transplant recipients who are seronegative is an effective way of minimizing the risk for subsequent CMV infection in this setting. Betts and associates have advocated use of the donor's serologic status as a major determinant in selecting a donor kidney for a seronegative recipient.[220] Similar arguments have been made for selecting both bone marrow donor sources and the sources for blood and blood products that are to be administered to CMV-seronegative bone marrow transplant recipients.

Winston and colleagues have suggested that seronegative donors be given priority as potential leukocyte donors because of evidence that CMV is leukocyte associated and that the development of CMV infection in recipients of leukocytes is often a serious problem.[190]

Both Lang and colleagues[219] and Tolkoff-Rubin and coworkers[217] have recommended transfusion of patients at high risk for CMV infection with either leukocyte-depleted blood or washed, frozen red cells to reduce the risk of CMV transmission. In addition, several studies have demonstrated a decreased risk for primary CMV infection associated with the transfusion of frozen, deglycerolized red blood cells.[217, 220, 224, 225] Brady and colleagues have extended their earlier studies to demonstrate that transfusion of either blood from CMV-seronegative donors or frozen, deglycerolized red blood cells was associated with significantly lower CMV excretion rates in preterm infants receiving these transfusions than was found in similar infants who received either saline-washed red blood cells or conventionally processed whole blood.[224] Despite the proven clinical efficacy, one study detected only a minor and statistically insignificant reduction in CMV DNA after freezing/thawing of red cells.[226] Thus, the risk for transfusion-associated CMV disease can be reduced and effectively eliminated by using CMV-seronegative donors,[227] by using frozen, deglycerolized red blood cells, and by using products that have been treated with leukocyte filters.[227–237] The relative efficacy of these three approaches remains somewhat controversial. Some investigators have suggested that adding back potentially cytotoxic donor T-lymphocytes a month or more after transplantation may help control graft-versus-host disease, help preserve a graft-versus-leukemia effect, and help reduce the risk for serious CMV infections in allogeneic bone marrow transplant patients.[238–241] Finally, the use of specific anti-CMV immune globulin has been associated with a reduction in CMV-associated morbidity in organ transplant recipients and patients at risk for CMV disease.[242, 243]

Yeager and colleagues[180] and Benson and associates[181] have demonstrated the efficacy of transfusing blood from seronegative donors into seronegative recipients to prevent the transmission of CMV to neonates. In one study, CMV infections were entirely prevented by administering seronegative blood to neonates.[180] One of these approaches would also be advisable if a seronegative transplant recipient who has received an organ from a seronegative donor requires transfusion. Because human milk may also be a reservoir for CMV infection in neonates,[176, 195, 197, 198] Yeager and coworkers have recommended that donors of milk be screened and that a premature infant of a seronegative mother receive milk from the mother or from seronegative donors.[180]

Because most pregnant women secreting CMV in cervical mucus are asymptomatic and—unlike infection with the herpes simplex viruses—because perinatal infection with CMV is not associated with symptomatic illness in the newborn, no precautions are advocated for mothers known to be secreting CMV at delivery.

Immunosuppressed patients who are infected with CMV (e.g., patients with AIDS, transplant recipients, or babies with congenital infection) excrete large quantities of virus in many different body fluids.[218] Appropriate precautions for such patients should include gloves for contact with wounds or lesions or for contact with blood, secretions, or excreta. Also, infected patients in the neonatal ICU should be segregated from noninfected babies. Other precautions advisable in caring for such patients would include handling linens and other reusable patient care items as isolation materials and emphasizing hand washing after each patient contact. In general, strict adherence to universal[55] or standard[56] infection control precautions should minimize the already small risk for occupational or nosocomial infection.

Management of Infected, Exposed, and Potentially Exposed Personnel

The risk for staff-to-patient transmission of CMV has received little attention in the literature, with only one study attempting to assess this risk. Demmler and colleagues found no evidence of CMV transmission among patients cared for by four CMV-shedding health care workers.[196] These investigators concluded that although a theoretical possibility, the risk for staff-to-patient transmission of CMV was sufficiently small to allow infected health care workers to continue working.[196] Based on currently available evidence regarding the transmission and transmissibility of CMV, such an approach seems entirely reasonable.

The issue of limiting exposure of pregnant health care workers to CMV-infected patients remains somewhat controversial. Although, as noted earlier, data documenting CMV transmission from patient to staff are nonexistent, a commonsense approach to the care of infected patients is appropriate. In an earlier edition of this text[244] I recommended that pregnant health care workers be restricted from taking care of patients with CMV infection, an approach previously advocated by Valenti and colleagues.[218] Several factors have caused our hospital infections committee to reassess this difficult and controversial issue; in a later publication, Valenti also modified his recommendations.[112]

First, a number of additional articles (see "Risk for Nosocomial Transmission," earlier) further documenting that the risk for occupational or nosocomial infection with CMV is quite small have been published. Because the number of seroconversions in these studies is small, a very large study would be required to precisely measure the magnitude of the small risk of CMV transmission to health care workers. Nonetheless, the expanded, consistent database is reassuring.

Second, numerous investigators have pointed out that many patients who are excreting CMV (e.g., immunosuppressed patients, AIDS patients, dialysis patients, transplant recipients, pediatric patients) have no signs or symptoms of CMV infection. Such patients are frequently not identified as being infected or infectious during the course of hospitalization. Presumably, most patients shedding CMV who are hospitalized will not be specifically identified as having CMV infection; for this reason, a broader approach to our patient population seems prudent.

Third, because the magnitude of risk to pregnant health care workers is currently below the limits of detection, the administrative problems associated with a more restrictive policy (i.e., if pregnant health care workers are restricted, how should one manage health care workers who "think they might be" or "are trying to become" or "are not trying to prevent becoming" pregnant?) may not be justified.

Fourth, the issuance by the CDC[55, 56] and the subsequent requirement for implementation of universal precautions guidelines by the U.S. Department of Labor's Occupational Safety and Health Administration[245] should reduce the already small risk for CMV transmission from patients to health care workers.

An initial clarification of the universal precautions policy noted that these precautions do not apply to feces, urine, saliva, sweat, sputum, or tears.[54] In this update, the CDC emphasizes that universal precautions are supplementary or baseline precautions and that these new precautions are not designed to replace standard infection control policy. Specifically, this update notes that prior CDC recommendations[122] recommend wearing gloves to prevent gross microbial contamination of hands. This latter recommendation deserves careful consideration when handling urine from any patient. Although universal precautions do not apply to saliva, the previous recommendation for gloving before digital examination of mucous membranes remains in effect. The subsequent "standard precautions" guidelines[56] issued by the CDC underscore the importance of using barriers for contact with all body fluids.

These new recommendations also allow the health care worker to use judgment in deciding whether barriers (such as gloves) are needed. These new guidelines emphasize the importance of hand washing, which if practiced appropriately, should minimize the risk for occupational CMV infection.

Finally, the issue of routine screening of health care workers for antibody to CMV is also controversial. Several articles have addressed this complex issue[52, 112, 121, 206, 246–248]; the lack of consensus is apparent. The CDC has not advocated routine screening.[20, 121, 246] Conversely, Adler[248] and Plotkin[247] support periodic serologic testing for "potentially pregnant" employees whose jobs entail exposure to CMV-infected patients. Brady[206] argues that on the basis of the magnitude of risk, serologic testing is not warranted and may in fact cause increased anxiety. Onorato and colleagues argue that no data indicate that routine testing will have any impact on the risk of congenital CMV infection.[246] Our hospital infections committee and occupational medical service have decided not to offer routine screening of employees. Because the risk for patient-to-staff transmission is as yet unmeasurable and because adherence to universal precautions will further reduce this risk, we do not recommend reassignment of pregnant health care workers. Rather, we have chosen to educate staff aggressively regarding CMV and other occupational risks and to emphasize the importance of good hygiene and universal precautions during pregnancy. For all these reasons, we do not recommend reassignment of pregnant health care workers.

EPSTEIN-BARR VIRUS

Risk for Nosocomial Transmission

The risk of nosocomial transmission of EBV appears to be very small. Several instances of nosocomial transmission of EBV to patients have been identified.[249–259] Secondary infections (most of which appear to be reactivation of latent infection in an immunosuppressed transplant recipient) are associated with a lymphoproliferative disorder.[260–270] Because the overwhelming majority of these infections represent recrudescence rather than acquired infection, they are discussed in more detail in Chapter 128.

Transmission of EBV from patient to staff or staff to patient has not been described, although Ginsburg and colleagues have described an outbreak of infectious mononucleosis in personnel working in an outpatient clinic[257] and Chang and coworkers have described the apparent transmissibility of EBV in a relatively crowded nursery providing domiciliary care.[258] A recent epidemiologic study found a possible risk for occupational acquisition of EBV in dentists and dental students.[48]

Mechanisms of Transmission

Patients who have been shown to have acquired nosocomial EBV infection have been recipients of blood or plasma transfusions,[249–256] solid organ transplants,[271] and bone marrow allografts[259, 272] apparently infected with EBV. In addition, one study has demonstrated evidence of EBV DNA in breast milk.[273] EBV appears to be one of the least contagious of the herpesviruses, and most authorities believe that intravenous inoculation or intimate contact is required for transmission of the virus.[274]

Prevention of Nosocomial Transmission

Patients known to have EBV in their secretions may be a reservoir for infection if health care workers follow extremely poor hygiene practices. In 1975, the CDC recommended that secretion precautions be used for patients with infectious mononucleosis.[275] In more recent recommendations, the CDC states that isolation precautions are not necessary but adds the codicil that oral secretions may be infectious.[122] Adherence to universal or standard precautions, use of appropriate barriers, and attention to hand washing and hygiene practices will further reduce the risk for occupational infection. As is the case for CMV infection in transplantation, some investigators have a found a benefit of infusing donor-specific lymphocytes as "adoptive immunotherapy"[265, 276–280] or interferon-α[264] to treat the EBV-associated lymphoproliferative disorders.

Management of Infected or Exposed Personnel

Staff members who acquire infection with EBV (e.g., infectious mononucleosis) may excrete virus much longer than symptoms persist,[281] but if good hygienic practices are followed (e.g., hand washing), such personnel presumably have an extremely small risk of transmitting the infection.

HUMAN HERPESVIRUS 6 AND HUMAN HERPESVIRUS 7

Risk for Nosocomial Transmission

HHV-6 and HHV-7 are somewhat similar β-subgroup herpesviruses that are most closely related to CMV.[11] HHV-6 (first called human B-lymphotropic virus[1]) was identified as a human pathogen in the mid and late 1980s.[2] Subsequently, this virus has been shown to be a cause of *roseola infantum (exanthem subitum)*[282] (see Chapter 129). This childhood exanthem is reasonably contagious and may represent a risk for nosocomial transmission, particularly in pediatric hospitals. Acute HHV-6 infection has also been associated with both a mononucleosis-like syndrome and a self-limited hepatitis.[283] More recently, a clear association between HHV-6 infection and acute febrile seizures has been established.[284] In addition, HHV-6 has been associated with several less common syndromes, including encephalitis, disseminated infection, and perhaps pneumonia. This virus may also complicate solid organ transplantation as well as bone marrow transplantation. HHV-6 has been found (presumably as an opportunist) in the peripheral blood of AIDS patients.[2]

HHV-7 was first identified in 1990.[285] Initial studies failed to identify a disease process associated with HHV-7 infection.[6, 21–25] HHV-7 is frequently found in human saliva[25] and, similar to HHV-6, is a T-lymphotropic virus.[21] Although HHV-7 infection has clearly been associated with a syndrome similar to roseola (usually occurring in children older than 2 years), studies have yet to identify a definitive infection syndrome in most children infected with this newly identified herpesvirus.[11]

Mechanisms of Transmission

Although it demonstrates a reasonably high level of contagion, HHV-6 is probably transmitted from oral secretions. Data describing the epidemiology and putative routes of transmission of HHV-6 remain somewhat ambiguous. Although the nosocomial epidemiology of infection with HHV-6 remains indistinct, a conservative approach to the management of this infection in the hospital seems prudent. As suggested by the "standard precautions" guidelines, secretions (including oral secretions) from all patients should be considered potentially infectious, and pediatric health care providers should pay special attention to the potential for cross-contamination in nurseries. Most care providers are likely to be immune to HHV-6 infection because of prior infection.

Prevention of Nosocomial Transmission

Virtually nothing is known about the nosocomial epidemiology of HHV-6 and HHV-7. Because of the apparent contagiousness of roseola, hospitalized patients who have roseola should be treated similarly to patients with VZV infection (see the earlier section on preventing nosocomial VZV transmission). Until definitive data are available to address the nosocomial transmissibility of HHV-6, using the VZV model for prevention seems reasonable. Techniques for establishing the diagnosis of HHV-7 infection are in their infancy and not generally available.

In the unusual instance in which the diagnosis of HHV-7 is established, use of standard precautions for such patients seems prudent. Based on the fact that children who acquire HHV-7 infection are generally older than those who acquire HHV-6 infection, HHV-7 appears to be less transmissible than HHV-6. At a minimum, in the absence of defined infection syndromes associated with HHV-7 infection, use of standard precautions for these patients should provide adequate protection.

HUMAN HERPESVIRUS 8

HHV-8 is a γ-subgroup herpesvirus that is most closely related to EBV. HHV-8 has been closely associated with Kaposi's sarcoma and (in combination with EBV) body cavity lymphoma in patients who have HIV infection. Initially identified in 1994,[286, 287] HHV-8 is also known as Kaposi's sarcoma–associated herpesvirus. The viral DNA sequence has been isolated from patients who have Kaposi's sarcomas that are both HIV related and unrelated to HIV infection or infection risk (i.e., patients who have classic Mediterranean Kaposi's sarcoma). Little is known about the epidemiology of HHV-8, and almost nothing is known about the potential for nosocomial transmission. Initial data suggest that the virus is most likely acquired during or after adolescence. By analogy, the epidemiology of HHV-8 may be similar to that of EBV. Based on these preliminary data, standard precautions should also be an effective management strategy for patients infected with HHV-8.

REFERENCES

1. Salahuddin S, Ablashi D, Markham P, et al. Isolation of a new virus, HBLV, in patients with lymphoproliferative disorders. Science. 1986;225:69–72.
2. Lopez C, Pellett P, Steward J, et al. Characterizations of human herpesvirus-6. J Infect Dis. 1988;157:1271–1273.

3. Levy JA. Three new human herpesviruses (HHV6, 7, and 8). Lancet. 1997;349:558–563.
4. Levy JA, Ferro F, Greenspan D, et al. Frequent isolation of HHV-6 from saliva and high seroprevalence of the virus in the population. Lancet. 1990;335:1047–1050.
5. Portolani M, Cermelli C, Moroni A, et al. Human herpesvirus-6 infections in infants admitted to hospital. J Med Virol. 1993;39:146–151.
6. Frenkel N, Wyatt LS. HHV-6 and HHV-7 as exogenous agents in human lymphocytes. Dev Biol Stand. 1992;76:259–265.
7. Ablashi DV, Bernbaum J, DiPaolo JA. Human herpesvirus 6 as a potential copathogen. Trends Microbiol. 1995;3:324–327.
8. Braun DK, Dominguez G, Pellett PE. Human herpesvirus 6. Clin Microbiol Rev. 1997;10:521–567.
9. Cone RW. Human herpesvirus 6 as a possible cause of pneumonia. Semin Respir Infect. 1995;10:254–258.
10. Di Luca D, Mirandola P, Ravaioli T, et al. Distribution of HHV-6 variants in human tissues. Infect Agents Dis. 1996;5:203–214.
11. Grose C. Childhood infections with human herpesviruses types 6, 7, and 8. Adv Pediatr Infect Dis. 1996;12:181–208.
12. Jones CA, Isaacs D. Human herpesvirus-6 infections. Arch Dis Child. 1996;74:98–100.
13. Kamei A, Ichinohe S, Onuma R, et al. Acute disseminated demyelination due to primary human herpesvirus-6 infection. Eur J Pediatr. 1997;156:709–712.
14. Kimberlin DW. Human herpesviruses 6 and 7: Identification of newly recognized viral pathogens and their association with human disease. Pediatr Infect Dis J. 1998;17:59–68.
15. Luppi M, Torelli G. The new lymphotropic herpesviruses (HHV-6, HHV-7, HHV-8) and hepatitis C virus (HCV) in human lymphoproliferative diseases: An overview. Haematologica. 1996;81:265–281.
16. Lusso P, Gallo RC. Human herpesvirus 6. Baillieres Clin Haematol. 1995;8:201–223.
17. Lusso P, Gallo RC. Human herpesvirus 6 in AIDS. Immunol Today. 1995;16:67–71.
18. Lusso P. Human herpesvirus 6 (HHV-6). Antiviral Res. 1996;31:1–21.
19. Lyall EG. Human herpesvirus 6: Primary infection and the central nervous system. Pediatr Infect Dis J. 1996;15:693–696.
20. Singh N, Carrigan DR. Human herpesvirus-6 in transplantation: An emerging pathogen. Ann Intern Med. 1996;124:1065–1071.
21. Berneman ZN, Ablashi DV, Li G, et al. Human herpesvirus 7 is a T-lymphotropic virus and is related to, but significantly different from, human herpesvirus 6 and human cytomegalovirus. Proc Natl Acad Sci U S A. 1992;89:10552–10556.
22. Berneman ZN, Gallo RC, Ablashi DV, et al. Human herpesvirus 7 (HHV-7) strain JI: Independent confirmation of HHV-7. J Infect Dis. 1992;166:690–691.
23. Peterslund NA. Herpesvirus infection: An overview of the clinical manifestations. Scand J Infect Dis Suppl. 1991;80:15–20.
24. Wyatt LS, Rodriguez WJ, Balachandran N, et al. Human herpesvirus 7: Antigenic properties and prevalence in children and adults. J Virol. 1991;65:6260–6265.
25. Wyatt LS, Frenkel N. Human herpesvirus 7 is a constitutive inhabitant of adult human saliva. J Virol. 1992;66:3206–3209.
26. Bart B, Fisher I. Primary herpes simplex infection of the hand: Report of a case. J Am Dent Assoc. 1965;71:74–77.
27. Brooks S, Rowe N, Drach J, et al. Prevalence of herpes simplex virus disease in a professional population. J Am Dent Assoc. 1981;102:31–34.
28. Crane L, Lerner A. Herpetic whitlow: A manifestation of primary infection with herpes simplex virus type 1 or type 2. J Infect Dis. 1978;137:855–856.
29. Gunbay T, Gunbay S, Kandemir S. Herpetic whitlow. Quintessence Int. 1993;24:363–364.
30. Gill M, Arlette J, Buchan K. Herpes simplex virus infections of the hand. A profile of 79 cases. Am J Med. 1988;84:89–93.
31. Hendricks A, Shapiro E. Primary herpes simplex infection following mouth-to-mouth resuscitation. JAMA. 1980;243:257–259.
32. Stern H, Eleck S, Millar D, et al. Herpetic whitlow: A form of cross-infection in hospitals. Lancet. 1959;2:871–874.
33. Rodu B, Tate AL, Lakeman AF, et al. Prevalence of herpes simplex virus antibodies in dental students. J Dent Educ. 1992;56:206–208.
34. Hanbrick GJ, Cox R, Senior J. Primary herpes infection of the finger in medical personnel. Arch Dermatol. 1962;85:583–589.
35. Rosato F, Rosato E, Plotkin S. Herpetic paronychia—an occupational hazard of medical personnel. N Engl J Med. 1964;270:979–982.
36. Adams G, Stover B, Keenlyside R, et al. Nosocomial herpetic infections in a pediatric intensive care unit. Am J Epidemiol. 1981;113:126–132.
37. Perl TM, Haugen TH, Pfaller MA, et al. Transmission of herpes simplex virus type 1 infection in an intensive care unit. Ann Intern Med. 1992;117:584–586.
38. Haburchak D. Recurrent herpetic whitlow due to herpes simplex virus type 2. Arch Intern Med. 1978;138:1418–1419.
39. Nahmias A, Roizman R. Infection with herpes-simplex viruses 1 and 2 (first of three parts). N Engl J Med. 1973;289:667–674.
40. Glogau R, Hanna L. Herpetic whitlow as part of genital virus infection. J Infect Dis. 1977;136:689–692.
41. Amir J, Nussinovitch M, Kleper R, et al. Primary herpes simplex virus type 1 gingivostomatitis in pediatric personnel. Infection. 1997;25:310–312.
42. Light I. Postnatal acquisition of herpes simplex virus by the newborn infant: A review of the literature. Pediatrics. 1979;63:480–482.
43. Linneman CJ, Buchman T, Light I, et al. Transmission of herpes simplex virus, type 1 in a nursery for the newborn: Identification of viral isolates by DNA fingerprinting. Lancet. 1978;1:964–966.
44. Sakadka H, Saheki Y, Uzuki K, et al. Two outbreaks of herpes simplex virus, type 1 nosocomial infection among newborns. J Clin Microbiol. 1986;24:36–40.
45. Blank H, Haines H. Experimental reinfection with herpes simplex virus. J Invest Dermatol. 1973;61:223–225.
46. Anders PL, Drinnan AJ, Thines TJ. Infectious diseases and the dental office. N Y State Dent J. 1998;64(4):29–34.
47. Blondeau JM, Embil JA. Herpes simplex virus infection: What to look for. What to do! J Can Dent Assoc. 1990;56:785–787.
48. Herbert AM, Bagg J, Walker DM, et al. Seroepidemiology of herpes virus infections among dental personnel. J Dent. 1995;23:339–342.
49. Molinari JA. Infection-control accomplishments: Learning the lessons of history. Compend Contin Educ Dent. 1996;17:114–116.
50. Daniels C, LeGoff S. Shedding of infectious virus/antibody complexes from vesicular lesions of patients with recurrent herpes labialis. Lancet. 1975;2:524–528.
51. Turner R, Shehab Z, Osborne K, et al. Shedding and survival of herpes simplex virus from "fever blisters." Pediatrics. 1982;70:547–549.
52. Hatherly L, Hayes K, Jack I. Herpes virus in an obstetric hospital: II. Asymptomatic virus excretion in staff members. Med J Aust. 1980;2:273–275.
53. Dunkle L, Schmidt R, O'Connor D. Neonatal herpes simplex infection possibly acquired via maternal breast milk. Pediatrics. 1979;63:250–251.
54. Centers for Disease Control. Update: Universal precautions for prevention of transmission of human immunodeficiency virus, hepatitis B virus, an other blood-borne pathogens in health care settings. MMWR Morb Mortal Wkly Rep. 1988;37:277–282, 287–288.
55. Centers for Disease Control. Recommendation for prevention of HIV transmission in health-care settings. MMWR Morb Mortal Wkly Rep. 1987;36(Suppl 2):S1–S18.
56. Garner JS. Guideline for isolation precautions in hospitals. The Hospital Infection Control Practices Advisory Committee. Infect Control Hosp Epidemiol. 1996;17:53–80.
57. Kibrick S. Herpes simplex infection at term: What to do with mother, newborn, and nursery personnel. JAMA. 1980;243:157–160.
58. Smith JR, Cowan FM, Munday P. The management of herpes simplex virus infection in pregnancy. Br J Obstet Gynaecol. 1998;105:255–260.
59. Whitley RJ, Kimberlin DW. Treatment of viral infections during pregnancy and the neonatal period. Clin Perinatol. 1997;24:267–283.
60. Jacobs RF. Neonatal herpes simplex virus infections. Semin Perinatol. 1998;22:64–71.
61. Forsgren M, Malm G. Herpes simplex virus and pregnancy. Scand J Infect Dis Suppl. 1996;100:14–19.
62. Brown ZA, Selke S, Zeh J, et al. The acquisition of herpes simplex virus during pregnancy. N Engl J Med. 1997;337:509–515.
63. Annunziato PW, Gershon A. Herpes simplex virus infections. Pediatr Rev. 1996;17:415–424.
64. Brown ZA, Benedetti J, Selke S, et al. Asymptomatic maternal shedding of herpes simplex virus at the onset of labor: Relationship to preterm labor. Obstet Gynecol. 1996;87:483–488.
65. Forsgren M, Sterner G, Anzen B, et al. Management of women at term with pregnancy complicated by herpes simplex. Scand J Infect Dis Suppl. 1990;71:58–66.
66. Garland SM. Neonatal herpes simplex: Royal Women's Hospital 10-year experience with management guidelines for herpes in pregnancy. Aust N Z J Obstet Gynaecol. 1992;32:331–334.
67. Arvin AM. Relationships between maternal immunity to herpes simplex virus and the risk of neonatal herpesvirus infection. Rev Infect Dis. 1991;13(Suppl):S953–S956.
68. Gibbs RS, Mead PB. Preventing neonatal herpes—current strategies. N Engl J Med. 1992;326:946–947.
69. Gibbs R. Infection control of herpes simplex virus in obstetrics and gynecology. J Reprod Med. 1986;31(Suppl):S395–S398.
70. Kaye E, Dooling E. Neonatal herpes simplex meningoencephalitis associated with fetal scalp monitor electrodes. Neurology. 1981;31:1045–1047.
71. Gerberding JL, Littell C, Tarkington A, et al. Risk of exposure of surgical personnel to patients' blood during surgery at San Francisco General Hospital. N Engl J Med. 1990;322:1788–1793.
72. Buchman T, Roizman B, Adams G, et al. Restriction endonuclease fingerprinting of herpes simplex virus DNA: A novel epidemiological tool applied to a nosocomial outbreak. J Infect Dis. 1978;138:488–498.
73. Nassar N, Touma H. Brief report: Susceptibility of Filipino nurses to the varicella zoster virus. Infect Control. 1986;7:71–72.
74. Feldman S, Hughes W, Daniel C. Varicella in children with cancer: Seventy-seven cases. Pediatrics. 1975;56:388–397.
75. Myers M. Viremia caused by varicella-zoster virus: Association with malignant progressive varicella. J Infect Dis. 1979;140:229–233.
76. Dolin R, Reichman R, Mazur M, et al. Herpes zoster-varicella infections in immunosuppressed patients. Ann Intern Med. 1978;89:375–388.
77. Feldman S, Hughes W, Kim H. Herpes zoster in children with cancer. Am J Dis Child. 1973;126:178–184.
78. Feldman S, Chaudary S, Ossi M, et al. A viremic phase for herpes zoster in children with cancer. J Pediatr. 1977;91:597–600.
79. Fish S. Maternal death due to disseminated varicella. JAMA. 1960;173:978–981.
80. Triebwasser J, Harris R, Bryant R, et al. Varicella pneumonia in adults. Report of seven cases and a review of the literature. Medicine (Baltimore). 1967;46:409–423.
81. Brunell P. Varicella-zoster infections in pregnancy. JAMA. 1967;199:93–95.
82. Brunell P. Varicella zoster virus. In: Mandell G, Douglas R, Bennett J, eds.

Principles and Practice of Infectious Diseases. New York: Churchill Livingstone; 1979:1295–1306.
83. Morens D, Bregman D, West M, et al. An outbreak of varicella-zoster virus infection among cancer patients. Ann Intern Med. 1980;93:414–419.
84. Gershon A, Steinberg S, Gelb L. Clinical reinfection with varicella zoster virus. J Infect Dis. 1984;149:137–142.
85. Schimpff S, Serpick A, Stoler B, et al. Varicella-zoster infection in patients with cancer. Ann Intern Med. 1972;76:241–254.
86. Henderson DK, Laniak J, Myers R, et al. Varicella-zoster virus infection among cancer patients. Ann Intern Med. 1981;95:655–656.
87. Henderson DK, Laniak J, Myers R, et al. Prevention of nosocomial varicella zoster disease. Ann Intern Med. 1981;95:515–516.
88. Wreghitt TG, Whipp PJ, Bagnall J. Transmission of chickenpox to two intensive care unit nurses from a liver transplant patient with zoster (Letter). J Hosp Infect. 1992;20:125–126.
89. Gerner HM, Staab AS, Ivey FD, et al. Controlling the spread of varicella zoster in the hospitalized patient. J Am Acad Nurse Pract. 1992;4:156–159.
90. Gurevich I, Jensen L, Kalter R, et al. Chickenpox in apparently "immune" hospital workers (Letter). Infect Control Hosp Epidemiol. 1990;11:510, 512.
91. Leclair J, Zaia J, Levin M, et al. Airborne transmission of chickenpox in a hospital. N Engl J Med. 1980;302:450–453.
92. Krasinski K, Holtzman R, LaCoufure R, et al. Hospital experience with varicella-zoster virus. Infect Control. 1986;7:312–316.
93. Gustafson T, Lavely G, Brawner E, et al. An outbreak of airborne nosocomial varicella. Pediatrics. 1982;70:550–556.
94. Josephson A, Karanfil L, Gombert ME. Strategies for the management of varicella-susceptible healthcare workers after a known exposure. Infect Control Hosp Epidemiol. 1990;11:309–313.
95. Rado J, Tako J, Geder L, et al. Herpes zoster house epidemic in steroid-treated patients. Arch Intern Med. 1965;116:329–335.
96. Berlin B, Campbell T. Hospital-acquired herpes zoster following exposure to chickenpox. JAMA. 1970;211:1831–1833.
97. Feinstein A, Trau H, Schewach-Millet M. Herpes zoster in a husband and wife. Int J Dermatol. 1980;19:514–516.
98. Haynes R. Varicella zoster infections in normal and compromised hosts. In: Galasso G, ed. Antiviral Agents and Viral Diseases of Man. New York: Raven; 1979:647–679.
99. Miller L, Brunell P. Zoster, reinfection or activation of latent virus? Observations on the antibody response. Am J Med. 1970;49:480–483.
100. Glynn C, Crockford G, Gavaghan D, et al. Epidemiology of shingles. J R Soc Med. 1990;83:617–619.
101. Garnett GP, Grenfell BT. The epidemiology of varicella-zoster virus infections: The influence of varicella on the prevalence of herpes zoster. Epidemiol Infect. 1992;108:513–528.
102. Asano Y, Iwayama S, Miyata T, et al. Spread of varicella in hospitalized children having no direct contact with an indicator zoster case and its prevention by a live vaccine. Biken J. 1980;23:157–161.
103. Centers for Disease Control. Varicella zoster immune globulin. MMWR Morb Mortal Wkly Rep. 1981;30:15–16, 21–23.
104. Anderson J, Bonner M, Scheifele D, et al. Lack of nosocomial spread of varicella in a pediatric hospital with negative pressure ventilated rooms. Infect Control. 1985;6:120–121.
105. Ferson MJ, Bell SM, Robertson PW. Determination and importance of varicella immune status of nursing staff in a children's hospital. J Hosp Infect. 1990;15:347–351.
106. Frank E, Wilson N, Casey KK. Chickenpox in "immune" hospital employees (Letter). Infect Control Hosp Epidemiol. 1991;12:76.
107. Goldmann DA. Transmission of infectious diseases in children. Pediatr Rev. 1992;13:283–293.
108. Hayden G, Meyers J, Dixon R. Nosocomial varicella: II. Suggested guidelines for management. West J Med. 1979;130:300–303.
109. Laniak J, Myers R, Henderson D. Algorithm for the control of nosocomial varicella zoster virus infections. In: Proceedings of the 82nd Annual Meeting of the American Society for Microbiology. Washington, DC: American Society for Microbiology; 1982:87.
110. Myers M, Rasley D, Hierholzer W. Hospital infection control for varicella zoster virus infection. Pediatrics. 1982;70:199–202.
111. Steele R, Coleman M, Fiser M, et al. Varicella zoster in hospital personnel: Skin test reactivity to monitor susceptibility. Pediatrics. 1982;70:604–608.
112. Valenti W. Infection control and the pregnant health care worker. Am J Infect Control. 1986;14:20–27.
113. Weitekamp M, Schan P, Aber R. An algorithm for the control of nosocomial varicella zoster virus infection. Am J Infect Control. 1985;13:193–198.
114. Centers for Disease Control and Prevention. Prevention of varicella: Recommendations of the Advisory Committee on Immunization Practices (ACIP). Centers for Disease Control and Prevention. MMWR Morb Mortal Wkly Rep. 1996;45(RR-11):1–36.
115. Antela A, Fortun J, Navas E, et al. Nosocomial varicella: Study of an epidemic outbreak among immunosuppressed patients. Enferm Infec Microbiol Clin. 1991;9:357–360.
116. Haiduven-Griffiths D, Fecko H. Varicella in hospital personnel: A challenge for the infection control practitioner. Am J Infect Control. 1987;15:207–211.
117. McGrath NE. Children with chickenpox: Emergency department care and teaching. J Emerg Nurs. 1992;18:353–354.
118. Mendelson M, Legg E, Hirschman S. Program for preventing nosocomial varicella-zoster virus infection: Application and implications (Abstract). In: Proceedings of the 26th Interscience Conference on Antimicrobial Agents and Chemotherapy. Washington, DC: American Society for Microbiology; 1986:307.
119. Menkhaus NA, Lanphear B, Linnemann CC. Airborne transmission of varicella-zoster virus in hospitals (Letter). Lancet. 1990;336:1315.
120. Murray A, Kangro HO, Heath RB. Screening hospital staff for antibodies to varicella-zoster virus (Letter). Lancet. 1990;336:192.
121. Williams W. Guidelines for infection control in hospital personnel. Infect Control. 1983;4(Suppl):S326–S349.
122. Garner J, Simmons B. Guidelines for isolation precautions in hospitals. Infect Control. 1983;4(Suppl):S245–S325.
123. Gallagher J, Quaid B, Cryan B. Susceptibility to varicella zoster virus infection in health care workers. Occup Med (Oxf). 1996;46:289–292.
124. Weber DJ, Rutala WA, Hamilton H. Prevention and control of varicella-zoster infections in healthcare facilities. Infect Control Hosp Epidemiol. 1996;17:694–705.
125. Sepkowitz KA. Occupationally acquired infections in health care workers. Part I. Ann Intern Med. 1996;125:826–834.
126. Casto DT. Varicella vaccination of health care workers. Am J Health Syst Pharm. 1996;53:2628–2635.
127. AMA Council on Scientific Affairs. Immunization of health care workers with varicella vaccine. J Okla State Med Assoc. 1997;90:376–382.
128. Meyers J, MacQuarrie M, Merigan T, et al. Nosocomial varicella: I. Outbreak in oncology patients at a children's hospital. West J Med. 1979;130:196–198.
129. Weber D, Rutala W, Parnam C. Impact and costs of varicella prevention in a university hospital. Am J Public Health. 1988;78:19–23.
130. Alter S, Hammond J, McVey C, et al. Susceptibility to varicella zoster virus among adults at high-risk for exposure. Infect Control. 1986;7:448–451.
131. Arvin AM. Varicella-zoster virus. Clin Microbiol Rev. 1996;9:361–381.
132. Brody MB, Moyer D. Varicella-zoster virus infection. The complex prevention-treatment picture. Postgrad Med. 1997;102:187–190, 192–194.
133. Cirelli R, Herne K, McCrary M, et al. Famciclovir: Review of clinical efficacy and safety. Antiviral Res. 1996;29:141–151.
134. De Clercq E. Therapeutic potential of cidofovir (HPMPC, Vistide) for the treatment of DNA virus (i.e. herpes-, papova-, pox- and adenovirus) infections. Verh K Acad Geneeskd Belg. 1996;58:19–49.
135. Erlich KS. Management of herpes simplex and varicella-zoster virus infections. West J Med. 1997;166:211–215.
136. Gershon AA. Varicella-zoster virus: Prospects for control. Adv Pediatr Infect Dis. 1995;10:93–124.
137. Johnson RW. Herpes zoster and postherpetic neuralgia. Optimal treatment. Drugs Aging. 1997;10:80–94.
138. Morrison Y. Varicella-zoster virus: Recent therapeutic advances. J Pediatr Health Care. 1995;9:81–86.
139. Ogilvie MM. Antiviral prophylaxis and treatment in chickenpox. A review prepared for the UK Advisory Group on Chickenpox on behalf of the British Society for the Study of Infection. J Infect. 1998;36 (Suppl 1):S31–S38.
140. Perry CM, Faulds D. Valaciclovir. A review of its antiviral activity, pharmacokinetic properties and therapeutic efficacy in herpesvirus infections. Drugs. 1996;52:754–772.
141. Reusser P. Current concepts and challenges in the prevention and treatment of viral infections in immunocompromised cancer patients. Support Care Cancer. 1998;6:39–45.
142. Safrin S. Treatment of acyclovir-resistant herpes simplex and varicella zoster virus infections. Adv Exp Med Biol. 1996;394:59–66.
143. Soltz-Szots J, Tyring S, Andersen PL, et al. A randomized controlled trial of acyclovir versus netivudine for treatment of herpes zoster. International Zoster Study Group. J Antimicrob Chemother. 1998;41:549–556.
144. Wallace MR, Chamberlin CJ, Sawyer MH, et al. Treatment of adult varicella with sorivudine: A randomized, placebo-controlled trial. J Infect Dis. 1996;174:249–255.
145. Whitley RJ. Sorivudine: A promising drug for the treatment of varicella-zoster virus infection. Neurology. 1995;45(Suppl 8):S73–S75.
146. Wallace MR, Bowler WA, Murray NB, et al. Treatment of adult varicella with oral acyclovir. A randomized, placebo-controlled trial. Ann Intern Med. 1992;117:358–363.
147. Lynfield R, Herrin JT, Rubin RH. Varicella in pediatric renal transplant recipients. Pediatrics. 1992;90:216–220.
148. Balfour HJ, Kelly JM, Suarez CS, et al. Acyclovir treatment of varicella in otherwise healthy children. J Pediatr. 1990;116:633–639.
149. Balfour HJ, Rotbart HA, Feldman S, et al. Acyclovir treatment of varicella in otherwise healthy adolescents. The Collaborative Acyclovir Varicella Study Group. J Pediatr. 1992;120:627–633.
150. Shortage of varicella zoster immunoglobulin prompts restriction on use. Commun Dis Rep CDR Wkly. 1996;6:433.
151. Balfour H, Groth K, McCullough J, et al. Prevention or modification of varicella using zoster immune plasma. Am J Dis Child. 1977;131:693–696.
152. Williams V, Gershon A, Brunell P. Serologic response to varicella-zoster membrane antigens measured by indirect immunofluorescence. J Infect Dis. 1974;130:669–672.
153. Gershon A, Kalter Z, Steinberg S. Detection of antibody to varicella-zoster virus by immune adherence hemagglutination. Proc Soc Exp Biol Med. 1976;151:762.
154. Stanley J, Myers M, Edmond B, et al. An enzyme-linked immunosorbent assay for detection of antibody to varicella zoster virus. J Clin Microbiol. 1982;15:205–211.

155. Brunell P, Gershon A, Uduman S, et al. Varicella-zoster immunoglobulins during varicella, latency, and zoster. J Infect Dis. 1975;132:49–54.
156. Varicella supplement 1998 and consensus guidelines for management. United Kingdom Advisory Group on Chickenpox. J Infect. 1998;36(Suppl 1):i–ii, S1–S83.
157. Arbeter AM. Clinical trials of varicella vaccine in healthy adolescents and adults. Infect Dis Clin North Am. 1996;10:609–615.
158. Brunell P, Shehab Z, Geiser C, et al. Administration of live varicella vaccine to children with leukaemia. Lancet. 1982;2:1069–1072.
159. Drwal KL, O'Donovan CA. Varicella in pediatric patients. Ann Pharmacother. 1993;27:938–949.
160. Faoagali JL, Darcy D. Chickenpox outbreak among the staff of a large, urban adult hospital: Costs of monitoring and control. Am J Infect Control. 1995;23:247–250.
161. Gray GC, Palinkas LA, Kelley PW. Increasing incidence of varicella hospitalizations in United States Army and Navy personnel: Are today's teenagers more susceptible? Should recruits be vaccinated? Pediatrics. 1990;86:867–873.
162. Hardy IR, Gershon AA. Prospects for use of a varicella vaccine in adults. Infect Dis Clin North Am. 1990;4:159–173.
163. Izawa T, Ihara T, Hattori A, et al. Application of live varicella vaccine in children with acute leukemia or other malignant diseases. Pediatrics. 1977;60:805–809.
164. Ng PC, Lyon DJ, Wong MY, et al. Varicella exposure in a neonatal intensive care unit: Emergency management and control measures. J Hosp Infect. 1996;32:229–236.
165. Shortridge-McCauley LA. Reproductive hazards: An overview of exposures to health care workers. AAOHN J. 1995;43:614–621.
166. Takahashi M. Current status and prospects of live varicella vaccine. Vaccine. 1992;10:1007–1014.
167. Tsolia M, Gershon AA, Steinberg SP, et al. Live attenuated varicella vaccine: Evidence that the virus is attenuated and the importance of skin lesions in transmission of varicella-zoster virus. National Institute of Allergy and Infectious Diseases Varicella Vaccine Collaborative Study Group. J Pediatr. 1990;116:184–189.
168. Lin TY, Huang YC, Ning HC, et al. Oral acyclovir prophylaxis of varicella after intimate contact. Pediatr Infect Dis J. 1997;16:1162–1165.
169. Huang YC, Lin TY, Chiu CH. Acyclovir prophylaxis of varicella after household exposure. Pediatr Infect Dis J. 1995;14:152–154.
170. Yoshikawa T, Suga S, Kozawa T, et al. Persistence of protective immunity after postexposure prophylaxis of varicella with oral aciclovir in the family setting. Arch Dis Child. 1998;78:61–63.
171. Andrei G, Snoeck R, Reymen D, et al. Comparative activity of selected antiviral compounds against clinical isolates of varicella-zoster virus. Eur J Clin Microbiol Infect Dis. 1995;14:318–329.
172. Kuzushima K, Kimura H, Shibata M, et al. Prophylactic oral acyclovir in outbreaks of primary herpes simplex virus 1 infection (Letter). Lancet. 1990;335:1043.
173. Mutalik S, Gupte A, Gupte S. Oral acyclovir therapy for varicella in pregnancy. Int J Dermatol. 1997;36:49–51.
174. Spector S, Schmidt W, Ticknor W, et al. Cytomegaloviruria in older infants in intensive care units. J Pediatr. 1979;59:444–446.
175. Spector S, Edwards D, Coen R. Association of acquired cytomegalovirus infections and bronchopulmonary dysplasia in premature infants. Pediatr Res. 1982;16:309.
176. Spector S, Spector D. Molecular epidemiology of cytomegalovirus infection in premature twin infants and their mother. Pediatr Infect Dis. 1982;1:405–409.
177. Ballard R, Drew L, Hufnagle K, et al. Acquired cytomegalovirus infection in preterm infants. Am J Dis Child. 1979;133:482–485.
178. Yeager A, Jacobs H, Clark J. Nursery-acquired cytomegalovirus infection in two preterm infants. J Pediatr. 1972;81:332–335.
179. Yeager A. Transfusion-acquired cytomegalovirus infection in newborn infants. Am J Dis Child. 1974;128:478–483.
180. Yeager A, Grumet F, Hufleigh E, et al. Prevention of transfusion-acquired cytomegalovirus infections in newborn infants. J Pediatr. 1981;98:281–287.
181. Benson J, Bodden S, Tobin J. Cytomegalovirus and blood transfusion in neonates. Arch Dis Child. 1979;54:538–541.
182. Singh N, Gayowski T, Wagener M, et al. Pulmonary infections in liver transplant recipients receiving tacrolimus. Changing pattern of microbial etiologies. Transplantation. 1996;61:396–401.
183. Glenn J. Cytomegalovirus infections following renal transplantation. Infect Dis. 1981;3:1151–1178.
184. Pollard R, Arvin A, Gamberg P, et al. Specific cell-mediated immunity and infections with herpes viruses in cardiac transplant recipients. Am J Med. 1982;73:679–687.
185. Thaler SJ, Rubin RH. Opportunistic infections in the cardiac transplant patient. Curr Opin Cardiol. 1996;11:191–203.
186. Harbarth S, Pittet D, Romand J. Fatal concomitant nosocomial legionnaires' disease and cytomegalovirus pneumonitis after cardiac transplantation. Intensive Care Med. 1996;22:1133–1134.
187. Avery RK, Longworth DL. Viral pulmonary infections in thoracic and cardiovascular surgery. Semin Thorac Cardiovasc Surg. 1995;7:88–94.
188. Serody JS, Shea TC. Prevention of infections in bone marrow transplant recipients. Infect Dis Clin North Am. 1997;11:459–477.
189. Hersman J, Meyers J, Thomas E, et al. The effect of granulocyte transfusions on the incidence of cytomegalovirus infection after allogeneic marrow transplantation. Ann Intern Med. 1982;96:149–152.
190. Winston D, Winston S, Howell C, et al. Cytomegalovirus infections associated with leukocyte transfusions. Ann Intern Med. 1980;93:671–675.
191. Armstrong J, Tarr G, Youngblood L, et al. Cytomegalovirus infection in children undergoing open heart surgery. Yale J Biol Med. 1976;49:83–91.
192. Prince A, Szmuness W, Millian S, et al. A serologic study of cytomegalovirus infections associated with blood transfusions. N Engl J Med. 1971;284:1125–1132.
193. Gurevich I, Cunha B. Non-parenteral transmission of cytomegalovirus in a neonatal intensive care unit. Lancet. 1981;2:222–224.
194. Spector S. Transmission of cytomegalovirus among infants in hospital documented by restriction-endonuclease-digestion analyses. Lancet. 1983;1:378–381.
195. Stagno S, Reynolds D, Pass R, et al. Breast milk and the risk of cytomegalovirus infection. N Engl J Med. 1980;302:1073–1077.
196. Demmler G, Yow M, Spector S, et al. Nosocomial cytomegalovirus infections within two hospitals caring for infants and children. J Infect Dis. 1987;156:9–16.
197. Alford C. Breast milk transmission of cytomegalovirus (CMV) infection. Adv Exp Med Biol. 1991;310:293–299.
198. Hayes K, Danks D, Gibas H. Brief recordings: Cytomegalovirus in human milk. N Engl J Med. 1972;287:177–178.
199. Aitken C, Booth J, Booth M, et al. Molecular epidemiology and significance of a cluster of cases of CMV infection occurring on a special care baby unit. J Hosp Infect. 1996;34:183–189.
200. Yeager A. Longitudinal, serological study of cytomegalovirus infections in nurses and in personnel without patient contact. J Clin Microbiol. 1975;2:448–452.
201. Ahlfors K, Ivarsson S, Johnsson T, et al. Risk of cytomegalovirus infection in nurses and congenital infection in their offspring. Acta Paediatr Scand. 1981;70:819–823.
202. Ahlfors K. Epidemiological studies of congenital cytomegalovirus infection. Scand J Infect Dis. 1982;34(Suppl):S1–S36.
203. Yow M, Lakeman A, Stagno S, et al. Use of restriction enzymes to investigate the source of a primary cytomegalovirus infection in a pediatric nurse. Pediatrics. 1982;70:713–716.
204. Wilfert C, Huang E, Stagno S. Restriction endonuclease analysis of cytomegalovirus deoxyribonucleic acid as an epidemiologic tool. Pediatrics. 1982;70:717–721.
205. Balfour C, Balfour H Jr. Cytomegalovirus is not an occupational risk for nurses in renal transplant and neonatal units. Results of a prospective surveillance study. JAMA. 1986;256:1909–1914.
206. Brady M. Cytomegalovirus infections: Occupational risk for health professionals. Am J Infect Control. 1986;14:197–203.
207. Brady M, Demmler G, Anderson D. Cytomegalovirus infection in pediatric house officers: Susceptibility to and rates of primary infection. Infect Control. 1987;8:329–332.
208. Adler S, Baggett J, Wilson M, et al. Molecular epidemiology of cytomegalovirus in a nursery: Lack of evidence for nosocomial transmission. Pediatrics. 1986;108:117–123.
209. Blackman J, Murph J, Bale JJ. Risk of cytomegalovirus infection among educators and health-care personnel serving disabled children. Pediatr Infect Dis J. 1987;6:725–729.
210. Gerberding J, Bryant-LeBlanc C, Nelson K, et al. Risk of transmitting the human immunodeficiency virus, cytomegalovirus, and hepatitis B virus to health-care workers exposed to AIDS patients and AIDS-related conditions. J Infect Dis. 1987;156:1–8.
211. Gerberding JL. Incidence and prevalence of human immunodeficiency virus, hepatitis B virus, hepatitis C virus, and cytomegalovirus among health care personnel at risk for blood exposure: Final report from a longitudinal study. J Infect Dis. 1994;170:1410–1417.
212. Hatherly L. Is primary cytomegalovirus infection an occupational hazard for obstetric nurses? A serologic study. Infect Control. 1986;7:452–455.
213. Kuhls T, Viker S, Parris N, et al. Occupational risk of HIV, HBV and HSV-2 infections in health care personnel caring for AIDS patients. Am J Public Health. 1987;77:1306–1309.
214. Dworsky M, Welch K, Cassady G, et al. Occupational risk for primary cytomegalovirus infection among pediatric health-care workers. N Engl J Med. 1983;309:950–953.
215. Murph JR, Souza IE, Dawson JD, et al. Epidemiology of congenital cytomegalovirus infection: Maternal risk factors and molecular analysis of cytomegalovirus strains. Am J Epidemiol. 1998;147:940–947.
216. Pass R. Epidemiology and transmission of cytomegalovirus. J Infect Dis. 1985;152:243–248.
217. Tolkoff-Rubin N, Rubin R, Keller E, et al. Cytomegalovirus infection in dialysis patients and personnel. Ann Intern Med. 1978;89:625–628.
218. Valenti W, Betts R, Breese-Hall C, et al. Nosocomial viral infections: II. Guidelines for prevention and control of respiratory viruses, herpesviruses, and hepatitis viruses. Infect Control. 1980;1:165–178.
219. Lang D, Ebert P, Rodgers B, et al. Reduction of post-transfusion cytomegalovirus infection following use of leukocyte-depleted blood. Transfusion. 1977;17:391–395.
220. Betts R, Cestero R, Freeman R, et al. Epidemiology of cytomegalovirus in end-stage renal disease. J Med Virol. 1979;4:89–96.
221. Ho M, Suwausirikul S, Dowling J, et al. The transplanted kidney as a source of cytomegalovirus infection. N Engl J Med. 1975;293:1109–1112.
222. Ho M. Epidemiology of cytomegalovirus infections. Rev Infect Dis. 1990;12(Suppl):S701–S710.
223. Weller T. The cytomegaloviruses: Ubiquitous agents with protean clinical manifestations. N Engl J Med. 1971;285:203–214.
224. Brady M, Demmler G, Seavy D, et al. Method of blood processing affects cytomegalovirus excretion in newborn nurseries. Am J Infect Control. 1987;15:245–248.
225. Brady M, Milan J, Anderson D, et al. Use of deglycerolized red blood cells to

prevent post-transfusion infection with cytomegalovirus in neonates. J Infect Dis. 1984;150:334–339.

226. Arseniev L, Battmer K, Andres J, et al. Influence of the freezing-thawing-washing procedure on the cytomegalovirus DNA content of cellular blood products. Infusionsther Transfusionsmed. 1992;19:199–201.
227. Bowden RA, Slichter SJ, Sayers M, et al. A comparison of filtered leukocyte-reduced and cytomegalovirus (CMV) seronegative blood products for the prevention of transfusion-associated CMV infection after marrow transplant. Blood. 1995;86:3598–3603.
228. Podnos YD, Williams RA. Current risks for blood borne viral illness in blood transfusions. West J Med. 1998;168:36–37.
229. Lane TA. Leukocyte depletion of cellular blood components. Curr Opin Hematol. 1994;1:443–451.
230. Sarkodee-Adoo C, Schiffer CA. Platelet transfusion support for patients with cancer and hematologic malignancies. Curr Opin Hematol. 1996;3:347–354.
231. Sloand EM. Viral risks associated with blood transfusion. Photochem Photobiol. 1997;65:428–431.
232. Dumont LJ, Schuyler R. Prevention of transfusion-associated cytomegalovirus infection: Defining the method of preparation for leukocyte-reduced blood products. Blood. 1996;88:1515.
233. Landaw EM, Kanter M, Petz LD. Safety of filtered leukocyte-reduced blood products for prevention of transfusion-associated cytomegalovirus infection. Blood. 1996;87:4910.
234. Norfolk DR, Williamson LM. Leucodepletion of blood products by filtration. Blood Rev. 1995;9:7–14.
235. Popovsky MA, Benson K, Glassman AB, et al. Transfusion practices in human immunodeficiency virus–infected patients. Transfusion. 1995;35:612–616.
236. Bowden RA. Transfusion-transmitted cytomegalovirus infection. Hematol Oncol Clin North Am. 1995;9:155–166.
237. Dzieczkowski JS, Barrett BB, Nester D, et al. Characterization of reactions after exclusive transfusion of white cell–reduced cellular blood components. Transfusion. 1995;35:20–25.
238. Dazzi F, Goldman JM. Adoptive immunotherapy following allogeneic bone marrow transplantation. Annu Rev Med. 1998;49:329–340.
239. Barrett AJ, Mavroudis D, Tisdale J, et al. T cell–depleted bone marrow transplantation and delayed T cell add-back to control acute GVHD and conserve a graft-versus-leukemia effect. Bone Marrow Transplant. 1998;21:543–551.
240. Couriel D, Canosa J, Engler H, et al. Early reactivation of cytomegalovirus and high risk of interstitial pneumonitis following T-depleted BMT for adults with hematological malignancies. Bone Marrow Transplant. 1996;18:347–353.
241. Mavroudis DA, Read EJ, Molldrem J, et al. T cell–depleted granulocyte colony-stimulating factor (G-CSF) modified allogenic bone marrow transplantation for hematological malignancy improves graft CD34+ cell content but is associated with delayed pancytopenia. Bone Marrow Transplant. 1998;21:431–440.
242. Falagas ME, Snydman DR, Ruthazer R, et al. Cytomegalovirus immune globulin (CMVIG) prophylaxis is associated with increased survival after orthotopic liver transplantation. The Boston Center for Liver Transplantation CMVIG Study Group. Clin Transplant. 1997;11:432–437.
243. Snydman DR, Werner BG, Meissner HC, et al. Use of cytomegalovirus immunoglobulin in multiply transfused premature neonates. Pediatr Infect Dis J. 1995;14:34–40.
244. Henderson DK. Nosocomial herpesvirus infections. In: Mandell G, Douglas R, Bennett J, eds. Principles and Practice of Infectious Diseases. New York: Churchill Livingstone; 1985:1630–1637.
245. Department of Labor (OSHA). Occupational exposure to bloodborne pathogens; final rule. Fed Register. 1991;56:64175–64182.
246. Onorato I, Morens D, Martone W, et al. Epidemiology of cytomegalovirus infections: Recommendations for prevention and control. Rev Infect Dis. 1985;7:479–497.
247. Plotkin S. Cytomegalovirus in hospitals. Pediatr Infect Dis. 1986;5:177–178.
248. Adler S. Nosocomial transmission of cytomegalovirus. Pediatr Infect Dis. 1986;5:239–246.
249. Gerber P, Walsh J, Rosenblum E, et al. Association of Epstein-Barr infection with the post-perfusion syndrome. Lancet. 1969;1:593–595.
250. Purtilo D, Paquin L, Sakamota K, et al. Persistent transfusion-associated infectious mononucleosis with transient acquired immunodeficiency. Am J Med. 1980;68:437–440.
251. Corey L, Stamm W, Feorino P, et al. HBsAg-negative hepatitis in a hemodialysis unit: Relation of Epstein-Barr virus. N Engl J Med. 1975;293:1273–1278.
252. Blacklow N, Watson B, Miller G, et al. Mononucleosis with heterophil antibodies: Epstein-Barr virus infection acquisition by an elderly patient in hospital. Am J Med. 1971;51:549–552.
253. Solem J, Jorgensen W. Accidentally transmitted infectious mononucleosis: Report of a case. Acta Med Scand. 1969;186:433–437.
254. Turner A, MacDonald R, Cooper B. Transmission of infectious mononucleosis by transfusion of pre-illness plasma. Ann Intern Med. 1972;77:751–753.
255. Virolainen M, Anderson L, Lalla M, et al. T-lymphocyte proliferation in mononucleosis. Clin Immunol Immunopathol. 1973;2:114–120.
256. Henle W, Henle G, Harrison F, et al. Antibody responses to the Epstein-Barr virus and cytomegalovirus after open-heart and other surgery. N Engl J Med. 1970;282:1068–1074.
257. Ginsburg C, Henle G, Henle W. An outbreak of infectious mononucleosis among the personnel in an outpatient clinic. Am J Epidemiol. 1976;104:571–575.
258. Chang R, Rosen L, Kapikian A. Epstein-Barr virus infections in a nursery. Am J Epidemiol. 1981;113:22–29.
259. Sullivan J, Wallen W, Johnson F. Epstein-Barr virus infection following bone-marrow transplantation. Int J Cancer. 1978;22:132–135.
260. Deeg HJ, Socie G. Malignancies after hematopoietic stem cell transplantation: Many questions, some answers. Blood. 1998;91:1833–1844.
261. Locasciulli A, Nava S, Sparano P, et al. Infections with hepatotropic viruses in children treated with allogeneic bone marrow transplantation. Bone Marrow Transplant. 1998;21(Suppl 2):S75–S77.
262. Lucas KG, Pollok KE, Emanuel DJ. Post-transplant EBV induced lymphoproliferative disorders. Leuk Lymphoma. 1997;25:1–8.
263. Nalesnik MA. Posttransplantation lymphoproliferative disorders (PTLD): Current perspectives. Semin Thorac Cardiovasc Surg. 1996;8:139–148.
264. O'Brien S, Bernert RA, Logan JL, et al. Remission of posttransplant lymphoproliferative disorder after interferon alfa therapy. J Am Soc Nephrol. 1997;8:1483–1489.
265. O'Reilly RJ, Small TN, Papadopoulos E, et al. Biology and adoptive cell therapy of Epstein-Barr virus–associated lymphoproliferative disorders in recipients of marrow allografts. Immunol Rev. 1997;157:195–216.
266. Patel R, Paya CV. Infections in solid-organ transplant recipients. Clin Microbiol Rev. 1997;10:86–124.
267. Raymond E, Tricottet V, Samuel D, et al. Epstein-Barr virus–related localized hepatic lymphoproliferative disorders after liver transplantation. Cancer. 1995;76:1344–1351.
268. Rustgi VK. Epstein-Barr viral infection and posttransplantation lymphoproliferative disorders. Liver Transpl Surg. 1995;1(Suppl 1):S100–S108.
269. Savage P, Waxman J. Post-transplantation lymphoproliferative disease. Q J Med. 1997;90:497–503.
270. Tosato G, Taga K, Angiolillo AL, et al. Epstein-Barr virus as an agent of haematological disease. Baillieres Clin Haematol. 1995;8:165–199.
271. Cen H, Breinig MC, Atchison RW, et al. Epstein-Barr virus transmission via the donor organs in solid organ transplantation: Polymerase chain reaction and restriction fragment length polymorphism analysis of IR2, IR3, and IR4. J Virol. 1991;65:976–980.
272. Epstein JB, Phillips K, Sherlock CH. Viral serology after bone marrow transplantation. Viral Immunol. 1991;4:133–137.
273. Junker AK, Thomas EE, Radcliffe A, et al. Epstein-Barr virus shedding in breast milk. Am J Med Sci. 1991;302:220–223.
274. Hoaglund R. The transmission of infectious mononucleosis. Am J Med Sci. 1955;229:262–272.
275. Centers for Disease Control. Isolation Techniques for Use in Hospitals. 2nd ed. US Department of Health, Education, and Welfare Publication No. (CDC) 76-8314. Washington, DC: Government Printing Office, 1975.
276. Ballen K, Stewart FM. Adoptive immunotherapy. Curr Opin Oncol. 1997;9:579–583.
277. Emanuel DJ, Lucas KG, Mallory GB Jr, et al. Treatment of posttransplant lymphoproliferative disease in the central nervous system of a lung transplant recipient using allogeneic leukocytes. Transplantation. 1997;63:1691–1694.
278. Heslop HF, Rooney CM. Adoptive cellular immunotherapy for EBV lymphoproliferative disease. Immunol Rev. 1997;157:217–222.
279. Imashuku S, Goto T, Matsumura T, et al. Unsuccessful CTL transfusion in a case of post-BMT Epstein-Barr virus–associated lymphoproliferative disorder (EBV-LPD). Bone Marrow Transplant. 1997;20:337–340.
280. O'Reilly RJ, Lacerda JF, Lucas KG, et al. Adoptive cell therapy with donor lymphocytes for EBV-associated lymphomas developing after allogeneic marrow transplants. Important Adv Oncol. 1996;149–166.
281. Miller G, Niederman J, Andrews L. Prolonged oropharyngeal excretion of Epstein-Barr virus after infectious mononucleosis. N Engl J Med. 1973;288:229–232.
282. Yamanishi K, Shiraki K, Kondo T, et al. Identification of human herpesvirus-6 as a causal agent for exanthem subitum. Lancet. 1988;1:1065–1067.
283. Irving WL, Cunningham AL. Serological diagnosis of infection with human herpesvirus type 6. BMJ. 1990;300:156–159.
284. Hall CB, Long CE, Schnabel KC, et al. Human herpesvirus-6 infection in children. A prospective study of complications and reactivation. N Engl J Med. 1994;331:432–438.
285. Frenkel N, Schirmer EC, Wyatt LS, et al. Isolation of a new herpesvirus from human CD4+ T cells. Proc Natl Acad Sci U S A. 1990;87:748–752.
286. Chang Y, Cesarman E, Pessin MS, et al. Identification of herpesvirus-like DNA sequences in AIDS-associated Kaposi's sarcoma. Science. 1994;266:1865–1869.
287. Ambroziak JA, Blackbourn DJ, Herndier BG, et al. Herpes-like sequences in HIV-infected and uninfected Kaposi's sarcoma patients. Science. 1995;268:582–583.

SECTION B

INFECTIONS IN SPECIAL HOSTS

Chapter 298

Infections in the Immunocompromised Host: General Principles

BEN E. DE PAUW
J. PETER DONNELLY

Infection is always the result of a negative balance between the capacity of the host defense system and the virulence of invading microorganisms, and therefore, dependent on multiple factors. An intact defense system offers protection against most microbial aggressors through a complex interrelationship of protecting surfaces, cells, and soluble factors. A good general condition, optimal nutritional status, and normal organ function, together with granulocytes and other components of the cellular and humoral immune system, provide adequate protection against potentially pathogenic microorganisms. All components of the defense system are more or less dependent on another for attaining maximum efficacy. For instance, mucous membranes can only exert optimal protection in conjunction with IgA and other secretory substances, which in turn influence interactions between the surfaces of the human body and colonizing microorganisms. The resident flora normally does not cause infection and may protect against pathogens by competing for binding sites on the surfaces and for the available nutrients.

Predisposition to infection as a consequence of any qualitative or quantitative defect in one of the natural defense mechanisms of the body has long been recognized. Until arrival of the acquired immunodeficiency syndrome, the term *immunocompromised host* was used more or less exclusively to describe infectious complications either in a rather small group of patients with congenital deficiencies of the immune system or, mainly, in patients suffering from a malignant disease, particularly hematologic malignancies. Much of the expertise on the management of infectious complications is derived from clinical studies performed in the latter group of patients, and the data obtained are not necessarily applicable to other categories of patients.

Infection promises to remain a principal cause of morbidity and mortality in immunocompromised patients. Hence, a comprehensive understanding of the possible causes of infectious complications and the predisposing factors involved, as well as a comprehensive anti-infective strategy, is imperative when offering these patients care. The attending physician has to be particularly aware of all potential risk factors for infection, including those related to the underlying disease and its treatment, because although susceptibility to infection is increased, timely diagnosis of the cause is seldom possible in immunocompromised patients. Ideally, there should be close cooperation among all disciplines involved in diagnosis, including nurses, hematologists or oncologists, radiologists, respiratory physicians, microbiologists, pathologists, and specialists in infectious diseases. The optimal clinical care afforded by such a team approach has made fulminating, rapidly fatal microbial sepsis a rare event during the 1990s in patients brought into remission of their underlying disease, despite the greater intensification of immunosuppressive treatment. In fact, the relationship is reciprocal insofar as better supportive care allows more aggressive therapy to achieve better cure rates, which in turn results in more infectious complications, often of a quite different character.

COMPONENTS OF HOST DEFENSES

Appreciation of the predisposing risk factors is an essential but perplexing exercise in that it suggests that the respective factors each play an independent role. Theoretically, a specific deficiency increases the patient's susceptibility to the very pathogens that are eradicated by that particular host defense mechanism (Table 298–1).

TABLE 298–1 Host Defects and Associated Prevalent Pathogens

Defect	Pathogen
Granulocytopenia	*Staphylococcus aureus*
	Coagulase-negative staphylococci
	Viridans streptococci
	Enterococcus spp.
	Escherichia coli
	Pseudomonas aeruginosa
	Klebsiella pneumoniae
	Enterobacter and *Citrobacter* spp.
	Aspergillus spp.
	Fusarium spp.
Damaged integument	
Skin—central venous catheter related	Coagulase negative staphylococci
	Staphylococcus aureus
	Stenotrophomonas maltophilia
	Pseudomonas aeruginosa
	Acinetobacter spp.
	Corynebacterium and *Bacillus* spp.
	Candida spp.
	Agents of mucormycosis
Oral mucositis	Viridans streptococci
	Enterococcus spp.
	Capnocytophaga spp.
	Stomatococcus mucilaginosus
	Candida spp.
	Herpes simplex virus
Impaired cellular immunity	Herpes simplex, herpes zoster, and Epstein-Barr virus and cytomegalovirus
	Adenovirus
	Respiratory syncytial virus, influenza, and parainfluenza virus
	Listeria monocytogenes
	Nocardia spp.
	Human papillomavirus
	Mycobacterium tuberculosis
	Nontuberculous mycobacteria
	Pneumocystis carinii
	Aspergillus spp.
	Cryptococcus neoformans
	Histoplasma capsulatum
	Coccidioides immitis
	Penicillium marneffei
	Toxoplasma gondii
Impaired humoral immunity	*Streptococcus pneumoniae*
	Haemophilus influenzae
Compromised organ function	
Spleen	*Streptococcus pneumoniae*
	Haemophilus influenzae
	Neisseria meningitidis
Deferoxamine therapy for iron or aluminum overload	Agents of mucormycosis

Although a basic pattern is recognizable, the types and severity of infectious complications are often unpredictable. Single, isolated deficiencies are virtually never encountered, and malfunction of one part of the system influences several other components. Moreover, therapeutic interventions and the underlying disease itself will perturb a range of defense mechanisms. Although the risks associated with granulocytopenia are well known, other toxicity, especially that affecting the mucosal barrier, has come to assume greater importance than was the case previously. The advent of aggressive treatment methods has changed the classic concept of specific defects of host defense mechanisms in the various types of diseases, the effects of chemotherapy and irradiation now being the primary factors determining the nature and depth of the defect. Patients with impaired humoral immunity as manifested by defective opsonization and phagocytosis of bacteria will also be exposed to chemotherapy-induced neutropenia or deficient cellular immunity as a result of treatment with purine analogues. To complicate things further, hazardous events are not static but rather exert their impact dynamically in as much as the degree of disturbance varies with time during the course of treatment and thereafter.

Granulocytes

Under normal circumstances, neutrophils, sometimes accompanied by eosinophils, congregate at the site of inflammation and are followed by macrophages. Formation of this inflammatory exudate is the result of activation of humoral factors and the vascular endothelium (see Chapter 8). Meanwhile, in the peripheral blood, granulocytosis evolves as a consequence of release of the marrow reserve and increased granulocytopoiesis, which is regulated by hematopoietic growth factors such as interleukin-3, granulocyte-macrophage colony-stimulating factor, and granulocyte colony-stimulating factor.

Virtually all cytotoxic drugs used in the treatment of malignant diseases have a deleterious effect on the proliferation of normal hematopoietic progenitor cells. Therefore, after destruction of the mitotic pool and depletion of the marrow pool reserve, granulocytopenia ensues. Likewise, therapeutic radiation can induce a clinically relevant granulocytopenia, depending on the dose rate, total dose given, and irradiated area of the body. Total body irradiation, as used in hematopoietic stem cell transplant procedures, is the most obvious illustration of the possible negative impact of irradiation. Thus, profound neutropenia is an unavoidable consequence of the treatment of malignancy and may persist for 3 to 4 weeks or even longer. Granulocytopenia or a treatment-related decrease in the granulocyte count is probably the most important primary risk factor for infection. Fever develops in nearly all patients with a granulocyte count less than 100/mm^3 for more than 3 weeks, whereas only one fifth of the febrile episodes in cancer patients occur when granulocyte counts are normal.[1] Moreover, during iatrogenic granulocytopenia, the risk of infection and infection-related mortality increases proportionally with time.

The presence of granulocytes at the infected site is irrelevant if they are not able to function normally. Both chemotherapeutic drugs and irradiation also interfere with nonproliferating cells and their function. Such interference may result in decreased chemotaxis, diminished phagocytotic capacity, and defective intracellular killing by granulocytes. Glucocorticosteroids seem to enhance granulocytopoiesis and mobilize the marginal and the marrow pool reserve, but these supposedly positive effects on neutrophilic granulocytes are counterbalanced by numerous disadvantages. These drugs curb the accumulation of neutrophils at the site of inflammation by reducing their adherent capacity and diminishing their chemotactic activity. Furthermore, they decrease phagocytosis and intracellular killing of microorganisms. The lack of functioning neutrophils deprives the host of a primary defense mechanism against invading microorganisms, which are consequently able to readily establish themselves, initiate local infection, disseminate unhindered, and eventually lead to fulminant sepsis and death unless treated promptly and effectively.

Cellular and Humoral Immunity

The cellular immune system serves to eliminate intracellular pathogens and virus-infected cells from the body (see Chapter 9). Normal macrophages have a limited capacity for killing ingested microorganisms, and various organisms are even able to survive and replicate inside the cell, unless the macrophage becomes activated. Activation of macrophages is a complex process primarily under the control of cytokines. Both antigen-specific and antigen-nonspecific cells contribute to the development of cellular immunity. The antigen-specific branch of cell-mediated immunity can be divided into two major categories. One category involves cytotoxic effector cells, which are able to lyse virus-infected or foreign lymphocytes and macrophages. The second category involves subpopulations of T cells that mediate delayed-type hypersensitivity reactions after antigen recognition when an antigen is displayed together with the major histocompatibility complex on the surface of specialized antigen-presenting cells.

This fine-tuned system can easily be deregulated by congenital defects or defects acquired as a result of a disease or its treatment. Long-term cytotoxic therapy, extensive irradiation, corticosteroids, and other more specific agents such as azathioprine and cyclosporine suppress cellular immunity, mainly by interacting with helper T cells and natural killer cells. The relatively recently introduced purine analogues, including fludarabine and cladribine, are particularly detrimental to cellular immunity and create a situation similar to acquired immunodeficiency syndrome. Likewise, malignant lymphomas, particularly Hodgkin's disease, are associated with impaired cellular immunity. Allogeneic hematopoietic stem cell transplantation brings about a long-lasting dysfunction of T and B cells, especially in association with graft-versus-host disease and its treatment (Table 298–2). The coordination of cellular immunity is often lost, and when aided and abetted by suppressed humoral immunity, the paracrine mediators released go on to induce the sepsis cascade, which may culminate in multiorgan failure instead of arresting infection.[2]

TABLE 298–2 Sequence of Infective Events in Relation to Phases of Allogeneic Bone Marrow Transplantation

	Early Phase	Mid-recovery Phase
Host defense mechanisms *without* graft-versus-host disease		
Phagocytes	Absent	Deficient
Integument		
Skin	Normal	Damaged
Mucous membranes	Severely damaged	Damaged
Cellular immunity	Slightly impaired	Impaired
Humoral immunity	Normal	Impaired
Host defense mechanisms *with* graft-versus-host disease		
Phagocytes	Absent	Deficient
Integument		
Skin	Damaged	Damaged
Mucous membranes	Damaged	Severely damaged
Cellular immunity	Slightly impaired	Severely impaired
Humoral immunity	Normal	Impaired
Prevalent infections		
Mucositis	Herpes simplex virus type 1 Viridans streptococci	Herpes simplex virus type 1 *Candida* spp.
Pneumonia	Gram-negative bacilli *Aspergillus* spp.	Cytomegalovirus *Aspergillus* spp.
Septicemia	Viridans streptococci Staphylococci Gram-negative bacilli *Candida* spp.	Staphylococci *Streptococcus pneumoniae* *Candida* spp.

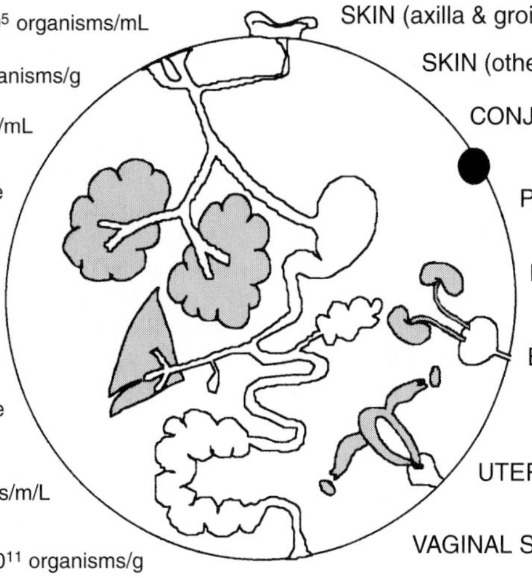

FIGURE 298–1. Body surfaces and their resident microbial flora. The integument comprises the skin; the respiratory tract, including the nasal cavity, ears, and conjunctivae; the alimentary tract; and the genitourinary tract and provides the first line of defense against microbial invasion. These body surfaces are normally colonized with a variety of microorganisms, including many different genera of bacteria and yeasts, but the range, number of species, and microbial biomass associated with the mucosal surfaces of the alimentary tract far exceed those of the skin. (From Noskin GA, ed. Management of Infectious Complications in Cancer Patients. Boston: Kluwer Academic Publishers; 1998.)

The humoral branch of the immune system, which is primarily responsible for clearing extracellular bacteria, involves the interaction of B cells with antigen and their subsequent proliferation and differentiation into antibody-secreting plasma cells (see Chapter 6). An important difference in antigen recognition by T cells and B cells is that the latter can recognize some antigens without the help of an antigen-presenting cell. The humoral system can identify a plethora of bacterial or viral microorganisms, as well as the soluble proteins that they release. On challenge with an antigen, immunoglobulins are produced that bind to the antigen. The specific functions of IgG and IgM include neutralization of the antigen, as well as complement activation and opsonization, that is, enhancement of phagocytosis of the antigen by neutrophils and macrophages. Secretory IgA, which is found on mucosal surfaces, is not an opsonin but nonetheless inhibits the motility of bacteria and prevents them from adhering to epithelial cells. The production of immunoglobulins is decreased in lymphoproliferative disorders such as chronic lymphocytic leukemia and multiple myeloma, whereas humoral immunity is generally well preserved in patients with acute leukemia. However, intensive radiotherapy and chemotherapy will lead not only to neutropenia but ultimately also to hypogammaglobulinemia.

The spleen is the principal organ for eliminating particles that are not opsonized, and it is left to the macrophages that occupy strategic positions within the organ to remove them. The primary immunoglobulin response also takes places in the spleen. Spleen-produced specific opsonizing antibodies are necessary for efficient phagocytosis of encapsulated bacteria. Splenectomy may result in a reduced level of the complement factor properdin and thereby lead to suboptimal opsonization,[3] a decrease in functional tuftsin, and low levels of circulating IgM.[4] The lack of opsonizing antibodies in serum against common encapsulated bacteria impairs the activity of all phagocytic cells, including granulocytes, monocytes, and macrophages. As a consequence, infections with *Streptococcus pneumoniae* and *Haemophilus influenzae* are often more severe in splenectomized patients, as well as in those who have received a hematopoietic stem cell transplant and are functionally asplenic.

Physical Barriers

The Integument

The skin, the respiratory tract including the nasal cavity, the ears and conjunctiva, the alimentary tract, and the genitourinary tract are in contact with the environment (Fig. 298–1) and provide a first line of defense against microbial invasion. The skin and the mucosal surfaces of the alimentary tract form the two principal barriers against microbial invasion. Both surfaces are normally colonized with a variety of microorganisms, including many different genera of bacteria and yeast that have an intimate association with a particular ecologic niche and help maintain the function and integrity of this first line of defense. When intact and healthy, both the mucosa and skin are capable of resisting colonization with the allochthonous organisms found in the immediate environment, as long as an ecologic balance is maintained within the indigenous microbial flora. Acidity plays a crucial role both in disinfecting the stomach and in regulating the microbial milieu of the vagina. The integrity of the mucosa, production of saliva and mucus, peristalsis, bile acids, digestive enzymes, and levels of secretory IgA also play an important role in maintaining a favorable microecology.[5, 6] Elimination of an inoculum is achieved by sneezing and coughing of microbes trapped in mucus, whereas flushing of the mouth and esophagus by saliva, as well as micturition and peristalsis, inhibits continuous intimate contact between a given surface area and unattached invasive microorganisms.

The Skin

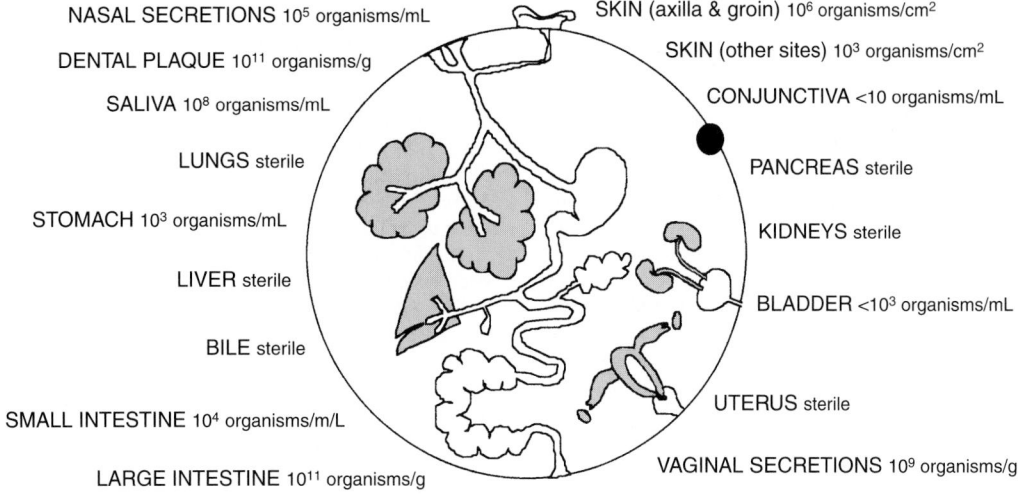

Healthy skin provides an effective barrier against invasion by microorganisms, mainly by remaining intact. Desquamation helps limit the opportunities for transient organisms to establish residence. Normally, very little water is present on the skin surface. Colonization with organisms sensitive to desiccation, such as gram-negative bacilli, is not favored. The skin also forms an acid mantle with a pH of 5.0 to 6.0, and its surface temperature is on average about 5°C lower than the core body temperature.[7] Besides containing secretory IgA, sweat also possesses sufficient salt to create a high osmotic pressure. Organisms that can withstand these conditions and compete successfully for binding sites and nutrients include staphylococci, corynebacteria, and the lipophilic yeast *Malassezia furfur.*[7] These organisms further modulate the microecology of the skin by releasing fatty acids from sebaceous secretions to produce a hydrophobic milieu, as well as short-chain lactic and propionic acid, which help maintain a low pH. Many of the bacteria also elaborate bacteriocins that inhibit other microorganisms.

The composition of the skin microflora is influenced by general factors including climate, body location, age, sex, race, and occupation, as well as by the use of soaps, detergents, and disinfectants. Antibiotics secreted in sweat disturb the balance within the commensal flora and leave the surface vulnerable to colonization by exogenous gram-negative bacilli. Antibiotics also exert selective pressure on the skin flora and cause resistance to emerge, as has been observed during treatment with ciprofloxacin.[8] Moreover, ciprofloxacin is both excreted in sweat and induces resistance among skin staphylococci within a few days of exposure.[9, 10] Chemotherapy and irradiation can bring about radical changes in healthy skin that cause hair loss, dryness, and loss of sweat production.

Needle punctures and catheters provide a ready means of access for microorganisms through the stratum corneum and into the blood stream. When the skin is broken, the release of fibronectin is thought to assist colonization with *Staphylococcus aureus,* whereas other changes facilitate colonization with gram-negative bacilli such as *Acinetobacter baumannii* and enteric bacteria. Abraded skin can lead to local infection, which can be a reservoir that promotes further spread to entry sites of intravenous catheters. When the balance is lost between host defenses and commensal flora around hair follicles, the follicles can become inflamed and necrotic and form a potential nidus of infection. Clinical infection therefore results from breaks in the skin, loss of local immunity, and disturbances within the resident flora. Vascular devices have gained widespread acceptance as a safe form of long-term venous access, but regular use is associated with a marked increase in the incidence of bacteremia with coagulase-negative staphylococci, which frequently colonize the catheter lumen.[11, 12] These staphylococci are commonly resistant to tobramycin, trimethoprim-sulfamethoxazole, and methicillin and may also be resistant to ciprofloxacin.[13] Unless the catheter ends in an implanted port, skin commensal flora have open access directly into the blood stream, depending on how frequently it is used[14] because the hub is the most likely source of contamination.[15] Infections related to the external surface of the catheter (exit-site infections and tunnel infections) can result in serious soft tissue infection, most notably by *S. aureus.* Exit-site infections occur much less frequently than does intraluminal colonization with an any one of an extraordinarily large variety of bacteria, many of which have relatively low virulence in other body sites. Once established, these infections can be very difficult to treat without removing the device, particularly those caused by *Bacillus* spp., *Candida* spp., and *Pseudomonas aeruginosa.*[16–19]

The Alimentary Tract

The surfaces of the alimentary tract are very different and range from the hard enamel of the teeth to the microvilli of the bowel. They are essentially composed of epithelial cells interspersed with cells that produce several host factors to support the protective properties of the mucosal surfaces. They also contain inhibitory substances, such as the iron-binding lactoferrin, lysozyme, and peroxidase, as well as secretory IgA. Oral commensal bacteria are also affected by antimicrobial agents. Very susceptible bacteria such as the oral *Neisseria* spp. are suppressed by a wide range of antimicrobial agents, whereas oral viridans streptococci such as *Streptococcus mitis* and *Streptococcus oralis* (formerly *sanguis* II) and other unusual oral commensal flora such as *Stomatococcus mucilaginosus* and *Capnocytophaga* spp. are likely to be selected for by antimicrobial agents such as a quinolone, to which the bacteria are only marginally susceptible, if at all. The chlorhexidine mouthwashes used to minimize infective complications arising from the oral toxicity induced by cytostatic agents also influence the microflora.[20–22]

Nausea and vomiting are frequent side effects of chemotherapy and irradiation and can be ameliorated by antiemetics. Dyspepsia is sufficiently commonplace for antacids such as H_2 histamine receptor antagonists to be regularly prescribed. Reduced gastric acidity inadvertently destroys the natural barrier that prevents transit and bowel colonization by oral commensal flora, many of which are resistant to most of the antimicrobial agents used for prophylaxis. When patients swallow large amounts of mucus as a result of severe mucositis, any oral commensal flora may survive passage to the bowel. Loss of the gastric barrier therefore effectively extends the area of potential sites for colonization to the full length of the alimentary tract, which may explain the pathogenesis of α-hemolytic streptococcal bacteremia.[23–25] Viridans streptococci, usually *S. mitis,* can cause life-threatening infections, including septic shock and pneumonitis with an often fatal respiratory distress syndrome. High-dose cytarabine predisposes to this infection.[24, 26–28] Finally, the ecology of the bowel flora is markedly altered by diarrhea induced by treatment with certain cytostatic agents such as cytarabine,[29] by graft-versus host disease,[30] and by total body irradiation.[31]

It is likely that severe mucositis leads to a commensurate increase in the number of unusual bacteria causing infection by providing them with a portal of entry, which may explain the increase in bacteremia caused by oral commensal gram-positive cocci such as the "viridans" streptococci, *S. mucilaginosus,* and *Capnocytophaga* spp.[24, 32–36] Besides damage to the oropharyngeal, esophageal, and gastric mucosa, chemotherapy and irradiation impair gut function and lead to rapid alterations in permeability. The increased absorption of sugars such as rhamnose, mannose, and lactulose and the decreased uptake of xylose after chemotherapy, irradiation, or a combination of both indicate a loss of integrity and damage to tight junctions.[37–41] Perturbed gut function has been shown to be one of the factors that together with antibiotic usage and colonization with *Candida* spp. predisposes patients with leukemia to invasive candidiasis and also appears to be a risk factor for neutropenic enterocolitis.[38] Impaired gut function and integrity may also facilitate translocation, particularly translocation of gram-negative bacilli such as *P. aeruginosa,* into the blood stream of patients colonized with the organism.[42] Gut toxicity has also been shown to be responsible for the reduced absorption of quinolones[43, 44] and has been implicated in the erratic bioavailability of the antifungal agent itraconazole.[45] Finally, a dysfunctional gut will have a marked effect on the nutritional status of the patient.

The alimentary tract is the major reservoir of gram-negative bacilli and *Candida* spp. Normally, the alimentary tract flora contains in excess of 10^{14} microorganisms amounting to several grams, only very few of which are capable of causing limited local infection and far fewer of which can cause disseminated infection, even in the most profoundly immunosuppressed patient. Most of the microbial flora is densely distributed around the surfaces of the oral cavity and the large bowel, where scores of different bacteria, including spirochetes, spore formers, bacilli, cocci, and yeasts, compete for the available surfaces and nutrients supplied to them daily.

Modern remission induction therapy and hematopoietic stem cell transplant conditioning regimens often induce substantial injury to the mucosa. Combinations containing melphalan, etoposide, methotrexate, cytarabine, and idarubicin have all been show to induce mucositis,[37, 38, 46] which can be very severe when anthracyclines are combined with total body irradiation and cyclophosphamide to condition patients for hematopoietic stem cell transplantation[47] or reinfusion. Widespread implementation of the hematopoietic growth factors granulocyte and granulocyte-macrophage colony-stimulating factor[48, 49] probably allows for the use of even higher doses of cytostatic drugs, which in turn further aggravate the oral mucositis.

Extensive mucosal damage is often accompanied by a decline in saliva production leading to a dry mouth. Any mucus produced may be extremely viscous and difficult to either swallow or cough up.[47, 50, 51] Periodontal disease may be exacerbated, and minor oral cuts and abrasions may become inflamed and ulcerated. The nonkeratinized surfaces of the mouth, including the underside of the tongue, the roof of the mouth, and the cheeks, may become red, inflamed, and swollen and thus limit the intake of both food and drink with the risk of malnutrition and catabolism.[52] Moreover, mucosal changes normally progress to a peak severity and coincide with the nadir of bone marrow aplasia and then begin to recover as hematopoiesis returns.[21, 52–54]

Anaerobic bacteria predominate among the resident flora of the oral cavity and large intestine population and play a crucial role in maintaining a healthy commensal flora by providing the facility to withstand the establishment of exogenous or allochthonous organisms, which is known as colonization resistance.[55] However, the microbial flora are not the only participants in the establishment and maintenance of colonization resistance.

Many antibiotics also exert a negative influence on the commensal flora. In particular, penicillins, rifamycin, clindamycin, erythromycin, bacitracin, and vancomycin significantly impair colonization resistance, probably because they inhibit the gram-positive nonsporulating, lactic acid–producing bacilli such as bifidobacteria.[54] Certain cephalosporins are also detrimental, whereas trimethoprim-sulfamethoxazole and the quinolones have been declared "friendly," hence their frequent use as prophylaxis.[54] Unexpectedly, imipenem used at higher doses led to an increase in *Clostridium difficile*.[56]

Because the normal commensal flora attach to the surfaces of the epithelium, their loss creates an ecologic vacuum that allows other organisms to establish colonization by occupying the vacant cell surfaces or by taking advantage of the surfeit of nutrients. Collapse of the ecology is invariably manifested by yeast overgrowth and colonization with nosocomial bacteria such as *Klebsiella pneumoniae* and *P. aeruginosa*[57, 58] and failure to detect viable anaerobes directly or indirectly.[59, 60] Recent examples of infectious complications associated with disturbance of the normal microbial equilibrium include the selection of previously uncommon species such as *Enterococcus faecium* and *Clostridium septicum*.

Other Organ Dysfunction

Tumors themselves may predispose to infection by local organ dysfunction. In patients with solid tumors, obstruction of natural passages can lead to inadequate drainage of secretory or excretory fluids from nasal sinuses, bronchi, bile ducts, and so forth. Furthermore, tissue invasion may create connections between normally sterile spaces and the outside world through disruption of epithelial surfaces. Examples include perforation of the esophagus by mediastinal tumors, invasive gynecologic malignancies with local pelvic abscesses caused by gram-negative bacilli and anaerobes, skin ulceration with cellulitis and even deep soft tissue infections, and invasion of the bowel wall by tumors of the lower gastrointestinal tract with seeding of bacteria into the blood stream. Central nervous system tumors, spinal cord compression, and paraneoplastic neuropathy are associated with an increased risk of infection because of a diminished ability to cough and swallow or vomit and incomplete emptying of the bladder.[61]

Treatment of malignancy inevitably damages healthy tissue. Even when the tumor is localized in a single area, relatively superficial, and readily removed, any surgery and local irradiation will nonetheless extend impairment of the normal defenses.

The lung appears to be very vulnerable to damage by cytostatic chemotherapy and irradiation and is exquisitely susceptible to infection. Immunopathologic reactions mediated by pulmonary macrophages that survive chemotherapy can lead to various other syndromes, including respiratory distress. Lung hemorrhage as a result of profound thrombocytopenia further imperils the lung and thereby increases the risk of infection. Inhalation of spores of *Aspergillus* spp. and other molds may lead to infection of the sinuses, bronchi, and lungs.

Herpesviruses may play a role in this process not only as direct pathogens but also because infection leads to impaired lymphocyte function and, in the case of herpes simplex virus, damage to mucosal surfaces.[62, 63] Dead or dying tissue alters the local microbial ecology and thereby creates a nidus for infection. Resident flora such as *Candida* spp. can establish a superficial infection[62, 63] marked by the presence of pseudomembranes over the ulcerated tissue, but they can also initiate local invasion and progressive spread to the esophagus and gastrointestinal tract culminating in disseminated candidiasis. In a healthy host, these conditions rarely prove fatal, are usually readily apparent and relatively short lived, and can generally be managed simply. However, when hypoplastic bone marrow is present at the same time, the lack of neutrophils allows any potential pathogen that has invaded the tissues or translocated to the blood stream to disseminate readily. Consequently, the transition from colonization to disseminated infection is likely to require fewer steps and involve much lower inocula than is necessary in patients whose immunity is not so comprehensively compromised. The trend toward more intensive chemotherapy and the increasing use of allogeneic and autologous hematopoietic stem cell transplantation augments the number of patients who will experience the double jeopardy of profound neutropenia and damage to the natural barriers of the skin and mucosa.

Platelets

The protective role of platelets in healthy individuals is often underestimated but becomes obvious during treatment of a malignant disease. Thrombocytopenia is an almost inevitable repercussion of intensive chemotherapy and irradiation, but decreased thrombocyte function is a similar matter of concern. Thrombocytopathy is either disease related or caused by concurrent medication. The consequences of both increased susceptibility to infection and decreased capacity to repair damaged tissues can be considerable and may have an impact on the eventual outcome of a treatment episode. Thrombocytopenia also appears to be an independent risk factor for bacteremia,[64] and the incidence of major hemorrhage at autopsy of patients who die with or of an infection is striking.

Nutritional Status

That patients need adequate nutritional support during the treatment of cancer has remained an aphorism that has yet to be fully supported scientifically. Patients who weigh less than 75% of their ideal body weight or who have experienced rapid weight loss and have hypoalbuminemia are severely nutritionally deficient, which correlates inversely with survival. Poor nutritional status endangers the integrity of host defenses because of the catabolic state induced by cachexia and the malnutrition that results from anorexia, therapy-induced nausea and vomiting, gastrointestinal obstruction, altered permeability, mucositis, and metabolic derangements. A state of iron deficiency reduces the microbicidal capacity of neutrophils and T-lymphocyte function in vitro. Nutrition may be given parenterally or via a nasogastric tube to redress the balance, but neither is entirely without risk because each introduces yet another breach in the normal barriers and increases the risk of aspiration, particularly when consciousness is impaired.

Concurrent Illnesses

Psychological stress is thought to suppress host defense mechanisms. This general assumption has been corroborated by the observations that psychological stress has a negative influence on the function of T cells and natural killer cells. Indeed, stress appears to be connected with an increased risk of acute viral respiratory illness, a risk that was related to the amount of stress, most likely mediated by endogenous opioids, hormones from the hypothalamic-pituitary-adrenal axis, catecholamines, and cytokines. Concomitant chronic illnesses enhance the risk of infection. Patients with a preexistent immune disturbance, such as a congenital immunodeficiency syndrome, are doubly jeopardized. The negative impact of smoking on patients with primary lung tumors is obvious and due to colonization of their airways with virulent encapsulated microorganisms and impaired clearance of secretions.[61] Patients with diabetes mellitus are prone to genitourinary tract and wound infections, and they frequently suffer from concurrent vascular disease and neuropathy. The proclivity to infection in patients with poorly controlled diabetes mellitus is not difficult to explain in view of aberrations such as impaired opsonization and decreased chemotactic activity of granulocytes and monocytes. Diabetes mellitus also predisposes to infections such as malignant external otitis[65] caused by *P. aeruginosa.* Treatment of iron overload with deferoxamine predisposes to rhinocerebral and pulmonary mucormycosis by providing the fungus with an available source of iron.[66]

ORIGIN OF FEVER AND INFECTIONS

An infectious origin of a fever can be confirmed microbiologically or clinically in only 30 to 50% of all febrile neutropenic patients (Fig. 298–2). Infectious complications usually arise insidiously in these patients because of a muted inflammatory response and the lack of pus, which can be attributed to the absence of granulocytes; even the presence of chills or rigors does not always correspond with bacteremia.[67] Yet, foci of infections can remain undetected because the physical examination was too cursory, specimens were either inappropriate or not collected at all, or the microbiologic investigations were incomplete or too insensitive. Obtaining a careful recent medical history and examining the patient thoroughly for any evidence of inflammation or infection should be considered obligatory, but getting a proper specimen is much more difficult because aspiration or biopsy is usually required which is ill advised for thrombocytopenic patients. Besides, even when a specimen is obtained from a normally sterile site, the yield is generally low. Consequently, failure to undertake an adequate physical examination and to obtain appropriate samples will result in fever being unexplained. Yet, the fact that most patients without any proven infection improve clinically after treatment with broad-spectrum antibacterial agents suggests the presence of an occult bacterial infection in many cases.

SITES OF INFECTION AND POTENTIAL PATHOGENS

The most common sites of infection are the oral cavity, the lung, and the skin with its underlying soft tissues. Oral infections are difficult to diagnose by appearance in patients with mucositis. Culture of oral lesions for herpes simplex virus and smears of scrapings for *Candida* pseudohyphae can be helpful.

Identifying the cause of skin and underlying soft tissue infections is equally difficult because culturing swabs of lesions rarely discriminates between pathogens and commensal flora. As an exception, Gram stain and culture from pus expressed from a catheter exit site can be useful. Culture and histologic examination of skin punch biopsy specimens is very helpful in the diagnosis of isolated maculopapular or ulcerated lesions. Disseminated infections by *Candida* spp., *Trichosporon* spp., and *Fusarium* spp., in a neutropenic patient may be manifested by skin lesions while blood cultures remain negative. Ecthyma gangrenosum from *P. aeruginosa* may be accompanied by positive blood cultures, but lesions with the same appearance in a neutropenic patient can be caused by *Aspergillus* spp. or the agents of mucormycosis. These fungal lesions require biopsy for diagnosis. Cellulitis can often be treated empirically with an agent that is active against *S. aureus* and *Streptococcus pyogenes,* such as an antistaphylococcal penicillin. Aspiration of skin lesions is seldom successful unless pus is present.

It is even more difficult to diagnose enteric infection, especially when nausea, vomiting, diarrhea, bowel cramps, and melena can all be due to toxicity related to chemotherapy, irradiation, or graft-versus-host disease. Endoscopy can be critical in the diagnosis of herpes simplex, *Candida* spp., and cytomegalovirus infection. The bowel flora can become the major reservoir of vancomycin-resistant enterococci, *Candida albicans, K. pneumoniae,* and *P. aeruginosa.*[57, 58, 68] Organisms can be spread from the bowel onto the skin and, by the fecal-oral route, into the mouth. Skin organisms can be spread to other patients by the hands of health care workers and, through intravenous catheters, into the patient's blood stream. Oral flora can be aspirated into the airway, particularly when the patient is intubated. Passage of bowel organisms into the blood stream can occur through chemotherapy-induced ulcers. Recovery of *C. septicum* from

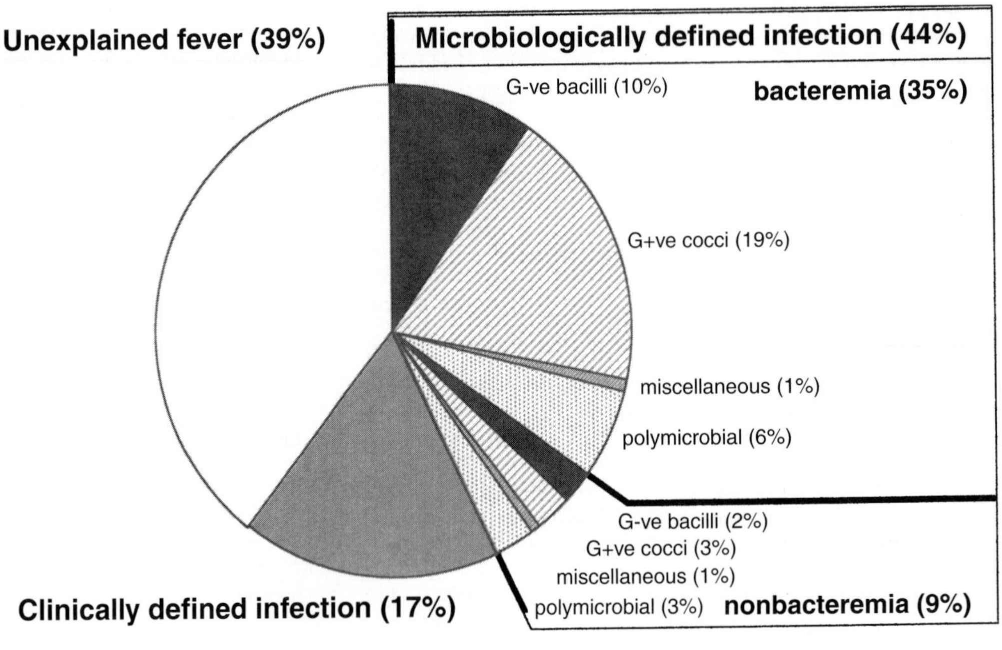

FIGURE 298–2. Causes of infection in 968 episodes of fever and neutropenia. (Unpublished data derived from the study of De Pauw BE, Deresinski SC, Feld R, et al. Ceftazidime compared with piperacillin and tobramycin for the empiric treatment of fever in neutropenic patients with cancer. A multicenter randomized trial. Ann Intern Med. 1994;120:834–844.)

the blood stream usually portends neutropenic enterocolitis.[69] Urinary tract infections, although rare in the absence of a Foley catheter, can also be initiated via perianal or vaginal contamination, as well as through hematogenous spread from the gut.

Infections associated with intravenous catheters usually originate from contamination of the catheter hub. Bacteria, typically coagulase-negative staphylococci, can be cultured from the blood drawn back through intravenous catheters, and yet the patient's condition does not appear septic when the culture becomes positive. The contaminated catheter may have already been removed since the culture was obtained, or the culture may have been contaminated by surface organisms at the time that blood was withdrawn. In afebrile patients, repeating blood cultures may be all that is indicated. In other cases, the organism can be cultured repeatedly from blood drawn through the same catheter port but not from blood drawn peripherally, thus suggesting that the organism has not yet been able to cause sepsis but has colonized the catheter. Removing the device or administering antibiotics through the same port may be indicated to circumvent future sepsis.

DIAGNOSIS

Despite the attenuation of physical signs and symptoms of infection in an immunocompromised patient, it is still essential to conduct a careful physical examination, with particular attention paid to vital signs (pulse, respiration rate, blood pressure), to the course of the patient's temperature during the preceding days, and to the oropharynx including the dentition, the lungs, the skin and exit sites of venous access devices, and the perirectal area and perianal region.

Apparently trivial complaints such as a persistent dry cough may prove to be an early sign of impending pneumonia from *Aspergillus* spp.,[70] respiratory syncytial virus, or influenza virus. Thoracic computed tomographic scans are more sensitive in detecting pulmonary infiltrates compatible with aspergillosis than are plain chest radiographs.[71] Bronchoalveolar lavage specimens from patients with pulmonary infiltrates should have a battery of tests that usually includes smears for *Pneumocystis carinii,* the acid-fast bacilli and *Nocardia* spp., bacteria, and molds, as well as culture for fungi and bacteria, including *Legionella* spp., *Mycobacterium* spp., *Nocardia* spp., and respiratory viruses (influenza and parainfluenza viruses, adenovirus, respiratory syncytial virus, and cytomegalovirus). Rapid assays by enzyme-linked immunosorbent assay, direct fluorescent antibody, or dot blot are also available for some of these viruses. Nasopharyngeal swabs can detect respiratory syncytial virus and can be tested by one of the rapid methods.

Fever in the presence of diarrhea or abdominal pain should prompt a cytotoxicity assay on stool for *C. difficile* toxin. Neutropenic patients with right lower quadrant pain may have typhlitis, the diagnosis of which can be supported by an edematous colonic wall on abdominal computed tomography with oral contrast. Urine from bone marrow transplant recipients with hemorrhagic cystitis should be tested for adenovirus and BK virus. Determination of C-reactive protein and cytokines such as interleukin-6 is recommended by some for diagnosing bacterial infection,[72–75] whereas others remain unconvinced.[76, 77]

Blood cultures are usually the most productive microbiologic investigation and help explain 10 to 40% of fevers, but the sensitivity of blood cultures is crucially dependent on the volume of blood cultured, with 30 to 40 ml per session being recommended for optimal results.[78] It has become common practice to draw at least 10 ml of blood for culture by venipuncture when investigating fever immediately before starting empirical therapy, together with at least 10 ml through each lumen of a central vascular catheter when one is present. Infusion of the antibiotic through catheter ports that are culture positive may be helpful in clearing colonized catheters. Once therapy is started, the value of further blood cultures is small if the patient is responding clinically. Patients with catheter-acquired sepsis who remain febrile with positive blood cultures usually need their catheters removed. In recent years, at least in clinical trials, blood cultures have been repeated 3 to 4 days after starting empirical therapy as a means of detecting persistent bacteremia.

The role of nonculture methods for diagnosis is small but expanding. *Legionella* antigen detection in urine is specific but detects only *Legionella pneumophila* type 1 or approximately 70% of patients with *Legionella* pneumonia. Detection of cytomegalovirus DNA is probably too sensitive unless done quantitatively, but measurement of pp65 antigen in peripheral blood neutrophils is being used routinely in bone marrow transplant recipients whose leukocyte counts have recovered sufficiently to permit this measurement. Detection of fungal DNA and *Candida* metabolites in blood and urine remains investigational.[79–82] Kits for the detection of *Aspergillus* antigen in serum by latex agglutination or enzyme-linked immunosorbent assay are commercially available, but their sensitivity and specificity have yet to be established accurately in patients at risk of aspergillosis.

Given the lack of sensitivity of cultures in general, many clinicians restrict microbiologic investigations in patients with no localizing signs to culture of blood and urine. They then treat empirically and rely only on the development, progress, and resolution of clinical signs and symptoms to further guide their actions (see Chapter 300).

The value of serodiagnosis for viral infections in an acutely ill patient is limited by the lag time between the infection and the immunologic response and by the immunosuppressive state that might decrease antibody production. Because information on this issue may become important during the further course of the disease, especially in poorly responding patients, samples should be obtained and stored for future testing when clinically indicated.

Microbiologically Defined Infections

Bacteremia

Bacteremia accounts for the vast majority of culture-documented infections. During the last decade a change from gram-negative to gram-positive bacteria has occurred,[83] but virtually any microorganism can cause infection in severely immunosuppressed patients. Worldwide, no single bacterial pathogen is presently predominant; variations between centers are considerable and depend on differences in chemotherapeutic and transplant conditioning regimens, prophylactic antibacterial and antifungal agents, management of central venous catheters, hospital environment, climate, and so forth.

Bacteremia Related to Intravascular Catheters. Coagulase-negative staphylococci are the most common cause of catheter-acquired sepsis,[10–13] but they are also recovered from catheter blood under circumstances suggesting that they are not causing the fever that prompted the blood culture. It is always easier to interpret the results of culturing of blood drawn from a peripheral vein. Simultaneous quantitative blood cultures from the catheter and a peripheral vein have been advocated but have not convincingly discriminated between catheter-acquired sepsis, sepsis from another source, asymptomatic intraluminal colonization of the catheter, and accidental contamination while drawing blood from the catheter hub. In all cases, the decision to treat is based not just on the blood culture but also on the clinical findings.

Bacteremia Related to Damaged Mucosa. With the increasing importance of mucositis, several investigators have drawn attention to the significance of viridans streptococci,[84] especially in patients who prophylactically receive oral quinolones, which enhance the survival of these bacteria on damaged mucous membranes.[24–28, 32] On the other hand, the signs and symptoms of viridans streptococcal infection might be inconspicuous to completely absent. In view of the direct correlation between the rate of positive blood cultures and the severity of damage to the mucosal surface, the normal habitat for these organisms, it is questionable whether viridans streptococci are true pathogens in all cases or whether they represent only an epiphenomenon.[6, 85] In fact, during the course of a normal day, the acts of chewing and teeth brushing lead to transient bacteremia caused mainly by viridans streptococci. In view of the extent of the damage in many cases, it is not surprising that next to streptococci, *Clostridium perfringens* and *C. septicum* septicemia, classically with massive hemolysis and diffuse intravascular coagulation, can arise during mucositis.[69] In patients with profuse diarrhea and severe abdominal pain in combination with virtually absent audible bowel sounds, recovery of *C. septicum* from the blood may confirm the diagnosis of typhlitis.[86]

Miscellaneous Infections

The risk of overwhelming sepsis some time during life in patients with a hematologic malignancy who have undergone splenectomy and in those who are long-term survivors of a bone marrow transplant is approximately 5%. Children are especially at high risk for life-threatening sepsis. Encapsulated bacteria such as *S. pneumoniae* and *H. influenzae* are the prevalent pathogens because they are able to elude phagocytosis; *Neisseria meningitidis* and staphylococci are occasionally encountered under these circumstances.

Patients with deficient cell-mediated immunity may be unable to cope with intracellular pathogens such as *Listeria monocytogenes, P. carinii*, or *Toxoplasma gondii*. Furthermore, reactivation of dormant organisms such as herpesviruses has been observed, as well as increased susceptibility to other viruses, mycobacteria including *Mycobacterium avium* and *M. kansasii, Cryptococcus neoformans, Aspergillus* spp., and in the United States, *Histoplasma capsulatum* and *Coccidioides immitis*. Higher awareness and better diagnostic capabilities have been important factors in recognizing the increased incidence of these hitherto infrequently reported infections. Varicella-zoster virus infections range from dermatomal localization to widely disseminated infection. A recently treated patient with Hodgkin's disease has a nearly 25% likelihood of the development of dermatomal lesions from herpes zoster, and some patients will have disseminated infection.

The Systemic Inflammatory Response Syndrome and Sepsis

Although neutropenic patients cannot mount a normal host response to tissue injury, the systemic inflammatory response syndrome and sepsis can and do develop when inflammation is uncontrolled and proinflammatory substances spread to other distant sites, ultimately leading to multiple organ dysfunction.[87]

Sepsis syndromes are not always the result of endotoxemia or even infection and can be brought about by noninfective tissue injury such as severe burns, acute pancreatitis, elective surgery and trauma.[2] They might also result from extensive mucositis inasmuch as the levels of some proinflammatory cytokines, particularly interleukin-6, are elevated after chemotherapy and conditioning therapy for hematopoietic stem cell transplantation; tumor necrosis factor-α levels may not be elevated under these conditions.[88]

SEQUENTIAL INFECTIVE EVENTS

The sequence of risk factors (Fig. 298–3) determines to a large extent the order of infectious events in granulocytopenic cancer

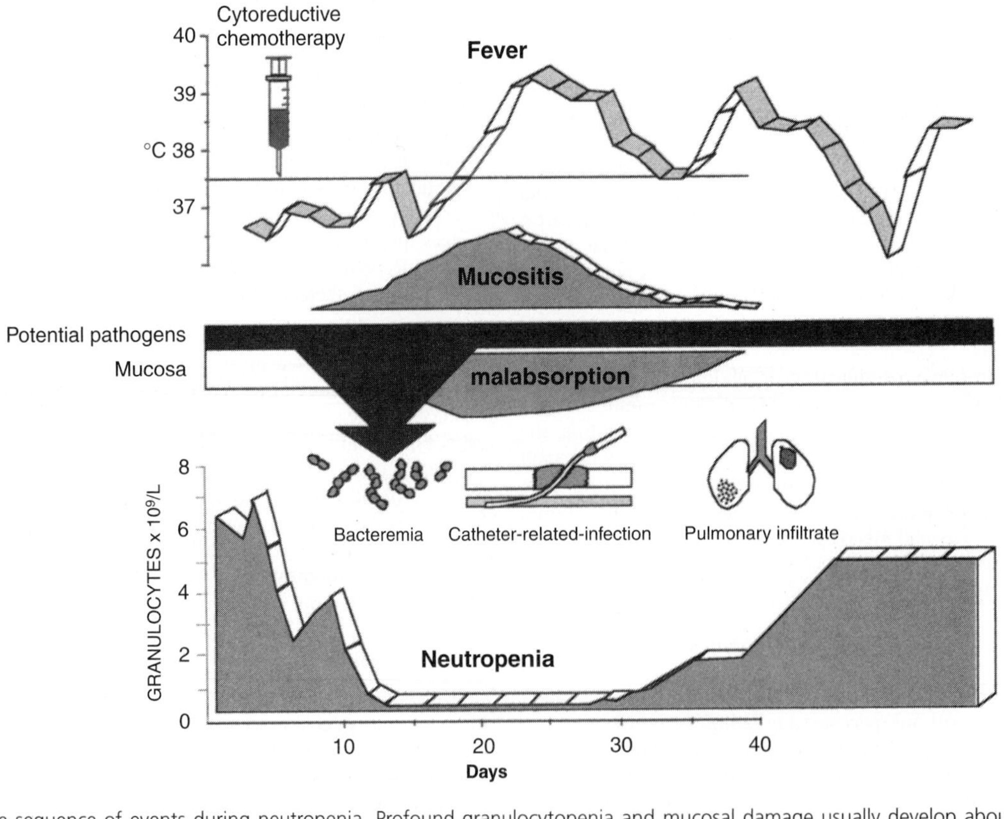

FIGURE 298–3. The sequence of events during neutropenia. Profound granulocytopenia and mucosal damage usually develop about a week after the start of cytoreductive chemotherapy. Thereafter, infectious and other complications tend to coincide with one another, placing the patient at most risk. Fever develops around a week later, and, if there is bacteremia, it mostly occurs at this time. The risk of infections related to the central venous catheters increases with the length of time that the catheter is left in place, but signs and symptoms usually manifest themselves during the first few days of fever, that is, during the third week after starting chemotherapy. Infectious complications related to the lung tend to occur a few days later, often being recognized only after 5 to 6 days of fever. The period of risk of bacterial and fungal infection diminishes with recovery of the granulocytes when the clinical manifestations of tissue infections may be temporarily exacerbated before finally resolving.

patients, which means that the types of infection occurring early in the granulocytopenic period differ from late infectious complications. Profound granulocytopenia and mucosal damage usually ensue about 10 days after initiating a course of chemotherapy and are followed by fever and bacteremia within a few days when toxicity is at its most pronounced. Clinically defined infections usually lag behind by a few days. Invasive pulmonary aspergillosis develops in few patients early in the course of granulocytopenia.[89] Infections related to central venous catheters have to be considered about 10 days after their insertion, with the risk increasing with the length of time that the catheter is left in place.[12]

The initial risk period resolves with recovery of the granulocyte count. Very intensively treated patients are still at risk because of other impaired defense mechanisms such as granulocytopathy, deficient cell-mediated immunity, and hypogammaglobulinemia. The kind of infectious complications for such patients is determined by the pace of reconstitution of these other components of the immune system. The major factor that influences immunologic reconstitution after allogeneic bone marrow transplantation is acute graft-versus-host disease and its treatment.[90] Cytomegalovirus, adenovirus, and fungi, including *P. carinii,* constitute the major pathogens during this episode. A third major risk period in these patients begins approximately 3 months after the procedure, at the time that chronic graft-versus-host disease develops. Sinopulmonary infections and cutaneous infections are common and probably related to the IgA deficiency with or without sicca syndrome and severely impaired cellular immunity. Varicella zoster is probably the most frequent cutaneous infection, and pulmonary infections caused by cytomegalovirus and *P. carinii* are regularly encountered. Months, if not years after successful engraftment or recovery from other very aggressive treatment, encapsulated organisms can cause rapidly fatal bacteremia and severe respiratory infections because of the lack of opsonizing antibodies.

PREVENTION OF INFECTION

Hygiene

High concentrations of pathogens in combination with poor hygiene are the traditional sources of infection, but isolation of patients in a sterile environment in combination with total decontamination and sterile food has been abandoned. It is expensive and a burden to the patients' quality of life, does not improve the survival rate, and discourages attempts at proper diagnosis. Organisms such as *L. pneumophila, P. aeruginosa,* and *Aeromonas hydrophila* can reach potentially dangerous concentrations in watery environments such as air-conditioning systems, sinks, bathrooms, and water for cut flowers and plants. Many centers do not allow flowers or home-cooked food in patients' rooms. Regular surveillance cultures of the environment may help identify reservoirs for potential pathogens such as *Pseudomonas* spp. in sink drains or enteric bacteria in foodstuffs, although such cultures are of value only when done in the context of an infection-control program that has clear goals. Ordinarily, this measure is prompted by prior nosocomial infections thought to be from that source. Laminar airflow or high-efficiency particulate air–filtered rooms can be recommended as an adjunct to care, particularly in bone marrow transplant units and oncology units with an increased incidence of mold infections. Recognition of possible transmission of infectious agents by blood products should lead to prudent use and careful screening of donors. Although it is obvious that sources of infection within the hospital and the patient's home should be eliminated as far as possible, masks, gowns, and gloves are not required unless a given individual has a specific indication, such as the carriage of resistant, virulent organisms. On the other hand, adequate hand washing or disinfection by visitors, nurses, doctors, and other personnel remains of paramount importance for reducing infection, and its neglect undermines all other, more sophisticated means of achieving optimal hygiene. Signs at oncology or bone marrow transplant ward entrances asking visitors not to enter if they have a cough or rhinorrhea may be indicated, particularly when viral influenza is in the community.

Prophylaxis

Whether patients with hypogammaglobulinemia from chronic lymphocytic leukemia should routinely receive replacement with intravenous immune globulin has been a matter of debate. A cost-effectiveness analysis has suggested that indiscriminate substitution might not result in improved quality or length of life in this patient group and that it is extraordinarily expensive.[91] However, such a decision analysis model cannot be applied to an individual patient who has actually suffered from recurrent bacterial infections. It seems reasonable to institute immune globulin prophylaxis in patients who have recovered from *S. pneumoniae* or *H. influenzae* infections and who have greatly decreased serum IgG concentrations.

Because of the risk of pneumococcal infection after splenectomy, immunization with a polyvalent pneumococcal vaccine is recommended, preferably before splenectomy to ensure a better immune response. Vaccination against pneumococcal, *H. influenzae,* and hepatitis B infection is feasible in patients with hematologic malignancies, but the response to vaccines may be suboptimal in those with preexisting immune deficiencies. Patient-initiated treatment with oral amoxicillin at the onset of fever is considered a suitable alternative or useful addition to vaccination in splenectomized patients.

Intravenous immune globulin, which is hyperimmune against herpes zoster, can be used to protect immunosuppressed patients who have been exposed to chickenpox or a dermatomal zoster if the patient has no history of chickenpox or no serum antibody (see Chapter 297). Commercially available hyperimmune antibody against respiratory syncytial virus is useful to protect children after a known hospital exposure. Although the globulin is only approved for otherwise healthy children younger than 2 years, it seems reasonable to use it for older immunosuppressed children known to have been exposed to the virus (see Chapter 148).

Hematopoietic growth factors do not prevent neutropenia per se but can shorten its duration. Usage should be restricted to high-risk populations, as detailed in Chapter 37.

Chemoprophylaxis is a compelling option to many, given the limitations in diagnosing an infection in an immunocompromised host at an early, easily curable stage. However, this issue is far from straightforward and divides opinions of specialists into two extremes ranging from those who believe that the benefit far outweighs the costs and those who remain skeptical and eschew any form of prophylaxis. Large, randomized trials on this subject are still scarce, and historical controls are wholly unsuitable for assessing the efficacy of prophylaxis strategies because the risk of infection, antitumor regimens, and ancillary medical practices fluctuate with time. It is also often the case that the centers with a high incidence of a particular infection are those most interested in developing new prophylactic schemes, which makes the results obtained look more impressive than they actually are.

Although mupirocin ointment is very effective against nasal carriage of *S. aureus* and skin colonization by gram-negative bacilli can be suppressed by applying povidone-iodine or chlorhexidine, the efficacy of specific chemoprophylaxis of the skin has never been demonstrated and is therefore rarely practiced.

The use of antibiotics for prophylaxis against bacterial infections has gained wide acceptance. In spite of an apparent reduction in the number of cases with bacteremia, morbidity and mortality at the end of a prolonged granulocytopenic episode are similar regardless of whether prophylactic antibacterial agents are given (Fig. 298–4). Furthermore, oral mucositis and gastritis often reduce the patient's compliance with all oral antibiotics. The occurrence of resistance should encourage a more circumspect attitude rather than the unrestricted, impetuous administration of prophylactic agents.[92]

Two major studies in patients undergoing bone marrow trans-

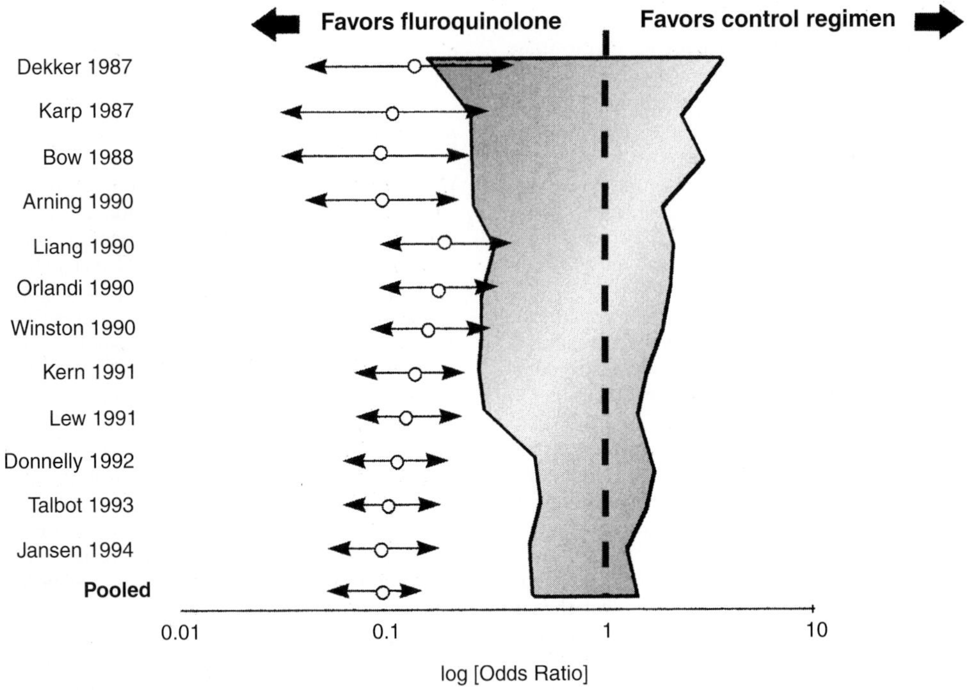

FIGURE 298–4. A meta-analysis of the effect of fluoroquinolone prophylaxis on bacterial infections in neutropenic patients. The effectiveness of fluoroquinolones in preventing bacterial infections in granulocytopenic patients who received chemotherapy for malignancies was assessed by Cruciani et al. The results depicted are based on the results of the 19 randomized studies that compared a fluoroquinolone (n = 619) with a control regimen (n = 536; trimethoprim-sulfamethoxazole, oral nonabsorbable antibiotics, or placebo). The fluoroquinolones alone were effective in preventing gram-negative *(open circles)* bacteremia but not gram-positive bacteremia (odds ratio [OR] = 1.05; 0.76–1.45; P = 0.7), fever-related morbidity (OR = 0.76; 0.56–1.04; P = 0.09), or infection-related mortality (OR = 0.79; 0.47–1.34; P = 0.4) (all points within the shaded area). (From Cruciani M, Rampazzo R, Malena M, et al. Prophylaxis with fluoroquinolones for bacterial infections in neutropenic patients: A meta-analysis. Clin Infect Dis. 1996;23:795–805. Copyright 1996, Infectious Diseases Society of America.)

plantation showed that fluconazole at a dose of 400 mg once daily was effective in preventing superficial and deep candidiasis and in one study it also reduced overall mortality.[93, 94] Other, smaller studies suggest that a lower dose of 150 to 200 mg might also be effective.[95, 96] Fluconazole treatment was free of serious adverse events apart from the tendency to select resistant *Candida* spp.[97, 98] However, the benefits of fluconazole were not evident in adults receiving remission induction therapy for acute leukemia.[99, 100] Fluconazole offers no protection against *Aspergillus* spp. and other molds. Itraconazole is often considered as an alternative, but little evidence supports its use for the prevention of either candidiasis or aspergillosis in neutropenic patients. In a randomized double-blind study, the capsule form at a dosage of 400 mg daily neither reduced the incidence of *Aspergillus* infections nor influenced the perceived need for treatment with intravenous amphotericin B in leukemic patients.[101] Amphotericin B sprays and inhalation, as well as reduced intravenous doses, have been used for prophylaxis. Although tolerance seems to be acceptable, the efficacy of these strategies is not convincing.[102, 103]

In the absence of supporting data, one could attempt to identify patients who are at increased risk of a deep mycosis and use a prophylactic regimen that might be effective against the anticipated mycosis. Risk groups for deep candidiasis include, but are not limited to patients who are heavily colonized by *Candida* spp.,[104] patients with long-standing mucosal lesions, and those who are being treated with broad-spectrum antibacterial agents. Patients with a history of an invasive fungal infection during a previous neutropenic episode are at risk of relapse, and febrile adult recipients of allogeneic bone marrow transplants who are seropositive for cytomegalovirus and suffer from graft-versus-host disease are prone to deep mycoses.[19, 105] Therapeutic doses of intravenous amphotericin B are required to protect patients with previous aspergillosis against recrudescence during hematopoietic stem cell transplantation.[106] Whether the increased bioavailability of itraconazole suspension as compared with the capsule formulation will permit the drug to be used in a more immunocompetent patient remains to be determined. Increased itraconazole blood levels come at the price of increased interactions with cyclosporine and tacrolimus and necessitate vigilance to prevent toxicity.

P. carinii has virtually been eliminated as a significant pathogen by the use of prophylactic trimethoprim-sulfamethoxazole 2 days a week.[107]

Acyclovir given orally as 400 mg four times daily constitutes effective prophylaxis against herpes simplex virus and varicella-zoster virus infections. Use is often restricted to immunosuppressed patients with serologic or clinical evidence of prior herpes simplex or varicella-zoster virus infection. It is not clear whether such use really represents an advantage for the prevention of varicella-zoster virus infections because reactivation frequently happens after cessation of acyclovir therapy. There is a suggestion that infections might be less severe in patients who had previously taken acyclovir prophylaxis. Prophylaxis with acyclovir against herpesviruses is advocated by many centers for the first 9 months after bone marrow transplantation or during chronic graft-versus-host disease and concomitant administration of the immunosuppressive agents used for its treatment.

REFERENCES

1. Bodey GP, Buckley M, Sathe YS, Freireich EJ: Quantitative relationships between circulating leukocytes and infection in patients with acute leukemia. Ann Intern Med. 1966;64:328–340.
2. Bone RC. The pathogenesis of sepsis. Ann Intern Med. 1991;115:457–469.

3. Carlisle H, Saslaw S: Properdin levels in splenectomized persons. Proc Soc Exp Biol Med. 1959;102:150–155.
4. Van der Meer J: Defects in host defense mechanisms. In: Rubin R, Young LS, eds. Current Approaches to Infection in the Compromised Host. New York: Plenum; 1994:33–66.
5. Van der Waaij D: Effect of antibiotics on colonization resistance. In: Easmon CS, ed. Medical Microbiology. London: Academic; 1984:227–237.
6. Donnelly JP: Chemoprophylaxis for the prevention of bacterial and fungal infections. Cancer Treat Res. 1995;79:45–81.
7. Roth RR, James WD: Microbial ecology of the skin. Annu Rev Microbiol. 1988;42:441–464.
8. Kotilainen P, Nikoskelainen J, Huovinen P: Emergence of ciprofloxacin-resistant coagulase-negative staphylococcal skin flora in immunocompromised patients receiving ciprofloxacin. J Infect Dis. 1990;161:41–44.
9. Høiby N, Johansen HK. Ciprofloxacin in sweat and antibiotic resistance. The Copenhagen Study Group on Antibiotics in Sweat (Letter). Lancet. 1995;346:1235.
10. Høiby N, Jarløv JO, Kemp M, et al. Excretion of ciprofloxacin in sweat and multiresistant *Staphylococcus epidermidis.* Lancet. 1997;349:167–169.
11. Weightman NC, Simpson EM, Speller DCE, et al. Bacteraemia related to indwelling central venous catheters: Prevention, diagnosis and treatment. Eur J Clin Microbiol Infect Dis. 1988;7:125–129.
12. Raad II, Bodey GP: Infectious complications of indwelling vascular catheters. Clin Infect Dis. 1992;15:197–208.
13. Hedin G, Hambraeus A: Multiply antibiotic-resistant *Staphylococcus epidermidis* in patients, staff and environment—a one-week survey in a bone marrow transplant unit. J Hosp Infect. 1991;17:95–106.
14. Groeger JS, Lucas AB, Thaler HT, et al. Infectious morbidity associated with long-term use of venous access devices in patients with cancer. Ann Intern Med. 1993;119:1168–1174.
15. Salzman MB, Isenberg HD, Shapiro JF, et al. A prospective study of the catheter hub as the portal of entry for microorganisms causing catheter-related sepsis in neonates. J Infect Dis. 1993;167:487–490.
16. De Pauw BE, Novakova IR, Donnelly JP: Options and limitations of teicoplanin in febrile granulocytopenic patients. Br J Haematol. 1990;2:1–5.
17. Weems JJ: *Candida parapsilosis:* Epidemiology, pathogenicity, clinical manifestations and antibiotic susceptibility. Clin Infect Dis. 1992;14:756–766.
18. Lecciones JA, Lee JW, Navarro EE, et al. Vascular catheter–associated fungemia in patients with cancer: Analysis of 155 episodes. Clin Infect Dis. 1992;14:875–883.
19. Morrison VA, Haake RJ, Weisdorf DJ: Non-*Candida* fungal infections after bone marrow transplantation: Risk factors and outcome. Am J Med. 1994;96:497–503.
20. Meurman JH, Laine P, Murtomaa H, et al. Effect of antiseptic mouthwashes on some clinical and microbiological findings in the mouths of lymphoma patients receiving cytostatic drugs. J Clin Periodontol. 1991;18:587–591.
21. Weisdorf DJ, Bostrom B, Raether D, et al. Oropharyngeal mucositis complicating bone marrow transplantation: Prognostic factors and the effect of chlorhexidine mouth rinse. Bone Marrow Transplant. 1989;4:89–95.
22. Ferretti GA, Ash RC, Brown AT, et al. Chlorhexidine for prophylaxis against oral infections and associated complications in patients receiving bone marrow transplants. J Am Dent Assoc. 1987;114:461–467.
23. Van der Lelie H, Van Ketel RJ, Von dem Borne AEGK, et al. Incidence and clinical epidemiology of streptococcal septicemia during treatment of acute myeloid leukemia. Scand J Infect Dis. 1991;23:163–168.
24. Bochud PY, Calandra T, Francioli P: Bacteremia due to viridans streptococci in neutropenic patients: A review. Am J Med. 1994;97:256–264.
25. Elting LS, Bodey GP, Keefe BH: Septicemia and shock syndrome due to viridans streptococci: A case-control study of predisposing factors. Clin Infect Dis. 1992;14:1201–1207.
26. Dybedal I, Lamvik J: Respiratory insufficiency in acute leukemia following treatment with cytosine arabinoside and septicemia with *Streptococcus viridans.* Eur J Haematol. 1989;42:405–406.
27. Kern W, Kurrle E, Schmeiser T: Streptococcal bacteremia in adult patients with leukemia undergoing aggressive chemotherapy: A review of 55 cases. Infection. 1990;18:138–145.
28. Dompeling EC, Donnelly JP, Raemaekers JM, De Pauw BE: Pre-emptive administration of corticosteroids prevents the development of ARDS associated with *Streptococcus mitis* bacteremia following chemotherapy with high-dose cytarabine. Ann Hematol. 1994;69:69–71.
29. Peters WG, Willemze R, Colly LP, Guiot HFL: Side effects of intermediate- and high-dose cytosine arabinoside in the treatment of refractory or relapsed acute leukaemia and non-Hodgkins lymphoma. Neth J Med. 1987;30:64–74.
30. Guiot HFL, Biemond J, Klasen E, et al. Protein loss during acute graft-versus-host disease: Diagnostics and clinical significance. Eur J Haematol. 1987;38:187–196.
31. Callum JL, Brandwein JM, Sutcliffe SB, et al. Influence of total body irradiation on infections after autologous bone marrow transplantation. Bone Marrow Transplant. 1991;8:245–251.
32. De Pauw BE, Donnelly JP, De Witte T, et al. Options and limitations of long-term oral ciprofloxacin as antibacterial prophylaxis in allogeneic bone marrow transplant recipients. Bone Marrow Transplant. 1990;5:179–182.
33. Classen DC, Burke JP, Ford CD, et al. *Streptococcus mitis* sepsis in bone marrow transplant patients receiving oral antimicrobial prophylaxis. Am J Med. 1990;89:441–446.
34. McWhinney PHM, Gillespie SH, Kibbler CC, et al. *Streptococcus mitis* and ARDS in neutropenic patients. Lancet 1991;337:429.
35. Bilgrami S, Bergstrom SK, Peterson DE, et al. *Capnocytophaga* bacteremia in a patient with Hodgkin's disease following bone marrow transplantation: Case report and review. Clin Infect Dis. 1992;14:1045–1049.
36. Weers-Pothoff G, Novakova IR, Donnelly JP, Muytjens HL: Bacteraemia caused by *Stomatococcus mucilaginosus* in a granulocytopenic patient with acute lymphocytic leukaemia. Neth J Med. 1989;35:143–146.
37. Bow EJ, Loewen R, Cheang MS, et al. Cytotoxic therapy–induced D-xylose malabsorption and invasive infection during remission-induction therapy for acute myeloid leukemia in adults. J Clin Oncol. 1997;15:2254–2261.
38. Bow EJ, Loewen R, Cheang MS, Schacter B: Invasive fungal disease in adults undergoing remission-induction therapy for acute myeloid leukemia: The pathogenetic role of the antileukemic regimen. Clin Infect Dis. 1995;21:361–369.
39. Fegan C, Poynton JA, Whittaker JA: The gut mucosal barrier in bone marrow transplantation. Bone Marrow Transplant. 1990;5:373–377.
40. Johansson JE, Ekman T: Gastro-intestinal toxicity related to bone marrow transplantation: Disruption of the intestinal barrier precedes clinical findings. Bone Marrow Transplant. 1997;19:921–925.
41. Keefe DM, Cummins AG, Dale BM, et al. Effect of high-dose chemotherapy on intestinal permeability in humans. Clin Sci. 1997;92:385–389.
42. Tancrede CH, Andremont AO: Bacterial translocation and gram-negative bacteremia in patients with hematological malignancies. J Infect Dis. 1985;152:99–103.
43. Brown NM, White LO, Blundell EL, et al. Absorption of oral ofloxacin after cytotoxic chemotherapy for haematological malignancy. J Antimicrob Chemother. 1993;32:117–122.
44. Johnson EJ, MacGowan AP, Potter MN, et al. Reduced absorption of oral ciprofloxacin after chemotherapy for haematological malignancy. J Antimicrob Chemother. 1990;25:837–842.
45. Prentice AG, Warnock DW, Johnson SA, et al. Multiple dose pharmacokinetics of an oral solution of itraconazole in autologous bone marrow transplant recipients. J Antimicrob Chemother. 1994;34:247–252.
46. Donnelly JP, Muus P, Schattenberg A, et al. A scheme for daily monitoring of oral mucositis in allogeneic BMT recipients. Bone Marrow Transplant. 1992;9:409–413.
47. Raemaekers J, De Witte T, Schattenberg A, Van Der Lely N: Prevention of leukaemic relapse after transplantation with lymphocyte-depleted marrow by intensification of the conditioning regimen with a 6-day continuous infusion of anthracyclines. Bone Marrow Transplant. 1989;4:167–171.
48. Schuster MW: Granulocyte-macrophage colony-stimulating factor (GM-CSF)—what role in bone marrow transplantation. Infection. 1992;20(Suppl):S95–S99.
49. Bronchud M: Can hematopoietic growth factors be used to improve the success of cytotoxic chemotherapy. Anticancer Drugs. 1993;4:127–139.
50. McGuire DB, Altomonte V, Peterson DE, et al. Patterns of mucositis and pain in patients receiving preparative chemotherapy and bone marrow transplantation. Oncol Nurs Forum. 1993;20:1493–1502.
51. Sable CA, Donowitz GR: Infections in bone marrow transplant recipients. Clin Infect Dis. 1994;18:273–281.
52. Kolbinson DA, Schubert MM, Fluornoy N, Truelove EL: Early oral changes following bone marrow transplantation. Oral Surg Oral Med Oral Pathol. 1988;66:130–138.
53. Rocke LK, Loprinzi CL, Lee JK, et al. A randomized clinical trial of two different durations of oral cryotherapy for prevention of 5-fluorouracil related stomatitis. Cancer. 1993;72:2234–2238.
54. Donnelly JP, Maschmeyer G, Daenen S: Selective oral antimicrobial prophylaxis for the prevention of infection in acute leukaemia—ciprofloxacin versus co-trimoxazole plus colistin. The EORTC-Gnotobiotic Project Group. Eur J Cancer. 1992;28A:873–878.
55. Van der Waaij D: The ecology of the human intestine and its consequences for overgrowth by pathogens such as *Clostridium difficile.* Annu Rev Microbiol. 1989;43:69–87.
56. Freifeld AG, Walsh T, Marshall D, et al. Monotherapy for fever and neutropenia in cancer patients: A randomized comparison of ceftazidime versus imipenem. J Clin Oncol. 1995;13:165–176.
57. Schimpff SC: Infection prevention during profound granulocytopenia: New approaches to alimentary canal microbial suppression. Ann Intern Med. 1980;93:358–361.
58. Van Der Waaij D: The colonization resistance of the digestive tract of man and animals. In: Fliedner TM, ed. Clinical and Experimental Gnotobiotics, Zbl Bakt. New York: Gustav Fischer Verlag; 1979.
59. Louie TJ, Chubb H, Bow EJ, et al. Preservation of colonization resistance parameters during empiric therapy with aztreonam in febrile neutropenic patient. Rev Infect Dis. 1985;7(Suppl):S747–S761.
60. Meijer-Severs GJ, Van Santen E: Short-chain fatty acids and succinate in feces of healthy human volunteers and their correlation with anaerobic cultural counts. J Gastroenterol. 1987;22:672–676.
61. McGeer A, Feld R: Epidemiology of infection in immunocompromised oncological patients. In: Glauser M, Calandra T, eds. Baillière's Clinical Infectious Diseases. Philadelphia: Ballière Tindall; 1994:415–438.
62. Beattie G, Whelan J, Cassidy J, et al. Herpes simplex virus, *Candida albicans* and mouth ulcers in neutropenic patients with non-haematological malignancy. Cancer Chemother Pharmacol. 1989;25:75–76.
63. Bergmann OJ: Oral infections in haematological patients—pathogenesis and clinical significance. Dan Med Bull. 1992;39:15–29.
64. Viscoli C, Bruzzi P, Castagnola E, et al. Factors associated with bacteraemia in febrile, granulocytopenic cancer patients. The International Antimicrobial Therapy Cooperative Group (IATCG) of the European Organization for Research and Treatment of Cancer (EORTC). Eur J Cancer. 1994;4:430–437.

65. Rubin J, Yu VL: Malignant external otitis: Insights into pathogenesis, clinical manifestations, diagnosis, and therapy. Am J Med. 1988;85:391–398.
66. Boelaert J, de Locht M, Van Cutsem J: Mucormycosis during desferrioxamine therapy is a siderophore-mediated infection. In vitro and in vivo animal studies. J Clin Invest. 1993;91:1979–1986.
67. Sickles EA, Greene WH, Wiernik PH: Clinical presentation of infection in granulocytopenic patients. Arch Intern Med. 1975;135:715–719.
68. Young LS: Antimicrobial prophylaxis against infection in neutropenic patients. J Infect Dis. 1983;147:611–614.
69. Pouwels MJ, Donnelly JP, Raemaekers JM, et al. *Clostridium septicum* sepsis and neutropenic enterocolitis in a patient treated with intensive chemotherapy for acute myeloid leukemia. Ann Hematol. 1997;74:143–147.
70. Novakova IR, Donnelly JP, De Pauw B: Potential sites of infection that develop in febrile neutropenic patients. Leuk Lymphoma. 1993;10:461–467.
71. Caillot D, Casasnovas O, Bernard A, et al. Improved management of invasive pulmonary aspergillosis in neutropenic patients using early thoracic computed tomographic scan and surgery. J Clin Oncol. 1997;15:139–147.
72. Manian FA: A prospective study of daily measurement of C-reactive protein in serum of adults with neutropenia. Clin Infect Dis. 1995;21:114–121.
73. De Bel C, Gerritsen E, De Maaker G, et al. C-reactive protein in the management of children with fever after allogeneic bone marrow transplantation. Infection. 1991;19:92–96.
74. Rintala E, Irjala K, Nikoskelainen J: Value of measurement of C-reactive protein in febrile patients with hematological malignancies. Eur J Clin Microbial Infect Dis. 1992;11:973–978.
75. Santolaya ME, Cofre J, Beresi V: C-reactive protein: A valuable aid for the management of febrile children with cancer and neutropenia. Clin Infect Dis. 1994;18:589–595.
76. Ligtenberg PC, Hoepelman IM, Oude Sogtoen GAC, et al. C-reactive protein in the diagnosis and management of infections in granulocytopenic and non-granulocytopenic patients. Eur J Clin Microbiol Infect Dis. 1991;10:25–31.
77. Riikonen P, Saarinen UM, Teppo AM, et al. Cytokine and acute-phase reactant levels in serum of children with cancer admitted for fever and neutropenia. J Infect Dis. 1992;166:432–436.
78. Mermel LA, Maki DG: Detection of bacteremia in adults: Consequences of culturing an inadequate volume of blood. Ann Intern Med. 1993;119:270–272.
79. Verweij PE, Donnelly JP, De Pauw BE, Meis JFGM: Prospects for the early diagnosis of invasive aspergillosis in the immunocompromised host. Rev Med Microbiol. 1996;7:105–113.
80. Walsh TJ, Lee JW, Sien T, et al. Serum D-arabinitol measured by automated quantitative enzymatic assay for detection and therapeutic monitoring of experimental disseminated candidiasis: Correlation with tissue concentrations of *Candida albicans*. J Med Vet Mycol. 1994;32:205–215.
81. Walsh TJ, Hathorn JW, Sobel JD, et al. Detection of circulating candida enolase by immunoassay in patients with cancer and invasive candidiasis. N Engl J Med. 1991;324:1026–1031.
82. Obayashi T, Yoshida M, Mori T, et al. Plasma (1⟶3)-beta-D-glucan measurement in diagnosis of invasive deep mycosis and fungal febrile episodes. Lancet. 1995;345:17–20.
83. The EORTC International Antimicrobial Therapy Cooperative Group: Gram-positive bacteraemia in granulocytopenic cancer patients. Eur J Cancer. 1990;26:569–574.
84. Villablanca JG, Steiner M, Kersey J, et al. The clinical spectrum of infections with viridans streptococci in bone marrow transplant patients. Bone Marrow Transplant. 1990;5:387–393.
85. Donnelly JP, Muus P, Horrevorts AM, et al. Failure of clindamycin to influence the course of severe oromucositis associated with streptococcal bacteraemia in allogeneic bone marrow transplant recipients. Scand J Infect Dis. 1993;25:43–50.
86. Johnson S, Driks MR, Tweten RK, et al. Clinical courses of seven survivors of *Clostridium septicum* infection and their immunologic responses to α-toxin. Clin Infect Dis. 1994;19:761–764.
87. Soto A, Evans TJ, Cohen J: Proinflammatory cytokine production by human peripheral blood mononuclear cells stimulated with cell-free supernatants of viridans streptococci. Cytokine. 1996;8:300–304.
88. Pechumer H, Wilhelm M, Zieglerheitbrock HWL: Interleukin-6 (IL-6) levels in febrile children during maximal aplasia after bone marrow transplantation (BMT) are similar to those in children with normal hematopoiesis. Ann Hematol. 1995;70:309–312.
89. Gerson SL, Talbot GH, Hurwitz S, et al. Prolonged granulocytopenia: The major risk factor for invasive pulmonary aspergillosis in patients with acute leukemia. Ann Intern Med. 1984;100:345–351.
90. Meyers JD: Infection in bone marrow transplant recipients. Am J Med. 1986;81:27–38.
91. Weeks JC, Tierney MR, Weinstein MC: Cost effectiveness of prophylactic intravenous immune globulin in chronic lymphocytic leukemia. N Engl J Med. 1991;325:81–86.
92. Cruciani M, Rampazzo R, Malena M, et al. Prophylaxis with fluoroquinolones for bacterial infections in neutropenic patients: A meta-analysis. Clin Infect Dis. 1996;23:795–805.
93. Slavin MA, Osborne B, Adams R, et al. Efficacy and safety of fluconazole prophylaxis for fungal infections after marrow transplantation—a prospective, randomized, double-blind study. J Infect Dis. 1995;171:1545–1552.
94. Goodman JL, Winston DJ, Greenfield RA, et al. A controlled trial of fluconazole to prevent fungal infections in patients undergoing bone marrow transplantation. N Engl J Med. 1992;326:845–851.
95. Alangaden G, Chandrasekar PH, Bailey E, Khaliq Y: Antifungal prophylaxis with low-dose fluconazole during bone marrow transplantation. The Bone Marrow Transplantation Team. Bone Marrow Transplant. 1994;14:919–924.
96. Ellis ME, Clink H, Ernst P, et al. Controlled study of fluconazole in the prevention of fungal infections in neutropenic patients with haematological malignancies and bone marrow transplant recipients. Eur J Clin Microbiol Infect Dis. 1994;13:3–11.
97. Wingard JR, Merz WG, Rinaldi MG, et al. Increase in *Candida krusei* infection among patients with bone marrow transplantation and neutropenia treated prophylactically with fluconazole. N Engl J Med. 1991;325:1274–1277.
98. Wingard JR, Merz WG, Rinaldi MG, et al. Association of *Torulopsis glabrata* infections with fluconazole prophylaxis in neutropenic bone marrow transplant patients. Antimicrob Agents Chemother. 1993;37:1847–1849.
99. Winston DJ, Chandrasekar PH, Lazarus HM, et al. Fluconazole prophylaxis of fungal infections in patients with acute leukemia. Results of a randomized placebo-controlled, double-blind, multicenter trial. Ann Intern Med. 1993;118:495–503.
100. Menichetti F, Del Favero A, Martino P, et al. Preventing fungal infection in neutropenic patients with acute leukemia: Fluconazole compared with oral amphotericin B. The GIMEMA Infection Program. Ann Intern Med. 1994;120:913–918.
101. Vreugdenhil G, Van Dijke BJ, Donnelly JP, et al. Efficacy of itraconazole in the prevention of fungal infections among neutropenic patients with hematologic malignancies and intensive chemotherapy. A double blind, placebo controlled study. Leuk Lymphoma. 1993;11:353–358.
102. Behre GF, Schwartz S, Lenz K, et al. Aerosol amphotericin B inhalations for prevention of invasive pulmonary aspergillosis in neutropenic cancer patients. Ann Hematol. 1995;71:287–291.
103. Perfect JR, Klotman ME, Gilbert CC, et al. Prophylactic intravenous amphotericin B in neutropenic autologous bone marrow transplant recipients. J Infect Dis. 1992;165:891–897.
104. Guiot HF, Fibbe WE, van't Wout JW: Risk factors for fungal infection in patients with malignant hematologic disorders: Implications for empirical therapy and prophylaxis. Clin Infect Dis. 1994;18:525–532.
105. Robertson MJ, Larson RA: Recurrent fungal pneumonias in patients with acute nonlymphocytic leukemia undergoing multiple courses of intensive chemotherapy. Am J Med. 1988;84:233–239.
106. Karp JE, Burch PA, Merz WG: An approach to intensive antileukemia therapy in patients with previous invasive aspergillosis. Am J Med. 1988;85:203–206.
107. Hughes WT, Rivera GK, Schell MJ, et al. Successful intermittent chemoprophylaxis for *Pneumocystis carinii* pneumonitis. N Engl J Med. 1987;316:1627–1632.

Chapter 299

Infections in Patients with Acute Leukemia and Lymphoma

BEN E. DE PAUW
FRANÇOISE MEUNIER

The better prognosis of patients with acute leukemia and lymphoma over the last decade is at least partly due to the possibility of administering more intensive chemotherapy and to the successful introduction of novel procedures such as allogeneic bone marrow transplantation, autologous stem cell reinfusion, platelet transfusion, granulocyte colony-stimulating factor, implanted central venous catheters, a wider array of antimicrobials, and improvements in diagnostic imaging. Lengthened survival during periods of profound immunosuppression has made infections a common complication and expanded the number of potential pathogens.[1]

Fundamental differences between hematologic malignancies and solid tumors affect the incidence and severity of the infectious complications concerned (Table 299–1). Leukemias and lymphomas reside by definition within the immune system itself and exert a dual deleterious effect. The malignant population interferes with and supplants the immunocompetent elements at their original location. The residue of normal cells is exposed to aggressive chemotherapy, and as a result, prolonged and profound granulocytopenia emerges rapidly.[2] Within a week after the initiation of chemotherapy, fever will have developed in more than 50% of patients.[3] Mucositis has become debilitating with the implementation of new antileukemic regimens, particularly in conjunction with the use of hematopoietic

TABLE 299–1 Characteristics of Susceptibility to Infections in Patients with Acute Leukemia or Lymphoma in Contrast to Solid Tumors

Prolonged granulocytopenia
More profound granulocytopenia
Rapid onset of severe granulocytopenia
Simultaneous occurrence of granulocytopenia, mucositis, and impaired cellular immunity
More severe mucositis
More hemorrhagic diathesis of skin and mucosal tissue
More skin-penetrating venous catheters
Unpredictable pharmacokinetics of antimicrobial drugs
Changed distribution volumes
Leakage of drugs via damaged mucosal tissue
Possible concurrent impaired kidney function
Less deep organ dysfunction as result of local tumor growth
More allergic reactions to drugs, including antibiotics
More interactions with concomitant drugs

granulocyte and granulocyte-macrophage growth factors. These factors are used to ameliorate bone marrow toxicity, but in practice they allow for the prescription of high doses of cytotoxic drugs.[4] The magnitude of the risk of infection is directly related to the severity and duration of damage incurred.[5] Severe injury to the mucosa is also thought to be responsible for leakage of antibiotics and other drugs from tissue into the gastrointestinal tract. Thus, doses higher than usual are constantly needed to secure therapeutic plasma levels.[3] Hemorrhage, inevitable during the course of acute leukemia, may impede organ function and facilitate the growth of microorganisms that are coincidentally present. Hemorrhage is also a potential complication of surgical implantation of a central venous catheter in thrombocytopenic patients, and these catheters also provide an additional portal of infection.[6, 7] Deterioration of the normal immune system is presumed to be responsible for the high drug allergy rate in patients with active acute leukemia; the allergy may abate when complete remission is achieved.[8] The same phenomenon can be witnessed in patients with infectious mononucleosis or acquired immunodeficiency syndrome.

The types of infection and the offending pathogens have been well characterized. Theoretically, they ought to be quite predictable given the relationship with predisposing factors such as granulocytopenia, defects in cell-mediated immunity, splenectomy, breaks in the mucocutaneous integument, or other deficiencies in host defense mechanisms (see Chapter 298). During the 1990s, a proportional increase in the incidence of gram-positive infections has occurred along with a decrease in bacterial infection–related mortality and a worrisome increase in lethal invasive fungal infections.[9, 10] Such changes are the result of alterations in the treatment of hematologic malignancies, as well as adjusted anti-infective programs. Virtually all the modern centers that offer care for these patients now have special units to treat the most vulnerable patients, and have specialists who inform patients and their families, hospital personnel, and medical staff about measures to reduce the risk of infection. Guidelines written to instruct all people involved on what to do in case of fever or after contact with possibly infectious sources have proved useful, and higher awareness of the risk associated with negligence of fever has certainly contributed to better survival.

Remarkably, the mortality attributed to gram-negative sepsis appears to be lower in patients who are treated for leukemia than in those with an intermediate grade of malignant lymphoma or solid tumor.[11, 12] This difference could be explained by the fact that the latter patients are often treated on an outpatient basis and neither they nor their relatives might react quickly enough to fever or other symptoms indicative of infection, which could lead to a potentially hazardous delay in instituting appropriate antimicrobial therapy.

The various sites of infection, the organisms, and current approach to diagnosis and prevention are described in Chapter 298, whereas empirical therapy is discussed in detail in Chapter 300.

OCCURRENCE OF INFECTIONS IN PATIENTS WITH GRANULOCYTOPENIA AND IMPAIRED CELL-MEDIATED IMMUNITY

Patients with polymorphonuclear cell counts less than $500/mm^3$ are at immediate risk of infection, the rate of occurrence being directly correlated to the granulocyte count and the duration of granulocytopenia.[5, 13] In virtually every patient who remains granulocytopenic for more than 10 days fever will develop, and those with polymorphonuclear neutrophil counts of less than $100/mm^3$ have a direct risk of acquiring life-threatening infectious complications.[14] Therefore, close medical surveillance is essential for this category of patients. Prompt initiation of empirical antimicrobial therapy at the onset of fever is compulsory.[11, 12] Ideally, antibiotics should be administered within an hour of the first signs or symptoms of infection.[15] This systematic approach has been shown to decrease early mortality from rapidly fatal sepsis.[16]

It is impossible to reliably predict the causative pathogen at the onset of fever. In a large survey, only 17 bacteremias among a total of 909 episodes were caused by an organism that was involved in a serious infection during a previous febrile episode.[9] Despite extensive cultures, only around 30% of all febrile patients will be shown to have microbiologically defined infections[17, 18] (see Chapter 298). The first fever during a neutropenic episode often represents bacteremia by pathogens originating from the gastrointestinal tract. They may be part of the original indigenous flora or, more commonly, have been acquired during hospitalization.[19] The possibility of a febrile episode being associated with drugs such as allopurinol, antibiotics, bleomycin, and cytarabine or with the underlying disease should always be considered, but such an association is usually quite apparent.[8, 20] The course of viral infections such as hepatitis B or C or cytomegalovirus transmitted with blood products is seldom fulminant. Acute fever after transfusion is more likely to be a consequence of irregular blood group antigens or cytotoxic antibodies acquired during previous transfusions or pregnancies. Extended storage of platelets and erythrocyte suspensions, as well as inappropriate handling, has been found to be responsible for sudden fever from contamination of the blood product by bacteria.[21] If disseminated fungal infections are encountered in an early stage, they are most likely the result of a colonized central venous catheter or paranasal sinus. Fungal infections, as well as infections with resistant or unusual bacteria, do occur more often during the later phases of prolonged and profound episodes of granulocytopenia,[22, 23] which can be partly attributed to better control of regular bacterial infections so that patients live longer and can acquire other less common pathogens.

Pathogens

Bacteria and Granulocytopenia

Until the early 1980s, most observations from large studies evaluating febrile episodes in granulocytopenic patients emphasized the predominance of aerobic gram-negative bacilli.[24–27] Although the pathogens associated with the highest mortality rate are still the Enterobacteriaceae (*Escherichia coli, Klebsiella* spp., *Proteus* spp.) and *Pseudomonas aeruginosa*,[28, 29] gram-positive pathogens seem to have largely superseded gram-negative bacilli. This worldwide observation is illustrated by data derived from a series of consecutive studies with thousands of patients by the International Antimicrobial Trial Cooperative Group of the European Organization for Research and Treatment of Cancer[26, 30–35] (Table 299–2). Coagulase-negative staphylococci and streptococci principally account for the steady increase in infections with gram-positive cocci.[26, 36–40] Several factors, which vary in different circumstances, play an interchangeable dominant role in these epidemiologic changes. Prompt empirical antimicrobial therapy and prophylaxis against gram-negative rods, for example, may have caused the decrease in the rate of recovery of these

TABLE 299-2 Evolution of the Incidence of Single Gram-Negative and Single Gram-Positive Bacteremia in Febrile Granulocytopenic Patients

EORTC Trial	Bacteremia (%)	
	Gram-Negative	*Gram-Positive*
Trial I (1973–1978)	15.7	5.8
Trial II (1978–1980)	15.7	7.8
Trial III (1980–1983)	12.9	9.0
Trial IV (1983–1986)	14.5	10.1
Trial V (1986–1988)	10.5	17.7
Trial VIII (1988–1990)	6.8	15.0
Trial IX (1991–1992)	6.2	12.6
Trial X (1993–1994)	6.4	14.4

Abbreviation: EORTC, European Organization for Research in Cancer Therapy.

pathogens from blood cultures,[41, 42] whereas selective pressure by these antimicrobial agents could have facilitated the recovery of previously obscure pathogens.[43–47] The emergence of viridans streptococci may be at least partially the result of selective pressure brought about by the extensive use of fluoroquinolones.[41] In addition, most patients treated for a hematologic malignancy have at least one intravascular device, and these catheters constitute a major source of infection with skin flora, principally staphylococci.[6, 7] Severe oral mucositis has made the mouth an important origin of infection, particularly by streptococci. Indeed, a connection has been noted between high-dose cytosine arabinoside therapy for acute leukemia and the occurrence of bacteremia by viridans streptococci, often identified as *Streptococcus mitis*.[40, 48] Despite a lower overall mortality in comparison with gram-negative bacilliary sepsis, the morbidity from infections with gram-positive organisms can be substantial. *S. mitis* bacteremia may even run a rapidly fatal course when it is accompanied by shock or followed by adult respiratory distress syndrome.[48–50]

Anaerobes represent less than 1% of the bacteremic isolates in febrile granulocytopenic patients and are often part of polymicrobial infections.[51]

Bacteria Associated with Impaired Cell-Mediated Immunity

Certain pathogens are more common in patients with deficient cell-mediated immunity (see Chapter 298). The occurrence of sepsis and meningitis caused by *Listeria monocytogenes*–contaminated milk and cheese does suggest an increased risk for individuals with defective cell-mediated immunity, but hitherto a clearly increased incidence of listeriosis in patients with Hodgkin's disease or lymphoma has not been confirmed.[52] *Legionella pneumophila* is a gram-negative bacillus that requires specific staining methods and culture media for identification. Outbreaks of infection with this organism have been observed among compromised patients in units with contaminated water systems.[53] The most common signs of nocardiosis are infiltrates in the lungs and abscesses in the skin, soft tissues, or brain.[54] Infections with *Mycobacterium tuberculosis* in patients with impaired cell-mediated immunity are manifested as either localized pulmonary disease or devastating miliary tuberculosis. Nontuberculous mycobacteria are still rather rare in patients with lymphoma or leukemia, but the introduction of purine analogues such as cladribine and fludarabine, which cause severe and prolonged depression of cellular immunity, may change this picture in the near future. The impact of purine analogues on the immune system at the end of a treatment course shows a striking congruence with the deficiencies seen in patients with acquired immunodeficiency syndrome or in those who are treated for graft-versus-host disease after allogeneic bone marrow transplantation.

Fungi and Granulocytopenia

Invasive fungal infections are encountered in up to 40% of autopsies in patients with hematologic malignancies.[55] Fungi have been found to be responsible for two thirds of all superinfections, which are infections emerging during broad-spectrum antibiotic treatment of neutropenic patients.[23] Nowadays, in several centers candidemia appears more frequently than does gram-negative bacilliary bacteremia. Previous exposure to antimicrobial agents, corticosteroid therapy, central venous catheters, total parenteral nutrition, and impaired cell-mediated immunity have all been recognized as predisposing factors. Invasive mycoses in patients with acute leukemia or lymphoma are mainly the result of persisting granulocytopenia because polymorphonuclear leukocytes play a crucial role in controlling these infections.[22, 56–58]

The most common initial characteristic of invasive aspergillosis is unremitting fever despite broad-spectrum antibacterial treatment, eventually accompanied in most patients by pulmonary infiltrates. In approximately 90% of cases the lungs are the portal of entry.[58] Clinicians should suspect the diagnosis in a patient with pleuritic pain, hemoptysis, localized wheezing and rubbing, or radiographic evidence of a pleural effusion or localized pulmonary infiltrates. A distinct halo of low attenuation surrounding a pulmonary infiltrate on a computed tomographic scan of a profoundly neutropenic patient is highly suggestive but not diagnostic of aspergillosis.[59, 60] As the neutrophil count returns toward normal, cavitation within the infiltrate, the so-called air-crescent sign, on a chest radiograph is similarly suggestive of aspergillosis, although mucormycosis and other agents may cause an identical appearance. Isolation of *Aspergillus* species from sputum or bronchoalveolar lavage specimens connotes either invasive infection or bronchial colonization, the latter conferring high risk for invasive aspergillosis. This finding is thought sufficient enough to initiate systemic antifungal therapy pending further documentation in granulocytopenic patients with an unexplained and unresponsive pneumonia.[61, 62] The frustrating lack of adequate diagnostic tools for pulmonary aspergillosis is demonstrated by the fact that not more than 25% of patients in whom the disease is shown at autopsy have had any positive sputum culture or microscopic finding antemortem. Infection of the paranasal sinuses may extend rapidly to surrounding bone structures and the brain. The use of nasal surveillance cultures positive for *Aspergillus* spp. to forecast threatening invasive infection remains contentious. Direct inspection of the nasal mucosa for focal lesions, particularly the nasal turbinates, can assist early diagnosis.

Candida species can cause superficial infections limited to the oropharynx and esophagus, as well as major organ infections.[57] Patients with esophagitis typically complain of a burning retrosternal or subxiphoid pain that becomes worse on swallowing. On endoscopy, brushings and biopsies from lesions should not only be cultured for herpes simplex virus (HSV) and cytomegalovirus but also examined by histopathology or smear for *Candida* pseudohyphae. Candidemia is characteristically manifested by a sudden onset of fever, tachycardia, tachypnea, chills, and hypotension during treatment with broad-spectrum antibacterials. Additional clinical clues to disseminated *Candida* infection in a profoundly neutropenic patient are fever unresponsive to antibacterial antibiotics, polymyalgia, and polyarthralgia, with or without azotemia. The most characteristic skin manifestation is a few small pinkish purple nodules with or without a central gray necrotic area. Erythematous subcutaneous nodules can also occur. *Trichosporon beigelii* and *Fusarium* spp. can cause identical lesions in profoundly neutropenic patients. Blurred vision or scotomas, late symptoms of *Candida* ophthalmitis, seldom occur in granulocytopenic patients but may occur in patients whose granulocyte count has returned toward normal. Chronic hepatic candidiasis is being recognized with increasing frequency. Typically, the patient has an irregular fever, hepatosplenomegaly, abdominal discomfort, and elevation of alkaline phosphatase levels after recovery from granulocytopenia. An abdominal ultrasound or computed tomography may show multiple abscesses in the liver, spleen, or kidney. The lesions have been called "bull's eyes."[63] Thrombocytopenia makes biopsies high-risk procedures, and cultures from biopsy specimens seldom yield growth. If the clinical picture is unclear, liver biopsy and painstaking examination of Gomori–methenamine silver–stained tissue sections should be performed to establish a correct diagnosis. Organisms may be largely pseudohyphae and easily confused with *Aspergillus* hyphae. The clinical relevance of culturing *Candida albicans* from any source other than blood is a matter of controversy. Positive cultures from natural secretions such as sputum, urine, saliva, and stool should never be accepted as definite proof of invasive candidiasis.[64] Only in patients with other evidence suggestive of candidiasis was a single positive blood culture traditionally regarded as indicative of a serious infection. Despite uncertainty about the diagnosis, neutropenic patients with a single positive blood culture for *Candida* spp. should be treated immediately, at least until organ involvement can be reliably ruled out. Experience has taught us that patients with a single positive blood culture without further clinical symptoms should not be classified as having benign transient candidemia. All cases must be monitored meticulously because an apparently transient candidemia may reemerge as acute or chronic disseminated candidiasis. On the other hand, it has to be underscored that many a granulocytopenic patient in whom unequivocal signs of invasive candidiasis eventually develop has never had any antecedent positive blood culture. Negative cultures may be due to an inadequate number of samples taken or suboptimal procedures in the microbiology laboratory.

Even within the fungal pathogens a shift in causative agents has been observed. *C. albicans* continues to be one of the most frequently isolated species,[57] followed by *Candida tropicalis, Candida glabrata,* and *Candida parapsilosis,* the last often in association with central venous catheters.[65] Over the last 10 years new *Candida* species have emerged, such as *Candida krusei, Candida lusitaniae, Candida utilis, Candida dubliniensis,* and *Candida gulliermondii.* The introduction of fluconazole for prophylaxis has undoubtedly reduced the proportion of *C. albicans* isolates in favor of strains such as *C. glabrata* and *C. krusei,* which are less susceptible to the drug. However, this attractive hypothesis does not provide the only explanation for this phenomenon inasmuch as the selection of non-*albicans* strains was not corroborated by several prospective, randomized multicenter studies of fluconazole prophylaxis (see Chapter 247). Moreover, an increased incidence of *C. krusei* was already seen in certain cancer centers long before fluconazole was introduced. Therefore, other mechanisms cannot be excluded, such as the distinct potential of non–*C. albicans* species to exploit the deficits in host defense mechanisms imposed by aggressive chemotherapeutic regimens or local cross-infection incidents.

Other fungi such as *T. beigelii, Blastoschizomyces capitatus, Saccharomyces cerevisiae, Rhodotorula,* and *Malassezia furfur* have been identified as the cause of fungemia in humans, intravenous and peritoneal catheters being the major risk factors.[66] *Fusarium* is the only mold infection frequently accompanied by fungemia. The diagnosis is seldom suspected until the organism is recovered from blood or a skin lesion. Histoplasmosis, coccidioidomycosis, blastomycosis, paracoccidioidomycosis, and *Penicillium marneffei* infection, so-called endemic mycoses, can now emerge anywhere as a result of air travel. Granulocytopenia does not appear to predispose to these endemic mycoses. If a peculiar fungus is isolated from any body site other than the skin in a patient with acute leukemia or a lymphoma during granulocytopenia, it must never be ignored and certainly not discarded as a contaminant without thorough clinical assessment. The molds *Pseudallescheria, Fusarium,* and *Alternaria* and the agents of mucormycosis constitute a growing problem in granulocytopenic patients and bone marrow transplant recipients.[67–70] The clinical picture of mucormycosis, fusariosis, pseudallescheriasis, and alternariosis can resemble aspergillosis, although differences do exist (see Chapter 259). In mucormycosis, the rhinocerebral form is manifested as painful unilateral facial swelling and ophthalmoplegia in combination with a serosanguineous nasal discharge. *Pseudallescheria boydii* can cause a wide range of clinical syndromes varying from esophagitis to pneumonitis and disseminated sepsis-like infections. Severe myalgias and disseminated tender reddish purple skin papules or nodules, which can resemble ecthyma gangrenosum, occur in 70% of patients with disseminated fusariosis, many of whom are fungemic. Skin lesions may also occur with alternariosis and phaeohyphomycosis. Invasive sinusitis may occur with fusariosis or pseudallescheriasis. In the past these pathogens might have been underreported inasmuch as the histologic demonstration of septate hyphae in pulmonary tissue can easily be misinterpreted as belonging to *Aspergillus* species. Because it is virtually impossible to adequately identify some of those fungal species by histology, confirmation by culture should be attempted in every case.

No commercially available, reliable test is yet available to enable an accurate diagnosis early in the evolution of invasive fungal infections by detecting either specific antibodies, circulating fungal antigens, or fungal metabolites.[71, 72]

Fungi Associated with Impaired Cell-Mediated Immunity

Defects in cell-mediated immunity predispose patients to cryptococcal meningitis and to severe infections caused by *Pneumocystis carinii.* The latter pathogen can be responsible for life-threatening pneumonitis.[73] Intermittent chemoprophylaxis with trimethoprim-sulfamethoxazole has proved very effective in reducing the incidence of pneumocystosis.[74]

Viruses

The predominant viral pathogens in patients with leukemia and lymphoma are herpes simplex, herpes zoster, and cytomegalovirus.[75] Numerous studies have documented the high incidence of HSV stomatitis in patients receiving antineoplastic chemotherapy for acute leukemia or lymphoma.[76] Isolating the virus by culture of swabs from mouth lesions is the best diagnostic test. Immunoperoxidase staining of tissue culture monolayers provides a result in a few days. HSV lesions are most commonly white painful plaques on the gums, tongue, buccal mucosa, or oropharynx. Swallowing can be so painful that saliva is expectorated and intake of food and fluids drastically reduced. It is not uncommon for an oropharyngeal HSV infection to extend to the esophagus with signs and symptoms mimicking *Candida* esophagitis. Accurate discrimination between these infections is very difficult, and coinfections are possible. Diagnosis requires endoscopy to collect a tissue sample for histologic examination and culture. HSV infections restricted to the genital or perineal areas and esophagitis without oropharyngeal involvement occur sporadically. Dissemination to the liver, spleen, lungs, and kidneys occurs but is rare.

Reactivation of herpes zoster virus is common in patients with decreased cell-mediated immunity. Lesions often remain confined to the dermatome but can spread to other skin sites and deep organs, including the brain and liver. The occurrence of acute abdominal pain resembling gut perforation or pancreatitis, frequently without any vesicular rash, is an unusual variant. In children and young adults who have never had chickenpox, severe and even lethal chickenpox can complicate the treatment of acute lymphoblastic leukemia or lymphoma.[77] Pneumonia caused by varicella-zoster virus may be seen in such children. Prophylactic vaccination with attenuated varicella-zoster virus has been recommended inasmuch as vaccinated children have been shown to have a lower incidence and severity of zoster.[78]

Measles, often without its typical rash, can also cause severe infections in children during treatment of acute leukemia.[79]

Viral hepatitis caused by hepatitis B or hepatitis C virus can occur, and both viruses are considered to be transfusion associated in most cases. Careful screening of donors is lessening this problem. Cytomegalovirus infection is usually reactivation disease and can be transmitted by blood or organ transplantation. Cytomegalovirus can cause hepatitis and has been found to be the culprit in interstitial pneumonia and ulcerations in the esophagus or gastrointestinal tract, particularly in patients with graft-versus-host disease after hematopoietic stem cell transplantation (see Chapter 303).

Evidence has been accumulating that community respiratory viruses such as respiratory syncytial virus, influenza virus, parainfluenza virus, adenovirus, and picornavirus play an underestimated role in the etiology of respiratory diseases in patients with deficient cellular immunity.[80, 81]

Parasites and Protozoa

Compromised cell-mediated immunity predisposes to parasitic and protozoan infections, but their incidence is surprisingly low in patients with hematologic malignancies. Nevertheless, epidemiologic factors such as a history of travel or previous symptomatic disease should be considered in patients who have persistent unexplained fever.

Reactivated *Toxoplasma gondii* can lead to cerebral abscesses. *Cryptosporidium* has been recognized as a rare cause of enteropathy in these patients.[82] *Strongyloides stercoralis* may induce diarrhea, as well as a dangerous hyperinfection.[83] In patients who have lived where strongyloidiasis is endemic, stool examination to rule out asymptomatic carriage should be considered before immunosuppressive chemotherapy is started.

Characteristics of Common Clinical Infections

The distribution of the different infections and symptoms characteristic of the various sites of infection are described in Chapter 298. During treatment of acute leukemia or lymphoma, problems pertinent to the underlying disease and the class of chemotherapy require special attention. It is important to discriminate between the miscellaneous types of infection because they each carry a different prognosis that might be favorably influenced by selection of the most appropriate therapy as early as possible.[84] Clinically documented infections that emerge later during the course of febrile granulocytopenia carry a dismal prognosis, probably because of the occurrence of fungi. Correspondingly, several studies have demonstrated a lower response rate in patients suffering from a clinically documented infection independent of microbiologic confirmation than in those with an uncomplicated bacteremia or unexplained fever.[9, 85, 86]

Sepsis and Bacteremia

Blood stream infections are life threatening unless the granulocyte count rises and the underlying disease is controlled. In most patients with a positive blood culture, the source of bacteremia will never be documented.[12, 17, 18, 86] Clinical manifestations of bacteremia are not pathognomonic, not even when the most notorious pathogens are involved. Therefore, blood should be cultured whenever fever, that is, a body temperature above 38.5°C, is registered or when infection is suspected on the basis of other clinical findings. Such a strategy also applies to patients already receiving antimicrobial therapy because breakthrough bacteremia or fungal infection may develop. Roughly 5% of patient with bacteremia caused by gram-negative bacilli and 10% of those with a polymicrobial bacteremia will present with shock. Shock at the onset of bacteremia is an ominous clinical sign, as is the concurrent presence of major organ infection or extensive tissue involvement.[9, 23] An initial response rate of about 35% may be expected in patients with shock, as compared with 70% in patients without shock.

Although the clinical relevance of a blood culture positive for gram-negative bacilli is not a matter of controversy, the significance of recovery of some gram-positive cocci is questionable.[87] Single blood cultures positive for *Staphylococcus aureus, Streptococcus pneumoniae,* or *Enterococcus faecalis* in granulocytopenic patients should be considered significant. Viridans group streptococci, with an average mortality of 15 to 20% are perhaps the most feared among the bacteremias today.[48–50] Although viridans streptococci are common blood contaminants in the general population, positive blood cultures in patients with oromucositis should not be disregarded, certainly not when it concerns *S. mitis.*

Even if they have an adequate granulocyte count, sepsis caused by *S. pneumoniae* infection can carry a mortality of 30% in splenectomized patients. Immediate antimicrobial therapy is obligatory. Attempts to protect these patients by vaccination before or after splenectomy are often unsuccessful.[88] Experimental protein-conjugate vaccines against pneumococcus will, we hope, be more successful. *Salmonella* spp. have sporadically been isolated from the blood of patients with severely impaired cell-mediated immunity. Similarly, *L. monocytogenes* and *Cryptococcus neoformans* have been isolated from blood cultures before the eventual advent of neurologic symptoms. Recovery of one of these pathogens should always prompt a lumbar puncture, provided that no intracranial hypertension or focal signs are detected or magnetic resonance imaging is performed.

Oropharyngeal Infections

Gingivostomatitis and periodontal lesions occur frequently in patients with acute leukemia.[89] Optimal dental care and appropriate hygienic measures before the initiation of antineoplastic chemotherapy are important. Lesions of mucosal ulcerations are usually colonized by oropharyngeal flora, and in turn, colonization is easily followed by local invasion and dissemination.

The principal pathogens in granulocytopenic patients with mucositis are numerous and include HSV, gram-negative bacilli, streptococci, anaerobes, and *Candida* spp. Mixed and polymicrobial infections are more or less standard.[90] Asymptomatic excretion of HSV can occur and appears to be predictive of imminent oropharyngeal infection. The course of herpes simplex stomatitis is usually extensive and protracted in patients treated for leukemia or lymphoma, and relapses are common. With the introduction of more aggressive chemotherapeutic regimens, hitherto unusual pathogens such as *Stomatococcus* and *Aerococcus* are increasingly met in patients with mucositis.[91] Oropharyngeal candidiasis or thrush that later extends to the esophagus has become a common dilemma. If *Candida* esophagitis, gastritis, or duodenitis is diagnosed endoscopically in a persistently febrile granulocytopenic patient, evidence of disseminated candidiasis should be sought. Unusual manifestations of candidiasis in the oropharyngeal area are epiglottitis, laryngitis, and reactive cervical lymphadenitis.[92]

Pulmonary Infections

Pulmonary infections, either as the primary focus or as a complication of septicemia, present a gloomy prospect for granulocytopenic patients inasmuch as they have been blamed for 70% of all fatal infections.[84, 93, 94] All causative agents found in nonimmunocompromised hosts can be encountered in patients who acquire pneumonia during treatment of acute leukemia or lymphoma. Typically, chest radiographs performed early in the evolution of infection in patients with profound granulocytopenia fail to show infiltrates. It may take more than 3 days for the infection to generate enough necrosis with hemorrhage and edema to produce an infiltrate on normal chest radiographs, although computed tomographic scans are positive earlier. Patients who present with pulmonary infections caused by organisms such as *P. aeruginosa* and *S. aureus* or fungi have a poor prognosis, as do those with adult respiratory distress syndrome that evolves in association with viridans streptococcal bacteremia or septicemia.[40, 48]

The high incidence of fungi, notably aspergillosis, among microbiologically defined lung infiltrates is a matter of apprehension.[95] The outcome depends on prompt diagnosis, an aggressive therapeutic approach, adequate control of the underlying disease, and most of all, recovery of the granulocyte count. Pulmonary aspergillosis has to be distinguished from infections with other molds and, especially in patients with impaired cell-mediated immunity, from tuberculosis. *P. carinii* pneumonia is manifested in patients with deficient cellular immunity as fever, progressive hypoxemia with dry cough, and dyspnea.[73] Early in its evolution, the chest radiograph shows discrete infiltrates advancing to interstitial pneumonia. Clinical signs and symptoms often begin after discontinuation of corticosteroid therapy given for other reasons. The diagnosis of pneumocystosis and tuberculosis in immunosuppressed patients is more difficult because of the absence of cough. Induced sputum, bronchoalveolar lavage, computed tomography–guided transthoracic fine-needle aspirates, or thoracoscopy-guided lung biopsy may be required. Fluorescent microscopy with auramine-rhodamine stains for mycobacteria and fluorescein-conjugated antibody for *P. carinii* has improved diagnostic sensitivity.

Legionella pneumonia is characterized by fever, cough, and a chest radiograph with signs of consolidation and is occasionally accompanied by headache, gastrointestinal symptoms, and renal insufficiency. The diagnosis is based on detection of urine antigen by enzyme-linked immunosorbent assay and culture of bronchoalveolar lavage fluid on special medium.[96]

Cytomegalovirus has been identified as an etiologic agent in pulmonary infections characterized by diffuse infiltrates, dry cough, and shortness of breath in patients undergoing allogeneic bone marrow transplantation.[97] Infections with respiratory syncytial virus, influenza, adenoviruses, and picornaviruses are often complicated by either viral pneumonitis or secondary bacterial pneumonia. Respiratory syncytial virus is manifested by rhinorrhea, nasal congestion, sore throat, and cough. This infection is highly communicable among children and immunosuppressed adults. Influenza A virus can cause serious and fatal infections in allogeneic bone marrow transplant recipients, but in most immunosuppressed patients, a clinical course comparable to that in immunocompetent adults is seen.[80, 81, 98] Parainfluenza virus, particularly type 3, may cause pneumonia in immunosuppressed adults as well as children. *Mycoplasma pneumoniae* is remarkably infrequent in patients treated for leukemia or lymphoma, but even in the absence of cold agglutinins this disease has to be kept in mind during differential diagnostic considerations.

Management of pulmonary infiltrates is complex. Many infiltrates do have a noninfectious etiology and can be secondary to radiation pneumonitis, fluid overload, cardiac or pulmonary toxicity of cytotoxic drugs, or pulmonary hemorrhage. The critical decision faced by the clinician at the bedside of patients with pulmonary infiltrates is whether to undertake invasive procedures such as bronchoscopy with or without bronchoalveolar lavage, transbronchial biopsy, transthoracic aspiration, thoracoscopy-guided biopsy, or open lung biopsy. The exact role of these diagnostic approaches in the optimal management of patients is still controversial because the yield depends on the collaboration and skill of various specialists. Moreover, concurrent thrombocytopenia precludes invasive diagnostic procedures in most patients unless adequate platelet transfusion can be given. Treating these patients empirically is a reasonable alternative as long as one realizes the limitations of blind escalation of antimicrobial therapy with multiple, potentially toxic agents.[18, 99, 100]

Skin, Soft Tissue, and Catheter-Related Infections

Cutaneous infections in granulocytopenic patients can be both localized and widespread and can represent either a primary focus of infection with or without cellulitis or septic emboli from a focus elsewhere.

Without adequate hygienic measures, venipuncture, bone marrow aspiration, and other skin perforations can lead to local infection and to bacteremia or fungemia in high-risk patients. Staphylococci, *Corynebacterium jeikeium,* Enterobacteriaceae, and *P. aeruginosa* have all been incriminated. Surgically implanted intravascular devices such as the Hickman, Grushong, or Broviac catheters and Port-a-Caths have become the leading source of infection. For shorter duration of use, percutaneously implanted central venous catheters have been used in nongranulocytopenic patients. The clinical spectrum of these catheter-related infections (see Chapter 292) ranges from asymptomatic bacteremia as a manifestation of intraluminal colonization or a process confined to the site of insertion to marked inflammation of the tunnel tract and septicemia with metastatic emboli in the skin and other organs. Malfunction of the catheter as illustrated by the impossibility of drawing blood from the line is often the first sign of an infectious problem. Coagulase-negative staphylococci are the most frequently found isolates, but sometimes organisms such as *P. aeruginosa, Pseudomonas putida, Burkholderia cepacia, Stenotrophomonas maltophilia, C. jeikeium, Bacillus* spp., Enterobacteriaceae, and *Candida* spp. can be encountered.[43–47] Although the incidence of endocarditis appears to be extremely low in granulocytopenic patients with chronic right atrial catheters, endocarditis has been reported after *Staphylococcus epidermidis* bacteremia.[101] Recognition of these complications and identification of the causative pathogen to provide the means for individually tailored antibiotic therapy are important.

Widespread papules or subcutaneous nodules may be indicative of disseminated candidiasis or fusariosis.[102–104] Ecthyma gangrenosum with extensive necrosis is a characteristic entity in patients with *P. aeruginosa* sepsis, but these cutaneous manifestations were reported in only 2% of cases.[105] Because pathogens such as *Candida* spp. and Mucorales can cause similar lesions, needle aspiration or biopsy should be performed to make a definite and accurate diagnosis as early as possible in the course of the disease.[104, 106] Ecthyma gangrenosum should be distinguished from pyoderma gangrenosum, a noninfectious cutaneous process in patients with myeloid malignancy or inflammatory bowel disease.[107] The sudden appearance of tender, reddish brown cutaneous plaques, fever, and leukocytosis should suggest the possibility of Sweet's syndrome.[108] Lesions tend to appear on the head, neck, and upper extremities, and biopsy will show dense infiltration of the dermis by neutrophils.

Localized infections on the face are usually caused by *S. aureus* or other gram-positive bacteria. Cutaneous lesions caused by cryptococcosis or nocardiosis have been described, but herpes zoster is the major dermatologic complication in patients with defects in cell-mediated immunity.[109–111] In patients with severe HSV stomatitis, lesions may also involve the lips with spread around the mouth. Autoinoculation by the patient's fingers can seed open skin lesions elsewhere on the body, such as weeping lesions of basal cell or squamous carcinoma. Vulvovaginal HSV can seed intertriginous skin in the perineum and perirectal area.

Perianal cellulitis with painful lesions but no abscess formation used to be a well-known complication during the treatment of acute nonlymphoblastic leukemia. The incidence of this clinical entity has decreased, probably as a result of higher awareness combined with better local care and, possibly, improved antibacterial chemoprophylaxis.

Other Sites of Infection

Hepatosplenic candidiasis has mainly been reported in patients with leukemia and resolving granulocytopenia. Trichosporonosis, fusariosis, and aspergillosis may cause a similar clinical syndrome.

Diarrhea is common in leukemic patients. The cause is not explained easily because diarrhea can be the result of many different disorders. Diagnostic problems are held accountable for underrating enteric viruses as causative agents in gastrointestinal infections. Fecal carriage of *Clostridium difficile* varies considerably among institutions, perhaps reflecting nosocomial acquisition under the influence of the local antibiotic policy.[47, 112–114] Pseudomembranous colitis from *C. difficile* can be severe and even fatal. Stool should be tested immediately for *C. difficile* toxin if the diagnosis is suspected. Relapses are frequent and may follow cancer chemotherapy or courses with antibiotics such as clindamycin and imipenem-cilastatin.[115] Relapse is harder to document because toxin may persist in the stool of successfully treated patients, particularly those who continue to receive broad-spectrum antibacterial agents. Disproportional bacterial overgrowth in the gastrointestinal tract of patients with damaged mucosa can serve as a source of bacteremia by normally exclusively enteric pathogens such as *Clostridium septicum*.[44, 116] Chemotherapy-induced colitis or typhlitis in patients with acute leukemia is accompanied by a combination of profuse diarrhea and severe abdominal pain with virtually no bowel movements. It may create a very alarming situation, and because unnecessary surgical interventions could be detrimental, it is essential for physicians to be aware of the existence and symptomatology of this entity.

An insidious onset of fever accompanied by headache and confusion is indicative of meningitis in patients with lymphoma or otherwise perturbed cellular immunity. The cerebrospinal fluid (CSF) is usually clear with a slight increase in white blood cells and a moderate elevation in protein concentration. In patients with a low glucose level, tuberculous meningitis should be taken into account. The prevalent pathogens, however, are *L. monocytogenes, C. neoformans* and *Toxoplasma gondii. L. monocytogenes,* a gram-positive bacillus, should not be discarded as a contaminant and should also not be mistaken for *Corynebacterium.* Because of significantly lower inoculum of yeast in CSF, the diagnosis of cryptococcal meningitis is more difficult to ascertain than in patients with acquired immunodeficiency syndrome. In patients with malignant diseases, the sensitivity of India ink examination is only 50%, in contrast to the 95% sensitivity of antigen detection in CSF. Efforts to grow *C. neoformans* should be pursued in patients whose CSF is abnormal, even if large amounts of CSF and repeated punctures are required for culture of this organism. If a patient has complaints of seizures and headaches, localization of the leukemia or lymphoma has to first be pursued by CSF cytology. Brain biopsy may be necessary to distinguish malignancy from cerebral abscesses caused by *Nocardia* spp., *T. gondii,* and other agents.

MANAGEMENT OF INFECTIONS IN PATIENTS WITH ACUTE LEUKEMIA AND LYMPHOMA

A single oral temperature of 38.5°C (101°F) or higher in the absence of obvious environmental causes is considered fever, and a temperature of 38.0°C (100.4°F) indicates a febrile state. Self-limiting infection is virtually nonexistent in patients who have been treated for acute leukemia or lymphoma. Medical intervention and administration of antimicrobials are indispensable to avoid premature death or unnecessary morbidity.

Empirical Antimicrobial Therapy

The introduction of empirical strategies in combination with the implementation of more powerful antibiotics fostered tremendous progress in the management of infections in these patients. The rationale behind empirical antimicrobial therapy, which was introduced for febrile granulocytopenic patients in the 1970s, was to prevent early death from sepsis caused by gram-negative bacilli or *S. aureus*.[15] This approach, extensively discussed in Chapter 300, proved very successful and was embraced by many study groups and, especially, the pharmaceutical companies. The latter recognized an easily accessible and possibly lucrative study population for their newly developed broad-spectrum antibiotics. Numerous trials were performed, and the results found their way into the literature.[117] However, by extending the study period from the truly empirical episode, namely, the first 48 to 72 hours, to the entire granulocytopenic episode, many of these clinical studies addressed the options and limitations of antibacterials rather than the value of a given regimen to protect the patient until the results of cultures and other investigations are available. Unfortunately, in many studies, scientific rigor and commercial interest have made interpretation of the results for practical clinical purposes difficult or even impossible. Too much emphasis has been put on assessment of the potency of the antibacterial agents tested. Such a goal prohibits a change in antibiotics, whereas adjustments to an initial regimen on the basis of the results of cultures and the clinical course are fully accepted in routine daily practice. At the onset of fever, approximately 20% of patients will have a clinical focus of infection to guide the selection of a certain regimen, and a clinically defined infection will develop in an additional 10% within 72 hours. Thirty percent of all patients will be shown to have positive blood cultures. In all these patients, who constitute about 50% of the total febrile population, antimicrobial therapy can be adjusted objectively on the basis of clinical or microbiologic findings. Such objective adjustment is in fact good clinical practice, whereas according to rigorous criteria from many clinical trial protocols, such cases would be deemed failures. Furthermore, about 65% of patients with unexplained fever will respond within a few days to the antibiotics administered. So, ultimately only 15 to 20% of patients with a persisting unexplained fever would require a continued empirical approach after 72 hours. Even in these patients a series of subsequent empirical therapeutic interventions should be avoided because they are basically futile and often imply neglect of diagnostic procedures, whereas diagnostic interventions, including repeated physical examination, are particularly warranted under these circumstances.

The major randomized trials of the last decade failed to show any substantial difference in efficacy of the antibacterial agents or regimens compared. There is no reason to foresee another conclusion in the near future because most of the episodes treated actually represent a low enough risk to assume guaranteed success for virtually all modern broad-spectrum antibacterial agents. Analysis of the various risk groups separately is usually frustrated by a lack of sufficient numbers to allow reliable conclusions. Because aminoglycoside-related nephrotoxicity poses a real issue in patients who receive cyclosporine, amphotericin B, or cisplatin concomitantly, monotherapy became deliberately or unwittingly fashionable. The latter refers to the use of a standard, low, and in fact, ineffective dose of aminoglycoside without monitoring of serum levels when toxicity was anticipated. Monotherapy was shown to be equally effective as traditional combinations, caused fewer adverse events, and appeared less expensive.[12, 34, 118–120]

Common sense dictates selection of an empirical antimicrobial regimen with the history of the individual patient in mind to cover locally prevalent pathogens. In addition, the more favorable overall prognosis of children with fever should not lead to a less strict antibiotic policy than in adults.[120–122]

Whatever regimen is used in both adults and children, the response rate will never be 100%. When the efficacy of the actual regimen is evaluated, it has to be remembered that even in ultimately successful cases the median time to defervescence is between 4 and 5 days.[12] Some patients will clearly fail to respond to the initial antibiotics; these patients and others in whom new fevers develop indicate a genuine need for modification in many cases. It is essential to consider patients as individuals under all circumstances, but without guidelines for adjusting an empirical regimen, precipitate actions wherein antibiotics will be overused and prescribed in a haphazard fashion are almost inevitable.[18, 99]

Treatment of Documented Infections

When results from blood cultures started before the initiation of empirical therapy become available, changes should be considered in accordance with the susceptibility pattern of the offending pathogen. Decisions should be guided by the evolving clinical condition of the patient. For patients with a microbiologically defined infection, antimicrobial coverage should never be restricted to antibiotics active only against the isolated pathogen as long as the patient remains febrile. Appropriate coverage against infections with gram-negative bacilli should be maintained until the granulocytopenia has resolved to avoid rapidly fatal breakthrough bacteremia.

Bacterial Infections

Most infections caused by aerobic gram-negative bacilli, *P. aeruginosa* being the most dangerous example, will respond adequately to treatment with a single broad-spectrum β-lactam antibiotic. Nonetheless, in such cases many a physician will perceive the need to add an aminoglycoside, either in three divided doses or as a single daily dose. Although aminoglycosides are redundant in most cases, no decisive arguments have been raised against this strategy when serum levels and kidney function are monitored closely and if the aminoglycoside is not given to compensate for resistance to the β-lactam. In the latter situation, the antibiotic concerned should be replaced by a more suitable β-lactam on the basis of the isolates' in vitro susceptibility. The risk of emerging resistance under monotherapy appears minimal if adequate doses are given, but the selection of resistant *Enterobacter, Citrobacter, Acinetobacter,* and *Klebsiella* spp. in some centers has been ascribed to the extensive use of third-generation cephalosporins.[43] In this respect, cefepime and cefpirome offer a theoretically attractive alternative, given their enhanced potential against mutant strains of Enterobacteriaceae.[123] Carbapenems have the broadest spectrum of activity of all antibiotics, but concomitant treatment with drugs such as ganciclovir and cyclosporine may predispose to seizures in imipenem-cilastatin recipients.[115, 118] Ceftazidime remains the β-lactam of choice against susceptible *P. aeruginosa,* non-*aeruginosa Pseudomonas* spp., and *S. maltophilia.*

If not used for prophylaxis, aztreonam and fluoroquinolones or trimethoprim-sulfamethoxazole may prove useful in patients allergic to β-lactams if combined with an aminoglycoside or a specific anti–gram-positive agent.[124, 125] Trials of anti-endotoxin monoclonal antibodies against gram-negative bacteremia have never been successful in granulocytopenic patients.

Many studies have demonstrated that response rates in patients with pneumonia caused by gram-negative bacilli and in patients with perirectal infections do not exceed 30 to 45% regardless of the initial use of a single agent or combination therapy. Improved survival in these patients is unlikely to occur solely by changing antibiotic therapy. Another ominous finding, especially if pneumonia is present, is polymicrobial bacteremia.[126] If in any organ, infection with or without bacteremic involvement of an anaerobic organism such as *Bacteroides fragilis* becomes likely, change to a carbapenem or the addition of metronidazole or clindamycin is highly recommended.

None of the common empirical regimens provide the optimal choice for treating infection by gram-positive cocci. However, the results of several prospective studies do not indicate a general need for a glycopeptide such as vancomycin as part of the front-line therapeutic regimen unless one has a particular reason to suspect the presence of methicillin-resistant *S. aureus* on the basis of local patterns of resistance.[31, 127–129] It would be prudent to incorporate a glycopeptide in the initial regimen in centers with a resistance problem and in selected cases with clinically obvious catheter-related infections or with mucositis and known colonization by resistant streptococci. Glycopeptides given empirically should be discontinued if the cultures taken at the onset of fever are negative for gram-positive organisms. Indeed, in view of the increasing occurrence of vancomycin-resistant enterococci as a result of the widespread use of glycopeptide antibiotics, empirical expansion of standard antimicrobial regimens with glycopeptides deserves caution. Because glycopeptides barely contribute to the chance of survival, these drugs can be added later when gram-positive bacteria have been isolated and no clinical response is attained.[100] On the other hand, the morbidity from infections caused by gram-positive cocci should not be underestimated because these infections can postpone the administration of maintenance or consolidation antineoplastic therapy and they can prolong hospitalization for many patients. In many countries, teicoplanin is regarded as a safe alternative to vancomycin for most febrile granulocytopenic patients.[100, 128, 130]

Most catheter-related uncomplicated gram-positive coccus bacteremias can be easily eradicated by a glycopeptide-containing regimen, but one should be prepared for relapses. In patients with tunnel infections caused by *S. aureus,* rapid progression is the rule and removal is a surgical emergency. In other tunnel infections and septic emboli, removal of the line is usually required.[6] It is also advisable to remove the catheter in patients with atypical mycobacterial infections, fungemias, and bacteremias caused by *P. aeruginosa, Bacillus* spp., *S. maltophilia, Acinetobacter* spp., and other pathogens causing persistent bacteremia despite appropriate therapy or rapidly progressive illness. Infections with *Clostridium* spp. require the addition of drugs such as penicillin G and vancomycin to ensure antibiotic coverage. Rotating the administration of antibiotics through each lumen is a judicious measure to avoid microbial sequestration in one of the lines of multilumen catheters.

Adaptation of an empirical regimen with antimicrobials such as penicillin and clindamycin to treat mucositis-related infections is commonly advocated. In about 10% of cases with viridans streptococcal septicemia adult respiratory distress syndrome may evolve with a mortality of around 60% in spite of aggressive supportive therapy. The pathophysiology of this serious complication is not fully understood. Probably many factors are involved, such as a deleterious effect of microorganisms superimposed on preexisting tissue damage. Indeed, even patients who had received vancomycin before their first positive culture were reported to experience shock and death.[49] Therefore, corticosteroids rather than supplementary antibiotics alone should be considered in the management of patients affected by this complication.[131, 132]

Therapy for *S. pneumoniae* is now changing because of the appearance of intermediate (penicillin minimal inhibitory concentration, 0.1 to 1.0 μg/ml) and high-level (minimal inhibitory concentration, >1 μg/ml) penicillin resistance. Ceftriaxone, cefotaxime, or high-dose penicillin G (2 to 3 million units every 4 hours) is currently the treatment of choice for serious infections with intermediately resistant pneumococcal strains. Vancomycin is preferred for the treatment of serious infections by highly penicillin-resistant strains. Levofloxacin or trovafloxacin can be given orally for less severe infections or intravenously for more severe infections with either intermediate or high-level penicillin resistance. Cefepime and cefpirome are also active against many intermediately resistant strains of *S. pneumoniae.* Clindamycin and other agents selected by in vitro susceptibility testing may be considered. Up to 20% of *S. pneumoniae* strains are resistant to macrolides.

The optimal antimicrobial regimen for *L. monocytogenes* consists of 2 to 4 weeks of ampicillin plus short courses of an aminoglycoside. Trimethoprim-sulfamethoxazole is another useful agent against both *Listeria* meningitis and nocardiosis. For immunocompromised patients with an infection caused by *Nocardia* spp., therapy should be continued for 12 months. Intravenous erythromycin, alone or in combination with rifampin, or a fluoroquinolone is the preferred therapy for legionellosis.

Fungal Infections

Empirical antifungal therapy for febrile granulocytopenic patients in whom fever persists in spite of treatment with adequate broad-spectrum antibacterials has become a widely accepted practice. This approach is based on two statistically feeble studies[133, 134] that suggested a reduction in the number of deaths from systemic fungal infections in those who were given amphotericin B empirically. Originally, the addition of antifungals was considered in cases with antibiotic-refractory fever for more than 5 days, but at present some centers start empirical antifungal therapy after 3 days without any evidence that such a strategy might be advantageous. In fact, starting too early will lead to overtreatment and unnecessary toxicity because it is obvious that not all unresponsive febrile episodes represent occult fungal infections. Besides, some pathogens may even escape the cover provided by an intermediate dose of intravenous amphotericin B.[135] Given its broad spectrum of activity, amphotericin B given intravenously is still the drug of choice for empirical purposes; lipid preparations should be reserved for patients who are unable to tolerate the conventional formulation and fluconazole for cases with a low risk of invasive mold infections.

Whereas the response rate of patients with unexplained persisting fever to systemically active antifungals is about 80% if the granulocytopenia resolves, successful outcome of documented invasive fungal infection may not exceed 20% even under optimal circumstances.[136] This figure is heavily dependent on the state of the underlying disease and recovery of the granulocyte count.

The clinical efficacy of fluconazole for oropharyngeal candidiasis has been documented in patients with malignancy. Amphotericin B with or without 5-flucytosine is the standard therapy for invasive candidiasis and cryptococcal meningitis; at least 50 to 70% of patients are expected to respond to this regimen. *C. lusitaniae* and *C. guilliermondii* may become resistant to amphotericin B during the course of therapy. Because 5-flucytosine may be toxic to bone marrow, the drug should be used with caution in patients who are treated for acute leukemia and lymphomas. Such patients and others with an invasive infection by susceptible *C. albicans* strains may benefit from fluconazole, but superinfections with *Aspergillus* spp. can emerge when fluconazole alone is given during granulocytopenia.[137–139] Given the variable susceptibilities of *Candida* spp. to fluconazole, an intravenous dose of 800 mg/day is often used as primary therapy for hematogenous candidiasis.[64] When a clinical response is noted and the results of cultures are available, the dose can be tapered to 400 mg/day and the drug given orally.

Removal of a central venous catheter appears justified when a patient with candidemia fails to respond to antifungal therapy within 96 hours or when the candidemia persists for more than 48 hours.[138, 140] Treatment of leukemic patients with hepatosplenic candidiasis who are no longer granulocytopenic may often be changed from amphotericin B to fluconazole to enable more convenient outpatient therapy.

Conventional amphotericin B remains the standard therapy for most invasive fungal infections in granulocytopenic patients. The target dose from the first day should be between 1 and 1.25 mg/kg/day for at least the first 10 to 14 days. In patients receiving cyclosporine or those with renal impairment, the maximum tolerated dose should be explored; alternatively, a lipid preparation should be chosen.[141–144] The other agent used successfully for the treatment of invasive aspergillosis is itraconazole. In a large, open multicenter study of proven and probable invasive aspergillosis performed by the Mycosis Study Group in the United States, 41% of patients showed a response by the end of therapy. In this study, all patients were treated with an oral loading dose of 600 mg/day itraconazole for 4 days, followed by 400 mg/day thereafter.[145–147] Many highly immunocompromised patients require a longer duration of therapy than their period of hospitalization. For these cases, oral itraconazole after a course of amphotericin B offers the opportunity of treatment on an outpatient basis if adequate serum levels can be attained. In this context, it is important to know that the oral solution of itraconazole is better absorbed than the capsulated formulation.

Liposomal amphotericin B, amphotericin B lipid complex, and amphotericin B colloidal dispersion are much better tolerated than conventional amphotericin; doses up to 5 mg/kg/day can be given without major complications.[141–144] A number of patients with fusariosis and mucormycosis have been treated successfully with such high doses of lipid-based forms of amphotericin B.[148]

Surgery is indicated for patients in whom lesions near the pulmonary hilum pose a direct threat of invasion of a major vessel with the risk of fatal hemorrhage or for débridement of dead tissue after a period of antifungal therapy.[136] Otherwise, lung or lung segment resection should be restricted to patients with persisting shadows confined to a single lobe who still have to undergo bone marrow transplantation or further aggressive chemotherapy.[60, 149] Some case reports have described improvement in patients refractory to all other antifungal regimens after granulocyte transfusions harvested from growth factor–pretreated donors in combination with amphotericin B, but this expensive, labor-intensive approach is still experimental.[150]

It is essential to see a clinical and preferably a radiologic response before therapy is discontinued in established cases. Patients with proven disseminated disease or those with diffuse pulmonary disease fare worse than do patients with localized disease. When the criteria for commencing treatment are simply fever unresponsive to antibiotics, without any evidence of invasive mycosis, treatment can be discontinued when the neutrophil count recovers and fever subsides. This approach applies when the diagnosis becomes questionable during the course of granulocytopenia.

Many studies have shown satisfactory results in the treatment of *P. carinii* pneumonitis with high-dose trimethoprim-sulfamethoxazole.[151] Alternatives include intravenous pentamidine, oral dapsone in combination with trimethoprim, or oral atovaquone suspension alone. Adjuvant therapy with corticosteroids is widely practiced, but its definite value is clearly established only for the initial treatment of hypoxemic patients (Po_2 < 70 mmHg) with pneumocystosis and acquired immunodeficiency syndrome[152] (see Chapter 260).

Viral Infections

Since the 1980s, great progress has been achieved in the treatment of viral infections. Intravenous acyclovir is the preferred treatment for immunocompromised patients with esophageal or progressive mucocutaneous herpes simplex. Shortening of the duration of virus shedding, resolution of pain, and better healing of lesions have all been demonstrated in controlled trials.[153–155] Acyclovir is superior to vidarabine for herpes simplex encephalitis. Moreover, acyclovir is less toxic and easier to administer. Relapses of mucocutaneous herpes simplex do occur, so prolonged therapy may be necessary in both compromised adults and children.[155] Doses of 10 mg/kg intravenously are recommended every 8 hours for 7 to 10 days or until crusting. Oral therapy for mucocutaneous herpes simplex in an immunocompromised patient with 400 mg five times daily should be attempted only if the patient can be monitored very closely, if the infection is mild, and if no other medical illnesses would make this approach hazardous. Seropositive bone marrow transplant recipients are often given oral acyclovir prophylaxis for 1 to 3 months post-transplant (see Chapter 303). Dermatomal herpes zoster, with or without dissemination, is treated with intravenous acyclovir, 10 mg/kg every 8 hours. The dose should be adjusted in azotemic patients. Foscarnet can be useful for patients with infections caused by herpes zoster virus resistant to acyclovir.[156]

Patients with pneumonia caused by respiratory syncytial virus, a uniformly fatal disease if not treated promptly, are candidates for therapy with aerosolized ribavirin. Efficacy has been most clearly documented in children when treatment was begun early in the course of disease. Intravenous immune globulin or immune globulin selected for its high titer against respiratory syncytial virus has been used with ribavirin aerosol, but the additional benefit is controversial. A single dose of the latter immune globulin has been approved for use in the prophylaxis of children younger than 2 years but may be considered for prophylaxis in older immunosuppressed children after a documented exposure. Either amantadine or rimantadine can decrease illness if begun in the first 48 hours of influenza with influenza A. Neither is effective in pneumonia caused by influenza B. Rimantidine has slightly less central nervous system toxicity. Neither drug is available parenterally. Although the use of rimantidine has not been shown to improve the ultimate outcome, it can be regarded as an option against severe influenza virus infections. Both respiratory syncytial virus and influenza virus infection have to be treated without delay in severely immunocompromised patients.[157]

Several noncontrolled trials have shown the combination of ganciclovir and immune globulin to achieve both an antiviral effect against cytomegalovirus pneumonia and a clinical benefit with survival rates of 50 to 70%.[97] Although randomized controlled trials are lacking, this combined therapy has been widely accepted as the treatment of choice for bone marrow transplant recipients with cytomegalovirus pneumonitis because the results are vastly better than those of other alternatives. Foscarnet is an alternative agent with anticytomegalovirus activity for patients who do not tolerate ganciclovir.

More recently developed antiviral compounds have not been sufficiently tested in patients with acute leukemia and lymphoma to endorse their use.

Miscellaneous Issues

Management of *S. stercoralis* hyperinfection can be extremely difficult. Thiabendazole is the usual drug, but ivermectin may also be useful.[83] Treatment of toxoplasmosis requires prolonged administration of sulfonamides with pyrimethamine. Folinic acid is often given to decrease the myelosuppression associated with pyrimethamine. Trimethoprim-sulfamethoxazole prophylaxis for pneumocystosis has led to a decreased incidence of toxoplasmosis in patients with acquired immunodeficiency syndrome, but it is not thought to be useful for the treatment of toxoplasmosis.

Granulocyte and granulocyte-macrophage colony-stimulating factors are now commonly used to shorten the duration of granulocytopenia after cytotoxic therapy. Prevention of infection does not necessarily imply value in treating infection. No significant difference between colony-stimulating factor and placebo was found with respect to infectious mortality in any of the studies on febrile leukemic patients.[4, 158] Therefore, overall there is no scientific reason to deviate from the guidelines presented by the American Society of Oncology and the European Organization for Research and Treatment of Cancer.[159, 160] However, the results of the studies do not exclude a possible benefit from the use of a colony-stimulating factor for subgroups of patients such as granulocytopenic patients with pneumonia, sepsis syndrome, severe cellulitis, or fungal infection.[158] If used, these factors should be discontinued once the granulocyte count has stabilized at greater than 500/mm^3. Furthermore, colony-stimulating factors seem to offer new therapeutic modalities such as the aforementioned harvest of leukocytes from healthy donors for patients with otherwise intractable infections. By contrast, conventional granulocyte transfusions have become almost obsolete.

The use of devices impregnated or coated with antimicrobial agents to reduce the risk of development of catheter-related infections has produced encouraging results, but this approach has to be seen as experimental until further evidence on long-term safety and efficacy are available.[161, 162] Moreover, lasting beneficial effects can only be expected if normal hygienic measures are maintained. Intravenous vancomycin for prophylactic purposes must be strongly discouraged because of the potential for emergence of resistant organisms.

Oral ambulatory treatment of patients who are not critically ill has been tested.[11, 163–165] A substantial proportion of successfully treated patients in these studies had received chemotherapy for a solid tumor when the granulocytopenia was not expected to last more than a week. Therefore, the results should be interpreted with prudence. Treatment as an outpatient appears to pose an acceptable risk and can improve quality of life if patients suffering from leukemia or lymphoma can be adequately instructed and if they can rely on family members or acquaintances. Moreover, easy access to a hospital in the case of emergency has to be guaranteed.[166–169] Alternatively, in the absence of discernible infectious disease and positive cultures, compliant patients may be discharged from the hospital after a few days, thereby stepping down from a standard intravenous regimen to oral agents or intravenous antibiotics through a home program.[170, 171]

Another important issue in the management of infections in patients with acute leukemia or lymphoma is the optimal duration of antibiotic therapy in patients who are still markedly granulocytopenic after normalization of the temperature or disappearance of the signs and symptoms of infection. If the patient has been treated adequately for 7 to 9 days, watchful waiting may be preferred over prolonged antimicrobial therapy with the inherent risk of superinfections with either resistant bacteria or opportunistic fungi. If antimicrobial therapy is stopped during granulocytopenia, the patient must be monitored closely and intravenous treatment restarted immediately if fever recurs or if any other evidence of infection is observed.[172]

Finally, little attention has been focused in the literature on the occurrence of fever in leukemic patients immediately after recovery from myelosuppression,[173] which is seen in approximately 15% of patients, fungal infection being the leading cause. About 10% of these episodes result in death of the patient after recovery of the bone marrow.[174]

Modern chemotherapy offers hope of a cure to many patients, but it confronts both the scientific community and practitioners with continuous new challenges in the field of infectious complications. With so many basic questions remaining, participation in clinical trials conducted by independent cooperative groups has to be stimulated to obtain more objective data necessary to support vital decisions. Optimal care can be delivered only by those who pay scrupulous attention to the patient's clinical condition and are aware of the evolving therapeutic and diagnostic modalities. Fixed treatment protocols are only acceptable if they allow reasoned deviations. Diagnostic considerations should prevail whenever patients do not respond adequately to the antimicrobial therapy administered.

REFERENCES

1. Sickles EA, Greene WH, Wiernik PH. Clinical presentation of infection in granulocytopenic patients. Arch Intern Med. 1975;135:715–719.
2. Nosanchuk JD, Sepkowitz KA, Pearse RN, et al. Infectious complications of autologous bone marrow and peripheral stem cell transplantation for refractory leukemia and lymphoma. Bone Marrow Transplant. 1996;18:355–359.
3. Bow EJ, Loewen R, Cheang MS, et al. Cytotoxic therapy–induced D-xylose malabsorption and invasive infection during remission-induction therapy for acute myeloid leukemia in adults. J Clin Oncol. 1997;15:2254–2261.
4. Maher DW, Lieschke GJ, Green M, et al. Filgrastim in patients with chemotherapy-induced febrile neutropenia. A double-blind, placebo controlled trial. Ann Intern Med. 1994;121:292–501.
5. Bodey GP, Buckley M, Sathe YS, Freireich EJ. Quantitative relationships between circulating leukocytes and infection in patients with acute leukemia. Ann Intern Med. 1966;64:328–340.
6. Press OW, Ramsey PG, Larson EB, et al. Hickman catheter infections in patients with malignancies. Medicine (Baltimore). 1984;63:189–200.
7. Raad II, Bodey GP. Infectious complications of indwelling vascular catheters. Clin Infect Dis. 1992;15:197–210.
8. Verhagen C, Stalpers LJA, De Pauw BE, Haanen C. Drug induced skin reactions in patients with acute non-lymphocytic leukaemia. Eur J Haematol. 1987;38:225–230.
9. Elting LS, Rubenstein EB, Rolston KVI, Bodey GP. Outcomes of bacteremia in patients with cancer and neutropenia: Observations from two decades of epidemiological and clinical trials. Clin Infect Dis. 1997;25:247–259.
10. Fridkin SK, Jarvis WR. Epidemiology of nosocomial fungal infections. Clin Microbiol Rev. 1996;9:499–511.
11. Meunier F, Zinner SH, Gaya H, et al. Prospective randomized evaluation of ciprofloxacin versus piperacillin plus amikacin for empiric antibiotic therapy of febrile granulocytopenic cancer patients with lymphomas and solid tumors. Antimicrob Agents Chemother. 1991;35:873–878.
12. De Pauw BE, Deresinski SC, Feld R, et al. Ceftazidime compared with piperacillin and tobramycin for the empiric treatment of fever in neutropenic patients with cancer. A multicenter randomized trial. The Intercontinental Antimicrobial Study Group. Ann Intern Med. 1994;120:834–844.
13. Schimpff SC, Young VM, Greene WH, et al. Origin of infection in acute nonlymphocytic leukemia: Significance of hospital acquisition of potential pathogens. Ann Intern Med. 1972;77:707–714.
14. Bodey GP, Rodriguez V, Chang HY, et al. Fever and infection in leukemic patients. Cancer. 1978;41:1610–1622.
15. Schimpff SC, Satterlee W, Young VM, Serpick A. Empiric therapy with carbenicillin and gentamicin for febrile patients with cancer and granulocytopenia. N Engl J Med. 1971;284:1061–1065.
16. Love LJ, Schimpff SC, Schiffer CA, et al. Improved prognosis for granulocytopenic patients with gram-negative bacteremia. Am J Med. 1980;68:643–648.
17. Pizzo PA. Management of fever in patients with cancer and treatment-induced neutropenia. N Engl J Med. 1993;328:1323–1332.
18. De Pauw BE, Dompeling EC. Antibiotic strategy after the empiric phase in patients treated for a hematological malignancy. Ann Hematol. 1996;72:273–279.
19. Fainstein V, Rodriguez V, Turck M, et al. Patterns of oropharyngeal and fecal flora in patients with acute leukemia. J Infect Dis. 1981;144:82–86.
20. Klastersky J. Non-infectious causes of fever in cancer patients. In: Glauser MP,

Calandra T, eds. Baillière's Clinical Infectious Diseases. Philadelphia: Baillière Tindall; 1994:439–453.
21. Anderson KC, Lew MA, Gorgone BC, et al. Transfusion-related sepsis after prolonged platelet storage. Am J Med. 1986;81:405–411.
22. Gerson SL, Talbot GH, Hurwitz S, et al. Prolonged granulocytopenia: The major risk factor for invasive pulmonary aspergillosis in patients with acute leukemia. Ann Intern Med. 1984;100:345–351.
23. Nucci M, Spector N, Bueno AP, et al. Risk factors and attributable mortality associated with superinfection in neutropenic patients with cancer. Clin Infect Dis. 1997;25:572–579.
24. Schimpff SC. Therapy of infection in patients with granulocytopenia. Med Clin North Am. 1978;61:1101–1118.
25. EORTC International Antimicrobial Therapy Cooperative Group. Three antibiotic regimens in the treatment of infection in febrile granulocytopenic patients with cancer. J Infect Dis. 1978;137:14–29.
26. Klastersky J, Zinner SH, Calandra T, et al. Empiric antimicrobial therapy for febrile granulocytopenic cancer patients: Lessons from four EORTC trials. Eur J Cancer Clin Oncol. 1988;24(Suppl):S35–S45.
27. Singer C, Kaplan MH, Armstrong D. Bacteremia and fungemia complicating neoplastic disease. A study of 364 cases. Am J Med. 1977;62:731–742.
28. Schimpff SC, Greene WH, Young VM, et al. *Pseudomonas* septicemia: Incidence, epidemiology, prevention and therapy in patients with advanced cancer. Eur J Cancer. 1973;9:449–455.
29. Vidal F, Mensa J, Almela M, et al. Epidemiology and outcome of *Pseudomonas aeruginosa* bacteremia, with special emphasis in the influence of antibiotic treatment. Analysis of 189 episodes. Arch Intern Med. 1996;156:2121–2126.
30. The EORTC International Antimicrobial Therapy Cooperative Group. Ceftazidime combined with a short or long course of amikacin for empiric therapy of gram-negative bacteremia in cancer patients with granulocytopenia. N Engl J Med. 1987;317:1692–1698.
31. The EORTC International Antimicrobial Therapy Cooperative Group and National Cancer Institute of Canada. Vancomycin added to empirical combination antibiotic therapy for fever in granulocytopenic cancer patients. J Infect Dis. 1991;163:951–958.
32. The International Antimicrobial Therapy Cooperative Group of the European Organization for Research and Treatment of Cancer. Efficacy and toxicity of single daily doses of amikacin and ceftriaxone versus multiple daily doses of amikacin and ceftazidime for infection in patients with cancer and neutropenia. Ann Intern Med. 1993;119:584–593.
33. The EORTC International Antimicrobial Therapy Cooperative Group and National Cancer Institute of Canada. Vancomycin added to empirical combination antibiotic therapy for fever in granulocytopenic cancer patients. J Infect Dis. 1991;163:951–958.
34. Cometta A, Calandra T, Gaya H, et al. Monotherapy with meropenem versus combination therapy with ceftazidime plus amikacin as empiric therapy for fever in granulocytopenic patients with cancer. Antimicrob Agents Chemother. 1996;40:1108–1115.
35. Cometta A, Zinner S, De Bock R, et al. Piperacillin-tazobactam plus amikacin versus ceftazidime plus amikacin as empiric therapy for fever in granulocytopenic patients with cancer. Antimicrob Agents Chemother. 1995;39:445–452.
36. Cohen J, Donnelly JP, Worsley AM, et al. Septicaemia caused by viridans streptococci in neutropenic patient with leukaemia. Lancet. 1983;2:981–983.
37. Winston DJ, Dudnick DV, Chapin M, et al. Coagulase negative staphylococcal bacteremia in patients receiving immunosuppressive therapy. Arch Intern Med. 1983;143:32–36.
38. Whimbey E, Kiehn TE, Brannon P, et al. Bacteremia and fungemia in patients with neoplastic disease. Am J Med. 1987;82:723–729.
39. Viscoli C, van der Auwera P, Meunier F. Gram-positive infections in granulocytopenic patients: An important issue? J Antimicrob Chemother. 1988;21(Suppl C):S149–S156.
40. Kern W, Jurrie E, Schmeiser T. Streptococcal bacteremia in adult patients with leukemia undergoing aggressive chemotherapy. A review of 55 cases. Infection. 1990;18:138–145.
41. Donnelly JP, Maschmeyer G, Daenen S, EORTC Gnotobiotic Project Group. Selective oral antimicrobial prophylaxis for the prevention of infection in acute leukemia: Ciprofloxacin versus co-trimoxazole plus colistin. Eur J Cancer. 1992;28A:873–878.
42. Awada A, van der Auwera P, Meunier F, et al. Streptococcal and enterococcal bacteremia in patients with cancer. Clin Infect Dis. 1992;15:33–48.
43. Sanders CC. New β-lactams: New problems for the internist. Ann Intern Med. 1991;115:650–651.
44. Pouwels MJM, Donnelly JP, Raemaekers JMM, et al. *Clostridium septicum* sepsis and neutropenic enterocolitis in a patient treated with intensive chemotherapy for acute myeloid leukemia. Ann Hematol. 1997;74:153–157.
45. Muder RR, Harris AP, Muller S, et al. Bacteremia due to *Stenotrophomonas (Xanthomonas) maltophilia:* A prospective multicenter study of 91 episodes. Clin Infect Dis. 1996;22:508–512.
46. Aoun M, van der Auwera, Devleeschouwer C, et al. Bacteraemia caused by non-*aeruginosa Pseudomonas* species in a cancer centre. J Hosp Infect. 1992;22:307–316.
47. Gerard M, Defresne N, Daneau D, et al. Incidence and significance of *Clostridium difficile* in hospitalized cancer patients. Eur J Clin Microbiol Infect Dis. 1988;7:274–278.
48. Sotiropoulos SV, Jackson MA, Woods GM, et al. Alpha-streptococcal septicemia in leukemic children treated with continuous or large dosage intermittent cytosine arabinoside. Pediatr Infect Dis J. 1989;8:755–758.
49. Engelhard D, Elishoov H, Or R, et al. Cytosine arabinoside as a major risk factor for *Streptococcus viridans* septicemia following bone marrow transplantation: A 5-year prospective study. Bone Marrow Transplant. 1995;16:565–570.
50. Bochut P-Y, Calandra T, Francioli P. Bacteremia due to viridans streptococci in neutropenic patients: A review. Am J Med. 1994;97:256–264.
51. Noriega LM, van der Auwera P, Phan M, et al. Anaerobic bacteremia in a cancer center. Support Care Cancer. 1993;1:250–255.
52. Chang J, Powles R, Mehta J, et al. Listeriosis in bone marrow transplant recipients: Incidence, clinical features, and treatment. Clin Infect Dis. 1995;21:1289–1290.
53. Ampel NM, Wing EJ. Legionellosis in the compromised host. In: Rubin RH, Young LS, eds. Clinical Approach to Infection in the Compromised Host. 2nd ed. New York: Plenum; 1988:305–319.
54. Young LS, Armstrong D, Blevins A, et al. *Nocardia asteroides* infection complicating neoplastic disease. Am J Med. 1971;50:356–367.
55. Bodey GP, Bueltmann B, Duguid W, et al. Fungal infections in cancer patients: An international autopsy survey. Eur J Clin Microbiol Infect Dis. 1992;11:99–109.
56. Horn R, Wong B, Kiehn TE, et al. Fungemia in a cancer hospital: Changing frequency, earlier onset, and results of therapy. Rev Infect Dis. 1985;7:646–655.
57. Meunier F, Aoun M, Bitar N. Candidemia in immunocompromised patients. Clin Infect Dis. 1992;14(Suppl 1):S120–S125.
58. Young RC, Bennett JE, Vogel CL, et al. Aspergillosis: The spectrum of the disease in 98 patients. Medicine (Baltimore). 1970;49:143–147.
59. Kuhlman JE, Fishman EK, Siegelman SS. Invasive pulmonary aspergillosis in acute leukemia: Characteristic findings on CT, the CT halo sign, and the role of CT in early diagnosis. Radiology. 1985;157:611–614.
60. Caillot D, Casasnovas O, Bernard A, et al. Improved management of invasive pulmonary aspergillosis in neutropenic patients using early thoracic computed tomographic scan and surgery. J Clin Oncol. 1997;15:139–147.
61. Yu VL, Muder RR, Poorsattar A. Significance of isolation of *Aspergillus* from the respiratory tract in diagnosis of invasive pulmonary aspergillosis. Am J Med. 1986;81:249–254.
62. Aisner J, Schimpff SC, Wiernik PH. Treatment of invasive aspergillosis: Relation of early diagnosis and treatment to response. Ann Intern Med. 1977;86:539–543.
63. Thaler M, Pastakia B, Shawker TH, et al. Hepatic candidiasis in cancer patients: The evolving picture of the syndrome. Ann Intern Med 1988;108:88–100.
64. Edwards JE, Bodey GP, Bowden RA, et al. International conference for the development of a consensus on the management and prevention of severe candidal infections. Clin Infect Dis. 1997;25:43–59.
65. Girmenia C, Martino P, De Bernardis F, et al. Rising incidence of *Candida parapsilosis* fungemia in patients with hematologic malignancies: Clinical aspects, predisposing factors, and differential pathogenicity of the causative strains. Clin Infect Dis. 1996;23:506–514.
66. Walsh TJ, Pizzo PA. Fungal infections in granulocytopenic patients: Current approaches to classification, diagnosis, and treatment. In: Holmberg K, Meyer R, eds. Diagnosis and Therapy of Systemic Fungal Infections. New York: Raven; 1989:47–70.
67. Krcmery V, Jesenska Z, Spanik S, et al. Fungemia due to *Fusarium* spp in cancer patients. J Hosp Infect. 1997;36:223–228.
68. Boutati EI, Anaissie EJ. *Fusarium,* a significant emerging pathogen in patients with hematologic malignancy: Ten years' experience at a cancer center and implications for management. Blood. 1997;90:999–1008.
69. Morrison VA, Weisdorf DJ. *Alternaria:* A sinonasal pathogen of immunocompromised hosts. Clin Infect Dis. 1993;16:265–270.
70. Pagano L, Ricci P, Tonso A, et al. Mucormycosis in patients with haematological malignancies: A retrospective clinical study of 37 cases. Br J Haematol. 1997;99:331–336.
71. Walsh TJ, Hathorn JW, Sobel JD, et al. Detection of circulating candida enolase by immunoassay in patients with cancer and invasive candidiasis. N Engl J Med. 1991;324:1026–1031.
72. Verweij PE, Stynen D, Rijs AJMM, et al. Sandwich enzyme-linked immunosorbent assay compared with Pastorex latex agglutination test for diagnosing invasive aspergillosis in immunocompromised patients. J Clin Microbiol. 1995;33:1912–1914.
73. Varthalitis I, Meunier F. *Pneumocystis carinii* pneumonia in cancer patients. Cancer Treat Rev. 1993;19:387–413.
74. Hughes WT, Rivera GK, Schell MJ, et al. Successful intermittent chemoprophylaxis for *Pneumocystis carinii* pneumonitis. N Engl J Med. 1987;316:1627–1632.
75. Carrigan DR, Drobyski WR, Russler SK, et al. Interstitial pneumonitis associated with human herpesvirus 6 after marrow transplantation. Lancet. 1991;338:147–149.
76. Corey L, Spear PG. Infections with herpes simplex viruses. N Engl J Med. 1986;314:686–691, 749–757.
77. Locksley RM, Flournoy N, Sullivan KM, Meyers JD. Infection with varicella-zoster virus in immunocompromised patients. J Infect Dis. 1986;153:840–847.
78. Hardy J, Gershon AA, Steinberg SP, et al. Varicella Vaccine Collaborative Study Group. The incidence of zoster after immunization with live attenuated varicella vaccine. N Engl J Med. 1991;325:1545–1550.
79. Kaplan LJ, Daum RS, Smaron M, et al. Severe measles in immunocompromised patients. JAMA. 1992;267:1237–1241.
80. Whimbey E, Couch RB, Englund JA, et al. Respiratory syncytial virus pneumonia in hospitalized adult patients with leukemia. Clin Infect Dis. 1995;21:376–379.
81. Whimbey E, Champlin RE, Couch RB, et al. Community respiratory virus infections among hospitalized adult bone marrow transplant recipients. Clin Infect Dis. 1996;22:778–782.

82. Luft BJ, Remington JS. Toxoplasmosis of the central nervous system. Curr Clin Top Infect Dis. 1985;6:315–358.
83. Longworth DL, Weller PF. Hyperinfection syndrome with strongyloidiasis. Curr Clin Top Infect Dis. 1986;7:1–26.
84. Donnelly JP, Nováková IRO, Raemaekers JMM, De Pauw BE. Empiric treatment of localized infections in the febrile neutropenic patients with monotherapy. Leuk Lymphoma. 1993;9:193–203.
85. Viscoli C, Bruzzi P, Castagnola E, et al. Factors associated with bacteremia in febrile granulocytopenic cancer patients. Eur J Cancer. 1994;30:430–437.
86. De Pauw BE, Raemaekers JMM, Schattenberg T, et al. Empirical and subsequent use of antibacterial agents in the febrile neutropenic patient. J Intern Med. 1997;242:69–77.
87. Rintala E. Incidence and clinical significance of positive blood cultures in febrile episodes of patients with hematological malignancies. Scand J Infect Dis. 1994;26:77–84.
88. Molrine DC, George S, Tarbell N, et al. Antibody responses to polysaccharide and polysaccharide-conjugate vaccines after treatment of Hodgkin's disease. Ann Intern Med. 1995;123:828–834.
89. Overholser CD, Peterson DE, William LT, et al. Periodontal infections in patients with acute nonlymphocytic leukemia: Prevalence of acute exacerbations. Arch Intern Med. 1982;142:551–554.
90. Bergmann OJ. Oral infections and fever in immunocompromised patients with haematologic malignancies. Eur J Clin Microbiol Infect Dis. 1989;8:207–213.
91. Weers-Pothof G, Nováková IRO, Donnelly JP, Muytjens HL. Bacteraemia caused by *Stomatococcus mucilaginosus* in a granulocytopenic patient with acute lymphocytic leukaemia. Neth J Med. 1989;35:143–146.
92. Shenep JL, Kalwinski DK, Feldman S, et al. Mycotic cervical lymphadenitis following oral mucositis in children with leukemia. J Pediatr. 1985;106:243–246.
93. Shelhamer JH, Toews GB, Masur H, et al. Respiratory disease in the immunosuppressed patient. Am Intern Med. 1992;117:415–431.
94. Nováková IRO, Donnelly JP, De Pauw B. Potential sites of infection that develop in febrile neutropenic patients. Leuk Lymphoma. 1993;10:461–467.
95. Maschmeyer G, Link H, Hiddeman W, et al. Pulmonary infiltrates in febrile patients with neutropenia. Risk factors and outcome under empirical antimicrobial therapy in a randomized multicenter study. Cancer. 1994;73:2296–2304.
96. Kovatch AL, Jardine DS, Dowling JN, et al. Legionellosis in children with leukemia in relapse. Pediatrics. 1984;73:811–815.
97. Goodrich JM, Mori M, Gleaves CA, et al. Early treatment with ganciclovir to prevent cytomegalovirus disease after allogeneic bone marrow transplantation. N Engl J Med. 1991;325:1601–1607.
98. Ljungman P, Andersson J, Aschan J, et al. Influenza A in immunocompromised patients. Clin Infect Dis. 1993;17:244–247.
99. O'Hanley P, Easaw J, Rugo H, Easaw S. Infectious disease management of adult leukemic patients undergoing chemotherapy: 1982 to 1986 experience at Stanford University hospital. Am J Med. 1989;87:605–613.
100. Nováková IRO, Donnelly JP, Verhagen C, De Pauw BE. Teicoplanin as modification of initial empirical therapy in febrile granulocytopenic patients. J Antimicrob Chemother. 1990;15:985–993.
101. Liepman MK, Jones PG, Kauffman CA. Endocarditis as a complication of indwelling right atrial catheters in leukemic patients. Cancer. 1984;54:804–807.
102. Allo MD, Miller J, Townsend T, et al. Primary cutaneous aspergillosis associated with Hickman intravenous catheters. N Engl J Med. 1987;317:1105–1108.
103. Fine JD, Miller JA, Harrist TJ, et al. Cutaneous lesions in disseminated candidiasis mimicking ecthyma gangrenosum. Am J Med. 1981;70:1133–1135.
104. Anaissie E. Opportunistic mycoses in the immunocompromised host: Experience at a cancer center and review. Clin Infect Dis. 1992;14(Suppl 1):S43–S53.
105. Bodey GP, Jadeja L, Elting L. *Pseudomonas* bacteremia: Retrospective analysis of 410 episodes. Arch Intern Med. 1985;145:1621–1629.
106. Suster S, Rose LB. Intradermal bullous dermatitis due to candidiasis in an immunocompromised patient. JAMA. 1987;258:2106–2107.
107. Hay CRM, Messenger AG, Cotton DWK, et al. Atypical bullous pyoderma gangrenosum associated with myeloid malignancies. J Clin Pathol. 1987;40:387–392.
108. Cohen PR, Kurzrock R. Sweet's syndrome and malignancy. Am J Med. 1987;82:1120–1126.
109. Bookman MA, Longo DL. Concomitant illness in patients treated for Hodgkin's disease. Cancer Treat Rev. 1986;13:77–111.
110. Miliauskas JR, Webber BL. Disseminated varicella at autopsy in children with cancer. Cancer. 1984;53:1518–1525.
111. Strauss SE. Varicella zoster virus infections: Biology, natural history, treatment and prevention. Ann Intern Med. 1988;108:221–237.
112. Rampling A, Warren RE, Bevan PC, et al. *Clostridium difficile* in haematological malignancy. J Clin Pathol. 1985;38:445–451.
113. Delmé M, Vandercam B, Avesani V, et al. Epidemiology and prevention of *Clostridium difficile* infection in a leukemia unit. Eur J Clin Microbiol. 1987;6:623–627.
114. Heard SR, O'Farrell S, Holland D, et al. The epidemiology of *Clostridium difficile* with use of a typing scheme: Nosocomial acquisition and cross-infection among immunocompromised patients. J Infect Dis. 1986;153:159–162.
115. Freifeld AG, Walsh T, Marshall D, et al. Monotherapy for fever and neutropenia in cancer patients: A randomized comparison of ceftazidime versus imipenem. J Clin Oncol. 1995;13:165–176.
116. Tikko SK, Distenfield A, Davidson M. *Clostridium septicum* septicemia with identical metastatic myonecroses in a granulocytopenic patient. Am J Med. 1985;79:256–258.
117. Hughes WT, Armstrong D, Bodey GP, et al. 1997 Guidelines for the use of antimicrobial agents in neutropenic patients with unexplained fever. Clin Infect Dis. 1997;25:551–573.
118. De Pauw BE, Meropenem Study Group of Leuven-London-Nijmegen. Meropenem and ceftazidime are equally effective as single agents for empirical therapy of the febrile neutropenic patient. J Antimicrob Chemother. 1995;36:185–200.
119. De Pauw BE, Kauw F, Muytjens H, et al. Randomized study of ceftazidime versus gentamicin plus cefotaxime for infections in severe granulocytopenic patients. J Antimicrob Chemother. 1983;12(Suppl A):S93–S99.
120. Pizzo PA, Hathorn JW, Hiemenz J, et al. A randomized trial comparing ceftazidime alone with combination antibiotic therapy in cancer patients with fever and neutropenia. N Engl J Med. 1986;315:552–558.
121. Viscoli C, Castagnola E, Rogers DD. Infections in the compromised child. Clin Haematol. 1991;2:511–543.
122. Hahn IM, Viscoli C, Paesmans M, et al. A comparison of outcome from febrile neutropenic episodes in children compared with adults: Results from four EORTC studies. Br J Haematol. 1997;99:580–588.
123. Eggiman P, Glauser MP, Aoun M, et al. Cefepime monotherapy for empirical treatment of fever in granulocytopenic patients. J Antimicrob Chemother. 1993;32:151–163.
124. Kelsey SM, Wood ME, Shaw E, et al. A comparative study of intravenous ciprofloxacin and benzylpenicillin versus netelmicin and piperacillin for the empirical treatment of fever in neutropenic patients. J Antimicrob Chemother. 1990;25:149–157.
125. Engervall PA, Stiernstedt GT, Günther G, Bjorkholm MJ: Trimethoprim-sulfamethoxazole plus amikacin as first-line therapy and imipenem/cilastatin as second empirical therapy in febrile neutropenic patients with hematological disorders. J Chemother. 1992;4:99–106.
126. Elting LS, Bodey GP, Fainstein V, et al. Polymicrobial septicemia in the cancer patient. Medicine (Baltimore). 1986;65:218–225.
127. Dompeling EC, Donnelly JP, Deresinski SC, et al. Early identification of neutropenic patients at risk of gram-positive bacteraemia and the impact of empirical administration of vancomycin. Eur J Cancer. 1996;32A:1332–1339.
128. Nováková I, Donnelly JP, De Pauw B. Ceftazidime as monotherapy or combined with teicoplanin for initial empirical treatment of presumed bacteremia in febrile granulocytopenic patients. Antimicrob Agents Chemother. 1991;35:672–678.
129. Ramphal R, Bolger M, Oblon DJ, et al. Vancomycin is not an essential component of the initial empiric treatment regimen for febrile neutropenic patients receiving ceftazidime—a randomized prospective study. Antimicrob Agents Chemother. 1992;36:445–452.
130. Kureishi A, Jewesson PJ, Rubinger M, et al. Double-blind comparison of teicoplanin versus vancomycin in febrile neutropenic patients receiving concomitant tobramycin and piperacillin: Effect on cyclosporin A–associated nephrotoxicity. Antimicrob Agents Chemother. 1991;35:2246–2252.
131. Donnelly JP, Muus P, Horrevorts AM, et al. Failure of clindamycin to influence the course of severe oromucositis associated with streptococcal bacteraemia in allogeneic bone marrow transplant recipients. Scand J Infect Dis. 1993;25:43–50.
132. Dompeling EC, Donnelly JP, Raemaekers JMM, De Pauw BE. Pre-emptive administration of corticosteroids prevents the development of ARDS associated with *Streptococcus mitis* bacteremia following chemotherapy with high-dose cytarabine. Ann Hematol. 1994;69:69–72.
133. Pizzo PA, Robichaud KJ, Gill FA, Witebsky FG. Empiric antibiotic and antifungal therapy for cancer patients with prolonged fever and granulocytopenia. Am J Med. 1982;2:101–110.
134. EORTC International Antimicrobial Therapy Cooperative Group. Empiric antifungal therapy in febrile neutropenic patients. Am J Med. 1989;86:668–672.
135. Blumberg EA, Reboli AC. Failure of systemic empirical treatment with amphotericin B to prevent candidemia in neutropenic patients with cancer. Clin Infect Dis. 1996;22:462–466.
136. Denning DW, Stevens DA. Antifungal and surgical treatment of invasive aspergillosis: Review of 2121 published cases. Rev Infect Dis. 1992;24:1147–1201.
137. Anaissie EJ, Vartivarian SE, Abi-Said D, et al. Fluconazole versus amphotericin B in the treatment of hematogenous candidiasis: A matched cohort study. Am J Med. 1996;101:170–176.
138. Anaissie EJ, Darouiche RO, Abi-Said D, et al. Management of invasive candidal infections: Results of a prospective, randomized, multicenter study of fluconazole versus amphotericin B and a review of the literature. Clin Infect Dis. 1996;23:964–972.
139. De Pauw BE, Raemaekers JMM, Donnelly JP, et al. An open study on the safety and efficacy of fluconazole in the treatment of disseminated *Candida* infections in patients treated for a hematological malignancy. Ann Hematol. 1995;70:83–87.
140. Lecciones JA, Lee JW, Navarro EE, et al. Vascular catheter–associated fungemia in patients with cancer: Analysis of 155 episodes. Clin Infect Dis. 1992;14:875–883.
141. Ringden O, Meunier F, Tollemar J, et al. Efficacy of amphotericin B encapsulated in liposomes (AmBisome) in the treatment of invasive fungal infections in immunocompromised patients. J Antimicrob Chemother. 1991;28(Suppl B):S73–S82.
142. Oppenheim BA, Herbrecht R, Kusne S. The safety and efficacy of amphotericin B colloidal dispersion in the treatment of invasive mycoses. Clin Infect Dis. 1995;21:1145–1153.
143. White MH, Anaissie EJ, Kusne S, et al. Amphotericin B colloidal dispersion vs. amphotericin B as therapy for invasive aspergillosis. Clin Infect Dis. 1997;24:635–642.
144. Anaissie EJ, Mattiuzzi GN, Miller CB, et al. Treatment of invasive fungal infections in renally impaired patients with amphotericin B colloidal dispersion. Antimicrob Agents Chemother. 1998;42:606–611.
145. Van't Wout JW, Novakova I, Verhagen CAH, et al. The efficacy of itraconazole

against systemic fungal infections in neutropenic patients: A randomised comparative with amphotericin B. J Infect. 1991;22:45–52.
146. Denning DW, Lee JY, Hostetler JS, et al. NIAID mycosis study group multicenter trial of oral itraconazole therapy for invasive aspergillosis. Am J Med. 1994;97:135–144.
147. Stevens DA, Lee JY. Analysis of compassionate use itraconazole therapy for invasive aspergillosis by the NIAID Mycosis Study Group criteria. Arch Intern Med. 1997;157:1857–1862.
148. Lister J. Amphotericin B lipid complex (Abelcet) in the treatment of invasive mycoses: The North American experience. Eur J Haematol. 1996;56(Suppl 57):S18–S23.
149. McWhinney PHM, Kibbler CC, Hamon MD, et al. Progress in the diagnosis and management of aspergillosis in bone marrow transplantation: Thirteen years experience. Clin Infect Dis. 1993;17:397–404.
150. Dignani MC, Anaissie EJ, Hester JP, et al. Treatment of neutropenia-related fungal infections with granulocyte colony-stimulating factor–elicited white blood cell transfusions: A pilot study. Leukemia. 1997;11:1621–1630.
151. Bernard EM, Sepkowitz KA, Telzak EE, et al. Pneumocystosis. Med Clin North Am. 1992;76:107–119.
152. Bozzette SA. The use of corticosteroids in *Pneumocystis carinii* pneumonia. J Infect Dis. 1990;162:1365–1369.
153. Bergman OJ, Mogensen SC, Ellermann-Eriksen S, Ellegaard J. Acyclovir prophylaxis and fever during remission-induction therapy of patients with acute myeloid leukemia: A randomized double-blind, placebo-controlled trial. J Clin Oncol. 1997;15:2269–2274.
154. Reusser P. Current concepts and challenges in the prevention and treatment of viral infections in immunocompromised cancer patients. Support Care Cancer. 1998;6:39–45.
155. Whitley RJ, Alford CA, Hirsch MS, et al. Vidarabine versus acyclovir therapy in herpes simplex encephalitis. N Engl J Med. 1986;314:144–149.
156. Naik HR, Siddique N, Chandrasekar PH. Foscarnet therapy for acyclovir resistant herpes simplex virus 1 infection in allogeneic bone marrow transplant recipients. Clin Infect Dis. 1995;21:1514–1515.
157. Heming VG, Prince GA, Groothuis JR, Siber GR. Hyperimmune globulins in prevention and treatment of respiratory syncytial virus infections. Clin Microbiol Rev. 1995;8:22–33.
158. Anaissie EJ, Vartivarian S, Bodey GP, et al. Randomized comparison between antibiotics alone and antibiotics plus granulocyte-macrophage colony-stimulating factor (*Escherichia coli*–derived) in cancer patients with fever and neutropenia. Am J Med. 1996;100:17–23.
159. American Society of Clinical Oncology. Update of recommendations for the use of hematopoietic colony-stimulating factors: Evidence-based clinical practice guidelines. J Clin Oncol. 1996;14:1957–1960.
160. Croockewit AJ, Bronchud MH, Aapro MS, et al. A European perspective on haematopoietic growth factors in haemato-oncology: Report of an expert meeting of the EORTC. Eur J Cancer. 1997;33:1732–1746.
161. Maki DG, Stolz SM, Wheeler S, Mermel LA. Prevention of central venous catheter–related bloodstream infection by use of an antiseptic-impregnated catheter. A randomized, controlled trial. Ann Intern Med. 1997;127:257–266.
162. Raad I, Darouiche R, Dupuis J, et al. Central venous catheters coated with minocycline and rifampin for the prevention of catheter-related colonization and bloodstream infections. A randomized double-blind trial. Ann Intern Med. 1997;127:267–274.
163. Talcott JA, Siegel RD, Finberg R, Goldman L. Risk assessment in cancer patients with fever and neutropenia: A prospective, two-center validation of a prediction rule. J Clin Oncol. 1992;10:316–322.
164. Jones GR, Konsler GK, Dunaway RP, et al. Risk factors for recurrent fever after discontinuation of empiric antibiotic therapy for fever and neutropenia in pediatric patients with a malignancy or hematologic condition. J Pediatr. 1994;124:703–708.
165. Lucas KG, Brown AE, Armstrong D, et al. The identification of febrile, neutropenic children with neoplastic disease at low risk for bacteremia and complications of sepsis. Cancer. 1996;77:791–798.
166. Malik IA, Abbas Z, Karim M. Randomised comparison of oral ofloxacin alone with a combination of parenteral antibiotics in neutropenic febrile patients. Lancet. 1992;339:1092–1096.
167. Rubenstein EB, Rolston K, Benjamin RS. Outpatient treatment of febrile episodes in low-risk neutropenic patients with cancer. Cancer. 1993;71:3640–3646.
168. Talcott JA, Whalen A, Clark J, et al. Home antibiotic therapy for low-risk cancer patients with fever and neutropenia: A pilot study of 30 patients based on a validated prediction rule. J Clin Oncol. 1994;12:107–114.
169. Malik IA, Khan WA, Karim M, et al. Feasibility of outpatient management of fever in cancer patient with low-risk neutropenia: Results of a prospective randomized trial. Am J Med. 1995;98:224–231.
170. Horowitz DW, Holmgren D, Seiter K. Stepdown single antibiotic therapy for the management of the high risk adult with hematologic malignancies. Leuk Lymphoma. 1996;23:159–163.
171. Aquino VM, Tkaczewski I, Buchanan GR. Early discharge of low-risk febrile neutropenic children and adolescents with cancer. Clin Infect Dis. 1997;25:74–78.
172. Joshi JH, Schimpff SC, Tenney JH, et al. Can antibacterial therapy be discontinued in persistently febrile granulocytopenic cancer patients? Am J Med. 1984;76:450–457.
173. Talbot GH, Provencher M, Cassileth PA. Persistent fever after recovery from granulocytopenia in acute leukemia. Arch Intern Med. 1988;148:129–135.
174. Barton TD, Schuster MG. The cause of fever following resolution of neutropenia in patients with acute leukemia. Clin Infect Dis. 1996;22:1064–1068.

Chapter 300

Empirical Therapy and Prevention of Infection in the Immunocompromised Host

PHILIP A. PIZZO

RATIONALE AND EVOLVING CONCEPTS FOR EMPIRICAL ANTIBIOTIC THERAPY

Empirical antibiotic therapy in febrile granulocytopenic cancer patients became well established during the early 1970s because of the high mortality observed when antibiotics were withheld until an infectious cause could be proved.[1] Although this approach has reduced infectious morbidity and mortality, the changes in the organisms responsible for infection, the hosts susceptible to them, and the antimicrobial agents and biologic response modifiers available to treat or prevent them have expanded the use of empirical therapy and have prompted the need for a continuing critical evaluation.[2, 3]

The original targets of empirical antibiotics were gram-negative bacteria, particularly *Pseudomonas aeruginosa.* Although gram-negative bacillary infections (especially *Escherichia coli* and *Klebsiella* spp.) still predominate in some cancer centers, infections due to *P. aeruginosa* now remain low. At the National Cancer Institute, for example, *P. aeruginosa* accounted for less than a dozen of the episodes of the fever and neutropenia that occurred in the more than 1200 adults and children enrolled in clinical trials. This change in the incidence of *Pseudomonas* infections has significant implications for patient outcomes and for the selection of empirical antibiotic regimens. At the same time, some treatment centers have observed a significant increase in the frequency of infections due to *Enterobacter*[4] or to *Stenotrophomonas maltophilia.*

In contrast, infections due to gram-positive cocci (*Staphylococcus aureus, Staphylococcus epidermidis*) are now substantial, particularly with the use of indwelling intravenous catheters, and in many centers are the most common isolates.[5–8] These organisms are less adequately covered by many empirical regimens. Vancomycin usage has steadily increased in many centers because coagulase-negative staphylococci are common, methicillin-resistant *S. aureus* infections are occurring, and α-hemolytic streptococcal infections seem to respond poorly to third-generation cephalosporins. However, pressure to use more vancomycin is certain to increase the problem of vancomycin-resistant enterococci and to raise the specter that vancomycin-resistant *S. aureus* will emerge as a much more serious problem. Some of these shifts in infection are related to changes in the care of patients. For example, patients with acute leukemia who receive high-dose cytosine arabinoside and who develop oral mucositis (with or without associated herpetic gingivostomatitis) appear to be more vulnerable to bacteremia with α-hemolytic streptococci (especially *Streptococcus mitis*), not infrequently accompanied by adult respiratory distress syndrome.[9, 10] Patients receiving oral quinolones for prophylaxis have also had breakthrough infections with α-hemolytic streptococci.[11]

Although anaerobes infrequently account for primary infection, they are associated with mixed infections affecting the oral cavity, gastrointestinal tract, or perianal area.

For several years, the incidence of tuberculosis, including multidrug-resistant tubercular infections, increased in a number of cities, especially in patients with the acquired immunodeficiency syndrome.[12, 13] This increased incidence has declined with better public health practices, increased use of directly observed therapy, and better antiviral control with highly active antiretroviral therapy. Although the impact of tuberculosis in immunosuppressed cancer patients appears to be low, it is important to include mycobacterial infection in the differential diagnosis of patients with cancer. The distribution of predominant pathogens often varies at different hospitals and may change at the same hospital over time, influencing both the selection and the success of empirical antibiotic therapy.

Empirical antimicrobial management was originally formulated for patients with acute leukemia. Modern cancer therapy and bone marrow transplantation regimens now render patients with lymphomas and solid tumors as granulocytopenic as patients with leukemia, making it important to extend the principles of empirical therapy to an ever-widening population of patients (Table 300–1). Because of the variety of organisms potentially responsible for infection, many centers have employed combination regimens to encompass gram-positive and gram-negative bacteria. The development of the newer cephalosporins, carbapenems, and quinolones offers new therapeutic options for simplifying in vitro empirical therapy for certain febrile neutropenic patients.[14]

Empirical therapy was initially focused on preventing death from an undiagnosed bacterial infection. Patients who remain granulocytopenic for extended periods are also at risk for second infections or even multiple infections, particularly with invasive mycoses. In the older literature, deep fungal infections were found at postmortem examination in 8 to 69% of patients who died with prolonged granulocytopenia, often without antemortem evidence of infection.[15–17] Whether these invasive fungal infections were a consequence of broad-spectrum antibiotics, prolonged granulocytopenia, or both remains unclear. Nonetheless, the excessive mortality related to these infections promoted empirical antifungal therapy in some high-risk patients, although the toxicity must be weighed against the benefits.[18]

Empirical antibiotics have also been used for patients who have clinically defined sites of infection when the risks of establishing a microbiologic diagnosis with an invasive diagnostic procedure appear prohibitive. The granulocytopenic patient with a new pulmonary infiltrate is such an example, because a trial of antibiotics may be preferable to biopsy.[19]

Currently relevant questions about empirical therapy include the following: Who should receive empirical therapy and when should it be started? What constitutes appropriate initial empirical therapy? How should the initial therapy be modified for patients who remain granulocytopenic or who do not respond to the initial regimen? How long should empirical antibiotic therapy be continued?

TABLE 300–1 General Principles of Management of Febrile Neutropenic Patients

Instruct patients and families to seek medical help if the patients develop a fever when their neutrophil count is falling or low.
Examine patients at least daily while they are febrile and neutropenic.
Initiate prompt therapy with broad-spectrum antibiotic or antibiotics when a neutropenic patient (polymorphonuclear leukocytes $<500/m^3$) becomes febrile (single oral-equivalent elevation >38.5°C or three elevations above 38°C during a 24-hour period).
If the patient has an indwelling intravenous catheter, obtain samples for culture from each port and lumen as well as peripherally. Also, rotate antibiotics so they are delivered to each lumen of double- or triple-lumen catheters.
Monitor patients who are receiving antibiotics closely for breakthrough or superinfections that require additions or modifications of the primary empirical regimen.
Continue empirical antibiotics in neutropenic patients with protracted (i.e., >1 week) periods of neutropenia, particularly in those who remain persistently febrile.
Add empirical antifungal therapy in neutropenic patients who remain febrile after 1 week of therapy with broad-spectrum antibiotic or antibiotics or in neutropenic patients who recrudesce after having initially become afebrile.
Discontinue antibiotic therapy when the neutrophil count has risen above $500/mm^3$ in high-risk patients or is recovering in low-risk patients.
Although most infections in neutropenic patients can be treated with conventional 10- to 14-day courses of therapy, more protracted therapy is necessary for neutropenic patients with a residual focus of infection or patients with invasive mycoses (e.g., hepatosplenic candidiasis).
Exercise careful hand washing in the care and management of hospitalized neutropenic patients.

From Pizzo PA. Management of fever in patients with cancer and treatment-induced neutropenia. N Engl J Med. 1993;328:1323–1332. Copyright © 1993 Massachusetts Medical Society. All rights reserved.

GUIDELINES FOR EMPIRICAL THERAPY

Candidates

As detailed in Chapter 298, granulocytopenia is the single most important risk factor for infection in patients with a hematologic malignancy. This risk is, however, influenced not only by the depth and duration of the granulocytopenia but also by qualitative abnormalities in phagocyte function, alterations in cellular or humoral immunity, and changes in physical defense barriers. Because more than 80% of the microbiologically defined primary bacterial infections arise from the patient's endogenous microbial flora,[20] the spectrum and virulence of the host's colonizing flora can influence the risk of developing an infection as well as the need, selection, and success of empirically administered antibiotics.[21, 22]

The level of granulocytopenia that should prompt empirical therapy is somewhat arbitrarily interpreted. Although some recommend starting antibiotics when the neutrophil count falls below $1000/mm^3$, most would wait until the granulocyte count is less than $500/mm^3$. Some studies have suggested that the incidence of bacteremia is significantly increased only when the neutrophil count is less than $200/mm^3$. Perhaps more important than the absolute nadir is the rate at which the counts are falling. For example, only 17% of the fevers that occurred in cancer patients whose neutrophil counts were greater than $500/mm^3$ could be attributed to infection. In contrast, the likelihood of an infectious cause of a fever was increased if the patient's neutrophil count was falling rapidly because of antecedent chemotherapy.[23]

The level of fever that should prompt therapy is also arbitrarily defined. In general, two or three low-grade elevations above 38°C, in concert with a granulocyte count of less than $500/mm^3$, is a sufficient criterion to begin empirical therapy. Fever should not be attributable to blood products, cancer, or medications, and note should be taken as to whether the patient is receiving drugs that might mask a febrile response (e.g., steroids, antipyretic-containing analgesics). It is optimal to have institutional criteria for fever and granulocytopenia both predefined and rigidly adhered to. Such a policy plays an important role in reducing infection-related morbidity (e.g., shock, perianal cellulitis) and mortality.

All patients who become febrile while neutropenic are at risk for infection and should receive prompt empirical broad-spectrum therapy. The anticipated severity of their infectious complications can be delineated according to their presumed duration of neutropenia.[3] Patients who are neutropenic for less than 7 to 10 days can be considered *low risk* and generally have an uncomplicated outcome.[24] However, patients remaining neutropenic beyond 10 days should be considered *high risk* and require scrupulous observation for multiple infectious complications.[25]

Preantibiotic Evaluation

The diminished inflammatory capability of the granulocytopenic patient can mask the usual signs and symptoms of infection.[26] In a prospective evaluation of 140 febrile granulocytopenic patients,[23] it was not possible to differentiate patients with bacteremia from those with unexplained fever according to their age, sex, underlying malignancy, or types of therapeutic modalities or invasive diagnostic procedures they had received. The absence of physical findings suggestive of infection did not exclude a potentially life-threatening bacteremia. More than half of the bacteremic patients in this study exhibited no specific physical findings. Alternatively, even minimal signs suggesting infection must be carefully pursued.

Patients about to receive empirical therapy should be questioned and examined for new symptoms and signs. They should also have a baseline chest radiograph if they have any respiratory symptoms;[27] a urinalysis; at least two sets of preantibiotic blood cultures; and aspirate (or biopsy) cultures from any accessible sites suggestive of infection. If material for blood cultures is obtained from an indwelling intravascular catheter, it is important to also obtain a sample or samples for culture percutaneously from a peripheral vein. Furthermore, it is important to obtain material for blood cultures from each port in patients with multilumen catheters.

Although the organisms ultimately responsible for infection are frequently part of the patient's colonizing flora, routine surveillance cultures from asymptomatic body sites are not helpful in guiding initial empirical therapy.[28] This is because no one body site is consistently positive and because multiple organisms are usually isolated from any one site, making prospective predictions of the true pathogen difficult. Moreover, the time lag for surveillance cultures to become positive does not make them prospectively useful or cost-effective. The role of surveillance cultures in guiding management decisions in patients already receiving antibiotics is also limited. Specific exceptions may be patients in protected isolation (where stool cultures may be of use) or centers with a high incidence of *Aspergillus flavus* infections, where nasal swabs may be helpful in identifying high-risk patients.[6, 18, 29, 30]

Despite careful preantibiotic evaluation, a clinical or microbiologic cause of the patient's fever can be discerned in less than 40% of febrile neutropenic episodes. Careful and frequent physical examination of the patient with persistent fever is essential, focusing particularly on the most common foci of infections (e.g., oral cavity, lungs, perianal area). It is hoped that refinements and developments in more sensitive diagnostic studies (e.g., polymerase chain reaction) will enhance the ability to detect subtle or occult sites of infection. Although the use of radionuclide imaging techniques to localize sites of infection has been disappointing, refinements in computed tomography and magnetic resonance imaging have improved diagnosis.[31]

Antibiotic Foundations for Initial Therapy

Because both gram-positive and gram-negative bacteria (as well as mixed infections) can be responsible for these initial infections, the empirical regimen must have a broad spectrum, ideally achieve high bactericidal levels, and be as nontoxic and simple to administer as possible. This has usually necessitated the combination of two or more antibiotics. The availability of third-generation cephalosporins and carbapenems has offered an alternative to combination regimens, because a number of these antibiotics provide, as single agents, an exceedingly broad range of activity (including both gram-positive and gram-negative bacteria).[4, 14] Unlike the aminoglycosides, these newer β-lactam antibiotics do not require the monitoring of serum levels and have minimal toxicity (Table 300–2).[32] Fortunately, once-daily aminoglycoside therapy has decreased aminoglycoside toxicity without compromising efficacy in empirical therapy of neutropenic patients (see Chapter 23).

An aminoglycoside plus a β-lactam–containing regimen (e.g., ceftazidime plus amikacin) is considered by many to be the standard of care, particularly for patients with documented gram-negative infection.[33] However, no particular combination regimen has been shown to be clearly superior, and the one that is chosen at a given institution should reflect specific epidemiologic considerations (e.g., local resistance patterns) as well as cost.

Despite the proven efficacy of combination therapy, the potential of a single antibiotic (monotherapy) for the empirical management of the febrile neutropenic patient is attractive for its ease of administration, cost, and lack of toxicity. To assess the efficacy of a monotherapeutic regimen, a series of prospective randomized trials were

TABLE 300–2 Antimicrobial Issues for the Neutropenic Patient

Antibiotics	
Third-generation cephalosporins	Only ceftazidime and cefepime are appropriate in neutropenic patients when coverage of *Pseudomonas aeruginosa* is desired.
Carbapenems	If *P. aeruginosa* is suspected or cultured, an aminoglycoside should be added to imipenem or meropenem.
Extended-spectrum penicillins	Because of the potential for resistance, piperacillin, ticarcillin, and mezlocillin should be administered with either an aminoglycoside or a third-generation cephalosporin.
Monobactams	Aztreonam provides an important alternative for β-lactam–allergic patients but should be combined with vancomycin if being used for empirical therapy.
Quinolones	Important for gram-negative infection and possibly for use in low-risk neutropenic patients. But to avoid resistance, use for prophylaxis is best avoided.
Vancomycin	Pathogen-directed therapy generally suffices. Empirical use can be restricted to centers with a high incidence of methicillin-resistant *Staphylococcus aureus*. Strains of vancomycin-resistant enterococci are increasingly common.
Antifungals	
Amphotericin B	Still the "gold standard." With the deoxycholate formulation, a dose of 0.6 mg/kg/day suffices for *Candida albicans* and *Cryptococcus;* 1 mg/kg/day is preferred for *Candida tropicalis,* and 1.5 mg/kg/day for *Aspergillus*. Lipid formulations are also available.
Ketoconazole	Useful for thrush and *Candida* esophagitis.
Fluconazole	Very effective for thrush, esophagitis. Effective in candidemia of nonneutropenic patients. No activity against *Aspergillus*.
Itraconazole	Active against *Aspergillus* but has variable bioavailability.
Antivirals	
Acyclovir	Oral therapy is not advised for severely compromised hosts with varicella. For patients with VZV, 1500 $mg/m^2/day$ in 3 divided doses is included. For patients with HSV, oral or parenteral therapy (750 $mg/m^2/day$ in 3 divided doses) is satisfactory.
Ganciclovir	Effective in CMV retinitis, prevention of pneumonitis and, in combination with IGIV, for treatment of pneumonitis.
Foscarnet	Alternative therapy for CMV, either alone or in combination therapy
Pneumocystis	
Trimethoprim-sulfamethoxazole	Remains drug of choice for PCP prophylaxis but not required in all cancer patients. Three times a week schedule is satisfactory.
Aerosolized pentamidine	Expensive and not as effective as trimethoprim-sulfamethoxazole from studies performed in HIV-infected adults.

Abbreviations: CMV, Cytomegalovirus; HSV, herpes simplex virus; HIV, human immunodeficiency virus; IGIV, intravenous immune globulin; PCP, *Pneumocystis carinii* pneumonia; VZV, varicella-zoster virus.
From Pizzo PA. Management of fever in patients with cancer and treatment-induced neutropenia. N Engl J Med. 1993;328:1323–1333. Copyright © 1993 Massachusetts Medical Society. All rights reserved.

conducted at the National Cancer Institute. The first of these compared ceftazidime monotherapy to a combination of cephalothin, gentamicin, and carbenicillin.[34] The antibiotic regimens were evaluated at both an *early* and an *overall* evaluation point. The early evaluation (at 72 hours) was specifically performed to assess the efficacy of the antibiotics during the period when they were truly used in an empirical manner (i.e., before the availability of definitive microbiologic data). The overall evaluation was performed at the resolution of the neutropenic episode. The responses were categorized as *successful* (with or without modification of the initial regimen) if the patient survived the episode of neutropenia and as *failures* if the patient died while neutropenic.

In this study, there was no significant difference in terms of success (with or without modifications) for patients randomized to ceftazidime or the combination regimen among patients classified as having either a fever of unknown origin (FUO) or a clinically or microbiologically documented infection. The results at the *overall evaluation* demonstrated equivalent success rates for the two regimens for patients classified as having either an FUO or a documented infection. The percentage of patients treated successfully without the need for modification of the initial antimicrobial therapy was predictably less at the final evaluation than at the early evaluation. Patients with documented infections required changes in antimicrobial therapy more often than those with FUO, but the overall need for modification of the initial therapy for all patients randomized to monotherapy (59%) and those randomized to combination therapy (59%) was similar. Therefore, in terms of the overall outcome and the frequency with which modifications of the initial empirical regimen were necessary, monotherapy with ceftazidime was as effective as combination therapy with cephalothin, carbenicillin, and gentamicin for this population of patients.

A second study at the National Cancer Institute compared initial empirical therapy with ceftazidime to that with imipenem-cilastatin.[35] Both antibiotics proved successful in the initial empirical management of adults and children with fever and neutropenia. The overall survival was greater than 98% in patients who began either ceftazidime or imipenem monotherapy. Again, additions to or modifications of this regimen were necessary for patients with documented infections or with prolonged neutropenia but were not significantly different from those of patients who started on either ceftazidime or imipenem. Although outcomes were similar with ceftazidime and imipenem-cilastatin, greater toxicity in the form of nausea, vomiting, and diarrhea, especially diarrhea due to *Clostridium difficile,* was observed with imipenem. Nonetheless, the principle of using either a third-generation cephalosporin or a carbapenem as monotherapy was clearly demonstrated with these and other studies. Further options with both an increased antimicrobial spectrum and decreased toxicity can be achieved with the newer third-generation cephalosporins (i.e., cefepime) or carbapenems (i.e., meropenem).[36, 37]

In addition to demonstrating that monotherapy is a viable option for patients who became febrile while neutropenic (a finding that has been confirmed by other studies and a meta-analysis), these clinical trials have affirmed that neutropenic patients can be divided into low- and high-risk groups. Most low-risk patients can be successfully treated without the need for frequent additions or modifications of their initial antibiotic regimen.[24] In contrast, high-risk patients (i.e., those remaining neutropenic beyond 7 to 10 days) have a significantly greater requirement for antimicrobial additions or modifications.[25, 34, 38] It becomes possible, therefore, to configure therapeutic strategies that take these risk categories into account. For example, low-risk patients can be more simply treated and may even be candidates for oral antibiotic therapy and possibly outpatient management.[24] High-risk patients, on the other hand, require careful inpatient management and are likely to require a number of antimicrobial additions or modifications. The criteria that help guide these modifications are best dictated by careful observation of the patients' evolving clinical course, including the persistence of fever, new clinical manifestations of infection, or the isolation of a new organism. Some of the more common criteria for considering a modification of the initial regimen are included in Table 300–3.

Regardless of whether the initial choice of antibiotic therapy is a third-generation cephalosporin or carbapenem alone, or their combination with an aminoglycoside, most authorities concur that vancomycin should not be added empirically because of the increased frequency of gram-positive infections (especially enterococci) in this patient population. In fact, a number of randomized clinical trials have demonstrated that there is no survival advantage to including vancomycin in the initial management of every neutropenic patient who becomes febrile.[39–41] Indeed, with rare exception, patients (even those with indwelling catheters) can be treated successfully without empirical vancomycin therapy, reserving it for the identification of a site or origin that requires its use. Of course, in centers where methicillin-resistant *S. aureus,* vancomycin-susceptible enterococci, or *S. mitis* are frequent, vancomycin may be included in the initial regimen.

Ultimately, the decision regarding the appropriate regimen must be individualized at each institution. Hospitals have different patterns of microbial isolates and antibiotic resistance patterns that must be taken into account. Nevertheless, there is mounting evidence that the initial empirical management of a febrile neutropenic cancer patient may be accomplished with a single antibiotic. Furthermore, for low-risk patients, observational data as well as a double-blind placebo-controlled trial performed at the National Cancer Institute has demonstrated that oral therapy (with ciprofloxacin plus amoxicillin-clavulanate) is comparable to parenteral therapy (with ceftazidime) for this subset of neutropenic patients who become febrile.[42–45] Regardless of the empirical regimen chosen, however, the clinician must recognize the indications for, and appropriately employ, the modifications of therapy essential to ensure a successful outcome for a neutropenic patient (see Table 300–3). The importance of including these modifications in the assessment and management of neutropenic patients has been underscored in consensus conferences.[46]

Empirical Antifungal Therapy

The rationale for the empirical use of an antifungal compound is based on several lines of reasoning. First, the antemortem diagnosis of disseminated fungal disease is difficult in an immunocompromised host. Withholding antifungal therapy until the establishment of a definitive diagnosis frequently allows dissemination to occur before the institution of therapy.[19, 47] It also appears that the outcome of a fungal infection in an immunocompromised patient is favorably improved with the early institution of effective therapy. Finally, it is possible to identify patients who are at greatest risk for the development of an invasive mycosis. Thus, neutropenic patients who remain febrile despite a 4- to 7-day trial of broad-spectrum antimicrobial therapy are particularly prone to fungal disease.

Support for the empirical institution of antifungal therapy comes from retrospective and prospective studies. Burke and coworkers used amphotericin B in patients with acute leukemia with recurrent or persistent fever despite antibiotic coverage with gentamicin and carbenicillin.[48] Stein and colleagues employed amphotericin B for patients with persistent or recrudescent fever after a week of antimicrobial therapy during induction therapy for acute myelogenous leukemia.[49] Both these studies reported a decrease in deaths due to deep mycoses relative to historical control groups. Studies performed at the National Cancer Institute[50] and by the European Organization for Research in the Treatment of Cancer[51] have demonstrated that empirical antifungal therapy with amphotericin B can decrease the incidence of invasive mycoses, especially with *Candida.* However, the toxicity of amphotericin B remains substantial, and breakthrough infection with *Aspergillus* can still occur when patients are receiving the usual empirical dosage of 0.5 to 0.6 mg/kg/day.[52] Whether these *Aspergillus* infections can be prevented by higher dosages of amphotericin B (1 to 1.5 mg/kg/day) is unclear, although toxicity is certainly more likely to occur.[53] Safer, more tolerable, and effective

TABLE 300-3 Common Modifications or Additions to Initial Empirical Therapy in Neutropenic Patients

Patient Status or Symptoms	Modifications of Primary Regimen
Fever	
Persistent for >1 wk	Add empirical antifungal therapy. Amphotericin B remains current "gold standard."
Recrudescence 1 wk or later in persistently neutropenic patient	Add empirical antifungal therapy.
Persistent or recurrent fever at time of recovery from neutropenia	Evaluate liver and spleen by CT, ultrasonography, or MRI for hepatosplenic candidiasis and need for antifungal therapy.
Blood stream	
Preantibiotic cultures	
Gram-positive isolate	Add vancomycin pending further identification.
Gram-negative isolate	Maintain regimen if patient is stable and isolate is sensitive. If *Pseudomonas aeruginosa, Enterobacter,* or *Citrobacter* is isolated, add an aminoglycoside and/or an additional β-lactam.
Organism isolated while on antibiotics	
Gram-positive	Add vancomycin.
Gram-negative	Change to new combination regimen (e.g., imipenem or meropenem plus gentamicin, or gentamicin plus piperacillin).
Head, ear, eye, nose, and throat sites	
Necrotizing or marginal gingivitis	Add specific antianaerobic agent (clindamycin or metronidazole) to empirical therapy.
Vesicular or ulcerative lesions	Suspect herpes simplex. Culture and begin acyclovir therapy.
Sinus tenderness or nasal ulcerative lesions	Suspect fungal infection with *Aspergillus* or *Mucor.*
Gastrointestinal	
Retrosternal burning pain	Suspect *Candida,* HSV, or both. Add antifungal therapy and if no response, acyclovir. Bacterial esophagitis also possibility. For patients who do not respond within 48 hr, endoscopy should be considered.
Acute abdominal pain	Suspect typhlitis, as well as appendicitis, if right lower quadrant pain. Add specific antianaerobic coverage to empirical regimen and monitor closely for surgical intervention.
Perianal tenderness	Add specific antianaerobic agent to empirical regimen. Monitor for surgical intervention especially when recovering from neutropenia.
Respiratory	
New focal lesion in patients recovering from neutropenia	Observe carefully because this may be consequence of inflammatory response in concert with neutrophil recovery.
New focal lesion in patients still neutropenic	*Aspergillus* is major concern. Attempt to heighten diagnostic index by culture or biopsy. If not candidate for procedure, administer high-dose amphotericin B (1.5 mg/kg/day).
New interstitial pneumonitis	Attempt diagnosis by induced sputum or BAL. If not feasible, begin empirical trimethoprim-sulfamethoxazole or pentamidine therapy. Consider noninfectious causes and need for open-lung biopsy if patients have not improved after 4 days of empirical therapy.
Central venous catheter	
Positive culture with organisms other than *Bacillus, Candida*	Attempt to treat. Be sure to rotate infusion port for antibiotics when using multilumen catheters.
Positive with *Bacillus, Candida*	Remove catheter and treat appropriately.
Exit site infection with mycobacteria, *Aspergillus*	Remove catheter and treat appropriately.
Tunnel infection	Remove catheter and treat appropriately.

Abbreviations: BAL, Bronchoalveolar lavage; CT, computed tomography; HSV, herpes simplex virus; MRI, magnetic resonance imaging.
Modified from Pizzo PA. Management of fever in patients with cancer and treatment-induced neutropenia. N Engl J Med. 1993;328:1323–1332. Copyright © 1993 Massachusetts Medical Society. All rights reserved.

alternatives to amphotericin B are needed. Ketoconazole and itraconazole have been evaluated, but neither is a clear replacement for amphotericin B.[54] Placebo-controlled trials in patients undergoing bone marrow transplantation have shown that fluconazole, administered prophylactically, decreased the incidence of superficial and deep candidiasis.[55] However, fluconazole is unlikely to prevent infection with *Candida krusei,* and its spectrum of activity does not include *Aspergillus* or *Mucor.* The use of a liposomal preparation of amphotericin (AmBisome) has been compared with amphotericin B deoxycholate, the old formulation. A multicenter randomized trial compared the two formulations for empirical therapy of neutropenic patients who remained febrile after at least 96 hours of broad-spectrum antibiotic therapy. With AmBisome, the efficacy was the same but the toxicity less. It is important to note that there are a number of differences among the lipid-associated formulations of amphotericin. Amphotericin B colloidal dispersion demonstrated an efficacy comparable to that of amphotericin B deoxycholate. Although there was little renal toxicity with amphotericin B colloidal dispersion, there were substantial infusion-related toxicity with that formulation.[56, 57]

Empirical antifungal therapy is indicated for those patients who remain neutropenic and febrile (or whose fever recrudesces) despite 1 week of broad-spectrum antibiotic therapy. The optimal duration of antibiotic antifungal therapy is based on the dictum of clinical experience. For patients who remain neutropenic, antifungal therapy should be continued until the resolution of granulocytopenia. The persistence or recrudescence of fever should prompt a meticulous investigation for nonfungal infectious causes (e.g., bacterial or viral superinfection). Patients who develop a documented fungal infection should be treated according to established clinical guidelines for the offending pathogen. Neutropenic patients with *Aspergillus* pneumonia may benefit from daily doses of amphotericin in the range of 1 to 1.5 mg/kg.[53]

In addition to antibiotics and antifungal agents, it may also be necessary to add antiviral and antiparasitic agents to the therapeutic regimen. Acyclovir is the drug of choice for immunocompromised patients with varicella-zoster virus and herpes simplex virus infections. For patients who develop pneumonitis or other serious disease manifestations of cytomegalovirus (CMV), ganciclovir should be used, perhaps with intravenous immunoglobulin. Foscarnet has been used for herpes simplex virus, varicella-zoster virus, or CMV infections that are resistant to acyclovir or ganciclovir. In some situations, the combination of ganciclovir plus foscarnet may be beneficial.

Duration of Empirical Antibacterial Therapy

When antibiotic therapy has been started empirically, the question of how long to continue it when a site of infection has not been defined is often problematic. Discontinuing antibiotic therapy too early can lead to clinical deterioration in patients who remain granulocytopenic, particularly when they are persistently febrile.[50, 58, 59]

Low-risk patients with unexplained fever in whom the granulocytopenia resolves within 1 week of starting antibiotic therapy can receive abbreviated courses of therapy, especially if no infectious cause is identified or bone marrow recovery is evident (e.g., rising neutrophil count) after therapy is initiated.[60–62]

High-risk FUO patients who remain neutropenic for more than 1 week pose more of a challenge. The management of these patients has been addressed in a series of prospective clinical studies, stratifying them according to whether they had defervesced after the initiation of broad-spectrum therapy or whether they remained persistently febrile in spite of empirical antibiotic therapy.[50, 59] Within 3 days after antibiotic therapy was discontinued on day 7 in patients who had defervesced on therapy but who remained afebrile, 41% again became febrile; the isolate or isolates obtained when these patients became febrile again were sensitive to the antibiotics that had been discontinued. By contrast, no subsequent infections were observed in the patients who simply continued receiving antibiotic therapy. However, these data did not define whether antibiotic therapy should be continued until the final resolution of neutropenia or whether a defined but limited course of antibiotic therapy, as if the patient had an occult site of infection, might suffice. In a subsequent study, the appropriate duration of therapy was evaluated by continuing antibiotic therapy for afebrile but persistently granulocytopenic FUO patients for a full 14-day treatment course (as if their fever had an occult infectious cause) and then randomizing them either to discontinue antibiotic therapy or to continue treatment until the resolution of the granulocytopenia. After day 14, approximately one third of the patients either discontinuing or continuing antibiotic therapy became febrile again; because patients randomized to discontinue antibiotic therapy responded to the reinstitution of therapy when the new fever developed, it seems reasonable simply to continue FUO patients on a standard 14-day treatment course if they remain febrile but granulocytopenic and then to discontinue any antibiotic therapy, recognizing that approximately 30% of the patients will require further intervention.

Empirical Therapy for Patients with Clinically Defined Infection

Antibiotics are also administered empirically to granulocytopenic patients who have clinically defined sites of infection (e.g., a pulmonary infiltrate) but for whom a microbiologic diagnosis cannot be established without an invasive procedure. Two caveats should guide such therapy. First, a defined end point for empirical trial of antibiotics should be established. For example, if broad-spectrum antibiotics are begun in a granulocytopenic patient with a localized pulmonary infiltrate, a trial lasting 48 to 72 hours is generally appropriate. If the patient has not stabilized or improved by that time, an aggressive attempt to establish the diagnosis should be pursued, even if this requires an open lung biopsy. Second, the choice of empirical antibiotics should closely approximate the probable causes of the putative infectious process. For example, a diffuse interstitial pneumonitis in a nongranulocytopenic child with leukemia in remission who is not taking effective prophylaxis is most likely due to *Pneumocystis carinii*. If bronchoalveolar lavage is inadvisable, a trial of trimethoprim-sulfamethoxazole (TMP-SMX) might be appropriate. If, however, the patient was neutropenic when the infiltrate appeared, the empirical regimen should include broad-spectrum antibiotics to cover possible bacterial causes of the diffuse pulmonary infiltrate in addition to TMP-SMX and erythromycin.[63] If the patient was granulocytopenic and had already been receiving antibiotics when the infiltrate appeared, empirical therapy would have to include TMP-SMX, erythromycin, broad-spectrum antibiotics, and antifungal therapy. The appearance of a halo sign on computed tomography would support that choice, as would the presence of *Aspergillus* either in sputum or, especially, in bronchoalveolar lavage. If the patient had had a prior fungal pneumonia and was again rendered neutropenic, the risk of recurrence of a fungal pneumonia might be high. Clearly, the merits of such empirical management must be balanced against the risks of polypharmacy. The likely yield and liability of an invasive diagnostic procedure are additional considerations.

PREVENTION OF INFECTION

Despite a multitude of clinical trials investigating the efficacy of various measures to prevent or reduce the occurrence of infection, the most important anti-infective measure identified has been the simplest: careful hand-washing practices.[64] A number of approaches have been taken to decrease the acquisition of new organisms or suppress those already colonizing the cancer patient (Table 300–4). Unfortunately, no method has stood out as singularly effective, each having promise and problems (see Tables 300–3 and 300–4). As new preventive strategies are evaluated, they initially appear promising, but as additional studies are conducted, their beneficial results become less convincing.

Preventing the Acquisition of New Organisms

It has been well documented that nearly 85% of the organisms responsible for infections among patients with cancer are derived from the endogenous flora. Nearly half of these are acquired from the hospital environment. Much attention has been directed toward mechanisms to prevent the acquisition of potential pathogens.

Inanimate objects within the hospital environment (i.e., faucet aerators, shower heads, respirators, plants, floor) are reservoirs of pathogenic organisms. However, most epidemiologic studies (albeit most commonly investigating nonimmunocompromised patients) suggest that transmission from such inanimate sources usually requires a human vector. Therefore, the simplest yet most efficacious intervention that can be performed is adherence to strict hand-washing precautions. In reality, the easiest way to enforce such a policy is to educate the patient or family to disallow contact with individuals who have neglected to wash their hands.

A second maneuver that has been advocated by some clinicians to decrease the acquisition of new organisms is to maintain a cooked diet during periods of granulocytopenia, with avoidance of fresh fruits and vegetables and nonprocessed dairy products, because these

TABLE 300–4 Strategies for Preventing Infection in Cancer Patients

Prevent Acquisition and/or Suppress or Eliminate Microbial Flora	Improve or Modify Host Defenses
Isolation	Immunization
Simple or reverse isolation	Active
Isolation with HEPA air filtration	*Haemophilus influenzae* vaccine
Prophylactic antibiotics	*Pneumococcus* vaccine
Nonabsorbable antibiotics	Passive
Trimethoprim-sulfamethoxazole	Pooled immune globulins
Selective decontamination	Specific immune globulin (e.g., RSV)
Quinolones	Acceleration of granulocyte recovery
Prophylactic antivirals	GM-CSF
Acyclovir	G-CSF
Ganciclovir	M-CSF
Amantadine	
Prophylactic antifungals	
Nystatin	
Imidazoles or azoles	
Prophylactic anti-*Pneumocystis*	
Trimethoprim-sulfamethoxazole	
Dapsone	
Atovaquone	
Aerosolized pentamidine	
Combination-comprehensive	
Total protected isolation	

Abbreviations: CSF, Colony-stimulating factor; G, granulocyte; GM, granulocyte-macrophage; HEPA, high-efficiency particulate air filters; M, macrophage, RSV, respiratory syncytial virus.

TABLE 300-5 Efficacy of Preventive Regimens in Reducing Acquisition of New Organisms or Suppressing Endogenous Microflora

	Total Protected Environment	Nonabsorbable Antibiotics	Trimethoprim-Sulfamethoxazole	Selected Decontamination	Quinolones
Exogenous sources (air, food, water, contacts)	Yes	No	No	No	No
Endogenous sources					
Nares	Yes	No	No	No	Yes
Oropharynx	Yes	±	No	Yes	Yes
Lower respiratory tract	±	No	±	±	Yes
Gastrointestinal tract	Yes	Yes	Yes	Yes	Yes
Perianal area	Yes	±	±	±	±
Skin	Yes	No	No	No	No
Central venous catheter	No	No	No	No	No
Peripheral catheters	No	No	No	No	No
Systemic effect	±	No	Yes	Yes	Yes

Key: Yes: the regimen is effective; No: the regimen is not effective; ±: the regimen is partially effective or effectiveness is debatable.

foods are naturally contaminated with gram-negative bacteria (especially *Klebsiella pneumoniae, E. coli,* and *P. aeruginosa*).

Environmental sources can contribute to fungal (especially *Aspergillus* spp.) and bacterial (*Legionella*) colonization and infection. In centers where *Aspergillus* is a significant problem, special air filtration systems (e.g., high-efficiency particulate air filters) or water purification systems may prove helpful.

Although the technique of *reverse isolation* has often been used, it does not significantly reduce the acquisition of new organisms in an environment where hand-washing techniques are strictly followed.[65] Therefore, there is no compelling reason to enforce this policy, particularly because the extra expense, time consumption, and inconvenience are not balanced by a beneficial effect.

The total protective environment is a comprehensive anti-infective regimen that was designed to reduce the patient's endogenous microbial burden while preventing the acquisition of new organisms (Table 300–5). A sterile environment is created in a clean-air room with constant positive airflow and is maintained by an aggressive program of surface decontamination, sterilization of all objects that enter the room, and an intensive regimen to disinfect the patient (including oral nonabsorbable antibiotics, skin antiseptics, antibiotic sprays and ointments, and a low-microbial diet). Indeed, a number of studies have documented that the total protective environment can reduce the number of infections in profoundly granulocytopenic individuals. However, the total protective environment is expensive, and because of improvements in treating established infections, it does not offer a clear survival advantage to patients. Thus, protected isolation is not necessary for the routine care of cancer patients (Table 300–6).

Prophylactic Antibiotics

A large number of clinical trials have been conducted to investigate the utility of prophylactic antibiotic regimens in immunocompromised patients. A number of strategies have been explored, including systemic prophylaxis, gastrointestinal decontamination, and selective gastrointestinal decontamination (i.e., maintenance of *colonization resistance*). Unfortunately, the interpretation of many of these trials is difficult as a result of poor study design (many are not controlled trials), nonuniform patient groupings, and failure to report or document compliance with the prophylactic regimens.

Because the gastrointestinal tract is the source of many of the pathogens causing microbiologically defined infections, investigators have evaluated the efficacy of reducing the endogenous gastrointestinal flora by the administration of oral nonabsorbable antibiotics. This technique has been found not to be especially valuable and is fraught with a number of problems. The antimicrobial agents used (e.g., vancomycin, gentamicin, polymyxin B, nystatin, framycetin, and colistin) are unpalatable and are generally poorly tolerated, making compliance a significant liability (especially among patients receiving emetogenic chemotherapy) (see Table 300–5). Equally disturbing has been the emergence of resistant bacterial strains when aminoglycoside-containing regimens have been used. Therefore, prophylactic regimens aimed solely at reducing the endogenous gastrointestinal flora cannot be recommended (see Table 300–6).

A modified technique is the *selective decontamination* of the gastrointestinal tract, employing antibiotics that preserve the anaerobic flora while reducing the numbers of aerobic bacteria. This is

TABLE 300-6 Effectiveness of Preventive Strategies Rated for Usefulness, Tolerance, Safety, and Cost Effectiveness

	Total Protected Environment	Nonabsorbable Antibiotics	Trimethoprim-Sulfamethoxazole	Selected Decontamination	Quinolones
Reduced infection	Yes	No	±	±	Yes
Decreased fever	Yes	No	No	No	No
Decreased or shortened need for antibiotics and antifungals	No	No	No	±	Yes
Contributed to survival	No	No	No	No	No
Compliance					
Well tolerated	No	No	±	±	Yes
Impact on efficacy	Yes	Yes	Yes	±	No
Liabilities					
Emergence of resistant organisms	Yes	Yes	Yes	Yes	Yes
Organ side effects					
Interference with other drugs	Yes	Yes	Yes	No	No
Bone marrow suppression	No	No	Yes	Yes	No
Specific organ toxicity	No	No	Yes	Yes	Yes
Cost					
For drugs or regimens	Yes	Yes	No	Yes	Yes
For surveillance or monitoring	Yes	Yes	Yes	Yes	Yes
Reducing need for hospitalization or drugs	No	No	No	±	?

Key: Yes: the regimen is effective; No: the regimen is not effective; ±: the regimen is partially effective or effectiveness is debatable.

based on experimental data showing that the preservation of the anaerobic flora of the gastrointestinal tract provides a colonization resistance against aerobic and fungal organisms.[66, 67] Although initial clinical trials provided evidence of a reduction of infections in patients undergoing induction therapy for acute leukemia, clearly defined efficacy has not been definitely established. The most commonly investigated agent used for selective decontamination has been TMP-SMX. Early trials investigating the utility of this antibiotic in children and adults demonstrate a reduction in all infections and in bacteremic episodes. However, a large number of follow-up clinical trials have yielded conflicting results.[63, 68] The reasons for the contradictory results are unclear, although factors such as variability in study design, nonuniform patient populations, and failure to properly monitor compliance have played a part. The potential for a reduction in infectious morbidity and mortality must be balanced against the prolongation of granulocytopenia and the emergence of resistant organisms noted with the prophylactic use of TMP-SMX. Successful use of this approach requires close microbiologic monitoring to adjust the antimicrobial regimen properly for resistant or newly emerging species. Such surveillance is costly in terms of both time and money.

Prophylactic trials with fluoroquinolones have received considerable attention. Although a number of investigators have suggested that the prophylactic administration of ciprofloxacin to neutropenic patients can delay the time to fever and need for parenteral empirical antibiotic therapy, two problems require consideration. First, breakthrough infections with gram-positive infection can occur, although this can be addressed by the addition of penicillin, clindamycin, or amoxicillin plus clavulanate. Of more concern, however, is the emergence of ciprofloxacin-resistant organisms.[69, 70] Indeed, the indiscriminate use of these agents can compromise their utility in more therapeutically appropriate clinical settings.[71] Accordingly, the Infectious Disease Society of America has not endorsed the use of prophylactic antimicrobials for bacterial infections and has specifically advised against the use of fluoroquinolones for routine prophylaxis.[72]

Antifungal Prophylaxis

Because of the increasing incidence of invasive mycoses in immunocompromised hosts, antifungal prophylaxis has also been studied.[18] Most prophylactic regimens have been aimed at a reduction of invasive infections due to *Candida* spp. and, by virtue of the antifungal activity of the agents employed, would not be expected to have a significant impact against *Aspergillus* infection or mucormycosis.

As with antibiotic prophylaxis, the interpretation of existing data is difficult, because studies suffer from variable patient inclusion criteria, disparate dosage regimens, differing response criteria, and a lack of appropriate controls. An added problem is the inherent difficulty in the definitive diagnosis of a fungal infection in an immunocompromised host.

Within the context of these limitations, however, several conclusions regarding antifungal prophylaxis can be put forth. First, when an adequate dose of an antifungal agent has been administered (e.g., oral amphotericin B, fluconazole, or clotrimazole), there has been a consistent decrease in fungal colonization (especially due to *Candida* spp.) Decreased colonization has not clearly resulted, however, in a decreased incidence of invasive mycotic disease (although a decrease in superficial infection has been noted in some studies). Second, several studies employing prophylactic (and empirical) antifungal regimens have noted a shift in the colonization pattern of fungal organisms. In general, these shifts have been toward more resistant fungi. Thus, the prophylactic regimens may successfully eradicate the susceptible fungi (particularly *C. albicans*) but may permit the overgrowth and ultimate invasion by more resistant species, especially *Aspergillus*. This trend was again noted when fluconazole was administered to patients undergoing bone marrow transplantation. Whether or not an increase in *C. krusei* infections also occurs remains in dispute.[73]

Overall, the potential benefits of prophylactic antifungal therapy must be balanced against toxicity, epidemiologic considerations, and the relative efficacy of the regimen employed.

Antiviral Prophylaxis

Either intravenous or oral formulations of acyclovir can prevent reactivation of herpes simplex virus and resultant stomatitis among patients undergoing induction therapy for leukemia or lymphoma or marrow allografting.[31] Twice-daily administration of intravenous acyclovir appears to be nearly as effective prophylaxis as three-times-daily use and is both more convenient and less expensive. Prevention of CMV infection has been more problematic. Primary CMV infection among seronegative patients can be prevented by the use of screened seronegative or leukocyte-depleted blood products. When used prophylactically, high-dose acyclovir and especially ganciclovir appear to prevent CMV infection.[74–77]

Pneumocystis Prophylaxis

In centers where *P. carinii* occurs with some frequency, the administration of TMP-SMX has been convincingly demonstrated to reduce the incidence of infection. Effective prophylaxis is accomplished with intermittent administration. For children, an effective prophylactic dose is 150 mg/m^2 (of the trimethoprim component) in two divided doses on 3 consecutive days (e.g., Monday, Tuesday, Wednesday). For adults, one double-strength tablet administered twice daily for 3 consecutive days is the preferred schedule.

Alternative prophylactic agents include aerosolized pentamidine or dapsone. Atovaquone, licensed for treatment of *P. carinii* pneumonia, has proved less useful for prophylaxis.

Improvement of Host Defenses with Immunoglobulin and Hematopoietic Growth Factors

Several agents that stimulate hematopoiesis or improve deficient immune functions have become available (Table 300–7). These include polyclonal and monoclonal antibodies; interleukins and interleukin-receptor antagonists; interferons; and several cytokines and growth factors.[78, 79] It is hoped that these agents may serve as adjuncts to antimicrobial therapy that will eventually simplify and improve the management of neutropenia and fever.

Hematopoietic growth factors (i.e., granulocyte-macrophage and granulocyte colony-stimulating factor) were all too rapidly embraced into the management of neutropenic patients.[79, 80] These glycoproteins stimulate the proliferation and maturation of bone marrow progenitor cells and increase the number and function of these committed cell populations. Treatment with either colony-stimulating factor has

TABLE 300–7 Caveats Regarding Biological and Immunomodulating Agents

Biologicals	Comments and Caveats
Intravenous immune globulin (IGIV)	No benefit in preventing fever or infection in neutropenic patients. Modest benefit for patients with antibody deficiencies (e.g., CLL), but not cost-effective.
Interferon-γ	Benefit for patients with neutrophil deficiencies other than CGD is of interest, but unproven.
G-CSF and GM-CSF	Although these agents can shorten duration of neutropenia by days, they do not by themselves eliminate neutropenic nadir. Side effects are dose related.

Abbreviations: CGD, Chronic granulomatous disease; CLL, chronic lymphocytic leukemia; CSF, colony-stimulating factor; G, granulocyte; GM, granulocyte-macrophage.

From Pizzo PA. Management of fever in patients with cancer and treatment-induced neutropenia. N Engl J Med. 1993;328:1323–1332. Copyright © 1993 Massachusetts Medical Society. All rights reserved.

reduced the duration and severity of neutropenia in patients receiving chemotherapy for a variety of hematopoietic cancers and nonhematopoietic malignancies and after bone marrow transplantation.[81–87] These cytokines do not prevent neutropenia per se but can reduce its duration. Importantly, the use of these agents has been associated with fewer infections, including a decrease in the incidence of oral mucositis in patients receiving chemotherapy for small-cell lung cancer.[81, 84] However, a number of more recent clinical trials have been less encouraging than the initial studies.[88] Recommendations for the use of the hematopoietic cytokines have been published by the American Society of Clinical Oncology and endorsed by the Infectious Disease Society of America.[72, 89, 90] In addition, the use of a colony-stimulating factor, although safe and well tolerated, can add to the cost of care. For patients with prolonged neutropenia, the use of such an agent may be beneficial and can be justified. For patients with low-risk neutropenia (i.e., less than 1 week), in whom the risk of infection is low, these agents are unnecessary. These cytokines do not, however, have a significant impact on the adjunctive treatment of patients with extant neutropenia.[91–93]

The role of other cytokines (e.g., macrophage colony-stimulating factor[80, 87] and interferon-γ) as adjuncts to the treatment of patients with neutropenia who have defined infections has been studied with no conclusive result.[79, 94] In vitro, the combination of granulocyte colony-stimulating factor and interferon-γ enhances the fungicidal activity of neutrophils against *Candida* and *Aspergillus*.[95, 96]

The potential value of passive immunization was stimulated by the report that antibody against the core glycolipid of the Enterobacteriaceae (J5 antiserum) could reduce mortality associated with *Pseudomonas* and other gram-negative infections in neutropenic animals. When polyclonal J5 antiserum was administered to patients with gram-negative infections, mortality was decreased, especially in patients who were hypotensive.[97] However, it is important to note that a benefit of passive immunization was not observed in neutropenic patients. Treatment with human monoclonal antiendotoxin antibodies (HA-IA) was reported to reduce mortality in patients ultimately found to have gram-negative bacteremia. The value of HA-IA therapy was subsequently cast into doubt and further studies halted.

Intravenous immunoglobulins have been used to reduce the frequency of respiratory infections in patients with chronic lymphocytic leukemia in whom antibody production is deficient.[98] A critical review of the data did not demonstrate that such therapy was cost-effective.[99] Similarly, in a randomized trial performed at the National Cancer Institute, compared with placebo, weekly administration of intravenous immunoglobulins did not reduce the incidence of fever or infection in patients with neutropenia that lasted more than 1 week. Neither polyclonal nor monoclonal antibacterial antibodies have a clearly defined role in empirical treatment of patients with neutropenia.[80] Usage of intravenous immunoglobulin in bone marrow transplant recipients is discussed in Chapter 303.

Goals for the Future

It is clear that the risk of infection can be decreased if the severity and duration of neutropenia are reduced. The current strategy is therefore to use cytokines to ameliorate chemotherapy-induced neutropenia in order to reduce that risk. Such treatment has several advantages. Decreasing the duration of neutropenia with granulocyte or granulocyte-macrophage colony-stimulating factor reduces the need for antibiotic therapy, the risk of second infections, and the complications of multidrug therapy. Patients in whom the duration of neutropenia is shortened can be treated with simpler antimicrobial regimens if fever develops.[100]

Cytokines, as well as certain cytotoxic agents (e.g., cyclophosphamide), can also increase the number of circulating progenitor cells. Harvesting these peripheral stem cells before the administration of cytotoxic chemotherapy and then administering them after treatment can limit the duration and severity of neutropenia.[101–104] Alternatively, administering cytokines such as granulocyte colony-stimulating factor to blood donors may permit the harvesting of sufficient leukocytes[105] to replace the depleted reserves of neutropenic patients with refractory infections. Such strategies may permit the use of chemotherapy regimens that could not otherwise be tolerated, ideally with improvement in tumoricidal activity. As more cytokines become available, their use in combination is likely to hasten hematologic recovery even more. The insertion of drug-resistance genes into hematopoietic stem cells that can then be administered to the patient, potentially eliminating the risk that neutropenia will develop after chemotherapy, is also being studied. In this way, neutropenia as a consequence of cancer treatment may be truly avoidable.

REFERENCES

1. Schimpff SC, Saterlee W, Young VM, et al. Empiric therapy with carbenicillin and gentamicin for febrile patients with cancer and granulocytopenia. N Engl J Med. 1971;284:1061.
2. Pizzo PA, Rubin M, Freifeld A, et al. The child with cancer and infection. I. Empiric therapy for fever and neutropenia, and preventive strategies. J Pediatr. 1991;119:679–694.
3. Pizzo PA. Management of fever in patients with cancer and treatment-induced neutropenia. N Engl J Med. 1993;328:1323–1332.
4. Chow JW, Fine MJ, Shlaes DM, et al. Enterobacter bacteremia: Clinical features and emergence of antibiotic resistance drug therapy. Ann Intern Med. 1991;115:585–590.
5. Pizzo PA, Ladisch S, Simon R, et al. Increasing incidence of gram positive sepsis in cancer patients. Med Pediatr Oncol. 1978;5:241.
6. Aquino VM, Pappo A, Buchman GR, et al. The changing epidemiology of bacteremia in neutropenic children with cancer. Pediatr Infect Dis J. 1995;14:140–143.
7. Walsh TJ, Vlahov D, Hansen SL, et al. Prospective surveillance in control of nosocomial methicillin-resistant *Staphylococcus aureus*. Infect Control. 1987;8:7.
8. Schwabe RS, Stapleton JT. Emergence of vancomycin resistance in coagulase-negative staphylococci. N Engl J Med. 1987;316:927.
9. Dybedal I, Lamvik J. Respiratory insufficiency in acute leukemia following treatment with cytosine arabinoside and septicemia with streptococcus viridans. Eur J Haematol. 1989;42:405–406.
10. Karp JE, Merz WG, Hendricksen C, et al. Oral norfloxacin for prevention of gram-negative bacterial infections in patients with acute leukemia and granulocytopenia. Ann Intern Med. 1987;106:1–7.
11. Dekker AW, Rozenberg-Arska M, Verhoef J. Infection prophylaxis in acute leukemia: A comparison of ciprofloxacin with trimethoprim-sulfamethoxazole and colistin. Ann Intern Med. 1987;106:7–12.
12. Barnes PF, Bloch AB, Davidson PT, et al. Tuberculosis in patients with human immunodeficiency virus infection. N Engl J Med. 1991;324:1644–1650.
13. Daley CL, Small PM, Schecter GF, et al. An outbreak of tuberculosis with accelerated progression among persons infected with the human immunodeficiency virus: An analysis using restriction-fragment-length polymorphisms. N Engl J Med. 1992;326:231–235.
14. Freifeld AG. The antimicrobial armamentarium. Hematol Oncol Clin North Am. 1993;813–839.
15. Cho SY, Choi HY. Opportunistic fungal infection among cancer patients. Am J Clin Pathol. 1979;72:617.
16. Krick JA, Remington JS. Opportunistic invasive fungal infections in patients with leukemia and lymphoma. Clin Haematol. 1976;5:249.
17. Meunier-Carpentier F, Kiehm T, Armstrong D. Fungemia in the immunocompromised host: Changing patterns, antigenemia, high mortality. Am J Med. 1981;71:363.
18. Walsh, TJ. Management of the immunocompromised patient who develops evidence of an invasive mycosis. Hematol Oncol Clin North Am. 1993;7:1003–1026.
19. Walsh TJ, Rubin M, Pizzo PA. Respiratory diseases in patients with malignant neoplasms. In: Shelhamer J, Pizzo PA, Parrillo JE, et al, eds. Respiratory Disease in the Immunocompromised Host. Philadelphia: JB Lippincott; 1991:640–663.
20. Schimpff SC, Young VM, Greene WH, et al. Origin of infection in acute nonlymphocytic leukemia: Significance of hospital acquisition of potential pathogens. Ann Intern Med. 1972;77:707.
21. Schimpff SC, Greene WH, Young VM, et al. Significance of *Pseudomonas aeruginosa* in the patient with leukemia or lymphoma. J Infect Dis. 1974;130:524.
22. Kurrie E, Bhaduri S, Krieger D, et al. Risk factors for infections of the oropharynx and the respiratory tract in patients with acute leukemia. J Infect Dis. 1981;144:128.
23. Pizzo PA, Robichaud KJ, Wesley R, et al. Fever in the pediatric and young adult patient with cancer: A prospective study of 1001 episodes. Medicine. 1982;61:153.
24. Buchanan GR. Approach to treatment of the febrile cancer patient with low risk neutropenia. Hematol Oncol Clin North Am. 1993;7:919–936.
25. Lee JW, Pizzo PA. Management of the cancer patient with fever and prolonged neutropenia. Hematol Oncol Clin North Am. 1993;7:937–960.
26. Chanock S. Evolving risk factors for infectious complications of cancer therapy. Hematol Oncol Clin North Am. 1993:771–793.
27. Kerones DN, Hussony MR, Gallace MA. Routine chest radiography of children with cancer hospitalized with fever and neutropenia: Is it really necessary? Cancer. 1997;80:1160–1164.

28. Kramer BS, Pizzo PA, Robichaud KJ, et al. Role of serial microbiologic surveillance and clinical evaluation in the management of cancer patients with fever and granulocytopenia. Am J Med. 1982;72:561.
29. Aisner J, Murillo J, Schimpff SC, et al. Invasive aspergillosis in acute leukemia: Correlation with more cultures and antibiotic use. Ann Intern Med. 1979;90:4.
30. Schimpff SC. Surveillance cultures. J Infect Dis. 1981;144:81.
31. Rubin RH, Ferraro MJ. Understanding and diagnosing infectious complications in the immunocompromised host. Hematol Oncol Clin North Am. 1993:795–812.
32. Pizzo PA, Thaler M, Hathorn J, et al. New β-lactam antibiotics in the granulocytopenic patient: New options and new questions. Am J Med. 1985;79:75.
33. The EORTC International Antimicrobial Therapy Cooperative Group. Ceftazidime combined with a short or long course of amikacin for empiric therapy of gram-negative bacteremia in cancer patients with granulocytopenia. N Engl J Med. 1987;317:1692.
34. Pizzo PA, Hathorn JW, Hiemenz JW, et al. A randomized trial comparing ceftazidime alone with combination antibiotic therapy in cancer patients with fever and neutropenia. N Engl J Med. 1986;315:552.
35. Freifeld A, Walsh T, Marshall D. Monotherapy for fever and neutropenia in cancer patients. A randomized comparison of ceftazidime versus imipenem. J Clin Oncol. 1995;165–176.
36. The Meropenen Study Group of Leuven, London and Nijmegen. Equivalent efficacies of meropenem and ceftazidime as empirical monotherapy of febrile neutropenic patients. J Anticrob Chemother. 1995;36:185–200.
37. Cometta A, Calandra T, Gaya H, et al. Monotherapy with meropenem versus combination therapy with ceftazidime plus amikacin as empiric therapy for fever in granulocytopenic patients with cancer. Antimicrob Agents Chemother. 1996;40:1108–1115.
38. Pizzo PA. After empiric therapy: What to do until the granulocyte comes back. Rev Infect Dis. 1987;9:214.
39. Shenep JL, Hughes WT, Roberson PK, et al. Vancomycin, ticarcillin, and amikacin compared with ticarcillin-clavulanate and amikacin in the empirical treatment of febrile, neutropenic children with cancer. N Engl J Med. 1988;319:1053–1058.
40. Rubin M, Hathorn JW, Marshall D, et al. Gram-positive infections and the use of vancomycin in 550 episodes of fever and neutropenia. Ann Intern Med. 1988;108:30–35.
41. European Organization for Research and Treatment of Cancer (EORTC), International Antimicrobial Therapy Cooperative Group and the National Cancer Institute of Canada-Clinical Trials Group. Vancomycin added to empirical combination antibiotic therapy for fever in granulocytopenic cancer patients. J Infect Dis. 1991;163:951–958 (Erratum, J Infect Dis. 1991;164:832).
42. Freifeld A, Pizzo PA. Use of fluoroquinolones for empirical management of febrile neutropenia in pediatric cancer patients. Pediatr Infect Dis J. 1997;16:140–146.
43. Freifeld A, Marchigiani D, Walsh T, et al. A double-blind comparison of empirical oral and intravenous antibiotic therapy for low-risk febrile patients with neutropenia during cancer chemotherapy. N Engl J Med. 1999;341:305–311.
44. Malik IA, Khan WA, Karo M. Feasibility of outpatient management of fever in cancer patients with low risk neutropenia: Results of a prospective randomized trial. Am J Med. 1995;98:224–231.
45. Mufsta MM, Aquino VM, Pappo A, et al. A study of outpatient management of febrile neutropenic children with cancer at low risk of bacteremia. J Pediatr. 1996;128:847–849.
46. Pizzo PA, Armstrong D, Bodey G, et al. The design, analysis, and reporting of clinical trials on the empirical antibiotic management of the neutropenic patient: Report of a consensus panel. J Infect Dis. 1990;161:397–401.
47. Pennington JE. Successful treatment of *Aspergillus* pneumonia in hematologic neoplasia. N Engl J Med. 1976;295:426.
48. Burke PJ, Branine HG, Rathbun HK, et al. The clinical significance and management of fever in acute myelocytic leukemia. Johns Hopkins Med J. 1976;139:1.
49. Stein RS, Kayser J, Flexner J. Clinical value of empirical amphotericin B in patients with acute myelogenous leukemia. Cancer. 1982;50:2247.
50. Pizzo PA, Robichaud KJ, Gill FA, et al. Empiric antibiotic and antifungal therapy for cancer patients with prolonged fever and granulocytopenia. Am J Med. 1982;72:101–111.
51. EORTC International Antimicrobial Therapy Cooperative Group. Empiric antifungal therapy in febrile granulocytopenic patients. Am J Med. 1989;86:668–672.
52. Walsh TJ, Gonzalez C, Lyman CA, et al. Invasive fungal infections in children: Recent advances in diagnosis and treatment. Adv Pediatric Infect Dis. 1996;11: 187–290.
53. Burch PA, Karp JE, Merz WG, et al. Favorable outcome of invasive aspergillosis in patients with acute leukemia. J Clin Oncol. 1987;5:1985–1993.
54. Walsh TJ, Rubin M, Hathorn J, et al. Amphotericin B vs. high-dose ketoconazole for empirical antifungal therapy among febrile, granulocytopenic cancer patients: A prospective, randomized study. Arch Intern Med. 1991;151:765–770.
55. Goodman JL, Winston DJ, Greenfield RA, et al. A controlled trial of fluconazole to prevent fungal infections in patients undergoing bone marrow transplantation. N Engl J Med. 1992;326:845–851.
56. Walsh TJ, Finberg RW, Arndt C, et al. Liposomal amphotericin B for empirical therapy in patients with persistent fever and neutropenia. N Engl J Med. 1999;340:764–771.
57. White MH, Bowden RA, Sandler ES, et al. Randomized double blind clinical trial of amphotericin B in the empirical treatment of fever and neutropenia. Clin Infect Dis. 1998;27:296–302.
58. Pizzo PA, Commers J, Cotton D, et al. Approaching the controversies in the antibacterial management of cancer patients. Am J Med. 1984;76:436–449.
59. Pizzo PA, Robichaud KJ, Gill FA, et al. Duration of empiric antibiotic therapy in granulocytopenic patients with cancer. Am J Med. 1979;67:194–200.
60. Aquino VM, Thaczewski I, Buchman GR. Early discharge of low risk febrile neutropenic children and adolescents with cancer. Clin Infect Dis. 1997;25:74–78.
61. Santolaya ME, Villarroel M, Avendano LF, Cofre J. Discontinuation of antimicrobial therapy for febrile neutropenic children with cancer: A prospective study. Clin Infect Dis. 1997;25:92–97.
62. Cohen KJ, Leamer K, Odom L, et al. Cessation of antibiotics regardless of ANC is safe in children with febrile neutropenia. J Pediatr Hematol Oncol. 1995;17:325–330.
63. Dichter JR, Levine SJ, Shelhamer JH. Approach to the immunocompromised host with pulmonary symptoms. Hematol Oncol Clin North Am. 1993:887–912.
64. Hathorn JW. A critical appraisal of antimicrobials for the prevention of infections in immunocompromised hosts. Hematol Oncol Clin North Am. 1993;7:1051–1101.
65. Nauseef WM, Maki DG. A study of the value of simple protective isolation in patients with granulocytopenia. N Engl J Med. 1981;304:448.
66. Van der Waaij D, Berghuis de Vries JN, Lekkerkerrk JEC, et al. Colonization resistance of the digestive tract in conventional and antibiotic treated mice. J Hyg (Lond). 1971;69:405.
67. Van der Waaij D, Berghuis de Vries J. Selective elimination of Enterobacteriaceae species from the digestive tract in mice and monkeys. J Hyg (Lond). 1974;72:205.
68. Hiemenz JW, Greene JN. Special considerations for the patient undergoing allogeneic or autologous bone marrow transplantation. Hematol Oncol Clin North Am. 1993;7:961–1002.
69. Cruciani M, Rampazzo R, Malena M, et al. Prophylaxis with fluoroquinolones for bacterial infections in neutropenic patients: A meta-analysis. Clin Infect Dis. 1996;23:795–805.
70. Carratala J, Fernandez-Sevilla A, Tabau F, et al. Emergence of quinolone resistant *Escherichia coli* bacteremia in neutropenic patients with cancer who have received prophylactic norfloxacin. Clin Infect Dis. 1995;20:557–560.
71. Kotilainen P, Nikoskelaimen J, Huovinen P. Emergence of ciprofloxacin-resistant coagulase-negative staphylococcal skin flora in immunocompromised patients receiving ciprofloxacin. J Infect Dis. 1990;161:41–44.
72. Fever and Neutropenia Guideline Panel, Infectious Disease Society of America. Guidelines for the use of antimicrobial agents in neutropenic patients with unexplained fever. Clin Infect Dis. 1997;25:551–573.
73. Viscoli C, Custagnola E, von Lindt MT. Fluconazole versus amphotericin B as empirical antifungal of unexplained fever in granulocytopenic cancer patients. A pragmatic, multicenter, prospective randomized clinical trial. Eur J Cancer. 1996;32:814–820.
74. Schmidt GM, Horak DA, Niland JC, et al. A randomized, controlled trial of prophylactic ganciclovir for cytomegalovirus pulmonary infection in recipients of allogeneic bone marrow transplants. N Engl J Med. 1991;324:1005–1011.
75. Merigan TC, Renlund DG, Keay S, et al. A controlled trial of ganciclovir to prevent cytomegalovirus disease after heart transplantation. N Engl J Med. 1992;326:1182–1186.
76. Emmanuel D, Cunningham I, Jules-Elysee K, et al. Cytomegalovirus pneumonia after bone marrow transplantation successfully treated with the combination of ganciclovir and high-dose intravenous immune globulin. Ann Intern Med. 1988;109:777–782.
77. Reed EC, Bowden RA, Dandliker PS, et al. Treatment of cytomegalovirus pneumonia with ganciclovir and intravenous cytomegalovirus immunoglobulin in patients with bone marrow transplantation. Ann Intern Med. 1988;109:783–788.
78. Ambrosino DM, Molrine DC. A critical appraisal of the use of immunization strategies for the prevention of infection in the compromised host. Hematol Oncol Clin North Am. 1993;7:1027–1050.
79. Roilides E, Pizzo PA. Biologicals and hematopoietic cytokines in prevention or treatment of infection in immunocompromised hosts. Hematol Oncol Clin North Am. 1993;7:841–864.
80. Dwyer JM. Manipulating the immune system with immune globulin. N Engl J Med. 1992;326:107–116.
81. Lieschke GJ, Burgess AW. Granulocyte colony-stimulating factor and granulocyte-macrophage colony-stimulating factor. N Engl J Med. 1992;327:28–35, 99–106.
82. Antman KS, Griffin JD, Elias A, et al. Effect of recombinant human granulocyte-macrophage colony-stimulating factor on chemotherapy-induced myelosuppression. N Engl J Med. 1988;319:593–598.
83. Gabrilove JL, Jakubowski A, Scher H, et al. Effect of granulocyte colony-stimulating factor on neutropenia and associated morbidity due to chemotherapy for transitional-cell carcinoma of the urothelium. N Engl J Med. 1988;318:1412–1422.
84. Bronchaud MH, Scarffe JH, Thatcher N, et al. Phase I/II study of recombinant human granulocyte colony-stimulating factor in patients receiving intensive chemotherapy for small cell lung cancer. Br J Cancer. 1987;56:809–813.
85. Brandt SJ, Peters WP, Atwater SK, et al. Effect of recombinant human granulocyte-macrophage colony-stimulating factor on hematopoietic reconstitution after high-dose chemotherapy and autologous bone marrow transplantation. N Engl J Med. 1988;318:869–876.
86. Nemunaitis J, Rabinowe SN, Singer JW, et al. Recombinant granulocyte-macrophage colony-stimulating factor after autologous bone marrow transplantation for lymphoid cancer. N Engl J Med. 1991;324:1773–1778.
87. Nemunaitis J, Meyers JD, Buckner CD, et al. Phase I trial of recombinant human macrophage colony-stimulating factor in patients with invasive fungal infections. Blood. 1991;78:907–913.

88. Pui CH, Boyett JM, Hughes WT, et al. Human granulocyte colony stimulating factor after induction chemotherapy in children with acute lymphoblastic leukemia. N Engl J Med. 1997;336:1781–1787.
89. ASCO Ad Hoc Colony stimulating factor guidelines expert panel: American Society of Clinical Oncology recommendations for the use of hematopoietic colony stimulating factor: Evidence based, clinical practice guidelines. J Clin Oncol. 1994;12:2471–2508.
90. ASCO Ad Hoc Colony stimulating factor guidelines expert panel: Update of recommendations for the use of hematopoietic colony-stimulating factors: Evidence based clinical practice guidelines. J Clin Oncol. 1996;14:1957–1960.
91. Mahar DW, Lieschle GJ, Green M, et al. Filgrastim in patients with chemotherapy induced febrile neutropenia. A double blind placebo controlled trial. Ann Intern Med. 1994;121:492–501.
92. Anaissie EJ, Vartivarian S, Bodey G, et al. Randomized comparison between antibiotics alone and antibiotics plus granulocyte-macrophage colony stimulating factor (*E. coli* derived) in cancer patients with fever and neutropenia. Am J Med. 1996;100:17–23.
93. Mitchell LR, Machoud B, Stevens MGC, et al. Granulocyte colony stimulating factor in established febrile neutropenia: A randomized study of pediatric patients. J Clin Oncol. 1997;15:1163–1170.
94. Roilides E, Pizzo PA. Modulation of host defenses by cytokines: Evolving adjuncts in prevention and treatment of serious infections in immunocompromised hosts. Clin Infect Dis. 1992;15:508–524.
95. Roilides E, Uhlig K, Venzon D, et al. Neutrophil oxidative burst in response to blastoconidia and pseudohyphae of *Candida albicans:* Augmentation by granulocyte colony-stimulating factor and interferon-γ. J Infect Dis. 1992;166:668–673.
96. Roilides E, Walsh TJ, Pizzo PA, et al. Granulocyte colony-stimulating factor enhances the phagocytic and bactericidal activity of normal and defective human neutrophils. J Infect Dis. 1991;63:579–583.
97. Ziegler EJ, Fisher CJ Jr, Sprung CL, et al. Treatment of gram-negative bacteremia and septic shock with HA-1A human monoclonal antibody against endotoxin: A randomized, double-blind, placebo-controlled trial. N Engl J Med. 1991;324:429–436.
98. The International Chronic Granulomatous Disease Cooperative Study Group. A controlled trial of interferon gamma to prevent infection in chronic granulomatous disease. N Engl J Med. 1991;324:509–516.
99. Weeks JC, Tierney MR, Weinstein MC. Cost effectiveness of prophylactic intravenous immune globulin in chronic lymphocytic leukemia. N Engl J Med. 1991;325:81–86.
100. Talcott JA, Siegel RD, Finberg R, et al. Risk assessment in cancer patients with fever and neutropenia: A prospective, two-year validation of a prediction rule. J Clin Oncol. 1992;10:316–322.
101. Duhrsen U, Villeval J-L, Boyd J, et al. Effects of recombinant human granulocyte colony-stimulating factor on hematopoietic progenitor cells in cancer patients. Blood. 1988;72:2074–2081.
102. Socinski MA, Cannistra S, Elias A, et al. Granulocyte-macrophage colony stimulating factor expands the circulating hematopoietic progenitor cell compartment in man. Lancet. 1988;1:1194–1198.
103. Peters W, Kurtzberg J, Kirkpatrick G, et al. GM-CSF primed peripheral blood progenitor cells coupled with autologous bone marrow transplantation will eliminate absolute leukopenia following high dose chemotherapy (Abstract). Blood. 1989;74(Suppl 1):50a.
104. Haas R, Ho AD, Bredthauer U, et al. Successful autologous transplantation of blood stem cells mobilized with recombinant human granulocyte-macrophage colony-stimulating factor. Exp Hematol. 1990;18:94–98.
105. Bensinger WI, Price TH, Dale DC, et al. The effects of daily recombinant human granulocyte colony-stimulating factor administration on normal granulocyte donors undergoing leukapheresis. Blood. 1993;81:1883–1888.

Chapter 301

Infections in Injection Drug Users

DONALD P. LEVINE
PATRICIA D. BROWN

Infections in injection drug users (IDUs) present a variety of challenges to the clinician, not only because of the complex nature of these patients' medical problems but also because of the unique psychosocial issues associated with their care. Infection is the most common cause of death in IDUs.[1] Management of infectious complications in these patients requires an understanding of the behavior of addicts and development of an approach that will help ensure a successful therapeutic regimen.

Drug users are notorious for their antisocial behaviors, which in the hospital setting may be manifested by acting out on the ward, disagreements with the staff, drug-seeking behaviors, and cutting the treatment regimen short by leaving the hospital against medical advice. These problems can be minimized by establishing at the outset the goal of the therapeutic plan, which is treatment of the infection. Too often there is an attempt to treat the patient's addiction, whereas the patient may not have agreed to that aspect of the approach. If the physician can establish a "therapeutic alliance" by gaining the acceptance of the patient on specific treatment objectives, which generally do not include withdrawal from illegal substances but may include abiding by routine hospital policies and procedures, the chances of success are high.[2] Not all drug users are sociopaths, and regarding them as such is likely to induce a mindset among the treatment team that will interfere with the physician-patient relationship and preclude effective management of the infection. One should not assume that all drug users are faking pain to obtain pain medication and support for their habit. A frequent response to presumed drug-seeking behavior is to underdose pain medication. This is viewed as punishment, it is unrelated to the infection problem, and it presents an obstacle to successful treatment.

The management of illness in the hospitalized IDU must be dictated by its severity. The only aspects of the narcotic addiction that should be addressed are those that are relevant to the infectious problem at hand.[3] Recognition that attempts to influence the problem of drug abuse during the acute phase of an infectious disease not only may be fruitless but in some cases are contraindicated helps the clinician focus on the medical aspects of the illness, which provide sufficient challenge to require complete attention.

The treatment of infections in drug abusers is complicated by a number of factors. First, a febrile reaction in an IDU may be caused by toxins or impurities in the injected substance rather than an infection. If there is an infection, the clinical features may be indistinct, making it difficult to determine the true nature of the disease.[4,5] In addition, nonprescribed antibiotic use is common among addicts as they try to self-treat or to prevent infection.[6] As a result, cultures may be negative, or positive for only some of the infecting organisms. In addition, such use of antibiotics undoubtedly has contributed to the broad prevalence of resistant organisms, most notably methicillin-resistant *Staphylococcus aureus*. Finally, a variety of associated conditions (e.g., intercurrent viral infections) may obfuscate the clinical presentation. The prevalence of human immunodeficiency virus (HIV)–related disease in this population, with all of its attendant problems, has introduced an entire spectrum of disorders that must be added to the already lengthy differential diagnosis of infection in the IDU. Combinations of diseases are the rule rather than the exception.

HOST DEFENSES

Relatively little is known about host defenses in IDUs. Most of the information available is based on studies of the effects of narcotics on animals or in vitro on tissue cultures. Many human studies have been limited to hospitalized IDUs or those enrolled in methadone programs. Another drawback is that, for studies performed before the availability of serologic diagnosis for HIV infection, the contribution of concomitant immunodeficiency due to HIV cannot be assessed. Many authors have concluded that immunologic dysfunction plays a relatively minor role in the pathogenesis of infection in IDUs, compared with the repeated parenteral introduction or injection of nonsterile material.[7] Abnormal skin colonization with *S. aureus* is reported to be common by some authors,[8–10] possibly as a result of repeated skin puncture, although another contributing factor may be ready access to self-administered β-lactam antibiotics.[11]

There has been a paucity of evidence to suggest a depression of the humoral immune system in IDUs. Depression of the blastogenic response of human peripheral blood mononuclear cells to pokeweed mitogen (PWM), a polyclonal B-cell activator, was reported in drug users who were seronegative for HIV and for human T-cell lymphotrophic virus I (HTLV-I).[12] Morphine (the major metabolite of heroin) has been shown not to effect PWM-stimulated immunoglobulin G (IgG) synthesis in vitro, suggesting that the drug does not directly influence B-cells in vivo but may exert immune modulatory effects via indirect mechanisms.[13] Serum levels of IgM and, to a lesser extent, IgG are frequently elevated in IDUs, whereas serum IgA levels are usually normal.[14] Increased immunoglobulin levels tend to normalize after prolonged opiate withdrawal. Elevated immunoglobulin concentrations are accompanied by a high frequency of autoantibodies, such as rheumatoid factor, as well as those directed against various microorganisms. The latter phenomenon often manifests as a biologic false-positive Venereal Disease Research Laboratory (VDRL) test, which may create diagnostic confusion in IDUs who are at high risk of acquiring sexually transmitted diseases. Hypergammaglobulinemia due to polyclonal B-cell activation may be the result of recurrent immunologic stimulation by injected foreign antigens as well as associated chronic liver disease and chronic infections with other pathogens.

A number of effects of morphine on T-lymphocyte function have been demonstrated, as summarized by Peterson and colleagues.[15] In vitro, morphine has been shown to decrease E-rosette marker formation, increase proliferation in response to phytohemagglutinin, decrease proliferation in response to concanavalin A (con A), and decrease production of interferon-γ in response to con A. Morphine has also been shown to decrease respiratory burst activity in monocytes both in vitro and in vivo. Many of these same effects have also been demonstrated with methadone. Delayed hypersensitivity skin test reactions are sometimes diminished or absent in IDUs. Various investigators have reported conflicting results regarding T-lymphocyte cell populations in IDUs. Both an increase and a decrease in absolute T-lymphocyte numbers has been observed, as has an increased number of T-helper cells, an increased number of T-suppressor cells, and a decrease in the ratio of T-helper to T-suppressor cells.[15] Klimas and associates studied HIV-negative IDUs receiving methadone and reported elevations in T-cell helper and suppressor subpopulations accompanied by suppression of lymphocyte function.[16] Moreover, natural killer (NK)–cell cytotoxicity was significantly reduced in the methadone group. None of the observed effects could be attributed to HTLV serostatus. Morphine has been shown to stimulate the replication of HIV in peripheral blood mononuclear cells.[17] Stoll-Keller and coworkers demonstrated that morphine depresses a number of monocyte functions essential for antiviral defense and inhibits their response to activating stimuli.[18] These alterations may contribute to the high efficiency of transmission in IDUs of HIV and other viral pathogens, including hepatitis B (HBV) and hepatitis C (HCV). In spite of the depressed cell-mediated immunity demonstrated in IDUs, opportunistic infections characteristic of T-cell deficiency were rarely reported before the HIV epidemic.

There have been relatively few studies evaluating the effects of morphine on the neutrophil-monocyte system. Nickerson and colleagues found no impairment in phagocytosis or killing of *S. aureus* and enterobacteriaceae.[19] In contrast, Tabara and associates showed highly significant depression of phagocytosis, superoxide production, and bactericidal activity of polymorphonuclear cells from IDUs using morphine.[20] These functions were suppressed to a lesser extent in patients receiving methadone. In the animal model, these authors also demonstrated a lesser effect of methadone compared with morphine on phagocyte function.[21] Peterson and associates, using cultured human peripheral mononuclear cells, demonstrated that morphine markedly suppressed superoxide and hydrogen peroxide production, an effect that was dependent on morphine-opiate receptor interaction.[22] The clinical significance of these in vitro observations is unknown.

SKIN AND SOFT TISSUE INFECTIONS

Although endocarditis is the infection most often attributed to the intravenous injection of illicit substances, skin and soft tissue infections represent the most common reason for admission.[23, 24] Over a 6-month study period, of a cohort of addicts, only 1% were treated for endocarditis, compared with 10% for abscesses.[25]

In the Detroit Medical Center, in a 1-year period, 1399 addicts were admitted for infection; 180 were bacteremic, and of these only 5% had endocarditis.[6, 26] The distribution of soft tissue lesions is as varied as the sites used for injection and tends to reflect both the duration of drug use and local practices among drug users. In Glasgow, up to 75% of soft tissue sepsis sites are found on the upper extremity.[27] In the United States, many addicts prefer to inject into the groin to avoid detection of the stigmata of drug abuse.[6, 26] Alternatively, after periods of extended drug use when there are no remaining accessible veins in the arms, users frequently resort to groin injections or other easily reached locations, such as the neck or subclavian veins. As a result of repeated injections into a single site, frequently without benefit of sterile technique,[25] the tissues develop local ischemia or necrosis and become susceptible to infection. In addition, the substances injected frequently contain impurities or materials added as diluents. These chemicals commonly cause norepinephrine release and vasospasm or local damage to the vascular intima that leads to thrombosis and further compromise of the soft tissues.[28, 29] Cocaine use may be associated with vascular thrombus at sites distant from injections and may cause muscle and skin infections after inhalational use.[30, 31] HIV infection is now recognized as an important risk factor for skin abscesses, undoubtedly because of the associated altered immune state. Women are also at greater risk, presumably related to the greater difficulty they have accessing veins and the consequent injury to skin and subcutaneous tissues.[32]

Most often cellulitis results, but when the deeper layers of the skin and its supporting structures are involved the patient may develop an abscess that may then erode into a superficial or deep abscess.[33] Synergy between streptococcal infection and cocaine-induced tissue ischemia may lead to large necrotic ulcerations and extensive tissue loss.[34] Alternatively, skin ulcerations may be a direct result of necrosis induced by the illicit substance injected.[35–37] Cellulitis may be extensive and can lead to overwhelming sepsis and death.[23, 38] In Detroit, 47 of 180 bacteremic drug users had either cellulitis, an abscess, or both. Abscesses may spread to adjacent tissues, frequently with disastrous consequences.[39] Mediastinitis may result from the extension of a cervical abscess, whereas lesions in the carotid triangle can erode into the carotid arteries, resulting in massive hemorrhage. Thrombosis of the internal jugular vein has been reported as a complication of a deep neck abscess, as has acute vocal cord paralysis.[40, 41] This can lead to acute, severe airway obstruction and may necessitate immediate tracheostomy. Cellulitis in HIV-positive IDUs is no different from that in non–HIV-infected addicts, with identical pathogens, including mixed infections. Patients respond to drainage and antibiotic administration in the same fashion as non–HIV-infected addicts do.[42]

S. aureus is the most common pathogen, followed by streptococci, either as the sole pathogen[26, 39, 43] or in combination with other organisms. Coagulase-negative staphylococci and α-hemolytic streptococci are also seen.[39, 43] Among the latter, *Streptococcus* of the *milleri* group is most important, especially in addicts in Scotland who inject tablets of buphenorphine and tamazepam after crushing them between their teeth.[34, 44] Other oral flora have been reported, in particular *Eikenella corrodens*, which in some centers has become the third most common pathogen. IDUs who lick their needles or contaminate their drugs with saliva are particularly prone to this infection.[45] The pneumococcus is also occasionally found in this setting.[46] Gram-negative bacilli are found with variable frequency,[43] and anaerobes may be encountered, usually in combination with other bacteria and occasionally as the most important pathogen.[26, 47]

The diagnosis of cellulitis is seldom obscure, and most patients present with signs and symptoms referable to the involved site; however, blood cultures should be obtained, because it is difficult to predict bacteremia.[26] In contrast, the diagnosis of an abscess can be difficult. Patients routinely present with erythema, pain, and tenderness of the involved site, but fluctuance is often absent.[48] Computed tomography (CT) is useful for cervical abscesses[44, 49] and is probably effective for detecting abscesses in the groin and femoral region. Ultrasonography has been reported to be useful but is of variable accuracy, particularly when diagnosing lesions in the groin.[50]

Antibiotic therapy is directed at the organisms recovered from the blood or purulent material. Early surgical drainage of abscesses is essential, and, because of the tendency of these lesions to spread to adjacent or even distant regions, multiple drainage procedures may be required.[39, 43] Deep infections of the hand are far more common in IDUs than in nonusers, and they mandate a unique approach. The microbiology of the infection varies depending on the injected substances. Patients who primarily inject cocaine have a high frequency of mixed anaerobic infection,[48] whereas heroin users are more likely to harbor streptococci and staphylococci.[51] In either case, surgical débridement is far more likely to be required in IDUs than in nonusers.[51] Some caution is indicated before incising a lesion in the vicinity of blood vessels, because a mycotic pseudoaneurysm can easily be misdiagnosed as an abscess. Inadvertent entry into such a lesion can have disastrous consequences.

Skin ulcers are extremely common in IDUs and are found at every conceivable site. The microbiology of these lesions is similar to that of other soft tissue infections in addicts, although they more frequently contain more than one organism.[37] *S. aureus* and β-hemolytic streptococci remain the most common isolates, with gram-negative bacilli, most often *Klebsiella*, *Pseudomonas*, *Escherichia coli*, and *Proteus*, playing an important role. They present particularly difficult management problems when ulcers involve the hands and feet and may ultimately lead to loss of function.[37] Treatment of skin ulcers requires administration of systemic antibiotics and prolonged local wound care, including gentle washing, wet-to-dry dressings, and application of topical antibacterial creams. Parenteral antibiotics are generally continued until the wound is covered by granulation tissue. Very large lesions may require skin grafting or muscle flaps, but these are only effective after all necrotic tissue has been removed and the wound is clean and granulating. With time, most skin ulcers heal completely, leaving circular, punched-out scars. The most important complication is contiguous osteomyelitis, which may be difficult to diagnose because frequently there is radiologic evidence of periosteal reaction in bones immediately beneath large ulcers. When there is still a question of osteomyelitis, a triple-phase bone scan may be helpful. Ultimately diagnosis of osteomyelitis may be impossible without a bone biopsy, which may be difficult to obtain without traversing infected superficial tissues. In such cases, prolonged antibiotic parenteral therapy directed at the organism cultured from the ulcer and careful radiographic follow-up may be the best approach. Recurrent and chronic infections are occasionally complicated by renal amyloidosis.

Necrotizing fasciitis, without or with myositis, is the single infection in IDUs that is most likely to need immediate and appropriate treatment; however, the clinical picture is subtle and rarely elicits the emergency response required. The classic findings of high fever, bullae, crepitance, and skin necrosis are usually absent initially, and the impression may be that of mild cellulitis.[51] In some cases, the true nature of the disease may be so subtle as to be missed during a procedure to débride an abscess or cellulitis. Alternatively, infection may spread after apparently effective incision and drainage.[52] The major indication of the true nature of the infection is the fact that signs and symptoms, such as pain and hemodynamic instability, are disproportionate to the apparent extent of the local process.[51] Because addicts are frequently viewed as complainers, what appears to be excessive complaint for minor disease may be interpreted as narcotic-seeking behavior, further delaying recognition of the need for aggressive and rapid action. Diagnostic accuracy can be increased by use of CT. Characteristic findings include asymmetric fascial thickening and fat stranding, followed by gas tracking along fascial planes. Abscesses may also be seen.[53] Contrast enhancement contributes no additional information. As with most addict-related infections, gram-positive organisms are usually found. However, β-hemolytic streptococci predominate in approximately 50% of cases, followed by *S. aureus*, α-hemolytic streptococci, and coagulase-negative staphylococci. Gram-negative organisms are infrequent and are usually represented by enteric pathogens, especially *E. coli*, *Klebsiella*, *Proteus mirabilis*, *Pseudomonas*, and *Enterobacter*. Anaerobes are recovered in 12% of cases; yeasts *(Candida)* are uncommon.[51, 52, 54]

Attempted management of necrotizing fasciitis by antibiotics alone is associated with progression of the infection in 75% of patients. A combined approach of parenteral antibiotics and aggressive surgery coupled with reexploration at 24 hours and as often as necessary afterward to ensure complete removal of all necrotic tissue offers the best prognosis. Ancillary measures, such as aggressive nutritional support and early coverage of the soft tissue defect, have been shown to improve the outcome,[54] which for addicts, who tend to be young and relatively healthy, is the best of any patient group with this disease.[55]

A less serious infection involving the musculature may be increasing in incidence among IDUs. At the Detroit Receiving Hospital, an increasing number of patients with pyomyositis are being seen. A 1996 review indicated an increase of this infection among IDUs.[56] Direct inoculation of bacteria into the musculature has been implicated, but hematogenous spread also occurs. Most patients with pyomyositis present with pain and swelling of the involved area, which is usually an extremity. Ultrasound or CT reveals the underlying defect within the muscle. *S. aureus* is the most common pathogen. Patients respond well to drainage and antibiotic therapy. A rare but related condition, uterine pyomyoma, has also been reported. The cause appears to be hematogenous dissemination to an infarcted leiomyoma.[57]

BONE AND JOINT INFECTIONS

Skeletal infections are common in IDUs, most occurring via hematogenous seeding by bacteria or fungi.[58] Target sites for infection are determined by the blood supply and predominantly affect the axial skeleton. The original source of these infections may be inapparent, or they may represent metastatic complications of endocarditis. In addition, bone and joint infections frequently result from contiguous spread from adjacent, often neglected areas of infection in skin and soft tissues. IDUs with hematogenous infection often have multiple sites involved simultaneously, and blood cultures frequently are negative at the time of presentation. In contrast, bone and joint infection caused by contiguous spread may lead to concomitant secondary bacteremia. IDUs with HIV infection do not appear to be at increased risk for osteoarticular infections.[59]

IDUs with skeletal infection tend to be young and otherwise healthy. Clinical findings include constitutional manifestations as well as local signs and symptoms depending on the site involved. Patients with osteitis often have a paucity of findings, presenting with local pain and tenderness only. Lack of signs and symptoms frequently results in delay in diagnosis. Fever is absent in one third of patients.[58] Similarly, signs of sepsis, leukocytosis, and radiologic signs may be absent in patients with osteomyelitis.

Pyogenic infections predominate, with almost 90% being bacterial in origin, although skeletal infections can be caused by virtually any organism. The predominant pathogens isolated are *S. aureus* and group A and group G streptococci. Gram-negative bacilli, particularly *Pseudomonas aeruginosa*, although less common, are well known, as are polymicrobial infections.

Joint infections usually involve the extremities, most commonly the knee. Left-sided involvement exceeds right-sided knee arthritis, possibly related to the tendency of right-handed IDUs to inject into the left groin veins; this suggests a relation between site of injection and infection.[58] IDUs are particularly susceptible to vertebral osteomyelitis. The lumbosacral spine is the most common site of infection, and a higher incidence of cervical spine involvement is seen in IDUs than in non-IDUs with vertebral osteomyelitis.[60] IDUs with vertebral osteomyelitis present with symptoms of a shorter duration than do other patients with infection of the spine.[60] Primary sternal osteomyelitis, often associated with an antecedent history of blunt trauma to the sternum, is reported in IDUs.[61, 62] This group is also prone to septic arthritis in unusual sites, such as the sternoclavicular and costochondral joints and the pubic symphysis.[60, 63] Other sites frequently involved include wrist, shoulder, hip, and sacroiliac joints. Vertebral osteomyelitis may extend into the subdural or epidural spaces and may cause formation of an abscess, with consequent cord compression and paraplegia.[58, 60, 64]

Because of the wide spectrum of organisms that may be involved, diagnostic needle aspiration for smear and culture is necessary in all cases. Even when blood cultures are positive, invasive diagnostic steps are advised, because skeletal and blood-stream infection may represent two separate processes and infections are frequently polymicrobial. Frequent arthrocentesis, arthroscopic or open drainage and débridement of nonviable bone is also advised if clinically indicated. Intravenous antibiotics are required for 4 to 6 weeks, selection being based on the identity of the responsible microorganisms. Overall, with early diagnosis, the immediate prognosis of bone and joint infection in IDUs is excellent, but long-term follow-up data are lacking.[58] Many IDUs present late in the clinical course, and delays in diagnosis and institution of therapy are accompanied by a high likelihood of chronic osteomyelitis and late relapse of disease. Also contributing to this late but frequent complication is the problem of noncompliance. IDUs tend to leave the hospital against medical advice when confronted with prolonged inpatient intravenous antibiotic therapy and a tendency for medical personnel to underappreciate and undertreat the pain associated with skeletal infection.

Nonpyogenic skeletal infections include those caused by mycobacteria and fungi. *Candida albicans* has been described particularly in cases of spondylodiscitis and vertebral osteomyelitis.[65] Tuberculous spondylodiscitis must be considered in any drug abuser with radiologic evidence of vertebral destruction,[66] and a biopsy should be performed. Mycobacterial skeletal infections, including those caused by atypical species, are frequently associated with extravertebral involvement of the lungs, adrenals, or pelvic organs. A characteristic form of systemic candidiasis in IDUs has been reported among users of heroin that included folliculitis, usually of the scalp and beard; endophthalmitis; and bone and joint lesions, most often costochondritis.[67]

A rare musculoskeletal syndrome, characterized by fever, arthralgia, myalgia (especially of paraspinal muscles), and periarticular tissue swelling, has been described and is thought to represent hypersensitivity to heroin contaminants.[68]

INFECTIVE ENDOCARDITIS

Infective endocarditis is a common cause of bacteremia in IDUs. In the Detroit Medical Center, 74 of 180 addicts with bacteremia had endocarditis.[26] The most common single organism is *S. aureus.* Since 1970 coagulase-negative staphylococci have become an uncommon cause of endocarditis in IDUs. Streptococci, particularly groups A, B, and G, are the second most common type.[26, 69] These two organisms account for up to 75% of cases in large series.[26] Enterococcus played a major role in the past, but its prevalence may be decreasing.[26, 69] Gram-negative organisms are infrequent causes, although *P. aeruginosa* endocarditis occurs in intermittent epidemics in Detroit and Chicago,[26, 70–72] and *Serratia marcescens* was responsible for a sustained epidemic in the Oakland, California, area.[73, 74] Fungi, especially non-*albicans* candida, account for approximately 5% of cases.[75] Polymicrobial endocarditis is being observed with increasing frequency among drug users.[76–78] Usually only a few organisms are involved, but rarely there may be numerous pathogens.[77, 78] In such cases, standard laboratory techniques may be inadequate to isolate and identify the full microbial spectrum, placing a burden on the clinician to suspect polymicrobial endocarditis caused by salivary contamination of needles or injection sites whenever uncommon oropharyngeal organisms are cultured from the blood.[78]

There are numerous reports describing endocarditis in IDUs involving a variety of organisms that are frequently considered nonpathogens. These infections may be related to altered host immunity resulting from HIV infection[79] or to unusual practices among addicts, such as licking of needles before use, or "cleaning" of the injection site with saliva. Among these unusual causes are *Bacillus* spp.,[80] *Pseudomonas cepacia*,[81] *Lactobacillus*,[82] *Haemophilus influenzae*,[83] diphtheroids,[84] *Corynebacterium diphtheriae* (including nontoxigenic strains),[85] *Corynebacterium xerosis*, *Arcanobacterium haemolyticum (Corynebacterium hemolyticum)*,[86] *Stenotrophomonas (Pseudomonas) maltophilia*,[87] *Comamonas acidovorans (Pseudomonas acidovorans)*,[88] *Neisseria subflava*,[89] *Neisseria sicca*, *Neisseria flavescens*, *Neisseria mucosa*,[90] *E. corrodens*,[91] *Stomatococcus mucilaginosus*,[92] *Citrobacter freundii*,[93] *Staphylococcus xylosus*,[94] *Staphylococcus saprophyticus*,[95] *Haemophilus parahaemolyticus*,[96] *Gamella morbillorum*,[97] and *Mycobacterium avium-intracellulare*, the last of these being in an HIV-negative patient.[98]

The pathophysiology of endocarditis in addicts is poorly understood. The organism is most often part of the patient's own flora,[26, 99] although injection paraphernalia have been implicated in the case of *P. aeruginosa* endocarditis.[100, 101] Environmental contamination was also considered in the initial outbreak of *Serratia* endocarditis in California when it was learned that years earlier *Serratia* had been sprayed into the air to study wind currents. However, these strains were not the same ones that caused disease, and the regional predilection for this infection remains a mystery.[73, 74] It is known that, unlike native valve endocarditis in nonaddicts, the affected cardiac valve is almost always previously normal.[26, 70, 102] In an autopsy study of addicts who died from endocarditis, Dressler and Roberts reported that 81% of the valves were normal, including all right-side valves.[102] Early reports of endocarditis in addicts noted a predominance of tricuspid valve involvement,[103, 104] and with few exceptions this predilection appears to hold true today.[26] However, there may be differences between the sexes, with mitral valve involvement exceeding that of the tricuspid valve in women.[105] One possible explanation for this difference is the greater prevalence of mitral valve prolapse in women. *S. aureus* predominantly affects the tricuspid valve, but it may also involve the mitral or aortic valves. *Serratia marcescens*, *Streptococcus pyogenes*, and enterococci are found almost exclusively on the left-side valves.[26, 73, 84] The incidence of left-sided infection may be increasing, with up to half of cases affecting the aortic or mitral valve.[69, 106] Some patients have multiple valves infected. One proposed explanation for the involvement of the tricuspid valve in addicts is microscopic damage to the endothelium caused by bombardment of the tricuspid valve by impurities in the injected illicit drugs.[70] The greater need for oxygen has been suggested as the reason certain organisms are found on the left side.

IDUs are also far more susceptible to recurrent bouts of endocarditis. The median interval between episodes is far shorter in addicts than in nonaddicts, and *S. aureus* remains the most common pathogen, affecting the tricuspid or pulmonary valve in approximately 90% of cases.[102]

Most addicts with endocarditis present within the first week of illness with constitutional signs indicative of severe, acute infection.[26, 69, 107] When there is right-sided infection, the patient most often presents with respiratory symptoms caused by septic pulmonary emboli.[26] The overall severity of the clinical picture depends on the valve or valves involved and whether there is any associated damage to the heart itself, such as valve ring abscess or valve rupture, or metastatic infection involving other organs. Classic findings such as Osler's nodes and Janeway's lesions are rare in addicts, and heart murmurs are found with variable frequency. When the infection is confined to the tricuspid valve, murmurs are detected in the minority of patients (35%).[26] In fact, there is an inverse relation between the number of patients with right-sided infection and the number of patients with murmurs.[108] The absence of signs specific for endocarditis makes the diagnosis difficult,[109] requiring a high index of suspicion. At the time of the initial presentation, there are no differences in age, sex, maximum temperature, or leukocyte count between addicts with and without endocarditis. Those with endocarditis account for only 13% of addicts admitted for infection, and only positive echocardiogram findings, pulmonary or systemic emboli, and bacteremia distinguish patients with endocarditis from those without.[110] The most sensitive indicator of endocarditis in the IDU is a blood culture, which is positive in 80 to 100% of cases.[69, 70, 107, 111] Many addicts take oral antibiotics before admission in an attempt to prevent hospitalization. This practice may cause initial cultures to be negative, but subsequent blood cultures will reveal the pathogen.[112] Even after several days of appropriate parenteral therapy, blood cultures are still likely to be positive.[113, 114] The echocardiogram has a relatively high sensitivity (approximately 90%), and false-positive results are unusual,[110] although the value of a two-dimensional echocardiogram for determining which valve is infected has been questioned.[26, 105] To decrease the number of unnecessary echocardiograms, Weisse and colleagues recommended that only IDUs with positive blood cultures and those with pulmonary emboli or cardiac complications be studied by this method.[110]

Because of the high-grade bacteremia and acute nature of endocarditis in addicts, every organ tends to be affected to some degree. Complications involving the heart, although infrequent, may be life-threatening. When cardiac problems dominate the picture, which is most likely with mitral or aortic valve infections, the prognosis is poor, especially if valve damage causes congestive heart failure. As has been noted, recurrent endocarditis is common in addicts. Most patients survive the first episode, but with such severely damaged valves that dysfunction occurs in almost 70%. Previous valve damage predisposes to subsequent episodes, which frequently are fatal. Additional cardiac lesions include left-ventricular abscesses, which are multifocal and are found in conjunction with clusters of bacteria in intramural arteries, and myocardial infarction. Valve ring abscesses and, rarely, focal, acute interstitial myocarditis are also found.[102] Cardiac abscesses may also lead to further serious complications, such as a pseudoaneurysm of the heart, which might be demonstrated by magnetic resonance imaging and color Doppler ultrasound.[115] As with nonaddicts, left-sided infection predisposes to systemic emboli and acute pericarditis, which may necessitate immediate drainage. Certain organisms, notably *Serratia* and *Candida*, are notable for their tendency to induce large, systemic emboli, and their isolation in a patient with endocarditis should alert the clinician to the probability of left-sided infection and the likelihood of a serious embolic event.[73, 75]

Most addicts with right-sided endocarditis present with signs and symptoms related to septic pulmonary emboli.[26] Typically, patients have acute onset of fever, chills, dyspnea, and chest pain that is often pleuritic in nature. Cough is frequently present; it may be nonproductive or associated with blood-streaked sputum. Pneumothorax, occasionally bilateral, occurs as a complication of septic pulmonary embolism.[116] Involvement of other organ systems is similar to that observed in endocarditis in nonaddicts. Central nervous system involvement may initially be confused with toxic effects of illicit drugs, but the diagnosis usually becomes rapidly apparent when blood cultures become positive.

Addicts with endocarditis who are stable and only moderately ill can be safely observed without antibiotic therapy while the results of blood cultures are awaited. Transient fevers and bacteremias occur in this population, and because bacteremia is the most sensitive indicator of endocarditis, a commitment to therapy before the nature of the septic condition is documented can lead to unnecessary and prolonged hospitalization for administration of antibiotics. Even when the patient is acutely ill, several blood cultures should be obtained before antibiotic therapy is initiated. The initial empiric regimen is based in part on knowledge of the organisms most likely to cause endocarditis in that geographic location. In most settings, coverage is directed against *S. aureus*. Where methicillin-resistant *S. aureus* is prevalent, vancomycin is the preferred agent. In settings where methicillin-resistant organisms account for few cases, nafcillin or a similar β-lactamase–resistant penicillin is preferred. When vancomycin is used to treat patients with methicillin-resistant *S. aureus*, both fever and bacteremia are considerably prolonged, compared with treatment with nafcillin.[114]

Trimethoprim-sulfamethoxazole has been used as an alternative for both methicillin-sensitive and methicillin-resistant *S. aureus* soft tissue infections, but its efficacy in endocarditis is questionable.[117] Traditionally, endocarditis in IDUs was treated with 4- to 6-week courses of parenteral antibiotics. However, it is now recognized that patients with uncomplicated right-sided endocarditis may be successfully treated with a 2-week regimen of nafcillin plus an aminoglycoside[118] or even cloxacillin alone.[119] In some cases, when quinolones are used, therapy may consist entirely of oral medication.[120] Whether an aminoglycoside should be added to an initial empiric regimen to provide coverage against a gram-negative pathogen is controversial. The standard dose of an aminoglycoside used with an antistaphylococcal penicillin is likely to have little effect against the most worrisome gram-negative organisms, particularly *Pseudomonas*; it has been reported that an aminoglycoside dose of 8 mg/kg is required to achieve acceptable antipseudomonal activity.[121, 122] With a combination of a high-dose aminoglycoside and a synergistic β-lactam antibiotic, the outcome in *Pseudomonas* endocarditis is much more favorable than with any other initial regimen.[123] Quinolones also have demonstrated utility against *Pseudomonas*, but the data are insufficient to permit a recommendation for their use.[124]

Combined therapy with penicillin (or vancomycin) plus an aminoglycoside is standard against enterococcal endocarditis, but resistance to multiple antibiotics is spreading, making such a selection less reliable without first screening for susceptibility.[125] Frequently, gentamicin-resistant enterococci are susceptible to streptomycin and synergy can be obtained with use of the latter.[125] Teicoplanin, which is not available in the United States, retains activity against some strains of vancomycin-resistant enterococci and is also active against methicillin-resistant *S. aureus*. However, the pharmacokinetics of this agent in drug addicts, particularly those who are acutely ill, are different from the kinetics observed in other populations. Clinicians unaware of this fact may underdose such patients by a considerable margin.[126]

In general, regardless of the infecting organism, antibiotic management should be based on susceptibility data and, when indicated, pharmacokinetic information. In most cases, the survival rate is good with antibiotics alone, despite complications and prolonged fever.[127] Septic emboli frequently occur after the initiation of therapy but do not affect the prognosis and are not necessarily an indication for removal or replacement of the infected valve.[26, 127] There is no correlation between vegetation size, as determined by echocardiography, and the likelihood of an embolus. However, vegetations larger than 2 cm are associated with a 33% mortality rate, compared with 1.3% for patients with vegetations smaller than 2 cm ($p < .001$).[127]

Prognosis is not affected by the duration of symptoms before initiation of therapy, antibiotic use before admission, right-sided heart failure, pulmonary embolism, or results of the following laboratory tests: leukocyte count, hemoglobin, and serum creatinine.[127] There are no differences in the presentation, clinical manifestations, or bacteriology of endocarditis in IDUs based solely on their being seropositive for HIV-1. However, IDUs with HIV infection are at much greater risk of acquiring endocarditis than are their HIV-negative counterparts.[128] Furthermore, there is a clear inverse relation between the CD4+ T-lymphocyte count and mortality.[129] Patients with the lowest CD4 counts may have a predisposition for left-sided infection, which also increases the mortality rate.[129]

The indications for surgery and the final result are the same in IDUs with endocarditis as in the general population.[130] Although surgical treatment carries substantial risk, the expected mortality rate in patients in whom medical management has failed approaches 100%, so surgical treatment is indicated and clearly improves survival.[131] The patient's HIV-1 status may play a significant role in the outcome. Some studies have detected a significant drop in the CD4 count after cardiopulmonary bypass, which led to an acceleration of the progress toward the acquired immunodeficiency syndrome (AIDS).[132] Addicts with HIV-1 infection whose endocarditis is poorly controlled at the time of cardiac surgery and those with advanced AIDS also seem to have a poor prognosis.[130] The major problem after cardiac surgery for endocarditis in IDUs is probably their propensity to continue illicit drug use. In one study, only 4 of 57 addicts remained drug-free, and the 10-year survival rate was only 10%.[130] For this reason, some authors advocate excision of the tricuspid valve or repair of the left-side valves rather than replacement for IDUs in need of surgical intervention.[133] This may represent a safer approach for patients who are likely to have recurrent bouts of endocarditis.

NONCARDIAC VASCULAR INFECTIONS

Peripheral and central vessels used for injection frequently become injured or infected, leading to the formation of hematoma, thrombosis, septic thrombophlebitis, mycotic aneurysm, or traumatic arteriovenous fistula.[134, 135] Clinical findings include local pain, swelling, and fever together with bacteremia and clinical sepsis. The predominant pathogens are gram-positive cocci, usually *S. aureus*, although gram-negative pathogens, particularly *P. aeruginosa*, are not infrequently found.[134–137]

As arm and leg veins become thrombosed, sclerosed, and unusable, femoral, axillary, and neck vessels are increasingly used. Local signs of infection may be masked when deep vessels are involved. Infection or sclerosis of proximal large veins is frequently complicated by venous stasis and supervening thrombosis. Septic pulmonary embolization follows and closely resembles right-sided bacterial endocarditis with septic or bland emboli originating from the tricuspid valve.[26] The management of septic thrombophlebitis, which most frequently involves the femoral veins, remains controversial. In addition to parenteral antimicrobial agents, the value of anticoagulant use has not been established in reducing pulmonary emboli. Furthermore, hemorrhagic complications from unrecognized coexistent femoral and cerebral mycotic aneurysms may occur. Difficulties of performing venography in IDUs has precluded controlled studies evaluating efficacy and complications of anticoagulant use. Some experienced clinicians have concluded that the risks of short-term anticoagulation are outweighed by the risk of major pulmonary emboli.

A major vascular complication in IDUs is the formation of mycotic aneurysms, most frequently involving femoral and less commonly neck vessels. True aneurysm, in which the abnormal localized dilatation contains all three layers of arterial wall, is rare. In the drug abuser, frequent direct trauma to peripheral vessels produces an initial sterile perivascular hematoma and damage to the vessel wall. Injection of chemical agents that are constituents of illicit drugs also causes tissue necrosis. The vascular wall usually becomes infected by contiguous spread from adjacent subcutaneous abscesses or areas of cellulitis. Infection causes liquefaction of the central portion of the hematoma in communication with the arterial, or less commonly the venous, wall, forming a secondary (false) pseudoaneurysm.[134, 138] The common femoral artery is the most frequent location, followed by the deep femoral and superficial femoral arteries. Because most IDUs are right handed, left-sided groin infections and aneurysms are more common. Primary mycotic aneurysms in which the damaged vessel wall is infected secondary to unrelated bacteremia are rare and are more likely to involve cerebral vessels as a complication of bacterial endocarditis. Pathogenesis includes septic embolization from valvular vegetations to the vasa vasorum of smaller vessels, such as the middle or posterior cerebral and visceral intra-abdominal arteries, which are more frequently involved than the aorta.

Clinical manifestations of a mycotic aneurysm include a painful, often enlarging, tender, and frequently pulsatile mass, accompanied by variable constitutional symptoms.[139] Evidence of ischemia of the associated distal extremity and nerve compression is often present, and detection of a bruit or thrill over the mass strongly supports the diagnosis. Because drug abusers usually present with associated cellulitis and accompanying edema and induration, the pulsatile mass may be masked, obscuring the diagnosis of aneurysm. Rupture of the aneurysm is usually preceded by severe pain and may be diagnosed as thrombophlebitis or soft tissue abscess. In contrast to the lower limb, distal ischemia in the upper extremity (hand) from induced arterial spasm occurs commonly.

Successful management of mycotic aneurysms requires early diagnosis before rupture occurs. Anemia, leukocytosis, and an elevated sedimentation rate, although frequently present, are of limited value in diagnosis. A high index of suspicion together with angiographic confirmation is essential, because misdiagnosis is common and cellulitis, abscess, or infected hematoma may mimic or mask an aneurysm (Fig. 301–1).

Ultrasonography, although useful, may fail to differentiate an abscess from an aneurysm.[137] In one study ultrasound had a false-negative rate of 54%.[140] CT, especially with injected contrast material, has proved extremely useful and delineates the pathology in the adjacent soft tissues. However, angiography remains the definitive diagnostic procedure, not only in delineating the lesion but in planning the approach to surgery. Digital subtraction angiography may replace traditional arteriography in diagnosing femoral and other peripheral aneurysms.[141] Needle aspiration, incision, and drainage should be avoided in noninvestigated inguinal masses, even if nonpulsatile, because of the risk of uncontrolled bleeding from an unrecognized mycotic aneurysm.[137]

Because *S. aureus* is the most common pathogen, initial empiric antibiotic therapy should include a β-lactamase–resistant penicillin such as nafcillin, and, where methicillin-resistant *S. aureus* is prominent, vancomycin should be started. An aminoglycoside is added initially if there is suspicion or evidence of gram-negative bacilli on gram staining of sanguinopurulent drainage. Subsequent cultures obtained from blood and local exudate influence antibiotic selection. Recommended therapy is 4 to 6 weeks intravenously. Surgical treatment should not be delayed, because rupture is frequent; it consists of proximal and distal ligation of the mycotic aneurysm followed by excision of all necrotic and infected material, including the infected vessel.[142] Vascular reconstruction as a delayed procedure is recommended only in patients who develop ischemia after excision of the aneurysm, and then only when a graft can be positioned through an uninfected tissue plane.

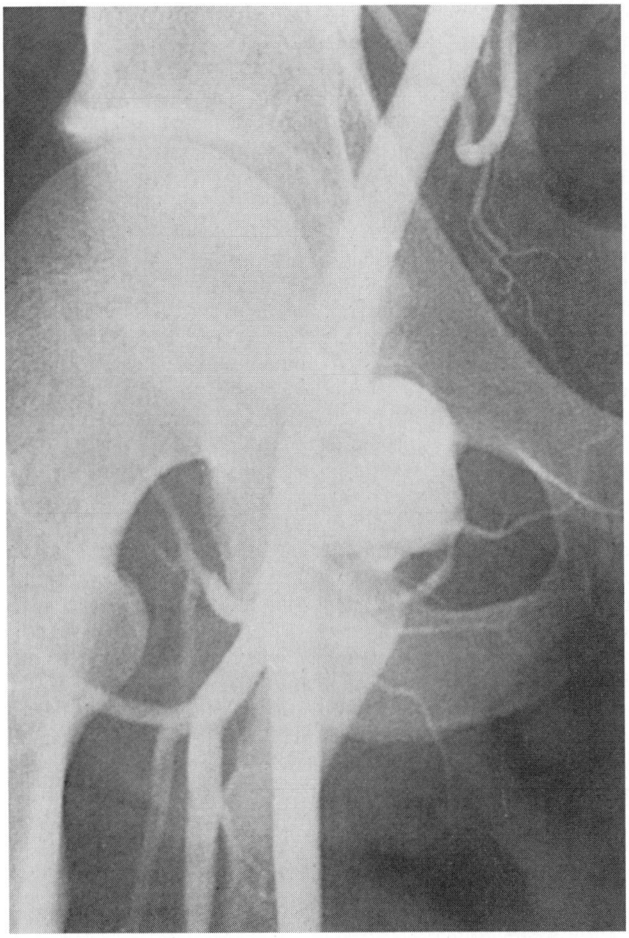

FIGURE 301–1. Arteriogram demonstrating a mycotic aneurysm of right common iliac artery in IVDA.

PULMONARY INFECTIONS

Pulmonary manifestations are extremely common in IDUs. The lung is the target of numerous infectious and noninfectious insults. The latter include drug-induced bronchospasm, acute pulmonary edema, and talc granulomatosis.[143] Heroin overdose may be associated with unilateral or bilateral pulmonary edema as a consequence of capillary-alveolar leak and may be accompanied by fever and leukocytosis.[143, 144] Starch can cause mild transient pulmonary granuloma formation, whereas cotton fibers from drug filters and talc (used as a filter) can cause permanent intravascular and perivascular granulomas in pulmonary arteries and arterioles.[145] The resultant baseline-abnormalities of chest x-ray films and blood gases may cause diagnostic confusion in febrile IDUs. It has been noted that former IDUs have reductions in pulmonary function, especially in the diffusing capacity; however, after adjustment for the effects of cigarette smoking these differences were shown to be insignificant.[146] The incidence of pneumonia is increased in IDUs for a number of reasons, including impaired clearance of secretions, aspiration, increased exposure, decreased immune function, and the higher prevalence of HIV infection. In a series of pulmonary complications of intravenous drug use, septic pulmonary emboli were the most common complication, followed by community-acquired pneumonia and *Mycobacterium tuberculosis* infection.[147]

Most pulmonary infections are community-acquired episodes of pneumonia caused by common respiratory pathogens.[144] In one series of febrile IDUs, pneumonia was the most common cause of fever[4]; in a second series, pneumonia was second only to cellulitis as a cause of fever in IDUs.[5] Bacterial pneumonia must be distinguished from septic emboli originating from right-sided endocarditis or more distal thrombophlebitis and resultant pulmonary infarcts. Septic emboli result in multiple round or wedge-shaped lesions that may cavitate (Fig. 301–2). Pleural involvement is common in both conditions and results in chest pain, pleural effusion, or empyema. Recurrent pulmonary emboli may also result in pulmonary hypertension. The usual pathogens in bacterial pneumonia include *Streptococcus pneumoniae*, oral anaerobes by the bronchogenic route, and *S. aureus* or *P. aeruginosa* by the hematogenous route. A high incidence of bacterial pneumonia caused by *H. influenzae* has been described in IDUs with concomitant HIV infection.[148–151] Lung abscesses may arise from aspiration pneumonia, necrotizing pneumonitis, or septic emboli. Opportunistic pulmonary infections, especially *Pneumocystis carinii* pneumonia, must also be considered in febrile IDUs.

Pulmonary tuberculosis is a major problem in non–HIV-1-infected drug users. Homelessness and medication noncompliance further complicate the problem.[152] IDUs are also at increased risk of drug-resistant disease.[153] Tuberculosis is especially a problem in IDUs with underlying HIV infection. An investigation in a New York methadone maintenance program showed that 15% of HIV-1–infected tuberculin-positive IDUs developed active tuberculosis during 2-year follow-up, whereas none of the tuberculin-positive HIV-1–negative patients did so.[154] Tuberculosis in IDUs with AIDS is more frequently extrapulmonary, and patients present with less cavitary pulmonary disease and fewer AFB-positive organisms in sputum

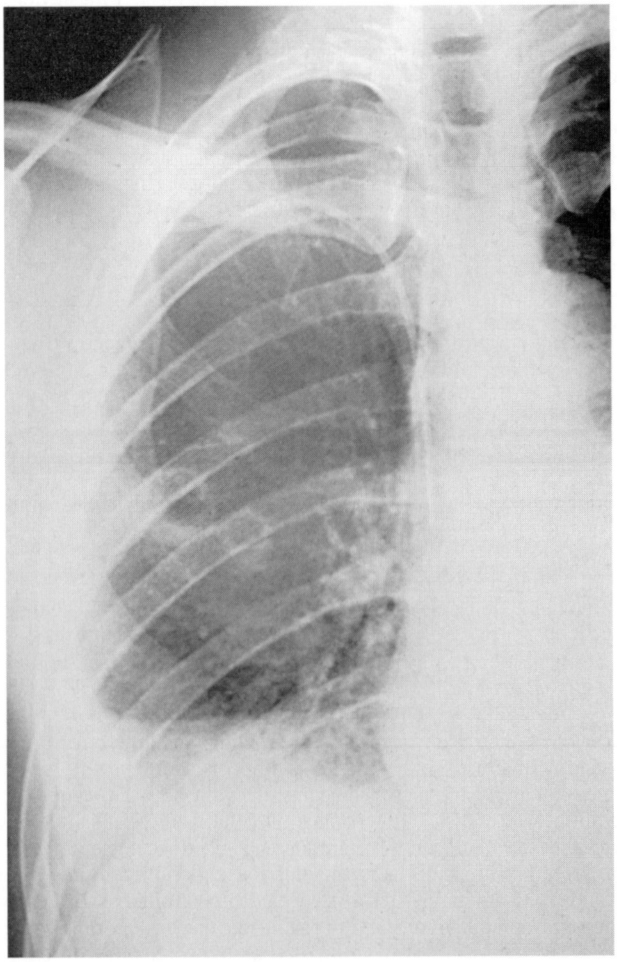

FIGURE 301–2. Anteroposterior radiograph of chest demonstrating pleural effusion and multiple cavitating nodular infarcts due to septic emboli in a patient with tricuspid endocarditis.

than other tuberculosis patients. IDUs with AIDS and pulmonary tuberculosis are just as capable of transmitting tuberculosis infection to their contacts as are tuberculosis patients without AIDS. Coughing induced by use of marijuana or crack cocaine may increase transmission of tuberculosis. IDUs should receive chemoprophylaxis with isoniazid if the tuberculin skin test reaction (TST) is larger than 10 mm. The duration of chemoprophylaxis should be at least 6 months; 12 months is recommended for those with chest roentgenograms suggestive of previously healed tuberculosis.[155] IDUs with HIV infection should receive prophylaxis as recommended for other HIV-infected persons—that is, if the TST is larger than 5 mm or if the patient is a close contact of persons who have active tuberculosis, regardless of skin test results or previous courses of chemoprophylaxis.[156] The recommended duration of chemoprophylaxis in HIV-infected patients is 12 months. Some experts also recommend that TST-negative and anergic HIV-infected persons from risk groups (such as IDUs) or geographic areas with a high prevalence of *M. tuberculosis* infection receive chemoprophylaxis.[156] The potential risk of isoniazid-induced hepatotoxicity in IDUs, who have a higher frequency of background hepatitis and who may also be abusing other hepatotoxic agents such as alcohol and cocaine, should be considered. IDUs have been conspicuous among HIV-infected persons who have been infected with and died from multidrug-resistant tuberculosis.[154]

The febrile IDU with pulmonary infiltrates constitutes an enormous diagnostic challenge given the wide differentiated diagnosis that includes noninfectious causes. Accordingly, initial treatment often involves multiple therapeutic agents to cover several pathogens, and empiric coverage for tuberculosis may be needed in critically ill patients.[154]

HEPATITIS

Hepatitis has long been recognized as a complication of injection drug use. Dual addiction to alcohol and narcotics increases the difficulty of determining the cause of liver disease in this population. The combination of alcohol plus HBV infection results in more severe liver disease than either alone and is associated with rapid acceleration to cirrhosis.[157, 158] Heroin itself is not known to be hepatotoxic,[159, 160] but cocaine can cause severe liver injury.[161]

In the 1950s HBV was the presumed cause of viral hepatitis in IDUs, although there were no confirmatory serologic markers among needle-sharing and sexual partners. In the 1970s non-A, non-B hepatitis, now known to be caused by hepatitis C virus (HCV), was recognized.[162] Subsequently the delta agent (hepatitis D virus; HDV) was recognized and was found to be a major pathogen among IDUs.[163–166] Hepatitis A virus (HAV) is also important in IDUs. The proportion of patients with HAV infection who are IDUs has increased from 4 to 16%, although the incidence of HAV has remained constant in the general population.[167] There is evidence that HAV can be transmitted by intravenous injection,[163] although poor hygiene probably plays a greater role.[168]

IDUs account for 10 to 15% of cases of acute HBV in the United States.[169] Most acquire infection within the first few years of beginning injection drug use, and exposure is promoted by needle sharing and participation in "shooting galleries," which are places an addict can go to have an individual with expertise assist them with injection into difficult-to-find veins.[170] Clinically apparent infection is uncommon, and most IDUs end up with a serologic pattern indicative of naturally acquired immunity. In the United States and in Europe, 25 to 50% of IDUs have serum antibody against HBV surface antigen[171]; however, only 5 to 10% become chronic carriers.[171] Spontaneous reactivation of chronic HBV infection has been described in IDUs, but the diagnosis may be difficult because the clinical presentation is indistinguishable from that of acute hepatitis and information on the patient's previous serologic status usually is unknown.[172, 173] HIV-infected persons with HBV infection are more likely to become chronic carriers.[174] Although both HIV-seropositive and -seronegative IDUs may have a suboptimal response to HBV vaccine,[170, 175, 176] vaccination is recommended for all IDUs who are without evidence of previous infection.[177]

HDV is a defective RNA virus that can replicate and cause hepatitis only in the presence of active HBV infection. HDV may be acquired along with HBV as a primary co-infection or as a superinfection in persons who are carriers of HBV. Because of the interdependent nature of the two viruses, immunity to HBV provides protection against HDV, although there has been one report of an IDU who had evidence of HDV infection without HBV.[178] In some areas where HBV is prevalent, HDV is also seen with relatively high frequency. In nonendemic areas, such as the United States, HDV infection is confined almost exclusively to particular high-risk groups, such as IDUs.[163, 169, 179] The incidence of HDV in IDUs who are hepatitis B surface antigen (HBsAg) carriers approaches 80%, but it is less than 10% in IDUs who have serum antibody to HBsAg.[164] The association of IDU with HBV and HDV was further clarified in a study comparing the transmission and carriage of each agent in two populations known to be at risk, IDUs and homosexuals.[180] Among 372 IDUs, 52.4% had evidence of current or past HBV infection; of these, 8.7% were chronic carriers of HBV. Among the chronic carriers, 70.6% were also chronic carriers of HDV. In contrast, only 27.4% of male homosexuals had serologic evidence of HBV infection (current or remote), of whom 7.9% were chronic carriers. Only a third of these chronic HBV carriers had evidence of HDV infection, a significant difference from the IDUs ($p < .0005$), demonstrating that intravenous drug use is a much more efficient means of transmission of HDV infection than is sexual contact.

Superinfection of HDV on previous HBV infection is the most common pattern of dual infection.[163] Simultaneous acquisition of both viruses is more common among IDUs and is more likely to result in fulminant infection.[179] IDUs who experience co-infection frequently have a biphasic illness.[180] The initial phase of the disease is caused by HDV, and the second by HBV.[178] The closer the proximity of the biphasic peaks, the greater is the risk of a fatal outcome. IDUs who survive such a illness usually have a complete recovery and clear both viruses.[181] Treatment of chronic HDV infection with recombinant interferon-α has shown transient effects; the role of interferon therapy in this infection is not clear.[182] Prevention of HDV can be accomplished by vaccination of IDUs against HBV.

Intravenous drug use is a major risk factor for HCV infection. IDUs accounted for 42% of cases of community-acquired HCV infection in four Centers for Disease Control and Prevention sentinel centers in the United States.[183] The seroprevalence of anti-HCV among IDUs ranges from 64 to 90%.[184] IDUs may be an important reservoir of HCV infection in the general population now that the incidence of transfusion-associated disease is decreasing.[185] The majority of patients with HCV infection develop some form of chronic liver disease. An increased severity of chronic liver disease due to HCV is seen in persons who abuse alcohol.[184] Intravenous drug use is also more efficient at transmitting HCV infection than is homosexual or heterosexual contact.[186, 187] IDUs tend to acquire HCV after a brief interval of drug use.[168]

Hepatitis G virus (GBV-C virus, HGV) is a newly recognized member of the flaviviridae family to which HCV belongs.[188] The prevalence of HGV infection among IDUs differs by geographic areas, varying from 9.7% of long-term IDUs in Los Angeles[189] to 24% of IDUs in Japan[190] and 35% of long-term IDUs in Switzerland.[191] Almost all persons with HGV infection in these studies were also infected with HCV. Although much about the epidemiology, natural history, and role in co-infection of HGV is currently unknown, several studies have failed to demonstrate an influence of HGV infection on the clinical or virologic course of infection with HCV (see Chapter 143).[189, 191, 192]

IDUs are also at risk for HAV infection, and fulminant, fatal hepatitis from HAV in IDUs with chronic liver disease has been reported.[193] Non-immune IDUs should be considered for vaccination against HAV.[177]

SPLENIC ABSCESS

Abscess of the spleen is a major complication of intravenous drug abuse. The splenic arteries are end arteries; any occlusion leads to ischemia or infarction. The ischemic or infarcted areas are highly susceptible to infection and serve as a nidus for abscess formation in the event of bacteremia. Trauma, including blunt trauma, also may lead to splenic injury and is an antecedent condition in some addicts who develop splenic abscess.[194] Bacteremia is the final common pathway. In the pre-antibiotic area, 10% of patients with bacterial endocarditis developed splenic abscess as a complication. Endocarditis is the most common underlying infection in IDUs,[194, 195] although splenic involvement also may result from spread of local infection directly to the splenic artery or extension of an adjacent process with erosion and thrombosis of the splenic artery.[196]

Splenic lesions may be multiple and small or solitary, occasionally becoming large.[194–196] Solitary lesions commonly accompany infection in the viscera. Lesions within the spleen are most often found in the upper pole (53.1%). Lower-pole lesions (21.9%) and midspleen lesions (15.6%) are found less often.[196] Staphylococci and streptococci are the organisms most often implicated; however, gram-negative bacilli and anaerobes are isolated in approximately 25 and 5% of cases, respectively.[196] Addicts who lick their needles are susceptible to splenic abscesses caused by mouth anaerobes, in particular *Fusobacterium* spp.[197] Bacteremia is common in patients with splenic abscess, and usually the same organism is cultured from the blood and from the splenic cavity. However, addicts have a tendency to have multiple infected sites that contain different organisms. Therefore, isolation of an organism from the blood is not assurance that the same organism will be found in the spleen.[195]

The signs and symptoms of splenic abscess may be vague or overshadowed by underlying endocarditis. Almost all patients have fever and some degree of abdominal pain or discomfort.[194–196] Pleuritic chest pain is common.[194–196] Left shoulder pain has also been described. Abdominal tenderness, which is frequently confined to the left upper quadrant, is found in approximately 50% of patients.[194–196] Splenomegaly may be present, but a splenic rub is unusual.[194] Abnormalities within the thorax are detected in two thirds of cases, including one third with pleural effusion. The differential diagnosis includes subphrenic abscess, pulmonary empyema, perinephric abscess, and bland splenic infarct. There are no characteristic laboratory abnormalities, although an extremely high leukocyte count has been correlated with a poor prognosis.[196] The chest radiograph may reveal an elevated hemidiaphragm or a pleural effusion; however, abdominal radiography is seldom useful. The most reliable diagnostic tests are ultrasound and CT of the abdomen,[194] which also define the extent and location of the lesions and hence are useful postoperatively to exclude any residual collections or intra-abdominal abscesses.

Treatment of splenic abscess requires splenectomy and antibiotics directed against the involved pathogens. Removal of the spleen may be difficult if it adheres to adjacent structures; removal or partial resection of these organs may be required.[194–197] Percutaneous aspiration is worth consideration.

The complications of splenic abscess include spontaneous rupture, which can be so subtle in some cases that the patient has no signs of generalized peritonitis or purulence in the abdominal cavity.[194] Other manifestations include recurrent bacteremia and intestinal obstruction.[196] Splenic abscess detected early and treated promptly results in a good prognosis.

CENTRAL NERVOUS SYSTEM INFECTIONS

IDUs may present with a variety of CNS manifestations that may or may not be infectious in origin. The differential diagnosis is extensive and frequently difficult. Complications related to the injection of illicit drugs include coma caused by overdose or intoxication, postanoxic encephalopathy, delirium, and acute confusion states. Seizures, cerebral edema, and dementia may result from noninfectious as well as infectious causes. Hemorrhage and infarction may be secondary to infection or compromise of the neurovascular system. Parkinsonism is most often the result of drug effects but has been reported in infection.[198] The etiology of these disorders may be obscure, necessitating a thorough work-up to exclude an infectious cause. Infections of the CNS may be local or secondary to an infectious process elsewhere. Where an infection is the primary problem, there are usually focal findings and fever. Furthermore, the presence of focal findings suggests the possibility of a mass lesion requiring immediate surgical intervention. Therefore, when faced with an IDU with neurologic findings, it is helpful to construct a differential diagnosis that includes both infectious and noninfectious causes and to differentiate between a local process and a complication of a distant primary infection.

CNS manifestations are found in up to 25% of individuals with endocarditis.[199] Nevertheless, because addicts tend to have right-sided endocarditis, CNS complications may occur less frequently in IDUs.[107] Endocarditis is the most common cause of CNS disease in IDUs, and it also accounts for the most serious complications, including brain abscess, meningitis, and hemorrhage from ruptured mycotic aneurysms.[26, 199] Mycotic aneurysms may manifest as a progressive focal neurologic deficit owing to expansion of the aneurysm or as an acute subarachnoid or intracerebral hemorrhage.[200] Focal abnormalities also result from septic emboli (which frequently result in transient focal neurologic deficits) and multiple cerebral abscesses. These lesions tend to resolve in 1 to 2 weeks with appropriate antibiotic therapy.[26] It is also common for IDUs to develop a diffuse encephalopathy. Although they are as susceptible as the general population to the usual viral causes of encephalitis, more often addicts who present with signs of diffuse cerebral infection have cerebritis attributable to the high-grade bacteremia associated with endocarditis.[26]

Focal neurologic infections represent the third most likely presentation of CNS infection in IDUs. Localized CNS infection in this population is confined primarily to brain abscess and subdural empyema. Brain abscess is usually caused by pyogenic bacteria; *Nocardia* has also been reported.[21] Fungi, including *Aspergillus* spp.,[201] *Chaetomium strumarium*,[202] and mucormycosis,[203] have also been reported. Mucormycosis in IDUs is rarely associated with HIV infection and presents as focal cerebritis or abscess, in contrast to the more extensive aggressive process observed in immunocompromised hosts. There may be a predilection for multifocal involvement and, in particular, involvement of the basal ganglia, with this region being affected far more often in addicts compared with nonaddicts.[202] Cerebral mucormycosis is not caused by spread from sinuses but it appears that the organism is either a contaminant in the illicit drugs or enters the blood stream from an infected injection site, finding its way to areas of the brain predisposed by earlier drug-induced injury. The patient usually presents with signs and symptoms of a mass lesion. The differential diagnosis of such lesions includes toxoplasmosis, lymphoma, tuberculosis, and cryptococcosis. Isolated involvement of the basal ganglia is uncommon in toxoplasmosis and lymphoma. Radiologic contrast enhancement may or may not be seen in patients with mucormycosis and therefore lends little to the diagnosis. Biopsy of the lesion is required to establish the diagnosis; failure to do so is associated with a very high mortality rate.[202] Remarkably, the outcome of this disease is very good, with survival in most cases after prolonged amphotericin B therapy and excision of as much of the infected tissue as possible.[198, 203, 204]

Brain abscesses in IDUs are usually the result of infected cerebral emboli in patients with mitral or aortic valve endocarditis.[26, 107, 199, 205] Rarely, emboli travel through or originate in the pulmonary circulation. Alternatively, pathogens may seed the brain after an inadvertent injection into the arterial system during an attempted jugular vein injection. Tuberculous brain abscesses may also be seen, particularly in IDUs who are co-infected with HIV. The lesions are typically solitary, multiloculated, and contrast-enhancing. They must be distinguished from *Toxoplasma*, which usually causes multiple lesions that are not multiloculated, and lymphoma, which can be necrotic with multiple loculations but is more often located near an ependymal surface.[206] IDUs with HIV infection who have characteristic lesions may be treated empirically for toxoplasmosis, but failure to respond within 2 weeks should prompt a biopsy, which will lead to the correct diagnosis. Subdural empyema is also seen in IDUs and may be secondary to direct extension from a local infectious process or complicated bacteremia.

Meningitis in IDUs is most often secondary to endocarditis[199] and hence is frequently caused by unusual pathogens.[207] Spinal epidural abscess should be considered in any addict presenting with spinal ache or back pain, especially if there are focal neurologic signs.[208] The patients tend to have a prolonged symptomatic course, often as long as several months, and frequently present without fever. One report described two IDUs, one of whom had not used drugs in several years, with extensive spinal epidural abscesses. Neither patient noted back pain before experiencing some minor trauma shortly before presentation. In each case the diagnosis was not considered until the patient later returned for medical attention with neurologic complaints accompanied by signs of infection.[209] Typically, complaints of addicts are minimized by clinicians, and the diagnosis may be overlooked even after admission to the hospital. The thoracic or lumbar spine is most often involved,[208] although cervical spine lesions are also seen. *S. aureus* is the most common cause, but other gram-positive and gram-negative organisms have been reported, occasionally in combination with other organisms. *M. tuberculosis* also causes spinal epidural abscess, and it too may be found in combination with other organisms,[207] making careful definition of the microbial etiology imperative. The pathophysiology is usually direct spread to the epidural space from adjacent disk or vertebral body infection or hematogenous dissemination from a distant focus of infection. In most cases immediate drainage relieves symptoms, although once a chronic condition ensues there may be nothing but granulation tissue, requiring multiple-level laminectomy to relieve pressure on the spinal cord.

Intramedullary spinal cord abscess has been reported in an IDU with symptoms resembling those of an epidural abscess. Myelography demonstrated cord enlargement that was confirmed to be a result of intramedullary pus. The infection was caused by *Pseudomonas cepacia* but failed to respond to antibiotic therapy to which the organism was susceptible in vitro.[210]

Toxin-mediated diseases, specifically wound botulism and tetanus, are being seen with increasing frequency among IDUs and must be considered in addicts who have neurologic symptoms. Epidemics of both tetanus and wound botulism have occurred in California,[211, 212] and cases are likely to be found elsewhere. The patient with tetanus is likely to be a long-time user who has poor venous access and multiple skin lesions caused by failed attempts at intravenous injections or by "skin popping" (intentional injection into the subcutaneous tissues). These lesions become colonized by multiple pathogens, including *Clostridium* spp., and in the proper anaerobic environment toxin is generated and produces disease.[213] Most IDUs with tetanus are Hispanic; this may be explained by a study that found that only 58% of Mexican-Americans had protective levels of antibody to tetanus toxoid, compared with 73% of non-Hispanic whites.[211] Wound botulism in IDUs was first described in New York City in 1982. Subsequently, sporadic cases were reported from different locations. Since 1990, a dramatic increase in the number of wound botulism cases has occurred in California.[213] With rare exceptions, patients have all been IDUs who inject "black tar" heroin, a black, gummy form of the drug that is synthesized in Mexico and distributed widely throughout the western United States. Skin popping of black tar heroin is the major risk factor for acquisition of wound botulism, and given the widespread distribution of this drug, additional cases should be anticipated throughout the western states. The greatest risk is seen among heavy users, but disease also occurs in occasional subcutaneous or intramuscular injection users. Most likely the drug is contaminated during the dilution process, when substances are added to the heroin to increase the amount of the product and thereby increase the seller's profits. The symptoms of wound botulism in IDUs are similar to those of botulism in nonaddicts. Unlike the latter, who usually have a dietary history to suggest the diagnosis, in IDUs the organism can usually be recovered from wound cultures. Serum assays for botulism toxin are rarely positive; administration of antitoxin, which is helpful only if given within the first 24 hours, must be done on the basis of a high index of suspicion, rather than waiting for culture identification.[212, 213]

Drug users were once the most common population in the United States to develop tetanus; now they account for only 40% of cases.[211] As noted previously, skin popping plays a major role, providing the lesions with an environment conducive to toxin production. Skin popping probably also accounts for the higher mortality rate in addicts than in nonaddicts. One proposed reason is that, because of the number and severity of skin lesions in addicts, there is greater opportunity for large amounts of toxin to be produced. In addition, an addict presenting with the typical symptoms of tetanus may be thought to be manifesting the effects of illicit drug toxicity, overdose or drug withdrawal.[214] In view of the risk for tetanus associated with intravenous drug use, it is worthwhile to consider giving a tetanus booster to any addict who is being treated for any other condition unless the patient has been immunized recently.

OCULAR MANIFESTATIONS

Endophthalmitis is a common and serious complication of intravenous drug use.[215–219] Both fungal and bacterial endophthalmitis are hematogenous in origin and frequently manifest as a complication of infective endocarditis. *Candida* is the most common fungal cause, and endophthalmitis may also occur as part of a disseminated syndrome involving eyes, bone, and skin in heroin users. Symptoms include blurred vision, pain, and decreased visual acuity. White, cotton-like exudative lesions are found in the choroid and retina with vitreous haziness. Diagnosis requires a high index of suspicion, and because blood cultures are usually negative at the time of ocular symptoms, definitive diagnosis often involves vitreous sampling. Treatment has traditionally consisted of parenteral amphotericin B together with flucytosine; the use of intraocular amphotericin B is controversial, and occasionally there is need for pars plana vitrectomy.[220, 221] Although data from prospective, controlled trials are lacking, a number of case reports have suggested that fluconazole is efficacious in the treatment of *Candida* endophthalmitis, as long as treatment is begun before extension into the vitreous occurs.[222–224]

Aspergillus spp. are the second most common cause of fungal endophthalmitis in IDUs. As with *Candida*, the pathogenesis reflects mycotic contamination of drug paraphernalia or of the heroin injected, rather than host immunosuppression. Physical findings and treatment are similar to those of *Candida* infection.

Bacterial endophthalmitis is less common, and the presentation is often acute with rapid progression of symptoms. Inflammation usually is present in the anterior and posterior chambers. In addition to pain, redness, and lid swelling, flame-shaped hemorrhages and cotton-wool spots may be present. Treatment includes use of subconjunctival and systemic antibiotics. Surgical aspiration may be required for both diagnosis and treatment. *S. aureus* is the organism most frequently isolated. A rapidly destructive form of endophthalmitis has been reported for *Bacillus cereus*, which has been cultured from heroin and drug paraphernalia.[225] In both mycotic and bacterial endophthalmitis, early diagnosis and intervention increase the chance of a favorable outcome. Whereas bacterial endophthalmitis is rare, ocular peripheral emboli are frequent complications of infective endocarditis in the IDU. These include conjunctival and retinal emboli (Roth's spots), which manifest as petechiae, retinal hemorrhage, ischemia, and papilledema.

ACQUIRED IMMUNODEFICIENCY SYNDROME

Early in the AIDS epidemic, injection drug use was identified as being associated with a high risk of contracting the disease.[226] Injection drug use accounts for 25% of the reported adult cases of AIDS in the United States—22% in males and 47% in females.[227] In addition, sexual contact with IDUs accounts for a significant number of cases among persons whose primary risk is heterosexual contact. The rapid increase in heterosexually acquired HIV infection among women is attributed primarily to sexual contact with male IDUs.[228, 229] HIV-infected women, regardless of their source of infection, may transmit the infection to their offspring. Shooting galleries have been shown to play an important role in the transmission of HIV infection.[230–232] Among 22 shooting galleries surveyed in Miami, 50% provided rooms for sexual activity for an additional fee.[233] Needle exchange programs have been shown to be an effective means of reducing the incidence of new HIV infections.[234, 235]; however, there remains intense political opposition to such programs, and needle exchange is illegal in many parts of the United States. In areas where needle exchange is illegal, IDUs can be taught to clean their injection equipment with household bleach before use, a technique that has been demonstrated to reduce the recovery of HIV virus from contaminated needles and syringes.[236] Providing medical care for HIV-infected IDUs can present a formidable challenge to the physician. A multidisciplinary approach that includes the diagnosis and treatment of substance abuse is essential.[237]

HIV-infected IDUs appear to progress to AIDS at rates comparable to those of other risk groups. No difference in the decline in the CD4 count could be demonstrated between HIV-infected IDUs and homosexual men.[238, 239] The rate of decline appears unaffected by the frequency of injection[240–242] or by alcohol use.[243] Cohort studies have failed to demonstrate any difference in the rate of progression to AIDS among IDUs, homosexual men, and heterosexuals.[244, 245] HIV-infected IDUs appear to be at substantial risk for pre-AIDS morbidity and mortality from bacterial infections.[246] In New York City, deaths from infections including bacterial pneumonia, endocarditis, and pulmonary tuberculosis were reported more frequently among HIV-positive IDUs than among those who were not infected.[247] In a study of pre-AIDS deaths in HIV-infected IDUs in Edinburgh, drug overdose was found to be the most common cause, followed by bacterial sepsis and liver disease.[248]

The spectrum of disease in persons with HIV infection appears to be identical at comparable CD4 counts regardless of risk behavior.[249] There is no difference in survival in IDUs from the time of AIDS diagnosis; prognosis is more strongly associated with initial AIDS diagnosis than with risk behavior.[250]

OTHER SEXUALLY TRANSMITTED DISEASES

A major contributing factor to the prevalence of sexually transmitted diseases (STDs) including syphilis and gonorrhea is unsafe sexual practices associated with the use of illicit drugs.[251, 252] Among almost 3000 active IDUs in Baltimore, 60% reported a history of an STD; 24.1% were HIV seropositive.[253] A history of syphilis was found to be independently associated with HIV seropositivity in homosexual and bisexual male IDUs, 90% of whom reported a history of sexual intercourse with women.[253] Studies that rely mainly on self-report of STD history may underestimate the true incidence of STDs in this population. Kleyn and associates found large discrepancies between results of serologic testing and self-reports of STDs among IDUs, with a general tendency toward underreporting.[254] In a sample of men who were actively using drugs, commonly reported high-risk behaviors included multiple recent sexual partners in 62% and not using condoms in 50%.[255] Among patients evaluated at an STD clinic, those who reported heavy drug use (including alcohol) were more likely to report high-risk sexual practices and to have HIV infection or syphilis than those who used drugs less frequently.[256] In a study of female IDUs in Los Angeles, 85% reported having had sex without using condoms.[257] Among female IDUs, those who trade sex for drugs are less likely to use condoms than those who trade sex for money.[258]

In contrast to previous years, more newly diagnosed syphilis patients report a history of intravenous drug use, mainly cocaine, and intercourse with commercial sex workers. The diagnosis and treatment of syphilis in IDUs may be complicated by the high rate of biologic false-positive, nonspecific serologic screening tests. In a study of IDUs in Baltimore, only 46% of reactive RPR tests could be confirmed as indicative of past or present syphilis, with a reactive FTA-ABS. Biologic false-positive tests were more common among heterosexual than among homosexual or bisexual IDUs.[254] A study of syphilis in HIV-infected IDUs revealed that HIV did not alter the stage of presentation, clinical course, serologic manifestations, or response to conventional treatment of syphilis.[260]

Given the importance of STDs as cofactors in the sexual transmission of HIV in both homosexuals and heterosexuals, reducing the prevalence of STDs in IDUs is an additional strategy to diminish the spread of HIV among IDUs and from them to their non–drug-using sexual contacts.

REFERENCES

1. Klatt EC, Mills NZ, Noguchi TT. Causes of death in hospitalized intravenous drug abusers. J Forensic Sci. 1990;35:1143–1148.
2. Niccolini R, Rubenstein R. Psychiatric aspects in the management of the hospitalized intravenous drug abusers. In: Levine DP, Sobel JD, eds. Infections in Intravenous Drug Abusers. New York: Oxford University Press; 1991;68–80.
3. Fultz JM Jr, Senay EC. Guidelines for the management of hospitalized narcotic addicts. Ann Intern Med. 1975;82:815–818.
4. Marantz PR, Linzer M, Feiner CJ, et al. Inability to predict diagnosis in febrile intravenous drug abusers. Ann Intern Med. 1987;106:823–828.
5. Samet JH, Shevitz A, Fowle J, et al. Hospitalization decision in febrile intravenous drug users. Am J Med. 1990;89:53–57.
6. Crane LR, Levine DP, Zervos MJ, et al. Bacteremia in narcotic addicts at the Detroit Medical Center: I. Microbiology, epidemiology, risk factors, and empiric therapy. Rev Infect Dis. 1986;8:364–373.
7. Peterson PK, Sharp B, Gekker G, et al. Opiate-mediated suppression of interferon gamma produced by cultured peripheral blood mononuclear cells. J Clin Invest. 1987;80:824–831.
8. Wybran J, Appelboom T, Famaey JP, et al. Suggestive evidence for receptors for morphine and methadone-encephalon on normal human blood T lymphocytes. J Immunol. 1979;123:1068–1070.
7. Des Jarlais FC, Friedman SR, Stoneburner RL. HIV infection and intravenous drug use: Critical issues in transmission dynamics, infection outcome and prevention. Rev Infect Dis. 1988;10:151–158.
8. Saravolatz LD, Markowitz N, Arking L, et al. Methicillin-resistant *Staphylococcus aureus*: Epidemiologic observations during a community-acquired outbreak. Ann Intern Med. 1982;96:364–373.
9. Tuazon CU, Sheagren JN. Increased rate of carriage of *Staphylococcus aureus* among narcotic addicts. J Infect Dis. 1974;129:725–727.
10. Berman DS, Schaefler S, Simberkoff M, et al. *Staphylococcus aureus* colonization in intravenous drug abusers, dialysis patients and diabetics. J Infect Dis. 1987;155:829–831.
11. Novik DM, Ness GL. Abuse of antibiotics by abusers of parenteral heroin or cocaine. South Med J. 1984;77:302–303.
12. Deshazo RD, Chadha N, Morgan JE et al. Immunologic assessment of a cluster of asymptomatic HTLV-1 infected individuals in New Orleans. Am J Med. 1989;86:65–70.
13. Martinez F, Watson RR. Effects of cocaine and morphine on IgG production by human peripheral blood lymphocytes in vitro. Life Sci. 1990;47:59–64.
14. Brown SM, Stimmel B, Taub RN, et al. Immunologic dysfunction in heroin addicts. Arch Intern Med. 1974;134:1001–1006.
15. Peterson PK, Sharp BM, Gekker G, et al. Opiates, human peripheral blood mononuclear cells, and HIV. In: Friedman, et al, eds. Drugs of Abuse, Immunity and Immunodeficiency. New York: Plenum Press; 1991:171–178.
16. Klimas NG, Blaney NT, Morgan RO, et al. Immune function and anti-HTLV-I/II status in anti-HIV-1–negative intravenous drug users receiving methadone. Am J Med. 1991;90:163–170.
17. Peterson PK, Sharp BM, Gekker G, et al. Morphine promotes the growth of HIV-1 in human peripheral blood mononuclear cell cultures. AIDS. 1990;4:869–873.
18. Stoll-Keller F, Schmitt C, Thumann C, et al. Effects of morphine on purified human blood monocytes: Modifications of properties involved in antiviral defenses. Int J Immunopharmacol. 1997;19:95–100.
19. Nickerson DS, Williams RC, Boxmeyer M, et al. Increased opsonic capacity of serum in chronic heroin addiction. South Med J. 1974;67:193–197.
20. Tabara E, Borelli G, Croce C, et al. Effect of morphine on resistance to infection. J Infect Dis. 1983;148:656–666.

21. Tabara E, Santiagneli C, Belogi L, et al. Methadone vs. morphine: Comparison of their effect on phagocytic functions. Int J Immunopharmacol. 1987;9:79–88.
22. Peterson PK, Gekker G, Brumm HC, et al. Suppression of human peripheral blood mononuclear cell function by methadone or morphine. J Infect Dis. 1989;159:480–487.
23. Organ CH. Surgical procedures upon the drug addict. Surg Gynecol Obstet. 1972;134:947–952.
24. Orangio GR, Pitlick SD, Della Latta P, et al. Soft tissue infection in parenteral drug abusers. Ann Surg. 1984;199:97–100.
25. Vlahov D, Sullivan M, Astembocski J, et al. Bacterial infections and skin cleaning prior to injection among intravenous drug abusers. Public Health Rep. 1992;5:595–598.
26. Levine DP, Crane LR, Zervos MJ. Bacteremia in narcotic addicts at the Detroit Medical Center: II. Infectious endocarditis: A prospective comparative study. Rev Infect Dis. 1986;8:374–395.
27. Stone MH, Stone PH, MacGregor WAR. Anatomical distributions of soft-tissue sepsis sites. Br J Addict. 1990;85:1495–1496.
28. Yeager RA, Hobson RW, Padberg FT, et al. Vascular complications related to drug abuse. J Trauma. 1987;27:305–308.
29. Wright CB, Lamoy RE, Hobson RW. Hemodynamic effects of intra-arterial injection of drugs of abuse. Surgery. 1976;79:425–431.
30. Creglar LL, Mark H. Medical complications of cocaine abuse. N Engl J Med. 1986;315:1495–1500.
31. Zamora-Quezada JC, Dinerman H, Stadecker MJ, et al. Muscle and skin infarction after free-basing cocaine (crack). Ann Intern Med. 1988;108:564–566.
32. Spijkerman IJ, van Ameijden EJ, Mientjes GH, et al. Human immunodeficiency virus infection and other risk factors for skin abscesses and endocarditis among injection drug users [see comments]. J Clin Epidemiol. 1996;49:1149–1154.
33. Rho YM. Infections as fatal complications of narcotism. N Y State J Med. 1972;72:823–830.
34. Hoeger PH, Haupt G, Hoelzle E. Acute multifocal skin necrosis: Synergism between invasive streptococcal infection and cocaine-induced tissue ischaemia? Acta Derm Venereol. 1996;76:239–241.
35. Hahn HH, Schwerd AI, Beaty HN. Complications of injecting dissolved methylphenidate tablets. Arch Intern Med. 1969;123:656–659.
36. Palestene RF, Millins JD, Spigel GT, et al. Skin manifestations of pentazocine abuse. J Am Acad Dermatol. 1980;2:47–55.
37. Kirchenbaum SE, Midenberg ML. Pedal and lower extremity complications of substance abuse. J Am Podiatr Assoc. 1982;72:380–387.
38. Whittiker DM. A fatal case of toxic shock associated with group A streptococcal cellulitis. J Am Board Fam Pract. 1992;5:523–526.
39. Wallace JR, Lucas CE, Ledgerwood A. Social, economic, and surgical anatomy of a drug-related abscess. Am Surg. 1986;52:398–401.
40. Tom MB, Rice DH. Presentation and management of neck abscess: A retrospective analysis. Laryngoscope. 1988;98:877–880.
41. Hillstrom RP, Cohn AM, McCarroll KA. Vocal cord paralysis resulting from neck injections in the intravenous drug use population. Laryngoscope. 1990;100:503–506.
42. Lee C, Tami TA, Echavez M, et al. Deep neck infections in patients at risk for acquired immunodeficiency syndrome. Laryngoscope. 1990;100:915–919.
43. Hasan SB, Albu E, Gerst PH. Infectious complications in IV drug abusers. Infect Surg. 1988;7:218–232.
44. Hemingway DM, Balfour AE, McCartney AC, et al. Streptococcus milleri complex groin abscess in intravenous drug abusers. Scott Med J. 1992;37:116–117.
45. Armstrong O, Fisher M. The treatment of *Eikenella corrodens* soft tissue infection in an injection drug user. W V Med J. 1996;92:138–139.
46. Lewis RJ, Richmons AS, McGrory JP. *Diplococcus pneumoniae* cellulitis in drug addicts. JAMA. 1975;232:54–55.
47. Summanen PH, Talan DA, Strong C, et al. Bacteriology of skin and soft-tissue infections: Comparison of infections in intravenous drug users and individuals with no history of intravenous drug use. Clin Infect Dis. 1995;20(Suppl 2):S279–S282.
48. Bergstein JM, Baker EJ, Aprahamian C, et al. Soft tissue abscesses associated with parenteral drug abuse: Presentation, microbiology, and treatment. Am Surg. 1995;61:1105–1108.
49. Myers EM, Kirkland LK, Mickey R. The head and neck sequelae of cervical intravenous drug abuse. Laryngoscope. 1988;98:213–218.
50. Yiengpruksawan A, Ganepola AP, Freeman HP. Acute soft tissue infection in intravenous drug abusers: Its differential diagnosis by ultrasonography. J Natl Med Assoc. 1986;78:1193–1196.
51. Simmen HP, Giovanoli P, Battaglia H, et al. Soft tissue infections of the upper extremities with special consideration of abscesses in parenteral drug abusers: A prospective study. J Hand Surg [Br]. 1995;20:797–800.
52. Gonzalez MH, Kay T, Weinzweig N, et al. Necrotizing fasciitis of the upper extremity. J Hand Surg [Am]. 1996;21:689–692.
53. Wysoki MG, Santora TA, Shah RM, Friedman AC. Necrotizing fasciitis: CT characteristics. Radiology. 1997;203:859–863.
54. Sunarsky LA, Laschinager JC, Coppa GF, et al. Improved results from a standardized approach in treating patients with necrotizing fasciitis. Ann Surg. 1987;206:661–665.
55. Clark DD. Surgical management of infections and other complications resulting from drug abuse. Arch Surg. 1970;101:619–623.
56. Hsueh PR, Hsiue TR, Hsieh WC. Pyomyositis in intravenous drug abusers: Report of a unique case and review of the literature. Clin Infect Dis. 1996;22:858–860.
57. Prahlow JA, Cappellari JO, Washburn SA. Uterine pyomyoma as a complication of pregnancy in an intravenous drug user. South Med J. 1996;89:892–895.
58. Chandrasekar PH, Narula AP. Bone and joint infections in intravenous drug abusers. Rev Infect Dis. 1986;8:904–910.
59. Meinoz-Fernandez V, Macia MA, Pantoja ML, et al. Osteoarticular infection in intravenous drug abusers: Influence of HIV infection and differences with non-drug abusers. Ann Rheum Dis. 1993;52:570–574.
60. Sapico FL, Montgomerie JZ. Vertebral osteomyelitis in intravenous drug abusers: Report of three cases and review of the literature. Rev Infect Dis. 1980;2:196–206.
61. Classen JA, Dales RL, Davies RS. Primary sternal osteomyelitis. South Med J. 1987;80:1054–1060.
62. Boll KL, Jurik AG. Sternal osteomyelitis in drug addicts. J Bone Joint Surg Br. 1990;72:328–329.
63. Magarian GJ, Reuler JB. Septic arthritis and osteomyelitis of the symphysis pubis (osteitis pubis) from intravenous drug use. West J Med. 1985;142:691–694.
64. Koppel BS, Tuchman AJ, Mangiardi J, et al. Epidural spinal infection in intravenous drug abusers. Arch Neurol. 1988;45:1331–1337.
65. Lafont A, Olive M, Gelman J, et al. *Candida albicans* spondylodiscitis and vertebral osteomyelitis in patients with intravenous heroin drug addiction: Report of three new cases. J Rheumatol. 1994;21:953–956.
66. Forlenza SW, Axelrod JL, Grieco MH. Potts disease in heroin addicts. JAMA. 1979;241:379–380.
67. Dupont B, Drouhet E. Cutaneous ocular and osteo-orticular candidiasis in heroin addicts: New clinical and therapeutic aspects in 38 patients. J Infect Dis. 1985;152:577.
68. Pastan RS, Silverman SL, Goldenberg DL. A musculo-skeletal syndrome in intravenous heroin users: Association with brown heroin. Ann Intern Med. 1977;87:22.
69. Mathew J, Addai T, Anand A, et al. Clinical features, site of involvement, bacteriologic findings, and outcome of infective endocarditis in intravenous drug users. Arch Intern Med. 1995;155:1641–1648.
70. Reyes MP, Palutke WA, Wylin RF, et al. *Pseudomonas* endocarditis in the Detroit Medical Center, 1969–1972. Medicine (Baltimore). 1973;52:173–194.
71. Archer G, Fekety FR, Supena R. *Pseudomonas aeruginosa* endocarditis in drug addicts. Am Heart J. 1974;88:570–578.
72. Shekar R, Rice TW, Zierot CH, et al. Outbreak of endocarditis caused by *Pseudomonas aeruginosa* serotype 011 among pentazocine and tripelennamine abusers in Chicago. J Infect Dis. 1985;151:203–208.
73. Mills J, Drew D. *Serratia marcescens* endocarditis: A regional illness associated with intravenous drug abuse. Ann Intern Med. 1976;84:29–35.
74. Cooper R, Mills J. Serratia endocarditis. A follow-up report. Arch Intern Med. 1980;140:199–202.
75. Rubinstein E, Noriega EB, Simberkoff MS, et al. Fungal endocarditis: Analysis of 24 cases and review of the literature. Medicine (Baltimore). 1975;54:331–334.
76. Baddour LM, Meyer J, Henry B. Polymicrobial infective endocarditis in the 1980's. Rev Infect Dis. 1991;13:963–970.
77. Mah MW, Shafran SD. Polymicrobial endocarditis with eight pathogens in an intravenous drug abuser. Scand J Infect Dis. 1990;22:735–737.
78. Adler AG, Blumberg EA, Schwartz DA, et al. Seven-pathogen tricuspid endocarditis in an intravenous drug abuser: Pitfalls in laboratory diagnosis. Chest. 1991;99:490–491.
79. Szabo S, Lieberman JP, Lue YA. Unusual pathogen in narcotic-associated endocarditis. Rev Infect Dis. 1990;12:412–415.
80. Weller PF, Nicholson A, Braslos N. The spectrum of bacillus bacteremia in heroin addicts. Arch Intern Med. 1979;139:293–294.
81. Neu HC, Garvey GJ, Beach MP. Successful treatment of *Pseudomonas cepacia* endocarditis in a heroin addict with trimethoprim-sulfamethoxazole. J Infect Dis. 1973;128(Suppl):S769–S770.
82. Sussman JI, Baron EJ, Goldberg SM, et al. Clinical manifestations and therapy of *Lactobacillus* endocarditis: Report of a case and review of the literature. Rev Infect Dis. 1986;8:771–776.
83. Dall L, Barnes WB, Gibbs HR, et al. Endocarditis caused by β-lactamase-producing *Haemophilus influenzae*. South Med J. 1987;80:405–406.
84. El-Khatib MR, Wilson FM, Lerner AM. Characteristics of bacterial endocarditis in heroin addicts in Detroit. Am J Med Sci. 1976;271:197–201.
85. Zuber PLF, Gruner E, Altwegg M, et al. Invasive infection with non-toxigenic *Corynebacterium diphtheriae* among drug users. Lancet. 1992;339:1359.
86. Alos JI, Barros C, Gomez-Garces JL. Endocarditis caused by *Arcanobacterium haemolyticum*. Eur J Clin Microbiol Infect Dis. 1995;14:1085–1088.
87. Yu VL, Romans LW, Wing EJ, et al. *Pseudomonas maltophilia* causing heroin-associated infective endocarditis. Arch Intern Med. 1978;138:1667–1671.
88. Horowitz H, Gilroy S, Feinstein S, et al. Endocarditis associated with *Comamonas acidovorans*. J Clin Microbiol. 1990;28:143–145.
89. Pollack S, Mogtader A, Lange M. *Neisseria subflava* endocarditis: Case report and review of the literature. Am J Med. 1984;76:752–758.
90. Bacon AG III, Pal PG, Schaberg DR. *Neisseria mucosa* endocarditis. J Infect Dis. 1990;162:1199–1201.
91. Sobel JD, Carrizosa J, Ziobrowski TF, et al. Case report. Polymicrobial endocarditis involving *Eikenella corrodens*. Am J Med Sci. 1981;282:41–44.
92. Coudron PE, Markowitz SM, Mohanty LB, et al. Isolation of *Stomatococcus mucilaginosus* from drug user with endocarditis. J Clin Microbiol. 1987;25:1359–1363.
93. Plantholt SJ, Troga AF. *Citrobacter freundii* endocarditis in an intravenous drug abuser. South Med J. 1987;80:1439–1441.
94. Conrad SA, West BG. Endocarditis caused by *Staphylococcus xylosus* associated with intravenous drug abuse. J Infect Dis. 1984;5:826–827.
95. Singh VR, Raad I. Fatal *Staphylococcus saprophyticus* native valve endocarditis in an intravenous drug addict. J Infect Dis. 1990;162:783–784.

96. Olle-Goig JE, Mildvan D. Possible pathogenic implications of right-sided polymicrobial endocarditis in a heroin abuser. Eur J Clin Microbiol. 1986;5:449–451.
97. Bell E, McCartney AC. *Gamella morbillorum* endocarditis in an intravenous drug abuser. J Infect Dis. 1992;25:110–112.
98. Landymore RW, Murphy DA, Marrie TJ, et al. *Mycobacterium avium-intracellulare* endocarditis causing rupture: Replacement and repair with aortic homograft. Can J Cardiol. 1992;8:729–732.
99. Tuazon CU, Sheagren JN. Staphylococcal endocarditis in parenteral drug abusers: Source of the organism. Ann Intern Med. 1975;82:788–790.
100. Rajashekaraiah KR, Rice TW, Kallick CA. Recovery of *Pseudomonas aeruginosa* from syringes of drug addicts with endocarditis. J Infect Dis. 1981;144:482.
101. Botsford KB, Weinstein RA, Nathan CR, et al. Selective survival in pentazocine and tripelennamine of *Pseudomonas aeruginosa* serotype O11 from drug addicts. J Infect Dis. 1985;151:209–216.
102. Dressler FA, Roberts WC. Infective endocarditis in opiate addicts: Analysis of 80 cases studied at necropsy. Am J Cardiol. 1989;63:1240–1257.
103. Hussey HH, Keliher TF, Schaefer BF, et al. Septicemia and bacterial endocarditis resulting from heroin addiction. JAMA. 1944;126:535–538.
104. Wilhelm F, Hirsh HL, Hussey HH, et al. The treatment of acute bacterial endocarditis with penicillin. Ann Intern Med. 1947;26:221–230.
105. Graves MK, Soto L. Left-sided endocarditis in parenteral drug abusers: Recent experience at a large community hospital. South Med J. 1992;85:378–380.
106. Faber M, Frimodt-Moller N, Espersen F, et al. *Staphylococcus aureus* endocarditis in Danish intravenous drug users: High proportion of left-sided endocarditis. Scand J Infect Dis. 1995;27:483–487.
107. Chambers HF, Korzeniowski OM, Sande MA, with the National Collaborative Endocarditis Study Group. *Staphylococcus aureus* endocarditis: Clinical manifestations in addicts and nonaddicts. Medicine (Baltimore). 1983;62:170–177.
108. Delaney KA. Endocarditis in the emergency department. Ann Emerg Med. 1991;20:405–414.
109. Young GP, Hedges JR, Dixon L, et al. Inability to validate a predictive score for infective endocarditis in intravenous drug users. J Emerg Med. 1993;11:1–7.
110. Weisse AB, Heller DR, Schimenti RJ, et al. The febrile parenteral drug user: A prospective study in 121 patients. Am J Med. 1993;94:274–280.
111. Tuazon CU, Cardella TA, Sheagren JN. Staphylococcal endocarditis in drug users. Arch Intern Med. 1975;135:1555–1561.
112. Pazin GJ, Saul S, Thompson ME. Blood culture positivity: Suppression by outpatient antibiotic therapy in patients with bacterial endocarditis. Arch Intern Med. 1982;142:263–268.
113. Korzeniowski O, Sande MA, and The National Collaborative Endocarditis Study Group. Combination antimicrobial therapy for *Staphylococcus aureus* endocarditis in patients addicted to parenteral drugs and in nonaddicts. Ann Intern Med. 1982;97:496–503.
114. Levine DP, Fromm BS, Reddy BR. Slow response to vancomycin or vancomycin plus rifampin in methicillin-resistant *Staphylococcus aureus* endocarditis. Ann Intern Med. 1991;115:674–680.
115. Roberts JH, Aponte V, Naidich DP, et al. Myocardial abscess resulting in a pseudoaneurysm: Case report. Cardiovasc Intervent Radiol. 1991;14:307–310.
116. Corzo JE, de Leon FL, Gomez-Mateos J, et al. Pneumothorax secondary to septic pulmonary emboli in tricuspid endocarditis. Thorax. 1992;47:1080–1081.
117. Markowitz N, Quinn EL, Saravolitz LD. Trimethoprim-sulfamethoxazole compared with vancomycin for the treatment of *Staphylococcus aureus* infection. Ann Intern Med. 1992;117:390–398.
118. Chambers H, Miller RT, Newman MD. Right-sided *Staphylococcus aureus* endocarditis in intravenous drug abusers: Two-week combination therapy. Ann Intern Med. 1988;109:619–624.
119. Ribera E, Gomez-Jimenez J, Cortes E, et al. Effectiveness of cloxacillin with and without gentamicin in short-term therapy for right-sided *Staphylococcus aureus* endocarditis: A randomized, controlled trial. Ann Intern Med. 1996;125:969–974.
120. Heldman AW, Hartert TV, Ray SC, et al. Oral antibiotic treatment of right-sided staphylococcal endocarditis in injection drug users: Prospective randomized comparison with parenteral therapy. Am J Med. 1996;101:68–76.
121. Reyes MP, Brown WJ, Lerner AM. Treatment of patients with pseudomonas endocarditis with high dose aminoglycoside and carbenicillin therapy. Medicine (Baltimore). 1978;57:57–67.
122. Reyes MP, El-Khatib MR, Brown WJ, et al. Synergy between carbenicillin and an aminoglycoside (gentamicin or tobramycin) against *Pseudomonas aeruginosa* isolated from patients with endocarditis and sensitivity of isolates to normal human serum. J Infect Dis. 1979;140:192–202.
123. Wieland M, Lederman MM, Kline-King C, et al. Left-sided endocarditis due to *Pseudomonas aeruginosa*: A report of 10 cases and review of the literature. Medicine (Baltimore). 1986;65:180–189.
124. Daikos GL, Kathpalia SB, Lolans VT. Long-term oral ciprofloxacin: Experience in the treatment of incurable infective endocarditis. Am J Med. 1988;84:786–790.
125. Libertin CR, McKinley KM. Gentamicin-resistant enterococcal endocarditis: The need for routine screening for high-level resistance to aminoglycosides. South Med J. 1990;83:458–460.
126. Rybak MJ, Lerner SA, Levine DP, et al. Teicoplanin pharmacokinetics in intravenous drug abusers being treated for bacterial endocarditis. Antimicrob Agents Chemother. 1991;35:696–700.
127. Hecht SR, Berger M. Right-sided endocarditis in intravenous drug users. Ann Intern Med. 1992;117:560–566.
128. Manoff SB, Vlahov D, Herskowitz A, et al. Human immunodeficiency virus infection and infective endocarditis among injecting drug users [see comments]. Epidemiology. 1996;7:566–570.
129. Pulvirenti JJ, Kerns E, Benson C, et al. Infective endocarditis in injection drug users: Importance of human immunodeficiency virus serostatus and degree of immunosuppression. Clin Infect Dis. 1996;22:40–45.
130. Frater RWM. Surgical management of endocarditis in drug addicts and long-term results. J Card Surg. 1990;5:63–67.
131. Mathew J, Abreo G, Namburi K, et al. Results of surgical treatment for infective endocarditis in intravenous drug users. Chest. 1995;108:73–77.
132. Lemma M, Vanelli P, Beretta L, et al. Cardiac surgery in HIV-positive intravenous drug addicts: Influence of cardiopulmonary bypass on the progression to AIDS. Thorac Cardiovasc Surg. 1992;40:279–282.
133. Monsuez JJ, Vittecoq D, Acar C, et al. Recurrent infective endocarditis one year after mitral repair in a woman addicted to drugs. J Thorac Cardiovasc Surg. 1997;114:864–866.
134. Yeager RA, Hobson RW, Padberg FT, et al. Vascular complications related to drug abuse. J Trauma. 1987;27:305–308.
135. Benitez RR, Newell MA. Vascular trauma in drug abuse: Patterns in injury. Ann Vasc Surg. 1986;1:175–180.
136. Tickson W, Anderson BB. Mycotic aneurysm in intravenous drug addicts: Diagnosis and management. J Natl Med Assoc. 1985;77:99–102.
137. Berguer R, Benitez P. Surgical emergencies from intravascular injection of drugs. In: Bergan J, Yao JST, eds. Vascular Surgical Emergencies. New York: Grune & Stratton; 1987:309–316.
138. Reddy DJ, Smith RF, Elliott JP Jr, et al. Infected femoral artery false aneurysms in drug addicts: Evolution of selective vascular reconstruction. J Vasc Surg. 1986;3:718–725.
139. Kaufman SL, White UR, Harrington DP, et al. Protean manifestations of mycotic aneurysms. AJR Am J Roentgenol. 1978;131:1019–1025.
140. McIlroy MA, Reddy D, Markowitz N, et al. Infected false aneurysms of the femoral artery in intravenous drug abusers. Rev Infect Dis. 1989;11:578–585.
141. Shetty PC, Kasicky GA, Sharma RP, et al. Mycotic aneurysms in IVDA: The utility of intravenous digital substraction angiography. Radiology. 1985;155:319–321.
142. Johnson JR, Ledgerwood AM, Lucas CE. Mycotic aneurysm: New concepts in therapy. Arch Surg. 1983;118:577–587.
143. Cherubin CE. Infectious disease problems of narcotic addicts. Arch Intern Med. 1971;128:309.
144. Louria DB, Hensle T, Rose J. The major medical complications of heroin addiction. Ann Intern Med. 1967;67:10.
145. Pare JP, Fraser RG, Hagg JC, et al. Pulmonary "mainline" granulomatosis: Talcosis of intravenous methadone abuse. Medicine (Baltimore). 1979;58:229–239.
146. Miller A, Taub H, Spinak A, et al. Lung function in former intravenous drug abusers: The effects of ubiquitous cigarette smoking. Am J Med. 1991;90:678–684.
147. O'Donnell AE, Pappas LS. Pulmonary complications of intravenous drug abuse. Chest. 1988;92:251–253.
148. Schlamm HT, Yancovitz SR. Haemophilus influenza pneumonia in young adults with AIDS: ARC or risk of AIDS. Am J Med. 1989;86:11–14.
149. Casadevall A, Dobrozycki J, Small C, et al. *Haemophilus influenzae* type B bacteremia in adults with AIDS. Am J Med. 1992;92:587–590.
150. Witt DJ, Craven DE, McCabe WR. Bacterial infections in adult patients with the acquired immune deficiency syndrome (AIDS) and AIDS-related complex. Am J Med. 1987;82:900–906.
151. Polsky B, Gold JW, Whimsbey E, et al. Bacterial pneumonia in patients with acquired immunodeficiency syndrome. Ann Intern Med. 1986;104:38–41.
152. Pitchenik AE, Fertel D, Bloch AB. Mycobacterial disease: Epidemiology, diagnosis, treatment, and prevention. Clin Chest Med. 1988;9:425–441.
153. Frieden TR, Sterling T, Pablos-Mendez A, et al. The emergence of drug-resistant tuberculosis in New York City. N Engl J Med. 1993;328:521–526.
154. Selwyn PA, Hortel D, Leivis VA, et al. A prospective study of the risk of tuberculosis among intravenous drug users with human immunodeficiency virus infection. N Engl J Med. 1989;320:545–550.
155. American Thoracic Society. Treatment of tuberculosis and tuberculosis infection in adults and children. Am Rev Respir Dis. 1986;134:355–363.
156. USPHS/IDSA Prevention of Opportunistic Infection Working Group. 1997 USPHS/IDSA Guidelines for the Prevention of Opportunistic Infection in Persons Infected with Human Immunodeficiency Virus. Ann Intern Med. 1997;127:922–946.
157. Novick DM, Gelb AM, Stenger RJ, et al. Hepatitis B serologic studies in narcotic users with chronic liver disease. Am J Gastroenterol. 1981;75:111–115.
158. Villa E, Barchi T, Grisendi A, et al. Susceptibility of chronic symptomless HB_SAg carriers to ethanol-induced damage. Lancet. 1982;2:1243–1244.
159. Gorodetzky CW, Sapira JD, Jasinski P, et al. Liver disease in narcotic addicts: The role of the drug. Clin Pharmacol Ther. 1968;9:720–724.
160. Kreek MJ, Dodes L, Kane S, et al. Long-term methadone maintenance therapy: Effects on liver function. Ann Intern Med. 1972;77:598–602.
161. Perino LE, Warren GH, Levine JS. Cocaine-induced hepatotoxicity in humans. Gastroenterology. 1987;93:176–180.
162. Francis DP, Hadler SC, Prendergast TJ, et al. Occurrence of hepatitis A, B, and non-A/non-B in the United States. Am J Med. 1984;76:69–74.
163. DeCock KM, Govindarajin S, Chin KP, et al. Delta hepatitis in the Los Angeles area: A report of 126 cases. Ann Intern Med. 1986;105:108–114.
164. Ponzetto A, Seeff LB, Buskell-Bales Z, et al. Hepatitis B markers in United States drug addicts with special emphasis on the delta hepatitis virus. Hepatology. 1984;4:1111–1115.
165. Govindarajan SM, Chin KP, Redeker AG, et al. Fulminant B viral hepatitis: Role of delta agent. Gastroenterology. 1984;86:1417–1420.
166. Shiels MT, Czaja AJ, Taswell HF, et al. Frequency and significance of delta antibody in acute and chronic hepatitis B. Gastroenterology. 1985;89:1230–1234.
167. Jenkerson SA, Middaugh JP, Pittman SL, et al. Hepatitis A among drug abusers. JAMA. 1988;259:3235–3236.

168. Bortolotti F, Bertaggia A, Cadrobbi P, et al. Epidemiological aspects of acute viral hepatitis in drug abusers. Infection. 1982;10:277–279.
169. Hoffman IF, Stratton JD, Lemon SM, et al. Hepatitis B among parenteral drug abusers–North Carolina. JAMA. 1986;256:1262–1269.
170. Piot P, Goilav C, Kegels E. Hepatitis B: Transmission by sexual contact and needle sharing. Vaccine. 1990;8s:S37–S40.
171. Novick DM. The medically ill substance abuser, In: Lowinson JH, Ruiz P, Millman R, et al, eds. Substance Abuse: A Comprehensive Textbook. Baltimore: Williams & Wilkins; 1992:657–674.
172. Davis GL, Hoofnagle JH, Waggoner JG. Spontaneous reactivation of chronic hepatitis B virus infection. Gastroenterology. 1985;86:230–235.
173. Davis GL, Hoofnagle JH. Reactivation of chronic type B hepatitis presenting as acute viral hepatitis. Ann Intern Med. 1985;102:762–765.
174. Drogsgaard K, Lindhardt BO, Nielsen JO, et al. The influence of HTLV-III infection on the natural history of hepatitis B virus infection in male homosexual HbsAg carriers. Hepatology. 1987;7:37–41.
175. Rumi M, Colombo M, Romeo R, et al. Suboptimal response to hepatitis B vaccine in drug users. Arch Intern Med. 1991;151:574–578.
176. Lugoboni F, Migliozzis, Schiesasi F. Immunoresponse to hepatitis B vaccination and adherence campaign among injecting drug users. Vaccine. 1997;15:1014–1016.
177. Lemon SM, Thomas DL. Vaccines to prevent viral hepatitis. N Engl J Med. 1997;336:196–204.
178. Kelly MG, Fielding J, Arthurs Y. Epidemic hepatitis B with delta antigenemia among Dublin drug-abusers. Ir J Med Sci. 1982;151:333–338.
179. Lettau LA, McCarthy JG, Smith MH, et al. Outbreak of severe hepatitis due to delta and hepatitis B viruses in parenteral drug abusers and their contacts. N Engl J Med. 1987;317:1256–1262.
180. Smith HM, Alexander GJM, Webb G, et al. Hepatitis B and delta virus infection among "at risk" populations in south east London. J Epidemiol Community Health. 1992;46:144–147.
181. Bonino F, Smedile A. Delta agent (type D) hepatitis. Semin Liver Dis. 1986;6:28–33.
182. Rosina F, Pinter C, Meschievitz C, et al. A randomized controlled trial of a 1 month course of recombinant interferon-α in chronic delta (type D) hepatitis: A multicenter Italian study. Hepatology. 1991;13:1052–1053.
183. Alter M. Epidemiology of community-acquired hepatitis C. In: Hollinger FB, Lemon SM, Margolis HS, eds. Viral hepatitis and liver disease. Baltimore: Williams & Wilkins; 1991:410–413.
184. Novick DM, Reagan KJ, Croxson TS, et al. Hepatitis C virus serology in parenteral drug users with chronic liver disease. Addiction. 1997;92:167–171.
185. Rall CJ, dirnstag JL. Epidemiology of hepatitis C virus infection. Semin Gastrointest Dis. 1995;6:3–12.
186. Osmond DH, Charlebois E, Sheppard HW, et al. Comparison of risk factors for hepatitis C and hepatitis B virus infection in homosexual men. J Infect Dis. 1993;167:766–771.
187. Shev S, Wejstal R, Wahl M, et al. The lack of transmission of NANB/C hepatitis between acute and chronically infected patients and their heterosexual partners. Scand J Infect Dis. 1991;23:407–411.
188. Linnen J, Wages J, Zhang-keck ZY, et al. Molecular cloning and disease association of hepatitis G virus: A transfusion transmissible agent. Science. 1996;271:505–508.
189. Fong T, Lee S, Kim JP, et al. Prevalence of hepatitis G virus among intravenous drug abusers in Los Angeles. Clin Infect Dis. 1997;25:165–166.
190. Aikawa T, Sugai Y, Okamoto H. Hepatitis G infection in drug abusers with chronic hepatitis C. N Engl J Med. 1996;334:195–196.
191. Diamantis I, Bassetti S, Erb P, et al. High prevalence and co-infection of hepatitis G and C infection in intravenous drug addicts. J Hepatol. 1997;26:794–797.
192. Tanaka E, Alter H, Nakatsuji, et al. Effect of hepatitis G virus infection of chronic hepatitis C. Ann Intern Med. 1996;125:740–743.
193. Akriviadis EA, Redeker AG. Fulminant hepatitis A in intravenous drug users with chronic liver disease. Ann Intern Med. 1989;110:838–839.
194. Nallathambi MN, Ivaturly RR, Lankin DH, et al. Pyogenic splenic abscess in intravenous drug addiction. Am Surg. 1987;53:342–346.
195. Fry DE, Richardson JD, Flint LM. Occult splenic abscess: An unrecognized complication of heroin abuse. Surgery. 1978;84:650–654.
196. Chun CH, Raff MJ, Varghese R, et al. Splenic abscess. Medicine (Baltimore). 1980;59:50–65.
197. Sastre J, Casas E, Sierra J, et al. Splenic abscess due to *Fusobacterium necrophorum*. Rev Infect Dis. 1991;13:1249–1250.
198. Adler CH, Stern MB, Brooks ML. Parkinsonism secondary to bilateral striated fungal abscesses. Mov Disord. 1989;4:333–337.
199. Lerner PI. Neurologic complications of infective endocarditis. Med Clin North Am. 1985;69:385–398.
200. Gilroy J, Andaya L, Thomas VS. Intracranial mycotic aneurysms and subacute bacterial endocarditis in heroin addiction. Neurology. 1973;23:1193–1198.
201. Caplan LR, Chinnamma T, Banks G. Central nervous system complications of addiction to "T's and blues". Neurology. 1982;32:623.
202. Abbott SP, Sigler L, McAleer R, et al. Fatal cerebral mycoses caused by the ascomycete *Chaetomium strumarium*. J Clin Microbiol. 1995;33:2692–2698.
203. Hopkins RJ, Rothman M, Fiore A, Goldblum SE. Cerebral mucormycosis associated with intravenous drug use: Three case reports and review [see comments]. Clin Infect Dis. 1994;19:1133–1137.
204. Blazquez R, Pinedo A, Cosin J, et al. Nonsurgical cure of isolated cerebral mucormycosis in an intravenous drug user. Eur J Clin Microbiol Infect Dis. 1996;15:598–599.
205. Pruitt AA, Rubin RH, Karchmer AW, et al. Neurologic complications of bacterial endocarditis. Medicine (Baltimore). 1978;57:329–343.
206. Farrar DJ, Flanigan TP, Gordon NM, et al. Tuberculous brain abscess in a patient with HIV infection: Case report and review. Am J Med. 1997;102:297–301.
207. Fraimow HS, Wormser GP, Coburn KD, et al. Salmonella meningitis and infection with HIV. AIDS. 1990;4:1271–1273.
208. Koppel BS, Tuchman AJ, Mangiardi JR, et al. Epidural spinal infection in intravenous drug users. Arch Neurol. 1988;45:1331–1337.
209. Prendergast H, Jerrard D, O'Connell J. Atypical presentations of epidural abscess in intravenous drug abusers. Am J Emerg Med. 1997;15:158–160.
210. Koppel BS, Daras M, Duffy KR. Intramedullary spinal cord abscess. Neurosurgery. 1990;26:145–146.
211. Centers for Disease Control and Prevention. Tetanus among injecting-drug users—California, 1997. JAMA. 1998;279:987.
212. Center for Disease Control and Prevention. Wound botulism—California, 1995. JAMA. 1996;275:95–96.
213. Passaro DJ, Werner SB, McGee J, et al. Wound botulism associated with black tar heroin among injecting drug users. JAMA. 1998;279:859–863.
214. Redmond J, Stritch M, Blaney P. Severe tetanus in a narcotic addict. Ir Med J. 1984;77:325–326.
215. Sugar HS, Mandell GH, Shale VJ. Metastatic endophthalmitis associated with injection of addictive drugs. Am J Ophthalmol. 1971;71:1055–1058.
216. Sorrell TC, Dunlop C, Collignon PJ, et al. Exogenous ocular candidiasis associated with intravenous heroin abuse. Br J Ophthalmol. 1984;68:841–845.
217. Kreeger R, Pearson PA, Bullock JD, et al. Endophthalmitis associated with intravenous drug abuse. Ann Emerg Med. 1987;16:585–595.
218. Atlee WE Jr. Talc and cornstarch emboli in eyes of drug abusers. JAMA. 1972;219:49–51.
219. Lederer CU, Sabates FN. Ocular findings in the intravenous drug abuser. Ann Ophthalmol. 1982;14:436–442.
220. Stern GA, Fetkenhour CL, O'Grady RB. Intravitreal amphotericin B treatment of *Candida* endophthalmitis. Arch Ophthalmol. 1977;95:89–93.
221. Mames RN, Soor TC. Ocular manifestations of intravenous drug abuse. In: Levine DP, Sobel JD, eds. Infections in Intravenous Drug Abusers. New York: Oxford University Press; 1991:167–181.
222. Akler ME, Vellend H, McNeely DM, et al. Use of fluconazole in the treatment of *Candida* endophthalmitis. Clin Infect Dis. 1995;20:657–664.
223. Luttrul JK, Wan WL, Kubak BM, et al. Treatment of ocular fungal infections with oral fluconazole. Am J Ophthalmol. 1995;179:477–481.
224. Christmas NJ, Smidely WE. Vitrectomy and systemic fluconazole for treatment of endogenous fungal endophthalmitis. Ophthalmic Surg Lasers. 1996;27:1012–1018.
225. Young EJ, Wallace RJ Jr, Ericsson CD, et al. Panophthalmitis due to *Bacillus cereus*. Arch Intern Med. 1984;140:559–560.
226. Small CB, Klein RS, Friedland GH, et al. Community-acquired opportunistic infections and defective cellular immunity in heterosexual drug abusers and homosexual men. Am J Med. 1983;74:433–441.
227. Centers for Disease Control and Prevention. HIV/AIDS surveillance report: Year-end edition. Atlanta: US Department of Health and Human Services, Public Health Services; 1996:7.
228. Centers for Disease Control and Prevention. Update: AIDS among women—United States, 1994. MMWR Morb Mortal Wkly Rep. 1995;44:81–84.
229. Prevots DR, Ancelle-Park RA, Neal JJ, et al. The epidemiology of heterosexually acquired HIV infection and AIDS in western industrialized countries. AIDS. 1994;8:S109–S117.
230. Nemoto T. Behavior characteristics of seroconverted intravenous drug users. Int J Addict. 1992;27:1413–1421.
231. Van Ameijden ETC, Van den Hoek JAR, Von Hoastrecht HJA, et al. The harm reduction approach and risk factors for human immunodeficiency virus (HIV) seroconversion in injecting drug users, Amsterdam. Am J Epidemiol. 1992;136:236–243.
232. Vlahov D, Munoz A, Anthony JC, et al. Association of drug injection patterns with antibody to human immunodeficiency virus type I among intravenous drug users in Baltimore, Maryland. Am J Epidemiol. 1990;132:847–856.
233. McCoy CB, Metch LR, Page JB, et al. Injection drug users' practices and attitudes toward intervention and potential for reducing the transmission of HIV. Med Anthropol. 1997;18:35–60.
234. Kaplan EH, Heimer R. HIV incidence among New Haven needle exchange participants: Updated estimates from syringe tracking and testing data. J Acquir Immune Defic Syndr. 1995;10:175–176.
235. Centers for Disease Control and Prevention. Syringe exchange programs: United States, 1994–1995. JAMA. 1996;274:1660–1662.
236. McCoy CB, Shapshak P, Metsch LR, et al. HIV-1 prevention: Interdisciplinary studies on the efficacy of bleach and development of prevention protocols. Arch Immunol Ther Exp (Warsz). 1995;43:1–9.
237. O'Connor PG, Selwyn PA, Schottenfeld RS. Medical care for injection-drug users with human immunodeficiency virus infection. N Engl J Med. 1994;331:450–459.
238. Margolick JB, Munoz A, Vlahov D, et al. Analysis of changes in CD_4+ lymphocytes in HIV-positive homosexual men and injecting drug users studied in a single laboratory. Arch Intern Med. 1994;154:869–875.
239. Galai N, Vlahov D, Margolick JB, et al. Changes in markers of disease progression in HIV-I seroconverters: A comparison between cohorts of injecting drug users and homosexual men. J Acquir Immune Defic Syndr. 1995;8:66–74.
240. Alcabes P, Schoenbaum EE, Klein RS. Correlates of the rate of decline of CD_4+ lymphocytes among injecting drug users infected with the human immunodeficiency virus. Am J Epidemiol. 1993;137:989–1000.

241. Margolick JB, Munoz A, Vlahov D, et al. Changes in T-lymphocyte subsets in intravenous drug users with HIV-1 infection. JAMA. 1992;267:1631–1636.
242. Montella F, DiSora F, Perucci C, et al. T-lymphocytes subsets in intravenous drug users with HIV-1 infection. JAMA. 1992;268:2516–2517.
243. Crum RM, Galai N, Cohn S, et al. Alcohol use and T-lymphocyte subsets among injecting drug users with HIV-1 infection: A prospective analysis. Alcohol Clin Exp Res. 1996;20:367–371.
244. Oelwyn PA, Alcabes P, Hartel D, et al. Clinical manifestations and predictors of disease progression in drug users with human immunodeficiency virus infection. N Engl J Med. 1992;327:1697–1703.
245. Munoz A, Vlahov D, Solomon L, et al. Prognostic indicators for development of AIDS among intravenous drug users. J Acquir Immune Defic Syndr. 1992;5:694–708.
246. Selwyn PA, Alcabes P, Hartel D, et al. Clinical manifestations and predictors of disease progression in drug users with human immunodeficiency virus infection. N Engl J Med. 1992;327:1697–1703.
247. Khabbaz RT, Onorato IM, Cannon RO, et al. Seroprevalence of HTLV-I and HTLV-II among intravenous drug users and persons in clinics for sexually transmitted diseases. N Engl J Med. 1992;326:375–380.
248. Brettle RP, Chiswick A, Bell J, et al. Pre-AIDS deaths in HIV infection related to intravenous drug use. QJM. 1997;90:617–629.
249. Farizo KM, Buehler JW, Chamberland ME, et al. Spectrum of disease in persons with human immunodeficiency virus infection in the United States. JAMA. 1992;267:1798–1805.
250. Friedland GH, Saltzman B, Vilena J, et al. Survival differences in patients with AIDS. J Acquir Immun Defic Syndr. 1991;4:144–153.
251. Goldsmith MT. Sex tied to drugs = STD spread. JAMA. 1988;260:2009.
252. Ross MW, Gold J, Wodak A, et al. Sexually transmissible disease in injecting drug users. Genitourin Med. 1991;67:32–36.
253. Nelson KE, Vlahov D, Cohn S, et al. Sexually transmitted diseases in a population of intravenous drug users: Association with seropositivity to human immunodeficiency virus (HIV). J Infect Dis. 1991;164:457–463.
254. Kleyn J, Schwebke J, Holmes KK. The validity of injecting drug users' self-reports about sexually transmitted diseases: A comparison of survey and serologic data. Addiction. 1993;88:673–680.
255. Seidman SN, Sterk-Elifson C, Aral SO. High-risk sexual behavior among drug-using men. Sex Transm Dis. 1994;21:173–180.
256. Zenilman JM, Hook EW III, Shepherd M, et al. Alcohol and other substance use in STD clinic patients: Relationships with STDs and prevalent HIV infection. Sex Transm Dis. 1994;21:220–225.
257. Nyamathi AM, Lewis C, Leake B, et al. Barriers to condom use and needle cleaning among impoverished minority female injection drug users and partners of injection drug users. Public Health Rep. 1995;110:116–172.
258. Seigal HA, Falck RS, Wang J, et al. History of sexually transmitted diseases infection, drug-sex behaviors, and the use of condoms among mid-western users of injection drugs and crack cocaine. Sex Transm Dis. 1996;23:277–282.
259. Gourevitch MN, Selwyn PA, Davenny K, et al. Effects of HIV infection on the serologic manifestation and response to treatment of syphilis in intravenous drug users. Ann Intern Med. 1993;118:350–355.

Chapter 302

Risk Factors and Approaches to Infections in Transplant Recipients

J. STEPHEN DUMMER
MONTO HO

The first patient to achieve long-term survival with a transplanted organ received a kidney in 1954 from his human leukocyte antigen (HLA)–identical twin without the use of immunosuppression.[1] Later, attempts were made to transplant organs from genetically different individuals with the use of total lymphoid irradiation to suppress the recipient's immune response to the allograft, but these efforts met with only occasional success. The introduction of drug regimens using azathioprine and corticosteroids in the early 1960s provided improved immunosuppression and catapulted human transplantation beyond the experimental stage, with the result that both living-related and cadaveric renal transplantation became part of regular clinical practice. Heart and liver transplantation were also attempted but proved more difficult to sustain, and clinical efforts remained limited to a few small, dedicated programs for more than a decade. The major watershed in the development of transplantation was the introduction of cyclosporine in the early 1980s.[2] This development ushered in a marked expansion of heart, liver, and lung transplantation and further growth of renal transplantation. Currently, about 16,000 solid organ transplantations are performed in the United States yearly, and most patients retain their grafts and survive many years after transplantation.[3] It is now likely that a physician will be called on to evaluate and manage patients with various types of transplants as part of general practice.

Except for medical and surgical problems related to the function and rejection of the transplanted organ, infections are the most important problem after transplantation. The clinical manifestations of infection are variable and depend on the infecting pathogen, the prior immune status of the host, the time after transplantation, the level of pharmacologic immunosuppression, and many other factors. With this complexity in mind, it is useful to address some general principles that may aid in the diagnosis, management, and understanding of infections after transplantation.

Infections require a susceptible host and an available pathogen. The susceptibility of transplant recipients is not the same for all pathogens. For instance, most enteroviruses do not appear to infect the transplant recipient with greater frequency or severity than a normal host. On the other hand, a transplant recipient may be quite susceptible to a given pathogen but have a low risk of infection because of lack of exposure. For this reason, tuberculosis is a relatively minor problem at most transplantation centers, yet, as illustrated by a recent outbreak and the experience at transplantation centers in developing countries, the vulnerability to infection in this population is high.[4, 5] Likewise, kidney recipients with no past exposure to cytomegalovirus (CMV) who receive kidneys from CMV-seronegative donors and have no blood transfusions are at very low risk for CMV infection.[6] In practice, the clinician can and should assess each patient's susceptibility to important pathogens.

Most important infections occur during the first 4 to 6 months after transplantation.[7–10] This is the period when all the risk factors for infection (Table 302–1) are fully operative. Patients may still be affected by direct or indirect effects of their underlying disease. They will have undergone major surgery and possibly intensive care with the attendant risks of wound and other nosocomial infections. Large amounts of immunosuppressive drugs will have been given, and the allograft may be malfunctioning as a result of rejection or other factors. This early period also covers the time of highest risk for infection by herpesviruses (CMV, herpes simplex virus [HSV], Epstein-Barr virus [EBV]), *Pneumocystis*, and *Toxoplasma*. After the first few months, infections related to surgery and the reactivation of latent pathogens become less important. Meanwhile, allograft reactions become less frequent and immunosuppression can be kept at lower maintenance levels. Although the risk of serious infection never disappears, infectious mortality declines to acceptable levels 6 months or more after surgery.[2, 8]

HOST FACTORS OF INFECTION

Underlying chronic diseases of the transplant recipient may contribute to infections after transplantation (see Table 302–1). The basic disease or organ dysfunction that led to transplantation may be corrected by the procedure, but occasionally it is not. In patients with fulminant hepatitis caused by hepatitis B virus (HBV), the virus is usually cleared by the immune system after the procedure, but chronic infection caused by HBV or hepatitis C virus (HCV) persists in most patients.[11, 12] Diabetes mellitus and its end-organ effects of vasculopathy and neuropathy continue to be a major problem in the diabetic renal transplant recipient and predispose such patients to the development of soft tissue and urinary tract infections.[13] Single lung transplant recipients are at significant risk for infection in the re-

TABLE 302–1 Factors That Contribute to Infection after Transplantation

Category	Examples and Comments
Pretransplant host factors	
Underlying medical condition	Conditions that persist or recur (hepatitis B, hepatitis C, diabetes mellitus)
	Conditions that exacerbate (chronic bronchitis, gallbladder disease)
Lack of specific immunity	Leads to important primary infections (i.e., CMV, EBV, HSV, toxoplasmosis)
Prior colonization	Nosocomial gram-negative agents, *Candida,* staphylococci, VRE
Prior latent infection	Activation produces tuberculosis, ?pneumocystis, CMV, VZV, HSV
Prior medications	Immunosuppressive drugs and antibiotics affect post-transplantation susceptibility to colonization
Transplantation factors	
Type of organ or tissue transplanted	Site of transplantation and allograft are most common sites of infection
	Allograft may carry infection or be affected by ischemia, injury, poor function, or allograft reaction
Trauma of surgery	Surgical stress, duration of surgery
Immunosuppression	
Immunosuppressive agents	Corticosteroids, azathioprine, and other cytotoxic agents; cyclosporine; tacrolimus, mycophenylate, polyclonal and monoclonal antilymphocyte serums
Other measures	Pretransplantation blood, total body irradiation
Infective immunosuppression	Primary CMV infection and chronic HCV infection contribute to more bacterial and fungal infection
Allograft reactions	
Graft-versus-host reaction	Cofactor in CMV pneumonitis in bone marrow recipients
Host-versus-graft reaction	? Cofactor in allograft infections

Abbreviations: CMV, Cytomegalovirus; EBV, Epstein-Barr virus; HCV, hepatitis C virus; HSV, herpes simplex virus; VRE, vancomycin-resistant enterococcus; VZV, varicella-zoster virus.

maining abnormal native lung.[14] Underlying medical conditions such as gallbladder disease, diverticulosis, or chronic bronchitis may be clinically quiescent before transplantation and first become manifest in the post-transplantation period, when their detection and management is complicated by chronic immunosuppressive therapy.

Along with the patient's underlying condition, medications, particularly antibiotics and immunosuppressive agents, have an effect on the type and severity of infections in the early post-transplantation period. For example, liver transplant recipients who receive antibiotics or corticosteroids before transplantation are more likely to develop systemic *Candida* infections after transplantation.[15]

EFFECT OF TYPE OF TRANSPLANTATION

The type of transplantation is an important determinant of the type of infection occurring after transplantation. Sites of major surgery are particularly vulnerable to bacterial and fungal infection either during or shortly after surgery. The transplanted organ must establish a vascular supply and regain its functional integrity. Ischemia and improper function are potent factors contributing to infection. Allograft reactions of the host-versus-graft or graft-versus-host type may occur (see Table 302–1). These reactions are known to reduce resistance to infection by viruses and to contribute to the graft's being a *locus minoris resistentiae*.[16] The most common site of infection in renal transplant recipients is the urinary tract. The abdomen, including the liver and biliary tree, is the most commonly infected site in liver recipients, as is the lung and chest cavity in heart and lung recipients.[17, 18] Bone marrow transplant recipients do not have surgical sites, but they are unique because leukopenia and depressed humoral immunity are superimposed on the depressed T-cell immunity common to other types of transplantation. This leads to a heightened vulnerability to many varieties of infection.

The contribution of surgical factors to infection is best illustrated by hepatic transplantation.[19–21] With this type of surgery, the Achilles' heel is viable function of the biliary and vascular anastomoses. For example, most liver abscesses in liver transplant recipients occur as a result of liver ischemia from hepatic artery thrombosis or obstruction to bile flow from biliary strictures.[20] The type of biliary drainage constructed at surgery is an important determinant of abdominal infection. Cholodochojejunostomy is associated with a higher rate of biliary leaks and infectious risk than is choledochocholedochostomy.[19–21] There is also a striking correlation between total hours spent in the operating room and mean episodes of infection per patient (Fig. 302–1).[20] Patients who spent more than 25 hours in the operating room had three episodes, whereas those who spent 5 to 10 hours in the operating room had less than one episode of infection on average. The duration of operation undoubtedly reflects the combined effects of surgical trauma and stress resulting from blood and body fluid loss, reduced tissue perfusion during bypass procedures, direct tissue damage from the operation, and the various metabolic derangements that may occur during a prolonged operation. In kidney transplantation, complications of surgery may lead to anastomotic or perinephric infection. Lymphoceles may result from interruption of lymphatic drainage, and they may become superinfected. In transplantation of the lung, peritracheal or peribronchial infection may follow breakdown of end-to-end anastomoses. Anastomotic infections may then predispose to bacterial infections of the lung, either directly or secondary to obstruction after placement of a bronchial stent.[14]

The susceptibility of the grafted organ to CMV and other viral infections is a striking example of the vulnerability of allografts to infection. Lung infection by CMV is more frequent and more severe in lung and heart-lung transplant recipients.[22] Table 302–2 summarizes data on four different types of transplant recipients in Pittsburgh, all of whom were prescribed similar immunosuppressive regimens and underwent transplantation before the manifestations of CMV disease could be modified by antiviral prophylaxis. Although the rates of CMV infection were high in all four groups, the numbers of symptomatic patients were quite different. The frequency of CMV pneumonia was 4 to 16 times higher in heart-lung recipients than in

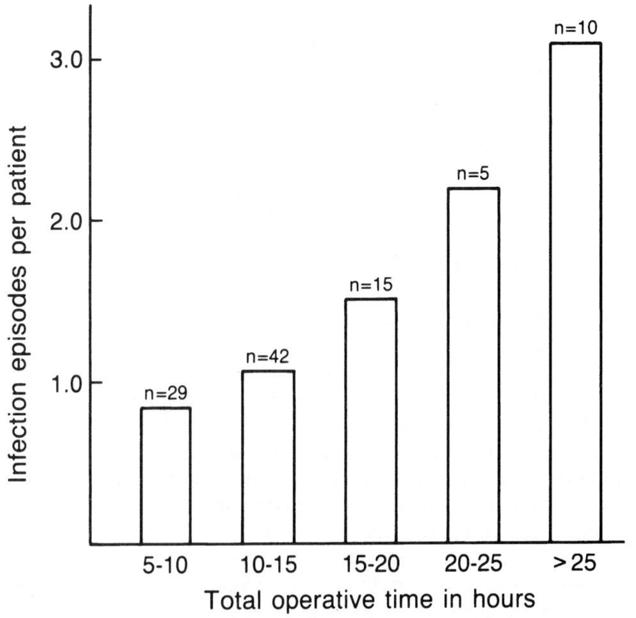

FIGURE 302–1. Frequency of severe infections in relation to time spent in liver transplant surgery. (From Kusne S, Dummer JS, Singh N, et al. Infections after liver transplantation: An analysis of 101 consecutive cases. Medicine [Baltimore]. 1988;67:132.)

TABLE 302–2 Infection and Morbidity of Cytomegalovirus (CMV) Infection in Transplant Groups in Pittsburgh after 1981

Group	N	Infected Patients (% of total)	Symptomatic Patients		Patients with CMV Pneumonia	
			% of Infected	*% of Total*	*% of Infected*	*% of Total*
Kidney	131	79/131 (60)	13	8	4	2
Liver	93	55/93 (59)	49	29	5	3
Heart	48	44/48 (92)	27	25	9	8
Heart-lung	31	22/31 (71)	55	39	45	32

Data from Dummer JS, Hardy A, Poorsattar A, Ho M. Early infections in kidney, heart, and liver transplant recipients on cyclosporine. Transplantation. 1983;36:259; and Ho M, Wajszczuk CP, Hardy A, et al. Infections in kidney, heart, and liver transplant recipients on cyclosporine. Transplant Proc. 1983;15:2768.

patients in the other groups. The reason the transplanted lung is so vulnerable to CMV infection has not been elucidated but may relate to the presence of ongoing allograft reactions in the lung, in analogy to the increased risk of CMV pneumonia after bone marrow transplantation in patients with graft-versus-host disease.[16] In any event, the vulnerability of the transplanted lung to viral infection may extend beyond CMV. Lung recipients also appear to be susceptible to frequent and severe infections with paramyxoviruses, such as respiratory syncytial virus (RSV).[23]

CMV hepatitis has been identified as a major problem in patients who undergo liver transplantation. In other patients with CMV infection, hepatitis is a common manifestation of infection, but it is almost always mild, causing an elevation of transaminases without jaundice. Before the availability of effective antiviral therapy, CMV hepatitis in liver transplant recipients was occasionally severe enough to necessitate retransplantation.[24] Other viruses to which the transplanted liver appears more susceptible are HBV, HSV, and possibly adenovirus.[25–27]

IMMUNOSUPPRESSION

Of all the factors contributing to the occurrence of infections in transplant recipients, the most obvious and probably the most important is iatrogenic immunosuppression.[28] The impact of immunosuppressive agents has become even more apparent as surgical techniques have improved and infections caused by surgical trauma, whether local or general in nature, have declined. Despite significant broadening of available immunosuppressive agents after the introduction of cyclosporine in 1983, tacrolimus in 1994, and mycophenylate mofetil (MMF) in 1995, the ideal suppressive regimen that prevents rejection but preserves antimicrobial immunity remains elusive.

The major immunosuppressive agents may be divided into several categories. Corticosteroids broadly inhibit the immune response, including innate inflammatory responses, cellular immunity, and to a lesser extent antibody formation.[29] Although they are inadequate to sustain graft survival, they have remained a part of most immunosuppressive regimens. High doses of prednisone and hyperglycemia have been found to be significant factors in the frequency of infections and deaths from infection in kidney transplant recipients.[30] Doses of prednisone greater than 60 mg/day have been associated with the occurrence of clinical fungal infection in kidney recipients.[31, 32] The general reduction of the dosage of prednisone in immunosuppressive regimens after 1966 was associated with reduction of significant infections in renal transplant recipients.[33] In a effort to free patients from the undesirable side effects of corticosteroid therapy, some transplant physicians have experimented with steroid-free regimens, but these are not widely used.[34]

A major advance in immunosuppression was the introduction of cytotoxic drugs, such as methotrexate, cyclophosphamide, actinomycin D, and azathioprine. All of these drugs suppress the bone marrow and produce leukopenia when administered in large doses. Azathioprine became the mainstay and was often effective in doses of 2 mg/kg/day or less without producing leukopenia. Higher doses were associated with leukopenia ($<3000/mm^3$) and produced more bacterial and fungal infections.[30] Azathioprine also may cause pancreatitis, a reversible hepatitis, rash, and gastrointestinal disturbances. Its metabolism is blocked by allopurinol. Major bone marrow depression can result when allopurinol is prescribed for the management of gout.

Cyclosporine was approved in 1983 and opened a new era in transplant immunosuppression.[2, 35] This cyclic peptide, which consists of 11 amino acids, does not inhibit cell proliferation in the manner of the cytotoxic drugs. Rather, it has a focused effect on T-helper cell function in that it inhibits cytokines normally produced when these T cells are exposed to antigens. The primary cytokine inhibited is interleukin-2.[36] Suppressor cells and B cells are relatively spared. Concentrations of the drug as low as 100 ng/ml effectively inhibit mixed lymphocyte reactions. Patients treated with cyclosporine alone for various autoimmune diseases show very low rates of clinical infection, suggesting the importance of corticosteroids and other cofactors for infection (see Table 302–1).[37] Most studies, whether randomized or historically controlled, demonstrate lower rates of infection in cyclosporine-treated heart and kidney recipients. For example, studies in renal recipients comparing azathioprine and cyclosporine showed reduction of bacterial infections in Pittsburgh and reduction of CMV infection in Minnesota and in Canada.[17, 38, 39] However, no differences were found in bacterial and viral infections in a European renal transplantation trial.[40]

Hofflin and colleagues compared the infectious morbidity and mortality of heart transplant recipients receiving immunosuppressive regimens based on azathioprine with those based on cyclosporine. Patients receiving cyclosporine had lower rates of infection (71% versus 89%) and a lower infectious mortality rate (11% versus 39%).[41] Although there have been no direct comparisons of rates of infection in liver recipients receiving azathioprine- versus cyclosporine-based regimens, most deaths in liver recipients are associated with infection.[20] The substantial decline in mortality in liver transplant patients that occurred after cyclosporine was introduced implies an associated reduction in infectious mortality.

Tacrolimus (FK-506) was approved in 1994. It is a macrolide produced by *Streptomyces tsukubaensis*. Despite some differences in the pathway, its mode of action is strikingly similar to that of cyclosporine in that it inhibits production of interleukin-2 and other cytokines by CD4-positive T cells.[42] Its potency is about 10 to 100 times greater than of cyclosporine. A comprehensive, randomized comparison of tacrolimus with cyclosporine as primary immunosuppression in 539 liver recipients showed equivalent patient and graft survival rates with the two regimens. Patients receiving tacrolimus had less rejection overall and less rejection resistant to steroid therapy, but they also had a higher rate of drug discontinuation due to adverse effects (14% versus 5%), of which nephrotoxicity and neurotoxicity were the most common events.[43] Other controlled studies of tacrolimus have shown similar results.[42] Use of tacrolimus as primary immunosuppression has not been shown convincingly to either increase or decrease the risk of infection.[21]

A new immunosuppressant, MMF, was approved in 1995 for renal recipients and in 1997 for heart recipients. It is a cytotoxic drug with an antiproliferative effect on T and B lymphocytes. It is not intended to compete with cyclosporine or tacrolimus as primary immunosuppression but rather to replace azathioprine in triple-drug regimens. A blinded, randomized, three-armed study in renal transplant recipients showed superiority of MMF over azathioprine, with biopsy-proven rejection occurring in 38% of azathioprine recipients compared with 19.8% and 17.5% in the two MMF arms.[44] The number of patients developing infections was similar across the three groups.

Antilymphocyte serums (ALSs) and antithymocyte globulins (ATGs) have been popular adjuncts for the prophylaxis or treatment of rejection. Excellent results for graft survival after their routine use as immunosuppressants have been reported. Mason and colleagues showed a significant increase in infection rates during the first 3 months after use of ATG for treatment of rejection of the heart.[45] There are also many reports testifying to the enhancing role of ALS or ATG on CMV disease in renal transplant recipients, and other reports describe an increased rate of post-transplantation lymphoproliferative disease in heart patients receiving high-dose cyclosporine and rabbit ATG or OKT3.[46–49]

The effect of monoclonal anti–T-cell globulins on infections appears to be similar. Liver transplant recipients who received OKT3 monoclonal antibodies for rejection had more instances of HSV superinfection, disseminated CMV disease, *Pneumocystis* infection, and lymphoproliferative disease.[20, 49, 50] Comparisons of monoclonal versus polyclonal anti–T-cell globulins have not shown consistent superiority of either regimen in terms of associated infections.[51–54]

It appears unlikely that polyclonal or monoclonal antilymphocyte serums will be displaced in the near future, because they are the most potent agents for treating severe rejections and can be used to reduce the dose of other immunosuppressive drugs and their associated toxicity. Part of the "cost" of their use may be a higher frequency of CMV disease and other infections. The history of use of immunosuppressants demonstrates that dosages are as important as the agent itself. It is possible that such agents may be used with relative safety if restricted in dosage and frequency.[22] Only careful prospective clinical studies can provide the necessary data on which to make such decisions. A number of other immunosuppressive drugs are being evaluated, and some have been used in patients. These include rapamycin, brequinar, 15-deoxyspergulin, and a variety of new monoclonal antibodies that attach to cell surface molecules involved in the immune response. Each of these agents is promising, but whether any of them will improve long-term graft survival or alter the infection risk of transplant recipients is not yet clear.[55]

INFECTING MICROBIAL AGENTS

The sources of microbial agents and their methods of transmission in transplant recipients are listed in Table 302–3, and the major infecting organisms are shown in Table 302–4.

There are two types of endogenous flora. One represents flora of extracorporeal lumina that colonize the mucous membranes of the gastrointestinal tract, including the oropharynx, the mouth, and the skin adjacent to the oral and anal orifices. This is the source of the most important potential pathogens, represented by some of the more common gram-negative and gram-positive organisms listed in Table 302–4. These organisms may produce local infections by contaminating adjacent wound sites, or they may infect systemically by invading blood vessels or lymphatics. They may also be transmitted from one site to another in the same patient by a surgical procedure or on contaminated instruments and hands.

Candida, a frequent component of normal gastrointestinal tract flora, is the most important fungal pathogen. Superficial mucosal infection is common in the mouth and urinary tract. Candidemia and visceral infection are common after liver transplantation and are occasionally seen in other transplant recipients in an intensive care setting. Another type of colonizing flora that has become important in the 1990s is enterococci resistant to vancomycin and other antibiotics. These organisms have been a particular problem in liver transplant patients, who have many risk factors for colonization, such as the prolonged used of broad-spectrum antibiotics.[56] Prevention of the spread of these organisms from patient to patient is possible but requires a concerted effort in infection control.

The other type of endogenous flora comes from latent tissue

TABLE 302–4 Common Types of Infecting Microbial Agents after Transplantation

Category	Examples and Comments
Bacteria	
Gram-negative bacteria	This group of organisms can cause superficial wound infections or infections of the blood and deeper tissues of the urinary tract, lung, thorax, and abdomen. Despite a succession of highly effective antibiotics, these remain among the most frequent causes of bacterial infection.
Enteric bacteria (*Escherichia coli*, other Enterobacteriaceae)	
Pseudomonas	
Acinetobacter	
Serratia	
Bacteroides and other anaerobes	
Legionella	Nosocomial from water supply.
Gram-positive aerobes	*S. epidermidis* has increased in frequency as other gram-positive organisms have been controlled by antibiotics. *Listeria* is an important cause of meningitis. Vancomycin-resistant enterococcus has become a major pathogen, especially in liver patients.
Staphylococcus aureus	
Staphylococcus epidermidis	
Streptococcus	
Enterococcus	
Pneumococcus	
Listeria monocytogenes	
Nocardia	
Gram-negative coccobacilli	
Haemophilus influenzae	Infection often seen with underlying lung disease.
Moraxella	
Fungi	
Candida spp.	*Candida* are the most common endogenous fungi. Deep *Candida* infection may be a particular problem after liver transplantation.
Aspergillus	
Cryptococcus	
Agents of mucormycoses	
Histoplasma capsulatum	Important in endemic areas.
Coccidioides immitis	Important in the southwestern United States.
Pneumocystis carinii	Probably latent in humans.
Viruses	
Herpesvirus group	Herpesviruses are most common after transplantation because subjects are latently infected with one or more species that reactivate. CMV, EBV, HSV and HIV-1 may also be transmitted by organs.
Herpes simplex (HSV)	
Cytomegalovirus (CMV)	
Varicella-zoster virus	
Epstein-Barr virus (EBV)	
Human herpesvirus-6	
Human immunodeficiency virus 1 (HIV-1)	
Adenovirus	Pediatric, occasionally in adults.
Rotavirus	Pediatric.
BK virus (papovavirus)	
Human papillomavirus	
Hepatitis B virus	
Hepatitis C virus	
Respiratory syncytial virus	During community outbreaks.
Influenza A and B viruses	
Parainfluenza viruses	
Mycoplasmas	
Mycoplasma hominis	*M. hominis* can cause severe mediastinal wound infection after heart transplantation as well as other types of systemic infection, including arthritis, meningitis, and peritonitis.
Protozoa and parasites	
Toxoplasma gondii	
Strongyloides stercoralis	Prior infection may intensify during immunosuppression.

TABLE 302–3 Sources of Microbial Agents and Methods of Transmission

Endogenous sources
- Colonization of the mucous membranes (*Candida*, enteric bacteria)
- Latent tissue infection (herpesviruses, ?pneumocystis, toxoplasma, tubercle bacillus)

Exogenous sources
- Physical environment (*Aspergillus, Nocardia, Legionella*)
- Human environment (all respiratory and enteric agents and viruses)
- Transmission by donated organs
- Transmission by blood and blood products

infection. Such infections may reactivate, and the latent microbial agents may proliferate when the patient is immunosuppressed. The existence of this type of "flora" is best demonstrated by herpesviruses, *Toxoplasma*, and the tubercle bacilli. Their latency in tissues may be detected by serologic or immunologic tests. The presence of immunoglobulin G (IgG) antibodies against herpesvirus and *Toxoplasma* accurately indicates latent infection by these organisms. A positive purified protein derivative (PPD) skin test signals probable latent tissue infection by *Mycobacterium tuberculosis*. The situation is less clear in the case of *Pneumocystis carinii*, because validated microbiologic or serologic tests for latent infection are still not available. In the absence of an environmental source for this organism, and in view of the remarkable frequency of *Pneumocystis* pneumonia in patients with the acquired immunodeficiency syndrome (AIDS), it is reasonable to assume that latent infection by this organism is common if not ubiquitous.

A number of organisms are transmitted through the air from the physical environment, particularly fungi such as *Aspergillus*, *Coccidioides*, *Histoplasma*, and *Cryptococcus*. *Aspergillus*, cryptococcal, and nocardial infections are seen in all geographic regions, but post-transplantation coccidioidomycosis is uniquely a problem of certain endemic regions, such as the arid deserts of the southwest United States, and most reported cases of histoplasmosis after transplantation have also occurred in endemic areas.[57, 58]

The most frequent source of infectious agents in the patient's environment is still other human beings. In the postoperative period, nosocomial transmission of RSV and of common gram-positive and gram-negative organisms occurs via contaminated hands and hospital vectors such as respiratory equipment, endoscopes, intravascular lines, and urinary catheters. Such equipment may at times amplify the agent if organisms are permitted to grow in reservoirs such as water baths and humidifiers. More virulent and fastidious microbial agents, such as encapsulated bacteria, viruses, and protozoa, are not likely to infect via the physical environment or to be transmitted in the hospital setting, but they are transmitted directly from other human beings.

Some bacteria listed in Table 302–4 probably have exogenous sources, but these are often undefined. *Pseudomonas* may come from environmental water sources or raw vegetables.[59] *Listeria* may arise from contaminated food sources, but a source is rarely identified in the sporadic cases of meningitis that are seen in the transplantation population.[60] The *Legionella* organisms, including *Legionella pneumophila* and *Legionella micdadei*, are important and well-described causes of pneumonia in transplant recipients.[61] *Legionella* can be isolated from hospital water sources, particularly the hot water reservoirs. It has been advocated that control of nosocomial legionellosis can be improved by hyperchlorination or periodic superheating of the hot water supply.[61, 62]

Transfused blood products and the donated organ have been important sources of infection in transplant recipients, but the impact of transfusion-transmitted infection is declining as a result of better screening for infectious agents, especially hepatitis C virus (HCV).[63] A large number of pathogens have been transmitted by allografts.[64] The most important agents and references are listed in Table 302–5. CMV is among the most important of these pathogens in terms of frequency of transmission by organs and blood products, and it is desirable to provide seronegative transplant recipients with organs only from seronegative donors.[6, 65] However, in view of the shortage of donors, the varying morbidity of CMV, and logistic problems involved with maintaining organ survival, selection of donors is difficult. Selection is practiced at some centers for high-risk recipients, such as marrow recipients, lung recipients, and pediatric CMV-seronegative renal recipients. In order to prevent transmission of CMV, seronegative transplant recipients are given blood transfusions from CMV-seronegative blood donors or the blood is run through in-line leukocyte filters to remove the white blood cells, which are the component in the blood that carries the latent virus.[66]

Toxoplasma has been transmitted by seropositive heart donors, but transmission with other organs is rare.[67] HSV infections have occasionally been transmitted from seropositive donors to seronegative recipients, and it is likely that seropositive donors are a major source of primary EBV in seronegative recipients.[68, 69] Donors who have antibodies to HCV transmit the virus to recipients at a high rate that approaches 100% if the donor is viremic.[70] However, the clinical significance of this transmitted infection is controversial, even though post-transplantation hepatitis is increased.[71] As opposed to organ recipients who were anti-HCV positive before transplantation, organ recipients who acquired their infection from the donor were not adversely affected in terms of survival or graft survival after a follow-up of 3 to 5 years.[72] For these reasons, there is, as yet, no consensus regarding donor selection.[73]

TABLE 302–5 Transmission of Infective Agents by Donated Tissues, Blood, and Blood Products

Type of Tissue	Infective Agent	References
Kidney, heart, liver, bone marrow	Cytomegalovirus	6, 16, 50, 64
Heart, kidney	Toxoplasmosis	67
Kidney	Herpes simplex virus	69
Kidney, heart, liver	HIV	77–79, 85, 86
Kidney, heart, liver	HBV	74–76
Kidney, heart, liver	HCV	70–72
Blood*	CMV, EBV, HIV, HBV, HAV, HDV, HCV, HTLV-I	63
Leukocytes	CMV, HIV	63

*On rare occasion, Chagas' disease, malaria, babesiosis, and syphilis have been transmitted by blood transfusion.
Abbreviations: CMV, Cytomegalovirus; EBV, Epstein-Barr virus; HAV, hepatitis A virus; HBV, hepatitis B virus; HCV, hepatitis C virus; HDV, delta hepatitis virus; HIV, Human immunodeficiency virus; HTLV-I, human T-cell lymphotrophic virus I.

The risk of transmitting hepatitis B depends on the serologic status of the donor and the recipient and the type of organ transplanted. Organs from donors positive for hepatitis B surface antigen (HbsAg) can transmit the infection, but the frequency is not well defined because of the small number of observations.[74] The organs of donors who are negative for HBsAg but positive for core antibody (HBcAb) also may transmit HBV.[75, 76] The risk of infection after receipt of these organs appears to be high for liver (25 to 83%) but low (about 2%) for other organs.[75, 76] The presence of anti-HBsAb in donor serum appears to decrease but not eliminate this risk.[76] Another uncertainty is the degree to which immunity to hepatitis B in the recipient is protective after transplantation with an organ carrying the virus. The decision to use an organ from a donor with serology positive for HBV involves a complicated assessment of risks and benefits for the intended recipient; this assessment varies with the type of transplant, the specific results of donor and recipient serologies, and whether the intended recipient is in immediate danger of dying from the underlying disease.[77]

Human immunodeficiency virus (HIV-1) is efficiently transmitted by donor organs, tissues, and blood products.[77–79] There is a general consensus that organs from donors seropositive for HIV-1 should not be transplanted. The Centers for Disease Control and Prevention has developed guidelines mandating that organ procurement personnel obtain from all potential donors a history of any risk factors for HIV-1 infection that could signal the possibility of transmission of HIV-1 despite negative antibody tests. The mandate includes the responsibility of sharing any relevant information with the intended recipient and family.[77]

DIAGNOSIS AND CONTROL OF INFECTION

Evaluation of the patient for infectious risks before transplantation has proved to be extremely valuable, and many transplantation centers have set up formal screening mechanisms.[7, 8] The first goal of such screening should be to detect the presence of active infection in the candidate that might amplify and prove to be a major problem after transplantation. Examples are a history of chronic bronchitis or the presence of active dental infection. The second step is to take an exposure history. The patient should be questioned about occupational exposures and hobbies, and a brief travel history should be obtained to explore possible exposure to tropical illnesses or endemic mycoses. As part of this history, routine inquiry should be made about a past history of tuberculosis, previous tuberculin skin test results, and any exposure that might have placed the patient at high risk of acquiring tuberculosis, such as extended travel in developing countries or work as a prison guard. Third, a battery of infectious disease screening tests should be performed, as outlined in Table 302–6. The results establish the presence of chronic viral pathogens (HIV, HCV, HBV) and help assess susceptibility to reactivation or infection by key transplant pathogens such the herpesviruses and *Toxoplasma gondii*. If negative, they also form an important baseline for future reference and testing. Tuberculin skin testing should be done for all patients unless they have a history of a definite positive test in the past. We also recommend coccidioidomycosis antibody tests for individuals with residence or significant exposure over the last 2 years in endemic areas of the southwestern United States. Patients with residence outside the United States may require specialized testing for *Trypanosoma cruzi*, malaria, or lumenal parasites such as strongyloides.[80]

The most useful tests before transplantation are the herpesvirus serologies, because they predict whether the patient is at risk for reactivation or for primary infection. An example would be knowledge of a patient's varicella status: few patients are seronegative, but these few are at high risk of potentially fatal varicella after transplantation. Knowledge of risk status allows intensive counseling of these patients and consideration of immunization.[81] Seropositive patients, on the other hand, can be told that they are at no significant risk from chickenpox exposure and require no intervention after exposure. CMV antibody status before transplantation is an important way of stratifying risk for significant illness due to CMV after transplantation, and many transplantation centers modify their management of seronegative patients (with seropositive donors) by instituting closer follow-up or giving more aggressive antiviral prophylaxis.[82]

The risk of active tuberculosis in transplant recipients is 30 to 50 times higher than in the general population.[5, 83] The management of a transplantation patient who has a positive skin test is controversial. Not all experts recommend a course of isoniazid because of a concern for hepatotoxicity.[33] But the risk of hepatotoxicity from isoniazid prophylaxis appears to be low in transplantation patients without preexisting liver disease.[84] We believe that most patients with positive tuberculin skin tests should be treated, but assessment of risks and benefits in individual patients is also important, and the optimal timing of prophylaxis should be considered. For instance, liver transplantation candidates may be at high risk for decompensation if they develop hepatic injury from isoniazid. If a decision is made for prophylaxis, it might best be delayed until a few weeks after transplantation, when the patient's hepatic function is stable.

Most transplantation centers have not transplanted HIV-1 infected patients, so little prospective information is available on the outcome of such procedures. Retrospective information suggests that, although survival may not be demonstrably worse than in HIV-negative transplant recipients, the progression to AIDS-defining diseases may be more rapid than in HIV-infected patients who do not undergo transplantation.[78, 85, 86] The introduction of highly active antiretroviral therapy and the ability to dramatically reduce viral load may increase enthusiasm for offering transplantation to stable HIV-1–positive patients without AIDS. A significant hurdle to overcome in such an undertaking may be drug interactions between currently available antiretroviral medications and the complicated drug regimens most transplantation patients must follow.

TABLE 302–6 Routine Laboratory Studies before and after Transplantation

Before Transplantation*	After Transplantation
Cytomegalovirus Immunoglobulin G (IgG) antibody	Viral surveillance cultures
Epstein-Barr virus IgG antibody	Antibody studies (as indicated)
Herpes simplex (types 1 and 2) antibody	
Varicella-zoster IgG antibody	
Toxoplasma IgG antibody (heart recipients)	
Hepatitis B screen†	
Hepatitis C ELISA‡	
Human immunodeficiency virus antibody	
Tuberculin skin test	
Stool for ova and parasites§	

*For serologic studies, it is most important to collect serum before transplantation. Studies may then be done as clinically indicated. Not all tests need to be done on all patients.
†Should include at least surface antigen, core antibody, and surface antibody.
‡Second-generation enzyme-linked immunosorbent assay. Liver candidates and patients with laboratory or clinical evidence of liver disease should also have a hepatitis C polymerase chain reaction assay performed.
§Particularly useful for residents of tropical and subtropical regions.

MONITORING FOR INFECTION

Routine surveillance for bacteria or fungi is probably of limited benefit, at least in most solid organ transplant recipients. One exception might be the routine surveillance of sputum of heart-lung and lung recipients who are intubated in the intensive care unit. Such patients have a substantial risk of pneumonia, and it may be easier to assess changes in chest radiographs or respiratory status when serial results are available. Routine surveillance for CMV is commonly obtained in the first 3 to 4 months after transplantation. In recent years, blood antigenemia testing and polymerase chain reaction (PCR) testing for CMV have replaced conventional and shell vial cultures for CMV at many centers. These tests are more sensitive, and in most studies the tests turn positive about 1 to 2 weeks earlier.[87–91] CMV antigenemia provides semiquantitative information that correlates with symptom development; PCR can also be run quantitatively, with a gain in specificity.[92] In marrow transplant populations, virologic tests for CMV, including shell vial culture, PCR, and antigenemia, have successfully triggered the use of prophylactic antiviral therapy and prevented progression to overt CMV disease.[87, 91, 93] This approach to management of CMV disease has also been taken in solid organ transplant recipients.[94]

Monitoring of the viral load has also been studied for other important viral infections in transplantation patients. For instance, the amount of HCV RNA in the serum of liver transplantation patients with active HCV infection can be quantified, but this has not been shown to predict the presence or severity of hepatitis.[95] Measurement of the viral load has proved useful as a way to monitor antiviral therapy with lamuvidine in liver recipients with chronic HBV infection.[96]

PROPHYLACTIC MEASURES

The use of prophylactic regimens to prevent infection in transplant recipients has become a widespread practice. Immunization is potentially the most cost-effective way to prevent infection. Although trials large enough to demonstrate clinical effectiveness of vaccines have not been done in transplantation populations, numerous smaller studies have looked at antibody responses. The response of renal recipients to booster doses of tetanus and diphtheria toxoids appears to be adequate, though reduced compared with the response in immunocompetent persons.[97] Renal recipients also respond to pneumococcal vaccine, but the peak antibody titers achieved are less than in patients receiving hemodialysis. The seroconversion rates of transplant recipients to influenza vaccine are also generally less than in control populations.[98–102]

There is an understandable reluctance to use live vaccines in transplantation patients, but measles and varicella vaccines have been used safely in small groups of transplant recipients with seroconversion rates of 65% and 47%, respectively.[103, 104] More studies need to be done with live vaccines before they can be recommended for general use in this group of patients. We advocate that transplantation patients receive those killed vaccines that are recommended for patients in the general population who have chronic diseases, including pneumococcal, influenza, and HBV vaccines. In practice, we often postpone immunization when the patient is heavily immunosuppressed, such as during the first 3 months after transplantation or when therapy for rejection has been recently given, because of a concern that the response will be poor in this setting. Concerns in the transplant community that vaccines may cause rejection have not been substantiated by available studies. Before transplantation, routine immunizations should be brought up to date. Serious consideration should also be given to immunization of transplant recipients against varicella, if they are seronegative. Current evidence suggests that this practice is moderately effective and safe.[81]

Antimicrobial agents commonly used for prophylaxis are listed in Table 302–7. Most surgeons give a short course of parenteral antibiotics to prevent intraoperative sepsis and wound infections immediately before and shortly after surgery. The type of antibiotic used varies greatly. The use of oral antibiotics to prevent infection has been advocated by some groups. The most commonly used prophylactic antimicrobial agent is trimethoprim-sulfamethoxazole (TMP-SMX). TMP-SMX provides superior prophylaxis against *P. carinii* pneumonia in all populations that have been studied, and it has become part of the standard care at many transplantation centers. Doses as small as three double-strength tablets a week appear to be effective. TMP-SMX has also been shown to be effective in the reduction of urinary tract infections in renal recipients when taken in a dose of 160 mg of trimethoprim and 800 mg of sulfamethoxazole daily for the first 4 months after transplantation.[105] Another blinded, randomized prophylactic trial of TMP-SMX in which the treatment group received 320 mg of trimethoprim and 1600 mg of sulfamethoxazole in the hospital followed by one half the dose after discharge, showed that the patients receiving TMP-SMX not only had significantly fewer urinary infections but also fewer blood-stream infections and fewer infections caused by enteric gram-negative bacteria, enterococci, and *S. aureus*.[106] The drug was well tolerated, but in the presence of cyclosporine, drug recipients had 25% higher creatinine levels, which, however, were fully reversible on discontinuation. It is claimed, but unproved, that TMP-SMX prophylaxis also decreases the rate of infections caused by other serious opportunistic pathogens that are susceptible to the drug, including *Legionella*, *Nocardia*, and *Listeria*.[107]

TABLE 302–7 Antimicrobial Prophylactic Regimens in Transplantation

Pathogen	Prophylactic Agents
Protozoa	
Toxoplasmosis	Pyrimethamine
Viral	
Herpes simplex	Acyclovir
Cytomegalovirus	Acyclovir Immunoglobulin Ganciclovir Foscarnet*
Fungal	
Candida	Fluconazole Nystatin Clotrimazole
Aspergillus	Amphotericin B Liposomal amphotericin
Pneumocystis	Trimethoprim-sulfamethoxazole (TMP-SMX)
Bacterial	
Wound infection	Variable
Urinary tract infection	TMP-SMX
Neutropenic infection	Quinolones
Tuberculosis	Isoniazid
Pneumococcus	Penicillin (bone marrow transplants)

*Foscarnet is mostly used in bone marrow recipients who have low blood counts.

Prophylactic quinolones are used at some marrow transplantation centers. They have been shown to reliably decrease the rate of gram-negative but not gram-positive infections during the neutropenic phase of chemotherapy.[108] No effect on mortality has been demonstrated. It is not yet known whether resistance will become a major problem in this population.

Antiviral prophylaxis is desirable in transplantation patients because of the clinical importance of the herpesviruses. Acyclovir is effective in preventing HSV infection in the early post-transplantation period. It is indicated in seropositive marrow and lung transplant recipients, because of their significant risk of visceral disease[109, 110]; it is also commonly used in other solid organ recipients because of their risk for mucocutaneous HSV infection. Although acyclovir has little therapeutic activity against CMV, it has been shown to provide some protection when given prophylactically in controlled studies. Acyclovir given intravenously at 500 mg/m^2 three times a day for 1 month after marrow transplantation reduced the frequency of CMV disease by about one third, and high-dose oral acyclovir (800 mg four times daily) given for 3 months to renal recipients significantly reduced their incidence of CMV disease.[111, 112] Subsequent studies, however, showed numerous breakthroughs of CMV disease in transplantation patients receiving acyclovir and many physicians have sought more potent agents.[82, 94]

Ganciclovir's greater activity against CMV makes it an attractive candidate for prophylaxis. The most impressive results have been in marrow transplantation, where ganciclovir has been shown to be effective prophylaxis when administered after engraftment to patients who are at risk for CMV disease based either on positive cultures or on seropositive status.[113, 114] Maintenance doses (5 to 6 mg/kg daily for 5 to 7 days/week) were continued intravenously for 100 to 120 days after transplantation. Significant problems with this prophylactic regimen were the requirement for frequent intravenous infusions, a high rate of neutropenia, and in one study an increase in bacterial infections.[114] "Preemptive" use of ganciclovir in liver transplant recipients with positive CMV cultures was reported to be successful.[94] A randomized study of ganciclovir prophylaxis for the first 4 weeks after transplantation in heart recipients produced interesting results, in that seropositive patients benefited but seronegative recipients of organs from seropositive donors did not.[115] It may be that the effective inhibition of viral replication by ganciclovir prevented an adequate primary immune response from being generated in seronegative subjects. However, Winston and associates were able to show a dramatic reduction of CMV disease in liver recipients in a controlled trial in which the treatment group received extended treatment with intravenous ganciclovir until 100 days after transplantation.[116] This strategy also appeared to be effective in seronegative patients. Although few adverse events were reported in this trial, many centers would not want to commit their patients to such long-term intravenous therapy, only to ensure a very low rate of CMV disease.

Two trials of CMV prophylaxis have demonstrated encouraging results with oral regimens. A randomized trial comparing 12 weeks of oral ganciclovir (1 g three times daily) with placebo in liver transplant recipients showed a significant reduction in CMV disease, from 17% to 4% in the treatment group.[117] The cases of CMV disease in ganciclovir recipients were not life-threatening and included only CMV syndromes and CMV hepatitis. Valacyclovir, a prodrug of acyclovir that yields serum levels of acyclovir in the range of those achieved with intravenous dosing, was compared with placebo in 616 renal recipients.[118] The frequency of CMV disease was reduced from 5% to 1% in seropositive patients and from 39% to 14% in seronegative recipients with seropositive donors. Only 1% of patients developed CMV disease while taking valacyclovir.

Immune control is the mechanism of the other major modality in CMV prophylaxis. Intravenous immunoglobulin has been widely studied for the prophylaxis of CMV disease after marrow transplantation. The results of these studies have been mixed but suggest some activity, perhaps through an effect on graft-versus-host disease.[119] A well-designed, prospective study showed that infusions of an immunoglobulin preparation with high titers of CMV antibodies significantly reduced the incidence of CMV disease and associated opportunistic infections in seronegative renal transplant recipients receiving seropositive donor organs.[120] A subsequent study in liver transplant recipients also showed positive results, but the effect was less striking and only seropositive patients benefited.[121]

The decision when and how to provide prophylaxis for CMV infection in transplantation patients is complex and is best made after careful consideration of the efficacy, side effects, and cost of the regimen under consideration and the severity of CMV disease in the intended recipient.

Thrush and other forms of mucocutaneous candidiasis occur in a high percentage of patients in the early post-transplantation period but are effectively prevented by treatment with oral nystatin or clotrimazole troches.[122] Oral systemic azoles are also effective and may be preferred in intubated patients because topical preparations cannot reliably be delivered to the pharynx and esophagus. Prophylaxis can usually be discontinued when prednisone doses drop to 20 mg/day or less, but they may need to be restarted during treatment of rejection with high-dose steroids or intercurrent antibiotic treatment. Prophylaxis for systemic fungal infection is now being used in some centers for high-risk patients such as marrow, liver, and lung recipients. Large studies in marrow recipients have shown that fluconazole (400 mg/day) significantly reduces the rate of deep *Candida* infections.[123] A trial of low-dose amphotericin (0.1 mg/kg/day) in neutropenic autologous marrow recipients also showed reduced mortality in the treatment arm, but it was not clear whether this was a result of reduced fungal infections.[124] A small controlled trial of fluconazole prophylaxis in liver recipients showed a trend toward reduced fungal infections in patients receiving fluconazole.[125] Likewise, intravenous lipid-based amphotericin given at 1 mg/kg/day during the first 5 days after liver transplantation was thought to have reduced invasive fungal infection in another small study.[126] All of the agents currently available for fungal prophylaxis in transplantation patients have some drawbacks in terms of spectrum of activity, side effects, interactions with immunosuppressive medications, or cost.

Another form of prophylaxis that has been proposed is pyrimethamine (25 mg/day for 6 weeks) for heart recipients who are seronegative for *Toxoplasma* and receive an organ from a *Toxoplasma*-seropositive donor.[127] However, patients receiving TMP-SMX appear to be protected from infection with *Toxoplasma*, and it is unclear whether the addition of pyrimethamine provides an additional benefit.[128] Some bone marrow units also employ long-term oral penicillin prophylaxis in allogenic transplant recipients because of the high rate of pneumococcal infection late after transplantation.

Because liver transplantation involves opening the potentially infected gastrointestinal tract, some groups advocate decontamination of the gut as a method to decrease bacterial and fungal sepsis. Selective decontamination was achieved by oral administration of nonabsorbable polymyxin E, gentamicin, and nystatin and a diet free of raw foods and cheese for 3 days before donor search and 21 days after transplantation.[129] Surveillance cultures showed reduction of bacteria and fungi. The reported infection rates were low but were difficult to evaluate in the absence of controls.

APPROACH TO FEVER IN THE TRANSPLANTATION PATIENT

Although immunosuppressive drugs can blunt the febrile response to infection, most transplant recipients with clinical infections have temperature elevations; often this is the first indication that something is awry.[130] When faced with a febrile patient, the first task is to identify possible sites and sources of infection and assess the severity of illness. Patients with typical upper respiratory tract infections and low-grade fevers (<38.0°C) can generally be observed clinically. Cyclosporine seems to predispose patients to sinus infections. If sinus infection is suspected, it is often wise to order sinus radiographs or computed tomographic scans. If the patient becomes febrile with a temperature higher than 38.0°C, a medical evaluation should be made. If there are symptoms suggesting a serious localized infection, the patient should be evaluated even in the absence of demonstrable fever.

The most important parts of this workup are a careful history and physical examination. A chest radiograph should be obtained to establish whether there is evidence for infection in the lungs. Patients with pulmonary infiltrates, or with persistent fevers higher than 38.5°C usually need to be hospitalized for further workup. Most patients who cannot go about their normal daily activities should probably be evaluated in the hospital unless the cause of their dysfunction is apparent and can be managed at home. Initial evaluation should include blood and urine cultures, examination of respiratory secretions (if pneumonia is suspected), white blood cell count and differential, liver function tests, and microscopic examination of the urine. Viral screening tests should be ordered if there is a clinical suspicion of CMV disease, if the patient has recently been treated for rejection, or if the patient is still in the high-risk early post-transplantation period (1 to 4 months). Antibiotics may be withheld from patients who appear well and in whom no source of infection has emerged from the preliminary workup. Although lumbar puncture need not be a routine part of the workup of febrile transplantation patients, the physician should have a low threshold for obtaining a sample of spinal fluid for culture and analysis in patients with headache and other neurologic complaints.

In a patient with a clear site of infection, evaluation should focus on quickly obtaining adequate samples for culture and smears from that site. The patient who has persistent fever (≥7 days) without positive cultures or an apparent site of infection presents a diagnostic and therapeutic problem.

Relatively few clinical entities appear to account for the majority of these fevers of unknown origin (FUO), the most important of which are viral syndromes caused by CMV or occasionally by EBV. In recent years, human herpesvirus-6 (HHV-6) has also emerged as a possible cause of FUO in the early post-transplantation period.[131] Other infections that manifest in this fashion are systemic toxoplasmosis and smoldering *Pneumocystis* infection with a normal chest radiograph. Deep tissue abscesses almost always occur in or near the anatomic site of previous surgery, or they may be caused by deep candidiasis. Disseminated candidiasis occurs largely in patients who are either neutropenic or long-term residents of the intensive care unit and who have received broad-spectrum antibiotics and have multiple intravenous lines. The risk for deep candidiasis is highest in liver recipients, moderate in lung and heart-lung recipients, and low in kidney and heart recipients. Disseminated coccidioidomycosis and histoplasmosis may cause FUO, but most of these cases occur in patients who are resident in or have traveled in the recent past to endemic areas.

Not all fevers are caused by infections. The most common causes of noninfectious fevers in transplant recipients in our experience are drug reactions (especially reactions to anti–T-cell globulins) and rejection. The frequency with which rejection causes fever appears to vary widely among different transplant recipient groups. For instance, heart rejection rarely causes fever, but acute lung rejection is often associated with temperature elevations. Renal and hepatic transplant recipients appear to have an intermediate risk of fever during episodes of rejection.

Other noninfectious causes of fever are deep venous thrombosis (or pulmonary embolism), organ ischemia from infarction or inadequate preservation, lymphoproliferative tumors, and hemolytic reactions.

Finally, it must be also be conceded that infections in transplantation patients may occur without any fever. At times this appears to be related to the use of high-dose corticosteroids; at other times severe organ failure (heart, liver, or kidney) appears to be implicated. Some infections, such as progressive multifocal leukoencephalopathy, never cause fever, and others frequently do not. *Pneumocystis* pneumonia may manifest with cough and dyspnea only. Fungal infections are frequently afebrile, particularly cryptococcal meningitis, which may manifest with only chronic headache and subtle neurologic symptoms. A good caveat for the physician approaching the transplant recipient is always to consider infection a possible cause of any new symptom or sign.

REFERENCES

1. Murray JE: Human organ transplantation: Background and consequences. Science. 1992;256:1411.
2. Starzl TE, Klintmalm GB, Porter KA, et al. Liver transplantation with use of cyclosporin A and prednisone. N Engl J Med. 1981;305:266.
3. United Network for Organ Sharing. 1997 Report of Center Specific Graft and Patient Survival Rates. Richmond, VA: UNOS and Rockville, MD: Division of Transplantation, Office of Special Programs, Health Resources and Services Administration, US Department of Health and Human Services. (The data and analyses in the 1997 Report of Center Specific Graft and Patient Survival Rates have been supplied by UNOS. The authors alone are responsible for the reporting and interpretation of the data.)
4. Sundberg R, Shapiro R, Darras F, et al. A tuberculosis outbreak in a renal transplant program. Transplant Proc. 1991;23:3091.
5. Qunibi WY, Al-Sibai MB, Taher S, et al. Mycobacterial infection after renal transplantation: Report of 14 cases and review of the literature. QJM. 1990;77:1039.
6. Ho M. Cytomegalovirus: Biology and Infection. 2nd ed. New York: Plenum Press; 1991:249–256.
7. Patel R, Paya CV. Infections in solid-organ transplant recipients. Clin Microbiol Rev. 1997;10:86.
8. Boden MD, Dummer JS. Infections after organ transplantation. J Intensive Care Med. 1997;12:166.
9. Rubin RH, Wolfson JS, Cosimi AB, Tolkoff-Rubin NE. Infection in the renal transplant recipient. Am J Med. 1981;70:405.
10. Peterson PK, Balfour HH Jr, Fryd DS, et al. Fever in renal transplant recipients: Causes, prognostic significance and changing patterns at the University of Minnesota Hospital. Am J Med. 1981;71:345.
11. Samuel D, Muller R, Alexander G, et al. Liver transplantation in European patients with the hepatitis B surface antigen. N Engl J Med. 1993;329:1842.
12. Terrault NA, Wright TL, Pereira BJ. Hepatitis C infection in the transplant recipient. Infect Dis Clin North Am. 1995;9:943.
13. Tolkoff-Rubin NE, Rubin RH. The infectious disease problems of the diabetic renal transplant recipient. Infect Dis Clin North Am. 1995;9:117.
14. Horvath J, Dummer S, Loyd J, et al. Infection in the transplanted and native lung after single lung transplantation. Chest. 1993;104:681.
15. Wajszczuk CP, Dummer JS, Ho M, et al. Fungal infections in liver transplant recipients. Transplantation. 1985;40:347.
16. Meyers JD, Flournoy N, Thomas ED. Risk factors for cytomegalovirus infection after human marrow transplantation. J Infect Dis. 1986;153:478.
17. Dummer JS, Hardy A, Poorsattar A, Ho M. Early infections in kidney, heart, and liver transplant recipients on cyclosporine. Transplantation. 1983;36:259.
18. Ho M, Wajszczuk CP, Hardy A, et al. Infections in kidney, heart, and liver transplant recipients on cyclosporine. Transplant Proc. 1983;15:2768.
19. Lebeau G, Yanaga K, Marsh JW, et al. Analysis of surgical complications after 397 hepatic transplantations. Surg Gynecol Obstet. 1990;170:317.
20. Kusne S, Dummer JS, Singh N, et al. Infections after liver transplantation: An analysis of 101 consecutive cases. Medicine (Baltimore). 1988;67:132.
21. Hadley S, Samore MH, Lewis WD, et al. Major infectious complications after orthotopic liver transplantation and comparison of outcomes in patients receiving cyclosporine or FK506 as primary immunosuppression. Transplantation. 1995;59:851.
22. Dummer JS, White LT, Ho M, et al. Morbidity of cytomegalovirus infection in recipients of heart or heart-lung transplants who received cyclosporine. J Infect Dis. 1985;152:1182.
23. Wendt CH, Fox JMK, Hertz MI. Paramyxovirus infection in lung transplant recipients. J Heart Lung Transplant. 1995;14:479.
24. Bronsther O, Makowka L, Jaffe R, et al. Occurrence of cytomegalovirus hepatitis in liver transplant patients. J Med Virol. 1988;24:423.
25. Kusne S, Schwartz M, Breinig MK, et al. Herpes simplex virus hepatitis after solid organ transplantation in adults. J Infect Dis. 1991;163:1001.
26. Michaels MG, Green M, Wald ER, Starzl TE. Adenovirus infection in pediatric liver transplant recipients. J Infect Dis. 1992;165:170.
27. Davies SE, Portmann BC, O'Grady JG, et al. Hepatic histological findings after transplantation for chronic hepatitis B virus infection, including a unique pattern of fibrosing cholestatic hepatitis. Hepatology. 1991;13:150.
28. Ho M. Virus infections after transplantation in man: Brief review. Arch Virol. 1977;55:1.
29. Meuleman J, Katz P. The immunologic effects, kinetics, and use of glucocorticoids. Med Clin North Am. 1985;69:805.
30. Anderson RJ, Schafer LA, Olin DB, Eickhoff TC. Infectious risk factors in the immunosuppressed host. Am J Med. 1973;54:453.
31. Rifkind D, Marchioro TL, Schneck SA, Hill RB Jr. Systemic fungal infections complicating renal transplantation and immunosuppressive therapy: Clinical, microbiologic, neurologic and pathologic features. Am J Med. 1967;43:28.
32. Gustafson TL, Schaffner W, Lavely GB, et al. Invasive aspergillosis in renal transplant recipients: Correlation with corticosteroid therapy. J Infect Dis. 1983;148:230.
33. Rubin R. Infection in the renal and liver transplant patient. In: Rubin RH, Young LS, eds. Clinical Approach to Infection in the Immunocompromised Host. 2nd ed. New York: Plenum Press; 1988:557.
34. Renlund DG, O'Connell JB, Gilbert EM, et al. Feasibility of discontinuation of corticosteroid maintenance therapy in heart transplantation. J Heart Transplant. 1987;6:71.
35. Starzl TE, Weil RD, Iwatsuki S, et al. The use of cyclosporin A and prednisone in cadaver kidney transplantation. Surg Gynecol Obstet. 1980;151:17.
36. Kahan BD. Cyclosporine. N Engl J Med. 1989;321:1725.
37. Palestine AG, Nussenblatt RB, Chan CC. Side effects of systemic cyclosporine in patients not undergoing transplantation. Am J Med. 1984;77:652.
38. Najarian JS, Fryd DS, Strand M, et al. A single institution, randomized, prospective trial of cyclosporin versus azathioprine-antilymphocyte globulin for immunosuppression in renal allograft recipients. Ann Surg. 1985;201:142.
39. Anonymous. A randomized clinical trial of cyclosporine in cadaveric renal transplantation: Analysis at three years. The Canadian Multicentre Transplant Study Group. N Engl J Med. 1986;314:1219.
40. Anonymous. Cyclosporin as sole immunosuppressive agent in recipients of kidney allografts from cadaver donors: Preliminary results of a European multicentre trial. Lancet. 1982;2:57.
41. Hofflin JM, Potasman I, Baldwin JC, et al. Infectious complications in heart transplant patients receiving cyclosporine and corticosteroids. Ann Intern Med. 1987;106:209.
42. Spencer CM, Goa KL, Gillis JC. Tacrolimus: An update of its pharmacology and clinical efficacy in the management of organ transplantation. Drugs. 1997;54:925.
43. Anonymous. A comparison of tacrolimus (FK 506) and cyclosporine for immunosuppression in liver transplantation. The US Multicenter FK506 Liver Study Group. N Engl J Med. 1994;331:1110.
44. Sollinger HW. Mycophenolate mofetil for the prevention of acute rejection in primary cadaveric renal allograft recipients. US Renal Transplant Mycophenolate Mofetil Study Group. Transplantation. 1995;60:225.
45. Mason JW, Stinson EB, Hunt SA, et al. Infections after cardiac transplantation: relation to rejection therapy. Ann Intern Med. 1976;85:69.
46. Peterson PK, Balfour HH Jr, Marker SC, et al. Cytomegalovirus disease in renal allograft recipients: A prospective study of the clinical features, risk factors and impact on renal transplantation. Medicine (Baltimore). 1980;59:283.
47. Bia MJ, Andiman W, Gaudio K, et al. Effect of treatment with cyclosporine versus azathioprine on incidence and severity of cytomegalovirus infection posttransplantation. Transplantation. 1985;40:610.
48. Bieber CP, Heberling RL, Jamieson SW, et al. Lymphoma in cardiac transplant recipients: Association with use of cyclosporin A, prednisone and antithymocyte globulin (ATG). In: Purtilo DT, ed. Immune Deficiency and Cancer. New York: Plenum Press; 1984:309.
49. Swinnen LJ, Costanzo-Nordin MR, Fisher SG, et al. Increased incidence of lymphoproliferative disorder after immunosuppression with the monoclonal antibody OKT3 in cardiac-transplant recipients. N Engl J Med. 1990;323:1723.
50. Singh N, Dummer JS, Kusne S, et al. Infections with cytomegalovirus and other herpesviruses in 121 liver transplant recipients: Transmission by donated organ and the effect of OKT3 antibodies. J Infect Dis. 1988;158:124.
51. Frey DJ, Matas AJ, Gillingham KJ, et al. Sequential therapy: A prospective randomized trial of MALG versus OKT3 for prophylactic immunosuppression in cadaver renal allograft recipients. Transplantation. 1992;54:50.
52. Kormos RL, Armitage JM, Dummer JS, et al. Optimal perioperative immunosuppression in cardiac transplantation using rabbit antithymocyte globulin. Transplantation. 1990;49:306.
53. Menkis AH, Powell AM, Novick RJ, et al. A prospective randomized controlled trial of initial immunosuppression with ALG versus OKT3 in recipients of cardiac allografts. J Heart Lung Transplant. 1992;11:569.
54. Renlund DG, O'Connell JB, Gilbert EM, et al. A prospective comparison of murine monoclonal CD-3 (OKT3) antibody-based and equine antithymocyte globulin-based rejection prophylaxis in cardiac transplantation: Decreased rejection and less corticosteroid use with OKT3. Transplantation. 1989;47:599.
55. First MR. An update on new immunosuppressive drugs undergoing preclinical and clinical trials: Potential applications in organ transplantation. Am J Kidney Dis. 1997;29:303.
56. Linden PK, Pasculle AW, Manez R, et al. Differences in outcomes for patients with bacteremia due to vancomycin-resistant *Enterococcus faecium* or vancomycin-susceptible *E. faecium*. Clin Infect Dis. 1996;22:663.
57. Cohen MI, Galgiani JN, Potter D, Ogden DA. Coccidioidomycosis in renal replacement therapy. Arch Intern Med. 1982;142:489.
58. Wheat J, Smith EJ, Sathapatayavongs B, et al. Histoplasmosis in renal allograft recipients: Two large urban outbreaks. Arch Intern Med. 1983;143:703.
59. Kominos SD, Copeland CE, Grosiak B, Postic B. Introduction of *Pseudomonas aeruginosa* into a hospital via vegetables. Appl Microbiol. 1992;24:567.
60. Schlech WF 3d, Lavigne PM, Bortolussi RA, et al. Epidemic listeriosis: Evidence for transmission by food. N Engl J Med. 1983;308:203.
61. Stout JE, Yu VL. Legionellosis. N Engl J Med. 1997;337:682.
62. Muder RR, Yu VL, Woo AH. Mode of transmission of *Legionella pneumophila*: A critical review. Arch Intern Med. 1986;146:1607.
63. Rossi EC, Simon TL, Moss GS, Gould SA. Principles of Transfusion Medicine. 2nd ed. Baltimore: Williams & Wilkins; 1996.

64. Gottesdiener KM. Transplanted infections: Donor-to-host transmission with the allograft. Ann Intern Med. 1989;110:1001.
65. Ho M, Suwansirikul S, Dowling JN, et al. The transplanted kidney as a source of cytomegalovirus infection. N Engl J Med. 1975;293:1109.
66. Gilbert GL, Hayes K, Hudson IL, James J. Prevention of transfusion-acquired cytomegalovirus infection in infants by blood filtration to remove leucocytes. Neonatal Cytomegalovirus Infection Study Group. Lancet. 1989;1:1228.
67. Luft BJ, Naot Y, Araujo FG, et al. Primary and reactivated toxoplasma infection in patients with cardiac transplants: Clinical spectrum and problems in diagnosis in a defined population. Ann Intern Med. 1983;99:27.
68. Cen H, Breinig MC, Atchison RW, et al. Epstein-Barr virus transmission via the donor organs in solid organ transplantation: Polymerase chain reaction and restriction fragment length polymorphism analysis of IR2, IR3, and IR4. J Virol. 1991;65:976.
69. Dummer JS, Armstrong J, Somers J, et al. Transmission of infection with herpes simplex virus by renal transplantation. J Infect Dis. 1987;155:202.
70. Pereira BJ, Milford EL, Kirkman RL, et al. Prevalence of hepatitis C virus RNA in organ donors positive for hepatitis C antibody and in the recipients of their organs. N Engl J Med. 1992;327:910.
71. Pereira BJ, Wright TL, Schmid CH, Levey AS. A controlled study of hepatitis C transmission by organ transplantation. Lancet. 1995;345:1174.
72. Bouthot BA, Murthy BV, Schmid CH, et al. Long-term follow-up of hepatitis C virus infection among organ transplant recipients: Implications for policies on organ procurement. Transplantation. 1997;63:849.
73. Lake KD, Smith CI, LaForest SK, et al. Policies regarding the transplantation of hepatitis C–positive candidates and donor organs. J Heart Lung Transplant. 1997;16:917.
74. Wolf JL, Perkins HA, Schreeder MT, Vincenti F. The transplanted kidney as a source of hepatitis B infection. Ann Intern Med. 1979;91:412.
75. Wachs ME, Amend WJ, Ascher NL, et al. The risk of transmission of hepatitis B from HBsAg(−), HBcAb(+), HBIgM(−) organ donors. Transplantation. 1995;59:230.
76. Dodson SF, Issa S, Araya V, et al. Infectivity of hepatic allografts with antibodies to hepatitis B virus. Transplantation. 1997;64:1582.
77. Delmonico FL, Snydman DR. Organ donor screening for infectious diseases. Transplantation. 1998;65:603.
78. Erice A, Rhame FS, Heussner RC, et al. Human immunodeficiency virus infection in patients with solid-organ transplants: Report of five cases and review. Rev Infect Dis. 1991;13.
79. Anonymous. Human immunodeficiency virus infection transmitted from an organ donor screened for HIV antibody—North Carolina. MMWR Morb Mortal Wkly Rep. 1987;36:306:537.
80. Cantarovich F, Vazquez M, Garcia WD, et al. Special infections in organ transplantation in South America. Transplant Proc. 1992;24:1902.
81. Broyer M, Tete MJ, Guest G, et al. Varicella and zoster in children after kidney transplantation: Long-term results of vaccination. Pediatrics. 1997;99:35.
82. Patel R, Snydman DR, Rubin RH, et al. Cytomegalovirus prophylaxis in solid organ transplant recipients. Transplantation. 1996;61:1279.
83. Lichtenstein IH, MacGregor RR. Mycobacterial infections in renal transplant recipients: Report of five cases and review of the literature. Rev Infect Dis. 1983;5:216.
84. Antony SJ, Ynares C, Dummer JS. Isoniazid hepatotoxicity in renal transplant recipients. Clin Transplant. 1997;11:34.
85. Dummer JS, Erb S, Breinig MK, et al. Infection with human immunodeficiency virus in the Pittsburgh transplant population: A study of 583 donors and 1043 recipients, 1981–1986. Transplantation. 1989;47:134.
86. Tzakis AG, Cooper MH, Dummer JS, et al. Transplantation in HIV+ patients. Transplantation. 1990;49:354.
87. Boeckh M, Bowden RA, Goodrich JM, et al. Cytomegalovirus antigen detection in peripheral blood leukocytes after allogeneic marrow transplantation. Blood. 1992;80:1358.
88. Abecassis MM, Koffron AJ, Kaplan B, et al. The role of PCR in the diagnosis and management of CMV in solid organ recipients: What is the predictive value for the development of disease and should PCR be used to guide antiviral therapy? Transplantation. 1997;63:275.
89. The TH, Van der Ploeg M, Van den Berg AP, et al. Direct detection of cytomegalovirus in peripheral blood leukocytes: A review of the antigenemia assay and polymerase chain reaction. Transplantation. 1992;54:193.
90. Erice A, Holm MA, Gill PC, et al. Cytomegalovirus (CMV) antigenemia assay is more sensitive than shell vial cultures for rapid detection of CMV in polymorphonuclear blood leukocytes. J Clin Microbiol. 1992;30:2822.
91. Einsele H, Ehninger G, Hebart H, et al. Polymerase chain reaction monitoring reduces the incidence of cytomegalovirus disease and the duration and side effects of antiviral therapy after bone marrow transplantation. Blood. 1995;86:2815.
92. Fox JC, Kidd IM, Griffiths PD, et al. Longitudinal analysis of cytomegalovirus load in renal transplant recipients using a quantitative polymerase chain reaction: Correlation with disease. J Gen Virol. 1995;76:309.
93. Goodrich JM, Mori M, Gleaves CA, et al. Early treatment with ganciclovir to prevent cytomegalovirus disease after allogeneic bone marrow transplantation. N Engl J Med. 1991;325:1601.
94. Singh N, Yu VL, Mieles L. High dose acyclovir compared with short course preemptive ganciclovir therapy to prevent cytomegalovirus disease in liver transplant recipients. Ann Intern Med. 1994;120:375.
95. Chazouilleres O, Kim M, Combs C, et al. Quantitation of hepatitis C virus RNA in liver transplant recipients. Gastroenterology. 1994.106:994.
96. Grellier L, Mutimer D, Ahmed M, et al. Lamivudine prophylaxis against reinfection in liver transplantation for hepatitis B cirrhosis. Lancet. 1996;348:1212.
97. Huzly D, Neifer S, Reinke P, et al. Routine immunizations in adult renal transplant recipients. Transplantation. 1997;63:839.
98. Grekas D, Alivanis P, Kiriazopoulou V, et al. Influenza vaccination in renal transplant patients is safe and serologically effective. Int J Clin Pharmacol Ther Toxicol. 1993;31:553.
99. Pabico RC, Douglas RG, Betts RF, et al. Antibody response to influenza vaccination in renal transplant patients: Correlation with allograft function. Ann Intern Med. 1976;85:431.
100. Huang KL, Armstrong JA, Ho M. Antibody response after influenza immunization in renal transplant patients receiving cyclosporin A or azathioprine. Infect Immun. 1983;40:421.
101. Blumberg EA, Albano C, Pruett T, et al. The immunogenicity of influenza virus vaccine in solid organ transplant recipients. Clin Infect Dis. 1996;22:295.
102. Briggs WA, Rozek RJ, Migdal SD, et al. Influenza vaccination in kidney transplant recipients: Cellular and humoral immune responses. Ann Intern Med. 1980;92:471.
103. Rand EB, McCarthy CA, Whitington PF. Measles vaccination after orthotopic liver transplantation. J Pediatr. 1993;123:87.
104. Zamora I, Simon JM, Da Silva ME, Piqueras AI. Attenuated varicella virus vaccine in children with renal transplants. Pediatr Nephrol. 1994;8:190.
105. Tolkoff-Rubin NE, Cosimi AB, Russell PS, Rubin RH. A controlled study of trimethoprim-sulfamethoxazole prophylaxis of urinary tract infection in renal transplant recipients. Rev Infect Dis. 1982;4:614.
106. Fox BC, Sollinger HW, Belzer FO, Maki DG. A prospective, randomized, double-blind study of trimethoprim-sulfamethoxazole for prophylaxis of infection in renal transplantation: Clinical efficacy, absorption of trimethoprim-sulfamethoxazole, effects on the microflora, and the cost-benefit of prophylaxis. Am J Med. 1990;89:255.
107. Andreone PA, Olivari MT, Elick B, et al. Reduction of infectious complications following heart transplantation with triple-drug immunotherapy. J Heart Transplant. 1986;5:13.
108. Cruciani M, Rampazzo R, Malena M, et al. Prophylaxis with fluoroquinolones for bacterial infections in neutropenic patients: A meta-analysis. Clin Infect Dis. 1996;23:795.
109. Smyth RL, Higenbottam TW, Scott JP, et al. Herpes simplex virus infection in heart-lung transplant recipients. Transplantation. 1990;49:735.
110. Saral R, Burns WH, Laskin OL, et al. Acyclovir prophylaxis of herpes-simplex-virus infections. N Engl J Med. 1981;305:63.
111. Meyers JD, Reed EC, Shepp DH, et al. Acyclovir for prevention of cytomegalovirus infection and disease after allogeneic marrow transplantation. N Engl J Med. 1988;318:70.
112. Balfour HH, Jr, Chace BA, Stapleton JT, et al. A randomized, placebo-controlled trial of oral acyclovir for the prevention of cytomegalovirus disease in recipients of renal allografts. N Engl J Med. 1989;320:1381.
113. Winston DJ, Ho WG, Bartoni K, et al. Ganciclovir prophylaxis of cytomegalovirus infection and disease in allogeneic bone marrow transplant recipients: Results of a placebo-controlled, double-blind trial. Ann Intern Med. 1993;118:179.
114. Goodrich JM, Bowden RA, Fisher L, et al. Ganciclovir prophylaxis to prevent cytomegalovirus disease after allogeneic marrow transplant. Ann Intern Med. 1993;118:173.
115. Merigan TC, Renlund DG, Keay S, et al. A controlled trial of ganciclovir to prevent cytomegalovirus disease after heart transplantation. N Engl J Med. 1992;326:1182.
116. Winston DJ, Wirin D, Shaked A, Busuttil RW. Randomised comparison of ganciclovir and high-dose acyclovir for long-term cytomegalovirus prophylaxis in liver-transplant recipients. Lancet. 1995;346:69.
117. Gane E, Saliba F, Valdecasas GJ, et al. Randomised trial of efficacy and safety of oral ganciclovir in the prevention of cytomegalovirus disease in liver-transplant recipients. Lancet. 1997;350:1729.
118. Lowance D, Neumayer H-H, Legendre CM, et al. Valacyclovir for the prevention of cytomegalovirus disease after renal transplantation. N Engl J Med. 1999;340:1462.
119. Stiehm ER, Ashida E, Kim KS, et al. Intravenous immunoglobulins as therapeutic agents. Ann Intern Med. 1987;107:367.
120. Snydman DR, Werner BG, Heinze-Lacey B, et al. Use of cytomegalovirus immune globulin to prevent cytomegalovirus disease in renal-transplant recipients. N Engl J Med. 1987;317:1049.
121. Snydman DR, Werner BG, Dougherty NN, et al. Cytomegalovirus immune globulin prophylaxis in liver transplantation: A randomized, double-blind, placebo-controlled trial. The Boston Center for Liver Transplantation CMVIG Study Group. Ann Intern Med. 1993;119:984.
122. Gombert ME, DuBouchet L, Aulicino TM, Butt KM. A comparative trial of clotrimazole troches and oral nystatin suspension in recipients of renal transplants: Use in prophylaxis of oropharyngeal candidiasis. JAMA. 1987;258:2553.
123. Goodman JL, Winston DJ, Greenfield RA, et al. A controlled trial of fluconazole to prevent fungal infections in patients undergoing bone marrow transplantation. N Engl J Med. 1992;326:845.
124. Perfect JR, Klotman ME, Gilbert CC, et al. Prophylactic intravenous amphotericin B in neutropenic autologous bone marrow transplant recipients. J Infect Dis. 1992;165:891.
125. Lumbreras C, Cuervas-Mons V, Jara P, et al. Randomized trial of fluconazole versus nystatin for the prophylaxis of *Candida* infection following liver transplantation. J Infect Dis. 1996;174:583.
126. Tollemar J, Hockerstedt K, Ericzon BG, et al. Liposomal amphotericin B prevents

invasive fungal infections in liver transplant recipients: A randomized, placebo-controlled study. Transplantation. 1995;59:45.
127. Wreghitt TG, Gray JJ, Pavel P, et al. Efficacy of pyrimethamine for the prevention of donor-acquired *Toxoplasma gondii* infection in heart and heart-lung transplant patients. Transpl Int. 1992;5:197.
128. Carr A, Tindall B, Brew BJ, et al. Low-dose trimethoprim-sulfmethoxazole for toxoplasmic encephalitis in patients with AIDS. Ann Intern Med. 1992;117:106.
129. Wiesner RH, Hermans PE, Rakela J, et al. Selective bowel decontamination to decrease gram-negative aerobic bacterial and *Candida* colonization and prevent infection after orthotopic liver transplantation. Transplantation. 1988;45:570.
130. Peterson PK, Anderson RC. Infection in renal transplant recipients: Current approaches to diagnosis, therapy, and prevention. Am J Med. 1986;81:2.
131. Singh NS, Carrigan DR. Human herpesvirus-6 in transplantation: An emerging pathogen. Ann Intern Med. 1996;124:1065.

Chapter 303

Infections in Recipients of Blood and Marrow Transplantation

JO-ANNE VAN BURIK
DANIEL WEISDORF

The clinical approach to infections in the bone marrow transplantation (BMT) patient involves an understanding of basic transplantation techniques, clinical syndromes, patterns of immunosuppression at different time points after transplantation, the natural history of individual infections, and the mechanisms underlying immune system reconstitution after transplantation. In general, the dominant elements of infectious risks for bacterial, viral, fungal, and parasitic infections after BMT depend on the pre-transplantation exposure history (viral serostatus), whether the transplant is from an autologous or an allogeneic donor source, and the day after transplantation on which the infection occurs. The distinguishing determinant of infectious risk between autologous and allogeneic grafts is the associated risk incurred by ongoing immunosuppression from graft-versus-host disease (GVHD) and its therapy; differing means of humoral and cellular immune reconstitution also affect the risk. The time period after transplantation defines eras of differing transplantation complications and the evolution of the slowly resolving post-transplantation immunologic deficiency: neutropenia, lymphopenia, and/or hypogammaglobulinemia. Many post-transplantation complications mimic infectious processes, and multiple infections may occur in the same patient at the same time. Therefore, the BMT patient should be examined in the context of pre-transplantation infectious disease serologies, conditioning regimen, available culture data from nonsterile mucosal surfaces, contemporary transplant complications, previous and recent infections, and the current degree and duration of neutropenia and cellular immunodeficiency.

BASIC TRANSPLANTATION TECHNIQUES

The technique of blood stem cell or bone marrow transplantation involves the intravenous delivery of hematopoietic stem cells to a recipient whose hematopoietic and immune systems have been ablated by a cytotoxic preparative regimen given over the 4 to 10 days before transplantation, commonly referred to as the conditioning regimen. Stem cells are obtained from bone marrow, peripheral blood, or umbilical cord blood.[1] In the last decade, the traditional expression *bone marrow transplantation* (BMT) has been replaced by the term *blood and marrow transplantation* (also abbreviated BMT). BMT is a treatment option for hematologic and oncologic syndromes including aplastic anemia, leukemias, lymphomas, immunodeficiency syndromes, inborn errors of metabolism, and some solid tumors (e.g., breast cancer), and it is currently used investigationally for diseases such as scleroderma and multiple sclerosis.

The conditioning regimen used to prepare the host is a major determinant of outcome, because of variable host tissue injury and the potential for induction of prolonged immunodeficiency. Conditioning regimens may consist of chemotherapeutic agents alone or of combined radiochemotherapy that damages mucosal surfaces, facilitating transmucosal origin of blood-stream infections. The transplantation complications that affect the infectious morbidity and mortality of the BMT recipient include the effects of high-dose cytoreductive therapy, such as mucositis, hemorrhagic cystitis, and diarrhea, and veno-occlusive disease (VOD); GVHD; and relapse of the underlying oncologic disease.

Chemotherapy. Busulfan is a commonly used oral alkylating agent that is toxic to myeloid stem cells and is associated with skin hyperpigmentation, nausea, vomiting, interstitial pneumonitis, and seizures.[2] When busulfan is combined with two other alkylating agents, melphalan and thiotepa, the metabolism of these agents is altered, resulting in accentuation of the expected skin and gut toxicity and late-onset VOD.[3, 4] Cytoxan-containing regimens predispose to hemorrhagic cystitis.[5] Horse anti-thymocyte globulin (ATG), which alters the function of or eliminates T lymphocytes, is used for the conditioning regimen for aplastic anemia and for GVHD treatment.[6, 7] Chills and fever commonly occur among patients receiving ATG and can be managed by symptomatic treatment and slowing of the infusion. Serum sickness, a syndrome of fever, arthralgias, and rash, can occur with subsequent ATG doses; it is treated with corticosteroid therapy.

Irradiation. Total body irradiation (TBI) may be administered as a single dose, "fractionated" in multiple doses given once daily over 6 or 7 days, or "hyperfractionated" in multiple doses given two or more times a day over several days. Diarrhea occurs in virtually all patients in the first week after irradiation; it may be treated symptomatically while stool culture is pending to exclude infectious causes. Severe mucositis occurs in most irradiated patients and is aggravated by prolonged neutropenia and the use of methotrexate. As long as the bleeding and oral inflammation do not compromise the patient's airway, mucositis is treated symptomatically. Single-dose TBI is currently given only in exceptional cases, but these patients may be febrile in the hours after treatment and may develop symptomatic parotitis or pancreatitis.[8, 9]

Human Leukocyte Antigen Matching. In general, engraftment is most rapid when the patient and donor are completely matched at all genetic human leukocyte antigen (HLA) loci (i.e., the transplanted cells are from an identical twin [syngeneic] or from the patient being transplanted [autologous]). Allogeneic BMT (sibling or unrelated donor) has the highest chance of success when fully matched HLA sibling donors are used, but less than 30% of intended recipients in North America have a matched sibling donor available. For HLA-mismatched family or unrelated donors, incompatibility and risk of infection can be described in terms of vectors. Incompatibility in the donor defines the genetic risk of rejection, which may result in delayed engraftment or graft failure.[10] Incompatibility in the recipient defines the genetic risk of GVHD, resulting in continued immunosuppression and its attendant complications. Both vectors of incompatibility may be present for a single transplanted patient in varying degrees, proportional to the number of mismatched immunodominant alleles.

Prevention of Infection. Preventative strategies include prevention of exposure, enhancement of host immune reconstitution, prophylaxis during high-risk periods with targeted antimicrobial chemotherapy, and suppression of subclinical infection with preemptive therapy. Prophylaxis or preemptive strategies are more effective than treatment after infection is established, and the mortality rate for patients with established infections continues to be high despite available therapy. After mucositis has cleared, oral therapy is preferred.

CLINICAL SYNDROMES UNIQUE TO THE BONE MARROW TRANSPLANTATION PATIENT

Hemorrhagic Cystitis. Hemorrhagic cystitis is a frequent complication and has both noninfectious and infectious causes.[5] Cystitis within 1 week after marrow infusion is usually caused by the administration of high-dose cyclophosphamide in the conditioning regimen. Much later after transplantation, GVHD can be a contributing cause.[11] The majority of infectious agents are viral, either the polyomaviruses BK or JC[12, 13] or adenovirus,[14–16] although herpes simplex virus (HSV) and cytomegalovirus (CMV)[17] occur with lower frequencies. Polyomaviruses are shed in the urine in up to 44% of BMT patients without clinical symptoms (see Chapter 134).[18] There is currently no specific treatment other than supportive care for viruria caused by BK or JC virus or adenovirus.

Veno-occlusive Disease. VOD refers to a syndrome of liver toxicity that occurs at any time after the onset of the conditioning regimen until approximately day 20; it is characterized by hepatomegaly, 5% or greater weight gain, and hyperbilirubinemia greater than 2 mg/dL.[19] The risk of severe VOD is increased by preexisting liver dysfunction, and death occurs in approximately 5 to 10% of patients with VOD. Severe VOD, with marked hyperbilirubinemia or ascites, leads to multiorgan failure involving the kidneys, heart, and lungs. Clinical predictors of severe VOD include higher-dose cytoreductive therapy (radiation regimens containing >13 Gy), hepatitis present before cytoreductive therapy, and previous radiation therapy to the liver. Conditions that may mimic VOD include cholestasis in patients with septicemia, hepatic infiltration secondary to infection or tumor, pericarditis, and intra-abdominal disease such as pancreatitis, peritonitis, or cholecystitis. Additionally, early GVHD and cyclosporine cholestasis are noninfectious causes of liver toxicity that may coexist with VOD. If there is doubt about the diagnosis and the disease is severe enough to warrant aggressive diagnostic measures, then liver biopsy with immunohistochemical staining and culture to rule out infectious causes may be indicated. Hepatotoxic and nephrotoxic drugs should be avoided in patients with VOD.

Graft-versus-Host Disease. GVHD is the chief complication after allogeneic transplantation. Donor T lymphocytes mount an immune attack against the recipient's tissues. Clinical manifestations of this disorder include fever, rash, cholestatic hepatitis, diarrhea, and pancytopenia. Cyclosporine is an effective immunosuppressive agent for the prevention of GVHD and is usually started before transplantation. GVHD itself can compound and prolong post-BMT immunodeficiency. The corticosteroids used for prevention or treatment of GVHD may impair phagocytic function and may lead to lymphoid immune suppression. Patients with chronic GVHD have an added risk for infection with encapsulated bacteria such as *Streptococcus pneumoniae*,[20] *Neisseria* spp., and *Haemophilus influenzae*.

Hepatitis. Clinical hepatitis in BMT recipients can range from fever associated with abdominal pain to fulminant hepatitis.[21] Infectious hepatitis must be distinguished from several common noninfectious causes, including liver dysfunction related to the conditioning regimen (i.e., VOD), acute GVHD, cholestatic liver injury related to sepsis, and chemical hepatitis related to either drugs or hyperalimentation. Clinically important viral hepatitis syndromes after transplantation include acquisition or reactivation of infection with hepatitis B virus (HBV),[22] hepatitis C virus (HCV),[23–25] HSV,[26] varicella-zoster virus (VZV),[27, 28] adenovirus,[29, 30] and, rarely, CMV. Disseminated VZV and adenovirus infections may be associated with elevations in the serum aminotransferase levels that precede the appearance of other disease manifestations by several days. In the short term, HCV infection may lead to an increased incidence of VOD early after transplantation.

In the long term, reactivation of HBV is more likely than HCV to result in fulminant hepatitis, although this outcome occurs in the minority of infected patients. Therefore, the finding of a positive hepatitis B surface antigen is not considered a contraindication to marrow transplantation.[22, 31] These patients should be monitored for hepatitis B DNA by polymerase chain reaction (PCR) after transplantation. For recipients who have transient hepatitis or a persistently positive HBV DNA PCR study after transplantation, the risk of fatal liver disease is approximately 12%.[32] Among patients with a negative hepatitis B surface antigen but a positive core antibody, reactivation of latent infection can rarely occur. In addition, HBV can be transmitted from a surface antigen– or core antibody–positive donor to either a naïve or a surface antibody–positive recipient. If the recipient had no serologic markers of HBV infection before transplantation, the subsequent infection is more likely to have severe consequences.[31] Experimental antiviral prophylaxis strategies for a positive donor include administration of interferon-α[33] or vaccination; for a surface antigen–positive recipient, one of the nucleoside analogues lamivudine[34] or famiciclovir[35] may be used.

Pneumonia Syndromes. Infectious pneumonias must be distinguished from noninfectious pulmonary complications after BMT, which can include pulmonary edema, alveolar hemorrhage, drug reactions, adult respiratory distress syndrome, idiopathic pneumonia syndrome, bronchiolitis obliterans, and chronic GVHD.[36] Management of noninfectious pneumonias requires exclusion of lower respiratory tract infection, and their pathophysiology may be distinct in that the therapeutic response to high-dose corticosteroids may be more likely.[37, 38] Diffuse alveolar hemorrhage begins insidiously with dyspnea and is distinguished from other non-infectious pneumonias by repeated bloody return washings during bronchoscopic examination.[39, 40] Idiopathic pneumonia syndrome is a process of widespread alveolar injury that is characterized clinically by diffuse interstitial infiltrates and varying degrees of respiratory failure in the absence of active lower respiratory tract infection. It is thought to be related to the chemotherapy and/or TBI used as part of the conditioning regimen.[41] Idiopathic pneumonia syndrome occurs in 8 to 17% of patients, has an equal frequency after autologous and allogeneic transplantation, and is associated with a mortality rate of 60 to 80%. Idiopathic pneumonia syndrome occurs classically in two peaks, one in the first few weeks and the other in the second and third month after transplantation.[42–44]

Diarrhea. Diarrhea after transplantation is primarily a result of noninfectious causes such as regimen-related toxicity and GVHD.[45] Diarrhea is associated with infection in less than 15% of cases,[46] the common infectious agents being *Clostridium difficile*, adenovirus, rotavirus, or coxsackievirus.[47, 48] *C. difficile* is seen with increasing frequency.[49] Outbreaks of diarrhea have been reported for *Cryptosporidia*[50] and enterovirus.[48]

Rash. Skin eruptions are often noninfectious, occurring as a direct result of radiation effect from conditioning therapy or secondary to GVHD or drug allergy. Rashes from conditioning regimens can result in the sudden onset of marked erythema over large areas of the body and blistering on the hands and feet. A skin biopsy can assist in distinguishing infectious from noninfectious causes of rash, and all lesions suspected to be infectious should be cultured or biopsied. The most common infectious causes are VZV, catheter-related exit site or tunnel infections, primary cutaneous fungal infections,[51] and secondary cutaneous manifestations of disseminated bacterial or fungal[52] infections. Focal areas of bacterial cellulitis may occur on the lower extremities in the setting of fluid gain from VOD with secondary lymphedema and impaired venous return.

Osteomyelitis. Osteomyelitis can rarely follow marrow aspiration from the sternum[53] or marrow harvest from the iliac crest.[54] When prolonged pain and fever occur after bone marrow harvest, osteomyelitis caused by *Staphylococcus aureus* should be considered.

PATTERNS OF IMMUNOSUPPRESSION AT DIFFERENT TIME POINTS AFTER BONE MARROW TRANSPLANTATION

Historically, three risk periods of immunologic deficiency occur predictably in recipients of BMT. They are the pre-engraftment period, the early postengraftment period (until day 100), and the late period (after day 100). An understanding of the immune deficiencies in each risk period and the period of peak risk for individual infections that are observed with standard infection prophylaxis helps the clinician recognize uncommon presentations of these infectious pathogens (Table 303–1).

Pre-engraftment Risk Period. The pre-engraftment risk period begins with the onset of conditioning therapy and continues until approximately day 30 after transplantation. Bacterial infections are common during this time of profound neutropenia and lymphopenia, requiring prophylactic and promptly administered empiric systemic antibiotic therapy (see Chapter 300). Prophylactic systemic antibiotics (e.g., trimethoprim-sulfamethoxazole [TMP-SMX], ciprofloxacin, penicillin) can be administered when the neutrophil count drops to less than 500/mm^3 and continued until the neutrophil count recovers to prevent bacterial infection (see Chapter 298). Gastrointestinal decontamination with nonabsorbable antibiotics was used in the past but is now rarely done.

Prophylactic antibiotic use has shifted the spectrum of gastrointestinal flora to potentially pathogenic organisms such as *C. difficile*, and the etiologic agents of bacteremia have shifted to include less common gram-negative bacilli (e.g., *Escherichia coli*, *Klebsiella*, *Enterobacter*, *Pseudomonas*, *Citrobacter*, *Acinetobacter*). Gram-positive organisms, especially coagulase-negative staphylococci and viridans streptococci, are even more often isolated from febrile neutropenic BMT recipients. Mechanical barrier defects caused by mucositis and central catheters predispose patients to blood-stream infections by allowing access for skin-colonizing organisms and gastrointestinal mucosal flora to otherwise sterile body sites. Recipients of autologous/syngeneic and allogeneic grafts develop a similar spectrum of infections during the pre-engraftment period; the major transplant-related complications occurring in this risk period (mucositis, severe neutropenia, and VOD) are similarly frequent in all types of transplants. However, the less frequent use of TBI and the more rapid neutrophil recovery often observed after autologous peripheral blood stem cell transplantation have markedly decreased the risks of serious bacteremia for this subpopulation of patients.

Adjunctive therapy with granulocyte transfusions has been used in some centers for treatment of infections that develop during neutropenia. Although the technology of granulocyte transfusion is improving, evidence for efficacy and therefore the indications for use of this expensive and labor-intensive supportive measure are not available.

Routine culture of hematopoietic progenitor cell products yields low rates of recovery of bacterial organisms. The American Association of Blood Banks requires routine culture of hematopoietic progenitor cells before BMT, but patients receiving culture-positive harvests usually do so without clinically adverse outcomes.[55, 56]

HSV predictably reactivates during this risk period in 80% of those patients who are HSV-seropositive, with most infections occurring before week 4 after transplantation, although use of prophylactic acyclovir at 400 to 800 mg/day (5 mg/kg twice daily for children) has minimized this clinical infection.[57] Fungal infection with blood-stream and hepatosplenic candidiasis and early-onset aspergillosis also occur in approximately 10% of patients during neu-

TABLE 303–1 Infections after Blood Stem Cell or Marrow Transplantation, in Order of Occurrence

Organism	Peak Time Period of Risk (weeks after BMT)	Usual Prophylaxis	Incidence (%)
Pre-engraftment risk period (1–4 wk)			
Herpes simplex virus (seropositive)	1–2[88, 89]	Acyclovir	5–9[90]
Herpes simplex virus (seronegative)	—	—	<2[57]
Gram-positive bacteremia (most commonly coagulase-negative staphylococci, *Streptococcus viridans*)	1–4	Prophylactic broad-spectrum antibiotics	20–30
Gram-negative bacteremia	1–4	Prophylactic broad-spectrum antibiotics	5–10
Candida	1–4[150]	Fluconazole	<1 (systemic infection),[143, 144] 30 (colonization)
Aspergillus	1–4, 12–15[160]	—	4–12[160–163]
Respiratory viruses	2–5[124]	Isolation, hand washing	15[122–128]
Idiopathic pneumonia syndrome	2–4[42]	—	8–17[42]
Postengraftment risk period (4–12 wk)			
Cytomegalovirus (seropositive)	7–15[68, 95, 101]	Ganciclovir or foscarnet	<5 (disease)[68, 93] 5–10 (viremia), up to 40 (antigenemia)[95, 96]
Cytomegalovirus (seronegative)	—	Blood product screening or filtration	1–3[87]
BK virus	—	—	44–47 (shedding)[12, 18]
Toxoplasma gondii (seropositive)	2–8[189, 192]	—*	2–7[189, 190]
Late risk period (12–52 wk)			
Varicella zoster virus (seropositive)	12–52[115, 116]	—	38–50[115–117]
Varicella zoster virus (seronegative)	—	—	<3[115]
Streptococcus pneumoniae†	—	Vaccination, penicillin‡	—
Haemophilus influenzae†	—	Vaccination, penicillin‡	—
Neisseria meningitidis†	—	Penicillin‡	—
Infections that span multiple risk periods			
Pneumocystis carinii	4–104[59]	Trimethoprim/sulfamethoxazole	<1
Adenovirus	—	—	4–5[14, 121]
Human herpesvirus-6	—	Ganciclovir or foscarnet	<2[136]
Epstein-Barr virus	—	—	<1[130]
Nocardia	—	—	<1[79, 80]
Legionella	—	—	<1[77]
Mycobacterium spp.	—	PPD screening	<1[73–75]
Listeria monocytogenes	—	—	<1[83, 84]

*Prophylaxis with pyrimethamine/sulfadoxine[193] may be used for seropositive patients in countries with a high rate of seroprevalence.
†Risk increased in patients with chronic graft-versus-host disease.
‡Undetermined efficacy for transplant recipients.

tropenia. The risk is greater for patients with slow engraftment or extended neutropenia before transplantation. With fluconazole prophylaxis (200 to 400 mg/day), *Candida albicans* infections have been for the most part eliminated during this risk period, although *Candida krusei* and *Candida glabrata* have emerged as fluconazole-resistant pathogens. Use of the hematopoietic growth factors granulocyte and granulocyte-macrophage colony-stimulating factors has reduced the incidence of bacteremia by shortening the duration of neutropenia, but it has not been clearly shown to improve outcome in established infections.

Postengraftment Risk Period. The postengraftment period begins with neutrophil recovery and continues until day 100, when early B- and T-lymphocyte functional recovery is apparent. Reconstituted T lymphocytes have abnormal function for approximately 18 months, as evidenced by in vitro antigen and mitogen proliferative responses. However, T-lymphocyte reconstitution may be blunted by the effects of GVHD or CMV and their attendant treatments (corticosteroids, cyclosporine, anti–T-lymphocyte therapy, and ganciclovir[58]). As a result, the rate of infection during this risk period is higher among recipients of allogeneic grafts, who are more likely to develop GVHD or CMV, than among recipients of autologous/syngeneic grafts. Another consequence of GVHD during this risk period is disruption of the gastrointestinal mucosa, potentially leading to bacteremia or fungemia from transmural entry of pathogens.

Prophylaxis of *Pneumocystis carinii* infection with TMP-SMX, dapsone, or pentamidine is required for 6 to 12 months, or longer if chronic GVHD is continuing.[59]

Reactivation of CMV predictably occurs in 20 to 40% of patients who are CMV-seropositive and in seronegative recipients who have seropositive donors. Surveillance for reactivation of CMV has been improved by the use of scheduled testing of peripheral blood leukocytes for CMV, using sensitive diagnostic methods such as pp65 antigenemia or plasma PCR.[60–64] Antiviral prophylaxis or ganciclovir therapy initiated preemptively at subclinical indications of reactivation has reduced the incidence of end-organ disease caused by CMV.[61] Finally, late-onset aspergillosis may also occur during this risk period in 10 to 15% of patients, especially those with continuing GVHD, those receiving high-dose corticosteroids, and those with poor graft function. No effective prophylaxis regimen directed toward molds has been developed to date for this risk period.

Late Risk Period. The late post-transplantation risk period begins at approximately day 100 and ends when the patient regains normal immunity, 18 to 36 months after BMT.[65–67] In general, immune recovery is substantial by the end of the first year after transplantation as long as the patient is no longer taking immunosuppressive medication and remains free from GVHD. For patients with continuing chronic GVHD, this period persists for as long as therapy for chronic GVHD is required and includes dysfunction of cellular and humoral immunity as well as macrophage function. VZV reactivation, infections with encapsulated bacteria (*S. pneumoniae*, *Neisseria*, and *H. influenzae*), and invasive aspergillosis may develop in this late risk period. The most common clinical syndromes include sinusitis, bronchitis, pneumonia, and otitis media caused by respiratory viruses or bacteria. With use of extended ganciclovir prophylaxis in the postengraftment period, CMV disease may develop in this late period, suggesting the need for continuing CMV surveillance (pp65 antigenemia or plasma PCR) in the seropositive recipient with chronic GVHD.[68] Late infections may be more common among patients with unrelated donors compared with patients whose donors were family members, even in the absence of GVHD.[65] Approximately 50% of late pneumonias in patients with ongoing chronic GVHD are caused by noninfectious interstitial pneumonitis. Lung histopathology shows obliterative bronchitis that responds to corticosteroid therapy.

NATURAL HISTORY OF INDIVIDUAL INFECTIONS AFTER BONE MARROW TRANSPLANTATION

With advances in infection prevention strategies, the risk periods for some infections are changing. Therefore it is important to understand the natural history of individual infections as they occur in the BMT recipient and how the natural history differs from that in other immunocompromised patient populations. Infections that occur with a high incidence among BMT recipients justify prophylaxis during the applicable risk period or empiric treatment during the course of applicable clinical scenarios of infection (see Table 303–1).

Bacterial Infections

Gram-positive organisms account for half of bacteremias occurring after BMT.[69] Although the skin has been thought to be the primary reservoir for these organisms, the gastrointestinal tract may be an additional source. *Staphylococcus epidermidis* is the most common species recovered in culture, followed closely by *Streptococcus pyogenes*, *Streptococcus mitis*, *Streptococcus pneumoniae*, and *Enterococcus* spp. Unlike catheter-associated infections with *S. aureus*, *Candida* spp., or some gram-negative bacilli, most gram-positive bacteremias can be successfully managed without removal of the intravascular device. If the patient is not responding to initial antibiotic management or if there is tenderness or erythema along the tunnel tract, the catheter may have to be removed. Rarely, adjunctive surgical débridement of the skin tunnel is needed. Catheter removal and surgical débridement are often required when the infection is caused by nontuberculous mycobacteria.

Gram-negative organisms are the second most frequent cause of blood-stream infection. The incidence of infection with *Pseudomonas* spp. is low, presumably because of the use of antipseudomonal antibiotics for prophylactic therapy. Although bacteremias have historically occurred during the neutropenic period, bacteremias continue to develop in patients with long-term central intravenous catheters, in those patients with ongoing immunosuppression resulting from GVHD or its therapy, and in those with neutropenia secondary to graft failure or drug-related marrow suppression (e.g., ganciclovir).

Encapsulated Bacteria. For patients who experience chronic GVHD or are otherwise asplenic, the risk for bacterial infection with encapsulated organisms is increased, and penicillin or macrolide prophylaxis may be indicated until immunosuppression is discontinued.[66]

Viridans Streptococci. Viridans streptococcal bacteremias may carry a high mortality rate, especially in children early after BMT.[70, 71] However, these highly antibiotic-sensitive organisms require therapy and should be viewed as virulent, even in the absence of marked clinical symptoms. Oral ulcerations caused by HSV reactivation during conditioning are thought to be an entry point, corroborated by a decreased incidence of viridans streptococcal septicemia after active prophylaxis of HSV infections with acyclovir.[72]

Mycobacteria. Mycobacteria are an infrequent cause of infection after BMT but are important to identify because treatment requires medication that would not be used empirically. The rapidly growing nontuberculous mycobacteria are responsible for catheter exit site infections, tunnel infections, bacteremia, or pneumonia, whereas infection with *M. tuberculosis* rarely occurs as pneumonia.[73–75] Clinically significant infection can be prevented by antituberculous prophylaxis for patients having reactive purified protein derivative (PPD) tests. Potential transplantation patients and their donors should receive PPD screening if they are from countries where tuberculosis is common, or if they have a history of abnormal chest radiographic findings before transplantation, recent travel to a foreign country for longer than 3 months, close contact with another person with known or suspected tuberculosis, employment in an institution with tuberculous clients, alcoholism or intravenous drug use, or HIV-seropositivity. PPD screening should be deferred if there is a history of past documented tuberculosis, past treatment for tuberculosis, or a well-documented positive PPD. For patients with no signs of active tuberculosis and no previous antituberculous therapy but a reactive PPD, a chest radiograph and liver function tests should be obtained in addition to peritransplantation and post-transplantation prophylaxis with 1 year of isoniazid and pyridoxine.

Intracellular Bacteria. Legionellosis[76–78] and nocardiosis[79, 80] can both manifest as lung nodules in the BMT patient. Detection of *Legionella* by direct fluorescent antibody (DFA) assays has proved unreliable in the BMT setting owing to a high proportion of disease caused by rare *Legionella* species not detectable by DFA. These species include *Legionella feeleii*, *Legionella (Tatlockia) micdadei* and *Legionella bozemanii*. Infection can persist or relapse after 3 weeks of appropriate antimicrobial therapy, suggesting that prolonged antibiotic treatment is indicated for BMT recipients with legionellosis.[76, 77] Medical therapy for nocardiosis often consists of administration of sulfonamide in combination with a synergistic agent; adjunctive surgical débridement may be useful for catheter-related infections with this organism. The role of other intracellular bacterial agents as pathogens has not been well defined, but *Chlamydia trachomatis*[81] and *Mycoplasma hominis*[82] may manifest as interstitial pneumonia, and *Listeria monocytogenes* may manifest as bacteremia or meningitis.[83–85]

Viral Infections

Certain viral infections are preventable. Administration of acyclovir for HSV-seropositive patients during the pre-engraftment period is generally widely accepted. Screened or filtered blood product transfusions for CMV-seronegative patients have proved especially effective in preventing transfusion-acquired CMV infections.[86, 87] Periodic CMV diagnostic surveillance (e.g., weekly) for CMV-seropositive patients during the postengraftment period and prompt institution of antiviral therapy are essential. Strict hand washing and avoidance of crowds to prevent transmission of respiratory viral and other infections (in the hospital or ambulatory clinic) remain the mainstay of effective infection control practice for this vulnerable population.

Herpes Simplex Virus. HSV reactivation can be reduced from 80% to less than 5% in HSV-seropositive recipients during the first month after transplantation through the use of acyclovir initiated at the time of conditioning and continued until mucositis has diminished.[57, 88, 89] The majority of postengraftment HSV infections are confined to the oropharynx, although occasionally the infection extends directly to the esophagus, larynx, or skin in the perioral or perianal areas. Patients who fail to respond to acyclovir beyond engraftment, and particularly those who have received prolonged or repeated courses of acyclovir, may have acyclovir-resistant HSV. Foscarnet may be beneficial in that setting.[90, 91] Uncommonly, HSV infection causes Bell's palsy, hepatitis, or encephalitis. Valacyclovir gives predictably higher drug levels than acyclovir, but it is available only for oral administration.

Cytomegalovirus. Primary CMV infection can be reduced from a historical incidence rate of 40% to 1 to 3% in the CMV-seronegative BMT recipient by use of either seronegative or leukocyte-filtered blood products during transfusions.[86, 87] CMV reactivation can be reduced from 70% in CMV-seropositive allogeneic[92] and 45% in autologous[93, 94] patients to 5 to 20% viremia or up to 40% antigenemia by the use of preemptive antiviral therapy with ganciclovir[95, 96] or foscarnet.[98] Results with acyclovir have varied.[97, 99, 100] With the current practice of use of preemptive early ganciclovir as prophylaxis, the median time of onset of CMV end-organ disease has been delayed from 1.5 to 3 to 4 months after BMT, indicating a need for longer duration CMV surveillance in high-risk groups.[68, 95, 101]

End-organ manifestations of CMV disease include pneumonia (63%), enteritis (26%), and retinitis (5%).[68] CMV pneumonia now occurs in less than 5% of CMV-seropositive allogeneic patients who receive ganciclovir prophylaxis during the first 100 days.[99, 100] For a patient with CMV pneumonia, the mortality rate remains higher than 50%, even when prompt ganciclovir treatment is combined with intravenous immune globulin (IVIG).[68, 102, 103] CMV pneumonia is rare before engraftment.[104] Anorexia, nausea, vomiting, and sometimes diarrhea characterize CMV gastroenteritis; the diagnosis is made by endoscopy and biopsy and is often associated with GVHD of the gastrointestinal tract.[105] Although it is common in patients infected with HIV, CMV retinitis is quite uncommon among BMT recipients.[106]

Weekly screening allows identification of patients who might benefit most from preemptive therapy with ganciclovir. CMV leukocyte antigen[107] and quantitative PCR testing[63] are excellent methods for early CMV detection. Antigen testing identifies pp65, a late structural protein of CMV, in leukocytes of infected patients and can be used to guide preemptive therapy with ganciclovir[61] or foscarnet.[108] Patients must have circulating leukocytes for the test to be performed, so it is not helpful in identifying subclinical CMV infection in neutropenic patients. These patients should be screened by PCR. Some centers use PCR testing for all weekly screening; however, PCR is not quantitative and remains positive longer than antigen after ganciclovir therapy is initiated. Shell vial technology rapidly identifies CMV from clinical specimens, especially bronchoalveolar lavage and biopsy material.[109] The rapidity of shell viral centrifugation cultures may be compromised by lower sensitivity compared with conventional viral tube cultures.

Once CMV is identified by an early detection method, patients are treated with 7 to 14 days of induction ganciclovir therapy (5 mg/kg twice daily), followed by maintenance therapy (5 mg/kg once daily) for several weeks beyond negative CMV tests (Table 303–2). Maintenance therapy may need to be continued for patients with persistent antigenemia and those with profound immunosuppression from active GVHD. Oral ganciclovir has not yet been shown to be a safe and effective alternative to intravenous therapy in the BMT setting, but it could be considered for the patient who needs long-term maintenance and is otherwise taking oral medications without difficulty.

End-organ CMV disease is difficult to treat. CMV pneumonia is treated with a combination of ganciclovir at induction doses for 14 to 21 days plus IVIG, 500 mg/kg every other day for 14 to 21 days, then maintenance ganciclovir.[102] Standard IVIG is generally used, because CMV-specific immune globulin has not been shown to improve outcome. CMV enteritis is treated with intravenous ganciclovir at induction doses for 3 or more weeks without IVIG.[110] Treatment of protracted CMV enteritis might include ganciclovir plus IVIG or a longer duration of ganciclovir maintenance therapy to facilitate gastrointestinal healing.

Development of a CMV-specific cytotoxic T-lymphocyte response is critical for the reconstitution of normal immunity and protection from late CMV disease.[68, 111, 112] For patients who remain at risk for late disease, CMV monitoring should be continued beyond day 100. Patients who are treated with acyclovir followed by ganciclovir may be at increased risk of genotypic resistance; consideration should be given to assays for UL97 CMV mutations associated with ganciclovir resistance.[113] Ganciclovir therapy appears to delay recovery of cytotoxic T-lymphocyte activity, either by a direct affect on lymphocytes or by limitation of the amount of antigen exposure to lymphocytes. This immunodeficiency can be reversed when cytotoxic T lymphocytes are given adoptively, but this technology is available only at tertiary centers.[111]

Varicella-Zoster Virus. VZV occurs as primary infection (5%) or as reactivation (95%) in 40% of patients at any time point in the first year after transplantation. VZV can be effectively prevented with acyclovir prophylaxis,[114] but VZV prophylaxis is not employed at all transplantation centers because only 30% to 50% of adult patients and 25% of pediatric patients develop this infection during the first year after transplantation.[115–119] The median time of onset is 5 months after transplantation, although prolonged antiviral prophylaxis may delay the onset of VZV. Localized zoster may present atypically with a few vesicles, or skin lesions may appear as atypical vesicles, so laboratory confirmation of VZV reactivation is recommended.

Disseminated varicelliform zoster may manifest as low back pain

TABLE 303-2 Suggestions for Management of Cytomegalovirus Infection after Bone Marrow Transplantation

Indication	Strategy	Comment
Prevention		
Allogeneic transplant		
Seropositive recipient	Antigenemia- or PCR-guided early ganciclovir treatment: 5 mg/kg bid for 7–14 d, followed by 5 mg/kg daily until day 100 (or until negative PCR or antigenemia)	Some cases of CMV disease may occur shortly after ganciclovir discontinuation if based on negative PCR or antigenemia results.[61]
	or	
	Ganciclovir prophylaxis at engraftment: 5 mg/kg bid for 5 d, followed by 5 mg/kg daily on 5–6 d/wk until day 100	Recommended approach if neither PCR nor antigenemia testing is available. CMV reactivation might be delayed to later after BMT.
Seronegative recipient with seropositive donor	Antigenemia- or PCR-guided early ganciclovir treatment: 5 mg/kg bid for 7–14 d, followed by 5 mg/kg daily until day 100 (or until negative PCR or antigenemia)	Prophylaxis at engraftment is not recommended because of the low incidence of post-transplantation infection.
	and	
	Seronegative or filtered blood products	
Seronegative recipient with seronegative donor	Seronegative or filtered blood products	
Autologous transplant		
Seropositive recipient	Antigenemia- or PCR-guided early ganciclovir treatment: 5 mg/kg ganciclovir bid for 7 d, followed by 5 mg/kg daily for 14 d	Monitoring is not uniformly advocated owing to the very low risk in some settings.
Seronegative recipient	Seronegative or filtered blood products	
Treatment of disease		
CMV pneumonia	Ganciclovir: 5 mg/kg bid for 14–21 d, followed by 5 mg/kg daily for at least 3–4 wk *plus* IVIG	Extended maintenance throughout periods of severe immunosuppression (i.e., GVHD treatment) may be considered.
Gastrointestinal disease	Ganciclovir: 5 mg/kg bid for 14–21 d, followed by 5 mg/kg daily for at least 3–4 wk	If deep ulcerations are present, maintenance may be required for a longer time.
Marrow failure	Foscarnet: 90 mg/kg bid for 14 d, followed by 90 mg/kg daily for 2 weeks *plus* G-CSF	Ganciclovir *plus* IVIG has also been used.
Retinitis	Ganciclovir: 5 mg/kg bid for 14–21 d, followed by 5 mg/kg daily for at least 3–4 wk	Extended maintenance may be required.

Abbreviations: CMV, Cytomegalovirus; G-CSF, granulocyte colony-stimulating factor; GVHD, graft-versus-host disease; IVIG, intravenous immune globulin; PCR, polymerase chain reaction.
From Boeckh M. Management of cytomegalovirus infections in blood and marrow transplant recipients. In: Mills J, Volberding PA, Corey L, eds. Antiviral Chemotherapy V. Advances in Experimental Biology and Medicine, vol 458. New York: Plenum; 1999:89–110.

or acute abdominal pain preceding the appearance of skin lesions.[27] GVHD is a strong predictor of VZV dissemination, which involves visceral organs in 40 to 50% of patients.[116] Most fatal cases of disseminated or abdominal zoster occur in patients who were treated with suboptimal doses of acyclovir or for whom therapy was initiated relatively late in the course of infection.[27, 116, 118] High-dose acyclovir (10 mg/kg intravenously every 8 hours) has been the treatment of choice for disseminated VZV infection. Patients who are already seropositive can acquire a second primary VZV infection. VZV vaccination is recommended for patients who have been free of immunosuppressive medications for several months unless the underlying oncologic disease is in relapse.

VZV is a fastidious virus and may not withstand the time required to transport the specimen to the diagnostic laboratory. Lesions of herpes zoster and chickenpox are best diagnosed by scraping the base of a vesicle and examining the cells by DFA with VZV-specific monoclonal antibodies. The Tzanck smear is less sensitive and is no longer recommended. Tissue diagnosis can be made by histology, immunohistochemical techniques, or culture.

Adenovirus. Adenovirus infection reactivates in approximately 5% of allogeneic BMT patients. Chronic shedding can occur in the absence of clinical disease, but adenovirus can also be acquired from respiratory droplet transmission. Support for reactivation as the major source of infection comes from the onset of infection at 1 to 2 months after transplantation, which is similar to that of CMV. In its most common manifestation in this setting, adenovirus is a cause of hemorrhagic cystitis.[14, 15] Systemic infection in the lung, liver, and kidney occurs in 18 to 20% of infected patients.[120] GVHD is a risk factor for the occurrence of adenovirus infection after BMT.[121] Immunofluorescence, shell vial, or conventional tube culture of blood, urine, stool, or tissue can be used to diagnose adenovirus. PCR testing is unavailable for adenovirus. No effective therapy is available for adenoviral infections.

Respiratory Viruses. BMT patients who develop a respiratory viral infection typically present with rhinorrhea and nasal congestion and may also have fever, cough, throat pain, headache, or myalgias. The common pathogens in BMT patients include respiratory syncytial virus (RSV),[122, 123] parainfluenza virus,[124, 125] and, to a lesser extent, influenza virus[126] and rhinovirus. Respiratory virus infections commonly occur during the winter season and cause pneumonia in up to 50% of patients.[120–128] In contrast, parainfluenza 3 virus infections may occur throughout the year, and nosocomial outbreaks of RSV have occurred outside the established winter season. Influenza, most often type A, infrequently progresses to pneumonia. Prophylactic or early initiation of amantadine or rimantadine therapy during outbreaks seems reasonable, although evidence of efficacy in the immunosuppressed host is not available.[126, 128] The role of rhinovirus has not been well described.

RSV and parainfluenza are associated with the highest incidence of progression from upper to lower tract disease among infected patients, with a mortality rate after BMT for lower tract infection of approximately 50% for RSV.[122] Upper respiratory tract illness with parainfluenza usually resolves without serious sequelae.[124, 125] Lower tract infection has a mortality rate of 80% for RSV[120] and 30 to 35% for parainfluenza virus.[124, 125] Therapy with aerosolized ribavirin[122] or a combination of ribavirin and IVIG have been used for RSV.[129] The survival rate appears to be higher when treatment is initiated before significant hypoxia is present.[129] There are only anecdotal case reports regarding the effectiveness of ribavirin for treatment of respiratory viruses other than RSV, including parainfluenza, adenovirus, and influenza. Preemptive therapy with aerosolized ribavarin in patients with positive nasopharyngeal cultures for RSV appears promising. Patients who develop respiratory viral pneumonia before engraftment have poorer outcomes.

Prevention of exposure is critical, because treatment is not always effective. Protection involves the use of frequent hand washing by hospital staff and isolation of patients with cold symptoms. In addition, family members and health care workers with upper respiratory tract symptoms should be separated from patients. Vaccination of family members against influenza may help control exposures. Amantadine or rimantadine prophylaxis may be useful during significant outbreaks. Rapid development of resistance has occurred in patients treated with these drugs. Immunoglobulin prophylaxis with RSV-specific polyclonal or monoclonal antibody, which is useful in high-risk infants, has not been studied in the BMT setting. During the respiratory virus season, all patients with respiratory symptoms should have a sample taken from the nasopharynx to look for respiratory viruses with DFA staining and shell vial and conventional tube culture.

Epstein-Barr Virus. EBV is a cause of a post-transplantation lymphoproliferative disorder that arises when anti–T-lymphocyte immunosuppressive therapy is ongoing.[130] Infusions of nonirradiated donor leukocytes may be an effective treatment for allograft recipients.[131]

Human Herpesvirus-6. HHV-6 has been implicated as a possible cause of bone marrow suppression,[132] fatal meningoencephalitis,[133] and interstitial pneumonitis[134, 135] in less than 2% of BMT patients.[136] HHV-6 appears to reactivate commonly, occurring in 46% of BMT patients by culture diagnosis[137] and as many as 100% of patients by PCR of blood. Most strains of HHV-6 identified after BMT appear to be caused by the B variant in blood or urine, although the A variant has been correlated with pneumonitis.[138]

Parvovirus. Parvovirus B19 is a rare cause of anemia after BMT.[139–141] Antibody or PCR tests detect parvovirus, although PCR may remain positive for months after the acute infection.[141] Use of individual patient rooms on BMT wards may be preventing transmission of this contagious virus to other BMT recipients, and the administration of IVIG for other reasons may be treating subclinical infections.[142]

Fungal Infections

Invasive fungal infections are becoming increasingly important causes of morbidity and mortality. The major causes of invasive fungal disease include *Candida* spp., *Aspergillus* spp., and less frequently the non-*Aspergillus* filamentous molds. Patients undergoing allogeneic transplantation are at 10-fold increased risk for invasive fungal infection compared with patients receiving an autologous graft. Systemic fluconazole prophylaxis[143, 144] or low-dose amphotericin B[145, 146] (0.1 to 0.3 mg/kg daily) can decrease the incidence of deep candidiasis.[147, 148] Empirical therapy of febrile neutropenic patients is discussed in Chapter 300.

Pneumocystis. *P. carinii* usually manifests as pneumonia with dyspnea, cough, fever, and bilateral infiltrates in the majority of infected patients.[59] It can be seen after both allogeneic and autologous transplantation, although the frequency is lower for the former. Before the use of routine prophylaxis, *Pneumocystis* had an incidence among allogeneic BMT recipients of approximately 7%, had a median time of onset of 1 to 3 months after transplantation, and was associated with a risk of death of 5%. Prophylaxis with TMP-SMX has resulted in negligible rates of infection. For patients who are intolerant of medications containing sulfa, prophylaxis options include desensitization with TMP-SMX, use of dapsone,[149] or inhaled pentamidine. The treatment of choice for *P. carinii* infection is TMP-SMX.

Candida. Candidiasis is an infection acquired from endogenous organisms colonizing the gastrointestinal tract; it usually manifests as fungemia or visceral candidiasis[150, 151] (see Chapter 247). *Candida* is second in frequency to *Aspergillus* spp. as the cause of brain abscess after BMT.[152] Onset of candidiasis occurs at a median of 2 to 3 weeks after transplantation.[150] Risk factors for invasive candidiasis include neutropenia, breakdown of the normal mucosal barriers, and the use of broad-spectrum antibiotics or corticosteroids. *C. albicans* infections are successfully prevented when fluconazole is given as prophylaxis from the time of conditioning until either engraftment or until day 75; the latter strategy has been associated with improved survival.[143, 144] The benefit of fluconazole prophylaxis is less clear for autologous transplants, for which the degree of mucositis is less. With the use of fluconazole over the last decade, the number of *Candida* infections has decreased.[153, 154] The spectrum of colonizing and infecting *Candida* organisms has shifted from *C. albicans* and *Candida tropicalis* to *C. krusei*, *C. glabrata*, and *Candida parapsilosis*.[155–158] *C. krusei* is innately resistant to fluconazole and therefore should be treated with amphotericin. Infections with *C. glabrata* or *C. parapsilosis* that manifest despite fluconazole prophylaxis should be treated with amphotericin. Patients entering transplantation with a history of treated hepatosplenic candidiasis should receive antifungal prophylaxis with a minimum of 0.5 mg/kg daily amphotericin B from conditioning through marrow engraftment, in place of fluconazole.[159]

Aspergillus. With the use of fluconazole prophylaxis, invasive aspergillosis has emerged as the leading fungal infection found at autopsy among BMT recipients.[153] *Aspergillus* infections are acquired exogenously, by inhalation of spores into the respiratory tract from the environment, and may occur with higher frequency during the summer in some localities.[160] Common sites of initial infection include the lung and sinuses, although contiguous or hematogenous extension to the central nervous system or other internal organs may occur.

In nonoutbreak settings, the incidence of invasive aspergillosis ranges from 4% to 12%.[160–163] The onset of *Aspergillus* infection after BMT occurs in a bimodal distribution, with the first peak at a median of 16 days and the second at a median of 96 days after BMT.[160] Aspergillosis is temporally associated with neutropenia. Therefore, infection among autologous BMT patients is rare after engraftment. Older age and increasing severity of the underlying oncologic disease are risk factors for the acquisition of aspergillosis during either peak. Donor type, male gender, summer season, and transplantation outside of a laminar air flow environment are specific risk factors for early aspergillosis, and construction in the vicinity of the hospital, acute GVHD, and corticosteroid therapy are significant risk factors for the development of late aspergillosis. The 1-year survival estimate for patients with invasive aspergillosis is 7%.

Preventive strategies should focus on reducing both environmental and host risk factors. Use of high-efficiency particulate air (HEPA)–filtered air systems or laminar air flow rooms during the pre-engraftment risk period are important to the prevention of infection, particularly for allograft recipients. Other prevention strategies, including nasal and aerosolized amphotericin B, have not been studied in controlled trials. Most patients who have had aspergillosis in the year before BMT do not survive transplantation, although the cause of death may not be related to recurrence of aspergillosis.

Blood cultures for molds are rarely positive[164] except in the case of *Fusarium*. Culture and histologic evaluation of tissue may be the only way to adequately diagnose an invasive infection, although fungal organisms that are identified by histopathology may not grow in the microbiology laboratory. A high index of suspicion in persistently febrile neutropenic patients and computed tomography of the chest to detect new infiltrates are important in early detection of invasive pulmonary aspergillosis. A small "ground-glass" halo around the lung lesion on computed tomography is highly suggestive of aspergillosis or mucormycosis in this setting. BMT patients with suspected invasive mold infections should be given amphotericin B deoxycholate, 1.0 to 1.5 mg/kg daily. Nephrotoxicity in patients receiving cyclosporine may necessitate a switch to one of the lipid formulations of amphotericin B, although much less evidence exists concerning their efficacy in aspergillosis.

The availability of accurate early diagnostic tests for invasive fungal infections lags behind those for other types of infections. Antigen-[165, 166] and nucleic acid–based[167, 168] diagnostic tests have been studied for early diagnosis of invasive tissue mold infection, but they have not been routinely adopted in the clinical laboratory.

TABLE 303–3. Suggested Schedule for Vaccination of Bone Marrow Transplantation Recipients

Vaccine	Time Period for Immunization after BMT		
	12 months	*14 months*	*24 months*
Inactivated Vaccines			
Diphtheria, tetanus, pertussis			
<7 years old*	X	X	X
>7 years old	X	X	X
Haemophilus influenzae type B conjugate	X	X	X
Hepatitis B	X	X	X
Pneumococcal 23-valent	X		(X)†
Inactivated polio	X	X	X
Hepatitis A	Routine administration is not indicated. If given, hepatitis A vaccination requires two doses given 6–12 months apart.		
Influenza	Lifelong, seasonal administration, beginning before BMT and resuming ≥6 months after BMT is recommended.		
Meningococcal	Routine administration is not indicated.		
Rabies	Routine administration is not indicated.		
Live Vaccines			
Measles-mumps-rubella			X‡
Varicella			X†‡

*Acellular pertussis optional.
†Optional dose.
‡In patients with no active graft-versus-host disease or immunosuppressive therapy.
Adapted from ref. 194.

At present they have not been tested in large numbers of clinical samples from BMT recipients.

Amphotericin B therapy is usually continued until lesions are stable, immunosuppression has decreased, and the patient is afebrile. Subsequent maintenance with itraconazole for the duration of immunosuppression has been advocated to reduce the risk of reactivation. However, multiple drug-drug interactions and the inability to achieve therapeutic drug levels complicate the administration of itraconazole. Itraconazole solution has improved oral bioavailability over the capsule and can be used, although blood level monitoring may be needed to ensure adequate absorption.

Other Yeasts. Pityrosporum folliculitis manifests in the early weeks after transplantation as erythematous macules and papules distributed on the chest, shoulders, and upper back; these lesions can also develop into pustules and crusts in some patients.[51] Response to either topical or systemic therapy is slow; recovery of granulocyte counts is usually associated with resolution. Trichosporonosis has manifested as fungemia, skin lesions, pneumonitis,[169] and arthritis.[170] Fungemia, usually acquired via an intravenous catheter, has been reported with *Rhodotorula*,[171] *Cryptococcus laurentii*,[172] and *Hansenula anomala*.[173] Meningitis with *Cryptococcus neoformans*[174] is unusual, in contrast to its frequent occurrence among patients infected with HIV.

Other Molds. Non-*Aspergillus* molds are infrequent causes of invasive tissue mold infections that appear clinically as similar to *Aspergillus*.[175, 176] Disseminated fusariosis is generally a fatal infection for BMT recipients, manifesting as positive blood cultures, skin lesions, or endophthalmitis.[177, 178] Successful recovery is usually associated with engraftment in addition to amphotericin B therapy. In the case of endophthalmitis, enucleation of the affected eye may be required.[178] Zygomycete infections mimic aspergillosis and may occur long after BMT.[179] Clinically significant infections caused by the dimorphic fungi, including coccidioidomycosis, histoplasmosis and blastomycosis, are unusual even in hyperendemic areas of the United States.

Parasitic Infections

Parasitic infection after BMT usually manifests as reactivation of toxoplasmosis, although Chagas' disease,[180–183] and *Plasmodium*[184–187] and *Clonorchis sinensis*[188] infection have also been reported. Routine blood smears before BMT cannot be used to exclude malarial transmission. In Hong Kong, *C. sinensis* infection was rarely identified in 1% of screening stool examinations performed 7 days before BMT.[188] None of the patients had symptoms related to clonorchiasis; patients received praziquantel (25 mg/kg orally three times daily for 1 day) before BMT, and subsequent stool examinations were negative for ova.

Toxoplasmosis is infrequent after transplant, occurring in 2 to 7% of patients who are seropositive before transplantation.[189, 190] Although the parasite can be transmitted as a primary infection via marrow, blood products, or donor solid organs, toxoplasmosis in the BMT recipient is almost always the result of reactivation of prior infection. GVHD is a risk factor relating to the suppression of cell-mediated immunity that is critical for host defense against *T. gondii*.[189] The clinical presentation includes fever, encephalitis with focal cerebral lesions, pneumonitis, dysrhythmias, or hypotension. Parasitemia is a feature of reactivation that may be identified in peripheral blood buffy-coat cells inoculated into fibroblast tissue culture and incubated for 10 to 40 days.[191] The identifiable risk period occurs 2 to 8 weeks after BMT.[189, 192] In countries with a high seropositivity rate, prophylaxis seems logical and justifies the use of pyrimethamine/sulfadoxine among seropositive BMT recipients.[193] However, in countries where the seroprevalence is low, prophylaxis is not routinely justified.

METHODS OF IMMUNE SYSTEM RECONSTITUTION AFTER BONE MARROW TRANSPLANTATION

Vaccination

Patients undergoing autologous or allogeneic BMT eventually lose immunity to the common childhood diseases and should be reimmunized between the first and second year after transplant (Table 303–3).[194] Use of combination vaccines in encouraged. There have been no reports of exacerbation of GVHD following immunization of BMT recipients.

All indicated non-live vaccines should be administered to BMT recipients regardless of BMT type or presence of GVHD. BMT recipients should be revaccinated with the combined tetanus-diphtheria toxoid, absorbed, every 10 years. No data are available on safety and immunogenicity of pertussis vaccination in BMT recipients. At 1 year, they should also be immunized against polio by the inactivated intramuscular vaccine,[195, 196] *H. influenzae* type B, hepatitis B, and *S. pneumoniae*.[197] If previously immunized, only one dose of hepatitis B vaccine should be given. At 2 years, a second dose of pneumococcal vaccine is optional, providing a second opportunity to vaccinate persons who failed to respond to the first dose, especially patients with chronic GVHD. Lifelong, seasonal administration of influenza vaccine should begin before BMT and resume more than 6 months after BMT. Children younger than 9 years who are receiving influenza vaccination for the first time require two doses. Children younger than 12 years should receive only split-virus influenza vaccine. Persons older than 12 years may receive whole- or split-virus influenza vaccine.

Live virus vaccines such as MMR[198–202] and varicella should not be given to BMT recipients with active GVHD or ongoing immunosuppressive therapy; the first doses are given to BMT recipients more than 24 months after BMT who are presumed immunocompetent.[194] A second MMR dose should be given 6 to 12 months later; however, the benefit of a second dose in this population has not been evaluated.

Vaccination with the live-attenuated VZV vaccine is used for VZV-seronegative patients no longer requiring immunosuppressive therapy, but no controlled study has demonstrated its safety in the BMT setting. Therefore, use of varicella vaccine in BMT recipients is restricted to research protocols for recipients older than 24 months after BMT and who are presumed immunocompetent. When varicella vaccination is given to persons older than 13 years of age, two doses given 4 to 8 weeks apart are required. No controlled study has demonstrated the safety of the live-attentuated VZV vaccine in the BMT setting. Susceptible family members should receive VZV vaccine to minimize chickenpox exposure for VZV-seronegative transplant recipients.

Routine adminstration of hepatitis A, meningococcal, and rabies vaccines is not indicated. Hepatitis A vaccine is recommended for BMT recipients with chronic liver disease, including hepatitis C infection or chronic GVHD, or who are from hepatitis A–endemic areas or areas experiencing outbreaks. If given, hepatitis A vaccination requires two doses given 6 to 12 months apart. For BMT recipients with potential occupational exposure to rabies, pre-exposure rabies vaccination should be delayed until at least 12 months, if not 24 months, after BMT.

Immunoglobulin Replacement

The major defect in humoral immunity is the absence of specific antibody production. Among patients with chronic GVHD, reduced production of opsonizing antibody and all classes of IgG and IgA antibodies is seen.[203] This immunodeficiency is further complicated by poor splenic function and is associated with recurrent pneumococcal infections and obstructive lung disease.[67] IVIG does not prevent infections when given weekly during the pre-engraftment or late risk periods[204, 205] but leads to reduced rates of septicemia and localized infection when given in the postengraftment risk period after transplantation.[206] Replacement IVIG, 200 to 500 mg/kg every 1 to 2 weeks, is recommended for BMT recipients with IgG levels lower than 400 mg/dl.

The role of hyperimmune globulin for prevention of specific infections is less clear. High-titer CMV globulin for prevention of CMV infection and treatment of CMV end-organ disease has proved to be of clear benefit compared with IVIG. However, antiviral drugs are effective in providing protection against CMV disease, and for resource as well as cost considerations the use of CMV globulin has therefore decreased at many transplantation centers. Hyperimmune RSV globulin is available but has not been studied in the BMT setting. Use of virus-specific monoclonal antibodies as preventative measures against RSV and CMV is currently under investigation. Hepatitis B, human rabies, and tetanus immune globulin should be used as needed for exposures. Variclla zoster immune globulin (VZIG) should be administered to VZV-seronegative BMT recipients within 96 hours of close contact with a person with varicella or shingles, although VZIG adminstration may extend the varicella incubation period from 10 to 21 days to 28 days.

REFERENCES

1. Rubinstein P, Carrier C, Scaradavou A, et al. Outcomes among 562 recipients of placental-blood transplants from unrelated donors. N Engl J Med. 1998;339:1565–1577.
2. Bandini G, Belardinelli A, Rosti G, et al. Toxicity of high-dose busulphan and cyclophosphamide as conditioning therapy for allogeneic bone marrow transplantation in adults with haematological malignancies. Bone Marrow Transplant. 1994;13:577–581.
3. Schiffman KS, Bensinger WI, Appelbaum FR, et al. Phase II study of high-dose busulfan, melphalan and thiotepa with autologous peripheral blood stem cell support in patients with malignant disease. Bone Marrow Transplant. 1996;17:943–950.
4. Weaver CH, Bensinger WI, Appelbaum FR, et al. Phase I study of high-dose busulfan, melphalan and thiotepa with autologous stem cell support in patients with refractory malignancies. Bone Marrow Transplant. 1994;14:813–819.
5. Sencer SF, Haake RJ, Weisdorf DJ. Hemorrhagic cystitis after bone marrow transplantation: Risk factors and complications. Transplantation. 1993;56:875–879.
6. Doney K, Storb R, Buckner CD, et al. Treatment of aplastic anemia with antithymocyte globulin, high-dose corticosteroids, and androgens. Exp Hematol. 1987;15:239–242.
7. Miller WJ, Branda RF, Flynn PJ, et al. Antithymocyte globulin treatment of severe aplastic anaemia. Br J Haematol. 1983;55:17–25.
8. Brattstrom C, Tollemar J, Ringden O, et al. Isoamylase levels in bone marrow transplant patients are affected by total body irradiation and not by graft-versus-host disease. Transpl Int. 1991;4:96–98.
9. Junglee D, Katrak A, Mohiuddin J, et al. Salivary amylase and pancreatic enzymes in serum after total body irradiation. Clin Chem. 1986;32:609–610.
10. Anasetti C, Amos D, Beatty PG, et al. Effect of HLA compatibility on engraftment of bone marrow transplants in patients with leukemia or lymphoma. N Engl J Med. 1989;320:197–204.
11. Ost L, Lonnqvist B, Eriksson L, et al. Hemorrhagic cystitis: A manifestation of graft versus host disease? Bone Marrow Transplant. 1987;2:19–25.
12. Arthur RR, Shah KV, Baust SJ, et al. Association of BK viruria with hemorrhagic cystitis in recipients of bone marrow transplants. N Engl J Med. 1986;315:230–234.
13. Bedi A, Miller CB, Hanson JL, et al. Association of BK virus with failure of prophylaxis against hemorrhagic cystitis following bone marrow transplantation. J Clin Oncol. 1995;13:1103–1109.
14. Ambinder RF, Burns W, Forman M, et al. Hemorrhagic cystitis associated with adenovirus infection in bone marrow transplantation. Arch Intern Med. 1986;146:1400–1401.
15. Miyamura K, Minami S, Matsuyama T, et al. Adenovirus-induced late onset hemorrhagic cystitis following allogeneic bone marrow transplantation. Bone Marrow Transplant. 1987;2:109–110.
16. Miyamura K, Takeyama K, Kojima S, et al. Hemorrhagic cystitis associated with urinary excretion of adenovirus type 11 following allogeneic bone marrow transplantation. Bone Marrow Transplant. 1989;4:533–535.
17. Spach DH, Bauwens JE, Myerson D, et al. Cytomegalovirus-induced hemorrhagic cystitis following bone marrow transplantation. Clin Infect Dis. 1993;16:142–144.
18. Drummond JE, Shah KV, Saral R, et al. BK virus specific humoral and cell-mediated immunity in allogeneic bone marrow transplant recipients. J Med Virol. 1987;23:331–344.
19. Jones RJ, Lee KS, Beschorner WE, et al. Venoocclusive disease of the liver following bone marrow transplantation. Transplantation. 1987;44:778–783.
20. Winston DJ, Schiffman G, Wang DC, et al. Pneumococcal infections after human bone marrow transplantation. Ann Intern Med. 1979;91:835–841.
21. Strasser SI, McDonald GB. Hepatitis viruses and hematopoietic cell transplantation: A guide to patient and donor management. Blood. 1999;93:1127–1136.
22. Reed EC, Myerson D, Corey L, Meyers JD. Allogeneic marrow transplantation in patients positive for hepatitis B surface antigen. Blood. 1991;77:195–200.
23. Locasciulli A, Bacigalupo A, Vanlint MT, et al. Hepatitis C virus infection in patients undergoing allogeneic bone marrow transplantation. Transplantation. 1991;52:315–318.
24. Shuhart MC, Myerson D, Spurgeon CL, et al. Hepatitis C virus (HCV) infection in bone marrow transplant patients after transfusions from anti-HCV–positive blood donors. Bone Marrow Transplant. 1996;17:601–606.
25. Shuhart MC, Myerson D, Childs BH, et al. Marrow transplantation from hepatitis C virus seropositive donors: Transmission rate and clinical course. Blood. 1994;84:3229–3235.
26. Johnson JR, Egaas S, Gleaves CA, et al. Hepatitis due to herpes simplex virus in marrow transplant recipients. Clin Infect Dis. 1992;14:38–45.
27. Schiller GJ, Nimer SD, Gajewski JL, Golde DW. Abdominal presentation of varicella zoster infection in recipients of allogeneic bone marrow transplantation. Bone Marrow Transplant. 1991;7:489–491.
28. Verdonck LF, Cornelissen JJ, Dekker AW, Rozenberg-Arska M. Acute abdominal pain as a presenting symptom of varicella zoster virus infection in recipients of bone marrow transplants. Clin Infect Dis. 1993;16:190–191.
29. Johnson PR, Yin JA, Morris DJ, et al. Fulminant hepatic necrosis caused by adenovirus type 5 following bone marrow transplantation. Bone Marrow Transplant. 1990;5:345–347.
30. Bertheau P, Parquet N, Ferchal F, et al. Fulminant adenovirus hepatitis after allogeneic bone marrow transplantation. Bone Marrow Transplant. 1996;17:295–298.
31. Locasciulli A, Alberti A, Bandini G, et al. Allogeneic bone marrow transplantation

from HBsAg+ donors: A multicenter study from the Gruppo Italiano Trapianto di Midollo Osseo (GITMO). Blood. 1995;86:3236–3240.
32. Lau GK, Liang R, Chiu EK, Lee CK, Lam SK. Hepatic events after bone marrow transplantation in patients with hepatitis B infection: A case controlled study. Bone Marrow Transplant. 1997;19:795–799.
33. Vance EA, Soiffer RJ, McDonald GB, et al. Prevention of transmission of hepatitis C virus in bone marrow transplantation by treating the donor with alpha-interferon. Transplantation. 1996;62:1358–1360.
34. Picardi M, Selleri C, De Rosa G, et al. Lamivudine treatment for chronic replicative hepatitis B virus infection after allogeneic bone marrow transplantation. Bone Marrow Transplant. 1998;21:1267–1269.
35. Lau GK, Liang R, Wu PC, et al. Use of famciclovir to prevent HBV reactivation in HBsAg-positive recipients after allogeneic bone marrow transplantation. J Hepatol. 1998;28:359–368.
36. Crawford SW. Supportive care in bone marrow transplantation: Pulmonary complications. Cancer Treat Res. 1997;77:231–254.
37. Metcalf JP, Rennard SI, Reed EC, et al. Corticosteroids as adjunctive therapy for diffuse alveolar hemorrhage associated with bone marrow transplantation. University of Nebraska Medical Center Bone Marrow Transplant Group. Am J Med. 1994;96:327–334.
38. Chao NJ, Duncan SR, Long GD, et al. Corticosteroid therapy for diffuse alveolar hemorrhage in autologous bone marrow transplant recipients. Ann Intern Med. 1991;114:145–146.
39. Agusti C, Ramirez J, Picado C, et al. Diffuse alveolar hemorrhage in allogeneic bone marrow transplantation: A postmortem study. Am J Respir Crit Care Med. 1995;151:1006–1010.
40. Robbins RA, Linder J, Stahl MG, et al. Diffuse alveolar hemorrhage in autologous bone marrow transplant recipients. Am J Med. 1989;87:511–518.
41. Crawford SW, Hackman RC. Clinical course of idiopathic pneumonia after bone marrow transplantation. Am Rev Respir Dis. 1993;147:1393–1400.
42. Kantrow SP, Hackman RC, Boeckh M, et al. Idiopathic pneumonia syndrome: Changing spectrum of lung injury after marrow transplantation. Transplantation. 1997;63:1079–1086.
43. Meyers JD, Flournoy N, Thomas ED. Nonbacterial pneumonia after allogeneic marrow transplantation: A review of ten years' experience. Rev Infect Dis. 1982;4:1119–1132.
44. Crawford SW, Longton G, Storb R. Acute graft-versus-host disease and the risks for idiopathic pneumonia after marrow transplantation for severe aplastic anemia. Bone Marrow Transplant. 1993;12:225–231.
45. Papadopoulou A, Nathavitharana KA, Williams MD, et al. Diarrhea and weight loss after bone marrow transplantation in children. Pediatr Hematol Oncol. 1994;11:601–611.
46. Cox GJ, Matsui SM, Lo RS, et al. Etiology and outcome of diarrhea after marrow transplantation: A prospective study. Gastroenterology. 1994;107:1398–1407.
47. Yolken RH, Bishop CA, Townsend TR, et al. Infectious gastroenteritis in bone marrow transplant recipients. N Engl J Med. 1982;306:1010–1012.
48. Townsend TR, Bolyard EA, Yolken RH, et al. Outbreak of coxsackie A1 gastroenteritis: A complication of bone marrow transplantation. Lancet. 1982;1:820–823.
49. Yuen KY, Woo PC, Liang RH, et al. Clinical significance of alimentary tract microbes in bone marrow transplant recipients. Diagn Microbiol Infect Dis. 1998;30:75–81.
50. Collier AC, Miller RA, Meyers JD. Cryptosporidiosis after marrow transplantation: Person-to-person transmission and treatment with spiramycin. Ann Intern Med. 1984;101:205–206.
51. Bufill JA, Lum LG, Caya JG, et al. Pityrosporum folliculitis after bone marrow transplantation: Clinical observations in five patients. Ann Intern Med. 1988;108:560–563.
52. Van Burik J-A, Colven R, Spach D. Cutaneous aspergillosis. J Clin Microbiol. 1998;36:3115–3121.
53. Shah M, Watanakunakorn C. *Staphylococcus aureus* sternal osteomyelitis complicating bone marrow aspiration. South Med J. 1978;71:348–349.
54. Riley D, Evans TG. Osteomyelitis complicating bone marrow harvest. Clin Infect Dis. 1992;14:980–981.
55. Lazarus HM, Magalhaes-Silverman M, Fox RM, et al. Contamination during in vitro processing of bone marrow for transplantation: Clinical significance. Bone Marrow Transplant. 1991;7:241–246.
56. Nasser RM, Hajjar I, Sandhaus LM, et al. Routine cultures of bone marrow and peripheral stem cell harvests: Clinical impact, cost analysis, and review. Clin Infect Dis. 1998;27:886–888.
57. Meyers JD, Flournoy N, Thomas ED. Infection with herpes simplex virus and cell-mediated immunity after marrow transplant. J Infect Dis. 1980;142:338–346.
58. Salzberger B, Bowden RA, Hackman RC, et al. Neutropenia in allogeneic marrow transplant recipients receiving ganciclovir for prevention of cytomegalovirus disease: Risk factors and outcome. Blood. 1997;90:2502–2508.
59. Tuan IZ, Dennison D, Weisdorf DJ. *Pneumocystis carinii* pneumonitis following bone marrow transplantation. Bone Marrow Transplant. 1992;10:267–272.
60. Boeckh M, Gallez-Hawkins GM, Myerson D, et al. Plasma polymerase chain reaction for cytomegalovirus DNA after allogeneic marrow transplantation: Comparison with polymerase chain reaction using peripheral blood leukocytes, pp65 antigenemia, and viral culture. Transplantation. 1997;64:108–113.
61. Boeckh M, Gooley TA, Myerson D, et al. Cytomegalovirus pp65 antigenemia-guided early treatment with ganciclovir versus ganciclovir at engraftment after allogeneic marrow transplantation: A randomized double-blind study. Blood. 1996;88:4063–4071.
62. Boeckh M, Stevens-Ayers T, Bowden RA. Cytomegalovirus pp65 antigenemia after autologous marrow and peripheral blood stem cell transplantation. J Infect Dis. 1996;174:907–912.
63. Einsele H, Ehninger G, Hebart H, et al. Polymerase chain reaction monitoring reduces the incidence of cytomegalovirus disease and the duration and side effects of antiviral therapy after bone marrow transplantation. Blood. 1995;86:2815–2820.
64. Boeckh M. Management of cytomegalovirus infections in blood and marrow transplant recipients. In: Mills J, Volberding PA, Corey L, eds. Antiviral Chemotherapy V. New York: Plenum; 1998:89–110.
65. Ochs L, Shu XO, Miller J, et al. Late infections after allogeneic bone marrow transplantations: Comparison of incidence in related and unrelated donor transplant recipients. Blood. 1995;86:3979–3986.
66. Roy V, Ochs L, Weisdorf D. Late infections following allogeneic bone marrow transplantation: Suggested strategies for prophylaxis. Leuk Lymphoma. 1997;26:1–15.
67. Sullivan KM, Mori M, Sanders J, et al. Late complications of allogeneic and autologous marrow transplantation. Bone Marrow Transplant. 1992;10:127–134.
68. Boeckh M, Riddell SR, Cunningham T, et al. Increased incidence of late CMV disease in allogeneic marrow transplant recipients after ganciclovir prophylaxis is due to a lack of CMV-specific T cell responses. Abstract no. 1195. Blood. 1996;88(Suppl. 1):302a.
69. Elishoov H, Or R, Strauss N, Engelhard D. Nosocomial colonization, septicemia, and Hickman/Broviac catheter-related infections in bone marrow transplant recipients. A 5-year prospective study. Medicine (Baltimore). 1998;77:83–101.
70. Steiner M, Villablanca J, Kersey J, et al. Viridans streptococcal shock in bone marrow transplantation patients. Am J Hematol. 1993;42:354–358.
71. Villablanca JG, Steiner M, Kersey J, et al. The clinical spectrum of infections with viridans streptococci in bone marrow transplant patients. Bone Marrow Transplant. 1990;5:387–393.
72. Ringden O, Heimdahl A, Lonnqvist B, et al. Decreased incidence of viridans streptococcal septicaemia in allogeneic bone marrow transplant recipients after the introduction of acyclovir. Lancet. 1984;314:744.
73. Kurzrock R, Zander A, Vellekoop L, et al. Mycobacterial pulmonary infections after allogeneic bone marrow transplantation. Am J Med. 1984;77:35–40.
74. Roy V, Weisdorf D. Mycobacterial infections following bone marrow transplantation: A 20 year retrospective review. Bone Marrow Transplant. 1997;19:467–470.
75. Navari RM, Sullivan KM, Springmeyer SC, et al. Mycobacterial infections in marrow transplant patients. Transplantation. 1983;36:509–513.
76. Kugler JW, Armitage JO, Helms CM, et al. Nosocomial legionnaires' disease: Occurrence in recipients of bone marrow transplants. Am J Med. 1983;74:281–288.
77. Harrington RD, Woolfrey AE, Bowden R, et al. Legionellosis in a bone marrow transplant center. Bone Marrow Transplant. 1996;18:361–368.
78. Benz-Lemoine E, Delwail V, Castel O, et al. Nosocomial legionnaires' disease in a bone marrow transplant unit. Bone Marrow Transplant. 1991;7:61–63.
79. Van Burik J-A, Hackman R, Nadeem S, et al. Nocardiosis after bone marrow transplantation: A retrospective study. Clin Infect Dis. 1997;24:1154–1160.
80. Choucino C, Goodman SA, Greer JP, et al. Nocardial infections in bone marrow transplant recipients. Clin Infect Dis. 1996;23:1012–1019.
81. Meyers JD, Hackman RC, Stamm WE. *Chlamydia trachomatis* infection as a cause of pneumonia after human marrow transplantation. Transplantation. 1983;36:130–134.
82. Kane JR, Shenep JL, Krance RA, Hurwitz CA. Diffuse alveolar hemorrhage associated with *Mycoplasma hominis* respiratory tract infection in a bone marrow transplant recipient. Chest. 1994;105:1891–1892.
83. Martino R, Lopez R, Pericas R, et al. Listeriosis in bone marrow transplant recipient. Clin Infect Dis. 1996;23:419–420.
84. Chang J, Powles R, Mehta J, et al. Listeriosis in the bone marrow transplant recipient. Clin Infect Dis. 1995:1289–1290.
85. Long SG, Leyland MJ, Milligan DW. *Listeria* meningitis after bone marrow transplantation. Bone Marrow Transplant. 1993;12:537–539.
86. Bowden RA, Sayers M, Flournoy N, et al. Cytomegalovirus immune globulin and seronegative blood products to prevent primary cytomegalovirus infection after marrow transplantation. N Engl J Med. 1986;314:1006–1010.
87. Bowden RA, Slichter SJ, Sayers M, et al. A comparison of filtered leukocyte-reduced and cytomegalovirus seronegative blood products for the prevention of transfusion-associated CMV infection after marrow transplant. Blood. 1995;86:3598–3603.
88. Wade JC, Newton B, Flournoy N, Meyers JD. Oral acyclovir for prevention of herpes simplex virus reactivation after marrow transplantation. Ann Intern Med. 1984;100:823–828.
89. Saral R, Burns WH, Laskin OL, et al. Acyclovir prophylaxis of herpes simplex virus infections: A randomized, double-blind, controlled trial in bone marrow transplant recipients. N Engl J Med. 1981;305:63–67.
90. Wade JC, McLaren C, Meyers JD. Frequency and significance of acyclovir-resistant herpes simplex virus isolated from marrow transplant patients receiving multiple courses of treatment with acyclovir. J Infect Dis. 1983;148:1077–1082.
91. Ljungman P, Ellis MN, Hackman RC, et al. Acyclovir-resistant herpes simplex virus causing pneumonia after marrow transplantation. J Infect Dis. 1990;162:244–248.
92. Meyers JD, Flournoy N, Thomas ED. Risk factors for cytomegalovirus infection after human marrow transplantation. J Infect Dis. 1986;153:478–488.
93. Wingard JR, Chen DY-H, Burns WH, et al. Cytomegalovirus infection after autologous bone marrow transplantation: Comparison to infection after allogeneic bone marrow transplantation. Blood. 1988;71:143–147.
94. Reusser P, Fisher LD, Buckner CD, et al. Cytomegalovirus infection after autolo-

gous bone marrow transplantation: Occurrence of cytomegalovirus disease and effect on engraftment. Blood. 1990;75:1888–1894.
95. Goodrich JM, Bowden RA, Fisher L, et al. Ganciclovir prophylaxis to prevent cytomegalovirus disease after allogeneic marrow transplant. Ann Intern Med. 1993;118:173–178.
96. Winston DJ, Ho WG, Bartoni K, et al. Ganciclovir prophylaxis of cytomegalovirus infection and disease in allogeneic bone marrow transplant recipients: Results of a placebo-controlled, double-blind trial. Ann Intern Med. 1993;118:179–184.
97. Prentice HG, Gluckman E, Powles RL, et al. Impact of long-term acyclovir on cytomegalovirus infection and survival after allogeneic bone marrow transplantation. European Acyclovir for CMV Prophylaxis Study Group. Lancet. 1994;343:749–753.
98. Reusser P, Gambertoglio JG, Lilleby K, Meyers JD. Phase I–II trial of foscarnet for prevention of cytomegalovirus infection in autologous and allogeneic marrow transplant recipients. J Infect Dis. 1992;166:473–479.
99. Goodrich JM, Mori M, Gleaves CA, et al. Early treatment with ganciclovir to prevent cytomegalovirus disease after allogeneic bone marrow transplantation. N Engl J Med. 1991;325:1601–1607.
100. Enright H, Haake R, Weisdorf D, et al. Cytomegalovirus pneumonia after bone marrow transplantation: Risk factors and response to therapy. Transplantation. 1993;55:1339–1346.
101. Meyers JD, Leszczynski J, Zaia JA, et al. Prevention of cytomegalovirus infection by cytomegalovirus immune globulin after marrow transplantation. Ann Intern Med. 1983;98:442–446.
102. Reed EC, Bowden RA, Dandliker PS, et al. Treatment of cytomegalovirus pneumonia with ganciclovir and intravenous cytomegalovirus immunoglobulin in patients with bone marrow transplants. Ann Intern Med. 1988;109:783–788.
103. Schmidt GM, Horak DA, Niland JC, et al. A randomized, controlled trial of prophylactic ganciclovir for cytomegalovirus pulmonary infection for recipients of allogeneic bone marrow transplant. N Engl J Med. 1991;324:1005–1011.
104. Limaye AP, Bowden RA, Myerson D, Boeckh M. Cytomegalovirus disease occurring before engraftment in marrow transplant recipients. Clin Infect Dis. 1997;24:830–835.
105. Hackman RC, Wolford JL, Gleaves CA, et al. Recognition and rapid diagnosis of upper gastrointestinal cytomegalovirus infection in marrow transplant recipients: A comparison of seven virologic methods. Transplantation. 1994;57:231–237.
106. Okamoto T, Okada M, Mori A, et al. Successful treatment of severe cytomegalovirus retinitis with foscarnet and intraocular injection of ganciclovir in a myelosuppressed unrelated bone marrow transplant patient. Bone Marrow Transplant. 1997;20:801–803.
107. Boeckh M, Bowden RA, Goodrich JM, et al. Cytomegalovirus antigen detection in peripheral blood leukocytes after allogeneic marrow transplantation. Blood. 1992;80:1358–1364.
108. Moretti S, Zikos P, Van Lint MT, et al. Foscarnet vs ganciclovir for cytomegalovirus antigenemia after allogeneic hemopoietic stem cell transplantation: A randomized study. Bone Marrow Transplant. 1998;22:175–180.
109. Gleaves CA, Reed EC, Hackman RC, Meyers JD. Rapid diagnosis of invasive cytomegalovirus infection by examination of tissue specimens in centrifugation culture. Am J Clin Pathol. 1987;88:354–358.
110. Reed EC, Wolford JL, Kopecky KJ, et al. Ganciclovir for the treatment of cytomegalovirus gastroenteritis in bone marrow transplant patients: A randomized, placebo-controlled trial. Ann Intern Med. 1990;112:505–510.
111. Walter EA, Greenberg PD, Gilbert MJ, et al. Reconstitution of cellular immunity against cytomegalovirus in recipients of allogeneic bone marrow by transfer of T-cell clones from the donor. N Engl J Med. 1995;333:1038–1044.
112. Reusser P, Riddell SR, Meyers JD, Greenberg PD. Cytotoxic T-lymphocyte response to cytomegalovirus after human allogeneic bone marrow transplantation: Pattern of recovery and correlation with cytomegalovirus infection and disease. Blood. 1991;78:1373–1380.
113. Erice A, Borrell N, Li W, et al. Ganciclovir susceptibilities and analysis of UL97 region in cytomegalovirus isolates from bone marrow recipients with CMV disease after antiviral prophylaxis. J Infect Dis. 1998;178:531–534.
114. Ljungman P, Wilczek H, Gahrton G, et al. Long-term acyclovir prophylaxis in bone marrow transplant recipients and lymphocyte proliferation responses to herpes virus antigens in vitro. Bone Marrow Transplant. 1986;1:185–192.
115. Atkinson K, Meyers JD, Storb R, et al. Varicella zoster virus infection after marrow transplantation for aplastic anemia or leukemia. Transplantation. 1980;29:47–50.
116. Locksley RM, Flournoy N, Sullivan KM, Meyers JD. Infection with varicella zoster virus after marrow transplantation. J Infect Dis. 1985;152:1172–1181.
117. Han CS, Miller W, Haake R, Weisdorf D. Varicella zoster infection after bone marrow transplantation: Incidence, risk factors and complications. Bone Marrow Transplant. 1994;13:277–283.
118. Schuchter LM, Wingard JR, Piantadosi S, et al. Herpes zoster infection after autologous bone marrow transplantation. Blood. 1989;74:1424–1427.
119. Wacker P, Hartmann O, Benhamou E, et al. Varicella zoster virus infections after autologous bone marrow transplantation in children. Bone Marrow Transplant. 1989;4:191–194.
120. Wasserman R, August CS, Plotkin SA. Viral infections in pediatric bone marrow transplant patients. Pediatr Infect Dis J. 1988;7:109–115.
121. Shields AF, Hackman RC, Fife KH, et al. Adenovirus infections in patients undergoing bone marrow transplantation. N Engl J Med. 1985;312:529–533.
122. Harrington RD, Hooton TM, Hackman RC, et al. An outbreak of respiratory syncytial virus in a bone marrow transplant center. J Infect Dis. 1992;165:987–993.
123. Garcia R, Raad I, Abi-Said D, et al. Nosocomial respiratory syncytial virus infections: Prevention and control in bone marrow transplant patients. Infect Control Hosp Epidemiol. 1997;18:412–416.
124. Wendt CH, Weisdorf DJ, Jordan MC, et al. Parainfluenza virus respiratory infection after bone marrow transplantation. N Engl J Med. 1992;326:921–926.
125. Lewis VA, Champlin R, Englund J, et al. Respiratory disease due to parainfluenza virus in adult bone marrow transplant recipients. Clin Infect Dis. 1996;23:1033–1037.
126. Whimbey E, Elting LS, Couch RB, et al. Influenza A virus infections among hospitalized adult bone marrow transplant recipients. Bone Marrow Transplant. 1994;13:437–440.
127. Whimbey E, Vartivarian SE, Champlin RE, et al. Parainfluenza virus infection in adult bone marrow transplant recipients. Eur J Clin Microbiol Infect Dis. 1993;12:699–701.
128. Whimbey E, Champlin RE, Couch RB, et al. Community respiratory virus infections among hospitalized adult bone marrow transplant recipients. Clin Infect Dis. 1996;22:778–782.
129. Whimbey E, Champlin RE, Englund JA, et al. Combination therapy with aerosolized ribavirin and intravenous immunoglobulin for respiratory syncytial virus disease in adult bone marrow transplant recipients. Bone Marrow Transplant. 1995;16:393–399.
130. Zutter MM, Martin PJ, Sale GE, et al. Epstein-Barr virus lymphoproliferation after bone marrow transplantation. Blood. 1988;72:520–529.
131. Papadopoulos EB, Ladanyi M, Emanuel D, et al. Infusions of donor leukocytes to treat Epstein-Barr virus-associated lymphoproliferative disorders after allogeneic bone marrow transplantation. N Engl J Med. 1994;330:1185–1191.
132. Drobyski WR, Dunne WM, Burd EM, et al. Human herpesvirus-6 (HHV-6) infection in allogeneic bone marrow transplant recipients: Evidence of a marrow-suppressive role for HHV-6 in vivo. J Infect Dis. 1993;167:735–739.
133. Bosi A, Zazzi M, Amantini A, et al. Fatal herpesvirus 6 encephalitis after unrelated bone marrow transplant. Bone Marrow Transplant. 1998;22:285–288.
134. Carrigan DR, Drobyski WR, Russler SK, et al. Interstitial pneumonitis associated with human herpesvirus-6 infection after marrow transplantation. Lancet. 1991;338:147–149.
135. Cone RW. Human herpesvirus 6 as a possible cause of pneumonia. Semin Respir Infect. 1995;10:254–258.
136. Wang F-Z, Linde A, Hagglund H, et al. Human herpesvirus-6 DNA in cerebrospinal fluid from allogeneic bone marrow transplant patients: Does it have clinical significance? Clin Infect Dis. 1999;28:562–568.
137. Kadakia MP, Rybka WB, Stewart JA, et al. Human herpesvirus 6: Infection and disease following autologous and allogeneic bone marrow transplantation. Blood. 1996;87:5341–5344.
138. Cone RW, Hackman RC, Huang ML, et al. Human herpesvirus 6 in lung tissue from patients with pneumonitis after bone marrow transplantation. N Engl J Med. 1993;329:156–161.
139. Weiland HT, Salimans MM, Fibbe WE, et al. Prolonged parvovirus B19 infection with severe anaemia in a bone marrow transplant patient. Br J Haematol. 1989;71:300.
140. Cohen BJ, Beard S, Knowles WA, et al. Chronic anemia due to parvovirus B19 infection in a bone marrow transplant patient after platelet transfusion. Transfusion. 1997;37:947–952.
141. Corbett TJ, Saw H, Popat U, et al. Successful treatment of parvovirus B19 infection and red cell aplasia occurring after an allogeneic bone marrow transplant. Bone Marrow Transplant. 1995;16:711–713.
142. Azzi A, Fanci R, Ciappi S, et al. Human parvovirus B19 infection in bone marrow transplantation patients. Am J Hematol. 1993;44:207–209.
143. Goodman JL, Winston DJ, Greenfield RA, et al. A controlled trial of fluconazole to prevent fungal infections in patients undergoing bone marrow transplantation. N Engl J Med. 1992;326:845–851.
144. Slavin MA, Osborne B, Adams R, et al. Efficacy and safety of fluconazole prophylaxis for fungal infections after marrow transplantation: A prospective, randomized, double-blind study. J Infect Dis. 1995;171:1545–1552.
145. Rousey SR, Russler S, Gottlieb M, Ash RC. Low-dose amphotericin B prophylaxis against invasive *Aspergillus* infections in allogeneic marrow transplantation. Am J Med. 1991;91:484–492.
146. Riley DK, Pavia AT, Beatty PG, et al. The prophylactic use of low-dose amphotericin B in bone marrow transplant patients. Am J Med. 1994;97:509–514.
147. White MH, Bowden RA, Sandler E, et al. Amphotericin B colloidal dispersion vs. amphotericin B in the empiric treatment of fever in neutropenic patients: A randomized, double-blind clinical trial. Clin Infect Dis. 1997;27:296–302.
148. Walsh TJ, Lee J, Lecciones J, et al. Empiric therapy with amphotericin B in febrile granulocytopenic patients. Rev Infect Dis. 1991;13:496–503.
149. Maltezou HC, Petropoulos D, Choroszy M, et al. Dapsone for *Pneumocystis carinii* prophylaxis in children undergoing bone marrow transplantation. Bone Marrow Transplant. 1997;20:879–881.
150. Goodrich JM, Reed EC, Mori M, et al. Clinical features and analysis of risk factors for invasive candidal infection after marrow transplantation. J Infect Dis. 1991;164:731–740.
151. Meyers JD. Fungal infections in bone marrow transplant patients. Semin Oncol. 1990;17(Suppl 6):10–13.
152. Hagensee ME, Bauwens JE, Kjos B, Bowden RA. Brain abscess following marrow transplantation: Experience at the Fred Hutchinson Cancer Research Center, 1984–1992. Clin Infect Dis. 1994;19:402–408.
153. Van Burik J-A, Leisenring W, Myerson D, et al. The effect of prophylactic fluconazole on the clinical spectrum of fungal diseases in bone marrow transplant

recipients with special attention to hepatic candidiasis: An autopsy study of 355 patients. Medicine (Baltimore). 1998;77:246–254.
154. Rossetti F, Brawner DL, Bowden R, et al. Fungal liver infection in marrow transplant patients: Prevalence at autopsy, predisposing factors, and clinical features. Clin Infect Dis. 1995;20:801–811.
155. Morrison VA, Haake RJ, Weisdorf DJ. Non-candidal fungal infections after bone marrow transplantation: Risk factors and outcome. Am J Med. 1994;96:497–503.
156. Hoppe JE, Klingebiel T, Niethammer D. Selection of *Candida glabrata* in pediatric bone marrow transplant recipients receiving fluconazole. Pediatr Hematol Oncol. 1994;11:207–210.
157. Klingspor L, Stintzing G, Fasth A, Tollemar J. Deep *Candida* infection in children receiving allogeneic bone marrow transplants: Incidence, risk factors and diagnosis. Bone Marrow Transplant. 1996;17:1043–1049.
158. Wingard JR. Importance of *Candida* species other than *C. albicans* as pathogens in oncology patients. Clin Infect Dis. 1995;20:115–125.
159. Bjerke JW, Meyers JD, Bowden RA. Hepatosplenic candidiasis: A contraindication to marrow transplantation? Blood. 1994;84:2811–2814.
160. Wald A, Leisenring W, van Burik J-A, Bowden RA. Natural history of *Aspergillus* infections in a large cohort of patients undergoing bone marrow transplantation. J Infect Dis. 1997;175:1459–1466.
161. Saugier-Veber P, Devergie A, Sulahian A, et al. Epidemiology and diagnosis of invasive pulmonary aspergillosis in bone marrow transplant patients: Results of a 5 year retrospective study. Bone Marrow Transplant. 1993;12:121–124.
162. Wingard JR, Beals SU, Santos GW, et al. *Aspergillus* infections in bone marrow transplant recipients. Bone Marrow Transplant. 1987;2:175–181.
163. Morrison VA, Haake RJ, Weisdorf DJ. The spectrum of non-*Candida* fungal infections following bone marrow transplantation. Medicine (Baltimore). 1993;72:78–89.
164. Duthie R, Denning DW. *Aspergillus* fungemia: Report of two cases and review. Clin Infect Dis. 1995;20:598–605.
165. Rodgers TR, Haynes KA, Barnes RA. Value of antigen detection in predicting invasive pulmonary aspergillosis. Lancet. 1990;330:1210–1213.
166. Verweij PE, Latge JP, Rijs AJMM, et al. Comparison of antigen detection and PCR assay with bronchoalveolar lavage fluid for diagnosing invasive aspergillosis in patients receiving treatment for hematological malignancies. J Clin Microbiol. 1995;33:3150–3153.
167. Van Burik J-A, Myerson D, Schreckhise RW, Bowden RA. Panfungal PCR assay for detection of fungal infection in human blood specimens. J Clin Microbiol. 1998;36:1169–1175.
168. Einsele H, Hebart H, Roller G, et al. Detection and identification of fungal pathogens in blood by using molecular probes. J Clin Microbiol. 1997;35:1353–1360.
169. Lowenthal RM, Atkinson K, Challis DR, et al. Invasive *Trichosporon cutaneum* infection: An increasing problem in immunosuppressed patients. Bone Marrow Transplant. 1987;2:321–327.
170. Gardella S, Nomdedeu B, Bombi JA, et al. Fatal fungemia with arthritic involvement caused by *Trichosporon beigelii* in a bone marrow transplant recipient. J Infect Dis. 1985;151:566.
171. Sheu MJ, Wang CC, Shi WJ, Chu ML. *Rhodotorula* septicemia: Report of a case. J Formos Med Assoc. 1994;93:645–647.
172. Krcmery V Jr, Kunova A, Mardiak J. Nosocomial *Cryptococcus laurentii* fungemia in a bone marrow transplant patient after prophylaxis with ketoconazole successfully treated with oral fluconazole. Infection. 1997;25:130.
173. Goss G, Grigg A, Rathbone P, Slavin M. *Hansenula anomala* infection after bone marrow transplantation. Bone Marrow Transplant. 1994;14:995–997.
174. Miniero R, Nesi F, Vai S, et al. Cryptococcal meningitis following a thrombotic microangiopathy in an unrelated donor bone marrow transplant recipient. Pediatr Hematol Oncol. 1997;14:469–474.
175. Lundstrom TS, Fairfax MR, Dugan MC, et al. *Phialophora verrucosa* infection in a BMT patient. Bone Marrow Transplant. 1997;20:789–791.
176. de la Camara R, Pinilla I, Munoz E, et al. *Penicillium brevicompactum* as the cause of a necrotic lung ball in an allogeneic bone marrow transplant recipient. Bone Marrow Transplant. 1996;18:1189–1193.
177. Gamis AS, Gudnason T, Giebink GS, Ramsay NK. Disseminated infection with *Fusarium* in recipients of bone marrow transplants. Rev Infect Dis. 1991;13:1077–1088.
178. Robertson MJ, Socinski MA, Soiffer RJ, et al. Successful treatment of disseminated *Fusarium* infection after autologous bone marrow transplantation for acute myeloid leukemia. Bone Marrow Transplant. 1991;8:143–145.
179. Morrison VA, McGlave PB. Mucormycosis in the BMT population. Bone Marrow Transplant. 1993;11:383.
180. Altclas J, Jaimovich G, Milovic V, et al. Chagas' disease after bone marrow transplantation. Bone Marrow Transplant. 1996;18:447–448.
181. Villalba R, Fornes G, Alvarez MA, et al. Acute Chagas' disease in a recipient of a bone marrow transplant in Spain: Case report. Clin Infect Dis. 1992;14:594–595.
182. Dictar M, Sinagra A, Veron MT, et al. Recipients and donors of bone marrow transplants suffering from Chagas' disease: Management and preemptive therapy of parasitemia. Bone Marrow Transplant. 1998;21:391–393.
183. Pasternak J, Amato Neto V, Hammerschlack N. Chagas' disease after bone marrow transplantation. Bone Marrow Transplant. 1997;19:958.
184. Salutari P, Sica S, Chiusolo P, et al. *Plasmodium vivax* malaria after autologous bone marrow transplantation: An unusual complication. Bone Marrow Transplant. 1996;18:805–806.
185. O'Donnell J, Goldman JM, Wagner K, et al. Donor-derived *Plasmodium vivax* infection following volunteer unrelated bone marrow transplantation. Bone Marrow Transplant. 1998;21:313–314.
186. Lefrere F, Besson C, Datry A, et al. Transmission of *Plasmodium falciparum* by allogeneic bone marrow transplantation. Bone Marrow Transplant. 1996;18:473–474.
187. Dharmasena F, Gordon-Smith EC. Transmission of malaria by bone marrow transplantation. Transplantation. 1986;42:228.
188. Woo PC, Lie AK, Yuen K, et al. Clonorchiasis in bone marrow transplant recipients. Clin Infect Dis. 1998;27:382–384.
189. Slavin MA, Meyers JD, Remington JS, Hackman RC. *Toxoplasma gondii* infection in marrow transplant recipients: A 20 year experience. Bone Marrow Transplant. 1994;13:549–557.
190. Derouin F, Gluckman E, Beauvais B, et al. *Toxoplasma* infection after human allogeneic bone marrow transplantation: Clinical and serological study of 80 patients. Bone Marrow Transplant. 1986;1:67–73.
191. Shepp DH, Hackman RC, Conley FK, et al. *Toxoplasma gondii* reactivation identified by detection of parasitemia in tissue culture. Ann Intern Med. 1985;103:218–221.
192. Derouin F, Devergie A, Auber P, et al. Toxoplasmosis in bone marrow-transplant recipients: Report of seven cases and review. Clin Infect Dis. 1992;15:267–270.
193. Foot AB, Garin YJ, Ribaud P, et al. Prophylaxis of toxoplasmosis infection with pyrimethamine/sulfadoxine (Fansidar) in bone marrow transplant recipients. Bone Marrow Transplant. 1994;14:241–245.
194. Centers for Disease Control and Prevention. Recommendations for immunization of bone marrow transplant recipients. MMWR Morb Mortal Wkly Rep. 1999. In press.
195. Ljungman P, Duraj V, Magnius L. Response to immunization against polio after allogeneic marrow transplantation. Bone Marrow Transplant. 1991;7:89–93.
196. Pauksen K, Hammarstrom V, Ljungman P, et al. Immunity to poliovirus and immunization with inactivated poliovirus vaccine after autologous bone marrow transplantation. Clin Infect Dis. 1994;18:547–552.
197. Giebink GS, Warkentin PI, Ramsay NK, Kersey JH. Titers of antibody to pneumococci in allogeneic bone marrow transplant recipients before and after vaccination with pneumococcal vaccine. J Infect Dis. 1986;154:590–596.
198. Ljungman P, Fridell E, Lonnqvist B, et al. Efficacy and safety of vaccination of marrow transplant recipients with a live attenuated measles, mumps, and rubella vaccine. J Infect Dis. 1989;159:610–615.
199. Pauksen K, Linde A, Lonnerholm G, et al. Influence of the specific T cell response on seroconversion after measles vaccination in autologous bone marrow transplant patients. Bone Marrow Transplant. 1996;18:969–973.
200. Pauksen K, Sjolin J, Linde A, et al. Th1 and Th2 cytokine responses after measles antigen stimulation in vitro in bone marrow transplant patients: Response to measles vaccination. Bone Marrow Transplant. 1997;20:317–323.
201. Pauksen K, Linde A, Ljungman P, et al. Specific T and B cell immunity to measles after allogeneic and autologous bone marrow transplantation. Bone Marrow Transplant. 1995;16:807–813.
202. Pauksen K, Duraj V, Ljungman P, et al. Immunity to and immunization against measles, rubella and mumps in patients after autologous bone marrow transplantation. Bone Marrow Transplant. 1992;9:427–432.
203. Witherspoon RP, Storb R, Ochs HD, et al. Recovery of antibody production in human allogeneic marrow graft recipients: Influence of time posttransplantation, the presence or absence of chronic graft-versus-host disease, and antithymocyte globulin treatment. Blood. 1981;58:360–368.
204. Wolff SN, Fay JW, Herzig RH, et al. High-dose weekly intravenous immunoglobulin to prevent infections in patients undergoing autologous bone marrow transplantation or severe myelosuppressive therapy: A study of the American Bone Marrow Transplant Group. Ann Intern Med. 1993;118:937–942.
205. Sullivan KM, Storek J, Kopecky KJ, et al. A controlled trial of long-term administration of intravenous immunoglobulin to prevent late infection and chronic graft-vs.-host disease after marrow transplantation: Clinical outcome and effect on subsequent immune recovery. Biol Blood Marrow Transplant. 1996;2:44–53.
206. Sullivan KM, Kopecky KJ, Jocom J, et al. Immunomodulatory and antimicrobial efficacy of intravenous immunoglobulin in bone marrow transplantation. N Engl J Med. 1990;323:705–712.

Chapter 304

Infections in Solid Organ Transplant Recipients

J. STEPHEN DUMMER
MONTO HO

After the introduction of cyclosporine as a major immunosuppressive agent, there was a marked increase in the transplantation of solid organs. The outlook improved for recipients of all types of organs, and liver, heart, and lung transplantation advanced from being experimental procedures to established therapeutic modalities similar to transplantation of the kidney. Table 304–1 shows the most recent data available on graft and patient survival released by the United Network of Organ Sharing.[1] The best results are in kidney transplantation, where 94% of recipients are alive and 83% have functioning allografts 1 year after transplantation. Perhaps the greatest progress has been in liver transplantation. Before the availability of cyclosporine, the 1-year survival rate after liver transplantation was only 32%, compared with a 3-year survival rate of 71% in the current era. The survival rates for lung and heart-lung transplant recipients have lagged somewhat behind the other groups, but these procedures were only introduced in the 1980s, and experience has been gained slowly because of the limited availability of donor organs.

Improvements in graft and patient survival have been paralleled by a decline in mortality from infections.[2, 3] For instance, the risk of death from infection in heart recipients transplanted in Pittsburgh fell significantly between 1981 and 1990 (Fig. 304–1). In the patients studied most recently, infectious mortality was only about 1.5% per year for the first 3 years after transplantation. Likewise, early post-transplantation mortality rate from infection in liver recipients decreased significantly, from 47% in the early 1980s[4] to 23% in the late 1980s[5] and 7% in the early 1990s.[6]

TIME OF OCCURRENCE OF INFECTIONS AFTER TRANSPLANTATION

Most infections occur in the first few months after transplantation, when the patient is still under close medical surveillance. Peterson and colleagues pointed out that 64% (125/194) of all febrile episodes were seen within the first 14 to 120 days after kidney transplantation.[8] The kinds of infections seen within this high-risk period are not uniform but follow a typical time schema.[7, 8] During the first post-transplantation month, common infections are those that might be seen after any surgical procedure: pneumonias and urinary, wound, and intravascular catheter infections caused by nosocomial bacteria. Except for the reactivation of herpes simplex virus (HSV), infections related to deficient T-cell immunity are not encountered. After 1 month, surgical infections decline in importance and typical opportunistic infections associated with the immunosuppressed state emerge. These include *Pneumocystis* pneumonia, opportunistic fungal infections, nocardiosis, and, most importantly, cytomegalovirus (CMV) infection. This time schema of infections is applicable to other types of transplantation with a few minor alterations.[5, 9–12] For instance, in liver transplant recipients, postsurgical infection may extend into the second and third month because of reoperation for technical complications or retransplantation.[5, 13] Also, opportunistic fungal infections often occur in the first month in some liver and lung transplant recipients because of their high susceptibility.[5, 14, 15]

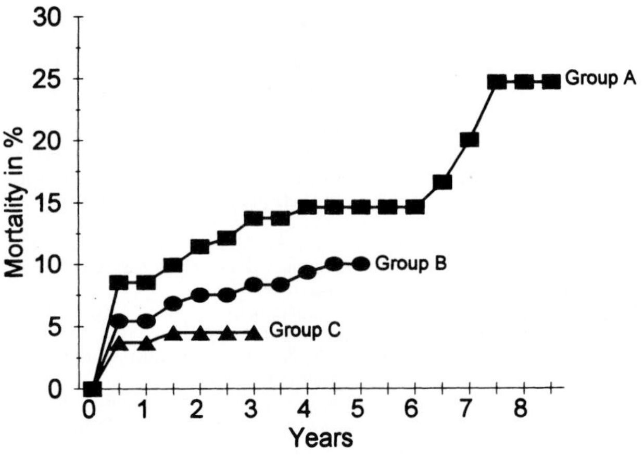

FIGURE 304–1. Mortality due to infections in heart transplant recipients in three different time periods. Group A: 1980–1985 (179 patients); group B: 1985–1987 (179 patients); group C: 1987–1990 (180 patients). Group A vs. group C, $p = 0.015$; mortality from other causes has been censored. (Data from ref. 2.)

Figure 304–2 illustrates the incidence of severe infections at various times after liver transplantation.[5] The figure excludes minor infections such as afebrile cystitis or localized HSV infection. It is apparent that the frequency of severe infections was quite high during the first or second month. Bacterial and fungal infections were most common in the first month and viral infections (mostly CMV) in the second month. Infections caused by "protozoa," most of which were actually *Pneumocystis*, occurred at a steady frequency during the first 6 months but were not seen thereafter. After 6 months, the rate of severe infections fell off to about one infection for every 4 patient years. All were caused by bacteria or fungi. This rate of late infection is similar to the frequency of severe, late infections seen in heart transplant recipients.[10]

Of the infections that occur after the first 6 months of transplantation, the most frequent are simply the common infections found in any population. Community-acquired pneumonia, diverticulitis, and cholecystitis are not unique for transplant recipients, but because of immune suppression these infections may manifest in an altered fashion or have more severe sequelae.[16]

Other late manifestations may represent reactivated or chronic viral infections. Eruptions of herpes zoster may occur at any time after transplantation.[10, 17] Subacute or chronic hepatitis, particularly that caused by hepatitis C virus (HCV), may become manifest many years after transplantation.[18] A number of tumors related to viral infection may also occur late, the most frequent being warts (verruca vulgaris). And some Epstein-Barr virus (EBV)–related lymphomas and lymphoproliferative syndromes occur after more than 1 year.[19–21]

A third type of late infection relates to chronic graft dysfunction. Lung transplant recipients with chronic rejection develop obliterative bronchiolitis and are susceptible to recurrent bacterial bronchitis and pneumonia.[9, 22] Liver transplant recipients may have recurrent cholangitis, often in association with biliary stricture.[5]

Finally, the risk for "opportunistic" infection declines, but never

TABLE 304–1 Overall Graft and Patient Survival Rates by Organ Transplanted

Organ	Graft Survival (%) 1 yr	Graft Survival (%) 3 yr	Patient Survival (%) 1 yr	Patient Survival (%) 3 yr
Kidney	83	76	94	89
Pancreas	74	67	91	84
Heart	82	74	83	75
Liver	79	62	79	71
Lung	70	53	72	55
Heart-Lung	62	50	62	50

Adapted from the 1997 Report of Center Specific Graft and Patient Survival Rates, UNOS, Richmond, VA, the Office of Special Programs, Health Resources and Services Administration, US Department of Health and Human Services, Rockville, MD.

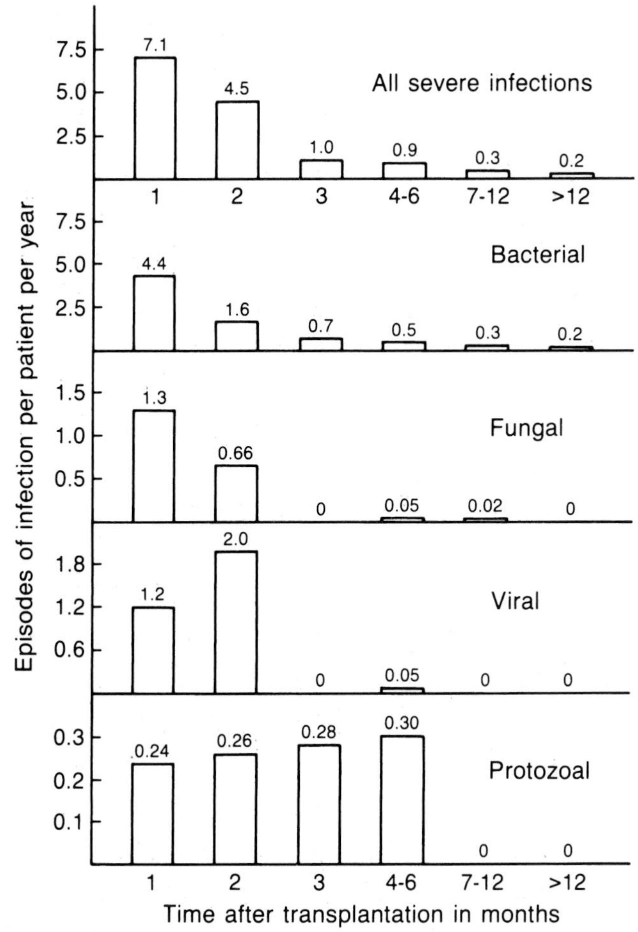

FIGURE 304–2. Incidence and timing of severe infections expressed in episodes of infection per liver transplant patient per year at different times after transplantation. Data on all severe, bacterial, fungal, viral, and "protozoal" (mostly *Pneumocystis*) infections are included.

completely disappears. Cryptococcal infection, for instance, often manifests late and without any inciting event.[23]

TYPES OF TRANSPLANTS AND CHARACTERISTIC INFECTIONS

Table 304–2 presents the type, severity, and characteristic sites of infections in 315 kidney, heart, heart-lung, and liver transplant recipients observed during the first year after transplantation.[5, 10, 24–26] These data were collected at the University of Pittsburgh from patients receiving very similar immunosuppressive regimens and before the advent of the complex prophylactic antimicrobial regimens used today. Therefore, they highlight intrinsic differences in the epidemiology of infections in different organ groups.

Although the number of infections was high in all transplant recipients, the type of infection, the severity, and the mortality varied widely with the organ or organs transplanted. The mean number of episodes of infection per patient was lowest in the renal group (0.98), and none of these patients died of infection. The heart-lung recipients had the largest number of episodes (3.19) and the largest number of deaths associated with infection (45%). The frequency of bacteremia may be used as an indicator of serious bacterial infection. It was highest in the liver transplantation group, and the most common origin of bacteremia in this group was the abdomen and biliary tract. As many as 75% of the heart-lung recipients had serious lung infections, and 32% of these patients became ill with CMV pneumonia. In comparison, symptomatic CMV disease, including CMV pneumonia, was relatively uncommon in renal transplant recipients. It is particularly striking how much better the outcome was for heart recipients than for heart-lung recipients, even though they were managed by the same physicians and were similar in having many serious pulmonary infections after transplantation. Invasive fungal infections, mostly caused by *Candida* and *Aspergillus*, are rarely a serious problem in renal recipients now, but in the 1960s half of the deaths in one series of renal transplant recipients were associated with serious fungal infection.[27] However, they were and still are a frequent serious problem in lung, heart-lung, and liver transplant recipients. Finally, Table 304–2 shows that the sites of infection after transplantation were closely related to the site of surgery.

Kidney Transplant Recipients

The most common site of infection in renal transplant recipients is the urinary tract.[28] The incidence has varied from 35 to 79% in several series.[7, 29, 30] In 1972, Myerowitz and colleagues found that 60% of bacteremias in kidney recipients arose from the urinary tract or adjacent sites.[31] One half of these patients had technical surgical complications such as ureteral leak or perinephric hematoma. Since then, surgical problems have decreased in frequency, but urosepsis still is an important problem. For example, in the study by Wagener and Yu, 40% of bacteremias in kidney recipients arose from the urinary tract.[32]

Most isolates are similar to those seen in urinary tract infections in other groups: *Escherichia coli*, other Enterobacteriaceae, *Pseudomonas aeruginosa*, *Enterococcus*, and *Candida*.[7, 31, 32] Avoidance of surgical complications and use of antimicrobial prophylaxis are the most important means of minimizing the impact of urinary infection.[33] Chronic and recurrent urinary tract infections remain problematic. Abnormalities such as ureteral reflux, strictures at the ureterovesicle junction, or neurogenic bladder should be sought in patients with recurrent infections. However, many of the late urinary tract infections seen in renal transplant recipients are benign. Griffin and Salaman[34] assessed the effect of urinary tract infections in 86 patients who had functional grafts for more than 1 year. One fifth of the patients acquired infection during the first 6 months, and a further fifth acquired it later. Recurrent or persistent infection was common

TABLE 304–2 Frequency, Severity, and Type of Infections Occurring in the First Year after Transplantation

Type of Transplant	N	Infections per Patient	Infectious Mortality (%)	Bacteremic Patients (%)	CMV Disease (%)*	Deep Fungal Infection (%)	Most Common Site	
							Site	*Proportion of All Infections (%)*
Renal	64	0.98	0	5	8 (5)	0	Urinary tract	41
Heart	119	1.36	15	13	16 (5)	8	Lung	27
Heart-lung	31	3.19	45	19	39 (32)	23	Lung	57
Liver	101	1.86	23	23	22 (5)	16	Abdomen and biliary	23

*Numbers in parentheses indicate percentage of all patients with CMV pneumonia.
Abbreviations: CMV, Cytomegalovirus.
Data on the four transplant groups are from the Pittsburgh experience, compiled from Ho,[25] Dummer,[10, 24] Kusne et al,[5] and Singh et al.[26]

but was usually asymptomatic and had no observable effect on graft function or the survival of patients. On the other hand, acute pyelonephritis that is not related to rejection may occur in a stable transplanted patient and cause acute renal failure. Renal shutdown resulting from infection is usually reversible with antibiotic treatment.[35] An extended course of antibiotics (6 weeks) is recommended to achieve eradication of the infecting bacterium. Extended courses of antibiotics may also be useful in patients who relapse with the same infecting organism after short-term treatment of cystitis and in those with special risk factors, such as diabetes or urinary retention.

Viral infections of the urinary tract are common but frequently asymptomatic. Infection by papovaviruses, either BK or JC, may occur after renal transplantation as a result of primary infection or reactivation. Papovaviruses are best detected by the polymerase chain reaction (PCR).[36–38] Unlike CMV, these viruses may reactivate or cause primary infection more than 3 months after transplantation. In a prospective study of 48 patients, Gardner and colleagues found that half of the BK and JC virus infections occurred during the first 3 months after transplantation and the remainder as long as 1 or 2 years thereafter.[36] Ureteral stenosis and hemorrhagic cystitis have been associated with papovavirus infection, but the viral infection has not been firmly established as a cause. Adenovirus may occasionally cause hemorrhagic cystitis in kidney recipients. The diagnosis can be made by isolating the virus or detecting adenoviral antigen in the urine.[39]

The clinician also must be alert also to other unusual pathogens. We have seen urinary tract tuberculosis that occurred during the first 2 weeks after transplantation and arose from a focus in the native kidneys. We have also seen *Mycoplasma hominis* infection cause a breakdown of a ureterovesicle anastomosis with subsequent graft loss.[40] Histoplasmosis may involve the transplanted kidney and cause renal failure.[41]

Historically, pneumonia occurred in 25 to 30% of renal transplant recipients and was the most common infectious cause of death.[42, 43] In the past, bacteria were a less common cause of transplantation-associated pneumonia than were cytomegalovirus and opportunists such as fungi, *Nocardia*, and *Pneumocystis*.[43, 44] More recently, CMV and other opportunistic infections have come under better control, and conventional bacterial pathogens have become relatively more common in transplantation populations.[45] Also, community-acquired viral infections caused by influenza, respiratory syncytial virus (RSV), and parainfluenza have been increasingly recognized in transplantation patients.[46]

Wound infections are relatively infrequent but are a serious problem when they occur, particularly if they involve the perinephric space. In the 1970s Kyriakides[46a] documented wound infection in 27 (6.1%) of 439 kidney recipients transplanted over a 6-year period. The mortality rate was 30%, and another 56% of patients survived but lost their grafts. Most infections were associated with surgical complications such as hematomas or urinary leaks. First-time transplantation patients without diabetes or surgical complications had a wound infection rate of only 0.7%. By the beginning of the cyclosporine era, a reduction in surgical complications and introduction of antibiotic prophylaxis had led to a fall in wound infection rates to 1 or 2%.[42, 47]

Although Table 304–2 lists no deaths from infections in renal transplant recipients, some such deaths may be expected after renal transplantation. In a survey of 604 renal transplant recipients at Minnesota, patients with infection had an 88% 3-year survival rate, compared with a 92% rate in patients without infection, revealing a small but significant increase in mortality.

Some renal transplant recipients continue to have infectious problems even after the first 6 months. Rubin identified these patients as those with a serum creatinine concentration higher than 2 mg/dl, a daily prednisone dose greater than 20 mg, a history of receiving multiple antirejection therapies, or a high incidence of chronic viral infection (e.g., HCV).[48]

Heart Transplant Recipients

Heart transplant recipients have more infections and are more affected by them than are kidney transplant recipients.[10, 28] In one multicenter study with long-term follow-up, infections accounted for one third to one half of all deaths.[49] The most common infections were CMV disease, bacteremia, soft tissue infections, and bacterial pneumonia. Most pneumonias in heart transplant recipients are caused by common pathogenic bacteria, both hospital-acquired and community-acquired (Table 304–3).[10] Although most infections occur in the first few months after transplantation, bacterial pneumonias continue to occur sporadically in the late post-transplantation period, after the immediate trauma of surgery is past.

Mediastinitis is a postoperative complication unique to heart, heart-lung, and lung transplant recipients. The pathogens seen are similar to those observed in other patients undergoing cardiothoracic surgery, with *Staphylococcus aureus* and *Staphylococcus epidermidis* predominating. The incidence in a large series from the Texas Heart Institute was 2.5% (9/361), which is in the range seen after conventional heart surgery.[50, 51] The clinical presentation may be subtle, with clinical signs such as low-grade fever or an elevated leukocyte count occurring for a number of days before more specific signs such as erythema, tenderness, or drainage along the sternal incision develop.[52] Infection by unusual organisms such as *M. hominis* or *Legionella* species should be considered when there is clinical mediastinitis and cultures for routine bacteria are negative.[53, 54] These species are likely to be missed if specific media such as A8 mycoplasma agar and buffered charcoal yeast agar are not used. Other unusual pathogens that have caused mediastinitis include *Aspergillus* and *Nocardia*.[16] Factors that are thought to predispose to mediastinitis in this population are repeat operations for hemorrhage, use of antirejection therapy, and the presence of diabetes mellitus.[51, 52] Surgical drainage is crucial to the success of treatment of any type of mediastinitis in the transplantation patient. There is considerable controversy regarding the best mode of drainage.

Griffith and coworkers reported a high rate of mediastinitis among patients in whom a Jarvik artificial heart device was used as a bridge to transplantation.[55] Most cases did not occur while the device was in place but only after it was removed and replaced with a transplant. The left ventricular assist devices that are currently preferred for mechanical support before heart transplantation seem to carry a much lower risk of infection.[56]

A number of other infections appear to be more common in heart recipients than in those receiving other types of transplants. These include systemic toxoplasmosis, nocardiosis, and Chagas' disease.[57–59] The importance of toxoplasmosis in heart transplant recipients is due to transmission of the infection by organisms encysted in the donated heart. Clinical toxoplasmosis usually occurs from a few

TABLE 304–3 Microbial Causes of Pneumonia in Transplant Recipients

Early Pneumonia (≤30 d)	Late Pneumonia (>30 d)
Common causes	
Gram-negative enteric bacilli	Pneumococcus
Staphylococcus aureus	*Haemophilus influenzae*
Aspiration	Cytomegalovirus
	No cause identified
Less common causes	
Aspergillus	*Pneumocystis*
Herpes simplex virus	*Nocardia*
Legionella	*Legionella*
Toxoplasma gondii	*Aspergillus*
	Gram-negative enteric bacilli
	Staphylococcus aureus
	Aspiration
	Varicella-zoster virus
	Tuberculosis
	Coccidioidomycosis
	Respiratory syncytial and other viruses
	Histoplasmosis

weeks to a few months after transplantation and is manifested by necrotizing pneumonitis, myocarditis, and encephalitis. The diagnosis may occasionally be made by identifying *Toxoplasma* cysts or tachyzoites on endomyocardial biopsy.[60] Heart transplantation patients at risk are *Toxoplasma*-seronegative recipients who receive hearts from seropositive donors. Prophylaxis with pyrimethamine (25 mg/day for 6 weeks) can reduce the frequency of toxoplasmosis in this population.[61] Routine use of *Pneumocystis* prophylaxis with trimethoprim-sulfamethoxazole (TMP-SMX) prevents toxoplasmosis in patients with the acquired immunodeficiency syndrome (AIDS) and may also be effective in transplantation patients.[62]

Patients with cardiomyopathy caused by chronic *Trypanosoma cruzi* infection who undergo transplantation may have relapses of acute Chagas' disease with clinical manifestations of fever, myocarditis, and skin lesions.[63] The disease can usually be controlled with chemotherapy.[57] *Nocardia* infections are also more frequently reported in heart transplant recipients than in recipients of kidney or liver transplants,[64] but the biologic reason for this increased rate of nocardiosis is unknown.

Despite frequent trauma to the tricuspid valve and right ventricular endocardium from repeated endomyocardial biopsies, a common post-transplantation practice, heart transplant recipients do not appear to be at substantial risk of endocarditis.

Heart-Lung and Lung Transplant Recipients

As a result of the shortage of suitable donors, the field of heart-lung and lung transplantation has progressed at a slower rate than others. In many respects, the heart-lung transplant recipients have infectious problems similar to those of heart transplant recipients, but the infections are more frequent and more severe. Infections cause about 75% of the deaths in heart-lung transplantation and 50% of deaths in lung transplantation.[15, 65] Early reports of heart-lung transplantation stressed the high rate of bacterial lung infections during the first few weeks after transplantation.[24, 66] These patients also have higher rates of mediastinitis, invasive fungal infections, *Pneumocystis* infection, and CMV pneumonia than comparable heart recipients.[9, 24, 67] Heart-lung and lung transplant recipients also experience rates of invasive aspergillosis that are greater than those of any other solid organ transplant group.[65, 68]

The exaggerated vulnerability of the transplanted lung to infection is probably multifactorial. In addition to the factors related to immunosuppression, allograft reactions, and anastomotic complications, other local factors such as ablation of the cough reflex below the tracheal or bronchial anastomosis are implicated. In the late post-transplantation period, as many as 65% of patients develop obliterative bronchiolitis.[69] This process is thought to be the main pathologic manifestation of chronic rejection of the lung, and it is often associated with recurrent pulmonary infections.[22]

The first success in transplanting lungs was achieved with combined heart-lung transplantation. Single and double lung transplantations have now largely replaced heart-lung transplantation as the procedures of choice for most patients with end-stage lung disease. The only major exception are patients who have severe cardiac anomalies that cannot be surgically repaired. Single and double lung procedures also allow the heart to be used for another patient with intrinsic heart disease. The types of infections seen in lung transplant recipients are similar to those in heart-lung recipients, although the overall survival rate is better.[1, 15] An interesting aspect of single lung transplantation is the occurrence of infections in the remaining native lung, which may be predisposed because of defects of ventilation or perfusion caused by the underlying lung disease.[11]

Donors for lung transplantation generally are intubated in intensive care units before harvest of their organs. The airways of these donors are often colonized with microorganisms, and occult parenchymal infection may be present.[70] It is useful to obtain cultures and gram stains of the donor bronchus or trachea to guide antibiotic therapy. Initial antibiotic prophylaxis should be aimed at common nosocomial pathogens, including *S. aureus* and enteric gram-negative bacilli. Another major problem in lung transplantation has been dehiscence of the airway anastomosis. This occurs during the first few weeks after transplantation, and it is often associated with bacterial or fungal infection at the anastomotic site.[11, 65] The incidence of severe airway complications appears to be declining and is only a few percent at many transplantation centers.[71]

Liver Transplant Recipients

Liver transplant recipients have higher rates of infection than renal or heart transplant recipients, and most deaths are associated with infection, either as a primary or secondary cause. Despite a decline in mortality in recent years, infections are still a major threat. In a study of 101 patients, most had at least one bacterial infection, and two thirds had at least one severe infection.[5] Most of the serious infections in liver transplant recipients are bacterial and fungal infections arising in the abdomen.[72, 73]

Bacteria are the most common pathogens causing serious infection after liver transplantation. The reported incidence has varied from 35 to 70%.[5, 72, 74] About half of these infections occur within 2 weeks after the transplant operation.[73] Identified risk factors include a prolonged duration of surgery, transfusion of large quantities of blood, use of a cholodochojejunostomy (Roux-en-Y) procedure for bile drainage, repeat transplantation, and CMV infection.[5, 73, 75] The most important sites of infection are the abdomen and biliary tract, the surgical wound, the lungs, and the blood stream, with or without associated catheter infection.

Fungal infections are encountered more often in liver transplant recipients than in recipients of other solid organ transplants. The reported incidence has been 20 to 42%, with a case fatality rate of 25 to 69%.[4, 72, 76] Eighty percent of fungal infections occur in the first month and 90% in the first 2 months.[4] *Candida* is the predominant pathogen. Risk factors noted in one retrospective analysis included elevated serum creatinine, longer operative time, retransplantation, and colonization with *Candida* at the time of transplantation.[77] Two thirds of patients with all four risk factors had invasive fungal infection. Other identified risk factors in this and other studies were administration of steroids before or after operation, duration of broad-spectrum antibiotic use, and CMV infection.[4, 5, 77]

Aspergillus infections occur in 1.5 to 4% of liver transplant recipients and are fatal in 80 to 100% of cases.[4, 14, 78] The average time of onset is somewhat later than for *Candida* infections, with 50% of cases occurring within 38 days after transplantation. Some of the important identified risk factors are severe hepatic injury before transplantation, use of augmented immunosuppression after transplantation, renal dysfunction, and CMV infection.

Abdominal Infections in Liver Transplant Recipients

Transplantation of the liver differs from other transplantation operations in the length and technical difficulty of the surgery and the frequency of severe bleeding problems. In addition, many liver transplant recipients have poor nutrition and severe metabolic difficulties. Abdominal infections after liver transplantation may be a result of technical aspects of the operation and their complications.[13] For example, a choledochojejunostomy with anastomosis of the biliary duct to a Roux-en-Y loop of jejunum is associated with more intra-abdominal infections, especially invasive fungal infections, than is choledochocholedochostomy with primary anastomosis of the donor's to the recipient's common bile duct.[5, 77]

Most *liver abscesses* in the transplanted liver are related to surgical problems such as biliary stricture or hepatic artery thrombosis.[5] The abscesses may be either solitary or multiple. They manifest as a febrile illness with bacteremia and leukocytosis. The organisms responsible are gram-negative enteric bacilli, enterococci, and anaerobes. The diagnosis is usually made by ultrasound or computed tomography (CT). Treatment with drainage and intravenous antibiotics is usually successful, if the source is biliary infection and any structural abnormalities can be corrected. In the case of hepatic artery thrombosis, the infectious symptoms can usually be controlled with antibiotics, but retransplantation ultimately is necessary.

Cholangitis is common after liver transplantation and often results from technical problems. Two situations predispose to cholangitis. The first is biliary stricture. Patients with strictures may have periodic bouts of cholangitis. Some improve after dilatation procedures, but in others operative repair is necessary. The second situation is that of cholangitis after radiologic study of the biliary tract, such as T-tube cholangiography and endoscopic retrograde cholangiopancreatography (ERCP).

It may not be easy to make a firm diagnosis of cholangitis, because many patients do not present with the classic "Charcot triad" of fever, abdominal pain, and jaundice. The clinical presentation may be difficult to distinguish from that of hepatic rejection. The diagnosis is more reliable if there is bacteremia or if a liver biopsy indicates pericholangitis with aggregates of neutrophils around bile ducts. It is important to choose antibiotics to cover gram-negative enteric and anaerobic bacteria when cholangitis is suspected. Because procedures such as T-tube cholangiography and ERCP may be followed by cholangitis and bacteremia, prophylactic antibiotics are recommended.

Peritonitis can accompany other abdominal infections, such as abdominal abscesses and cholangitis, and frequently complicates biliary leaks or disruption of an abdominal viscus. Bile peritonitis may occur after extraction of a T-tube. This is often well tolerated and may resolve by itself, but occasionally the leak persists and the chemical peritonitis becomes secondarily infected. The most common organisms involved in peritonitis are enterococcus and aerobic enteric gram-negative rods, but staphylococcal and candidal infections are not infrequent. In established peritonitis, prolonged antibiotic therapy is indicated together with drainage of associated abscesses and repair of technical problems such as biliary leaks.

Abdominal abscesses are more common in patients who have had frequent or lengthy abdominal operations. Only about one third of abdominal abscesses are associated with bacteremia. The location is frequently in the vicinity of the liver, but splenic, pericolic, and pelvic abscesses are also seen. Most patients with abscesses have had transplantation or another abdominal operation within the preceding 30 days.[5] One third of abscesses are polymicrobial, and although anaerobes and gram-negative enteric organisms cause most abscesses, they also may be caused by coagulase-positive or coagulase-negative staphylococci. Usually radiologic studies (CT, ultrasound) define the location of the abscess, but occasionally the abscess is discovered only at laparotomy. As with any other abscesses, the appropriate treatment is a combination of drainage and antibiotics directed against the responsible pathogens. Fever is part of the clinical presentation in most cases, but some abscesses, especially those caused by *Candida*, may not cause significant fever.

Pancreas Transplant Recipients

About 500 pancreas transplant operations are performed in the United States annually, or about 1 for every 20 renal transplantations.[1] Pancreas transplantation can improve quality of life and may prevent some of the secondary complications of type I diabetes mellitus by restoring physiologic titration of insulin in accordance with metabolic needs.[79] In exchange for possible perfect diabetic management and prevention of complications, however, patients assume the risks of a major operation and the problems of long-term immunosuppression. The experience so far comes largely from patients who have undergone or require kidney transplantation for diabetic nephropathy, and most patients have both pancreas and kidney implanted in a single operation. Current patient and graft survival rates approach those for kidney transplantation alone, but morbidity, especially infectious morbidity, is higher.[1, 80]

The main technical problem associated with pancreas transplantation has been adequate and safe drainage of exocrine secretions. The current practice of draining these secretions into the bladder using a conduit of duodenum is an advance over the older forms of enteric, percutaneous, or peritoneal drainage,[12, 81] but infectious complications are still a problem. In a series of 100 pancreas transplant patients from Wisconsin, 18% had surgical infections, 25% had opportunistic infections, and there were 71 readmissions to the hospital for infection.[81] A formal comparison of infections after isolated kidney and combined kidney-pancreas transplantation showed similar patient and graft survival rates, but more wound complications and CMV disease occurred among the patients receiving combined organs.[80] Pancreas transplant recipients also share with liver recipients a high rate of fungal infection. In a small but well detailed observation of 34 pancreas recipients from the Mayo Clinic, 35% had invasive fungal infections, most of which were caused by *Candida*.[82]

Small Bowel Transplantation

Small bowel transplantation is in the early stages of clinical development. It is used in patients who are dependent on parenteral nutrition to survive because of congenital or acquired intestinal disease or short gut syndrome after intestinal resection.[83] Although the mortality rate appears to be acceptably low, many patients have had very slow return of bowel function after the procedure, resulting in prolonged hospitalization. Rejection episodes cause mucosal injury, and some have led to breakdown of the "bowel-blood" barrier with subsequent septic syndromes.[84] More than 90% of patients develop significant infections, and the reported rates of infection are higher than in other transplantation groups.[85] Intra-abdominal pyogenic infections and blood-stream infections predominate; but the transplanted gut, like the transplanted liver and lung, appears to be very susceptible to CMV infection, including a tendency to relapse after successful antiviral treatment.[86] This form of transplantation may also be complicated by graft-versus-host disease presumably as a result of the large amount of lymphoid tissue transplanted with the gut.[84] EBV-associated lymphoproliferative disorders also seem to be a major problem, with rates as high as 11% reported in pediatric patients.[83]

SITES AND TYPES OF INFECTION

Infections of the Skin and Wound Infections

Infections of the skin are common after transplantation but are rarely life-threatening. They constitute a significant nuisance to the transplant recipient, and they may indicate the presence of serious systemic infection. The most frequent pathogens are listed in Table 304–4.

All transplant recipients who undergo surgical procedures are at risk for wound infections. The reported incidence of wound infections after transplantation varies widely from center to center; it appears to be highest among liver and pancreas transplant recipients, lower in heart and heart-lung transplant recipients, and lowest in renal transplant recipients.[5, 12, 47, 51] The most common isolate is *S. aureus*, but infections with gram-negative enteric bacteria, *S. epidermidis*, *Candida* spp., and *M. hominis* may also be seen.[54] Rarely, mucormycosis occurs in surgical wounds of transplantation

TABLE 304–4 Common Skin Manifestations of Infection in Transplant Recipients

Staphylococcus aureus
Herpes simplex virus
Varicella-zoster virus
Papillomavirus
Mycobacterium chelonae
Candida spp.
Dermatophytes

patients.[4] The wounds typically are black from tissue infarction caused by invasion of the blood vessels by the fungus. Tissue biopsy usually is required for a definitive diagnosis, and therapy should include wide surgical débridement.

The most common viral infections manifested in the skin are those caused by HSV and varicella-zoster virus. These are discussed later. Warts usually are treated with surgery, including electrosurgery or cryosurgery, or by the application of agents such as podophyllin. *Mycobacterium chelonae* causes pigmented nodular skin lesions that occur singly or in groups, often on extremities. About half of the cases are multifocal at presentation.[87] Dermatophyte infections usually respond to topical antifungals such as clotrimazole and miconazole; griseofulvin and oral azoles may be used for severe cases.

The skin is a target organ for many systemic infections. Systemic bacterial, fungal, nocardial, mycobacterial, and CMV infections may include skin manifestations. As a rule, one should be aggressive about investigating any new and unusual skin lesion with a biopsy.

Infections of the Urinary Tract

Urinary tract infections are discussed in the section on "Kidney Transplant Recipients."

Infections of the Blood Stream

Bacteremia. The basic approach to bacteremia is the same whether or not the patient has undergone transplantation. The first step is to ascertain the source of the bacteremia. The most common sites producing bacterial blood-stream infections are the lung, the urinary tract, the abdomen (including the biliary tract), soft tissues, and intravenous catheters. Inability to pinpoint a source is not rare, especially in liver transplant recipients.[5, 32] In one large study of bacteremia in multiple transplant groups at a single institution, the overall mortality rate was 23%.[32] Mortality was highest in heart recipients and lowest in kidney recipients. Risk factors for mortality were the presence of gram-negative or polymicrobial infection, early onset of infection after transplantation, the presence of pneumonia, and impaired kidney and liver function.

The source of bacteremia varies with the type of transplantation and is most commonly related to the transplantation site (see Table 304–1). For example, 41 to 60% of the bacteremias in kidney recipients come from the urinary tract or from perinephric sources.[8, 32, 88] Bacteremia in kidney recipients is relatively uncommon in the very early post-transplantation period (14 days) but relatively more common in the late post-transplantation period. Many of these late bacteremias are caused by urinary infection.[32]

Among 101 liver recipients monitored for more than 1 year, 33 bacteremias occurred in 26 patients.[5] Thirty-six percent of the bacteremias had a fatal outcome. The most common source was the abdomen (33%), followed by the urinary tract (21%). The other bacteremias with a known source arose from wound infection (9%), intravenous catheters (6%), pneumonia (6%), and endocarditis (3%). Twenty-one percent of the bacteremias had no documented source, but most of these probably originated in the abdomen. Gram-negative enteric bacilli were the most common isolates in this and other series.[32, 73] The use of an oral bowel decontamination regimen to suppress gram-negative flora led to a preponderance of gram-positive isolates at one liver transplantation center.[89] The emergence of vancomycin-resistant enterococcus has also increased the frequency of gram-positive blood-stream isolates in some liver transplantation units.[90]

Hofflin and colleagues compared the infectious complications of heart transplant recipients receiving either azathioprine or cyclosporine supplemented with corticosteroids and noted that the incidence of bacteremia declined from 29% to 15% in those receiving cyclosporine.[3] The isolates were equally divided between gram-positive and gram-negative bacteria and included only one opportunistic infection (*Listeria monocytogenes*).

Blood-Borne Infection with Nonbacterial Agents. The only fungi that are isolated from the blood stream of transplantation patients with any frequency are *Candida* and cryptococci. Catheter-related sepsis with *Candida* is a well-recognized entity in normal hosts that can often be treated by catheter removal and administration of fluconazole. However, the isolation of *Candida* from the blood stream of transplant recipients usually signals severe infection and necessitates a concerted search for a source and therapy with amphotericin. Cryptococcemia is frequently associated with cryptococcal infection elsewhere, most often in the central nervous system (CNS), and carries a poor prognosis.[91] If routine viral cultures of buffy-coat specimens are performed on transplant recipients, viremia with CMV will be found in 25 to 50% of the patients during the first 2 months after transplantation.[92] Less than half of these patients have a clinical illness caused by CMV, so the detection of CMV in the blood does not have a high positive predictive value for CMV disease.[28] However, significant CMV disease usually is accompanied by CMV viremia. Both varicella-zoster virus and HSV may be detected in buffy-coat cultures during disseminated disease with these agents. Viremia with HSV usually is associated with fulminant and often fatal disease.[93]

Infections in the Chest

Pulmonary Infections. The usual microbial causes of pneumonia in the transplant recipient are listed in Table 304–3. They are subdivided according to whether the pneumonia occurs during the first month after transplantation or later and whether they are common or less common causes. The key to the management of pneumonia in transplant recipients is rapid identification of the responsible pathogen and initiation of specific therapy. Patients with a brief duration of symptoms ($\leq$3 days) who have a focal chest infiltrate and are producing sputum with neutrophils and a predominant bacterial population on gram stain are likely to have a routine bacterial pneumonia. Therapy to cover the bacteria found in the sputum usually can be started while culture results are pending. The presence of diffuse infiltrates (or nodular lesions), a nonproductive cough, or a long duration of symptoms ($>$7 days) favors the presence of an unusual or "opportunistic" pathogen, and consideration should be given to the early use of invasive techniques to make the diagnosis.

Transtracheal aspiration was used for many years to obtain uncontaminated respiratory secretions for diagnosis, but it has been supplanted by bronchoscopy employing bronchoalveolar lavage (BAL) with or without tissue biopsy. BAL provides access to cells and fluid from the alveoli and therefore has excellent sensitivity ($>$90%) in the diagnosis of *Pneumocystis* infection.[94] Cytologic analysis of the cellular material returned from BAL is also helpful for detecting inclusion bodies of CMV and other viruses.

Patients who present with new peripheral lung nodules or cavities on chest radiography may undergo percutaneous aspiration of these lesions with radiographic guidance (CT or fluoroscopy) to obtain diagnostic material. Open or thoracoscopic lung biopsy usually is reserved for those patients in whom these procedures do not yield a strong presumptive diagnosis. Lung biopsy might be used initially in patients in whom the suspicion of lung tumor (e.g., post-transplant lymphoma) is high.

The frequency of *Legionella* infection varies widely, depending on its endemicity in the hospital and the sensitivity of diagnostic methods.[95] Even when *Legionella* organisms are absent from the nosocomial environment, sporadic community-acquired cases will continue to occur among transplantation patients, because *Legionella* infection is responsible for 2 to 15% of community-acquired pneumonias.[95] Special laboratory measures are necessary for the diagnosis of *Legionella* pneumonia. The most specific method of diagnosis is isolation of the organism on special media, but detection of urinary antigen is also helpful. Even with specific treatment, a fatal outcome may result.[96] The radiographic presentation is variable and may include focal infiltrates spreading to multiple lobes, globular pleural-based lesions, lung abscess, pleural effusion, or pericardial effusion. Any one of the serotypes of *Legionella pneumophila* or *Legionella micdadei* may be responsible.[31] Erythromycin, with or without rifampin, has been the treatment of choice, but these drugs interfere with the metabolism of cyclosporine and tacrolimus. Quinolones are very active and have been recommended as a suitable alternative in transplant recipients.[95, 97]

Aspergillus or *Nocardia* infection may also be relatively common in some localities. The environmental factors determining these occurrences are poorly understood. Community-acquired respiratory viruses may cause pneumonia in transplant recipients. This is best documented for respiratory syncytial virus and influenza.[46]

Abdominal and Gastrointestinal Infections

Abdominal infections in liver transplant recipients have already been discussed. They also occur at increased frequency among recipients of pancreas and small bowel transplants.[81, 85] They are less common after transplant operations that do not involve the abdomen. When they do occur, they are usually related to preexisting medical conditions such as biliary stones or diverticulosis.

Studies in developing countries show that transplant recipients are very susceptible to *Salmonella* infection.[98] *Clostridium difficile* infections are common in some populations who are heavily treated with antibiotics. For instance, symptomatic *C. difficile* infections were seen in 3 to 6% of liver transplant recipients.[5, 73] Infections caused by *Shigella*, *Campylobacter*, or *Helicobacter* do not appear to be increased in transplant recipients.[99]

Hyperinfection and disseminated infection with *Strongyloides stercoralis* were substantial problems in the past but appear to have virtually disappeared.[100, 101] One reason may be the ability of cyclosporine to inhibit this parasite, as has been shown in an animal model.[102] Tacrolimus does not seem to have this antiparasitic effect.[103] Universal pretransplantation screening of stools for parasites is probably not cost-effective, but vigilance for this infection should be maintained in patients from endemic areas.

Hepatitis. The most important causes of hepatitis in transplantation patients are HBV, HCV, and CMV. In many respects, CMV is the least important cause of hepatitis because it never leads to chronic hepatitis. The presence of chronic HBV infection adversely affects survival after transplantation.[104, 105] Certain subgroups of patients with HBV infection may have worse prognoses. For example, 63% of renal recipients with circulating HBV DNA or hepatitis E antigen died of liver disease during 10 years of follow-up, compared with only 33% of those without such markers.[106] Likewise, liver transplant candidates with HBV DNA in their blood are more likely to have recurrent infection and liver disease after transplantation than are candidates with HBV infection but without HBV DNA.[107] An exception is patients with fulminant HBV infection, who have lower rates of recurrence. Some liver transplant recipients with recurrent HBV infection develop a rapidly fatal liver disease called *fibrosing cytolytic hepatitis*, in which the pathology of the liver shows hepatocyte drop-out, fibrosis, and a very high viral load, but only sparse inflammatory infiltrates.[108] The situation with hepatitis D is less clear because of complex interactions between the hepatitis D virus and HBV. Preliminary data suggest that recurrence of hepatitis D may be less common than recurrence of HBV infection,[107] and the combined presence of the delta agent and HBV infection in the same liver transplantation candidate may actually lower the rate of HBV recurrence.[109]

The recurrence rate of HBV infection after liver transplantation can be reduced by regimens employing serial infusions of hepatitis B immune globulin (HBIG).[110] Large doses are required and this adds a major expense to the cost of transplantation. Two antiviral drugs, lamuvidine and famciclovir, have been found to inhibit the replication of HBV. Both agents are well tolerated and have antiviral effect in vivo, as demonstrated by lowering of HBV DNA or clearance of hepatitis B surface antigen in small numbers of infected patients, either before or after transplantation.[111, 112] Development of resistance has also been described, so long-term benefit of these agents is uncertain and requires further study.[111]

Information on HCV infection after transplantation is rapidly emerging. It is clear that the virus can cause liver disease in patients with either normal or transplanted livers.[113–116] Candidates who have HCV viremia before liver transplantation almost always reinfect their livers after transplantation, and 43 to 75% develop hepatitis during the first year after transplantation.[114] Gane and colleagues found that liver transplant recipients with recurrent HCV infection retained their grafts and survived as well as patients without HCV infection for 5 years after transplantation. However 27% of HCV-infected patients developed moderate chronic active hepatitis, and 8% developed cirrhosis during follow-up.[117] Ynares and associates found that HCV infection did not affect patient or graft survival in two cohorts of renal transplant recipients monitored for 5 and 10 years after transplantation.[118] Other authors, however, found worse outcomes in HCV-infected renal transplant recipients. Pereira and coworkers reported that HCV-infected kidney recipients had a five times higher rate of liver disease and a three times higher rate of death than uninfected recipients.[119] Many of the deaths occurred as a result of septic complications. There is great interest in discovering factors that predict the progression of liver disease from HCV infection in transplant recipients, but available studies have not produced uniform results. Infection with HCV type 1b has been frequently but not universally recognized as a risk factor.[117, 120, 121] The occurrence of hepatitis after transplantation has not correlated with the quantity of HCV RNA in the blood.[122]

Antiviral treatment of HCV infection with interferon is commonly used in nontransplantation patients, but in transplant recipients interferon therapy has had only weak and transient effects.[123] It also may precipitate rejection.[124] In a small pilot study of ribivirin treatment in 9 liver recipients, liver injury test results improved in all patients, but the amount of HCV detected by quantitative PCR fell only slightly and biochemical relapse occurred when ribivirin was discontinued.[125] At present, there is no consensus on how to best treat HCV infection after transplantation, and better therapy is clearly needed.

Infections of the Central Nervous System

Infections of the CNS in transplantation patients require prompt evaluation and diagnosis and early, appropriate therapy. Table 304–5 lists the most commonly seen agents.[8, 126] Notably absent on the list are the pyogenic bacteria and HSV, which are common pathogens at other sites in such patients. The highest risk for opportunistic CNS infection is present for 1 to 6 months after transplantation; an exception is cryptococcal meningitis, which is usually a "late" event.[23]

L. monocytogenes is a motile, gram-positive rod that typically causes bacteremia, meningitis, and at times cerebritis in the immunosuppressed transplantation patient.[23, 127] The gram stain of the spinal fluid is negative in more than half of the cases. Usually the diagnosis is made by culturing the organism from cerebrospinal fluid or blood. All patients with *Listeria* bacteremia should have lumbar punctures,

TABLE 304–5 Pathogens of the Central Nervous System in Transplantation Patients

Listeria monocytogenes
Aspergillus fumigatus
Cryptococcus neoformans
Toxoplasma gondii
Nocardia spp.
Agents of mucormycosis
Polyomavirus
Candida
Varicella-zoster virus

even in the absence of CNS signs, because the mortality is much higher when CNS disease is present.

Aspergillus fumigatus is a ubiquitous fungus that is an important cause of infection in immunocompromised patients. The most common portal of entry is the lung; invasive sinus infection also occurs but is less common. Patients with *Aspergillus* infection usually have been recently transplanted or are receiving high doses of corticosteroids.[128] *Aspergillus* invades blood vessels, and metastatic spread to the brain may occur early in the course of the infection. Examination of the cerebrospinal fluid is rarely helpful in establishing the diagnosis.[129] The CT scan reveals single or multiple low-density lesions. The prognosis of CNS *Aspergillus* infections is dismal, and the only hope is to begin high-dose amphotericin B therapy as early as possible.[130]

Cryptococcal meningitis usually manifests subacutely, often with only headache or low-grade fever.[23, 48] Pulmonary disease caused by *Cryptococcus* coexists in about 40% of the cases. A lumbar puncture should be performed in any patient with cryptococcal infection even if no CNS signs are present. The spinal fluid usually has a white blood cell count lower than 500 cells/mm^3 with lymphocyte predominance, and a positive cryptococcal antigen test. India ink preparations reveal positive findings in about 50% of patients.

Toxoplasma gondii is a protozoan that can cause a nonspecific encephalopathy, diffuse meningoencephalitis, or progressive single or multiple brain lesions. *Toxoplasma* infection has been reported in renal, cardiac, liver, and bone marrow transplant recipients.[58, 131–133] Toxoplasmosis usually results from primary infection in solid organ transplant recipients, but reactivation is the usual mechanism in bone marrow recipients. The cardiac allograft has been shown to be a source of infection.[58, 134] The neurologic manifestations of a *Toxoplasma* infection are seizures, visual disturbances, headache, photophobia, and focal neurologic findings. Serology should be performed on cardiac donors and recipients to identify patients at risk for disease transmitted by the allograft. Definitive diagnosis usually requires tissue biopsy, although occasionally the organism may be isolated from peripheral blood cells in tissue culture.[131, 133] The fatality rate is high, and often the diagnosis is not established until autopsy. The treatment of choice is pyrimethamine (50 to 75 mg/day) and sulfadiazine (4 to 6 g/day).

Nocardia asteroides is a gram-positive, beaded, branching rod that may cause CNS lesions. For unknown reasons, pulmonary nocardiosis may occur more commonly in certain centers than others.[59, 64] The primary route of infection is pulmonary, with metastatic spread to bone, skin, and CNS. It is possible to have single or multiple brain abscesses, but meningitis is rare. *Nocardia* brain abscesses may benefit from stereotactic aspiration biopsy and surgical drainage in addition to long-term (9-month) antimicrobial therapy. Sulfonamides are the mainstay of treatment, because they penetrate the CNS well and most isolates are sensitive. In the presence of disseminated disease, it may be prudent to use more than one drug and obtain sensitivity testing on isolates.[135] Agents such as amikacin, imipenem, and cefotaxime have shown good activity in animal models, with more rapid killing than sulfonamides.[136] Also, isolates with resistance to commonly used antibiotics, including sulfonamides, have been described.[135]

SPECIFIC PROBLEMS OF HERPESVIRUS INFECTIONS

Herpes Simplex Virus and Varicella-Zoster Virus Infections

HSV reactivates after transplantation in approximately 60% of recipients not given antiviral prophylaxis.[10, 26, 28] As many as half of these persons develop symptomatic oral or genital lesions. Genital herpes may become clinically evident for the first time after transplantation and may be very distressing for the patient. If the patient is not receiving antiviral prophylaxis, reactivation usually occurs early, about 1 to 2 weeks after transplantation. Visceral infection has been reported in a small number of patients; most cases have been HSV hepatitis after liver transplantation or HSV pneumonia after lung transplantation.[15, 137] A rare event is primary HSV occurring early after transplantation. The donor organ has been shown to be the source in a few patients.[93, 138] These primary HSV infections may produce a severe septic syndrome with hypotension and disseminated intravascular coagulation.

Most cases of reactivated HSV infection can be reliably diagnosed and respond well to antiviral therapy. Use of antiviral prophylaxis prevents HSV infection; it is a reasonable approach and is preferable in patients who are at risk for visceral HSV infection, such as lung or liver transplant recipients. Low-dose acyclovir (400 mg twice daily) for the first 3 to 4 weeks after transplantation is usually sufficient.[101]

Herpes zoster occurs in 7 to 16% of patients during the first year after transplantation, and further cases occur sporadically during long-term follow-up.[10, 17, 26, 139, 140] Antiviral therapy is indicated, because healing is slow and transplantation patients occasionally develop disseminated infection. We usually use oral therapy with acyclovir, valaciclovir, or famciclovir for dermatomal zoster. If the patient has ophthalmic zoster or there is evidence of dissemination, intravenous acyclovir is used initially. Chickenpox in a transplantation patient is a medical emergency and requires admission to hospital and treatment with intravenous acyclovir. It is useful to perform serology for varicella-zoster virus before transplantation to identify patients at risk for chickenpox so that they can be counseled and considered for vaccination.[140] Varicella-seronegative transplant recipients who have exposure to chickenpox may benefit from the use of varicella-zoster immunoglobulin (VZIG) if it can be given within 72 hours.[101]

Cytomegalovirus Infections

Almost all seropositive graft recipients experience reactivation of latent CMV infections, and most seronegative recipients develop primary infections. Primary infections are more likely to be symptomatic.[26, 141, 142] The proportion of infected patients who become symptomatic is also a function of the intensity of immunosuppression.

The most common and least serious type of CMV disease is a mononucleosis syndrome characterized by fever, frequently of prolonged duration, with few or no focal symptoms. There may be abnormalities of the liver function tests, although rarely jaundice, and leukopenia is often present. Interstitial pneumonia is the most serious complication of CMV infection and is present in most fatal cases. Fever, breathlessness, hypoxemia, and diffuse infiltrates on chest radiographs are typical findings but are not pathognomonic, and a tissue diagnosis by BAL or lung biopsy is required for diagnosis.[94] CMV pneumonia may coexist with other pathogens, particularly *Pneumocystis.*

One of the more troublesome manifestations of CMV disease is ulcerations in the gastrointestinal tract. These ulcerations are often multiple and may be found anywhere from the esophagus to the rectum. Severe complications such as bleeding or perforation occur in some patients. CMV disease should be considered in the differential diagnosis of transplantation patients who have fever and acute or subacute abdominal symptoms, especially if transplantation occurred within the last 4 months or there was a recent intensification of immunosuppression. The exact frequency with which CMV causes gastrointestinal disease is difficult to determine, because a definite diagnosis depends on endoscopy and CMV may involve inaccessible parts of the bowel.[99]

CMV hepatitis occurs in up to 17% of liver transplant recipients and is more common with primary than with reactivation infection.[143] The pathologic finding is microabscesses scattered around the liver lobule. Inclusion bodies may be easy to find or scant.[144] The disease is typically mild and may even be an incidental finding in an asymptomatic patient undergoing liver biopsy for elevated liver enzyme concentrations.[143]

Controlled trials of antiviral therapy for CMV disease in solid organ transplant recipients have never been performed, but considerable experience has led to a consensus that antiviral therapy is beneficial, unless started very late in the course of the disease. Intravenous ganciclovir is the drug of choice and is well tolerated. The duration of therapy is usually 2 to 3 weeks. Foscarnet is also very active, but it is infrequently used in solid organ recipients because of its potential for nephrotoxicity.

Other Viral Infections

Infection with human herpesvirus-6 (HHV-6) has been described as a possible cause of fever and leukopenia in transplant recipients.[145] Most cases are caused by reactivation, and the timing of the infection overlaps to a large extent with that of CMV infection, although the onset may be somewhat earlier. It may be difficult to reach a definite diagnosis because there are no characteristic pathologic lesions and the symptoms may be similar to those seen in CMV infection. Adenovirus and respiratory syncytial virus are important pathogens in pediatric transplant recipients and occasionally are seen in adults.[46, 67, 146, 147] As with CMV, adenoviral infections may be asymptomatic, but they also may cause diffuse pneumonia, necrotizing hepatitis, and hemorrhagic cystitis. In one series, the mortality rate was 45% when invasive infection occurred.[147] Biopsy of an involved organ may reveal characteristic pathologic findings and may facilitate a rapid diagnosis, but there is no known effective treatment. Respiratory syncytial virus infection should be considered when a transplantation patient has a respiratory tract illness between November and April. Therapy with aerosolized ribivirin may be helpful and is usually well tolerated, but is also expensive and has not been scientifically evaluated in immunosuppressed populations.[148]

Lymphoproliferative Disease and Epstein-Barr Virus Infection

EBV infection may occur as a primary or a reactivation infection in transplant recipients. Primary infection occurs in about three fourths of seronegative children or adults.[25, 149, 150] Reactivation infection, defined by fourfold or greater rise in IgG antibodies to viral capsid antigen, is detected in about one third of seropositive persons. Most infections occur within the first 4 months after transplantation.[151] The most important disease associated with EBV infections in transplantation patients is EBV-related post-transplantation lymphoproliferative disorder (PTLD). The risk for PTLD is high in EBV-seronegative persons. We found that 35% of 40 EBV-seronegative adult liver transplant recipients developed PTLD during follow-up.[21] These results compare with a PTLD rate of 2% in EBV-seropositive adult liver transplant recipients.[150] They underscore the importance of obtaining pretransplantation EBV serology to assess susceptibility to primary infection. Most EBV-seropositive patients with PTLD also have evidence of reactivation of EBV infection. This has been shown by the detection of serologic rises to EBV antigens or, more recently, by measurement of EBV viral load with quantitative molecular studies.[149, 152] The mechanism by which EBV promotes PTLD is unknown but is under active investigation.

PTLD comprises three general clinical types.[19, 150, 153] First, it may be a mononucleosis-like syndrome without evidence of tissue involvement except in tonsils and peripheral lymph nodes. The second manifestation is a diffuse polymorphous B-cell infiltration in many visceral organs. This type may be preceded by a mononucleosus-like episode that either evolves directly into the tissue infiltrative process or is temporally separated from it. It may resemble the lethal X-linked lymphoproliferative syndrome described in children with a congenital susceptibility to EBV.[154] Terminal hepatitis with disseminated intravascular coagulation, other clotting defects, and deficient immunoglobulin levels have been seen.[150] The third clinical presentation is the appearance of localized extranodal tumors in the gastrointestinal tract, neck, thorax, or other parts of the body. Tumors in the brain have also been described.[19] These tumors have the microscopic appearance of lymphomas and contain EBV genome detectable by nucleic acid hybridization or EBV-specific antigens (e.g., nuclear antigen). The tumors may be either monoclonal or oligoclonal, as determined by IgG light-chain phenotype or immunoglobulin gene rearrangement. Involved tissues of the other two clinical types of PTLD also contain evidence of EBV infection, demonstrated by presence of EBV nuclear antigen or EBV genome.[153, 155] Acyclovir inhibits the production of EBV virions in the lytic phase of EBV production, but does not affect the replication of cells latently infected with EBV.[156] Acyclovir has no proven efficacy either in the mononucleosis syndrome or in prevention or amelioration of these lymphoproliferative syndromes. It has, however, been used empirically.

Mononucleosis syndromes may resolve and tumors may regress after reduction or elimination of immunosuppression.[153] This regression occurs in about one half of cases. It is more common with tumors that appear during the first year after transplantation and in those that are polymorphous in appearance or have cells that contain more than a single clone by immunohistologic or immunoglobulin gene rearrangement studies.[157] However, there is no prognostic indicator that is entirely reliable. Other modalities of treatment, including chemotherapy, interferon, antilymphocyte serums, and specific cytotoxic cells, have been described in small series. The most promising at this time is infusion of HLA-compatible, EBV-specific cytotoxic T cells (CTLs). This has been found to be feasible and effective in cases of PTLD in marrow recipients, where the PTLD is of donor origin and proper CTLs from the donor can be prepared and infused.[158] It is more difficult to apply this treatment for PTLD in solid organ recipients.

REFERENCES

1. 1997 Report of Center Specific Graft and Patient Survival Rates, UNOS, Richmond, VA, and the Division of Transplantation, Office of Special Programs, Health Resources and Services Administration, U.S. Department of Health and Human Services, Rockville, Md. (The data and analyses in the 1997 Report of Center Specific Graft and Patient Survival Rates have been supplied by UNOS. The authors alone are responsible for the reporting and interpretation of the data.)
2. Dummer JS. Antibiotic prophylaxis and management of infectious complications. In: Kaye MP, O'Connell JB, eds. Heart and Lung Transplantation 2000. Austin, TX: R. G. Landes; 1993:78.
3. Hofflin JM, Potasman I, Baldwin JC, et al. Infectious complications in heart transplant patients receiving cyclosporine and corticosteroids. Ann Intern Med. 1987;106:209.
4. Wajszczuk CP, Dummer JS, Ho M, et al. Fungal infections in liver transplant recipients. Transplantation. 1985;40:347.
5. Kusne S, Dummer JS, Singh N, et al. Infections after liver transplantation: An analysis of 101 consecutive cases. Medicine (Baltimore). 1988;67:132.
6. Kusne S, Fung J, Alessiani M, et al. Infections during a randomized trial comparing cyclosporine to FK 506 immunosuppression in liver transplantation. Transplant Proc. 1992;24:429.
7. Rubin RH, Wolfson JS, Cosimi AB, Tolkoff-Rubin NE. Infection in the renal transplant recipient. Am J Med. 1981;70:405.
8. Peterson PK, Anderson RC. Infection in renal transplant recipients: Current approaches to diagnosis, therapy, and prevention. Am J Med. 1986;81:2.
9. Dummer JS, Montero CG, Griffith BP, et al. Infections in heart-lung transplant recipients. Transplantation. 1986;41:725.
10. Dummer JS. Infectious complications of transplantation. Cardiovasc Clin. 1990;20:163.
11. Horvath J, Dummer S, Loyd J, et al. Infection in the transplanted and native lung after single lung transplantation. Chest. 1993;104:681.
12. Hesse UJ, Sutherland DE, Simmons RL, Najarian JS. Intra-abdominal infections in pancreas transplant recipients. Ann Surg. 1986;203:153.
13. Lebeau G, Yanaga K, Marsh JW, et al. Analysis of surgical complications after 397 hepatic transplantations. Surg Gynecol Obstet. 1990;170:317.
14. Kusne S, Torre-Cisneros J, Manez R, et al. Factors associated with invasive lung aspergillosis and the significance of positive *Aspergillus* culture after liver transplantation. J Infect Dis. 1992;166:1379.
15. Maurer JR, Tullis E, Grossman RF, et al. Infectious complications following lung transplantation. Chest. 1992;101:1056.
16. Boden MD, Dummer JS. Infections after organ transplantation. J Intensive Care Med. 1997;12:166.

17. Rifkind D. The activation of varicella-zoster virus infections by immunosuppressive therapy. J Lab Clin Med. 1966;68:463.
18. Terrault NA, Wright TL, Pereira BJ. Hepatitis C infection in the transplant recipient. Infect Dis Clin North Am. 1995;9:943.
19. Hanto DW, Frizzera G, Purtilo DT, et al. Clinical spectrum of lymphoproliferative disorders in renal transplant recipients and evidence for the role of Epstein-Barr virus. Cancer Res. 1981;41:4253.
20. Manez R, Breinig MC, Linden P, et al. Posttransplant lymphoproliferative disease in primary Epstein-Barr virus infection after liver transplantation: The role of cytomegalovirus disease. J Infect Dis. 1997;176:1462.
21. Armitage JM, Kormos RL, Stuart RS, et al. Posttransplant lymphoproliferative disease in thoracic organ transplant patients: Ten years of cyclosporine-based immunosuppression. J Heart Lung Transplant. 1991;10:877.
22. Duncan AJ, Dummer JS, Paradis IL, et al. Cytomegalovirus infection and survival in lung transplant recipients. J Heart Lung Transplant. 1991;10:638.
23. Hooper DC, Pruitt AA, Rubin RH. Central nervous system infection in the chronically immunosuppressed. Medicine (Baltimore). 1982;61:166.
24. Dummer JS. Infectious complications of heart-lung recipients. In: Cooper DKC, Novitzky D, eds. The Transplantation and Replacement of Thoracic Organs. Lancaster, England: Kluwer Academic Publishers; 1990:325–332.
25. Ho M. Infection and organ transplantation. In: Gelman S, ed. Anesthesia and Organ Transplantation. Philadelphia: WB Saunders; 1987:47.
26. Singh N, Dummer JS, Kusne S, et al. Infections with cytomegalovirus and other herpesviruses in 121 liver transplant recipients: Transmission by donated organ and the effect of OKT3 antibodies. J Infect Dis. 1988;158:124.
27. Rifkind D, Marchioro TL, Schneck SA, Hill RB Jr. Systemic fungal infections complicating renal transplantation and immunosuppressive therapy: Clinical, microbiologic, neurologic and pathologic features. Am J Med. 1967;43:28.
28. Ho M, Wajszczuk CP, Hardy A, et al. Infections in kidney, heart, and liver transplant recipients on cyclosporine. Transplant Proc. 1983;15:2768.
29. Hinman FJ, Schmaelzle JF, Belzer FO. Urinary tract infection in renal homotransplant recipients. J Urol. 1969;101:673.
30. Peterson PK, Ferguson R, Fryd DS, et al. Infectious diseases in hospitalized renal transplant recipients: A prospective study of a complex and evolving problem. Medicine (Baltimore). 1982;61:360.
31. Myerowitz RL, Pasculle AW, Dowling JN, et al. Opportunistic lung infection due to "Pittsburgh Pneumonia Agent." N Engl J Med. 1979;301:953.
32. Wagener MM, Yu VL. Bacteremia in transplant recipients: A prospective study of demographics, etiologic agents, risk factors and outcomes. Am J Infect Control. 1992;20:239.
33. Fox BC, Sollinger HW, Belzer FO, Maki DG. A prospective, randomized, double-blind study of trimethoprim-sulfamethoxazole for prophylaxis of infection in renal transplantation: Clinical efficacy, absorption of trimethoprim-sulfamethoxazole, effects on the microflora, and the cost-benefit of prophylaxis. Am J Med. 1990;89:255.
34. Griffin PJ, Salaman JR. Urinary tract infections after renal transplantation: Do they matter? Br Med J. 1979;1:710.
35. Gillum DM, Kelleher SP. Acute pyelonephritis as a cause of late transplant dysfunction. Am J Med. 1985;78:156.
36. Gardner SD, Mackenzie EFD, Smith C, Porter AA. Prospective study of the human polyoma viruses BK and JC cytomegalovirus in renal transplant recipients. J Clin Pathol. 1984;37:578.
37. Hogan TF, Borden EC, McBain JA, et al. Human polyomavirus infections with JC virus and BK virus in renal transplant patients. Ann Intern Med. 1980;92:373.
38. Bogdanovic G, Ljungman P, Wang F, Dalianis T. Presence of human polyomavirus DNA in the peripheral circulation of bone marrow transplant patients with and without hemorrhagic cystitis. Bone Marrow Transplant. 1996;17:573.
39. Buchanan WJ, Bowman JS, Jaffers G. Adenoviral acute hemorrhagic cystitis following renal transplantation. Am J Nephrol. 1990;10:350.
40. McMahon DK, Dummer JS, Pasculle AW, Cassell G. Extragenital *Mycoplasma hominis* infections in adults. Am J Med. 1990;89:275.
41. Superdock KR, Dummer JS, Koch MO, et al. Disseminated histoplasmosis presenting as urinary tract obstruction in a renal transplant recipient. Am J Kidney Dis. 1994;23:600.
42. Tilney NL, Strom TB, Vineyard GC, Merrill JP. Factors contributing to the declining mortality rate in renal transplantation. N Engl J Med. 1978;299:1321.
43. Ramsey PG, Rubin RH, Tolkoff-Rubin NE, et al. The renal transplant patient with fever and pulmonary infiltrates: Etiology, clinical manifestations, and management. Medicine (Baltimore). 1980;59:206.
44. Heurlin N, Brattstrom C, Tyden G, et al. Cytomegalovirus the predominant cause of pneumonia in renal transplant patients: A two-year study of pneumonia in renal transplant recipients with evaluation of fiberoptic bronchoscopy. Scand J Infect Dis. 1989;21:245.
45. Chang FY, Singh N, Gayowski T, et al. Fever in liver transplant recipients: Changing spectrum of etiologic agents. Clin Infect Dis. 1998;26:59.
46. Sable CA, Hayden FG. Orthomyxoviral and paramyxoviral infections in transplant patients. Infect Dis Clin North Am. 1995;9:987.
46a. Kyriakides GK, Simmons RL, Najarian JS. Wound infection in renal transplant wounds: Pathogenic and prognostic factors. Ann Surg. 1975;182:770.
47. Novick AC. The value of intraoperative antibiotics in preventing renal transplant wound infections. J Urol. 1981;125:151.
48. Rubin R. Infection in the renal and liver transplant patient. In: Rubin RH, Young LS, eds. Clinical Approach to Infection in the Immunocompromised Host. 2nd ed. New York: Plenum Press; 1988:557.
49. Fragomeni LS, Kaye MP. The registry of the international society for heart transplantation: Fifth official report—1988. J Heart Transplant. 1988;7:249.
50. Sarr MG, Gott VL, Townsend TR. Mediastinal infection after cardiac surgery. Ann Thorac Surg. 1984;38:415.
51. Baldwin RT, Radovancevic B, Sweeney MS, et al. Bacterial mediastinitis after heart transplantation. J Heart Lung Transplant. 1992;11:545.
52. Trento A, Dummer JS, Hardesty RL, et al. Mediastinitis following heart transplantation: Incidence, treatment and complications. J Heart Transplant. 1984;3:336.
53. Lowry PW, Blankenship RJ, Gridley W, et al. A cluster of legionella sternal-wound infections due to postoperative topical exposure to contaminated tap water. N Engl J Med. 1991;324:109.
54. Steffenson DO, Dummer JS, Granick MS, et al. Sternotomy infections with *Mycoplasma hominis*. Ann Intern Med. 1987;106:204.
55. Griffith BP, Kormos RL, Hardesty RL, et al. The artificial heart: Infection-related morbidity and its effect on transplantation. Ann Thorac Surg. 1988;45:409.
56. Farrar DJ, Hill JD, Gray LA Jr, et al. Heterotopic prosthetic ventricles as a bridge to cardiac transplantation: A multicenter study in 29 patients. N Engl J Med. 1988;318:333.
57. de Carvalho VB, Sousa EF, Vila JH, et al. Heart transplantation in Chagas' disease 10 years after the initial experience. Circulation. 1996;94:1815.
58. Luft BJ, Naot Y, Araujo FG, et al. Primary and reactivated toxoplasma infection in patients with cardiac transplants: Clinical spectrum and problems in diagnosis in a defined population. Ann Intern Med. 1983;99:27.
59. Simpson GL, Stinson EB, Egger MJ, Remington JS. Nocardial infections in the immunocompromised host: A detailed study in a defined population. Rev Infect Dis. 1981;3:492.
60. Luft BJ, Billingham M, Remington JS. Endomyocardial biopsy in the diagnosis of toxoplasmic myocarditis. Transplant Proc. 1986;18:1871.
61. Wreghitt TG, Gray JJ, Pavel P, et al. Efficacy of pyrimethamine for the prevention of donor-acquired *Toxoplasma gondii* infection in heart and heart-lung transplant patients. Transpl Int. 1992;5:197.
62. Carr A, Tindall B, Brew BJ, et al. Low-dose trimethoprim-sulfamethoxazole prophylaxis for toxoplasmic encephalitis in patients with AIDS. Ann Intern Med. 1992;117:106.
63. Bocchi EA, Bellotti G, Mocelin AO, et al. Heart transplantation for chronic Chagas' heart disease. Ann Thorac Surg. 1996;61:1727.
64. Chapman SW, Wilson JP. Nocardiosis in transplant recipients. Semin Respir Infect. 1990;5:74.
65. Dauber JH, Paradis IL, Dummer JS. Infectious complications in pulmonary allograft recipients. Clin Chest Med. 1990;11:291.
66. Brooks RG, Hofflin JM, Jamieson SW, et al. Infectious complications in heart-lung transplant recipients. Am J Med. 1985;79:412.
67. Kramer MR, Marshall SE, Starnes VA, et al. Infectious complications in heart-lung transplantation: Analysis of 200 episodes. Arch Intern Med. 1993;153:2010.
68. Westney GE, Kesten S, De Hoyos A, et al. Aspergillus infection in single and double lung transplant recipients. Transplantation. 1996;61:915.
69. Girgis RE, Tu I, Berry GJ, et al. Risk factors for the development of obliterative bronchiolitis after lung transplantation. J Heart Lung Transplant. 1996;15:1200.
70. Zenati M, Dowling RD, Dummer JS, et al. Influence of the donor lung on development of early infections in lung transplant recipients. J Heart Transplant. 1990;9:502.
71. Wilson IC, Hasan A, Healey M, et al. Healing of the bronchus in pulmonary transplantation. Eur J Card Thorac Surg. 1996;10:521.
72. Paya CV, Hermans PE, Washington JA II, et al. Incidence, distribution and outcome of episodes of infection in 100 liver transplantations. Mayo Clin Proc. 1989;64:355.
73. George DL, Arnow PM, Fox AS, et al. Bacterial infection as a complication of liver transplantation: Epidemiology and risk factors. Rev Infect Dis. 1991;13:387.
74. Colonna JO II, Winston DJ, Brill JE, et al. Infectious complications in liver transplantation. Arch Surg. 1988;123:360.
75. Dummer S, Kusne S. Liver transplantation and related infections. Semin Respir Infect. 1993;8:191.
76. Castaldo P, Stratta R, Wood P. Clinical spectrum of fungal infections complicating liver transplantation. Arch Surg. 1991;126:149.
77. Collins LA, Samore MH, Roberts MS, et al. Risk factors for invasive fungal infections complicating orthotopic liver transplantation. J Infect Dis. 1994;170:644.
78. Paya CV. Fungal infections in solid-organ transplantation. Clin Infect Dis. 1993;16:677.
79. Sollinger HW, Geffner SR. Pancreas transplantation. Surg Clin North Am. 1994;74:1182.
80. Rosen CB, Frohnert PP, Velosa JA, et al. Morbidity of pancreas transplantation during cadaveric renal transplantation. Transplantation. 1991;51:123.
81. Sollinger HW, Knechtle SJ, Reed A, et al. Experience with 100 consecutive simultaneous kidney-pancreas transplants with bladder drainage. Ann Surg. 1991;214:703.
82. Lumbreras C, Fernandez I, Velosa J, et al. Infectious complications following pancreatic transplantation: Incidence, microbiological and clinical characteristics, and outcome. Clin Infect Dis. 1995;20:514.
83. Asfar S, Zhong R, Grant D. Small bowel transplantation. Surg Clin North Am. 1994;74:1197.
84. Grant D, Wall W, Mimeault R, et al. Successful small-bowel/liver transplantation. Lancet. 1990;335:181.
85. Kusne S, Funukawa H, Abu-Elmagd K, et al. Infectious complications after small bowel transplantation in adults: An update. Transplant Proc. 1996;28:2761.
86. Kusne S, Manez R, Frye BL, et al. Use of DNA amplification for diagnosis of

cytomegalovirus enteritis after intestinal transplantation. Gastroenterology. 1997; 112:1121.
87. Wallace RJJ, Brown BA, Onyi GO. Skin, soft tissue and bone infections due to *Mycobacterium chelonae chelonae*: Importance of prior corticosteroid therapy, frequency of disseminated infections and resistance to antimicrobials other than clarithromycin. J Infect Dis. 1992;166:405–412.
88. Myerowitz RL, Medeiros AA, O'Brien TF. Bacterial infection in renal homograft recipients: A study of 53 bacteremic episodes. Am J Med. 1992;53:308.
89. Paya CV, Hermans PE. Bacterial infections after liver transplantation. Eur J Clin Microbiol Infect Dis. 1989;8:499.
90. Linden PK, Pasculle AW, Manez R, et al. Differences in outcomes for patients with bacteremia due to vancomycin-resistant *Enterococcus faecium* or vancomycin-susceptible *E. faecium*. Clin Infect Dis. 1996;22:663.
91. Diamond RD, Bennett JE. Prognostic factors in cryptococcal meningitis: A study in 111 cases. Ann Intern Med. 1974;80:176.
92. Dummer JS, Hardy A, Poorsattar A, Ho M. Early infections in kidney, heart, and liver transplant recipients on cyclosporine. Transplantation. 1983;36:259.
93. Koneru B, Tzakis AG, DePuydt LE, et al. Transmission of fatal herpes simplex infection through renal transplantation. Transplantation. 1988;45:653.
94. Stover DE, Zaman MB, Hajdu SI, et al. Bronchoalveolar lavage in the diagnosis of diffuse pulmonary infiltrates in the immunosuppressed host. Ann Intern Med. 1984;101:1.
95. Stout JE, Yu VL. Legionellosis. N Engl J Med. 1997;337:682.
96. Kugler JW, Armitage JO, Helms CM, et al. Nosocomial legionnaires' disease: Occurrence in recipients of bone marrow transplants. Am J Med. 1983;74:281.
97. Edelstein PH. Antimicrobial chemotherapy for legionnaires' disease: A review. Clin Infect Dis. 1995;21:5265.
98. Berk MR, Meyers AM, Cassal W, et al. Non-typhoid salmonella infections after renal transplantation. Nephron. 1984;37:186.
99. Dummer JS, Allos BM. Gastrointestinal infections in transplant patients. In: Blaser MJ, Smith PD, Ravidin JI, et al., eds. Infections of the Gastrointestinal Tract. New York: Raven Press, 1995:511.
100. Stone WJ, Schaffner W. *Strongyloides* infections in transplant recipients. Semin Respir Infect. 1990;5:58.
101. Patel R, Paya CV. Infections in solid-organ transplant recipients. Clin Microbiol Rev. 1997;10:86.
102. Schad GA. Cyclosporine may eliminate the threat of overwhelming strongyloidiasis in immunosuppressed patients. J Infect Dis. 1986;153:178.
103. Nolan TJ, Schad GA. Tacrolimus allows autoinfective development of the parasitic nematode *Strongyloides stercoralis*. Transplantation. 1996;62:1038.
104. Harnett JD, Zeldis JB, Parfrey PS, et al. Hepatitis B disease in dialysis and transplant patients: Further epidemiologic and serologic studies. Transplantation. 1987;44:369.
105. Starzl TE, Demetris AJ, Van Thiel D. Liver transplantation (2). N Engl J Med. 1989;321:1092.
106. Fairley CK, Mijch A, Gust ID, et al. The increased risk of fatal liver disease in renal transplant patients who are hepatitis Be antigen and/or HBV DNA positive. Transplantation. 1991;52:497.
107. Samuel D, Muller R, Alexander G, et al. Liver transplantation in European patients with the hepatitis B surface antigen. N Engl J Med. 1993;329:1842.
108. Davies SE, Portmann BC, O'Grady JG, et al. Hepatic histological findings after transplantation for chronic hepatitis B virus infection, including a unique pattern of fibrosing cholestatic hepatitis. Hepatology. 1991;13:150.
109. Lucey MR, Graham DM, Martin P, et al. Recurrence of hepatitis B, and delta hepatitis after orthotopic liver transplantation. Gut. 1992;33:1390.
110. Terrault NA, Zhou S, Combs C, et al. Prophylaxis in liver transplant recipients using a fixed dosing schedule of hepatitis B immunoglobulin. Hepatology. 1996;24:1327.
111. Grellier L, Mutimer D, Ahmed M, et al. Lamivudine prophylaxis against reinfection in liver transplantation for hepatitis B cirrhosis. Lancet. 1996;348:1212.
112. Kruger M, Tillmann HL, Trautwein C, et al. Famciclovir treatment of hepatitis B virus recurrence after liver transplantation: A pilot study. Liver Transpl Surg. 1996;2:253.
113. Kliem V, van den Hoff U, Brunkhorst R, et al. The long-term course of hepatitis C after kidney transplantation. Transplantation. 1996;62:1417.
114. Araya V, Rakela J, Wright T. Hepatitis C after orthotopic liver transplantation. Gastroenterology. 1997;112:575.
115. Konig V, Bauditz J, Lobeck H, et al. Hepatitis C virus reinfection in allografts after orthotopic liver transplantation. Hepatology. 1992;16:1137.
116. Huang CC, Liaw YF, Lai MK, et al. The clinical outcome of hepatitis C virus antibody-positive renal allograft recipients. Transplantation. 1992;53:763.
117. Gane EJ, Portmann BC, Naoumov NV, et al. Long-term outcome of hepatitis C infection after liver transplantation. N Engl J Med. 1996;334:815.
118. Ynares C, Johnson HK, Kerlin T, et al. Impact of pretransplant hepatitis C antibody status upon long-term patient and renal allograft survival: A 5- and 10-year follow-up. Transplant Proc. 1993;25:1466.
119. Pereira BJG, Wright TL, Schmid CH, Levey AS. The impact of pretransplantation hepatitis C infection on the outcome of renal transplantation. Transplantation. 1995;60:799.
120. Gordon FD, Poterucha JJ, Germer J, et al. Relationship between hepatitis C genotype and severity of recurrent hepatitis C after liver transplantation. Transplantation. 1997;63:1419.
121. Zhou S, Terrault NA, Ferrell L, et al. Severity of liver disease in liver transplantation recipients with hepatitis C virus infection: Relationship to genotype and level of viremia. Hepatology. 1996;24:1041.
122. Chazouilleres O, Kim M, Combs C, et al. Quantitation of hepatitis C virus RNA in liver transplant recipients. Gastroenterology. 1994;106:994.
123. Brumage LK, Wright TL. Treatment for recurrent viral hepatitis after liver transplantation. J Hepatol. 1997;26:440.
124. Feray C, Samuel D, Gigou M, et al. An open trial of interferon alfa recombinant for hepatitis C after liver transplantation: Antiviral effects and risk of rejection. Hepatology. 1995;22:1084.
125. Cattral MS, Krajden M, Wanless IR, et al. A pilot study of ribivirin therapy for recurrent hepatitis C virus infection after liver transplantation. Transplantation. 1996;61:1483.
126. Hall WA, Martinez AJ, Dummer JS, et al. Central nervous system infections in heart and heart-lung transplant recipients. Arch Neurol. 1989;46:173.
127. Stamm AM, Dismukes WE, Simmons BP, et al. Listeriosis in renal transplant recipients: Report of an outbreak and review of 102 cases. Rev Infect Dis. 1982;4:665.
128. Gustafson TL, Schaffner W, Lavely GB, et al. Invasive aspergillosis in renal transplant recipients: Correlation with corticosteroid therapy. J Infect Dis. 1983;148:230.
129. Weiland D, Ferguson RM, Peterson PK, et al. Aspergillosis in 25 renal transplant patients: Epidemiology, clinical presentation, diagnosis, and management. Ann Surg. 1983;198:622.
130. Denning DW. Invasive aspergillosis. Clin Infect Dis. 1998;26:781.
131. Kusne S, Dummer JS, Ho M, et al. Self-limited *Toxoplasma* parasitemia after liver transplantation. Transplantation. 1987;44:457.
132. Mason JC, Ordelheide KS, Grames GM, et al. Toxoplasmosis in two renal transplant recipients from a single donor. Transplantation. 1987;44:588.
133. Shepp DH, Hackman RC, Conley FK, et al. *Toxoplasma gondii* reactivation identified by detection of parasitemia in tissue culture. Ann Intern Med. 1985;103:218.
134. Wreghitt TG, Hakim M, Gray JJ, et al. Toxoplasmosis in heart and heart and lung transplant recipients. J Clin Pathol. 1989;42:194.
135. Beaman BL, Beaman L. *Nocardia* species: Host-parasite relationships. Clin Microbiol Rev. 1994;7:213.
136. Gombert ME, Aulicino TM, duBouchet L, et al. Therapy of experimental cerebral nocardiosis with imipenem, amikacin, trimethoprim-sulfamethoxazole, and minocycline. Antimicrob Agents Chemother. 1986;30:270.
137. Kusne S, Schwartz M, Breinig MK, et al. Herpes simplex virus hepatitis after solid organ transplantation in adults. J Infect Dis. 1991;163:1001.
138. Dummer JS, Armstrong J, Somers J, et al. Transmission of infection with herpes simplex virus by renal transplantation. J Infect Dis. 1987;155:202.
139. Copeland JG, Stinson EB. Human heart transplantation. In: Harvey WP, ed. Current Problems in Cardiology. Chicago: Year Book Medical Publishers; 1980:3.
140. Broyer M, Tete MJ, Guest G, et al. Varicella and zoster in children after kidney transplantation: Long-term results of vaccination. Pediatrics. 1997;99:35.
141. Suwansirikul S, Rao N, Dowling JN, Ho M. Primary and secondary cytomegalovirus infection. Arch Intern Med. 1977;137:1026.
142. Dummer JS, White LT, Ho M, et al. Morbidity of cytomegalovirus infection in recipients of heart or heart-lung transplants who received cyclosporine. J Infect Dis. 1985;152:1182.
143. Paya CV, Hermans PE, Wiesner RH, et al. Cytomegalovirus hepatitis in liver transplantation: Prospective analysis of 93 consecutive orthotopic liver transplantations. J Infect Dis. 1989;160:752.
144. Bronsther O, Makowka L, Jaffe R, et al. Occurrence of cytomegalovirus hepatitis in liver transplant patients. J Med Virol. 1988;24:423.
145. Singh NS, Carrigan DR. Human herpesvirus-6 in transplantation: An emerging pathogen. Ann Intern Med. 1996;124:1065.
146. Pohl C, Green M, Wald ER, Ledesma-Medina J. Respiratory syncytial virus infections in pediatric liver transplant recipients. J Infect Dis. 1992;165:166.
147. Michaels MG, Green M, Wald ER, Starzl TE. Adenovirus infection in pediatric liver transplant recipients. J Infect Dis. 1992;165:170.
148. Englund JA, Piedra PA, Whimbey E. Prevention and treatment of respiratory virus and parainfluenza viruses in immunocompromised adults. Am J Med. 1997;102 (3A):61.
149. Ho M, Miller G, Atchison RW, et al. Epstein-Barr virus infections and DNA hybridization studies in posttransplantation lymphoma and lymphoproliferative lesions: The role of primary infection. J Infect Dis. 1985;152:876.
150. Ho M, Jaffe R, Miller G, et al. The frequency of Epstein-Barr virus infection and associated lymphoproliferative syndrome after transplantation and its manifestations in children. Transplantation. 1988;45:719.
151. Breinig MK, Zitelli B, Ho M. Epstein-Barr virus, cytomegalovirus and other viral infections in children after liver transplantation. J Infect Dis. 1987;156:273.
152. Preiksaitis JK, Diaz-Mitoma F, Mirzayans F, et al. Quantitative oropharyngeal Epstein-Barr virus shedding in renal and cardiac transplant recipients: Relationship to immunosuppressive therapy, serologic responses, and the risk of posttransplant lymphoproliferative disorder. J Infect Dis. 1992;166:986.
153. Starzl TE, Nalesnik MA, Porter KA, et al. Reversibility of lymphomas and lymphoproliferative lesions developing under cyclosporin-steroid therapy. Lancet. 1984;1:583.
154. Purtilo DT, Sakamoto K, Saemundsen AK, et al. Documentation of Epstein-Barr virus infection in immunodeficient patients with life-threatening lymphoproliferative diseases by clinical, virological, and immunopathological studies. Cancer Res. 1981;41:4226.
155. Cleary ML, Sklar J. Lymphoproliferative disorders in cardiac transplant recipients are multiclonal lymphomas. Lancet. 1984;2:489.

156. Pagano JS, Sixbey JW, Lin J-C. Acyclovir and Epstein-Barr virus infection. J Antimicrob Chemother. 1983;12(Suppl B):113.
157. Nalesnik MA. Lymphoproliferative disease in organ transplant recipients. Springer Seminars in Immunopathology. 1991;13:199.
158. Papadopoulos EB, Ladanyi M, Emanuel D, et al. Infusions of donor leukocytes to treat Epstein-Barr virus-associated lymphoproliferative disorders after allogeneic bone marrow transplantation. N Engl J Med. 1994;330:1231.

Chapter 305

Infections in Patients with Spinal Cord Injury

RABIH O. DAROUICHE

About 11,000 Americans survive spinal cord injury (SCI) each year. More than 230,000 persons with SCI reside in the United States, and as they have life expectancies approaching normal levels, this number is expected to increase.[1] Trauma is the most common cause of SCI. As with other patients who survive trauma, patients with SCI are particularly predisposed to infection in the acute setting of the injury. However, because of the almost-normal life expectancy of SCI patients, the vast majority of infections occur long after the injury. Infections of the urinary tract, pulmonary tract, pressure sores, and bone predominate in this population and are a major cause of morbidity and mortality.[2, 3]

FACTORS THAT PREDISPOSE TO INFECTION

Despite important interactions between the central nervous system and the immune system, there is no convincing evidence that SCI by itself suppresses immunity. For instance, noninfected individuals with SCI have been shown to have normal function of T and B lymphocytes.[4] Patients with SCI usually have higher levels of complement and acute-phase reactants than able-bodied cohorts[4, 5]; however, this difference may be attributed to undetected inflammation or occult infection. Nevertheless, SCI patients may suffer from complicating conditions (e.g., malnutrition, stress, renal failure)[6] or receive medications (e.g., high-dose glucocorticosteroids in the acute setting of SCI) that can impair the immune response to infection.

More important, there are unique factors in the SCI population that predispose to infection of specific body organs. Most SCI patients have a neurogenic bladder and suffer from frequent episodes of urinary tract infection that are largely due to urinary stasis and bladder catheterization.[7] Urinary stasis greatly impairs the naturally protective mechanisms of the urinary tract such as the washout effect of voiding and the phagocytic capacity of bladder epithelial cells. Even though some techniques of bladder catheterization are safer than others, none can be carried out without introducing organisms into the urinary tract. Paralytic ileus is a usual event in the acute stage of SCI and predisposes to aspiration of gastric contents. Aspiration pneumonia is also likely to occur in SCI patients who have an abnormal state of consciousness that is due to associated head injury or illicit drug ingestion.[8] In persons with cervical or high thoracic cord lesions, weakness of the diaphragmatic and intercostal muscles impairs the capacity to clear respiratory secretions. Muscle paralysis and breakdown of skin in anesthetic areas together with urinary leakage and fecal contamination help establish infection of pressure sores. Frequent hospitalization and insertion of prosthetic devices (e.g., vascular, orthopedic, urinary) predispose these patients to a variety of device-related infections.

IMPORTANT ISSUES RELATED TO EVALUATION FOR INFECTION

Spinal cord–injured patients may have manifestations of infection that differ from those in the general population (Table 305–1). By possibly masking symptoms of an infection, absent or altered sensations constitute the single most important obstacle in the diagnosis of infection in this population. For instance, dysuria, which is a regular finding in able-bodied patients who have urinary tract infection, is usually absent in infected patients with SCI.[7] Similarly, the inability to recognize the signs and symptoms of cord damage or bone infection contributes to delays in the diagnosis of spinal epidural abscess[9] or osteomyelitis of the spine[10] below the level of injury. The diagnostic dilemma caused by the paucity of clinical findings can be heightened by the presence of neurogenic or referred pain that may have no relation to an infection. Furthermore, more than one source of fever may be found in patients with SCI, particularly those with medical or surgical complications.[2] What may be more problematic than identifying the source of an infection is determining whether fever is due to an infection. In general, one fifth of episodes of fever in SCI patients may be caused by noninfectious conditions,[4] some of which may closely mimic infections, as discussed later in the sections on specific infections.

Treatment of infection in SCI patients also poses special challenges. For example, changes in gross body composition that follow SCI alter the disposition of aminoglycosides,[11] vancomycin,[12] and other drugs that primarily distribute into the extracellular fluid. Patients with SCI have an expanded extracellular volume, which is due to retention of extracellular water as subclinical edema and replacement of eroded skeletal muscle mass by extracellular water. As a result, SCI patients have a larger weight-adjusted volume of distribution for aminoglycosides and may require larger weight-adjusted loading and maintenance doses than able-bodied counterparts to achieve similar drug concentrations. Not only can drug distribution be altered in the SCI population, but the estimation of creatinine clearance is especially susceptible to error; various equations that are used in non-SCI persons to predict creatinine clearance from serum creatinine levels tend to yield results that overestimate the true creatinine clearance.[13] This prompted the evaluation of simple meth-

TABLE 305–1 Important Issues to Be Considered during Evaluation of Spinal Cord–Injured Patients for Infection

General
Absent or altered sensations and paucity of clinical findings
Interference of neurogenic pain with localization of source
Coexistence of multiple infections
Mimicry of infection by noninfectious conditions
Unique dosing of aminoglycosides and vancomycin because of altered distribution of drugs and erroneous estimation of creatinine clearance
Urinary tract infection
Almost universal prevalence of bacteriuria
Value of pyuria as indicator of infection
Nonspecific manifestations of symptomatic infection
Investigation of urine cultures growing several bacterial species
Pneumonia
Impact of ineffective cough on determining microbial cause
Defective perception of dyspnea and need to evaluate gas exchange
Eligibility for and efficacy of immunization
Infections of skin and soft tissue
Limitations of history provided by patient
Supreme importance of physical findings in diagnosing ulcer infection
Universal bacterial colonization of pressure sores and unreliability of cultures of swab specimens
Potential reasons for failure to respond to therapy
Deceptive appearance of sinus tract
Osteomyelitis
Representative nature of cultured samples
Possible variations of findings from bones beneath different sores
Significance of organisms growing from cultures of bone
Poor predictive value of clinical evaluation
Appropriateness of imaging studies for diagnosis and for follow-up

ods to properly administer vancomycin and other antibiotics in the SCI population.[12]

URINARY TRACT INFECTION

Bacteriuria is almost universal in SCI patients who depend on bladder catheterization. Chronic indwelling catheters (urethral and suprapubic) are associated with the highest rate of bacteriuria (culture of a randomly obtained urine sample is positive in almost 98% of instances).[14] Patients with SCI who undergo intermittent bladder catheterization have a somewhat lower rate (approximately 70%) of bacteriuria,[15] which may be influenced by the frequency of catheterization. A longer time interval between bladder catheterization may be associated with a higher incidence of bacteriuria. Although sterile insertion of new catheters may be associated with a lower rate of bacteriuria than insertion of clean reusable catheters in a nonsterile fashion,[16] the latter technique is more practical for outpatients.

The distinction between colonization and asymptomatic infection of the urinary tract is made based, respectively, on the absence or presence of pyuria (a white blood cell count of $>10^4$/ml of uncentrifuged urine), reflecting inflammation of the mucosal lining. Colonization may progress to symptomatic infection but often does not; in contrast, asymptomatic infection, if untreated, frequently progresses to symptomatic infection.[17] Typical manifestations of symptomatic urinary tract infection (including dysuria, urgency, frequency, suprapubic discomfort, and in patients with pyelonephritis, costovertebral angle tenderness) are usually lacking in patients with SCI. Instead, a change in voiding habits, an increase in the residual volume of urine in the bladder, foul-smelling urine, a worsening of muscular spasticity, or aggravation of autonomic dysreflexia, or all of these, is often the only clinical clue to the presence of a symptomatic urinary tract infection. Because of the nonspecificity of these clinical manifestations, other causes should be excluded before diagnosing symptomatic urinary tract infection.

Although the lack of pyuria reasonably predicts the absence of urinary tract infection in SCI patients, pyuria may be also be observed in uninfected individuals who have inflammation of the urinary tract that is due to a recent invasive procedure or other condition such as a renal calculus. As with other subjects who require bladder catheterization, quantification of bacteriuria in SCI patients may not help differentiate between colonization and asymptomatic infection of the urinary tract. A consensus of investigators for the National Institute on Disability and Rehabilitation Research determined that bacterial growth of as few as 10^2 CFU/ml of urine from catheter-dependent patients or 10^4 CFU/ml of urine from catheter-free males using external condoms can be associated with symptomatic urinary tract infection.[18]

The vast majority of cases of urinary tract infection in SCI patients are caused by gram-negative bacilli and enterococci, commensal organisms of the bowel and perineum. The patient's gender and level of injury may affect the microbiology of organisms residing in the bladder. For instance, *Escherichia coli* and *Enterococcus* spp. have been reported to cause more than two thirds of the cases of urinary tract infection in female patients undergoing intermittent catheterization.[19] In contrast, *Klebsiella pneumoniae* has emerged as one of the most common causes of urinary tract infection in hospitalized SCI patients,[20, 21] with particularly high prevalence of bacterial strains that exhibit strong type 1 fimbrial–mediated adherence to uroepithelial cells.[21]

Almost half of positive urine cultures at our SCI facility grow more than one organism,[22] and polymicrobial bacteriuria is reportedly even more common in patients who have chronic indwelling urethral catheters.[14] Although isolation of multiple bacterial species is often viewed as indicative of contamination, such a finding in SCI patients should not be disregarded. Isolation of several uropathogens can be associated with symptomatic UTI that fails to respond to antibiotic therapy directed against only one or some of the organisms but is eradicated after additional antimicrobial therapy for other isolated organisms. Although the majority of urine cultures are obtained from patients with only lower urinary tract infection and in whom the yield of blood cultures is extremely low, the detection of concurrent bacteremia confirms the pathogenicity of organisms isolated from urine culture. Even in patients who have pyelonephritis in association with polymicrobial bacteriuria, isolation of only one organism from blood cultures may not negate the role of other bacteria in causing urinary tract infection.

Because asymptomatic infection or, to a lesser extent, colonization of the urine, can progress to symptomatic infection, approaches have been devised to prevent or eradicate colonization or asymptomatic infection. In general, however, neither the use of antiseptics or antibiotics for prophylaxis nor the antibiotic treatment of asymptomatic bacteriuria has proved beneficial in SCI patients[23]; in fact, such approaches may induce the emergence of resistant organisms and expose patients to adverse effects of drugs. In those instances in which asymptomatic bacteriuria might be associated with significant complications, such as during pregnancy or in patients with struvite urinary stones associated with urea-splitting organisms, treatment of asymptomatic bacteriuria may be indicated.

The optimal management of symptomatic urinary tract infection depends on the location of the infection and the host. Analysis of urine samples obtained by ureteral catheterization, the definitive procedure for distinguishing between upper and lower urinary tract infection, is not practical in the clinical setting. Moreover, neither sequential analysis of urine specimens after irrigation of the bladder (bladder washout test) nor examination for antibody coating of urinary bacteria is reliable in localizing the site of urinary tract infection in SCI patients.[24, 25] The frequent occurrence of vesicoureteral reflux and the potential stimulation of local antibody production by the bladder in the presence of a foreign body (catheter), respectively, may help explain the inaccuracy of these two tests in the SCI population. In the absence of literature that provides full support of this concept in the SCI population, most physicians suspect pyelonephritis in the presence of high fever, chills, systemic toxicity, or leukocyte casts in urinary sediment, or all of these. Results of studies in otherwise healthy individuals[26] indicating that short courses of oral antibiotics (one large dose or a 3-day course) are efficacious in eradicating uncomplicated lower urinary tract infections should not be extrapolated to the SCI population. In the absence of supportive clinical trials, catheter-related infections of the neurogenic bladder are generally treated with a 7- to 10-day course of antibiotics. In SCI patients with vesicoureteral reflux, pyelonephritis is likely to occur and is usually treated with a 2-week course of antibiotics. A longer duration of antibiotic therapy (4 to 6 weeks) is advocated in patients with persistent infection, documented relapse of infection, or prostatitis.

Although pyuria regresses to normal values ($\leq 10^4$ white blood cells/ml of uncentrifuged urine) after the completion of successful treatment of urinary tract infection in SCI patients with intermittent bladder catheterization, above-normal levels of pyuria may persist after treatment in SCI patients with indwelling bladder catheters.[27] In patients with persistent infection, documented relapse of infection (by the same bacterial strain), or frequent reinfections (by different organisms), the urinary tract should be investigated for anatomic abnormalities such as a stone, an abscess, stricture, or functional alterations, including vesicoureteral reflux, and high residual volume of urine in bladder. Although intentional colonization of the neurogenic bladder with a nonpathogenic strain of *E. coli* has been reported anecdotally to prevent symptomatic infection,[28, 28a] studies examining the utility of this principle of bacterial interference in SCI patients with recurrent infections are limited.[28b]

PNEUMONIA

Although less than 10% of infections in SCI patients affect the respiratory tract,[2] the high mortality associated with pneumonia makes it the leading cause of death due to infection in this population.[3] Pneumonia is the most common pulmonary complication in the immediate postinjury period[29] and is particularly likely to occur in the first few months after cervical or high thoracic SCI and among quadriplegics and persons at least 55 years of age.[3] In patients who aspirate gastric contents, infections caused by gram-negative and anaerobic bacteria are most common. In the absence of aspiration, community-acquired infections due to *Streptococcus pneumoniae* and *Haemophilus influenzae* probably predominate. *Staphylococcus aureus* and gram-negative bacilli (particularly *Pseudomonas aeruginosa*) commonly cause pneumonia or tracheitis in mechanically ventilated patients and in those with tracheostomy.

The same circumstances that predispose to the development of pneumonia in SCI patients can also favor the occurrence of noninfectious pulmonary complications, including atelectasis, pulmonary embolism, chemical pneumonitis, fat embolism, and pulmonary contusion. Such noninfectious pulmonary complications can be clinically confused with pneumonia and pose serious diagnostic and therapeutic problems. For instance, atelectasis, like pneumonia, commonly occurs because of retained pulmonary secretions early after injury to the cervical or high thoracic cord. In such patients with absent sensations of chest pain and dyspnea and ineffective cough, the only clinical clues that suggest the diagnosis of pneumonia may include tachypnea, tachycardia, fever, and leukocytosis. However, atelectasis may also be accompanied by an element of fever and leukocytosis. The site of pulmonary involvement may not help differentiate atelectasis from pneumonia because both conditions predominantly involve the left lung owing to the difficulty in suctioning the left main stem bronchus, which branches off at a more acute angle than the right bronchus. Occasionally, bronchoscopy is required for both diagnostic and therapeutic purposes. Mucus plugging may also simulate pulmonary embolism,[30] another disease that can be clinically confused with pneumonia. Pulmonary embolism occurs in about 5% of SCI patients; however, a thrombotic source for pulmonary embolism is not detected in the majority of cases.[31] Although pulmonary embolism can ordinarily be diagnosed by a ventilation-perfusion lung scan, the observed defects on scanning may be uninterpretable in patients who also have roentgenographic abnormalities in corresponding areas of lungs as a result of atelectasis or other causes. In those instances a pulmonary angiogram is required for definitive diagnosis. Aspiration of gastric contents may occur because of paralytic ileus and an ineffective cough reflex, leading to chemical pneumonitis that mimics bacterial pneumonia; evaluation of an adequate sample of respiratory secretions may help differentiate between these two clinical entities. In the acute stage of SCI, associated fracture of a long bone may lead to fat embolism; the presence of petechiae and cerebral dysfunction helps diagnose this entity. Finally, pulmonary contusion can be confused with pneumonia in the acute setting of SCI.

Because respiratory muscles may become fatigued and SCI patients can have a defective perception of dyspnea, evaluation of gas exchange, preferably by analysis of arterial blood gases, is strongly recommended if pneumonia is suspected. Transcutaneous measurement of oxygen saturation may also be employed, but with caution because heated electrodes can produce burns on anesthetized skin.

Because patients with SCI may be at a greater risk of developing pneumonia than able-bodied subjects, it is important to assess the immunization status in such patients. By virtue of old age (older than 65 years), chronic respiratory disease, or residence in chronic care facilities, or all of these, almost two thirds of SCI patients are eligible for vaccination against *S. pneumoniae* and influenza viruses. The antibody response to pneumococcal vaccination of SCI patients appears adequate,[32] and unpublished findings by the author suggest similar results with the influenza vaccination. Notwithstanding the lack of studies that examine the clinical benefit of these vaccinations in SCI patients, it may be justifiable to administer pneumococcal and influenza vaccines to all SCI patients.

INFECTIONS OF SKIN AND SOFT TISSUE

The majority of pressure sores in SCI patients develop in areas adjacent to the ischium, sacrum, and greater trochanter. Local factors that contribute to cellulitis and soft tissue infection in the vicinity of pressure sores include breaks in the integrity of the skin barrier, pressure-induced changes, and contamination from contiguous dirty areas. The latter factor may explain the predominance of gram-negative and anaerobic bacteria, usually in combination, in cultures from pressure sores.[33] Because of the inadequacy of sensation, physical findings are usually relied on to diagnose infection of the ulcer, including fever, purulent drainage, and surrounding inflammatory changes such as erythema, swelling, and warmth. In paralyzed individuals who cannot directly visualize the ulcers, a history provided by patients is usually incomplete, and infection has already progressed to an advanced stage by the time of presentation. It is remarkable how often the extent of the infection is not appreciated.

Because of the universal colonization of pressure sores by bacteria, samples for culture should not be obtained unless infection is clinically evident. In patients with seemingly infected decubitus ulcers, biopsy of deep tissue may constitute the most reliable means for determining the infectious cause. Cultures of swab specimens from the ulcer or the sinus tract are generally unreliable, and cultures of material obtained by needle aspiration tend to overestimate the number of bacterial isolates.[34] If cellulitis is recognized adjacent to a decubitus ulcer, the challenge to the clinician is to discern the infecting organism or organisms. Because the decubitus ulcer can serve as the potential source of bacteria causing contiguous cellulitis, cultures obtained by irrigation followed by aspiration from beneath the margins of the ulcer may help resolve this problem.[35] In non-SCI patients with cellulitis adjacent to a cutaneous ulcer, skin biopsy has been demonstrated to yield only staphylococci or streptococci in most cases, with clinical response resulting from treatment directed specifically against these organisms.[36] Similar studies of decubitus ulcers in SCI patients have not been reported.

Treatment of infected pressure sores usually requires a combination of appropriate antibiotics and surgery. Clearly, necrotic tissue and eschar need to be removed and collections of pus drained. Although antibiotic levels in tissues adjacent to diabetic ulcers can be subtherapeutic,[37] penetration of antibiotics into paralyzed soft tissue was demonstrated in a rat model to be adequate.[38] A lack of response of infected ulcers to therapy may be due to inadequate antibiotic therapy, unrecognized soft tissue abscess, communication of the ulcer with an infected bone or joint, or a fistula with the gastrointestinal or urinary tract. The appearance of newly isolated bacterial species soon after the initiation of therapy probably indicates colonization, and unless there has been an initial response followed by recurrence of fever, these organisms may be ignored.

Even in patients with apparently healed ulcers, deep soft tissue abscesses may exist, sometimes causing fever or even bacteremia.[33] Although the sensitivity of the gallium scan for the detection of soft tissue abscesses is generally very high, this test can also be positive in SCI patients who have an infected pressure sore without an associated abscess.[39] Soft tissue abscess in association with an infected sore can be more accurately diagnosed by computed tomography.[39] In SCI patients with a sinus tract, the opening of the sinus tract onto the skin may appear deceptively small because pressure necrosis affects subcutaneous tissues and muscles more than skin; although generally helpful, probing may not reveal the full depth of the tract. Sinography delineates the full depth of the tract and the potential communication with bone, joint, intra-abdominal abscess, or visceral organs. Injection of dye into the intestines or bladder may also help establish fistulous connections.

Several noninfectious conditions may clinically mimic infections of skin and soft tissue in SCI patients. Asymmetric, warm swelling of lower extremities may be caused by deep vein thrombosis, which occurs in about 15% of SCI patients, usually within the first 3 months of complete paralysis.[31] Abnormalities in vascular perfusion can be assessed by venous Doppler studies, nuclear perfusion scanning, or impedance plethysmograms. If the results of these studies are nonconfirmatory, deep vein thrombosis can be ultimately diagnosed by a radiocontrast venogram.

Heterotopic ossification may also cause warm, erythematous

swelling of soft tissues, primarily in areas adjacent to the hip and knee. This complication appears in 16 to 53% of SCI patients, particularly those who are completely paralyzed or have pressure sores,[40] usually in the first year after injury unless other inciting phenomena, such as infection or surgery, occur. Roentgenographic changes are often absent for 1 to 2 weeks after clinical signs appear, but by then, a technetium bone scan should reveal increased uptake. Although the serum alkaline phosphatase level can be elevated early, it is not diagnostic of heterotopic ossification because many other proliferative bone processes may also cause an abnormal elevation. Osteoporotic bone in patients with SCI can easily fracture and cause swelling; plain roentgenograms should disclose this process. Concurrent with what may seem as a minor trauma to SCI patients, swelling of soft tissue or joint space may be due to a hematoma that can be detected by ultrasound examination. If a pertinent history is not obtained, erythematous swelling after sun exposure of extremities that lack sensation may also be misdiagnosed as cellulitis.

OSTEOMYELITIS

The vast majority of cases of osteomyelitis in SCI patients occur beneath pressure sores. Other types of infections, including vertebral, prosthesis-related, postoperative, and hematogenous osteomyelitis, are seen less frequently.[41] Although failure of decubitus ulcers to heal can result from underlying osteomyelitis,[33, 42] it is more likely to be due to noninfectious causes such as pressure-related changes, heterotopic ossification, spasticity, and malnutrition.

In general, it is difficult to determine whether bone beneath a decubitus ulcer is infected and, if infected, what organism or organisms are responsible. The definitive diagnosis of osteomyelitis beneath pressure sores requires histopathologic examination of bone tissue.[43, 44] Histopathologic examination of bone specimens obtained by percutaneous needle biopsy demonstrates osteomyelitis beneath about one fifth to one third of pressure sores.[43, 44] Because osteomyelitis is likely to be a focal process and percutaneous bone biopsy may fail to sample infected foci, bone infection can be documented more frequently in patients in whom intraoperative bone biopsy is performed.[42, 45] In patients with multiple pressure ulcers, histopathologic evaluation of a bone specimen from one site may not necessarily reflect the same findings beneath the other ulcers. In addition, even if pathologic findings are similar, bone cultures from various sites may grow different organisms.

Cultures of a swab specimen from the ulcer are of little value in predicting causative organisms of osteomyelitis.[42] Because of the high frequency of bacterial colonization of fibrotic tissue adherent to bone, semiquantitative cultures of bone specimens are positive in at least two thirds of patients in whom histopathologic examination of bone tissue is not compatible with osteomyelitis.[42] Moreover, quantitative bone cultures do not differentiate osteomyelitis from colonization or infection of overlying soft tissue.[44] Therefore, in patients with histopathologic evidence of osteomyelitis, it may be reasonable to direct antibiotic treatment against all organisms that grow from cultures of bone, except those that are usual colonizers such as *Staphylococcus epidermidis* and diphtheroids. Most cases of osteomyelitis are thought to be caused by two or more bacterial species, including facultative organisms (mainly *S. aureus, Streptococcus* spp., and Enterobacteriaceae), aerobic bacteria (e.g., *P. aeruginosa*), and anaerobes (particularly *Bacteroides* spp.).[42]

In SCI patients with deep nonhealing pressure sores, clinical evaluation poorly predicts the presence of underlying osteomyelitis. In particular, clinical information (duration of ulcer, bone exposure, purulent drainage, and fever), laboratory data (white blood cell count and erythrocyte sedimentation rate), and radiologic findings (plain roentgenograms and technetium bone scans) do not correlate well with the likelihood of finding histopathologic evidence of infection of bone.[42–44] Bone scanning is very sensitive (100%) but poorly specific (<33%) for diagnosing osteomyelitis beneath pressure sores.[43] This low specificity is attributed to the capacity of technetium to concentrate in areas of bone where pressure-induced changes exist or in foci of heterotopic ossification. The only value of a bone scan in the context of a pressure sore in patients with SCI is a negative result that would essentially exclude the diagnosis of osteomyelitis and obviate the need for bone biopsy.

Patients with SCI who have osteomyelitis beneath pressure sores are usually treated with antibiotics and, when indicated, surgery. Even though the ideal duration of antibiotic therapy is not clear, most patients receive at least 4 to 6 weeks of antibiotic therapy; some authorities suggest that a 3-week course of antibiotics suffices.[42] Although parenteral antibiotics have traditionally been used, oral administration of effective drugs may be preferred. If all infected bone is excised at the time of surgery, a shorter course of antibiotics may suffice. Musculocutaneous flap surgery is preferable to débridement alone because the transposition of a well-vascularized muscle allows more extensive removal of devitalized tissue, enhances the host's defense against infection, and provides a better vascular supply to facilitate bone healing. Diligent care should be given to prevent postoperative flap wound infections that can impair the vitality of the musculocutaneous flap.[46] Recurrent infection or very extensive disease indicates a possible need for amputation.[41] Changes on plain roentgenograms and bone scans may persist after what clinically seems to be successful treatment of osteomyelitis.[44] Gallium scanning and leukocyte scintigraphy with indium may be more useful in monitoring a patient's response to treatment.[47]

INTRA-ABDOMINAL INFECTIONS

Cholelithiasis occurs more commonly in SCI patients than in the general population.[48] Although the majority of gallstones may remain asymptomatic, some may cause cholecystitis or migrate down the common bile duct to cause cholangitis or pancreatitis. Intra-abdominal abscesses that are due to ruptured viscus or fistulous connection with a pressure sore are also frequently seen in SCI patients. These intra-abdominal infections may be misdiagnosed, particularly in patients with high cord lesions, because they frequently present with abdominal distension, diffuse spasm of abdominal wall musculature, and rigidity on palpation, but no localized abdominal pain or tenderness.[2, 49] Ultrasound examination or computed tomography of the abdomen should help establish the correct diagnosis.[49]

BACTEREMIA

Infections of the urinary tract, pressure sores, lungs, and vascular access are the most common identifiable sources of bacteremia in patients with SCI.[2, 6, 50, 51] In bacteremic patients without an apparent focus, a search for a deep-seated abscess may be rewarding. Gram-negative bacilli are responsible for most cases of bacteremia, particularly those associated with infections of the urinary tract[50] and vascular shunts or grafts in patients with chronic renal failure undergoing hemodialysis.[6] In contrast, anaerobic bacteria and *S. aureus* are the most frequent isolates from blood cultures of patients with infected pressure sores.[50] Except for patients with chronic renal failure in whom bacteremia can be fatal in half the occasions,[6] the mortality from bacteremia in SCI patients (9 to 17%) is not higher than in the general population.[50, 51]

FEVER WITHOUT DETECTABLE INFECTION

Because of the imbalance between heat production and heat loss, patients with SCI above T8 may not be able to maintain a normal body temperature in response to heating or cooling (poikilothermia). This phenomenon of altered thermoregulation is attributed to the loss of sweating and muscular activity below the spinal cord lesion. These factors may contribute to the occurrence of self-limited febrile episodes in SCI patients that resolve spontaneously within hours to days.[2] However, neither alterations in environmental temperature nor changes in a subject's sweating and muscular activity may explain the occurrence of prolonged fever in recently injured quadriplegic patients who have no identifiable focus of infection.[52] This unique syndrome, so-called quadriplegia fever, lasts weeks to months and is problematic because it may incite repeated evaluation for infection and multiple courses of antibiotics but to no avail. Rarely, fever may occur in the context of autonomic dysreflexia, a paroxysmal syndrome characterized mainly by hypertension, sweating, facial flushing, and headache.[53] Occasionally, bradycardia may also be present and can help differentiate febrile episodes of autonomic dysreflexia from infection. This type of autonomic hyperactivity is seen only in patients with SCI above T6 and is usually triggered by distention of viscera (bladder and rectum), cutaneous stimulation (e.g., ingrown toenails), or even infection.

REFERENCES

1. Ergas Z. Spinal cord injury in the United States: A statistical update. Cent Nerv Syst Trauma. 1985;2:19–32.
2. Sugarman B, Brown D, Musher D. Fever and infection in spinal cord injury patients. JAMA. 1982;248:66–70.
3. DeVivo MJ, Kartus PL, Stover SL, et al. Cause of death for patients with spinal cord injuries. Arch Intern Med. 1989;149:1761–1766.
4. Lyons M. Immune function in spinal cord injured males. J Neurosci Nurs. 1987;19:18–23.
5. Rebhun J, Madorsky JGB, Glovsky MM. Proteins of the complement system and acute phase reactants in sera of patients with spinal cord injury. Ann Allergy. 1991;66:335–338.
6. Vaziri ND, Cesario T, Mootoo K, et al. Bacterial infections in patients with chronic renal failure: Occurrence with spinal cord injury. Arch Intern Med. 1982;142:1273–1276.
7. Stover SL, Lloyd LK, Waites KB, et al. Urinary tract infection in spinal cord injury. Arch Phys Med Rehabil. 1989;70:47–54.
8. Reines HD, Harris RC. Pulmonary complications of acute spinal cord injuries. Neurosurgery. 1987;21:193–196.
9. Darouiche RO, Hamill RJ, Greenberg SB, et al. Bacterial spinal epidural abscess: Review of 43 cases and literature survey. Medicine. 1992;71:369–385.
10. Malik GM, Sapico FL, Montgomerie JZ. Severe vertebral osteomyelitis in patients with spinal cord injury. Arch Intern Med. 1982;142:807–808.
11. Gilman TM, Brunnemann SR, Segal JL. Comparison of population pharmacokinetic models for gentamicin in spinal cord–injured and able-bodied patients. Antimicrob Agents Chemother. 1993;37:93–99.
12. Griver AR, Prince RA, Darouiche RO. A simple method for administering vancomycin in the spinal cord injured population. Arch Phys Med Rehabil. 1997;78:459–462.
13. Mirahmadi MK, Byrne C, Barton C, et al. Prediction of creatinine clearance from serum creatinine in spinal cord injury patients. Paraplegia. 1983;21:23–29.
14. Warren JW, Tenney JH, Hoopes JM, et al. A prospective microbiologic study of bacteriuria in patients with chronic indwelling urethral catheters. J Infect Dis. 1982;146:719–723.
15. McGuire EJ, Savastano JA. Long-term followup of spinal cord injury patients managed by intermittent catheterization. J Urol. 1983;129:775–776.
16. Anderson RU. Non-sterile intermittent catheterization with antibiotic prophylaxis in the acute spinal cord injured male patient. J Urol. 1980;124:392–394.
17. Peterson JR, Roth EJ. Fever, bacteriuria, and pyuria in spinal cord injured patients with indwelling urethral catheters. Arch Phys Med Rehabil. 1989;70:839–841.
18. National Institute on Disability and Rehabilitation Research (NIDRR) Consensus Statement. The prevention and management of urinary tract infection among people with spinal cord injuries. J Am Paraplegia Soc. 1992;15:194–207.
19. Bennett CJ, Young MN, Darrington H. Differences in urinary tract infection in male and female spinal cord injury patients on intermittent catheterization. Paraplegia. 1995;33:69–72.
20. Darouiche R, Cadle R, Zenon G, et al. Progression from asymptomatic to symptomatic urinary tract infection in patients with SCI: A preliminary study. J Am Paraplegia Soc. 1993:16:221–226.
21. Kil KS, Darouiche RO, Hull RA, et al. Identification of a *Klebsiella pneumoniae* strain associated with nosocomial urinary tract infection. J Clin Microbiol. 1997;35:2370–2374.
22. Darouiche RO, Priebe M, Clarridge JE. Limited vs full microbiological investigation for the management of symptomatic polymicrobial urinary tract infection in adult spinal cord–injured patients. Spinal Cord. 1997;35:534–539.
23. Mohler JL, Cowen DL, Flanigan RC. Suppression and treatment of urinary tract infection in patients with an intermittently catheterized neurogenic bladder. J Urol. 1987;138:336–340.
24. Kuhlemeier KV, Lloyd LK, Stover SL. Failure of antibody-coated bacteria and bladder washout tests to localize infection in spinal cord injury patients. J Urol. 1983;130:729–731.
25. Hooton TM, O'shaughnessy EJ, Clowers D, et al. Localization of urinary tract infection in patients with spinal cord injury. J Infect Dis. 1984;150:85–91.
26. Kunin CM. Duration of treatment of urinary tract infections. Am J Med. 1981;71:849–854.
27. Joshi A, Darouiche RO. Regression of pyuria during the treatment of symptomatic urinary tract infection in patients with spinal cord injury. Spinal Cord. 1996;34:742–744.
28. Andersson P, Engberg I, Lidin-Janson G, Lincoln K, Hull R, Hull S, Svanborg C. Persistence of *Escherichia coli* bacteriuria is not determined by bacterial adherence. Infect Immun. 1991;59:2915–2921.

28a. Hull RA, Rudy DC, Donovan WH, et al. Virulence properties of *Escherichia coli* 83972, a prototype strain associated with asymptomatic bacteriuria. Infect Immun. 1999;67:429–432.

28b. Wullt B, Connell H, Röllano P, et al. Urodynamic factors influence the duration of *Escherichia coli* bacteriuria in deliberately colonized cases. J Urol. 1998;159:2057–2062.

29. Fishburn MJ, Marino RJ, Ditunno JF Jr. Atelectasis and pneumonia in acute spinal cord injury. Arch Phys Med Rehabil. 1990;71:197–200.
30. Dee PM, Suratt PM, Bray ST, et al. Mucous plugging simulating pulmonary embolism in patients with quadriplegia. Chest. 1984;85:363–366.
31. Waring WP, Karunas RS. Acute spinal cord injuries and the incidence of clinically occurring thromboembolic disease. Paraplegia. 1991;29:8–16.
32. Darouiche RO, Groover J, Rowland J, et al. Pneumococcal vaccination for patients with spinal cord injury. Arch Phys Med Rehabil. 1993;74:1354–1357.
33. Sugarman B. Infection and pressure sores. Arch Phys Med Rehabil. 1985;66:177–179.
34. Rudensky B, Lipschits M, Isaacsohn M, et al. Infected pressure sores: Comparison of methods for bacterial identification. South Med J. 1992;85:901–903.
35. Ehrenkranz NJ, Alfonso B, Nerenberg D. Irrigation-aspiration for culturing draining decubitus ulcers: Correlation of bacteriological findings with a clinical inflammatory scoring index. J Clin Microbiol. 1990;28:2389–2393.
36. Hook EW III, Hooton TM, Horton CA, et al. Microbiologic evaluation of cutaneous cellulitis in adults. Arch Intern Med. 1986;146:295–297.
37. Seabrook GR, Edmiston CE, Schmitt DD, et al. Comparison of serum and tissue antibiotic levels in diabetes-related foot infections. Surgery. 1991;110:671–677.
38. Darouiche R, Musher D, Hamill R, et al. Cephalosporin penetration into soft tissue of paralyzed limbs. Antimicrob Agents Chemother. 1989;33:1326–1328.
39. Firooznia H, Rafii M, Golimbu C, et al. Computerized tomography of pelvic osteomyelitis in patients with spinal cord injuries. Clin Orthop. 1983;126–131.
40. Lal S, Hamilton BB, Heinemann A, et al. Risk factors for heterotopic ossification in spinal cord injury. Arch Phys Med Rehabil. 1989;70:387–390.
41. Sugarman B. Osteomyelitis in spinal cord injury. Arch Phys Med Rehabil. 1984;65:132–134.
42. Thornhill-Joynes M, Gonzales F, Stewart CA, et al. Osteomyelitis associated with pressure ulcers. Arch Phys Med Rehabil. 1986;67:314–318.
43. Sugarman B. Pressure sores and underlying bone infection. Arch Intern Med. 1987;147:553–555.
44. Darouiche RO, Landon GC, Klima M, et al. Osteomyelitis associated with pressure sores. Arch Intern Med. 1994;154:753–758.
45. Lewis VL Jr, Bailey MH, Pulawski G, et al. The diagnosis of osteomyelitis in patients with pressure sores. Plast Reconstr Surg. 1988;81:229–232.
46. Garg M, Rubayi S, Montgomerie JZ. Postoperative wound infections following mycocutaneous flap surgery in spinal injury patients. Paraplegia. 1992;30:734–739.
47. McCarthy K, Velchik MG, Alavi A, et al. Indium-III–labeled white blood cells in the detection of osteomyelitis complicated by a pre-existing condition. J Nucl Med. 1988;29:1015–1021.
48. Apstein MD, Dalecki-Chipperfield K. Spinal cord injury is a risk factor for gallstone disease. Gastroenterology. 1987;92:966–968.
49. Neumayer LA, Bull DA, Mohr JD, et al. The acutely affected abdomen in paraplegic spinal cord injury patients. Ann Surg. 1990;212:561–566.
50. Montgomerie JZ, Chan E, Gilmore D, et al. Low mortality among patients with spinal cord injury and bacteremia. Rev Infect Dis. 1991;13:867–871.
51. Bhatt K, Cid E, Maiman D. Bacteremia in the spinal cord injury population. J Am Paraplegia Soc. 1987;10:11–14.
52. Sugarman B. Fever in recently injured quadriplegic persons. Arch Phys Med Rehabil. 1982;63:639–640.
53. Kewalramani LS. Autonomic dysreflexia in traumatic myelopathy. Am J Phys Med. 1980;59:1–21.

Chapter 306

Infections in the Elderly

KENT B. CROSSLEY
PHILLIP K. PETERSON

The extremes of age are appreciated as periods of increased susceptibility to infection. In the elderly (which we define as people 65 years of age or older), there are many reasons for more frequent infection. These include impairment of cell-mediated and humoral immunity[1] and reduced physiologic functions such as cough reflex, circulation, and wound healing.[2] Increased prevalence of many chronic illnesses associated with infection, use of immunosuppressive drugs, and communal living are probably also each partly responsible for the increased frequency of infection in the elderly. It is well established that many infections are both more frequent (e.g., herpes zoster, listeriosis, urinary tract infection) and more often associated with mortality (e.g., bacteremia, meningitis) in older individuals. Conversely, some infections (e.g., sexually transmitted diseases) are less common in the elderly.

Infections in the aged must be viewed from the perspective of how best (and most economically) to provide therapy in an era of growing cost containment. The elderly are a large and increasing segment of the population worldwide. It is estimated that of all human beings who have ever lived to be 65 years or older, half are currently alive.[3] In 1900, only 15 million people were age 65 years or older (1% of the global population). In 1992, 342 million people were in this age group (6.2% of the world population), and by the year 2050 this number is projected to expand to 2.5 billion (about 20% of the world population)! Similar demographics characterize population growth in the United States.[4]

A high proportion of lifetime health care costs are expended in the last few months before death. Older patients have longer hospital stays, higher mortality, and higher total hospital costs than younger patients.[5] Infections are one of the most common reasons for the elderly to be transferred from a nursing home to an acute care hospital.[6] Developing better ways to treat infections in aged patients in long-term care facilities (thus avoiding transfer to an acute care institution) could potentially both improve the quality of their care and save substantial amounts of money.

In this chapter, we discuss infections that are disproportionately common in the elderly. Many infections in the aged share a common denominator of muted clinical signs and symptoms. It is key to remember that most physiologic responses to infection are blunted in the aged.[7] Peak temperatures, maximal white blood cell counts, and intensity of many clinical symptoms and signs are less marked in the elderly. Understanding this is crucial to caring for aged individuals adequately.

URINARY TRACT INFECTIONS

Urinary tract infections (UTIs) are more common in women until advanced age. The incidence of asymptomatic bacteriuria (defined as the presence of $>10^5$ organisms per milliliter of urine in the absence of symptoms) in women increases by about 1% per decade so that women 70 to 80 years old have a 7 to 8% annual incidence of bacteriuria. In men, bacteriuria becomes increasingly prevalent with age, largely as a result of urethral obstruction caused by prostatic hypertrophy. The prevalence of bacteriuria in the elderly is approximately 10% in men and 20% in women.[8] In residents of nursing homes and in the hospitalized elderly, bacteriuria is more common, and the frequencies in men and women become similar.[9] Bacteriuria often disappears spontaneously in the aged without any intervention.[10]

Asymptomatic bacteriuria in the elderly does not require antibiotic therapy. The frequency of death attributed to diseases that might in some way be causally associated with bacteriuria (e.g., sepsis, pyelonephritis, renal failure, hypertension) has been shown in several studies to be no different in patients with or without bacteriuria. Functionally disabled elderly individuals are more prone to have bacteriuria, and they are also more apt to die from the cause of their primary disability.[11] Controlled studies of antibiotic treatment of elderly bacteriuric men and women have not shown decreased survival in the untreated population. Nicolle and colleagues[12] have demonstrated that treatment of bacteriuria in elderly men or women usually results in only transient clearing and is often complicated by drug-related side effects. Even though the majority of elderly institutionalized women with asymptomatic bacteriuria may have upper tract involvement, there are no clear guidelines for determining who should be treated, and there is no good evidence that treatment is associated with any benefit.[13]

The etiology of UTIs in the elderly largely depends on where the infection was acquired. Among individuals living in the community, the distribution of organisms causing infection in the elderly is similar to that seen in younger persons. In institutionalized aged individuals, there is a marked change in pathogens, with one third of cases of UTI or bacteriuria caused by *Escherichia coli* and about as many caused by *Proteus* spp. There is more than a sixfold increase in the frequency of *Klebsiella* spp. and *Pseudomonas aeruginosa* compared with that in noninstitutionalized persons. Up to 25% of these infections may be polymicrobial.[10] A significant excess of gram-positive infections in elderly men with UTIs has also been observed.[11] In several studies, bacteriuria has been reported to be transient and the responsible organisms to change frequently.[10, 14–18] The common use of antibiotics in long-term care institutions is undoubtedly one factor altering the etiology of these infections. Both the organisms recovered and the antibiotic susceptibility of the isolate may be a function of the patient's exposure to antibiotics.

Pyuria is not a reliable marker for bacteriuria. In the studies of Baldassarre and Kaye,[11] 60.9% of 133 women with pyuria did not have bacteriuria. Of 184 women who did not have pyuria, on the other hand, only 4.3% were bacteriuric.[11]

Symptomatic UTI should always be treated in older individuals. Antibiotic selection should be guided by a Gram-stained specimen of urine and the patient's history. Residence in a nursing home, recent hospital stays, previous antibiotic therapy, and a history of multiple UTIs are all associated with more resistant organisms. Enterococci and *Staphylococcus aureus* cause a significant minority of infections in older patients. Because many drugs used to treat gram-negative infection are not active against these organisms, it is important to exclude them by the urine Gram stain.

For elderly patients with apparent acute upper tract disease, hemodynamic instability is more common than in younger patients,[19] and parenteral antimicrobial therapy and hospitalization are usually appropriate. If gram-positive organisms are present in urine, vancomycin is probably the best empirical therapy. For gram-negative infection, a third-generation cephalosporin or another β-lactam (e.g., ticarcillin-clavulanate), trimethoprim-sulfamethoxazole, or ciprofloxacin is a good initial choice. Patients at high risk of having resistant organisms are best treated initially with a broad-spectrum β-lactam or a carbapenem and an aminoglycoside beginning with a low dose (e.g., 1 mg/kg/day) until blood aminoglycoside levels can be obtained. With both gram-negative and gram-positive infections, final therapy should be guided by susceptibility studies. As with younger patients, failure of symptoms (e.g., chills or fever) to resolve, any persisting back pain, or continuing positive urine cultures require careful evaluation to exclude obstruction or a perinephric abscess.

Prevention of recurrent UTIs in elderly women has been evaluated in two studies. Raz and Stamm[20] found that intravaginal estriol in postmenopausal women results in decreased colonization with Enterobacteriaceae and fewer infections. Avorn and colleagues[21] showed in a placebo-controlled trial that regular ingestion of cranberry juice reduced both bacteriuria and pyuria in elderly women.

Urinary catheters are a significant cause of UTI in the elderly.[22] These devices should be avoided whenever possible. Virtually all patients with indwelling catheters present for 30 days or longer are bacteriuric, but only a small percentage of these patients develop symptomatic infection. Conversely, about two thirds of febrile illnesses in elderly patients with indwelling catheters are the result of UTI.[23] Warren and coworkers[24] have shown that infection-related mortality in elderly bacteriuric women is limited to severely debilitated patients. When symptomatic infections develop in patients with indwelling catheters, they should be treated empirically as described previously. Although catheter removal is usually recommended, there is little evidence that it is needed as part of the treatment of a catheter-associated UTI. It is also unclear whether intermittent catheterization is associated with a reduction in the frequency of either bacteriuria or symptomatic infections.[25]

Cystitis (manifest by dysuria, urgency, and frequency in a patient who is usually afebrile) is probably best managed with short-course (3-day) antibiotic therapy. Although more data about the efficacy of short-course therapy of lower urinary tract infections in the elderly are needed, cost and complications are reduced and cure rates appear to be similar to those achieved with longer periods of therapy.[26] This regimen is only for women; men (because of the potential of a prostatic focus of infection) should be treated for at least 10 to 14 days.[9] Appropriate drugs include trimethoprim-sulfamethoxazole and one of the quinolones.

PNEUMONIA

The association between aging and pneumonia has been recognized for many years. Sir William Osler (who himself was to die of bacterial pneumonia) described the disease in his textbook as "a friend of the elderly."[27] Marrie[28] reported that community-acquired pneumonia occurred 50 times as frequently in individuals older than 75 as in 15- to 19-year-olds. In addition to their significant associated mortality, pneumonic infections are difficult and expensive to treat. Although one study found that two thirds of patients with bronchitis or pneumonia were not hospitalized, pneumonia was the third most frequent diagnosis accounting for hospitalization of the elderly in 1988.[29] Efforts to reduce the occurrence of nosocomial pneumonia and the associated morbidity and mortality are especially important because this is the most costly of the common hospital-acquired infections.[30]

The etiology of pulmonary infections in elderly individuals is somewhat different from that in younger adults. Respiratory syncytial virus is a more common cause of pneumonia in older individuals than is generally appreciated. These viral infections, which occur primarily in nursing homes, are often of rapid onset; bronchospasm may be a frequent and prominent feature.[31] Some studies have recognized that rhinoviruses may be associated with lower respiratory tract disease in the elderly, but their overall importance is uncertain.[32] *Chlamydia pneumoniae* has also been noted to cause an outbreak of respiratory infection in a nursing home.[33]

Streptococcus pneumoniae, gram-negative bacilli, and *Haemophilus influenzae* were the most commonly identified bacterial pathogens in a study of hospitalized elderly individuals with pneumonia.[34] Although most studies of the etiology of pneumonia in the elderly are limited by the use of expectorated sputum as the source of culture, in general, in both community and institutional settings, the risk of gram-negative and *S. aureus* pulmonary infection appears to be increased in the elderly.[35]

As with other infections in the aged, the clinical presentation of pneumonia is usually muted. Temperatures of patients with bacteremic pneumococcal pneumonia who are elderly are lower than those of younger individuals, and cough and fever may be absent in elderly patients with pneumonia.[36] As with other severe infections, confusion and obtundation may be valuable early clues to the presence of life-threatening pneumonia.

It is important to culture the blood and sputum of elderly patients with apparent pneumonia. However, sputum is often difficult to collect, and in some seriously ill elderly individuals, it may be appropriate to attempt to obtain a specimen for culture that does not pass through the oropharynx (e.g., by bronchoalveolar lavage or by use of a covered brush). Such invasive procedures for obtaining sputum for special stains and cultures are generally reserved for circumstances in which microorganisms other than common bacterial pathogens are being considered.

Empirical management of pneumonia in aged individuals requires treatment with an antimicrobial agent that is effective against a broad range of possible causative organisms.[37] One of the third-generation cephalosporins that has good activity against *S. pneumoniae, S. aureus, H. influenzae,* and common gram-negative organisms (e.g., cefotaxime or ceftriaxone) is appropriate for community-acquired infections. In hospital-acquired infections, initial broad-spectrum coverage that includes *P. aeruginosa* (e.g., a carbapenem or a broad-spectrum β-lactam with an aminoglycoside) is appropriate. Although published data from studies of the elderly are limited so far, the newer broad-spectrum quinolones (e.g., trovafloxacin and levofloxacin) are promising agents for nursing home–acquired pneumonia. Improved clinical outcome may result from treatment that avoids hospital transfer.[38]

Among hospitalized patients, those older than 65 developed pneumonia twice as often as younger patients.[39] Risk factors included poor nutrition, endotracheal intubation, and neuromuscular disease. Interestingly, mortality of patients with respiratory disease in intensive care units is not predictable on the basis of age alone but requires examination of comorbid conditions.[40]

Efforts to prevent pneumonia are very important, particularly in the frail elderly. These should include immunization with the pneumococcal polysaccharide vaccine as well as influenza vaccine.[41] Pneumococcal polysaccharide vaccine is dramatically underused; a study in Washington State found that only 7% of residents of a nursing home had received vaccine. Quick and colleagues[42] reported that the major impediments to vaccine use were a low priority among physicians and difficulty in determining residents' immunization history. In addition, limiting contact between patients or employees with respiratory illness and elderly individuals during an influenza outbreak is appropriate. Use of amantadine or rimantadine may reduce the severity of influenza virus infection and may prevent the development of influenza when it is given as prophylaxis to patients in nursing homes.[43]

TUBERCULOSIS

Tuberculosis is the most common reportable disease among persons older than 65 years.[44] Nearly a quarter of cases of tuberculosis in the United States in 1995 were in patients in this age group. Among elderly in the community, the incidence is twice that in the general population, and in residents of nursing homes, the incidence is four times that in the community.

Usually, development of disease in the elderly reflects reactivation of infection acquired at a younger age and is due to declining cellular immunity associated with aging. In addition, poor nutrition, the increased occurrence of diabetes and other diseases common to the elderly, and use of corticosteroid therapy may be associated with reactivation of *Mycobacterium tuberculosis* infection. The disease is of particular importance in nursing homes, where outbreaks may occur.

Tuberculin testing is widely carried out in the elderly and is commonly required on admission to long-term care facilities. Testing should be done using intradermal (the Mantoux technique) administration of purified protein derivative. The use of a two-step technique is probably appropriate in older patients.[45] For individuals who have positive purified protein derivative tests, chest roentgenograms should be obtained and then repeated on a regular basis. Follow-up tuberculin testing and chest roentgenograms are recommended at a frequency determined by the prevalence of tuberculous disease in the community (typically at 6- to 24-month intervals).

Tuberculin-positive patients need to be followed up closely.[46] Unexplained weight loss or fever, pulmonary symptoms, unexplained lymphadenopathy, or changes in renal function should be clues to the possible presence of active tuberculosis.

The key to diagnosing tuberculosis in the elderly is to maintain a high index of suspicion. It is also imperative to remember that some manifestations may be atypical.[47] In one study, fever, weight loss, night sweats, sputum production, and hemoptysis were all significantly less common in elderly patients than in younger subjects.[48]

Preventive therapy with isoniazid is not indicated for an elderly individual who has a history of a positive tuberculin test and no other risk factors. On the other hand, individuals with a recently converted tuberculin test, regardless of age, should be given isoniazid prophylaxis (see Chapter 240). Studies in Arkansas demonstrated that toxicity in an older population is uncommon. Dutt and Stead[46] reported a 4.5% incidence of nonfatal hepatitis in a group of 2000 elderly individuals. Preventive therapy should be the same as for younger individuals: administration of isoniazid at 300 mg once daily for 6 to 12 months. Patients who develop symptoms of possible isoniazid toxicity (e.g., nausea, malaise, vomiting) should stop taking the drug and have liver function tests immediately. If the transaminase level is more than five times the upper limit of normal, the drug should be discontinued permanently. If the serum transminase is elevated to a lesser degree, the patient can be challenged with 150 mg/day for 3 days, and if this is tolerated, the regular regimen can be resumed.[46]

PRESSURE SORES AND SKIN INFECTIONS

Pressure sores are most common in the seriously disabled elderly and are typically quite difficult to treat. In a study in 1990 of nearly 20,000 nursing home patients, the prevalence of pressure sores was 10.4% after a 1-year stay in a nursing home.[49] Pressure sores occur primarily in individuals with impaired mobility, and the usual cause is skin necrosis resulting from ischemia.[50] The ulcer that develops may be associated with a number of infectious complications. In order of frequency, these are local infection, cellulitis of surrounding tissue, contiguous osteomyelitis, and bacteremia.[51]

Guidelines to preventing the development of pressure lesions in adults have been published by the Agency for Health Care Policy and Research.[52] Key components include monitoring patients who are at risk, reducing exposure of the skin to pressure, maintaining the skin in a clean and dry condition, and maintaining good nutritional status. Therapy of pressure ulcers should include pressure relief, appropriate nutrition, and débridement. A variety of treatments have been used topically, and there is no clear evidence to favor one over another. Povidone-iodine, hydrogen peroxide, and other agents have been used. Povidone-iodine use has been associated with thyrotoxicosis.[53] Topical antimicrobial agents have not been shown to be effective. Systemic antibiotic therapy should be reserved for infected ulcers. Most pressure ulcers in the elderly yield multiple organisms when cultured. Aerobes that are commonly recovered include staphylococci, enterococci, *Proteus mirabilis, E. coli,* and *Pseudomonas* spp. In addition, anaerobic *Peptostreptococcus, Bacteroides fragilis,* and *Clostridium* spp. are frequently isolated in these infections.

Making an accurate bacteriologic diagnosis is difficult. Many of the issues involved in determining the bacteriology of an infected pressure sore are similar to those confronted in the assessment of infected diabetic foot ulcers. Swabbing the wound often yields organisms that are colonizers and not actually causes of infection. It may be most appropriate to aspirate material from the margin or base of the ulcer, directing the needle through intact skin.

A variety of empirical antibiotic regimens have been suggested for patients with pressure ulcer–associated cellulitis, osteomyelitis, or bacteremia. Bacteremia in this situation is usually caused by *P. mirabilis, S. aureus,* or *B. fragilis.*[51] In general, any regimen that is active against the majority of organisms that are usually causal is appropriate. Although a 10- to 14-day course is commonly prescribed, no studies have carefully defined the duration of therapy. Although advanced inanition is the most common cause of failure of these lesions to heal, osteomyelitis needs to be ruled out by physical examination and roentgenography. If osteomyelitis is present, it requires a more extended course of therapy. A comprehensive review of the management of pressure sores has been published.[54]

Some common types of cellulitis may be more severe and associated with increased mortality in elderly individuals compared with younger patients. In particular, outbreaks of skin infection caused by group A β-hemolytic streptococci associated with bacteremia have been reported in nursing homes in the United States.[55] Because many of these infections are fatal and because of the high costs of inpatient management, cutaneous infections in elderly patients need to be treated promptly. Skin and soft tissue infections are common in the nursing home setting; a prevalence of 5% is a reasonable estimate. Herpes zoster is also particularly common in the elderly and often associated with severe and protracted pain. Pathogenesis and therapy of this disease are discussed elsewhere in this volume (see Chapter 126).

BACTEREMIA

Probably because of the increased prevalence of chronic diseases in older individuals, bacteremic illnesses appear to be more frequent and more often associated with death in the elderly. In both the hospital and the community, bacteremia is more common in the aged.[56] The presence of comorbid conditions is clearly a determinant of the mortality associated with bacteremic illness.[57]

A number of studies have pointed out the blunted clinical responses to bacteremia in aged patients. It is clear that elderly patients may be bacteremic and afebrile.[58] A significant proportion of patients may not have neutrophilia.[59] Weakness and altered mental status may be the presenting symptoms.

The main sources of community-acquired bacteremia in the elderly in order of decreasing frequency are the urinary tract, intra-abdominal sites, and lungs.[60] In long-term care facilities, the urinary tract is the most frequent source, followed by skin and subcutaneous tissue and the respiratory tract.[61] Organisms most commonly recovered from patients with bacteremia associated with skin sources are *S. aureus, Staphylococcus epidermidis,* gram-negative enteric bacteria, and anaerobes.[60] Bacteria from the urinary tract are usually gram-negative enterics or enterococci; from the biliary tract, gram-negative enterics or anaerobes; and from the respiratory tract, *H. influenzae, S. pneumoniae,* group B *streptococci,* or gram-negative enterics.

Because of their increased risk of complications and higher mortality, elderly patients should be treated as soon as a presumptive diagnosis of bacteremia is considered. Selection of a proper antibiotic regimen is guided by the same principles as for younger individuals. It is important to remember that aged patients eliminate most antibiotics more slowly than younger individuals; dosages should be adjusted accordingly. Aminoglycosides, because of the increasing potential for toxicity with age, are best used with caution.[62]

INFECTIVE ENDOCARDITIS

Infective endocarditis is especially common in elderly individuals. In most of the recent studies of endocarditis, more than 50% of patients were 60 or more years of age.[63–65] The increased incidence of endocarditis in the elderly seems to be related to prolonged survival of patients with cardiac valvular disease and the use of prosthetic heart valves, intravascular monitoring devices, and surgically implanted materials.

The diagnosis of infective endocarditis may be particularly difficult in the elderly. Often, presenting signs and symptoms are nonspecific, and development of weakness, malaise, weight loss, confusion, and so on may be the only evidence of infection. Peripheral vascular signs and splenomegaly are both less common in the elderly than in younger patients.[66] In one study, more than two thirds of cases of endocarditis in aged patients were misdiagnosed at the time of admission.[67] Musculoskeletal manifestations are often mistakenly ascribed to primary rheumatologic disorders, and heart murmurs are considered benign or thought to result from calcific lesions associated with aging.

Several studies suggest that older patients have an increased frequency of endocarditis caused by gram-positive organisms.[63, 64] These include *Enterococcus faecalis* (usually from the urinary tract) and *Streptococcus bovis* (usually from a colonic source).[68] It is important to remember the association of *S. bovis* with gastrointestinal carcinoma. In individuals with prosthetic valves, the likelihood is high that the infection is caused by staphylococci or enterococci.

As in younger individuals, prompt empirical therapy is needed for patients with presumed endocarditis who appear to be seriously ill. A regimen that might be used for initial therapy consists of vancomycin and gentamicin. Subsequently, therapy should be guided by results of blood culture and antibiotic susceptibility tests. As in younger patients, careful observation is required for possible complications including recurrent episodes of fever and congestive heart failure. Although the therapy of infective endocarditis in an elderly individual is not different from that in a younger person (see Chapter 65), two points need to be emphasized. First, because of less rapid elimination of many antimicrobials in elderly patients, care needs to be taken in dosing and monitoring levels of drugs that are potentially toxic. Second, because elderly patients do not tolerate long hospital stays well, every effort should be made to administer parenteral therapy on an outpatient basis.

In the elderly, cardiac complications of endocarditis such as congestive heart failure are increased by nonvalvular causes of decompensation such as myocardial infarction, conduction abnormalities, arrhythmias, myocarditis, or myocardial abscess. Elderly persons are prone to arterial embolization, the second most common complication of infective endocarditis. The mortality associated with infective endocarditis is substantially greater in elderly than in younger patients, and permanent disability and a need for long-term care are common outcomes.[68]

Antibiotic prophylaxis to prevent development of endocarditis is important in older individuals. The topic has been reviewed in a statement regarding prevention published by the American Heart Association[69] (see Chapter 67).

INFECTIOUS DIARRHEA

Diarrhea is a significant cause of morbidity and mortality in the elderly. One study found that 51% of deaths caused by diarrhea over a 9-year period occurred in individuals older than 74.[70] A disproportionate share of diarrheal deaths occurred in elderly nursing home residents.[70]

Older patients may be at increased risk for *Salmonella* infections because of achlorhydria, decreased intestinal motility associated with medications, other coexistent gastrointestinal diseases, and more frequent use of antibiotics. Some authors have suggested that patients older than 50 should be considered for antibiotic therapy for uncomplicated *Salmonella* gastroenteritis. This assumes that older patients may not tolerate these infections well and that, if bacteremic, they may be at increased risk for vascular infection caused by salmonellae. The quinolones have assumed an important role in the empirical therapy of acute gastroenteritis when a bacterial etiology is suspected, and this class of agents is usually active against *Salmonella* spp.

Because antibiotics shorten the duration of *Shigella* gastroenteritis, therapy is indicated to reduce the risk of fluid and electrolyte imbalance in the elderly. Antibiotic therapy is also recommended for diarrhea caused by *Campylobacter jejuni,* invasive *E. coli, Vibrio parahaemolyticus,* and *Yersinia enterocolitica* (see Chapter 85).

In the nursing home setting, outbreaks of diarrhea occur relatively commonly during the winter months. Both the Norwalk agent and rotavirus have been implicated in these episodes.[71] There are also substantial data associating *Clostridium difficile* diarrhea with residence in a long-term care institution.[72] This organism is increasingly recognized as a cause of sporadic cases of diarrhea in the elderly. It is the most common reportable cause of diarrhea in the elderly in Great Britain.[73] Enterohemorrhagic *E. coli* (O157-H7) has been reported to cause outbreaks of gastroenteritis in long-term care institutions.[74] *Cryptosporidium* is also newly appreciated as a cause of diarrhea in the aged.[75] Although *Candida* spp. have been implicated as a cause of diarrhea in elderly patients,[76] isolation of this fungus from stool, even in high colony counts, appears to indicate colonization and not infection.

MENINGITIS

As is true of other serious infections in the aged, the case-fatality ratio of meningitis is higher than in younger individuals. In one study using data from hospital discharges in Rhode Island, the case-fatality rate was 54.8%, compared with an overall fatality rate of 10.3%.[77]

It is also well established that the organisms that cause meningitis in aged individuals differ from the distribution of bacteria seen in younger adults.[78] As suggested in a number of studies, viral meningitis is relatively uncommon in the elderly. The major causes of meningitis in the aged are *S. pneumoniae, Listeria monocytogenes,* gram-negative bacilli, and *M. tuberculosis.* Disease caused by *Neisseria meningitidis* and *H. influenzae* are uncommon in elderly patients.[79, 80]

It should be remembered that *S. pneumoniae* may be penicillin resistant and that isolated cases of meningitis in the elderly may be caused by penicillin-resistant strains of *S. pneumoniae.* It is important that susceptibility testing be performed on all *S. pneumoniae* isolates from cerebrospinal fluid or blood. Cases of *L. monocytogenes* meningitis are usually sporadic and are most common in patients with compromised cell-mediated immunity or a history of alcoholism.

The signs and symptoms of bacterial meningitis in the elderly are muted. Nuchal rigidity is often found on examination of elderly patients who do not have bacterial meningitis.[80] Usually, these patients have coexistent neurologic deficits. Elderly patients who have nuchal rigidity in the absence of other neurologic problems should not be dismissed as having "osteoarthritis of the cervical spine" but should be intensively investigated for possible meningitis. Several reviews of meningitis suggest that the laboratory findings for elderly people do not differ from those for younger individuals. Complications, however, are more frequent in older individuals.[79, 80] Gorse and coworkers[80] found that the frequency of complications (including neurologic complications, pneumonia, and UTIs) was approximately twice as high in patients older than 65 as in younger patients.

The empirical treatment of meningitis in older patients needs to cover *S. pneumoniae, L. monocytogenes,* and gram-negative bacilli. Because *L. monocytogenes* is not susceptible to cephalosporins, an appropriate initial regimen includes ampicillin with cefotaxime or ceftriaxone. In areas where cephalosporin-resistant *S. pneumoniae* have been encountered, vancomycin should be used empirically until culture and antibiotic susceptibility results are known.

SEPTIC ARTHRITIS

About 25% of persons with septic arthritis are older than 60. The mortality in the elderly is higher, and recovery of joint function is less satisfactory. Septic arthritis is commonly associated with preexisting rheumatoid arthritis, prosthetic joints, or degenerative arthritis.[81] These associations, as well as that with diseases such as diabetes mellitus and malignancy and with cytotoxic or systemic corticosteroid therapy, suggests that immunologic defects may play an important role in the pathogenesis of septic arthritis in the elderly.

The knee is the joint most frequently involved, followed by the wrist and shoulder. Although most elderly patients with septic arthritis complain of a painful, swollen joint, in contrast to younger patients, they are seldom totally immobilized by pain, and muscle spasm is infrequent. As in younger patients, the most commonly isolated organism is *S. aureus,* but gram-negative rods are also frequent causes in the elderly. In addition, septic arthritis is associated more frequently with osteomyelitis in the older patient.

FEVER AND FEVER OF UNDETERMINED ORIGIN

Many elderly persons appear to have lower body temperatures than are traditionally accepted as normal and consequently have a diminished febrile response to infection.[82, 83] However, 95% of elderly patients who have infection show some febrile response.[84] One study examined the importance of fever in 470 consecutive elderly patients who were seen in an emergency room with temperatures of 100.0°F or greater.[85] Three quarters of these patients were classified by the authors as seriously ill. The most frequent diagnoses included pneumonia (24%), UTI (21.7%), and septicemia (12.8%). Many of these patients did not have high fever, tachycardia, leukocytosis, or tachypnea.

Esposito and Gleckman[86] found that 36% of their elderly patients with fever of undetermined origin had infection. Intraabdominal infection was the most common infectious cause in their series. Fifty percent of these fevers of undetermined origin were caused by neoplasm and connective tissue disorders in about equal numbers.[86] Over half of the neoplasms were lymphomas, two thirds of which were diagnosed on laparotomy. Most other neoplasms were renal or hepatobiliary in origin. Sixty-five percent of the connective tissue diseases were giant cell arteritis, predominantly in women. Polyarteritis nodosa was diagnosed in 20%.

PHARMACOLOGIC CONSIDERATIONS

Although the elderly are the group most likely to receive antibiotic therapy when hospitalized and in nursing homes, there has been little accurate information about the effects of aging on the pharmacokinetics and toxicity of antimicrobial agents until the past decade.[87, 88] Physiologic changes that accompany advanced age may significantly affect the absorption, distribution, plasma protein binding, metabolism, and elimination of many antibiotics. The risk of toxicity of some antimicrobials is also increased in the elderly. Newer antibiotics have been studied more extensively in older patients. The phenomenon of "polypharmacy," which is so common in this age group, greatly increases the chances of drug interactions. Extensive information about use of antibiotics in nursing homes has been published.[89–91]

PREVENTION

A number of studies suggest that age per se is no longer an independent risk factor for many types of infection. Whereas many studies of infections in elderly populations comprise patients who have suffered the consequences of age-related physiologic impairment (i.e., senescence), a majority of elderly people are healthy and living independently at home. Of Americans who are in the age group 65 to 74, 89% are fully functioning and robust. Of those 75 to 84 years of age, 73% enjoy this health status, and 40% of individuals 85 years of age or older continue to have aged successfully.[3]

Prevention of infection in the aged is increasingly viewed as a need to prevent comorbidities and nutritional deficiencies that contribute to the pathogenesis of infection. In addition to immunizations (with influenza, pneumococcal, and tetanus vaccines), mounting evidence supports the value of adequate nutrition, exercise, social engagement, and continued involvement in productive activities in the attainment of a long and qualitatively rich life.[3]

REFERENCES

1. Saltzman RL, Peterson PK. Immunodeficiency of the elderly. Rev Infect Dis. 1987;9:1127–1139.
2. Ben-Yehuda A, Weksler ME. Host resistance and the immune system. Clin Geriatr Med. 1992;8:701–711.
3. Rowe JW, Kahn RL. Successful Aging. New York: Pantheon; 1990.
4. Crossley K, Peterson PK. Infections in the elderly—New developments. In: Remington JS, Swartz MN, eds. Current Clinical Topics in Infectious Diseases. Malden, Mass: Blackwell Science; 1998:75–100.
5. Munoz E, Rosner F, Chalfin D, et al. Financial risk and hospital cost for elderly patients. Age- and non-age-stratified medical diagnosis related groups. Arch Intern Med. 1988;148:909–912.
6. Irvine PW, Van Buren N, Crossley K. Causes for hospitalization of nursing home residents: The role of infection. J Am Geriatr Soc. 1984;32:103–107.
7. Norman DC, Toledo SD. Infections in elderly persons. Clin Geriatr Med. 1992;8:713–719.
8. Sobel JD, Kaye D. Urinary tract infections. In: Mandell GL, Douglas RG Jr, Bennett JE, eds. Principles and Practice of Infectious Diseases. 3rd ed. New York: Churchill Livingstone; 1990:582–611.
9. Lipsky BA. Urinary tract infections in men. Epidemiology, pathophysiology, diagnosis, and treatment. Ann Intern Med. 1989;110:138–150.
10. Nicolle LE. Asymptomatic bacteriuria in the elderly. Infect Dis Clin North Am. 1997;11:647.
11. Baldassarre JS, Kaye D. Special problems of urinary tract infection in the elderly. Med Clin North Am. 1991;75:375–390.
12. Nicolle LE, Bjornson J, Harding GKM, et al. Bacteriuria in elderly institutionalized men. N Engl J Med. 1983;309:1420–1425.
13. Nicolle LE, Mayhew WJ, Bryan L. Prospective randomized comparison of therapy and no therapy for asymptomatic bacteriuria in institutionalized elderly women. Am J Med. 1987;83:27–33.
14. Mims AD, Norman DC, Yamamura RH, et al. Clinically inapparent (asymptomatic) bacteriuria in ambulatory elderly men: Epidemiological, clinical, and microbiological findings. J Am Geriatr Soc. 1990;38:1209.
15. Boscia JA, Kobasa WD, Knight RA, et al. Epidemiology of bacteriuria in an elderly ambulatory population. Am J Med. 1986;80:208–214.
16. Gleckman RA. Urinary tract infection. Clin Geriatr Med. 1992;8:793–819.
17. Kasviki-Charvati P, Drolette-Kefakis B, Papanayiotou PC, et al. Turnover of bacteriuria in old age. Age Ageing. 1982;11:169–174.
18. Sourander LB, Kasanen A. A 5-year follow-up of bacteriuria in the aged. Gerontol Clin. 1972;14:274–281.
19. Gleckman R, Blagg N, Hibert D, et al. Acute pyelonephritis in the elderly. South Med J. 1982;75:551–554.
20. Raz R, Stamm WE. A controlled trial of intravaginal estriol in postmenopausal women with recurrent urinary tract infections. N Engl J Med. 1993;329:753–756.
21. Avorn J, Monane M, Gurwitz JH, et al. Reduction of bacteriuria and pyuria after ingestion of cranberry juice. JAMA. 1994;271:751–754.
22. Warren HW. Catheter-associated urinary tract infections. Infect Dis Clin North Am. 1997;11:609–622.
23. Ouslander JG, Schapira M, Schnelle JF, Fingold S. Pyuria and asymptomatic bacteriuria in elderly ambulatory women. Ann Intern Med. 1989;110:404–405.
24. Warren JW, Damron D, Tenney JH, et al. Fever, bacteremia, and death as complications of bacteriuria in women with long-term urethral catheters. J Infect Dis. 1987;155:1151–1158.
25. Nicolle LE. Prevention and treatment of urinary catheter–related infections in older patients. Drugs Aging. 1994;4:379–391.
26. Saginur R, Nicolle LE. Single-dose compared with 3-day norfloxacin treatment of uncomplicated urinary tract infection in women. Canadian Infectious Diseases Society Clinical Trials Study Group. Arch Intern Med. 1992;152:1233–1237.
27. Osler W, ed. The Principles and Practice of Medicine. 3rd ed. New York: D Appleton; 1898:109.
28. Marrie TJ. Epidemiology of community-acquired pneumonia in the elderly. Semin Respir Infect. 1990;5:260.
29. May DS, Kelly JJ, Mendlein JM, et al. Surveillance of major causes of hospitalization among the elderly, 1988. MMWR Morb Mortal Wkly Rep. 1991;40:7–21.
30. Haley RW, Schaberg DR, Crossley KB, et al. Extra charges and prolongation of stay attributable to nosocomial infections: A prospective interhospital comparison. Am J Med. 1981;70:51–57.
31. Mlinaric-Galinovic G, Falsey AR, Walsh EE. Respiratory synctial virus infection in the elderly. Eur J Clin Microbiol Infect Dis. 1996;15:777–781.
32. Nicholson KG, Kent J, Hammersley V, Cancio E. Risk factors for lower respiratory complications of rhinovirus infections in elderly people living in the community: Prospective cohort study. Br Med J. 1996;313:1119–1123.
33. Troy CJ, Peeling RW, Ellis AG, et al. *Chlamydia pneumoniae* as a new source of infectious outbreaks in nursing homes. JAMA. 1997;277:1214–1218.
34. Rello J, Rodriguez R, Jubert P, Alvarez B. Severe community-acquired pneumonia in the elderly: Epidemiology and prognosis. Study Group for Severe Community-Acquired Pneumonia. Clin Infect Dis. 1996;23:723–728.

35. Crossley KB, Thurn JR. Nursing home–acquired pneumonia. Semin Respir Infect. 1989;4:64–72.
36. Bentley DW. Bacterial pneumonia in the elderly: Clinical features, diagnosis, etiology, and treatment. Gerontology. 1984;30:297–307.
37. Norman DC. Pneumonia in the elderly: Empiric antimicrobial therapy. Geriatrics. 1991;46:26–32.
38. Fried TR, Gillick MR, Lipsitz LA. Short-term functional outcomes of long-term care residents with pneumonia treated with and without hospital transfer. J Am Geriatr Soc. 1997;45:302–306.
39. Hanson LC, Weber DJ, Rutala WA, et al. Risk factors for nosocomial pneumonia in the elderly. Am J Med. 1992;92:161–166.
40. Heuser MD, Case LD, Ettinger WH. Mortality in intensive care patients with respiratory disease: Is age important? Arch Intern Med. 1992;152:1683–1688.
41. Monto AS, Terpenning MS. The value of influenza and pneumococcal vaccines in the elderly. Drugs Aging. 1996;6:445–451.
42. Quick RE, Hoge CW, Hamilton DJ, et al. Underutilization of pneumococcal vaccine in ursing homes in Washington State: Report of a serotype-specific outbreak and a survey. Am J Med. 1993;94:149–152.
43. Arden NH, Patriarca PA, Fasano MB, et al. The roles of vaccination and amantadine prophylaxis in controlling an outbreak of influenza A (H3N2) in a nursing home. Arch Intern Med. 1988;148:865–868.
44. Ten leading nationally notifiable infectious diseases—United States, 1995. MMWR Morb Mortal Wkly Rep. 1996;45:883–884.
45. Stead WW, Dutt AK. Tuberculosis in elderly persons. Annu Rev Med. 1991;42:267–276.
46. Dutt AK, Stead WW. Tuberculosis. Clin Geriatr Med. 1992;8:761–775.
47. Davies P. Tuberculosis in the elderly. Epidemiology and optimal management. Drugs Aging. 1996;8:436–444.
48. Alvarez S, Shell C, Berk SL. Pulmonary tuberculosis in elderly men. Am J Med. 1987;82:602–606.
49. Brandeis GH, Morris JN, Nash DJ, et al. The epidemiology and natural history of pressure ulcers in elderly nursing home residents. JAMA. 1990;264:2905.
50. Kertesz D, Chow AW. Infected pressure and diabetic ulcers. Clin Geriatr Med. 1992;8:835–852.
51. Bryan CS, Dew CE, Reynolds KL. Bacteremia associated with decubitus ulcers. Arch Intern Med. 1983;143:2093.
52. AGS Clinical Practice Committee. Pressure ulcers in adults: Prediction and prevention. J Am Geriatr Soc. 1996;44:1118–1119.
53. Shetty KR, Duthie EH Jr. Thyrotoxicosis induced by topical iodine application. Arch Intern Med. 1990;150:2400–2401.
54. Smith DM, Winsemius DK, Besdine RW. Pressure sores in the elderly: Can this outcome be improved? J Gen Intern Med. 1991;6:81–93.
55. Auerbach SB, Schwartz B, Williams D, et al. Outbreak of invasive group A streptococcal infections in a nursing home. Lessons on prevention and control. Arch Intern Med. 1992;152:1017–1022.
56. Grandsen WR, Eykyn SJ, Phillips I. Septicaemia in the newborn and elderly. J Antimicrob Chemother. 1994;34:101–119.
57. Meyers BR, Sherman E, Mendelson MH, et al. Bloodstream infections in the elderly. Am J Med. 1989;86:379–384.
58. Gleckman R, Hibert D. Afebrile bacteremia: A phenomenon in geriatric patients. JAMA. 1982;248:1478–1481.
59. Chassagne P, Perol M-B, Doucet J, et al. Is presentation of bacteremia in the elderly the same as in younger patients? Am J Med. 1996;100:65–70.
60. Leibovici L. Bacteraemia in the very old. Drugs Aging. 1995;6:456–464.
61. Setia U, Serventi I, Lorenz P. Bacteremia in a long-term care facility. Arch Intern Med. 1984;144:1633–1635.
62. Morike K, Schwab M, Klotz U. Use of aminoglycosides in elderly patients. Drugs Aging. 1997;10:259–277.
63. Terpenning MS, Buggy BP, Kauffman CA. Infective endocarditis: Clinical features in young and elderly patients. Am J Med. 1987;83:626–634.
64. Watanakunakorn C, Burkert T. Infective endocarditis at a large community teaching hospital, 1980–1990. A review of 210 episodes. Medicine (Baltimore). 1993;72:90–102.
65. Van der Meer JTM, Thompson J, Valkenburg HA, Michel MF. Epidemiology of bacterial endocarditis in The Netherlands. Arch Intern Med. 1992;152:1863–1868.
66. Cantrell M, Yoshikawa TT. Aging and infective endocarditis. J Am Geriatr Soc. 1983;31:216–222.
67. Terpenning MS, Buggy BP, Kauffman CA. Infective endocarditis: Clinical features in young and elderly patients. Am J Med. 1987;83:626.
68. Selton-Suty C, Hoen B, Grentzinger A, et al. Clinical and bacteriological characteristics of infective endocarditis in the elderly. Heart. 1997;77:260–263.
69. Dajani AS, Taubert KA, Wilson W, et al: Prevention of bacterial endocarditis: Recommendations by the American Heart Association. JAMA. 1997;277:1794–1801.
70. Lew JF, Glass RI, Gangarosa RE, et al. Diarrheal deaths in the United States, 1979 through 1987. JAMA. 1991;265:3280–3284.
71. Augustin AK, Simor ASE, Shorrock C, McCausland J. Outbreaks of gastroenteritis due to Norwalk-like virus in two long-term care facilities for the elderly. Can J Infect Control. 1995;10(4):111–113.
72. Bentley DW. *Clostridium difficile*–associated disease in long-term care facilities. Infect Control Hosp Epidemiol. 1990;11:434–438.
73. Wilcox MH. Cleaning up *Clostridium difficile* infection. Lancet. 1996;348:767–769.
74. Ryan CA, Tauxe RV, Hosek GW, et al. *Escherichia coli* O157:H7 diarrhea in a nursing home: Clinical, epidemiological, and pathological findings. J Infect Dis. 1986;154:631–638.
75. Neill MA, Rice SK, Ahmad NV, Flanigan TP. Cryptosporidiosis: An unrecognized cause of diarrhea in elderly hospitalized patients. Clin Infect Dis. 1996;22:168–170.
76. Danna PL, Urban C, Bellin E, et al. Role of *Candida* in pathogenesis of antibiotic-associated diarrhoea in elderly inpatients. Lancet. 1991;337:511–514.
77. Aronson SM, DeBuono BA, Buechner JS. Acute bacterial meningitis in Rhode Island: A survey of the years 1976 to 1985. RI Med J. 1991;74:33.
78. Choi C. Bacterial meningitis. Clin Geriatr Med. 1992;8:889–901.
79. Behrman RE, Meyers BR, Mendelson MH, et al. Central nervous system infections in the elderly. Arch Intern Med. 1989;149:1596–1599.
80. Gorse GJ, Thrupp LD, Nudleman KL, et al. Bacterial meningitis in the elderly. Arch Intern Med. 1984;144:1603–1607.
81. McGuire NM, Kauffman CA. Septic arthritis in the elderly. J Am Geriatr Soc. 1985;33:170–174.
82. Downton JH, Andrews K, Puxty JAH. "Silent" pyrexia in the elderly. Age Ageing. 1987;16:41–44.
83. Fox RH, MacGibbon R, Davies L, et al. Problem of the old and the cold. Br Med J. 1973;1:21–24.
84. McAlpine CH, Martin BJ, Lennox IM, et al. Pyrexia in infection in the elderly. Age Ageing. 1986;15:230–234.
85. Marco CA, Schoenfeld CN, Hansen KN, et al. Fever in geriatric emergency patients: Clinical features associated with serious illness. Ann Emerg Med. 1995;26:18–24.
86. Esposito AL, Gleckman RA. Fever of unknown origin in the elderly. J Am Geriatr Soc. 1978;26:498–505.
87. Borrego F, Gleckman R. Principles of antibiotic prescribing in the elderly. Drugs Aging. 1997;11:7–18.
88. Norrby SR. Antibiotic therapy in aging patients. Bull NY Acad Med. 1987;63:519–532.
89. Beers MH, Ouslander JG, Rollingher I, et al. Explicit criteria for determining inappropriate medication use in nursing home residents. Arch Intern Med. 1991;151:1825–1832.
90. Warren JW, Palumbo FB, Fitterman L, et al. Incidence and characteristics of antibiotic use in aged nursing home patients. J Am Geriatr Soc. 1991;39:963–972.
91. Mulligan T. Parenteral antibiotic therapy for patients in nursing homes. Rev Infect Dis. 1991;13 (Suppl 2):S180–S183.

Chapter 307

Infections in Asplenic Patients

LARRY I. LUTWICK

This member hath propritie by itself sometimes, to hinder a man's running; whereupon professed runners in the race that be troubled with the splene have a devise to burne and waste it with a hot iron. . . . They say that the splene may be taken out of the body by way of incision, and yet the creature lives nevertheless.

C. Plinius Secundus[1]

Pliny's words reflect the many difficulties in understanding splenic function that have plagued humankind for more than 25 centuries. The once-popular theory of bodily humors deemed the spleen's black bile to be a source of melancholia, giving rise to the concept of "venting one's spleen." An association with laughter, a putative therapeutic process, led to the prophetic idea that the spleen "cleanses the blood and spirit from unclean and obscuring matter."[2] Overall, however, the spleen was relegated to a role as an nonessential organ that could be removed without any adverse effects.

As early as 1919, animal studies suggested that spleen removal resulted in problems with serious infection.[3] Interest was not truly aroused until King and Schmacher's 1952 report, which highlighted life-threatening infection after splenectomy in infants younger than 6 months of age.[4] The relation between splenectomy (or a hypofunctioning spleen) and severe infection, called *postsplenectomy sepsis* (PSS) or *overwhelming postsplenectomy infection*, is now well documented by illnesses evolving from good health to death within a single day. Although they are not common, such septic deaths may occur at an incidence 600 times greater than in the eusplenic population,[5] influenced by factors including age at, and underlying cause of, splenectomy.

EPIDEMIOLOGY OF SPLENECTOMY

With an enlightened approach toward the spleen's role in PSS prevention, the indications for splenectomy have been reassessed. This has resulted in an increasingly conservative approach toward resection and greater efforts to preserve splenic tissue. This is particularly true in regard to splenic trauma and malignant conditions. A variety of splenic salvage procedures are being performed in trauma cases,[6] and splenectomy is no longer a usual procedure in Hodgkin's disease.[7]

Overall, the National Center for Health Statistics estimated that the number of splenectomies performed in the United States was 27,000 in 1993, 22,000 in 1994, and 26,000 in 1995,[8] indicating a per capita decrease in splenectomy. The procedure remains significant in the management of patients with hereditary hemolytic anemias, spherocytosis in particular. It may be used in the management of a number of conditions such as those shown in Table 307–1.

NONSURGICAL EQUIVALENTS OF SPLENECTOMY

Congenital Asplenia

Splenic absence can be congenital rather than surgically acquired. In infants, asplenia usually is linked to serious organ malformations (Ivemark's syndrome), but isolated congenital asplenia diagnosed in adults can occur. Of ten adult patients,[9] one had a fatal PSS-like illness and another died of malaria. As such, congenital asplenia may be first diagnosed at autopsy in a person succumbing to fulminant infection. Classic pneumococcal PSS-like disease has also been very rarely reported in previously healthy persons with histologically normal spleens.[10]

Functional Hyposplenism

PSS may occur with an anatomically present, poorly performing organ. Called *functional hyposplenism*, it is associated with a wide variety of disorders (Table 307–2). Among the mechanisms responsible for splenic dysfunction are repeated infarction, infiltration, intrasplenic redistribution of blood flow, and antigen-antibody complex blockade.

Functional hyposplenism may be partially reversible, as shown by improved splenic function in celiac disease with the use of a gluten-free diet.[15] Similarly, alcohol abstinence has improved splenic activity in ethanol abusers,[16] and hydroxyurea or transfusions have had some effect in patients with sickle hemoglobinopathies.[17] Transient splenic dysfunction has been described as occurring secondary to pneumococcemia, perhaps a consequence of low fibronectin levels.[18]

ASSESSMENT OF SPLENIC FUNCTION

As the body's largest lymphoid organ, the spleen has a variety of immunologic functions (Table 307–3).[19, 20] Encamped in the midst of the blood's antigenic superhighway as the main production site of opsonizing antibody, it is particularly important for the efficient clearance of encapsulated bacteria. Increased amounts of specific antibody may be needed in asplenia for the remaining reticuloendothelial system (e.g., the liver) to effectively clear intravascular opsonized material.[21] For more virulent organisms such as pneumococci, the splenic absence cannot be as well compensated by the liver.[22]

The splenic architecture functions as a sieve for the blood, removing blood cells, microorganisms and immune complexes. Red blood cells (RBCs) that contain inclusions, after circulating through the splenic microvasculature, may be returned to the blood stream after remodeling (pitting).[14] Howell-Jolly bodies (nuclear remnants) and/or "pocked" RBCs are measures of decreased splenic clearance that are used to assess hyposplenic states.

The presence of Howell-Jolly bodies (Figure 307–1*A*) has been used as a simple screening test for asplenia, but it is relatively insensitive in the hyposplenic patient without severe impairment of function.[23] Clearance of chromium-tagged heat-damaged RBCs is more sensitive, but this test is invasive and is less available. Although spleen size on technetium 99m sulfur colloid scan does correlate with damaged RBC clearance, there is substantial discordance. The "pocked" RBC count (pit count) is a more sensitive indicator of splenic clearance,[24] with RBCs vacuoles visualized by interference phase microscopy (Figure 307–1*B*).

Additional immunologic defects occurring concurrently with asplenia do not necessarily add to the PSS risk. Although Hodgkin's disease carries a higher PSS incidence (see later discussion), the combination of cytotoxic medication and corticosteroids in the asplenic renal transplant recipient does not seem to contribute to a higher PSS risk than in incidental surgical splenectomy alone.[25]

TABLE 307–1 Conditions That Are Associated with Need for Splenectomy

Trauma	Hypersplenism
Community acquired	Agnogenic myeloid metaplasia
Incidental surgical	Portal hypertension
Immunologic conditions	Type 1 Gaucher's disease
Idiopathic thrombocytopenic purpura	Thalassemia
Autoimmune hemolytic anemia	Malignancy
	Hodgkin's disease
	Hairy cell leukemia
	Ovarian carcinoma

TABLE 307–2 Conditions That Are Associated with Functional Hyposplenism

Autoimmune disorders	Infiltrative diseases
Biliary cirrhosis	Amyloidosis
Chronic active hepatitis	Sarcoidosis
Grave's disease	Intestinal disorders
Hashimoto's thyroiditis	Celiac disease
Rheumatoid arthritis	Crohn's disease
Sjögren's syndrome	Dermatitis herpetiformis
Systemic lupus erythematosus	Intestinal lymphangiectasis
Vasculitis	Ulcerative colitis
Hematologic diseases	Whipple's disease
Essential thrombocythemia	Miscellaneous
Fanconi's syndrome	Alcoholism
Hemophilia	Age
Sickle cell hemoglobinopathies	Elderly (>70 y)
SS	Neonates, premature infant
SC	Bone marrow transplantation
S-β thalassemia	Graft-versus-host reaction
Neoplasias	Hypopituitarism
Breast carcinoma	Parenteral nutrition (chronic)
Chronic myelogenous leukemia	Splenic irradiation
	External
Hemangiosarcoma of the spleen	Thoratrast
	Thrombosis of splenic vessels
Non-Hodgkin's lymphoma	
Sézary's syndrome	

Data from refs. 11–14.

TABLE 307–3 Immunologic Functions of the Spleen

- Immune regulatory activities
  - Development of B- and T-cell memories
  - Maturation of T-suppressor cells
  - Termination of autoantibody production
  - Regulation of idiotype-antiidiotype network
- Immune clearance
  - Opsonization
    - Production of specific antibody
    - Production of complement
    - Production of tuftsin (tetrapeptide phagocytic adjuvant)
- Phagocytosis
  - Removal of circulating microorganisms
  - Uptake of immune complexes
  - Disposal of senescent cells
- Immune surveillance
  - Delivery of antigenic information
  - B- and T-cell trafficking

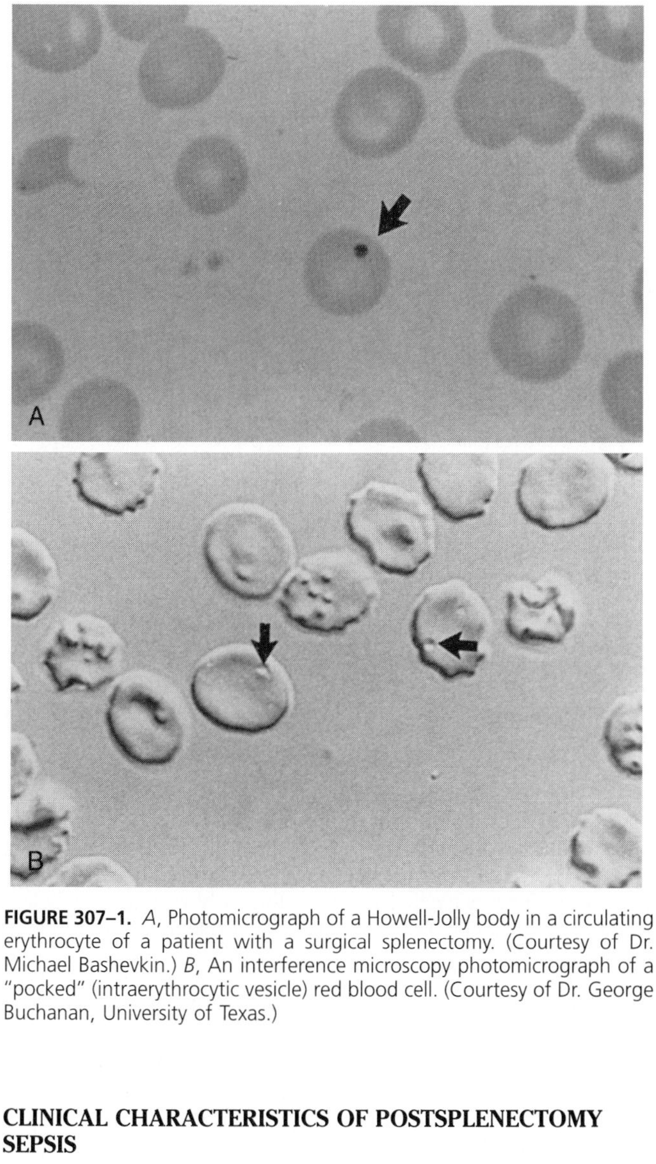

FIGURE 307–1. *A*, Photomicrograph of a Howell-Jolly body in a circulating erythrocyte of a patient with a surgical splenectomy. (Courtesy of Dr. Michael Bashevkin.) *B*, An interference microscopy photomicrograph of a "pocked" (intraerythrocytic vesicle) red blood cell. (Courtesy of Dr. George Buchanan, University of Texas.)

CLINICAL CHARACTERISTICS OF POSTSPLENECTOMY SEPSIS

Frequency

Factors contributing to difficulties in estimating PSS frequency[26, 27] include a variable disease definition (whether any bacteremia or serious infection is included despite the lack of prototypical presentation), duration of follow-up, and stratification for age and splenectomy cause. Styrt[26] assessed reports for the risk of fatal PSS to factor out milder, nonclassic infections. In children, an incidence density of 1 fatal case per 350 patient-years of follow-up was found, equivalent (assuming a 50% case fatality rate) to 1 case of PSS per 175 patient-years. The risk can also be stratified by splenectomy cause (Table 307–4). The lowest risk is related to trauma, intermediate risk to spherocytosis; idiopathic thrombocytic purpura, or portal hypertension; and highest risk in thalassemia or Hodgkin's disease. Some 5.7% of total PSS cases occurred in hyposplenic hosts.[27]

PSS frequency is more variable after adult splenectomy, probably because of the more diverse reasons for the procedure. Styrt found an incidence density of 1 fatal case per 137 to more than 1,190 patient-years, concluding that the risk is lower than after childhood splenectomy.[26] She estimated an overall risk of 1 fatal case in 800 to 1000 patient-years, or 1 case of PSS every 400–500 patient-years. In 5491 patient-years of follow-up after splenectomy for hereditary spherocytosis, a risk of 1 case per 910 patient-years, or 1 fatal case per 1365 patient-years, was found.[28] Some 2.6% of the splenectomized group developed PSS in this report.

TABLE 307–4 Attack Rates of Postsplenectomy Sepsis Related to Splenectomy Cause

	Rate (n)	
Cause	***Singer***[5]	***Styrt***[26]
Low attack rate		
Trauma	1.5% (688)	1.5% (1358)
Incidental surgical	2.1% (333)	1.2% (420)
Intermediate attack rate		
Idiopathic thrombocytopenic purpura	2.1% (489)	3.3% (484)
Spherocytosis*	3.5% (850)	2.4% (932)
Portal hypertension	5.9% (221)	4.1% (122)
High attack rate		
Hodgkin's disease	11.6% (69)	7.1% (451)
Thalassemia	24.8% (109)	7.0% (185)

*Also, 2.6% (n = 226) in the study by Holdsworth et al.[27]

Timing Related to Splenectomy

Because of this low incidence, it is difficult to assess the time for greatest risk after splenectomy. Early cases may be underreported owing to consideration as surgical complications rather than consequences of the asplenic state, and late cases may be underrepresented by loss to follow-up or overreported because of novelty value.[26] It is generally thought that the risk is highest in the first few years.[26, 27] However, PSS has manifested many years after loss of the spleen, with intervals of more than four decades.[29]

Styrt[26] found that 9 of 46 fatal cases of PSS occurred within the first year, followed by 4 to 5 in each subsequent year from 2 to 7 years as a linear incidence curve. In a more extensive review of 288 PSS cases,[27] 32% occurred within the first year and 52% within 2 years (Fig. 307–2). The younger the patient was at the time of splenectomy, the shorter the interval to PSS.

Typical Presentation

PSS may have a short prodrome of low-grade fever with chills, pharyngitis, muscle aches, vomiting, or diarrhea. Whether these symptoms represent a predisposing viral illness is unclear. Styrt[26] noted that, if enough detail is reported, true rigors is frequently present for 1 to 2 days before clinical deterioration. In the setting of known asplenia or significant hyposplenism, a febrile illness with gastrointestinal or other focal symptoms must not lead the clinician away from consideration of PSS. In general, no clinically demonstrable site of infection is found in adult PSS patients. In children younger than 5 years of age, focal infections, particularly meningitis, are more prominent.[27]

The onset of overt deterioration is abrupt, and progression, measured in hours rather than days, has a picture that remains disturbingly unchanged.[2] An asplenic patient may walk into a facility complaining about fever and diarrhea only to be hypotensive and unresponsive several hours later. Rapid deterioration is often accompanied by disseminated intravascular coagulation, seizures, coma, and cardiovascular collapse. Tissue damage can be compounded by the development of purpura fulminans,[30] in which hypotension, endovascular injury, and coagulopathy contribute to extremity gangrene, resulting in the need for multiple amputations.

Diagnosis

Early consideration of PSS must occur so that aggressive intervention can be instituted. A high index of clinical suspicion should be maintained for febrile presentations in the splenectomized patient and the patient with a chronic disease that can produce hyposplenism. Diagnostic workup must never delay the use of empiric antimicrobial therapy.

The presence of an extremely high level of bacteremia, although contributing to morbidity and mortality, allows a diagnosis to be made quickly, before the availability of culture results. Bacteria can

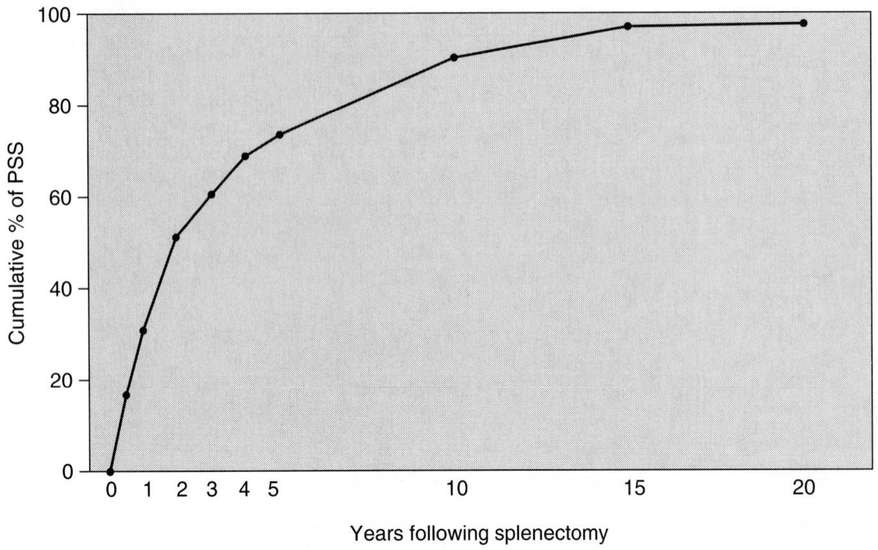

FIGURE 307–2. The interval from splenectomy to postsplenectomy sepsis based on data from reference 27 from 288 individual patients; 3.1% of the total occurred more than 20 years following splenectomy.

be visualized on Gram or Wright staining of the peripheral blood buffy coat (Fig. 307–3*A*) and may even be seen on a stained peripheral blood smear (Fig. 307–3*B*). This latter finding reflects a level of bacteremia of more than 10^6/ml, at least 4 logs greater than a usual bacteremia. Gram stain and culture should also be performed on an aspirate of any petechiae or purpurae that have developed. A positive result from any of these sites assists in tailoring antimicrobial therapy. Acridine orange stain,[31] if available, can be used if standard stains are not helpful. Blood cultures are usually positive within 24 hours and should always be performed to assist in guiding changes in antimicrobial treatment. Cultures and Gram stains should also be obtained from any identified site of overt infection. Cerebrospinal fluid examination may be needed, particularly in children.

Examination of the peripheral blood for evidence of malaria or babesiosis may be required, guided by the patient's history. Furthermore, Howell-Jolly bodies or other evidence for hyposplenism should be sought, especially in the patient with a history of an illness predisposing to hyposplenism.

Mortality

PSS is particularly problematic because of high mortality rates, usually 50 to 70% despite appropriate antimicrobial therapy and intensive medical support.[26, 27] In large review by Holdsworth and colleagues,[27] an overall fatality rate of 55.3% in 349 episodes was found. The dramatic nature of the illness is further reflected by the time from initial symptoms to death, with 68% of the deaths occurring within 24 hours and 80% with 48 hours. This course underscores the need for prevention and emergency intervention strategies.

Mortality is generally higher in cases occurring in patients older than 16 years of age, reflecting their somewhat different presentation of illness. Holdsworth reported a lower mortality rate (31.8%) in the small number of *H. influenzae* cases, compared with pneumococcal PSS.[27] In total, however, the mortality rate of pneumococcal cases (57.6%) did not differ from that of cases of nonpneumococcal origin (52.3%). Unlike incidence, the PSS case fatality rate does not correlate with the principal indication for splenectomy.

MICROBIOLOGY OF POSTSPLENECTOMY SEPSIS

Streptococcus pneumoniae

The pneumococcus is the single most important organism implicated in PSS; it is involved in 50 to 90% of cases.[26, 27] In a review of 349 PSS cases,[27] *Streptococcus pneumoniae* was causative in 67% of episodes in which an organism was identified (Fig. 307–4). Common in all age groups, the percentage of pneumococcal PSS cases tends to increase with age. A predominant polysaccharide serotype is not found, and no evidence exists to suggest that the distribution of serotypes involved in PSS differs from that in other forms of pneumococcal infection.

Lacking the endotoxin of gram-negative organisms, *S. pneumoniae* can still activate inflammatory cascades leading to disseminated intravascular coagulation and irreversible shock. The mechanism may be related to endovascular injury from the high-grade bacteremia or to direct activation by circulating polysaccharide capsule.[32] Antigen-antibody complexes can also play a role in the activation of complement.

Increases in pneumococcal antimicrobial drug resistance have occurred in recent years. In some areas of the United States, a significant percentage of pneumococci demonstrate penicillin resistance, either relative or absolute.[33] These isolates may also be resistant to the extended-spectrum cephalosporins (e.g., ceftriaxone). Penicillin-resistant pneumococci (PRP) must be considered in the empiric therapy of PSS.

Haemophilus influenzae

Type B *H. influenzae* is the second most common organism related to PSS.[26, 27] Most PSS cases associated with this organism have occurred in children younger than 15 years of age, 86% in one review.[27] Such cases have been about 10 times less frequent than pneumococcal PSS. The use of the conjugated *H. influenzae* type B vaccine has dramatically decreased the overall incidence of invasive disease.[34] The consequences of this vaccine-associated protection should be a decrease in the overall number of PSS cases associated with *H. influenzae*, with more of the remaining infections occurring in older, nonvaccinated persons. Nontypable strains predominate among *H. influenzae* bacteremias in cancer patients[35] but are not significant in PSS. Invasive infection by non-b capsular strains (a and c through f) exists, but these bacilli appear to be of low virulence[36] and, to date, have not been relevant in PSS. β-lactamase production by many *H. influenzae* strains must be accounted for during planning of empiric PSS therapy.

Other Bacterial Organisms

Neisseria meningitidis, the meningococcus, has been cited as the third most common cause of PSS. Although meningococcemia occurs in the asplenic host[37, 38] and was reported in King and Schmack-

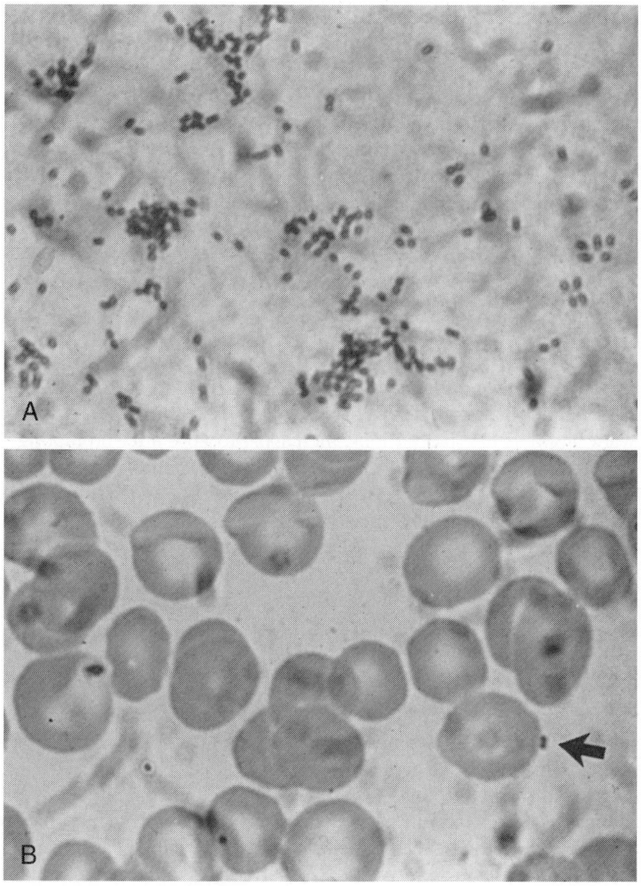

FIGURE 307–3. *A*, The Gram stain of a buffy coat smear of a patient with rapidly fatal pneumococcal postsplenectomy sepsis 7 years following a staging laparotomy for Hodgkin's disease with many gram-positive diplococci. *B*, A Wright-stained peripheral blood smear from the same patient showing extracellular diplococci. (From Lynch AM, Kapila R. Overwhelming postsplenectomy infection. Infect Dis Clin North Am. 1996;10:693–707.)

er's original publication,[4] it is not clear that meningococcemia is either more frequent or more severe in asplenic/hyposplenic patients than in healthy persons. Certainly fulminant meningococcal infection occurs in the eusplenic host. Data from asplenic mice further support this lack of association.[39]

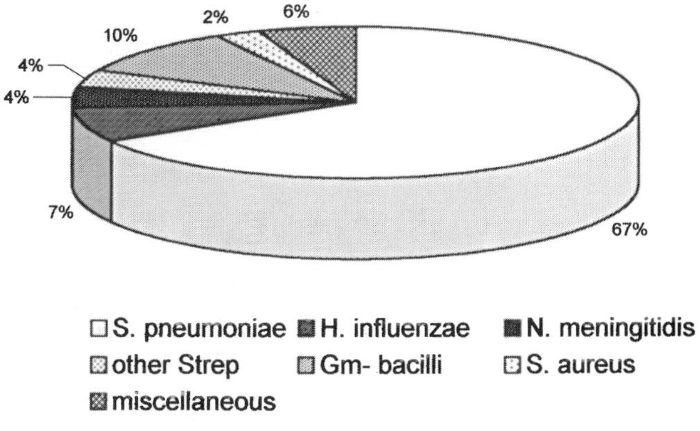

FIGURE 307–4. The microbiology of postsplenectomy sepsis adapted from reference 27 based on 298 culture-positive episodes including those due to the meningococcus; 51 (14.6%) additional episodes did not have a reported organism. Data not stratified by age or cause of splenectomy.

Capnocytophaga canimorsus, a fastidious gram-negative rod formerly known as CDC group DF-2, is part of the normal oral flora of dogs and cats. It is typically transmitted to humans through contact with an animal, usually a bite or scratch. Severe *C. canimorsus* infection can occur in healthy immunocompetent persons, but in 80% of reported cases there is a predisposing condition, primarily asplenia or hyposplenic state.[40] The consequences of *C. canimorsus* infection in such hosts also appear to be more severe. PSS related to this bacillus may not be differentiable from that caused by the pneumococcus. The finding of gram-negative bacilli in the buffy coat or peripheral blood smear[41, 42] and/or an eschar at the bite site[43] suggests infection by *C. canimorsus*, which manifests 1 to 7 days after exposure. Some 30% of these organisms produce a β-lactamase.[44]

Salmonella species have also been associated with PSS.[45, 46] Severe infection with this bacillus can be associated with the hyposplenism of chronic reticuloendothelial blockage in bartonellosis[47] and *Salmonella* is a prominent pathogen in children with sickle cell anemia and splenic dysfunction,[48] so it is surprising that *Salmonella* does not play a larger role in PSS. Most cases have occurred in persons with illnesses in which defects in cell-mediated immunity, from either the disease or its treatment, predispose to salmonellosis.

A wide collection of other bacterial organisms have been reported as occasional pathogens in PSS. These include nonpneumococcal streptococci, *Staphylococcus aureus*, *Escherichia coli*, and other Enterobacteriaceae, *Campylobacter*, *Bacteroides*, *Pseudomonas*, and *Plesiomonas shigelloides*. As unusual causes of an uncommon entity, consideration of these or other organisms is required only if specific epidemiologic circumstances exist.

RELATION OF SPLENECTOMY TO OTHER INFECTIONS

Overall, there is no strong evidence that the asplenic host has a higher frequency or severity of most infections. A case report of an asplenic patient with widespread influenza A infection in association with pneumococcal PSS exists,[49] but the cohort does not appear to have more frequent or more severe respiratory virus infections. One study reported an increase in varicella-zoster virus infections in Hodgkin's disease patients after splenectomy, but there was no survival difference.[50]

Postoperative Period

Early postoperative infections after splenectomy are related to pulmonary, urinary, or intra-abdominal sites. In splenectomized trauma patients, both focal infections and bacteremias are more common in patients with additional injuries.[51] The microbiologic causes of these infections are primarily staphylococci and enteric gram-negative bacilli, not the usual PSS organisms. Whether splenectomy is an independent risk factor for postoperative infection is not clear.[52, 53] Any increased risk is probably related to the cause of the splenectomy rather than the procedure itself.

Babesiosis and Malaria

The asplenic host seems to be more susceptible to more serious infections with certain intra-erythrocytic protozoa. In babesiosis, a significant percentage of the morbidity and mortality in human cases has been found in asplenic hosts.[54] Animal malaria is clearly exacerbated by splenectomy. As examples, spleen removal allows adaptation of human malaria to primates, and spontaneous resolution ("crisis") of malaria is spleen-mediated in a number of species.[55] Whether human malaria is as clinically affected by splenectomy is unclear, and most evidence is based on only a few cases[56] of an infection that kills millions each year. In persons who are partially immune to malaria, the course of *Plasmodium falciparum* infection was not affected by splenectomy, but parasite clearance was delayed in the nonimmune asplenic patient.[57]

Human Immunodeficiency Virus Infection

Splenectomy may be necessary in the treatment of refractory thrombocytopenia in human immunodeficiency virus (HIV) infection and can be associated with PSS. After spleen removal, absolute counts of CD4- and CD8-positive T lymphocyte levels rise,[58] as also occurs in the non-HIV infected person. However, the CD4/CD8 ratio remains low and becomes more important in therapeutic decision-making processes for the splenectomized HIV-infected person.

The effect of splenectomy on the natural history of HIV infection has been studied. There is no information to suggest that the surgery adversely affects patients with the acquired immunodeficiency syndrome (AIDS). Favorable effects of splenectomy on HIV-related events was observed in a study with a median 51-month follow-up.[59] Another report also found a statistically lower risk of progression to AIDS in patients splenectomized before HIV infection or during the asymptomatic phase.[60] This effect may be the equivalent of debulking of the lymphatic tissue, a significant site of viral sequestration and replication.

THERAPEUTIC STRATEGIES

Immediate Self-Treatment

Because of the potential for fulminant disease, self-administration of antimicrobials at the first sign of a suspicious illness, although not supported by any controlled studies, is a commonly advised practice. Such treatment must never be substituted for immediate medical evaluation but should be instituted especially if any delay in the delivery of medical care is to occur. Indications for treatment could be fever and rigors or any febrile illness with prostration.

Many clinicians prescribe a small amount of an antibiotic such as amoxicillin to be kept at home (and taken along when traveling) for this purpose. Alternative choices, based on drug allergy and local antimicrobial resistance patterns, include amoxicillin-clavulanic acid, trimethoprim-sulfamethoxazole, and newer macrolides such as azithromycin. The β-lactamase inhibitor facilitates activity against β-lactamase–producing *H. influenzae* or *C. canimorsus* but not against PRP. Neither trimethoprim-sulfamethoxazole nor azithromycin may be effective against PRP. A newer quinolone with activity against this organism could also be considered in adults.

Antimicrobial Interventions

If a patient with suspected PSS is seen in a physician's office, an antimicrobial agent such as ceftriaxone should be given parenterally before transfer to the hospital, whether or not blood cultures can be obtained. Empirical antimicrobial options for suspected PSS are shown in Table 307–5. Unless an organism with pneumococcal-like morphology is visualized, coverage for selected gram-negative organisms must be part of the regimen.

Potential Immunologic Interventions

Immunologic manipulations could have benefit in PSS as adjuvants to prompt antimicrobial therapy and cardiovascular support. Because there is a lack or relative lack of opsonizing antibody in the absence of the spleen, intravenous human immunoglobulin (IG) may be useful. In asplenic animal studies, IG decreased mortality from infection.[61, 62] The administration of tuftsin, cleaved from the Fc portion of immunoglobulin by splenic endocarboxypeptidase, decreased mortality from infection in splenectomized mice.[63] A natural immunomodulating tetrapeptide, tuftsin can stimulate activity of circulating phagocytes and hepatic Kupffer's cells,[64] helping to compensate for splenic loss.

PREVENTION STRATEGIES

Patient and Family Education

Patients may have a low level of knowledge regarding PSS risk. One study found that only 16% of 89 postsplenectomy patients were aware of any health precautions, increasing to 40% after prompting.[65] Important issues to impart to the patient and family are listed in Table 307–6 and should be delivered in both oral and written form. Because awareness was decreased with increasing age, emphasis on long-term follow-up is vital. The patient should wear a medical alert bracelet or necklace and carry a card documenting immunization, any prophylactic antimicrobials in use, and a plan for emergencies.[66]

Vaccination

Pneumococcal immunization with the polyvalent capsular polysaccharide vaccine is uniformly recommended for the asplenic or hyposplenic host. The specific antibody response (IgM and IgG) to immunization in this cohort is delayed, and the magnitude of the response is lower than in normal persons,[67] although wide variation in response from patient to patient and among vaccine capsule types is seen. The hyporesponsiveness is partially related to underlying disease. In Hodgkin's disease, response improves as the time after chemotherapy or radiation increases, but it can still be subnormal after 4 years.[68]

For patients undergoing elective splenectomy, the vaccine should be given at least 2 weeks before the procedure to optimize the antibody response. After emergency splenectomy, immunization is usually given at the time of hospital discharge. It remains unclear whether the timing of vaccination affects efficacy, but it is reasonable to allow the host to recover from perioperative catabolism before immunization. Vaccine use is also often delayed for 6 months or longer after chemotherapy or therapeutic irradiation. The current vaccine is poorly immunogenic in children younger than 2 years old.

How efficacious pneumococcal vaccination is in the asplenic host is not known, and anecdotal reports of failures exist. Failures have been related to both vaccine-associated[69] and non–vaccine-associated[70] strains. A small study of patients with hyposplenic sickle cell anemia did show protection by the vaccine over a 2-year interval.[71] A 1997 retrospective study from Norway in Hodgkin's disease patients also suggested protective efficacy,[72] and a similar conclusion was reached in a Danish study of splenectomized children receiving vaccine and antibiotic prophylaxis.[73] Reimmunization in this cohort

TABLE 307–5 Empiric Postsplenectomy Sepsis Antimicrobial Treatment*

Setting	Antimicrobial
Gram-stain evidence of *Streptococcus pneumoniae*	
Areas without concern for penicillin-resistant PRP	Penicillin or ceftriaxone
Areas with concern for moderately resistant PRP (MIC 0.1–1.0 μg/ml)	Ceftriaxone ± vancomycin
Areas with concern for highly resistant PRP (MIC ≥ 2.0 μg/ml)	Vancomycin (with or without rifampin) ± ceftriaxone
Gram-stain evidence of a gram-negative bacillus or diplococcus	Ceftriaxone (if clinical circumstances suggest the possibility of a pseudomonad, use ceftazidime instead)
No organism seen on Gram stain	Combination of both approaches

*Adult dosages: penicillin, 4 million units IV every 4 h; ceftriaxone, 2 g IV every 24 h; vancomycin, 1 g IV every 12 h; ceftazidime, 2 g IV every 8 h. These regimens may need modification in patients with renal or hepatic disease. Many patients with IgE-mediated penicillin allergy can tolerate cephalosporins, but they ought to be given with caution or an alternative sought. Higher doses of vancomycin may be needed if meningitis is present. Modifications of the regimen chosen should be made when culture and sensitivity data are available.

Abbreviations: MIC, Minimal inhibitory concentration; PRP, penicillin-resistant pneumococci.

seems reasonable.[74] Because specific antibody levels can decrease more rapidly in the asplenic patient,[75] revaccination as frequently as every 2 or 3 years has been suggested.[74, 76] A protein-linked capsular vaccine may be useful in facilitating a response in young children and augmenting the response in asplenics.

H. influenzae type B conjugated polysaccharide vaccination should also be given to at risk individuals.[74] This vaccine is now part of universal immunization in infants in the developed world, so the target population is asplenics/hyposplenics who are old enough not to have been immunized. Many adults already have specific antibody to this organism, explaining why PSS related to *H. influenzae* type B has been much less common in adults than in children. In pediatric sickle cell anemia patients, the conjugated vaccine is immunogenic.[77] As with pneumococci, a higher level of specific antibody may be needed for protection in the absence of a functional spleen.[77] The role of boosters for this vaccine is unknown.

Quadrivalent meningococcal vaccine (types A, C, Y and W135) is also immunogenic in asplenic patients but less so in those with diseases treated with chemotherapy and radiotherapy.[78] Lack of a clearly increased risk, the absence of type B in the vaccine, and the short duration of protection in normal persons suggest that this vaccine may not be useful in the asplenic host. It should be given, however, before high-risk travel or in the setting of an epidemic.

Yearly influenza vaccination is recommended in the asplenic/hyposplenic patient who falls into the usual high-risk groups for complications of influenza. It is reasonable to use influenza immunization for all asplenic/hyposplenic persons.

Use of Prophylactic Antimicrobials

It has been commonplace for asplenic pediatric patients to receive oral phenoxymethyl penicillin prophylaxis for the first few years after splenectomy. Studies in children with sickle hemoglobinopathies have revealed a 84% reduction in pneumococcal bacteremia with the use of such prophylaxis.[79] The efficacy in the asplenic child, however, is not clear. Failures are reported, and the degree of protection against PSS has not been quantified. In a 1986 review, 14 reports of prophylaxis failure were cited,[80] none of the isolates being penicillin resistant. This, however, was before the more recent increase in PRP isolates.

Penicillin prophylaxis has been discontinued in children with sickle cell anemia after at least 2 years of treatment and pneumococcal vaccination. No increased incidence of pneumococcal events was found, compared with similar patients still receiving penicillin.[81] A similar approach may be taken in the asplenic child who has not had PSS, although lifelong prophylaxis in those with underlying immune defects has been suggested.[74]

Little information is available on the utility of this modality in asplenic adults. Because of the rarity of PSS in adults, the possibility of adverse effects from therapy, selection of resistant strains, compliance issues, and the psychosocial burden of lifelong therapy, long-term prophylaxis in adults is not generally recommended.[26, 74] The role of antibiotic prophylaxis in hyposplenic patients without S-hemoglobinopathies is unknown.

Antimicrobial prophylaxis of the asplenic/hyposplenic patient undergoing bacteremia-associated dental procedures has been discussed.[82] No routine prophylaxis is suggested, although it is recommended for consideration by some.

TABLE 307–6 Educational Issues for the Asplenic/Hyposplenic Host

Persons without a functioning spleen are more susceptible to certain infections.
The infection can be very rapidly progressive and life-threatening.
The risk of infection is lifelong, but it is highest in the first year or two after the surgery.
All physicians tending the patient should be informed of the condition, no matter how long after the splenectomy.
Both vaccination and antimicrobial agents may be used for prevention.

Spleen-Sparing Treatments

The risk of fulminant infection has focused attention on alternatives to total splenectomy. Various methods of splenic preservation after traumatic rupture has been successful, including conservative management, splenic repair, and partial splenectomy.[83] One report found that salvage could be accomplished in more than 90% of transcapsular splenic injuries.[84] The finding of some return of splenic clearance function after traumatic rupture has led to the suggestion that splenosis, growth of peritoneal implants of splenic tissue, explains the lower risk of PSS after trauma. One study reported the presence of such "born again" spleen function in 13 of 22 cases.[85] Surgeons may autotransplant splenic tissue during splenectomy to facilitate splenosis.

Observed splenic function is greater after partial splenectomy or splenic repair than after autotransplantation, but the latter patients retained more function than did those undergoing total splenectomy.[86] Fatal pneumococcal PSS was reported, however, in a patient with 92 g of splenosis, leading to the suggestion that splenic blood supply alterations may also play a role in PSS risk.[87] Conservative approaches to splenectomy for Hodgkin's disease staging, tropical splenomegaly, hypersplenism, and splenic cysts have also been more frequently used.[26, 83, 88]

Potential Immunologic Preventive Interventions

Granulocyte-macrophage colony-stimulating factor (GM-CSF), used to augment defenses in the neutropenic host, stimulates macrophage progenitors as well. GM-CSF increases macrophage bactericidal activity in eusplenic and asplenic mice, and treated animals had improved survival after pneumococcal challenge.[89] *Corynebacterium parvum*, a nonspecific adjuvant that stimulates the reticuloendothelial system, produced a splenomimetic effect in an asplenic rat model that decreased mortality after pneumococcal infection.[90]

REFERENCES

1. Plinius Secundus C. The Historie of the World. Translated by Philemon Holland. Book 30. London: A. Islip; 1634:381. Cited by: Coon WW. The spleen and splenectomy. Surg Gynecol Obstet. 1991;173:407–414.
2. Lynch AM, Kapila R. Overwhelming postsplenectomy infection. Infect Dis Clin North Am. 1996;10:693–707.
3. Morris DH, Bullock FD. The importance of the spleen in resistance to infection. Ann Surg. 1919;70:513–20.
4. King H, Schmacker HB. Splenic studies: I. Susceptibility to infection after splenectomy performed in infancy. Ann Surg. 1952;136:239–242.
5. Singer DB. Postsplenectomy sepsis. In: Rosenberg HS, Bolande RP, eds. Perspectives in Pediatric Pathology. Vol 1. Chicago: Year Book Medical Publishers; 1973:285–311.
6. Clancy TV, Ramshaw DG, Maxwell JG, et al. Management outcomes in splenic injury: A statewide trauma center review. Ann Surg. 1997;226:17–24.
7. Jameson JS, Thomas WM, Dawson S, et al. Splenectomy for haematological disease. J R Coll Surg Edin. 1996;41:307–311.
8. National Center for Health Statistics. Health, United States, 1995. Hyattsville, MD: Public Health Service, 1996.
9. Myerson RM, Koelle WA. Congenital absence of the spleen in an adult: Report of a case with recurrent Waterhouse-Friderichsen syndrome. N Engl J Med. 1956;254:1131–1132.
10. Bramely PN, Shah P, Williams DJ, Losowsky MS. Pneumococcal Waterhouse-Friderichsen syndrome despite a normal spleen. Postgrad Med J. 1989;65:687–688.
11. Foster PN, Losowsky MS. Hyposplenism: A review. J R Coll Phys Lond. 1987;21:188–191.
12. Doll DC, List AF, Yarbro JW. Functional hyposplenism. South Med J. 1987;80:999–1006.
13. Muller AF, Toghill PJ. Hyposplenism in gastrointestinal disease. Gut. 1995;36:165–167.
14. Zago MA. The evaluation of spleen function in man. Braz J Med Biol Res. 1989;22:159–169.
15. Corazza GR, Frisoni M, Vaira D, Gasbarrini G. Effect of gluten-free diet on splenic hypofunction of adult coeliac disease. Gut. 1983;24:228–230.
16. Muller AF, Toghill PJ. Functional hyposplenism in alcoholic liver disease: A toxic effect of alcohol? Gut. 1994;35:679–682.
17. Closter S, Vichinsky E. First report of reversal of organ dysfunction in sickle cell anemia by the use of hydroxyurea: Splenic regeneration. Blood. 1996;88:1951–1953.
18. Boughton BJ, Simpson A, Chandler S. Functional hyposplenism during pneumococcal septicaemia. Lancet. 1983;1:121–122.

19. Lockwood CM. Immunological functions of the spleen. Clin Haematol. 1983;12:449–465.
20. Bohnsack JF, Brown EJ. The role of the spleen in resistance to infection. Ann Rev Med. 1986;37:49–59.
21. Hosea SW, Brown EJ, Hamburger MI, Frank MM. Opsonic requirements for intravascular clearance after splenectomy. N Engl J Med. 1981;304:245–250.
22. Brown EJ, Hosea SW, Frank MM. The role of the spleen in experimental pneumococcal bacteremia. J Clin Invest. 1981;67:975–982.
23. Robertson DAF, Bullen AW, Hall R, Losowsky MS. Blood film appearances in the hyposplenism of coeliac disease. Br J Clin Pract. 1983;37:19–22.
24. Buchanan GR, Holtkamp CA, Horton JA. Formation and disappearance of pocked erythrocytes: Studies in human subjects and laboratory animals. Am J Hematol. 1987;25:243–251.
25. Bourgault A-M, Van Scoy RE, Wilkowske CJ, et al. Severe infection due to *Streptococcus pneumoniae* in asplenic renal transplant patients. Mayo Clin Proc. 1979;54:123–126.
26. Styrt B. Infection associated with asplenia: Risks, mechanisms, and prevention. Am J Med. 1990;88:5-33N–5-42N.
27. Holdsworth RJ, Irving AD, Cuschieri A. Postsplenectomy sepsis and its mortality rate: Actual *versus* perceived risks. Br J Surg. 1991;78:1031–1038.
28. Schilling RF. Estimating the risk for sepsis after splenectomy in hereditary spherocytosis. Ann Inern Med. 1995;122:187–188.
29. Evans DIK. Postsplenectomy sepsis 10 years or more after operation. J Clin Pathol. 1985;38:309–311.
30. Carpenter CT, Kaiser AB. Purpura fulminans in pneumococcal sepsis: Case report and review. Scand J Infect Dis. 1997;29:479–483.
31. Burdash NM, Manos JP, Bannister ER, Welborn AL. Acridine orange staining and radiometric detection of microorganisms in blood cultures. J Clin Microbiol. 1983;17:463–465.
32. Rytel MW, Dee TH, Ferstenfeld JE, Hensley GT. Possible pathogenic role of capsular antigens in fulminant pneumococcal disease with disseminated intravascular coagulation. Am J Med. 1974;57:889–896.
33. Hofmann J, Cetron MS, Farley MM, et al. The prevalence of drug-resistant *Streptococcus pneumoniae* in Atlanta. N Engl J Med. 1995;333:481–486.
34. Vadheim CM, Greenberg DP, Eriksen E, et al. Eradication of *Haemophilus influenzae* type b disease in southern California. Arch Pediatr Adolesc Med. 1994;148:51–56.
35. Fainstein V, Berkey P, Elting L, Bodey GP. *Haemophilus* species bacteremia in patients with cancer: A 13-year experience. Arch Intern Med. 1989;149:1341–1345.
36. Rutherford GW, Wilfert CM. Invasive *Haemophilus influenzae* type a infections: A report of two cases and a review of the literature. Pediatr Infect Dis. 1984;3:575–577.
37. Holmes FF, Weyandt T, Glazier J, et al. Fulminant meningococcemia after splenectomy. JAMA. 1981;246:1119–1120.
38. Condon RJ, Riley TV, Kelly H. Invasive meningococcal infection after splenectomy. BMJ. 1994;308:792–793.
39. Loggie BW, Hinchey EJ. Does splenectomy predispose to meningococcal sepsis? An experimental study and clinical review. J Pediatr Surg. 1986;21:326–330.
40. Zumla A, Lipscomb G, Corbett M, et al. Dysgonic fermenter, type 2: A zoonosis. Report of two cases and review. Q J Med. 1988;68:741–752.
41. Case Records of the Massachusetts General Hospital (Case 29-1986). N Engl J Med. 1986;315:241–249.
42. Martone WJ, Zuehl RW, Minson GE, Scheld WM. Postsplenectomy sepsis with DF-2: Report of a case with isolation of the organism from the patient's dog. Ann Intern Med. 1980;93:457–458.
43. Kalb R, Kaplan MH, Tenebaum MJ, et al. Cutaneous infection at dog bite wounds associated with fulminant DF-2 septicemia. Am J Med. 1985;78:687–690.
44. Roscoe DL, Zemcov SJV, Thornber D, et al. Antimicrobial susceptibilities and β-lactamase characterization of *Capnocytophaga* species. Antimicrob Agent Chemother. 1992;36:2197–2200.
45. Donaldson SS, Moore MR, Rosenberg SA, Vosti KL. Characterization of postsplenectomy bacteremia among patients with and without lymphoma. N Engl J Med. 1972;287:69–71.
46. Baccarani M, Fiacchini M, Galieni P, et al. Meningitis and septicemia in adults splenectomized for Hodgkin's disease. Scand J Haematol. 1986;36:492–498.
47. Dooley JR. Haemotropic bacteria in man. Lancet. 1980;2:1237–1239.
48. Onwubalili JK. Sickle cell disease and infection. J Infect. 1983;7:2–20.
49. Roberts GT, Roberts JT. Postsplenectomy sepsis due to influenzal viremia and pneumococcemia. Can Med Assoc J. 1976;115:435–437.
50. Goffinet DR, Glatstein EJ, Merigan TC. Herpes zoster-varicella infections and lymphoma. Ann Intern Med. 1972;76:235–240.
51. Malangoni MA, Dillon LD, Klamer TW, Condon RE. Factors influencing the risk of early and late serious infection in adults after splenectomy for trauma. Surgery. 1984;96:775–783.
52. Sekikawa T, Shatney CH. Septic sequelae after splenectomy for trauma in adults. Am J Surg. 1983;145:667–673.
53. Fujita T, Matai K, Kohno S, Itsubo K. Impact of splenectomy on circulatory immunoglobulin levels and the development of postoperative infection following total gastrectomy for gastric cancer. Br J Surg. 1996;83:1776–1778.
54. Rosner F, Zarrabi MH, Benach JL, Habicht GS. Babesiosis in splenectomized adults: Review of 22 reported cases. Am J Med. 1984;76:696–701.
55. Quinn TC, Wyler DJ. Resolution of acute malaria (*Plasmodium berghei* in the rat): Reversibility and spleen dependence. Am J Trop Med Hyg. 1980;29:1–4.
56. Tapper ML, Armstrong D. Malaria complicating neoplastic disease. Arch Intern Med. 1976;136:807–810.
57. Looareesuwan S, Suntharasamai P, Webster HK, Ho M. Malaria in splenectomized patients: Report of four cases and review. Clin Infect Dis. 1993;16:361–366.
58. Domingo P, Fuster M, Muñiz-Diaz E, et al. Spurious post-splenectomy CD4 and CD8 lymphocytosis in HIV-infected patients. AIDS. 1996;10:106–107.
59. Morlat P, Dequae-Merchadou L, Dobis F, et al. Splenectomy and prognosis of HIV infection. AIDS. 1996;10:1170–1172.
60. Tsoukas CM, Bernard NF, Abrahamowicz M, et al. Effect of splenectomy on slowing human immunodeficiency virus disease progression. Arch Surg. 1998;133:25–31.
61. Camel JE, Kim KS, Tchejeyan GH, Mahour GH. Efficacy of passive immunotherapy in experimental postsplenectomy sepsis due to *Haemophilus influenzae* type b. J Pediatr Surg. 1993;28:1441–1445.
62. Offenbartl K, Christensen P, Gullstrand P, et al. Treatment of pneumococcal postsplenectomy sepsis in the rat with human γ-globulin. J Surg Res. 1986;40:198–201.
63. Chu DZJ, Nishioka K, El-Hagin T, et al. Effects of tuftsin on postsplenectomy sepsis. Surgery. 1985;97:701–706.
64. Kubo S, Rodriguez T, Roh MS, et al. Stimulation of phagocytic activity of murine Kupffer cells by tuftsin. Hepatology. 1994;19:1044–1049.
65. White KS, Covington D, Churchill P, et al. Patient awareness of health precautions after splenectomy. Am J Infect Control. 1991;19:36–41.
66. Canadian Paediatric Society. Prevention and therapy of bacterial infections of the child with asplenia/hyposplenia. Can J Paediatr. 1995;2:371–375.
67. Hosea SW, Burch CG, Brown EJ, et al. Impaired immune response of splenectomized patients to polyvalent pneumococcal vaccine. Lancet. 1981;1:804–807.
68. Siber GR, Weitzman SA, Aisenberg AC, et al. Impaired antibody response to pneumococcal vaccine after treatment for Hodgkin's disease. N Engl J Med. 1978;299:422–428.
69. Evans DIK. Fatal post-splenectomy sepsis despite prophylaxis with penicillin and pneumococcal vaccine. Lancet. 1984;1:1124.
70. Appelbaum PC, Shaikh BS, Widome MD, et al. Fatal pneumococcal bacteremia in a vaccinated, splenectomized child. N Engl J Med. 1979;300:203–204.
71. Ammann AJ, Addiego J, Wara DW, et al. Polyvalent pneumococcal-polysaccharide immunization of patients with sickle-cell anemia and patients with splenectomy. N Engl J Med. 1977;297:897–900.
72. Foss Abrahamsen A, Hoiby EA, Hannisdol E, et al. Systemic pneumococcal disease after staging for Hodgkin's disease 1969–1980 without pneumococcal vaccine protection: A follow-up study 1994. Eur J Haematol. 1997;58:73–77.
73. Konradsen HB, Henrichsen J. Pneumococcal infections in splenectomized children are preventable. Acta Paediatr Scand. 1991;80:423–427.
74. Working Party of the British Committee for Standards in Haematology Clinical Haematology Task Force. Guidelines for the prevention and treatment of infection in patients with an absent or dysfunctional spleen. BMJ. 1996;312:430–434.
75. Giebink GS, Le CT, Cosio FG, et al. Serum antibody responses of high-risk children and adults to vaccination with capsular polysaccharide of *Streptococcus pneumoniae*. Rev Infect Dis. 1981;3(Suppl):168–178.
76. Rutherford EJ, Livengood J, Higginbotham M, et al. Efficacy and safety of pneumococcal revaccination after splenectomy for trauma. J Trauma. 1995;39:448–452.
77. Rubin LG, Voulalas D, Carmody L. Immunogenicity of *Haemophilus influenzae* type b conjugate vaccine in children with sickle cell anemia. Am J Dis Child. 1992;146:340–342.
78. Ruben FL, Hankins WA, Zeigler Z, et al. Antibody responses to meningococcal polysaccharide vaccine in adults without a spleen. Am J Med. 1984;76:115–121.
79. Gaston MH, Verter JI, Woods G, et al. Prophylaxis with oral penicillin in children with sickle cell anemia: A randomized trial. N Engl J Med. 1986;314:1593–1539.
80. Zarrabi MH, Rosner F. Rarity of failure of penicillin prophylaxis to prevent postsplenectomy sepsis. Arch Intern Med. 1986;146:1207–1208.
81. Falletta JM, Woods GM, Verter JI, et al. Discontinuing penicillin prophylaxis in children with sickle cell anemia. J Pediatr. 1995;127:685–690.
82. De Rossi SS, Glick M. Dental considerations in asplenic patients. J Am Dent Assoc. 1996;127:1359–1363.
83. Cooper MJ, Williamson RCN. Splenectomy: Indications, hazards and alternatives. Br J Surg. 1984;71:173–180.
84. Rozinov VM, Salel'ev SB, Keshishyan RA, et al. Organ-sparing treatment for closed spleen injuries in children. Clin Orthop. 1995;320:34–39.
85. Pearson HA, Johnston D, Smith KA, Touloukian RJ. The born-again spleen: Return of splenic function after splenectomy for trauma. N Engl J Med. 1978;298:1389–1392.
86. Traub A, Giebink GS, Smith C, et al. Splenic reticuloendothelial function after splenectomy, spleen repair, and spleen autotransplantation. N Engl J Med. 1987;317:1559–1564.
87. Rice HM, James PD. Ectopic splenic tissue failed to prevent fatal pneumococcal septicaemia after splenectomy for trauma. Lancet. 1980;1:565–566.
88. Hoestra HJ, Tamminga RY, Timens W. Partial splenectomy in children: An alternative for splenectomy in the pathological staging of Hodgkin's disease. Ann Surg Oncol. 1994;1:480–486.
89. Hebert JC, O'Reilly M. Granulocyte-macrophage colony-stimulating factor (GM-CSF) enhances pulmonary defenses against pneumococcal infections after splenectomy. J Trauma. 1996;41:663–666.
90. Wellish KL, Witte MH, Witte CL, et al. Splenomimetic effect of *Corynebacterium parvum* in fulminant pneumococcemia. J Infect Dis. 1987;156:130–135.

S E C T I O N C

SURGICAL AND TRAUMA-RELATED INFECTIONS

Chapter 308

Postoperative Infections and Antimicrobial Prophylaxis

DOUGLAS S. KERNODLE
ALLEN B. KAISER

In 1862, Louis Pasteur's ingenious experiments into the nature of putrefaction were officially endorsed by the Paris Academy of Science. The endorsement signaled an end to the long-held belief that the exposure of organic material to air brought about the "spontaneous generation" of microorganisms, and the concepts of "sepsis" and "asepsis" became firmly established. A scant 3 years later, in what must be regarded as a paradigm of applied science, Joseph Lister demonstrated the incredible implications of antisepsis in his practice of orthopedic surgery. For the first time in recorded history, major surgical procedures could be performed with a reasonable expectation of primary wound healing and recovery. Essential enhancements for preventing and controlling wound "sepsis" were provided by the antibiotic revolution of the 1940s, ushering in the highly technical, highly invasive, and highly successful era of modern surgery. As noted by McDermott and Rogers,[1] a major impact of the antibiotic revolution is its essential role in supporting the advancements of modern surgery. Indeed, surgery as we know it today would be impossible in an environment in which infection was likely or, once established, untreatable. As a case in point, further advances in the implantation of the artificial heart—the epitome of applied technology in surgery—must await improved methods of infection control.[2]

Despite the fundamental role of antisepsis and antibiotics in the development of modern surgery, implementation of these discoveries in the practice of surgery has not occurred without opposition. As late as 1880, for example, William Halstead was ordered from the operating theater when he challenged a senior surgeon's disregard for antiseptic techniques. The early use of antibiotics for prophylaxis in surgical procedures was also questioned as respected academicians freely voiced their disapproval of antibiotic prophylaxis in clean surgical procedures.[3] For a number of years the value of prophylactic antibiotics in preventing infections of the surgical wound remained in doubt.

A consensus in favor of their use did not emerge until two concepts of perioperative prophylaxis and infection were established. First, investigators in Cincinnati and Boston demonstrated that, despite the use of standard aseptic techniques, *Staphylococcus aureus* could be regularly isolated from the operative field.[4–6] It became apparent that aseptic technique could decrease but not eliminate bacterial contamination of the surgical field. Therefore, it appeared plausible that the use of perioperative antibiotics could supplement aseptic techniques in containing the inevitable contamination of the operative wound. The second major finding involved the timing of the administration of the prophylactic antibiotic. As early as 1946, Howes[7] had noted a correlation between the amelioration of infection and the interval between the contamination of the wounds and the administration of antibiotics. Several years later, Miles and colleagues[8] and Burke,[9] working in a guinea pig model of wound infection, demonstrated the remarkable brevity of the "window" of prophylactic efficacy. They noted that antibiotics given shortly before or at the time of bacterial inoculation of the subcutaneous tissue of the guinea pig produced a notable diminution in the size of the subsequent wound induration compared with lesions in animals not receiving antibiotic prophylaxis (Fig. 308–1). By delaying the administration of antibiotics by only 3 or 4 hours, resulting lesions were identical in size to those of animals receiving no antibiotic prophylaxis whatsoever. Thus, "failures" of antimicrobial prophylaxis noted in earlier clinical studies could be traced to the fact that preoperative or intraoperative antibiotics had not been given.[10–12] The efficacy of prophylactic antibiotics for most major surgical procedures has now been verified for a wide variety of antimicrobials when care has been given to provide adequate serum and tissue levels of antibiotics during the surgical procedure. Perioperative antibiotics and aseptic techniques have become routine aspects of care in most major surgical procedures. Despite efforts to prevent infection, however, analysis of data from the National Center for Health Statistics[13] and the National Nosocomial Infections Survey[14] suggests that between 300,000 and 800,000 surgical wound infections complicate the approximately 34 million surgical procedures performed annually in the United States. Much remains to be learned regarding the pathophysiology of surgical wound infections and optimal measures for prevention.

PRINCIPLES OF PREVENTION AND CONTROL OF POSTOPERATIVE INFECTION

Determinants and Pathophysiology of Surgical Wound Infection

Whether a wound infection occurs after surgery depends on a complex interaction among (1) patient-related factors such as host immunity, nutritional status, and the presence or absence of diabetes; (2) procedure-related factors such as whether foreign bodies are used

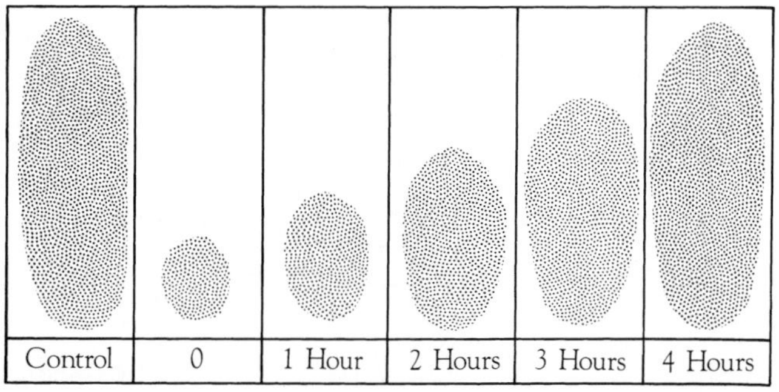

FIGURE 308–1. Relationship between the timing of antimicrobial administration and the effectiveness of prophylaxis as shown by the size of wound infection in an animal model. Lesion sizes were measured as mean diameter (mm) of induration developing 24 hours after intradermal inoculation of *Staphylococcus aureus.*

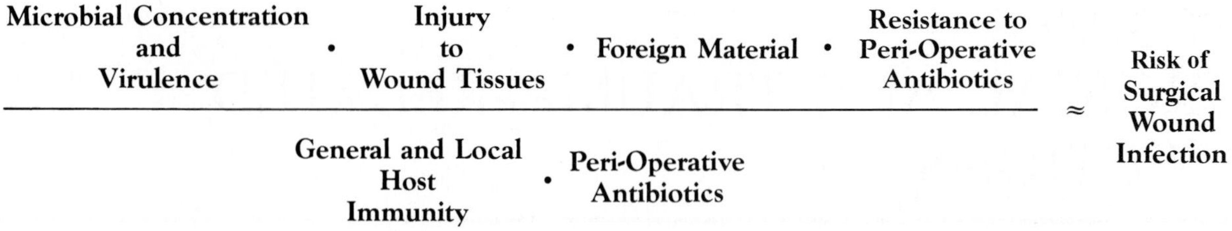

FIGURE 308–2. Determinants of surgical wound infection. As the number and virulence of contaminating bacteria increase, so does the chance for the development of a postoperative infection. Surgical trauma to the tissues and the use of foreign material act as adjuvants to further potentiate the risk of infection, whereas systemic and local host immune mechanisms function to contain inoculated bacteria and prevent infection. Antibiotics in the tissues provide a pharmacologic means of defense that augments the natural host immunity. Bacterial resistance mechanisms may contribute to the pathogenesis of wound infection by enabling organisms to evade the prophylactically administered antibiotics.

TABLE 308–1 Classification of Operative Wounds by Level of Bacterial Contamination

	% Infection Rate	
	Preoperative Antibiotics *Routinely Administered*	
Classification Criteria[16]	*No**	*Yes†*
Clean wound A nontraumatic wound in which no inflammation was encountered; no break in technique occurred; and respiratory, alimentary, and genitourinary tracts were not entered.	5.1	0.8
Clean-contaminated wound A nontraumatic wound in which a minor break in technique occurred or in which the gastrointestinal, genitourinary, or respiratory tracts were entered without significant spillage. This category includes transection of the appendix or cystic duct in the absence of acute inflammation and entrance into the biliary or genitourinary tracts in the absence of infected bile or urine.	10.1	1.3
Contaminated wound A fresh, traumatic wound from a relatively clean source or an operative wound in which there is a major break in technique, gross spillage from the gastrointestinal tract, or entrance into the genitourinary or biliary tract in the presence of infected urine or bile. This includes incisions encountering acute nonpurulent inflammation. Also included in this contaminated category are dirty wounds, such as traumatic wounds from a dirty source or with delayed treatment, fecal contamination, foreign bodies, a devitalized viscus, or pus from any source that is encountered.	21.9	10.2

*Data obtained from a multicenter study performed at a time (1960–1961) when antibiotic prophylaxis, if administered, was usually initiated postoperatively.[17] Classification criteria in 1960–1961 were less restrictive in that cholecystectomies, appendectomies, hysterectomies, and urinary tract operations were included as clean if no inflammation was present at the time of operation. Contaminated wounds were also subdivided into contaminated and dirty; the latter included old traumatic wounds and wounds involving abscesses or perforated viscus.

†Data obtained from a prospective single-center study of 20,000 wounds[18] in which a fall in infection rates over a 5-year period was attributable to an increasing use of preoperative antibiotics.

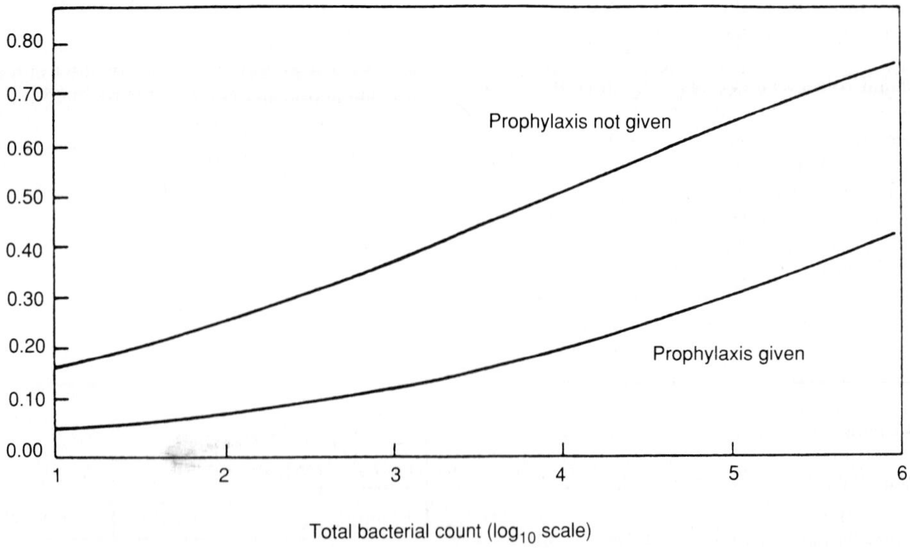

FIGURE 308–3. Plot of the probability of wound infection and/or febrile morbidity according to total bacterial counts at the operative site in patients undergoing abdominal hysterectomy. The administration of antimicrobial prophylaxis reduces the likelihood of infection or fever for a given level of bacterial contamination of the wound. Stated another way, the administration of prophylaxis increases the magnitude of the bacterial inoculum needed to produce infection. (From Houang ET, Ahmet Z. Intraoperative wound contamination during abdominal hysterectomy. J Hosp Infect. 1991;19:181–189.)

TABLE 308–2 Major Pathogens in Surgical Wound Infections

Pathogen	Percent of Infections*
Staphylococcus aureus	20
Coagulase-negative staphylococci	14
Enterococci	12
Escherichia coli	8
Pseudomona aeruginosa	8
Enterobacter spp.	7
Proteus mirabilis	3
Klebsiella pneumoniae	3
Other streptococcal spp.	3
Candida albicans	2
Group D streptococci	2
Bacteroides fragilis	2
Other gram-positive aerobes	2
Citrobacter spp.	1
Serratia marcescens	1
Candida spp.	1
Gram-positive anaerobes	1
Group B streptococci	1
Acinetobacter spp.	1

*From a total of 17,671 isolates, as reported by the National Nosocomial Infections Surveillance System, January 1990 to March 1996.
From Hospital Infections Program, National Center for Infectious Diseases, Centers for Disease Control and Prevention. National nosocomial infections surveillance (NNIS) report, data summary from October 1986–April 1996, issued May 1996: A report from the NNIS system. Am J Infect Control. 1996;24:380–388.

and the magnitude of trauma to the host tissues during the surgical procedure; (3) microbial factors that mediate tissue adherence and invasion or that enable the bacterium to survive the host immune response and antibiotics in the tissue; and (4) perioperative antimicrobial prophylaxis. The milieu of the surgical wound may be viewed as a balance of opposing forces (Fig. 308–2).

Species and Sources of Wound Bacteria. It is axiomatic to appreciate the inevitability of bacterial contamination of the surgical wound. State-of-the-art aseptic technique has been associated with a dramatic drop in, but not the elimination of, this phenomenon. Even under laminar flow operating room environments, bacteria can be predictably isolated from wound surfaces at the close of the surgical procedure.[15]

The importance of the microbial load in determining whether a wound becomes infected has been appreciated for decades and is relevant even in the era of the routine administration of antimicrobial prophylaxis for most major surgical procedures (Fig. 308–3). Historically, surgeons and hospital epidemiologists have stratified operations into clean, clean-contaminated, and contaminated procedures on the basis of the expected quantity of bacteria introduced into the operative site during surgery (Table 308–1). Although the magnitude of bacterial inoculation into the wound still has some predictive value regarding the risk of developing a wound infection, patient and procedure-related risk factors have also been identified that contribute greatly to this risk.[19, 20]

Numerous species have been described as wound pathogens, and the most common organisms are listed in Table 308–2. Unusual and hard-to-culture species as well as species generally considered to be contaminants that occasionally cause surgical site infections include nontuberculous mycobacteria, *Nocardia, Mycoplasma hominis,* and *Propionibacterium acnes.*

Different species are important in different procedures. For clean surgical procedures, staphylococcal species are the most common wound pathogens. Although *S. aureus* and *Staphylococcus epidermidis* wound infections can occur in clusters, sometimes with a particular surgeon or nurse implicated in their spread, the origin of the inoculum is not established with certainty for most infections. The patient's endogenous flora has been implicated as a source of the infecting bacteria. Selected populations such as diabetic individuals and recipients of hemodialysis are colonized with *S. aureus* at frequencies in excess of 50%. Even with the application of modern aseptic techniques and the use of antibiotic prophylaxis, *S. aureus* colonization of the nares appears to be a major risk factor for developing a *S. aureus* wound infection. Sternotomy infection rates have been estimated at 8 for carriers versus 1.1% for noncarriers among patients undergoing cardiac surgery.[21]

Modern methods of antisepsis can reduce but not eliminate the skin-associated bacteria of surgical patients. This limitation derives, in part, from the localization of up to 20% of skin-associated bacteria in skin appendages, including hair follicles and sebaceous glands[22] (Fig. 308–4). Because these sites are beneath the skin's surface, bacteria residing there are not eliminated by topical antisepsis. Transection of these skin structures by surgical incision may carry the patient's resident bacteria deep into the wound and set the stage for subsequent infection.

For contaminated procedures, wound pathogens frequently are among the bacterial species that comprise the normal flora of the

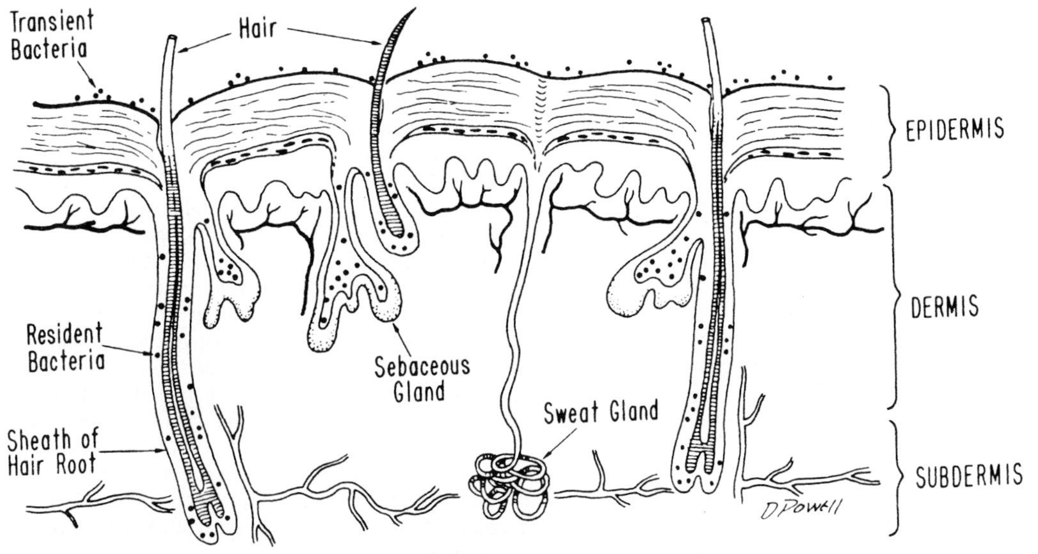

FIGURE 308–4. Schematic diagram of the skin demonstrating the location of the transient bacteria on the skin surface, which are easily removed, and the deep resident bacteria, which cannot be destroyed by skin antiseptics. (From Postlethwaite RW. Principles of operative surgery: Antisepsis, technique, sutures, and drains. In: Sabistan DC, ed. Davis-Christopher Textbook of Surgery. 11th ed. Philadelphia: WB Saunders; 1977.)

viscus entered during the surgical procedure. Polymicrobial infections are common in wound infections complicating colorectal procedures, in which an average of five species are recovered. The association of a particular species with infection does not correlate directly with its quantitative presence among the normal flora, however; the particular virulence attributes of bacteria are the major determinants of which species infect the wound. *Escherichia coli* and *Bacteroides fragilis* are common pathogens of wounds after colonic procedures. It is a basic tenet of antimicrobial prophylaxis that the regimen should be active against the major "pathogens," and it is not necessary to cover those species among the normal flora that have little pathogenic potential.

Although numerous sources of bacterial contamination of surgical wounds have been described (Table 308–3), it is virtually impossible to identify, with certainty, the sources and routes of contamination. The direct inoculation of a patient's endogenous flora at the time of surgery is believed to be the most common mechanism; however, others undoubtedly occur. Outbreaks of group A streptococcal wound infection have been traced to the anal or vaginal carriage of this organism by operating room personnel.[23, 24] Epidemiologic investigation of these outbreaks indicated that airborne contamination of the operative field had occurred. More important, the prospective controlled study by Lidwell and colleagues[25] demonstrated a remarkable decrease in infection rates in total hip and knee procedures associated with operating in an ultraclean operating room environment. However, the value of ultraclean or laminar flow environments in decreasing wound infections may be lessened when surgery occurs in modern operating room environments in which high rates of air exchange and perioperative antibiotic use are routine.[26]

TABLE 308–3 Sources of Microbial Contamination of Surgical Wounds

Source	Estimated Frequency of Occurrence
Direct inoculation	
At time of surgery	
Residual flora of patient's skin	Common
Hands of surgical team members (via torn gloves)	Occasional
Contaminated surgical material	Rare
Contaminated or infected host tissues (during contaminated procedures)	Common
During the postoperative period*	
Drains and irrigating catheters	Occasional
Transient and residual skin flora of patient (via unstable incision sites, e.g., unstable sternum)	Rare
Contaminated or infected tissues (after contaminated procedures)	Occasional
Airborne contamination	
At time of surgery	
Skin, mucous membranes, and clothing of patient	Occasional
Skin, mucous membranes, and clothing of operating room staff	Occasional
Inanimate operating room environment	Rare
Air filtration equipment (malfunctioning)	Rare
During postoperative period	
Theoretically unimportant except for open wounds and burns	
Hematogenous-lymphatic seeding	
At time of surgery	
Preexisting infection of nonwound sites (e.g., pneumonia, urinary tract infection)	Rare
Intravenous lines or equipment with intravascular access (e.g., bypass perfusion apparatus, cell-saver devices)	Rare
During the postoperative period†	Rare
Intravenous lines or equipment with intravascular access (e.g., Swan-Ganz catheter)	
Postoperative infection involving nonwound sites	Rare

*Sources of contamination are evaluated only for primarily closed wounds. Wounds left open (secondary closure) and burn wounds are also vulnerable to contamination from a variety of personnel and environmental sources.

†Incidental or transient bacteremia from a variety of sources (e.g., mucous membranes, superficial skin infections) has been implicated in the late hematogenous seeding of implanted prosthetic material.

More controversial still is the relative importance of hematogenous seeding of the surgical wound. Postoperative infections associated with the intraoperative use of the anesthetic agent, propofol, suggests the importance of this route of contamination.[27] Epidemiologic studies suggest that extrinsic contamination followed by rapid microbial growth in the lipid-based drug formulation before intravenous infusion was responsible for the infections. It is generally accepted that after surgery, prosthetic valves and hips are at risk for an indefinite period of time for hematogenous seeding and infection. It is difficult, however, to be certain if a late postoperative infection results from intraoperative bacterial seeding of the prosthetic device with prolonged dormancy or from a true postoperative hematogenous event. In a random prospective controlled study of antibiotic prophylaxis in total hip replacement, Carlsson and associates[28] demonstrated that deep wound infections that developed more than 2.5 years after surgery were more likely to have occurred among placebo rather than cloxacillin recipients (13.7% versus 3.3%, respectively, $p <$ 0.05, one-tailed Fisher's exact test). These data strongly suggest that bacteria inoculated into wounds at the time of surgery lie dormant for years, rendering differentiation of the precise source of late wound infection virtually impossible.

Information regarding the hematogenous seeding of surgical wounds during the postoperative period is mainly anecdotal. Postoperative urinary tract infections were implicated as a source of postoperative surgical wound infection in one study.[29] A report of acute pneumococcal osteomyelitis of the sternum occurring 3 months after coronary artery bypass surgery supports the concept that a surgical incision that does not contain a prosthetic device can also be seeded hematogenously during the postoperative period.[30] If late hematogenous seeding of a surgical wound with or without prosthetic material can occur, it is reasonable to assume that wounds are even more vulnerable to seeding and secondary infection during the immediate postoperative periods. During this time, surgical incisions are hyperemic from the trauma of the surgery and endothelialization of intravascular prosthetic materials has not yet had time to occur. Moreover, the regular use of indwelling intravascular access devices likely increases the risk of bacteremia. However, information with which to judge the relative contribution of intraoperative versus postoperative hematogenous seeding of the surgical incision is unavailable.

Virulence Factors of Major Wound Pathogens

Clean Wound Infections. The requirement for large inocula in the early models of *S. aureus* soft tissue infection gave the misleading impression that cooperative interaction among bacteria may be required to establish a wound infection.[8, 9, 31] More recent models involving foreign bodies have demonstrated ID_{50} values less than 100 colony-forming units (CFUs) with polytetrafluoroethylene (PTFE) tissue cages,[32] 10 CFUs with PTFE vascular grafts,[33] and as low as 1 CFU with dextran microbeads.[37] These data demonstrate the pathogenic potential of a single bacterium to produce wound infection, provided that it is inoculated into a suitable niche.

Determinants of *S. aureus* virulence have been studied for decades and include a wide variety of enzymes and toxins with diverse effects on the host. Which staphylococcal virulence factors contribute to the development of a wound infection is poorly understood. *S. aureus* and the coagulase-negative staphylococci bind to a variety of biologic molecules including fibronectin, fibrinogen, vitronectin, collagen, laminin, and platelet thrombospondin.[35, 36] Fibronectin and collagen receptors in *S. aureus* have been identified.[35, 37] Blood clots and the subendothelium are rich in fibronectin, and adherence to such sites may be the first step in the pathogenesis of a clean surgical wound infection.

Once in the wound, several staphylococcal exoenzymes can damage host tissues, including hyaluronidase, lipase, proteases, nucleases, and four membrane-damaging toxins.[38] Under some conditions protein A competes with phagocytic cells for Fc receptors,

TABLE 308–4 Surgical Site Infection Rates, by Operative Procedure and Risk Index Category, 1986–1996*

Operative Procedure Category	Duration Cutpoint (h)	Infection Rates† (No. of Procedures) for NNIS Risk Index = 0	1	2	3
CABG—chest and leg	5	0.84 (830)	3.29 (65595)	5.56 (14178)	17.86 (28)
Thoracic surgery	3	0.50 (1197)	1.50 (3028)	3.49 (1060)	
Appendectomy	1	1.30 (4472)	3.11 (4177)	6.25 (1664)	
Cholecystectomy (open)	2	0.60 (5129)	2.22 (4454)	3.98 (2010)	
Cholecystectomy (laparoscopic)	2	0.51 (11348)	0.81 (5893)	2.36 (1100)	
Colon surgery	3	4.32 (5606)	6.51 (9352)	10.53 (4171)	13.90 (581)
Gastric surgery	3	2.79 (1469)	5.57 (2461)	12.37 (1067)	
Small bowel surgery	3	5.28 (758)	7.70 (1519)	10.65 (1005)	
Laparotomy	2	1.94 (4030)	3.32 (4151)	6.92 (1966)	9.89 (283)
Prostatectomy	4	1.05 (1524)	2.56 (1134)	5.21 (211)	
Genitourinary other than prostatectomy or nephrectomy	2	0.52 (12185)	1.29 (4747)	4.29 (1025)	
Head and neck surgery	5	1.99 (804)	4.17 (816)	12.74 (369)	
Herniorrhaphy	2	0.93 (7307)	2.06 (3941)	3.10 (743)	
Mastectomy	2	1.72 (9486)		4.96 (665)	
Craniotomy	5	0.99 (2029)	1.55 (5992)		
Ventricular shunt	2	3.57 (1289)	4.80 (2918)		
Cesarean section	1	3.36 (45441)	4.45 (16610)	7.21 (1221)	
Abdominal hysterectomy	2	1.60 (16035)	2.84 (8445)	6.12 (1633)	
Vaginal hysterectomy	2	1.02 (6497)	1.70 (3235)		
Limb amputation	1	4.57 (6260)			
Open reduction of fracture	2	0.81 (8309)	1.44 (11588)	2.91 (2615)	
Hip prosthesis	2	0.69 (4504)	1.70 (10873)		
Knee prosthesis	2	0.87 (5601)	1.23 (7510)	1.77 (2314)	
Laminectomy	2	0.67 (9702)	1.36 (6686)	2.40 (1919)	
Vascular surgery	3	1.34 (3819)	2.01 (24031)	5.15 (9649)	8.83 (283)

*As reported by the National Nosocomial Infection Surveillance System.[46]
†Surgical site infection rates for adjacent risk index groupings that were not significantly different are grouped together.

thereby reducing antibody-mediated opsonization.[39] Coagulase may also interfere with phagocytosis.

Contaminated Wound Infections. The role of coliforms and anaerobes in abdominal sepsis has been elucidated in a model that involves inserting a gelatin capsule containing a standardized inoculum of pooled cecal contents into the peritoneal cavities of rats.[40, 41] Acute peritonitis and septicemia from coliforms caused rapid death in 37% of the animals, and all of the survivors developed abscesses with anaerobes as the predominant organisms. The capsular polysaccharide of *B. fragilis* promotes abscess formation and may reduce phagocytosis. In experimental models, immunization against capsular polysaccharide can protect against abscess formation after inoculation with *B. fragilis* by a T-cell–dependent mechanism, except in the presence of foreign material.[42] Also, *B. fragilis* produces a variety of tissue-damaging enzymes including fibrinolysin, chondroitin sulfatase, collagenase, and hyaluronidase.

General Host Immunity and Risk Factors for Infection. Various host factors have been associated with an increased risk of infection: extremes of age, diabetes, concomitant steroid therapy, prior site irradiation, hypoxemia, cigarette smoking, early shaving of the surgical site, a low preoperative serum albumin level, skin test anergy, a long preoperative hospitalization, severe obesity or malnutrition, and the presence of remote infection at the time of surgery.[17, 43]

Many patient risk factors for infection are interrelated, A patient who exhibits one risk factor is likely to have others. An index that takes into account both a traditional assessment of the level of wound contamination (see Table 308–1) and with three patient and procedure-related risk factors was developed and tested on more than 58,000 patients during the Centers for Disease Control and Prevention's Study on the Efficacy of Nosocomial Infection Control (SENIC).[19] Using multivariate analysis, it was found that an operation involving the abdomen, a procedure lasting longer than 2 hours, and the presence of three or more discharge diagnoses (as a surrogate for identifying the complicated patient) were independent risk factors for a wound infection. Their inclusion with the traditional wound classification system predicted the risk of wound infection about twice as well as the wound classification system alone, and the addition of other factors did not improve the predictive capability of the model. This model has subsequently been simplified further, resulting in the National Nosocomial Infections Study (NNIS) risk index, which contains only three variables: (1) a patient with an American Society of Anesthesiologists preoperative assessment score of 3, 4, or 5; (2) an operation classified as contaminated or dirty-infected; and (3) an operation lasting longer than T hours, when T depends on the procedure.[20, 44, 45] Over the past decade, very detailed information related to surgical site infection rates associated with specific procedures has been generated (Table 308–4).[46]

The Wound Microenvironment. Much of our understanding of the pathophysiology of wound infection and the nature of the surgical wound derives from investigational models (Table 308–5). The demonstration that the efficacy of antibiotics in preventing wound infection is limited to only a few hours after the moment of bacterial inoculation[7, 8] implies that the wound microenvironment is not static. What changes occur during this "decisive period" are poorly understood, however. It is unclear whether the decisive period is attributable to microbial factors, such as a shift from exponential to stationary phase growth with an accompanying decrease in bacterial susceptibility to antibiotics and possibly the expression of different microbial virulence factors, or to wound-related factors, such as gradually diminishing tissue perfusion and antibiotic delivery related to increased tissue oncotic pressure brought about by the effect of inflammatory mediators on vascular permeability. Both or neither of these examples may be important. It is likely, however, that the elucidation of the pathophysiology of the decisive period will have a profound effect on developing strategies for improving the efficacy of antibiotic prophylaxis.

TABLE 308-5 Contributions of Investigational Models to an Understanding of the Pathophysiology of Surgical Wound Infection

Investigative Findings	Model	Author(s) (Date)
Adverse effect of dehydration, adrenalin, and heparin on infection resistance of contaminated wounds	Subcutaneous infection in guinea pigs using a variety of aerobic and anaerobic bacteria	Miles and Niven[47] (1950) Burke and Miles[48] (1958)
Importance of early administration of antibiotics in preventing wound infection	Subcutaneous and intradermal infection in guinea pigs with *S. aureus*	Howes[7] (1946) Miles et al.[8] (1957) Burke[9] (1961)
Importance of foreign material in enhancing *Staphylococcus aureus* infections	Intradermal and subcutaneous infection in human volunteers	Elek and Conen[31] (1958)
Development of muscle infection model and exploring the role of iron in enhancing the infectious process	Muscle infection in mice using *Escherichia coli* with nonreplicating phage	Polk and Miles[49] (1971)
Development of intra-abdominal abscess model	Intraperitoneal infection in rats with *E. coli* and *Bacteroides fragilis*	Weinstein et al.[46] (1974)
Role of lymphatic clearance of bacteria in host defenses	Subcutaneous infection in rabbits with *S. aureus* and anaerobic gram-negative rods	DeLong and Simmons[50] (1982)
Development of a model of subcutaneous tissue cage infection	Subcutaneous infection in guinea pigs with *S. aureus*	Zimmerli et al.[32] (1982)
Importance of early administration of topical antiseptics and antibiotics in preventing wound infection	Subcutaneous infection in guinea pigs with *S. aureus, E. coli,* and *B. fragilis*	Platt and Bucknall[51] (1984)
Importance of oxygen in preventing wound infection	Intradermal infection in guinea pigs with *E. coli*	Knighton et al.[52] (1984)
Role of fibrin in enhancing abscess formation	Intraperitoneal infection in rats with *E. coli* and *B. fragilis*	Hau et al.[53] (1986)
Importance of granulocytes in antibiotic prophylaxis	Muscle infection of mice with *S. aureus*	Hoogeterp et al.[54] (1987)
Quantitation of *S. aureus* capsular polysaccharide	Subcutaneous graft infection in guinea pigs with *S. aureus*	Arbeit and Dunn[33] (1987)
Quantification of *S. aureus* exopolymers	Subcutaneous tissue cage infection in guinea pigs with *S. aureus*	Falcieri et al.[55] (1987)
Use of dextran microcarrier beads as an adjuvant, permitting production of an abscess with small numbers of staphylococci	Subcutaneous abscess model in mice	Ford et al.[56] (1989)
Low-inoculum model with the sensitivity to compare different regimens of antibiotic prophylaxis in preventing infection	Intramuscular *S. aureus* abscess model in guinea pigs	Kaiser et al.[34] (1992)

Multiple host defense mechanisms are involved in the response to bacteria inoculated at the surgical site. Neutrophils are probably the most important effector cells, and the most common wound pathogens are highly susceptible to killing by reactive oxygen intermediates. Opsonization by antibodies and complement facilitate phagocytosis. An additional host defense mechanism against abscess formation by *S. aureus* has been described by Dye and Kapral.[57] Abscess homogenates are bactericidal for staphylococci, and this activity is mediated by 2-monoglycerides and unsaturated free fatty acids. Most strains of *S. aureus* produce fatty acid metabolizing enzyme (FAME), which inactivates the bactericidal lipids. Strains deficient in this enzyme are eliminated rapidly from intraperitoneal abscesses in mice, whereas strains producing FAME are capable of prolonged survival in vivo. More recently, phospholipase A_2 has been found in inflammatory exudates and has potent antistaphylococcal activity.[58] T-cell–dependent immune mechanisms have been shown to be important in protection against *B. fragilis* infection,[42] but their importance with other common wound pathogens is not as well established.

Foreign Material and Surgical Trauma to Tissue. Investigations of *S. aureus* infection in the skin of human volunteers by Elek and Conen[3] established conclusively the role of foreign material in potentiating wound infection. By including suture material with the intradermal staphylococcal inoculum, the number of organisms required to establish a skin pustule could be reduced 10,000-fold relative to lesions without sutures (i.e., a fall from 5×10^6 organisms to 3×10^2 organisms in the inoculum). These investigators further suggested that "other circumstances may lead to the unhindered growth of small inocula, including heavily traumatized tissues, burns, or devitalized tissues distal to the ligated vessels. This may be the explanation of the traditional surgical view that untidy operative techniques predispose to infection."[31] In clean and clean-contaminated surgical procedures, it is generally believed that the quantitative bacterial inoculation into the wound is small. Tissue devitalization at a gross or microscopic level, by providing a niche wherein a small bacterial inoculum may grow in relative isolation from the host's defenses, plays a major role in the pathogenesis of clean wound infection.

Investigational models have demonstrated how technical variables of the surgical procedure influence the risk of infection. Some suture materials appear to have a stronger adjuvant effect on infection than others.[59] Whether the use of the electrosurgical knife, which can damage host tissues via the transfer of heat, is an adjuvant for infection is controversial.[60, 61] In an in vitro system, thermally killed fibroblasts activate the alternative complement pathway, leading ultimately to impaired neutrophilic activity against bacteria.[62]

The Effect of Surgery on Systemic and Local Immunity. Surgery induces systemic and local changes in the immune defense mechanisms of the host. Operative procedures impair neutrophil function and serum opsonizing capacity. The microbicidal activity of neutrophils obtained postoperatively from patients undergoing abdominal hysterectomy is 25% less than that of neutrophils harvested from the same patients preoperatively, and it takes 9 days to return to normal.[63] The depletion of opsonizing factors within the abscess milieu also may contribute to decreased neutrophilic bactericidal function.[64, 65]

Major surgical procedures compromise the host defenses in other ways. Surface levels of HLA-DR antigens on the circulating monocytes of patients are reduced following major surgery.[66] However, it has been shown that defects in T-cell proliferation and cytokine secretion after major surgery involve an inability of T cells to respond to T-cell receptor–and CD28 coreceptor–mediated signals rather than problems with antigen presentation by monocytes-macrophages.[67] Perioperative hypothermia induced by anesthetic-induced impairment of thermoregulation and exposure to the low ambient temperatures of the operating room may accompany major surgery and are believed to trigger vasoconstriction and decrease oxygen tension in the tissues. Low subcutaneous oxygen tension is a risk factor for a surgical site infection.[68] In the setting of perioperative hypothermia, neutrophils have reduced chemotaxis, impaired ingestion of staphylococci, and diminished superoxide production.[69] In colorectal surgery, active measures to maintain normothermia during surgery were associated with a reduction in wound infections compared with patients allowed to experience routine mild perioperative hypothermia.[70] Allogeneic but not autologous blood transfusion has been associated with an increased rate of postoperative infection at nonwound and wound sites.[71, 72] This has been attributed to a generalized immunosuppressive effect. More data are needed, however, before general conclusions regarding the relative merits of autologous blood transfusions can be determined.

In cardiac surgery the patient may be exposed to hypothermia, cardiopulmonary bypass, and relative arterial hypotension throughout much of the procedure as well as the use of one or both internal mammary arteries for grafting. Exposure of blood to cardiopulmonary bypass depletes serum complement and immunoglobulins and adversely affects neutrophilic function.[73, 74] Furthermore, protein denaturation and chylomicron aggregation may contribute to small vessel occlusion and tissue hypoxia as well as overwhelm the capacity of the reticuloendothelial system to clear infectious agents from the blood.[75] This raises the possibility that postbypass patients may be predisposed to develop infections via hematogenous bacterial seeding, which may originate from intravascular catheters, as a result of reduced reticuloendothelial clearance.

The release of cytokines at the wound site may have a protective effect against infection. Pretreatment of tissue cages with tumor necrosis factor, either administered directly or generated in vivo by exposure to staphylococcal cell wall components, inhibited abscess formation by an inoculum of *S. aureus* that under normal circumstances would have produced infection 100% of the time.[76] Also, the use of fibrinolytic agents prevents abscess formation in investigational models.[77] This is consistent with the hypothesis that the adherence of bacteria to fibrinous exudates is an essential step in the pathogenesis of a wound infection.

Perioperative Antibiotics. The in vivo interaction between inoculated bacteria and prophylactically administered antibiotic is one of the most important determinants of the fate of the wound. For example, without antibiotic prophylaxis the reported risk of developing a *S. aureus* wound infection after cardiac surgery is 15 to 44%,[78–80] an incidence that approximates the frequency of skin/nares colonization with *S. aureus*. Infection rates are generally lower for clean procedures involving less tissue trauma and better hemostasis. Over the past 20 years, the efficacy of antibiotic prophylaxis in clean surgery has been clearly established. The principle on which most systemic antibiotic prophylaxis is based is the belief that antibiotics in the host tissues can augment natural immune defense mechanisms and help to kill bacteria that are inoculated into the wound. The rationale for the administration of oral antibiotics in colonic surgery differs in that although some agents exhibit systemic absorption and penetrate into host tissues (e.g., erythromycin and metronidazole, but not neomycin), the primary goal in this setting is a reduction in potential pathogens among the normal gut flora at the time of surgery. Oral prophylaxis is generally combined with mechanical preparation of the bowel to reduce colonic flora, including the use of cathartics, isotonic lavage solutions, or both.

Every effort should be made to ensure that adequate antibiotic levels are maintained throughout the surgical procedure. Although a number of studies in the past have indicated that prolonged surgical procedures are associated with a higher infection rate, it is not clear whether this increased risk is inevitable or it is attributable primarily to the greater likelihood of there being low or undetectable concentrations of antibiotics during long procedures.

Resistance to Perioperative Antibiotics. The success of prophylaxis in clean surgery correlates directly with the susceptibility of bacteria to the antibiotic in vitro (Fig. 308–5), with some failures of prophylaxis attributable to bacterial resistance. Furthermore, some *S. aureus* wound infections are caused by strains that are reported by the clinical laboratory to be susceptible to cephalosporin but that produce the type A variant of staphylococcal β-lactamase and can degrade less stable cephalosporins such as cefazolin relatively rapidly.[81] Studies involving a guinea pig model of wound infection and isogeneic strains of *S. aureus* that differ only in the presence or absence of the

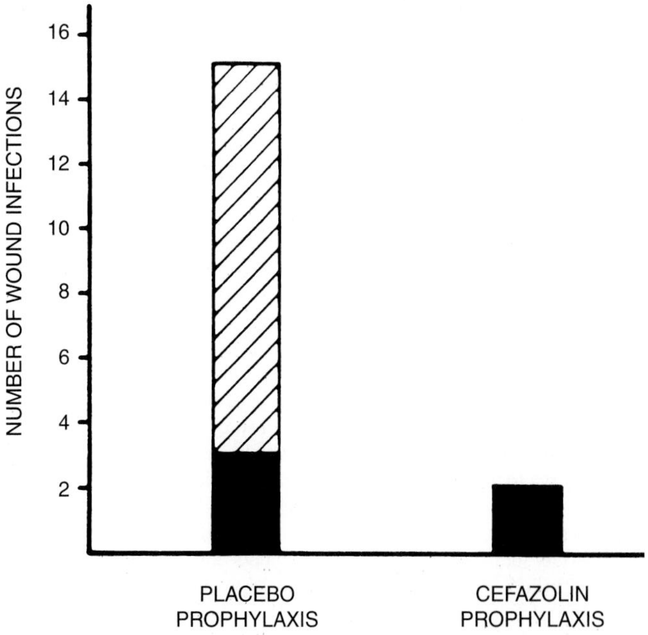

FIGURE 308–5. Susceptibility to cefazolin of pathogens isolated from 17 wound infections among patients receiving placebo (saline) or cefazolin for prophylaxis of vascular surgical procedures. The striped area indicates cefazolin-susceptible bacteria, and the shaded area indicates cefazolin-resistant bacteria. Infection rates were 6.8% and 0.9% for patients receiving placebo and cefazolin, respectively. This difference was attributable entirely to the prevention of infection by cefazolin-susceptible pathogens, mainly *Staphylococcus aureus,* among patients receiving cefazolin. The incidence of infection by cefazolin-resistant pathogens was similar in both regimens. (From Kaiser AB, Clayson KR, Mulherin JL Jr, et al. Antibiotic prophylaxis in vascular surgery. Ann Surg. 1978;188:283–289.)

gene encoding type A staphylococcal β-lactamase have shown that when cefazolin is administered as prophylaxis the number of CFU required to establish infection 50% of the time (ID_{50}) is significantly smaller for the β-lactamase–producing isolate than for the non–β-lactamase–producing isolate.[82] A subpopulation of *S. aureus* belonging to phage group 94/96 and characterized by borderline susceptibility to oxacillin, the presence of a unique 17.2-kb plasmid, and the production of large quantities of type A staphylococcal β-lactamase has been associated with deep wound infections among surgical patients receiving cefazolin as perioperative prophylaxis.[83] β-Lactamase–mediated degradation of cephalosporins in vivo appears to enable a bacterium to survive beyond the time of its initial lodgement in antibiotic-containing tissues, ultimately contributing to the development of a wound infection.[81–83]

Because cephalosporins have become the mainstay of prophylaxis, the increasing prevalence of cephalosporin-resistant pathogens has important implications for prophylaxis. The proportion of *S. aureus* organisms causing nosocomial infection that are methicillin-resistant (and cephalosporin resistant) has increased from 14.3% in 1987 to 39.7% in 1997.[84] Furthermore, infections caused by methicillin-resistant coagulase-negative staphylococci, cephalosporin- and gentamicin-resistant gram-negative rods, vancomycin-resistant enterococci, and fungi are being reported with increasing frequency, including surgical procedures traditionally regarded as clean.[85, 86] It is increasingly clear that strategies must be devised to contain these pathogens.

Nonwound Infections in the Surgical Patient

As many as 71% of all nosocomial infections occur in surgical patients.[87] Infections at the operative site account for 40% of these, with the urinary tract (42%), respiratory tract (14%), and blood stream (4%) representing the other major foci. Catheters inserted into vessels and the bladder as well as intubation and anesthesia impair the ability of normal host defense mechanisms to prevent infection at these sites.

PRACTICE OF PREVENTION OF POSTOPERATIVE INFECTION

Stemming from these concepts of wound infection pathogenesis have been a number of interventions that have been put into practice over the past century to reduce the risk of wound infection. These interventions can be grouped into two major categories (Table 308–6). The first line of defense involves measures that reduce bacterial inoculation into the wound site. These include familiar rituals such as the application of antiseptics to the skin of the patient, the washing and gloving of the surgeon's hands, the use of sterile drapes, airflow control, and the use of gowns and masks by operating room personnel. Efforts to reduce patient colonization with staphylococci may also be of benefit. A recent unblinded study found that mupirocin applied to the nares of patients undergoing cardiac surgery beginning on the day before surgery and continued for 5 consecutive days resulted in a *S. aureus* surgical site infection rate of 0.9% compared with one of 2.9% for historical controls.[88] Randomized prospective studies to further evaluate this issue are needed. Preoperative showering with a solution containing chlorhexidine suppresses bacterial colonization of the skin[89]; however, it is not clear whether this practice results in a reduction in infection rates. To minimize the acquisition of resistant hospital flora before surgery, the preoperative hospital stay should be as short as possible and the use of antibiotics in the preoperative period should be avoided whenever possible. If shaving for hair removal at the operative site is required, it should be performed as close to the time of surgery as possible. Infection at sites remote from the operative field is a host risk factor for postoperative infection that is potentially correctable before surgery.[90] Drains and intravascular devices should be removed as quickly as possible to avoid the risk of, respectively, direct and hematogenous seeding of the operative site.

TABLE 308-6 Interventional Maneuvers of Proved or Theoretical Benefit in Diminishing the Risk of Surgical Wound Infection

Maneuvers to diminish inoculation of virulent or antimicrobial-resistant bacteria into wound
- Preoperative factors
  - Avoid preoperative antibiotic use
  - Minimize preoperative hospitalization
  - Eliminate nasal colonization with *Staphylococcus aureus*
  - Treat remote sites of infection
  - Avoid shaving or delay shaving at operative site until time of surgery
  - Routinely have patient shower or bathe preoperatively with chlorhexidine-containing soap
- Intraoperative and postoperative factors
  - Carefully prepare patient's skin with povidone-iodine or chlorhexidine-containing solution
  - Rigorously adhere to routine aseptic techniques
  - Maintain high flow of filtered air
  - Consider laminar flow environment
  - Consider irrigation of wound with antibiotic-containing solution
  - Isolate clean from contaminated surgical fields (e.g., reglove and change instruments used to harvest saphenous vein before participating in intrathoracic field)
  - Minimize use of drains
  - Drains, if used, should be brought through a separate stab wound
  - Minimize use of catheters and intravascular lines postoperatively

Maneuvers to improve host containment of contaminating bacteria
- Preoperative factors
  - Resolve malnutrition or obesity
  - Discontinue cigarette smoking
  - Maximize diabetes control
- Intraoperative and postoperative factors
  - Minimize dead space, devitalized tissue, and hematomas
  - Maintain adequate hydration, oxygenation, and nutrition

Second-line measures are directed toward improving host containment and elimination of bacteria that have circumvented the front line of defense and have been inoculated into the wound. Most authorities have emphasized that the single most important factor in preventing wound infection is surgical technique. Gentle handling of wound tissues; avoidance of dead space, devitalized tissues, and hematomas; and careful approximation of tissue planes are believed to be critical in maintaining an infection-free incision. Good surgical technique along with minimizing hypothermia and minimizing the use of vasoconstrictive medications help to improve tissue perfusion and oxygenation, thereby improving the delivery and function of neutrophils. Avoiding malnourishment and achieving tight control of glucose levels in diabetics also appear to reduce the risk of postoperative infection.[91, 92]

On the other hand, investigations of mechanisms to directly modify the host immune system (administration of granulocyte-macrophage colony stimulating factor,[93] exclusive use of autologous blood transfusions,[93] exclusive use of autologous blood transfusions,[71] or administration of H_2 receptor antagonist[94]) are either too preliminary or too inconclusive to provide guidelines for clinical practice.

Perioperative Antimicrobial Prophylaxis

The efficacy of perioperative prophylaxis in preventing wound infection after many surgical procedures is unquestioned. Not only have the benefits of early antibiotic administration been duplicated by numerous investigators using different animal models, different pathogens, and different antibiotics, literally hundreds of clinical trials have verified the efficacy of perioperative antibiotics. Nevertheless, issues regarding the optimal choice, frequency, and duration of perioperative antibiotic prophylaxis are unresolved.

Selection of Prophylactic Regimen. It is important to realize that the current practice of antimicrobial prophylaxis is based largely on the results of clinical trials that are, for the most part, too underpowered to detect differences in efficacy between prophylactic regimens.[95] For example, in clean elective surgical procedures, infection rates with routine cephalosporin prophylaxis are already low, 5% or lower. In attempting to evaluate clinically the superiority of a different antibiotic regimen, randomization of approximately 900 patients would be necessary before a 50% reduction in infection rate could be demonstrated at the $p = 0.05$ level. Many more patients would require study to demonstrate reliably that differences did not exist.

Based on their antibacterial spectrum and low incidence of allergy and side effects, the cephalosporins have emerged as the drugs of choice for the vast majority of operative procedures. Because of its reasonably long half-life and low cost, cefazolin has been the dominant choice for clean procedures. Even in clean-contaminated procedures such as hysterectomy and cholecystectomy in which cephalosporins with improved in vitro activity against anaerobic bacteria are often advocated, most clinical studies indicate that cefazolin is equivalent in its prophylactic efficacy.

The prevalence of methicillin-resistant *S. aureus* (MRSA) in some medical centers has resulted in the increased use of vancomycin for perioperative prophylaxis of clean procedures. In one institution, surgical prophylaxis was reported to account for 35% of intravenous vancomycin use.[96] Studies comparing prophylaxis with vancomycin and cephalosporins have shown vancomycin to be equivalent or superior in preventing wound infection.[97, 98] However, theoretical concerns remain about a possible increased risk of infection from gram-negative aerobic pathogens. In a guinea pig model of intramuscular abscess formation and antimicrobial prophylaxis, prophylaxis with vancomycin increases the number of bacteria needed to establish infection to greater than 100,000 CFU compared with less than 1000 CFU for cefazolin prophylaxis.[99] Practical limitations that may affect the use of vancomycin in surgery include its narrow spectrum of antimicrobial activity and the need for a slow rate of infusion. Furthermore, the growing prevalence of vancomycin-resistant enterococci and reports of *S. aureus* with intermediate resistance to vancomycin (VISA) raise concerns about potential adverse effects on the antimicrobial susceptibility of nosocomial pathogens induced by the selective pressure of surgical antibiotic prophylaxis.[100] It is currently recommended that the use of vancomycin for perioperative prophylaxis should be considered only in patients with a life-threatening allergy to β-lactam antibiotics or at institutions with a high rate of infections due to MRSA or MRSE.[101]

With regard to contaminated procedures, whether a few doses of systemic prophylaxis should be added to oral antibiotics in colorectal surgery remains unresolved, although it appears prudent to do so in certain circumstances. These include when surgery has been delayed longer than 10 to 12 hours after the last oral dose, when there is spillage of colonic contents intraoperatively, and when procedures last longer than 3.5 hours.[102]

It should not be presumed that cephalosporins will remain the prophylactic agents of choice in the future. Over the past decade, various classes of antibiotics have been shown to differ appreciably in activity against bacteria in the stationary phase of growth, in a postantibiotic effect, in diffusibility into devitalized tissue or fibrin clots, in resistance to enzymatic degradation, in activity within abscesses, and in the penetration of and activity within neutrophils that may have ingested but be unable to kill wound bacteria. Each of these variables may affect the efficacy of an agent used for prophylaxis, and it is likely that preferred prophylactic regimens will change over time in response to an improved understanding of the pathophysiology of infection and to antimicrobial resistance among wound pathogens. Animal models may be especially valuable in helping to define improved regimens of antimicrobial prophylaxis and in determining whether immunomodulation can further reduce the risk of wound infection.[99, 103]

Timing and Duration of Prophylaxis. Except in elective colonic surgical procedures in which oral antibiotics must be administered several hours before the procedure, there is general agreement that the initial dose of systemically administered antibiotics need not be given until the onset of the procedure. The induction of anesthesia represents a convenient point for initiating antibiotic prophylaxis in major surgical procedures.

It is generally recommended that antibiotics be readministered during long surgical procedures so as to maintain serum concentrations well above the minimal inhibitory concentration values of common pathogens.[43, 104, 105] Theoretical reasons to ensure that adequate serum and tissue levels of antibiotics are maintained throughout the surgical procedure include the probability that the introduction of bacteria into the surgical wound occurs not only at the time of incision but continuously throughout the surgical procedure. The period of highest risk for bacterial contamination may be the close, not the beginning, of surgery. In prolonged procedures or with antibiotics with short half-lives, patients may be inadequately protected if redosing is not routinely provided.[106]

Historically, it has proved to be more difficult to administer pre- and intraoperative antimicrobial prophylaxis at the optimal times than might be supposed. Retrospective studies to determine the proportion of surgical patients who received an appropriate antibiotic within an hour before surgery suggest that 30 to 70% of patients do not receive prophylaxis in a timely fashion.[107–109] Quality standards for antimicrobial prophylaxis in surgery recommend incorporating the administration of the perioperative antimicrobial into the routine procedures executed within the operating room by either the anesthesiologist or the circulating nurse.[105]

Whether and for how long antibiotics should be given postoperatively is a subject of considerable disagreement. This issue is complicated by the targeting of surgical prophylaxis by many hospitals as an area in which significant cost savings can be achieved.

In general, studies comparing short-course versus long-course prophylaxis have reflected no increase in infection rates among the short-course recipients.[110–115] However, one comparative study of cesarian sections did detect a significantly higher incidence of endometritis in patients randomized to receive the short (18 hour) versus the long (3 day) course of perioperative ampicillin prophylaxis.[116] Also, Gatell and colleagues[117] noted a significantly higher infection rate in major joint repairs among patients receiving one versus five doses of perioperative cefamandole. Surgeons have justified continuing postoperative antibiotics for 2 or 3 days in patients who have undergone major surgical procedures and are being monitored with invasive devices on the basis that hematogenous seeding of the operative wound may occur. A study comparing vascular surgery patients receiving pre- and intraoperative prophylaxis only versus a group that continued antibiotics until intravascular lines and drain tubes were removed (but not exceeding 5 days) found the infection rate of the short-course group was twice that of the long-course group.[118] The ultimate implications of the duration of postoperative antibiotics remain to be determined. Data are simply not available to quantify the relative risk and benefits of prolonged postoperative antibiotic prophylaxis. Large-scale studies with careful attention to infection rates and antimicrobial resistance patterns of infecting pathogens are clearly needed to resolve this issue.

Recommendations for Prophylaxis. Based on prospective studies of antibiotic prophylaxis, prophylactic regimens can be recommended for a wide variety of surgical procedures (Table 308–7). However, marked variations in the spectrum of infecting pathogens and in the degree of antimicrobial resistance exist among various hospitals. Moreover, variations in infecting pathogens and resistance patterns can and do occur over time within a given institution. Physicians and individual health care institutions must tailor routine prophylactic regimens based on carefully collected epidemiologic data regarding surgical wound infection. Equally important, many surgical procedures are far from routine, and numerous variations in perioperative circumstances will dictate deviations from established prophylactic regimens. Early reexplorations for postoperative bleeding, a history of penicillin or cephalosporin allergy, trauma and other emergency surgery, and existing preoperative infections of nonwound sites (e.g., urinary tract infections, decubitus ulcers) are important variables that may influence the choice and duration of perioperative prophylaxis. Studies are not available that can provide guidelines for such situations. A continuous assessment of failures of prophylaxis and a willingness to alter antiseptic and perioperative antibiotic protocols based on local observations or published data are essential aspects of surgical wound prevention and antimicrobial prophylaxis.

Side Effects of Prophylaxis. Adverse effects for the patient include allergic reactions ranging in severity from minor skin rashes to anaphylaxis. Pseudomembranous colitis has been noted with a wide variety of prophylactic agents including oral erythromycin and neomycin, parenteral aminoglycosides, metronidazole, cephradine, cephaloridine, and cefoxitin.[189] However, in view of the extensive use of prophylaxis in the United States and judging from the infrequency of published reports, pseudomembranous colitis remains an unusual complication of prophylactic therapy.

Another notable side effect is profound hypotension associated with vancomycin prophylaxis.[190] Although the risk of this potentially reversible complication has been associated with rapid infusions of the antibiotic, others have encountered clinically significant hypotension despite exercising care to maintain slow vancomycin infusion rates.[191]

The use of prophylactic antibiotics has consequences for the institution as well as the individual patient. Antibiotic use, and specifically prophylactic antibiotic use, has been shown to have a critical role in the selection of antibiotic-resistant bacteria to become the dominant colonizing flora as well as nosocomial pathogens of hospitalized patients.[192] At least two mechanisms for this process have been documented. First, the antibiotic-resistant flora may be endemic within the institution and transferred to the patient during the course of hospitalization.[193] Second, a small population of antibiotic-resistant bacteria that are part of the patient's endogenous flora

TABLE 308–7 Recommended Antibiotic Prophylaxis for the Most Commonly Performed Surgical Procedures

Surgical Procedure*	Recommended Prophylactic Regimen†
Gynecologic Surgery	
Cesarean section[119–124]	Cefazolin,‡ 1 g IV after clamping the cord and 6 and 12 h later. Prophylaxis is not required in elective, uncomplicated cases. Uterine irrigation with antibiotics may be comparable to systemic therapy. If irrigating antibiotics are used, 2 g of cefoxitin§ in 1 L of normal saline is effective. With β-lactam allergy, metronidazole, 500 mg IV after clamping cord, is effective.
Dilation and curettage and abortion[125–127]	Prophylactic antimicrobials are not recommended for uncomplicated dilation and curettage. In second-trimester instillation abortion, 1 g of cefazolin‡ preprocedure and 1 g q6h for 2 doses is effective. With β-lactam allergy, metronidazole, 400 mg PO preprocedure and q4h for 2 doses, is effective. For induced abortion in the first trimester in patients with a history of pelvic inflammatory disease, 2 million IU of penicillin G IM before and 3 h after the procedure is effective.‖
Hysterectomy, abdominal or vaginal[128, 129]	Cefotetan, 1 g IV preoperatively. With β-lactam allergy, doxycycline, 200 mg IV, preoperatively as a single dose is effective in vaginal hysterectomy.
Bilateral occlusion of fallopian tubes	Data to recommend prophylaxis are not available.
Repair of cystocele and rectocele[130]	Prophylactic antibiotics have not proved to be effective.
Orthopaedic Surgery	
Arthroplasty of joints, including replacement[111, 131, 132]	For major joint (hip, knee) repair, cefazolin,‡ 1 g IV preoperatively and every 6 h for 3 doses. A higher cefazolin dose (2 g) should be considered in knee replacement when a tourniquet is used.
Arthroscopic surgery[133]	Available data indicate that antimicrobial prophylaxis will not improve the already low infection rate.
Open reduction of fracture[134, 135]	Cefazolin,‡ 1 g IV preoperatively and every 6 h for 3 doses. Complex (open) fractures are considered contaminated and cefazolin therapy, 1 g every 8 h for 10 d, beginning on admission, is indicated.
Laminectomy and spinal fusion[136, 137]	Prophylactic antimicrobials have not proved beneficial.
Lower limb amputation[138]	Cefoxitin,§ 2 g IV preoperatively and every 6 h for 4 doses.
Ophthalmic Surgery	
Extraction of lens, including insertion of prosthesis[139]	There are no adequately controlled trials in ophthalmic surgery. Retrospective review of data suggests that antibiotics or topical antiseptics may be efficacious, but there is no consensus regarding efficacy or choice of therapy.
General Surgery	
Cholecystectomy,[140–142] open or laparoscopic[143]	Cefazolin,‡ 2 g IV preoperatively in high-risk patients: age >60, previous biliary surgery, history of acute symptoms, or presence of jaundice. With β-lactam allergy, gentamicin, 80 mg IV preoperatively and every 8 h IV for 3 doses, is effective in open cholecystectomy.
Inguinal hernia repair[144, 145]	Available data indicate marginal to no benefit from routine antimicrobial prophylaxis.
Colon surgery[146–148]	Neomycin and erythromycin base, 1 g of each PO at 1, 2, and 11 PM on the day before surgery. For emergency colon surgery or situations precluding preoperative oral prophylaxis, cefoxitin,§ 2 g IV preoperatively and every 4 h for 3 doses, is effective. With β-lactam allergy, metronidazole, 500 mg IV, and gentamicin, 1.7 mg/kg IV, preoperatively and every 8 h postoperatively for 3 doses are effective.
Division of adhesions, laparotomy, and abdominal surgery not involving a viscus	Data to recommend prophylaxis are not available.
Primary appendectomy[130, 149–152]	Cefoxitin,§ 2 g IV preoperatively and every 6 h or 3 doses in nonperforated appendices; in perforated appendices, continue therapy for 3–5 d. Although combined aerobic and anaerobic coverage appears preferable, with β-lactam allergy, metronidazole, 500 mg IV preoperatively, is effective. With perforated appendices, continue metronidazole every 8 h IV or PO for 3–5 d.
Mastectomy, total or partial[144, 145, 153]	Data are limited. The routine use of prophylaxis is not recommended.¶
Gastric resection[154–156]	Cefazolin,‡ 1 g preoperatively in high-risk patients only: bleeding gastric or duodenal ulcer, obstructive duodenal ulcer, gastric ulcer, gastric malignancy, or morbid obesity (i.e., prophylaxis is not indicated in chronic uncomplicated duodenal ulcer). With β-lactam allergy, a single preoperative IV dose of gentamicin, 120 mg, and clindamycin, 600 mg, may be effective, but data are limited.
Surgery for penetrating abdominal trauma[157, 158]	Cefoxitin,§ 2 g IV on admission to the hospital. For patients found to have intestinal perforation, 2 g of cefoxitin§ IV q6h for 2–5 d is effective.
Urologic Surgery	
Prostatectomy, transurethral and peritoneal[159–161]	Antimicrobial prophylaxis is not recommended in patients with sterile preoperative urine cultures. Prophylactic antibiotics have not proven effective in transperitoneal needle biopsy of prostate with sterile preprocedure cultures.
Dilatation of urethra	Data to recommend prophylaxis are not available.
Surgery on Nose, Mouth, and Pharynx	
Tonsillectomy with or without adenoidectomy	Data to recommend prophylaxis are not available.
Major head, neck, and oral surgery[162–164]	In major surgical procedures involving an incision through oral or pharyngeal mucosa, a combination of gentamicin, 1.7 mg/kg, and clindamycin, 300 mg IV, preoperatively and every 8 h for 2 doses. Cefazolin and third-generation cephalosporins have also demonstrated effectiveness when given over a 24-h period perioperatively.
Rhinoplasty and repair of nose[165]	Prophylactic antimicrobials have not proved effective.
Cardiothoracic Surgery and Vascular Surgery	
Median sternotomy, coronary artery bypass grafting, and valve surgery[97, 166–168]	Although cefazolin,‡ 1 g IV preoperatively, followed by 1 g IV every 4 to 6 h intraoperatively, is commonly used, persistent *S. aureus* wound infections have been reported to be a problem in some institutions despite use of cefazolin prophylaxis. Cefuroxime, cefamandole, and vancomycin alternatives as outlined in the footnote should be considered in institutions in which *S. aureus* wound infections continue to occur despite cefazolin prophylaxis. Antibiotic administration is often continued into the postoperative period for 48 or 72 h although there are data indicating that prolonged administration does not improve efficacy.
Pacemaker insertion[169]	Cefazolin,‡ 1 g preoperatively and every 6 h postoperatively for 24 h. With β-lactam allergy, no prophylaxis may be a reasonable alternative given the low incidence of infection.
Thoracic surgery procedure, including lobectomy and pneumonectomy[170–173]	Cefazolin,‡ 1 g preoperatively and every 6 h postoperatively for 24 h. The optimal duration of postoperative prophylaxis has not been established. In penetrating thoracic trauma and in the placement of chest tubes in trauma management, prophylactic antibiotics have not been effective.
Chest tube insertion[174]	A meta-analysis suggests that prophylactic antimicrobials that focus on *S. aureus* may be warranted.
Peripheral vascular surgery[97, 175, 176]	Cefazolin,‡ 1 g preoperatively and every 6 h postoperatively for 24 h. Vancomycin is also effective. The utility of antibiotic prophylaxis in carotid artery surgery has not been established, but when infection rates are high, cefazolin‡ as mentioned above should be used. Oral ciprofloxacin was shown to be as effective as intravenous cefuroxime in one trial.

TABLE 308–7 Recommended Antibiotic Prophylaxis for the Most Commonly Performed Surgical Procedures *Continued*

Neurosurgical Procedures	
(See section on orthopedic surgery for recommendations regarding laminectomy and spinal fusion)	
Cerebrospinal fluid shunting procedures[177–179]	Antibiotic prophylaxis is not indicated in institutions with low infection rates (<10%). Trimethoprim (160 mg)-sulfamethoxazole (800 mg) IV preoperatively and every 12 h for 3 doses has proved beneficial in institutions with high infection rates (>20%).
Craniotomy[180–183]	For high-risk procedures (e.g., reexploration, microsurgery), clindamycin, 300 mg IV preoperatively and at 4 h, has proved effective. Vancomycin, 10 mg/kg (maximum of 500 mg) IV, and gentamicin, 2 mg/kg (maximum of 120 mg) IV, plus an aminoglycoside irrigating solution, has also proved effective.
Miscellaneous Procedures	
Simple hand laceration[184–186]	Prophylactic antibiotics have not proved effective. However, in animal (cat) bites, amoxicillin/clavulanate** (250 mg/125 mg) PO every 6 h for 5 d may be effective.
Percutaneous endoscopic gastrostomy (PEG)[187]	Ampicillin-sulbactam††, 1.5 g (1.0 g ampicillin, 0.5 g sulbactam), 3 doses over 24 h, has proven effective.

*Procedures are ranked in approximately descending order of frequency with which they were performed in patients discharged from federal short-stay hospitals and ambulatory facilities, 1995.[13]
†Unless otherwise noted, the preoperative dose of intravenous (IV) antibiotic should be administered at the approximate time of the operative incision. Preoperative intramuscular (IM) antibiotic should be administered ½ to 1 h before the time of the operative incision.
‡Because of its superior half-life, cefazolin is recommended at the indicated dosing schedule, although another dose of cefazolin, another cephalosporin, or a semisynthetic penicillin was evaluated in the referenced article. However, if methicillin-sensitive *S. aureus* infections continue to occur despite cefazolin prophylaxis, consider substituting cefuroxime, 1500 mg IV at the induction of anesthesia and 750 mg q4–6h throughout the procedure. If coagulase-negative or methicillin-resistant staphylococcal infections become frequent, vancomycin, 15 mg/kg preoperatively, 10 mg/kg during surgery, and q8h thereafter, should be considered.[188]
§Cefotetan or cefmetazole may be substituted for cefoxitin.
||In the referenced article, pivampicillin, 350 mg tid for 4 d, was also given postprocedure to patients in the prophylaxis group. Whether ampicillin, 500 mg PO tid, can be substituted or whether a postprocedure oral antibiotic is necessary at all is not known.
¶In a randomized, prospective study, prophylaxis with cefonicid was comparable in efficacy to placebo in preventing wound infections following herniorrhaphy or surgery involving the breast. When nonwound infections were considered together with wound infections, a slight benefit of prophylaxis was observed.[143]
**Amoxicillin-clavulanate is recommended, although oxacillin was used in the reference article.
††Ampicillin-sulbactam is recommended, although amoxicillin-clavulanate was used in the referenced article.
Adapted from Kaiser AB. Drug therapy: Antimicrobial prophylaxis in surgery. N Engl J Med. 1986;315:1129–1138. Copyright © 1986 Massachusetts Medical Society. All rights reserved.

at the time of hospitalization may emerge under the selective pressure of perioperative prophylaxis to become the dominant flora.[194] The increasing prevalence of MRSA and methicillin-resistant coagulase-negative staphylococci has profound implications for a continued or expanded role of prophylactic antibiotics in surgery. In view of the improvement in overall surgical wound infection rates over recent decades (see Table 308–1), the consensus is that prophylactic antibiotics are clearly worth this risk.

Over recent years several other multiple antibiotic-resistant bacteria have become important nosocomial pathogens, including strains of *Enterococcus faecium* that are resistant to vancomycin, ampicillin, and/or gentamicin; *S. aureus* organisms that are resistant to β-lactams and the quinolones; and *E. coli* and *Klebsiella* isolates that are resistant to cefotaxime and ceftazidime.[85] One would predict that increasing reliance on our most potent antibiotics in prophylaxis will be associated in time with further increases in the prevalence of these antibiotic-resistant strains. Genetic exchange of plasmid DNA between the enterococci and *S. aureus* has been documented,[195] and the possibility of the transfer of vancomycin resistance to *S. aureus* has ominous implications.

Cost-Benefit Analysis of Prophylaxis. Prophylactic antibiotics add considerable cost to the routine care of surgical patients. In major surgical centers, the perioperative use of antibiotics may represent almost half of the pharmacy's expenditures for antibiotics, and surgeons are often encouraged to reduce or eliminate antibiotics given for prophylaxis in certain settings. For example, in carotid endarterectomy and cholecystectomy, infections develop only infrequently, are seldom life-threatening, and may cost more to prevent than to treat. However, it seems inappropriate to evaluate antibiotic use on the basis of cost alone. When prophylaxis or a particular form of prophylaxis offers a clear advantage to the patient, the health care system should advocate the better treatment without consideration of its cost. Moreover, an analysis of the cost of prophylactic antibiotics can be complicated. The cost not only of the antibiotic per se but also of preparing, transporting, and administering multiple doses of antibiotic must be included. Perhaps of more importance, the cost in terms of mortality, morbidity, and resources of managing wound infections that develop when using inadequate prophylaxis must be considered.[196] The 6-month mortality rate of patients who develop a deep wound infection is 2.5-fold that of patients who do not develop a deep wound infection.[197] Case-matched studies show that a postoperative wound infection doubles the length of postoperative hospitalization.[198]

Surgical Wound Infection Surveillance

An effective infection control program is an essential part of surgical wound prevention. Such a program should provide accurate analysis of pathogens and their antibiograms. A surveillance system must be in place to readily identify epidemiologic foci of surgical wound infection. Ideally, representatives from the surgical attending staff should be involved in the analysis of surveillance data for appropriate input and response. Data from surveillance activities must be evaluated critically, often with the aid of computerization, so that variations and trends in the antimicrobial susceptibility pattern of surgical wound pathogens can be detected.

In collecting information on surgical wound infections, criteria for the definition of a wound infection must be established and endorsed by both infection control and surgical advisory committees. The presence of purulence within a surgical incision generally serves as evidence of a surgical wound infection. Culture results of surgical wounds or exudates should not be used as guides to the presence or absence of infection. Surgeons and hospital epidemiologists have recently emphasized the importance of stratifying surgical wound infections according to the depth of the infection. For example, delineation of surgical wound infection into four classes or degrees of infection has been recommended.[199]

In health care settings associated with a high volume of surgical procedures, surgical wound isolates should be maintained, if possible, for 2 to 3 weeks after isolation. Clusters or outbreaks of surgical wound infections due to a common pathogen are usually identified retrospectively, and the availability of infecting pathogens such as *S. aureus* or coagulase-negative staphylococci for pulsed-field gel electrophoresis or another means of molecular typing may be instrumental in identifying and eliminating the cause of the outbreak.

There have been recommendations to maintain and even publicize surgeon-specific infection rates in an effort to cause a decrease in surgical wound infections indirectly.[200] Such data may identify unsuspected problems among the surgical staff or may encourage individual surgeons to adhere rigorously to standards of perioperative aseptic techniques. If such a program is used, it is vital that any analysis include an assessment of procedure-specific infection rates. Wide differences in infection rates exist among surgical procedures, even among procedures within the same surgical subspecialty and category of bacterial contamination. For example, infection rates in vascular surgery after carotid endarterectomy are exceedingly low, less than one tenth of 1%. On the other hand, bypass grafting in the femoral popliteal area may be associated with an infection rate of 2 to 3% despite the fact that both procedures are clean and may be performed by the same vascular surgeons. Other important variables such as the age and condition of the patients must also be considered before comparing infection rates among surgeons.

REFERENCES

1. McDermott W, Rogers DE. Social ramifications of control of microbial disease. Johns Hopkins Med J. 1982;151:301–312.
2. Rice LB, Karchmer AW. Artificial heart implantation: What limitations are imposed by infectious complications? JAMA. 1988;259:894–895.
3. Finland M. Antibacterial agents: Uses and abuses in treatment and prophylaxis. Rhode Island Med J. 1960;43:499–520.
4. Culbertson WR, Altemeier WA, Gonzalez LL, et al. Studies on the epidemiology of postoperative infection of clean operative wounds. Ann Surg. 1961;154:599–610.
5. Howe CW, Marston AT. A study on sources of postoperative staphylococcal infection. Surg Gynecol Obstet. 1962;115:266–275.
6. Burke JF. Identification of the sources of staphylococci contaminating the surgical wound during operation. Ann Surg. 1963;158:898–904.
7. Howes EL. Prevention of wound infection by the injection of nontoxic antibacterial substances. Ann Surg. 1946;124:268–276.
8. Miles AA, Miles EM, Burke J. The value and duration of defense mechanisms to the primary lodgement of bacteria. Br J Exp Pathol. 1957;38:79–86.
9. Burke JF. The effective period of preventive antibiotic action in experimental incisions and dermal lesions. Surgery. 1961;50:161–167.
10. Sanchez-Ubeda R, Fernand E, Rousselot LM. Complication rate in general surgical cases: The value of penicillin and streptomycin as postoperative prophylaxis—a study of 511 cases. N Engl J Med. 1958;259:1045–1050.
11. Johnstone FRC. An assessment of prophylactic antibiotics in general surgery. Surg Gynecol Obstet. 1963;116:1–10.
12. Classen DC, Evans RS, Pestotnik SL, et al. The timing of prophylactic administration of antibiotics and the risk of surgical-wound infection. N Engl J Med. 1992;326:281–286.
13. Vital and Health Statistics. Ambulatory and in-patient procedures in the United States, 1995. Series 13: Data from the National Health Care Survey, No. 135, DHHS Publication No. (PHS) 98-1796. Hyattsville, MD. U.S. Department of Health and Human Services, Centers for Disease Control and Prevention, National Center for Health Statistics, 1998.
14. Weinstein RA. Nosocomial infection update. Emerg Infect Dis. 1998;4:416–420.
15. Aglietti P, Salvati EA, Wilson PD Jr, et al. Effect of a surgical horizontal unidirectional filtered air flow unit on wound bacterial contamination and wound healing. Clin Orthop. 1974;101:99–104.
16. Altemeier WA, Burke JF, Pluitt BA Jr, et al. Manual on Control of Infection in Surgical Patients. Philadelphia: JB Lippincott; 1976:29–30.
17. Ad Hoc Committee of the Committee on Trauma, National Research Council Division of Medical Sciences. Postoperative wound infections: The influence of ultraviolet irradiation of the operating room and of various other factors. Ann Surg. 1964;160(Suppl 2):1–132.
18. Olson M, O'Connor M, Schwartz ML. Surgical wound infections: A 5-year prospective study of 20,193 wounds at the Minneapolis VA Medical Center. Ann Surg. 1984;199:253–259.
19. Haley RW, Culver DH, Morgan WM, et al. Identifying patients at high risk of surgical wound infection: A simple multivariate index of patient susceptibility and wound contamination. Am J Epidemiol. 1985;121:206–215.
20. Culver DH, Horan TC, Gaynes RP, et al. Surgical wound infection rates by wound class, operative procedure, and patient risk index. Am J Med. 1991;91(Suppl 3B):152S–1527S.
21. Kluytmans JAJW, Mouton JW, Ijzerman EPF, et al: Nasal carriage of *Staphylococcus aureus* as a major risk factor for wound infections after cardiac surgery. J Infect Dis. 1995;171:216–219.
22. Tuazon CU. Skin and skin structure infections in the patient at risk: Carrier state of *Staphylococcus aureus*. Am J Med. 1984;76:166–71.
23. Schaffner W, Lefkowitz LB, Goodman JS. Hospital outbreak of infections with group A streptococci traced to an asymptomatic anal carrier. N Engl J Med. 1969;280:1224–1225.
24. Stamm WE, Feeley JC, Facklam RR. Wound infections due to group A *Streptococcus* traced to a vaginal carrier. J Infect Dis. 1978;138:287–292.
25. Lidwell OM, Lowbury EJL, Whyte W, et al. Effect of ultraclean air in operating rooms on deep sepsis in the joint after total hip or knee replacement: A randomized study. BMJ. 1982;185:10–14.
26. Marotte JH, Lord GA, Blanchard JP, et al. Infection rate in total hip arthroplasty as a function of air cleanliness and antibiotic prophylaxis: 10-year experience with 2,384 cementless Lord Madreporic prostheses. J Arthroplasty. 1987;2:77–82.
27. Bennett SN, McNeil MM, Bland LA, et al. Postoperative infections traced to contamination of an intravenous anesthetic, propofol. N Engl J Med. 1995;333:147–154.
28. Carlsson AS, Lidgren L, Lindberg L. Prophylactic antibiotics against early and late deep infections after total hip replacements. Acta Orthop Scand. 1977;48:405–410.
29. Krieger JN, Kaiser DL, Wenzel RP. Nosocomial urinary tract infections cause wound infections postoperatively in surgical patients. Surg Gynecol Obstet. 1983;156:313–318.
30. Kaiser AB. Overview of cephalosporin prophylaxis. Am J Surg. 1988;155(Suppl 5A):52–55.
31. Elek SD, Conen PE. The virulence of *Staphylococcus pyogenes* for man. A study of the problems of wound infection. Br J Exp Pathol. 1958;38:573–586.
32. Zimmerli W, Waldvogel FA, Vaudaux P, et al. Pathogenesis of foreign body infection: Description and characteristics of an animal model. J Infect Dis. 1982;146:487–497.
33. Arbeit RD, Dunn RM. Expression of capsular polysaccharide during experimental focal infection with *Staphylococcus aureus*. J Infect Dis. 1987;156:947–952.
34. Kaiser AB, Kernodle DS, Parker RA. A low-inoculum animal model of subcutaneous abscess formation and antimicrobial prophylaxis. J Infect Dis. 1992;166:393–399.
35. Patti JM, Jonsson H, Guss B, et al. Molecular characterization and expression of a gene encoding a *Staphylococcus aureus* collagen adhesin. J Biol Chem. 1992;267:4766–4772.
36. Paulsson M, Ljungh Å, Wadström T. Rapid identification of fibronectin, vitronectin, laminin, and collagen cell surface binding proteins on coagulase-negative staphylococci by particle agglutination assays. J Clin Microbiol. 1992;30:2006–2012.
37. Fröman G, Switalski LM, Speziale P, et al. Isolation and characterization of a fibronectin receptor from *Staphylococcus aureus*. J Biol Chem. 1987;262:6564–6571.
38. Rogolsky M. Nonenteric toxins of *Staphylococcus aureus*. Microbiol Rev. 1979;43:320–360.
39. Dossett JH, Kronvall G, Williams RC Jr, et al. Antiphagocytic effects of staphylococcal protein A. J Immunol. 1969;103:1405–1410.
40. Weinstein WM, Onderdonk AB, Bartlett JG, et al. Experimental intra-abdominal abscesses in rats: Development of an experimental model. Infect Immun. 1974;10:1250–1255.
41. Onderdonk AB, Bartlett JG, Louie T, et al. Microbial synergy in experimental abscess. Infect Immun. 1976;13:22–26.
42. Onderdonk AB, Markham RB, Zaleznik DF, et al. Evidence of T cell-dependent immunity to *Bacteroides fragilis* in an intraabdominal abscess model. J Clin Invest. 1982;69:9–16.
43. Page CP, Bohnen JMA, Fletcher JR, et al. Antimicrobial prophylaxis for surgical wounds: Guidelines for clinical care. Arch Surg. 1993;128:79–88.
44. Owens WD, Felts JA, Spitznagel EL. ASA physical status classifications: A study of consistency of ratings. Anesthesiology. 1978;49:239–243.
45. Emori TG, Culver DH, Horan TC, et al. National nosocomial infection surveillance system (NNIS): description of surveillance methods. Am J Infect Control. 1991;19:19–35.
46. National nosocomial infections surveillance (NNIS) report, data summary from October 1986–April 1997, issued May 1997: A report from the NNIS system. Atlanta: Hospital Infections Program, National Center for Infectious Diseases, Centers for Disease Control and Prevention, Public Health Service, U.S. Department of Health and Human Services.
47. Miles AA, Niven JSF. The enhancement of infection during shock produced by bacterial toxins and other agents. Br J Exp Pathol. 1950;31:73.
48. Burke JF, Miles AA. The significance of vascular events in early infective inflammation. J Pathol Bacteriol. 1958;76:1–19.
49. Polk HC Jr, Miles AA. Enhancement of bacterial infection by ferric iron: Kinetics, mechanisms, and surgical significance. Surgery. 1971;70:71–77.
50. DeLong TG, Simmons RL. Role of lymphatic vessels in bacterial clearance from early soft tissue infection. Arch Surg. 1982;117:123–128.
51. Platt J, Bucknall RA. An experimental evaluation of antiseptic wound irrigation. J Hosp Infect. 1984;5:181–188.
52. Knighton DR, Halliday B, Hunt TK. Oxygen as an antibiotic. Arch Surg. 1984;119:199–204.
53. Hau T, Jacobs DE, Hawkins NL. Antibiotics fail to prevent abscess formation secondary to bacteria trapped in fibrin clots. Arch Surg. 1986;121:163–167.
54. Hoogeterp JJ, Mattie H, Krul AM, et al. Quantitative effect of granulocytes on antibiotic treatment of experimental staphylococcal infection. Antimicrob Agents Chemother. 1987;31:930–934.
55. Falcieri E, Vandaux P, Huggler E, et al. Role of bacterial exopolymers and host factors on adherence and phagocytosis of *Staphylococcus aureus* in foreign body infections. J Infect Dis. 1987;155:524–531.
56. Ford CW, Hamel JC, Stapert D, et al. Establishment of an experimental model of a *Staphylococcus aureus* abscess in mice by use of dextran and gelatin microcarriers. J Med Microbiol. 1989;28:259–266.
57. Dye ES, Kapral FA. Partial characterization of a bactericidal system in staphylococcal abscesses. Infect Immun. 1980;30:198–203.
58. Weinrauch Y, Elsback P, Madsen LM, et al. The potent anti-*Staphylococcus aureus*

activity of a sterile rabbit inflammatory fluid is due to a 14-kD phospholipase A2. J Clin Invest. 1996;97:250–257.
59. McGeehan D, Hunt D, Chaudhuri A, et al. An experimental study of the relationship between synergistic wound sepsis and suture materials. Br J Surg. 1980;67:636–638.
60. Nishida H, Grooters RK, Merkley DF, et al. Postoperative mediastinitis: A comparison of two electrocautery techniques on presternal soft tissues. J Thorac Cardiovasc Surg. 1990;99:969–976.
61. Kumagai SG, Rosales RF, Hunter GC, et al. Effects of electrocautery on midline laparotomy wound infection. Am J Surg 1991;162:620–622.
62. Yamada Y, Hefter K, Burke JE, et al. An in vitro model of the wound microenvironment: Local phagocytic cell abnormalities associated with in situ complement activation. J Infect Dis. 1987;155:998–1004.
63. El-Maallem H, Fletcher J. Effects of surgery on neutrophil granulocyte function. Infect Immun. 1981;32:38–41.
64. Bamberger DM, Herndon BL. Bactericidal capacity of neutrophils in rabbits with experimental acute and chronic abscesses. J Infect Dis. 1990;162:186–192.
65. Zimmerli W, Lew PD, Waldvogel FA. Pathogenesis of foreign body infection. Evidence for a local granulocyte defect. J Clin Invest. 1984;73:1191–1200.
66. Cheadle WG, Hershman MJ, Wellhausen SR, Polk HC Jr. HLA-DR antigen expression on peripheral blood monocytes correlates with surgical infection. Am J Surg. 1991;161:639–645.
67. Hensler T, Hecker H, Heeg K, Heidecke C-D, et al. Distinct mechanisms of immunosuppression as a consequence of major surgery. Infect Immun. 1997;65:2283–2291.
68. Hopf HW, Hunt TK, West JM, et al. Wound tissue oxygen tension predicts the risk of wound infection in surgical patients. Arch Surg. 1997;132:997–1004.
69. Clardy CW, Edwards KM, Gay JC. Increased susceptibility to infection in hypothermic children: Possible role of acquired neutrophil dysfunction. Pediatr Infect. 1985;4:379–382.
70. Kurz A, Sessler DI, Lenhardt R for the Study of Wound Infection and Temperature Group. Perioperative normothermia to reduce the incidence of surgical-wound infection and shorten hospitalization. N Engl J Med. 1996;334:1209–1215.
71. Jensen LS, Kissmeyer-Nielsen P, Wolff B, Qvist N. Randomized comparison of leucocyte-depleted versus buffy-coat-poor blood transfusion and complications after colorectal surgery. Lancet. 1996;348:841–845.
72. Houbiers JG, van de Velde CJ, van de Watering LM, et al. Transfusion of red cells is associated with increased incidence of bacterial infection after colorectal surgery: A prospective study. Transfusion. 1997;37:126–134.
73. Silva J, Hoeksema H, Fekety FR. Transient defects in phagocytic functions during cardiopulmonary bypass. J Thorac Cardiovasc Surg. 1974;67:175–183.
74. Parker DJ, Cantrell JW, Karp RB, et al. Changes in serum complement and immunoglobulins following cardiopulmonary bypass. Surgery. 1972;71:824–827.
75. Subramanian VA, Gay WA, Dineen PAP. Effect of cardiopulmonary bypass on in vivo clearance of live *Klebsiella aerogenes*. Surg Forum. 1977;28:255–257.
76. Vaudaux P, Grau GE, Huggler E, et al. Contribution of tumor necrosis factor to host defense against staphylococci in a guinea pig model of foreign body infections. J Infect Dis. 1992;166:58–64.
77. Rotstein OD, Kao J. Prevention of intra-abdominal abscesses by fibrinolysis using recombinant tissue plasminogen activator. J Infect Dis. 1988;158:766–772.
78. Fong IW, Baker CB, McKee DC. The value of prophylactic antibiotics in aorta-coronary bypass operations: A double-blind randomized trial. J Thorac Cardiovasc Surg. 1979;78:908–913.
79. Penketh ARL, Wansbrough-Jones MH, Wright E, et al. Antibiotic prophylaxis for coronary artery bypass surgery. Lancet. 1985;1:1500.
80. Austin TW, Coles JC, Burnett R, et al. Aortocoronary bypass procedures and sternotomy infections: A study of antistaphylococcal prophylaxis. Can J Surg. 1980;23:483–485.
81. Kernodle DS, Classen DC, Burke JP, et al. Failure of cephalosporins to prevent *Staphylococcus aureus* surgical wound infections. JAMA. 1990;263:961–966.
82. Kernodle DS, Voladri RKR, Kaiser AB. β-lactamase production diminishes the prophylactic efficacy of ampicillin and cefazolin in a guinea pig model of *Staphylococcus aureus* wound infection. J Infect Dis. 1998;177:701–706.
83. Kernodle DS, Classen DC, Stratton CW, Kaiser AB. Association of borderline oxacillin-susceptible strains of *Staphylococcus aureus* with surgical wound infections. J Clin Microbiol. 1998;36:219–222.
84. Gaynes R, Culver D, and the National Nosocomial Infection Surveillance (NNIS) System. Emergence of nosocomial methicillin-resistant *Staphylococcus aureus* (MRSA) in the United States, 1987–1997. Emerging Infectious Diseases Conference, Atlanta, GA, March 8–12, 1998.
85. Archibald L, Phillips L, Monnet D, et al. Antimicrobial resistance in isolates from inpatients and outpatients in the United States: increasing importance of the intensive care unit. Clin Infect Dis. 1997;24:211–215.
86. Neu HC. Emergence and mechanisms of bacterial resistance in surgical infections. Am J Surg. 1995;169:13S–20S.
87. Tetteroo GWM, Wagenvoort JHT, Bruining HA. Role of selective decontamination in surgery. Br J Surg. 1992;79:300–304.
88. Kluytmans JAJW, Mouton JW, VanderBergh MFQ, et al. Reduction of surgical-site infections in cardiothoracic surgery by elimination of nasal carraige of *Staphylococcus aureus*. Infect Control Hosp Epidemiol. 1996;17:780–785.
89. Kaul AF, Jewett JF. Agents and techniques for disinfection of the skin. Surg Gynecol Obstet. 1981;152:677–685.
90. Valentine RJ, Weigelt JA, Dryer D, et al. Effect of remote infections on clean wound infection rates. Am J Infect Control. 1986;14:64–68.
91. Klein JD, Hey LA, Yu CS, et al. Perioperative nutrition and postoperative complications in patients undergoing spinal surgery. Spine. 1996;21:2676–2682.
92. Zerr KJ, Furnary AP, Grunkemeier GL, et al. Glucose control lowers the risk of wound infection in diabetics after open heart operations. Ann Thorac Surg. 1997;63:356–361.
93. Meropol NJ, Wood DE, Nemunaitis J, et al. Randomized, placebo-controlled, multicenter trial of granulocyte-machrophage colony-stimulating factor as infection prophylaxis in oncologic surgery. J Clin Onc. 1998;16:1167–1173.
94. Moesgaard F, Jensen LS, Christiansen PM, et al. The effect of ranitidine on postoperative infectious complications following emergency colorectal surgery: A randomized, placebo-controlled, double-blind trial. Inflamm Res. 1998;47:12–17.
95. Evans M, Pollock AV. Trials on trials: A review of trials of antibiotic prophylaxis. Arch Surg. 1984;119:109–113.
96. Ena J, Dick RW, Jones RN, et al. The epidemiology of intravenous vancomycin usage in a university hospital: A 10-year study. JAMA. 1993;269:598–602.
97. Maki DG, Bohn MJ, Stolz SM, et al. Comparative study of cefazolin, cefamandole, and vancomycin for surgical prophylaxis in cardiac and vascular operations. A double-blind randomized trial. J Thorac Cardiovasc Surg. 1992;104:1423–1434.
98. Vuorisalo S, Haukipuro K, Pokela R, Syrjala H. Comparison of vancomycin and cefuroxime for infection prophylaxis in coronary artery bypass surgery. Infect Control Hosp Epidemiol. 1998;19:234–239.
99. Kernodle DS, Kaiser AB. Comparative prophylactic efficacy of cefazolin and vancomycin in a guinea pig model of *Staphylococcus aureus* wound infection. J Infect Dis. 1993;168:152–157.
100. Centers for Disease Control and Prevention. Update: *Staphylococcus aureus* with reduced susceptibility to vancomycin—United States, 1997. MMWR Morb Mortal Wkly Rep. 1997;46:813–815.
101. Hospital Infection Control Advisory Committee, Centers for Disease Control and Prevention. Recommendations for preventing the spread of vancomycin resistance. Infect Control Hosp Epidemiol. 1995;16:105–113.
102. Gorbach SL. Antimicrobial prophylaxis for appendectomy and colorectal surgery. Rev Infect Dis. 1991;13(Suppl 10):S815–S820.
103. Kernodle DS, Gates H, Kaiser AB. Prophylactic anti-infective activity of poly-[1, 6]-β-D-glucopyranosyl-[1, 3]-β-D-glucopyranose glucan in a guinea pig model of staphylococcal wound infection. Antimicrob Agents Chemother. 1998;42:545–549.
104. Antimicrobial prophylaxis in surgery. Med Lett Drugs Ther. 1997;39:97–101.
105. Dellinger EP, Gross PA, Barrett TL, et al. Quality standard for antimicrobial prophylaxis in surgical procedures. Clin Infect Dis. 1994;18:422–427.
106. Platt R, Munoz A, Stella J, et al. Antibiotic prophylaxis for cardiovascular surgery: Efficacy with coronary artery bypass. Ann Intern Med. 1984;101:770–774.
107. Currier JS, Campbell H, Platt R, Kaiser AB. Perioperative antimicrobial prophylaxis in middle Tennessee, 1989–1990. Rev Infect Dis. 1991;13(Suppl 10):S874–S878.
108. Silver A, Eichorn A, Kral J, et al. Timeliness and use of antibiotic prophylaxis in selected inpatient surgical procedures: The antibiotic prophylaxis study group. Am J Surg. 1996;171:548–552.
109. Matuschka PR, Cheadle WG, Burke JD, Garrison RN. A new standard of care: Administration of preoperative antibiotics in the operating room. Am Surg. 1997;63:500–503.
110. Goldmann DA, Hopkins CC, Karchmer AW. Cephalothin prophylaxis in cardiac valve surgery: A prospective, double-blind comparison of two-day and six-day regimen. J Thorac Cardiovasc Surg. 1977;73:470–479.
111. Nelson CL, Green TG, Porter RA, et al. One day versus seven days of preventive antibiotic therapy in orthopedic surgery. Clin Orthop. 1983;176:258–263.
112. Scarpignato C, Caltabiano M, Condemi V, et al. Short-term versus long-term cefuroxime prophylaxis in patients undergoing emergency cesarean section. Clin Ther. 1982;5:186–192.
113. Soper DE, Yarwood RL. Single-dose antibiotic prophylaxis in women undergoing vaginal hysterectomy. Obstet Gynecol. 1987;69:879–882.
114. Conte JE Jr, Cohen SN, Roe BB, et al. Antibiotic prophylaxis and cardiac surgery: A prospective double-blind comparison of single-dose versus multiple-dose regimens. Ann Intern Med. 1972;76:943–949.
115. Hillis DJ, Rosenfeldt FL, Spicer WJ, et al. Antibiotic prophylaxis for coronary bypass grafting: Comparison of a five-day and a two-day course. J Thorac Cardiovasc Surg. 1983;86:217.
116. Elliott JP, Freeman RK, Dorchester W. Short versus long course of prophylactic antibiotics in cesarean section. Am J Obstet Gynecol. 1982;143:740–744.
117. Gatell JM, Garcia S, Lozano L, et al. Perioperative cefamandole prophylaxis against infections. J Bone Joint Surg. 1987;8:1189–1193.
118. Hall JC, Christiansen KJ, Goodman M, et al. Duration of antimicrobial prophylaxis in vascular surgery. Am J Surg. 1998;175:87–90.
119. Elyan A, Mahran M, el-Maraghy M, et al. Prophylactic intravenous metronidazole in cesarean section. Chemioterapia. 1984;3:67–70.
120. Stiver HG, Forward KR, Livingstone RA, et al. Multicenter comparison of cefoxitin versus cefazolin for prevention of infectious morbidity after nonelective cesarean section. Am J Obstet Gynecol. 1983;145:158–163.
121. Harger JH, English DH. Selection of patients for antibiotic prophylaxis in cesarean section. Am J Obstet Gynecol. 1981;141:752–758.
122. Hawrylyshyn PA, Bernstein P, Papsin FR. Short-term antibiotic prophylaxis in high-risk patients following cesarean section. Am J Obstet Gynecol. 1983;145:285–289.
123. Elliott JP, Flaherty JF. Comparison of lavage or intravenous antibiotics at cesarean section. Obstet Gynecol. 1986;67:29–32.

124. Conover WB, Moore TR. Comparison of irrigation and intravenous antibiotics prophylaxis at cesarean section. Obstet Gynecol. 1984;63:787–791.
125. Heisterbert L, Petersen K. Metronidazole prophylaxis in elective first trimester abortion. Obstet Gynecol. 1985;65:371–374.
126. Sonne-Holm S, Heisterberg L, Hebjorn S, et al. Prophylactic antibiotics in first-trimester abortions: A clinical, controlled trial. Am J Obstet Gynecol. 1981;139:693–696.
127. Spence MR, King TM, Burkman RT, et al. Cephalothin prophylaxis for midtrimester abortion. Obstet Gynecol. 1982;60:502–505.
128. Hemsell DL, Hemsell PG, Nobles BJ. Doxycycline and cefamandole prophylaxis for premenopausal women undergoing vaginal hysterectomy. Surg Gynecol Obstet. 1985;161:462–464.
129. Hemsell DL, Johnson ER, Hemsell PG, et al. Cefazolin is inferior to Cefotetan as single-dose prophylaxis for women undergoing elective total abdominal hysterectomy. Clin Infect Dis. 1995;20:677–684.
130. Lau WY, Fan ST, Yui TF, et al. Prophylaxis of postappendicectomy sepsis by metronidazole and cefotaxime; a randomized, prospective and double blind trial. Br J Surg. 1983;70:670–672.
131. Cunha BA, Gossling HR, Pasternak HS, et al. Penetration of cephalosporins into bone. Infection. 1984;12:80–84.
132. Hill C, Flamant R, Mazas F, et al. Prophylactic cefazolin versus placebo in total hip replacement. Lancet. 1981;1:795–797.
133. Wieck JA, Jackson JK, O'Brien TJ, et al. Efficacy of prophylactic antibiotics in arthroscopic surgery. Orthopedics. 1997;20:133–134.
134. Gatell JM, Riba J, Lozano ML, et al. Prophylactic cefamandole in orthopaedic surgery. J Bone Joint Surg. 1984;66:1219–1222.
135. Patzakis MJ, Harvey P, Ivler D. The role of antibiotics in the management of open fractures. J Bone Joint Surg. 1974;56:532–541.
136. Geraghty J, Feely M. Antibiotic prophylaxis in neurosurgery: A randomized controlled trial. J Neurosurg. 1984;60:724–726.
137. Strohecker J, Piotrowski WP, Lametschwandtner A. The intra-operative application of povidone-iodine in neurosurgery. J Hosp Infect. 1985;6:532–541.
138. Sonne-Holm S, Boeckstyns M, Mench H, et al. Prophylactic antibiotics in amputation of the lower extremity for ischemia. J Bone Joint Surg. 1985;67:800–803.
139. Starr MB. Prophylactic antibiotics for ophthalmic surgery. Surv Ophthalmol. 1983;27:353–373.
140. Kaufman Z, Engelberg M, Eliashiv A, et al. Systemic prophylactic antibiotics in elective biliary surgery. Arch Surg. 1984;119:1002–1004.
141. Lewis RT, Allan CM, Goodall RG, et al. A single preoperative dose of cefazolin prevents postoperative sepsis in high-risk biliary surgery. Can J Surg. 1984;27:44–47.
142. Lykkegaard Nielsen M, Moesgaard F, Justesen T, et al. Wound sepsis after elective cholecystectomy: Restriction of prophylactic antibiotics to risk groups. Scand J Gastroenterol. 1981;16:937–940.
143. Illig KA, Schmidt E, Cavanaugh J, et al. Are prophylactic antibiotics required for elective laparoscopic cholecystectomy. J Am Coll Surg. 1997;184:353–356.
144. Platt R, Zucker JR, Zaleznik DF, et al. Prophylaxis against wound infection following herniorrhaphy or breast surgery. J Infect Dis. 1992;166:556–560.
145. Taylor EW, Byrne DJ, Leaper DJ, et al. Antibiotic prophylaxis and open groin hernia repair. World J Surg. 1997;21:811–815.
146. Kaiser AB, Herrington JL Jr, Jacobs JK, et al. Cefoxitin versus erythromycin, neomycin, and cefazolin in colorectal operations: Importance of the duration of the surgical procedure. Ann Surg. 1983;198:525–530.
147. McDonald PJ, Karran SJ. A comparison of intravenous cefoxitin and a combination of gentamicin and metronidazole as prophylaxis in colorectal surgery. Dis Colon Rectum. 1983;26:661–664.
148. Clarke JS, Condon RE, Bartlett JG, et al. Preoperative oral antibiotics reduce septic complications of colon operations: Results of prospective randomized, double-blind clinical study. Ann Surg. 1977;186:251–259.
149. Chant AD, Turner DTL, Machin D. Metronidazole v ampicillin: Differing effects on the postoperative recovery. Ann R Coll Surg Engl. 1984;66:96–97.
150. Greenall MJ, Bakran A, Pickford IR, et al. A double-blind trial of a single intravenous dose of metronidazole as prophylaxis against wound infection following appendicectomy. Br J Surg. 1979;66:428–429.
151. Morris WT, Innes DB, Richardson RA, et al. Prevention of post-appendicectomy sepsis by metronidazole and cefazolin: A controlled double blind trial. Aust NZ J Surg. 1980;50:429–433.
152. Winslow RE, Dean RE, Harley JW. Acute nonperforating appendicitis. Arch Surg. 1983;118:651–655.
153. Wagman LD, Tegtmeier B, Beatty JD, et al. A prospective, randomized double-blind study of the use of antibiotics at the time of mastectomy. Surg Gynecol Obstet. 1990;170:12–16.
154. LoCicero J III, Nichols RL. Sepsis after gastroduodenal operations: Relationship to gastric acid, motility, and endogenous microflora. South Med J. 1980;73:878–890.
155. Richards DG, Clark RG, Rowland BJ, et al. Antibiotic prophylaxis against wound infection in emergency abdominal surgery. J R Coll Surg Edinb. 1981;26:232–237.
156. Stone HH, Hooper CA, Kolb LD, et al. Antibiotic prophylaxis in gastric, biliary and colonic surgery. Ann Surg. 1976;184:443–452.
157. Gentry LO, Feliciano DV, Lea AS, et al. Perioperative antibiotic therapy for penetrating injuries of the abdomen. Ann Surg. 1984;200:561–566.
158. Nichols RL, Smith JW, Klein DB, et al. Risk of infection after penetrating abdominal trauma. N Engl J Med. 1984;311:1065–1070.
159. Ferrie BG, Scott R. Prophylactic cefuroxime in transurethral resection. Urol Res. 1984;12:279–281.
160. Quist N, Christiansen HM, Ehlers D. Severe *Vibrio cholerae* sepsis and meningitis in a young infant. Urol Res. 1984;12:275–277.
161. Packer MG, Russo P, Fair WR. Prophylactic antibiotics and Foley catheter use in transperineal needle biopsy of the prostate. J Urol. 1984;131:687–689.
162. Johnson JR, YU VL, Myers EN, et al. Efficacy of two third-generation cephalosporins in prophylaxis for head and neck surgery. Arch Otolaryngol. 1984;110:224–227.
163. Seagle MB, Duberstein LE, Gross CW, et al. Efficacy of cefazolin as prophylactic antibiotic in head and neck surgery. Otolaryngology. 1979;85:568–572.
164. Slight PH, Gundling K, Plotkin SA, et al. A trial of vancomycin for prophylaxis of infections after neurosurgical shunts. N Engl J Med. 1985;312:921.
165. Weimert TA, Yoder MG. Antibiotics and nasal surgery. Laryngoscope. 1980;90:667–672.
166. Kaiser AB, Petracek MR, Lea JW IV, et al. Efficacy of cefazolin, cefamandole, and gentamicin as prophylactic agents in cardiac surgery. Ann Surg. 1987;206:791–797.
167. Slama TG, Sklar SJ, Misinski J, et al. Randomized comparison of cefamandole, cefazolin, and cefuroxime prophylaxis in open-heart surgery. Antimicrob Agents Chemother. 1986;29:744–747.
168. Nooyen SM, Overbeek BP, Brutel de la Riviere A, et al. Prospective randomised comparison of single-dose versus multiple-dose cefuroxime for prophylaxis in coronary artery bypass grafting. Eur J Clin Microbiol Infect Dis. 1994;13:1033–1037.
169. Muers MF, Arnold AG, Sleight P. Prophylactic antibiotics for cardiac pacemaker implantation: A prospective trial. Br Heart J. 1981;46:539–544.
170. Frimodt-Moller N, Ostri P, Pendersen IBK, et al. Antibiotic prophylaxis in pulmonary surgery: A double-blind study of penicillin versus placebo. Ann Surg. 1982;195:444–450.
171. Kvale PA, Ranga V, Kopacz M, et al. Pulmonary resection. South Med J. 1977;70:64–68.
172. LeBlanc KA, Tucker WY. Prophylactic antibiotics and closed tube thoracostomy. Surg Gynecol Obstet. 1985;160:259–263.
173. Mandal AK, Montano J, Thadepalli H. Prophylactic antibiotics and no antibiotics compared in penetrating chest trauma. J Trauma. 1985;25:639–643.
174. Evans JT, Green JD, Carlin PE, Barrett LO. Meta-analysis of antibiotics in tube thoracostomy. Am Surg. 1995;61:215–219.
175. Kaiser AB, Clayson KR, Mulherin JL Jr, et al. Antibiotic prophylaxis in vascular surgery. Ann Surgery. 1978;188:283–289.
176. Risberg B, Drott C, Dalman P, Holm J, et al. Oral ciprofloxacin versus intravenous cefuroxime as prophylaxis against postoperative infection in vascular surgery: A randomised double-blind, prospective multicenter study. Eur J Vasc Endovasc Surg. 1995;10:345–351.
177. Blomstedt GC. Results of trimethoprim-sulfamethoxazole prophylaxis in ventriculotomy and shunting procedures: A double-blind randomized trial. J Neurosurg. 1985;62:694–697.
178. Wang EEL, Prober CG, Hendrick BE, et al. Prophylactic sulfamethoxazole and trimethoprim in ventriculoperitoneal shunt surgery: A double-blind, randomized, placebo-controlled trial. JAMA. 1984;251:1174–1177.
179. Schmidt K, Gjerris F, Osgaard O, et al. Antibiotic prophylaxis in cerebrospinal fluid shunting: A prospective randomized trial in 152 hydrocephalic patients. Neurosurg. 1985;17:1–5.
180. Blomstedt GC, Kytta J. Results of a randomized trial of vancomycin prophylaxis in craniotomy. J Neurosurg. 1988;69:216–220.
181. Shapiro M, Wald U, Simchen E, et al. Randomized clinical trial of intra-operative antimicrobial prophylaxis of infection after neurosurgical procedures. J Hosp Infect. 1986;8:283–295.
182. Geraghty J, Feely M. Antibiotic prophylaxis in neurosurgery. A randomized controlled trial. J Neurosurg. 1984;60:724–726.
183. Savitz MH, Malis LI. Prophylactic clindamycin for neurosurgical patients. N Y State J Med. 1976;76:64–67.
184. Elenbaas RM, McNabney WK, Robinson WA. Evaluation of prophylactic oxacillin in cat bite wounds. Ann Emerg Med. 1984;13:155–157.
185. Grossman JAI, Adams JP, Kunec J. Prophylactic antibiotics in simple hand lacerations. JAMA. 1981;245:1055–1056.
186. Haughey RE, Lammers RL, Wagner DK. Use of antibiotics in the initial management of soft tissue hand wounds. Ann Emerg Med. 1981;10:187–192.
187. Akkersdijk WL, van Bergeijk JD, van Egmond T, et al. Percutaneous endoscopic gastrostomy (PEG): Comparison of push and pull methods and evaluation of antibiotic prophylaxis. Endoscopy. 1995;27:313–316.
188. Farber BF, Karchmer AW, Buckley MJ, et al. Vancomycin prophylaxis in cardiac operations: Determination of an optimal dosage regimen. J Thorac Cardiovasc Surg. 1983;85:933–940.
189. Block BS, Mercer LJ, Ismail MA, et al. *Clostridium difficile*-associated diarrhea follows perioperative prophylaxis with cefoxitin. Am J Obstet Gynecol. 1986;153:835–838.
190. Dajee H, Laks H, Miller J, et al. Profound hypotension from rapid vancomycin administration during cardiac operation. J Thorac Cardiovasc Surg. 1984;87:145–146.
191. Odio C, Mohs E, Sklar FH, et al. Adverse reactions to vancomycin used as prophylaxis for CSF shunt procedures. Am J Dis Child. 1984;138:17–19.
192. Roberts NJ Jr, Douglas RG Jr. Gentamicin use and *Pseudomonas* and *Serratia* resistance: Effect of a surgical prophylaxis regimen. Antimicrob Agents Chemother. 1978;13:214–220.
193. Archer GL, Armstrong BC. Alteration of staphylococcal flora in cardiac patients receiving antibiotic prophylaxis. J Infect Dis. 1983;147:642–649.
194. Kernodle DS, Barg NL, Kaiser AB. Low-level colonization of hospitalized patients

with methicillin-resistant coagulase-negative staphylococci and their emergence during surgical antimicrobial prophylaxis. Antimicrob Agents Chemother. 1988;32:202–208.
195. Schaberg DR, Clewell DB, Glatzer L. Conjugative transfer of R-plasmids from *Streptococcus faecalis* to *Staphylococcus aureus*. Antimicrob Agents Chemother. 1982;22:204–207.
196. Roach AL, Kernodle DS, Kaiser AB. Selecting cost-effective antimicrobial prophylaxis in surgery: Are we getting what we pay for? Ann Pharmacother. 1990;24:183–185.
197. Poulsen KB, Wachmann CH, Bremmelgaard A, et al. Survival of patients with surgical wound infection: A case-control study of common surgical interventions. Br J Surg. 1995;82:208–209.
198. Green JW, Wenzel RP. Postoperative wound infection: A controlled study of the increased duration of hospital stay and direct cost of hospitalization. Ann Surg. 1977;185:264–268.
199. Kaiser AB. The use of antibiotics in cardiac and thoracic surgery. In: Sabistan DC, Spencer FC, eds. Gibbon's Surgery of the Chest. 5th ed. Philadelphia: WB Saunders; 1989.
200. Condon RE, Haley RW, Lee JT Jr, et al. Does infection control control infections? Arch Surg. 1988;123:250–256.

Chapter 309

Multiple Trauma

RONALD P. RABINOWITZ
ANTHONY E. FIORE
MANJARI JOSHI
ELLIS S. CAPLAN

Trauma remains a leading cause of morbidity, mortality, and health care expenditures despite remarkable achievements in treatment over the past several decades. Traumatic injury is the nation's second largest source of health care expenditures and the largest source in the working age population.[1, 2] Advances in rapid transport and resuscitation of trauma victims have resulted in prolonged survival of even the most profoundly injured, and the role of infection in subsequent morbidity and mortality is substantial. Numerous studies of victims of both blunt and penetrating trauma document that infection is responsible for 30 to 88% of deaths occurring in those who survive the initial injury.[3–6]

MECHANISMS FOR INCREASED RISK OF INFECTION

Trauma patients are at increased risk for infection for a number of reasons. Broken skin and mucosal surfaces are immediately contaminated as part of the mechanism of injury, and pathogens can bypass the first-line defenses. Devitalized or ischemic integument is exploited by microbes, and surgical drains, intravenous lines, urinary catheters, and endotracheal tubes allow these pathogens to bypass even healthy skin and mucosa. Colonization with nosocomial pathogens occurs quickly in the intensive care settings necessary for treatment of multiple trauma and correlates well with the severity of injury and presence of invasive devices.[7, 8] Once colonized, wounds, drains, and catheters are resistant to microbial clearance by host immune defenses. Patients who remain longer in the intensive care unit (ICU) have these problems further complicated by tracheostomies, bedsores, immobilization, intravascular monitoring, and implanted prosthetic devices. A critically injured patient loses the protective colonization immunity provided by normal gut flora as a result of disruption of the normal microenvironment by injury, ischemia, impaired motility, pH changes, fasting, and antibiotics. Traumatic injury produces a hypermetabolic state that results in a relative nutritional deficiency, potentially compromising wound healing and host immunity.[9] This "relative state of malnutrition" can also lead to an increased susceptibility to infection, decreased protein levels, and decreased wound healing. Nutritional support plays a critical role in the care of a multiply traumatized patient. New immune-enhancing diets with a variety of supplements, including arginine, glutamine, and ω-3 and ω-6 fatty acids, have recently been introduced. Some evidence supports their ability to decrease infection rates and decrease multisystem organ dysfunction.[10–14] No data to date, however, have suggested that these new formulations can decrease overall mortality.[12, 13] ICUs are reservoirs for virulent, often highly resistant bacteria that are easily spread between patients by personnel or shared equipment.[7] Transfusions may introduce pathogenic and potentially immunosuppressive viral agents such as cytomegalovirus, Epstein-Barr virus, and hepatitis viruses.[15]

Transfusion can also lead to iron overload. Certain organisms, such as *Vibrio vulnificus*, *Pseudomonas aeruginosa*, *Escherichia coli*, *Klebsiella pneumoniae,* and the agents of mucormycosis,[16] show increased virulence when exposed to free iron. Normally, most iron in the body is tightly bound. Acute-phase reactants and fever have been shown to decrease free iron concentrations, which may theoretically aid host defense. This scenario becomes clinically relevant in patients who have experienced abdominal trauma with intraperitoneal spillage of bacteria and blood, which can lead to increased iron concentrations that could potentially increase the virulence of gut organisms.[16, 17] Along with packed red blood cells, cell-free hemoglobin products are being studied for use in trauma patients. Cell-free hemoglobin disaggregates endotoxin. This "free" endotoxin has increased in vitro activity.[18] In a mouse model, hemoglobin given with intraperitoneal lipopolysaccharide injections substantially increased mortality. This effect was also noted with cell-free hemoglobin and cross-linked hemoglobin.[18] Along with the previously discussed effects of free iron on bacterial growth, increased endotoxin activity could be potentially clinically important in victims of penetrating or blunt abdominal trauma.

Evidence continues to accumulate that traumatic injury or hemorrhage can cause a degree of immunodeficiency. Corticosteroid administration necessitated by head trauma may further impair immunity. Corticosteroids given to spinal cord–injured patients may improve motor outcome but may increase risks for nosocomial infection.[19] Macrophages isolated from trauma patients show an impaired ability to present antigen, depression of interleukin-1 production,[20] and enhanced synthesis of prostaglandin E_2[21] and interleukin-6.[22] Extensive wounds may lead to systemic release of these latter macrophage products.[23] Interferon-γ restores some antigen-presenting capacity in vitro[24] and has recently been used in patients with what was considered to be a beneficial effect.[25] Interferon-γ may alleviate the T-cell immunosuppression seen in trauma patients.[25, 26] Neutrophil chemotaxis and adherence are also impaired,[27] and increased neutrophil oxidative burst activation is predictive of subsequent fulminant adult respiratory distress syndrome,[28] possibly mediated by tumor necrosis factor.[29]

Post-traumatic auto-oxidation may reduce neutrophil opsonic receptor expression, chemotaxis, and phagocytosis.[30] This phenomenon could increase the risks for infection, particularly nosocomial pneumonia.[30] Unfortunately, in no way can one predict a priori in whom the sequelae of post-traumatic auto-oxidation could be a problem. These data at least suggest a biologic rationale for exogenous antioxidant supplementation or for developing methods of increasing tissue oxygenation.

Massive neutrophil accumulations are found even in uninfected organs at autopsy.[31] Injured tissue activates complement[32] and serum complement levels are decreased after trauma, whereas the increase in activated complement products[33] correlates with injury severity and the continued presence of undrained abscesses or necrotic tissue.[34] Specific antibody production, particularly IgM, is decreased after blunt trauma[35] and is partially restored by the addition of normal T lymphocytes.[36] Prophylactic intravenous immune globulin given to high-risk surgical patients does not influence mortality or the incidence of shock.[37] Injured patients are frequently anergic[38]; however, debate regarding whether this predicts septic complications continues. Antithrombin III levels decrease initially after trauma and return to normal quickly in patients who suffer no infections. In patients in whom infections subsequently develop, levels stay abnormal. This factor may allow clinicians to predict high-risk patients.[39] Likewise elevated CD14 T-cell measurements may be used prognostically but not diagnostically for bacterial sepsis.[40]

Immune cellular abnormalities after trauma are reflected by cytokine dysregulation. Tumor necrosis factor,[41] interleukin-1,[42] and interleukin-6[43] levels are elevated, whereas serum interleukin-2[44] and interferon-γ[45] levels are reduced. Transfusion of allogeneic blood products, in addition to the risk of transfusion-associated viral infection, may disturb normal lymphocyte blastogenesis, suppress natural killer cell and serum opsonic activity, and alter T-cell subset ratios.[41, 46] However, the extent, if any, to which this immunosuppression contributes to infection remains uncertain. Finally, hypothermia is a common occurrence in almost all surgical patients and potentially more so in victims of trauma who may have been exposed to the elements. Except in cases where hypothermia is protective (cardiothoracic surgery and neurosurgery), every effort should be made to keep patients normothermic because of evidence that hypothermia can increase the incidence of coagulopathy and surgical infection.[47, 48]

SIGNS AND SYMPTOMS OF INFECTION

The usual signs and symptoms of infection lose much of their predictive value in a multiply traumatized patient. Fever, leukocytosis, and a hyperdynamic state are frequently present within hours of injury, but this condition rarely heralds an infection at this stage. These signs may persist beyond the first few days, however, and can be the result of noninfectious inflammation, massive hematoma, atelectasis, pulmonary contusion, deep venous thrombosis, drug or alcohol withdrawal, drug fever, hypovolemia, transfusion reactions, or heterotopic ossification. Diagnostic examination is hindered by patient immobility, pain, impaired mental status, paralysis, mechanical ventilators, monitors, cumbersome bandages, and orthopedic devices. Sending a critically ill, unstable patient for diagnostic radiologic or other studies is also problematic. Newer portable diagnostic equipment such as portable computed tomography scanners will certainly help in the management of critically injured patients. Retrospectively assessing which signs, symptoms, laboratory values, or radiologic findings are suggestive of infection is also hampered by the lack of a "gold standard" for diagnosis of many of the most important nosocomial infections. Although it may be relatively easy to determine the sites and identity of colonizing organisms, as with other nosocomial infections, the difficulty lies in determining where on the continuum from colonization to infection each culture result should be considered. At present, diagnosis of infection in a trauma patient depends on the clinician's ability to assimilate the information at hand into a cohesive assessment of the patient's likelihood of having a given infection. Injudicious use of antimicrobial agents may ultimately result in colonization by resistant organisms, both in the patient being considered and in others in the ICU.

CAUSATIVE ORGANISMS

The spectrum of microbial pathogens that cause nosocomial infection in trauma patients has changed over the past decade. Gram-negative facultative aerobes and staphylococcal species are the most common causes of post-traumatic infections. Recent data from the Shock Trauma Center of the University of Maryland Medical Systems indicate that 47% of infections in the trauma population were caused by gram-positive organisms led by *Staphylococcus aureus* (20%), 29% of which were methicillin resistant (6% of the total). Coagulase-negative *Staphylococcus* and *Enterococcus* species caused 10 and 8% of infections, respectively. Gram-negative organisms were found in 53% of the infections. *Haemophilus influenzae* caused 11% (all isolates were from the respiratory tract), followed by *P. aeruginosa* (9%), *Enterobacter* species (9%), and *E. coli* (6%) (E. S. Caplan, unpublished data). The use of broad-spectrum antimicrobial agents has resulted in the ascendance of antibiotic-resistant pathogens such as methicillin-resistant *S. aureus*, coagulase-negative staphylococci, and multiresistant Enterobacteriaceae and *Enterococcus* spp.[49, 50] Analysis of a national database compiled from 1980 to 1989 by the National Nosocomial Surveillance System demonstrates a declining proportion of gram-negative infections, but an increase in staphylococcal and fungal infections.[51] Of note, most of these studies have examined a mix of surgical and medical patients, but data from the Maryland Institute for Emergency Medical Services Systems (MIEMSS) suggest that fungal infections can be avoided with judicious antibiotic use.[6] Clinicians need to be alert to the possibility of human immunodeficiency virus type 1 (HIV-1) infection in trauma patients because the pathogen profile may be expanded. HIV-positive asymptomatic individuals may be at increased risk of wound infections at both open and closed fracture sites in comparison to non–HIV-infected controls.[52] However, other studies have shown no overall increased risk of infection in HIV-infected individuals with CD4 counts greater than 200.[53] One hypothesis is that the polyclonal B-cell activation and subsequent increase in immunoglobulin levels may compensate for the trauma-associated decrease in B-cell function and may actually confer some protection against common post-trauma infections. Conversely, patients who meet the Centers for Disease Control and Prevention definition of AIDS may be at increased risk for infection because this effect may not be as pronounced.[54]

Pneumonia

Table 309–1 delineates infections by site among trauma patients admitted to MIEMSS during two different periods (E. S. Caplan unpublished data).[6] Nosocomial pneumonia is a leading cause of morbidity and mortality in trauma patients. Estimates of incidence have ranged from 15% in a heterogeneous population of all patients admitted for traumatic injury[6] to 44% of those requiring intubation after injury.[55] Associated risks for pneumonia include head injury, chest trauma, immobilization, corticosteroid use, hypotension, and the need for emergency intubation on admission.[19, 56] Comatose patients are at particularly high risk, presumably because of aspiration, and one series documented a 42% incidence in this population.[57] One study demonstrated a pneumonia incidence of 27.8% in 180 mechanically ventilated trauma patients, with the incidence rising to 69% in those requiring 30 or more days of ventilatory support.[58] Pneumonia in an intubated trauma patient is probably both underdiagnosed and overdiagnosed because familiar signs and symptoms of pneumonia may be unreliable. Chest radiographs are poor predictors

TABLE 309–1 Infections by Site Occurring among 13,754 Multiply Traumatized Patients*

Site	Infections (%) (1977–1984)	Infections (%) (1995)
Primary bacteremia	8	12
Vascular line associated	14	11
Respiratory tract	29	32
Urinary tract	17	15
Central nervous system	4	2
Intra-abdominal	9	7
Surgical wound	12	13
Other	7	<8

*From November 1977 to December 1984 (10,308 patients) and 1995 (3446 patients) at the Maryland Institute for Emergency Medical Services Systems Shock Trauma Center (present name, RA Cowley Shock Trauma Center).

of autopsy-proven nosocomial pneumonia,[59] particularly in patients with thoracic trauma.[60] Pulmonary contusions, hemorrhage, emboli, aspiration, adult respiratory distress syndrome, atelectasis, and fluid overload can all mimic pulmonary infection, and these conditions predispose patients to the subsequent development of pneumonia. Cultures that grow pathogens may reflect colonization rather than actual infection. The diagnosis of pulmonary infection has always been difficult inasmuch as standardized criteria can be easily fulfilled by noninfectious problems. Bronchoalveolar lavage or protected brush specimens have been advocated to improve diagnosis and decrease inappropriate antibiotic use.[61] These procedures, however, probably do not decrease overall mortality.[62] Quantitative bronchoalveolar lavage has been shown to be able to differentiate between the systemic inflammatory response syndrome and nosocomial pneumonia.[63] Blood cultures are of no added diagnostic importance in the diagnosis of nosocomial pneumonia under most circumstances.[64] Many clinicians rely on compatible clinical findings (purulent sputum and changes in ventilatory function) combined with a positive Gram stain.

Management of these infections is similar to that of any nosocomial pneumonia. Some infiltrates represent atelectasis and mucus plugging, and in stable patients, the infiltrate may clear with chest physiotherapy and aggressive pulmonary toilet, occasionally supplemented by bronchoscopy. Pneumonias developing within the first several days are often the result of aspiration at the time of injury. *H. influenzae* is the most common cause of pneumonia in the first few days.[63, 65] Antibiotic-resistant *Streptococcus pneumoniae* has become an increasingly difficult problem, and infections with this organism can also develop in trauma patients early in their hospital stay.[66] Later in the hospitalization, gram-negative rods and *S. aureus* predominate, and the mortality rate for gram-negative pneumonias is considerably higher.[6] Examination of the Gram stain and results from previous cultures dictate the specific antibiotic regimen. Given that diagnosis and treatment of pneumonia are problematic, prevention, if possible, would be beneficial. The American Thoracic Society and the Centers for Disease Control and Prevention have published guidelines for the prevention of nosocomial pneumonia.[67, 68] In specific situations the following may decrease the incidence of hospital-associated pneumonia: influenza and pneumococcal vaccination, hand washing, careful manipulation of ventilator tubing, nutritional support, and subglottic secretion drainage. One attractive modality, selective decontamination of the digestive tract with oral and occasionally brief parenteral antibiotic regimens, is as yet an unproven intervention. A recent study in trauma patients showed a decrease in pneumonias but no change in days in the ICU or ventilator requirements and an increase in methicillin-resistant *Staphylococcus epidermidis* infections.[69] The effect on hospital flora when selective decontamination of the digestive tract is being used is not known, but one study suggests that the impact is minimal.[70] Use of agents that do not alter gastric pH lowers the incidence of pneumonia in ICU patients,[71] as confirmed in a recent meta-analysis,[72] although the applicability of this finding to trauma patients has been disputed.[73] Above all, early extubation is the most important factor in preventing pneumonia. Prolonging intubation for staff convenience (upcoming surgery, sedation, or excessive concern about aspiration risk) places the patient at an increasing cumulative risk for nosocomial pneumonia.[58]

Sinusitis

Sinusitis has recently been recognized as a source of cryptic fever in trauma patients, who are at particular risk because of the frequent presence of facial fractures, nasal packing, and nasotracheal and nasogastric tubes, coupled with depressed mental status and immobility in a supine position. Patients with hospital-acquired sinusitis will most often *not* have a purulent nasal discharge; thus diagnosis relies on clinical suspicion and radiologic studies.[74] Although computed tomographic scanning of the sinuses may be a more sensitive test, portable plain radiographs are often easier and safer to obtain. Removal and avoidance of nasogastric and nasotracheal tubes is suggested to avoid sinusitis and, in fact, may be curative.[74, 75] Antral puncture with irrigation is a relatively simple procedure that drains the infection and provides material for Gram stain and culture. Nosocomial sinusitis is most often polymicrobial, with gram-negative rods and *S. aureus* frequently involved; thus, Gram-stain results guide initial therapy.[74] Persistent signs of infection in a patient with head injury warrant investigation of the paranasal sinuses,[76] and sinusitis may be present concomitantly with pneumonia or tracheobronchitis.[77] The finding of otitis media is a marker for occult sinusitis in victims of head trauma.[78]

Central Nervous System Infection

Central nervous system (CNS) infection is surprisingly uncommon even in patients with head trauma and a cerebrospinal fluid (CSF) leak. Stillwell and Caplan found that only 4% of infections in trauma patients were in the CNS, most being meningitis (67%), ventriculitis (17%), or brain abscess (15%).[6] Those with a CSF leak and basilar skull fracture are at higher risk of infection.[79] Diagnosis is complicated by the fact that post-traumatic cerebral edema often precludes sampling of CSF, and empirical CNS coverage is mandated in the setting of head trauma, known or suspected dural tear, and fever without other apparent sources. *S. pneumoniae* and gram-negative rods constituted the most common pathogens in one series,[80] although empirical regimens must include antistaphylococcal coverage in patients with recent neurosurgical procedures or a documented CSF leak.[6]

Infection rates as high as 22% have been reported with ventriculostomy catheters, although epidural catheters are less frequently implicated.[6] Factors related to the development of infection include the duration of monitoring,[81–83] requirement for more than two monitors,[81] and irrigation of the drainage system.[82, 83] Routine catheter change does not appear to decrease the infection rate.[84] In few patients monitored for less than 72 hours does an infectious complication develop. Neither prophylactic antibiotics nor surveillance CSF cultures are useful in preventing or predicting infection.[81–83] Treatment consists of removal of the catheter and administration of antibiotics appropriate for the suspected pathogen and capable of CNS penetration.

Urinary Tract Infection

Urinary tract infections are the most frequent infections encountered in trauma patients. These infections are usually catheter associated, and the organisms isolated are nearly always gram-negative rods or *Enterococcus* spp.[6] Many of these infections are relatively benign, but 3% in the MIEMSS series resulted in bacteremia,[6] a figure in accord with that cited by Stamm.[85] Removing catheters or substituting condom or intermittent straight catheterization should be an early consideration in trauma patients. Because colonization and bacteriuria are common in these patients, pyuria and clinical symptoms are also required to secure the diagnosis. The importance of funguria without pyuria in a catheterized patient has yet to be determined,[86] and the optimal antifungal therapy, if any, is controversial.[87] Modification of predisposing factors such as broad-spectrum antibiotics, glucosuria, and urinary catheters may be as effective as specific treatment.

Catheter-Acquired Bacteremia

Intravascular lines, a major source of infectious complications in a multiply injured patient, were the leading cause of bacteremia in one series,[6] with *S. aureus* and coagulase-negative staphylococci being the most common blood isolates (E. S. Caplan, unpublished data). Intravascular line infections may be a particular problem in trauma patients because of emergency conditions during placement, proximity to wounds, and frequent manipulation of the catheter. Furthermore, replacing these devices is problematic in patients with extremity injuries. Although newer catheters coated with antimicrobial agents in an attempt to extend their "useful" lives are promising, most critically ill trauma patients have multiple noninfectious fevers prompting multiple workups for infections and multiple line changes that negate the potential benefits of these catheters.[88, 89] Vascular infections are discussed in Chapter 292.

Wound Infection

All traumatic wounds must be considered contaminated, and the need for tetanus prophylaxis should be assessed on admission. Considerable debris may be present within traumatic lacerations, and early, thorough irrigation, removal of foreign bodies, and débridement of devitalized tissue represent the most effective prophylaxis against infection. Many of the wounds encountered are too contaminated or complicated to undergo primary closure. Some authors have proposed quantitative wound cultures as a means of determining which wounds can be closed primarily,[90] but in the setting of emergency care such culturing has not been of practical use. Other risk factors for wound infection include shock, colon injury, and massive hemorrhage, and *S. aureus* and Enterobacteriaceae are the most commonly implicated organisms.[6, 91] Patients who deteriorate rapidly or who appear to be in a toxic state may have streptococcal or clostridial infections, and emergency débridement combined with parenteral antibiotics is indicated. Necrotizing fasciitis and clostridial myonecrosis are dreaded complications of trauma wounds.

Several unusual pathogens have been described in traumatic wound infections. *Aeromonas hydrophila* is capable of causing a rapidly progressive cellulitis or myositis after exposure to fresh or brackish water, sometimes within hours of injury.[92, 93] A similar manifestation caused by *V. vulnificus* has been seen after salt water injuries.[94] Inoculation of soil fungi of the class *zygomycetes* and *Aspergillus* spp. has been reported to cause aggressive and occasionally fatal wound infections.[95, 96] Standard culture and staining techniques may not identify these unusual infections.

Blunt and penetrating injuries often involve the abdomen. The distal end of the gastrointestinal tract, especially the colon, is home to extraordinarily high concentrations of bacteria. Spillage of these potential pathogens into the peritoneal cavity predisposes the patient to abscess formation, even with timely surgical repair. One large series retrospectively examined 2416 patients with penetrating trauma and found an overall abscess rate of 2.4%.[97] Knife wounds are less prone to result in abscess,[98] whereas blunt trauma severe enough to require laparotomy is associated with a considerably higher incidence (4.6%).[99] Colon injury, especially when combined with pancreatic, duodenal, or splenic injury, increases the incidence of abscess formation.[97–99] Drains or packs placed in patients with liver trauma may themselves lead to intra-abdominal abscess.[100] In the absence of splenic injury, advanced age, massive transfusion requirements, and severe extra-abdominal injuries, primary repair or anastomosis of colon injury is associated with a lower rate of infectious complications than is the traditional approach of colostomy and diversion of the fecal stream.[101] Trauma patients who received enteral instead of parenteral feeding postoperatively had reduced infectious complications.[102] Gross peritoneal contamination, when combined with delayed operative repair, may require a course of treatment beyond the usual antibiotic prophylaxis.

Computed tomography has emerged as the most sensitive test for detection of an intra-abdominal abscess, with some series reporting sensitivities of 95% or more.[103] Although less sensitive, ultrasonography can be performed rapidly and safely at the bedside. Radionuclide imaging is reserved for workups in which an occult abscess is suspected but not visualized by computed tomography or ultrasonography. Open surgical drainage of identified abscesses has, in many cases, been supplanted by radiographically guided percutaneous catheter drainage, which has a similar success rate with less morbidity.[104, 105] Multiple, loculated, or fungal abscesses are primarily managed with operative drainage. Most infections are polymicrobial, and coverage of anaerobes, gram-negative facultative aerobes, and *S. aureus* is recommended.

Acute acalculous cholecystitis is another recognized entity that may be manifested in trauma patients as cryptic fever.[106] Recognized factors predisposing patients to this rare, but lethal complication are usually noninfectious and include visceral hypoperfusion, mechanical ventilation with positive end-expiratory pressure, and biliary stasis, as seen with narcotic or total parenteral nutrition administration. Clinical signs may be absent or misleading, and liver function tests may be nonspecifically elevated or normal. Diagnosis depends on clinical suspicion and computed tomography or ultrasonography.[107, 108] Antibiotics are recommended pending results from intraoperative cultures.

Splenic trauma necessitating splenectomy has been an area of particular concern,[109] although the risk of postsplenectomy sepsis appears to be lower than that seen in patients splenectomized for other reasons.[110] In the postoperative period, patients undergoing splenectomy necessitated by trauma had a reduced ability to mount an immunoglobulin response to infection.[111, 112] Splenic salvage is now deemed desirable whenever possible, and infectious complications are actually reduced in patients with both spleen and colon trauma when the spleen is repaired rather than removed.[113] Patients undergoing total or nearly total splenectomy should receive pneumococcal vaccination in the postoperative period because their immune response to the vaccine is not impaired.[114] Most patients are unaware of the increased risk for certain infections that they face after splenectomy or even that they have received vaccines.[115] Fortunately, pneumococcal revaccination appears to be safe and can increase antibody titers. Whether routine periodic revaccination in trauma patients needs to be done is unknown.[115] Although prophylactic antibiotics have been advocated by some, the relatively low risk of postsplenectomy sepsis in trauma patients suggests that this measure is unwarranted. No current recommendations exist regarding the use of vaccines for *Neisseria meningitidis* or *H. influenzae*. A transient, but at times impressive leukocytosis is commonly observed after splenectomy, and deciding whether occult infection is present in this setting can be problematic.

Sepsis

Critically injured patients often meet the criteria for sepsis syndrome,[116] and infection is one common cause. It has been recognized that an identical clinical picture can be seen in the absence of an identifiable source of infection. Distinguishing infection from the hyperdynamic, hyperadrenergic state often seen in injured patients requires attention to detail combined with clinical judgment. One of the most difficult decisions in treating victims of trauma is differentiating sepsis from other causes of the systemic inflammatory response syndrome. A variety of researchers have attempted to assay lipopolysaccharide and tumor necrosis factor monocyte responses in vitro that may help clinicians more accurately diagnose sepsis and treat their patients.[117] These assays are still experimental.

Signs of infection may include worsening respiratory failure and acidosis, glucose intolerance, renal failure, thrombocytopenia, a rising lactate dehydrogenase, bilirubin, or alkaline phosphatase concentration, and leukocytosis with a shift to immature forms. A change in the level of consciousness may be the only sign of serious infection in an elderly or brain-injured patient. Taken individually, any one marker may have relatively little value; however, when examined in the aggregate, trends in these measurements often prove helpful. Any patient who "falls off the curve" of normal recovery must be carefully evaluated for occult infection, the signs of which may be remarkably subtle. Signs of infection may be mimicked by a normal, previously healthy person's response to severe injury because inflammatory mediators are released by injured, yet uninfected tissue.[118] Conversely, therapeutic interventions such as corticosteroids, anesthesia, transfusion products, and paralytic agents blunt the host reaction to infection. Hypotension may be caused by hypovolemia and, if caused by infection, may be disguised by the administration of vasoactive amines.

Hemodynamic instability in the absence of hypovolemia mandates consideration of empirical antibiotic therapy, even in the absence of other signs of infection. Empirical regimens should combine an antistaphylococcal agent with broad gram-negative coverage. When intra-abdominal injury is present, anaerobic coverage should be included. Significant head injury warrants the use of both an antistaphylococcal and an antipseudomonal agent with adequate CNS penetration. Recent MIEMSS data (1995–1997) reveal that 350 bacteremias occurred over a 3-year period, with 69% caused by gram-positive organisms and 30% caused by gram-negative organisms. Of the gram-positive organisms, 33% were coagulase-negative staphylococci, 18% were *S. aureus* (13% of all the *S. aureus* isolates were oxacillin resistant), and 12% were *Enterococcus* spp. *Enterobacter* spp. and *P. aeruginosa* accounted for 26 and 14% of gram-negative bacteremias, respectively. Only 11 episodes of fungemia were seen in this 3-year period (E. S. Caplan, R. P. Rabinowitz, unpublished data).

Long-term residents of the ICU may have previously been colonized with an unusual or multiresistant pathogen, and the empirical regimen should be appropriately customized to cover these organisms. Many physicians advocate routine surveillance cultures for this reason.[119, 120] Even in settings in which routine surveillance cultures are not collected formally, culture results from previous fever workups often provide a microbial colonization profile that proves useful if an indication for empirical antibiotics should arise. If the patient responds favorably to antibiotics but no source of infection can be identified, an antibiotic course of at least 1 week is suggested. In the event that no source is identified, no new culture result is diagnostic, and the patient has not responded, an abbreviated course is recommended. The need for empirical antibiotic therapy mandates an aggressive search for infection inasmuch as drainage of a closed-space infection or débridement of necrotic tissue remains the most important therapeutic intervention for these patients. Other causes for treatment failure must also be examined, such as inadequate or inappropriate antibiotics, failure to remove infected intravascular lines, poor antibiotic penetration into potentially infected areas, or absence of infection.

The concept of sepsis as a syndrome at least partially driven by the host response has resulted in the notion of "culture-negative sepsis." Many authors suggest that the gastrointestinal tract may be the source of this inflammatory stimulus, even in the absence of detectable bacteremia. Bacterial translocation to mesenteric lymph nodes has been shown to occur after experimental hemorrhagic shock in rats[121, 122] and after intestinal obstruction in humans, although patients in whom such translocation was demonstrated were not clinically infected.[123] Bacterial translocation may represent an antigen-sampling function of normal gut lymphoid tissue that leads to infection in a traumatized or immunocompromised host.[124] Translocation is an accepted phenomenon, but its clinical significance remains unproven.

PREVENTION OF INFECTION

Although widely used, antibiotic prophylaxis given on admission in the hope of averting infection is of proven value in only certain specific situations.[125, 126] Use of perioperative antibiotics as prophylaxis against infection in a patient with abdominal trauma and a suspected ruptured hollow viscus is widely accepted.[125–127] In a sense, this practice is actually an adjunct to surgical drainage and repair, and peritoneal soilage at the time of injury means that a potential infective process is already under way. Antibiotic regimens should be directed toward normal fecal flora, including both anaerobes and the *Enterobacteriaceae*. The rising incidence of enterococcal and staphylococcal infections has led to concern that standard regimens fail to control these organisms; however, their role in intra-abdominal infection is as yet unclear. The optimal duration of treatment is also undetermined; most authors advocate 1 to 3 days of parenteral antibiotics once disruption of a hollow viscus has been demonstrated.[125–128] Patients with open fractures are routinely given antibiotic prophylaxis.[125] A 24-hour course of antistaphylococcal therapy was as efficacious as the traditional 3- to 5-day regimen.[129] Local factors such as severity and location of the open fracture and the type of fixation used may be more important than antibiotics.[130] Some orthopedic surgeons advocate the use of antibiotic-impregnated beads,[131, 132] although prospective, randomized studies are lacking. Antibiotic prophylaxis for facial fractures may also be of benefit. Cefazolin, 1 g intravenously 1 hour before surgery and again 8 hours later, reduced the incidence of infectious complications, but only in those with mandibular or compound fractures.[133] Others advocate the use of penicillin when intraoral contamination has occurred.[6, 127] A recent meta-analysis suggests that prophylactic antibiotics in patients with basilar skull fracture are not efficacious, although a prospective controlled study of this issue has never been published.[134] Vaccines against surface polysaccharides of gram-negative bacilli have been formulated and been shown to be antigenic in victims of trauma. These vaccines could have future implications in the prevention of infections in trauma patients.[135]

PROTECTION OF HEALTH CARE PERSONNEL

Protection of personnel who care for trauma patients is an important part of infectious disease practice. The incidence of HIV-1 infection continues to rise, and the seroprevalence of HIV-1 in trauma patients reflects the infection rate in the surrounding community.[136] However, the overall incidence of HIV infection and hepatitis B surface antigen–positive patients seen in urban emergency rooms is 3 to 4% each. These numbers are significantly higher than those in the general population and may be attributable to urban drug-related violence.[137–139]

Standard precautions, although adequate to reduce transmission risk in most instances, may need to be supplemented by protective eyewear, aprons, and leg coverings in an admitting area where emergency surgery is commonplace. Caregiver compliance with universal precautions may substantially increase with improved access to barrier devices and education.[140] Anyone involved in the care of trauma patients should receive hepatitis B vaccination.

GENERAL MANAGEMENT OF INFECTION IN TRAUMA PATIENTS

Victims of multiple trauma, because of the nature of their injuries and resuscitation efforts, are subjected to multiple intravascular lines and other invasive instrumentation. Careful attention to indwelling devices, surgical wounds, and the respiratory system is particularly important when investigating the possibility of infection. Empirical antibiotic choices should be based not only on the site of infection and Gram stain but also on previous culture results. Trauma patients are often young and previously healthy, and the antibiotic volume of distribution in these patients may be surprisingly large and necessitate supranormal doses and careful attention to serum levels.[141, 142] As stated earlier, trauma patients have many noninfectious causes for fever, and judicious use of short courses of antibiotics helps avoid future problems with multiresistant organisms. Finally, we advocate monitoring of all victims of multiple trauma requiring ICU care on a prospective basis so that the infectious disease practitioner can have the opportunity to note subtle changes in clinical status suggestive of infection and avoid the use of antibiotics in patients febrile for other reasons.

REFERENCES

1. Harlan LC, Harlan WR, Parsons PE. The economic impact of injuries: A major source of medical costs. Am J Public Health. 1990;80:453–459.

2. Rice DP, MacKenzie EJ, et al. Cost of Injury in the United States: A Report to Congress. San Francisco: Institute for Health & Aging, University of California, and Injury Prevention Center, The Johns Hopkins University; 1989.
3. Baker CC, Oppenheimer L, Stephens B, et al. Epidemiology of trauma deaths. Am J Surg. 1980;140:144–150.
4. Goris RJA, Draaisma J. Causes of death after blunt trauma. J Trauma. 1982;22:141–146.
5. Allgower M, Durig M, Wolff G. Infection and trauma. Surg Clin North Am. 1980;60:133–144.
6. Stillwell M, Caplan ES. The septic multiple-trauma patient. Infect Dis Clin North Am. 1989;3:155–183.
7. Northey D, Adess M, Hartsuck J, et al. Microbial surveillance in a surgical intensive care unit. Surg Gynecol Obstet. 1974;139:321–325.
8. Wenzel RP, Osterman CA, Hunting KJ. Hospital-acquired infections: II. Infection rates by site, service, and common procedures in a university hospital. Am J Epidemiol. 1976;104:645–651.
9. Polk HC, Fry D, Flint LM. Dissemination and causes of infection. Surg Clin North Am. 1976;56:817–829.
10. Moore FA, Moore EE, Kudsk KA, et al. Clinical results of an immune-enhancing diet for early postinjury enteral feeding. J Trauma. 1994;37:607–615.
11. Brown RO, Hunt H, Mowatt-Larssen CA, et al. Comparison of specialized and standard enteral formulas in trauma patients. Pharmacotherapy. 1994;14:314–320.
12. Bower RH, Cerra FB, Bershadsky B, et al. Early enteral administration of a formula (Impact) supplemented with arginine, nucleotides, and fish oil in intensive care unit patients: Results of a multicenter, prospective, randomized, clinical trial. Crit Care Med. 1995;23:436–449.
13. Heyland DK, Cook DJ, Guyuatt GH. Does the formulation of enteral feeding products influence infectious morbidity and mortality rates in the critically ill patient? A critical review of the evidence. Crit Care Med. 1994;22:1192–1202.
14. Gianotti L, Alexander JW, Gennari R, et al. Oral glutamine decreased bacterial translocation and improves survival in experimental gut-origin sepsis. JPEN J Parenter Enteral Nutr. 1995;19:69–74.
15. Langdale LA. Infectious complications of blood transfusions. Infect Dis Clin North Am. 1992;6:731–744.
16. Brown RB. Serum iron and infection. Infect Dis Pract. 1994;18:49–56.
17. Ward CG, Bullen JJ, Rogers HJ. Iron and infection: New developments and their implications. J Trauma. 1996;41:356–364.
18. Donghui SU, Roth RI, Yoshida M, et al. Hemogloblin increases mortality from bacterial endotoxin. Infect Immun. 1997;65:1258–1266.
19. Bracken MB, Shepard MJ, Holford TR, et al. Administration of methyprednisolone for 24 or 48 hours or tirilazad mesylate for 48 hours in the treatment of acute spinal injury. JAMA. 1997;277:1597–1604.
20. Rodrick ML, Wood JJ, O'Mahoney JB, et al. Mechanisms of immunosuppression associated with severe nonthermal traumatic injuries in man: Production of interleukin-1 and 2. J Clin Immunol. 1986;6:310–318.
21. Faist E, Mewes A, Strasser T, et al. Alteration of monocyte function following major injury. Arch Surg. 1988;123:287–292.
22. Szabo G, Kodys K, Miller-Graziano CL. Elevated monocyte interleukin-6 (IL-6) production in immunosuppressed trauma patients. II. Downregulation by IL-4. J Clin Immunol. 1991;11:336–344.
23. Border JR. Hypothesis: Sepsis, multiple systems organ failure, and the macrophage. Arch Surg. 1988;123:285–286.
24. Redmond HP, Hofmann K, Shou J, et al. Effects of laparotomy on systemic macrophage function. Surgery. 1992;111:647–655.
25. Dries DJ. Interferon gamma in trauma-related infections. Intensive Care Med. 1996;22(Suppl):S462–S467.
26. Murray HW. Current and future clinical applications of interferon-gamma in host antimicrobial defense. Intensive Care Med. 1996;22(Suppl):S456–S461.
27. Maderazo EG, Woronick CL, Albana SD, et al. Inappropriate activation, deactivation, and probable autooxidative damage as a mechanism of neutrophil locomotory defect in trauma. J Infect Dis. 1986;154:471–477.
28. Rivkind AL, Seigel JH, Guadalupi P, et al. Sequential patterns of eicosanoid, platelet, and neutrophil interactions in the evolution of the fulminant post-traumatic adult respiratory distress syndrome. Ann Surg. 1989;210:355–373.
29. Tanaka H, Ogura H, Yokota J, et al. Acceleration of superoxide production from leukocytes in trauma patients. Ann Surg. 1991;214:187–192.
30. Simms HH, D'Amico R. Posttraumatic auto-oxidative polymorphonuclear neutrophil receptor injury predicts the development of noscocomial infection. Arch Surg. 1997;132:171–177.
31. Nuytinck HK, Offermans XJ, Kubat K, et al. Whole-body inflammation in trauma patients: An autopsy study. Arch Surg. 1988;123:1519–1524.
32. Heideman M, Saravis C, Clowes GHA. Effect of non-viable tissue and abscesses on complement depletion and the development of bacteremia. J Trauma. 1982;22:527–532.
33. Maderazo EG, Moore M, Woronick CL. Characterization of the regulation of complement-derived chemotactic factors in blunt trauma. J Infect Dis. 1988;157:364–367.
34. Kapur MM, Jain P, Gidh M. The effect of trauma on serum C3 activation and its correlation with injury severity score in man. J Trauma. 1986;26:464–466.
35. Faist E, Ertel W, Baker C, et al. Terminal B-cell maturation and immunoglobulin (Ig) synthesis in vitro in patients with major injury. J Trauma. 1989;29:2–9.
McRitchie DI, Girotti MJ, Rotstein OD, et al. Impaired antibody production in nt trauma: Possible role for T cell dysfunction. Arch Surg. 1990;125:91–96.
enous Immunoglobulin Collaborative Study Group. Prophylactic intravenous tration of standard immune globulin as compared with core lipopolysaccharide immune globulin in patients at high risk of postsurgical infection. N Engl J Med. 1992;327:234–240.
38. Hershman MJ, Cheadle WG, Appel SH, et al. Comparison of antibody response with delayed hypersensitivity in severely injured patients. Arch Surg. 1989;124:339–341.
39. Wilson RF, Mammen EF, Tyburski JG, et al. Antithrombin levels related to infections and outcome. J Trauma. 1996;40:384–387.
40. Burgmann H, Winkler S, Locker GJ, et al. Increased serum concentration of soluble CD14 is a prognostic marker in gram-positive sepsis. Clin Immun Immunopathol. 1996;80:307–310.
41. Chaudry IH, Ayala A, Ertel W, et al. Hemorrhage and resuscitation: Immunologic aspects. Am J Physiol. 1990;259:R663–R674.
42. Ertel W, Faist E, Nestle C, et al. Kinetics of interleukin-2 and interleukin-6 synthesis following major mechanical trauma. J Surg Res. 1990;48:622–628.
43. Kaplan E, Dinarello CA, Gelfand JA. Interleukin-1 and the response to injury. Immunol Res. 1989;8:118–129.
44. Abraham E, Regan R. The effects of hemorrhage and trauma on interleukin-2 production. Arch Surg. 1985;120:1341–1344.
45. Livingston DH, Appel SH, Wellhausen SR, et al. Depressed interferon gamma production and monocyte HLA-DR expression after severe injury. Arch Surg. 1988;123:1309–1312.
46. Agarwal N, Murphy JG, Cayten CG, et al. Blood transfusion increases the risk of infection after trauma. Arch Surg. 1993;128:171–177.
47. Kurz A, Sesslerl DI, Lenhardt R. Perioperative normothermia to reduce the incidence of surgical-wound infection and shorten hospitalization. N Engl J Med. 1996;334:1209–1215.
48. Sessler DI. Mild perioperative hypothermia. N Engl J Med. 1997;336:1730–1737.
49. Nathens AB, Chu PTY, Marshall JC. Nosocomial infection in the surgical intensive care unit. Infect Dis Clin North Am. 1992;6:657–675.
50. Donowitz LG, Wenzel RP, Hoyt JW. High risk of hospital-acquired infection in the ICU. Crit Care Med. 1982;10:355–357.
51. National nosocomial infections surveillance (NNIS) report, data summary from October 1986–April 1997, issued May 1977. A report from the NNIS system. Am J Infect Control. 1997;25:477–487.
52. Paiement GD, Hymes RA, LaDouceur MS, et al. Postoperative infections in asymptomatic HIV-seropositive orthopedic trauma patients. J Trauma. 1994;37:545–551.
53. Guth AA, Hofsetttner SR, Patcher HL. Human immunodeficiency virus and the trauma patient: Factors influencing postoperative infectious complications. J Trauma. 1996;41:251–256.
54. Weber DJ, Becherer PR, Rutala WA, et al. Nosocomial infection as a function of human immunodeficiency virus type 1 status in hemophiliacs. Am J Med. 1991;91(Suppl):S206–S212.
55. Antonelli M, Moro ML, Capelli O, et al. Risk factors for early onset pneumonia in trauma patients. Chest. 1994;105:224–228.
56. Rodriguez JL, Gibbons KJ, Bitzer LG, et al. Pneumonia: Incidence, risk factors, and outcome in injured patients. J Trauma. 1991;31:907–914.
57. Rello J, Ausina V, Castella J, et al. Nosocomial respiratory tract infections in multiple trauma patients: Influence of level of consciousness with implications for therapy. Chest. 1992;102:525–529.
58. Langer M, Mosconi P, Cigada M, et al. Long-term respiratory support and risk of pneumonia in critically ill patients. Am Rev Respir Dis. 1989;140:302–305.
59. Wunderink RG, Woldenberg LS, Zeiss J, et al. The radiologic diagnosis of autopsy-proven ventilator-associated pneumonia. Chest. 1992;101:458–463.
60. Andrews CP, Coalson JJ, Smith JD, et al. Diagnosis of nosocomial bacterial pneumonia in acute, diffuse lung injury. Chest. 1981;80:254–258.
61. Baker AM, Meredith W, Hapoink EF. Pneumonia in intubated trauma patients. Am J Respir Crit Care Med. 1996;153:343–349.
62. Bregon F, Papazian L, Viconti A, et al. Relationship of microbiologic diagnostic criteria to morbidity and mortality in patients with ventilator-associated pneumonia. JAMA. 1997;227:655–662.
63. Croce MA, Fabian TC, Schurr MJ, et al. Using bronchoalveolar lavage to distinguish nosocomial pneumonia from systemic inflammatory response syndrome: A prospective analysis. J Trauma Injury. 1995;39:1134–1140.
64. Chensdrasekhar A. Are routine blood cultures effective in the evaluation of patients clinically diagnosed to have nosocomial pneumonia? Am Surg. 1996;62:373–376.
65. Spain DA, Wilson MA, Bozas PW, et al. *Haemophilus* pneumonia is a common cause of early pulmonary dysfunction following trauma. Arch Surg. 1995;130:1228–1232.
66. Campbell GD, Silberman R. Drug-resistant *Streptococcus pneumoniae*. Clin Infect Dis. 1998;26:1188–1195.
67. Campbell GD, Niederman MS, American Thoracic Society. Hospital-acquired pneumonia in adults: Diagnosis, assessment of severity, initial antimicrobial therapy, and preventative strategies. A consensus statement. Am J Respir Crit Care Med. 1995;153:1711–1725.
68. Centers for Disease Control and Prevention. Guidelines for prevention of nosocomial pneumonia. MMWR Morb Mortal Wkly Rep. 1997;46:1–79.
69. Quinio B, Albanese J, Charbit M, et al. Selective decontamination of the digestive tract in multiple trauma patients. Chest. 1996;109:765.
70. Hammond JMJ, Potgieter PD. Long-term effects of selective decontamination on antimicrobial resistance. Crit Care Med. 1995;23:637–645.
71. Craven DE, Kunches LM, Kilinsky V, et al. Risk factors for pneumonia and fatality in patients receiving continuous mechanical ventilation. Am Rev Respir Dis. 1986;133:792–796.

72. Cook DJ, Laine LA, Guyat GH, et al. Nosocomial pneumonia and the role of gastric pH: A meta-analysis. Chest. 1991;100:7–13.
73. Simms HH, DeMaria E, McDonald L, et al. Role of gastric colonization in the development of pneumonia in critically ill trauma patients: Results of a prospective randomized trial. J Trauma. 1991;31:531–537.
74. Caplan ES, Hoyt NJ. Nosocomial sinusitis. JAMA. 1982;247:639–641.
75. Bach A, Boehrer H, Schmidt H, et al. Nosocomial sinusitis in ventilated patients. Nasotracheal versus orotracheal intubation. Anaesthesia. 1992;47:335–338.
76. Kulber DA, Santora TA, Shabot MM, et al. Early diagnosis and treatment of sinusitis in the critically ill trauma patient. Am Surg. 1991;57:775–779.
77. Humphrey MA, Simpson GT, Grindlinger GA. Clinical characteristics of nosocomial sinusitis. Ann Otol Rhinol Laryngol. 1987;96:687–690.
78. Christensen L, Schaffer S, Ross SE. Otitis media in adult trauma patients: Incidence and clinical significance. J Trauma. 1991;31:1543–1545.
79. Applebaum E. Meningitis following trauma to the head and face. JAMA. 1960;173:1818–1822.
80. Hand W, Sanford J. Posttraumatic bacterial meningitis. Ann Intern Med. 1970;72:869–874.
81. Clark WC, Muhlbauer MS, Lowrey R, et al. Complications of intracranial pressure monitoring in trauma patients. Neurosurgery. 1989;25:20–24.
82. Mayhall CG, Archer NH, Lamb VA, et al. Ventriculostomy-related infections: A prospective epidemiologic study. N Engl J Med. 1984;310:553–559.
83. Aucoin PJ, Kotilainen HR, Gantz NM, et al. Intracranial pressure monitors: Epidemiologic study of risk factors and infections. Am J Med. 1986;80:369–376.
84. Holloway KL, Barnes T, Choi S, et al. Ventriculostomy infections: The effect of monitoring duration and catheter exchange in 584 patients. J Neurosurg. 1996;85:419–424.
85. Stamm WE. Catheter-associated urinary tract infections: Epidemiology, pathogenesis, and prevention. Am J Med. 1991;91(Suppl):S65–S70.
86. Wong-Beringer A, Jacobs RA, Gugliemo BJ. Treatment of funguria. JAMA. 1992;267:2780–2785.
87. Sanford JP. The enigma of candiduria: Evolution of bladder irrigation with amphotericin B for management from anecdote to dogma and a lesson from Machiavelli. Clin Infect Dis. 1993;16:145–147.
88. Raad IS, Darouiche R, Dupuis J, et al. Central venous catheters coated with minocycline and rifampin for the prevention of catheter-related colonization and bloodstream infections. A randomized double-blind trial. Ann Intern Med. 1997;127:267–274.
89. Marr KA, Sexton DJ, Conlon PJ, et al. Catheter-related bacteremia and outcome of attempted catheter salvage in patients undergoing hemodialysis. Ann Intern Med. 1997;127:275–280.
90. Krizek TJ, Robson MC. Evolution of quantitative bacteriology in wound management. Am J Surg. 1975;130:579–584.
91. Fildes J, Bannon MP, Barret J. Soft-tissue infections after trauma. Surg Clin North Am. 1991;71:371–384.
92. Semel JD, Trenholme G. *Aeromonas hydrophila* water-associated traumatic wound infections: A review. J Trauma. 1990;30:324–327.
93. Gold WL, Salit IE. *Aeromonas hydrophila* infections of skin and soft tissue: Report of 11 cases and review. Clin Infect Dis. 1993;16:69–73.
94. Tacket CO, Brenner F, Blake PA. Clinical features and an epidemiologic study of *Vibrio vulnificus* infections. J Infect Dis. 1984;149:558–561.
95. Vainrub B, Macareno A, Mandel S, et al. Wound zygomycosis (mucormycosis) in otherwise healthy adults. Am J Med. 1988;84:546–548.
96. Cone JB, Bradsher R, Golladay S. Atypical surgical infections. Am J Surg. 1988;156:522–523.
97. Gibson DM, Feliciano DV, Mattox KL, et al. Intraabdominal abscess after penetrating abdominal trauma. Am J Surg. 1981;142:699–703.
98. Ivatory RR, Zubowski R, Psarras P, et al. Intraabdominal abscess after penetrating abdominal trauma. J Trauma. 1988;28:1238–1243.
99. Goins WA, Rodriguez A, Joshi M, et al. Intra-abdominal abscess after blunt abdominal trauma. Ann Surg. 1990;212:60–65.
100. Noyes LD, Doyle DJ, McSwain NE. Septic complications associated with the use of peritoneal drains in liver trauma. J Trauma. 1988;28:337–346.
101. Dawes LG, Aprahamian C, Condon RE, et al. The risk of infection after colon injury. Surgery. 1986;100:796–803.
102. Kudsk KA, Croce MA, Fabian TC, et al. Enteral versus parenteral feeding: Effects of septic morbidity after blunt and penetrating abdominal trauma. Ann Surg. 1992;215:503–513.
103. Gerzof SG, Oates ME. Imaging techniques for infections in the surgical patient. Surg Clin North Am. 1988;68:147–165.
104. Lambiase RE, Deyoe L, Cronan JJ, et al. Percutaneous drainage of 335 consecutive abscesses: Results of primary drainage with 1-year follow-up. Radiology. 1992;184:167–179.
105. Pruett TL, Simmons RL. Status of percutaneous catheter drainage of abscesses. Surg Clin North Am. 1988;68:89–105.
106. DuPriest RW Jr, Khaneja SC, Cowley RA. Acute cholecystitis complicating trauma. Ann Surg. 1979;189:84–89.
107. Frazee RC, Nagorney DM, Mucha P. Acute acalculous cholecystitis. Mayo Clin Proc. 1989;64:163–167.
108. Cornwell EE, Rodriguez A, Mirvis SE, et al. Acute acalculous cholecystitis in critically injured patients. Ann Surg. 1989;210:52–55.
109. Sekikawa T, Shatney CH. Septic sequelae after splenectomy for trauma in adults. Am J Surg. 1983;145:667–672.
110. Cullingford GL, Watkins DN, Watts AD, et al. Severe late postsplenectomy infection. Br J Surg. 1991;78:716–721.
111. Blackwood JM, Hurd T, Suval W, et al. Intra-abdominal infection following combined spleen-colon trauma. Am Surg. 1988;54:212–214.
112. Carroll A. Decision-making in splenectomy. Br J Hosp Med. 1995;54:147–149.
113. O'Sullivan ST, Reardon CM, O'Donnell JA, et al. How safe is splenectomy? Ir J Med Sci. 1994;163:374–378.
114. Caplan ES, Boltansky H, Snyder MJ, et al. Response of traumatized splenectomized patients to immediate vaccination with polyvalent pneumococcal vaccine. J Trauma. 1983;23:801–805.
115. Rutherford EJ, Livengood J, Higginbotham M, et al. Efficacy and safety of pneumococcal revaccination after splenectomy for trauma. J Trauma. 1995;39:448–452.
116. Bone RC. The pathogenesis of sepsis. Ann Intern Med. 1991;115:457–469.
117. Wilson CS, Seatter SC, Rodriquez, et al. In vivo tolerance: Impaired LPS-stimulated TNF release of monocytes from patients with sepsis, but not SIRS. J Surg Res. 1997;69:101–106.
118. Waydhas C, Nast-Kolb D, Jochum M, et al. Inflammatory mediators, infection, sepsis, and multiple organ failure after severe trauma. Arch Surg. 1992;127:460–467.
119. Caplan ES, Hoyt N. Infection surveillance and control in the severely traumatized patient. Am J Med. 1981;70:638–640.
120. Penin GB, Ehrenkranz NJ. Priorities of surveillance and cost-effective control of postoperative infection. Arch Surg. 1988;123:1305–1308.
121. Baker JW, Deitch EA, Berg RD, et al. Hemorrhagic shock induces bacterial translocation from the gut. J Trauma. 1988;28:896–906.
122. Sori AJ, Rush BF, Lysz TW, et al. The gut as source of sepsis after hemorrhagic shock. Am J Surg. 1988;155:187–191.
123. Deitch EA. Simple intestinal obstruction causes bacterial translocation in man. Arch Surg. 1989;124:699–701.
124. Wells CL, Maddaus MA, Simmons RL. Proposed mechanisms for the translocation of intestinal bacteria. Rev Infect Dis. 1988;10:958–979.
125. Dellinger EP. Antibiotic prophylaxis in trauma: Penetrating abdominal injuries and open fractures. Rev Infect Dis. 1991;13(Suppl):S847–S857.
126. Page CP, Bohnen JM, Fletcher R, et al. Antimicrobial prophylaxis for surgical wounds. Arch Surg. 1993;128:79–88.
127. Malangoni MA, Jacobs DG. Antibiotic prophylaxis for injured patients. Infect Dis Clin North Am. 1992;6:627–642.
128. Fabian TC, Patton JH. Infections associated with penetrating intra-abdominal trauma. Oscher Clin Rep. 1996;8(4):1–8.
129. Dellinger EP, Caplan ES, Weaver LD, et al. Duration of preventive antibiotic administration for open extremity fractures. Arch Surg. 1988;123:333–339.
130. Dellinger EP, Miller SD, Wertz MJ, et al. Risk of infection after open fracture of the arm or leg. Arch Surg. 1988;123:1320–1327.
131. Henry SL, Ostermann PAW, Seligson D. The prophylactic use of antibiotic impregnated beads in open fractures. J Trauma. 1990;30:1231–1238.
132. Wininger DA, Fass RJ. Antibiotic-impregnated cement and beads for orthopaedic infections. Antimicrob Agents Chemother. 1996;40:2675–2679.
133. Chole RA, Yee J. Antibiotic prophylaxis for facial fractures: A prospective, randomized clinical trial. Arch Otolaryngol Head Neck Surg. 1987;113:1055–1057.
134. Rathore MH. Do prophylactic antibiotics prevent meningitis after basilar skull fractures? Pediatr Infect Dis J. 1991;10:87–88.
135. Campbell WN, Hendrix E, Cryz S, et al. Immunogenicity of a 24-valent klebsiella capsular polysaccharide vaccine and an eight-valent pseudomonas *o*-polysaccharide conjugate vaccine administered to victims of acute trauma. Clin Infect Dis. 1996;23:179–181.
136. Soderstom CA, Furth PA, Glasser D, et al. HIV infection rates in a trauma center treating predominantly rural blunt trauma victims. J Trauma. 1989;29:1526–1530.
137. Caplan ES, Preas MA, Kerns T, et al. Seroprevalence of human immunodeficiency virus, hepatitis B virus, hepatitis C virus, and rapid plasma reagin in a trauma population. J Trauma. 1995;39:533–538.
138. Sloan EP, McGill BA, Zalenski R, et al. Human immunodeficiency virus and hepatitis B virus seroprevalance in an urban trauma population. J Trauma. 1995;38:736–741.
139. Nagachinta T, Gold CR, Cheng F, et al. Unrecognized HIV-1 infection in innercity hospital emergency department patients. Infect Control Hosp Epidemiol. 1996;174–177.
140. Hammond JS, Eckes JM, Gomez GA, et al. HIV, trauma, and infection control: Universal precautions are universally ignored. J Trauma. 1990;30:555–561.
141. Ericcson CD, Fischer RP, Rowlands BJ, et al. Prophylactic antibiotics in trauma: The hazards of underdosing. J Trauma. 1989;29:1356–1361.
142. Reed RL, Ericcson CD, Wu A, et al. The pharmacodynamics of prophylactic antibiotics in trauma. J Trauma. 1992;32:21–27.

Chapter 310

Burns

ROGER W. YURT

The disruption of homeostasis associated with severe burn injury exceeds that of any other injury or disease. Since the advent of aggressive early resuscitation measures, mortality in the acute phase after injury is rare.[1, 2] However, the mortality rate after burns over more than 40% of the body surface area (BSA), which is primarily attributed to infection, continues to be high. Because the risk of infection relates directly to the extent of injury, the initial therapeutic approach is oriented toward limiting the progression of the injury by stabilizing the patient and maintaining blood flow to the wound. The development and progression of the burn wound is well characterized as a dynamic process in which there are irreversible changes in the zone of coagulative necrosis and potentially reversible changes for as long as 3 days in the zones of stasis and hyperemia.[3, 4] Because methods of manipulating the inflammatory response that may mediate progression of the injury are not yet available, the primary goal of early burn therapy is to ensure adequate delivery of oxygen, nutrients, and circulating cells to the wound. Therefore, immediate burn care focuses on prevention of progression of injury and maintenance of a viable interface at which both specific and nonspecific defenses against infection can be mounted.[5]

WOUND AND INFLAMMATORY PATHOPHYSIOLOGY

The evolution of the burn wound is dramatically seen in the conversion of partial- to full-thickness wounds during difficult resuscitations, particularly in patients at the extremes of age in whom cardiac output cannot meet the circulatory demand of large BSA injury. In such patients with progressive necrosis and limited defense at the viable tissue interface, early microbial invasion of wounds is to be anticipated. Similarly, decreases in body temperature caused by heat loss to the environment or application of cool solutions or ice to the wound may lead to progressive deterioration of the wounds. Although circulating factors that depress myocardial function after burn injury have been postulated to exist,[6] the primary problem in maintenance of cardiovascular stability is ongoing intravascular volume depletion. Efforts are therefore directed at volume repletion, and adrenergic agents in particular are avoided in view of the deleterious result of further diminution of wound blood flow. Likewise, meticulous evaluation of blood flow in extremities with circumferential full-thickness injury is necessary to avoid additional compromise of wound and muscular blood flow. When signs of compromised blood flow first appear, escharotomy is performed to diminish the developing pressure in the extremity.

In addition to the culture medium provided by the necrotic tissue, the patient with large burns is predisposed to infection because of depression of nonspecific, humoral, and cellular immune function.[7] Circulating levels of immunoglobulins are inversely proportional to the extent of injury,[8] and persistently decreased levels of immunoglobulin G (IgG) have been related to mortality.[9] The ratio of T-helper to T-suppressor lymphocytes is decreased.[10, 11] In addition, monocyte defects have been reported,[12] leading to the hypothesis that depressed immune response in these patients is caused by an imbalance in the cellular immune system. That multiple cascades are involved is supported by the finding that tumor necrosis factor (TNF) is produced after burn injury,[13] as are other cytokines.[14] It has been shown that plasma levels of interleukin-1 β, interleukin-6, and TNF-α are elevated in severely burned patients.[15–17] Increased levels of these cytokines were associated with increased rates of mortality and infection. Numerous theories regarding the initiation of the exaggerated inflammatory response have been proposed, including the possibility that activation of Hageman's factor and generation of kinin are primary in the process.[18] Although it has been documented that intestinal permeability increases in association with infection in burn patients,[19] it is not known whether this is a primary or a secondary event. Based on prospective study of patients with large burns, however, it has been suggested that disorders of neutrophil function appear to be the major factors predisposing to the development of sepsis.[20]

That the response of the neutrophil to a site of injury and antigen challenge was depressed in patients with 40% or greater total BSA burn was shown by McCabe and colleagues[21] by the skin window technique. Such findings of depressed neutrophil response in vivo have been confirmed by quantitating the response to heat-killed *Staphylococcus* in burn-injured patients.[22] Study of the mechanism of decreased neutrophil response to microbial invasion and injury has centered on in vitro neutrophil function. The chemotactic response of peripheral blood neutrophils after thermal injury is depressed early after injury in proportion to the extent of tissue damage[23] and correlates with mortality, presumably because of sepsis.[23, 24] Neutrophils have a decreased production of superoxide anion and decreased oxygen consumption. This finding was associated with a decrease in oxidase activity in cells isolated from patients who had sustained thermal injury.[25] The decrease in oxidase activity has been associated with previous in vivo stimulation of the neutrophil.[26, 27] Furthermore, it has been suggested that inhibition of apoptosis, as found in patients with burn injury,[28] may regulate the inflammatory response to injury. Consumption of complement components might account for depressed neutrophil response after burn injury[29]; however, even low levels of complement were sufficient to opsonize the invading bacteria.[30] Data from an animal model suggest that neutrophils do not respond to the burn wound as well after large burns. However, in vivo evaluation of neutrophil activity indicated that the cells were more responsive than after lesser injury.[31] These findings suggest that "indiscriminant" margination may be occurring after injury. Such a response would lead to depressed appropriate wound response and potentially to distant tissue damage. These earlier findings are supported by data[32–34] indicating that neutrophil surface receptors are altered after burn injury in patients. Furthermore, infusion of low levels of exogenous chemotaxins led to increased mortality from burn wound sepsis in a rat model.[35] Others have described similar events in infected patients and have correlated release of leukocyte enzymes with levels of chemotactic factors produced by complement activation.[36]

PREVENTION OF INFECTION

Although it is common practice to give prophylactic systemic antibiotics (penicillin) to outpatients with burns, current data do not support their general use in the inpatient population.[37, 38] Frequent evaluation of the wound and surrounding tissue allows early and appropriate therapy of cellulitis while sparing most patients exposure to unnecessary antibiotics. Although it was documented[39] that manipulation of the burn wound leads to bacteremia, and therefore antibiotics were administered immediately before and during burn wound excision, more recent data[40] suggest that the incidence of bacteremia may be as low as 15%. Therefore, a selective approach to use of prophylactic antibiotics is advocated. The choice of antibiotics is dictated by knowledge of the current flora in the burn center or more specifically by the burn wound flora of the individual patient. The cyclic nature of particular microorganisms causing burn wound invasion in our center was documented by the results of surveillance and specifically indicated wound biopsies over a 6-month period (Table 310–1). *Enterobacter cloacae* was frequently isolated but was most prominent in March, April, and June. *Staphylococcus aureus*, which was methicillin resistant, was most prominent in May, but no isolates were found in April. The cyclic nature of wound infection revealed in these data from 15 years ago was supported by data from the

TABLE 310–1 Distribution of Organisms in Burn Wound Biopsies

Parameter	January		February		March		April		May		June	
	1982	*1997*	*1982*	*1997*	*1982*	*1997*	*1982*	*1997*	*1998*	*1997*	*1982*	*1997*
No. biopsies	189	27	141	9	244	6	201	12	162	20	69	12
No. biopsies with $\geq 10^5$ organisms per gram of tissue	84	0	39	0	85	2	84	2	70	3	41	8
Organisms identified (% of total positive biopsies)												
Enterobacter cloacae	29.8	—	18.0	—	37.7	0	82.1	0	25.7	33.3	39.0	0
Staphylococcus aureus	27.4	—	28.2	—	22.4	50	0	100	42.9	33.3	17.1	0
Staphylococcus epidermidis	14.3	—	5.1	—	0	0	3.6	0	0	33.3	0	12.5
Enterococcus faecalis	10.7	—	12.8	—	4.7	—	2.4	—	11.4	0	17.1	25
Escherichia coli	7.1	—	7.6	—	11.8	0	6.0	0	4.3	0	12.2	0
Pseudomonas aeruginosa	2.4	—	5.1	—	20.0	50.0	6.0	0	8.6	0	12.2	25
Klebsiella pneumoniae	0	—	0	—	0	0	0	0	0	0	0	25
Acinetobacter baumanii	0	—	0	—	0	0	0	0	0	0	0	12.5

same months in 1997 (Table 310–1) at the same center. However, the decrease in incidence of wound infection between these two periods should be noted. In the earlier study there were 1006 biopsies, of which 40% were positive, and in the later studies only 21% of a total of 86 biopsies were positive. Patient admissions were twice the number in the more recent period, and *Klebsiella pneumoniae* and *Acinetobacter baumanii* emerged as new pathogens. Based on such data, the regimen for wound manipulation prophylaxis consisted of intravenous vancomycin and amikacin during the earlier study and currently consists of vancomycin and a third-generation cephalosporin.

The advent of effective topical antimicrobial therapy has decreased the incidence of conversion of partial-thickness to full-thickness wounds by local infection. In addition, these agents may prolong the sterility of the full-thickness burn wound. However, they have not eliminated the need for aggressive removal of the necrotic tissue and closure of the wound with autograft. Silver nitrate in a 0.5% solution is an effective topical agent when used before wound colonization. However, because this agent does not penetrate eschar, its broad-spectrum gram-negative effectiveness is diminished once bacterial proliferation has occurred in the eschar. Additional disadvantages of this agent include the need for continuous occlusive dressings, which limit evaluation of wounds and range of motion. The black discoloration of the wound and the environment contributes to a decrease in use of silver nitrate.

Topical burn wound creams allow for open wound therapy and, except in an outpatient setting, are most commonly used without dressings. Mafenide acetate (Sulfamylon) cream has a broad spectrum of activity against gram-negative organisms but little activity against staphylococci. A significant advantage of this agent is that it penetrates the burn eschar and therefore is effective in the colonized wound. The disadvantages of Sulfamylon are a transient burning sensation, an accentuation of postinjury hyperventilation, and inhibition of carbonic anhydrase activity. Silver sulfadiazine, on the other hand, is a soothing cream with good activity against gram-negative organisms. Because it does not penetrate the wound, it is best used as a prophylactic antimicrobial. Bacterial resistance to silver sulfadiazine has been reported.[41] Some centers have adopted an approach of alternating agents to take advantage of the attributes of both, with silver sulfadiazine being applied at night and Sulfamylon during the day.[41] The current approach in our center is to initiate topical prophylaxis with silver sulfadiazine and to switch to Sulfamylon if wounds appear to deteriorate based on clinical and laboratory criteria. A promising but as yet unproved approach to prevention of infection is through stimulation of neutrophil production by recombinant granulocyte colony-stimulating factor (G-CSF). Initial animal studies suggest that G-CSF may be of benefit[42]; however, concern exists that a larger circulating neutrophil pool may amplify the inflammatory response.

The goal of burn therapy is to prevent burn wound infection by permanent closure of the wound as rapidly as possible. Recognition of the advantages of early removal of necrotic tissue and wound closure has led to an aggressive surgical approach in selected patients.[1] In such cases, full-thickness wounds are excised as soon after injury as cardiovascular stability has been achieved. The advantages of this approach include removal of eschar before colonization, which typically is appreciated at 5 to 7 days after injury, and reduction of the overall extent of injury. The extent of excision of burn wound is usually limited to 20% of the BSA at any one time, and blood loss is limited to one blood volume. Such an approach is most easily achieved by excision of full-thickness injury to the level of the fascia, because blood loss is minimized under these conditions. The open wound is covered with autograft if donor sites are available or with allograft. This is repeated until the entire wound is closed. This aggressive surgical approach is modified by the age of the patient (ideally 15 to 35 years) and by factors such as significant preexisting disease and inhalation injury, which require a more conservative approach.

An additional difficulty with early excisional therapy is the possibility of excision of burned tissue that may heal if left alone for 2 to 3 weeks. If such a question arises, initial tangential excision of the eschar or biopsy may assist in evaluating the depth and the possibility of healing of the burn wound. Data suggest that a more conservative approach, in which operative time is limited to 2 hours and blood loss to four units, may contribute to improved survival from extensive burn injury.[43] In an effort to achieve burn wound closure more rapidly, Burke and colleagues[44] advocated the use of immunosuppressive therapy to enhance allograft acceptance in children with extensive burns. These patients were kept in bacteria-controlled nursing units to minimize the possibility of infection during immunosuppression. Attempts to follow a similar protocol in adults have been discouraging.[41]

Throughout the course of hospitalization, efforts are directed toward minimizing contamination of the patient's wounds. Cross-contamination is avoided through the use of gowns, gloves, and masks by nursing and medical staff and visitors. The patient is not touched except with a gloved hand, and each patient is restricted to his or her own monitoring and diagnostic equipment. Concern about the potential for cross-contamination in large burn centers has led to diminished use of the traditional Hubbard tanking of patients. A satisfactory alternative is showering and débridement on a covered or readily disinfected plinth. If adequate nursing care can be provided, it is preferable to isolate patients who have large open wounds in individual rooms. Cohort patient care has been shown to be effective in eliminating endemic infections.[45] The bacteria-controlled nursing unit[46] has been advocated as a means of protecting the patient and the environment. Such elaborate systems are not generally available.

DIAGNOSIS AND TREATMENT OF INFECTION

Wound Infection

Although surface cultures of burn wounds are helpful from the standpoint of evaluating the potential pathogens that exist on the patient and on a burn ward, they give no indication of the actual status of the wound itself. Biopsy of the wound has been shown to provide an accurate indication on its status.[47] Pruitt and Foley reported that quantitative cultures of 10^5 or more bacteria per gram of tissue or histologic evidence of bacterial invasion of viable tissue correlated with a high (75%) mortality rate.[48] In addition, serial biopsies that indicated advancing wound infection were associated with a mortality rate of 85%, whereas stable or improving wounds were associated with an overall mortality rate of 55%. Direct correlation between biopsy and autopsy diagnosis was found in 26 of 32 patients. These data and those of others[49] support systematic evaluation of burn wounds with biopsy of all areas of wound change. Routine biopsy of full-thickness burn wounds on an every-other-day schedule has allowed detection of progressive wound infections.[50] The rapid fixation technique allows histologic diagnosis of invasive infection within 3 hours, whereas quantitative counts and identification of the organism are available within 24 hours. The combined use of histologic and culture techniques provides early diagnosis as well as the identity of the organism and its sensitivity to antimicrobials. However, the only way to conclusively determine burn wound invasion by bacteria or fungi is by histologic methods.[51]

A change in wound appearance or character provokes the clinician to modify therapy and stimulates an aggressive diagnostic approach. Hemorrhage, rapid eschar separation, or greenish discoloration of eschar or subeschar fat suggests bacterial colonization or invasion of the wound. If clinical or biopsy data support a diagnosis of colonization, then a change in topical therapy and plans for excision are entertained (Table 310–2). However, if the findings are consistent with invasive infection, then more aggressive therapy is instituted. In addition, if bacteremia is documented and other sources are eliminated, urgent surgical intervention is necessary. In the absence of documented bacteremia, signs of sepsis such as hypothermia or hyperthermia, hypotension, decreased urinary output, hyperglycemia, neutropenia or neutrophilia, or thrombocytopenia support early intervention. When the wound is invaded with gram-negative organisms, surgical excision to the level of the fascia is the procedure of choice. In preparation for surgery and in those patients who require stabilization before general anesthesia is given, a penetrating topical agent (Sulfamylon) is used, and subeschar clysis is initiated with the use of an appropriate antibiotic. The choice of antibiotic is based on previous biopsy sensitivity data or data accumulated on sensitivities of the current flora in the patient population. Such a preoperative approach is based on evidence that Sulfamylon pulse therapy is effective in decreasing wound colony counts[52] and on the previous data of Baxter and colleagues[50] supporting the efficacy of subeschar clysis. In general, systemic antimicrobials are not necessary, because the full daily dose of antibiotic administered by clysis is absorbed into the circulation. The direct administration of antibiotic into the viable/nonviable tissue interface is supported by concern that systemically administered antibiotics may not reach sufficient levels in tissues with poor or absent vascularity. However, some data suggest that antibiotics administered at a distant site are effective[52] and that systemically administered antibiotics reach these tissues. Whether activity of the antimicrobial is maintained in these foci is not known.

In distinction to gram-negative invasion, gram-positive infection often manifests as suppurative foci in the tissue or is associated with rapid eschar separation. In such cases, simple débridement with unroofing of involved areas, under the umbrella of appropriate systemic antibiotics, is sufficient acute therapy. Because surgical débridement should arrest this process, topical agents are of lesser importance; however, the wound should not be allowed to dessicate. Silver sulfadiazine, Dakin solution, Sulfamylon solution, and triple-antibiotic solutions have been used for this purpose.

Although gram-positive burn wound infection is anticipated to be primarily a suppurative type of infection, there appears to be a growing number of patients who present with primary nonsuppurative gram-positive infections. These infections are caused by methicillin-resistant *S. aureus* (personal observation). Whether diminished neutrophil response or a change in the nature or virulence of such organisms[53] explains this phenomenon is unknown. Burn wound invasion of this type seems to be best treated as are gram-negative invasive infections (see Table 310–2).

Over the past 10 years there has been a decrease in bacterial wound infections after burn injury, but during this period there has been an increase in fungal burn wound infection.[54] Blackened discoloration of the burn wound should arouse suspicion of fungal infection. Such changes are more typical of the agents of mucormycosis.[41] Confirmation of such organisms is best made on histologic sections of wound biopsies, where, in addition, a determination of invasion of viable tissue can be made. Reliance on culture data prolongs the time to diagnosis. Although silver sulfadiazine is active against *Candida* spp., a mixture of this agent or Sulfamylon with Nystatin may be more effective for topical treatment of superficial fungal infections. Because fungal infection is often preceded by bacterial infection and multiple antibiotic therapy, the use of Sulfamylon in such a mixture is preferred.[41] The treatment of fungal invasion is surgical excision to the level of noninvaded viable tissue. When invasion extends to the level of the investing fascia, the excision is carried deep to this level to viable muscle.[55] The cytotoxicity of currently available antifungal agents mitigates against their use for preoperative clysis. Recovery of the fungus from the blood mandates systemic therapy, which is often used even without positive blood cultures if invasion is documented and clinical signs are present.

Pulmonary Infection

With the advent of effective topical therapy for the burn wound, pulmonary complications have become a prominent problem in the burn-injured patient.[51, 56] In addition, the ability to salvage an increasing number of patients from the shock phase immediately after injury has led to a greater number of patients' surviving to the time (2 to 3 days after injury) when the effects of inhalation injury become clinically prominent.[57] In patients without inhalation injury but with large burns, postinjury hyperventilation and subsequent decreases in tidal volume may lead to atelectasis and pneumonia. Furthermore, a recognized complication of circumferential full-thickness chest burns is a decrease in compliance of the chest wall. Aggressive pulmonary toilet and escharotomy are necessary to maintain pulmonary function.

TABLE 310–2 Prophylaxis and Treatment of Burn Wound Infection

Diagnosis	Topical	Clysis	Systemic Therapy	Surgical
"Clean" burn	Silver sulfadiazine/silver nitrate	No	No	Excision/débridement
Superficial infection or colonization	Silver sulfadiazine/Sulfamylon	No	No	Excision/débridement
Gram-negative invasion	Sulfamylon	Yes	No	Excision to fascia
Gram-positive invasion	Silver sulfadiazine	No	Yes	Unroof
Suppurative				
Nonsuppurative		Yes	No	Excision to fascia
Fungal infection	Sulfamylon plus Mycostatin	No	No	Excision
Superficial				
Invasive	Sulfamylon plus Mycostatin	No	Yes	Excision to or deep to fascia

Because these patients frequently require large-volume feedings via nasogastric or nasojejunal tubes, aspiration must be guarded against. Diminished mucociliary functions and destruction of airways by inhalation of products of combustion lead to airway obstruction and infection.[58] Frequent diagnostic and therapeutic bronchoscopy is necessary in this group of patients.

Attempts at specific prophylaxis of the sequelae of inhalation injury, such as nebulization of antibiotics[59] and treatment with steroids,[60] have failed to show any benefit. Although hematogenous pneumonia is less common than in the past,[56] it remains a significant problem in the patient with burns. When it occurs, the source (most commonly wound or suppurative vein) must be defined and eradicated. Prophylactic antibiotics are not used for either bronchopneumonia or hematogenous pneumonia; specific therapy is based on knowledge of previous endobronchial culture, and sensitivity is substantiated by repeat cultures at the time of diagnosis.

Miscellaneous Infections

Several additional types of infection are significant in burn-injured patients and should be mentioned because of their frequency and peculiarities of clinical presentation. The diagnosis of suppurative thrombophlebitis in the presence of normal tissue is often difficult to make. In the burned patient, the addition of injured and necrotic tissue compounds this difficulty. Less than 35% of suppurative veins in burned patients result in local findings.[61] The incidence of this disease is at least 5%, and the mortality rate, even in treated suppurative thrombophlebitis, reaches 60%.[61] In the absence of a septic venous source, persistent positive blood cultures in the burned patient should be attributed to endocarditis until proven otherwise.

In addition to superficial tissue damaged by direct heat, deeper tissue can be injured and can provide a focus for infection. The vascular compromise associated with circumferential full-thickness injury, if not decompressed early, leads to muscle necrosis and subsequent pyomyositis. A high index of suspicion is necessary to detect these changes in an already edematous extremity. Direct electrical contact can lead to deep muscular necrosis with delayed infection. Furthermore, significant visceral damage may occur after electrical injury, with subsequent abscess formation.[62]

CONCLUSIONS

The combination of injury-associated immunosuppression and the large area of nonviable tissue in the patient with more than 30% BSA burns inevitably leads to infection. Success in treatment of these patients rests more with removal of necrotic tissue and achievement of wound closure than with use of antimicrobials. Current data support the judicious use of systemic antibiotics for treatment of documented infection and for prophylaxis during burn wound manipulation. The cyclic nature of exposure to various bacteria and the rapid emergence of resistance to antibiotics in this population supplies ample evidence that there is always a niche that will be filled. Although contamination of the wound must be minimized and surveillance must be adequate to detect organisms before they invade the wound, closure of the wound is the primary prophylactic and therapeutic maneuver in the care of the burned patient.

REFERENCES

1. Saffle JR, Davis B, Williams P. Recent outcomes in the treatment of burn injury in the United States: A report from the American Burn Association Patient Registry. J Burn Care Rehabil. 1995;16:219–232.
2. Monafo WW. Initial management of burns. N Engl J Med. 1996;335:1581–1586.
3. Jackson DM. The diagnosis of the depth of burning. Br J Surg. 1953;40:558–596.
4. Noble HGS, Robson MC, Krizek TJ. Dermal ischemia in the burn wound. J Surg Res. 1977;23:117–125.
5. Yurt RW. Burns. In: Polk HC, Gardner B, Stone HH, eds. Basic Surgery. St. Louis: Quality Medical Publishing; 1995;750–761.
6. Baxter CR, Cook WA, Shires GT. Serum myocardial depressant factor of burn shock. Surg Forum. 1966;17:1–2.
7. Heideman M, Bengtsson A. The immunologic response to injury. World J Surg. 1992;16:53–56.
8. Arturson G, Hogman CF, Johansson SGO, et al. Changes in immunoglobulin levels in severely burned patients. Lancet. 1969;1:546–548.
9. Munster AM, Hoagland HC, Pruitt BA Jr. The effect of thermal injury on serum immunoglobulins. Ann Surg. 1970;172:965–969.
10. Burleson DG, Mason AD Jr, Pruitt BA Jr. Lymphoid subpopulation changes after thermal injury and thermal injury with infection in an experimental model. Ann Surg. 1987;207:208–212.
11. Antonacci AC, Reaves LE, Calvano SE, et al. Flow cytometric analysis of lymphoid cell subpopulations after thermal injury in human beings. Surg Gynecol Obstet. 1984;159:1–8.
12. Shelby J, Merrell SW. In vivo monitoring of postburn immune response. J Trauma. 1987;27:213–216.
13. Marano M, Moldawer L, Fong Y, et al. Cachectin tumor necrosis factor production in experimental burns and pseudomonas infection. Arch Surg. 1988;123:1383–1388.
14. Struzyna J, Pojda Z, Braun B, et al. Serum cytokine levels (IL-4, IL-6, IL-8, G-CSF, GM-CSF) in burned patients. Burns. 1995;21:437–440.
15. Drost AC, Burleson DG, Cioffi WG Jr, et al. Plasma cytokines following thermal injury and their relationship with patient mortality, burn size, and time postburn. J Trauma. 1993;35:335–339.
16. Drost AC, Lasen B, Aulick LH. The effects of thermal injury on serum interleukin 1 activity in rats. Lymphokine Cytokine Res. 1993;12:181–185.
17. Drost AC, Burleson DG, Cioffi WG Jr, et al. Plasma cytokines following thermal injury and their relationship to infection. Ann Surg. 1993;218:74–78.
18. Holder IA, Neeley AN. Hageman factor-dependent kinin activation in burns and its theoretical relationship to postburn immunosuppression syndrome and infection. J Burn Care Rehabil. 1990;11:496–503.
19. Ziegler TR, Smith RJ, O'Dwyer ST, et al. Increased permeability associated with infection in burn patients. Arch Surg. 1988;123:1313–1319.
20. Alexander JW, Ogle CK, Stinnett JD, et al. A sequential prospective analysis of immunologic abnormalities and infection following severe thermal injury. Ann Surg. 1978;188:809–816.
21. McCabe WP, Rebuck JW, Kelly AP Jr, et al. Leukocyte response as a monitor of immunodepression in burn patients. Arch Surg. 1973;106:155–159.
22. Balch HH, Watters BS, Kelly D. Resistance to infection in burned patients. Ann Surg. 1963;157:1–19.
23. Warden GD, Mason AD Jr, Pruitt BA Jr. Evaluation of leukocyte chemotaxis in vitro in thermally injured patients. J Clin Invest. 1974;54:1001–1014.
24. Grogan JB. Suppressed in vitro chemotaxis of burn neutrophils. J Trauma. 1976;16:985–988.
25. Rosenthal J, Thurman GW, Cusack N, et al. Neutrophils from patients after burn injury express a deficiency of the oxidase components p47-phox and p-67-phox. Blood. 1996;88:4321–4329.
26. Cioffi WG Jr, Burleson DG, Jordan BS, et al. Granulocyte oxidative activity after thermal injury. Surgery. 1992;112:860–865.
27. Sparkes BG. Immunological response to thermal injury. Burns. 1997;23:106–113.
28. Chitnis D, Dickerson C, Munster AM, Winchurch RA. Inhibition of apoptosis in polymorphonuclear neutrophils from burn patients. J Leukoc Biol. 1996;59:835–839.
29. Bjornson AB, Altemeier WA, Bjornson HS, et al. Host defense against opportunist microorganisms following trauma: I. Studies to determine the association between changes in humoral components of host defense and septicemia in burned patients. Ann Surg. 1978;188:93–101.
30. Bjornson AB, Altemeier WA, Bjornson HS. Complement, opsonins, and the immune response to bacterial infection in burned patients. Ann Surg. 1980;191:323–329.
31. Yurt RW, Pruitt BA. Decreased wound neutrophils and indiscriminate margination in the pathogenesis of wound infection. Surgery. 1985;95:191–198.
32. Bjerknes R, Vindenes H, Laerum OD. Altered neutrophil function in patients with large burns. Blood Cells. 1990;16:127–143.
33. Rodeberg DA, Bass RC, Alexander JW, et al. Neutrophils from burn patients are unable to increase the expression of CD11b/CD18 in response to inflammatory stimuli. J Leukoc Biol. 1997;61:575–582.
34. Mileski W, Borgstrom D, Lightfoot E, et al. Inhibition of leukocyte endothelial adherence following thermal injury. J Surg Res. 1992;52:334–339.
35. Yurt RW, Shires GT. Increased susceptibility to infection due to infusion of exogenous chemotaxin. Arch Surg. 1987;122:111–116.
36. Solomkin JS, Jenkins MK, Nelson RD, et al. Neutrophil dysfunction in sepsis: II. Evidence for the role of complement activation products in cellular deactivation. Surgery. 1981;90:319–327.
37. Alexander JW. Prophylactic antibiotics in trauma. Am Surg. 1982;48:45–48.
38. Durtschi MB, Orgain C, Counts GW, et al. A prospective study of prophylactic penicillin in acutely burned hospitalized patients. J Trauma. 1982;22:11–14.
39. Sasaki TM, Welch GW, Herndon DN, et al. Burn wound manipulation-induced bacteremia. J Trauma. 1979;19:46–48.
40. Mozingo DW, McManus AT, Kim SH, Pruitt BA Jr. Incidence of bacteremia after burn wound manipulation in the early postburn period. J Trauma. 1997;42:1006–1010.
41. Pruitt BA Jr. The burn patient: II. Later care and complications of thermal injury. Curr Probl Surg. 1979;16:1–95.
42. Mooney DP, Gamelli RL, O'Reilly M, et al. Recombinant human granulocyte colony-stimulating factor and *Pseudomonas* burn wound sepsis. Arch Surg. 1988;123:1353–1357.
43. Demling RH. Improved survival after massive burns. J Trauma. 1983;23:179–184.

44. Burke JF, Quinby WC, Bondoc CC, et al. Immunosuppression and temporary skin transplantation in the treatment of massive third degree burns. Ann Surg. 1975;182:183–197.
45. McManus AT, McManus WF, Mason AD Jr, et al. Microbial colonization in a new intensive care burn unit. Arch Surg. 1985;120:217–221.
46. Burke JF, Quinby WC, Bondoc CC, et al. The contribution of a bacterially isolated environment to the prevention of infection in seriously burned patients. Ann Surg. 1977;186:377–387.
47. McManus AT, Kim SH, Mason AD, et al. A comparison of quantitative microbiology and histopathology in divided burn wound biopsies. Arch Surg. 1987;122:64–66.
48. Pruitt BA, Foley FD. The use of biopsies in burn patient care. Surgery. 1973;73:887–897.
49. Loebl EC, Marvin JA, Heck EL, et al. The method of quantitative burn wound biopsy cultures and its routine use in the care of the burned patient. Am J Clin Pathol. 1974;61:20–24.
50. Baxter CR, Curreri PW, Marvin JA. The control of burn wound sepsis by the use of quantitative bacterial studies and subeschar clysis with antibiotics. Surg Clin North Am. 1973;53:1509–1518.
51. Pruitt BA Jr, McManus AT. The changing epidemiology of infection in burn patients. World J Surg. 1992;16:57–67.
52. McManus WF, Mason AD Jr. Subeschar antibiotic infusion in the treatment of burn wound infection. J Trauma. 1980;20:1021–1023.
53. Lacey RW, Chopra I. Effect of plasmid carriage on the virulence of *Staphylococcus aureus*. J Med Microbiol. 1975;8:137–147.
54. Becker WK, Cioffi WG, McManus AT, et al. Fungal burn wound infection. Arch Surg. 1991;126:44–48.
55. Levine BA, Sirinek KR, Pruitt BA Jr. Wound excision to fascia in burned patients. Arch Surg. 1978;113:403–407.
56. Pruitt BA Jr, Flemma RJ, Divincenti FC, et al. Pulmonary complications in burn patients: A comparative study of 697 patients. J Thorac Cardiovasc Surg. 1970;59:7–20.
57. Bingham HG, Gallagher TJ, Powell MD. Early bronchoscopy as a predictor of ventilatory support for burned patients. J Trauma. 1987;27:1286–1288.
58. Hunt JL, Agee RN, Pruitt BA Jr. Fiberoptic bronchoscopy in acute inhalation injury. J Trauma. 1975;15:641–649.
59. Levine BA, Petroff PA, Slade CL, et al. Prospective trials of dexamethasone and aerosolized gentamicin in the treatment of inhalation injury in the burned patient. J Trauma. 1978;145:539–544.
60. Welch GW, Lull RJ, Petroff PA, et al. The use of steroids in inhalation injury. Surg Gynecol Obstet. 1977;145:539–544.
61. Pruitt BA Jr, McManus WF, Kim SH, et al. Diagnosis and treatment of cannula-related intravenous sepsis in burn patients. Ann Surg. 1980;191:546–554.
62. Newsome TW, Curreri PW, Eurenius K. Visceral injuries: An unusual complication of an electrical burn. Arch Surg. 1972;105:494–497.

Chapter 311

Bites

ELLIE J. C. GOLDSTEIN

Bite wounds are common injuries that are often mistakenly considered innocuous by both patients and physicians. Most data on the incidence of infection, bacteriology, and the value of various medical and surgical methods of treatment come from small studies or anecdotal case reports that are further biased by the types of patients who elect to seek medical attention. Bite wounds consist of lacerations, evulsions, punctures, and scratches. Although 80% of patients never seek and do not need medical care, awareness of the magnitude of the infectious complications from bites is growing. The bacteria associated with bite infections may come from the environment, from the victim's skin flora, or most frequently, from the "normal" flora of the biter (Table 311–1).

ANIMAL BITES

In 1992 the U.S. government estimated that 52.4 million dogs and 54.6 million cats were kept as pets in 38.2 million and 30.5 million households with dogs and cats, respectively.[1] Previously, it was estimated that one of every two Americans will be bitten in their lifetime, usually by a dog. Bites occur in 4.7 million Americans yearly[2] and account for 800,000 medical visits, including approximately 1% of all emergency department visits.[3] Most dog bites (85%) are provoked attacks by either the victim's own pet or a dog known to the victim and occur during the warm weather months.[4] Bite wounds that require attention are often those to the extremities, especially the dominant hand. Facial bites are more frequent in children younger than 10 years and lead to 5 to 10 deaths per year, often because of exsanguination.[5] Larger dogs can exert more than 450 pounds/inch^2 of pressure with their jaws, which can lead to extensive crush injury.

TABLE 311–1 Common Bacterial Isolates from Dog and Cat Bite Wounds

Pasteurella multocida subsp. *multocida*	*Actinobacillus actinomycetemcomitans*
Pasteurella multocida subsp. *septica*	*Eikenella corrodens*
Pasteurella dagmatis	*Weeksella zoohelcum*
Pasteurella canis	Peptostreptococci
Pasteurella stomatis	*Fusobacterium nucleatum*
Capnocytophaga canimorsus	*Fusobacterium russii*
Capnocytophaga cynodegmi	*Prevotella melaninogenica*
α-Hemolytic streptococci	*Prevotella intermedia*
β-Hemolytic streptococci	*Porphyromonas salivosa*
Enterococci	*Porphyromonas asaccharolytica*
Staphylococcus aureus	*Veillonella parvula*
Staphylococcus intermedius	*Prevotella heparinolytica*
Staphylococcus epidermidis	*Leptotrichia buccalis*
Haemophilus felis	*Porphyromonas gingivalis*
Haemophilus aphrophilus	*Porphyromonas canoris*
Corynebacterium spp.	*Bacteroides tectum*
Micrococcus luteus	*Prevotella zoogleoformans*
Neisseria canis	*Moraxella* spp.
Neisseria weaveri	*Corynebacterium aquaticum*
Acinetobacter spp.	*Corynebacterium minutissimum*

Patients who present within 8 hours after injury are usually concerned with crush injury, care of disfiguring wounds, or the need for rabies or tetanus therapy.[4] These wounds are frequently contaminated with multiple strains of aerobic and anaerobic bacteria, similar to the spectrum found in documented bite infections. Between 2 and 30% of "treated" wounds will become infected and may require hospitalization.[6–10] Patients presenting longer than 8 hours after injury usually have established infection.[4, 6, 8, 9, 11] Infection is usually manifested by localized cellulitis, pain at the site of injury, and a purulent discharge, often gray and malodorous.[12] Temperature greater than 37.2°C, regional adenopathy, and lymphangitis occur in less than 10% of patients. Puncture wounds may become infected more frequently than evulsions and lead to abscess formation. Wounds close to bones or joints may penetrate these structures and cause septic arthritis, osteomyelitis, tenosynovitis, or local abscesses in any potential anatomic space. Osteomyelitis is a frequent and severe complication of bite wounds and should always be considered in the presence of pain in a joint or limited range of motion.

Rarely, sepsis, endocarditis, meningitis, or brain abscesses may develop after a bite injury. Fatal infection caused by *Capnocytophaga canimorsus* (formerly designated DF2) in association with asplenia or liver disease has been noted.[13–15] This organism may be difficult to isolate and identify and may require up to 14 days of incubation to grow on blood culture. It is generally susceptible to penicillin, cephalosporins, and fluoroquinolones but variably resistant to aztreonam and aminoglycosides[16] (Table 311–2).

Women who have undergone radical or modified radical mastectomy, patients with edema of an extremity of any cause, patients with lupus erythematosus, especially if taking steroids, and compromised hosts (e.g., patients with acute leukemia) may be prone to more severe infections, including sepsis, from the usual isolates that cause only limited cellulitis in immunocompetent patients.

Dog bite wound infections are considered to be predominantly related to the dog's oral flora.[4, 7, 11, 12, 17–19] Although most attention has

TABLE 311–2 Antimicrobial Susceptibilities of Bacteria Frequently Isolated from Animal Bite Wounds*

Agent	Percentages of Isolates Susceptible					
	Staphylococcus aureus	Eikenella corrodens	*Anaerobes*	Pasteurella multocida	Capnocytophaga canimorsus	Staphylococcus intermedius
Penicillin	10	99	50/95†	95	95	70
Dicloxacillin	99	5	50	30	NS	100
Amoxicillin/clavulanic acid	100	100	100	100	95	100
Cephalexin	100	20	40	30	NS	95
Cefuroxime	100	70	40	90	NS	NS
Cefoxitin	100	95	100	95	95	NS
Erythromycin	100	20	40	20	95	95
Tetracycline	95	85	60	90	95	NS
TMP-SMX	100	95	0	95	V	NS
Ciprofloxacin	100	100	40	95	100	100
Levofloxacin	100	100	60	100	100	100
Trovafloxacin	100	100	85‡	100	100	100
Moxifloxacin	100	100	85‡	100	100	100
Azithromycin	100	80	70‡§	100	100	NS
Clarithromycin	100	60	70‡§	70	100	NS
Ketolides (HMR 3647)	100	100	85‡	100	NS	100
Clindamycin	95	0	100	0	95	95

* Data are compiled from various studies.
† Percentage of human bite isolates/percentage of animal bite isolates.
‡ Many fusobacteria are resistant.
§Some peptostreptococci are resistant.
Abbreviations: NS, Not studied; TMP-SMX, trimethoprim-sulfamethoxazole; V, variable.

been focused on *Pasteurella multocida,* the spectrum of organisms associated with bite wound infections is much greater. Based on DNA hybridization studies, the genus *Pasteurella* has been reclassified to comprise 13 taxa. Holst and colleagues[20] noted the following distribution of 159 *P. multocida* strains isolated over a period of 3 years from human infections, mostly from bite wounds: *P. multocida* (60%), which was the isolate in all bacteremia cases; *P. multocida* subsp. *septica* (13%), which has a greater prevalence in cats than in dogs and may have a preferential affinity for the central nervous system; *P. canis* biotype 1 (18%), which was isolated exclusively from dog bite infections; *P. stomatis* (6%); and *P. dagmatis* (3%), which may cause systemic infections. A study[12] of 107 dog and cat bite wounds showed that 75% of cat bites grew *Pasteurella* species on culturing (*P. multocida* subsp. *multocida*, 54%), as did 50% of the dog bites (*P. canis*, 26%; *P. multocida* subsp. *multocida*, 12%). Other common isolates include streptococci (50%), *Staphylococcus aureus* (20 to 40%), and anaerobes (70%). Table 311–1 lists common bite pathogens. A number of newly described or reclassified organisms have become associated with animal bite wounds. *Staphylococcus intermedius* can be coagulase positive and mistaken for *S. aureus* and is fourfold more common in canine flora.[21, 22] It is often susceptible to penicillin (55%) and possesses β-galactosidase activity, which differentiates it from *S. aureus.* Dysgonic fermenter 2 (DF2) has been named *C. canimorsus*[15]; it is difficult to grow on most routine solid media but can grow on chocolate agar and heart infusion agar with 5% rabbit blood when incubated in CO_2 and a variety of liquid media, including BACTEC aerobic medium.[14] This species can be differentiated from other *Capnocytophaga* spp. by the presence of positive oxidase and catalase reactions.[15] "DF2-like" strains have been classified as *Capnocytophaga cynodegmi.* M5 has been classified as *Neisseria weaveri*[23] and has been associated with dog bites. *Haemophilus felis* was previously confused with *Haemophilus paraphrophilus,* requires factor V and CO_2 for growth, and is common in cat nasopharyngeal flora.[24] IIj has been named *Weeksella zoohelcum* and has been associated with bite cellulitis, sepsis, and meningitis.[25] Other new aerobic species include *Neisseria canis* from a cat bite,[26] *Flavobacterium* IIb–like isolates from a pig bite,[27] *Actinobacillus lignieresii and Actinobacillus equi*–like bacterium from horse bites,[28] and NO1, a nonoxidative gram-negative rod[29] different from *Acinetobacter* spp. Anaerobic bacteria have undergone major reclassification. Many of the old "oral *Bacteroides*" spp. are now in the genera *Prevotella* and *Porphyromonas.* Anaerobes are isolated in up to 70% of animal bite wounds, always in mixed culture.[4, 9, 11] Approximately 50 to 60% of cat and dog bite wounds contain *Bacteroides tectum*, *Prevotella heparinolytica*, *Prevotella zoogleoformans*, *Prevotella bivia*, *Porphyromonas salivosa*, *Porphyromonas gingivalis*, *Porphyromonas canoris*, fusobacteria, and peptostreptococci.[30–33]

Gram stains of bite wounds are specific but nonsensitive indicators of bacterial growth. When compared, little difference was noted in the types of bacteria isolated from noninfected wounds seen early and infected wounds seen later.[4] All moderate to severe dog bite wounds, except those not clinically infected and more than 1 day old, should be considered contaminated with potential pathogens.

Wounds inflicted by cats are frequently scratches or tiny punctures located on the extremities and are likely to become infected.[33] *P. multocida* has been isolated from 50 to 70% of healthy cats and is a frequent pathogen in cat-associated wounds.[12, 20, 34] *Erysipelothrix rhusiopathiae* has been isolated from cat bite wounds.[12] Punctures over or near a joint, especially on the hands, should be treated aggressively with antibiotics and elevation because of a high incidence of osteomyelitis and septic arthritis. Cougar, tiger, and other feline bites also yield *P. multocida.*[35] Tularemia has likewise been transmitted by cat bites.[36] People are also bitten by a variety of other animals, including unusual domestic pets, farm animals, wild animals, aquatic animals, and laboratory animals.[3, 37–40] Monkey bites cause more swelling and infection than do many other animal bites[41] and may transmit subtype B virus (herpes simiae virus).[42] The bacteriology of most of these wounds is based on single case reports.

Management of Animal Bites

Table 311–3 notes the elements for treatment of animal bite wounds. The most problematic elements of the management of wounds seen early include the following:

1. The use of "prophylactic" antibiotics in wounds that are seen early but as yet are uninfected. Because 85% of such wounds harbor potential pathogens and one cannot reliably predict which wounds will become infected, selected wounds should be treated with 3 to 5 days of oral therapy (see Table 311–2).

2. The decision to suture the wound. Facial wounds are usually sutured after copious irrigation and the use of antibiotics in all but the most trivial wounds. No prospective studies are available to

TABLE 311–3 Management of Bite Wounds

History
- Animal bite: ascertain the type of animal, whether the bite was provoked or unprovoked, and the situation/environment when the bite occurred. If the species can be rabid, locate the animal for 10 days' observation or sacrifice
- Patient: obtain information on antimicrobial allergies, current medications, splenectomy, mastectomy, liver disease, and immunosuppression

Physical examination
- Record a diagram of the wound with the location, type, and depth of injury, range of motion, possibility of joint penetration, presence of edema or crush injury, nerve and tendon function, signs of infection, and odor of exudate

Cultures
- Infected wounds should be cultured and a Gram stain performed. Anaerobic cultures should be obtained in the presence of abscesses, sepsis, serious cellulitis, devitalized tissue, or foul odor of the exudate. Small tears and infected punctures should be cultured with a minitipped (nasopharyngeal) swab

Irrigation
- Copious amounts of normal saline should be used for irrigation. Puncture wounds should be irrigated with a "high-pressure jet" from a 20-ml syringe and an 18-gauge needle or catheter tip

Débridement
- Devitalized or necrotic tissue should be cautiously débrided. Debris and foreign bodies should be removed

Radiographs
- Radiographs should be obtained if fracture or bone penetration is possible to provide a baseline to judge future osteomyelitis

Wound closure
- Wound closure may be necessary for selected, fresh uninfected wounds, especially facial wounds, but primary wound closure is not usually indicated. Wound edges should be approximated with adhesive strips in selected cases

Antimicrobial therapy
- Prophylaxis: Consider prophylaxis (1) for moderate to severe injury less than 8 hours old, especially if edema or crush injury is present, (2) if bone or joint penetration is possible, (3) for hand wounds, (4) for immunocompromised patients (including those with mastectomy, liver disease, or steroid therapy), (5) if the wound is adjacent to a prosthetic joint, and (6) if the wound is in the genital area. Coverage should include *Pasteurella multocida, Staphylococcus aureus,* and anaerobes (see Table 311–2)
- Treatment: cover *P. multocida, S. aureus,* and anaerobes (see Table 311–2). Use oral medication if the patient is seen early after a bite and only mild to moderate signs of infection are present. Amoxicillin/clavulanic acid, 875/125 mg bid or 500/125 mg tid with food, will cover most bite pathogens. No alternative has been established for penicillin-allergic patients. Upon emergency department discharge, a single starting dose of parenteral antibiotic may be useful in selected cases. If hospitalization or closely monitored outpatient follow-up is required, intravenous agents should be used. Choices could include ampicillin/sulbactam or cefoxitin

Hospitalization
- Indications include fever, sepsis, spread of cellulitis, significant edema or crush injury, loss of function, compromised host, patient noncompliance

Immunizations
- Give tetanus booster if original three-dose series has been given, but none in the past 5 years. Give a primary series and tetanus immune globulin if the patient was never immunized (see Chapter 312)
- Rabies vaccine (days 0, 3, 7, 14, and 28) with hyperimmune globulin (40 IU/kg or 18 IU/lb) may be required, depending on the type of animal, ability to observe the animal, and locality (see Chapter 151)

Elevation
- Elevation may be required if any edema is present. Lack of elevation is a common cause of therapeutic failure

Immobilization
- Immobilize the extremity, especially hands, with a splint

Follow-up
- Follow-up should occur at 24 and perhaps 48 hours for outpatients

Reporting
- Reporting the incident to a local health department may be required

determine whether the risk of infection is increased. It is my experience and recommendation that other wounds not be primarily closed, but after irrigation and débridement they can be approximated and be closed by delayed primary or secondary intention.

The most common causes of therapeutic failure are the following:

1. Failure to stress the importance of or noncompliance of the patient in elevating an edematous wound. If the wound is on the hands, slings must be recommended because compliance is unlikely unless passively accomplished.

2. Selection of the incorrect antimicrobial agent (see Table 311–2). Most fastidious animal pathogens are susceptible to penicillin/amoxicillin. Because of resistance of certain bacteria, including *P. multocida,* first-generation cephalosporins, dicloxacillin, and erythromycin should be avoided or used cautiously. In vitro data suggest that some fluoroquinolones (ciprofloxacin, levofloxacin, and trovafloxacin), sulfamethoxazole-trimethoprim, and second-generation oral cephalosporins (cefuroxime) are active against many bite isolates.[43–47]

3. Failure to recognize joint penetration. Pain, diminished range of motion, local edema, and proximity of the puncture wound to a joint should alert one to the possibility of septic arthritis.

VENOMOUS SNAKEBITES

Venomous snakes, usually vipers (rattlesnakes, copperheads, cottonmouths, or water moccasins), bite approximately 8000 people in the United States yearly.[48] Envenomation can cause extensive tissue destruction and devitalization that predisposes to infection from the snake's normal oral flora. Sparse data exist on the incidence and bacteriology of snakebite infections. In rattlesnakes, the oral flora appears to be fecal in nature because the live prey usually defecates in the snake's mouth coincident with ingestion. Common oral isolates include *Pseudomonas aeruginosa, Proteus* spp., coagulase-negative staphylococci, and *Clostridium* spp.[49, 50] Other potential pathogens isolated from rattlesnakes' mouths include *Bacteroides fragilis* and *Salmonella arizonae* (*Salmonella* groups IIIa and IIIb). *Crotalus* rattlesnake venom has innate broad activity against aerobic gram-positive and gram-negative bacteria but not against anaerobes.[51, 52] The role of empirical antimicrobial therapy for noninfected wounds is not well defined. Specific therapy based on culturing of infected wounds should be instituted.

HUMAN BITES

Human bites have a higher complication and infection rate than do animal bites. Wounds of the lip and paronychia and infections of the structure surrounding the nail account for most self-inflicted bite wounds that come to medical attention. Paronychia is more frequent in children who suck their fingers and results from direct inoculation of the oral flora into the fingers. Brook[53] took cultures from 33 children with paronychia. Aerobes and anaerobes were each found in pure culture in 27% of cases, whereas mixed infection was found in 46% of cases. The most frequent aerobic organisms isolated were viridans streptococci, group A streptococci, *S. aureus, Haemophilus parainfluenzae, Klebsiella pneumoniae,* and *Eikenella corrodens.* The most frequently isolated anaerobic bacteria were *Bacteroides* spp., *Fusobacterium* spp., and gram-positive cocci. Therapy should include drainage, appropriate antibiotics, and avoidance of further bacterial contamination.

Occlusional human bites may affect any part of the body but most often involve the distal phalanx of the long or index fingers of the dominant hand. About 10 to 20% of wounds are "love nips" to the breasts and genital areas.[17, 54, 55] Bites to the hand are more serious and more frequently become infected than do bites to other areas.[56] Bites may also be caused by or be harbingers of child abuse.[57]

Important prognostic factors for the development of infection include the extent of tissue damage, the depth of the wound and which compartments are entered, and the pathogenicity of the inoculated oral bacteria.[58–60] Viridans streptococci were the most common wound isolates. *S. aureus* infection occurred in 40% of wounds and was usually present in patients who had attempted self-débridement and presented 3 to 4 days after injury. Although *H. influenzae* was occasionally isolated, no other penicillin-resistant gram-negative rods were isolated. *Bacteroides* spp., excluding *B. fragilis, Peptostreptococcus* spp., and *Fusobacterium nucleatum,* were also frequent isolates.[58] Up to 45% of the anaerobic gram-negative bacilli isolated from human bite wounds may be penicillin resistant and β-lactamase positive.[45, 61]

Management of Human Bites

A Gram stain and aerobic and anaerobic cultures should be obtained for all infected wounds before any therapy. Wounds should be copiously irrigated, surgically débrided, and diagrammed, photographed, or both. Immobilization of the affected area, including splinting if necessary, and elevation should be instituted. Empirical antimicrobial therapy should be based on the Gram stain (specific but not sensitive) or knowledge of the susceptibility of the oral flora. Patients who present early with uninfected wounds should also be given antimicrobial therapy of shorter duration and may be considered for outpatient management. Amoxicillin/clavulanic acid or penicillin plus a penicillinase-resistant penicillin or cephalosporin should be used. First-generation cephalosporins are not as effective as monotherapy because of resistance of some anaerobic bacteria and *E. corrodens*. Many patients require hospitalization. Baseline radiographs should be taken of wounds close to the bone to check for osteomyelitis. Most physicians advise against primary closure, even for uninfected human bite wounds, especially those on the hands. Facial wounds may present a special situation because of the possibility of scarring and disfigurement, and many investigators recommend primary closure. Approximation of the wound margins or delayed primary closure (3 to 5 days) is often possible even in infected cases.

CLENCHED-FIST INJURIES

Clenched-fist injuries are traumatic lacerations that occur when one person strikes another in the mouth with a clenched fist. These injuries are most common over the third and fourth metacarpophalangeal joints of the dominant hand, but they may also occur over the proximal interphalangeal joints. These lacerations are often only 12 to 14 cm long but, despite their innocuous appearance, frequently lead to serious complications because of the proximity of the skin over the knuckles to the joint capsule and the potential spread of infection into subcutaneous, subfascial, subtendinous, subaponeurotic, and web spaces.

Typically, patients sustain a clenched-fist injury and attempt to cleanse it or, more often, ignore it until 3 to 24 hours postinjury, when they awaken with a painful, throbbing, and swollen hand. The swelling usually spreads proximally but not distally and results in decreased range of motion. A purulent discharge is often present. Lymphangitis, adenopathy, fever, or other signs of systemic infection are infrequent.

The bacteriology of clenched-fist injuries is similar to that of human bites and usually consists of the normal oral flora. Viridans streptococci are the most frequent isolates, but *S. aureus* may be present in 20 to 40% of cases. Anaerobic bacteria can be recovered in more than 55% of clenched-fist injuries, including *Bacteroides* spp., *Fusobacterium* spp., and peptostreptococci. *E. corrodens* is an often overlooked but especially important pathogen in clenched-fist injury infections.[62–64] It has a prevalence rate of 59% in human gingival plaque[65] and may be isolated in 25% of clenched-fist injuries.[62] It can act synergistically with viridans streptococci and is a common cause of osteomyelitis. Although *E. corrodens* is susceptible to penicillin, it is resistant to penicillinase-resistant penicillins, clindamycin, and metronidazole and is variably resistant to cephalosporins.[45–47]

Management should include examination by an experienced hand surgeon to evaluate nerve and muscular function and the extent of injury to tendons, bones, and joints. Débridement and copious irrigation are often required. Elevation and immobilization with a plaster splint from the fingers to the elbow are essential and should be continued until marked improvement is noted. Aerobic and anaerobic cultures and x-ray films (to check for fracture and osteomyelitis) should be obtained. Many authors suggest the use of tetanus toxoid or both toxoid and antitoxin when indicated. Secondary débridement to remove necrotic bone and tissue or to drain abscesses may be advisable.

Empirical antimicrobial therapy is often intravenous and should include either cefoxitin or ampicillin/sulbactam or ticarcillin/clavulanate until culture results are known. Failure of first-generation cephalosporins and penicillinase-resistant penicillins, when used alone, has been reported and is often due to *E. corrodens*.[62–67] If resistant gram-negative rods are isolated, therapy should be altered according to the results of culture. What role β-lactamase–positive *Prevotella* and *Porphyromonas* spp. will have in the selection of antimicrobial therapy remains to be determined.

REFERENCES

1. U.S. Department of Commerce. Statistical Abstracts of the United States—1992. 112th ed. Table No. 392, p. 328.
2. Sacks JJ, Kresnow M, Houston B. Dog bites: How big a problem? Inj Prev. 1996;2:52–54.
3. Weiss HB, Friedman DJ, Cohen JH. Incidence of dog bite injuries treated in emergency departments. JAMA. 1998;279:51–53.
4. Goldstein EJC, Citron DM, Finegold SM. Dog bite wounds and infection: A prospective clinical study. Ann Emerg Med. 1980;9:508–512.
5. Lockwood R. Dog-bite–related fatalities—United States 1995–1996. MMWR Morb Mortal Wkly Rep. 1997;46:463–467.
6. Brakenbury PH, Muwanga C. A comparative double blind study of amoxycillin/clavulanate vs placebo in the prevention of infection after animal bites. Arch Emerg Med. 1989;6:251–256.
7. Feder HM, Shanley JD, Barbera JA. Review of 59 patients hospitalized with animal bites. Pediatr Infect Dis J. 1987;6:24–28.
8. Goldstein EJC. Bite wounds and infection. Clin Infect Dis. 1992;14:633–640.
9. Goldstein EJC, Citron DM, Nesbit C, et al. Prevalence and characterization of anaerobic bacteria from 50 patients with infected dog and cat bite wounds. In: Ely A, Bennett K, eds. Anaerobic Pathogens. Sheffield, England: Sheffield Academic; 1997:177–185.
10. Zook EG, Miller M, Van Beek AL, et al. Successful treatment protocol of canine fang injuries. J Trauma. 1980;20:243–247.
11. Brook I. Microbiology of human and animal bite wounds in children. Pediatr Infect Dis J. 1987;6:29–32.
12. Talan DA, Citron DM, Abrahamian FM, et al. Bacteriologic analysis of infected dog and cat bites. Emergency Medicine Animal Bite Infection Study Group. N Engl J Med. 1999;340:85–92.
13. Gallen IW, Ispahani P. Fulminant *Capnocytophaga canimorsus* (DF-2) septicaemia. Lancet. 1991;337:308.
14. Hicklin H, Verghese A, Alvarez S. Dysgonic fermenter 2 septicemia. Rev Infect Dis. 1987;9:884–890.
15. Brenner DJ, Hollis DG, Fanning GR, et al. *Capnocytophaga canimorsus* sp. nov. (formerly CDC group DF2), a cause of septicemia following dog bite, and *C. cynodegmi* sp. nov., a cause of localized wound infection following dog bite. J Clin Microbiol. 1989;27:231–235.
16. Verghese A, Hamati F, Berk S, et al. Susceptibility of dysgonic fermenter 2 to antimicrobial agents in vitro. Antimicrob Agents Chemother. 1988;32:78–80.
17. Goldstein EJC, Citron DM, Finegold SM. Role of anaerobic bacteria in bite wound infections. Rev Infect Dis. 1984;6(Suppl 1):S177–S183.
18. Stucker FJ, Shaw GY, Boyd S, et al. Management of animal and human bites in the head and neck. Arch Otolaryngol Head Neck Surg. 1990;116:789–793.
19. Brook I. Human and animal bite infections. J Fam Pract. 1989;28:713–718.
20. Holst E, Rollof J, Larsson L, et al. Characterization and distribution of *Pasteurella* species recovered from human infections. J Clin Microbiol. 1992;30:2984–2987.
21. Talan DA, Staatz D, Staatz A, et al. *Staphylococcus intermedius* in canine gingiva and canine inflicted human wound infections: Laboratory characterization of a newly recognized zoonotic pathogen. J Clin Microbiol. 1989;27:78–81.
22. Talan DA, Goldstein EJC, Staatz D, et al. *Staphylococcus intermedius:* Clinical presentation of a new human dog bite pathogen. Ann Emerg Med. 1989;18:410–413.
23. Andersen BM, Steigerwalt AG, O'Conner SP, et al. *Neisseria weaveri* sp. nov., formerly CDC group M-5, a gram-negative bacterium associated with dog bite wounds. J Clin Microbiol. 1993;31:2456–2466.
24. Inzana TJ, Johnson JL, Shell L, et al. Isolation and characterization of a newly identified *Haemophilus* species from cats: *Haemophilus felis*. J Clin Microbiol. 1992;30:2108–2112.
25. Holmes B, Steigerwalt AG, Weaver RE, et al. *Weeksella zoohelcum* sp. nov. (formerly group IIj) from human clinical specimens. Syst Appl Microbiol. 1986;8:191–196.
26. Guibourdenche M, Lamber T, Riou JY. Isolation of *Neisseria canis* in mixed culture from a patient after a cat bite. J Clin Microbiol. 1989;27:1673–1674.
27. Goldstein EJC, Citron DM, Merkin TE, et al. Recovery of an unusual *Flavobacterium* IIb-like isolate from a hand infection following pig bite. J Clin Microbiol. 1990;28:1709–1781.
28. Peel NM, Hornridge KA, Luppino M, et al. *Actinobacillus* spp. and related bacteria in infected wounds of humans bitten by horses and sheep. J Clin Microbiol. 1991;29:2535–2538.
29. Hollis DG, Moss CW, Daneshaver MI, et al. Characterization of Centers for Disease Control group NO1, a fastidious, nonoxidative, gram negative organism associated with dog and cat bites. J Clin Microbiol. 1993;31:746–748.

30. Citron DM, Gerardo SH, Claros MC, et al. Frequency of isolation of *Porphyromonas* species from infected dog and cat bite wounds in humans and their characterization by biochemical tests and arbitrarily primed-polymerase chain reaction fingerprinting. Clin Infect Dis. 1996;23(Suppl 1):S78–S82.
31. Alexander CJ, Citron DM, Gerardo SH, et al. Characterization of saccharolytic *Bacteroides* and *Prevotella* isolates from infected dog and cat bite wounds in humans. J Clin Microbiol. 1997;35:406–411.
32. Hudspeth MK, Gerardo SH, Citron DM, et al. Growth characteristics and a novel method of identification (the WEE-TAB system) of *Porphyromonas* species isolated from infected dog and cat bite wounds in humans. J Clin Microbiol. 1997;35:2450–2453.
33. Love DN, Cato EP, Johnson JL, et al. Deoxyribonucleic acid hybridization among strains of fusobacteria isolated from soft tissue infections of cats: Comparison with the human and animal type strains from oral and other sites. Int J Syst Bacteriol. 1987;37:23–26.
34. Lucas GL, Bartlett DH. *Pasteurella multocida* infection in the hand. Plast Reconstr Surg. 1981;67:49–53.
35. Burdge DR, Scheifele D, Speert DP. Serious *Pasteurella multocida* infections from lion and tiger bites. JAMA. 1985;253:3296–3297.
36. Capellan J, Fong IW. Tularemia from a cat bite: Case report and review. Clin Infect Dis. 1993;16:472–475.
37. Ordog GJ, Balasubramianium S, Wasserberger J. Rat bites: Fifty cases. Ann Emerg Med. 1985;14:126–130.
38. Paisley JW, Lauer BA. Severe facial injuries to infants due to unprovoked attacks by pet ferrets. JAMA. 1988;259:2005–2006.
39. Barnham M. Pig bite injuries and infection: Report of seven human cases. Epidemiol Infect. 1988;101:641–645.
40. Flandry F, Lisecki EJ, Domingue GJ, et al. Initial antibiotic therapy for alligator bites. South Med J. 1989;82:262–266.
41. Goldstein EJC, Pryor EP III, Citron DM. Simian bites and bacterial infection. Clin Infect Dis. 1995;20:1551–1552.
42. Holmes GP, Chapman LE, Stewart J, et al. Guidelines for the prevention and treatment of B virus infections in exposed persons. Clin Infect Dis. 1995;20:421–439.
43. Goldstein EJC, Citron DM, Richwald GA. Lack of in vitro efficacy of oral forms of certain cephalosporins, erythromycin and oxacillin against *Pasteurella multocida.* Antimicrob Agents Chemother. 1988;32:213–215.
44. Gaillot O, Guilbert L, Maruejouls C, et al. In vitro susceptibility to thirteen of *Pasteurella* spp. and related bacteria isolated from humans. J Antimicrob Chemother. 1995;36:878–880.
45. Goldstein EJC, Citron DM, Hudspeth M, et al. In vitro activity of Bay 12-8039, a new 8-methoxy-quinolone, compared to the activities of 11 other oral antimicrobial agents against 390 aerobic and anaerobic bacteria isolated from human and animal bite wounds in skin and soft tissue infections in humans. Antimicrob Agents Chemother. 1997;41:1552–1557.
46. Goldstein EJC, Citron DM, Hudspeth M, et al. Trovafloxacin compared with levofloxacin, ofloxacin, ciprofloxacin, azithromycin and clarithromycin against unusual aerobic and anaerobic human and animal bite-wound pathogens. J Antimicrob Chemother. 1998;41:391–396.
47. Goldstein EJC, Citron DM, Gerardo SH, et al. Activities of HMR 3004 (RU 64004) and HMR 3647 (RU 6647) compared to those of erythromycin, azithromycin, clarithromycin, roxithromycin and eight other antimicrobial agents against unusual aerobic and anaerobic human and animal bite pathogens isolated from skin and soft tissue. Antimicrob Agents Chemother. 1998;42:1127–1132.
48. Parish HM. Incidence of treated snake bites in the United States. Public Health Rep. 1966;81:269–276.
49. Russell FE. Clinical aspects of snake venom poisoning in North America. Toxicon. 1969;7:33–37.
50. Goldstein EJC, Citron DM, Gonzalez H, et al. Bacteriology of rattlesnake venom and implications for therapy. J Infect Dis. 1979;140:818–821.
51. Williams FE, Freeman M, Kennedy E. The bacterial flora of the mouths of Australian venomous snakes in captivity. Med J Aust. 1934;2:190–193.
52. Talan D, Citron DM, Overturf GD, et al. Antibacterial activity of crotalid venoms against oral snake flora and other clinical bacteria. J Infect Dis. 1991;164:195–198.
53. Brook I. Bacteriology study of paronychia in children. Am J Surg. 1981;141:703.
54. Al Fallouji M. Traumatic love bites. Br J Surg. 1990;77:100–101.
55. Wolf JS, Gomez R, McAninch JW. Human bites to the penis. J Urol. 1992;147:2065–2067.
56. Mann RJ, Hoffeld TA, Farmer CB. Human bites of the hand: Twenty years of experience. J Hand Surg. 1977;2:97–104.
57. Sperber ND. Bite marks, oral and facial injuries. Harbingers of severe child abuse? Pediatrician. 1989;16:207–211.
58. Goldstein EJC, Citron DM, Wield B, et al. Bacteriology of human and animal bite wounds. J Clin Microbiol. 1978;8:667–672.
59. Chuinard RG, D'Ambrosia RD. Human bite infections of the hand. J Bone Joint Surg Am. 1977;59:416–418.
60. Zubowicz VN, Gravier M. Management of early human bites of the hand: A prospective randomized study. Plastic Reconstr Surg. 1991;88:111–114.
61. Brook I. Microbiology of human and animal bite wounds in children. Pediatr Infect Dis. 1987;6:29–32.
62. Goldstein EJC, Miller TA, Citron DM, et al. Infections following clenched-fist injury: A new perspective. J Hand Surg. 1978;3:455–457.
63. Goldstein EJC, Barone M, Miller TA. *Eikenella corrodens* in hand infections. J Hand Surg. 1983;8:563–567.
64. McDonald I. *Eikenella corrodens* infections of the hand. Hand. 1979;11:224–227.
65. Goldstein EJC, Tarenzi LA, Agyare EO, et al. Prevalence of *Eikenella corrodens* in dental plaque. J Clin Microbiol. 1983;17:636–639.
66. Goldstein EJC, Sutter VL, Finegold SM. Susceptibility of *Eikenella corrodens* to ten cephalosporins. Antimicrob Agents Chemother. 1978;14:639–641.
67. Goldstein EJC, Gombert ME, Agyare EO. Susceptibility of *Eikenella corrodens* to newer beta-lactam antibiotics. Antimicrob Agents Chemother. 1980;18:832–833.

SECTION D

Chapter 312

Immunization

WALTER A. ORENSTEIN
MELINDA WHARTON
KENNETH J. BART
ALAN R. HINMAN

The two most effective means of preventing disease, disability, and death from infectious diseases have been sanitation and immunization. Both these approaches antedated understanding of the germ theory of disease. Artificial induction of immunity began centuries ago with variolation, the practice of inoculating fluid from smallpox lesions into the skin of susceptible persons. Although this technique usually produced mild illness without complications, spread of disease did occur, with occasional complications. In 1796, Jenner demonstrated that milk maids who had contracted cowpox (vaccinia) were immune to smallpox. He inoculated the vesicular fluid from cowpox lesions into the skin of susceptible individuals and induced protection against smallpox, thus beginning the era of immunization.

Immunization is the act of artificially inducing immunity or providing protection from disease; it can be active or passive. Active immunization consists of inducing the body to develop defenses against disease. This is usually accomplished by the administration of vaccines or toxoids that stimulate the body's immune system to produce antibodies or cell-mediated immunity, or both, that protects against the infectious agent. Passive immunization consists of providing temporary protection through the administration of exogenously produced antibody. Two situations in which passive immunization commonly occurs are through the transplacental transfer of antibodies to the fetus, which may provide protection against certain diseases for the first 3 to 6 months of life, and the injection of immunoglobulin for specific preventive purposes. A more detailed description of the immune mechanisms involved follows.

Immunizing agents include vaccines, toxoids, and antibody-containing preparations from human or animal donors. Some important definitions follow.[1]

1. Vaccine: A suspension of attenuated live or killed microorganisms (bacteria, viruses, or rickettsiae), or fractions thereof, administered to induce immunity and thereby prevent infectious disease.
2. Toxoid: A modified bacterial toxin that has been rendered nontoxic but retains the ability to stimulate the formation of antitoxin.
3. Immunoglobulin (IG): A sterile solution for intramuscular administration containing antibody from human blood. It contains 10 to 18% protein obtained by cold ethanol fractionation of large pools of blood plasma. It is primarily indicated for routine protection of certain immunodeficient persons and for passive immunization against measles and hepatitis A. Immunoglobulin intravenous (IGIV), a specialized preparation allowing intravenous administration, contains approximately 5% protein and is indicated primarily for replacement therapy in IgG deficiency, treatment of Kawasaki disease, and idiopathic thrombocytopenic purpura.
4. Specific immunoglobulin: Special preparations obtained from donor pools preselected for a high antibody content against a specific disease, for example, hepatitis B immune globulin (HBIG), varicella-zoster immune globulin (VZIG), rabies immune globulin (RIG), and tetanus immune globulin (TIG).

The constituents of immunizing agents include:

1. Suspending fluid: This frequently is as simple as sterile water or saline, but it may be a complex fluid containing small amounts of proteins or other constituents derived from the medium or biologic system in which the immunizing agent is produced (serum proteins, egg antigens, cell culture–derived antigens).
2. Preservatives, stabilizers, antibiotics: These components of vaccines are used (1) to inhibit or prevent bacterial growth in viral culture or the final product or (2) to stabilize the antigen. They include materials such as mercurials (thimerosal), gelatin, and specific antibiotics. Allergic reactions may occur if the recipient is sensitive to any of these additives. Because of the results of a review of the mercury content of vaccines, an effort is under way to develop thimerosal-free vaccines that contain other preservatives or do not need a preservative because they are packaged as single doses.[1a]
3. Adjuvants: An aluminum salt is used in some vaccines to enhance the immune response to vaccines containing inactivated microorganisms or their products (e.g., toxoids and hepatitis B vaccine). Vaccines with such adjuvants should usually be injected deeply into muscle masses because subcutaneous or intracutaneous administration can cause local irritation, inflammation, granuloma formation, or necrosis.

IMMUNOLOGIC BASIS OF VACCINATION

Two major approaches to active immunization have been employed: the use of live (generally attenuated) infectious agents or the use of inactivated, or detoxified, agents or their extracts. For many diseases (including influenza, poliomyelitis, typhoid, and measles) both approaches have been employed. Live, attenuated vaccines are believed to induce an immunologic response more similar to that resulting from natural infection than do killed vaccines. Inactivated or killed vaccines can consist of inactivated whole organisms (e.g., cholera, pertussis), detoxified exotoxin (e.g., diphtheria and tetanus toxoids), soluble capsular material either alone (e.g., pneumococcal polysaccharide) or covalently linked to carrier proteins (e.g., *Haemophilus influenzae* type B conjugate vaccines), or purified extracts of some component or components of the organism (e.g., hepatitis B, subunit influenza, and acellular pertussis vaccines).

DETERMINANTS OF IMMUNOGENICITY

The immune system is complex, and antigen composition and presentation are critical for stimulation of the desired immune response. Immunogenicity is determined not only by the chemical and physical states of the antigen and degree of purity (e.g., whole cell pertussis vaccine versus acellular pertussis vaccine) but also by the genetic characteristics of the responding individual (major histocompatibility complex [MHC] polymorphism), the physiologic condition of the individual (e.g., age, nutrition, gender, pregnancy status, stress, infections, immune status), and the manner in which the antigen is presented (route of administration, dose or doses and timing of doses, presence of adjuvants).[2]

Major Histocompatibility Complex Polymorphism

The extensive polymorphism of the MHC in human populations contributes to the recognition by different individuals of different

All material in this chapter is in the public domain, with the exception of any borrowed figures or tables.

epitopes in a complex protein antigen. To vaccinate a population effectively, a vaccine must contain epitopes that can be processed and bind to the product of at least one allele in every individual.[3]

Live versus Killed or Subunit Vaccines

Because the organisms in live vaccines multiply in the recipient, antigen production generally increases logarithmically until checked by the onset of the immune response it is intended to induce. The live, attenuated viruses (e.g., measles, mumps, rubella) generally are believed to confer lifelong protection with one dose in those who respond. By contrast, killed vaccines generally do not induce permanent immunity with one dose, making repeated vaccination and boosters necessary to develop and maintain high levels of antibody (e.g., diphtheria, tetanus, rabies, typhoid). Exceptions to this general rule may include hepatitis B vaccine, for which long-term immunologic memory has been demonstrated for at least 10 years after vaccination, and inactivated polio vaccine (IPV), for which the duration of immunity is unknown. Although the amount of antigen initially introduced is greater with inactivated vaccines, multiplication of organisms in the host results in a cumulatively greater antigenic input with live vaccines.

Polysaccharide vaccines tend to induce T-cell–independent immune responses that do not produce booster responses on repeated injections and have poor immunogenicity in infants and young children. In contrast, protein antigens tend to generate a T-cell–dependent immune response with induction of immunologic memory, booster effects on repeat administration, and good immunogenicity in infants and young children. Covalent linkage of *H. influenzae* type B capsular polysaccharide to carrier proteins converts them from T-cell–independent to T-cell–dependent antigens.

Dose

The amount of antigen is important. The presentation of an insufficient amount may result in an absence of immune responsiveness. There is usually a dose response curve relationship between antigen dose and peak response obtained beyond a threshold; however, responsiveness may reach a plateau, failing to increase beyond a certain level despite increasing doses of vaccine.

Adjuvants

The degree of "foreignness" of the antigen and its purity determines the extent and specificity of the response. More complex antigens are more immunogenic. The immune response to some vaccines or toxoids can be potentiated by the addition of adjuvants, such as aluminum salts. They are particularly useful with inactivated products such as diphtheria and tetanus toxoids and whole cell or acellular pertussis vaccines (DTP or DTaP) and hepatitis B vaccine. The mechanism of enhancement of antigenicity by adjuvants is not totally defined; however, adjuvants render a soluble antigen immunogenic, mobilize phagocytes to the site of antigen deposition, and delay the release of antigen.

Route of Administration

The route of administration may determine the rapidity and nature of the immune response to a vaccine or toxoid. Inoculation into or on organs of external secretion (e.g., nasal or gastrointestinal mucosa) is more likely to result in production of local IgA compared with that after intramuscular injection. The immunogenicity of some vaccines is reduced when not given by the recommended route. For example, administration of hepatitis B vaccine subcutaneously into the fatty tissue of the buttock was associated with substantially lower seroconversion rates than injection intramuscularly into the deltoid.[4]

Age

The immune response to a vaccine may be age-dependent. Although children and young adults usually respond well to all vaccines, differences in response capability exist during early infancy and old age. The presence of high levels of passively acquired maternal antibody in the first few months of life impairs the initial immune response to some killed vaccines (hepatitis A vaccine,[5] diphtheria toxoid) and many live vaccines. In the elderly, the response to antigenic stimulation may be diminished (e.g., influenza, hepatitis B vaccines).

MOBILIZATION OF THE IMMUNE RESPONSE

Many of the structural constituents of microorganisms as well as exotoxins are antigenic. At rest, the lymphoid immune system consists of quiescent cells—B and T lymphocytes—each potentially responsive to a unique, specific antigen. When an antigen is presented or recognized, these lymphocytes proliferate into a clonal population of cells that directs an immune response against the foreign antigen. Antigens usually require the interaction of B and T cells (T-cell–dependent) to generate an immune response (e.g., measles, varicella) (also see Chapter 9) T cells can recognize polypeptides of a relatively small length (8 to 20 amino acids) in association with a specific MHC molecule.[6] On occasion, antigen may initiate B cell proliferation and antibody production without the help of T cells (T-cell–independent, e.g., pneumococcal polysaccharide).

The first step in the induction of a T-cell–dependent antibody response is the activation of T-helper cells by presentation of antigen by mononuclear phagocytes or dendritic cells, a step that may be facilitated by the use of an adjuvant. Presentation of an antigen triggers the secretion of a cascade of mediators (cytokines), which are made by or act on elements of the immune system to stimulate the maturation of naive T-helper cells, and communicate between leukocytes (interleukins [IL], intercellular messengers which activate lymphocyte cellular differentiation) to regulate the immune response. Depending on the stimulus (thymus-dependent or -independent), T lymphocytes are stimulated by IL-12 to differentiate into one of two subsets: T helper 1 (T_H1), which execute cell-mediated immune responses or by IL-4 to differentiate into T helper 2 cells (T_H2), which assist in antibody production for humoral immunity. Each of the subsets in turn produces interleukins: T_H1 produces IL-2 and interferon; T_H2 produces IL-4, IL-5, IL-6, and IL-10.[7, 8]

The antibody molecules formed after immunization may express a variety of antigen binding specificities (i.e., recognize different structures on a complex multideterminant antigen).[9, 10]

The most important protective antibodies include those that inactivate soluble toxic protein products of bacteria (antitoxins), facilitate phagocytosis and intracellular digestion of bacteria (opsonins), interact with components of serum complement to damage the bacterial membrane with resultant bacteriolysis (lysins), prevent proliferation of infectious virus (neutralizing antibodies), or interact with components of the bacterial surface to prevent adhesion to mucosal surfaces (antiadhesins) (also see Chapter 2).

Antigens react with antibody in the blood stream and extracellular fluid and at mucosal surfaces. Antibodies cannot readily reach intracellular sites of infection, the sites of viral and some bacterial replication. However, antibodies are effective against many viral diseases by (1) interacting with virus before initial intracellular penetration occurs, and (2) preventing locally replicating virus from disseminating from the site of entry to an important target organ, as in the spread of poliovirus from the gut to the central nervous system or of rabies from a puncture wound to peripheral neural tissue.

UNANTICIPATED RESPONSES

Independent of antibody production, the stimulation of the immune system by vaccination may, on occasion, elicit a hypersensitivity response. Killed measles vaccine, in use in the United States between 1963 and 1967, induced incomplete humoral immunity and cell-mediated hypersensitivity, resulting in the development of a syndrome of atypical measles in some children on subsequent challenge.[11] In addition, some antibodies produced may not be protective but "block" the reaction of protective antibodies with antigens, inhibiting the body's defenses. Some vaccines may induce immunologic tolerance that results in blunting of the immune response on subsequent exposure to the antigen (e.g., meningococcal polysaccharide vaccine[12]).

TEMPORAL COURSE OF THE IMMUNE RESPONSE

The "primary response" occurs after first exposure to a vaccine antigen. After a latent period, humoral and cell-mediated immunity can be detected. Circulating antibodies do not usually appear for 7 to 10 days. The immunoglobulin class of the response changes over time. Early-appearing antibodies are usually IgM class and of low affinity; late-appearing antibodies are usually IgG and display a high affinity. When the antigen is thymus-dependent, IgM and IgG classes of antibody are initially secreted by B cells, with IgM appearing first. IgM antibodies may fix complement, making lysis and phagocytosis possible. As the titer of IgG rises during the second week (or later) after immunogenic stimulation, the IgM titer falls. IgG antibodies are produced in large amounts and function in the neutralization, precipitation, and fixation of complement. The antibody titer frequently reaches a peak in approximately 2 to 6 weeks and then falls gradually. The switch from IgM synthesis to predominantly IgG synthesis in B cells requires T-cell cooperation. Uncommonly, individuals may not respond to a vaccine, experiencing a "primary vaccine failure." Such individuals may lack the MHC determinants required to recognize the antigen, but other mechanisms exist as well; for example, almost all children who do not respond immunologically to the first dose of measles, mumps, rubella MMR vaccine will acquire measles immunity following a second dose.[13]

Many pathogens replicate at mucosal surfaces before host invasion and may induce secretory IgA along the respiratory and gastrointestinal mucous membranes and at other localized sites (e.g., polio, rubella, influenza). IgA antibodies are efficient at virus neutralization (e.g., polio), fix complement through the alternative pathway (e.g., cholera), prevent absorption of organisms to the intestinal wall (e.g., *Escherichia coli,* cholera), and can lyse gram-negative bacteria (with the aid of both complement and lysozyme).[14] Current parenteral, especially inactivated, vaccines rarely induce high levels of secretory IgA antibodies.

After a second exposure to the same antigen, a heightened humoral or cell-mediated responses, an "anamnestic response," is observed. These "secondary responses" occur sooner than the primary response, usually within 4 to 5 days, and depend on a marked proliferation of antibody-producing cells or effector T cells. The secondary response depends on immunologic memory after the first exposure mediated by both T and B cells. Infection with measles or varicella vaccine strains has been shown to evoke a cell-mediated as well as humoral response.

Some immune responses may not in themselves confer immunity but may be sufficiently associated with protection that they remain useful proxy measures of protective immunity (e.g., vibriocidal serum antibodies in cholera).

MEASUREMENT OF THE IMMUNE RESPONSE

Response to vaccines is often gauged by measuring the appearance and concentration of the specific antibody in the serum.[15] For some viral vaccines, such as those for measles, rubella, and hepatitis B, the presence of circulating antibodies correlates with clinical protection. Although this has served as a dependable indicator of immunity, seroconversion measures only the humoral parameter of the immune response. Secondary vaccine failure occurs when an individual who had previously had an adequate immune response loses that immunity over time. Evaluating persistence of antibody has been used to determine duration of vaccine-induced immunity. However, the absence of measurable antibody may not mean that the individual is unprotected. Although a fall in titer takes place for some vaccines over time (e.g., measles, rubella, hepatitis B) on revaccination or challenge, a rapid secondary response is observed in IgG antibodies with little or no detectable IgM response, suggesting persistent protection. With some vaccines and toxoids, the mere presence of antibodies is not sufficient to ensure clinical protection, but rather a minimal circulating level of antibody is required (e.g., 0.01 IU/ml of tetanus antitoxin). The measurement of cell-mediated immunity, which would be helpful in assessing the degree of ongoing protection, is usually limited to research laboratories and to only a few vaccines.

VACCINE DEVELOPMENT

Most vaccines in use today have been developed by conventional techniques.[16] For live attenuated viral vaccines, organisms are repeatedly passaged in various tissue culture cell lines to reduce virulent properties while maintaining immunogenicity. Inactivated vaccines usually have been developed by growing microorganisms, followed by concentration, purification, and inactivation, not necessarily in that order. Component vaccines usually are derived from chemical separation of the needed component from the parent organism.

Future vaccines are likely to be derived from new methods of biotechnology—especially recombinant techniques. Currently available hepatitis B vaccines were developed by cloning the hepatitis B surface antigen (HBsAg) gene into yeast, leading to synthesis of HBsAg within the yeast cell. Other new approaches for producing vaccines include live vectors, in which one or more genes encoding for critical determinants of immunity from pathogenic microorganisms are inserted into the genome of the vector. Such vectors may include viruses such as pox viruses (vaccinia or canarypox) or bacteria such as salmonella or bacillus Calmette-Guérin (BCG). Other newer techniques include microencapsulation of critical antigens in polymers that can lead to sustained release or pulse release over prolonged periods, mimicking the effect of multiple injections of an antigen over a several-month interval. New technologies also include use of nucleic acids, which encodes critical antigens. Injection of the DNA leads to production of antigen without risk of producing whole infectious organisms. Rotavirus vaccine was developed using genetic reassortment of the genes encoding one of the surface glycoproteins from human isolates with 10 other genes contributed from a rhesus monkey strain. Similar techniques have been used in the development of live attenuated influenza vaccines.

General Principles of Immunization

The introduction and widespread use of vaccines has resulted in global eradication of smallpox, elimination of poliomyelitis caused by wild viruses in the United States, and dramatic reductions in the incidence rates of other diseases (Table 312–1). Measles, diphtheria, and rubella have been greatly reduced in developed countries (>90%) and, if global vaccination efforts can be sustained, may eventually be eliminated from the United States and many other countries.[17] The World Health Assembly has established a goal to eradicate polio from the world by the end of 2000. The last case of polio due to wild virus in the Western Hemisphere was in 1991, and major progress toward polio eradication has been made worldwide.[18, 19] Global use of hepatitis B vaccine in infants will potentially have an impact comparable to that of other vaccines in childhood, although impact has been suboptimal due to limited use to date. *H. influenzae* type B vaccines have only recently come into widespread use, but disease incidence has been markedly reduced in many developed countries.[20, 21]

TABLE 312–1 Baseline 20th Century Annual Morbidity and 1998 Provisional Morbidity from Nine Diseases with Vaccines Recommended before 1990 for Universal Use in Children—United States

Disease	Baseline 20th Century Annual Morbidity	1998 Provisional Morbidity	% Decrease
Smallpox	48,164*	0	100%
Diphtheria	175,885†	1	100%‡
Pertussis	147,271§	6279	95.7%
Tetanus	1314‖	34	97.4%
Poliomyelitis (paralytic)	16,316¶	0**	100%
Measles	503,282††	89	100%‡
Mumps	152,209‡‡	606	99.6%
Rubella	47,745§§	345	99.3%
Congenital rubella syndrome	823‖‖	5	99.4%
Haemophilus influenzae type B	20,000¶¶	54***	99.7%

*Average annual number of cases during 1900–1904.
†Average annual number of reported cases during 1920–1922, 3 years before vaccine development.
‡Rounded to nearest tenth.
§Average annual number of reported cases during 1922–1925, 4 years before vaccine development.
‖Estimated number of cases based on reported number of deaths during 1922–1926 assuming a case-fatality rate of 90%.
¶Average annual number of reported cases during 1951–1954, 4 years before vaccine licensure.
**Excludes one case of vaccine-associated polio reported in 1998.
††Average number of reported cases during 1958–1962, 5 years before vaccine licensure.
‡‡Number of reported cases in 1968, the first year reporting began and the first year after vaccine licensure.
§§Average annual number of reported cases during 1966–1968, 3 years before vaccine licensure.
‖‖Estimated number of cases based on seroprevalence data in the population and on the risk that women infected during a childbearing year would have a fetus with congenital rubella syndrome.
¶¶Estimated number of cases from population-based surveillance studies before vaccine licensure in 1985.
***Excludes 71 cases of *Haemophilus influenzae* disease of unknown serotype.
Adapted from Centers for Disease Control and Prevention. Ten great public health achievements—United States, 1900–1999. MMWR Morb Mortal Wkly Rep. 1999;48 (12):245.

Modern vaccines are very safe and effective; however, they are not completely so. Each vaccine is associated with some adverse effects, which may range from very mild to life-threatening, and each vaccine falls short of 100% effectiveness. Consequently, some persons who have received a full course of vaccine or toxoid may acquire disease on exposure. The effectiveness of vaccines recommended for universal use in children is well defined, ranging from about 50% (rotavirus vaccine) to more than 90 to 95% for most of the other vaccines. Acellular pertussis vaccines range in efficacy from 71 to 89% in most studies.[22] Varicella vaccine is 95% or more effective against severe varicella but is less effective against varicella of any severity.[23, 24] In 1998, reductions of 95% or more from baseline 20th-century morbidity have been reported in the United States for smallpox, diphtheria, tetanus, pertussis, polio, measles, mumps, and rubella (see Table 312–1). Similar reductions, based on historical estimates, have been achieved for congenital rubella syndrome and *H. influenzae* type B invasive disease.[24a]

Although the high efficacy of each of these vaccines is readily apparent, there has been substantial controversy over reported adverse events temporally associated with vaccination. Because of these controversies, the Institute of Medicine (IOM) reviewed available information regarding 9 of the 11 vaccines universally recommended for children and the serious adverse effects that have been reported in association with them.[25–27] For most events, the available evidence was insufficient to make a causal evaluation. However, evidence related to several events was sufficient to (1) support a rejection of vaccine playing a causal role, (2) support vaccine playing a causal role, or (3) more definitively establish that vaccine has a causal role. Table 312–2 summarizes events associated with vaccines about which the IOM could reach a conclusion. The IOM review provides the best and most comprehensive compilation of data on vaccine safety to date. The Advisory Committee on Immunization Practices (ACIP) subsequently reviewed the IOM findings along with new data available regarding Guillain-Barré syndrome (GBS). Most of the IOM conclusions were accepted. However, new data from population-based studies of GBS and vaccines as well as new information from a Finnish study do not support a causal relationship between oral polio vaccine, DTP, or tetanus toxoid and GBS.[28, 29] Likewise, more recent studies have found no evidence of increased risk for new onset of chronic arthropathies among women vaccinated with RA27/3 vaccine, arguing against RA27/3 rubella vaccine as a cause of chronic arthropathy.[30–32]

In the development of vaccines, the initial studies are typically carried out in animal models to demonstrate protection (or at least production of antibodies) and relative safety and then limited numbers of doses are administered to humans to demonstrate antibody production and safety (phase I). After this stage, clinical trials in humans are typically carried out in a limited number of individuals to select optimal vaccine schedules and to demonstrate further safety (phase II). Larger trials are carried out to demonstrate efficacy (phase III). Because of their limited size, these field trials can only be expected to detect adverse events that occur relatively frequently (1/1000 doses or higher). After clinical trials, licensure may be sought. In the United States, vaccine production is strictly regulated by the Center for Biologics Evaluation and Research of the Food and Drug Administration. Only after a vaccine is found to be safe and effective is it licensed for use. Postmarketing surveillance (phase IV) is necessary to detect rare adverse events associated with vaccination and to monitor safety of vaccination practices such as simultaneous immunization.

Although there is no direct evidence of risk to the fetus when pregnant women are given a particular vaccine, most live virus vaccines induce viremia, which can result in infection of the fetus.

TABLE 312–2 Summary of Institute of Medicine Findings on the Relationship of Adverse Events to Individual Vaccines

Vaccine	Establishes Causation	Favors Causation	Favors Rejection of Causation
DT/Td/T	Anaphylaxis	Guillain-Barré syndrome; brachial neuritis	Encephalopathy, infantile spasms, SIDS
Pertussis* (DTP)	Anaphylaxis; protracted, inconsolable crying	Acute encephalopathy; shock and unusual shocklike state (hypotonic-hyporesponsive episodes)	Infantile spasms, hypsarrhythmia, Reye syndrome, SIDS
Measles		Anaphylaxis; death from measles vaccine strain in primarily immunocompromised	
MMR (see also measles and rubella)	Anaphylaxis; thrombocytopenia		
Mumps (see MMR)			
OPV	Poliomyelitis; death from polio vaccine strain (mainly in immunocompromised individuals)	Guillain-Barré syndrome	
IPV			
Hepatitis B	Anaphylaxis		
HIB conjugate			Early onset *Haemophilus influenzae* type B disease
Rubella* (see also MMR)	Acute arthritis	Chronic arthritis	

*Reviewed by an earlier committee. Initial report categories corresponding to those table headings were "Evidence indicates a causal relationship," "Evidence is consistent with a causal relationship," and "Evidence does not indicate a causal relationship."
Abbreviations: DT, Diphtheria and tetanus toxoids; HIB, *Haemophilus influenzae* type B; IPV, inactivated polio vaccine; MMR, measles, mumps, and rubella; OPV, oral polio vaccine; P, pertussis; SIDS, sudden infant death syndrome; Td, tetanus and diphtheria toxoids adsorbed.

TABLE 312–3 Currently Available Vaccines and Toxoids and Year Licensed*

Product	Year Licensed
Anthrax vaccine absorbed	1970
Bacillus Calmette Guérin vaccine	1950
Cholera vaccine	1917
Diphtheria and tetanus toxoids and pertussis vaccine adsorbed	1949
Diphtheria and tetanus toxoids and acellular pertussis vaccine	1991
Diphtheria and tetanus toxoids adsorbed (pediatric use, DT)	1949
Diphtheria and tetanus toxoids and pertussis vaccine and *Haemophilus* B conjugate vaccine	1993
Diphtheria and tetanus toxoids and acellular pertussis vaccine reconstituted with *Haemophilus* B conjugate vaccine	1996
Diphtheria toxoid	1927
Diphtheria toxoid adsorbed	1952
Hepatitis A vaccine	1995
Haemophilus B polysaccharide vaccine	1985
Haemophilus B conjugate vaccine	1987
Haemophilus B conjugate reconstituted with DTP	1993
Hepatitis B vaccine—plasma-derived	1981
Hepatitis B recombinant vaccine	1987
Hepatitis B recombinant vaccine and *Haemophilus* B conjugate vaccine	1996
Influenza virus vaccine	1945
Japanese encephalitis vaccine	1993
Lyme disease vaccine	1998
Measles and mumps virus vaccine, live	1973
Measles and rubella virus vaccine, live	1971
Measles virus vaccine, live, attenuated	1963
Measles, mumps, and rubella virus vaccine, live	1971
Meningococcal polysaccharide vaccine, group A	1975
Meningococcal polysaccharide vaccine, group C	1975
Meningococcal polysaccharide vaccine, groups A and C combined	1975
Meningococcal polysaccharide vaccine, groups A, C, Y, W135 combined	1981
Mumps virus vaccine, live	1967
Pertussis vaccine adsorbed	1948
Plague vaccine	1911
Pneumococcal vaccine, 23 valent	1983
Poliomyelitis vaccine (inactivated, enhanced potency)	1987
Poliovirus vaccine, live, oral, trivalent*	1963
Rabies vaccine (human diploid)	1980
Rotavirus vaccine	1998
Rubella and mumps virus vaccine, live	1970
Rubella virus vaccine, live	1969
Smallpox vaccine	1903
Tetanus and diphtheria toxoids adsorbed (adult use, Td)	1955
Tetanus toxoid	1933
Tetanus toxoid adsorbed	1949
Typhoid vaccine (parenteral)	1917
Typhoid vaccine (oral)	1990
Varicella vaccine	1995
Yellow fever vaccine	1953

*As of December 31, 1998.
†Monovalent forms licensed 1961.
Prepared by Bob Snyder, National Immunization Program, Centers for Disease Control and Prevention, Atlanta, Ga.

For this reason, live virus vaccines are not generally administered to pregnant women except in unusual circumstances.

The decision to use a vaccine involves assessment of the risks of disease, the benefits of vaccination, and the risks associated with vaccination. The relative balance of risks and benefits may change over time; consequently, continuing assessment of vaccines is essential. Recommendations for vaccine use are developed by several different bodies: The Centers for Disease Control and Prevention (CDC) ACIP develops recommendations for vaccines with primary orientation toward the public health sector. These recommendations are available on the World Wide Web at http://www.cdc.gov/nip/publications/ACIP_list.htm. The Committee on Infectious Diseases of the American Academy of Pediatrics (the "Red Book" committee) develops recommendations for vaccine use in private pediatric practice.[33] The Task Force on Adult Immunization of the American College of Physicians and the Infectious Diseases Society of America have developed recommendations for vaccination of adults in the private sector.[34] Since 1995, the ACIP, the American Academy of Pediatrics, and the American Academy of Family Physicians have collaborated to issue a harmonized childhood immunization schedule, which is updated annually.[35]

CURRENTLY AVAILABLE IMMUNIZING AGENTS

Tables 312–3 and 312–4 list currently licensed immunizing agents and immunoglobulins. This section presents brief information about most, including the type of immunizing agent it represents, the primary indications for its use, its relative efficacy, the number and spacing of doses required, known adverse effects, and precautions and contraindications for use. Package inserts and specific references and recommendations should be consulted for more detailed information. In addition to these licensed products, several other vaccines are under development and may soon become available (e.g., pneumococcal polysaccharide conjugate vaccine, meningococcal polysaccharide conjugate vaccine, live attenuated influenza vaccine, respiratory syncytial virus vaccine, and parainfluenza virus vaccine).

Vaccines

Anthrax Vaccine. Anthrax vaccine is prepared from microaerophilic cultures of an avirulent nonencapsulated strain of *Bacillus anthracis.* The cultures are grown in a synthetic medium, and during the growth period the organism elaborates the antigen that induces protective antibodies. The vaccine is indicated only for those at high risk of exposure to anthrax, such as persons who may come into contact with the following materials imported from anthrax-endemic areas: animal hides, furs, bone meal, wool, hair (especially goat hair), and bristles; for all personnel in factories handling these materials; laboratory workers planning investigational studies with the organism; and the military, who may be exposed to anthrax spores used as a biologic warfare agent. In 1998, vaccination of all members of the United States Armed Forces was begun. Concerns that *B. anthracis* could be an agent for biological warfare or bioterrorism have stimulated interest in use of vaccine along with antibiotics in exposed civilians. Efficacy has been demonstrated in protection against cutaneous disease. Clinical efficacy is not known with certainty against inhaled anthrax, but the vaccine induces antibodies in 90% or more of those who received the primary course of six subcutaneous injections given at time zero, 2 weeks, 4 weeks, 6 months, 12 months, and 18 months. A controlled study of a vaccine similar to the currently available vaccine demonstrated protective efficacy against cutaneous disease of 92.5% among mill workers.[36] Experience suggests that two doses of vaccine confer some protection.[37] Annual boosters are recommended to maintain immunity. Mild local reactions at the site of injection occur in about 30% of recipients. More severe local reactions occur infrequently (<4%) and systemic reactions are rare (0.2%). Availability of the vaccine is currently limited. The vaccine is manufactured by Bio Port (Lansing, Mich.).

Bacille Calmette-Guérin Vaccine. BCG vaccine contains living Calmette-Guérin bacillus, an attenuated strain of *Mycobacterium bovis.*

TABLE 312–4 Currently Available Immune Globulins and Year First Licensed*

Product	Year Licensed
Cytomegalovirus immunoglobulin	1990
Hepatitis B immunoglobulin (human)	1977
Immune globulin intravenous (human)	1981
Immune serum globulin (human)	1943
Monoclonal antibody respiratory syncytial virus (palivizumab)	1998
Rabies immunoglobulin (human)	1974
Respiratory syncytial virus immune globulin intravenous (human) (RSV-IGIV)	1996
Rh$_0$ (D) immunoglobulin (human)	1968
Tetanus immunoglobulin (human)	1957
Vaccinia immunoglobulin (human)	1968
Varicella zoster immune globulin (human)	1980

*As of December 31, 1998.
Prepared by Bob Snyder, National Immunization Program, Centers for Disease Control and Prevention, Atlanta, Ga.

In many countries, it is widely used in infants and young children to prevent disseminated tuberculosis infection. In the United States, use of the vaccine is recommended only in special circumstances because the general risk of infection is low and because BCG vaccination results in conversion of the tuberculin skin test, thereby removing one of the most important indicators of tuberculosis infection (tuberculin conversion). Although it is widely used throughout the world, there has been much controversy regarding its efficacy. Recent studies suggest that the vaccine is effective particularly for preventing complications of disseminated tuberculosis in young children.[38–40] In the United States use of BCG should be considered for individuals, such as infants, whose skin test results are negative and who have prolonged, close contact with patients with active tuberculosis who are untreated, are ineffectively treated, or have antibiotic-resistant infection. BCG may also be considered for health care workers in areas in which multiple drug–resistant *M. tuberculosis* infection has become a significant problem.[41]

A single dose of vaccine is administered intradermally or by the percutaneous route. Known adverse effects include regional adenitis, disseminated BCG infection, and osteitis due to the BCG organism. Adenitis occurs in approximately 1 to 10% of vaccinees, whereas disseminated infections and osteitis are apparently quite rare (approximately one case/million vaccinees). Hypertrophic scars at the injection site occur in up to one third of vaccinated persons, and keloids occur in 2 to 4%. Immunocompromised individuals should not receive the vaccine because of increased risk of disseminated BCG infection.[41]

Cholera Vaccine. Cholera vaccine is a killed suspension of *Vibrio cholerae* that can be administered intramuscularly, subcutaneously (for persons 6 months of age or older), or intradermally (for persons 5 years of age or older). The immunizing course consists of two doses given at least 1 week apart. Boosters are required every 6 months to maintain protection. Dosage varies, depending on the route of administration and age of the recipient. The efficacy of this vaccine is on the order of 50%, and protection lasts only about 6 months. It is currently recommended for use only to satisfy the immunization requirements for entry into certain countries. For these purposes, a single dose is sufficient. The traveler's best protection against cholera (and many other enteric diseases) is to avoid food and water that might be contaminated. Frequent adverse effects from cholera vaccine include local reactions and fever. Serious side effects are very rare.[42]

Diphtheria Toxoid. Diphtheria toxoid is a purified preparation of inactivated diphtheria toxin. It is highly effective in inducing antibodies that will prevent disease, although they may not prevent acquisition or carriage of the organism. The toxoid is available in adsorbed form, combined with tetanus toxoid (adult formulation Td and pediatric formulation DT) or with tetanus toxoid and whole cell or acellular pertussis vaccine (DTP or DTaP). Single-antigen diphtheria toxoid is not distributed in the United States. Two dosage formulations are generally available, one for use up to the seventh year of life and one for use in older children and adults. The adult formulation has a lower concentration of diphtheria toxoid (<2 Lf) than the pediatric formulation (6.7 to 25 Lf), because local reactions are thought to relate to both age and dosage. With all formulations, levels of antitoxin considered protective are induced in excess of more than 90% of recipients who complete the schedule.[22, 43]

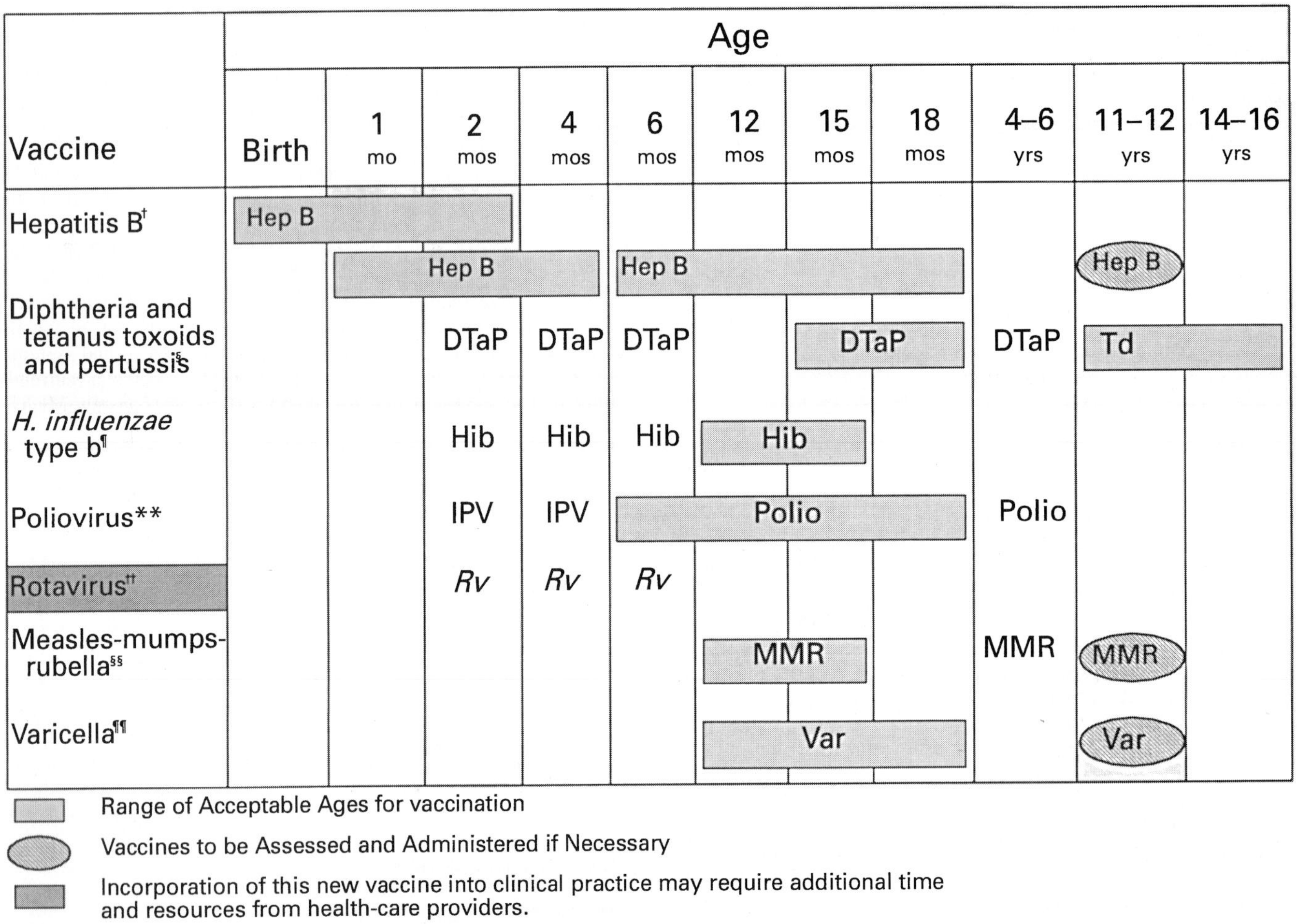

FIGURE 312–1. *See legend on opposite page*

Immunization against diphtheria is recommended for all residents in the United States. For children younger than 7 years of age with no contraindication to pertussis immunization, DTaP is recommended, and the primary series is three doses administered 4 to 8 weeks apart followed by a fourth dose 6 to 12 months later and a booster dose at school entry (4 to 6 years of age). For infants with contraindications to pertussis vaccine, DT is administered in the same schedule as DTaP (see "Pertussis Vaccine," Fig. 312–1, Table 312–5). The primary immunizing series of DT (for children 1 to 6 years of age) or Td (for older children and adults) consists of at least two doses administered 4 to 8 weeks apart followed by a third dose 6 to 12 months later. There is no need to restart a series if the schedule is interrupted; the next dose in the series should be given. Booster doses of Td should be given every 10 years. Known adverse effects include local reactions and mild or moderate systemic reactions such as fever; anaphylaxis occurs rarely. Brachial neuritis appears to be a rare consequence of immunization and is most likely due to tetanus antigen.[26] GBS may also be related to the tetanus toxoid component, but population-based studies do not support a causal relationship.[28, 29] The only known contraindication is in individuals who have previously had neurologic or severe hypersensitivity reactions after diphtheria or tetanus toxoids because all diphtheria toxoid in the United States is combined with tetanus toxoid.

***Haemophilus Influenzae* Type B Vaccine.** Conjugated vaccines to prevent *H. influenzae* type B (HIB) invasive disease were first licensed at the end of 1987 and have replaced the earlier polysaccharide vaccines because they elicit substantially higher antibody titers and are effective in young infants.[44] The polysaccharide in these vaccines is covalently linked to protein carriers converting them from T-cell–independent antigens to T-cell–dependent antigens. At present, there are four available conjugate vaccines, three of which are licensed for use in infants.[45] Carrier proteins include a mutant, nontoxic diphtheria toxin (CRM) (HbOC), *Neisseria meningitidis* outer membrane protein complex (PRP-OMP), tetanus toxoid (PRP-T), and diphtheria toxoid (PRP-D). All except the last are immunogenic in infants. HbOC and PRP-OMP have been demonstrated to be 93 to 100% effective in clinical trials in infants. PRP-T has been licensed for use in infants because it elicits comparable antibody responses to the other two vaccines. PRP-D should not be used in infants because of diminished immunogenicity and variable efficacy in clinical trials.

PRP-OMP behaves differently from the other conjugates, inducing high levels of antibody after a single dose. A second dose 2 months later increases those levels; less benefit appears to be derived from a third dose. The basic series for PRP-OMP is two doses given 2 months apart beginning at 2 months of age followed by a reinforc-

FIGURE 312–1. Recommended childhood immunization schedule*—United States, January–December 1999.

*This schedule indicates the recommended ages for routine administration of currently licensed childhood vaccines. Any dose not given at the recommended age should be given as a "catch-up" vaccination at any subsequent visit when indicated and feasible. Combination vaccines may be used whenever any components of the combination are indicated and its other components are not contraindicated. Providers should consult the manufacturers' package inserts for detailed recommendations.

†**Infants born to hepatitis B surface antigen (HBsAg)-negative mothers** should receive the second dose of hepatitis B (Hep B) vaccine at least 1 month after the first dose. The third dose should be administered at least 4 months after the first dose and at least 2 months after the second dose, but not before age 6 months. **Infants born to HBsAg-positive mothers** should receive Hep B vaccine and 0.5 ml hepatitis B immune globulin (HBIG) within 12 hours of birth at separate injection sites. The second dose is recommended at age 1–2 months and the third dose at age 6 months. **Infants born to mothers whose HBsAg status is unknown** should receive Hep B vaccine within 12 hours of birth. Maternal blood should be drawn at the time of delivery to determine the mother's HBsAg status; if the HBsAg test is positive, the infant should receive HBIG as soon as possible (no later than age 1 week). All children and adolescents (through age 18 years) who have not been vaccinated against hepatitis B may begin the series during any visit. Special efforts should be made to vaccinate children who were born in or whose parents were born in areas of the world where hepatitis B virus infection is moderately or highly endemic.

§Diphtheria and tetanus toxoids and acellular pertussis vaccine (DTaP) is the preferred vaccine for all doses in the vaccination series, including completion of the series in children who have received one or more doses of whole-cell diphtheria and tetanus toxoids and pertussis vaccine (DTP). Whole-cell DTP is an acceptable alternative to DTaP. The fourth dose (DTP or DTaP) may be administered as early as age 12 months, provided 6 months have elapsed since the third dose and if the child is unlikely to return at age 15–18 months. Tetanus and diphtheria toxoids (Td) is recommended at age 11–12 years if at least 5 years have elapsed since the last dose of DTP, DTaP, or DT. Subsequent routine Td boosters are recommended every 10 years.

¶Three *Haemophilus influenzae* type B (HIB) conjugate vaccines are licensed for infant use. If HIB conjugate vaccine (PRP-OMP) (PedvaxHIB or ComVax [Merck]) is administered at ages 2 and 4 months, a dose at age 6 months is not required. Because clinical studies in infants have demonstrated that using some combination products may induce a lower immune response to the HIB vaccine component, DTaP/HIB combination products should not be used for primary vaccination in infants at ages 2, 4, or 6 months unless approved by the Food and Drug Administration for these ages.

**Two poliovirus vaccines are licensed in the United States: inactivated poliovirus vaccine (IPV) and oral poliovirus vaccine (OPV). The ACIP, AAFP, and AAP recommend that the first two doses of poliovirus vaccine should be IPV. The ACIP continues to recommend a sequential schedule of two doses of IPV administered at ages 2 and 4 months followed by two doses of OPV at age 12–18 months and age 4–6 years. Use of IPV for all doses also is acceptable and is recommended for immunocompromised persons and their household contacts. OPV is no longer recommended for the first two doses of the schedule and is acceptable only for special circumstances (e.g., children of parents who do not accept the recommended number of injections, late initiation of vaccination that would require an unacceptable number of injections, and imminent travel to areas where poliomyelitis is endemic). OPV remains the vaccine of choice for mass vaccination campaigns to control outbreaks of wild poliovirus. As of January 2000, the ACIP will recommend an all IPV schedule.

††The first dose of Rv vaccine should not be administered before age 6 weeks, and the minimum interval between doses is 3 weeks. The Rv vaccine series should not be initiated at age 7 months or older, and all doses should be completed by the first birthday. The AAFP opinion is that the decision to use rotavirus vaccine should be made by the parent or guardian in consultation with the physician or other health-care provider.

§§The second dose of measles, mumps, and rubella vaccine (MMR) is recommended routinely at age 4–6 years but may be administered during any visit provided at least 4 weeks have elapsed since receipt of the first dose and that both doses are administered beginning at or after age 12 months. Those who have not previously received the second dose should complete the schedule no later than the routine visit to a health-care provider at age 11–12 years.

¶¶Varicella (Var) vaccine is recommended at any visit on or after the first birthday for susceptible children (i.e., those who lack a reliable history of chickenpox [as judged by a health-care provider] and who have not been vaccinated). Susceptible persons aged ≥13 years should receive two doses given at least 4 weeks apart.

Use of trade names and commercial sources is for identification only and does not imply endorsement by CDC or the U.S. Department of Health and Human Services.

Source: Advisory Committee on Immunization Practices (ACIP), American Academy of Family Physicians (AAFP), and American Academy of Pediatrics (AAP).

From Centers for Disease Control and Prevention. MMWR Morb Mortal Wkly Rep. 1999;48(1):12–16.

TABLE 312–5 Recommended Immunization Schedules for Children Not Immunized in the First Year of Life*

Recommended Time/Age	Immunization†‡	Comments
	Younger than 7 Years	
First visit	DTaP (or DTP), HIB, HBV, MMR, IPV	If indicated, tuberculin testing may be done at the same visit
Interval after first visit		
1 mo (4 wk)	DTaP (or DTP), HBV, Var‖	The second dose of IPV may be given if accelerated poliomyelitis vaccination is necessary, such as for travelers to areas where polio is endemic
2 mo	DTaP (or DTP), HIB, IPV	Second dose of HIB is indicated only if the first dose was received before 15 mo of age
≥8 mo	DTaP (or DTP), HBV, IPV	IPV and HBV are not given if the third doses were given earlier
Age 4–6 yr (at or before school entry)	DTaP (or DTP), IPV, MMR**	DTaP (DTP) is not necessary if the fourth dose was given after the fourth birthday; IPV is not necessary if the third dose was given after the fourth birthday
	7 to 12 Years	
First visit	HBV, MMR, Td, IPV	
Interval after first visit		
2 mo (8 wk)	HBV, MMR**, Var¶, IPV	IPV may also be given 1 mo after the first visit if accelerated poliomyelitis vaccination is necessary
8–14 mo	HBV,†† Td, IPV	IPV and HBV are not given if the third doses were given earlier
Age 11–12 yr	See Fig. 312–1	

*The table is not completely consistent with all package inserts. For products used, also consult manufacturer's package insert for instructions on storage, handling, dosage, and administration. Biologicals prepared by different manufacturers may vary, and package inserts of the same manufacturer may change from time to time. Therefore, the physician should be aware of the contents of the current package insert.

†If all needed vaccines cannot be administered simultaneously, priority should be given to protecting the child against those diseases that pose the greatest immediate risk. In the United States, these diseases for children younger than 2 yr are usually measles and *Haemophilus influenzae* type B infection; for children older than 7 yr, they are measles, mumps, and rubella. Before 13 yr of age, immunity against hepatitis B and varicella should be ensured.

‡DTaP, HBV, Hib, MMR, and Var can be given simultaneously at separate sites if failure of the patient to return for future immunizations is a concern.

‖Varicella vaccine can be administered to susceptible children any time after 12 mo of age. Unvaccinated children who lack a reliable history of chickenpox should be vaccinated before their 13th birthday.

**Minimal interval between doses of MMR is 1 mo (4 wk).

††HBV may be given earlier in a 0-, 2-, and 4-mo schedule.

Abbreviations: DTaP, Diphtheria and inactivated poliovirus vaccine; DTP, diphtheria and tetanus toxoids and pertussis vaccine; HBV, hepatitis B virus vaccine; HIB, *Haemophilus influenzae* type B conjugate vaccine; IPV, inactivated poliovirus vaccine; MMR, live measles-mumps-rubella vaccine; Td, adult tetanus toxoid and diphtheria toxoid, for children 7 yr and older and adults; Var, varicella vaccine.

Used with permission of the American Academy of Pediatrics, 1997 Red Book: Report of the Committee on Infectious Diseases. 24th ed. Elk Grove, Ill: American Academy of Pediatrics; 1997:20.

ing dose at 12 to 15 months of age.[45] In contrast, HbOC and PRP-T do not induce substantial antibody levels until dose 2, and high levels of protection are achieved only after three doses 2 months apart. The basic series for HbOC and PRP-T starts at 2 months of age with three doses 2 months apart followed by a booster dose at 12 to 15 months of age.[45] Although use of a single conjugate vaccine for the primary series has been recommended, several studies suggest that mixed sequences of HIB conjugate vaccines induce an adequate immune response.[46–48] Thus, for infants younger than 6 months of age, three doses of any licensed HIB vaccine administered at 2-month intervals should confer protection; a fourth dose is given at 12 to 15 months. For infants starting immunization between 7 and 11 months, two doses of any of the three HIB vaccines licensed for infants should be given 2 months apart followed by a reinforcing dose at 12 to 15 months provided that at least 2 months have elapsed since the second dose. Any of the four conjugates, including PRP-D, can be used for the booster dose.[45]

Children beginning immunization between 12 and 14 months can receive two doses of any conjugate, with the second dose given after age 15 months, at least 2 months after dose 1. Children who are initially immunized at 15 months of age need only one dose of any of the four conjugate vaccines. Three combination vaccines are available—DTP-HbOC and DTP-PRP-T, which contain whole cell pertussis vaccine,[45, 49] and can be used for the primary series of DTP and HIB vaccines,[45] as well as DTaP-PRP-T, which, as of July 1999, is licensed only for dose 4 of the primary series.[22] Decreased immune responses to the HIB component when it is combined with acellular vaccines have slowed approval for infant indications.[50] Except as already noted, combination products are comparable in immunogenicity and safety to the individual vaccines.

On the basis of the epidemiology of invasive *H. influenzae* type B infection in the United States, vaccination is not routinely recommended beyond the fifth year of life, except for specific risk groups. Although vaccine is not indicated for children who had documented invasive *H. influenzae* type B infection at 2 years of age or older, it is indicated for younger children because of their inadequate antibody response after natural infection.

The vaccines appear to be quite safe. Local reactions at the injection site and fever have been noted in less than 4% of vaccinees. They can be administered simultaneously with measles, mumps, rubella (MMR), DTP or DTaP, and oral polio vaccine (OPV) or inactivated polio vaccine (IPV) with no increased risk of adverse reactions or compromise in efficacy of any of the vaccines. The vaccines should not be administered if there is a history of anaphylaxis to the specific vaccine or to other vaccine components such as thimerosal. Although a slight increase in risk of invasive *H. influenzae* type B disease was observed shortly after receipt of the original unconjugated polysaccharide vaccine, available data show no such association with conjugate vaccines.

Hepatitis A Vaccine. There are two inactivated hepatitis A vaccines available in the United States, HAVRIX from SmithKline Beecham Biologicals and VAQTA from Merck and Company. More than 97% of persons 2 years of age and older acquire antibody titers considered protective after a single dose of either vaccine. More than 85% of children and adults acquire protective levels within 15 days of a dose of HAVRIX. An efficacy trial of HAVRIX using 360-enzyme-linked immunosorbent assay (ELISA) unit doses 1 month apart in children 1 to 16 years of age demonstrated a 94% efficacy against hepatitis A.[51] Efficacy of one 25-unit dose of VAQTA in children 2 to 16 years of age was 100%.[52]

The vaccine is currently recommended for use among populations known to be at increased risk of infection, including persons traveling to hepatitis A–endemic areas; children in communities with high rates of hepatitis A; men who have sex with men; illegal drug users; persons who work with hepatitis A virus-infected primates or who do research with the virus; and recipients of clotting factors. Persons with chronic liver disease may be at increased risk of fulminant hepatitis A and should be vaccinated as well.[53] Nonetheless, most cases of hepatitis A occur among persons who are not among these risk groups, but instead are acquired as part of community-wide outbreaks. Preventing hepatitis A at the community level will require widespread vaccination of children and adults.[54] The ACIP has recently recommended that children living in states, counties, or communities with reported annual rates of hepatitis A of 20 per 100,000 or higher between 1987 and 1997 be routinely vaccinated beginning at 2 years of age or older. Vaccination should be considered for all children living in states, counties, or communities with reported rates of hepatitis A of 10 per 100,000 or higher but lower than 20 per 100,000 between 1987 and 1999.[54a] As of December 1998 one state, Oklahoma, enacted a school immunization requirement for hepatitis A vaccine. HAVRIX is recommended in a two-dose schedule with doses separated by 6 to 12 months. The dose for children 2 to 18 years is 720 ELISA units and for adults is 1440 ELISA units. Two doses of 25 units of VAQTA 6 to 18 months apart are recommended for persons 2 to 17 years, and two doses of 50 units 6 months apart are recommended for persons 18 years of age or older. Hepatitis A vaccine is not licensed for use in children younger than 2 years of age. The vaccine is poorly immunogenic in infants born to women who are seropositive for hepatitis A.[5, 55] Simultaneous administration with IG may decrease immunogenicity slightly, but should not cause any decrease in protection.[56] The ACIP recommends simultaneous IG if the interval between dose 1 and travel to a high risk area is less than 4 weeks, although some authorities have questioned the need for IG.

No serious adverse events have been attributed to either hepatitis A vaccine. The most frequent side effects are local reactions. The only contraindication is for persons sensitive to vaccine components.[53]

Hepatitis B Vaccine. Hepatitis B vaccine consists of purified inactivated HBsAg particles obtained either from the plasma of chronic carriers or from yeast through recombinant DNA technology. In the United States, plasma-derived vaccines have been replaced by recombinant vaccines, although the former are still available abroad. There are two hepatitis B vaccines currently available in the United States—Recombivax HB (Merck & Company) and Engerix-B (SmithKline Beecham). Because recommended doses vary by age, the package insert should be consulted for the proper dose of each product. When initially licensed, use of vaccine was targeted to individuals at high risk of exposure to hepatitis B, including certain categories of health care workers (those with risk of exposure to blood or blood products), hemodialysis patients, recipients of certain blood products, homosexual males, certain institutionalized individuals, and household or sexual contacts of chronic carriers of HBsAg. Vaccine continues to be indicated for these groups and federal regulations now mandate that the vaccine be made available at no charge to all health care and public safety workers who anticipate exposure to human blood or body fluids during work.[57] Failure of vaccination targeted only to high-risk groups to have substantial impact on disease incidence, along with the appreciation that hepatitis B affects larger groups in the general population (such as heterosexuals with multiple partners), has led to the development of population-based control strategies.[58, 59]

Currently, hepatitis B vaccine is recommended for all infants in the United States. Acceptable schedules include (1) doses at birth, 1 to 2 months, and 6 to 18 months of age or (2) doses at 1 to 2 months, 4 months, and 6 to 18 months. The former schedule minimizes the need for simultaneous injections with other vaccines but potentially requires more visits to the health care provider. The latter schedule requires more injections at a given visit but fewer visits because it is integrated with the current immunization schedule. It is anticipated that those immunized as infants will still be protected when they become adolescents and young adults, the greatest risk period in the United States.[58] Because of the concern about the thimerosal content of vaccines for infants, a recommendation was made that until thimerosal-free hepatitis B vaccines become available, the first dose should be postponed until 2 to 6 months of age, with completion of the three-dose series by 18 months of age.[1a] When thimerosal-free hepatitis B vaccine becomes available, the birth dose should be reinstituted. The birth dose is still recommended for infants born to HBsAg-positive mothers and for others whose status is unknown as well as for children born into high-risk populations, in which horizontal transmission has been a problem.

To protect infants at highest risk for the development of chronic hepatitis B infection, all pregnant women should be routinely screened for HBsAg, preferably during an early prenatal visit. The vaccine should be administered within 12 hours of birth along with hepatitis B IG to infants born of HBsAg-positive mothers. The immunizing course consists of three doses given intramuscularly at birth, 1 month, and 6 months.[58]

For adolescents and adults, the usual schedule is doses at 0, 1, and 6 months. All adolescents who have not previously been vaccinated should receive three doses of vaccine. The second and third doses should be administered 1 to 2 months and 4 to 6 months, respectively, after the first dose. A good time to begin adolescent immunization is at 11 to 12 years of age when other immunizations are also recommended.[60]

The vaccine should be administered intramuscularly to infants in the anterolateral thigh and to children and adults in the deltoid region. Gluteal administration is associated with poorer antibody responses.[4] A series of three intramuscular doses produces a protective antibody response (antibody to HbsAg >10 mIU/ml) in more than 95% of infants and children, more than 90% of adults younger than 40 years of age, and 75 to 90% of adults greater than 40 years of age. Host factors such as smoking and obesity contribute to decreased immunogenicity of the primary vaccine series, but age is the major determinant of vaccine response. Vaccine immunogenicity may also be lower in immunocompromised patients. Follow-up for up to 12 years has shown the virtual absence of clinically significant infections in persons who initially achieved a protective antibody titer. Persons who lose detectable antibody appear to retain immunologic memory against significant infections. Thus, there is no indication for booster doses of vaccine in the first decade after immunization of immunocompetent children or adults. Additional experience will be necessary to know whether there will be any need for booster doses in the second decade after immunization.

Adverse effects associated with hepatitis B vaccine have been few; they consist primarily of local reactions of low-grade fever. Serious reactions have been very rare and, aside from anaphylaxis, have not convincingly been established to be caused by vaccination. Recent reports suggest that hepatitis B vaccine may rarely cause alopecia. The condition has been reported primarily in adults and has been reversible in most cases.[61] A number of case reports have linked hepatitis B vaccine to demyelinating syndromes including multiple sclerosis.[62] However, data available thus far do not support a causal relationship.[63]

There are no known contraindications to the use of hepatitis B vaccine. It is not effective in eliminating the carrier state, but there is no known risk of vaccinating individuals who are carriers or who are already immune.[58]

Influenza Virus Vaccine. Influenza virus vaccine is composed of inactivated whole or disrupted ("split") influenza viruses. Because of the frequent antigenic changes in influenza viruses, the antigenic content of influenza virus vaccine is changed annually to reflect the influenza A and B virus strains in circulation. Annual immunization is recommended for those who receive influenza vaccine. The efficacy of the vaccine in protecting against influenza is directly related to the degree of concordance between the virus strains included in the vaccine and the strains that are circulating in the community. When periodic major shifts in antigenic structure of influenza viruses occur, vaccine that contains antigens representative of prior viruses has little or no effectiveness. In recent years, influenza vaccine has been estimated to be 60 to 80% effective, except in nursing home settings, where efficacy has often been substantially lower, on the order of 20 to 30%. However, prevention of complications of influenza in such settings has been considerably higher, averaging from about 50 to 60% in preventing pneumonia to 80% in preventing death.[64]

Influenza immunization strategy in the United States is directed at reducing the complications and mortality associated with influenza. Because these occur primarily in the chronically ill and elderly, these groups are most strongly advised to receive vaccine. Specifically, annual immunization is recommended for all persons 65 years of age or older; residents of nursing homes and other chronic care facilities with chronic medical conditions regardless of age; persons with chronic cardiovascular or pulmonary disorders, including children with asthma; and persons requiring regular medical follow-up or those hospitalized in the preceding year with chronic metabolic disease (including diabetes mellitus), renal dysfunction, hemoglobinopathies, or immunosuppression; and children and teenagers on long-term aspirin therapy. Pregnant women who will be in the second or third trimester during the influenza season (usually December through March) should be vaccinated. Physicians and other personnel caring for high-risk persons should be vaccinated to reduce the chances that such patients will be exposed to influenza. Similar recommendations apply to employees in nursing homes, those who provide home care, and household members of persons with high-risk conditions. Many of the persons in need of influenza vaccine are hospitalized frequently and should be vaccinated on discharge if hospitalized during the autumn.[65]

If a child 6 months to 8 years of age is thought not to have had any prior exposure to influenza virus of the type circulating, two doses of vaccine are recommended with an interval of at least 4 weeks between them; otherwise, only a single dose is needed. Children younger than 13 years should receive only split virus vaccines because reactions to whole virus vaccines are more frequent in this age group. Older individuals can receive any vaccine. In the United States, the optimal time for vaccination is between October and mid-November.[65]

Adverse events associated with current influenza vaccines are infrequent. Three to 5% of recipients report local tenderness or low-grade fever. During the swine influenza immunization program of 1976, an elevated incidence rate of GBS was noted in recipients of the swine flu vaccine.[66] The risk of GBS after influenza vaccine during six subsequent seasons that were studied was not significantly elevated compared with expected rates. However, studies during the 1992 to 1993 and 1993 to 1994 influenza seasons suggest that influenza vaccines may have been associated with GBS at an attributable risk of about 1/million doses in those years.[65, 67] No cases of GBS within 6 weeks of vaccination were detected in persons 18 to 44 years of age despite administration of approximately 4 million doses of vaccine over the two flu seasons studied.[67] The overall risk of GBS in these studies was about one-tenth the risk of GBS after swine flu vaccine. If GBS is ever caused by current influenza vaccines, it is very rare. In contrast, the risk of hospitalization from influenza disease and its complications ranges from 200 to 300 hospitalizations per million in persons 5 to 44 years of age to 2000 to 10,000 or more/million in persons 65 years or older.[65] Given the substantial benefits of influenza vaccine among the targeted populations, the risk of GBS, if any, is exceeded by the benefits. Persons with an immediate hypersensitivity reaction to a prior dose or those with anaphylactic hypersensitivity to eggs, in which vaccine viruses are grown, should be vaccinated only after careful assessment that the benefits are likely to outweight the risks.[65] Protocols have been developed for vaccinating such patients.[68] Concerns have been raised regarding vaccination of human immunodeficiency virus (HIV)-infected individuals. Persons with severe immunocompromise do not respond well, and some studies have shown a transient increase in HIV-1 in the plasma in the 2 to 4 weeks after vaccination, which has not been associated with clinical deterioration. Because many patients may still benefit from vaccine, influenza vaccine should be considered for HIV-infected persons.[65]

Japanese Encephalitis. Japanese encephalitis vaccine is a whole virus vaccine grown in mouse brains and inactivated and purified in at least a five-step process. No myelin basic protein has been detected in the vaccine. The vaccine has proved 91% effective in a large-scale trial in Thailand.[69] The vaccine is indicated for some persons traveling to or residing in endemic or epidemic areas, particularly those spending 30 or more days in high-risk areas (especially rural areas) in Asia during transmission season. Persons traveling to such areas for shorter periods may warrant vaccine under special circumstances. The primary immunization schedule for persons 4 years of age or older consists of three 1-ml doses administered subcutaneously on days 0, 7, and 30. An abbreviated schedule with the third dose at 14 days may be used if time constraints do not permit the full schedule. The dose is 0.5 ml for children 1 to 3 years of age given by the same schedule. Antibody persists at least 2 years and the need, if any, for boosters is uncertain. About 20% of vaccinees experience local reactions, and about 10% have minor systemic symptoms such as fever, malaise, nausea, and vomiting. Although serious neurologic events have been reported rarely in temporal association with Japanese encephalitis vaccination, a causal role for the vaccine has not been established. The major significant adverse events appear to be allergic in nature, consisting of generalized urticaria or angioedema, or both. Respiratory distress and hypotension have also occurred. The incidence of these adverse events in studies of United States citizens varies from 15 to 62/10,000 vaccines. Prior history of allergic reactions (especially urticaria) is associated with increased risks of allergic reactions to the vaccine.[70]

Lyme Disease Vaccine. On December 21, 1998, the Food and Drug Administration licensed the first vaccine designed to prevent Lyme disease in the United States—LYMErix, manufactured by SmithKline Beecham Biologicals.[71] The vaccine is made from lipidated recombinant outer surface protein A (OspA) of *Borrelia burgdorferi.* OspA is expressed on spirochetes in the gut of tick vectors. The antigen is substantially reduced or eliminated after ingestion of a blood meal from a human host.[72] Organisms that infect humans do not appear to induce immune responses against OspA. The vaccine works because ticks ingest human blood with antibodies to OspA that aid in killing the organisms prior to regurgitation by the tick, which would otherwise lead to human infection. After two doses of vaccine administered at 0 and 1 month to persons 15 to 70 years of age, the efficacy against definite Lyme disease was 49% (95% confidence intervals 15 to 69%). After a third dose, 12 months after the first, efficacy improved to 76% (58 to 86%).[73] The efficacy against asymptomatic infection was 83% after two doses and 100% after three doses. The duration of immunity is unknown, and hence the need for boosters is unclear. In contrast to most vaccines, the immunity induced by Lyme disease vaccine is completely dependent on the amount of antibody ingested by the tick. Immunologic memory in the host may reduce the number of boosters required, but memory alone presumably will not be adequate to prevent disease. Adverse reactions consist primarily of local reactions such as soreness (24.1% in vaccinees versus 7.6% in placebo recipients) and mild systemic reactions within 30 days of a dose (19.4% in vaccinees versus 15.1% in placebo recipients). Statistically significant systemic reactions included myalgias, achiness, influenza-like illness, fever, and chills. The attributable risk from vaccine was 1.5% or less for each of those systemic reactions. There were no significant differences in occurrence of severe or late adverse events. A second Lyme disease vaccine, manufactured by Pasteur-Mérieux-Connaught, showed an efficacy of 68% after two doses and 92% after three doses.[74] As of August 15, 1999, the Pasteur-Mérieux-Connaught vaccine had not been licensed.

The vaccine should be targeted to persons who are at risk of exposure to infected ticks.[74a] This can be determined by evaluation of the known geographic distribution of Lyme disease and the extent that a person's activities place them in contact with ticks. The vaccine is licensed only for use in persons 15 to 70 years of age in a schedule at 0, 1, and 12 months. The second and third doses should be timed, ideally, to precede the *B. burgdorferi* transmission season, which usually begins in April, by several weeks.

Measles Vaccine. Measles vaccine is a live attenuated virus vaccine recommended for use in all children 12 months of age and older who do not have contraindications. When administered to a child 12 to 15 months of age or older, efficacy is greater than 95%. Only a single dose is needed to provide long lasting, probably lifelong, immunity in those who respond to the vaccine.

Evidence suggests that measles transmission can be sustained among the 2 to 5% of vaccinated persons who fail to seroconvert after an initial dose of vaccine. Therefore, beginning in 1989, a two-dose schedule is recommended in the United States. The first dose should be administered at 12 to 15 months of age. The 12-month age is especially indicated for areas at high risk of measles among preschool-aged children, including inner cities with large numbers of unvaccinated children and areas that have either had a recent outbreak among preschoolers or persistent transmission in that age group. Lower levels of maternal antibody from today's vaccinated mothers may allow higher rates of seroconversion at 12 months than in the past when most maternal antibody came from mothers with naturally acquired disease.[75]

The second dose should be administered at 1 month or more after the first dose, typically at entry to school (4 to 6 years of age). All children who have not received a second dose by the time of entry to middle or junior high school (approximately 12 years of age) should be vaccinated. The ACIP has established a goal of ensuring that all children, kindergarten through 12th grade, receive a second dose by 2001. Both doses should routinely be given as combined MMR vaccine.[76]

All college entrants who have not received two doses on or after the first birthday should receive them. If necessary, the two doses can be given at a minimum of 1 month apart. Immunization is recommended for all individuals not known to be immune. Because individuals born before 1957 are likely to have been infected naturally, they are usually considered to be immune. Other acceptable evidence of measles immunity is documentation of adequate vaccination, laboratory evidence of immunity to measles, or documentation of prior physician-diagnosed measles. Similar recommendations apply to health care workers. Health care facilities should consider recommending a dose of MMR to unvaccinated workers born before 1957 who do not have a history of physician-diagnosed measles or laboratory evidence of immunity to both measles and rubella.[76, 77]

Because measles is much more prevalent outside the United States, adequate vaccination is recommended for all travelers born after 1956. Such persons should receive a second dose if they have not previously been vaccinated and lack other evidence of measles immunity.[76]

Untoward reactions associated with measles vaccine include fever of 39.4°C or greater in 5% of recipients and transient rashes in approximately 5% of vaccines. Fever and rash generally begin 7 to 12 days after vaccination and last 1 to 2 days. Because measles vaccine causes fever, it can be associated with febrile convulsions.[78] Children with prior personal histories of convulsions or histories of convulsions in the immediate family may be at increased risk of febrile convulsions following MMR vaccination.[79] Antipyretics may prevent febrile seizures after MMR vaccination if administered before onset of fever and continued for 5 to 7 days. However, fever is difficult to anticipate, making use of antipyretics impractical in many situations. Aspirin should not be used to prevent or control fever beause of its association with Reye's syndrome. Anaphylaxis and thrombocytopenic purpura also appear to be caused rarely by MMR.[26] Encephalopathy with onset approximately 10 days after vaccination has been reported in vaccine recipients, with a frequency of approximately 1 in 2 million vaccinations, although a causal role for measles vaccine has not been established.[80]

Measles vaccine is contraindicated for pregnant women and in persons who are immunocompromised because of either congenital or acquired disorders (e.g., leukemia or immunosuppressive drugs), with the exception of those infected with HIV. Because measles may cause severe disease in HIV-infected persons, asymptomatic and mildly symptomatic HIV-infected persons may be vaccinated if measles vaccination is otherwise indicated. However, vaccination is contraindicated for those who are severely immunocompromised. Persons with a history of anaphylactic reactions to eggs may be vaccinated and observed for at least 20 minutes because most persons with such histories do not have serious reactions to vaccine. Skin testing of persons with such histories is no longer recommended because such tests appear not to predict severe reactions.[76]

Meningococcal Polysaccharide Vaccine. A vaccine containing purified meningococcal capsular polysaccharides of groups A, C, Y, and W135 is available for use in the United States. The vaccine is routinely indicated for control of outbreaks of serogroup C meningococcal disease and for use among certain high-risk groups such as persons with terminal complement component deficiencies, anatomic or functional asplenia, and laboratory personnel who routinely are exposed to *N. meningitidis* in solutions that may be aerosolized. Military recruits, who previously had high rates of meningococcal disease, are also routinely vaccinated with the quadrivalent vaccine. It may be of benefit to travelers to countries with endemic or hyperendemic disease who are expected to have prolonged contact with the local population. Frequent epidemics, generally between December and June, occur in the "meningitis belt" of sub-Saharan Africa (which stretches from Senegal to Ethiopia).[81] A single intramuscular injection induces protective levels of antibody in 90% or more of recipients 2 years of age and older. Vaccine is recommended as a single dose for persons 2 years of age or older. The vaccine is not effective for children younger than 2 years of age with the exception of group A. Short-term protection may be achieved against this group in children as young as 3 months of age. When vaccinating 3- to 18-month-old children, two doses 3 months apart are recommended. Booster doses after 2 to 3 years may be indicated for high-risk children, especially those vaccinated before 4 years of age. Because antibody titers decline rapidly in the 2 to 3 years after vaccination, revaccination may be considered 3 to 5 years after initial vaccination in those with persistent risk. Adverse effects associated with meningococcal polysaccharide vaccine are mild and consist primarily of pain and redness at the injection site. More than 40% of recipients have reported local reactions in some studies, but in others reactions have been much more infrequent.[82, 83] Up to 2% of children experience fever. There are no known contraindications to the use of this vaccine.[84]

Mumps Vaccine. Mumps vaccine is a live attenuated virus vaccine that is recommended for use in all children 12 months of age or older who do not have contraindications. Mumps vaccine is routinely administered as MMR at 12 to 15 months of age. When administered on or after the first birthday, 90% or more of recipients can be expected to acquire protective antibodies. Protection is thought to be lifelong. Only a single dose is generally recommended, although most persons will receive two doses as part of the two-dose MMR policy to prevent measles. As with measles, most persons born before 1957 are likely to have been infected naturally by mumps virus and can generally be considered immune; otherwise, individuals should be considered susceptible unless they have documentation of having received live mumps vaccine on or after the first birthday, laboratory evidence of mumps immunity, or documentation of physician-diagnosed mumps disease.[76]

Contraindications to mumps vaccine are pregnancy and an immunocompromised state (see "Measles Vaccine"). Persons with a history of anaphylactic reactions to eggs may be vaccinated. Adverse events associated with mumps vaccine are very few. Parotitis and orchitis have been reported rarely. Thrombocytopenic purpura and anaphylaxis appear to be caused rarely by MMR.[26] Aseptic meningitis has been associated with the Urabe strain of mumps vaccine, a strain not available in the United States.[85] The Jeryl Lynn strain used in U.S. vaccines has not been proved to cause aseptic meningitis.[26]

Pertussis Vaccine. Two types of pertussis vaccines are currently available in the United States: (1) suspensions of killed whole *Bordetella pertussis* (whole cell vaccines) and (2) combinations of purified components of the organism and detoxified pertussis toxin PT (acellular vaccines).[22, 43, 86] In addition to the toxoid, acellular vaccines may contain one or more of the following: (1) filamentous hemagglutinin (FHA), (2) fimbriae, and (3) pertactin (69-kD protein). Pertussis vaccines are usually combined with diphtheria and tetanus toxoids as DTP (whole cell pertussis vaccines) or DTaP (acellular pertussis vaccines). The primary immunizing course consists of three doses of DTaP or DTP administered intramuscularly at 4- to 8-week intervals typically given at 2, 4, and 6 months of age. A fourth dose is given approximately 6 to 12 months later (15 to 18 months of age) and a fifth dose at 4 to 6 years of age. DTaP is preferred over DTP because the efficacy of acellular vaccines is comparable to whole cell vaccines and because the incidence of adverse events after acellular vaccines is significantly lower than after whole cell vaccines. As of August 15, 1999, four acellular vaccines were licensed in the United States: ACEL-IMUNE (Wyeth-Lederle Vaccines and Pediatrics), which contains PT, FHA, fimbriae, and pertactin; Tripedia (Connaught Laboratories, Inc.), which contains PT and FHA; Infanrix (SmithKline Beecham Biologicals), which contains PT, FHA, and pertactin; and Certiva (North American Vaccines), which contains only PT. Efficacy in preventing classic pertussis, consisting of 21 or more days of paroxysmal cough, has ranged from 71 to 89% for three doses.[22] This is considerably higher than the efficacy found for one of the U.S. whole cell vaccines after three doses in clinical trials in Europe (36 to 48%).[87, 88] However, in comparative trials, most acellular vaccines have had slightly lower efficacy than whole cell vaccines. Overall, U.S. whole cell vaccines have had an estimated efficacy of 83 to 90% with the recommended schedule of four doses in the first 2 years of life.[89, 90]

Symptoms and signs of local reactions occur about one-tenth to one-half as frequently after acellular vaccines compared with whole cell vaccines. For example, the incidence of erythema by the third evening after any of the first three doses of acellular vaccines ranged from 26.3% to 39.2% in one large comparative trial, compared with 72.7% in those who received the whole cell vaccine. In that study, the incidence of fever (>39.4°C) after acellular vaccines was 3.3 to 5.2% compared with 15.9% after receipt of whole cell vaccine.[22, 91] More serious adverse events such as seizures and hypotonic hyporesponsive episodes also appear to occur less frequently after acellular vaccine than after whole cell vaccines.[92, 93] The lower incidence of fever associated with acellular vaccines would be expected to decrease febrile seizures, especially after the fourth dose.

The IOM has completed an extensive review of the adverse consequences of whole cell pertussis vaccines (see Table 312–2).[25] Pertussis vaccine was implicated as a cause of acute encephalopathy.[94] The excess risk has been estimated to range from 0 to 10.5/million immunizations.[95] In a more recent evaluation, the IOM concluded that the balance of evidence was consistent with a causal relationship between DTP and some forms of chronic nervous system disorders in children who acquired an acute neurologic disorder within 7 days after DTP administration. However, the IOM also concluded that the data are insufficient to indicate whether DTP increases the overall risk of chronic nervous system dysfunction in children. Other adverse events causally related to whole cell pertussis vaccines included hypotonic, hyporesponsive episodes; anaphylaxis; and protracted, inconsolable crying. The evidence indicated that whole cell vaccines did not play a causal role in infantile spasms, hypsarrhythmia, Reye's syndrome, and sudden infant death syndrome. There was either no evidence or insufficient evidence to evaluate the role of whole cell vaccines in a variety of other syndromes.

Contraindications to pertussis-containing vaccines include an immediate anaphylactic reaction or encephalopathy within the 7 days after a prior dose. Although formerly contraindications, the following events are now considered precautions: (1) temperature greater than or equal to 40.5°C within 48 hours of a prior dose without other identifiable cause, (2) collapse or shocklike state (hypotonic hyporesponsive episode) within 48 hours, (3) persistent inconsolable crying lasting 3 hours or more within 48 hours, and (4) convulsions with or without fever occurring within 3 days. Although under most circumstances such children will not be vaccinated, the physician may elect to continue pertussis vaccination if the benefits are judged to outweigh the risks, such as when there is a pertussis outbreak in the community. If pertussis vaccine is used in the preceeding situation, DTaP and not DTP should be administered. Children with evolving neurologic disorders should have immunization deferred until the situation is clarified. Once stable, they can receive pertussis vaccine. Decisions about vaccinating children with underlying neurologic disease should be made no later than the first birthday. If pertussis vaccine is not used, the pediatric preparation of combined diphtheria and tetanus toxoids (DT) is indicated.

Combined DTP-HbOC or PRP-T reconstituted with DTP (Connaught only) can be used when both whole cell pertussis vaccine and HIB vaccine are indicated; however, because DTaP is preferred over DTP, it is best to use separate DTaP and HIB vaccines. As of August 15, 1999, a combined DTaP-PRP-T vaccine (Connaught Laboratories, Inc.) has been licensed for use as a fourth dose only.[22] Combinations of acellular vaccines with HIB have generally resulted in diminished antibody response to the HIB component when administered to infants.[50] However, it is expected that this interference will be overcome and combined preparations of DTaP and HIB will be available in the future for infant immunization.

Children with a personal or family history of convulsions appear to be at higher risk of seizures after pertussis vaccination than the general population. However, the benefits of vaccination outweigh the risks. Children with stable seizure disorders or with family histories of seizures may be vaccinated. Use of acetaminophen, 15 mg/kg, at the time of vaccination, and subsequently every 4 hours for 24 hours, and then as needed reduces the risk of fever after pertussis vaccination and may decrease the likelihood of postvaccination seizures. Such children should always receive DTaP instead of DTP.

Because of the adverse reactions known or suspected to be associated with whole cell pertussis vaccines, there has been considerable controversy about their continuing routine use in some countries. As a result, pertussis vaccine uptake in the United Kingdom declined markedly in the period 1974 to 1978. The result was a major epidemic of pertussis in the years 1977 to 1979, with a second epidemic in 1982. This experience and similar ones in Japan and other countries illustrate the necessity for maintaining protection against pertussis, even while evaluating the effectiveness of improved vaccines.[96]

Pertussis vaccines are not recommended for administration to individuals older than 7 years because the risk of pertussis and pertussis complications appears to be substantially lower and reactions to whole cell vaccines may be more frequent in older individuals. Efforts are under way to evaluate the use of acellular vaccines in the adult population. Recent studies of pertussis epidemiology suggest that adults may play an important role in sustaining transmission.[97, 98] Of adults with an acute-cough illness of 6 or more day's duration, 12% or more will have serologic evidence of pertussis infection.[99–101] Small studies suggest acellular vaccines are safe and immunogenic in adults.[102] It is likely that vaccines to immunize adolescents and adults will become available in the near future.

Plague Vaccine. Plague vaccine is a suspension of killed *Yersinia pestis.* It is recommended for use only in individuals who are at substantial risk of plague infection, such as those who work in laboratories with plague organisms or those who work with wild animals in plague enzootic areas (e.g., parts of New Mexico, Arizona). The efficacy of plague vaccine has never been measured precisely. After a primary immunizing course of three doses administered at time zero, 4 weeks, and 6 months, about 93% of recipients acquire antibody to fraction 1 capsular antigen. A few fail to acquire a reciprocal titer of 128 or more, the level that correlates with immunity in experimental animals. Three booster doses can be given at 6-month intervals after the primary series and may be given every 1 to 2 years thereafter, especially for those who have titers less than 1:128. Adverse effects, including local reactions, are common, occurring in more than 70% of recipients after the first dose and more than 18% after the second dose. Severe reactions are rare. Mild systemic complaints such as headache have been reported in more than 19% of persons after dose 1 and more than 6% after dose 2. Hypersensitivity reactions have been reported rarely. Sterile abscesses have not been reported with the current preparation. Contraindications to its use include known hypersensitivity to any of the constituents and severe reactions to a previous dose.[103]

Pneumococcal Polysaccharide Vaccine. Pneumococcal polysaccharide vaccine was initially licensed as a purified preparation of 14 different serotypes of pneumococcal capsular polysaccharide in 1979. Since 1983, vaccine containing 23 types has replaced the earlier version. The types included in the current vaccine and immunologically related types are responsible for approximately 85 to 90% of all bacteremic pneumococcal disease in the United States. Demonstrable antibody rises to the serotypes contained in the vaccine are noted in

80 to 95% or more of healthy recipients. The vaccine has been highly effective in reducing pneumococcal disease among South African gold miners (a group at particularly high risk) and among military recruits.[104–106] In randomized trials in some populations at high risk of pneumococcal infections, such as the elderly and those with high-risk medical conditions, efficacy against nonbacteremic pneumococcal pneumonia has not been convincingly demonstrated, in part because determining the cause of pneumonia from sputum specimens may be difficult and because the studies were too small to detect a difference in the incidence of laboratory-confirmed, nonbacteremic pneumococcal pneumonia between the vaccinated and unvaccinated groups.[107] However, studies of patients with isolates from normally sterile body fluids have generally reported efficacies of 60 to 80% overall, with lower efficacy in persons who have compromised immune systems.[108–110] Vaccine is primarily recommended for adults at high risk of complications from respiratory infections, particularly those with cardiovascular and chronic pulmonary disease, adults and children 2 years of age or older at high risk of pneumococcal disease (e.g., splenic dysfunction or anatomic asplenia, Hodgkin's disease, multiple myeloma, chronic liver disease, including cirrhosis, alcoholism, renal failure, cerebrospinal fluid leaks, and immunocompromised state), and the otherwise healthy elderly (≥65 years of age).[110]

A single dose is administered by intramuscular injection. Revaccination is recommended for persons 65 years of age or older who received an initial vaccination prior to age 65, if at least 5 years has elapsed since that dose. Revaccination is also recommended for persons less than 65 years of age with anatomic or functional asplenia or those who are immunocompromised, including patients with chronic renal failure and nephrotic syndrome. For such patients who are older than 10 years of age, revaccination should take place 5 years or more after the first dose. For younger patients, revaccination should be considered 3 years after the first dose.[110]

In some studies, mild reactions such as erythema and mild pain at the site of injection occurred in approximately one half of recipients. Anaphylactic reactions have rarely been reported. Revaccination at intervals of 4 years may be associated with an increased risk of local reactions after vaccination, but these reactions tend to be self-limited and would not be a contraindication.[110a] No contraindications are known, although its safety in pregnant women has not been evaluated.[110] Transient increases in plasma HIV levels have been documented after vaccination in some studies, although the clinical significance is unknown.[111] Conversely, risk of pneumococcal disease is increased in HIV-infected persons and therefore they should be vaccinated as soon as possible after diagnosis to optimize immune response to the vaccine.[110]

Polysaccharide vaccines are not effective in children younger than 2 years of age. Efforts are under way to develop conjugate vaccines in which pneumococcal capsular polysaccharide is covalently linked to protein carriers. A conjugate vaccine containing seven polysaccharide types covering about three fourths of invasive isolates in children has been demonstrated to be immunogenic. Preliminary results of a large-scale efficacy trial in northern California showed 100% efficacy against invasive disease caused by serotypes in the vaccine in a three-dose schedule at 2, 4, and 6 months with a booster at 12 to 15 months.[112] Should conjugate vaccines be licensed, it is likely they will be recommended for routine vaccination of infants.

Polio Vaccine. Two types of polio vaccine are available in the United States: live attenuated oral polio vaccine (OPV) and inactivated polio vaccine (IPV), which is administered by injection. The schedule consists of two doses of IPV at 2 and 4 months of age followed by OPV or IPV at 6 to 18 months and 4 to 6 years. Through 1999 the ACIP currently recommends a sequential schedule of two doses of IPV followed by two doses of OPV, although four doses of IPV are acceptable. The first OPV dose in the sequential schedule should be administered at 12 to 18 months of age. Through 1999, OPV is recommended for the first two doses of the polio schedule only in special circumstances such as parental refusal to accept increased injections, imminent international travel to endemic or epidemic areas, and catch-up of children seriously behind schedule, for whom extra injections might be a problem. With any of the schedules, there is no need to restart a series if the primary immunization schedule is interrupted; the next dose in the series should be given.[28] Beginning in 2000, the ACIP will recommend an all IPV schedule. The first three doses should be administered by 18 months of age, with doses at 2 and 4 months followed by a third dose at 6 to 18 months.[112a] OPV use will be limited to (1) mass vaccinations to control outbreaks, (2) unvaccinated children who are traveling to polio-endemic areas and present less than 4 weeks before departure, and (3) children of parents who object to the additional injections of IPV, but only for doses three and four.

IPV is the vaccine of choice for individuals beyond secondary school age (generally 18 years of age and older) who have never previously been vaccinated because the risk of vaccine-associated polio is somewhat higher in adults. However, during control of an epidemic, OPV should be used for all age groups. Before 1997, the United States relied primarily on OPV. Use of OPV eliminated indigenous transmission of wild polio since 1979 and induced intestinal immunity to serve as a barrier to spread within a community should wild virus be introduced. In addition, vaccine viruses are shed in the stools of recipients, leading to immunization of contacts who might not have been reached in routine immunization programs. However, on rare occasions, OPV is associated with paralysis either in the vaccine recipient or in contacts of vaccine recipients (overall risk about 1 in every 2.4 million doses distributed). Approximately eight cases of vaccine-associated paralytic polio (VAPP) were reported annually from 1980 to 1994, about three cases in immunologically normal recipients, three cases in healthy close contacts of vaccine recipients, and two cases in immunodeficient persons. Most risk to both recipients and contacts is associated with administration of the first dose to the recipient (overall risk 1 in every 750,000 first doses).[28] The risk of paralysis is increased if OPV is given to an immunocompromised individual. Infants with primary immunodeficiency, primarily B-cell abnormalities, have a risk approximately 3200 times that of other infants.[113]

The IOM has reviewed adverse reactions after OPV and concluded that OPV viruses could cause nonparalytic poliomyelitis and even very rarely death, mainly in immunocompromised individuals.[26] Although the IOM indicated OPV might cause GBS, more recent population-based data as well as a reanalysis of the data reviewed by the IOM do not support a causal relationship.[28, 29] Contraindications to the use of OPV are an immunocompromised state (congenital or acquired), pregnancy (on theoretic grounds), or living in the same household with an immunocompromised individual. Children whose siblings were immunodeficient but no longer living in the household should not receive OPV until it is ensured that they are not also immunodeficient. No significant adverse effects have been reported with current IPV, and there are no known contraindications to its use. Vaccination in pregnancy should be avoided on theoretic grounds, although IPV or OPV can be used if needed.[28]

In 1988, the World Health Assembly endorsed a goal to eradicate polio from the world by the end of the year 2000. Extensive efforts in the Americas, including mass campaigns with OPV twice a year targeted to all children under 5 years regardless of prior immunization status, have led to the elimination of polio in the Western Hemisphere. The last known case of polio due to wild poliovirus in the Americas had onset in Peru in 1991, and the Western Hemisphere was certified free of polio in 1994.[18] Since 1988, almost all countries with endemic polio have conducted National Immunization Days, and even with greatly improved surveillance, reported cases of polio have decreased about 85% from 1988 to 1997.[19]

With progress in the global effort to eradicate polio by the year 2000, the risk from wild virus in the United States has decreased while VAPP continued to occur. Thus, a change in policy was advocated by all major immunization groups to enhance use of IPV and facilitate choice. All acceptable schedules induce individual protection against all three serotypes of polio in more than 95% of recipients. The major advantage of using only IPV is the elimination of VAPP. There are no known risks from IPV, but it clearly induces less intestinal immunity than OPV. The ACIP preferred a sequential schedule as the best policy for public health for the following reasons:

1. The benefits of both vaccines are gained: high levels of individual immunity, intestinal immunity, and vaccine virus spread.
2. The sequential schedule should prevent VAPP in recipients and reduce VAPP in contacts because IPV decreases shedding compared with no vaccine and because fewer doses of OPV are used.
3. The sequential schedule may reduce VAPP in immunodeficient persons because OPV is not given until 12 months of age, which gives more time to make the diagnosis of immunodeficiency, which would contraindicate OPV.
4. Overall, the sequential schedule is estimated to reduce VAPP by 50 to 75%.
5. Stocking of both IPV and OPV facilitates parent and provider choice.

With further progress in global polio eradication, a switch to IPV only is anticipated in the near future before stopping all vaccination after polio is eradicated.

Polio vaccine is not routinely recommended for persons 18 years of age or older in the United States because the risk from wild virus is low. However, if vaccine is needed, such as for persons traveling to polio-endemic areas, previously unvaccinated adults should receive two doses of IPV at intervals of 4 to 8 weeks and a third dose 6 to 12 months after the second. Adults who have had a primary series of OPV or IPV and who are at increased risk for exposure to poliovirus may receive an additional dose of either OPV or IPV. Adults who have not been adequately vaccinated against poliomyelitis have a minimal risk for the development of OPV-associated paralytic poliomyelitis when OPV is administered to children in their households; children in such households should be vaccinated with IPV.[28]

Rabies Vaccine. Rabies vaccine is an inactivated virus vaccine prepared either in human or fetal rhesus lung diploid cell culture (HDCV and RVA, respectively) or in purified chick embryo cell culture (PCEC). HDCV can be used by either the intramuscular or intradermal routes. In contrast, RVA and the PCEC vaccine can be administered only intramuscularly. Rabies vaccination is recommended in two situations: as a routine in individuals likely to be exposed to rabies (e.g., veterinarians, forest rangers) and after exposure to animals known or suspected to be rabid. The primary preexposure immunizing course is three doses of rabies vaccine given intramuscularly or intradermally (HDCV only) at time 0, 7 days, and 21 to 28 days. The intradermal preparation is prepackaged by the manufacturer to be reconstituted in the syringe. The three-dose course results in formation of protective levels of antibodies in virtually 100% of vaccinees. Serologic testing every 2 years is recommended to ensure that high-risk vaccinees maintain protective levels of antibody. Those whose titer falls to less than the recommended level should receive a booster. Alternatively, boosters may be administered every 2 years without serologic testing for those at high risk of exposure. In the postexposure setting, five doses of rabies vaccine are given intramuscularly in a relatively short period (on days 0, 3, 7, 14, and 28) to previously unimmunized persons. The intradermal route is not indicated for postexposure prophylaxis. Previously fully vaccinated persons who are exposed to rabies should receive intramuscular doses of rabies vaccine on days 0 and 3. In all postexposure settings for previously unimmunized persons, rabies vaccine should always be used in conjunction with rabies IG (see "Rabies Immune Globulin"). Adverse events associated with current rabies vaccines include local reactions in 30 to 74% of recipients and systemic reactions including headache, nausea, myalgia, abdominal pain, and dizziness in 5 to 40% of recipients. As many as 6% of persons may acquire illnesses 2 to 21 days after boosters; these conditions include arthralgia, arthritis, angioedema, nausea, vomiting, fever, and malaise. There have been rare reports of transient neurologic reactions in association with the current vaccine; however, a causal relationship has not been demonstrated. There are no known contraindications to rabies vaccination in persons at risk or exposed[114] (see Chapter 151 for more details.)

Rotavirus Vaccine. Tetravalent rotavirus vaccine consists of live attenuated viruses from a rhesus rotavirus strain (MMU 18006) and three reassortants of human and rhesus rotaviruses at a concentration of 10^5 plaque-forming units of each type (total dose 4×10^5 pfu). The parent rhesus strain has a similar VP7 capsid surface protein to the human G3 serotype. The G1, G2, and G4 serotypes were developed by reassortment and retain 10 genes from the rhesus strain with human genes for the VP7 protein.

Three orally administered doses of vaccine at 2, 4, and 6 months of age have resulted in point estimates of vaccine efficacy of 49 to 68% against all diarrhea during four randomized placebo-controlled trials. The efficacy was greater against severe diarrhea, ranging from 69 to 91%.[115, 118] The only study large enough to evaluate prevention of rotavirus hospitalization found an efficacy of 100% (13 cases in placebo recipients and 0 cases in vaccines).[118] Extended follow-up in Finland demonstrated that protection against severe rotavirus disease continued through three rotavirus seasons.[119] Adverse events are almost exclusively related to the first dose and consist primarily of fever on the third to fifth day after vaccination. A summary of data from the four trials reported an incidence of fever greater than 38°C in 21% of vaccines after dose 1 versus 6% of placebo recipients. Fever higher than 39°C was also greater—2% in vaccines versus 1% in controls. After the second dose, fever greater than 38°C was significantly higher in vaccine recipients, but the differences were small—11% in vaccines versus 9% in controls.[120] Intussusception was reported in five vaccine recipients, but the rate was not significantly higher than expected in an unvaccinated population.[121]

In the United States, the vaccine is recommended for all children at 2, 4, and 6 months of age. The minimal interval between doses is 3 weeks. Because rotavirus is primarily confined to the months between November and May with early activity in the Southwest United States and later progression to the Northeast United States consideration for more rapid immunization should be given for infants approaching the expected seasonal peaks in a given area. All doses should be administered before the first birthday because of the absence of data on safety and efficacy in older children. Very limited information suggests that infants who start immunization at 7 months of age or older may be at greater risk for adverse events. Thus, children who have not received at least one dose of vaccine prior to 7 months of age should not be vaccinated. Children who are breastfeeding or are receiving simultaneous OPV should be vaccinated. The vaccine is contraindicated in children with known or suspected immunodeficiency, hypersensitivity to a prior dose, or acute moderate to severe febrile illness. Premature infants (<37 weeks) may be at increased risk from rotavirus disease, but the safety and efficacy of the vaccine have not been established in this population. Although data are limited, premature infants may receive rotavirus vaccine at or after discharge from the hospital nursery if they are at least 6 weeks old.[122] Other precautions include infants living in households with immunocompromised persons, although most experts believe the benefits of vaccination outweigh the theoretical risks of transmission and disease. There are no data on efficacy and safety in children with acute diarrhea or chronic gastrointestinal disease. Children who regurgitate vaccine do not need to be revaccinated. Blood or blood products are not expected to interfere with this vaccine.[120] The efficacy of this vaccine in developing countries has yet to be well established, although it was found to be highly efficacious in preventing dehydrating illness in Venezuela.[123, 124] More data on the use of rotavirus vaccine in developing countries are needed, but cost will likely remain a major barrier to use of this vaccine in these settings.

Recommendations were made in July 1999 to postpone rotavirus vaccination until a more scientifically rigorous evaluation could be made regarding whether the vaccine might be playing a role in intussusception in infants.[124a] Such an evaluation to help determine whether routine vaccination should be reinstituted was expected by November 1999.

Rubella Vaccine. Rubella vaccine contains live attenuated rubella virus grown in human diploid cells (RA 27/3). Other substrates, such as duck embryo cells or rabbit kidney cells, have also been used for rubella vaccines, but these vaccines are no longer licensed in the United States. When administered to a person on or after the first birthday, 95% or more of recipients can be expected to become immune. Immunity after a single dose is long-lasting and appears likely to be lifelong. Boosters are not necessary, although many persons will receive a second dose as part of the two-dose MMR schedule to prevent measles. Rubella vaccine is recommended for all individuals on or after the first birthday except those who have documentation of having received live rubella vaccine and those who have laboratory documentation of immunity to rubella. Most persons born before 1957 can be considered immune. However, it is particularly important to ensure that women of childbearing age including those born before 1957 are immune to rubella. Rubella vaccine virus is known to be able to cross the placenta and infect fetal tissue. Nonetheless, there have been no instances of congenital rubella syndrome in the offspring of 226 susceptible women who received RA 27/3 rubella vaccine within 3 months of conception and who carried their pregnancies to term.[125] This indicates that the risk of congenital rubella syndrome from vaccine virus is so small as to be negligible. CDC's ACIP has stated that rubella vaccination during pregnancy should not ordinarily be a reason to consider termination of pregnancy. Notwithstanding the fact that no observable risk has been associated with rubella vaccine administered during pregnancy, rubella vaccine should not knowingly be administered to a pregnant woman. A reasonable approach is to ask women whether they are pregnant or may become pregnant within the next 3 months, exclude those who answer affirmatively, and vaccinate the others, after explaining the theoretical risk to them.[76]

Known adverse events associated with rubella vaccine include low-grade fever and rash in 5 to 10% of recipients and joint pains with or without objective manifestations of arthritis. The latter occur with increasing frequency in older individuals; about 25% of susceptible adult females may have transient arthralgia after rubella vaccination.[126, 127] Acute arthritis is seen in approximately 10% of susceptible women. The risk of arthritis after rubella vaccine is substantially lower than the risk after natural rubella. The IOM reviewed the adverse consequences of rubella vaccination and concluded that the vaccine was an established cause of acute arthritis and that the evidence was consistent with a causal role of vaccine in rare cases of chronic arthritis.[25] However, more recent studies have found no evidence of increased risk for new onset of chronic arthropathies among women vaccinated with RA 27/3 vaccine.[30–32] With regard to other illnesses temporally related to rubella vaccine, the IOM concluded that the evidence was insufficient to implicate rubella vaccine as a cause of thrombocytopenic purpura, radiculoneuritis, and other neuropathies. Thrombocytopenic purpura has been associated with MMR vaccine.[26]

Previous experience with programs involving serologic screening and subsequent vaccination of susceptible individuals has demonstrated a low success rate in delivering vaccinations to identified susceptible persons (typically on the order of 30 to 50%). Because of the importance of ensuring that adult women are immune to rubella and because reactions appear to occur only in susceptible individuals, it is recommended that women be vaccinated without serologic testing unless it can be ensured that they can be successfully contacted and recalled for vaccination if serologic testing indicates they are susceptible. Contraindications to rubella vaccination are pregnancy and an immunocompromised state (see "Measles Vaccine").[76]

Smallpox Vaccine. Effective use of smallpox vaccine has eradicated smallpox disease from the earth. The vaccine is a live unattenuated preparation of vaccinia virus that induces protection against smallpox virus in 95% or more of recipients. It is also highly effective in providing protection against vaccinia and other orthopoxviruses. The only indication for the use of smallpox vaccine in the United States is for individuals working with vaccinia or other orthopoxviruses. Smallpox vaccine is not effective in the treatment of herpes simplex infections. Vaccinia vector vaccines, in which DNA coding for antigens from various microorganisms is integrated into vaccinia virus DNA, may lead to greater use of these types of vaccines in the future. Vaccination may also be considered for health care workers who may directly contact recombinant vaccinia viruses during clinical vaccine trials. Known adverse events associated with smallpox vaccine are rare and include disseminated vaccinia, vaccinia necrosum, encephalitis, and death. Although rare, the fact that smallpox no longer exists makes these reactions unacceptable and contravenes the use of smallpox vaccine in any but the limited circumstances already described. In May 1983, Wyeth Laboratories, Inc., the only active licensed producer in the United States, discontinued general distribution of smallpox vaccine, making it no longer available for general civilian use.[128] Because of concerns that smallpox may become an agent for bioterrorism, discussions are under way about stockpiling vaccine to be used in the unlikely event of a terrorist incident.

Tetanus Toxoid. Tetanus toxoid, a purified preparation of inactivated tetanus toxin, is one of the most effective immunizing agents known. The preferred preparation is adsorbed (alum-precipitated) because it is more immunogenic than the fluid preparation. A primary course of two doses administered 4 to 8 weeks apart with a third dose given 6 to 12 months later induces protective antibodies in more than 95% of recipients and is recommended for all unvaccinated older children and adults. When it is given to children younger than 7 years of age as DTaP or DTP, five doses are given beginning at 2 months of age. For unvaccinated children in the first year of life, for whom pertussis vaccine is contraindicated, pediatric DT should be substituted for DTaP or DTP. For unvaccinated children in the second year of life for whom pertussis vaccine is contraindicated, two doses of DT should be administered 4 to 8 weeks apart with a third dose 6 to 12 months later. (See "Pertussis Vaccine," see Table 312–5.) Tetanus toxoid is recommended for use in all residents of the United States for whom contraindications do not exist. It should always be used in combination with diphtheria toxoid to ensure protection against both diseases. Common adverse effects include local reactions and fever. In some individuals who have received multiple doses of tetanus toxoid, Arthus-like reactions have been described.[129] Consequently, it is recommended that individuals receive boosters only every 10 years, unless a particularly tetanus-prone wound has been incurred (see "Tetanus Immune Globulin" farther on). Tetanus toxoid has been suggested as a rare cause of brachial plexus neuropathy. The IOM concluded tetanus toxoid caused brachial neuritis in the 1 month after immunization at a rate of 0.5 to 1 case/100,000 toxoid recipients.[26] Tetanus toxoid has also been implicated as a cause of GBS. The most convincing evidence comes from a case report of one individual who acquired GBS three times with successive administrations of toxoid.[130] However, population-based studies in both children and adults have revealed an incidence of GBS within expected limits and do not support a causal role.[29, 131] If tetanus toxoid causes GBS, it does so very rarely. The only contraindication is in individuals who have previously had neurologic or severe hypersensitivity reactions after tetanus toxoid. Table 312–6 summarizes the ACIP recommended approach to postexposure prophylaxis of tetanus.[43]

Typhoid Vaccine. Three preparations of typhoid vaccine are available in the United States: an oral live attenuated strain of *Salmonella typhi* (Ty21a), a Vi capsular polysaccharide vaccine (ViCPS), and a parenteral heat-phenol inactivated vaccine. The three vaccines provide between 50 and 80% protection after a primary series. An acetone-inactivated preparation, available to the armed forces only, ranges in efficacy between 75 and 94%. Typhoid vaccines are indicated for travelers who will have prolonged exposure to contaminated food and drinks in developing countries, those with prolonged exposure to typhoid carriers, and laboratory workers who work with *S. typhi.*

The oral vaccine comes as an enteric-coated capsule that should be taken on alternate days with cool liquid approximately 1 hour before a meal. The four recommended doses should be refrigerated

TABLE 312-6 Summary Guide to Tetanus Prophylaxis in Routine Wound Management: United States*

History of Adsorbed Tetanus Toxoid (Doses)	Clean, Minor Wounds		All Other Wounds†	
	Td‡	TIG	Td‡	TIG
Unknown or less than three	Yes	No	Yes	Yes
Three§	No‖	No	No**	No

*Important details are in the text.
†Such as, but not limited to, wounds contaminated with dirt, feces, soil, saliva, and so on; puncture wounds; avulsions; and wounds resulting from missiles, crushing, burns, and frostbite.
‡For children less than 7 yr, DTaP or DTP (DT if pertussis vaccine is contraindicated) is preferred to tetanus toxoid alone. For persons 7 yr and older, Td is preferred to tetanus toxoid alone.
§If only three doses of fluid toxoid have been received, a fourth dose of toxoid, preferably an adsorbed toxoid, should be given.
‖Yes, if more than 10 yr since last dose.
**Yes, if more than 5 yr since last dose. (More frequent boosters are not needed and can accentuate side effects.)

until needed. Data are not available to make recommendations about the need for boosters with the oral vaccine, although the manufacturer recommends a new complete series every 5 years. The ViCPS is recommended as a single 0.5-ml dose. Boosters are recommended every 2 years. The heat-phenol inactivated vaccine should be administered in two doses 4 or more weeks apart. The dose for children 10 years of age or older and adults, 0.5 ml, is twice the dose for younger children, 0.25 ml. For those who received the heat-phenol vaccine, boosters are indicated every 3 years for those at continued risk. Heat-phenol vaccines commonly produce fever (14 to 24%), headache (9 to 30%), and severe local pain (up to 40%). Intradermal injection, which can be used for booster doses, reduces the incidence of systemic side effects. The Ty21a vaccine is not recommended for children less than 6 years of age. The ViCPS is recommended for persons 2 years of age or older, whereas the heat-phenol inactivated vaccine can be administered to children as young as 6 months. The Ty21a and the ViCPS vaccines cause fever and headache in less than 6% of recipients. Other adverse reactions to the oral preparation are rare and consist of abdominal discomfort, nausea, and vomiting. Local reactions to the ViCPS have been reported in 7% of recipients. In contrast, heat-phenol inactivated vaccines have been associated with rates of fever of 7 to 24% and local reactions have been seen in as many as 35% of recipients. The major contraindication to the heat-phenol preparation is a prior serious reaction. The oral vaccine should not be given to persons who are immunocompromised, including those with HIV infection. Ty21a should not be given to a person taking the antimalarial mefloquine or antibiotics, especially sulfonamides, unless at least 24 hours has elapsed since the last dose. Because of (1) the marked increase in safety with use of Ty21a and ViCPS vaccines and (2) comparable efficacy of these vaccines to the heat-phenol inactivated product, ViCPS and Ty21a are preferred.[132]

Varicella Vaccine. A live attenuated varicella vaccine (Oka strain) was licensed in the United States in March 1995. Efficacy estimates vary with potency of the preparation and the severity of illness prevented. The efficacy in preventing any varicella has ranged from 67% for a preparation of lower potency than used today to 95% with a preparation of higher potency than that used now.[23, 133] Studies have shown protection against severe disease is usually 95% or greater. A recent postlicensure evaluation of the current vaccine estimated effectiveness to be 86% against any varicella and 100% against severe disease.[24] Most vaccinees who acquire varicella tend to have mild illness with fewer than 50 lesions compared with 250 to 500 lesions in unvaccinated persons with disease.[134–136] Immunity appears to be long lasting. With the current vaccine, varicella occurs at a rate of 2 to 4% per year with no evidence for increasing severity with increasing time since vaccination.[137] The vaccine is recommended routinely for all children at 12 to 18 months of age and can be given to any susceptible older child or adult. Persons 13 years of age and older require two doses 4 to 8 weeks apart. Vaccination is recommended for susceptible persons who have contact with persons at high risk of complications such as health care workers and family contacts of immunocompromised persons. Vaccination should be considered for susceptible persons who (1) work in institutions where varicella transmission is likely or can occur such as schools, day care centers, colleges, prisons, and the military; (2) are nonpregnant females of childbearing age; and (3) are international travelers. Because adults are at higher risk of complications from varicella than are children, vaccination of all susceptible adolescents and adults is desirable. Persons with a reliable history of varicella can be considered immune. Although a negative or uncertain history of varicella in young children is predictive of susceptibility, most young adults with such histories are immune. In some settings, serologic screening of persons with negative or unknown prior histories of varicella is cost-effective.[138] However, recalling and vaccinating identified susceptible persons may be difficult, making vaccination using history as the determinant of need more attractive.

The most common adverse events are local reactions and rash. In children, approximately 3% acquire a varicella-like rash at the injection site with a median of two lesions and 4% acquire a generalized rash with a median of five lesions. For adults, 3% and 1% acquire localized rashes after doses 1 and 2, respectively, whereas 6% and 1% acquire more generalized rashes.[23] Transmission of vaccine virus has been reported rarely and only from persons with rash. There is no evidence that vaccination increases the risk of zoster. In fact, zoster incidence after vaccination appears lower than would be expected after natural infection. Vaccine is contraindicated in persons with anaphylactic hypersensitivity to vaccine components, including neomycin and gelatin, and in immunocompromised persons. Patients with acute lymphoblastic leukemia in remission may qualify for vaccine under an investigational new drug protocol (phone number 215-283-0897). Pregnant women should not be vaccinated and women should be warned not to become pregnant for 1 month after vaccination.[23]

Varicella vaccine is more thermolabile than other vaccines. It must be stored frozen at an average temperature of −15°C or less.

Yellow Fever Vaccine. Yellow fever vaccine is a live attenuated virus preparation that is highly effective in inducing protection in recipients. It is indicated for use in travelers going to yellow fever–endemic areas and may be required for entry into some countries. Only a single dose of vaccine is required; it is administered by subcutaneous inoculation. Boosters are recommended every 10 years, although their need has not been conclusively established. Local and mild systemic reactions occur in 2 to 5% of recipients 5 to 10 days after vaccination; more severe reactions, primarily encephalitis and encephalopathy, are rare. Children less than 4 months of age appear to be at highest risk of severe reactions and vaccine is contraindicated in this age group. Other contraindications include anaphylactic hypersensitivity to eggs and immunocompromised states. If possible, vaccination of infants should be delayed until 9 months of age. Pregnancy is not considered an absolute contraindication; however, it is recommended that administration of the vaccine be postponed until after completion of pregnancy, if possible. Because the immune response to yellow fever vaccine may be inhibited by cholera vaccine administered simultaneously or within 3 weeks of yellow fever vaccine, it is best to separate them by at least 3 weeks.[139] Given the little benefit derived from cholera vaccine, if it is needed it should be administered after yellow fever vaccine whenever possible.

Immunoglobulins

Immune Globulin. (also see Chapter 36). IG is a preparation of pooled human immunoglobulins containing antibodies against infectious agents that cause several diseases, including hepatitis A and measles. IG is effective in preventing hepatitis A when administered within 14 days of exposure (a dose of 0.02 ml/kg) or when given before exposure in somewhat larger quantities (dose of 0.02 ml/kg for trips of 1 to 2 months, 0.06 ml/kg every 5 months for longer trips).[53] It may also prevent or modify measles if administered within 6 days of exposure (a dose of 0.25 ml/kg for normal persons, 0.5 ml/kg for those who are immunocompromised, up to a maximum of 15 ml). Adverse effects include local tenderness and, rarely, Arthus-type or anaphylactic reactions. Anaphylaxis has been reported after repeated administration to IgA-deficient persons.[140] Other than prior anaphylactic reactions, there are no known contraindications to use of the product. IG inhibits response to certain live virus vaccines (i.e., measles and rubella vaccines) for between 3 and 9 months, depending on the dose administered (3 months for hepatitis dose; 5 months for measles prevention doses).[141] Simultaneous administration of IG with hepatitis A vaccine may result in a decrease of the ultimate titer of hepatitis A antibody achieved but does not influence seroconversion and presumed protection.[56]

Ordinary IG should not be administered intravenously.[142] IGIV is formulated for intravenous use primarily as a maintenance preparation for individuals with hypogammaglobulinemia. In addition, it may also be useful to decrease risk of infection in other immunodeficiency states such as HIV infection in children and may provide postexposure protection against measles and other infections. IGIV is also used to treat immune thrombocytopenic purpura and Kawasaki's disease.

IG and specific IG products prepared by Cohn fractionation pose no risk of transmitting hepatitis B, HIV, or other known infectious agents. Hepatitis C has been transmitted by IGIV in both Europe and the United States and by an intravenous Rh IG preparation in Ireland.[143–145] Hepatitis C virus RNA has been detected by polymerase chain reaction in various IG preparations,[146] but the significance of this finding is unclear; disease has not been associated with products other than those noted previously. In response to these findings, manufacturing procedures are being modified to add new viral inactivation steps.[147]

Hepatitis B Immune Globulin. HBIG is prepared from plasma preselected for high titer of antibody to HBsAg. In the United States, HBIG has an anti-HBsAg titer of more than 1:100,000 by radioimmunoassay. It is recommended for use in postexposure settings for susceptible individuals who have been exposed by known hepatitis B virus–infected sexual partners or to blood containing HBsAg by the percutaneous or mucous membrane route. The dose is 0.06 ml/kg given immediately for both sexual contacts and those exposed percutaneously. The hepatitis B vaccine series should be started simultaneously in those who have not previously been vaccinated. Alternatively, a second dose of HBIG may be given 1 month later for persons for whom hepatitis B vaccine is not indicated. HBIG is also recommended for infants born to HBsAg-positive women. A dose of 0.5 ml should be given within 12 hours of delivery in conjunction with a dose of hepatitis B vaccine. Additional doses of vaccine are indicated at 1 month and 6 months. The only known adverse effect is local discomfort at the site of injection. There are no known precautions or contraindications.[58]

Rabies Immune Globulin. RIG is a hyperimmune globulin prepared from humans who have been immunized against rabies and have very high titers of antibodies to rabies. It is designed for management of individuals who have been exposed to rabid animals. RIG should always be used in conjunction with rabies vaccine in previously unvaccinated persons. However, if more than 8 days has elapsed since the first dose of rabies vaccine, RIG is unnecessary because an active antibody response to the vaccine has presumably begun. Experience to date indicates that administration of a full course of human diploid cell rabies vaccine with rabies immunoglobulin is 100% effective in preventing the development of rabies after exposure to known rabid animals. As much as possible of the 20 IU/kg dose should be infiltrated into and around the wound. Any remaining RIG should be administered intramuscularly at a different site from vaccine. Adverse effects include minor local discomfort. There are no known contraindications.[114]

Respiratory Syncytial Virus Immune Globulin and Palivizumab. Two products are licensed in the United States for administration to infants and children at high risk of severe disease due to respiratory syncytial virus (RSV); groups at high risk include infants and children younger than 24 months of age with chronic lung disease or a history of premature birth (≤35 weeks' gestation). Respiratory syncytial virus immune globulin intravenous (RSV-IGIV) is a hyperimmune globulin formulated for intravenous administration. It is administered monthly during the RSV season (November through April in the Northern Hemisphere). RSV-IGIV has been demonstrated to be effective in reducing the risk of RSV hospitalization.[148] The recommended maximal dose is 750 mg/kg. However, an unexpected increase in adverse events was observed in RSV-IGIV–treated children with cyanotic congenital heart disease.[149] RSV-IGIV, like other IG products, may interfere with the immune response to live virus vaccines.[141] Palivizumab is a humanized monoclonal antibody against the F protein of RSV and is produced by recombinant DNA technology. The recommended dosage is 15 mg/kg administered intramuscularly monthly throughout the RSV season. Palivizumab has been demonstrated to be effective in reducing the risk of RSV hospitalization.[150] No significant adverse events have been associated with palivizumab, and there is no interference with the immune response to live virus vaccines. The American Academy of Pediatrics has recommended that palivizumab or RSV-IGIV prophylaxis be considered for infants and children younger than 2 years of age with chronic lung disease who have required medical therapy for lung disease within the 6 months preceding RSV season.[151]

Rh Immune Globulin. Rh IG is a hyperimmune globulin prepared for use in Rh-negative women who have just delivered Rh-positive babies or have had a miscarriage or abortion of an Rh-positive fetus. When administered within 24 hours of the time of delivery or abortion, it is highly effective in preventing sensitization of the mother to Rh-positive red blood cells that might be present in a future pregnancy. Appropriate administration of Rh IG has reduced the occurrence of Rh hemolytic disease of the newborn in the United States to very low levels. Further reductions will require more careful attention to the administration of the product after abortion or delivery in all women for whom it is indicated. There are essentially no adverse effects associated with the product, and there are no known contraindications.[152]

Tetanus Immune Globulin. TIG is a hyperimmune globulin indicated for management of tetanus-prone wounds in individuals who have no prior history of tetanus immunization. The standard dose is 250 units intramuscularly, although some groups recommend doses as high as 500 units. Local reactions are rare, and there are no known contraindications. If used, it should be administered simultaneously with, but at a different site from, combined tetanus-diphtheria toxoids. Primary immunization against tetanus and diphtheria should then be completed using the routine schedule. Table 312–6 summarizes the ACIP-recommended approach to postexposure prophylaxis of tetanus.[43] TIG in large doses (3000 to 6000 units) may also be used in the treatment of tetanus.

Vaccinia Immune Globulin. Vaccinia immune globulin (VIG) is a hyperimmune globulin prepared for treatment of complications of vaccinia vaccination (eczema vaccinatum, severe generalized vaccinia, ocular vaccinia). The need for this product should be very limited in the United States because smallpox vaccine should be used only in very rare circumstances.[128]

Varicella-Zoster Immune Globulin. VZIG is prepared by selection of serum containing high titers of varicella-zoster antibodies. It is indicated for administration to susceptible immunocompromised individuals and certain others who have recently been exposed to varicella, including newborns whose mothers acquire varicella within 5 days before to 48 hours after delivery. It should be administered within 96 hours of exposure, but ideally as soon after exposure as possible. Some believe it may also be useful in ameliorating the expression of varicella in susceptible adults, particularly susceptible pregnant females who are at increased risk of complications from varicella infection after exposure to the virus. The product may not prevent infection; however, if infection occurs it is usually subclinical or mild. Local reactions are rare, and there are no known contraindications.[23]

USE OF VACCINES

Routine

Children. The recommended schedules for administration of vaccines to infants and children are shown in Figure 312–1 and Table 312–5. It is currently recommended that all children receive DTaP, polio, measles, mumps, rubella, HIB, hepatitis B, varicella, and rotavirus vaccines unless contraindications exist.[35] Five doses of DTaP and four doses of polio-containing vaccines are recommended. The fifth dose of DTaP and the fourth dose of polio vaccine are recommended at 4 to 6 years of age.[22, 28] DTaP is preferred over DTP for all doses of the five-dose schedule. Td boosters should be administered at 11 to 12 years of age and every 10 years thereafter.[60] A single dose of combined measles, mumps, and rubella vaccine at 12 to 15 months of age or older provides long-lasting, probably lifelong, immunity in more than 95% of recipients. The second dose of MMR at school entry should provide immunity to most of those not protected by the first dose.[76] DTaP, MMR, HIB, hepatitis B, polio, and varicella vaccines may be given simultaneously if necessary. Similarly, rotavirus vaccine can be administered in the first year of life simultaneously with DTaP, HIB, hepatitis B, and polio vaccines. Although all potential simultaneous administration schemes have not been evaluated, experience to date suggests that simultaneous administration of most vaccines does not increase reaction rates nor interfere with the immune responses.[153] Stress for infants, as measured by serum cortisol, does not increase when a second injection is given.[154, 155] HIB should be given in two doses (PRP-OMP) or three doses (HbOC, PRP-T) in the first year of life followed by a reinforcing dose at 12 to 15 months.[45] Hepatitis B vaccine can be given as early as birth, and the three-dose series should be completed by 18 months of age; hepatitis B vaccine can be given simultaneously with all other childhood vaccines.[58] Combined DTP-HbOC or PRP-T reconstituted with DTP (Connaught) can be given any time both DTP and HIB are indicated simultaneously,[45, 49] although their use should be limited because DTaP is preferred over DTP.[35] A combined DTaP–PRP-T is available for dose four of the schedule as of August 15, 1999.[22] The three-dose rotavirus vaccine series should be begun before 7 months of age and completed by the first birthday.[120] As of August 15, 1999, routine vaccination against rotavirus has been postponed pending an investigation into the relationship between rotavirus vaccine and intussusception.[124a] Children should receive varicella vaccine routinely at 12 to 18 months of age.[23]

Adolescents. An adolescent immunization visit has been established at 11 to 12 years of age.[60] This is the appropriate time to administer (1) a booster dose of Td for those persons who completed a primary series and received their last dose of a vaccine containing tetanus and diphtheria toxoids at school entry, (2) a second dose of MMR if not previously received, and (3) a dose of varicella vaccine if the patient is susceptible. The three-dose hepatitis B vaccination series should be administered if not previously received. A schedule of doses of hepatitis B vaccine at 0, 1 to 2 months, and 4 to 6 months is recommended. Other immunizations such as pneumococcal vaccine, influenza vaccine, and hepatitis A vaccine should be given, if indicated.

Adults. Routine immunizations for adults have received increasing attention in recent years with recognition of the large burden of vaccine-preventable diseases in this age group. All adults should be immune to diphtheria and tetanus and if not previously immunized should be given a primary immunizing course (three doses of Td administered at time zero, 4 to 8 weeks, and 6 to 12 months) with boosters administered every 10 years thereafter.[43] Routine immunization against polio is not recommended for adults unless they are at particular risk of exposure.[28] All individuals should be immune to measles, mumps, and rubella. For practical purposes, those born before 1957 can generally be considered immune to measles, mumps, and rubella. All other individuals should be vaccinated unless it can be documented that they have either received vaccine on or after the first birthday or have had physician-diagnosed disease. Rubella vaccine should be administered to women of childbearing age even if they were born before 1957 unless they have documented proof of having received rubella vaccine on or after the first birthday or laboratory evidence of immunity. A history of prior rubella disease is unreliable and should not be accepted.[76] Influenza vaccine is recommended for routine annual administration to adults 65 years of age and older and to individuals at any age who have chronic illness.[65] Pneumococcal polysaccharide vaccine is recommended for administration to the elderly and the chronically ill.[110] Hepatitis B virus vaccine is recommended for individuals at high risk of exposure to hepatitis B virus. These include primarily health care and emergency responder personnel who anticipate contact with blood or blood-containing body fluids, homosexual men and sexually active heterosexuals with multiple sexual partners, users of illicit injectable drugs, individuals living and working in institutions for the developmentally disabled, and household contacts of carriers of HBsAg.[34, 156] All susceptible adults should be vaccinated against chickenpox.[23] Table 312–7 summarizes recommended adult immunizations.

Special Circumstances

Travel (also see Chapter 315). The International Health Regulations allow countries to impose requirements for yellow fever vaccine as a condition for admission. Consequently, travelers should be aware of whether this vaccine is required for entry into the country of their destination. This information is summarized in *Health Information for International Travel*[157] (see "Sources of Information" farther on) and can also be obtained by calling local health departments or the Centers for Disease Control and Prevention Travel Information System at 404-332-4559. Other vaccines commonly considered for travelers include measles vaccine, polio vaccine, and boosters for tetanus and diphtheria. In addition, travelers to specified areas may wish to consider plague, typhoid, rabies, Japanese encephalitis, yellow fever, and hepatitis B vaccines, and hepatitis A prophylaxis.

Occupational Exposure. A complete set of recommendations for vaccination for most occupational groups has not been developed. Specific recommendations are available for health care workers.[77] Federal regulations require that health care and public safety workers who anticipate exposure to human blood or blood-derived body fluids are offered hepatitis B vaccination free of charge.[57] It is clear that transmission of rubella in medical facilities can occur to or from health care workers. Consequently, it is important that all health care workers who might transmit rubella to pregnant patients be immune to rubella. Documentation of a single dose of a rubella-containing vaccine on or after the first birthday or serologic evidence of immunity is acceptable. Health care workers are at greater risk from measles than the general public. All workers likely to come in contact with measles patients should be immune, defined as documentation of receipt of two doses of live measles vaccine on or after the first birthday, at least 1 month apart, physician-diagnosed measles, or serologic evidence of immunity. Although most persons born before 1957 have been considered to be immune to measles, approximately 4% of cases in health care workers in recent years were in persons born before this date. Therefore, in health care settings, it may be worthwhile to ensure that all persons have documented evidence of immunity regardless of age. Although mumps has not been a major problem in health care settings, mumps transmission in such settings has been reported and mumps immunity can be ensured at the same time as measles and rubella if MMR is used.[76] Because health care workers caring for patients with chronic

TABLE 312–7 Recommended Immunizations for Adults

	Routine—Age Group (Yr)*				Special Circumstances						
Vaccine	*18–24*	*25–49*	*50–64*	*≥65*	*Military Recruits*	*Travelers*	*Health Care Workers*	*Occupation*	*Immunocompromised*	*Pregnancy*	*Chronic Illness*
Anthrax								S			
Bacillus Calmette-Guérin							S±		O		
Cholera						S					
Diphtheria	X	X	X	X	X	X	X	X	X	X	X
Haemophilus influenzae type B									S±		
Hepatitis B						S	X	S			
Influenza				X	X	S	X	S	X	X	X
Japanese encephalitis						S					
Measles	X	X†			X	X†	X†		O‡	O	
Meningococcal					X	S					
Mumps	X	X†				X†	X†		O‡	O	
Plague						S		S			
Pneumococcal				X					X		X
Inactivated polio					X	S	S				
Oral polio§					X‖	S	S		O		
Rabies						S		S			
Rubella	X	X¶			X	X¶	X¶		O‡	O	
Smallpox (vaccinia)								S	O	O	
Tetanus	X	X	X	X	X	X	X	X	X	X	X
Typhoid						S		S			
Varicella**	X	X	X	X	X	X	X	X	O	O	X
Yellow fever						S			O		

*Unless contraindications exist.
†If susceptible; persons born before 1957 are generally considered immune.
‡Measles, mumps, and rubella vaccines should be considered for persons with symptomatic human immunodeficiency virus (HIV) infection without severe immunocompromise. They are routinely indicated for persons with asymptomatic HIV infection and contraindicated in persons with severe immunocompromise.
§After January 1, 2000, OPV use is likely to be limited to control of outbreaks. IPV will be the vaccine of choice in virtually all settings.
‖OPV is used only for recruits who have been previously vaccinated so they are ready to travel to polio endemic areas. With expected decrease in OPV availability in 2000, policy may switch to IPV.
¶If susceptible; persons born before 1957 are generally considered immune (except women of childbearing age who could become pregnant in whom immunity should be ensured.)
**If susceptible.
Symbols: X, recommended; ±, divided opinion; O, contraindicated; S, selected risk situation.

diseases may transmit influenza to their patients, such workers should be vaccinated annually.[65] Health care workers should also be immune to varicella.[23]

Pregnancy. Because of unknown but theoretical risks to the fetus, immunization of pregnant women is generally avoided. However, it is important to ensure that pregnant women are immune to tetanus, because transfer of maternal antibodies to tetanus toxin is an important means of preventing neonatal tetanus. Pregnant women can receive combined tetanus-diphtheria toxoids. In general, live virus vaccines are contraindicated in pregnancy with the exceptions of polio and yellow fever virus vaccines, which may be administered if the risk of exposure to the disease is great. If indicated, some inactivated vaccines, such as influenza and hepatitis B, can be administered to pregnant women under the same circumstances they are administered to nonpregnant individuals.[1] Women likely to be in the second or third trimester of pregnancy during the upcoming influenza season should receive influenza vaccines.[65]

Immunocompromised States. Immunocompromised individuals (congenital, acquired, or due to drug therapy) are particularly susceptible to many infections. They may also be more susceptible to adverse effects from live virus vaccines, although severe complications have been documented only rarely.[25, 26] Consequently, in general live virus vaccines are not administered to immunocompromised individuals, although inactivated vaccines are safe and are indicated. It is particularly important to avoid administration of OPV vaccine to immunocompromised individuals or their household contacts. IPV should be used under those circumstances. Rotavirus and varicella vaccines are also contraindicated in immunocompromised persons. The efficacy of inactivated vaccines in immunocompromised individuals may be less than that in healthy patients.[158, 159]

Human Immunodeficiency Virus. Live attenuated vaccines are generally contraindicated in immunocompromised persons, including those with symptomatic HIV infection. Limited studies in HIV-infected persons have generally failed to show an increased risk of adverse events from live or inactivated vaccines. Exceptions include BCG given to patients with acquired immunodeficiency syndrome and measles-containing vaccine in a patient with severe immunodeficiency.[160–162] A single case of vaccine-associated polio has been reported in an HIV-infected person.[163] Whether this represents a chance occurrence or significant increased risk is uncertain. Regardless, IPV should be used in place of OPV for all HIV-infected persons in the United States.[28] Known HIV-infected persons who are asymptomatic should receive live attenuated MMR vaccine (Table 312–8). Because of reports of severe measles disease, including death, in symptomatic HIV-infected children, measles vaccine, alone or preferably with mumps and rubella vaccines, can be considered for symptomatic HIV-infected persons.[76] However, measles vaccine has been documented to cause death when given to a severely immunocompromised HIV-infected adult.[162] Therefore, vaccine is contraindicated in persons with severe immunodeficiency. Because measles has occurred even after vaccination in HIV-infected children, it is recommended that symptomatic HIV-infected children receive IG or IGIV after an exposure to measles[76] (see Chapter 149). For asymptomatic persons presenting for immunization, serologic testing to determine HIV infection is not necessary for making decisions about immunization. Recommendations for administration of other vaccines are listed in Table 312–8. Although transient increases of HIV in the blood of patients have been documented in the month after receipt of both pneumococcal and influenza vaccines, their clinical significance is unknown. In contrast, HIV-infected persons are known to be at significantly higher risk of pneumococcal disease. Pneumococcal vaccine is recommended for infected persons 2 years of age or older, and many HIV-infected persons may benefit from influenza vaccination as well.[65, 110] Although a protective immune response to vaccines and toxoids cannot be ensured in these patients, some protection may be provided.

Postexposure Immunization. For certain diseases, administration of vaccine or IG soon after exposure can prevent or attenuate the expression of the disease.[142] For example, administration of IG within

TABLE 312–8 Recommendations for Routine Immunization of Human Immunodeficiency Virus–Infected Persons—United States

	Human Immunodeficiency Virus Infection	
Vaccine	*Asymptomatic*	*Symptomatic*
DTaP/DTP*	Yes	Yes
OPV†	No	No
IPV‡	Yes	Yes
MMR§	Yes	Yes‖
HIB**	Yes	Yes
HBV††	Yes	Yes
Rotavirus	No	No
Varicella	No	No
Pneumococcal‡‡	Yes	Yes‖‖
Influenza§§	Yes	Yes‖‖
Hepatitis A vaccine	Yes***	Yes***

*DTaP: diphtheria and tetanus toxoids and acellular pertussis vaccine, DTP, diphtheria and tetanus toxoids and pertussis vaccine. Not recommended for persons ≥7 yr of age.
†OPV: oral, attenuated poliovirus vaccine; contains poliovirus types 1, 2, and 3.
‡IPV: inactivated poliovirus vaccine; contains poliovirus types 1, 2, and 3.
§MMR: live, attenuated measles, mumps, and rubella vaccines in a combined vaccine.
‖Vaccine should be considered, except for persons with severe immunocompromise.
**HIB: *Haemophilus* B conjugate vaccine.
††Hepatitis B vaccine.
‡‡Pneumococcal polysaccharide vaccine recommended for persons ≥2 yr of age.
§§Not recommended for infants <6 mo of age.
‖‖Vaccine should be considered.
***If otherwise indicated.
Updated from Centers for Disease Control and Prevention. Recommendation of the Immunization Practices Advisory Committee (ACIP): Immunization of children infected with human immunodeficiency virus—supplementary ACIP statement. MMWR Morb Mortal Wkly Rep. 1988, 37:181–183 and Centers for Disease Control and Prevention. Recommendations of the Advisory Committee on Immunization Practices (ACIP): Use of vaccines and immune globulins in persons with altered immunocompetence. MMWR Morb Mortal Wkly Rep. 1993;42:1–18.

2 weeks of exposure to hepatitis A is likely to prevent clinical illness. Similarly, the administration of RIG and rabies vaccine in the immediate postexposure period is highly effective in preventing the development of rabies. Individuals who have received a complete course of immunization against tetanus are in general well protected against the development of tetanus, particularly if a booster dose has been administered within 10 years. More problematic is the situation with individuals who cannot recall their immune status or who have not been immunized at all. Table 312–6 shows the ACIP recommended approach to postexposure prophylaxis of tetanus. IG administered within 6 days of exposure may be effective in preventing measles or modifying it so that the illness is very mild. There is also evidence that administration of measles vaccine within the first few days after exposure may prevent manifestations of the illness. In addition, if the exposure did not result in infection, the vaccination will provide protection against future exposure. Although overt manifestations of rubella can be minimized by postexposure administration of IG, this may not prevent viremia and fetal infection with rubella. Therefore, the administration of IG is recommended only for individuals who acquire rubella during pregnancy and will not consider induced abortion under any circumstances. Data are limited on postexposure use of the licensed formulation of varicella vaccine, but studies in both the United States and Japan suggest that the vaccine may be useful in postexposure prophylaxis.[164, 165]

Other Considerations

Assessing the Need for Immunization. Immunization has traditionally been viewed as the task of the pediatrician and general practitioner caring for children, but all health care providers should assess the immunization status of their patients at first contact and, depending on immunization status and age, at selected contacts thereafter. In general, individuals should be viewed as susceptible unless they can prove immunity through documentation of having received vaccine, laboratory evidence of immunity or, for some diseases, documentation of physician-diagnosed disease.

A high proportion of elderly individuals in the United States have never been immunized against tetanus or diphtheria. This is reflected in the fact that 35% of all cases of tetanus in the United States in the period 1995 to 1997 have occurred in individuals older than the age of 60 years.[166] Internists and other physicians caring for adults and elderly individuals should be particularly attuned to the need for administering tetanus and diphtheria toxoids to these individuals. Similarly, studies repeatedly demonstrate that no more than 66% of targeted individuals receive influenza immunization in a given year, only an estimated 45% have received pneumococcal vaccine, and only about 20% of target populations have received hepatitis B vaccine. It is vital that internists and family practitioners remind themselves and their patients of the need for annual influenza immunization of the chronically ill and elderly.

Immunization Records. Every individual should have an immunization record that is up to date and that contains information about each dose of vaccine received, including the date. Patients should be asked to bring this record with them to all health care visits, and the record should be reviewed to ensure that it is up to date. Official immunization record cards should be used; they are available through local or state health departments. The National Childhood Vaccine Injury Act requires that all providers of DTP or components, OPV or IPV, MMR or components, Hib, hepatitis B, varicella, and rotavirus vaccines record on the patient's permanent medical record the date, manufacturer, and lot number of each dose of vaccine administered and the name of the person giving the vaccine. This information should be recorded for other vaccines as well.

Parent and Patient Education. All patients (or their parents or guardians) should be informed of the benefits and the risks associated with vaccination. The discussion should be carried out in language that is comprehensible to the recipient (or parent or guardian), and ample opportunity for questions and discussion should be given. Vaccine Information Statements have been developed for (1) MMR or components, (2) diphtheria and tetanus toxoids and pertussis vaccine or components, (3) oral and inactivated polio vaccines, (4) HIB vaccine, (5) hepatitis B vaccine, and (6) varicella vaccine. As of August 15, 1999, a statement for rotavirus was under development. The National Childhood Vaccine Injury Act requires use of these statements with these vaccines. In addition, the Public Health Service has developed forms that explain the benefits as well as the risks of vaccination for use with pneumococcal and influenza vaccines. Interested health care providers can receive copies of these forms through local health departments or from the Internet (http://www.cdc.gov/nip/publications/vis/default.htm).

Simultaneous Administration and Intervals between Immunizations. Most of the widely used antigens can be given safely and effectively at the same time. In general, inactivated vaccines can be administered simultaneously at separate sites, and field observations indicate that simultaneous administration of the most widely used live virus vaccines has not resulted in impaired antibody responses or increased rates of adverse reactions.[153] When vaccines are administered simultaneously, they should be given in separate limbs. When this is not feasible, they should be separated by at least 1 to 2 inches. However, simultaneous administration of IG and MMR vaccines should be avoided because this may result in interference with antibody responses. With those vaccines, IG should not be given for at least 2 weeks after vaccination. Persons receiving high doses of IG or other blood products may have impaired responses to vaccines for as long as 11 months depending on the dose received.[1, 141] Persons who received standard doses of IG for hepatitis A prophylaxis can receive live vaccines 3 months after IG, whereas children treated for Kawasaki's disease with intravenous IG in a dose of 2 g/kg should be vaccinated ideally 11 months after the dose. Similar recommendations apply to varicella vaccine. IG does not appear to interfere with the response to OPV or yellow fever vaccines.[167] In general, the antigenic mass of inactivated vaccines is so great that IG will not interfere with the antibody response.

With live vaccines, there is the theoretical possibility of interference in the development of antibody responses when live vaccines are administered at intervals of 3 to 14 days. If more than one live vaccine is needed, the vaccines should be administered simultaneously or at intervals of approximately 1 month between different vaccines. This does not apply to OPV and parenterally administered live viral vaccines. OPV and those vaccines can be administered regardless of interval between vaccines. In general, there are no restrictions on intervals between doses of different inactivated vaccines or between different inactivated and live vaccines. The only exceptions are cholera and yellow fever vaccines, which should ideally be administered at least 3 weeks apart to achieve maximal immune responses to both vaccines.

Interrupted Schedules. Immunologic memory induced by vaccines is usually long term. Therefore, when doses in a schedule of doses are missed, there is no need to restart the series. Instead, continue from where the schedule left off.

Reporting of Disease and Adverse Events. Each state has laws requiring the reporting of certain communicable diseases. The list of reportable diseases generally includes all or most of the diseases preventable by vaccination.[168] Health care providers should ensure that each suspected case of vaccine-preventable disease is reported promptly to the local health department. Similarly, serious adverse events after immunization should be reported to the Vaccine Adverse Events Reporting System (VAERS). Forms for VAERS can be obtained by calling 800-822-7967. The National Childhood Vaccine Injury Act requires providers to report specified adverse events if they occur within a designated time frame following immunization (Table 312–9).[169, 170] However, all serious events temporally related to vaccination should be reported regardless of whether or not they are thought to be caused by the vaccine. Only through accurate reporting and follow-up of both disease and adverse vaccine effects can the changing balance of benefits and risks of vaccination be properly assessed.

Compensation for Vaccine Injuries. The National Childhood Vaccine Injury Act of 1986 established a no-fault compensation program for persons injured by vaccines.[170] Table 312–9 lists the covered vaccines, conditions, and time frames for which persons are eligible for compensation in the absence of other known causes for the events. All persons with alleged injuries from covered vaccines must file first under the compensation program. Persons who meet the criteria of the table (and other legal requirements) are entitled to compensation without proving that vaccine caused the injury. Persons alleging a condition not included in the table or who otherwise do not meet criteria in the table must prove that the vaccine was the cause. Individuals may accept decisions of the program or reject those decisions and go to the tort system. If compensation decisions are accepted, manufacturers and vaccine administrators are protected from litigation. More information on the compensation program can be obtained by calling 800-338-2382 or through the Division of Vaccine Injury Compensation's Home Page: (http://www.hrsa.gov/bhpr/vicp).

Standards for Immunization Practices. Investigation into the resurgence of measles in the United States from 1989 to 1991 during which more than 55,000 cases were reported, more than 11,000 persons were hospitalized, and more than 130 persons died indicated that failure to vaccinate preschool children on time was the major cause of the epidemic.[171] Immunization coverage for four DTP, three OPV, and one MMR in some inner cities ranged as low as 10%.[172] These investigations also documented that other significant reasons for the low vaccination rates in children by their second birthday were barriers and obstacles to immunizations that parents faced in getting their children immunized and opportunities missed by health care providers to provide vaccines.

At least three types of missed opportunities exist: (1) the patient receives some but not all indicated vaccines because the provider is unaware that many vaccines can be administered simultaneously, (2) inappropriate contraindications are used to deny vaccinations to children in need, and (3) the patient presents for another reason such as trauma, and immunization status is not reviewed. To minimize the barriers to immunization and to ensure that all opportunities to vaccinate are taken, in 1992 the National Vaccine Advisory Committee issued 18 Standards for Pediatric Immunization Practices (Table 312–10), which should be followed by both public and private health care providers.[173] These have been endorsed by the U.S. Public Health Service, the American Academy of Pediatrics, and many other professional groups.

Some of the more critical standards include providing vaccines in all health care settings; minimizing prevaccination requirements such as full physician evaluation when those services are not readily obtainable; screening for contraindications including, at a minimum, observation of the child, soliciting illness history from the parents, and verbally asking questions about contraindications; use of simultaneous immunization except when, in the judgment of the provider, nonsimultaneous vaccination will not compromise the immunization status of the patient; and regular audits of patient records to determine the vaccination levels of the patients in each provider's practice. To assist in using only valid contraindications, Table 312–10, taken from the standards and updated, is reproduced here.

Similar standards have been produced for adult immunization.[174] The Infectious Diseases Society of America has established 14 guidelines that combine relevant aspects of both the pediatric and adult standards.[175]

Methods to Improve Immunization Coverage. In the wake of the resurgence of measles, a Childhood Immunization Initiative was undertaken to improve delivery of immunizations to infants and young children and to ensure that they completed the primary immunization series by their second birthday, as recommended. Supported by unprecedented levels of federal resources and activities spearheaded by community-wide coalitions, record high levels of coverage have now been achieved in preschool children.

Several approaches have been shown to be useful in improving immunization coverage.[176] Two of the most important include assessment of immunization levels in a given practice with provision of information back to the provider and use of reminder-recall systems.

Studies have shown that providers (as well as parents) tend to overestimate the level of coverage in their patients (or children), and formal review of records can be very useful in making practitioners aware of the need to continue to pay attention. Bushnell asked physicians and nurses from both public and private sectors in Massachusetts to estimate immunization coverage of their patient populations. Estimates ranged from 85 to 100%. Record reviews documented a median coverage of 61% (range 19 to 93%).[177] Providing this information back to providers has been shown to lead to improvements in coverage.[178]

Reminder systems entail providing reminders to patients and parents or providers that an individual is due for an immunization. Recall systems notify individuals that they are past due for an immunization. Both patient and provider reminder-recall systems have been extensively studied and demonstrated effective.[176] The ACIP American Academy of Pediatrics, and American Academy of Family Physicians have recently recommended "the regular use of R-R (reminder-recall) systems by public and private health-care providers in settings that have not achieved high documented levels of age-appropriate vaccinations."[179]

Immunization registries are information systems that can automate assessment, reminder and recall, and a number of other activities, such as assisting the practitioner in deciding whether a vaccine

TABLE 312–9 National Vaccine Childhood Vaccine Injury Act Reporting and Compensation Tables*

Vaccine	Adverse Event	Interval from Vaccination to Onset of Event: For Reporting†	Interval from Vaccination to Onset of Event: For Compensation†
I. Tetanus toxoid–containing vaccines (e.g., DTaP, DTP, DT, Td or TT)	A. Anaphylaxis or anaphylactic shock	0–7 d	0–4 hr
	B. Brachial neuritis	0–28 d	2–28 d
	C. Any acute complication or sequela (including death) of above events	No limit	No limit
	D. Events described in manufacturer's package insert as contraindications to additional doses of vaccine	No limit	Not applicable
II. Pertussis antigen-containing vaccines (e.g., DTaP, DTP, P, DTP-Hib)	A. Anaphylaxis or anaphylactic shock	0–7 d	0–4 hr
	B. Encephalopathy (or encephalitis)	0–7 d	0–72 hr
	C. Any acute complication or sequela (including death) of above events	No limit	No limit
	D. Events described in manufacturer's package insert as contraindications to additional doses of vaccine	No limit	Not applicable
III. Measles, mumps, and rubella virus-containing vaccines in any combination (e.g., MMR, MR, M, R)	A. Anaphylaxis or anaphylactic shock	0–7 d	0–4 hr
	B. Encephalopathy (or encephalitis)	0–15 d	5–15 d
	C. Any acute complication or sequela (including death) of above events	No limit	No limit
	D. Events described in manufacturer's package insert as contraindications to additional doses of vaccine	No limit	Not applicable
IV. Rubella virus–containing vaccines (e.g., MMR, MR, R)	A. Chronic arthritis	0–42 d	7–42 d
	B. Any acute complication or sequela (including death) of above events	No limit	No limit
	C. Events described in manufacturer's package insert as contraindications to additional doses of vaccine	No limit	Not applicable
V. Measles virus–containing vaccines (e.g., MMR, MR, M)	A. Thrombocytopenic purpura	0–30 d	7–30 d
	B. Vaccine-strain measles viral infection in an immunodeficient recipient	0–6 mo	0–6 mo
	C. Any acute complication or sequela (including death) of above events	No limit	No limit
	D. Events described in manufacturer's package insert as contraindications to additional doses of vaccine	No limit	Not applicable
VI. Polio live virus–containing vaccines (OPV)	A. Paralytic polio		
	In a nonimmunodeficient recipient	0–30 d	0–30 d
	In an immunodeficient recipient	0–6 mo	0–6 mo
	In a vaccine-associated community case	No limit	No limit
	B. Vaccine-strain polio viral infection		
	In a nonimmunodeficient recipient	0–30 d	0–30 d
	In an immunodeficient recipient	0–6 mo	0–6 mo
	In a vaccine-associated community case	No limit	No limit
	C. Any acute complication or sequela (including death) of above events	No limit	No limit
	D. Events described in manufacturer's package insert as contraindications to additional doses of vaccine	No limit	Not applicable
VII. Polio inactivated virus–containing vaccines (e.g., IPV)	A. Anaphylaxis or anaphylactic shock	0–7 d	0–4 hr
	B. Any acute complication or sequela (including death) of above events	No limit	No limit
	C. Events described in manufacturer's package insert as contraindications to additional doses of vaccine	No limit	Not applicable
VIII. Hepatitis B antigen–containing vaccines	A. Anaphylaxis or anaphylactic shock	0–7 d	0–4 hr
	B. Any acute complication or sequela (including death) of above events	No limit	No limit
	C. Events described in manufacturer's package insert as contraindications to additional doses of vaccine	No limit	Not applicable
IX. *Haemophilus influenzae* type B (HIB) polysaccharide vaccines (unconjugated vaccines)	A. Early-onset HIB disease	0–7 d	0–4 hr
	B. Any acute complication or sequela (including death) of above events	No limit	No limit
	C. Events described in manufacturer's package insert as contraindications to additional doses of vaccine	No limit	Not applicable
X. HIB polysaccharide conjugate vaccines	A. No condition specified for compensation	Not applicable	Not applicable
	B. Events described in manufacturer's package insert as contraindications to additional doses of vaccine	No limit	Not applicable
XI. Varicella-zoster virus–containing vaccine	A. No condition specified for compensation	Not applicable	Not applicable
	B. Events described in manufacturer's package insert as contraindications to additional doses of vaccine	No limit	Not applicable
XII. Any new vaccine recommended by the Centers for Disease Control and Prevention for routine administration to children, after publication by the Secretary of the Department of Health and Human Services of a notice of coverage	A. No condition specified for compensation	Not applicable	Not applicable
	B. Events described in manufacturer's package insert as contraindications to additional doses of vaccine	No limit	Not applicable

Table continued on opposite page

*Qualifications and aids to interpretation

(1) *Anaphylaxis and anaphylactic shock* mean an acute, severe, and potentially lethal systemic allergic reaction. Most cases resolve without sequelae. Signs and symptoms begin minutes to a few hours after exposure. Death, if it occurs, usually results from airway obstruction caused by laryngeal edema or bronchospasm and may be associated with cardiovascular collapse. Other significant clinical signs and symptoms may include the following: cyanosis, hypotension, bradycardia, tachycardia, arrhythmia, edema of the pharynx and/or trachea and/or larynx with stridor and dyspnea. Autopsy findings may include acute emphysema, which results from lower respiratory tract obstruction, edema of the hypopharynx, epiglottis, larynx, or trachea and minimal findings of eosinophilia in the liver, spleen, and lungs. When death occurs within minutes of exposure and without signs of respiratory distress, there may not be significant pathologic findings.

(2) *Encephalopathy.* For purposes of the Vaccine Injury Table, a vaccine recipient shall be considered to have suffered an encephalopathy only if such recipient manifests, within the applicable period, an injury meeting the description below of an acute encephalopathy, and then a chronic encephalopathy persists in such person for more than 6 mo beyond the date of vaccination.

(i) An *acute encephalopathy* is one that is sufficiently severe so as to require hospitalization (whether or not hospitalization occurred).

(A) *For children younger than 18 mo* who present without an associated seizure event, an acute encephalopathy is indicated by a "significantly decreased level of consciousness" (see D, below) lasting for at least 24 hr. Those children younger than 18 mo who present following a seizure shall be viewed as having an acute encephalopathy if their significantly decreased level of consciousness persists beyond 24 hr and cannot be attributed to a postictal state (seizure) or medication.

(B) *For adults and children 18 mo of age or older,* an acute encephalopathy is one that persists for at least 24 hr and characterized by at least two of the following:

(1) A significant change in mental status that is not medication related; specifically a confusional state, or a delirium, or a psychosis

(2) A significantly decreased level of consciousness, which is independent of a seizure and cannot be attributed to the effects of medication.

(3) A seizure associated with loss of consciousness.

(C) Increased intracranial pressure may be a clinical feature of acute encephalopathy in any age group.

(D) A "significantly decreased level of consciousness" is indicated by the presence of at least one of the following clinical signs for at least 24 hours or greater (see paragraphs (2)(1)(A) and (2)(1)(B) of this section for applicable time frames):

(1) Decreased or absent response to environment (responds, if at all, only to loud voice or painful stimuli)

(2) Decreased or absent eye contact (does not fix gaze upon family members or other individuals)

(3) Inconsistent or absent response to external stimuli (does not recognize familiar people or things)

(E) The following clinical features alone, or in combination, do not demonstrate an acute encephalopathy or a significant change in either mental status or level of consciousness as described above: sleepiness, irritability (fussiness), high-pitched and unusual screaming, persistent inconsolable crying, and bulging fontanelle. Seizures in themselves are not sufficient to constitute a diagnosis of encephalopathy. In the absence of other evidence of an acute encephalopathy, seizures shall not be viewed as the first symptom or manifestation of the onset of an acute encephalopathy.

(ii) *Chronic encephalopathy* occurs when a change in mental or neurologic status, first manifested during the applicable time period, persists for a period of at least 6 mo from the date of vaccination. Individuals who return to a normal neurologic state after the acute encephalopathy shall not be presumed to have suffered residual neurologic damage from that event; any subsequent chronic encephalopathy shall not be presumed to be a sequela of the acute encephalopathy. If a preponderance of the evidence indicates that a child's chronic encephalopathy is secondary to genetic, prenatal, or perinatal factors, that chronic encephalopathy shall not be considered to be a condition set forth in the Table.

(iii) An encephalopathy shall not be considered to be a condition set forth in the Table if in a proceeding on a petition, it is shown by a preponderance of the evidence that the encephalopathy was caused by an infection, a toxin, a metabolic disturbance, a structural lesion, a genetic disorder or trauma (without regard to whether the cause of the infection, toxin, trauma, metabolic disturbance, structural lesion, or genetic disorder is known). If at the time a decision is made on a petition filed under section 2111(b) of the Act for a vaccine-related injury or death, it is not possible to determine the cause by a preponderance of the evidence of an encephalopathy, the encephalopathy shall be considered to be a condition set forth in the Table.

(iv) In determining whether or not an encephalopathy is a condition set forth in the Table, the Court shall consider the entire medical record.

(3) *Residual seizure disorder:* A petitioner may be considered to have suffered a residual seizure disorder for purposes of the Vaccine Injury Table if the first seizure or convulsion occurred 5–15 days (not less than 5 days and not more than 15 days) after administration of the vaccine and two or more additional distinct seizure or convulsion episodes occurred within 1 yr after the administration of the vaccine, which were unaccompanied by fever (defined as a rectal temperature equal to or greater than 101.0°F or an oral temperature equal to or greater than 100.0°F). A distinct seizure or convulsion episode is ordinarily defined as including all seizure or convulsive activity occurring within a 24-hr period, unless competent and qualified expert neurologic testimony is presented to the contrary in a particular case. For purposes of the Vaccine Injury Table, a petitioner shall not be considered to have suffered a residual seizure disorder, if the petitioner suffered a seizure or convulsion unaccompanied by fever (as defined above) before the fifth day after the administration of the vaccine involved.

(4) *Seizure and convulsion.* For purposes of paragraphs (2) and (3) of this section, the terms "seizure" and "convulsion" include myoclonic, generalized tonic-clonic (grand mal), and simple and complex partial seizures. Absence (petit mal) seizures shall not be considered to be a condition set forth in the Table. Jerking movements or staring episodes alone are not necessarily an indication of seizure activity.

(5) *Sequela.* The term *sequela* means a condition or event that was actually caused by a condition listed in the Vaccine Injury Table.

(6) *Chronic arthritis.* For purposes of the Vaccine Injury Table, chronic arthritis may be found in a person with no history in the 3 yr prior to vaccination of arthropathy (joint disease) on the basis of:

(A) Medical documentation, recorded within 30 days after the onset, of objective signs of acute arthritis (joint swelling) that occurred between 7 and 42 d after a rubella vaccination

(B) Medical documentation (recorded within 3 yr after the onset of acute arthritis) of the persistence of objective signs of intermittent or continuous arthritis for more than 6 mo following vaccination

(C) Medical documentation of an antibody response to the rubella virus

For purposes of the Vaccine Injury Table, the following shall not be considered as chronic arthritis: musculoskeletal disorders such as diffuse connective tissue diseases (including but not limited to rheumatoid arthritis, juvenile rheumatoid arthritis, systemic lupus erythematosus, systemic sclerosis, mixed connective tissue disease, polymyositis/dermatomyositis, fibromyalgia, necrotizing vasculitis and vasculopathies, and Sjögren's syndrome), degenerative joint disease, infectious agents other than rubella (whether by direct invasion or as an immune reaction), metabolic and endocrine diseases, trauma, neoplasms, neuropathic disorders, bone and cartilage disorders, and arthritis associated with ankylosing spondylitis, psoriasis, inflammatory bowel disease, Reiter's syndrome, or blood disorders.

Arthralgia (joint pain) or stiffness without joint swelling shall not be viewed as chronic arthritis for purposes of the Vaccine Injury Table.

(7) *Brachial neuritis* is defined as dysfunction limited to the upper extremity nerve plexus (i.e., its trunks, divisions, or cords) without involvement of other peripheral (e.g., nerve roots or a single peripheral nerve) or central (e.g., spinal cord) nervous system structures. A deep, steady, often severe aching pain in the shoulder and upper arm usually heralds onset of the condition. The pain is followed in days or weeks by weakness and atrophy in upper extremity muscle groups. Sensory loss may accompany the motor deficits, but is generally a less notable clinical feature. The neuritis, or plexopathy, may be present on the same side as or the opposite side of the injection; it is sometimes bilateral, affecting both upper extremities. Weakness is required before the diagnosis can be made. Motor, sensory, and reflex findings on physical examination and the results of nerve conduction and electromyographic studies must be consistent in confirming that dysfunction is attributable to the brachial plexus. The condition should thereby be distinguishable from conditions that may give rise to dysfunction of nerve roots (i.e., radiculopathies) and peripheral nerves (i.e., including multiple mononeuropathies), as well as other peripheral and central nervous system structures (e.g., cranial neuropathies and myelopathies).

(8) *Thrombocytopenic purpura* is defined by a serum platelet count less than 50,000/mm. Thrombocytopenic purpura does not include cases of thrombocytopenia associated with other causes such as hypersplenism, autoimmune disorders (including alloantibodies from previous transfusions), myelodysplasias, lymphoproliferative disorders, congenital thrombocytopenia, or hemolytic uremic syndrome. This does not include cases of immune (formerly called idiopathic) thrombocytopenic purpura (ITP) that are mediated, for example, by viral or fungal infections, toxins, or drugs. Thrombocytopenic purpura does not include cases of thrombocytopenia associated with disseminated intravascular coagulation, as observed with bacterial and viral infections. Viral infections include, for example, those infections secondary to Epstein-Barr virus, cytomegalovirus, hepatitis A and B, rhinovirus, human immunodeficiency virus (HIV), adenovirus, and dengue virus. An antecedent viral infection may be demonstrated by clinical signs and symptoms and need not be confirmed by culture or serologic testing. Bone marrow examination, if performed, must reveal a normal or an increased number of megakaryocytes in an otherwise normal marrow.

(9) *Vaccine-strain measles viral infection* is defined as a disease caused by the vaccine strain that should be determined by vaccine-specific monoclonal antibody or polymerase chain reaction tests.

(10) *Vaccine-strain polio viral infection* is defined as a disease caused by poliovirus that is isolated from the affected tissue and should be determined to be the vaccine-strain by oligonucleotide or polymerase chain reaction. Isolation of poliovirus from the stool is not sufficient to establish a tissue specific infection or disease caused by vaccine-strain poliovirus.

(11) *Early-onset Hib disease* is defined as invasive bacterial illness associated with the presence of Hib organism on culture of normally sterile body fluids or tissue, or clinical findings consistent with the diagnosis of epiglottitis. Hib pneumonia qualifies as invasive Hib disease when radiographic findings consistent with the diagnosis of pneumonitis are accompanied by a blood culture positive for the Hib organism. Otitis media, in the absence of the above findings, does not qualify as invasive bacterial disease. A child is considered to have suffered this injury only if the vaccine was the first Hib immunization received by the child.

*Tables effective as of March 24, 1997.

†Taken from the Reportable Events Table (RET), which lists conditions reportable by law (42 USC 300aa-25) to the Vaccine Adverse Event Reporting System (VAERS), including conditions found in the manufacturer's package insert. In addition, individuals are encouraged to report *ANY* clinically significant or unexpected events (even if you are not certain the vaccine caused the event) for *ANY* vaccine, whether or not it is listed on the RET. Manufacturers are also required by regulation (21 CFR 600.80) to report to the VAERS program all adverse events made known to them for any vaccine. VAERS reporting forms and information can be obtained by calling 1-800-822-7967.

‡Taken from the Vaccine Injury Table (VIT) used in adjudication of claims filed with the National Vaccine Injury Compensation Program. Claims may also be filed for a condition with onset outside the designated time intervals or a condition not included in the Table. The Qualifications and Aids to Interpretation define conditions or injuries listed on the VIT. Information on filing a claim can be obtained by calling 1-800-338-2382 or through the Division of Vaccine Injury Compensation's Home Page: (http://www.hrsa.gov/bhpr/vicp).

Abbreviations: DTaP, Diphtheria, tetanus, and acellular pertussis; DTP, diphtheria, tetanus, and pertussis; HIB, *Haemophilus influenzae* type B; OPV, oral polio vaccine; Td, tetanus and diphtheria toxoids; TT, tetanus toxoid.

From Kitch EW, Evans G, Gopin R. U.S. Law. In: Plotkin SA, Orenstein WA, eds. Vaccines. 3rd ed. Philadelphia: WB Saunders; 1999:1165–1186.

TABLE 312-10 Standards for Pediatric Immunization Practices

1. Immunization services are readily available.
2. There are no barriers or unnecessary prerequisites to the receipt of vaccines.
3. Immunization services are available free or for a minimal fee.
4. Providers use all clinical encounters to screen and, when indicated, vaccinate children.
5. Providers educate parents and guardians about immunization in general terms.
6. Providers question parents or guardians about contraindications and, before vaccinating a child, inform them in specific terms about the risks and benefits of the vaccinations their child is to receive.
7. Providers follow only true contraindications.
8. Providers administer simultaneously all vaccine doses for which a child is eligible at the time of each visit.
9. Providers use accurate and complete recording procedures.
10. Providers co-schedule immunization appointments in conjunction with appointments for other child health services.
11. Providers report adverse events following vaccination promptly, accurately, and completely.
12. Providers operate a tracking system.
13. Providers adhere to appropriate procedures for vaccine management.
14. Providers conduct semiannual audits to assess immunization coverage levels and to review immunization records in the patient populations they serve.
15. Providers maintain up-to-date, easily retrievable medical protocols at all locations where vaccines are administered.
16. Providers practice patient-oriented and community-based approaches.
17. Vaccines are administered by properly trained persons.
18. Providers receive ongoing education and training regarding current immunization recommendations.

From Ad Hoc Working Group for the Development of Standards for Pediatric Immunization Practices. JAMA. 1993;269:1817–1822.

is needed, consolidating multiple records into a single complete record for a given individual, generating immunization records, and generating immunization coverage information for reports such as those called for in managed care settings by the Health Plan Employer Data Information System.[180] Registries are increasingly being developed and used throughout the United States and there is a proposed Healthy People 2010 objective to "increase to 95% the number of children enrolled in a fully functional population-based immunization registry (birth through age 5)."[181] Many public health authorities believe that a nationwide network of community-state population-based registries capable of exchanging information while maintaining privacy and confidentiality is essential to maintain the improvements in vaccine coverage that have been achieved.

Sources of Information. Important sources for information about vaccines include the following:

Official Package Circular. Manufacturers provide product-specific information along with each vaccine; some of these are reproduced in their entirety in the *Physicians' Desk Reference* and are dated.

***Morbidity and Mortality Weekly Report* (MMWR).** This report is published weekly by the Centers for Disease Control and Prevention (CDC) and contains vaccine recommendations, reports of specific disease activity, policy statements, and regular and special recommendations of the ACIP. The MMWR will contain any necessary updated information on the ACIP recommendations. Subscription information is available from MMWR, Superintendent of Documents, U.S. Government Printing Office, Washington, D.C. 20402-9235 (202-783-3238). The MMWR is also available from MMS Publications, C.S.P.O. Box 9120, Waltham, MA 02254-9120 (800-843-6356) or on the Internet at http://www.cdc.gov/epo/mmwr/mmwr.html. ACIP recommendations are also available at http://www.cdc.gov/nip/publications/ACIP_list.htm.

Health Information for International Travel. The CDC publishes an annual booklet as a guide to requirements and recommendations for specific immunizations and health practices for travel to various countries. This publication is available on the Internet at http://www.cdc.gov/travel/yellowbk99.pdf or may be purchased from the U.S. Government Printing Office (stock number 017-023-00197-3) for $20. To purchase a copy, send your request with title, stock number, and payment to: Superintendent of Documents, P.O. Box 371954, Washington, DC 15250-7954. Orders may also be placed by telephone (202-512-1800).

Travelers' health information can also be obtained through a 24-hour hotline operated by the CDC (404-332-4559). In addition, travel information can be accessed at http://www.cdc.gov/travel/travel.html. Hard copies of specific recommendations can be received from the CDC FAX Information Service (404-332-4565).

Advisory Memoranda. Memoranda are published when necessary by the CDC to advise international travelers or those who provide information to travelers about specific outbreaks of communicable diseases abroad. These memoranda include health information for prevention and specific recommendations for immunization and may currently be obtained at no cost by writing to the Travelers Health Section, Division of Quarantine, Centers for Disease Control and Prevention, Atlanta, GA 30333, to request placement on the mailing list (888-232-3228).

Report of the Committee on Infectious Diseases of the American Academy of Pediatrics (Red Book). The full report containing recommendations on all licensed vaccines is usually updated every 3 years. The most recent Red Book was published in 1997. It can be ordered from American Academy of Pediatrics, 141 Northwest Point Boulevard, P.O. Box 927, Elk Grove Village, IL 60009-0927.

Control of Communicable Diseases Manual. The American Public Health Association publishes this manual at approximately 5-year intervals. The 16th edition (1995) is currently available and a revision is in progress. The manual contains valuable information concerning infectious diseases; their occurrence worldwide; immunization, diagnostic, and therapeutic information; and up-to-date recommendations on isolation and other control measures for each disease presented. It can be ordered from the American Public Health Association, 1015 Fifteenth Street, N.W., Washington, DC 20005.

Guide for Adult Immunization. The American College of Physicians and the Infectious Diseases Society of America produce a guide for physicians caring for adults. The third edition was published in 1994. It can be ordered from Subscriber Services, the American College of Physicians, Independence Mall West, 6th Street at Race, Philadelphia, PA 19106-1572 (800-523-1546, ext. 2600).

Technical Bulletins of the American College of Obstetricians and Gynecologists (ACOG). ACOG bulletins, which are updated periodically, contain important information on immunization of women. A set can be ordered from American College of Obstetricians and Gynecologists, Attention: Resource Center, 409 12th Street, SW, Washington, DC 20024-2188.

Health Departments. Most state and many local health departments provide routine immunizations, immunization cards, and schedules to patients. They also send out routine reports of disease incidence.

Centers for Disease Control and Prevention National Immunization Program. Toll free numbers are available for inquiries from both providers and the general public (800-232-2522, English; 800-232-0233, Spanish). Inquiries can also be sent to the CDC by electronic mail (nipinfo@cdc.gov). The National Immunization Program operates an Internet site to provide information to both the general public and professionals (http://www.cdc.gov/nip). Specific vaccine safety issues are addressed at http://www.cdc.gov/nip/vacsafe.

Additional Information. Additional information can be obtained from city, county, or state health departments, medical schools, and large hospitals. Specific questions can be addressed to the National Immunization Program, Centers for Disease Control and Prevention, Atlanta, GA 30333. CDC Immunization Voice/FAX Information System: Voice—404-332-4553. Documents FAX—404-332-4565.

TABLE 312–11 Guide to Contraindications and Precautions to Immunizations

Vaccine	True Contraindications and Precautions	Not True (Vaccines May Be Given)
General for all vaccines	Anaphylactic reaction to a vaccine contraindicates further doses of that vaccine	Mild to moderate local reaction (soreness, redness, swelling) after a dose of an injectable antigen
	Anaphylactic reaction to a vaccine constituent contraindicates the use of vaccines containing that substance	Low-grade or moderate fever after a prior vaccine dose
	Moderate or severe illnesses with or without a fever	Mild acute illness with or without low-grade fever
(DTP/DTaP, OPV, IPV, MMR, Hib, HBV, Var, Rota)		Current antimicrobial therapy
		Convalescent phase of illnesses
		Prematurity (same dosage and indications as for normal, full-term infants)
		Pregnancy of mother or household contact
		Unvaccinated household contact
		Recent exposure to an infectious disease
		History of penicillin or other nonspecific allergies or fact that relatives have such allergies
DTP, DTaP	Encephalopathy within 7 d of prior dose of DTP or DTaP	
Precautions*	Fever of ≥40.5°C (105°F) within 48 hr after vaccination with a prior dose of DTP/DTaP and not attributable to another identifiable cause	Family history of convulsions†
	Collapse or shocklike state (hypotonic-hyporesponsive episode) within 48 hr of receiving a prior dose of DTP/DTaP	Family history of sudden infant death syndrome (SIDS)
	Seizures within 3 d of receiving a prior dose of DTP/DTaP (see † regarding management of children with a personal history of seizures at any time)	Family history of an adverse event after DTP/DTaP administration
	Persistent, inconsolable crying lasting 3 hr, within 48 hr of receiving a prior dose of DTP/DTaP	Fever of <40.5°C (105°F) following a previous dose of DTP or DTaP
	Guillain-Barré syndrome (GBS) within 6 wk after a dose‡	
IPV	Anaphylactic reaction to neomycin, streptomycin, or polymyxin B	
Precaution*	Pregnancy	
OPV	Infection with human immunodeficiency virus (HIV) or a household contact with HIV infection	Breast-feeding
	Known immunodeficiency (hematologic and solid tumors; congenital immunodeficiency; and long-term immunosuppressive therapy)	Current antimicrobial therapy
	Immunodeficiency household contact	Mild diarrhea
Precaution*	Pregnancy	
MMR§	Anaphylactic reactions to neomycin or gelatin	Tuberculosis or positive purified protein derivative (PPD) test result
	Pregnancy	Simultaneous tuberculosis skin testing§
	Known immunodeficiency (hematologic and solid tumors; congenital immunodeficiency; and long-term immunosuppressive therapy; HIV infection with evidence of severe immunosuppression)	Breast-feeding Pregnancy of mother or household contact of vaccine recipient
Precaution*	Recent (within 3–11 mo, depending on product and dose) administration of a blood product or immune globulin preparation	Immunodeficient family member or household contact HIV infection without evidence of severe immunosuppression
	Thrombocytopenia‖	Allergic reaction to eggs**
	History of thrombocytopenic purpura‖	Nonanaphylactic reactions to neomycin
HIB	None	
Hepatitis B HBV	Anaphylactic reaction to baker's yeast	Pregnancy
Rotavirus	Known or suspected immunodeficiency	Breast-feeding
	Age ≥7 mo at first dose	Receiving OPV
	Age ≥12 mo	
Precaution*	Anaphylactic reaction to aminoglycoside antibiotics, monosodium glutamate, or amphotericin B	
	Acute gastrointestinal disorder	
	Prematurity‖‖	
	Persons living in households with immunocompromised***	
Varicella††	Anaphylactic reaction to neomycin or gelatin	Immunodeficiency of a household contact
	Pregnancy	HIV infection in a household contact
	Known immunodeficiency (hematologic and solid tumors; congenital immunodeficiency; long-term immunosuppressive therapy)	Pregnancy in the mother or other household contact of the recipient
Precaution*	Recent (within 5 mo) administration of an immune globulin preparation‡‡	
	Family history of immunodeficiency§§	

Note: This information is based on the recommendations of the Advisory Committee on Immunization Practices (ACIP) and those of the Committee on Infectious Diseases (Red Book Committee) of the American Academy of Pediatrics (AAP). Sometimes these recommendations vary from those contained in the manufacturers' package inserts. For more detailed information, providers should consult the published recommendations of the ACIP, AAP, the AAFP, and the manufacturers' package inserts.

*The events or conditions listed as precautions, although not contraindications, should be carefully reviewed. The benefits and risks of administering a specific vaccine to an individual under the circumstances should be considered. If the risks are believed to outweigh the benefits, the immunization should be withheld; if the benefits are believed to outweigh the risks (e.g., during an outbreak or foreign travel), the immunization should be given. Whether and when to administer DTP/DTaP to children with proven or suspected underlying neurologic disorders should be decided on an individual basis. Avoiding administration of certain vaccines to pregnant women is prudent on theoretic grounds.

†Acetaminophen given before administering DTP/DTaP and thereafter every 4 hr for 24 hr should be considered for children with a personal or a family history of convulsions in siblings or parents.

‡The decision to give additional doses of DTP/DTaP should be based on consideration of the benefit of further vaccination versus the risk of recurrence of GBS. For example, completion of the primary series in children is justified.

§Measles vaccination may temporarily suppress tuberculin reactivity. MMR vaccine may be given after, or on the same day as, TB testing. If MMR has been given recently, postpone the TB test until 4–6 wk after administration of MMR. If giving MMR simultaneously with tuberculin skin test, use the Mantoux test and not multiple puncture tests, because the latter require confirmation if positive, which would have to be postponed 4–6 wk.

‖The decision to vaccinate should be based on consideration of the benefits of immunity to measles, mumps, and rubella versus the risk of recurrence or exacerbation of thrombocytopenia after vaccination, or from natural infections of measles or rubella. In most instances, the benefits of vaccination will be much greater than the potential risks and justify giving MMR, particularly in view of the even greater risk of thrombocytopenia after measles or rubella disease. However, if a prior episode of thrombocytopenia occurred in close temporal proximity to vaccination, it might be prudent to avoid a subsequent dose.

**Recent data suggest that most anaphylactic reactions to measles- and mumps-containing vaccines are associated with hypersensitivity not to egg antigens but to other components of the vaccines. Because the risk of anaphylactic reactions after administration of measles- or mumps-containing vaccines in persons who are allergic to eggs is extremely low and skin testing with vaccine is not predictive of allergic reactions to these vaccines, skin testing and desensitization are no longer required before administration of MMR vaccine to persons who are allergic to eggs.

††Varicella virus vaccine preferably should be administered routinely to children at the same time as MMR vaccine. Varicella virus vaccine is safe and effective in healthy children ≥12 mo age when administered at the same time as MMR vaccine at separate sites and with separate syringes or when administered separately ≥30 days apart.

‡‡Varicella vaccine should not be given for at least 5 mo after administration of blood (except washed red blood cells), or plasma transfusions, immune globulin, or VZIG. Immune globulin or VZIG should not be given for 3 wk after vaccination unless the benefits exceed those of the vaccination. In such cases, the vaccine should either be revaccinated 5 mo later or tested for immunity 6 mo later and revaccinated if seronegative.

§§Varicella vaccine should not be given to a member of a household with a family history of immunodeficiency until the immune status of the recipient and other children in the family is documented.

‖‖Premature infants (<37 wk) may be at increased risk of severe rotavirus disease. However, safety and efficacy of vaccine have not been established in this population.

***Most experts believe benefits will outweigh risks in this situation.

Abbreviations: DTP/DTaP, Diphtheria, tetanus, and pertussis/diphtheria, tetanus, and acellular pertussis; HBV, hepatitis B virus; HIB, *Haemophilus influenzae* type B; IPV, inactivated poliovirus vaccine; MMR, measles, mumps, and rubella; OPV, oral polio vaccine; Rota, rotavirus; Var, varicella; VZIG, varicella-zoster immune globulin.

REFERENCES

1. Centers for Disease Control and Prevention. Recommendation of the Immunization Practices Advisory Committee (ACIP); General recommendations on immunization. MMWR Morb Mortal Wkly Rep. 1994;43(RR1):1–38.
1a. Centers for Disease Control and Prevention. Thimerosal in vaccines: A joint statement of the American Academy of Pediatrics and the Public Health Service. MMWR Morb Mortal Wkly Rep. 1999;48:563–565.
2. Claman HN. The biology of the immune response. JAMA. 1992;268:2790–2796.
3. McDevitt HO. Regulation of the immune response by the major histocompatibility complex system. N Engl J Med 1980;303:1514–1517.
4. Shaw FE, Guess HA, Roets JM, et al. Effect of anatomic injection site, age and smoking on the immune response to hepatitis B vaccination. Vaccine 1989;7:425–430.
5. Lieberman JM, Marcy SM, Partridge S, Ward JI. Evaluation of a hepatitis A vaccine in infants: Effect of maternal antibodies on the antibody response. Abstracts of the Infectious Diseases Society of America 36th Annual Meeting, November 12–15, 1998, Denver, Colo.
6. Lanzavecchia A. Antigen-specific interaction between T and B cells. Nature: 1985;314:537–539.
7. Arai K, Lee F, Miyajima A, et al. Cytokines: Coordinators of immune and inflammatory responses. Ann Rev Biochem. 1990;59:783–836.
8. Reinherz EL, Schlossman SF. Regulation of the immune response—inducer and suppressor T lymphocyte subsets in human beings. N Engl J Med. 1980;303:370–373.
9. William AF, Barclay AN. The immune globulin super-family-domains for cell surface recognition. Ann Rev Immunol. 1988;6:381–405.
10. Baker PJ. Homeostatic control of antibody responses. A model based on the recognition of cell-associated antibody by regulatory T-cells. Transplant Rev. 1974;26:1–20.
11. Fulginiti VA, Eller JJ, Donnie AW, et al. Altered reactivity to measles virus: Atypical measles in children previously immunized with inactivated measles virus vaccines. JAMA. 1967;202:1075–1080.
12. MacDonald NE, Halperin SA, Law BJ, et al. Induction of immunologic memory by conjugated vs. plain meningococcal C polysaccharide vaccine in toddlers: A randomized controlled trial. JAMA. 1998;280:1685–1689.
13. Watson JC, Pearson JA, Markowitz LE, et al. An evaluation of measles revaccination among school-entry-aged children. Pediatrics. 1996;97:613–618.
14. McGee JR, Mestecky J, Dertzbaugh MT, et al. The mucosal immune system: From fundamental concepts to vaccine development. Vaccine. 1992;10:75–88.
15. Milgrom F, Abeyounis CJ, Kano K. Principles of Immunological Diagnosis in Medicine. Philadelphia: Lea & Febiger; 1981.
16. Ellis RW. New technologies for making vaccines. In: Plotkin SA, Orenstein WA eds. Vaccines. 3rd ed. Philadelphia: WB Saunders; 1999:881–901.
17. Centers for Disease Control and Prevention. Recommendations of the International Task Force for Disease Eradication. MMWR Morb Mortal Wkly Rep. 1993;42:1–38.
18. Centers for Disease Control and Prevention. Certification of poliomyelitis eradication—the Americas, 1994. MMWR Morb Mortal Wkly Rep. 1994;43:720–722.
19. Centers for Disease Control and Prevention. Progress toward global poliomyelitis eradication—1997–1998. MMWR Morb Mortal Wkly Rep. 1999;48:416–421.
20. Peltola H, Kilpi T, Anttila M. Rapid disappearance of *Haemophilus influenzae* type b meningitis after routine childhood immunization with conjugate vaccines. Lancet. 1992;340:592–594.
21. Centers for Disease Control and Prevention. Progress toward eliminating *Haemophilus influenzae* type b disease among infants and children—United States, 1987–1997. MMWR Morb Mortal Wkly Rep. 1998;47:993–998.
22. Centers for Disease Control and Prevention. Pertussis vaccination: Use of acellular pertussis vaccines among infants and young children: Recommendations of the Advisory Committee on Immunization Practices (ACIP). MMWR Morb Mortal Wkly Rep. 1997;46:1–25.
23. Centers for Disease Control and Prevention. Prevention of varicella: Recommendations of the Advisory Committee on Immunization Practices (ACIP). MMWR Morb Mortal Wkly Rep. 1996;45:1–36.
24. Izurieta HS, Strebel PM, Blake PA. Postlicensure effectiveness of varicella vaccine during an outbreak in a child care center. JAMA. 1997;278:1495–1499.
24a. Centers for Disease Control and Prevention. Impact of vaccines universally recommended for children—United States, 1990–1998. MMWR Morb Mortal Wkly Rep. 1999;48:243–248.
25. Howson CP, Howe CJ, Fineberg HV, eds. Institute of Medicine. Adverse Effects of Pertussis and Rubella Vaccines. Washington, DC: National Academy Press; 1991.
26. Stratton KR, Howe CJ, Johnston RB Jr, eds. Institute of Medicine. Adverse Events Associated with Childhood Vaccines. Evidence Bearing on Causation. Washington, DC: National Academy Press; 1994.
27. Howson CP, Fineberg HV. Adverse events following pertussis and rubella vaccines: Summary of a report by the Institute of Medicine. JAMA. 1992;267:392–396.
28. Centers for Disease Control and Prevention. Poliomyelitis prevention in the United States: Introduction of a sequential vaccination schedule of inactivated poliovirus vaccine followed by oral poliovirus vacine. MMWR Morb Mortal Wkly Rep. 1997;46:1–25.
29. Rantala H, Cherry JD, Shields WD, Uhari M. Epidemiology of Guillain-Barré syndrome in children: Relationship of oral polio vaccine administration to occurrence. J Pediatr. 1994;124:220–223.
30. Slater PE, Ben-Zvi T, Fogel A, et al. Absence of an association between rubella vaccination and arthritis in underimmune postpartum women. Vaccine. 1995;13:1529–1532.
31. Frenkel LM, Nielson K, Garakian A, et al. A search for persistent rubella virus infection in persons with chronic symptoms after rubella and rubella immunization and in patients with juvenile rheumatoid arthritis. Clin Infect Dis. 1996;22:287–294.
32. Ray R, Black S, Shinefield H, et al. Risk of chronic arthropathy among women after rubella vaccination. JAMA. 1997;278:551–556.
33. Committee on Infectious Diseases. American Academy of Pediatrics, Report of the Committee on Infectious Diseases. 24th ed. Elk Grove Village, Ill: American Academy of Pediatrics; 1997.
34. American College of Physicians Task Force on Adult Immunization and Infectious Diseases Society of America. Guide for Adult Immunization. 3rd ed. Philadelphia: American College of Physicians; 1994.
35. Centers for Disease Control and Prevention. Recommended childhood immunization schedule—United States, 1999. MMWR Morb Mortal Wkly Rep. 1999;48:12–16.
36. Brachman PS, Gold H, Plotkin SA, et al. Field evaluation of a human anthrax vaccine. Am J Public Health. 1962;52:632–645.
37. Abramowicz M. Anthrax vaccine. Med Letter. 1998;40:52–53.
38. Snider DE, Rieder HL, Combs D, et al. Tuberculosis in children. Pediatr Infect Dis J. 1988;7:271–278.
39. Rodrigues LC, Diwan K, Wheeler JG. Protective effect of BCG against tuberculous meningitis and miliary tuberculosis: A metaanalysis. Int J Epidemiol. 1993;22:1154–1158.
40. Colditz GA, Brewer TF, Berkey CS, et al. Efficacy of BCG vaccine in prevention of tuberculosis: Metaanalysis of the published literature. JAMA. 1994;271:698–702.
41. Centers for Disease Control and Prevention. The role of BCG vaccine in the prevention and control of tuberculosis in the United States. A joint statement by the Advisory Council for the Elimination of Tuberculosis and the Advisory Committee on Immunization Practices. MMWR Morb Mortal Wkly Rep. 1996;45:1–18.
42. Centers for Disease Control and Prevention. Recommendations of the Immunization Practices Advisory Committee (ACIP): Cholera vaccine. MMWR Morb Mortal Wkly Rep. 1988;37:617–624.
43. Centers for Disease Control and Prevention. Recommendation of the Immunization Practices Advisory Committee (ACIP): Diphtheria, tetanus, and pertussis: Guidelines for vaccine prophylaxis and other preventive measures. MMWR Morb Mortal Wkly Rep. 1991;40:1–28.
44. Centers for Disease Control and Prevention. Recommendations of the Immunization Practices Advisory Committee (ACIP): *Haemophilus* b conjugate vaccines for prevention of *Haemophilus influenzae* type b disease among infants and children two months of age and older. MMWR Morb Mortal Wkly Rep. 1991;40:1–17.
45. Centers for Disease Control and Prevention. Recommendations of the Immunization Practices Advisory Committee (ACIP): Recommendations for use of *Haemophilus b* conjugate vaccines and a combined diphtheria tetanus pertussis and *Haemophilus b* vaccine. MMWR Morb Mortal Wkly Rep. 1993;42:(No. RR-13): 1–15.
46. Anderson EL, Decker MD, Englund JA, et al. Interchangeability of conjugated *Haemophilus influenzae* type b vaccines in infants. JAMA. 1995;273:849–853.
47. Greenberg DP, Lieberman JM, Marcy SM, et al. Enhanced antibody responses in infants given different sequences of heterogeneous *Haemophilus influenzae* type b conjugate vaccines. J Pediatr. 1995;126:206–211.
48. Bewley KM, Schwab JG, Ballanco GA, Daum RS. Interchangeability of *Haemophilus influenzae* type b vaccines in the primary series: Evaluation of a two-dose mixed regimen. Pediatrics. 1996;98:898–904.
49. Centers for Disease Control and Prevention. FDA approval of use of *Haemophilus b* conjugate vaccine reconstituted with diphtheria-tetanus-pertussis vaccine for infants and children. MMWR Morb Mortal Wkly Rep. 1993;42:964–965.
50. Centers for Disease Control and Prevention. Unlicensed use of combination of *Haemophilus influenzae* type b conjugate vaccine and diphtheria and tetanus toxoid and acellular pertussis vaccine for infants. MMWR Morb Mortal Wkly Rep. 1998;47:787.
51. Innis BL, Snitbhan R, Kunasol P, et al. Protection against hepatitis A by an inactivated vaccine. JAMA. 1994;271:1328–1334.
52. Werzberger A, Mensch B, Kuter B, et al. A controlled trial of a formalin-inactivated hepatitis A vaccine in healthy children. N Engl J Med. 1992;327:453–457.
53. Centers for Disease Control and Prevention. Prevention of hepatitis A through active or passive immunization: Recommendations of the Advisory Committee on Immunization Practices (ACIP). MMWR Morb Mortal Wkly Rep. 1996;45:1–30.
54. Bell BP, Shapiro CN, Alter MJ, et al. The diverse patterns of hepatitis A epidemiology in the United States—implications for vaccination strategies. J Infect Dis. 1998;178:1579–1584.
54a. Centers for Disease Control and Prevention. Prevention of hepatitis A through active or passive immunization: Recommendations of the Advisory Committee on Immunization Practices (ACIP). MMWR Morb Mortal Wkly Rep. 1999;48(RR-12). In press.
55. Shapiro CN, Letson GW, Kuehn D, et al. Effect of maternal antibody on immunogenicity of hepatitis A vaccine in infants. Abstract H61 in Abstracts of the 35th Interscience Conference on Antimicrobial Agents and Chemotherapy, San Francisco, Calif, September 17–20, 1995.
56. Green MS, Cohen D, Lerman Y, et al. Depression of the immune response to an inactivated hepatitis A vaccine administered concomitantly with immune globulin. J Infect Dis. 1993;168:740–743.
57. 29 CFR 1910.1030
58. Centers for Disease Control and Prevention. Recommendations of the Immunization Practices Advisory Committee: Hepatitis B virus: A comprehensive strategy

for eliminating transmission in the United States through universal childhood vaccination. MMWR Morb Mortal Wkly Rep. 1991;40:1–25.
59. Centers for Disease Control and Prevention. Update: Recommendations to prevent hepatitis B virus transmission—United States. MMWR Morb Mortal Wkly Rep. 1995;44:574–575.
60. Centers for Disease Control and Prevention. Immunization of adolescents: Recommendations of the Advisory Committee on Immunization Practices, the American Academy of Pediatrics, the American Academy of Family Physicians, and the American Medical Association. MMWR Morb Mortal Wkly Rep. 1996;45:1–16.
61. Wise RP, Kiminyo KP, Salive ME. Hair loss after routine immunizations. JAMA. 1997;278:1176–1178.
62. Pirmohamed M, Winstanley P. Hepatitis B vaccine and neurotoxicity. Postgrad Med J. 1997;73:462–463.
63. Expanded Programme on Immunization (EPI). Lack of evidence that hepatitis B vaccine causes multiple sclerosis. Wkly Epidemiol Rec. 1997;72:149–152.
64. Patriarca PA, Arden NH, Koplan JP, et al. Prevention and control of type A influenza infections in nursing homes: Benefits and costs of four approaches using vaccination and amantadine. Ann Intern Med. 1987;107:732–740.
65. Centers for Disease Control and Prevention. Prevention and control of influenza. Recommendations of the Advisory Committee on Immunization Practices (ACIP). MMWR Morb Mortal Wkly Rep. 1998;47:1–26.
66. Schonberger LB, Bregman DJ, Sullivan-Bolyai JZ, et al. Guillain-Barré syndrome following vaccination in the National Influenza Immunization Program, United States, 1976–1977. Am J Epidemiol. 1979;110:105–123.
67. Lasky T, Terracciano GJ, Magder L, et al. The Guillain-Barré syndrome and the 1992–1993 and 1993–1994 influenza vaccines. N Engl J Med. 1998;339:1797–1802.
68. Murphy KR, Strunk RC. Safe administration of influenza vaccine in asthmatic children hypersensitive to egg proteins. J Pediatr. 1985;106:931–933.
69. Hoke CH, Nisalak A, Sangawhipa N, et al. Protection against Japanese encephalitis by inactivated vaccines. N Engl J Med. 1988;319:609–614.
70. Centers for Disease Control and Prevention. Recommendations of the Immunization Practices Advisory Committee (ACIP): Inactivated Japanese encephalitis virus vaccine. MMWR Morb Mortal Wkly Rep. 1993;42:1–15.
71. Centers for Disease Control and Prevention. Lyme disease vaccine. MMWR Morb Mortal Wkly Rep. 1999;48:35–36, 43.
72. Steigbigel RT, Benach JL. Immunization against Lyme disease—an important first step. N Engl J Med. 1998;339:263–264.
73. Steere AC, Sikand VK, Meurice F, et al. Vaccination against Lyme disease with recombinant *Borrelia burgdorferi* outer-surface lipoprotein A with adjuvant. N Engl J Med. 1998;339:209–215.
74. Sigal LH, Zhradnik JM, Lavin P, et al. A vaccine consisting of recombinant *Borrelia burgdorferi* outer-surface protein A to prevent Lyme disease. N Engl J Med. 1998;339:216–222.
74a. Centers for Disease Control and Prevention. Recommendations for the use of Lyme disease vaccine: Recommendations of the Advisory Committee on Immunization Practices (ACIP). MMWR Morbid Mortal Wkly Rep. 1999;48 (No. RR-7):1–25.
75. Pabst HF, Spady DW, Marusyk RG, et al. Reduced measles immunity in infants in a well-vaccinated population. Pediatr Infect Dis J. 1992;11:525–529.
76. Centers for Disease Control and Prevention. Measles, mumps and rubella—vaccine use and strategies for elimination of measles, rubella, and congenital rubella syndrome and control of mumps: Recommendations of the Advisory Committee on Immunization Practices (ACIP). MMWR Morb Mortal Wkly Rep. 1998;47:1–57.
77. Centers for Disease Control and Prevention. Immunization of health-care workers. MMWR Morb Mortal Wkly Rep. 1997;46:1–42.
78. Griffin MR, Ray WA, Mortimer ER, et al. Risk of seizures after measles-mumps-rubella immunization. Pediatrics. 1991;88:881–885.
79. Centers for Disease Control and Prevention. Adverse events following immunization. Atlanta: U.S. Department of Health and Human Services, Public Health Service, CDC, 1989. (Surveillance Report No. 3, 1985–1986.)
80. Weibel RE, Caserta V, Benor DE, Evans G. Acute encephalopathy followed by permanent brain injury or death associated with further attenuated measles vaccines: A review of claims submitted to the National Vaccine Injury Compensation Program. Pediatrics. 1998;101:383–387.
81. Riedo FX, Plikaytis BD, Broome CV. Epidemiology and prevention of meningococcal disease. Pediatr Infect Dis J. 1995;14:643–657.
82. Schiefle DW, Bjornson G, Boraston S. Local adverse effects of meningococcal vaccine. Can Med Assoc J. 1994;150:14–15.
83. Lepow ML, Beeler J, Randolph M, et al. Reactogenicity and immunogenicity of a quadrivalent combined meningococcal vaccine in children. J Infect Dis. 1986;154:1033–1036.
84. Centers for Disease Control and Prevention. Control and prevention of meningococcal disease and control and prevention of serogroup C meningococcal disease: Evaluation and management of suspected outbreaks: Recommendations of the Advisory Committee on Immunization Practices (ACIP). MMWR Morb Mortal Wkly Rep. 1997;46:1–21.
85. Miller E, Goldacre M, Pugh S, et al. Risk of aseptic meningitis after measles, mumps, and rubella vaccine in UK children. Lancet. 1993;341:979–982.
86. Centers for Disease Control and Prevention. FDA approval of a fourth acellular pertussis vaccine for use among infants and young children. MMWR Morb Mortal Wkly Rep. 1998;47:934–936.
87. Gustafsson L, Hallander HO, Olin P, et al. A controlled trial of a two-component acellular, a five-component acellular, and a whole-cell pertussis vaccine. N Engl J Med. 1996;334:349–355.
88. Greco D, Salmaso S, Mastrantonio P, et al. A controlled trial of two acellular vaccines and one whole-cell vaccine against pertussis. N Engl J Med. 1996;334:341–348.
89. Onorato IM, Wassilak SG, Meade B. Efficacy of whole-cell pertussis vaccine in preschool children in the United States. JAMA. 1992;267:2745–2749.
90. Guris D, Strebel PM, Tachdjian R, et al. Effectiveness of the pertussis vaccination program as determined by use of the screening method: United States, 1992–1994. J Infect Dis. 1997;176:456–463.
91. Decker MD, Edwards KM, Steinhoff MC, et al. Comparison of 13 acellular pertussis vaccines: Adverse reactions. Pediatrics. 1995;96(suppl):557–566.
92. Heijbel H, Rasmussen F, Olin P. Safety evaluation of one whole-cell and three acellular pertussis vaccines in Stockholm Trial II. Dev Biol Stand. 1997;89:99–100.
93. Heijbel H, Ciofi degli Atti M, Harzer E, et al. Hypotonic hyporesponsive episodes in eight pertussis vaccine studies. Dev Biol Stand. 1997;89:101–103.
94. Miller D, Wadsworth J, Diamond J, et al. Pertussis vaccine and whooping cough as risk factors in acute neurological illness and death in young children. Dev Biol Stand. 1985;61:389–394.
95. Stratton KR, Howe CJ, Johnston RB, Jr, eds. DPT Vaccine and Chronic Nervous System Dysfunction. A New Analysis. Washington, DC: National Academy Press; 1994.
96. Gangarosa EJ, Galazka AM, Wolfe CR, et al. Impact of anti-vaccine movements on pertussis control: The untold story. Lancet. 1998;351:356–361.
97. Deen JL, Mink CM, Cherry JD, et al. Household contact study of *Bordetella pertussis* infection. Clin Infect Dis. 1995;21:1211–1219.
98. Izurieta HS, Kenyon TA, Strebel PM, et al. Risk factors for pertussis in young infants during an outbreak in Chicago in 1993. Clin Infect Dis. 1996;22:503–507.
99. Mink CM, Cherry JD, Christenson P, et al. A search for *Bordetella pertussis* infection in university students. Clin Infect Dis. 1992;14:464–471.
100. Wright SW, Edwards KM, Decker MD, Zeldin MH. Pertussis infection in adults with persistent cough. JAMA. 1996;273:1044–1046.
101. Nennig ME, Shinefield HR, Edwards KM, et al. Prevalence and incidence of adult pertussis in an urban population. JAMA. 1996;275:1672–1674.
102. Edwards KM, Decker MD, Graham BS, et al. Adult immunization with acellular pertussis vaccine. JAMA. 1993;269:53–56.
103. Centers for Disease Control and Prevention. Prevention of plague. Recommendations of the Advisory Committee on Immunization Practices. MMWR Morb Mortal Wkly Rep. 1996;45:1–15.
104. MacLeod CM, Hodges RG, Heidelberger M, Bernhard WG. Prevention of pneumococcal pneumonia by immunization with specific capsular polysaccharides. J Exp Med. 1945;82:445–465.
105. Austrian R, Douglas RM, Schiffman G, et al. Prevention of pneumococcal pneumonia by vaccination. Trans Assoc Am Phys. 1976;89:184–189.
106. Smit P, Oberholzer D, Hayden-Smith S, et al. Protective efficacy of pneumococcal polysaccharide vaccines. JAMA. 1977;238:2613–2616.
107. Spika JS, Fedson DS, Facklam RR. Pneumococcal vaccination—controversies and opportunities. Infect Dis Clin North Am. 1990;4:11–27.
108. Shapiro ED, Berg AT, Austrian R, et al. The protective efficacy of polyvalent pneumococcal polysaccharide vaccine. N Engl J Med. 1991;325:1453–1460.
109. Butler JC, Breiman RF, Campbell JF, et al. Pneumococcal polysaccharide vaccine efficacy; an evaluation of current recommendations. JAMA. 1993;270:1826–1831.
110. Centers for Disease Control and Prevention. Prevention of pneumococcal disease: Recommendations of the Advisory Committee on Immunization Practices (ACIP). MMWR Morb Mortal Wkly Rep. 1997;46:1–24.
110a. Jackson LA, Benson P, Sneller VP, et al. Safety of revaccination with pneumococcal polysaccharide vaccine. JAMA. 1999;281:243–248.
111. Brichacek B, Swindells S, Janoff EN, et al. Increased plasma HIV-1 burden following antigenic challenge with pneumococcal vaccine. J Infect Dis. 1996;174:1191–1199.
112. Black S, Shinefield H, Ray P, et al. Efficacy of heptavalent conjugate pneumococcal vaccine (Wyeth Lederle) in 37,000 infants and children: Results of the Northern California Kaiser Permanente Efficacy Trial. 38th Interscience Conference on Antimicrobial Agents and Chemotherapy Final Program, Abstracts and Exhibits Addendum, Abstract LB-9.
112a. Centers for Disease Control and Prevention. Recommendations of the Advisory Committee on Immunization Practices (ACIP). Revised recommendations for routine poliomyelitis vaccination. MMWR Morb Mortal Wkly Rep. 1999;48:590.
113. Sutter RW, Prevots DR. Vaccine-associated paralytic poliomyelitis among immunodeficient persons. Infect Med. 1994;11:426, 429–430, 435–438.
114. Centers for Disease Control and Prevention. Recommendation of the Immunization Practices Advisory Committee (ACIP): Rabies prevention—United States. MMWR Morb Mortal Wkly Rep. 1998;48:1–21.
115. Rennels MB, Glass RI, Dennehy PH, et al. Safety and efficacy of high-dose rhesus-human reassortant rotavirus vaccines—report of the National Multicenter Trial. For the United States Rotavirus Vaccine Efficacy Group. Pediatrics 1996;97:7–13.
116. Santosham M, Moulton LH, Reid R, et al. Efficacy and safety of high-dose rhesus-human reassortant rotavirus vaccine in Native American populations. J Pediatr. 1997;131:632–638.
117. Bernstein DI, Glass RI, Rodgers G, et al. Evaluation of rhesus rotavirus monovalent and tetravalent reassortant vaccines in US children. For the US Rotavirus Vaccine Efficacy Group. JAMA. 1995;273:1191–1196.
118. Joensuu J, Koskenniemi E, Pang XL, Vesikari T. Randomised placebo-controlled trial of rhesus-human reassortant rotavirus vaccine for prevention of severe rotavirus gastroenteritis. Lancet. 1997;350:1205–1209.
119. Joensuu J, Koskenniemi E, Vesikari T. Prolonged efficacy of rhesus-human reassortant rotavirus vaccine. Pediatr Infect Dis J. 1998;17:427–429.
120. Centers for Disease Control and Prevention. Rotavirus vaccine for the prevention of rotavirus gastroenteritis in children. Recommendations of the Advisory Committee on Immunization Practices. MMWR Morb Mortal Wkly Rep. 1999. In press.

121. Rennels MB, Parashar UD, Holman RC, et al. Lack of an apparent association between intussusception and wild or vaccine rotavirus infection. Pediatr Infect Dis J. 1998;924–925.
122. Committee on Infectious Diseases. Prevention of rotavirus disease: Guidelines for use of rotavirus vaccine. Pediatrics. 1998;102:1483–1491.
123. Keusch GT, Cash RA. A vaccine against rotavirus—when is too much too much? N Engl J Med. 1997;337:1228–1229.
124. Pérez-Schal I, Gutiñas MJ, Pérez M, et al. Efficacy of the rhesus rotavirus-based quadrivalent vaccine in infants and young children in Venezuela. N Engl J Med. 1997;337:1181–1187.
124a. Centers for Disease Control and Prevention. Intussusception among recipients of rotavirus vaccine—United States 1998–1999. MMWR Morb Mortal Wkly Rep. 1999;48:577–581.
125. Centers for Disease Control and Prevention. Rubella vaccination during pregnancy—United States, 1971–88. MMWR Morb Mortal Wkly Rep. 1989; 38:289–293.
126. Freestone DS, Prydie J, Smith SG, Laurence G. Vaccination of adults with Wistar RA 27/3 rubella vaccine. J Hygiene. 1971;69:471–477.
127. Polk BF, Modlin JF, White JA, DeGirolami PC. A controlled comparison of joint reactions among women receiving one of two rubella vaccines. Am J Epidemiol. 1982;115:19–25.
128. Centers for Disease Control and Prevention. Recommendation of the Immunization Practices Advisory Committee (ACIP): Vaccinia (smallpox) vaccine. MMWR Morb Mortal Wkly Rep. 1991;40:1–10.
129. Relyveld EH, Henocq E, Bizzini B. Studies on untoward reactions to diphtheria and tetanus toxoids. Dev Biol Stand 1979;43:33–37.
130. Pollard JD, Selby G. Relapsing polyneuropathy due to tetanus toxoid: Report of a case. J Neurol Sci. 1978;37:113–125.
131. Centers for Disease Control and Prevention. Update: Vaccine side effects, adverse reactions, contraindications, and precautions. Recommendations of the Advisory Committee on Immunization Practices. MMWR Morb Mortal Wkly Rep. 1996;45:1–35.
132. Centers for Disease Control and Prevention. Typhoid immunization. Recommendations of the Advisory Committee on Immunization Practices. MMWR Morb Mortal Wkly Rep. 1994;43:1–7.
133. Kuter BJ, Weibel RE, Guess HA, et al. Oka/Merck varicella vaccine in healthy children: Final report of a 2-year efficacy study and 7-year follow-up studies. Vaccine. 1991;9:643–647.
134. White CJ, Kuter BJ, Ngai A, et al. Modified cases of chickenpox after varicella vaccination: Correlation of protection with antibody response. Pediatr Infect Dis J. 1992;11:19–23.
135. Watson BM, Piercy SA, Plotkin SA, Starr SE. Modified chickenpox in children immunized with the Oka/Merck varicella vaccine. Pediatrics. 1993;91:17–22.
136. Bernstein HH, Rothstein EP, Pennridge Pediatric Associates, et al. Clinical survey of natural varicella compared with breakthrough varicella after immunization with live attenuated Oka/Merck varicella vaccine. Pediatrics. 1993;92:833–837.
137. Clements DA, Armstrong CB, Ursano AM, et al. Over five-year follow-up of Oka/Merck varicella vaccine recipients in 465 infants and adolescents. Pediatr Infect Dis J. 1995;14:874–879.
138. Lieu TA, Finkler LJ, Sorel ME, et al. Cost effectiveness of varicella serotesting vs. presumptive vaccination of school-age children and adolescents. Pediatrics. 1995;96:632–638.
139. Centers for Disease Control and Prevention. Recommendation of the Immunization Practices Advisory Committee (ACIP): Yellow fever vaccine. MMWR Morb Mortal Wkly Rep. 1990;39:1–6.
140. Ellis EF, Henney CS. Adverse reactions following administration of human gamma globulin. J Allergy Clin Immunol. 1969;43:45–54.
141. Siber GR, Werner BC, Halsey NA. Interference of immune globulin with measles and rubella immunization. J Pediatr. 1993;122:204–211.
142. Siber GB, Snydman DR. Use of immune globulins in the prevention and treatment of infections. In: Remington JJ, Swartz MN, eds. Current Clinical Topics in Infectious Diseases. Boston: Blackwell Scientific Publications; 1992:208–256.
143. Schiff RI. Transmission of viral infections through intravenous immune globulin. N Engl J Med. 1994;331:1649–1650.
144. Centers for Disease Control and Prevention. Outbreak of hepatitis C associated with intravenous immunoglobulin administration—United States, October 1993–June 1994. MMWR Morb Mortal Wkly Rep. 1994;43:505–509.
145. PHLS Communicable Disease Surveillance Centre. Hepatitis C virus and intravenous anti-D immunoglobulin. Commun Dis Rep CDR Wkly. 1995;5:1–2.
146. Yu MY, Mason BL, Tankersley DL. Detection and characterization of hepatitis C virus RNA in immune globulins. Transfusion. 1994;34:596–602.
147. Khabbaz RF, Chamberland M. From prions to parasites: Issues and concerns in blood safety. In: Scheld WM, Craig WA, Hughes JM, eds. Emerging Infections 2. Washington, DC: ASM Press; 1998:295–309.
148. PREVENT Study Group. Reduction of respiratory syncytial virus hospitalization among premature infants and infants with bronchopulmonary dysplasia using respiratory syncytial virus immune globulin prophylaxis. Pediatrics. 1997;99:93–99.
149. Simoes EA, Sondheimer HM, Top FH, et al. Respiratory syncytial virus immune globulin for prophylaxis against respiratory syncytial virus disease in infants and children with congenital heart disease. The Cardiac Study Group. J Pediatr. 1998;133:492–499.
150. The IMpact-RSV Study Group. Palivizumab, a humanized respiratory syncytial virus monoclonal antibody, reduces hospitalization from respiratory syncytial virus infection in high-risk infants. Pediatrics. 1998;102:531–537.
151. Committee on Infectious Diseases and Committee on Fetus and Newborn. Prevention of respiratory syncytial virus infections: Indications for the use of palivizumab and update on the use of RSV-IGIV. Pediatrics. 1998;102:1211–1216.
152. American College of Obstetricians and Gynecologists (ACOG). Selective Rho (D) immune globulin (RHIG). Technical Bulletin No. 61. Chicago: American College of Obstetricians and Gynecologists; 1981.
153. King GE, Hadler SC. Simultaneous administration of childhood vaccines: An important public health policy that is safe and efficacious. Pediatr Infect Dis J. 1994;13:394–407.
153a. Centers for Disease Control and Prevention. Combination vaccines for childhood immunization: Recommendations of the Advisory Committee on Immunization Practices (ACIP), the American Academy of Pediatrics (AAP), and the American Academy of Family Physicians (AAFP). MMWR Morb Mortal Wkly Rep. 1999;48 (No. RR-5):1–15.
154. Lewis M, Ramsey DS. Validating current immunization practice with young infants. Pediatrics. 1992;90:771–773.
155. Ramsey DS, Lewis M. Developmental change in infant cortisol and behavioral response to inoculation. Child Dev. 1994;65:1491–1502.
156. Centers for Disease Control and Prevention. Recommendation of the Immunization Practices Advisory Committee (ACIP): Update on adult immunization. MMWR Morb Mortal Wkly Rep. 1991;40:1–94.
157. Centers for Disease Control and Prevention. Health Information for International Travel, 1996–97. Washington, DC: U.S. Government Printing Office; 1996.
158. Centers for Disease Control and Prevention. Recommendations of the Advisory Committee on Immunization Practices (ACIP): Use of vaccines and immune globulins in persons with altered immunocompetence. MMWR Morb Mortal Wkly Rep. 1993;42:1–18.
159. Pirofski LA, Casadevall A. Use of licensed vaccines for active immunization of the immunocompromised host. Clin Microbiol Rev. 1998;11:1–26.
160. Ninane J, Grymonprez A, Burtonboy G, et al. Disseminated BCG in HIV infection. Arch Dis Child. 1988;63:1268–1269.
161. Centers for Disease Control and Prevention. Disseminated *Mycobacterium bovis* infection from BCG vaccination of a patient with acquired immunodeficiency syndrome. MMWR Morb Mortal Wkly Rep. 1985;34:227–228.
162. Centers for Disease Control and Prevention. Measles pneumonitis following measles-mumps-rubella vaccination of a patient with HIV infection, 1993. MMWR Morb Mortal Wkly Rep. 1996;45:603–606.
163. Ion-Nedelcu N, Dobrescu A, Strebel PM, Sutter RW. Vaccine-associated paralytic poliomyelitis and HIV infection. Lancet. 1994;343:51–52.
164. Asano Y, Hirose S, Iwayama S, et al. Protective effect of immediate inoculation of a live varicella vaccine in household contacts in relation to the viral dose and interval between exposure and vaccination. Biken J. 1982;25:43–45.
165. Salzman MB, Garcia C. Postexposure varicella vaccination in siblings of children with active varicella. Pediatr Infect Dis J. 1998;17:256–257.
166. Bardenheier B, Prevots DR, Khetsuriani N, Wharton M. Tetanus surveillance—United States, 1995–1997. In: CDC Surveillance Summaries, July 3, 1998. MMWR Morb Mortal Wkly Rep. 1998;47:1–13.
167. Kaplan JE, Nelson DB, Schonberger LB, et al. The effect of immune globulin on trivalent oral polio and yellow fever vaccinations. Bull World Health Organ. 1984;62:585–590.
168. Chorba TL, Berkelman RL, Safford SK, et al. Mandatory reporting of infectious diseases by clinicians. MMWR Morb Mortal Wkly Rep. 1990;39:1–17.
169. Centers for Disease Control and Prevention. National Childhood Vaccine Injury Act: Requirements for permanent vaccination records and for reporting of selected events for vaccination. MMWR Morb Mortal Wkly Rep. 1988;37:197–200.
170. Kitch EW, Evans G, Gopin R. U.S. Law. In: Plotkin SA, Orenstein WA, eds. Vaccines. 3rd ed. Philadelphia: WB Saunders; 1999:1165–1186.
171. The National Vaccine Advisory Committee. The measles epidemic: The problems, barriers, and recommendations. JAMA. 1991;266:1547–1552.
172. Centers for Disease Control and Prevention. Retrospective assessment of vaccination coverage among school-aged children—selected U.S. cities, 1991. MMWR Morb Mortal Wkly Rep. 1992;41:103–107.
173. Ad Hoc Working Group for the Development of Standards for Pediatric Immunization Practices. Standards for pediatric immunization practices. JAMA. 1993;269:1817–1822.
174. Centers for Disease Control and Prevention. Public health burden of vaccine-preventable diseases among adults: Standards for adult immunization practice. MMWR Morb Mortal Wkly Rep. 1990;39:725–729.
175. Gershon AA, Gardner P, Peter G, et al. Quality standards for immunization. Clin Infect Dis. 1997;25:782–786.
176. Shefer A, Briss P, Rodewald L, et al. Improving immunization coverage rates: An evidence-based review of the literature. Epidemiol Rev. In press.
177. Bushnell CJ. The ABCs of practice-based immunization assessments. Proceedings of the 28th National Immunization Conference. Washington, DC: U.S. Department of Health and Human Services; 1994:207–209.
178. Dini EF, Chaney M, Moolenaar RL, LeBaron CW. Information as intervention: How Georgia used vaccination coverage data to double public sector vaccination coverage in seven years. J Public Health Manag Pract. 1996;2:45–49.
179. Advisory Committee on Immunization Practices. Recommendations of the Advisory Committee on Immunization Practices, the American Academy of Pediatrics, and the American Academy of Family Physicians: Use of reminder and recall by vaccination providers to increase vaccination rates. MMWR Morb Mortal Wkly Rep. 1998;47:715–717.
180. Linkins RW, Feikema SM. Immunization registries: The cornerstone of childhood immunization in the 21st century. Pediatr Ann. 1998;27:349–354.
181. Department of Health and Human Services. Healthy People 2010 Objectives: Draft for Public Comment. Washington, DC, 1998.

SECTION E

BIOLOGICAL WARFARE

Chapter 313

Biological Warfare and Bioterrorism

JOSHUA LEDERBERG

Biological warfare, by treaty definition, is the use of "microbial . . . agents . . . for hostile purposes or in armed conflict." The treaty definition applies to states under international law; equally cogent is customary and intrastate law as it applies to groups and individuals, notably terrorists who pursue political aims, revenge, or other idiosyncratic agenda through the use of violence. During the Cold War, superpower states sustained major biological warfare technology programs, at least until 1975. Since then, the burden of concern has shifted to bioterrorism, either state sponsored or in the pursuit of fanatical aims of smaller groups.

Biological warfare has a long but sporadic history associated with the almost inevitable accompaniment of epidemic disease in military operations through the centuries. The possibly inadvertent accompaniment of smallpox and measles with the Conquistadors played a large part in the European conquest of the Western Hemisphere and likewise the Australian continent and Pacific Islands. However, recent episodes of the systematic use of microbial weapons have been rare—in contrast to the major involvement of their cousins, chemical weapons, in the trench warfare of World War I.

Since the advent of the Biological Warfare Convention, formally in force in 1975, the major task facing containment of biological warfare has been promulgation and enforcement of the Biological Warfare Convention—the most egregious recent challenge having come from Iraq. Saddam Hussein has not hesitated to use chemical weapons against Iran and against dissidents in Iraq and has often threatened to use biological warfare, but he never did even under the stresses of the Persian Gulf War (1990–1991). As governed the stalemate of the Cold War, an even larger framework of deterrence was operative. At this writing, the United Nations Special Commission is spasmodically investigating Iraq and seeking reassurance that its stockpiles and production facilities—notably of anthrax—had indeed been fully declared and demolished.

Today, as a result of deterrence, the principal threats of biological warfare are attributed to non-state actors, including state-sponsored terrorists and new breeds of sociopathic individuals and groups prepared to make war against society using motives that are hard to fathom. The scale of violence of such terrorist acts has escalated from demonstrative theater to the downing of jumbo aircraft and attacks on major buildings, as in Oklahoma City and New York City's World Trade Center. Had the World Trade Center collapsed, as was intended by the culprits, 100,000 citizens would have been at risk—an event on the scale of wartime Hiroshima or Nagasaki. Abroad, U.S. embassies have been targeted in Africa, with incidents thus far being limited to savage explosive attacks that have produced many civilian and bystander casualties.

The consideration of biological warfare has thus moved from the conventional military theater to a bioterrorism that puts millions of people in cities under the threat of artificially acquired infectious disease. Working in collaboration with every level of government and especially at the local and regional level, infectious disease specialists can play many instrumental roles:

1. Anticipation of threat agents and modalities of dissemination and their impact on public health
2. Assistance to local emergency authorities in planning for management of the consequences of a biological warfare attack
3. Participating in local public health teams in the epidemiologic investigation and definitive diagnosis of suspicious outbreaks
4. Acting as central agents in the medical and public health management of outbreaks and their further consequences for the life of the community
5. Assisting other branches of government in authentic assurance and guidance to the public to avert panic and chaos
6. Assisting when appropriate in taking measures to limit the further spread of contagious agents and to decontaminate affected facilities
7. Undertaking ongoing basic and translational research to sharpen the tools available for all these functions and further training of colleagues and supporting personnel
8. Instilling a globally shared ethos in condemnation of any possible use of biological warfare or offensive planning and preparation therefor
9. Maintaining networks of expertise that are available to public health and defense officials in confronting exotic agents for which such expertise is scarce and may be unavailable within government

The United States is on the verge of establishing a fully coordinated framework for responses on the part of government (President Bill Clinton's Presidential Decision Directive #62, May 22, 1998); as this framework is spelled out by further legislation and executive orders, infectious disease specialists in every major community will have no trouble locating where they can be of assistance.

ANTICIPATION OF THREAT AGENTS

Under conventional military doctrine, a biological warfare agent should be highly reliable, able to be targeted precisely at an enemy, cheap to produce, enjoy long shelf life and aerosol durability, and show limited epidemic spread. These criteria have converged to form a fairly short list of tier 1 agents (Table 313–1) that can be artificially aerosolized to deadly effect, regardless of their natural mode of transmission.

Most of these diseases are expected to follow a clinical course after biological warfare inoculation similar to that of the natural infections and to have limited capacity for person-to-person spread. (This objective cannot be ensured for the very large group subsumed

TABLE 313–1 Tier 1 Agents/Diseases

Anthrax
Plague
Tularemia
Brucellosis
Q fever
Alphaviruses
Venezuelan equine encephalitis
Western equine encephalitis
Eastern equine encephalitis
Viral hemorrhagic fevers
Smallpox—special category

under viral hemorrhagic fevers.) Empirical data are limited, but every expectation is that early antibiotic treatment will be effective against any of the bacterial culprits. (See other chapters for details.)

Aerosolized anthrax induces a disease quite distinct from the more usual and often survivable cutaneous variety. With intense involvement of mediastinal lymph nodes, it has a mortality approaching 100% if untreated before overt symptoms develop. Studies with primates suggest that early treatment with penicillin or doxycycline may be effective but may have to be prolonged for weeks and supplemented with vaccination or boostering. With heavy inocula, it is thought that some inhaled spores may remain dormant for long periods before germinating and becoming exposed to administered antibiotic.

No ex post facto specific treatment is known for the viral disorders, and for many of them there remain lacunae in our understanding of their natural history.

In a military defense setting, physical protection (masks and suits) plays the largest role—the same defense as against chemical weapons. In addition, mass prophylactic vaccination (e.g., against anthrax and some viral agents) is feasible in principle and has been adopted as routine for the U.S. Armed Forces. Likewise, routine monitoring of suspected clouds in the theater of operations should be conducted to provide early warning of chemical and biological warfare threats.

The changing threat, with special apprehension about vengeful individuals, forces our attention to agents and media beyond those of tactical military consequence. We can hardly monitor every civil airspace, although special attention has been paid to spectacular sites and events such as the Olympics—recalling the attacks at Munich in 1972. Massive outbreaks of foodborne and waterborne disease remind us of these vehicles for intentional infection. Other consumer product tampering has occurred on a minor scale for homicidal purposes; such tampering might be escalated manyfold for harassment of a corporation or a nation. Toxic tampering of a few grapes led to great economic losses for Chile in 1989. Similar harassment against domestic products, farm animals, or crops might be motivated for crass gains in the futures markets. Some terrorist mentalities may be undeterred by the untold havoc that would ensue from the reintroduction of smallpox into a global herd, the younger half of which is by now unvaccinated.[1] Smallpox had been discounted as a "rational" weapon because its spread might be uncontrollable. Now, our policy dilemmas about the merits (and hazards) of reintroducing vaccination are compounded by the technical ones of rediscovering and authenticating reliable seed stock and reconstituting the capacity for production of vaccine.

All things considered, anthrax has long held pride of place as an agent fairly easily grown and whose spores have long-lasting durability. Efficient dissemination is another matter: to produce a cloud of 1- to 5-μm particles takes more than a garden sprayer, and its action is subject to many vagaries of wind, rain, sunshine, and atmospheric turbulence. The oft-quoted figures of a potential for 10,000 casualties per kilogram of spore suspension are within the envelope of possibility, but as an optimal case combining substantial technical expertise, including meteorologic insight. The requisite technology remains within the reach of any determined state and requires investments in the low millions of dollars. That the reliability of outcome probably remains low may be less consequential to a clandestine terrorist, who can always try again, than to a military planner in a moment of tactical crisis. State-sponsored terrorism remains the most strident threat, and we should be particularly alert in connection with military confrontations with the states (mainly in the Middle East) that have had a history of use of such instrumentalities. Even if the principal state actors remain influenced by our deterrence strategies, others are often eager to precipitate hostilities in furtherance of their domestic political conflicts. The looming nuclear arms race on the Indian subcontinent also raises new alarms that these and other parties will look to biological warfare as a means of influencing the strategic balance there.

PLANNING FOR CONSEQUENCE MANAGEMENT

Absent a major catastrophic incident, it has been difficult to mobilize much attention to prior planning for a biological warfare attack. That nonchalance was strained by the Aum Shinrikyo nerve gas attack (1995) on the Tokyo subway system and by subsequent revelations that the cult had also stockpiled many agents and had attempted to deploy anthrax. New York City and metropolitan Washington, D.C., have taken the lead to organize themselves locally, with modest assistance from federal agencies and funding under the Nunn-Lugar-Domenici legislation (1996). In many cities, as in New York, fire departments also have emergency medical service and hazardous material release responsibilities. Their principals have rightly expressed concern for the welfare of the first responders, who play a vital role in situational assessment and in damage limitation and rescue services. Without special training and equipment, they could readily be booby-trapped and remain oblivious to an infectious presence for hours and days until symptoms develop, whereupon it may be too late for effective intervention. Coordination with law enforcement—the police department locally, the FBI with jurisdiction for criminal terrorism and eager to apprehend culprits and collect and preserve evidence—must also be planned and exercised in advance. Then, health providers must be mobilized for diagnosis, triage, emergency medical treatment, and disposition for further follow-up, in settings likely to strain all available hospital capacities. Professionals must also be responsible for certifying decontamination and for signaling all clear or ongoing vigilance to the public.

Infectious disease experts will play an indispensable role in motivating sober attention to these contingencies and in assisting at every stage of the planning for mitigation. They must weigh the risks and benefits of arousing public attention, but not hysteria. Attention must always be paid to the risk that every constructive step, when publicly displayed, may also inspire a culprit to circumvent the progress made. It would be well to not publicize technical details of methods of cultivation of prospective agents or their effective dissemination. Microaerosol generating equipment may also have to be put under special license, much as the distribution of cultures of special pathogens is now subject to Public Health Service registration in the United States.

EPIDEMIOLOGIC INVESTIGATION AND DEFINITIVE DIAGNOSIS

Terrorist theater (which includes hoaxes) apart, serious malefactors are unlikely to give advance, specific warning. Any major explosion may be contaminated with "bioshrapnel" to complicate the tasks of salvage and rescue, a caution that the first responders have begun to internalize. However, the first indicator of a major outbreak may well be a cluster of symptomatic or soon moribund cases. Isolated fatalities from undiagnosed febrile illness are not so uncommon, especially among immunocompromised individuals, who could be the most sensitive indicators. Special efforts must be applied to collect statistics, on a day-to-day basis, that might be evidence of suspected clustering and attract particularly energetic efforts at prompt diagnosis. The event might be an outbreak of natural viral disease, perhaps an import. So even a laboratory or pathologic diagnosis may not at first reveal man-made versus natural provenance. (If it is pulmonic anthrax, there would be little doubt.) In either event, prompt epidemiologic inquiry is indispensable to define the bounds of the outbreak in order to identify the most effective interventions to save others not yet symptomatic. The hope is that the earliest cases might reflect the persons most heavily dosed. They may be beyond saving, but the bulk of the exposed population would have longer incubation periods and could be reached for, say, antibiotic treatment. Effective consequence management relies on epidemiologic modeling of the outbreak and calls on meteorologic as well as infectious disease insights. Moreover, all this must be done within hours!

Waterborne outbreaks, in principle, have similar features—and the added imperative to shut down continued sources of infection. Emergency disinfection of water is easiest—by boiling; how that would apply to anthrax spores has probably not been studied. The bioterror threat is just one additional argument for more diligent monitoring of municipal water supplies, not just at the treatment plant (if any) but at major terminal distribution points as well.

Food and other media could be more widespread, especially in light of the relentless international commerce—consider the *Cyclospora* outbreak eventually traced to Guatemalan raspberries. In 1995, more than 200,000 Americans were infected with *Salmonella enteritidis* from ice cream connected with a premix contaminated with unpasteurized egg yolks. This national outbreak was presumably unintentional. Another local one in 1984 in Oregon affected 751 people; this outbreak was traced to malicious inoculation of salad bars and was intended to influence a local election.

Definitive diagnosis may require special skills and reagents, for which the ultimate resort may be the Centers for Disease Control and Prevention in Atlanta or the U.S. Army Research Institute for Infectious Diseases located at Fort Detrick, Maryland. Local preparedness will be enhanced either by pre-established confidence of communication with these centers or by the qualification of a local infectious disease laboratory and an alert to invoke these resources at a reasonably early stage.

MEDICAL AND PUBLIC HEALTH MANAGEMENT OF OUTBREAKS

Establishment of the diagnosis and epidemiologic model, as best as possible from the available data, opens the way for active management. We have no historical precedent to draw on; the nearest analogue would be natural disasters such as earthquakes and hurricanes. The additional opportunity, as well as burden, is the utility of prompt, well-targeted interventions if instituted within hours. With the likelihood of limited resources of time and medicinals, some form of triage is inevitable to focus these resources on persons who will achieve the most benefit. The worried (and angry and resentful) well are likely to greatly outnumber those needful of treatment—and that criterion may be difficult to authenticate at the earliest and hence most treatable stages. As with other emergencies, a host of practical problems from record keeping to who will pay the bills will also confound optimal treatment. Interim facilities outside of hospitals will need to be established and staffed. Little wonder that there is a universal expectation of calling in federal resources—Public Health Service, specialized Marine Corps units—but at best these resources will take time to mobilize and transport and themselves have limited further scope. Plans have been initiated for training National Guard units in several states to provide for rapidly mobilizable, but local reserves.

One of the immediate issues is the choice and availability of antibiotics. Given the possibility of drug-resistant pathogens, a cocktail might be prescribed—but such a combination may face poorly understood details of drug interactions and enhance the possibility of adverse side effects. Detailed, advance planning should be implemented to locate stockpiles of antibiotics, most effectively planned boluses in the normal distribution pipeline, and make arrangements for their transport, safeguarding, and orderly distribution. Even so, shortages are inevitable, and difficult decisions may be in the offing about stretching out the doses, mixing drugs, and whether to use material aged beyond the nominal expiration date.

This kind of planning is still at a developmental stage, and it is obvious that infectious disease experts need to be at the center from planning through execution.

ASSURANCE AND GUIDANCE TO THE PUBLIC IN AVERTING PANIC AND CHAOS

The media will not be silent during such episodes, and their far-flung intelligence could be invaluable in assembling important information. They will be disseminating what they learn or surmise to wide audiences, near and far. It would be most helpful if they can get that information from well-informed professionals and best if they could speak with a consistent voice in collaboration with operating governmental officials about the implications of an outbreak and the measures entailed for citizens. The same applies to the precautionary planning and exercises that are being mounted in major cities.

Caregivers may need special attention: their services are crucial and they must be sustained, and they may be at the brunt of hazardous exposure and psychic trauma from caring for the victims. The disposition of remains will be a further stress, materially and psychically.

Meanwhile, there will be no holiday for other civic functions, including health providers for other ailments, not to mention the personal, social, and economic life of the city—all functions that need to be restored promptly.

LIMITING THE FURTHER SPREAD OF CONTAGIOUS AGENTS

From a public health perspective, high priority must be given to the decision about the hazards of spreading infection further and, if it does spread, what can be done to persuade victims to limit their movements. In any event, those potentially exposed need advice and resources about initial and follow-up treatment and whether it can be acquired away from the initial treatment sites. Other implications of mass out-migration—and whether or how to avert it—leap to mind. Nor can it be assumed that the first attack will be the last one or at the same site.

Although the greatest hazards derive from the primary aerosol, spores residual on interior surfaces or vehicles or in heavily trafficked areas have some small chance of reaerosolization and continued threat. Exposed food and water supplies will need special validation. Decontamination protocols will have to be reassessed for the local contingency and some measure of laboratory verification invoked for the safe use of such sites.

ONGOING BASIC AND TRANSLATIONAL RESEARCH

Innumerable challenges to skilled judgment have already been posed throughout this discussion. They call for additional translational research to sharpen the tools available for all these functions: optimum treatment modalities for exotic diseases and assessment of the compromises necessitated by the exigencies of a crisis. In addition, infectious disease specialists by the very nature of their work are deeply involved in the underlying research on pathogenesis, immunity, and treatment. We are particularly frustrated in the treatment of viral infections, which cries out for further discovery in small-molecule antivirals, in interventions in pathogenetic mechanisms, in the acceleration of active immunity, and in the possible use of preformed antibodies.

Unhappily, the same biotechnological science that can lead to therapeutic advances can be diverted to making further mischief with genetically engineered constructs. Published work from Russia already points to the prospects of augmenting the virulence and offering vaccine escape for anthrax by importing toxins from other species.[2] Such research, if continued—and it may have to be to enable defenses to be contrived—must be carefully regulated and utterly transparent to provide some reassurance about its purposes.

All these research programs also entail further specialized training of colleagues and supporting personnel.

GLOBALLY SHARED ETHOS IN CONDEMNATION OF BIOLOGICAL WARFARE

The infectious disease worker knows better than anyone else how hard we have to work to keep up with natural disease outbreaks.

The contemplation of malicious compounding of nature's hazards is almost unbearable. The infectious disease community is also aware of the indivisible hazards to all humanity if biological warfare were to be routinized in the realm of human conflict. Technically, defense against biological warfare is already speculative; the recipes in this article are for damage mitigation, and the net of the most effective defense of a city may still be the death of thousands of victims. This awareness may alert professionals to the need to build a network of resolve that cuts across national boundaries to forfend the thought of biological warfare. They can exert their influence to reinforce that moral resolve with the consolidation of national policies and the institutionalization of international law. The same professionals may first need to enhance their own familiarity with these issues. This distasteful necessity is immediately derived from infectious disease specialists' unique understanding of the relentless competition between the human and micropredatory species.

REFERENCES

1. Breman JG, Henderson DA. Poxvirus dilemmas—monkeypox, smallpox, and biological terrorism. N Engl J Med. 1998;339:556–557.
2. Pomerantsev AP, Staritsin NA, Mockov YV, et al. Expression of cereolysine AB genes in *Bacillus anthracis* vaccine strain ensures protection against experimental hemolytic anthrax infection. Vaccine. 1997;15:1846–1850.

BIBLIOGRAPHY

Ali J, Rodrigues L, Moodie M. Chemical-Biological Defense Handbook. Alexandria, Va: Jane's Information Group; 1997.

Carus WS. Bioterrorism and Biocrimes: The Illicit Use of Biological Agents in the 20th Century. Washington, DC: Center for Counterproliferation Research, National Defense University; 1998.

Falkenrath RA, Newman RD, Thayer BA. America's Achilles' Heel: Nuclear, Biological, and Chemical Terrorism and Covert Attack. (BCSIA Studies in International Security). Cambridge, Mass: MIT; 1998.

Lederberg J, ed. Biological Weapons: Limiting the Threat (BCSIA Studies in International Security). Cambridge, Mass: MIT; 1999.

Office of Technology Assessment. Proliferation of weapons of mass destruction: Assessing the risks. Publication No. OTA-ISC-559. Washington, DC: US Government Printing Office; August 1993.

Office of Technology Assessment. Technologies Underlying Weapons of Mass Destruction. Publication No. OTA-BP-ISC-115. Washington, DC: US Government Printing Office; December 1993.

Poupard JA, Miller LA. Biological warfare. In: Lederberg J, ed. Encyclopedia of Microbiology, v. 1. San Diego: Academic Press; 1992:297–308.

Sidell FR, Takafuji ET, Franz DR, eds. Medical Aspects of Chemical and Biological Warfare. Washington, DC: Office of the Surgeon General; 1997.

World Wide Web. Visit http://oep-ndm.dhss.gov and http://mediccom.org/public for information on further access to servers pertaining to this topic.

SECTION F
ZOONOSES

Chapter 314

Zoonoses

ARNOLD N. WEINBERG

Zoonoses are a complex group of diseases caused by a remarkable diversity of pathogenic microorganisms that ordinarily reside and cause disease in the nonhuman animal world.[1] Criteria used to define a zoonotic infection vary, depending on how strictly the definition includes a vertebrate intermediate, other than humans, in the natural cycle of distribution. Thus, in this chapter malaria has been omitted because of a cycle between mosquitoes and humans. Babesiosis, a disease caused by an animal protozoan, is included since transmission occurs from vertebrate nonhuman hosts via infected *Ixodes* ticks. Yellow fever is also recognized by virtue of known reservoirs in nonhuman primates and transmission via arthropod vectors to people. In this heterogeneous group are agents that are transmitted by all of the accepted mechanisms—direct contact, ingestion, inhalation, arthropod intermediates, and animal bites. Some microbes, such as *Francisella tularensis,* can spread to humans or to other animals via all five of these routes of transmission! Inadvertently, zoonoses can be spread from one infected person to another, although rarely, through blood transfusions (e.g., babesiosis) or tissue transplants (e.g., rabies following corneal transplants).[2, 3] Ordinarily excluded from the group of zoonotic diseases are environmental microbes, such as *Burkholderia pseudomallei* and *Legionella* spp.

The defining criteria for the selection of pathogens and diseases recognized in this introduction to the zoonoses include the following: (1) a vertebrate reservoir exclusive of humans; (2) transmission of the agent directly to people *or* from products derived from the host animal *or* through an arthropod intermediate; and (3) a recognized infectious disease syndrome in susceptible individuals.[1] Many, if not most, animals that carry zoonotic pathogens can develop clinical disease.

The diversity of the zoonoses, their global distribution in mundane and exotic niches, the glamorous or complex names given to some diseases (e.g., Kyasanur Forest disease), and the enthusiasm that people have for travel and outdoor adventure all contribute to the aura and complexity surrounding this group of diseases. To these realities add domestic and laboratory animal contacts and varied household pet populations,[4, 5] with their economic and emotional implications, and it should be apparent that animal infections that can be transmitted to humans have a significant potential and real impact on everyone, including physicians and veterinarians. Few areas of our specialty demand the precision in extracting details of a travel, occupation, or exposure history than that which is required when we confront a patient ill with a perplexing fever who has been roughing it in the United States or abroad or who has had an animal, animal product, or arthropod encounter.

The association of animal and human disease with profound effects on human emotions, economics, and politics and with global reverberations reached a new dimension with the emergence of bovine spongiform encephalopathy in the United Kingdom in 1986. Farmers fought to preserve their herds, the beef-eating public became increasingly upset as human cases of a new variant of Creutzfeldt-Jakob disease were discovered, and political turmoil intensified as other European countries recognized the disease in native or imported cattle. The efforts of basic scientists and epidemiologists and the involvement of the World Health Organization (WHO) have resulted in considerable clarification of the etiology of the disease and its probable initiation in cattle feed containing ruminant carcasses (see Chapter 165). As a result of this experience, the WHO has taken on a greater responsibility for surveillance and protocol development, an indication of the globalization of concern, organization, and action in approaching emerging and reemerging infectious diseases.[6]

IMPORTANCE OF ZOONOSES IN CONTEMPORARY INFECTIOUS DISEASE PRACTICE

Perusal of Tables 314–1 to 314–3 reinforces the global significance of animal-associated infectious agents as well as the large proportion that are indigenous to North America in wild and domestic animal reservoirs. In absolute numbers, zoonotic pathogens are common. Documented illness in humans is unusual in the United States but constitutes a significant worldwide impact on morbidity and mortality. Without reviewing historical reports on epidemic bubonic plague, typhus fever, or woolsorter's disease, numerous contemporary examples illustrate the real and potential impact of zoonotic diseases in urban and rural settings. The possibility of spread in the animal and arthropod vector planes and subsequently to humans often cannot be anticipated. The history of Lyme borreliosis and Rocky Mountain spotted fever suggests how far reaching the impact of zoonoses can be in numbers of cases and extension of a geographic range.

Continental United States

Before 1991 the average yearly number of endemic and imported zoonotic infections (excluding salmonellosis) reported in *Morbidity and Mortality Weekly Report* (MMWR) of the Centers for Disease Control was approximately 2400 cases.[7] Lyme borreliosis, recognized in the late 1970s, became a reportable disease in 1991 and has contributed an additional approximately 10,000 to 15,000 cases per reporting year subsequently, reflecting the dissemination and greater awareness of the disease. Regrowth of forests in the northeastern United State has resulted in ballooning populations of white-tailed deer, white-footed mice, and *Ixodes scapularis* ticks. The agents of Lyme disease and ehrlichiosis have been identified in parks, including an urban park on the edge of New York City.[8] Babesiosis, a rare protozoan zoonotic disease primarily afflicting elderly and splenectomized individuals, and cryptosporidiosis, responsible for sporadic and epidemic gastroenteritis, are being reported with increasing frequency in patients ill with the acquired immunodeficiency syndrome (AIDS).[9, 10] *Babesia microti* is transmitted naturally via the feeding of *Ixodes* ticks that may simultaneously transmit Lyme borreliosis. Cryptosporidia are spread during contact with infected animals or ingestion of contaminated water supplies.[11] Importation of a few subclinically infected rabid raccoons from Florida to stock hunting camps in West Virginia in 1978 initiated a rapidly spreading rabies epizootic, primarily into contiguous Middle Atlantic states.[12] Since 1990 New York and New England states have been invaded. Other terrestrial wild animals, especially skunks, have been infected, and the epizootic has also spread to a wide variety of domestic animals, such as unvaccinated cats and pet rabbits. The impact on public health resources has been enormous, including a significant expenditure for vaccination programs for domestic animals, postexposure

TABLE 314–1 Diseases Acquired Directly or Indirectly from Animals or from Arthropod Vectors*

Disease	Pathogen	Mode Spread†	Persons at Risk‡
Viral			
B virus	Herpesvirus simiae	C	II,III,IV
California encephalitis	**Bunyavirus**	**A**	**I,II,public**
Colorado tick fever	**Orbivirus**	**A**	**I,II**
Contagious ecthyma (Orf)	**Parapoxvirus**	**C**	**I**
Dengue fever	**Flavivirus sp (dengue)**	**A**	**II,public**
Eastern equine encephalitis	**Alphavirus**	**A**	**II,IV,public**
Eastern hemisphere tick-borne encephalitis	Flavivirus	A,I	II
Equine morbillivirus	Bat paramyxovirus	C,R	I,II
Hantavirus pulmonary syndrome	**Sin Nombre virus**	**C,R**	**I,II**
Hemorrhagic fever renal syndrome	Hantavirus spp	C,R,I	I,II,IV
Japanese encephalitis	Flavivirus	A	II
Kyasanur Forest disease	Flavivirus	A	II
Lassa fever	Arenavirus	C	I,II
LCM meningitis	**Lymphocytic choriomeningitis virus**	**C,R**	**I,III,IV,public**
Mayaro virus disease	Alphavirus	A	II
Milker's nodule	**Parapoxvirus**	**C**	**I**
Monkey pox	Orthopoxvirus	C	II
Murray Valley encephalitis	Flavivirus	A	II
Creutzfeldt-Jakob encephalitis	Prion	I	public
Omsk hemorrhagic fever	Flavivirus	A,C,R	II,IV
Oropouche virus	Alphavirus	A	II
Powassan virus encephalitis	**Flavivirus**	**A,I**	**I,II,III**
Rabies	**Rhabdovirus**	**C**	**II,IV,public**
Rift Valley fever	Phlebovirus	C,R,A,I	I,II,IV,public
Ross River polyarthritis	Alphavirus	A	II
Semliki Forest	Alphavirus	A	II
St. Louis encephalitis	**Flavivirus**	**A**	**I,public**
Venezuelan equine encephalitis	**Alphavirus**	**A,R**	**II,III,IV**
West Nile fever	Flavivirus	A	II
Yellow fever	Flavivirus	A	II
Bacterial			
Anthrax	***Bacillis anthracis***	**C,R,I**	**I,III**
Brucellosis	***Brucella* spp**	**C,I,R**	**I,II,III,IV**
Campylobacteriosis	***Campylobacter jejuni***	**I**	**I,II,III,IV**
Cat-scratch disease, bacillary angiomatosis	***Bartonella henselae***	**C**	**II,III,VI,public**
Cholera	***Vibrio cholerae***	**I**	**V,public**
Eastern hemisphere spotted fevers	*Rickettsia* spp	A	II,III
***Edwardsiella* infection**	***Edwardsiella tarda***	**I**	**II,III,IV**
Ehrlichiosis, granulocytic	***Ehrlichia phagocytophila equi***	**A**	**II,III**
Ehrlichiosis, monocytic	***Ehrlichia chaffeensis***	**A**	**II,III**
Erysipeloid	***Erysipelothrix rhusiopathiae***	**C**	**I,II,V**
Gastroenteritis	***Vibrio parahemolyticus***	**I**	**II,V,public**
Glanders	*Burkholderia mallei*	R,C,I	I,III,IV
Leptospirosis	***Leptospira interrogans* spp**	**C,I**	**I,II,III,IV**
Listeriosis	***Listeria monocytogenes***	**I**	**I,VI,public**
Lyme borreliosis	***Borrelia burgdorferi***	**A**	**I,II,III**
Murine typhus	***Rickettsia typhi***	**A**	**I,II,III**
Pasteurellosis	***Pasteurella multocida***	**C,R**	**II,III**
Plague	***Yersinia pestis***	**A,C,R**	**II,III,IV,V**
***Plesiomonas* gastroenteritis**	***Plesiomonas shigelloides***	**I**	**V,public**
Psittacosis, ornithosis	***Chlamydia psittaci***	**R**	**I,III,IV,public**
Q fever	***Coxiella burnetii***	**R,A**	**I,II,III,IV,public**
Rat-bite fever (H)	***Streptobacillus moniliformis***	**C,I**	**I,III,IV,public**
Rat-bite fever (S)	***Spirillum minor***	**C**	**I,II,III**
Relapsing fever	***Borrelia* spp**	**A**	**I,III**
***Rhodococcus* pneumonia**	***Rhodococcus equi***	**R**	**III,VI**
Rickettsialpox	***Rickettsia akari***	**A**	**III,IV**
Rocky Mountain spotted fever	***Rickettsia rickettsii***	**A,C**	**I,II,III,IV,VI**
Salmonellosis	***Salmonella enteriditis***	**I**	**I,II,III,IV,VI**
Scrub typhus	*Orientia tsutsugamushi*	A	II,V
Septicemia—canine bite associated	***Capnocytophaga canimorsus***	**C**	**II,III,VI**
Skin gangrene sepsis—salt water associated	***Vibrio vulnificus,* other vibrios**	**C,I**	**V,VI**
Streptococcal cellulitis	***Streptococcus iniae***	**C**	**I,V**
Trench fever	***Bartonella quintana***	**A,C**	**VI,public**
Tuberculosis	***Mycobacterium bovis, M. tuberculosis***	**I**	**I,III,IV,VI**
Tularemia	***Francisella tularensis***	**C,I,A,R**	**I,II,III,IV,public**
Yersiniosis	***Yersinia enterocolitica***	**I**	**I,II,III,IV,V,public**
Yersiniosis	***Yersinia pseudotuberculosis***	**I**	**I,II,III,V,public**

TABLE 314-1 Diseases Acquired Directly or Indirectly from Animals or from Arthropod Vectors* *Continued*

Disease	Pathogen	Mode Spread†	Persons at Risk‡
Parasitic			
Angiostrongyliasis	*Parastrongylus cantonensis*	I,C	II
African trypanosomiasis	*Trypanosoma brucei*	A	II
Babesiosis	***Babesia microti***	**A**	**II,VI**
Chagas' disease	*Trypanosoma cruzi*	A	II
Cyclosporiasis	***Cyclospora cayetanensis***	**I**	**II,III**
Clinorchiasis	*Clonorchis sinensis*	I	II
Cryptosporidiosis	***Cryptosporidis* spp**	**I**	**I,II,VI**
Cysticercosis	***Taenia solium***	**I**	**public**
Dirofilariasis	***Dirofilaria immitis***	**A**	**II**
Echinococcosis	***Echinococcus granulosus***	**I**	**I**
Fascioliasis	*Fasciola hepatica*	I	I,II
Giardiasis	***Giardia lamblia***	**I**	**I,II,III**
Leishmaniasis, cutaneous	*Leishmania mexicana*	A	II
Leishmaniasis, visceral (kala-azar)	*Leishmania donovani*	A	II,VI
Microsporidial diarrhea, chronic	**Microsporidia**	**I**	**I,II,VI**
Paragonimiasis	*Paragonimus westermani*	I	II,V
Toxocariasis	***Toxocara canis, cati***	**I**	**III**
Toxoplasmosis	***Toxoplasma gondii***	**I**	**III,VI**
Trichinosis	***Trichinella spiralis***	**I**	**public**

*Bold type indicates indigenous to North America, although the disease may have a wider distribution.
†*Mode of Spread:* C = contact (direct including bite, water); I = ingestion; A = arthropod vector (mosquito, tick, flea, mite, etc.); R = respiratory.
‡*At Risk:* I = farmers, livestock and animal processing workers; II = outdoor recreational or vocational activities in wild or underdeveloped regions; III = persons in contact with pets, other animals in urban areas; IV = health care and laboratory personnel (human and veterinary); V = fisherman and others working in aquatic environment; VI = immunocompromised hosts; public = anyone, any place.

prophylaxis for humans, and strategies to contain spread in wildlife by means such as baited oral vaccines. Isolation, containment, and sacrifice of companion pets and the threat posed to individuals have added an emotional burden to the monetary drain placed on communities.

Hantaviruses have been documented, by serologic and virologic methods, to occur in the United States in a variety of New World rodents.[13] No clinical human disease had been recognized, although globally hemorrhagic fever with renal syndrome (e.g., Korean hemorrhagic fever) and nephropathia epidemica (milder Scandinavian nephropathy) are familiar illnesses caused by members of the Bunyaviridae family. The dramatic appearance of an acute respiratory distress syndrome (ARDS) that afflicts primarily outdoor-oriented young adults and that carries significant mortality was first described in newspapers and in MMWR in 1993 in the Four Corners area of four southwestern states.[14] This virulent respiratory disease, caused by a number of previously unidentified Hantaviruses, has now been identified throughout the United States and in Central and South America in a variety of rodent reservoirs.[15] The clinical syndrome of hemorrhage and nephropathy, typical of Hantavirus infections reported from Asia and Europe, has not been identified in the Western Hemisphere cases. The epidemiology of this new viral respiratory syndrome appears to be exposure to wild rodent excrement. The route of spread to humans is probably inhalation of virus in dried excreta or via contact. A new clinical syndrome—Hantavirus pulmonary syndrome—has emerged throughout the United States and in Central and South America, afflicting active healthy individuals.[15] Factors influencing pathogenicity, modes of spread, and temporal characteristics of Hantavirus respiratory disease are being elucidated. This recently discovered zoonosis graphically illustrates the uncer-

TABLE 314-2 Animal Reservoirs of Zoonoses in North America

Disease	Cat	Cattle	Dog	Fish and Shellfish	Fowl and Other Birds	Goats and Sheep	Horse	Rabbit	Rodent	Swine	Wildlife
Anthrax	x	x	x			x	x			x	x
Babesiosis		x							x		x
Brucellosis		x	x			x	x			x	
Campylobacteriosis	x	x	x		x	x			x	x	x
Cryptosporidiosis	x	x	x	x	x	x	x		x	x	x
Erysipeloid		x		x	x	x				x	
Giardiasis	x		x			x					x
Leptospirosis		x	x			x	x		x	x	x
Listeriosis		x			x	x		x		x	x
Lyme borreliosis		x	x				x		x		x
Lymphocytic choriomeningitis									x		
Murine typhus									x		x
Ornithosis, psittacosis					x	x					
Pasteurellosis	x	x	x		x						
Plague	x							x	x		x
Q fever	x	x				x					x
Rabies	x	x	x			x	x	x	x	x	x
Rat-bite fever	x		x						x		x
Rocky Mountain spotted fever			x			x		x			x
Salmonellosis	x	x	x	x	x	x	x	x	x	x	x
Toxoplasmosis	x	x				x					x
Tularemia	x	x	x		x	x	x	x	x	x	x
Vibriosis				x							
Viral encephalitis					x	x	x		x		x
Yersiniosis		x	x		x	x			x	x	x

TABLE 314–3 Animal Associations and Zoonotic Disease Risk

Animal	Anthrax	Bartonellosis	Brucellosis	Campylobacteriosis	*Capnocytophaga canimorsus* infection	Cryptosporidiosis	Erysipeloid	Giardiasis	Hantavirus Pulmonary Syndrome	Hepatitis A	Herpes B	Histoplasmosis	Lymphocytic Choriomeningitis	Leptospirosis	Listeriosis	*Mycobacterium tuberculosis* or *M. bovi*
Aquatic mammal							x	x								
Birds				x			x					x			x	
Cat	x	x	x	x		x								x		
Cattle	x		x	x		x								x	x	x
Dog	x		x	x	x	x								x	x	
Fish/Shellfish						x	x									
Goats/Sheep	x		x	x		x								x	x	
Horse	x		x			x								x		
Nonhuman primate				x				x		x	x				x	x
Rabbit/Hare			x												x	
Rodent									x				x	x	x	
Snakes/Lizards																
Swine	x		x	x		x	x							x	x	x
Wildlife	x										x	x	x	x		x

Animal	*ORF*	Ornithosis	Pasteurellosis	Rat-Bite Fever	Plague	Q fever	Rabies	*Salmonellosis/Edwardsiella* infection	*Streptococcus iniae* cellulitis	Shigellosis	Toxoplasmosis	Tularemia	Vibriosis	Viral Hemorrhagic fever	Yersiniosis
Aquatic mammal															
Birds		x	x					x				x			
Cat			x		x	x	x	x			x	x			
Cattle						x	x	x							x
Dog			x		x		x	x	x			x	x		x
Fish/Shellfish													x		
Goats/Sheep	x					x	x	x							x
Horse							x	x							x
Nonhuman primate								x		x					x
Rabbit/Hare					x	x	x	x				x			
Rodent				x	x		x	x			x	x		x	
Snakes/Lizards								x							
Swine			x				x	x				x			x
Wildlife					x		x	x			x	x		x	

tainty of events in nature and the need for continued vigilance and respect for the impact of zoonotic pathogens on human health, including the factors that influence their emergence.[16]

Global Experiences

Our responsibility for patients' well-being often includes travel advice. The distribution of zoonotic diseases and their modes of spread often dictate the choice of protective immunizations, medications, and specific instructions about food and drink. Theoretically, many problems can be avoided through doctor-patient interaction. In practical terms, many problems result from failed communication or incomplete advice. For example, in Boston and some other cities in the United States more cases of Eastern Hemisphere spotted fever (e.g., South African tick bite fever) are seen in a decade than of indigenous Rocky Mountain spotted fever. Analysis of most of these cases reveals that no precautionary measures were discussed by the physician during the pretravel visit even though the patient's itinerary included a walking safari in an endemic region. The incubation period may influence the timing of an emerging zoonotic infection.

Movement of large numbers of susceptible young soldiers to areas of the world endemic for contagious diseases, including infectious zoonoses, has always been is a problem. Korean hemorrhagic fever emerged as an acute clinical problem among United Nations' troops in the Korean conflict, as well as for practicing physicians in the West dealing with returning soldiers. The editor of *Reviews of Infectious Diseases* demonstrated his prescience by inviting experts to prepare a monograph supplement in the autumn of 1990 on the subject of infectious disease problems related to the Persian Gulf area.[17] A wide circulation of this supplement reached infectious disease specialists just as the Desert Storm conflict erupted. The major zoonoses endemic in the region were reviewed thoughtfully. In the aftermath of that brief conflict, rare reports of animal-associated diseases, such as Q fever, that had become clinically active after a period of latency, appeared in the literature. Conflicts continue to erupt in other regions of the globe, and responsible reporting in the medical literature has been timely in bringing regional zoonoses to the attention of physicians.[18]

The reemergence of dengue and dengue hemorrhagic fever as a global health problem is another illustration of the unpredictability of arbovirus dissemination and the many factors influencing local outbreaks and epidemics.[19] In the Western Hemisphere its resurgence clearly relates to failure of mosquito control, urbanization and population growth, and lack of proper water and waste removal procedures. Competent mosquitoes, including *Aedes aegypti* and *Aedes albopictus,* have spread dengue virus throughout the Caribbean and

Central and South America. The presence of these arthropod vectors in the southern United States increases the likelihood of dengue outbreaks locally, not only among tourists returning from vacationing in endemic areas.

At a time when people seek adventure in the outdoors, when travel time around the globe is shorter than the incubation period of many zoonotic diseases, and when patients who are immunocompromised by illness or therapy crowd foreign travel experiences into brief periods of wellness, our efforts must be assiduous in providing advance warning and in investigating new clinical symptoms in returning travelers. A useful text that covers worldwide distribution of infections is available,[20] and the Centers for Disease Control and Prevention continues to provide physicians with a weekly summary of health information for international travelers.

DISTRIBUTION OF ZOONOTIC PATHOGENS IN NATURE

During the past several decades a number of new diseases have emerged globally, and some previously recognized infections have been identified in regions where they had not been reported heretofore. Table 314–4 lists the natural and human factors that individually and collectively are known to affect the environment and therefore potentially influence where certain zoonoses emerge, persist, or spread locally or globally.

Geoclimatic Conditions

Numerous examples can be cited to illustrate the influence of temperature, moisture, and soil conditions on the distribution of zoonotic agents and diseases. "Tropical" diseases implies that an environment is extant that supports the growth and transmission of infectious agents requiring high temperatures and abundant rainfall in which arthropod vectors thrive and appropriate animal hosts exist. Global warming is an example of a geoclimatic issue that may result in major changes in zoonotic disease distribution.[21] Arthropod vectors, such as mosquitoes and ticks, enhanced growth and distribution of plants, and animal migrations are intimately tied to changes in ambient temperature. The presence of anopheles mosquitoes and the increasing number of cases of malaria at higher elevations support scientists who argue that climate change is already occuring.[22] Counterarguments include the observations that centuries ago many diseases currently described as "tropical" regularly occurred in temperate regions, even in epidemic proportions.

Bacillus anthracis spores and vegetative growth of organisms are strongly influenced by ambient temperatures, "incubator" areas where plant decay adds warmth and moisture, and the presence of a supportive alkaline soil containing adequate calcium salts.[23] The halophilic and nonhalophilic vibrios of the Northern Hemisphere winter in estuarine mud and appear in significant numbers only as water temperatures warm to approximately 20°C. Cases of gastroenteritis, necrotizing cellulitis, and septicemia are being diagnosed in individuals exposed to New England and the Danish coastal sea waters, regions traditionally considered too cold to support the growth of these organisms.[24] Does this change indicate the wider distribution of pathogens adapting to colder temperatures or a change in water temperatures associated with global warming? Ticks responsible for the transmission of Rocky Mountain spotted fever and Lyme borreliosis are strongly influenced in distribution and activity by temperature and precipitation. The extreme cold of Alaska has prohibited the extension of the range of these tick-associated diseases into our most northern state. Of course, the influence of population expansion and migration, socioeconomic conditions, customs, housing, nutrition, sanitation, potable water, and mosquito control contribute to the susceptibility and spread of diseases in tandem with geoclimatic characteristics.

TABLE 314-4 Factors Associated with the Distribution of Zoonotic Pathogens in Nature

Geoclimatic conditions
Temperature extremes—terrestrial and water
Rainfall
Soil characteristics
Animal, avian, and aquatic hosts
Migration patterns of animals and birds
Arthropod reservoirs and vectors
Human influence on ecosystem and biosystem

Animal, Avian, and Aquatic Hosts

Human and animal susceptibility factors, including genetic characteristics and natural and acquired immunity, influence the patterns of spread of zoonoses. Interactions with domestic animals can be a major factor. Rabies vaccination of dogs in developed countries has all but eliminated rabies acquired from these pets, but in the developing world rabies is almost always the result of dog bites.[12] When domestic animals are allowed to stray or to become feral, they can acquire many zoonotic infections such as tularemia, plague, and rabies.[25] Household pets can carry infected arthropod vectors into homes or to other geographic areas. The penchant of raccoons for suburban areas has clearly facilitated the spread of rabies to domestic animals in the Middle Atlantic and New England states, primarily to cats, but also to dogs, cattle, horses, and even to pet rabbits.[26] The Hantavirus pulmonary syndrome, first described in the southwestern United States, probably has become clinically apparent owing to the proximity of susceptible humans to a variety of wild rodent species, each infected with a unique strain of virus. Conditions appropriate for spread—burgeoning numbers of rodents and contamination of local environments—have resulted in numerous cases, primarily in the United States and South America.[15] Migrating and overwintering sedentary birds provide a reservoir for arboviruses, and aquatic mammals, such as beaver and muskrat, are sources of multiplication and dissemination of *Giardia lamblia*[27] and *F. tularensis.*[28]

Not unexpectedly, new zoonotic diseases continue to be recognized. Our ability to marshall observation and communication skills, clinical and epidemiologic surveillance, sophisticated scientific and laboratory methodology, and the collaboration of veterinarians, physicians, and biologists augers well for future discoveries. The recent description of equine morbillivirus disease in horses and humans in Queensland, Australia, illustrates the necessity for constant vigil and cooperation.[29] The need for surveillance and cooperation is essential for the health of people and the health of our planet as expressed in a recent WHO report.[6]

Migration Patterns of Animals and Birds

Tularemia appeared in Vermont for the first time in the late 1960s, brought there by infected muskrats migrating via a water route from Canada and New York State.[28] Cases of Rocky Mountain spotted fever appear in new and unexpected places, such as a small park surrounded by concrete and asphalt in Bronx, New York.[30] Did a dog bring the rickettsiae in dog ticks acquired from a visit to eastern Long Island? Did a hawk carry an infected rabbit from an endemic area? Can *Rickettsia rickettsii* be transported by migrating birds carrying infected arthropods? In nature, when considering the potential for emergence of zoonosis, no haven is a safe haven. Even in a verdant park in New York City ticks have been discovered carrying *Borrelia burgdorferi* and *Ehrlichia phagocytophila,* probably transported by roaming white-footed mice.[8] The questions are many, the answers are few. However, observations of zoonotic disease spread confirms the influence of animal reservior movements, the necessity of co-hosts for long-term survival of some pathogens (e.g., *B. burgdorferi*),[31] and the importance of overwintering sedentary birds as well as migratory patterns for persistence and dissemination of selected zoonoses (e.g., arboviruses). The presence of favorable conditions for growth, survival, and multiplication of ticks, biting flies, and mosquitoes, important vectors of many zoonotic pathogens (see Table 314–1), illustrates the potential for widespread movements of microorganisms carried by these vectors to new geographic regions. The current raccoon rabies epizootic can be traced to the march of animals over a 15-year period from a locale in West Virginia, south to Georgia, west to Ohio, and especially north and east to New Jersey, New York, and the New England states.[26]

Arthropod Reservoirs and Vectors

Vectorial capacity, the summation of many factors that contribute to the ability of a pathogen to perpetuate in an arthropod host, is often enhanced by actions that increase survival and multiplication of the arthropod and vertebrate host intermediates.[32] Although incompletely understood, it appears that the spread of Lyme borreliosis to the majority of the lower 48 states resulted from a population explosion of white-tailed deer and white-footed mice, which allowed overwintering of the pathogen and enhanced distribution of the dependent *Ixodes* ticks. A provocative report linking eastern United States oak forests to a chain reaction involving gypsy moth activity, white-footed mouse density, acorn production, and white-tailed deer presence illustrates the delicate balance that can eventuate in the distribution and prevalence of Lyme disease.[33] The appearance in the southern and eastern United States of a mosquito vector from Asia, the Asian tiger mosquito *A. albopictus,* corresponded to the commercial stockpiling of used tire casings imported into the Houston, Texas, area in the early 1980s.[34] This mosquito, a competent laboratory vector for at least 22 arboviruses, including dengue, eastern equine encephalitis, and yellow fever, has now been identified in 25 states, including Hawaii.[35] In a surveillance effort initiated in Polk County, Florida, 14 strains of eastern equine encephalitis virus have been isolated from these mosquitoes.[36]

Human Influence on Ecosystem and Biosystem

The ability of humans to exert significant influence on wind velocity, rainfall, temperature extremes, and soil conditions pales when compared with the natural forces operating around the globe. However, there are numerous small- and large-scale examples in irrigation practices, waste distribution, water purification, agricultural technologies, insecticide usage, and incursions into areas of virgin vegetation that illustrate the profound effects of human activities on the establishment and spread of zoonoses.

Dramatic examples can be found in epidemics following pollution of water supplies, the most contemporary being the massive outbreak of cryptosporidial gastroenteritis that affected approximately 400,000 Milwaukee, Wisconsin, residents drinking water from their faucets in April 1993. Groundwater pollution by domestic animal excrement overwhelmed the purification system handling Lake Michigan water that was being removed close to where the contamination occurred. Waterborne cryptosporidiosis remains a major threat, especially among immunocompromised individuals.[37] The first microbiologically documented *Giardia lamblia* epidemic, reported in 1993, spread from wild beavers through fecally contaminated water supplied to residents of several towns in western Canada.[27] We are not protecting our water systems adequately to kill and remove selected pathogens that encyst and therefore avoid methods used in purification.

Recreational swimming holes can be contaminated by *Leptospira* sp brought downstream from neighboring farms.[38] Raccoons infected with rabies virus, imported into a region where animals were highly susceptible, initiated an epizootic rapidly spreading in the eastern United States. Airplanes can facilitate the inadvertent transport of potentially infectious arthropod vectors of zoonoses in the wheel bays of intercontinental and transcontinental flights.[39] Indiscriminate use of insecticides has influenced avian populations instrumental in the control of various disease-carrying arthropod vectors. Perhaps the most devastating influence affecting the distribution of zoonotic pathogens occurs when virgin forests are cleared or are invaded by new roads and new towns in the name of economic development.[40] It has been theorized that many undiscovered potentially pathogenic viruses and bacteria reside in animal hosts that are inaccessible to humans in remote ecosystems until such areas are developed and susceptible people begin moving to and fro. An example often quoted is the recognition of the viral disease Oropouche several years after a new road was built connecting Belem with Brasilia in Brazil.[41] A variety of prospective studies are under way to learn more about the relationship of alterations in biosystems and ecosystems and the emergence of "new" infectious diseases including zoonoses.[41, 42]

DIAGNOSTIC APPROACH TO ZOONOSES

There are more than 200 well-described zoonotic diseases, of which 87 are included in Table 314–1. A majority of those that are included (bold type) are indigenous to North America. Some of those pathogens and diseases are also found in other parts of the world.

The possibility of a zoonotic infection may surface quickly from even a superficial history or features of the physical examination, or both. Included are residence and travel history, occupation (e.g., abattoir worker, veterinarian, farmer), outside interests (e.g., hunting, trapping, other outdoor activities), or the presence of a characteristic skin lesion (e.g., erythema migrans of Lyme borreliosis, peripheral petechial lesions of Rocky Mountain spotted fever, tache noire of eastern hemisphere spotted fever). A characteristic illness, such as St. Louis encephalitis in Texas or eastern equine encephalitis in New Jersey, may alert a physician to similar diagnoses in other patients being seen with central nervous system symptoms.

By using Tables 314–1 through 314–3 as cross-referencing guides, an individual's at-risk activity or animal contacts can help narrow the etiologic possibilities, and potential modes of spread can be evaluated through careful attention to historical details. Geographic considerations and clinical data can then help in selecting possible etiologic diagnoses. Laboratory studies, including appropriate cultures, paired serologic specimens, chemistries selected to evaluate target organ involvement, and search for specific parasites, can help to confirm a suspected diagnosis. In acute circumstances, therapy should be instituted before confirming a specific diagnosis, guided by the available data.

If a positive history of animal exposure is elicited, information contained in Tables 314–2 and 314–3 can be helpful in identifying possible zoonotic diseases that could account for the clinical picture. The epidemic of Q fever that occurred after a group of poker players were exposed to a parturient cat in urban Halifax, Nova Scotia, attests to the usefulness of this type of table in identifying diseases specific to selected animal species that should be considered based on the clinical data available.[43] The multiplicity of possible etiologies for a cluster of patients, for example, with an acute respiratory disease, allows greater precision in diagnosis by having a reference to animal reservoirs characteristic for specific pathogens.[44]

Zoonotic diseases can be severe, life-threatening, and contagious and can even warn of an emerging epidemic. Many of these infections can be suspected from information obtained in a detailed history. Rapid noncultural diagnostic tests, such as enzyme-linked immunosorbent assay methodology, polymerase chain reaction, and DNA probes, are being developed and are in use to identify selected zoonoses.[45, 46] Therapy is currently available for the majority of nonviral zoonotic infections and even for a few viral zoonoses, such as Lassa fever, some Hantavirus hemorrhagic fevers with renal syndromes, and possibly Herpesvirus simiae infections. Most of the sophisticated studies to unravel the identity of a zoonotic infectious disease ultimately rely on a detailed and accurate history from which specific tests and effective therapy emerge.

REFERENCES

1. Waltner-Toews D. Caught in the causal web: Analytical problems in the epidemiology of zoonoses. Acta Vet Scand Supp. 1988;84:296–298.

2. Smith PS, Evans AT, Popovsky M, et al. Transfusion-acquired babesiosis and failure of antibiotic treatment. JAMA. 1986;256:2726–2727.
3. Centers for Disease Control. Human-to-human transmission of rabies via a corneal transplant—France. MMWR Morb Mortal Wkly Rep. 1980;29:25–26.
4. Fox JG, Lipman NS. Infections transmitted by large and small laboratory animals. Infect Dis Clin North Am. 1991;5:131–163.
5. Goldstein EJC. Household pets and human infections. Infect Dis Clin North Am. 1991;5:117–130.
6. Meslin FX. Global aspects of emerging and potential zoonoses: A WHO perspective. Emerg Infect Dis. 1997;3:223–228.
7. Centers for Disease Control. Summary of notifiable diseases, United States. MMWR Morb Mortal Wkly Rep. 1991;40(53):1–63.
8. Daniels TJ, Falco RC, Schwartz I, et al. Deer ticks (*Ixodes scapularis*) and the agents of Lyme disease and human granulocytic ehrlichiosis in a New York City park. Emerg Infect Dis. 1997;3:353–355.
9. Benezra D, Brown AE, Polsky B, et al. Babesiosis and infection with human immunodeficiency virus (HIV). Ann Intern Med. 1987;107:944.
10. Wittner M, Tanowitz HB, Weiss LM. Parasitic infections in AIDS patients: Cryptosporidiosis, isosporiasis, microsporidiosis, cyclosporiasis. Infect Dis Clin North Am. 1993;7:569–586.
11. Guerrant RL. Cryptosporidiosis: An emerging, highly infectious threat. Emerg Infect Dis. 1997;3:51–57.
12. Fishbein DB. Rabies. Infect Dis Clin North Am. 1991;5:53–71.
13. Tsai TF, Bauer SP, Sasso DR, et al. Serological and virological evidence of a Hantaan virus–related enzootic in the United States. J Infect Dis. 1985;152:126–136.
14. Centers for Disease Control. Update: Hantavirus infection—United States, 1993. MMWR Morb Mortal Wkly Rep. 1993;42:517–519.
15. Schmaljohn C, Hjelle B. Hantaviruses: A global disease problem. Emerg Infect Dis. 1997;3:95–104.
16. Murphy FA. Emerging zoonoses. Emerg Infect Dis. 1998;4:429–435.
17. Oldfield EC III, Wallace MR, Hyams KC, et al. Endemic infectious diseases of the Middle East. Rev Infect Dis. 1991;13(Suppl 3):S199–S217.
18. Deresinski S. Health hazards in Somalia. Infect Dis Alert. 1993;12:69–72.
19. Gubler DJ, Clark GC. Dengue/dengue hemorrhagic fever: The emergence of a global health problem. Emerg Infect Dis. 1995;1:55–57.
20. Wilson ME. A World Guide to Infections: Disease, Distribution, Diagnosis. New York: Oxford University Press; 1991.
21. Colwell R, Epstein P, Gubler D, et al. Emerg Infect Dis. 1998;4:451–452.
22. Epstein RP, Diaz HF, Elias S, et al. Biological and physical signs of climate change: Focus on mosquito-borne disease. Bull Am Meteorol Soc. 1998;78:409–417.
23. Van Ness GB. Ecology of anthrax. Science. 1971;172:1303–1307.
24. Hill MK, Sanders CV. Localized and systemic infection due to vibrio species. Infect Dis Clin North Am. 1987;1:687–707.
25. Capellan J, Fong IW. Tularemia from a cat bite: Case report and review of feline-associated tularemia. Clin Infect Dis. 1993;16:472–475.
26. Centers for Disease Control. Extension of the raccoon rabies epizootic—United States 1992. MMWR Morb Mortal Wkly Rep. 1992;41:661–664.
27. Isaac-Renton JL, Cordeiro C, Sarafis K, Shahriari H. Characterization of *Giardia duodenalis* isolates from a waterborne outbreak. J Infect Dis. 1993;167:431–440.
28. Young LS, Bicknell DS, Archer BG, et al. Tularemia epidemic: Vermont 1968. N Engl J Med. 1969;280:1253–1260.
29. Paterson DL, Murray PK, McCormack JG. Zoonotic disease in Australia caused by a novel member of the Paramyxoviridae. Clin Infect Dis. 1998;27:112–118.
30. Salgo MP, Telzak EE, Currie B, et al. A focus of Rocky Mountain spotted fever within New York City. N Engl J Med. 1988;318:1345–1348.
31. Steere AC. Lyme disease. N Engl J Med. 1989;321:586–596.
32. Telford SR III, Pollack RJ, Spielman A. Emerging vector-borne infections. Infect Dis Clin North Am. 1991;5:7–18.
33. Jones CG, Ostfeld RS, Richard MP, et al. Chain reactions linking acorns to gypsy moth outbreaks and Lyme disease risk. Science. 1998;279:1023–1026.
34. Centers for Disease Control. Update: *Aedes albopictus* infestation—United States. MMWR Morb Mortal Wkly Rep. 1987;36:769–773.
35. Moore CG, Mitchell CJ. *Aedes albopictus* in the United States: Ten-year presence and public health implications. Emerg Infect Dis. 1997;3:329–334.
36. Mitchell CJ, Niebylski ML, Smith GC, et al. Isolation of eastern equine encephalitis virus from *Aedes albopictus* in Florida. Science. 1992;257:526–527.
37. Juranek DD. Cryptosporidiosis: Sources of infection and guidelines for prevention. Clin Infect Dis. 1995;21(Suppl 1):S57–S61.
38. Jackson LA, Kaufmann AF, Adams WG, et al. Outbreak of leptospirosis associated with swimming. Pediatr Infect Dis J. 1993;12:48–54.
39. Russell RC. Survival of insects in the wheel bays of a Boeing 747B aircraft on flights between tropical and temperate airports. Bull World Health Organ. 1987;65:659–662.
40. Coid CR. Diseases of animals transmissible to man (zoonoses). Br J Obstet Gynaecol. 1988;95:209–210.
41. Gibbons A. Where are "new" diseases born? Science. 1993;261:680–681.
42. Momen H. Emerging infectious diseases—Brazil. Emerg Infect Dis. 1998;4:1–3.
43. Langley JM, Marrie TJ, Covert A, et al. Poker players pneumonia: An urban outbreak of Q fever following exposure to a parturient cat. N Engl J Med. 1988;319:354–356.
44. Weinberg AN. Respiratory infections transmitted from animals. In: Infect Dis Clin North Am. 1991;5:649–661.
45. Keller TL, Halperin JJ, Whitman M. PCR detection of *Borrelia burgdorferi* DNA in cerebrospinal fluid of Lyme neuroborreliosis patients. Neurology. 1992;42:32–42.
46. Relman DA. Detection and identification of previously unrecognized microbial pathogens. Emerg Infect Dis. 1998;4:382–389.

SECTION G

PROTECTION OF TRAVELERS

Chapter 315

Protection of Travelers

MARTIN S. WOLFE

Physicians dealing with traveling patients should be familiar with the potential diseases to which the traveler might be exposed. Advice on immunizations and general preventive measures must be given before travel, and on the traveler's return the physician must be aware of and recognize problems resulting from travel.

PRETRAVEL ADVICE

Preparations for Travel

Anyone with a preexisting medical condition should be examined by, or at least have a consultation with, his or her physician approximately 1 month before beginning a trip. Special precautions are necessary for those with allergies, gastrointestinal conditions, diabetes, or cardiovascular or pulmonary disease. A brief medical summary and a recent copy of the patient's electrocardiogram or chest radiography, if pertinent, should be taken along. Engraved bracelets with a brief description of a potentially dangerous medical condition are available from a number of sources. For those requiring care by a particular specialist while abroad, a directory of that specialty should be consulted. A pocket directory is available from the nonprofit International Association for Medical Assistance to Travelers (IAMAT, 40 Regal Road, Guelph, Ontario N1K 1B5, Quebec, Canada), listing doctors worldwide who speak English, have attained respected qualifications, and understand U.S. medical techniques and practices. A regular visit to the dentist should be scheduled before traveling. If glasses or contact lenses are worn, an extra pair should be taken, as well as a prescription for replacement of eyeglasses. Travelers should be certain that their health insurance policy covers medical care, hospitalization, or medical evacuation in foreign countries. If not, special policies are available for such coverage.

Supply of Necessary Drugs

Patients with chronic illnesses who are taking medications such as digitalis, insulin, or anticoagulants should carry a sufficient supply. Because drugs sold abroad may have different names and may vary in potency, prescriptions should be clearly written, giving the trade, generic, and chemical names of the drug and the dosage.

Many drugs may be purchased over the counter in foreign countries, and these often lack label warnings. Travelers should be warned that potentially dangerous drugs such as chloramphenicol, sulfas, butazolidine, and aminopyrine may be included in cold or antidiarrheal preparations. In some countries injections are given in pharmacies, and it is important to avoid needles and syringes of questionable sterility and, when possible, to purchase or bring along disposable needles and syringes.

Components of a traveler's medical kit might include a thermometer, bandages and gauze, adhesive tape, an antiseptic or bactericidal soap solution, aspirin, antacids, an antimotion sickness drug such as dimenhydrinate, and a mild oral laxative or suppository for constipation. A decongestant should be carried while in the aircraft cabin for those prone to nasal congestion, and saline nose drops are useful to prevent nasal dryness from the low humidity of aircraft cabins. An antihistamine should be taken for allergies. Cough medication and other liquids should be carried in a tightly stoppered plastic bottle. A small amount of a nonnarcotic pain medication, or perhaps a codeine preparation, should be carried. Antibiotic and antifungal ointments and perhaps a foot powder should be included. In general, broad-spectrum antibiotics should not be given to travelers, because if they are sufficiently ill to require these medications, they would be better served by consulting a recommended physician. An exception to this may be made for travelers who will be in remote areas in which immediate medical assistance may be unavailable; a tetracycline, a fluoroquinolone, or trimethoprim-sulfamethoxazole may then be given with clearly written instructions on indications, dosage, and possible side effects. Salt tablets may be useful in hot, humid climates.

Particularly useful drugs such as antimalarials and antidiarrheals, water purification materials, insect repellents, and sunscreens will be discussed in detail in appropriate sections.

IMMUNIZATIONS

Required Immunizations

Only yellow fever vaccine is compulsory for entry into certain countries. Vaccination certificate requirements of various countries are listed in a Centers for Disease Control and Prevention (CDC) Publication, 1999–2000, DHHS, Atlanta, Ga, 1999 *Health Information for International Travel.*[1] This is revised yearly and is available from the Superintendent of Documents, U.S. Government Printing Office, Washington, DC 20402. The CDC, in Atlanta, has a FAX service for information on various aspects of travelers' health. Access is by dialing 1-888-232-3299 to obtain a listing of available documents in the Travelers' Health Directory. The CDC also has a website for travelers' health at http://www.cdc.gov/travel/travel.htm. The World Health Organization (WHO), in Geneva, also publishes a booklet each January, *International Travel and Health: Vaccination Requirements and Health Advice,*[2] which gives a country-by-country listing of the required yellow fever immunization and the malaria situation. This information is supplemented on a weekly basis by the WHO *Weekly Epidemiological Record.* Subscriptions for these publications may be ordered in the United States from the WHO Publications Center USA, 49 Sheridan Avenue, Albany, NY 12210. Because vaccination certificate requirements can change, physicians who are frequently required to advise travelers should subscribe to these publications. Advice is also available from local health departments and travel clinics.

International Certificates of Vaccination are individual certificates and cannot be used collectively. Thus, separate certificates must be issued for children; the information cannot be incorporated into the parent's certificate. Travelers who do not have required yellow fever vaccination on entering a country may be subject to vaccination, medical follow-up, and/or isolation, and in some countries they may be denied entry. The date of vaccination should be recorded on the certificate in the following sequence: day, month (spelled out), year. Certificates of children who cannot write must be signed by a parent. The origin and batch number of the vaccine and the validation stamp of the center where the vaccine was given must be recorded on the certificate.

Yellow Fever

Yellow fever occurs in parts of tropical Africa and South America. Immunization can be required both for protection against infection and for entry when traveling to countries in these regions. A valid yellow fever vaccination certificate may also be required for entry into other countries from all travelers coming from a yellow-fever–infected area or, in some cases, from a country in which any part is infected (e.g., travelers crossing tropical Africa en route to India or Pakistan). Children below age 1 year are usually exempt from these requirements, but vaccine can be given to children 9 months of age if they are traveling to or living in areas where yellow fever is officially reported. Single primary or booster doses are valid for 10 years beginning 10 days after primary vaccination or on the date of revaccination if within 10 years of first injection. Unlike other immunizations, yellow fever vaccine must be administered at a designated yellow fever vaccination center, the locations of which can be obtained from local health departments.

From 2 to 10% of vaccinees have mild headache, myalgias, low-grade fever, or other minor symptoms 5 to 10 days after vaccination. Yellow fever vaccine should not be administered to anyone with a documented hypersensitivity to eggs or with an altered immune state. These people, as well as children younger than 9 months and pregnant women who are not at risk for infection, should receive a letter of contraindication. Ideally, yellow fever vaccine should not be given to a known pregnant woman, but if she travels to an area in which there is any risk of infection, it should be administered.[1] See Table 315–1 for vaccine doses.

Cholera

Since 1988, the WHO has dropped the requirement for cholera vaccine, and International Certificates of Vaccination no longer have a special section for cholera vaccine. Cholera vaccine is not recommended for most travelers, as the available injectable inactivated vaccine is not very effective in preventing cholera. Local reactions may occur, but serious reactions are very rare. Travelers to areas of epidemic outbreaks of cholera, such as South America, should practice appropriate food and water hygiene rather than obtain a false sense of security from a vaccination.[1, 2] New oral cholera vaccines appear to be much more effective and well tolerated. These could prove useful for travelers to areas of epidemic and endemic cholera.[3]

TABLE 315–1 Doses of Commonly Used Vaccines for International Travel

Vaccine	Age	Dose	Booster
Yellow fever	>9 mo	0.5 ml	0.5 ml, q10yr
Polio			
OPV	Up to 18 yr	4 doses	1 dose*
EIPV	All ages	4 doses	1 dose*
Varicella	<13 yr	1 dose	None
	≥13 yr	2 doses	None
Tetanus-diphtheria	>7 yr	3 doses	q10yr
Measles	>15 mo	1 dose	1 dose (see ref. 1)
Typhoid			
Oral	>6 yr	4 caps	Same doses, q5yr
Injectable	>2 yr	0.5 ml	Same dose, q2yr
Rabies (preexposure)	All ages	1.0 ml	See ref. 1
Meningococcus	>2 yr	0.5 ml	See ref. 1
Japanese B encephalitis	1–3 yr	0.5 ml	Same doses, q3yr
	>3 yr	1.0 ml	
Plague	See ref. 1		
Immunoglobulin	Travel <3 mo:	>3 mo:	For long term, same doses as for >3 mo, repeat q4–6 mo
<23 kg	0.5 ml	1.0 ml	
23–45 kg	1.0 ml	2.5 ml	
<45 kg	2.0 ml	5.0 ml	
Hepatitis A	>2 yr	1 dose	1 dose 6–12 mo later
Hepatitis B Recombivax or Engerix-B	All ages	3 doses: 0, 1, and 6 mo	Need not known
Engerix-B accelerated		3 doses: days 0, 30, and 60	Dose 4 at 12 mo

*Give one dose to persons traveling to developing countries.
Abbreviations: EIPV, Enhanced potency, inactivated, injectable polio vaccine; im, intramuscular; OPV, oral polio vaccine.

Smallpox

The last reported case of endemic smallpox occurred in October 1977. The WHO has amended the International Health Regulations to remove smallpox from the diseases subject to the regulations. All countries have advised the WHO that a smallpox vaccination certificate is not required from any traveler. As the risk of contracting smallpox is virtually nil and because smallpox vaccine may rarely cause very serious or even fatal reactions, there is no justification for administering smallpox vaccine to any traveler.[4] The risk of vaccination clearly exceeds any benefit.

RECOMMENDED IMMUNIZATIONS

Although not required by international regulations, several other vaccines are recommended for protection against diseases more prevalent in certain areas of the world. For children, routine childhood vaccines should be up to date before traveling.

Poliomyelitis

In 1994, the Pan American Health Organization certified that non–vaccine-related poliovirus transmission no longer was occurring in the Americas. Polio remains a definite hazard to travelers to other parts of the developing world, and unprotected adults are particularly susceptible to paralytic complications. Many travelers have had the basic series of trivalent oral polio vaccine or inactivated polio vaccine. A single booster dose of the oral or inactivated vaccine is recommended in this situation before traveling to areas of increased polio risk. The need for further supplementary booster doses has not been established. Those who have been unvaccinated or partially vaccinated should complete a polio vaccination series. Four doses of enhanced-potency inactivated polio vaccine are recommended for adults in the United States.[5] Sequential vaccination with two doses of enhanced-potency inactivated polio vaccine followed by two doses of oral polio vaccine is now recommended for children. Oral polio vaccine is still recommended for outbreaks of poliomyelitis. If less than 4 weeks are available before protection is needed for an unvaccinated person, a single dose of enhanced-potency inactivated polio vaccine is recommended. When time permits, the remaining doses can be administered.

Varicella

Vaccination should be considered for international travelers who do not have evidence of immunity to varicella virus, especially if the traveler expects to have close personal contact with local populations, as varicella is endemic in most countries. A single dose is given for children younger than 13 years of age. Two doses given 4 to 8 weeks apart are recommended for individuals 13 years of age and older.[6]

Tetanus-Diphtheria

Most travelers will have received the basic series with diphtheria, pertussis, and tetanus (DPT) during childhood, and boosters are recommended every 10 years to offer continued protection against tetanus and diphtheria. Tetanus and diphtheria toxoid (Td) is the vaccine of choice for children older than 7 years and adults, because it has only 10 to 20% of the amount of diphtheria toxoid present in standard DPT preparations and leads to fewer febrile reactions in those older than 7 years. In recent years there have been outbreaks of diphtheria in Russia and the new independent states of the former Soviet Union.[7] Travelers to these regions must be protected against this disease.

Measles

Persons born in or after 1957 who travel abroad should be protected against measles, which is endemic in many parts of the world. Adults born in the United States before 1957 are considered immune because measles was endemic here as well. Consideration should be given to providing one dose of measles vaccine to persons who have not previously received two doses of measles vaccine and who do not have a history of measles.[8] Measles immunity is particularly important for adults, who have greater probability of serious complications and death. Vaccination is contraindicated in pregnant women and persons with immune deficiency. If indicated, patients with acquired immunodeficiency syndrome (AIDS) may be vaccinated. In the United States, children are routinely vaccinated against measles, usually the measles-mumps-rubella (MMR) vaccine, at age 15 months. The risk of contracting measles is much greater in the developing world than in the United States, and the age of vaccination should be lowered to 6 months for younger children traveling to measles endemic or epidemic areas. A dose of single-antigen measles or MMR vaccine should be given, and children who have received this dose should then be revaccinated with an additional dose of MMR vaccine at age 12 to 15 months and at entry into school.

Typhoid

Typhoid fever is endemic in much of the developing world, and typhoid vaccine is recommended for travelers to areas in which it is difficult to follow good water and food hygiene. Certainly, travelers to typhoid epidemic areas and those traveling overland to remote areas should receive this vaccine. Both an oral live attenuated Ty21a strain vaccine and a parenteral inactivated vaccine are available.[9] The oral vaccine is taken as four separate doses, one every other day, and gives protection for 5 years, after which reimmunization is indicated for those still at risk for typhoid infection.[10] This vaccine is about 70% protective and is very well tolerated. A parenteral capsular polysaccharide Vi-antigen vaccine is also available. A single dose offers approximately 70% protection and is of particular value for persons who must travel immediately and have not previously received a basic typhoid vaccine series.

Rabies

Relatively few countries can be considered rabies free. Preexposure vaccination is recommended for high-risk groups for possible rabies exposure in rabies endemic areas, in which the disease is a constant threat. These might include young children, joggers, veterinarians, animal handlers, field workers, and persons in remote areas who are distant from facilities in which postexposure treatment can be obtained.[11] Although adequate preexposure vaccination offers very valuable added protection when rabies exposure occurs, it does not eliminate the need for additional vaccine therapy. It does eliminate the need for human rabies immune globulin, which is often difficult to obtain. Preexposure recommendations call for a series of three 1-ml intramuscular (administered over the deltoid) doses of human diploid cell vaccine (HDCV) or the new purified chick embryo cell cultures (PCEC) vaccine[12] on days 0, 7, and 21 or 28. Local reactions such as redness, pain, and itching are common. Systemic effects may also occur, and allergic reactions and neurologic complications have been very rarely reported with the HDCV vaccine.[13] Hypersensitivity reactions from booster doses of PCEC vaccine appear to be less common than with HDCV vaccine.[12]

Meningococcal Meningitis

Meningococcal disease is endemic throughout the world. In the sub-Saharan Sahel region of Africa, epidemics of *Neisseria meningitidis* serogroups A and C infection occur almost yearly in the winter and early spring months.[14] Although meningitis is extremely uncommon in travelers or resident expatriates to these areas, even in epidemic situations, vaccination is often a more reasonable protective measure than drug prophylaxis.[15] A quadrivalent A/C/Y/W135 vaccine is available. A single dose in the volume indicated by the manufacturer is administered. The duration of immunity is unknown but appears to be at least 3 years in those 4 years of age or older. Serogroup A vaccine has not been shown to be effective in children younger than 3 months and may be less than fully effective in children 3 to 11 months. Serogroup C vaccine is not considered efficacious in children younger than 2 years. Adverse reactions, consisting of localized erythema for 1 to 2 days, are uncommon. Although not proven to be dangerous to pregnant women, it is prudent not to use this vaccine unless there is a substantial risk of infection. Saudi Arabia requires proof of immunization for meningococcal meningitis from all visa applicants. Outbreaks of meningococcal meningitis due to serogroup B also occur, but there is currently no available vaccine against this serogroup.

RARELY INDICATED IMMUNIZATIONS

Certain vaccines are indicated only for very particular situations or for travel to specific remote locations.

Japanese B Encephalitis

Rare cases of Japanese B encephalitis have occurred in resident expatriates in certain endemic areas of the Far East and Southeast Asia. The risk to short-term travelers to urban areas is quite low. Persons who will travel or reside in rural agricultural areas of that have high rates of infection countries are at greater risk.[16, 17] A three-dose series of injections is necessary, on days 0, 7, and 30. A booster dose should be given after 3 years for those at continued risk. The vaccine is manufactured in Japan and is marketed in the United States and other countries. It is recommended that, in general, vaccine should be offered to persons spending a month or longer in endemic areas during the transmission season, especially if travel includes rural areas. Certain circumstances may also make the vaccine indicated for travelers spending less than 30 days in an endemic area in which there is epidemic transmission in the specific area to be visited and those camping or hiking in rural areas. Japanese encephalitis vaccine is associated with a moderate frequency of local and mild systemic adverse effects. More serious adverse reactions have occurred, characterized by urticaria, angioedema, itching, and, rarely, respiratory distress. Studies among U.S. citizens receiving the Japanese encephalitis vaccine have given rates of these reactions of up to 6/1000 recipients.[16] The reactions may have a delayed onset of hours to as long as 2 weeks, and it is recommended that the last dose be administered at least 10 days before travel. The vaccine constituents and the immunologic mechanism of these reactions have not yet been defined. Whether or not the vaccine is taken, the conscientious use of precautions against insects should be followed, as described later under "Insects."

Plague

Plague vaccination is not required for entry into any country and is recommended only for plague-infected areas. Plague is sporadically reported from the former Indochina area of Southeast Asia and Burma and in remote areas of enzootic plague in Asia, South America, and Africa. Vaccination is not indicated for most travelers to countries reporting cases, particularly if their travel is limited to urban areas with modern accommodations. Selected people engaged in field work in plague-enzootic or plague-epidemic rural areas might benefit from vaccination.[18] Plague vaccine is not effective against pneumonic plague; a series of doses and periodic booster doses are required to maintain immunity; and reactions occur frequently.

Typhus

No epidemic typhus cases have been reported in U.S. travelers since 1950. Production of typhus vaccine has been discontinued in the United States, and the vaccine is no longer available or recommended.

Influenza and Pneumococcus

Those considered at high risk for contracting influenza and traveling to parts of the world in which influenza is epidemic should receive influenza vaccine. The pneumococcal capsular polysaccharide vaccine is recommended for the prevention of pneumococcal infection only in high-risk patients. These two vaccines can be given simultaneously, with no decrease in effectiveness or increases in adverse reactions.[19]

Calmette-Guérin Bacillus

Tuberculosis is a potential hazard to visitors to the developing world, and Calmette-Guérin bacillus (BCG) is sometimes recommended for travelers to highly endemic areas. However, its use in this situation remains controversial, and the weight of expert opinion is presently against its use. The troublesome side effects of BCG, the questionable efficacy of certain batches, and the possible loss of skin test sensitivity lead the majority of workers to rely on skin test screening and treatment of the relatively few people infected.[20]

Tick-Borne Encephalitis

Tick-borne encephalitis is a viral infection of the central nervous system occurring in forested areas of central and eastern Europe and Russia. No tick-borne encephalitis vaccine is approved for use in the United States, but an effective vaccine may be obtained in Europe.[21] Present data do not support a recommendation for its routine use in travelers to endemic countries, but it can be considered in certain longer-term travelers or residents with exposure risk in forested areas of countries in which the disease is endemic.[22]

HEPATITIS PREVENTION

Hepatitis A is the most common type of hepatitis contracted by unprotected travelers to areas of endemicity.[23] Two hepatitis A vaccines are now available in the United States. Havrix (SmithKline Beecham, Philadelphia, Pa.) was approved in 1995 and Vaqta (Merck, West Point, Pa.) became available in 1996. Havrix is marketed in a 1440-unit formulation for adults and a 720-unit formulation for children and adolescents 2 to 18 years of age. Vaqta is supplied as a dose of 50 units/ml for adults and as a dose of 25 units/0.5 ml for children and adolescents 2 to 17 years of age. Following administration of an initial single dose of either vaccine, protective immunity can be assumed to be present by 4 weeks. Because protection may not be complete until 4 weeks after vaccination, persons traveling to a high-risk area less than 4 weeks after administration of the initial dose should receive an injection of immune globulin (0.02 mU/kg) at a different site. A second booster dose of hepatitis A vaccine, given 6 to 12 months after the initial dose, is expected to give long-term protection (possibly for ~20 years). Immune globulin is an alternative protective measure and can be used in children younger than 2 years of age. It is very uncommon for a traveler or long-term resident to develop symptomatic hepatitis A when the appropriate dose of immune globulin is taken. Persons undertaking short-term travel (<3 months) will be protected by a single intramuscular dose (0.02 mU/kg). Persons undertaking travel for longer periods, as well as residents, should receive an intramuscular dose of 0.06 mU/kg at 4-month to no more than 6-month intervals. No transmission of hepatitis B virus, human immunodeficiency virus (HIV), hepatitis C virus, or other viruses have been reported with the use of intramuscular immune globulin. Immune globulin is not protective against hepatitis types B, C, and E.[24]

Hepatitis B is more prevalent in the developing world and is transmitted through intimate contact with contaminated blood or body secretions. Travelers who might have close contact with blood or sexual contact with local residents should consider taking the hepatitis B vaccine series. Two recombinant vaccines are available in the United States, Recombivax HB and Engerix-B. Both can be given in a three-dose series, with doses 1 and 2 given 1 month apart and dose 3 given 6 months after dose 1. An accelerated course of 3 monthly doses is approved only for Engerix-B; with this regimen, a fourth booster dose is necessary 12 months after dose 1 to ensure immunity. Hepatitis B vaccine is safe and effective, but major inhibitions to wider use in travelers are its relatively high cost and extended course of doses. For children and adults whose immune status is normal, booster doses of vaccines are not recommended, nor is serologic testing to assess antibody levels necessary.[1, 25]

VACCINATION DURING PREGNANCY

Pregnancy is a theoretical contraindication to all live virus vaccines. However, if there is a substantial risk of exposure to natural infection with polio and yellow fever, vaccines should be administered. If there is no risk of yellow fever, it is best to give a letter of contraindication. Pregnancy and breast-feeding are not contraindications to administration of immune globulin, toxoid vaccines, or killed or inactivated vaccines.[1]

GENERAL VACCINE RECOMMENDATIONS

People who have anaphylactic reactions to avian products should not receive vaccines containing egg products.

Some vaccines contain preservatives or trace amounts of antibiotics, such as neomycin or streptomycin, to which certain people may be hypersensitive. Vaccine label information should be reviewed with this in mind before deciding whether these vaccines should be administered to those with known hypersensitivity to these products.

An inactivated and a live attenuated virus vaccine can be administered simultaneously at separate sites.

Adults with HIV infection or other immunosuppressed states have reduced response rates to immunization. However, immunization with most travel-related vaccines is considered indicated, the exceptions being live vaccines, including oral polio, varicella, oral typhoid, and yellow fever.[26]

Vaccination of people with a severe febrile illness should generally be deferred until recovery. Minor illnesses, such as upper respiratory tract infections, do not necessarily preclude vaccination.

Vaccines for routine preventable diseases in childhood (measles, mumps, rubella, polio, diphtheria, tetanus, pertussis, varicella, and *Haemophilus influenzae* type B meningitis) should be administered to children going abroad according to recommended schedules for the United States.

ADVICE WHILE TRAVELING

General Advice

Flying. Because long distance travel today is almost always by air, the traveler must be prepared for the effects of jet lag, which are due to disturbance in circadian body rhythm. The average traveler requires about 1 day to readjust for every 1 or 2 hours of time change. Mild sedatives may be required to assist sleeping on the first night or two after arrival at the destination. Motion sickness may be prevented by agents such as dimenhydrinate (Dramamine) or meclizine (Bonine). A small plastic disk for continuous administration of scopolamine (Transderm-Scōp) through the skin is available for treatment of motion sickness, but it takes several hours or longer to be effective and can cause dry mouth and drowsiness.[27] Moderation in the intake of alcoholic and carbonated beverages and avoidance of excessive food intake lead to a more comfortable trip. Prolonged sitting should be avoided because this can lead to postural hypotension, abdominal distention, or venous stasis. The last can predispose to pulmonary embolization.[28] It is therefore essential for the traveler to walk about the plane periodically. If flying is necessary with a cold, nasal decongestants should be used.

Acclimatization. Going to high altitudes requires time for acclimatization, and it is best to avoid alcoholic beverages, tobacco, excessive food, and exercise; take more frequent rests for the first few days at altitude; and increase water intake. Acetazolamide (Diamox) can be taken on the day of ascent and continued for 2 days after arrival at altitude to treat altitude-related problems.[29]

Water. A great hazard to the traveler to the developing world is contaminated water and ice. Unless it is absolutely certain that piped water is potable or that the water in a major chain hotel is safe, it is necessary to boil water for 3 minutes or to treat all water chemically for drinking or making ice. Iodine compounds such as Potable Aqua tablets, 2% iodine tincture or Lugol's solution, or liquid chlorine bleach are satisfactory under most conditions but may be less effective in cloudy or very cold water, and an increased amount of disinfectant or contact time may be required.[30] Various personal water purification devices containing microfilters and iodine resins are available and are very effective.[31] Hot water from the tap, although relatively safer than cold water, may still contain dangerous organisms and cannot be considered completely safe for drinking or for brushing teeth. It is possible for community-treated water to be coliform free but yet capable of transmitting protozoa such as *Giardia lamblia* or *Cryptosporidium* spp. Bottled commercial water is generally safer than untreated tap water, but this water is occasionally contaminated also.

Food and Beverages. If well-cooked hot foods are eaten, most foodborne infections can be avoided. Cold foods and salads are much more easily contaminated by infected food handlers or may be prepared with contaminated water. Raw fruits should be eaten only when they have an unbroken skin and are peeled by the eater. Raw vegetables and green salads are often contaminated with bacteria, protozoan cysts, and helminth eggs from night soil used as fertilizer or from contaminated water used in growing or in preparation. Scrubbing green leafy vegetables with a detergent solution and then soaking them in strong iodine or chlorine solutions can eliminate most but not all organisms. Dairy products should be eaten only if they are known to be prepared hygienically and properly refrigerated. Custards, cream pastries, salads made with mayonnaise, and raw or poorly cooked shellfish should be avoided, because these are excellent vehicles for propagation of pathogenic organisms. Eating raw or undercooked local beef, pork, sausage, or fish can lead to trichinosis, tapeworms, or fluke infections. Smoking, salting, pickling, or drying meat or fish alone is not effective, but heating these to at least 55°C for 1 hour or freezing at −10°C for 20 days will kill infective stage parasites. Ciguatera and scombroid fish poisoning and shellfish poisoning may occur from eating apparently normal large marine fishes and shellfish in tropical areas and occasionally in temperate areas.[32, 33] When fresh fruits and vegetables cannot be obtained or eaten, multivitamins should be taken.

Iced drinks, juices mixed with water, and noncarbonated bottled fluids should be avoided. Canned or bottled name-brand carbonated beverages are usually safe, as are coffee and tea made with boiled water and hot milk, beer, and wine.

Sunstroke and Heat Exhaustion. These can be avoided by abstaining from prolonged exposure to the sun or overly strenuous exercises. It is important to drink more salt-containing solutions and to add salt to food. Protection against a strong sun can be obtained by applying a broad-spectrum sunscreen (against both ultraviolet A and B) to the skin 30 to 60 minutes before sun exposure. Water-resistant preparations are available, and sunscreens with a higher sun protective factor (SPF), approximately 15, offer a longer period of protection.[34] Sunscreen should be reapplied every 1 to 3 hours and after swimming or sweating.

Insects. Mosquitoes, in particular, are carriers of important infectious diseases, including malaria, Japanese encephalitis, dengue fever, and yellow fever. All residence windows and doors should be well screened. Beds should be covered with mosquito nets, preferably impregnated with permethrin repellent. Exposed parts of the body should be protected by applying insect repellents containing diethyltoluamide (DEET) in a 20 to 35% concentration.[35] A pyrethrin-containing flying insect spray should be used in living areas. Long sleeve shirts and pants impregnated or sprayed with permethrin help to protect against bites of disease-carrying ticks when in vegetated areas.[36]

Snakes. Snakes are usually nocturnal in their habits and will generally bite during the day only if they are attacked or surprised. When walking in areas in which snakes are commonly found, boots with long trousers tucked into them should be worn. When going into remote areas, a snakebite kit containing antivenom against local snakes or scorpions should be taken along.

Schistosomiasis and Other Waterborne Organisms. Where schistosomiasis occurs, in parts of Africa, the Middle East, South America, and the Caribbean, all bodies of fresh water must be considered to be infected with these parasites, and contact with this water must be avoided. However, these parasites cannot be contracted in salt water or adequately chlorinated swimming pools. Some attractive bathing beaches, particularly in urban areas, may be highly polluted. Corals, jelly fish, and other biting and stinging aquatic creatures are a hazard to bathers.[37, 38]

Sleeping Sickness. Only a handful of cases of sleeping sickness have occurred in U.S. travelers, and most of these have been contracted in the game parks of East Africa and northern Botswana.[39] Drug prophylaxis with pentamidine injections is not recommended, but wearing long sleeves and trousers and using insect repellent may decrease the risk of bites from the tsetse fly vector.

Malaria Prophylaxis

One of the greatest risks to travelers in many parts of the developing world is malaria, and appropriate prophylactic drugs must always be taken and mosquito protection measures used when going to an area in which malaria transmission occurs. Country-by-country guides to the need for malaria prophylaxis and specific areas of chloroquine-resistant falciparum malaria are published by the CDC[1] and the WHO.[2]

Chloroquine-resistant *Plasmodium falciparum* malaria occurs in most of tropical Africa, Southeast Asia, Oceania, the para-Amazon region of South America, and South Asia.[40] The continued extension of chloroquine-resistant *P. falciparum* and the development of resistance against other antimalarials have reduced the number of effective drugs for malaria prophylaxis. Also, some alternative drugs to chloroquine have been associated with serious side effects, which limits their usefulness. Guidelines for prophylaxis must consider the exposure risk to malaria, the safety and effectiveness of available antimalarial drugs, and the use of personal protective measures (see "Insects").

Recommendations for the prevention of malaria must be revised periodically because of the geographic spread of parasite resistance to various drugs, new information on the efficacy and safety of prophylactic drugs, and the availability of new drugs. At this time, there is no available drug or combination of drugs with proven efficacy or safety to prevent all malaria infections. A variety of recommendations made in different countries has resulted, which has led to confusion. The following recommendations are considered most appropriate at the present time, as offering the best combinations of safety and relative effectiveness. It must also be emphasized to travelers that regardless of the methods employed, malaria can still be contracted. Those who have symptoms of malaria must seek prompt medical attention. (See also Chapter 264 for a discussion of prophylaxis.)

For areas with chloroquine-sensitive malaria species (Haiti, Dominican Republic, Central America, and parts of the Middle East), the drug of choice is chloroquine (Aralen). This is taken in an adult dose of 300 mg of base (equal to 500 mg of salt) once weekly, beginning 2 weeks before departure to ensure tolerance, regularly while in the malarious area, and for 4 weeks after leaving. For young children, the dose is 5 mg/kg of base weekly. Liquid chloroquine preparations are available overseas but not in the United States. Although minor side effects are common, marked intolerance is unusual. Chloroquine is considered safe for infants and pregnant women.[41] Serious eye damage has not been confirmed in those taking the recommended dose for malaria prophylaxis.[42] Only rarely should malaria develop in those taking regular suppressive chloroquine in areas in which resistance to it does not occur; most malaria infections occur in those who have either not taken any suppressive medicine, have taken it irregularly, or have ceased taking it prematurely on leaving the malarious area. It should be emphasized that all malaria prophylactic drugs must be continued for 4 weeks after the last malaria exposure.

For malarious areas with chloroquine-resistant *P. falciparum,* the most effective prophylactic drug in most situations is mefloquine (Lariam) in an adult dose of 250 mg weekly beginning 2 to 3 weeks before travel. Comparative studies indicate that mefloquine's adverse effects are similar in frequency and quality to those seen with other antimalarial drugs.[40] Reported adverse effects include insomnia, bad dreams, dizziness, headache, irritability, and gastrointestinal symptoms. More serious neuropsychiatric reactions, including toxic psychosis and seizures, occur in approximately one of every 10,000 users.[43] A study of long-term mefloquine use in Peace Corps volunteers in Africa showed this drug to be well tolerated.[44] With higher doses of mefloquine used for treatment of malaria, the frequency of these more severe reactions is in the order of 1/1000. Mefloquine is not recommended for self-treatment of malaria. Mefloquine is contraindicated in those with a psychiatric or epileptic history. It should not be used by those with cardiac conduction disturbances. Available data indicate that mefloquine is well tolerated in children of all ages including those weighing less than 15 kg. It also appears to be safe in all stages of pregnancy.[1, 40]

For those unable to tolerate mefloquine or who have a contraindication, doxycycline, 100 mg daily, can be recommended.[45] Some areas have multidrug resistance, including resistance to mefloquine. These include border areas of Thailand and in Cambodia. In these situations doxycycline is presently the drug of choice. Doxycycline cannot be used by pregnant women or children younger than 8 years. It may also cause photosensitivity, gastrointestinal effects, and moniliasis.[43]

In chloroquine-resistant *P. falciparum* areas in which mefloquine and doxycycline cannot be used, the addition of daily proguanil (Paludrine) in an adult dose of 200 mg daily (reduced dosages for children) can be added to weekly chloroquine.[40, 43] This combination has proved to be effective only in tropical Africa but to a lesser extent than mefloquine or doxycycline. Except for the occurrence of mouth ulcers and gastrointestinal symptoms, proguanil is a safe drug. It can be used in pregnancy. Proguanil is not licensed in the United States but is widely available in Europe and in tropical Africa. Travelers using chloroquine plus proguanil should carry Fansidar for self-treatment with this combination,[1, 40] if medical attention is not available when a malaria breakthrough occurs.

Amodiaquine and pyrimethamine plus dapsone (Maloprim) are available abroad and are recommended by some experts. Neither is available in the United States. Both have been associated with bone marrow toxicity and are not recommended.[46, 47] Fansidar is not recommended for prophylaxis because of a high incidence of fatal Stevens-Johnson syndrome associated with its use as a prophylactic.[48]

Newer antimalarial prophylactic regimens under evaluation include daily primaquine[49] and a daily combination of atovaquone plus proguanil (Malarone).[50]

To prevent potentially later relapsing malaria from persisting liver forms of *Plasmodium vivax* and *Plasmodium ovale,* which can occur for up to 3 years after leaving most malarious areas, primaquine can be considered. This possibility is particularly important to consider for those who have prolonged exposure in malarious areas. The drug is taken after the conclusion of terminal suppressive therapy with chloroquine and/or other drugs. The dose of primaquine is 15 mg of base daily for 14 days (0.3 mg of base/kg/day, not to exceed 15 mg, in young children). As primaquine may cause severe hemolysis in glucose-6-phosphate dehydrogenase deficiency, this deficiency must be ruled out before using primaquine.[51] Primaquine is not recommended in pregnancy. In recent years, resistance to chloroquine and standard doses of primaquine has been seen in *P. vivax* cases. This is particularly common in Papua New Guinea, Indonesia, and the Solomon Islands but has also been reported in parts of Southeast Asia, India, Latin America, and Somalia.[52, 53]

Traveler's Diarrhea

Some of the diarrheas that affect travelers during or shortly after their trip may be noninfectious and self-limited, related to eating strange foods, nervous tension, fatigue, altitude, or other factors. Acute viral infections, caused mainly by rotavirus and Norwalk agent, are other common causes of undiagnosed diarrhea. Enterotoxigenic *Escherichia coli* is the leading cause of traveler's diarrhea, causing more cases than all other infective agents combined. *Campylobacter* infections may cause more diarrhea in travelers than *Shigella* and *Salmonella* infections combined. Amebiasis and giardiasis are less likely causes of acute traveler's diarrhea and more commonly present following return.[54]

The most important factor in treating any diarrhea is the replacement of lost fluids by drinking water, tea, broth, and carbonated beverages. Electrolyte replacement is also important, and commercial oral rehydration solutions can be mixed with a liter of potable water to prepare a satisfactory replacement fluid.[55] Bananas and oranges are a good source of potassium. The accompanying diet should be bland, with particular avoidance of alcohol and fats.

Useful drugs to relieve excessive diarrhea or cramps include loperamide (Imodium) and diphenoxylate (Lomotil). These drugs are not recommended for young children and should be stopped if diarrhea becomes intractable after 2 days, if blood or mucus occurs in the stool, or if there is fever, chills, or severe cramps. A physician must then be contacted for appropriate diagnosis and treatment. Bismuth subsalicylate liquid (Pepto-Bismol), taken in a dose of 30 ml every half hour until eight doses are taken, has been shown to have a favorable effect on the course of diarrhea caused by enterotoxigenic *E. coli.*[56] Antibiotics are usually not required with acute watery diarrheas, which are usually self-limited with supportive treatment. If it is important to shorten the course or decrease the severity of moderate to severe traveler's diarrhea, antimicrobial agents may be taken. After three or more loose stools with symptoms, consideration can be given to a short course of a fluoroquinolone or trimethoprim-sulfamethoxazole plus loperamide.[55]

Preventive measures for traveler's diarrhea include food and beverage hygiene, use of nonantimicrobial medications, and prophylactic antimicrobial drugs. Meticulous attention to food and beverage preparation can decrease the likelihood of developing traveler's diarrhea, but this is admittedly difficult to accomplish. No specific vaccines are available to prevent traveler's diarrhea caused by enterotoxigenic *E. coli.* The only nonantimicrobial agent found useful in preventing traveler's diarrhea is bismuth subsalicylate; the dosage of two tablets four times daily (2.4 g/day) appears to be a safe and effective means of reducing by about 65% the occurrence of traveler's diarrhea among persons at risk for periods of up to 3 weeks.[57] On the basis of apparent risk/benefit ratios, prophylactic antimicrobial agents are not recommended for travelers.[58] Some travelers may wish to consult with their physician and may elect to use prophylactic antimicrobial agents for travel under special circumstances once the risks and benefits are clearly understood.[55] The use of halogenated hydroxyquinolone derivatives (e.g., Enterovioform, Mexaform, clioquinol, and others) as a prophylactic is not recommended, because these drugs have never been proven to be effective for this purpose and their use has been associated with a syndrome of subacute myelo-optic neuropathy.[59] Enterovioform has been removed from the U.S. market, but it and related drugs are still available over the counter in some foreign countries.

ADVICE ON RETURN FROM TRAVEL

Even though apparently healthy, the traveler returning from exotic parts of the world should have certain routine screening procedures performed for exotic infections. These include a urinalysis, liver function tests, tuberculosis skin test or chest radiographic examination, and a complete blood cell count for evidence of anemia, leucocytosis, leukopenia, or eosinophilia. The last is an indicator of possible intestinal or systemic helminthic infection and seldom indicates protozoal infections. A series of three stool tests should be carried out, including direct saline and iodine smears, concentration examination, and a stained slide examination. Stool specimens should be collected in a preservative, such as merthiolate formalin (MF), formalin, or polyvinyl-alcohol (PVA). In interpreting a negative stool result, it must be remembered that many preparations can cause a transient disappearance of parasites from the stool or can interfere with their recognition. These include antibiotics, sulfa drugs, antacids, kaolin products, barium, most enema products, and oily laxatives. It is necessary to wait for at least a week after a course of antibiotics and for at least 3 to 4 days after the use of other products, particularly when searching for protozoal parasites. A single negative stool is not sufficient to rule out parasitic infection, but three adequately performed negative examinations carried out on alternate days indicate approximately 70% certainty of the absence of infection. In certain clinically suggested protozoal infections without parasitologic proof from stool examinations, empirical treatment should be considered.

In the febrile returnee, leading considerations are malaria, enteric fever, dengue fever, hepatitis, and amebic liver abscess. Returnees with significant eosinophilia and a possible exposure history for helminths should be evaluated for infections such as filariasis, schistosomiasis, strongyloidiasis, and other intestinal helminths. When there is a history of possible exposure, serologic screening tests are available for certain parasitic infections; those for schistosomiasis, strongyloidiasis, and amebiasis are particularly useful. Serologic testing may not be routinely available but can be obtained through some state health laboratories or at the CDC.

As certain exotic infections, including malaria, hepatitis, schistosomiasis, and intestinal parasites, may manifest themselves months or, rarely, years after the traveler's return, it is necessary for both the traveler and his or her physician to consider the possible relationship of the symptoms to earlier travel.[60]

REFERENCES

1. Centers for Disease Control and Prevention. Health Information for International Travel, 1999–2000. Atlanta, Ga: Department of Health and Human Services; 1999.
2. World Health Organization. International Travel and Health, Vaccination Requirements, and Health Advice 1999. Geneva: World Health Organization; 1999.
3. Levine MM. Oral vaccines against cholera: Lessons from Vietnam and elsewhere. Lancet. 1997;349:220.
4. Centers for Disease Control and Prevention. Vaccinia (smallpox) vaccine. MMWR Morb Mortal Wkly Rep. 1991;40(RR-14):1–10.
5. Centers for Disease Control and Prevention. Poliomyelitis prevention in the United States: Introduction of a sequential vaccination schedule of inactivated poliovirus vaccine followed by oral poliovirus vaccine. MMWR Morb Mortal Wkly Rep. 1996;46(No. RR-3).
6. Centers for Disease Control and Prevention. Prevention of varicella. MMWR Morb Mortal Wkly Rep. 1996;45(No. RR-11).
7. Centers for Disease Control and Prevention. Diphtheria acquired by U.S. citizens in the Russian Federation and Ukraine—1994. MMWR Morb Mortal Wkly Rep. 1995;44:237–244.
8. Hill DR, Pearson RD. Measles prophylaxis for international travel. Ann Intern Med. 1989;111:699–701.
9. Bennish ML. Immunization against *Salmonella typhi.* Infect Dis Clin Pract. 1995;4:114–122.
10. Cryz SJ. Post-marketing experience with live Ty 21a vaccine. Lancet. 1993;341:49–50.
11. Centers for Disease Control and Prevention. Human rabies prevention—United States—1999. MMWR Morb Mortal Wkly Rep. 1999;48(RR-1).
12. Centers for Disease Control and Prevention. Availability of new rabies vaccine for human use. MMWR Morb Mortal Wkly Rep. 1998;47:12–19.
13. Dreesen DW, Bernard KW, Parker RA, et al. Immune complex–like disease in 23 persons following a booster dose of rabies human diploid cell vaccine. Vaccine. 1986;4:45–49.
14. Centers for Disease Control and Prevention. Control and prevention of meningococcal disease. MMWR Morb Mortal Wkly Rep. 1997;46(No. RR-5).
15. Koch S, Steffen R. Meningococcal disease in travelers: Vaccination recommendations. J Travel Med. 1994;1:4–7.
16. Centers for Disease Control and Prevention. Inactivated Japanese encephalitis virus vaccine. MMWR Morb Mortal Wkly Rep. 1993;42(No. RR-1).
17. Thisyakorn U, Thisyakorn C, Wilde H. Japanese encephalitis and international travel. J Travel Med. 1995;2:37–40.
18. Wolfe MS, Tuazon C, Schultz R. Imported bubonic plague—District of Columbia. MMWR Morb Mortal Wkly Rep. 1990;39:895–901.
19. Centers for Disease Control. Prevention and control of influenza. MMWR Morb Mortal Wkly Rep. 1999;48(RR-4).
20. Centers for Disease Control and Prevention. The role of BCG vaccine in the prevention and control of tuberculosis in the United States. MMWR Morb Mortal Wkly Rep. 1996;45(No. RR-4).
21. Barrett PN, Donner F. Tick-borne encephalitis vaccine. In: Plotkin SA, Mortimer EA Jr, eds. Vaccines. 2nd ed. Philadelphia: WB Saunders; 1994:715–727.
22. McNeil JG, Lednar WM, Stansfield SK, et al. Central European tick-borne encephalitis: Assessment of risk for persons in the armed forces and vacationers. J Infect Dis. 1985;152:650–651.
23. Wolfe MS. Hepatitis A and the American traveler. J Infect Dis. 1995;171(Suppl 1):S29–S32.
24. Centers for Disease Control and Prevention. Prevention of Hepatitis A through active or passive immunization. MMWR Morb Mortal Wkly Rep. 1996;45(No. RR-15).
25. Tilzey AJ. Hepatitis B vaccine boosting: The debate continues. Lancet. 1995;345:1000.
26. Wilson M, von Reyn CF, Fineberg HV. Infections in HIV-infected travelers: Risks and prevention. Ann Int Med. 1991;114:582–592.
27. Bezruchka SA. Disequilibrium: Jet lag, motion sickness, and heat illness. In: Jong EC, McMullen R. The Travel and Tropical Medicine Manual. 2nd ed. Philadelphia: WB. Saunders; 1995:117–130.
28. Cruickshank HM, Gorlin R, Jennett B. Air travel and thrombotic episodes: The economy class syndrome. Lancet. 1988;2:497–498.
29. Bezruchka SA. High altitude medicine. Med Clin North Am. 1992;76:1481–1487.
30. Jarroll EL, Bingham AK, Meyer EA. *Giardia* cyst destruction: Effectiveness of six small-quantity water disinfection methods. Am J Trop Med Hyg. 1980;29:8–11.
31. Backer HD. Water disinfection. In: Jong EC, McMullen R. The Travel and Tropical Medicine Manual. 2nd ed. Philadelphia: WB Saunders, 1995;80–116.
32. Dembert ML. Common diseases of fish and shellfish ingestion: Hazards of overseas travel and an underseas appetite. Travel Med Int. 1988;6:1–9.
33. Lange WR, Snyder FR, Fudala PJ. Travel and ciguatera fish poisoning. Arch Intern Med. 1992;152:2049–2053.
34. Potts JF. Sunlight, sunburn, and sunscreen. Postgrad Med. 1990;87:52–63.
35. Fradin MS. Mosquitoes and mosquito repellants: A clinician's guide. Ann Intern Med. 1998;128:931–940.
36. Newman K. Strategies for outwitting insects. Travel Med Int. 1997;15:137–141.

37. Rosson CL, Tolle SW. Management of marine stings and scrapes. West J Med. 1989;150:97–100.
38. Wong DE, Meinking TL, Rosen LB, et al. Seabather's eruption: Clinical, histologic, and immunologic features. J Am Acad Dermatol. 1994;30:399–406.
39. Bryan RT, Waskin HA, Richards FO, et al. African trypanosomiasis in American travelers: A 20 year review. In: Steffen R, Lobel HO, Haworth J, et al., eds. Travel Medicine (Proceedings of the First Conference on International Travel Medicine, Zurich, Switzerland, 1988). Berlin: Springer-Verlag; 1989.
40. Lobel HO, Kozarsky PE. Update on prevention of malaria for travelers. JAMA. 1997;278:1767–1771.
41. Wolfe MS, Cordero JF. Safety of chloroquine in chemosuppression of malaria during pregnancy. BMJ. 1985;290:1466–1467.
42. Appleton B, Wolfe MS, Mishtowt GI. Chloroquine as a malarial suppressive: Absence of visual effects. Milit Med. 1973:138:225–226.
43. Bradley DJ, Warhurst DC. Guidelines for prevention of malaria in travelers from the United Kingdom. Commun Dis Rep CDC Rev. 1997;7:R137–152.
44. Lobel HO, Miani M, Eng T, et al. Long-term malaria prophylaxis with weekly mefloquine. Lancet. 1993;341:848–851.
45. Orht C, Richie TL, Widjaya H, et al. Mefloquine compared with doxycycline for the prophylaxis of malaria in Indonesian soldiers. Ann Intern Med. 1997;126:963–972.
46. Centers for Disease Control. Agranulocytosis associated with the use of amodiaquine for malaria prophylaxis. MMWR Morb Mortal Wkly Rep. 1986;35:165–166.
47. Bruce-Chwatt LJ, Hutchinson DBA. Maloprim and agranulocytosis. Lancet. 1983;2:1487–1488.
48. Miller KD, Lobel HO, Satriale RF, et al. Severe cutaneous reactions among American travelers using pyrimethamine-sulfadoxine (Fansidar) for malaria prophylaxis. Am J Trop Med Hyg. 1986;35:451–458.
49. Baird JK, Fryauff DJ, Basri H, et al. Primaquine for prophylaxis against malaria among nonimmune transmigrants in Irian Jaya, Indonesia. Am J Trop Med Hyg. 1995;52:479–484.
50. Lell B, Luckner D, Ndjavé M, et al. Randomised placebo-controlled study of atovaquone plus proguanil for malaria prophylaxis in children. Lancet. 1998;351:709–713.
51. Clyde DF. Clinical problems associated with the use of primaquine as a tissue schizonticidal and gametocytocidal drug. Bull World Health Organ. 1981;59:391–395.
52. Murphy GS, Basri H, Purnomo, et al. Vivax malaria resistant to treatment and prophylaxis with chloroquine. Lancet. 1993;341:96–100.
53. Smoak BL, DeFraites RF, Magill AJ, et al. *Plasmodium vivax* infections in U.S. Army troops: Failure of primaquine to prevent relapse in studies from Somalia. Am J Trop Med Hyg. 1997;56:231–234.
54. Wolfe MS. Acute diarrhea associated with travel. Am J Med. 1990;88(Suppl 6A):34S–37S.
55. Ericsson CD, DuPont HL. Travelers' diarrhea: Approaches to prevention and treatment. Clin Infect Dis. 1993;16:616–626.
56. Johnson PC, Ericsson CD, DuPont HL, et al. Comparison of loperamide with bismuth subsalicylate for treatment of acute travelers' diarrhea. JAMA. 1986;255:757–760.
57. DuPont HL, Ericsson CD, Johnson PC, et al. Prevention of travelers' diarrhea by the tablet formulation of bismuth subsalicylate. JAMA. 1987;257:1347–1350.
58. Gorbach SL, Edelman R, eds. Traveler's diarrhea: National Institutes of Health Consensus Development Conference. J Infect Dis. 1986;8:S109–S227.
59. Wolfe MS, Mishtowt GI. Enterovioform in travelers' diarrhea. JAMA. 1972;220:275–276.
60. Wolfe MS. Medical evaluation of the returning traveler. In: Jong EC, Keystone JS, eds. Travel Medicine Advisor. Atlanta, Ga: American Health Consultants; 1991:26.1–26.15.

SECTION H

MANAGED CARE

Chapter 316

Health Care Reform and the Specialist in Infectious Diseases

RICHARD P. WENZEL

The specialty of infectious diseases is young, and only in the second half of the 20th century has it clearly emerged from the parent field of internal medicine, in parallel with establishment of the antibiotic era. When to prescribe specific antibiotics, how long to treat, and what specific markers of improvement were the areas of interest of our professional society's founding fathers. Subspecialty training itself was initially an apprenticeship, but formal fellowship programs evolved coincident with the complexities of critical care and the emergence of new infections and treatment options. Since its inception, the Infectious Diseases Society of America continued to expand its membership, and our subspecialty journals flourished. The fee-for-service system for reimbursement of medical care was a critical factor that stimulated growth of the field of clinical infectious diseases.

Poised at the door to a new century with barely 60 years of antibiotic history, we specialists in infectious diseases face remarkable turbulence in our practices. The recognition of new infections is stunning, the rate of antibiotic resistance among common pathogens is staggering, and we are still disoriented by the evolving changes in the delivery system for health care. The specific question before us is "What is the impact of modern health care reform?"

To begin to address the question, it is important to understand the place of medicine in our society. Although it is tempting to view medicine as an independent segment or even a central part of society, such perceptions are flawed. The delivery of medical care is in fact a part of a much larger social fabric, and the changes we note in medicine directly follow the major social, economic, and ethical revolutions that have altered not only the delivery and financing of medical care but also the doctor-patient relationship. What we perceive as the newest medical revolution is popularly labeled "health care reform," and the term implies some constraints to access to medical care. This chapter focuses on recent revolutions and briefly reviews their impact on the specialist in infectious diseases.

THE SOCIAL REVOLUTION: MODERNITY TO THE POSTMODERN ERA

Coincident with the social revolution of modernity with its reliance and trust in science and technology was an expansive use of resources for medical care, a close doctor-patient relationship, and an ethical approach to patient care that focused almost exclusively on patient needs and preferences (Fig. 316–1). Subsequently, with the postmodern era of doubt about the value of science and technology, an increased emphasis was placed on cost containment and accountability, and the direct doctor-patient relationship was lost.[1–4] With societal issues considered more prominently, the relationship triangularized to involve the doctor, patient, and society. Even in ethical considerations, an enhanced role for the interest of society evolved, with less advocacy for the individual patient.

It should not be surprising that in the postmodern era, general respect for physicians has diminished and complementary ("alternative") medicine is being increasingly exploited. Untested remedies are being touted in lay journals, the news media, and the information web. Much of the information available undergoes no rigor of evaluation, and medicine is increasingly viewed as a commodity.[5, 6] This viewpoint is probably enhanced at a time when medicine is being subjected to changes related to market-based forces.

THE VIEW OF MEDICINE AS A COMMODITY

A commodity market such as the automobile sales market can be differentiated only on the basis of price. It matters little to a buyer of a Volvo if the sales agent is an automotive engineer, an experienced sales representative with no science background, or a young novice with 2 weeks of training. In the purchase of a new car, the prospective owner seeks the best "deal." If medicine were a pure commodity, imagine a patient with fever, headache, and a petechial rash presenting either to an experienced infectious diseases specialist, a primary care physician, a nurse practitioner, or a modern-day shaman. To most of us, the advantages of an infectious diseases specialist are obvious, and we may find alternative ideas ludicrous. However, in the current era of doubt and loss of trust in science, some "consumers" of medical care view the management of fever and rash as a simple commodity, and the least costly approach to illness may be seen as desirable and acceptable.

If this scenario were not serious enough, once a patient decides that medical care is needed, the immediate issue is access. In an era of market-based health care reform, access to an infectious diseases specialist is difficult even from Monday to Friday during daylight hours. The idea that a patient could navigate the health delivery system to a specialist at night or over the weekend seems questionable. One might ask, do the bureaucratic barriers to infectious diseases specialists imposed by managed care companies support the public's perception of medicine as a commodity? Have we as a society of specialists responded to such barriers to our patients with appropriate public education and efforts for reform? Simply stated, can our patients find us on Saturday night?

In observing the social and economic landscape in the United States, one concludes that infectious diseases specialists must seek to develop and maintain exceptional skills and the highest possible standards of care to distinguish us from those less well trained and able. We also need to show value-favorable outcome per dollar spent on care. All this relates to cost savings, quality of care, and accountability—critical investments for the infectious diseases specialist.

THE IMPERATIVE FOR VALUES-BASED LEADERSHIP

Other byproducts of the postmodern era and parallel market-based health delivery system are an emphasis on caring (increased doubt about cure) and an increasing popularity of complementary or alternative medicine. Some medical schools have responded with programs on alternative medicine, and the National Institutes of Health has sponsored such programs intramurally. The field of medical ethics has blossomed, and in a market-based era the opinions of

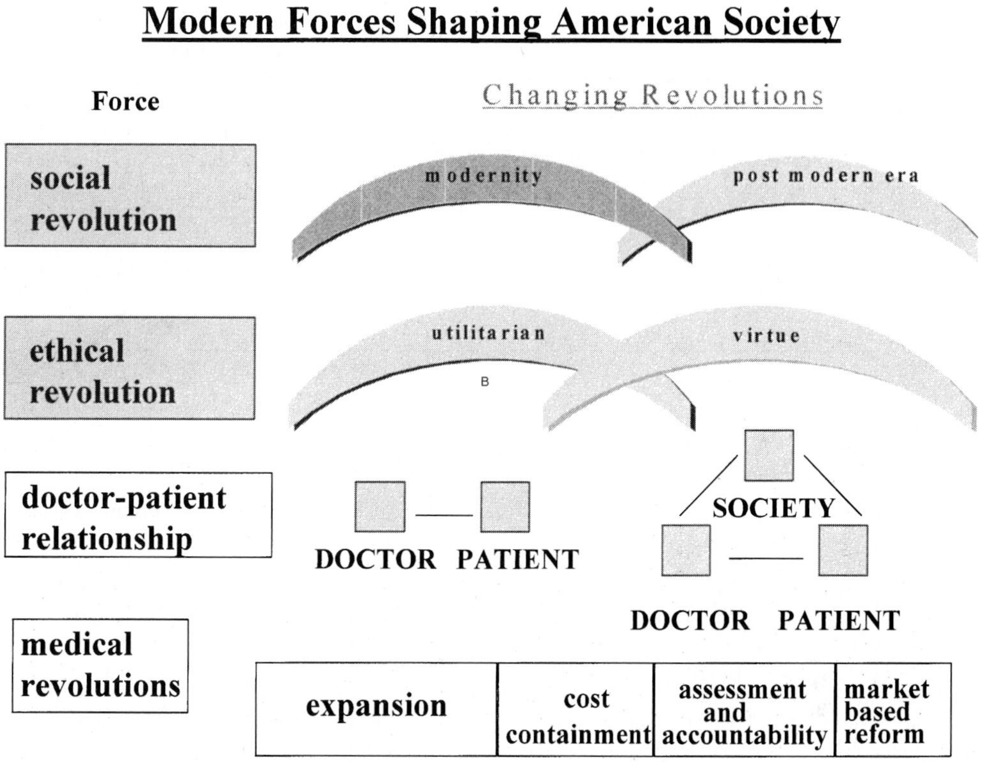

FIGURE 316–1. Various overlapping revolutions are shown to illustrate the concept that recent medical revolutions (after Relman A, N Engl J Med. 1990;319:1220–1222) are in fact occurring as part of underlying, larger, and more powerful social and ethical revolutions that also have affected the doctor-patient relationship.

bioethicists are sought on many issues by a society willing to pay thousands of dollars in honoraria for public statements. No longer is extending life the major focus. Instead, the quality of living and even the quality of dying have become important and often paramount, perhaps highlighted by the front-page news stories and debates on physician-assisted suicide.

Physicians in our discipline must be familiar with measures of quality of life and outcomes and have the ability to communicate therapeutic options to patients and their families. While performing those duties, individual practitioners of infectious diseases need to maintain the highest ethical standards possible. We need to regain the confidence and trust of our patients.[7] Specifically, our patient interaction should include the strict avoidance of financial conflicts of interest and a redoubled dedication to build an active partnership with our communities to solve unfair social and medical care inequities.

HEALTH MANAGEMENT ORGANIZATIONS

Managed care has saved money, primarily by imposing barriers to open and unfettered access to specialists, and the national cost of delivering medicine has declined. Health management organizations (HMOs) "manage" care and thus costs by requiring patients to meet established criteria before primary care physicians can refer them to specialists. However, patient dissatisfaction can be seen in repeated late-breaking news stories and analyses. Lack of physician choice, reduced access to specialists, increased out-of-pocket copayment by patients, and the need to go to court and sue the insurer to cover expensive procedures that were considered necessary are all cited as examples of disappointments and acute concerns. Although the market has cut costs, it has not clearly and favorably influenced access, quality, or outcomes. It nevertheless needs to be stated that many population-based studies have shown no *decrease* in outcomes of care related to HMOs.

In early 1998, increasing concerns about HMOs were fueled by newspaper reports about financial conflicts of interest by large insurers. Unfortunately, such ethical breeches of large administrative entities tarnish all of medicine, including the physicians who deliver health care. Current legislative responses have included mandates for minimal lengths of stay for specific diseases, clearly an incremental approach, yet no overriding plan for reform has surfaced. Because neither patients nor physicians have had much voice in the market-based health care era, it is likely that any meaningful change will have to come from more comprehensive legislative reform. However, optimism for the latter should be guarded because government and industry have accrued great savings under the market-based system and currently have no great incentive to change. Only when employees cry loudly to their employers or when citizens speak directly with their votes will we see sympathy for those distressed by the negative aspects of HMO care. The Infectious Diseases Society of America should seriously consider efforts to lobby legislators forcefully for patients' rights in seeking access to consultation of experts in infectious diseases.

NEW OPPORTUNITIES: QUALITY OF CARE AND THE INTEGRATED DELIVERY SYSTEM EPIDEMIOLOGIST

The opportunities afforded us in the current era involve a special need for clinical and epidemiologic studies in some areas and a need for special expertise and new services. With the "commoditization" of medicine, outcomes studies are needed to show specific areas of value of the infectious diseases specialist. Some examples of effective translation of science to patient care include the value of preoperative antibiotics, the timing of prophylactic antibiotics relative to the surgical incision, the relationship of surgical volume to outcome (incisional wound infection), the relationship of surgical experience to outcome, and others.[8] Clearly, we specialists have shown value. Similarly, with respect to complementary medicine it will be important to test the value of touted remedies with the same rigor and open-mindedness that we have developed for any new drug. There is no question that we have growth areas in our field (Table 316–1), but we may need to reexamine the way we are doing our day-to-day work. For example, today's hospital epidemiologists still have opportunities in infection control, but more opportunities exist in

TABLE 316-1 Growth Areas for the Infectious Diseases Specialist in the Era of Managed Care

Outcomes evaluations
Clinical trials of new drugs and alternative therapies
Basic science
The molecular basis of disease, risk of adverse events, and new therapies
New roles for hospital epidemiology: the integrated delivery system epidemiologist
Quality of care
Travel medicine
Nursing home and home care
Management of HIV infection
The importance of patient volume to favorable outcomes
Health care policy and administration
New roles in industry, government, public health

combining infection control, outcomes, and quality measurement.[1] Alternatively, some hospital epidemiologists will be asked to oversee employee health care[9] or travel medicine.[10]

Because managed care seeks to discourage patients from using expensive resources associated with inpatient stays, more emphasis on outpatient care and home care continues to occur. Taken to its logical conclusion, greater emphasis will be placed on healthy communities, and the hospital epidemiologist is poised to participate actively. Such activities will involve preventive services in schools, places of worship, employment, and athletic and community facilities—in short, anywhere that groups of people congregate. As a result, instead of a hospital epidemiologist, the concept of an integrated delivery system epidemiologist will emerge. Infection control, health promotion, and quality-of-care programs of several hospitals and clinics would come under the purview of the integrated delivery system epidemiologist (Fig. 316–2). For the first time, health promotion and disease prevention could be integrated from the home to the hospital and, if needed, to extended care facilities. It is quite possible that a new alliance could be forged with public health authorities, who traditionally have had some of these responsibilities.

MANAGING HUMAN IMMUNODEFICIENCY VIRUS INFECTION

With the proliferation of new drugs and drug combinations available for treating human immunodeficiency virus (HIV) infection, we have de facto created a subspecialty within our field. Program directors will have to train the appropriate number of highly skilled experts needed to combat this pandemic with unparalleled skill, efficiency, and compassion. Such experts will probably work in a team committed to HIV management: physician, nurse, social worker, pharmacist, psychologist, and others. The key point is that therapy is sufficiently complicated that only those with larger patient volumes will be comfortable and skillful in managing difficult clinical problems. Moreover, in the information age, the era of accountability, and the competitive managed care arena, such experts and their colleagues will need to *measure* the quality of their care.[11] Furthermore, as a result of increasingly complicated therapies and drug-drug interactions, the design and conduct of proper clinical trials and postmarketing follow-up studies become more complicated. Those with special skills in clinical trials and analysis of data will be in great demand.

BASIC SCIENCE

Enormous opportunities are evolving for basic scientists not only because of the likelihood of increased funding from both the National Institutes of Health[12] and Veterans Affairs but also because of policy needs related to the development of new information. For example, as a result of advances in molecular biology, it is becoming more feasible to identify genetic predispositions to diseases and possibly to adverse events related to specific therapies. Basic scientists will not only be able to do more but will also be in increasing demand to translate their findings to the public and to those who influence public policy. In part, the enthusiasm in Congress for basic science may reflect better times economically or the sense that health care costs have been contained. Such optimism may in fact reflect a new attitude emerging from the postmodern era. It is also possible that enlightened leaders of HMOs will envision financial advantages as new technology is transferred from the laboratory to the clinic.

EDUCATIONAL NEEDS

The director of a modern division of infectious diseases needs to be acutely aware of current changes in health care and prepare for its continued evolution. In addition to the traditional training in clinical infectious diseases, the director should emphasize information management, including MEDLINE and web searches, critique of the

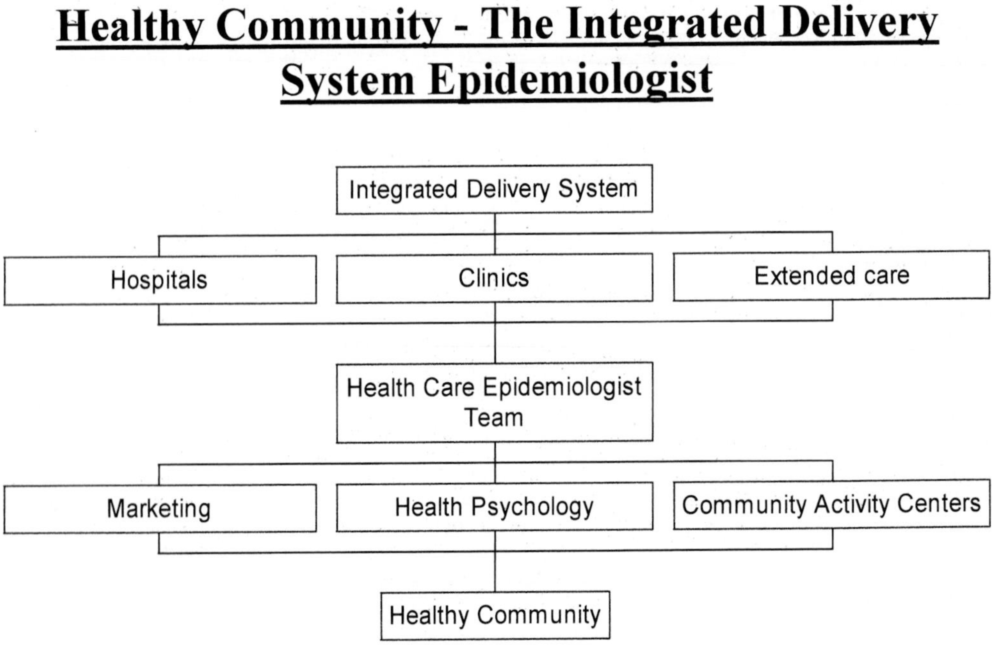

FIGURE 316–2. My concept of an integrated delivery system epidemiologist, forging relationships with more than one hospital or clinic as well as various community services for health promotion and disease prevention. The integrated delivery system epidemiologist would be the leader of a health care epidemiologist team with responsibilities for promoting health in the community and the integrated delivery system.

literature, excellent bedside diagnostic skills, and excellent communication skills. Some fellows interested in clinical research should be encouraged to obtain an advanced degree: a Master of Public Health (M.P.H.), a Master of Science (M.S.) in epidemiology, or an M.S. in clinical trials or biostatistics. Those who wish to become leaders in administration should pursue an advanced degree in health administration or in business administration—an M.S.H.A. or M.B.A. Trainees who wish to remain competitive in basic science should be encouraged to get an M.S. or a Ph.D. in their field of interest. This recommendation derives from my view that increasingly formal training creates value, differentiates the subspecialist, and is advantageous to tomorrow's infectious diseases experts. All groups should be well versed on the basics of study design, quality-of-life measurements, ethical principles, and outcomes evaluation.

SUMMARY

Although it is popular to speak of the revolutions in medicine or of the changes wrought by health care reform, it is argued that the primary change has been a social revolution. The era of modernity with its optimism for science and medicine has given way to the postmodern era characterized by doubts about the value of medicine and science. Such social changes in attitude have triangularized the doctor-patient relationship to include the needs of society at large. In turn, that triangularization has helped reframe ethical issues surrounding the delivery of care. The conclusion is that current market-based concepts for financing medical care reflect the underlying beliefs and concerns of our society.

The infectious diseases specialist needs to be aware of the added skills needed to compete in the current era, the need to show value, and the imperative to maintain high ethical standards. New opportunities do in fact exist in both basic and applied areas in infectious diseases, and a new era of optimism for medicine may be emerging.

REFERENCES

1. Wenzel RP. Instituting health care reform and preserving quality: Role of the hospital epidemiologist. Clin Infect Dis. 1993;17:831–834.
2. Wenzel RP. Health care reform and the hospital epidemiologist. In: Wenzel RP, ed. Prevention and Control of Nosocomial Infections. 3rd ed. Baltimore: Williams & Wilkins; 1997:47–54.
3. Wenzel RP. Managed health care: Outcomes and update. In: Remington J, Schwartz, M, eds. Current Clinical Topics in Infectious Diseases. Malden, Mass: Blackwell; 1999. In press.
4. Wenzel RP. Modern perspectives—the revolution in health care delivery. In: Wenzel RP, ed. Assessing Quality Care: Perspectives for Clinicians. Baltimore: Williams & Wilkins; 1992:3–16.
5. Hurley R, Thompson J. Schmoozing with the enemy: Conversations with employee benefits managers. Hosp Health Services Admin. 1993;38:197–214.
6. Hurley R. The purchaser-driven reformation in health care: Alternative approaches to leveling our cathedrals. Front Health Service Manage. 1993;9:3–35.
7. Mechanic D, Schlesinger M. The impact of managed care on patients' trust in medical care and their physicians. JAMA. 1996;275:1693–1697.
8. Wenzel RP. The Lobury lecture. The economics of nosocomial infection. J Hosp Infect. 1995;31:79–87.
9. Doebbeling BN. Protecting the healthcare worker from infection and injury. In: Wenzel RP, ed. Prevention and Control of Nosocomial Infections. 3rd ed. Baltimore: Williams & Wilkins; 1997:397–435.
10. Nettleman MD. Emporiatics, Introduction to Travel Medicine. 2nd ed. Iowa City, Iowa: University of Iowa; 1995.
11. Franchi D, Wenzel RP. Measuring health-related quality of life among patients infected with human immunodeficiency virus. Clin Infect Dis. 1998;26:20–26.
12. Medical research funding (Editorial). NY Times. 1988, Jan 6:A20.

SECTION I
THE INTERNET

Chapter 317

The Infectious Diseases Physician and the Internet

EDWARD H. SHORTLIFFE
LAWRENCE M. FAGAN
VICTOR L. YU

The last decade has witnessed a remarkable transition in the penetration of computing and communications concepts into the everyday life of both professionals and the public. It is arguable that no other innovative 20th century technology (such as radio, television, video recorders, or fax machines) has affected the societal consciousness as rapidly and pervasively as has the Internet and its most famous application, the World Wide Web.[1] As recently as 1990, the Web was unknown and the Internet remained largely the domain of academics, scientists, and government agencies.

The national networking concept had first emerged from government and university research laboratories in the late 1960s, a product of the U.S. Department of Defense Advanced Research Projects Agency (ARPA). Initially conceived as a method for interconnecting military computers to share data and computer programs, that early ARPANET (as it was known) was never expected to have the remarkably broad societal impact that we experienced in the 1990s. Nor was there any expectation that the Internet would in time become a commercial entity; however, it was totally privatized in the United States by April 1995.

The Web was originally conceived in the early 1990s by research physicists who sought a mechanism for sharing publications, including images, on the Internet. It was then rapidly popularized with the introduction of software known as *browsers*, the first of which (Mosaic) was developed and placed in the public domain by the National Center for Supercomputing Applications in Illinois. These programs, subsequently commercialized by companies such as Netscape and Microsoft, easily allowed even a computer novice to access and share useful information by following an intuitive "point and click" navigation method on the computer screen. Today, it is rare to see a television commercial that does not provide a web address for the company; commerce constitutes a multibillion dollar economy on the Internet. The Web has penetrated the educational system at all levels (including kindergarten to 12th grade classrooms in the public schools), and it is common for individuals to turn first to the Internet for information that they once would have sought from friends or from libraries—or failed to look for at all.

It is hardly surprising that the Internet and the Web should also begin to affect the health care system in a variety of ways. Many patients have access to the Web from their home or offices and regularly seek health-related information on the Internet. By late 1998, requests for health information were the most frequent type of network-based query documented by the major Internet search-engine companies. Major resources for health professionals have also become available on the Web and offer marvelous new opportunities for enhanced access to data and information while creating new and challenging issues regarding currency, quality, and confidentiality of the information that is distributed by this mechanism. The infectious diseases physician has a wide variety of important resources available to support both research and practice in the field. This chapter provides some suggestions regarding useful starting points and strategies for making the most of the Internet's potential when addressing problems in infectious diseases. Physicians must become familiar with these resources, both because they can enhance the quality of patient care and also because patients and the public are increasingly assuming that health care providers will be familiar with the information and tools that are now readily available in this networked age.

A BRIEF TUTORIAL ON THE INTERNET

Like the international telephone networks and the banking infrastructure for funds transfer, the Internet is technically complex. Yet, like the telephone and automated teller machines used to access those other networks, the basic user interface for the Internet (and especially the browser concept used for the Web) is simple and requires no detailed understanding of the network's technical underpinnings. A few basic principles can support a robust conceptual grasp of the Internet and the Web; once a user understands these notions, conquering the Internet and the Web can be straightforward.

It often amazes Internet initiates when they learn that no single organization is in charge of the network. The Internet is made possible by collegial agreements on standards for networking connectivity and information exchange; individual networks can connect to the Internet (and access machines on all other networks that are connected to the Internet) if they agree to abide by the standards that ensure compatibility. Thus, the Internet is actually a "network of networks," with individual networks within organizations, businesses, or geographic regions independently owned and managed.

When information is sent from one machine on the Internet to another (such as a cross-country electronic mail [e-mail] message or a web page from a company's server when viewed on a desktop personal computer), it is segmented into small pieces of digital information known as *packets*. One of the clever aspects of the Internet's underlying technology is the notion of *packet switching*, whereby interconnecting nodes on the Internet can dynamically decide, for each packet in a message, what the instantaneously optimal way is to send that packet to the intended destination. Each packet carries the destination address with it, and even if all the packets in a message take different routes when traveling from one machine to the other, they are appropriately reassembled at the other end. This approach helps to avoid bottlenecks on heavily used network segments and ensures balanced use of available network connections.

The individual networks in the Internet must use a standard protocol known as the *Internet protocol* (IP) for exchanging these packets of information. The IP is coupled with another transmission protocol known as TCP, and these two standards are now the dominant communications protocols for all networking. References to TCP/IP merely indicate that a network has adopted the Internet standard for communications.

If a message is going to move efficiently from one computer to another, often spanning many networks, it is necessary to have a convention for identifying a computer's address on the Internet. To help make this addressing scheme understandable to all Internet users, a naming system has been developed for networking *domains*. Addresses are broken up with "dots" (or periods) between the increasingly general elements in the subdomain and domain specifications. Thus, the Internet address *nlm.nih.gov* refers to the National

Library of Medicine's machines (*nlm*) within the National Institutes of Health domain (*nih*), which is a part of the government's master domain (*gov*). The domain naming system is undergoing expansion, but the most common domains are educational (*.edu*), commercial (*.com*), organizational (*.org*), and governmental (*.gov*). In addition, international sites on the Internet generally add a two-character domain to the end of their addresses to specify the country (such as *.uk* for the United Kingdom).

The World Wide Web is only one application on the Internet. Others include e-mail, file transfers, news groups, and remote login to computers. The basic protocol that supports the Web is known as the HyperText Transfer Protocol (*HTTP*). Thus, addresses for sites on the World Wide Web generally augment the machine's Internet address with a specification of the fact that a web application is being used. The syntax for such addresses requires the protocol specification, followed by a colon and two backslashes, by *www*, and then by the machine's domain name. For example, *http://www.cdc.gov* is the address* for the main web page at the Centers for Disease Control and Prevention (CDC) in Atlanta (Fig. 317–1). Such addresses are known as *uniform resource locators* (URLs). If you know the URL for a site of interest, it is trivial to "visit" that site via a web browser on a machine that has been connected to the Internet. Connections can be achieved through direct wiring to a local area network or by accessing a commercial Internet service provider via a telephone modem connection. Most browsers support a type-in field (named "location" or "address") for entering the URL. Once the characters for the URL are typed in and the "enter" key is pressed, the browser starts to communicate with the remote site to obtain the information requested and display it on your own computer's screen. Access to web pages can also be simplified by allowing a user to click on an active area or *link* on one page, which automatically requests the retrieval of the associated page, even if it is on a different computer somewhere else on the Internet.

*All Internet addresses provided in this chapter are valid at the time of writing, but the nature of the Web makes it inevitable that some sites will move to new locations or disappear altogether. The search engines provide a mechanism for locating sites and resources if a cited URL becomes outdated after publication of this volume.

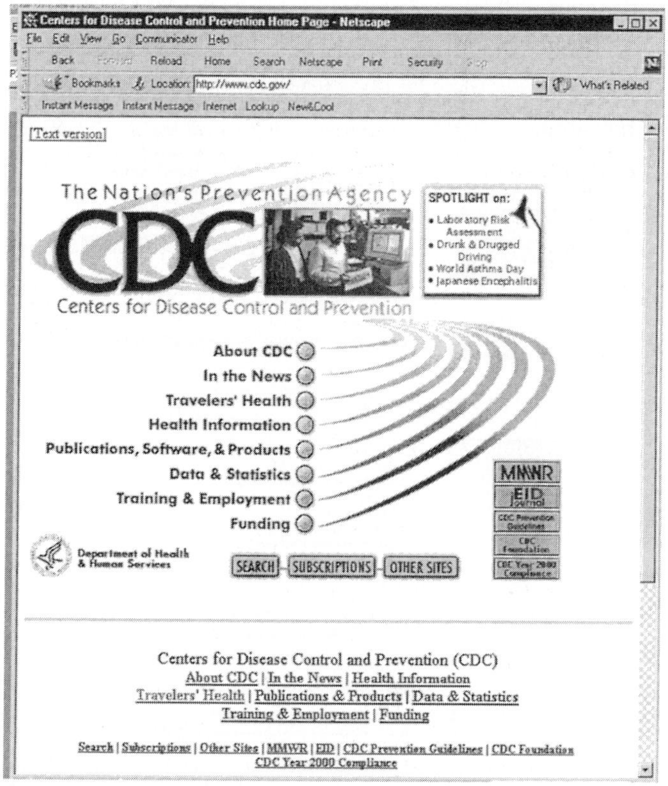

FIGURE 317–1. The home page for the Centers for Disease Control and Prevention in Atlanta, viewed with a Web browser.

Many people are puzzled when they first discover the existence of web-based search engines such as Yahoo or AltaVista; they wonder how it is possible to index a vast resource like the World Wide Web. One key notion is called *web crawling*. A web crawler is software that exhaustively searches the Internet for web pages by following links on pages and analyzing the contents of each page to determine the words that occur there. Such crawlers run in the background all the time, constantly updating and expanding the word indices for existing pages on the Web. For example, this process is the basis for the AltaVista search engine (*http://www.altavista.com*).

A second method for indexing information has emerged as well. This method involves building a taxonomy of concepts (e.g., a structured description of organizations or diseases) and associating specific URLs with the taxonomy, often through a process of manual review and indexing. Yahoo has taken this approach, which means that only a small number of the existing URLs have been indexed (see Yahoo Health at *http://www.yahoo.com/Health*). In general, if you wish to get focused information on a well-structured concept such as medical centers in a particular geographic area, it is preferable to go to one of the sites that has used the taxonomy approach. If you are looking for a document that contains multiple concepts that may be obscure, you are better off to search one of the systems derived from the web crawler approach.

Many people worry about the security of information that is moved over the Internet, but a variety of methods are available for protecting such data. Not only is this issue important for the biomedical community, in which confidential patient data are a particular concern, but it is also important in electronic commerce applications so that consumers may have confidence that it is safe to conduct business and provide confidential financial information on the Internet. The key central notions in networking security are those of *encryption* (encoding information by using secret codes that prevent unauthorized individuals from interpreting the data, even if they manage to "listen in") and *authentication* (implementing technologies that make it difficult for one individual to access information while pretending to be another individual who may have valid access to that information). An excellent summary of both the technical and policy issues, as they relate to protection of confidential patient data, is available in a 1997 report from the National Research Council.[2]

PHYSICIANS, PATIENTS, AND THE INTERNET

As the number of Internet users grows (current estimates suggest more than 50 million users in the United States alone), it is not surprising that increasing numbers of patients, as well as healthy individuals, are turning to the Internet for health information. It is a rare North American physician who has not encountered a patient who comes to an appointment armed with a question or a stack of laser-printed pages that arose from medically related searches on the Web. On the one hand, some of the information is timely and excellent; in this sense, physicians can often learn about innovations from their patients and will increasingly need to be open to the kinds of questions that this enhanced access to information will generate from patients in their practices. On the other hand, much of the health information on the Web lacks peer review or is purely anecdotal. People who lack medical training can be misled by such information, just as they have been in the past by printed information in books and magazines dealing with fad treatments from anecdotal sources. In addition, some sites provide personalized advice, often for a fee, with all the attendant concerns about the quality of the suggestions and the ability to give valid advice based solely on an e-mail or a web-based interaction.

In a more positive light, the new communications technologies offer creative ways to interact with patients and to provide higher-quality care. For example, there has been rapid growth in the use of e-mail as a mechanism for avoiding telephone tag and allowing simple questions to be answered asynchronously (the telephone requires synchronous communication; e-mail does not). More exploratory, but extremely promising, are communications methods based on the technology of the World Wide Web. For example, some young companies work with managed care organizations and health care systems to provide web-based facilities for disease management. Patients access a private website, provide information about the status of their chronic disease (for example, blood glucose readings in diabetes), and later obtain feedback from their physician or from disease managers who seek to keep the patients healthy at home, thereby decreasing the need for emergency department or clinic visits.

The Web, however, is far from a panacea for the busy physician. Web browsers are generally poorly integrated with clinical information systems in hospitals and offices, thus creating disincentives for taking the time to search the Web for information in the midst of a harried practice day. Even if a user has facile access, search mechanisms are generally incapable of selecting sites that give the most accurate or specific information. Finding the answer to a particular clinical question can be time consuming, difficult, and tedious. For example, a request in one search engine for the string "HIV/AIDS" returned over 96,000 web addresses in January 1999.

However, with more physicians learning to use the Web and accessing it from home or office outside regular practice hours, it has become clear that the Internet provides marvelous resources that are simpler to access and more up to date than those to which practitioners have had to turn for assistance in the past. A prime example, now available both to health personnel and to the public at large, is no-cost web-based searching of MEDLINE provided by the National Library of Medicine. Using very simple search procedures implemented and refined by the National Library of Medicine, a physician can search MEDLINE and other key knowledge bases with assurance that the collection is up to date and complete.

Many geographic areas have only limited access to the Internet. Yet even in countries where Internet access is readily available, use by physicians in their practices remains low.[3] For example, one article reported that only 8% of Canadian physicians used the Internet regularly in 1997.[4] Only a third of the members of the Society of Healthcare Epidemiology of America listed an e-mail address in the 1997 directory.[5] Although these numbers are increasing rapidly, current use is still limited. Some studies have shown that physicians tend to find retrieval of information from MEDLINE to be time consuming (30 minutes per search on average); those who do not become facile with searching often find that their use of the technology declines as the novelty fades.[6] Similar results would be likely for Internet use in general.

A variety of professional medical organizations now offer websites that include access to specialized health information aimed at clinicians, patients, or both. There is a growing notion of a *portal* to the Internet, a specialized site that provides pointers to other key websites for a specific topic area and allows people to avoid dependence on the more generic and unscreened search engines. Some examples of portals in the area of medicine and infectious diseases are provided later in this chapter.

The sudden growth in the Internet and in the level of use of the Web has created challenging new issues, some of which are particularly relevant in the fields of health care and biomedical research. The promise of the Internet—and its ability to integrate information from disparate sources—will be seriously threatened if users do not think that they can trust the network, especially in areas related to security and confidentiality. Furthermore, questions still need to be resolved regarding liability associated with providing health information on the Web, as well as issues of ownership and copyright in a world in which making a copy of someone else's intellectual property is as easy as pointing and clicking with one's desktop mouse.[7]

The world of scientific publishing is in particular turmoil because of questions raised by the new information technologies in areas ranging from copyright protection to business models for maintaining income streams when information is sold on the Internet. In the last 2 years, many clinical and research journals, including most of the major infectious diseases journals, began making the transition from a completely paper-based delivery system to partly electronic delivery over the Internet. Many of the electronic versions of the journals have maintained the same content and format as the paper versions, but it is possible that significant changes in format will be able to reduce printing costs while providing increased access to the medical content and experimental results. A pertinent perspective was provided in 1998 by the *British Medical Journal* (BMJ): "Three years ago, it was hard to find a medical journal on the Internet. Now most have websites, providing selections from their paper journals in electronic form. This week the *BMJ* joins the *Lancet* and a host of specialist journals in taking the obvious next step: providing the full text of the paper journal online. Soon most other medical journals interested in their long term survival will follow suit." [8]

Publishers are also struggling with the implications of the Internet for monographs and textbooks. Until recently, the main method for creating electronic versions of textbooks had been to develop a CD-ROM version combining formatted text files with a search engine that could find sections of the text containing the words or concepts of interest. Typically, such CD-ROMs contain a single reference book or occasionally several related textbooks. It was inevitable that electronic textbooks would begin to move to the World Wide Web. Of special interest are websites that provide access to multiple information sources that can be searched in parallel. Examples of these sites are MD Consult (*http://www.mdconsult.com*) and Primary Care Online (*http://www.lrponline.com*).

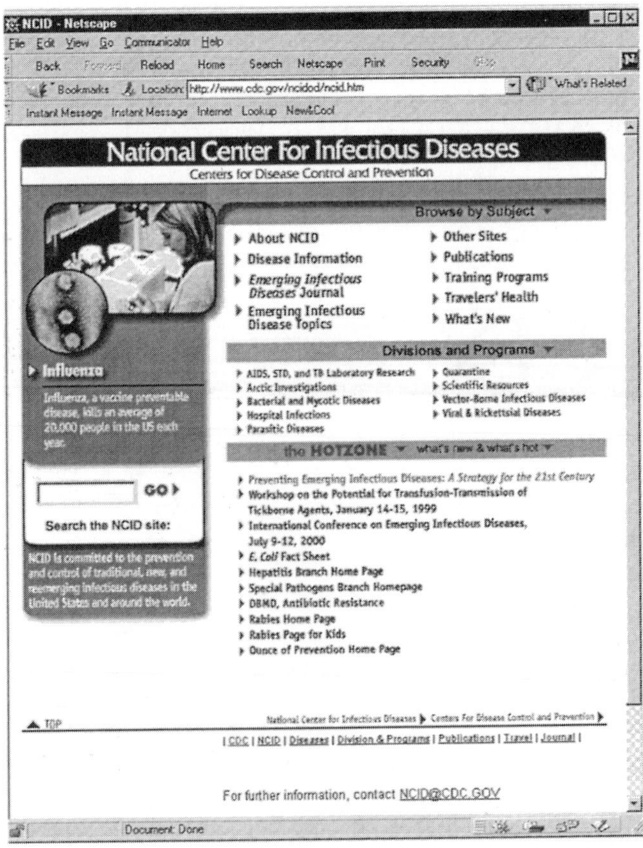

FIGURE 317–2. The Centers for Disease Control and Prevention has a special site, maintained by the National Center for Infectious Diseases, which provides a useful entry to many of the other infectious diseases resources on the World Wide Web.

TABLE 317–1 Some General Health Resources on the Internet

Source	Internet Address	Description
National Library of Medicine (PubMed and Internet Grateful Med)	<http://www.nlm.nih.gov/databases/freemedl.html>	The NLM provides two free search environments for retrieving information from Medline and other databases. *PubMed* requires no user training, whereas *Internet Grateful Med* is more powerful but somewhat more complicated to use. Both are accessible via this single URL
Biomednet	<http://www.biomednet.com/>	Biomednet is a general resource for biomedical researchers. It serves as a useful portal to a variety of research databases
CliniWeb	<http://www.ohsu.edu/cliniweb/>	Developed at Oregon Health Sciences University, this portal provides a general search interface to medical sites on the Internet. Sites are screened for quality and then indexed with the use of specialized controlled terminology from the National Library of Medicine
Medical Matrix	<http://www.medmatrix.org>	Another Internet portal aimed at physicians and other health workers
	<http://www.medmatrix.org/SPages/Infectious_Diseases.asp>	A specific subset of pointers for the field of infectious diseases
Medscape	<http://www.medscape.com/>	Another general resource of health professionals
	<http://www.medscape.com/Home/Topics/ID/InfectiousDiseases.html>	Medscape's infectious diseases subsite

Abbreviation: URL, Uniform resource locator.

Electronic versions of textbooks can provide indexing capabilities beyond those available in hard-copy textbooks. For certain areas of medicine where well-structured documents exist, it is possible to define a set of questions that the physician is likely to ask about the document. Once this set of questions is defined, indexers can go line by line through the documents to identify how the text addresses this list of key questions.

SPECIAL ISSUES IN INFECTIOUS DISEASES

Generic web-based resources that are of use to all physicians are of course valuable to infectious diseases practitioners and researchers as well. However, a growing number of sites are specific to problems in infection and communicable disease and are accordingly of particular value to infectious diseases experts. For the infectious diseases physician, the Internet provides a number of new opportunities and advantages, but some caveats apply as well.

The general public often searches for health information of all kinds by using one of the health-oriented Internet search engines such as Yahoo Health (*http://www.yahoo.com/Health*). The National Library of Medicine has also created a consumer-oriented health portal (*http://medlineplus.nlm.nih.gov/medlineplus*). Of particular interest to patients and also valuable to physicians are the sites that provide detailed information on international travel and immunizations. The CDC's own travel site is perhaps the best and most popular of these resources (*http://www.cdc.gov/travel/index.htm*). Patients often seek information on specific infectious diseases from on-line government resources such as the National Library of Medicine's pages regarding human immunodeficiency virus and acquired immunodeficiency syndrome (AIDS) (*http://sis.nlm.nih.gov/aidswww.htm*).

For health professionals, the CDC has developed an extensive set of web pages related to infectious diseases, with an entry home page for the National Center for Infectious Diseases (*http://www.cdc.gov/ncidod/ncid.htm*) that provides links to a variety of other resources (Fig. 317–2). An earlier on-line CDC resource, CDC Wonder,[9] provides facile access to CDC documents and newsletters, including the *Morbidity and Mortality Weekly Report*, and has been converted for access by practitioners using the Web.[10]

Academicians and researchers in infectious diseases have exploited the Internet as well. Numerous research groups have their own websites, which allow them to make known their expertise and the availability of laboratory and clinical services. The Internet has also been used to facilitate the recruitment of patients for controlled studies and for the rapid dissemination and exchange of information to other researchers. Training programs are increasingly using the Web to recruit faculty and research fellows and to serve as a communications link among faculty and trainees.

The promise of the Internet is particularly exciting in areas of infection, in which traditional methods have been limited or ineffective. The Internet offers remarkable abilities to support disease surveillance as professionals work to link regional testing laboratories with local health care institutions and patient care practices while they seek to pool data within states and nationally. Early recognition of emerging infections and epidemics may be greatly enhanced as automated surveillance methods based on Internet technologies are put in place. Already, significant state and regional efforts have been

TABLE 317–2 Some General Internet Resources for Infectious Diseases Physicians

Source	Internet Address	Description
Centers for Disease Control and Prevention (CDC)	http://www.cdc.gov/	The main home page for the CDC
	http://www.cdc.gov/ncidod/id_links.htm	This CDC subsite provides an excellent set of links related to infectious diseases research and practice
World Health Organization	http://www.who.ch/	Home page for the WHO, from which information about a wide variety of programs can be obtained
	http://www.who.int/emc/	Subsite provides excerpts from the *Disease Outbreak News* and *Weekly Epidemiological Record,* travel information, and disease-specific information on emerging infections
APEC Emerging Infections Network	http://www.apec.org/infectious/	Information from the University of Washington and CDC on emerging infections
MedNet Infectious Diseases Connections	http://www.sermed.com/infect.htm	Access to on-line journals, epidemiologic data, and related ID sites

TABLE 317–3 Internet Resources on Specific Infectious Diseases Topics

Topic	Internet Address	Description
AIDS	http://www.ama-assn.org/special/hiv/hivhome.htm	*JAMA:* Excellent site for clinicians and researchers with guidelines, updates and news, policy issues, and links to other AIDS sites that have been evaluated by *JAMA* consultants
	http://www.iapac.org/	International Association of AIDS Physicians: Covers international conferences and updates in AIDS therapy and policy
	http://www.healthcg.com/hiv/	*Clinical Care Options for HIV:* Billed as a state-of-the-art HIV medical resource for health care professionals
	http://sis.nlm.nih.gov/aidswww.htm	National Library of Medicine AIDS-Related Online Databases: Contains on-line databases to journals, books, and abstracts
Online journals	http://www.newslettersonline.com	American Healthcare Communications: *Infectious Disease Alert*
	http://www.asmusa.org http://intl-journals.asm.org (for European and Asian readers)	American Society for Microbiology: Contains full text of 10 ASM journals, including *Antimicrobial Agents and Chemotherapy, Journal of Clinical Microbiology, Journal of Virology*
	http://www.mosby.com	Association for Practioners in Infection Control (Mosby): *American Journal of Infection Control*
	http://www.oup.co.uk/jac/	British Society of Antimicrobial Chemotherapy: *Journal of Antimicrobial Chemotherapy*
	http://www.cdc.gov/ncidod/eid/index.htm	CDC: *Emerging Infectious Diseases*
	www.hbuk.co.uk/wbs/jhi/	Hospital Infection Society: *Journal of Hospital Infection*
	http://www.journals.uchicago.edu	Infectious Disease Society of America: *Journal of Infectious Diseases, Clinical Infectious Diseases*
	http://www.chez.com/malaria/edito.html	*Tropical Medicine:* Malaria and Infectious Diseases in Africa
	http://www.slackinc.com/general/iche/ichehome.htm	Society for Healthcare Epidemiology America (Slack): *Infection Control and Hospital Epidemiology*
Professional societies	http://www.idsociety.org/index.html	Infectious Disease Society of America
	http://www.idlinks.com/international_id/int_soc.html	Infectious disease societies worldwide
	http://idis.org	International Society for Infectious Diseases
	http://www.nfid.org	National Foundation for Infectious Diseases
	http://www.asmusa.org	American Society for Microbiology
Disease specific	http://www.lshtm.ac.uk/mp/bcu/enta/home.htm	Amebiasis
	http://www.helicobacter.org	European Helicobacter Pylori Study Group
	http://www.helicobacter.com	The Helicobacter Foundation
	http://www.hepnet.com	Hepatitis Information Network, with research, news articles, and links to other websites for all viruses
	http://www.viridae.com	Herpes
	http://www.iupui.edu/it/histodgn	Histoplasmosis (Indiana University)
	http://www.cdc.gov/ncidod/diseases/legion/legion.htm	Legionnaires' disease: CDC
	http://www.legionella.org	Legionnaires' disease: University of Pittsburgh (VA)
	http://www.who.int/lep	Leprosy
	http://www.lymenet.org	Lyme Disease Network of New Jersey: Excellent website of scientific, legal, and societal news of Lyme disease
	http://www.med.monash.edu.au/micro/malaria/	Monash University, Australia, and WHO
	http://www.ulst.ac.uk/faculty/science/bms/	Mycology (British Mycological Society)
	http://www.cdfound.to.it/html/atlas.htm	Parasitology
	http://www.rabies.com	Rabies
	http://www.tmvc.com.au	Australian Travelers Medical and Vaccination Center
	http://www.cdc.gov/nchstp/tb	CDC Division of Tuberculosis Elimination
	http://www.who.int/gtb	WHO Global Tuberculosis Program

made in this area,[11] although the problems are inherently complicated by the lack of standards in electronic medical record systems, which confounds attempts to pool data from a variety of organizations. Similarly, the Internet can support the dissemination of crucial information to providers and patients as new infectious agents emerge and the criteria for their diagnosis and treatment are better understood.

We can anticipate a role for the Internet in acute crisis management, including such emergencies as domestic accidents with biologicals or terrorist attacks.[12] The communications infrastructure will play a crucial role in allowing coordination among local, state, and federal response teams while also providing a mechanism for specialized expertise to be made available to those on site who may be faced with severe problems in containment and diagnosis. The Internet may augment traditional telephone resources for accessing and disseminating crucial information in such circumstances.

INTERNET RESOURCES FOR INFECTIOUS DISEASES

Tables 317–1 through 317–3 summarize some additional Internet resources that will be of interest to infectious diseases physicians. AIDS management, emerging infections, and issues regarding vaccination are particularly well covered on Internet sites. The listing here is by no means exhaustive or complete, and for some sites the specific Internet addresses may change over time, but it does provide a set of useful starting points for those who may wish to explore the available information that is pertinent to their research or to clinical activities in infectious diseases.

LOOKING TO THE FUTURE

Many Internet users long for the day when their connections to the Web will be faster so that large amounts of information and images will load onto their machines more quickly than is typically possible today. We clearly need higher speeds (*bandwidth*), and remarkable changes in technology are occurring regularly to help to satisfy society's appetite for this new resource. Yet many applications will fail to be effective or accepted if the *quality* of that bandwidth is also not adequate. Certain critical applications need to have guaranteed, reliable transmission speeds, even if they are only needed for a short period. Moreover, faster connections do not necessarily solve the problems of latency, or inherent delays caused by the time required for transmission of signals. A long pause after information is requested can be frustrating to busy computer users, even if the information then arrives quickly once the transmission begins. Simulations that require feedback from a distant site are especially limited by problems with latency.

The research agenda for the next-generation Internet is being defined and will require an effective partnership between government and academia that is informed by and coordinated with the changes occurring in the industry. Many observers are eager to see new technical and logistic capabilities developed that will enable new kinds of health applications on the Internet.[1] The forces that are shrinking the world in other societal arenas, such as use of the Internet in entertainment, in scientific collaboration, and in travel planning, will also allow globalization of health care and health information exchange. Internet efforts will in turn influence the global information infrastructure and our ability both to provide advanced health care services to others and to benefit from the information and experience that they will make available to us via the same technologies. International public health stands to benefit greatly from the networking innovations and applications that are already under way.

REFERENCES

1. Shortliffe E. Health care and the next generation Internet (Editorial). Ann Intern Med. 1998;129:138–140.
2. National Research Council. For the Record: Protecting Electronic Health Information. Washington, DC: National Academy Press; 1997.
3. Krause G, Dauschner F. Guidelines, policies, and the Internet. Curr Opin Infect Dis. 1998;11:445–448.
4. Lampitt W. Why should physicians use e-mail? Can Med Assoc J. 1997;156:1325.
5. Sellick J. Electronic mail: An imperative for health care epidemiologists. Infect Control Hosp Epidemiol. 1997;18:337–381.
6. Hersh W, Hickam D. How well do physicians use electronic information retrieval systems? A framework for investigation and systematic review. JAMA. 1998;280:1347–1352.
7. Shapiro C, Varian H. Information Rules: A Strategic Guide to the Network Economy. Cambridge, Mass: Harvard Business School Press; 1998.
8. Delamothe T, Smith R. The BMJ's website scales up. BMJ. 1998;316:1109–1110.
9. Friede A, Reid J, Ory H. CDC Wonder: A comprehensive on-line public health information system of the Centers for Disease Control and Prevention. Am J Public Health. 1993;83:1289–1294.
10. Friede A, O'Carroll P, Thralls R, et al. CDC Wonder on the Web. In: Cimino JJ, ed. Annual Symposium of the American Medical Informatics Association. Washington, DC: Hanley & Belfus; 1996:408–412.
11. Bean N, Martin S, Bradford H. PHLIS: An electronic system for reporting public health data from remote sites. Am J Public Health. 1992;82:1273–1276.
12. Lederberg J. Infectious disease and biological weapons: Prophylaxis and mitigation. JAMA. 1997;278:435–436.

Index

Note: Page numbers in *italics* refer to illustrations; page numbers followed by t refer to tables.

B

C

E

F

G

H

I

J

K

L

N

O

P

Q

R

S

W

X

Y

Z

ISBN 0-443-07524-7
90071
9 780443 075247